International WHO'S WHO of Authors AND Writers

2013

International WHO'S WHO of Authors AND Writers 2013

28th Edition

Routledge
Taylor & Francis Group

LONDON AND NEW YORK

Twenty-eighth edition published 2012
by Routledge
2 Park Square, Milton Park, Abingdon, Oxon., OX14 4RN, United Kingdom

Simultaneously published in the USA and Canada
by Routledge
711 Third Avenue, New York, NY 10017

www.routledge.com

Routledge is an imprint of the Taylor & Francis Group, an informa business

© 2012 Routledge

All rights reserved. No part of this book may be reprinted or reproduced or utilised in any form or by any electronic, mechanical, or other means, now known or hereafter invented, including photocopying and recording, or in any information storage or retrieval system, without permission in writing from the publishers.

Trademark notice: Product or corporate names may be trademarks or registered trademarks, and are used only for identification and explanation without intent to infringe.

First published 1934

ISBN: 978-1-85743-651-8
ISSN: 1740-018X

Typeset in Frome by Data Standards Limited

Senior Editor: Robert J. Elster
Editorial Researchers: Anuradha Ravindra (Team Leader), Ankita Baruah (Senior Researcher), Jubi Borkakoti, Divya Joy
Consulting Editors: Gerard Delaney, Annabella Gabb, Sue Leckey, Justin Lewis
Editorial Director: Paul Kelly

The Publishers make no representation, express or implied, with regard to the accuracy of the information contained in this book and cannot accept any legal responsibility for any errors or omissions that may take place.

Printed and bound in Great Britain by
CPI Antony Rowe, Chippenham, Wiltshire

FOREWORD

The 28th edition of the INTERNATIONAL WHO'S WHO OF AUTHORS AND WRITERS provides biographical information on novelists, journalists, essayists, dramatists, poets and editors, as well as literary agents and publishers. The biographies include, where available, personal and contact details, information on career and awards, publications, and contributions to books and periodicals.

For each edition entrants are given the opportunity to make necessary amendments and additions to their biographies. Supplementary research is done by the editorial group in order to ensure that the book is as up to date as possible on publication.

In addition to the biographical information, a directory section provides details of literary awards and prizes, literary organizations and literary festivals and national libraries of the world. The introduction contains a list of abbreviations and international telephone codes. The names of entrants whose death has been reported over the past year are included in the obituary.

Readers are referred to the book's companion title in The Europa Biographical Reference Series, the INTERNATIONAL WHO'S WHO IN POETRY, for a comprehensive collection of information on the most prominent international poets.

The biographical information contained in this edition, as well as information on past entrants, deceased entrants and entrants from the wide range of other Europa biographical sources, is provided online in WORLD WHO'S WHO. Using the product's sophisticated search functions, researchers can quickly and easily access the rich biographical data in the comprehensive Europa biographical database. As well, online users can take advantage of the quarterly updating cycle that ensures the data is as current as possible. Details of this resource are available at www.worldwhoswho.com

The assistance of the individuals and organizations included in this publication in providing up-to-date material is invaluable, and the editors would like to take this opportunity to express their appreciation.

August 2012

ALPHABETIZATION AND THE TRANSCRIPTION OF NAMES

The list of names is alphabetical, with the entrants listed under their family name. If part of an entrant's family name is in parentheses, indicating that this part is not usually used, this will be ignored for the purposes of the alphabetical listing.

If an entrant's name is spelt in a variety of ways, a cross-reference is provided. An entrant who is known by a pseudonym or by an abbreviation of their name is either listed under this name or a cross-reference is provided. Multiple pseudonyms are cross-referenced where considered necessary.

Titles as part of a pseudonym, such as DJ, are ignored for the purposes of the alphabetical listing. Pseudonyms that include numbers as part of the name are listed alphabetically under the spelling of that number.

All names beginning Mc and Mac are listed as if they began Mac, e.g. McDevitt before MacDonald.

In the case of surnames beginning De, Des, Du, van or von the entries are normally found under the prefix. Names beginning St are listed as if they began Saint, e.g. St Germain before Salamun.

It should be noted that in some countries (including The People's Republic of China, The Republic of Korea, The Democratic People's Republic of Korea, Cambodia and Viet Nam) the family name is given first, followed by the given name; however, this does not affect alphabetization.

In Indonesia some people have only one name, under which their entries are alphabetized. In Thailand people often have two names, but these do not always equate to Western usage. We alphabetize the entries under the better-known name, providing the full name in the entry and cross-references where considered necessary.

Arabic names have been transliterated from the written form, rather than from pronunciation (which can vary from place to place). However, in Arabic pronunciation, when the word to which the definite article, al, is attached begins with one of certain letters called 'Sun-letters', the l of the article changes to the initial letter in question, e.g. al-shamsu (the sun) is pronounced ash-shamsu. Accordingly, where the article is attached to a name beginning with a Sun-letter, it has been rendered phonetically. Names beginning with 'Moon-letters', however, retain the l of the definite article. Names with Arabic prefixes are alphabetized after the prefix, unless requested otherwise by the entrant.

In a few cases consistency of transliteration has been sacrificed in order to avoid replacing a familiar and accepted form of a name by another which, although more accurate, would be unrecognizable.

CONTENTS

	page
Abbreviations	viii
International Telephone Codes	xviii
Obituary	xx

PART ONE

Biographies ... 3

PART TWO

Directory

Appendix A: Literary Awards and Prizes	877
Appendix B: Literary Organizations	884
Appendix C: Literary Festivals	890
Appendix D: National Libraries	892

ABBREVIATIONS

AA	Associate in Arts		AM	amplitude modulation
AAA	Agricultural Adjustment Administration		AM	Master of Arts
AAAS	American Association for the Advancement of Science		AM	Member of the Order of Australia
AAF	Army Air Force		Amb.	Ambassador
AASA	Associate of the Australian Society of Accountants		AMICE	Associate Member of the Institution of Civil Engineers
AB	Aktiebolag		AMIEE	Associate Member of the Institution of Electrical Engineers
AB	Alberta		AMIMechE	Associate Member of the Institution of Mechanical Engineers
AB	Bachelor of Arts		ANC	African National Congress
ABA	American Bar Association		ANU	Australian National University
ABC	American Broadcasting Company		AO	Officer of the Order of Australia
ABC	Australian Broadcasting Corporation		AP	Andhra Pradesh (India)
ABRSM	Associated Board for the Royal Schools of Music		Apdo	Apartado (Post Box)
AC	Companion of the Order of Australia		APEC	Asia and Pacific Economic Co-operation
ACA	American Composers' Alliance		approx.	approximately
ACA	Associate of the Institute of Chartered Accountants		appt	appointment
Acad.	Académie, Academy		apptd	appointed
Acad.	Académie		APRA	Australian Performing Rights Association
Acad.	Academy		apt	apartment
ACCA	Associate of the Association of Certified Accountants		apto	apartamento
Accad.	Accademia		A&R	Artists and Repertoire
accred	accredited		AR	Arkansas
ACIS	Associate of the Chartered Institute of Secretaries		ARA	Associate of the Royal Academy
ACLS	American Council of Learned Societies		ARAM	Associate of the Royal Academy of Music
ACM	Academy of Country Music		ARAS	Associate of the Royal Astronomical Society
ACP	American College of Physicians		ARC	Agriculture Research Council
ACS	American Chemical Society		ARCA	Associate of the Royal College of Art
ACT	Australian Capital Territory		ARCM	Associate of the Royal College of Music
ADB	African Development Bank		ARCO	Associate of the Royal College of Organists
ADC	Aide-de-camp		ARCS	Associate of the Royal College of Science
Adm.	Admiral		ARIBA	Associate of the Royal Institute of British Architects
Admin.	Administration, Administrative, Administrator		Ariz.	Arizona
Admin	Administration		Ark.	Arkansas
Admin.	Administrative		ARSA	Associate of the Royal Scottish Academy, Associate of the Royal Society of Arts
Admin.	Administrator			
AE	Air Efficiency Award		ARSA	Associate of the Royal Scottish Academy
AERE	Atomic Energy Research Establishment		ARSA	Associate of the Royal Society of Arts
AF	Air Force		ASCAP	American Society of Composers, Authors and Publishers
AFC	Air Force Cross		ASEAN	Association of South-East Asian Nations
affil.	affiliated		ASLIB	Association of Special Libraries and Information Bureaux
AFL	American Federation of Labor		ASME	American Society of Mechanical Engineers
AFM	Air Force Medal		Asoc.	Asociación
AFofM	American Federation of Musicians		Ass.	Assembly
AFtrA	American Federation of Television and Radio Artists		Asscn	Association
AG	Aktiengesellschaft (Joint Stock Company)		Assoc.	Associate
AGMA	American Guild of Musical Artists		ASSR	Autonomous Soviet Socialist Republic
Agric.	Agriculture		Asst	Assistant
a.i.	ad interim		Atd	Art Teacher's Diploma
AIA	American Institute of Architects, Associate of the Institute of Actuaries		ATV	Associated Television
			Aug.	August
AIA	American Institute of Architects		autobiog.	autobiography
AIA	Associate of the Institute of Actuaries		Avda	Avenida (Avenue)
AIAA	American Institute of Aeronautics and Astronautics		AZ	Arizona
AIB	Associate of the Institute of Bankers			
AICC	All-India Congress Committee		b.	born
AICE	Associate of the Institute of Civil Engineers		BA	Bachelor of Arts, British Airways
AIChE	American Institute of Chemical Engineers		BA	Bachelor of Arts
AIDS	Acquired Immune Deficiency Syndrome		BA	British Airways
AIEE	American Institute of Electrical Engineers		BAAS	British Association for the Advancement of Science
AIME	American Institute of Mining Engineers, Associate of the Institution of Mining Engineers		BAC&S	British Academy of Composers and Songwriters
			BAFTA	British Academy of Film and Television Arts
AIME	American Institute of Mining Engineers		BAgr	Bachelor of Agriculture
AIME	Associate of the Institution of Mining Engineers		BAgrSc	Bachelor of Agricultural Science
AIMechE	Associate of the Institution of Mechanical Engineers		BAO	Bachelor of Obstetrics
AIR	All-India Radio		BAOR	British Army of the Rhine
AK	Alaska		BArch	Bachelor of Architecture
AK	Knight of the Order of Australia		Bart	Baronet
aka	also known as		BAS	Bachelor in Agricultural Science
Akad.	Akademie		BASc	Bachelor of Applied Science
AL	Alabama		BASCA	British Association of Songwriters, Composers and Authors (now BAC&S)
Ala	Alabama			
ALCS	Authors' Lending and Copyright Society		BBA	Bachelor of Business Administration
ALS	Associate of the Linnaean Society		BBC	British Broadcasting Corporation
Alt.	Alternate		BC	British Columbia
AM	Albert Medal, Alpes Maritimes, Master of Arts, Member of the Order of Australia		BCC	British Council of Churches
			BCE	Bachelor of Civil Engineering
AM	Albert Medal		BChir	Bachelor of Surgery
AM	Alpes Maritimes		BCL	Bachelor of Canon Law, Bachelor of Civil Law

ABBREVIATIONS

BCL	Bachelor of Canon Law		CBS	Columbia Broadcasting System
BCL	Bachelor of Civil Law		CBSO	City of Birmingham Symphony Orchestra
BCom	Bachelor of Commerce		CC	Companion of the Order of Canada
BComm	Bachelor of Commerce		CChem	Chartered Chemist
BCS	Bachelor of Commercial Sciences		CCMA	Canadian Country Music Association
BD	Bachelor of Divinity		CCMI	Companion of the Chartered Management Institute (formerly CIMgt)
Bd	Board			
BDS	Bachelor of Dental Surgery		CCP	Chinese Communist Party
Bdwy	Broadway		CD	Canadian Forces Decoration, Commander Order of Distinction
BE	Bachelor of Education, Bachelor of Engineering			
BE	Bachelor of Education		CD	Canadian Forces Decoration
BE	Bachelor of Engineering		CD	Commander Order of Distinction
BEA	British European Airways		CD	compact disc
BEcons	Bachelor of Economics		Cdre	Commodore
BEd	Bachelor of Education		CD-ROM	compact disc read-only memory
Beds.	Bedfordshire		CDU	Christlich-Demokratische Union
BEE	Bachelor of Electrical Engineering		CE	Chartered Engineer, Civil Engineer
BEM	British Empire Medal		CE	Chartered Engineer
BEng	Bachelor of Engineering		CE	Civil Engineer
Berks.	Berkshire		CEAO	Communauté Economique de l'Afrique de l'Ouest
BET	Black Entertainment Television		Cen.	Central
BFA	Bachelor of Fine Arts		CEng	Chartered Engineer
BFI	British Film Institute		CENTO	Central Treaty Organization
BIM	British Institute of Management		CEO	Chief Executive Officer
biog.	biography		CERN	Conseil (now Organisation) Européen(ne) pour la Recherche Nucléaire
BIS	Bank for International Settlements			
BJ	Bachelor of Journalism		CFR	Commander of the Federal Republic of Nigeria
BL	Bachelor of Laws		CGM	Conspicuous Gallantry Medal
BLA	Bachelor of Landscape Architecture		CGT	Confédération Général du Travail
Bldg	Building		CH	Companion of Honour
BLit	Bachelor of Letters		Chair.	Chairman, Chairwoman, Chairperson
BLit	Bachelor of Literature		Chair.	Chairman
BLit(t)	Bachelor of Letters		Chair.	Chairperson
BLitt	Bachelor of Letters		Chair.	Chairwoman
BLitt	Bachelor of Literature		ChB	Bachelor of Surgery
BLL	Bachelor of Laws		CHB	Companion of Honour of Barbados
BLS	Bachelor in Library Science		Chem.	Chemistry
blvd	boulevard		ChM	Master of Surgery
BM	Bachelor of Medicine		CI	Channel Islands
BM	Bachelor of Music		CIA	Central Intelligence Agency
BMA	British Medical Association		Cia	Compagnia, Companhia (Company)
BME	Bachelor of Music Education		Cía	Compañía (Company)
BMEd	Bachelor of Music Education		CID	Criminal Investigation Department
BMI	Broadcast Music Incorporated		Cie	Compagnie (Company)
BMus	Bachelor of Music		CIE	Companion of (the Order of) the Indian Empire
Bn	Battalion		CIEE	Companion of the Institution of Electrical Engineers
BNOC	British National Oil Corporation		CIMgt	Companion of the Institute of Management (now CCMI)
BOAC	British Overseas Airways Corporation		C-in-C	Commander-in-Chief
BP	Boîte Postale (Post Box)		CIO	Congress of Industrial Organizations
BPA	Bachelor of Public Administration		CIOMS	Council of International Organizations of Medical Science
BPharm	Bachelor of Pharmacy		circ.	circulation
BPhil	Bachelor of Philosophy		CIS	Commonwealth of Independent States
Br.	Branch		CLD	Doctor of Civil Law (USA)
Brig.	Brigadier		CLit	Companion of Literature
BS	Bachelor of Science, Bachelor of Surgery		CM	Canada Medal, Master of Surgery
BS	Bachelor of Science		CM	Canada Medal
BS	Bachelor of Surgery		CM	Master of Surgery
BSA	Bachelor of Scientific Agriculture		CMA	Country Music Association
BSc	Bachelor of Science		CMEA	Council for Mutual Economic Assistance
BSE	Bachelor of Science in Engineering (USA)		CMG	Companion of (the Order of) St Michael and St George
BSFA	British Science Fiction Association		CNAA	Council for National Academic Awards
Bt	Baronet		CNRS	Centre National de la Recherche Scientifique
BTh	Bachelor of Theology		CO	Chamber Orchestra
BTI	British Theatre Institute		CO	Colorado
Bucks.	Buckinghamshire		CO	Commanding Officer
			Co.	Company, County
c.	circa		Co.	Company
c.	child(ren)		Co.	County
c/o	care of		COI	Central Office of Information
CA	California		Col	Colonel
CA	Chartered Accountant		Col.	Colonia, Colima (hill)
Calif.	California		Coll.	College
Cambs.	Cambridgeshire		Colo	Colorado
CAMI	Columbia Artists Management International		COMECON	Council for Mutual Economic Assistance
Cand.	Candidate, Candidature		COMESA	Common Market for Eastern and Southern Asia
Cand.	Candidate		Comm.	Commission
Cand.	Candidature		Commdg	Commanding
Cantab.	of Cambridge University		Commdr	Commander, Commandeur
Capt.	Captain		Commdr	Commander
Cards.	Cardiganshire		Commdr	Commandeur
CB	Companion of (the Order of) the Bath		Commdt	Commandant
CBC	Canadian Broadcasting Corporation		Commr	Commissioner
CBE	Commander of (the Order of) the British Empire		CON	Commander of Order of Nigeria
CBI	Confederation of British Industry		Conf.	Conference
CBIM	Companion of the British Institute of Management		Confed.	Confederation
CBiol	Chartered Biologist		Conn.	Connecticut

ABBREVIATIONS

Contrib.	contribution, Contributor
Contrib.	contribution
Contrib.	Contributor
COO	Chief Operating Officer
Corp.	Corporate
Corpn	Corporation
Corresp.	Correspondent, Corresponding
Corresp.	Correspondent
Corresp.	Corresponding
CP	Caixa Postal (Post Box), Communist Party
CP	Caixa Postal, Case Postale, Casella Postale (Post Box)
CP	Communist Party
CPA	Certified Public Accountant
CPA	Commonwealth Parliamentary Association
CPhys	Chartered Physicist
CPP	Convention People's Party (Ghana)
CPPCC	Chinese People's Political Consultative Conference
CPSU	Communist Party of the Soviet Union
cr.	created
CRNCM	Companion of the Royal Northern College of Music
CSc	Candidate of Sciences
CSCE	Conference on Security and Co-operation in Europe
CSI	Companion of (the Order of) the Star of India
CSIRO	Commonwealth Scientific and Industrial Research Organization
CSSR	Czechoslovak Socialist Republic
CStJ	Commander of (the Order of) St John of Jerusalem
CT	Connecticut
Cttee	Committee
CUNY	City University of New York
CV	Commanditaire Vennootschap
CVO	Commander of the Royal Victorian Order
CWA	(British) Crime Writers' Association
d.	daughter(s)
DArch	Doctor of Architecture
DB	Bachelor of Divinity
DBA	Doctor of Business Administration
DBE	Dame Commander of (the Order of) the British Empire
DC	District of Columbia
DC	Distrito Central
DCE	Doctor of Civil Engineering
DCL	Doctor of Canon Law, Doctor of Civil Law
DCL	Doctor of Canon Law
DCL	Doctor of Civil Law
DCM	Distinguished Conduct Medal
DCMG	Dame Commander of (the Order of) St Michael and St George
DCnL	Doctor of Canon Law
DComm	Doctor of Commerce
DCS	Doctor of Commercial Sciences
DCT	Doctor of Christian Theology
DCVO	Dame Commander of the Royal Victorian Order
DD	Doctor of Divinity
Dd'ES	Diplôme d'études supérieures
DDR	Deutsche Demokratische Republik (German Democratic Republic)
DDS	Doctor of Dental Surgery
DE	Delaware
Dec.	December
DEcon	Doctor of Economics
DEd	Doctor of Education
DEFRA	Department for Environment, Food and Rural Affairs
Del.	Delaware, Delegate, Delegation
Del.	Delaware
Del.	Delegate
Del.	Delegation
Denbighs.	Denbighshire
DenD	Docteur en Droit
DEng	Doctor of Engineering
DenM	Docteur en Medicine
Dep.	Deputy
Dept	Department
DES	Department of Education and Science
Desig.	Designate
DèsL	Docteur ès Lettres
DèsSc	Docteur ès Sciences
Devt	Development
DF	Distrito Federal
DFA	Diploma of Fine Arts, Doctor of Fine Arts
DFA	Diploma of Fine Arts
DFA	Doctor of Fine Arts
DFC	Distinguished Flying Cross
DFM	Distinguished Flying Medal
DH	Doctor of Humanities
DHist	Doctor of History
DHL	Doctor of Hebrew Literature
DHSS	Department of Health and Social Security
DHumLitt	Doctor of Humane Letters
DIC	Diploma of Imperial College
DipAD	Diploma in Art and Design
DipAgr	Diploma in Agriculture
DipArch	Diploma in Architecture
DipEd	Diploma in Education
DipEng	Diploma in Engineering
DipMus	Diploma in Music
DipScEconSc	Diploma of Social and Economic Science
DipTh	Diploma in Theology
Dir	Director
Dist	District
DIur	Doctor of Law
DIurUtr	Doctor of both Civil and Canon Law
Div.	Division, Divisional
Div.	Division
Div.	Divisional
DJ	disc jockey
DJur	Doctor of Law
DK	Most Esteemed Family (Malaysia)
DL	Deputy Lieutenant
DLit	Doctor of Letters
DLit	Doctor of Literature
DLit(t)	Doctor of Letters, Doctor of Literature
DLitt	Doctor of Letters
DLitt	Doctor of Literature
DLS	Doctor of Library Science
DM	Doctor of Medicine (Oxford)
DM	Doctor of Music
DMA	Doctor of Musical Arts
DMD	Doctor of Dental Medicine
DME	Doctor of Musical Education
DMEd	Doctor of Musical Education
DMedSc	Doctor of Medical Science
DMilSc	Doctor of Military Science
DMinSci	Doctor of Municipal Science
DMS	Director of Medical Services
DMus	Doctor of Music
DMusEd	Doctor of Music Education
DMV	Doctor of Veterinary Medicine
DN	Distrito Nacional
DO	Doctor of Ophthalmology
DPH	Diploma in Public Health
DPhil	Doctor of Philosophy
DPM	Diploma in Psychological Medicine
DPS	Doctor of Public Service
dpto	departamento
Dr	Doctor
Dr(a)	Doctor(a)
Dr rer. nat	Doctor of Natural Sciences
Dr rer. pol	Doctor of Political Science
DrAgr	Doctor of Agriculture
DrIng	Doctor of Engineering
DrIur	Doctor of Laws
DrMed	Doctor of Medicine
DrOecPol	Doctor of Political Economy
DrOecPubl	Doctor of (Public) Economy
DrPhilNat	Doctor of Natural Philosophy
DrSc	Doctor of Sciences
DrSci	Doctor of Sciences
DrScNat	Doctor of Natural Sciences
DS	Doctor of Science
DSC	Distinguished Service Cross
DSc	Doctor of Science
DSci	Doctor of Sciences
DScS	Doctor of Social Science
DSM	Distinguished Service Medal
DSO	Companion of the Distinguished Service Order
DSocSc	Doctor of Social Science
DSocSci	Doctor of Social Science
DST	Doctor of Sacred Theology
DTech	Doctor of Technology
DTechSc	Doctor of Technical Sciences
DTechSci	Doctor of Technical Sciences
DTh	Doctor of Theology
DTheol	Doctor of Theology
DTM	Diploma in Tropical Medicine
DTM&H	Diploma in Tropical Medicine and Hygiene
DUniv	Doctor of the University
DUP	Diploma of the University of Paris
DVD	digital versatile disc
E	East, Eastern
EBRD	European Bank for Reconstruction and Development
EC	European Commission, European Community

ABBREVIATIONS

EC	European Commission
EC	European Community
ECA	Economic Commission for Africa, Economic Co-operation Administration
ECA	Economic Commission for Africa
ECA	Economic Co-operation Administration
ECAFE	Economic Commission for Asia and the Far East
ECE	Economic Commission for Europe
ECLA	Economic Commission for Latin America
ECLAC	Economic Commission for Latin America and the Caribbean
ECO	Economic Co-operation Organization
Econ.	Economic
Econ(s)	Economic(s)
Econs	Economics
ECOSOC	Economic and Social Council
ECSC	European Coal and Steel Community
ECWA	Economic Commission for Western Asia
ED	Doctor of Engineering (USA), Efficiency Decoration
ED	Doctor of Engineering (USA)
ED	Efficiency Decoration
ed	educated
ed.	edited, editor
ed	edited
Ed.	Editor
ed.	editor
EdD	Doctor of Education
Edif.	Edificio (Building)
Edin.	Edinburgh
EdM	Master of Education
Edn	Edition
edn	edition
Educ.	Education
EEC	European Economic Community
EFTA	European Free Trade Association
e.g.	exempli gratia (for example)
eh	Ehrenhalben (Honorary)
EIB	European Investment Bank
EM	Edward Medal, Master of Engineering (USA)
EM	Edward Medal
EM	Master of Engineering (USA)
Emer.	Emerita, Emeritus
EMI	Electrical and Musical Industries
Eng	Engineering
EngD	Doctor of Engineering
ENO	English National Opera
EP	extended-play (record)
EPLF	Eritrean People's Liberation Front
ESA	European Space Agency
ESCAP	Economic and Social Commission for Asia and the Pacific
ESCWA	Economic and Social Commission for Western Asia
esq.	esquina (corner)
est.	established
etc.	et cetera
ETH	Eidgenössische Technische Hochschule (Swiss Federal Institute of Technology)
Ets	Etablissements
EU	European Union
EURATOM	European Atomic Energy Community
eV	eingetragener Verein
Exec.	Executive
Exhbn	Exhibition
Ext.	Extension
f.	founded
FAA	Fellow of the Australian Academy of Science
FAAS	Fellow of the American Association for the Advancement of Science
FAATS	Fellow of the Australian Academy of Technological Sciences
FACC	Fellow of the American College of Cardiology
FACCA	Fellow of the Association of Certified and Corporate Accountants
FACE	Fellow of the Australian College of Education
FACP	Fellow of the American College of Physicians
FACS	Fellow of the American College of Surgeons
FAHA	Fellow of the Australian Academy of the Humanities
FAIA	Fellow of the American Institute of Architects
FAIAS	Fellow of the Australian Institute of Agricultural Science
FAIM	Fellow of the Australian Institute of Management
FAO	Food and Agriculture Organization
FAS	Fellow of the Antiquarian Society
FASE	Fellow of the Antiquarian Society of Edinburgh
FASSA	Fellow of the Academy of Social Sciences of Australia
FBA	Fellow of the British Academy
FBI	Federal Bureau of Investigation
FBIM	Fellow of the British Institute of Management
FBIP	Fellow of the British Institute of Physics
FCA	Fellow of the Institute of Chartered Accountants
FCAE	Fellow of the Canadian Academy of Engineering
FCGI	Fellow of the City and Guilds of London Institute
FCIA	Fellow of the Chartered Institute of Arbitrators
FCIB	Fellow of the Chartered Institute of Bankers
FCIC	Fellow of the Chemical Institute of Canada
FCIM	Fellow of the Chartered Institute of Management
FCIS	Fellow of the Chartered Institute of Secretaries
FCMA	Fellow of the Chartered Institute of Management Accountants
FCO	Foreign and Commonwealth Office
FCSD	Fellow of the Chartered Society of Designers
FCT	Federal Capital Territory
FCWA	Fellow of the Institute of Cost and Works Accountants (now FCMA)
FDGB	Freier Deutscher Gewerkschaftsbund
FDP	Freier Demokratische Partei
Feb.	February
Fed.	Federal, Federation
Fed.	Federal
Fed.	Federation
FEng	Fellow(ship) of Engineering
FFCM	Fellow of the Faculty of Community Medicine
FFPHM	Fellow of the Faculty of Public Health Medicine
FGCM	Fellow of the Guild of Church Musicians
FGS	Fellow of the Geological Society
FGSM	Fellow of the Guildhall School of Music and Drama
FIA	Fellow of the Institute of Actuaries
FIAL	Fellow of the International Institute of Arts and Letters
FIAM	Fellow of the International Academy of Management
FIAMS	Fellow of the Indian Academy of Medical Sciences
FIAP	Fellow of the Institution of Analysts and Programmers
FIArb	Fellow of the Institute of Arbitrators
FIB	Fellow of the Institute of Bankers
FIBA	Fellow of the Institute of Banking Associations
FIBiol	Fellow of the Institute of Biologists
FICE	Fellow of the Institution of Civil Engineers
FIChemE	Fellow of the Institute of Chemical Engineers
FID	Fellow of the Institute of Directors
FIE	Fellow of the Institute of Engineers
FIEE	Fellow of the Institution of Electrical Engineers
FIEEE	Fellow of the Institute of Electrical and Electronics Engineers
FIFA	Fédération Internationale de Football Association
FIJ	Fellow of the Institute of Journalists
FilLic	Licentiate in Philosophy
FIM	Fellow of the Institute of Metallurgists
FIME	Fellow of the Institute of Mining Engineers
FIMechE	Fellow of the Institute of Mechanical Engineers
FIMI	Fellow of the Institute of the Motor Industry
FInstF	Fellow of the Institute of Fuel
FInstM	Fellow of the Institute of Marketing
FInstP	Fellow of the Institute of Physics
FInstPet	Fellow of the Institute of Petroleum
FIPM	Fellow of the Institute of Personnel Management
FIRE	Fellow of the Institution of Radio Engineers
FItd	Fellow of the Institute of Training and Development
FL	Florida
FLA	Fellow of the Library Association
Fla	Florida
FLN	Front de Libération Nationale
FLS	Fellow of the Linnaean Society
FM	frequency modulation
FMA	Florida Music Association
FMedSci	Fellow of the Academy of Medical Sciences
fmr	former
fmrly	formerly
FNI	Fellow of the National Institute of Sciences of India
FNZIA	Fellow of the New Zealand Institute of Architects
FRACP	Fellow of the Royal Australasian College of Physicians
FRACS	Fellow of the Royal Australasian College of Surgeons
FRAeS	Fellow of the Royal Aeronautical Society
FRAI	Fellow of the Royal Anthropological Institute
FRAIA	Fellow of the Royal Australian Institute of Architects
FRAIC	Fellow of the Royal Architectural Institute of Canada
FRAM	Fellow of the Royal Academy of Music
FRAS	Fellow of the Royal Asiatic Society, Fellow of the Royal Astronomical Society
FRAS	Fellow of the Royal Asiatic Society
FRAS	Fellow of the Royal Astronomical Society
FRBS	Fellow of the Royal Society of British Sculptors
FRCA	Fellow of the Royal College of Anaesthetists
FRCM	Fellow of the Royal College of Music
FRCO	Fellow of the Royal College of Organists
FRCOG	Fellow of the Royal College of Obstetricians and Gynaecologists
FRCP	Fellow of the Royal College of Physicians (UK)

ABBREVIATIONS

FRCPath	Fellow of the Royal College of Pathologists	HE	His (or Her) Excellency
FRCP(E)	Fellow of the Royal College of Physicians (Edinburgh)	Herefords.	Herefordshire
FRCPE	Fellow of the Royal College of Physicians, Edinburgh	Herts.	Hertfordshire
FRCPGlas	Fellow of the Royal College of Physicians (Glasgow)	HH	His (or Her) Highness
FRCPI	Fellow of the Royal College of Physicians of Ireland	HHD	Doctor of Humanities
FRCR	Fellow of the Royal College of Radiology	HI	Hawaii
FRCS	Fellow of the Royal College of Surgeons	HIV	human immunodeficiency virus
FRCS(E)	Fellow of the Royal College of Surgeons (Edinburgh)	HLD	Doctor of Humane Letters
FRCSE	Fellow of the Royal College of Surgeons, Edinburgh	HM	His (or Her) Majesty
FRCVS	Fellow of the Royal College of Veterinary Surgeons	HMS	His (or Her) Majesty's Ship
FREconS	Fellow of the Royal Economic Society	Hon.	Honorary, Honourable
FREng	Fellow of the Royal Academy of Engineering	Hon.	Honorary
FRES	Fellow of the Royal Entomological Society	Hon.	Honourable
FRFPS	Fellow of the Royal Faculty of Physicians and Surgeons	Hons	Honours
FRG	Federal Republic of Germany	Hosp.	Hospital
FRGS	Fellow of the Royal Geographical Society	HQ	Headquarters
FRHistS	Fellow of the Royal Historical Society	HRH	His (or Her) Royal Highness
FRHortS	Fellow of the Royal Horticultural Society	HS	Heraldry Society
FRIBA	Fellow of the Royal Institute of British Architects	HSH	His (or Her) Serene Highness
FRIC	Fellow of the Royal Institute of Chemists	HSP	Hungarian Socialist Party
FRICS	Fellow of the Royal Institute of Chartered Surveyors	HSWP	Hungarian Socialist Workers' Party
FRMetS	Fellow of the Royal Meteorological Society	Hunts.	Huntingdonshire
FRNCM	Fellow of the Royal Northern College of Music		
FRPS	Fellow of the Royal Photographic Society	IA	Iowa
FRS	Fellow of the Royal Society	Ia	Iowa
FRSA	Fellow of the Royal Society of Arts	IAAF	International Association of Athletics Federations
FRSAMD	Fellow of the Royal Scottish Academy of Music and Drama	IAEA	International Atomic Energy Agency
FRSC	Fellow of the Royal Society of Canada, Fellow of the Royal Society of Chemistry	IATA	International Air Transport Association
		IBA	Independent Broadcasting Authority
FRSC	Fellow of the Royal Society of Canada	IBRD	International Bank for Reconstruction and Development (World Bank)
FRSC	Fellow of the Royal Society of Chemistry		
FRSE	Fellow of the Royal Society of Edinburgh	ICAO	International Civil Aviation Organization
FRSL	Fellow of the Royal Society of Literature	ICC	International Chamber of Commerce
FRSM	Fellow of the Royal Society of Medicine	ICE	Institution of Civil Engineers
FRSNZ	Fellow of the Royal Society of New Zealand	ICEM	Intergovernmental Committee for European Migration
FRSS	Fellow of the Royal Statistical Society	ICFTU	International Confederation of Free Trade Unions
FRSSA	Fellow of the Royal Society of South Africa	ICI	Imperial Chemical Industries
FRTS	Fellow of the Royal Television Society	ICOM	International Council of Museums
FSA	Fellow of the Society of Antiquaries	ICRC	International Committee for the Red Cross
FSIAD	Fellow of the Society of Industrial Artists and Designers	ICS	Indian Civil Service
FTCL	Fellow of Trinity College London	ICSID	International Centre for Settlement of Investment Disputes
FTI	Fellow of the Textile Institute	ICSU	International Council of Scientific Unions
FTS	Fellow of Technological Sciences	ID	Idaho
FWAAS	Fellow of the World Academy of Arts and Sciences	Ida	Idaho
FZS	Fellow of the Zoological Society	IDA	International Development Association
		IDB	Inter-American Development Bank
GA	Georgia	i.e.	id est (that is to say)
Ga	Georgia	IEA	International Energy Agency
GATT	General Agreement on Tariffs and Trade	IEE	Institution of Electrical Engineers
GB	Great Britain	IEEE	Institution of Electrical and Electronic Engineers
GBE	Knight (or Dame) Grand Cross of (the Order of) the British Empire	IFAD	International Fund for Agricultural Development
		IFC	International Finance Corporation
GC	George Cross	IGAD	Intergovernmental Authority on Development
GCB	Knight Grand Cross of (the Order of) the Bath	IISS	International Institute for Strategic Studies
GCIE	Knight Grand Commander of (the Order of) the Indian Empire	IL	Illinois
		Ill.	Illinois
GCMG	Knight (or Dame) Grand Cross of (the Order of) St Michael and St George	ILO	International Labour Organization
		IMC	International Music Council
GCSI	Knight Grand Commander of (the Order of) the Star of India	IMCO	Inter-Governmental Maritime Consultative Organization
GCVO	Knight (or Dame) Grand Cross of the Royal Victorian Order	IMechE	Institution of Mechanical Engineers
GDR	German Democratic Republic	IMF	International Monetary Fund
Gen.	General	IMMIE	Indian Music Excellence (award)
GHQ	General Headquarters	IMO	International Maritime Organization
GLA	Greater London Authority	IN	Indiana
Glam.	Glamorganshire	Inc.	Incorporated
GLC	Greater London Council	incl.	including
Glos.	Gloucestershire	Ind.	Independent, Indiana
GM	George Medal	Ind.	Independent
GmbH	Gesellschaft mit beschränkter Haftung (Limited Liability Company)	Ind.	Indiana
		Insp.	Inspector
GMT	Greenwich Mean Time	Inst.	Institute, Institution
GOC	General Officer Commanding	Inst.	Institute
GOC-in-C	General Officer Commanding-in-Chief	Inst.	Institution
Gov.	Governor	Int.	International
Govt	Government	INTERPOL	International Criminal Police Organization
GP	General Practitioner	INTUC	Indian National Trades Union Congress
GPO	General Post Office	IOC	International Olympic Committee
Grad.	Graduate	IPC	Institute of Professional Critics
GRSM	Graduate of the Royal School of Music	IPU	Inter-Parliamentary Union
GSMD	Guildhall School of Music and Drama, London	IRCAM	Institut de Recherche et Coordination Acoustique/Musique
GSO	General Staff Officer	ISCM	International Society for Contemporary Music
		ISM	Incorporated Society of Musicians
Hants.	Hampshire	ISO	Companion of the Imperial Service Order
hc	honoris causa	ITA	Independent Television Authority
HE	His Eminence, His (or Her) Excellency	ITN	Independent Television News
HE	His Eminence	ITU	International Telecommunications Union

ABBREVIATIONS

ITV	Independent Television	Ltd(a)	Limited, Limitada
IUPAC	International Union of Pure and Applied Chemistry	Ltda	Limitada
IUPAP	International Union of Pure and Applied Physics	LTh	Licentiate in Theology
		LVO	Lieutenant, Royal Victorian Order
Jan.	January	LW	long wave
JCB	Bachelor of Canon Law	LWT	London Weekend Television
JCD	Doctor of Canon Law		
JD	Doctor of Jurisprudence		
JMK	Johan Mangku Negara (Malaysia)	m.	marriage, married, metre(s)
JP	Justice of the Peace	m.	marriage
Jr	Junior	m.	married
JSD	Doctor of Juristic Science	m.	metre(s)
Jt	Joint	MA	Massachusetts
Jtly	Jointly	MA	Master of Arts
JuD	Doctor of Law	MAgr	Master of Agriculture (USA)
JUD	Juris utriusque Doctor (Doctor of both Civil and Canon Law)	Maj.	Major
JUDr	Juris utriusque Doctor (Doctor of both Civil and Canon Law), Doctor of Law	MALD	Master of Arts in Law and Diplomacy
		Man.	Management, Manager, Managing, Manitoba
		Man.	Management
Kan.	Kansas	Man.	Manager
KBE	Knight Commander of (the Order of) the British Empire	Man.	Managing
KC	King's Counsel	Man.	Manitoba
KCB	Knight Commander of (the Order of) the Bath	MArch	Master of Architecture
KCIE	Knight Commander of (the Order of) the Indian Empire	Mass	Massachusetts
KCMG	Knight Commander of (the Order of) St Michael and St George	MAT	Master of Arts and Teaching
		Math.	Mathematical, Mathematics
KCSI	Knight Commander of (the Order of) the Star of India	Math.	Mathematical
KCVO	Knight Commander of the Royal Victorian Order	Math.	Mathematics
KG	Royal Knight of the Most Noble Order of the Garter	MB	Bachelor of Medicine
KGB	Committee of State Security (USSR)	MB	Manitoba
KK	Kaien Kaisha	MBA	Master of Business Administration
KLM	Koninklijke Luchtvaart Maatschappij (Royal Dutch Airlines)	MBE	Member of (the Order of) the British Empire
km	kilometre(s)	MBS	Master of Business Studies
KNZM	Knight of the New Zealand Order of Merit	MC	master of ceremonies
KP	Knight of (the Order of) St Patrick	MCC	Military Cross
KS	Kansas	MCC	Marylebone Cricket Club
KStJ	Knight of (the Order of) St John of Jerusalem	MCE	Master of Civil Engineering
Kt	Knight	MCh	Master of Surgery
KT	Knight of (the Order of) the Thistle	MChD	Master of Dental Surgery
KY	Kentucky	MCL	Master of Civil Law
Ky	Kentucky	MCom	Master of Commerce
		MComm	Master of Commerce
LA	Los Angeles	MCP	Master of City Planning
LA	Louisiana	MD	Doctor of Medicine
La	Louisiana	MD	Maryland
Lab.	Laboratory	Md	Maryland
LAMDA	London Academy of Music and Dramatic Art	MD	Music Director
Lancs.	Lancashire	MDiv	Master of Divinity
LDP	Liberal Democratic Party	MDS	Master of Dental Surgery
LDS	Licentiate in Dental Surgery	Me	Maine
LEA	Local Education Authority	ME	Maine
Legis.	Legislative	ME	Myalgic Encephalomyehtis
Leics.	Leicestershire	MEconSc	Master of Economic Sciences
LenD	Licencié en Droit	MEd	Master of Education
LèsL	Licencié ès Lettres	mem.	member
LèsSc	Licencié ès Sciences	MEng	Master of Engineering (Dublin)
LG	Lady of (the Order of) the Garter	MEngSc	Master of Engineering
LHD	Doctor of Humane Letters	MEP	Member of European Parliament
LI	Long Island	Met	Metropolitan Opera House, New York
LicenDer	Licenciado en Derecho	MFA	Master of Fine Arts
LicenFil	Licenciado en Filosofía	Mfg	Manufacturing
LicenLet	Licenciado en Letras	Mfrs	Manufacturers
LicMed	Licentiate in Medicine	Mgr	Monseigneur, Monsignor
Lincs.	Lincolnshire	Mgr	Monseigneur
LittD	Doctor of Letters	Mgr	Monsignor
LLB	Bachelor of Laws	MHRA	Modern Humanities Research Association
LLC	Limited Liability Company	MHz	megahertz (megacycles)
LLD	Doctor of Laws	MI	Marshall Islands
LLL	Licentiate of Laws	MI	Michigan
LLM	Master of Laws	MIA	Master of International Affairs
LLP	Limited Liability Partnership	MICE	Member of the Institution of Civil Engineers
LM	Licentiate of Medicine, Licentiate of Midwifery	Mich.	Michigan
LM	Licentiate of Medicine	MIChemE	Member of the Institution of Chemical Engineers
LM	Licentiate of Midwifery	Middx	Middlesex
LN	League of Nations	MIDI	Musical Instrument Digital Interface
LP	long-playing (record)	MIEE	Member of the Institution of Electrical Engineers
LPh	Licentiate of Philosophy	Mil.	Military
LPO	London Philharmonic Orchestra	MIMarE	Member of the Institute of Marine Engineers
LRAM	Licentiate of the Royal Academy of Music	MIMechE	Member of the Institution of Mechanical Engineers
LRCP	Licentiate of the Royal College of Physicians	MIMinE	Member of the Institution of Mining Engineers
LRSM	Licentiate of the Royal Schools of Music	Minn.	Minnesota
LSE	London School of Economics and Political Science	MInstT	Member of the Institute of Transport
LSO	London Symphony Orchestra	Miss.	Mississippi
Lt	Lieutenant	MIStructE	Member of the Institution of Structural Engineers
LTCL	Licentiate of Trinity College of Music, London	MIT	Massachusetts Institute of Technology
Ltd	Limited	MJ	Master of Jurisprudence

ABBREVIATIONS

MLA	Master of Landscape Architecture, Member of the Legislative Assembly
MLA	Master of Landscape Architecture
MLA	Member of the Legislative Assembly
MLA	Modern Language Association
MLC	Member of the Legislative Council
MLitt	Master of Letters
MLitt	Master of Literature
MLS	Master of Library Science
MM	Master of Music
MM	Military Medal
MME	Master of Music Education
MMEd	Master of Music Education
MMus	Master of Music
MN	Minnesota
MNOC	Movement of Non-Aligned Countries
MO	Missouri
Mo.	Missouri
MOBO	Music of Black Origin
MOH	Medical Officer of Health
Mon.	Monmouthshire
Mont.	Montana
Movt	Movement
MP	Madhya Pradesh (India), Member of Parliament
MP	Madhya Pradesh (India)
MP	Member of Parliament
MP3	MPEG-1 Audio Layer-3 (audio compression format)
MPA	Master of Public Administration (Harvard)
MPEG	Moving Picture Experts Group
MPh	Master of Philosophy (USA)
MPhil	Master of Philosophy
MPolSci	Master of Political Science
MPP	Member of Provincial Parliament (Canada)
MRAS	Member of the Royal Asiatic Society
MRC	Medical Research Council
MRCP	Member of the Royal College of Physicians
MRCP(E)	Member of the Royal College of Physicians (Edinburgh)
MRCPE	Member of the Royal College of Physicians, Edinburgh
MRCS	Member of the Royal College of Surgeons of England
MRCSE	Member of the Royal College of Surgeons, Edinburgh
MRCVS	Member of the Royal College of Veterinary Surgeons
MRI	Member of the Royal Institution
MRIA	Member of the Royal Irish Academy
MRIC	Member of the Royal Institute of Chemistry
MRP	Mouvement Républicain Populaire
MS	manuscript
MS	Master of Science, Master of Surgery
MS	Master of Science
MS	Master of Surgery
MS	Mississippi
MSA	Memphis Songwriters' Association
MSc	Master of Science
MScS	Master of Social Science
MSO	Melbourne Symphony Orchestra
MSP	Member Scottish Parliament
MT	Montana
MTh	Master of Theology
MTS	Master of Theological Studies
MTV	Music Television
MUDr	Doctor of Medicine
MusB	Bachelor of Music
MusBac	Bachelor of Music
MusD	Doctor of Music
MusDoc	Doctor of Music
MusM	Master of Music (Cambridge)
MVD	Master of Veterinary Medicine
MVO	Member of the Royal Victorian Order
MW	Master of Wine
MW	medium wave
MWA	Mystery Writers of America
N	North, Northern
NABOB	National Association of Black-Owned Broadcasters
NARAS	National Academy of Recording Arts and Sciences
NAS	National Academy of Sciences (USA)
NAS	National Academy of Songwriters
NASA	National Aeronautics and Space Administration
Nat.	National
NATO	North Atlantic Treaty Organization
Naz.	Nazionale
NB	New Brunswick
NBC	National Broadcasting Company
NC	North Carolina
ND	North Dakota
NDD	National Diploma in Design
NE	Nebraska
NE	North East
NEA	National Endowment for the Arts
Neb.	Nebraska
NEDC	National Economic Development Council
NEH	National Endowment for the Humanities
NERC	Natural Environment Research Council
Nev.	Nevada
NF	Newfoundland
NFSPS	National Federation of State Poetry Societies
NGO	non-governmental organization
NH	New Hampshire
NHK	Nippon Hoso Kyokai (Japanese broadcasting system)
NHS	National Health Service
NI	Northern Ireland
NIH	National Institutes of Health
NJ	New Jersey
NL	Newfoundland and Labrador
NM	New Mexico
NME	New Musical Express
no.	number
Northants.	Northamptonshire
Notts.	Nottinghamshire
Nov.	November
NPC	National People's Congress
nr	near
NRC	Nuclear Research Council
NRK	Norsk Rikskringkasting (Norwegian broadcasting system)
NS	Nova Scotia
NSAI	Nashville Songwriters' Association International
NSF	National Science Foundation
NSW	New South Wales
NT	Northern Territory
NT	Northwest Territories
NU	Nunavut Territory
NUJ	National Union of Journalists
NV	Naamloze Vennootschap
NV	Nevada
NW	North West
NWT	North West Territories
NY	New York (State)
NYPO	New York Philharmonic Orchestra
NYSO	New York Symphony Orchestra
NZ	New Zealand
NZIC	New Zealand Institute of Chemistry
NZSA	New Zealand Society of Authors
O	Ohio
OAPEC	Organization of Arab Petroleum Exporting Countries
OAS	Organization of American States
OAU	Organization of African Unity
OBE	Officer of (the Order of) the British Empire
OC	Officer of the Order of Canada
Oct.	October
OE	Order of Excellence (Guyana)
OECD	Organisation for Economic Co-operation and Development
OEEC	Organization for European Economic Co-operation
Of.	Oficina (Office)
OFS	Orange Free State
OH	Ohio
OHCHR	Office of the United Nations High Commissioner for Human Rights
OIC	Organization of the Islamic Conference
OJ	Order of Jamaica
OK	Oklahoma
Okla	Oklahoma
OM	Member of the Order of Merit
ON	Ontario
ON	Order of Nigeria
Ont.	Ontario
ONZ	Order of New Zealand
ONZM	Officer of the New Zealand Order of Merit
OP	Ordo Praedicatorum (Dominicans)
OPCW	Organization for the Prohibition of Chemical Weapons
OPEC	Organization of the Petroleum Exporting Countries
OPM	Office of Production Management
OQ	Officer National Order of Québec
OR	Oregon
Ore.	Oregon
Org.	Organization
ORTF	Office de Radiodiffusion-Télévision Française
OSB	Order of St Benedict
OSCE	Organization for Security and Co-operation in Europe
OST	original soundtrack
Oxon.	of Oxford University, Oxfordshire
Oxon.	of Oxford University
Oxon.	Oxfordshire

ABBREVIATIONS

PA	Pennsylvania	QSO	Queensland Symphony Orchestra
Pa.	Pennsylvania	q.v.	quod vide (to which refer)
Parl.	Parliament, Parliamentary		
Parl.	Parliament	RA	Royal Academician, Royal Academy, Royal Artillery
Parl.	Parliamentary	RA	Royal Academician
PBS	Public Broadcasting Service	RA	Royal Academy
PC	Privy Councillor	RA	Royal Artillery
PCC	Provincial Congress Committee	RAAF	Royal Australian Air Force
PdB	Bachelor of Pedagogy	RAC	Royal Armoured Corps
PdD	Doctor of Pedagogy	RACP	Royal Australasian College of Physicians
PdM	Master of Pedagogy	RADA	Royal Academy of Dramatic Art
PDS	Partei des Demokratischen Sozialismus	RAF	Royal Air Force
PE	Prince Edward Island	RAFVR	Royal Air Force Volunteer Reserve
PEI	Prince Edward Island	RAH	Royal Albert Hall, London
Pembs.	Pembrokeshire	RAI	Radio Audizioni Italiane
PEN	Poets, Playwrights, Essayists, Editors and Novelists (Club)	RAM	Royal Academy of Music
Perm.	Permanent	RAMC	Royal Army Medical Corps
PETA	People for the Ethical Treatment of Animals	RAOC	Royal Army Ordnance Corps
PF	Postfach (Post Box)	R&B	Rhythm and Blues
PGCE	Postgraduate Certificate of Education	RC	Roman Catholic
PharmD	Docteur en Pharmacie	RCA	Radio Corporation of America, Royal Canadian Academy, Royal College of Art
PhB	Bachelor of Philosophy		
PhD	Doctor of Philosophy	RCA	Radio Corporation of America
PhDr	Doctor of Philosophy	RCA	Royal Canadian Academy
Phila	Philadelphia	RCA	Royal College of Art
PhL	Licentiate of Philosophy	RCAF	Royal Canadian Air Force
PLA	People's Liberation Army, Port of London Authority	RCM	Royal College of Music
PLA	People's Liberation Army	RCO	Royal College of Organists
PLA	Port of London Authority	RCP	Romanian Communist Party
PLC	Public Limited Company	RCP	Royal College of Physicians
PLO	Palestine Liberation Organization	RCPI	Royal College of Physicians of Ireland
PMB	Private Mail Bag	Regt	Regiment
pnr	partner	REME	Royal Electric and Mechanical Engineers
PO	Philharmonia Orchestra	Rep.	Representative, Represented
PO	Post Office	Rep.	Representative
PO Box	Post Office Box	Rep.	Represented
POB	Post Office Box	Repub.	Republic
POW	Prisoner of War	resgnd	resigned
PPR	Polish Workers' Party	retd	retired
PPRA	Past President of the Royal Academy	Rev.	Reverend
PPRNCM	Professsional Performer of the Royal Northern College of Music	rev. edn	revised edition
		RFH	Royal Festival Hall, London
PQ	Province of Québec	RGS	Royal Geographical Society
PR	Puerto Rico	RI	Rhode Island
PR(O)	Public Relations (Officer)	RIAS	Radio im Amerikanischen Sektor
PRA	President of the Royal Academy	RIBA	Royal Institute of British Architects
Pref.	Prefecture	RLPO	Royal Liverpool Philharmonic Orchestra
Prep.	Preparatory	RMA	Royal Military Academy
Pres.	President	RMA	Royal Musical Association
PRI	President of the Royal Institute (of Painters in Water Colours)	RN	Royal Navy
		RNCM	Royal Northern College of Music (formerly Royal Manchester College of Music)
PRIBA	President of the Royal Institute of British Architects		
Prin.	Principal	RNLI	Royal National Life-boat Institution
Priv Doz	Privat Dozent (recognized teacher not on the regular staff)	RNR	Royal Naval Reserve
PRO	Public Relations Officer	RNVR	Royal Naval Volunteer Reserve
Proc.	Proceedings	RNZAF	Royal New Zealand Air Force
Prod.	Producer	RO	Radio Orchestra
Prof.	Professor	ROC	Rock Out Censorship
promo	promotional	ROH	Royal Opera House, London
Propr	Proprietor	RP	Member Royal Society of Portrait Painters
Prov.	Province, Provincial	rpm	revolutions per minute
Prov.	Province	RPO	Royal Philharmonic Orchestra
Prov.	Provincial	RPR	Rassemblement pour la République
PRS	Performing Right Society	RSA	Royal Scottish Academy, Royal Society of Arts
PRS	President of the Royal Society	RSA	Royal Scottish Academy
PRSA	President of the Royal Scottish Academy	RSA	Royal Society of Arts
PSM	Panglima Setia Mahkota (Malaysia)	RSAMD	Royal Scottish Academy of Music and Drama
pt	part	RSC	Royal Shakespeare Company, Royal Society of Canada
Pty	Proprietary	RSC	Royal Shakespeare Company
Publ.	Publication	RSC	Royal Society of Canada
publ.	publication	RSDr	Doctor of Social Sciences
Publr	Publisher	RSFSR	Russian Soviet Federative Socialist Republic
Publ(s)	Publication(s)	RSL	Royal Society of Literature
Publs	Publications	RSNO	Royal Scottish National Orchestra (formerly SNO)
publs	publications	RSO	Radio Symphony Orchestra
Pvt.	Private	RSPB	Royal Society for Protection of Birds
PZPR	Polish United Workers' Party	Rt Hon.	Right Honourable
		Rt Rev.	Right Reverend
		RTÉ	Radio Telefís Éireann
QC	Province of Québec	RTF	Radiodiffusion-Télévision Française
QC	Queen's Counsel	RTS	Royal Television Society
QEH	Queen Elizabeth Hall, London	RVO	Royal Victorian Order
QGM	Queen's Gallantry Medal	RWS	Royal Society of Painters in Water Colours
Qld	Queensland		
QPM	Queen's Police Medal	S	South, Southern
QSO	Queen's Service Order	S.	San

ABBREVIATIONS

s.	son(s)
SA	Sociedad Anónima, Société Anonyme, South Africa
SA	Sociedad Anónima (Limited Company)
SA	Société Anonyme (Limited Company)
SA	South Africa
SA	South Australia
SAARC	South Asian Association for Regional Co-operation
SACEM	Société d'Auteurs, Compositeurs et Editeurs de Musique
SADC	South African Development Community
SAE	Society of Aeronautical Engineers
SAG	Screen Actors' Guild
Salop.	Shropshire
SALT	Strategic Arms Limitation Treaty
Sask.	Saskatchewan
SATB	soprano, alto, tenor, bass
SB	Bachelor of Science (USA)
SC	Senior Counsel
SC	South Carolina
SCAP	Supreme Command Allied Powers
ScB	Bachelor of Science
ScD	Doctor of Science
SD	South Dakota
SDak	South Dakota
SDLP	Social and Democratic Liberal Party
SDP	Social Democratic Party
SE	South East
SEATO	South East Asia Treaty Organization
SEC	Securities and Exchange Commission
Sec.	Secretary
Secr.	Secretariat
SED	Sozialistische Einheitspartei Deutschlands (Socialist Unity Party of the German Democratic Republic)
Sept.	September
S-et-O	Seine-et-Oise
SFWA	Science Fiction and Fantasy Writers of America
SGA	Songwriters' Guild of America
SHAEF	Supreme Headquarters Allied Expeditionary Force
SHAPE	Supreme Headquarters Allied Powers in Europe
SJ	Society of Jesus (Jesuits)
SJD	Doctor of Juristic Science
SK	Saskatchewan
SL	Sociedad Limitada
SLD	Social and Liberal Democrats
SM	Master of Science
SO	Symphony Orchestra
SOAS	School of Oriental and African Studies
Soc.	Société, Society
Soc.	Société
Soc.	Society
SOCAN	Society of Composers, Authors and Music Publishers of Canada
SOSA	State Opera of South Australia
SpA	Società per Azioni
SPD	Sozialdemokratische Partei Deutschlands
SPNM	Society for the Promotion of New Music
Sr	Senior
SRC	Science Research Council
Srl	Società a responsabilità
SSM	Seria Seta Mahkota (Malaysia)
SSR	Soviet Socialist Republic
St	Saint
Sta	Santa
Staffs.	Staffordshire
STB	Bachelor of Sacred Theology
Std	Doctor of Sacred Theology
Ste	Sainte
STL	Licentiate of Sacred Theology
STM	Master of Sacred Theology
str.	strasse
SUNY	State University of New York
Supt	Superintendent
SVSA	South West Virginia Songwriters' Association
SW	short wave
SW	South West
SWAPO	South West Africa People's Organization
TA	Territorial Army
TCL	Trinity College of Music, London
td	Teachta Dála (mem. of the Dáil), Territorial Decoration
td	Teachta Dála (mem. of the Dáil)
td	Territorial Decoration
Tech.	Technical, Technology
Tech.	Technical
Tech.	Technology
Temp.	Temporary
Tenn.	Tennessee
Tex.	Texas
ThB	Bachelor of Theology
ThD	Doctor of Theology
THDr	Doctor of Theology
ThM	Master of Theology
TLS	Times Literary Supplement
TN	Tennessee
trans.	translated
Trans.	Translation, translator
Trans.	Translation
Trans.	translator
Treas.	Treasurer
TU(C)	Trades Union (Congress)
TV	television
TX	Texas
u.	utca (street)
UAE	United Arab Emirates
UAR	United Arab Republic
UCLA	University of California at Los Angeles
UDEAC	L'Union Douanière et Economique de l'Afrique Centrale
UDR	Union des Démocrates pour la République
UED	University Education Diploma
UHF	ultra-high frequency
UK	United Kingdom (of Great Britain and Northern Ireland)
UKAEA	United Kingdom Atomic Energy Authority
ul.	ulitsa (street)
UMIST	University of Manchester Institute of Science and Technology
UMNO	United Malays National Organization
UN(O)	United Nations (Organization)
UNA	United Nations Association
UNCED	United Nations Council for Education and Development
UNCHS	United Nations Centre for Human Settlements (Habitat)
UNCTAD	United Nations Conference on Trade and Development
UNDCP	United Nations International Drug Control Programme
UNDP	United Nations Development Programme
UNDRO	United Nations Disaster Relief Office
UNEF	United Nations Emergency Force
UNEP	United Nations Environment Programme
UNESCO	United Nations Educational, Scientific and Cultural Organization
UNFPA	United Nations Population Fund
UNHCR	United Nations High Commissioner for Refugees
UNICEF	United Nations International Children's Emergency Fund
UNIDO	United Nations Industrial Development Organization
UNIFEM	United Nations Development Fund for Women
UNITAR	United Nations Institute for Training and Research
Univ.	University
UNKRA	United Nations Korean Relief Administration
UNRRA	United Nations Relief and Rehabilitation Administration
UNRWA	United Nations Relief and Works Agency
UNU	United Nations University
UP	United Provinces, Uttar Pradesh (India)
UP	United Provinces
UP	Uttar Pradesh (India)
UPU	Universal Postal Union
Urb.	Urbanización (urban district)
US	United States
USA	United States of America
USAAF	United States Army Air Force
USAF	United States Air Force
USAID	United States Agency for International Development
USN	United States Navy
USNR	United States Navy Reserve
USPHS	United States Public Health Service
USS	United States Ship
USSR	Union of Soviet Socialist Republics
UT	Utah
UWI	University of the West Indies
VA	Virginia
Va	Virginia
VC	Victoria Cross
VHF	very high frequency
VI	(US) Virgin Islands
Vic.	Victoria
Vol.	Volume
vol.	volume
Vol(s)	Volume(s)
Vols	Volumes
vols	volumes
VSO	Victoria State Opera
VSO	Voluntary Service Overseas
VT	Vermont
Vt	Vermont

ABBREVIATIONS

W	West, Western	WNO	Welsh National Opera
WA	Washington (State)	WOMAD	World of Music, Arts and Dance
WA	Western Australia	Worcs.	Worcestershire
Warwicks.	Warwickshire	WRAC	Women's Royal Army Corps
Wash.	Washington (State)	WRNS	Women's Royal Naval Service
WCC	World Council of Churches	WTO	World Trade Organization
WCMD	Welsh College of Music and Drama, Cardiff	WV	West Virginia
WCT	World Championship Tennis	WVa	West Virginia
WEU	Western European Union	WWF	World Wildlife Fund
WFP	World Food Programme	WY	Wyoming
WFTU	World Federation of Trade Unions	Wyo.	Wyoming
WHO	World Health Organization		
WI	Wisconsin		
Wilts.	Wiltshire	YMCA	Young Men's Christian Association
WIPO	World Intellectual Property Organization	Yorks.	Yorkshire
Wis.	Wisconsin	YT	Yukon Territory
WMO	World Meteorological Organization	YWCA	Young Women's Christian Association

INTERNATIONAL TELEPHONE CODES

To make international calls to telephone and fax numbers listed in the book, dial the international code of the country from which you are calling, followed by the appropriate code for the country you wish to call (listed below), followed by the area code (if applicable) and telephone or fax number listed in the entry.

	Country code	+ or − GMT*
Abkhazia	7	+4
Afghanistan	93	+4½
Åland Islands	358	+2
Albania	355	+1
Algeria	213	+1
American Samoa	1 684	−11
Andorra	376	+1
Angola	244	+1
Anguilla	1 264	−4
Antigua and Barbuda	1 268	−4
Argentina	54	−3
Armenia	374	+4
Aruba	297	−4
Ascension Island	247	0
Australia	61	+8 to +10
Austria	43	+1
Azerbaijan	994	+5
Bahamas	1 242	−5
Bahrain	973	+3
Bangladesh	880	+6
Barbados	1 246	−4
Belarus	375	+2
Belgium	32	+1
Belize	501	−6
Benin	229	+1
Bermuda	1 441	−4
Bhutan	975	+6
Bolivia	591	−4
Bonaire	599	−4
Bosnia and Herzegovina	387	+1
Botswana	267	+2
Brazil	55	−3 to −4
British Indian Ocean Territory (Diego Garcia)	246	+5
British Virgin Islands	1 284	−4
Brunei	673	+8
Bulgaria	359	+2
Burkina Faso	226	0
Burundi	257	+2
Cambodia	855	+7
Cameroon	237	+1
Canada	1	−3 to −8
Cape Verde	238	−1
Cayman Islands	1 345	−5
Central African Republic	236	+1
Ceuta	34	+1
Chad	235	+1
Chile	56	−4
China, People's Republic	86	+8
Christmas Island	61	+7
Cocos (Keeling) Islands	61	+6½
Colombia	57	−5
Comoros	269	+3
Congo, Democratic Republic	243	+1
Congo, Republic	242	+1
Cook Islands	682	−10
Costa Rica	506	−6
Côte d'Ivoire	225	0
Croatia	385	+1
Cuba	53	−5
Curaçao	599	−4
Cyprus	357	+2
Czech Republic	420	+1
Denmark	45	+1
Djibouti	253	+3

	Country code	+ or − GMT*
Dominica	1 767	−4
Dominican Republic	1 809	−4
Ecuador	593	−5
Egypt	20	+2
El Salvador	503	−6
Equatorial Guinea	240	+1
Eritrea	291	+3
Estonia	372	+2
Ethiopia	251	+3
Falkland Islands	500	−4
Faroe Islands	298	0
Fiji	679	+12
Finland	358	+2
France	33	+1
French Guiana	594	−3
French Polynesia	689	−9 to −10
Gabon	241	+1
Gambia	220	0
Georgia	995	+4
Germany	49	+1
Ghana	233	0
Gibraltar	350	+1
Greece	30	+2
Greenland	299	−1 to −4
Grenada	1 473	−4
Guadeloupe	590	−4
Guam	1 671	+10
Guatemala	502	−6
Guernsey	44	0
Guinea	224	0
Guinea-Bissau	245	0
Guyana	592	−4
Haiti	509	−5
Honduras	504	−6
Hong Kong	852	+8
Hungary	36	+1
Iceland	354	0
India	91	+5½
Indonesia	62	+7 to +9
Iran	98	+3½
Iraq	964	+3
Ireland	353	0
Isle of Man	44	0
Israel	972	+2
Italy	39	+1
Jamaica	1 876	−5
Japan	81	+9
Jersey	44	0
Jordan	962	+2
Kazakhstan	7	+6
Kenya	254	+3
Kiribati	686	+12 to +13
Korea, Democratic People's Republic (North Korea)	850	+9
Korea, Republic (South Korea)	82	+9
Kosovo	381†	+3
Kuwait	965	+3
Kyrgyzstan	996	+5
Laos	856	+7
Latvia	371	+2
Lebanon	961	+2
Lesotho	266	+2
Liberia	231	0
Libya	218	+1
Liechtenstein	423	+1

INTERNATIONAL TELEPHONE CODES

	Country code	+ or − GMT*
Lithuania	370	+2
Luxembourg	352	+1
Macao	853	+8
Macedonia, former Yugoslav republic	389	+1
Madagascar	261	+3
Malawi	265	+2
Malaysia	60	+8
Maldives	960	+5
Mali	223	0
Malta	356	+1
Marshall Islands	692	+12
Martinique	596	−4
Mauritania	222	0
Mauritius	230	+4
Mayotte	262	+3
Melilla	34	+1
Mexico	52	−6 to −7
Micronesia, Federated States	691	+10 to +11
Moldova	373	+2
Monaco	377	+1
Mongolia	976	+7 to +9
Montenegro	382	+1
Montserrat	1 664	−4
Morocco	212	0
Mozambique	258	+2
Myanmar	95	+6½
Nagornyi Karabakh	374	+4
Namibia	264	+2
Nauru	674	+12
Nepal	977	+5¾
Netherlands	31	+1
New Caledonia	687	+11
New Zealand	64	+12
Nicaragua	505	−6
Niger	227	+1
Nigeria	234	+1
Niue	683	−11
Norfolk Island	672	+11½
Northern Mariana Islands	1 670	+10
Norway	47	+1
Oman	968	+4
Pakistan	92	+5
Palau	680	+9
Palestinian Autonomous Areas	970 or 972	+2
Panama	507	−5
Papua New Guinea	675	+10
Paraguay	595	−4
Peru	51	−5
Philippines	63	+8
Pitcairn Islands	872	−8
Poland	48	+1
Portugal	351	0
Puerto Rico	1 787	−4
Qatar	974	+3
Réunion	262	+4
Romania	40	+2
Russian Federation	7	+3 to +12
Rwanda	250	+2
Saba	599	−4
Saint-Barthélemy	590	−4
Saint Christopher and Nevis	1 869	−4
Saint Helena	290	0
Saint Lucia	1 758	−4
Saint-Martin	590	−4
Saint Pierre and Miquelon	508	−3
Saint Vincent and the Grenadines	1 784	−4
Samoa	685	+13
San Marino	378	+1
São Tomé and Príncipe	239	0
Saudi Arabia	966	+3
Senegal	221	0
Serbia	381	+1
Seychelles	248	+4
Sierra Leone	232	0
Singapore	65	+8
Sint Eustatius	1721	−4
Sint Maarten	599	−4
Slovakia	421	+1
Slovenia	386	+1
Solomon Islands	677	+11
Somalia	252	+3
South Africa	27	+2
South Ossetia	7	+4
South Sudan	211‡	+2
Spain	34	+1
Sri Lanka	94	+5½
Sudan	249	+2
Suriname	597	−3
Svalbard	47	+1
Swaziland	268	+2
Sweden	46	+1
Switzerland	41	+1
Syria	963	+2
Taiwan	886	+8
Tajikistan	992	+5
Tanzania	255	+3
Thailand	66	+7
Timor-Leste	670	+9
Togo	228	0
Tokelau	690	+15
Tonga	676	+13
Transnistria	373	+2
Trinidad and Tobago	1 868	−4
Tristan da Cunha	290	0
Tunisia	216	+1
Turkey	90	+2
'Turkish Republic of Northern Cyprus'	90 392	+2
Turkmenistan	993	+5
Turks and Caicos Islands	1 649	−5
Tuvalu	688	+12
Uganda	256	+3
Ukraine	380	+2
United Arab Emirates	971	+4
United Kingdom	44	0
United States of America	1	−5 to −10
United States Virgin Islands	1 340	−4
Uruguay	598	−3
Uzbekistan	998	+5
Vanuatu	678	+11
Vatican City	39	+1
Venezuela	58	−4½
Viet Nam	84	+7
Wallis and Futuna Islands	681	+12
Yemen	967	+3
Zambia	260	+2
Zimbabwe	263	+2

* The times listed compare the standard (winter) times in the various countries. Some countries adopt Summer (Daylight Saving) Time—i.e. +1 hour—for part of the year.

† Mobile telephone numbers for Kosovo use either the country code for Monaco (377) or the country code for Slovenia (386).

‡ Although South Sudan was assigned the international telephone code 211 by the International Telecommunication Union in July 2011, many mobile and fixed line telephone services continue to use either Sudanese (249) or Ugandan (256) networks. Therefore, all telephone numbers given for South Sudan include the full international dialling code.

Note: Telephone and fax numbers using the Inmarsat ocean region code 870 are listed in full. No country or area code is required, but it is necessary to precede the number with the international access code of the country from which the call is made.

OBITUARY

Adair, Gilbert	8 December 2011	Hill, Reginald Charles	12 January 2012
Arden, John	28 March 2012	Hitchens, Christopher Eric	15 December 2011
Barstow, Stanley	1 August 2011	Hoban, Russell Conwell	13 December 2011
Blair, Iain John	3 July 2011	Holbrook, David Kenneth	11 August 2011
Borge, Tomas Martinez	30 April 2012	Horowitz, Irving Louis	21 March 2012
Born, Anne Rosemary	27 July 2011	Joensuu, Matti Yrjana	4 December 2011
Brooke-Rose, Christine	21 March 2012	Johnston, William	12 October 2010
Burke, John Frederick	20 September 2011	Kaufmann, Myron S.	29 January 2010
Collinson, Patrick	28 September 2011	Kerner, Fred	24 December 2011
Colvin, Marie Catherine	22 February 2012	Komrij, Gerrit	5 June 2012
Courtemanche, Gil	19 August 2011	Lambert, Derek William	10 April 2001
Crews, Harry Eugene	28 March 2012	Litvinoff, Emanuel	24 September 2011
Daniel, Jean	12 January 2010	Logue, Christopher John	2 December 2011
Darke, Marjorie Shiela	21 July 2009	Lomas, Herbert	9 September 2011
D'arzille, Juliette	18 December 2011	Low, Lois Dorothea	8 November 2002
Delaney, Shelagh	20 November 2011	McCaffrey, Anne Inez	21 November 2011
Denniston, Robin Alastair	6 April 2012	McCredie, Andrew Dalgarno	7 June 2006
Denker, Henry	15 May 2012	Marceau, Felicien	7 March 2012
Dovring, Karin	7 August 2011	Marcus, Ruth Barcan	19 February 2012
Durr, Alfred	7 April 2011	Mayhar, Ardath	1 February 2012
Ephron, Nora	26 June 2012	Morrison, Bill	7 December 2011
Enslin, Theodore Vernon	21 November 2011	Muhringer, Doris Agathe Annemarie	26 May 2009
Fillioud, Georges	15 September 2011	Neill, William	5 April 2010
Fuentes, Carlos	15 May 2012	Norling, Bernard	17 September 2003
Fussell, Paul	23 May 2012	Nourissier, Francois	15 February 2011
Forrester, Helen	24 November 2011	Osers, Ewald	10 October 2011
Gebauer, Phyllis	15 June 2011	Peters, Richard Stanley	30 December 2011
George, Jean Craighead	15 May 2012	Rich, Adrienne	28 March 2012
Gersovitz, Sarah Valerie	22 September 2007	Robinson, Robert Henry	12 August 2011
Gheorghiu, Mihnea	11 December 2011	Rosset, Barnet Lee	21 February 2012
Ghellab, Abdelkarim	2006	Sabatier, Robert	28 June 2012
Gilbert, Bentley Brinkerhoff	5 April 2008	Saint, Dora Jessie	11 April 2012
Gilman, Dorothy	2 February 2012	Sanden, Einar	18 April 2007
Gordon, Donald Ramsay	2006	Scalapino, Robert Anthony	1 November 2011
Goswami, Indira	29 November 2011	Searle, Ronald	30 December 2011
Graver, Lawrence Stanley	28 February 2010	Segovia, Tomas	7 November 2011
Gray, Dulcie Winifred Catherine	15 November 2011	Sendak, Maurice Bernard	8 May 2012
Greene, Alvin Carl	5 April 2002	Sereny, Gitta	14 June 2012
Gregor-Dellin, Martin	23 June 1988	Shalaby, Khairy	9 September 2011
Grusa, Jiri	28 October 2011	Simpson, Norman Frederick	27 August 2011
Guy, Rosa Cuthbert	3 June 2012	Skvorecky, Josef Vaclav	3 January 2012
Hall, James Byron	28 February 2008	Smith, Bernard William	2 September 2011
Hamburger, Philip Paul	23 April 2004	Szymborska, Wislawa	1 February 2012
Hampson, Norman	8 July 2011	Tabucchi, Antonio	25 March 2012
Handlin, Oscar	20 September 2011	Unsworth, Barry	5 June 2012
Harrison, Elizabeth Fancourt	26 February 2008	Varas Morel, Jose Miguel	23 September 2011
Hartcup, Adeline	7 November 2011	Vinken, Pierre	4 November 2011
Hartman, Jan	9 November 2006	Wicker, Thomas (Tom) Grey	25 November 2011
Hastings, Michael Gerald	19 November 2011	Wilson, Donald M.	29 November 2011
Haugaard, Erik Christian	2009	Wolf, Christa	1 December 2011
Havel, Václav	18 December 2011	Woodring, Carl Ray	12 September 2009
Hepburn, Ronald William	23 December 2008	Young-Bruehl, Elisabeth	1 December 2011

Biographies

A

AARON, Hugh, (Max Barnet), BA; American writer; b. 30 Nov. 1924, Worcester, Mass; m. Ann Stein 1989; one s. two d. *Education:* Univ. of Chicago. *Plays include:* Family Agendas, A Son's Father, A Father's Son: A Tale of Two Wars. *Publications:* Business Not as Usual 1993, When Wars Were Won 1995, It's All Chaos 1996, Letters from the Good War 1997, Films in Review 1998, Suzy, Fair Suzy 1998, Quintet 2005; as Max Barnet: Driven: Notes of a Neurotic Entrepreneur 1995, Go West Old Man 1996, Stories from a Lifetime 2010; contrib. to Sail Magazine, Wall Street Journal. *Address:* Stones Point Press, 6 Henderson Lane, Cushing, ME 04563, USA (office). *Telephone:* (207) 354-0735 (office). *E-mail:* stones49@gmail.com (office); books@stonespointbooks.com (office). *Website:* www.stonespointbooks.com (office); www.zoofky.com; www.businesswisdom.blogspot.com.

ABANI, Chris, BA, MA, PhD; Nigerian poet and writer; *Professor, Department of Creative Writing, University of California, Riverside*; b. 27 Dec. 1966, Afikpo. *Education:* Imo State Univ., Nigeria, Birkbeck Coll., London, UK, Univ. of Southern California, USA. *Career:* political prisoner in Nigeria 1985–91; fmr Middleton Fellow, Univ. of Southern California; Assoc. Prof., Creative Writing, Antioch Univ. 2001–04; Visiting Asst Prof., Dept of Creative Writing, Univ. of California, Riverside 2003–04, Prof. 2004–; Stanford Distinguished Prof., Center for Humanities, Univ. of Miami 2010–11; Fellow, Guggenheim Foundation 2009; founding ed., Black Goat poetry series; mem. Bd Calif. Council for Humanities. *Plays:* Room at the Top 1985, Song of a Broken Flute 1990, The Poet, The Soldier, The Lover and The Paper-Kite Maker 2003. *Publications:* poetry: Kalakuta Republic 2001, Daphne's Lot 2003, Dog Woman 2004, Hands Washing Water 2006, Sanctificum 2010; prose: Masters of the Board (novel) (Delta Fiction Award, Nigeria) 1985, GraceLand (novel) (Hurston/Wright Legacy Award, PEN Hemingway Book Prize 2005) 2004, Becoming Abigail (novella) 2006, The Virgin of Flames (novel) 2007, Song For Night (novella) (PEN Beyond the Margins Award 2008) 2007. *Honours:* PEN USA Freedom-to-Write Award 2001, Prince Claus Award, Netherlands 2001, Imbonge Yesizwe Poetry Int. Award, South Africa 2002, Lannan Literary Fellowship 2003, Calif. Book Award, Distinguished Humanist Award, Univ. of California, Riverside 2008. *Literary Agent:* c/o Ellen Levine, Trident Media Group, 41 Madison Avenue, 36th Floor, New York, NY 10010, USA. *Telephone:* (212) 333-1517. *Fax:* (212) 725-4501. *E-mail:* levine.assistant@tridentmediagroup.com. *Website:* www.tridentmediagroup.com. *Address:* Department of Creative Writing, University of California, 3400 Humanities and Social Sciences Building, Riverside, CA 92521, USA (office). *Telephone:* (951) 827-3360 (office). *E-mail:* chris.abani@ucr.edu (office); abani@chrisabani.com (office). *Website:* www.creativewriting.ucr.edu (office); www.chrisabani.com.

ABBATE, Florencia, PhD; Argentine writer; b. 24 Dec. 1976, Buenos Aires. *Education:* Univ. of Buenos Aires. *Career:* columnist, Ñ magazine (Clarín newspaper); also contrib. to newspapers La Nación, Perfil, Página 12 (Argentina), El País (Uruguay), Taz (Germany), and magazines Surcos en America Latina (Chile), Día Siete (Mexico), Clarín (Spain), Quimera (Spain), Diario de poesia (Argentina); Dir, Tantalia publishing house. *Publications:* novels: El grito 2004, Magic Resort 2007; non-fiction: El, ella, ella? Apuntes sobre transexualidad masculina 1998, Deleuze para principiantes (co-author) 2001, Shhh, Lamentables documentos 2002, Literatura latinoamericana para principiantes 2003; short stories: Las siete maravillas del mundo 2006, Una terraza propia (Nuevas narradoras argentinas) 2006; poetry: Puntos de fuga 1996, Los transparentes 2000, Pisa con suavidad 2008. *Literary Agent:* Guillermo Schavelzon y Asociados, Muntaner 339, 5°, 08021 Barcelona, Spain. *Telephone:* (93) 2011310. *Fax:* (93) 2003886. *E-mail:* info@schavelzon.com. *Website:* www.schavelzon.com. *Address:* Lavalleja 529, CP 1414, Buenos Aires, Argentina (office). *Telephone:* (11) 4856-6055 (office). *E-mail:* fabbate24@yahoo.com.ar (office). *Website:* www.magicresort.com.ar (office).

ABBENSETTS, Michael John; British writer; b. 8 June 1938, Guyana; s. of Dr N. J. Abbensetts and Elaine Abbensetts; m. Liz Abbensetts; one d. *Education:* Queen's Coll., Guyana, Stanstead Coll., QC, Canada and Sir George Williams Univ., Montréal. *Career:* security attendant, Tower of London 1963–67; staff mem. Sir John Soane's Museum, London 1968–71; resident playwright, Royal Court Theatre, London 1974; Visiting Prof. of Drama, Carnegie Mellon Univ., Pittsburgh 1981; Fellow, Royal Literary Fund, Univ. of North London, City and Guilds of London School of Art; writer for radio and TV. *Plays:* Sweet Talk (London 1973, New York 1974), Alterations (London and New York 1978, revised production London 1985), Samba (London 1980), In the Mood (London 1981), Outlaw (Leicester and London 1983), Royston's Day (London 1988), The Street Party (London 1988), El Dorado (London 1984), The Lion (London 1993), Inner City Blues, Crime and Passion, Roadrunner, The Museum Attendant. *Television include:* Little Napoleons, Empire Road. *Radio:* Summer Passions, The Dark Horse, Brothers of the Sword, The Sunny Side of the Street, Home Again. *Publication:* Empire Road (novel, from TV series) 1979, Four Plays. *Honours:* George Devine Award 1973, Arts Council Bursary 1977, Afro-Caribbean Award 1979. *Literary Agent:* c/o Julian Friedmann, Blake Friedmann Agency, 122 Arlington Road, London, NW1 7HP, England. *Telephone:* (20) 7284-0408. *Fax:* (20) 7284-0442. *E-mail:* info@blakefriedmann.co.uk. *Website:* www.blakefriedmann.co.uk. *E-mail:* abbensem@gmail.com.

ABBOTT, Elizabeth, BA, MA, PhD; Canadian historian and writer; b. 27 Sept. 1946, Ottawa, Ont.; d. of William Richard Abbott and Margaret Abbott; one s. *Education:* Concordia and McGill Univs. *Career:* Prof. of History, Dawson Coll., Montréal 1972–84; reporter, Reuters, Haiti 1986–88; Ed.-in-Chief Chronicle Publications, Canada 1989–91, The Urban Pet 1991–93; Research Assoc. in Arts 2004–10, Trinity Coll., Univ. of Toronto, Dean of Women Students and Dean of St Hilda's Coll. 1991–2004; Dir St Patrick's Benevolent Soc.; co-f. Riverdale Historical Soc. 1999; mem. Editorial Bd Canadian Human Rights Foundation; volunteer for Tafelmusik; mem. The Writers' Union of Canada, Antigua and Barbuda Asscn Toronto, PEN Canada. *Publications include:* Tropical Observation (play) 1986, Haiti: The Duvaliers and Their Legacy 1988, Chronicle of Canada 1990, A History of Celibacy 1999, A History of Mistresses 2003, Sugar: A Bittersweet History 2008, A History of Marriage 2010; contribs to Equinox, Harrowsmith, The Globe and Mail, Toronto Star, The Ottawa Citizen, The Gazette (Montreal), Quill and Quire, London Free Press. *Honours:* Lt-Gov.'s Silver Medal for History, Sir George Williams Univ. 1963, Nat. Magazine Award for Environmental Writing 1991, Mount Sinai Hospital Volunteer Service Award, City of Toronto Community Service Volunteer Award, Volunteer Service Award. *Address:* c/o Heide Lange, Sanford J. Greenburger Associates, 55 Fifth Avenue, New York, NY 10003, USA. *Website:* www.elizabethabbott.ca.

ABBS, Peter Francis, BA, DPhil; British writer, poet, editor and academic; *Professor of Creative Writing, University of Sussex*; b. 22 Feb. 1942, Cromer, Norfolk, England; m. Barbara Beazeley 1963 (divorced 2002); one s. two d. *Education:* Univ. of Bristol, Univ. of Sussex. *Career:* Lecturer in Education, Univ. of Sussex 1976–85, Reader 1985–99, Prof. of Creative Writing 1999–; Founding mem. New Metaphysical Art 1996; mem. Soc. of Authors, Asscn of Univ. Teachers; Fellow, English Asscn, Aegean Center for Fine Arts. *Publications:* English for Diversity: A Polemic 1969, The Forms of Narrative: A Practical Guide (with John Richardson) 1970, Autobiography in Education 1974, The Black Rainbow: Essays on the Present Breakdown of Culture (ed.) 1975, Root and Blossom: Essays on the Philosophy, Practice and Politics of English Teaching 1976, Proposal for a New College (with Graham Carey) 1977, For Man and Islands (poems) 1978, Reclamations: Essays on Culture, Mass-Culture and the Curriculum 1979, Songs of a New Taliesin (poems) 1979, English Within the Arts: A Radical Alternative 1982, Living Powers: The Arts in Education (ed.) 1987, A is for Aesthetic: Essays on Creative and Aesthetic Education 1988, The Symbolic Order: A Contemporary Reader on the Arts Debate (ed.) 1989, The Forms of Poetry: A Practical Guide (with John Richardson) 1991, Icons of Time: An Experiment in Autobiography 1991, The Educational Imperative 1994, The Polemics of Imagination: Essays on Art, Culture and Society 1996, Love After Sappho (poems) 1999, Selected Poems 2001, Earth Songs: an anthology of contemporary eco-poetry 2002, Against the Flow: Education, the Arts and Postmodern Culture 2003, Viva la Vida (poems) 2005, The Flowering of Flint (poems) 2007, Voyaging Out (poems) 2009; contrib. to scholarly and literary periodicals. *Address:* Graduate Research Centre in the Humanities, Arts Bldg B, University of Sussex, Falmer, Brighton, BN1 9QN, England (office). *Telephone:* (1273) 606755 (office). *Fax:* (1273) 625972 (office). *E-mail:* p.f.abbs@sussex.ac.uk (office). *Website:* www.sussex.ac.uk/education (office).

ABDEL-MALEK, Anouar I., DLit, PhD; Egyptian academic and writer; *Adviser, National Centre for Middle East Studies*; b. 23 Oct. 1924, Cairo; s. of Iskandar Abdel-Malek and Alice Zaki Ibrahim; m. Karin Konigseider 1961; one d. *Education:* Coll. de la Sainte Famille, British Inst., Ain Shams Univ., Cairo and Univ. de Paris-Sorbonne. *Career:* leading mem. Egyptian Nat. and Progressive Movt 1941–; official, Nat. Bank of Egypt, Cairo 1941–42, Crédit Foncier Egyptien, Cairo 1943–46; Jt Ed. Actualité, Cairo 1950–59; journalist, Le Journal d'Egypte, Cairo 1950–59; contrib. to Rose el-Yusef, Al-Magallah, Al-Masa, Cairo 1950–59; teacher of philosophy, Lycée Al-Hurriya, Cairo 1958–59; Research Asst, Ecole Pratique des Hautes Etudes, Paris 1959–60; Research Lecturer, later Research Reader, Research Prof., CNRS, Paris 1960–, Dir of Research 1970–90, Hon. Dir 1990–; Project Co-ordinator, The UN Univ., Tokyo 1976–86; Prof. of Sociology and Politics, Faculty of Int. Relations, Ristumeikan Univ., Kyoto 1989–92; Prof. Emer. of Philosophy, Ain Shams Univ. 1998–; Adviser Nat. Centre for Middle East Studies, Cairo 1990–; mem. Bd and Adviser, Centre for Asian Studies, Cairo Univ. 1994–; writer, Al-Ahram 1995; mem. exec. cttee, EEC Int. Sociological Asscn 1970–74 (vice-pres. 1974–78), Egyptian Council for Foreign Affairs 2002–, IISS, Int. Political Science Asscn, Royal Inst. for Int. Affairs, Chatham House, London 2007–; Visiting Prof., Univ. of Santiago, Chile 1969, Ain Shams 1975, Québec 1986, Cairo 1992; Visiting Fellow, Clare Coll., Cambridge 1985, Life Assoc. 1986–; Ed. Library of the Contemporary Orient 1989, Ideas of the New World 1991. *Publications include:* Egypte, société militaire 1962, Studies on National Culture 1967, Idéologie et renaissance nationale: l'Egypte moderne 1969, La pensée politique arabe contemporaine 1970, Sociologie de l'impérialisme 1970, La dialectique sociale 1972, The Army and National Movements 1974, Spécificité et Théorie sociale 1977, Intellectual Creativity in Endogenous Culture 1983, East Wind 1983, The Transformation of the World 1985, The Egyptian Street and Thought 1989, Creativity and the Civilizational Project 1991, Endogenous Intellectual Creativity in the Arab World 1994, Towards a Civilizational Strategy 2005, On the Origins of the Civilizational Question

2005, Along the Path Towards a New Egypt 2005, China in the Eyes of Egyptians 2006, Patriotism is the Solution 2006. *Honours:* Prix du Jury de l'Amitié Franco-Arabe, Paris 1965, Gold Medal, Nasser Higher Mil. Acad. 1976, State Prize in the Social Sciences 1996, Prize for Best Book, Cairo 2001, Gold Medal, Faculty of Econs and Political Sciences, Cairo Univ. 2003. *Address:* 48 Nehru Street, 11351 Heliopolis, Cairo, Egypt (home). *Telephone:* (2) 634-3977 (home). *Fax:* (2) 634-3977 (home). *E-mail:* anouarmalek@hotmail.com (home).

ABEL, Sam, BA, MA, PhD; American writer, editor and academic; *Professor, Dartmouth College;* b. 5 Oct. 1957, Norwood, Mass; pnr Craig B. Palmer 1994. *Education:* Dartmouth Coll., Indiana Univ. *Career:* Assoc. Instructor, Indiana Univ., Bloomington 1981–82; Instructor, Moorhead State Univ., Moorhead, MN 1983–84, Asst Prof., DePauw Univ., Greencastle, Ind. 1985–90, Dartmouth Coll., Hanover, NH 1990–; book review ed., reader New England Theatre Journal 1990–93, Co-ed. 1993–; Consulting Ed., Theatre History Studies 1996; consultant for Oxford University Press, Univ. of Michigan Press, Indiana Univ., Warner Bentley Theatre; dir various stage productions; mem. Asscn for Theatre in Higher Education, Modern Language Asscn, American Soc. for Theatre Research, Popular Culture Asscn. *Publications:* Opera in the Flesh: Sexuality in Operatic Performance 1996, Irrational Entertainment: Reflections on Opera for the Twenty-First Century 1998; contributed articles and reviews to periodicals, journals and anthologies, including Journal of Dramatic Theory and Criticism, Journal of Popular Culture, Memory, Practice, Desire: Gay Performances, New England Theatre Journal, A Night at the Opera, Media Representation of Opera, Notable Gays and Lesbians in American Theatre History, Opera News, Terrance McNally: A Casebook, Theatre Annual: A Journal of Performance Studies, Theatre History Studies, Theatre Journal, Theatre Survey, Theatre Topics, Western European Studies. *Honours:* Dartmouth Coll. Marcus Heiman Award for the Creative and Performing Arts 1979, Burke Research Grant 1990–93, Indiana Univ. Graduate Fellow 1979–80, American Coll. Theatre Festival Regional Award for Dramatic Criticism 1980, American Coll. Theatre Festival Regional Award for Playwriting 1981, DePauw Univ. Creative Project Grant 1988, DePauw Univ. Course Devt Grant 1989. *Address:* Dartmouth College, Hanover, NH 03755, USA (office). *Telephone:* (603) 646-1110 (office). *Website:* www.dartmouth.edu (office).

ABISH, Walter; American writer; b. (Walter Abisch), 24 Dec. 1931, Vienna, Austria; s. of Adolph Abish and Frieda Abish; m. Cecile Abish. *Career:* Fellow, American Acad. of Arts and Sciences; taught at Empire State Coll., Wheaton Coll., State Univ. of New York, Brown Univ., Yale Univ.; mem. PEN American Centre (exec. bd 1982–88), New York Foundation for the Arts (mem. Bd of Govs 1990–93). *Art exhibition:* The Writer's Brush (Shapolsky Gallery, New York) 2007, The Writer's Brush (Pierre Menard Gallery, Cambridge) 2008. *Publications:* Duel Site 1970, Alphabetical Africa 1974, Minds Meet 1975, In the Future Perfect 1977, How German Is It 1980, 99 – The New Meaning 1990, Eclipse Fever 1993, Double Vision – A Self-Portrait 2004; contrib. to Antaeus, Conjunctions, Granta, Manuskripte, New Directions Annual, Paris Review, Partisan Review, Tri-Quarterly, Salmagundi. *Honours:* Hon. DLitt (State Univ. of NY at Oneonta) 1996; Ingram Merrill Foundation Grant 1977, Nat. Endowment for the Arts Fellowships 1979, 1985, PEN-Faulkner Award 1981, Guggenheim Fellowship 1981, Deutscher Akademischer Austauschdienst Residency, Berlin 1987, John D. and Catherine T. MacArthur Foundation Fellowship 1987–92, American Acad. of Arts and Letters Medal of Merit 1991, Lila Wallace-Reader's Digest Fellowship 1992–95. *Address:* PO Box 485, Cooper Station, NY 10276, USA (home).

ABOULELA, Leila, MSc; Sudanese writer; b. 1964, Cairo, Egypt; m.; three c. *Education:* The Sisters' School, Khartoum, Univ. of Khartoum and London School of Econs, UK. *Career:* lived in Aberdeen, Scotland 1990–2000; fmr lecturer in statistics and part-time research asst in Scotland; began writing 1992; co-writer of plays broadcast on BBC Radio 4; currently lives in Abu Dhabi. *Publications:* The Translator (novel) 1999, The Museum (short story) (Caine Prize for African Writing) 2000, Coloured Lights (novel) 2001, Minaret (novel) 2005; work included in anthologies Scottish Short Stories 1996, Ahead of its Time 1998. *Literary Agent:* c/o Stephanie Cabot, The Gernert Company, 136 East 57th Street, New York, NY 10022, USA. *Telephone:* (212) 838-7777. *Fax:* (212) 838-6020. *E-mail:* info@thegernertco.com. *Website:* www.thegernertco.com.

ABOUZEÏD, Leïla; Moroccan novelist and journalist; b. 1950, al-Ksiba, Middle Atlas Mountains. *Education:* Mohamed V Univ., Rabat, Univ. of Texas at Austin, World Press Inst., St Paul, Minn., USA, London School of Journalism, UK. *Career:* worked as radio and TV journalist; press asst in govt ministries and Prime Minister's Office 1970s, 1983, 1991; full-time fiction writer 1992–; fmr Fellow, World Press Inst. *Publications include:* Bid' Sanābil Khudr (articles, short stories, Few Green Wheat Stalks) 1978, 'Am al-Fil (novel, trans. as Year of the Elephant: A Moroccan Woman's Journey Toward Independence) 1983, Rujū' ilā at-Tufula (autobiography, trans. as Return to Childhood) 1993, The Last Chapter (semi-autobiography, in trans.) 2003, The Director and Other Stories from Morocco 2006. *Address:* The American University in Cairo Press, 113 Sharia Kasr al-Aini Street, Cairo 11511, Egypt (office). *E-mail:* aucpress@aucegypt.edu (office). *Website:* www.aucpress.com (office).

ABRAHAM, Henry Julian, BA, MA, PhD; American political scientist and academic; *James Hart Professor Emeritus in Government and Foreign Affairs, University of Virginia;* b. 25 Aug. 1921, Offenbach am Main, Germany; m. Mildred K. Kosches 1954; two s. *Education:* Kenyon Coll., Columbia Univ., Univ. of Pennsylvania. *Career:* instructor, Univ. of Pennsylvania 1949–53, Asst Prof. 1953–57, Assoc. Prof. 1957–62, Prof. of Political Science 1962–72; Henry L. and Grace Doherty Memorial Foundation Prof. in Govt and Foreign Affairs, Univ. of Virginia 1972–78, James Hart Prof. in Govt and Foreign Affairs, now Prof. Emer. 1978–; Visiting Lecturer and Visiting Prof. at many univs and colls in USA and abroad; Fulbright Lecturer 1959–60; Fellow, American Philosophical Soc. 1960–61, 1970–71, 1979; Rockefeller Foundation Resident Scholar, Bellagio, Italy 1978; mem. American Judicature Soc., American Political Science Asscn (vice-pres. 1980–82), American Soc. for Legal History, English-Speaking Union, Int. Political Science Asscn, Nat. Asscn of Scholars, Southern Political Science Asscn. *Publications:* Elements of Democratic Government (with J.A. Corry, fourth edn) 1964, The Judicial Process: An Introductory Analysis of the Courts of the United States, England, and France 1962, The Judiciary: The Supreme Court in the Governmental Process 1965, Freedom and the Court: Civil Rights and Liberties in the United States 1967, Essentials of American National Government (with J.C. Phillips, third edn) 1971, Justices and Presidents: A Political History of Appointments to the Supreme Court 1974, American Democracy 1983, Justices, President and Senators: A History of Supreme Court Appointments from Washington to Bush II 2008; numerous chapters in books, articles, monographs and essays. *Honours:* Hon. LLD 1972, 1982, 1982, 1987; Hon. LHD 1996; Thomas Jefferson Award, Univ. of Virginia 1983, First Lifetime Achievement Award, Organized Section on Law and Courts, American Political Science Asscn 1996, Annual Award, Daughters of American Revolution 2007. *Address:* Apt 5311, 250 Pantops Mountain Road, Charlottesville, VA 22911-8704 (home); Department of Politics, PO Box 400787, University of Virginia, Charlottesville, VA 22904, USA (office). *Telephone:* (434) 972-2482 (home); (434) 924-3192 (office). *Fax:* (434) 924-3359 (office).

ABRAHAMS, Peter Henry; South African novelist (retired); b. 19 March 1919, Vrededorp, Johannesburg; s. of the late James Henry Abrahams and of Angelina DuPlessis; m. 1st Dorothy Pennington (divorced 1948); m. 2nd Daphne Elizabeth Miller; three c. *Education:* Church of England mission schools, St Peter's Coll., Johannesburg, Teachers' Training Coll., Petersburg. *Career:* Controller, West Indian News, Jamaica 1955–64; Chair., Radio Jamaica, Kingston 1977–80; journalist, West Indian Economist 1958–62; mem. Soc. of Authors, Int. PEN, Authors League. *Publications:* fiction: Song of the City 1945, Mine Boy 1946, The Path of Thunder 1948, Wild Conquest 1950, Tell Freedom 1954, A Wreath for Undomo 1956, A Night of Their Own 1965, This Island Now 1966, The View from Coyaba 1985, The Coyoba Chronicles: Reflections on the Black Experience in the Twentieth Century 2000; short story collection: Dark Testament 1942; poetry: A Black Man Speaks of Freedom 1938. *Address:* Red Hills, PO Box 20, St Andrew, Jamaica. *Telephone:* 9444420.

ABRAHAMS, Roger David, BA, MA, PhD; American academic and writer; *Hum Rosen Professor Emeritus of Humanities, University of Pennsylvania;* b. 12 June 1933, Philadelphia, Pa; s. of Robert D. Abrahams and Florence Kohn Abrahams. *Education:* Swarthmore Coll., Columbia Univ., Univ. of Pennsylvania. *Career:* Instructor, Univ. of Texas at Austin 1960–63, Asst Prof. 1963–66, Assoc. Prof. 1966–69, Prof. of English and Anthropology 1969–79, Chair. English Dept 1974–79; Alexander H. Kenan Prof. of Humanities and Anthropology, Pitzer Coll. and Scripps Coll., Claremont, Calif. 1979–85; Prof. of Folklore and Folklife, Univ. of Pennsylvania 1985–2002 (Founder and Dir Center for Folklore and Ethnography 1998–2001), teaching graduate-level courses in Folklore and Folklife 2002–, currently Hum Rosen Prof. Emer. of Humanities; various visiting professorships; Fellow, American Folklore Soc. 1970, Nat. Humanities Inst. 1976–77; fmr Chair. Univ. of Pennsylvania Press; fmr consultant Texas Educational Agency, Roanoke Coll., Mt Senario Coll., Univ. of Louisville; mem. Bd of Advisors Encyclopedia of American Ethnicity, Wayne State Publications in Folklore; mem. American Folklore Soc. (Pres. 1978–79), Int. Soc. for Folk Narrative Research. *Publications include:* Deep Down in the Jungle: Negro Narrative Folklore from the Streets of Philadelphia 1964, Anglo-American Folksong Style (with George W. Foss Jr) 1968, Positively Black 1970, Deep the Water, Shallow the Shore: Three Essays on Shantying in the West Indies 1974, Talking Black 1976, Afro-American Folk Culture: An Annotated Bibliography 1977, Between the Living and the Dead: Riddles Which Tell Stories 1980, The Man-of-Words in the West Indies 1983, Singing the Master: The Emergence of African-American Culture in the Plantation South 1992, Everyday Life 2005, Blues for New Orleans 2006, The Ethnography of Performance (ed.). *Honours:* Guggenheim Fellowship 1965–66, American Folklore Soc. Lifetime Achievement Award 1989, Kenneth Goldstein Award for Lifetime Academic Leadership, American Folklore Soc. 2005.

ABRAMS, Meyer Howard, BA, MA, PhD; American writer and academic; *Professor Emeritus, Cornell University;* b. 23 July 1912, Long Branch, NJ; m. Ruth Gaynes 1937; two d. *Education:* Harvard Univ., Univ. of Cambridge, UK. *Career:* instructor in English 1938–42, Research Assoc., Psycho-Acoustic Laboratory 1942–45, Harvard Univ.; Asst Prof. Cornell Univ. 1945–47, Assoc. Prof. 1947–53, Prof. of English 1953–61, Frederic J. Whiton Prof. 1961–73, Class of 1916 Prof. 1973–83, Prof. Emer. 1983–; Visiting Lecturer at several insts of higher learning; Corresp. Fellow, British Acad.; mem. American Acad. of Arts and Sciences, American Acad. of Arts and Letters, American Asscn of Univ. Profs, American Philosophical Soc., Modern Language Asscn of

America, Nat. Humanities Center Founders' Group, Council of Scholars, Library of Congress. *Publications:* The Milk of Paradise: The Effects of Opium Visions on the Works of De Quincey, Crabbe, Francis Thompson and Coleridge 1934, The Mirror and the Lamp: Romantic Theory and the Critical Tradition 1953, A Glossary of Literary Terms 1957, Natural Supernaturalism: Tradition and Revolution in Romantic Literature 1971, The Correspondent Breeze: Essays in English Romanticism 1984, Doing Things With Texts: Essays in Criticism and Critical Theory 1989; editor: The Poetry of Pope 1954, Literature and Belief 1958, English Romantic Poets: Modern Essays in Criticism 1960, The Norton Anthology of English Literature 1962, Wordsworth: A Collection of Critical Essays 1972, William Wordsworth: Prelude 1979; contrib. to several vols. *Honours:* Rockefeller Foundation Fellowship 1946–47, Ford Foundation Fellowship 1953, Fulbright Scholarship 1954, Guggenheim Fellowships 1958, 1960, Fellow, Center for Advanced Study in the Behavioral Sciences 1967, Christian Gauss Prize 1954, MLA of America James Russell Lowell Prize 1971, Visiting Fellow, All Souls Coll., Oxford 1977, American Acad. of Arts and Sciences Award in Humanistic Studies 1984, Keats-Shelley Asscn Distinguished Scholar Award 1987, American Acad. and Inst. of Arts and Letters Award 1990. *Address:* 378 Savage Farm Drive, Ithaca, NY 14850, USA (home). *Telephone:* (607) 257-7012 (home). *E-mail:* mha5@cornell.edu.

ABRAMSKY, Dame Jennifer (Jenny), DBE, CBE, BA; British radio producer, editor and broadcasting industry executive; *Chair, Heritage Lottery Fund and National Heritage Memorial Fund*; b. 7 Oct. 1946, d. of the late Chimen Abramsky and Miriam Abramsky (née Nirenstein); m. Alasdair D. MacDuff Liddell 1976; one s. one d. *Education:* Holland Park School and Univ. of East Anglia. *Career:* joined BBC Radio as Programme Operations Asst 1969, Producer, The World at One 1973, Ed. PM 1978–81, Producer Radio Four Budget Programmes 1979–86, The World at One 1981–86, Ed. Today programme 1986–87, News and Current Affairs Radio 1987–93, est. Radio Four News FM 1991, Controller BBC Radio Five Live 1993–96, Dir Continuous News Services, BBC (including Radio Five Live, BBC News 24, BBC World, BBC News Online, Ceefax) 1996–98, Dir BBC Radio 1998–2000, BBC Radio and Music 2000–06, Head, Audio and Music Group 2006–08, also in charge of BBC Radio Drama and Popular Music TV 2007–08, mem. Exec. Bd; Chair., Heritage Lottery Fund and Nat. Heritage Memorial Fund 2008–; Chair. Univ. of London 2008–; News Int. Visiting Prof. of Broadcast Media, Exeter Coll., Oxford 2002; mem. Econ. and Social Research Council 1992–96, Editorial Bd British Journalism Review 1993–; Vice-Chair. Digital Radio Devt Bureau 2002–08, RAM; mem. Bd of Dirs Hampstead Theatre 2003–, Chair. 2005–; mem. Bd of Govs BFI 2000–06; Gov. Royal Ballet; Trustee, Shakespeare Schools Festival, Central School of Ballet; Radio Acad. Fellowship 1998; Fellow, Central School of Speech and Drama. *Honours:* Hon. Prof., Thames Valley Univ. 1994; Hon. RAM 2002; Hon. MA (Salford) 1997; Dr hc (Westminster), (East Anglia); Woman of Distinction, Jewish Care 1990, Sony Radio Acad. Award 1995. *Address:* Heritage Lottery Fund, 7 Holbein Place, London, SW1W 8NR, England (office). *Telephone:* (20) 7591-6000 (office). *Fax:* (20) 7591-6001 (office). *E-mail:* enquire@hlf.org.uk (office). *Website:* www.hlf.org.uk (office).

ABRAMSON, Jill Ellen, BA; American newspaper editor; *Executive Editor, New York Times*; b. 1954, d. of Norman L. Abramson and Dovie Abramson; m. Henry Griggs; two c. *Education:* Harvard Univ. *Career:* covered 1976 US presidential election for Time Magazine; Editorial Consultant, The American Lawyer 1976; Ed.-in-Chief Legal Times, Washington, DC 1986–88; Deputy Bureau Chief and investigative reporter, Wall Street Journal 1988–97; joined New York Times 1997, Enterprise Ed., Washington Bureau 1997–99, Washington Ed. 1999–2000, Washington Bureau Chief 2000–03, News Man. Ed. 2003–11, Exec. Ed. 2011–. *Publications include:* Where They Are Now 1986, Strange Justice (with Jane Mayer) 1994, The Puppy Diaries: Raising a Dog Named Scout 2011. *Honours:* Nat. Press Club Award 1992, ranked by Forbes magazine amongst The World's 100 Most Powerful Women (12th) 2011, ranked by Forbes magazine amongst The World's Most Powerful People (64th) 2011. *Address:* New York Times, 620 Eighth Avenue, New York, NY 10018, USA (office). *Telephone:* (212) 556-8000 (office). *E-mail:* managing-editor@nytimes.com (office). *Website:* www.nytimes.com (office).

ABSE, Dannie, CBE, DLitt, LRCP, MRCS, FRSL; British writer, poet and physician; b. 22 Sept. 1923, Cardiff, Wales; s. of Rudolph Abse and Kate Shepherd; m. Joan Mercer 1951 (died 2005); one s. two d. *Education:* St Illtyd's Coll. Cardiff, Univ. Coll. Cardiff, King's Coll., London and Westminster Hosp., London. *Career:* first book of poems published while still a medical student 1948; qualified as doctor 1950; Squadron-Leader RAF 1951–55; doctor in charge of chest clinic at Cen. Medical Establishment, Cleveland Street, London 1954–89; Writer-in-Residence, Princeton Univ., NJ, USA 1973–74; Pres. Poetry Soc. 1979–92; Fellow, Welsh Acad. 1993; Council Mem. Royal Soc. of Literature. *Publications:* poetry: After Every Green Thing 1948, Walking Under Water 1952, Ash on a Young Man's Sleeve 1954, Fire in Heaven 1956, Some Corner of an English Field 1956, Tenants of the House: Poems 1951–1956 1957, Poems, Golders Green 1962, Poems! Dannie Abse: A Selection 1963, Medicine on Trial 1967, Three Questor Plays 1967, A Small Desperation 1968, Demo Sceptre 1969, O. Jones, O. Jones 1970, Selected Poems 1970, Funland and Other Poems 1973, Way Out in the Centre 1981, A Strong Dose of Myself 1983, One-legged on Ice: Poems 1983, Ask the Bloody Horse 1986, Journals From the Ant Heap 1986, White Coat, Purple Coat: Collected Poems 1948–1988 1989, People (contrib.) 1990, Remembrance of Crimes Past: Poems 1986–1989 1990, The View from Row G: Three Plays 1990, Intermittent Journals Seren 1994, On the Evening Road 1994, Selected Poems 1994, Welsh Retrospective 1997, Arcadia, One Mile 1998, Be Seated, Thou: Poems 1989–1998 1999, Encounters Hearing Eye 2001, Goodbye, Twentieth Century: An Autobiography 2001, There Was a Young Man from Cardiff 2001, New and Collected Poems 2002, The Two Roads Taken: A Prose Miscellany 2003, Yellow Bird 2004, Running Late (Roland Mathias Award 2007) 2006, New Selected Poems 1949–2009: Anniversary Collection 2009, Two For Joy – Scenes from Married Life 2010; editor: Mavericks: An Anthology (co-ed. with Howard Sergeant) 1957, Modern European Verse 1964, Modern Poets in Focus 1 1971, Modern Poets in Focus 3 1971, Thirteen Poets 1972, Doctors and Patients 1984, Voices in the Gallery: Poems and Pictures (co-ed. with Joan Abse) 1986, The Music Lover's Literary Companion (co-ed. with Joan Abse) 1989, The Hutchinson Book of Post-War British Poets 1989, The Gregory Anthology 1991–93 (co-ed. with A. Stevenson) 1994, Twentieth-Century Anglo-Welsh Poetry 1997, New and Collected Poems 2003, 100 Great Poems of Love and Lust: Homage to Eros (compiler and ed.) 2007; fiction: Pythagoras (a play), Ash on a Young Man's Sleeve 1954, Some Corner of an English Field 1956, O Jones, O Jones 1970, Ask the Bloody Horse 1986, The View from Row G (three plays) 1990, There Was a Young Man from Cardiff 2001, The Strange Case of Dr Simmonds and Dr Glas 2002; other: Journals from the Ant Heap 1986, Intermittent Journals 1994, A Welsh Retrospective 1997, Goodbye, Twentieth Century 2001, The Two Roads Taken 2003, The Presence (memoir) (Wales Book of the Year English Language Prize 2008) 2007; contribs to BBC and various publs in the UK and USA. *Honours:* Hon. Fellow, Univ. of Wales Coll. of Medicine 1999; Hon. DLitt (Univ. of Wales) 1989, (Glamorgan) 1997; Welsh Arts Council Literature Prize 1971, 1987, Henry Foyle Award 1964, Jewish Chronicle Award, Cholmondeley Award 1983, 1985. *Literary Agent:* c/o United Agents, 12–26 Lexington Street, London, W1F 0LE. *Telephone:* (20) 3214-0800. *Fax:* (20) 3214-0801. *E-mail:* info@unitedagents.co.uk. *Website:* www.unitedagents.co.uk. *Address:* 85 Hodford Road, London, NW11 8NH, England (home). *Website:* www.dannieabse.com.

ABU-JABER, Diana, BA, MA, PhD; Jordanian/American author and academic; *Professor of English, Portland State University*; b. 1960, Syracuse, NY. *Education:* State Univ. of New York, Oswego and Binghamton, Univ. of Windsor. *Career:* Visiting Asst Prof. in English, Iowa State Univ. 1990; Asst Prof. of English, Univ. of Oregon 1990–95; Prof. of English, Portland State Univ. 1996–. *Radio:* frequent contrib. to Nat. Public Radio. *Publications:* fiction: Arabian Jazz (Oregon Book Award 1994) 1993, Crescent (PEN Center USA Award for Literary Fiction 2004, Before Columbus Foundation American Book Award 2004, Willamette Writers Northwest Distinguished Author Award 2004) 2003, Origin (Arab-American Book Award 2008, Florida Book Award Bronze Medal 2008) 2007, Birds of Paradise 2011; non-fiction: The Language of Baklava (Northwest Bookseller's Award 2005) 2005; contrib. of short fiction to many journals including Northwest Review, Left Bank, Story, Many Mountains Moving, Kenyon Review, Salt Hill Journal, Middle East Report, Tin House Magazine, Good Housekeeping magazine, Flyway Literary Magazine, Southern Review. *Honours:* Nat. Endowment for the Arts Writing Fellowship 1994–96, Int. Writers Nat. Endowment for the Arts Fellowship in Fiction 1996–98, Fulbright Research Award, Amman, Jordan 1996. *Literary Agent:* c/o Miriam Feuerle and Kate Gannon, Lyceum Agency, 915 SE 35th Avenue, #205, Portland, OR 97214, USA. *Telephone:* (503) 467-4622. *Website:* www.lyceumagency.com. *Address:* c/o Department of English, Neuberger Hall M403, Portland State University, Portland, OR 97207, USA (office). *Telephone:* (503) 267-2918 (office). *Fax:* (503) 725-3554 (office). *E-mail:* abujaber@pdx.edu (office); abujaber@aol.com. *Website:* www.english.pdx.edu/faculty/abu-jaber_d.php (office); www.dianaabujaber.com.

ABU KHALID, Fawziyya, MA; Saudi Arabian poet and essayist; *Lecturer in Sociology, King Saud University*; b. 1955, Riyadh. *Education:* American Univ. of Beirut, Lebanon, Lewis and Clark Coll., Portland, OR, USA. *Career:* taught at Women's Coll. King Saud Univ., Riyadh, now Lecturer in Sociology. *Publications:* poetry: Ila Mata Yakhtatifunaki Laylalt al-'Urs (How Long Will They Keep Raping You on Your Wedding Night) 1973, Oira' a fi as-Sirr li-Tarikh as-samt al-'Arabi (Secret Reading in the History of Arab Silence) 1985, Ma' as-Sarab (Water of the Mirage) 1995; also stories for children. *Address:* Department of Sociology, King Saud University, POB 2454, Riyadh 11451, Saudi Arabia (office). *Website:* www.ksu.edu.sa (office).

ABU ZAYD, Layla (see Abouzeïd, Leïla)

ACAR, Özgen; Turkish journalist; b. 29 Sept. 1938, Bor; s. of Mihilmi Acar and Naciye Acar (née Eren); m. Inci Güven 1980; one s. *Education:* Ankara Univ. *Career:* Parl. Corresp. Cumhuriyet Daily Newspaper 1960–61, Econ. Corresp. 1961–63, Diplomatic Corresp. 1963–65, 1967–72, Investigative Corresp. 1990–92, 1994–, Ed.-in-Chief Istanbul 1992–94; Corresp. Reuters, Ankara 1972–74; Bureau Chief Milliyet Daily Newspaper Athens 1980–84, Ankara 1984–86, New York 1986–88; TV and radio reporter; mem. Exec. Cttee of Int. Fed. of Journalists (IFJ) 1971, Adviser 1972–78. *Publications:* numerous investigative reports. *Honours:* several journalism awards. *Address:* Cumhuriyet Gazetesi, Ahmet Rasim Sokak, 06550 Cankaya, Ankara, Turkey. *Telephone:* (312) 4427989 (office). *Fax:* (312) 4427990 (office). *E-mail:* postakutusu@cumhuriyet.com.tr (office). *Website:* www.cumhuriyet.com.tr (office).

ACCAD, Evelyne, MA, PhD; Lebanese/Swiss/American academic and writer; *Professor Emerita, University of Illinois at Urbana-Champaign and Lebanese American University*; b. 6 Oct. 1943, Beirut, Lebanon; pnr Paul Vieille. *Education:* Beirut Coll. for Women, Anderson Coll., Ball State Univ., Indiana Univ. *Career:* Prof., Univ. of Illinois at Urbana-Champaign, now Prof. Emer., mem. core faculty African Center, Women's Studies Center, Middle East Studies Program, Campus Honors Faculty 1974–; Prof. Emer., Lebanese American Univ.; teacher, Beirut Univ. Coll. 1978–84, Northwestern Univ. 1991; mem. of jury, Int. Neustadt Prize for Literature. *Publications:* Veil of Shame: The Role of Women in the Modern Fiction of North Africa and the Arab World (Delta Kappa Gamma Soc. Int. Educator's Award) 1978, Montjoie Palestine! or Last Year in Jerusalem 1980, L'Excisée 1982, Coquelicot du Massacre 1988, Sexuality and War: Literary Masks of the Middle East 1990, Des femmes, des hommes et la guerre: Fiction et Réalité au Proche-Orient (France-Lebanon Literary Award ADELF) 1993, Blessures des Mots 1993, Wounding Words: A Woman's Journal in Tunisia 1996, Voyages en Cancer (translated as The Wounded Breast: Intimate Journeys Through Cancer) (Prix Phénix 2001) 2000, Femmes de Crépuscule 2008; other: four edited vols, 15 book chapters and 76 articles. *Honours:* Florence Howard Award (Hon. Mention) 1975, special recognition Illinois Arts Council Creative Writing Fellowship 1979, Fulbright Awards 1983–85, 2002, Social Science Research Council Fellowship 1988–89, Studies of Cultural Values and Ethics Program Award 1992, 1996–97, Emmanuel Robles Poetry Award 2006. *Address:* Department of French, 2090 Foreign Languages Bldg, University of Illinois, Urbana, IL 61801 (office); 306 W Michigan, Urbana, IL 61801, USA (home). *Telephone:* (217) 333-2020 (office). *Fax:* (217) 244-2223 (office). *E-mail:* evaccad@yahoo.fr; e-accad@illinois.edu (office).

ACHAARI, Mohammad; Moroccan writer; b. 1951, Moulay Idriss Zerhoun. *Education:* Mohammed V Univ. *Career:* fmr contrib. to several Moroccan newspapers including Al-Alam, Al Ittihad Al Ichtiraki; mem. Union des Écrivains du Maroc (Moroccan Union of Writers) 1975–, Pres. 1989–96; Sec.-Gen. Syndicat nat. de l'agriculture 1979–84; Bureau Chief, Al Ittihad Al Ichtiraki (daily newspaper) 1983–98; Minister of Culture 1998; mem. Union socialiste des forces populaires, mem. Poltical Bureau; mem. Syndicat nat. de la Presse, Fondation Mohammed V pour la Solidarité. *Publications:* six collections of poetry, short-story collection; El Jardin de la Soledad/The Garden of Solitude (collected poems in English and Spanish translation) 2005; novels: South of the Soul, The Arch and the Butterfly (co-recipient Int. Prize for Arabic Fiction 2011). *Address:* c/o Ministry of Culture, 1 rue Ghandi, Rabat, Morocco (office).

ACHCAR, Gilbert; Lebanese/French author and academic; *Professor of Development Studies and International Relations, School of Oriental and African Studies, London*; b. 1951, Senegal. *Education:* Univ. of Lebanon, Beirut, Univ. of Paris VIII. *Career:* Prof. of Politics and Int. Relations, Univ. of Paris VIII –2003; worked at Marcel Bloch Inst., Berlin 2003–07; Prof. of Devt Studies and Int. Relations, School of Oriental and African Studies, London 2007–; Fellow, Int. Inst. for Research and Educ. *Publications:* La Nouvelle Guerre Froide: le monde après le Kosovo 1999, Le Marxisme d'Ernest Mandel 1999, Eastern Cauldron: Islam, Afghanistan, Palestine and Iraq in a Marxist Mirror 2004, The Israeli Dilemma: A Debate between Two Left-Wing Jews 2006, The Clash of Barbarisms: The Making of the New World Disorder 2006, The 33-Day War: Israel's War on Hezbollah in Lebanon and its Consequences (with Michel Warschawski) 2007, Perilous Power: The Middle East and US Foreign Policy (with Noam Chomsky) 2007, The Arabs and the Holocaust: The Arab-Israeli War of Narratives 2010; contrib. to Le Monde Diplomatique, ZNet, International Viewpoint, other contribs include numerous chapters in books and articles in journals. *Address:* Office No. 292b, School of Oriental and African Studies, University of London, Thornhaugh Street, Russell Square, London, WC1H 0XG, England (office); International Institute for Research and Education, Lombokstraat 40, 1094 Amsterdam, Netherlands (office). *Telephone:* (20) 7898-4557 (London) (office); (20) 6717263 (Amsterdam) (office). *E-mail:* ga3@soas.ac.uk (office). *Website:* www.soas.ac.uk (office); www.iire.org (office).

ACHEBE, (Albert Chinualumogu) Chinua, BA, FRSL; Nigerian writer, poet and academic; *Charles P. Stevenson Jr Professor of Languages and Literature, Bard College*; b. 16 Nov. 1930, Ogidi, Anambra State; s. of the late Isaiah O. Achebe and Janet N. Achebe; m. Christie C. Okoli 1961; two s. two d. *Education:* Govt Coll., Umuahia and Univ. Coll., Ibadan. *Career:* Producer, Nigerian Broadcasting Corpn, Lagos 1954–58, Regional Controller, Enugu 1958–61, Dir Voice of Nigeria, Lagos 1961–66; Sr Research Fellow, Univ. of Nigeria, Nsukka 1967–72; Rockefeller Fellowship 1960–61; UNESCO Fellowship 1963; Foundation mem. Asscn of Nigerian Authors 1982–, Pres. 1981–86; mem. Gov. Council, Lagos Univ. 1966, mem. E. Cen. State Library Bd 1971–72; Founding Ed., Okike 1971–; Prof. of English, Univ. of Mass 1972–75, Univ. of Conn. 1975–76, Univ. of Nigeria, Nsukka 1976–81, Prof. Emer. 1985–; Charles P. Stevenson Jr Prof. of Languages and Literature, Bard Coll. 1991–; Pro-Chancellor and Chair. of Council, Anambra State Univ. of Tech., Enugu, Nigeria 1986–88; Regents Lecturer, UCLA 1984; Founding Ed. African Writers' Series (Heinemann) 1962–72; Dir Heinemann Educational Books (Nigeria) Ltd, Nwamife (Publishers), Enugu; mem. Tokyo Colloquium 1981; Visiting Distinguished Prof. of English, City Coll., New York 1989; Montgomery Fellow and Visiting Prof., Dartmouth Coll., Hanover 1990; Visiting Fellow, Ashby Lecturer, Clare Hall, Cambridge 1993; Scottish Arts Council Neil Gunn Int. Fellow 1975; Fellow, Ghana Asscn of Writers 1975; Goodwill Amb. (UN Population Fund) 1998–. *Publications:* fiction: Things Fall Apart 1958, No Longer at Ease 1960, The Sacrificial Egg and Other Stories (short stories) 1962, Arrow of God 1964, A Man of the People 1966, Chike and the River (juvenile) 1966, How the Leopard Got his Claws (juvenile, with John Iroaganachi) 1972, Girls at War (short stories) 1973, The Flute (juvenile) 1978, The Drum (juvenile) 1978, African Short Stories (ed., with C. L. Innes) 1984, Anthills of the Savannah 1987, The Heinemann Book of Contemporary African Short Stories (ed., with C. L. Innes) 1992, Telling Tales (contrib. to charity anthology) 2004; poetry: Beware, Soul-Brother and Other Poems 1971, Christmas in Biafra and Other Poems 1973, Don't Let him Die: An Anthology of Memorial Poems for Christopher Okigbo (ed., with Dubem Okafor) 1978, Aka Weta: An Anthology of Igbo Poetry (ed., with Obiora Udechukwu) 1982, Home and Exile 2000, Collected Poems 2004; non-fiction: Morning Yet on Creation Day (essays) 1975, The Trouble with Nigeria (essays) 1983, Hopes and Impediments: Selected Essays 1965–87 1988, Essays and Poems: Another Africa (ed., with Robert Lyons) 1998, Home and Exile (essays) 2000, The Education of a British-Protected Child: Essays 2009; contrib. to New York Review of Books, Transition, Callaloo. *Honours:* Hon. mem. American Acad. of Arts and Letters 1982; Hon. Fellow, Modern Language Asscn of America 1974; Hon. DUniv, Hon. DLitt (16 times), Hon. DHL (eight times), Hon. LLD (three times), Dr hc (Open Univ.) 1989; Margaret Wrong Memorial Prize 1959, Nigerian Nat. Trophy 1960, Jock Campbell New Statesman Award 1965, Commonwealth Poetry Prize 1972, The Lotus Prize (Afro-Asian writers) 1975, Order of the Federal Republic (Nigeria) 1979, Nigerian Nat. Merit Award 1979, Nonino Prize (Italy) 1994, Campion Medal, New York 1996, Nat. Creativity Award 1999, Friedenspreis (Germany) 2002, Man Booker Int. Prize 2007, Dorothy and Lillian Gish Prize 2010. *Literary Agent:* David Higham Associates, 5–8 Lower John Street, Golden Square, London, W1F 9HA, England. *Address:* Bard College, PO Box 41, Annandale-on-Hudson, NY 12504, USA (office). *Telephone:* (845) 758-7325 (office). *E-mail:* achebe@bard.edu (office). *Website:* www.bard.edu/academics/programs/langlit (office).

ACHOLONU, Catherine Obianuju, MA, PhD; Nigerian poet, playwright, literary critic, essayist and academic; *Director, Catherine Acholonu Research Centre*; b. 26 Oct. 1956, Orlu; d. of Chief Lazarus Emejuru Olumba; four c. *Education:* Univ. of Düsseldorf, Germany. *Career:* Lecturer, Alvan Ikoku Coll., Owerri 1980–96; Fulbright Scholar and Visiting Prof., Manhattanville Coll., NY, USA 1990–91; Sr Special Asst to Nigerian Pres. for Arts and Culture 1999–2002; Founder-Dir Catherine Acholonu Research Centre; Founder Let's Help Humanitarian Project; currently Nigeria Country Amb., Forum of Arts and Culture to UN Convention to Combat Desertification; Prof. of African History and Philosophy, Pilgrim's Univ. and Theological Seminary (Aba Campus), NC, USA; Fellow, Nigerian Inst. of Corp. Admin, Nigerian Chartered Inst. of Public Admin, Worldwide Services – Worldwide Finance Ltd. *Plays include:* Into the Heart of Biafra 1985, Trial of the Beautiful Ones 1985 (presented at Manhattanville Coll., Purchase, NY 1991), The Deal and Who is the Head of State 1986. *Publications include:* poetry: Nigeria in the Year 1999 1985, The Spring's Last Drop 1985; essays: The Earth Unchained: A Quantum Leap in Consciousness 1995, Motherism: The Afrocentric Alternative to Feminism 1995, Africa the New Frontier 2002; research works on anthropology, linguistics, prehistory, indigenous culture: The Igbo Roots of Olaudah Equiano 1989, The Gram Code of African Adam 2005, They Lived Before Adam (Int. Book Awards (USA) 2009) 2009, The Lost Testament of the Ancestors of Adam 2010; children's books and poems: Recite and Learn – Poetry for Senior Primary 1986, Recite and Learn Poetry for Junior Primary 1986, Abu Umu Praimari (in Igbo language) 1987; contrib. of poems and short stories to anthologies, articles and chapters to magazines and journals worldwide. *Honours:* Grand Fellow of Ife Poets, OAU Univ.; Fulbright Scholar-Writer-in-Residency Award 1990 and numerous literary awards, including Flora Nwapa Award at Harlem Book Fair (USA) 2009, Nigerian Nat. Merit Award 2011. *Address:* Catherine Acholonu Research Centre, PMB 5197, Abuja, Nigeria (office). *Telephone:* (9) 8707887 (office); (9) 2906360 (office). *E-mail:* ikomgram@yahoo.com (office); unfacnigeria@yahoo.com (office). *Website:* www.carcafriculture.org (office).

ACKERMAN, Diane, BA, MFA, PhD; American poet, writer and educator; b. 7 Oct. 1948, Waukegan, Ill. *Education:* Boston Univ., Pennsylvania State Univ., Cornell Univ. *Career:* Teaching Asst, Cornell Univ. 1971–78, Lecturer 1978, Visiting Writer 1987, Visiting Prof. 1998–2000; Asst Prof., Univ. of Pittsburgh 1980–83; Writer-in-Residence, Coll. of William and Mary 1982–83, Ohio Univ. 1983, New York Univ. 1986, Columbia Univ. 1986–87; Writer-in-Residence, Washington Univ. 1983–86, Dir Writers' Program 1984–86; staff writer, New Yorker magazine 1988–94; Visiting Prof., Soc. for the Humanities, Cornell Univ. 1998–2000; Nat. Endowment for the Humanities Distinguished Prof. of English, Univ. of Richmond 2001. *Television:* A Natural History of the Senses. *Publications include:* The Planets: A Cosmic Pastoral 1976, Wife of Light 1978, Twilight of the Tenderfoot 1980, Lady Faustus 1983, On Extended Wings 1985, Reverse Thunder 1988, A Natural History of the Senses 1990, Jaguar of Sweet Laughter: New and Selected Poems 1991, The Moon by Whale Light and Other Adventures Among Bats, Crocodilians, Penguins and Whales 1991, A Natural History of Love 1994, The Rarest of the Rare 1995, Monk Seal Hideaway 1995, A Slender Thread 1997, Bats: Shadows in the Night 1997, I Praise My Destroyer 1998, The Norton Book of Love (ed. with Jeanne Mackin) 1998, Deep Play 1999, Cultivating Delight: A Natural History of My Garden 2001, Origami Bridges 2002, Animal Sense 2003, An Alchemy of Mind: the Marvel and Mystery of the Mind 2004, The Zookeeper's Wife, a War Story (Orion Book Award 2008) 2007, Dawn Light 2009, One Hundred Names for

Love: A Stroke, a Marriage, and the Language of Healing 2011; contrib. to numerous anthologies, books, newspapers, journals and magazines. *Honours:* Hon. DLit (Kenyon Coll.); Abbie Copps Poetry Prize 1974, Nat. Endowment for the Arts Creative Writing Fellowships 1976, 1986, Black Warrior Review Poetry Prize 1981, Pushcart Prize 1984, Acad. of American Poets Peter I. B. Lavan Award 1985, Lowell Thomas Award 1990, New York Times Book Review Notable Books of the Year 1991, 1992, and New and Noteworthy Books of the Year 1993, 1997, Wordsmith Award 1992, New York Public Library Literary Lion 1994, John Burroughs Nature Award 1997, Art of Fact Award 2000, Best American Essays Citation 2001, Guggenheim Fellowship 2003. *Literary Agent:* c/o Suzanne Gluck, William Morris Agency, 1325 Avenue of the Americas, New York, NY 10019, USA. *E-mail:* SGasst@wma.com. *Website:* www.wma.com. *E-mail:* inkdream@hotmail.com (home). *Website:* www.dianeackerman.com.

ACKERMAN, Susan Yoder, BA; American teacher and writer; b. 2 Nov. 1945, Newport News, Va; d. of Lauren Aquilla Yoder and Nina Viola Stemen Yoder; m. Robert W. Ackerman II 1969; one s. two d. *Education:* Eastern Mennonite Coll., Coll. of William and Mary, Univ. of Virginia, Longwood Coll. and Hampton Univ. *Career:* elementary school teacher, Newport News, Va 1966–67, 1972; teacher of English as a foreign language, Lubumbashi, Zaïre 1969–70, Kongolo, Zaïre 1979–80; middle and high school French teacher, Newport News 1984–86, 1989–96; Day Care Dir, Newport News 1989–90; elementary school prin. 2000–03; Writer-in-Residence, Island Inst., Sitka, Alaska April 2000; speaker on African experiences and on writing; leader, workshops on writing children's fiction; mem. Soc. of Children's Book Writers and Illustrators. *Publications:* Copper Moons 1990, The Flying Pie and Other Stories 1996, Zane the Train 2006, Kindermusik; contrib. of educational testing material, stories and articles to periodicals, including Cricket, On the Line, With, Instructor, Story Friends, Christian Living, Purpose, Together, Live, Mothering, Click, Cicada, Spider, Primary Treasure, USArt, Zootles; lyrics to two CDs by Do, Re, Mi, and You. *Address:* 524 Marlin Drive, Newport News, VA 23602, USA (home). *Telephone:* (757) 877-9113 (home). *E-mail:* susan@ackerman.net (office).

ACKLIN, Jürg; Swiss psychoanalyst and writer; b. 20 Feb. 1945, Zurich; m. Beate Acklin-Schönegger 2008; one s. two d. *Education:* Univs of Zürich and Bremen. *Career:* Leader, Literturclub, Swiss TV. *Publications:* collection of poems 1967; fiction: Michael Häuptli 1969, Alias 1971, Das Uberhandnehmen 1973, Der Aufstieg des Fesselballons 1980, Der Känguruhmann 1992, Das Tangopaar 1994, Froschgesang 1996, Der Vater 1998, Defekt 2002, Vertrauen ist gut 2009. *Honours:* C. F. Meyer Prize 1971, Bremer Literature Prize 1972, Zürcher Buch Prize 1997, Literarische Auszeichnung des Kantons Zürich 2009. *Address:* c/o Verlag Nagel & Kimche AG, V-Nr. 1320 506, Nordstr. 9, 8006 Zurich, Switzerland (office).

ACKROYD, Peter, CBE, MA, FRSL; British writer; b. 5 Oct. 1949, London; s. of Graham Ackroyd and Audrey Whiteside. *Education:* St Benedict's School, Ealing, Clare Coll., Cambridge and Yale Univ., USA. *Career:* Literary Ed. The Spectator 1973–77, Jt Man. Ed. 1978–82; Chief Book Reviewer The Times 1986–; Mellon Fellow, Yale Univ. *Play:* The Mystery of Charles Dickens 2000. *Television:* Charles Dickens (BBC 2), Peter Ackroyd's London (BBC 2) 2004, The Romantics (BBC 2) 2006, London Visions (Artsworld) 2007, Peter Ackroyd's Venice (BBC 2) 2009. *Publications:* fiction: The Great Fire of London 1982, The Last Testament of Oscar Wilde (Somerset Maugham Prize 1984) 1983, Hawksmoor (Whitbread Award for Fiction 1986, Guardian Fiction Award 1986) 1985, Chatterton 1987, First Light 1989, English Music 1992, The House of Doctor Dee 1993, Dan Leno and the Limehouse Golem 1994, Milton in America 1996, The Plato Papers 1999, The Clerkenwell Tales (short stories) 2003, The Lambs of London 2004, The Fall of Troy 2006, The Casebook of Victor Frankenstein 2009, The Canterbury Tales: A Retelling 2009, The Death of King Arthur: The Immortal Legend 2010; non-fiction: Notes for a New Culture 1976, Dressing Up: Transvestism and Drag: The History of an Obsession 1979, Ezra Pound and His World 1980, T. S. Eliot (RSL W. H. Heinemann Award 1985, Whitbread Award for Biography 1985) 1984, Dickens 1990, Introduction to Dickens 1991, Blake 1995, The Life of Thomas More 1998, London: The Biography 2000, Dickens: Public Life and Private Passion 2002, The Collection 2002, Albion: The Origins of the English Imagination 2002, Illustrated London 2003, The Beginning: Voyages Through Time (juvenile) 2003, Chaucer 2004, Shakespeare: The Biography 2005, Brief Lives – Newton 2006, Thames: Sacred River 2007, Poe: A Life Cut Short 2008, Venice: Pure City 2009, The English Ghost: Spectres through Time 2010, London Under 2011, Foundation: The History of England (Vol. 1) 2011, Wilkie Collins 2012, London: The Concise Biography 2012; poetry: London Lickpenny 1973, Country Life 1978, The Diversions of Purley 1987. *Honours:* Hon. Fellow, Clare Coll., Univ. of Cambridge 2008, Hon. Fellow, RIBA 2009; Hon. DLitt (Univ. of Exeter), (London Guildhall), (City Univ.), (Univ. Coll., London), (Brunel Univ.) 2006. *Literary Agent:* c/o Anthony Sheil Associates Ltd, 43 Doughty Street, London, WC1N 2LF, England. *Telephone:* (20) 7405-9351.

ACOSTA, Devashish Donald, MFA; American writer; b. 9 Nov. 1956, New York, NY. *Education:* San Diego State Univ. *Publications:* Felicitavia: A Spiritual Journey 1997, When the Time Comes 1998, Sadvipra 2000, The Ashram 2004, Devi 2010, Anandamurti: The Jamalpur Years 2010.

ÁCS, Margit; Hungarian writer and editor; b. 11 June 1941, Újpest; d. of Ferenc Ács and Margit Ács (née Baracsi); m. Mátyás Domokos 1967; two s. *Education:* Loránd Eötvös Univ. *Career:* Ed. Szépirodalmi Publishing 1964–87, Magvető Publishing 1987. *Publications:* short stories: Only Air and Water 1977, Whip and Alms 1983; novels: Initiation 1979, Chance 1988, The Unsuspecting Traveller 1988. *Honours:* Füst Milán Prize 1989, József Attila Prize 1991. *Address:* c/o Magvető Könyvkiadó, 1806 Budapest, Vörösmarty tér 1 (office); 1085 Budapest, Somogyi Béla u 24, Hungary (home). *Telephone:* (1) 118-5109 (office); (1) 114-3610 (home).

ADALJA, Varsha Mahendra, MA; Indian writer and editor; b. 1940, Bombay (now Mumbai). *Education:* Bombay (now Mumbai) Univ. *Career:* Gujarati writer; Ed., Sudha magazine 1973–76, Gujarati Femina magazine 1989–90; mem. Advisory Bd Sahitya Akademi. *Television:* as producer: Ansaar. *Publications include:* more than forty books including: Shravan tara sarvada 1967, Avaj no Akar 1975, Anand dhara 1976, Neelima Mrityu Paami Chhey 1977, Paccha fartan 1981, Pagalan 1983, Khari Padelo Tahuko 1983, Gantha chutyani vela 1984, Ananddhara 1984, Mare pan ek ghar hoy 1986, Eni sugandh 1990, Matinun 1991, Bandivan 1991, Varsha adaljani shresttha vartao 1992, Gantha chutyani vela.1994, Khari padelo tahuko 1995, Anasara 1997, Mandodari 1998, Ganthe bandhyun akash 1998, Sabdasrshti 2000, Shag re sankoru 2003. *Honours:* Gujarati Sahitya Parishad Award 1972, 1975, Soviet Land Nehru Award 1976, Gujarati Sahitya Academy Award 1977, 1979, 1980, Sahitya Akademi Award 1995. *Address:* 110-112 Princess Street, Keshav Baug, Mumbai 400 002 (office); Dwarkesh, Nr. Royal Apartment, Nehru Bridge Corner, Khanpur, Ahmedabad 380 001, India (office). *Telephone:* (22) 22013441 (Mumbai) (office); (22) 22058293 (Mumbai) (office); (79) 25506573 (Ahmedabad) (office); (79) 25501732 (Ahmedabad) (office). *E-mail:* authors@rrsheth.com (office). *Website:* www.rrsheth.com (office).

ADAMESTEANU, Gabriela; Romanian writer, journalist and translator; b. 2 April 1942, Targu Ocna; d. of Mircea Adameșteanu and Elena Adameșteanu; m. Gheorghe-Mihai Ionescu; one s. *Education:* Univ. of Bucharest. *Career:* apptd Ed.-in-Chief 22 magazine 1991–95; mem. Romanian PEN Centre (Pres. 2004–06), Women's Edn 1998–2001; Guest Author, 7th New Literature, Europe Festival USA 2010. *Publications:* Drumul egal al fiecarei zile (novel) 1975, Daruieste-ti o zi de vacanta (short stories) 1979, Dimineata pierduta (novel) 1983, Vara-primavara (short stories) 1989, Obsesia politicii (interviews) 1995, Cele doua Romanii 2000, Întâlnirea (novel) 2003, The Encounter (novel) 2007, Provisional (novel) 2010. *Honours:* Romanian Acad. Award for Fiction 1975, Romanian Writers Union Award 1984, Human Rights Watch Hellman Hammett Grant 2002, Ziarul de Iasi Nat. Award for Fiction 2004. *Address:* c/o Romanian PEN Centre, S.F. Voievozi 29, Apartment 19, Sector 1, 010964 Bucharest, Romania.

ADAMS, Daniel (see NICOLE, Christopher Robin)

ADAMS, Deborah; American writer and poet; b. 22 Jan. 1956, Tenn.; m.; three c. *Education:* Univ. of Tennessee at Martin, Austin Peay Univ. *Career:* Adjunct Faculty, Nashville State Technical Inst.; mem. Appalachian Writers' Asscn, Mystery Writers of America, Sisters in Crime. *Publications:* fiction: All the Great Pretenders 1992, All the Crazy Winters 1992, All the Dark Disguises 1993, All the Hungry Mothers 1994, All the Deadly Beloved 1995, All the Blood Relatives 1997, All the Dirty Cowards 2000, Kudzu and Corpses (e-book) 2010; poetry: Propriety 1976, Looking for Heroes 1984. *Honours:* Flair and Macavity Award. *E-mail:* rrcommunications@aol.com (office).

ADAMS, Harold, BA; American writer; b. 20 Feb. 1923, Clark, SDak; m. Betty E. Skogsberg 1959 (divorced 1965); one d. *Education:* Univ. of Minnesota. *Career:* fmr Operations Man. Minneapolis Better Business Bureau; fmr mem. Bd of Dirs Minnesota Charities Review Council; mem. Authors' Guild, Mystery Writers of America. *Publications:* Murder 1981, Paint the Town Red 1982, The Missing Moon 1983, The Naked Liar 1985, The Fourth Widow 1986, When Rich Men Die 1987, The Barbed Wire Noose 1987, The Man Who Met the Train 1988, The Man Who Missed the Party 1989, The Man Who was Taller than God 1992, A Perfectly Proper Murder 1993, A Way with Widows 1994, The Ditched Blonde 1995, The Hatchet Job 1996, The Ice Pick Artist 1997, No Badge, No Gun 1998, Lead, so I Can Follow 2000, The Fourth of July Wake 2002. *Honours:* Shamus Award, Best Private Eye Novel 1992, Minnesota Book Award, Mystery and Detective 1993.

ADAMS, Hazard Simeon, BA, MA, PhD; American writer, poet, editor and academic; *Byron W. and Alice L. Lockwood Professor Emeritus of Humanities, University of Washington*; b. 15 Feb. 1926, Cleveland, Ohio; s. of Robert Simeon Adams and Mary Thurness Adams; m. Diana White 1949; two s. *Education:* Princeton Univ., Univ. of Washington. *Career:* mil. service in Marine Corps 1943–45, 1951; Instructor, Asst Prof., Cornell Univ. 1952–56; Asst Prof., Univ. of Texas 1956–59; Assoc. Prof. to Prof., Michigan State Univ. 1959–64; Fulbright Lecturer, Trinity Coll., Dublin 1961–62; Prof., Univ. of California, Irvine 1964–77, Dean of Humanities 1970–72, Vice-Chancellor 1972–75; Prof. of English and Comparative Literature, Univ. of Washington 1977–97, Byron W. and Alice L. Lockwood Prof. of Humanities 1987–97, Prof. Emer. 1997–. *Publications:* Blake and Yeats – The Contrary Vision 1955, William Blake – A Reading of the Shorter Poems 1963, The Contexts of Poetry 1963, The Horses of Instruction – A Novel 1968, The Interests of Criticism 1969, The Truth About Dragons – An Anti-Romance 1971, Lady Gregory 1973, The Academic Tribes 1976, Philosophy of the Literary Symbolic 1983, Joyce Cary's Trilogies – Pursuit of the Particular Real 1983, Antithetical Essays in Literary Criticism and Liberal Education 1990, The Book of Yeats's Poems 1990, The Book of Yeats's Vision 1995, The Farm at Richwood and Other

Poems 1997, Many Pretty Toys – A Novel 1999, Four Lectures on the History of Criticism in the West 2000, Home – A Novel 2001, The Offensive of Poetry 2007, Academic Child 2008, Blake's Margins 2009, William Blake on His Poetry and Painting 2010, The Day the Dogs Talked 2011; ed.: Poems by Robert Simeon Adams 1952, Poetry – An Introductory Anthology 1968, Fiction as Process (with Carl Hartman) 1968, William Blake–Jerusalem, Selected Poems and Prose 1970, Critical Theory Since Plato 1971 (third edn 2003), Critical Theory Since 1965 (with Leroy Searle) 1986, Critical Essays on William Blake 1991; contribs to numerous poetry, scholarly and critical journals. *Honours:* Guggenheim Fellowship 1974. *Address:* 3930 NE 157th Place, Lake Forest Park, WA 98155, USA (home). *Telephone:* (206) 364-4302 (home). *E-mail:* HAdams3048@aol.com (office).

ADAMS, James MacGregor David; British journalist and writer; b. 22 April 1951, Newcastle upon Tyne, England; m. Renee Thatcher Riley 1990; two d. *Education:* Harrow School, Neuchâtel Univ., Switzerland. *Career:* began career at Evening Chronicle, Newcastle; reporter and News Ed., 8 Days magazine, London; Foreign Man., Defence Corresp., Man. Ed. and Washington Bureau Chief, Sunday Times 1981–97; CEO United Press International 1997–2001; Founder Ashland Inst. for Strategic Studies 2001–05; presenter, Jefferson Exchange radio show. *Publications:* The Unnatural Alliance 1984, The Financing of Terror 1986, Secret Armies 1988, Ambush (the War Between the SAS and the IRA) with Robin, Morgan and Anthony Bambridge 1988, Merchants of Death 1990, The Final Terror 1991, Bull's Eye 1992, Taking the Tunnel 1993, Full Service Bank 1993, The Next World War 2001; contribs to Sunday Times, Washington Post, Los Angeles Times, Atlantic. *Address:* 4880 Highway 66, Ashland, OR 97520-9712, USA (home). *Telephone:* (541) 482-2273 (home).

ADAMS, Joanna Z. (see KOCH, Joanne Barbara)

ADAMS, Perseus, BA; South African writer, journalist, poet and teacher (retd); b. (Peter Robert Charles Adams), 11 March 1933, Cape Town; m. 1958. *Education:* Univ. of Cape Town. *Career:* worked as journalist, psychologist, clerk, and teacher in seven countries. *Publications:* The Land at My Door 1965, Grass for the Unicorn 1975, Cries and Silences: Selected Poems 1996; contribs: numerous, mostly to Contrast, Cape Town. *Honours:* South Africa State Poetry Prize 1963, Festival of Rhodesia Prize 1970, Keats Memorial Int. Prize 1971, Bridport Arts Festival Prize 1984, co-winner, Writing Section, Bard of the Year 1993.

ADAMS, Phillip Andrew, AO, AM, FRSA; Australian writer, broadcaster and film maker; b. 12 July 1939; m. 1st (divorced); three d.; m. 2nd Patrice Newell; one d. *Education:* Eltham High School. *Career:* columnist and critic 1956–; Chair. Film, Radio and TV Bd 1972–75; Founder-mem. Australia Council 1972–75; Vic. Govt Rep., Australian Children's TV Foundation 1981–87; Pres. Vic. Council for Arts 1982–86; Chair. Australian Film Inst. 1975–80, Australian Film Comm. 1983–90, Comm. for the Future 1985–90, Nat. Australia Day Council 1992–96; Foundation Chair., Australian Centre for Social Innovation 2009–; mem. Bd Ausflag 1990–, Cttee for the Centenary of Fed. 1994; worked with Families in Distress 1985–, Montsalvat Artists' Soc. 1986–, CARE Australia 1995–97; Sr ANZAC Fellow 1981; mem. Bd Nat. Museum of Australia 1996–97, Festival of Ideas 1999; mem. Council, Adelaide Festival 1996. *Films include:* Jack and Jill: A Postscript 1970, The Naked Bunyip 1971, The Adventures of Barry McKenzie 1972, Don's Party 1975, The Getting of Wisdom 1976, Grendel Grendel Grendel 1980, We of the Never Never 1982, Lonely Hearts 1982, Fighting Back 1983. *Radio includes:* Compere, Late Night Live (ABC). *Television includes:* Death and Destiny, Short and Sweet (ABC), Adam's Australia (BBC), The Big Question, Face the Press (SBS). *Publications:* Adams With Added Enzymes 1970, The Unspeakable Adams 1977, More Unspeakable Adams 1979, The Uncensored Adams 1981, The Inflammable Adams 1983, Adams Versus God 1985, Harold Cazneaux: The Quiet Observer (with H. Ennis) 1994, Classic Columns 1994, The Penguin Book of Australian Jokes (with P. Newell) 1994, The Penguin Book of Jokes from Cyberspace (with P. Newell) 1995, The Big Questions (with P. Davies) 1996, The Penguin Book of More Australian Jokes 1996, Kookaburra 1996, Emperors of the Air 1997, Retreat from Tolerance? 1997, More Big Questions (with P. Davies) 1998, The Penguin Book of Schoolyard Jokes (with P. Newell) 1998, A Billion Voices 1999, The Penguin Book of All New Australian Jokes (with P. Newell) 2000, Adams Ark 2004, Adams vs. God: The Rematch 2007, Backstage Politics 2011. *Honours:* Hon. FAHA 2008; Hon. DUniv (Griffith Univ.) 1998, (Univ. of South Australia) 2004, Hon. DLitt (Edith Cowan Univ.) 2003, (Univ. of Sydney); Raymond Longford Award 1981, Australian Arts Award 1987, Australian Humanist of the Year 1987, CSICOP Award for Responsibility in Media (New York) 1996, Australian Republican of the Year 2006, Human Rights and Equal Opportunity Comm. Human Rights Medal 2006. *Address:* c/o Radio National, ABC, GPO Box 9994, Sydney, NSW 2001, Australia (office). *E-mail:* philadams@ozemail.com.au (home).

ADAMS, Richard George, MA, FRSA, FRSL; British novelist; b. 9 May 1920, Newbury, Berks., England; s. of Dr E. G. B. Adams, FRCS and Lilian Rosa Adams (née Button); m. Barbara Elizabeth Acland 1949; two d. *Education:* Bradfield Coll., Berks. and Worcester Coll., Oxford. *Career:* army service 1940–46; Home Civil Service 1948–74; Pres. Royal Soc. for the Prevention of Cruelty to Animals 1980–82; Writer-in-Residence, Univ. of Florida, USA 1975, Hollins Coll., Va, USA 1976. *Publications:* Watership Down 1972 (filmed 1974), Shardik 1974, Nature Through the Seasons, The Tyger Voyage 1976, The Plague Dogs 1977 (filmed 1982), The Ship's Cat 1977, Nature Day and Night 1978, The Girl in a Swing 1980 (filmed 1988), The Unbroken Web (The Iron Wolf) 1980, Voyage Through the Antarctic 1982, Maia 1984, The Bureaucats 1985, A Nature Diary 1985, Occasional Poets: anthology (ed. and contrib.) 1986, The Legend of Te Tuna 1986, Traveller 1988, The Day Gone By (autobiog.) 1990, Tales From Watership Down 1996, The Outlandish Knight 2000, Daniel 2006. *Honours:* Carnegie Medal 1972, Guardian Award for Children's Fiction 1972, Medal of California Young Readers' Asscn 1977. *Address:* 26 Church Street, Whitchurch, Hants., RG28 7AR, England (home). *E-mail:* water.bow@virgin.net (office).

ADAMSON, Donald, JP, MA, MLitt, DPhil, FRSL, FSA, FRHistS, FCIL; British critic, biographer and historian; b. 30 March 1939, Culcheth, Cheshire, England; s. of Donald Adamson and Hannah Mary Booth; m. Helen Freda Griffiths 1966; two s. *Education:* Magdalen Coll., Oxford, Univ. of Paris, France. *Career:* taught at Manchester Grammar School; Prin. Lecturer, Goldsmiths Coll., London; Chair. Bd of Examiners 1983–86; Visiting Fellow, Wolfson Coll., Cambridge; Fellow, Chartered Inst. of Linguists, Soc. of Antiquaries, London; Renter Warden, Worshipful Co. of Curriers of City of London 2010, Upper Warden 2011. *Publications:* The Genesis of Le Cousin Pons 1966, T. S. Eliot: A Memoir 1971, The House of Nell Gwyn (co-author) 1974, Balzac: Illusions perdues 1981, Les Romantiques Français devant la Peinture espagnole 1989, Blaise Pascal: Mathematician, Physicist, And Thinker About God 1995, Rides Round Britain, The Travel Journals of John Byng, 5th Viscount Torrington 1996, The Curriers' Company: A Modern History 2000, Pascal's Views on Mathematics and the Divine 2005, Oskar Kokoschka at Polperro 2009, William Golding Remembered 2010, Researching Kokoschka 2010, St John in Cornwall 2011; studies of Balzac's Comédie Humaine and various translations of Balzac and Maupassant; contrib. to Oxford Dictionary of National Biography. *Honours:* KStJ, Chevalier, Ordre des Palmes académiques 1986. *Address:* Dodmore House, The Street, Meopham, Kent, DA13 0AJ, England (office). *Telephone:* 7747-733931 (mobile) (office); 7890-824213 (mobile) (office). *E-mail:* aimsworthy@tesco.net (home); aimsworthy@aol.com (home). *Website:* www.dodmore.co.uk.

ADAMSON, Gil; Canadian writer; b. 1 Jan. 1961; pnr Kevin Connolly. *Publications:* Primitive (poetry) 1991, Help Me, Jacques Cousteau (short stories) 1995, Ashland (poetry) 2003, The Outlander (novel) (Drummer General's Award, Hammett Award, ReLit Award) 2007. *Address:* c/o House of Anansi Press, 110 Spadina Avenue, Suite 801, Toronto, ON M5V 2K4, Canada. *Website:* www.anansi.ca.

ADAMSON, Robert Harry; Australian poet, writer and publisher; b. 17 May 1943, Sydney, NSW; m. 1st Cheryl Adamson 1973; m. 2nd Juno Adamson 1989; one s. *Education:* Crows Nest Tech. Coll. *Career:* Assoc. Ed., New Poetry magazine, Sydney 1968–70, Ed. 1970–75, Asst Ed. 1975–77; Ed. and Dir, Prism Books, Sydney 1970–77; Founding Ed. and Dir (with Dorothy Hewett), Big Smoke Books, Sydney 1979–; Founder (with Michael Wilding), Paper Bark Press 1988–; mem. Australian Soc. of Authors, Poetry Soc. of Australia (Pres. 1970–80). *Publications include:* poetry: Canticles on the Skin 1970, The Rumour 1971, Swamp Riddles 1974, Theatre I–XIX 1976, Cross the Border 1977, Selected Poems (Grace Leven Prize for Poetry) 1977, Where I Come From 1979, The Law at Heart's Desire 1982, The Clean Dark (Kenneth Slessor Award for Poetry, C. J. Dennis Award for Poetry, Turnbull-Fox-Phillips Award 1990) 1989, Robert Adamson Selected Poems 1970–1989 1990, Waving to Hart Crane 1994, Mulberry Leaves: New and Selected Poems 1970–2001 2002, Reading the River: Selected Poems 2004, The Goldfinches of Baghdad (Grace Leven Prize for Poetry 2007) 2006, The Best Australian Poems 2010 (ed.) 2010; prose: Zimmer's Essay (with Bruce Hanford) 1974, Australian Writing Now (co-ed. with Manfred Jurgensen) 1988, Wards of the State: An Autobiographical Novella 1992, Inside Out (autobiog.) 2004; contrib. to periodicals. *Honours:* Australia Council Fellowships 1976, 1977. *Address:* PO Box 59, Brooklyn, NSW 2083, Australia (home). *Website:* www.robertadamson.com.

ADCOCK, Fleur, OBE, CNZM, MA, FRSL; British writer; b. 10 Feb. 1934, Papakura, New Zealand; d. of Cyril John Adcock and Irene Robinson; m. 1st Alistair Teariki Campbell 1952 (divorced 1958); two s.; m. 2nd Barry Crump 1962 (divorced 1966). *Education:* Victoria Univ., Wellington. *Career:* Asst Lecturer, Univ. of Otago 1958, Asst Librarian 1959–61; with Alexander Turnbull Library 1962; with FCO 1963–79; freelance writer 1979–; Northern Arts Fellowship in Literature, Newcastle and Durham Univs 1979–81; Eastern Arts Fellowship, Univ. of East Anglia 1984; Writer-in-Residence, Univ. of Adelaide, NZ 1986; mem. Poetry Soc. *Publications:* The Eye of the Hurricane 1964, Tigers 1967, High Tide in the Garden 1971, The Scenic Route 1974, The Inner Harbour 1979, Below Loughrigg 1979, The Oxford Book of Contemporary New Zealand Poetry (ed.) 1982, Selected Poems 1983, The Virgin and the Nightingale: Medieval Latin Poems 1983, Hotspur: A Ballad for Music 1986, The Incident Book 1986, The Faber Book of 20th Century Women's Poetry 1987, Orient Express: Poems by Grete Tartler (trans.) 1989, Time Zones 1991, Letters from Darkness: Poems by Daniela Crasnaru (trans.) 1991, High Primas and the Archpoet (ed. and trans.) 1994, The Oxford Book of Creatures (ed. with Jacqueline Simms) 1995, Looking Back 1997, Poems 1960–2000 (Queen's Gold Medal for Poetry 2006) 2000, Dragon Talk 2010. *Honours:* Festival of Wellington Poetry Award 1961, NZ State Literary Fund Award 1964, Buckland Award 1967, 1979, Jessie MacKay Award 1968, 1972, Cholmondeley Award 1976, NZ Nat. Book Award 1984, Arts Council Writers' Award 1988. *Address:* 14 Lincoln Road, London, N2 9DL, England (home). *Telephone:* (20) 8444-7881 (home).

ADDINGTON, Larry Holbrook, BA, MA, PhD; American writer and academic; *Professor Emeritus of History, The Citadel*; b. 16 Nov. 1932, Charlotte, NC. *Education:* Univ. of North Carolina at Chapel Hill, Duke Univ. *Career:* Asst Prof., San Jose State Coll. 1962–64; Asst Prof. 1964–66, Assoc. Prof. 1966–70, Prof. 1970–94, Head of Dept 1989–94, Prof. Emeritus 1994–, of History, The Citadel; Visiting Prof., Duke Univ. 1976–77; Charter Mem. The Citadel Chapter 1974, Nat. Honor Soc.; Guest Lecturer, Naval War Coll., Marine Command and Staff Coll.; mem. Soc. for Mil. History. *Publications:* From Moltke to Hitler: The Evolution of German Military Doctrine, 1865–1939 1966, Firepower and Maneuver: The European Inheritance in the Two World Wars 1967, Firepower and Maneuver: Historical Case Studies 1969, The Blitzkrieg Era and the German General Staff, 1865–1941 1971, The Patterns of War Since the Eighteenth Century 1984, The Patterns of War Through the Eighteenth Century 1990, America's War in Vietnam: A Short Narrative History 2000; contrib. to encyclopedias, books and scholarly journals. *Honours:* AMI Award for Best Seminal Work 1984. *Address:* 1341 New Castle Street, Charleston, SC 29407, USA (office). *E-mail:* larrya103@aol.com (office).

ADDIS, Richard James, MA; British journalist, newspaper editor, writer and entrepreneur; *Founder and CEO, The Day*; b. 23 Aug. 1956, s. of Richard Thomas Addis and Jane Addis; m. Eunice Minogue 1983 (divorced 2000); one s. two d.; two s. by Helen Slater. *Education:* Rugby School, Downing Coll., Cambridge. *Career:* Asst Ed. Evening Standard 1985–89; Deputy Ed. Sunday Telegraph 1989–91; Exec. Ed. Daily Mail 1991–95; Ed. Daily Express 1995–98, The Express on Sunday 1996–98; Ed. Mail on Sunday Review 1998–99; Ed. The Globe and Mail, Toronto 1999–2002; Ed. Financial Times Weekend 2002–06; Founder and Man. Dir Shakeup Media, London 2006; Founder and CEO The Day, London 2010–. *Telephone:* 7899-968427 (mobile) (office). *E-mail:* richard@theday.co.uk (office). *Website:* www.theday.co.uk (office).

ADEBAYO, Diran, FRSL; Nigerian novelist, critic and journalist; b. 1968, London, England. *Education:* Malvern Public School, Univ. of Oxford. *Career:* fmr journalist, The Voice newspaper; broadcaster for LWT; Writer-in-Residence, First Story; mem. Arts Council England. *Publications:* novels: Some Kind of Black (New Writer of Year Award, Saga Prize 1996, Betty Trask Award, Best First Novel Award) 1996, My Once Upon a Time 2000; New Writing 12 (co-ed.) 2004; contrib. to The Guardian, Daily Mail, Daily Express, The Voice. *Address:* c/o Little, Brown Book Group, 100 Victoria Embankment, London, EC4Y 0DY, England. *Website:* www.littlebrown.co.uk; www.theblessedmonkey.com.

ADESANMI, Pius Adebola Oota, BA, MA, PhD; Nigerian writer, critic and academic; *Associate Professor, Department of English Language and Literature, Carleton University*; b. 27 Feb. 1972, Egbe; s. of Alfred Dare Adesanmi and Lois Olufunke Adesanmi; two d. *Education:* Univ. of Ilorin, Univ. of Ibadan, Univ. of British Columbia, Canada. *Career:* Asst Prof. of Comparative Literature, Pennsylvania State Univ., USA 2002–06; Assoc. Prof. of Literature, Carleton Univ., Ottawa, Canada 2006–, also Dir Project on New African Literatures; fmr Fellow, French Inst. of South Africa. *Publications:* The Wayfarer and Other Poems (Assen of Nigerian Authors Poetry Prize 2001) 2001, You're Not a Country, Africa (Penguin Prize for African Writing 2010) 2011; has also contributed essays on literature and culture to journals, literary reviews, newspapers and edited books. *Honours:* Erasmus Teaching Award, Pennsylvania State Univ. 2006. *Address:* 1916 Dunton Tower, Carleton University, 1125 Colonel By Drive, Ottawa, ON K1S 5B6, Canada (office). *Telephone:* (613) 520-2600 (ext. 1175) (office). *E-mail:* piusadesanmi@gmail.com (office). *Website:* www.carleton.ca/english (office).

ADHIKARI, Santosh Kumar; Indian university administrator (retd), writer and poet; b. 24 Nov. 1923, West Bengal; m. 1948; one s. two d. *Education:* Univ. of Calcutta, Indian Inst. of Bankers, Mumbai, Indian Inst. of Man. *Career:* Prin., Staff Coll., United Bank of India, Kolkata –1983; Vidyasagar Lecturer, Univ. of Calcutta 1979; Speaker, Bengal Studies Conf., Univ. of Chicago, USA 1990; Ed. Spark 1975–96; Founder and fmr Sec. Vidyasagar Research Centre; mem. Asiatic Soc., Akhil Bharat, Bhasa Sahitya Sammelan, PEN West Bengal Br. (Sec. 1985–87). *Publications include:* fiction: Rakta-Kamal 1967, Nirjan Shikhar 1971, Panka-Lipi 1985, Durer Desh Durer Manus 1988; poetry: Ekla Chalore 1948, Diganter Megh 1960, Anya Kono Khane 1973, Blossoms in the Dust (in English) 1980, Paari 1986; non-fiction: Vidya Sagar 1970, Santrasbad O' Bhagat Singh 1979, Vidyasagar and the Regeneration of Bengal (in English) 1980, Vidyasagarer Jiboner Seshdinguli 1985, Vidyasagarer Sikshaneeti 1987, Durer Desh Durer Manush 1988, Vidyasagar and the New Nat. Consciousness 1990, Netaji Subhas Chandra 1990, Vidyasagar: Educator, Reformer and Humanist (in English) 1995; contrib. to All India Radio and major journals. *Honours:* Hon. Bharat Bhasa Bhusan 1991; Prasad Puraskar for Poetry 1986. *Address:* c/o Vidyasagar Research Centre, 81 Raja Basanta Roy Road, Kolkata 700 029, India (office). *Telephone:* (33) 24008393 (home); (33) 9874168632 (home).

ADICHIE, Chimamanda Ngozi, BSc, MA; Nigerian writer; b. 1977, Abba, Anambra State. *Education:* Univ. of Nigeria, Eastern Connecticut State Univ., Johns Hopkins Univ. and Yale Univ., USA. *Career:* Hodder Fellow, Princeton Univ. 2005–06. *Publications:* novels: Purple Hibiscus (Commonwealth Writers' Best First Book Award) 2004, Half of a Yellow Sun (Orange Broadband Prize for Fiction 2007) 2006; short stories: Lye, The American Embassy, My Mother The Crazy African, You in America 2001, The Thing Around Your Neck 2009; poetry: Decisions 1997; play: For Love of Biafra 1998; contrib. to Prism International, Poetry Magazine, Posse Review, Zoetrope All-Story, Allegheny Review of Undergraduate Literature, Iowa Review, Granta, New Yorker, Virginia Quarterly Review, Conjunctions. *Honours:* International PEN/David Wong Award 2003, Hurston/Wright Legacy Award 2004, Commonwealth Writers Prize 2005, MacArthur Fellowship 2008. *Literary Agent:* c/o The Wylie Agency, 17 Bedford Square, London, WC1B 3JA, England. *Telephone:* (20) 7908-5900. *E-mail:* mail@wylieagency.com. *Website:* www.wylieagency.com. *E-mail:* chimamanda.adichie@gmail.com. *Website:* www.halfofayellowsun.com.

ADICKES, Sandra, BA, MA, PhD; American academic and writer; *Professor Emerita, Winona State University*; b. 14 July 1933, New York, NY; three d. *Education:* Douglass Coll., Hunter Coll., City Univ. of New York, , New York Univ. *Career:* Prof. of English 1988–98, Winona State Univ., Prof. Emer. 1998–. *Publications:* The Social Quest 1991, Legends of Good Women (novel) 1992, To Be Young Was Very Heaven: Women in New York Before the First World War 1997, The Legacy of a Freedom School 2005, Arrows of Desire (novel) 2010; contribs to reference books and journals. *Address:* 93 Renaissance Lane, New Brunswick, NJ 08901-3179, USA (home). *Telephone:* (732) 993-1275 (home). *E-mail:* sadickes@optonline.net.

ADIE, Kathryn (Kate), OBE, BA; British journalist, broadcaster and author; b. 19 Sept. 1945, d. of Babe Dunnett (née Issit) and adopted d. of the late John Wilfrid Adie and of Maud Adie (née Fambely). *Education:* Sunderland Church High School, Univ. of Newcastle. *Career:* technician and producer BBC Radio 1969–76; reporter BBC TV South 1977–78, BBC TV News 1979–81, corresp. 1982–89, Chief News Corresp. 1989–2003, presenter, From Our Own Correspondent, BBC Radio 4; freelance journalist, broadcaster and TV presenter 2003–; Visiting Fellow, Univ. of Bournemouth 1998–. *Publications:* The Kindness of Strangers (autobiog.) 2002, Corsets to Camouflage: Women and War 2003, Nobody's Child: The Lives of Abandoned Children 2005, Into Danger 2008. *Honours:* Hon. Prof., Sunderland Univ. 1995; Hon. Fellow, Royal Holloway, Univ. of London 1996; Freeman of Sunderland 1990; Hon. MA (Bath) 1987, (Newcastle) 1990; Hon. DLitt (City Univ.) 1989, (Loughborough) 1991, (Sunderland) 1993, (Robert Gordon) 1996, (Nottingham) 1998, (Nottingham Trent) 1998; Hon. MUniv (Open Univ.) 1996; Royal Television Soc. News Award 1981, 1987, Monte Carlo Int. News Award 1981, 1990, BAFTA Richard Dimbleby Award 1989. *Address:* POB 317, Brentford, London, TW8 8WX, England (office). *Telephone:* (20) 8838-2871 (office).

ADIGA, Aravind; Indian author and journalist; b. 23 Oct. 1974, Chennai; s. of Dr K. Madhava Adiga and Usha Adiga. *Education:* Univ. of Oxford, UK and Columbia Univ., USA. *Career:* corresp. for Time magazine 2003–07. *Publications include:* The White Tiger (Man Booker Prize) 2008, Between the Assassinations (short stories) 2009, Last Man in the Tower 2011; contrib. to The Independent, Financial Times, The New Yorker, The Guardian, The Times, The Daily Beast, Time, Tehelka, Sunday Times, The Times of India. *Honours:* British Book Award for Author of the Year 2009. *Address:* c/o Atlantic Books, Ormond House, 26–27 Boswell Street, London, WC1N 3JZ, England. *E-mail:* enquiries@groveatlantic.co.uk. *Website:* www.groveatlantic.co.uk; www.aravindadiga.com.

ADISA, Opal Palmer, BA, MA, PhD; Jamaican/American writer, poet, educator and consultant, storyteller, performer and photographer; *Professor of Literature and Creative Writing, California College of the Arts*; b. 6 Nov. 1954, Jamaica; d. of Orlando Palmer and Catherine Palmer; three c. *Education:* Hunter Coll., New York, San Francisco State Univ., Calif., Univ. of California, Berkeley. *Career:* co-founder and fmr Artistic Dir, Bay Area Children's group, Watoto Wa Kuumba; taught Caribbean and African Literature at San Francisco State Univ.; also taught at Stanford Univ. and Univ. of Calif., Berkeley; currently Full Prof. of Literature and Creative Writing, Calif. Coll. of the Arts, fmr Chair. Ethnic Studies/Cultural Diversity Program; Lecturer, Univ. of Virgin Islands; Ed. The Caribbean Writer; Pres. and Ind. Consultant, Opalwriter Consultancy; Consultant/Writer Developmental Studies Center; has taught storytelling workshops in Oakland and San Francisco Unified School Dists; numerous live storytelling performances, broadcasts on TV and radio, writer-in-residences. *Exhibitions:* (Richmond Art Center, Calif.) 2002, Juried Group Show (Pro Arts, Oakland) 2002–03, four pieces in Conversations/Conversaciones: Women Collaborate (de Saisset Museum, Santa Clara Univ.) 2004, Working Man (photo/poem), Art of Living Black 2004, two mixed-media pieces, Inside the Teeth of Love and So This is It (travelling exhbn, Afetos Roubados No Tempo, Bahía, Brazil and in different cites throughout Brazil before travelling to S Africa) 2006, Swimming with Yemanja in Brazil, mixed media, (Faculty Group Show, California Coll. of the Arts) 2006, six black and white photographs from the Cuba series and six colour photographs from Brazil (Group Show, A Celebration of Latin Art, Health & Community, at WCRC Gallery, Oakland, Calif.) 2006. *Recordings:* Fierce/Love (with Devorah Major) 1992, The Tongue is a Drum (with Devorah Major) 2002. *Publications include:* Pina, The Many-Eyed Fruit (juvenile) 1985, Bake-Face and Other Guava Stories 1986, Traveling Women (poems) 1989, Tamarind and Mango Women (poems) (PEN Oakland/Josephine Miles Award) 1991, It Begins with Years (novel) 1997, Leaf-of-Life (poems) 2000, Saucy Caribbean Tales (stories CD) 2003, Caribbean Passion (poems) 2004, Eros Muse–Poetry and Essays 2006, Until Judgment Comes (short stories) 2007, I Name Me Name (poems/prose) 2008, Painting Away Regrets (fiction) 2011; contrib. poems, fiction and essays to anthologies, chapbooks and magazines, including The Caribbean Writer, Go, Tell Michelle. *Honours:*

Calif. Arts Council Master Folk Artist for Storytelling, City of Oakland Creative Artist Fellowship Award for Storytelling 2002–03, Nat. Women's Political Caucus Distinguished Bay Area Woman Writer Award, Univ. of the Virgin Islands Daily News Prize for Best Poems in The Caribbean Writer, Canute A. Brodhurst Prize, Distinguished Writer for the Middle Atlantic Writers Asscn, Caribbean-American Heritage Legacy Award 2008. *Address:* PO Box 10625, Oakland, CA 94610, USA (home). *Telephone:* (510) 219-0704 (home). *Fax:* (510) 383-9883 (office). *E-mail:* opalwrites@sbcglobal.net. *Website:* www.opalpalmeradisa.com (home).

ADJMI, David, BA; American playwright; b. 1973, New York. *Education:* Sarah Lawrence Coll., Iowa Playwrights Workshop, Juilliard School. *Career:* received comms from Lincoln Center, the Royal Court, Yale Repertory Theater, Berkeley Repertory Theater; mem. New Dramatists, Dramatists Guild, MCC Playwrights Coalition, Vinegar Tom Players. *Plays:* 3C, Caligula, Marie Antoinette, Strange Attractors 2002, Tennis Pro, Woody Allen's Fall Project, The Evildoers 2008, Stunning 2009, Elective Affinities 2009, Stunning and Other Plays 2011. *Honours:* Helen Merill Award, McKnight Advancement Grant, Marian Seldes-Kanin Award, Jerome Fellowship, Lecomte du Nouy Award, Kesselring Fellowship 2008–09, Steinberg Distinguished Playwright Award 2009, Whiting Writers' Award 2010. *Literary Agent:* c/o Creative Artists Agency, 162 Fifth Avenue, New York, NY 10010, USA. *Telephone:* (212) 277-9000. *Fax:* (212) 277-9099. *Website:* www.caa.com. *E-mail:* dadjmi@earthlink.net (office).

ADLER, Carole Schwerdtfeger, BA, MS; American writer; b. 23 Feb. 1932, Long Island, NY; m. Arnold R. Adler 1952; three s. *Education:* Hunter Coll., City Univ. of New York, Russell Sage Coll. *Career:* mem. Soc. of Children's Book Writers, Authors' Guild, Gila Gang. *Publications include:* The Magic of the Glits 1979, The Silver Coach 1979, In Our House Scott is My Brother 1980, The Cat That Was Left Behind 1981, Down By the River 1981, Shelter on Blue Barns Road 1981, Footsteps on the Stairs 1982, The Evidence That Wasn't There 1982, The Once in a While Hero 1982, Some Other Summer 1982, The Shell Lady's Daughter 1983, Get Lost Little Brother 1983, Roadside Valentine 1983, Shadows on Little Reef Bay 1984, Fly Free 1984, Binding Ties 1985, With Westie and the Tin Man 1985, Good-Bye Pink Pig 1985, Split Sisters 1986, Kiss the Clown 1986, Carly's Buck 1987, Always and Forever Friends 1988, If You Need Me 1988, Eddie's Blue Winged Dragon 1988, One Sister Too Many 1989, The Lump in the Middle 1989, Help Pink Pig! 1990, Ghost Brother 1990, Mismatched Summer 1991, A Tribe for Lexi 1991, Tuna Fish Thanksgiving 1992, Daddy's Climbing Tree 1993, Willie, the Frog Prince 1994, That Horse Whiskey 1994, Youn Hee and Me 1995, Court Yard Cat 1995, What's to be Scared of, Suki? 1996, More Than a Horse 1997, Her Blue Straw Hat 1997, Not Just A Summer Crush 1998, Winning 1999, One Unhappy Horse 2001, No Place Cat 2002, Saving Dove: One Unhappy Horse 2003, Timothy and Jacob the Two Trumpet Players, Taylor Giais the Girl. *Honours:* William Allen White Award 1980, Golden Kite Award 1980, American Library Asscn Best Young Adult Book 1984, Children's Book Award, Child Study Cttee 1986, IRA Children's Selections 1987, 1991, ASPCA Henry Berg Award 2001. *Address:* 7041 N Cathedral Rock Place, Tucson, AZ 85718, USA (home). *E-mail:* csawrite@mindspring.com (office). *Website:* www.c-s-adler.com.

ADLER, Laure, MA; French journalist, historian and writer; b. 11 March 1950, Caen; m. 1st Fred Adler 1968; m. 2nd Alain Veinstein. *Career:* sec. France Culture radio station 1974, Dir 1999–2005; responsible for essays and documents, Grasset 1997; responsible for literature dept, Editions du Seuil 2005–; taught at Institut d'Etudes Politiques de Paris; mem. Bd of Dirs City Theatre, Univ. of Avignon, Pays de Vaucluse; mem. Policy Bd Asscn Realtime. *Film:* actress in Des nouvelles du bon Dieu 1996. *Publications:* non-fiction: A laube du féminisme: les premières journalistes (1830–1850) 1979, L'amour à l'arsenic: Histoire de Marie Lafarge 1985, Avignon: 40 ans de festival 1987, La Vie quotidienne dans les maisons closes: 1830–1930 1990, Les femmes politiques 1993, L'année des adieux 1995, Marguerite Duras 2000, A ce soir 2001, Les Maisons closes 2002, Bis heute abend 2004, Dans les pas de Hannah Arendt 2005, Les Femmes qui lisent sont dangereuses (with Stefan Bollmann) 2006, Les Femmes qui écrivent vivent dangereusement (with Stefan Bollmann) 2007, L'Insoumise 2008, Histoire de notre collection de tableaux (with Pierre Bergé) 2009. *Address:* c/o Editions du Seuil, 27 rue Jacob, 75006 Paris, France. *E-mail:* contact@seuil.com. *Website:* www.seuil.com.

ADLER, Margot Susanna, BA, MS; American journalist and broadcaster; *Correspondent, National Public Radio*; b. 16 April 1946, Little Rock, Ark.; d. of Dr Kurt Alfred Adler and Freyda Nacque Adler; m. John Lowell Gliedman; one s. *Education:* Univ. of California, Berkeley, Columbia School of Journalism, Harvard Univ. *Career:* Corresp., Nat. Public Radio 1979–; mem. Authors' Guild, American Fed. of Television and Radio Artists, Covenant of Unitarian Universalist Pagans. *Radio:* drama: War Day (co-producer). *Publications:* Drawing Down the Moon: Witches, Druids, Goddess-Worshippers and Other Pagans in America Today 1979, Heretic's Heart: A Journey Through Spirit and Revolution 1997. *Honours:* Neman Fellow, Harvard Univ. 1982. *Address:* National Public Radio, 635 Massachusetts Avenue NW, Washington, DC 20001, USA (office). *Telephone:* (212) 880-4435 (office); (212) 222-6298 (home). *E-mail:* madler@npr.org.

ADLER, Renata, AB, Dd'ES, MA, JD; American writer; b. 19 Oct. 1938, Milan, Italy; one s. *Education:* Bryn Mawr Coll., Sorbonne Univ., Paris, Harvard Univ., Yale Univ. Law School. *Career:* writer-reporter, New Yorker 1962–68, 1970–82; Fellow, Trubull Coll., Yale Univ. 1969–72; Assoc. Prof. of Theatre and Cinema, Hunter Coll., CUNY 1972–73; Guggenheim Fellowship 1973–74; Woodrow Wilson and Fulbright Fellowships; fmr Chief Film Critic, The New York Times; Fellow of the Univ. Profs and Visiting Prof. of Journalism, Coll. of Communication, Boston Univ. –2007; Media Fellow, Hoover Inst., Stanford Univ. 2004; elected mem. American Acad. and Inst. of Arts and Letters 1987; mem. PEN. *Publications:* Toward a Radical Middle: Fourteen Pieces of Reporting and Criticism 1969, A Year in the Dark: Journal of a Film Critic, 1968–69 1970, Speedboat (novel) (Ernest Hemingway Prize) 1976, Pitch Dark (novel) 1983, Reckless Disregard: Westmoreland v. CBS et al: Sharon v. Time 1986, Politics and Media: Essays 1988, Gone: The Last Days of the New Yorker 1999, Private Capacity 2000, Canaries in the Mineshaft: Essays on Politics and Media 2001, Irreparable Harm: The US Supreme Court and the Decision That Made George W. Bush President 2004. *Honours:* Hon. LLD (Georgetown Univ. Law School) 1989; O. Henry Short Story Award 1974, American Acad. and Inst. of Arts and Letters Award 1976, New York Newswomen's Club Front Page Award. *Address:* c/o Department of Journalism, College of Communication, Boston University, 640 Commonwealth Avenue, Boston, MA 02215, USA.

ADLER, Warren, BA; American writer and playwright; b. 16 Dec. 1927, New York, NY; s. of Sol Adler and Fritzie Adler; m. Sonia Kline 1951; three s. *Education:* Brooklyn Tech. Coll., New York Univ., New School Univ., New York. *Career:* Washington Corresp., Armed Forces Press Service in the Pentagon 1951–53; Ed. Queens Post, Forest Hills, NY; Pres. Warren Adler Ltd, advertising and public relations agency, Washington, DC 1959–78; Chair. Jackson Hole Public Library 2003; mem. Century Asscn, Lotos Club, PEN, Authors' Guild. *Plays:* The War of the Roses, The Sunset Gang Musical, Libido, Family Business, Father Glory. *Films:* The War of the Roses 1989, Random Hearts 1999. *Television:* The Sunset Gang (trilogy) 1991. *Publications:* Undertow 1974, Banquet Before Dawn 1976, The Henderson Equation 1976, Trans-Siberian Express 1977, The Sunset Gang 1978, The Casanova Embrace 1978, Blood Ties 1979, Natural Enemies 1980, The War of the Roses 1981, American Quartet 1982, American Sextet 1983, Random Hearts 1984, Twilight Child 1989, Immaculate Deception 1991, Senator Love 1991, Private Lies 1992, The Witch of Watergate 1992, The Ties That Bind 1994, Never Too Late for Love 1996, Jackson Hole Uneasy Eden 1997, Mourning Glory 1997, Cult: A Novel of Brainwashing and Death 2002, Death of a Washington Madame 2005, New York Echoes 2007, Funny Boys 2008, The David Embrace 2010, Flanagan's Dolls 2010, The Womanizer 2010, Residue 2010, Empty Treasures 2010. *Honours:* New York Univ. Alumni of the Year 2009. *Address:* Stonehouse Press, 300 E 56th Street, New York, NY 10022, USA (home). *Telephone:* (212) 350-9357 (home). *E-mail:* adlernovel@aol.com. *Website:* www.warrenadler.com.

ADNAN, Etel; American artist and writer; b. 24 Feb. 1925, Beirut, Lebanon. *Education:* Univ. of Paris (Sorbonne) and Univs of Berkeley and Harvard, USA. *Career:* Prof. of Aesthetics, Dominican Coll., San Rafael, Calif., USA – 1972; artist *c* 1960–, more than 30 solo exhbns in USA, Europe, Middle East; Cultural Ed. Al-Safa, Lebanon 1972–74, L'Orient-Le Jour 1974–79; mem. Poetry Center, San Francisco. *Publications include:* poetry: Moonshots 1966, Five Senses for One Death 1971, From A to Z 1982, The Indian Never Had a Horse and Other Poems 1985, The Arab Apocalypse 1989, The Spring Flowers Own and the Manifestations of the Voyage 1990, In/somnia 2002; novel: Sitt Marie Rose 1982; other: Journey to Mount Tamalpais 1986, Paris When It's Naked 1993, Of Cities and Women: Letters to Fawazz 1993, There: In the Light and the Darkness of the Self and of the Other 1995, To Write in a Foreign Language 1996, In the Heart of the Heart of Another Country 2005, Master of the Eclipse (Arab American Book Award 2010) 2009. *Honours:* France-Pays Arabes Prize 1978. *Address:* 35 Marie Street, Sausalito, CA 94965, USA (home); 29 rue Madame, Paris 75006, France (home). *Telephone:* (415) 332-1458 (USA) (home); 1-45-44-33-31 (France) (home). *E-mail:* sifattal@yahoo.com.

ADOFF, Arnold, BA; American poet, writer and literary agent; b. 16 July 1935, New York, NY; m. Virginia Hamilton 1960; two c. *Education:* City Coll., City Univ. of New York, Columbia Univ., New School for Social Research Poetry Workshops, New York. *Career:* teacher, New York City Public Schools 1957–69; literary agent, Yellow Springs, Ohio 1977–; Distinguished Visiting Prof., Queens Coll., CUNY 1986–87; guest lecturer in many US venues. *Publications include:* poetry: Black Is Brown Is Tan 1973, Make a Circle Keep Us In: Poems for a Good Day 1975, Big Sister Tells Me That I'm Black 1976, Tornado!: Poems 1977, Under the Early Morning Trees 1978, Where Wild Willie 1978, Eats: Poems 1979, I Am the Running Girl 1979, Friend Dog 1980, OUTside INside Poems 1981, Today We Are Brother and Sister 1981, Birds 1982, All the Colors of the Race 1982, The Cabbages are Chasing the Rabbits 1985, Sports Pages 1986, Flamboyan 1988, Greens 1988, Chocolate Dreams 1989, Hard to Be Six 1990, In for Winter, Out for Spring 1991, Touch The Poem 2000; other: Malcolm X (biog.) 1970, MA nDA LA (picture book) 1971, Daring Dog and Captain Cat 2003; ed.: I Am the Darker Brother: An Anthology of Modern Poems by Negro Americans 1968, Black on Black: Commentaries by Negro Americans 1968, City in All Directions: An Anthology of Modern Poems by Black Americans 1970, Brothers and Sisters: Modern Stories by Black Americans 1970, It is the Poem Singing into Your Eyes: An Anthology of New Young Poets 1971, The Poetry of Black America: An Anthology of the 20th Century 1973, My Black Me: A Beginning Book of Black Poetry 1974, Celebrations: A New Anthology of Black American Poetry 1978; contrib.: articles and reviews to periodicals. *Honours:* Child Study Asscn of

America Children's Book of the Year Citations 1968, 1969, 1986, American Library Asscn Notable Book Awards 1968, 1970, 1971, 1972, 1979, School Library Journal Best Children's Book Citations 1971, 1973, Nat. Council for Social Studies Notable Children's Trade Book Citation, Children's Book Council 1974, Jane Addams Peace Asscn Special Certificate 1983, Children's Book Council Children's Choice Citation, Int. Reading Asscn 1985, Poetry Award, Nat. Council of Teachers of English 1988. *Address:* Arnold Adoff Agency, 750 Union Street, Yellow Springs, OH 45387-1740, USA (office). *E-mail:* arnoldadoff@aol.com (office). *Website:* www.arnoldadoff.com.

ADRIAN, Chris, BA, MFA, MD, MDiv; American writer and doctor; b. 7 Nov. 1970, Washington DC. *Education:* Univ. of Florida, Eastern Virginia Medical School, Univ. of California, San Francisco, Harvard Divinity School, Iowa Writers' Workshop. *Career:* resident doctor, Univ. of California, San Francisco 2001–05; attending physician in paediatric oncology, Boston Children's Hosp. 2005–08. *Publications:* novels: Gob's Grief 2001, The Children's Hospital 2007, The Great Night 2011; short stories: A Better Angel 2008. *Honours:* Guggenheim Foundation Fellowship 2009. *Address:* c/o Farrar, Strauss and Giroux, 18 West 18th Street, New York, NY 10011, USA. *Website:* us.macmillan.com/fsg.aspx.

ADRIAN, Frances (see POLLAND, Madelaine Angela)

AFOLABI, Segun A.; Nigerian writer; b. 1966, Kaduna; s. of James Afolabi and Christine Afolabi. *Education:* Brighton Coll., Univ. Coll., Wales. *Career:* has lived in various countries, including the Congo, Canada, East Germany and Indonesia; fmrly worked for the BBC, London. *Publications:* Monday Morning (short story) (Caine Prize 2005) 2004, A Life Elsewhere (short stories) 2006, Goodbye Lucille (novel) (Authors' Club Best First Novel Award 2008) 2007; contrib. to Wasafiri, The Edinburgh Review, Granta, New Welsh Review, The Interpreter's House, Dream Catcher, Salamander, Prism International, Pretext, London Magazine, The Kenyon Review, Tampa Review, Pretext, The Malahat Review, Msafiri. *Address:* c/o Jonathan Cape, 20 Vauxhall Bridge Road, London, SW1V 2SA, England. *E-mail:* capepublicity@randomhouse.co.uk.

AFRICANO, Lillian, (Nora Ashby, Lila Cook, Jessica March), BA; American writer and columnist; *President-Elect, Society of American Travel Writers*; b. 7 June 1935, Paterson, NJ; m. (divorced); two s. one d. *Education:* Barnard Coll., Columbia Univ. Graduate School. *Career:* Arts Ed. The Villager 1971; News Ed., Penthouse/Forum 1973; columnist New York Times Syndicate 1977, Woman's World 1980; Pres. International Food, Wine and Travel Writers Asscn 2003–08, currently mem. Bd of Dirs and Exec. Ed. Global Writes; Ed.-in-Chief, Worldwide Spa Review magazine 2004–; apptd Chair. (Northeast Chapter) Soc. of American Travel Writers 2006, currently Pres.-Elect; Cruise Ed. JAX FAX 2009–; Ed. AOL Travel 2010–; currently also Sr Ed. Elegant Accents Magazine; also Ed.-in-chief of SpaReviewMag.com, LuxuryLifeReview.com; mem. Drama Desk (Vice-Pres., Sec.), Outer Critics' Circle, American Soc. of Journalists and Authors, Authors' Guild. *Publications include:* Businessman's Guide to the Middle East 1977, Doctor's Walking Book (co-author) 1980, Something Old, Something New 1983, Passions 1985, The Insiders' Guide to the Jersey Shore 2004, You Know You're in New Jersey When …2006, New York Off the Beaten Path 2007; as Nora Ashby: Gone From Breezy Hill 1985; as Lila Cook: Consenting Adults 1988; as Jessica March: Illusions 1988, Temptations 1989, Obsessions 1990, Sensations 1993, Visions 1995; contribs: New York Times, New York News, Reader's Digest, Harper's Bazaar, Woman's Day, Woman's World, National Review, Nation. *Address:* Society of American Travel Writers, 11950 W. Lake Park Drive, Suite 320, Milwaukee, WI 53224-3049, USA (office). *Telephone:* (414) 359-1625 (office). *Fax:* (414) 359-1671 (office). *E-mail:* info@satw.org (office); author@lillianafricano.com. *Website:* www.satw.org (office); www.lillianafricano.com.

AĞAOĞLU, Adalet; Turkish writer; b. 23 Oct. 1929, Ankara; d. of Mustafa Sümer and İsmet Sümer; m. Halim Ağaoğlu 1954. *Education:* Univ. of Ankara. *Career:* worked for Türkiye Radyo Televizyon Kurumu (TRT) 1953–73; freelance writer 1973–; co-founder Arena Theatre Co. *Publications include:* (in Turkish) novels: Lying Down to Die 1973, The Fine Rose of My Mind 1976, A Wedding Night (Sedat Simavi Literature Award 1979, Orhan Kemal Novel Award 1980, Madaralı Novel Award 1980) 1979, The End of Summer 1980, A Few People 1984, Migration Cleansing 1985, No… 1987, Cold in Spirit 1991, A Romantic Viennese Summer (Aydın Doğan Novel Award 1997) 1993; short stories: High Tension (Sait Faik Prize 1975) 1974, The First Sound of Silence 1978, Come On, Let's Go 1982, Ways to Defend Life 1997; essays: Crossing 1986, My Life at Night 1992, Encounters 1993, Other Encounters 1996; plays: Three Play (Prize of Turkish Language Inst.) 1956, Playing Mum and Dad 1964, Bingo 1967, The Crack in The Roof 1969, The Death of a Hero 1973, Cocoons 1973, The Song that Wrote Itself 1977, Plays 1982, Too Far Too Close 1991 (Is Bankasi Grand Award for the Theatre) 1991, The Story of the Wall 1992, The Poem and the Fly 1992. *Honours:* Hon. PhD (Anadolu Univ.) 1998, Dr hc (Ohio State Univ.) 1998; TDK Theatre Award 1974, Pres. of the Turkish Repub. Grand Prize for Culture and the Arts 1995. *Address:* Piyasa Cad, Bülbül Sok, 10/5 Ceviz Apt, Büyükdere, Istanbul, Turkey. *Telephone:* (1) 1422636.

AGARD, John; Guyanese poet, children's writer and editor; b. 21 June 1949; pnr Grace Nichols. *Career:* sub-ed. and feature writer, Guyana Sunday Chronicle newspaper; moved to UK 1977; touring lecturer with Commonwealth Inst.; Writer-in-Residence, South Bank Centre London 1993; Poet-in-Residence, BBC Educ. Dept 1997–98. *Publications include:* Shoot Me with Flowers 1974, Letters for Lettie and Other Stories 1979, Dig Away Two-Hole Tim 1981, Man to Pan (Casa de las Américas Prize, Cuba) 1982, I Din Do Nuttin and Other Poems 1983, Limbo Dancer in Dark Glasses 1983, Livingroom 1983, Mangoes and Bullets: Selected and New Poems 1972-84 1985, Say it Again, Granny! 1986, Lend Me Your Wings 1987, Life Doesn't Frighten Me At All (ed.) 1989, Go Noah Go! 1990, Laughter is an Egg 1990, The Calypso Alphabet 1990, No Hickory, No Dockory, No Dock (with Grace Nichols) 1991, The Emperor's Dan-dan 1992, A Stone's Throw from Embankment: The South Bank Collection 1993, The Great Snakeskin (play for children) 1993, Grandfather's Old Bruk-a-Down Car 1994, Oriki and the Monster Who Hated Balloons 1994, The Monster Who Loved Cameras 1994, The Monster Who Loved Telephones 1994, The Monster Who Loved Toothbrushes 1994, A Caribbean Dozen (co-ed.) 1994, Poems in My Earphone (ed.) 1995, Eat a Poem, Wear a Poem 1995, Get Back, Pimple! 1996, Why is the Sky? (ed.) 1996, We Animals Would Like a Word With You (Bronze Award, Nestle Smarties Book Prize) 1996, From the Devil's Pulpit 1997, Brer Rabbit: The Great Tug-o-War 1998, Points of View with Professor Peekaboo 2000, Weblines 2000, A Child's Year of Stories and Poems (with Michael Rosen and Robert Frost) 2000, Hello New: New Poems for a New Century (ed.) 2000, Come Back to Me My Boomerang (with Lydia Monks) 2001, Number Parade: Number Poems from 0–100 (with Jackie Kay, Grace Nichols, Nick Toczek and Michael Rosen) 2002, Under The Moon and Over the Sea (co-ed.) 2002, Einstein, The Girl Who Hated Maths 2002, Hello H2O 2003, From Mouth to Mouth 2004, Baby Poems 2005, Half-Caste 2005, Butter-Finger (with Bob Cattell) 2006, We Brits 2006, Wriggle Piggy Toes 2006, The Young Inferno (CLPE Poetry Award 2009) 2008, Tiger Dead! Tiger Dead!: Stories from the Caribbean (co-ed.) 2008, Alternative Anthem: Selected Poems 2009, Clever Backbone 2009; contrib. to Caribbean Poetry Now 1984, The Penguin Book of Caribbean Verse (ed.) 1986, Border Country: Poems in Progress 1991, Grandchildren of Albion 1992, The Heinemann Book of Caribbean Poetry 1992, Another Day on your Foot and I Would Have Died 1996. *Honours:* Arts Council Bursary 1989, Paul Hamlyn Award for Poetry 1997, Cholmondley Award 2004. *Address:* c/o Bloodaxe Books Ltd, Highgreen, Tarset, Northumberland, NE48 1RP, England. *E-mail:* publicity@bloodaxebooks.com. *Website:* www.bloodaxebooks.com.

AGARWAL, Purushottam, MA, PhD; Indian academic, author and critic; b. 25 Aug. 1955; m.; one s., one d. *Education:* Gwalior Univ., Jawharlal Nehru Univ. *Career:* Lecturer, Ramjas Coll., Univ. of Delhi 1982–90; Assoc. Prof., Center of Indian Languages, School of Language, Literature and Cultural Studies, Jawharlal Nehru Univ. 1990–2003, Prof. of Hindi Literature 2003–07, Chair., Center of Indian Languages 2005–07; Visiting Prof., El Colegio de Mexico 2002, Univ. of Cambridge 2002; Consultant to Oxfam, India 1998–2002; Chief Advisor to Aman Trust, Delhi 2003–06; mem. Union Public Service Comm. 2007–, Chair. 2008–. *Publications:* Teesra Rukh (Devi Shankar Awasthy Samman Award) (essays) 1996, Sanskriti: Varchswa aur Pratiroadh (essays) 1995, Vichar Ka Ananta 2000, Ji Pradhanmantriji (two vols) 2002, Nij Brahm Vichar: Dharm, Samaj aur Dharmetar Adhyatma (essays) 2004, Shivdan Singh Chauhan – a Biography 2006, Kabir – Sakhi Aur Sabad 2007, Akath Kahani Prem Ki: Kabir Ki Kavita aur Unka Samay (An Ineffable Tale of Love: Kabir's Poetry and his Times) (Rajkamal Kriti Samman Award 2009) 2009. *Address:* c/o Union Public Service Commission (UPSC), Dholpur House, Shahjahan Road, New Delhi 110 011, India (office). *E-mail:* mail@purushottamagrawal.com (home). *Website:* www.upsc.gov.in (office); www.purushottamagrawal.com (home).

AGBABI, Patience Ayibaifie, MA; British poet; *Fellow in Creative Writing, Oxford Brookes University*; b. 26 Aug. 1965, UK; pnr, two c. *Education:* Univs of Oxford and Sussex. *Career:* performance poet, worldwide projects include British Council/Apples & Snakes tour (India), Crossing Border (Netherlands), Diggante Festival (Sweden), Rough Talk Sweet Song tour (South Africa), British Council tour (Namibia), Rome Poetry Festival (Italy), Aldeburgh Festival, Soho Jazz Festival, Royal Albert Hall, Poetry Int., Cheltenham Festival, London Palladium, Edinburgh Book Festival, Glastonbury Festival, Spit Lit Festival, Brixton Acad., Bittersweet tour 1999–2000, Modern Love tour 2001, Dream Tour 2007 (all UK); resident poet, tattoo parlour, Flamin' 8 2000; poet-in-residence, Oxford Brookes Univ. –2001, Eton Coll. 2005; Lecturer, Univ. of Greenwich 2002–03, Cardiff Univ. 2002–04, Univ. of Kent 2004–05; Assoc. Creative Writing Lecturer, Univ. of Wales 2002–04; Fellow in Creative Writing, Oxford Brookes Univ. 2008–; co-judge 2005 Forward Prize for Poetry; mem. Atomic Lip. *Radio:* presenter: Blood, Sweat, Tears and Poetry (BBC Radio 4) 2008. *Television:* Litpop (three shorts, Channel 4) 1998. *Publications include:* R.A.W. 1995, Transformatrix 2000, Bloodshot Monochrome 2008; contrib. to anthologies and journals, including Bittersweet 1998, The Fire People 1998, Wasafiri 2000, Here to Eternity 2001, New Poems on the Underground 2003, 2006, Poetry Review 2006, Earth Shattering: Eco Poems 2007, The Forward Book of Poetry 2009. *Honours:* Excelle Literary Award for Poetry, Canterbury Poet Laureate 2010. *Literary Agent:* c/o Paul Beasley, 57 Productions. *E-mail:* paul@57productions.com. *Website:* www.57productions.com. *Address:* c/o Canongate Books, 14 High Street, Edinburgh, EH1 1TE, Scotland. *Telephone:* (131) 557-5111. *Website:* www.canongate.net.

AGBOLUAJE, Oladipo (Dipo), PhD; Nigerian playwright; b. (Oladipupo Olugbolahan Agboluaje), 15 June 1968, UK; s. of Niyi Agboluaje and Iyabo Agboluaje. *Education:* Univ. of Benin, London Metropolitan Univ., Open Univ. *Career:* involved in Eclipse Writers' Lab; Writer-in-Residence, New Wolsey

Theatre, Ipswich 2005–06; Pearson Writer-in-Residence, Soho Theatre 2007; mem. Talawa Writers Group 2005, Tricycle Theatre Writers Group, Breakthrough Brits 2009; writing tutor, New Vision Theatre, Unicorn Theatre; mem. Bd Soho Theatre, Oval House Theatre; mem. African Theatre Asscn. *Film:* Area Boys 2007. *Plays:* Early Morning 2003, Mother Courage and her Children (adaptation) 2004, Sight-Seeing (with Sophie Woolley) 2005, For One Night Only 2005–08, British-ish 2005, Captain Britain 2006, The Estate 2006, The Christ of Coldharbour Lane 2007, The Wish Collector 2008, Knock Against My Heart 2008, The Hounding of David Oluwale (adaptation) 2009, Iya Ile (The First Wife) 2009, The Garbage King, (adaptation) 2010, The Jero Plays (adaptation, BBC World Service), The Estate (adaptation, BBC World Service). *Radio:* Say Goodbye Twice (BBC Radio 3) 2010. *Honours:* Alfred Fagon Award 2009.

AGEE, Jonis, BA, MA, PhD; American writer, poet and academic; *Adele Hall Professor of English, University of Nebraska at Lincoln*; b. 31 May 1943, Omaha, Neb.; m. Paul McDonough; one d. *Education:* Univ. of Iowa, State Univ. of NY, Binghamton. *Career:* teacher, Coll. of St Catherine, St Paul, Minn. 1975–95; literary consultant, Walker Arts Center, Minneapolis 1978–84; adjunct teacher, Macalester Coll., St Paul, Minn. 1980–88; teacher and Ed., Literary Post Program for Sr Citizen Writers 1986–89; Prof., Univ. of Michigan 1995; currently Adele Hall Prof. of English, Univ. of Nebraska at Lincoln; many poetry readings; mem. Literary Guild. *Films (screenplays):* Full Throttle 2007, Baghdad Rules (co-writer) (California Film Award 2010). *Publications include:* Houses (chapbook) 1976, Mercury (chapbook) 1981, Two Poems 1982, Border Crossings (ed.) 1984, Stiller's Pond (ed.) 1988, Bend This Heart (short stories) 1989, Pretend We've Never Met (short stories) 1989, Sweet Eyes (novel) 1991, My Mother's Hands 1994, Strange Angels (novel) 1994, A .38 Special and a Broken Heart (short stories) 1995, South of Resurrection (novel) 1997, The Weight of Dreams 1999, Taking the Wall 1999, Acts of Love on Indigo Road: New and Selected Stories (ForeWord magazine Gold Book of the Year Award 2004, Nebraska Book Award for Fiction 2004) 2003, The River Wife (John Gardner Fiction Book Award 2008) 2007; contrib. to anthologies and periodicals. *Honours:* Minnesota State Arts Board Award 1977, NEA Fellowship 1978, Loft-McKnight Awards 1987, 1991, Mark Twain Award 2008, Outstanding Research and Creativity Award, Univ. of Nebraska 2010, George Garrett Award, Asscn of Writers and Writing Programs 2010. *Address:* 13202 North River Road, Omaha, NE 68112 (home); Department of English, University of Nebraska, 215 Andrews Hall, Lincoln, NE 68588-0333, USA (office). *Telephone:* (402) 472-1834 (office). *Fax:* (402) 455-1500 (office). *E-mail:* jagee@unl.edu (office). *Website:* english.unl.edu/faculty/profs/jagee.html (office); www.jonisagee.com.

AGOSÍN, Marjorie, PhD; Chilean human rights activist, writer, poet and professor of Spanish; *Professor of Spanish, Wellesley College*; b. 15 June 1955, Bethesda, Md, USA; d. of Moises Agosín and Frida Agosín. *Education:* Univ. of Georgia, Indiana Univ., Bloomington. *Career:* grew up in Chile, moved to USA aged 16 to escape mil. coup; currently Prof. of Spanish, Wellesley Coll. *Publications include:* Zones of Pain 1988, Circles of Madness: Mothers of the Plaza de Mayo 1992, Dear Anne Frank (poems), Tapestries of Hope, Threads of Love, A Cross and a Star: Memoirs of a Jewish Girl in Chile 1994, Always From Somewhere Else, Secrets in the Sand: The Young Women of Juárez 2007, The Light of Desire 2009; more than 40 vols of fiction, non-fiction, poetry and essays; contrib. articles to newspapers and magazines like Cuadernos Americanos, Arbor: Ciencia, Pensamiento y Cultura, Latin American Theater Review. *Honours:* Letras de Oro Award 1995, Latino Literature Prize 1995, Conf. of Christians and Jews Good Neighbor Award 1995, Jeanette Rankin Award 1995, UNA of Greater Boston Leadership Award for contrib. to int. understanding and human rights 1998. *Address:* Spanish Department, Wellesley College, Green Hall, Room 332, 106 Central Street, Wellesley, MA 02481, USA (office). *Telephone:* (781) 283-2425 (office). *E-mail:* magosin@wellesley.edu (office). *Website:* www.wellesley.edu/Spanish (office).

AGUALUSA, José Eduardo; Angolan novelist and poet; b. 13 Dec. 1960, Huambo. *Education:* Instituto Superior de Agronomia, Lisbon, Portugal. *Career:* newspaper and radio journalist, journal Público; Founder Língua Geral publishing co. 2006; mem. União dos Escritores Angolanos; lives between Angola, Brazil and Portugal. *Plays:* as writer: W generation, O monólogo, Chovem amores na Rua do Matador, A Caixa Preta. *Television:* A Hora das Cigarras (series, Antena 1, RDP Africa). *Publications include:* novels: A Conjura 1989, A Feira dos Assombrados (novella) 1992, Estação das Chuvas 1996, Nação crioula (trans. as Creole) 1997, Um estranho em Goa 2000, O Ano em que Zumbi Tomou o Rio 2002, O Vendedor de Passados 2004, As Mulheres do meu Pai 2007, Barroco tropical 2009, Milagrário Pessoal 2010; short stories: D. Nicolau Água-Rosada e outras estórias verdadeiras e inverosímeis 1990, Fronteiras Perdidas, contos para viajar 1999, A Substância do Amor e Outras Crónicas 2000, Estranhões e Bizarrocos 2000, O Homem que Parecia um Domingo 2002, Catálogo de Sombras 2003, Manual prático de levitação 2005, A girafa que comia estrelas 2005, Passageiros em Trânsito 2006, O filho do vento 2006; poetry: Coração dos Bosques 1980–1990 1991; non-fiction: Lisboa Africana (co-author) 1993, O lugar do morto 2011. *Honours:* Grand Prize for Literature, Portugal 1997, Ind. Foreign Fiction Prize 2007. *Address:* Editora Língua Geral, Rua Jardim Botânico, 600, cj. 502, 22461-000 Rio de Janerio, RJ Brazil (office). *Telephone:* (21) 2279-6165 (office). *Fax:* (21) 2279-6184 (office). *E-mail:* info@linguageral.com.br (office). *Website:* www.linguageral.com.br (office).

AGUILAR, Mila D., (Clarita Roja), BA, MA; Philippine poet and journalist; b. 31 March 1949, La Paz, Iloilo; d. of Dr Jose V. Aguilar and Ramona D. Aguilar; m. Magtanggol Roque; one s. *Education:* Univ. of the Philippines. *Career:* taught at Univ. of the Philippines at Diliman 1969–71, 2000–06; regular writer, Graphic magazine 1969–71; active in fighting to topple Marcos govt 1970–83; worked at St Joseph's Coll., Quezon City 1983–84, 1986–88; detained in govt prison 1984–86; Pres. Inst. for Filipino Cinema 1989–91; freelance writer, video documentarist, web weaver 1992–. *Films:* approx. 50 video documentaries 1989–91. *Publications:* Dare to Struggle, Dare to Win! 1974, The Mass Line 1997, A Comrade is as Precious as a Rice Seedling (poems) 1984, Why Cage Pigeons (poems) 1984, Pall Hanging over Manila 1984, Journey: An Autobiography in Verse (1964–1995) 1996; contrib. poems to anthologies including Pintig 1985. *Honours:* Pres.'s Award 1985, Freedom-to-Write Award 1991, Gawad Chancellor Award, Univ. of the Philippines, Diliman 2002, Gawad Leopoldo Yabes, Univ. of the Philippines, Diliman, Pinakamahusay na Instruktor sa Taong, Coll. of Arts and Letters 2002. *Address:* Philippine Center of International PEN, 531 Padre Faura, Ermita, Manila 1000, Philippines (office). *E-mail:* philippinepen@yahoo.com (office). *Website:* www.mda.ph.

AGUILAR-CARIÑO, Ma. Luisa B. (see IGLORIA, Luisa A.)

AGUIRRE RAMIREZ DE AGUILAR, Eugenio, BA, MA; Mexican writer; b. 31 July 1944, México, DF; m. 1st 1971; one s. one d.; m. 2nd María Silanes 2002. *Education:* Univ. Nacional Autónoma de México. *Career:* Lecturer, Univ. of Kansas, USA, Wabash Coll., USA, Univ. of Cambridge, UK, Instituto Cervantes, London, UK; mem. Writers' Asscn of Panama; Past Pres. Asociación de Escritores de México; Bd mem. Sociedad General de Escritores de México; mem. International PEN. *Publications:* fiction: Jesucristo Perez 1973, Pajar de Imaginación 1975, El caballero de las espadas 1978, Gonzalo Guerrero 1980, El testamento del diablo 1982, En el campo 1983, Cadaver exquisito 1984, Cuentos de tierra y asfalto (short stories) 1984, El rumor que llegó del mar 1985, Pájaros de fuego 1986, La suerte de la fea 1986, Un mundo de niño lleno de mar 1986, Pasos de sangre 1988, Amor de mis amores 1988, Los siete pecados capitales (short stories) 1989, El guerrero del sur 1991, Cosas de ángeles y otros cuentos (short stories) 1992, Los niños de colores 1993, Elena o el laberinto de la lujuria 1994, El demonio me visita 1994, La fascinación de la bestia 1994, Desierto ardiente 1995, Ruiz Massieu: el mejor enemigo 1995, Cuarto cerrado 1996, El hombre baldío 1998, Los perros de Angagua (short stories) 1998, El silencio de los pequeños secretos (short stories) 1999, La lotería del deseo 2003, La fotografía del hombre colgado 2005, Hidalgo, entre la virtud y el vicio 2009; biographical novels: Valentín Gómez Farías 1982, Leona Vicario 1986, Victoria 2005, The Maya Cross 2006, Isabel Moctezuma 2008, Pecar como dios manda 2010, La gran traición 2011; non-fiction: Eugenio Aguirre: De cuerpo entero (autobiog.) 1991; contrib. to Mexican and foreign publs. *Honours:* Int. Acad. of Lutece Great Silver Medal, Paris 1981, Premio Nacional de literatura José Fuentes Mares, Univ. Autónoma de Chihuahua 1986. *Address:* Paseo de la Reforma 2233, edificio Sauces, depto. 302. Col. Lomas Reforma. Delegación miguel Hidalgo. CP 11930 México DF (home); c/o Editorial Planeta, Presidente Masaryk esquina con Petrarca, Col. Polanco, 11540 México DF, Mexico (office). *Telephone:* 5292-4619 (office); 5292-4621 (office). *Fax:* 3000-6200 (ext.247) (office). *E-mail:* aguirre_eugenio@yahoo.com.

AHAMED, Liaquat, BSc; American investment manager and writer; b. 1964, Kenya. *Education:* Harvard Univ., Trinity Coll., Cambridge, UK. *Career:* fmr Head of Investment Div., World Bank, Washington, DC; CEO Fischer Francis Trees and Watts, New York 2001–04; adviser to hedge fund groups including Rock Creek Group and Rohatyn Group 2004–; mem. Bd of Dirs Rohatyn Group, Aspen Insurance Co. 2007–; mem. Bd of Trustees, The Brookings Inst. *Publications:* Lords of Finance: The Bankers Who Broke the World (Financial Times/Goldman Sachs Business Book of the Year 2009, Pulitzer Prize for History 2010, Spear's Book Award for Financial History Book of the Year 2010, Arthur Ross Book Award Gold Medal 2010) 2009. *Address:* c/o Aspen Insurance Company, 260 Madison Avenue, 8th Floor, New York, NY 10016 (office); c/o The Penguin Press Publicity, Penguin Group (USA) Inc., 375 Hudson Street, New York, NY 10014, USA (office). *E-mail:* liaquatahamed.theboard@aspen.bm (office). *Website:* us.penguingroup.com (office).

AHARONI, Ada Andrée, PhD; Israeli/French writer, poet, educationalist, lecturer and translator and researcher; *President, International Forum for the Literature and Culture of Peace (IFLAC)*; b. 30 July 1933, Cairo, Egypt; d. of Nessim Yadid and Fortunée Hemsi; m. Chaim Aharoni 1951 (died 2006); one s. one d. *Education:* Hebrew Univ., Jerusalem, Univ. of London, UK. *Career:* Lecturer, Dept of English, Haifa Univ. 1967–77; Sr Lecturer in Peace and Conflict Studies, Technion-Israel Inst. of Tech., Haifa 1977–93; Prof. of Literature, Univ. of Pennsylvania, USA; Ed. Galim: Anthology for the Literature and Culture of Peace 1985–2003, Horizon and Poetry Israel 1997–98; f. Story Telling Festival in Haifa 2009–10; Pres. 13th World Congress of Poets 1992, Writers' and Poets' Asscn 1984–2010, To Pave a World Beyond War Through Literature (PAVE) 1985–96, Int. Friends of Literature (IFLA) 1995–99; f. IFLAC (Int. Forum for the Literature and Culture of Peace), Pres. 1999–, Exec. Dir World IFLAC and IFLAC in the Middle East; f. The Bridge: Jewish and Arab Women for Peace in the Middle East, Pres. 1978–90; Vice-Pres., Hebrew Writers' Asscn in Israel 2003–05; Ed. of Chapter of EOLSS, UNESCO Encyclopedia, on The Culture of Peace; Founder-Pres. World Congress of Jews from Egypt 2004–10; mem. PEN, IWA Writers Asscn, Cttee of Hebrew Writers' Org.; Head of Northern Br. of ANI –

Creative Women in Israel Asscn. *Plays:* Inbar, The Second Exodus. *Radio:* numerous interviews for BBC, Kol Yisrael, Al Jazeera (and reading of her Peace Poems), US stations and also in Paris. *Television:* Festival of Storytelling: The Second Exodus of the Jews from Egypt, interviews on her historical novel From the Nile to the Jordan. *Publications:* 27 books (historical novels, biographies, poetry collections, chidlren's books and Peace Culture anthologies (GALIM, ten vols)), including Poems From Israel and Other Poems 1974, From the Pyramids to Mount Carmel 1980, Love Poems 1980, The Second Exodus: A Historical Novel 1983, Shin Shalom: Poems 1984, Shin Shalom: New Poems 1986, A Green Week 1988, Métal et Violettes 1989, Selected Poems from Israel and Around the World 1992, Saul Bellow: A Mosaic 1992, Selected Poems: In My Carmel Woods 1993, Memoirs from Alexandria 1993, In the Curve of Your Palm 1994, From the Nile to the Jordan 1995, The Peace Flower 1996, Waves of Peace 1997, Peace Poems 1997, Not in Vain: An Extraordinary Life (co-author) 1998, You and I Can Change the World: New and Selected Poems 2000, Culture of Peace Poetry Anthology 2000, Women Creating a World Beyond War and Violence 2001, The Pomegranate 2002, Moznaim 2004, Muestros 2004, Chosen Verse: English and Chinese – Bilingual 2004, Peace Poems 2010, A Wonderful Mosaic: Stories about the Jews of Egypt 2010; contrib. to Poetry Nippon, Jewish Chronicle, Voices, Arc, New Society, International Poetry Review, El Shark, Poet, Galim 10 Poetry Anthology 2003; ed.: various online magazines: Horizon Pave Peace; JAC: Jews from Arab Countries. *Honours:* British Council Poetry Award 1972, Haifa and Bremen Poetry Award 1975, Pres. of Israel's Literature Award, Keren Amos 1977, Bank Discount Literary Award 1979, Boston Forum Prize 1981, Haifa Culture Poetry Prize 1984, The Bemaaracha Jerusalem Poetry Grant 1987, Pennsylvania Poetry Award 1989, World Acad. of Arts and Culture, UNESCO Prize 1991, Yunus Imri Poetry Award 1992, Korean World Poetry Crown Award 1993, Shin Shalom Peace Poetry Award 1993, Int. Poetry Prize 1994, Merit Award, Historical Soc. of Jews from Egypt 1997, Best of the Planet Award (for website) 1998, 100 Global Heroines Award 1998, UNESCO Italy Poetry Contest 2003, Turkish-Ataturk Literary Award 2003, IFLAC Prize 2009. *Address:* PO Box 16077, Givat Amos, Nesher (office); 18A Amos Street, Apt 77, Nesher, Israel (home). *Telephone:* (77) 3202818 (home). *Fax:* (77) 4007835 (home). *E-mail:* ada@tx.technion.ac.il (office); iflac@bezeqint.net. *Website:* www.iflac.com/horizon (office); www.iflac.wordpress.com (office); www.iflac.com/ada (home).

AHERN, Cecelia; Irish novelist; b. 30 Sept. 1981, Dublin; d. of Bertie Ahern; m. 1st Nicky Byrne; one s.; m. 2nd David Keoghan; one d. *Education:* Griffith Coll., Dublin. *Television:* co-producer: Samantha Who?. *Publications:* P.S. I Love You 2004, Where Rainbows End (Corine Award, Germany 2005) 2004, If You Could See Me Now 2005, A Place Called Here 2006, Thanks for the Memories 2007, The Gift 2008, The Book of Tomorrow 2009, The Time of My Life 2011; contrib.: short stories to anthologies. *Honours:* Irish Post Award for Literature 2005, voted Author of Year in Glamour Women of the Year Awards 2008, Literary Award 2009. *Address:* c/o HarperCollins Publishers Ltd, 77–85 Fulham Palace Road, London, W6 8JB, England. *Website:* www.ceceliaahern.ie.

AHLBERG, Allan; British writer; b. 1938, Croydon, South London, England; m. Janet Ahlberg (nèe Hall) 1969 (died 1994); one d. *Career:* primary school teacher for ten years; formed successful author/illustrator partnership with his late wife, Janet; also worked with illustrators Fritz Wegner, Andre Amstultz, Colin McNaughton, Faith Jaques, Joe Wright, Emma Chichester-Clarke. *Publications include:* juvenile: with Janet Ahlberg: The Old Joke Book 1977, The Vanishment of Thomas Tull 1977, Burglar Bill 1977, Jeremiah in the Dark Woods 1977, Cops and Robbers 1978, Each Peach Pear Plum 1978, One and Only Two Heads 1979, The Baby's Catalogue 1982, See the Rabbit 1982, Peepo 1983, Poorly Pig 1984, Yum Yum 1984, Playmates 1984, The Jolly Postman (Kate Greenaway Medal, Emil/Kurt Maschler Award) 1986, The Cinderella Show 1986, Starting School 1988, Bye Bye Baby 1989, The Bear Nobody Wanted 1992, It was a Dark and Stormy Night 1993, The Jolly Pocket Postman 1995, Janet's Last Book 1996; with Colin McNaughton: Mr and Mrs Hay the Horse 1981, Big Bad Pig 1985, Fee Fi Fo Fum 1985, Happy Worm 1985, Help! 1985; with Andre Amstultz: Master Salt the Sailor's Son 1982, Hip-hippo-ray 1984, Dinosaur Dreams 1991, The Black Cat 1993, Monkey Do! 1998; with Fritz Wegner: Woof! 1987, The Giant Baby 1994, The Better Brown Stories 1995; with other illustrators: The Adventures of Bert (with Robert Briggs) 2001, Happy Families series (with various illustrators), The Children who Smelled a Rat 2005, The Runaway Dinner (with Bruce Ingman) 2006, The Boyhood of Burglar Bill 2007, Previously 2007, The Pencil (with Bruce Ingman) 2008; poetry: Heard it in the Playground, Please, Mrs Butler. *Honours:* several awards including Children's Book Award 1987, Blue Peter Book Award 2001, Children's Book Awards for a Book for Younger Children 2002, 2009. *Address:* c/o Puffin Publicity, 80 Strand, London, WC2R 0RL, England.

AHLMARK, Per, BA; Swedish politician, journalist, novelist and poet; *Adviser, Elie Wiesel Foundation for Humanity*; b. 15 Jan. 1939, Stockholm; s. of Prof. Axel Ahlmark; m. 1st (divorced); one s. one d.; m. 2nd Bibi Andersson 1978 (divorced); m. 3rd Lilian Edström; one s. *Career:* Leader of Young Liberals 1960–62; columnist for Expressen 1961–95, for Dagens Nyheter 1997–; mem. Parl. 1967–78; Deputy Chair. Swedish-Israeli Friendship Org. 1970–97; mem. Council of Europe 1971–76; mem. Royal Comms. on Literature, Human Rights, etc. in the 1970s; Leader, Folkpartiet (Liberal Party) 1975–78; Deputy Prime Minister and Minister of Labour 1976–78; Deputy Chair. Martin Luther King Fund 1968–73; Chair. Swedish Film Inst. 1978–81; Founder and Deputy Chair. Swedish Comm. Against Antisemitism 1983–95; Adviser to Elie Wiesel Foundation for Humanity, New York 1987–; mem. UN Watch, Geneva 1993–; mem. Acad. Universelle des Cultures, Paris; Fellow Wissenschaftskolleg zu Berlin 1998–99. *Publications:* An Open Sore, Tyranny and the Left, many political books, essays and numerous articles, three books of poetry, one novel. *Honours:* Hon. Fellow, Hebrew Univ., Jerusalem 1992; Defender of Jerusalem Award, New York 1986. *Address:* Folkungag 61, 11622 Stockholm, Sweden.

AHLSEN, Leopold; German writer; b. 12 Jan. 1927, Munich; s. of Max Alzmann and Margaret; m. Ruth Gehwald 1964; one s. one d. *Television:* series: The Old Man 1978–89, Cruise of a Globetrotter 1980, Deep Water 1983, From the Loom to a World Power 1983, The Wiesinger 1984, Island of Dreams 1991; movie: Philemon and Baucis 1956, Crime and Punishment 1959, All Power to the Earth 1962, Clothes Make the Man 1963, You Will Die, Sire 1964, The Poor Man Luther 1965, The Ruepp 1965, Berlin Antigone 1968, Boredom 1969, People 1970, Deaths 1971, Pear and Elderberry Shrubs 1971, Fat Eyes - An Idyll of the Small German Town 1972, A Weekend of Alfred Berger 1972, A Selfish Love 1973, Death in Astapovo 1974, The Wittiber 1975, The Hard Trade 1978, The Big Carp Ferdinand and Other Christmas Stories 1978, Defects 1980, François Villon 1981, The Good-Natured Grantler 1982, In This Town Home 1994, The Broken Jug 2003. *Honours:* Gerhart Hauptmann Prize 1955, Schiller-Förderungspreis 1957, Goldener Bildschirm 1968, Silver Nymph of Monte Carlo 1971, Bundesverdienstkreuz and other awards 1990. *Address:* Waldschulstrasse 58, 81827 Munich, Germany (home). *Telephone:* (89) 4301466 (home). *Fax:* (89) 4301466 (home).

AHMAD, Datuk Shahnon, BA, MA; Malaysian writer; *Professor Emeritus, School of Humanities, University of Science, Penang*; b. 13 Jan. 1933, Sik, Kedah; m. Wan Fatimah Wan Salleh. *Education:* studied in Australia and at Univ. of Science, Penang. *Career:* Head of Islamic Centre, Univ. of Science, Penang –1996; taught literature, Dean School of Humanities, Univ. of Science, Penang –1999, currently Prof. Emer.; mem. of Parl. for Sik, Kedah 1999–2004; Life mem. Nat. Literary Laureate. *Publications include:* Anjing-anjing 1964, Debu merah 1965, Terdedah 1965, Rentong (Rope of Ash) 1965, Ranjau Sepanjang Jalan (No Harvest but a Thorn) 1966, Protes 1967, Menteri 1967, Perdana 1969, Srengenge 1973, Sampah 1974, Kemelut 1977, Selasai sudah 1977, Seluang menolak Baung 1978, Penglibatan dalam puisi 1978, Gubahan novel 1979, The Third Notch and Other Stories 1980, Kesusasteraan dan etika Islam 1981, Al-syiqaq 1985, Tok Guru 1988, Ummi dan Abang Syeikhul 1992, Pongang sastera: gema karya kreatif dan kesannya terhadap khalayak 1995, Shit 1999. *Honours:* several awards including Nat. Literary Award 1982, Malaysian Nat. Laureate 1984, Malaysian Literary Prize 1999. *Address:* Universiti Sains Malaysia, 11800 Pulau Pinang (office); 61, Cangkat Minden, Jalan 1, 11700 Gelugor, Pulau Pinang, Malaysia (home). *Telephone:* (4) 6533888 (office). *Fax:* (4) 6589666 (office). *Website:* www.usm.my (office).

AHRENS, Bridget, BA, MPh, MFA; American writer; b. 9 Jan. 1958, Buffalo, NY; m. 1981; one s. one d. *Education:* State Univ. of NY, Univ. of California, Vermont Coll. *Career:* fmr instructor in fiction and non-fiction writing, Lebanon Coll.; Assoc. Ed., AIDS and Society: An International Research and Policy Bulletin; mem. Poets and Writers. *Publications:* Our Lady of the Keyboard 1989, The Problems and Pitfalls of Writing about Sex 1989, A Woman's Place is Intuition 1990, The Art of Baking, The Politics of Love 1991, The Eye of the Needle 1991, Atlas's Revenge 1992. *Honours:* Fellowship, Vermont Council on the Arts 1992. *Address:* 48 Lafountain Street, Winooski, VT 05404-1846, USA (home). *Telephone:* (802) 655-1106 (home).

AICHINGER, Ilse; Austrian writer; b. 1 Nov. 1921, Vienna; m. Günter Eich (died 1972). *Education:* Universität Wien. *Career:* fmrly worked with Inge Scholl at Hochschule für Gestaltung, Ulm; later worked as a reader for S. Fischer (publrs), Frankfurt and Vienna. *Publications include:* Die Grössere Hoffnung (novel) 1948, Knöpfe (radio play) 1952, Der Gefesselte (short stories) 1953, Zu keiner Stunde (dialogues) 1957, Besuch im Pfarrhaus (radio play) 1961, Wo ich wohne (stories, dialogues, poems) 1963, Eliza, Eliza (stories) 1965, Nachricht von Tag (stories) 1970, Schlechte Worter 1976, Meine Sprache und Ich Erzählungen 1978, Radio Plays, Selected Poetry and Prose by Ilse Aichinger 1983, Kleist, Moos, Fasane 1987, Collected Works (eight vols) 1991, Film und Verhängnis 2001. *Honours:* Förderungspreis des Österreichischen Staatspreises 1952, Preis der Gruppe 47 1952, Literaturpreis der Freien und Hansestadt Bremen 1954, Immermannpreis der Stadt Düsseldorf 1955, Literaturpreis der Bayerischen Akad. 1961, Nyell Sachs-Preis, Dortmund 1971, City of Vienna Literature Prize 1974, Georg Tracke Prize 1979, Petrarca Prize 1982, Belgian Europe Festival Prize 1987, Town of Solothurn Prize 1991, Joseph-Breitbach-Preis 2000. *Address:* c/o Fischer Verlag, POB 700480, 60008 Frankfurt, Germany.

AIDOO, Ama Ata; Ghanaian writer and academic; *Visiting Professor of Africana Studies and Creative Writing, Brown University*; b. Abeadzi Kyiakor, Gold Coast (now Ghana); one d. *Career:* Lecturer, Cape Coast Univ. 1970–73; Consultant Prof., Phelps-Stokes Fund Ethnic Studies Program, Washington 1974–75; consultant at univs, acads and research insts in Africa, Europe and USA; Prof. of English, Univ. of Ghana; Minister of Educ. 1982–83; fmr Fellow of Advanced Creative Writing Program, Stanford Univ.; currently Visiting Prof. of Africana Studies and Creative Writing, Brown Univ., also Writer-in-Residence; Chair. African Regional Panel of the Commonwealth Writers' Prize 1990, 1991; fmr mem. Bd of Dirs Ghana Broadcasting Corpn, Arts Council of

Ghana, Ghana Medical and Dental Council; Fellow, Inst. for African Studies. *Publications include:* novels: Our Sister Killjoy or Reflections from a Black-Eyed Squint 1977, Changes: A Love Story (Commonwealth Writers' Prize for the Africa region 1993) 1991; poetry: Someone Talking to Sometime 1985, Birds and Other Poems; plays: The Dilemma of a Ghost 1965, Anowa 1970, Changes: A Love Story 1991; short stories: No Sweetness Here 1970, The Eagle and The Chicken and Other Stories 1987, The Girl Who Can and Other Stories 1999; numerous contribs to magazines and journals. *Honours:* Millennium Award for Literary Excellence, Ghana's Excellence Awards Foundation 2005, Woman of Substance Award, African Women's Devt Fund 2005. *Address:* Department of Africana Studies, Brown University, Box 1904, 155 Angell Street, Providence, RI 02912, USA (office). *Telephone:* (401) 863-3137 (office). *Fax:* (401) 863-3559 (office). *E-mail:* Ama_Ata_Aidoo@brown.edu (office). *Website:* www.brown.edu/Departments/Africana_Studies (office).

AIDT, Naja Marie; Danish poet and author; b. 24 Dec. 1963, Egedesminde, Greenland; d. of Leif Aidt and Lene Aidt; m. Eigil Bryld; four s. *Plays:* Rundt på gulvet 1999, Siska 2000, Åsted 2006. *Music:* Den lille havfrue (libretto) 2000. *Film:* Strings 2005. *Radio:* Ubrydeligt 1996, Tjenende ånder 1998. *Publications:* poetry: Så længe jeg er ung 1991, Et vanskeligt møde 1992, Det tredje landskab 1994, Huset overfor 1996, Rejse for en fremmed 1999, Begyndelsen til en historie 2002, Balladen om Bianca 2002, Poesibog 2008, Alting blinker 2009; short story collections: Vandmærket 1993, Tilgang 1995, Bavian (Danish Critics' Choice Award 2006, Literature Prize, Nordic Council 2008) 2006; juvenile: Zakarias 1-5 2005, Hvor er Villy? 2006, Huset 2009; books have been translated into several languages. *Honours:* Martin Andersen Nexø-prisen 1996, Herman Bangs mindelegat 1996, Morten Nielsens mindelegat 1997, Otto Rungs forfatterlegat 2003, Beatrice Prize, Danish Acad. 2004, Lifetime grant from Statens Kunstfond 2006, Søren Gyldendal Prize 2011. *Literary Agent:* c/o Anneli Høier, Leonhardt & Høier A/S, Studiestræde 35A, 1455 Copenhagen K, Denmark. *Telephone:* 33-13-25-23. *Fax:* 33-13-49-92. *E-mail:* anneli@leonhardt-hoier.dk. *Website:* www.leonhardt-hoier.dk. *Address:* c/o Gyldendal, Klareboderne 3, 1001 Copenhagen, Denmark. *Telephone:* 33-75-55-55. *E-mail:* gyldendal@gyldendal.dk; SRSP@gyldendal.dk. *Website:* www.najamarieaidt.com; www.gyldendal.dk.

AINI, Lea; Israeli writer and poet; b. 1962, Tel-Aviv; d. of Yitzhak Aini. *Play:* Mi-Alma, staged by Habima Nat. Theater 2006–07. *Publications:* Diokan (poems) 1988, Keisarit Ha-Pirion Ha-Medumeh (poems) 1991, Gibborei Kayitz (short stories and novella, The Sea Horse Race) 1991, Geut Ha-Hol (novel) 1992, Tikrah Li Mi-Lemata (juvenile) 1994, Mar Arnav Mehapes Avoda (juvenile) 1994, Hei, Yuli (juvenile) 1995, Mishehi Tzerikha Lehiyot Kan (novel, Someone Must Be Here) 1995, Hetzi ve-ananas: Tamnunina (juvenile) 1996, Hardufim O Sipurim Mur'alim Al Ahava (short stories) 1997, Ashtoret (novel) 1999, Shir Ani, Shir Imma (poems for children) 2000, Anak, Malka, Ve'aman Hamischakim (novel), Sdommel (novella and short stories) 2001, The Giant, the Queen and the Master of Games (novel) 2004, Rose of Lebanon (novel) 2009. *Honours:* Wertheim Prize 1988, Adler Prize 1988, Tel-Aviv Foundation Award 1994, Prime Minister's Prize 1994, 2004, Bernstein's Prize for Drama 2006, Bialik Prize for Literature 2010. *Address:* c/o Hakibbutz Hameuchad Publishing House Ltd, PO Box 1432, Bnei Brak, Tel-Aviv 51114, Israel. *E-mail:* iradscharss@013.net.il.

AIRA, César; Argentine novelist, essayist and dramatist; b. 23 Feb. 1949, Coronel Pringles; m.; two c. *Career:* fmr Lecturer, Universidad de Buenos Aires, Universidad de Rosario. *Plays:* El mensajero 1996, Madre e hijo 1993. *Publications include:* novels: Moreira 1975, Ema, la cautiva 1981, La luz argentina 1983, Las ovejas 1984, Canto Castrato 1984, Una novela china 1987, Los fantasmas 1990, El bautismo 1991, La liebre 1991, Copi 1991, Embalse 1992, La guerra de los gimnasios 1992, La prueba 1992, El llanto 1992, El volante 1992, Cómo me hice monja 1993, El infinito 1994, La costurera y el viento 1994, Los misterios de Rosario 1994, La fuente 1995, Los dos payasos 1995, El mensajero 1996, Dante y Reina, Abeja 1996, La serpiente 1997, El Mago, Cumpleaños, La villa, La pastilla de hormona, El juego de los mundos, El Sueño 1998, Alejandra Pizarnik 1998, Las curas milagrosas del Dr Aira 1998, La mendiga 1998, El congreso de literatura 1999, Un episodio en la vida del pintor viajero 2000, Las tres fechas 2001, La Villa 2001, El Mago 2002, Varamo 2002, La Liebre 2002, Fragmento de un diario en los Alpes 2002, Canto Castrado 2003, Diario de la hepatitis 2003, El tilo 2003, Una novela china 2004, El Bautismo 2004, La Noches de 2004, Yo era una chica moderna 2004, Edward Lear 2004, Yo era una niña de siete años 2005; short stories: El vestido rosa 1984, Cecil Taylor, La trompeta de mimbre 1998; essays: Copi 1991, Nouvelles impressions du Petit Maroc 1991, Taxol: precedido de Duchamp en México y La broma 1997, La cena 2006, Las conversaciones 2007, La confesión 2008, Las aventuras de Barbaverde 2009, Ghosts 2009; non-fiction: Diccionario de autores latinoamericanos, Alejandra Pizarnik 1998, Haikus 2004; contrib. to numerous periodicals and books world-wide. *Address:* c/o Interzona Editora, Arabe Siria 3040 P.B. I, C1425EYJ Buenos Aires, Argentina. *E-mail:* info@interzonaeditora.com. *Website:* www.interzonaeditora.com.

AKAEKE ONWUEME, Tess (see ONWUEME, Osonye Tess)

AKAGAWA, Jiro; Japanese writer; b. 29 Feb. 1948, Fukuoka; m. Fumiko Serita 1973; one d. *Education:* Toho-gakuen High School. *Career:* fmr proof-reader for Japan Soc. of Mechanical Engineers; mem. Japanese Mystery Writers' Assn 1977–. *Publications:* more than 500 works including novels: The School Festival for the Dead 1977, Ghost Train (All Yomimono New Mystery Writers' Prize) 1976, The Deduction of Tortoise-shell Holmes 1978, High School Girl with a Machine Gun 1978, The Requiem Dedicated to the Bad Wife 1980, Virgin Road 1983, Chizuko's Younger Sister 1989, The Ghost Story of the Hitokoizaka-Slope 1995, The Ball at Castle Dracula 2008, Calico Cat Holmes' Tea Party 2008, Yurei Basu Tsua: AI Ni Omakase 1 2011, A Detective Story, Two, Incident in the Bedroom Suburb, Voice From Heaven, Sailor Suit, Machine Gun. *Honours:* Kadokawa Publishing Book Award 1980. *Address:* 40-16-201 Ohyama-cho, Sibuya-ku, Tokyo 151-0065, Japan (home).

AKAVIA, Miriam; Israeli (b. Polish) writer and translator; b. 20 Nov. 1927, Kraków, Poland; m. 1946; two d. *Education:* Univ. of Tel-Aviv, Israel. *Career:* licensed nurse; went through Holocaust in Kraków Ghetto, Plaszów and Auschwitz and later in Bergen-Belsen; arrived in Israel via Sweden 1946; worked at Jewish Agency; served as Israel's Social and Cultural Attaché in Stockholm; began publishing in 1975, describing her childhood, Holocaust and post-war experiences; translates Polish literature into Hebrew and Hebrew into Polish; Pres. Platform for Jewish-Polish Dialogue; fmr Pres., Israel-Poland Asscn. *Publications:* An End To Childhood (novel, translated into several languages) 1975, Adolescence of Autumn 1975, The Price (stories) 1977, Ha mechir 1978, Galia and Miklosh – Severance of Relations (for young people) 1982, (in Polish) 2000, Karmi Sheli (My Own Vineyard) (novel, translated into several languages) 1984, Bus Adventure (for children) 1986, Ma Vigne A Moi 1992, Ha-Derech Ha-Aheret: Sipur Ha-Kevutza (The Other Way: The Story of a Group) (novel) 1992, Jurek and Ania 2000, Lomhullas 2000, Short Stories (translated into German and Polish) 2000, Build a House with Love (for children) 2001, In the Land of Janusz Korczak 2006, My Life in the Shadow of the Holocaust (autobiog.) 2006; contribs to various literary magazines. *Honours:* Yakir Tel-Aviv 2000; Yad Va-Shem Prize 1978, Sec Prize 1985, Korczak Prize (Germany) (1988), Gold Medal (Poland) 1991, Prime Minister's Prize (Israel) 1993, Wizo Prize (Tel-Aviv) 1998. *Address:* PO Box 53050, Tel-Aviv 61530 (office); K. Zytomir 11, Tel-Aviv, 69405 Israel (home). *Telephone:* (3) 6479833 (home). *Fax:* (3) 6479833 (home). *E-mail:* akavie@inter.net.il.

AKELLO, Grace; Ugandan politician, poet, essayist and folklorist; m. 2nd; four s. *Education:* Makerere Univ. *Career:* fmr Deputy Ed. Viva magazine; mem. Parl. 1996–2006; Minister of State in Ministry of Gender, Labour and Social Devt (Entandikwa) 1999–2005, Minister of State for Northern Uganda Rehabilitation 2005–06; f. Nile Book Service; advised on setting up of Pres. Comm. to help resolve armed conflict in Teso area of Uganda, Sec., then Chair.; f. mem. Teso Devt Trust; Bd mem. Christian Aid; lives in Kenya. *Publications include:* My Dear Brother (poem) 1977, Iteso Thought Patterns in Tales 1975, My Barren Song (poems) 1979, Self Twice-Removed: Ugandan Woman (non-fiction) 1982, Problems Women Face (essay) 1995, Girl Soldier: A Story of Hope for Northern Uganda's Children (co-author) 2007. *Address:* c/o Ministry of Gender, Labour and Social Development, Plot 2, Lumumba Avenue, Simbamanyo House, 7136 Kampala, Uganda.

AKENSON, Donald Harman, BA, MEd, PhD, DLitt, DHum, FRSA, FRSC, FRHistS; Canadian historian and academic; *Douglas Professor of Canadian and Colonial History, Queen's University*; b. 22 May 1941, Minneapolis, Minn.; s. of Donald Nels Akenson and Fern L. Harman Akenson. *Education:* Yale and Harvard Univs. *Career:* Allston Burr Sr Tutor, Dunster House, Harvard Coll. 1966–67; Assoc. Prof. of History, Queen's Univ., Kingston, Ont. 1970–74, Prof. 1974–, currently Douglas Prof. of Canadian and Colonial History; Beamish Research Prof., Inst. of Irish Studies, Univ. of Liverpool 1998–2002; Guggenheim Fellow 1984–85. *Publications:* The Irish Education Experiment 1970, The Church of Ireland: Ecclesiastical Reform and Revolution 1800–1885 1971, Education and Enmity: The Control of Schooling in Northern Ireland 1920–50 1973, The United States and Ireland 1973, A Mirror to Kathleen's Face: Education in Independent Ireland 1922–60 1975, Local Poets and Social History: James Orr, Bard of Ballycarry 1977, Between Two Revolutions: Islandmagee, Co. Antrim 1798–1920 1979, A Protestant in Purgatory: Richard Whately: Archbishop of Dublin 1981, The Irish in Ontario: A Study of Rural History 1984, Being Had: Historians, Evidence and the Irish in North America 1985, The Life and Times of Ogle Gowan 1986, Small Differences: Irish Catholics and Irish Protestants, 1815–1921 1988, Half the World from Home: Perspectives on the Irish in New Zealand 1990, Occasional Papers on the Irish in South Africa 1991, God's Peoples: Covenant and Land in South Africa, Israel and Ulster 1992, The Irish Diaspora, A Primer 1993, Conor: A Biography of Conor Cruise O'Brien 1994, If the Irish Ran the World: Montserrat 1630–1730, Surpassing Wonder: The Invention of the Bible and the Talmuds 1998, Saint Saul: A Skeleton Key to the Historical Jesus 2000, Intolerance: The E. Coli of the Human Mind 2004, An Irish History of Civilization (two vols) 2006, Some Family – The Mormons and How Humanity Keeps Track of Itself 2007, Ireland, Sweden and the Great European Migration 1815–1914 2011; novels: The Lazar House Notebooks 1981, Brotherhood Week in Belfast 1984, The Orangeman: The Edgerston Audit 1987, At Face Value: The Life and Times of Eliza McCormack 1990. *Honours:* Hon. DLitt (McMaster) 1995, (Guelph) 2000; Hon. DHumLitt (Lethbridge) 1996; Hon. LLD (Regina) 2002; Hon. DLH (Queen's Univ. Belfast) 2008, (Victoria Univ., Wellington, NZ) 2010; Chalmers Prize 1985, Landon Prize 1987, Grawemeyer World Peace Prize 1993, Molson Laureate 1996 and many other awards and distinctions. *Address:* Department of History, Queen's University, Kingston, ON, K7L 3N6, Canada (office). *Telephone:* (613) 533-2155 (office). *Fax:* (613) 533-6822 (office). *Website:* www.queensu.ca/history (office).

AKHTAR, Javed; Indian scriptwriter, poet and songwriter; b. 17 Jan. 1945, Gwalior, Madhya Pradesh; s. of Jan Nisar Akhtar and Safia Akhtar; m. 1st Honey Irani (divorced 1983); m. 2nd Shabana Azmi 1984; one s. one d. (from previous m.). *Education:* Colvin Taluqedar Coll. *Career:* Urdu writer; formed scriptwriting partnership with Salim Khan 1971–1980; began writing poetry 1980–; Pres. Muslims for Secular Democracy; mem. Advisory Bd Asian Acad. of Film and TV; Chair. Jury, Uninor Mirchi Music Awards 2010; Founder-mem. Muslim Intelligentsia group; mem. Citizens for Justice and Peace. *Films include:* writer: Andaz 1971, Haathi mere Saathi 1971, Seeta aur Geeta 1972, Yaadon ki Baraat 1973, Zanzeer 1973, Haath ki Safai 1974, Aakri Dao 1975, Deewar 1975, Sholay 1975, Chacha Bhatija 1977, Imaan Dharam 1977, Don 1978, Trishul 1978, Kaala Patthar 1979, Dostana 1980, Shaan 1980, Kranti 1981, Shakti 1982, Betaab 1983, Duniya 1984, Mashaal 1984, Meri Jung 1985, Saagar 1985, Zamaana 1985, Dacait 1987, Mr India 1987, Joshilay 1989, Main Azaad Hoon 1989, Roop ki Rani Choron ka Raja 1993, Prem 1995, Kabhi na Kabhi 1998, Lakshya 2004, Don 2006. *Compositions include:* numerous film soundtracks. *Publications include:* Tarkash (poetry) 1995; contrib. to Talking Films & Talking Songs: Conversations with Javed Akhtar. *Honours:* 14 Filmfare Awards, Screen Videocon Awards 1995, 1997, Nat. Award for Best Lyricist 1996–98, 2000–01, Padma Shri 1999, Avadh Ratan, Uttar Pradesh Govt 2000, Nat. Integration Award, All India Anti-Terrorist Asscn 2001, Nagrik Samman, Mayor of Bhopal 2002, Zee Lux Cine Award 2002, 2005, Hakim Khan Sur Sammaan Award, Maharana Mewar Foundation Udaipur, 2003, Best Lyricist, Int. Indian Film Acad. 2005, 2008, Padma Bhushan 2007, has been named by India Today amongst India's 50 Most Powerful People. *E-mail:* javed@javedakhtar.com (office); jaduakhtar@gmail.com (home). *Website:* www.javedakhtar.com (home).

AKMAKJIAN, Alan Paul, BA, MA, PhD; American educator, poet and writer; b. 18 July 1948, Highland Park, Mich. *Education:* Eastern Michigan Univ., Univ. of Texas at Dallas, St John's Univ., New York, Wayne State Univ., Detroit, California State Univ., San Francisco. *Career:* teacher, California State Univ., San Francisco 1985, St John's Univ., New York 1994–95, Univ. of Texas at Dallas 1995–; instructor, Poets in the Schools, Calif. 1986–91; mem. Acad. of American Poets, Associated Writing Programs, Modern Language Asscn, PEN, Poetry Soc. of America. *Publications:* Treading Pages of Water 1992, Let the Sun Go 1992, California Picnic 1992, Grounded Angels 1993, Breaking the Silence 1994, California Picnic and Other Poems 1997, And what Rough Beast: Poems at the end of the Century 1999; contrib. to anthologies, journals, reviews and magazines. *Honours:* Nat. Endowment for the Arts Grant 1984, California Arts Council Grant 1984, St John's Univ. Fellowship 1994–95, Univ. of Texas Fellowships 1994–95, 1995–96, 1996–97, Texas Public Educational Grant 1996–97. *Address:* 2200 Waterview Parkway, Apt 2134, Richardson, TX 75080-2268, USA (home). *Telephone:* (972) 497-9412 (home).

AKPAN, Uwem, MFA; Nigerian priest and writer; b. 19 May 1971, Ikot Akpan Eda. *Education:* Creighton Univ and Gonzaga Univ, Univ. of Michigan, USA, Catholic Univ. of Eastern Africa. *Career:* ordained as Jesuit priest 2003; taught in Jesuit school in Harare, Zimbabwe 2007; currently teacher, Christ the King Church, Ilasamaja-Lagos. *Publications:* Say You're One of Them (short stories) (Hurston/Wright Legacy Award 2009, Commonwealth Writers' Prize for Best First Book, Africa region 2009, PEN/Beyond Margins Award 2009) 2008. *Literary Agent:* c/o Maria Massie, Lippincott Massie McQuilkin, 27 West 20th Street, Suite 305, New York, NY 10011, USA. *Telephone:* (212) 352-2055. *E-mail:* maria@lmqlit.com. *Website:* www.lmqlit.com; www.uwemakpan.com.

AKUNIN, Boris; Russian (b. Georgian) writer; b. (Grigory Shalvovich Chkhartishvili), 1956, Georgia. *Education:* Moscow State Univ. *Career:* Deputy Ed.-in-Chief Inostrannaya Literatura (magazine) –2000; Ed.-in-Chief Anthology of Japanese Literature (20 vols); Chair. Exec. Bd Pushkin Library (Soros Foundation). *Publications:* (names in trans.) fiction: Azazel, Special Errands, Counsellor of State, Coronation or the Last of the Novels, Lover of Death Vol One, Lover of Death Vol Two, Pelagia and the White Bulldog, Pelagia and the Black Monkey, Pelagia and the Red Rooster, The Winter Queen, Leviathan, Turkish Gambit, The Death of Achilles, Jack of Spades, The Decorator, The Diamond Chariot, F.M. 2006, Special Assignments 2007, Pelagia and the Black Monk 2007, The State Counsellor 2008, Sister Pelagia and the Red Cockerel 2009, The Coronation 2009; non-fiction: Tales for Idiots (essays), The Writer and Suicide; contrib. to numerous reviews and criticisms, numerous trans of Japanese, American and English literature. *Address:* Poema Press Publications, Zvezdny blvd 23, 129075 Moscow, Russia (office). *Telephone:* (495) 925-42-05 (home). *E-mail:* erikavoronova@mtu-net.ru (office). *Website:* www.akunin.ru (office).

ALAGIAH, George, OBE; British journalist, broadcaster and writer; *Presenter, Six O'Clock News and World News Today, British Broadcasting Corporation (BBC);* b. 22 Nov. 1955, Sri Lanka; m. Frances Robathan; two s. *Education:* St John's Coll., Portsmouth and Univ. of Durham. *Career:* family moved to Ghana 1960; worked in print journalism for South Magazine 1982–89; joined the BBC 1989, Leading Foreign Corresp. specializing in Africa and the developing world, BBC's Africa Corresp., Johannesburg 1994–98, Presenter The World News on BBC 4 2002, Presenter BBC Six O'Clock News 2003–, World News Today (rebranded as GMT with George Alagiah 2010) 2006–, BBC World; has interviewed many internationally prominent figures; has contributed to The Guardian, Daily Telegraph, The Independent and Daily Express newspapers; Bd mem. Royal Shakespeare Co.; Patron NAZ Project, Parenting UK 2000–, Fairtrade Foundation 2002–09. *Publications:* A Passage to Africa 2001, The Day That Shook the World, A Home from Home (autobiography) 2006. *Honours:* Critics' Award and Golden Nymph Award, Monte Carlo TV Festival 1992, Best Int. Report, Royal TV Soc. 1993, Best TV Journalist Award, Amnesty Int. 1994, One World Broadcasting Trust Award 1994, James Cameron Memorial Trust Award 1995, Bayeux Award for War Reporting 1996, Media Personality of the Year, Ethnic Minority Media Awards 1998, BAFTA Award (part of BBC Team) for coverage of Kosovo conflict 2000, Asian Award for Outstanding Achievement in TV 2010. *Address:* BBC, Room 1640, Television Centre, Wood Lane, London, W12 7RJ, England (office). *Telephone:* (20) 8743-8000 (office). *Fax:* (20) 8743-7882 (office). *Website:* www.bbc.co.uk (office).

ALARCÓN, Daniel, BA, MFA; Peruvian writer; b. 1977, Lima. *Education:* Columbia Univ., New York and Iowa Creative Writing Workshop, USA. *Career:* moved to USA as a child; Assoc. Ed., Etiqueta Negra magazine; Distinguished Visiting Writer, Mills Coll., Calif. 2005–07; Visiting Scholar, Center for Latin American Studies, Univ. of California at Berkeley. *Publications:* War by Candlelight 2006, Lost City Radio 2006, El rey siempre esta por encima del pueblo 2009, The Secret Miracle: The Novelist's Handbook (ed.) 2010; contribs to The New Yorker, Harper's, Virginia Quarterly Review, Salon, Eyeshot. *Honours:* Whiting Award 2004, Guggenheim Fellowship 2007, Lannan Literary Award 2007, Nat. Magazine Award 2008, PEN USA Award 2008, Int. Literature Award 2009. *Address:* c/o Author Mail, 7th Floor, HarperCollins Publishers, 10 East 53rd Street, New York, NY 10022, USA. *E-mail:* web@etiquetanegra.com.pe. *Website:* etiquetanegra.com.pe; www.danielalarcon.com.

ALBAHARI, David; Serbian writer; b. 1948, Pec; m.; two c. *Education:* Univ. of Belgrade. *Career:* moved to Calgary, Canada 1994; Markin-Flanagan Distinguished Writer-in-Residence, Univ. of Calgary 1995–96; Ed.-in-Chief Pismo magazine; mem. Fed. of Jewish Communities of Yugoslavia (Pres. 1991); mem. Serbian Acad. of Science and Arts. *Publications include:* novels: Sudija Dimitrijevic (trans. as Judge Dimitrijevic) 1978, Cink (trans. as Tsing) 1988, Kratka knjiga 1993, Snezni covek (trans. as Man of Snow) 1995, Mamac (trans. as Bait) (NIN Prize) 1996, Mrak (trans. as Darkness) 1997, Gec i Majer (trans. as Götz and Meyer) 1998, Svetski Putnik (trans. as Globetrotter) 2001, Pijavice (trans. as Leeches) 2005, Marke (trans. as Stamps) 2006, Ludvig 2007, Brat (trans. as Brother) 2008; short stories: Porodicno vreme (trans. as Family Time) 1978, Obicne price (trans. as Ordinary Stories) 1978, Opis smrti (trans. as Description of Death) (Ivo Andric Prize) 1982, Fras u supi (trans. as Shock in the Shed) 1984, Jednostavnost (trans. as Simplicity) 1988, Pelerina (trans. as Cloak) (Stanislav Winaver Prize) 1993, Izabrane price 1994, Words are Something Else (trans.) 1996, Neobicne price (trans. as Unusual Stories) 1999, Najlepse price (trans. as The Best Stories) 2001, Drugi Jezik (trans. as Second Language) 2003, Senke (trans. as Shadows) 2006, Ema I Jez Koji Nestaje (trans. as Ema and the Disappearing Hedgehog) 2008, Svake noci u drugom gradu (trans. as Every Night in Another City) 2008; essays: Prepisivanje Sveta (trans. as Rewriting the World) 1997, Teret (trans. as Burden) 2004, Dijaspora i Druge Stvari (trans. as Diaspora and Other Things) 2008. *Literary Agent:* c/o Liepmann AG Literary Agency, Englischviertelstrasse 59, 8032 Zurich, Switzerland. *Telephone:* (43) 2682380. *Fax:* (43) 2682381. *E-mail:* info@liepmanagency.com. *Website:* www.liepmanagency.com; www.davidalbahari.com.

ALBANY, James (see RAE, Hugh Crauford)

ALBEE, Edward Franklin, III; American playwright; b. 12 March 1928, Virginia, VA; adopted s. of Reed Albee and Frances Cotter. *Education:* Lawrenceville and Choate Schools, Washington, DC, Valley Forge Mil. Acad., Trinity Coll., Hartford. *Career:* Comm. Chair. Brandeis Univ. Creative Arts Awards 1983, 1984; Founder-Pres. The Edward F. Albee Foundation 1967–; Distinguished Prof., Univ. of Houston 1988–2003; mem. Dramatists Guild Council, PEN America, The American Acad., Nat. Inst. of Arts and Letters; Fellow, American Acad. of Arts and Sciences 1972. *Plays include:* The Zoo Story (Vernon Rice Award 1960) 1958, The Death of Bessie Smith 1959, The Sandbox 1959, Fam and Yam 1959, The American Dream (Foreign Press Asscn Award 1961) 1960, Who's Afraid of Virginia Woolf? (Drama Critics' Circle Award for Best Play) 1962, stage adaptation of The Ballad of the Sad Café (Carson McCuller) 1963, Tiny Alice 1964, Malcolm (from novel by James Purdy) 1965, A Delicate Balance (Pulitzer Prize 1966) 1966, Everything in the Garden (after a play by Giles Cooper) 1967, Box 1968, Quotations from Chairman Mao Tse-tung 1968, All Over 1971, Seascape (Pulitzer Prize 1975) 1974, Listening 1975, Counting the Ways 1976, The Lady from Dubuque 1977–79, Lolita (adapted from Vladimir Nabokov) 1979, The Man Who Had Three Arms 1981, Finding the Sun 1982, Marriage Play 1986–87, Three Tall Women (Pulitzer Prize 1994) 1990–91, Fragments 1993, The Play About the Baby 1996, The Goat, or, Who is Sylvia? 2000, Occupant 2001, Peter and Jerry (Act 1: Home Life, Act 2: The Zoo Story) 2004, Me, Myself and I 2007, At Home at the Zoo 2009; essays: Stretching My Mind: Essays 1960–2005 2005. *Honours:* Dr hc (Bulgarian Nat. Acad. of Theater and Film Arts) 2009; Tony Awards 1963, 1996, 2002, Gold Medal, American Acad. and Inst. of Arts and Letters 1980, inducted into Theater Hall of Fame 1985, Kennedy Center Award 1996, Nat. Medal of Arts 1996, Special Tony Award for Lifetime Achievement 2005. *Address:* 14 Harrison Street, New York, NY 10013 (office); PO Box 697, Montauk, NY 11954, USA (home). *Telephone:* (212) 226-2020 (office). *Fax:* (212)226-5551 (office). *E-mail:* albee@albeefoundation.org (office); info@albeefoundation.org (office). *Website:* www.albeefoundation.org (office).

ALBERT, Bill, BA, PhD; American writer and economist; b. (William Gombert), 16 Dec. 1942, New York, NY, USA; s. of Matthrews Gombert and Ruth Buchman; m. 1st Ada Rapoport (divorced 1990); m. 2nd Gillian Ann Albert 1990; one s. two d. *Education:* Univ. of California, Berkeley, London School of Econs. *Career:* Reader in Econ. History, Univ. of East Anglia, Norwich, UK 1968–93; CEO Norfolk Coalition of Disabled People 2006–08. *Publications:* fiction: Et Rodriguez alors? 1990, Desert Blues 1994, Castle Garden 1996; contribs to magazines. *Literary Agent:* c/o Agence Littéraire Lora Fountain, 7 rue de Belfort, 75011 Paris, France. *Website:* billalbert.me.uk.

ALBERT, Gábor; Hungarian writer and editor; b. 30 Oct. 1929; m. Zsuzsanna Marek 1954; one s. one d. *Education:* Eötvös Lorand Univ. *Career:* librarian, Széchényi Nat. Library 1955–64, Inst. of Musicology 1964–95; Ed.-in-Chief, Új Magyarország 1991–92, Magyarok Világlapja 1992–96; mem. Asscn of Hungarian Writers, Hungarian Acad. of Arts. *Publications:* Dragon and Octahedron (short stories), After Scattering (essays), Where Are Those Columns (novel), In a Shell (novel), Book of Kings (novel), Heroes of the Failures (essays), Atheist (short stories), Final Settlement of a Wedding (short stories), Stephen King's Tart Wine (essays) 1993, ...We Have Survived Him (novel) 1996, The Stone Don't Feel It (essays) 1998, I am Reading the Letters of B. Szemere (essay) 1999, The Old Dog Is About To Cast His Coat (essays) 2001, Vaults, Gargoyles, Rosettes (memoirs) 2002, In the Belly of the Fish (novel) 2002, Initiation Ceremonies (essays) 2003, Waves and the Shore (short stories) 2004, Suspension Corridors (novel) 2006, In the Shadow of Death–Socrates and Bakunin (essay) 2007, At the Mercy of the Truth (essays) 2007, Notwithstanding! (essays) 2009, Under the Leaves of Strawberry (essays) 2010, For Whom Tolls the Hidas Bell? (essay) 2011; contribs to periodicals. *Honours:* Book of the Year 1990, Attila József Award 1996, Arany János Award 2003. *Address:* Erdö u 150, 2092 Budakeszi, Hungary (home). *Telephone:* (23) 453438 (home). *E-mail:* galbert29@gmail.com. *Website:* www.albertgabor.hu.

ALBERT, Neil, BS, MA, JD; American attorney and writer; b. 12 May 1950, Los Angeles, Calif.; m. Linda Kling 1979. *Education:* Univ. of Oregon, Villanova Law School. *Career:* Assoc. Ed. Villanova Law Review 1975–76; attorney, Lancaster, Pa 1976–; Law Clerk to Hon. Paul A. Mueller Court of Common Pleas of Lancaster Co. 1976–77; Fellow, Acad. of Advocacy; mem. Mystery Writers of America. *Publications include:* The January Corpse 1991, The February Trouble 1992, Burning March 1993, Cruel April 1994, Appointment in May 1996, Tangled June 1997. *Address:* 2226 Main Street, Narvon, PA 17602, USA. *E-mail:* nalbert@epix.net.

ALBERT, Susan Wittig, (Robin Paige, Susan Blake, Carolyn Keene), BA, PhD; American writer; b. 2 Jan. 1940, Maywood, Ill.; m. 1st (divorced); three c.; m. 2nd William Albert 1986. *Education:* Univ. of Illinois, Univ. of California, Berkeley. *Career:* instructor, Univ. of San Francisco 1969–71; Asst Prof., Univ. of Texas at Austin 1972–77, Assoc. Prof. 1977–79, Assoc. Dean of Grad. School 1977–79; Dean, Sophie Newcomb Coll. 1979–81; Grad. Dean, Southwest Texas State Univ. 1981–82, Prof. of English 1981–87, Vice-Pres. for Academic Affairs 1982–86; mem. Garden Writers of America, Herb Soc. of America, Mystery Writers of America, Sisters in Crime, Story Circle Network (Founder, Pres. and journal ed. 1997–2003), Texas Inst. of Letters. *Publications include:* fiction: Thyme of Death 1992, Witches' Bane 1993, Hangman's Root 1994, Rosemary Remembered 1995, Rueful Death 1996, Love Lies Bleeding 1997, Chile Death 1998, Lavender Lies 1999, Mistletoe Man 2000, Bloodroot 2001, Indigo Dying 2003, A Dilly of a Death 2004, Dead Man's Bones 2004, Bleeding Hearts 2006, The China Bayles Book of Days 2006, Spanish Dagger 2007, What Wildness is this: Women Write about the Southwest (co-ed.) (Willa Award for Creative Non-fiction 2009) 2007, Nightshade 2008, Wormwood 2009, Together, Alone: A Memoir of Marriage and Place (autobiog.) 2009, Holly Blues 2010, Mourning Gloria 2011; co-author as Robin Paige: Death at Bishop's Keep 1994, Death at Gallow's Green 1995, Death at Daisy's Folly 1997, Death at Devil's Bridge 1998, Death at Rottingdean 1999, Death at Whitechapel 2000, Death at Epsom Downs 2001, Death at Dartmoor 2002, Death at Glamis Castle 2003, Death in Hyde Park 2004, Death at Blenheim Palace 2005, Death on the Lizard 2006; The Cottage Tales of Beatrix Potter series: The Tale of Hill Top Farm 2004, The Tale of Holly How 2005, The Tale of Cuckoo Brow Wood 2006, The Tale of Hawthorn House 2007, The Tale of Briar Bank 2008, The Tale of Applebeck Orchard 2009, The Tale of Oat Cake Crag 2010, The Tale of Castle Cottage 2011, The Darling Dahlias and the Cucumber Tree 2010, The Darling Dahlias and the Naked Ladies 2011; author or co-author of more than 60 juvenile books; non-fiction: Stylistic and Narrative Structures in the Middle English Verse Romances 1977, The Participating Reader (co-author) 1979, Work of Her Own: How Women Create Success and Fulfillment off the Traditonal Career Track 1992, Writing from Life: Telling Your Soul's Story 1997, An Extraordinary Year of Ordinary Days 2010. *Address:* PO Box 1616, Bertram, TX 78605, USA (home). *E-mail:* susan@susanalbert.com (office). *Website:* www.mysterypartners.com; www.aboutthyme.com; www.susanalbert.com.

ALBEVERIO-MANZONI, Solvejg Giovanna Maria; Swiss artist and writer; b. 9 Nov. 1939, Arogno; d. of Cesco Manzoni and Madi Manzoni (née Angioletti); m. Sergio Albeverio 1970; one d. *Education:* textile design, Como, Italy, Kunstgewerbeschule, Zürich, Switzerland and Statens Handverk og Kunstindustriskole, Oslo, Norway. *Career:* has given poetry readings at int. meetings at Ferrara, Italy 1987, Poesia dell'Europa latina, Fano, Italy 1987, World Conf. for Poets, Crete, Greece 1991, Sintra, Portugal 1995, The Gerard Manley Hopkins Soc. Summer School, Monasterevin, Co. Kildare, Ireland 2002; mem. Cttee Associazione degli Scrittori della Svizzera Italiana (ASSI) (Pres. 1991–95), PEN. *Exhibitions include:* solo: Campione d'Italia, Bielefeld, Bochum, Berlin, Bonn, Remagen-Kripp and Wilhelmshaven (Germany), Marseille and Paris (France), Zürich, Biasca and Bellinzona (Switzerland), Salzburg (Austria); group: Fredrikstad (Norway), New York (USA), Bielefeld, Essen (Germany), Maastricht (Netherlands) and Zürich, Ascona, Basel, Lugano, Locarno and Bellinzona (Switzerland). *Publications include:* Da stanze chiuse (poetry and drawings) 1987, Il pensatore con il mantello come meteora (novel) 1990, Controcanto al chiuso (drawings, with poetry by B. M. Frabotta) 1991, Il fiore e il frutto. Triandro donna (poetry) (with K. Fusco and C. Ragni) 1993, Frange di solitudine (novel) 1994, Spiagge confinanti (poetry) (with K. Fusco and C. Ragni) 1996, All'ombra delle farfalle in fiore (drawings with poetry by Folco Portinari) 1998, La carcassa color del cielo (novel) 2001, Il castello, le autostrade, i boschi, la ronda (novel) 2001, Contrappunto (poetry) 2005, Gestation infinie (with Annie Richard) 2007; numerous stories, poetry and drawings in magazines, journals and anthologies. *Honours:* Premio Ascona for unpublished narrative 1987, Pro Helvetia Scholarship 1995. *Address:* Liebfrauenweg 5B, 53125 Bonn, Germany (home). *Telephone:* (228) 2599991 (home).

ALBINATI, Edoardo; Italian novelist, poet and translator; b. 1956, Rome. *Career:* fmr Ed. cultural review, Nuovi Argomenti; fmr Visiting Writer Columbia Univ., New York, USA; teaches at Rebibbia Penitentiary, Rome 1994–. *Publications include:* Arabeschi della vita morale (novel) 1988, Il polacco lavatore dei vetri (novel) 1989, Elegie e proverbi (poems) 1989, La comunione dei beni (poems) 1995, Mare o monti (poem) 1997, Orti di guerra (novel) 1997, Maggio selvaggio (autobiog.) 1999, 19 (novel) 2000, Sintassi italiana (poems) 2001, Il ritorno 2002, Svenimenti (Premio Viareggio) 2004, Tuttalpiù muoio (co-author) 2006, L'Italie telle qu'elle est 2010, Svenimenti 2010. *Address:* c/o Giulio Einaudi Editore SpA, Via Biancamano 2, 10121 Turin, Italy. *E-mail:* einaudi@einaudi.it. *Website:* www.einaudi.it.

ALBOM, Mitch, MA, MBA; American writer and journalist; b. 23 May 1958, Passaic, NJ; m. Janine Sabino 1995. *Education:* Brandeis Univ., Columbia Univ. *Career:* sports columnist, Detroit Free Press newspaper 1985–; f. charities, The Dream Fund 1989, A Time to Help 1998, S.A.Y Detroit; Contributing Ed. Parade magazine; Bd mem. CATCH, Forgotten Harvest, Michigan Hospice Org.; mem. Rock Bottom Remainders Band. *Plays:* has written numerous plays including off-Broadway version of Tuesdays With Morrie (co-written with Jeffrey Hatcher). *Films:* Tuesdays with Morrie (book) 1999, The Five People You Meet in Heaven 2004 (screenwriter and producer). *Radio:* presenter The Mitch Albom Show, The Monday Sports Albom. *Publications:* Live Albom I 1987, Bo (with Bo Schembechler) 1989, Live Albom II 1990, Live Albom III 1992, Fab Five 1993, Live Albom IV 1995, Tuesdays with Morrie 1997, The Five People You Meet in Heaven 2003, For One More Day 2006, Have a Little Faith 2009; contrib. to Sports Illustrated, GQ, Sport, The New York Times, TV Guide, USA Today, GEO Magazine. *Honours:* APSE No. 1 Sports Columnist in the Nation, seven APSE awards for feature writing, writing awards from AP, UPI, Headliners Club, Nat. Sportswriters and Broadcasters Asscns, Nat. Hospice Org. Man of the Year 1999, Red Smith Award for Lifetime Achievement, Press Sports Eds 2010. *Address:* The Detroit Free Press, 615 West Lafayette, Detroit, MI 48226, USA (office). *Telephone:* (313) 222-6400 (office). *E-mail:* malbom@freepress.com (office). *Website:* www.freep.com (office); mitchalbom.com.

ALBRIGHT, Daniel, BA, MPhil, PhD; American academic and writer; *Ernest Bernbaum Professor of Literature, Harvard University*; b. 29 Oct. 1945, Chicago, Ill.; m. Karin Larson 1977, one d. *Education:* Rice Univ., Yale Univ. *Career:* Asst Prof., Univ. of Virginia 1970–75, Assoc. Prof. 1975–81, Prof. 1981–87; Visiting Prof., Univ. of Munich 1986–87; Prof., Univ. of Rochester 1987–, Richard L. Turner Prof. in the Humanities 1995; now Ernest Bernbaum Prof. of Literature, Harvard Univ. *Publications:* The Myth Against Myth: A Study of Yeats' Imagination in Old Age 1972, Personality and Impersonality: Lawrence, Woolf, Mann 1978, Representation and the Imagination: Beckett, Kafka, Nabokov and Schoenberg 1981, Lyricality in English Literature 1985, Tennyson: The Muses' Tug-of-War 1986, Poetries of America: Essays in the Relation of Character to Style, by Irvin Ehrenpreis (ed.) 1988, Stravinsky: The Music-Box and the Nightingale 1989, Amerikanische Lyrik: Texte und Deutungen (ed. and co-trans.) 1989, W. B. Yeats: The Poems (ed.) 1990, Quantum Poetics: Yeats, Pound, Eliot, and the Science of Modernism 1997, Untwisting the Serpent: Modernism in Music, Literature, and the Visual Arts 2000, Berlioz's Semi-Operas: Roméo et Juliette and La Damnation de Faust 2001, Beckett and Aesthetics 2003, Modernism and Music: An Anthology of Sources 2004, Musicking Shakespeare: A Conflict of Theatres 2007, Evasions (co-author) 2011. *Honours:* NEA Fellowship 1973–74, Guggenheim Fellowship 1976–77. *Address:* Harvard University Department of English and American Literature and Language, Barker Center, 12 Quincy Street, Cambridge, MA 02138, USA (office). *Telephone:* (617) 384-9395 (office). *E-mail:* albright@fas.harvard.edu (office). *Website:* www.fas.harvard.edu (office).

ALCALÁ, Kathleen, BA, MA; American writer and editor; b. 29 Aug. 1954, Compton, Calif.; m. Wayne C. Roth 1979; one s. *Education:* Stanford Univ., Univ. of Washington. *Career:* grantwriter, administrator, public broadcasting, other non-profit groups 1976–89; teaches fiction Northwest Inst. of Literary Arts; Bd mem., Seattle Review; fmr Contributing Ed., Raven Chronicles; mem. PEN West, Authors' Guild, Artist Trust, Clarion West. *Publications:* Mrs Vargas and the Dead Naturalist 1992, Spirits of the Ordinary 1997, The Flower in the Skull 1998, Treasures in Heaven 2000, Cities of Gold 2005, The Desert Remembers My Name (Latino Int. Book Award 2008) 2007; contribs to journals and periodicals, including: Americas Review, American Voice, Calyx, Seattle Review, Before Columbus Review, Black Ice, Chiricu, Seattle Times, Ploughshares, The Colorado Review, Hopscotch; anthologies, including Women and Aging, Dreams in a Minor Key: Magic Realism by Women, Mirrors Beneath the Earth, Dreamers and Desperadoes, A Writer's Journal, Cracking the Earth, Fantasmas, Norton's Anthology of Latino Literature. *Honours:* Milliman Scholar of Creative Writing, Univ. of Washington 1984, Artist Trust GAP Grants 1989, 1991, Invitational Residency at Cottages at Hedgebrook, King County Fiction Publication Project 1990, Authors' Award, Brandeis Univ. Women's Cttee 1994, Pacific NW Booksellers Asscn Award 1998, Western States Book Award and Govs Writing Award 1999, Washington State Book Award 2000, Washington State-Artist Trust Fellowship 2007. *E-mail:* kjalcala@gmail.com (office). *Website:* www.kathleenalcala.com.

ALDERSEY-WILLIAMS, Hugh Arthur, BA, MA, FRSA; British journalist and writer; b. 17 June 1959, London, England; m. Moira Morrissey 1989; one s. *Education:* St John's Coll., Cambridge. *Career:* mem. Soc. of Authors, European Acad. of Design. *Publications:* New American Design 1988, Hollington Industrial Design 1990, King and Miranda: Poetry of the Machine 1991, World Design: Nationalism and Globalism in Design 1992, The Most Beautiful Molecule: An Adventure in Chemistry (aka The Most Beautiful Molecule: The Discovery of the Buckyball) 1994, Zoomorphic: New Animal Architecture 2003, Findings: Hidden Stories in first-hand accounts of Scientific Discovery 2005, Panicology (with Simon Briscoe) 2008, Periodic Tales: The Curious Lives of the Elements 2011; contrib.: monographs on leading designers, various book chapters, articles to The Independent, Independent on Sunday. *E-mail:* hugh@hughalderseywilliams.com (office). *Website:* www.hughalderseywilliams.com.

ALDERSON, Margaret (Maggie) Hanne, MA; British journalist, editor, novelist and children's writer; b. 31 July 1959, London, England; d. of Douglas Arthur Alderson and Margaret Dura Alderson (née Mackay); m. 1st Geoffrey Francis Laurence 1991 (divorced 1996); m. 2nd Radenko Popovic 2002; one d. *Education:* St Dominic's Priory and Alleynes School, Stone, Staffs., Univ. of St Andrews. *Career:* writer and features Ed., several magazines and newspapers including Honey, You and London Evening Standard 1983–88; Ed., ES (London Evening Standard Magazine) 1988–89, Elle 1989–92, Mode 1994–95; Deputy Ed., Cleo 1993–94; journalist and Sr Writer, Sydney Morning Herald 1996–2001. *Publications include:* Shoe Money 1998, Pants On Fire 2000, Handbag Heaven 2001, Big Night Out 2002 (co-ed.), Mad About the Boy 2003, Handbags and Gladrags 2004, Ladies' Night (co-ed.) 2005, Cents and Sensibility 2006, Gravity Sucks 2007, In Bed With (co-ed.) 2009, How To Break Your Own Heart 2009, Shall We Dance 2010, Ten Short Stories You Must Read In 2010 2010, Evangeline The Wish Keeper's Helper 2010. *Honours:* Ed. of the Year (Colour Supplements), British Soc. of Magazine Editors 1989. *Literary Agent:* c/o Curtis Brown Ltd, 28–29 Haymarket, London, SW1Y 4SP, England. *Telephone:* (20) 7393-4400. *Fax:* (20) 7393-4401. *E-mail:* info@curtisbrown.co.uk. *Website:* www.curtisbrown.co.uk; www .maggiealderson.com; maggiealdersonstylenotes.wordpress.com.

ALDERSON, Sue Ann, MA; American academic; b. 11 Sept. 1940, New York; d. of Eugene Leonard Hartley and Ruth Edith Hartley (née Schuchowsky); m. Evan Alderson 1965 (divorced); two c. *Education:* Antioch Coll., Ohio State Univ. and Univ. of California, Berkeley. *Career:* moved to Vancouver, BC, Canada in 1967; English Instructor, Simon Fraser Univ., BC 1967–71, Capilano Coll. 1973–80; Asst Prof., Univ. of British Columbia 1980–84, Assoc. Prof. of Creative Writing 1984–92, Prof. 1992 (sole instructor on writing for children); mem. Writer's Union of Canada; juror, Canadian Council on Children's Literary Prize 1981–83. *Publications include:* for children: Bonnie McSmithers, You're Driving Me Dithers 1974, The Finding Princess 1977, The Adventures of Prince Paul 1977, Hurry Up, Bonnie! 1977, Bonnie McSmithers Is At It Again! 1979, Anne-Marie Maginol tu me rends folle 1981, Ida and the Wool Smugglers 1987; jr fiction: Comet's Tale 1983, The Not Impossible Summer 1983, The Something in Thurlo Darby's House 1984, Maybe You Had To Be There, By Duncan 1989, Chapter One 1990, Sure as Strawberries 1992, A Ride for Martha 1993, Ten for Lots of Boxes 1995, Pond Seasons 1997, The Not Impossible Summer 1998, Wherever Bears Be 1999, The Eco-Diary of Kiran Singer (ASPCA Henry Bergh Children's Book Award 2008) 2007. *Address:* 4004 West 32nd Street Vancouver, BC V6S 1Z6, Canada (home). *E-mail:* salderso@shaw.ca.

ALDING, Peter (see JEFFRIES, Roderic Graeme)

ALDISS, Brian Wilson, OBE, FRSL; British writer, critic and actor; b. 18 Aug. 1925, Norfolk; m. 2nd Margaret Manson 1965 (died 1997); two s. two d. *Education:* Framlingham Coll. and West Buckland School. *Career:* fmr soldier, draughtsman, bookseller and film critic; Literary Ed. Oxford Mail 1957–69; Pres. British Science Fiction Asscn 1960–65; Jt-Pres. European Science Fiction Cttees 1976–80; Chair. John W. Campbell Memorial Award 1976–77; Chair. Cttee of Man. Soc. of Authors 1977–78; mem. Literature Advisory Panel, Arts Council 1978–80; Chair. Cultural Exchanges Cttee of Authors 1978; Judge, Booker McConnell Prize 1981; Pres. World SF 1982–84; Ed. S.F. Horizons 1964–; Vice-Pres. H. G. Wells Soc., W. Buckland School 1997–. *Opera:* Oedipus on Mars. *Plays (author):* SF Blues, Kindred Blood in Kensington Gore, Monsters of Every Day (Oxford Literary Festival) 2000, Drinks with The Spider King (Florida) 2000; acted in own productions 1985–2002. *Art exhibition:* The Other Hemisphere, The Jam Factory Gallery, Oxford 2010. *Publications:* The Brightfount Diaries 1955, Space, Time & Nathaniel 1957, Non-Stop (Jules Verne Award 1977) 1958, The Male Response 1959, Hothouse (Hugo Award 1962) 1962, The Airs of Earth 1963, The Dark Light Years 1964, Greybeard 1964, Earthworks 1965, Best Science Fiction Stories of Brian W. Aldiss 1965, The Saliva Tree (Nebula Award) 1965, Cities and Stones: A Traveller's Jugoslavia 1966, Report on Probability A 1968, Barefoot in the Head 1969, Intangibles Inc., 1969, A Brian Aldiss Omnibus 1969, The Hand-Reared Boy 1970, The Shape of Further Things 1970, A Soldier Erect 1971, The Moment of Eclipse (British Science Fiction Asscn Award 1972) 1971, Brian Aldiss Omnibus 2 1971, Penguin Science Fiction Omnibus (ed.) 1973, Comic Inferno 1973, Billion Year Spree (III Merit Award 1976) 1973, Frankenstein Unbound (made into film directed by Roger Corman) 1973, The Eighty-Minute Hour 1974, Hell's Cartographers (ed.) 1975, Space Odysseys, Evil Earths, Science Fiction Art 1975, The Malacia Tapestry, Galactic Empires (two vols) 1976, Last Orders, Brothers of the Head 1977, Perilous Planets 1977, A Rude Awakening 1978, Enemies of the System 1978, This World and Nearer Ones 1979, Pile 1979, New Arrivals, Old Encounters 1979, Moreau's Other Island 1980, Life in the West 1980, An Island Called Moreau 1981, Foreign Bodies 1981, Helliconia Spring 1982, Science Fiction Quiz 1983, Helliconia Summer 1983, Seasons in Flight 1984, Helliconia Winter 1985, The Pale Shadow of Science 1985, ... And the Lurid Glare of the Comet 1986, Trillion Year Spree (Hugo Award 1987) 1986, Ruins 1987, Forgotten Life 1988, Science Fiction Blues 1988, Best SF Stories of Brian W. Aldiss 1988, Cracken at Critical 1989, A Romance of the Equator 1990, Bury My Heart at W. H. Smith's 1990, Dracula Unbound 1991, Remembrance Day 1993, A Tupolev Too Far 1993, Somewhere East of Life 1994, The Detached Retina 1995, At the Caligula Hotel (poems) 1995, The Secret of this Book 1995, Songs from the Steppes of Central Asia 1996, The Twinkling of an Eye 1998, The Squire Quartet (four vols) 1998, When the Feast is Finished 1999, White Mars 1999, Supertoys Last All Summer Long (made into Kubrick–Spielberg film A.I. 2001) 2001, The Cretan Teat 2001, Super-State 2002, Researches and Churches in Serbia 2002, The Dark Sun Rises (poems) 2002, Affairs in Hampden Ferrers 2004, Jocasta 2005, Sanity and the Lady 2005, Cultural Breaks 2006, Harm 2007, A Science Fiction Omnibus (ed) 2007, A Prehistory of Mind 2008, Walcot 2010, Mortal Morning (poetry) 2011, An Exile on Planet Earth 2012, The Friday Project 2012; contributions: TLS, Nature. *Honours:* Hon. DLitt 2000; Ditmar Award for World's Best Contemporary Science Fiction Writer 1969, first James Blish Award for Excellence in Criticism 1977, Pilgrim Award 1978, John W. Campbell Award 1983, Kurt Lasswitz Award 1984, IAFA Distinguished Scholarship Award 1986, J. Lloyd Eaton Award 1988, Prix Utopie (France) 1999, Grand Master of Science Fiction 2000. *Address:* Hambleden, 39 St Andrew's Road, Old Headington, Oxford, OX3 9DL, England. *Telephone:* (1865) 762464. *E-mail:* aldiss.brian@gmail.com. *Website:* www.brianwaldiss .co.uk.

ALDRIDGE, (Harold Edward) James; British author and journalist; b. 10 July 1918, White Hills, Vic., Australia; s. of William Thomas Aldridge and Edith Quayle Aldridge; m. Dina Mitchnik 1942; two s. *Career:* with Herald and Sun, Melbourne, Australia 1937–38, Daily Sketch and Sunday Dispatch, London 1939; with Australian Newspaper Service and North American Newspaper Alliance (as war corresp.), Finland, Norway, Middle East, Greece, USSR 1939–45; corresp. for Time and Life, Tehran 1944. *Plays:* 49th State 1947, One Last Glimpse 1981. *Publications:* Signed with Their Honour 1942, The Sea Eagle 1944, Of Many Men 1946, The Diplomat 1950, The Hunter 1951, Heroes of the Empty View 1954, Underwater Hunting for Inexperienced Englishmen 1955, I Wish He Would Not Die 1958, Gold and Sand (short stories) 1960, The Last Exile 1961, A Captive in the Land 1962, The Statesman's Game 1966, My Brother Tom 1966, The Flying 19 1966, Living Egypt (with Paul Strand) 1969, Cairo: Biography of a City 1970, A Sporting Proposition 1973, The Marvellous Mongolian 1974, Mockery in Arms 1974, The Untouchable Juli 1975, One Last Glimpse 1977, Goodbye Un-America 1979, The Broken Saddle 1982, The True Story of Lilli Stubek (Australian Children's Book of the Year 1985) 1984, The True Story of Spit MacPhee (Guardian Children's Fiction Prize) 1985, The True Story of Lola MacKellar 1993, The Girl From the Sea 2003, The Wings of Kitty St Clair 2006. *Honours:* Rhys Memorial Award 1945, New South Wales Premier's Literary Award 1986; Lenin Peace Prize 1972. *Literary Agent:* Curtis Brown Ltd, Haymarket House, 28–29 Haymarket, London, SW1Y 4SP, England. *Telephone:* (20) 7393-4400. *Fax:* (20) 7393-4401. *E-mail:* info@curtisbrown.co.uk. *Website:* www .curtisbrown.co.uk.

ALDUY, Dominique, MA; French newspaper executive and economist; b. 23 Feb. 1944, Paris; d. of Maurice Daumas and Madeleine Daumas (née Colas); m. Jean-Paul Alduy 1969; one s. two d. *Education:* Univ. of Paris, Inst. d'Etudes Politiques de Paris and Pennsylvania State Univ., USA. *Career:* in charge of local community financial studies, Ministry of Equipment 1972–76; Rep. to Secr.-Gen. for New Towns 1976–78; in charge of Habitat and Environment Comm., Comm. Gen. du Plan 1979–81; Social Policies Rep. to Cabinet of the Prime Minister 1981–83; Dir of Programmes, Caisse des Dépôts et Consignations 1983–86, Dir Devt of Deposits-Devt 1986, Pres., Dir-Gen. of Communication Devt 1986–89; Dir-Gen. Soc. Nationale de Programmes—

France Régions 3 (FR3) 1989–93, apptd Dir-Gen. Film 3 production 1989; Dir-Gen. Centre Nat. d'Art et de Culture Georges Pompidou 1993–94; Dir-Gen. Le Monde newspaper 1994–2005, mem. Bd of Dirs Le Monde and Le Monde SA 1995–2004; mem. Bd of Dirs and Pres. Théâtre de la Ville, Paris 2006–; Co-Man. Cahiers du Cinéma; Pres. European Newspapers Publrs' Asscn (ENPA) 2000–04, Hon. Pres. 2006–. *Honours:* Chevalier de la Légion d'honneur. *Address:* 74A rue Lecourbe, 75015 Paris, France (home). *E-mail:* dalduy@noos.fr.

ALEGRÍA, Claribel, BA; Salvadorean/Nicaraguan writer and poet; b. 12 May 1924, Estelí, Nicaragua; d. of Daniel Alegría and Ana Maria Alegría (née Vides); m. Darwin J. Flakoll 1947 (died 1995); one s. three d. *Education:* George Washington Univ., USA. *Career:* extensive travelling in USA, S America and Europe 1943–; writer 1943–. *Publications include:* poetry: Anillo de Silencio 1948, Acuario 1955, Huésped de mi tiempo 1961, Aprendizaje 1970, Sobrevivo (Casa de las Américas Award, Cuba) 1978, Flores del volcano 1982, Umbrales 1997; prose: Fuga de canto grande (with Darwin J. Flakoll) 1992, Death of Somoza (with Darwin J. Flakoll, title in trans.), The Sandinista Revolution (with Darwin J. Flakoll, title in trans.), They'll Never Take Me Alive (with Darwin J. Flakoll, title in trans.), Ashes of Izalco (novel, with Darwin J. Flakoll), Mitos y delitos 2008. *Honours:* Dr hc (East Connecticut State Univ.) 1998, (León) 2005; Ind. Publr Book Award 2000, Book Sense Choice 2001, Neustadt Int. Prize for Literature 2006. *Address:* Apdo Postal A-36, Managua, Nicaragua (home). *Telephone:* 88844795 (home). *E-mail:* claribel@ibw.com.ni (home).

ALEKAR, Satish; Indian playwright, actor, director and academic; b. 30 Jan. 1949, Delhi; m. Anita Alekar; one s. *Career:* Marathi writer; Founder-mem. Theatre Acad., Pune 1973–92; fmr Fulbright Scholar, Dept of Performance Studies, Tisch School of the Arts, New York, USA; fmr Vice-Chair. Nat. School of Drama, New Delhi; Prof. and Dir Lalit Kala Kendra (Centre for Performing Arts), Univ. of Pune 1996–2009; Pres. Int. Playwrights' Forum 2006–08; mem. Theatre Advisory Cttee Sangeet Natak Akademi, Delhi 2001–05. *Films include:* Jait Re Jait (scriptwriter) 1977, Katha Don Ganpatravanchi (dialogues) 1995–96. *Plays include:* Jhulta Pool 1969, Miki ani memsaheb 1974, Mahanirvan 1973, Mahapoor 1975, Begum Barve 1979, Shanivar-ravivar 1982, Dusra samna 1987, Atireki 1990, Pidhijat 2003. *Honours:* Nandikar Sanman 1992 Nat. Award for Playwriting, Sangeet Natak Akademi 1994–95, V.K. Joag Award 2004–05. *Address:* c/o Lalit Kala Kendra, University of Pune, Ganeshkhind Road, Pune 411 007, India. *Website:* www.satishalekar.com.

ALEKSANDROWICZ, Piotr, MSc, MBA; Polish editor; *Business Editor, Newsweek Polska*; b. 4 Oct. 1953, Warsaw. *Education:* Warsaw Tech. Univ., Warsaw Univ. and Univ. of Illinois, USA. *Career:* reporter, Polish Press Agency 1981–82; reporter, ITD (weekly) 1982–86; Business Ed., Przegląd Tygodniowy 1986–88; journalist, Gazeta Bankowa 1988–89; Deputy Ed.-in-Chief Rzeczpospolita daily 1989–96, Ed.-in-Chief 1996–2001; Ed. Business Week Polish edn 2002–06; Business Ed., Newsweek Polska 2006–. *Address:* Newsweek Polska, 02-672 Warsaw, ul. Domaniewska 52, Poland (office). *Telephone:* (22) 2321052 (home). *E-mail:* piotr.aleksandrowicz@newsweek.pl (office). *Website:* www.newsweek.pl (office).

ALEKSEJEV, Tiit, MA; Estonian writer, historical novelist and fmr diplomat; b. 1968. *Education:* Univ. of Tartu. *Career:* joined Foreign Service, served in Embassies in Paris and Brussels. *Publications include:* Tartu rahu (short story) (Award from literary magazine Looming) 1999, Valge kuningriik (The White Kingdom) (novel) (Betti Alver Award for Best Debut Novel) 2006, Palveränd (Pilgrimage) (novel) (EU Prize for Literature 2010) 2008, Leegionärid (Legionaries) (play) 2010; also short stories. *Address:* c/o AS Varrak, Pärnu mnt 67A, 7 korrus, Tallinn 10134, Estonia (office). *Telephone:* 6161038 (office). *E-mail:* varrak@varrak.ee (office). *Website:* www.varrak.ee.

ALEKSIEVICH, Svetlana; Belarusian journalist and writer; b. 31 May 1948, Minsk, Ukraine. *Education:* Minsk Univ. *Career:* worked as journalist on local newspaper in early 1970s. *Publications include:* non-fiction: Aposhniya svedki. kniga nedzitsyachyh raskaza? 1985, U voyny ne zhenskoe litso (The War's Unwomanly Face) 1985, Tsinkovye mal'chiki (Zinky Boys: Soviet Voices from a Forgotten War) 1991, Zacharavanyya smertsu (Enchanted with Death) 1993, Poslednie svideteli (The Last Witnesses), Charnobyl'skaya malitva (trans. as Chernobyl Prayer: A Chronicle of the Future) 1997. *Honours:* Kurt Tucholsky Prize, Swedish PEN Club, Stockholm 1996, Andrej Sinjavskij Prize, Moscow 1997, Triumph Prize 1998, European Understanding Prize for contrib. to a better understanding among European nations 1998, 'Témoin du Monde', Paris 1999, Erich Maria Remarque Peace Prize (Germany) 2001, Nat. Book Critics' Circle Award, New York 2006, Oxfam Novib PEN Award 2007. *Address:* c/o Galina Dursthoff, Marsiliusstr. 70, 50937 Cologne, Germany. *E-mail:* svett_al@hotmail.com; galina@dursthoff.de. *Website:* alexievich.info.

ALEM, Raja, BA; Saudi Arabian author and poet; b. Mecca. *Education:* King Abdel Aziz Univ., Jeddah. *Career:* work first published in cultural supplement of Riyadh newspaper; has worked on cultural projects for UNESCO; collaborations with her sister Shadia Alem; participant, Women Writers of the Arab World, Hedgebrook Writers' Retreat, USA 2005. *Publications include:* novels: Silk Road, Final Death of the Actor, Hyattombs Hyattombs 1997, Fatma 2002, My Thousand and One Nights 2007, The Doves' Necklace (Int. Prize for Arabic Fiction 2011) 2011; other: Holes in the Back (drama), Ring (drama), Animal River (short stories), Jinniyat Lar (with Shadia Alem) (poems) 2001, children's books. *Honours:* Arabic Women's Creative Writing Prize 2005, Lebanese Literary Club Prize 2008. *Address:* c/o Syracuse University Press, 621 Skytop Road, Suite 110, Syracuse, NY 13244-5290, USA.

ALEXAKIS, Vassilis; French/Greek author; b. 25 Dec. 1943, Athens, Greece; s. of Yannis Alexakis. *Education:* École Supérieure de Journalisme, Lille. *Career:* studied journalism in Lille, France 1961, returned to Greece for mil. service 1964, after mil. coup d'état in Greece moved to Paris 1967; writes in both Greek and French. *Publications include:* fiction in French: Le Sandwich 1974, Les Girls de City-Boum-Boum 1975, La Tête du chat 1978, Mon amour! 1978, Contrôle d'Identité 1985, Le fils de King Kong 1987, Paris-Athènes 1989, Avant (Prix Albert Camus, Prix Charles-Exbrayat, Prix Alexandre-Vialat) 1992, La Langue Maternelle (Médicis Prize) 1995, Papa (short stories) (Erzählung, Prix de la Nouvelle de l' Acad. française) 1997, L'invention du baiser 1997, Le colin d'Alaska 1999, Les mots étrangers (trans. as Foreign Words) 2002, Je t'oublierai tous les jours 2005, Paroles du coeur de l'Afrique 2007, Ap. J.-C. (Grand prix du roman de l' Acad. française 2007) 2007, Le premier mot 2010; fiction in Greek: Talgo 1980, Le cœur de Marguerite 1999. *Honours:* Officier, Ordre des Arts et des Lettres, Commdr, Ordre du Phénix; Prix Edouard Glissant 2003. *Address:* c/o Éditions Stock, 31 rue de Fleurus, 75278 Paris Cedex 06, France. *Website:* www.editions-stock.fr.

ALEXANDER, Brooke, BA; American art dealer and publisher; b. 26 April 1937, Los Angeles; s. of Richard H. Alexander and Marion C. Alexander; m. Carolyn Rankin 1967; two d. *Education:* Yale Univ. *Career:* f. Brooke Alexander Inc. to publish and distribute graphic art 1968, expanded co. 1975; f. Brooke Alexander Editions, opened separate gallery for graphics 1989; partner in Madrid gallery, Galería Weber, Alexander y Cobo 1991–; mem. Governing Bd Yale Univ. Art Gallery 1988–. *Address:* Brooke Alexander Editions, 59 Wooster Street, New York, NY 10012-4349, USA (office). *Telephone:* (212) 925-4338 (office). *Fax:* (212) 941-9565 (office). *E-mail:* info@baeditions.com (office). *Website:* www.baeditions.com (office).

ALEXANDER, Caroline Elizabeth, BA, PhD; American writer; b. 13 March 1956, Fla. *Education:* Florida State Univ., Univ. of Oxford, UK, Columbia Univ., New York. *Career:* est. Classics Dept, Univ. of Malawi 1982–85; mem. American Philological Soc., RGS. *Publications:* One Dry Season: In the Footsteps of Mary Kingsley 1990, The Way to Xanadu 1994, Battle's End, Mrs Chippy's Last Expedition 1997, The Endurance 1998, The Bounty: The True Story of the Mutiny on the Bounty 2003, The War that Killed Achilles: The True Story of Homer's Iliad and the Trojan War 2009; contribs: New Yorker, Smithsonian, Independent, Sunday Telegraph Weekend Magazine. *Honours:* Mellon Fellowship, Rhodes Scholarship. *Literary Agent:* c/o Aitken Alexander Associates Ltd, 18–21 Cavaye Place, London, SW10 9PT, England. *Telephone:* (20) 7373-8672. *Fax:* (20) 7373-6002. *E-mail:* reception@aitkenalexander.co.uk. *Website:* www.aitkenalexander.co.uk.

ALEXANDER, Christine Anne, PhD, FAHA; New Zealand academic and writer; *Scientia Professor, School of English, Media and Performing Arts, University of New South Wales*; b. 9 July 1949, Hastings; d. of Bruce Bird and June Bird; m. Peter Fraser Alexander 1977; one s. one d. *Education:* Univ. of Canterbury, Univ. of Cambridge, UK. *Career:* Asst Lectureship, Univ. of Canterbury 1972; Tutor, Univ. of New South Wales, Australia 1978–83, Lecturer 1986–88, Sr Lecturer 1988–92, Assoc. Prof. 1993–97, Prof. 1998–2007, Scientia Prof. 2008–; Fellow, Inst. of the Arts and Humanities, Univ. of North Carolina, Chapel Hill 1996; Visiting Fellowship, Dept of English, Duke Univ. 1996, Clare Hall, Cambridge 2003–04; Malcolm Bowie Distinguished Visiting Scholar, Christ's Coll., Cambridge 2007; currently Dir and Gen. Ed., Juvenilia Press; mem. Brontë Soc., Australian Brontë Asscn (Patron), Australasian Language and Literature Asscn, Australian Victorian Studies Asscn, Australian and South Pacific Asscn for Comparative Literary Studies, Cambridge Soc., Jane Austen Soc. (of UK, America, Australia), Asscn for the Study of Australian Literature, Bibliographical Soc. of Australia and New Zealand, Soc. for Textual Scholarship, Soc. for the History of Authorship, Reading and Publishing, Int. Asscn of Univ. Profs in English. *Publications include:* Bibliography of the Manuscripts of Charlotte Brontë 1982, The Early Writings of Charlotte Brontë 1983, An Edition of the Early Writings of Charlotte Brontë, three vols 1987–, The Art of the Brontës 1994, High Life in Verdopolis: A Tale from the Glass Town Saga 1995, The Oxford Companion to the Brontës 2003, The Child Writer from Austen to Woolf 2005, Jane Austen's Lady Susan (ed.) 2005, The Gipsy Dancer & Early Poems by Dorothy Hewett (ed.) 2009, Tales of Glass Town, Angria, and Gondal: Selected Early Writings 2010; contrib. to books and journals. *Honours:* New Zealand Postgraduate Scholarships, New Zealand Univ. Women's Fellowship, British Acad. Rose Mary Crawshay Prize 1984, Visiting Scholarship Pembroke Coll., Cambridge 1990–91, Australian Research Council Senior Research Fellowship 1995–97, Library Fellowship, Princeton Univ. 1996, Centenary Medal for Service to Australian Soc. and the Humanities 2003; travel grants, special research grants. *Address:* School of English, Media & Performing Arts, University of New South Wales, Sydney, NSW 2052, Australia (office). *Telephone:* (2) 93852310 (office). *E-mail:* c.alexander@unsw.edu.au (office). *Website:* www.arts.unsw.edu.au/juvenilia (office).

ALEXANDER, Clare; British literary agent; *Director, Aitken Alexander Associates Ltd. Career:* ed. with Penguin Books 1981–90; Publishing Dir Viking 1990–97; Ed.-in-Chief, Macmillan 1997–98; literary agent, later Dir Gillon Aitken Assocs (now Aitken Alexander Associates Ltd) 1998–; Vice-Pres.

Asscn of Authors' Agents 2004–06, Pres. 2006–08; mem. Women's Cttee of Orange Prize. *Honours:* Kim Scott Walwyn Award 2008. *Address:* Aitken Alexander Associates Ltd, 18–21 Cavaye Place, London, SW10 9PT, England (office). *Telephone:* (20) 7373-8672 (office). *Fax:* (20) 7373-6002 (office). *E-mail:* clare@aitkenalexander.co.uk (office). *Website:* www.aitkenalexander.co.uk (office).

ALEXANDER, Doris Muriel, BA, MA, PhD; American academic and writer; b. 14 Dec. 1922, Newark, NJ. *Education:* Univ. of Missouri, Univ. of Pennsylvania, New York Univ. *Career:* Instructor, Rutgers Univ. 1950–56; Assoc. Prof., then Dept Chair, CUNY 1956–62; mem. Asscn of Literary Scholars and Critics, Eugene O'Neill Soc. *Publications include:* The Tempering of Eugene O'Neill 1962, Creating Characters with Charles Dickens 1991, Eugene O'Neill's Creative Struggle 1992, Creating Literature Out of Life 1996, Eugene O'Neill's Last Plays: Separating Art from Autobiography 2004; contrib. to many journals. *Honours:* Penfield Fellowship, New York Univ. 1946, Fulbright Prof., Univ. of Athens 1966–67. *Address:* San Trovaso 1116, Dorsoduro, 30123 Venice, Italy (home). *Telephone:* (041) 5207719 (home). *E-mail:* dalex1@tin.it.

ALEXANDER, Gary Roy; American writer; b. 18 Jan. 1941, Bremerton, Wash.; m. Shari 1969; three d. *Education:* Olympic Community Coll., Univ. of Washington. *Career:* mem. Mystery Writers of America. *Publications:* Pigeon Blood 1988, Unfunny Money 1989, Kiet and the Golden Peacock 1989, Kiet and the Opium War 1990, Deadly Drought 1991, Dead Dinosaurs 1994, Kiet Goes West 1992, Blood Sacrifice 1993, Disappeared 2010, Dragon Lady 2011; contrib. of many stories and travel articles in magazines. *Address:* 6709 South 238th Place, H-102, Kent, WA 98032-2644, USA (home). *E-mail:* alexagr61@hotmail.com.

ALEXANDER, Dame Helen Anne, DBE, CBE, MA, MBA; British business executive; *Chairman, Port of London Authority;* b. 10 Feb. 1957, d. of the late Bernard Alexander and Tania Alexander (née Benckendorff); m. Tim Suter 1985; two s. one d. *Education:* Hertford Coll. Oxford, INSEAD, France. *Career:* with Gerald Duckworth 1978–79, Faber & Faber 1979–83; joined The Economist Group 1984, Man. Dir Economist Intelligence Unit 1993–96, Group CEO 1997–2008; Sr Adviser, Bain Capital 2008–; Chair. Incisive Media 2009–; Chair. Port of London Authority 2010–; Deputy Pres. CBI 2008, 2011–, Pres. 2009–11; Dir (non-exec.) Northern Foods 1994–2003, British Telecom 1998–2002, Centrica, Rolls-Royce; Chair. Said Business School Advisory Council; Trustee Tate Gallery, WWW Foundation; Gov. St Paul's Girls' School. *Honours:* Hon. Fellow, Hertford Coll., Oxford. *Address:* Port of London Authority, The Lock House, Ranelagh Drive, Twickenham, TW1 1QZ, England (office). *Telephone:* (20) 8843-7210 (office). *Website:* www.pla.co.uk (office).

ALEXANDER, Meena, BA, PhD; American (b. Indian) poet, writer and academic; *Distinguished Professor of English and Women's Studies, Hunter College and the Graduate School and University Center, City University of New York;* b. 17 Feb. 1951, Allahabad, India; d. of George Alexander and Mary Kuruvilla Alexander; m. David Lelyveld 1979; one s. one d. *Education:* Univ. of Khartoum, Sudan, Univ. of Nottingham, UK. *Career:* Lecturer, Univ. of Hyderabad 1977–79, Reader 1979; Asst Prof., Fordham Univ. 1980–87; Asst Prof., Hunter Coll. and the Grad. School and Univ. Center, CUNY 1987–89, Assoc. Prof. 1989–92, Prof. of English 1992–99, Distinguished Prof. of English and Women's Studies 1999–; Visiting Prof., School of the Arts, Columbia Univ. 2005; Poet-in-Residence, Univ. of Hyderabad 2010; mem. Jury, Fifteenth Neustadt Int. Award in Literature 1997–98; mem. Modern Language Asscn, PEN American Center. *Publications include:* poetry: The Bird's Bright Wing 1976, Stone Roots 1980, House of a Thousand Doors 1988, The Storm: A Poem in Five Parts 1989, Night-Scene: The Garden 1992, River and Bridge 1995, Illiterate Heart (PEN Open Book Award) 2002, Raw Silk 2004, Indian Love Poems (ed.) 2005, Quickly Changing River 2008; poetry and essays: The Shock of Arrival: Reflections on Postcolonial Experience 1996, Poetics of Dislocation 2009; fiction: Nampally Road 1991, Manhattan Music 1997; non-fiction: The Poetic Self: Towards a Phenomenology of Romanticism 1979 (criticism), Women in Romanticism: Mary Wollstonecraft, Dorothy Wordsworth and Mary Shelley 1989, Fault Lines 1993 (new expanded edn 2003); contribs to books, anthologies and periodicals. *Honours:* numerous awards including Altrusa Int. Award 1973, MacDowell Fellow 1993, 1998, Poet-in-Residence, American Coll., Madurai 1994, Artist/Humanist-in-Residence, Intercultural Resource Centre, Columbia Univ. 1995, Int. Writer in Residence, Arts Council of England 1995, Poetry Award, New York State Foundation for the Arts 1999, Poet-in-Residence, Nat. Univ. of Singapore 1999, Imbongi Yesizwe Poetry Int. Award (S Africa) 2002, Hunter Coll. Faculty Fellowship 2002, Fulbright Sr Scholar Award, Mahatma Gandhi Univ., India 2002–03, Bellagio Award, Rockefeller Foundation 2003, Martha Walsh Pulver Residency for a Poet, Yaddo 2005, Fulbright Sr Specialist Award, Elector, American Poet's Corner, Cathedral of St John the Divine, New York 2006–, John Simon Guggenheim Fellowship 2008, Camargo Foundation Fellowship 2008, S Asian Literary Asscn Distinguished Achievement Award in Literature 2009, also awards from Fulbright Foundation, Arts Council of England, Nat. Endowment for the Humanities, American Council of Learned Societies, Nat. Council for Research on Women, New York State Council on the Arts, New York Foundation for the Arts, Ledig-Rowohlt Foundation. *Address:* PhD Program in English, CUNY Graduate Center, 365 Fifth Avenue, New York, NY 10016 (office); English Department, Hunter College, City University of New York, 695 Park Avenue, New York, NY 10065, USA (office). *Telephone:* (212) 772-5164 (office); (212) 772-5200 (office). *Fax:* (212) 772-5411 (office). *E-mail:* malexander@gc.cuny.edu (office). *Website:* web.gc.cuny.edu/English/faculty/alexander.html (office); www.meenaalexander.com.

ALEXANDER, Phil; British editor; *Editor-in-Chief, Mojo.* *Career:* Man. Ed. Kerrang! –2002; Man. Ed. Q magazine 2002; currently Ed.-in-Chief Mojo magazine; Assoc. Publr, Bauer Media 2011–. *Television includes:* presenter of rock show, Raw Power 1990, presenter of Popped In, Crashed Out (series) 1999. *Address:* MOJO, Mappin House, 4 Winsley Street, London, W1W 8HF, England (office). *E-mail:* mojo@bauermedia.co.uk (office). *Website:* www.mojo4music.com.

ALEXIE, Sherman, BA; American poet and novelist; b. 7 Oct. 1966, Spokane, Wash.; m. Diane Tomhave 1994; two s. *Education:* Washington State Univ., Pullman. *Career:* Spokane/Coeur d'Alene Indian; stand-up comedian, poet, songwriter, writer; Founding Bd mem. Longhouse Media. *Films:* Smoke Signals 1968, The Business of Fancydancing 2002, The Exiles 2008. *Publications:* The Business of Fancydancing (short stories and poetry, also screenplay) 1991, The Lone Ranger and Tonto Fist Fight in Heaven (short stories) 1993, Old Shirts and New Skins (poetry) 1993, I Would Steal Horses (poetry) 1993, First Indian on the Moon (poetry) 1993, Reservation Blues (novel) 1995, Water Flowing Home (poetry) 1995, The Summer of Black Widows (poetry) 1996, Indian Killer (novel) 1996, Smoke Signals (screenplay) 1998, The Man Who Loves Salmon (poetry) 1998, The Toughest Indian in the World (short stories) 2000, One Stick Song (poetry) 2000, Ten Little Indians (short stories) 2003, Flight (novel) 2007, The Absolutely True Diary of a Part-Time Indian (novel) (Nat. Book Award for Young People's Literature, Pacific Northwest Book Award, Boston Globe-Horn Book Award) 2007, Face (poetry) 2009, War Dances (short stories) (PEN/Faulkner Award for Fiction 2010) 2009; contrib. to The Stranger, Indiana Review, New Yorker. *Honours:* Dr hc (Columbia Coll., Seattle) 1999, (Seattle Univ.) 2000; Nat. Endowment for the Arts Fellowship 1992, PEN/Hemingway Best First Book Award 1993, Lila Wallace-Readers Digest Writers' Award 1994, Chad Walsh Poetry Award 1995, PEN/Malamud short story award (co-recipient) 2001, Pushcart Prize 2005, Lifetime Achievement Award, Native Writers' Circle of the Americas 2010, Puterbaugh Award 2010. *Address:* FallsApart Productions Inc., PMB 2294, 10002 Aurora Avenue N, Suite 36, Seattle, WA 98133, USA (office). *E-mail:* christyc@fallsapart.com (office). *Website:* www.fallsapart.com (office).

ALFERI, Pierre; French poet and writer; *Professor of Poetry, European Graduate School;* b. 10 April 1963, Paris. *Career:* co-f. Détail magazine (with Suzanne Doppelt), Revue de Littérature générale (with Olivier Cadiot); Writer-in-Residence, French Acad., Rome 1987–88, Fondation Royaumont 1991–92; currently Prof. of Poetry, European Grad. School, Switzerland. *Publications:* poetry: Les allures naturelles 1991, Le Chemin familier du poisson combatif 1992, Kub Or 1994, Sentimentale journée 1997, La Voie des airs 2004; novels: Fmn 1994, Le Cinéma des familles 1999, Ça commence à Séoul 2007, Les Jumelles 2009, Après vous 2010; essays: Le Singulair 1989, Chercher une phrase 1991, Guillaume d'Ockham, Des Enfants et des monstres 2004. *Address:* European Graduate School, Media and Communication Division, Alter Kehr 20, 3953 Leuk-Stadt, Switzerland (office); c/o Éditions P.O.L., 33, rue Saint-André-des-Arts, 75006 Paris, France. *Telephone:* (27) 4749917 (office). *Fax:* (27) 4749969 (office). *E-mail:* auteurs@pol-editeur.fr. *Website:* www.pol-editeur.fr.

ALFTAN, Maija Kyllikki; Finnish journalist; *Reporter, Helsingin Sanomat;* b. 17 Dec. 1948, Alatornio; d. of Oskar Tallgren and Henni Tallgren; m. Robert Alftan 1976; two d. *Education:* Sanoma School of Journalism, Helsinki. *Career:* reporter on Ilta-Sanomat 1969–78, Kotiliesi 1978–83; Man. Ed. Avotakka 1983–85, Kodin Kuvalehti magazine 1986–89; apptd Ed.-in-Chief Kodin Kuvalehti 1989–94; reporter, Helsingin Sanomat 1994–. *Address:* Helsingin Sanomat, Töölönlahdenkatu 2, PO Box 77, 00089 Sanomat, Finland (office). *E-mail:* maija.alftan@hs.fi (office). *Website:* www.hs.fi (office).

ALI, Bachtyar; Iraqi writer and critic; b. 1960, Slemani, Kurdistan. *Education:* Univ. of Sulaimani, Salah al-Din Univ. *Career:* Kurdish writer. *Publications include:* novels: Maegi Taqaney Duwem 1997, Ewarey Perwane 1998, Duwahemin Henari Dnya 2002, Shari Mosiqare Spiyekan (trans. as The City of the White Musician) 2005, Ghezelnus u Baxekani Xeyal (trans. as Ghazalnus and the Gardens of Imagination) 2008, Koshki Balinde Xemginekan (trans. as Mansion of the Sad Birds) 2009, Jemşîd xanî mamim: ke hemîşe ba legel xoyda deybird 2010; poetry: Gunah u Kerneval, Sewi Seyem 2009. *Website:* www.bachtyar-ali.com.

ALI, Monica; British novelist; b. 20 Oct. 1967, Dhaka, East Pakistan (now Bangladesh); m. Simon Torrance; one s. one d. *Education:* Wadham Coll., Oxford. *Career:* family moved to Bolton, UK 1971; worked in publishing, design and branding; judge, Man Asian Literary Prize 2010. *Publications include:* Brick Lane (WH Smith People's Choice Award for Best Debut Novel 2003, British Book Awards Newcomer of the Year 2003) 2003, Knife (short story in The Weekenders: Adventures in Calcutta) 2004, Alentejo Blue 2006, In the Kitchen 2009, Untold Story 2011; contrib. of essays to Free Expression Is No Offence. *Honours:* Granta's Best of Young British Novelists list 2003. *Literary Agent:* c/o A.P. Watt Ltd, 20 John Street, London, WC1N 2DR, England. *Telephone:* (20) 7405-6774. *Fax:* (20) 7831-2154. *Website:* www.apwatt.co.uk.

ALI, Tariq; Pakistani political activist and writer; b. 21 Oct. 1943, Lahore; pnr Susan Watkins; two d. one s. *Education:* Punjab Univ., Univ. of Oxford.

Career: Editorial Dir Verso 1999–; mem. editorial bd New Left Review 1982–; mem. Fourth International. *Publications:* fiction: Redemption 1990, Shadows of the Pomegranate Tree 1992, Fear of Mirrors 1998, The Book of Saladin 1999, The Stone Woman 2000, The Illustrious Corpse 2003, A Sultan in Palermo 2005, Night of the Golden Butterfly 2010; non-fiction: The Thoughts of Chairman Harold (compiler) 1967, The New Revolutionaries: A Handbook of the International Radical Left (ed.) 1969, Pakistan: Military Rule or People's Power? 1970, The Coming British Revolution 1972, Chile: Lessons of the Coup: Which Way to Workers' Power? (with Gerry Hedley) 1974, 1968 and After: Inside the Revolution 1978, Trotsky for Beginners 1980, Can Pakistan Survive? 1983, What is Stalinism? (ed.) 1984, The Stalinist Legacy: Its Impact on Twentieth-Century World Politics (ed.) 1984, An Indian Dynasty: The Story of the Nehru-Gandhi Family 1985, Street Fighting Years: An Autobiography of the Sixties 1987, Revolution from Above: Where is the Soviet Union Going? 1988, Moscow Gold (with Howard Brenton) 1990, 1968: Marching in the Streets (with Susan Watkins) 1998, Ugly Rumours (with Howard Brenton) 1998, Masters of the Universe?: NATO's Balkan Crusade (ed.) 2000, The Clash of Fundamentalisms: Crusades, Jihads and Modernity 2002, The Clash of Fundamentalisms: Bush in Babylon: Recolonising Iraq 2003, Rough Music 2005, Conversations with Edward Said 2006, Pirates of the Caribbean: Axis of Hope 2006, The Leopard and the Fox 2007, A Banker for All Seasons: Crooks and Cheats Inc. 2007, The Assassination 2008, The Duel: Pakistan on the Flight Path of American Power 2009, The Protocols of the Elders of Sodom 2009, The Obama Syndrome 2010; contribs to periodicals, including London Review of Books. *Address:* c/o Verso, 6 Meard Street, London, W1F 0EG, England (office). *E-mail:* tariq.ali3@btinternet.com (office). *Website:* www.tariqali.org.

ALIA, Josette, (Josette de Benbrahem); French journalist; b. 25 Nov. 1929, Ferté-Bernard; d. of Jack David and Germaine David (née Legeay); m. Raouf Benbrahem 1952; one s. *Education:* Inst. d'Etudes Politiques de Paris and Univ. of Paris (Paris-Sorbonne). *Career:* journalist, Jeune Afrique 1960–62; Corresp., Le Monde newspaper 1962–67; apptd Sr Reporter, then Ed.-in-Chief, then Deputy Editorial Dir, then Editorial Dir Le Nouvel Observateur magazine 1985; Pres. Jury Prix Albert Londres 2006–. *Publications include:* La guerre de Mitterrand: La dernière grande illusion 1991, Quand le soleil était chaud (Prix des Maisons de la Presse) 1993, Étoile Bleue, Chapeaux Noirs 1999, Impossible Israel 1999, Le Pensionnat 2005. *Honours:* Echo de la Presse et de la Publicité Best Journalist Award 1980, Personality of the Year 1985, Prix Mumm 1993. *Address:* c/o Le Nouvel Observateur, 12 place de la Bourse, 75002 Paris; 169 rue de Rennes, 75006 Paris, France (home). *Telephone:* 1-44-88-34-33; 1-45-48-96-72. *E-mail:* josette.alia@nouvelobs.com.

ALIOTH, Gabrielle, Lic.rer.pol.; Swiss novelist; b. 21 April 1955, Basel; m. Martin Alioth. *Career:* Writer-in-Residence, Univ. of Southern California, USA 1997, California State Univ. 1997, Case Western Reserve Univ., Cleveland, OH, USA 2002, Univ. Coll., Dublin, Ireland 2005–06; Lecturer, Coll. of Design and Art, Lucerne; mem. Irish del. 1996, Swiss del. 1998 at Frankfurt Book Fair; mem. PEN, AdS, Asscn of Authors of Switzerland. *Publications include:* novels: Der Narr (The Fool) 1990, Wie ein kostbarer Stein (Like a Precious Stone) 1994, Die Arche der Frauen (Women's Arch) 1996, Die Stumme Reiterin (The Silent Rider) 1998, Die Erfindung von Liebe und Tod (The Invention of Love and Death) 2003, Der prüfende Blick (The Searching Gaze) 2007, Die Braut aus Byzanz (The Bride from Byzantium) 2008, Die griechische Kaiserin (The Greek Empress) 2011; children's books: Das magische Licht (The Magic Light) 2001, Im Tal der Schatten (In the Valley of Shadows) 2002; travel books: Ireland – A Journey Through the Land of the Rainbows 2003, Ireland 2007. *Honours:* Hamburg Literary Award for Best First Novel. *Literary Agent:* c/o Verlag Nagel & Kimche AG, V-Nr. 1320 506, Nordstr. 9, 8035, Zürich, Switzerland. *Telephone:* (44) 3666680. *Fax:* (44) 3666688. *E-mail:* info@nagel-kimche.ch. *Website:* www.nagel-kimche.ch. *Address:* Rosemount, Julianstown, Co. Meath, Ireland (office). *Telephone:* (41) 9829302 (office). *Fax:* (41) 9829612 (office). *E-mail:* info@gabriellealioth .com (office). *Website:* www.gabriellealioth.com.

ALKALI, Zaynab, BA, MA, PhD; Nigerian academic, novelist and essayist; *Deputy Vice-Chancellor, Nasarawa State University*; b. 1950, Garkida; m. Dr Mohammed Nur Alkali (divorced); five c. *Education:* Ahmadu Bello Univ., Zaira, Bayero Univ., Kano. *Career:* Headmistress, Shekara Girl's Primary Boarding School, Kano 1974–76; Asst Lecturer, Univ. of Maiduguri 1981–83, Dir of Gen. Studies Programme 1987, Assoc. Prof. of African Literature and Creative Writing 1988–92, 1996–98, Patron, Women's Asscn 1988–92, News Flash Agency; Assoc. Prof., Bayero Univ., Kano 1992–95; Coordinator Gen. Studies Programme, Modibbo Adama Coll. 1984–86; Admin. Sec. Women's Rights Advancement and Protection Alternative 1999; Deputy Dir and Head of Resources Centre, Nat. Primary Health Care Agency 2000–03; Assoc. Prof. of African Literature and Creative Writing, Nasarawa State Univ. 2003, Prof. 2004–, currently Deputy Vice-Chancellor; Pres. Asscn of Nigerian Authors 1988–92; Fellow, Cambridge Seminar 1997, Stiftung Kulfursfond, Germany 1998. *Publications include:* The Stillborn (Asscn of Nigerian Authors' Prose Prize for Best Novel 1985) 1984, The Virtuous Woman (novel) 1987, Salzolose Asche (co-author) 1989, Saltless Ash (short story), The Vagabond (short story), The Cobwebs (short story) 1990, Vultures in the Air: Voices from Northern Nigeria (co-ed. with Al Imfeld) 1995, The Cobwebs and Other Stories (Best Short Stories of the Year) 1997, Ganga: A Journal of Language and Literature (ed.-in-chief) 1998, Primary Health Care, NPHCDA, News Magazine, The Road (co-ed.) 2001–03, The Matriarch 2003, The House Guest 2003, The Descendants 2005, The Initiates 2007. *Honours:* Magiran Garkida (traditional title); Roll of Honour Award, Creative Writer's Asscn of ABU Zaria 1987, Asscn of Nigerian Authors' Best Short Story of the Year Prize 1997, Award of Excellence, Leo Club Univ. of Maiduguri 1997, Merit Award for Letters, Nat. Council for Women Socs 1997, Merit Award for Literature Nat. Council for Women Socs 2000, Merit Award Nat. Council for Arts and Culture 2001, Icon of Hope, African Leadership Forum 2002, Award of Excellence in African Literature, Int. Conf. on African Literature and the English Language 2004, Merit Award Per-Excellence, Open Creative Forum, Nasarawa State Univ. 2005, Asell Award of Excellence 2005, Merit Award, Old Students of Queen Elizabeth School 2006, Award of Excellence, Nat. Asscn of Nigerian Students 2007, Professional Novelist Award, Nat. Asscn of Faculty of Educ. Students 2008, Award of Excellence 2008, Arewa Literary Excellence Award 2008. *Address:* Faculty of Arts, Nasarawa State University, PMB 1022, Keffi, Nasarawa State, Nigeria (office). *Website:* www.nsukonline.net (office).

ALKHATIB, Burhan, BEng, MA; Iraqi writer, translator, journalist and engineer; b. 10 Oct. 1944, Mosaib, Babel; m. 1st 1978 (divorced 1982); m. 2nd 1988 (divorced 1994); two s. one d. *Education:* Univ. of Baghdad, Literary Inst., Moscow. *Career:* mem. Writers' Union of Sweden, Journalists' Union of Iraq. *Publications include:* Khutwat ila Alufq Albaid (Steps Toward a Distant Horizon) 1967, Dabab fi Addahira (Mist at Midday) 1968, Shiqqatun fi Shari' Abi Nuwas (An Apartment on Abi Nuwas Street) 1972, Ajusur Azujajiyya (Bridges of Glass) 1975, Ashari 'aljadid (A New Street) 1980, Nujum Oldhuhr (Under the Heat of Midday) 1986, Suqut Sparta (The Fall of Sparta) 1992, Layla Baghdadia (A Baghdad Night) 1993, Babel alfaiha (The Aromatic Babylon) 1995, Thalik assaif fi Iskendria (That Summer in Alexandria) 1998, Aljanain Almuglaqa (The Closed Gardens) 2000, Liali Aluns Fi Shari Abi Nuwas (Pleasure Nights on Abi Nuwas Street) 2009, Ala tukhum Alelfein (on the ages of the 2000) 2011; trans. of 13 books; contrib. to Arab magazines and journals. *Address:* ÖsterV. 10, tr 5, 19631 Kungsangen, Sweden (home). *Telephone:* (8) 581-70-89-9 (office). *E-mail:* alburhan@hotmail.com (office). *Website:* www.authorsden.com/visit/author.asp?AuthorID=39468.

ALLABY, (John) Michael; British writer and editor; b. 18 Sept. 1933, Belper, Derbyshire, England; s. of Albert Theodore Allaby and Jessica May King; m. Ailsa Marthe McGregor 1957; one s. one d. *Career:* mem. Asscn of British Science Writers, Soc. of Authors. *Publications include:* The Eco-Activists 1971, Who Will Eat? 1972, Robots Behind the Plow 1974, Ecology 1975, Inventing Tomorrow 1976, World Food Resources, Actual and Potential 1977, Dictionary of the Environment 1977, 1983, 1988, 1994, Making and Managing a Smallholding 1979, Animals that Hunt 1979, Wildlife of North America 1979, The Politics of Self-Sufficency 1980, Le Foreste Tropicali 1981, A Year in the Life of a Field 1981, The Curious Cat 1982, Animal Artisans 1982, The Great Extinction 1983, The Food Chain 1984, The Greening of Mars 1984, The Oxford Dictionary of Natural History 1985, Your Child and the Computer 1985, Nine Lives 1985, 2040: Our World in the Future 1985, A Dog's Life 1986, The Woodland Trust Book of British Woodlands 1986, Ecology Facts 1986, The Concise Oxford Dictionary of Earth Sciences 1986, The Ordnance Survey Outdoor Handbook 1987, A Pony's Tale 1987, Conservation at Home 1988, Green Facts 1989, Thinking Green: An Anthology of Essential Ecological Writing 1989, Guide to Gaia 1989, Into Harmony with the Planet 1990, Living in the Greenhouse 1990, Concise Oxford Dictionary of Zoology 1991, Concise Oxford Dictionary of Botany 1992, Elements: Water 1992, Elements: Air 1993, Elements: Fire 1993, Elements: Earth 1993, Planet Earth: A Visual Factfinder 1993, The Concise Oxford Dictionary of Ecology 1994, Facing the Future 1995, How it Works: The Environment 1996, Basics of Environmental Science 1996, Dangerous Weather (six vols) 1997–98, (eight vols) 2003–04, Temperate Forests 1999, Biomes of the World (nine vols) 1999, DK Guide to Weather (Aventis Jr Prize for Science Books 2001) 2000, Plants and Plant Life (five vols) 2001, Deserts 2001, Encyclopedia of Weather and Climate 2002, Facts on File: Weather and Climate Handbook 2002, How it Works: The World's Weather 2002, Countries of the World: India 2005, A Change in the Weather 2004, Temperate Forests 2005, Tropical Forests 2006, Deserts 2006, Grasslands 2006, Children's Encyclopedia of Earth 2007, Earth: A Visual Guide 2007, Planet Earth 2008, Dictionary of Earth Sciences 2008, The Encyclopedia of Earth 2008, Atmosphere: A Scientific History of Air, Weather and Climate 2009, Earth Science: A Scientific History of the Solid Earth 2009, Oceans: A Scientific History of Oceans and Marine Life 2009, Ecology: Plants, Animals and the Environment 2010, Animals: From Mythology to Zoology 2010, Plants: Foods, Medicines and the Green Earth 2010, Exploration: New Lands, New Worlds 2010; contribs to newspapers and magazines. *Address:* Braehead Cottage, Tighnabruaich, Argyll, PA21 2ED, Scotland (home). *Telephone:* (1700) 811322 (office). *E-mail:* m.allaby@ btinternet.com. *Website:* www.michaelallaby.com.

ALLAN, Keith, BA, MLitt, PhD, FAHA; Australian/British academic, writer and editor; *Professor Emeritus of Linguistics, Monash University*; b. 27 March 1943, London, England; m. Wendy F. Allen 1993; two d. *Education:* Univs of Leeds and Edinburgh. *Career:* Research Assoc., Nuffield Language Devt Research Project, Dept of Child Life and Health, Univ. of Edinburgh 1967–70; Lecturer in English Language, Ahmadu Bello Univ., Zaria, Nigeria 1970–73; Lecturer in Linguistics, Univ. of Essex 1973–74, Univ. of Nairobi, Kenya 1975–77; Guest Prof. in Linguistics, Gesamthochschule, Paderborn, Germany 1975; Sr Tutor in Linguistics, Monash Univ., Australia 1978–81, Lecturer in Linguistics 1982–87, Sr Lecturer in Linguistics 1988–91, Acting Prof. and Head, Dept of Linguistics 1992–93, Reader in Linguistics 1992–2007, fmr

Prof. of Linguistics, now Prof. Emer.; Visiting Prof. in Linguistics, Univ. of Arizona, USA 1990; Visiting Fellow, Research Centre for English and Applied Linguistics and Clare Hall, Cambridge 2000, St Catherine's Coll., Oxford 2005; Chair. Linguistics and Philology Section, Australian Acad. of Humanities 1997–2000; Ed. Australian Journal of Linguistics. *Publications include:* Linguistic Meaning (two vols) 1986, Oxford International Encyclopedia of Linguistics (semantics ed.) 1991, Euphemism and Dysphemism: Language Used as Shield and Weapon (with Kate Burridge) 1991, Natural Language Semantics 2001, Encyclopedia of Languages and Linguistics (second edn, semantics ed.) 2005, Forbidden Words (with Kate Burridge) 2006, The Western Classical Tradition in Linguistics 2007, The Concise Encyclopedia of Semantics 2009, The English Language and Linguistics Companion (with Julie Bradshaw) 2010, Salience and Defaults in Utterance Processing (with Kasia Jaszczolt) 2011, Cambridge Handbook of Pragmatics (with Kasia Jaszczolt) 2012; contribs to reference works, scholarly books and professional journals. *Honours:* Hon. Assoc. Prof., Univ. of Queensland; Centenary Medal for Services to Linguistics and Philology, Australian Govt . *Address:* Linguistics Program, Building 11, Monash University, Clayton, Vic. 3800, Australia (office). *E-mail:* keith.allan@monash.edu (office). *Website:* www.arts.monash .edu.au/linguistics/staff/kallan.php (office).

ALLASON, Rupert William Simon, (Nigel West); British writer and editor; b. 8 Nov. 1951, London, England; m. Nicole Van Moppes 1979 (divorced 1996); one s. one d. *Education:* Univ. of Grenoble, France, Univ. of London. *Career:* Ed. World Intelligence Review 1985–; MP for Torbay, Conservative Party 1987–97; Lecturer, Center for Counterintelligence and Security Studies, Washington, DC, USA; Editorial Dir St Ermin's Press, Judge, St Ermin's Intelligence Book of the Year; mem. Special Forces Club. *Publications include:* Spy! (with Richard Deacon) 1980, British Security Service Operations 1909–45 1981, A Matter of Trust: MI5 1945–72 1982, MI6: British Secret Intelligence Service Operations 1909–45 1983, The Branch: A History of the Metropolitan Police Special Branch 1983, Unreliable Witness: Espionage Myths of the Second World War 1984, GARBO (with Juan Pujol) 1985, GCHQ: The Secret Wireless War 1986, Molehunt 1987, The Friends: Britain's Postwar Secret Intelligence Operations 1988, Games of Intelligence 1989, Seven Spies Who Changed the World 1991, Secret War: The Story of SOE 1992, The Faber Book of Espionage 1993, The Illegals 1993, Mortal Crimes 1994, The Faber Book of Treachery 1995, The Secret War for the Falklands 1997, Counterfeit Spies 1998, Crown Jewels 1998, Venona 1999, The Third Secret 2000, Mortal Crimes 2004, Mask 2005, The Guy Liddell Diaries (ed.) 2005, Historical Dictionary of British Intelligence 2005, Mask: MI5's Penetration of the Communist Party of Great Britain 2005, At Her Majesty's Secret Service 2006, Historical Dictionary of World War II Intelligence 2007, Historical Dictionary of Cold War Counterintelligence 2007, Historical Dictionary of Sexspionage 2009, Historical Dictionary of Naval Intelligence 2010, Snow: The Double Life of a World War II Spy 2011, Historical Dictionary of Chinese Intelligence 2012. *Honours:* Asscn of Former Intelligence Officers Lifetime Literature Achievement Award 2004. *Address:* 6 Burton Mews, London, SW1W 9EP, England (home). *Telephone:* 7836-200600 (mobile) (home). *Fax:* (20) 7352-1111 (office). *E-mail:* nigel@westintel.co.uk (office). *Website:* www.nigelwest.com.

ALLDRITT, Keith, BA, MA, FRSL; British academic and writer; b. 10 Dec. 1935, Wolverhampton, England; m. Joan Hardwick 1980; one s. one d. *Education:* St Catharine's Coll., Cambridge. *Career:* Prof. of English, Univ. of British Columbia, now Prof. Emer.; mem. Arnold Bennett Soc., Soc. of Authors, D. H. Lawrence Soc., Int. Churchill Soc., Modern Language Asscn, Academi. *Publications include:* The Making of George Orwell 1969, The Visual Imagination of D. H. Lawrence 1970, The Good Pit Man 1975, The Lover Next Door 1977, Elgar on the Journey to Hanley 1978, Poetry as Chamber Music 1978, Modernism in the Second World War 1989, Churchill the Writer: His Life as a Man of Letters 1992, The Greatest of Friends: Franklin Roosevelt and Winston Churchill 1939–45 1995, W. B. Yeats: The Man and the Milieu 1997, Poet as Spy: The Life and Wild Times of Basil Bunting 1998, David Jones: A Life 2003. *Address:* c/o Academi, 3rd Floor, Mount Stuart House, Mount Stuart Square, Cardiff, CF10 5FQ, Wales.

ALLEN, Blair H., (Ghosthand), AA, BA; American writer, poet, editor, artist and photographer; *Special Feature Editor, Cerulean Press and Kent Publications*; b. 2 July 1933, Los Angeles, Calif.; s. of Wendall Boyd and Ethel Rose Allen; m. Juanita Aguilar Raya 1968; one s. one d. *Education:* San Diego City Coll., Univ. of Washington, San Diego State Univ. *Career:* book reviewer, Los Angeles Times, 1977–78; Special Feature Ed., Cerulean Press and Kent Publs 1982–; mem. Asscn for Applied Poetry, Beyond Baroque Foundation, California State Poetry Soc., Medina Foundation, Acad. of American Poets, Poets and Writers (US). *Art exhibitions:* at San Diego State Art Gallery, Unicorn Gallery, La Jolla, Chatterton's Bookstore Gallery, Los Angeles. *Publications include:* Televisual Poems for Bloodshot Eyeballs 1973, Malice in Blunderland 1974, N/Z 1979, The Atlantis Trilogy 1982, Dreamwish of the Magician 1983, Right Through the Silver Lined 1984 Looking Glass 1984, The Magical World of David Cole (ed.) 1984, Snow Summits in the Sun (anthology, ed.) 1988, Trapped in a Cold War Travelogue 1991, May Burning into August 1992, The Subway Poems 1993, Bonfire on the Beach, by John Brander (ed.) 1993, The Cerulean Anthology of Sci-Fi/Outer Space/Fantasy/Poetry and Prose Poems (ed.) 1995, When the Ghost of Cassandra Whispers in My Ears 1996, Ashes Ashes All Fall Down 1997, Around the World in 56 Days 1998, Thunderclouds from the Door 1999, Jabberbunglemerkeltoy 1999, The Athens Café 2000, The Day of the Jamberee Call 2001, Assembled I Stand 2002, Wine of Starlight 2002, Hour of Iced Wheels 2003, Snow Birds in Cloud Hands (ed. anthology) 2003, Trek into Yellowstone's Cascade Corner Wilderness 2003, Light in the Crossroads 2004, Shot Doves 2005, What Time Does: One Man Show (art book retrospective) 2006, Moon Hiding in the Orange Tree 2007, In the Face of Gateless High Walls the Sound of Purple Horns 2007, Opossum in the Fig Tree 2008, When Morning is Still Night 2008, Rain Hiking in Nikko 2009, Flight to the Green Dream 2009; contribs to numerous periodicals and anthologies. *Honours:* First Prize for Poetry, Pacificus Foundation Competition 1992, Pacificus Foundation Literary Prize for Lifetime Achievement in Poetry and Story Writing 2003, various other honours and awards. *Address:* PO Box 162, Colton, CA 92324-0162, USA.

ALLEN, Rev. Diogenes, BA, BD, MA, PhD; American academic and writer; *Professor Emeritus, Princeton Theological Seminary*; b. 17 Oct. 1932, Lexington, Ky; m. Jane Mary Billing 1958, three s. one d. *Education:* Univ. of Kentucky, Princeton Univ., Univ. of Oxford, UK, Yale Univ. *Career:* ordained, Presbyterian Church 1959; Pastor, Windham Presbyterian Church, NH 1958–61; Asst Prof., York Univ., Toronto 1964–66, Assoc. Prof. 1966–67; Assoc. Prof., Princeton Theological Seminary 1967–74, Prof. of Philosophy 1974–81, Chair. Dept of Theology 1977–79, 1988–91, Stuart Prof. of Philosophy 1981–2002, Prof. Emer. 2002–; ordained deacon and priest, Episcopal Church, 2002; currently Priest Assoc. All Saints Church, Princeton, NJ; Fellow, St Deiniol's Library, Hawarden, North Wales 2003; mem. American Philosophical Asscn, American Theological Soc., American Weil Soc. (Co-founder and Exec. Bd mem.), Asscn étude pensées S. Weil, Canadian Philosophical Asscn, Leibniz Gesellschaft, Soc. of Christian Philosophers, American Acad. of Religion. *Publications include:* Leibniz' Theodicy (ed.) 1966, The Reasonableness of Faith 1968, Finding Our Father (aka The Path of Perfect Love) 1974, Between Two Worlds (aka Temptation) 1977, Traces of God in a Frequently Hostile World 1981, Three Outsiders: Pascal, Kierkegaard and Simone Weil 1983, Mechanical Explanations and the Ultimate Origin of the Universe According to Leibniz 1983, Philosophy for Understanding Theology 1985, Love: Christian Romance, Marriage and Friendship 1987, Christian Belief in a Postmodern World: The Full Wealth of Conviction 1989, Quest: The Search for Meaning Through Christ 1990, Primary Reading in Philosophy for Understanding Theology (co-ed. with Eric Springsted) 1992, Nature, Spirit, and Community: Issues in the Thought of Simone Weil (with Eric Springsted) 1997, Spiritual Theology 1997, Steps Along the Way 2002, Theology for a Troubled Believer 2010. *Honours:* Rhodes Scholar 1955–57, 1963–64, Rockefeller Doctoral Fellow 1962–64, Asscn of Theological Schools Research Fellowship 1975–76, Center of Theological Inquiry Research Fellowship 1985–86, 1994–95, Pew Evangelical Scholarship 1991–92, John Templeton Awards in Science and Theology 1992, 1993, Best Courses in Science and Religion 1995. *Address:* Princeton Theological Seminary, PO Box 821, Princeton, NJ 08542-0803, USA (office).

ALLEN, Edward Hathaway, MA, PhD; American writer and poet; *Associate Professor of English, University of South Dakota*; b. 20 Oct. 1948, New Haven, Conn. *Education:* Goddard Coll., Univ. of Iowa, Ohio Univ. *Career:* Asst Prof., Rhodes Coll., Memphis, Tenn. 1989–91; Writer-in-Residence, Univ. of Central Oklahoma 1992–94; Sr Fulbright Lecturer, Jagiellonian Univ., Poland 1994–95; Asst Prof. of English, San Jose State Univ. 1995–96; Assoc. Prof. of English, Univ. of South Dakota 1996–; mem. Acad. of American Poets, Associated Writing Programs, Modern Language Asscn, Poets and Writers, Writers' Guild of America. *Publications include:* fiction: Straight Through the Night 1989, Mustang Sally 1992, Verso La Notte 1998, Ate It Anyway (short stories) (Flannery O'Connor Award for Short Fiction) 2002; poetry: 67 Mixed Messages 2005, contrib. to newspapers and periodicals. *Address:* Department of English, University of South Dakota, Dakota Hall 218, 414 East Clark Street, Vermillion, SD 57069-5229, USA (office). *Telephone:* (605) 677-5967 (office). *E-mail:* eallen@usd.edu (office). *Website:* www.usd.edu/engl/faculty/ allen.cfm (office).

ALLEN, John (see PERRY, Ritchie)

ALLEN, Judy; British writer; b. 8 July 1941, Old Sarum, Wilts.; d. of the late Maj. Jack Turner Allen and Janet Marion Beall. *Education:* privately. *Career:* writer 1976–; dramatized The Secret Garden (by Frances Hodgson-Burnett) for BBC Radio 5, Tom's Midnight Garden, The River. *Radio plays:* Survival, The Sailor's Return, Squatter's Rights, Unicorn Calling. *Publications include:* adult fiction: December Flower (Christopher Award, USA for TV version 1987) 1982, Bag and Baggage 1988, The Book of the Dragon, Wildlife in the Country 1995, Wildlife in the City 1999; jr fiction: Auntie Billie's Greatest Invention, Seven Weird Days at Number 31, Rainforest, What is a Wall, After All?, The Most Brilliant Trick Ever, Five Weird Days at Aunt Carly's, Frogs and Toads, Something Rare and Special 1985, Travelling Hopefully 1987, Awaiting Developments (Whitbread Children's Novel Award 1988, Friends of the Earth Earthworm Award 1989) 1988, Stones of the Moon, Lord of the Dance, Between the Moon and the Rock, Something Rare and Special, The Blue Death, The Last Green Book on Earth, The Spring on the Mountain, The Burning, Storm-Voice, The Dream Thing, Anthology for the Earth, Animals at Risk series (Eagle, Panda, Tiger, Elephant, Seal, Whale), City Farm series (The Great Pig Sprint, The Cheap Sheep Shock, The Dim Thin Ducks, The Long Loan Llama) 1990, Endangered Species series 1991–92, Between the Moon and the Rock 1992, Highfliers series (Paris Quest, Sydney Quest, Spanish Quest, Amsterdam Quest, New York Quest, Highland Quest) 1996, Up the Garden Path series (Are you a Ladybird?, Are You a Butterfly?, Are

You a Bee?, Are You an Ant?, Are You a Snail?, Are You a Spider?, Are You a Dragonfly?, Are You a Grasshopper?) 1999–2002; non-fiction: The Last Green Book on Earth 1994; guide books: London Arts Guide (Best Specialist Guidebook Award, London Tourist Bd) 1984, The Guide to London by Bus and Tube 1987, London Docklands Street Atlas and Guide 1988; other: The Diary of Minnie Gorrie (abridgement for BBC Radio 4). *Honours:* Washington State Children's Choice Award 1995. *Literary Agent:* c/o Laurence Fitch Ltd, 483 Southbank House, Black Prince Road, Albert Embankment, London, SE1 7SJ; c/o Rogers, Coleridge & White, 20 Powis Mews, London, W11 1JN, England. *Telephone:* (20) 7735-8171 (Fitch); (20) 7221-3717 (Rogers, Coleridge & White). *E-mail:* contactjudyallen@beeb.net. *Website:* www.judyallen.co.uk.

ALLEN, (Mary) Darina; Irish cookery writer and teacher; Founder and Principal, *Ballymaloe Cookery School;* b. 30 July 1948, Dublin; d. of William and Elizabeth O'Connell; m. Timothy Allen; two s. two d. *Education:* Dominican Convent, Wicklow and Dublin Coll. of Catering. *Career:* Cook at Ballymaloe House Hotel 1968–83; Founder and Prin. Ballymaloe Cookery School (with Timothy Allen) 1983–; Presenter, Radio Telefis Eireann (RTE) Simply Delicious Series on TV 1989–96; featured in BBC Hot Chefs Series 1992; columnist, The Irish Examiner; responsible for setting up Ireland's first Farmers' Markets; mem. Bd BIM (Irish Sea Fisheries Bd) 1989; mem. Int. Asscn of Culinary Professionals (IACP), Eurotoques, Slow Food Movement, Ireland; Certified Teacher, Culinary Professional and Food Professional, IACP. *Television:* A Year at Ballymaloe Cookery School (26-part series for Carlton Food Network) 1998, Ballymaloe Cookery School (RTE) 2002; guest appearances on numerous TV shows, including judging BBC's Masterchef and Junior Masterchef, Food and Drink Show, The Holiday Programme, Wish You Were Here, Good Morning America, NBC Weekend Today Show. *Publications include:* Simply Delicious (series of five titles) 1989–92, Darina Allen's Simply Delicious Recipes 1992, Simply Delicious Versatile Vegetables 1994, Irish Traditional Cooking 1995, A Year at Ballymaloe Cookery School 1997, Festive Food of Ireland 2001, Darina Allen's Simply Delicious Suppers 2001, Ballymaloe Cookery Course 2001, Healthy Gluten-Free Eating (co-author) 2004, Easy Entertaining 2005, Forgotten Skills of Cooking 2009; contribs to Sainsbury's Magazine, Irish Examiner, Irish Times, BBC Good Food. *Honours:* Dr hc (Univ. of Ulster) 2003; Waterford Wedgwood Hospitality Award 2000, Veuve Clicquot Irish Businesswoman of the Year Award 2001, Cooking Teacher of the Year Award 2005, Mike Butt Award 2010, co-recipient, Premios Verdes Awards (Green Awards), José Navarro Foundation, Valencia, Spain 2011. *Address:* Ballymaloe Cookery School, Shanagarry, Midleton, Co. Cork, Ireland (office). *Telephone:* (21) 4646785 (office). *Fax:* (21) 4646909 (office). *E-mail:* info@cookingisfun.ie (office). *Website:* www.cookingisfun.ie (office).

ALLEN, Roberta L.; American writer, artist and teacher; b. 6 Oct. 1945, New York; d. of Sol Allen and Jeanette Allen (née Waldner). *Education:* Fashion Inst. of Tech., New York. *Career:* Lecturer, Corcoran School of Art 1975, Kutztown State Coll., Pa 1979; Instructor in Creative Writing, Parsons School of Design 1986, The Writer's Voice 1992–97, The New School 1993–2009, School of Continuing Educ., New York Univ. 1993–2000, Columbia Univ. School of the Arts 1998–99; Tennessee Williams Fellow in Creative Writing, Univ. of the South, Sewanee, Tenn. 1998; Fellow, Eugene Lang Coll., The New School 2000. *Solo exhibitions include:* Galerie 845, Amsterdam, Netherlands 1967, John Weber Gallery, New York 1974, 1977, 1979, Galerie Maier-Hahn, Düsseldorf, Germany 1977, Galleria Primo Piano, Italy 1981, Galerie Walter Storms, Munich, Germany 1981, PSI Museum, MOMA, New York 1977, 1981, Perth Inst. of Contemporary Arts, Australia 1989, Art Resources Transfer, New York 2001, State Univ. of New York, Binghamton, NY 2001, New Arts Program, Kutztown, Pa 2001. *Publications include:* Pointless Arrows 1976, Possibilities 1977, The Traveling Woman 1986, The Daughter 1992, Pointless Acts 1976, Amazon Dream 1993, Certain People 1997, Fast Fiction 1997, The Dreaming Girl 2000, The Playful Way to Serious Writing 2002, The Playful Way to Knowing Yourself 2003. *Honours:* MacDowell Colony Residency 1971, 1972, Ossabaw Island Project Residency 1972, Creative Artists Public Service Grant 1978–79, Yaddo Residency 1983, 1987, 1993, LINE (NEA and NYS Council) Grant 1985, Virginia Center for Creative Arts Residency 1985, 1994, 2005, Artist-in-Residence Fellowship, Art Gallery of Western Australia, Perth 1989. *Address:* 5 West 16th Street, New York, NY 10011, USA (home). *Telephone:* (646) 241-4648 (home). *E-mail:* roleea@gmail.com. *Website:* www.robertaallen.com.

ALLEN, William L.; American editor, executive and photographer; *Editor-in-Chief Emeritus, National Geographic Magazine;* b. 28 Dec. 1940, Tyler, Tex. *Education:* Georgia Tech, Louisiana State Univ. *Career:* served in US army as lieutenant late 1960s, ran several military newspapers; became freelance photographer; joined Nat. Geographic magazine 1969, Illustrations Ed. 1985–92, Sr Asst Ed., then Assoc. Ed. 1992–95, Ed.-in-Chief 1995–2005 (also Bd mem.), currently Ed.-in-Chief Emer.; contrib. to The Huffington Post; Bd mem. Nat. Geographic Editorial Foundation, Nat. Space Biomedical Research Inst., Inst. of Nautical Archaeology, Teton Science School, Nat. Council of the World Wildlife Fund, Council on Foreign Relations; mem. Cosmos Club. *Honours:* Nat. Magazine Award 2000. *Address:* PO Box 7410, Alexandria, VA 22307, USA (office). *E-mail:* bill@billallenphotography.com (office). *Website:* www.billallenphotography.com (office).

ALLEN, Woody; American actor, writer, producer and director; b. (Allen Stewart Konigsberg), 1 Dec. 1935, Brooklyn, NY; s. of the late Martin Konigsberg and of Nettie Konigsberg (née Cherry); m. 1st Harlene Rosen 1956 (divorced 1962); m. 2nd Louise Lasser 1966 (divorced 1970); m. 3rd Soon-Yi Previn 1997; two adopted d.; one s. with Mia Farrow. *Education:* City Coll. of New York and New York Univ. *Career:* made his debut as a performer in 1961 at the Duplex in Greenwich Village; has performed in a variety of nightclubs across the USA; produced the play Don't Drink the Water 1966, Morosco Theater 1966, Broadhurst Theatre 1969; made his Broadway debut as Allan Felix in Play it Again, Sam, which he also wrote; during the 1950s wrote for TV performers Herb Shriner 1953, Sid Caesar 1957, Art Carney 1958–59, Jack Paar and Carol Channing, also wrote for the Tonight Show and the Gary Moore Show. *Films include:* What's New Pussycat? 1965, Casino Royale 1967, What's Up, Tiger Lily? 1967, Take the Money and Run 1969, Bananas 1971, Everything You Always Wanted to Know About Sex 1972, Play it Again, Sam 1972, Sleeper 1973, Love and Death 1976, The Front 1976, Annie Hall (Acad. Awards for Best Dir and Best Writer 1978, BAFTA Film Awards for Best Screenplay and Best Direction 1978) 1977, Interiors 1978, Manhattan 1979 (BAFTA Film Award for Best Screenplay – Original 1980), Stardust Memories 1980, A Midsummer Night's Sex Comedy 1982, Zelig 1983, Broadway Danny Rose (BAFTA Film Award for Best Screenplay – Original 1985) 1984, The Purple Rose of Cairo (BAFTA Film Awards for Best Film and Best Screenplay – Original 1986, Golden Globe Award for Best Screenplay 1986) 1985 , Hannah and Her Sisters (BAFTA Film Award for Best Direction 1987, Acad. Award for Best Writing, Screenplay Written Directly for the Screen 1987) 1986, Radio Days 1987, September 1987, Another Woman 1988, Oedipus Wrecks 1989, Crimes and Misdemeanors 1989, Alice 1990, Scenes from a Mall, Shadows and Fog 1991, Husbands and Wives (BAFTA Award Film Award for Best Screenplay – Original 1993) 1992, Manhattan Murder Mystery 1993, Bullets Over Broadway 1995, Mighty Aphrodite 1995, Everyone Says I Love You 1996, Deconstructing Harry 1997, Celebrity 1998, Antz (voice only) 1998, Wild Man Blues 1998, Stuck on You 1998, Company Men 1999, Sweet and Lowdown 1999, Small Town Crooks 2000, The Curse of the Jade Scorpion 2001, Hail Sid Caesar! 2001, Hollywood Ending 2002, Anything Else 2003, Melinda and Melinda 2004, Match Point 2005, Scoop 2006, Cassandra's Dream 2007, Vicky Cristina Barcelona 2008, Whatever Works 2009, You Will Meet a Tall Dark Stranger 2010, Midnight in Paris (Golden Globe Award for Best Screenplay 2012, Acad. Award for Best Writing, Screenplay Written Directly for the Screen 2012) 2011, To Rome With Love 2012. *Television:* Sounds from a Town I Love 2001. *Plays written include:* Don't Drink the Water 1966, The Floating Lightbulb 1981, Death Defying Acts (one act) 1995. *Opera:* as producer: Gianni Schicchi, Los Angeles Opera 2008. *Publications include:* Getting Even 1971, Without Feathers 1975, Side Effects 1980, The Complete Prose 1994, Telling Tales (contrib. to charity anthology) 2004, Mere Anarchy 2007, The Insanity Defense 2007; contribs to Playboy and New Yorker. *Honours:* Dr hc (Universitat Pompeu Fabra, Spain) 2007; Laurel Award for Screen Writing Achievement 1987, D.W. Griffith Award 1996, Directors Guild of America Lifetime Achievement Award 1996, San Sebastian Film Festival Donosti a Prize 2004. *Address:* 930 Fifth Avenue, New York, NY 10021, USA.

ALLENDE, Isabel; Chilean (b. Peruvian) writer; b. 2 Aug. 1942, Lima, Peru; d. of Tomás Allende and Francisca Llona Barros; m. 1st Miguel Frias 1962; one s. one d.; m. 2nd William Gordon 1988. *Career:* journalist, Paula women's magazine 1967–74, Mampato children's magazine 1969–74, TV shows and film documentaries 1970–74, El Nacional newspaper, Caracas, Venezuela 1975–84; taught literature at Montclair State Coll., NJ 1985, Univ. of Virginia, Charlottesville 1988, Univ. of California, Berkeley 1989; Goodwill Amb. for Hans Christian Andersen Bicentenary 2004; lecture tours in USA and Europe, speech tours in univs and cols, numerous literature workshops; mem. Academia de Artes y Ciencias, Puerto Rico 1995, Academia de la Lengua, Chile 1989, American Acad. of Arts and Letters 2004. *Plays:* El Embajador 1971, La balada del medio pelo 1973, Los siete espejos 1974. *Publications:* La casa de los espíritus (novel, trans. as The House of the Spirits) 1982, La gorda de porcelana (juvenile short stories) 1983, De amor y de sombra (novel, trans. as Of Love and Shadows) 1984, Cuentos de Eva Luna (short stories, trans. as Stories of Eva Luna) 1989, El plan infinito (novel, trans. as The Infinite Plan) 1991, Paula (memoir) 1994, Afrodita (trans. as Aphrodite) 1998, Hija de la fortuna (novel, trans. as Daughter of Fortune) 1999, Retrato en sepia (novel, trans. as Portrait in Sepia) 2000, La ciudad de las bestias (juvenile novel, trans. as City of the Beasts) 2002, Mi país inventado (memoir, trans. as My Invented Country) (Latino Literacy Now Award for Best Biography 2004) 2003, El reino del dragón de oro (juvenile novel, trans. as Kingdom of the Golden Dragon) (Latino Literacy Now Award for Best Young Adult Fiction 2004) 2003, El Zorro (novel) 2005, El Bosque de los Pigmeos (juvenile novel, trans. as Forest of the Pygmies) 2005, Inés del alma mía (novel, trans. as Inés of My Soul) 2006, La Suma de los Días (memoirs, trans. as The Sum of Our Days) 2007, La Isla Bajo el Mar (novel, trans. as Island Beneath the Sea) 2009. *Honours:* Hon. Citizen of Austin, Tex. USA 1995; Hon. Prof. of Literature, Univ. of Chile 1991; Hon. mem. Acad. of Devt and Peace, Austria 2000; Chevalier, Ordre des Arts et Lettres 1994, Condecoracion Gabriela Mistral (Chile) 1994; Hon. DLitt (New York State Univ.) 1991, (Bates Coll., USA) 1994, (Dominican Coll., USA) 1994, (Columbia Coll., USA) 1996; Hon. DHumLitt (Florida Atlantic Univ.) 1996; Dr hc (Lawrence Univ., USA) 2000, (Mills Coll., USA) 2000, (Illinois Wesleyan Univ.) 2002; Best Novel of the Year (Chile) 1983, Panorama Literario Award (Chile) 1983, Author of the Year (Germany) 1984, Book of the Year (Germany) 1984, Grand Prix d'Evasion Award (France) 1984, Point de Mire Award, Belgian Radio and TV 1985, Quality Paperback Book Club New Voice (USA) 1986, Premio Literario Colima Award (Mexico) 1986, XV Premio Internazionale I Migliori Dell'Anno (Italy) 1987, Mulheres Best Foreign Novel Award (Portugal) 1987, Quimera Libros (Chile) 1987, Book of the Year (Switzerland) 1987, Library Journal's Best Book (USA) 1988, Before Columbus Foundation Award (USA) 1988, Best Novel (Mexico) 1985, Author of the Year (Germany) 1986, Freedom to Write Pen Club (USA) 1991, XLI Bancarella Literary Award (Italy) 1993, Ind. Foreign Fiction Award (UK) 1993, Brandeis Univ. Major Book Collection Award (USA) 1993, Marin Women's Hall of Fame (USA) 1994, Feminist of the Year Award, The Feminist Majority Foundation (USA) 1994, Read About Me Literary Award (USA) 1996, Critics' Choice Award (USA) 1996, Books to Remember Award, American Library Asscn 1996, Gift of HOPE Award, HOPE Educ. and Leadership Fund (USA) 1996, Harold Washington Literary Award, City of Chicago 1996, Malaparte Award, Amici di Capri (Italy) 1998, Donna Città Di Roma Literary Award, Italy 1998, Dorothy and Lillian Gish Prize (USA) 1998, Sara Lee Frontrunner Award (USA) 1998, GEMS Women of the Year Award (USA) 1999, Donna Dell'Anno 1999 Award (Italy) 1999, Books to Remember, The New York Public Library WILLA Literary Award 2000, Excellence in Int. Literature and Arts Award (USA) 2002, The Celebration of Books Amb. Award (USA) 2002, Int. Women's Forum Award (Mexico) 2002, Nopal Award, Cal Poly Pomona (USA) 2003, Cyril Magnin Lifetime Achievement Award (USA) 2003, Premios Iberoamericano de Letrasjose Donoso (Chile) 2003, Premio Personalidad Distinguida, Universdidad del Pacifico (Chile) 2004, Commonwealth Award of Distinguished Service for Literature (USA) 2004, Premio Nacional de Literatura 2010. *Literary Agent:* Carmen Balcells, Diagonal 580, Barcelona 21, Spain. *Address:* 116 Caledonia Street, Sausalito, CA 94965, USA (office). *Fax:* (415) 332-4149 (office). *E-mail:* assistant@isabelallende.com (office). *Website:* www.isabelallende.com.

ALLISON, Dorothy, BA, MA; American writer, poet, teacher and lecturer; b. 11 April 1949, Greenville, SC; pnr Alexis Layman; one s. *Education:* Florida Presbyterian Coll., New School for Social Research. *Career:* Writer-in-Residence, Columbia Coll., Chicago 2006, Emory Coll., Atlanta 2008; Distinguished Visiting Prof., Emory Univ. Center for Humanistic Inquiry 2008; McGee Prof., Davidson Coll., NC 2009; mem. Authors' Guild, PEN, Writers' Union, Feminists Against Censorship; mem. Bd Fellowship of Southern Writers. *Films:* Bastard Out Of Carolina 1995, Two or Three Things and Nothing for Sure 1997, Cavedweller 2003. *Publications include:* fiction: Trash 1988, Bastard Out of Carolina 1992, Cavedweller 1998, Trash and Other Stories 2002; poetry: The Women Who Hate Me 1983; non-fiction: Skin: Talking About Sex, Class and Literature 1994, Two or Three Things I Know for Sure 1995, The Writer's Notebook: Craft Essays from Tin House (co-author) 2009. *Honours:* Lambda Literary Award for Best Small Press Book and Best Lesbian Book 1989, Tanner Prize In Ethics and Community, Stanford Univ. 2001, Robert Penn Warren Award for Fiction 2007. *Literary Agent:* Frances Goldin Literary Agency, 57 East Eleventh Street, 5B, New York, NY 10003, USA. *Telephone:* (212) 777-0047 (office). *E-mail:* fg@goldinlit.com (office). *Address:* PO Box 136, Guerneville, CA 95446, USA (home). *E-mail:* rydab@aol.com (office). *Website:* www.dorothyallison.net.

ALLISON, John, BMus, PhD, ARCO; British editor and critic; *Editor, Opera*; b. 20 May 1965, Cape Town, S Africa; s. of David Allison and Adele Allison; m. Nicole Galgut. *Education:* Univ. of Cape Town. *Career:* fmr organist at Cape Town Cathedral; music critic for The Times; Ed. Opera magazine 2000–. *Publications include:* Edward Elgar: Sacred Music 1994, Mitchell Beazley Pocket Guide to Opera 1998, A Way of Seeing: Perception, Imagination, and Poetry 2003, The English Historical Constitution: Continuity, Change and European Effects 2007, Dropped Stitches in Tennessee History 2010; contrib. to Opera News, BBC Music Magazine, Classic FM Magazine, Financial Times, London Evening Standard, The Observer, The Australian, New Grove Dictionary of Music and Musicians, The New Penguin Opera Guide, Music and Words – Essays in Honour of Andrew Porter. *Address:* Opera Magazine, 36 Black Lion Lane, London, W6 9BE, England (office). *Telephone:* (20) 8563-8893 (office). *Fax:* (20) 8563-8635 (office). *E-mail:* editor@opera.co.uk (office). *Website:* www.opera.co.uk (office).

ALLOUACHE, Merzak; Algerian film director and writer; b. 6 Oct. 1944, Algiers; s. of Omar Allouache and Fatma Allouache; m. Lazib Anissa 1962; one d. *Career:* worked in Nat. Inst. of Cinema, Algiers, later in Inst. of Film, Paris; after return to Algeria worked as Adviser, Ministry of Culture. *Films include:* Our Agrarian Revolution (documentary) 1973, Omar Gatlato, Les aventures d'un héros, L'homme qui regardait les fenêtres 1982, Bab El-Oued City 1994, Lumiére et Compagnie 1995, Salut Cousin! 1996, Dans la décapotable 1996, Alger–Beyrouth: Pour Mémoire 1998, Pepe Carvalho: La Solitude du Manager (TV) 1999, À bicyclette (TV) 2001, L'Autre Monde 2001, Chouchou 2003, Bab el seb 2005. *Publications:* Bab El-Oued (novel) 1994. *Honours:* Silver Prize, Moscow Festival; Tanit D'Or Prize, Carthage 1979.

ALMODÓVAR, Pedro; Spanish film director and screenwriter; b. 25 Sept. 1951, Calzada de Calatrava, Ciudad Real, Castilla La Mancha. *Career:* fronted a rock band; worked at Telefónica for ten years; started career with full-length super-8 films; made 16mm short films 1974–83; f. El Deseo SA (film production co.). *Films as writer and director:* Film político 1974, Dos putas, o historia de amor que termina en boda 1974, El Sueño, o la estrella 1975, Homenaje 1975, La caída de Sódoma 1975, Blancor 1975, Sea caritativo 1976, Muerte en la carretera 1976, Sexo va, sexo viene 1977, Salomé 1978, ¡Folle... folle... fólleme Tim! 1978, Pepe, Luci, Bom y otras chicas del montón 1980, Laberinto de pasiones 1982, Entre tinieblas 1983, ¿Qué he hecho yo para merecer esto? 1985, Matador 1986, La ley del deseo 1987, Mujeres al borde de un ataque de nervios (Felix Award) 1988, ¡Atame! 1990, Tacones lejanos 1991, Kika 1993, La flor de mi secreto 1995, Carne trémula 1997, Todo sobre mi madre (Acad. Award for Best Foreign Language Film) 1999, Hable con ella (BAFTA Award for Best Film not in the English language 2003, Acad. Award for Best Original Screenplay 2003) 2002, La mala educación 2004, Volver (Best Foreign Film Nat. Bd of Review 2006, Goya Award for Best Film, Best Dir 2007, Best Foreign Film, London Film Critics' Circle Awards 2007) 2006, Los abrazos rotos 2009, La piel que habito 2011. *Films as producer:* Laberinto de pasiones 1982, Mujeres al borde de un ataque de nervios 1988, Acción mutante 1993, Mi nombre es sombra (assoc. producer) 1996, Cuernos de espuma 1996, El Espinazo del diablo 2001, Mi vida sin mí (exec. producer) 2003, La Mala educación 2004, La niña santa 2004, La Vida secreta de las palabras 2005, La Mujer sin Cabeza 2008, El último verano de la Boyita 2009, La piel que habito 2011. *Publications:* Fuego en las entrañas 1982, The Patty Diphusa Stories and Other Writings 1992. *Honours:* Prince of Asturias Award for the Arts 2006. *Address:* c/o El Deseo SA, Ruiz Perelló 15, Madrid 28028, Spain (office); Miramax Films, 18 E 48th Street, New York, NY 10017, USA (office).

ALMOG, Ruth; Israeli novelist and journalist; b. 1936, Petach Tikva; m. Aharon Almog; two d. *Education:* Tel-Aviv Univ. *Career:* taught in schools and Depts of Philosophy and Film, Tel-Aviv Univ.; Deputy Ed. Literary Section, Ha'aretz daily newspaper 1967–; Writer-in-Residence and Tutor in Creative Writing, Hebrew Univ. of Jerusalem; also taught creative writing at Ben-Gurion Univ., Beersheba. *Publications include:* short stories: Hasdei Ha-Laila Shel Margerita 1969, Aharei Tu Bi-Shvat 1979, Nashim 1986, Tikun Omanuti (novella and stories) 1993, All This Exaggerated Happiness 2001, Kol Ha-Osher Ha-Mufraz Haze 2003; novels: Be-Eretz Gezirah 1971, Mavet Ba-Geshem 1982, Shorshei Avir (Brenner Prize 1989) 1987, Meahev Mushlam (with Esther Ettinger) 1995, Estelina Ahuvati (with Esther Ettinger) 2002, Love, Natalia 2005, Stranger in Paradise 2008; juvenile: Naphy Nasich Ha-Karnafim 1979, Gilgil 1986, Tzoanim Ba-Pardes 1986, Kadur Ha-Kesef 1986, Hasibor 1991, Rakefet, Ahavati Ha-Rishonah 1992, Gilgil Rotza Kelev 1998, Hamasa Sheli Im Alex (trans. as My Journey with Alex) (Yad Vashem Prize, Andersen Honor Citation) 1999, Balut Ha-pele shel Kamila 1999, Od Chibuk Echad 2003, Be-Ahava, Natalia 2005, Meil Katon 2008, Zara Be-Gan Eden 2008; other: Et Ha-Zar Ve-Ha-Oyev 1980, Ha-Agam Ha-pnimi 2000. *Honours:* Yad Vashem Prize, Agnon Prize 2001, Newman Prize 2004, Prime Minister's Prize 1995, 2007, German Gerty Spies Prize for Literature, Rheinland-Pfalz 2004, Bialik Prize for Lifetime Achievement 2006, ACUM Literary Award 2010. *Address:* 4 Haneriim Street, Tel-Aviv 64356, Israel (home). *Telephone:* (3) 5282451 (home). *E-mail:* ruth66@bezegint.net.

ALMOND, David John, BA, PGCE; British writer; b. 15 May 1951, Felling-on-Tyne, England; s. of James Arthur Almond and Catherine Almond; pnr; one d. *Education:* Univ. of East Anglia. *Career:* fmr teacher; Ed. Panurge magazine 1987–93; Visiting Prof., Nottingham Trent Univ. *Plays:* Wild Girl Wild Boy 2001, Skellig 2002, My Dad's a Birdman 2003, Noah and The Fludd 2010. *Opera:* libretto: Skellig (music by Tod Machover) 2008. *Films for television:* Clay (BBC 1) 2008, Skellig (Sky1) 2009. *Publications include:* short story collections: Sleepless Nights 1985, A Kind of Heaven 1997, Counting Stars 2000; juvenile fiction: Skellig (Carnegie Medal, Whitbread Children's Book of the Year) 1998, Kit's Wilderness (Smarties Prize Silver Medal 2000) 1999, Heaven Eyes 2000, Secret Heart 2001, Where Your Wings Were 2002, The Fire-Eaters (Nestlé Smarties Prize Gold Award, Whitbread Children's Book of the Year) 2003, Clay 2005, My Dad's a Birdman 2007, Jackdaw Summer 2008, My Name is Mina 2010; picture books: Kate, the Cat and the Moon (illustrated by Stephen Lambert) 2004, The Savage (illustrated by Dave McKean) 2008, The Boy Who Climbed into the Moon (illustrated by Polly Dunbar) 2010, Slog's Dad; The True Tale of the Monster Billy Dean (fiction) 2011, The Boy Who Swam with Piranhas (illustrated by Oliver Jeffers) 2012, Mouse Bird Snake Wolf (illustrated by Dave McKean) 2012. *Honours:* Hon. DLitt (Newcastle), (Leicester), (Sunderland); Michael L. Printz Award 2001, Boston Globe-Horn Book Award 2004, Hans Christian Andersen Award 2010. *Literary Agent:* c/o Catherine Clarke, Felicity Bryan Literary Agency, 2A North Parade Avenue, Oxford, OX2 6LX, England. *Telephone:* (1865) 513816. *Fax:* (1865) 310055. *E-mail:* agency@felicitybryan.com. *Website:* www.felicitybryan.com; www.davidalmond.com.

ALPHONSO-KARKALA, John B., BA, MA, PhD; Indian writer, poet and academic; *Professor Emeritus, Comparative World Literature, SUNY New Paltz*; b. 30 May 1923, South Kanara, Mysore State; m. Leena Anneli Hakalehto 1964; three c. *Education:* Mumbai Univ., Univ. of London, UK, Columbia Univ., USA. *Career:* Visiting Lecturer, City Coll., CUNY 1963; Asst Prof., State Univ. of NY (SUNY) New Paltz 1964–65, Assoc. Prof. 1965–68, Prof. of Literature 1969, currently Prof. Emer., Comparative World Literature, Asian Studies Program; Visiting Prof., Columbia Univ. 1969–70; mem. American Oriental Soc., Asscn for Asian Studies, Int. Congress of Comparative Literature, Int. Congress of Orientalists, Modern Language Asscn; fmr mem. Seminars on Shakespeare/Renaissance and Indology/South Asia, Columbia Univ. *Publications include:* Indo-English Literature in the Nineteenth Century 1970, Anthology of Indian Literature (ed., aka Ages of Rishis, Buddha, Acharyas, Bhaktas and Mahatma) 1971, Bibliography of Indo-English Literature, 1800–1966 (co-ed. with Leena Karkala) 1974, Comparative World Literature: Seven Essays 1974, Passions of the Nightless Night (novel) 1974, Jawaharlal Nehru: A Literary Portrait 1975, When Night Falls (poems) 1980, Vedic Vision (ed.) 1980, Joys of Jayanagara (novel) 1981, Indo-English Literature: Essays (with Leena Karkala) 1994. *Address:* Asian

Studies Program, SUNY New Paltz, 600 Hawk Drive, New Paltz, NY 12561-2443 (office); 20 Millrock Road, New Paltz, NY 12561, USA (home). *E-mail:* jakarkala@aol.com. *Website:* www.newpaltz.edu/asianstudies/index.html (office).

ALTER, Robert Bernard, BA, MA, PhD; American literary critic and academic; *Class of 1937 Professor, University of California at Berkeley*; b. 2 April 1935, New York, NY; m. Carol Cosman 1974; three s. one d. *Education:* Columbia Coll., Harvard Univ. *Career:* instructor, Asst Prof. of English, Columbia Univ., New York 1962–66; Assoc. Prof. of Hebrew and Comparative Literature, Univ. of California, Berkeley 1967–69, Prof. of Hebrew and Comparative Literature 1969–89, Class of 1937 Prof. 1989–; mem. American Comparative Literature Asscn, Asscn of Literary Scholars and Critics, Council of Scholars of the Library of Congress, American Acad. of Arts and Sciences, American Philosophical Soc.; fmr Pres. Asscn of Literary Scholars and Critics; Fellow, Guggenheim Foundation, Inst. for Advanced Studies in Jerusalem, American Acad. of Jewish Research; Sr Fellow, Nat. Endowment for Humanities; Old Dominion Fellow, Univ. of Princeton. *Publications include:* Rogue's Progress 1965, After the Tradition 1968, Modern Hebrew Literature 1975, Partial Magic 1975, Defenses of the Imagination 1978, Stendhal: A Biography 1979, The Art of Biblical Narrative 1981, Motives for Fiction 1984, The Art of Biblical Poetry 1985, The Invention of Hebrew Prose 1988, The Pleasures of Reading in an Ideological Age 1989, Necessary Angels 1991, The World of Biblical Literature 1992, Hebrew and Modernity 1994, Genesis: Translation and Commentary 1996, Canon and Creativity: Modern Writing and the Authority of Scripture 2000, The Five Books of Moses 2004, Imagined Cities 2005, Psalms: A Translation with Commentary 2007, Pen of Iron: American Prose and the King James Bible 2010, The Wisdom Books: Translation and Commentary 2011; contrib. to Commentary, New Republic, New York Times Book Review, London Review of Books, Times Literary Supplement. *Honours:* Dr hc (Yale) 2010; English Inst. Essay Prize 1965, Nat. Jewish Book Award for Jewish Thought 1982, Present Tense Award for Religious Thought 1986, Nat. Foundation for Jewish Culture Award for Scholarship 1995, Koret Trans. Award 2005, PEN-USA Trans. Award 2005, Robert Kirsch Award 2009. *Address:* 1475 Le Roy Avenue, Berkeley, CA 94708, USA (office). *Telephone:* (510) 642-6457 (office); (510) 845-2640 (home). *Fax:* (510) 841-4085 (home). *E-mail:* altcos@berkeley.edu (office).

ALTHER, Lisa, BA; American writer, academic and journalist; b. 23 July 1944, Kingsport, Tenn.; d. of John Shelton Reed and Alice Greene Reed; m. Richard Alther 1966 (divorced); one d. *Education:* Wellesley Coll. *Career:* editorial asst, Atheneum Publrs, New York 1967–68; freelance writer 1968–; Lecturer, St Michael's Coll., Winooski, Vt 1980–81; Prof., East Tennessee State Univ. 1999–2000. *Publications:* Kinflicks 1975, Original Sins 1980, Other Women 1984, Bedrock 1990, Birdman and the Dancer 1993, Five Minutes in Heaven 1995, Kinfolks 2007, Washed in the Blood 2011; contrib. to periodicals. *Honours:* Basler Chair, East Tennessee State Univ. *Literary Agent:* c/o Martha Kaplan Agency, 115 West 29th Street, New York, NY 10001, USA. *E-mail:* kaplanagency@sprynet.com (office). *E-mail:* lisaalther@lisaalther.com (office). *Website:* www.lisaalther.com.

ALTON, Roger Martin; British journalist; *Executive Editor, The Times*; b. 20 Dec. 1947, Oxford; s. of the late Reggie Alton and Jeanine Alton; m. (divorced); one d. *Education:* Clifton Coll., Exeter Coll., Oxford. *Career:* grad. trainee, Liverpool Post, then Gen. Reporter and Deputy Features Ed. 1969–74; Sub-Ed. News The Guardian 1974–76, Chief Sub-Ed. News 1976–81, Deputy Sports Ed. 1981–85, Arts Ed. 1985–90, Weekend Magazine Ed. 1990–93, Features Ed. 1993–96, Asst Ed. 1996–98, Ed. The Observer 1998–2007, The Independent 2008–10; Exec. Ed. The Times 2010–. *Honours:* Editor of the Year, What the Papers Say Awards 2000, GQ Editor of the Year 2005. *Address:* The Times, 1 Pennington Street, London E98 1TT, England (office). *Telephone:* (20) 7782-5000 (office). *Fax:* (20) 7782-5046 (office). *Website:* www.timesonline.co.uk (office).

ALUNAN, Merlie M., MA; Philippine poet; b. 1943. *Education:* Univ. of the Visayas, Cebu City, Silliman Univ. Grad. School. *Career:* Prof. of Literature and Communication Tacloban Coll., Univ. of the Philippines in the Visayas, also involved in creative writing workshops; Writing Fellow, Silliman Univ. *Publications include:* Mater Dolorosa in Two Voices (poems) (First Prize English of Home Life poetry competition), Fern Garden: Anthology of Women Writing in the South, Hearthstone, Sacred Tree (poems) 1993, Kabilin: 100 Years of Negros Oriental (non-fiction) 1993, Amina Among Angels (poems) 1997, Tales of the Spiderwoman (poems) (Palanca Award 2010). *Honours:* Palanca, Free Press, Home Life UMPIL Gawad Alagad ni Balagtas, Chancellor's Award for Excellence in Creative Work, Lillian Jerome Thornton Award for Nonfiction, Likhaan Workshop Award. *Address:* c/o University of the Philippines in the Visayas, Miagao, Iloilo 5023-A, Philippines. *Website:* merliealunan.blogspot.com.

ALVAREZ, Alfred (Al), BA, MA; British poet and writer; b. 5 Aug. 1929, London, England; m. 1966; two s. one d. *Education:* Oundle School, Corpus Christi Coll., Oxford. *Career:* poetry critic and Ed., Observer 1956–66; Advisory Ed., Penguin Modern European Poets 1964–76. *Publications include:* The Shaping Spirit 1958, The School of Donne 1961, The New Poetry 1962, Under Pressure 1965, Beyond All This Fiddle 1968, Lost 1968, Penguin Modern Poets No. 18 1970, Apparition 1971, The Savage God 1971, Beckett 1973, Hers 1974, Autumn to Autumn and Selected Poems 1978, Hunt 1978, Life After Marriage 1982, The Biggest Game in Town 1983, Offshore 1986, Feeding the Rat 1988, Rain Forest 1988, Day of Atonement 1991, Faber Book of Modern European Poetry 1992, Night 1995, Where Did It All Go Right? 1999, Poker: Bets, Bluffs and Bad Beats 2001, New and Selected Poems 2002, The Writer's Voice 2005, Risky Business 2007; contrib. to numerous magazines and journals. *Honours:* Hon. DLitt (Univ. of East London) 1998, Hon. Fellow, Corpus Christi Coll., Oxford 2001; Vachel Lindsay Prize for Poetry 1961, A.C. Benson Medal 2009. *Literary Agent:* c/o Aitken Alexander Associates Ltd, 18–21 Cavaye Place, London, SW10 9PT, England. *Telephone:* (20) 7373-8672. *Fax:* (20) 7373-6002. *E-mail:* reception@aitkenalexander.co.uk. *Website:* www.aitkenalexander.co.uk.

ALVAREZ, Julia, MA; American writer, poet and academic; b. 27 March 1950, Dominican Republic; m. Bill Eichner 1989. *Education:* Connecticut Coll., Middlebury Coll., Syracuse Univ., Bread Loaf School of English. *Career:* Visiting Asst Prof. of Creative Writing, Univ. of Vermont 1981–83; Jenny McKean Moore Visiting Writer, George Washington Univ. 1984–85; Asst Prof. of English, Univ. of Illinois 1985–88; Asst Prof. of English, Middlebury Coll. 1988–91, Assoc. Prof. 1991–93, Prof. 1993–96, Writer-in-Residence 1996–; council mem. PEN American Center 1997–99. *Publications:* fiction: How the García Girls Lost Their Accents 1991 (one of NY Librarians' 21 classics for the 21st Century 1999), In the Time of the Butterflies 1994, !Yo! 1997, Something to Declare 1988, In the Name of Salomé 2000, The Secret Footprints (for children) 2000, How Tía Lola Came to Visit Stay (for children, Child Magazine Best Children's Book) 2001, A Cafecito Story (Nebraska Book Award for Fiction 2002) 2001, Before We Were Free (for children, Americas Award for Young Adult Literature 2002, Miami Herald best book of the year 2002, American Library Asscn Pura Belpre Award 2003) 2002, finding miracles (for young adults) 2004, A Gift of Gracias: The Legend of Altagracia (for children) 2005, Saving the World 2006, Return to Sender 2009; non-fiction: Something to Declare 1998, Once Upon a Quinceañera: Coming of Age in the USA 2007; poetry: Old Age Ain't for Sissies (ed.) 1979, The Housekeeping Book 1984, Homecoming 1984, The Other Side/El otro lado 1995, Seven Trees 1998, The Woman I Kept to Myself 2004; contributions: many anthologies and periodicals. *Honours:* Hon. DHumLitt (CUNY) 1996, Hon. DLit (Union Coll., Schenectady NY) 2004; La Reina Press Poetry Award 1982, Robert Frost Poetry Fellowship, Bread Loaf Writers Conference 1986, National Endowment for the Arts Grant 1987–88, Ingram Merrill Foundation Grant 1990, American Library Asscn Notable Book Citation 1992, American Poetry Review Jessica Nobel-Maxwell Poetry Prize 1995, Latina Magazine's Woman of the Year 2000, Mexican Fine Arts Museum Sor Juana Award (USA), Hispanic Heritage Award in Literature (USA) 2002. *Literary Agent:* Susan Bergholz Literary Services, 17 West 10th Street, No. 5B, New York, NY 10011, USA. *Telephone:* (212) 387-0545. *Fax:* (212) 387-0546. *Website:* www.juliaalvarez.com.

ALVES, Miriam, BA; Brazilian writer, poet and literary critic; b. 1952, São Paulo. *Career:* assoc. with Quilombhoge black writers group, which edits Cadernos negros anthology 1983–; employed as social worker. *Publications include:* Momentos de Busca (poems) 1983, Estrelas no dedo (poems) 1985, Terramar (play), Enfim... Nos (ed, trans. as Finally... Us: Contemporary Black Brazilian Women Writers) 1995, Women Righting/Mulheres escrevendo 2005; contrib. to numerous collections of poetry and critical essays. *Address:* c/o Mango Publishing, PO Box 13378, London, SE27 0ZN, England.

ALVI, Moniza; British poet; b. 2 Feb. 1954, Lahore, Pakistan. *Education:* Univs of York and London. *Career:* school teacher; tutor at Open Coll. of the Arts and the Poetry School, London. *Publications include:* poetry: Peacock Luggage (with Peter Daniels) 1992, The Country at My Shoulder 1993, A Bowl of Warm Air 1996, Carrying My Wife 2000, Souls 2002, How the Stone Found its Voice 2005, Split World: Poems 1990–2005 2008, Europa 2008; contrib. to A Dragonfly in the Sun: An Anthology of Pakistani Writing in English 1998, The Poetry Quartets: 6 2000. *Honours:* The Poetry Business Prize 1991, Cholmondeley Award 2002. *Address:* c/o Bloodaxe Books Ltd, Highgreen, Tarset, Northumberland, NE48 1RP, England. *Website:* www.bloodaxebooks.com.

AMABILE, George, BA, MA, PhD; Canadian academic, poet and writer; b. 29 May 1936, Jersey City, NJ, USA. *Education:* Amherst Coll., Univ. of Minnesota, Univ. of Connecticut. *Career:* Lecturer, Univ. of Manitoba 1963, Asst Prof. 1966–68, 1969–71, Assoc. Prof. 1972–86, Prof. of English 1987–97; Visiting Writer-in-Residence, Univ. of British Columbia 1968–69; Writer-in-Residence, Winnipeg Centennial Library 2000–01; various readings, Manitoba Theatre Centre, radio and TV; mem. League of Canadian Poets, Western Canadian Publrs' Asscn. *Publications include:* Blood Ties 1972, Open Country 1976, Flower and Song 1977, Ideas of Shelter 1981, The Presence of Fire 1982, Four of a Kind 1994, Rumours of Paradise/Rumours of War 1995, Tasting the Dark: New and Selected Poems 2001; contribs: many anthologies, journals and periodicals. *Honours:* Canada Council Grants 1968, 1969, 1981, 1982, 1995, 1996, Canadian Authors' Asscn Nat. Prize for Poetry, 1983, Third Prize, CBC Nat. Literary Competition 1992. *Address:* 908 Merriam Boulevard, Winnipeg, MB R3T 0V2, Canada (home). *Telephone:* (204) 453-3107 (home). *E-mail:* gamabile@home.com.

AMADI, Capt. Elechi, BSc; Nigerian writer and fmr teacher and fmr army officer and government administrator; *Chairman, Rivers State Scholarships Board*; b. 12 May 1934, Aluu, Rivers State; s. of Chief Wonuchukwu Amadi and Enwere Amadi; m. 1st Dorah Nwonne Ohale 1957; m. 2nd Priye Iyalla 1991; four s. eight d. *Education:* Govt Coll. Umuahia, Survey School, Oyo,

Univ. Coll. Ibadan, Univ. of Pittsburgh, Brookings Inst., USA. *Career:* worked as land surveyor, East Regional Govt of Nigeria 1959–60; physics/maths teacher 1960–63; army officer (capt.) 1963–66, with 3rd Marine Commandos during civil war 1968–69, Officer with 14th Brigade, retd with rank of Capt.; Prin. Asa Grammar School 1967–68; Perm. Sec. Rivers State Govt 1973–83, Commr of Educ. 1987–88, of Lands and Housing 1989–90; Writer-in-Residence and Lecturer, Rivers State Coll. of Educ. 1984–85, Dean of Arts 1985–86, Head of Dept of Literature 1991–93; Founder and Dir Elechi Amadi School of Creative Writing 1997–; Chair. Asscn of Nigerian Authors (Rivers State Br.); Fellow, Nigerian Acad. of Educ. 2003–; Chair. Rivers State Scholarships Bd 2008–. *Publications:* novels: The Concubine 1966, The Great Ponds 1969, The Slave 1977, Estrangement 1987; plays: Isiburu 1973, Peppersoup 1977, The Road to Ibadan 1977, Dancer of Johannesburg 1977, The Woman of Calabar 2002; Sunset in Biafra (war diary) 1973; Ethics in Nigerian Culture (philosophy) 1982; Speaking and Singing (essays and poems) 2003. *Honours:* mem. Order of Fed. Repub. (Nigeria) 2003; Hon. DSc (Rivers State Univ. of Science and Tech.) 2003;. *Address:* PO Box 331, Port Harcourt, Rivers State, Nigeria (home). *Telephone:* (803) 339-8036 (home). *E-mail:* info@elechiamadi.org (office); amadielechi@yahoo.com (home). *Website:* www.elechiamadi.org.

AMADIUME, Ifi, PhD; Nigerian poet, ethnographer and essayist; *Professor of Religion, Dartmouth College*; b. 23 April 1947, Kaduna. *Education:* School of Oriental and African Studies, Univ. of London, UK. *Career:* moved to UK in 1971; fmr Ed. Pan-African Liberation Platform journal; taught African Studies, Univ. of Nigeria, SOAS; moved to USA 1993; Assoc. Prof. of Religion and African Studies, Dartmouth Coll. 1993–2000, Chair. African and African-American Studies program, Prof. of Religion 2000–; mem. Advisory Bd Centre for Democracy and Devt. *Publications include:* non-fiction: Male Daughters, Female Husbands: Gender and Sex in an African Society 1987, African Matriarchal Foundations: The Igbo Case 1987, Reinventing Africa: Matriarchy, Religion and Culture 1997, Daughters of the Goddess, Daughters of Imperialism 2000, The Politics of Memory: Truth, Healing and Social Justice (co-ed. with Abdullahi An Na'im) 2000, Black Womanhood: Images, Icons, and Ideologies of the African Body (co-author) 2008; poetry: Passion Waves 1985, Ecstasy 1995, Circle of Love 2006, Voice Draped in Black 2007. *Address:* Department of Religion, Dartmouth College, 6036 Thornton Hall, Hanover, NH 03755, USA (office). *E-mail:* religion@dartmouth.edu (office). *Website:* www.dartmouth.edu/~religion (office).

AMAL, Nukila; Indonesian novelist; b. Dec. 1971, Ternate, North Maluku. *Education:* Bandung Tourism Acad. *Career:* participated in Int. Writers Program, Univ. of Iowa, USA 2006; Visiting Writer, Int. Writers Workshop, Hong Kong Baptist Univ. 2007; mem. Literature Cttee, Jakarta Arts Council. *Publications include:* novel: Cala Ibi 2003; short stories: Laluba 2005; Tahun-tahun yang menentukan: Babullah Datu Syah menamatkan kehadiran Portugis di Maluku (co-author); contrib. to Kalam. *Literary Agent:* c/o Pena Gaia Klasik, Jakarta, Indonesia. *Address:* c/o Metropoli d'Asia P.le Principessa, Clotilde n. 6, 20121 Milan, Italy.

AMANN, Jürg, PhD; Swiss writer and dramatist; b. 2 July 1947, Winterthur. *Education:* Univs of Zürich and Berlin. *Career:* mem. Authors of Switzerland AdS, PEN. *Theatre includes:* Das Fenster, Zürich 1975, Das Ende von Venedig, Zürich 1976, Der Traum des Seiltänzers vom freien Fall, Zürich 1978, Die Korrektur, Zürich 1980, Die deutsche Nacht, St Gallen 1982, Nachgerufen, Regensburg 1984, Cologne 1995, Büchners Lenz, Staatstheater Darmstadt 1984, ÖE Vienna 1991, Gruppe 80 Vienna 2002, Ach, diese Wege sind sehr dunkel, Staatstheater Karlsruhe 1985, SE Zürich 1985, Zürich 1993, Memmingen, Graz, Stuttgart, Vienna, Bremen, Bonn, Innsbruck, Würzburg, Krefeld etc, Der Rücktritt, Schauspielhaus, Zürich 1989, Nach dem Fest, Theater Forum Stadtpark, Graz 1989, IE Teatro Due, Rome 1992, SE Zürich 1995, Zweite Liebe, Basel 1992, Liebe Frau Mermet, Ensemble Theatre, Berlin 1992, SE Zürich 1992, Jugend ohne Gott (after Horvath), Neumarkt Theater, Zürich 1993, Staatstheater Braunschweig 1994, Ich bin nicht Ihre Luise (after Nachgerufen), Theater am Sachsenring, Cologne 1995, Sit well, Edith, Zürich 1996, ÖE Vienna 1997, Ach, diese Wege sind sehr dunkel (opera, music by Roger Matscheizik), Badisches Staatstheater, Karlsruhe 1996, Reise zum Nordpol, Zürich 1997, Hotel, Sils-Maria 1997, Weil immer das Meer vor der Liebe ist. Elegie für und nach Hertha Kräftner, Vienna 2000, SE Zürich 2000, Synchronisation in Birkenwald (after Viktor E. Frankl), Odeon Theater, Vienna 2003. *Radio plays:* productions by Radio Bremen, Bayerischer Rundfunk, Südwestrundfunk, WDR, ORF, Radio DRS, RSI. *Publications include:* Das Symbol Kafka 1974, Hardenberg 1978, Verirren oder das plötzliche Schweigen des Robert Walser 1978, Die Kunst des wirkungsvollen Abgangs 1979, Die Baumschule 1982, Franz Kafka 1983, Nachgerufen 1983, Ach, diese Wege sind sehr dunkel 1985, Patagonien 1985, Robert Walser 1985, Fort 1987, Aus dem Hohen Lied 1987, Nach dem Fest 1988, Tod Weidigs 1989, Der Rücktritt 1989, Der Vater der Mutter und der Vater des Vaters 1990, Der Anfang der Angst 1991, Der Lauf der Zeit 1993, Zwei oder drei Dinge 1993, Über die Jahre 1994, Und über die Liebe wäre wieder zu sprechen 1994, Robert Walser 1995, Rondo 1996, Schöne Aussicht 1997, Iphigenie oder Operation Meereswind 1998, Ikarus 1998, Golomir 1999, Kafka 2000, Am Ufer des Flusses 2001, Kein Weg nach Rom 2001, Mutter töten 2003, Sternendrift 2003, Wind und Weh 2005, Pornographische Novelle 2005, Übermalungen, Überspitzungen: Van Gogh Variationen (with Urs Amann) 2005, Zimmer zum Hof 2006, Pekinger Passion 2008, Nichtsangst 2008, Die kalabrische Hochzeit 2009, Die Reise zum Horizont 2010, Das Märchen von der Welt 2010, Der Kommandant 2011, Die Briefe der Puppe 2011. *Honours:* Ingeborg Bachmann Prize 1982, Conrad Ferdinand Meyer Prize 1983, Schiller Foundation Award 1989, Art Prize of Winterthur 1989, int. awards for radio plays 1998 1999, 2000, Schiller Prize 2001, Floriana Prize 2004. *Address:* Haus zum Spiegel, Napfgasse, 3, 8001 Zürich, Switzerland (home). *Telephone:* (44) 252-43-23 (home). *Fax:* (44) 252-43-23 (home).

AMAT, Nuria, PhD; Spanish writer; b. 1950, Barcelona. *Career:* has lived in Colombia, Mexico, Germany, France and USA; fmr Prof. of Library Studies, Univ. of Barcelona. *Play:* Pat's Room 1997. *Publications include:* novels: El ladrón de libros 1988, Amor breve 1990, Monstruos 1991, Todos somos Kafka 1993, Viajar es muy difícil 1995, La intimidad 1997, El país del alma 1999, El siglo de las mujeres 2000, Reina de América (Premio Ciudad de Barcelona 2002) 2001, Deja que la vida llueva sobre mí 2008, Amor i guerra (Ramon Llull Award for Catalan Literature 2011); poetry: Pan de boda 1979, Amor infiel 2004, Poemas impuros 2008; non-fiction: De la información al saber 1990, El libro mudo 1994, Letra herida 1998, Juan Rulfo: El arte del silencio 2003, Escribir y callar 2010. *Address:* Editorial Lumen, Random House Mondadori, Travessera de Gràcia 47–49, 08021 Barcelona, Spain. *Website:* www.editoriallumen.com; www.nuriaamat.com.

AMATAYA, Zakariya; Thai author and poet; b. 25 May 1975, Bacho, Narathiwat. *Education:* Attarkiah Islamiah Inst., Islamic Coll. of Bangkok, Darul Uloom Nadwatul Ulama Coll., India, Mahidol Univ. *Career:* regular contrib. to newspapers and periodicals 2004–. *Publications:* Duay-Jit-Winyarn-Aun-Piemsook (Happy Soul), No Women in Poetry (South East Asian Write Award 2010) 2010. *Address:* c/o 1001 Nights Editions, 666 Charoen Nakorn, Bang lampu lang, Klongsan, Bangkok, 10600, Thailand (office). *E-mail:* 1001nightseditions@gmail.com (office). *Website:* www.1001nightseditions.wordpress.com (office).

AMBARTSUMOV, Yevgeniy Arshakovich, CandHistSc; Russian politician, social scientist, political analyst and journalist; *Professor, Universidad La Salle*; b. 19 Aug. 1929, Moscow; s. of Arshak Ambartsumov and Alexandra Vassilevskaia; m. Nina Ignatovskaia 1978; one s. *Education:* Moscow Inst. of Int. Relations. *Career:* with Novoye Vremya 1954–59, Problems of Peace and Socialism 1959–63; Sr Scientific Researcher, Inst. of World Econs and Int. Relations 1956–59, Head of Dept Inst. of World Int. Labour Movt 1966–69; Head of Dept, Inst. of Sociology 1969–73; Head of Dept of Politics, Inst. of Economics of World Socialist System (now Inst. of Int. Economic and Political Studies) 1973–90; Russian People's Deputy 1990–93; Chair. Foreign Affairs Cttee of Russian Supreme Soviet 1992–93; mem. State Duma (Parl.) 1993–94; mem. Presidential Council 1993–95; Amb. to Mexico, also accred to Belize 1994–99; Prof. Universidad La Salle, Mexico 1999–. *Publications include:* How Socialism Began: Russia under Lenin 1978, NEP: A Modern View 1988, Socialism: Past and Present (ed.) 1990. *Honours:* Order of Aguila Azteca con banda Mexico 1999. *Address:* Universidad La Salle, Benjamin Franklin 47, Col Condesa, Del. Cuauhtémoc, 06140 México, DF, Mexico. *Telephone:* (55) 26-14-40-79 (Mexico) (home); (495) 332-64-25 (Russia) (home). *Website:* www.ulsa.edu.mx.

AMBERT, Alba, BA, MEd, DEd; American writer and poet; b. 10 Oct. 1946, San Juan, PR; m. 1st Walter McCann 1984; one d.; m. 2nd Norman Smith. *Education:* Univ. of Puerto Rico, Harvard Univ. *Career:* bilingual teacher, Boston Public Schools 1975–80; Asst Prof. and Dir Bilingual Special Educ. Teacher Training Program, Univ. of Hartford 1980–84; Visiting Scientist, MIT 1984–85; Sr Research Scholar, Athens Coll., Greece 1985–93; Writer-in-Residence, Richmond, The American Int. Univ. in London 1993–2002; mem. Authors' Guild, Writers' Union. *Publications include:* fiction: Porque hay silencio 1989, A Perfect Silence (Carey McWilliams Award 1996) 1995, The Eighth Continent and Other Stories 1997, An Inclination of Mirrors 1997, The Passion of Maria Magdalena Stein 2004, The Seven Powers of Spiritual Evolution 2008, The Anarchist's Daughter 2009; poetry: Gotas sobre el columpio 1980, The Fifth Sun 1989, Habito tu nombre 1994, At Dawn We Start Again 1997, Alphabets of Seeds: Poems by Alba Ambert 2004; children's books: Thunder from the Earth 1997, Why the Wild Winds Blow 1997, Face to Sky 1998. *Honours:* Hon. DLit (Richmond, The American Int. Univ. in London) 2002; Ford Foundation Fellowship 1984, Inst. of Puerto Rican Literature Award 1989, Pres.'s Award, Massachusetts Asscn for Bilingual Educ. 1997. *Address:* c/o Mango Publishing, PO Box 13378, London, SE27 OZN, England.

AMBROSE, David Edwin, LLB; British playwright, screenwriter and writer; b. 21 Feb. 1943, Chorley, Lancs., England; m. Laurence Huguette Hammerli 1979. *Education:* Merton Coll., Oxford. *Career:* mem. Dramatists' Club, London. *Publications include:* fiction: Siege (play, Cambridge Theatre, London) 1972, The Man Who Turned into Himself 1993, Mother of God 1995, Hollywood Lies, Superstition 1997, Coincidence 2002, A Memory of Demons 2003; numerous TV plays and screenplays world-wide. *Honours:* Sitges Film Festival First Prize for Screenplay 1980. *Literary Agent:* c/o William Morris Agency (UK) Ltd, Centre Point, 103 New Oxford Street, London, WC1A 1DD, England. *Telephone:* (20) 7534-6800. *Fax:* (20) 7534-6900. *E-mail:* info@wma.com. *Website:* www.wma.com; www.davidambrose.com.

AMES, Jonathan; American writer; b. 23 March 1964. *Education:* Princeton Univ., Columbia Univ. *Career:* Visiting Faculty mem. Columbia Univ., The New School, Iowa Writers' Workshop; fmr columnist, New York Press. *Television includes:* Late Show with David Letterman 2003, Bored to Death 2009. *Publications include:* I Pass Like Night 1989, The Extra Man 1998, What's Not to Love?: The Adventures of a Mildly Perverted Young Writer

2000, My Less Than Secret Life 2002, Wake Up, Sir! 2004, Sexual Metamorphosis 2005, I Love you More than You Know 2006, The Alcoholic 2008, The Double Life is Twice as Good: Essays and Fiction 2009; contrib. to McSweeny's, boldtype. *Address:* c/o Scribner Publicity Department, Simon & Schuster Inc., 1230 Avenue of the Americas, New York, NY 10020, USA. *E-mail:* jonathanames3@aol.com (office). *Website:* www.jonathanames.com.

AMETTE, Jacques-Pierre, (Paul Clément); French novelist and playwright; b. 18 May 1943, Normandy. *Career:* French Corresp., New York Times, numerous French newspapers. *Plays include:* Les sables mouvants 1974, Le maître-nageur 1989, Les environs de Heilbronn 1989, La Waldstein 1991, Après nous 1991, Singe 1992, Le mal du pays 1992, Passions secrètes, crimes d'avril 1993, Appassionata 1993, La clarière 1997, Le Tableau de Poussin 2005. *Publications include:* novels: La congé 1965, Élisabeth Skerla 1966, Un voyage en province 1970, Les lumières de l'Antarctique 1973, La vie comme ça 1974, Bermuda 1977, La nuit tombante 1978, Jeunesse dans une ville normande 1981, Enquête d'hiver 1985, Confessions d'un enfant gâté 1986, L'après-midi 1987, La peau du monde 1992, L'adieu à la raison 1993, Stendhal: 3 juin 1819 1994, Province 1995, L'Homme du silence 1999, Jeunesse dans ville normande 2000, Ma vie, son oeuvre 2001, La maîtresse de Brecht (Prix Goncourt) 2003, Un été chez Voltaire 2007, Le lac d'or 2008; as Paul Clément: Exit 1981, Je tue à la campagne 1982. *Honours:* Prix Roger Nimier 1986, Prix CIC du Théâtre 1992, Prix Contre-point 1997. *E-mail:* amette@free.fr. *Website:* amette.free.fr.

AMICOLA, José, LèsL, PhD; Argentine academic and writer; *Professor, Universidad Nacional de la Plata;* b. 15 Feb. 1942, Buenos Aires. *Education:* Univ. de Buenos Aires, Univ. Göttingen, Germany. *Career:* Prof., Univ. Nacional de la Plata 1986–; mem. Instituto Int. de Literatura Iberoamericana, Univ. of Pittsburgh. *Publications include:* Sobre Cortázar 1969, Astrología y fascismo en la obra de Arlt 1984, Manuel Puig y la tela que atrapa al lector 1992, Dostoievski 1994, De la forma a la información 1997, Camp y postvanguardia 2000, Manuel Puig's El beso de la mujer araña (critical edn) 2002, Batalla de los géneros: Novela gótica versus novela de educación 2003, Autobiografía como Autofiguración 2007. *Honours:* Premio Banco Mercantil 1992. *Address:* Las Heras, 3794-11A, 1425 Buenos Aires, Argentina (home).

AMIEL, Barbara, Lady Black of Crossharbour, BA; Canadian/British journalist and writer; b. 4 Dec. 1940, Watford, Herts., England; d. of Harold Joffre Amiel and Vera Isserles Amiel (née Barnett); m. 1st Gary Smith 1959; m. 2nd George Jonas 1974 (divorced 1979); m. 3rd David Graham 1984 (divorced 1988); m. 4th Conrad Black (now Lord Black of Crossharbour) 1992. *Education:* North London Collegiate School and Univ. of Toronto. *Career:* family moved to Canada and settled in Hamilton, Ont. 1952; joined CBC as a typist, later script asst, story ed. and TV presenter; columnist, Maclean's 1976–2004, 2005–, The Times, UK 1986–90, The Sunday Times 1986–94, The Daily Telegraph 1994–2004; Ed. Toronto Sun 1983–85 (first female ed.), Assoc. Ed. 1985; Vice-Pres. Editorial, Hollinger International 1995, Dir 1996; fmr mem. Bd of Dirs The Spectator, Jerusalem Post, Saturday Night, Southam Inc., Hollinger Int. *Publications include:* By Person Unknown (co-author) (Mystery Writers of America Edgar Award for Best Non-Fiction 1978) 1977, Confessions (essays) (Canadian Periodical Publrs' Prize) 1980. *Honours:* Media Club of Canada Award 1976, Periodical Publrs' Asscn Award 1977, Mystery Writers of America Edgar Allan Poe Award 1978, British Press Award 1987, Women of Distinction, UK 1989. *Address:* c/o Maclean's, 1 Mount Pleasant Road, 11th Floor, Toronto, ON N4Y 2Y5, Canada. *Website:* www.macleans.ca.

AMIN, Haji Khalidah Adibah; Malaysian columnist, essayist and scriptwriter; b. 19 Feb. 1936, Johor Bahru, Johor. *Education:* Univ. of Malaya, Singapore. *Career:* columnist English daily newspaper 1970s; fmr Advisory Ed. Majalah Jelita. *Publications include:* As I Was Passing (essays, two vols) 1976, 1978, This End of the Rainbow (novel) 2006; contrib. to newspaper columns and magazine features. *Honours:* Asian Journalist of the Year 1979, Southeast Asia Writer Award 1983, Esso-Gapena Award 1991, NSW Literary Award 1996, Tun Razak Award 1998. *Address:* c/o Karisma Publications, No. 5, Jalan Pengeluaran U1/78, Glenmarie Industrial Park, 40150 Shah Alam, Selangor, Malaysia.

AMĪR, Daisy al-; Iraqi short story writer, poet and novelist; b. 1935, Alexandria, Egypt. *Education:* Baghdad Univ., Inst. for Fine Arts. *Career:* Dir Iraqi Cultural Centre, Beirut 1970–85; returned to Iraq in 1985–89; spent two years in USA; returned to Beirut 1991–. *Publications include:* short story collections: Al-Balad al-Ba'īd Alladhī Tuhibb (The Distant Land She Loves) 1964, Fī Dawwāmat al-Hubb wa-al-Karāhiya (The Vortex of Love and Hate) 1978, Ala La'ihat al-Intizar (trans. as The Waiting List: An Iraqi Woman's Tales of Alienation) 1988, Amaliyyat Tajmīl li-al-Zaman (Plastic Surgery for Time) 1997; other short stories: The Eyes in the Mirror, An Andalusian Tale. *Address:* c/o Modern Middle East Literature in Translation series, University of Texas Press, POB 7819, Austin, TX 78713-7819, USA.

AMIREDJIBI, Chabua; Georgian writer, editor and politician; b. (Mzechabuk I. Amiredjibi), 18 Nov. 1921, Tbilisi; s. of Irakli Amiredjibi and Maria Nakashidze; m. Tamar Djavakhishvili 1966; four s. (one deceased) two d. *Education:* Tbilisi State Univ., A. Pushkin Tbilisi Pedagogical Inst. *Career:* as student of Tbilisi State Univ. arrested for anti-Soviet activities 1944, sentenced to 25 years' imprisonment in Gulag, released 1959; Dir Advertising-Information Bureau Goskinoprokat 1965–70; Chief Ed. Kino anthology 1970–83; Dir Mematiane documentary film studio 1983–89; mem. Parl. 1992–96; Chair. Defence Fund of Georgia 1992–96; f. PEN Centre of Georgia, Pres. 1994–97, Hon. Chair. 1998–; Publr and Ed.-in-Chief Ganakhlebuli Iveria newspaper 1999–2003; mem. Writers' Union of Georgia 1964–; mem. editorial bds of several journals and newspapers. *Screenplay:* Data Tutashkhia 1979. *Publications:* Road (short stories) 1964, Tales for Children 1966, Data Tutashkhia (novel) 1973, Gora Mborgali (novel) 1994, King George the Excellent (novel) 2003, From the Thoughts 2007. *Honours:* Honoured Art Worker of Georgia 1987, Order of Honour 1994, Order of King Vakhtang Gorgasili (First Class) 2001; USSR State Prize 1979, Sh. Rustaveli Prize 1994. *Address:* 8/45 Tamarashvili Street, 0162 Tbilisi, Georgia (home). *E-mail:* kutsna@posta.ge (office).

AMIRSHAHI, Mahshid, MA; Iranian writer; b. 1940, Qazvin. *Education:* Univ. of Oxford, UK. *Career:* educated in UK, returned to Iran; self-exile after Islamic Revolution 1979–; Rockefeller Fellow in Middle Eastern Studies, Univ. of Michigan, USA 1990–91. *Publications include:* short stories: Kushehye Bonbast (The Blind Alley & Other Stories) 1966, Sar-e Bibi Khanom (Bibi Khanom's Starling & Other Stories) 1968, Badaz Ruz-e Akher (After the Last Day & Other Stories) 1969, Be-Sigheh-ye Avval Shakhas-e Mofrad (First Person Singular) 1970, An Anthology of Short Stories 1972, Tales of A Persian Teenage Girl (in trans.) 1995, Short Stories 1998, Persian Fables for Our Time 2010; novels: Dar Hazar (At Home) 1987, Dar Safar (Away) 1995, Mothers and Daughters quartet: Abbass Khan's Wedding 1998, Dadeh Good Omen 1999, Shahrbanoo's Honey Moon 2001, Reminiscences of Mehr-e-Olia 2010; other: Hezaar Bishe (miscellaneous, anthology of views, reviews and interviews in Persian, English and French) 2000. *E-mail:* mamirshahy@aol.com (office). *Website:* www.amirshahi.org.

AMIS, Martin Louis, BA; British writer; b. 25 Aug. 1949, Oxford; s. of the late Kingsley Amis and of Hilary Bardwell; m. 1st Antonia Phillips 1984 (divorced 1996); two s.; m. 2nd Isabel Fonseca 1998; two d. *Education:* Exeter Coll., Oxford. *Career:* Asst Ed., TLS 1971, Fiction and Poetry Ed. TLS 1974–75; Asst Literary Ed., New Statesman 1975–77, Literary Ed. 1977–79; special writer for The Observer newspaper 1980–; Prof., Centre for New Writing, Univ. of Manchester 2007–. *Publications:* fiction: The Rachel Papers (Somerset Maugham Award 1974) 1973, Dead Babies 1975, new edn as Dark Secrets 1977, Success 1978, Other People: A Mystery Story 1981, Money: A Suicide Note 1984, Einstein's Monsters (short stories) 1987, London Fields 1989, Time's Arrow, or, the Nature of the Offence 1991, God's Dice 1995, The Information 1995, Night Train 1997, Heavy Water and Other Stories 1999, Yellow Dog 2003, The Last Days of Muhammad Atta (short stories, novella, essay) 2006, House of Meetings (novella) 2006, The Pregnant Widow 2010, Lionel Asbo 2012; non-fiction: My Oxford (with others) 1977, Invasion of the Space Invaders 1982, The Moronic Inferno and Other Visits to America 1986, Visiting Mrs Nabokov and Other Excursions 1993, Experience: A Memoir (James Tait Black Memorial Prize for Biography 2001) 2000, The War Against Cliché (essays and reviews 1971–2000) 2001, Koba the Dread: Laughter and Twenty Million 2002, The Second Plane 2008; contrib. to many publs. *Honours:* Galaxy Nat. Book Award for Outstanding Achievement 2010. *Literary Agent:* Wylie Agency (UK) Ltd, 17 Bedford Square, London, WC1B 3JA, England. *Telephone:* (20) 7908-5900 (office). *Fax:* (20) 7908-5901 (office). *E-mail:* mail@wylieagency.co.uk.

AMMANITI, Niccolò; Italian writer; b. 25 Sept. 1966, Rome. *Publications include:* La figlia di Siva (short story in La giungla sotto l'asfalto) 1993, Branchie! 1994, Nel nome del figlio (essays, with Massimo Ammaniti) 1995, Fango (short stories) 1996, Seratina (short story in Gioventù Cannibale, with Luisa Brancaccio) 1996, Alba tragica (short story in Tutti i denti del mostro sono perfetti) 1997, Anche il sole fa schifo 1997, Enchanted Music & Light Records (short story in Il fagiano Jonathan Livingstone, with Jaime D'Alessandro) 1998, Ti prendo e ti porto via 1999, L'amico di Jeffrey Dahmer è l'amico mio (short story in Italia odia) 2000, Io non ho paura 2001, Fa un po' male 2002, Sei il mio tesoro (short story in Crimini) 2005, Como Dio Comande (Premio Strega 2007) 2006, As God Commands (co-author) 2009. *Honours:* Viareggio-Repaci Prize. *Address:* c/o Einaudi, via Biancamano 2, 10121 Turin, Italy. *E-mail:* francesca@niccoloammaniti.com. *Website:* www.niccoloammaniti.com.

AMOR, Anne Clark, (Anne Clark), BA; British writer; b. 4 Feb. 1933, London, England; m. 1982; one s. one d. *Education:* Birkbeck Coll., London. *Career:* mem. Lewis Carroll Soc. (Founder-mem., Trustee 1969–, currently Pres.), Oscar Wilde Soc. (Cttee mem. 1993–). *Publications include:* Beasts and Bawdy 1975, Lewis Carroll: A Biography 1979, The Real Alice 1981, Mrs Oscar Wilde: A Woman of Some Importance 1983, William Holman Hunt: The True Pre-Raphaelite 1989, Lewis Carroll: Child of the North 1995, Wonderland Come True to Alice in Lyndhurst 1996, Charles Dodgson and Alice Liddell Go to Paris 1997; ed.: Letters to Skeffington Dodgson from His Father, The Carrollian; contribs to books, periodicals, including Washington Post, Los Angeles Times, The Lady, Literary Review, Books and Bookmen, The Wildean.

ANAGNOSTAKI, Loula, LLB; Greek playwright; b. Thessaloniki; m. Yiorgos Chimonas (divorced). *Education:* Aristotle Univ., Thessaloniki. *Career:* plays staged in Italy, France, London, New York and on Cyprus TV. *Plays include:* Staying Overnight (one-act play, Carolos Koun's Theatre Co. Art Theatre) 1965, The City (one-act play, Carolos Koun's Theatre Co. Art Theatre) 1965, The Parade (one-act play, Carolos Koun's Theatre Co. Art Theatre) 1965, Antonio e to menyma (Antonio or the Message) 1972, He Nike (The Victory)

1978, He Kaseta (The Cassette) 1982, Ho Ecos tou Hoplou (The Sound of the Gun) 1987, He Synanastrophe (The Gathering, Nat. Theatre of Greece) 1967, Diamantia kai Blues (Diamonds and Blues, Karezi-Kazakos theatre group) 1990, To Taxidi Makria (The Journey Far Away) 1995, The Sky is Scarlet (Contemporary Stage of the Nat. Theatre of Greece) 1998, To You Who Listen to Me (Theatre of Cyclades Street, Athens) 2003. *Address:* c/o Art Theatre Company, 25 Tzavela Street, 10681 Athens, Greece.

ANANTHAMURTHY, U. R., MA PhD; Indian academic and writer; b. 21 Dec. 1932, Melige, Karnataka. *Education:* Mysore Univ., Univ. of Birmingham, UK. *Career:* writer in Kannada; Prof. of English Literature, Mysore Univ. 1970–80; Vice-Chancellor, Mahatma Gandhi Univ., Kottayam 1987–91; Visiting Prof., Univ. of Iowa 1975, Shivaji Univ. 1982, Univ. of Tubingen, Germany 1992, Univ. of Pennsylvania 2000, Cornell Univ. 2001, Univ. of Hyderabad 2001; Ed. and Publr, Rujuvathu 1981; Chair. State Level Cttee on Drug Addiction, Kerala 1988, Review Cttee Indian Inst. of Advanced Study Shimla 1994, Nat. Book Trust 1992–93, Indian Inst. of Social Sciences 1998, Film Inst. of India, Pune 2002; Pres. Sahitya Akademi, Delhi 1993–98; Commonwealth Fellowship (to study in UK 1963–66, Homi Bhabha Fellowship 1972–74, Fellowship, Univ. of Iowa 1975. *Publications include:* novels: Samskara 1966, Bharatipura 1973, Awashte 1986, Bhava 1998, Divya 2001; short stories: Endendhigu Mugiyada Kathe 1955, Prashne 1962, Mouni 1967, Ghata Shradda, Aakaasha Mattu Bekku 1983, Mooru Dashakada Kategalu 1989, Suryana Kudure 1995, Aidu Dashakada Kathegalu 2001; several books of poetry and essays. *Honours:* Hon. DLitt, Kendriya uchcha Tibatti Shiksha Samsthanam, Varanasi 2002, Rabindra Bharati Univ., Calcutta Univ. 1995; Poorna Krishna Rao Gold Medal for Highest Rank in MA 1956, Best Story Award—Samskara, Ghatashradda, Bara, Karnataka Film Devt Corpn 1970, 1978, 1989, Fiction Award, Karnataka Sahitya Akademi 1983, Award for Literary Distinction, Govt of Karnataka 1984, Award for Literary Achievement, Karnataka Sahitya Akademi 1984, Rajyothsava Award 1984, Samaj Bhushan Award 1988, Harmony Award 1990, Bharatiya Jnanpith 1994, Masti Award 1994, Padma Bhushan 1998, Bapureddi Puraskaram, Hyderabad 2001, Ganakrishti Award 2002, Keladi Shivappa Nayaka Prashasti, Village Keladi 2002. *Address:* c/o Arvind Kumar Publishers, C1-324, Palam Villas, Palam Vihar, Gurgaon 122 017, India (office). *Telephone:* (124) 4256103 (office). *Fax:* (124) 4256103 (office). *E-mail:* arvind@arvindkumarpublishers.com (office). *Website:* www.arvindkumarpublishers.com (office); www.urananthamurthy.com.

ANAYA, Rudolfo, MA; American academic and author; *Professor Emeritus, University of New Mexico*; b. 30 Oct. 1937, Pastura, NM; s. of Martin Anaya and Rafaelita Mares; m. Patricia Lawless 1966. *Education:* Albuquerque High School, Browning Business School, Univ. of New Mexico. *Career:* teacher, Albuquerque public schools 1963–70; Dir Counseling Center, Univ. of Albuquerque 1971–73; Lecturer, Univ. Anahuac, Mexico City 1974; Prof., Dept of Language and Literature, Univ. of New Mexico 1974–93, Prof. Emer. 1993–; Founder, Ed. Blue Mesa Review 1989–93; Martin Luther King, Jr/César Chávez, Rosa Parks Visiting Prof., Univ. of Michigan, Ann Arbor 1996; currently Assoc. Ed. The American Book Review; Bd Contributing Ed. The Americas Review; Advisory Ed. Great Plains Quarterly; f. PEN-NM, Teachers of English and Chicano Language Arts 1991; Founder, Pres. NM Rio Grande Writers Asscn; mem. Bd Before Columbus Foundation; mem. Nat. Asscn of Chicano Studies. *Plays:* Billy the Kid, Who Killed Don José?, Matachines, Angie, Ay, Compadre, The Farolitos of Christmas, Bless Me, Ultima 2009. *Publications include:* Bless Me, Ultima 1972 (Premio Quinto Sol Award 1971), Heart of Aztlan 1976, Tortuga 1979 (American Book Award, Before Columbus Foundation 1979), Cuentos: Tales from the Hispanic Southwest (trans.) 1980, The Silence of the Llano (short stories) 1982, The Legend of La Llorona 1984, The Adventures of Juan Chicaspatas (poem) 1985, A Chicano in China 1986, Lord of the Dawn, The Legend of Quetzalcoatl 1987, Alburquerque 1992 (PEN-WEST Fiction Award 1993), The Anaya Reader (anthology) 1994, Zia Summer 1995, The Farolitos of Christmas (children's fiction) 1995, Jalamanta, A Message from the Desert 1996, Rio Grande Fall 1996, Maya's Children (children's fiction) 1997, Descansos: An Interrupted Journey (with Estevan Arellano and Denise Chávez) 1997, Isis in the Heart 1998, Shaman Winter 1999, Farolitos for Abuelo (children's fiction) 1999, My Land Sings 1999, Roadrunner's Dance 2000, Elegy for Cesar Chavez 2000, The Santero's Miracle (children's fiction) 2004, Serafina's Stories 2004, Jemez Spring 2005, The Man who Could Fly and other stories 2006, ChupaCabra and the Roswell UFO (children's fiction) 2008; short stories in literary magazines in USA and internationally; has also edited various collections of short stories. *Honours:* Hon. DHumLitt (Albuquerque) 1981, (Marycrest Coll.) 1984, (New England) 1992, (Calif. Lutheran Univ.) 1994, (New Hampshire) 1997; Hon. PhD (Santa Fe) 1991; Hon. DLitt (New Hampshire) 1996; recipient of numerous awards, including Nat. Endowment for the Arts Fellowship 1980, NM Gov.'s Award for Excellence and Achievement in Literature 1980, W.K. Kellogg Foundation Fellowship 1983–86, New Mexico Eminent Scholar Award 1989, Rockefeller Foundation Residency Bellagio, Italy 1991, Excellence in the Humanities Award, New Mexico Endowment for the Humanities 1995, Tomás Rivera Mexican American Children's Book Awards 1995, 2000, Distinguished Achievement Award, Western Literature Asscn 1997, Ariz. Adult Authors Award, Arizona Library Asscn 2000, Wallace Stegner Award Center of the American West 2001, Nat. Medal of Arts 2001, Nat. Asscn of Chicano/Chicana Studies Scholar 2002. *Address:* 5324 Cañada Vista NW, Albuquerque, NM 87120-2412, USA (home). *Fax:* (505) 899-0014 (home).

ANDAHAZI, Federico, BSc; Argentine writer; b. 6 June 1963, Buenos Aires; s. of Bela Andahazi and Juana Merlín; pnr Aída Pippo; one s. one d. *Education:* Univ. de Buenos Aires. *Career:* fmr psychoanalyst. *Publications include:* short stories: Por encargo (CAMED Prize) 1995, Almas misericordias (First Prize, Segunda Bienal de Arte Joven de Buenos Aires) 1996, El sueño de los justos (Concurso Anual Literario Desde la Gente) 1996, La trilliza 1996; novels: El anatomista (Premio de la Fundación Amalia Lacrozede Fortabat) 1997, Las piadosas 1998, El príncipe 2000, El secreto de los flamencos 2002, Errante en la sombra 2004, La ciudad de los herejes 2005, El conquistador 2006; non-fiction: Pecar como Dios manda, Historia sexual de los argentinos 2008, Argentina con Pecado Concebida 2009. *Honours:* Premio Fortabat 1996, Premio Buenos Artes Joven 1996, Premio Concurso Anual Literario Desde la Gente 1996, Premio Planeta Argentina 2006. *Literary Agent:* Guillermo Schavelzon y Asociados, Muntaner, 339-5°, 08021 Barcelona, Spain. *Telephone:* (93) 011310. *Fax:* (93) 2003886. *E-mail:* info@schavelzon.com. *Website:* www.schavelzon.com. *Address:* CP 1430, Washington 1816, Buenos Aires, Argentina (office). *E-mail:* federico.andahazi@gmail.com. *Website:* www.andahazi.com.

ANDERKA, Johanna; German writer; b. 12 Jan. 1933, Mährisch-Ostrau, Czechoslovakia; d. of Leo Anderka and Margarete Anderka (née Kutschera). *Education:* Volksschule and Lyzeum, Mährisch-Ostrau and other towns in E and W Germany and Handelsschule, Flensburg. *Career:* office and admin. work 1950–. *Publications include:* Ergebnis eines Tages 1977, Herr, halte meine Hände 1979, Heilige Zeit 1981, Über die Freude 1983, Zweierlei Dinge 1983, Für L 1986, Blaue Wolke meiner Träume 1987, Ich werfe meine Fragen aus 1989, Sprachlos mein Schrei 1991, Nachtstadt 1992, Gegen die Fermdheit gesprochen 1994, Vertauschte Gezeiten 1995, Ausgefahren d. Brucken 1997, Bewahrte Landschaft 1999, Silbenhaus 2000, Zugeteilte Zeit 2003, Namen geben den Zeichen 2007; radio plays: Der Mann im Lift 1983, Beginn einer Freundschaft 1984; numerous publs in anthologies and literary journals. *Honours:* Kulturpreis für Schrifttum, Sudetendeutsche Landsmannschaft 1988, Hafizpreis Prosa 1988, prize in GEDOK Rhein-Main-Taunus Prose competition 1990, Nikolaus-Lenau-Preis, Künstlergilde Esslingen 1991, Ehrengabe zum Andreas-Gryphius-Preis, Lyrische Gesamtwerk 1992, Inge-Czernik-Förderpreis für Lyrik 1995, A. Launhardt Lyrikpreis 1998. *Address:* Tannenäcker 52, 89079 Ulm, Germany (home). *Telephone:* (731) 42112 (home).

ANDERSEN, Benny Allan; Danish writer, poet and composer; b. 7 Nov. 1929, Copenhagen; m. 2nd Elisabeth Ehmer 2004. *Career:* began as young person writing poems, later songs and compositions, has produced works for film, theatre and TV; still active, tours with artists including Danish singer Povl Dissing; recently visited Barbados where he wrote collection of poems; mem. numerous Danish orgs. *Recordings include:* Svantes Viser, Rosalina sangene repræsenteret i den danske højskolebog, Adskillige indspilninger på. *Publications include:* Den Musikalske ål 1960, Kamera med Køkkenadgang 1962, Den indre bowlerhat 1964, Puderne (short stories) 1965, Portrætgalleri 1966, Tykke-Olsen m. fl. (short stories) 1968, Det Sidste Øh 1969, Her i reservatet 1971, Man burde burde 1971, Svantes viser 1972, Personlige papirer 1974, Under begge øjne 1978, Himmelspræt – eller Kunsten at komme til Verden 1979, Tiden og Storken 1985, Andre Sider 1987, Chagall og skorpiondans 1991, Denne Kommen og Gåen 1993, Verdensborger i Danmark 1995, Verden udenfor Syltetøjsglasset 1996, Samlede digte 1960–1996 (poems) 1998, Sjælen marineret 2001, Spredte digte 2005, Kram 2009. *Honours:* decorated by Queen Margrethe II; Louisiana-Prisen 1964, Tildelt Carl Møllers Humoristlegat 1965, Arbejdernes Fællesorganisations Kulturpris 1965, Kritiker-Prisen 1966, Ministeriet for Kulturelle Anliggenders Forfatterpris for børne- og ungdomsbøger 1971, H.C. Andersen Legatet 1974, Boghandlernes Ærespris De Gyldne Laurbær 1975, Otto Rungs Forfatterlegat 1975, IFPIs Jubilæumspris 1980, Aarestrup Medaljen 1984, PH-Fondens Fødselsdagspris 1984, Modersmål-Selskabets Pris 1985, LOs Kulturpris 1985, Ejner Hansen Fondens Hæderspris 1985, Henri Nathansens Mindelagt 1989, BMFs Børnebogspris 1989, Kunst og Kulturhøjskolens Kulturpris 1990, Hovedstadens Oplysningsforbunds Pris 1990, Den Folkelige Sangs Pris 1991, Morten Nielsens Mindelegat 1992, Weekendavisens Litteraturpris 1994, Niels-Prisen af Niels Matthiasens Mindefond 1995, Værkets Kulturpris 1995, Dansk Forfatterforenings Jubilæumslegat 1995, Hartmann-Prisen 1996, Landsforeningen af Danske Flygtningevenners Pris 1997, Dansk AFS Interkulturpris 1998, Nordisk Populærautorunions Pris 1999, Den Gyldne Grundtvig 2000, Foreningen Nordens Hæderspris 2001, Holberg-Medaljen 2001, Blicher-prisen 2003, Krebs Skoles Pris 2004, Lumbye Prisen 2004, Poul Sørensen og fru Susanne Sørensens legat 2004, Hammerich Prisen 2006, Jens August Schade Prisen 2010, Berlingske Fonds Hæderspris 2011, Bibliotekernes Pris 2011. *Address:* Nybrovej 401 A, 2800 Kgs. Lyngby, Denmark (office). *Telephone:* 75-81-58-65 (office). *E-mail:* bobenon@maiol.dk (office). *Literary Agent:* c/o Borgens Forlag, Valbygårdsvej 33, 2500 Valby, Denmark. *E-mail:* post@borgen.dk (office). *Website:* www.borgen.dk (office).

ANDERSON, Annelise Graebner, PhD; American economist; *Senior Research Fellow, Hoover Institute on War, Revolution and Peace, Stanford University*; b. 19 Nov. 1938, Oklahoma City, Okla; d. of Ellmer Graebner and Dorothy Graebner (née Zilisch); m. Martin Anderson 1965. *Education:* Wellesley Coll., Mass and Columbia Univ., New York. *Career:* Assoc. Ed., McKinsey and Co. Inc. 1963–65; researcher, Nixon Campaign Staff 1968–69; Project Man., Dept of Justice 1970–71; Asst Prof. of Business Admin, then Assoc. Prof., Calif. State Univ. at Hayward 1975–80; Sr Policy Advisor,

Reagan Presidential Campaign and Transition, Washington, DC 1980; Assoc. Dir of Econs and Govt, Office of Man. and Budget, Washington, DC 1981–83; adviser on econ. reform to govts of Russia, Romania, and Repub. of Georgia; Sr Research Fellow, Hoover Inst. on War, Revolution and Peace, Stanford Univ., CA 1983–, Assoc. Dir 1989–90; mem. Bd Overseers RAND/UCLA Center for Soviet Studies 1987–91; fmr mem. Advisory Bd RAND Center for the Study of Immigration Policy, Gov. Wilson's Council of Econ. Advisers, Gov.'s Task Force on California Tax Reform and Reduction; mem. Nat. Science Bd 1985–90. *Publications include:* The Business of Organized Crime: A Cosa Nostra Family 1979, Illegal Aliens and Employer Sanctions: Solving the Wrong Problem 1986, Thinking About America: The United States in the 1990s (co-ed.) 1988, Political Money: Deregulating American Politics 2000, Reagan, In His Own Hand: The Writings of Ronald Reagan That Reveal His Revolutionary Vision for America (co-ed.) 2001, Free BSD: An Open Source Operating System for Your Personal Computer 2001, Reagan: A Life in Letters (co-ed.) 2003, Reagan's Path to Victory (co-ed.) 2004, Stories in His Own Hand: The Everyday Wisdom of Ronald Reagan (co-ed.) 2007, Reagan's Secret War: The Untold Story of His Fight to Save the World from Nuclear Disaster (co-author) 2010; numerous contribs to professional journals. *Address:* Stanford University, Hoover Institution on War, Revolution and Peace, HHMB – Room 301, Stanford, CA 94305-6010, USA (office). *Telephone:* (650) 723-3139 (office). *E-mail:* andrsn@hoover.stanford.edu (office). *Website:* www.stanford.edu/~andrsn (office).

ANDERSON, Barbara, BSc, BA; New Zealand writer and dramatist; b. 14 April 1926; m. Neil Anderson; two s. *Education:* Univ. of Otago, Victoria Univ., Wellington. *Career:* mem. PEN New Zealand (Cttee mem. 1992–94). *Publications include:* Uncollected Short Stories 1985, I Think We Should Go into the Jungle (short stories) 1989, Girls High 1990, We Could Celebrate 1991, Portrait of the Artist's Wife 1992, All the Nice Girls 1993, The House Guest 1995, Proud Garments 1996, The Peacocks and Other Stories (aka Glorious Things) 1997, Beginnings (essay) 1998, Long Hot Summer 1999, The Swing Around 2002, Change of Heart 2003, Getting There 2008; several radio plays, short stories. *Honours:* Hon. DLit (Univ. of Otago) 2009; John Cowie Reid Memorial Award (play) 1986, Ansett/Sunday Star Short Story Award 1988, Timaru Herald/Aoraki Short Story Award 1990, Victoria Fellowship 1991, Goodman Fielder Wattie Award 1992, Scholarship of Letters 1994. *Literary Agent:* United Agents, 12–26 Lexington Street, London, W1F 0LE, England. *Telephone:* (20) 3214-0800. *Fax:* (20) 3214-0801. *E-mail:* info@unitedagents.co.uk. *Website:* unitedagents.co.uk. *Address:* 10 Pukeko Street, Woodlands, Waikanae 5036, New Zealand (home). *Telephone:* (4) 293-2939 (home). *E-mail:* b.and.n.anderson@gmail.com (home).

ANDERSON, Christopher (Chris), BEcons; Australian journalist; b. 9 Dec. 1944, s. of C. F. Anderson and L. A. Anderson; m. Gabriella Douglas 1969; one s. one d. *Education:* Picton High School, NSW, Univ. of Sydney, Columbia Univ., New York. *Career:* journalist and political commentator 1962–76; Deputy Ed., later Ed., The Sun-Herald 1976–79; Deputy Ed., later Ed., The Sydney Morning Herald 1980–83, Ed.-in-Chief 1983–88; Man. Dir and Group Ed. Dir John Fairfax Ltd 1987–90, Chief Exec. 1990–91; Man. Ed. Australian Broadcasting Corpn 1993–95; Chief Exec. TV New Zealand Ltd 1995–97; CEO Optus Communications 1997–2004; mem. Bd, Austrade 2004–07.

ANDERSON, David Daniel, BS, MA, PhD; American academic, writer and editor; b. 8 June 1924, Lorain, Ohio; m. Patricia Ann Rittenhour 1953. *Education:* Bowling Green State Univ., Michigan State Univ. *Career:* Distinguished Univ. Prof., Dept of American Thought and Language, Michigan State Univ., East Lansing 1957–93, Distinguished Prof. Emer. 1993–; Ed. Midwestern Miscellany Annual; Exec. Sec. Soc. for the Study of Midwestern Literature 1971–73. *Publications include:* Louis Bromfield 1964, Critical Studies in American Literature 1964, Sherwood Anderson 1967, Sherwood Anderson's Winesburg, Ohio 1967, Brand Whitlock 1968, The Black Experience (ed.-in-chief) 1969, Abraham Lincoln 1970, The Literary Works of Abraham Lincoln 1970, The Dark and Tangled Path (with R. Wright) 1971, Sunshine and Smoke 1971, Robert Ingersoll 1972, Mid-America I–XIV 1974–87, Sherwood Anderson: Dimensions of his Literary Art (essays) 1976, Woodrow Wilson 1978, Sherwood Anderson: The Writer at his Craft 1979, Ignatius Donnelly 1980, William Jennings Bryan 1981, Critical Essays on Sherwood Anderson 1981, Michigan: A State Anthology 1982, Route Two, Titus, Ohio 1993, The Path in the Shadow 1998, The Durability of Raintree County 1998, Ohio in Myth, Memory and Imagination 2004. *Honours:* Hon. DLitt (Wittenburg Univ.) 1989; Ohioana Career Award 2009. *Address:* c/o Department of American Thought and Language, Michigan State University, East Lansing, MI 48821, USA.

ANDERSON, Kevin James, (Gabriel Mesta), BS; American writer and editor; b. 27 March 1962, Racine, Wis.; m. 1st Mary Franco Nijhuis 1983 (divorced 1987); m. 2nd Rebecca Moesta 1991; one step-s. *Education:* Univ. of Wisconsin-Madison. *Career:* Tech. Writer-Ed., Lawrence Livermore Nat. Lab. 1983–96; columnist, Materials Research Soc. 1988–96; copy ed., Int. Soc. for Respiratory Protection 1989–95; mem. Science Fiction and Fantasy Writers of America, Horror Writers of America. *Publications include:* novels (author or co-author): Resurrection Inc 1988, Lifeline 1991, The Trinity Paradox 1991, Afterimage 1992, Assemblers of Infinity 1993, Climbing Olympus 1994, Ill Wind 1995, Blindfold 1995, Born of Elven Blood 1995, Virtual Destruction 1996, Ignition 1997, Fallout 1997, Hidden Empire 2002, Captain Nemo 2002 A Forest of Stars 2003, Horizon Storms 2004; X-Files series: Ground Zero 1995, Ruins 1996, War of the Worlds: Global Dispatches (anthology, ed.) 1996; Gamearth series: Gamearth 1989, Gameplay 1989, Game's End 1990; Star Wars series: Darksaber 1995, Dark Lords 1997, Delusions of Grandeur 1997, Diversity Alliance 1997, Jedi Bounty 1997; Star Wars: Jedi Academy trilogy: Jedi Search 1994, Dark Apprentice 1994, Champions of the Force 1994; Star Wars: Young Jedi Knights series: The Lost Ones 1995, Shadow Academy 1995, Heirs of the Force 1995, Darkest Knight 1996, Lightsabers 1996, Jedi under Siege 1996, Shards of Alderaan 1997; Star Wars anthologies (ed.): Star Wars: Tales from the Mos Eisley Cantina 1995, Star Wars: Tales from Jabba's Palace 1995, Star Wars: Tales of the Bounty Hunters 1996; Star Wars: Tales of the Jedi series: Dark Lords of the Sith 1996, Golden Age of Sith 1997; non-fiction: The Illustrated Star Wars Universe 1995, Star Wars: The Mos Eisley Cantina Pop-Up Book 1995, Star Wars: Jabba's Palace Pop-Up Book 1995; Dune series: Dune: House Atreides 1999, Dune: House Harkonnen 2000, Dune: House Corrino 2001, Dune: The Butterian Jihad 2002, Dune: The Machine Crusade 2003, Dune: The Battle of Corrin 2004, Hunters of Dune (with Brian Herbert) 2006, Sandworms of Dune 2007, Paul of Dune 2008, Winds of Dune 2009; contribs to anthologies and periodicals. *Honours:* Bram Stoker Award 1988. *Literary Agent:* c/o John Silbersack, Trident Media Group LLC, 41 Madison Avenue, New York, NY 10010, USA.

ANDERSON, Michael Falconer; British writer and journalist; b. 16 Jan. 1947, Aberdeen, Scotland; m. Hildegarde Becze 1970; two s. *Career:* newspaper and magazine ed.; chief sub-ed. of a nat. weekly; sub-ed. of a daily newspaper; showbusiness writer; reporter; corresp. in newspapers, TV and radio; mem. Soc. of Authors, Nat. Union of Journalists. *Publications include:* The Woodsmen 1986, Blood Rite 1986, The Unholy 1987, God of a Thousand Faces 1987, The Covenant 1988, Black Trinity 1989, The Clan of Golgotha Scalp 1990; numerous short stories and plays for radio and TV; contrib.: feature articles on subjects including travel, history, the environment and books, in newspapers and magazines world-wide.

ANDERSON, Rachel; British writer and dramatist; b. 18 March 1943, Hampton Court, Surrey, England; d. of Verily Anderson; m. David Bradby; four c. *Publications include:* Pineapple 1965, The Purple Heart Throbs: A Survey of Popular Romantic Fiction 1850–1972, 1974, Dream Lovers 1978, For the Love of Sang 1990; young children's fiction: Tim Walks 1985, The Cat's Tale 1985, Wild Goose Chase 1986, Jessy Runs Away 1988, Best Friends 1991, Jessy and the Long-Short Dress 1992, Tough as Old Boots 1991, Little Lost Fox 1992; older children's fiction: Moffatt's Road 1978, The Poacher's Son 1982, The War Orphan 1984, Little Angel Comes to Stay 1985, Renard the Fox (with David Bradby) 1986, Little Angel Bonjour 1988, French Lessons 1988, The Boy Who Laughed 1989, The Bus People 1989, Paper Faces 1991, When Mum Went to Work 1992, The Working Class 1993, Blackwater 1994, Ollie and the Trainers 1999, The Scavenger's Tale 2000, The War Orphan 2000, Moving Times Trilogy 1999–2000, Joe's Story 2001, The Flight of the Emu 2001, Paper Faces 2002, The Rattletrap Trip 2003, Pizza on Saturday 2004, Hugo and the Long Red Arm 2004, This Strange New Life 2006, Red Moon 2006, Warlands 2006, This Strange New Life 2006, The Poacher's Son 2006, Big Ben 2007, Stronger than Mountains 2009, Grandmother's Footsteps 2009, Bloom of Youth 2009. *Honours:* Medical Journalists' Asscn Award 1990, 25th Anniversary Guardian Children's Fiction Award 1992. *Literary Agent:* c/o Aitken Alexander Associates, 18–21 Cavaye Place, London, SW10 9PT, England. *Telephone:* (20) 7373-8672. *Fax:* (20) 7373-6002. *E-mail:* kate@aitkenalexander.co.uk. *Website:* www.aitkenalexander.co.uk.

ANDERSON, Robert David, MA, FSA; British conductor, writer and editor; b. 20 Aug. 1927, Shillong, Assam, India; s. of Robert David Anderson and Gladys Anderson (née Clayton). *Education:* Gonville and Caius Coll., Cambridge. *Career:* Asst Ed. Record News 1954–56; Asst Master and Dir of Music Gordonstoun School 1956–62; Conductor Moray Choral Union; Asst Conductor Spoleto Festival 1962; Conductor St Bartholomew's Hosp. Choral Soc. 1965–90; Extra-Mural Lecturer, Univ. of London 1966–77; Assoc. Ed. The Musical Times 1967–85; critic, The Times 1967–72; Visiting Lecturer, City Univ. 1983–92; Co-ordinating Ed. Elgar Complete Edition 1983–2003; mem. Egypt Exploration Soc. (Hon. Sec. 1971–82), Royal Musical Asscn. *Publications include:* Egyptian Antiquities in the British Museum III: Musical Instruments 1976, Wagner 1980, Egypt in 1800 (co-ed.) 1988, Wagner, in Heritage of Music III 1989, Elgar in Manuscript 1990, Elgar 1993, Music and Dance in Pharaonic Egypt in Civilisations of the Ancient Near East IV 1995, Elgar and Chivalry 2002, Baalbek, Heliopolis and Rome 2006. *Honours:* Hon. Prof. of History, State Univ. of Rostov-on-Don 2002; Hon. DMus (City Univ.) 1985, Hon. DHist (Russian State Univ. for Humanities, Moscow) 2000; Liveryman Worshipful Co. of Musicians 1977. *Address:* 54 Hornton Street, London, W8 4NT, England (home). *Telephone:* (20) 7937-5146 (home).

ANDERSON-DARGATZ, Gail, BA; Canadian writer and academic; *Adjunct Professor, University of British Columbia*; b. 14 Nov. 1963, Kamloops, BC. *Education:* Univ. of Victoria. *Career:* fmr reporter, Salmon Arm Observer; currently Adjunct Prof., Creative Writing Program, Univ. of British Columbia; mem. Canadian Writers' Union; lives on Manitoulin Island, Ont. *Publications include:* The Miss Hereford Stories 1994, The Cure for Death by Lightning (Betty Trask Prize) 1996, A Recipe for Bees 1999, A Rhinestone Button 2003, Turtle Valley 2007; contrib. to periodicals. *Literary Agent:* c/o Westwood Creative Artists, 94 Harbord Street, Toronto, ON M5S 1G6, Canada. *E-mail:* jackie@wcaltd.com. *Website:* www.wcaltd.com; www.gailanderson-dargatz.ca.

ANDERSSON, Claes, DMed; Finnish politician, psychiatrist, writer and poet; b. 30 May 1937, Helsinki; s. of Oscar Andersson and Ethel Hjelt; m. Katriina

Kuusi 1970; six c. *Career:* novelist and poet 1974–; mem. Parl. 1987–99, 2007–08; Minister, Ministry of Educ. 1995–98; fmrly mem. Finnish People's Democratic League 1970–90, mem. Left-Wing Alliance 1990–, Chair. 1990; Chair. Finland's Swedish Union of Writers; Vice-Pres. Information Centre of Finnish Literature 1985–. *Music:* album: Claes Andersson Trio: These Foolish Things - Jazz! 2011. *Publications include:* novels: Bakom bilderna 1972, Den fagraste vår 1976, En mänske börjar likna sin själ 1983, Mina tolv politiska år 2000, Har de sett öknen blomma? 2006, Ottos liv 2011; poetry: Ventil 1962, Som om ingenting hänt 1964, Staden heter Helsingfors 1965, Samhället vi dör i 1967, Det är inte lätt att vara villaägare i dessa tider 1969, Bli, tillsammans 1970, Rumskamrater 1974, Jag har mött dem 1976, Genom sprickorna i vårt ansikte 1977, Trädens sånger 1979, Tillkortakommanden 1981, Under 1984, Det som blev ord i mig 1987, Mina bästa dagar 1987, Som lyser mellan gallren 1989, Huden där den är som tunnasi 1991, Dikter från havets botten 1993, En lycklig mänska 1996, Dessa underbara stränder, förber glidande 2002, Mörkret regnar stjärnor 2002, Det är kallt, det brinner 2004, Tidens framfart 2005, Lust 2008, Mörkrets klarhet 2010, Oton elämä 2011; 20 stage plays and several radio plays and an opera libretto. *Honours:* Eino-Leino Prize 1985, five times recipient of State Prize of Literature, Bellmanpriset 2007.

ANDIIEVSKA, Emma; Ukrainian poet, writer and artist; b. 19 March 1931, Donetsk; m. Ivan Koshelivets (died 1999). *Career:* settled in Munich, Germany after World War II; exhibited her artistic work in USA, Canada, Australia, Brazil, Ukraine; mem. PEN, Ukrainian Acad. of Arts and Sciences (Germany). *Publications include:* Poeziia (poems) 1951, Podorozh (short stories) 1955, Narodzhennia idola (poems) 1958, Ryba i rozmir (poems) 1961, Kuty opostin' (poems) 1962, Tyhry (short stories) 1962, Dzhalapita (short stories) 1962, Roman pro dobru liudyny (novel) 1973, Roman pro liudske pryznachennia (novel) (Tatiana and Omelan Antonovych Award 1984) 1982, Kavarnia (poems) 1983, Vigilii (poems) 1987, Arkkhitekturni Ansambli 1989, Znaky Tarok 1995, Mezhyrichchia 1998, Segmenty Snu 1998, Villi nad Morem 2000, Problema Holovy (short stories) 2000, Kazky (novel) 2004, The Look from Cliff 2006, Hemispheres and Cones 2006, Pink Caldrons 2007, Fulgurites 2008, Idylls 2009. *Address:* Ukrainian Academy of Arts and Sciences, c/o Embassy of Ukraine, Albrechtstr. 26, 10117 Berlin, Germany.

ANDRÉE, Alice (see CLUYSENAAR, Anne)

ANDREW, Prudence Hastings, BA; British writer; b. 23 May 1924, London, England. *Education:* St Anne's Coll., Oxford. *Publications include:* The Hooded Falcon 1960, Ordeal by Silence 1961, Ginger Over the Wall 1962, A Question of Choice 1963, Ginger and Batty Billy 1963, The Earthworms 1964, Ginger and No. 10 1964, The Constant Star 1964, A Sparkle from the Coal 1964, Christmas Card 1966, Mr Morgan's Marrow 1967, Mister O'Brien 1972, Rodge, Sylvie and Munch 1973, Una and Grubstreet 1973, Goodbye to the Rat 1974, The Heroic Deeds of Jason Jones 1975, Where Are You Going To, My Pretty Maid? 1977, Robinson Daniel Crusoe 1978 (in USA as Close Within My Own Circle 1980), The Other Side of the Park 1984.

ANDREWS, Graham, BA; Northern Irish writer; b. 3 Feb. 1948, Belfast; m. Agnes Helena Ferguson 1982. *Education:* Open Univ., Milton Keynes, England. *Career:* Assoc. Ed., Extro Science Fiction Magazine, 1980–81; Staff Writer, World Asscn for Orphans and Abandoned Children, 1990–91; mem. Soc. of Authors, RSL, British Science Fiction Asscn. *Publications include:* The Fragile Future 1990, The WAO Vocational Training Programme 1990, Darkness Audible (science fiction novel) 1991, St James Guide to Fantasy Writers (contrib.) 1996, Dr Kilcasey in Space: A Bio-Bibliography of James White 2000, Gideon's Day/Gideon of Scotland Yard 2003, The Man Who Met His Maker (play) 2004, Two Just Men: Richard S. Prather and Shell Scott; contrib. to Belfast Telegraph, Brussels Bulletin, The Guardian, F & SF, Interzone, Million, Vector, Foundation, Locus, Book and Magazine Collector. *Honours:* Aisling Gheal (Bright Vision) Award, Irish Science Fiction Asscn 1980, First Prize in playwriting, American Theatre Co. of Brussels, 2001. *Address:* Avenue du Merle 37, 1640 Rhode-Saint-Genese, Belgium (home).

ANDREWS, Kenneth Raymond, PhD, FBA; British academic and author; *Professor Emeritus of History, University of Hull;* b. 26 Aug. 1921, London, England; s. of Arthur Walter Andrews and Marion Gertrude Andrews; m. Ottilie Kalman 1969; two step-s. *Education:* Henry Thornton School, Clapham, London and King's Coll., London. *Career:* Southend Polytechnic 1954–56; Chiswick Polytechnic 1956–63; Lecturer, Univ. of Liverpool 1963–64; Lecturer then Sr Lecturer, Univ. of Hull 1964–79, Prof. of History 1979–88 (part time 1986–88), Prof. Emer. 1988–; conducting research in English maritime history; Vice-Pres. Hakluyt Soc. 1983–90. *Publications include:* English Privateering Voyages to the West Indies 1588–95 1959, Elizabethan Privateering 1964, Drake's Voyages 1967, Last Voyage of Drake and Hawkins (ed.) 1972, The Spanish Caribbean 1978, The Westward Enterprise: English Activities in Ireland, the Atlantic and America 1480–1650 (ed.) 1979, Trade, Plunder and Settlement: Maritime Enterprise and the Genesis of the British Empire 1480–1630 1984, Ships, Money and Politics 1991, Freedom is a Constant Struggle: The Mississippi Civil Rights Movement and its Consequences 2004, Elizabethan Privateering: English Privateering During the Spanish War 1585–1603 2011. *Address:* 8 Grange Drive, Cottingham, North Humberside, HU16 5RE, England (home).

ANDRUKHOVYCH, Yuriy; Ukrainian novelist and poet; b. 13 March 1960, Ivano-Frankivsk. *Education:* Ukrainian Inst. of Polygraphy, Maxim Gorky Literary Inst., Moscow. *Career:* mil. service 1983–84; Co-founder literary performance group 'The Bu-Ba-Bu' (Burlesque-Bluster-Buffoonery) 1985; literary readings in American univs, including Harvard, Yale, Columbia, Pennsylvania State Univ. and La Salle Univ. 1998; Fulbright Scholar in Residence Dept of Germanic and Slavic Languages, Penn State Univ.; mem. Bd periodicals, Krytyka, Potyah 76; mem. Polish experimental jazz group, Karbido. *Film screenplay:* A Military March for an Angel 1989. *Plays:* Orpheus, Illegal 2006. *Recording:* album with Karbido: Samogon 2006. *Publications include:* poetry: The Sky and Squares 1985, Downtown 1989, Exotic Birds and Plants 1991, Songs for the Dead Rooster 2004; fiction: Army Stories (short stories) 1989, Rekreatsii (trans. as Recreations) 1992, Moscoviada 1993, Perverzion 1996, Twelve Rings 2003, The Secret 2007; non-fiction: Disorientation on Location (essays) 1999, 'Central-Eastern Revision' essay in anthology, My Europe 2001, The Last Territory 2003; contribs in trans. to Agni, Salt Hill, Exquisite Corpse. *Honours:* Blahovist 1993, Helen Shcherban-Lapika Foundation Award 1996, Novel of the Year Prize, Suchasnist 1997, Lesia & Petro Kovalev Award 1998, Leipzig Book Prize for European Understanding 2005, Angelus Prize 2006. *Address:* c/o The National Writers' Union of Ukraine, Bankova Street 2, 01024 Kiev, Ukraine. *E-mail:* nspu@i.kiev.ua.

ANEIROS, Rosa; Spanish writer; b. 1976, Valdoviño. *Education:* Univ. of Santiago de Compostela. *Career:* regular contributor to various print and digital media including culturagalega.org, Radio Galega, Diário de São Paulo, Folha Online, Grails; journalist, Galician Council for Culture. *Publications:* Relatos 1999, Eu de maior quero ser 1999, Corazóns amolecidos en salitre 2002, Resistencia 2002, Seis ferroláns 2003, Alma de beiramar perdida 2003, Botella ao mar 2003, ou Narradio 2003, Veu visitarme o mar 2004, O xardín da media lúa 2004, Ao pé do abismo 2007, Os ourizos cachos e o gran río gris 2008, Sol de inverno 2009, Ás de bolboreta 2009. *Honours:* Lueiro Manuel Rey 1996, Pedron Gold 1998, Manuel Murguia 2001, Carvalho Calero 2001, Archbishop of St John Clement Award 2003, Losada Diéguez Critics Award 2005, Careón Award 2006, Award Francisco Fernández del Riego Caixanova 2007, Gerais Prize 2009, Foundation Award Caixa Galicia for Youth Literature 2009, Literary Award for Best Juvenile Waterfalls year book 2009, Award of Romance General Waterfalls Literary Award 2009, Winter Sun (General Romance Award) 2009, The White Raven Award (Internationale Jugend Bibliothek) 2010. *Address:* Edicións Xerais of Galicia, 12 Doutor Marañón, 36211 Vigo, Spain. *Telephone:* (98) 6214888. *Fax:* (98) 6201366. *E-mail:* xerais@xerais.es. *Website:* www.xerais.es.

ANGEL, Albalucía Marulanda; Colombian novelist and playwright; b. 27 Sept. 1939, Pereira, Risaralda. *Education:* Univ. de los Andes, Bogotá. *Plays:* La manzaza de piedra 1983, Siete lunas y un espejo 1991. *Publications include:* Los girasoles en invierno (novel) 1970, Dos veces Alicia (novel) 1972, Estaba la pájara pinta sentada en el verde limón (novel) (Best Novel of the Year Award) 1975, Oh, Gloria inmarcesible! 1979, Misiá señora (novel) 1982, Las andariegas (poetic prose) 1984, No Man's Land 2002. *Honours:* Premio Vivencias 1975.

ANGEL, Leonard Jay, BA, MA, PhD; Canadian writer, dramatist and lecturer; b. 20 Sept. 1945; m. Susan Angel; one s. two d. *Education:* McGill Univ., Univ. of British Columbia. *Career:* Dept of Creative Writing, Univ. of British Columbia 1981–82, Univ. of Victoria 1984–86; Instructor, Dept of Philosophy and Humanities, Douglas Coll. 1992–; mem. Playwrights Canada 1976–88, Guild of Canadian Playwrights, Chair., British Columbia region 1978–79, Regional Representative 1980–81, Writers' Guild of Canada 1993. *Plays:* Unveiling, Eleanor Marx. *Publications include:* Antietam 1975, Isadora and G. B. 1976, The Unveiling 1981, The Silence of the Mystic 1983, Eleanor Marx 1985, How to Build a Conscious Machine 1989, Englightenment East and West 1994, The Book of Miriam 1997; contribs to The British Journal for the Philosophy of Science, Religious Studies. *Honours:* First Prize, Short Fiction, McGill Daily 1963, First Prize (joint), Playhouse Theatre Award 1971, Canada Council Artist Grants 1979, 1982. *Address:* 865 Durward Avenue, Vancouver, BC V5V 2Z1, Canada (home). *Telephone:* (604) 527-5427 (office). *E-mail:* leonard_angel@douglas.bc.ca. *Website:* www.douglas.bc.ca (office).

ANGELOU, Maya; American writer, poet and academic; b. (Marguerite Johnson), 4 April 1928, St Louis, Mo.; d. of Bailey Johnson and Vivian Baxter; one s. *Career:* Assoc. Ed. Arab Observer 1961–62; Asst Admin., teacher, School of Music and Drama, Univ. of Ghana 1963–66; Feature Ed. African Review, Accra 1964–66; Reynolds Prof. of American Studies, Wake Forest Univ. 1981–; teacher of modern dance, Rome Opera House, Hambina Theatre, Tel-Aviv; has written several film scores; contrib. to numerous periodicals; Woman of Year in Communication 1976; numerous TV acting appearances; mem. Bd of Govs Maya Angelou Inst. for the Improvement of Child and Family Educ., Winston-Salem State Univ., NC 1998–; distinguished visiting prof. at several univs; mem. various arts orgs. *Plays:* Cabaret for Freedom 1960, The Least of These 1966, Gettin' Up Stayed On My Mind 1967, Ajax 1974, And Still I Rise 1976, Moon On a Rainbow Shawl (producer) 1988. *Theatre appearances include:* Porgy and Bess 1954–55, Calypso 19576, The Blacks 1960, Mother Courage 1964, Look Away 1973, Roots 1977, How To Make an American Quilt 1995 (feature film 1996). *Films directed include:* Down in the Delta 1998. *Publications include:* I Know Why the Caged Bird Sings 1970, Just Give Me A Cool Drink of Water 'Fore I Die 1971, Georgia, Georgia (screenplay) 1972, Gather Together In My Name 1974, All Day Long (screenplay) 1974, Oh Pray My Wings Are Gonna Fit Me Well 1975, Singin' and Swingin' and Gettin' Merry Like Christmas 1976, And Still I Rise 1976, The Heart of a Woman 1981, Shaker, Why Don't You Sing 1983, All God's Children Need Travelling Shoes 1986, Now Sheba Sings the Song 1987, I Shall Not Be Moved 1990,

Gathered Together in My Name 1991, Wouldn't Take Nothing for my Journey Now 1993, Life Doesn't Frighten Me 1993, Collected Poems 1994, My Painted House, My Friendly Chicken and Me 1994, Phenomenal Woman 1995, Kofi and His Magic 1996, Even the Stars Look Lonesome 1997, Making Magic in the World 1998, A Song Flung up to Heaven 2002, Hallelujah! The Welcome Table 2005, Amazing Peace (long poem) (Quill Award for Poetry 2006) 2005, Letter to My Daughter 2008. *Honours:* Hon. Amb. to UNICEF 1996–; more than 50 hon. degrees; Horatio Alger Award 1992, Grammy Award Best Spoken Word or Non-Traditional Album 1994, Lifetime Achievement Award for Literature 1999, Presidential Medal for the Arts 2000, Lincoln Ledal 2008, Presidential Medal of Freedom 2010, numerous other awards. *Literary Agent:* Lordly and Dame Inc., 1344 Main Street, Waltham, MA 02451, USA. *Telephone:* (781) 373-3680. *Fax:* (781) 373-3681. *E-mail:* kwheeler@lordly.com. *Website:* www.lordly.com; www.mayaangelou.com.

ANGHELAKI-ROOKE, Katerina; Greek poet and translator; b. 22 Feb. 1939, Athens. *Education:* Univs of Nice, Athens and Geneva. *Career:* freelance trans. 1962–; Visiting Prof. (Fulbright), Harvard Univ. 1980; Visiting Fellow, Princeton Univ. 1987. *Publications include:* Wolves and Clouds 1963, Poems 63–69 1971, Magdalene the Vast Mammal 1974, The Body is the Victory and the Defeat of Dreams (in English) 1975, The Scattered Papers of Penelope 1977, The Triumph of Constant Loss 1978, Counter Love 1982, The Suitors 1984, Beings and Things on Their Own (in English) 1986, When the Body 1988, Wind Epilogue 1990, Empty Nature 1993, Tristiu 1995, The Flesh is a Beautiful Desert 1996, From Purple into Night (in English) 1997, Poems 1963–1977 1997, Poems 1978–1985 1998, Poems 1986–1996 1999, Matter Alone 2001, La Chair beau désert (in French and Greek) 2001, Translating into Love Life's End (in English) 2004; trans. of works by Shakespeare, Albee, Dylan Thomas, Beckett, and from Russian of Pushkin, Mayiakorski, Lermontov. *Honours:* Greek Nat. Poetry Prize 1985, Greek Acad. Ouranis Prize 2000. *Address:* Synesiou Kyrenes 4, 114 71 Athens, Greece (home).

ANGIER, Natalie; American journalist; b. 16 Feb. 1958, New York; d. of Keith Angier and Adele Angier; m. Richard S. Weiss 1991; one d. *Education:* Univ. of Michigan and Barnard Coll., New York. *Career:* writer on Discover Magazine, New York 1980–83, Time Magazine, New York 1984–86; Ed. Savvy Magazine, New York 1983–84; Prof., New York Univ. Grad. Program in Science and Environmental Reporting 1987–89; joined New York Times as Reporter 1990, currently Science Corresp., Washington, DC. *Publications include:* Natural Obsessions (Notable Book of the Year, New York Times and AAAS) 1988, The Beauty of the Beastly (cited as one of notable science books of the year by New York Times and Library Journal) 1995, Woman: An Intimate Geography 1999, The Best American Science and Nature Writing (ed.) 2002, The Canon: A Whirligig Tour of the Beautiful Basics of Science 2007, Best American Science Writing (co-ed.) 2009; contribs to Parade, Washington Monthly, Reader's Digest, Fox TV Network, CBC and several other publs. *Honours:* Pulitzer Prize for Reporting 1991, Journalism Award, GM Ind. Bd 1991, Lewis Thomas Award for Distinguished Writing in the Life Sciences, Marine Biology Labs 1990, Journalism Award, AAAS Award for Excellence in Journalism 1992, Distinguished Alumna Award, Barnard Coll. 1993, General Motors Int. Award, named by Forbes MediaGuide amongst seven journalists awarded its top rating of four stars. *Literary Agent:* c/o Anne Sibbald, Janklow & Nesbit, 445 Park Avenue, New York, NY 10022-2606. *Telephone:* (212) 421-1700. *E-mail:* asibbald@janklow.com. *Address:* New York Times, Washington Bureau, 1627 I Street, NW, 7th Floor, Washington, DC 20006, USA (office). *E-mail:* angier58@comcast.net. *Website:* www.natalieangier.com.

ANGLUND, Joan Walsh; American children's writer; b. 3 Jan. 1926, Hinsdale, Ill. *Education:* Chicago Art Inst. *Publications include:* A Friend is Someone Who Likes You 1958, Look Out the Window 1959, The Brave Cowboy 1959, Love is a Special Way of Feeling 1960, In a Pumpkin Shell: A Mother Goose ABC 1960, Christmas Is a Time of Giving 1961, Cowboy and his Friend 1961, Nibble Nible Mousekin: A Tale of Hansel and Gretel 1962, Cowboy's Secret Life 1963, Spring is a New Beginning 1963, Childhood Is a Time of Innocence 1964, A Pocketful of Proverbs (verse) 1964, A Book of Good Tidings from the Bible 1965, What Color is Love? 1966, A Year is Round 1966, A Cup of Sun: A Book of Poems 1967, A Is for Always: An ABC Book 1968, Morning Is a Little Child (verse) 1969, A Slice of Snow: A Book of Poems 1970, Do You Love Someone? 1971, The Cowboy's Christmas 1972, A Child's Book of Old Nursery Rhymes 1973, Goodbye, Yesterday: A Book of Poems 1974, Storybook 1978, Emily and Adam 1979, Almost a Rainbow 1980, A Gift of Love (five vols) 1980, A Christmas Cookie Book 1982, Rainbow Love 1982, Christmas Candy Book (co-author) 1983, A Christmas Book 1983, See the Year 1984, Coloring Book 1984, Memories of the Heart 1984, Teddy Bear Tales 1985, Baby Brother 1985, All About Me! 1986, Christmas is Here! 1986, Tubtime for Thaddeus 1986, A Mother Goose Book 1991, A Child's Year 1992, Love is a Baby 1992, The Way of Love 1992, Bedtime Book 1993, The Friend We Have Not Met 1993, Peace is a Circle of Love 1993, Be My Friend 2000, A Christmas Sampler 2001, You Are Loved 2003, Love Is the Best Teacher 2004, Baby Dear 2005, Faith Is a Flower 2006.

ANGOT, Christine, BA, DEA; French writer; b. 7 Feb. 1959, Châteauroux; m. *Education:* Reims Univ. *Publications include:* Vu du ciel 1990, Léonore, toujours 1994, Interview 1995, Les Autres 1997, Sujet Angot 1998, L'Inceste 1999, Quitter la Ville 2000, Normalement 2001, Pourquoi le Brésil? 2002, Peau d'Ane 2003, Les Désaxés 2004, Une Partie de Coeur 2004, Rendez-vous (Prix de Flore) 2006, Le Marché des Amants 2008. *Address:* c/o Editions du Seuil, La Martinière Groupe, 27 rue Jacob, 75261 Paris, France. *E-mail:* contact@seuil.com. *Website:* www.editionsduseuil.com.

ANMAR, Frank (see NOLAN, William Francis)

ANNWN, David, BA, PGCE, PhD; British poet, critic and lecturer; *Assistant Lecturer, Open University;* b. (David Jones), 9 May 1953, Congleton, Cheshire, England; m. 1994. *Education:* Wigan Tech. Coll., Univ. Coll. of Wales, Aberystwyth, Univ. of Bath. *Career:* Postgraduate Tutor, Univ. of Aberystwyth 1975–78; Lecturer, Wakefield Coll. 1981–88, Head of English Degree Work 1988–95; Lecturer, Tutor and Examiner, Open Univ. 1995–96, currently Asst Lecturer; Lecturer in Creative Writing, Univ. of Leeds 1996; Symposium Poet, Univ. of Sunderland 2011; mem. Humanities and Arts Higher Educ. Network, Northern Asscn of Writers in Educ., Welsh Acad. *Publications include:* poetry: Foster the Ghost 1984, King Saturn's Book 1986, The Other 1988, Primavera Violin 1990, The Spirit/That Kiss 1993, Dantean Designs 1995, Danse Macabre, Death and the Printers (with Kelvin Corcoran, Alan Halsey and Gavin Selerie) 1997; prose: Inhabited Voices: Myth and History in the Poetry of Seamus Heaney, Geoffrey Hill and George Mackay Brown 1984, Catgut and Blossom: Jonathon Williams in England (ed.) 1989, A Different Can of Words (ed.) 1992, Presence, Spacing Sign: The Graphic Art of Peterjon Skelt 1993, Hear the Voice of the Bard!: The Early Bards, William Blake and Robert Duncan 1995, Poetry in the British Isles: Non-Metropolitan Perspectives 1995, Inner Celtia (with Alan Richardson) 1996, A Breton Herbal: Translations of Poems by Eugene Guillevic 1998, Gothic Machine 2011; contrib. to anthologies and to Anglo-Welsh Review, Poetry Wales, Ambit, Iron, Scintilla, David Jones Soc. Journal. *Honours:* Winner Int. Collegiate Eisteddfod 1975, Ilkley Arts Festival Prize 1982, Yorkshire Arts Bursary 1985, First Prize, Cardiff Int. Poetry Competition 1996, Ferguson Centre Award 2004–07. *Address:* c/o West House Books, 40 Crescent Road, Sheffield, S7 1HN, England. *Website:* www.davidannwn.co.uk.

ANTHONY, Evelyn; British writer; b. 3 July 1928, d. of Henry Christian Stephens and Elizabeth Stephens (née Sharkey); m. Michael Ward-Thomas 1955 (deceased); four s. two d. (and one d. deceased). *Education:* Convent of the Sacred Heart, Roehampton. *Career:* started writing short stories under the name Anthony Evelyn 1949; emerged as female author 1953. *Publications include:* Imperial Highness 1953, Curse Not the King 1954, Far Fly the Eagles 1955, Anne Boleyn (US Literary Guild Award) 1956, Victoria (US Literary Guild Award) 1957, Elizabeth 1959, Charles the King 1961, The Heiress 1964, The Rendezvous 1966, The Assassin 1970, The Tamarind Seed 1971 (filmed 1974), The Occupying Power (Yorkshire Post Fiction Prize 1973) 1973, The Persian Ransom 1975, The Silver Falcon 1977, The Grave of Truth 1979, The Defector 1980, The Avenue of the Dead 1981, Albatross 1982, The Company of Saints 1983, Voices On the Wind 1985, No Enemy But Time 1987, The House of Vandekar 1988, The Scarlet Thread 1989, The Doll's House 1990, Exposure 1992, Bloodstones 1994, The Legacy 1997, A Dubious Legacy 2002, Codeword Janus 2003, Sleeping with the Enemy 2003, Mind Games 2005. *Honours:* Freeman City of London 1989, Liveryman of Needlemakers Co. 1989, High Sheriff of Essex (first woman) 1994–95, DL (Essex) 1995. *Address:* Horham Hall, Thaxted, Essex, CM6 2NN, England (home).

ANTHONY, Michael; Trinidad and Tobago writer; b. 10 Feb. 1930, Mayaro; m. Yvette Francesca 1958; two s. two d. *Education:* Junior Tech. Coll., San Fernando, Trinidad. *Career:* Sub-Ed., Reuters News Agency, London 1964–68; Asst Ed., Texas Star, Texaco Trinidad, Pointe-a-Pierre, Trinidad and Tobago 1972–88; Teacher of Creative Writing, Univ. of Richmond, Va, USA 1992. *Publications include:* fiction: The Games Were Coming 1963, The Year in San Fernando 1965, Green Days by the River 1967, Streets of Conflict 1976, All That Glitters 1981, Bright Road to Eldorado 1982, Mass Casualties: A Young Medic's True Story of Death, Deception, and Dishonor in Iraq 2009; short stories: Cricket in the Road and Other Stories 1973, Sandra Street and Other Stories 1973, Folk Tales and Fantasies 1976, The Chieftain's Carnival and Other Stories 1993; other: Glimpses of Trinidad and Tobago, with a Glance at the West Indies 1974, King of the Masquerade 1974, Profile Trinidad: A Historical Survey from the Discovery to 1900 1975, The Making of Port-of-Spain, 1757–1939 1978, Port-of-Spain in a World War, 1939–1945 1984, First in Trinidad 1985, Heroes of the People of Trinidad and Tobago 1986, A Brighter and Better Day 1987, Towns and Villages of Trinidad and Tobago 1988, Parade of the Carnivals of Trinidad, 1839–1989 1989, The Golden Quest: The Four Voyages of Christopher Columbus 1992, In the Heat of the Day 1996, Historical Dictionary of Trinidad and Tobago 1997, The High Tide of Intrigue 2001, Butler, Till the Final Bell 2002; ed.: The History of Aviation in Trinidad and Tobago, 1913–1962 1987; contribs: various periodicals. *Honours:* Dr hc (Univ. of the West Indies) 2003. *E-mail:* manthony@tstt.net.tt (office). *Website:* michaelanthonytrinidad.com.

ANTHONY, Patricia, BA; American writer and educator; b. 29 March 1947, San Antonio, Tex.; d. of Raymond Anthony and Evelyn Anthony; m. Dennis John Hunt April 1967 (divorced 1974); one s. one d. *Education:* Univ. of Texas, Austin, Universidade Fed. de Santa Catarina, Florianopolis, Brazil. *Career:* Visiting Prof. of English Literature, Univ. of Lisbon, Portugal; Assoc. Prof. of English, Universidade Fed. de Santa Catarina, Florianopolis; Adjunct Prof. of Creative Writing, Southern Methodist Univ., Dallas, Tex. *Publications include:* fiction: Cold Allies (Best First Novel Award, Locus 1993) 1993, Brother Termite 1993, Conscience of the Beagle 1993, Happy Policeman 1994, Cradle of Splendor 1996, God's Fires 1997, Flanders 1998; short stories: Eating Memories 1997; contribs short stories to magazines including Aboriginal SF. *Literary Agent:* c/o Meredith Bernstein Literary Agency, 2112 Broadway, Suite 503A, New York, NY 10023, USA. *Address:* 9712 Amberton Parkway, Dallas, TX 75243, USA (home). *Telephone:* (972) 231-6155 (home). *E-mail:* patanthony@mindspring.com; patriciaanthony@sbcglobal.net (office).

ANTHONY, Piers, BA; American writer; b. (Piers Anthony Dillingham Jacob), 6 Aug. 1934, Oxford, England; m. Carol Marble 1956; two d. *Education:* Goddard Coll., Univ. of South Florida. *Career:* mil. service 1955–59. *Publications include:* Chthon 1967, Omnivore 1968, Sos the Rope 1968, The Ring (with Robert E. Margroff) 1968, Macroscope 1969, The E.S.P. Worm (with Robert E. Margroff) 1970, Orn 1971, Prostho Plus 1971, Var the Stick 1972, Kiai! 1974, Mistress of Death 1974, Rings of Ice 1974, Triple Détente 1974, The Bamboo Bloodbath 1975, Neq the Sword 1975, Ninja's Revenge 1975, Phthor 1975, Amazon Slaughter 1976, Ox 1976, But What of Earth? (with Robert Coulson) 1976, Steppe 1976, Cluster 1977, Hasan 1977, A Spell for Chameleon 1977, Chaining the Lady 1978, Kirlian Quest 1978, The Source of Magic 1979, Castle Roogna 1979, God of Tarot 1979, The Pretender (with Frances Hall) 1979, Split Infinity 1980, Vision of Tarot 1980, Faith of Tarot 1980, Thousandstar 1980, Blue Adept 1981, Centaur Aisle 1981, Mute 1981, Juxtaposition 1982, Ogre, Ogre 1982, Viscous Circle 1982, Night Mare 1983, Dragon on a Pedestal 1983, On a Pale Horse 1983, Refugee 1983, Mercenary 1984, Bearing an Hourglass 1984, Anthonology 1985, Crewel Lye: A Caustic Yarn 1985, With a Tangled Skein 1985, Politician 1985, Executive 1985, Ghost 1986, Golem in the Gears 1986, Shade of the Tree 1986, Statesman 1986, Out of Phaze 1987, Vale of the Vole 1987, Wielding a Red Sword 1987, Being a Green Mother 1987, Dragon's Gold (with Robert E. Margroff) 1987, Bio of an Ogre 1988, For Love of Evil 1988, Heaven Cent 1988, Robot Adept 1988, Serpent's Silver (with Robert E. Margroff) 1988, Pornucopia 1988, Dead Morn 1988, Total Recall 1989, Unicorn Point 1989, And Eternity 1990, Isle of View 1990, Firefly 1990, Hard Sell 1990, Phaze Doubt 1990, Through the Ice (with Robert Kornwise) 1990, Orc's Opal (with Robert E. Margroff) 1990, Chimaera's Copper (with Robert E. Margroff) 1990, Tatham Mound 1991, Virtual Mode 1991, MerCycle 1991, Question Quest 1991, Alien Plot 1992, The Color of Her Panties 1992, Fractal Mode 1992, The Caterpillar's Question (with Jose Farmer) 1992, If I Pay Thee Not in Gold 1993, Killobyte 1993, Letters to Jenny 1993, Demons Don't Dream 1993, Chaos Mode 1993, Isle of Woman 1993, Mouvar's Magic (with Robert E. Margroff) 1993, Harpy Thyme 1994, Shame of Man 1994, Tales from the Great Turtle 1994, Geis of the Gargoyle 1995, Roc and a Hard Place 1995, Yon Ill Wind 1996, The Willing Spirit (with Alfred Tells) 1996, The Continuing Xanth Saga 1997, Hope of Earth 1997, Faun and Games 1997, Quest for the Fallen Star (with James Richey and Alan Riggs) 1998, Zombie Lover 1998, Xone of Contention 1999, Realty Check 1999, How Precious Was That While 1999, Muse of Art 1999, The Dastard 2000, Swell Foop 2001, DoOon Mode 2001, Up in a Heaval 2002, The Iron Maiden 2002, Cube Route 2003, The Magic Fart 2003, Currant Events 2004, Pet Peeve 2005, Stork Naked 2006, Relationships 2006, Air Apparent 2007, Tortoise Reform 2007, Alfred 2007, Relationships 2 2008, Two to the Fifth 2008, Jumper Cable 2009, Relationships 3 2009, Relationships 4 2010. *Honours:* Science Fiction Award, Pyramid Books/ Magazine of Fantasy and Science Fiction/Kent Productions 1967, British Fantasy Award 1977. *E-mail:* PiersAnthony@hipiers.com (home). *Website:* www.hipiers.com.

ANTIN, David, BA, MA; American academic and poet; *Professor Emeritus, Department of Visual Arts, University of California at San Diego*; b. 1 Feb. 1932, New York, NY; m. Eleanor Fineman 1960; one s. *Education:* City Coll., City Univ. of New York, New York Univ. *Career:* Chief Ed. and Scientific Dir, Research Information Service 1958–60; Curator, Inst. of Contemporary Art, Boston 1967; Dir Univ. Art Gallery, Dept of Visual Arts, Univ. of California, San Diego 1968–72, Asst Prof. 1968–72, fmr Prof. of Visual Arts, currently Prof. Emer. *Publications include:* Definitions 1967, Autobiography 1967, Code of Flag Behavior 1968, Meditiations 1971, Talking 1972, After the War 1973, Talking at the Boundaries 1976, Who's Listening Out There? 1980, Tuning 1984, Poèmes Parlés 1984, Selected Poems 1963–73 1991, What it Means to be Avant Garde 1993, A Conversation with David Antin (with Charles Bernstein) 2002, I Never Knew What Time it Was 2005, John Cage Uncaged is Still Cagey 2005; contrib. to periodicals. *Honours:* Longview Award 1960, Univ. of California Creative Arts Award 1972, Guggenheim Fellowship 1976, Nat. Endowment for the Humanities Fellowship 1983, PEN Award for Poetry 1984, Getty Research Fellow 2002. *Address:* Visual Arts Department, University of California at San Diego, 9500 Gilman Drive, La Jolla, CA 92093-0327, USA (office). *Telephone:* (858) 534-2860 (office). *E-mail:* dantin@ucsd.edu (office). *Website:* visarts.ucsd.edu (office).

ANTOINE, Yves, MEd, DLitt; Haitian academic, writer, poet and novelist; b. 12 Dec. 1941, Port-au-Prince, Haiti; one d. *Education:* Univ. of Ottawa, Univ. of Montréal. *Career:* taught at Algonquin Coll., Outaouais Coll. 1981–2002; mem. Union of Writers, QC, Ligue des Droits et Liberté, Asscn des auteurs de l'Outaouais québécois, Asscn des Auteurs de l'Ontario français. *Publications include:* La Veillée 1964, Témoin Oculaire 1970, Au gré des heures 1972, Les sabots de la nuit 1974, Alliage 1979, Libations pour le soleil 1985, Sémiologie et personnage romanesque chez Jacques S. Alexis 1993, Polyphonie (poems and prose) 1996, Inventeurs et savants noirs 1998, La mémoire à fleur de peau 2002, Les Sentiers Parallèles 2008; contrib. to Une affligeante réalité, Le Droit, Ottawa 1987, L'indélébile, Symbiosis, Ottawa 1992, Inventeurs et savants noirs 1998, 2004, 2012. *Honours:* Guest Harambee Foundation Soc. 1988, Carter G. Woodson Award Intercultural Council of Outaouais (Québec, Canada) 1999, Student Fed. of the Univ. of Ottawa Award 2010, Efficience Award, Paris (France) 2010. *Address:* 6 rue de la Sablière, Apt 3, Gatineau, QC J8Z 2V4, Canada (home). *Telephone:* (819) 595-1360 (home).

ANTOKOLETZ, Elliott Maxim, BA, MA, PhD; American musicologist, academic and writer; *Professor of Musicology, University of Texas, Austin*; b. 3 Aug. 1942, Jersey City, NJ; s. of Jack Antokoletz and Esther Antokoletz; m. Juana Canabal 1972; one s. *Education:* Juilliard School of Music, Hunter Coll., Graduate School and Univ. Center, City Univ. of New York. *Career:* Lecturer and mem. of faculty string quartet, Queens Coll., CUNY 1973–76; Prof. of Musicology, Univ. of Texas, Austin 1976–, Head of Musicology Div. 1992–94, Tacquard Endowed Centennial Chair. 1983–84, E.W. Doty Prof. in Fine Arts 1994–95; Co-ed. International Journal of Musicology 1992–; mem. American Musicological Soc. *Publications include:* The Music of Béla Bartók: A Study of Tonality and Progression in Twentieth-Century Music 1984, Béla Bartók: A Guide to Research 1988, Twentieth-Century Music 1992, Bartók Perspectives (co-ed. with V. Fischer and B. Suchoff) 2000, Musical Symbolism in the Operas of Debussy and Bartók 2004; contrib. three chapters to The Bartók Companion, one chapter to Sibelius Studies, one chapter to Copland and his World; contrib. to scholarly books and professional journals. *Honours:* Nat. Endowment for the Humanities Grants 1980, 1982, Béla Bartók Memorial Plaque and Diploma 1981, Teaching Excellence Award 1981, PhD Alumni Award, CUNY 1987. *Address:* School of Music, University of Texas, 1 University Station, E3100, Austin, TX 78712, USA (office). *Telephone:* (512) 471-7764 (office). *Fax:* (512) 441-7520 (office). *E-mail:* antokoletz@mail.utexas.edu (office). *Website:* www.music.utexas.edu (office).

ANTROBUS, John; British dramatist, writer and screenwriter; b. 2 July 1933, London, England; m. Margaret McCormick 1958 (divorced 1980); two s. one d. *Education:* King Edward VII Nautical Coll., Royal Mil. Acad., Sandhurst. *Career:* mem. Writers' Guild of America West, Writers' Guild of GB. *Plays include:* The Bed-Sitting Room (with Spike Milligan) 1963, Sperm Test 1965, Captain Oates' Left Sock 1969, Walton on Thames (revised edn as The Bed-Sitting Room 2) 1970, Crete and Sergeant Pepper 1972, An Apple a Day 1974, The Illegal Immigrant 1974, Mrs Grabowski's Academy 1975, City Delights 1978, Jonah 1979, Hitler in Liverpool 1980, One Orange for the Baby 1980, Up in the Hide 1980, When Did You Last See Your Trousers? (with Ray Galton) 1986, That Woman 1994, Of Good Report 2004, Steptoe and Son in Murder at Oil Drum Lane 2005, It's All in the Mind, Folks. *Film screenplays:* Carry on Sergeant (with Norman Hudis) 1958, Idol on Parade 1959, The Wrong Arm of the Law (with others) 1962, The Big Job (with Talbot Rothwell) 1965, The Bed-Sitting Room (with Charles Wood) 1969. *Publications include:* juvenile: The Boy with Illuminating Measles 1978, Help! I'm a Prisoner in a Toothpaste Factory 1978, Ronnie and the Haunted Rolls Royce 1982, Ronnie and the Great Knitted Robbery 1982, Ronnie and the High Rise 1992, Ronnie and the Flying Carpet 1992, non-fiction: Of Good Report, Parental Wisdom Or the Philosophy and Social Bearings of Education: With Historical Illustrations of Its Power, Its Political Importance, Etc. (1849) 2009, The Wrongs of Poland, a Poem, with Historical Notes, by the Author of 'Parental Wisdom' 2009. *Honours:* George Devine Award 1970, Writers' Guild Award 1971, Arts Council bursaries 1973, 1976, 1980, 1982, Banff Television Festival Award for Best Comedy 1987.

ANTUNES, Arnaldo; Brazilian singer, songwriter, poet and writer; b. (Arnaldo Augusto Nora Antunes Filho), 2 Sept. 1960, São Paulo; s. of Arnaldo Augusto Nora Antunes and Dora Leme Ferreira Antunes; m. 1st Go Antunes 1980; m. 2nd Zaba Moreau 1987; four c. *Education:* Pontifical Catholic Univ. of Rio de Janeiro. *Career:* mem. Titãs do Iêlê 1981–92; solo artist 1992–; mem. Tribalistas (with Carlinhos Brown and Marisa Monte) 2002–03. *Recordings:* albums: with Titãs do IêIê: Titãs 1984, Televisão 1985, Cabeça Dinossauro 1986, Jesus não tem Dentes no País dos Banguelas 1987, Go Back 1988, Õ Blesq Blom 1989, Tudo as Mesmo Tempo Agora 1991; solo: Nome 1993, Ninguém 1995, O Silêncio 1996, Um som 1998, O Corpo 2000, Paradeiro 2001, Saiba 2004, Qualquer 2006, Iê-Iê-Iê 2009; with Tribalistas: Tribalistas 2003. *Publications include:* poetry: Ou E 1983, Psia 1986, 2 ou + corpos no mesmo espaço 1997, Doble Duplo 2000, Outro 2001, ET et Tu 2003, Antologia 2006; other: Tudos 1990, As Coisas 1992, Nome 1993, 40 escritos 2000, Palavra Desordem 2002, Frases do Tomé aos Três Anos 2006, Como é que chamo o Nome Disso 2006. *Address:* c/o Biscoito Fino, Rua Sarapuí, no. 8, Botafogo, Rio de Janeiro, RJ 22260-170, Brazil. *Telephone:* (21) 2266-9300. *Fax:* (21) 2240-5144. *E-mail:* sidimir@biscoitofino.com.br. *Website:* www.biscoitofino.com.br; www.arnaldoantunes.com.br.

ANTUNES, Xana, BA; British publishing executive; *Editor, Crain's New York Business*; b. 1965. *Education:* Univ. of Leeds and City Univ., London. *Career:* postgraduate diploma in journalism; began career in journalism as reporter with The Independent (newspaper) business section 1988; TV journalist on Business Daily (Channel 4); Business News Ed., Evening Standard 1992–93, est. Wall Street bureau 1993, New York Corresp. 1993–95; Deputy Business Ed. New York Post 1995–96, Business Ed. 1996–98, Deputy Ed. 1998–99, Ed. 1999–2001; host of feature writing seminars and consultant to various magazines and newspapers 2002–03; Exec. Ed. Fortune magazine 2003–05, Exec. Ed. CNNMoney.com 2005–08; Ed. Crain's New York Business 2008–. *Address:* Crain's New York Business, 711 Third Avenue, New York, NY 10017, USA (office). *Telephone:* (212) 210-0100 (office). *E-mail:* xantunes@crainsnewyork.com (office). *Website:* www.crainsnewyork.com (office).

ANVIL, Christopher (see CROSBY, Harry Clifton)

ANYANWU, Christina, BA, MSc; Nigerian journalist; b. 29 Oct. 1951, Ahiazu Mbaise Local Govt Area; m. Dr Casmir Anyanwu; one s. one d. *Education:* Owerri Girls Secondary School, Univs of Missouri and Florida, USA. *Career:* Newsweek Corresp. at Nat. Ass. 1979; with Nat. TV Authority 1979, Producer Newsline Magazine 1986; Commr of Information, Imo State 1989; Founder, Dir and Ed.-in-Chief The Sunday Magazine 1989; sentenced by special mil. tribunal in camera to life imprisonment for "spreading false news" July 1995, sentence reduced to 15 years' imprisonment Oct. 1995, released June 1998; with Nigerian TV Authority (NTA) hosting NEWSLINE show and covering activities of OPEC as petroleum corresp.; Owner HOT 98.3 FM radio station, Abuja; elected to Senate representing Owerri dist (People's Democratic Party) 2007–. *Honours:* Nat. Nigerian Award for Women Journalists, Ford Foundation Garnet Award, Int. Women's Media Foundation Prize for Courage 1995, Reporters Sans Frontières Award 1995, African Women's Media Center Courage in Journalism Award, Cttee to Protect Journalism Int. Press Freedom Award 1997, UNESCO/Guillermo Cano World Press Freedom Prize 1998, mem. of the Fed. Repub. (MFR), Govt of Nigeria 2004. *Address:* 21B, MCC Road, Owerri, Imo State, Nigeria (office). *Telephone:* (33) 081944 (office). *E-mail:* nigerkris@hotmail.com (office). *Website:* www.nassnig.org/senate (office).

AO, Temsula, BA, MA; Indian writer and academic; *Dean, School of Humanities and Education, North-Eastern Hill University*; b. 25 Oct. 1945. *Education:* Guwahati Univ., Assam. *Career:* fmr Prof. of English, North-Eastern Hill Univ., Shillong, currently Dean, School of Humanities and Educ.; Fulbright Fellowship, Univ. of Minnesota 1985–86; mem. Bd of Dirs North East Zone Cultural Centre 1992–97. *Publications include:* five books of poetry including Songs that Tell 1988, Songs of Many Moods 1995, Ao-Naga Oral Tradition 1999, Laburnum for my Head; short stories: These Hills Called Home: Stories from a War Zone 2006, Laburnum For My Head: Stories 2009; contrib. numerous articles to journals and encyclopedias. *Honours:* Shakespeare Prize, Guwahati Univ. 1973, Padma Shri 2007, Gov.'s Gold Medal 2009. *Address:* School of Humanities and Education, North-Eastern Hill University, Umshing Mawkynroh, Shillong 793 022, India (office). *Telephone:* (364) 2723501 (office); (364) 2726505 (home); (364) 2550642 (home). *Fax:* (364) 2551722 (office). *E-mail:* deanshe@nehu.ac.in (office). *Website:* www.nehu.ac.in (office).

APPACHANA, Anjana, MFA; Indian novelist and short story writer; b. Coorg, Karnataka; m.; one d. *Education:* Scindia Kanya Vidyalaya, Delhi Univ., Jawaharlal Nehru Univ., Pennsylvania State Univ. *Career:* moved to USA 1984; Visiting Prof., Arizona State Univ. 1998–99, 2006–07; has taught creative writing at Univ. of Pennsylvania and YMCA Writer's Voice; Nat. Endowment for the Arts Fellowship. *Publications include:* Her Mother (short story) (O. Henry Festival Prize for Fiction) 1989, Incantations and Other Stories 1991, Sharmaji (short story), Listening Now (novel) 1998, Bahu (novel) 2009; contrib. short stories to several journals, magazines and anthologies. *Address:* c/o Zulma, 122, boulevard Haussman, 75008 Paris, France.

APPELFELD, Aharon; Israeli novelist; b. 16 Feb. 1932, Czernowitz, Poland. *Education:* Hebrew Univ., Jerusalem. *Career:* fmr Prof., Ben Gurion Univ. of the Negev. *Publications (in Hebrew) include:* Smoke (stories) 1962, In the Fertile Valley (stories) 1963, Frost on the Land (stories) 1965, On the Ground Floor (stories) 1968, Pillars of the River (stories) 1971, The Skin and the Gown (novel) 1971, As an Apple of his Eye (novella) 1973, A Hundred Witnesses (stories selection) 1975, Years and Hours (novellas) 1975, The Age of Wonders (novel) 1978, First Person Essays (essays) 1979, Badenheim 1939 (novel) 1979, Searing Light (novel) 1980, The Shirt and the Stripes (novella) 1983, Tzili: The Story of a Life (novel) 1983, At One and the Same Time (novel) 1985, Tongue of Fire 1988, Katerina (novel) 1989, The Railway (novel) 1991, Laish 1994, Lost 1995, Until the Dawn's Light 1995, The Ice Mine 1997, All Whom I Have Loved 1999, The Story of a Life: A Memoir (Prix Médicis, France) 1999, A Table for One (memoir) 2008, Laish (novel) 2009, Blooms of Darkness (novel) 2010. *Honours:* Dr hc (Hebrew Univ., Brandeis Univ., Bar-Ilan Univ., Yeshiva Univ.); Anne Frank Prize, Brenner Prize, Bialik Prize, Israel Prize 1983, H. H. Wingate Literary Award 1989, Nelly Sachs Prize, Dortmund, Germany 2005. *Address:* c/o Schocken Books Publicity Department, Random House, 1745 Broadway, New York, NY 10019, USA. *Website:* schocken.knopfdoubleday.com.

APPELGREN, Anne Marie; Finnish writer and translator; b. 12 March 1956, Ekenaes; m.; two c. *Publications include:* novels: Salto Mortal 1990, Skuggan av Saturnus 1992; non-fiction: Astrologi i dag. Självkännedom genom symboler 1994; other: trans. of various books into Swedish. *Address:* Vikingavagen 17, Nynashamm, Sweden (home). *E-mail:* annemarie.appelgren@bredband.net (office).

APPIAH, Kwame Anthony Akroma-Ampim Kusi, PhD; American (b. British) academic and writer; *Laurance S. Rockefeller University Professor of Philosophy and the University Center for Human Values, Princeton University*; b. 8 May 1954, London, England, UK; s. of Joe Appiah and Peggy Appiah; partner, Henry David Finder. *Education:* Ullenwod Manor School for Boys, Port Regis and Bryanston School, UK, Kwame Nkrumah Univ. of Science and Tech., Ghana, Univ. of Cambridge, UK. *Career:* raised in Ghana; taught at Univ. of Ghana; has held position of Prof. of Philosophy and/or Prof. of African Studies and African-American Studies at Univ. of Cambridge, Yale Univ., Cornell Univ., Duke Univ., Harvard Univ. 1991–2002; Laurance S. Rockefeller Univ. Prof. of Philosophy and Univ. Center for Human Values, Princeton Univ. 2002–; Juror, Neustadt Prize, Univ. of Oklahoma 2001; mem. American Philosophical Soc. 2001, American Acad. of Arts and Letters 2008. *Publications include:* Assertion and Conditionals 1985, For Truth in Semantics 1986, Necessary Questions: An Introduction to Philosophy 1989, Avenging Angel (novel) 1991, In My Father's House: Africa in the Philosophy of Culture (essays) (Annisfield-Wolf Book Award 1993, African Studies Asscn Herskovits Award 1993) 1992, Nobody Likes Letitia (novel) 1994, Color Consciousness: The Political Morality of Race (with Amy Gutman) (North American Soc. for Social Philosophy Annual Book Award) 1996, The Ethics of Identity 2005, Cosmopolitanism: Ethics in a World of Strangers (Council on Foreign Relations Arthur Ross Award) 2006, Experiments in Ethics 2007, The Honor Code: How Moral Revolutions Happen 2010; Ed.: Early African-American Classics 1990; Co-Ed. with Henry Louis Gates, Jr: Critical Perspectives Past and Present (series) 1993, The Dictionary of Global Culture 1996, Africana: The Encyclopedia of African and African American Experience 1999; with Peggy Appiah: Bu Me Bé: The Proverbs of the Akan; with Martin Bunzl: Buying Freedom 2007. *Honours:* Hon. DLitt (Richmond) 2000, (Colgate) 2003, (Bard Coll.) 2004, (Fairleigh Dickinson) 2006, (Swarthmore Coll.) 2006, (Dickinson Coll.) 2008, (Columbia) 2009, (The New School) 2009; Hon. LLD (Colby Coll.) 2010; Hon. DHum (Berea Coll.) 2010; Annisfield-Wolf Book Award 1993, Herskovits Award, African Studies Asscn 1993, Annual Book Award, N American Soc. for Social Philosophy 1996, Ralph J. Bunche Award, American Political Science Asscn 1997, Gustavus Myers Center Award 1997, Phi Beta Kappa Speaker, Harvard Commencement 2000, Tanner Lecturer, Univ. of California, San Diego and Univ. of Cambridge 2001, Morehouse Coll. Candle in the Dark Award in Educ. 2003, Arthur Ross Book Award, Council on Foreign Relations 2007, Joseph B. and Toby Gittler Prize 2008, Book Award, NJ Council of Humanities 2011. *Address:* Department of Philosophy, 208 Marx Hall, Princeton University, Princeton, NJ 08544-1006, USA (office). *Telephone:* (609) 258-4302 (office). *Fax:* (609) 258-1502 (office). *E-mail:* kappiah@princeton.edu (office); anthony.appiah@gmail.com (home). *Website:* web.princeton.edu/sites/philosph (office); www.appiah.net (home).

APPIGNANESI, Lisa, BA, MA, DPhil; British writer; b. 4 Jan. 1946, Łodź, Poland; two c.; partner Prof. John Forrester. *Education:* McGill Univ., Canada, Univ. of Sussex. *Career:* brought up in Canada and France, also lived and worked in USA, now based in London, England; staff writer, Center for Community Research, New York 1970–71; fmr Lecturer in European Studies, Univ. of Essex; Founding mem. and fmr Editorial Dir, Writers and Readers Publishing Cooperative in 1970s; Dir of Talks and Seminars, Inst. of Contemporary Arts (ICA), London 1980–86, Deputy Dir ICA 1986–90, Series Ed. ICA's Writers in Conversation 1983–90; full-time writer 1990–; Deputy Pres. English PEN 2004–07, Pres. 2008–10; Chair. Freud Museum, London; producer, writer or presenter of numerous TV and radio programmes; Visiting Prof. in Literature and the Medical Humanities, King's Coll., London. *Television:* No Place Quite Like It (BBC) 1987, The World of Gypsy Music (BBC) 1988, Intruders at the Palace (BBC) 1988, England's Henry Moore (Channel 4, UK) 1988, Seductions (series of short plays, Channel 4, UK) 1991, A Portrait of Salman Rushdie (FR3, France) 1999. *Radio:* The Case of Sigmund Freud, Freudian Slips (BBC Radio 4), Night Waves (BBC Radio 3). *Publications include:* non-fiction: Proust, Musil and Henry James: Femininity and the Creative Imagination 1973, Cabaret: The First Hundred Years 1984, Science and Beyond (ed.) 1986, Simone De Beauvoir 1988, Dismantling Truth: Reality in the Post-Modern World (ed.) 1989, Ideas From France: The Legacy of French Theory (ed.) 1989, Postmodernism (ed.) 1989, The Rushdie File (ed.) 1989, Losing the Dead 1999, Freud's Women 2000, The Cabaret 2004, Free Expression is No Offence (ed.) 2005, Mad, Bad and Sad (BMA Award for Public Understanding of Science) 2008, All About Love: Anatomy of an Unruly Emotion 2011; novels: Memory and Desire 1991, Dreams of Innocence 1994, A Good Woman 1996, The Things We Do For Love 1997, The Dead of Winter 1998, Sanctuary 2001, Paris Requiem 2001, Kicking Fifty 2003, The Memory Man (Canadian Holocaust Fiction Award) 2004, Unholy Loves 2006; trans.: Little Girls, The Year is 42 (Scott Moncrieff Prize for literary translation 2005), The Diary of Ma Yan by Ma Yan, My Forbidden Face: Growing Up Under the Taliban by Latifa. *Honours:* Chevalier, Ordre des Arts et des Lettres. *Literary Agent:* c/o Clare Alexander, Aitken Alexander Associates, 18–21 Cavaye Place, London SW10 9PT, England. *Telephone:* (20) 7373-8672. *Fax:* (20) 7373-6002. *E-mail:* reception@aitkenalexander.co.uk. *Website:* www.aitkenalexander.co.uk; lisaappignanesi.com.

APPLE, Max Isaac, BA, PhD; American academic and writer; *Teacher of Creative Writing, University of Pennsylvania*; b. 22 Oct. 1941, Grand Rapids, Mich.; one s. one d. *Education:* Michigan Univ. and Stanford Univ. *Career:* Asst Prof., Reed Coll., Portland, Ore. 1970–71; Asst Prof., Rice Univ. 1972–76, Assoc. Prof. 1976–80, Prof. of English 1980–2001, Prof. Emer. 2001–; teacher of creative writing, Univ. of Pennsylvania 2001–; mem. Modern Language Asscn, PEN, Texas Inst. of Letters. *Publications include:* Studies in English (with others) 1975, The Oranging of America and Other Stories 1976, Zip: A Novel of the Left and the Right 1978, Southwest Fiction (ed.) 1980, Three Stories 1983, Free Agents 1984, The Propheteers: A Novel 1987, Roomates: My Grandfather's Story (memoir) 1994, I Love Gootie: My Grandmother's Story 1998, The Jew of Home Depot 2008. *Honours:* Nat. Endowment for the Humanities Fellowship 1971, Texas Inst. of Letters Jesse Jones Award 1976, 1985, Hadassah Magazine Ribalous Award 1985.

APPLEBAUM, Anne; American writer and journalist; b. 25 July 1964, Washington, DC; d. of Harvey M. Applebaum and Elizabeth Applebaum; m.

Radek Sikorski; two c. *Education:* Univ. of Yale, London School of Econs and Univ. of Oxford, UK. *Career:* Warsaw Corresp., The Economist 1988; journalist, numerous journals in Cen. and Eastern Europe 1988–92; Foreign Ed. and Deputy Ed. The Spectator, London; fmr columnist, The Daily Telegraph, The Sunday Telegraph, Evening Standard; Political Ed., Evening Standard 1997; mem. Editorial Bd The Washington Post 2002–06, currently columnist; columnist, Slate; George Herbert Walker Bush/Axel Springer Fellow, American Acad., Germany 2008; broadcasting work includes Newsnight (BBC 2), Today (BBC Radio 4), Week in Westminster (BBC Radio 4), CNN, MSNBC, CBS, Sky News. *Publications include:* non-fiction: Between East and West: Across the Borderlands of Europe 1995, Gulag: A History 2003; contrib. to Wall Street Journal, International Herald Tribune, Foreign Affairs, Boston Globe, Independent, Guardian, Commentaire, Suddeutsche Zeitung, Newsweek, New Criterion, Weekly Standard, New Republic, New York Review of Books, National Review, New Statesman, TLS, Literary Review. *Honours:* Order of the Cross of Terra Mariana (Estonia) 2008; Charles Douglas-Home Memorial Trust Award for Journalism 1992, Adolph Bentnick Prize for European non-fiction 1996, Petőfi Award 2010. *Address:* The Washington Post, 1150 15th Street NW, Washington, DC 20071, USA (office). *E-mail:* applebaumanne@washpost.com (office). *Website:* www.washingtonpost.com (office); www.anneapplebaum.com.

APPLEMAN, Marjorie H., BA, MA; American dramatist and poet; b. Fort Wayne, Ind.; m. Philip Appleman. *Education:* Northwestern Univ., Indiana Univ., Univ. of Paris (Sorbonne), France. *Career:* Prof. of English and Playwriting, New York Univ., Columbia Univ.; Int. Honors Program, Indiana Univ.; mem. Authors' League of America, Circle East Theater Co., Dramatists' Guild, League of Professional Theatre Women, PEN American Center, Poets and Writers, Acad. of American Poets. *Publications include:* plays: Seduction Duet 1982, The Commuter 1985, more than 60 plays given in full productions or staged readings 1971–2006, Against Time (poems) 1994, Let's Not Talk About Lenny Anymore (opera libretto) 1989; contrib. to numerous anthologies and journals. *Honours:* several playwriting awards. *Address:* PO Box 5058, East Hampton, NY 11937, USA (home). *E-mail:* applemanmh@yahoo.com (home).

APPLEMAN, Philip Dean, BS, AM, PhD; American writer, poet and academic; *Distinguished Professor Emeritus, Indiana University;* b. 8 Feb. 1926, Kendallville, Ind.; s. of William Russell Appleman and Gertrude Collins Keller Appleman; m. Marjorie Ann Haberkorn 1950. *Education:* Northwestern Univ., Univ. of Michigan. *Career:* Fulbright Scholar, Univ. of Lyon, France 1951–52; Instructor to Prof., Indiana Univ. 1955–67, Prof. 1967–84, Distinguished Prof. of English 1984–86, Distinguished Prof. Emer. 1986–; Dir and Instructor, Int. School of America 1960–61, 1962–63; Visiting Prof., State Univ. of NY at Purchase 1973, Columbia Univ., New York 1974; Visiting Scholar, New York Univ., UCLA; John Steinbeck Visiting Writer, Long Island Univ. at Southampton 1992; mem. Acad. of American Poets, American Asscn of Univ. Profs, Authors' Guild of America, Modern Language Asscn, Nat. Council of Teachers of English, PEN American Center, Poetry Soc. of America, Poets and Writers. *Publications include:* fiction: In the Twelfth Year of the War 1970, Shame the Devil 1981, Apes and Angels 1989; poetry: Kites on a Windy Day 1967, Summer Love and Surf 1968, Open Doorways 1976, Darwin's Ark 1984, Darwin's Bestiary 1986, Let There Be Light 1991, New and Selected Poems 1956–1996 1996, Karma, Dharma, Pudding & Pie 2009; non-fiction: The Silent Explosion 1965; ed.: 1859: Entering an Age of Crisis 1959, Darwin 1970, The Origin of Species 1975, An Essay on the Principle of Population 1976; contribs to numerous publs. *Honours:* Ferguson Memorial Award, Friends of Literature Soc. 1969, Christopher Morley Awards, Poetry Soc. of America 1970, 1975, Castanola Award, Poetry Soc. of America 1975, Nat. Endowment for the Arts Fellowship 1975, Pushcart Prize 1985, Humanist Arts Award, American Humanist Asscn 1994, Friend of Darwin Award, Nat. Center for Science Educ. 2002. *Address:* PO Box 5058, East Hampton, NY 11937, USA (home). *Fax:* (631) 324-1252 (home). *E-mail:* applemanmp@yahoo.com; phil.appleman@gmail.com.

APT, Bryan Andrew, BLS, MS, MPh; American writer; b. 30 May 1965, Fort Collins, Colo. *Education:* Princeton Univ., Iowa State Univ., Indiana Univ., Johns Hopkins Univ. *Publications include:* Case of the Missing Detective: Mystery Down Under 1995, Search for Freedom – Distinctions between Illusory and Actual Human Freedom: Dickens and Engels 1999, Tragic Time and Comic Time in Shakespeare's Plays 1999, Under the Apple Tree: Musings and Poetry 2001, Othello: A Tragic Passage from Light to Darkness 2002, Images of Light and Darkness in Heart of Darkness: Undermining Nineteenth-Century Idealism 2003. *Honours:* Nat. Merit Scholar, US Tennis Asscn ranked player. *Address:* c/o Harper Benton Press, 1017 Burnett Avenue, Ames, IA 50010, USA.

ARAC DE NYEKO, Monica, BA, MA; Ugandan writer; b. 1979, Kitgum dist. *Education:* Makerere Univ., Groningen Univ., Netherlands. *Career:* taught Literature and English at St Mary's Coll., Kisubi; Chief Ed. TAP Voices (journal); writer for Sunday Monitor (newspaper); mem. Uganda Women Writers Asscn (FEMRITE), Transcend Art and Peace network (TAP); currently based in Kenya. *Publications include:* Children of the Fields 2005; numerous essays and short stories in anthologies and journals including In the Stars (First Prize, Women's World Voices in War Zones) 2006, Jambula Tree (Caine Prize for African Writing 2007) 2006. *Address:* c/o Uganda Women Writers Association (FEMRITE), PO Box 705, Kampala, Uganda.

ARBASINO, Alberto; Italian author, essayist and critic; b. 22 Jan. 1930, Voghera. *Education:* Univ. of Milan. *Career:* Ed. Italo Calvino 1957–59; began literary career writing reports for the weekly Il Mondo from Paris and London; also worked for newspapers Il Giorno and later Il Corriere della sera; has collaborated with la Repubblica 1975–; mem. Group 63; hosted programme Match on RAI2 1977, Che tempo che fa by Fabio Fazio 2006; Deputy, Italian Parl. (elected as ind. for Italian Republican Party) 1983–87. *Publications include:* Le piccole vacanze 1957, L'Anonimo lombardo 1959, Parigi o cara 1960, Fratelli d'Italia 1963, La narcisata – La controra 1964, Grazie per le magnifiche rose 1966, La maleducazione teatrale 1966, Off-Off 1968, Super Eliogabalo 1969, Sessanta posizioni 1971, I Turchi 1971, Certi romanzi – La Belle Epoque per le scuole 1977, Il principe costante 1972, La bella di Lodi 1972, Amate Sponde (con Mario Missiroli) 1974, La narcisata 1975, Un paese senza 1980, Matine 1983, Il meraviglioso, anzi 1985, Lettere da Londra 1997, Passeggiando tra i draghi addormentati 1997, Paesaggi italiani con zombi 1998, Le muse a Los Angeles 2000, Rap! 2001, Marescialle e libertini 2004, Dall'Ellade a Bisanzio 2006, L'Ingegnere in blu 2008, La vita bassa 2008, Romanzi e Racconti 2009, 2010; contrib. to L'illustrazione italiana, Officina, Il Mondo, Tempo presente, Il Verri, Espresso, il Giorno, la Repubblica. *Honours:* Cavaliere di Gran Croce Ordine al Merito della Repubblica Italiana 1995, Commandeur des Arts et des Lettres 2010. *Address:* Gruppo Editoriale L'Espresso, Div. La Repubblica, Via C. Colombo 90, 00147 Rome, Italy (office). *Telephone:* (06) 49822499 (office). *Fax:* (06) 49822651 (office). *E-mail:* segreteria_cultura@repubblica.it (office). *Website:* www.repubblica.it (office).

ARBATOVA, Maria Ivanovna; Russian novelist, playwright and poet; b. (Maria Ivanova Gavrilina), 17 July 1957, Murom, Vladimir region; d. of Ivan Gavrilovich Gavrilin and Ludmila Ilyinichna Aisenstadt; m. 2nd Oleg Tumayevich Vitte; two s. *Education:* Moscow State Univ. and Moscow Literary Inst. (workshop of Victor Rozov). *Career:* active participant in feminist movt and other political activities 1991–; Founder Psychological Club Garmonia 1991–96; Dir Women Involved with Politics Club 1996–; columnist, Obshchaya Gazeta; Cand. for State Duma 1999; Co-Chair. Partiya prav Cheloveka pressure group; commentator for Ya Sama TV talk show; mem. Union of Writers of Moscow, Union of Theatrical Artistes of Russia. *TV appearances:* I-Myself (regular appearances). *Plays:* Victoria Vassilyeva in the Eye of Strangers (USSR Competition of Young Dramatists Prize 1985), Dreams on the Bank of Dnieper (Festival of Young Dramatists Prize 1990), Detailed Interview on the Subject of Freedom (Bonn Theatre Festival Prize, Germany) 1996, Russian Mirror: Three Plays by Russian Women (Russian Theatre Archive) 1998. *Radio plays:* Late Crew, Initiation Ceremony (Europe Prize 1998). *Publications include:* more than 20 books including I Am 40 (autobiographical novel), I Am a Woman (stories), A Will and a Way: Russian Women's Writing in the 1990s (co-author) 2002; numerous articles and essays. *Address:* EKSMO Publishers, Narognogo Opolcheniya str. 38, 1232298 Moscow, Russia (office). *Telephone:* (495) 246-81-55 (home). *E-mail:* arbatova@cityline.ru. *Website:* www.arbatova.ru.

ARCHER, Geoffrey Wilson; British writer; b. 21 May 1944, London, England; m. Eva Janson; one s. one d. *Education:* Highgate School, London. *Career:* researcher, Southern TV 1964; reporter, Anglia TV, Norwich 1965–69, Tyne-Tees TV, Newcastle 1969, ITN 1969–95 (Defence Corresp.) 1980–95; mem. Soc. of Authors. *Publications include:* fiction: Skydancer 1987, Shadow Hunter 1989, Eagle Trap 1992, Scorpion Trail 1995, Java Spider 1997, Fire Hawk 1998, The Lucifer Network 2001, The Burma Legacy 2002, Dark Angel 2004. *E-mail:* author@geoffreyarcher.com (home). *Website:* www.geoffreyarcher.com.

ARCHER OF WESTON-SUPER-MARE, Baron (Life Peer), cr. 1992, of Mark in the County of Somerset; **Jeffrey Howard Archer;** British writer and fmr politician; b. 15 April 1940, London, England; s. of William Archer and Lola Archer (née Cook); m. Mary Doreen Archer (née Weeden) 1966; two s. *Education:* Wellington School, Brasenose Coll., Oxford. *Career:* mem. GLC for Havering 1966–70; MP for Louth (Conservative) 1969–74; Deputy Chair. Conservative Party 1985–86; mem. House of Lords 1992–. *Plays:* Beyond Reasonable Doubt 1987, Exclusive 1989, The Accused (writer and actor) 2000. *Film:* Bridget Jones's Diary (as himself) 2001. *Publications include:* Not a Penny More, Not a Penny Less 1975, Shall We Tell the President? 1977, Kane and Abel 1979, A Quiver Full of Arrows 1980, The First Miracle (with Craigie Aitchison) 1980, The Prodigal Daughter 1982, First Among Equals 1984, A Matter of Honour 1985, A Twist in the Tale (short stories) 1988, Honour Among Thieves 1993, The Fourth Estate 1996, The Collected Short Stories 1997, To Cut a Long Story Short (short stories) 2000, A Prison Diary Vols I and II 2002, Sons of Fortune 2003, A Prison Diary Vol. III 2004, Cat O' Nine Tales (short stories) 2006, The Gospel According to Judas 2007, A Prisoner of Birth (Prix Polar Int. Prize 2009) 2008, Paths of Glory (Prix Relay du roman d'evasion 2010) 2009, 30th Anniversary revised edn of Kane and Abel 2009, And Thereby Hangs a Tale (short stories) 2010, Only Time Will Tell 2011, The Sins of the Father 2012. *Address:* 93 Albert Embankment, London, SE1 7TY, England (office). *E-mail:* questions@jeffreyarcher.co.uk (office). *Website:* www.jeffreyarcher.com (home).

ARDAI, Charles, BA; American writer and editor; *Chairman, Schrödinger LLC;* b. 25 Oct. 1969, New York, NY; m. Naomi Novik. *Education:* Columbia Univ. *Career:* Contributing Ed., Computer Entertainment and K-Power 1985; Ed., Davis Publications 1990–91; co-f. Hard Case Crime; Founder and fmr CEO Juno Online Services Inc.; currently Chair. Schrödinger LLC; mem. Bd of Dirs D.E. Shaw Tech. LLC; mem. Mystery Writers of America. *Television:*

Haven (writer, producer) 2010. *Publications include:* Great Tales of Madness and the Macabre 1990, Kingpins 1992, Futurecrime 1992, Death Do Us Part 2006, Little Girl Lost, Songs of Innocence, Fifty to One 2008; contrib.: Alfred Hitchcock's Mystery Magazine, Ellery Queen's Mystery Magazine, Twilight Zone, The Year's Best Horror Stories, Computer Gaming World, and others. *Honours:* Pearlman Prize for Fiction, Columbia Univ. 1991, Edgar Award for Best Short Story (for The Home Front) 2007. *Address:* Schrödinger LLC, 120 West, 45th Street, 17th Floor, Tower 45, New York, NY 10036, USA (office). *Telephone:* (212) 295-5800 (office). *Fax:* (212) 295-5801 (office). *E-mail:* info@hardcasecrime.com (office). *Website:* www.schrodinger.com (office); www.hardcasecrime.com.

ARGUELLES, Ivan Wallace, BA, MLS; American poet, publisher and librarian; b. 24 Jan. 1939, Rochester, Minn.; m. 1st Claire Birnbaum 1958 (divorced 1960); m. 2nd Marilla Calhourn Elder 1962; two s. *Education:* Univ. of Minnesota, Univ. of Chicago, New York Univ., Vanderbilt Univ. *Career:* Guest Lecturer, Rampo Coll., NJ 1978; Co-founder Rock Steady Press, San Francisco, Calif. 1988, Pantograph Press, Berkeley, Calif. 1992. *Publications include:* Instamatic Reconditioning 1978, The Invention of Spain 1978, Captive of the Vision of Paradise 1983, The Tattooed Heart of the Drunken Sailor 1983, Manicomio 1984, Nailed to the Coffin of Life 1985, What Are They Doing to My Animal? 1986, The Structure of Hell 1986, Pieces of the Bone-Text Still There 1987, Baudelaire's Brain 1988, Looking for Mary Lou: Illegal Syntax (William Carlos Williams Award, Poetry Soc. of America) 1989, 'THAT' Goddess 1992, Hapax Legomenon 1993, The Tragedy of Momus 1993, Enigma and Variations: Paradise is Persian for Park 1996, Madonna Septet (two vols) 2000, Chac Prostibulario (with John M. Bennett) 2002, Triloka 2003, Inferno 2005, Comedy Divine The 2009, The Death of Stalin (American Book Award, Before Columbus Foundation) 2010, Ulterior Vision(s) 2011; contribs to various anthologies and magazines. *Address:* 1740 Walnut Street, No. 4, Berkeley, CA 94709, USA (home). *E-mail:* iarguell@hotmail.com.

ARGUETA, Manlio; Salvadorean writer and librarian; b. 24 Nov. 1935, San Miguel. *Career:* lived in exile in Costa Rica for many years since 1973; Dir Biblioteca Nacional de El Salvador 1996. *Publications:* En el costado de la luz (poetry) 1968, Un hombre por la patria 1968, El valle de las Hamacas 1977, Caperucita en la zona roja 1977, Un día en la vida (Univ. of Cen. America Prize) 1980, Cuscatlán (novel) 1987, Milagro de la Paz (novel) 1996, Siglo de O(g)ro 1997. *Address:* Biblioteca Nacional, 4ta Calle Oriente y Avda Mons. Oscar A. Romero #124, San Salvador, El Salvador (office). *Telephone:* 2221-2099 (office). *Fax:* 2221-8847 (office). *Website:* www.binaes.gob.sv (office).

ARGULLOL, Rafael, DPhil; Spanish writer and academic; *Professor of Aesthetics and Art Theory, Universitat Pompeu Fabra*; b. (Rafael Argullol i Murgadas), 1949, Barcelona. *Education:* Univ. of Barcelona, Univ. of Rome, Warburg Inst., London, Free Univ. of Berlin. *Career:* Prof. of Aesthetics and Art Theory, Faculty of Humanities, Universitat Pompeu Fabra, Dir Inst. for Culture 2002–08. *Publications include:* poetry: Disturbios del conocimiento 1980, Duelo en el Valle de la Muerte 1986, L'esmolador de ganivets 1998, El afilador de cuchillo 1999; novel: Leopardi: infelicidad y titanismo 1985, Tres miradas sobre el arte 1985, Lampedusa: una historia mediterránea 1987, Territorio del nómada 1987, El Quattrocento: arte y cultura en el renacimiento italiano 1988, Desciende, río invisible 1990, La razón del mal (Nadal Prize) 1993, El cansancio de Occidente: una conversación 1993, Sabiduría de la ilusión: quince escenarios 1994, Naturaleza: la conquista de la soledad 1995, Transeuropa 1998, Davalú o el dolor: crònica d'un duel 2001, El cazador de instantes: cuaderno de travesía 1990–95 2002, Una educación sensorial: historia personal del desnudo femenino en la pintura (Fondo de Cultura Económica Essay Prize) 2002, Del Ganges al Mediterránea: un diálogo entre las culturas de India y Europa 2004, El pont de foc 2004, Wolfgang Amadeus Mozart. Las últimas sinfonías 2004, Lampedusa 2008, Visión desde el fondo del mar (City of Barcelona Prize 2010, Cálamo Prize 2010) 2010; essays: La atracción del abismo: un itinerario por el paisaje romántico 1983, El Héroe y el Único: el espíritu trágico del Romanticismo 1984, El fin del mundo como obra de arte: un relato occidental 1991, Aventura. Una filosofía nómada 2000, Manifiesto contra la servidumbre, Escritos frente a la Guerra 2003, Cazador de instants, El puente del fuego 2004, Enciclopedia del crepúsculo, Breviario the aurora 2006. *Address:* Universitat Pompeu Fabra, 25–27 Ramon Trias Fargas, 08005 Barcelona, Spain (office). *Telephone:* (93) 5422585 (office). *Fax:* (93) 5421620 (office). *E-mail:* rafael.argullol@upf.edu (office). *Website:* www.upf.edu/huma/directori/argullol.html (office); www.rafaelargullol.com.

ARIAS, Arturo, PhD; Guatemalan novelist and literary critic; *Professor, Department of Spanish and Portuguese, University of Texas at Austin*; b. 22 June 1950, Guatemala City. *Education:* École des Hautes Études en Sciences Sociales, Paris, France. *Career:* Pres., Latin American Studies Asscn 2001–03; fmr Dir of Latin American Studies, Univ. of Redlands; Richard E. Greenleaf Chair in Latin American Studies, Tulane Univ. 2007; currently Prof., Dept of Spanish and Portuguese, Univ. of Texas, Austin. *Film screenplays include:* El Norte 1984. *Publications include:* novels: Despues de las bombas (trans. as After the Bombs) 1979, Itzam Na 1981, Jaguar en Llamas 1989, Los caminos de Paxil 1990, Cascabel (trans. as Rattlesnake) 1998, Sopa de caracol 2003; criticism: La identidad de la palabra (trans. as The Identity of the Word) 1998, Gestos ceremoniales (trans. as Ceremonial Gestures) 1998, Miguel Angel Asturias's Mulata 2001, The Rigoberta Menchu Controversy 2001, Taking Their Word: Literature and the Signs of Central America 2007. *Honours:* Casa de las Americas Prize (twice), Anna Seghers Scholarship, Miguel Angel Asturias Nat. Literary Award 2008. *Address:* Department of Spanish and Portuguese, University of Texas at Austin, BEN 4.130, 1 University Station B3700, Austin, TX 78712-1155, USA (office). *Telephone:* (512) 232-4549 (office). *Fax:* (512) 471-8073 (office). *E-mail:* arturo_arias@austin.utexas.edu (office). *Website:* www.utexas.edu (office).

ARIDJIS, Homero; Mexican author, poet and diplomatist; *Ambassador to UNESCO*; b. 6 April 1940, Contepec, Michoacán; m. Betty Ferber 1965, two d. *Education:* Autonomous Univ. of Mexico 1961. *Career:* lecturer in Mexican literature at univs in USA; Cultural Attaché, Embassy in Netherlands 1972, later Amb. to Switzerland and the Netherlands; Man. Cultural Inst., Michoacán, Dir Festival Int. de Poesia 1981, 1982, 1987; f. Review Correspondencias; Chief Ed. Dialogos; Visiting Prof., Univ. of Indiana and New York Univ.; Poet-in-Residence, Columbia Univ. Translation Center, New York; co-f. Pres. Grupo de los Cien 1985 (100 internationally renowned artists and intellectuals active in environmental affairs); Nichols Chair in the Humanities and the Public Sphere, Univ. of Calif. at Irvine; Pres. International PEN 1997–2003, Pres. Emer. 2003–; Amb. to UNESCO 2007–. *Publications include:* poetry: Los ojos desdoblados 1960, Antes del reino 1963, Ajedrez-Navegaciones 1969, Los espacios azules 1969 (Blue Spaces 1974), Quemar las naves 1975, Vivir para ver 1977, Construir la muerte 1982, Obra poética 1960–86 1987, Imágenes para el fin del milenio 1990, Nueva expulsión del paraíso 1990, El poeta en peligro de extinción 1992, Tiempo de ángeles 1994, Ojos de otro mirar 1998 (Eyes to See Otherwise: Selected Poems of Homero Aridjis 2002), El ojo de la ballena 2001; prose: La tumba de Filidor 1961, Mirándola dormir 1964, Perséfone 1967 (Persephone 1986), El poeta niño 1971, Noche de independencia 1978, Espectáculo del año dos mil 1981, Playa nudista y otros relatos 1982, 1492 vida y tiempos de Juan Cabezón de Castilla 1985, El último Adán 1986, Memorias del nuevo mundo 1988, Gran teatro del fin del mundo 1989, La leyenda de los soles 1993, El Señor de los últimos días: Visiones del año dos mil 1994, ¿En quién piensas cuando haces el amor? 1996, Apocalipsis con figuras 1997, La montaña de las mariposas 2000, El silencio de Orlando 2000, La zona del silencio 2002, El hombre que amaba el Sol 2005. *Honours:* Guggenheim Fellow 1966–67, 1979–80; Hon. DHumLitt (Indiana) 1993; Global 500 Award 1987, Novedades Novela Prize 1988, Grinzane Cavour Prize for Best Foreign Fiction 1992, Prix Roger Caillois, France 1997, Presea Generalisimo José María Morelos, City of Morelia 1998, Environmentalist of the Year Award, Latin Trade Magazine 1999, John Hay Award, Orion Soc. 2000, Forces for Nature Award, National Resources Defense Council 2001, Green Cross Millennium Award for Int. Environmental Leadership, Global Green, USA 2002. *Address:* Permanent Delegation of Mexico to UNESCO, Maison de l'UNESCO, Bureaux M7.45, 1 rue Miollis, 75732 Paris, France (office). *Telephone:* 1-45-68-33-55 (office). *Fax:* 1-47-34-92-45 (office). *E-mail:* dl.mexique@unesco.org (office).

ARJOUNI, Jakob; German novelist and playwright; b. 8 Oct. 1964, Frankfurt am Main. *Plays:* The Garage 1988, Nobleman Daughter 1996. *Publications include:* novels: Happy Birthday Turk 1987, More Beer 1987, One Man One Murder 1991, And Still Drink More! 1994, Magic Hoffman 1996, One Death to Die 1997, Kismet 2001, Hausaufgaben 2004, Chez Max 2006, Der Heilige Eddy 2009; short story collections: A Friend 1998. *Honours:* Golden Diogenes Owl Award 2011. *Address:* Diogenes Verlag, Sprecherstrasse 8, 8032 Zürich, Switzerland (office). *E-mail:* info@diogenes.ch (office). *Website:* www.diogenes.ch (office).

ARLEN, Leslie (see NICOLE, Christopher Robin)

ARLEN, Michael John, BA; American writer; b. 9 Dec. 1930, London, England; m. Alice Albright 1972; four d. *Education:* Harvard Univ. *Career:* mem. Authors' Guild, PEN. *Publications include:* Living-Room War 1969, Exiles 1970, An American Verdist 1972, Passage to Ararat (Nat. Book Award 1976) 1974, The View from Highway One 1975, Thirty Seconds 1980, The Camera Age 1982, Say Goodbye to Sam 1984, New Yorker Anatomy: An Index to Departments: Affairs of State to Onward and Upward With the Arts 1975–1989 1989; contrib. to New Yorker magazine. *Honours:* Hon. DLitt 1984; Nat. Book Award 1975, Le Prix Bremond 1976. *Address:* 1120 Fifth Avenue, Apartment 9A, New York, NY 10128-0144, USA (home). *Telephone:* (212) 289-0788 (home).

ARMAH, Ayi Kwei, MFA; Ghanaian novelist and poet; b. 1939, Sekondi Takoradi. *Education:* Harvard Univ. and Columbia Univ., USA. *Career:* fmr trans., Révolution Africaine magazine; scriptwriter, Ghana TV 1964; Ed., Jeune Afrique magazine, Paris 1967–68; teacher, Coll. of Nat. Education, Chamg'omge, Tanzania, Nat. Univ. of Lesotho, various other insts; currently lives in Senegal. *Publications include:* novels: The Beautyful Ones are Not Yet Born 1968, Fragments 1970, Why Are We So Blest? 1972, Two Thousand Seasons 1973, The Healers 1978, Osiris Rising 1995, Kmt: In the House of Life, The Silence of the Elders; contrib.: short stories and articles to Présense Africaine, Okyeame, Harper's, Atlantic Monthly, New African, West Africa. *Address:* c/o Per Ankh Publishing Company, B.P. 2, Popenguine, Senegal. *E-mail:* perankheditions@arc.sn. *Website:* www.perankhbooks.com.

ARMEL, Aliette; French writer; b. 23 Feb. 1951. *Career:* critic, Magazine littéraire 1984–. *Publications include:* non-fiction: Marguerita Duras et l'autobiographie 1990, Michel Leiris 1997; fiction: L'enfant abandonné (short stories) 1998, Le voyage de Bilqîs (novel, trans. as Love, The Painter's Wife and The Queen of Sheba) 2002, Le Disparu de Salonique (novel) 2005, Le Pianiste de Trieste 2008, Pondicherry, at Dawn 2010; contrib. of essays to Marguierite Duras: Les trois lieux de l'écrit 1998, Les itinéraires de Michel Ragon 1999, Antigone 1999, Sylvie 2001. *Address:* 5 rue Nicolas Roret, 75013

Paris, France (home). *Telephone:* 1-55-43-99-30 (home). *Fax:* 1-55-43-99-30 (home). *E-mail:* aliette.armel@libertysurf.fr. *Website:* www.magazine-litteraire.com (office).

ARMES, Roy Philip, BA, PhD; British writer and academic; b. 16 March 1937, Norwich, Norfolk, England; m. Margaret Anne Johnson 1960; one s. two d. *Education:* Univs of Bristol, Exeter and London. *Career:* teacher, Royal Liberty School, Romford 1960–69; Assoc. Lecturer in Film, Univ. of Surrey 1969–72; Research Fellow, Hornsey Coll. of Art 1969–72, Lecturer 1972–73; Sr Lecturer, Middlesex Polytechnic (later Middlesex Univ.) 1973–78, fmr Reader in Film and Television, now Prof. Emer.; visiting lecturer at many colls and univs. *Publications include:* French Cinema Since 1946 (two vols) 1966, The Cinema of Alain Resnais 1968, French Film 1970, Patterns of Realism 1972, Film and Reality: An Historical Survey 1974, The Ambiguous Image 1976, A Critical History of British Cinema 1978, The Films of Alain Robbe-Grillet 1981, French Cinema 1984, Third World Film Making and the West 1987, Action and Image: Dramatic Structure in Cinema 1994, Postcolonial Images: Studies in North African Film 2005, African Filmmaking: North and South of the Sahara 2006, Arab and African Film Making (with Lizbeth Malkmus), Dictionary of North African Film Makers; contrib. to many books and periodicals. *Address:* Middlesex University, The Burroughs, London, NW4 4BT, England (office). *Telephone:* (20) 8411-5555 (office). *Website:* www.mdx.ac.uk (office).

ARMITAGE, Gary Edric, (Robert Edric), BA, PhD; British writer; b. 14 April 1956, Sheffield, England; m. Sara Jones 1978. *Education:* Univ. of Hull. *Publications include:* Winter Garden 1985, A Season of Peace 1985, A New Ice Age 1986, Across the Autumn Grass 1986; as Robert Edric: A Lunar Eclipse 1989, In the Days of the American Museum 1990, The Broken Lands 1992, Hallowed Ground 1993, The Earth Made of Glass 1994, Elysium 1995, In Desolate Heaven 1997, The Sword Cabinet 1999, The Book of the Heathen 2000, Peacetime 2002, Cradle Song 2003, Siren Song 2004, Swan Song 2005, Gathering the Water 2006, The Kingdom of Ashes (novel) 2007, In Zodiac Light 2008, Salvage 2010, The London Satyr 2011, The Lives Of The Savages 2011, The Devil's Beat 2012; contrib. to various periodicals. *Honours:* James Tait Black Memorial Prize 1985, Trask Award 1985, Soc. of Authors Award 1994, Arts Council Bursary 1995. *Address:* Glenfinnan, Springbank Avenue, Hornsea, HU18 1ED, England (home). *Telephone:* (1964) 532069 (home).

ARMITAGE, Ronda Jacqueline, DipEd; New Zealand writer, teacher and family therapist; b. 11 March 1943, Kaikoura; m. David Armitage 1966, two c. *Education:* Univ. of Auckland, Massey Univ., Hamilton Teacher's Coll. *Career:* school teacher, Duvauchelle 1964–66, London, UK 1966, Auckland 1968–69; adviser on children's books, Dorothy Butler Ltd, Auckland 1970–71; Asst Librarian, Lewes Priory Comprehensive School, Sussex, UK 1976–77; teacher, East Sussex Co. Council 1978–; mem. Soc. of Authors. *Publications:* Let's Talk About Drinking 1982, New Zealand 1983; children's fiction: The Lighthouse Keeper's Lunch (New Zealand Library Asscn Esther Glen Award 1978) 1977, The Trouble With Mr Harris 1978, Don't Forget, Matilda! 1978, The Bossing of Josie (aka The Birthday Spell) 1980, Ice Creams for Rosie 1981, One Moonlit Night 1983, Grandma Goes Shopping 1984, The Lighthouse Keeper's Catastrophe 1986, The Lighthouse Keeper's Rescue 1989, When Dad Did the Washing 1990, Watch the Baby, Daisy 1991, Looking After Chocolates 1992, A Quarrel of Koalas 1992, The Lighthouse Keeper's Picnic 1993, The Lighthouse Keeper's Cat 1996, Flora and the Strawberry Red Birthday Party 1997, Queen of the Night 1999, Family Violence 1999, Queen of the Night 1999, The Lighthouse Keeper's Favourite Stories 1999, The Lighthouse Keeper's Breakfast 2000, The Lighthouse Keeper's Tea 2001, The Lighthouse Keeper's Christmas 2002, Violence in Society 2003, A New Home for Pirate 2007, Small Knight and George 2007, The Lighthouse Keeper's New Friend 2007, Small Knight and George and the Royal Chocolate Cake 2008, The Bungle Jungle Bedtime Kiss 2008, A Very Strange Creature 2009, The Lighthouse Keeper's Surprise 2009; contrib. of features in children's magazine Aquila 1998, 1999, 2000. *Literary Agent:* c/o Miles Stott Children's Literary Agency, East Hook Farm, Lower Quay Road, Hook, Haverfordwest, SA62 4LR, Wales. *Telephone:* (1437) 890570. *E-mail:* miles.stott@virgin.net.

ARMITAGE, Simon Robert, CBE, BA, MA; British poet and writer; *Professor of Poetry, University of Sheffield*; b. 26 May 1963, Huddersfield, West Yorks., England. *Education:* Portsmouth Polytechnic, Univ. of Manchester. *Career:* Probation Officer, Greater Manchester Probation Service 1988–93; Poetry Ed., Chatto and Windus 1993–95; Sr Lecturer, Manchester Metropolitan Univ. 1999–2011; Prof. of Poetry, Univ. of Sheffield 2011–. *Publications include:* Human Geography 1986, The Distance Between Stars 1987, The Walking Horses 1988, Zoom! 1989, Around Robinson 1991, Xanadu 1992, Kid 1992, Book of Matches 1993, The Anaesthetist 1994, The Dead Sea Poems 1995, Moon Country 1996, CloudCuckooLand 1997, All Points North (essays) 1998, Mister Heracles 2000, Little Green Man (novel) 2001, Selected Poems 2001, Travelling Songs 2002, The Universal Home Doctor 2002, The White Stuff (novel) 2004, Homer's Odyssey (trans.) 2006, Tyrannosaurus Rex Versus the Corduroy Kid 2006, Sir Gawain and the Green Knight (trans.) 2007, Gig 2008, The Not Dead 2008, Seeing Stars 2010; contrib. to Sunday Times, TLS, Guardian, Observer, Independent. *Honours:* Hon. DLitt (Portsmouth) 1996, (Huddersfield) 1996; Dr hc (Sheffield Hallam) 2009; Eric Gregory Award 1988, Sunday Times Young Writer of the Year 1993, Forward Poetry Prize 1993, Lannan Award 1994, Ivor Novello Award 2005, BAFTA Award 2005, Keats-Shelley Poetry Prize (for The Present) 2011. *Literary Agent:* c/o David Godwin Associates, 55 Monmouth Street, London, WC2H 9DG, England. *Telephone:* (20) 7240-9992. *Fax:* (20) 7395-6110. *Website:* www.davidgodwinassociates.co.uk; www.simonarmitage.com.

ARMSTRONG, David John, BA; Australian journalist and media executive; *Adviser to Senior Management, Post Publishing, Bangkok*; b. 25 Nov. 1947, Sydney; s. of Allan E. Armstrong and Mary P. Armstrong; m. Deborah Bailey 1980 (deceased); two d. *Education:* Marist Brothers High School, Parramatta, Univ. of NSW. *Career:* Ed. The Bulletin 1985–86; Deputy Ed. The Daily Telegraph 1988–89; Ed. The Australian 1989–92, Ed.-in-Chief 1996–2002; Ed. The Canberra Times 1992–93; Ed. South China Morning Post, Hong Kong 1993–94, Ed.-in-Chief 1994–96; Ed.-in-Chief, South China Morning Post 2003–05; mem. Bd Dirs Post Publishing 2004–09, Pres. and COO 2005–08, mem. Exec. Cttee 2006–08, currently Adviser to Sr Man.; mem. Bd Dirs HFP-Post 2006–09; mem. Asian Bd Int. News Media Asscn 2006–. *Honours:* Australian Centenary Medal 2003. *Address:* Bangkok Post Building, 136 Na Ranong Road, off Sunthorn Kosa Road, Klong Toey, Bangkok 10110, Thailand (office). *Telephone:* (2) 712-0396 (office). *E-mail:* david@bangkokpost.co.th (office); wansao365@gmail.com (office). *Website:* www.bangkokpost.com (office).

ARMSTRONG, David Malet, AO, BA, BPhil, PhD, FAHA, FBA; Australian academic and writer; *Professor Emeritus of Philosophy, University of Sydney*; b. 8 July 1926, Melbourne; s. of Cdre J. M. Armstrong and Philippa Suzanne Marett; m. Jennifer Mary de Bohun Clark 1982. *Education:* Dragon School, Oxford, UK, Geelong Grammar School, Sydney Univ., Exeter Coll., Oxford, Univ. of Melbourne. *Career:* Asst Lecturer in Philosophy, Birkbeck Coll., London, UK 1954–55; Lecturer, Sr Lecturer in Philosophy, Univ. of Melbourne 1956–63; Challis Prof. of Philosophy, Univ. of Sydney 1964–91, Prof. Emer. 1992–; mem. Bd Quadrant magazine; mem. US Acad. of Arts and Science. *Publications:* Berkeley's Theory of Vision 1961, Perception and the Physical World 1961, Bodily Sensations 1962, A Materialist Theory of the Mind 1968, Belief, Truth and Knowledge 1973, Universals and Scientific Realism 1978, The Nature of the Mind and Other Essays 1983, What is a Law of Nature? 1983, Consciousness and Causality (with Norman Malcolm) 1984, A Combinatorial Theory of Possibility 1989, Universals: An Opinionated Instruction 1989, Dispositions: A Debate (with C. B. Martin and U. T. Place) 1996, A World of States of Affairs 1997, The Mind-Body Problem: An Opinionated Introduction 1999, Truth and Truthmakers 2004; contribs to scholarly books and journals. *Honours:* Hon. DLitt (Nottingham). *Address:* 206 Glebe Point Road, Glebe, NSW 2037, Australia (home). *Telephone:* (2) 9660-1435 (home). *Fax:* (2) 9660-8846 (home). *E-mail:* armo.dm@gmail.com (office).

ARMSTRONG, Jeannette Christine, DFA, BFA, LLD, PhD; Canadian (Okanagan, Penticton Indian Band) writer, poet and academic; b. 5 Feb. 1948; one s. one d. *Education:* Okanagan Coll., Univ. of Victoria, Univ. of Greifswald, Germany. *Career:* Exec. Dir En'owkin Centre 1986–, Adjunct Prof., En'owkin School of Writing, Univ. of Victoria 1989–; Asst Prof. Indigenous Studies, Univ. of British Columbia, Okanagan; mem. Nat. Aboriginal Traditional Knowledge Sub-cttee of Cttee on Status of Endangered Wildlife in Canada; Vice-Chair. Indigenous Adult and Higher Learning Asscn, BC; mem. PEN International, Writers' Union of Canada; Okanagan mem. Penticton Indian Band. *Publications include:* novels: Slash 1985, Whispering in Shadows 2000; poetry: Breath Tracks 1991, Native Poetry in Canada: A Contemporary Anthology (ed with Lally Grauer) 2001; children's books: Enwhisteetkwa (Walk in Water) 1982, Neekna and Chemai 1984, Dancing with Cranes 2004; ed The Native Creative Process 1991 (with Douglas Cardinal), Looking at the Words of Our People: First Nations Analysis of Literature 1993; contribs to This is a Story, All My Relations: An Anthology of Contemporary Canadian Native Fiction 1990, Aboriginal Perspectives of the Natural Environment 1991, Give Back: First Nations Perspectives on Cultural Practice 1992, We Get Our Living Like Milk from the Land 1993, Looking at the Words of Our People: First Nations Analysis of Literature 1993. *Honours:* Hon. Fellow, Okanagan Coll. 2008; Dr hc (St Thomas Univ.) 2000, Hon. LLD (Univ. of British Columbia Okanagan) 2006; Mungo Martin Award 1974, Helen Pitt Memorial Award 1978, Children's Book Centre Choice Award 1983, Buffett Award for Aboriginal Leadership 2003. *Address:* En'owkin Centre, Lot 45, Green Mountain Road, Penticton, BC V2A 6J7, Canada (office). *Telephone:* (250) 493-7181 (office). *Fax:* (250) 493-5302 (office). *E-mail:* enowkin@vip.net (office). *Website:* www.enowkincentre.ca (office).

ARMSTRONG, Karen Andersen, MA, MLitt; British writer and broadcaster; b. 14 Nov. 1944, Stourbridge, West Midlands, England; d. of John O. S. Armstrong and Eileen H. MacHale. *Education:* Convent of the Holy Child Jesus, Birmingham, St Anne's Coll., Oxford. *Career:* nun 1962–69; Research Fellow, Bedford Coll., London 1973–76; Head of English, James Allen's Girls' School, London 1976–82; writer and broadcaster 1982–; regular columnist, The Guardian. *Publications include:* Through the Narrow Gate 1981, The Gospel According to Women 1986, Holy War 1988, Muhammaed, A Biography of the Prophet 1991, A History of God 1993, Jerusalem: One City, Three Faiths 1996, In the Beginning, A New Reading of Genesis 1996, The Battle for God – A History of Fundamentalism 2000, Islam: A Short History 2000, Buddha 2001, The Spiral Staircase: A Memoir 2004, The Great Transformation: The World in the Time of Buddha, Socrates, Confucius and Jeremiah 2006, Muhammad 2006, A Short History of Myth 2006, The Bible: A Biography 2007, The Case for God 2009, Twelve Steps to a Compassionate Life 2010. *Honours:* First Class Decoration for Art and Literature, Govt of Egypt; Hon. DLitt (Aston, Exeter), Hon. PhD (Georgetown); Muslim Public Affairs Council

Media Award 1999, Asscn of Muslim Social Scientists (UK) Award 2004, Open Center New York City Award 2004, The TED Prize 2008, Franklin D. Roosevelt Four Freedoms Medal 2008, Tübingen Univ. Leopold-Lucas Prize 2009. *Literary Agent:* c/o Felicity Bryan, 2A North Parade, Banbury Road, Oxford, OX2 6PE, England. *Telephone:* (1865) 513816. *Fax:* (1865) 310055. *E-mail:* mt@felicitybryan.com.

ARMSTRONG, Patrick Hamilton, BSc, MA, PhD, DipEd; Australian (b. British) academic and writer; *Adjunct Professor, University of Western Australia;* b. 10 Oct. 1941, Leeds, Yorks., England; s. of Edward Armstrong and Eunice Joan Armstrong (née Uttley); m. Moyra E. J. Irvine 1964; two s. *Education:* Univ. of Durham, UK. *Career:* mem. Faculty, School of Earth and Environment, Univ. of Western Australia, currently Adjunct Prof.; Adjunct Prof., Edith Cowan Univ.; fmr Chief Examiner, Int. Baccalaureate Org.; lately Ed. Geographers-Biobibliographical Studies; has broadcast for Australian Broadcasting Corpn, BBC World Service; Fellow, Inst. of Australian Geographers. *Publications include:* Discovering Ecology 1973, Discovering Geology 1974, The Changing Landscape 1975, series of children's books for Ladybird Books 1976–79, Ecology 1977, Reading and Interpretation of Australian and New Zealand Maps 1981, Living in the Environment 1982, The Earth: Home of Humanity 1984, Charles Darwin in Western Australia 1985, A Sketch Map Geography of Australia 1988, A Sketch Map Physical Geography for Australia 1989, Darwin's Desolate Islands 1992, The English Parson-Naturalist: A Companionship Between Science and Religion 2000, Darwin's Other Islands 2004, All Things Darwin 2007, Darwin's Luck 2009; contribs to New Scientist, Geographical Magazine, East Anglian Magazine, Geography, Cambridgeshire Life, Eastern Daily Press, Work and Travel Abroad, West Australian Newspaper, Sydney Morning Herald, Weekly Telegraph; numerous articles in scholarly and scientific journals. *Address:* School of Earth and Environment, University of Western Australia, Nedlands, WA 6009, Australia (office).

ARMSTRONG OF ILMINSTER, Baron (Life Peer), cr. 1988, of Ashill in the County of Somerset; **Robert Temple Armstrong,** GCB, CVO, MA; British fmr civil servant; b. 30 March 1927, Oxford; s. of Sir Thomas Armstrong and of Lady Armstrong (née Draper); m. 1st Serena Mary Benedicta Chance 1953 (divorced 1985); two d.; m. 2nd (Mary) Patricia Carlow 1985. *Education:* Eton Coll. and Christ Church, Oxford. *Career:* Asst Prin. Treasury 1950–55, Pvt. Sec. to Econ. Sec. 1953–54; Pvt. Sec. to Chancellor of the Exchequer (Rt Hon. R. A. Butler) 1954–55; Prin. Treasury 1955–64; Asst Sec. Cabinet Office 1964–66; Asst Sec. Treasury 1966–68; Prin. Pvt. Sec. to Chancellor of the Exchequer (Rt Hon. Roy Jenkins) 1968; Under-Sec. Treasury 1968–70; Prin. Pvt. Sec. to the Prime Minister 1970–75; Deputy Under-Sec. of State, Home Office 1975–77, Perm. Under-Sec. of State 1977–79; Sec. of the Cabinet 1979–87; Perm. Sec. Man. and Personnel Office 1981–87; Head, Home Civil Service 1981–87; Chair. Biotechnology Investments Ltd 1989–2000; Chair. Forensic Investigative Assocs PLC 1997–2003; Chair. Hestercombe Gardens Trust 1995–2005, Bd of Govs Royal Northern Coll. of Music 2000–05; Sec. Radcliffe Cttee on Monetary System 1957–59; Sec. to the Dirs, Royal Opera House, Covent Garden 1968–87, Dir 1988–93; Dir Bristol and West Bldg Soc. 1988–97 (Chair. 1993–97), Bank of Ireland and other cos; Chair. Bd of Trustees, Victoria and Albert Museum 1988–98; mem. Rhodes Trust 1975–97; Fellow, Eton Coll. 1979–94; Chancellor, Univ. of Hull 1994–2006; Pres. The Literary Soc. 2004–; Trustee Leeds Castle Foundation 1987– (Chair. 2001–). *Honours:* Hon. Student, Christ Church 1985; Hon. Bencher, Inner Temple 1986; Hon. LLD. *Address:* House of Lords, Westminster, London, SW1A 0PW, England (office). *Telephone:* (20) 7219-4983 (office). *Fax:* (20) 7219-1259 (office).

ARNDT, Angelica, BA; Chilean journalist; b. 19 Aug. 1937, Santiago; d. of Eduardo Arndt and Eleonora Arndt (née Garay); m. Georges de Bourguignon 1958; two s. *Education:* Dunalastair School, Santiago, Catholic Univ. of Santiago and Colegio de Periodistas de Chile. *Career:* Ed. El Mercurio, Santiago 1974–76; int. relations columnist La Tercera 1976–77; int. relations reporter, Ercilla 1977–80, Revista Negocios 1980–81, Paula 1980–81, Chilean nat. TV 1980–81; dir, producer and ed. political and cultural programmes, Chilean nat. TV 1980–83; political interviewer, Cosas int. magazine 1982–; Research Archive Asst Hoover Inst., Stanford, CA, USA 1991, 1994; freelance political analyst, interviewer and journalist; contribs to int. journals. *Address:* Arnex, Casilia 19039, Correo 19, Lo Castillo, Santiago, Chile (office).

ARNOLD, Emily (see McCULLY, Emily Arnold)

ARNOLD, Heinz Ludwig; German writer, critic and editor; b. 29 March 1940, Essen, Ruhr. *Education:* Univ. of Göttingen. *Career:* Ed. Text und Kritik 1963, Kritisches Lexikon zur Deutschsprachigen Gegenwartsliteratur 1978, Kritisches Lexikon zur Fremdsprachigen Gegenwartsliteratur 1983–2007; mem. Asscn of German Writers, PEN, Deutsche Akad. für Sprache und Dichtung, Darmstadt, OH Tulip Order. *Publications include:* Brauchen wir noch die Literatur? 1972, Gespräche mit Schriftstellern 1975, Gespräch mit F. Dürrenmatt 1976, Handbuch der Deutschen Arbeiterliteratur 1977, Als Schriftsteller leben 1979, Vom Verlust der Scham und dem allmählichen Verschwinden der Demokratie 1988, Krieger, Waldgänger, Anarch. Versuch über E. Jünger 1990, Querfahrt mit Dürrenmatt 1990–96, Die Drei Sprünge der Westdeutschen Gegenwartsliteratur 1993, Die Deutsche Literatur 1945–1960 (11 vols) 1995–2000, Grundzüge der Literaturwissenschaft 1996, F. Dürrenmatt, Gespräche 1996, Einigkeit und aus Ruinen 1999, Arthur Schnitzler: Ausgewählte Werke (eight vols) 1999–2002, Da schwimmen manchmal ein paar Sätze vorbei... 2001, 'Was bin ich?' Über Max Frisch 2002, Arbeiterlyrik 1842–1932 2003, Von Unvollendeten Literarische Porträts 2005, Kindler Literatur Lexikon (18 vols) 2009, Ein abenteuerliches Herz. Ernst-Jünger-Lesebuch 2011; contrib. to Die Zeit, Frankfurter Rundschau, Frankfurter Allgemeine Zeitung, various radio stations. *Honours:* Hon. Prof., Univ. of Göttingen. *Address:* Tuckermannweg 10, 37085 Göttingen, Germany (home).

ARNOLD, Margot (see COOK, Petronelle Marguerite Mary)

ARNOTHY, Christine; French journalist and writer; b. 20 Nov. 1934, Budapest, Hungary; d. of Mr and Mrs Kovach de Szendrö; m. Claude Bellanger 1964 (died 1978); one s. one d. *Education:* Lycée Français, Austria and Univ. of Paris (Sorbonne). *Career:* literary critic, Le Parisien Libéré, Paris 1961–78, Head of Literary Column 1978–2004; literary column in La Suisse, Geneva, Switzerland 1982–94; contribs to other newspapers and magazines. *Publications:* J'ai quinze ans et je ne veux pas mourir (autobiog., Grand Prix Vérité) 1955, Dieu est en retard 1955, Il n'est pas si facile de vivre (autobiog.) 1957, Le Guérisseur 1958, Femmes du Japon 1959, Pique-nique en Sologne 1960, Le cardinal prisonnier 1962, La saison des Américains 1964, Le jardin noir 1966, Jouer à l'été 1967, Aviva 1968, Chiche! 1970, Un type merveilleux 1972, Lettre ouverte aux rois nus 1974, Clodomir Free, Le Grand Complot 1975, Le cavalier mongol (Grand Prix de la Nouvelle, Acad. française) 1976, J'aime la vie 1976, Le bonheur d'une manière ou d'une autre 1978, Toutes les chances plus une (Prix Interallié) 1980, Jeux de mémoire 1981, Un paradis sur mesure 1983, L'ami de la famille 1984, Les trouble-fête 1986, Vent africain (Prix des Maisons de la Presse, Prix Bernanos-Artois, Lacouture) 1989, Une affaire d'héritage 1991, Désert brûlant 1992, Voyage de noces 1994, Une question de chance 1995, La piste africaine 1997, La Dernière Nuit avant l'an 2000 1997, Malins plaisirs 1999, Complot de femmes 2000, Embrasser la vie 2001, On ne fait jamais vraiment ce que l'on veut 2002, Aller-retour, tous frais payés 2004, Une rentrée littéraire 2004, Relations inquiétantes 2005, L'Homme aux yeux de diamant 2006, Donnant Donnant 2007, Les Années Cannibales 2008, Une Valse à Vienne 2009; Clodomir Free ou le grand complot (cartoon text) 1975; also short stories in numerous magazines, and plays for TV and radio; works have been translated into many languages. *Honours:* Commdr, Légion d'honneur, des Arts et des Lettres; Officier, Ordre nat. du Mérite; Golden Cross of Merit (Hungary) 1991. *Address:* c/o Fayard, 13 rue du Montparnasse, 75006 Paris, France; 2 rue Pedro Meylan, 1208 Genea, Switzerland (home). *Telephone:* (22) 7005833 (home). *Website:* www.fayard.fr; www.arnothy.ch.

ARNOULT, Erik, (Erik Orsenna), DèsScEcon, PhD; French civil servant and writer; b. 22 March 1947, Paris; s. of Claude Arnoult and Janine Arnoult (née Bodé); m. 2nd Catherine Clavier; one s. one d.; m. 3rd Isabelle de Saint Aubin. *Education:* Ecole Saint-Jean de Béthune, Versailles, Institut d'Etudes Politiques, Paris, Univ. of Paris I, London School of Economics. *Career:* Lecturer, Inst. d'Etudes Politiques, Paris 1975–80, Ecole Normale Supérieure 1977–81; Literary Ed. Editions Ramsay 1977–81; Sr Lecturer, Université de Paris I 1978–81; Tech. Adviser to Ministry of Co-operation and Devt 1981–83, to Minister of Foreign Affairs 1990–92; Cultural Adviser to Pres. of Repub. 1983–90; Maître des Requêtes, Conseil d'Etat 1985–, Sr mem. 2000–; Pres. Centre Int. de la Mer 1991–, Ecole Nat. Supérieure du Paysage 1995–; Vice-Pres. Cytale Soc. 2000–03; mem. Foundation for World Agric. and Rural Life 2006–, Acad. Française. *Film screenplay:* Indochine (co-writer) (Acad. Award for Best Foreign Film). *Publications:* Loyola's blues 1974, Espace national et déséquilibre monétaire 1977, La Vie comme à Lausanne 1977 (Prix Roger Nimier), Une comédie française 1980, L'Exposition coloniale (novel) (Prix Goncourt) 1988, Grand Amour 1993, Histoire du monde en neuf guitares 1996, Deux Etés (novel) 1996, Longtemps (novel) 1998, Portrait d'un homme heureux, André Le Nôtre 1613–1700 2000, La Grammaire est une chanson donce 2001, Madame Bâ 2003, Les Chevaliers du Subjonctif 2004, Portrait du Gulf Stream 2005, Voyage aux pays du coton (Prix du livre d'économie) 2006, La révolte des accents 2007, L'avenir de l'eau 2009. *Address:* Conseil d'Etat, 1 place du Palais Royal, 75001 Paris (office); 8 passage Sigaud, 75013 Paris, France (home).

ARPAIA, Bruno; Italian novelist, editor and translator; b. 1957, Ottaviano, Naples. *Education:* Univ. of Naples. *Career:* fmr journalist, Il Mattino and La Repubblica; now freelance; trans. of Spanish and Latin American literature. *Publications include:* novels: I forestieri (Bagutta Opera Prima Prize) 1990, Il futuro in punta di piedi 1994, Tempo perso (Premio Hammett Italia) 1997, L'angelo della storia (trans. as The Angel of History) (Premio Campielli, Premio Alassio Centolibri) 2001, Il Passato davanti a noi (Premio Napoli, Premio Letterario Giovanni Comisso) 2006, Per una sinistra reazionaria 2007, L'energia del vuoto 2011. *Address:* c/o Ugo Guanda Editore, Via Gherardini 10, 20145 Milan, Italy. *E-mail:* info@guanda.it. *Website:* www.guanda.it.

ARRABAL, Fernando; Spanish writer; b. 11 Aug. 1932, Melilla; s. of Fernando Arrabal and Carmen Terán González; m. Luce Moreau 1958; one s. one d. *Education:* Univ. of Madrid. *Career:* political prisoner in Spain 1967; Founder Panique Movt with Topor, Jodorowsky, others. *Exhibition:* Kalédescopies, Musée de Bayeux 2000. *Publications include:* plays: numerous plays including Le cimetière des voitures, Guernica, Le grand cérémonial, L'architecte et l'Empereur d'Assyrie, Le jardin des délices, Et ils passèrent des menottes aux fleurs, Le ciel et la merde, Bella ciao, La Tour de Babel, L'extravagante réussite de Jésus-Christ, Karl Marx et William Shakespeare, Les délices de la chair, La traversée de l'empire, Luly, Cielito, Fando et Lis, Lettre d'amour; novels: Baal Babylone 1959, L'enterrement de la sardine

1962, Fêtes et rites de la confusion 1965, La tour prends garde, La reverdie, La vierge rouge, Bréviaire d'amour d'un haltérophile, L'extravagante croisade d'un castrat amoureux 1991, La tueuse du jardin d'hiver 1994, El Mono 1994, Le Funambule de Dieu 1998, Ceremonia por un teniente abandonado 1998, Porté disparu 2000, Champagne pour tous 2002, Como un paraíso de locos 2008; poetry includes: La pierre de la folie 1963, 100 sonnets 1966, Humbles paradis 1983, Liberté couleur de femme 1993, Arrabalesques 1994, Passion, Passions 1997, Le Frénétique du Spasme 1997; essays: numerous, including Le Panique, Le New York d'Arrabal, Lettre au Général Franco, Greco 1970, Lettre à Fidel Castro 1983, Goya-Dali 1992, La Dudosa Luz del Día 1994. *Films:* directed and written: Viva la Muerte, J'irai comme un cheval fou, L'arbre de Guernica, L'odyssée de la Pacific, Le cimetière des voitures, Adieu Babylone!, J.-L. Borges (Una Vida de Poesía) 1998. *Honours:* Officier, Ordre des Arts et des Lettres 1984, Chevalier, Légion d'honneur 2005; Superdotado Award 1942, Ford Foundation Award 1959, Grand Prix du Théâtre 1967, Grand Prix Humour Noir 1968, Obie Award 1976, Premio Nadal (Spain) 1983, World's Theater Prize 1984, Medalla de Oro de Bellas Artes (Spain) 1989, Prix du Théâtre (Acad. Française) 1993, Prix Int. Vladimir Nabokov 1994, Premio de Ensayo Espasa 1994, Grand Prix Soc. des Gens de Lettres 1996, Grand Prix de la Méditerranée 1996, Medal of Centre for French Civilization and Culture, New York 1997, Prix de la Francophonie 1998, Premio Mariano de Cavia 1998, Prix Alessandro Manzoni di Poesia 1999, Premio Nacional de las Letras, Premio Eninci Cine y Literatura 2000, Premio Nacional de Teatro 2001, Premio Ercilla Teatro 2001. *Address:* 22 rue Jouffroy d'Abbans, Paris 75017, France (home). *Fax:* 1-42-67-01-26 (home). *E-mail:* fernando.arrabal@orange.fr (home); arrabalf@gmail.com (home). *Website:* www.arrabal.org.

ARRIAGA JORDÁN, Guillermo; Mexican scriptwriter; b. 13 March 1958, Mexico City. *Career:* Prof. of Film, Instituto Tecnológico de Estudios Superiores de Monterrey. *Films:* Campeones sin límite (writer, dir) 1997, ABC discapacidad (series writer) 1999, Amores Perros (writer) 2000, Rogelio (dir) 2000, Powder Keg (writer) 2001, 21 Grams (writer, assoc. producer) (Satellite Award for Best Original Screenplay) 2003, Los elefantes nunca olvidan (producer) 2004, The Three Burials of Melquiades Estrada (writer, actor) 2005, Babel (writer) 2006, El Búfalo de la noche (writer, producer) 2007, La Hora Cero (writer) 2008, The Burning Plain (writer) 2008. *Publications include:* novels: Escuádron guillotina 1991, Un dulce olor a muerte (trans. as A Sweet Scent of Death) 1994, El Búfalo de la noche 2000, Amores Perros 2001, 21 Grams 2004. *Address:* c/o Faber and Faber Ltd, Bloomsbury House, 74–77 Great Russell Street, London, WC1B 3DA, England.

ARROW, Kenneth Joseph, BS, MA, PhD; American economist and academic; *Professor Emeritus of Economics and Operations Research, Stanford University;* b. 23 Aug. 1921, New York, NY; s. of Harry I. Arrow and Lillian Arrow; m. Selma Schweitzer 1947; two s. *Education:* The City College, Columbia Univ. *Career:* Capt. in USAF 1942–46; Research Assoc., Cowles Comm. for Research in Econ., Univ. of Chicago 1947–49; Asst Prof., then Assoc. Prof. of Econs, Statistics and Operations Research, Stanford Univ. 1949–68, Prof. of Econs and Operations Research 1979–91, Prof. Emer. 1991–; Prof. of Econs, Harvard Univ. 1968–79; mem. NAS, American Acad. of Arts and Sciences, American Philosophical Soc., Finnish Acad. of Sciences, British Acad., Inst. of Medicine, Pontifical Acad. of Social Sciences; Pres. Int. Soc. for Inventory Research 1983–90, Int. Econ. Assen, Econometric Soc., American Econ. Assen, Soc. for Social Choice and Welfare; Dir various cos. *Publications:* Social Choice and Individual Values 1951, 1963, Studies in the Mathematical Theory of Inventory and Production (with S. Karlin and H. Scarf) 1958, Studies in Linear and Nonlinear Programming (with L. Hurwicz and H. Uzawa) 1958, A Time Series Analysis of Inter-industry Demands (with M. Hoffenberg) 1959, Public Investment, The Rate of Return and Optimal Fiscal Policy (with M. Kurz) 1970, Essays in the Theory of Risk-Bearing 1971, General Competitive Analysis (with F. H. Hahn) 1971, The Limits of Organization 1973, Studies in Resource Allocation Processes (with L. Hurwicz) 1977, Collected Papers 1983–85, Social Choice and Multicriterion Decision Making (with H. Raynaud) 1985; more than 240 articles in learned journals. *Honours:* Order of the Rising Sun (Japan); Hon. LLD (City Univ., Univ. of Chicago, Washington Univ., Univ. of Pennsylvania, Ben-Gurion Univ., Harvard Univ., Univ. of Cyprus, Univ. of Buenos Aires), Hon. Dr of Social and Econ. Sciences (Vienna), Hon. ScD (Columbia Univ.) 1973, Hon. DSocSci (Yale) 1974, Hon. LLD (Hebrew Univ. Jerusalem) 1975, Hon. DPolSci (Helsinki) 1976, Hon. DLitt (Cambridge) 1985, (Harvard) 1999, Hon. DUniv (Uppsala) 1995, Hon. PhD (Univ. of Tel-Aviv) 2001, Dr hc (Univ. René Descartes) 1974, (Univ. Aix-Marseille III) 1985, (Univ. of Cyprus) 2000; Nobel Memorial Prize in Econ. Science 1972, John Bates Clark Medal, Von Neumann Prize, Medal of Univ. of Paris 1998, Nat. Medal of Science 2006. *Address:* Room 342, Landau Economics, Department of Economics, Stanford University, Stanford, CA 94305-6072 (office); 620 Sand Hill Road, Apartment 406C, Palo Alto, CA 94304, USA (home). *Telephone:* (650) 723-9165 (office). *Fax:* (650) 725-5702 (office). *E-mail:* arrow@stanford.edu (office). *Website:* economics.stanford.edu/faculty/arrow (office).

ARROWSMITH, Pat, BA; British writer and peace activist; b. 2 March 1930. *Education:* Cheltenham Ladies' Coll., Newnham Coll., Cambridge, Univ. of Ohio, USA, Univ. of Liverpool. *Career:* staff mem., Amnesty International 1972–94; mem. Ver Poets, London Poetry Soc.; Vice-Pres. Campaign for Nuclear Disarmament. *Publications include:* poetry: Breakout 1975, On the Brink 1981, Thin Ice 1984, Nine Lives 1990, Drawing to Extinction 2000, Going On 2005, Dark Light 2009; novels: Jericho 1965, Somewhere Like This 1970, The Prisoner 1982, I Should Have Been a Hornby Train (fiction/memoir) 1995, Many are Called 1998; non-fiction: To Asia in Peace 1972, The Colour of Six Schools 1972. *Honours:* Second Prize, Hornsey, London Competition 1977, Highly Commended, Westminster, London Competition 1978, Americans Removing Injustice, Suppression and Exploitation (ARISE) Peace Prize 1991, Ver Poets Competition Prize 1993.

ARSAND, Daniel; French novelist and publisher; b. 9 July 1950, Avignon. *Career:* bookseller, publr; est. Les Editions de la Sphere 1979–. *Publications include:* novels: La Province des ténèbres (trans. as The Land of Darkness) (Prix Fémina) 1998, En silence 2000, Lily 2002, Drunken son 2004, Black Horses 2006, Lovers 2008, Alberto 2008. *Address:* c/o Éditions Phébus, 7 rue des Canettes, 75006 Paris, France. *Telephone:* (1) 46-33-36-36. *E-mail:* informations@editions-phebus.fr. *Website:* www.phebus-editions.com.

ARTEAGA SERRANO, Rosalía, PhD; Ecuadorean politician, lawyer, journalist and writer; b. 5 Dec. 1956, Cuerca; m. Pedro Fernández de Córdova 1978; three c. *Career:* graduated in political and social sciences, holds a Master's degree in Basic Educ. and Recovery of Latin American Cultural Values; Minister of Educ. and Culture 1994–96; Vice-Pres. of Ecuador 1996–98; Interim Pres. of Ecuador 9–11 Feb. 1997; fmr Chair. Nat. Devt Council (Conade); Sec.-Gen. Amazon Cooperation Treaty Org., Brasilia 2004–07; Dir Fundación Natura Regional 2007–; mem. Editorial Bd Encyclopædia Britannica 2005–07. *Publications include:* Horas 1982, Árboles de Cuenca 1985, Alto Cenepa 1985, La Presidenta, el secuestro de una protesta 1997, Jerónimo 1999. *Address:* Fundación Natura Quito, Elia Liut N45-10 y Telégrafo Primero, Quito, Ecuador (office). *E-mail:* natura@fnatura.org.ec (office). *Website:* www.fnatura.org (office).

ARTHUR, Elizabeth Ann, BA; American writer; b. 15 Nov. 1953, New York, NY; d. of Robert Arthur and Joan Vaczek Arthur; m. Steven Bauer 1982. *Education:* Univ. of Victoria. *Career:* Visiting Instructor, Creative Writing, Univ. of Cincinnati 1983–84; Visiting Asst Prof. of English, Miami Univ. 1984–85, Visiting Assoc. Prof. of English 1996; Asst Prof. of English, Indiana Univ.-Purdue Univ., Indianapolis 1985–92, Assoc. Prof. 1992–96; mem. Poets and Writers. *Publications include:* Island Sojourn (memoir) 1980, Beyond the Mountain (novel) 1983, Bad Guys (novel) 1986, Binding Spell (novel) 1988, Looking for the Klondike Stone (memoir) 1993, Antarctic Navigation (novel) 1995, Bring Deeps (novel) 2003; contribs: New York Times, Outside, Backpacker, Ski-XC, Shenandoah. *Honours:* William Sloane Fellowship, Bread Loaf Writers' Conf. 1980, Writing Fellowship, Ossabaw Island Project 1981, Grant in Aid, Vermont Council on the Arts 1982, Fellowship in Prose, Nat. Endowment for the Arts 1982–83, Master Artist Fellowship, Indiana Arts Comm., Indianapolis 1988, Fellowship in Fiction, Nat. Endowment for Arts 1989–90, Antarctic Artists' and Writers' Grant, Nat. Science Foundation 1990, Critics' Choice Award for Antarctic Navigation 1995, Notable Book, New York Times Book Review 1995. *E-mail:* contact@elizabetharthur.org (office). *Website:* www.elizabetharthur.org.

ARTHUR, Rasjid Arthur James, MA; British journalist; b. 7 June 1928, Stirling, Scotland. *Education:* Edinburgh Univ. *Career:* Nat. Service, RAF 1950–52; local reporter, Stirling 1952–54; sub-ed., The Scotsman 1954–55, leader writer 1955–64; Features Ed., News Ed. and writer, Central Office of Information, London 1965–78; freelance writer on environment, development and related topics 1978–; mem. Chartered Inst. of Journalists. *Publications include:* many articles on environmental subjects for British and int. magazines of the water industry and for the London Press Service of the Press Assen. *Address:* 32 Midway, Middleton Cheney, Banbury, Oxon., OX17 2QW, England (home). *Telephone:* (1295) 712099 (office). *E-mail:* rasjid_arthur@yahoo.co.uk (office).

ASANTE, Molefi Kete, BA, MA, PhD; American academic and poet; *Professor, Department of African American Studies, Temple University;* b. 14 Aug. 1942, Vaidosta, Calif.; m. Kariamu Welsh 1981; two s. one d. *Education:* Oklahoma Christian Univ., Pepperdine Univ., Univ. of California, Los Angeles. *Career:* Prof., UCLA 1969–73, State Univ. of NY at Buffalo 1973–84; worked in Zimbabwe training journalists 1980–82; Prof., Dept of African American Studies, Temple Univ. 1984–; Guest Prof., Zhejiang Univ.; Chair. Diaspora Intellectuals 2009–; mem. African Writers' Union (Vice-Pres. 1994–). *Publications include:* Break of Dawn 1964, Epic in Search of African Kings 1979, Afrocentricity 1980, The Afrocentric Idea 1987, African Culture 1989, The Book of African Names 1991, Kemet, Afrocentricity and Knowledge 1992, Classical Africa 1992, Thunder and Silence 1992, Malcolm X as Cultural Hero and Afrocentric Essays 1993, African American History 1995, African Intellectual Heritage 1996, Love Dance 1997, African American Atlas 1998, Scream of Blood: Desettlerism in Southern Africa 1998, The Painful Demise of Eurocentricism 2000, Transcultural Realities 2001, Handbook of International and Intercultural Communication 2002, Culture and Customs of Egypt 2002, Erasing Racism 2003, 100 Greatest African Americans 2003, Encyclopedia of Black Studies 2004, Race, Rhetoric and Identity 2005, Handbook of Black Studies 2006, The History of Africa 2007, An Afrocentric Manifesto 2007, Encyclopedia of African Religion 2008, Erasing Racism: The Survival of the American Nation 2010, Rooming in the Mater's House: Power and Privilege in the Rise of Black Conservatism 2010, Maulana Karenga: An Intellectual Portrait 2010; contribs to journals. *Honours:* hon. degrees, citations and awards. *Literary Agent:* c/o Jay Acton, Spartan Literary Agency, 55 Fifth Avenue, New York, NY 10003, USA. *E-mail:* jacton@timeequities.com. *Address:* c/o Ana Yenenga, Asante and Associates, PO Box 30004, Elkins

Park, PA 19027, USA. *Telephone:* (215) 782-3214. *E-mail:* anaroot@cs.com. *Website:* www.asante.net.

ASARE, Meshack; Ghanaian children's writer and illustrator; b. 18 Sept. 1945; m. Angela Asare. *Career:* fmr teacher. *Publications include:* Tawia Goes to Sea 1970, I am Kofi 1972, Mansa Helps at Home 1973, The Brassman's Secret 1981, The Canoe's Story 1982, Chipo and the Bird on the Hill 1984, Cat: In Search of a Friend 1986, Seeing the World 1989, Bury my Bones but Keep my Words: African Tales for Retelling 1991, Halima's Dilemma 1992, The Frightened Thief 1993, The Magic Goat 1997, Sosu's Call 1998, Children of the Tree 1999, Meliga's Day 2000, Nana's Son 2000, Kwajo and the Brassman's Secret: A Tale of Old Ashanti Wisdom and Gold 2002, Noma's Sand: A Tale from Lesotho 2002, L'appel de Sosu 2002, Tawia Goes to Sea 2007, The Cross Drums 2008. *Honours:* Noma Award for Publishing in Africa 1982, Austrian Nat. Book Prize 1985, UNESCO Prize for Children and Young People's Literature in the Service of Tolerance 1999. *Address:* c/o African Books Collective, PO Box 721, Oxford, OX1 9EN, England. *E-mail:* meshack@globalnet.co.uk. *Website:* www.africanbookscollective.com.

ASARO, Catherine, BS, MA, PhD; American astrophysicist, writer and music producer; *President, Starflight Music;* b. Oakland, Calif.; m. John Kendall Cannizzo 1986; one d. *Education:* Univ. of California, Los Angeles, Harvard Univ., Univ. of Toronto, Canada. *Career:* consultant to Lawrence Livermore Lab. 1978–83, Biodesign 1987, Harvard-Smithsonian Center for Astrophysics 1991; Asst Prof. of Physics, Kenyon Coll., Gambier, Ohio 1987–90, Affiliated Scholar 1990–91; Pres., Molecudyne Research, Laurel, Md 1990–; Visiting Scientist, Max Planck Inst. for Astrophysics 1991–92; Ed., Publr Mindsparks: The Magazine of Science and Science Fiction 1993–; columnist, Tangent periodical; Founder Howard Area Homeschoolers; Pres. Starflight Music; mem. Science Fiction and Fantasy Writers of America (SWFA), American Asscn of Physics Teachers, American Physicists Soc. *Recordings include:* Diamond Star 2009, Goodbye Note 2010. *Publications include:* Primary Inversion 1995, Catch the Lightning 1996, The Last Hawk 1997, The Radiant Seas 1998, The Veiled Web 1999, The Quantum Rose 2000 (Nebula Award), The Phoenix Code 2000, Ascendant Sun 2000, Spherical Harmonic 2001, The Moon's Shadow 2003, Skyfall 2003, Schism 2004, The Charmed Sphere 2004, Sunrise Alley 2004, The Final Key 2005, The Misted Cliffs 2005, The Dawn Star 2006, Alpha 2006, The Fire Opal 2007, The Night Bird 2008, The Spacetime Pool (Nebula Award) 2008, The Ruby Dice 2008, Diamond Star 2009; contribs: anthologies including Christmas Forever, Analog, periodicals and scholarly journals including Analog, Journal of Chemical Physics, New York Review of Science Fiction, American Journal of Physics, International Journal of Quantitative Chemistry, SFWA Bulletin, Science Fiction Age, Pirate Writings, Physical Review Letters. *Honours:* AnLab Analog Readers Poll, Homer Award, Sapphire Award, Nat. Readers Choice Award, Prism Award, UTC Award, Nebula Award. *Literary Agent:* Binnie Syril Braunstein, Press Kit Communications, 7504 Labyrinth Road, Baltimore, MD 21208-45417, USA. *Telephone:* (410) 486-6178. *Fax:* (410) 486-6178. *E-mail:* BSBGC@aol.com. *E-mail:* mail@catherineasaro.net (office). *Website:* www.catherineasaro.net.

ASBAR, Ali Ahmad Said, (Adonis), PhD; Syrian poet and academic; b. 1930, Kassabin, nr Latakia; two d. *Education:* Univ. of Damascus, Univ. of St Joseph, Beirut. *Career:* Prof. of Arabic Literature, Lebanese Univ., Beirut 1971–85; PhD Adviser, Univ. of St Joseph, Beirut 1971–85; Visiting Lecturer, Collège de France, Paris 1983, Georgetown Univ., Washington, DC 1985; Assoc. Prof. of Arab Poetry, Univ. of Geneva 1989–95; mem. Acad. Stéphane Mallarmé, Paris, Haut Conseil de Réflexion du Collège Int. de Philosophie, Paris. *Publications include:* Songs of Mihyar, the Damascene 1961, The Book of Changes and Migration to the Regions of Day and Night 1965, A Time Between Ashes and Roses 1970, Introduction to Arab Poetry 1971, A Tomb for New York 1971, The Blood of Adonis 1971, Singular in the Form of Plural 1974, Further Songs of Mihyar, the Damascene 1975, The Shock of Modernity 1978, The Book of Five Poems 1980, Manifesto of Modernity 1980, Transformations of the Lover 1982, Mémoire du Vent 1991, La Prière et L'Épée 1992, Soleils Seconds 1994, The Pages of Day and Night 2001, Chants de Mihyar le Damascène 2002, If Only the Sea Could Sleep 2003, Commencement du Corps, Fin de l'Océan 2004, Histoire qui se Déchire sue le Corps d'une Femme 2008, Selected Poems 2010. *Honours:* Officier, Ordre des Arts et des Lettres 1993; Prix des Amis du Livre, Beirut 1968, Syria-Lebanon Award, Int. Poetry Forum 1971, Nat. Prize for Poetry, Lebanon 1974, Grand Prix des Biennales Internationales de la Poésie de Liège, Belgium 1986, Prix Jean Malrieu-Etranger, Marseille 1991, Feronia-Cita di Fiano, Rome 1993, Nazim Hikmat Prize, Istanbul 1994, Prix Méditerranée-Etranger, France 1995, Bjørnson Prize 2007, Goethe Prize 2011. *Address:* 1 sq Henri Regnault, 92400 Courbevoie, France (home).

ASCHERSON, (Charles) Neal, MA; British journalist, editor and writer; *Honorary Editor, Public Archaeology;* b. 5 Oct. 1932, Edinburgh, Scotland; m. 1st Corinna Adam 1958 (divorced 1984); two d.; m. 2nd Isabel Hilton 1984; one s. one d. *Education:* Eton Coll., King's Coll., Cambridge. *Career:* reporter and leader writer, Manchester Guardian 1956–58; Commonwealth Corresp., The Scotsman 1959–60, Eastern Europe Corresp. 1968–75, Scottish Politics Corresp. 1975–79; reporter, The Observer 1960–63, Cen. Europe Corresp. 1963–68, Foreign Writer 1979–85, Assoc. Ed. 1985–89, columnist 1985–90; columnist, The Independent on Sunday 1990–98; Ed. Public Archaeology 1998–2010, Hon. Ed. 2010–. *Publications include:* The King Incorporated 1963, The Polish August: The Self-Limiting Revolution 1981, The Struggles for Poland 1987, Games with Shadows 1988, Black Sea 1995, Stone Voices 2002. *Honours:* Golden Insignia, Order of Merit, Poland 1992; Hon. Fellow, King's Coll., Cambridge 1993, Univ. Coll. London 2010, Hon. Prof., Inst. of Archaeology, Univ. Coll. London 2009; Dr hc (Strathclyde, Edinburgh, St Andrews, Open Univ., Paisley, Bradford, Aberdeen, Highlands & Islands); Reporter of the Year 1982, Journalist of the Year 1987, Granada Awards James Cameron Award 1989, David Watt Memorial Prize 1991, George Orwell Award Political Quarterly 1993, Saltire Award for Literature 1995, 50th Anniversary Award of the Political Studies Asscn 2000. *Address:* 27 Corsica Street, London, N5 1JT, England.

ASH, John, BA; British writer, poet and teacher; b. 29 June 1948, Manchester, England. *Education:* Univ. of Birmingham. *Publications include:* The Golden Hordes: International Tourism and the Pleasure Periphery (with Louis Turner) 1975, Casino: A Poem in Three Parts 1978, The Bed and Other Poems 1981, The Goodbyes 1982, The Branching Stairs 1984, Disbelief 1987, The Burnt Pages 1991, A Byzantine Journey 1995, Selected Poems 1996, The Anatolikon 2002, To the City 2002, The Parthian Stations 2007, In the Wake of the Day 2010. *Honours:* Ingram Merrill Foundation Grant 1985, Writing Foundation Award 1986. *Address:* Memutiyet Cod No. 68, Cagdas Apt 1E 5D7, 34440 Tunel-Beyoglu, Istanbul, Turkey (office).

ASHBERY, John Lawrence, MA; American poet, author, critic and academic; *Charles P. Stevenson, Jr Professor of Languages and Literature, Bard College;* b. 28 July 1927, Rochester, NY; s. of Chester F. Ashbery and Helen L. Ashbery. *Education:* Deerfield Acad., Mass, Harvard, Columbia and New York Univs. *Career:* asst, Literature Dept, Brooklyn (NY) Public Library 1949; copywriter, Oxford Univ. Press, New York 1951–54, McGraw-Hill Book Co. 1954–55; went to France as a Fulbright Scholar 1955–56, 1956–57, lived there 1958–65; Art Critic, Int. edn New York Herald-Tribune, Paris 1960–65; Co-Ed. Locus Solus, Lans-en-Vercors, France 1960–62, Art and Literature, Paris 1964–67; Art Critic, Art International, Lugano 1961–63, New York Magazine 1978–80, Newsweek 1980–85; Paris corresp. Art News, New York 1964–65, Exec. Ed. 1965–72; Prof. of English and Co-Dir MFA Program in Creative Writing, Brooklyn Coll., NY (CUNY) 1974–90, Distinguished Prof. 1980–90, Distinguished Prof. Emer. 1990–; Poetry Ed. Partisan Review, New York 1976–80; Charles Eliot Norton Prof. of Poetry, Harvard Univ. 1989–90; Charles P. Stevenson, Jr Prof. of Languages and Literature, Bard Coll., Annandale-on-Hudson, NY 1990–; Chancellor Acad. of American Poets 1988–99; Leader, Fondation d'Art de La Napoule 1989; Poet Laureate, New York State 2001–03, MtvU (to promote poetry in US universities) 2007–; mem. American Acad. of Arts and Letters 1980–, American Acad. of Arts and Sciences 1983–; works translated into more than 20 languages. *Plays:* The Heroes 1952, The Compromise 1956, The Philosopher 1963, Three Plays 1978. *Publications include:* poetry: Turandot and Other Poems 1953, Some Trees 1956, The Tennis Court Oath 1962, Rivers and Mountains 1966, The Double Dream of Spring 1970, Three Poems 1972, The Vermont Notebook 1975, Self-Portrait in a Convex Mirror (Pulitzer Prize 1975, Nat. Book Award 1975, Nat. Book Critics' Circle Award 1975) 1975, Houseboat Days 1979, As We Know 1979, Shadow Train 1981, A Wave 1984, Selected Poems 1985, April Galleons 1987, Flow Chart 1991, Hotel Lautréamont 1992, And the Stars Were Shining 1994, Can You Hear, Bird 1995, Wakefulness 1998, Girls on the Run 1999, Your Name Here 2000, As Umbrellas Follow Rain 2001, Chinese Whispers 2002, Where Shall I Wander 2005, Notes from the Air: Selected Later Poems (Griffin Prize for Poetry 2008) 2007, Planisphere 2009; novel: A Nest of Ninnies (with J. Schuyler) 1969; essays and criticism: Fairfield Porter 1983, R. B. Kitaj (with others) 1983, Reported Sightings: Art Chronicles 1957–1987 1989, Other Traditions (The Charles Eliot Norton Lectures at Harvard) 2000; numerous translations from French including works by Raymond Roussel, Max Jacob, Alfred Jarry, Antonin Artaud and Pierre Martory, including Every Question but One 1990, The Landscape is behind the Door 1994. *Honours:* Chevalier des Arts et Lettres 1993; Officier, Légion d'honneur 2002; Hon. DLitt (Southampton Coll. of Long Island Univ.) 1979, (Univ. of Rochester, NY) 1994, (Harvard Univ.) 2001; recipient of numerous awards, grants and honours, including two Guggenheim Fellowships 1967, 1973, MacArthur Fellow 1985–90, Horst Bienek Prize for Poetry (Bavarian Acad. of Fine Arts) 1991, Ruth Lilly Prize for Poetry 1992, Antonio Fraternelli Int. Prize for Poetry (Accad. Nazionale dei Lincei, Rome) 1992, Robert Frost Medal (Poetry Soc. of America) 1995, Grand Prix de Biennales Internationales de Poésie (Brussels) 1996, Gold Medal for Poetry (American Acad. of Arts and Letters) 1997, Bingham Poetry Prize 1998, Walt Whitman Citation of Merit (State of New York and New York State Writers' Inst.) 2000, Signet Soc. Medal for Achievement in the Arts 2001, Wallace Stevens Award (Acad. of American Poets) 2001. *Address:* c/o George Borchardt Inc., 136 East 57th Street, New York, NY 10022-2707; Bard College, Department of Languages and Literature, PO Box 5000, Annandale-on-Hudson, NY 12504-5000, USA (office). *Telephone:* (845) 758-7290 (office). *Website:* www.bard.edu/academics/programs/langlit (office).

ASHBY, Nora (see AFRICANO, Lillian)

ASHCROFT, Frances Mary, BA, PhD, ScD, FRS, FMedSci; British physiologist and academic; *Royal Society GlaxoSmithKline Research Professor of Physiology, University of Oxford;* b. 15 Feb. 1952, d. of John Ashcroft and Kathleen Ashcroft. *Education:* Talbot Heath School, Bournemouth, Girton Coll., Cambridge. *Career:* MRC Training Fellow in Physiology, Univ. of Leicester 1978–82; Demonstrator in Physiology, Univ. of Oxford 1982–85, EPA Cephalosporin Jr Research Fellow, Linacre Coll. 1983–85, Royal Soc. Univ.

Research Fellow in Physiology 1985–90, Lecturer in Physiology, Christ Church 1986–87, Trinity Coll. 1988–89 (Sr Research Fellow 1992–); Tutorial Fellow in Medicine, St Hilda's Coll. 1990–91, Univ. Lecturer in Physiology 1990–96, Prof. of Physiology 1996–2001, Royal Soc. GlaxoSmithKline Research Prof. 2001–, Dir, Oxford Centre for Gene Function; mem. European Molecular Biology Org. *Television:* appeared (as a diner) on Masterchef, along with several other Fellows of the Royal Soc. 2011. *Publications:* Insulin-Molecular Biology to Pathology (co-author) 1992, Ion Channels and Disease 2000, Life at the Extremes: The Science of Survival 2000, and numerous articles in scientific journals. *Honours:* Dr hc (Open Univ.) 2003, (Univ. of Leicester) 2007; Frank Smart Prize, Univ. of Cambridge 1974, Andrew Culworth Memorial Prize 1990, G.B. Morgagni Young Investigator Award 1991, G.L. Brown Prize Lecturer, Yale Univ. 1997, Peter Curran Lecturer 1999, Charter Award, Inst. of Biology 2004, Walter B. Cannon Award, American Physiological Soc. 2007, L'Oréal-UNESCO For Women in Science Award (Europe) for her discovery of an ATP-sensitive potassium channel linking glucose metabolism and insulin secretion and its role in neonatal diabetes 2012. *Address:* Department of Physiology, Anatomy and Genetics, Sherrington Building, Parks Road, Oxford, OX1 3PT, England (office). *Telephone:* (1865) 285810 (office). *Fax:* (1865) 285812 (office). *E-mail:* frances.ashcroft@dpag.ox.ac.uk (office). *Website:* www.dpag.ox.ac.uk/academic_staff/frances_ashcroft (office); oxion.dpag.ox.ac.uk (office).

ASHE, Geoffrey Thomas Leslie, MBE, BA, MA, FRSL; British author and lecturer; b. 29 March 1923, London, England; s. of Arthur William Ashe and Thelma Sydney Hoodless Ashe; m. 1st Dorothy Irene Train 1946 (deceased); four s. one d.; m. 2nd Maxine Lefever 1992 (divorced); m. 3rd Patricia Chandler 1998. *Education:* Univ. of British Columbia, Canada, Trinity Coll., Cambridge. *Career:* Assoc. Ed. Arthurian Encyclopedia 1986; mem. Medieval Acad. of America, Int. Arthurian Soc.; Co-founder and Sec. Camelot Research Cttee 1965–70. *Publications include:* King Arthur's Avalon 1957 (re-issued on 50th anniversary 2007), From Caesar to Arthur 1960, Land to the West 1962, The Land and the Book 1965, Gandhi 1968, The Quest for Arthur's Britain 1968, Camelot and the Vision of Albion 1971, The Art of Writing Made Simple 1972, The Finger and the Moon 1973, The Virgin 1976, The Ancient Wisdom 1977, Miracles 1978, Guidebook to Arthurian Britain 1980, Kings and Queens of Early Britain 1982, Avalonian Quest 1982, The Discovery of King Arthur 1985, Landscape of King Arthur 1987, Mythology of the British Isles 1990, King Arthur: The Dream of a Golden Age 1990, Dawn Behind the Dawn 1992, Atlantis 1992, The Traveller's Guide to Arthurian Britain 1997, The Book of Prophecy 1999, The Hell-Fire Clubs 2000, Merlin 2001, Labyrinths and Mazes 2003, Merlin: The Prophet and his History 2006, The Offbeat Radicals: The British Tradition of Alternative Dissent 2007; contrib. to numerous magazines and journals. *Literary Agent:* c/o Rogers, Coleridge & White Literary Agency, 20 Powis Mews, London, W11 1JN, England. *Telephone:* (20) 7221-3717. *Fax:* (20) 7229-9084. *Website:* www.rcwlitagency.co.uk. *Address:* Chalice Orchard, Well House Lane, Glastonbury, Somerset, BA6 8BJ, England (home). *Telephone:* (1458) 832485 (home). *E-mail:* ashemail@tinyworld.co.uk (home).

ASHER, Harry (see FREEMANTLE, Brian Harry)

ASHER, Neal Lewis; British writer; b. 4 Feb. 1961, Billericay, Essex, England. *Education:* mechanical and production eng ONC. *Publications include:* Another England 1989, Out of the Leaflight 1991, Mason's Rats 1992, The Thrake 1993, Woodsmith 1993, Dragon in the Flower 1993, Blue Holes and Bloody Waters 1994, Mason's Rats II 1994, Stinging Things 1994, Adaptogenic 1994, The Flame 1994, Great African Vampire 1994, Stones of Straw 1994, Oceana Foods 1994, Jable Sharks 1994, Cavefish 1995, Spatterjay 1995, Jack O'Gravestones 1995, Snairls 1995, The Bacon 1996, Page Dow 1996, The Devil You Know 1996, The Berserker Captain 1996, Alternative Hospital 1996, Floundering 1996, Plastipak 1996, The Gurnard 1997, Snow in the Desert 1997, Conversations 1998, Cowl 2004, The Voyage of the Sable Keech 2006, Hilldiggers 2007, Prador Moon 2007, The Gabble and Other Stories 2008, The Shadow of the Scorpion 2009, The Technician 2010. *Address:* 22 Snoreham Gardens, Latchingdon, Chelmsford, Essex, CM3 6UN, England.

ASHFORD, Jeffrey (see JEFFRIES, Roderic Graeme)

ASHLEY, Bernard, DipEd; British writer; b. 2 April 1935, London, England; s. of Alfred Walter Ashley and Vera Ashley; m. Iris Frances Ashley; three s. *Education:* Cambridge Inst. of Educ. *Career:* mem. Writers' Guild, BAFTA. *Plays:* The Secret of Theodore Brown, The Old Woman who Lived in a Cola Can, Little Soldier. *Television:* Running Scared, The Country Boy, Dodgem, 3-7-11, Justin and the Demon Drop Kick. *Publications include:* The Trouble with Donovan Croft 1974, Terry on the Fence 1975, All My Men 1977, A Kind of Wild Justice 1978, Break in the Sun 1980, Dinner Ladies Don't Count 1981, Dodgem 1982, High Pavement Blues 1983, Janey 1985, Running Scared 1986, Bad Blood 1988, The Country Boy 1989, The Secret of Theodore Brown 1989, Clipper Street 1990, Seeing off Uncle Jack 1992, Cleversticks 1993, Three Seven Eleven 1993, Johnnie's Blitz 1995, I Forgot, Said Troy 1996, A Present for Paul 1996, City Limits 1997, Tiger Without Teeth 1998, Growing Good 1999, Little Soldier 1999, Revenge House 2002, Double the Love 2002, The Bush 2003, Freedom Flight 2003, Torrent 2004, Ten Days to Zero 2005, Smokescreen, Down to the Wire 2007, Flashpoint, Angel Boy, Solitaire 2008, No Way to Go 2009, Ronnie's War 2010, Aftershock 2011, Dive Bombing 2012; contribs to Books for Your Children, Junior Education, Books for Keeps, Times Educational Supplement, School Librarian. *Honours:* Hon. EdD (Greenwich) 2002, Hon. DLit (Leicester) 2004; The Other Award 1976, RTS Best Children's Entertainment Programme 1993. *Address:* 128 Heathwood Gardens, London, SE7 8ER, England (office). *Telephone:* (20) 8854-5785 (office). *E-mail:* bernardashley@talktalk.net (office). *Website:* www.bashley.com.

ASHOKAMITRAN, BSc; Indian editor and writer; b. (Jagadisa Thyagarajan), 22 Sept. 1931, Secunderabad, Andhra Pradesh; m. Rajeswari 1963; three s. *Career:* Tutor, Popular Tutorials, Secunderabad, 1950–52; Public Relations Officer, Gemini Studios, Chennai, 1952–66; Exec. Ed. Kanaiyazhi (monthly), 1966–88; Ed. Munril (literary journal) 1989–; Founding mem. Ilakkia Sangam (literary forum), Creative Forum (writers and painters); mem. PEN India. *Publications include:* Anbin Parisu (play) 1953, Karainda Nizhalgal 1969, Vaazhvilay Oru Murai 1971, Innum Sila Naatkal 1972, Thanneer 1973, Kaalamum 5 Kuzhan Daigalum 1974, 18th Parallel 1977, Viduthalai 1979, Unmai Vetkai 1979, Akaya Thamarai 1980, En Payanam 1981, Vimochanam 1982, Thanthaikkaka 1983, Indru 1984, Muraippen 1984, Moonru Paarvaigal (co-author) 1984, Otran! 1985, Sila Asiriyargal Noolgal 1987, Padaippu Kalai 1987, Uttara Ramayanam 1988, Manasarovar 1989, Oru Gramattu Adyayam 1990, Appavin Snehidar (Sahitya Akademi Award 1996) 1991, Water 1993, 18-Vadhu Atchakkodu (RamaKrishna Dalmia Award 1995, Ilakkiya Chinthanai Book of the Year Award 1977) 1993, Iruvarukka Podum 1995, Ellame Sari 1997, Colours of Evil (in English) 1998, Most Truthful Picture (in English) 1998, Adhunik Tamil Kahaniyan 1998, Complete Short Stories 2000, Complete Novellas 2000, Sila India Mozhigalil Mudal Novelgal 2001, Sand and Other Stories 2002, My Years With Boss 2002, My Father's Friend 2002, Collected Short Stories (two vols) 2004, Collected Essays (two vols) 2005, Mole! 2005, Tandeya Snehita 2006, Star-crossed 2007, Today 2007, Between the Wars 2009, Manasarovar 2010; contribs to Illustrated Weekly of India, Indian Literature, Poet, Hindu Deccan Herald, India Today, Outlook, The Hindu, Indian Express, Times of India. *Honours:* Hon. DLitt (World Acad. of Art and Culture) 1990; Story of the Month Award (five times), Ilakkiya Chinthanai Book of the Year Award 1985, Story of the Year Award 1985, Govt of Tamil Nadu Fiction of the Year Award 1985, 1987, 1990, Lily Memorial Award 1992, Harmony Award 1995, Agnri Akshara Award 1996, MGR Award 2006, Saaral Award 2011. *Address:* 1A, Ninth Cross Avenue, Dandeeswaranagar, Velachery, Chennai 600 042, India (home). *Telephone:* (44) 22432703 (home); 9444608686 (mobile). *E-mail:* ashoka_mitran@yahoo.co.in.

ASHTON, Dore, BA, MA; American writer; *Professor of Art History*, *The Cooper Union*; b. 21 May 1928, Newark, NJ; m. 1st Adja Yunkers 1952 (died 1983); two d.; m. 2nd Matti Megged (died 2003). *Education:* Univ. of Wisconsin, Harvard Univ. *Career:* Assoc. Ed. Art Digest 1951–54, Arts, 1974–92; Art Critic, New York Times, 1955–60; Lecturer, Pratt Inst. 1962–63; Head, Dept of Humanities, School of Visual Arts 1965–68; Prof. of Art History, The Cooper Union 1969–; Adjunct Prof. of Art History, CUNY 1973, Columbia Univ. 1975, New School for Social Research 1986; Sr Lecturer, Yale Univ. 1995–; mem. Int. Asscn of Art Critics. *Publications include:* Abstract Art Before Columbus 1957, Poets and the Past 1959, Philip Guston 1960, Redon, Moreau, Bresdin (co-author) 1961, The Unknown Shore 1962, Rauschenberg's Dante 1964, Richard Lindner 1969, Pol Bury 1971, Picasso on Art 1972, Cultural Guide New York 1972, The New York School: A Cultural Reckoning 1973, A Joseph Cornell Album 1974, Yes, But: A Critical Biography of Philip Guston 1976, A Fable of Modern Art 1980, Rosa Bonheur: A Life and Legend (with Denise Browne Hare) 1981, American Art Since 1945 1982, About Rothko 1983, 20th Century Artists on Art 1985, Out of the Whirlwind 1987, Fragonard in the Universe of Painting 1988, Noguchi East and West 1992, The Delicate Thread: Hiroshi Teshigahara 1997, William Tucker 2001, The Walls of the Heart: Life and Work of David Rankin 2002, The Black Rainbow: Fernando de Szyszlo 2003, Miguel Barceló: Una Vida en el medio de camino 2008; contribs: journals and magazines. *Honours:* Ford Foundation Fellow 1960, Graham Fellow 1963, Mather Award for Art Criticism, College Art Asscn 1963, Guggenheim Fellowship 1964, Nat. Endowment for the Humanities Grant 1980, Art Criticism Prize, St Louis Art Museum 1988, Int. Sculpture Center's Award 2010, Archives of American Art Award 2011. *Address:* The Cooper Union, Cooper Square, New York, NY 10003 (office); 217 East 11th Street, New York, NY 10003, USA (home). *Telephone:* (212) 477-6911 (home). *Fax:* (212) 353-4398 (office); (212) 477-6911 (home).

ASHTON, Robert, BA, PhD, FRHistS; British fmr academic; *Professor Emeritus, University of East Anglia*; b. 21 July 1924, Chester, England; s. of Joseph Ashton and Edith Frances Ashton; m. Margaret Alice Sedgwick 1946; two d. *Education:* Magdalen Coll. School, Oxford, Univ. Coll., Southampton, London School of Econs. *Career:* Asst Lecturer, Univ. of Nottingham, later Lecturer, Sr Lecturer 1952–63; Visiting Assoc. Prof., Univ. of California, Berkeley 1962–63; Prof., Univ. of East Anglia 1963–89, Prof. Emer. 1989–; Visiting Fellow, All Souls Coll., Oxford, 1974–75, 1987; Vice-Pres. Royal Historical Soc. 1983–84, Leverhulme Emer. Fellow 1989–91. *Publications include:* The Crown and the Money Market 1603–40 1960, James I by his Contemporaries 1969, The English Civil War: Conservatism and Revolution 1603–49 1978, The City and the Court 1603–1643 1979, Reformation and Revolution, 1558–1660 1984, Counter Revolution: The Second Civil War and its Origins 1646–1648 1994; contribs to Economic History Review, Bulletin of Institute of Historical Research, Past and Present, historical journals. *Address:* The Manor House, Brundall, Norwich, NR13 5JY, England (home). *Telephone:* (1603) 713368 (home). *E-mail:* robert.ashton@uea.ac.uk.

'ĀSHŪR, Radwā, MA, PhD; Egyptian novelist, short-story writer, literary critic and academic; b. 1946, Cairo; m. Murīd Barghūthī; one s. *Education:*

Cairo Univ., Univ. of Massachusetts, USA. *Career:* resided in USA 1973–75; joined Faculty, Ain Shams Univ., Cairo 1967, later Prof. of English and Comparative Literature; mem. Cttee for the Defence of Nat. Culture. *Publications:* Al-Rihla (travel memoir) 1983, Hajar Dāfi (novel) 1985, Khadīja wa-Sawsan (novel) 1989, Gharnāta (novel trilogy, part trans. as Granada: A Novel) (Int. Cairo Book Fair Best Novel Award 1994, Arab Women's Book Fair First Prize 1995) 1994 (second and third parts published as Maryama, Wa al-rahil 1995), Taqarir sayyida ra 2001, Qatal nazif (short story, trans. as A Clean Kill) 2001, Siraaj (short story) 2006, Atyaaf (trans. as Spectres) 2007; other: Sayyadu al-dhakira (critical essays); has published critical studies on West African literature, on Palestinian writer Ghassan Kanafani, on Kahlil Gibran and on William Blake; several short stories have been translated into English. *Honours:* Constantine Cavafi Prize for Literature 2007. *Address:* c/o Faculty of Al-Alsun, English Department, Ain Shams University, Elkhalifa Elmaamoon Street, Abbassia, Cairo, Egypt. *Website:* www.radwaashour.net.

ASIMOV, Janet O. Jeppson, BA, MD; American physician and writer; b. 6 Aug. 1926, Ashland, Pa; m. Isaac Asimov 1973 (died 1992). *Education:* Stanford Univ., New York Univ. Coll. of Medicine, William Alanson White Inst. *Career:* mem. Science Fiction and Fantasy Writers of America, William Alanson White Soc., American Acad. of Psychoanalysis, American Psychiatric Asscn. *Publications include:* The Second Experiment 1974; The Last Immortal 1980, Laughing Space 1982, Norby, the Mixed-Up Robot 1983, Norby's Other Secret 1984, Norby and the Lost Princess 1985, Norby and the Invaders 1985, The Mysterious Cure 1985, Norby and the Queen's Necklace 1986, Norby Finds a Villain 1987, The Package in Hyperspace 1988, Mind Transfer 1988, Norby and Yobo's Great Adventure 1989, Norby and the Oldest Dragon 1990, Norby Down to Earth 1991, Norby and the Court Jester 1991, Norby and the Terrified Taxi 1993, Murder at the Galactic Writers' Society 1995, Norby and the Terrified Taxi 1997, It's Been a Good Life by Isaac Asimov (ed.) 2002, Notes for a Memoir 2006, The House Where Isadora Danced 2009; contribs to several journals, science columns in various newspapers.

ASLAM, Nadeem; British writer; b. 1966, Gujranwala, Pakistan. *Education:* Univ. of Manchester. *Career:* wrote first short story (in Urdu) aged 13, published in Pakistani newspaper; moved to UK aged 14. *Publications include:* Season of the Rainbirds (Betty Trask Award, Author's Club Best First Novel Award) 1993, Maps for Lost Lovers (Kiriyama Prize 2005, Encore Award 2005) 2004, The Wasted Vigil 2008, Leila in the Wilderness 2010. *Honours:* Royal Literary Fund grant. *Address:* c/o Faber and Faber Ltd, Bloomsbury House, 74-77 Great Russell Street, London, WC1B 3DA, England. *Website:* www.faber.co.uk.

ASMUNDSDOTTIR, Steinunn; Icelandic journalist, writer, poet, photographer and translator; b. 1 March 1966, Reykjavík; d. of Asmundur Matthiasson and Ragnhildur Petursdottir; m. Thorsteinn Ingi Steinthorsson; two d. *Education:* Univ. of Iceland. *Career:* Ed. Andblaer (Breeze) magazine 1995–2000; journalist, Morgunbladid newspaper 2003–06; Ed. Austurgluggin weekly 2007–10; now freelance. *Publications include:* Frimanns Postilla (children's book) 1982, Solo on the Rainbow (poems) 1989, Words of a Goddess (poems) 1993, House on the Moor (poems) 1996; contribs to various publs. *Website:* www.mbl.is (office).

ASPLER, Tony, CM, BA; Canadian writer and broadcaster; b. (Anthony Elliott), 12 May 1939, London, England; s. of Moses Elliott and Mimi Young; one s. one d. *Education:* McGill Univ. *Career:* mem. Crime Writers of Canada (Founding Chair. 1982–84), Wine Writers Circle of Canada. *Publications include:* Streets of Askelon 1972, One of My Marionettes 1973, Chain Reaction (with Gordon Pape) 1978, The Scorpion Sanction (with Gordon Pape) 1980, Vintage Canada 1983, The Music Wars (with Gordon Pape) 1983, Titanic (novel) 1989, Blood is Thicker than Beaujolais (novel) 1993, Cellar and Silver (with Rose Murray) 1993, Aligoté to Zinfandel 1994, The Beast of Barbaresco (novel) 1996, Death on the Douro (novel) 1997, Travels With My Corkscrew (non-fiction) 1998, The Wine Lover Cooks (with Kathleen Sloan) 1999, Canadian Wine for Dummies 2000, The Wine Atlas of Canada 2006, North American Wine Routes (with Dan Beger) 2010; contribs to periodicals. *Address:* 1402-900 Mount Pleasant Road, Toronto, ON M4P 3J9, Canada (home). *Telephone:* (416) 488-8597 (home). *E-mail:* tony.aspler@rogers.com (home). *Website:* www.iwineanddine.com; www.tonyaspler.com.

ASSAD, Rifat al-, PhD; Syrian politician, newspaper publisher and fmr army officer; b. 22 Aug. 1937, Kerdaha; s. of Ali Al-Assad and Na'issa Ibad; m. Lyn Al-Khayer 1973; eight s. eight d. *Career:* officer in Syrian Army 1963–94, Founder and Commdr of Defence Regts 1965–84, mem. Regional Command of Syria 1975; Prof., Coll. of Law, Damascus Univ. 1976; Vice-Pres. of Syria 1984; Founder and Publr Al-Forsan magazine, Damascus 1966–84, Paris and London 1984–92, Al-Shah daily newspaper, Paris 1988, Shaza magazine, Paris 1986 and Memo magazine, Cyprus 1986; Founder and Pres. League of Higher Studies, Grads and Research 1974. *Publications include:* many econ. and political articles in Arabic newspapers and magazines. *Honours:* many Syrian decorations, Légion d'honneur, Hon. Decoration of Morocco. *Address:* c/o Mezzeh, Jabal, Damascus, Syria.

ASSAYESH, Shahin, MPhil; Iranian publishing executive; b. 11 March 1939, Mashhad; d. of Zabihollah Assayesh and Afsaneh Shamlou Assayesh; m. Nasser Meh 1959 (divorced 1987); two s. *Education:* Univ. of London, UK and Tehran and Mashhad Univs. *Career:* secondary school teacher, Tehran 1964–76; moved to UK 1976, to Canada 1983; Founder Iranian Women's Quarterly Journal 1986, then Ed. and Publisher; Pres. Iranian Women's Publications 1991–. *Address:* 278 Bloor Street, Suite 809, Toronto, ON M4W 3M4, Canada (home). *Telephone:* (416) 926-9401 (home).

ASSOULINE, Pierre; French writer and editor; b. 1953, Casablanca, Morocco. *Career:* Ed. Lire magazine, France. *Publications include:* Gaston Gallimard: Un demi-siècle d'edition française 1984, English trans. as Gaston Gallimard: A Half-Century of French Publishing 1988, Une éminence grise: Jean Jardin (1904–1976) 1986, L'homme de l'art: D. H. Kahnweiler, 1884–1979 1988, English trans. as An Artful Life: A Biography of D. H. Kahnweiler, 1884–1979 1990, Albert Londres: Vie et mort d'un grand reporter, 1884–1932 1989, Monsieur Dassault 1993, Trois hommes d'influence 1994, Hergé: Biographie 1996, Simenon: Biographie 1992, English trans. as Simenon: A Biography 1997, Germinal: l'aventure d'un film 1993, Hergé : biographie 1996, Le dernier des Camondo 1997, Le fleuve Combelle 1997, La cliente 1997, Cartier-Bresson: l'oeil du siècle 1999, Double vie 2000, Grâces lui soient rendues: Paul Durand-Ruel, le marchand des impressionnistes 2002, État limite 2003, Lutetia 2005, Rosebud: éclats de biographies 2006, Desiree Dolron: exaltation, gaze, xteriors (with Mark Haworth-Booth) 2006, Le Portrait 2007, Les Invités 2009, Das Bildnis der Baronin 2010, Portret 2010, A la recherche de Winston Churchill 2011, Vies de Job 2011; Other: De nos envoyés spéciaux: les coulisses du reportage (co-author) 1977, Lourdes: Histoires d'eau 1980, Les nouveaux convertis: Enquête sur les chrétiens, des juifs et des musulmans pas comme les autres 1982, L'épuration des intellectuels 1944–1945 1985, Le fleuve combelle 1997. *Address:* c/o Éditions Gallimard, 5 rue Sébastian-Bottin, 75328 Paris, France. *Website:* www .gallimard.fr; passouline.blog.lemonde.fr.

ASSUNÇÃO, Leilah; Brazilian playwright and novelist; b. (Maria de Lourdes Torres de Assunção), 1943, Botucatu, São Paulo. *Education:* São Paulo Univ. *Plays:* Vejo um Vulto na Janela, me Acudam que Sou Donzela 1963–64, Use Pó de Arroz Bijou 1968, Fala Baixo, senão Eu Grito (Moliere Theatre Prize) 1969, Jorginho, o Machão 1970, Amanhã, Amélia, de Manhã 1973, (later renamed Roda côr de roda), A kuka de Kamaiorá 1975, Feira Brasileira de Opinião 1976, Seda Pura e Alfinetadas 1981, Boca Molhada de Paixão Calada 1984, Lua Nua 1987, Adorável Desgraçada 1994, O Momento de Mariana Martins 1999. *Television:* screenplays: Venha Ver o Sol na Estrada 1974, Um Sonho a Mais 1984, Avenida Paulista 1985. *Publications include:* Sorriso na Alvorada (novel) 1955. *Honours:* São Paulo Drama Critics' Award for best Brazilian playwright 1969. *Address:* c/o Ministry of Culture, Esplanada dos Ministérios, Bloco B, 3 andar, 70068-900 Brasília, DF, Brazil.

ASTLEY, Neil, BA; British writer and poetry publisher; *Editor, Bloodaxe Books*; b. 12 May 1953. *Education:* Univ. of Newcastle upon Tyne. *Career:* Co-ed., Stand magazine 1976–78; Founder-Ed. Bloodaxe Books 1978–. *Publications include:* poetry: Darwin Survivor 1988, Biting My Tongue 1995; novels: The End of My Tether 2002, The Sheep Who Changed the World 2005; ed. anthologies: Ten North-East Poets 1980, Poetry with an Edge 1988, Tony Harrison 1991, New Blood 1999, Staying Alive: Real Poems for Unreal Times 2002, Pleased to See Me: 69 Very Sexy Poems 2002, Do Not Go Gentle: Poems for Funerals 2003, Being Alive 2004, Passionfood: 100 Love Poems 2005, Bloodaxe Poetry Introductions 1, 2 & 3 2006–07, Soul Food: Nourishing Poems for Starved Minds (with Pamela Robertson-Pearce) 2007, Earth Shattering: Ecopoems 2007, In Person: 30 Poets (DVD and book, with Pamela Robertson-Pearce) 2008, Being Human 2011. *Honours:* Hon. DLitt (Newcastle); Eric Gregory Award. *Address:* Bloodaxe Books Ltd, Highgreen, Tarset, Northumberland, NE48 1RP, England (office). *E-mail:* editor@bloodaxebooks.com (office). *Website:* www.bloodaxebooks.com (office).

ASTRUC, Alexandre, LèsL; French film director, writer and journalist; b. 13 July 1923, Paris; s. of Marcel Astruc and Huguette Haendel; m. Elyette Helies 1983. *Education:* Lycée de Saint-Germain-en-Laye, Lycée Henri IV and Faculté des Lettres, Paris. *Career:* journalist and film critic 1945–; film dir 1952–; TV reporter for Radio Luxembourg 1969–72; film critic, Paris Match 1970–72; contributor to Figaro-Dimanche 1977–. *Films directed include:* Le rideau cramoisi 1952, Les mauvaises rencontres 1955, Une vie 1958, La proie pour l'ombre 1960, Education sentimentale 1961, Evariste galois 1965, La longue marche 1966, Flammes sur l'Adriatique 1968, Sartre par lui-même 1976; also TV films and series. *Publications:* Les vacances 1945, La tête la première, Ciel de cendres 1975, Le serpent jaune 1976, Quand la chouette s'envole 1978, Le permissionnaire 1982, Le roman de Descartes 1989, De la caméra au stylo 1992, L'autre versant de la colline 1993, Evariste Galois 1994, Le montreur d'ombres 1996, La France au coeur 2000, Un rose en hiver 2006, Les secrets de Mademoiselle Fechtenbaum 2008. *Honours:* Chevalier, Légion d'honneur; Officier, Ordre nat. du Mérite; Commdr des Arts et des Lettres; various film prizes and other awards. *Address:* 168 rue de Grenelle, 75007 Paris, France (home). *Telephone:* 6-24-60-87-82 (home).

ASWANY, Alaa al-; Egyptian writer and dentist; b. 26 May 1957, Cairo. *Education:* Lycee Français, Cairo, Cairo Univ., Univ. of Illinois, USA. *Career:* own dental clinic. *Publications include:* The Papers of Essam Abdel 1989, The Man who got Closer and Saw 1990, Waiting for the Leader 1998, Umaret Yacoubian (trans. as The Yacoubian Building) 2002, Niran Sadiqa (Friendly Fire, short stories) 2004, Chicago 2007, Limatha la Yathour El Masriyoon 2010, Hal nastahiqq al-dimoqratiyya? 2011. *Address:* c/o Dar El Shorouk, 8 Sibaweh El Masri, Cairo (Nasr City) 11371, Egypt. *Telephone:* (2) 24023399. *Fax:* (2) 24037567. *E-mail:* dar@shorouk.com. *Website:* www.shorouk.com.

ASZYK, Urszula, PhD; Polish academic; *Professor, Department of Iberic Studies, University of Warsaw*; b. 26 Sept. 1944, Jedrzejów, Kielce; d. of Feliks

Aszyk and Helena Aszyk (née Sutor); m. Paul Bangs 1994; two d. *Education:* Univ. of Łódź. *Career:* Lecturer in Literary and Theatrical Theory, Univ. of Łódź 1968–76; Lecturer in Polish Language and Literature, Univ. Autónoma, Madrid 1976–81; Asst Prof. of Spanish Literature, Dept of Iberian Studies, Univ. of Warsaw 1981–90, Assoc. Prof. 1992–98, Prof. 2000–, Deputy Head of Dept 1982–83, Head of Section of Spanish Language and Literature 1985–1991, 1994–98, Head of Section of Spanish Literature 2009–; Assoc. Prof., State Univ. of New York at Stony Brook 1987–88; Visiting Prof., Univ. of San Sebastian, Spain 1989, Univ. of Mainz, Germany 1991–92, Univ. of São Paulo, Brazil 1993, Univ. of Stockholm, Sweden 1996; Sr Research Fellow, Univ. of Bristol, UK 1995–2003; Prof., Univ. of Silesia 1998–2000; mem. Int. Inst. of Theater, UNESCO 1981–, Int. Asscn of Hispanistas, Polish Asscn Polaca de Hispanistas (Pres. 1985–87, 1989–94, 2004–10). *Publications include:* Iwo Gall's Theatre Searching (Ministry of Educ. and Science Award 1979) 1978, Spanish Contemporary Theatre (Ministry of Culture and Theatre Club Awards 1989) 1988, Iwo Gall's Works About Theatre 1993, Entre la crisis y la vanguardia. Estudios sobre el teatro español del siglo XX 1995, Federico García Lorca and the Theatre of His Time (in Polish) 1997, Federico García Lorca, Unfinished Theatre, Open Theatre (in Polish) (trans. and ed.) 1998, The Theatre of Calderon: Tradition and Modernity (in Polish) 2002, Espacio Dramático frente al Espacio Escénico (ed.) 2003, Corrales de Comedias (Theatre Critics Award 2007) 2005, Lope de Vega, Arte nuevo de hacer comedias (in Polish) (trans. and ed.) 2008, Nowa sztuka pisania komedii w dzisiejszych czasach Lopego de Vega w czterechsetlecie wydania (Ed.) 2009; numerous contribs to professional journals including articles on Calderon's Theatre and Spanish Golden Age 2000. *Honours:* Gold Medal "for long service" 2011, numerous awards for research and for published works. *Address:* University of Warsaw, Department of Iberic Studies, ul Obozna 8, 00 332 Warsaw, Poland (office); 2 Kenton Close, Bracknell, Berks., RG12 9AZ, England (home). *Telephone:* (22) 8282962 (Warsaw) (office); (22) 5520429 (office); (1344) 429307 (home). *E-mail:* uaszyk@aol.com.

ATHILL, Diana, OBE; British writer and editor; b. 21 Dec. 1917, Norfolk, England. *Education:* Lady Margaret Hall, Oxford. *Career:* worked for News Information Dept, BBC Overseas Service during World War II; helped set up publishing co. with André Deutsch; Ed., Allan Wingate and André Deutsch publrs –1993; worked with authors including V. S. Naipaul, Philip Roth, John Updike, Norman Mailer and Jean Rhys. *Publications include:* memoirs: After A Funeral 1986, Make Believe 1993, Stet 2000, Instead of a Letter 2001, Yesterday Morning 2003, Somewhere Towards the End (Costa Book Award for Biography, Nat. Book Critics' Circle Award for Autobiography 2009) 2008, Life Class: The Selected Memoirs of Diana Athill 2009; other: An Unavoidable Delay (short stories) 1962, Don't Look at Me Like That (novel) 2001. *Address:* c/o Granta Books, 12 Addison Avenue, London, W11 4QR, England. *E-mail:* info@granta.com. *Website:* www.granta.com.

ATIYAH, Sir Michael Francis, Kt, OM, MA, PhD, ScD, FRS, FRSE; British mathematician and academic; b. 22 April 1929, London; s. of Edward Selim Atiyah and Jean Atiyah (née Levens); m. Lily Brown 1955; three s. *Education:* Victoria Coll., Egypt, Manchester Grammar School and Trinity Coll. Cambridge. *Career:* Research Fellow, Trinity Coll., Cambridge 1954–58, Hon. Fellow 1976, Master 1990–97, Fellow 1997–; Fellow, Pembroke Coll., Cambridge 1958–61 (Hon. Fellow 1983), Univ. Lecturer 1957–61; Reader, Oxford Univ. and Fellow St Catherine's Coll., Oxford 1961–63, Hon. Fellow 1991; Savilian Prof. of Geometry, Univ. of Oxford and Fellow, New Coll., Oxford 1963–69, Hon. Fellow 1999; Prof. of Mathematics, Inst. for Advanced Study, Princeton, NJ 1969–72; Royal Soc. Research Prof., Oxford Univ. 1973–90, Fellow, St Catherine's Coll., Oxford 1973–90; Dir Isaac Newton Inst. of Math. Sciences, Cambridge 1990–96; Chancellor Univ. of Leicester 1995–2005; Pres. Royal Soc. of Edinburgh 2005–08; Pres. London Math. Soc. 1974–76, Pres. Math. Asscn 1981; mem. Science and Eng Research Council 1984–89; Pres. Pugwash Confs 1997–2002; mem. Council Royal Soc. 1984–85, Pres. 1990–95; Foreign mem. American Acad. of Arts and Sciences, Swedish Acad. of Sciences, Leopoldina Acad. (Germany), NAS, Acad. des Sciences (France), Royal Irish Acad., Third World Acad. of Science, Indian Nat. Science Acad., Australian Acad. of Sciences, Chinese Acad. of Sciences, American Philosophical Soc., Ukrainian Acad. of Sciences, Russian Acad. of Sciences, Georgian Acad. of Sciences, Venezuelan Acad. of Sciences, Accad. Nazionale dei Lincei, Royal Spanish Acad. of Sciences, Norwegian Acad. of Science and Letters. *Publications:* K-Theory 1966, Commutative Algebra 1969, Geometry and Dynamics of Magnetic Monopoles 1988, Collected Works (five vols) 1988, vol. 6 2005, The Geometry and Physics of Knots 1990. *Honours:* Hon. Prof., Univ. of Edinburgh 1997–; Hon. Fellow, Darwin Coll., Cambridge 1992, Hon. FREng 1993, Hon. Faculty of Actuaries 1999, Univ. of Wales Swansea 1999; Commdr Order of the Cedars, Gold Order of Merit, Lebanon, Order of Andreas Bello (Venezuela); Hon. DSc (Bonn, Warwick, Durham, St Andrew's, Dublin, Chicago, Edinburgh, Cambridge, Essex, London, Sussex, Ghent, Reading, Helsinki, Leicester, Rutgers, Salamanca, Montreal, Waterloo, Wales, Queen's-Kingston, Keele, Birmingham, Lebanon, Open, Brown, Oxford, Prague, Chinese, Hong Kong, Heriot-Watt, York Univs, American Univ. of Beirut, Scuola Normale Pisa, Polytechnic Univ. of Catalonia), Dr hc (UMIST) 1996; Fields Medal, Int. Congress of Mathematicians, Moscow 1966, Royal Medal of Royal Soc. 1968, De Morgan Medal, London Math. Soc. 1980, Copley Medal of Royal Soc. 1988, Feltrinelli Prize, Accad. Nazionale dei Lincei 1981, King Faisal Int. Prize for Science 1987, Benjamin Franklin Medal, American Philosophical Soc., Nehru Medal, Indian Nat. Science Acad., Abel Prize, Norwegian Acad. of Sciences (jtly with Isadore Singer) 2004. *Address:* University of Edinburgh, Room 6319, School of Mathematics, Mayfield Road, Edinburgh, EH9 3JZ (office); 3/8 West Grange Gardens, Edinburgh, EH9 2RA, Scotland (home). *Telephone:* (131) 650-6018 (office); (131) 667-0898 (home). *E-mail:* m.atiyah@ed.ac.uk (home). *Website:* www.maths.ed.ac.uk (office).

ATKINS, Ace; American author and fmr journalist; b. 28 June 1970, Troy, Ala; m. Angela Moore Atkins; two c. *Education:* Auburn Univ. *Career:* fmr crime reporter, Tampa Tribune; became full-time writer 2000; chosen by Robert B. Parker estate to take over writing Spenser private eye series of books 2011. *Publications:* novels: Crossroad Blues 1998, Leavin' Trunk Blues 2000, Dark End of the Street 2002, Dirty South 2004, White Shadow 2006, Wicked City 2008, Devil's Garden 2009, Infamous 2010, The Ranger 2011, The Lost Ones 2012, Lullaby 2012; work appears in several anthologies. *Honours:* First Arts Advancement Award, Auburn Univ. *Address:* c/o Michael Barson, G. P. Putnam's Sons, Penguin Group USA, 375 Hudson Street, New York, NY 10014, USA (office). *Telephone:* (212) 366-2547 (office). *E-mail:* aceatkinsbooks@gmail.com. *Website:* www.aceatkins.com.

ATKINSON, Kate, BA, MBE; British writer and playwright; b. 1951, York, England; m. (divorced); two d. *Education:* Univ. of Dundee. *Career:* fmrly home help, teacher and short story writer for women's magazines; writer 1988–. *Plays include:* Nice 1996, Abandonment 2000. *Publications:* Behind the Scences at the Museum (novel) (Whitbread First Novel award and Book of the Year 1996, Boeker Prize, SA, Livre Book of the Year, France) 1995, Human Croquet (novel) 1997, Emotionally Weird (novel) 2001, Not the End of the World (short stories) 2002, Case Histories (novel) 2004, One Good Turn (novel) 2006, When Will There be Good News? (British Book Award for Best Read of the Year 2009) 2008, Started Early, Took My Dog 2010; contrib. of short stories to Daily Telegraph, BBC 2, BBC Radio 4, Daily Express, Daily Mail, Scotsman. *Honours:* Woman's Own Short Story Competition 1986, Ian St James Award 1993, E.M. Forster Award, American Acad. of Arts and Letters 1997. *Address:* c/o Transworld Publishers Ltd, 61–63 Uxbridge Road, London, W5 5SA, England (office). *Website:* www.booksattransworld.co.uk (office); www.kateatkinson.co.uk.

ATLAS, Ronald M., BS, MS, PhD; American academic and writer; *Dean, Graduate School and Professor of Biology, University of Louisville*; b. 1946, New York, NY. *Education:* New York State Univ., Rutgers Univ. *Career:* Nat. Research Council Research Assoc., Jet Propulsion Lab. 1972–73; Faculty mem. Univ. of Louisville 1973–, currently Prof. of Biology, Dean, Grad. School, Co-Dir Center for the Deterrence of Biowarfare and Bioterrorism, School of Public Health and Information Sciences; Pres. American Soc. for Microbiology; Ed. CRC Critical Reviews in Microbiology. *Publications include:* Handbook of Media for Environmental Microbiology 1993, Handbook of Media for Clinical Microbiology (co-author) 1995, Handbook of Microbiological Media (second edn) 1996, Microbial Ecology: Fundamentals and Applications 1997, Bioremediation: Applied microbial solutions for real-world environmental clean-up 2005. *Address:* Graduate School, Houchens Building, Room 105, Louisville, Ky 40292, USA (office). *Telephone:* (502) 852-6495 (office). *Fax:* (502) 852-2365 (office). *E-mail:* r.atlas@louisville.edu (office). *Website:* louisville.edu/bioethics/faculty (office); www.asm.org (office).

ATSUMI, Ikuko, MA, PhD; Japanese poet, writer and business consultant; *President, Intercultural Business Center, Inc. Career:* fmr Prof. of English Literature, Aoyama Gakuin Univ.; published journal Feminist: The New Bluestocking 1977–80, issued reports on women's issues and int. feminist movts; presentations on Japanese women's movt at academic insts including Reischauer Inst. of Japanese Studies 1982; moved to USA 1981; fmr Research Fellow and Invited Scholar, Harvard Univ.; Founder and Pres. New England Japanese Center; currently Pres. Intercultural Business Center, Inc.; Rep. Multicultural Playing Field LLC 2003–. *Publications include:* Mother Is (translator) 1975, The Burning Heart: Women Poets of Japan (co-author with Kenneth Rexroth) 1977, Seasons of Sacred Lust: Selected Poems of Kazuko Shiraishi (translator), Ariake (translator) 2000, Law of Success: Doing Business Globally; papers on feminism and Japanese women's movt. *Address:* Intercultural Business Center, Inc., 17 Ridge Road, Atlantic Highlands, NJ 07716, USA (office). *Telephone:* (732) 872-2948 (office). *Fax:* (732) 872-7516 (office). *E-mail:* iatsumi@ikukoatsumi.com (office).

ATTALI, Jacques; French international bank official and writer; *President, Attali et Associés*; b. 1 Nov. 1943, Algiers; s. of the late Simon Attali and of Fernande Abecassis; twin brother of Bernard Attali; m. Elisabeth Allain 1981; one s. one d. *Education:* Ecole Polytechnique, Inst. d'Etudes Politiques de Paris, Ecoles des Mines de Paris, Ecole Nat. d' Admin. *Career:* started career as mining engineer, then Lecturer in Econs, Ecole Polytechnique; Auditeur, Council of State; Adviser to the Pres. 1981–91; State Councillor 1989–91; Pres. EBRD, London 1991–93; Pres. Attali et Associés (ACA) 1994–; mem. Council of State 1981–90, 1993–; Admin. KeeBoo 2000–; Pres. Attali Comm. (est. to evaluate means of liberalising econ. growth in France) 2007–; columnist for L'Express magazine. *Publications:* Analyse économique de la vie politique 1972, Modèles politiques 1973, Anti-économique (with Marc Guillaume) 1974, La parole et l'outil 1975, Bruits, Essai sur l'économie politique de la musique 1976, La nouvelle économie française 1977, L'ordre cannibale 1979, Les trois mondes 1981, Histoires du temps 1982, La figure de Fraser 1984, Un homme d'influence 1985, Au propre et au Figuré 1988, La vie éternelle (novel) 1989, Millennium: Winners and Losers in the Coming World Order 1991, 1492 1991, Verbatim (Tome I) 1993, Europe(s) 1994, Verbatim (Tome II) 1995, Economie de l'Apocalypse 1995, Tome III 1996, Chemins de Sagesse 1996, Au delà de nulle part 1997, Dictionnaire du XXIe siècle 1998, Les portes du ciel 1999, La femme du menteur 1999 (novel), Fraternités 1999, Blaise Pascal ou le génie français 2000, Bruits 2001, Nouv'Elles 2002 (novel), L'homme nomade 2003, La Confrérie des Eveillés 2004 (novel), Karl Marx ou l'esprit du Monde 2004, Une brève histoire de l'avenir 2007. *Honours:* Dr hc (Univ. of Kent, Univ. of Haifa). *Address:* Attali et Associés 27, rue Vernet, 75008 Paris, France (office). *Telephone:* 1-53-57-38-38 (office). *Fax:* 1-47-23-09-91 (office). *Website:* www .aeta.net/fr (office).

ATTALLAH, Naim Ibrahim, FRSA; British publisher and financial adviser; *Chairman, Namara Group*; b. 1 May 1931, Haifa, Palestine; s. of Ibrahim Attallah and Genevieve Attallah; m. Maria Nykolyn 1957; one s. *Education:* Coll. des Frères, Haifa and Battersea Polytechnic, London. *Career:* Propr Quartet Books 1976–, Women's Press 1977–, Robin Clark 1980–, Pipeline Books 1978–2000, The Literary Review 1981–2001, The Wire 1984–2000, Acad. Club 1989–96, The Oldie 1991–2001; Group Chief Exec. Asprey PLC 1992–96, Deputy Chair. Asprey (Bond Street) 1992–98; Man. Dir Mappin and Webb 1990–95; Exec. Dir Garrard 1990–95; Chair. Namara Group of cos 1973–, launched Parfums Namara 1985, Avant L'Amour and Après L'Amour 1985, Naïdor 1987, L'Amour de Namara 1990. *Films produced:* The Slipper and the Rose (with David Frost q.v.) 1975, Brimstone and Treacle (Exec. Producer) 1982 and several TV documentaries. *Theatre:* Happy End (Co-Presenter) 1975, The Beastly Beatitudes of Balthazar B. (Presenter and Producer) 1981, Trafford Tanzi (Co-Producer) 1982. *Publications:* Women 1987, Singular Encounters 1990, Of a Certain Age 1992, More of a Certain Age 1993, Speaking for the Oldie 1994, A Timeless Passion 1995, Tara and Claire (novel) 1996, Asking Questions 1996, A Woman a Week 1998, In Conversation with Naim Attalah 1998, Insights 1999, Dialogues 2001, The Old Ladies of Nazareth 2004, The Boy in England (memoir) 2005, In Touch with His Roots: a Second Memoir 2006, Fulfilment & Betrayal 2007. *Honours:* Hon. MA (Surrey) 1993; Retail Personality of the Year, UK Jewellery Awards 1993. *Address:* 25 Shepherd Market, London, W1J 7PP, England (home). *Telephone:* (20) 7499-2901 (home). *Fax:* (20) 7499-2914 (home). *E-mail:* nattallah@aol.com (office).

ATTAR, Samar al-, PhD; Syrian novelist and translator; *Professor of Arabic Studies, University of Sydney*; b. 1945, Damascus; m.; one d. *Education:* Damascus Univ., Dalhousie Univ., Canada, State Univ. of NY, Binghamton, USA. *Career:* taught Arabic and English in Canada, USA, Algeria, Germany; currently Prof. of Arabic Studies, Univ. of Sydney, Australia. *Publications include:* Lina: A Portrait of Damascene Girl (novel) 1982, The House on Arnus Square 1988, The Vital Roots of European Enlightenment: Ibn Tufayl's Influence on Modern Western Thought (co-author) 2007; also scholarly studies, textbooks for teaching Arabic, trans. of Arabic poetry. *Address:* Department of Arabic and Islamic Studies, University of Sydney, Sydney, NSW 2006, Australia (office). *Website:* www.sydney.edu.au (office).

ATTENBOROUGH, Sir David Frederick, Kt, OM, CH, CVO, CBE, MA, FRS; British broadcaster, naturalist and writer; b. 8 May 1926, London; s. of the late Frederick Attenborough and of Mary Attenborough; brother of Lord Attenborough; m. Jane Elizabeth Ebsworth Oriel 1950 (died 1997); one s. one d. *Education:* Wyggeston Grammar School, Leicester and Clare Coll., Cambridge. *Career:* served with RN 1947–49; editorial asst in publishing house 1949–52; with BBC Television 1952–73, Producer of zoological, archaeological, travel, political and other programmes 1952–64, Controller BBC 2 1964–68, Dir of Programmes, TV 1969–73; writer, presenter BBC series: Tribal Eye 1976, Wildlife on One, annually 1977–2004, Life on Earth 1979, The Living Planet 1984, The First Eden 1987, Lost World, Vanished Lives 1989, The Trials of Life 1990, Life in the Freezer 1993, The Private Life of Plants 1995, The Life of Birds 1998, State of the Planet 2000, The Blue Planet (narrator) 2001, The Life of Mammals 2002, Life in Cold Blood 2008, Charles Darwin and the Tree of Life (writer) 2009, First Life (writer) 2010, Frozen Planet 2011, Kingdom of Plants 3D 2012; Huw Wheldon Memorial Lecturer, RTS 1987; Pres. BAAS 1990–91, Royal Soc. for Nature Conservation 1991–96; mem. Nature Conservancy Council 1975–82; Fellow, Soc. of Film and Television Arts 1980; Int. Trustee, World Wild Life Fund 1979–86; Trustee, British Museum 1980–2000, Science Museum 1984–87, Royal Botanical Gardens, Kew 1986–92. *Publications:* Zoo Quest to Guiana 1956, Zoo Quest for a Dragon 1957, Zoo Quest in Paraguay 1959, Quest in Paradise 1960, Zoo Quest to Madagascar 1961, Quest under Capricorn 1963, The Tribal Eye 1976, Life on Earth 1979, The Zoo Quest Expeditions 1982; The Living Planet 1984, The First Eden, The Mediterranean World and Man 1987, The Trials of Life 1990, The Private Life of Plants 1994, The Life of Birds (BP Natural World Book Prize) 1998, The Life of Mammals 2002, Life on Air (memoirs) 2002, Life in the Undergrowth 2005, Life in Cold Blood 2008, Life Stories 2009, Frozen Planet 2011. *Honours:* Hon. Fellow, Clare Coll., Cambridge 1980, UMIST 1980, Inst. of Biology; Order of Merit; Hon. DLitt (Leicester, London, Birmingham, City); Hon. DSc (Liverpool, Ulster, Sussex, Bath, Durham, Keele, Heriot-Watt, Bradford, Nottingham); Hon. LLD (Bristol, Glasgow) 1977; Hon. DUniv (Open Univ.) 1980, (Essex) 1987, Antwerp 1993; Dr hc (Edin.) 1994; Special Award, Guild of TV Producers 1961, Silver Medal, Royal TV Soc. 1966, Silver Medal, Zoological Soc. of London 1966, Desmond Davis Award, Soc. of Film and TV Arts 1970, UNESCO Kalinga Prize 1982, Medallist, Acad. of Natural Sciences, Philadelphia 1982, Founders Gold Medal, Royal Geographical Soc. 1985, Int. Emmy Award 1985, Encyclopedia Britannica Award 1987, Kew Award 1996, Edin. Medal, Edin. Science Festival 1998, BP Natural World Book Prize 1998, Faraday Prize, Royal Soc. 2003, Int. Documentary Asscn Career Achievement Award 2003, Raffles Medal, Zoological Soc. of London 2004, Caird Medal, Nat. Maritime Museum 2004, British Book Awards Lifetime Achievement Award 2004. *Address:* 5 Park Road, Richmond, Surrey, TW10 6NS, England. *Website:* www.davidattenborough.co.uk.

ATWOOD, Margaret Eleanor, CC, AM, FRSC; Canadian writer; b. 18 Nov. 1939, Ottawa, Ont.; m. Graeme Gibson; one d. *Education:* Victoria Coll., Univ. of Toronto, Radcliffe Coll. and Harvard Univ., Cambridge, Mass. *Career:* Lecturer in English, Univ. of British Columbia, Vancouver 1964–65; Instructor in English, Sir George Williams Univ., Montreal 1967–68, Univ. of Alberta 1969–70; Asst Prof. of English, York Univ., Toronto 1971; Writer-in-Residence, Univ. of Toronto 1972–73, Maquarie Univ., Australia 1987, Trinity Univ., San Antonio, Tex. 1989; Berg Chair, New York Univ. 1986; Pres. Writers' Union of Canada 1981–82, International PEN (Canadian Centre—English Speaking) 1984–86. *Play:* The Penelopiad – The Play 2007. *Radio script:* The Trumpets of Summer (CBC Radio) 1964. *Television screenplays:* The Servant Girl (CBC) 1974, Snowbird 1981, Heaven on Earth (with Peter Pearson) 1986. *Recordings:* The Poetry and Voice of Margaret Atwood 1977, Margaret Atwood Reads From A Handmaid's Tale, Margaret Atwood Reads Unearthing Suite 1985, audio edns of her novels. *Publications:* poetry: Double Persephone 1961, The Circle Game (Gov.-Gen.'s Award 1966) 1964, Kaleidoscopes Baroque 1965, Talismans for Children 1965, Speeches for Doctor Frankenstein 1966, The Animals in That Country 1968, The Journals of Susanna Moodie 1970, Procedures for Underground 1970, Power Politics 1971, You Are Happy 1974, Selected Poems 1976, Marsh, Hawk 1977, Two-Headed Poems 1978, True Stories 1981, Notes Towards a Poem That Can Never Be Written 1981, Snake Poems 1983, Interlunar 1984, Selected Poems II: Poems Selected and New 1976–1986 1986, Selected Poems 1966–1984 1990, Margaret Atwood Poems 1965–1975 1991, Morning in the Burned House (Trillium Award for Excellence in Ontario Writing) 1995, The Door 2007; fiction: The Edible Woman 1969, Surfacing 1972, Lady Oracle 1976, Dancing Girls (short stories) 1977, Life Before Man 1979, Bodily Harm 1981, Encounters with the Element Man 1982, Murder in the Dark (short stories) 1983, Bluebeard's Egg (short stories) (Periodical Distributors of Canada/ Foundation for The Advancement of Canadian Letters Book of the Year Award) 1983, Unearthing Suite 1983, The Handmaid's Tale (Gov.-Gen.'s Award 1986) (adapted for the screen by Harold Pinter and directed by Volker Schlöndorf 1990) 1985, Cat's Eye (Torgi Talking Book—CNIB 1989, City of Toronto Book Award 1989, Coles Book of the Year 1989, Foundation for the Advancement of Canadian Letters/Periodical Marketers of Canada Book of the Year 1989) 1988, Wilderness Tips (short stories) (Govt of Ont. Trillium Award (with Jane Urquhart) for Excellence in Ontario Writing 1992, Periodical Marketers of Canada Book of the Year Award 1992) 1991, Good Bones (short stories) 1992, The Robber Bride (Canadian Authors' Asscn Novel of the Year 1993, Trillium Award for Excellence in Ontario Writing 1994, Commonwealth Writers' Prize for the Canadian and Caribbean Region 1994, Sunday Times Award for Literary Excellence 1994, Swedish Humour Asscn's Int. Humorous Writer Award 1995) 1993, Bones and Murder 1995, The Labrador Fiasco 1996, Alias Grace (Giller Prize 1996, Premio Mondello 1997, Salon Magazine Best Fiction of the Year 1997) 1996, The Blind Assassin (Booker Prize) 2000, Oryx and Crake 2003, Telling Tales (contrib. to charity anthology) 2004, Bottle 2004, The Penelopaid 2005, The Tent (short stories) 2006, Moral Disorder (short stories) 2006, The Year of the Flood 2009; juvenile: Up in the Tree 1978, 2006, Anna's Pet 1980, For the Birds 1990, Princess Prunella and the Purple Peanut 1995, Rude Ramsay and the Roaring Radishes 2003, Bashful Bob and Doleful Dorinda 2004, Wandering Wenda 2011; non-fiction: Survival: A Thematic Guide to Canadian Literature 1972, Days of the Rebels 1815–1840 1977, Second Words: Selected Critical Prose 1982, Strange Things: The Malevolent North in Canadian Literature 1995, Negotiating with the Dead: A Writer on Writing 2002, Moving Targets: Writing With Intent 1982–2004 2004, Curious Pursuits: Occasional Writing 2005, Writing with Intent: Essays, Reviews, Personal Prose 1983–2005 2005, Payback: Debt and the Shadow Side of Wealth (Libris Award for Best Non-Fiction Book 2009) 2008, In Other Worlds: SF and the Human Imagination 2011; editor: The New Oxford Book of Canadian Verse in English (ed.) 1982, The Oxford Book of Canadian Short Stories in English (with Robert Weaver) 1986, The Canlit Foodbook 1987, The Best American Short Stories (with Shannon Ravenel) 1989, The New Oxford Book of Canadian Short Stories in English (with Robert Weaver) 1995; reviews and critical articles have appeared in Canadian Literature, Maclean's, Saturday Night, This Magazine, New York Times Book Review, Globe and Mail, National Post, The Nation, Books In Canada, Washington Post, Harvard Educational Review, and many others; works have been translated into many languages, including French, German, Italian, Urdu, Estonian, Romanian, Serbo-Croatian, Catalan, Turkish, Russian, Finnish, Dutch, Danish, Norwegian, Swedish, Portuguese, Greek, Polish, Japanese, Icelandic, Spanish, Hebrew. *Honours:* MFA Hon. Chair, Univ. of Alabama, Tuscaloosa 1985, Foreign Hon. mem. American Acad. of Arts and Sciences 1988; Order of Ont. 1990, 125th Anniversary of Canadian Confederation Commemorative Medal 1992, Chevalier, Ordre des Arts et des Lettres 1994, Order of Literary Merit (Norway) 1996, Markets Initiative Order of the Forest 2006; Hon. DLitt (Trent) 1973, (Concordia) 1980, (Smith Coll., Mass) 1982, (Toronto) 1983, (Mount Holyoke) 1985, (Waterloo) 1985, (Guelph) 1985, (Oxford) 1998, (Ontario Coll. of Art and Design) 2009; Hon. LLD (Queen's Univ.) 1974; Dr hc (Victoria Coll.) 1987, (Université de

Montréal) 1991, (Leeds) 1994, (McMaster) 1996, (Lakehead) 1998, (Oxford) 1998, (Cambridge) 2001, (Algoma) 2001, (Harvard) 2004, (Sorbonne Nouvelle) 2005, (Literary and Historical Soc., Univ. Coll. Dublin) 2005, (Ontario Coll. of Art and Design) 2009; E.J. Pratt Medal 1961, Pres.'s Medal, Univ. of Western Ontario 1965, First Prize, Centennial Comm. Poetry Competition 1967, Union Poetry Prize, Chicago 1969, Bess Hoskins Prize for Poetry, Chicago 1974, City of Toronto Book Award 1977, Canadian Bookseller's Asscn Award 1977, Periodical Distributors of Canada Short Fiction Award 1977, St Lawrence Award for Fiction 1978, Radcliffe Grad. Medal 1980, Molson Award 1981, Guggenheim Fellowship 1981, Welsh Arts Council Int. Writer's Prize 1982, Ida Nudel Humanitarian Award 1986, Toronto Arts Award 1986, Los Angeles Times Fiction Award 1986, Ms. Magazine Woman of the Year 1986, Arthur C. Clarke Award for Best Science Fiction 1987, Commonwealth Literary Prize (regional winner) 1987, 1994, Silver Medal for Best Article of the Year, Council for Advancement and Support of Educ. 1987, Humanist of the Year Award 1987, YWCA Women of Distinction Award 1988, First Prize, Nat. Magazine Award for Environmental Journalism 1988, Canadian Booksellers Asscn Author of the Year 1989, 1996, Harvard Univ. Centennial Medal 1990, John Hughes Prize, Welsh Devt Bd 1992, Commemorative Medal for the 125th Anniversary of Canadian Confed. 1992, Best Local Author, NOW Magazine Readers' Poll 1995, 1997, 1998, 1999, 2000, 2003, 2004, Nat. Arts Club Medal of Honor for Literature 1997, London Literature Award 1999, Int. Crime Writers' Asscn Dashiell Hammett Award 2001, Canadian Booksellers Asscn People's Choice Award 2001, Radcliffe Medal 2003, Harold Washington Literary Award 2003, Banff Centre Nat. Arts Award 2005, Edinburgh Int. Book Festival Enlightenment Award 2005, Chicago Tribune Literary Prize 2005, Premio Príncipe de Asturias, Spain 2008, Dan David Prize 2010, Crystal Award, World Econ. Forum 2010, Sun Life Financial Arts & Communications Award: Canada's Most Powerful Women 2011. *Literary Agent:* c/o McClelland & Stewart, 75 Sherbourne Street, 5th Floor, Toronto, ON M5A 2P9, Canada. *Telephone:* (416) 598-1114. *Fax:* (416) 598-7764. *E-mail:* mail@mcclelland.com. *Website:* www.mcclelland.com; www.margaretatwood.ca (home).

ATXAGA, Bernardo; Spanish writer and academic; b. (Joseba Irazu Garmendia), 27 July 1951, Guipúzcoa, Basque Autonomous Community. *Education:* Univ. of Bilbao, Univ. of Barcelona. *Career:* has worked as economist, bookseller, teacher of Basque language, publisher and radio scriptwriter; writes in Euskera, the Basque language; has published novels, short stories, essays, plays, children's fiction; fmr Eusko Ikaskuntza Visiting Prof. of Basque Culture, Stanford Univ.; mem. Jakiunde, Acad. of Sciences, Arts and Letters 2010. *Play:* Lezio berri bat ostrukari buruz 1994. *Publications include:* novels: Obabakoak (Nat. Literature Prize, Spain 1989) 1988, Behi euskaldun baten memoriak (Memoirs of a Basque Cow) 1991, Gizona bere bakardadean (trans. as The Lone Man) 1993, Zeru horiek (trans. as The Lone Woman) 1996, Soinujolearen semea (trans. as The Accordionist's Son) (Grinzane Cavour Prize, Mondello Prize 2008) 2003, Zazpi etxe Frantzian 2009; short stories: Bi anai (trans. as Two Brothers) 1985, Bi letter jaso nituen oso denbora gutxian 1985, Sugeak txoriak begiratzen dionean 1985, Zeru horiek 1995, Sara izeneko gizona 1996; poetry: Etiopia 1978, Henry Bengoa inventarium 1986, Nueva Etiopia 1997; poems in journals including Jahbuch der Lyrik, Die horen, Lichtungen (Germany), Lyrikklubbss bibliotek (Sweden), Vuelta (Mexico), Linea d'ombra (Italy); children's fiction: Nikolasaren abenturak eta kalenturak 1979, Ramuntxo detektibea 1979, Antonino apreta 1982, Jimmy Potxolo 1984, Asto bat hipodromoan 1984, Txitoen istorioak 1984, Chuck Aranberri dentista baten etxean 1985, La cacería 1986, Astakiloak Arabian 1987, Flannery eta bere astakiloak 1991, Astakiloak jo eta jo 1993, Mundua eta Markoni 1995, Xolak badu lehoien berri 1995, Xola eta basurdeak (Basque Children's Literature Prize 1997) 1996, Markonitar handien ekintza handiak 1997, Bambulo: Lehen urratsak 1998, Bambulo: Krisia 1998, Bambulo: Ternuako penak 1999, Xola ehitzan 2000, Xola eta Angelito 2004; other: Ziutateaz I (short story) 1976, Ziutateaz II (short story) 1976, Groenlandiako lezioa (essay) 1998, Alfabeto sobre la literatura infantil (essay) 2002, Lekuak (essay) 2005, Markak: Gernika 1937 (essay) 2007. *Address:* c/o Editorial Pamiela, Polígono Agustinos, Soltxate, Calle G, nave B6, 31013 Pamplona, Spain. *E-mail:* soltxate@pamiela.org. *Website:* www.pamiela.org; www.atxaga.org.

AUBERT, Alvin Bernard, BA, MA; American academic and poet; *Professor Emeritus, Wayne State University*; b. 12 March 1930, Lutcher, La; m. 1st Olga Alexis 1948 (divorced); one d.; m. 2nd Bernardine Tenant 1960; two d. *Education:* Southern Univ., Baton Rouge, Univ. of Michigan, Univ. of Illinois at Urbana-Champaign. *Career:* Instructor, Southern Univ. 1960–62, Asst Prof. 1962–65, Assoc. Prof. of English 1965–70; Visiting Prof. of English, Univ. of Oregon at Eugene 1970; Assoc. Prof., SUNY at Fredonia 1970–74, Prof. of English 1974–79; founder-Ed., Obsidian magazine 1975–85; Prof. of English, Wayne State Univ., Detroit 1980–92, Prof. Emer. 1992–; mem. Modern Language Asscn of America, Nat. Council of Teachers of English, African Heritage Studies Asscn, Nat. Council for Black Studies. *Publications include:* Against the Blues 1972, Feeling Through 1975, South Louisiana: New and Selected Poems 1985, If Winter Come: Collected Poems 1994, Harlem Wrestler 1995. *Honours:* Bread Loaf Writers Conf. Scholarship 1968, NEA grants 1973, 1981, Co-ordinating Council of Literary Magazines Grant 1979, Callaloo Award 1989. *Address:* 55 Gervin Road, Lawrenceville, NJ 08648, USA (home). *Telephone:* (313) 268-1771 (home). *E-mail:* ad8722@wayne.edu (office).

AUBRY, Gwenaëlle, BA, MA, MPhil, DEA, PhD; French writer and academic; *Researcher, Centre National de la Recherche Scientifique*; b. 2 April 1971, d. of François-Xavier Aubry. *Education:* École Normale Supérieure, Paris, Univ. of Cambridge, UK, Univ. of Paris – Sorbonne. *Career:* Lecturer in Philosophy and Ancient Philosophy, Univ. of Nancy 1999–2002; Researcher, CNRS 2002–; Lecturer, Univ. of Paris-Sorbonne 2005–; Lecturer, École Normale Supérieure, Ulm 2010–. *Publications include:* novels: Le Diable Détacheur 1999, L'Isolée 2002, L'Isolement 2003, Notre vie s'use en transfigurations 2007, Le (dé)goût de la laideur 2007, Personne (Prix Femina) 2009; non-fiction: Plotin: Traite 53 I.i: Traduction et commentale 2004, Dieu sans la puissance. Dunamis et Energeia chez Aristotle et chez Plotin 2006, Le moi et l'intériorité (with Frédérique Ildefonse) 2008. *Address:* Editions Mercure de France, 26 rue de Condé, 75006 Paris (office); 17 rue Emile Durkheim, 75013 Paris, France (home). *E-mail:* g.aubry@vjf.cnrs.fr (office); gwenaelle.aubry@club-internet.fr (home). *Website:* upr_76.vjf.cnrs.fr (office).

AUDE, MA, PhD; Canadian novelist; b. (Claudette Charbonneau-Tissot), 22 June 1947, Montréal, Québec. *Education:* Laval Univ. *Career:* fmr teacher in Québec. *Publications include:* as Claudette Charbonneau: L'Enigme du coude 1973, Les Petits trains 1973, Contes pour hydrocéphales adultes (short stories) 1974, La contrainte (short stories) 1976, L'Orient de l'esprit 1985, Compulsion: short stories 1989; as Aude: La chaise au fond de l'oeil (novel) 1979, Les petites boîtes (juvenile, two vols short stories) 1983, L'Assembleur (novel) 1985, Banc de brume, ou les aventures de la petite fille que l'on croyait partie avec l'eau du bain (short stories) 1987, Cet imperceptible mouvement (short stories) (Prix littéraire du Gouverneur Général 1997) 1997, L'enfant migrateur (novel) (Prix des lectrices Elle-Québec 1999) 1998, L'homme au complet (novel) 1999, Quelqu'un (novel) 2002, Chrysalide (novel) 2006; contribs: short stories in trans. in anthologies and journals. *Address:* c/o Dundurn Books, 500-3 Church Street, Suite 500, Toronto, ON M5E 1M2, Canada.

AUDOUARD, Antoine; French writer; b. 6 Aug. 1956, Paris; s. of Yvan Audouard; m. Susanna Lea. *Education:* Pasteur de Neuilly school. *Career:* Publishing Dir Laffont-Fixot 1994–2000. *Publications include:* Marie en quelques mots (novel) 1977, Le Voyage au liban (novel) 1979, Abeilles, vous avez changé de maître (novel) 1981, Passage de l'Eden, Adieu, mon unique (novel, trans. as Farewell, My Only One) 2000, Une Maison au bord du monde (non-fiction) 2001, La Peau à l'envers 2003, Un Pont d'Oisaux 2006, L'Arabe , L'Olivier 2009, Le rendez-vous de Saigon 2011. *Address:* c/o Éditions Gallimard, 5 rue Sébastien-Bottin, 75328 Paris, France. *E-mail:* pub@gallimard.fr. *Website:* www.gallimard.fr.

AUEL, Jean Marie, MBA; American writer; b. 18 Feb. 1936, Chicago, Ill.; m. Ray Bernard Auel 1954; two s. three d. *Education:* Univ. of Portland. *Career:* mem. Authors' Guild, Int. Women's Forum (mem. Bd Dirs 1985–93), Mensa (Hon. Vice-Pres. 1990–), Oregon Museum of Science and Industry (mem. Bd Dirs 1993–96), Oregon Writers' Colony, PEN. *Publications include:* The Clan of the Cave Bear 1980, The Valley of Horses 1982, The Mammoth Hunters 1985, The Plains of Passage 1990, The Shelters of Stone 2002, The Land of Painted Caves 2011. *Honours:* Ordre des Arts et des Lettres 2008; Hon. DLitt (Univ. of Portland) 1984, Hon. HHD (Univ. of Maine) 1986, (Pacific Univ.) 1995, Hon. LHD (Mount Vernon Coll.) 1986; Pacific North West Booksellers Asscn Excellence in Writing Award 1980, Friends of Literature Vicki Penziner Matson Memorial Award, Chicago 1980, American Acad. of Achievement Golden Plate Award for Notable Author 1986, Smithsonian Inst. Centennial Medal 1990, Award for Contribs to Cultural Resource Man., Dept of the Interior, Sec. Manuel Lujan and the Soc. for American Archaeology 1990, Williamette Writers Distinguished Northwest Writer Award 1995, Publieksprijs voor het Nederlandse Boek for most popular foreign language novel (Netherlands). *Literary Agent:* c/o Jean V. Naggar Literary Agency, 216 E 75th Street, New York, NY 10021, USA. *Telephone:* (212) 794-1082. *Website:* www.jvnla.com.

AUERBACH, Nina Joan, BA, MA, PhD; American academic and writer; *John Welsh Centennial Professor of English, University of Pennsylvania*; b. 24 May 1943, New York, NY. *Education:* Univ. of Wisconsin, Madison, Columbia Univ. *Career:* Adjunct Prof., Hunter Coll., CUNY 1969–70; Asst Prof. of English, California State Univ. at Los Angeles 1970–72; Asst Prof. of English, Univ. of Pennsylvania 1972–77, Assoc. Prof. 1977–83, Prof. 1983–, currently John Welsh Centennial Prof. of English; mem. Modern Language Asscn, Victorian Soc. of America. *Publications include:* Communities of Women: An Idea in Fiction 1978, Woman and the Demon: The Life of a Victorian Myth 1982, Romantic Imprisonment: Women and Other Glorified Outcasts 1985, Ellen Terry: Player in Her Time 1987, Private Theatrical: The Lives of the Victorians 1990, Forbidden Journeys: Fairy Tales and Fantasies by Victorian Women Writers (co-ed. with U. C. Knoepflmacher) 1992, Our Vampires, Ourselves 1995, Daphne Du Maurier: Haunted Heiress 2000; contrib. to books and periodicals, including London Review of Books. *Honours:* Ford Foundation Fellowship 1975–76, Radcliffe Inst. Fellowship 1975–76, Guggenheim Fellowship 1979–80, Distinguished Scholarship Award, Int. Asscn of the Fantastic in Arts 2000. *Address:* Department of English, University of Pennsylvania, Fisher Bennett Hall 115, 3340 Walnut Street, Philadelphia, PA 19104-6273, USA (office). *Telephone:* (215) 898-6332 (office). *E-mail:* nauerbac@english.upenn.edu (office). *Website:* www.english.upenn.edu/~nauerbac (office).

AUFFARTH, Susanne; German writer; b. 8 Sept. 1920, Gr Malchau. *Education:* secondary school in Uelzen. *Publications include:* Olympias (drama) 1979, Lofoten (poems to Else Winter's watercolours) 1985, Der Knabe mit der Geige (fairy tales) 1989, Unvergessenes Leben (poems) 1990, Zwölf Märchen 1998, Zwischenzeit (poems) 2003, Acht Märchen, Vier Erzählungen, Dorfchronik, Der Knabe mit der Geige. *Honours:* Herta-Bläschke Gedächtnispreis, Klagenfurt 1983 and Edition L. Lyrikpreis, Bayreuth 1988. *Address:* Gr Malchau, 29597 Stoetze, Germany.

AUNG SAN SUU KYI, BA; Myanma politician; b. 19 June 1945, Rangoon; d. of the late Gen. Aung San and of Khin Kyi; m. Michael Aris 1972 (died 1999); two s. *Education:* St Francis Convent, Methodist English High School, Lady Shri Ram Coll., Delhi Univ., St Hugh's Coll., Oxford. *Career:* Asst Sec. Advisory Cttee on Admin. and Budgetary Questions UN Secr., New York 1969–71; Resident Officer, Ministry of Foreign Affairs, Bhutan 1972; Visiting Scholar Centre for SE Asian Studies, Kyoto Univ., Japan 1985–86; Fellow, Indian Inst. of Advanced Studies 1987; Co-founder and Gen. Sec. Nat. League for Democracy 1988 (expelled from party), reinstated as Gen. Sec. Oct. 1995; returned from UK 1988, under house arrest 1989–95, house arrest lifted July 1995, placed under de facto house arrest Sept. 2000, released unconditionally May 2002, arrested following Depayin massacre 30 May 2003, held in secret detention for over three months before being returned to house arrest, house arrest extended by one year 25 May 2007, mil. junta extended her house arrest another year 27 May 2008, release date set by court ruling Aug. 2009, released from house arrest 13 Nov. 2010; elected to Parl. 2012. *Publications:* Tibetan Studies in Honour of Hugh Richardson (co-ed.) 1979, Aung San 1984, Burma (Let's Visit Series) 1985, Nepal (Let's Visit Series) 1985, Bhutan (Let's Visit Series) 1986, Burma and India: Some Aspects of Intellectual Life Under Colonialism 1990, Aung San (Leaders of Asia Series) 1990, Aung San of Burma: A Biographical Portrait by His Daughter 1991, Freedom from Fear 1991, Towards a True Refuge 1993, Burma's Revolution of the Spirit: The Struggle for Democratic Freedom and Dignity (co-author) 1994, Freedom from Fear and Other Writings (co-author) 1995, Letter to Daniel: Despatches from the Heart by Fergal Keane (foreword by Aung San Suu Kyi) 1996, The Voice of Hope (with Alan Clements) 1998 (revised edn 2008), Letters from Burma (with Fergal Keane) 1998, Der Weg zur Freiheit (with U Kyi Maung and U Tin O) 1999. *Honours:* Freeman, City of Dublin, Ireland 1999, Hon. mem. Bd Council Int. Inst. for Democracy and Electoral Assistance 2003, Hon. Canadian citizenship 2007, Hon. Pres. LSE Students' Union 2007, Freeman, City of Glasgow, Scotland 2009; Hon. AC 1996; numerous hon. degrees, including Hon. LLD (Memorial Univ. of Newfoundland) 2004, (Colgate Univ.) 2008, (Univ. of Ulster) 2009; Thorolf Rafto Memorial Prize 1990, Sakharov Prize 1990, European Parl. Human Rights Prize 1991, Nobel Peace Prize 1991, Simón Bolívar Int. Prize 1992, Liberal Int. Prize for Freedom 1995, Jawaharlal Nehru Award for Int. Understanding 1995, Freedom Award of Int. Rescue Cttee 1995, Presidential Medal of Freedom 2000, UNESCO Madanjeet Singh Prize for the Promotion of Tolerance and Non-Violence 2002, Free Spirit Prize, Freedom Forum USA 2003, Gwangju Prize for Human Rights 2004, ranked by Forbes magazine amongst The World's 100 Most Powerful Women (45th) 2004, (15th) 2005, (47th) 2006, (71st) 2007, (38th) 2008, (26th) 2011, Olof Palme Prize 2005, Freedom from Fear Award 2006, US Congressional Gold Medal 2008, Premi Internacional Catalunya 2008, Mahatma Gandhi Int. Award for Peace and Reconciliation 2009, Amb. of Conscience Award, Amnesty International 2009, Int. Bhagwan Mahavir World Peace Award 2012. *Address:* c/o National League for Democracy, 97B West Shwegondine Road, Bahan Township, Yangon, Myanmar. *Website:* www.dassk.com.

AUST, Stefan; German journalist and writer; b. 1 July 1946, Stade; m. Ulrike Meinhof. *Career:* Ed. Concrete magazine 1966–69; staff mem. NDR TV 1970–72; journalist Panorama (political magazine) 1972–86; Chief Ed. Der Spiegel TV 1988–94, Ed.-in-Chief Der Spiegel 1994–2008; Man. Dir Der Spiegel TV GmbH 1995–; fmr TV host with talkshow Talk in the Tower, currently Host Spiegel-TV. *Publications include:* Kennwort 100 Blumen – Verwicklung des Verfassungsschutzes in den Mordfall Ulrich Schmücker 1980, Brokdorf: Symbol Einer Politischen Wende 1981, Der Baader Meinhof Komplex 1985, Stammheim (film script) 1986, Werner Mauss – Ein Deutscher Agent 1988, Der Pirat: Die Drogenkarriere des Jan C. 1990, Die Flucht: Über die Vertreibung der Deutschen aus dem Osten 2002, Der Lockvogel. 2002, Irak: Geschichte eines modernen Krieges 2003, Die Gegenwart der Vergangenheit: Der lange Schatten des Dritten Reichs 2004, Wettlauf um die Welt: Die Globalisierung und wir 2007, Deutschland, Deutschland: Expedition durch die Wendezeit 2011. *Honours:* Goldenen Kamera 2005. *Address:* Der Spiegel, Brandstwiete 19/Ost-West-Strasse 23, 20457 Hamburg, Germany (office). *Telephone:* (40) 30070 (office). *Fax:* (40) 30072247 (office). *E-mail:* spiegel@spiegel.de (office). *Website:* www.spiegel.de (office).

AUSTER, Paul, BA, MA; American writer, poet and film director; b. 3 Feb. 1947, Newark, NJ; s. of the late Sam Auster and Queenie Auster; m. 1st Lydia Davis 1974 (divorced 1982); one s.; m. 2nd Siri Hustvedt 1982; one d. *Education:* Columbia High School, NJ, Columbia Coll., New York, Columbia Univ., New York. *Career:* worked as census taker; oil tanker utility man. on the Esso Florence; moved to Paris, France 1971, returned to USA 1974; worked as translator; Lecturer in Creative Writing and Translation, Princeton Univ. 1986–90; juror, Cannes Film Festival 1997; mem. PEN (fmr Sec. and Vice-Pres. PEN American Center). *Films:* screenplays: Smoke 1995, Blue in the Face (co-dir) 1995, Lulu on the Bridge (also dir) 1998, The Inner Life of Martin Frost (also dir) 2007. *Publications:* fiction: City of Glass 1985, Ghosts 1986, The Locked Room 1986, In the Country of Last Things 1987, Moon Palace 1989, The Music of Chance 1990, Leviathan 1992, Mr Vertigo 1994, Timbuktu 1999, The Book of Illusions 2002, Oracle Night 2003, The Brooklyn Follies 2005, Travels in the Scriptorium 2006, Man in the Dark 2008, Invisible 2009, Sunset Park 2010; non-fiction: White Spaces 1980, The Invention of Solitude 1982, The Art of Hunger 1982, Hand to Mouth (memoir) 1989, The Red Notebook 1995, Why Write? 1996, Translations 1996, Collected Prose 2003, Winter Journal 2012; poetry: Unearth 1974, Wall Writing 1976, Fragments From Cold 1977, Facing the Music 1980, Disappearances: Selected Poems 1988, Collected Poems 2003; editor: The Random House Book of Twentieth-Century French Poetry 1982, True Tales of American Life 2001, Samuel Beckett: The Grove Centenary Edn 2006. *Honours:* Nat. Endowment for the Arts fellowships 1979, 1985; Prix Médicis Étranger 1993, Prince of Asturias Prize for Literature 2006, Premio di Napoli 2011; Commandeur, Ordre des Arts et des Lettres. *Literary Agent:* Carol Mann Agency, 55 Fifth Avenue, New York, NY 10003, USA. *Website:* www.paulauster.co.uk.

AVERY, Gillian Elise; British writer and editor; b. 30 Sept. 1926, England; m. Anthony Oliver John Cockshut 1952; one d. *Career:* jr reporter, Surrey Mirror, Redhill, Surrey 1944–47; staff, Chambers's Encyclopaedia, London 1947–50; Asst Illustrations Ed., Clarendon Press, Oxford 1950–54. *Publications include:* juvenile fiction: The Warden's Niece 1957, Trespassers at Charlcote 1958, James Without Thomas 1959, The Elephant War 1960, To Tame a Sister 1961, The Greatest Gresham 1962, The Peacock House 1963, The Italian Spring 1964, The Call of the Valley 1966, A Likely Lad 1971, Huck and her Time Machine 1977; adult fiction: The Lost Railway 1980, Onlookers 1983; non-fiction: Nineteenth-Century Children: Heroes and Heroines in English Children's Stories (with Angela Bull) 1965, Victorian People in Life and Literature 1970, The Echoing Green: Memories of Regency and Victorian Youth 1974, Childhood's Pattern 1975, Children and Their Books: a Celebration of the Work of Iona and Peter Opie (co-ed. with Julia Briggs) 1989, The Best Type of Girl: a History of Girls' Independent Schools 1991, Behold the Child: American Children and Their Books, 1621–1922 1994, Representations of Childhood Death (co-ed. with Kimberley Reynolds) 1999, Cheltenham Ladies: A History of the Cheltenham Ladies' College 2003; ed. of many other books. *Honours:* Guardian Award 1972. *Address:* 32 Charlbury Road, Oxford, OX2 6UU, England (office).

AVI (see WORTIS, Avi)

AVIA, Rodrigo Munoz, PhB; Spanish writer; b. 1967, Madrid; s. of Lucio Muñoz and Amalia Avia. *Education:* Universidad Complutense de Madrid. *Career:* columnist, ABC Cultural. *Publications:* Lo que no sabemos (Premio Jaén de Literatura Juvenil) 1996, El portero de hockey 1998, Alfonso Vizán. Un pirata en la montaña 2004, Julia y Gus visitan el top manta 2005, Psiquiatras, psicólogos y otros enfermos 2005, Los perfectos (Edebé Children's Literature Prize) 2007, Vidas terrestres 2007, El gato de guardia 2008, Mi hermano el genio 2010. *Address:* Santillana Ediciones Generales SL, 60 Calle Torrelaguna, 28043 Madrid, Spain. *Telephone:* (91) 7449060. *Fax:* (91) 7449224. *E-mail:* alfaguara@santillana.es. *Website:* www.alfaguara.com.

AVRIL, Nicole, LèsL; French novelist and writer; b. 15 Aug. 1939, Rambouillet; m. Jean-Pierre Elkabbach 1974. *Education:* Univ. of Lyon. *Career:* fmr actress, model, teacher of literature. *Publications include:* novels: L'Été de la Saint Valentin 1972, Les Gens de Misar (Prix des Quatre Jurys au Maroc) 1972, Les Remparts d'Adrien 1975, Le Jardin des absents 1977, Monsieur de Lyon 1979, La Disgrâce (also TV adaptation 1997) 1981, Jeanne (also TV adaptation 1995) 1984, Dans les jardins de mon père (memoirs) 1989, La Première alliance 1992, Sur la peau du diable 1992, L'Impératrice 1995, Une Personne déplacé 1996, Le Roman d'un inconnu (also video documentary for ARTE 2002) 1998, Il y a longtemps que je t'aime 1999, Le Roman du visage 1999, Moi, Dora Maar 2002, Le Regard de la grenouille 2003, Dernière mise en scène 2005, Dictionnaire de la passion amoureuse 2007, Voyage en Avril 2010. *Honours:* Ordre supérieure autrichien (pour l'Impératrice) 1996. *Address:* c/o Mme Muriel Beyer, Editions Plon, 76 rue Bonaparte, 75006 Paris. *Telephone:* 1-47-34-80-62 (home); 6-69-04-41-61 (mobile) (home). *E-mail:* nicoleavril@orange.fr.

AW, Tash, LLM; Malaysian writer; b. (Aw Ta-Shii), Taipei, Taiwan. *Education:* Univ. of Cambridge, Univ. of East Anglia, UK. *Career:* moved to UK aged 18; trained as lawyer; currently full-time writer. *Publications include:* The Harmony Silk Factory (Whitbread First Novel Award, Commonwealth Writers Prize for Best First Novel, Asia Pacific region) 2005, Map of the Invisible World 2009. *Address:* c/o Harper Perennial, 77–85 Fulham Palace Road, London, W6 8JB, England. *Website:* www.tash-aw.com.

AWERBUCK, Diane, BA, HDipEd, MA, PhD; South African writer, teacher and reviewer; b. Kimberley. *Education:* Rhodes Univ., Grahamstown, Univ. of Cape Town. *Career:* Head of English, Rustenburg High School for Girls, Cape Town 1997–2002; Freelance publr and writer 2003–; Dir of Content Devt, Electric Book Works 2005–09; Fellow, Univ. of Cape Town 2007–08; ad hoc Lecturer, AFDA Film School, Cape Town. *Exhibitions include:* with Lisa Firer and Marlise Keith (porcelain and brushwork) 2005, Horror Lounge 2009. *Radio:* Otherwise (with Nancy Richards) 2006. *Television:* Good Morning South Africa 2004. *Publications include:* Gardening at Night (novel) 2003, The Portable Pilgrim (online column) 2003–08, Laugh It Off (anthology) 2004, 2005, 180 Degrees (anthology) 2005, Yizo Yizo (anthology) 2005, En stereo i Soweto (anthology) 2005, Sylt Kunst:raum (anthology) 2005, Something Wicked (anthology) 2006, Nice Times (anthology) 2006, Crossing the Universe (anthology) 2007, Ons Klyntjie (anthology) 2007–11, Imago (anthology) 2008, Elf (anthology) 2009, Cabin Fever (short story collection) 2011; works translated into German, Russian, Swedish and Chinese; contrib. to magazines including The Sunday Times, Leadership, Glamour, House and Garden, Design Indaba, Real Simple, Oprah Magazine. *Honours:* Mellon Foundation Fellow; Best First Book Award (Africa and Caribbean) 2004. *Address:* c/o Umuzi Books, PO Box 1144, Cape Town 8000, South Africa. *Telephone:* (21) 4605400.

AWOONOR, Kofi Nyidevu, PhD; Ghanaian writer, teacher, diplomatist and politician; b. (George Awoonor-Williams), 13 March 1935, Wheta; s. of Kosiwo Awoonor and Atsu Awoonor; m.; five s. one d. *Education:* Univ. of Ghana, Univ. Coll., London and State Univ. of NY, Stony Brook. *Career:* Research Fellow, Inst. of African Studies; Man. Dir Film Corpn, Accra; Longmans Fellow, Univ. of London; Asst Prof. and later Chair. Comparative Literature Program, State Univ. of NY; Visiting Prof., Univ. of Texas, Austin and New School of Social Research, New York; detained in Ghana for allegedly harbouring leader of coup 1975, on trial 1976, sentenced to one year's imprisonment Oct. 1976, pardoned Oct. 1976; fmr Chair. Dept of English and Dean of Faculty of Arts, Univ. of Cape Coast; Sec.-Gen. Action Congress Party; Amb. to Brazil 1984–90 (also accred to Cuba 1988–90); Perm. Rep. to UN, New York 1990–94; currently Minister of State; Contributing Ed. Transition and Alcheringa; Longmans and Fairfield Fellowships. *Publications:* poetry: Rediscovery 1964, Messages 1970, Night of My Blood 1971, House by the Sea 1978, Until the Morning After (collected poems); prose: This Earth My Brother 1971, Guardians of the Sacred Word 1973, Ride Me Memory 1973, Breast of the Earth 1974 (history of African literature), Traditional African Literature (series, ed.), Alien Corn (novel) 1974, Where is the Mississippi Panorama 1974, Fire in the Valley: Folktales of the Ewes 1980, The Ghana Revolution, Ghana: A Political History 1990, Comes the Voyage at Last 1991, The Caribbean and Latin American Notebook 1992, Africa the Marginalized Continent. *Honours:* Gurrey Prize for Poetry, Nat. Book Council Award for Poetry 1979, Dillons Commonwealth Prize for Poetry (Africa Div.) 1989, Order of the Volta 1977, Agbonugla of ANLO 1997, Agbaledzigla of the Wheta Traditional Area 1998.

AXTON, David (see KOONTZ, Dean Ray)

AYCKBOURN, Sir Alan, Kt, CBE, FRSA; British playwright and theatre director; b. 12 April 1939, London, England; s. of Horace Ayckbourn and Irene Maud Ayckbourn (née Worley); m. 1st Christine Helen Roland 1959 (divorced 1997); two s.; m. 2nd Heather Elizabeth Stoney 1997. *Education:* Haileybury. *Career:* on leaving school went straight into the theatre as stage manager and actor with various repertory cos in England; Founder-mem. Victoria Theatre Co., Stoke on Trent 1962–64; Drama Producer, BBC Radio 1964–70; Artistic Dir Stephen Joseph Theatre, Scarborough 1971–2009; Prof. of Contemporary Theatre, Univ. of Oxford 1992. *Plays:* Mr Whatnot 1963, Relatively Speaking 1965, How the Other Half Loves 1969, Ernie's Incredible Illucinations 1969, Family Circles 1970, Time and Time Again 1971, Absurd Person Singular (Evening Standard Award for Best New Comedy 1973) 1972, The Norman Conquests (Evening Standard Award for Best New Play 1974, Plays and Players Award for Best New Play 1974, New York Drama Critics' Circle Special Citation 2009, Outer Critics' Circle Award for Outstanding Revival 2009, Drama Desk Award for Outstanding Revival 2009, Tony Award for Best Revival of a Play 2010) 1973, Jeeves (book and lyrics for Andrew Lloyd Webber musical) 1975 (rewritten as By Jeeves – TMA Regional Theatre Awards for Best Musical 1996), Absent Friends 1974, Confusions 1974, Bedroom Farce 1975, Just Between Ourselves (Evening Standard Award for Best New Play 1977) 1976, Ten Times Table 1977, Joking Apart (Co-winner Plays and Players Award for Best New Comedy 1979) 1978, Family Circles 1978, Sisterly Feelings 1979, Taking Steps 1979, Suburban Strains (musical play with music by Paul Todd) 1980, Season's Greetings 1980, Me, Myself & I (with Paul Todd) 1981, Way Upstream 1981, Intimate Exchanges 1982, It Could Be Any One Of Us 1983, A Chorus of Disapproval (London Evening Standard Award, Olivier Award and DRAMA Award for Best Comedy 1985) 1984 (film 1988), Woman in Mind 1985, A Small Family Business (London Evening Standard Award for Best New Play 1987) 1987, Henceforward (London Evening Standard Award for Best Comedy 1989) 1987, A View from the Bridge (Plays and Players Director of the Year Award) 1987, Man of the Moment (Evening Standard Best Comedy Award 1990) 1988, Mr A's Amazing Maze Plays (TMA/Martini Regional Theatre Award for Best Show for Children and Young People 1993) 1988, The Revengers' Comedies 1989, Invisible Friends 1989, Body Language 1990, This Is Where We Came In 1990, Callisto 5 1990 (rewritten as Callisto 7 1999), Wildest Dreams 1991, My Very Own Story 1991, Henceforward… (Drama-Logue Critic Award) 1991, Time of My Life 1992, Dreams From a Summer House (with music by John Pattison) 1992, Communicating Doors (Writers' Guild of GB Award for Best West End Play 1996, Moliere for Best Comedy 1997) 1994, Haunting Julia 1994, A Word from Our Sponsor (with music by John Pattison) 1995, The Champion of Paribanou 1996, Things We Do For Love (Lloyds Pvt. Banking Playwright of the Year Award 1997, Moliere for Best Comedy 2003) 1997, Comic Potential 1998, The Boy Who Fell into a Book 1998, House & Garden 1999, Whenever (with music by Denis King) 2000, Damsels in Distress (trilogy: GamePlan, FlatSpin, RolePlay) 2001, Snake in the Grass 2002, The Jollies 2002, Sugar Daddies 2003, Orvin – Champion of Champions (with music by Denis King) 2003, My Sister Sadie 2003, Drowning on Dry Land 2004, Private Fears in Public Places 2004, Miss Yesterday 2004, Improbable Fiction 2005, The Girl Who Lost Her Voice 2005, If I Were You 2006, Life and Beth 2008, My Wonderful Day 2009, Uncle Vanya – Dear Uncle 2009, Neighbourhood Watch 2010; as director: A View from the Bridge (Plays and Players Director of the Year Award) 1987. *Publications:* fiction: majority of plays have been published; non-fiction: Conversations with Ayckbourn (with I. Watson) 1981, The Crafty Art of Playmaking 2002. *Honours:* Hon. Fellow, Bretton Hall Coll. 1982, Cardiff Univ. 1995, Hon. Prof., Univ. of Hull 2007; Hon. DLitt (Hull) 1981, (Keele, Leeds) 1987, (Bradford) 1994, (York St John) 2011; Hon. DUniv (York) 1992, (Open Univ.) 1998, (Manchester) 2003; Variety Club of GB Playwright of the Year 1974, Lifetime Achievement Award, Writers' Guild of GB 1993, John Ederyn Hughes Rural Wales Award for Literature 1993, Birmingham Press Club Personality of the Year Award 1993, Yorkshire Man of the Year 1994, Montblanc de la Culture Award for Europe 1994, Sunday Times Award for Literary Excellence 2001, Variety Club of GB Lifetime Achievement Award 2004, Yorkshire Arts and Entertainment Personality Award, Yorkshire Awards 2005, Soc. of West End Theatre's Special Award (Olivier) 2009, inducted into Hall of Fame for Achievements in American Theatre 2009, Laurence Olivier Awards Special Award 2009, Critics' Circle Award for Services to the Arts 2010, Special Tony Award for Lifetime Achievement in the Theatre 2010. *Literary Agent:* c/o Casarotto Ramsay & Associates Ltd, Waverley House, 7–12 Noel Street, London, W1F 8GQ, England. *Telephone:* (20) 7287-4450 (office). *Fax:* (20) 7287-9128 (office). *E-mail:* info@casarotto.uk.com. *Website:* www.casarotto.uk.com (office); www.alanayckbourn.net (home).

AYRE, Richard James, BA; British journalist; b. 1 Aug. 1949, Newcastle-upon-Tyne, England; s. of Thomas Henry Ayre and Beth Carson; partner Guy Douglas Burch. *Education:* Univ. Coll., Durham. *Career:* Pres. Durham Univ. Students' Union 1969–70; producer and reporter, BBC NI 1973–76, Home News Ed., TV News 1979–84, Head of BBC Westminster 1989–92, Controller of Editorial Policy 1993–96, Deputy Chief Exec., BBC News 1996–2000; Chair. Asian & Afro-Carribean Reporters' Trust 1997–2000; mem. Bd Food Standards Agency 2000–07; Freedom of Information Adjudicator, Law Soc. 2001–; Chair. Article 19 2002–05; Civil Service Commr 2005–06; Bd mem. for England, Ofcom Content Bd 2006–10; Chair. Dairy Partnership 2008–10; mem. Bd BBC Trust 2010–; Benton Fellow, Univ. of Chicago, USA 1984–85. *Address:* 88 Cumberland Mills, London, E14 3BJ, England (home). *E-mail:* richardayre@whats2hide.com (office).

AYRES, Pamela (Pam), MBE; British writer, poet and broadcaster; b. 14 March 1947, Stanford-in-the-Vale, Berks. (now in Oxfordshire), England; d. of Stanley William Ayres and Phyllis Evelyn Loder; m. Dudley Russell 1982; two s. *Education:* Faringdon Secondary Modern School, Berks. *Career:* served in Women's RAF 1965–69; writer and performer, solo shows in the UK, Ireland, Middle East, Hong Kong, France, Kenya, Canada, NZ, Australia. *Radio includes:* Pam Ayres Radio Show 1995, Pam Ayres on Sunday (BBC Radio 2) 1996–99, Ayres On The Air (four series, BBC Radio 4) 2004, 2007, 2009, 2012, Potting On (sitcom, BBC Radio 4) 2008. *Television includes:* Opportunity Knocks 1975, The World of Pam Ayres 1977, numerous specials in UK, Hong Kong and Canada; guest on British TV shows, including QI, Paul O'Grady, Countdown, The One Show, My Life in Books. *Publications include:* poetry: Some of Me Poetry 1975, Some More of Me Poetry 1976, Thoughts of a Late-Night Knitter 1978, All Pam's Poems 1978, The Ballad of Bill Spinks' Bedstead and Other Poems 1981, Dear Mum 1985; other: Pam Ayres – The Works 1992 (revised hardback edn 2008), With These Hands: A Collection of Work 1997, Surgically Enhanced 2006, The Necessary Aptitude (autobiog.) (Best-Selling Female Autobiography of the Year 2011) 2011; children's books: Bertha and the Racing Pigeon 1979, Guess Who? 1987, Guess What? 1987, When Dad Fills in the Garden Pond 1988, When Dad Cuts Down the Chestnut Tree 1988, Piggo and the Nosebag 1990, Piggo Has a Train Ride 1990, The Bear Who Was Left Behind 1991, Guess Why? 1994, The Nubbler 1997. *Address:* c/o Acorn Entertainments Ltd, PO Box 64, Cirencester, GL7 5YD, England. *Telephone:* (1285) 644622. *Fax:* (1285) 642291. *E-mail:* drussell@acornents.co.uk. *Website:* www.pamayres.com.

AYRES, Philip James, BA, PhD, FRHistS, FAHA; Australian writer and academic; b. 28 July 1944, S Australia; m. 1st Maruta Sudrabs 1965 (divorced 1981); m. 2nd Patricia San Martin 1981; one s. *Education:* Univ. of Adelaide. *Career:* Lecturer, Monash Univ. 1972–79, Sr Lecturer 1979–93, Assoc. Prof. 1993–2006, Professorial Fellow 2006–08; Visiting Prof., Vassar Coll., New York, USA 1993; Visiting Fellow, Boston Univ., USA 2001; mem. Australian Council, Deputy Chair. Literature Bd 2000–02. *Publications include:* The Revenger's Tragedy 1977, The English Roman Life 1980, Malcolm Fraser: A Biography 1987, Classical Culture and the Idea of Rome in Eighteenth Century England 1997, Douglas Mawson 1999, Owen Dixon 2002, Prince of the Church: Patrick Francis Moran, 1839–1911 2007; ed.: Ben Jonson: Sejanus His Fall 1990, 3rd Earl of Shaftesbury, Characteristics 1999; contribs to English Literary Renaissance, Modern Philology, Studies in Bibliography, Studies in English Literature, Studies in Philology. *Address:* 13 Harris Avenue, Glen Iris, Vic. 3146, Australia (home).

AZINA CHRONIDES, Myrto, Dr med; Cypriot physician and novelist; b. (Myrto Azina), 26 Dec. 1961, Nicosia; d. of Andreas Azinas; m. Antonis Chronides; one s. one d. *Education:* Univ. of Bonn and Academic Hosp. Euskirchen, Germany (specialized in Family Medicine), Royal Coll. of Gen. Practitioners, London, UK. *Career:* currently with Ministry of Health. *Publications include:* Diary 1974, Pathology, Rachel, To Peirama (The Experiment) (EU Prize for Literature 2010) 2009; contrib. essays, poems and stories to anthologies and journals; short stories included in bilingual anthologies and literature teaching books of the Ministry of Educ. *Address:* Armida Publications, Valesta 36A, 2370 Ayios Dhometios, Nicosia (office);

Ministry of Health, Prodromou 1, 1448 Nicosia, Cyprus (office). *Telephone:* (22) 358028 (office). *Fax:* (22) 358028 (office). *Website:* armidapublications.com (office).

AZÚA, Félix de, MPh, DPhil; Spanish writer; b. 30 April 1944, Barcelona. *Career:* fmr mem. Faculty of Philosophy, Zorroaga (San Sebastian) (part of Univ. of the Basque Country); fmr mem. Bd of Dirs Cervantes Inst., Paris; fmr Prof. of Aesthetics, School of Architecture, Polytechnic Univ. of Catalonia; currently journalist, El Periódico de Catalunya. *Publications:* poems: Cepo de nutria 1968, El velo en el rostro de Agamenón 1971, Edgar en Stéphane 1971, La lengua de cal 1972, Pasar y siete canciones 1977, Poesía (1968–78) 1979, Farra 1983, Poesía (1968–89) 1989, Demasiadas preguntas 1994, Última sangre (Poesía 1968–2007) 2007; novels: Las lecciones de Jena 1972, Tres cuentos didácticos 1975, Las lecciones suspendidas 1978, Los ensayos de Baudelaire 1978, Última lección 1981, Mansura 1984, Historia de un idiota contada por él mismo 1986, Diario de un hombre humillado (Premio Herralde) 1987, Cambio de bandera 1991, Demasiadas preguntas 1994, Momentos decisivos 2000; juvenile literature: El largo viaje del mensajero 1991; test: Conocer Baudelaire y su obra 1978, La paradoja del primitivo 1983, El aprendizaje de la decepción 1989, La Venecia de Casanova 1990, Salidas de tono 1997, Lecturas compulsivas 1998, Baudelaire (el artista de la vida moderna) 1999, La invención de Caín 1999, Diccionario de las Artes 2002, Cortocircuitos 2004, Esplendor y nada 2006, Abierto a todas horas 2007, Ovejas negras 2007, La pasión domesticada. Las reinas de Persia y el nacimiento de la pintura moderna 2007, Autobiografía sin vida 2010, Abierto a todas horas 2010. *Address:* Arnoldo Mondadori Editore, Via Privata Mondadori 1, 20090 Segrate-Milano, Italy. *Telephone:* (02) 75421. *Fax:* (07) 5423047. *E-mail:* stampalibri@mondadori.it. *Website:* www.mondadori.it.

AZZOPARDI, Trezza, MA; British writer; b. 1961, Cardiff, Wales. *Education:* Univ. of East Anglia. *Career:* examiner for Norwich School of Art; Lecturer in Creative Writing, Univ. of East Anglia. *Publications include:* novels: The Hiding Place (Geoffrey Faber Memorial Prize) 2000, Remember Me 2004, Winterton Blue 2007, The Song House 2010; contrib. to Neon Lit 1, Take Twenty, New Writing 9. *Literary Agent:* c/o A.P. Watt Ltd, 20 John Street, London, WC1N 2DR, England. *Telephone:* (20) 7405-6774. *Fax:* (20) 7831-2154. *E-mail:* apw@apwatt.co.uk. *Website:* www.apwatt.co.uk.

B

BAALBAKI, Layla; Lebanese writer and journalist; b. 1936, Beirut. *Education:* Jesuit Univ., Beirut. *Career:* began writing aged 14; began career as journalist on local newspapers and magazines; fmr sec. in Lebanese parl.; scholarship to Paris, France 1960. *Publications:* Anā Ahyā (I Am Alive) (novel) 1958, al-Aliha al-mamsukha (The Disfigured Gods) 1958, Safīnat Hanān ilā al-Qamar (Spaceship of Tenderness to the Moon) (short stories) 1963; currently contrib. of articles to newspapers.

BABATUNDE, Rotimi; Nigerian author, poet and playwright; *Chair, Nigerian PEN Centre's Writers for Peace Committee. Career:* stories published in several journals including Mirabilia Review, Die Aussenseite des Elementes, Fiction on the Web; wrote short story Bombay's Republic (shortlisted for Caine Prize for African Writing) 2012; currently Chair. Nigerian PEN Centre's Writers for Peace Cttee. *Plays:* A Shroud for Lazarus, Royal Court, Theatre Upstairs, London 2004, The Bonfire of the Innocents, Swedish tour (under title of Elddopet) 2008. *Publications:* featured in several anthologies including: Daybreak on the Land 1997, A Volcano of Voices 1999, Little Drops 2000, African Violet: The 2012 Caine Prize Anthology 2012. *Honours:* Winner, BBC World Service Meridian Tragic Love Story Competition 1999, Ledig House Fellowship 2001, MacDowell Colony Fellowship, USA 2002, Ludwig Vogelstein Foundation Writing Award 2005, Fondazione Pistoletto Unidee Award 2007, Rockefeller Foundation's Bellagio Centre Fellowship, Italy 2009, Abuja Writers Forum Cyprian Ekwensi Prize for Short Stories. *Address:* c/o Ropo Ewenla, Nigerian PEN, Cora House, 70 Bode Thomas, Surulere, Lagos, Nigeria (office). *Telephone:* 8032311574 (Lagos) (office). *E-mail:* firo_po@yahoo.co.uk (office). *Website:* www.pen-international.org/centres/nigerian-centre (office).

BABINEAU, Jean Joseph, BA, BEd, MA; Canadian teacher and writer; b. 10 Aug. 1952, Moncton, NB; m. Gisèle Ouellette 1993; one s. *Career:* mem. AAAPNB, CEAD. *Publications:* Bloupe 1993, Gîte 1998, Vortex 2003; contribs to Quai des lettres, Éloizes, Mœbius, Mots en Volet, Littéréalité, Satellite, Nouvelles d'Amérique, Virages, Le Front. *Honours:* Canada Council Exploration Grant 1989, New Brunswick Arts Br. Creation Grant 1998, 2002, Prix Antonine Maillet-Acadie Vie, Institut des études acadiennes Grant 2008. *Address:* 12 allée Gîte, Grand-Barachois, NB, E4P 7N9, Canada.

BACHMAN, Richard (see King, Stephen Edwin)

BACIGALUPI, Paolo Tadini; American science fiction and fantasy author; b. 6 Aug. 1972, Paonia, Colo. *Career:* fiction published in numerous periodicals including Magazine of Fantasy and Science Fiction, Asimov's Science Fiction, High Country News; non-fiction published at Salon.com, in High Country News, and in numerous newspapers including Idaho Statesman, Albuquerque Journal, Salt Lake Tribune. *Publications:* short fiction collection: Pump Six and Other Stories 2008; novels: The Windup Girl (Hugo Award for Best Novel 2010, Locus Award for Best First Novel 2010, Compton Crook Award for Best First Novel 2010, Nebula Award 2010, John W. Campbell Memorial Award 2010) 2009, Ship Breaker (Michael L. Printz Award for Best Young Adult Novel 2011) 2010, The Drowned Cities 2012; novella: The Alchemist (co-author) 2011; numerous short stories. *Honours:* Theodore Sturgeon Award 2006. *Literary Agent:* c/o Martha Millard Literary Agency, 420 Central Park West, #5H, New York, NY 10025, USA. *Telephone:* (212) 787-7769. *E-mail:* marmillink@aol.com. *Address:* PO Box 222, Paonia, CO 81428, USA (home). *E-mail:* ladyarlyn@windupstories.com. *Website:* windupstories.com.

BACK, Jean; Luxembourg photographer and novelist; b. 1953, Dudelange. *Career:* fmr civil servant, served at Ministry of Labour and Ministry of Culture; Dir Centre Nat. de l'Audiovisuel, Dudelange 1989–. *Photo exhibition:* Lieux et Portraits du Bassin Minier 1990. *Publications include:* Wollekestel 2003, Mon amour schwein 2007, Amateur (EU Prize for Literature 2010) 2009. *Address:* c/o Editions Ultimomondo, 35 rue de Dondelange, 8391 Nospelt, Luxembourg (office). *Telephone:* 308701 (office). *E-mail:* info@umo.lu (office). *Website:* www.umo.lu/ultimomondo (office).

BACKSCHEIDER, Paula, BA, MS, PhD; American academic, writer and editor; *Stevens Eminent Scholar, Auburn University;* b. 31 March 1943, Brownsville, Tenn.; m. Nickolas Andrew Backscheider 1964; one s. one d. *Education:* Purdue Univ., Southern Connecticut State Univ. *Career:* Asst Prof., Rollins Coll., Winter Park, Fla 1973–75; Asst Prof., Univ. of Rochester 1975–78, Assoc. Prof. 1978–87, Prof. of English 1987–1990, Roswell Burrows Prof. 1991–92; Philpott-Stevens Eminent Scholar, Auburn Univ. 1992–; William Andrews Clark Fellow, UCLA 1974; Sr Fellow, Nat. Endowment for the Humanities 1983; Fellow, Inst. for Advanced Studies, Univ. of Edinburgh 1980–; mem. American Soc. for Eighteenth-Century Studies (Pres. 1992), Inst. for Advanced Studies, Univ. of Edinburgh, Modern Language Asscn, Coll. of Liberal Arts Acad. of Teaching and Outstanding Teachers 2003. *Publications include:* An Annotated Bibliography of Twentieth-Century Studies of Women and Literature 1660–1800 (with Felicity Nussbaum and Philip Anderson) 1977, Probability, Time, and Space in Eighteenth-Century Literature (ed.) 1979, The Plays of Charles Gildon (ed.) 1979, Eighteenth-Century Drama (ed.), 69 vols 1979–83, The Plays of Elizabeth Inchbald (ed.) 1980, The Plays of Samuel Foote (co-ed.) 1983, A Being More Intense: The Prose Works of Bunyan, Swift, and Defoe 1984, Daniel Defoe: Ambition and Innovation 1986, Daniel Defoe: His Life (British Council Prize 1990) 1989, Moll Flanders: The Making of a Criminal Mind 1990, Spectacular Politics: Theatrical Power and Mass Culture in Early Modern England 1993, Popular Fiction by Women 1660–1730: An Anthology (co-ed. with John J. Richetti) 1996, The Intersections of the Public and Private Spheres in Early Modern England (co-ed. with Timothy Dykstal) 1996, Reflections on Biography 1999, Revising Women: Eighteenth-Century 'Women's Fiction' and Social Engagement (ed.) 2000, A Companion to the Eighteenth-Century Novel and Culture (co-ed. with Catherine Ingrassia) 2005, Eighteenth-Century Women Poets and Their Poetry: Inventing Agency, Inventing Genre (Lowell Prize, Modern Language Asscn 2006) 2005, British Women Poets of the Long Eighteenth-Century: An Anthology ((co-ed.) 2009; contrib. to reference works, scholarly books and professional journals. *Honours:* American Philosophical Soc. Grants 1975, 1980, 1986, American Antiquarian Soc. Fellowship 1987, John Simon Guggenheim Fellowship 1991, Distinguished Alumna Award, Purdue Univ. 2001, Outstanding Service Award, Office of Multicultural Affairs 2001, Creative Research Award, Auburn Univ. 2001, 2010, Distinguished Teaching Award, Omicron Delta Kappa Hon. Soc. 2003, World Women's Literature Center Award (Korea) 2003, Presidential Award of Excellence, Auburn Univ. 2007. *Address:* Department of English, Auburn University, Auburn, AL 36849 (office); 1930 Canary Drive, Auburn, AL 36830, USA (home). *Telephone:* (334) 844-9091 (office); (334) 821-8874 (home). *Fax:* (334) 844-9027 (office). *E-mail:* pkrb@auburn.edu (office). *Website:* www.auburn.edu/~pkrb (office).

BADAWI, (Mohamed) Mustafa, BA, PhD; British lecturer and writer; *Emeritus Fellow, St Antony's College, Oxford;* b. 10 June 1925, Alexandria, Egypt. *Education:* Alexandria Univ., Univ. of London. *Career:* Research Fellow, Alexandria Univ., Egypt 1947–54, Lecturer 1954–60, Asst Prof. of English 1960–64; Lecturer, Univ. of Oxford and Brasenose Coll. 1964–92; Fellow, St Antony's Coll., Oxford 1967, currently Emer. Fellow; Ed. Journal of Arabic Literature, Leiden 1970–96; mem. Advisory Bd Cambridge History of Arabic Literature, Cttees of Ministry of Culture, Egypt 1961; UNESCO Expert on Modern Arabic Culture 1974. *Publications include:* An Anthology of Modern Arabic Verse (ed.) 1970, Coleridge as Critic of Shakespeare 1973, A Critical Introduction to Modern Arabic Poetry 1975, Background to Shakespeare 1981, Modern Arabic Literature and the West 1985, Modern Arabic Drama: An Anthology, Modern Arabic Drama in Egypt 1987, Early Arabic Drama 1988, Modern Arabic Literature: Cambridge History of Arabic Literature (ed.) 1992, A Short History of Modern Arabic Literature 1993, Print Politics: The Press and Radical Opposition in Early Nineteenth-Century England; several books and vols of verse in Arabic, including Arabic trans. of Shakespeare's Macbeth 2001, King Lear 2003, Othello 2004, Hamlet 2005. *Honours:* King Faisal Int. Prize for Arabic Literature 1992, Supreme Council Award for promoting knowledge of Arabic culture, Egypt 2006. *Address:* St Antony's College, 62 Woodstock Road, Oxford, OX2 6JF, England (office). *Telephone:* (1865) 284700 (office). *Fax:* (1865) 274526 (office). *Website:* www.sant.ox.ac.uk (office).

BADCOCK, Gary David, BA, MA, BD, PhD; Canadian academic, writer and editor; *Associate Professor, Faculty of Theology, Huron University College;* b. 13 Jan. 1961, Bay Roberts; m. Susan Dorothy Greig 1988; two d. *Education:* Memorial Univ., Univ. of Edinburgh, Scotland. *Career:* Teaching Fellow, Univ. of Aberdeen 1991–92; Meldrum Lecturer in Dogmatic Theology, Univ. of Edinburgh 1993–99, Assoc. Dean, Faculty of Divinity 1997; Asst Prof., Faculty of Theology, Huron Univ. Coll., London, Ontario 1999–2002, Assoc. Prof. 2002–. *Publications include:* Disruption to Diversity: Edinburgh Divinity 1846–1996 (ed. with D. F. Wright) 1996, Theology After the Storm, by John McIntyre (ed.) 1996, Light of Truth and Fire of Love 1997, The Way of Life: A Theology of Christian Vocation 1998, The House Where God Lives: The Doctrine of the Church 2009; contribs to books and scholarly journals. *Honours:* Leslie Tarr Award 1998. *Address:* Faculty of Theology, Huron University College, 1349 Western Road, London, ON, N6G 1H3, Canada (office). *Telephone:* (519) 438-7224 (office). *Fax:* (519) 438-3938 (office). *E-mail:* gbadcock@uwo.ca (office). *Website:* www.huronuc.ca/faculty_of_theology (office).

BADR, Liana, BA, MA; Palestinian writer, journalist and film maker; *Advisor for Cinematic Archive, Ministry of Culture;* b. Jerusalem; m.; two s. *Education:* Univ. of Jordan, Beirut Arab Univ., Birzeit Univ. *Career:* fmr volunteer in various Palestinian women's orgs; Culture Ed. Al Hurriyya review; after Palestinian exodus from Lebanon in 1982, lived in Damascus, Tunis and Amman, before returning to Palestine in 1994; Head, Cinema and Audio-Visual Dept, Palestine Ministry of Culture 1994–2004, currently adviser, Cinema Archive; Founder and fmr Ed., Ministry of Culture periodical Dafater Thaqafiyya); Cultural Ed., Attareek magazine (published by Peace Coalition and Palestine Media Center); Ed.-in-Chief, Awraq Thaqafia; Founder, Creative Women Platform, Palestine; bd mem. Palestinian Nat. Theatre. *Films:* Fadwa (A Tale of a Palestinian Poetess) 1999, Zeitounat 2001, The Green Bird 2002, Siege (A Writer's Diary) 2003, The Gates are Open, Sometimes! 2006, A Football Match on Thursday Afternoon 2006, Rana's Wedding, Al Quds My City 2011. *Publications include:* A Compass for the Sunflower (novel, in trans.) 1979, Stories of Love and Pursuit (short stories) 1983, A Balcony Over the Fakahani (three novellas, in trans.) 1983, I Want the Day (short stories) 1989, The Eye of the Mirror (novel, in trans.) 1991, Golden

Hell (short stories) 1991, Stars of Jericho (novel) 1993 (trans. into Italian 2011), Fadwa Touqan – the shadow of narrated words (memoir of the poet) 1996; ten children's books 1980–91, two collections of poems 1997, 1998, One Sky (collected stories); story published in Freedom (anthology published by Amnesty International in English and Spanish) 2009. *Honours:* Sigilio de la Pace Film Award (Italy) 2007, several awards at int. film festivals, named as one of the 100 Most Powerful Women in Arabic Countries 2011. *Address:* Ramallah, Al Bireh, Palestinian Autonomous Areas (office). *Telephone:* (2) 2407721 (office). *Fax:* (2) 2407730 (office). *E-mail:* creatf@yahoo.com (office).

BADRINATH, Tulsi, BA, MBA; Indian writer and dancer; b. 1967, Madras; d. of Chaturvedi Badrinath and Seeta Badrinath. *Education:* Stella Maris Coll. Chennai, Ohio Univ., USA. *Career:* trained in Bharata Natyam dance since age eight, has performed widely in India and abroad; mem. Dhananjayan's Bharata Kalanjali Troupe; worked at Standard Chartered Bank 1992–95; full-time writer and dancer 1995–; solo performances: Natyanjali Festival, Chidambaram, Nishagandhi Festival, Trivandrum, Palghat Festival, Spirit of Youth Festival, Music Acad., Chennai, Poompuhar Exhibition, The Maidan, Kolkata, India Int. Centre, New Delhi, ICCR, Azad Bhavan, New Delhi, Ghunghroo Festival, Bharat Bhavan, Bhopal, Brihadeeswara Temple, Thanjavur, Krishna Gana Sabha, Narada Gana Sabha, Karthik Fine Arts, Natyarangam, Mylapore Fine Arts, Sri Thyaga Brahma Gana Sabha, Int. Dance Alliance, Bharat Kalachar, Sri Varasiddhi Vinayaka Temple, Chennai. *Publications include:* Meeting Lives (trans. as The Living God) 2008, Melting Love (Man of A Thousand Chances) 2008, contribs. to newspapers and journals. *Address:* Niyogi Books, D-78, Okhla Industrial Area Phase 1, New Delhi 110 020, India. *Telephone:* (11) 26813350; (11) 26813351. *Fax:* (11) 26810483; (11) 26813830. *E-mail:* niyogibooks@gmail.com; tulsibadrinath@hotmail.com. *Website:* www.niyogibooks.com; tulsibadrinath.com.

BAGDIKIAN, Ben Haig, AB; Turkish academic and writer; *Professor and Dean Emeritus, Graduate School of Journalism, University of California, Berkeley*; b. 30 Jan. 1920, Marash; m. Marlene Griffith Bagdikian 1983; two s. *Education:* Clark Univ. *Career:* Asst Man. Ed. National News, The Washington Post; fmr Prof. and Dean, Grad. School of Journalism, Univ. of California, Berkeley, currently Prof. and Dean Emer.; Fellow, John Simon Guggenheim Memorial Foundation 1962. *Publications include:* In the Midst of Plenty: The Poor in America 1964, The Information Machines 1973, The Effete Conspiracy and Other Crimes of the Press 1973, Caged: Eight Prisoners and Their Keepers 1976, The Media Monopoly 1983, 7th edn as The New Media Monopoly, Double Vision: Reflections on My Heritage, Life and Profession 1995, The Memoir of Lydia Bagdikian (ed.) 1997, War, Media, And Propaganda: A Global Perspective 2004; contrib. to more than 200 to nat. magazines and journals. *Honours:* Hon. LHD (Brown Univ.) 1961, (Univ. of Rhode Island) 1992, Hon. LittD (Clark Univ.) 1963; Peabody Award 1951, Sidney Hillman Award 1955, Berkeley Citation 1990, James Madison Award, American Library Asscn Coalition on Govt Information 1998. *Address:* Berkeley Graduate School of Journalism, University of California, 121 North Gate Hall 5860, Berkeley, CA 94720-5860 (office); 25 Stonewall Road, Berkeley, CA 94705, USA (home). *Telephone:* (510) 642-3383 (office). *Fax:* (510) 643-9136 (office). *Website:* journalism.berkeley.edu (office).

BAHN, Paul Gerard, BA, MA, PhD; British archaeologist and writer; b. 29 July 1953, Hull. *Education:* Univ. of Cambridge. *Career:* Research Fellow, Univ. of Liverpool 1979–82; Sr Research Fellow, Univ. of London 1982–83; J. Paul Getty Postdoctoral Fellow 1985–86; Fellow, Soc. of Antiquaries; Corresp. mem. Archaeological Inst. of America; contrib. to Archaeology magazine published by Archaeological Inst. of America. *Publications include:* Pyrenean Prehistory 1984, Ancient Places (co-author) 1986, Images of the Ice Age (co-author) 1988, The Bluffer's Guide to Archaeology (second edn) 1989, Archaeology: Theories, Methods and Practice 1991, Easter Island, Earth Island 1992, Mammoths 1994, The Story of Archaeology 1995, Archaeology: A Very Short Introduction 1996, The Cambridge Illustrated History of Archaeology 1996, Tombs, Graves and Mummies 1996, Journey Through the Ice Age 1997, Lost Cities 1997, The Cambridge Illustrated History of Prehistoric Art 1998, Disgraceful Archaeology 1999, Wonderful Things (ed.) 1999, Atlas of World Archaeology 2000, The Archaeology Detectives 2001, The Penguin Guide to Archaeology 2001, Archaeology: The Definitive Guide 2002, Written in Bones 2003, The Enigmas of Easter Island 2003, Archaeology: The Key Concepts 2004, The New Penguin Dictionary of Archaeology 2004, Waking the Trance Fixed 2005, Unearthing the Past 2005, Chamanismes et Arts Prehistoriques 2006, Archaeology Essentials 2007, Palaeolithic Cave Art at Creswell Crags in European Context 2007, Ancient Obscenities 2007, Ancient World in Your Pocket 2007, Cave Art: A Guide to the Decorated Ice Age Caves of Europe 2007, Exploring the Ancient World 2008, Britain's Oldest Art: The Ice age Cave Art of Creswell Crags 2009, An Enquiring Mind: Studies in Honor of Alexander Marshack 2009, Prehistoric Rock Art: Polemics and Progress 2010; contribs to periodicals. *Literary Agent:* Watson, Little Ltd, 48–56 Bayham Place, London, NW1 0EU, England. *Address:* Archaeology Magazine, 36-36 33rd Street, Long Island City, New York, NY 11106, USA (office). *Telephone:* (718) 472-3050 (office). *Fax:* (718) 472-3051 (office). *E-mail:* general@archaeology.org (office); editorial@archaeology.org (office); pgbahn@anlabyrd.karoo.co.uk. *Website:* www.archaeology.org (office).

BAI, Fengxi; Chinese feminist, actress and playwright; b. 1934, Wen'an, Hebei Prov.; m. Yan Zhongying; one d. *Education:* N China People's Revolutionary Univ. *Career:* became actress China Youth Theater 1954; began writing plays after 1976. *Plays:* Liu Hulai 1951, Prince Wencheng 1960. *Publications:* The Women Trilogy: First Bathed in Moonlight 1981, An Old Friend Returning in a Stormy Night 1983, Where is Longing in Autumn? 1986. *Address:* c/o Chinese Literature Press, 24 Baiwanzhuang Road, Beijing 1000037, People's Republic of China.

BAIGELL, Matthew, BA, MA, PhD; American academic and writer; *Professor Emeritus, Department of Art History, Rutgers University*; b. 27 April 1933, New York, NY; m. Renee Moses 1959; two d. *Education:* Univ. of Vermont, Columbia Univ., Univ. of Pennsylvania. *Career:* Lieutenant US Air Force 1955–57; Instructor, Ohio State Univ. 1961–65, Asst Prof. 1965–67, Assoc. Prof. of Art 1967–68; Assoc. Prof., Dept of Art History, Rutgers Univ. 1968–72, Prof. 1972–78, currently Prof. Emer. *Publications:* A History of American Painting 1971, A Thomas Hart Benton Miscellany (ed.) 1971, The American Scene: American Painting in the 1930s 1974, Thomas Hart Benton 1974, Charles Burchfield 1976, The Western Art of Frederic Remington 1976, Dictionary of American Art 1979, Albert Bierstadt 1981, Thomas Cole 1981, A Concise History of American Painting and Sculpture 1984, The Papers of the American Artists' Congress (1936) 1985, Artists Against War and Fascism (ed. with J. Williams) 1986, Soviet Dissident Artists: Interviews After Perestroika (co-author) 1995, Jewish-American Artists and the Holocaust 1997, Artist and Identity in Twentieth-Century America 2001, Complex Identities: Jewish Consciousness and Modern Art (co-editor) 2001, Peeling Potatoes, Painting Pictures: Women Artists in Post-Soviet Russia, Estonia, and Latvia (co-author) 2001, Jewish Artists in New York: The Holocaust Years 2002, Jewish Art in America: An Introduction 2006, American Artists, Jewish Images 2006, Ruth Weisberg Unfurled (co-author) 2007, Jewish Dimensions in Modern Visual Culture: Antisemitism, Assimilation, Affirmation (co-editor) 2009. *Address:* Department of Art History, Rutgers University, Voorhees Hall, 71 Hamilton Street, New Brunswick, NJ 08901, USA (office). *Telephone:* (732) 932-7041 (office). *Fax:* (732) 932-1261 (office). *Website:* arthistory.rutgers.edu (office).

BAIGENT, Beryl, (Snowdon), BA, MA; British/Canadian teacher, writer and poet; b. (Beryl Jones), 16 Dec. 1937, Llay, Wrexham, North Wales; d. of Edmund Ivor Jones and Mary Elizabeth Bewley; m. Alan H. Baigent 1963; three d. *Education:* Univ. of Western Ontario, London, Canada. *Career:* Teacher of T'ai Chi and Sacred Dance 1971–; mem. Celtic Arts Asscn, Canadian Poetry Asscn, League of Canadian Poets (Ont. Representative) 1994–96; Poetry Contests Judge, Libraries & Poetry Organ. *Publications include:* The Quiet Village 1972, Pause 1974, In Counterpoint 1976, Ancestral Dreams 1981, The Sacred Beech 1985, Mystic Animals 1988, Absorbing the Dark 1990, Hiraeth: In Search of Celtic Origins 1994, Triptych: Virgins, Victims, Votives 1996, The Celtic Tree Calendar 1999, The Mary Poems 2000, And a Branch Shall Grow: The Irish Connection 2006, In Praise of Darkness 2010; contribs to various anthologies and periodicals including Northern Spirit: A Pagan Anthology 1988, Bite to Eat Place 1995, Spirit of the Circle 1998, Poetry and Spiritual Practice 2002. *Honours:* Ontario Weekly Newspaper Award 1979, June Fritch Memorial Award, Canadian Authors Asscn 1982, Ontario Arts Council Awards 1983, 1985, 1987, Kent Writers Award 1986, Black Mountain Award 1986, Canada Council Touring Awards 1990, 1992, 1993, 1994, 1998, Forest City Poetry Award 1991, Int. Affairs Touring Award 1991, Writers on Tour Award, North Wales Arts Asscn 1993, 1995, 1997, 1998, Welsh Arts Council Awards 1993, 1994, 1996, 1998, 1999, 2000, 2002–09, Muse Journal Award 1994. *Address:* The League of Canadian Poets, 312-192 Spadina Avenue, Toronto, ON M5T 2C2 (office); 137 Byron Avenue, Thamesford, ON N0M 2M0, Canada (home). *Telephone:* (416) 504-1657 (office); (519) 285-2441 (home). *Fax:* (416) 504-0096 (office). *E-mail:* berylbaigent@yahoo.ca. *Website:* www.poets.ca (office).

BAIL, Murray; Australian writer; b. 22 Sept. 1941, Adelaide; m. Margaret Wordsworth 1965. *Education:* Norwood Technical High School, Adelaide. *Career:* lived in India 1968–70, in England and Europe 1970–74; Trustee, Nat. Gallery of Australia 1976–81. *Publications include:* novels: Homesickness (Age Book of the Year Award (jtly 1980), Nat. Book Council Award) 1980, Holden's Performance (Victorian Premier's Literary Award Vance Palmer Prize 1988) 1987, Eucalyptus (ALS Gold Medal 1998, Miles Franklin Award 1999, Commonwealth Writers Prize 1999) 1998, The Pages 2008; short stories: Contemporary Portraits and Other Stories 1975, The Faber Book of Contemporary Australian Short Stories (ed.) 1988, Fairweather (ed.) 1994, Camouflage 2001; non-fiction: Ian Fairweather 1981, Longhand: A Writer's Notebook 1989, Notebooks 1970–2003 2005. *Address:* Random House Australia, 100 Pacific Highway, North Sydney, NSW 2060, Australia (office). *Telephone:* (2) 9954-9966 (office). *Fax:* (2) 9954-4562 (office). *E-mail:* random@randomhouse.com.au (office). *Website:* www.randomhouse.com.au (office).

BAILEY, Anthony Cowper, BA, MA; British writer and journalist; b. 5 Jan. 1933, Portsmouth; s. of Goldsmith Bailey Cowper and Phyllis Bailey Cowper; m. Margot Bailey; four d. *Education:* Merton Coll., Oxford. *Career:* staff writer, New Yorker magazine 1956–92; Chair. Burney Street Garden Project Greenwich 1981–90; Vice-Pres. The Turner Soc. 1999; speaker and visiting lecturer at various univs; Visiting Fellow, Yale Center for British Art 2002; mem. Bd of Govs Greenwich Theatre 1985–89; mem. Authors' Guild, Int. PEN, Soc. of Authors. *Publications include:* Making Progress 1959, The Mother Tongue 1961, The Inside Passage 1965, Through the Great City 1967, The Thousand Dollar Yacht 1968, The Light in Holland 1970, In the Village 1971, A Concise History of the Low Countries 1972, Rembrandt's House 1978, Acts of Union: Reports on Ireland 1973–79 1980, America, Lost and Found 1980, Along the Edge of the Forest: An Iron Curtain Journey 1983, England, First and Last 1985, Spring Jaunts: Some Walks, Excursions, and Personal Explorations of City, Country and Seashore 1986, Major André 1987, The Outer Banks 1989, A Walk Through Wales 1992, Responses to Rembrandt 1994, A Coast of Summer: Sailing New England Waters from Shelter Island to Cape Cod 1994, Standing in the Sun-A Life of JMW Turner 1997, A View of Delft-Vermeer Then and Now 2001, John Constable: A Kingdom of His Own 2006. *Honours:* Hon. Citizen, Oakwood Ohio 1982; Overeas Press Club Award 1974, Lowell Thomas Award 1994.

BAILEY, Glenda Adrianne, MA, OBE; British magazine editor; *Editor-in-Chief, Harper's Bazaar*; b. 16 Nov. 1958, Derbyshire, England; d. of John Ernest Bailey and Constance Bailey (née Groome); pnr Steve Sumner. *Education:* Noel Baker Grammar School, Derby and Kingston Polytechnic, Kingston Univ. *Career:* fmr consultant, Fashion Forecast, Design Direction; produced collection for Guisi Slaverio, Italy 1983; Ed. Honey 1986–88; launched Folio quarterly fashion magazine; launch Ed. Marie Claire, UK 1988–1996, Int. Editorial Consultant of all 26 editions of Marie Claire 1995, Marie Claire, USA 1996–2001; Ed.-in-Chief Harper's Bazaar, USA 2001–. *Honours:* Chevalier des Artes et des Lettres 2011; three Magazine Editor of the Year Awards, five Magazine of the Year Awards, two Amnesty Int. Awards 1988–96, Women's Magazine Ed. of the Year, British Soc. of Magazine Eds 1990, Media Week Press Award, Periodical Publrs Award, Consumer Magazine of the Year 1991, Amnesty Int. Award 1997, Community Action Network Award 1998, 1999, named Editor of the Year by Adweek 2001, ASME Best Celebrity Cover Award 2006, OCRF Legends Award 2006, ASME Best Fashion Cover 2007, FFANY Journalism Excellence 2008, Gem Award Excellence in Journalism 2009. *Address:* Harper's Bazaar Magazine, 300 West 57th Street, New York, NY 10019-3799, USA (office). *Telephone:* (212) 903-5000 (office). *Fax:* (212) 262-7101 (office). *E-mail:* bazaar@hearst.com (office). *Website:* www.harpersbazaar.com (office).

BAILEY, Martin, PhD; British journalist; b. 26 Oct. 1947, London. *Education:* LSE. *Career:* journalist, The Observer 1983–93; currently Corresp. The Art Newspaper. *Publications include:* Freedom Railway 1976, Oilgate: The Sanctions Scandal 1979, A Green Part of the World 1984, Young Vincent: Van Gogh's Years in England 1992, Van Gogh in England: Portrait of the Artist as a Young Man 1992, Van Gogh: Letters from Provence 1995, Durer 1995, Vermeer 1995, The Folio Society Book of the 100 Greatest Paintings, 2001, P J Crook 2003, The Folio Society Book of the 100 Greatest Portraits 2004, Van Gogh and Britain: Pioneer Collectors 2006. *Honours:* Journalist of the Year 1979. *Address:* The Art Newspaper, Third Floor, 70 South Lambeth Road, London, SW8 1RL, England (office). *Telephone:* (20) 3416-9000 (office). *Website:* www.theartnewspaper.com (office).

BAILEY, Paul, FRSL; British writer; b. (Peter Harry Bailey), 16 Feb. 1937, s. of Arthur Oswald Bailey and Helen Maud Burgess. *Education:* Sir Walter St John's School, London. *Career:* actor 1956–64, appearing in The Sport of My Mad Mother 1958 and Epitaph for George Dillon 1958; Literary Fellow at Univs of Newcastle and Durham 1972–74; Bicentennial Fellowship 1976; Visiting Lecturer in English Literature, North Dakota State Univ. 1977–79. *Publications:* At the Jerusalem (Author's Club First Novel Award, Somerset Maugham Award 1968) 1967, Trespasses 1970, A Distant Likeness 1973, Peter Smart's Confessions 1977, Old Soldiers 1980, An English Madam 1982, Gabriel's Lament 1986, An Immaculate Mistake (autobiography) 1990, Hearth and Home 1990, Sugar Cane 1993, The Oxford Book of London (ed.) 1995, First Love (ed.) 1997, Kitty and Virgil 1998, The Stately Homo: A Celebration of the Life of Quentin Crisp (ed.) 2000, Three Queer Lives: An Alternative Biography of Naomi Jacob, Fred Barnes and Arthur Marshall 2001, Uncle Rudolf (novel) 2002, A Dog's Life 2003, Chapman's Odyssey 2011; numerous newspaper articles. *Honours:* Somerset Maugham Award 1968, E.M. Forster Award 1978, George Orwell Memorial Prize 1978. *Literary Agent:* Rogers, Coleridge and White Ltd., 20 Powis Mews, London W11 1JN, England. *Telephone:* (20) 7221-3717. *Fax:* (20) 7229-9084. *E-mail:* info@rcwlitagency.com. *Website:* www.rcwlitagency.com. *Address:* 2/79 Davisville Road, London, W12 9SH, England (home). *Telephone:* (20) 8248-2127 (home).

BAILEY, Sly; British publishing and media executive; *CEO, Trinity Mirror PLC*; b. (Sylvia Grice), 24 Jan. 1962, London; d. of Thomas Lewis and Sylvia Grice (née Bantick); m. Peter Bailey 1998. *Education:* St Saviours and St Olaves Grammar School for Girls. *Career:* telephone sales exec. at The Guardian 1984–87; Advertisement Sales Man., The Independent 1987–89; moved to IPC Magazines 1989, Advertising Sales Exec. 1994, mem. Bd of Dirs 1994–2003, Man. Dir TX 1997, CEO 1999–2003; mem. Bd of Dirs and CEO Trinity Mirror PLC 2003–, (announced she would be leaving post at end of 2012); Dir (non-exec.) Littlewoods PLC April–Sept. 2002, EMI 2004– (Sr Ind. Dir 2007–); mem. Ind. Panel on BBC Charter Review 2004; Dir The Press Asscn; Pres. NewstrAid Benevolent Soc. *Honours:* Periodical Publrs Asscn Marcus Morris Award for Outstanding Contrib. to Publishing Industry 2002, named as one of 50 Most Powerful Women in Britain by Management Today 2002, named as one of Britain's Most Influential Women by Daily Mail 2003, ranked amongst top 20 of MediaGuardian's 100 Most Influential Figures in Media 2003, ranked by Fortune magazine amongst 50 Most Powerful Women in Business outside the US (23rd) 2003, (23rd) 2004, (33rd) 2005, (45th) 2006, ranked by the Financial Times amongst Top 25 Businesswomen in Europe (12th) 2005, (18th) 2006, (25th) 2007. *Address:* Trinity Mirror PLC, 1 Canada Square, Canary Wharf, London, E14 5AP, England (office). *Telephone:* (20) 7293-2203 (office). *Fax:* (20) 7293-3360 (office). *E-mail:* sly.bailey@trinitymirror.com (office). *Website:* www.trinitymirror.com (office).

BAILYN, Bernard, PhD; American historian, author and professor of history; *Professor Emeritus of History, Harvard University*; b. 10 Sept. 1922, Hartford, Conn.; s. of Charles Manuel Bailyn and Esther Schloss; m. Lotte Lazarsfeld 1952; two s. *Education:* Williams Coll. and Harvard Univ. *Career:* mem. Faculty, Harvard Univ. 1953–, Prof. of History 1961–66, Winthrop Prof. of History 1966–81, Adams Univ. Prof. 1981–93, Prof. Emer. 1993–, James Duncan Phillips Prof. in Early American History 1991–93, Prof. Emer. 1993–; Dir Charles Warren Center for Studies in American History 1983–94; Pitt Prof. of American Hist., Cambridge Univ. 1986–87; Dir Int. Seminar on History of Atlantic World 1995–; Ed.-in-Chief John Harvard Library 1962–70; Co-Ed. Perspectives in American History (journal) 1967–77, 1984–86; mem. American Historical Asscn (Pres. 1981), American Acad. of Arts and Sciences, Nat. Acad. of Educ., American Philosophical Soc.; Foreign mem. Russian Acad. of Sciences, Academia Europaea, Mexican Acad. of History and Geography; Sr Fellow, Soc. of Fellows; Hon. Fellow Christ's Coll., Cambridge Univ.; Corresp. Fellow, British Acad. 1989, Royal Historial Soc.; Trustee, Inst. of Advanced Study, Princeton 1989–94; Trevelyan Lecturer, Cambridge Univ. 1971; Jefferson Lecturer, Nat. Endowment for the Humanities 1998. *Publications:* The New England Merchants in the 17th Century 1955, Massachusetts Shipping 1697–1714: A Statistical Study (jtly) 1959, Education in the Forming of American Society 1960, Pamphlets of the American Revolution 1750–1776, Vol. I (ed.) (Faculty Prize, Harvard Univ. Press) 1965, The Apologia of Robert Keayne (ed.) 1965, The Ideological Origins of the American Revolution (Pulitzer and Bancroft Prizes 1968) 1967, The Origins of American Politics 1968, The Intellectual Migration 1930–1960 (co-ed.) 1969, Law in American History (co-ed.) 1972, The Ordeal of Thomas Hutchinson (Nat. Book Award 1975) 1974, The Great Republic (co-author) 1977, The Press and the American Revolution (co-ed.) 1980, The Peopling of British North America 1986, Voyagers to the West (Pulitzer Prize 1986) 1986, Faces of Revolution 1990, Strangers Within the Realm (co-ed.) 1991, The Debate on the Constitution (two vols, ed.) 1993, On the Teaching and Writing of History 1994, To Begin the World Anew: The Genius and Ambiguities of the American Founders 2003, Atlantic History 2005. *Honours:* 15 hon. degrees; Robert H. Lord Award, Emmanuel Coll. 1967, Pulitzer Prize for History 1968, 1987, Thomas Jefferson Medal 1993, Henry Allen Moe Prize, American Philosophical Soc. 1994, Foreign Policy Asscn Medal 1998; Catton Prize, Soc. American Historians 2000, Nat. Humanities Medal 2010, Samuel Eliot Morison Award 2011. *Address:* Department of History, Harvard University, Cambridge, MA 02138 (office); 170 Clifton Street, Belmont, MA 02478-2604, USA (home). *Website:* fas-www.harvard.edu/~atlantic/bailyn.html (home).

BAINBRIDGE, Cyril; British writer and journalist; b. 15 Nov. 1928, Bradford, West Yorkshire; m. Barbara Hannah Crook 1953; one s. two d. *Education:* Negus Coll., Bradford. *Career:* reporter, Bingley Guardian 1944–45, Yorkshire Observer & Bradford Telegraph 1945–54, Press Asscn 1954–63; Asst News Ed., The Times 1963–67, Deputy News Ed. 1967–69, Regional News Ed. 1969–77, Man. News Ed. 1977–82, Asst Man. Ed. 1982–88; mem. Brontë Soc., Chartered Inst. of Journalists (fmr Pres. and Fellow), Soc. of Authors. *Publications include:* Taught With Care: A Century of Church Schooling in Whetstone 1974, Brass Triumphant 1980, One Hundred Years of Journalism: Social Aspects of the Press 1984, Pavilions on the Sea 1986, The Brontës and Their Country, North Yorkshire and North Humberside 1989, The News of the World Story 1993; contrib. to newspapers, magazines and periodicals. *Address:* 6 Lea Road, Hemingford Grey, Huntingdon, PE28 9ED, England (home).

BAINES, John (see Salas Sommer, Dario)

BAITZ, Jon Robin; American playwright, scriptwriter and producer; b. 4 Nov. 1961, Los Angeles; s. of Edward Baitz; pnr Joe Mantello 1990–2002. *Education:* Beverly Hills High School. *Career:* Fellow, American Acad. and Inst. of Arts and Letters 1994; Fellow, Guggenheim Foundation; Artist-in-Residence, New School for Drama 2009–10. *Film:* Last Summer in the Hamptons 1995, One Fine Day 1996, People I Know 2003, The Substance of Fire 1996. *Television:* as writer: Three Hotels 1990, The Frightening Frammis (co-scriptwriter), Brothers and Sisters (also exec. producer) 2006–08, The West Wing, Alias. *Publications include:* plays: The Film Society 1987, Dutch Landscape 1989, The Substance of Fire 1991, Mizlansky/Zilinsky, The End of the Day 1993, A Fair Country 1996, Ten Unknowns 2001, My Beautiful Goddam City 2004, The Paris Letter 2005; contribs to The Huffington Post. *Honours:* Rockefeller Foundation Award, Drama Desk Award, Humanitas Award. *Literary Agent:* Creative Artists Agency, 162 Fifth Avenue, 6th Floor, New York, NY 10010, USA. *Telephone:* (212) 277-9000. *Fax:* (212) 277-9099. *Website:* www.caa.com.

BAJWA, Rupa; Indian writer; b. 1976, Amritsar, Punjab; d. of Swarn Singh Bajwa. *Publications include:* The Sari Shop (Grinzane Cavour Prize 2005, Best First Book Award, Commonwealth Writers Prize, Eurasia region 2005, Sahitya Akademi Award 2006) 2004; contribs to The Telegraph and India Today. *Address:* Marketing and Promotions Department, Penguin Books India Private Limited, 11, Community Centre, Panchsheel Park, New Delhi, 110 017, India. *E-mail:* publicity@in.penguingroup.com (office). *Website:* www.penguinbooksindia.com (office).

BAKER, Alison, BA; American writer; b. 7 Aug. 1953, Lancaster, Pa; m. Hans Rilling. *Education:* Reed Coll., Indiana Univ. *Career:* worked as medical librarian and library activist; fmr Resident Ragdale Foundation; fmr Fellow, Virginia Center for the Creative Arts; fmr mem. Advisory Bd Writers@?Work;

mem. Editorial Bd Wabash Magazine. *Publications include:* How I Came West, and Why I Stayed 1993, Loving Wanda Beaver 1995; contrib. to anthologies and periodicals. *Honours:* George Garrett Fiction Award 1992, First Prize, O. Henry Collection 1994, Gettysburg Review Award, named Oregon Library Supporter of the Year, Oregon Library Asscn 2001. *Literary Agent:* Gail Hochman, Brandt and Hochman Literary Agents, 1501 Broadway, Suite 2310, New York, NY 10036, USA. *Telephone:* (212) 840-5760. *Fax:* (212) 840-5776. *E-mail:* alison@alisonbaker.com (office). *Website:* www.alisonbaker.com.

BAKER, David Anthony, BSE, MA, PhD; American academic, poet and editor; *Poetry Editor, The Kenyon Review;* b. 27 Dec. 1954, Bangor, Me; s. of Donald Dayle Baker and Martha Baker; m. Ann Townsend 1987 (divorced 2007); one d. *Education:* Central Missouri State Univ., Univ. of Utah. *Career:* Poetry Ed. Quarterly West 1980–81, Ed.-in-Chief 1981–83; Visiting Asst Prof., Kenyon Coll. 1983–84; Asst Ed. Kenyon Review 1983–89, Poetry Ed./Consulting Poetry Ed. 1989–94, Poetry Ed. 1994–; Asst Prof. of English, Denison Univ. 1984–90, Assoc. Prof. of English 1990–97, Thomas B. Fordham Endowed Chair in Creative Writing 1996, Prof. of English 1997–; Visiting Telluride Prof., Cornell Univ. 1985; Visiting Assoc. Prof., Univ. of Michigan 1996; Visiting Prof., Ohio State Univ. 2005; Contributing Ed. The Pushcart Prize 1992–; mem. Associated Writing Programs, Modern Language Asscn, Nat. Book Critics Circle, Poetry Soc. of America, Poets and Writers. *Publications include:* poetry: Looking Ahead 1975, Rivers in the Sea 1977, Laws of the Land 1981, Summer Sleep 1984, Haunts 1985, The Soil is Suited to the Seed: A Miscellany in Honor of Paul Bennett (Ed.) 1986, Sweet Home, Saturday Night 1991, Echo for an Anniversary 1992, After the Reunion 1994, Holding Katherine 1997, The Truth About Small Towns 1998, Changeable Thunder 2001, Midwest Eclogue 2005, Treatise on Touch: Selected Poems 2007, Never-Ending Birds 2009; criticism: Meter in English: A Critical Engagement 1996, Heresy and the Ideal: On Contemporary Poetry 2000, Radiant Lyre: Essays on Lyric Poetry 2007; contribs to periodicals, including The Atlantic, The Nation, The New Yorker, Poetry, The Yale Review, reviews to The Georgia Review, The Kenyon Review, Poetry. *Honours:* Bread Loaf Poetry Fellow 1989, Nat. Endowment for the Arts Fellowship 1985, 2006, Ohio Arts Council Fellowship 2000, 2008, Guggenheim Fellowship 2000; Bread Loaf Margaret Bridgman Scholar of Poetry 1982, Pushcart Press Outstanding Writer 1982, 1984, 1985, 1986, 1990, 1991, 1994, 1995, Mid-American Review James Wright Prize for Poetry 1983, Pushcart Prize 1992, 2004, 2005, 2008, Poetry Soc. of America Mary Carolyn Davies Award 1995. *Address:* The Kenyon Review, Finn House, 102 West Wiggin Street, Kenyon College, Gambier, OH 43022-9623 (office); Department of English, Denison University, Granville, OH 43023, USA (office). *Telephone:* (740) 427-5208 (Kenyon Review) (office). *Fax:* (740) 427-5417 (Kenyon Review) (office). *E-mail:* kenyonreview@kenyon.edu (office). *Website:* www.kenyonreview.org (office).

BAKER, Houston Alfred, Jr, BA, MA, PhD; American academic, writer, editor and poet; *Professor of English and Distinguished University Professor, Vanderbilt University;* b. 22 March 1943, Louisville, Ky; m. Charlotte Pierce-Baker 1966; one s. *Education:* Howard Univ., Univ. of California, Los Angeles, Univ. of Edinburgh. *Career:* Instructor, Howard Univ. 1966; Instructor, Yale Univ. 1968–69, Asst Prof. of English 1969–70; Assoc. Prof. and mem. Center for Advanced Studies, Univ. of Virginia 1970–73, Prof. of English 1973–74; Prof. of English, Univ. of Pennsylvania 1974–, Dir, Afro-American Studies Program 1974–77, Albert M. Greenfield Prof. of Human Relations 1982–99, Dir Center for the Study of Black Literature and Culture 1987–99; George D. and Susan Fox Beischer Prof. of English, Duke Univ. 1999–2006; Prof. of English and Distinguished Univ. Prof., Vanderbilt Univ. 2006–; Fellow, Center for Advanced Study in the Behavioral Sciences 1977–78, Nat. Humanities Center 1982–83; Bucknell Distinguished Scholar, Univ. of Vermont 1992; Berg Visiting Prof. of English, New York Univ. 1994; Fulbright 50th Anniversary Distinguished Fellow, Brazil 1996; Sr Fellow, School of Criticism and Theory, Cornell Univ. 1996–2002; Visiting Fellow, Inst. for the Humanities, Univ. of Illinois, Chicago 2008; mem. Coll. Language Asscn, English Inst. (Bd of Supervisors 1989–91), Modern Language Asscn (Pres. 1992). *Publications include:* Long Black Song 1972, Singers of Daybreak 1974, A Many-Colored Coat of Dreams: The Poetry of Countee Cullen 1974, The Journey Back: Issues in Black Literature and Criticism 1980, Blues, Ideology, and Afro-American Literature: A Vernacular Theory 1984, Modernism and Harlem Renaissance 1987, Afro-American Poetics: Revisions of Harlem and the Black Aesthetic 1988, Workings of the Spirit: The Poetics of Afro-American Women's Writing 1991, Black Studies, Rap, and the Academy 1993, Turning South Again: Re-Thinking Modernism/Re-Reading Booker T. 2001, I Don't Hate the South: Reflections on Faulkner, Family, and the South 2007, Betrayal: How Black Intellectuals Have Abandoned the Ideals of the Civil Rights Era (American Book Award 2009) 2008; poetry: No Matter Where You Travel, You Still Be Black 1979, Spirit Run 1982, Blues Journeys Home 1985, Passing Over 2000; ed various books; contrib. to scholarly books and journals. *Honours:* several hon. doctorates; Alumni Award for Distinguished Achievement in Literature and the Humanities, Howard Univ. 1985, Distinguished Writer of the Year Award, Middle Atlantic Writers Asscn 1986, Creative Scholarship Award, Coll. Language Asscn of America 1988, Pennsylvania Gov.'s Award for Excellence in the Humanities 1990, Lifetime Achievement Award, 25th Anniversary Celebration of Black Writing, Philadelphia 2009, Lifetime Achievement Award, MELUS 2012. *Address:* Department of English, Vanderbilt University, 2301 Vanderbilt Place, 331 Benson Hall, PMB 351654, Nashville, TN 37235, USA (office). *Telephone:* (615) 343-7355 (office). *Fax:* (615) 322-8672 (office). *E-mail:* houston.a.baker@vanderbilt.edu (office). *Website:* sitemason.vanderbilt.edu/english (office).

BAKER, Baron (Life Peer), cr. 1997, of Dorking in the County of Surrey; **Kenneth Wilfred Baker,** PC, CH; British politician and writer; b. 3 Nov. 1934, Newport, Wales; s. of the late W. M. Baker; m. Mary Elizabeth Gray-Muir 1963; one s. two d. *Education:* St Paul's School and Magdalen Coll., Oxford. *Career:* nat. service 1953–55; served Twickenham Borough Council 1960–62; as Conservative cand. contested Poplar 1964, Acton 1966; Conservative MP for Acton 1968–70, St Marylebone 1970–83, Mole Valley 1983–97; Parl. Sec. Civil Service Dept 1972–74, Parl. Pvt. Sec. to Leader of Opposition 1974–75; Minister of State and Minister for Information Tech., Dept of Trade and Industry 1981–84; Sec. of State for the Environment 1985–86, for Educ. and Science 1986–89; Chancellor of the Duchy of Lancaster and Chair. Conservative Party 1989–90; Sec. of State for the Home Dept 1990–92; mem. Public Accounts Cttee 1969–70; mem. Exec. 1922 Cttee 1978–81; Chair. Hansard Soc. 1978–81, MTT PLC 1996–97, Business Serve PLC, Northern Edge Ltd, Museum of British History, Belmont Press (London) Ltd, Monstermob, Teather & Greenwood 2003–; Pres. Royal London Soc. for the Blind; Sec. Gen. UN Conf. of Parliamentarians on World Population and Devt 1978; Chair. (non-exec.) Teather & Greenwood PLC, Monstermob, Business Serve; Dir (non-exec.) Hanson 1992–, Stanley Leisure PLC; Chair. Information Cttee, House of Lords 2002–. *Publications:* I Have No Gun But I Can Spit 1980, London Lines (ed.) 1982, The Faber Book of English History in Verse (ed.) 1988, The Faber Book of English Parodies (ed.) 1990, Unauthorized Versions (ed.) 1990, The Faber Book of Conservatism (ed.) 1993, The Turbulent Years: My Life in Politics 1993, The Prime Ministers: An Irreverent Political History in Cartoons 1995, The Kings and Queens: An Irreverent Cartoon History of the British Monarchy 1995, The Faber Book of War Poetry (ed.) 1996, Children's English History in Verse (ed.) 2000, The Faber Book of Landscape Poetry (ed.) 2000, George III: A Life in Caricature 2007. *Honours:* Companion of Honour 1997. *Address:* House of Lords, Westminster, London, SW1A 0PW, England (office). *Telephone:* (20) 7219-3000 (office).

BAKER, Maureen, BA, MA, PhD, FRSNZ, FNZAH; Canadian/New Zealand sociologist, academic and author; *Professor of Sociology, University of Auckland;* b. 9 March 1948, Toronto, Ont.; d. of Albert Baker and Irene Baker; m. David J. Tippin 1983. *Education:* Univ. of Toronto, Univ. of Alberta. *Career:* Asst Prof. of Sociology, Acadia Univ. 1974–76; Lecturer, Warrnambool Inst. and Kuringai Coll., Australia 1976–78; Asst Prof. of Sociology, Univ. of Toronto 1978–83; Researcher, Parl. of Canada 1983–90; Assoc. Prof. and Prof. of Social Work, McGill Univ., Montreal 1990–97; Prof. of Sociology, Univ. of Auckland, NZ 1998–, Head, Dept of Sociology 1998–2004; mem. Australian Sociology Asscn, Canadian Sociology Asscn, Sociological Asscn for Aotearoa/NZ; Fellow, NZ Acad. of the Humanities 2008. *Publications include:* Families: Changing Trends in Canada 1984 (sixth edn) 2009, What will Tomorrow Bring? 1985, Aging in Canadian Society 1988, Families in Canadian Society 1989, Canada's Changing Families: Challenges to Public Policy 1994, Canadian Family Policies: Cross-National Comparisons 1995, Poverty, Social Assistance and the Employability of Mothers: Restructuring Welfare States (with D. Tippin) 1999, Families, Labour and Love 2001, Restructuring Family Policies 2006, Choices and Constraints in Family Life 2007, (new edn) 2010, Perpetuating the Academic Gender Gap? 2012; contribs to numerous scholarly books and journals. *Honours:* numerous research grants. *Address:* Department of Sociology, University of Auckland, Level 9, Human Sciences Building, 10 Symonds Street, Auckland 1142, New Zealand (office). *Telephone:* (9) 373-7599 (ext. 88610) (office). *Fax:* (9) 373-7439 (office). *E-mail:* ma.baker@auckland.ac.nz (office). *Website:* www.arts.auckland.ac.nz (office).

BAKER, Nicholson, BA; American writer; b. 7 Jan. 1957, Rochester, NY; m. Margaret Brentano 1985; two c. *Education:* The School Without Walls, Rochester, Eastman Music School, Rochester, Haverford Coll., Pa. *Publications include:* fiction: The Mezzanine 1988, Room Temperature 1990, Vox 1993, The Fermata 1995, The Everlasting Story of Nory 1999, A Box of Matches 2003, Checkpoint 2004, The Anthologist 2009; non-fiction: 'Weeds: A Talk at the Library', in Reclaiming San Francisco: history, politics, culture (anthology) 1998, U and I 1992, The Size of Thoughts 1997, Double Fold (Nat. Book Critics Circle Award 2002) 2002, Human Smoke: The Beginnings of World War II, the End of Civilization 2008, The Anthologist 2009; contrib. to periodicals, including New Yorker, Atlantic Monthly, New York Review of Books, Esquire, American Scholar, New York Times, London Review of Books, Literary Outtakes, Little Magazine, StoryQuarterly. *Honours:* James Madison Freedom of Information Award. *Address:* c/o Simon and Schuster Publicity Department, Simon and Schuster, Inc., 1230 Avenue of the Americas, New York, NY 10020, USA. *Website:* www.simonsays.com.

BAKER, Paul Raymond, AB, MA, PhD; American historian and academic; *Professor Emeritus of History, New York University;* b. 28 Sept. 1927, Everett, Wash.; s. of Loren R. Baker and Alma I. Baker; m. Elizabeth Kemp; one c. *Education:* Stanford, Columbia and Harvard Univs. *Career:* Prof. of History, New York Univ. 1965–99, Prof. Emer. 1999–, Dir of American Civilization Program 1972–92. *Publications include:* Views of Society and Manners in America (ed) 1963, The Fortunate Pilgrims: Americans in Italy 1800–1860 1964, The Atomic Bomb: The Great Decision (ed) 1968, The American Experience (five vols) 1976–79, Richard Morris Hunt 1980, Stanny: The Gilded Life of Stanford White 1989; contrib. to Around the Square 1982, Master Builders 1985, The Architecture of Richard Morris Hunt 1986, Insight and Inspiration: The Italian Presence in American Art 1860–1920 1992,

Henry Adams and His World 1993, Greenwich Village: Culture and Counterculture 1993. *Honours:* Turpie Award in American Studies 1994, New Jersey Literary Hall of Fame Authors' Award. *Address:* Department of History, New York University, King Juan Carlos I of Spain Center, 7th Floor, 53 Washington Square S, New York, NY 10012 (office); 90 Hillside Avenue, Glen Ridge, NJ 07028, USA (home). *Telephone:* (212) 998-8600 (office); (212) 995-4017 (office). *E-mail:* prb2@nyu.edu (office).

BAKER, Peter Gorton; British writer; b. 28 March 1924, Eastbourne, Sussex. *Career:* reporter, Sussex Daily News 1944–45; chief reporter, Kinematograph Weekly 1945–53; Ed. Films and Filming magazine; British rep. on film festival juries at Cannes, Venice, Moscow, Berlin 1953–70. *Television plays:* The Offence, Little Girl Blue, contrib. to many TV drama series. *Publications include:* Cruise 1968, The Antibodies 1969, Minnie Swan 1969, The Bedroom Sailors 1971, Babel Beach 1972, Jesus, Casino, Clinic, To Win a Prize on Sunday. *Address:* Calle Don Juan de Málaga 6, Málaga 29015, Spain.

BAKER, Russell Wayne, BA, DLitt; American journalist and author; b. 14 Aug. 1925, London Co., Va; s. of Benjamin R. Baker and Lucy E. Robinson; m. Miriam E. Nash 1950; two s. one d. *Education:* Johns Hopkins Univ. *Career:* served USNR 1943–45; with Baltimore Sun 1947–64; mem. Washington Bureau, New York Times 1954–62, author-columnist, editorial page 1962–98; Fellow, American Acad., Inst. of Arts and Letters 1993. *Television:* Masterpiece Theatre (host) 1993–2004. *Publications:* American in Washington 1961, No Cause for Panic 1964, All Things Considered 1965, Our Next President 1968, Poor Russell's Almanac 1972, The Upside Down Man 1977, Home Again, Home Again 1979, So This is Depravity 1980, Growing Up (Pulitzer Prize) 1982, The Rescue of Miss Yaskell and Other Pipe Dreams 1983, The Good Times (memories) 1989, There's a Country in My Cellar 1990, Russell Baker's Book of American Humor 1993, Looking Back 2004; contrib. to The New York Times Magazine, Sports Illustrated, Saturday Evening Post, McCalls. *Honours:* several hon. degrees; Pulitzer Prize for distinguished commentary 1979, and other awards.

BAKER, William, BA, MPhil, MLS, PhD; American/British academic and writer; *Board of Trustees Professor and Distinguished Research Professor, Northern Illinois University;* b. 6 July 1944, Shipston, Warwicks., England; s. of the late Stanley Cohen Baker and Mabel Baker (née Woolf); m. 1969; two d. *Education:* Univs of Sussex, London, Loughborough. *Career:* Lecturer, Thurrock Tech. Coll., Essex 1969–71, Ben-Gurion Univ., Israel 1971–77, Univ. of Kent, Canterbury 1977–78, West Midlands Coll. 1978–85; Prof., Pitzer Coll., Claremont, Calif. 1981–82; Housemaster, Clifton Coll. 1986–89; Prof., Northern Illinois Univ. 1989–2003, Presidential Research Prof. 2003–07, Distinguished Research Prof. 2007–, Bd of Trustees Prof. 2009–; Visiting Prof., Sheffield Hallam Univ. 2005–08; Ed. George Eliot–George Henry Lewes Studies 1981, The Year's Work in English Studies 2000–; Co-Ed. Year's Work in English Studies, Oxford Univ. Press; Fellow, English Asscn 2003–, Humanities Inst., Univ. of Lyon III, France 2006–07; mem. Bibliographical Soc. of America (Council mem. 2000–08), American Library Asscn, Modern Language Asscn. *Publications include:* Harold Pinter 1973, George Eliot and Judaism 1975, The Early History of the London Library 1992, Literary Theories: A Case Study in Critical Performance 1996, Nineteenth Century British Book Collectors and Bibliographers 1997, Twentieth Century British Book Collectors and Bibliographers 1999, Pre-Nineteenth Century British Book Collectors and Bibliographers 1999, The Letters of Wilkie Collins 1999, Twentieth Century Bibliography and Textual Criticism 2000, A Companion to the Victorian Novel 2002, Wilkie Collins's Library: A Reconstruction 2002, George Eliot: A Bibliographical History 2002, Nineteenth-Century Travels, Exploration and Empires–North America 2003, Middle East 2004, Redefining the Modern: Essays on Literature and Society in Honor of Joseph Wiensenfarth 2004, Harold Pinter: A Bibliographical History 2005, Shakespeare: The Critical Tradition, The Merchant of Venice 2005, History of the English Association 2007, A Wilkie Collins Chronology 2007, Jane Austen – A Critical Companion 2008, David Daiches A Celebration of his Life and Work 2008, Harold Pinter (Writers' Lives Series) 2008, Shakespeare (Writers' Lives Series) 2009; edns of letters by George Henry Lewes, George Eliot and Wilkie Collins, and four vols of George Eliot's notebooks; contrib. to ODNB, Book and Magazine Collector, over 150 articles and many reviews. *Honours:* Indiana Univ. Lilly Library Ball Brothers Foundation Fellowship 1993, Bibliographical Soc. of America Fellowship 1994–95, American Philosophical Soc. grant 1997, 'Choice' Outstanding Academic Book of the Year Awards 2000, 2006, Nat. Endowment of the Humanities Sr Fellowship 2002–03, Mellon Fellowship, Harry Ransom Humanities Research Center, Univ. of Texas 2006–07. *Address:* Department of English, Room FO 207B, Northern Illinois University, Dekalb, IL 60115, USA (office). *Telephone:* (815) 753-1857 (office). *Fax:* (815) 753-2003 (office). *E-mail:* wbaker@niu.edu (office). *Website:* www.engl.niu.edu (office).

BAKEWELL, Baroness (Life Peer), cr. 2011, of Stockport in the County of Greater Manchester; **Joan Dawson Bakewell,** DBE, BA; British broadcaster and author; b. 16 April 1933, Stockport, Cheshire (now Greater Manchester), England; d. of John Rowlands and Rose Bland; m. 1st Michael Bakewell 1955 (divorced 1972); one s. one d.; m. 2nd Jack Emery 1975 (divorced 2001). *Education:* Stockport High School for Girls and Newnham Coll., Cambridge. *Career:* TV Critic, The Times 1978–81, columnist, Sunday Times 1988–90; columnist ('Just Seventy'), The Guardian 2003; began fortnightly column in Times2 section of The Times 2008; currently has a weekly column in The Independent; Assoc. Newnham Coll., Cambridge 1980–91, Assoc. Fellow 1984–87; Council mem. Aldeburgh Foundation 1985–99; Gov. BFI 1994–99, Chair. 2000–02; Govt-apptd Voice of Older People 2008–10; Chair. and Trustee, Shared Experience theatre co.; mem. (Labour) House of Lords 2011–. *Radio includes:* Artist of the Week 1998–99, The Brains Trust 1999–, Belief (BBC Radio 3) 2000–, Saturday Live (BBC Radio 4). *Television includes:* Sunday Break 1962, Home at 4.30 (writer and producer) 1964, Meeting Point, The Second Sex 1964, Late Night Line Up 1965–72, 2008, The Youthful Eye 1968, Moviemakers at the National Film Theatre 1971, Film 72, Film 73, Holiday 74, 75, 76, 77, 78 (series), Reports Action (series) 1976–78, Arts UK: OK? 1980, Heart of the Matter (BBC 1) 1988–2000, My Generation 2000, One Foot in the Past 2000, Taboo (series) 2001, Daily Politics (BBC 1), Permissive Night (BBC Parliament) 2008, GMTV's Sunday programme, Panorama (BBC 1) 2010. *Publications:* The New Priesthood: British Television Today (co-author) 1970, A Fine and Private Place (co-author) 1977, The Complete Traveller 1977, The Heart of the Matter 1996, The Centre of the Bed: An Autobiography 2004, selection of her interviews for radio series Belief published 2005, The View from Here: Life at 70 2007, All the Nice Girls (novel) 2009; contribs to journals. *Honours:* Dimbleby Award, BAFTA 1995, Journalist of the Year, Stonewall Awards 2009. *Literary Agent:* c/o Knight Ayton Management, 35 Great James Street, London, WC1N 3HB, England. *Telephone:* (20) 7831-4400. *Fax:* (20) 7831-4455. *E-mail:* info@knightayton.co.uk. *Website:* knightayton.co.uk. *Address:* House of Lords, Westminster, London, SW1A 0PW, England. *Telephone:* (20) 7219-5353 (House of Lords).

BAKHTARI, Ustad Wasef, BA; Afghan poet and academic; b. 1942, Balkh; m. Soriya Bakhtari. *Education:* Kabul Univ., Columbia Univ., USA. *Career:* Leader, Shole Jawed party, sent to prison 1978, left politics after release from prison 1980; wrote and translated text books for Ministry of Educ.; fmr Prof. of Literature, Kabul Univ.; Ed.-in-Chief Zhwandoon Magazine 1978; exiled from Afghanistan 1996, later settled in New Port Richey, Florida. *Publications:* poems include: Calamity 1972.

BAKKER, Gerbrand, PhD; Dutch writer; b. 28 April 1962, Wieringerwaard, Noord-Holland. *Education:* Univ. of Amsterdam. *Career:* etymologist; subtitle trans. on documentary nature films 1995–2002; trained as professional gardener 2003–06; writes weekly column, De Groene Amsterdammer 2007–. *Publications include:* fiction: Perenbomen Bloeien wit 1999, Boven is het Stil (trans. as The Twin) (Golden Dog-Ear Award, Int. IMPAC Dublin Literary Award 2010) 2006, Juni 2009; non-fiction: Het Etymologisch Woordenboek voor Beginners of Hoe het mannetje mannequin werd 1997, Het Tweede Etymologisch Woordenboek voor Beginners of Hoe het karretje carrière maakte 1998, Woordenboek voor Aankomende Brugklassers 2000, Junior Etymologisch Woordenboek 2006, Ezel, schaap en tureluur 2009, De omweg 2010. *Honours:* Prix Millepages 2009, Prix Initiales 2010. *Address:* Uitgeverij Cossee BV, Postbus 15548, 1001 Amsterdam, Netherlands (office); c/o Archipelago Books, 232 3rd Street, A111 Brooklyn, NY 11215, USA. *Telephone:* (718) 852-6134. *Fax:* (718) 852-6135. *E-mail:* info@archipelagobooks.org; gerbrand.bakker@hetnet.nl (office). *Website:* www.archipelagobooks.org; www.gerbrandsdingetje.nl.

BAKR, Salwā, BA; Egyptian short story writer and novelist; b. June 1949, Cairo; m. Mourir Al Shaarani; two c. *Education:* Ayn Shams Univ., Cairo. *Career:* film and theatre critic for Arabian language publs; concentrated on creative writing 1985–; Founder Hagar journal 1993; Visiting Prof., American Univ. in Cairo 2001–. *Publications include:* short stories: Zinat fi Janasat ar-Ra'is (Zinat at the President's Funeral) 1986, Atiyyah's Shrine 1987, About the Soul that was Spirited Away 1989, The Wiles of Men and Other Stories (trans. by Denys Johnson Davies) 1992, Such A Beautiful Voice, Monkey Business 1992, The Peasant Woman's Dough 1992, My Grandmother's Cactus (in trans.) 1993, Rabbits 1994, Inverse Rhythms 1996, Night and Day 1997, Streams of Time 2003, The Diamond Edematous; other: Wasf al-Bulbul (novel, trans. as Depicting the Nightingale 1993), al-'Araba al-dhahabiya la Tas'ad ila-l-Sama (novel, trans. as The Golden Chariot 1995) 1991, El-Bashmouri (novel) Vol. 1 1998, Vol. 2 2000 (trans. as The Man from Bashmour 2007), Dream of Years (play) 2002. *Honours:* Fiction Prize, German Nat. Radio. *Address:* c/o Atelier of Writers, Karim al-Dawla Street, Talat Harb Square, Cairo, Egypt.

BA'LABAKKI, Laila (see Layla Baalbaki)

BALABAN, John, BA, AM; American academic, writer, poet and translator; *Professor of English and Poet-in-Residence, North Carolina State University*; b. 2 Dec. 1943, Philadelphia; m. 1970; one d. *Education:* Pennsylvania State Univ., Harvard Univ. *Career:* Instructor in Linguistics, Univ. of Can Tho, South Viet Nam 1967–68; Instructor Pennsylvania State Univ. 1970–73, Asst Prof. 1973–76, Assoc. Prof. 1976–82, Prof. 1982–92; Nat. Endowment for the Humanities Younger Humanist Fellow 1971–72; Fulbright Distinguished Visiting Lecturer, Romania 1979; Prof. of English and Dir of Creative Writing, Univ. of Miami 1992–2000; Prof. of English and Poet-in-Residence, North Carolina State Univ., Raleigh 2000–; Founder and fmr Pres. Vietnamese Nôm Preservation Foundation, currently Pres. Emer.; mem. American Literary Trans. Asscn (Pres. 1994–97); Chair. Nat. Endowment for the Arts Trans. Panel 1993–94. *Publications include:* Vietnam Poems 1970, Vietnamese Folk Poetry (ed. and trans.) 1974, After Our War (poems) 1974, Letters From Across the Sea (poems) 1978, Blue Mountain (poems) 1982, Coming Down Again (novel) 1985, The Hawk's Tale (children's fiction) 1988, Three Poems 1989, Vietnam: The Land We Never Knew 1989, Coming Down Again 1989,

Words for My Daughter (poems) 1991, Remembering Heaven's Face: A Story of Rescue in Wartime Vietnam (memoir) 2002, Vietnam: A Traveler's Literary Companion (ed. with Nguyen Qui Duc) 1996, Locusts at the Edge of Summer: New and Selected Poems and Translations 1997, Spring Essence: The Poetry of Ho Xuan Huong (ed. and trans.) 2000, Ca Dao Vietnam: A Bilingual Anthology of Vietnamese Folk Poetry (ed. and trans.) 2003, Path, Crooked Path 2006; contrib. to anthologies, books, scholarly journals and periodicals. *Honours:* Lamont Selection, Acad. of American Poets 1974, Fulbright-Hays Senior Lectureship in Romania 1976–77, Steaua Prize, Romanian Writers Union 1978, Nat. Endowment for the Arts Fellowships 1978, 1985, Vaptsarov Medal, Union of Bulgarian Writers 1980, Nat. Poetry Series Book Selection 1990, Pushcart Prize XV 1990, William Carlos Williams Award 1997, Guggenheim Fellowship 2003, named Nat. Artist for Phi Kappa Phi Honor Soc. 2001–04. *Address:* Department of English, North Carolina State University, Tompkins Hall 256, Box 8105, Raleigh, NC 27695 (office); The Vietnamese Nôm Preservation Foundation, 229 Beachers Brook Lane, Cary, NC 27511, USA (office). *Telephone:* (919) 515-4147 (office). *Fax:* (919) 515-1836 (office). *E-mail:* tbalaban@earthlink.net (office); jbalaba@ncsu.edu (office); balaban@johnbalaban.com. *Website:* www.ncsu.edu (office); www.nomfoundation.org (office); www.johnbalaban.com.

BALABANOV, Alexei O.; Russian film director, producer and scriptwriter; b. 25 Feb. 1959, Sverdlovsk. *Education:* Gorky State Pedagogical Inst. *Career:* asst dir Sverdlovsk Film Studio 1983–87; freelance 1987–; co-founder film co. STV. *Films:* dir: Yegor and Nastya 1989, From the History of Aerostatics in Russia 1990; dir and scriptwriter: Happy Days 1991, The Castle 1994, The Arrival of a Train 1995, Brother 1997, Of Freaks and Men 1998, Brother 2 2000, War (Voyna) (main prize Golden Rose 2002, film festival Kinotavr, Sochi) 2002, River (Reka) 2002, The American (Amerikanets) 2004, Blindman's-Buff (Zhmurki) 2005 (with S. Mokhnachev), It Doesn't Hurt Me (Mne ne bolno) (with S. Mokhnachev) 2006, Burden 200 (Gruz 200) 2007 (prize of the Russian Guild of Film Critics 2007, film festival Kinotavr, Sochi), Morfiy 2008; other: Secrets Shared with a Stranger (producer) 1994, Sergey Eisenstein (producer) 1995. *Honours:* Youth Film Festival Prize, Kiev 1991, Moscow Film Festival Debut Jury Prize 1992, Kinotaur Film Festival, Sochi, Jury Prize 1994 and Best Movie Prize 1997. *Address:* STV, Kamennoostrovskii prospect 10, St Petersburg 197101, Russia (office). *E-mail:* kino@ctb.ru (office). *Website:* www.ctb.ru (office).

BALCOMB, Mary Nelson, BFA, MFA; American painter/etcher and writer; b. 29 April 1928, Ontonagon, Mich.; m. Robert S. Balcomb 1948; one s. one d. *Education:* American Acad. of Art, Univ. of New Mexico, Univ. of Washington. *Career:* Founder-mem. Children's Arts Center Foundation Inc., Seattle; mem. Authors' Guild Inc., New York; contrib. American Artist and Southwest Art; etchings shown at Fine Impressions Gallery, Seattle, Amy Burnett Gallery, Bremerton, The Gallery, Bainbridge Island. *Exhibitions:* solo shows: Kansas Wesleyan Univ., Frye Art Museum, Nordic Heritage Museum, Seattle, Olympic Coll., Sidney, Blue Heron Art Galleries, Kitsap County. *Publications include:* Nicolai Fechin: Russian and American Artist 1975, Les Perhacs Sculptor 1978, William F. Reese: American Artist 1984, Robin-Robin: A Journal 1995, Sergei-Bongart: Russian American Artist 2002; contribs to periodicals. *Honours:* Frye Art Museum Seattle Painting Award 1994, Honorarium Prix de West, Western Heritage Museum, Oklahoma City. *Address:* 4981 NW Eldorado Boulevard, Bremerton, WA 98312-1121, USA (home). *Telephone:* (360) 692-3686 (home). *Website:* www.marynbalcomb.com.

BALDACCI, David, BA, JD; American writer; b. 1960, Richmond, Va; m. Michelle Baldacci; two c. *Education:* Virginia Commonwealth Univ., Univ. of Virginia. *Career:* Co-founder Wish You Well Foundation 2002, currently Bd mem.; also Nat. Amb. Nat. Multiple Sclerosis Soc.; associated with Barbara Bush Foundation for Family Literacy, American Cancer Soc., Cystic Fibrosis Foundation. *Publications include:* Absolute Power 1996, Total Control (Gold Medal Award, Southern Writers Guild) 1997, The Winner 1997, The Simple Truth 1998, Saving Faith 1999, Wish You Well 2000, Last Man Standing 2001, The Christmas Train, Split Second 2003, Hour Game, Hell's Corner, Office Hours, Freddy and the French Fries: Fries Alive! 2005, The Camel Club 2006, The Collectors 2006, Freddy and the French Fries: The Adventures of Silas Finklebean 2006, Simple Genius 2007, Stone Cold 2007, The Whole Truth 2008, Divine Justice 2008, First Family 2009, True Blue 2010, Deliver Us from Evil 2010, One Summer 2011, Zero Day 2011; contrib. to periodicals. *Honours:* WHSmith Thumping Good Read Award for Fiction 1997. *Literary Agent:* c/o Aaron Priest Literary Agency, 708 Third Avenue, New York, NY 10017, USA. *Website:* www.davidbaldacci.com.

BALDEOSINGH, Kevin, BA; Trinidad andTobago writer and journalist; b. 1963. *Education:* Univ. of the West Indies. *Career:* fmr teacher; fmr reporter, columnist and ed. for various newspapers in Trinidad and Tobago; Regional Chair. (Canada/Caribbean), Commonwealth Writers Prize 2000–01; Founding mem. Trinidad and Tobago Humanist Asscn; currently staff writer, Trinidad Express Newspapers. *Publications include:* novels: The Autobiography of Paras P 1996, Virgin's Triangle 1997, The Ten Incarnations of Adam Avatar 2005, Caribbean History for CSEC 2011; contrib. to Tobago Newsday, Weekend Independent. *Address:* #3 Ali Lane, Freeport Todds Road, Upper Carapichaima, Trinidad and Tobago, West Indies (home). *E-mail:* kbaldeosingh@hotmail.com. *Website:* www.humanist.org.tt (office).

BALESTRINI, Nanni; Italian poet, author and artist; b. 2 July 1935, Milan. *Career:* mem. group of poets called Novissimi and co-founder of Gruppo 63 in Palermo 1963; one of prin. eds of literary magazine Il Verri; co-editor (with Alfredo Giuliani) Quindici magazine 1966–68; has organized numerous confs and exhbns; also a figurative artist, exhibiting in many galleries in Italy and abroad, and at Venice Biennale in 1993. *Publications include:* poetry: Come si agisce 1963, Ma noi facciamone un'altra 1966, Le ballate della signorina Richmond 1977, Blackout 1980, Ipocalisse 1986, Il ritorno della signorina 1987, Osservazioni sul volo degli uccelli, poesie 1954–56 1988, The Unseen 1989, Il pubblico del labirinto 1992, Estremi rimedi 1995, Le avventure complete della signorina 1999, Elettra, operapoesia 2001, Sfinimondo 2003, Sconnessioni 2008, Blackout e altro 2009, Lo sventramento della storia 2009, Caosmogonia 2010; novels: Tristano 1964, Vogliamo tutto 1971, La violenza illustrata 1976, Gli invisibili 1987, L'editore 1989, I furiosi 1994, Una mattina ci siam svegliati 1995, La Grande Rivolta (comprising Vogliamo tutto, Gli invisibili, L'editore) 1999, Sandokan, storia di camorra 2004, Liberamilano seguito da Una mattina ci siam svegliati 2011; other works: Gruppo 63. Il romanzo sperimentale 1965, L'Opera di Pechino (with Letizia Paolozzi) 1966, L'orda d'oro (with Primo Moroni) 1988, Paladino 2002, Parma 1922 (radio drama) 2002, Con gli occhi del linguaggio 2006, Les yeux invisibles 2008, Qualcosaper tutti 2010; contrib. to many periodicals and journals. *E-mail:* info@nannibalestrini.it (office). *Website:* www.nannibalestrini.it (office).

BALL, Brian Neville, BA, MA; British writer; b. 19 June 1932, Cheshire. *Education:* Univ. of London, Univ. of Sheffield. *Career:* Staff mem. to Sr Lecturer in English, Doncaster Coll. of Educ. 1965–81. *Publications include:* Mr Tofat's Term 1964, Tales of Science Fiction (ed) 1964, Escape Velocity (short stories) 1964, Sundog 1965, Basic Linguistics for Secondary Schools, 3 vols 1966–67, Paris adventure 1967, Timepiece 1968, Timepivot 1970, Lay Down Your Wife for Another 1971, Timepit 1971, Lesson for the Damned 1971, Devil's Peak 1972, Night of the Robots (in the USA as The Regiments of Night) 1972, The Probability Man 1972, Singularity Station 1973, Planet Probability 1973, The No-Option Contract 1975, The Venomous Serpent (in the USA as The Night Creature) 1974, Death of a Low-Handicap Man 1974, Montenegrin Gold 1974, Jackson's Friend 1975, Jackson's House 1975, Princess Priscilla 1975, Witchfinder: The Mark of the Beast 1976, The One-Way Deal 1976, Witchfinder: The Evil at Monteine 1977, Jackson's Holiday 1977, Jackson and the Magpies 1978, The Witch in Our Attic 1979, Young Person's Guide to UFOs 1979, Dennis and the Flying Saucer 1980, The Starbuggy 1983, The Baker Street Boys 1983, The Doomship of Drax 1985, Truant From Space 1985, Frog Island Summer 1987, The Quest for Queenie 1988, Stone Age Magic 1989, Magic on the Tide 1995, Malice of the Soul 2008, Death on the Driving Range 2009; contribs to anthologies, newspapers, radio, and television.

BALL, Philip, BA, PhD; British science writer and editor; *Science Writer-in-Residence, Department of Chemistry, University College, London*; b. 30 Oct. 1962, Newport, Isle of Wight; s. of David Ball and Jennifer Ball; m.; one d. *Education:* Univs of Oxford and Bristol. *Career:* Ed. for Physical Sciences, Nature magazine, later Consultant Ed., now writes for Nature's online news; has delivered lectures at various venues, including Victoria & Albert Museum, NASA, Ames Research Center, LSE; writes regularly for News@Nature; currently Science Writer-in-Residence, Dept of Chem., Univ. Coll., London; mem. European Comm. Expert Group on Synthetic Biology; mem. Advisory Council, Inst. of Advanced Study, Durham Univ. *Play:* Paracelsus the Great, London 2000. *Radio:* presenter, Small Worlds (three-part series on nano tech., BBC Radio 4). *Publications include:* Designing the Molecular World: Chemistry at the Frontier (Asscn of American Publishers Award) 1994, Made to Measure: New Materials for the 21st Century 1997, The Self-Made Tapestry: Pattern Formation in Nature 1998, H_2O: A Biography of Water (Premio Acqua Scrittura, Italy 2000) 1999, Life's Matrix 2000, Stories of the Invisible: A Guided Tour of Molecules 2001, Bright Earth: Art and the Invention of Colour (Soc. for the History of Tech. Sally Hacker Prize 2003) 2001, More Than Meets the Eye (V&A museum exhbn booklet) (Asscn of British Science Writers Award 2001) 2001, The Ingredients: A Guided Tour of the Elements 2002, Critical Mass: How One Thing Leads to Another (Aventis Prize 2005) 2004, The Devil's Doctor: Paracelsus and the World of Renaissance Magic and Science 2006, Elegant Solutions: Ten Beautiful Experiments in Chemistry (Dingle Prize, British Soc. for the History of Science 2007) 2006, The Sun and Moon Corrupted (novel) 2008, Universe of Stone 2008, Nature's Patterns 2009, Branches 2010, The Music Instinct 2010, Unnatural 2011; contrib. to journals, including Nature, Nature Materials, Journal of Materials Education, Chemistry in Britain, V&A Conservation Journal, Technology Review, Interdisciplinary Science, Physics World, Chemistry World, Angewandte Chemie Int. Edn, New Scientist, New York Times, Guardian, Financial Times, New Statesman. *Honours:* Hon. DSc (Union Coll., Schenectady, NY) 2003, Hon. DLit (Bristol) 2009; numerous prizes including Asscn of British Science Writers Award 2001, James T. Grady-James H. Stack Award, ACS 2006, Lagrange Prize, ISI and CRT Foundations, Italy 2008. *Address:* Department of Chemistry, University College, 20 Gordon Street, London, WC1H 0AJ (office); Nature, 4–6 Crinan Street, London, N1 9XW, England (office). *Telephone:* (20) 7679-1003 (office). *E-mail:* p.ball@nature.com (office). *Website:* www.ucl.ac.uk (office); www.philipball.com.

BALLE, Solvej; Danish writer; b. 16 Aug. 1962, S Jutland. *Education:* Univ. of Copenhagen, The Writer's School, Copenhagen. *Publications include:* Lyrefugl (novel) 1984, & (short prose) 1990, Ifølge loven (short stories) 1993, According to the Law 1993, Eller (prose poetry) 1998, Det umuliges kunst (essay) 2005, Frydendal 2008. *Address:* c/o Gyldendal, Klareboderne 3, 1001

Copenhagen K, Denmark. *E-mail:* gyldendal@gyldendal.dk. *Website:* www.gyldendal.dk.

BALMER, Josephine, BA, PhD; British poet, translator, literary critic and literary scholar; b. 1 June 1959, Hants., England; m. Paul Dunn 1982. *Education:* Univ. Coll. London, Univ. of East Anglia. *Career:* Reviews Ed., Modern Poetry in Translation; Chair., Translators' Asscn (UK) 2001–05; judge, Stephen Spender Prize for Poetry in Translation 2006–. *Publications include:* Sappho: Poems and Fragments 1984, 1988, 1992, Classical Women Poets 1996, Catullus: Poems of Love and Hate 2004, Chasing Catullus 2004, The Word for Sorrow 2009; books chapters in Living Classics: Greece and Rome in Contemporary Poetry in English 2009, The Translator as Writer 2006, Translation Right or Wrong 2012, Classical Receptions: Transgressions 2012; contribs to The Times, The Times Literary Supplement, The New Statesman, Modern Poetry in Translation, Women's Review, The Guardian, Independent on Sunday, The Observer, Agenda. *Honours:* Univ. Coll. London Platt Prize for Greek 1978, Lambda Literary Foundation Poetry Award (USA) 1988, Arts Council Write Out Loud Award 1994, Southeast Arts Writers Bursary 1997, Authors Foundation Award 1994, 2004, Wingate Foundation Scholarship 2004–05. *E-mail:* mail@jobalmer.fsnet.co.uk (office).

BALOGH, Mary, BA; Welsh/Canadian writer and teacher; b. 24 March 1944, Swansea, Wales; d. of Arthur Jenkins and Mildred Jenkins; m. Robert Balogh 1969; one s. two d. *Education:* Univ. of Wales. *Career:* English Teacher, Kipling High School, Sask., Canada 1967–82; Principal, English Teacher, Windthorst High School, Sask. 1982–88; mem. Sask. Writers' Guild. *Publications include:* fiction: A Masked Deception 1985, The Double Wager 1985, Red Rose 1985, A Chance Encounter 1986, The Trysting Place 1986, The First Snowdrop 1986, The Wood Nymph 1987, The Constant Heart 1987, Gentle Conquest 1987, Secrets of the Heart 1988, The Ungrateful Governess 1988, An Unacceptable Offer 1988, A Daring Masquerade 1989, A Gift of Daisies 1989, The Obedient Bride 1989, Lady with a Black Umbrella 1989, The Gilded Web 1989, A Promise of Spring 1990, Web of Love 1990, The Incurable Matchmaker 1990, Devil's Web 1990, An Unlikely Duchess 1990, A Certain Magic 1991, Snow Angel 1991, The Secret Pearl 1991, The Ideal Wife 1991, Christmas Beau 1991, The Counterfeit Betrothal 1992, The Notorious Rake 1992, A Christmas Promise 1992, Beyond the Sunrise 1992, A Precious Jewel 1993, Deceived 1993, Courting Julia 1993, Dancing with Clara 1994, Tangled 1994, Tempting Harriet 1994, Dark Angel 1994, A Christmas Belle 1994, Longing 1994, Lord Carew's Bride 1995, Heartless 1995, The Famous Heroine 1996, Truly 1996, The Plumed Bonnet 1996, Indiscreet 1997, Temporary Wife 1997, Silent Melody 1997, A Christmas Bride 1997, Unforgiven 1998, Thief of Dreams 1998, Irresistible 1998, The Last Waltz 1998, One Night for Love 1999, More than a Mistress 2000, No Man's Mistress 2001, A Summer to Remember 2002, Slightly Married 2003, Slightly Wicked 2003, Slightly Scandalous 2003, Slightly Tempted 2004, Slightly Sinful 2004, Slightly Dangerous 2004, Simply Unforgettable 2005, Simply Love 2006, Simply Magic 2007, Simply Perfect 2008, Devil's Web 2008, Ideal Wife 2008, First Comes Marriage 2009, Then Comes Seduction 2009, At Last Comes Love 2009, Seducing an Angel 2009, A Precious Jewel 2009, A Matter of Class 2009, A Matter of Class 2009, Bespelling Jane Austen 2010, Dark Angel/Lord Carew's Bride 2010, A Secret Affair 2010, A Christmas Promise 2010; novellas in collections including A Regency Christmas series; short stories: Full Moon Magic 1992, Tokens of Love 1993, Rakes and Rogues 1993, Moonlight Lovers 1993. *Honours:* Best New Regency Author Award 1985, Best Regency Author Award 1988, Career Achievement Award 1989, Best Regency Novel Award 1991, Best Regency Romance Award 1992, Career Achievement for Short Stories Award 1993, Romantic Times; Northern Lights Best Historical Novella Award 1996. *Literary Agent:* Maria Carvainis, 1350 Avenue of the Americas, New York, NY 10019, USA. *Address:* Box 571, Kipling, SK S0G 2S0 Canada (home). *Telephone:* (306) 736-2246 (home). *Fax:* (306) 736-2246 (home). *E-mail:* author@marybalogh.com. *Website:* www.marybalogh.com.

BANDA-AAKU, Ellen, BA, MA; Zambian writer; b. 1965, Woking, Surrey, England; two d. *Education:* Univ. of Zambia, Middlesex Univ., UK, Univ. of Cape Town, South Africa. *Career:* moved to Ghana 2000; fmr Asst Admin. Officer, Overseas Processing Entity (NGO), Accra, Ghana; has worked as a tutor in Literary Studies and as a Writing Consultant, Univ. of Cape Town. *Publications:* Wandi's Little Voice (Macmillan Writer's Prize for Africa 2004) 2004, Sozi's Box (winner, Commonwealth Short Story Competition 2007) 2007, Yours Faithfully Yogi 2008, Twelve Months 2010, Patchwork (novel) (Penguin Prize for African Writing 2010) 2011. *Address:* c/o Penguin Group (South Africa), 24 Sturdee Avenue, Rosebank, Johannesburg 2196, South Africa. *Website:* www.ellenbandaaaku.com.

BANDELE, Biyi; Nigerian playwright and novelist; b. 13 Oct. 1967, Kafanchan. *Education:* Obafemi Awolowo Univ., Ile-Ife. *Career:* Assoc. Writer, Royal Court Theatre, London; Writer-in-Residence, Talawa Theatre Co. 1994–95; also worked with Royal Shakespeare Co.; Resident Dramatist, Royal Nat. Theatre Studio 1996; Judith E. Wilson Fellow, Churchill Coll., Cambridge 2000–02; Royal Literary Fund Resident Playwright, Bush Theatre 2002–03; mem. Soc. of Authors, Writers' Guild, PEN. *Publications include:* fiction: The Man Who Came in from the Back of Beyond 1991, The Sympathetic Undertaker and Other Dreams 1991, The Street 1999, Burma Boy 2007, The King's Rifle 2009; plays: Rain (Int. Student Playscript Competition Award) 1991, Marching for Fausa 1993, Two Horsemen 1994, Resurrections in the Season of the Longest Drought 1994, Death Catches the Hunter and Me and the Boys 1995, Things Fall Apart 1997, Oroonoko (Ethnic and Multicultural Media Award 2000) 1999, Thieves Like Us 1998, Happy Birthday Mister Deka 1999; screenplays: Not Even God Is Wise Enough 1993, Bad Boy Blues 1996. *Honours:* British Council Lagos Award 1989–90, Commonwealth Prize, Black Young Writers Competition, London New Play Festival Award 1994, Wingate Scholarship Award 1995, Peggy Ramsay Award 1998. *Literary Agent:* The Wylie Agency (UK) Ltd, 17 Bedford Square, London, WC1B 3JA, England. *Telephone:* (20) 7908-5900. *Fax:* (20) 7908-5901. *E-mail:* mail@wylieagency.co.uk. *Website:* www.wylieagency.co.uk. *Address:* c/o Jonathan Cape Ltd, Random House (UK) Ltd, 20 Vauxhall Bridge Road, London, SW1V 2SA, England. *Telephone:* (20) 7840-8579. *Fax:* (20) 7932-0077. *Website:* www.randomhouse.co.uk.

BANERJEE DIVAKARUNI, Chitralekha (Chitra), BA, MA, PhD; Indian/American author, poet and teacher; *Betty and Gene McDavid Professor of Writing, Creative Writing Program, University of Houston*; b. 1956, Kolkata, India; m. Murthy Divakaruni; two s. *Education:* Univ. of Calcutta, Wright State Univ., USA, Univ. of California, Berkeley. *Career:* fmr teacher, Foothill Coll., Los Altos, Calif. and Diablo Valley Coll.; currently Betty and Gene McDavid Prof. of Writing, Creative Writing Program, Univ. of Houston; author for adults and children; books translated into nearly 30 languages; contrib. to numerous journals; Co-founder and Bd mem. Maitri (helpline for S Asian women dealing with domestic abuse) 1991– (fmr Pres.). *Publications:* poetry: The Reason for Nasturtiums 1990, Black Candle 1991, Leaving Yuba City 1997; short stories: Arranged Marriage (American Book Award 1995) 1995, The Unknown Errors of our Lives 2001; novels: The Mistress of Spices 1997, Sister of My Heart 1999, Neela: Victory Song 2002, The Vine of Desire 2002, The Conch Bearer 2003, Queen of Dreams 2004, The Mirror of Fire and Dreaming 2005, The Palace of Illusions 2008, Shadowland 2009, One Amazing Thing 2010. *Honours:* Allen Ginsberg Poetry Prize 1997, Pushcart Prize 1997, 2003, S Asian Literary Asscn Distinguished Writer Award 2007, Int. House Alumna of the Year Award, Univ. of California, Berkeley 2008, Indian Culture Center Cultural Jewel Award, Houston 2009, Light of India Jury's Award for Journalism and Literature 2011. *Literary Agent:* c/o Sandra Dijkstra, Dijkstra Agency, 1155 Camino del Mar, PMB 515, Del Mar, CA 92014, USA. *Telephone:* (858) 755-3115. *E-mail:* sandy@dijkstraagency.com. *Website:* www.dijkstraagency.com. *Address:* c/o The Creative Writing Program, Department of English, College of Liberal Arts and Social Sciences, University of Houston, 229 Roy Cullen Building, Houston, TX 77204-5008, USA (office). *Telephone:* (713) 743-2967 (office). *E-mail:* chitradivakaruni@hotmail.com (home). *Website:* www.uh.edu (office); www.chitradivakaruni.com (home).

BANERJI, Sara Ann; British writer; *Lecturer in Creative Writing, Department of Continuing Education, University of Oxford*; b. 6 June 1932, Bucks., England; d. of Sir Basil Mostyn and Anita Mostyn; m. Ranjit Banerji 1951; three d. *Education:* schools and convents in UK and Southern Rhodesia (now Zimbabwe). *Career:* fmr teacher, jockey, waitress, gardener and riding instructor; currently Lecturer in Creative Writing, Dept of Continuing Educ., Univ. of Oxford. *Publications include:* Cobwebwalking 1987, The Wedding of Jayanthi Mandel 1988, The Teaplanter's Daughter 1989, Shining Agnes 1990, Absolute Hush 1991, Writing on Skin 1993, Shining Hero 2002, The Waiting Time 2005, Blood Precious 2007. *Honours:* Arts Council Award for Literature, Write Out Loud Award (for radio writing). *Literary Agent:* c/o United Agents, 12–26 Lexington Street, London, W1F 0LE, England. *Telephone:* (20) 3214-0800. *Fax:* (20) 3214-0801. *E-mail:* info@unitedagents.co.uk. *Website:* unitedagents.co.uk; www.banerji.info; www.myspace.com/ladyacs.

BANFIELD, Stephen David, BA, DPhil, FRCO; British academic and writer; *Stanley Hugh Badock Professor of Music, University of Bristol*; b. 15 July 1951, Dulwich, London. *Education:* Clare Coll., Cambridge, Harvard Univ., USA, St John's Coll., Oxford. *Career:* Lecturer, Univ. of Keele 1978–88, Sr Lecturer 1988–92; Elgar Prof. of Music, Univ. of Birmingham 1992–2003, Head, School of Performance Studies 1992–97, Head, Dept of Music 1996–98; Visiting Prof. of Musicology, Univ. of Minnesota, USA 1998; Stanley Hugh Badock Prof. of Music, Univ. of Bristol 2003–; Hon. Prin. Fellow, Univ. of Melbourne 2007–; Vice-Pres. British Music Soc.; mem. American Musicological Soc., Royal Musical Asscn, Kurt Weill Foundation. *Publications include:* Sensibility and English Song 1985, Sondheim's Broadway Musicals 1993, The Blackwell History of Music in Britain, Vol. VI: The Twentieth Century (ed.) 1995, Gerald Finzi 1997, Jerome Kern 2006, The Sounds of Stonehenge 2009, Music and the Wesleys 2010; contribs to scholarly books and journals. *Honours:* First Kurt Weill Prize, USA, Irving Lowens Award, USA 1995. *Address:* Department of Music, University of Bristol, Victoria Rooms, Queens Road, Bristol, BS8 1SA, England (office). *Telephone:* (117) 954-5045 (office). *Fax:* (117) 954-5027 (office). *E-mail:* s.d.banfield@bristol.ac.uk (office). *Website:* www.bris.ac.uk/music (office).

BANKS, Brian Robert; British teacher, writer and poet; b. 4 Oct. 1956, Carshalton, Surrey; m.; two s. two d. *Education:* Westminster Coll., Middlesex Polytechnic, Worthing Coll. *Publications include:* The Image of J-K Huysmans 1990, Phantoms of the Belle Epoque 1993, Atmosphere and Attitudes 1993, Trajectory of a Comet: S. Przybyszewski, Muse & Messiah–Life, Imagination and Legacy of Bruno Schulz 2006, Pilgrim of the Absolute: Stefan Zechowski 2010; contribs to journals worldwide including Teksty Drugie, Discover Poland, BookWorld, Wormwood, R2, Golden Dawn, Aklo. *Address:* c/o Inkermen Press, Loughborough, England. *E-mail:* durtal51@hotmail.com.

BANKS, Iain Menzies, BA; British writer; b. 16 Feb. 1954, Fife, Scotland. *Education:* Univ. of Stirling. *Career:* worked as technician, British Steel 1976, IBM, Greenock 1978; writes fiction as Iain Banks and science fiction as Iain M. Banks. *Publications:* as Iain Banks: The Wasp Factory 1984, Walking on Glass 1985, The Bridge 1986, Espedair Street 1987, Canal Dreams 1989, The Crow Road 1992, Complicity 1993, Whit 1995, A Song of Stone 1997, The Business 1999, Dead Air 2002, Raw Spirit: In Search of the Perfect Dram (non-fiction) 2003, The Steep Approach to Garbadale 2007, Transition 2009; as Iain M. Banks: Consider Phlebas 1987, The Player of Games 1988, The State of the Art 1989, Use of Weapons 1990, Against a Dark Background 1993, Feersum Endjinn 1994, Excession 1996, Inversions 1998, Look to Windward 2000, The Algebraist 2004, Matter 2008, Surface Detail 2010. *Honours:* Hon. DUniv (Stirling) 1997, (St Andrews) 1997, (Middlesex) 2009, (Open Univ.) 2010; Hon. DLitt (Napier) 2003, (Glasgow) 2005; British Science Fiction Asscn Best Novel 1997. *Literary Agent:* c/o Ms Mic Cheetham, Mic Cheetham Literary Agency, 50 Albemarle Street, London, W1S 4BD, England. *Telephone:* (20) 7495-2002. *Fax:* (20) 7399-2801. *E-mail:* info@miccheetham.com. *Website:* www.miccheetham.com. *Address:* c/o Publicity Department, Time Warner Books UK, Brettenham House, Lancaster Place, London, WC2E 7EN, England. *Telephone:* (20) 7911-8000. *Fax:* (20) 7911-8100. *E-mail:* mail@iain-banks.net. *Website:* www.iain-banks.net.

BANKS, Lynne Reid; British writer; b. (Belinda Gillian Reid Banks), 31 July 1929, London; d. of James Reid Banks and Pat Reid Banks; m. Chaim Stephenson 1965; three s. *Education:* Royal Acad. of Dramatic Art, London. *Career:* stage career 1949–54; freelance journalist 1954–55; TV news reporter (first woman in UK), Independent TV News (ITN) 1955–62; taught English as a foreign language in Israel 1962–71; writer, playwright and journalist 1971–. *Plays:* It Never Rains, and others. *Films:* The L-Shaped Room 1961, The Indian in the Cupboard 1995. *Television plays:* Last Word on Julie, The Eye of the Beholder and others. *Radio:* Lame Duck, Purely from Principle and others. *Publications include:* 40 published books: The L-Shaped Room (film 1962) 1960, An End to Running 1962, Children at the Gate 1968, The Backward Shadow 1970, One More River (juvenile) 1973, Two Is Lonely 1974, Sarah and After: The Matriarchs 1975, The Adventures of King Midas 1976, Dark Quartet: the story of the Brontës (Yorkshire Arts Literature Award 1977) 1976, The Farthest-Away Mountain 1976, Path to the Silent Country: Charlotte Brontë's Years of Fame 1977, My Darling Villain 1977, I, Houdini 1978, Letters to My Israeli Sons (history) 1979, The Indian in the Cupboard (numerous children's book awards, USA, made into feature film, released 1995) 1980, Torn Country: An Oral History of the Israeli War of Independence 1980, Defy the Wilderness 1981, The Writing on the Wall 1981, Return of the Indian 1982, Maura's Angel 1984, The Warning Bell 1984, Secret of the Indian 1985, The Fairy Rebel 1985, Casualties 1986, Melusine, A Mystery 1988, The Magic Hare 1991, Travels of Yoshi and the Tea-Kettle (children's play) 1991, The Mystery of the Cupboard 1993, Broken Bridge 1994, Key to the Indian 1996, Harry the Poisonous Centipede 1997, Angela and Diabola 1997, Moses in Egypt 1998, Fair Exchange (for adults) 1999, Alice-by-Accident 2000, Harry the Poisonous Centipede's Big Adventure 2000, The Dungeon 2002, Stealing Stacey 2004, Tiger, Tiger 2004, Harry the Poisonous Centipede Goes to Sea 2005, Bad Cat, Good Cat 2011; several picture-books with son Omri Stephenson, works translated into 20 languages; plays, anthologies, short stories; other: An L-Shaped Life (autobiog.) 2009; contrib. articles to newspapers including The Times, The Sunday Telegraph, The Guardian, Observer, Times Literary and Educational Supplements, The Independent, Saga Magazine, The Oldie. *Honours:* awards for children's literature (Australia, Italy and USA), Smarties Prize, UK . *Literary Agent:* Abner Stein, 10 Roland Gardens, London, SW10 3PH, England. *Telephone:* (20) 7373-0456. *E-mail:* lynne.stephenson@ukgateway.net (office). *Website:* www.lynnereidbanks.com (office).

BANKS, Russell, BA; American writer; b. 28 March 1940, Barnstead, NH; s. of Earl Banks and Florence Banks; m. 1st Darlene Bennett (divorced 1962); one d.; m. 2nd Mary Gunst (divorced 1977); three d.; m. 3rd Kathy Walton (divorced 1988); m. 4th Chase Twichell. *Education:* Colgate Univ. and Univ. of North Carolina. *Career:* fmr teacher of creative writing at Emerson Coll. Boston, Univ. of NH at Durham, Univ. of Ala, New England Coll.; teacher of creative writing, Princeton Univ. 1982–97; Pres. Parl. Int. des Écrivains 2001–. *Publications include:* poetry: Waiting to Freeze 1967, 30/6 1969, Snow: Meditations of a Cautious Man in Winter 1974; novels: Family Life 1975, Hamilton Stark 1978, The Book of Jamaica 1980, The Relation of My Imprisonment 1984, Continental Drift 1985, Affliction 1989, The Sweet Hereafter 1991, Rule of the Bone 1995, Cloudsplitter 1998, The Angel on the Roof 2000, The Darling 2004, The Reserve 2008, Outer Banks 2008, Lost Memory of Skin 2011; collected short stories: Searching for Survivors 1975, The New World 1978, Trailerpark 1981, Success Stories 1986; contrib. short stories to magazines and periodicals, including New York Times Book Review, Washington Post, American Review, Vanity Fair, Antaeus, Partisan Review, New England Review, Fiction International, Boston Globe Magazine. *Honours:* Best American Short Stories Awards 1971, 1985, Fels Award for Fiction 1974, O. Henry Awards 1975, St Lawrence Award for Fiction 1976, Guggenheim Fellowship 1976, Nat. Endowment for the Arts Fellowships 1977, 1983, John Dos Passos Award 1985, American Acad. of Arts and Letters Award 1985. *Literary Agent:* Steven Barclay Agency, 12 Western Avenue, Petaluma, CA 94952, USA. *Telephone:* (707) 773-0654. *Fax:* (707) 778-1868. *Website:* www.barclayagency.com. *Address:* 1000 Park Avenue, New York, NY 10028, USA.

BANNERMAN, Mark (see Lewing, Anthony Charles)

BANNISTER, Jo; British writer; b. 31 July 1951, Rochdale; d. of Alan Bannister and Marjorie Bannister. *Education:* studied in Birmingham, Nottingham, Bangor, Northern Ireland. *Career:* fmr Ed. County Down Spectator; mem. Soc. of Authors, Crime Writers Asscn. *Publications include:* The Matrix 1981, The Winter Plain 1982, A Cactus Garden 1983, Striving With Gods (revised edn as An Unknown Death) 1984, Mosaic 1987, The Mason Codex 1988, Gilgamesh 1989, The Going Down of the Sun 1989, Shards (revised edn as Critical Angle) 1990, Death and Other Lovers 1991, A Bleeding of Innocents 1993, Sins of the Heart (aka Charisma) 1994, A Taste for Burning 1995, The Lazarus Hotel 1996, No Birds Sing 1996, The Primrose Convention 1997, Broken Lines 1999, The Hireling's Tale 1999, Changelings 2000, The Primrose Switchback 2000, Echoes of Lies 2001, True Witness 2002, Reflections 2003, The Depths of Solitude 2004, Breaking Faith 2005, The Fifth Cataract 2005, Requiem for a Dealer 2006, The Tinderbox 2006, From Fire and Flood 2007, Flawed 2007, Fathers and Sins 2008, Closer Still 2008, Liars All 2009, Death in High Places 2011. *Honours:* British Press Award 1976, NI Press Award 1982, Ellery Queen Readers Award 1994, Mary Higgins Clark Award 2006. *Literary Agent:* c/o Jane Gregory, Gregory & Company Authors' Agents, 3 Barb Mews, Hammersmith, London, W6 7PA, England. *Telephone:* (20) 7610-4676. *E-mail:* info@gregoryandcompany.co.uk. *Website:* www.gregoryandcompany.co.uk.

BANTOCK, Gavin Marcus August, BA, DipEd, MA; British poet, writer and stage director; *Director, Meitoku International Players*; b. 4 July 1939, Barnt Green, Worcs.; s. of Raymond Bantock and Margaret More; m. Kyoko Oshima 1976. *Education:* Univ. of Oxford. *Career:* educator in British schools 1964–69; faculty mem. Dept of English, Reitaku Univ., Chiba-ken, Japan 1969–94; currently Dir Meitoku Int. Players, Meitoku Gikuku Acad., Kochi-ken, Japan. *Publications include:* Christ: A Poem in Twenty-Six Parts 1965, Juggernaut: Selected Poems 1968, A New Thing Breathing 1969, Anhaga 1970, Gleeman 1972, Eirenikon 1973, Isles 1974, Dragons 1979, Just Think of It 2002, Floating World 2002, SeaManShip 2003; essay collections; contribs to anthologies and numerous magazines. *Honours:* Richard Hillary Memorial Prize 1964, Alice-Hunt-Bartlett Prize 1966, Eric Gregory Award 1969, Arvon Foundation Prize 1998, Cardiff Int. Poetry Prize 1999. *Address:* c/o Peter Jay, Anvil Press Poetry, 69 King George Street, London, SE10 8PX, England (office). *E-mail:* gb@gol.com (office). *Website:* web.me.com/gavinbantock.

BANVILLE, John; Irish writer; b. 8 Dec. 1945, Wexford; m. Janet Dunham; two s. *Education:* St Peter's Coll., Wexford. *Career:* fmrly night copy ed., The Irish Times, Literary Ed. 1988–99, Chief Literary Critic and Assoc. Literary Ed. 1999–2002. *Film script:* The Last September 1998. *Plays:* The Broken Jug (after Kleist) 1994, God's Gift (after Kleist's 'Amphitryon') 2000. *Publications include:* novels: Nightspawn 1971, Birchwood 1973, Dr Copernicus 1976, Kepler 1983, The Newton Letter 1985, Mefisto 1987, The Book of Evidence (Guinness Peat Aviation Prize 1989) 1989, Ghosts 1993, Athena 1995, The Untouchable 1996, Eclipse 2000, Shroud 2003, The Sea (Man Booker Prize, Irish Novel of the Year) 2005, The Infinities 2009; as Benjamin Black: Christine Falls 2006, The Silver Swan 2007, The Lemur 2008, Elegy for April 2010, A Death in Summer 2011, Ancient Light 2012; non-fiction: Prague Pictures: Portraits of a City 2003; short stories: Imagined Lives: Portraits of Unknown People 2011; contribs to New York Review of Books, Irish Times, Guardian, New Republic. *Honours:* Lannan Foundation Award 1998, Franz Kafka Prize 2011. *Literary Agent:* c/o Ed Victor Ltd, 6 Bayley Street, Bedford Square, London, WC1B 3HE, England. *Telephone:* (20) 7304-4100. *Fax:* (20) 7304-4111.

BAPTISTE, Eric; French radio executive and writer; *CEO, Society of Composers, Authors and Music Publishers of Canada*. *Education:* Institut d'Études Politiques, École nationale d'administration. *Career:* Gen. Man., Radio France Int. 1990–95; Exec. Pres. Musiques France Plus 1995–98; CEO Radio 95.2 Paris 1996–98; Vice-Pres., Radio Néo; Dir-Gen., Int. Confed. of Socs of Authors and Composers (CISAC) 1999–2010; CEO Society of Composers, Authors and Music Publrs of Canada (SOCAN) 2010–; Chair. Vive la Radio asscn 1994–98, of govt think tank on digital convergence 2001–02. *Publications include:* Rapport sur les relations entre les diffuseurs télévisuels et les producteurs cinématographiques et audiovisuels 1989, L'infosphère: stratégies des médias et rôle de l'État 2000. *Honours:* Chevalier, Ordre des Arts et des Lettres 2006. *Address:* Society of Composers, Authors and Music Publishers of Canada, 41 Valleybrook Drive, Toronto, ON M3B 2S6, Canada (office). *Website:* www.socan.ca (office).

BAQUET, Dean Paul; American journalist and editor; *Assistant Managing Editor and Washington Bureau Chief, New York Times*; b. 21 Sept. 1956, New Orleans; s. of Edward Joseph Baquet and Myrtle Baquet (née Romano); m. Dylan Landis 1986; one s. *Education:* Columbia Univ., New York. *Career:* investigative reporter, New Orleans 1978–84; investigative reporter, Chicago Tribune 1984–87, Chief Investigative Reporter 1987–90; investigative reporter, New York Times 1990–92, Projects Ed. 1992–95, Deputy Metropolitan Ed. 1995, Nat. Ed. 1995–2000, Asst Man. Ed. and Washington Bureau Chief 2007–; Man. Ed. Los Angeles Times 2000–05, Ed. 2005–06; mem. Bd of Dirs Cttee to Protect Journalists. *Honours:* Pulitzer Prize for Investigative Reporting 1988. *Address:* New York Times, 1627 Eye Street, NW, 7th Floor, Washington, DC 20006, USA (office). *Telephone:* (202) 862-0300 (office). *Fax:* (202) 862-0340 (office). *Website:* www.nytimes.com (office).

BARAKA, Amiri; American writer and poet; *Professor Emeritus, State University of New York*; b. (Everett LeRoi Jones), 7 Oct. 1934, Newark, NJ; m. 1st Hettie Cohen 1958 (divorced 1965); m. 2nd Amina Baraka 1966; five c. *Education:* Rutgers, Howard and Columbia Univs, New School for Social Research. *Career:* served in USAF 1954–57; settled in New York in late 1950s; f. Totem Press 1958; mem. Black Arts Movement, f. Black Arts Repertory Theatre/School 1964; f. Spirithouse (arts and cultural org.), Newark; Asst Prof. of African Studies, State Univ. of New York 1980–82, Assoc. Prof. 1983–84, Prof. 1985–2000, Prof. Emer. 2000–; Poet Laureate of New Jersey 1999–2001; Chair. Cttee for Unified Newark 1968–75; Founder and fmr Sec.-Gen. Nat. Black Political Ass.; fmr Chair. Congress of African People; co-ed. (with Diane Di Prima) The Floating Bear (literary newsletter). *Plays:* The Slave 1962, The Toilet 1962, The Dutchman and the Slave (Obie Award) 1964, The Baptism and the Toilet 1967, Arm Yrself or Harm Yrself 1967, Home on the Range 1968, Police 1968, The Death of Malcolm X 1969, Rockgroup 1969, Four Black Revolutionary Plays 1969, Junkies are Full of SHHH 1970, Jello 1970, BA-RA-KA 1972, Black Power Chant 1972, The Motion of History and Other Plays 1978, The Sidney Poet Heroical, in 29 Scenes 1979, General Hag's Skeezag 1992, Slave Ship. *Publications include:* poetry: Preface to a Twenty Volume Suicide Note 1961, The Dead Lecturer 1964, Black Art 1969, Black Magic 1969, In Our Terribleness 1970, It's Nation Time 1970, Spirit Reach 1972, Hard Facts 1975, Poetry for the Advanced 1979, reggae or not! 1981, Confirmation: An Anthology of African-American Women (ed) (American Book Award, Before Columbus Foundation) 1983, Transbluesency: The Selected Poems of Amiri Baraka/LeRoi Jones 1995, Wise Why's Y's: The Griot's Tale 1995, Funk Lore: New Poems 1996, Somebody Blew Up America 2003; essays: Blues People: Negro Music in White America 1963, Home: Social Essays 1966, Raise Race Rays Raize: Essays Since 1965 1971, Black Fire: An Anthology of Afro-American Writing (ed) 1968, Daggers and Javelins: Essays 1974–1979 1984, The Music: Reflections on Jazz and Blues 1987, Jesse Jackson and Black People 1996, You Ever Hear Albert Ayler?, Black Reconstruction: DuBois and the US Struggle for Democracy and Socialism, The Essence of Reparations 2003, Tales of the Out and the Gone 2006; novels: The System of Dante's Hell 1965, Tales 1967; other: The Autobiography of Leroi Jones 1984. *Honours:* PEN/Faulkner Award, Rockefeller Foundation Award for Drama, American Book Award, Langston Hughes Award, Before Columbus Foundation Lifetime Achievement Award, Guggenheim Foundation Fellowship. *Literary Agent:* Celeste Bateman and Associates, PO Box 4071, Newark, NJ 07114-4071, USA. *Telephone:* (973) 705-8253. *E-mail:* celestebateman@aol.com. *Website:* www.celestebateman.com; www.amiribaraka.com.

BARAKAT, Hoda, BA; Lebanese/French writer and journalist; b. 1952, Beirut; m.; two c. *Education:* Lebanese Univ., Beirut. *Career:* worked as teacher and journalist during civil war; worked at Center for Lebanese Research, Beirut 1985–86; moved to Paris, France 1989. *Plays:* Viva la Diva 2009, The Last Quart of The Night 2010. *Publications include:* Za'irat (short stories, Visitors) 1985, Hajar al-Dahik (The Stones of Laughter, novel) (Al-Naqid Award) 1990, Ahl el-Hawa (Disciples of Passion) 1993, Harith al-Miyah (The Tiller of Waters, novel) (Naguib Mahfouz Award 2000) 1999, Sayyidi wa habibi (My Master and Beloved, novel) 2004, Stanger's Letters, Chroniques/Rassaïlou L'gharibah 2004, Malakoutou hazihi l'ard (The Kingdom of This Land, novel). *Honours:* Chevalier, Ordre des Arts et des Lettres 2001, Chevalier, Ordre du Mérite 2004; numerous literary prizes. *Address:* 7 rue des Partants, 75020 Paris, France (home). *Telephone:* 9-51-72-85-10 (mobile) (home). *E-mail:* barakath@hotmail.fr (home).

BARAŃCZAK, Stanisław, PhD; Polish poet, translator, literary critic and academic; *Alfred Jurzykowski Professor of Polish Language and Literature, Harvard University;* b. 13 Nov. 1946, Poznań; m.; one s. one d. *Education:* Adam Mickiewicz Univ., Poznań. *Career:* on staff, Nurt magazine, Poznań 1967–71; Asst Lecturer, later Prof., Adam Mickiewicz Univ. 1969–80; Co-Founder Committee for the Defence of the Workers (and of clandestine quarterly Zapis) 1976; in the USA 1981–; Prof. of Slavic Languages and Literatures, Harvard Univ. 1981–84, Alfred Jurzykowski Prof. of Polish Language and Literature 1984–; Co-Founder and Co-Ed. Zeszyty Literackie, Paris 1983–; Assoc. Ed. The Polish Review 1986–87, Ed.-in-Chief 1987–90; mem. American Asscn for Polish-Jewish Studies, American Asscn for Advancement of Slavic Studies, PEN Polish Center, Polish Inst. of Arts and Sciences in America, Polish Writers' Asscn, Union of Polish Authors, Union of Polish Writers Abroad. *Publications:* poetry collections: Korekta twarzy (Face Correction) 1968, Jednym tchem (In One breath) 1970, Dziennik poranny (Morning Diary) 1972, Sztuczne oddychanie (Breathing Underwater) 1974, Ja wiem, że to niesłuszne (I know That It's Wrong) 1977, Atlantyda (Atlantis) 1986, Widokówka z tego świata (A Postcard from This World) 1988, The Weight of the Body 1989, Podróż zimowa (Winter Journey) 1994, Zimy i podroze (Winter and Journeys) 1997, Chirurgiczna precyzja (Surgical Precision) (Nike Prize 1999) 1998, Wiersze zebrane 2006; criticism includes: Ironia i Harmonia (Irony and Harmony) 1973, Etyka i poetyka (Ethics and Poetry) 1979, Przed i po (Before and After) 1988, Tablica z Macondo (Board from Macondo) 1990, Ocalone w tłumaczeniu (Saved in Translation) 1992, Fioletowa krowa (Violet Cow) 1993, Poezja i duch h uogólnienia. Wybor esejow 1970–1995 (Poetry and the Spirit of Generalization: Selected Essays) 1996; essays: Breathing Under Water and Other East European Essays 1990; numerous trans of English, American and Russian poetry and of William Shakespeare, including A Fugitive From Utopia: The Poetry of Zbigniew Herbert 1987, The Weight of the Body: Selected Poems 1989, Panorama der polnischen Literatur des 20. Jahrhunderts (in German) 1997, Polnische Lyrik aus 100 Jahren (in German) 1997; regular contrib. to Teksty Drugie. *Honours:* Chivalric Cross of the Order of Polonia Restituta 1991; Alfred Jurzykowski Foundation Literary Award 1980, Guggenheim Fellowship 1989, Terrence Des Pres Poetry Prize 1989, Special Diploma for Lifetime Achievement in Promoting Polish Culture Abroad, Polish Minister of Foreign Affairs 1993, Co-Winner PEN Best Trans. Award 1996, Award for Lifetime Achievement, Wrocław Silesius Poetry Awards 2009. *Address:* Department of Slavic Languages and Literatures, Barker Center 374, 12 Quincy Street, Cambridge, MA 02138, USA (office). *Telephone:* (617) 495-4065 (office). *Fax:* (617) 496-4466 (office). *E-mail:* abarancz@fas.harvard.edu (office). *Website:* www.fas.harvard.edu/~slavic (office).

BARBALET, Margaret, MA; Australian diplomatist and writer; b. Adelaide, SA; m. Jack Barbalet 1970 (divorced 1989); three s. *Education:* Univ. of Adelaide. *Career:* Historian, Adelaide Children's Hosp. 1973–74; Research Officer, Adelaide City Council 1973–75; Research Consultant, Commonwealth Schools Comm. 1984–88; mem. staff, Dept of Foreign Affairs and Trade 1990–2008, Second Sec., High Comm. in Kuala Lumpur 1996, posted to Abu Dhabi 2005–08; H.C. Coombs Creative Arts Fellow, ANU 1998; Harold White Fellow, Nat. Library of Australia 2001; mem. Australian Soc. of Authors, Seven Writers. *Publications include:* The Adelaide Children's Hospital 1975, Far From a Low Gutter Girl: The Forgotten World of State Wards 1983, Blood in the Rain (novel) 1986, Steel Beach (novel) 1988, Canberra Tales (short stories) 1988, The Wolf (children's book) (Human Rights Award 1993) 1991, Lady, Baby, Gypsy, Queen (novel) 1992, Paradise Hotel, The Presence of Angels (novel) 2001, Reflecting Canberra 2001, Reggie, Queen of the Street (children's book) 2003, Mouth to Mouth (short stories) 2009, The Rain Beginning (short stories) 2010. *Honours:* Australia Council Literature Grant, ACT Arts Fellowship 1999, ACT Literature Fellowship 2001, Australia Council Literature Grant 2002. *Address:* c/o Penguin Group, 250 Camberwell Road, Camberwell, Vic. 3124; c/o Publicity Department, Penguin Books, PO Box 701, Hawthorn, Vic. 3122, Australia. *Telephone:* (3) 9811-2400. *Fax:* (3) 9811-2620. *Website:* www.penguin.com.au.

BARBER, Elizabeth Jane Wayland, BA, PhD; American academic and writer; *Professor Emerita of Linguistics and Archaeology, Occidental College;* b. 2 Dec. 1940, Pasadena, Calif.; d. of Dr J. Harold Wayland and Virginia Wayland; m. Paul Thomas Barber 1965. *Education:* Bryn Mawr Coll., Yale Univ. *Career:* Research Assoc., Princeton Univ. 1968–69; Asst Prof., Occidental Coll., LA, Calif. 1970, then Assoc. Prof., Full Prof. of Linguistics and Archaeology –2007, Prof. Emer. 2007–; Consultant to Asia Foundation on Chinese machine translation project 1974; Lecturer, Archaeological Inst. of America, 1974–76, 1983–84, 1993–99, 2002–03; Lecturer, Phi Beta Kappa 2001–02; fmr Research Assoc., Cotsen Inst. of Archaeology, UCLA. *Dance theatre:* The Frog Princess, The Faerie Changeling, Legend of Rag Rock, Stoyan and Radka. *Publications include:* Archaeological Decipherment 1974, Prehistoric Textiles 1991, The Development of Cloth in the Neolithic and Bronze Ages 1991, Women's Work: The First 20,000 Years 1994, The Mummies of Ürümchi 1998, When They Severed Earth From Sky: How the Human Mind Shapes Myth 2005, The Dancing Goddesses 2012; contrib. to scholarly books and journals. *Honours:* Guggenheim Fellowship 1979–80, Davenport Book Prize, Costume Soc. of America, Breasted Prize in Ancient History, American Historical Asscn, Nat. Endowment for the Humanities and Wenner-Gren Fellowships. *E-mail:* barber@oxy.edu (office). *Website:* www.oxy.edu (office); elizabethwaylandbarber.com.

BARBER, Lionel, BA; British journalist; *Editor, Financial Times;* b. 1955, London; m.; two c. *Education:* Univ. of Oxford. *Career:* journalist, The Scotsman 1978–81; Business Corresp., The Times (London) 1981–85; Washington Corresp. and US Ed. Financial Times 1986–92, Brussels bureau chief 1992–98, News Ed. 1998–2000, Ed. Continental European Edn 2000–02, US Man. Ed. 2002–05, Ed. Financial Times 2005–; Visiting Fellow, European Univ. Inst., Florence, Italy 1996; mem. Bd of Dirs Int. Center for Journalists; mem. Bd of Trustees Tate Gallery; Woodrow Wilson Foundation Fellow 1991, Eliot-Winant Fellow, British-American-Canadian Foundation 1994; Laurence Stern Fellowship, Washington Post 1985. *Publications include:* Price of Truth: Story of the Reuters Millions (with John Lawrenson) 1984, Not With Honour: Inside the Westland Scandal (co-author) 1986, Britain and the New European Agenda 1998. *Address:* Financial Times, One Southwark Bridge, London, SE1 9HL, England (office). *Telephone:* (20) 7873-4222 (office). *Fax:* (20) 7873-3924 (office). *Website:* www.ft.com (office).

BARBER, Richard William, BA, MA, PhD; British publisher and writer; b. 30 Oct. 1941, Dunmow, Essex; m. Helen Tolson 1970; one s. one d. *Education:* Corpus Christi Coll., Cambridge. *Career:* f. The Boydell Press (later Boydell & Brewer Ltd) 1969, later group Man. Dir; mem. RSL, Royal Historical Soc., Soc. of Antiquaries. *Publications include:* Arthur of Albion 1961, Henry Plantagenet 1964, The Knight and Chivalry (Somerset Maugham Prize) 1972, The Figure of Arthur 1972, King Arthur: in Legend and History 1973, Edward Prince of Wales and Aquitaine 1976, Companion Guide to South West France 1977, Tournaments 1978, The Arthurian Legends 1979, Life and Campaigns of the Black Prince 1979, The Penguin Guide to Medieval Europe 1984, Fuller's Worthies 1987, The Worlds of John Aubrey 1988, Pilgrimages 1991, Myths and Legends of the British Isles (ed) 1998, Legends of Arthur 2000, The Holy Grail: Imagination and Belief 2004, The Holy Grail, The History of a Legend 2004, The Reign of Chivalry (second edn) 2005, A Strong Land & a Sturdy: England in the Middle Ages, King Arthur: Hero and Legend, King Arthur in Music, A Companion to World Mythology (co-author), The Devil's

Crown: Henry II, Richard I, John (co-author); contribs to Arthurian Literature. *Honours:* Somerset Maugham Award 1972, Times Higher Educational Supplement Book Award 1978. *Address:* Stangrove Hall, The Street, Alderton, Nr Woodbridge, Suffolk, IP12 3BL (office); Boydell & Brewer Ltd, Whitwell House, St Audry's Park Road, Melton, Woodbridge, IP12 1SY, England (office). *Telephone:* (1394) 610600 (office). *Fax:* (1394) 610316 (office). *Website:* www.boydellandbrewer.com (office).

BARBERY, Muriel, DEA; French writer; b. 28 May 1969, Casablanca, Morocco. *Education:* École Normale Supérieure de Fontenay-Saint-Cloud. *Career:* moved to France to study; taught philosophy in a lycée, Univ. de Bourgogne, and Inst. Universitaire de Formation des Maîtres (teacher training coll.), St Lô; lives in Japan. *Publications include:* Une Gourmandise (trans. as The Gourmet and Gourmet Rhapsody) (Bacchus-Bsn Prize) 2000, L'Élégance du Hérisson (trans. as The Elegance of the Hedgehog) (Prix des Libraires, Prix des Bibliothèques, Prix Georges Brassens, Prix Rotary Int.) 2006. *Address:* c/o Éditions Gallimard, 5 rue Sébastien-Bottin, 75328 Paris Cedex 07, France. *Telephone:* 1-49-54-42-00. *Fax:* 1-45-44-94-03. *Website:* www.gallimard.fr.

BARBOSA, Miguel; Portuguese writer, dramatist, poet and painter; b. 22 Nov. 1925, Lisbon. *Education:* Univ. of Lisbon. *Career:* mem. Accad. Internazionale Greci-Marino di Lettere, Arti e Scienze, Soc. of Portuguese Authors, Grupo de Arujos do Museu de Angueologia de Lisbon, da Umáe Brasileira de Escritos do Rio de Janeiro, Brazil; Second Sec., Institut de Sintra. *Publications include:* fiction: Jrineu do Morro 1972, Mulher Mancumba 1973, A Pileca no Poleiro 1976, As Confissoes de Um Cacador de Dinossauros 1981, Esta Louca Profissao de Escritor 1983, Cartas a Um Fogo-Fatuo 1985, O Grito de Silêncio Ferido 2007; poetry: Dans un Cri de Couleurs 1991, Um Gesto no Rosto da Utopia 1994, Prima del Verbo 1995, Mare di Illusioni Naufragate 1995, Preludio Poético de um Vagabundo da Madrugada 1996, Mouthfuls of Red Confetti and the Hunt for God's Skull 1996, O Teu Corpo na Minha Alma 1996, A Eternidade de Un Segundo de Amor 2002, A Ninha Amante Lisboa 2003, Apologia do Silêncio 2004; Chiça! Estou farto 2006; other: plays and short stories, contribs to various publs. *Honours:* several awards for art. *Address:* Rua Mateus Vicente de Oliveira, N° 14-2E, 2745-167, Queluz, Portugal (home). *Telephone:* (214) 367438 (home).

BARBOUR, Douglas Fleming, BA, MA, PhD; Canadian poet, writer and academic; *Professor Emeritus, Department of English and Film Studies, University of Alberta;* b. 21 March 1940, Winnipeg; s. of Harold D Barbour and E Phyllis; m. M. Sharon Nicoll 1966. *Education:* Acadia Univ., Dalhousie Univ., Queen's Univ., Kingston. *Career:* teacher, Alderwood Collegiate Inst. 1968–69; Asst Prof., Univ. of Alberta 1969–77, Assoc. Prof. 1977–82, Prof. of English and Film Studies 1982, currently Prof. Emer.; fmr Pres. League of Canadian Poets; mem. Asscn of Canadian Univ. Teachers. *Publications include:* poetry: Land Fall 1971, A Poem as Long as the Highway 1971, White 1972, Song Book 1973, He and She and 1974, Visions of My Grandfather 1977, Shore Lines 1979, Vision/Sounding 1980, The Pirates of Pen's Chance (with Stephen Scobie) 1981, The Harbingers 1984, Visible Visions: Selected Poems (Stephan Spehansson Award for Poetry) 1984, Canadian Poetry Chronicle 1985, Story for a Saskatchewan Night 1989, Fragmenting Body 2000, Breath Takes 2002, A Flame on the Spanish Stairs 2003, Continuations 2006; other: Worlds Out of Words: The Science Fiction Novels of Samuel R. Delany 1978, The Story So Far Five (ed) 1978, The Maple Laugh Forever: An Anthology of Canadian Comic Poetry (ed. with Stephen Scobie) 1981, Writing Right: New Poetry by Canadian Women (ed. with Marni Stanley) 1982, Three Times Five: Short Stories by Beverly Harris, Gloria Sawai, Fred Stenson (ed) 1983, Richard Sommer. Selected and New Poems (ed) 1983, Tesseracts 2 (ed. with Phyllis Gotlieb) 1987, Beyond Tish (ed) 1991, Carnivocal: A Celebration of Sound Poetry (ed) 1999, B. P. Nichol and His Works 1992, Daphne Marlatt and Her Works 1992, John Newlove and His Works 1992, Michael Ondaatje 1993, Lyric/Anti-lyric: Essays on Contemporary Poetry 2001, Transformations of Contemporary Canadian Poetry in English 2005. *Address:* 11655, 72 Avenue NW, Edmonton, AB T6G 0B9, Canada (home). *Telephone:* (780) 436-3320 (home).

BARBOUR, Ian Graeme, BD, PhD; American (b. British) physicist, theologian and academic; *Carleton Professor Emeritus, Department of Religion, Carleton College;* b. 5 Oct. 1923, Peking (now Beijing), (People's Repub. of) China; m. Deane Kern Barbour; four c. *Education:* Swarthmore Coll., Duke Univ., Univ. of Chicago, Yale Univ. *Career:* Asst Prof., Assoc. Prof. of Physics, Kalamazoo Coll. 1949–53; Asst Prof. of Physics, Assoc. Prof. of Religion, Carleton Coll., Northfield, Minn. 1955–73, Prof. of Religion 1974–86, Winifred and Atherton Bean Prof. of Science, Tech. and Soc. 1981–86, Carleton Prof. Emer., Dept of Religion 1986–; Lilly Visiting Prof. of Science, Theology and Human Values Purdue Univ. 1973–74; Gifford Lecturer Univ. of Aberdeen, Scotland 1989–91; mem. American Acad. of Religion, Soc. for Values in Higher Educ. *Publications:* Christianity and the Scientist 1960, Issues in Science and Religion 1966, Science and Religion: New Perspectives on the Dialogue (ed) 1968, Science and Secularity: The Ethics of Technology 1970, Earth Might Be Fair (ed) 1971, Western Man and Environmental Ethics (ed) 1972, Myths, Models and Paradigms 1974, Finite Resources and the Human Future (ed) 1976, Technology, Environment and Human Values 1980, Energy and American Values (co-author) 1982, Religion in an Age of Science (Gifford Lectures) 1990, Ethics in an Age of Technology 1993, Religion and Science: Historical and Contemporary Issues 1997, When Science Meets Religion 2000, Nature, Human Nature and God 2002; contribs to scientific and religious journals. *Honours:* Ford Faculty Fellowship 1953–54, Harbison Award for Distinguished Teaching, Danforth Foundation 1963–64, Guggenheim Fellowship 1967–68, Fulbright Fellowship 1967–68, ACLS Fellowship 1976–77, Nat. Endowment for the Humanities Fellowship 1976–77, Nat. Humanities Center Fellow 1980–81, American Acad. of Religion Book Award 1993, Templeton Prize for Progress in Religion 1999. *Address:* 301 West 7th St., Apt 1205, Northfield, MN 55057, USA (home). *E-mail:* ibarbour@carleton.edu (home).

BARCLAY, Linwood, BA; Canadian writer; b. 20 March 1955, New Haven, Conn., USA; m. Neetha Barclay; one s. one d. *Education:* Trent Univ., Peterborough, Ont. *Career:* moved from USA to Canada at aged three; spent early teen years helping run his family's cottage resort and trailer park; joined Peterborough Examiner aged 16; several editorial staff roles on Toronto Star 1981–93, humour columnist 1993–2008; full-time writer 2008–. *Publications include:* fiction: Bad Move 2004, Bad Guys 2005, Lone Wolf 2006, Stone Rain 2007, No Time For Goodbye 2007, Too Close to Home (Arthur Ellis Award) 2008, Fear the Worst 2009, Never Look Away 2010, Clouded Vision 2011, The Accident 2011; non-fiction: four books including Last Resort: Coming of Age in Cottage Country (memoir) 1996–2000. *Literary Agent:* The Helen Heller Agency Inc., 253 Eglinton Avenue West, Suite 202, Toronto, ON M4R 1B1, Canada. *Telephone:* (416) 489-0396. *E-mail:* info@helenhelleragency.com. *Website:* www.helenhelleragency.com. *E-mail:* linwoodbarclay@mac.com. *Website:* www.linwoodbarclay.com.

BARER, Burl; American writer; b. 8 Aug. 1947, Walla Walla, Wash.; m. Britt Johnsen 1974; one s. one d. *Education:* Univ. of Washington. *Career:* mem. Mystery Writers of America. *Radio:* Outlaw Radio 2007, True Crimes (In Cold Blog Detective Award 2009). *Films:* The Last Ride 1991. *Publications include:* Selections from the Holy Quran 1987, The Saint: A Complete History in Print, Radio, Film and Television (Edgar Award 1994) 1993, Man Overboard: The Counterfeit Resurrection of Phil Champagne 1994, The Saint 1997, Capture the Saint 1998, Murder In The Family 2000, Headlock 2000, Head Shot 2001, Body Count 2002, Broken Doll 2004, Mom Said Kill 2008, Fatal Beauty 2011; contrib. to books and periodicals. *Honours:* Edgar Award 1994. *E-mail:* burl@burlbarer.net (office). *Website:* www.adoraburl.typepad.com.

BARFOOT, Joan Louise, BA; Canadian novelist and journalist; b. 17 May 1946, Owen Sound, Ont.; d. of Robert Barfoot and Helen MacKinnon. *Education:* Univ. of Western Ontario. *Career:* reporter, Religion Ed. Windsor Star 1967–69; feature and news writer, Mirror Publications, Toronto 1969–73, Toronto Sunday Sun 1973–75; with London Free Press 1976–79, 1980–94; has taught both journalism and creative writing at Univ. of Western Ontario and creative writing through Humber Coll.; juror, Books in Canada First Novel Award 1987; mem. Writers' Union of Canada, PEN Canada. *Publications:* Abra 1978, Dancing in the Dark 1982, Duet for Three 1985, Family News 1989, Plain Jane 1992, Charlotte and Claudia Keeping in Touch 1994, Some Things About Flying 1997, Getting Over Edgar 1999, Critical Injuries 2001, Luck 2005, Exit Lines 2008. *Honours:* Books in Canada First Novel Award 1978, Marian Engel Award 1992. *E-mail:* jbarfoot@sympatico.ca (home). *Website:* www3.sympatico.ca/jbarfoot (home).

BARGHOUTI, Mourid; Palestinian poet; b. 8 July 1944, Deir Ghassanah, Israel; m. Radwa Ashour 1970; one s. *Education:* Univ. of Cairo. *Career:* emigrated to Egypt 1963; teacher, Kuwait 1971 and Egypt; Rep. Palestinian Liberation Org. (PLO), Budapest; journalist for Palestine Radio, Cairo and Beirut; returned to Palestine 1996. *Publications include:* poetry: The Palestinians, Qasa'id Al-Rasif 1980, Collected Works 1997, A Small Sun 2003, Muntasaf al-Lail (trans. as Midnight) 2005, Medianoche 2006, Midnight and Other Poems 2008, Transmission Interrupted (co-author) 2009, I Was Born There, I Was Born Here 2011; non-fiction: Ra'ytu Ramallah (trans. as I Saw Ramallah) (Naguib Mahfouz Award) 1997. *Honours:* Palestine Award for Poetry 2000. *E-mail:* tbohan@wylieagency.co.uk *Website:* www.mouridbarghouti.net.

BARICCO, Alessandro; Italian writer and playwright; b. 25 Jan. 1958, Turin. *Career:* music critic, La Repubblica; cultural correspondent, La Stampa; co-founder La Scuola Holden (narrative skills workshop) 1994; collaboration with French band, Air, to produce backing music for City 2003; Assoc. Fandango Libri Publishing House 2005–. *Television:* L'amore è un dardo 1993, Pickwick, del leggere e dello scrivere 1994, Totem. Letture, suoni, lezioni 1998–2001. *Plays:* Novecento 1994, Davila Roa 1996, Partita Spagnola 2003. *Film:* Lezione 21 2008. *Publications:* novels: Castelli di rabbia (trans. as Lands of Glass) (Premio Selezione Campiello, Prix Médicis étranger) 1991, Oceano Mare (trans. as Ocean Sea) (Premio Viareggio) 1993, Novecento. Un Monologo 1994, Seta (trans. as Silk) 1996, City 1999, Senza sangue (trans. as Without Blood) 2002, Omero, Iliade 2004, Questa Storia 2005; non-fiction: Il Genio in fuga 1988, L'anima di Hegel e le mucche del Wisconsin 1992, Barnum (collection of articles) 1995, Barnum 2 (collection of articles) 1998, Next 2002, I Barbari 2006. *Honours:* several literary prizes. *Address:* Fandango Libri, viale Gorizia 19, 00198, Rome, Italy (office); c/o Canongate Books, 14 High Street, Edinburgh, EH1 1TE, Scotland.

BARICH, Bill, BA; American writer; b. 23 Aug. 1943, Winona, Minn.; s. of Russell Barich and Lois Barich; pnr Imelda Healy. *Education:* Colgate Univ. *Career:* with US Peace Corps, Nigeria 1966–67; teacher, Somerset Hills School, NJ 1968–69; publicist, Alfred Knopf, New York 1971–75; staff writer, The New Yorker 1981–94; Adjunct Prof., Univ. of California, Berkeley 1988–89, 1999–; Fellow, Marin Co. Arts Council 1995; Literary Laureate, San Francisco Public Library 1998; scriptwriter, NYPD Blue, 20th Century

Fox 1999; mem. PEN. *Publications include:* Laughing in the Hills 1980, Travelling Light 1984, Hard to Be Good 1987, Big Dreams: Into the Heart of California 1994, Carson Valley 1997, Crazy for Rivers 1999, The Sporting Life 2000, A Fine Place to Daydream: Racehorses, Romance, and the Irish 2005, A Pint of Plain: Tradition, Change and the Fate of the Irish Pub 2009, Long Way Home: On the Trail of Steinbeck's America 2010; contribs to periodicals, magazines and journals. *Honours:* Guggenheim Fellowship 1985. *Literary Agent:* c/o Liz Darsanhoff, 236 West 26th Street, New York, NY 10001, USA. *E-mail:* barichbill@hotmail.com (home).

BARKER, Clive; British writer, dramatist and artist; b. 5 Oct. 1952, Liverpool. *Education:* Univ. of Liverpool. *Films:* as director: Salome 1973, The Forbidden 1978, Hellraiser 1987, Nightbreed 1990, Lord of Illusions 1995, Tortured Souls: Animae Damnatae 2011; as producer: Hellbound: Hellraiser II 1988, Hellraiser III: Hell on Earth 1992, Candyman 1992, Hellraiser: Bloodline 1996, Gods and Monsters 1998, The Plague 2006, The Midnight Meat Train 2008, Dread 2009; as writer: Rawhead Rex 1986, Transmutations 1987, Book of Blood 2008. *Publications include:* fiction: The Damnation Game 1985, The Inhuman Condition 1985, Lost Souls 1985, The Hellbound Heart 1986, Weaveworld 1987, Cabal 1988, Coming To Grief 1988, Whose Line Is It Anyway? 1988, The Great and Secret Show 1989, Imajica 1991, The Hellbound Heart 1991, On Amen's Shore 1992, The Thief of Always 1992, The Departed 1992, Hermione And The Moon 1992, Pidgin And Theresa 1993, Emerville 1994, Animal Life 1994, A Story With No Title, A Street With No Name 1995, Sacrament 1996, Chiliad 1997, Galilee 1998, The Essential Clive Barker 1999, Coldheart Canyon: A Hollywood Ghost Story 2001, Six Destinies 2001, The Wood On The Hill 2001, Abarat 2002, The Infernal Parade 2004, Abarat II: Days of Magic, Nights of War 2004, Jump Tribe 2005, Mr B Gone 2007, The Adventures of Mr. Maximillian Bacchus And His Travelling Circus 2009; poetry: Rare Flesh 2003; essays: The Painter, The Creature and The Father of Lies 2010; plays: Forms of Heaven: Three Plays 1996, Incarnations: Three Plays 1995. *Address:* c/o HarperCollins, 10 East 53rd Street, New York, NY 10022, USA. *E-mail:* philandsarah@clivebarker.info (office). *Website:* www.clivebarker.info.

BARKER, Dennis Malcolm; British journalist and author; b. 21 June 1929, Lowestoft, Suffolk; s. of George Walter Barker and Gertrude Edith Barker; m. Sarah Katherine Alwyn; one d. *Education:* Royal Grammar School, High Wycombe, Lowestoft Grammar School, Nat. Diploma in Journalism. *Career:* reporter and sub-ed., Suffolk Chronicle & Mercury, Ipswich 1947–48; reporter, feature writer, theatre and film critic, East Anglian Daily Times 1948–58; Ed. and Editorial Dir East Anglian Architecture & Building Review 1956–58; Estates and Property Ed. and theatre critic, Express & Star, Wolverhampton 1958–63; Midlands Corresp., The Guardian 1963–67, reporter, feature writer, columnist 1967–91; mem. Nat. Union of Journalists, Newspaper Press Fund, Writers' Guild of GB, Broadcasting Press Guild, Soc. of Authors. *Radio:* panellist, Stop the Week (BBC Radio 4) 1994–97. *Publications include:* fiction: Candidate of Promise 1969, The Scandalisers 1974, Winston Three Three Three 1987, Games with the General 2007, The Clients of Miss May 2008; non-fiction: Soldiering On (The People of the Forces Trilogy, Vol. I) 1981, One Man's Estate 1983, Parian Ware 1985, Ruling the Waves (The People of the Forces Trilogy, Vol. II) 1986, Guarding the Skies (The People of the Forces Trilogy, Vol. III) 1989, Fresh Start 1990, The Craft of the Media Interview 1998, How to Deal with the Media 2000, Seize the Day (contrib.) 2001, The Guardian Book of Obituaries (contrib.) 2003, Oxford Dictionary of National Biography (contrib.) 2004–, Tricks Journalists Play 2007; contrib. to BBC, Punch, The Guardian 1991–. *Address:* 67 Speldhurst Road, Chiswick, London, W4 1BY, England. *Telephone:* (20) 8994-5380.

BARKER, Elspeth; British writer; b. 16 Nov. 1940, Edinburgh; m. 1st George Granville Barker 1989 (deceased 1991); three s. two d.; m. 2nd Bill Troop 2007. *Education:* St Leonards School, Scotland; Univ. of Oxford. *Career:* tutor and lecturer in creative writing, Norwich School of Art 1992; Visiting Prof. of Fiction, Kansas State Univ., USA 1999. *Publications include:* O Caledonia 1991, Anthology of Loss 1997; short stories in various anthologies including New Writing 2000, A Distant Cry 2002, Dead Men Talking 2007, Dog Days: Selected Writings 2010; reviews and features in Independent on Sunday, Guardian, Harpers & Queen, TLS, LRB, Vogue, Big Issue, Sunday Times, Observer, Daily Mail, The Literary Review. *Honours:* David Higham Award, Scottish Arts Council Spring Book Award, Angel Literary Award, RSL Winifred Holtby Award, shortlisted for Whitbread First Novel Award 1991–92. *Address:* Bintry House, Itteringham, Aylsham, Norfolk, NR11 7AT, England (office). *E-mail:* elspethbarker2010@gmail.com (office).

BARKER, Howard, MA; British dramatist and poet; *Artistic Director, The Wrestling School*; b. 28 June 1946, London. *Education:* Univ. of Sussex. *Career:* resident dramatist, Open Space Theatre, London 1975; currently Artistic Dir The Wrestling School. *Radio:* plays: Henry V in two parts 1971, Herman, with Mille and Mick 1972, Scenes from an Execution 1984, Albertina, The Quick And The Dead 2004, The Road, The House, The Road 2006, Let Me 2006. *Television:* plays: Cows 1972, Mutinies 1974, The Chauffeur and the Lady 1974, Prowling Offensive 1975, Conrod, Heroes of Labour 1976, Credentials of a Sympathiser 1976, Pity in History 1984, The Blow, film 1985, Brutopia 1989. *Plays:* Cheek 1970, No One Was Saved 1970, Edward-the Final Days 1972, Alpha Alpha 1972, Rule Britannia 1973, My Sister and I 1973, Claw 1975, Stripwell 1975, Wax 1976, Fair Slaughter 1977, That Good Between Us 1977, Birth on a Hard Shoulder 1977, Downchild 1977, The Hang of the Gaol 1978, The Love of a Good Man 1978, The Loud Boy's Life 1980, Crimes in Hot Countries 1980 (also performed as Twice Dead), No End of Blame 1981, The Poor Man's Friend 1981, The Power of the Dog 1981, Victory 1983, A Passion in Six Days 1983, The Castle 1985, Women Beware Women 1986, The Possibilities 1986, The Bite of the Night 1986, The Europeans 1987, The Last Supper 1988, Rome 1989, Seven Lears 1989, Golgo 1989, (Uncle) Vanya, adaptation of Chekhov's Uncle Vanya 1991, Ten Dilemmas in the Life of a God 1992, Judith 1992, Ego in Arcadia 1992, A Hard Heart 1992, Minna, adaptation of Lessing's Minna von Barnhelm 1993, All He Fears, for marionettes 1993, The Early Hours of a Reviled Man, Stalingrad, 12 Encounters with a Prodigy, The Twelfth Battle of Isonzo, Found in the Ground, Hated Nightfall and Wounds to the Face 1995, The Gaoler's Ache for the Nearly Dead 1997, Ursula; Fear of the Estuary 1998, Und 1999, The Ecstatic Bible 2000, He Stumbled 2000, A House of Correction 2001, Gertrude-The Cry 2002, 13 Objects 2003, Dead Hands 2004, The Fence In Its Thousandth Year 2005, The Seduction of Almighty God by the Boy Priest Loftus in the Abbey of Calcetto 1539 2006, Christ's Dog 2006, I Saw Myself 2008, The Dying of Today 2008, A Wounded Knife 2009. *Publications include:* poetry: Don't Exaggerate, The Breath of the Crowd, Gary the Thief, Lullabies for the Impatient, The Ascent of Monte Grappa, The Tortman Diaries; essays: Arguments for a Theatre. *Literary Agent:* Judy Daish Associates, 2 St Charles Place, London, W10 6EG, England. *Telephone:* (20) 8964-8811. *Fax:* (20) 8964-8966. *E-mail:* howard@judydaish.com. *Address:* The Wrestling School, 42 Durlston Road, London, E5 8RR, England (office). *Website:* www.howardbarker.co.uk.

BARKER, Nicola; British writer; b. 30 March 1966, Ely, Cambs. *Education:* Univ. of Cambridge. *Publications include:* Love Your Enemies (short stories) (David Higham Prize for Fiction, PEN/Macmillan Silver Pen Award) 1992, Reversed Forecast (novel) 1994, Small Holdings (novel) 1995, Heading Inland (short stories) (Mail on Sunday/John Llewellyn Rhys Prize) 1996, Wide Open (novel) (Int. IMPAC Dublin Literary Award 2000) 1998, Five Miles From Outer Hope (novel) 2000, Behindlings (novel) 2002, The Three Button Trick (short stories) 2003, Clear: A Transparent Novel 2004, Darkmans (novel) (Hawthornden Prize 2008) 2007, Burley Cross Postbox Theft 2010; contrib. to Time Out Book of London Short Stories, Food With Feeling (story adapted for BBC Radio 4). *Honours:* David Higham Prize for Fiction, Jt winner, Macmillan Silver PEN Award for Fiction, Mail on Sunday/John Llewellyn Rhys Award 1997, IMPAC Dublin Literary Award 2000, one of Granta's Best of Young British Novelists 2003. *Literary Agent:* Rogers, Coleridge & White Ltd, 20 Powis Mews, London, W11 1JN, England. *Telephone:* (20) 7221-3717. *Fax:* (20) 7229-9084. *Website:* www.rcwlitagency.co.uk. *Address:* c/o HarperCollins Publishers, 77-85 Fulham Palace Road, London, W6 8JB, England. *Telephone:* (20) 8741-7070. *Fax:* (20 8307-4440. *Website:* www.harpercollins.co.uk.

BARKER, Patricia (Pat) Margaret, CBE, BSc (Econ), FRSL; British author; b. 8 May 1943, Thornaby-on-Tees; m. David Barker 1978; one s., one d. *Education:* London School of Econs. *Career:* taught in colls of further educ. 1965–70; Patron New Writing North; mem. Soc. of Authors, PEN. *Publications include:* novels: Union Street 1982, Blow Your House Down 1984, The Century's Daughter 1986 (retitled Liza's England 1996), The Man Who Wasn't There 1989; trilogy of First World War novels: Regeneration 1991, The Eye in the Door 1993, The Ghost Road (Booker Prize 1995) 1995, Toby's Room 2012; Another World 1998, Border Crossing 2001, Double Vision 2003, Life Class 2007. *Honours:* Hon. Fellow, LSE 1998; Hon. MLitt (Teesside) 1993; Hon. DLitt (Napier) 1996, (Durham) 1998, (Hertfordshire) 1998, (London) 2002; Dr hc (Open Univ.) 1997; Fawcett Prize 1983, Guardian Prize for Fiction 1993, Northern Electric Special Arts Award 1994. *Address:* 10 The Avenue, Durham, DH1 4ED, England.

BARKER, Paul, MA, FRSA; British writer and broadcaster; b. 24 Aug. 1935, Mytholmroyd, Yorks.; m. Sally Huddleston; three s. one d. *Education:* Univ. of Oxford. *Career:* Ed. New Society 1968–86; Social Policy Ed. Sunday Telegraph 1986–88; Visiting Fellow, Univ. of Bath 1986–2000; columnist, London Evening Standard 1987–92, Social Policy Commentator 1992–2007; Assoc. Ed. The Independent Magazine 1988–90; reviewer, Times Literary Supplement 1960–64, 1991–; columnist, New Statesman 1996–99; Leverhulme Research Fellow 1993–95; Fellowship in Built Environment 2000–02; Sr Research Fellow, The Young Foundation (fmrly Inst. of Community Studies). *Radio:* My Country, Right is Wrong (BBC Radio 4) (Broadcasting Press Guild Award for Outstanding Radio Programme) 1988. *Publications include:* A Sociological Portrait 1972, One for Sorrow, Two for Joy 1972, The Social Sciences Today 1975, Arts in Society 1977, The Other Britain 1982, Founders of the Welfare State 1985, Britain in the Eighties 1989, Towards a New Landscape 1993, Young at Eighty 1995, Gulliver and Beyond 1996, Living as Equals 1996, A Critic Writes 1997, Town and Country 1998, Non-Plan 2000, From Black Economy to Moment of Truth 2004, Porcupines in Winter 2005, The Rise and Rise of Meritocracy 2006, The Freedoms of Suburbia 2009; contrib. to The Banham Lectures 2010. *Address:* 15 Dartmouth Park Avenue, London, NW5 1JL, England (office). *Telephone:* (20) 7485-8861 (office).

BARKER, Ralph Hammond; British writer; b. 21 Oct. 1917, Feltham, Middx; m. 1st Joan Muriel Harris 1948 (died 1993); one adopted d.; m. 2nd Diana Darvey 1995 (died 2000). *Education:* Hounslow Coll. *Career:* with RAF 1940–46, 1949–61, retd as Flight Lt; mem. Cricket Soc., MCC, Savage Club. *Publications include:* Down in the Drink 1955, The Ship-Busters 1957, The Last Blue Mountain 1959, Strike Hard, Strike Sure 1963, Ten Great Innings 1964, The Thousand Plan 1965, Ten Great Bowlers 1967, Great Mysteries of the Air 1967, Verdict on a Lost Flyer 1969, Aviator Extraordinary 1969, Test Cricket: England v Australia (with Irving Rosenwater) 1969, The Schneider Trophy Races 1971, Against the Sea: True Stories of Survival and Disaster 1972, One Man's Jungle 1975, The Blockade Busters 1976, The Cricketing Family Edrich 1976, The Hurricats 1978, Not Here, But in Another Place 1980, The RAF at War 1981, Innings of a Lifetime 1982, Good-Night, Sorry for Sinking You 1984, Children of the Benares 1987, Purple Patches 1987, That Eternal Summer 1990, The Royal Flying Corps in France, two vols 1994–95, combined edn 2002, Men of the Bombers 2005; contrib. to Sunday Express 1955–88, The Cricketer. *Honours:* Buchpreis des Deutschen Alpenvereins 1982. *Literary Agent:* Peter Knight, 20 Crescent Grove, London, SW4 7AH, England. *Telephone:* (20) 7622-1467. *Address:* Old Timbers, 16 Aldercombe Lane, Caterham, Surrey, CR3 6ED, England (home). *Telephone:* (1883) 343842 (home).

BARKER, Rodney, BA; American writer; b. 9 Feb. 1946, Lewisburg, Pa; s. of Thomas Barker and Jean Barker; m. Star York 1989. *Education:* Knox Coll., San Francisco State Univ. *Career:* worked as newspaper ed., investigative reporter, feature writer for regional and nat. magazines; currently working as full-time author; mem. Int. PEN. *Publications include:* Political Ideas in Modern Britain 1978, The Hiroshima Maidens 1985, The Broken Circle 1992, Dancing with the Devil 1996, And the Waters Turned to Blood 1997, The Trail of Painted Ponies 2002. *Literary Agent:* Janklow & Nesbit Associates, 445 Park Avenue, New York, NY 10022, USA. *E-mail:* rod@trailofpaintedponies.com (home).

BARKLEM, Jill; British children's writer and illustrator; b. Epping; m. 1977; two c. *Education:* St Martin's School of Art. *Publications include:* Spring Story 1980, Summer Story 1980, Autumn Story 1980, Winter Story 1980, The Secret Staircase 1983, The High Hills 1986, Sea Story 1990, Poppy's Babies 1994, Primrose's Adventure, Wilfred's Birthday 1995, House for a Mouse, Nice for Mice 1999, The Snow Ball, Wilfred to the Rescue 2005, A Year In Brambly Hedge 2010. *Address:* Brambly Hedge, 3 Coastguard Cottages, Pinmill, Ipswich, IP9 1JR, England (office). *E-mail:* enquiries@bramblyhedge.co.uk (office). *Website:* www.bramblyhedge.co.uk (office).

BARLAS, Fevziye Rahgozar, MA, PhD; Afghan journalist, short story writer and poet; b. 1955, Balkh; d. of M. Shafee Rahgozar; m. Rai Barlas. *Education:* Istanbul Univ., Turkey, Univ. of Washington, USA. *Career:* lived in Turkey in early to mid-1970s; worked as writer and journalist in Ministry of Information and Culture, Kabul, and for Kabul State Radio and TV, and as trans. –1979; writings banned under Communist regime, fled to Turkey; fmr Sr Ed. and News Anchor Radio Free Europe/Radio Liberty, Munich, Germany; moved to USA 1996. *Publications include:* Deyar-e Shegeftiha (poems, Wonderland) 1999, The Heavens are my Father (poems) 2001, Wondering Eyes (short stories); contrib. short stories to Persian publs in USA and Europe. *Honours:* award from then US Pres. Bill Clinton. *Address:* c/o Interdisciplinary Programs, The Graduate School, POB 352192, University of Washington, Seattle, WA 98195-2192, USA.

BARNABY, Charles Frank, BSc, MSc, PhD; British physicist; *Consultant Emeritus, Oxford Research Group;* b. 27 Sept. 1927, Andover, Hants.; s. of Charles H. Barnaby and Lilian Sainsbury; m. Wendy Elizabeth Field 1972; one s. one d. *Education:* Andover Grammar School and Univ. of London. *Career:* Physicist, UK Atomic Energy Authority 1950–57; mem. Sr Scientific Staff, MRC, Univ. Coll. Medical School 1957–68; Exec. Sec. Pugwash Confs on Science and World Affairs 1968–70; Dir Stockholm Int. Peace Research Inst. (SIPRI) 1971–81; Prof. of Peace Studies, Free Univ., Amsterdam 1981–85; Dir and Scientific Adviser, World Disarmament Campaign (UK) 1982–; fmr Consultant, Oxford Research Group, currently Consultant Emer.; Ed. Int. Journal of Human Rights. *Publications:* Man and the Atom 1971, Preventing the Spread of Nuclear Weapons (ed.) 1971, Anti-ballistic Missile Systems (co-ed.) 1971, Disarmament and Arms Control 1973, Nuclear Energy 1975, The Nuclear Age 1976, Prospects for Peace 1980, Future Warfare (co-author and ed.) 1983, Space Weapons 1984, Star Wars Brought Down to Earth 1986, The Automated Battlefield 1986, The Invisible Bomb 1989, The Gaia Peace Atlas 1989, The Role and Control of Weapons in the 1990s 1992, How Nuclear Weapons Spread 1993, Instruments of Terror 1997, How to Build a Nuclear Bomb and Other Weapons of Mass Destruction 2003, The Furuire of Terrorism; articles in scientific journals. *Honours:* Hon. DSc (Frei Univ. Amsterdam) 1982, (Southampton) 1996, (Bradford) 2007. *Address:* Brandreth, Chilbolton, Stockbridge, Hants., SO20 6HW, England (home). *Telephone:* (1264) 860423 (home). *Fax:* (1264) 860868 (home). *E-mail:* frank.barnaby@btinternet.com (home).

BARNARD, Robert, (Bernard Bastable), BA, PhD; British writer; b. 23 Nov. 1936, Burnham on Crouch, Essex; s. of Leslie Thomas Barnard and Vera Barnard (née Nethercoat); m. Mary Louise Tabor 1963. *Education:* Balliol Coll., Oxford, Univ. of Bergen, Norway. *Career:* Lecturer in English, Univ. of New England, Armidale, NSW, Australia 1961–66; Lecturer, then Sr Lecturer in English, Univ. of Bergen 1966–76; Prof. of English, Univ. of Tromsø, Norway 1976–84; mem. Crime Writers Asscn (CWA), Brontë Soc. (Chair. 1996–99, 2002–05), Soc. of Authors. *Publications include:* Death of an Old Goat 1974, Imagery and Theme in the Novels of Dickens 1974, A Little Local Murder 1976, Death on the High C's 1977, Blood Brotherhood 1977, Unruly Son (Death of a Mystery Writer) 1978, Posthumous Papers (Death of a Literary Widow) 1979, Death in a Cold Climate 1980, A Talent to Deceive: Appreciation of Agatha Christie 1980, Mother's Boys (Death of a Perfect Mother) 1981, Sheer Torture (Death by Sheer Torture) 1981, Death and the Princess 1982, The Missing Brontë (The Case of the Missing Brontë) 1983, Little Victims (School for Murder) 1983, A Corpse in a Gilded Cage 1984, A Short History of English Literature 1984, Out of the Blackout 1985, The Disposal of the Living (Fête Fatale) 1985, Political Suicide 1986, Bodies 1986, Death in Purple Prose (The Cherry Blossom Corpse) 1987, The Skeleton in the Grass 1987, At Death's Door 1988, Death and the Chaste Apprentice 1989, A City of Strangers 1990, A Scandal in Belgravia 1991, A Fatal Attachment 1992, A Hovering of Vultures 1993, The Masters of the House 1994, The Bad Samaritan 1995, No Place of Safety 1997, The Corpse at the Haworth Tandoori 1998, Touched by the Dead 1999, The Corpse at the Haworth Tandoori 1999, Unholy Dying 2000, Emily Bronte 2000, The Mistress of Alderley 2002, The Bones in the Attic 2001, A Cry from the Dark 2003, The Graveyard Position 2004, Dying Flames 2005, Sins of Scarlet (short story) (CWA Award for Best Crime Short Story) 2006, A Fall from Grace 2007, A Brontë Encyclopedia (with Louise Barnard) 2007, Last Post 2008, The Killings on Jubilee Terrace 2009, A Stranger in the Family 2010; as Bernard Bastable: To Die Like a Gentleman 1993, Dead, Mr Mozart 1995, Too Many Notes, Mr Mozart 1995; contribs include short stories and essays. *Honours:* CWA Cartier Diamond Dagger 2003. *Address:* Hazeldene, Houghley Lane, Leeds, LS13 2DT, England (home). *Telephone:* (113) 263-8955 (home). *Fax:* (113) 263-8955 (home).

BARNES, Christopher John, BA, MA, PhD; British academic and writer; *Professor of Slavic Languages and Literatures, University of Toronto;* b. 10 March 1942, Sheffield, Yorks., England; m. Svetlana Tzapina 1994; two d. *Education:* Corpus Christi Coll., Cambridge. *Career:* Lecturer in Russian Language and Literature, Univ. of St Andrews 1967–89; Prof. and Chair. Dept of Slavic Languages and Literatures, Univ. of Toronto, Canada 1989–; mem. American Asscn for the Advancement of Slavic Studies, American Asscn of Teachers of Slavic and East European Languages, British Royal Musical Asscn, British Univs Asscn of Slavists, Canadian Asscn of Slavists, Modern Language Asscn of America. *Publications include:* Studies in Twentieth-Century Russian Literature (ed.) 1976, Boris Pasternak: Collected Short Prose (ed. and trans.) 1977, Boris Pasternak: The Voice of Prose (ed. and trans., two vols) 1986, 1990, Boris Pasternak: A Literary Biography, Vol. 1, 1890–1928 1989, Vol. 2, 1928–1960 1998, Boris Pasternak and European Literature (ed.) 1990, The Moscow Piano School (ed.) 2007, Vadim Bytensky–Journey from St Petersburg (ed. and translator) 2007; contribs to scholarly journals. *Address:* Department of Slavic Languages and Literatures, University of Toronto, Alumni Hall, 121 St Joseph Street, Room 425, Toronto, ON M5S 1J4 (office); 53 Alberta Avenue, Toronto, ON M6H 2R5, Canada (home). *Telephone:* (416) 926-2075 (office); (416) 850-5102 (home). *Fax:* (416) 926-2076 (office). *E-mail:* chrjbarnes1942@yahoo.ca (home). *Website:* www.utoronto.ca (office).

BARNES, Jim Weaver, BA, MA, PhD; American writer, poet and teacher; b. 22 Dec. 1933, Summerfield, Okla; m. Carolyn 1973; two s. *Education:* Southeastern Oklahoma State Univ., Univ. of Arkansas. *Career:* Prof. and Writer-in-Residence, Truman State Univ. 1970–2003; Distinguished Prof. of English and Creative Writing, Brigham Young Univ. 2003–06; Oklahoma State Poet Laureate 2009–10; Ed. The Charlton Review, Founding Ed. Charlton Review Press; Poetry Ed. Truman State Univ. Press; contributing ed. to Pushcart Prize; Distinguished Writer-in-Residence, Univ. of Maryland Far East Div. 1992; Featured Poet, Paris Writers Workshop, 13th Franco-Anglais Poetry Translation Festival; Munich Translator-in-Residence, Villa Walberta, Germany 1995; mem. PEN Center West, Assoc. Writing Programs, Nat. Asscn for Ethnic Studies, Editorial Bd of Thomas Jefferson Univ. Press. *Publications include:* Fish on Poteau Mountain 1980, American Book of the Dead 1982, Season of Loss 1985, La Plata Canata 1989, Sawdust War (Oklahoma Book Award 1993) 1992, Paris 1997, On Native Ground (American Book Award 1998) 1997, Numbered Days 1999, On a Wing of the Sun 2001, Visiting Picasso 2007; contribs to Poetry Chicago, Nation, American Scholar, Georgia Review, Poetry Northwest, Quarterly West, Prairie Schooner, Mississippi Review, Plus 400. *Honours:* Nat. Endowment for the Arts Fellowship 1978, Columbia Univ. Translation Award 1980, Stanley Hanks Memorial Poetry Award 1989, Bellagio Residency Fellowship 1990, 2003, Sr Fulbright Fellowship 1993–94, Camargo Foundation Fellowships 1996, 2001. *Address:* c/o Truman State University Press, 100 East Normal Street, Kirksville, MO 63501-4221, USA.

BARNES, Jonathan, FBA, FAAS; British academic (retd); b. 26 Dec. 1942, Much Wenlock, Salop., England; s. of the late A. L. Barnes and K. M. Barnes; m. Jennifer Mary Postgate 1964; two d. *Education:* City of London School, Balliol Coll., Oxford. *Career:* Lecturer in Philosophy, Exeter Coll., Oxford 1967–68, Fellow, Oriel Coll., Oxford 1968–78, Balliol Coll., Oxford 1978–94; Prof. of Ancient Philosophy, Univ. of Oxford 1989–94, Univ. of Geneva 1994–2002, Univ. of Paris IV-Sorbonne 2003–06; visiting posts at Univ. of Chicago 1966–67, Inst. for Advanced Study, Princeton 1972, Univ. of Mass 1973, Univ. of Tex. 1981, Wissenschaftskolleg zu Berlin 1985, Univ. of Alberta 1986, Univ. of Zurich 1987, Istituto Italiano per la Storia della Filosofia 1989, 1994, 1999, Ecole Normale Supérieure, Paris 1996, Scuola Normale di Pisa 2002; mem. L' Acad. scientifique, Geneva, Aristotelian Soc., Mind Asscn. *Publications:* The Ontological Argument 1972, Aristotle's Posterior Analytics 1975, The Presocratic Philosophers 1979, Doubt and Dogmatism (with M. F. Burnyeat and M. Schofield) 1980, Aristotle 1982, Science and Speculation (with J. Brunschwig and M. F. Burnyeat) 1982, The Complete Works of Aristotle 1984, The Modes of Scepticism (with J. Annas) 1985, Early Greek

Philosophy 1987, Matter and Metaphysics (with M. Mignucci 1988, Philosophia Togata (with M. Griffin) Vol. I 1989, Vol. II 1997, The Toils of Scepticism 1991, Sextus Empiricus: Outlines of Scepticisim (with J. Annas) 1994, The Cambridge Companion to Aristotle 1995, Logic and the Imperial Stoa 1997, The Cambridge History of Hellenistic Philosophy (with K. Algra, J. Mansfield and M. Schofield) 1999, Porphyry: Introduction 2003, Coffee with Aristotle 2008. *Honours:* Hon. Fellow, Oriel Coll., Oxford 2008–, Hon. Citizen of Velia 2010; Dr hc (Université de Genève) 2010; Condorcet Medal 1996, John Locke Lecturer, Univ. of Oxford 2004. *Address:* Les Charmilles, 36200 Ceaulmont (home); 12 blvd Arago, 75013 Paris, France (home). *E-mail:* jonathanbarnes@wanadoo.fr (home).

BARNES, Julian Patrick, (Dan Kavanagh, Basil Seal), BA; British writer; b. 19 Jan. 1946, Leicester, England; m. Pat Kavanagh (died 2008). *Education:* City of London School, Magdalen Coll., Oxford. *Career:* lexicographer, Oxford English Dictionary Supplement 1969–72; Asst Literary Ed. New Statesman 1977–79, reviewer 1977–81, TV critic 1979–82; Contributing Ed. New Review, London 1977–78; Deputy Literary Ed. Sunday Times, London 1979–81; TV Critic The Observer 1982–86; Hon. Fellow Magdalen Coll., Oxford 1996–. *Publications:* Metroland (Somerset Maugham Award 1981) 1980, Before She Met Me 1982, Flaubert's Parrot (Geoffrey Faber Memorial Prize, Prix Médicis 1986) 1984, Staring at the Sun 1986, A History of the World in 10½ Chapters 1989, Talking it Over (Prix Femina Etranger 1992) 1991, The Porcupine 1992, Letters From London 1990–95 (articles) 1995, Cross Channel (short stories) 1996, England, England 1998, Love, etc. 2000, Something to Declare (essays) 2002, In the Land of Pain, by Alphonse Daudet (ed. and trans.) 2002, The Lemon Table (short stories) 2004, The Pedant in the Kitchen 2004, Arthur & George 2005, Nothing to be Frightened Of 2008, Pulse 2011, The Sense of the Ending (Man Booker Prize 2011) 2011; as Dan Kavanagh: Duffy 1980, Fiddle City 1981, Putting the Boot In 1985, Going to the Dogs 1987. *Honours:* E. M. Forster Award, US Acad. of Arts and Letters 1986, Gutenberg Prize 1987, Grinzane Cavour Prize, Italy 1988, Shakespeare Prize, Germany 1993, Austrian State Prize for European Literature 2004, David Cohen Prize for Literature 2011; Chevalier, Ordre des Arts et des Lettres 1988, Officier, Ordre des Arts et des Lettres 1995, Commdr, Ordre des Arts et des Lettres 2004. *Literary Agent:* United Agents, 12–26 Lexington Street, London, W1F 0LE, England. *Telephone:* (20) 3214-0800. *Fax:* (20) 3214-0801. *E-mail:* info@unitedagents.co.uk. *Website:* unitedagents.co.uk; www.julianbarnes.com.

BARNES, Richard John Black, FRGS, FRSA; British editor and writer; b. 13 Aug. 1950, Nyasaland, Malawi; s. of Harold Charles Vernon Black Barnes and Joan Augusta Gwynne Bird; m. Lucette Aylmer 1975; one s. one d. *Education:* Stonyhurst Coll., Royal Coll. of Agric., Polytechnic of Cen. London. *Career:* mem. Public Monuments and Sculpture Asscn. *Publications include:* The Sun in the East 1983, Eye on the Hill: Horse Travels in Britain 1987, John Bell, Sculptor 1999, The Year of Public Sculpture–Norfolk 2001, The Obelisk–A Monumental Feature in Britain 2004, British Sculpture in India-New Views and Old Memories 2011. *Address:* c/o Frontier Publishing, Windetts Farm, Long Lane, Kirstead, Norwich, NR15 1EG, England. *Telephone:* (1508) 558174. *E-mail:* contact@frontierpublishing.co.uk. *Website:* www.frontierpublishing.co.uk.

BARNET, Max (see Aaron, Hugh)

BARNET, Miguel; Cuban writer; b. 28 Jan. 1940, Havana. *Education:* Univ. of Havana. *Career:* Founder-Pres. Fernando Ortiz Foundation; Pres. UNEAC (Unión de Escitores y Artistas de Cuba) 2008–; mem. Honor Council, Extraordinary Staff of Nuestra América of Anthropological Sciences Faculty, Autonomous Univ., Yucatan, Mexico. *Publications include:* La piedrafina y el pavorreal 1963, Isla de güijes 1964, Biografía de un cimarrón 1966, La sagrada familia 1967, Cancion de Rachel (translated as Rachel's Song) 1969, Biography of a Runaway Slave 1970, Orikis y otros poemas 1980, Carta de noche 1982, Gallego 1983, La fuente viva 1983, La vida real 1986, Autógrafos cubanos 1989, Mapa del tiempo 1989, Oficio de ángel 1989, Poemas chinos 1993, Con pies de gato 1993, Los orejas del conejo 1995, Actas del final 2000, Reyes y sin coronas (translated as Kings Without Crowns) 2001, Afro-Cuban Religions 2001. *Honours:* Dr hc (Cuban Nat. Comm. of Scientific Degrees) 1997; Distinction for Nat. Culture, La Giraldillo de la Habana, Garcia Lorca Prize (Spain), Nat. Prize for Literature 1994, Int. Book Fair Honour 2002, Premio Jose Donoso, Chile 2007, Medal of Colony City (Germany), Medal of the French Senate. *E-mail:* ffo@cubarte.cult.cu (office); uneac@azurina.cult.cu (office). *Website:* www.fundacionfernandoortiz.org (office).

BARNETT, Anthony Peter John, MA; British writer, poet, publisher and music historian; b. 10 Sept. 1941, London. *Education:* Univ. of Essex. *Career:* Editorial Dir Allardyce, Barnett, Publishers; producer, AB Fable Recording; Visiting Scholar, Meiji Univ., Japan 2002. *Recordings:* Desert Sands: The Recordings and Performances of Stuff Smith 1995, Black Gypsy: The Recordings of Eddie South 1999, Listening for Henry Crowder 2007. *Publications include:* poetry: Blood Flow 1975, Fear and Misadventure 1977, The Resting Bell: Collected Poems 1987, Stuff Smith (ed) 1991, Prose and Poetry: Carp and Rubato 1995, Anti-Beauty 1999, Miscanthus: Selected and New Poems 2005; prose: Lisa Lisa 2000; contribs to New Grove Dictionary of Music and Musicians, New Grove Dictionary of Jazz, The Guardian, The Independent, TLS, The Use of English, anthologies, journals and periodicals. *Address:* c/o Allardyce, Barnett, Publishers, 14 Mount Street, Lewes, East Sussex, BN7 1HL, England. *Telephone:* (1273) 479393. *Fax:* (1273) 479393. *E-mail:* ab@abar.net. *Website:* www.abar.net.

BARNETT, Correlli Douglas, CBE, MA; British historian; *Fellow, Churchill College, Cambridge*; b. 28 June 1927, Norbury, Surrey; s. of Douglas A. Barnett and Kathleen M. Barnett; m. Ruth Murby 1950; two d. *Education:* Trinity School, Croydon and Exeter Coll. Oxford. *Career:* Intelligence Corps 1945–48; North Thames Gas Bd 1952–57; public relations 1957–63; Keeper of Archives, Churchill Coll. Cambridge 1977–95; Defence Lecturer, Univ. of Cambridge 1980–83; Fellow, Churchill Coll., Cambridge 1977–; mem. Council, Royal United Services Inst. for Defence Studies 1973–85; mem. Cttee London Library 1977–79, 1982–84; Winston Churchill Memorial Lecturer, Switzerland 1982. *Television includes:* The Great War (BBC TV) 1964, The Lost Peace (BBC TV) 1966, The Commanders (BBC TV) 1972. *Publications:* The Hump Organisation 1957, The Channel Tunnel (with Humphrey Slater) 1958, The Desert Generals 1960, The Swordbearers 1963, Britain and Her Army 1970, The Collapse of British Power 1972, Marlborough 1974, Bonaparte 1978, The Great War 1979, The Audit of War 1986, Hitler's Generals 1989, Engage the Enemy More Closely 1991 (Yorkshire Post Book of the Year Award 1991), The Lost Victory: British Dreams, British Realities 1945–1950 1995, The Verdict of Peace: Britain Between Her Yesterday and the Future 2001. *Honours:* Hon. DSc (Cranfield Univ.) 1993; Hon. Fellow, City and Guilds of London Inst. 2003; Screenwriters' Guild Award for Best British TV Documentary (The Great War) 1964; FRSL Award for Britain and Her Army 1971; Chesney Gold Medal Royal United Services Inst. for Defence Studies 1991. *Address:* Catbridge House, East Carleton, Norwich, Norfolk, NR14 8JX, England (home). *Telephone:* (1508) 570410 (home). *Fax:* (1508) 570410 (home).

BARNETT, Paul le Page, (Dennis Brezhnev, Eve Devereux, Freddie Duff-Ware, John Grant, Armytage Ware); British writer and editor; b. 22 Nov. 1949, Aberdeen, Scotland; m. Catherine Stewart 1974; two d. *Career:* moved to USA 1999; Commissioning Ed. Paper Tiger; currently Contributing Ed. to Artists' and Photographers' Press Ltd, also US Reviews Ed. Infinity Plus; mem. West Country Writers' Asscn. *Publications include:* as John Grant: Book of Time (with Colin Wilson) 1979, A Directory of Discarded Ideas 1981, A Book of Numbers 1982, Dreamers 1983, Sex Secrets of Ancient Atlantis 1985, The Depths of Cricket 1986, Earthdoom (with David Langford) 1987, The Advanced Trivia Quizbook 1987, Great Mysteries 1988, Great Unsolved Mysteries of Science 1989, Eclipse of the Kai 1989, The Dark Door Opens 1989, The Sword of the Sun 1989, Hunting Wolf 1990, Albion 1991, Unexplained Mysteries of the World 1991, The Claws of Helgedad 1991, The Sacrifice of Ruanon 1991, The World 1992, Monsters 1992, The Birthplace 1992, Encyclopedia of Walt Disney's Animated Characters: From Mickey Mouse to Aladdin 1992, The Hundredfold Problem 1994, Encyclopedia of Fantasy Art Techniques (with Ron Tiner) 1996, Encyclopedia of Fantasy (ed. with John Clute) 1997, The Far-Enough Window 2002, Dragonhenge 2002, Perceptualistics: Art of Jael 2002, Take No Prisoners 2004, Stardragons 2005, New Writings in the Fantastic (ed.) 2006, The Dragons of Manhattan 2008, The City In These Pages 2008, Discarded Science, Corrupted Science 2009; as Paul Barnett: Planet Earth: An Encyclopedia of Geology (ed. with A. Hallam and Peter Hutchinson), Phaidon Concise Encyclopedia of Science and Technology (contributing ed.) 1978, Strider's Galaxy 1997, Discarded Science 1999, Enchanted World 2000, Masters of Animation 2001, Dragonhenge 2002, The Hundredfold Problem 2003, Earthdoom 2003, Take no Prisoners 2004, The Stardragons 2005, Beer 2006, Corrupted Science 2007, Leaving Fortusa 2008, Bogus Science: Or Some People Believe In These Things 2009; as Eve Devereux: Book of World Flags 1992, Ultimate Card Trick Book 1994; as Armytage Ware (joint pseudonym with Ron Tiner): Parlour Games 1992, Conjuring Tricks 1992, Juggling and Feats of Dexterity 1992, Card Games 1992; as Freddie Duff-Ware (joint pseudonym with Ron Tiner): Practical Jokes 1993. *Honours:* Hugo Awards, World Fantasy Award, Locus Award, Chesley Award. *E-mail:* cb@aappl.com (office); aappl@optonline.net (office). *Website:* www.johngrantpaulbarnett.com.

BARNHARDT, Wilton, BA, MPhil; American writer; *Associate Professor of Creative Writing, North Carolina State University*; b. 25 July 1960, Winston-Salem, NC. *Education:* Michigan State Univ., Univ. of Oxford, UK. *Career:* fmr reporter, Sports Illustrated; currently Assoc. Prof. of Creative Writing and Dir MFA in Creative Writing, North Carolina State Univ. *Publications include:* Emma Who Saved My Life 1989, Gospel 1993, Show World 1998; contribs to magazines. *Address:* Department of English, North Carolina State University, 276 Tompkins Hall, Campus Box 8105, Raleigh, NC 27695-8105, USA (office). *Telephone:* (919) 515-4129 (office). *E-mail:* wwbarnha@unity.ncsu.edu (office). *Website:* english.chass.ncsu.edu (office).

BARNSLEY, Victoria, OBE; British publisher; *CEO, HarperCollins UK*; b. 4 March 1954, d. of the late Thomas E. Barnsley and Margaret Gwyneth Barnsley (née Llewellin); m. Nicholas Howard 1992; one d. one step-s. *Education:* Loughborough High School, Beech Lawn Tutorial Coll., Univ. of Edinburgh, Univ. Coll. London, Univ. of York. *Career:* with Junction Books 1980–83; Founder, Chair. and CEO Fourth Estate 1984–2000; CEO HarperCollins UK 2000–, also for Australia, New Zealand, India and South Africa 2008–; Trustee, Tate Gallery 1998–; Dir Tate Enterprises Ltd 1998–; council mem. Publishers Asscn 2001–, Vice-Pres. 2009–10, Pres. 2010–11. *Address:* HarperCollins, 77–85 Fulham Palace Road, London, W6 8JB, England (office). *Telephone:* (20) 8307-4000 (office). *Fax:* (20) 8307-4440 (office). *E-mail:* contact@harpercollins.co.uk (office). *Website:* www.harpercollins.co.uk (office).

BARNSTONE, Willis, BA, MA, PhD; American poet, novelist and academic; *Distinguished Professor Emeritus, Department of Comparative Literature, Indiana University*; b. 13 Nov. 1927, Lewiston, Me; two s. one d. *Education:* Bowdoin Coll., Columbia Univ., Yale Univ., Univ. of Mexico. *Career:* instructor in English and French, Anavryta Classical Lyceum, Greece 1949–50; Asst Prof. of Romance Languages, Wesleyan Univ. 1959–62; O'Connor Prof. of Greek, Colgate Univ.; fmr Prof., Dept of Comparative Literature and Dept of Spanish and Portuguese, Indiana Univ., currently Distinguished Prof. Emer.; Visiting Prof. at various univs 1967–73; Sr Fulbright Prof., English Literature, Instituto Superior del Profesorado, Profesorado de Lenguas Vivas, Buenos Aires 1975–76; Sr Fulbright Prof., English and American Literature, Peking Foreign Studies Univ. 1984–85; Fellow, Guggenheim Foundation, Spain 1961–62, American Council of Learned Socs, Greece 1968–69, Nat. Endowment for the Arts, Spain 1983–84; Sr Research Fellow, Nat. Endowment for the Humanities New York 1979–80; mem. PEN, Poetry Soc. of America. *Publications include:* Poems for Exchange 1951, From This White Island 1959, Modern European Poetry: French, German, Greek, Italian, Russian, Spanish (ed.) 1966, A Sky of Days 1967, Concrete Poetry: A World View (ed.) 1969, Spanish Poetry from the Beginning through the Nineteenth Century (ed.) 1970, A Day in the Country 1971, Eighteen Texts: Writings by Contemporary Greek Authors (ed.) 1972, China Poems 1976, Stickball on 88th Street 1978, Modern European Poetry 1978, Overheard 1979, A Book of Women Poets from Antiquity to Now (ed.) 1980, Ten Gospels and a Nightingale 1981, Borges at Eighty: Conversations 1981, The Poetics of Ecstasy: Varieties of Ekstasis from Sappho to Borges 1983, The Alphabet of Night 1984, The Other Bible: Jewish Pseudepigrapha, Christian Noncanonical Apocrypha, and Gnostic Scriptures (ed.) 1984, Five AM in Beijing 1987, Sappho and the Greek Lyric Poets 1988, With Borges on an Ordinary Evening in Buenos Aires 1992, ABC of Translating Poetry (illustrated) 1993, The Poetics of Translation 1993, Funny Ways of Staying Alive: Poems and Ink Drawings 1993, Sunday Morning in Fascist Spain: A European Memoir 1948–1953 1995 1994, The Secret Reader: 501 Sonnets 1996, The Poems of Sappho: A New Translation 1997, The Literatures of Asia, Africa and Latin America (co-ed. with Tony Barnstone) 1998, To Touch the Sky: Spiritual, Mystical and Philosophical Poems in Translation 1999, Algebra of Night: New and Selected Poems 1948–1998 1998, The Apocalypse (Revelation): A New Translation with Introduction 2000, The New Covenant: The Four Gospels and Apocalypse. Newly Translated from the Greek and Informed by Semitic Sources 2002, Literatures of the Middle East (ed. with Tony Barnstone) 2002, Literatures of Latin America (ed.) 2002, The Restored New Testament 2009. *Honours:* Cecil Hemley Memorial Award 1968, Indiana Univ. Writers Conf. Award 1971, Lucille Medwick Memorial Awards 1978, 1982, Colorado Quarterly Annual Poetry Award 1978, Gustav Davidson Memorial Awards 1980, 1988, Emily Dickinson Award 1985, Poetry Soc. of America, W. H. Auden Award, New York State Arts Council 1986, Nat. Poetry Competition Award 1988, Chester H. Jones Foundation 1988, Midland Authors Award in Poetry 2000, Lannan Literary Award 2003, Northern California Book Award 2004, American Literary Translators Asscn 2007. *Address:* Department of Comparative Literature, Indiana University, 1020 East Kirkwood Avenue, Ballantine Hall 914, Bloomington, IN 47405, USA (office). *Telephone:* (812) 855-2688. *E-mail:* willis.barnstone@sbcglobal.net (office); willis@barnstone .com. *Website:* www.indiana.edu (office); web.whittier.edu/barnstone.

BARON, Martin, BA, MBA; American journalist; *Editor, The Boston Globe*; b. Tampa, FL. *Education:* Lehigh Univ. *Career:* state reporter, business writer The Miami Herald 1976–79; joined Los Angeles Times 1979, apptd Business Ed. 1983, Asst . Man. Ed. for 'Column One' 1991, Ed. Orange Co. Edn 1993; joined The New York Times 1996, Assoc. Man. Ed. responsible for night-time news operations 1997–99; Exec. Ed. The Miami Herald 1999–2002; Ed. The Boston Globe 2002–. *Honours:* Pulitzer Prize 2001, Ed. of the Year, Editor & Publisher Magazine 2002. *Address:* The Boston Globe, 135 Morrissey Boulevard, POB 55819, Boston, MA 02205-5819, USA (office). *Telephone:* (617) 929-2000 (office). *Fax:* (617) 929-3192 (office). *E-mail:* letters@globe.com (office). *Website:* www.boston.com (office).

BARR, Patricia Miriam, BA, MA; British writer; b. 25 April 1934, Norwich. *Education:* Univ. of Birmingham, Univ. Coll. London. *Career:* mem. Soc. of Authors. *Publications include:* The Coming of the Barbarians 1967, The Deer Cry Pavilion 1968, Foreign Devils 1970, I Remember 1970, A Curious Life for a Lady 1970, To China with Love 1972, The Memsahibs 1976, Taming the Jungle 1978, Simla 1978, The Framing of the Female 1978, Japan 1980, Chinese Alice 1981, Jade: A Novel of China 1982, Uncut Jade 1983, Kenjiro 1985, Coromandel 1988, The Dust in the Balance 1989. *Honours:* Winston Churchill Fellowship for Historical Biography 1972. *Address:* 6 Mount Pleasant, Norwich, NR2 2DG, England (home).

BARRACK, Romana, (Carla Lane), OBE; British writer; b. 5 Aug. 1937, Liverpool; m. Arthur Hollins 1954 (divorced 1980); two s. *Career:* won a poetry prize aged seven; has written for radio and TV, first successes came in collaboration with Myra Taylor; contrib. to Northern Drift series; cr. and wrote numerous comedy series and plays for BBC TV. *TV series and plays include:* The Liver Birds (with Myra Taylor) 1969–79, 1996, Bless This House (with Myra Taylor and others) 1971–76, No Strings 1974, Going, Going, Gone… Free? 1975, Three Piece Suite 1977, Butterflies 1978–82, 2000, The Last Song 1981–83, Solo 1981–82, Leaving 1984–85, The Mistress 1985–87, I Woke Up One Morning 1985, Bread 1986–91, Screaming 1992, Luv (also producer) 1993–94, Searching (also producer) 1995, Happy Christmas, I Love You, The Last Supper. *Publications include:* Instead of Diamonds 1995, Dreams and Other Aggravations 2003, Somebody I'll Find Me (autobiography) 2006; several short stories and poems. *Honours:* Dr hc (Liverpool); Richard Martin Award, RSPCA. *Address:* c/o Jonathan Clowes Ltd, 10 Iron Bridge House, Bridge Approach, London, NW1 8BD; Broadhurst Manor, Broadhurst Manor Road, Horsted Keynes, West Sussex, RH17 7BG, England (home). *Telephone:* (1342) 811377 (home). *Fax:* (1342) 811377 (home). *E-mail:* office@ animaline.plus.com (office). *Website:* www.carlalane.com.

BARRERA TYSZKA, Alberto; Venezuelan writer, journalist and screenwriter; b. 1960, Caracas. *Education:* School of Arts, Universidad Central de Venezuela,. *Career:* columnist, El Nacional 1996–; writer of 'telenovelas'. *Film:* Zamuros Way (co-writer). *Television series as writer:* Déjate querer 1993, Nada personal 1996, Enséñame a querer 1998, Demasiado corazón 1998, La calle de las novias 2000, Agua y aceite 2002, Un nuevo amor 2003. *Publications include:* Edición de lujo (short stories) 1990, También el corazón es un descuido (novel) 2001, La enfermedad (novel) (Premio Herralde, Spain) 2006, Hugo Chavez (biog. with Cristina Marcano) 2007; poetry: Amor que por demás 1985, Coyote de ventanas 1993, Tal vez el frío 2000. *Address:* C.A. Editora El Nacional, Av. principal de Los Cortijos de Lourdes, con 3ra. Transversal, Caracas 1071, Venezuela (office). *Telephone:* (212) 203-3194. *E-mail:* contactenos@el-nacional.com (office). *Website:* www.el-nacional.com (office).

BARRETT, Andrea, BS; American writer and academic; *Lecturer in English, Williams College*; b. 16 Nov. 1954, Boston; d. of Norman F. Barrett Jr and Anne Tucker Jensen; pnr Barry M. Goldstein. *Education:* Union Coll., Schenectady, New York. *Career:* Lecturer in English, Williams Coll. 2004–; fmr Fellow, Center for Scholars and Writers, New York Public Library. *Publications include:* Lucid Stars 1988, Secret Harmonies 1989, The Middle Kingdom 1991, The Forms of Water 1993, Ship Fever & Other Stories (Nat. Book Award in Fiction) 1996, The Voyage of the Narwhal 1998, Servants of the Map 2002, The Air We Breathe 2007. *Honours:* Hon. LLD (Union Coll.) 1996, Hon. DHumLitt (Rochester) 2004; Pushcart Prize 1997, Guggenheim Fellowship 1997, MacArthur Fellowship 2001, American Acad. of Arts and Letters Award for Literature 2003. *Address:* Department of English, Williams College, Morey House, Room 4, Williamstown, MA 01267, USA (office). *Telephone:* (413) 597-3346 (office). *E-mail:* andrea.barrett@williams.edu (office). *Website:* www.williams.edu/English (office).

BARRETT, Charles Kingsley, DD, FBA; British academic (retd) and writer; *Professor Emeritus in Theology, Durham University*; b. 4 May 1917, Salford, Lancs.; s. of Rev. F. Barrett and Clara Barrett (née Seed); m. Margaret E. Heap 1944 (died 2008); one s. one d. *Education:* Shebbear Coll., Pembroke Coll., Cambridge and Wesley House, Cambridge. *Career:* Lecturer in Theology, Durham Univ. 1945–58, Prof. of Divinity 1958–82, currently Prof. Emer. in Theology; Visiting Lecturer and Prof. in various European countries, USA, Canada, Australia and NZ; Pres. Studiorum Novi Testamenti Societas 1973–74; mem. Royal Norwegian Soc. of Sciences and Letters 1991–. *Publications include:* The Holy Spirit and the Gospel Tradition 1947, The Gospel according to St John 1955, The Epistle to the Romans 1957, From First Adam to Last 1962, Jesus and the Gospel Tradition 1967, The First Epistle to the Corinthians 1968, The Signs of an Apostle 1970, The Second Epistle to the Corinthians 1973, Essays on Paul 1982, Essays on John 1982, Freedom and Obligation 1985, Church, Ministry and Sacraments in the New Testament 1985, Paul: An Introduction to his Thought 1994, The Acts of the Apostles, Vol. I 1994, Vol. II 1998, Jesus and the Word 1996, Jesus, Paul and John 1999, Acts: A Shorter Commentary 2002, On Paul: Aspects of his Life, Work and Influence in the Early Church 2003; several other books and many articles in learned journals and symposia. *Honours:* Hon. Fellow, Pembroke Coll. Cambridge, Hon. mem. Soc. of Biblical Literature (USA); Dr hc (Hull, Aberdeen, Hamburg); Burkitt Medal for Biblical Study 1966, Von Humboldt Forschungspreis 1988. *Address:* Department of Theology and Religion, Durham University, Abbey House, Palace Green, Durham, DH1 3RS (office); 22 Rosemount, Durham, DH1 5GA, England (home). *Telephone:* (19) 1386-1340 (home). *Fax:* (19) 1334-3941 (office).

BARRETT, Susan Mary, MA; British copywriter, novelist, counsellor and psychotherapist; *Author's Mentor, WritersReadersDirect*; b. 24 June 1938, Plymouth, Devon, England; d. of Richard Leigh Withington and Mary Richmond Withington; m. Peter Barrett 1960; one s. one d. *Education:* The Royal School, Bath, Bath Spa Univ. Coll. *Career:* e-book publr, WritersReadersDirect. *Television play:* The Portrait (LWT) 1977. *Publications include:* Louisa 1969, Moses 1970, The Circle Sarah Drew (with Peter Barrett) 1970, The Square Ben Drew (with Peter Barrett) 1970, Noah's Ark 1971, Private View 1972, Rubbish 1974, The Beacon 1981, Travels with a Wildlife Artist: Greek Landscape and Wildlife (with Peter Barrett) 1986, Stephen and Violet 1988, A Day in the Life of a Baby Deer: The Fawn's First Snowfall 1996, A Day in the Life of a Puppy, A Day in the Life of a Kitten (series with Peter Barrett) 1996, Making a Difference 2007, Take Care, Dear 2010. *Literary Agent:* c/o Toby Eady Associates Ltd, Third Floor, 9 Orme Court, London, W2 4RL, England. *Telephone:* (20) 7792-0092. *Fax:* (20) 7792-0879. *E-mail:* toby@ tobyeady.demon.co.uk; zaria@tobyeadyassociates.co.uk. *Website:* www .tobyeadyassociates.co.uk.

BARRINGTON, Judith Mary, BA, MA; British poet, memoirist, critic and academic; *Associate Professor, University of Alaska*; b. 7 July 1944, Brighton, Sussex; s. of Reginald Barrington and Violet Barrington. *Education:* St Mary's

Hall, Brighton, Marylhurst Univ., Ore. and Goddard Coll., USA. *Career:* West Coast Ed. Motheroot Journal 1985–93; Poet-in-the-Schools, Ore., and Wash. 1986–2000; Dir The Flight of the Mind Writing Workshops 1984–2000; f. Soapstone Inc. 1992, Dir 1992–95, Pres. 1997–2010, currently Bd mem.; currently Assoc. Prof., Univ. of Alaska; Fellow, Oregon Inst. of Literary Arts 1989, 1992, 1999; Resident Fellow, Tyrone Guthrie Centre, Annaghmakerrig, Ireland 1996; mem. PEN America, Poetry Soc. of America, Poetry Soc. *Publications include:* Deviation 1975, Why Children (co-author) 1980, Trying to Be an Honest Woman 1985, History and Geography 1989, An Intimate Wilderness (ed.) 1991, Writing the Memoir: From Truth to Art 1997, Lifesaving: A Memoir (Lambda Literary Award 2001) 2000, Horses and the Human Soul 2004, Postcard from the Bottom of the Sea 2009, Lost Lands (Robin Becker Chapbook Award) 2009, A Touch of Madness Chapbook 2011; contribs to anthologies, journals, and magazines. *Honours:* Fairlie Place Essay Prize 1963, Jeanette Rankin Award for Feminist Journalism 1983, Creative Nonfiction Grant, Oregon Inst. of Literary Arts 1989, 1993, Annual Nonfiction Award, Sonora Review 1993, Freedom of Expression Award, American Civil Liberties Union, Oregon 1994, Andres Berger Award in Creative Non-Fiction, Northwest Writers 1996, Dulwich Festival Poetry Prize 1996, Stuart H. Holbrook Award 1997, Literary Arts Inc. Award 1997, White Mice Award in Poetry, Lawrence Durrell Asscn 1997, Oregon Arts Commission Fellowship 1997, Robin Becker Chapbook Award 2009. *Address:* 622 SE 29th Avenue, Portland, OR 97214, USA (home). *E-mail:* judith@judithbarrington.com (office). *Website:* www.judithbarrington.com.

BARROW, Jedediah (see Benson, Gerard John)

BARROW, Robin St Clair, MA, PhD, FRSC; British author and academic; *Professor of Education, Simon Fraser University;* b. 18 Nov. 1944, Oxford, England. *Education:* Univ. of Oxford, Inst. of Educ., London, Univ. of London. *Career:* Lecturer in Philosophy of Educ., Univ. of Leicester 1972–80, Personal Readership in Educ. 1980–82; Visiting Prof. of Philosophy of Educ., Univ. of Western Ontario, Canada 1977–78; Prof. of Educ., Simon Fraser Univ., Burnaby, BC 1982–, Dean of Educ. 1992–2003; mem. Philosophy of Educ. Soc. of GB (Vice-Chair. 1980–83), Northwestern Philosophy of Educ. Soc. of N America (Pres. 1984–85), Canadian Philosophy of Educ. Soc. (Pres. 1990–91). *Publications include:* Athenian Democracy 1973, An Introduction to the Philosophy of Education 1974, Sparta 1975, Plato, Utilitarianism and Education 1975, Moral Philosophy for Education 1975, Greek and Roman Education 1976, Plato and Education 1976, Common Sense and the Curriculum 1976, Plato's Apology 1978, The Canadian Curriculum: A Personal View 1978, Radical Education 1978, Happiness 1979, The Philosophy of Schooling 1981, Injustice, Inequality and Ethics 1982, Language and Thought: Rethinking Language Across the Curriculum 1982, Giving Teaching Back to Teachers: A Critical Introduction to Curriculum Theory 1984, A Critical Dictionary of Educational Concepts: An Appraisal of Selected Ideas and Issues in Educational Theory and Practice 1986, Understanding Skills: Thinking, Feeling and Caring 1990, Utilitarianism: A Contemporary Statement 1991, Beyond Liberal Education (co-ed. with Patricia White) 1993, Language, Intelligence and Thought 1993, What Use is Educational Research? 2005, Academic Ethics (co-ed. with Patrick Keeney) 2006, An Introduction to Moral Philosophy and Moral Education 2007, Plato 2007, Plato, Utilitarianism and Education 2009, The Sage Handbook of Philosophy of Education (ed) 2010; contribs to books and scholarly journals. *Address:* Faculty of Education, Simon Fraser University, Building No 9507, Burnaby, BC V5A 1S6, Canada (office). *Telephone:* (778) 782-5890 (office). *E-mail:* robin_barrow@sfu.ca (office). *Website:* www.educ.sfu.ca (office).

BARRY, Edward William, BA; American publishing executive; b. 24 Nov. 1937, Stamford, Conn.; s. of Edward Barry and Elizabeth Cosgrove; m. Barbara H. Walker 1963; one s. one d. *Education:* Univ. of Conn. *Career:* Pres. The Free Press, New York 1972–82, Oxford Univ. Press Inc., New York 1982–2000; Sr Vice-Pres. Macmillan Publishing Co., New York 1973–82; mem. Exec. Council, Professional and Scholarly Publications 1993; mem. Advisory Bd Pace Univ. Grad. Program in Publishing 1990–; mem. Bd of Dirs Asscn of American Publrs 1995; Trustee Columbia Univ. Press 2000–. *Honours:* Hon. LittD (Univ. of Oxford) 2000. *Address:* 266 Old Poverty Road, Southbury, CT 06488-1769, USA (home). *Telephone:* (203) 267-7854 (home).

BARRY, James P., BA; American writer and editor; b. 23 Oct. 1918, Alton, IL; m. Anne Elizabeth Jackson 1966. *Education:* Ohio State Univ. *Career:* Dir Ohioana Library Asscn 1977–88; Ed. Ohioana Quarterly 1977–88; mem. Ohioana Library Asscn. *Publications include:* Georgian Bay: The Sixth Great Lake 1968, The Battle of Lake Erie 1970, Bloody Kansas 1972, The Noble Experiment 1972, The Fate of the Lakes 1972, The Louisiana Purchase 1973, Ships of the Great Lakes: 300 Years of Navigation 1973, Great Lakes 1976, Wrecks and Rescues of the Great Lakes 1981, Georgian Bay: An Illustrated History 1992, Old Forts of the Great Lakes 1994, American Powerboats 2003, Hackercraft 2009, Fidistoria 2010. *Honours:* American Soc. of State and Local History Award 1974, Marine History Soc. of Detroit Great Lakes Historian of the Year 1995. *Address:* 353 Fairway Blvd, Columbus, OH 43213, USA (home).

BARRY, Kevin; Irish author and journalist; b. 1969, Limerick. *Career:* fmr reporter, Limerick Tribune, Limerick Post; writes articles on travel and literature for, The Guardian, Sydney Morning Herald, Irish Times and others; columnist and sketch writer, Sunday Herald, Irish Examiner. *Publications:* short story collections: There Are Little Kingdoms (Rooney Prize for Irish Literature 2007) 2007, Dark Lies the Island 2012; novel: City of Bohane 2011. *Honours:* Sunday Times EFG Private Bank Short Story Award 2012. *Address:* c/o Jonathan Cape, Random House, 20 Vauxhall Bridge Road, London, SW1V 2SA, England (office). *Telephone:* (20) 7840-8400 (office). *Fax:* (20) 7840-8778 (office). *Website:* www.randomhouse.co.uk (office).

BARRY, Sebastian, BA; Irish writer, dramatist and poet; b. 5 July 1955, Dublin; m.; three c. *Education:* Trinity Coll., Dublin. *Career:* Writer-in-Asscn and Dir of Bd, Abbey Theatre, Dublin 1989–90; Writer Fellow, Trinity Coll., Dublin 1995–96; mem. Aosdána, Irish Writers' Union. *Publications include:* Macker's Garden 1982, The Water-Colourist (poetry) 1983, Time Out of Mind (novel) 1983, Strappado Square (novel) 1983, The Inherited Boundaries: Younger Poets of the Republic of Ireland (Ed.) 1984, Elsewhere: The Adventures of Belemus (children's fiction) 1985, The Rhetorical Town 1985, The Engine of Owl-Light 1987, Fanny Hawke Goes to the Mainland Forever (poetry) 1989, Boss Grady's Boys (play) (BBC/Stewart Parker Award 1989) 1989, Prayers of Sherkin (play) 1990, The Only True History of Lizzie Finn 1995, The Steward of Christendom (play) (Christopher Ewart-Biggs Memorial Prize, Ireland/America Literary Prize, Critics' Circle Award for Best New Play, Writers' Guild Award for Best Fringe Play) 1995, White Woman Street 1995, Our Lady of Sligo (play) (Peggy Ramsay Play Award) 1998, The Whereabouts of Eneas McNulty (novel) 1998, Annie Dunne (novel) 2002, Hinterland (play) 2002, The Pinkening Boy (poems) 2004, Whistling Psyche (play) 2004, Fred and Jane 2004, A Long, Long Way (novel) 2005, The Pride of Parnell Street (play) 2006, Andersen's English, The Secret Scripture (novel) (Costa Book of the Year Award 2008, James Tait Black Memorial Prize for Fiction, Ind. Booksellers' Award, Hughes & Hughes Irish Book of the Year Award) 2008, On Canaan's Side 2011; contribs to periodicals. *Honours:* Hon. Fellow in Writing, Univ. of Iowa 1984; Arts Council Bursary 1982, Iowa Int. Writing Fellowship 1984, Hawthornden Int. Fellowships 1985, 1988, Lloyds Private Banking Playwright of the Year 1995. *Literary Agent:* AP Watt Ltd, 20 John Street, London, WC1N 2DR, England. *Telephone:* (20) 7405-6774. *Fax:* (20) 7831-2154. *E-mail:* apw@apwatt.co.uk. *Website:* www.apwatt.co.uk.

BARSKY, Robert F., BA, MA, PhD; Canadian researcher, academic and writer; *Professor of English and French Literature, European Studies, Jewish Studies, Quebec and Canadian Studies, Vanderbilt University;* b. 18 May 1961, Montreal; m. Marsha Barsky; two s. *Education:* Vanier Coll., Brandeis Univ., McGill Univ., Free Univ., Brussels, Belgium. *Career:* content analysis researcher, Trans-Canada Social Policy Research Centre, Montreal 1985–91; ethnic studies and refugee studies researcher, Institut Québecois de Recherche sur la Culture, Montréal 1991–93; refugee studies researcher, Institut Nat. de la Recherche Scientifique, Montréal 1993–95; Assoc. Prof. of English, Univ. of Western Ontario, London 1995; currently Prof. of English and French Literature, European Studies, Jewish Studies, Quebec and Canadian Studies, Vanderbilt Univ., USA; Visiting Prof., IQRC/INRS 1991–96, Univ. of Western Ontario 1996, Université du Québec 2000–02; Visiting Fellow, Yale Univ. 2000, 2003, Canadian Bicentennial Prof. 2002; Founder-Ed., AmeriQuests; Founder and fmr Co-Ed., Discours social/Social Discourse: Discourse Analysis and Text Sociocriticism; Founder and fmr Ed., 415 South Street; Assoc. Ed., SubStance; mem. Scarlet Key 1992–. *Publications include:* Bakhtin and Otherness 1991, Constructing a Productive Other: Discourse Theory and the Convention Refugee Hearing 1994, Introduction à la théorie littéraire 1997, Noam Chomsky: A Life of Dissent 1997, Arguing and Justifying 2000, Philosophy and the Passions (trans.) 2000, French Theory Today (co-ed. with Eric Méchoulan) 2002, Workers' Councils, by Anton Pannekoek (ed.) 2003, Marc Angenot and the Scandal of History (ed.) 2004, The Chomsky Effect 2007, Zellig Harris: From American Linguistics to Socialist Zionism 2011; contrib. to periodicals. *Honours:* Chancellor Heard Prof. of the Year, Vanderbilt Univ. 2005. *Address:* Department of French and Italian, Furman Hall 219, Vanderbilt University, PO Box 6312 Station B, Nashville, TN 37235-0001, USA (office). *Telephone:* (615) 322-6910 (office). *Fax:* (615) 343-6909 (office). *E-mail:* robert.barsky@vanderbilt.edu (office). *Website:* www.vanderbilt.edu/french_ital/barsky (office); www.ameriquests.org (home).

BARTH, John Simmons, MA; American novelist and academic; *Professor Emeritus in the Writing Seminars, Johns Hopkins University;* b. 27 May 1930, Cambridge, Md; s. of John J. Barth and Georgia Simmons; m. 1st Harriette Anne Strickland 1950 (divorced 1969); two s. one d.; m. 2nd Shelly Rosenberg 1970. *Education:* Johns Hopkins Univ. *Career:* Instructor, Pennsylvania State Univ. 1953, Assoc. Prof. until 1965; Prof. of English, State Univ. of New York at Buffalo 1965–73, Johns Hopkins Univ. 1973–91, Prof. Emer. in the Writing Seminars 1991–; Rockefeller Foundation Grant. *Publications:* The Floating Opera 1956, The End of the Road 1958, The Sot-Weed Factor 1960, Giles Goat-Boy 1966; Lost in the Funhouse (stories) 1968, Chimera 1972, Letters 1979, Sabbatical 1982, The Friday Book (essays) 1984, The Tidewater Tales: A Novel 1987, The Last Voyage of Somebody the Sailor 1991, Once Upon a Time 1994, On With the Story (stories) 1996, Coming Soon!!! (novel) 2001, The Book of Ten Nights and a Night (stories) 2004, Three Roads Meet (novella) 2005, The Development (stories) 2008, Every Third Thought: A Novel in Five Seasons 2011. *Honours:* mem., American Acad. of Arts and Letters 1974, Fellow, American Acad. of Arts and Sciences 1974; Hon. LittD (Univ. of Maryland) 1969, (Salisbury Univ.) 1975; Hon. DHL (Pennsylvania State Univ.) 1996, (Western Maryland Coll.) 1973, (Towson Univ.) 1981, (Univ. of Colorado) 2009; Laurea hc in Letter (Univ. Macerata, Italy) 1990; Hon. LittD (Colby Coll.) 2007; Brandeis Univ. Citation in Literature, Nat. Acad. of Arts and

Letters Award, Nat. Book Award 1973, F. Scott Fitzgerald Award 1997, President's Medal, Johns Hopkins Univ. 1997, PEN/Malamud Award 1998, Lifetime Achievement Award, Lannan Foundation 1998, Lifetime Achievement in Letters Award, Enoch Pratt Soc. 1999, Roozi Rozegari (Iranian literature prize) 2008. *Address:* The Writing Seminars, 135 Gilman Hall, Johns Hopkins University, 3400 North Charles Street, Baltimore, MD 21218, USA (office). *Telephone:* (410) 167-563 (office). *Website:* www.jhu.edu/writsem (office).

BARTLETT, Christopher John, BA, PhD, FRHistS, FRSE; British writer; b. 12 Oct. 1931, Bournemouth, England; m. Shirley Maureen Briggs 1958; three s. *Education:* University Coll., Exeter and LSE. *Career:* Asst Lecturer, Univ. of Edinburgh 1957–59; Lecturer in Modern History, Univ. of the West Indies, Jamaica 1959–62, Queen's Coll., Dundee 1962–68; Reader in Int. History, Univ. of Dundee 1968–78, Prof. of Int. History 1978–96, Head, Dept of History 1983–88, Emer. and Hon. Prof. of Int. History 1996–2002. *Publications include:* Great Britain and Sea Power, 1815–53 1963, Castlereagh 1966, Britain Pre-eminent: Studies of British World Influence in the Nineteenth Century (ed.) 1969, The Long Retreat: A Short History of British Defence Policy, 1945–70 1972, The Rise and Fall of the Pax Americana: American Foreign Policy in the Twentieth Century 1974, A History of Postwar Britain, 1945–74 1977, The Global Conflict, 1880–1990: The International Rivalry of the Great Powers 1984, British Foreign Policy in the Twentieth Century 1989, 'The Special Relationship': A Political History or Anglo-American Relations Since 1945 1992, Defence and Diplomacy: Britain and the Great Powers 1815–1914 1993, Peace, War and the European Great Powers 1814–1914 1996; contrib. to scholarly books and journals. *Address:* c/o University of Dundee, Nethergate, Dundee, DD1 4HN, Scotland.

BARTLETT, Robert John, BA, MA, DPhil, FRHistS, FBA, FRSE, FSA; British academic, writer and editor; *Bishop Wardlaw Professor, University of St Andrews*; b. 27 Nov. 1950, London; m. Honora Elaine Hickey 1979; one s. one d. *Education:* Peterhouse, Cambridge, St John's Coll., Oxford. *Career:* Lecturer in History, Univ. of Edinburgh 1980–86; mem. Inst. for Advanced Study, Princeton, NJ and Visiting Fellow, Davis Center, Dept of History, Princeton Univ. 1983–84; Prof. of Medieval History, Univ. of Chicago 1986–92; Prof. of Mediaeval History, Univ. of St Andrews 1992–, Bishop Wardlaw Prof. 1997–; Assoc. Ed. New Dictionary of National Biography 1994–; British Acad. Reader 1995–97; Sackler Scholar, Mortimer and Raymond Sackler Inst. of Advanced Studies, Univ. of Tel-Aviv 2001; Jr Fellow, Univ. of Michigan Soc. of Fellows 1979–80; Alexander von Humboldt Fellow, Univ. of Göttingen 1988–89. *Television:* Inside the Medieval Mind, BBC4 2008, The Normans, BBC2 2010. *Publications include:* Gerald of Wales 1146–1223 1982, Trial by Fire and Water, The Medieval Judicial Ordeal 1986, Medieval Frontier Societies (ed. with Angus MacKay) 1989, The Making of Europe: Conquest, Colonization and Cultural Change 950–1350 (Wolfson Literary Prize) 1993, England Under the Norman and Angevin Kings 1075–1225 2000, Medieval Panorama (ed.) 2001, Life and Miracles of St Modwenna, by Geoffrey of Burton (ed and translated) 2002, The Miracles of St Aebbe of Coldingham and St Margaret of Scotland (ed and translated) 2003, The Hanged Man: A Story of Miracle, Memory and Colonialism in the Middle Ages 2004, The Natural and the Supernatural in the Middle Ages 2008; contribs to scholarly books and journals. *Honours:* Wolfson Literary Prize for History 1993, Leverhulme Trust Major Research Fellowship 2009. *Address:* School of History, University of St Andrews, 71 South Street, St Andrews, KY16 9QW, Scotland (office). *Telephone:* (1334) 463309 (office). *Fax:* (1334) 463334 (office). *E-mail:* rjb1@st-andrews.ac.uk (office). *Website:* www.st-andrews.ac.uk/history (office).

BARTON, Rev. John, MA, DPhil, DLitt, FBA; British academic; *Oriel and Laing Professor of the Interpretation of Holy Scripture, Oriel College, University of Oxford*; b. 17 June 1948, London; s. of Bernard A. Barton and Gwendolyn H. Barton; m. Mary Burn 1973; one d. *Education:* Latymer Upper School, London and Keble Coll. Oxford. *Career:* Jr Research Fellow, Merton Coll. Oxford 1973–74; Univ. Lecturer in Theology, Univ. of Oxford 1974–89, Reader in Biblical Studies 1989–91; Fellow, St Cross Coll. Oxford 1974–91; Oriel and Laing Prof. of the Interpretation of Holy Scripture and Fellow, Oriel Coll. Oxford 1991–; Canon Theologian of Winchester Cathedral 1991–2003; mem. Norwegian Acad. of Arts & Sciences 2008. *Publications:* Amos's Oracles Against the Nations 1980, Reading the Old Testament 1984, Oracles of God 1986, People of the Book? 1988, Love Unknown 1990, What is the Bible? 1991, Isaiah 1–39 1995, The Spirit and the Letter 1997, Making the Christian Bible 1997, Ethics and the Old Testament 1998, The Cambridge Companion to Biblical Interpretation 1998, Oxford Bible Commentary 2001, Joel and Obadiah 2001, The Biblical World 2003, Understanding Old Testament Ethics 2003, The Original Story (with J. Bowden) 2004, Living Belief 2005, The Nature of Biblical Criticism 2007, The Old Testament: Canon, Literature, Theology 2007. *Honours:* Hon. DrTheol (Bonn) 1998. *Address:* Oriel College, Oxford, OX1 4EW, England (office). *Telephone:* (1865) 276537 (office). *E-mail:* john.barton@oriel.ox.ac.uk (office). *Website:* www.oriel.ox.ac.uk (office).

BARTOV, Hanoch; Israeli writer, playwright and journalist; b. 13 Aug. 1926, Petah Tikva. *Education:* Hebrew Univ. of Jerusalem. *Career:* served in British Army's Jewish Brigade during World War II; fought in Arab–Israeli War 1948; Cultural Attaché to London 1966–68; regular columnist, Maariv newspaper. *Publications include:* Ha-Hesbon Ve-Ha-Nefesh (trans. as The Reckoning and the Soul) 1953, Shesh Knafaim Le-Ehad (trans. as Everyone Had Six Wings) 1973, Ha-Shuk Ha-Katan (trans. as The Little Market) 1957, Arba Yisrealim Ve-Col America (trans. as Four Israelis and All America) 1961, Sifriat Poalim (trans. as The Heart of the Wise) 1962, Pitzei Bagrut (trans. as The Brigade) 1965, Arba Yisraelim Be-Hatzer Saint James (trans. as Israelis at the Court of St James) 1969, Shel Mi ata Yeled (trans. as Whose Little Boy Are You?) 1970, Ahot Rehoka (trans. as A Distant Sister) 1973, Ha-Badai (trans. as The Dissembler) 1975, Dado, 48 Shanim Ve-Od 20 Yom (trans. as Dado, 48 Years and Another 20 Days) 1978, Yehudi Katan (trans. as Little Jew) 1981, Be-Emtza Ha-Roman (trans. as In the Middle of It All) 1984, Yerid Be-Moskva (trans. as A Fair in Moscow) 1988, Mazal Ayala 1988, Ze Ishel Medaber (trans. as This is Ishel Speaking) 1990, Mavet Be-Purim (trans. as Death on Purim) 1992, Regel Ahat Ba-Hutz (trans. as Halfway Out) 1994, Ani Lo Ha-Tzabar Ha-Mitologi (trans. as I am not the Mythological Sabra) 1995, Lev Shafuch (trans. as A Heart Poured Out) 2001, Mi-Tom Ad Tom (trans. as Hand in Hand, Locked for Life) 2003, Mi-huts La-Ofek, Me'ever La-rechov (trans. as Beyond the Street, Across the Horizon) 2006, Ligdol Ve-Lichtov Be-eretz Israel (trans. as To Be and to Write in the Land of Israel) 2008. *Honours:* Dr hc (Tel-Aviv) 2005; Bialik Prize 1995, President's Prize for Literature 1998, Agnon Prize 2005, Buchman Prize 2006, Prime Minister's Prize 2007, Yehuda Amichai-ACUM Prize for Lifetime Achievement 2007, Israel Prize for Literature 2010. *Address:* c/o Kinneret Zmora-Bitan Dvir Publishing House, 10 Hataasiya Street, Or-Yehuda 60210, Israel. *Telephone:* 3-6344977. *Fax:* 3-6340953. *Website:* www.kinbooks.co.il.

BARZUN, Jacques Martin, AB, PhD, FRSA, FRSL; American writer and academic; *Professor Emeritus, Columbia University*; b. 30 Nov. 1907, Créteil, France; s. of Henri Martin and Anna-Rose Barzun; m. 1st Mariana Lowell 1936 (died 1979); two s. one d.; m. 2nd Marguerite Lee Davenport 1980. *Education:* Lycée Janson de Sailly and Columbia Univ. *Career:* Instructor in History, Columbia Univ. 1929, Asst Prof. 1938, Assoc. Prof. 1942, Prof. 1945, Dean of Graduate Faculties 1955–58, Dean of Faculties and Provost 1958–67, Seth Low Prof. 1960–67, Univ. Prof. 1967–75; Prof. Emer. 1975–; Literary Adviser, Scribner's 1975–93; fmr Dir Council for Basic Educ., New York Soc. Library, Open Court Publications Inc., Peabody Inst.; mem. Advisory Council, Univ. Coll. at Buckingham, Editorial Bd Encyclopedia Britannica 1979–; mem. Acad. Delphinale (Grenoble), American Acad. of Arts and Letters (Pres. 1972–75, 1977–78), American Historical Asscn, Royal Soc. of Arts, American Arbitration Asscn, American Philosophical Soc., Royal Soc. of Literature, American Acad. of Arts and Sciences; Extraordinary Fellow, Churchill Coll., Cambridge 1961. *Publications:* The French Race: Theories of its Origins and their Social and Political Implications Prior to the Revolution 1932, Race: A Study in Modern Superstition 1937, Of Human Freedom 1939, Darwin, Marx, Wagner: Critique of a Heritage 1941, Romanticism and the Modern Ego (revised edn as Classic, Romantic, and Modern) 1943, Introduction to Naval History (with Paul H. Beik, George Crothers and E. O. Golob) 1944, Teacher in America 1945, Berlioz and the Romantic Century 1950, God's Country and Mine: A Declaration of Love Spiced with a Few Harsh Words 1954, Music in American Life 1956, The Energies of Art: Studies of Authors, Classic and Modern 1956, The Modern Researcher (with Henry F. Graff) 1957, Lincoln the Literary Genius 1959, The House of Intellect 1959, Science, the Glorious Entertainment 1964, The American University: How it Runs, Where it is Going 1968, On Writing, Editing and Publishing: Essays Explicative and Horatory 1971, A Catalogue of Crime (with Wendell Hertig Taylor) 1971, The Use and Abuse of Art 1974, Clio and the Doctors: Psycho-History, Quanto-History and History 1974, Simple and Direct: A Rhetoric for Writers 1975, Critical Questions 1982, A Stroll with William James 1983, A Word or Two Before You Go 1986, The Culture We Deserve 1989, Begin Here: On Teaching and Learning 1990, An Essay on French Verse for Readers of English Poetry 1991, From Dawn to Decadence: 500 Years of Western Cultural Life 2000, A Jacques Barzun Reader 2001; editor: Pleasures of Music 1950, The Selected Letters of Lord Byron 1953, New Letters of Berlioz (also trans.) 1954, The Selected Writings of John Jay Chapman 1957, Modern American Usage; translator: Diderot: Rameau's Nephew 1952, Flaubert's Dictionary of Accepted Ideas 1954, Evenings with the Orchestra 1956, Courteline: A Rule is a Rule 1960, Beaumarchais: The Marriage of Figaro 1961; contrib. of articles to various scholarly and non-scholarly periodicals and journals. *Honours:* Chevalier de la Légion d'honneur, Presidential Medal of Freedom 2004; Gold Medal for Criticism, American Acad. of Arts and Letters. *Address:* 18 Wolfeton Way, San Antonio, TX 78218-6045, USA (home).

BASARA, Svetislav; Serbian writer and fmr diplomatist; b. 21 Dec. 1953, Bajina Bašta. *Career:* fmr Amb. to Cyprus. *Publications include:* Bumerang, Dzon B. Malkovic, Fama o biciklistima (novel) 1988, Kinesko pismo (novel, trans. as Chinese Letters) 1984, Kratkodnevica, Looney Tunes, Mongolski bedeker, Na gralovom tragu, Najlepse price, Napuklo ogledalo, Peking by Night, Srce zemlje, Sveta mast, Ukleta zemlja, Le Pays Maudit 2005, Le Miroir Fêlé 2005, Histoires en disparition 2005, Phénomènes 2005, Uspon i pad Parkinsonove bolesti (NIN Prize for Best Novel) 2006, Izgubljen u samoposluzi 2008, Perdu Dans Un Supermarché 2008. *Address:* c/o Ministry of Foreign Affairs, 11000 Belgrade, Kneza Miloša 24–26, Serbia.

BASINGER, Jeanine Deyling, BS, MS; American academic, curator and writer; *Corwin-Fuller Professor of Film Studies, Wesleyan University*; b. 3 Feb. 1936, Ravenden, Ark.; m. John Peter Basinger 1967, one d. *Education:* South Dakota State Univ. *Career:* Instructor, South Dakota State Univ. 1958–59; Teaching Assoc., Wesleyan Univ. 1971–72, Adjunct Lecturer 1972–76, Adjunct Assoc. Prof. 1976–80, Assoc. Prof. 1980–84, Prof. 1984–88, Corwin-Fuller Prof. of Film Studies 1988–; Founder-Curator, Wesleyan Cinema Archives 1985–; Trustee, American Film Inst.; mem. Steering Cttee,

Nat. Center for Film and Video Preservation; mem. Bd of Advisors, Asscn of Ind. Video and Filmmakers. *Publications include:* Working with Kazan (ed. with John Frazer and Joseph W. Reed) 1973, Shirley Temple 1975, Gene Kelly 1976, Lana Turner 1977, Anthony Mann: A Critical Analysis 1979, Anatomy of a Genre: World War II Combat Films 1986, The It's A Wonderful Life Book (co-author) 1986, A Woman's View: How Hollywood Saw Women, 1930–1960 1993, American Cinema: 100 Years of Filmmaking 1994, Silent Stars 2000, The Star Machine 2007; contrib. to books and periodicals. *Honours:* Hon. PhD (South Dakota State Univ.) 1996, Hon. DHumLitt (American Film Inst.) 2006; Distinguished Alumni Award, South Dakota State Univ. 1994, Outstanding Teaching Award, Wesleyan Univ. 1996, William K. Everson Award, Best Film Book of the Year. *Address:* Film Studies Department, Room 152, Wesleyan University, 301 Washington Terrace, Middletown, CT 06459, USA (office). *Telephone:* (860) 685-3542 (office). *Fax:* (860) 685-2221 (office). *E-mail:* jbasinger@wesleyan.edu (home). *Website:* www.wesleyan.edu/filmstudies (office).

BASS, Cynthia, BA, MA; American writer; b. 17 Oct. 1949, Washington, DC; m. Steven Seltzer. *Education:* Univ. of California, Berkeley. *Career:* columnist, San Francisco Examiner. *Publications include:* Sherman's March 1994, Maiden Voyage 1996, Beyond Our Wishes; contribs to periodicals. *E-mail:* cynthia@cynthiabass.com. *Website:* www.cynthiabass.com.

BASS, Jenna Cato, (Constance Myburgh); South African filmmaker, photographer and author; b. 15 Dec. 1986, London, England. *Education:* AFDA Film School, Cape Town. *Career:* raised in S Africa; numerous short films as writer/dir; dir of several music videos; story Hunter Emmanuel shortlisted for Caine Prize 2012; Ed. and Co-founder, Jungle Jim (literary magazine of pulp fiction). *Films include:* as writer, dir and producer: 5, 4, 3, 2, 1 2005, Yo! Elvis 2006, Ratcatcher 2006, Kite Dreams 2006, Weatherman 2006, Camp Wamkelikeli 2006, So Long to the City 2007, Jellyfish 2008, Already Gone 2009, The Tunnel 2009, Tok Tokkie (forthcoming feature film). *Publications:* as Constance Myburgh: featured in: African Violet: The 2012 Caine Prize Anthology (features story Hunter Emmanuel) 2012. *E-mail:* junglejimmag@gmail.com (office), jseebass@gmail.com (home). *Website:* www.junglejim.org (office), jseephoto.blogspot.com (home).

BASS, Rick, BS; American writer; b. 7 March 1958, Fort Worth, Tex.; m. Elizabeth Hughes Bass; two d. *Education:* Utah State Univ. *Career:* Bd mem. Yaak Valley Forest Council, Round River Conservation Studies. *Publications include:* The Deer Pasture 1985, Wild to the Heart 1987, Oil Notes 1989, The Watch 1989, Winter : Notes from Montana 1992, Platte River 1994, The Lost Grizzlies 1995, In the Loyal Mountains 1995, The Book of Yaak 1996, The Sky, the Stars, the Wilderness 1998, Where the Sea Used to Be 1998, Fiber 1998, The New Wolves 1998, Brown Dog of the YAAK 1999, Colter 2000, The Hermit's Story (short stories) 2002, The Ninemile Wolves 2003, The Diezmo: A Novel 2005, The Lives of Rocks (short stories) 2006, The New Wolves 2007, Why I Came West 2008, The Wild Marsh: Four Seasons at Home in Montana 2009, Nashville Chrome 2010; contribs to anthologies and periodicals. *Honours:* Pushcart Prize, O. Henry Award, PEN-Nelson Award 1988. *Address:* c/o Houghton Mifflin Company, Trade Division, Adult Editorial, 8th Floor, 222 Berkeley Street, Boston, MA 02116-3764, USA. *Website:* www.houghtonmifflinbooks.com.

BASS, Thomas Alden, AB, PhD; American writer and academic; *Professor of English, State University of New York, Albany*; b. 9 March 1951, Chagrin Falls, Ohio; m.; three c. *Education:* Univ. of Chicago, Univ. of California, Santa Cruz. *Career:* fmr Lecturer, Hamilton Coll., Clinton, NY and Univ. of California; currently Prof. of English, State Univ. of New York, Albany; Lecturer, Sciences Po, Paris; mem. Authors' Guild, PEN. *Publications include:* The Eudaemonic Pie (The Newtonian Casino) 1985, Camping with the Prince and Other Tales of Science in Africa 1990, Reinventing the Future: Conversations with the World's Leading Scientists 1993, Vietnamerica: The War Comes Home 1996, The Predictors 1999, The Spy Who Loved Us 2009; contribs to Smithsonian, Discover, Audubon, New York Times, New Yorker, Smithsonian, Wired. *Honours:* New York Foundation for the Arts Fellowship, Blue Mountain Center Fellowship, Ford Foundation Fellowship. *Address:* Department of English, State University of New York at Albany, Humanities Building 328, Albany, NY 12222, USA (office). *E-mail:* tbass@albany.edu (office). *Website:* www.albany.edu/english (office); www.thomasbass.com.

BASTABLE, Bernard (see Barnard, Robert)

BASU, Bani, MA; Indian writer; b. 11 March 1939, Calcutta (now Kolkata). *Education:* Lady Brabourne Coll., Scottish Church Coll., Univ. of Calcutta. *Career:* Bengali writer; fmr teacher, Bijay Krishna Girls Coll., Howrah; contrib. to various magazines, including Janmabhoomi Matribhoomi, Anandamala, Desh. *Publications include:* stories: Mohana, Samudra, Nana Swader Galpa, Varandah–O–Anyanya, Golper Sat Satero, Jakhan Chand Ebong, Bachhai Golpa 1, 2, 3, Golpa Samagra 1, 2, 3, Nandita (made into telefilm), Jakhan Chand (made into telefilm); novels: Janmabhumi Matribhumi 1987, Antarghaat (Tara Sankar Award 1991) 1989, Pancham Purush, Shet Phatharer Thala (made into film) 1991, Uttar Sadhak, Gandharbi (made into film and TV serial) 1993, Ekushe Paa (made into TV serial), Didi Maser Gens, Britter Baire 1995, Meyeli Adder Halchal, Moou; Radhanagar, Amrita (made into TV serial), Kharap Chhele, Timir Bidar, Jharer Kheya, Maitreya Jataka (Ananda Purashkar 1997), Ashtam Garbha, Ujan Jatra, Samudra Jatra, Khana Mihirer Dhipi, Je Jekhane Jai, Upanyas Panchak, Trekers, Shakambherir Dwip (made into TV serial), Ballyguange Court (made into film), Ashwajoni; juvenile literature: Operation Arindom, Rupar Gachh, Chotoder Golpo Samagra. *Honours:* Tara Sankar Award 1991, Sahitya Setu Award 1995, Siromoni Award 1997, Ananda Award 1997, Bankim Award 1998, Mahadevi Birla Award 1998, Katha Award 2003, Pratima Mitra Smriti Award 2007, Kabi Krittbas Sahitya Award 2008, Bhuban Mohini Dasi Swarna Padak, Calcutta Univ. 2008, Sushila Devi Birla Award, Sahitya Acad. Award 2010. *Address:* 30 Haripada Dutta Lane, Indrolok Apartments, Flat B/4, Kolkata 700 033, India (home). *Telephone:* (33) 24178359 (home); (98) 30494883 (home). *E-mail:* banibasu_cal@yahoo.co.in (home).

BASU, Kunal, PhD; Indian author and academic; *Reader in Marketing, Said Business School, University of Oxford*; b. 4 May 1956, Kolkata; s. of Sunil Kumar Basu and Chabi Basu; m. Susmita Basu 1982; one d. *Education:* Univ. of Florida, USA. *Career:* fmr Assoc. Prof., McGill Univ., Montreal, Canada 1986–99; worked at Indian Inst. of Man. 1989; Reader in Marketing, Said Business School and Templeton Coll., Univ. of Oxford 1999–; work published in numerous journals; fmr Dir Powercorp Centre for Int. Man. Studies, Montreal. *Films:* screenplays: Football 1980, The Magic Loom 1997. *Publications include:* novels: The Opium Clerk 2001, The Miniaturist 2003, Racists 2006, The Yellow Emperor's Cure 2011; short story collection: The Japanese Wife 2008; essays: Intimacies 2011. *Honours:* several teaching awards including Royal Bank Teaching Innovation Award. *Literary Agent:* c/o Philippa Brewster, Capel & Land Limited, 29 Wardour Street, London, W1D 6PS, England. *Telephone:* (20) 7734-2414. *E-mail:* philippabrewster@googlemail.com. *Website:* www.capelandland.com. *Address:* Said Business School, University of Oxford, Park End Street, Oxford, OX1 1HP (office); 12 Randolph House, 1 Hernes Road, Oxford, OX2 7PT, England (home). *Telephone:* (1865) 288907 (office); (7921) 603660 (mobile). *E-mail:* Kunal.Basu@sbs.ox.ac.uk (office); kunalbasu100@yahoo.co.uk (home). *Website:* www.sbs.ox.ac.uk (office); www.kunalbasu.com (home).

BASU, Samit; Indian author; b. 14 Dec. 1979, Kolkata. *Education:* Don Bosco School, Presidency Coll., Kolkata, Univ. of Westminster, London. *Career:* fantasy novelist and comics writer; fmrly worked for Virgin Comics; as novelist created The GameWorld Trilogy. *Publications:* novels: The Gameworld Trilogy: The Simoqin Prophecies 2004, The Manticore's Secret 2005, The Unwaba Revelations 2007, Turbulence 2010, Terror on the Titanic 2010; contrib. to several anthologies. *Address:* c/o Titan Books, 144 Southwark Street, London, SE1 0UP, England (office). *Telephone:* (20) 7620-0200 (office). *E-mail:* readerfeedback@titanemail.com (office). *Website:* titanbooks.com (office); samitbasu.com (home).

BAT-SHAHAR, Hannah, BA, MA; Israeli writer; b. 25 Oct. 1944, Jerusalem; m.; five c. *Education:* Hebrew Univ. *Publications include:* Sipurei Ha-Kos (short stories) 1987, Likroh La-Atalefim (short stories) 1990, Among the Geranium Pots (short story, in trans.) 1990, Rikud Ha-Parpar (short stories) 1993, Sham Sirot Ha-Dayig (three novellas) 1997, Yonkey Ha-Devash Ha-Metukim (short stories) 1999, Ha-Naara Mi-Agam Mishigan (novel) 2002, Nimfa Levana, Seira Meshugaat (novel) 2005, Tzlalim Ba-Rei (novel) 2008. *Honours:* Rachel & Mordachi Nyman Prize 1984, Prime Minister's Prize 1994. *Address:* The Institute for the Translation of Hebrew Literature, POB 10051, Ramat Gan 52001 (office); Chezkeyow 30, Jerusalem 93644, Israel (home). *Telephone:* 3-5796830 (office); 2-5661566 (home). *Fax:* 3-5796832 (office); 2-5630274 (home). *E-mail:* litscene@ithl.org.il (office); chana9@bezeqint.net. *Website:* www.ithl.org.il (office).

BATCHELOR, John Barham, MA, PhD; British academic, writer and editor; *Professor Emeritus, School of English Literature, Language and Linguistics, Newcastle University*; b. 15 March 1942, Farnborough, Hants., England; m. Henrietta Jane Letts 1968; two s. one d. *Education:* Magdalene Coll., Cambridge, Univ. of New Brunswick, Canada. *Career:* Lecturer in English, Univ. of Birmingham 1968–76; Fellow and Tutor, New Coll., Oxford 1976–90; Joseph Cowen Prof., School of English Literature, Language and Linguistics, Newcastle Univ. 1990–2007, Prof. Emer. 2009–; Visiting Prof. (in asscn with Ruskin Programme), Lancaster Univ. 2002–; Ed. Modern Language Review, Yearbook of English Studies; mem. Int. Asscn of Profs of English; Founding Fellow, English Asscn (UK). *Publications include:* Mervyn Peake 1974, Breathless Hush (novel) 1974, The Edwardian Novelists 1982, Lord Jim (ed) 1983, H. G. Wells 1985, Joseph Conrad's Victory 1986, Virginia Woolf: The Major Novels 1991, The Life of Joseph Conrad: A Critical Biography 1994, The Art of Literary Biography (ed.) 1995, Ruskin and Shakespeare (ed) 1997, Shakespearean Continuities (co-ed.) 1997, Conrad and Wells at the End of the Century 1998, John Ruskin: No Wealth But Life 2000, Lady Trevelyan and the Pre-Raphaelite Brotherhood 2006; contribs to TLS, Observer, Daily Telegraph, Economist, Articles in English, Yearbook of English Studies, Review of English Studies, Dictionary of National Biography. *Honours:* Hon. Life mem. Modern Humanities Research Asscn. *Literary Agent:* c/o Felicity Bryan, 2A North Parade, Oxford, OX2 6LX, England. *Address:* School of English Literature, Language and Linguistics, Newcastle University, Newcastle upon Tyne, NE1 7RU, England (office). *Telephone:* (191) 222-7764 (office). *E-mail:* j.b.batchelor@ncl.ac.uk (office). *Website:* www.ncl.ac.uk/elll (office).

BATE, (Andrew) Jonathan, CBE, PhD, FBA, FRSL; British academic; *Professor of Shakespeare and Renaissance Literature, University of Warwick*; b. 26 June 1958, Sevenoaks, Kent, England; s. of Ronald Montagu Bate and Sylvia Helen Bate; m. 1st Hilary Gaskin 1984 (divorced 1995); m. 2nd Paula Jayne Byrne 1996; two s. one d. *Education:* St Catharine's Coll., Cambridge. *Career:* Harkness Fellow, Harvard Univ. 1980–81; Research Fellow, St Catharine's

Coll., Cambridge 1983–85, Hon. Fellow 2000–; Fellow, Trinity Hall, Cambridge, Lecturer 1985–90; King Alfred Prof. of English Literature, Univ. of Liverpool 1991–2003; Prof. of Shakespeare and Renaissance Literature, Univ. of Warwick 2003–; Research Reader, British Acad. 1994–96; Leverhulme Personal Research Prof. 1999–2004; Gov. Bd RSC, Ed. Shakespeare Edition. *Radio:* features and reviews for BBC Radio 3 and Radio 4. *Television:* South Bank Show and other arts programmes. *Publications:* Shakespeare and the English Romantic Imagination 1986, Charles Lamb: Essays of Elia (ed.) 1987, Shakespearean Constitutions: Politics, Theatre, Criticism 1730–1830 1989, Romantic Ecology: Wordsworth and the Environmental Tradition 1991, The Romantics on Shakespeare (ed.) 1992, Shakespeare and Ovid 1993, The Arden Shakespeare: Titus Andronicus (ed.) 1995, Shakespeare: An Illustrated Stage History (ed.) 1996, The Genius of Shakespeare 1997, The Cure for Love (novel) 1998, The Song of the Earth 2000, John Clare: A Biography (Hawthornden Prize 2003, James Tait Black Memorial Prize 2004) 2003, I Am: The Selected Poetry of John Clare (ed.) 2003, Andrew Marvell: Complete Poems (ed.) 2005, William Shakespeare: Complete Works (ed.) 2007, Soul of the Age: The Life, Mind and World of William Shakespeare 2008. *Honours:* Hon. Fellow, St Catharine's Coll., Cambridge; Calvin & Rose Hoffman Prize 1996, NAMI NY Book Award 2003. *Literary Agent:* c/o Wylie Agency Ltd, 17 Bedford Square, London, WC1B 3JA, England. *Address:* Department of English, Room H513, University of Warwick, Coventry, CV4 7AL, England (office). *E-mail:* j.bate@warwick.ac.uk (office). *Website:* www2.warwick.ac.uk/fac/arts/english (office).

BATES, Harry (see Home, Stewart Ramsay)

BATES, Milton James, BA, MA, PhD; American academic and writer; b. 4 June 1945, Warrensburg, Mo.; m. 1972; one s. one d. *Education:* St Louis Univ., Univ. of California, Berkeley. *Career:* Asst Prof. of English, Williams Coll. 1975–81; Asst Prof., Marquette Univ. 1981–86, Assoc. Prof. 1986–91, Prof. of English 1991–2010; Fulbright Distinguished Lecturer, Beijing Foreign Studies Univ. 2000, Universidad Complutense de Madrid 2006; mem. Wallace Stevens Soc. (Sec. 1990–2010). *Publications include:* Wallace Stevens: A Mythology of Self 1985, Sur Plusieurs Beaux Sujects: Wallace Stevens' Commonplace Book 1989, Wallace Stevens: Opus Posthumous (revised edn) 1989, The Wars We Took to Vietnam: Cultural Conflict and Storytelling 1996, The Bark River Chronicles: Stories from a Wisconsin Watershed 2012; contrib.: articles and book reviews in journals and periodicals. *Honours:* New York Times Book Review Notable Book of the Year 1985, Wisconsin Library Asscn Outstanding Achievement in Literature 1985, Guggenheim Fellowship 1989–90, Nat. Jesuit Book Award 1999, Council for Wisconsin Writers Scholarly Book Award 1996. *Address:* 208 Eagles Nest Road, Marquette, MI 49855, USA.

BATES, Quentin, (Graskeggur), MA; British journalist and author; b. 1962. *Education:* Styrimannaskólinn á Dalvík, Iðnskólinn á Ísafirði, Iceland, Univ. of Portsmouth. *Career:* lived in Iceland 1979–90; moved back to UK 1990–; Tech. Ed. Fishing News International 2000–. *Publications:* novels: Frozen Out (US title: Frozen Assets) 2011, Cold Comfort 2012. *Literary Agent:* c/o Peter Buckman, Ampersand Agency, Ryman's Cottages, Little Tew, Oxfordshire, OX7 4JJ, England. *E-mail:* info@theampersandagency.co.uk. *Website:* www.theampersandagency.co.uk. *Address:* c/o Fishing News International, Nexus Place, 25 Farringdon Street, London, EC4A 4AB, England (office). *Telephone:* (20) 7029-5700 (office). *E-mail:* cuan.joannides@intrafish.com (office). *Website:* www.graskeggur.com (home).

BATTESTIN, Martin Carey, PhD; American academic and writer; b. 25 March 1930, New York, NY; m. Ruthe Rootes 1963; one s. (died 1999) one d. *Education:* Princeton Univ. *Career:* Instructor, Wesleyan Univ. 1956–58, Asst Prof. 1958–61; Asst Prof., Univ. of Virginia 1961–63, Assoc. Prof. 1963–67, Prof. 1967–75, William R. Kenan, Jr Prof. of English 1975–98, Chair. Dept of English 1983–86, later William R. Kenan, Jr Prof. Emer. of English; Visiting Prof., Rice Univ. 1967–68; Assoc., Clare Hall, Cambridge 1972; mem. Asscn of Literary Scholars and Critics, American Soc. for 18th Century Studies, Int. Asscn of Univ. Profs of English, The Johnsonians, Modern Language Asscn. *Publications include:* The Moral Basis of Fielding's Art: A Study of 'Joseph Andrews' 1959, The Providence of Wit: Aspects of Form in Augustan Literature and the Arts 1974, Dictionary of Literary Biography 1985, New Essays by Henry Fielding: His Contributions to 'The Craftsman' (1734–39) and Other Early Journalism 1989, Providence of Wit 1989, Henry Fielding: A Life (with Ruthe R. Battestin) 1993, A Henry Fielding Companion 2000, Henry Fielding: 'Joseph Andrews' and 'Shamela' (ed.) 1961, Henry Fielding: The History of the Adventures of Joseph Andrews (ed.) 1967, Tom Jones: A Collection of Critical Essays (ed.) 1968, Henry Fielding: The History of Tom Jones, a Foundling (co-ed. with Fredson Bowers) (two vols) 1974, Henry Fielding: Amelia (ed.) 1983, British Novelists, 1660–1800 (ed.) 1985, The Works of Tobias Smollett (ed., mem. editorial bd, Georgia edn) 1987–, The Correspondence of Henry and Sarah Fielding (co-ed. with Clive T. Probyn) 1993, Smollett's trans. of Cervantes' Don Quixote (co-ed. with O. M. Brack) 2003; contribs to books and scholarly journals. *Honours:* American Council of Learned Socs Fellowships 1960–61, 1972, Guggenheim Fellowship 1964–65, Council of the Humanities Sr Fellow, Princeton Univ. 1971, Center for Advanced Studies, Univ. of Virginia 1974–75, Nat. Endowment for the Humanities Bicentennial Research Fellow 1975–76, Festschrift 1997, Visiting Fellow, Lincoln Coll., Oxford 1999. *Address:* 1832 Westview Road, Charlottesville, VA 22903, USA (home). *E-mail:* mcb9g@virginia.edu (office).

BATTIN, B. W., (S. W. Bradford, Alexander Brinton, Warner Lee, Casey McAllister), BA; American writer and financial consultant; b. 15 Nov. 1941, Ridgewood, NJ; m. Sandra McCraw 1976. *Education:* Univ. of New Mexico. *Career:* works as insurance consultant; joined as Financial Consultant Financial Network Investment Corpn, Belen 2001; fmr Pres. Belen Library Bd; fmr Pres. Belen Kiwanis Clubs; mem. Belen Rotary Club, Los Lunas Chambers of Commerce. *Publications include:* Angel of the Night 1983, The Boogeyman 1984, Satan's Servant 1984, Mary, Mary 1985, Programmed for Terror 1985, The Attraction 1985, The Creep 1987, Smithereens 1987, Demented 1988, Into the Pit 1989, It's Loose 1990, Night Sounds 1992, Tender Prey 1990, Fair Game 1992, Serial Blood 1992, Catch Me if You Can 1993; contribs to Cat Crimes I, II, and III. *Address:* Financial Network Investment Corporation, 511 W. Reinken Avenue, Belen, NM 87002, USA (office). *Telephone:* (505) 864-6675 (office).

BATTLES, R(oxy) E(dith) B(aker), BA, MA; American writer, poet, children's author and teacher; b. 29 March 1921, Spokane, Wash.; m. Willis Ralph Battles 1941; one s. two d. *Education:* Bakersfield Junior Coll., California State Univ., Pepperdine Univ. *Career:* elementary school teacher, Torrance Unified Schools 1959–85; Instructor, Torrance Adult School 1968–88, Pepperdine Univ. 1976–79; Author-in-Residence, American School of Madrid, Spain 1991; Instructor in Creative Writing, Los Angeles Harbor Coll. 1995; mem. Southwest Manuscripters. *Plays:* The Lavender Castle 1996, The Sacred Submarine 2000. *Publications include:* Over the Rickety Fence 1967, The Terrible Trick or Treat 1970, 501 Balloons Sail East 1971, The Terrible Terrier 1972, One to Teeter Totter 1973, Eddie Couldn't Find the Elephants 1974, What Does the Rooster Say, Yoshio? 1978, The Secret of Castle Drai 1980, The Witch in Room 6 1987, The Chemistry of Whispering Caves 1989, Barking for Rebellion (monologue) 2001; contribs to numerous periodicals. *Honours:* Nat. Science Award 1971, United Nations Award 1978. *Address:* 2172 Halcyon Road, Arroyo Grande, CA 93420, USA (home). *Telephone:* (805) 574-8537 (home). *E-mail:* groxy@aol.com.

BAUER, Caroline Feller, BA, PhD; American author and lecturer; b. 12 May 1935, Washington, DC; m. 1969; one d. *Education:* Sarah Lawrence Coll., Columbia Univ., Univ. of Oregon. *Career:* mem. American Library Asscn, Soc. of Children's Book Writers. *Publications include:* My Mom Travels a Lot 1981, This Way to Books 1983, Too Many Books 1984, Celebrations 1985, Rainy Day 1986, Snowy Day 1986, Midnight Snowman 1987, Presenting Reader's Theater 1987, Windy Day 1988, Halloween 1989, Read for the Fun of It 1992, New Handbook for Storytellers 1993, Putting on a Play 1993, Valentine's Day 1993, Thanksgiving Day 1994, The Poetry Break 1995, Leading Kids to Books Through Magic 1996, Leading Kids to Books Through Crafts, Leading Kids to Books Through Puppets, Meet the Presidents, What to Read to Your Little Brother or Sister, Bangladesh At Work 2006. *Honours:* Ersted Award for Distinguished Teaching, Christopher Award, Dorothy McKenzie Award for Distinguished Contribution to Children's Literature.

BAUER, Douglas; American writer; b. 17 Aug. 1945, Cheyenne, Wyo. *Career:* Writer-in-Residence, New York State Writers Inst., State Univ. of New York; Ed. Prime Times. *Publications include:* Prairie City, IA: Three Seasons at Home 1979, Dexterity 1989, The Very Air 1993, The Book of Famous Iowans 1997, The Stuff of Fiction: Advice on Craft 2006, Death by Pad Thai (ed) 2006. *Honours:* Dr hc (Univ. at Albany) 1983; Nat. Endowment for the Arts Fellowship, Massachusetts Artists Foundation Fellowship, Boston Public Library Literary Light.

BAUER, Steven Albert, BA, MFA; American writer, poet and academic; *Professor Emeritus of English, Miami University*; b. 10 Sept. 1948, Newark, NJ; s. of Albert Henry Bauer and Alice Marian Horrocks; m. Elizabeth Arthur 1982. *Education:* Trinity Coll., Hartford, Conn., Univ. of Massachusetts, Amherst, Vassar Coll. *Career:* Instructor Colby Coll., Waterville, ME 1979–81, Asst Prof. 1981–82; Asst Prof. of English, Miami Univ., Oxford, Ohio 1982–86, Assoc. Prof. 1986–96, Prof. 1996–2009, Prof. Emer. 2009–, Dir of Creative Writing 1986–96, Internal Dir of Creative Writing 1996–2001; Writing Fellowship Fine Arts Work Center, Provincetown 1978–79; Allan Collins Fellowship in Prose, Bread Loaf Writers' Conf. 1981, Writing Fellowship Ossabaw Island Project 1982; Owner Hollow Tree Literary Services. *Publications include:* Satyrday (novel) 1980, The River (novel) 1985, Steven Spielberg's Amazing Stories (two vols) 1986, Daylight Savings (poems) 1989, The Strange and Wonderful Tale of Robert McDoodle (The Boy Who Wanted to be a Dog) (juvenile) 1999, A Cat of a Different Color (juvenile) 2000; contributed essays, stories and poems in many periodicals. *Honours:* Prairie Schooner Strousse Award for Poetry 1982, Indiana Arts Council Master Artist Fellowship Award 1988, Peregrine Smith Poetry Prize 1989, Parents' Choice Recommended Writer 2000. *Address:* Department of English, Miami University, 356 Bachelor Hall, Oxford, OH 45056 (office); 14100 Harmony Road, Bath, IN 47010-9701, USA (home). *Telephone:* (513) 529-5221 (office). *Fax:* (513) 529-1392 (office). *E-mail:* sbauer@muohio.edu (office); info@hollowtree (office). *Website:* www.units.muohio.edu/english/index.html (office).

BAUER, Yehuda, MA, PhD; Israeli historian, academic and writer; *Academic Adviser, International Center for Holocaust Studies*; b. (Yehuda Martin), 6 April 1926, Prague, Czechoslovakia; two d. *Education:* Univ. of Wales, Hebrew Univ., Jerusalem. *Career:* served in Palmach Forces of the Haganah (Jewish Underground) 1944–45, and in Israel's War of Independence 1948–49; Lecturer, Inst. of Contemporary Jewry, Hebrew Univ. 1961–73, Head of Div. of Holocaust Studies 1968–95, Assoc. Prof. 1973–77, Head 1973–75,

1977–79, Prof. 1977–95, Prof. Emer. 1995–; Founder-Chair., Vidal Sassoon Int. Center for the Study of Antisemitism, Hebrew Univ. 1982–95; Ed., Journal of Holocaust and Genocide Studies 1986–95; Visiting Prof., Univ. of Honolulu at Manoa 1992, Yale Univ. 1993; Distinguished Visiting Prof., Ida E. King Chair of Holocaust Studies, Richard Stockton Coll., New Jersey 1995–96, 2002; Dir Int. Center for Holocaust Studies, Yad Vashem, Jerusalem 1996–2001, Academic Adviser 2000–. *Publications include:* (in English): From Diplomacy to Resistance: A History of Jewish Palestine 1939–1945 1970, My Brother's Keeper 1974, Flight and Rescue 1975, The Holocaust in Historical Perspective 1978, The Jewish Emergence From Powerlessness 1979, The Holocaust as Historical Experience (ed.) 1981, American Jewry and the Holocaust 1982, History of the Holocaust 1984, Jewish Reactions to the Holocaust 1988, Out of the Ashes 1989, Jews for Sale?: Nazi–Jewish Negotiations 1939–1945 1994, Rethinking the Holocaust 2001, The Death of the Shtetl 2010; contribs to scholarly books, yearbooks and journals. *Address:* International Center for Holocaust Studies, Yad Vashem, PO Box 3477, Jerusalem 91034, Israel (office). *Telephone:* 2-6443482 (office). *Fax:* 2-6443479 (office). *E-mail:* research.institute@yadvashem.org.il (office). *Website:* www1.yadvashem.org (office).

BAUMAN, Zygmunt, MA, PhD; British academic and writer; *Professor Emeritus of Sociology, University of Leeds*; b. 19 Nov. 1925, Poznań, Poland; s. of Maurycy Bauman and Zofia Bauman (née Cohn); m. Janina Bauman (née Lewinson) 1948 (died 2009); three d. *Education:* Univ. of Warsaw. *Career:* held Chair of Gen. Sociology, Univ. of Warsaw 1964–68, Prof. Emer. 1968–; Prof. of Sociology, Tel-Aviv Univ. 1968–71; Prof. of Sociology, Univ. of Leeds 1971–91, Prof. Emer. 1991–; mem. British Sociological Asscn, Polish Sociological Asscn. *Publications:* Culture as Praxis 1972, Hermeneutics and Social Science 1977, Memories of Class 1982, Legislators and Interpreters 1987, Modernity and the Holocaust 1989, Modernity and Ambivalence 1990, Intimations of Postmodernity 1991, Thinking Sociologically 1991, Mortality, Immortality and Other Life Strategies 1992, Postmodern Ethics 1993, Life in Fragments 1995, Postmodernity and Its Discontents 1996, Globalization: The Human Consequences 1998, Work, Consumerism and the New Poor 1998, In Search of Politics 1999, Liquid Modernity 2000, Individualized Society 2000, Community: Seeking Safety in an Uncertain World 2001, Society Under Siege 2002, Liquid Love: On the Frailty of Human Bonds 2003, Wasted Lives: Modernity and its Outcasts 2003, Europe: An Unfinished Adventure 2004, Liquid Life 2005, Liquid – Modern Fears 2006, Has Ethics a Chance in a Society of Consumers? 2008, The Art of Life 2008, Living on Borrowed Time 2009, 44 Letters from the Liquid Modern World 2010; contrib. to scholarly journals and general periodicals. *Honours:* Krzyz Walecznych (Poland) 1945; Dr hc (Oslo) 1997, (Lapland) 1999, (Uppsala) 2000, (Prague) 2001, (Copenhagen) 2001, (Sofia) 2001, (West of England) 2002, (London) 2003, (Leeds) 2004, (Gotenburg) 2005, (Leeds, Metropolitan) 2007, (Kaunas) 2008, (New School, NY) 2008, (Aberdeen) 2009, (Copenhagen Business School) 2009; Amalfi Prize for Sociology and Social Sciences 1989, Theodor W. Adorno Prize 1998. *Address:* 1 Lawnswood Gardens, Leeds, LS16 6HF, England (home). *E-mail:* janzygbau@aol.com (home).

BAUMBACH, Jonathan, AB, MFA, PhD; American writer and professor of English; b. 5 July 1933, Brooklyn, NY; m. 1st Naomi Miller; m. 2nd Elinor Berkman; m. 3rd Georgia Brown; m. 4th Annette Grant 2004; three s. one d. *Education:* Brooklyn Coll., City Univ. of New York, Columbia Univ., Stanford Univ. *Career:* served in US Army 1956–58; Instructor, Stanford Univ. 1958–60; Instructor Ohio State Univ. 1961–62, Asst Prof. 1962–64; Asst Prof., New York Univ. 1964–66; Assoc. Prof. of English, Brooklyn Coll., CUNY 1966–72, Prof. 1972–; Co-founder Fiction Collective, New York 1974, Co-dir 1974–78, currently mem. Bd of Dirs; Visiting Prof., Tufts Univ. 1970–71, Univ. of Washington 1978–79, 1985–86, Brown Univ., Rhode Island 1994; Movie Critic, Partisan Review 1973–82; Chair. Nat. Soc. of Film Critics 1982–84; mem. Teachers and Writers Collaborative, Bd of Dirs. *Publications:* The One-Eyed Man Is King (play) 1956, The Landscape of Nightmare: Studies in the Contemporary American Novel 1965, A Man to Conjure With 1965, What Comes Next 1968, Moderns and Contemporaries: Nine Masters of the Short Story (co-ed.) 1968, Writers as Teachers/Teachers as Writers (ed.) 1970, Reruns 1974, Statements: New Fiction from the Fiction Collective (ed.) 1975, Babble 1976, Statements 2: New Fiction (ed.) 1977, Chez, Charlotte and Emily 1979, My Father More or Less 1984, Separate Hours 1990, Seven Wives 1994, D-Tours 1998, B, a novel 2002, On The Way To My Father's Funeral 2004, You, or the Invention of Memory 2007, Dreams of Molly 2011; short stories: You Better Watch Out 1978, The Return of Service 1979, Neglected Masterpieces III 1986, The Life and Times of Major Fiction 1987, The History of Elegance 1988, Low Light 1990, The Mother Murders 1990, The Man Who Invented the World 1991, Men at Lunch 1991, Stills from Imaginary Movies 1991, The Villa Mondare 1992, The Reading 1993, Outlaws 1993, Bright Is Innocent 1994, His View of Her View of Him 1995; contrib. of articles, fiction in Esquire, American Review, Tri Quarterly, Iowa Review, Open City, Boulevard. *Honours:* New Republic Award 1958, Nat. Endowment for the Arts Fellowship 1978, Guggenheim Fellowship 1980, O. Henry Prize Stories 1980, 1984, 1988. *Literary Agent:* c/o Ellen Levine Literary Agency, 432 Park Avenue South, Suite 1205, New York, NY 10016, USA. *Address:* 320 Stratford Road, New York, NY 11218, USA (home). *E-mail:* jquartz@panix.com.

BAUSCH, Richard Carl, BA, MFA; American author and academic; *Lillian and Morrie A. Moss Chair of Excellence, University of Memphis*; b. 18 April 1945, Fort Benning, Ga; m. Karen Miller 1969; two s. one d. *Education:* George Mason Univ., Univ. of Iowa. *Career:* fmr Prof. of English and Heritage and Chair. of Creative Writing, George Mason Univ.; currently Lillian and Morrie A. Moss Chair. of Excellence, Univ. of Memphis; mem. Associated Writing Programs. *Publications include:* Real Presence 1980, Take Me Back 1981, The Last Good Time 1984, Spirits and Other Stories 1987, Mr Field's Daughter 1989, The Fireman's Wife and Other Stories 1990, Violence 1992, Rebel Powers 1993, Rare and Endangered Species: A Novella and Stories 1994, The Selected Stories of Richard Bausch 1996, Good Evening Mr and Mrs America, and All the Ships at Sea 1996, In the Night Season 1998, Someone to Watch Over Me 1999, Hello to the Cannibals 2002, The Stories of Richard Bausch 2003, Wives and Lovers 2004, Thanksgiving Night 2006, Peace (Dayton Literary Peace Prize 2009) 2008, Something is Out There 2010. *Honours:* Guggenheim Fellowship 1984, Nat. Endowment for the Arts Fellowship, Lila Wallace-Reader's Digest Writer's Award, Acad. of Arts and Letters Award in Literature. *Address:* English Department, University of Memphis, Patterson Hall, Memphis, TN 38152, USA (office). *Telephone:* (901) 678-2651 (office). *Fax:* (901) 678-2226 (office). *E-mail:* rbausch@memphis.edu (office). *Website:* www.memphis.edu/english/bios/bausch.htm (office).

BAUSCH, Robert Charles, BA, MA, MFA; American writer and teacher; b. 18 April 1945, Fort Benning, Ga; m. 1st Geri Marrese 1970 (divorced 1982); three d.; m. 2nd Denise Natt 1982; one s. *Education:* George Mason Univ. *Career:* Instructor in Creative Writing, Northern Virginia Community Coll. 1975–, currently Prof., Dept of Communication and Humanities; taught at Univ. of Virginia, American Univ., George Mason Univ., Johns Hopkins Univ.; mem. Bd of Dirs Pen-Faulkner Foundation. *Publications include:* On the Way Home 1982, The Lives of Riley Chance 1984, Almighty Me 1991, The White Rooster and Other Stories 1995, A Hole in the Earth 2000, The Gypsy Man (Fellowship of Southern Writer's Hillsdale Award for fiction) 2002, Out of Season 2005; contribs to periodicals. *Honours:* John Dos Passos Prize 2009. *Address:* Northern Virginia Community College, Department of Communication and Humanities, Room No WC 402J, 15200 Neabsco Mills Road, Woodbridge, VA 22191-4099, USA (office). *Telephone:* (703) 878-5664 (office). *E-mail:* rbausch@nvcc.edu (office). *Website:* www.nvcc.edu (office); www.robertbausch.org.

BAWDEN, Nina Mary, CBE, MA, JP, FRSL; British novelist; b. 19 Jan. 1925, Ilford, Essex; d. of Charles Mabey and Ellaline Ursula May Mabey; m. 1st H. W. Bawden 1947; two s. (one deceased); m. 2nd Austen S. Kark 1954 (died 2002); one d. two step-d. *Education:* Ilford Co. High School, Somerville Coll., Oxford. *Career:* Asst, Town and Country Planning Asscn 1946–47; JP, Surrey 1968; Pres. Soc. of Women Writers and Journalists 1981–; Hon. Fellow, Somerville Coll., Oxford; mem. PEN; council mem. Soc. of Authors. *Publications:* Who Calls the Tune 1953, The Odd Flamingo 1954, The Solitary Child 1956, Devil by the Sea 1958, Just Like a Lady 1960, In Honour Bound 1961, Tortoise by Candlelight 1963, A Little Love, A Little Learning 1965, A Woman of My Age 1967, The Grain of Truth 1969, The Birds on the Trees 1970, Anna Apparent 1972, George Beneath a Paper Moon 1974, Afternoon of a Good Woman 1976, Familiar Passions 1979, Walking Naked 1981, The Ice House 1983, Circles of Deceit (also adapted for TV) 1987, Family Money (also adapted for TV) 1991, In My Own Time (autobiog.) 1994, A Nice Change 1997, Dear Austen 2005; for children: The Secret Passage 1963, The Runaway Summer 1969, Carrie's War (Phoenix Award 1993) (also adapted for BBC TV 2003) 1973, The Peppermint Pig (Guardian Prize for Children's Literature 1975) 1975, The Finding 1985, Princess Alice 1985, Keeping Henry 1988, The Outside Child 1989, Humbug 1992, The Real Plato Jones 1993, Granny the Pig 1995, Off the Road 1998, Ruffian on the Stair 2001. *Honours:* Yorkshire Post Novel of the Year Award 1976, Edgar Allan Poe Award, Phoenix Award 1993, S. T. Dupont Golden Pen Award for Services to Literature 2004. *Literary Agent:* c/o Curtis Brown Ltd, Haymarket House, 28–29 Haymarket, London, SW1Y 4SP. *Telephone:* (20) 7393-4400. *Fax:* (20) 7393-4401. *E-mail:* info@curtisbrown.co.uk. *Website:* www.curtisbrown.co.uk. *Address:* 22 Noel Road, London, N1 8HA, England (office); 19 Kapodistriou, Nauplion 21100, Greece (home). *Telephone:* (20) 7226-2839 (office). *Fax:* (20) 7359-7103 (office).

BAWER, Bruce, BA, MA, PhD; American poet and critic; b. 31 Oct. 1956, New York, NY; s. of Theodore Bawer and Nell Carol Thomas. *Education:* State Univ. of New York, Stony Brook. *Career:* Literary Ed. Arrival Magazine 1986–87; movie reviewer, American Spectator; columnist, Advocate magazine 1994–99; moved to Netherlands 1998, to Norway 1999–; mem. Bd of Dirs Nat. Book Critics Circle; mem. Poetry Soc. of America, PEN. *Publications include:* poetry: Innocence 1988, Coast to Coast 1993; non-fiction: The Middle Generation 1987, The Contemporary Stylize 1987, Diminishing Fictions 1988, The Screenplay's the Thing 1992, The Aspect of Eternity 1993, A Place at the Table: The Gay Individual in American Society 1993, Prophets and Professors 1995, Beyond Queer: Challenging Gay Left Orthodoxy (ed.) 1996, House and Home 1996, Stealing Jesus: How Fundamentalism Betrays Christianity 1997, While Europe Slept: How Radical Islam is Destroying the West from Within 2006, Surrender: Appeasing Islam, Sacrificing Freedom 2009; contribs to Poetry, Paris Review, New Criterion, Hudson Review, American Scholar, Poetry East, Poetry Northwest, Boulevard, Chelsea, Pequod, Agni, Crosscurrents, Verse, 2 Plus 2, Arizona Quarterly, Kansas Quarterly, Wall Street Journal. *Honours:* Residency, Djerassi Foundation 1987. *E-mail:* media.queries@gmail.com (office). *Website:* www.brucebawer.com.

BAXTER, Charles, BA, PhD; American academic, author and poet; *Edelstein-Keller Visiting Professor of Creative Writing, University of Minnesota*; b. 13 May 1947, Minneapolis, Minn.; s. of John and Mary Barber Baxter; m. Martha

Hauser; one s. *Education:* Macalester Coll., State Univ. of NY, Buffalo. *Career:* Asst Prof., Wayne State Univ. 1974–79, Assoc. Prof. 1979–85, Prof. of English 1985–89; Faculty, Warren Wilson Coll. 1986–; Visiting Faculty, Univ. of Michigan 1987, Prof. of English 1989–2003; currently Edelstein-Keller Visiting Prof. of Creative Writing, Univ. of Minnesota. *Publications include:* fiction: Harmony of the World (Associated Writing Programs Award) 1984, Through the Safety Net 1985, First Light 1987, A Relative Stranger 1990, Shadow Play (Daniel A. Pollack-Harvard Review Award 1994) 1993, Believers 1997, The Business of Memory (ed) 1999, The Feast of Love 2000, Bringing the Devil to His Knees: The Craft of Fiction and the Writing Life (ed) 2001, Best New American Voices 2001 (ed) 2001, Saul and Patsy 2004, A William Maxwell Portrait: Memories and Appreciations (ed) 2004, The Soul Thief 2008, Gryphon: New and Selected Stories 2011; non-fiction: Burning Down the House 1997, The Art of Subtext: Beyond Plot 2007; poetry: Chameleon 1970, The South Dakota Guidebook 1974, Imaginary Paintings and Other Poems 1990; contribs to numerous anthologies, journals, reviews, and newspapers. *Honours:* Lawrence Foundation Award 1982, Nat. Endowment for the Arts Grant 1983, Michigan Council for the Arts Grant 1984, Guggenheim Fellowship 1985–86, Arts Foundation of Michigan Award 1991, Lawrence Foundation Award 1991, Lila Wallace-Reader's Digest Foundation Fellowship 1992–95, Michigan Author of the Year Award 1993, American Acad. of Arts and Letters Award in Literature 1997, American Acad. of Arts and Letters Award of Merit for Short Stories 2007. *Address:* Department of Creative Writing, University of Minnesota, Room 207, LindH, 207 Church Street SE, Minneapolis, MN 55455 (office); 410 North 2nd Street, Apt 456, Minneapolis, MN 55401, USA (home). *E-mail:* baxte087@umn.edu (office). *Website:* www.umn.edu (office); www.charlesbaxter.com.

BAXTER, Craig, BA, AM, PhD; American academic, writer and consultant; b. 16 Feb. 1929, Elizabeth, NJ; m. Barbara T. Stevens 1984 (died 2003); one s. one d. *Education:* Univ. of Pennsylvania. *Career:* joined Foreign Service; Vice-Consul, Embassy in Mumbai 1958–60; Political Officer, Embassy in New Delhi 1961–64; Deputy Principal Officer and Political Officer, Embassy in Lahore 1965–68; Analyst for India 1968–69; Sr Political Officer for Pakistan and Afghanistan 1969–71; Visiting Assoc. Prof. in Social Sciences, United State Military Acad. 1971–74; Political Counselor, Embassy in Accra 1974–76, Dhaka 1976–78; Officer-in-Charge, Int. Scientific Relations for the Near East, South Asia, and Africa 1978–80; Lecturer, Mount Vernon Coll., Washington, DC 1981, Visiting Prof. of Political Science and Diplomat-in-Residence 1981–82, Prof. of Politics and History 1982–99; Chair. Dept of Political Science 1991–94, Juniata Coll., Huntingdon, Pennsylvania; consultant to various orgs; mem. American Foreign Service Asscn, Asscn for Asian Studies, American Inst. of Pakistan Studies (Pres. 1993–99), American Inst. of Bangladesh Studies (Pres. 1989–98). *Publications include:* The Jana Sangh: A Biography of an Indian Political Party 1969, Bangladesh: A New Nation in an Old Setting 1984, Zia's Pakistan: Politics and Stability in a Frontline State (ed. and contributor) 1985, From Martial Law to Martial Law: Politics in the Punjab 1919-1958 (with Syed Nur Ahmad, Craig Baxter, Mahmud Ali) 1985, Government and Politics in South Asia (with Yogendra K. Malik, Charles H. Kennedy and Robert C. Oberst) 1987, Historical Dictionary of Bangladesh (with Syedur Rahman) 1989, Pakistan Under the Military: Eleven Years of Zia ul-Haq (with Shahid Javed Burki) 1990, Pakistan, Authoritarianism in 1980s (with Syed Razi Wasti) 1991, Bangladesh: From a Nation to a State 1996, Pakistan 1997 (with Charles H. Kennedy) 1998, Pakistan 2000 (with Charles H. Kennedy) 2000, Pakistan on the Brink 2003, The Ministry of Pleasure 2004, Diaries of Field Marshal Mohammad Ayub Khan 1966-1972 (with Mohammad Ayub Khan) 2007; contribs to books, encyclopedias and scholarly journals. *Honours:* Outstanding Academic Book, American Library Asscn 1996, Distinguished Asianist Mid-Atlantic Region Asscn for Asian Studies 2002. *Address:* 10223 Tanglewood Drive, Huntingdon, PA 16652-7407, USA (home). *E-mail:* cbaxter@pennswoods.net.

BAXTER, John; Australian writer; b. 14 Dec. 1939, Sydney, NSW; m. Marie-Dominique Montel; one d. *Education:* Waverly Coll., Sydney. *Career:* Dir of Publicity, Australian Commonwealth Film Unit, Sydney 1968–70; Lecturer in Film and Theatre, Hollins Coll. 1974–78; freelance TV producer and screen-writer 1978–87; Visiting Lecturer, Mitchell Coll. 1987; Dean of Faculty, Paris Through Expatriate Eyes; Co-Dir Paris Writers Workshop 2007–. *Television:* Filmstruck, First Take, The Cutting Room. *Radio:* Books and Writing. *Publications include:* The Off Worlders 1966, in Australia as The God Killers: Hollywood in the Thirties 1968, The Pacific Book of Australian Science Fiction (ed) 1970, The Australian Cinema 1970, Science Fiction in the Cinema 1970, The Gangster Film 1970, The Cinema of Josef von Sternburg 1971, The Cinema of John Ford 1971, The Second Pacific Book of Australian Science Fiction (ed) 1971, Hollywood in the Sixties 1972, Sixty Years of Hollywood 1973, An Appalling Talent: Kent Russell 1973, Stunt: The Story of the Great Movie Stunt Men 1974, The Hollywood Exiles 1976, The Fire Came By (with Thomas R. Atkins) 1976, King Vidor 1976, Hollywood 1920–1970 1977, The Hermes Fall 1978, The Bidders (in UK as Bidding) 1979, The Kid 1981, The Video Handbook (with Brian Norris) 1982, The Black Yacht 1982, Who Burned Australia? The Ash Wednesday Fires 1982, Filmstruck 1987, Bondi Blues 1993, Fellini 1993, Luis Buñuel 1994, Steven Spielberg: The Unauthorised Biography 1996, Stanley Kubrick 1997, Woody Allen: A Biography 1998, George Lucas: A Biography 1999, Mythmaker: The Life and Work of George Lucas 1999, The Making of Dungeons and Dragons: The Movie; A Pound of Paper: Confessions of a Book Addict 2002, De Niro: A Biography 2002, We'll Always Have Paris: Sex and Love in the City of Light 2006, Immoveable Feast: A Paris Christmas 2008, Carnal Knowledge: Baxter's Concise Encyclopedia of Modern Sex 2009, Von Sternberg 2010, The Paris Mens' Salon 2010, The Most Beautiful Walk in the World: A Pedestrian in Paris 2011; screenplays: The Time Guardian 1988; TV Series: The Cutting Room 1986, First Take 1986, Filmstruck 1986. *E-mail:* genet@noos.fr. *Website:* www.johnbaxterparis.com.

BAXTER, Stephen, MA, PhD; British writer; b. 13 Nov. 1957, Liverpool, England. *Education:* Univ. of Cambridge, Univ. of Southampton, Henley Man. Coll. *Career:* Pres. British Science Fiction Asscn; Vice-Pres. HG Wells Soc.; Fellow, British Interplanetary Soc.; full-time author 1995–. *Publications include:* fiction: Raft 1991, Timelike Infinity 1992, Anti-Ice 1993, Flux 1993, Ring 1994, The Time Ships (John W. Campbell Award 1996, Philip K. Dick Award 1996, British Science Fiction Asscn Award) 1995, Voyage (Sidewise Award) 1996, Titan 1997, Vacuum Diagrams (short stories) (Philip K. Dick Award 1999) 1997, Gulliverzone 1997, Traces (short stories) 1998, Moonseed 1998, Webcrash 1998, Manifold 1: Time 1999, Silverhair 1999, Longtusk 2000, Manifold 2: Space 2000, The Light of Other Days (with Arthur C. Clarke) 2000, Icebones 2001, Manifold 3: Origin 2001, Evolution 2002, Phase Space (short stories) 2002, Destiny's Children 1: Coalescent 2003, Time's Eye (with Arthur C. Clarke) 2004, Exultant 2004, Hunters of Pangaea (short stories) 2004, Sunstorm (with Arthur C. Clarke) 2005, Transscendent 2005, Emperor 2006, Resplendent 2006, Conqueror 2007, The H Bomb Girl 2007, Weaver 2008, Flood 2008, Stone Spring 2010; non-fiction: Angular Distribution Analysis in Acoustics 1986, Reengineering Information Technology (with David Lisburn) 1994, The Role of the IT/IS Manager 1996, Deep Future 2001, Omegatropic (British Science Fiction Asscn Award) 2001, Revolutions in the Earth: James Hutton and the True Age of the Earth 2003; other: Irina (online publ.) 1996, numerous short stories, ed. of anthologies, articles and talks; contribs to anthologies, science and computing journals, science fiction magazines, radio and television. *Honours:* British Science Fiction Asscn Award for Best Short Story 1998, Kurd Lasswitz Award (Germany), Seiun Award (Japan). *Address:* Ralph Vicinanza, 303 West 18th Street, New York, NY 10011, USA. *E-mail:* christopher.schelling@vicinanzaltd.com. *Website:* www.stephen-baxter.com.

BAYARD, Pierre; French psychoanalyst, writer and academic; *Professor of French Literature, University of Paris VIII*; b. 1954. *Career:* currently Prof. of French Literature, Univ. of Paris VIII. *Publications include:* Balzac et le troc de l'imaginaire: Lecture de La Peau de chagrin 1978, Symptôme de Stendhal: Armance et l'aveu 1980, Il était deux fois Romain Gary 1990, Le Paradoxe du menteur: Sur Laclos 1993, Maupassant, juste avant Freud 1994, Le Hors-sujet: Proust et la digression 1996, Qui a tué Roger Ackroyd? (Who Killed Roger Ackroyd?) 1998, Lire avec Freud: Pour Jean Bellemin-Noël 1998, Comment améliorer les œuvres ratées? 2000, Enquête sur Hamlet: Le Dialogue de sourds 2002, Le Détour par les autres arts: Pour Marie-Claire Ropars (co-ed.) 2004, Peut-on appliquer la littérature à la psychanalyse 2004, Demain est écrit 2005, Comment parler des livres que l'on n'a pas lus? (How to talk about books you haven't read) 2007, L'Affaire du Chien des Baskerville (Sherlock Holmes was Wrong: Re-opening the Case of the Hound of the Baskervilles) 2008. *Address:* Département de Littérature Française, Université Paris 8, 2 rue de la Liberté, 93526 Saint Denis cedex 02, France (office). *Telephone:* 1-49-40-68-16 (office). *E-mail:* bayard.sakai@wanadoo.fr (office). *Website:* www.univ-paris8.fr/littfra (office).

BAYEN, Bruno; French writer, dramatist, theatre producer and translator; b. 1950, Paris; one s. one d. *Education:* Ecole Normale Supérieure. *Career:* f. La Fabrique. *Theatre includes:* Schliemann, épisodes ignorés 1982, Faut-il choisir? Faut-il rêver? 1984, Weimarland et Le'enfant bâtard 1992, À trois mains 1997, La Fuite en Égypte 1999, Stella de Goethe 2001, Plaidoyer en faveur des larmes d'Héraclite 2003, Georg Büchner – Parcours complet 2004, Les Névroses sexuelles de nos parents 2005, L'éclipse du onze août 2006, Les Provinciales - Une querelle 2007, Laissez-moi seule 2009, Les Femmes savantes de Molière 2010. *Films:* Swing Troubadour 1991. *Television:* Mary of Bernard Sobel: Inspector of the Militia 1980. *Publications include:* Jean 3 Locke 1987, Restent les voyages (novel) 1990, Eloge de l'aller simple (novel) 1991, Weimarland/L'Enfant bâtard 1992, Hernando Colón, enquête sur un bâtard (novel) 1992, À trois mains 1997, Le pli de la nappe au milieu du jour (essay) 1997, La Fuite en Égypte 1999, Plaidoyer en faveur des larmes d'Héraclite, Les Excédés, La Forêt de six mois d'hiver, La Vie sentimentale 2002, Pourquoi pas tout de suite (essay) 2004, L'éclipse du onze août 2006, Fugue et rendez-vous 2011. *Address:* c/o Editions Mercure de France, 26 rue de Condé, 75006 Paris, France. *E-mail:* b.bayen@free.fr.

BAYLEY, John Oliver, MA, FBA, CBE, FRSL; British writer and professor of English; b. 27 March 1925, s. of F. J. Bayley; m. 1st (Jean) Iris Murdoch 1956 (died 1999); m. 2nd Audi Villers 2000. *Education:* Eton Coll., New Coll., Oxford. *Career:* served in army 1943–47; mem. St Antony's and Magdalen Colls, Oxford 1951–55; Fellow and Tutor in English, New Coll., Oxford 1955–74; Warton Prof. of English Literature and Fellow, St Catherine's Coll., Oxford 1974–92. *Publications:* In Another Country (novel) 1954, The Romantic Survival: A Study in Poetic Evolution 1956, The Characters of Love 1961, Tolstoy and the Novel 1966, Keats and Reality 1969, Pushkin: A Comparative Commentary 1971, The Uses of Division: Unity and Disharmony in Literature 1976, An Essay on Hardy 1978, Shakespeare and Tragedy 1981, The Order of Battle at Trafalgar 1987, The Short Story: Henry James to Elizabeth Bowen 1988, Tolstoy and the Novel 1988, Housman's Poems 1992, Alice (novel) 1994, The Queer Captain (novel) 1995, George's Lair (novel) 1996, The Red Hat (novel) 1997, Iris and the Friends: A Year of Memories 1998, Elegy for Iris: A

Memoir (1999) 1999, Widower's House 2001, Hand Luggage – An Anthology 2001, The Power of Delight – A Lifetime in Literature: Essays 1962–2002 2005; The Wings of the Dove (by Henry James) (ed.). *Honours:* Heinemann Literary Award. *Address:* c/o St Catherine's College, Manor Road, Oxford, OX1 3UJ, England.

BAYLEY, Peter Charles, MA; British academic and writer; *Fellow Emeritus, University College Oxford*; b. 25 Jan. 1921, Gloucester, England; s. of William Charles Abell and Irene Evelyn Beatrice Bayley (née Heath); one s. two d. *Education:* Univ. Coll., Oxford. *Career:* Jr Research Fellow, Univ. of Oxford 1947–49, Fellow and Praelector in English 1949–72, Univ. Lecturer 1952–72; Fellow, Univ. Coll. Oxford 1962–67, currently Fellow Emer.; Master, Collingwood Coll., Univ. of Durham 1972–78; Berry Prof. and Head of English Dept, Univ. of St Andrews, Fife 1978–85, Berry Prof. Emer. 1985–. *Publications include:* York Notes on John Milton's Selected Poems, Book 1 1966, 1970, The Faerie Queene, by Spenser, (ed) 1970, 1975, Edmund Spenser, Prince of Poets 1971, Loves and Deaths 1972, A Casebook on Spenser's Faerie Queene 1977, Poems of Milton 1982, An ABC of Shakespeare 1985, Pits, Parachutes and Pulpits: Reminiscences from a Wheelchair 2005, French Pulpit Oratory 1598–1650 2010; contribs to Patterns of Love and Courtesy 1966, Oxford Bibliographical Guides 1971, C. S. Lewis at the Breakfast Table 1979, The Encyclopedia of Oxford 1988, University College Oxford: a Guide and Brief History, Sir William Jones 1746–94 1998. *Honours:* Hon. Ed., Univ. Coll. Oxford annual Record 1950–72. *Address:* University College, Oxford, OX1 4BH, England (office). *Telephone:* (1865) 276602 (office). *E-mail:* academic.office@univ.ox.ac.uk (office). *Website:* www.univ.ox.ac.uk (office).

BAYLY, Sir Christopher Alan, Kt, FBA; British historian; *Vere Harmsworth Professor of Imperial and Naval History, University of Cambridge*; b. Tunbridge Wells, Kent. *Education:* Balliol and St Antony's Colls, Oxford. *Career:* Fellow, St Catharine's Coll. 1970–, Pres. 2007–; Vere Harmsworth Prof. of Imperial and Naval History, Univ. of Cambridge 1991–, currently Dir Cambridge's Centre of South Asian Studies; co-ed. New Cambridge History of India. *Publications include:* The Local Roots of Indian Politics: Allahabad 1880–1920 1975, Rulers, Townsmen and Bazaars: North Indian Society in the Age of British Expansion 1780–1870 1983, Two Colonial Empires: The Java War 1825–30 and the Indian Mutiny' of 1857–59 (ed) 1986, The Peasant Armed: The Indian Rebellion of 1857 (ed) 1986, Indian Society and the Making of the British Empire (ed) 1988, Rulers, Townsmen, and Bazaars: North Indian Society in the Age of British Expansion 1770-1870 1988, Imperial Meridian: The British Empire and the World, 1780–1830 1989, The Raj: India and the British, 1600–1947 1990, Environment and Ethnicity in India 1200 (ed) 1991, Architecture of Mughal India (ed) 1992, Empire and Information: Intelligence Gathering and Social Communication in India 1780–1870 (ed) 1996, The Origins of Nationality in South Asia 1997, European Commercial Enterprise in Pre-Colonial India (ed) 1998, Women and Labour in Late Colonial India: The Bengal Jute Industry (ed) 1999, Traditional Industry in the Economy of Colonial India (ed) 1999, The Politics of the Urban Poor in Early Twentieth-Century India (ed) 2001, Modernity and Culture from the Mediterranean to the Indian Ocean 1890–1920 (ed) 2001, The Birth of the Modern World: Global Connections and Comparisons 1780–1914 2004, Forgotten Armies: The Fall of British Asia 1941–45 (with Tim Harper) 2004, Imperial Meridian: The British Empire and the World 1780–1830 2004, Forgotten Wars: Freedom and Revolution in Southeast Asia (with Tim Harper) 2007, Empire in Question: Reading, Writing, and Teaching British Imperialism (co-author) 2011. *Honours:* Royal Asiatic Soc. Medal 2008; Wolfson Prize for History 2005. *Literary Agent:* c/o Bruce Hunter, David Higham Associates, 5–8 Lower John Street, Golden Square, London, W1F 9HA, England. *Telephone:* (20) 7434-5900. *Fax:* (20) 7437-1072. *E-mail:* dha@davidhigham.co.uk. *Website:* www.davidhigham.co.uk. *Address:* St Catharine's College, Cambridge, CB2 1RL, England (office). *E-mail:* cab1002@cam.ac.uk (office). *Website:* www.hist.cam.ac.uk (office).

BAYLY LETTS, Jaime; Peruvian/American journalist, writer and broadcaster; b. 19 Feb. 1965, Lima; s. of Jaime Bayly Llona; m. Sandra Masías; two d. *Education:* Inmaculado Corazón, Markham Coll., Lima, Colegio San Agustín de Lima, Pontificia Universidad Católica del Perú. *Career:* began career as columnist La Prensa (newspaper) 1980; fmr political corresp., TV series Pulso, Canal 5; fmr presenter '1990 en America'; currently presenter, El Francotirador (TV show), Peru, Bayly (own chat show), Mega TV, Miami, Nuestra Tele Noticias (NTN) 24; columnist, The Miami Herald, Peru 21. *Publications:* 10 novels including No se lo digas a nadie (Don't Tell Anyone) 1994, Yo amo a mi mami (I Love my Mummy) 2000, Y de Repente, Un Angel (Suddenly, an Angel) 2005, El Cojo y el Loco (The Crippled and the Crazy) 2009. *Honours:* GLAAD Visibility Award, USA 2007. *Address:* c/o Frecuencia Latina, Canal 2 Avda San Felipe 968, Jesús María, Lima, Peru (office). *Website:* www.frecuencialatina.com.pe/noticias/el_francotirador (office).

BEACH, Eric; Australian poet and writer; b. 1947, New Zealand. *Publications include:* Lyrics and Blues 1971, Henry Lawson Petfoods 1974, St Kilda Meets Hugo Ball 1974, In Occupied Territory 1977, A Photo of Some People in a Football Stadium 1978, Fair Deal Express: Writing from Kids at the Parks (ed) 1984, Hey Hey Brass Buttons (ed) 1990, Weeping for Lost Babylon 1996, Red Heart My Country 2000; contribs to anthologies. *Honours:* NSW Premier's Literary Award, Age Poetry Book of the Year Award. *Address:* c/o Pardalote Press, 44 Bayside Drive, Lauderdale, Tasmania 7021, Australia. *Telephone:* (3) 6248-8496. *E-mail:* info@pardalote.com.au. *Website:* www.pardalote.com.au.

BEAGLE, Peter Soyer, BA; American writer, musician, singer and songwriter; b. 20 April 1939, New York, NY; s. of Simon Soyer Beagle and Rebecca Soyer Beagle; m. 1st Enid Nordeen 1964 (divorced 1980); one s. two d.; m. 2nd Padma Hejmadi 1989 (divorced 2001). *Education:* Univ. of Pittsburgh. *Career:* Visiting Asst Prof., Univ. of Washington 1988; mem. Friends of Davis Group. *Publications include:* A Fine and Private Place 1960, I See By My Outfit 1965, The Last Unicorn 1968, The California Feeling 1969, Lila the Werewolf 1974, American Denim: A New Folk Art 1975, The Lady and Her Tiger (with Pat Derby) 1976, The Fantasy Worlds of Peter S. Beagle 1978, The Garden of Earthly Delights 1982, The Folk of the Air (Locus Award, Mythopoetic Fantasy Award 1987) 1986, The Innkeeper's Song (Locus Award, Mythopoetic Fantasy Award 1994) 1993, The Midnight Angel 1993, Peter Beagle's Immortal Unicorn (co-ed.) (Locus Award 1996) 1995, In the Presence of Elephants (with Pat Derby) 1995, The Unicorn Sonata (Locus Award 1997) 1996, Giant Bones (Locus Award 1998) 1997, The Rhinoceros Who Quoted Nietzsche, and Other Odd Acquaintances 1997, Tamsin (Mythopoetic Fantasy Award 2000) 1999, A Dance for Emilia 2000, Two Hearts (Hugo Award 2006, Nebula Award 2007) 2005, The Line Between 2006, Your Friendly Neighbourhood Magician 2006, The Last Unicorn: The Lost Version 2007, Strange Roads 2008, We Never Talk About my Brother 2009, Return 2010, Two Hearts 2010, Mirror Kingdoms 2010, Summerlong 2010, The Secret History of Fantasy (ed.) 2010, The First Last Unicorn and Other Beginnings 2010, Three Faces of The Lady 2010, I'm Afraid You've Got Dragons 2010, Green-Eyed Boy: Three Schmendrick Stories 2010, Three Unicorns 2010, Four Years, Five Seasons 2010, Sweet Lightning 2011, Sleight of Hand 2011; contribs to anthologies, periodicals, films, and TV. *Honours:* Inkpot Award 2006. *Address:* 250 Whitmore Street, Apt 216, Oakland, CA 94611-4628, USA (home). *Telephone:* (510) 658-6163 (home). *Website:* www.peterbeagle.com.

BEALES, Derek Edward Dawson, BA, PhD, LittD, FBA; British historian and academic; *Professor Emeritus of Modern History, Sidney Sussex College, Cambridge*; b. 12 June 1931, Felixstowe, Suffolk, England; s. of Edward Beales and Dorothy K. Dawson; m. Sara J. Ledbury 1964; one s. one d. *Education:* Bishop's Stortford Coll. and Sidney Sussex Coll., Cambridge. *Career:* Research Fellow, Sidney Sussex Coll., Cambridge 1955–58, Fellow 1955–, Asst Lecturer in History, Univ. of Cambridge 1962–65, Lecturer 1965–80, Prof. of Modern History 1980–97, Prof. Emer. 1997–; Stenton Lecturer, Univ. of Reading 1992, Birkbeck Lecturer, Trinity Coll., Cambridge 1993; Recurring Visiting Prof., Cen. European Univ., Budapest 1995–; Ed. Historical Journal 1971–75; mem. Standing Cttee for Humanities, European Science Foundation 1994–99; Leverhulme 2000, Emer., Fellowship 2001–03. *Publications:* England and Italy 1859–60 1961, From Castlereagh to Gladstone 1969, History and Biography 1981, History, Society and the Churches (with G. Best) 1985, Joseph II, Vol. I: In the Shadow of Maria Theresa 1987, Mozart and the Habsburgs 1993, Sidney Sussex Quatercentenary Essays (with H. B. Nisbet) 1996, The Risorgimento and the Unification of Italy (second edn with E. Biagini) 2002, Prosperity and Plunder: European Catholic Monasteries in the Age of Revolution 2003, Enlightenment and Reform in the 18th Century 2005, Joseph II, Vol. II: Against the World 2009. *Honours:* Prince Consort Prize, Univ. of Cambridge 1960, Henry Paolucci/Walter Bagehot Prize, Intercollegiate Studies Inst., Wilmington, Del. 2004. *Address:* Sidney Sussex College, Cambridge, CB2 3HU, England (office). *Telephone:* (1223) 338833 (office). *E-mail:* derek@beales.ws (home).

BEAR, Carolyn Ann, (Chlöe Rayban), BA (Hons); British writer; b. 10 April 1944, Exeter, Devon, England; m. Peter Julian Bear; two d. *Education:* Univ. of Western Australia, Univ. of Newcastle upon Tyne. *Career:* author of books for children and teenagers. *Film:* Virtual Sexuality. *Publications include:* Under Different Stars 1988, Wild Child 1991, Virtual Sexual Reality (also film) 1994, Love in Cyberia 1996, Screen Kiss 1997, Clash on the Catwalk 1997, Havana to Hollywood 1997, Street to Stardom 1997, Models Move On 1998, Watching You, Watching Me 1999, Footprints in the Sand 2000, Terminal Chic 2000, Wrong Number 2004, Drama Queen 2004, My Life Starring Mum 2005, Hollywood Bliss – My Life So Far 2007, Mwah-Mwah 2008. *Literary Agent:* c/o Laura Cecil Literary Agency, 17 Alwyne Villas, London, N1 2HG, England. *E-mail:* info@lauracecil.co.uk. *Website:* www.lauracecil.co.uk; www.chloerayban.com.

BEAR, Gregory Dale, AB; American writer; b. 20 Aug. 1951, San Diego, Calif.; m. 1st Christina Nielsen 1975 (divorced 1981); m. 2nd Astrid Anderson 1983; one s. one d. *Education:* San Diego State Coll. *Career:* mem. Science Fiction and Fantasy Writers of America (Pres. 1988–90); adviser, Microsoft Corpn, US Army, CIA, Sandia Nat. Laboratories, Callison Architecture Inc., Homeland Security; mem. several political, scientific action cttees. *Publications include:* Hegira 1979, Psychlone 1979, Beyond Heaven's River 1980, Strength of Stones 1981, The Wind From a Burning Woman 1983, Corona 1984, The Infinity Concerto 1984, Eon 1985, Blood Music (Hugo Best Novellette Award, Nebula Best Novellette Award) 1985, The Serpent Mage 1986, The Forge of God 1987, Sleepside Story 1987, Eternity 1988, Hardfought (Nebula Best Novella Award 1984) 1988, Early Harvest 1988, Tangents (Hugo Best Short Story Award, Nebula Best Short Story Award) 1989, Queen of Angels 1990, Heads 1990, The Venging 1992, Bear's Fantasies 1992, Songs of Earth and Power 1992, Sisters 1992, Anvil of Stars 1992, Moving Mars (Nebula Best Novel Award) 1993, Legacy 1995, New Legends 1995, Slant 1997, Dinosaur Summer 1998, Greatest Science Fiction Stories of the 20th Century 1998, Foundation and Chaos 1998, Darwin's Radio (Nebula Best Novel Award) 1999, Rogue Planet 2000, Vitals 2002, The Collected Stories of

Greg Bear 2002, Darwin's Children 2003, W3 Women in Deep Time 2003, Sleepside: The Collected Fantasies of Greg Bear 2004, Dead Lines 2004, Quantico 2007, City at the End of Time 2008, Mariposa 2009, Hull Zero Three 2010, Halo: Cryptum 2011. *Honours:* Monty Award 2006, Heinlein Award 2006. *Address:* 506 Lakeview Road, Lynnwood, WA 98036, USA (home). *E-mail:* webmaster@gregbear.com (office). *Website:* www.gregbear.com.

BEARD, Mary, PhD; British lecturer in classics and writer; *Professor of Classics, Newnham College, University of Cambridge*; b. 1 Jan. 1955, Much Wenlock, Shropshire; d. of Roy Whitbread Beard and Joyce Emily Beard; m. Robin Sinclair Cormack 1985; one d. one s. *Education:* Shrewsbury High School and Newnham Coll., Cambridge. *Career:* research in Roman history 1977–79; Lecturer in Classics, King's Coll., London 1979–83; Univ. Lecturer in Classics and Fellow, Newnham Coll., Cambridge 1984–, Reader in Classics 1999–2004, Prof. of Classics 2004–; Classics Ed. Times Literary Supplement. *Publications include:* Rome in the Late Republic (co-author) 1985, The Good Working Mother's Guide 1989, Pagan Priests (co-author) 1990, Classics: A Very Short Introduction (co-author) 1995, Religions of Rome: (co-author) 1998, The Invention of Jane Harrison 2000, Classical Art: From Greece to Rome (co-author) 2001, The Parthenon 2002, The Invention of Jane Harrison 2002, The Colosseum (with Keith Hopkins) 2004, The Roman Triumph 2007, Pompeii: The Life of a Roman Town 2008, It's a Don's Life 2009. *Address:* Faculty of Classics, University of Cambridge, Sidgwick Avenue, Cambridge, CB3 9DA (office); Newnham College, Cambridge, CB3 9DF, England. *Telephone:* (1223) 335162 (office); (1223) 335712 (office). *Fax:* (1223) 335409 (office). *E-mail:* mb127@cam.ac.uk (office). *Website:* www.classics.cam.ac.uk (office).

BEARDSLEY, (John) Douglas, BA, MA; Canadian writer, poet, editor, reviewer and teacher; b. 27 April 1941, Montreal. *Education:* George Williams (now Concordia) Univ., Univ. of Victoria, York Univ., Toronto. *Career:* Chief Ed., Gregson Graham Ltd 1980–82; Sr Instructor, Dept of English, Univ. of Victoria 1981–2006; Writer, Ed. and Graphic Designer, Beardsley and Asscns, Victoria 1982–85, Writer, Ed. and Proofreader, 1985–. *Publications include:* Going Down into History 1976, The Only Country in the World Called Canada 1976, Six Saanich Poems 1977, Play on the Water: The Paul Klee Poems 1978, Premonitions and Gifts (with Theresa Kishkan) 1979, Poems (with Charles Lillard) 1979, Pacific Sands 1980, Kissing the Body of My Lord: The Marie Poems 1982, Country on Ice 1987, A Dancing Star 1988, The Rocket, the Flower, the Hammer and Me (ed.) 1988, Free to Talk 1992, Inside Passage 1994, Wrestling with Angels (Selected Poems, 1960–1995) 1996, My Friends the Strangers 1996, Our Game (ed.) 1998, No One Else is Lawrence! (with Al Purdy) 1998, The Man Who Outlived Himself (with Al Purdy) 2000, Nothing I Can Do to Stop the Sun From Sinking; contribs to anthologies, newspapers, magazines and periodicals. *Honours:* Canada Council Arts Award 1978, British Columbia Millennium Book Award 2000. *Address:* 1074 Lodge Avenue, Victoria, BC V8X 3A8, Canada (home). *Telephone:* (250) 384-6730 (home).

BEATTIE, Ann, MA; American writer and academic; *Edgar Allan Poe Professor of Literature and Creative Writing, University of Virginia*; b. 8 Sept. 1947, Washington; d. of James Beattie and Charlotte Crosby; m. Lincoln Perry. *Education:* American Univ., Univ. of Connecticut. *Career:* Visiting Asst Prof., Univ. of Virginia, Charlottesville 1976–77, Visiting Writer 1980; Briggs Copeland Lecturer in English, Harvard Univ. 1977; Guggenheim Fellow 1977; currently Edgar Allan Poe Prof. of Literature and Creative Writing, Univ. of Virginia; mem. American Acad. of Arts and Letters, PEN, Authors' Guild. *Publications:* Chilly Scenes of Winter 1976, Distortions 1976, Secrets and Surprises 1979, Falling in Place 1990, Jacklighting 1981, The Burning House 1982, Love Always 1985, Where You'll Find Me 1986, Alex Katz (art criticism) 1987, Picturing Will 1990, What Was Mine (story collection) 1991, My Life Starring Dara Falcon 1997, Park City: New and Selected Stories 1998, Perfect Recall 2001, The Doctor's House 2002, Follies 2005, Walks with Men 2010, The New Yorker Stories 2010, Mrs. Nixon: A Novelist Imagines a Life 2011. *Honours:* Hon. LHD (American Univ.); Award in Literature, American Acad. of Arts and Letters 1980, PEN/Bernard Malamud Award (co-recipient) 2000. *Address:* Department of English, University of Virginia, 219 Bryan Hall, PO Box 400121, Charlottesville, VA 22904-4121 (office); c/o Scribner, Simon & Schuster, 1230 Avenue of the Americas, New York, NY 10020, USA. *Website:* www.engl.virginia.edu (office).

BEAUCHEMIN, Yves, BA, LèsL; Canadian author; b. 26 June 1941, Noranda, PQ; s. of Jean-Marie Beauchemin and of the late Thérèse Maurice Beauchemin; m. Viviane St Onge 1973; two c. *Education:* Collège de Joliette, Univ. of Montréal. *Career:* taught literature at Collège Garneau, Université Laval; researcher at Radio-Québec 1969; mem. Amnesty Int., Int. PEN, Union des écrivaines et des écrivains québécois, Pres. 1986–87. *Publications include:* L'enfirouapé (Prix France-Québec) 1974, Le matou 1981 (translated as The Alley Cat) 1986, Du sommet d'un arbre 1986, Juliette Pomerleau (Prix Jean Giono) 1989, Finalement. . . les enfants 1991, Une histoire a faire japper 1991, Antoine et Alfred 1996, Alfred sauve Antoine 1996, Alfred et la lune cassée 1996, Le second violon 1996, Les Émois d'un marchand de café 1999, Charles le téméraire 2005, Charles le Téméraire 2007, Un pari très audacieux 2009, Renard Bleu 2009; contribs to newspapers, magazines, and radio. *Honours:* Officier, Ordre National de Québec 2003; Prix France-Quèbec 1975, Prix de la communauté urbaine, Montréal 1982, Prix des jeunes romanciers, Journal de Montréal 1982, Prix du roman de l'ete, Cannes, France 1982. *Address:* c/o McClelland and Stewart Ltd, 75 Sherbourne Street, 5th Floor, Toronto, ON M5A 2P9, Canada. *Telephone:* (416) 598-1114. *Fax:* (416) 598-7764. *E-mail:* editorial@mcclelland.com. *Website:* www.mcclelland.com (office).

BEAULIEU, Victor-Lévy; Canadian author and dramatist; b. 2 Sept. 1945, Saint-Paul-de-la-Croix, PQ; m. Francine Cantin; two d. *Education:* Univ. of Rallonge. *Career:* clerk, Canadian Nat. Bank 1965–66; chronicler, Montreal Perspectives (weekly) 1966–76, copy writer, La Presse, Petit Journal, Digest Éclair 1967, Maintenant 1970; Dir Lightning Digest magazine 1968–69; teacher of literature, Nat. Theatre School of Canada 1972–78; journalist and columnist, Le Devoir 1968–77; literary ed. Éditions du Jour 1969–73; full time writer 1985–. *Film:* Le Grand Voyage (screenplay) 1974. *Television:* Hamlet Quebec, Race de Monde 1978–81, L'héritage 1987–89, Montréal PQ 1991–94, Bouscotte 1997–2001. *Publications include:* Mémoires d'outre-tonneau' 1968, Race de monde 1969, La nuite de Malcomm Hudd 1969, Jos Connaissant 1970, Pour saluer Victor Hugo 1971, Les Grands-Pères (translated as The Grandfathers: A Novel) 1972, Jack Kerouac: Essai-poulet (translated as Don Quixote in Nighttown) 1972, Un rêve québécois 1972, Oh Miami Miami Miami 1973, Don Quichotte de la démanche (Gov.-Gen.'s Award for Fiction) 1974, Manuel de la petite littérature de Québec 1974, Blanche forcée 1975, Ma Corriveau, suivi de La sorcellerie en finale sexuée 1976, N'évoque plus que le désenchantement de ta ténèbre, mon si pauvre Abel 1976, Sagamo Job J 1977, Monsieur Melville, 3 vols, 1978, A Quebecois dream 1978, Don Quixote in Nighttown: A novel 1978, Jack Kerouac: a Chicken-Essay 1979, Una 1980, Satan Belhumeur (Molson Prize) 1981, Moi Pierre Leroy, prophète, martyr et un peu felé du chaudron 1982, Entre la sainteté et le terrorisme 1984, Steven Le Herault 1987, Docteur Ferron 1991, Two Solicitudes: Conversations (co-author) 1998, James Joyce, Je m'ennuie de michele viroly 2005, L'Irlande, le Québec, les Mots 2006, Mémoires d'outre-tonneau 2010, Bibi 2010; contribs to various publications. *Honours:* Grand Prix de la Ville de Montréal 1972, Prix France-Canada 1979, Beraud-Molson Prize 1981, Prix Canada-Belgique 1982, Prix Ludger-Duvernay 1982, Gemini Award 1988, 1990, 1997, Grand Prix, Montreal Theatre Journal 1993. *E-mail:* vlb@victor-levybeaulieu.com. *Website:* www.victor-levybeaulieu.com.

BEAUMAN, Sally Vanessa, (Vanessa James), MA; British writer and journalist; b. 25 July 1944, Torquay, Devon; d. of Ronald Kinsey-Miles and Gabrielle Kinsey-Miles (née Robinson); m. 1st Christopher Beauman 1966 (divorced 1973); m. 2nd Alan Howard 2004; one s. *Education:* Redland High School, Bristol and Girton Coll., Cambridge. *Career:* Assoc. Ed. New York Magazine, USA 1968–72; Features Ed. Vogue 1968–69, Harper's Bazaar 1969–71; Ed. Queen magazine (now Harper's & Queen) 1970; Arts Ed. Telegraph Magazine 1971–79; writer 1980–; mem. Soc. of Authors. *Publications include:* The Royal Shakespeare Company's Centenary Production of Henry V (ed.) 1976, The Royal Shakespeare Company: A History of Ten Decades 1982, Destiny 1987, Dark Angel 1990, Secret Lives 1994, Lovers and Liars 1994, Danger Zones 1996, Sextet 1998, Deception & Desire 1998, Rebecca's Tale 2001, The Landscape of Love 2005; contribs to newspapers and periodicals. *Honours:* Catherine Pakenham Memorial Award for Journalism 1970, Daphne du Maurier Prize 2005. *Literary Agent:* United Agents, 12–26 Lexington Street, London, W1F 0LE, England. *Telephone:* (20) 3214-0800. *Fax:* (20) 3214-0801. *E-mail:* info@unitedagents.co.uk. *Website:* unitedagents .co.uk.

BEAUMONT, Roger Alban, BS, MS, PhD; American academic and writer; *Professor Emeritus, Texas A & M University*; b. 2 Oct. 1935, Milwaukee, WI; m. Jean Beaumont 1974; one s. two d. *Education:* Univ. of Wisconsin, Madison and Kansas State Univ. *Career:* part-time Lecturer 1965–67, 1969–73, Assoc. Dir, Center for Advanced Study in Organization Science 1970–73, Assoc. Prof. of Organization Science, Univ. of Wisconsin, Milwaukee 1972–74; Instructor, Univ. of Wisconsin, Oshkosh 1968–69; Fellow, Inter-Univ. Seminar on the Armed Forces and Society 1969–; part-time Lecturer, Marquette Univ. 1970–73; Assoc. Prof., Texas A & M Univ. 1974–79, Prof. of History 1979–2003, Prof. Emer. 2003–; co-founder and N American Ed., Defense Analysis 1983–90; mem. American Military Inst. (trustee 1978–81, Chair. editorial advisory Bd 1984–85), Dept of the Army Historical Advisory Cttee 1983–87, Int. Inst. for Strategic Studies 1974–92. *Publications include:* War in the Next Decade (ed. with Martin Edmonds) 1974, Military Elites: Special Fighting Units in the Modern World 1974, Sword of the Raj: The British Army in India 1747–1947 1977, Special Operations and Elite Units 1939–1988: A Reference Guide 1988, Joint Military Operations: A Short History 1993, War, Chaos and History 1994, The Nazis' March to Chaos 2000, What's Your Name I'm Fine Thank You 2000, Right Backed by Might: The International Air Force Concept 2001; five monographs, 19 book chapters; contribs to reference works and many scholarly journals. *Honours:* Dept of the Army Patriotic Civilian Service Award 1987, Sec. of the Navy Fellow, History Dept, US Naval Acad. 1989–90, Faculty Teaching Award, Delta Delta Delta Sorority 1994, Research Award Coll. of Liberal Arts 1997. *Address:* 308 E Brookside Drive, Bryan, TX 77801, USA (home). *Telephone:* (979) 846-3282 (home); 9792182441 (mobile). *E-mail:* r-beaumont@tamu.edu (office). *Website:* http://history.tamu.edu/ (office).

BEAUSOLEIL, Claude, BA, MA, PhD; Canadian poet, writer, translator, editor and academic; b. 16 Nov. 1948, Montreal. *Education:* Collège Sainte-Marie, Univ. of Montréal; Bac Specialisé, Université du Québec a Montréal, Sherbrooke Univ. *Career:* Prof. of Québec Literature, Collège Edouard-Montpetit, Longueuil 1973–; Ed. Livrès urbaines. *Publications include:* poems: Intrusion ralentie 1972, Les Bracelets d'ombre 1973, Journal mobile 1974, Promenade modern style 1975, Sens interdit 1976, Les Marges du désir

1977, La surface du paysage 1979, Au milieu du corps l'attraction s'insinue 1980, Dans la matière revant comme une émeute 1982, Le livre du voyage 1983, Concrete City: Selected Poems 1972–82 1983, Une certaine fin de siècle, two vols (Literary Award 1991) 1983, 1991, Les livres parlent 1984, S'inscrit sous le ciel gris en graphiques de feu 1985, Découvertes des heures 1985, Il y a des nuits que nous habitons tous 1986, Grand hotel des étrangers 1988, Fureur de Mexico 1992, Montréal est une vill de poèmes vous savez 1992, Le Déchiffrement du monde 1993, L'Usage du temps 1994, Le Rythme des lieux 1995, La Ville aux yeux d'hiver 1998, Exilé 1999, La Parole jusqu'en ses envoûtements 2001, Les Passions extérieures 2002, Dépossessions 2003, Lecture des éblouissements 2004, Regarde, tu vois 2006, L'inscription lyrique 2007, Sonnets numériques 2007, La blessure du silence (Louise Labe Prize) 2009, Black Billie 2010; fiction: Dead line, récits 1974, Fort Sauvage 1996, Architecte des sentiments 2005, Alma 2006; essays: Extase et déchirure 1987, Librement dit, carnets parisiens 1997, Oscar Wilde, pour l'amour du Beau 2001. *Honours:* Ordre des francophones d'Amérique 1989; Prix Emile-Nelligan 1980, Prix Alain-Grandbois 1997. *Address:* c/o Union des écrivaines et des écrivains québécois, La Maison des Écrivains, 3492 Avenue Laval, Montréal H2X 3C8, Canada.

BEAVER, Paul Eli, FRSA, FRAeS; British writer, broadcaster and commentator on defence and security; b. 3 April 1953, Winchester; m. 1st Ann Middleton 1978 (divorced 1993); one s.; m. 2nd Cathryn Anne Pye 2006. *Education:* Sheffield City Polytechnic, Henley Man. Coll. *Career:* Ed. IPMS Magazine 1976–80, Helicopter World, 1981–86, Defence Helicopter World, 1982–86, Jane's Videotape 1986–87; Asst Compiler, Jane's Fighting Ships 1987–88; Man. Ed. Jane's Defence Yearbooks 1988–89; Publr Jane's Defence Weekly 1989–93; Defence Commentator, Sky News 1990–2001; Sr Publr Jane's SENTINEL 1993–94; Group Spokesman for Jane's 1994–2001; Defence and Aerospace Correspondent, CNBC Europe 1994–97; Research Fellow, Centre for Defence and Int. Security Studies, Lancaster Univ. 1997–2001; Defence Commentator, BBC 2001–; apptd Specialist Adviser to House of Commons Defence Cttee 2003; Founder-Dir Beaver Westminster Ltd 2004–. *Publications include:* Ark Royal: A Pictorial History 1979, U-Boats in the Atlantic 1979, German Capital Ships 1980, German Destroyers and Escorts 1981, Fleet Command 1984, The British Aircraft Carrier 1984, Modern Combat Ships: Invincible Class 1984, Encyclopaedia of the Modern Royal Navy Including the Fleet Air Arm and Royal Marines 1985, Encyclopaedia of Aviation 1986, Modern British Military Missiles (co-author) 1986, Encyclopaedia of the Fleet Air Arm Since 1945 1987, Attack Helicopters 1987, Today's Royal Marines 1988, Rescue: True-life Drama of Royal Air Force Search and Rescue 1990, The Gulf States Regional Security Assessment 1993, The Balkans Regional Security Assessment 1994, D-DAY: Private Lines 1994, The South China Sea Regional Security Assessment 1994, The CIS Regional Security Assessment 1994, The North Africa Regional Security Assessment 1994, The China and North East Asia Regional Security Assessment 1995, Baltics and Central Europe Regional Security Assessment 1996, The Modern Royal Navy 1996, Diary of an Amazon Jungle Guide: Amazing Encounters with Tropical Nature and Culture 2001; contribs to many journals. *Address:* Beaver Westminster Limited, 45 Great Peter Street, London, SW1P 3LT, England (office). *Telephone:* (20) 7799-4212 (office). *Fax:* (20) 7799-4217 (office). *E-mail:* paul@beaverwestminster.com (office); contact@beaverwestminster.com (office). *Website:* www.beaverwestminster.com (office).

BEBB, Prudence, BA, DipEd; British writer; b. 20 March 1939, Catterick, North Yorkshire; d. of the Rev. Dr and Mrs E. D. Bebb. *Education:* Sheffield Univ. *Career:* teacher, Snaith School 1961–63; History teacher, Howden School 1963–90; mem. PEN. *Publications include:* The Eleventh Emerald 1981, The Ridgeway Ruby 1983, The White Swan 1984, The Nabob's Nephew 1985, Life in Regency York 1992, Shopping in Regency York 1811 to 1820: Butcher, Baker, Candlestick Maker 1994, Georgian Poppleton 1994, Life in Regency Harrogate 1994, Life in Regency Scarborough 1997, Life in Regency Whitby 2000, Life in Regency Beverley 2003, Life in Regency Bridlington 2006, Life in Regency Halifax 2011; contribs to Impressions, Journal of the Northern Branch of the Jane Austen Soc. *Address:* 12 Bracken Hills, Upper Poppleton, York, YO26 6DH, England (home).

BECHMANN, Roland Philippe, LèsL, DipArch, DPLG; French architect, historian and writer; b. 1 April 1919, Paris; m. Martine Cohen 1942; six d. *Education:* Ecole Nat. Supérieure des Beaux-Arts, Paris, Univ. of the Sorbonne, Paris. *Career:* architect 1945–85; Chief Ed. Aménagement et Nature 1966–2000; mem. Asscn des Journalistes de l'Environnement, Soc. des gens de Lettre, AVISTA (USA); Pres. Asscn Jean Prévost, Asscn pour les Espaces Naturels. *Works include:* Banque Centrale, Cote d'Ivoire, Bouaké 1965, Lycée Agricole Pétrarque, Avignon (inscribed on Inventory of Historical Monuments 1989) 1969, Banque Centrale, Novakchott (Mauritania) 1963. *Publications include:* L'architecture gothique, expression des conditions du milieu 1981, Des Arbres et des Hommes: La foret au Moyen Age (translated as Trees and Man: The Forest in the Middle Ages) 1984, Carnet de Villard de Honnecourt XIII e siècle (co-author) 1986, Villard de Honnecourt Disegni (co-author) 1987, Villard de Honnecourt: La pensée technique au XIIIe siècle et sa communication 1991, Les Racines des Cathedrales 1996, L'Arbre du Ciel (novel) 1997, L'arbre du ciel 2000, Villard de Honnecourt's Portfolio (CD-ROM) 2000, Le radici delle cattedrali 2006, Vercors : Résistance en résonances (co-author) 2008; contribs to journals. *Honours:* Croix de guerre 1944, Chevalier, Légion d'honneur 1957; Prix du premier roman, Festival de Chambéry 1997, Prix Roberval, Université de Technologie de Compiègne 2002. *Address:* 7 Villa de Buzenval, 92100 Boulogne sur Seine, France (home). *Telephone:* 1-46-05-53-67 (home).

BECK, Albert (Al) William, BA, MFA; American artist, poet, writer and educator; *Artist-in-Residence, Culver-Stockton College*; b. 4 April 1931, Scranton, Pa; m. Carmen Federowich; two s. one d. *Education:* Northwestern Univ., US Army Admin. School, Univ. of Paris (Sorbonne), Clayton Univ., St Louis. *Career:* Dean of Students, Kansas City Art Inst., Mo. 1967–68; Assoc. Prof. of Art and Head of Art Dept, Culver-Stockton Coll. 1968–96, Artist-in-Residence 1996–; Dir Pyrapod Gallery 1996–; numerous exhbns 1956–2007; mem. Missouri Arts Council, Missouri Writers' Guild, Hannibal Arts Council, Monroe City Arts Council. *Publications include:* Gnomes and Poems 1992, Sight Lines 1996, Songs from the Rainbow Worm 1997, Beaucoup Haiku 1999, God is in the Glove Compartment 2000, Survival Weapons 2001, Warm Verse, Cold Turkey 2002, Rapping Paper, Mythic Thundermugs 2002, Conversations with Lizard Bones and Wizard Stones 2003, Lifepsychles 2004, Beyond the Stars and Gripes 2005, Eclectricity 2006; contribs to professional journals. *Honours:* various painting, pottery and poetry awards. *Address:* 5987 County Road 231, Monroe City, MO 63456-2207, USA (home). *Telephone:* (573) 439-5039 (home). *E-mail:* abeck@marktwain.net (home).

BECK-COULTER, (Eva Maria) Barbara, BSc, FRSA; British (b. German) journalist; b. 14 Oct. 1941, Berlin, Germany; d. of Wilhelm Beck and Ursula Beck; m. Ian Coulter 1971 (died 2008); two s. one d. *Education:* Victoria-Luise Gymnasium, Hamelin, Germany, Univs of Munich and London. *Career:* mem. editorial staff, The Economist 1965–74, European Ed. 1974–80, Asst Ed. 1980–81, Special Reports Ed. 1995–; Sec.-Gen. Anglo-German Foundation for the Study of Industrial Soc. 1981–91; Ed. International Management (monthly European business magazine) 1991–94; Head of Communications (Europe), Andersen Consulting 1994; broadcaster, writer and lecturer on current affairs in English and German; Chair. Reform Club 1992–93, Trustee 1995–; mem. Steering Cttee Anglo-German Koenigswinter Conf. 1982–91, Council Royal Inst. of Int. Affairs 1984–90, Int. Council Science Centre, Berlin 1990–95. *Publications include:* articles published in The Economist and other publs over the past three decades, including many special reports on a range of countries and subjects including the economics of ageing, demography, women and work. *Telephone:* 7894-521491 (mobile) (office). *Address:* The Economist, 25 St James's Street, London, SW1A 1HG (office); 9 Paget Street, London, EC1V 7PA, England (home). *Telephone:* (20) 7830-7168 (office). *E-mail:* barbarabeck@economist.com (office). *Website:* www.economist.com (office).

BECKER, Gary Stanley, PhD; American economist and academic; *University Professor of Economics and Sociology, University of Chicago*; b. 2 Dec. 1930, Pottsville, Pa; s. of Louis William Becker and Anna Siskind Becker; m. 1st Doria Slote 1954 (deceased); m. 2nd Guity Nashat 1979; two s. two d. *Education:* Princeton Univ., Univ. of Chicago. *Career:* Asst Prof., Univ. of Chicago 1954–57, Ford Foundation Visiting Prof. of Econs 1969–70, Univ. Prof., Dept of Econs 1970–83, Depts of Econs and Sociology 1983–, Chair. Dept of Econs 1984–85, Univ. Prof., Grad. School of Business 2002–; Asst and Assoc. Prof. of Econs, Columbia Univ. 1957–60, Prof. of Econs 1960, Arthur Lehman Prof. of Econs 1968–69; Research Assoc., Econs Research Center, Nat. Opinion Research Center, Chicago 1980–; mem. NAS, Int. Union for the Scientific Study of Population, American Philosophical Soc. and American Econ. Asscn (Pres. 1987), Mont Pelerin Soc. (Dir 1985–, Pres. 1990–92); Fellow, American Statistical Asscn, Econometric Soc., Nat. Acad. of Educ., American Acad. of Arts and Sciences; mem. Bd of Dirs UNext.com 1999–; affil., Lexecon Corpn 1990–2002; columnist, Business Week 1985–2004. *Publications:* The Economics of Discrimination 1957, Human Capital 1964, Human Capital and the Personal Distribution of Income: Analytical Approach 1967, Economic Theory 1971, Essays in the Economics of Crime and Punishment (co-ed. with William M. Landes) 1974, The Allocation of Time and Goods over the Life Cycle (with Gilbert Ghez) 1975, The Economic Approach to Human Behavior 1976, A Treatise on the Family 1991, Accounting for Tastes 1996, The Economics of Life 1996, Family, Society and State (in German) 1996, L'Approccio Economico al Comportamento Umano 1998, Social Economics 2000, Uncommon Sense: Economic Insights, from Marriage to Terrorism (with Richard Posner) 2009, The Challenge of Immigration 2011; numerous articles in professional journals. *Honours:* hon. degrees from Hebrew Univ. of Jerusalem 1985, Knox Coll., Galesburg, Ill. 1985, Univ. of Illinois, Chicago 1988, State Univ. of NY 1990, Princeton Univ. 1991, Univs of Palermo and Buenos Aires 1993, Columbia Univ. 1993, Warsaw School of Econs 1995, Univ. of Econs, Prague 1995, Univ. of Miami 1995, Univ. of Rochester 1995, Hofstra Univ. 1997, Univ. d'Aix-Marseille 1999, Univ. of Athens 2002, Harvard Univ. 2003, Hitotsubashi Univ. 2005; W.S. Woytinsky Award (Univ. of Michigan) 1964, John Bates Clark Medal, American Econ. Asscn 1967, Frank E. Seidman Distinguished Award in Political Econ. 1985, NIH Merit Award 1986, John R. Commons Award, Nobel Prize in Econ. Sciences 1992, Lord Foundation Award 1995, Irene Tauber Award 1997, Nat. Medal of Science 2000, Phoenix Prize, Univ. of Chicago 2000, American Acad. of Achievement 2001, Presidential Medal of Freedom 2007, Bradley Prize 2008, Alumni Medal, Univ. of Chicago 2010. *Address:* Department of Economics, University of Chicago, 1126 East 59th Street, Chicago, IL 60637, USA (office). *Telephone:* (312) 702-8168 (office). *Fax:* (773) 702-8496 (office); (312) 702-8490 (office). *E-mail:* gbecker@uchicago.edu (office). *Website:* www.uchicago.edu (office).

BECKER, Heinz, PhD; German musicologist, music educator and writer; b. 26 June 1922, Berlin. *Education:* Berlin Hochschule für Musik, Humboldt

Univ., Berlin. *Career:* Asst Lecturer, Inst. of Musicology 1956–66, Habilitation 1961, Univ. of Hamburg; Prof. of Musicology, Ruhr-Univ., Bochum 1966–87; mem. Gesellschaft für Musikforschung 1951–. *Publications include:* Klarinettenkonzerte des 18. Jahrhunderts 1957, Der Fall Heine-Meyerbeer 1958, Giacomo Meyerbeer: Briefwechsel und Tagebücher (ed four vols) 1960–85, Geschichte der Instrumentation 1964, Beitrage zur Geschichte der Musikkritik 1965, Studien zur Entwicklungsgeschichte der antiken und mittelalterlichen Rohrblattinstrumente 1966, Beiträge zur Geschichte der Oper 1969, Die Couleur locale in der Oper des 19 Jahrhunderts 1976, Giacomo Meyerbeer in Selbstzeugnissen und Bilddokumenten 1980, Giacomo Meyerbeer: Ein Leben in Briefen (ed) 1983, The Films Of Olivia De Havilland 1986, The 19th-century Legacy, Heritage of Music 1989, Giacomo Meyerbeer. Weltbürger der Musik 1991, Ausstellungskatalog zum 200 Geburtstag Meyerbeers (with Gudrun Becker), Im Auftrag de Staatsbibl. BLN, Preußischer Kulturbesitz 1991, Johannes Brahms 1993, Die Deutsche Schautaube 1997, Art Bridge (co-author) 2002; contribs to various music journals and other publications. *Honours:* Festschrift published in honour of 60th birthday 1982, G. Meyerbeer–Musik als Welterfahrung, Festschrift in honour of 70th birthday (ed Sieghart Döhring and Jürgen Schläder) 1992. *Address:* Wohnstift Augustinum, App 1242, Sterleyer Str 44, 23879 Mölln, Germany (home).

BECKER, Jürgen; German writer and editor; b. 10 July 1932, Cologne; s. of Robert Becker and Else Becker (née Schuchardt); m. 1st Mare Becker 1954 (divorced 1965); one s.; m. 2nd Rango Bohne 1965; one step-s. one step-d. *Education:* Univ. of Cologne. *Career:* various jobs until 1959; freelance writer and contrib. to West German Radio 1959–64; Reader, Rowohlt Verlag 1964–65; freelance writer living in Cologne, Berlin, Hamburg and Rome; Dir Suhrkamp-Theaterverlag 1974; Head of Drama Dept, Deutschlandfunk Cologne; Writer-in-Residence, Univ. of Warwick 1988; mem. Akademie der Künste Berlin, Deutsche Akademie für Sprache und Dichtung Darmstadt, PEN Club. *Publications include:* Felder (short stories) 1964, Ränder (short stories) 1968, Bilder, Häuser (Radio Play) 1969, Umgebungen (short stories) 1970, Schnee (poems) 1971, Das Ende der Landschaftsmalerei (poems) 1974, Erzähl mir nichts vom Krieg (poems) 1977, In der verbleibenden Zeit (poems) 1979, Erzählen bis Ostende (short stories) 1981, Fenster und Stimmen (poems with Rango Bohne) 1982, Odenthals Küste (poems) 1986, Das Gedicht von der wiedervereinigten Landschaft (poem) 1988, Das Englische Fenster (poems) 1990, Frauen mit dem Rücken zum Betrachter (short stories with Rango Bohne) 1989, Foxtrott im Erfurter Stadion 1993, Korrespondenzen mit Landschaft (poems with pictures from Rango Bohne) 1996, Der fehlende Rest 1997, Aus der Geschichte der Trennungen (novel) 1999, Schnee in den Ardennen (novel) 2003; Ed. Happenings (documentary with Wolf Vostell) 1965. *Honours:* Förderpreis des Landes Niedersachsen 1964, Stipendium Deutsche Akad. Villa Massimo, Rome 1965, 1966, Group 47 Prize 1967, Literaturpreis der Stadt Cologne 1968, Literaturpreis, Bavarian Acad. of Arts 1980, Kritikerpreis 1981, Bremer Literaturpreis 1986, Peter Huchel Prize 1994, Heinrich Böll Prize 1995, Rhein Literary Prize 1998, Uwe Johnson Prize 2001. *Address:* Am Klausenberg 84, 51109 Cologne, Germany (home). *Telephone:* 841139 (home).

BECKER, Lucille F., BA, MA, PhD; American academic and writer; *Professor Emerita of French, Drew University*; b. 4 Feb. 1929, New York City; d. of Mark Frackman and Sylvia Schwartz Frackman; m.; four s. *Education:* Univ. of Mexico, Barnard Coll., Columbia Univ., New York, Université d'Aix-Marseille, France. *Career:* Fulbright Scholar, France 1949–50; part-time instructor, Columbia Univ. 1954–58, Univ. Coll., Rutgers Univ. 1958–68; Assoc. Prof. of French, Drew Univ. 1968–77, Chair. Dept French 1976–81, Prof. of French 1977–93, Prof. Emer. of French 1993–; int. lecturer on French literature at univs in China, Hong Kong, India, Nepal, Sri Lanka, Thailand, Australia, NZ 1978–83; keynote speaker at Nat. Press Club Salute to Georges Simenon, Washington, DC 1987; mem. American Asscn of Teachers of French, American Asscn of Univ. Profs, French Inst./Alliance Française. *Television:* featured speaker in films Simenon in America, Simenon en Amerique (CBC 2002. *Publications include:* Le Maître de Santiago, Henry de Montherlant (co-ed.) 1965, Henry de Montherlant 1970, Louis Aragon 1971, Georges Simenon 1977, Françoise Mallet-Joris 1985, Twentieth-Century French Women Novelists 1989, Pierre Boulle 1996, Georges Simenon Revisited 1999, Cahiers Simenon 15: Sous les feux de la critique II (1945–1955) 2001, Georges Simenon – 'Maigrets' and the 'roman durs' 2006; contribs to scholarly books and journals. *Address:* French Department, Drew University, 36 Madison Avenue, Embury Hall, Madison, NJ 07940 (office); 82 Harding Drive, South Orange, NJ 07079, USA (home). *Telephone:* (973) 762-6672 (home). *Fax:* (973) 762-0567 (home). *E-mail:* lucillefbecker@cs.com.

BECKET, Henry S. A. (see Goulden, Joseph C.)

BECKETT, Wendy, (Sister Wendy), MA; British art writer and nun; b. 25 Feb. 1930, Johannesburg, SA. *Education:* Univ. of Oxford. *Career:* mem. Sacred Heart teaching order, currently living in solitude on the grounds of a Carmelite Monastery. *Television:* several series for BBC and Public Broadcasting Service including Sister Wendy's Grand Tour 1997, Sister Wendy's Story of Painting 1997. *Publications:* A Thousand Masterpieces, The Story of Painting, Meditations, My Favourite Things, Sister Wendy's American Collection 2000, Living the Lord's Prayer (with Rowan Williams) 2007. *Literary Agent:* Toby Eady Associates Ltd, Third Floor, 9 Orme Court, London, W2 4RL, England. *Telephone:* (20) 7792-0092. *Fax:* (20) 7792-0879. *E-mail:* toby@tobyeady.demon.co.uk. *Website:* www.tobyeadyassociates.co.uk.

BECKLES WILLSON, Robina Elizabeth, BA, MA; British writer; b. 26 Sept. 1930, London; m. Anthony Beckles Willson; one s. one d. *Education:* Univ. of Liverpool. *Career:* teacher, Liverpool School of Art 1952–56, Ballet Rambert Educational School, London 1956–58. *Publications include:* Leopards on the Loire 1961, A Time to Dance 1962, Musical Instruments 1964, A Reflection of Rachel 1967, The Leader of the Band 1967, Roundabout Ride 1968, Dancing Day 1971, The Last Harper 1972, The Shell on Your Back 1972, What a Noise 1974, The Voice of Music 1975, Musical Merry-go-Round 1977, The Beaver Book of Ballet 1979, Eyes Wide Open 1981, Anna Pavlova: A Legend Among Dancers 1981, Pocket Book of Ballet 1982, Secret Witch 1982, Square Bear 1983, Merry Christmas 1983, Holiday Witch 1983, Sophie and Nicky series, 2 vols, Hungry Witch 1984, Music Maker 1986, Sporty Witch 1986, The Haunting Music 1987, Mozart's Story 1991, Just Imagine 1993, Harry Stories in Animal World 1996, Ambulance! 1996, Very Best Friend 1998, Ballet, Pendulum Quest, Rainbow Pavement and Other Stories (co-author), Emperor's New Clothes 2008. *Address:* 44 Popes Avenue, Twickenham, Middx, TW2 5TL, England (home). *E-mail:* robinabw@gmail.com (home).

BEDAU, Hugo Adam, BA, MA, AM, PhD; American academic and writer; *Austin B. Fletcher Professor Emeritus of Philosophy, Tufts University*; b. 23 Sept. 1926, Portland, OR; m. 1st Jan Mastin 1952 (divorced 1988); three s. one d.; m. 2nd Constance Putnam 1990. *Education:* Univ. of Redlands, Boston Univ., Harvard Univ. *Career:* instructor, Dartmouth Coll. 1953–54; Lecturer, Princeton Univ. 1954–57, 1958–61; Assoc. Prof., Reed Coll. 1962–66; Prof. of Philosophy, Tufts Univ. 1966–99, Austin B. Fletcher Prof. Emer. of Philosophy 1999–; Visiting Life Fellow Clare Hall, Cambridge 1980–; Visiting Fellow, Max Planck Insts, Heidelberg and Freiburg im Breisgau 1988, Wolfson Coll., Oxford 1989; Romanell-Phi Beta Kappa Prof. of Philosophy 1994; mem. American Asscn of Univ. Profs, American Philosophical Asscn, American Soc. for Political and Legal Philosophy, American Civil Liberties Union. *Publications include:* The Death Penalty in America (ed.) 1964, Civil Disobedience: Theory and Practice (ed.) 1969, Justice and Equality (ed.) 1971, Victimless Crimes: Two Views (with Edwin M. Schur) 1974, Capital Punishment in the United States (co-ed.) 1976, The Courts, the Constitution, and Capital Punishment 1977, Current Issues and Enduring Questions (with Sylvan Barnet) 1987, Death is Different: Studies in the Morality, Law, and Politics of Capital Punishment 1987, Civil Disobedience in Focus (ed.) 1991, In Spite of Innocence (co-author) 1992, Critical Thinking, Reading, and Writing (with Sylvan Barnet) 1993, Thinking and Writing About Philosophy 1996, Making Mortal Choices 1996, Killing as Punishment 2004, Debating The Death Penalty (ed.) 2005, Ethics And Public Policy 2008; contribs to many books, journals and magazines. *Honours:* August Vollmer Award, American Soc. of Criminology 1995, Civil Liberties Union of Massachusetts Roger Baldwin Award 2003. *Address:* Department of Philosophy, Tufts University, Miner Hall 222, Medford, MA 02155 (office). *Telephone:* (617) 627-3230 (office). *Fax:* (617) 627-3899 (office). *E-mail:* hebedau@aol.com. *Website:* www.ase.tufts.edu/philosophy (office).

BEDFORD, Martyn Corby, MA; British writer and critic; *Associate Senior Lecturer in Creative Writing, Leeds Trinity University College*; b. 10 Oct. 1959, Croydon, Surrey; s. of Peter Bedford and Marjorie Bedford; m. Damaris Croxall 1994; two d. *Education:* Univ. of East Anglia. *Career:* Lecturer in Creative Writing, Univ. of Manchester 2001–06; Critic-in-Residence, www.youwriteon.com 2006–; Teaching Fellow in Creative Writing, Univ. of Leeds 2008; Visiting Lecturer, Leeds Metropolitan Univ.; Assoc. Sr Lecturer in Creative Writing, Leeds Trinity Univ. Coll. 2009–; mem. Nat. Asscn of Writers in Education. *Publications include:* Acts of Revision (Yorkshire Post Best First Work Award) 1996, Exit, Orange & Red 1997, The Houdini Girl 1999, Black Cat 2000, The Island of Lost Souls 2006, Flip 2011. *Literary Agent:* Curtis Brown Ltd, 5th Floor, Haymarket House, 28–29 Haymarket, London, SW1Y 4SP, England. *Telephone:* (20) 7393-4400. *Fax:* (20) 7393-4401. *E-mail:* cb@curtisbrown.co.uk. *Website:* www.curtisbrown.co.uk; www.martynbedford.com.

BEDOYA, Esteban; Paraguayan writer; b. 25 April 1958, Asunción. *Career:* moved to Argentina as a child with his family; mem. Paraguayan Soc. of Writers, PEN Club del Paraguay, Soc. of Writers of Fribourg, Switzerland. *Publications include:* La fosa de los osos 2003, Los Malqueridos 2006, El apocalipsis según Benedicto (PEN/Edward and Lily Tuck Award for Paraguayan Literature 2010) 2010. *Address:* c/o Arandurã Editorial, Tte. Fariña 1074, Asunción, Paraguay.

BEER, Dame Gillian Patricia Kempster, DBE, LittD, DLitt, FBA, FRSL; British academic, writer and fmr college president; *Professor Emerita, University of Cambridge*; b. 27 Jan. 1935, Bookham, Surrey, England; d. of Owen Kempster Thomas and Ruth Winifred Bell, fmrly Thomas; m. John Bernard Beer 1962; three s. *Education:* St Anne's Coll., Oxford. *Career:* Asst Lecturer, Bedford Coll., London 1959–62; Lecturer (part-time), Univ. of Liverpool 1962–64; Asst Lecturer, Univ. of Cambridge 1966–71, Lecturer, then Reader in Literature and Narrative 1971–89, Grace I Prof. of English 1989–94, King Edward VII Prof. of English Literature 1994–2002, Pres. Clare Hall 1994–2001, Prof. Emer. 2002–; Fellow, Girton Coll. 1965–94; Chair. Poetry Book Soc. 1992–96, Chair. of Judges, Booker Prize 1997; Pres. History of Science Section of BAAS, British Comparative Literature Asscn 2004–, British Soc. for Literature and Science 2005–; Vice-Pres. British Acad. 1994–96; Trustee, British Museum 1992–2002; mem. Bd Arts Council England East 2004–, New Writing Partnership (now Writers' Centre,

Norwich) 2005–. *Publications include:* Meredith: a change of masks 1970, The Romance 1970, Darwin's Plots 1983 (revised edn 2000, 3rd edn 2009), George Eliot 1986, Arguing with the Past 1989, Open Fields 1996, Virginia Woolf: The Common Ground 1996, Collected Poems of Lewis Carroll 2012. *Honours:* Hon. mem. American Acad. of Arts and Sciences, Int. Hon. mem. American Philosophical Soc., Hon. Fellow, Univ. of Wales (Cardiff) 1986, St Anne's Coll., Oxford 1989, Girton Coll., Cambridge 1994, Clare Hall, Cambridge 2001; Hon. DLitt (Liverpool) 1995, (Oxford) 2005, Hon. LittD (Leicester, ARU, London), Hon. DLit (Queens Univ., Belfast), Dr hc (Sorbonne, Paris); medals from MIT and Nat. Autonomous Univ., Mexico, Rose Mary Crawshay Prize, British Acad. 1984. *Address:* Clare Hall, Herschel Road, Cambridge, CB3 9AL (office); 44 Newton Road, Cambridge, CB2 8AL, England (home). *Telephone:* (1223) 356384 (office); (1223) 356384 (home). *Fax:* (1223) 332333 (office). *E-mail:* gpb1000@cam.ac.uk (office).

BEERS, Burton Floyd, AB, MA, PhD; American academic and writer; b. 13 Sept. 1927, Chemung, New York; m. Pauline Cone Beers 1952; one s. one d. *Education:* Hobart Coll., Duke Univ. *Career:* Instructor, North Carolina State Univ. 1955–57, Asst Prof. 1957–61, Assoc. Prof. 1961–66, Prof. 1966–96; mem. American Historical Asscn, Asscn for Asian Studies, Asscn of Historians in North Carolina, Historical Soc. of North Carolina, North Carolina Literary and Historical Soc., Soc. for Historians of American Foreign Relations, Southern Historical Asscn. *Publications include:* Vain Endeavor: Robert Lansing's Attempts to End the American-Japanese Rivalry 1962, The Far East: A History of Western Impacts and Eastern Responses 1830–1975 (co-author) (sixth edn 1975), China in Old Photographs 1981, North Carolina's China Connection 1840–1949 (co-author) 1981, World History: Patterns of Civilization 1984, North Carolina State University: A Pictorial History (co-author) 1986, The Vietnam War: An Historical Case Study (co-author) 1997, Living in our World (chief exec. ed.) 1998, World History: Connections to Today (consultant ed.) 2008; contribs to textbooks, books, scholarly journals, and periodicals. *Honours:* Alexander Quarles Holladay Medal for Excellence, North Carolina State Univ. Bd of Trustees 1992, Medal for Excellence, Hobart and William Smith Colls 1994, Watauga Medal, North Carolina State Univ. 1998. *Address:* 201 John Wesley Road, Greenville, NC 27858-1668, USA (home). *Telephone:* (252) 830-1118 (home).

BEEVOR, Antony, FRSL; British historian, writer and academic; b. 14 Dec. 1946, London; m. Artemis Cooper 1986; one s. one d. *Education:* Winchester Coll., Grenoble Univ., Royal Mil. Acad., Sandhurst. *Career:* Exec. Council French Theatre Season 1997; Lees-Knowles Lecturer, Univ. of Cambridge 2002–03; Visiting Prof., Birkbeck Coll., London 2002–, Univ. of Kent 2010–; Boeing Visiting Fellow, Australian War Memorial 2012; Cttee mem. Soc. of Authors 2001–05 (Chair. 2003–05), mem. of Council 2005–; mem. Steering Cttee Samuel Johnson Prize 2004–; judge, British Acad. Book Prize 2004, David Cohen Prize 2004; mem. Anglo Hellenic League, Friends of the British Libraries, London Library. *Publications include:* The Spanish Civil War 1982, The Enchantment of Christina Von Retzen (novel) 1988, Inside the British Army 1990, Crete: The Battle and the Resistance (Runciman Award 1992) 1991, Paris After the Liberation 1944–49 1994, Stalingrad (Samuel Johnson Prize for Non-Fiction 1999, Wolfson Prize for History 1999, Hawthornden Prize 1999) 1998, Berlin: The Downfall 1945 (Longman-History Today Trustees' Award 2003) 2002, The Mystery of Olga Chekhova 2004, A Writer at War: Vasily Grossman with the Red Army 1941–1945 (co-ed.) 2005, The Battle for Spain – The Spanish Civil War 1936–39 (Premio Vanguardia 2005) 2005, D-Day – The Battle for Normandy (Prix Henry Malherbe, Duke of Westminster Medal for Military Literature, Royal United Services Inst. 2010) 2009, The Second World War 2012; contribs to TLS, Times, Telegraph, Independent, Spectator, Guardian. *Honours:* Chevalier, Ordre des Arts et des Lettres 1997, Order of Cross of Terra Mariana (Estonia) 2008; Hon. DLitt (Kent) 2004, (Bath) 2010. *Literary Agent:* Andrew Nurnberg Associates, 20–23 Greville Street, London, EC1N 8SS, England. *Telephone:* (20) 3327-0400. *Fax:* (20) 7430-0801. *E-mail:* contact@andrewnurnberg.com. *Website:* www.andrewnurnberg.com; www.antonybeevor.com.

BEGLEY, Louis, AB, LLB; American lawyer and writer; b. (Ludwik Begleiter), 6 Oct. 1933, Stryj, Poland; s. of Edward D. Begley and Frances Hauser; m. 1st Sally Higginson 1956 (divorced 1970); two s. one d.; m. 2nd Anka Muhlstein 1974. *Education:* Harvard Univ. *Career:* specialist in int. corp. law; writer and lecturer; mem. Bar Asscn of the City of New York, Council on Foreign Relations, American Philosophical Soc. *Publications include:* fiction: Wartime Lies 1991, The Man Who Was Late 1993, As Max Saw It 1994, About Schmidt 1996, Mistler's Exit 1998, Schmidt Delivered 2000, Shipwreck 2003, Matters of Honor 2007, Schmidt Steps Bac 2012; non-fiction: Das Gelobte Land 2002, Venedig Unter Vier Augen (with Anka Muhlstein) 2003, The Tremendous World I Have Inside My Head: Franz Kafka 2008, Zwischen Fakten und Fiktionen 2008, Why the Dreyfus Affair Matters 2009; contribs to periodicals. *Honours:* Chevalier, Ordre des Art et des Lettres; Hon. PhD (Heidelberg); Irish Times-Aer Lingus Int. Fiction Prize 1991, PEN/Ernest Hemingway First Fiction Award 1992, Prix Médicis Étranger 1992, Jeanette-Schocken Preis, Bremerhaven Bürgerpreis für Literatur 1995, American Acad. of Arts and Letters Award in Literature 1995, Konrad-Adenauer Stiftung Literaturpreis 1999. *Literary Agent:* c/o Georges Borchardt, 136 East 57th Street, New York, NY 10022, USA. *Telephone:* (212) 753-5785. *Fax:* (212) 838-6518. *Address:* 919 Third Avenue, New York, NY 10022, USA (office). *Telephone:* (212) 628-4201 (office). *E-mail:* lbegley@louisbegley.com (office). *Website:* www.louisbegley.com.

BÉGUIN, Bernard, LèsL; Swiss journalist; b. 14 Feb. 1923, Sion, Valais; s. of Bernard Béguin and Clemence Welten; m. Antoinette Waelbroeck 1948; two s. two d. *Education:* Geneva High School, Geneva Univ. and Graduate Inst. of Int. Studies. *Career:* Swiss Sec. World Student Relief 1945–46; corresp. at UN European Headquarters; Journal de Geneva 1946–70, Foreign Ed. 1947, Ed.-in-Chief 1959–70; Diplomatic Commentator, Swiss Broadcasting System 1954–59, Swiss TV 1959–70; Head of Programmes, Swiss French-speaking TV 1970–73; Deputy Dir Radio and TV 1973–86; Cen. Pres. Swiss Press Asscn 1958–60, Hon. mem. 1974–; Visiting Prof. in Professional Ethics, Univ. of Neuchâtel 1984–88; Pres. Swiss Press Council 1985–90; Pres. Swiss Ind. Authority on Complaints concerning Broadcasting Programmes 1991–92; consultant with UNESCO (assessment of the media environment), Belarus 1994; mem. Fed. Comm. on Cartels 1964–80; mem. Bd, Swiss Telegraphic Agency 1968–71. *Publication:* Journaliste, qui t'a fait roi? Les médias entre droit et liberté, 1988. *Address:* 41 avenue de Budé, 1202 Geneva 1, Switzerland (home). *Telephone:* (22) 733-75-30 (home). *Fax:* (22) 733-75-30 (home). *E-mail:* beguinb@worldcom.ch (home).

BÉGUIN, Louis-Paul, BA; French writer and poet; b. 31 March 1923, Amiens. *Education:* Sorbonne, Univ. of Paris. *Career:* mem. PEN, Québec, Québec Writers Union. *Publications include:* Miroir de Janus 1966, Impromptu de Québec 1974, Un homme et son langage 1977, Problèmes de langage Au Quebec Et Ailleurs 1978, Vocabulaire Technique Des Assurances Sur La Vie 1979, Terminologie Des Rentes De Retraite (co-author) 1980, Yourcenar, Ou, Le Triomphe Des Femmes 1980, Idoles et Paraboles 1982, Yourcenar 1982, Poèmes et pastiches 1985, Parcours paralleles 1988, Lexique general des assurances 1990, Ange Pleureur 1991, Poèmes depuis la tendre enfance 1995, The Weeping Angel 1996, Écrits des trois pignans 1998; contribs to newspapers and magazines. *Honours:* Poetry Award 1967, Prix Montcalm 1974.

BEHAR, Ruth, BA, MA, PhD; American academic, poet and writer; *Victor Haim Perera Collegiate Professor of Anthropology, University of Michigan*; b. 12 Nov. 1956, Havana, Cuba; d. of Alberto Behar and Rebecca Behar; m. David Frye 1982; one s. *Education:* Wesleyan Univ., Princeton Univ. *Career:* Asst Prof., Univ. of Michigan, Ann Arbor 1986–89, Assoc. Prof. 1989–94, Victor Haim Perera Collegiate Prof. of Anthropology 1994–; Henry King Stanford Distinguished Prof. in Humanities, Univ. of Miami, Jan.–April 2008, Jan.–April 2009. *Film:* Adio Kerida: A Cuban Sephardic Journey (documentary). *Publications include:* Santa Maria del Monte: The Presence of the Past in a Spanish Village 1986 (revised edn as The Presence of the Past in a Spanish Village: Santa Maria del Monte 1991), Translated Woman: Crossing the Border with Esperanza's Story 1993, Bridges to Cuba (Puentes a Cuba) (ed.) 1995, Las Visiones de una Bruja Guachichil en 1599: Hacia una Perspectiva Indígena Sobre la Conquista de San Luis Potosal 1995, Women Writing Culture (co-ed.) 1995, The Vulnerable Observer: Anthropology That Breaks Your Heart 1996, An Island Called Home: Returning to Jewish Cuba 2007, The Portable Island: Cubans At Home in the World (co-ed.) 2008, Todo lo que guardé: Poemas en prosa; contribs to anthologies, scholarly journals and literary periodicals. *Honours:* Harry Frank Guggenheim Foundation Career Devt Award 1989–92, John D. and Catherine T. MacArthur Foundation Fellowship 1988–93, Faculty Fund Award, Univ. of Michigan 1991–92, Faculty Recognition Award 1992, Guggenheim Fellowship 1995–96, John Simon Guggenheim Memorial Foundation Award 1995–96, Excellence in Research Award 1996, Univ. of Michigan, D'Arms Faculty Award, Univ. of Michigan 1998, Recognition Award, American Psychological Asscn 2002, Excellence in Education Award, Univ. of Michigan 2006, Breaking the Glass Ceiling Award, Jewish Museum of Florida 2009, Circle Award, La Celebración Latina, Univ. of Michigan 2010. *Address:* Department of Anthropology, University of Michigan, 101 West Hall, 1085 South University Avenue, Ann Arbor, MI 48109-1107, USA (office). *Telephone:* (734) 936-0365 (office). *Fax:* (734) 763-6077 (office). *E-mail:* rbehar@umich.edu (office). *Website:* www.lsa.umich.edu/anthro (office); www.ruthbehar.com.

BEHBAHANI, Simin; Iranian poet; b. 20 July 1927, Tehran; d. of Abbas Khalili and Fakhr Azami Arghoon; m.; three c. *Career:* Pres. Iranian Writers' Asscn. *Publications include:* The Broken Lute 1951, Footprint 1954, Candelabrum 1955, Marble 1961, Resurrection 1971, A Line of Speed and Fire 1980, Wounded Rose: Three Iranian Poets (co-author) 1980, Arzhan Plain 1983, Guzinah-i Ash'ar (Selected Poems) 1988, An Mard Mard-i Hamraham (That Man, My Fellow Man) 1990, Simin Chilchiragh (Chandelier) 1991, Paper Dress 1992, A Windowful of Freedom 1995, A Cup of Sin: Selected Poems (co-author) 1999, Collected Poems 2003, Maybe It's the Messiah 2004, Collected Poems in Persian 2009. *Honours:* Human Rights Watch-Hellman/Hammet grant 1998, Carl von Ossietzky Medal 1999, Freedom of Expression Prize, Norwegian Authors' Union 2006, Bita Prize for Literature and Freedom, Stanford Univ. 2008. *Address:* c/o Ministry of Culture and Islamic Guidance, POB 5158, Baharestan Square, Tehran 11365, Iran.

BEHRENS, Katja; German writer; b. 18 Dec. 1942, Berlin; m. Peter Behrens 1960 (divorced 1971). *Career:* trans. of contemporary American literature (including William S. Burroughs and Henry Miller) 1960–73; ed., publishing house 1973–78; writer 1978–; Guest Prof., Washington Univ., St Louis, Mo. 1986, Dartmouth Coll., Hanover, NH 1991; mem. German PEN. *Publications include:* Die Weiße Frau 1978, Die Dreizehnte Fee 1983, Frauen der Romantik (ed) 1983, Weiches Wasser bricht den Stein (ed) 1984, Abschiedsbriefe (ed) 1987, Im Wasser tanzen 1990, Salomo und die anderen 1992, Die Vagantin 1997, Zorro–Im Jahr des Pferdes 1999, Sooft ich deiner gedenke… Briefe der

Romantik (ed) 1999, Alles Sehen Kommt von der Seele–Die Lebensgeschichte der Helen Keller 2001, Ich bin geblieben-warum? Juden in Deutschland-heute (ed) 2002, Hathaway Jones 2003, Alles aus Liebe, sonst geht die Welt unter 2005, Roman von einem Feld 2007, Der kleine Mausche aus Dessau-Moses Mendelssohns Reise nach Berlin im Jahre 1743 2009, Der Raub des Bücherschatzes 2012. *Honours:* Förderpreis zum Ingeborg Bachmann Preis 1978, Förderpreis der Märkischen Kulturkonferenz 1978, Thaddäus Troll Preis 1982, Villa Massimo Stipendium in Olevano 1986, Stadtschreiberin von Mainz 1992, Künstlerhaus Schloß Wiepersdorf 1996, Premio Internazionale 'Lo Stellato' 2000, Kinder-und Jugendbuchpreis Luchs 2002, Literaturpreis der Stadt Wiesbaden 2002, Ehrengabe der Deutschen Schillerstiftung 2003. *Address:* Park Rosenhöhe 23, 64287 Darmstadt, Germany (home). *Telephone:* (6151) 54762 (home). *Fax:* (6151) 54762 (home). *E-mail:* behrenskatja@aol.com (home). *Website:* www.katja-behrens.de.

BEHRENS, Peter Henry; Canadian/American writer and screenwriter; b. 7 Oct. 1954, Montréal; s. of Hermann Henry Behrens and Frances O'Brien Behrens; m. Basha Burwell; one s. *Education:* Lower Canada Coll., Concordia Univ., McGill Univ., Stanford Univ., USA. *Career:* Wallace Stegner Fellowship in Creative Writing, Stanford Univ.; Fellow, Fine Arts Work Center, Provincetown. *Screenplays:* Night Driving (TV) 1993, Cadillac Girls 1993, Promise the Moon (TV) 1997, Kayla 1999. *Publications include:* Night Driving (short stories) 1987, The Law of Dreams (novel) (Gov.-Gen.'s Literary Award) 2006, The O'Briens 2011; contrib. short stories and essays to magazines, including The Atlantic Monthly, Best Canadian Essays, Best Canadian Stories, Brick, Lost, Tin House, and to anthologies. *Literary Agent:* Sarah Burnes, The Gernert Company, 136 East 57th Street, New York, NY 10022, USA. *Telephone:* (212) 838-7777. *E-mail:* sburnes@thegernertco.com. *E-mail:* himself@peterbehrens.org. *Website:* www.peterbehrens.org.

BEIGBEDER, Frédéric; French writer; b. 21 Sept. 1965, Neuilly-sur-Seine; s. of Jean-Michel Beigbader and Christine de Chasteigner; one d. *Career:* Ed. Flammarion editions 2003–06. *Publications include:* Mémoire d'un jeune homme dérangé 1990, Vacances dans le coma 1994, L'Amour dure trois ans 1997, Nouvelles sous ecstasy 1999, Barbie (Barbie Universe of Fashion) 1998, 99 francs (£9.99, aka £6.99) 2000, Dernier inventaire avant liquidation (essay) 2001, 2002: Rester Normal Dargaud 2002, Windows on the World (Independent Foreign Fiction Prize 2005) 2004, Rester Normal à Saint-Tropez Dargaud 2004, L'égoiste romantique 2005, Au secours pardon 2007, Un Roman Français (Prix Renaudot) 2009. *Address:* Éditions Grasset, 61 rue des Saints-Pères, 75006 Paris, France. *Telephone:* 1-44-39-22-00. *Fax:* 1-42-22-64-18. *Website:* www.edition-grasset.fr.

BEILHARZ, Manfred; German director and producer; b. 13 July 1938, Böblingen. *Education:* Univ. of Tübingen, Univ. of Munich, Paris, London. *Career:* founded Studiobühne, Munich; Asst Dir Münchner Kammerspiele; Dir and head of literary Dept, Westfälisches Landestheater 1968; Artistic Dir, Tübingen Landestheater 1970–75, City Theatre of Freiburg 1976–83, City Theatre of Kassel 1983–91, Schauspiel, Bonn 1991–92; Genralintendant, Municipal Theatre of Bonn 1997–2002; Dir Hessisches Staatstheater Wiesbaden; mem. Acad. of Performing Arts, Frankfurt, European Theatre Convention, Brussels and Paris; Vice-Pres. Hessischen Theaterakademie, Frankfurt; Pres. Int. Theatre Inst. 2002–08; Chair. Dramaturgische Gesellschaft, Berlin –2007. *Plays and opera directed:* Marat Sade, The Mother, Threepenny Opera, Rise and Fall of the City of Mahagonny, A Romantic Woman, A Midsummer Night's Dream, Fidelio, The Hot Oven, L'enfant et les sortilèges, Love of Three Oranges, Falstaff, Spring Awakening, Schauspiel Bonn 1997, Wozzeck, Opera Bonn, Der Zerbrochne Krug. *Honours:* Federal Cross of Merit (Germany) 2007. *Address:* c/o International Theatre Institute, UNESCO, 1 rue Miollis, 75732 Paris Cedex 15, France.

BEISSEL, Henry Eric, BA, MA; Canadian (b. German) poet, dramatist, writer, translator and editor and academic; *Distinguished Professor Emeritus, Concordia University;* b. 12 April 1929, Cologne, Germany; s. of Walter Beissel and Johanna Dilgen; m. 1st Ruth Heydasch; two d.; m. 2nd Arlette Francière 1981; one d. *Education:* Univs of Cologne, Germany, London, UK and Toronto, Canada. *Career:* teacher, Univ. of Munich, Germany 1960–62, Univ. of Edmonton, Canada 1962–64, Univ. of Trinidad 1964–66; mem. Faculty, Concordia Univ., Montréal 1966–96, Prof. of English Emer. 1997–2000, Distinguished Prof. Emer. 2000–; Founder-Ed. Edge Journal 1963–69; Deutscher Akademischer Austauschdienst Fellowship 1977; Ed. Humanist Perspectives 2008–09; mem. League of Canadian Poets (Pres. 1980–81), PEN, Playwrights Canada, Writers' Union of Canada; Ed. Humanist Perspectives 2008–09. *Plays:* The Curve (trans. from Tankred Dorst, Univ. of Alberta Theatre, Edmonton) 1962, A Trumpet for Nap (trans. from Tankred Dorst, Little Angel Theatre, London, UK) 1968–70, Mister Skinflint (Jesu Theatre, Montréal) 1969, Inook and the Sun (Stratford Shakespeare Festival, Ont.) 1973, Inook and the Sun 1974, For Crying Out Loud (Char-Lan Theatre Workshop, Williamstown, Ont.) 1975, Goya (Montréal Theatre Lab) 1976, Under Coyote's Eye (The Other Theatre, Chicago) 1978, Goya 1978, Under Coyote's Eye 1980, The Emigrants (trans. from Slawomir Mrozek, Saidye Bronfman Centre Theatre, Montreal) 1981, Hedda Gabler (trans. from Henrik Ibsen, The Saidye Bronfman Centre Theatre, Montreal) 1982, The Noose (Univ. of Winnipeg Theatre) 1985, Improvisations for Mr X (Actors' Studio, New York) 1979, The Noose 1989, Improvisations for Mr X 1989, The Glass Mountain (trans. with Per Brask from Tor Age Bringsvaerd, Univ. of Winnipeg Theatre) 1990, Inuk 2000, Peer Gynt (trans. from Henrik Ibsen, Third Wall Theatre, Ottawa) 2009, Antigone 2011. *Radio:* The Double Take (trans. and adapted from Luigi Pirandello, CBC) 1985, The Apple Orchard (trans. and adapted from Walter Bauer, CBC) 1959, The Inseparable (trans. and adapted from Walter Bauer, CBC) 1959, The Curve (trans. and adapted from Tankred Dorst, CBC) 1968, All Corpses are Equal (trans. and adapted with Jia-Lin Peng from Shie Min, CKUT) 1988. *Publications include:* poetry: Witness the Heart 1963, New Wings for Icarus 1966, The World is a Rainbow 1968, Face on the Dark 1970, The Salt I Taste 1975, Cantos North 1980, Season of Blood 1984, Poems New and Selected 1987, Ammonite 1987, Dying I Was Born 1992, Stones to Harvest 1993, The Dragon and the Pearl 2002, Across the Sun's Warp 2003, A Meteorology of Love 2010, Coming to Terms with a Child 2011, Seasons of Blood 2011; other: Kanada: Romantik und Wirklichkeit 1981, Raging Like a Fire: A Celebration of Irving Layton (co-ed. with Joy Bennett) 1993; trans. of poetry and plays; contrib. to journals. *Honours:* Epstein Award 1958, Davidson Award 1959, Sr Canada Council Award 1969, DAAD Fellowship, Berlin 1977, Walter-Bauer Literaturpreis, Germany 1994, First Prize (Poetry), Surrey Int. Writers' Conf. 2006, Naji Naaman Literary Prize, Maison Naaman pour la culture, Beirut 2008. *Address:* 34 Woodview Crescent, Ottawa, ON K1B 3A9, Canada (home). *Telephone:* (613) 845-0676 (home). *E-mail:* hebe@rogers.com; beisselhenry@gmail.com.

BEJERANO, Maya, BA, MA; Israeli librarian, poet and writer; b. 23 Feb. 1949, Haifa; m. 1983 (divorced 1988); one d. *Education:* Bar-Ilan Univ. and Hebrew Univ. of Jerusalem. *Career:* librarian, Main Public Library, Tel-Aviv. *Publications include:* Bat Yaana (Ostrich) 1978, Ha-Chom Ve-Ha-Kor (The Heat and the Cold) 1981, Ibud Netunim 52 Shishah Maamarim u Maamar al Mosad Meen Makamah (Data Processing) 1982, Shirat Ha-Tsiporim (The Song of Birds) 1985, Retsef Ha-Shirim (Selected Poems) 1987, Voice 1987, Whale 1990, Ha-Simla Ha-Kehula Ve-Sochen Ha-Bituach (The Blue Dress and the Insurance Agent) 1992, Mizmorei Iyov (The Hymns of Job) 1993, Ha-Perah Ha-Sakran (The Curious Flower) 1993, Anase La-Gaat Be-Tabur Bitny (Trying to Touch my Belly Button) 1998, Optical Poems: Thirteen Poems of Maya Bejerano Produced to Interactive Media Works (CD ROM) 1999, Tedarim (Frequencies) 2005, Madrich Taiarim Ba-Ir Zara (A Tour Guide in a Foreign City) 2007, The Hymns of Job and Other Poems (trans.) 2008, Hitorarti be- Merkazu sel Ha- Alachsun (Waking at the Heart of the Diagonal) 2009; contribs to newspapers and journals. *Honours:* Harry Hershon Prize 1976, Levi Eschol Prize 1986, Bernstein Prize for Poetry 1989, Prime Minister Award 1986, 1996, Bialik Prize 2002, ACUM Literary Award 2010. *Address:* c/o Institute for the Translation of Hebrew Literature, PO Box 10051, Ramat Gan 52001, Israel.

BÉJI, Hélé; Tunisian essayist and novelist; b. 1948, Tunis. *Career:* fmr Prof. of French Literature, Univ. of Tunis; Int. Expert at UNESCO, Paris, France; Founder-Chair. Int. Coll. of Tunis 1998–. *Publications include:* Le Désenchantement national: essai sur la décolonisation 1982, L'Oeil du jour (novel) 1985, Itinéraire de Paris à Tunis, Satire 1992, L'Art contre la culture, Nûba 1994, La Fièvre identitaire 1997, L'Imposture culturelle 1997, Une Force qui demeure (essay) 2006, Nous, Décolonisés (essay) 2008, Islam Pride: Derriere le voile 2011; contribs to numerous journals, including Revue des Deux Mondes. *Honours:* Mediterranean Africa Prize 1982, Literary Creation Prize 1998, 2009, Association d'Amitié France-Tunisie Prize 2000. *Address:* Editions Arléa, 16 rue de l'Odéon, 75006 Paris, France (office). *Telephone:* 1-43-26-98-18. *Fax:* 1-44-07-04-88. *E-mail:* arlea@wanadoo.fr. *Website:* www.arlea.fr (office).

BÉKÉS, Pál; Hungarian author, playwright and translator. *Career:* Iowa Int. Writing Program, USA 1997; Artistic Dir Magyar Magic festival, UK 2003; Pres. IBBY, Hungary. *Publications include:* Darvak 1979, Szerelmem útközben 1983, Lakótelepi mítoszok 1984, Törzsi viszonyok 1990, Erzekeny utazasok Kozep-Europan at, avagy, Jorik Andras kulonos vanlorlasa volt es valo orszagok foldjen, mely tomerdek tanulsaggal szolgal mindazok szamara, ... kapott ezusttalca, s mire szolgal a historia 1991, A noi partorség szeme láttara 1992, Es very, very a dobot a rozsaszin plusselefant 1999. *Honours:* Fulbright Scholarship, USA 1992–93. *Address:* 1136 Budapest, Hegedűs Gy. u. 24, Hungary (home). *Telephone:* (1) 329-5145 (home). *E-mail:* bekespal@t-online.hu.

BEKRI, Tahar, PhD; Tunisian poet; *Lecturer, University of Paris X-Nanterre;* b. 7 July 1951, Gabès; m. Annick Le Thoër 1987. *Education:* Univ. of Tunisia, Sorbonne, Univ. of Paris. *Career:* Lecturer, Univ. of Paris X-Nanterre; mem. Soc. des Gens de Lettres de France, Maison des Ecrivains. *Publications:* Poèmes bilingues 1978, Exils 1979, Le laboureur du soleil 1983, Les lignes sont des arbres 1984, Le chant du roi errant 1985, Malek Haddad 1986, Le coeur rompu aux océans 1988, Poèmes à Selma 1989, La sève des jours 1991, Les chapelets d'attache 1993, Littératures de Tunisie et du Maghreb 1994, Les songes impatients 1997, Journal de neige et de feu 1997, Le pêcheur de lunes 1998, Inconnues saisons (translated as Unknown Seasons) 1999, De la littérature tunisienne et maghrébine 1999, Marcher sur l'oubli 2000, L'horizon incendié 2002, La brûlante rumeur de la mer 2004, Le vent sans abri 2005, Dernières nouvelles de l'été 2005, Si la musique doit mourir 2006, Le livre du souvenir 2007, Les Dits du fleuve 2009, Salam Gaza 2010, Je te nomme Tunisie 2011; contrib. to various publs. *Honours:* Officier, Mérite Culturel, Tunisia 1993; Prix Tunisie-France 2006. *Address:* 32 rue Pierre Nicole, 75005 Paris, France (home). *Telephone:* 1-43-29-33-39 (home). *Fax:* 1-43-29-33-39 (home); 1-40-97-71-51 (office). *E-mail:* taharbekri@wanadoo.fr (home); tahar.bekri@u_paris10.fr (office). *Website:* tahar.bekri.free.fr.

BELL, Antonia (see Rae-Ellis, Vivienne)

BELL, Edward; British publisher; *Partner, Bell Lomax Moreton Agency*; b. 2 Aug. 1949, s. of Eddie Bell and Jean Bell; m. Junette Bannatyne 1969; one s. two d. *Education:* Airdrie High School. *Career:* with Hodder & Stoughton 1970–85; Man. Dir Collins Gen. Div. 1985–89; launched Harper Paperbacks in USA 1989; Deputy Chief Exec., HarperCollins UK 1990–91, Chief Exec. 1991–92, Chair. 1992–2000; Chair. HarperCollins India 1994–2000; Dir (non-exec.) Haynes Publishing 2001–09, Sr Ind. non-exec. Dir 2009–; Dir (non-exec.) Be Cogent Ltd, Management Diagnostics Ltd; Chair. (non-exec.) OAG Worldwide Ltd 2001; Pnr, Bell Lomax Moreton Agency 2002–. *Address:* The Bell Lomax Moreton Agency, James House, 1 Babmaes Street, London, SW1Y 6HF, England (office). *Telephone:* (20) 7930-4447 (office). *Fax:* (20) 7925-0118 (office). *E-mail:* eddie@bell-lomax.co.uk.

BELL, Hilary; Australian playwright; b. 1966, d. of John Bell and Anna Volska; m. Phillip Johnston. *Education:* Australia's Nat. Inst. of Dramatic Art, Australia Film Television & Radio School, Juilliard School, New York, USA. *Career:* Tennessee Williams Fellow, Univ. of the South, Tenn. 2003–04. *Plays:* Pocketful of Hula Dreams 1968, Conversations with Jesus 1988, Fortune 1995, Wolf Lullaby 1997, The Falls 2001, The Anatomy Lesson of Doctor Ruysch 2002, Shot While Dancing 2004, The Eye of the Storm, Cheering up Mother, Memmie Le Blanc (Inscription Award) 2007, The Bloody Bride, Perfect Stranger, Mrs Satan (opera). *Television:* Echo Point (writer) 1995, Mirror, Mirror (writer) 1995. *Film:* Isabelle the Navigator (writer). *Publications include:* Fortune 1994, Wolf Lullaby 1996, Mirror Mirror (Aurealis Award) 1996. *Honours:* Philip Parsons Playwright Award 1994, Jill Blewett Playwright Award 1996, Bug'n'Bub Award, Eric Kocher Playwright Award 1997, Australian Writers' Guild Award 2003, AWGIE Award. *Literary Agent:* RGM Associates, PO Box 128, Surry Hills, NSW 2010, Australia. *Telephone:* (2) 9281-3911. *Fax:* (2) 9281-4705. *E-mail:* info@rgm.com.au. *Website:* www.rgm.com.au.

BELL, Madison Smartt, AB, MA; American writer and academic; *Director of Creative Writing Program, Department of English, Goucher College*; b. 1 Aug. 1957, Nashville, Tenn.; m. Elizabeth Spires 1985. *Education:* Princeton Univ., Hollins Coll. *Career:* Lecturer, Poetry Center of the 92nd Street YMHA, New York 1984–86; Writer-in-Residence and Dir Creative Writing Program, Dept of English, Goucher Coll. 1984–86, 1988–, Dir Kratz Center for Creative Writing 1999–2008, currently Prof. of English; Visiting Lecturer, Univ. of Iowa 1987–88; Visiting Assoc. Prof., Johns Hopkins Univ. 1989–95; Fellow, Soc. of American Historians 2005; mem. Fellowship of Southern Writers. *Publications include:* fiction: The Washington Square Ensemble 1983, Waiting for the End of the World 1985, Straight Cut 1986, Zero db 1987, The Year of Silence 1987, Soldier's Joy 1989, Barking Man 1990, Doctor Sleep 1991, Save Me, Joe Louis 1993, All Souls' Rising (Annisfield-Wolf Award 1996) 1995, Ten Indians 1996, Master of the Crossroads 2000, Anything Goes 2002, The Stone the Builder refused 2004, Devil's Dream 2009; non-fiction: readers' guides on various authors 1979–83, The History of the Owen Graduate School of Management 1988, Narrative Design: A Writer's Guide to Structure 1997, Narrative Design: Working with Imagination, Craft and Form 2000, The Stone that the Builder Refused (novel) 2004, Lavoisier in the Year One 2005, Toussaint Louverture: A Biography 2007, Charm City: A Walk Through Baltimore 2007, Devil's Dream (novel) 2009, The Color of Night 2011; contribs fiction in many anthologies and periodicals, also essays, book reviews, etc. *Honours:* Lillian Smith Award 1989, Guggenheim Fellowship 1991, George A. and Eliza Gardner Howard Foundation Award 1991–92, Maryland State Arts Council Award 1991, National Endowment for the Arts Literature Fellowship 1992, Strauss Living Award, American Acad. of Arts and Letters 2008. *Address:* Department of English, Goucher College, 1021 Dulaney Valley Road, Baltimore, MD 21204-2794, USA (office). *E-mail:* mbell@goucher.edu (office). *Website:* www.goucher.edu (office).

BELL, Marvin Hartley, BA, MA, MFA; American poet, writer and academic; *Flannery O'Connor Professor Emeritus of Letters, University of Iowa*; b. 3 Aug. 1937, New York, NY; s. of Saul Bell and Belle Spector Bell; m. 1st Mary Mammosser 1958; m. 2nd Dorothy Murphy 1961; two s. *Education:* Alfred Univ., Univ. of Chicago, Univ. of Iowa. *Career:* Prof., Faculty Writers' Workshop, Univ. of Iowa 1965–2005, Flannery O'Connor Prof. Emer. of Letters 2005–; mem. Faculty, Pacific Univ. MFA Program, Ore. 2004–; Distinguished Visiting Prof., Univ. of Hawaii 1981, Portland State Univ. 2007; Visiting Lecturer, Goddard Coll. 1970; Visiting Prof., Univ. of Washington 1982, Grinnell Coll. 1999, 2007; Distinguished Poet-in-Residence, Wichita State Univ. 2004; Lila Wallace-Reader's Digest Writing Fellow, Univ. of Redlands 1991–93; Woodrow Wilson Visiting Fellow, Saint Mary's Coll. of California 1994–95, Pacific Univ. 1996–97, Nebraska-Wesleyan Univ. 1996–97, Hampden-Sydney Coll. 1998–99, West Virginia Wesleyan Coll. 2000–01, Birmingham Southern Coll. 2000–01, Illinois Coll. 2002–03, Bethany Coll. 2003–04, Morningside Coll. 2008–09, Augustana Coll. 2008–09, Hiram Coll. 2008–09; Urban Teachers' Workshop for America Scores 2002–06; mem. Faculty, Rainier Writing Workshop, Pacific Lutheran Univ. 2004–05; Ed. and Publr Statements 1959–64; Poetry Ed. The North American Review 1964–69; Poetry Ed. The Iowa Review 1969–71, Guest Poetry Ed. 1980, 2005; Poetry Ed. Pushcart Prize 1991–92, 1996–97, Series Poetry Ed. 1997–2002; Series Ed. New Poets/Short Books, Lost Horse Press 2006–11; columnist, The American Poetry Review 1975–78, 1990–92. *Achievements include:* first Poet Laureate of the State of Iowa 2000–04. *Publications include:* poetry: Things We Dreamt We Died For 1966, A Probable Volume of Dreams 1969, The Escape Into You 1971, Residue of Song 1974, Stars Which See, Stars Which Do Not See 1977, These Green-Going-to-Yellow 1981, Segues: A Correspondence in Poetry (with William Stafford) 1983, Drawn by Stones, by Earth, by Things That Have Been in the Fire 1984, New and Selected Poems 1987, Iris of Creation 1990, The Book of the Dead Man 1994, Ardor: The Book of the Dead Man (vol. two) 1997, Poetry for a Midsummer's Night 1998, Wednesday: Selected Poems 1966–1997 1998, Nightworks: Poems 1962–2000 2000, Rampant 2004, Mars Being Red 2007, 7 Poets, 4 Days, 1 Book (with others) 2009, Vertigo: The Living Dead Man Poems 2011, Whiteout: Dead Man Poems by Marvin Bell in Response to Photographs by Nathan Lyons 2011, A Primer About the Flag (children's picture book illustrated by Chris Raschka) 2011; other: Old Snow Just Melting: Essays and Interviews 1983, A Marvin Bell Reader: Selected Prose and Poetry 1994; contrib. to many anthologies and periodicals. *Honours:* Hon. DLitt (Alfred Univ.) 1986, (Union Coll.) 2011; Acad. of American Poets Lamont Award 1969, Guggenheim Fellowship 1977, Nat. Endowment for the Arts Fellowships 1978, 1984, Sr Fulbright Scholar 1983, 1986, American Poetry Review Prize 1982, American Acad. of Arts and Letters Award in Literature 1994, American Poetry Review Shestack Prize 2003. *Address:* Writers' Workshop, Dey House, Univ. of Iowa, Iowa City, IA 52242, USA (office). *E-mail:* marvin-bell@uiowa.edu (office).

BELL, Robin, MA, MS; British writer, poet, broadcaster and artist; b. 4 Jan. 1945, Dundee; two d. *Education:* St Andrews Univ., Scotland, Columbia Univ., New York, USA. *Radio:* Strathinver: A Portrait Album 1945–1953 (Sony Award for Best British Radio Feature 1985); other broadcast drama and documentaries include The Other Thief, Melville Bay, Bittersweet Within My Heart. *Art exhibitions:* My River, Your River (sequence for UK G8) 2005, Drawing The Tay (solo, touring). *Publications include:* Sawing Logs 1980, Strathinver: A Portrait Album 1984, Radio Poems 1989, The Best of Scottish Poetry (ed.) 1989, Collected Poems of the Marquis of Montrose (ed.) 1990, Bittersweet Within My Heart, The Collected Poems of Mary, Queen of Scots (trans.) 1992, Scanning the Forth Bridge 1994, Le Château des Enfants 2000, Chapeau! 2002, Civil Warrior 2002, Tethering a Horse 2004, How to Tell Lies 2006, Behind You! 2011. *Honours:* Best Documentary, TV and Radio Industries of Scotland Award 1984, Creative Scotland Award 2005. *Address:* The Orchard Muirton, Auchterarder, Perthshire, PH3 1ND, Scotland. *Telephone:* (1764) 662211.

BELL BURNELL, Dame S(usan) Jocelyn, DBE, PhD, FRS, FRSE; British astrophysicist, academic and fmr university administrator; *Visiting Professor, University of Oxford*; b. 15 July 1943, d. of (George) Philip Bell and (Margaret) Allison Bell (née Kennedy); m. (divorced); one s. *Education:* Univs of Glasgow and Cambridge. *Career:* Lecturer, Univ. of Southampton 1968–73; part-time with Mullard Space Lab., Univ. Coll. London 1974–82; part-time with Royal Observatory, Edin. 1982–91; Chair. Physics Dept, Open Univ. 1991–99; Dean of Science, Univ. of Bath 2001–04; Visiting Prof. for Distinguished Teaching, Princeton Univ., USA 1999–2000; Visiting Prof., Univ. of Oxford 2004–; Pres. Royal Astronomical Soc. 2002–04; Pres. Inst. of Physics 2008–11; Foreign Assoc., NAS 2005; frequent radio and TV broadcaster on science, on being a woman in science, on astronomy and poetry and on science and religion. *Achievements include:* discovered the first four pulsars. *Radio:* Scientific Life 2011. *Television:* Beautiful Minds 2010. *Publications:* three books, three chapters in books, approx. 70 scientific papers and 35 Quaker publs; Dark Matter: Poems of Space (co-ed.) 2008. *Honours:* Hon. Fellow, New Hall, Cambridge 1996, British Science Asscn 2006, Singapore Inst. of Physics 2008, European Physical Soc. 2010, Science Museum London 2010, Glyndwr Univ. 2011; 26 hon. doctorates, including Univs of Cambridge, London, Michigan and Harvard; Joseph Black Medal and Cowie Book Prize, Univ. of Glasgow 1962, Michelson Medal, Franklin Inst., USA 1973, J. Robert Oppenheimer Memorial Prize, Center for Theoretical Studies, Fla 1978, Beatrice M. Tinsley Prize, American Astronomical Soc. (first recipient) 1987, Herschel Medal, Royal Astronomical Soc., London 1989, Edinburgh Medal 1999, Magellanic Premium, American Philosophical Soc. 2000, Joseph Priestly Award, Dickinson Coll., Pa 2002, Robinson Medal, Armagh Observatory 2004, Kelvin Medal 2007, Royal Soc. Faraday Award 2010, Reber Medal 2011. *Address:* University of Oxford, Astrophysics, Denys Wilkinson Building, Keble Road, Oxford, OX1 3RH, England (office). *Telephone:* (1865) 273306 (office). *Fax:* (1865) 273390 (office).

BELLAMY, David James, OBE, PhD, CBiol, FIBiol; British botanist, writer, broadcaster and environmental organization administrator; b. 18 Jan. 1933, London; s. of Thomas Bellamy and Winifred Green; m. Rosemary Froy 1959; two s. three d. *Education:* Sutton County Grammar School, Chelsea Coll. of Science and Tech., Bedford Coll., Univ. of London. *Career:* Lecturer, then Sr Lecturer, Dept of Botany, Univ. of Durham 1960–80, Hon. Prof. of Adult and Continuing Educ. 1980–82; Visiting Prof., Massey Univ., NZ 1988–89; Special Prof. of Botany, Univ. of Nottingham 1987–; TV and radio presenter and scriptwriter; Founder Dir Conservation Foundation; Pres. WATCH 1982, Youth Hostels Asscn 1983, Population Concern 1988–, Nat. Asscn of Environmental Educ. 1989–, Plantlife 1990–2005, Wildlife Trust's Partnership 1996–2005, British Inst. of Cleaning Science 1997–, Council Zoological Soc. of London 1991–94, BH&HPA 2000–, Camping and Caravanning Club 2002–; Vice-Pres. BTCV, Fauna and Flora International, Marine Conservation Soc., Australian Marine Conservation Soc.; Chair. Int. Cttee for the Tourism for Tomorrow Awards; Dir David Bellamy Assocs (environmental consultants) 1988–97, Bellamy & Nevard Environmental Consultants 2003–;

Trustee, Living Landscape Trust, World Land Trust 1992–2002; Patron Project AWARE Foundation, The Space Theatre, Dundee, Te Pua O Whirinaki Regeneration Trust, NZ. *Television series include:* Life in Our Sea 1970, Bellamy on Botany 1973, Bellamy's Britain 1975, Bellamy's Europe 1977, Botanic Man 1978, Up a Gum Tree 1980, Backyard Safari 1981, The Great Seasons 1982, Bellamy's New World 1983, End of the Rainbow Show 1986, S.W.A.L.L.O.W. 1986, Turning the Tide 1986, Bellamy's Bugle 1986, 1987, 1988, Bellamy on Top of the World 1987, Bellamy's Journey to the Centre of the World 1987, Bellamy's Bird's Eye View 1989, Wheat Today What Tomorrow? 1989, Moa's Ark 1990, Bellamy Rides Again 1992, Blooming Bellamy 1993, 1994, Routes of Wisdom 1993, The Peak 1994, Bellamy's Border Raids 1996, Westwatch 1997, A Welsh Herbal 1998, Salt Solutions 1999, The Challenge 1999. *Publications include:* more than 45 books, including Bellamy on Botany 1972, Peatlands 1974, Bellamy's Britain 1974, Life Giving Sea 1975, Green Worlds 1975, The World of Plants 1975, Bellamy's Europe 1976, Botanic Action 1978, Botanic Man 1978, Half of Paradise 1979, Forces of Life 1979, Bellamy's Backyard Safari 1981, The Great Seasons (with Sheila Mackie, illustrator) 1981, Il Libro Verde 1981, Discovering the Countryside with David Bellamy (Vols I, II) 1982, (Vols III, IV) 1983, The Mouse Book 1983, Bellamy's New World 1983, The Queen's Hidden Garden 1984, Bellamy's Bugle 1986, Bellamy's Ireland 1986, Turning the Tide 1986, Bellamy's Changing Countryside (four vols) 1987, England's Last Wilderness 1989, England's Lost Wilderness 1990, Wetlands 1990, Wilderness Britain 1990, How Green Are You? 1991, Tomorrow's Earth 1992, World Medicine: Plants, Patients and People 1992, Blooming Bellamy 1993, Trees of the World 1993, Poo, You and the Poteroo's Loo 1997, Bellamy's Changing Countryside 1998, The Glorious Trees of Great Britain 2002, Jolly Green Giant (autobiog.) 2002, A Natural Life (autobiog.) 2002, The Bellamy Herbal 2003, Conflicts in the Countryside: The New Battle for Britain 2005, and books connected with TV series; Consultant Ed. and contrib. for series published by Hamlyn in conjunction with Royal Soc. for Nature Conservation: Coastal Walks 1982, Woodland Walks 1982, Waterside Walks 1983, Grassland Walks 1983. *Honours:* Hon. Fellow, Chartered Inst. of Water and Environmental Man.; Hon. FLS; Hon. Prof., Central Queensland Univ.; Hon. mem. BSES Expeditions; Dutch Order of the Golden Ark 1989; Hon. DSc (Bournemouth); Hon. DUniv; Dr hc (CNAA) 1990; UNEP Global 500 Award 1990, Busk Medal, Royal Geographical Soc., Duke of Edinburgh's Award for Underwater Research, BAFTA Richard Dimbleby Award, BSAC Diver of the Year Award. *Address:* The Mill House, Bedburn, Bishop Auckland, Co. Durham, DL13 3NN, England (home).

BELLAMY, Joe David, BA, MFA; American writer, poet and academic; b. 29 Dec. 1941, Cincinnati, OH; m. Connie Sue Arendsee 1964; one s. one d. *Education:* Duke Univ., Antioch Coll., Univ. of Iowa. *Career:* Instructor, Mansfield State Coll., Pennsylvania 1969–70 Asst Prof. 1970–72; Publisher and Ed. Fiction International magazine and press 1972–84; Asst Prof., St Lawrence Univ., Canton, New York 1972–74, Assoc. Prof. 1974–80, Prof. of English 1980–; Program Consultant in American Literature, Divisions of Public Programs and Research Programs, Nat. Endowment for the Humanities 1976–90; Pres. and Chair. Co-ordinating Council of Literary Magazines 1979–81, Co-ordinating Council of Literary Magazines and Associated Writing Programs 1990; Distinguished Visiting Prof., George Mason Univ. 1987–88; Dir Literature Program, Nat. Endowment for the Arts 1990–92; Whichard Distinguished Prof. in the Humanities, East Carolina Univ. 1994–96; mem. Nat. Book Critics Circle. *Publications include:* Apocalypse: Dominant Contemporary Forms 1972, The New Fiction: Interviews with Innovative Writers 1974, Superfiction, or the American Story Transformed 1975, Olympic Gold Medallist (poems) 1978, Moral Fiction: An Anthology 1980, New Writers for the Eighties: An Anthology 1981, Love Stories/Love Poems: An Anthology (with Roger Weingarten) 1982, American Poetry Observed: Poets on Their Work, 1984, The Frozen Sea (poems) 1988, Suzi Sinzinnati (novel) (Editors' Book Award) 1989, Atomic Love (short stories) 1993, Literary Luxuries: American Writing at the End of the Millennium 1995, The Bellamys of Early Virginia 2005, The Lost Saranac Interviews (co-ed.) 2007, New World Extra 2009, Island in the Sky: Bellamy and Allied Families, Kindred Spirits: 400 Years of an American Family 2011; contribs to books, anthologies, journals and magazines. *Honours:* Bread Loaf Scholar-Bridgman Award 1973, Nat. Endowment for the Humanities Fellowship 1974, Fels Award 1976, Co-ordinating Council of Literary Magazine Award for Fiction 1977, Kansas Quarterly-Kansas Arts Comm. Fiction Prize 1982, New York State Council on the Arts Grant in Fiction 1984, Nat. Endowment for the Arts Fellowship for Creative Writers 1985. *Address:* 5318 Lake Bluff Terrace, Sanford, FL 32771, USA. *E-mail:* joedavid@joedavidbellamy.com. *Website:* www.joedavidbellamy.com.

BELLATIN, Mario, (Abdul Salaam); Mexican novelist; b. 23 July 1960, Mexico City. *Education:* Universidad de Lima, Peru, Escuela Internacional de Çine Latinoamericano de San Antonio de los Baños, Cuba. *Career:* fmr Dir Área de Literatura y Humanidades, Universidad del Claustro de Sor Juana; fmr mem. Sistema Nacional de Creadores de México 1999–2005; Founder-Dir Escuela Dinámica de Escritores, Ciudad de México 2000–. *Publications include:* novellas: Mujeres de sal 1986, Efecto invernadero 1992, Canon perpetuo 1993, Salón de belleza 1994, Damas chinas 1995, Tres novelas 1995, Poeta ciego 1998, El jardín de la señora Murakami 2000, Flores (Premio Xavier Villaurrutia) 2001, Shiki Nagaoka: Una nariz de ficción 2001, La escuela del dolor humano de Sechuán 2001, Jacobo el mutante 2002, Perros héroes 2003, Obra reunida 2005, Underwood portátil modelo 1915 2005, Lecciones para una liebre muerta 2005, Pájaro transparente 2006, El gran vidrio (Premio Mazatlán de Literatura 2008) 2007, La jornada de la mona y el paciente 2007, La Condición de las flores 2008, Los fantasmas del masajista 2009, Biografía ilustrada de Mishima 2009, El pasante de notario Murasaki Shikibu 2011, Disecado 2011; other: El arte de enseñar a escribir 2006, Las dos Fridas 2008; contribs to several anthologies. *Honours:* Guggenheim Fellowship 2002. *Literary Agent:* c/o Antonia Kerrigan Literary Agency, Travesera de Gracia 22, 1º, 2ª, 08021 Barcelona, Spain. *Telephone:* (93) 2093820. *Fax:* (93) 4144328. *E-mail:* antonia@antoniakerrigan.com. *Website:* www.antoniakerrigan.com.

BELLE, Pamela Dorothy Alice, BA; British author; b. 16 June 1952, Ipswich, Suffolk, England; m. Steve Thomas; two s. *Education:* Univ. of Sussex, Coventry Coll. of Educ. *Career:* mem. Soc. of Authors, Historical Novel Soc. *Publications include:* The Moon in the Water 1983, The Chains of Fate 1984, Alathea 1985, The Lodestar 1987, Wintercombe 1988, Herald of Joy 1989, A Falling Star 1990, Treason's Gift 1992, The Silver City 1994, The Wolf Within 1995, Blood Imperial 1996, Mermaid's Ground 1998, No Love Lost 1999; contribs to periodicals. *Literary Agent:* c/o Vivienne Schuster, Curtis Brown Group Ltd, Haymarket House, Haymarket, London, SW1Y 4SP, England. *Telephone:* (20) 7393-4400. *E-mail:* elfwyn@dsl.pipex.com (office).

BELLI, Gioconda; Nicaraguan poet and writer; b. 9 Dec. 1949, Managua; m. 2nd Charles Castaldi 1987; four c. *Education:* Charles Morris Price School, Philadelphia, INCAE (Harvard Univ. School of Business Admin in Cen. America), Georgetown Univ., Washington, DC. *Career:* mem. Political-Diplomatic Comm. 1978–79, Int. Press Liaison 1982–83, Exec. Sec. and Spokesperson for Electoral Campaign 1983–84, Sandinista Nat. Liberation Front; Dir of Communications and Public Relations, Ministry of Economic Planning 1979–82; Foreign Affairs Sec., Nicaragua Writer's Union 1983–88; Man. Dir Sistema Nacional de Publicidad 1984–86; mem. Royal Spanish Acad. of Letters, PEN. *Publications include:* poetry: Sobre la grama (translated as On the Grass) 1972, Línea de Fuego (translated as Line of Fire) (Casa de las Américas Poetry Prize, Cuba) 1978, Truenos y arco iris 1982, Amor insurrecto (anthology) 1985, De la costilla de Eva (translated. as From Eve's Rib) 1987, Poesía reunida 1989, El ojo de la mujer 1991, Sortilegio contra el frío 1992, Apogeo 1997; fiction: La mujer habitada (translated as The Inhabited Woman) 1988, Sofía de los Presagios (translated as Sophie and the Omens) 1990, El Taller de las mariposas (juvenile, translated as The Workshop of the Butterflies) (Luchs del Semanario Die Zeit a su libro Award) 1992, Waslala 1996, El país bajo mi piel: memorias de amor y guerra (autobiography) 2001, El pergamino de la seducción (novel) 2005, El Apretado abrazo de la enredadera 2006, Fuego soy, apartado y espada puesta lejos 2007, El infinito en la palma de la mano (Biblioteca Breve Award) 2008, El Pais de las Mujeres (Otra Orilla Hispano-American Prize) 2010; contribs to anthologies and periodicals. *Honours:* Nat. Univ. Poetry Prize 1972, Friedrich Ebhert Foundation Booksellers, Editors and Publishers Literary Prize, Germany 1989, Anna Seghers Literary Fellowship, Germany 1989, Internacional de Poesía Generación del 27 Award 2002, Premio Pluma de Plata 2005, Premio Sor Juana de la Cruz 2008. *Literary Agent:* c/o Paul Cirone, The Friederich Agency, 19 West 21st Street, Suite 201, New York, NY 10010, USA. *Telephone:* (212) 317-8810. *Fax:* (212) 317-8811. *E-mail:* giocondaIsHere@aol.com (office). *Website:* www.giocondabelli.com.

BELSHAW, Cyril Shirley, PhD, FRSC; Canadian anthropologist, writer and publisher; b. 3 Dec. 1921, Waddington, NZ; s. of Horace Belshaw and Marion L. S. Belshaw (née McHardie); m. Betty J. Sweetman 1943 (deceased); one s. one d. *Education:* Auckland Univ. Coll. and Victoria Coll., Wellington (Univ. of New Zealand), London School of Econs. *Career:* Dist Officer and Deputy Commr for Western Pacific, British Solomon Islands 1943–46; Sr Research Fellow, ANU 1950–53; Prof., Univ. of British Columbia 1953–86, Prof. Emer. 1986–; Dir Regional Training Centre for UN Fellows, Vancouver 1961–62; Ed. Current Anthropology 1974–84; mem. numerous UNESCO comms, working parties and consultancy groups; Pres. Int. Union of Anthropological and Ethnological Sciences 1978–83, XIth Int. Congress of Anthropological and Ethnological Sciences 1983; Exec. American Anthropological Assoc. 1969–70; Chair. Standing Cttee Social Sciences and Humanities Pacific Science Asscn 1968–76; Ed. The Anthroglobe Journal 1998–2000, 2004–06; Propr Webzines of Vancouver 2000–; Man. Ed. Adam's Vancouver Dining Guide 1997–2007, www.anthropologising.ca 2001–08. *Publications include:* Island Administration in the South West Pacific 1950, Changing Melanesia 1954, In Search of Wealth 1955, The Great Village 1957, The Indians of British Columbia (with others) 1958, Under the Ivi Tree 1964, Anatomy of a University 1964, Traditional Exchange and Modern Markets 1965, The Conditions of Social Performance 1970, Towers Besieged 1974, The Sorcerer's Apprentice 1976, The Complete Good Dining Guide to Restaurants in Greater Vancouver 1984, Choosing Our Destiny 2006, Remuera: Memories of a New Zealand Boy Between the Wars 2009, Bumps on a Long Road: Essays from an Anthropologist's Memory 2009, Fixing the World 2010. *Honours:* Hon. Life Fellow, Royal Anthropological Inst., Pacific Science Asscn, Asscn for the Social Anthropology of Oceania, Hon. Life mem. Royal Anthropological Inst. 1978, Pacific Science Asscn 1981; World Utopian Champion 2005. *Address:* Suite 2901, 969 Richards Street, Vancouver, BC V6B 1A8, Canada (home). *Telephone:* (604) 739-8130 (home). *E-mail:* cyril@anthropologising.ca. *Website:* www.anthropologising.ca (home).

BELTING, Hans, PhD; German writer and academic; *Mary Jane Crowe Professor of Art History, Northwestern University*; b. 7 July 1935, Andernach.

Education: Univ. of Mainz, Univ. of Rome. *Career:* Visiting Fellow, Harvard Univ.; Asst Prof. of Art History, Univ. of Hamburg 1966; Prof. of Art History, Univ. of Heidelberg 1970–80, Univ. of Munich 1980–93; Visiting Prof., Harvard Univ. 1984; Meyer Shapiro Visiting Prof., Columbia Univ. 1989, 1990; Prof. of Art History and New Media, School for New Media, Karlsruhe 1993–2002, Chair. Anthropology Programme 2000–02; Visiting Prof., Getty Inst., Buenos Aires 2002; European Chair., Collège de France, Paris 2002–03; Dir Int. Research Centre for Cultural Studies, Vienna 2004–07; Mary Jane Crowe Prof. of Art History, Northwestern Univ. 2003–; Fellow, Wissenschaftkolleg, Berlin; mem. American Acad. of Arts and Sciences, Medieval Acad. of America, Academia Europaea. *Publications include:* Die Basilica de SS Martiti in Cimitile und ihr frühmittelalterlicher Freskenzyklus 1962, Die Euphemia-Kirche am Hippodrom in Istabul und ihre Fresken (with Rudolf Naumann) 1966, Studien zur beneventanischen Malerei 1968, Das illuminierte Buch in der spätbyzantinischen Gesellschaft 1970, Die Oberkirche von San Francesco in Assisi: Ihre Dekoration als Aufgabe und die Genese einer neuen Wandmalerei 1977, The Mosaics and Frescoes of St Mary Pammakaritos (with Cyril Mango and Doula Mouriki) 1978, Patronage in 13th Century Constantinople: An Atelier of Later Byzantine Book Illumination and Calligraphy (with Hugo Buchthal) 1978, Die Bibel des Niketas: Ein Werk der höfischen Buchkunst in Byanz und sein antikes Vorbild (with Guglielmo Cavallo) 1979, Das bild und sein Publikum in Mittelalter: Form und Funktion früher Bildtafeln der Passion 1981, English trans. as The Image and Its Public in the Middle Ages 1990, Jan van Ecyk als Erzählet (with Dagmar Eichberger) 1983, Das Ende der Kunstgeschichte?: Überlegungen zur heutigen Kunsterfahrung und historischen Kunstforschung 1983, English trans. as The End of the History of Art? 1987, Max Beckmann: Die Tradition als Problem in der Kunst der Moderne 1984, English trans. 1989, Giovanni Bellini Pictà: Ikone und Bilderzählung in der venezianischen Malerei 1985, Alex Katz: Bilder und Zeichnungen 1989, Bild und Kult: Eine Geschichte des Bildes vor dem Zeitalter der Kunst 1990, English trans. as Likeness and Presence: A History of the Image Before the Era of Art 1993, Die Deutschen und ihre Kunst: Ein schwieriges Erbe 1992, English trans. as The Germans and Their Art 1998, Thomas Struth: Museums Photographs 1993, English trans. 1998, Der Ort der Bilder (with Boris Groys) 1993, Die Erfindung des Gemäldes: Das erste Jahrhundert der neiderländischen Malerei (with Christiane Kruse) 1994, Das unsichtbare Meisterwerk: Die modernen Mythen der Kunst 1998, English trans. as The Invisible Masterpiece 2001, Identität im Zweifel: Ansichten der deutschen Kunst 1999, Theatres: Interiors of Cinema Spaces (with Hiroshi Sugimoto) 2000, Bild-Anthropologie: Entwürfe für eine Bildwissenschaft 2001, Hieronymous Bosch: Der Garten der Lüste 2002, English trans. as Hieronymus Bosch: Gardens of Earthly Delights 2002, Art History after Modernism 2003, Das echte Bild 2005, Florenz und Bagdad 2008, Looking through Duchamp's Door 2010; contribs to scholarly books and journals. *Honours:* Hon. Chair., Univ. of Heidelberg; Orden pour le mérite für Wissenschaften und Künste; Hon. DLit (Univ. of London) 2003. *Address:* Department of Art History, Kresge Hall-Room 3-400, 1880 Campus Drive, Evanston, IL 60208-2208, USA (office). *Telephone:* (847) 491-3230 (office). *Fax:* (847) 467-1035 (office). *E-mail:* art-history@northwestern.edu (office). *Website:* www.wcas.northwestern.edu (office).

BELYANIN, Andrei; Russian writer; b. 24 Jan. 1967, Astrakhan; m.; one s. (died 2004). *Publications include:* Sword With No Name 1997, The Furious Landgrave 1998, The Age of Saint Skiminok 1998, Jack the Mad King 1999, My Wife Is a Witch 1999, Tsar Gorokh's Detective Agency 1999, The Redheaded Knight 2000, The Flying Ship 2000, Red and Striped 2000, The Return of Red and Striped 2000, The Order of Porcelain Knights 2000, The Little Sister from Hell 2001, Bride Elimination 2002, The Thief of Baghdad 2002, Professional Werewolf (co-author) 2002, Taste of the Vampire 2003, Werewolves' Vacation 2003, Bear Guard (poetry) 2003, Werewolves' Chronicles 2004, The Hunt for the Hussar 2004, The Case of the Sober Buffoons 2004, Cossack in Heaven 2005, Detectives on Vacation 2006, The Return of the Werewolves 2007, Diary of Cat with Lemonade Name (short stories) 2007, Aargh 2007, Aargh in the Elf-Nursery 2007, Aargh on the Throne 2007, The Wishes of Demons (short stories) 2008, Cossack in Hell 2008, To Merry and Neutralize 2009, Werewolves' Stories 2009.

BEN JELLOUN, Tahar; Moroccan writer and poet; b. 1 Dec. 1944, Fès; m. Aicha Ben Jelloun 1986; two s. two d. *Education:* Lycée Regnault de Tanger, Faculté de Lettres, Mohammed-V Univ., Rabat and Univ. of Paris. *Career:* worked as a prof. in Morocco, teaching philosophy first in Tetouan and then in Casablanca; emigrated to France 1971; columnist, Le Monde 1973–, La Repubblica (Italy) and La Vanguardia (Spain); mem. Conseil supérieur de la langue française; UN Goodwill Amb. for Human Rights. *Publications include:* fiction: Harrouda 1973, La Réclusion solitaire 1976 (trans. as Solitaire 1988), Moha le fou, Moha le sage 1978, La Prière de l'absent 1980, Muha al-ma'twah, Muha al-hakim 1982, L'Écrivain public 1983, L'Enfant de sable 1985 (trans. as The Sand Child 1987), La Nuit sacrée 1987 (trans. as The Sacred Night 1989), Jour de silence à Tanger 1990 (trans. as Silent Day in Tangier 1991), Les Yeux baissés 1991, L'Ange aveugle 1992, L'Homme rompu 1994, Corruption 1995, Le Premier amour est toujours le dernier 1995, Les Raisins de la galère 1995, La Soudure fraternelle 1995, La Nuit de l'erreur 1997, L'Auberge des pauvres 1999, Labyrinthe des Sentiments 1999, Cette aveuglante absence de lumière (trans. as This Blinding Absence of Light) (Int. IMPAC Dublin Literary Award 2004) 2001, Amours sorcières 2003, La Belle au bois dormant 2004, Le Dernier Ami (trans. as The Last Friend) 2004, Partir 2005, L'ecole perdue 2006, Yemma 2007, Sur ma mère 2008, Au pays 2009, Leaving Tangier 2009, A Palace in the Old Village 2010; poetry: Hommes sous linceul de silence 1970, Cicatrice du soleil 1972, Le Discours du chameau 1974, La Mémoire future: Anthologie de la nouvelle poésie du Maroc 1976, Les Amandiers sont morts de leurs blessures 1976, A l'insu du souvenir 1980, Sahara 1987, La Remontée des cendres 1991, Poésie Complète (1966–95) 1995, The Rising of the Ashes 2010; plays: Chronique d'une solitude 1976, Entretien avec Monsieur Said Hammadi, ouvrier algérien 1982, La Fiancée de l'eau 1984; non-fiction: La Plus haute des solitudes: Misère sexuelle d'émigrés nord-africains 1977, Haut Atlas: L'Exil de pierres 1982, Hospitalité française: Racisme et immigration maghrebine 1984, Marseille, comme un matin d'insomnie 1986, Giacometti 1991, Le Racisme expliqué à ma fille 1998, L'islam expliqué aux enfants 2002. *Honours:* Dr hc (Montréal); Chevalier des Arts et des Lettres 1983, Chevalier de la Légion d'honneur 1988, Grand Croix 2008; Prix de l'Amitié Franco-Arabe 1976, Médaille du Mérite Nat. (Morocco), Prix Goncourt 1987, Prix des Hemisphere 1991, UN Global Tolerance Award 1998, Prix Ulysse 2005, Special Prize for "peace and friendship between people" at Lazio between Europe and the Mediterranean Festival 2006, Prix de la ville Catania 2009, Argana Int. Poetry Award 2010, Erich Maria Remarque Peace Prize 2011, Prix de la Fondation Crans Montana 2011. *Address:* c/o Éditions Gallimard, 5 rue Sébastien-Bottin, 75328 Paris Cedex 07, France. *E-mail:* tbjweb@gmail.com (office). *Website:* www.taharbenjelloun.org.

BEN-RAFAEL, Eliezer, BA, MA, PhD; Israeli sociologist and academic; *Professor Emeritus, Department of Sociology and Anthropology, Tel-Aviv University*; b. 3 Oct. 1938, Brussels, Belgium; m. Miriam Neufeld 1960; two d. *Education:* Hebrew Univ., Jerusalem. *Career:* Research Fellow, Dept of Sociology, Harvard Univ. 1973–74; Lecturer, Dept of Sociology and Social Anthropology, Hebrew Univ. of Jerusalem; Sr Lecturer, Dept of Sociology, Univ. of Tel-Aviv, Head of Dept of Sociology and Anthropology 1985–87, Assoc. Prof. 1986, Prof. 1992–2006, Prof. Emer. 2006–, Jima and Zalman Weinberg Chair of Political Sociology 1997–2007; Directeur d'Études Associé, École des Hautes Études en Sciences Sociales 1984–85; Visiting Scholar, Oxford Centre for Postgraduate Hebrew Studies 1989–90; Co-Ed. Israel Social Sciences Review 1992–; Fellow, Int. Biographical Asscn 1994; mem. Israel Soc. of Sociology (Pres. 1994–97), Int. Inst. of Sociology (Vice-Pres. –2001, Pres. 2001–05), Asscn for Social Scientific Study of Jewry; Dir Klal Yisrael Project; Leading Researcher, Int. Research About Russian-Speaking Jews (Israel-Germany and Israel). *Publications include:* Social Aspects of Guerilla and Anti-Guerilla Warfare 1978, Le Nouveau Kibboutz 1979, The Emergence of Ethnicity: Cultural Groups and Social Conflict in Israel 1982, Le kibboutz 1983, The Kibbutz: Progress vs Equality 1987, Israel-Palestine: A Guerilla Conflict in International Politics 1987, Status, Power and Conflict in the Kibbutz 1988, Community in Transition: Mobility, Integration and Conflict 1993, Language, Identity and Social Division: The Case of Israel 1994, Crisis and Transformation: The Kibbutz at Century's End 1997, Language and Communication in Israel 2000, Identités Juives, 50 sages repondent à Ben-Gourion 2001, Identity, Culture and Globalization 2001, Sociology and Ideology 2003, Contemporary Jewries: Convergence and Divergence 2003, Comparing Modernities 2005, Is Israel One? 2005, Jewry Between Tradition and Secularism 2006, Jewish Identities in a Era of Multiple Modernities 2006, Cleavages in Israeli Society 2006 (co-author) 2006, Building a Diaspora: Russian Jews in Israel, Germany and the USA 2006, Ethnicity, Religion and Class in Israeli Society 2007, Identities in an Era of Globalization and Multiculturalism: Latin America in the Jewish World (co-ed.) 2008, Ha-Kibbutz al Drakhim Mitpatslot (The Kibbutz on Ways Apart) (co-author) 2009, Jews and Jewish Education in Germany Today (co-author) 2011; contribs to professional journals. *Honours:* Ordre des Arts et des Lettres 2010; Prize Landau 2009. *Address:* Hadror 11, Ramat Hasharon 47203 (home); Department of Sociology, University of Tel-Aviv, Naftali Building 629, Tel-Aviv 69978, Israel (office). *Telephone:* (3) 6408824 (office); (3) 5406297 (home). *Fax:* (3) 6409215 (office); (3) 5402291 (home). *E-mail:* saba@post.tau.ed.il (office). *Website:* spirit.tau.ac.il/socant/benRafael (office).

BÉNABOU, Marcel, PhD; French writer and academic; *Professor Emeritus of Roman History, Université de Paris VII (Denis Diderot)*; b. 29 June 1939, Meknès, Morocco; m. Isabelle Dubosc; one s. *Education:* Lycée Louis-le-Grand, Paris, Ecole Normale Supérieure, Sorbonne, Univ. of Paris. *Career:* Prof. of Roman History, Université de Paris VII (Denis Diderot) 1974–2002, now Prof. Emer.; mem. Ouvroir de Littérature Potentielle (Oulipo) (secrétaire définitivement provisoire 1970–) 1969–. *Publications include:* Suétone, les Césars et l'histoire dans Suétone 1975, La résistance africaine à la romanisation 1976, La vie de Tacfarinas dans Les Africains IX 1978, La vie de Juba II dans Les Africains XI 1979, Un aphorisme peut en cacher un autre 1980, Locutions introuvables 1984, Alexandre au greffoir 1986, Pourquoi je n'ai écrit aucun de mes livres (translated as Why I Have Not Written Any of my Books) (Prix de l'Humour noir Xavier Forneret) 1986, Bris de mots, Presbytères et prolétaires 1989, Jette ce livre avant qu'il soit trop tard! (translated as Dump This Book While You Still Can!) 1992, Rendre à Cézanne 1993, Jacob, Menahem et Mimoun, une épopée familiale (translated as Jacob, Menahem, and Mimoun: A Family Epic) (Nat. Jewish Book Award) 1995, L'Hannibal perdu 1997, Altitude et profondeur 1999, Un art simple et tout d'exécution (with Jacques Jouet, Harry Mathews and Jacques Roubaud) 2001, Résidence d'hiver 2001, 789 néologismes de Jacques Lacan 2002, Écrire sur Tamara (translated as To Write on Tamara?) 2002, La résistance africaine à la romanisation, L'Appentis revisité 2003, Presbytère et prolétaires (co-author), De but en blanc. *Address:*

67 rue de Rochechouart, 75009 Paris, France (home). *E-mail:* mbenabou@noos.fr. *Website:* www.oulipo.net/oulipiens/MB.

BENACQUISTA, Tonino; French novelist and screenwriter; b. 1 Sept. 1961, Choisy-le-Roi, Paris. *Career:* fmr museum night watchman and train guard. *Play:* Le Contrat: un western psychanalytique en deux actes et un épilogue. *Film and television screenplays:* La Souris noire (series) 1987, Couchettes express (TV) 1994, La Débandade 1999, Les Faux-fuyants (TV) 2000, Le Coeur à l'ouvrage 2000, Le Plafond 2001, Les Morsures de l'aube 2001, Sur mes lèvres 2001, L'Outremangeur 2003, De battre mon coeur s'est arrêté 2005, La Boîte noire 2005, A Crime 2006, Les Disparus 2006, Saga 2009. *Publications include:* novels: Impossible n'est pas français (juvenile), Victor Pigeon (juvenile), Epinglé comme une pin-up dans un placard de G.I. 1985, La Maldonne des sleepings 1989, Trois carrés rouges sur fond noir 1990, La Commedia des ratés (Grand Prix de Littérature Policière 1992) 1991, Les Morsures de l'aube 1992, Saga 1997, L'Outremangeur (Angoulême Int. Comics Festival René Goscinny Award) 2000, Tout à l'ego 2001, Quelqu'un d'autre 2003, Malavita 2004, Dieu n'a pas réponse à tout 2007, Le Serrurier Volant 2008, Malavita Encore 2009, Badfellas 2010, Les amours insolentes: 17 variations sur le couple (co-author) 2010, Le Grand Palais, catalogue Déraisonné (co-author) 2010, Homo Erectus 2011. *Honours:* Trophee 813, Grand Prix des lectrices de Elle, Prix Mystére de la Critique, César Award 2001, 2005. *Address:* c/o Éditions Gallimard, 5 rue Sébastien-Bottin, 75328 Paris cedex 07, France (office). *Website:* www.gallimard.fr (office).

BENEDICTUS, David Henry, BA; British writer, dramatist and reviewer; b. 16 Sept. 1938, London, England; m. Yvonne Daphne Antrobus 1971; one s. one d. *Education:* Balliol Coll., Oxford, Eton Coll. *Career:* BBC News and Current Affairs, BBC Radio 1961, Ed., Readings 1989–91, and Radio 3 Drama 1992, Sr Prod., Serial Readings 1992–95; Drama Dir, BBC TV 1962, Story Ed. 1965; Asst Dir, RSC 1970; Writer-in-Residence, Sutton Library, Surrey 1975, Kibbutz Gezer, Israel 1978, Bitterne Library, Southampton 1983–84; Antiques Correspondent, Evening Standard 1977–80; Judith E. Wilson Visiting Fellow, Cambridge, and Fellow Commoner, Churchill Coll., Cambridge 1981–82; Commissioning Ed., Drama Series, Channel 4 TV 1984–86. *Publications include:* The Fourth of June 1962, You're a Big Boy Now 1963, This Animal is Mischievous 1965, Hump, or Bone by Bone Alive 1967, The Guru and the Golf Club 1969, A World of Windows 1971, The Rabbi's Wife 1976, Junk: How and Where to Buy Beautiful Things at Next to Nothing Prices 1976, A Twentieth Century Man 1978, The Antique Collector's Guide 1980, Lloyd George (after Elaine Morgan's screenplay) 1981, Whose Life is it Anyway? (after Brian Clarke's screenplay) 1981, Who Killed the Prince Consort? 1982, Local Hero (after Bill Forsyth's screenplay) 1983, The Essential London Guide 1984, Floating Down to Camelot 1985, The Streets of London 1986, The Absolutely Essential London Guide 1986, Little Sir Nicholas 1990, Odyssey of a Scientist (with Hans Kalmus) 1991, Sunny Intervals and Showers 1992, The Stamp Collector 1994, How to Cope When the Money Runs Out 1998, Dropping Names (auto-biog.) 2005, Return to the Hundred Acre Wood 2009; plays: Betjemania 1976, The Golden Key 1982, What a Way to Run a Revolution! 1985, You Say Potato 1992; contribs to newspapers and magazines. *Telephone:* (7986) 041386. *E-mail:* davidbenedictus@hotmail.com (office). *Website:* www.davidbenedictus.co.uk.

BENFORD, Gregory Albert, BA, MS, PhD; American physicist, science fiction writer and academic; *Professor Emeritus, Department of Physics and Astronomy,, University of California, Irvine;* b. 30 Jan. 1941, Mobile, Ala; m. Joan Abbe 1967; one s. one d. *Education:* Univ. of Oklahoma, Univ. of California, San Diego. *Career:* Fellow, Lawrence Radiation Laboratory, Livermore 1967–69, Research Physicist 1969–71, Asst Prof., School of Physical Sciences, Univ. of California, Irvine 1971–73, Assoc. Prof. 1973–79, Prof. 1979–2005, Prof. Emer. 2006–; Founder-Chair. Genescient Corpn 2006–; Visiting Fellow, Univs of Cambridge 1976, Turin, Bologna; Fellow, American Physical Soc. 2004; Adviser to NASA, Defense Advanced Research Projects Agency, CIA; mem. Royal Astronomical Soc., Science Fiction and Fantasy Writers of America, Social Science Exploration. *Publications include:* Deeper Than the Darkness (revised edn as The Stars in the Shroud) 1970, If the Stars are Gods (with Gordon Eklund) 1977, In the Ocean of Night 1977, Find the Changeling (with Gordon Eklund) 1980, Shiva Descending (with William Rotsler) 1980, Timescape (Nebula Award) 1980, Against Infinity 1983, Across the Sea of Suns 1984, Artifact 1985, Of Space-Time and the River 1985, In Alien Flesh 1986, Heart of the Comet (with David Brin) 1986, Great Sky River 1987, Under the Wheel (with others) 1987, Hitler Victorious: Eleven Stories of the German Victory in World War II (ed. with Martin H. Greenberg) 1987, We Could Do Worse 1988, Tides of Light 1989, Beyond the Fall of Night (with Arthur C. Clarke) 1990, Centigrade 233 1990, Matter's End (ed.) 1991, Chiller 1993, Furious Gulf 1994, Far Futures 1995, Sailing Bright Eternity 1995, Foundation's Fear 1997, Immersion and Other Short Novels 2002, Beyond Infinity 2004, What Might have Been 2004, The Sunborn 2005, Beyond Human: Living with Robots and Cyborgs 2008, The Wonderful Future That Never Was (co-author) 2010. *Honours:* Woodrow Wilson Fellowship 1963, Nebula Award 1975, Australian Ditmar Award 1980, Int. Campbell Award 1980, UN Medal in Literature 1994, Lord Foundation Award in Science 1995, Isaac Asimov Memorial Award 2007. *Address:* Department of Physics and Astronomy, University of California, 4176 Frederick Reines Hall, Irvine, CA 92697 (office); Genescient Corporation, 11180 Warner Ave., Suite 165, Fountain Valley, CA 92708, USA (office). *Telephone:* (949) 824-6911 (Irvine) (office); (949) 954-7463 (Fountain Valley) (office). *Fax:* (949) 824-2174 (Irvine) (office). *E-mail:* gbenford@uci.edu (home). *Website:* www.physics.uci.edu/faculty/benford.html (office); www.genescient.com (office); www.gregorybenford.com.

BENÍTEZ, Sandra, BS, MA; American writer; b. 26 March 1941, Washington, DC; m. James F. Kondrick 1980; two s. *Education:* Northeast Missouri State Univ. *Career:* Distinguished Edelstein-Keller Writer-in-Residence, Univ. of Minnesota 1997; Knapp Chair in Humanities, Univ. of San Diego 2001; Judith Anderson Stoutland Writer-in-Residence, St Olaf Coll. 2004; mem. Authors' Guild, Poets and Writers. *Publications include:* A Place Where the Sea Remembers (Minnesota Book Award for Fiction 1993, Barnes and Noble Fiction Award 1994) 1993, Bitter Grounds (American Book Award) 1997, The Weight of All Things 2000, Night of the Radishes 2004, Bag Lady: A Memoir 2005. *Honours:* Loft-McKnight Award 1988, 1993, Bush Foundation Fellowship 2000, Nat. Hispanic Heritage Award 2004, USA Gund Fellow 2006. *Literary Agent:* Ellen Levine, The Ellen Levine Literary Agency, Trident Media Group, 41 Madison Avenue, 36th Floor, New York, NY 10010, USA. *Telephone:* (212) 333-1517. *Fax:* (212) 333-1518. *Website:* www.tridentmediagroup.com. *E-mail:* benitezbooks@msn.com (office). *Website:* www.sandrabenitez.com.

BENJAMIN, David (see Slavitt, David Rytman)

BENN, Rt Hon. Anthony (Tony) Neil Wedgwood, PC, MA; British politician, writer and broadcaster; b. 3 April 1925, London; s. of William Wedgwood Benn (1st Viscount Stansgate), PC and Margaret Eadie (née Holmes); m. Caroline de Camp 1949 (died 2000); three s. one d. *Education:* Westminster School and New Coll., Oxford. *Career:* RAF pilot 1943–45; Univ. of Oxford 1946–49; Producer, BBC 1949–50; Labour MP for Bristol SE 1950–60, compelled to leave House of Commons on inheriting peerage 1960, re-elected and unseated 1961, renounced peerage and re-elected 1963, contested and lost Bristol E seat in 1983, re-elected as mem. for Chesterfield 1984–2001; Nat. Exec. Labour Party 1959–94; Chair. Fabian Soc. 1964; Postmaster-Gen. 1964–66; Minister of Tech. 1966–70, of Power 1969–70; Shadow Minister of Trade and Industry 1970–74; Sec. of State for Industry and Minister of Posts and Telecommunications 1974–75; Sec. of State for Energy 1975–79; Vice-Chair. Labour Party 1970, Chair. 1971–72; Chair. Labour Party Home Policy Cttee 1974–82; cand. for Leadership of Labour Party 1976, 1988, for Deputy Leadership 1971, 1981; Pres. Socialist Campaign Group of Labour MPs, EEC Energy Council 1977, Labour Action for Peace 1997–2001, currently Pres. Stop the War Coalition; Visiting Prof. of Politics, LSE 2001–02; fmr mem. Bureau Confed. of Socialist Parties of the European Community; numerous TV and radio broadcasts. *Television:* Speaking Up in Parliament 1993, Westminster Behind Closed Doors 1995, New Labour in Focus 1998, Tony Benn Speaks 2001. *Recordings:* The BBC Benn Tapes 1994, 1995, Writings on the Wall (with Roy Bailey) 1996, Tony Benn's Greatest Hits 2003, An Audience with Tony Benn 2003. *Publications:* The Privy Council as a Second Chamber 1957, The Regeneration of Britain 1964, The New Politics 1970, Speeches by Tony Benn 1974, Arguments for Socialism 1979, Arguments for Democracy 1981, Parliament, People and Power 1982, The Sizewell Syndrome 1984, Writings on the Wall: A Radical and Socialist Anthology 1215–1984 (ed.) 1984, Out of the Wilderness: Diaries 1963–67 1987, Office Without Power: Diaries 1968–72 1988, Fighting Back: Speaking Out for Socialism in the Eighties 1988, Against the Tide: Diaries 1973–76 1989, Conflicts of Interest: Diaries 1977–80 1990, A Future for Socialism 1991, End of an Era: Diaries 1980–90 1992, Common Sense: A New Constitution for Britain (with Andrew Hood) 1993, Years of Hope: Diaries 1940–1962 1994, The Benn Diaries 1940–1990 1995, Free at Last: Diaries 1991–2001 2002, Free Radical: New Century Essays 2003, Dare to be a Daniel (memoir) 2004, More Time for Politics: Diaries 2001–07 2007, Letters to my Grandchildren 2009. *Honours:* Freeman of the City of Bristol 2003; Hon. Fellow, New Coll. Oxford 2005; Hon. LLD (Strathclyde, Williams Coll., USA, Brunel, Bristol, Univ. of West of England, Univ. of N London); Hon. DTech (Bradford); Hon. DSc (Aston); Dr hc (Paisley). *Address:* 12 Holland Park Avenue, London, W11 3QU, England (office). *Telephone:* (20) 7229-0779 (office). *E-mail:* tony@tbenn.fsnet.co.uk (office).

BENNACK, Frank Anthony, Jr; American publishing executive; *Vice-Chairman of the Board and CEO, Hearst Corporation;* b. 12 Feb. 1933, San Antonio; s. of Frank Bennack and Lula Connally; m. Luella Smith 1951; five d. *Education:* Univ. of Maryland and St Mary's Univ. *Career:* advertising account exec. San Antonio Light 1950–53, 1956–58, Advertising Man. 1961–65, Asst Publr 1965–67, Publr 1967–74; Gen. Man. (newspapers), Hearst Corpn New York 1974–76, Exec. Vice-Pres. and COO 1975–78, Pres. and CEO 1978–2002, Vice-Chair. Bd 2002–, Chair. Exec. Cttee 2002–08; Chair. Hearst-Argyle Television 2008–, CEO 2008–; Chair. Museum of TV and Radio, NY City 1991–; Pres. Tex. Daily Newspaper Asscn 1973–; mem. Bd of Dirs J.P. Morgan Chase & Co., Wyeth, Polo Ralph Lauren Corpn, Metropolitan Opera of New York; Dir, Vice-Chair. Lincoln Center for the Performing Arts; Dir Newspaper Asscn of American (fmrly American Newspaper Publrs Asscn), Chair. 1992–93; Gov., Vice-Chair. New York Presbyterian Hosp.; mem. Bd of Dirs Mfrs Hanover Trust Co., New York; mem. American Acad. of Arts and Sciences 2007–. *Address:* Hearst Corporation, Hearst Tower, 12th Floor, 300 West 57th Street, New York, NY 10019, USA (office). *Telephone:* (212) 649-4190 (office). *Fax:* (212) 649-2108 (office). *E-mail:* hearstnewspapers@hearst.com (office). *Website:* www.hearstcorp.com (office).

BENNASSAR, Bartolomé; French historian, novelist and academic; b. 8 April 1929, Nîmes; m. 1954; one s. two d. *Education:* Univ. of Montpellier, Univ. of Toulouse. *Career:* Prof. of History, High Schools of Rodez, Agen and Marseille; Asst Prof., Prof., then Pres., Univ. of Toulouse Le Mirail. *Publications include:* Le Coup de Midi 1964, Valladolid au siècle d'or 1967, Une fille on mars 1968, Recherches sur les grandes épidémies dans le Nord de l'Espagne 1969, L'Homme espagnol (translated as The Spanish Character) 1975, L'Inquisition espagnole XV–XIX 1979, Un siècle d'or espagnol 1982, Histoire d'Espagnols 1985, Les Chrétiens d'Allah 1989, 1492: Un monde nouveau? 1991, Histoire de la tauromachie 1993, Franco 1995, Le Voyage en Espagne 1998, Le Temps de l'Espagne VVI-XVIIe siècles 1999, Les chrétiens d'Allah (co-author) 2001, El galeote de argel 2005, Le Lit, le pouvoir et la mort 2006, Histoire du Brésil 1500–2000 2006, Histoire de la tauromachie-Une société du spectacle 2011; fiction: Le Baptême du Mort 1962, Picture: le dernier saut 1970, Les Tribulations de Mustafa des Six-Fours 1995, Don Juan de Austria. A Hero for an Empire 2000, Toute les Colombies 2002, Hernan Cortes. The consquistador of the Impossible 2002; contribs to Annales ESC, L'Histoire, Historia. *Honours:* Dr hc (Univ. of Valladolid, Spain); Bronze Medal, Centre National de la Recherche Scientifique. *Address:* 1 Allee du Val D'Aran, 31240 Saint Jean, France.

BENNETT, Alan, BA; British playwright and actor; b. 9 May 1934, Leeds; s. of Walter Bennett and Lilian Mary Peel. *Education:* Leeds Modern School, Exeter Coll., Oxford. *Career:* Jr Lecturer, Modern History, Magdalen Coll., Oxford 1960–62; co-author and actor Beyond the Fringe, Edin. 1960, London 1961, New York 1962; Trustee Nat. Gallery 1993–98. *Plays:* On the Margin (TV series, author and actor) 1966, Forty Years On (author and actor) 1968, Getting On 1971, Habeas Corpus 1973, The Old Country 1977, Enjoy 1980, Kafka's Dick 1986, Single Spies 1988, The Wind in the Willows (adapted for Nat. Theatre) 1990, The Madness of George III 1991, The Lady in the Van 1999, The History Boys (Royal Nat. Theatre, London) (Evening Standard Award for Best Play 2004, Critics Circle Theatre Award for Best New Play 2005, Olivier Award for Best New Play 2005, New York Drama Critics' Circle Play of the Year 2006, Drama Desk Award for Best Play 2006, Tony Award for Best Play 2006) 2004, The Habit of Art 2009. *Radio:* The Last of the Sun 2004. *Television scripts:* A Day Out (film) 1972, Sunset Across the Bay (TV film) 1975, A Little Outing, A Visit from Miss Prothero (plays) 1977, Doris and Doreen, The Old Crowd, Me! I'm Afraid of Virginia Woolf, All Day on the Sands, Afternoon Off, One Fine Day 1978–79, Intensive Care, Our Winnie, A Woman of No Importance, Rolling Home, Marks, Say Something Happened, An Englishman Abroad 1982, The Insurance Man 1986, Talking Heads (Olivier Award) 1992, 102 Boulevard Haussmann 1991, A Question of Attribution 1991, Talking Heads 2 1998. *Films:* A Private Function 1984, Prick Up Your Ears 1987, The Madness of King George 1994, The History Boys 2006. *Television documentaries:* Dinner at Noon 1988, Poetry in Motion 1990, Portrait or Bust 1994, The Abbey 1995, Telling Tales 1999. *Publications:* Beyond the Fringe (with Peter Cook, Jonathan Miller and Dudley Moore) 1962, Forty Years On 1969, Getting On 1972, Habeas Corpus 1973, The Old Country 1978, Enjoy 1980, Office Suite 1981, Objects of Affection 1982, The Writer in Disguise 1985, Two Kafka Plays 1987, Talking Heads 1988, Single Spies 1989, Poetry in Motion 1990, The Lady in the Van 1991, The Wind in the Willows (adaptation) 1991, The Madness of George III 1992, Writing Home (autobiog.) 1994, Diaries 1997, The Clothes They Stood Up In 1998, Talking Heads 2 1998, The Complete Talking Heads 1998, A Box of Alan Bennett 2000, Father, Father! Burning Bright 2000, The Laying on of Hands 2001, The History Boys 2004, Untold Stories 2005, The Uncommon Reader 2007, Smut (short stories) 2011; regular contrib. to London Review of Books. *Honours:* Hon. Fellow, Royal Acad. 2000; Hon. Fellow, Exeter Coll., Oxford; Freeman of Leeds 2004; Hon. DLitt (Leeds); Evening Standard Award 1961, 1969, Hawthornden Prize 1988, two Olivier Awards 1993, Evening Standard Film Award 1996, Lifetime Achievement Award, British Book Awards 2003, Evening Standard Best Play Award 2004, Olivier Award for outstanding contribution to British theatre 2005, British Book Awards Reader's Digest Author of the Year 2006, Bodley Medal 2008. *Literary Agent:* Chatto & Linnit, 123A Kings Road, London, SW3 4PL, England. *Telephone:* (20) 7352-7722 (office).

BENNETT, Amanda; American news editor and writer; *Executive Editor, Special Projects and Investigations, Bloomberg News*; m. 1st Terence Foley; two c.; m. 2nd Donald Graham 2012. *Education:* Harvard Univ. *Career:* worked 23 years with Wall Street Journal, positions included Auto Industry Reporter, Detroit 1970s–1980s, Pentagon and State Dept Reporter, Beijing Corresp., Man. Ed./Reporter, Nat. Econs Corresp., Atlanta Bureau Chief 1994–98; Man. Ed./Projects The Oregonian, Portland 2001; Ed. The Lexington Herald-Leader, Ky 2001–03; Ed. and Exec. Vice-Pres. The Philadelphia Enquirer 2003–06; Exec. Ed. of Enterprise Stories, Bloomberg News 2007, currently Exec. Ed., Projects and Investigations; fmr Pulitzer Prize juror, mem. Pulitzer Prize Bd 2002–08; fmr Nat. Headliners' Judge; mem. Bd of Dirs Temple Univ. Press, Rosenbach Museum; Bd mem. American Soc. of News Editors, Loeb Awards; mem. Pennsylvania Women's Forum, Nat. Asscn of Black Journalists. *Publications include:* Death of the Organization Man 1991, The Man Who Stayed Behind (co-author) 1993, Your Child's Symptoms (with John Garwood, M.D) 1995, In Memoriam (co-author) 1998, The Cost of Hope 2012. *Honours:* Pulitzer Prize for Nat. Reporting (co-recipient) 1997, Pulitzer Prize for Public Service (co-recipient) 2000. *Address:* Bloomberg News, 731 Lexington Avenue, New York, NY 10022, USA (office). *Telephone:* (212) 318-2000 (office). *Fax:* (212) 893-5999 (office). *Website:* www.bloomberg.com (office).

BENNETT, Bruce Harry, AO, BA, DipEd, MA, DLitt, FAHA; Australian editor, writer and academic; *Professor Emeritus, School of Humanities and Social Sciences, University of New South Wales*; b. 23 March 1941, Perth, WA; m. Patricia Ann Bennett 1967; one s. one d. *Education:* Univ. of Western Australia, Univ. of Oxford, Univ. of London, UK, Univ. of New South Wales. *Career:* Lecturer, Univ. of Western Australia 1968–75, Sr Lecturer 1975–85, Assoc. Prof. 1985–90; Co-Ed. Westerly: A Quarterly Review 1975–92; Prof. of English, School of Humanities and Social Sciences, Univ. of New South Wales, Australian Defence Force Acad., currently Prof. Emer.; Overseas Fellow, Churchill Coll. Cambridge, UK 2005; Visiting Prof. of Australian Studies, Georgetown Univ., Washington, DC, USA 2005–06; Chief Investigator, AustLit; mem. Asscn for the Study of Australian Literature (Pres. 1983–85), Australian Soc. of Authors, Asscn of Commonwealth Literature and Language Studies (also Vice-Chair.), MLA of America, PEN International, Australia-India Council 2002–08. *Publications include:* Place, Region and Community 1985, An Australian Compass: Essays on Place and Direction in Australian Literature 1991, Spirit in Exile: Peter Porter and his Poetry 1991, Dorothy Hewett: Selected Critical Essays 1995, Crossing Cultures: Essays on the Literature and Culture of the Asia-Pacific (ed) 1996, Oxford Literary History of Australia (co-ed.) 1998, Australian Short Fiction: A History 2002, Resistance and Reconciliation: Writing in the Commonwealth (co-ed) 2003, Homing In: Essays on Australian Literature and Selfhood (essays) 2006, Of Sadhus and Spinners: Australian Encounters with India (co-ed) 2009; contribs to many books and journals. *Honours:* Rhodes Scholar, Pembroke Coll., Oxford 1964–67, Western Australia Premier's Award, Historical and Critical Studies 1992. *Address:* School of Humanities and Social Sciences, University of New South Wales, Australian Defence Force Academy, Northcott Drive, Canberra, ACT 2600, Australia (office). *Telephone:* (2) 6268-8902 (office). *Fax:* (2) 6268-8879 (office). *E-mail:* b.bennett@adfa.edu.au (office). *Website:* www.unsw.edu.au (office).

BENNETT, John J.; American writer; b. 8 Aug. 1938, New York, NY. *Education:* George Washington Univ., Univ. of Munich. *Publications include:* Tripping in America 1984, Crime of the Century 1986, The New World Order 1991, Bodo (novel) 1995, Karmic Four-Star Buckaroo 1997; contribs to Chicago Review, Exquisite Corpse, Northwest Review, Transatlantic Review, New York Quarterly, Seattle Weekly. *Honours:* First Prize for Fiction, Iron Country 1978, William Wantling Award 1987, Darrell Bob Houston Award 1988.

BENNETT, Ronan, BA, PhD; British writer; b. 1956, Belfast, Northern Ireland; m. Georgina Henry. *Education:* King's Coll., London. *Television screenplays:* Love Lies Bleeding 1993, A Man You Don't Meet Every Day 1994, Rebel Heart 2001, Fields of Gold 2002, 10 Days in War 2008. *Film screenplays:* Face 1997, A Further Gesture (aka The Break) 1997, Lucky Break 2001, Face 1997, Do Armed Robbers Have Love Affairs? (short) 2002, The Hamburg Cell 2004, Public Enemies 2009. *Publications include:* novels: The Second Prison 1991, Overthrown by Strangers 1992, The Catastrophist 1998, Havoc, in its Third Year (Hughes & Hughes/Sunday Independent Irish Novel of the Year) 2004, Zugzwang 2006; non-fiction: Stolen Years: Before and After Guildford (co-author) 1990, Fire and Rain 1994. *Literary Agent:* David Godwin Associates, 55 Monmouth Street, London, WC2H 9DG, England. *Telephone:* (20) 7240-9992. *Fax:* (20) 7240-3007. *E-mail:* assistant@davidgodwinassociates.co.uk. *Website:* www.davidgodwinassociates.co.uk.

BENNETT, William John, BA, PhD, JD; American lawyer, broadcaster, academic and fmr government official; b. 31 July 1943, Brooklyn, New York; m. Elyane Glover 1982; two s. *Education:* Williams Coll., Univ. of Texas, Harvard Univ. Law School. *Career:* Asst Prof., Univ. of Southern Mississippi 1967–68, Univ. of Texas 1970, Univ. of Wisconsin 1973; Resident Adviser and Tutor, Harvard Univ. 1969–71; Asst Prof. and Asst to the Pres., Boston Univ. 1971–76; Exec. Dir Nat. Humanities Center, NC 1976–79, Pres. and Dir 1979–81; Adjunct Assoc. Prof., North Carolina State Univ., Raleigh 1979–81, Univ. of North Carolina 1979–81; Pres. Nat. Endowment for the Humanities, Washington, DC 1981–85; US Sec. of Educ., Washington, DC 1985–88; Pnr Dunnells, Duvall, Bennett and Porter, Washington, DC 1988; Dir Nat. Drug Policy, The White House 1989–90; Co-Dir Empower America 1993; host, Bill Bennett's Morning in America (radio talk show) 2004–; mem. American Soc. for Political and Legal Philosophy, Nat. Acad. of Education, Nat. Humanities Faculty, Soc. for Values in Higher Education, Southern Education Communications Asscn; Chair. Americans for Victory Over Terrorism; co-Chair. Partnership for a Drug-Free America; Washington Fellow, Claremont Inst.; Contrib. CNN; fmr Democrat, joined Republican Party 1986. *Publications include:* Counting by Race: Equality from the Founding Fathers to Bakke and Weber (with Terry Eastland) 1979, Our Children and Our Country: Improving America's Schools and Affirming the Common Culture 1988, The De-Valuing of America: The Fight for Our Culture and Our Children 1992, The Book of Virtues: A Treasury of Great Moral Stories 1993, The Index of Leading Cultural Indicators: Facts and Figures of the State of American Society 1994, The Moral Compass: Stories for a Life's Journey 1995, Our Sacred Honor 1997, Children's Book of Heroes 1997, Book of Virtures for Young People 1997, Children's Book of America 1998, Death of Outrage: Bill Clinton and the Assault on American Ideals 1998, Children's Book of Faith 2000, Broken Hearth: Reversing the Moral Collapse of the American Family 2001, Children's Book of Home and Family 2002, Why We Fight: Moral Clarity and the War on Terrorism 2003, America: The Last Best Hope Volume I 2006, Volume 2 2007, The American Patriot's Almanac (with John Cribb) 2008, A Century Turns: New Hopes, New Fears 2010. *Address:* c/o Salem Communications, 1901 North Moore Street, Suite 200, Arlington, VA 22209, USA. *Website:* www.bennettmornings.com.

BENNOUNA, Khnata; Moroccan writer; b. 1940. *Career:* fmr Prin., Lycée Ouallada, Casablanca. *Publications include:* fiction: Liyasqet Assamt (trans. as Down with Silence!) 1967, Annar wa Al-'ikhtiyar (trans. as Fire and Choice) (Morocco Literary Prize 1971) 1969, Assawt wa Assurah (trans. as Sound and Image) 1975, Al-A'asifah (trans. as The Tempest) 1979, Al-Ghad wa Al-Ghadab (novel, trans. as Tomorrow and Wrath) 1981, Assamt Annatiq (trans. as Talking Silence) 1987.

BENSLEY, Connie; British poet and writer; b. 28 July 1929, London, England; m. J. A. Bensley 1952 (divorced 1976); two s. *Career:* Poetry Ed., PEN Magazine 1984–85; mem. Poetry Soc.; judge, Forward Prizes for poetry 2003. *Publications include:* Progress Report 1981, Moving In 1984, Central Reservations 1990, Choosing to be a Swan 1994, The Back and the Front of It 2000, Private Pleasures 2007; contribs to Observer, Poetry Review, Spectator, TLS. *Honours:* Winner, TLS Poetry Competition 1986, Second Prize, Leek Poetry Competition 1988, Winner, Arvon/Observer Poetry Competition 1994, Second Proze, Tate Gallery Poetry Competition 1995. *Address:* 40 Ashleigh Road, London, SW14 8PX, England (home). *Telephone:* (20) 8878-6260 (home). *E-mail:* ConnieBensley@googlemail.com (home).

BENSON, Eugene, BA, MA, PhD; Canadian/Northern Irish writer and academic; *Professor Emeritus, School of English and Theatre Studies, University of Guelph*; b. 6 July 1928, Larne, Co. Down, Northern Ireland; m. Renate Niklaus 1968; two s. *Education:* Nat. Univ. of Ireland, Univ. of Western Ontario, Univ. of Toronto. *Career:* Lecturer, Royal Mil. Coll., Kingston, 1960–61; Asst Prof. of English, Laurentian Univ. 1961–64; Asst Prof., School of English and Theatre Studies, Univ. of Guelph 1965–67, Assoc. Prof. 1967–71, Prof. of English 1971–93, Univ. Prof. Emer. 1994–; mem. Asscn of Canadian Theatre Historians, Canadian Asscn of Irish Studies, Writers' Union of Canada (Chair. 1983–84, elected Life mem. 2001), PEN Canada (Co-Pres. 1984–85). *Publications include:* Encounter: Canadian Drama in Four Media (anthology, ed.) 1973, The Bulls of Ronda (novel) 1976, Power Game, or the Making of a Prime Minister (novel) 1980, J. M. Synge 1982, English-Canadian Theatre (co-author) 1987, Oxford Companion to Canadian Theatre (co-ed.) 1989, Encyclopedia of Post-Colonial Literatures in English (co-ed.) 1994, The Oxford Companion to Canadian Literature (co-ed.) 1997. *Address:* School of English and Theatre Studies, University of Guelph, 50 Stone Road East, Guelph, ON N1G 2W1 (office); 55 Palmer Street, Guelph, ON N1E 2P9, Canada (home). *Telephone:* (519) 821-0343 (office). *E-mail:* ebenson@uoguelph.ca (office). *Website:* www.uoguelph.ca (office).

BENSON, Gerard John, (Jedediah Barrow); British poet, writer, editor and actor; *Editor/Administrator, Poems on the Underground*; b. 9 April 1931, London, England; s. of Arthur Bayard Benson and Eileen Benson; m. 2nd; one s. one d. *Education:* Rendcomb Coll., Univ. of Exeter, Cen. School of Speech and Drama, Univ. of London, IPA. *Career:* Resident Tutor, Arvon Foundation and Taliesen Trust; Sr Lecturer, Cen. School of Speech and Drama; Co-originator and Admin. of Poems on the Underground 1986–; Arts Council Poet-in-Residence, Dove Cottage, Wordsworth Trust 1994–; British Council Poet-in-Residence, Cairo and Alexandria 1997; British Council Writer-in-Residence, Stavanger and Kristiansand 1998; Poetry in Practice, Poet-in-Residence, Ashwell Medical Centre, Bradford 2000–01; poet and lecturer, Aldeburgh Poetry Festival 2002, 2003, 2005; Poet Laureate of the City of Bradford, UK 2008–11; mem. Barrow Poets, Quaker Arts Network, Poems on the Underground, Poetry Soc. Educ. Advisory Panel, Nat. Asscn of Writers in Educ. (Chair. 1992), Soc. of Authors. *Publications include:* Name Game 1971, Gorgon 1983, This Poem Doesn't Rhyme (ed.) 1990, Tower Block Poet: Sequence of 15 poems commissioned by BBC Radio 1990, Poems on the Underground anthologies (co-ed.) 1991–2006, The Magnificent Callisto 1993, Does W Trouble You? (ed.) 1994, Evidence of Elephants 1995, In Wordsworth's Chair 1995, Love Poems on the Underground 1996, Bradford and Beyond 1997, Nemo's Almanac (ed. and author) 1997–2006, Help! (15 poems with woodcuts by Ros Cuthbert) 2001, The Poetry Business 2002, To Catch an Elephant (poems for children) 2002, The Carnival of the Animals – poems and music for children (co-ed.) 2005, Omba Bolomba (poems for children) 2005, Best Poems on the Underground (co-ed.) 2009, A Good Time 2010; contribs to newspapers, journals, reviews and the internet. *Honours:* Signal Award for Poetry 1991. *Address:* 46 Ashwell Road, Manningham, Bradford, West Yorks., BD8 9DU, England (home). *Telephone:* (1274) 541316 (office). *Fax:* (1274) 541316 (office). *E-mail:* gerardjbenson@hotmail.com (home).

BENTLEY, Eric, BA, BLitt, PhD; American (b. British) dramatist, critic and academic; b. 14 Sept. 1916, Bolton, Lancs., England; m. 1st Maja Tschernjakow (divorced); m. 2nd Joanne Davis 1953; two s. *Education:* Univ. of Oxford, Yale Univ. *Career:* drama critic, New Republic 1952–56; Brander Matthews Prof. of Dramatic Literature, Columbia Univ., New York 1953–69; Charles Eliot Norton Prof. of Poetry, Harvard Univ. 1960–61; Katharine Cornell Prof. of Theatre, State Univ. of New York at Buffalo 1975–82; Fulbright Prof., Belgrade 1980; Prof. of Comparative Literature, Univ. of Maryland, College Park 1982–89; mem. American Acad. of Arts and Sciences, American Acad. of Arts and Letters. *Publications include:* A Century of Hero-Worship 1944, The Playwright as Thinker 1946, Bernard Shaw 1947, In Search of Theatre 1953, The Dramatic Event 1954, What is Theatre? 1956, The Life of the Drama 1964, The Theatre of Commitment 1967, A Time to Die and a Time to Love 1070, The Red White and Black 1970, Are You Now or Have You Ever Been 1972, The Recantation of Galileo Galilei 1972, Theatre of War 1972, Expletive Deleted 1974, Memoirs of Pilate 1977, Rallying Cries (three plays) 1977, Lord Alfred's Lover 1978, Wannsee 1979, The Brecht Commentaries 1981, Concord 1981, The Fall of the Amazons 1982, The Kleist Variations (three plays) 1982, Monstrous Martyrdoms (three plays) 1985, The Pirandello Commentaries 1985, The Brecht Memoir 1986, Before Brecht: Four German Plays 1986, Thinking About the Playwright 1987, Galileo (ed) 1994, Bentley on Brecht 1999, The Good Woman of Setzuan (co-author) 1999, The Life of the Drama 2000, Spring's Awakening (ed) 2000, Inspector and Other Plays (ed) 2000, Life Is a Dream: And Other Spanish Classics 2000, Bernard Shaw (co-author) 2002. *Honours:* Hon. DFA (Wisconsin) 1975, Hon. LittD (East Anglia) 1979, Dr hc (New School for Social Research) 1992; Festschrift: The Play and its Critic 1986, Florida Theatre Festival named in his honour 1992, Robert Lewis Award for Life Achievement in the Theatre 1992, inducted into Theatre Hall of Fame 1997, Thalia Prize 2006. *Literary Agent:* c/o Jack Tantleff, William Morris Agency, 1325 Avenue of the Americas, New York, NY 10019, USA. *Telephone:* (212) 586-5100. *Fax:* (212) 246-3583. *Website:* www.wma.com. *Address:* 194 Riverside Drive, New York, NY 10025, USA (home). *E-mail:* ericbentley@verizon.net.

BERENBAUM, Michael, AB, PhD; American academic, museum and foundation executive and writer; *Professor of Jewish Studies and Director, Sigi Ziering Institute, American Jewish University*; b. 31 July 1945, Newark, NJ; s. of Saul Berenbaum and Rhea Kass Berenbaum; m. Melissa Patack Berenbaum 1995; four c. *Education:* Queens Coll., CUNY, Jewish Theological Seminary, Hebrew Univ., Boston Univ., Florida State Univ. *Career:* Hymen Goldman Prof. of Theology, Georgetown Univ. 1983–97; Sr Scholar, Religious Action Center 1986–89; Adjunct Prof. of Judaic Studies, American Univ. 1987; Project Dir, United States Holocaust Memorial Museum 1988–93; Dir, United States Holocaust Research Institute 1993–97; Pres. and CEO, Survivors of Shoah Visual History Foundation 1997–2000; Ida E. King Distinguished Prof. of Holocaust Studies, Richard Stockton Coll. 1999–2000; Adjunct Prof. of Theology, Univ. of Judaism, later renamed American Jewish Univ. 2002–07, Prof. of Jewish Studies and Dir, Sigi Ziering Inst. 2002–; Strassler Family Distinguished Visiting Prof. of Holocaust Studies, Clark Univ. 2000; Podlich Distinguished Visiting Prof., Claremont McKenna Coll. 2003; Gold-Weinstein Distinguished Visiting Prof., Chapman Univ. 2009, 2010; fmr Pres. and CEO The Survivors of the Shoah Visual History Foundation; Historical Consultant for The Last Days (documentary by Shoah Foundation); Chief Historical HConsultant, Conspiracy (HBO), Uprising (NBC), The Holocaust: The Untold Story (History Channel) 2001. *Films include:* Desperate Hours: Turkey and the Holocaust, Swimming in Australia, One Survivor Remembers: The Gerda Weissman Klein Story (co-producer) (Academy Award, Emmy Award 1995, Cable Ace Award), Imaginary Witness: Hollywood and the Holocaust, Blessed Be the Match: The Story of Hannah Senesch. *Publications include:* The Vision of the Void: Theological Reflections on the Works of Elie Wiesel 1979, A Mosaic of Victims: Non-Jews Persecuted and Murdered by the Nazis (ed.) 1990, The World Must Know: A History of the Holocaust 1993, Anatomy of the Auschwitz Death Camp (ed. with Israel Gutman) 1994, What Kind of God? (ed. with Betty Rogers Rubenstein) 1995, Witness to the Holocaust: An Illustrated Documentary History of the Holocaust in the Words of Its Victims, Perpetrators and Bystanders 1997, The Holocaust and History: The Known, the Unknown, the Disputed and the Reexamined (ed. with Abraham Peck) 1998, The Bombing of Auschwitz (ed. with Michael Neufeld) 2000, A Promise to Remember: The Holocaust in the Words and Voices of its Survivors 2003, After the Passion is Gone (with J. Shawn Landres) 2004, Murder Most Merciful: Essays on the Ethical Conundrum Occasioned by Sigi Ziering's The Judgement of Herbert Bierhoff (ed.) 2005, The World Must Know 2006, Not Your Father's Antisemitism: Antisemitism in the Early 21st Century (ed.) 2008, Memory and Legacy: The Shoah Narrative of the Illinois Holocaust Museum (with Yitzhak Mais) 2009, The Holocaust: Religious and Philosophical Implications (co-ed.); Encyclopaedia Judaica (exec. dir) (Dartmouth Medal for Best Reference Work, American Library Asscn 2006, 2007). *Honours:* Hon. DD (Nazareth Coll.) 1995, Hon. DHumLitt (Denison Univ.) 2000; Silver Angel Award 1981, Simon Rockower Memorial Award, American Jewish Press Asscn 1986, 1987, Danforth Fellowship, George Wise Fellowship, Charles E. Merrill Fellowship. *Address:* The Berenbaum Group, 1124 South Orlando Avenue, Los Angeles, CA 90035, USA (office). *Telephone:* (323) 930-9325 (office). *Fax:* (323) 935-9056 (office). *E-mail:* mberenbaum@ajula.edu (office); michael@berenbaumgroup.com (office). *Website:* www.berenbaumgroup.com (office).

BERENDT, John, BA; American writer and journalist; b. (John Lawrence Berendt), 5 Dec. 1939, Syracuse, NY; s. of Ralph Berendt and Carol Berendt (née Deschere). *Education:* Nottingham High School, Syracuse, NY and Harvard Univ., Cambridge, Mass. *Career:* Assoc. Ed. Esquire 1961–69, columnist 1982–94; Ed. New York magazine 1977–79; freelance writer 1979–; mem. PEN, The Century Asscn. *Publications:* Midnight in the Garden of Good and Evil (Southern Book Award for Non-fiction) 1994, The City of Falling Angels 2005. *Literary Agent:* c/o Suzanne Gluck, William Morris Agency, 1325 Avenue of the Americas, New York, NY 10019, USA. *Telephone:* (212) 903-1169. *E-mail:* sgluck@wmeentertainment.com. *Address:* c/o Hodder & Stoughton, 338 Euston Road, London, NW1 3BH, England. *Telephone:* (20) 7873-6000.

BERESFORD-HOWE, Constance, BA, MA, PhD; Canadian academic and novelist; b. 10 Nov. 1922, Montréal; d. of Russell Beresford-Howe and Marjory Mary Moore Beresford-Howe; m. 1960; one s. *Education:* McGill Univ., Brown Univ. *Career:* Lecturer, Dept of English, McGill Univ. 1949–71; Lecturer in English, Ryerson Polytechnical Inst. 1971–87; mem. International PEN, Writers in Prison Cttee. *Publications include:* The Unreasoning Heart 1946, Of This Day's Journey 1947, The Invisible Gate 1949, My Lady Greensleeves 1955, The Book of Eve 1973, A Population of One 1977, The Marriage Bed 1981, Night Studies 1985, Prospero's Daughter 1989, A Serious Widow 1990. *Honours:* Dodd Mead Intercollegiate Literary Fellowship 1948, Canadian Booksellers Award 1974.

BERG, Elizabeth; American writer; b. 2 Dec. 1948, Minnesota; m. Howard Berg 1974 (divorced); two d. *Education:* Univ. of Minnesota, St Mary's Coll. *Publications include:* Family Traditions: Celebrations for Holidays and Everyday 1992, Durable Goods 1993, Talk Before Sleep 1994, Range of Motion 1995, The Pull of the Moon 1996, Joy School 1997, What We Keep 1998, Until the Real Thing Comes Along 1999, Escaping Into the Open: The Art of Writing True 1999, Open House 2000, Escaping into the Open: The Art of Writing True 2000, Ordinary Life 2001, Never Change 2001, True to Form 2002, Say When 2003, The Art of Mending 2004, The Year of Pleasures 2005, The Handmaid and the Carpenter 2006, We are all Welcome Here 2006, Dream When You're Feeling Blue 2007, The Day I Ate Whatever I Wanted: and Other Small Acts of Liberation 2008, Home Safe 2009, The Last Time I Saw You 2010, Once Upon a Time, There Was You 2011; contribs to periodicals. *Honours:* New England Book Award for Fiction 1997, AMC Cancer Research Center's Illuminator Award. *Address:* PO Box 707, Oak Park, IL 60303, USA (home). *Website:* www.elizabeth-berg.net.

BERG, Stephen Walter, BA; American poet and writer; *Joint Editor, American Poetry Review*; b. 2 Aug. 1934, Philadelphia; m. Millie Lane 1959; two d. *Education:* Univ. of Pennsylvania, Boston Univ., Univ. of Iowa, Indiana Univ. *Career:* teacher, Temple Univ., Philadelphia, Princeton Univ., Haverford Coll., Pa; Prof., Philadelphia Coll. of Art; Poetry Ed. Saturday Evening Post 1961–62; Founding Ed. (with Stephen Parker and Rhoda Schwartz) American Poetry Review 1972–. *Publications include:* poetry: Berg Goodman Mezey 1957, Bearing Weapons 1963, The Queen's Triangle: A Romance 1970, The Daughters 1971, Nothing in the Word: Versions of Aztec Poetry 1972, Grief: Poems and Versions of Poems 1975, New Naked Poetry Recent American Poetry in Open Forms 1976, With Akmatova at the Black Gates: Variations 1981, In It 1986, Shaving 1988, First Song, Bankei, 1653 1989, Homage to the Afterlife 1991, New and Selected Poems 1992, Oblivion: Poems 1995; Naked Poetry: Recent American Poetry in Open Forms (with Robert Mezey) 1969, Between People (with S. J. Marks) 1972, About Women (with S. J. Marks) 1973, The New Naked Poetry (with Robert Mezey) 1976, In Praise of What Persists 1983, Singular Voices: American Poetry Today 1985, The Steel Cricket: Versions: 1958–1997 1997, Porno Diva Numero Uno: An Anonymous Confession 2000, Halo 2000, The Body Electric: America's Best Poetry from The American Poetry Review (co-ed.) 2001, Rimbaud Versions and Inventions: Still Unilluminated I... 2005, The Elegy on Hats 2005, Cuckoo's Blood: Versions of Zen Poetry (co-author) 2008; other: Sea Ice: Versions of Eskimo Songs 1988; contribs to periodicals. *Honours:* Rockefeller-Centro Mexicano de Escritores Grant 1959–61, Nat. Trans. Center Grant 1969, Frank O'Hara Prize, Poetry magazine 1970, Guggenheim Fellowship 1974, Nat. Endowment for the Arts Grant 1976, Columbia Univ. Trans. Center Award 1976. *Address:* The American Poetry Review, 1700 Samsom Street, Suite 800, Philadelphia, PA 19103, USA (office). *Telephone:* (215) 496-0439. *Fax:* (215) 569-0808. *E-mail:* sberg@aprweb.org. *Website:* www.aprweb.org.

BERGEL, Hans; German writer; b. 26 July 1925, Kronstadt, Romania. *Education:* Univ. of Cluj-Napoca. *Career:* mem. Die Künstlergilde, Esslingen, PEN International, Institut für deutsche Kultur und Geschichte Südosteuropas, Munich. *Publications include:* Fürst und Lautenschläger 1956, Die Abenteuer des Japps 1958, Rumanien, Portrait einer Nation 1969, Ten Southern European Short Stories 1972, Die Sachsen in Siebenburgen nach dreissig Jahren Kommunismus 1976, Der Tanz in Ketten 1977, Siebenburgen 1980, Gestalten und Gewalten 1982, Hermann Oberth oder Der mythische Traum vom Fliegen 1984, Der Tod des Hirten 1985, Literaturgeschichte der Deutschen in Siebenburgen 1987, Das Venusherz (short novel) 1987, Weihnacht ist uberall (eleven short stories) 1988, Wenn die Adler kommen 1996, Bukowiner Spuren 2002, Die Wiederkehr der Wölfe 2007, Wegkreuzungen. Dreizehn Lebensbilder 2009, Am Vorabend des Taifuns. Geschichten aus einem abenteuerlichen Leben 2010, Die Wildgans: Erzählungen aus Siebenbürgen 2011; contribs to periodicals. *Honours:* Federal Cross of Merit (Germany); Dr hc (Univ. of Bucharest); Short Story Prize, Bucharest 1957, Bonn 1972, Georg Dehio Prize, Esslingen 1972, Goethe Foundation Prize, Basel 1972, Medien Prizes, Bavarian Broadcasting Company 1983, 1989, Bundesverdienstkreuz 1987, Saxon of Transylvania Culture Prize 1988, Geyphius-Prize 1990. *Address:* c/o Herbig Buchverlage, Thomas-Wimmer-Ring 11, 80539 Munich, Germany (office). *Website:* www.herbig.net (office).

BERGEN, David, BEd; Canadian novelist; b. 1957, Port Edward, BC; s. of Fred Bergen and Eva Bergen; m. Dori Bergen; two s. *Career:* worked as a carpenter, bricklayer and orderly; English teacher in high school –2002; currently teaches creative writing, Humber Coll., Banff Centre for the Arts. *Publications include:* Sitting Opposite My Brother (short stories) 1993, A Year of Lesser (novel) (New York Times Notable Book, McNally Robinson Book of the Year Award) 1996, See the Child (novel) 1999, The Case of Lena S. (novel) (Carol Shields Winnipeg Book Award) 2002, The Time in Between (novel) (Scotiabank Giller Prize 2006) 2005, The Retreat (McNally Robinson Book of the Year Award, Margaret Laurence Award for Fiction) 2008, The Matter with Morris 2010. *Address:* Harper Collins Canada, 2 Bloor Street East, 20th Floor, Toronto, ON M4W 1A8, Canada. *Telephone:* (416) 975-9334. *E-mail:* david@davidbergen.org. *Website:* www.davidbergen.org; www.harpercollins.ca.

BERGER, François, LenD; Swiss barrister, poet and writer; b. 16 May 1950, Neuchâtel. *Education:* Neuchâtel Univ., Univ. of Vienna. *Career:* worked as a barrister, Neuchâtel; mem. Asscn des écrivains de langue française, Asscn des écrivains neuchâtelois et jurassiens; Pres. Canton of Neuchâtel Literature Cttee; Pres. Autrices et auteurs de Suisse; mem. Soc. Européenne de Culture. *Publications include:* poetry: Mémoire d'anges 1981, Gestes du veilleur 1984, Le Pré 1986, Les Indiennes 1988, Le Repos d'Ariane 1990; fiction: Le jour avant 1995, Le Voyage de l'Ange 1999, L'Anneau de sable 2001, L'Amour à Trieste 2004, Mariage de plaisir 2006, Revenir 2008; contribs to several anthologies and to L'Express/Feuille d'Avis de Neuchâtel (newspaper). *Honours:* Louise Labé Prize, Paris 1982, Citation of Distinction, Schiller Foundation, Zürich 1984, Auguste Bachelin Prize, Neuchâtel 1988, Prix du roman poétique, Soc. de poètes et d'écrivains d'expression française, Geneva 2002. *Address:* 7 rue de l'Hôpital, 2000 Neuchâtel, Switzerland (office). *Telephone:* (32) 724-03-71 (office). *Fax:* (32) 724-03-72 (office). *E-mail:* etudeberger@vtx.ch (office). *Website:* www.francois-berger.ch.

BERGER, John; British author and art critic; b. 5 Nov. 1926, London; s. of the late S. J. D. Berger and Miriam Berger (née Branson). *Education:* Cen. School of Art and Chelsea School of Art, London. *Career:* began career as painter and teacher of drawing; exhbns at Wildenstein, Redfern and Leicester Galleries, London; Art Critic Tribune, New Statesman; Visiting Fellow BFI 1990–; numerous TV appearances including Monitor, two series for Granada; Scenario: La Salamandre (with Alain Tanner), Le Milieu du Monde, Jonas (New York Critics Prize for Best Scenario of Year 1976). *Plays:* The Three Lives of Lucy Cabrol (with Simon McBurney) 1994, Isabelle (with Nella Bielski) 1998. *Radio:* Will It Be A Likeness? 1996. *Publications:* fiction: A Painter of Our Time 1958, The Foot of Clive 1962, Corker's Freedom 1964, G (Booker Prize, James Tait Black Memorial Prize) 1972, Pig Earth 1979, Once in Europa 1989, Lilac and Flag 1991, To The Wedding 1995, Photocopies 1996, King: A Street Story 1999, Here is Where we Meet 2005, From A to X: A Story in Letters 2008; theatre: Question of Geography (with Nella Bielski) 1984 (staged in Marseille, Paris and by RSC, Stratford), Francisco Goya's Last Portrait (with Nella Bielski) 1989, I Send You This Cadmium Red (with John Christie) 2000; non-fiction: Marcel Frishman 1958, Permanent Red 1960, The Success and Failure of Picasso 1965, A Fortunate Man: The Story of a Country Doctor (with J. Mohr) 1967, Art and Revolution, Moments of Cubism and Other Essays 1969, The Look of Things, Ways of Seeing 1972, The Seventh Man 1975 (Prize for Best Reportage, Union of Journalists and Writers, Paris 1977), About Looking 1980, Another Way of Telling (with J. Mohr) 1982, And Our Faces, My Heart, Brief as Photos 1984, The White Bird 1985 (USA as The Sense of Sight 1985), Keeping a Rendezvous (essays and poems) 1992, Titian: Nymph and Shepherd (with Katya Berger) 1996, Steps Towards a Small Theory of the Visible 1996, The Shape of a Pocket 2001, John Berger Selected Essays (ed. by Geoff Dyer) 2001, Hold Everything Dear: Dispatches on Survival and Resistance 2008; poetry: Pages of the Wound: Poems, Drawings, Photographs 1956–96 1996; translations: (with A. Bostock): Poems on the Theatre by B. Brecht 1960, Return to My Native Land by Aimé Césaire 1969; Oranges for the Son of Alexander Levy by Nella Bielski (with Lisa Appignanesi) 1982. *Honours:* George Orwell Memorial Prize 1977, Golden PEN Award 2009. *Address:* Quincy, Mieussy, 74440 Taninges, France (home). *Telephone:* 4-50-43-03-36 (home).

BERGER, Thomas Louis, BA; American writer; b. 20 July 1924, Cincinnati, OH; s. of Thomas C. Berger and Mildred Berger; m. Jeanne Redpath 1950. *Education:* Univ. of Cincinnati and Columbia Univ. Grad. School. *Career:* mil. service 1943–46; Assoc. Ed., Popular Science Monthly 1952–53; Distinguished Visiting Prof. Southampton Univ. 1975–76; Visiting Lecturer, Yale Univ. 1981, 1982; Regents Lecturer, Univ. of Calif. at Davis 1982; Dial Fellow 1962. *Play:* Other People 1970. *Publications:* Crazy in Berlin 1958, Reinhart in Love 1962, Little Big Man 1964, Killing Time 1967, Vital Parts 1970, Regiment of Women 1973, Sneaky People 1975, Who is Teddy Villanova? 1977, Arthur Rex 1978, Neighbors 1980, Reinhart's Women 1981, The Feud 1983, Nowhere 1985, Being Invisible 1987, The Houseguest 1988, Changing the Past 1989, Orrie's Story 1990, Meeting Evil 1992, Robert Crews 1994, Suspects 1996, The Return of Little Big Man 1999, Best Friends 2003, Adventures of the Artificial Woman 2004. *Honours:* Hon. LittD (Long Island) 1986; Rosenthal Award, Nat. Inst. of Arts and Letters 1965, Western Heritage Award 1965, Ohiona Book Award 1982. *Literary Agent:* Don Congdon Associates, 156 Fifth Avenue, Suite 625, New York, NY 10010-7002. *Telephone:* (212) 645-1229. *Fax:* (212) 727-2688. *E-mail:* doncongdon@aol.com. *Address:* 80 Rive Road, Nyack, NY 10960-4902, USA (home).

BERGON, Frank, BA, PhD; American novelist and academic; b. 24 Feb. 1943, Ely, Nev.; m. Holly St John Bergon 1979. *Education:* Boston Coll., Stanford Univ., Harvard Univ. *Career:* Teaching Fellow, Harvard Univ. 1968–70; Lecturer, Newton Coll. 1971–72; Prof. of English, Vassar Coll. 1972–2005, Dir American Culture Program 1982–85; Visiting Assoc. Prof., Univ. of Washington 1980–81; mem. Modern Language Asscn, Western Literature Asscn, Asscn of the Study of Literature and the Environment. *Publications include:* Stephen Crane's Artistry 1975, Looking Far West: The Search for the

American West in History, Myth and Literature (co-ed.) 1978, The Western Writings of Stephen Crane (ed.) 1979, The Wilderness Reader (ed.) 1980, Shoshone Mike (novel) 1987, A Sharp Lookout: Selected Nature Essays of John Burroughs (ed.) 1987, The Journals of Lewis & Clark (ed.) 1989, The Temptations of St Ed & Brother S (novel) 1993, Wild Game (novel) 1995, Jesse's Ghost 2011; contribs to American Literary History, Terra Nova, Journal of Nature and Culture. *Honours:* Wallace Stegner Fellowship 1965–66. *Telephone:* (914) 400-4147. *E-mail:* tracy@brownlit.com.

BERGONZI, Bernard, BLitt, MA; British writer, poet and academic; b. 13 April 1929, London. *Education:* Wadham Coll., Oxford. *Career:* Sr Lecturer, Univ. of Warwick 1966–71, Prof. of English 1971–92, Prof. Emer. 1992–. *Publications include:* The Early H. G. Wells 1961, Heroes' Twilight 1965, Innovations: Essays on Art and Ideas 1968, T. S. Eliot: Four Quartets: A Casebook 1969, The Situation of the Novel 1970, T. S. Eliot 1972, The Turn of a Century 1973, H. G. Wells: A Collection of Critical Essays 1975, Gerard Manley Hopkins 1977, Reading the Thirties 1978, Years: Sixteen Poems 1979, Poetry 1870–1914 1980, The Roman Persuasion (novel) 1981, The Myth of Modernism and Twentieth Century Literature 1986, Exploding English 1990, Wartime and Aftermath 1993, David Lodge 1995, War Poets and Other Subjects 1999, A Victorian Wanderer 2003, A Study in Greene 2006. *Address:* 19 St Mary's Crescent, Leamington Spa, CV31 1JL, England (home).

BERGOUNIOUX, Pierre; French writer, literary critic, teacher and sculptor; *Professor, Ecole Nationale Supérieure des Beaux Arts;* b. 25 May 1949, Brive-la-Gaillarde, Corrèze. *Education:* Ecole Normale Supérieure de Saint-Cloud. *Career:* teacher of French in Paris schools; currently Prof., Ecole Nat. Supérieure des Beaux Arts, Paris. *Publications include:* novels: Catherine 1984, Ce pas et le suivant 1985, La Bête faramineuse 1986, La Maison rose 1987, L'Arbre sur la rivière 1988, C'était nous 19889, La Mue 1991, L'Orphelin 1992, Le Matin des origines 1992, Le Grand Sylvain 1993, La Toussaint 1994, Miette 1996, La Mort de Brune 1996, La Ligne 1997, Les Forges de Syam 2001, Un Peu de bleu dans le paysage 2001, Le Premier mot 2001, François 2001; non-fiction: B-17 G 2001, Jusqu'à Faulkner (literary criticism) 2002, École: mission accomplie 2006, Années folles, Circa 1924 2008, Agir, écrire 2008, Couleurs 2008, Une chambre en Hollande 2009, Deux querelles 2009, Deux écrivains français 2009, Chasseur à la manque 2010, Les restes du monde 2010, Le Baiser de sorcière 2010. *Honours:* Prix François Mauriac 1986, Prix Alain Fournier, Grand Prix de littérature de la SGDL for lifetime achievement 2002, Prix Virgile 2002, Prix Charles Brisset 2002, Prix Roger Caillois 2009. *Address:* 11 bis, Chemin des Buttes, 91190 Gif sur Yvette, France (home). *Telephone:* (1) 69-07-38-32 (home). *E-mail:* bergounioux-pierre@orange.fr.

BERGSON, Leo (see Stebel, Sidney Leo)

BERKOFF, Steven; British actor, writer and director; b. 3 Aug. 1937, Stepney, London; s. of Alfred Berkoff and Pauline Berkoff; m. 1st Alison Minto 1970; m. 2nd Shelley Lee 1976 (divorced). *Education:* Hackney Downs Grammar School, Webber-Douglas School of Drama. *Films include:* Octopussy, First Blood 2, Beverly Hills Cop, Absolute Beginners, War and Remembrance (TV) 1988, The Krays 1990, Decadence 1994, Rancid Aluminium 2000, Head in the Clouds 2004, Brides 2004, Forest of the Gods 2005. *Plays/Productions include:* Agamemnon (London) 1973, The House of Usher 1974, The Trial 1976, East 1978, Hamlet 1980, 2001, Greek 1980, Decadence 1981, Agamemnon (USA) 1984, Harry's Xmas 1985, Kvetch 1986, 1991 (Evening Standard Award for Comedy of the Year 1991), Sink the Belgrano 1987, Coriolanus 1988, Metamorphosis 1988, Salome 1989, The Trial 1991, Brighton Beach Scumbags 1994; Dir West (London) 1983, Acapulco (LA) 1990, One Man (London) 1993, Coriolanus 1996, Mermaid 1996, Massage (LA and Edinburgh) 1997, Shakespeare's Villains 1998, Messiah 2000 (London 2003), Dir Sit and Shiver (Los Angeles) 2004, Dir Richard II (Ludlow Festival) 2005, Sit and Shiver (London) 2006, Biblical Tales (London) 2010. *Publications:* America 1988, I am Hamlet 1989, A Prisoner in Rio 1989, The Theatre of Steven Berkoff (photographic) 1992, Coriolanus in Deutschland 1992, Overview (collected essays) 1994, Free Association (autobiog.) 1996, Graft: Tales of an Actor 1998, Shopping in the Santa Monica Mall, Ritual in Blood, Messiah 2000 (Glasgow Herald Golden Angel Award, Edinburgh Festival Fringe First), Oedipus 2000, The Secret Love Life of Ophelia 2001 (Glasgow Herald Golden Angel Award), Tough Acts 2003, My Life in Food 2008. *Address:* East Productions, 1 Keepier Wharf, 12 Narrow Street, London, E14 8DH, England (office). *Telephone:* (20) 7790-6313 (office). *Fax:* (20) 7790-1752 (office). *E-mail:* eastproductions@stevenberkoff.com (office). *Website:* www.stevenberkoff.com.

BERKSON, William (Bill) Craig; American poet, critic, editor and academic; *Professor Emeritus, San Francisco Art Institute;* b. 30 Aug. 1939, New York, NY; s. of Seymour Berkson and Eleanor Lambert; m. 1st Lynn O'Hare 1975 (divorced); one s. one d.; m. 2nd Constance Lewallen 1998. *Education:* Brown Univ., Columbia Univ., New School for Social Research, New York, New York Univ. Inst. of Fine Arts. *Career:* Instructor, New School for Social Research 1964–69; Visiting Fellow, Yale Univ. 1969–70; Ed. and Publr Big Sky magazine and books 1971–78; Adjunct Prof., Southampton Coll., Long Island Univ. 1980, Marin Community Coll. 1983–84; Assoc. Prof., California Coll. of Arts and Crafts 1983–84; Prof., San Francisco Art Inst. 1984–2008, Prof. Emer. 2008–, Dir Letters and Science 1994–99; Visiting Artist/Scholar, American Acad. in Rome 1991. *Publications include:* Saturday Night: Poems, 1960–1961 1961, Shining Leaves 1969, Two Serious Poems and One Other (with Larry Fagin) 1972, Recent Visitors 1973, Hymns of St Bridget (with Frank O'Hara) 1975, Enigma Variations (with Philip Guston) 1975, Ants 1975, 100 Women 1975, Blue is the Hero: Poems, 1960–1975 1976, Red Devil 1983, Lush Life 1983, Start Over 1984, Serenade 2000, Fugue State 2001, Hymns of St Bridget and Other Writings (with Frank O'Hara) 2002, 25 Grand View 2002, The Sweet Singer of Modernism and Other Art Writings 2003, Gloria (with Alex Katz) 2005, What's Your Idea of a Good Time? (with Bernadette Mayer) 2006, Sudden Address 2008, BILL (with Colter Jacobsen) 2008, Goods and Services 2009, Portrait and Dream: New and Selected Poems 2009, Ted Berrigan (with George Schneeman) 2009, Not an Exit (with Leonie Guyer) 2010, Lady Air 2010, Les Parties du Corps 2011, For the Ordinary Artist 2011, Repeat after Me 2012; other: ed. or co-ed. of several books; contrib. to anthologies, periodicals, quarterlies and journals. *Honours:* Dylan Thomas Memorial Award 1959, Poets Foundation Grant 1968, Yaddo Fellowship 1968, Nat. Endowment for the Arts Fellowship 1980, Briarcombe Fellowship 1983, Artspace Award 1990, Fund for Poetry Awards 1995, 2001, Mellon Fellowship 2006, Goldie for Literature, San Francisco Bay Guardian 2008, Balcones Poetry Prize, Austin, Texas 2010. *Address:* 25 Grand View Avenue, San Francisco, CA 94114, USA (home). *Telephone:* (415) 826-2947 (home). *E-mail:* berkson@pacbell.net (home).

BERMAN, David, BA, MA, PhD; American writer and academic; *Associate Professor of Philosophy, Trinity College, Dublin;* b. 20 Nov. 1942, New York, NY; s. of Seymour Berman and Marion Berman; m. 1st Aileen Jill Mitchell 1970 (divorced 2001); two s. two d.; m. 2nd Patricia O'Riordan 2002. *Education:* New School for Social Research, New York, Univ. of Denver, Trinity Coll., Dublin, St Vincent's Hospital, Dublin. *Career:* Sr Lecturer in Philosophy, Trinity Coll., Dublin 1981–94, Fellow 1984, Assoc. Prof. of Philosophy 1994–, Head of Philosophy Dept 1997–2002. *Publications include:* A History of Atheism in Britain: From Hobbes to Russell 1988, George Berkeley's Alciphron or the Minute Philosopher in Focus (ed.) 1993, George Berkeley: Idealism and the Man 1994, Arthur Schopenhauer's World as Will and Idea (ed.) 1995, Berkeley: Experimental Philosophy 1997, The Irish Enlightenment and Counter-Enlightenment (co-ed. with P. O'Riordan, six vols) 2002, Berkeley and Irish Philosophy 2005, Schopenhauer's World as Will and Idea (ed.) 2005; contrib. to reference works, books, scholarly journals. *Address:* Department of Philosophy, Trinity College, College Green, Dublin 2, Ireland (office). *Telephone:* (1) 8961126 (office). *E-mail:* dberman@tcd.ie (office). *Website:* www.tcd.ie/Philosophy (office).

BERMAN, Sabina; Mexican playwright, poet and theatre director; b. 21 Aug. 1956, Mexico City. *Education:* Universidad Nacional Autónoma de México. *Film screenplay:* Tía Alejandra (Premio de la Academia de Artes y Ciencias Cinematográficas) 1974. *Plays:* Mariposa (Premio de Poesía Pluridimensional Juguete) 1974, El jardín de las delicias (aka El suplicio del placer) 1976, Yankee (aka Bill) (Premio de Teatro Instituto Nacional de Bellas Artes) 1979, Rompecabezas (aka Un buen trabajador de piolet) (Premio de Teatro Instituto Nacional de Bellas Artes) 1981, La maravillosa historia del niño pingüica, de cómo supo de su gran destino y de cómo comprobó su grandeza (Premio de Teatro Instituto Nacional de Bellas Artes) 1982, Herejía (aka Anatema) (Premio de Teatro Instituto Nacional de Bellas Artes) 1983, Aguila o sol 1985, Muerte súbita 1987, Volar la tecnología maharishi del campo unificado 1987, Caracol y colibrí 1990, La grieta 1990, La guerra culta 1991, Los ladrones del tiempo 1991, Entre Villa y una mujer desnuda 1993, El árbol de humo 1993, Krisis 1996, Los carvajales, En el nombre de Dios. *Publications include:* poetry: Año internacional de la mujer (poems) (Premio de Poesía Pluridimensional Máscaraz, Premio de Cuento Latinoamericano) 1975, Poemas de agua 1986, Shanik 1986, Lunas 1988, Katún 1988; prose: La bobe (novel) 1990, Mujeres y poder (collection of interviews) (Nat. Journalism Award) 2000, The Theatre of Sabina Berman: The Agony of Ecstasy and Other Plays 2002, Democracia cultural. Una conversación a cuatro manos (co-author) 2006. *Honours:* Fondo Nacional grants 1993, 1994.

BERNARD, David Kane, BA, JD; American pastor, author and editor; *Co-Pastor, New Life United Pentecostal Church;* b. 20 Nov. 1956, Baton Rouge; s. of Elton Bernard and Loretta Bernard; m. Connie Sharpe Bernard 1981; two s. one d. *Education:* Rice Univ., Wesley Biblical Seminary, Univ. of Texas, Univ. of South Africa. *Career:* Instructor, Administrator, Jackson Coll. of Ministries 1981–86; Assoc. Ed., United Pentecostal Church Int. 1986–, Supt 2009–; Founder and Co-Pastor, New Life United Pentecostal Church, Austin, Texas 1992–; currently Pres. Urshan Graduate School of Theology; mem. Soc. for Pentecostal Studies. *Publications include:* In Search of Holiness 1981, The Oneness of God 1983, The New Birth 1984, Practical Holiness 1985, The Message of Romans 1987, A Handbook of Basic Doctrines 1988, Oneness and Trinity, A.D. 100-300 1991, God's Infallible Word 1992, The Trinitarian Controversy in the Fourth Century 1993, A History of Christian Doctrine, 3 vols 1995–99, Spiritual Gifts 1997, Growing a Church: Seven Apostolic Principles 2001, The Apostolic Life 2006, Justification and the Holy Spirit 2007, Essentials of Oneness Theology 2010, Essentials of Holiness 2010; contribs to Pentecostal Herald, Forward. *Honours:* Word Aflame Press Writer of the Year 1987. *Address:* New Life Pentecostal Church, 4001 Adelphi Lane, Austin, TX 78727, USA (office). *Telephone:* (512) 832-5433 (office). *Fax:* (512) 832-9108 (office). *E-mail:* office@newlifeupc.org (office). *Website:* www.newlifeupc.org (office).

BERNARD, Oliver Owen, BA; British poet and translator; b. 6 Dec. 1925, Chalfont St Peter, Bucks.; s. of Oliver Percy Bernard and (Edith) Dora Hodges; two s. two d. *Education:* Westminster School, Goldsmiths Coll., Central School of Speech and Drama. *Career:* RAFVR 1943–47; teacher of English, Paris and Corsica 1947–56; copywriter, London 1957–64; teacher of English, Suffolk and

Norfolk 1964–74; advisory teacher of drama, Norfolk Education Cttee 1974–81; mem. British Actors' Equity Asscn, Speak-a-Poem (cttee mem.), William Morris Soc., Dominicans for Peace and Justice. *Film:* Rimbaud: A Season in Hell (video performance filmed by Martin Jones). *Publications include:* Country Matters 1960, Rimbaud: Collected Poems (translating ed.) 1961, Apollinaire: Selected Poems (trans.) 1965, Moons and Tides 1978, Poems 1983, Five Peace Poems 1985, The Finger Points at the Moon (trans.) 1989, Salvador Espriu: Forms and Words 1990, Getting Over It (autobiog.) 1992, Quia Amore Langueo (trans.) 1995, Verse Etc 2001; contribs to various publications. *Honours:* Poetry Soc. Gold Medal for Verse Speaking 1982. *Address:* 1 East Church Street, Kenninghall, Norwich, NR16 2EP, England (home). *Telephone:* (1953) 887768 (home).

BERNAYS, Anne Fleischman, BA; American writer and teacher; b. 14 Sept. 1930, New York, NY; d. of Edward L. Bernays and Doris E. Fleischman; m. Justin Kaplan 1954; three d. *Education:* Barnard Coll. *Career:* Jenks Prof. of Contemporary Letters, Coll. of the Holy Cross 1992–95; Writing Instructor, Nieman Foundation, Harvard Univ. 1993–; also taught at Coll. of Communications, Boston Univ.; Chair. Bd of Trustees, Fine Arts Work Center, Provincetown; Bd mem. Vilna Center for Jewish Heritage, Jewish Film Festival; mem. Advisory Bd, Nat. Writers Union; mem. PEN New England, Century Asscn, New York; teaches at Harvard's Nieman Foundation. *Publications include:* Short Pleasures 1962, Growing Up Rich (novel) (Edward Lewis Wallant Award) 1975, The School Book: A Novel 1980, Professor Romeo (novel) 1989, What If?: Writing Exercises for Fiction Writers (non-fiction, with Pamela Painter) 1990, The Language of Names (with Justin Kaplan) 1999, Back Then (non-fiction, with Justin Kaplan) 2003, Trophy House 2005, Domestic Partners: A Novel 2008, Breakup Girl to the Rescue! 2009 (co-author); contribs to New York Times Book Review, Nation, Sports Illustrated, Travel and Leisure, Sophisticated Traveller. *Honours:* Edward Lewis Wallant Award, Bellagio Study and Conf. Centre Residency. *Literary Agent:* Sterling Lord Literistic Inc., 65 Bleecker Street, New York, NY 10012, USA. *Address:* 16 Francis Avenue, Cambridge, MA 02138, USA (home). *Telephone:* (617) 354-2577 (home). *Fax:* (617) 868-3209 (home). *E-mail:* AFBernays@aol.com (home).

BERNE, Stanley, BS, MA, PhD; American writer and academic; *Research Professor Emeritus, Eastern New Mexico University;* b. 8 June 1923, Port Richmond, Staten Island, NY; s. of William Berne and Irene Berne; m. Arlene Zekowski 1952. *Education:* Rutgers Univ., New York Univ., Louisiana State Univ., Baton Rouge, Marlborough Univ., Univ. of Illinois, Syracuse Univ. *Career:* served in Philippines during World War II; mem. Army of Occupation of Japan 1942–46, one of first Americans to visit and report from ground of Hiroshima following dropping of atomic bomb 1945; Art Gallery Dir Carlebach Galleries, Manhattan, met numerous painters of Abstract Expressionism, mem. The Art Club of New York 1945–53; was associated with collectors and art gallery owners such as Peggy Guggenheim, and her sister, the painter Hazel McKinley; taught in school system of Dallas, Tex. 1953–55, organized first Dept for the Teaching of Exceptional Children in the State of Texas; Teaching Fellowship, Louisiana State Univ. 1955–60; Assoc. Prof. of English, Eastern New Mexico Univ., Portales 1960–80, Research Prof. Emer. of English 1980–; Chair. American-Canadian Publrs Inc. 1980–97; mem. Bd of Dirs New Arts Foundation Inc., Santa Fe 1990–; mem. PEN, New England Small Press Asscn, Rio Grande Writers' Asscn, Santa Fe Writers; included in Post-Beat Movt of Authors And Poets. *Television:* co-host and co-producer with Arlene Zekowski Future Writing Today (series on KENW-TV, PBS) 1984–85. *Publications include:* A First Book of the Neo-Narrative 1954, Cardinals and Saints: On the aims and purposes of the arts in our time 1958, The Dialogues 1962, The Multiple Modern Gods and Other Stories 1964, The Unconscious Victorious and Other Stories 1969, The New Rubaiyat of Stanley Berne (poems) 1973, Future Language 1976, The Great American Empire 1981, Every Person's Little Book of P-L-U-T-O-N-I-U-M (with Arlene Zekowski) 1992, Alphabet Soup: A Dictionary of Ideas 1993, To Hell with Optimism! 1996, Gravity Drag 1998, Swimming to Significance 1999, At One with Birds 2000, Extremely Urgent Messages 2000, Empire Sweets, or How I Learned to Live and Love in the Greatest Empire on Earth 2003, Legal Tender, or It's All About Money! 2003, You and Me, or How to Survive in the Greatest Empire on Earth! 2003, The Dark Vehicles 2007; contribs to anthologies and other publications. *Honours:* Medal of Philippine Liberation 1946; Eastern New Mexico Univ. literary research awards 1966–76, St-John Perse Award for Int. Prose 1998. *Address:* PO Box 4595, Santa Fe, NM 87502-4595 (home); Pamela Tree, Rising Tide Press, PO Box 6136, Santa Fe, NM 87502-6136, USA (office).

BERNSTEIN, Carl, LLD; American journalist and author; b. 14 Feb. 1944, Washington; s. of Alfred Bernstein and Sylvia Walker; m. 2nd Nora Ephron 1976 (divorced); two s.; m. 3rd Christine Bernstein. *Education:* Univ. of Maryland and Boston Univ. *Career:* copyboy, reporter, Washington Star 1960–65; reporter Elizabeth (NJ) Journal 1965–66, Washington Post 1966–77; Washington bureau chief, ABC 1979–81; corresp. ABC News, New York 1981–84; Corresp., contrib. Time Magazine 1990–91; Visiting Prof. New York Univ. 1992–93; Exec. Vice-Pres. and Exec. Dir Voter.com –2001; contributing ed. Vanity Fair 1997–; frequent political commentator on network TV; fmr rock and music critic for the Washington Post. *Publications:* All the President's Men (with Bob Woodward) (Pulitzer Prize 1977) 1974, The Final Days (with Bob Woodward) 1976, Loyalties: A Son's Memoir 1989, His Holiness: John Paul II and the Hidden History of Our Time (with Marco Politi) 1996, A Woman in Charge: the Life of Hillary Rodham Clinton 2007; numerous articles in The New Republic, Rolling Stone, The New York Times, Newsweek and Der Spiegel. *Honours:* Drew Pearson Prize for investigative reporting of Watergate 1972, George Polk Memorial Award and other awards for journalism. *Address:* c/o Knopf Publishing/Author Mail, 1745 Broadway, New York, NY 10019, USA (office). *Website:* www.carlbernstein.com.

BERNSTEIN, Charles, AB; American poet, writer, editor and academic; *Professor of English and Comparative Literature, University of Pennsylvania;* b. 4 April 1950, New York, NY; s. of Herman Bernstein and Sherry Bernstein; m. Susan Bee Laufer 1977; one s. one d. *Education:* Harvard Coll. *Career:* freelance writer in the medical field 1976–89; Visiting Lecturer in Literature, Univ. of California, San Diego 1987; Lecturer in Creative Writing, Princeton Univ. 1989, 1990; David Gray Prof. of Poetry and Letters, State Univ. of NY, Buffalo 1990–2003; Prof. of English and Comparative Literature, Univ. of Pennsylvania 2003–; Curator, Poetry Plastique exhbn; Fellow, American Acad. of Arts and Sciences. *Music:* libretto for Shadowtime (opera with music by Brian Ferneyhough), premiered Munich Biennalle 2004, Blind Witness: Three American Operas (libretti collection) 2008. *Radio:* Host and Producer of LINEbreak, Close Listening. *Publications include:* poetry: Asylums 1975, Parsing 1976, Shade 1978, Poetic Justice 1979, Senses of Responsibility 1979, Legend (with others) 1980, Controlling Interests 1980, Disfrutes 1981, The Occurrence of Tune 1981, Stigma 1981, Islets/Irritations 1983, Resistance 1983, Veil 1987, The Sophist 1987, Four Poems 1988, The Nude Formalism 1989, The Absent Father in Dumbo 1990, Fool's Gold (with Susan Bee) 1991, Rough Trades 1991, Dark City 1994, The Subject 1995, Republics of Reality: Poems 1975–1995 2000, With Strings 2001, Girly Man 2006, All the Whiskey in Heaven: Selected Poems 2010; essays: Content's Dream: Essays 1975–1984 1986, A Poetics 1992, My Way: Speeches and Poems 1999; editor: L=A=N=G=U=A=G=E Book (with Bruce Andrews, four vols) 1978–84, The Politics of Poetic Form: Poetry and Public Policy 1990, Close Listening: Poetry and the Performed Word 1998; contribs to numerous anthologies, collections and periodicals. *Honours:* William Lyon Mackenzie King Fellow, Simon Fraser Univ. 1973, Nat. Endowment for the Arts Fellowship 1980, Guggenheim Fellowship 1985, Foundation Fellowship, Univ. of Auckland, NZ 1986, New York Foundation for the Arts Fellowships 1990, 1995, Roy Harvey Pearce/Archive for New Poetry Prize 2000. *Address:* 119 Fisher-Bennet Hall, University of Pennsylvania, Philadelphia, PA 19104-6273, USA (office). *E-mail:* charles.bernstein@english.upenn.edu (office). *Website:* epc.buffalo.edu/authors/bernstein.html (office).

BERNSTEIN, Marcelle; British writer and journalist; b. 14 June 1945, Manchester; m. Eric Clark 1972; one s. two d. *Career:* mem. of staff, The Guardian, Daily Mirror, The Observer; Fellow, Royal Literary Fund; Creative Writing, Media and Communications Skills tutor, Univ. of Greenwich; mem. Soc. of Authors. *Publications include:* Nuns 1976, Sadie 1983, Salka 1986, The Russian Bride 1986, Lili 1988, Body and Soul (dramatised as a prizewinning six-part TV series) 1991, Sacred and Profane 1995 (filmed as Le Pacte du Silence 2003), Saints and Sinners 1998, The Vision 1998; contribs to The Times, Sunday Times, Guardian, Daily Telegraph, Daily Mail, New Statesman, Saga magazine, Jewish Chronicle, Catholic Herald, Washington Post, Melbourne Age, Woman's Journal (USA), New York Post. *Honours:* Arts Council Award for Best First Novel, Helene Heroys Award. *Literary Agent:* c/o Carole Blake, Blake Friedmann Agency, 122 Arlington Road, London, NW1 7HP, England.

BERNSTEIN, Robert Louis; American publisher; b. 5 Jan. 1923, New York, NY; s. of Alfred Bernstein and Sylvia Bernstein; m. Helen Walter 1950; three s. *Education:* Harvard Univ. *Career:* US Army Air Force 1943–46; with Simon & Schuster (book publrs) 1946–57, Gen. Sales Man. 1950–57; Random House Inc. 1958–61, Vice-Pres. (Sales) 1961–63, First Vice-Pres. 1963–65, Pres. and CEO 1966–89, Chair. 1975–89; Publr at Large, Adviser John Wiley & Sons Inc. 1991–98; Vice-Chair. Asscn of American Publrs 1970–72, Chair. 1972–73; Chair. Asscn of American Publrs Cttee on Soviet-American Publishing Relations 1973–74, on Int. Freedom to Publish 1975; Chair. US Helsinki Watch Cttee, New York, 1979–92, Founding Chair. 1992; Chair. Fund for Free Expression 1975–90, Founding Chair. 1990; Founding Chair. Human Rights Watch 1975–, now Emer. Bd Mem.; Co-Chair. Human Rights in China 1999–; fmr mem. Council on Foreign Relations, Nat. Advisory Cttee Amnesty Int.; mem. Americas Watch, Asia Watch, Middle East Watch, Africa Watch, Advisory Cttee Carter-Menil Human Rights Foundation, Advisory Bd Robert F. Kennedy Foundation Human Rights Award, Int. Liberal Education Bd Bard Coll.; Vice-Pres. Bd of Dirs Aaron Diamond Foundation, The Century Asscn. *Honours:* Hon. LLD (New School for Social Research) 1991, (Swarthmore Coll.) 1997; Hon. DHumLitt (Bard Coll.) 1998, (Hofstra) 1998, (Tougaloo Coll.) 2000, (Bates Coll.) 2000, (Yale) 2003; Human Rights Award (Lawyers' Cttee for Human Rights) 1987, Spirit of Liberty Award for the American Way 1989, Barnard Medal of Distinction, Barnard Coll. 1990, Liberty Award, Brandeis Univ. 1994, Eleanor Roosevelt Human Rights Award 1998, and other awards. *Address:* 277 Park Avenue, 49th Floor, New York, NY 10172-0003, USA (office). *E-mail:* r.l.bernstein@att.net (office).

BERRADA, Mohamed, PhD; Moroccan literary critic, translator and writer; *Professor of Arabic Literature, Mohammed V Souissi University;* b. 1938; m. Leïla Shahid. *Education:* Cairo Univ., Egypt, Paris-Sorbonne, France. *Career:* trans. of literary criticism of Roland Barthes, Bakhtin and Moroccan philosophers, and cultural critics Mohammed Aziz Lehbabi and Abdelkebir Khatibi; Prof. of Arabic Literature Mohammed V Souissi Univ., Rabat; teacher

Nat. Inst. of Dramatic Arts; judge, Arab Prize for Fiction 2008; f. mem. Union of Moroccan Writers (pres. 1976–83); mem. advisory Bd literary magazine Prologue. *Publications include:* Frantz Fanon 'aw Maa'rakatu Ashshua'ub Al-Mutakhallifah (co-author, trans. as Frantz Fanon and the Struggle of Developing Countries) 1963, Salkh Al-Jild (fiction, trans. as Skinning) 1979, Mohammed Mandur wa Tanthir Annaqd Al-A'rabi (trans. as Mohammed Mandur and the Theorization of Arab Criticism) 1986, Lua'bat Annisyan (fiction, trans. as The Game of Forgetting) 1987, Le Jeu de l'Oubli (novel, in trans.) 1990, Al-Daw' al-Harib (novel, trans. as The Fugitive Light and Lumière Fuyante) 1998, Le théâtre au Maroc: tradition, expérimentation et perspectives 1998, Maroc Musique de l'Ombre 2001, Comme un été qui ne reviendra pas: Le Caire 1955–1996 2001, Imra'at al-nisyān: riwāyah 2001, Faoā'āt riwā'īyah 2003, Siyāqāt thaqāfīyah: mawāqif, mudākhalāt, marāfi 2003, Nouvelles arabes du Maghreb (co-author); trans. of Mohammed Aziz Lehbabi's Mina Lmunghalaq 'ila Lmunfatah' (From the Closed to the Open), Tahar Ben Jelloun's H'adith Al-Jamal (Talk of the Camel) 1971, Abdellatif Laâbi's Aas'a-'id tah't Al-Kimamah (Muzzled Poems) 1982, Abdelkebir Khatibi's Fi Lkitaba wa Ttajriba (On Writing and Experience) 1990. *Honours:* numerous prizes including Prix du Mérite culturel (Belgium) 1999, Prix de la Critique (Belgium) 2004. *Address:* c/o Université Mohammed V Souissi, BP 8007, N. U. Agdal, Rabat, Morocco.

BERRY, Adrian Michael (see Camrose, 4th Viscount)

BERRY, James, OBE, FRSL; British poet, writer and editor; b. 1925, Fair Prospect, Jamaica. *Career:* emigrated to UK 1948. *Publications include:* Bluefoot Traveller: An Anthology of West Indian Poets in Britain (ed.) 1976, Fractured Circles 1979, Lucy's Letters and Loving 1982, News for Babylon: The Chatto Book of West Indian-British Poetry (ed.) 1984, Chain of Days 1985, The Girls and Yanga Marshall (short stories) 1987, A Thief in the Village and Other Stories (Smarties Prize Grand Prix 1987, Coretta Scott King Award 1989) 1988, Don't Leave an Elephant to Go and Chase a Bird 1990, When I Dance (poems) (Signal Poetry Award 1988) 1991, Ajeema and his Son 1992, Celebration Song 1994, Hot Earth, Cold Earth 1995, Playing a Dazzler 1996, Classic Poems to Read Aloud 1996, Around the World in Eighty Poems 2001, A Nest Full of Stars 2002, Only One of Me 2004, Windrush Songs 2007. *Honours:* C. Day-Lewis Fellowship, Greater London Arts Asscn Fellowship 1977, Nat. Poetry Competition Award 1981, Poetry Soc. Prize 1981, Soc. of Authors Cholmondeley Award for Poetry 1991, Boston Globe/Horn Book Award 1993; Hon. DUniv (Open Univ.) 2002; Hon. Fellow, Birkbeck Coll. 2001. *Literary Agent:* United Agents, 12–26 Lexington Street, London, W1F 0LE, England. *Telephone:* (20) 3214-0800. *Fax:* (20) 3214-0801. *E-mail:* info@unitedagents.co.uk. *Website:* unitedagents.co.uk.

BERRY, Wendell, MA; American writer; b. 5 Aug. 1934, Henry County, Ky; m. Tanya Amyx 1957; one s. one d. *Education:* Univ. of Kentucky. *Career:* mem. Faculty, Univ. of Kentucky 1964–77, 1987, Distinguished Prof. of English 1971–72. *Publications include:* novels: Nathan Coulter 1962, A Place on Earth 1967, The Memory of Old Jack 1974, Remembering 1988, The Discovery of Kentucky 1991, Fidelity 1992, A Consent 1993, Watch With Me 1994, A World Lost 1996, Jayber Crow 2001, Hannah Coulter 2004, Whitefoot 2009; short stories: The Wild Birds 1986; poetry: The Broken Ground 1964, Openings 1968, Findings 1969, Farming: A Handbook 1970, The Country of Marriage 1973, Clearing 1977, A Part 1980, The Wheel 1982, Collected Poems 1985, Sabbaths 1987, Sayings and Doings and an Eastward Look 1990, Entries 1994, The Farm 1995, A Timbered Choir: The Sabbath Poems 1979–1997 1999, Given 2005, The Mad Farmer Poems 2008, Leavings 2009; essays: The Long-Legged House 1969, The Hidden Wound 1970, The Unforseen Wilderness 1971, A Continuous Harmony 1972, The Unsettling of America 1977, Recollected Essays 1965–80 1981, The Gift of Good Land 1981, Standing by Words 1985, Standing on Earth 1991, Sex, Economy, Freedom and Community 1993, Another Turn of the Crank 1995, Life is a Miracle: An Essay Against Modern Superstition 2000, Citizenship Papers 2005, The Way of Ignorance 2006, Imagination in Place 2010; co-ed. Meeting the Expectations of the Land 1985, Home Economics 1987, What Are People For? 1990, Harland Hubbard: Life and Work 1990, Standing on Earth 1991, Another Turn of the Crank. *Address:* c/o Counterpoint Press, 2117 Fourth Street, Suite D, Berkeley, CA 94710 (office); 2803 Oak Ridge Road, Vanceburg, KY 41179-8447, USA (home). *Telephone:* (606) 796-2937 (home). *Website:* www.wendellberrybooks.com.

BERTI, Eduardo; Argentine writer and journalist; b. 1964, Buenos Aires. *Career:* lives in Paris, France; writes for TV documentaries, including La cueva, Rocanrol. *Publications include:* Los pájaros (short stories) 1979, Spinetta (essays) 1988, Rockología (essays) 1990, Agua (novel) 1997, La mujer de Wakefield (novel) 1999, La vida imposible (short stories) 2002, Todos los Funes 2004, Las pequeños espejos 2007, La sombra del púgil 2008, Lo inolvidable 2010, Fantasmas 2010, Lady Susan (ed.) 2010; contribs to short stories to numerous publications. *Address:* Pushkin Press, 12 Chester Terrace, London, NW1 4ND, England. *Telephone:* (20) 7730-0750. *E-mail:* contacto@eduardoberti.com.

BERTOLINO, James, BS, MFA; American poet, writer and academic; b. 4 Oct. 1942, Ironwood, Mich.; m. Anita K. Boyle. *Education:* Univ. of Wisconsin, Cornell Univ. *Career:* Teacher, Washington State Univ. 1970–71, Cornell Univ. 1971–74, Univ. of Cincinnati 1974–84, Washington Community Colleges 1984–91, Chapman Univ. 1989–96, Western Washington Univ. 1991–2005; Writer-in-Residence and Hallie Ford Chair. of Creative Writing, Willamette Univ. 2005–06; Co-founder, Whatcom Poetry Series; Resident Artist, Espy Foundation, Oysterville, Washington 2008. *Publications include:* poetry: Employed 1972, Soft Rock 1973, The Gestures 1975, Making Space for Our Living 1975, The Alleged Conception 1976, New & Selected Poems 1978, Precint Kali 1982, First Credo 1986, Snail River 1995, Poetry Comes Up Where it Can 2000, Urban Nature: Poems about Wildlife in the City 2000, Pocket Animals 2002, Finding Water, Holding Stone 2009; chapbooks: Drool 1968, Day of Change 1968, Stone Marrow 1969, Becoming Human 1970, Edging Through 1972, Terminal Placebos 1975, Are You Tough Enough for the Eighties? 1979, Like a Planet 1993, Greatest Hits: 1965–2000 2000, 26 Poems from Snail River 2000, Pub Proceedings 2001, Bar Exams 2004, The Path of Water 2008, Finding Water, Holding Stone 2009. *Honours:* Hart Crane Poetry Award 1969, Discovery Award 1972, Nat. Endowment for the Arts Fellowship 1974, Quarterly Review of Literature Int. Book Awards 1986, 1995, Djerassi Foundation Residency 1987, Bumbershoot Big Book Award 1994, Jeanne Lohmann Prize for Washington State Poets 2007. *Address:* PO Box 28907, Bellingham, WA 98228, USA (office). *Telephone:* (360) 398-7870 (office). *E-mail:* jimbertolino@yahoo.com (office); jim@jamesbertolino.com. *Website:* www.jamesbertolino.com; www.whatcompoetryseries.org (office).

BESS, Clayton (see Locke, Robert Howard)

BESSA-LUÍS, Agustina; Portuguese writer; b. 15 Oct. 1922, Vila Meã. *Career:* Dir O Primeiro de Janeiro (newspaper) 1986–87; Dir Teatro Nacional de Dona Maria II, Lisbon 1990–93; mem. Bd European Community of Writers 1961–62; mem. European Acad. of Sciences, European Acad. of Arts and Letters, Brazilian Acad. of Letters, Portuguese Acad. of Sciences. *Plays:* O Inseparável ou o Amigo por testamento 1958, Estados Eróticos Imediatos de Sören Kirkegaard 1992, Party: Garden Party dos Açores 1996. *Publications include:* Mundo Fechado 1948, Os Super-Homens 1950, Contos Impopulares 1951, A Sibila 1954, Os Incuráveis 1956, A Muralha 1957, O Susto 1958, Ternos Guarreiros 1960, Embaixada a Calígula 1961, O Manto 1961, O Sermão do Fogo 1962, As Relações Humanas: Vol. I, Os Quatro Rios 1964, Vol. II, A Dança das Espadas 1965, Vol. III, Canção Diante de Uma Porta Fechada 1966, A Bíblia dos Pobres: Vol. I, Homens e Mulheres 1967, Vol. II, As Categorias 1970, A Brusca 1971, Santo António 1973, As pessoas felizes 1975, Crónica do Cruzado Osb 1976, As Fúrias 1977, Conversações com Dimitri e Outras Fantasias 1979, A Vida e a Obra de Florbela Espanca 1979, O Mosteiro 1980, A Mãe de um Rio 1981, Sebastião José 1981, Dostoievski e a Peste Emocional 1981, António Cruz, o Pintor e a Cidade 1982, D. Sebastião, o Pícaro e o Heróico 1982, O Artista e o Pensador como Minoria Social 1982, Longos Dias Têm Cem Anos 1982, A Memória de Giz 1983, Adivinhas de Pedro e Inês 1983, Os Meninos de Ouro 1983, Um Bicho da Terra 1984, Um Presépio Aberto 1984, Menina e Moça 1984, A Monja de Lisboa 1985, Martha Telles 1986, A Bela Portuguesa 1986, Apocalipse de Albrecht Dürer 1986, A Corte do Norte 1987, Contos Amrantinos 1987, Dentes de Rato 1987, Aforismos 1988, Orazer e Glória 1988, A Torre 1989, Eugénia e Silvina 1989, Vento, Areia e Amoras Bravas 1990, Breviário do Brasil 1991, Vale Abraão 1991, Ordens Menores 1992, Camilo 1994, O Concerto dos Flamengos 1994, As Terras do Risco 1994, Um Outro Olhar sobre Portugal 1995, Aquário e Sagitário 1995, Alegria do Mundo I 1996, Memórias Laurentinas 1996, Um Cão que Sonha 1997, Douro 1997, O Comum dos Mortais 1998, Alegria do Mundo II 1998, Os Dezassete Brasões 1998, A Quinta Essência 1999, A Bela Adormecida 1999, Dominga 1999, As Meninas 2001, As Relações Humanas 2001, O Princípio da Incerteza I: Jóia da Família 2001, O Livro de Agustina 2002, O Princípio da Incerteza II: A Alma dos Ricos 2002, Azul 2002, As Estações da Vida 2002, O Princípio da Incerteza III: Os Espaços em Branco 2003, Antes do degelo 2004, A ronda de noite 2006, Fama e segredo no História de Portugal 2006, Metamorfoses 2007, La Ronde de nuit 2008. *Honours:* Ordem de Sant'Iago de Espada 1980, Officier, Ordre des Arts et des Lettres 1989; Medal of Honour, City of Porto 1988, Prémio Seiva de Literatura 1988, Prémio Camões 2004, Prémio Vergílio Ferreira 2004, numerous other prizes. *Address:* Dom Quixote, rua Ivane Silva 6, 2°, 1050-124 Lisbon, Portugal. *E-mail:* comunicacao@dquixote.pt. *Website:* www.dquixote.pt.

BESSON, Philippe; French writer and lawyer; b. 29 Jan. 1967, Barbezieux, Charente. *Education:* Lycée Montaigne de Bordeaux, École Supérieure de Commerce de Rouen. *Career:* lawyer and teacher of social law, Paris 1989. *Publications include:* En l'absence des hommes (translated as In the Absence of Men) (Prix Emmanuel-Roblès) 2001, Son frère 2001, L'arrière-saison (Grand Prix TRL-Lire 2003) 2002, Zeit der Abwesenheit 2002, Un garcon d'Italie 2003, Les Jours Fragiles 2004, L'enfant d'Octobre 2005, Les Amants 2005, Niepewne dni 2005, Un instant d'abandon 2006, Brüchige Tage 2006, Se résoudre aux adieux 2007, Nachsaison 2007, Un Homme Accidentel 2008, Einen Augenblick allein 2008, Arrière-saison 2009, Un ragazzo italiano 2009, La trahison de Thomas Spencer 2010, Retour parmi les hommes 2011. *Website:* www.philippebesson.com.

BETHEL, Marion, BA, MA, BL; Bahamian poet, writer and lawyer; b. 1953, Nassau; d. of Marcus H. Bethel and Jane F. Bethel; m. Alfred M. Sears; two c. *Education:* McGill Univ., Columbia Univ., Univ. of Cambridge. *Career:* has private law practice, Sears and Co.; teacher and consultant on education; Alice Naumburg Proskauer Fellow, Bunting Inst. of Radcliffe Coll. 1997–98; fmr Nat. Chair. Asscn for Feminist Research and Action (CAFRA), Bahamas; Guest Poet, Int. Writers Workshop, Hong Kong Baptist Univ. 2006, 16th Medellin Poetry Festival 2006, Granada Poetry Festival, Nicaragua 2008. *Publications include:* Guanahaní, mi amor (poems) (Casa de las Américas Prize) 1994, Bougainvillea Ringplay 2009; several essays; contribs to journals, including Callaloo, Caribbean Writer, Lignum Vitae, Massachusetts Review, Moving Beyond Boundaries, River City, WomanSpeak, and to anthologies. *Honours:* Univ. of Miami Writer's Summer Inst. James Michener Fellowship 1991, Bahamas Nat. Poetry Award 1996. *Address:* Sears & Company, POB N-3645, Nassau, NP, Bahamas (office). *Telephone:* 326-3481 (office). *Fax:* 326-3483 (office). *E-mail:* missma@batelnet.bs (home); info@searschambers.com (office); mbethel@searschambers.com (office). *Website:* www.searschambers.com (office).

BETTARINI, Mariella, DipEd; Italian writer, poet and teacher; b. 31 Jan. 1942, Florence. *Career:* elementary school teacher; co-founder, Ed. and Publisher, Salvo Imprevisti 1973; Ed. Poesia (monthly magazine) 1998–2000. *Publications include:* poetry: Il pudore e l'effondersi 1966, Il leccio 1968, La rivoluzione copernicana 1970, Terra di tutti e altre poesie 1972, Dal vero 1974, In bocca alla balena 1977, Diario fiorentino 1979, Ossessi oggetti-Spiritate materie 1981, Il viaggio-Il corpo 1982, La nostra gioventù 1982, Poesie vegetali 1982, Tre lustri ed oltre: Antologia poetica 1963–1981 1986, Delle Nuvole 1991, Diciotto acrostici 1992, Asimmetria 1994, Familiari parvenze 1995, Il silenzio scritto 1995, Zia Vera 1996, Case-luoghi – la parola 1998, Per mano d'un Guillotin qualunque 1998, L'amoroso dissenso 1998, Haiku di maggio 1999, Nursia 2000, La scelta – la sorte 2001, Trialogo 2006, Balestrucci 2006, A parole – in immagini, 1963–2007 2008; fiction: Storie d'Ortensia 1978, Psicographia 1982, Amorosa persona 1989, Lettera agli alberi 1997, L'albero che faceva l'uva 2000, La testa invasa 2003, Il libro degli avverbi 2005. *Address:* Via San Zanobi 36, 50129 Florence, Italy (home). *E-mail:* bettarini.broca@tin.it (office). *Website:* www.mariellabettarini.it.

BETTENCOURT-PINTO, Eduardo; Angolan accountant and poet; b. 23 April 1954, Gabela; m. Rosa Pinto 1980; two s. *Education:* studied commercial and accounting and labour law. *Career:* left Angola due to civil war 1975; lived in Zimbabwe, the Azores, moved to Canada 1983–; mem. Portuguese Writers' Asscn. *Publications include:* poetry: Emoção 1978, Poemas (with Jorge Arrimar) 1979, Razões 1979, Mão Tardia 1981, Emersos Vestígios 1985, A Deusa da Chuva 1991, Menina de Água 1997, Tango nos Pátios do Sul 1999, Um Dia qualquer em junho 2000; fiction: As Brancas Passagens do Silêncio 1988, Sombra duma Rosa 1998, O Principe dos Regressos 1999, A Casa das Rugas 2004, Viajar com Sombras 2008; Ed.: Os Nove Rumores do Mar 1996; contribs to Correio dos Acores, Diario Insular, Gavea Brown Magazine, Prism International Suplemento Agoriano de Cultura. *Honours:* Contexto, Poetry Award 1981, Portuguese Cultural Asscn, France 1986. *E-mail:* jecoeduardo@hotmail.com (home). *Website:* www.eduardobpinto.com.

BEUTLER, Maja; Swiss writer; b. (Meieli Maroni), 8 Dec. 1936, Berne; m. Urs Beutler 1961 (died 2007); two s. one d. *Education:* Dolmetscher Schule, Zürich, also in France, UK and Italy. *Career:* trans. for UNESCO, Rome; radio presenter (Italian and German) for Swiss Int. radio 1962–70; columnist, Radio DRS. *Dance:* Der Traum (libretto for ballet), Berne 1981. *Plays:* Das Blaue Gesetz (Solothurn 1977, Das Marmelspiel (Berne) 1985, Lady Macbeth wäscht sich die Hände nicht mehr (Zürich) 1994. *Radio:* features on Walter Mehring 1981, 1984. *Publications include:* novels: Fuss fassen 1980, Die Wortfalle (second edn) 1990, Die Stunde, da wir fliegen Lernen 1994; short stories: Flissingen fehlt auf der Karte 1976, Das Bildnis der Doña Quichotte 1989, Schwarzer Schnee 2009, Das Album der Signora 2009; plays: Das Blaue Gesetz 1979, Das Marmelspiel 1985, Lady Macbeth Wäscht Sich Die Hände Nicht Mehr 1994; collected radio contribs: Wärchtig 1986, Beiderlei 1991, Tagwärts 1996. *Honours:* Schillerstiftung Prize for works 1983, Weltipreis für Drama 1985, Literaturpreis, Stadt Berne 1989, Weiterschreiben 2011. *E-mail:* maja.beutler@hispeed.ch (office). *Website:* www.majabeutler.ch.

BEVERLEY, Jo, BA; British/Canadian writer; b. (Jo Dunn), 22 Sept. 1947, Morecambe, Lancs., England; m. Kenneth Beverley 1971; two s. *Education:* Univ. of Keele. *Career:* mem. Canadian Romance Authors Network, Romance Writers of America, SF Canada, Writers' Union of Canada, Novelists Inc. *Publications include:* Lord Wraybourne's Betrothed 1988, The Stanforth Secrets 1989, The Stolen Bride 1990, If Fancy Be the Food of Love 1991, Emily and the Dark Angel 1991, The Fortune Hunter 1991, An Arranged Marriage 1991, Deirdre and Don Juan 1992, The Christmas Angel 1992, An Unwilling Bride 1992, Lord of My Heart 1992, Dark Champion 1993, My Lady Notorious 1993, Forbidden 1994, Dangerous Joy 1995, Tempting Fortune 1995, The Shattered Rose 1996, Something Wicked 1997, Forbidden Magic 1998, Lord of Midnight 1998, Secrets of the Night, Devilish, The Dragon's Bride, The Devil's Heiress, Hazard, St Raven 2003, Winter Fire 2003, Skylark 2004, A Most Unsuitable Man 2005, The Rogue's Return 2006, To Rescue A Rogue 2006, Lady Beware 2007, A Lady's Secret 2008, The Secret Wedding 2009, The Secret Duke 2010, Stolen Bride 2010, Tempting Fortune 2010, An Unlikely Countess 2011; contribs to anthologies. *Honours:* Career Achievement for Regency Romance 1992, and for Regency Historical 1997, Romantic Times, five RITA awards, Sapphire Award for Best SF Romance 2006. *Literary Agent:* Jane Rotrosen Agency, 318 East 51st Street, New York, NY 10022, USA. *Telephone:* (212) 593-4330. *Fax:* (212) 935-6985. *Website:* www.janerotrosen.com. *E-mail:* jo@jobev.com (office). *Website:* www.jobev.com.

BEWES, Richard Thomas, OBE, MA; British ecclesiastic (retd), writer and broadcaster; b. 1 Dec. 1934, Nairobi, Kenya; s. of Cecil Bewes and Sylvia Bewes; m. Elisabeth Ingrid Jaques 1964 (died 2006); two s. one d. *Education:* Marlborough School, Emmanuel Coll., Cambridge, Ridley Hall Theological Coll., Cambridge. *Career:* Rector of All Souls Church, Langham Place, London 1983–2004; Prebendary St Paul's Cathedral, London 1986–; Int. Vice-Chair., African Enterprise; mem. Guild of British Songwriters. *Films:* Open Home Open Bible, Book by Book film series, The Sermon int. film series. *Television:* features in Loma Linda Broadcasting Network, Calif. and in The United Christian Broadcasters programmes in Europe. *Publications include:* Talking About Prayer 1979, The Pocket Handbook of Christian Truth 1981, The Church Reaches Out 1981, John Wesley's England 1981, The Church Overcomes 1983, On the Way 1984, Quest for Life 1985, The Church Marches On 1986, When God Surprises 1986, A New Beginning 1989, The Resurrection 1989, Does God Reign? 1995, Speaking in Public – Effectively 1998, Open Home Open Bible 2000, The Lamb Wins 2000, The Stone That Became a Mountain 2001, Ten Steps in Prayer 2001, Words That Circled the World 2001, The Top 100 Questions 2002, Wesley Country 2003, Beginning the Christian Life 2004, 150 Pocket Thoughts 2004, The Goodnight Book 2008. *Honours:* Freeman of the City of Charlotte, NC 1985. *Address:* Christian Focus, Geanies House, Fearn, Tain, IV20 1TW, Ross-shire, Scotland (office); African Enterprise, PO Box 453, Potters Bar, EN6 9DP, England (office). *Telephone:* (1862) 871011 (office); (1707) 663314 (office). *Fax:* (1862) 871699 (office); (1707) 662653 (office). *E-mail:* info@christianfocus.com (office); info@africanenterprise.co.uk (office). *Website:* www.christianfocus.com (office); www.richardbewes.com.

BEYALA, Calixthe, BA; Cameroonian novelist; b. 1961, Douala; m. (divorced); two c. *Career:* lives in Paris, France. *Publications include:* novels: C'est le soleil qui m'a brûlée 1987, Tu t'appelleras Tanga 1988, Seul le Diable le savait (aka La Négresse rousse) 1990, Le Petit prince de Belleville 1992, Maman a un amant (Grand Prix Littéraire de l'Afrique Noire) 1993, Asséze l'africaine (Prix François Mauriac de l'Académie française, Prix tropique) 1994, Les Honneurs perdus (Grand prix du roman de l'Académie française) 1996, La Petite fille du réverbère (Grand Prix de l'Unicef) 1997, Amours sauvages 1999, Comment cuisiner son mari à l'africaine 1999, Les Arbres en parlent encore 2002, Femme nue, femme noire 2003, La Plantation 2005, L'Homme qui m'offrait le ciel 2007, Le Roman de Pauline 2009, Uwe Ommer 2011; essays: Lettre d'une africaine à ses sœurs occidentales 1995, Lettre d'une afro-française à ses compatriotes 2000. *Honours:* Chevalier, Ordre des Arts et des Lettres; Prix de l'Action Communautaire 2000, Prix Genova 2002. *Address:* Collectif Egalité, 9 rue roger Gobaut, 93500 Pantin, France. *E-mail:* calixthe.beyala@online.fr. *Website:* www.calixthe.beyala.free.fr.

BEYDOUN, Abbas; Lebanese poet and author; *Cultural Editor, As-Safir*; b. 1945, Sour. *Education:* Lebanese Univ. Beirut, Sorbonne, Paris. *Career:* Cultural Ed., As-Safir newspaper, Beirut 1997–. *Publications include:* A Season in Berlin (poems), Tahlil damm (trans. as Blood Test) (novel) 2002, Le Poème de Tyr 2002, Al-Jasad bila Mu'alim (trans. as The Body without a Teacher) (poems) 2004; has published nine vols of poetry. *Address:* Riad Al-Rayyes Books, Sanayeh, Union Building, Beirut, Lebanon. *Telephone:* (1) 743640. *Fax:* (1) 743641. *E-mail:* info@elrayyesbooks.com; mail@assafir.com. *Website:* www.elrayyesbooks.com.

BEZMOZGIS, David, BA, MFA; Canadian (b. Latvian) writer; b. 1973, Riga, Latvia. *Education:* McGill Univ., Montréal, Univ. of California Film School. *Career:* emigrated with parents to Toronto, Canada 1980; currently Dorothy and Lewis B. Cullman Fellow, New York Public Library. *Films directed:* L. A. Mohel (documentary) 1999, The Diamond Nose 2000, Genuine Article: The First Trial 2003, Victoria Day 2009. *Play:* The Last Waltz: An Inheritance. *Publications include:* Natasha and Other Stories (Reform Judaism Prize for Jewish Fiction 2004, The Jewish Quarterly Wingate Literary Prize for fiction 2005) 2004, The Second Strongest Man (short story), Roman Berman, Massage Therapist (short story), Tapka (short story), The Free World (novel) 2011; contrib. short stories to Harper's, The New Yorker, Zoetrope: All Story. *Honours:* Guggenheim Fellowship, MacDowell Fellowship, Commonwealth First Book Prize for Caribbean/Canada 2004, City of Toronto Book Award 2005, Danuta Gleed Literary Award 2005, Helen and Stan Vine Canadian Jewish Book Award, Koffler Centre of the Arts 2005. *Literary Agent:* Ira Silverberg, Sterling Lord Literistic Inc., 65 Bleecker Street, New York, NY 10012, USA. *Telephone:* (212) 780-6050. *Address:* HarperCollins Canada, 2 Bloor Street East, 20th Floor, Toronto, ON M4W 1AB, Canada. *Telephone:* (416) 975-9334. *E-mail:* david@bezmozgis.com. *Website:* www.harpercollins.ca; www.bezmozgis.com.

BHABHA, Homi K., MA, DPhil; Indian writer and academic; *Anne F. Rothenberg Professor of the Humanities, Harvard University*; b. 1949. *Education:* Univ. of Bombay (now Mumbai), Christ Church Coll. Univ. of Oxford, UK. *Career:* Tutor, Wadham Coll., St Anne's Coll., Oxford, 1976–78; Lecturer in Creative Writing, Warwick Univ. 1977–78; Reader in English Literature, Sussex Univ. 1978–94; Visiting Scholar, Brown Univ. 1987, SUNY Stonybrook 1990, Univs of Pennsylvania and Queensland, Australia 1991, Princeton Univ. 1992, Dartmouth Coll. 1993; Distinguished Prof., Univ. of Edmonton, Canada 1992; Mellon Prof., Tulane Univ., New Orleans 1994; Prof. of English Literature, Univ. of Chicago 1994, Chester D. Tripp Distinguished Prof. in the Humanities 1996–2000; Chair. Program in History and Literature, Harvard Univ. 2001–04, Anne F. Rothenberg Prof. of English and American Literature and Language, Harvard Univ. 2001–06, Anne F. Rothenberg Prof. of the Humanities 2006–, Dir Humanities Center 2005–; Distinguished Visiting Prof., Univ. Coll. London 2004–; Faculty Advisor, World Econ. Forum, Davos; Fellow, Wissenschaftskolleg zu Berlin 2001–2002; British Council Scholarship 1976, Violet Vaughan-Morgan Grad. Fellowship Univ. of Oxford. *Publications include:* Nation and Narration (ed.) 1990, The Location of Culture 1993, Die Bhagavadgita 1997, Anish Kapoor (co-author)

1998, Die Verortung der Kultur 2000, Cosmopolitanism (ed.) 2002, Habitations of Modernity: Essays in the Wake of Subaltern Studies 2002, Edward Said: Continuing the Conversation (ed.) 2005, Without Boundary (co-author) 2006, The Urgency of Theory 2008; numerous essays and articles in professional journals. *Honours:* Asian American Inst. Milestone Award 2000. *Address:* Humanities Center, Harvard University, 12 Quincy Street, Barker Center 134, Cambridge, MA 02138, USA (office). *Telephone:* (617) 495-0739 (office). *Fax:* (617) 495-0730 (office). *E-mail:* hbhabha@fas.harvard.edu (office). *Website:* www.aaas.fas.harvard.edu (office).

BHAGAT, Chetan, MBA; Indian writer and fmr investment banker; b. 22 April 1974, New Delhi; m. Anusha; two s. *Education:* IIT Delhi, IIM Ahmedabad. *Career:* investment banker, Goldman Sachs, Hong Kong 1999–2008, Deutsche Bank, Mumbai 2008–09. *Films:* Hello (scriptwriter). *Publications include:* novels: Five Point Someone: What Not to Do at IIT (Soc. Young Achiever's Award 2004, Publr's Recognition Award 2005) 2004, One Night @ the Call Center 2005, The Three Mistakes of My Life 2008, 2 States: The Story of My Marriage 2009, contribs. to Dainik Bhaskar, Hindustan Times, The Times of India. *Address:* Rupa and Co., 7/16 Ansari Road, Darya ganj, New Delhi 110 002, India (office). *E-mail:* info@chetanbhagat.com (home); info@rupapublications.com (office). *Website:* www.rupapublications.com (office); www.chetanbhagat.com (home).

BHARTIA, Shobhana; Indian newspaper executive; *Chairperson and Editorial Director, The Hindustani Times;* b. 4 Jan. 1957, Calcutta (now Kolkata); d. of the late Dr Krishna Kumar Birla and Manorama Devi; m. Shyam Sunder Bhartia 1974; two s. *Education:* Loreto House, Calcutta. *Career:* Exec. Dir The Hindustani Times Ltd 1986, Chair. and Editorial Dir 2008–; Chair. HT Vision Ltd 1990–; nominated to Rajya Sabha (Parl.) 2006, Pres. FICCI (women's org.); Chair. and Treas. Bd of Govs Delhi Coll. of Arts and Commerce 1988–90; Chair. Bd of Govs Shyama Prasad Mukherjee Coll. (for Women) 1992; mem. Bd of Dirs Press Trust of India Ltd 1987– (Chair.), Indian Airlines Ltd, New Delhi 1988–90 (and currently), Air Travel Bureau Pvt. Ltd 1989, Shri Mata Vaishno Devi Shrine, Katra 1991, Hero Honda Ltd; Chair. Endeavor India; Deputy Chair. Exec. Cttee, Audit Bureau of Circulations; Pro-Chancellor, Birla Inst. of Tech. and Science, Pilani; Leader of dels to Australia, NZ, the Philippines and to World Congress of Women Conf. (Moscow, fmr USSR) 1987–88; mem. Bd North Regional Bd of Reserve Bank of India; mem. Exec. Cttee Indian Newspaper Soc. and Commonwealth Press Union, London; mem. Apex Cttee of Commonwealth Games 2010, Governing Council, India Habitat Centre, Alliance of Civilizations Bd of Govs., Nat. Inst. of Fashion Tech., Indian Public School Society (The Doon School); Trustee, Indira Gandhi Memorial Trust, Bhartiya Vidya Bhavan. *Honours:* Int. Cultural Devt Org. Award 1989, Mahila Shiromani Award 1990, Lok Shri Award, Inst. of Econ. Studies 1990, Vijaya Shri Award, Int. Friendship Soc. of India 1991, Nat. Press India Award 1992, Nat. Unity Award 1993, Global Leader for Tomorrow, World Econ. Forum 1996, Outstanding Businesswoman Award, PHD Chamber of Commerce & Industry, Punjab, Haryana, Delhi Chamber of Commerce and Industry 2001, Padma Shri 2005, Ernst and Young Entrepreneur of the Year Award 2005, Business Woman Award, The Economic Times Awards for Corp. Excellence 2007, ranked by Fortune magazine amongst the 50 Most Powerful Women in Business outside the US (34th) 2008, (43rd) 2009, (44th) 2010. *Address:* Hindustani Times House, 18–20 Kasturba Gandhi Marg, New Delhi, 110 001 (office); HT Media Ltd, Park Centra Building, 7th Floor, Sector-30, Delhi–Jaipur Highway, Gurgaon 122 001, India (office). *Telephone:* (11) 23361234 (office); (124) 3954700 (office); (11) 6830260 (home). *Fax:* (11) 66561270 (office). *E-mail:* feedback@hindustantimes.com (office). *Website:* www.hindustantimes.com (office); www.htmedia.in (office).

BHATTACHARYA, Nabarun; Indian writer and poet; b. 23 June 1948, Baharampur; s. of Bijon Bhattacharya and Mahasweta Devi; m. Pranati Bhattacharya; one s. *Career:* Chief Ed. Bengali literary monthly Bhashabandhan. *Publications include:* Herbert (Narsinha Das Award, Bankim Puraskar Award, Sahitya Akademi Award 1997) 1993, Kangal Maalsaat 2003, Ei Mrityu Upotyoka Aamaar Desh Na 2004, Lubdhak 2006, Halaljhanda o Onyanyo 2009, Mahajaaner Aayna 2010, Fatadu-r Bombachaak o onanyo golpo, Khelna Nagar. *Honours:* Sahitya Akademi Award.

BHATTACHARYA, Nalinaksha, BSc; Indian civil servant and writer; b. 2 April 1949, Kolkata; m. Manju Bhattacharya 1982. *Education:* Univ. of Calcutta, London School of Journalism. *Publications include:* Hem and Football (novel) 1992, Hem and Maxine (novel) 1995, A Fistful of Desire (novel) 1997; contribs to BBC World Service, London Magazine, New Writing 5. *Honours:* First Prize in Short Story Writing, American Univ. Centre, Kolkata 1977. *Address:* Sector 8/121, R. K. Puram, New Delhi 110 022, India (home).

BHUTTO, Fatima Murtaza, BA, MA; Pakistani writer; b. 29 May 1982, Kabul, Afghanistan; d. of Murtaza Bhutto and Fauzia Fasihudin Bhutto; grand-d. of Zulfikar Ali Bhutto (fmr Prime Minister of Pakistan); niece of Benazir Bhutto. *Education:* Columbia Univ., USA, SOAS, Univ. of London, UK. *Career:* fmr columnist, Jang (Urdu daily newspaper), The News (sister publ.); currently writes columns for The Daily Beast, The New Statesman, The Guardian, The Caravan Magazine. *Publications:* Whispers in the Desert (poetry) 1997, 8.50 a.m. 8 October 2005 2006, Songs of Blood and Sword: A Daughter's Memoir 2010. *Address:* 70 Clifton Road, Old Clifton, Karachi, Pakistan (office). *Website:* www.fatimabhutto.com.pk (office).

BI, Feiyu; Chinese author and screenwriter; b. 1964, Xinghua, Jiangsu Prov. *Career:* fmr journalist for a newspaper in Nanjing; Writer-in-Residence, Iowa Int. Writing Program 2006; Ed. Yu Hua (literary magazine). *Film:* Shanghai Triad (co-writer). *Publications include:* fiction: Yuyang (novella) 2003, Qingyi (Moon Opera) 2007, Yumi (Three Sisters) (Man Asian Literary Prize 2010), Tuina (Massage) 2008. *Honours:* Xu Lun Prize 1995–96. *Literary Agent:* The Susijin Agency Ltd, 3rd floor, 64 Great Titchfield Street, London, W1W 7QH, England. *Telephone:* (20) 7580-6341. *Fax:* (20) 7580-8626. *E-mail:* info@thesusijnagency.com. *Website:* www.thesusijnagency.com.

BIANCONI, Lorenzo Gennaro, PhD; Swiss/Italian musicologist and academic; *Professor of Musical Dramaturgy, University of Bologna;* b. 14 Jan. 1946, Muralto, Switzerland; m. Giuseppina La Face 1979; two s. *Education:* Univ. of Heidelberg, Germany, studied music theory with Luciano Sgrizzi in Lugano, Switzerland. *Career:* collaborator, Répertoire International des Sources Musicales, Italy 1969–70; mem., German Inst., Venice 1974–76; Guest Asst, German Historical Inst., Rome 1976; Guest Prof., Princeton Univ., USA 1977; Prof. of Musical Dramaturgy, Univ. of Bologna, Italy 1977–; Prof. of the History of Music, Siena Univ., Arezzo, Italy 1980–83; Co-Ed., Rivista Italiana di Musicologia 1973–79; Ed., Acta Musicologica 1987–91; Head of Programme Cttee, 14th Int. Musicological Congress, Bologna 1987; Co-Ed., Musica e Storia 1993–; Co-Ed., Il Saggiatore Musicale 1994–; Ed., Historiae Musicae Cultores 1999–; Head of Music Dept, Bologna Univ., Italy 1998–2001; coordinated School of Specialization for Secondary education, music education classes 2006–09; Hon. mem. Accademia Filarmonica, Bologna 2001; corresponding mem., American Musicological Soc. 1995, Acad. of Sciences of Turin 2006. *Publications include:* B. Marcello, Sonates pour clavecin (ed. with Luciano Sgrizzi) 1971, P. M. Marsolo, Madrigali a 4 voci (1614) 1973, A Il Verso, Madrigali a tre e a cinque voci (1605–19) 1978, Il Seicento 1982, La Drammaturgia Musicale 1986, Storia dell'Opera Italiana 1987, I Libretti Italiani di G. F. Händel (with G. La Face) 1992, Il Teatro d'Opera in Italia 1993, G. Frescobaldi, Madrigali a cinque voci (with M. Privitera) 1996, Opera Production and Its Resources (co-ed.) 1998, Opera on Stage (co-ed.) 2002, Opera in Theory and Practice, Image and Myth (co-ed.) 2003, Guida al percorso museale (Museo della Musica, Bologna) 2004. *Honours:* Dent Medal of the Royal Musical Asscn 1983, Premio Imola per la Critica 1994. *Address:* Dipartimento di Musica e Spettacolo, Università di Bologna, via Barberia 4/2, 40123, Bologna (office); via A. Frank 17, 40068 San Lazzaro di Savena, Bologna, Italy (home). *Telephone:* (20) 92000 (office). *E-mail:* lorenzo.bianconi@unibo.it (office). *Website:* www.unibo.it/docenti/lorenzo.bianconi (office).

BIBBY, Peter Leonard, BA, DipEd; British poet, writer, dramatist and screenwriter; b. 21 Dec. 1940, London; m. 1967; two s. two d. *Education:* Univ. of Western Australia, Murdoch Univ. *Career:* Ed., Fellowship of Australian Writers, Bagabala Books; mem. Australian Film Inst., Australian Writers' Guild, Computer Graphics Asscn, Fellowship of Australian Writers. *Publications:* Island Weekend 1960; contribs to various anthologies and journals. *Honours:* Tom Collins Literary Awards 1978, 1982, Lyndall Hadow Nat. Short Story Award 1983, Donald Stuart Nat. Short Story Award 1985.

BICHSEL, Peter; Swiss writer; b. 24 March 1935, Lucerne; m. Therese Spörri 1956; one s. one d. *Education:* Teacher's Coll., Solothurn. *Career:* Writer-in-Residence, Oberlin Coll., Ohio 1971–72; Visiting Lecturer, Univ. of Essen 1980, Univ. of Frankfurt am Main 1982, Dartmouth Coll., Hanover 1987, Middlebury Coll., Vermont 1989, CUNY 1992; mem. Akademie der Künste; Corresponding mem. Deutsche Akademie für Sprache und Dichtung, Darmstadt. *Publications include:* Eigentlich möchte Frau Blum den Milchmann kennenlernen 1964, Das Gästehaus 1965, Die Jahreszeiten 1967, Kindergeschichten 1969, Des Schweizers Schweiz 1969, Geschichten zur falschen Zeit 1979, Der Leser: Das Erzählen 1982, Der Busant: Von Trinkern, Polizisten und der schönen Magelone 1985, Schulmeistereien 1985, Irgendwo anderswo 1986, Im Gegenteil 1990, Zur Stadt Paris 1993, Die Totaldemokraten 1998, Cherubin Hammer und Cherubin Hammer 1999, Alles von mir gelernt 2000, Eisenbahnfatzen 2002, Kolumnen Kolumnen 2005, Geschichten 2005, Dezembergeschichten 2007, Heute kommt Johnson nicht 2008, Über Gott und die Welt: Schriften zur Religion (co-author) 2009, Hosenlupf Eine freche Kulturgeschichte des Schwingens (co-author) 2010. *Honours:* Hon. mem. American Asscn of Teachers of German; Hon. DTheol (Univ. of Basel) 2004; Gruppe 47 Prize 1965, Lessing Prize, Hamburg 1965, Deutscher Jugendbuchpreis 1970, Arts Prize, Solothurn 1979, Literature Prize, Bern 1979, Stadtschreiber von Bergen 1981, 1982, Johann Peter Hebel Prize 1986, Culture Prize, Lucerne 1989, Mainzer Stadtschreiber 1996, Gottfried Keller Prize, Zurich 1999, Veillon Prize, Lausanne 2000. *Address:* Nelkenweg 24, 4512 Bellach, Switzerland (home).

BIDART, Frank; American poet and academic; *Andrew W. Mellon Professor of English, Wellesley College;* b. 1939, Bakersfield, Calif. *Education:* Univ. of California, Harvard Univ. *Career:* teacher, Wellesley Coll. 1972–, currently Andrew W. Mellon Prof. of English; elected Chancellor, Acad. of American Poets 2003. *Publications include:* poetry: Golden State 1973, The Book of the Body 1977, The Sacrifice 1983, In the Western Night: Collected Poems 1965–90 1990, Desire (Theodore Roethke Memorial Prize) 1997, Music Like Dirt 2002, Robert Lowell: Collected Poems (co-ed.) 2003, Star Dust 2005, Watching the Spring Festival 2008. *Honours:* Lila Wallace–Reader's Digest Foundation Writer's Award, Bernard F. Conners Prize, American Acad. of Arts and Letters Morton Dauwen Zaubel Award, Shelley Award, Poetry Soc. of America, Bollingen Prize 2007. *Address:* Department of English, Wellesley

College, Founders Hall 103, 106 Central Hall, Wellesley, MA 02481, USA (office). *Telephone:* (781) 283-2590 (office). *Website:* www.wellesley.edu/english (office).

BIDDISS, Michael Denis, MA, PhD, FRHistS, FHA; British academic and writer; *Professor Emeritus of History, University of Reading*; b. 15 April 1942, Farnborough, Kent, England; s. of Daniel Biddiss and Eileen Biddiss (née Jones); m. Ruth Margaret Cartwright 1967; four d. *Education:* Queens' Coll., Cambridge, Centre des Hautes Etudes Européennes, Univ. of Strasbourg, France. *Career:* Fellow in History, Downing Coll., Cambridge and Dir of Studies in History, Social and Political Sciences 1966–73; Lecturer, then Reader in History, Univ. of Leicester 1973–79; Prof. of History, Univ. of Reading 1979–2004, Prof. Emer. 2004–, Dean, Faculty of Letters and Social Sciences 1982–85; Visiting Prof., Univ. of Victoria, Canada 1973, Univ. of Cape Town, South Africa 1976, 1978, Univ. of Cairo, Egypt 1985, Monash Univ., Australia 1989, Univ. of Nanjing, China 1997; Chair. History at the Univs Defence Group 1984–87; mem. Council, The Historical Asscn 1985– (Pres. 1991–94), Vice-Pres. Royal Historical Soc. 1995–99 (mem. Council 1988–92); Lister Lecturer, BAAS 1975. *Publications:* Father of Racist Ideology 1970, Gobineau: Selected Political Writings (ed.) 1970, Disease and History (co-author) 1972, The Age of the Masses 1977, Images of Race (ed.) 1979, Thatcherism (co-ed.) 1987, The Nuremberg Trial and the Third Reich (co-author) 1992, The Uses and Abuses of Antiquity (co-ed.) 1999, The Humanities in the New Millennium (co-ed.) 2000, Themes in Modern European History 1890–1945 (co-ed.) 2008, The Wiley-Blackwell Dictionary of Modern European History since 1789 (co-author) 2010. *Honours:* Hon. Fellow, Faculty of the History of Medicine (Pres. 1994–98), Soc. of Apothecaries 1986–; Osler Medallist, Soc. of Apothecaries of London 1989, Locke Medallist, Soc. of Apothecaries of London 1996, Sydenham Medallist, Soc. of Apothecaries of London 2000, Master's Medallist, Soc. of Apothecaries of London 2009. *Address:* Department of History, University of Reading, Whiteknights, Reading, RG6 6AA, England (office). *E-mail:* m.d.biddiss@reading.ac.uk (office).

BIDGOOD, Ruth, MA; Welsh poet and local historian; b. 20 July 1922, Seven Sisters, Glamorgan; m. David Edgar Bidgood 1946; two s. one d. *Education:* Univ. of Oxford. *Career:* coder, WRNS; Sub-Ed., Chambers Encyclopaedia; Fellow, Academi Gymreig, English Speaking Section. *Publications include:* The Given Time 1972, Not Without Homage 1975, The Print of Miracle 1978, Lighting Candles 1982, Kindred 1986, Selected Poems 1992, The Fluent Moment 1996, Singing to Wolves 2000, Parishes of the Buzzard (non-fiction) 2000, New and Selected Poems 2004, Symbols of Plenty 2006, Hearing Voices 2008, Time Being 2009 (Poetry Book Soc. Recommendation); contribs to literary and historical reviews, magazines and journals. *Honours:* Welsh Arts Council Awards 1976, 1993, 1997, Roland Mathias Prize 2011. *Address:* 2 Wylfa, Beulah, Llanwrtyd Wells, Powys, Wales (home).

BIEBER, Konrad, LèsL, PhD; American writer, translator and academic; *Professor Emeritus of French and Comparative Literature, State University of New York, Stony Brook*; b. 24 March 1916, Berlin, Germany; m. Tamara Siew 1939 (died 1995); one s. *Education:* Sorbonne, Univ. of Paris, Yale Univ. *Career:* instructor in French, Yale Univ. 1948–53; instructor, Middlebury French Summer School 1949–51, 1956; Visiting Lecturer in French and Comparative Literature, Univ. of Colorado at Boulder 1952; Asst Prof. 1953–57, Assoc. Prof. 1957–60, Prof. of French and Chair Dept of French 1959–68, Connecticut Coll., New London; Prof. of French and Comparative Literature, State University of New York, Stony Brook 1968–86, Prof. Emer. 1986–. *Publications include:* L'Allemagne vue par les Écrivains de la Résistance Française 1954, Simone de Beauvoir 1979, Outwitting the Gestapo (trans. of Lucie Aubrac's Ils partiront dans l'Ivresse) 1993; contribs to encyclopedias, dictionaries, books and journals. *Honours:* Chevalier, Ordre des Palmes Académiques 1970; Guggenheim Fellowship 1957–58, Book of the Month and History Club selections 1993. *Address:* 1211 Foulkeways, Gwynedd, PA 19436, USA (home).

BIEGMAN, Nicolaas H., PhD; Dutch historian, diplomatist and writer; b. 23 Sept. 1936, Apeldoorn; s. of Nicolaas Biegman and Aukje de Boer; m. Mirjana Cibilic; two s. *Education:* Univ. of Leiden. *Career:* Lecturer in Turkish and Persian, Univ. of Leiden 1960–62; various posts in Netherlands Foreign Service 1963–84; Amb. to Egypt 1984–88; Dir-Gen. for Int. Co-operation, Ministry of Foreign Affairs 1988–92; Perm. Rep. to UN 1992–97; Perm. Rep. to NATO 1998–2001 (retd from Dutch Foreign Service); Sr Civilian Rep. of NATO in Macedonia, Skopje 2002–04; Chair. Bd of Trustees East West Parl. Practice Project, Amsterdam; fmr mem. Bd of Dirs Int. Peace Acad. *Publications:* The Turco-Ragusan Relationship 1967, Egypt-Moulids, Saints, Sufis 1990, Egypt's Sideshows 1992, An Island of Bliss 1993, Mainly Manhattan 1997, God's Lovers 2006, Oil Wrestlers 2009, Living Sufism 2009. *Honours:* Order of The Netherlands Lion, Order of Merit, UAR. *Address:* c/o KIT Publishers, Mauritskade 63, 1092 AD Amsterdam, Netherlands.

BIELSKI, Alison Joy Prosser; Welsh poet, writer and fmr lecturer; b. 24 Nov. 1925, Newport, Gwent; m. 1st Dennis Ford Treverton Jones 1948; m. 2nd Anthony Edward Bielski 1955; one s. one d. *Career:* Lecturer, Writers on Tour, Welsh Arts Council; mem. Gwent Poetry Soc., Soc. of Women Writers and Journalists, Welsh Acad., Welsh Union of Writers. *Publications include:* The Story of the Welsh Dragon 1969, Across the Burning Sand 1970, Eve 1973, Flower Legends of the Wye Valley 1974, Shapes and Colours 1974, The Lovetree 1974, Mermaid Poems 1974, Seth 1980, Night Sequence 1981, Eagles 1983, The Story of St Mellons 1985, That Crimson Flame 1996, The Green-Eyed Pool 1997, Sacramental Sonnets 2003, One of Our Skylarks 2010; contrib. to anthologies and journals. *Honours:* Premium Prize, Poetry Soc. 1964, Anglo-Welsh Review Poetry Prize 1970, Arnold Vincent Bowen Poetry Prize 1971, Orbis Poetry Prize 1984, second, Soc. of Women Writers and Journalists Julia Cairns Trophy 1984, 1992.

BIELSKI, Nella; French (b. Russian) playwright and novelist; m. 1962. *Education:* Moscow Univ. *Career:* lives in Paris, writes in French. *Publications include:* Voronej, Oranges for the Son of Alexander Levy (novel) 1982, Last Portrait of Francisco Goya (theatre plays co-written with John Berger) 1989, After Arkadia (novel) 1992, Isabella (screenplay) 1998, A Question of Geography (play), The Year Is '42 (novel) 2004, Pulpe de l'étreinte (essay on poet Rainer Maria Rilke); contrib. to Granta magazine. *Address:* Bloomsbury Publishing plc, 38 Soho Square, London, W1D 3QY, England. *Telephone:* (20) 7494-2111. *Fax:* (20) 7434-0151. *Website:* www.bloomsbury.com.

BIERMANN, Wolf; German poet, songwriter and musician; b. 15 Nov. 1936, Hamburg; m. Pamela Rüsche; seven s. three d. *Education:* Humboldt Univ., Berlin. *Career:* Asst Dir Berliner Ensemble, 1957–59; song and guitar performances throughout Germany. *Recordings:* albums: Wolf Biermann (Ost) zu Gast bei Wolfgang Neuß (West) 1965, Vier neue Lieder 1968, Chausseestraße 131 1969, Warte nicht auf bessre Zeiten 1973, ah-jaa! 1974, Liebeslieder 1975, Es gibt ein Leben vor dem Tod 1976, Das geht sein' Sozialistischen Gang 1977, Der Friedensclown (Kinderlieder) 1977, Trotzalledem 1978, Halfte des Lebens 1979, Eins in die Fresse, mein Herzblatt 1980, Wir miissen vor Hoffnung verrückt sein 1982, Im Hamburger Federheft 1983, Die Welt ist schon 1985, Seelengeld 1986, VEB-volkseigener Biermann 1988, Gut Kirschenessen 1990, Nur wer sich andert, bleibt sich treu 1991, Süßes Leben – saures Leben 1996, Brecht, deine Nachgeborenen 1999, Paradies uff Erden – ein Berliner Bilderbogen 1999, Ermutigung im Steinbruch der Zeit 2001, Großer Gesang des Jizchak Katzenelson vom Ausgerotteten Jtidischen Volk 2004. *Publications include:* Die Drahtharfe: Balladen, Gedichte, Lieder 1965, Mit Marx-und Engelszungen 1968, Der Dra-Dra (play) 1970, Für meine Genossen 1972, Deutschland: Ein Wintermärchen 1972, Nachlass I 1977, Wolf Biermann, Poems and Ballads 1977, Preussischer Ikarus 1978, Verdrehte welt das seh'ich gerne 1982, Und als ich von Deutschland nach Deutschland: Three Contemporary German Poets 1985, Affenels und Barrikade 1986, Alle Lieder 1991, Der Sturz des Dadalus 1992, Großer Gesang des Jizchak Katzenelson vom ausgerotteten jiidischen volk 1994, Alle Gedichte 1995, Wie man Verse macht und Lieder – eine Poetik in acht Gangen 1997, Paradies uff Erden – ein Berliner Bilderbogen 1999, Wolf Biermann und andere Autoren: Die Ausbürgerung. Anfang vom Ende der DDR. Herausgegeben von Fritz Pleitgen 2001, Uber Deutschland Unter Deutschen. Essays, Kiepenheuer & Witsch 2002, Wolf Biermanns Nachdichtung ins Deutsche der 'Elf Entwiirfe für meinen Grabspruch' von Bob Dylan 2003, Das ist die feinste Liebeskunst – Die Sonette des William Shakespeares als Gedichte und Lieder von Wolf Biermann 2004. *Honours:* Büchner Prize 1991, Möricke Prize 1991, Heine Prize 1993. *Address:* c/o Verlag Kiepenheuer und Witsch, Rondorferstrasse 5, 5000 Cologne-Marienburg, Germany.

BIGSBY, Christopher William Edgar, BA, MA, PhD, FRSL, FRSA; British broadcaster, novelist and academic; *Professor of American Studies, University of East Anglia*; b. 27 June 1941, Dundee, Scotland; s. of Edgar Edward Leo Bigsby and Ivy May Bigsby. *Education:* Sheffield Univ., Nottingham Univ. *Career:* Lecturer in American Literature, Univ. Coll. of Wales 1966–69; Lecturer, Univ. of East Anglia, 1969–73, Sr Lecturer 1973–85, Prof. of American Studies 1985–, Founder-Dir Arthur Miller Centre for American Studies. *Publications include:* Confrontation and Commitment: A Study of Contemporary American Drama 1967, Edward Albee 1969, The Black American Writer (ed.) 1969, Three Negro Plays 1969, Dada and Surrealism 1972, Approaches to Popular Culture 1975, Tom Stoppard 1976, Superculture 1976, Edward Albee 1976, The Second Black Renaissance 1980, Contemporary English Drama 1981, Joe Orton 1982, A Critical Introduction to 20th Century American Drama, 3 vols 1982, 1984, 1985, The Radical Imagination and the Liberal Tradition 1982, David Mamet 1985, Cultural Change in the United States since World War II 1986, Plays by Susan Glaspell 1987, File on Miller 1988, Modern American Drama: 1945–1990 1992, revised edn as Modern American Drama: 1945–2000 2000, Hester (novel) 1994, Pearl (novel) 1995, 19th Century American Short Stories (ed.) 1995, Portable Arthur Miller (ed.) 1998, Cambridge History of American Theatre (joint ed.), three vols 1998, 1999, 2000, Contemporary American Playwrights 1999, Writers in Conversation (ed.) 2000, Beautiful Dreamer (novel) 2003, Arthur Miller: A Critical Study 2005, The Cambridge Companion to Modern American Culture (ed.) 2006, Remembering and Imagining the Holocaust: The Chain of Memory 2006, One Hundred Days: One Hundred Nights (novel) 2008, Arthur Miller 1915–1962 2008, Neil LaBute: Stage and Cinema 2008, Arthur Miller 1962-2005 2011; contribs to radio, TV, TLS, Times Higher Education Supplement, Sunday Independent, American Quarterly, Modern Drama, Theatre Quarterly, Guardian, Sunday Telegraph. *Honours:* George Freedly Jury Award, Bernard Hewitt Award for Outstanding Research in Theatre History, Betty Jean Jones Award, Sheridan Morley Award, George Freedly Memorial Award, American Studies Network Award (jtly). *Address:* School of American Studies, Faculty of Arts and Humanities, University of East Anglia, Norwich, NR4 7TJ, England (office). *Telephone:* (1603) 592789 (office). *E-mail:* c.bigsby@uea.ac.uk (office). *Website:* www.uea.ac.uk/ams (office).

BILGRAMI, Akeel, BA, PhD; Indian academic; *Johnsonian Professor of Philosophy and Director, Heyman Center for the Humanities, Columbia University*; b. 28 Feb. 1950, Hyderabad; m. Carol Rovane 1990; one d. *Education:* Univ. of Bombay, Univ. of Oxford, UK, Univ. of Chicago, USA. *Career:* Asst Prof., Univ. of Michigan, USA 1983–85; Prof. of Philosophy, Columbia Univ. 1985–, later Chair. of Philosophy Dept and Johnsonian Prof. of Philosophy, Dir Heyman Center for the Humanities; mem. Cttee on Global Thought; American Philosophical Soc.; Whitney Humanities Fellow 1992. *Publications include:* Belief and Meaning 1992, Self-Knowledge and Intentionality 1996, Internal Dialectics: The Moral Psychology of Identity, Self Knowledge and Resentment 2006, Politics and The Moral Psychology of Identity 2011; contrib. to Journal of Philosophy, Philosophical Quarterly, Philosophical Topics. *Address:* Department of Philosophy, Columbia University, 719 Philosophy Hall, 1150 Amsterdam Avenue, MC 4971, New York, NY 10027, USA (office). *Telephone:* (212) 854-1277 (office). *Fax:* (212) 316-2745 (office). *E-mail:* ab41@columbia.edu (office). *Website:* www.columbia.edu/cu/philosophy (office).

BILLETDOUX, Raphaële Marie; French novelist and film director; b. 28 Feb. 1951, Neuilly; d. of Francis Billetdoux. *Film:* La Femme enfant (screenplay writer and director) 1980. *Publications include:* Jeune fille en silence 1971, L'Ouverture des bras de l'homme 1973, Prends garde à la douceur des choses 1976, La Lettre d'excuse 1980, Mes nuits sont plus belles que vos jours (Night Without Day) (Prix Renaudot) 1985, Chère Madame ma fille cadette 1987, Entrez et fermez la porte 1991, Mélanie dans un vent terrible 1994, Je frémis en le racontant : horresco referens 2000, De l'air 2001, Un peu de désir sinon je meurs 2006, C'est fou, une fille 2007, C'est encore moi qui vous écris 2010.

BILLINGTON, James Hadley, PhD; American historian, academic and librarian; *Librarian of Congress*; b. 1 June 1929, Bryn Mawr, Pa; s. of Nelson Billington and Jane Coolbaugh; m. Marjorie A. Brennan 1957; two s. two d. *Education:* Princeton Univ. and Univ. of Oxford, UK. *Career:* army service 1953–56; Instructor in History, Harvard Univ. 1957–58, Fellow, Russian Research Center 1958–59, Asst Prof. of History 1958–61; Assoc. Prof. of History, Princeton Univ. 1962–64, Prof. 1964–73; Dir Woodrow Wilson Int. Center for Scholars, Washington, DC 1973–87; Librarian of Congress, Library of Congress, Washington, DC 1987–; Visiting Research Prof., Inst. of History, USSR Acad. of Sciences 1966–67, Univ. of Helsinki 1960–61, Ecole des Hautes Etudes en Sciences Sociales, Paris 1985, 1988; Guggenheim Fellow 1960–61; mem. Bd of Dirs John F. Kennedy Center for the Performing Arts; mem. American Acad. of Arts and Sciences, American Philosophical Soc.; Foreign mem. Russian Acad. Sciences; mem. Bd of Foreign Scholarships, Fulbright Program 1971–76 (Chair. 1973–75); writer/host, The Face of Russia (TV series) 1998. *Publications include:* Mikhailovsky and Russian Populism 1958, The Icon and the Axe: An Interpretive History of Russian Culture 1966, Fire in the Minds of Men: Origins of the Revolutionary Faith 1980, Russia Transformed: Breakthrough to Hope 1992, The Face of Russia 1998, Russia in Search of Itself 2004; contribs to books and journals. *Honours:* Chevalier des Arts et des Lettres, Légion d'honneur, Kt Commdr's Cross of the Order of Merit (Germany) 1996, Commdr Nat. Order of the Southern Cross (Brazil), Order of Merit (Italy), Order of Friendship (Russia) 2008; 40 hon. degrees; Gwangha Medal (Repub. of Korea), Woodrow Wilson Award 1992, UCLA Medal 1999, Pushkin Medal 2000, Karamzin Prize, Foreign Literature Library, Moscow 2005, Likhachev Prize, Likhachev Foundation, St Petersburg 2006, Lafayette Prize, French-American Cultural Foundation 2007, EastWest Inst. Outstanding Leadership Award 2007, Presidential Citizens Medal 2008. *Address:* Library of Congress, 101 Independence Avenue, SE, Washington, DC 20540-0002, USA (office). *Telephone:* (202) 707-5000 (office). *Fax:* (202) 707-1714 (office). *Website:* www.loc.gov (office).

BILLINGTON, Michael Keith, BA; British drama critic and author; b. 16 Nov. 1939, Leamington Spa; s. of Alfred R. Billington and Patricia Bradshaw; m. Jeanine Bradlaugh 1977; one d. *Education:* Warwick School and St Catherine's Coll., Oxford. *Career:* Public Liaison Officer, Theatre Royal, Lincoln 1962–64; writer on theatre, film and cinema, The Times 1965–71; Drama Critic, The Guardian 1971–, Country Life 1988–; presenter of various BBC Radio arts programmes including Options, Kaleidoscope, Meridian, etc. 1971–91; writer on London arts scene for The New York Times 1984–94; writer and presenter of TV profiles of Peter Hall, Alan Ayckbourn, Peggy Ashcroft 1988–90. *Publications:* The Modern Actor 1973, Alan Ayckbourn 1983, Tom Stoppard 1987, Peggy Ashcroft 1988, One Night Stands 1993, The Life and Work of Harold Pinter 1996, Stage and Screen Lives (Ed.) 2001, State of the Nation (Theatre Book Prize 2007) 2007. *Honours:* IPC Critic of the Year 1974, Theatre Critic of the Year 1993, 1995, 1997. *Address:* 15 Hearne Road, London, W4 3NJ, England (home). *Telephone:* (20) 8995-0455 (home). *Fax:* (20) 8742-3496 (home). *E-mail:* michael.billington@guardian.co.uk (office).

BILLINGTON, Rachel Mary, OBE, BA; British writer; b. 11 May 1942, Oxford, England; d. of Frank Billington and Elizabeth Pakenham; m. 1967; two s. two d. *Education:* Univ. of London. *Career:* fmr Pres. English PEN, later Vice-Pres.; Co-Ed. Inside Time (newspaper for prisoners); mem. Soc. of Authors. *Publications include:* novels: All Things Nice 1969, The Big Dipper 1970, Lilacs out of the Dead Land 1971, Cock Robin 1973, Beautiful 1974, A Painted Devil 1974, A Woman's Age 1979, Occasion of Sin 1982, The Garish Day 1986, Loving Attitudes 1988, Theo and Matilda 1990, Bodily Harm 1992, Magic and Fate 1996, Perfect Happiness (published in USA as Emma & Knightley) 1996, Tiger Sky 1998, A Woman's Life 2002, The Space Between 2004, One Summer 2006, Lies and Loyalties 2008, The Missing Boy 2010; juvenile: The Life of Jesus 1996, The Life of St Francis 1999, Far Out! 2002, There's More to Life 2006; other: The First Miracles (illustrated by Barbara Brown) 1990, The Family Year (illustrated by Clara Vulliamy) 1992, The Great Umbilical 1994; contrib. to various publs, radio and TV. *Literary Agent:* c/o David Higham Associates Ltd, 5–8 Lower John Street, Golden Square, London, W1F 9HA, England. *Telephone:* (20) 7434-7888. *Fax:* (20) 7437-1072. *E-mail:* dha@davidhigham.co.uk. *Website:* www.davidhigham.co.uk. *Address:* The Court House, Poyntington, nr Sherborne, Dorset, DT9 4LF, England (home). *Website:* www.rachelbillington.com.

BINCHY, Maeve, BA; Irish writer; b. 28 May 1940, Dalkey, Co Dublin; d. of William Binchy and Maureen Blackmore; m. Gordon Thomas Snell 1977. *Education:* Univ. Coll. Dublin. *Career:* teacher of history and French, Pembroke School, Dublin 1961–68; columnist, Irish Times 1968–2000. *Publications:* short story collections: Central Line 1978, Victoria Line 1980, Dublin Four 1982, Victoria Line/Central Line (revised edn of two earlier titles, aka London Transports) 1983, This Year it Will be Different 1996, The Return Journey 1998; novels: Silver Wedding 1979, Light a Penny Candle 1982, The Lilac Bus 1984, Echoes 1985, Firefly Summer 1987, Circle of Friends 1990, The Copper Beech 1992, The Glass Lake 1994, Evening Class 1996, Tara Road 1999, Scarlet Feather 2000, Quentins 2002, Nights of Rain and Stars 2004, Whitethorn Woods 2006, Heart and Soul 2008, Minding Frankie 2010; non-fiction: Aches and Pains 2000, The Maeve Binchy Writers' Club 2008; other: several plays. *Honours:* Hon. DLit (Nat. Univ. of Ireland) 1990, (Queen's Belfast) 1998; Int. Television Festival Golden Prague Award, Czech TV 1979, Jacobs Award 1979, WHSmith Fiction Award 2001, Irish PEN/A T Cross Award for Literature 2007, Lifetime Achievement Award, Romantic Novelists' Asscn 2010, Bob Hughes Lifetime Achievement Award, Bord Gáis Energy Irish Book Awards 2010. *Literary Agent:* Christine Green, 6 Whitehorse Mews, Westminster Bridge Road, London, SE1 7QD, England. *E-mail:* info@christinegreen.co.uk. *Website:* www.christinegreen.co.uk. *Address:* PO Box 6737, Dun Laoghaire, Co Dublin, Ireland (office). *Website:* www.maevebinchy.com.

BINDING, Tim; British writer and scriptwriter; b. 1947, Germany; m.; one d. *Career:* fmrly Editorial Dir Picador, Penguin Books; Commissioning Ed. Simon & Schuster. *Television:* The Last Salute (with Simon Nye), Men Behaving Badly. *Publications include:* fiction: In the Kingdom of Air 1993, A Perfect Execution 1996, Island Madness (aka Lying with the Enemy) 1998, Anthem 2003, Man Overboard 2005; non-fiction: Firebird: Writing Today (ed.) 1983, On Ilkley Moor: The Story of an English Town 2001; children's fiction: Sylvie and the Songman 2008; contrib. to Granta 56. *Honours:* Soc. of Authors Travelling Scholarship 2004. *Address:* c/o Picador, 20 New Wharf Road, London, N1 9RR, England.

BINEBINE, Mahi; Moroccan novelist and artist; b. 13 Feb. 1959, Marrakesh; m.; three d. *Career:* moved to Paris 1980; teacher of mathematics for eight years; lived in USA 1994–99; returned to Marrakesh 2002; paintings exhibited at Guggenheim Museum, New York, Venice Biennale, Aaart Foundation, Austria. *Publications include:* novels: Le Sommeil de l'esclave (Prix Méditerranée Maghreb 1993) 1992, Les Funérailles du lait 1994, L'Ombre du Poète 1997, Cannibales (trans. as Welcome to Paradise) 1999, Pollens (Prix de l'Amitié Franco-Arabe) 2001, Terre d'ombre brulée 2004, Le griot de Marrakech 2005, Les Étoiles de Sidi Moumen 2010; illustrator: L'Écriture au tournant by Abdellatif Laâbi 2000. *Literary Agent:* c/o Granta Books, 2–3 Hanover Yard, Noel Road, London, N1 8BE, England. *Website:* www.granta.co.uk. *Telephone:* (66) 1351959 (office). *Fax:* (52) 4493124 (office). *E-mail:* binebine@gmail.com (office); mahibinebine@hotmail.com (home). *Website:* www.mahibinebine.com.

BINGHAM, Hon. Charlotte Marie-Thérèse; British writer; b. 29 June 1942, Haywards Heath, Sussex; d. of John Michael Ward Bingham, 7th Baron Clanmorris and Madeleine Mary Bingham (née Ebel); m. Terence Brady 1964; one s. one d. *Education:* The Priory (Haywards Heath) and Univ. of Paris (Sorbonne). *Career:* writer of screenplays with Terence Brady. *Stage plays include:* I Wish, I Wish 1989. *TV includes:* Series: Boy Meets Girl, Take Three Girls, Upstairs Downstairs, Away From it All, No—Honestly, Yes—Honestly, Pig in the Middle, Thomas and Sarah, Father Matthew's Daughter, Oh Madeleine!, Forever Green, The Upper Hand; Films: Love With a Perfect Stranger 1986, Losing Control 1987, The Seventh Raven 1987, The Magic Moment 1988. *Publications include:* Coronet Among the Weeds 1963, Lucinda 1965, Coronet Among the Grass 1972, Victoria (jtly) 1972, Rose's Story (jtly) 1973, Victoria and Company (jtly) 1974, Belgravia 1983, Country Life 1986, At Home 1987, To Hear a Nightingale 1988, The Business 1989, In Sunshine or in Shadow 1991, Stardust 1992, By Invitation 1993, Nanny 1993, Change of Heart 1994, Debutantes 1995, The Nightingale Sings 1996, Grand Affair 1997, Love Song 1998, The Kissing Garden 1999, The Love Knot 2000, The Blue Note 2000, The Season 2001, Summertime 2001, Distant Music 2002, The Chestnut Tree 2002, The Moon at Midnight 2003, The Wind Off the Sea 2003, Daughters of Eden 2004, The House of Flowers 2004, Friday's Girl 2005, The Magic Hour 2005, Out of the Blue 2006, In Distant Fields 2006, The White Marriage 2007, Goodnight Sweetheart 2007, The Land of Summer 2008, Mums on the Run 2010. *Literary Agent:* Annabel Merullo, Peters Fraser and Dunlop, The Rights House, 34–43 Russell Street, London WC2B 5HA, England. *Telephone:* (20) 7344-1000. *Fax:* (20) 7836-9539. *E-mail:* info@pfd.co.uk. *Website:* www.pfd.co.uk. *E-mail:* charlottebrady@btconnect.com. *Website:* www.charlottebingham.com.

BINGHAM, Kate; British poet, novelist and screenwriter; b. 1971, London. *Education:* Univ. of Oxford. *Publications include:* novels: Mummy's Legs 1998, Slipstream 2000; poetry: Cohabitation 1998, Eighteenth 2003, Quicksand Beach 2006. *Honours:* Eric Gregory Award, Soc. of Authors 1996, Prizewinner, Nat. Poetry Competition 2003. *Address:* Seren Books, 57 Nolton Street, Bridgend, CF31 3AE, Wales. *Telephone:* (16) 5666-3018. *Website:* www.serenbooks.com.

BIRCH, Carol; British novelist; b. 3 Jan. 1951, Manchester; m. Martin Lucas Butler 1990; two s. *Education:* Univ. of Keele. *Career:* mem. Soc. of Authors. *Publications include:* Life in the Palace (David Higham Prize) 1988, The Fog Line (Geoffrey Faber Memorial Award) 1989, The Unmaking 1992, Songs of the West 1994, Little Sister 1998, Come Back Paddy Riley 2000, Turn Again Home 2003, In a Certain Light 2004, The Naming of Eliza Quinn 2005, Scapegallows (East Anglian Book of the Year Award 2008) 2007, Jamrach's Menagerie 2011; contrib. to TLS, Independent, New Statesman. *Literary Agent:* Mic Cheetham Agency, 11–12 Dover Street, Green Park, London, W1S 4LJ, England. *Telephone:* (20) 7495-2002. *Fax:* (20) 7399-2801. *E-mail:* info@miccheetham.com. *Website:* www.miccheetham.com.

BIRD, Charles (see Wittich, John Charles Bird)

BIRD, Kai, BA, MSc; American writer; b. 2 Sept. 1951, Eugene, Ore.; m. Susan Gloria Goldmark 1975; one s. *Education:* Carleton Coll., Northwestern Univ. *Publications include:* The Chairman: John J. McCloy, The Making of the American Establishment 1992, Hiroshima's Shadow: Writings on the Denial of History and the Smithsonian Controversy (ed. with Lawrence Lifshultz) 1998, The Color of Truth: McGeorge Bundy and William Bundy, Brothers in Arms: A Biography 1998, American Prometheus: The Triumph and Tragedy of J. Robert Oppenheimer (with Martin J. Sherwin) (Pulitzer Prize in Biography 2006, Duff Cooper Prize 2008) 2005, Crossing Mandelbaum Gate: Coming of Age Between the Arabs and Israelis, 1956–1978 2010; contribs to periodicals and journals. *Honours:* John D. and Catherine T. MacArthur Foundation Writing Fellowship, German Marshall Fund Fellow, Alicia Patterson Journalism Fellowship, John Simon Guggenheim Foundation Fellowship, Fellow, Woodrow Wilson Center for Int. Scholarship 2001–02. *Address:* 1914 Biltmore Street, NW, Washington, DC 20009, USA (home).

BIRDSELL, Sandra Louise; Canadian writer; b. 22 April 1942, Hamiota, Manitoba; m. Stanley Vivian Birdsell 1959 (divorced 1984); one s. two d. *Career:* several writer-in-residencies; instructor in English, Capilano Coll., N Vancouver; mem. Manitoba Writers' Guild, Saskatchewan Writers' Guild, PEN Int., Writers' Guild of Canada, Writers' Union of Canada. *Publications:* Night Travellers (short stories) 1982, Ladies of the House (short stories) 1984, The Missing Child (novel) 1989, The Chrome Suite (novel) 1992, The Two-Headed Calf (short stories) 1997, The Town That Floated Away (juvenile) 1997, The Russländer (novel) 2001, Katya (novel) 2004, Children of the Day (novel) 2005, Waiting for Joe (novel) 2010; contribs to various publications. *Honours:* Gerald Lampert Memorial Award 1982, WHSmith/Books in Canada First Novel Award 1989, McNally Robinson Award for Manitoba Book of the Year 1992, McNally Robinson Book of the Year 1993, Marion Engel Award 1993, City of Regina Book of the Year 2001, Saskatchewan Book Awards for Children's Literature and Fiction 2001, Saskatchewan Book of the Year 2001, 2005. *Literary Agent:* Anne McDermid, Anne McDermid and Associates, 83 Willcocks Street, Toronto, Ont. M5S 1C9, Canada. *Telephone:* (416) 324-8845. *Fax:* (416) 324-8870. *E-mail:* info@mcdermidagency.com. *Website:* www.mcdermidagency.com. *Address:* Random House of Canada Ltd, One Toronto Street, Unit 300, Toronto, Ont. M5C 2V6, Canada. *Telephone:* (416) 364-4449. *Fax:* (416) 364-6863. *Website:* www.randomhouse.ca; www.sandrabirdsell.com.

BIRLEY, Julia, BA; British writer; b. 13 May 1928, London; m. 1954; one s. three d. *Education:* Univ. of Oxford. *Career:* mem. PEN, Charlotte Yonge Soc. *Publications include:* fiction: The Children on the Shore 1958, The Time of the Cuckoo 1960, When You Were There 1963, A Serpent's Egg 1966, Dr Spicer 1988; also short stories and plays; contribs to The Guardian. *Address:* Upper Bryn, Longtown, HR2 0NA, England (home).

BIRMINGHAM, Stephen, BA; American writer; b. 28 May 1931, Hartford, Conn.; s. of Thomas Birmingham and Editha Gardner Birmingham; m. Janet Tillson 1951 (divorced); one s. two d. *Education:* Williams Coll., Univ. of Oxford, UK. *Career:* Advertising Copywriter, Needham, Harper & Steers Inc. 1953–67; fmr teacher of writing, Univ. of Cincinnati; mem. New England Soc. of the City of New York. *Publications include:* Young Mr Keefe 1958, Baraba Greer 1959, The Towers of Love 1961, Those Harper Women 1963, Fast Start, Fast Finish 1966, Our Crowd: The Great Jewish Families of New York 1967, The Right People 1968, Heart Troubles 1968, The Grandees 1971, The Late John Marquand 1972, The Right Places 1973, Real Lace 1973, Certain People: America's Black Elite 1977, The Golden Dream: Suburbia in the 1970s 1978, Jacqueline Bouvier Kennedy Onassis 1978, Life at the Dakota 1979, California Rich 1980, Duchess 1981, The Grandes Dames 1982, The Auerbach Will 1983, The Rest of Us 1984, The LeBaron Secret 1986, America's Secret Aristocracy 1987, Shades of Fortune 1989, The Rothman Scandal 1991, Carriage Trade 1993, The Grandees 1997, The Wrong Kind of Money 1998; contribs to periodicals. *Address:* 1247 Ida Street, Cincinnati, OH 45202-1525, USA (home).

BISATIE, Muhammad al-; Egyptian writer; b. 19 Nov. 1937, el-Gamalia, Dakahlia. *Education:* Cairo Univ. *Career:* fmr Accountancy Inspector; full-time writer 1962–. *Publications include:* Alkibar wa al-Sighar 1966, Al-Tajir wa-l-Naqqash 1976, Al Maqha az Zujaji (trans. as The Glass Cafe) 1978, Al Ayyam as Sa'bah (trans. as Hard Days) 1978, Beyout Wara' al-Ashgar 1993, Houses Behind the Trees (in trans.), Sakhab al-Buhayra (trans. as The Roaring of the Lake) (Cairo Int. Book Fair Award for Best Novel 1995) 1994, Sa'at Maghrib 1996, Aswat el-Leil 1998, Al-Tajir wa-l-Naqqash, Wa ya'ti al'-Qitar (trans. as And the Train Comes) 1999, Layal Ukhra 2000, Fardous 2003, Over the Bridge 2006, Hunger (in trans.) 2008, Drumbeat (Sawiris Foundation Award) 2010. *Honours:* Oweiss Prize 2001. *Address:* Dar al-Abad, PO Box 4123, Sakiet Al Janzie, Bayhom Building, Beirut, Lebanon.

BISCHOFF, David Frederick; American writer; b. 15 Dec. 1951, Washington, DC. *Career:* Assoc. Ed., Amazing Magazine; mem. Faculty, Masters Program for Popular Fiction, Seton Hill Univ., Pa. *Publications include:* fiction: The Seeker (with Christopher Lampton) 1976, Quest (ed.) 1977, Strange Encounters (ed.) 1977, The Phantom of the Opera (children's) 1977, The Woodman (with Dennis R. Bailey) 1979, Nightworld 1979, Star Fall 1980, The Vampires of the Nightworld 1981, Tin Woodman (with Dennis Bailey) 1982, Star Spring 1982, The Selkie 1982, War Games 1983, Mandala 1983, Day of the Dragonstar (with Thomas F. Monteleone) 1983, The Crunch Bunch 1985, Destiny Dice 1985, The Wraith Board 1985, Galactic Warriors 1985, The Infinite Battle 1985, Night of the Dragonstar 1985, A Personal Demon 1985, The Macrocosmic Conflict 1986, Manhattan Project 1986, The Unicorn Gambit 1986, Some Kind of Wonderful 1987, The Blob 1988, Dragonstar Destiny 1989, Abduction: The UFO Conspiracy 1990, Revelation: The UFO Conspiracy 1991, Deception: The UFO Conspiracy 1991, Mutant's Amok 1991, Mutant Hell 1991, Rebel Attack 1991, Holocaust Horror 1991, Dr Dimenson 1993, Masters of Springtime 1994, Aliens Versus Predator: Hunter's Planet 1994, The Judas Cross 1994, Hackers 1995, Philip K. Dick High 2000, J.R.R. Tolkien University 2000, Tripping the Dark Fantastic 2000, The Diplomatic Touch 2001, The H.P. Lovecraft Touch 2002, Jack London, Star Warrior 2002, The Tawdry Yellow Brick Road 2004; short fiction: The Most Dangerous Man in the World 1974, The Sky's an Oyster; the Stars Are Pearls 1975, Feeding Time 1976, Top Hat 1977, In Medias Res 1978, All the Stage, A World 1979, Outside 1980, Waterloo Sunset 1982, The Warmth of the Stars 1983, Copyright Infringement 1984, Cooking with Children 1989, Spare Change 1991, Dr. Dimension 1993, Santa Ritual Abuse 1995, Vicious Wishes 1996, Fade 1996, The Xaxrkling of J. Arnold Boysenberry 1997, The S-Files 1998, Tooth or Consequences 1998, Sittin' on the Dock 1999, Joy to the World 1999, Love After Death 2000, Fat Farm 2000, A Game of Swords 2000, The Whiteviper Scrolls 2001, The Tenth Wonder of the World 2001, Books 2002, The Sorcerer's Apprentice's Apprentice 2002, Die, Christmas, Die! 2004, Lonesome Diesel 2004, Enter All Abandon, Ye Who Hope Here 2005, Quoth the Screaming Chicken 2006, Further 2006, The Man Who Would Be Overlord 2007. *E-mail:* david.bischoff@gmail.com.

BISHER, Badrya al-; Saudi Arabian writer; b. 1967, Riyadh; m. *Education:* Univ. of Riyadh. *Career:* writer for Al-Yamama weekly literary magazine, Alhayat newspaper. *Publications include:* short story collections: Nihayat al-lu'ba (The End of the Game) 1992, Masa' al-arbia' (The Evening of the Weekend) 1994; contribs to Voices of Change: Short Stories by Saudi Arabian Women Writers 1997. *Address:* Dar al-Adab, PO Box 11-4123, Beirut, Lebanon (office). *E-mail:* d_aladab@cyberia.net.lb (office).

BISHOP, James Drew, BA; British journalist; b. 18 June 1929, London; s. of the late Sir Patrick Bishop and Vera Drew; m. Brenda Pearson 1959; two s. *Education:* Haileybury Coll., Hertford and Corpus Christi Coll., Cambridge. *Career:* reporter, Northampton Chronicle 1953; editorial staff of The Times (London) 1954–70, Foreign Corresp. 1957–64, Foreign News Ed. 1964–66, Features Ed. 1966–70; Ed. The Illustrated London News 1971–87, Newsweek Int. Diary 1977–88; Dir Int. Thomson Publishing Co. 1980–85; Editorial Dir Orient Express, Connections and Natural World Magazines 1981–94; Ed.-in-Chief Illustrated London News Publs 1987–94; contrib. to The Annual Register 1960–88, mem. Advisory Bd 1970–; Chair. Editorial Bd Natural World 1981–97, Asscn of British Eds 1987–95; Chair. Nat. Heritage 1998– (Trustee 1994–). *Publications:* A Social History of Edwardian Britain 1977, Social History of the First World War 1982, The Story of The Times (with O. Woods) 1983, Illustrated Counties of England (ed.) 1985, The Sedgwick Story 1998. *Address:* Black Fen, Stoke by Nayland, Suffolk, CO6 4QD, England (home). *Telephone:* (1206) 262315 (office). *Fax:* (1206) 262876 (office). *E-mail:* jamesbishop3@tiscali.co.uk (home).

BISHOP, Jan (see McConchie, Lyn)

BISHOP, Michael Lawson, (Philip Lawson (with Paul Di Filippo), MA; American writer, poet and teacher; b. 12 Nov. 1945, Lincoln, Neb.; s. of Lee O. Bishop and Maxine Elaine Matison; m. Jeri Whitaker 1969; one s. one d. *Education:* Univ. of Georgia. *Career:* Writer-in-Residence, LaGrange Coll. 1997–; mem. Science Fiction and Fantasy Writers of America Inc., Science Fiction Poetry Asscn, Georgia Writers Inc. *Publications include:* fiction: A Funeral for the Eyes of Fire (aka Eyes of Fire) 1975, And Strange at Ecbatan the Trees 1976, Stolen Faces 1977, A Little Knowledge 1977, Transfigurations 1979, Under Heaven's Bridge (with Ian Watson) 1981, No Enemy but Time 1982, Who Made Steve Cry? 1984, Ancient of Days 1985, The Secret Ascension, or, Philip K. Dick Is Dead, Alas 1987, Unicorn Mountain 1988, Apartheid, Superstrings and Mordecai Thubana 1989, Count Geiger's Blues 1992, Brittle Innings 1994; as Philip Lawson (jt pseudonym with Paul di Filippo): Would It Kill You to Smile? 1998, Muskrat Courage 2000; short stories: Catacomb Years 1979, Blooded on Arachne 1982, One Winter in Eden 1984, Close Encounters with the Deity 1986, Emphatically Not SF, Almost 1990, At the City Limits of Fate 1996, Brighten to Incandescence 2003; non-fiction: A Reverie for Mister Ray: Reflections on Life, Death and Speculative Fiction 2005; poetry: Windows and Mirrors 1977, Time Pieces 1999, Novella Collection: Blue Kansas Sky 2000, Brighten to Incandescence: 17 Stories 2003; editor: Changes (anthology) (with Ian Watson) 1982, Light Years and Dark (anthology) 1984, Nebula Awards: SFWA's Choices for the Best Science Fiction and Fantasy (Vols 23–25) 1989–91, Passing for Human (anthology) (with Steven Utley) 2009, A Cross of Centuries: 25 Imaginative Tales about the Christ 2007; contrib. to anthologies and periodicals. *Honours:* Hon. LHD (LaGrange Coll.) 2001; Phoenix Award 1977, Clark Ashton Smith Award 1978, Science Fiction Poetry Asscn Rhysling Award 1979, SFWA Nebula Awards 1981, 1982, Mythopoetic Fantasy Award 1988, Locus Award for Best Fantasy Novel 1994, Southeastern Science Fiction Asscn Award for Best Short Fiction 2004, 2006, Shirley Jackson Award 2009. *Address:* PO Box 646, Pine Mountain, GA 31822, USA (home). *Telephone:* (706) 663-4461 (home). *Fax:* (706) 880-8102 (home). *E-mail:* mlbishop@juno.com (home). *Website:* www.michaelbishop-writer.com.

BISHOP, Pike (see Obstfeld, Raymond)

BISKIND, Peter; American film critic and writer. *Career:* fmr documentarist; Exec. Ed. Premiere magazine for nine years; Ed.-in-Chief, American Film magazine for five years; fmr Contributing Ed. Vanity Fair. *Publications include:* Seeing is Believing: How Hollywood Taught Us to Stop Worrying and Love the Fifties 1983, The Godfather Companion 1991, Easy Riders, Raging Bulls: How the Sex, Drugs and Rock 'n' Roll Generation Saved Hollywood 1998, Down and Dirty Pictures: Miramax, Sundance and the Rise of Independent Film 2004, Gods and Monsters: Movers, Shakers, and Other Casualties of the Hollywood Machine 2004, Star: How Warren Beatty Seduced America 2010; contribs to New York Times, Washington Post, Rolling Stone. *Address:* c/o Kathy Robbins, The Robbins Office, Inc., 405 Park Avenue, New York, NY 10022, USA. *Telephone:* (212) 223-0720. *E-mail:* peb4@mac.com. *Website:* www.peterbiskind.com.

BISSETT, Bill; Canadian poet and artist; b. 23 Nov. 1939, Halifax, NS; m. Michelle Bissett. *Education:* Dalhousie Univ., Univ. of British Columbia. *Career:* Ed. Printer Blewointmentpress, Vancouver 1962–83. *Exhibitions:* art shows at Van Art Gallery, BC, Modern Art, Ont., Harbour Front, Ont., This Ain't the Rosedale Library Gallery, Ont. 2006–07. *Publications include:* The Jinx Ship and other Trips: Poems-drawings-collage 1966, We Sleep Inside Each Other All 1966, Fires in the Temple 1967, Where Is Miss Florence Riddle 1967, What Poetiks 1967, Gossamer Bed Pan 1967, Lebanon Voices 1967, Of the Land/Divine Service Poems 1968, Awake in the Red Desert 1968, Killer Whale 1969, Sunday Work? 1969, Liberating Skies 1969, The Lost Angel Mining Company 1969, The Outlaw 1970, Blew Trewz 1970, Nobody Owns the Earth 1971, Air 6 1971, Dragon Fly 1971, Four Parts Sand: Concrete Poems 1972, The Ice Bag 1972, Poems for Yoshi 1972, Drifting into War 1972, Air 10-11-12 1973, Pass the Food, Release the Spirit Book 1973, The First Sufi Line 1973, Vancouver Mainland Ice and Cold Storage 1973, Living with the Vishyan 1974, What 1974, Drawings 1974, Medicine My Mouths on Fire 1974, Space Travel 1974, You Can Eat it at the Opening 1974, The Fifth Sun 1975, The Wind up Tongue 1975, Stardust 1975, An Allusyun to Macbeth 1976, Plutonium Missing 1976, Sailor 1978, Beyond Even Faithful Legends 1979, Soul Arrow 1980, Northern Birds in Color 1981, Parlant 1982, Seagull on Yonge Street 1983, Canada Geese Mate for Life 1985, Animal Uproar 1987, What we Have 1989, Hard 2 Beleev 1990, Incorrect Thoughts 1992, Vocalist with the Luddites, Dreaming of the Night 1992, The Last Photo of the Human Soul 1993, Th Influenza uv Logik 1995, loving without being vulnrabul 1997, Offthroad (cassette) 1998, Skars on the Seehors 1999, B leev abul char ak trs 2000, Offthroad (with CD) 2000, rainbow mewsick (ed.) 2002, peter among th towring boxes 2002, unmatching phenomena I (with CD) 2002, rumours uv hurricane (CD) 2003, narrativ enigma 2004, northern wild roses 2005, deth interrupts th dansing (CD) 2006, ths is erth thees ar peopul 2007, ths is erth thees ar peopul cd 2008, sublingual 2008, griddle talk: a yeer uv bill n carol dewing brunch 2009. *Honours:* People's Poets 1992, Dorothy Livesay Poetry Award 1993, 2003, George Woodcott Award for Lifetime Achievement 2007. *Telephone:* (416) 924-4201. *E-mail:* centralianwings@sympatico.ca. *Website:* www.billbissett.com.

BISSON, Thomas Noel, PhD; American historian and academic; *Henry Charles Lea Professor Emeritus of Medieval History, Harvard University*; b. 30 March 1931, New York, NY; s. of Thomas A. Bisson and Faith W. Bisson; m. Margaretta C. Webb 1962; two d. *Education:* Port Washington High School, New York, Haverford Coll., Univ. of California, Berkeley and Princeton Univ. *Career:* Instructor in History, Amherst Coll. 1957–60; Asst Prof., Brown Univ. 1960–65; Assoc. Prof., Swarthmore Coll. 1965–67; Assoc. Prof., Univ. of California, Berkeley 1967–69, Prof. 1969–87; Prof., Harvard Univ. 1986–, Henry Charles Lea Prof. of Medieval History 1988–2005, Emer. 2005–, Chair. Dept of History 1991–95; mem. American Philosophical Soc., American Acad. of Arts and Sciences; Fellow, Medieval Acad. of America (Pres. 1994–95), Royal Historical Soc., British Acad., Institut d'Estudis Catalans etc. *Publications:* Assemblies and Representation in Languedoc in the Thirteenth Century 1964, Medieval Representative Institutions: Their Origins and Nature 1973, Conservation of Coinage: Monetary Exploitation and its Restraint in France, Catalonia and Aragon (c. AD 1000–c. AD 1225) 1979, Fiscal Accounts of Catalonia under the Early Count-Kings 1151–1213 (two vols) 1985, The Medieval Crown of Aragon: A Short History 1986, Medieval France and Her Pyrenean Neighbors 1989, Tormented Voices: Power, Crisis and Humanity in Rural Catalonia 1140–1200 1998, The Crisis of the Twelfth Century 2009; articles in journals. *Honours:* Creu de Sant Jordi (Generalitat of Catalonia) 2001; Dr hc (Barcelona) 1991; Guggenheim Fellow 1964–65. *Address:* 21 Hammond Street, Cambridge, MA 02138, USA (home). *Telephone:* (617) 354 0178 (home). *E-mail:* tnbisson@fas.harvard.edu (office). *Website:* www.fas.harvard.edu/~history (office).

BISSOONDATH, Neil Devindra, BA; Canadian writer and academic; *Professor, Department of Literature, Université Laval*; b. 19 April 1955, Arima, Trinidad; m. Anne Bissoondath; one d. *Education:* York Univ. *Career:* taught English and French, Inlingua School of Languages and Toronto Language Workshop; Prof., Dept of Literature, Université Laval 1999–. *Publications include:* Digging Up the Mountains (short stories) 1985, A Casual Brutality (novel) 1988, On the Eve of Uncertain Tomorrows (short stories) 1990, The Innocence of Age (novel) 1992, Selling Illusions: The Cult of Multiculturalism in Canada (Gordon Montador Award) 1994, The Worlds Within Her 1998, Doing the Heart Good 2001, The Unyielding Clamour of the Night 2005, The Soul of All Great Designs 2008, Postcards from Hell 2009; contribs to periodicals. *Honours:* Chevalier of the Ordre national du Québec 2010; McClelland and Stewart Award 1986, Nat. Magazine Award 1986, Literary Award, Canadian Authors' Asscn 1993, Hugh MacLennan Prize 2002, 2005. *Address:* Department of Literature, Université Laval, Pavillon Charles-De Koninck, Room 3300, 1030, avenue des Sciences-Humain, Québec City, PQ G1V 0A6, Canada. *Telephone:* (418) 656-2131, ext 7531. *Fax:* (418) 656-2991. *E-mail:* Neil.Bissoondath@lit.ulaval.ca. *Website:* www.lit.ulaval.ca/accueil.

BISWAS, Brian, BA, MS; American writer; b. 7 March 1957, Columbus, Ohio; m. Elizabeth Phelan 1977; one s. one d. *Education:* Antioch Coll., Univ. of Illinois. *Publications include:* short stories: The Bridge 1991, Solitary Confinement 1992, The Museum of North African Treasures 1992, A Sea Voyage 1992, The Nature of Love 1993, Fare-Thee-Well 1993, Others 1993, The Vulture 1997, A Betrayal 1999, Apologia Du Amore 2000, The Crystal 2000, A Soldier's Lament 2003, The Town That Went to Sleep 2004, Death in the Afternoon 2004, The Room at the End of the World 2005, The Moons of Jupiter 2005, Hoag's Object 2006, Happenstance 2006, Three Degrees above Absolute Zero 2007, The House in the Forest 2007, The Looking Glass 2008, A Love Story 2008, Secrets of Life 2008, The Astronomer 2009, The Garden of Love 2010, Ariel 2010, Mario Bakar 2010, Alpha Centauri 2010, Worms 2010, The Last Photon 2011, This Old Man 2011, Skipping Stones 2011, Julie's Murderer 2011; contribs to various literary journals. *Address:* 412 Holly Lane, Chapel Hill, NC 27517, USA (home). *E-mail:* bbiswas@email.unc.edu (office). *Website:* www.brianbiswas.com (office).

BJØRNSTAD, Ketil; Norwegian musician (piano), composer and writer; b. 25 April 1952, Oslo. *Education:* studied piano with Amalie Christie and Robert Riefling, Oslo, further studies in London and Paris. *Career:* professional debut with Oslo Philharmonic 1969; performed with experimental Svein Finnerud Trio 1971; music and literary critic, Aftenposten 1972–98; first recording of own music Åpning 1973; collaborations with numerous Norwegian and int. musicians from fields of jazz, folk, rock, avant-garde and classical music, including Ole Paus, Jon Christensen, Terje Rypdal, David Darling, Cornelis Vreeswijk, Randi Stene, Lars Anders Tomter, Anneli Drecker, Nora Taksdal, Lill Lindfors; has toured in Europe, Asia and USA and performed at jazz festivals in Frankfurt, Neuwied, Ingolstadt, Hamburg, Stans, Vienna, Voss, Molde, Modena, Ravenna, Nancy, Porto, Montreal, Shanghai, Warsaw and London; UK tour with Contemporary Music Network 2006; has published over 20 novels, also poetry, essays, literary and music criticism. *Recordings include:* Åpning 1973, Berget det blå (Spellemannsprisen) 1974, Tredje dag 1975, Lise Madsen, Moses & de Andre (with Ole Paus) 1975, Finnes du noensteds ikveld 1976, Selena 1977, Musikk for en lang natt 1977, Leve Patagonia 1978, Svart Piano 1979, Tidevann 1980, Och människor ser igen (with Lill Lindfors) 1980, 30-års-krigen (with Stavangerenseblet) 1981, Engler i sneen 1982, Bjørnstad/Paus/Hamsun 1982, Aniara (with Lindfors/Fristorp) 1983, Mine dager i Paris 1983, Preludes Vol. 1 1984, Människors makt (with Lill Lindfors) 1985, Natten (with Sissel I. Andersen) 1985, Preludes Vol. 2 1986, Three Ballets 1987, Karen Mowat-suite 1988, The Shadow (with Randi Stene) 1990, Odyssey 1991, Rift 1991, Messe for en såret jord (with Randi Stene and Lars Anders Tomter) 1992, Løsrivelse (with Kari Bremnes) 1993, Water Stories 1993, For den som elsker 1994, Sanger fra en klode 1995, Salomos Høysang 1995, The Sea 1995, Haugtussa 1996, The River (with David Darling) 1997, Reisetid 1997, The Sea II 1997, Ett Liv (with Lill Lindfors) 1998, The Rosenborg Tapes Vol. 1 1998, The Rosenborg Tapes Vol. 2 1999, Himmelrand – Tusenårsoratoriet 1999, Epigraphs (with David Darling) 2000, Grace 2001, Old 2001, The Nest 2003, Seafarer's Song 2004, Floating 2005, Rainbow Sessions 2007, Devotions 2007, Life in Leipzig 2008, The Light: Songs of Love and Fear 2008, Coastlines (with Lill Lindfords) 2008, Remembrance 2010, Hvalenes Sang 2010, Night Song 2011, Early Piano Music 2011. *Compositions:* Minotauros (ballet) 1997, IZZAT (youth opera) 2006. *Film soundtracks:* Engler i sneen 1983, Forever Mozart 1996, Nous sommes touts encore ici 1997, Emporte moi 1999, Museum of Modern Art 1999, Histoire du Cinéma 1999, Eloge d'Amour 2001, Trofast 2004, Ae Fond Kiss 2005, Samotnosc W Sieci 2006. *Plays:* Ildlandet (musical) 1984, Spill 1995, Forestillinger 1997, Minotauros 1997. *Publications include:* fiction: Nattsvermere 1974, Kråker og Krigere 1975, Pavane 1976, Vinterbyen 1977,

Landet på andre siden 1979, Bingo 1981, Oda! 1983, Det personlige motiv 1985, G-moll-balladen 1986, Oppstigning fra det usynlig 1988, Stormen 1989, Skumringsmulighetene 1990, Villa Europa 1992, Historien om Edvard Munch 1993, Barnevakt 1994, Drift 1996, Drømmen om havet 1996, Veien til Dhaka 1997, Nåde (Riksmålsprisen) 1998, Fall 1999, Ludvig Hassels tusenårsskifte 2000, Jæger 2001, Mannen som gikk på jorden (jtly) 2002, Tesman 2003, Til Musikken 2004, Elven 2007, Damen i Dalen 2009; poetry: Alene ut 1972, Nærmere 1973; non-fiction: Reisen til Gallia (essays, with Ole Paus) 1998, Flammeslukeren (biog.) 2005, Liv Ullmann: Livslinjer (biog.) 2005, Historier om sårbarhet (with Catherine Jacobsen) 2007, Elven 2007, Kolbein Falkeid - et naerbilde (biog.) 2008, Damen i Dalen 2009, De udødelige 2011. *Honours:* Priz des Lecteurs, France 2008. *Literary Agent:* Kjell Kalleklev Management, Georgernes Verft 3, 5011 Bergen, Norway. *Telephone:* 55-55-76-30. *Fax:* 55-55-76-31. *E-mail:* kjell@kalleklev.no. *Website:* www.kalleklev.no; www.ketilbjornstad.com.

BLACK, David, BA, MFA; American writer, scriptwriter and producer; b. 21 April 1945, Boston; m. Deborah Hughes Keehn 1968; one s. one d. *Education:* Amherst Coll., Columbia Univ. *Career:* Writer-in-Residence, Mt Holyoke Coll. 1982–86; Contributing Ed. Rolling Stone 1986–89; mem. Int. Asscn of Crime Writers, Mystery Writers of America, PEN, Writers' Guild-East. *Television:* as writer: Hill Street Blues 1986–87, Miami Vice 1987–88, Gideon Oliver 1989, Nasty Boys 1989, H.E.L.P. 1990, Law & Order 1990–2006, Legacy of Lies 1992, EZ Streets 1996–97, The Confession (Writers' Guild of America Award) 1999, 100 Centre Street 2001, The Education of Max Bickford 2002, Kojak 2005; as producer: Law & Order 1990–91, 1997–2001, The Good Policeman 1991, Legacy of Lies 1992, The Cosby Mysteries 1994, The Education of Max Bickford 2001, 100 Centre Street 2001–02, CSI: Miami 2003, Copshop 2004. *Publications include:* Mirrors 1968, Ekstasy 1975, Like Father 1978, The King of Fifth Avenue 1981, Minds 1982, Murder at the Met 1984, Medicine Man 1985, Peep Show 1986, The Plague Years 1986, An Impossible Life, The Extincton Event 2010; contribs to numerous magazines. *Honours:* Gold Medal for Excellence in Writing, Writers' Foundation of America 1992. *Address:* Tor/Forge Books, Macmillan, 175 Fifth Avenue, New York, NY 10010, USA. *Telephone:* (646) 307-5151. *Website:* us.macmillan.com/torforge.aspx; www.davidblackwriter.com.

BLACK OF CROSSHARBOUR, Baron (Life Peer), cr. 2001, of Crossharbour in the London Borough of Tower Hamlets; **Conrad Moffat Black,** Kt, PC, OC, BA, LLL, MA, LittD; British (b. Canadian) publisher, business executive, author, columnist and investor; *Chairman, Conrad Black Capital Corporation;* b. 25 Aug. 1944, Montreal, Quebec; s. of George Montegu and Jean Elizabeth Black (née Riley); m. 1st Joanna Catherine Louise Black 1978 (divorced 1991); two s. one d.; m. 2nd Barbara Amiel 1992. *Education:* Carleton, Laval, McGill Univs. *Career:* Chair. and CEO Ravelston Corpn Ltd; Chair. Hollinger Int. 1985–2004, acquired Daily Telegraph newspaper group 1985, Chair. Telegraph Group –2004; CEO Chair. Argus Corpn 1978–2005; Chair. Conrad Black Capital Corpn; mem. Advisory Bd, The Nat. Interest, Washington, DC; Patron, The Malcolm Muggeridge Foundation; charged with 17 counts of criminal offences by US Dept of Justice, which sought life imprisonment and fine of $140 million 2005, four counts dropped, nine led to acquittals, remaining four vacated unanimously by US Supreme Court after spending 29 months in a low security fed. prison, two counts revived by a lower court but US Supreme Court refused to grant leave to appeal these May 2011, resentenced to a reduced term of 42 months and a fine of $125,000, returned to prison to serve remaining 13 months of his sentence June 2011, released from prison and deported to Canada May 2012, granted a one-year temporary resident's permit to re-enter Canada as he had renounced his Canadian citizenship in 2001. *Publications:* Duplessis 1977, A Life in Progress (autobiog.) 1994, Franklin D. Roosevelt: Champion of Freedom 2003, Richard Milhous Nixon: The Invincible Quest 2007. *Honours:* Kt Commdr, Order of St Gregory the Great; Hon. LLD (St Francis Xavier) 1979, (McMaster) 1979, (Windsor) 1979, (Carleton) 1992. *Address:* 3044 Bloor Street West, Suite 296, Toronto, ON M8X 2Y8, Canada. *Telephone:* (416) 241-7758. *Fax:* (416) 241-5026. *E-mail:* jmaida@blackam.net (office).

BLACKBOURN, David Gordon, BA, PhD, FRHistS; British historian and academic; *Coolidge Professor of History and Director, Minda de Gunzburg Center for European Studies, Harvard University;* b. 1 Nov. 1949, Spilsby, Lincs.; s. of Harry Blackbourn and Pamela Jean Blackbourn; m. Deborah Frances Langton; one s. one d. *Education:* Leeds Modern Grammar School, Christ's Coll., Cambridge. *Career:* Research Fellow, Jesus Coll., Cambridge 1973–76; Lecturer in History, Queen Mary Coll., Univ. of London 1976–79, Birkbeck Coll. 1979–85, Reader in Modern History 1985–89, Prof. of Modern European History 1989–92; Coolidge Prof. of History, Harvard Univ., USA 1992–, Dir Minda de Gunzburg Center for European Studies 2007–; lectures and contribs to confs in UK, Ireland, Germany, France, Italy, fmr Yugoslavia, USA and Canada 1973–; Fellow, Inst. for European History, Mainz, FRG 1974–75; Research Fellow, Alexander von Humboldt Foundation, Bonn-Bad Godesberg, FRG 1984–85, 1994–95; Visiting Kratter Prof. of German History, Stanford Univ., Calif., USA 1989–90; Fellow, Guggenheim Foundation, New York 1994–95; Sec. German History Soc. 1978–81, mem. Cttee 1981–86; mem. Academic Advisory Bd, German Historical Inst., London 1983–92; mem. Editorial Bd Past and Present 1988–; mem. European Sub-cttee of Labour Party Nat. Exec. Cttee 1978–80, Academic Advisory Bd, Inst. for European History, Mainz, Germany 1995–2005, Cttee on Hon. Foreign mems, American Historical Asscn 2000–02; Pres. Conf. Group on Cen. European History, American Historical Asscn 2003–04; mem. Advisory Bd, Edmund Spevack Memorial Foundation 2003–06, mem. Bd, Friends of the German Historical Inst., Washington, DC 2004, Chair. Bd 2007–; mem. Academic Advisory Bd Lichtenberg Coll. Univ. of Goettingen 2007–; Ed. Penguin Custom Editions: The Western World Database 2000–; consultant to SMASH/The History Channel, USA; Fellow, American Acad. of Arts and Sciences 2007; gave Annual Lecture of German Historical Inst., London 1998, Malcolm Wynn Lecture, Stetson Univ., Fla. 2002, George C. Windell Memorial Lecture, Univ. of New Orleans 2006, Crayenborgh Lecture, Leiden Univ., Netherlands 2007, Jakob and Wilhelm Grimm Lecture, Univ. of Waterloo, Canada 2010. *Publications:* Class, Religion and Local Politics in Wilhelmine Germany 1980, The Peculiarities of German History (with Geoff Eley) 1984, Populists and Patricians: Essays in Modern German History 1987, Volksfrömmigkeit und Fortschrittsglaube im Kulturkampf 1988, The German Bourgeoisie (co-ed. with Richard J. Evans) 1991, Marpingen: Apparitions of the Virgin Mary in Bismarckian Germany 1993, The Fontana History of Germany: The Long Nineteenth Century, 1780–1918 1997, The Conquest of Nature: Water, Landscape and the Making of Modern Germany 2006; scholarly articles in English, German, French, Serbo-Croat, Japanese and Italian; contribs to several magazines and the BBC. *Honours:* American Historical Asscn Book Prize 1996, Walter Channing Cabot Fellow, Harvard Univ. 2003–04, George L. Mosse Prize, American Historical Asscn 2007, Charles A. Weyerhaeuser Prize, Forest History Soc. 2007. *Address:* Minda de Gunzburg Center for European Studies, Harvard University, 27 Kirkland Street, Cambridge, MA 02138, USA (office). *Telephone:* (617) 495-4303, ext. 228 (office). *Fax:* (617) 495-8509 (office). *E-mail:* dgblackb@fas.harvard.edu (office). *Website:* www.fas.harvard.edu/~history (office).

BLACKBURN, Alexander Lambert, MA, PhD; American writer, editor and academic; *Professor Emeritus of English, University of Colorado at Colorado Springs;* b. 6 Sept. 1929, Durham, NC; s. of William Maxwell Blackburn and Elizabeth Cheney Bayne Blackburn; m. Inés Dölz 1975; two s. one d. *Education:* Yale Univ., Univ. of North Carolina, Univ. of Cambridge, UK. *Career:* instructor, Hampden-Sydney Coll. 1960–61, Univ. of Pennsylvania 1963–65; Lecturer, Univ. of Maryland European Div. 1967–72; Prof. of English, Univ. of Colorado at Colorado Springs 1973–95, Prof. Emer. of English 1996–; Founder and Ed.-in-Chief Writers' Forum 1974–95; mem. Authors' Guild, PEN West, Colorado Authors' League. *Publications include:* The Myth of the Picaro 1979, The Cold War of Kitty Pentecost (novel) 1979, The Interior Country: Stories of the Modern West (ed.) 1987, A Sunrise Brighter Still: The Visionary Novels of Frank Waters 1991, Higher Elevations: Stories from the West (ed.) 1993, Suddenly a Mortal Splendor (novel) 1995, Creative Spirit: Towards a Better World 2001, Meeting the Professor: Growing Up in the William Blackburn Family 2004, Gifts From the Heart: Stories, Memories and Chronicles of Lou Gonzales Oller (ed.) 2009, Remembering Time: Stories and Novellas 2009, A Strange Joy 2009. *Honours:* Faculty Book Award Colorado Univ. 1993, Int. Peace Writing Award 2003, Frank Waters Award for Excellence in Literature 2005. *Address:* 6030 Twin Rock Court, Colorado Springs, CO 80918, USA (home). *Telephone:* (719) 599-4023 (home). *E-mail:* idb99@yahoo.com; iblackburn@me.com. *Website:* www.alexanderblackburn.com.

BLACKBURN, Julia, BA, FRSL; British writer; b. 12 Aug. 1948, London; d. of Thomas Blackburn and Rosalie de Meric; m. 1st Hein Bonger 1978 (divorced); one d. one s.; m. 2nd Herman Makkink 1999. *Education:* Univ. of York. *Radio:* plays for BBC Radio 3 and 4: A Good Death 2001, Betsy and Napoleon 2005, The Need for Nonsense 2010, The Spellbound Horses 2011. *Publications include:* The White Men 1979, Charles Waterton 1989, The Book of Colour 1991, Daisy Bates in the Desert 1994, The Emperor's Last Island 1997, The Leper's Companions 1999, For A Child: Selected Poems by Thomas Blackburn (ed and introduction) 2000, Old Man Goya 2002, With Billie (biog.) 2005, My Animals and Other Family: Radio Stories 2007, The Three of Us: A Memoir (PEN/Ackerley Prize 2009) 2008, Thin Paths 2011. *Address:* Green Pastures, Bramfield, Suffolk, IP19 9HD, England (home). *Telephone:* (1986) 784134 (home). *Fax:* (1986) 784665 (home). *E-mail:* blackburnmakkink@gmail.com (home). *Website:* www.juliablackburn.com.

BLACKBURN, Simon W., PhD, DPhil, FBA; British academic; *Professor of Philosophy, University of Cambridge;* b. 12 July 1944, Bristol; s. of Cuthbert Blackburn and Edna Blackburn; m. Angela Bowles 1968; one s. one d. *Education:* Clifton Coll. Bristol and Trinity Coll., Cambridge. *Career:* Research Fellow, Churchill Coll. Cambridge 1967–69; Fellow and Tutor in Philosophy, Pembroke Coll. Oxford 1969–90; Ed. Mind 1984–90; Edna J. Koury Distinguished Prof. of Philosophy, Univ. of NC 1990–2000; Adjunct Prof., ANU 1993–; Prof. of Philosophy, Univ. of Cambridge 2001–; Foreign mem. American Acad. of Arts and Sciences. *Publications:* Reason and Prediction 1970, Spreading the Word 1984, Essays in Quasi-Realism 1993, Oxford Dictionary of Philosophy 1994, Ruling Passions 1998, Think 1999, Being Good 2001, Lust 2004, Truth: A Guide for the Perplexed 2005, Plato's Republic: A Biography 2006, How to Read Hume 2008. *Honours:* Hon. LLD (Sunderland). *Address:* Faculty of Philosophy, University of Cambridge, Sidgwick Avenue, Cambridge, CB3 9DA (office); 141 Thornton Road, Cambridge, CB3 0NE, England (home). *Telephone:* (1223) 528278 (office). *E-mail:* swb24@cam.ac.uk (office). *Website:* www.phil.cam.ac.uk/~swb24/ (office).

BLACKMAN, Malorie, OBE; British writer; b. 1962, London; one d. *Education:* Honor Oak Grammar School, Thames Polytechnic. *Career:* database man. for Reuters; full-time writer 1990–. *Publications include:* Not

So Stupid! 1990, Elaine You're a Brat 1991, Girl Wonder and the Terrific Twins 1991, That New Dress 1991, A New Dress for Maya 1992, Hacker 1992, Girl Wonder's Winter Adventures 1992, Trust Me 1992, Betsey Biggalow the Detective 1992, Betsey Biggalow is Here! 1993, Operation Gadgetman! 1993, Hurricane Betsey 1993, Crazy Crocs 1994, Rachel and the Difference Thief 1994, Magic Betsey 1994, My Friend's a Gris-Quok! 1994, All Aboard 1995, Deadly Dare 1995, Truth! 1995, Jack Sweettooth the 73rd 1995, Whizziwig 1995, Mrs Spoon's Family 1995, A.N.T.I.D.O.T.E. 1996, Betsey's Birthday Surprise 1996, Grandma's Haunted Handbag 1996, Peril on Planet Pelia 1997, The Mellion Moon Mystery 1997, The Computer Ghost 1997, The Secret of the Terrible Hand 1997, Space Race 1997, Pig Heart Boy 1997, Quasar Quartz Quest 1997, Lie Detectives 1998, Aesop's Fables 1998, Words Last Forever 1998, Fangs 1998, Tell Me No Lies 1999, Dangerous Reality 1999, Forbidden Game 1999, Dizzy's Walk 1999, Whizziwig Returns 1999, Hostage 1999, Marty Monster 1999, Noughts and Crosses 2001, Snow Dog 2001, The Monster Crisp-Guzzler 2002, Dead Gorgeous 2002, I Want A Cuddle 2002, Jessica Strange 2002, The Amazing Adventures of Girl Wonder 2003, An Eye for an Eye 2003, Sinclair the Wonder Bear 2003, Cloud Busting 2004, Knife Edge 2004, Ellie and the Cat 2004, Unheard Voices (ed., stories and poems about slavery) 2007, Stuff of Nightmares 2007, The Big Bad Book of Betsey Biggalow 2007, Double Cross 2008, Boys Don't Cry 2011; contribs to A Christmas Tree of Stories 1999, Animal Avengers 1999. *Honours:* Young Telegraph's Fully Booked Award, WHSmith Mind Boggling Book Award 1994, Children's Book Award 2001, Children's Book Circle Eleanor Farjeon Award 2005. *Address:* c/o Random House UK Ltd, 20 Vauxhall Bridge Road, London, SW1V 2SA, England. *Telephone:* (20) 7840-8400. *Fax:* (20) 7840-8778. *Website:* www.randomhouse.co.uk; www.malorieblackman.co.uk.

BLACKWELL, Julian Toby; British bookseller; b. 10 Jan. 1929, s. of the late Sir Basil Henry Blackwell and Marion Christine Soans; m. Jennifer Jocelyn Darley Wykeham 1953; two s. one d. *Education:* Winchester Coll., Trinity Coll., Oxford. *Career:* served 5th Royal Tank Regt 1947–49; 21st SAS (TA) 1950–59; Dir and Chair. various Blackwell cos 1956–99; Chair. Blackwell Group Ltd 1980–94; Pres. Blackwell Ltd (retd) 1995–99, Chair. 1996–99 (retd); Chair. Council, ASLIB 1966–68; Pres. Booksellers' Asscn 1980–82; Chair. Thames Business Advice Centre 1986–97, Heart of England TEC 1989–94, Fox FM 1989–98, Cottontail Ltd 1990; apptd Chair. Son White Memorial Trust 1991, Milestone Group; DL (Oxfordshire) 1988. *Honours:* Hon. DLitt (Robert Gordon) 1997, DUniv (Sheffield Hallam) 1998. *Address:* c/o Blackwell UK, 50 Broad Street, Oxford, OX1 3BQ, England.

BLADES, Ann; Canadian writer, illustrator and teacher; b. 16 Nov. 1947, Vancouver, BC; d. of Arthur Sager and Dorothy Sager; m. David Morrison 1984 (divorced 1986); two s. *Education:* Croft House School, Vancouver and Univ. of British Columbia. *Career:* illustrator 1968–; elementary school teacher, nr Mile 18, BC 1967–71; Registered Nurse 1974–80; artist 1982–; kindergarten teacher, Surrey school district 2001–; exhbns include Vancouver Art Gallery 1971, Biennale of Illustrations, Bratislava, Czechoslovakia 1977, Art Gallery of Ontario 1977, Master Eagle Gallery, New York 1980, Dunlop Art Gallery 1982, Bau Xi Galleries, Toronto and Vancouver 1982–91, Canada at Bologna 1990. *Publications include:* writer and illustrator: Mary of Mile 18 (Book of the Year Award, CACL—Canadian Asscn of Children's Librarians, Hon. List German and Austrian Kinderbuchpreis 1976) 1971, A Boy of Taché (A Child Study Asscn Best Children's Book 1977) 1973, A Cottage at Crescent Beach 1977, By the Sea: An Alphabet Book (Elizabeth Mrazik-Cleaver Canadian Picture Book Award 1986) 1985, Seasons Board Books 1989, Back to the Cabin 1996, Wolf and the Seven Little Kids: Based on a Tale from the Brothers Grimm; illustrations: Jacques the Woodcutter 1977, A Salmon for Simon (Children's Literature Award for Illustration, Canada Council 1979, Amelia Frances Howard-Gibbon Award, CACL) 1978, Six Darn Cows 1979, Pettranella 1980, A Candle for Christmas 1986, Ida and the Wool Smugglers 1987, A Guide to Authors and Illustrators 1988, Anna's Pet 1989, Spring 1989, Summer 1989, Fall 1989, Winter 1989, The Singing Basket 1990, A Dog Came, Too 1992, A Ride for Martha 1993, Pond Seasons 1997, Too Small 2000. *Address:* McClelland and Stewart Ltd, 75 Sherbourne Street, 5th Floor, Toronto, ON M5A 2P9, Canada (office). *Website:* www.mcclelland.com (office).

BLAINEY, Geoffrey Norman, AC; Australian historian and author; b. 11 March 1930, Melbourne, Vic.; s. of Rev. Samuel C. Blainey and Hilda Blainey; m. Ann Heriot 1957; one d. *Education:* Ballarat High School, Wesley Coll., Univ. of Melbourne. *Career:* freelance historian 1951–61; Reader in Econ. History, Univ. of Melbourne 1963–68, Prof. 1968–76, Ernest Scott Prof. of History 1977–88, Dean of Faculty of Arts 1982–87; Prof. of Australian Studies, Harvard Univ., USA 1982–83; columnist in daily newspapers 1974–; Commr, Australian Heritage Comm. 1976–77, Chair. Australia Council 1977–81, Chair. Fed. Govt's Australia-China Council 1979–84, Chair. Commonwealth Literary Fund 1971–73; Pres. Council, Queen's Coll., Univ. of Melbourne 1971–89; Chair. Australian Selection Cttee Commonwealth Fund (Harkness) Fellowships 1983–90; Chancellor Univ. of Ballarat 1994–98; Dir Royal Humane Soc. 1996–2004; Gov. Ian Potter Foundation 1991–; Councillor, Nat. Council for the Centenary of Fed. 1997–2002 (Chair. 2001–02), Australian War Memorial 1997–2004; Del. to Australian Constitutional Convention 1998. *Publications include:* The Peaks of Lyell 1954, Centenary History of the University of Melbourne 1957, Gold and Paper: A History of the National Bank 1958, Mines in the Spinifex 1960, The Rush That Never Ended 1963, A History of Camberwell 1965, If I Remember Rightly: The Memoirs of W. S. Robinson 1966, The Tyranny of Distance 1966, Wesley College: The First Hundred Years (co-author and ed.) 1967, Across a Red World 1968, The Rise of Broken Hill 1968, The Steel Master 1971, The Causes of War 1973, Triumph of the Nomads: A History of Ancient Australia 1975, A Land Half Won 1980, Our Side of the Country 1984, All for Australia 1984, The Great Seesaw 1988, A Game of Our Own 1990, Eye on Australia 1991, Odd Fellows 1992, The Golden Mile 1993, Jumping over the Wheel 1993, A Shorter History of Australia 1994, White Gold 1997, A History of AMP 1999, In Our Time 1999, A Short History of the World 2000, This Land is All Horizons 2001, Black Kettle and Full Moon: Daily Life in a Vanished Australia 2003, A Very Short History of the World 2004, A Short History of the Twentieth Century 2005, A History of Victoria 2006, Sea of Dangers: Captain Cook and His Rivals 2009, A Short History of Christianity 2011. *Honours:* Hon. LLD (Melbourne, Ballarat); Gold Medal, Australian Literature Soc. 1963, Capt. Cook Bicentenary Literary Award 1970, Britannica Award for dissemination of learning, New York 1988, Dublin Prize 1986, Australian Authors' Soc. Book of the Year 2000, Centenary Medal 2003. *Address:* PO Box 257, East Melbourne, Vic. 3002, Australia (home). *Telephone:* (3) 9417-7782 (home). *E-mail:* ablainey@netlink.com.au.

BLAIR, David Chalmers Leslie, Jr, BA; American/British writer, composer and artist; b. 8 April 1951, Long Beach, Calif.; descendant of 13th Earl of Rothes, Scotland. *Education:* California State Univ. at Long Beach, Univ. of Aix-en-Provence; teaching certificate, English as a Second Language. *Career:* music has been performed in California and New York and worldwide in Denmark, Sweden, Ukraine and elsewhere. *Recordings:* 109 albums, including Her Garden of Earthly Delights, Sir Blair of Rothes, The Jack, Danish Pastry, San Francisco, Peace on the White House Lawn, Holocaust in Waco, Europe, St Luke Passion, The Seduction of Inga, My Only Link with Reality, Her Sexual Banquet, Journey of a Poor Man, Psychedelico Band, Brave New Girl, First Day of University. *Publications include:* Death of an Artist 1982, Vive la France 1993, Death of America 1994, Mother 1998, Evening in Wisconsin 2001, The Girls (& Women) I Have Known 2001, A Small Snack Shop in Stockholm-Sweden 2002. *Address:* 19331 105th Avenue, Cadott, WI 54727, USA (home). *Telephone:* (715) 382-4925 (home).

BLAIR, Jessica (see Spence, William John Duncan)

BLAIS, Marie-Claire, CC; Canadian writer; b. 5 Oct. 1939, Québec City; d. of Fernando Blais and Véronique Nolin. *Education:* studied in Québec, Paris, France and USA. *Career:* Guggenheim Foundation Fellowship, New York 1963, 1964; Hon. Prof. Calgary Univ. 1978; mem. Royal Soc. of Canada, Acad. Royale de Belgique, Acad. des Lettres françaises. *Publications:* La belle bête 1959, Tête blanche 1960, Le jour est noir 1962, Existences (poems), Pays voilés (poems) 1964, Une saison dans la vie d'Emmanuel 1965, L'insoumise 1966, Les voyageurs sacrés 1966, David Sterne 1967, L'océan 1967, L'exécution 1968, Manuscrits de Pauline Archange 1968, Vivre, vivre 1969, Les apparences 1970, Le loup 1972, Un Joualonais sa Joualonie 1973, Théâtre radiophonique 1974, Fièvre 1974, Une liaison parisienne 1976, La nef des sorcières 1976, Les nuits de l'underground 1978, Le sourd dans la ville 1980, Visions d'Anna 1982, Pierre 1984, Sommeil d'hiver 1985, Fière 1985, L'île 1988 (plays), L'ange de la solitude (novel) 1989, Un jardin dans la tempête (play) 1990, Parcours d'un Ecrivain: Notes Américaines (essay) 1993, L'Exile (short stories) 1993, Soifs (novel) 1995, Théâtre (Ed.), Des Rencontres Humaines 2002, Dans la foudre et la lumière (novel) 2002, Noces à midi au-dessus de l'abîme (play) 2004, Augustino et le choeur de la destruction (novel) 2007, Naissance de Rebecca à l'ère des Tourments (Gov. Gen's Award for Fiction) 2008, Mal au Bal des Prédateurs 2010. *Honours:* Hon. mem. Boivin Center of French Language and Culture, Univ. of Massachusetts, USA; Chevalier, Légion d'honneur; Dr hc (York Univ., Toronto) 1975, (Lyon) 2003, (Ottawa) 2004, (Lyon) 2005; Prix de la langue française 1961, Prix France-Québec 1964, Prix Médicis 1966, Prix de l'Acad. Française 1983, Prix Athanase-David (Québec) 1983, Prix Nessim Habif (Acad. Royale de Belgique) 1991, Prix de la Fondation Prince Pierre de Monaco, Prix du Gouverneur Général (Canada) (three times), Prix Gilles Corbeil 2006, and others. *Literary Agent:* Agence Goodwin, 839 Sherbrooke Estate, Suite 2, Montréal, H26 1K6, Canada. *Telephone:* (514) 598-5252. *Fax:* (514) 598-1878. *E-mail:* goodleim@qc.aira.com (office). *Address:* 717 Windsor Lane, Key West, FL 33040, USA (home). *Telephone:* (305) 292-9450 (home).

BLAISE, Clark Lee, OC, AB, MFA; American/Canadian writer and academic; *Professor Emeritus, University of Iowa*; b. 10 April 1940, Fargo, ND; s. of Leo Romeo Blaise and Anne Marion Blaise; m. Bharati Mukherjee 1963; two s. *Education:* Denison Univ., Univ. of Iowa. *Career:* Prof., Concordia Univ. 1966–78, York Univ. 1978–80, Skidmore Coll. 1980–81, 1982–83; Visiting Prof., Univ. of Iowa 1981–82, Prof. Emer. 1998–, Dir Int. Writing Program 1990–; Writer-in-Residence, David Thompson Univ. Center 1983, Emory Univ. 1985; Adjunct Prof., Columbia Univ., New York 1986; Visiting Prof., Univ. of California, Berkeley 1998–2000; Distinguished Writer, Long Island Univ. –2005, Southhampton Coll. 2005; mem. PEN. *Publications include:* A North American Education (short stories) 1973, Tribal Justice (short stories) 1974, Days and Nights in Calcutta (with B. Mukherjee) 1977, Here and Now (co-ed.) 1977, Lunar Attractions (Books in Canada First Novel Award 1980) 1978, Lusts 1983, Resident Alien (short stories) 1986, The Sorrow and the Terror: The Haunting Legacy of the Air India Tragedy 1987, Man and His World (short stories) 1992, I Had a Father: A Post-Modern Autobiography 1993, If I Were Me (novel) 1997, Southern Stories (short stories) 2000, New and Selected Stories (four vols) 2000–06, Time Lord: Sir Sandford Fleming and the Creation of Standard Time 2000, Pittsburgh Stories (short stories) 2001, Montreal Stories (short stories) 2003, World Body 2006; contribs to various publs. *Honours:* Hon. PhD (Denison Univ.) 1979, (McGill Univ.) 2005;

Nat. Endowment for the Arts grant 1982, Guggenheim Fellowship, Canada Council grants, Lifetime Achievement Award, American Acad. of Arts and Letters 2003. *Literary Agent:* Janklow & Nesbit Associates, 445 Park Avenue, New York, NY 10022, USA. *Address:* 130 Rivoli Street, San Francisco, CA 94117, USA (home). *Telephone:* (631) 804-7264 (home). *Fax:* (415) 759-9810 (home). *E-mail:* clarquito@aol.com.

BLAKE, James Carlos; American/Mexican writer; b. 26 May 1948, Tampico, Mexico. *Career:* mem. Texas Inst. of Letters. *Publications include:* I, Fierro (novella) 1991, The Pistoleer 1995, The Friends of Pancho Villa 1996, In the Rogue Blood (Los Angeles Times Book Prize) 1997, Red Grass River: A Legend (Chautauqua South Fiction Award 1999) 1998, The Outsider (memoir essay), Borderlands: Short Fiction (Southwest Book Award) 1999, Wildwood Boys: A Novel 2000, Shortcut (memoir essay) 2001, A World of Thieves 2002, Under the Skin (Falcon Award 2007) 2004, Handsome Henry 2005, The Killings of Stanley Ketchel 2006; short stories: Aliens in the Garden 1987, The House of Esperanza 1988, Soldadera 1990, Small Times 1991, The Sharks Below 1992, Three Tales of the Revolution 1993, Runaway Horses 1994, Referee 1998, Old Boys 2000, La Vida Loca 2001. *Honours:* First Prize, Quarterly West Novella Competition 1991, Authors in the Park National Short Story Competition Award 1993. *Address:* Author Mail, 7th Floor, HarperCollins Publishers, 10 East 53rd Street, New York, NY 10022, USA. *Website:* www.harpercollins.com.

BLAKE, Jennifer (see Maxwell, Patricia Anne)

BLAKE, Norman Francis, BA, BLitt, MA; British writer, editor, translator and academic; *Professor Emeritus of English Language and Linguistics, University of Sheffield;* b. 19 April 1934, Ceara, Brazil. *Education:* Univ. of Oxford. *Career:* Lecturer in English Language and Linguistics, Univ. of Sheffield 1959–68, Sr Lecturer 1968–73, Prof. 1973–2004, Prof. Emer. 2004–; Research Prof. De Montfort Univ., Leicester. *Publications include:* The Saga of the Jomsvikings 1962, The Phoenix 1964, Caxton and His World 1969, William Caxton's Reynard the Fox 1970, Middle English Religious Prose 1972, Selections from William Caxton 1973, Caxton's Quattuor Sermiones 1973, Caxton's Own Prose 1975, Caxton: England's First Publisher 1976, The English Language in Medieval Literature 1977, Non-Standard Language in English Literature 1981, Shakespeare's Language 1983, Textual Tradition of the Canterbury Tales 1985, William Caxton: A Bibliographical Guide 1985, Traditional English Grammar and Beyond 1988, Index of Printed Middle English Prose 1985, The Language of Shakespeare (with R. E. Lewis and A. S. G. Edwards) 1989, An Introduction to the Languages of Literature 1990, William Caxton and English Literary Culture 1991, The Cambridge History of the English Language, Vol. II: 1066–1476 1992, Introduction to English Language (with J. Moorhead) 1993, William Caxton 1996, Essays in Shakespeare's Language 1996, History of the English Language 1996, Shakespeare's Non-Standard English – A Dictionary of his Informal Language 2004. *Address:* The School of English Literature, Language and Linguistics, Jessop West, 1 Upper Hanover Street, Sheffield, S3 7RA, England (office). *Telephone:* (11) 4222-8480 (office). *Fax:* (11) 4222-8481 (office). *E-mail:* n.f.blake@sheffield.ac.uk (office); english@sheffield.ac.uk (office). *Website:* www.sheffield.ac.uk/english (office).

BLAKE, Quentin Saxby, OBE, CBE, RDI, MA, FCSD; British artist, writer, illustrator and teacher; b. 16 Dec. 1932, Sidcup, Kent; s. of William Blake and Evelyn Blake. *Education:* Downing Coll., Cambridge, London Inst. of Educ., Chelsea School of Art. *Career:* freelance illustrator 1957–; Tutor, RCA 1965–86, Head of Illustration Dept 1978–86, Sr Fellow RCA 1988, Visiting Prof. 1989–; first British Children's Laureate 1999–2001. *Exhibitions:* Quentin Blake – 50 Years of Illustration, The Gilbert Collection, Somerset House, London 2003–04, Quentin Blake at Christmas, Dulwich Picture Gallery, London 2004–05, In All Directions, Holborn Gallery, Bath, Les Demoiselles des bords de Seine, Le Petit Palais, Paris 2006, Quentin Blake at Kelvingrove, Edinburgh 2008. *Publications include:* Patrick 1968, Angelo 1970, Mister Magnolia 1980, Quentin Blake's Nursery Rhyme Book 1983, The Story of the Dancing Frog 1984, Mrs Armitage on Wheels 1987, Mrs Armitage Queen of the Road, Quentin Blake's ABC 1989, All Join In 1992, Cockatoos 1992, Simpkin 1993, La Vie de la Page 1995, The Puffin Book of Nonsense Verse 1996, Mrs Armitage and the Big Wave 1997, The Green Ship 1998, Clown 1998, Drawing for the Artistically Undiscovered (with John Cassidy) 1999, Fantastic Daisy Artichoke 1999, Words and Pictures 2000, The Laureate's Party 2000, Zagazoo 2000, Tell Me a Picture 2001, Loveykins 2002, A Sailing Boat in the Sky 2002, Laureate's Progress 2002, Angel Pavement 2004, The Life of Birds 2005; illustrations for over 250 works for children and adults, including collaborations with Roald Dahl, Russell Hoban, Joan Aiken, Michael Rosen, John Yeoman, Michael Morpurgo. *Honours:* Hon. Fellow, Univ. of Brighton 1996, Downing Coll. Cambridge 2000, Cardiff Univ. 2006, Hon. RA; Officier, Ordre des Arts et des Lettres 2002; Dr hc (London Inst.) 2000, (Northumbria) 2001, (RCA) 2001, (Open Univ.) 2006, (Loughborough) 2007, (Anglia Ruskin Univ.); Hon. DLitt (Cambridge) 2004. *Literary Agent:* c/o AP Watt Ltd, 20 John Street, London, WC1N 2DR, England. *Telephone:* (20) 7405-6774. *Fax:* (20) 7831-2154. *E-mail:* apw@apwatt.co.uk. *Website:* www.apwatt.co.uk. *Address:* Flat 8, 30 Bramham Gardens, London, SW5 0HF, England (home). *Website:* www.quentinblake.com.

BLAKE-HANNAH, Barbara Makeda; Jamaican/British author, cultural historian and filmmaker; *Managing Director, Jamaica Media Productions Ltd;* b. 5 June 1941, d. of Evon Blake and Veronica Stewart; m. Deeb Roy Hanna 1984; one s. *Education:* Hampton High School, Wolmers Girls' School and Inst. of Public Relations, London. *Career:* TV reporter and interviewer in UK 1968–72, Cuban Film Week 1975; Organizer Annual Festival of Black and Third World Films 1974–85; Special Asst to Minister of Information and Culture 1976–77; Dir of Public Relations Kingston 1978, Montego Bay 1980; mem. Senate (Ind.) 1984–87; Founder and Man. Dir Jamaica Media Productions Ltd 1982–; columnist and feature writer for numerous magazines and newspapers; reporter and interviewer, Jamaica Broadcasting Corpn, RJR-Radio Jamaica, KLAS-FM, IRIE-FM 1972–96; has been a Rastafarian for 30 years, considered an Elder Empress of the Jamaican faith; lecturer at Univ. of West Indies, Vienna, New York, Florida (FIU), USVI. *Film and TV includes:* documentaries and features: Kids Paradise – The Movie, Hotel Kids Paradise – the Great Lost Treasure Hunt, Race, Rhetoric, Rastafari, The Peaceful Gun, By The Land We Live, The Road through the Blue Mountains 2002. *Publications include:* Rastafari – The New Creation 1981, Joseph – A Rasta Reggae Fable 1992, Home – The First School 2006, Growing Out 2010. *Honours:* UN Peace Medal 1974, Gold Adowa Centenary Medal Ethiopian Crown Council 1997. *Address:* PO Box 727, Kingston 6, Jamaica (office). *Telephone:* (876) 384-2923 (office). *E-mail:* jamediapro@hotmail.com (office); i_makeda@yahoo.com.

BLAMIRES, Harry, BA, MA; British writer and academic; b. 6 Nov. 1916, Bradford, Yorks.; m. Nancy Bowles 1940; five s. *Education:* Univ. Coll., Oxford. *Career:* Head, English Dept, King Alfred's Coll., Winchester 1948–72, Dean Arts and Sciences 1972–76; Clyde Kilby Visiting Prof. of English, Wheaton Coll., Wheaton, Ill. 1987; mem. Soc. of Authors. *Publications include:* Repair the Ruins 1950, The Devil's Hunting Grounds 1954, Cold War in Hell 1955, Blessing Unbounded 1955, The Faith and Modern Error 1956, The Will and the Way 1957, The Kirkbride Conversations 1958, The Offering of Man 1959, The Christian Mind 1963, A Defence of Dogmatism 1965, The Bloomsday Book: Guide to Joyce's Ulysses 1966, Word Unheard: Guide Through Eliot's Four Quartets 1969, Milton's Creation 1971, A Short History of English Literature 1974, Where Do We Stand? 1980, Twentieth-Century English Literature 1982, Guide to 20th Century Literature in English 1983, On Christian Truth 1983, Words Made Flesh (aka The Marks of the Maker) 1985, The Victorian Age of Literature 1988, Meat Not Milk 1988, The Age of Romantic Literature 1989, A History of Literary Criticism 1991, The Queen's English 1994, The Cassell Guide to Common Errors in English 1997, The Penguin Guide to Plain English 2000, The Post-Christian Mind 2001, Compose Yourself – and Write Good English 2003, New Town: A Fable 2005. *Honours:* Hon. DLitt (Southampton) 1993. *Address:* Pinfold, 3 Glebe Close, Keswick, Cumbria, CA12 5QQ, England (home). *Telephone:* (1768) 775232 (home).

BLANCHARD, Stephen Thomas; British writer; b. 8 Dec. 1950, Hull, Yorkshire; m. Sarah Rookledge; two s. one d. *Education:* Univ. of Liverpool. *Career:* carpenter, antique dealer, postman; mem. Soc. of Authors. *Publications include:* fiction: Gagarin and I 1995, Wilson's Island 1997, The Paraffin Child 1999; contribs to magazines. *Honours:* McKitterick Prize, Soc. of Authors 1996, First Novel Award, Yorkshire Post 1996. *Literary Agent:* Rachel Calder, The Sayle Literary Agency, 1 Petersfield, Cambridge, CB1 1BB, England. *Telephone:* (1223) 303035. *Fax:* (1223) 301638. *E-mail:* info@sayleliteraryagency.com. *Website:* www.sayleliteraryagency.com. *Address:* 74 Rectory Grove, London, SW4 0ED, England (home). *Telephone:* (20) 7627-3639 (home).

BLAND, Peter; New Zealand poet, reviewer, actor and dramatist; b. 12 May 1934, Scarborough, Yorkshire; m. Beryl Matilda Connolly 1956; one s. two d. *Education:* Victoria Univ. of Wellington. *Career:* journalist, NZ Broadcasting Corpn 1960–64; Co-founder, dir, actor and dramatist, Downstage Theatre, Wellington 1964–68; actor, West End plays and numerous television productions, London; leading role, Came a Hot Friday (New Zealand film) 1985. *Publications include:* poetry: My Side of the Story 1964, The Man with the Carpet Bag 1972, Mr Maui 1976, Stone Tents 1981, The Crusoe Factor 1985, Selected Poems 1987, Paper Boats 1991, Selected Poems 1998, Ports of Call 2003, Night Kite (poems for children) 2004, Let's Meet 2004, Mr Maui's Monologues 2008; plays: Father's Day 1967, George the Mad Ad Man 1967; memoir: Sorry, I'm a Stranger Here Myself 2004. *Honours:* Macmillan-Brown Prize for Creative Writing, Victoria Univ. of Wellington 1958, Melbourne Arts Festival Literary Award 1960, Queen Elizabeth II Arts Council Drama Fellowship 1968, Cholmondeley Award for Poetry 1977, Best Film Actor Award, Guild of Film and TV Arts 1985, Poetry Book Soc. Recommendation 1987, Observer/Arvon Foundation Int. Poetry Prize 1990, NZ Post Children's Book Award 2004. *Address:* 17 Tower Road, Worthing, West Sussex, BN11 1DP (home); Carcanet Press, Fourth Floor, Alliance House, Cross Street, Manchester, M2 7AP, England (office). *Telephone:* (1903) 820401 (home).

BLANNING, Timothy Charles William, LittD, FBA; British academic; *Fellow in History, Sidney Sussex College, Cambridge;* b. 21 April 1942, Wells, Somerset, England; s. of Thomas Walter Blanning and Gwendolen Marchant-Jones; m. Nicky Susan Jones 1988; one s. one d. *Education:* King's School, Bruton, Somerset, Sidney Sussex Coll., Cambridge. *Career:* Research Fellow, Sidney Sussex Coll. 1965–68, Fellow 1968–, Asst Lecturer in History, Univ. of Cambridge 1972–76, Lecturer 1976–87, Reader in Modern European History 1987–92, Prof. of Modern European History 1992–2009. *Publications include:* Joseph II and Enlightened Despotism 1970, Reform and Revolution in Mainz 1743–1803 1974, The French Revolution in Germany 1983, The Origins of the French Revolutionary Wars 1986, The French Revolution: Aristocrats versus

Bourgeois? 1987, Joseph II 1994, The French Revolutionary Wars 1787–1802 1996, The French Revolution: Class War or Culture Clash? 1998, The Culture of Power and the Power of Culture 2002, The Pursuit of Glory: Europe 1648–1815 2007; Ed.: The Oxford Illustrated History of Modern Europe 1996, The Rise and Fall of the French Revolution 1996, History and Biography: Essays in Honour of Derek Beales (with Peter Wende), Reform in Great Britain and Germany 1750–1850 1999, The Short Oxford History of Europe: The Eighteenth Century 2000, The Short Oxford History of Europe: The Nineteenth Century 2000, Unity and Diversity in European Culture *c.* 1800 2006, The Triumph of Music 2008, The Romantic Revolution 2010. *Address:* Sidney Sussex College, Cambridge, CB2 3HU, England (office). *Telephone:* (1223) 338854 (office). *Fax:* (1223) 338884 (office). *E-mail:* tcb1000@cam.ac.uk (office).

BLAS DE ROBLÈS, Jean-Marie; French writer, poet and archaeologist; b. 1954, Sidi-Bel-Abbès, Algeria. *Education:* Univ. of Paris-Sorbonne, Coll. de France. *Career:* teacher and headmaster, Maison de la Culture Française, Univ. of Fortaleza, Brazil 1982; Lecturer in French Literature, Univ. of Tianjin, China, Univ. of Palermo, Italy, Alliance Française, Taipei, Taiwan; Ed. and Publisher Archéologies series, Edisud; Ed. Aouras (archaeological research journal); mem. French Archaeological Mission in Libya 1986–. *Publications include:* La mémoire de riz et autres contes (short stories) (Prix de la nouvelle, Académie Française) 1982, L'Impudeur des choses (novel) 1987, Le Rituel des dunes (novel) 1989, Une certaine façon de se taire (short stories) 1991, Là où les tigres sont chez eux (novel) (Prix du Roman FNAC, Prix du Jury Jean Giono, Prix Médicis) 2008, Méduse en son miroir (essays) 2008, La Montagne de minuit 2010; contrib. essays and poetry to literary and archaeological journals and anthologies. *Address:* Editions Zulma, 122 Boulevard Haussmann, 75008 Paris, France. *Telephone:* 1-58-22-19-90. *Fax:* 1-58-22-19-99. *E-mail:* zulma@zulma.fr; jeanmarie@blasderobles.com. *Website:* www.zulma.fr; www.blasderobles.com.

BLASHFORD-SNELL, Col John Nicholas, OBE, FRSGS; British explorer, writer and broadcaster; *President, Scientific Exploration Society*; b. 22 Oct. 1936, Hereford, Herefords.; s. of the late Rev. Prebendary Leland John Blashford-Snell and Gwendolen Ives Blashford-Snell (née Sadler); m. Judith Frances Sherman 1960; two d. *Education:* Victoria Coll., Jersey, Royal Mil. Acad., Sandhurst. *Career:* commissioned in Royal Engineers 1957; Commdr Operation Aphrodite (Expedition), Cyprus 1959–61; Instructor, Jr Leaders Regt Royal Engineers 1962–63; Instructor, RMA, Sandhurst 1963–66; Adjt, 3rd Div. Engineers 1966–67; Commdr The Great Abbai Expedition (Blue Nile) 1968; attended Staff Coll., Camberley 1969; Chair. Scientific Exploration Soc. 1969–2009, currently Pres.; Commdr Dahlak Quest Expedition 1969–70, British Trans-Americas Expedition (Darien Gap) 1971–72; Officer Commdg 48th Field Squadron, Royal Engineers 1972–74; Commdr, Zaïre River Expedition 1974–75; CO, Jr Leaders Regt, Royal Engineers 1976–78; Dir of Operations, Operation Drake 1978–81; Staff Officer, Ministry of Defence 1978–91, Consultant 1992–; Commdr, Fort George Volunteers 1982; Operations Dir, Operation Raleigh 1982–88, Dir-Gen. 1989–91; Dir SES Tibet Expedition 1987; Leader, Kalahari Quest Expedition 1990, Karnali Quest Expedition 1991, Karnali Gorges Expedition 1992, numerous exploration projects thereafter; Trustee, Operation New World 1995–; Chair. Just a Drop Charity 2001–04, Pres. 2004–, The Liverpool Construction-Crafts Guild 2003–05, Pres. 2005–; Pres. The British Travel Health Assn 2006–. *Publications include:* Weapons and Tactics (with T. Wintringham) 1970, The Expedition Organiser's Guide (with Richard Snailham) 1970, Where the Trails Run Out 1974, In the Steps of Stanley 1975, Expeditions the Experts' Way (with A. Ballantine) 1977, A Taste for Adventure 1978, Operation Drake (with M. Cable) 1981, In the Wake of Drake (with M. Cable) 1982, Mysteries: Encounters with the Unexplained 1983, Operation Raleigh, The Start of an Adventure 1987, Operation Raleigh, Adventure Challenge (with Ann Tweedy) 1988, Operation Raleigh, Adventure Unlimited (with Ann Tweedy) 1990, Something Lost Behind the Ranges 1994, Mammoth Hunt (with Rula Lenska) 1996, Kota Mama: Retracing the Lost Trade Routes of Ancient South American Peoples (with Richard Snailham) 2000, East to the Amazon (with Richard Snailham) 2002. *Honours:* Freeman of the City of Hereford; Hon. Pres. The Vole Club 1996–; Hon. Life Pres. The Centre for Fortean Zoology 2003–; Hon. Fellow, Liverpool John Moores Univ. 2010; Hon. DSc (Durham); Hon. DEng (Bournemouth) 1997; The Livingstone Medal, The Darien Medal (Colombia) 1972, The Segrave Trophy, Paul Harris Fellow, Rotary International, Royal Geographical Soc. Patrons' Medal 1993, Gold Medal, Inst. of Royal Engineers 1994, La Paz Medal (Bolivia) 2000. *Address:* Scientific Exploration Society, Expedition Base, Motcombe, nr Shaftesbury, Dorset, SP7 9PB, England (office). *Telephone:* (1747) 854456 (office). *E-mail:* jbs@ses-explore.org (office). *Website:* www.johnblashfordsnell.org.uk.

BLATNIK, Andrej, MA, PhD; Slovenian author, editor and academic; *Associate Professor, University of Ljubljana*; b. 22 May 1963, Ljubljana. *Education:* Univ. of Ljubljana. *Career:* mem. Editorial Bd Literatura (monthly journal) 1984–; Ed. Cankarjeva publishing house; Assoc. Prof., Univ. of Ljubljana; mem. Int. Writing Program, Univ. of Iowa, USA 1993, Int. Writers Center, Old Dominion Univ., Va, USA 1995, Ledig House Int. Writers Colony 1998; Pres. Jury, Vilenica Prize. *Publications include:* novels: Plamenice in solze (Torches and Tears) 1987, Tao ljubezni (Closer to Love) 1996, Spremeni me (Change Me) 2008; short stories: Šopki za Adama venijo (Bouquets for Adam Fade) 1983, Biografije brezimenih (Biographies of the Nameless) 1989, Menjave ko (Skinswaps) 1990, Zakon elje (Law of Desire) 2000, Saj razumeš? (Do You Understand?) 2009; non-fiction: Labirinti papirja (Paper Labyrinths) (essays) 1994, Gledanje čez ramo (Looking over the Shoulder) 1996, Neonski pečati (Neon Seals) 2005, Pisanje kratke zgodbe (Writing Short Stories) 2010; contribs include short stories in anthologies including The Day Tito Died 1993, The Imagination From Terra Incognita 1997, Afterwards 1999, Best European Short Stories 2010; trans.: Sylvia Plath's The Bell Jar, Paul Bowles' The Sheltering Sky. *Honours:* Prešernov sklad Nat. Award, Upančičeva Award, City of Ljubljana, Zlata ptica, Fulbright Fellowship. *Address:* Vošnjakova 4B, 1000 Ljubljana, Slovenia (home). *E-mail:* Andrej.Blatnik2@guest.arnes.si (office). *Website:* www.andrejblatnik.com.

BLATTY, William Peter, MA, DHumLitt; American writer and screenwriter; b. 7 Jan. 1928, New York, NY; s. of Peter Blatty and Mary (née Mouakad) Blatty; m. Julie Alicia Witbrodt 1983; three s. three d. *Education:* Georgetown Univ., George Washington Univ. and Seattle Univ. *Career:* served in USAF 1951–54; ed. with US Information Agency 1955–57; Publicity Dir Univ. Southern Calif. 1957–58; Public Relations Dir Loyola Univ., Los Angeles 1959–60. *Screenplays:* The Man from the Diner's Club 1961, Promise Her Anything 1962, John Goldfarb, Please Come Home 1963, A Shot in the Dark 1964, The Great Bank Robbery 1967, What Did You Do in the War, Daddy? 1965, Gunn 1967, Darling Lili 1968, Twinkle, Twinkle, 'Killer' Kane (Golden Globe for Best Movie Screenplay) 1973, Mastermind 1976, The Ninth Configuration (also dir) 1978, The Exorcist (Golden Globe for Best Movie Screenplay 1980) 1973, The Exorcist III 1990, Exorcist: The Beginning 2004. *Writing for television:* Watts Made Out of Thread (series episode) (American Film Festival Blue Ribbon and Gabriel Award). *Publications:* Which Way to Mecca, Jack? 1959, John Goldfarb, Please Come Home 1963, I, Billy Shakespeare 1965, Twinkle, Twinkle, 'Killer' Kane 1966, The Exorcist 1970, I'll Tell Them I Remember You (autobiog.) 1973, The Exorcist: From Novel to Film 1974, The Ninth Configuration 1978, Legion 1983, Demons Five, Exorcists Nothing 1996, Elsewhere 1999, Dimiter 2010. *Honours:* Acad. Award of Acad. Motion Picture, Arts and Sciences 1973, Acad. of Fantasy, Science Fiction and Horror award 1980, Stoker Award for Lifetime Achievement 1998. *Address:* c/o Tor/Forge, Tom Doherty Associates, LLC, 175 Fifth Avenue, New York, NY 10010, USA (office).

BLAYNE, Diana (see Kyle, Susan Eloise Spaeth)

BLAŽKOVÁ, Jaroslava; Slovak novelist and editor; b. 15 Nov. 1933, Valasské Mezirící, Moravia. *Education:* Comenius Univ., Bratislava. *Career:* moved between Slovakia and Czech lands in her youth; worked at Slovak Radio and later in culture section of Smena newspaper; started publishing short stories in various periodicals from 1956; settled in Canada after Soviet invasion of Czechoslovakia; worked for CBC and later for 68 Publishers. *Publications include:* Nylonový mesiac (novel) 1961, Tóno, ja a mravce 1961, Ostrov kapitána Hašašara 1962, Ohňostroj pre deduška (juvenile novel) (King Frana Price 1963, UNESCO Prize 1964) 1962, Poviedka plná snehu (short story, A Tale Full of Snow) 1964, Jahniatko a grandi (juvenile short stories) 1964, Daduška a jarabáč 1965, Ako si mačky kúpili televízor 1967, Môj skvelý brat Robinson (novel) 1968, Rozprávky z červenej ponožky 1969, Svadba v Káne Galilejskej (short stories) 2001, Minka a pyžaminka 2003, Traja nebojsovia a duch Miguel 2003, Happyendy 2005. *Honours:* Price Bibiana Triple Rose Award 1999.

BLEAKLEY, David Wylie, OBE, BA, MA; British politician, educator and writer; b. 11 Jan. 1925, Belfast; m. Winifred Wason 1949; three s. *Education:* Ruskin Coll., Oxford, Queen's Univ., Belfast. *Career:* Prin., Belfast Further Educ. Centre 1955–58; MP (Labour Party), Parl. of Northern Ireland, Belfast 1958–65; Lecturer in Industrial Relations, Kivukoni Coll., Dar-es-Salaam 1967–69; Head of Dept of Economics and Political Studies, Methodist Coll., Belfast 1969–79; Minister of Community Relations 1971; mem. Northern Ireland Labour Party, East Belfast, Northern Ireland Assembly 1973–75; Visiting Sr Lecturer in Peace Studies, Univ. of Bradford 1974–; Chief Exec. Irish Council of Churches 1980–92; apptd Privy Councillor 1971; mem. Church Mission Soc. (Pres. 1983–97). *Publications include:* Ulster Since 1800: Regional History Symposium 1958, Young Ulster and Religion in the Sixties 1964, Peace in Ulster 1972, Faulkner: A Biography 1974, Saidie Patterson: Irish Peacemaker 1980, In Place of Work 1981, The Shadow and Substance 1983, Beyond Work: Free to Be 1985, Will the Future Work? 1986, Europe: A Christian Vision 1992, Ageing and Ageism in a Technological Society 1994, Peace in Ireland: Two States, One People 1995, C. S. Lewis: At Home in Ireland 1998; contribs to BBC and periodicals. *Honours:* Hon. MA (Open Univ.) 1975.

BLEASDALE, Alan; British playwright and novelist; b. 23 March 1946, s. of George Bleasdale and Margaret Bleasdale; m. Julia Moses 1970; two s. one d. *Education:* Wade Deacon Grammar School, Widnes, Padgate Teachers Training Coll. *Career:* schoolteacher 1967–75. *Publications:* Scully 1975, Who's Been Sleeping in My Bed? 1977, No More Sitting on the Old School Bench 1979, Boys from the Blackstuff 1982, Are You Lonesome Tonight? (Best Musical, Evening Standard Drama Awards 1985) 1985, No Surrender (film script) 1986, Having a Ball 1986, It's a Madhouse 1986, The Monocled Mutineer (televised 1986) 1986, GBH (TV series) 1991, On the Ledge 1993, Jake's Progress (TV) 1995, Oliver Twist 1999 (Best Drama Series, TV and Radio Industries Club 2000). *Honours:* Hon. DLitt (Liverpool Polytechnic) 1991; BAFTA Writers Award 1982, Royal TV Soc. Writer of the Year 1982; Best Writer Monte Carlo Int. TV Festival 1996 (for Jake's Progress). *Literary Agent:* c/o The Agency, 24 Pottery Lane, Holland Park, London, W11 4LZ,

England. *Telephone:* (20) 7727-1346. *E-mail:* info@theagency.co.uk. *Website:* www.theagency.co.uk.

BLEDSOE, Lucy Jane, BA; American writer and editor; b. 1 Feb. 1957, Portland, OR; pnr Patricia E. Mullan. *Education:* Williams Coll., Univ. of California at Berkeley. *Career:* Instructor, Univ. of California Graduate Program of Creative Writing; Instructor, Creative Writing workshops in adult literacy programmes; mem. Media Alliance; Nat. Writers Union; PEN. *Publications include:* Sweat: Stories and a Novella 1995, The Big Bike Race 1995, Tracks in the Snow 1997, Working Parts 1997, Gay Travels (ed) 1998, Lesbian Travels (ed) 1998, Cougar Canyon 2001, Hoop Girlz 2002, This Wild Silence 2003, The Antarctic Scoop 2003, How to Survive in Antarctica 2006, Biting the Apple 2007, The Big Bang Symphony 2010; non-fiction: The Ice Cave; contribs to books and magazines. *Honours:* PEN Syndicated Fiction Award 1985, Creative Writing Fellowship, Money for Women/Barbara Deming Memorial Fund 1989, Gay/Lesbian/Bisexual Award for Literature 1998. *E-mail:* lucy@lucyjanebledsoe.com (office). *Website:* www.lucyjanebledsoe.com.

BLEGVAD, Peter; American singer, songwriter and cartoonist; b. 14 Aug. 1951, New York. *Career:* Founder-mem. Slapp Happy 1971–; collaborations with Henry Cow, Faust, Golden Palominos, John Greaves, Chris Cutler, Lisa Herman; creator of Leviathan cartoon strip, Independent on Sunday 1992–99. *Recordings include:* albums: with Slapp Happy: Sort Of 1973, Slapp Happy 1974, Ça Va 1998; with Slapp Happy and Henry Cow: Desperate Straights, In Praise Of Learning; solo: Kew Rhône (with John Greaves and Lisa Herman) 1977, Smell of a Friend by The Lodge (with John Greaves), Dr Huelsenbeck's Mentale Heilmethode (with John Greaves) 1992, The Naked Shakespeare 1983, Knights Like This 1985, Downtime 1989, King Strut & Other Stories 1990, Unearthed (with John Greaves) 1995, Just Woke Up (with John Greaves and Chris Cutler) 1995, Hangman's Hill 1998, Choices Under Pressure 2001, Orpheus the Lowdown (with Andy Partridge) 2004. *Publication:* The Book of Leviathan 2001. *Website:* www.leviathan.co.uk.

BLICKER, Seymour, BA; Canadian writer; b. 12 Feb. 1940, Montréal; m. Susan Wanda Colman 1963; three s. one d. *Education:* Loyola Coll. 1962. *Career:* Special Lecturer, Creative Writing, Concordia Univ. 1978–90; mem. Writers Guild of Canada, Playwrights Union of Canada, Acad. of Canadian Cinema and Television Writers' Guild of America West. *Film and television:* various works including episodes of Emmy Award-winning The Barney Miller Show, Side Street series (CBC), Urban Angel series and the film The Kid starring Rod Steiger. *Publications include:* fiction: Blues Chased a Rabbit 1969, Shmucks 1972, The Last Collection 1976; stage plays: Up Your Alley 1987, Never Judge a Book By Its Cover 1987, Pals 1995, Home Free 1998, Pipe Dreams 1999, Found Money 2003. *Honours:* Canada Council Sr Arts Fellowship 1974, British Council Int. New Playwriting Award for the Americas Region 1997. *Address:* 7460 Kingsley Road, No. 804, Montréal, PQ H4W 1P3, Canada (home). *Telephone:* (514) 485-8263 (home); (819) 322-6232 (office). *Fax:* (514) 485-8263 (home); (819) 322-6232 (office). *E-mail:* seymour.blicker@sympatico.ca (home).

BLISS, (John William) Michael, CM, PhD, FRSC; Canadian historian, academic and writer; *University Professor Emeritus of History, University of Toronto*; b. 18 Jan. 1941, Kingsville, Ont.; s. of Quartus Bliss and Anne L. Crow; m. Elizabeth J. Haslam 1963; one s. two d. *Education:* Kingsville Dist High School and Univ. of Toronto. *Career:* Teaching Asst, Harvard Univ. 1967–68; Dept of History, Univ. of Toronto 1968–72, Prof. 1975–99, Univ. Prof. 1999–2006, Prof. Emer. 2006–, also held cross-appointments to Faculty of Medicine and to Inst. for History and Philosophy of Science and Tech.; Sr Fellow, Massey Coll. *Publications include:* A Living Profit 1974, A Canadian Millionaire: The Life of Sir Joseph Flavelle (Sir John A. Macdonald Prize, Canadian Historical Asscn, F.-X. Garneau Medal) 1978, The Discovery of Insulin (William A. Welch Medal, American Asscn for the History of Medicine 1984, City of Toronto Book Award 1983) 1982, Banting: A Biography 1984, Northern Enterprise: Five Centuries of Canadian Business (Nat. Business Book Award for the best book about business published in Canada, Award of Merit of Asscn for Canadian Studies) 1987, Plague: A Story of Smallpox in Montreal 1991, Right Honourable Men: The Descent of Canadian Politics from Macdonald to Mulroney 1994, William Osler: A Life in Medicine (Canadian Historical Asscn Ferguson Prize for the best book of the year in a field of history other than Canadian, Jason Hannah Medical Award, RSC) 1999, Harvey Cushing: A Life in Surgery 2005, The Making of Modern Medicine: Turning Points in the Treatment of Disease 2010; essays in various newspapers and magazines. *Honours:* Hon. Fellow, Royal Coll. of Physicians and Surgeons of Canada; Hon. DLitt (McGill) 2001; numerous awards including Tyrrell Medal 1987, RSC 1988, Oswald T. Avery Medal, Dalhousie History of Medicine Soc. 1998. *Address:* Department of History, University of Toronto, Sidney Smith Hall, 100 St. George Street, Toronto, ON M5S 3G3, Canada (office). *Telephone:* (416) 978-3363 (office). *Fax:* (416) 978-6647 (office). *E-mail:* m.bliss@sympatico.ca; history@chass.utoronto.ca (office). *Website:* www.history.utoronto.ca (office).

BLOCH, Chana, BA, MA, PhD; American poet, translator, critic, essayist and academic; *Professor Emerita of English, Mills College*; b. 15 March 1940, New York, NY; d. of Benjamin Faerstein and Rose Rosenberg; m. 1st Ariel Bloch 1969 (divorced); two s.; m. 2nd David Sutter 2003. *Education:* Cornell Univ., Brandeis Univ., Univ. of California, Berkeley. *Career:* Instructor of English, Hebrew Univ., Jerusalem 1964–67; Assoc. in Near Eastern Studies, Univ. of California, Berkeley 1967–69; Instructor, Mills Coll., Oakland, Calif. 1973–75, Asst Prof. 1975–81, Assoc. Prof. 1981–87, Chair. Dept of English 1986–89, Prof. of English 1987–2002, Dir Creative Writing Program 1993–2001, Prof. Emer. 2002–; mem. PEN, Poetry Soc. of America, Modern Language Asscn, Asscn for Literary Scholars and Critics. *Publications:* poetry: The Secrets of the Tribe 1981, The Past Keeps Changing 1992, Mrs Dumpty 1998, Blood Honey 2009; literary criticism: Spelling the Word: George Herbert and the Bible 1985; trans.: Dahlia Ravikovitch: A Dress of Fire 1978, Yehuda Amichai: The Selected Poetry (with Stephen Mitchell) 1986, Dahlia Ravikovitch: The Window: New and Selected Poems (with Ariel Bloch) 1989, The Song of Songs: A New Translation, Introduction and Commentary (with Ariel Bloch) 1995, Open Closed Open, by Yehuda Amichai (with Chana Kronfeld) 2000, Hovering at a Low Altitude: The Collected Poetry of Dahlia Ravikovitch (with Chana Kronfeld) 2009; contribs poetry, trans, criticism and essays in various anthologies and periodicals. *Honours:* Discovery Award, Poetry Centre, New York 1974, Trans. Award, Columbia Univ. 1978, Nat. Endowment for the Humanities Fellowship 1980, Book of the Year Award, Conf. on Christianity and Literature 1986, Writers Exchange Award, Poets and Writers 1988, Rockefeller Foundation Residency, Bellagio Study Center 2004, Yaddo Residencies 1988, 1990, 1993, 1994, 1995, 1996, 1997, 1999, 2001, MacDowell Colony Residencies 1988, 1992, 1993, 2000, Djerassi Foundation Residencies 1989, 1991, Nat. Endowment for the Arts Fellowships 1989–90, 1999, Felix Pollak Prize 1998, California Book Award Silver Medal in Poetry 1999, PEN Award for Poetry in Trans. 2001, Alice Fay di Castagnola Award, Poetry Soc. of America 2004. *Literary Agent:* Georges Borchardt, Inc., 136 East 57th Street, New York, NY 10022, USA. *Telephone:* (212) 753-5785. *Fax:* (212) 838-6518. *E-mail:* barbara@gbagency.com. *Address:* 12 Menlo Place, Berkeley, CA 94707, USA (home). *Telephone:* (510) 524-8459 (home). *Fax:* (510) 524-8459 (home). *E-mail:* chana@mills.edu (office). *Website:* www.chanabloch.com.

BLOCK, Lawrence, (Jill Emerson); American novelist; m. Lynnen Block. *Career:* mem. Mystery Writers of America (fmr Pres.), Private Eye Writers of America (fmr Pres.). *Publications include:* novels: You Could Call it Murder 1961, Mona 1961, Cinderella Sims 1961, Coward's Kiss 1961, The Girl With the Long Green Heart 1965, Deadly Honeymoon 1967, After the First Death 1969, The Specialists 1969, Such Men are Dangerous 1969, The Triumph of Evil 1971, Ronald Rabbit is a Dirty Old Man 1971, Not Comin' Home to You 1974, Ariel 1980, Random Walk 1988, Small Town 2003, A Diet of Treacle 2008, Killing Castro 2009; Evan Tanner series: The Thief who Couldn't Sleep 1966, The Canceled Czech 1966, Tanner's Twelve Swingers 1967, Two for Tanner (aka The Scoreless Thai) 1968, Tanner's Tiger 1968, Here Comes a Hero 1968, Me Tanner, You Jane 1970, Tanner on Ice 1998; Matthew Scudder series: The Sins of the Fathers 1976, In the Midst of Death 1976, Time to Murder and Create 1977, A Stab in the Dark 1981, Eight Million Ways to Die 1982, When the Sacred Ginmill Closes 1986, Out on the Cutting Edge 1989, A Ticket to the Boneyard 1990, A Dance at the Slaughterhouse 1991, A Walk Among the Tombstones 1992, The Devil Knows You're Dead 1993, A Long Line of Dead Men 1994, Even the Wicked 1996, Everybody Dies 1998, Hope to Die 2001, All The Flowers Are Dying 2005, A Drop of The Hard Stuff 2011; Bernie Rhodenbarr series: Burglars Can't be Choosers 1977, The Burglar in the Closet 1978, The Burglar Who Liked to Quote Kipling 1979, The Burglar Who Studied Spinoza 1980, The Burglar Who Painted Like Mondrian 1983, The Burglar Who Traded Ted Williams 1994, The Burglar Who Thought he was Bogart 1995, The Burglar in the Library 1997, The Burglar in the Rye 1999, The Burglar on the Prowl 2004; Chip Harrison series: No Score 1970, Chip Harrison Scores Again 1971, Make Out With Murder (aka The Five Little Rich Girls) 1974, The Topless Tulip Caper 1975; Keller series: Hit Man 1998, Hit List 2000, Hit Parade 2006, Hit and Run 2008, Step by Step: A Pedestrian Memoir 2009, Hellcats and Honeygirls (with Donald E. Westlake) 2010; as Jill Emerson: Getting Off: A Novel of Sex & Violence 2011; short stories: Sometimes They Bite 1983, Like A Lamb To Slaughter 1984, Some Days You Get The Bear 1993, Ehrengraf for The Defense 1994, One Night Stands 1999, Enough Rope 2002, One Night Stands And Lost Weekends 2008; contribs to anthologies; articles and short stories in American Heritage, Redbook, Playboy, Cosmopolitan, GQ, New York Times. *Honours:* Nero Wolfe Award 1979, four Shamus Awards, Japanese Maltese Falcon awards 1986, 1989, four Edgar Awards, Philip Marlowe Award, Life Achievement award, Private Eye Writers of America, Mystery Writers of America Grand Master, two Société 813 trophies, presented with the key to the city of Muncie. *Address:* 299 W 12th Street, Suite 12-D, New York, NY 10014, USA (home). *E-mail:* LawBloc@aol.com (home). *Website:* www.lawrenceblock.com.

BLOEM, Marion; Dutch novelist, filmmaker and artist; b. 24 Aug. 1952, d. of the late Alexander Kouthoofd Flower and of Jacqueline Flower. *Education:* State Univ. of Utrecht. *Films include:* shorts: Feest (scriptwriter, dir, prod.) 1978, Buitenspel (scriptwriter, dir, prod.) 1979, Aanraken (script with Ivan Wolffers, dir, prod.) 1980, Nieuwsgierig (script with Ivan Wolffers, dir, prod.) 1980, Borsten (script with Ivan Wolffers, dir, prod.) 1981, De Tovenaarsleerling (scriptwriter, dir) (VPRO Kid Screen Award 1987) 1986; documentaries: Het land van mijn ouders (scriptwriter, dir) 1983, Wij komen als vrienden (scriptwriter, dir, producer) 1984. *Video and television includes:* Vrijheid (dir, producer), Lot (script, dir) 1984, Screentest (script, dir) 1985, Cursus voor beginners in de liefde (script with Ivan Wolffers, dir) 1988, Walden Place (script, dir, producer) 1993, De kunst van het vertellen (dir, prod.) 1999, Liefde is soms lastig, liefste 2002. *Radio:* De stem van mijn vader (scriptwriter) 1996. *Publications include:* Geen gewoon Indisch meisje (novel, trans. as Not an Ordinary Indonesian Girl) 1983, Kermis achter kerk (juvenile) 1984, Brieven van Souad (juvenile) 1986, Waar schuil je als het regent? (juvenile) 1987, Lange reizen korte liefdes (novel) 1987, Rio (novel) 1987, Meisjes vechten niet (novel) 1988, Vaders van betekenis (novel) 1989, Gezichten van Zon (poems) 1990, Matabia (juvenile) (Jenny Smelik IBBY Prize 1992) 1990, Vliegers onder het matras (short stories) 1990, Zwartwit in en achter kleuren (poems) 1992, Schilderijen en gedichten (poems) 1992, De honden van Slip (novel, trans. as Slipi's Dogs) 1992, Blauwen noemden ze ons (poems) 1993, De leugen van de kaketoe (novel, trans. as The Cockatoo's Lie) 1993, Op de brug naar de tempel (poems) 1994, Hoop op nieuwe woorden (poems and silk prints) 1995, De geheime plek (juvenile) 1995, Muggen mensen olifanten (short stories) 1995, De smaak van het onbekende (novel) 1995, De droom van de magere tijger (juvenile) 1996, Mooie meisjesmond (novel) 1997, Ver van familie (novel) 1999, Voor altijd moeder (short stories and poems) 2001, Games4Girls (novel) 2001, Amsterdam, A Traveller's Literary Companion 2001, Liefde is soms lastig liefste (poems) 2002, Thuis (art book) 2003, De V van Venus (novel) 2004, Zo groot als Hugo (illustrated biog., trans. as As Great as Hugo) 2004, De kleine krijger (juvenile, trans. as The Little Warrior) 2005, Vervlochten grenzen (novel) 2009, Geen Requiem (poem) 2010, Als je man verandert (non-fiction) 2010, Meer dan mannelijk 2011. *Honours:* Du Perron Prize 1993. *Address:* c/o Arbeiderspers, Herengracht 376, 1016 CH Amsterdam, Netherlands. *Website:* www.marionbloem.nl.

BLONDEL, Jean Fernand Pierre, BLitt; French political scientist, writer and academic; *Professorial Fellow, European University Institute*; b. 26 Oct. 1929, Toulon; m. 1st Michele Hadet 1954 (divorced); m. 2nd Teresa Ashton 1982; two d. *Education:* Institut d'etudes politiques, Paris, Univ. of Paris, St Antony's Coll., Oxford, Univ. of Manchester, UK. *Career:* Lecturer in Political Insts, Univ. of Keele, UK 1958–63; Fellow, American Council of Learned Socs 1963–64; Founding Prof., Dept of Govt, Univ. of Essex 1964–83; Co-founder and Dir European Consortium of Political Research 1970–78; Scholar, Russell Sage Foundation 1984–85; Prof. of Political Science, European Univ. Inst., Florence, Italy 1985–94, Professorial Fellow 1994–; Visiting Prof., Univ. of Siena 1995–; mem. American Political Science Asscn, Asscn Française de Science Politique, British Political Studies Asscn. *Publications include:* Voters, Parties and Leaders 1963, An Introduction to Conservative Government 1969, Comparative Legislatures 1973, Government of France 1974, Political Parties 1978, World Leaders 1980, The Discipline of Politics 1982, The Organisation of Governments 1982, Government Ministers in the Contemporary World 1985, Political Leadership 1993, Governing Together (ed. with F. Muller-Rommel) 1993, Comparative Government (second edn) 1995, Party and Government (ed. with M. Cotta) 1996, People and Parliament in the European Union (co-author) 1998, Democracy, Governance and Economic Performance (ed. with I. Marsh and T. Inoguchi) 1999, The Nature of Party Government (ed. with M. Cotta) 2000, Cabinets in Eastern Europe (with F. Muller-Rommel) 2001, Political Cultures in Asia and Europe (co-author) 2006, Governing New European Democracies (co-author) 2007; contribs to professional journals. *Honours:* Dr hc (Univ. of Salford) 1990, (Univ. of Essex) 1992, (Catholic Univ. of Louvain) 1992, (Univ. of Turku) 1995; Hon. mem. American Science Acad. 2004–, Swedish Royal Acad. of Sciences; Johan Skytte Prize 2004. *Address:* 15 Marloes Road, London, W8 6LQ, England (home); c/o European University Institute, Via dei Roccettini 9, 50016 San Domenico di Fiesole, Italy. *Telephone:* (20) 7370-6008 (home); (055) 21-00-38 (office). *E-mail:* jean.blondel@iue.it (office).

BLOOM, Harold, PhD; American academic and writer; *Sterling Professor of Humanities and English, Yale University*; b. 11 July 1930, New York; s. of William Bloom and Paula Lev; m. Jeanne Gould 1958; two s. *Education:* Cornell and Yale Univs, Pembroke Coll., Cambridge, UK. *Career:* mem. Faculty, Yale Univ. 1955–, Prof. of English 1965–77, DeVane Prof. of Humanities 1974–77, Prof. of Humanities 1977–, Sterling Prof. of Humanities and English 1983–; Visiting Prof., Hebrew Univ. Jerusalem 1959, Breadloaf Summer School 1965–66, Soc. for Humanities, Cornell Univ. 1968–69; Visiting Univ. Prof., New School of Social Research, New York 1982–84; Charles Eliot Norton Prof. of Poetry, Harvard Univ. 1987–88; Berg Visiting Prof. of English, New York Univ. 1988–2004; mem. American Acad. and Inst. of Arts and Letters, American Philosophical Soc.; Fulbright Fellow 1955, Guggenheim Fellow 1962. *Publications:* Shelley's Mythmaking 1959, The Visionary Company 1961, Blake's Apocalypse 1963, Commentary to Blake 1965, Yeats 1970, The Ringers in the Tower 1971, The Anxiety of Influence 1973, Wallace Stevens: The Poems of Our Climate 1977, A Map of Misreading 1975, Kabbalah and Criticism 1975, Poetry and Repression 1976, Figures of Capable Imagination 1976, The Flight to Lucifer: A Gnostic Fantasy 1979, Agon: Towards a Theory of Revisionism 1981, The Breaking of the Vessels 1981, The Strong Light of the Canonical 1987, Freud: Transference and Authority 1988, Poetics of Influence: New and Selected Criticism 1988, Ruin the Sacred Truths 1989, The Book of J 1990, The American Religion 1991, The Western Canon 1994, Omens of Millennium 1996, Shakespeare: The Invention of the Human 1998, How to Read and Why 2000, Stories and Poems for Extremely Intelligent Children of All Ages 2000, Genius: A Mosaic of One Hundred Exemplary Creative Minds 2002, Hamlet: Poem Unlimited 2003, Best Poems of the English Language: Chaucer to Hart Crane 2003, Where Shall Wisdom be Found? 2004, The Names Divine: Jesus and Yahweh 2005, Yetziat: Fallen Angels, Demons and Devils 2006, Till I End My Song: A Gathering of Last Poems 2010, The Anatomy of Influence: Literature as a Way of Life 2011, The King James Bible: A Literary Appreciation 2011. *Honours:* Dr hc (St Michael's Coll., Univ. of Rome, Univ. of Bologna, Univ. of Coimbra, Boston Coll., Yeshiva Univ., Univ. of Mass. at Dartmouth, Univ. of Buenos Aires); Newton Arvin Award 1967, Melville Cane Award, Poetry Soc. of America 1970, Zabel Prize, American Inst. of Arts and Letters 1982, MacArthur Foundation Fellowship 1985, Christian Gauss Prize 1989, Gold Medal for Criticism, American Acad. of Arts and Letters 1999, Int. Prize of Catalonia 2002, Alfonso Reyes Prize (Mexico) 2003, Hans Christian Anderson Bicentennial Prize (Denmark) 2005. *Address:* Department of English, WHC 202, Yale University, 63 High Street, POB 208302, New Haven, CT 06520-8302, USA (office). *Telephone:* (203) 432-0029 (office). *E-mail:* harold.bloom@yale.edu (office). *Website:* www.yale.edu/english (office).

BLOOM, Valerie, MBE, BA, MA; British/Jamaican poet and novelist; b. 15 Sept. 1956, Clarendon, Jamaica; d. of John Wright and Edna Wright; m. Douglas Bloom; one s. two d. *Education:* Univ. of Kent, Canterbury. *Career:* emigrated to England 1979; has worked in numerous jobs including librarian, steel band instructor, arts officer, teacher, Arvon Foundation; resident poet for numerous orgs; mem. Bd and Patron, Poetry Book Soc. *Radio:* producer and contrib. to various poetry and literature programmes. *Television:* various schools and entertainment programmes. *Publications include:* poems: Touch Mi! Tell Mi! 1983, Duppy Jamboree and Other Jamaican Poems 1992, Fruits (Smarties Bronze Award, Américas Honor Award) 1997, Ackee, Breadfruit, Callaloo: An Edible Alphabet 1999, Let me Touch the Sky 2000, New Baby 2000, The World is Sweet 2000, Hot Like Fire 2002, Whoop an' Shout 2003, On Good Form: Poetry Made Simple 2006; On a Camel to the Moon and other poems about journeys (ed.) 2001, Surprising Joy (novel) 2003, Many Creeks: Poems from Around the World (ed.) 2003, A Twist in the Tale (ed.) 2004, The Tribe (novel) 2008, One River (ed.); contribs to over 450 anthologies. *Honours:* Hon. MA (Univ. of Kent); Community Award for Literature, Voice (newspaper). *Literary Agent:* c/o Clare Pearson, Eddison Pearson Ltd, West Hill House, 6 Swains Lane, London, N6 6QS, England. *Telephone:* (20) 7700-7763. *Fax:* (20) 7700-7866. *E-mail:* clare@eddisonpearson.com. *Website:* www.eddisonpearson.com. *Address:* c/o Pan Macmillan Ltd, 20 New Wharf Road, London, N1 9RR, England. *Telephone:* (20) 7014-6000. *Fax:* (20) 7014-6001. *E-mail:* vblo@aol.com (home). *Website:* www.panmacmillan.com; www.valbloom.info.

BLOUNT, Roy Alton, Jr, (Noah Sanders, C. R. Ways), BA, MA; American writer, poet, screenwriter and broadcaster; b. 4 Oct. 1941, Indianapolis, Ind.; s. of Roy A. Blount, Sr and Louise Floyd Blount; m. 1st Ellen Pearson 1964 (divorced 1973); one s. one d.; m. 2nd Joan Ackermann 1976 (divorced 1990); m. 3rd Joan Griswold 2006. *Education:* Vanderbilt Univ., Harvard Univ. *Career:* mem. staff, Decatur-DeKalb News 1958–59, Morning Telegraph, New York 1961, New Orleans Times-Picayune 1963; reporter, editorial writer and columnist, Atlanta Journal 1966–68; staff writer, Sports Illustrated 1968–74, Assoc. Ed. 1974–75; Contributing Ed. Atlantic Monthly 1983–2008; columnist, Oxford American 1995–2008, Garden and Gun 2009–; Pres. Authors Guild 2006–10; mem. Fellowship of Southern Writers. *Film:* screenplay: Larger than Life. *Radio:* panellist, Wait, Wait…Don't Tell Me (NPR) 1998–. *Television:* Treme (cameo) 2010. *Publications include:* About Three Bricks Shy of a Load (revised edn as About Three Bricks Shy – and the Load Filled Up: The Story of the Greatest Football Team Ever) 1974, Crackers: This Whole Many-Sided Thing of Jimmy, More Carters, Ominous Little Animals, Sad-Singing Women, My Daddy and Me 1980, One Fell Soup, or, I'm Just a Bug on the Windshield of Life 1982, What Men Don't Tell Women 1984, Not Exactly What I Had in Mind 1985, It Grows on You: A Hair-Raising Survey of Human Plumage 1986, Soupsongs/Webster's Ark 1987, Now, Where Were We? 1989, First Hubby 1990, Camels Are Easy, Comedy's Hard 1991, Roy Blount's Book of Southern Humor 1994, Be Sweet: A Conditional Love Story 1998, If Only You Knew How Much I Smell You 1998, I Am Puppy, Hear Me Yap 2000, Am I Pig Enough For You Yet? 2001, Robert E. Lee 2003, I Am the Cat, Don't Forget That 2004, Feet on the Street: Rambles around New Orleans 2005, Long Time Leaving: Dispatches From Up South 2007, Alphabet Juice 2008, Hail, Hail, Euphoria! 2010, Alphabetter Juice 2011; contrib. to numerous anthologies and periodicals. *Honours:* Library Lion, New York Public Library, Thomas Wolfe Prize, Univ. of North Carolina. *Literary Agent:* c/o Esther Newberg, International Creative Management, 730 Fifth Avenue, New York, NY 10019, USA. *Telephone:* (212) 556-5600. *E-mail:* enewberg@icmtalent.com. *Website:* www.icmtalent.com; www.royblountjr.com.

BLUME, Judy, BS; American writer; b. 12 Feb. 1938, Elizabeth, NJ; d. of Rudolph and Esther (née Rosenfeld) Sussman; m. 1st John M. Blume 1959 (divorced 1975); one s. one d.; m. 2nd George Cooper 1987; one step-d. *Education:* New York Univ. *Career:* Founder and Trustee The Kids Fund 1981; mem. PEN Club, Authors' Guild, Nat. Coalition Against Censorship, Soc. of Children's Book Writers and Illustrators, Key West Literary Seminar, Nat. Coalition Against Censorship. *Publications:* juvenile fiction: The One in the Middle Is the Green Kangaroo 1969, Iggie's House 1970, Are You There God? It's Me, Margaret (Outstanding Book of the Year Award 1970, Nene Award 1975, Young Hoosier Award 1976, North Dakota Children's Choice Book Award 1979, Great Stone Face Award 1980) 1970, Then Again, Maybe I Won't 1971, Freckle Juice (Michigan Young Reader's Award 1980) 1971, It's Not the End of the World 1972, Tales of a Fourth Grade Nothing 1972, Otherwise Known as Sheila the Great (South Carolina Children's Book Award 1982) 1972, Deenie 1973, Blubber (Outstanding Book of the Year Award 1974, North Dakota Children's Choice Award 1983) 1974, Forever 1975, Starring Sally J. Freedman as Herself 1977, Superfudge (Golden Sower Award 1983, Iowa Children's Choice Award 1983, Arizona Young Readers' Award, Georgia Children's Book Award, California Young Reader Medal Reader's Choice

Award 1984, Great Stone Face Award 1985, 1986) 1980, Tiger Eyes (Buckeye Children's Book Award 1983, Iowa Teen Award 1985, Colorado Blue Spruce Young Adult Book Award 1985) 1981, Fudge-a-mania (California Young Reader Medal, Iowa Children's Choice Award, Nene Award, Nevada Young Reader's Award, Sunshine State Young Reader's Award, Pennsylvania Young Reader's Choice Award, Michigan Readers' Choice Award) 1983, The Pain and the Great One (Young Readers' Choice Award 1989) 1984, Just As Long As We're Together 1987, Here's to You, Rachel Robinson (Parents' Choice Award) 1993, Places I Never Meant To Be (ed) 1999, Double Fudge 2002, The Pain and the Great One: Soupy Saturdays 2008, The Pain and the Great One: Cool Zone 2008, The Pain and the Great One: Going, Going, Gone! 2009, The Pain and the Great One: Friend or Fiend? 2009; adult fiction: Wifey 1978, Smart Women 1983, Summer Sisters 1998; non-fiction: Letters to Judy: What Kids Wish They Could Tell You 1986, The Judy Blume Memory Book 1988. *Honours:* Hon. LHD (Kean Coll.) 1987; Chicago Public Library Carl Sandburg Freedom to Read Award 1984, Civil Liberties Award, American Civil Liberties Union of Atlanta 1986, American Library Asscn Margaret A. Edwards Award for Lifetime Achievement 1996, Library of Congress Living Legends Award, Medal for distinguished contrib. to American Letters, Nat. Book Foundation 2004; Nat. Book Foundation Medal for Distinguished Contribution to American Letters 2004. *Literary Agent:* c/o Suzanne Gluck, William Morris Agency, 1325 Avenue of the Americas, New York, NY 10022, USA. *Address:* c/o Tashmoo Productions, 1075 Duval Street, Suite C21 #236, Key West, FL 33040, USA. *E-mail:* JudyB@judyblume.com. *Website:* www.judyblume.com.

BLUMENTHAL, Michael Charles, BA, JD; American writer, poet and academic; *Mina Hohenberg Darden Endowed Chair of Creative Writing, Old Dominion University*; b. 8 March 1949, Vineland, NJ; m. Isabelle Leconte (divorced); one s. *Education:* State Univ. of New York, Binghamton, Cornell Univ. *Career:* Bingham Distinguished Poet-in-Residence, Univ. of Louisville, 1982; Briggs-Copeland Lecturer and Asst Prof. of Poetry, Harvard Univ. 1983–88, Assoc. Prof. of English and Dir of Creative Writing 1988–93; Sr Fulbright Lecturer in American Literature, Eötvös Lorand Univ., Budapest 1992–96; Distinguished Visiting Writer-in-Residence, Boise State Univ. 1996; Assoc. Prof. of English, Univ. of Haifa 1996; Visiting Writer, Southwest Texas State Univ. 1997–98; Distinguished Visiting Poet-in-Residence, Wichita State Univ. 1999; Distinguished Writer-in-Residence, Santa Clara Univ. 2001; Lecturer in Creative Non-Fiction, American Univ. of Paris 2001–02; Distinguished Visiting Prof. of American Literature, Université Jean Monnet, Saint-Etienne, France 2001; Acuff Distinguished Chair. of Excellence, Austin Peay State Univ., Clarksville 2004–05; Mina Hohenberg Darden Endowed Chair. of Creative Writing, Old Dominion Univ. 2006–; Copenhaver Distinguished Visiting Chair., Univ. of West Virginia 2009–11; mem. Associated Writing Programs, PEN American Center, Poetry Soc. of America, Poets and Writers. *Publications include:* Sympathetic Magic 1980, Days We Would Rather Know 1984, Laps 1984, Against Romance 1987, The Wages of Goodness 1992, To Wed & To Woo: Poets on Marriage (ed.) 1992, Weinstock Among the Dying (Harold U. Ribelow Prize for Jewish Fiction 1994) 1993, When History Enters the House: Central European Essays 1998, Dusty Angel 1999, All My Mothers and Fathers 2002, Connecting the World: Selected Poetry and Prose of Michael Blumenthal 2007, And 2009; contribs to reviews, quarterlies and journals. *Honours:* First Book Prize, Water Mark Poets of North America 1980, Juniper Prize, Univ. of Massachusetts 1984, Lavan Younger Poets Prize, Acad. of American Poets 1986, Guggenheim Fellowship 1989, Hadassah magazine 1994. *Literary Agent:* Nat Sobel, Sobel Weber Associates, 146 East 19th Street, New York, NY 10003-2404, USA. *Telephone:* (212) 420-8585. *E-mail:* nsobel@sobelweber.com. *Website:* www.sobelweber.com. *Address:* BOA Editions, Ltd. 250 North Goodman Street, Suite 306, Rochester, NY 14607, USA. *Telephone:* (585) 546-3410. *E-mail:* mcblume@attglobal.net (office). *Website:* www.michael-blumenthal.com.

BLUNDELL, Sue, BA, PhD; British writer and lecturer; b. 4 Aug. 1947, Manchester. *Education:* Westfield Coll., London, Goldsmiths Coll., London. *Career:* part-time Lecturer, Birkbeck Coll., London 1979–2004; Asst Lecturer of Classical Civilization, Open Univ. 1986–; academic tutor, Architectural Asscn, London 1994–. *Plays:* How to be Happy (British Museum, London) 2006, Goddesses (Pleasance Theatre, London) 2007. *Publications include:* The Origins of Civilisation in Greek and Roman Thought 1986, Women in Ancient Greece 1995, The Sacred and the Feminine in Ancient Greece (ed. with Margaret Williamson) 1998, Women in Classical Athens 1998, Epicurus on Happiness (dramatic monologue, performed at British Museum) 2001; contrib. to Women's Dress in the Ancient Greek World 2002, Greek Art in View: Studies in Honour of Brian Sparkes 2004, Gender and the Classics Curriculum 2008. *Address:* 59B Goodge Street, London, W1T 1TJ, England (home). *Telephone:* (20) 7580-4917 (office). *E-mail:* sblundell@aaschool.ac.uk (office).

BLY, Robert Elwood, MA; American writer and poet; b. 23 Dec. 1926, Madison, Minn.; s. of Jacob Thomas Bly and Alice Bly (née Aws); m. 1st Carolyn McLean 1955 (divorced 1979); m. 2nd Ruth Counsell 1980; five c. *Education:* Harvard Univ. and Univ. of Iowa. *Career:* served USN 1944–46; founder and Ed. The Fifties 1958–, later The Sixties and Seventies Press; f. American Writers Against the Vietnam War 1966. *Publications include:* poems: Silence in the Snowy Fields 1962, The Light Around the Body 1967, Chrysanthemums 1967, Ducks 1968, The Morning Glory: Another Thing That Will Never Be My Friend 1969, The Teeth Mother Naked at Last 1971, Poems for Tennessee (with William Stafford and William Matthews) 1971, Christmas Eve Service at Midnight at St Michael's 1972, Water Under the Earth 1972, The Dead Seal Near McClure's Beach 1973, Sleepers Joining Hands 1973, Jumping out of Bed 1973, The Hockey Poem 1974, Point Reyes Poems 1974, Old Man Rubbing his Eyes 1975, The Loon 1977, Visiting Emily Dickinson's Grave and Other Poems 1979, This Tree Will Be Here for a Thousand Years 1979, Finding An Old Ant Mansion 1981, The Man in the Black Coat Turns 1982, Four Ramages 1983, The Whole Moisty Night 1983, Out of the Rollling Ocean 1984, Mirabai Versions 1984, In the Month of May 1985, A Love of Minute Particulars 1985, Loving a Woman in Two Worlds 1985, Selected Poems (ed.) 1986, The Moon on the Fencepost 1988, The Apple Found in the Plowing 1989, What Have I Ever Lost By Dying?: Collected Prose Poems 1993, Gratitude to Old Teachers 1993, Meditations on the Insatiable Soul 1994, Morning Poems 1997, Eating the Honey of Words: New and Selected Poems 1999, The Best American Poetry (ed.) 1999, The Night Abraham Called to the Stars 2001, My Sentence was a Thousand Years of Joy 2005; prose poems: The Morning Glory 1973, This Body is Made of Camphor and Gopherwood 1977, This Body is Made of Eating the Honey of Words: New and Selected Poems 1999, The Best American Poetry (ed.) 1999; prose: Iron John 1990; criticism: A Poetry Reading Against the Vietnam War 1966, The Sea and the Honeycomb 1966, Forty Poems Touching on Recent American History (ed.) 1967, Leaping Poetry 1975, The Soul is Here for its Own Joy 1995; trans. of vols of poetry from Swedish, Norwegian, German, Spanish and Hindi. *Honours:* Fulbright Award 1956–57, Amy Lowell Fellow 1964–65, Guggenheim Fellow 1965–66, Rockefeller Foundation Fellow 1967, Nat. Book Award in Poetry 1968. *Address:* 1904 Girard Avenue South, Minneapolis, MN 55403, USA (home).

BLYTH, Myrna, BA; American writer and editor; *Editor-in-Chief, ThirdAge.com*; b. 22 March 1939, New York; d. of Benjamin Greenstein and Betty Greenstein (née Austin); m. Jeffrey Blyth 1962; two s. *Education:* Bennington Coll. *Career:* Sr Ed. Datebook 1960–62, Ingenue 1963–68; Book Ed. Family Health 1968–71; Book and Fiction Ed., then Assoc. Ed. Family Circle 1972–78, Exec. Ed. 1978–81; Ed.-in-Chief Ladies' Home Journal 1981–2002, Sr Vice-Pres. and Publishing Dir 1987–2002, Ed. Dir Meredith Corpn New York magazines 2002–03, Editorial Dir New Product Devt, Meredith Publishing Group 2002–03; Founding Ed.-in-Chief and Publishing Dir More magazine 1998; currently Ed.-in-Chief ThirdAge.com; Commr on Pres.'s Comm. on White House Fellows, fmr Chair.; mem. Advisory Cttee for the Office of Research in Women's Health, NIH; mem. Exec. Bd American Soc. of Magazine Eds; mem. Bd Govs Overseas Press Club, Child Care Action Campaign, Advisory Bd ThirdAge Media and Research America; mem. Authors' Guild, Women's Media Group; fmr Pres. New York Women in Communications Inc.; mem. Del. to UN Fourth World Conf. on Women, Beijing. *Publications include:* For Better and For Worse, Cousin Suzanne, Spin Sisters – How the Women of the Media Sell Unhappiness and Liberalism to the Women of America 2004, How to Raise an American 2007; contrib. of short stories and non-fiction articles to New Yorker, New York, McCall's, Redbook, The Reader's Digest. *Honours:* Matrix Award, New York Women in Communications Inc. 1988, Magazine of the Year Award, Clarion Award 1984, 1989, MagazineWeek Publishing Excellence Award 1991, Henry Johnson Fisher Award, Magazine Publr Asscn 1999, Women of Achievement Award, New York City Comm. on Status of Women 2000, Matrix Award, New York Women in Communications, Headliner Award, Women in Communications, Inc., Publishing Exec. of the Year Award, Advertising Age magazine 2001, Innovator Award, Isis Fund, Soc. for Women's Health Research, Athena Award, Partnership for Women's Health, Columbia Univ. *Address:* Third Age Media LLC, 230 Park Avenue, New York, NY 10169, USA (office). *Telephone:* (212) 684-0367 (office). *Website:* www.thirdage.com (office).

BLYTHE, Ronald George, FRSL, DLitt; British writer; b. 6 Nov. 1922, Acton, Suffolk; s. of George Blythe and Matilda Blythe. *Education:* St Peter's and St Gregory's School, Sudbury, Suffolk. *Career:* Lay Canon, St Edmundsbury Cathedral 2003; Pres. John Clare Soc., Kilvert Soc., Robert Bloomfield Soc.; Vice-Pres. William Hazlitt Soc.; f. Colchester Literary Soc.; Patron The Woodland Trust; mem. Soc. of Authors, Fabian Soc. *Films include:* Akenfield 1974; art films for BBC. *Publications include:* A Treasonable Growth 1960, Immediate Possession 1961, The Age of Illusion 1963, Akenfield 1969, William Hazlett: Selected Writings (ed.) 1970, The View in Winter 1979, From the Headlands 1982, The Stories of Ronald Blythe 1985, Divine Landscapes 1986, Each Returning Day 1989, Private Words 1991, Word from Wormingford 1997, First Friends 1998, Going to Meet George 1998, Talking About John Clare 1999, Out of the Valley 2000, The Circling Year 2001, Talking to the Neighbours 2002, The Assassin 2004, Borderland 2004, A Writer's Day Book 2006, Field Work 2007, A River Diary 2008, Outsiders: A Book of Garden Friends 2008, The Bookman's Tale 2009, Aftermath 2010; other: critical studies of Jane Austen, Thomas Hardy, Leo Tolstoy, Henry James, Literature of the Second World War; ed. of various authors' works; contrib. to Observer, Sunday Times, New York Times, Listener, Atlantic Monthly, London Magazine, Tablet, New Statesman, Bottegue Oscure, Guardian. *Honours:* Hon. MA (East Anglia) 1991, Hon. MLitt (Lambeth) 2001, Hon. DLitt (Anglia Ruskin Univ.) 2001, (Essex) 2002; Heinemann Award 1969, Soc. of Authors Travel Scholarship 1970, Angel Prize for Literature 1986, Benson Medal for Literature 2006. *Address:* Bottengoms Farm, Wormingford, Colchester, Essex, CO6 3AP, England (home). *Telephone:* (1206) 271308 (home).

BOADEN, Helen, BA,; British broadcasting executive; *Director, BBC News Group*; b. 1 March 1956, Colchester, Essex, England; d. of William John Boaden and Barbara Mary Boaden; m. Stephen Burley 1994. *Education:* Univ.

of Sussex. *Career:* Care Asst, Hackney Social Services, London 1978; Reporter, Radio WBAI, NY, USA 1979, Radio Tees and Radio Aire 1980–83; Producer, BBC Radio Leeds 1983–85; Reporter, File on 4, Radio 4 1985–91, Brass Tacks, BBC 2 1985–91; Presenter, Woman's Hour, Radio 4 1985–91, Verdict, Channel 4 1991–; Ed., File on 4, Radio 4 1991–94; Head of Network Current Affairs, BBC Manchester (first woman in position) 1994–97; Head of Business Programmes, BBC News 1997, Head of Current Affairs and Business Programmes 1998–2000; Controller, BBC Radio 4 2000–04, BBC 7 2002–04; Dir BBC News 2004–11, Dir BBC News Group, with additional responsibility for the Global News div., and mem. Exec. Bd 2011–; Fellow, Radio Acad., Chair. 2003–. *Honours:* Hon. Fellow, Univ. of the Arts, London; Dr hc (East Anglia, Sussex, York, Open Univ.); Sony Gold Award (File on 4 investigation into AIDS in Africa in 1987), Sony Gold Award (File on 4 investigation into bullying in Feltham Young Offenders Inst. 1993), Radio Station of the Year 2003, 2004, ranked by Forbes magazine amongst The World's 100 Most Powerful Women (51st) 2011. *Address:* BBC, Television Centre, Wood Lane, London, W12 7RJ, England (office). *Telephone:* (20) 8743-8000 (office). *Website:* www.bbc.co.uk (office).

BOARDMAN, Sir John, Kt, MA, FSA, FBA; British archaeologist and academic; *Professor Emeritus of Classical Archaeology and Art, University of Oxford*; b. 20 Aug. 1927, s. of the late Frederick Boardman and Clare Wells; m. Sheila Stanford 1952; one s. one d. *Education:* Chigwell School and Magdalene Coll., Cambridge. *Career:* Asst Dir British School, Athens 1952–55; Asst Keeper, Ashmolean Museum, Oxford 1955–59; Reader in Classical Archaeology, Univ. of Oxford 1959–78, Lincoln Prof. of Classical Archaeology and Art 1978–94, Hon. Fellow 1995, now Prof. Emer.; Fellow, Merton Coll. Oxford 1973–78, Hon. Fellow 1978–, Sub-Warden 1975–78; Prof. of Ancient History, Royal Acad. of Arts 1989–; conducted excavations on Chios 1953–55, Crete 1964–65, in Tocra, Libya 1964–65; Visiting Prof., Columbia Univ. 1965; Geddes-Harrower Prof., Univ. of Aberdeen 1974; Fellow, Inst. of Etruscan Studies, Florence 1983, Austrian and German Archaeological Insts; Foreign mem. Royal Danish Acad.; Assoc. mem. Acad. des Inscriptions et des Belles Lettres, Institut de France; Corresp. mem. Bavarian Acad. of Sciences; Foreign mem. American Philosophical Soc., Accad. dei Lincei, Rome, Russian Acad. of Sciences. *Publications include:* Cretan Collection in Oxford 1961, Island Gems 1963, Archaic Greek Gems 1968, Athenian Black Figure Vases 1974, Escarabeos de Piedra de Ibiza 1984, The Oxford History of the Classical World (with others) 1986, Athenian Red Figure Vases: Classical period 1989, Oxford History of Classical Art 1993, The Diffusion of Classical Art in Antiquity 1994, Greek Sculpture, Later Classical 1995, Runciman Prioxe 1995, Early Greek Vase Painting 1997, Persia and the West 2000, The History of Greek Vases 2001, Greek Gems and Finger Rings 2001, The Archaeology of Nostalgia 2002, Classical Phoenician Scarabs 2003, The World of Ancient Art 2006; articles in learned journals. *Honours:* Hon. RA; Hon. MRIA; Dr hc (Athens) 1991, (Sorbonne) 1994; Kenyon Medal (British Acad.) 1995, Onassis Prize for Humanities 2009. *Address:* 11 Park Street, Woodstock, Oxford, OX20 1SJ (home); Beazley Archive, Classics Centre, Oxford, OX1 3LU, England. *Telephone:* (1993) 811259 (home); (1865) 278084. *Fax:* (1865) 610237 (office). *E-mail:* john.boardman@ashmus.ox.ac.uk (office).

BOAST, Philip James; British writer; b. 30 April 1952, London, England; m. Rosalind Thorpe 1981; two s. one d. *Education:* Mill Hill School. *Publications include:* The Assassinators 1976, London's Child 1987, The Millionaire 1989, Watersmeet 1990, Pride 1991, The Londons of London 1992, Gloria 1993, London's Daughter 1994, City 1994, The Foundling 1995, Resurrection 1996, Deus 1997, Sion 1998, Era 2000, The Third Princess 2006, The Son of Heaven 2007; contribs to Science Fiction Monthly. *Address:* Upper Thornehill, 27 Church Road, St Marychurch, Torquay, Devon, TQ1 4QY, England (home). *E-mail:* philipboast@btinternet.com.

BOBIS, Merlinda Carullo, PhD; Philippine/Australian poet, novelist, dramatist and academic; *Senior Lecturer, Faculty of Creative Arts, University of Wollongong*; b. 25 Nov. 1959, Albay; d. of Nicolas Bobis and Amprao Carullo Bobis; m. *Education:* Bicol Univ. High School, Aquinas Univ., Legazpi City, Univ. of Sto Tomas, Univ. of Wollongong, Australia. *Career:* Lecturer in Creative Writing in Australia and the Philippines for over 17 years; currently Sr Lecturer Faculty of Creative Arts, Univ. of Wollongong; regularly performs plays and poetry on radio and at festivals. *Plays include:* Rita's Lullaby (Ian Reed Radio Drama Prize) 1995. *Publications include:* Cantata of the Warrior Woman Daragang Magayon (epic poem) 1993, Rituals (poems) 1990, Flight is Song on Four Winds (poems) 1990, Summer Was A Fast Train Without Terminals (poems) 1998, Rita's Lullaby (poetic drama) (Prix Italia, Australian Writers' Guild Award) 1998, White Turtle (short stories) (Philippine Nat. Book Award for Fiction 2000) 1999, Fish-Hair Woman (novel), Banana Heart Summer (novel, Gintong Aklat Award 2006) 2005, The Solemn Lantern Maker 2008. *Honours:* Steele Rudd Award for Best Collection of Australian Short Stories 2000, Ministry for the Arts Writers' Fellowship 2000. *Address:* Faculty of Creative Arts, University of Wollongong, Wollongong, NSW 2522, Australia (office). *E-mail:* merlinda_bobis@uow.edu.au (office). *Website:* www-static.uow.edu.au/crearts (office); www.merlindabobis.com.au.

BOCEK, Alois (see Vaniček, Zdeněk)

BOCHEŃSKI, Jacek; Polish writer and essayist; b. 29 July 1926, Lvov; m.; one d. *Education:* State Coll. of Theatrical Arts, Warsaw. *Career:* Co-founder and Ed. Zapis (first Polish underground periodical) 1977–81; Pres. Polish PEN Club 1996–99; currently Pres. Authors & Composers Asscn's Council. *Radio:* Post-Breakdown, Naso Poet, The Elderely Man's Fantasies 1998–2002. *Television and stage plays:* Taboo, Post-Breakdown. *Publications include:* fiction: Farewell to Miss Syngilu 1960, Roman Trilogy: Divine Julius 1961, Taboo 1965, Naso Poet 1969, Post-Breakdown 1987, The Elderely Man's Fantasies 2004, Tiberius Caesar 2009; non-fiction: Bloody Italian Rarities 1982, Thirteen European Exercises 2005, Antiquity after Antiquity 2010; several essays and contribs to magazines on politics and culture. *Honours:* Solidarity Prize 1987, Polish PEN Club Parandowski Prize 2006, Gloria Artis Golden Medal 2009. *Address:* ul. Sonaty 6 m. 801, 02-744 Warsaw, Poland (home). *E-mail:* jacek.bochenski@gazeta.pl. *Website:* www.jacekbochenski.blox.pl.

BOCOCK, Robert James, PhD; British sociologist, writer and academic; b. 29 Sept. 1940, Lincoln, Lincs. *Education:* Univ. of London, Brunel Univ. *Career:* Lecturer in Sociology, Brunel Univ. 1966–79, Open Univ., Bucks.; mem. Asscn of Univ. Teachers, British Sociological Asscn. *Publications include:* Ritual in Industrial Society 1974, Freud and Modern Society 1976, An Introduction to Sociology 1980, Sigmund Freud 1983, Religion and Ideology (ed.) 1985, Hegemony 1986, Consumption 1993; contribs to journals.

BODANIS, David; American writer and academic; b. Chicago; two c. *Education:* Univ. of Chicago. *Career:* copy boy, Int. Herald Tribune, Paris 1977; Sr Assoc. mem., St Antony's Coll., Oxford 1988, Lecturer in Social Science, Univ. of Oxford 1991–97; business consultant mid-1990s–, working with companies, including Accenture, BMW, General Motors, Microsoft, Pfizer and Shell, and with governments. *Television:* The Secret Family (documentary, Discovery Channel and CBC). *Publications include:* Being Human: A Day in the Life of the Human Body 1984, The Body Book: A Fantastic Voyage to the World Within 1984, The Secret House 1986, Web of Words: The Ideas Behind Politics 1988, The Secret Garden 1993, The Secret Family: 24 Hours Inside the Mysterious World of Our Minds and Bodies 1997, E=mc2: A Biography of the World's Most Famous Equation 2000, Electric Universe: How Electricity Switched on the Modern World (Royal Soc. Aventis Prize 2006) 2005, Passionate Minds: The Great Enlightenment Love Affair 2006; contribs to journals, including Popular Science. *E-mail:* d.bodanis@virgin.net (office). *Website:* www.davidbodanis.com.

BODEN, Group Captain (retd) Anthony Norman, BA; British writer; b. 21 April 1938, Altrincham, Cheshire, England; m. Elizabeth Anne Miles; one s. one d. *Education:* Open Univ. *Career:* served in RAF, retiring in the rank of Group Capt. 1957–89; Festival Admin. Three Choirs Festival, Gloucester 1989–99; mem. Ivor Gurney Soc. (Chair. 1995–2002). *Publications include:* Stars in a Dark Night: The Letters of Ivor Gurney to the Chapman Family 1986 (revised edn 2004), F. W. Harvey: Soldier Poet 1988 (revised edn 2011), Three Choirs: A History of the Festival 1992, The Parrys of the Golden Vale 1998, Thomas Tomkins: The Last Elizabethan 2005, F. W. Harvey: Selected Poems (co-ed. with R. K. R. Thornton) 2011. *Honours:* Officer (Brother) of the Order of St John 1987. *Address:* Chosen Hay, The Green, Churchdown, Gloucester, Glos., GL3 2LF, England (home).

BODEN, Margaret Ann, OBE, ScD, PhD, FBA; British cognitive scientist and professor of cognitive science; *Research Professor of Cognitive Science, Centre for Research in Cognitive Science, University of Sussex*; b. 26 Nov. 1936, London; d. of Leonard F. Boden and Violet Dorothy Boden (née Dawson); m. John R. Spiers 1967 (divorced 1981); one s. one d. *Education:* Newnham Coll., Cambridge (Major Scholar) and Harvard Grad. School (Harkness Fellow). *Career:* Lecturer in Philosophy, Univ. of Birmingham 1959–65; Lecturer, then Reader in Philosophy and Psychology, Univ. of Sussex 1965–80, Prof. 1980–, Founding Dean School of Cognitive and Computing Sciences 1987, Research Prof. of Cognitive Science, Centre for Research in Cognitive Science 2002–; Curator Univ. of London Inst. for Advanced Study 1995–; Co-founder, Harvester Press Ltd 1970, Dir 1970–85; Vice-Pres. British Acad. 1989–91, Royal Inst. of GB 1993–95, Chair. of Council 1993–95, mem. of Council 1992–95; mem. Advisory Bd for the Research Councils 1989–90, Academia Europaea 1993–, Animal Procedures Cttee 1995–99; Fellow, American Asscn for Artificial Intelligence 1993–, European Coordinating Cttee for Artificial Intelligence 1999–. *Publications:* Purposive Explanation in Psychology 1972, Artificial Intelligence and Natural Man 1977, Piaget 1979, Minds and Mechanisms 1981, Computer Models of Mind 1988, Artificial Intelligence in Psychology 1989, The Philosophy of Artificial Intelligence (ed.) 1990, Dimensions of Creativity (ed.) 1994, Artificial Intelligence and the Mind (co-ed.) 1994, The Philosophy of Artificial Life (ed.) 1996, Artificial Intelligence (ed.) 1996, The Creative Mind (2nd edn) 2004, Mind as Machine 2006, Creativity and Art 2010. *Honours:* Hon. DSc (Sussex) 2001, (Bristol) 2002, Hon. DUniv (Open) 2004. *Address:* Centre for Research in Cognitive Science, University of Sussex, Falmer, Brighton, BN1 9QJ, England (office). *Telephone:* (1273) 678386 (office). *Fax:* (1273) 671320 (office). *E-mail:* maggieb@cogs.susx.ac.uk (office). *Website:* www.cogs.susx.ac.uk (office).

BØDKER, Cecil; Danish novelist, poet and playwright; b. 27 March 1927, Fredericia; d. of the late Hans Peter Jacobsen and Gertrude Mathiesen; four c. *Career:* apprenticed and qualified as a silversmith 1948; worked for four years for Georg Jensen, Copenhagen and Markstroem's, Uppsala, Sweden; turned to writing full time in mid-1950s. *Publications include:* poetry: Luseblomster (Edith Rhodes grant 1956) 1955; juvenile: Silas og den sorte hoppe 1967, Silas og Ben-Godik 1969, Timmerlis 1969, Leoparden 1970, Dimma Gole 1971, Silas fanger et firspand 1972, Silas stifter familie 1976, Silas på Sebastiansbjerget 1977, Silas og Hestekragen mødes igen 1978, Silas møder Matti 1979, Syv år for Rakel 1982, Silas–livet i bjergbyen 1984, Silas–de blå heste 1985, Silas–Sebastians arv 1986, Ægget der voksede 1987, Silas–ulverejsen 1988, Silas–testamentet 1992, Silas og flodrøverne 1998, Silas–fortrøstningens tid 2001; fiction: Salthandlerskens hus 1972, Marias barn. Drengen 1983, Marias barn. Manden 1984, Maria fra Nazaret 1988, Hungerbarnet 1990, Men i hvert fald i live 1995, Siffrine 2003; also short stories, radio and theatre plays. *Honours:* Critics' Award 1961, Ministry of Culture Children's Book Prize 1968, Hans Christian Andersen Award 1976, Mildred L. Batchelder Award 1977, The Golden Laurels 1985, Danish Acad. Grand Prize 1998. *Address:* Gyldendal, Klareboderne 3, 1001 Copenhagen K, Denmark. *E-mail:* gyldendal@gyldendal.dk. *Website:* www.gyldendal.dk.

BOESCHE-ZACHAROW, Tilly, (Eva Trojan); German writer and publisher; b. 31 Jan. 1928, Elbing; d. of Ernst Großkopf and Maria Großkopf; m. Hans Boesche 1950 (divorced 1963); two s. two d. *Education:* in Berlin, also while living in Haifa, Israel. *Career:* fmr clerk and bookseller; writer 1950–; ed. and publr 1980–, ed. of four children's books, fairy tales, books on religious philosophy, feminism; has written 300 romantic thrillers (under various pseudonyms including Eva Trojan, Ilka Korff, Eve Jean); Co-founder M. & N. Boesche Verlag, Berlin and Haifa, Israel. *Publications include:* Dream of Jalna 2001, The Small Line Between Sky and Water 2001, The Rabbi 2001, Pintus of Seehausen 2001, O Israel, They Want to Kill You 2001, Nicht das letzte Wort 2005, Auf dem Thron Petri 2007, Aweyden 2008. *Honours:* Dr hc 1981, Dip. di merito, Dip. d'Honore, Hon. DLitt (World Univ., Ariz., USA) 1987; European Banner of Arts 1984, Studiosis Humanitas 1984. *Address:* M. & N. Boesche Verlag, Wollankstraße 99, 13359 Berlin, Germany (office); M. & N. Boesche Verlag, Hapoel 14, 33536 Haifa, Israel (office). *Telephone:* (30) 4019009 (Berlin) (office); 4-8620169 (Haifa) (office). *E-mail:* berlin@boesche-verlag.de (office); haifa@boesche-verlag.de (office). *Website:* www.boesche-verlag.de (office).

BOFF, Leonardo Genezio Darci, DPhil, DTheol; Brazilian academic, writer and editor; b. 14 Dec. 1938, Concórdia, SC; s. of Mansueto Boff and Regina Fontana Boff. *Education:* Inst. Teológico Franciscano, Petrópolis, Univ. of Munich, Germany. *Career:* Prof. of Systematic Theology and of Franciscan Spirituality, Inst. Teológico Franciscano, Petrópolis, Rio de Janeiro 1971–92, also Prof. of Theology of Liberation; Adviser to Latin American Conf. of Religions (CLAR) 1971–80, to Nat. Conf. of Brazilian Bishops (CNBB) 1971–80; mem. Editorial Bd of Revista Eclesiástica Brasileira 1971–92; mem. Bd of Dirs Vozes publishing house 1971–92; Pres. Bd of Eds, Theology and Liberation collection 1985–; mem. Editorial Bd Concilium; ordered by Roman Curia to begin unspecified period of 'obedient silence' 1985. *Publications:* over 60 books including Jesus Christ Liberator 1971, Die Kirche als Sakrament im Horizont der Welterfahrung 1972, Theology of Captivity and Liberation 1972, Ecclesiogenesis 1977, The Maternal Face of God 1979, Church: Charisma and Power 1980, Theology Listening to People 1981, St Francis: A Model for Human Liberation 1984, Trinity and Society 1988, The Gospel of the Cosmic Christ 1989, The New Evangelization: The Perspective of the Oppressed 1990, Ecology and Spirituality 1991, Mística e Espiritualidade 1994, Nova Era: a Consciência Planetária 1994. *Honours:* Dr hc (Turin, Lund); Paz y Justicia Award, Barcelona, Menschenrechte in der Kirche Award, Herbert Haag Foundation, FRG and Switzerland, Right Livelihood Award, Stockholm 2001. *E-mail:* contato@leonardoboff.com (office). *Website:* leonardoboff.com.

BOGAARDS, Carla; Dutch novelist and poet; b. 12 July 1947, Voorburg. *Publications include:* Ik kom op niets 1982, Lena en de mannen 1985, De reigers van Amsterdam (Agenda Award) 1987, De bruinvisvrouw 1989, Lillian sugar baby 1990, Meisjesgenade 1992, Eigen vlees en bloed 1995, God bewogen 1997, Het gezichtsbedrog 2000, Klein hittegolf in mei 2003, Roes 2005, De verdronken postbode 2009. *E-mail:* carlab@xs4all.nl (office). *Website:* www.carlabogaards.nl.

BOGDANOR, Vernon, CBE, MA, FRSA, FBA; British academic; *Research Professor, Institute of Contemporary History, King's College London;* b. 16 July 1943, London, England; s. of Harry Bogdanor and Rosa Weinger; m. Judith Beckett 1972 (divorced 2000); two s.; m. 2nd Sonia Robertson 2009. *Education:* Queen's Coll. and Nuffield Coll., Oxford. *Career:* Fellow, Brasenose Coll., Oxford 1966–2010, Sr Tutor 1979–85, 1996–97; mem. Council of Hansard Soc. for Parl. Govt 1981–97; Special Adviser, House of Lords Select Cttee on European Communities 1982–83; adviser to Govts of Czech Repub., Slovakia, Hungary and Israel on constitutional and electoral matters 1988–; Reader in Govt, Univ. of Oxford 1989–96, Prof. of Govt 1996–2010, Prof. Emer. 2010–; Gresham Prof. of Law, Gresham Coll., London 2004–07; Research Prof., Inst. of Contemporary History, King's Coll., London 2010–; mem. UK del. to CSCE Conf., Oslo 1991; Special Adviser, House of Commons Public Service Cttee 1996; mem. Int. Advisory Council, The Israel Democracy Inst. 2010–; Fellow, Acad. of Social Sciences 2009. *Publications:* Devolution 1979, The People and the Party System 1981, Multi-party Politics and the Constitution 1983, What is Proportional Representation? 1984, The Blackwell Encyclopaedia of Political Institutions (ed.) 1987, Comparing Constitutions (co-author) 1995, The Monarchy and the Constitution 1995, Politics and the Constitution 1996, Power and the People 1997, Devolution in the United Kingdom 1999, The British Constitution in the Twentieth Century (ed.) 2003, Joined-Up Government (ed.) 2005, The New British Constitution 2009, From New Jerusalem to New Labour: British Prime Ministers from Attlee to Blair (ed.) 2010, The Coalition and the Constitution 2011. *Honours:* Hon. Fellow, Soc. for Advanced Legal Studies 1997, Queen's Coll., Oxford 2009, Hon. Bencher, Middle Temple 2010; Chevalier, Légion d'honneur 2009; Hon. DLitt (Kent) 2010; Mishcon Lecturer 1994, Magna Carta Lecturer 2006, Sir Isaiah Berlin Prize for Lifetime Contribution to Political Studies. *Address:* Institute for Contemporary History, Strand Building, King's College, Strand, London, WC2R 2LS (office); 21 Edmunds Walk, East Finchley, London, N2 0HU, England (home).

BOGDANOV, Vsevolod Leonidovich; Russian journalist; *Chairman, Russian Union of Journalists;* b. 6 Feb. 1944, Arkhangelsk Region; m.; three d. *Education:* Leningrad State Univ. *Career:* corresp., ed. in newspapers, radio and TV Magadan 1961–76; Head of Dept of Periodicals, State Cttee of Publs 1976–89; Dir-Gen. TV programmes State Radio and TV Cttee 1989–92; Chair. Russian Union of Journalists 1992–; Pres. Nat. Journalist Trade Union 1999–; Pres. Int. Confed. of Journalists' Unions 1999–. *Address:* Russian Union of Journalists, Zubovsky blvd 4, 1199911 Moscow, Russia (office). *Telephone:* (495) 637-51-01 (office). *E-mail:* ruj@ruj.ru (office). *Website:* www.ruj.ru (office).

BOGDANOVICH, Peter; American film director, writer, producer and actor; b. 30 July 1939, Kingston, NY; s. of Borislav Bogdanovich and Herma Bogdanovich (née Robinson); m. 1st Polly Platt 1962 (divorced 1970); two d.; m. 2nd Louise Straten 1988 (divorced 2001). *Career:* actor, American Shakespeare Festival, Stratford, Conn. 1956, NY Shakespeare Festival 1958; Dir and Producer of off-Broadway plays The Big Knife 1959, Camino Real, Ten Little Indians, Rocket to the Moon 1961, Once in a Lifetime 1964; film feature writer for Esquire, New York Times, Village Voice, Cahiers du Cinéma, Los Angeles Times, New York Magazine, Vogue, Variety etc. 1961–; Owner The Holly Moon Co. Inc. 1992–; mem. Dirs Guild of America, Writers' Guild of America, Acad. of Motion Picture Arts and Sciences. *Films include:* The Wild Angels (2nd unit dir, co-writer, actor) 1966, Targets (dir, co-writer, producer, actor) 1968, The Last Picture Show (dir, co-writer) 1971, Directed by John Ford (dir, writer) 1971, What's Up Doc? (dir, co-writer, producer) 1972, Paper Moon (dir, producer) 1973, Daisy Miller (dir, producer) 1974, At Long Last Love (dir, writer, producer) 1975, Nickelodeon (dir, co-writer) 1976, Saint Jack (dir, co-writer, actor) 1979, They All Laughed (dir, writer) 1981, Mask (dir) 1985, Illegally Yours (dir, producer) 1988, Texasville (dir, producer, writer) 1990, Noises Off (dir, exec. producer) 1992, The Thing Called Love (dir) 1993, Who The Devil Made It (dir) 1997, Mr Jealousy (actor) 1997, Highball (actor) 1997, Coming Soon (actor) 1999, Rated X (actor) 2000, The Independent (actor) 2000, The Cat's Meow (dir) 2003, Scene Stealers (actor) 2003, Infamous (actor) 2006, The Doorman (actor) 2007, Broken English (actor) 2007, Dedication (actor) 2007, The Dukes (actor) 2007, The Fifth Patient (actor) 2007, Humboldt County (actor) 2008, The Doorman (actor) 2008, Queen of the Lot (actor) 2010, Abandoned (actor) 2010. *Television:* The Great Professional: Howard Hawks (co-dir, wrote), BBC 1967, The Sopranos 2000–07; dir: Saintly Switch 1999, The Sopranos 1999, Hustle 2004, The Mystery of Natalie Wood 2004; regular commentator for CBS This Morning 1987–89; actor: Northern Exposure, CBS 1993, Fallen Angels 1995, Painted Word 1995, To Sir With Love II 1996, Naked City: A Killer Christmas 1998. *Publications include:* The Cinema of Orson Welles 1961, The Cinema of Howard Hawks 1962, The Cinema of Alfred Hitchcock 1963, John Ford 1968, Fritz Lang in America 1969, Allan Dwan, the Last Pioneer 1971, Pieces of Time, Peter Bogdanovich on the Movies 1961–85, The Killing of the Unicorn: Dorothy Stratten (1960–80) 1984, A Year and a Day Calendar (ed.) 1991, This is Orson Welles (with Orson Welles) 1992, Who the Devil Made It 1997, Who the Hell's In It? 2004. *Honours:* NY Film Critics' Award 1971 and BAFTA Award for Best Screenplay (The Last Picture Show) 1971, Writers' Guild of America Award for Best Screenplay (What's Up, Doc?) 1972, Pasinetti Award, Critics' Prize, Venice Festival (Saint Jack) 1979 and other awards and prizes. *Address:* c/o William Pfeiffer, 30 Lane of Acres, Haddonfield, NJ 08033; c/o CAA, 9830 Wilshire Boulevard, Beverly Hills, CA 90212-1804, USA (office).

BOGUSLAVSKAYA, Zoya Borisovna, PhD; Russian writer, playwright and critic; b. 16 April 1929, Moscow; d. of Boris Lvovich Boguslavsky and Emma Iosifovna Boguslavskaya; m. Andrei Andreyevich Voznesensky; one s. *Education:* Moscow State Inst. of Arts and Inst. of History of Art, USSR Acad. of Sciences. *Career:* Ed. Sovetsky Pisatel publishing house; Lecturer, Moscow Higher School of Theatre Art; Head Div. of Literature, USSR State Cttee on Lenin's and State Prizes; Founder Festival of Arts Christmas Carousel (Moscow-Paris); Guest Writer, Columbia Univ., New York, USA, Catholic Acad., Stuttgart, Germany; mem. Editorial Bd several literary magazines and journals, including Elite, Rabotnitsa, Marina (American-Russian magazine published in USA); mem. Asscn of Women-Writers of Russia, Russian Writers' Union 1960, Int. Asscn of Women-Writers in Paris; mem. Bd Dirs Russian PEN-Centre; est. Russian Ind. Triumph and Foundation Prizes, currently Jury Coordinator; currently also Head, Triumph-Logovaz Foundation; juror, Neustadt Prize 1994. *Publications include:* novels and short stories: And Tomorrow 1959, Vera Panova 1963, Seven Hundred in New Banknotes, The Defence, Obsession, Kinship, Change, Ghost, Passing Through, Mediators, By Transit, Races 1981, Leonid Leonov, American Women (Bravo! TV-show Prize, Yunost journal Prize), American Women Plus, Ludmila Gutsko's Disappearance, or Change of Landmarks, A View to the South; plays: Windows Overlooking the South, Contact, A Promise (banned for political reasons); essays: Unthought-Up Stories, Time of Lubimov and Vysotsky, Lisa and Baryshnikov, One Way Ticket; nearly 100 articles on literature in the areas of theatre and cinema published in periodicals; collection of works in two vols, Mirrow-world, Imaginary and Unimaginary, Prediction; stories: Verunj and Gentlemen; Mistake; some works have been translated into English,

German, French, Japanese and other languages. *E-mail:* ZB1307875@yandex.ru (office). *Address:* Moscow, Krasnopresnenskaya nab. 12, Entrance No. 6, Office 807 (office); 109240 Moscow, Kotelnicheskaya nab 1/15, korpus B, apt 62, Russia (home). *Telephone:* (495) 258-21-30 (office); (495) 227-49-90 (home). *Fax:* (495) 258-21-31 (office). *E-mail:* triumph1@inbox.ru (office). *Website:* www.zoyaboguslavskaya.ru.

BOHAN, Edmund, MA; New Zealand singer (tenor) and writer; b. 5 Oct. 1935, Christchurch; m. Gillian Margaret Neason 1968; one s. one d. *Education:* Canterbury Univ., New Zealand; singing with Godfrey Stirling, Sydney, Eric Green and Gustave Sacher, London. *Career:* oratorio debut 1956, opera debut 1962; repertoire of more than 170 operas and major works, including oratorio, concerts in England, Europe, Australasia and Brazil; opera, English Opera Group, Dublin Grand Opera, London Chamber Opera, State Opera of South Australia, Canterbury Opera New Zealand; Wexford Festival, New Zealand Int. Festival of the Arts, Aldeburgh Festival, Norwich Triennial, Adelaide Festival; Nat. Opera of Wellington, New Zealand; TV includes Australian Broadcasting, BBC Proms, ABC, and New Zealand Radio; film, Barber of Seville; venues include Royal Festival Hall, Queen Elizabeth Hall and other major halls with Royal Philharmonic Orchestra, London Concert, BBC Concert and Ulster Orchestras; oratorio soloist with British, Australian and New Zealand Choral Socs. *Recordings:* A Gilbert and Sullivan Spectacular, When Song is Sweet, Sweet and Low, Gilbert and Sullivan with Band and Voice, The Olympians and Intaglio (Bliss). *Publications include:* The Buckler 1972, The Writ of Green Wax 1990, Edward Stafford – New Zealand's First Statesman 1994, The Opawa Affair 1996, The Dancing Man 1997, Blest Madman – FitzGerald of Canterbury 1998, To Be A Hero – Sir George Grey 1998, The Matter of Parihaka 2000, The Irish Yankee (runner-up, Richard Webster Popular Fiction Award) 2001, A Present for the Czar 2003, Burdon – A Man of Our Time 2004, The Story So Far – A Short Illustrated History of New Zealand, Climates of War: Conflict in New Zealand 1859–1869 2005, The House of Reed 1907–1983: Great Days in New Zealand Publishing 2005; contribs to The Theatre Royal Christchurch; An Illustrated History, Remembering Godley, The Irish in New Zealand, Historical Contexts and Perspectives, Ulster-New Zealand Migration and Cultural Transfers. *Address:* 5 Vincent Place, Opawa, Christchurch, New Zealand (home).

BOHJALIAN, Chris; American novelist and journalist; b. 12 Aug. 1961, White Plains, NY; m. Victoria Blewer 1984. *Career:* mem. PEN. *Publications include:* A Killing in the Real World 1988, Hangman 1990, Past the Bleachers 1992, Water Witches 1995, Midwives 1997, The Law of Similars 1999, Trans-Sister Radio 2000, The Buffalo Soldier 2002, Idyll Banter 2003, Before You Know Kindness 2004, The Double Bind 2007, Skeletons at the Feast 2008, Secrets of Eden 2010, The Night Strangers 2010. *Honours:* New England Booksellers Asscn Discovery Prize, New England Book Award 2002. *Address:* Crown Publishing Group, Random House Publicity, 1745 Broadway, New York, NY 10019, USA. *E-mail:* sbreivogel@randomhouse.com. *Website:* www.randomhouse.com; www.chrisbohjalian.com.

BOISVERT, France, BA, MLitt, PhD; Canadian teacher, writer and poet; *Directrice littéraire, Éditions de La Grenouillère;* b. (Marie Marguerite France Boisvert), 10 June 1959, Sherbrooke, QC; one s. *Career:* teacher of French and French Canadian literature; mem. Union des écrivaines et des écrivains québécois (elected mem. Conseil d' admin 1992–93, 1995); elected mem. Syndicat des Enseignantes et Enseignants du Cégep Lionel-Groulx (SEECLG), Vice-Pres. 2008–09, Pres. 2009–; Ed. and Directrice littéraire, Les Éditions de La Grenouillère. *Publications include:* Les Samourailles (fiction) 1987, Li Tsing-tao ou Le grand avoir (fiction) 1989, Massawippi (poem) 1992, Comme un vol de gerfauts (poem) 1993, Les Vents de l'Aube (prose) 1997, Le Voyageur aux yeux d'onyx (prose) 2002, Un vernis de culture (short stories) 2012; contribs to Liberté, Moebius, Arcade, La Vie en Rose, La Presse, Le Devoir. *Honours:* Minister of Culture, Québec bursaries 1989, 1990, 1991. *Address:* A/S Collège Lionel-Groulx, 100 rue Duquet, Sainte-Thérèse, PQ J7E 3G6, Canada (office). *Telephone:* (450) 430-3120 (office). *Fax:* (450) 971-7883 (office). *E-mail:* france59boisvert@yahoo.ca (home). *Website:* www.lagrenouillere.info (office); www.litterature.org/recherche/ecrivains/boisvert-france-80 (office); www.franceboisvert.com.

BOK, Derek, MA, JD; American legal scholar, university administrator and academic; *300th Anniversary University President Emeritus, Professor Emeritus and Faculty Chair, Hauser Center for Non-Profit Organizations, Harvard University;* b. 22 March 1930, Bryn Mawr, Pa; s. of late Curtis Bok and Margaret Plummer (now Mrs. W. S. Kiskadden); m. Sissela Ann Myrdal (d. of Karl Gunnar and Alva Myrdal) 1955; one s. two d. *Education:* Univs of Stanford, Harvard, George Washington and Inst. of Political Science, Paris Univ. *Career:* served US Army 1956–58; Asst Prof. of Law, Harvard Univ. 1958–61, Prof. 1961–, Dean 1968–71, 300th Anniversary Univ. Prof. 1991–, now Emer.; Pres. Harvard Univ. 1971–91, now Pres. Emer., Interim Pres. 2006–; Dir, Nat. Chair. Common Cause 1999–; Chair. Spencer Foundation 2002–; Faculty Chair. Hauser Center for Non-Profit Orgs 2002–. *Publications include:* The First Three Years of the Schuman Plan, Cases and Materials on Labor Law (with Archibald Cox), Labor and the American Community (with John Dunlop), The Federal Government and the University, Beyond the Ivory Tower: Social Responsibilities of the Modern University 1982, Higher Learning 1986, Universities and the Future of America 1990, The Cost of Talent 1993, The State of the Nation 1997, The Shape of the River (jtly) 1998, The Trouble with Government 2001, Universities in the Marketplace: the commercialization of higher education 2004, The Politics of Happiness: What Government Can Learn from the New Research on Well-Being 2010. *Address:* Hauser Center for Nonprofit Organizations, 5 Bennett Street, Cambridge, MA 02138 (office); John F. Kennedy School of Government, Harvard University, 79 John F. Kennedy Street, Cambridge, MA 02138, USA (office). *Telephone:* (617) 495-1199 (office). *Fax:* (617) 496-6886 (office). *E-mail:* derek_bok@harvard.edu (office). *Website:* www.ksg.harvard.edu/hauser (office).

BOK, Sissela, BA, MA, PhD; American (b. Swedish) philosopher, writer and academic; *Senior Visiting Fellow, Harvard Center for Population and Development Studies, School of Public Health, Harvard University;* b. (Sissela Myrdal), 2 Dec. 1934, Stockholm, Sweden; d. of Gunnar Myrdal and Alva Myrdal; m. Derek Bok 1955; one s. two d. *Education:* George Washington Univ., Harvard Univ. *Career:* Lecturer, Simmons Coll., Boston 1971–72, Harvard-MIT Div. of Health Sciences and Tech., Cambridge 1975–82, Harvard Univ. 1982–84; Assoc. Prof. 1985–89, Prof. of Philosophy 1989–92, Brandeis Univ.; Fellow, Center for Advanced Study, Stanford, Calif. 1991–92; Distinguished Fellow, Harvard Center for Population and Devt Studies 1993, currently Sr Visiting Fellow; mem. Pulitzer Prize Bd 1988–97, Chair. 1996–97; Fellow, Hasting Center 1972–2002, Dir 1976–84, 1994–97; mem. American Philosophical Asscn. *Publications include:* Lying: Moral Choice in Public and Private Life 1978, Secrets: On the Ethics of Concealment and Revelation 1982, Alva: Ett kvinnoliv 1987, A Strategy for Peace 1989, Alva Myrdal: A Daughter's Memoir 1991, Common Values 1996, Mayhem: Violence as Public Entertainment 1998, Euthanasia and Physician-Assisted Suicide (with Gerald Dworkin and Ray Frey) 1998, Exploring Happiness: From Aristotle to Brain Science 2010; contribs to scholarly publications. *Honours:* Dr hc (Mount Holyoke Coll.) 1985, (George Washington Univ.) 1986, (Clark Univ.) 1988, (Univ. of Massachusetts) 1991, (Georgetown Univ.) 1992; George Orwell Award 1978, Melcher Awards 1978, 1991, Abram L. Sacher Silver Medallion, Brandeis Univ. 1985, St Botolph Foundation Award 2002, Radcliffe Coll. Grad. Soc. Medal 1993, Barnard Coll. Medal of Distinction 1995, Centennial Medal, Grad. School of Arts and Sciences, Harvard Univ. 1998, Commonwealth Humanities Lecturer 2006. *Address:* Harvard Center for Population and Development Studies, 9 Bow Street, Cambridge, MA 02138, USA (office). *Telephone:* (617) 495-2021 (office). *E-mail:* sbok@hsph.harvard.edu (office).

BOKHARI, Salim; Pakistani journalist; *Editor, The Nation. Career:* correspondent for numerous publications and TV and radio broadcasts, including The International News and CNN; Ed. The News, The Muslim, The Sun, The National; Ed.-in-Chief, Amoon Media Group; Lahore Resident Ed. The Daily Mail; Ed. The Nation 2010–. *Honours:* Best English Reporting Award, All Pakistan Newspapers Soc. 1984–85, Pres.'s Award for Pride of Performance 2005. *Address:* The Nation, NIPCO House, 4 Shaarey Fatima Jinnah, Lahore, Pakistan (office). *Telephone:* (42) 6367580 (office). *Fax:* (42) 6367005 (office). *Website:* www.nation.com.pk (office).

BOLAM, Robyn, (Marion Lomax), BA, DPhil; British academic, poet and editor; *Professor of Literature, St Mary's College, University of Surrey;* b. (Marion Bolam), 20 Oct. 1953, Newcastle upon Tyne; m. Michael Lomax 1974 (divorced 1999). *Education:* Univ. of Kent; Univ. of York. *Career:* Part-time Lecturer, King Alfred's Coll. 1983–86; Creative Writing Fellow, Univ. of Reading 1987–88; Lecturer, later Sr Lecturer in English, St Mary's Coll., Univ. of Surrey 1988–95, Prof. of Literature 1995–; Writer-in-Residence, Univ. of Stockholm, March–May 1998; published as Marion Lomax –2000, as Robyn Bolam 2000–; mem. Nat. Asscn for Writers in Educ., Poetry Soc., Soc. of Authors, Higher Educ. Acad., English Asscn. *Opera:* libretto for Beyond Men and Dreams (composer Bennett Hogg), Royal Opera House Garden Venture 1991. *Publications include:* poetry: The Peepshow Girl 1989, Raiding the Borders 1996, New Wings: Poems 1977–2007 2007; non-fiction: Stage Images and Traditions: Shakespeare to Ford 1987, Eliza's Babes: Four Centuries of Women's Poetry in English, c. 1500–1900 2005, New Wings: Poems 1977–2007 2007, Stage Images and Traditions: Shakespeare to Ford 2009; editor: Time Present and Time Past: Poets at the University of Kent 1965–1985 1985, Four Plays by John Ford 1995, The Rover, by Aphra Behn 1995, Out of the Blue (with Steven Harman) 1998, Eliza's Babes: Four Centuries of Women's Poetry in English 2003; contribs to collections of essays, anthologies and periodicals. *Honours:* E.C. Gregory Award, Soc. of Authors 1981, First Prize, Cheltenham Festival Poetry Competition 1981, Hawthornden Fellowship 1993. *Address:* Bloodaxe Books Ltd, Highgreen, Tarset, NE48 1RP, England. *Telephone:* (1434) 240500. *Fax:* (1434) 240505. *E-mail:* publicity@bloodaxebooks.com. *Website:* www.bloodaxebooks.com.

BOLAND, Eavan Aisling, BA; Irish poet, critic and academic; *Melvin and Bill Lane Professor for the Director of the Creative Writing Program and Bella Mabury and Eloise Mabury Knapp Professor in Humanities, Stanford University;* b. 24 Sept. 1944, Dublin; d. of Frederick Boland and Frances Kelly; two d. *Education:* schools in London, New York, USA and Dublin, and Trinity Coll., Dublin. *Career:* Lecturer, Trinity Coll., Dublin 1967–68 and School of Irish Studies, Dublin; fmr Writer-in-Residence, Trinity Coll. and Univ. Coll. Dublin; Poet-in-Residence, Nat. Maternity Hosp. 1994; fmr Hurst Prof., Washington Univ., also mem. Advisory Bd Int. Writers' Center; fmr Regent's Lecturer, Univ. of California, Santa Barbara; Chair. of judging panel, Irish Times-Aer Lingus Irish Literature Prizes; Melvin and Bill Lane Prof. for the Dir of the Creative Writing Program, Stanford Univ., Calif. 1995–2000, 2002–, Bella Mabury and Eloise Mabury Knapp Prof. in Humanities 1995–; reviewer, Irish Times; mem. Bd Irish Arts Council; mem. Irish Acad. of Letters; Macaulay Fellowship 1967. *Publications include:* poetry: 23 Poems

1962, New Territory 1967, The War Horse 1976, In her Own Image 1980, Night Feed 1982, The Journey and Other Poems 1987, Selected Poems 1989, A Kind of Scar – The Woman Poet in a National Tradition 1989, Outside History – Selected Poems 1980–1990 1990, In a Time of Violence 1994, A Dozen Lips 1994, Collected Poems 1995, An Origin Like Water – Collected Poems 1967–1987 1996, The Lost Land 1998, Against Love Poetry 2001, Code 2001, Domestic Violence 2007, New Collected Poems 2008; prose: W. B. Yeats and his World (with Michael MacLiammoir) 1971, Object Lessons: The Life of the Woman and the Poet in Our Time 1995, A Journey with Two Maps 2011; other: The Making of a Poem: A Norton Anthology of Poetic Forms (ed. with Mark Strand) 2000, The Making of a Sonnet: A Norton Anthology (ed with Edward Hirsch) 2008, A Journey with Two Maps: Becoming A Woman Poet 2011. *Honours:* Dr hc (Nat. Univ. of Ireland), (Univ. of Strathclyde, UK), (Holy Cross Coll., Boston, USA), (Colby Coll., Maine, USA), Trinity Coll., Dublin, Ireland), (Bowdoin Coll., Maine); Irish-American Foundation Award 1983, Ingram Merrill Award 1989, Ireland-American Fund 1994, Lannan Award for Poetry 1994, Charity Hume Randall Award 1997, John Frederick Nims Award 2002. *Address:* English Department, Stanford University, 450 Serra Mall, Building 460, Room 201, Stanford, CA 94305-2087, USA (office). *Telephone:* (650) 725-1207 (office). *Fax:* (650) 723-3679 (office). *E-mail:* boland@stanford.edu (office). *Website:* www.stanford.edu (office).

BOLGER, Dermot; Irish writer, dramatist and poet; b. 6 Feb. 1959, Finglas, Dublin; s. of Roger Bolger and the late Bridie Flanagan; m. Bernadette Clifton 1988 (died 2010); two s. *Education:* St Canice's BNS, Finglas and Benevin Coll., Finglas. *Career:* worked as factory hand, library asst and professional author; Founder and Ed. Raven Arts Press 1979–92; Founder and Exec. Ed. New Island Books, Dublin 1992–; mem. Arts Council of Ireland 1989–93; elected mem. Aosdána 1991–; Playwright in Asscn, The Abbey (Nat.) Theatre 1997; Writer Fellow, Trinity Coll., Dublin 2003; Writer in Residence, Farmleigh House, Dublin 2008. *Plays:* The Lament for Arthur Cleary 1989, Blinded by the Light 1990, In High Germany 1990, The Holy Ground 1990, One Last White Horse 1991, A Dublin Bloom 1994, April Bright 1995, The Passion of Jerome 1999, Consenting Adults 2000, From These Green Heights 2004, The Townlands of Brazil 2006, Walking the Road 2007, The Consequences of Lightning 2008, The Parting Glass 2010, Tea Chests & Dreams 2012. *Radio:* The Woman's Daughter 2005, Hunger Again 2006, The Fortunestown Kid 2006, The Night Manager 2007, The Kerlogue 2007, Moving In Day 2008, Accident & Emergency 2010, Outline Permission 2012. *Television screenplay:* Edward No Hands 1996. *Publications:* novels: Night Shift 1985, The Woman's Daughter 1987, The Journey Home 1990, Emily's Shoes 1992, A Second Life 1994, Father's Music 1997, Finbar's Hotel (co-author) 1997, Ladies Night at Finbar's Hotel (co-author) 1999, Temptation 2000, The Valparaiso Voyage 2001, The Family on Paradise Pier 2005, The Journey Home 2008; poetry: The Habit of Flesh 1979, Finglas Lilies 1980, No Waiting America 1981, Internal Exile 1986, Leinster Street Ghosts 1989, Taking My Letters Back, New and Selected Poems 1998, The Chosen Moment 2004; editor: The Dolmen Book of Irish Christmas Stories 1986, The Bright Wave: Poetry in Irish Now 1986, 16 on 16: Irish Writers on the Easter Rising 1988, Invisible Cities: The New Dubliners: A Journey through Unofficial Dublin 1988, Invisible Dublin: A Journey through its Writers 1992, The Picador Book of Contemporary Irish Fiction 1993, 12 Bar Blues (with Aidan Murphy) 1993, The New Picador Book of Contemporary Irish Fiction 2000, Druids, Dudes and Beauty Queens: The Changing Face of Irish Theatre 2001, The Ledwidge Treasury 2007, Night & Day: 24 Hours in the Life of Dublin 2008, External Affairs 2008, The Ballymun Trilogy 2010, New Town Soul 2010, A Second Life: A Renewed Novel 2010. *Honours:* A.E. Memorial Prize 1986, Macauley Fellowship 1987, A.Z. Whitehead Prize 1987, Samuel Beckett Award 1991, Edinburgh Fringe First Awards 1991, 1995, Stewart Parker BBC Award 1991, The Hennessy Irish Literature Hall of Fame Award 2003, Irish Times/EBS Prize for Best New Irish Play of 2004, Worldplay Int. Radio Prize for Best Script 2005. *Literary Agent:* c/o AP Watt Ltd, 20 John Street, London, WC1N 2DR, England. *Telephone:* (20) 7405-6774. *Fax:* (20) 7831-2154. *E-mail:* apw@apwatt.co.uk. *Website:* www.apwatt.co.uk; www.dermotbolger.com (office).

BOLTSHAUSER, Patrick; Swiss author and playwright; b. 1971, St Gallen. *Education:* Univ. of Bern. *Career:* grew up in Schaan, Liechtenstein; studied biology and behavioural ecology; fmr actor, director and playwright for various theatre groups; plays performed in Austria, Germany, Switzerland; writer of short stories including Morgen in Deggendorf (Tomorrow It's Deggendorf), Die falschen Dinge (All the Wrong Things). *Publications:* as contrib.: Best European Fiction 2012. *Address:* c/o Dalkey Archive Press, University of Illinois, 1805 South Wright Street, MC-011, Champaign, IL 61820, USA (office). *Telephone:* (217) 244-5700 (office). *Fax:* (217) 244-9142 (office). *E-mail:* contact@dalkeyarchive.com (office). *Website:* www.dalkeyarchive.com (office).

BON, François; French writer; b. 22 May 1953, Luçon, Vendée. *Education:* École Nat. Supérieure d'Arts et Métiers. *Career:* Founder remue.net (literary collective website) 2001; Writer-in-Residence, Acad. de France, Rome 1984–85, Deutscher Akademischer Austauschdienst, Berlin 1987–88, Robert Bosch Stiftung, Stuttgart, 1991–92, Centre Dramatique Nat. de Nancy 1998–99, Théâtre Ouvert, Paris 1999–2000; Founder publie.net 2008; Visiting Prof., Univ. Laval, Univ. of Montreal 2009–10; Guest Artist, Univ. of Louvain-la-Neuve 2011–. *Plays:* Scène (Centre Dramatique Régional de Tours) 1998, Au buffet de la gare d'Angoulême (Centre Dramatique Régional de Tours) 1998, Vie de Myriam C. (Centre Dramatique Nat. de Nancy) 1998, Fariboles (Centre Dramatique Nat. de Nancy) 1999, Qui se déchire (France-Culture) 2000, Bruit (Théâtre Ouvert, Paris) 2000, Quatre avec le mort (Théâtre de la Comédie Française) 2002, Daewoo (Festival d'Avignon) 2004. *Publications include:* Sortie d'usine 1982, Limite 1985, Le Crime de Buzon 1986, Décor ciment 1988, Calvaire des chiens 1990, La Folie Rabelais (essay) 1990, L'Enterrement 1990, Temps Machine 1992, Un Fait divers 1993, Dans la ville invisible (juvenile) 1995, C'était toute une vie 1995, Parking 1996, Voleurs de feu, vies singulières des poètes (juvenile) 1996, 30, rue de la Poste (juvenile) 1996, Le Solitaire (non-fiction) 1996, Impatience 1998, Prison 1998, Dehors est la ville (non-fiction) 1998, Autoroute (juvenile) 1999, Pour Koltès (essay) 2000, Tous les mots sont adultes 2000, Paysage fer (Prix France Culture La Ville à Lire) 2000, Mécanique 2001, Quoi faire de son chien mort? et autres textes courts pour la scène 2002, Rolling Stones, une biographie (Soc. des Gens de Lettres Prix d'automne) 2002, Billancourt (non-fiction) 2003, Daewoo (novel) 2004, Tumulte 2006, Déplacements 2007, Bob Dylan, une biographie 2007, Jacques Villeglé (co-author) 2007, L'incendie du Hilton 2009, Préhistoire : La fabrique de l'homme 2009, Après le livre 2011. *Honours:* Chevalier, Ordre des Arts et des Lettres 1998. *Address:* Le Tiers Livre, BP 145, 37541 Saint-Cyr sur Loire, France (office). *E-mail:* fbon@tierslivre.net (office). *Website:* www.tierslivre.net (office).

BONA, Dominique Henriette Marie; French journalist and writer; b. 29 July 1953, Perpignan; d. of Arthur Conte and Colette Conte; m. Philippe Bona 1973; one s. one d. *Education:* Cours Dupanloup, Boulogne, Lycée Victor Duruy, Univ. of Paris IV (Paris-Sorbonne). *Career:* journalist, Le Quotidien de Paris 1980–85, Le Figaro 1985–; writer of novels and biographies; mem. Jury Prix Renaudot 1999–. *Publications include:* novels: Les heures volées 1981, Argentina 1984, Malika (Prix Interallié) 1992, Le manuscit de Port-Ebène (Prix Renaudot) 1998, La Ville d'Hiver 2005; biographies: Romain Gary (Grand Prix de la Biographie, Acad. Française) 1987, Les yeux noirs ou les vies extraordinaires des sœurs Hérédia (Grand Prix de la Femme, Prix Lutèce, Prix de l'Enclave des Papes 1990) 1989, Gala 1994, Stefan Zweig, l'ami blessé 1996, Berthe Morisot, Le Secret de la femme en noir (Prix Goncourt de la Biographie) 2000, Il n'y a qu'un amour 2003, Camille et Paul (Grand Prix des Lectrices d'Elle 2007) 2006, Clara Malraux : Nous avons été deux 2010, Stefan Zweig (Bona) 2010. *Honours:* Officier des Arts et Lettres, Chevalier de l'Ordre nat. du Mérite, Légion d'honneur. *Address:* Editions Grasset, 61 rue des Saints-Pères, 75006 Paris, France. *Telephone:* 1-44-39-22-00. *Fax:* 1-42-22-64-18. *E-mail:* hwarneke@grasset.fr. *Website:* www.grasset.fr (office).

BONALD, Jose Manuel Caballero; Spanish poet, novelist, academic and essayist; *President, Caballero Bonald Foundation;* b. 11 Nov. 1926, Jerez de la Frontera; s. of Placido Caballero and Julia Bonald. *Education:* Coll. of Marianist Jerez. *Career:* mil. service in Naval Militia Univ.; at Seminary of Lexicography, Royal Spanish Acad. 1971–75; taught at Universidad Nacional de Colombia; fmr Sec., currently Deputy Dir Papeles de Son Armadans (magazine); fmr Prof. of Literature in Bogotá; Literary Ed. Editions Júcar Officer 1973; Prof. of Contemporary Spanish Literature, Centre for Hispanic Studies, Bryn Mawr Coll., Pa, USA 1974–78; fmr Pres. PEN Club Spanish (resgnd 1980); currently Pres. Caballero Bonald Foundation; fmr mem. North American Spanish Language Acad. 1993. *Publications:* poems: Mendigo (Platero Poetry Award) 1950, Las adivinaciones 1952, Memorias de poco tiempo 1954, Anteo 1956, Las horas muertas (Boscan and Review, Critics' Award) 1959, Pliegos de cordel 1963, Descrédito del héroe (Critics' Award) 1977, Laberinto de Fortuna 1984, Doce poemas 1991, Descrédito del héroe y Laberinto de Fortuna 1993, Diario de Argónida 1997, Manual de infractores (International Award for Best Book Terenci Moix 2005, National Poetry Award 2006) 2005, Antídotos 2008, La noche no tiene paredes 2009; narrative: Dos días de setiembre (Biblioteca Breve) 1962, Ágata ojo de gato 1974, Toda la noche oyeron pasar pájaros 1981, En la casa del padre (Plaza and Janes) 1988, Campo de Agramante (Andalusian Literature prize 1994) 1992; memories: Tiempo de guerras perdidas 1995, La costumbre de vivir 2001, La novela de la memoria 2010; theatre adaptations: Abre el ojo 1959, Don Gil de las calzas verdes 1994, Fuenteovejuna 1995; other works: El baile andaluz 1957, Cádiz, Jerez y los Puertos 1963, Narrativa cubana de la Revolución 1968, Luces y sombras del flamenco 1975, Cuixart 1977, Breviario del vino 1980, Luis de Góngora: Poesía 1982, Los personajes de Fajardo 1986, De la sierra al mar de Cádiz 1988, Andalucía 1989, Botero: La corrida 1990, España: Fiestas y ritos 1992, Sevilla en tiempos de Cervantes 1992, España 1997, Copias del natural (selección de textos) 1999, Mar adentro 2002, José de Espronceda 2002, Miguel de Cervantes 2005, Copias rescatadas del natural 2006, Un Madrid literario 2009. *Honours:* Favorite Son of Andalucía 1996, Son of the Province of Cadiz 1999; Dr hc (Univ. of Cádiz) 2004; Pablo Iglesias Letters 1979, Ibn al-Khatib 1988, Gold Medal of Fine Arts Circle Award and the Julian Besteiro of Arts and Letters 1999, Queen Sofia of Poetry 2004, Nat. Literature Prize 2005, Nat. Poetry Award 2008, Int. Prize for Poetry Federico García Lorca Granada-City 2009. *Address:* Caballero Bonald Foundation, 17 Caballeros, 11403 Jerez de la Frontera, Spain (office). *Telephone:* (95) 6149140 (office). *Website:* www.fcbonald.com (office).

BONANNO, David; American editor; *Joint Editor, American Poetry Review;* m. Kathleen Sheeder Bonanno. *Career:* Joint Ed. American Poetry Review 1973–; teaches workshops on poetry and literary publishing; co-ordinator of poetry in the high schools programme in Philadelphia; mem. Literary Advisory Panel, Pennsylvania Council on the Arts. *Publications include:* The Body Electric: America's Best Poetry from The American Poetry Review (co-ed.) 2001. *Address:* The American Poetry Review, 1700 Sansom Street, Suite 800, Philadelphia, PA 19103, USA (office). *Telephone:* (215) 496-0439 (office). *E-mail:* dbonanno@aprweb.org (office). *Website:* www.aprweb.org (office).

BOND, Edward; British playwright, director and poet; b. 18 July 1934, London; m. Elisabeth Pablé 1971. *Career:* Northern Arts Literary Fellowship 1977–79; resident theatre writer, Univ. of Essex 1982–83. *Publications:* plays: The Pope's Wedding 1962, Saved 1965, Narrow Road to the Deep North 1968, Early Morning 1968, Passion 1971, Black Mass 1971, Lear 1972, The Sea 1973, Bingo 1974, The Fool 1976, A-A-America! (Grandma Faust and The Swing) 1976, Stone 1976, The Bundle 1978, The Woman 1979, The Worlds 1980, The Activist Papers 1980, Restoration 1981, Summer: A Play for Europe 1982, Derek 1983, Human Cannon 1985, The War Plays (Red Black and Ignorant, The Tin Can People, Great Peace) 1985, Jackets 1989, In the Company of Men 1990, September 1990, Olly's Prison 1993, Tuesday 1993, Coffee: A Tragedy 1994, At the Inland Sea (A Play for Young People) 1996, Eleven Vests (A Play for Young People) 1997, The Crime of the Twenty-first Century 1999, The Children (A Play for Two Adults and Sixteen Children) 2000, Chair 2000, Have I None 2000, Existence 2002, Born 2004, The Balancing Act 2004, The Short Electra 2004, My Day (Song Cycle for Children) 2005, The Under Room 2006, Arcade 2006, Tune 2007, People 2007, A Window 2009, There Will Be More 2010, Collected Plays (nine vols) 1977–2011 2011, Innocence 2011, The Broken Bowl 2011, The Edge 2012, The Chair Trilogy 2012; short stories: Fables 1982; opera librettos of music by Hans Werner Henze: We Come to the River 1977, The English Cat 1983; ballet libretto of music by Henze: Orpheus 1982; translations: Chekhov's The Three Sisters 1967, Wedekind's Spring Awakening 1974, Wedekind's Lulu: A Monster Tragedy (with Elisabeth Bond-Pablé) 1992; other: Theatre Poems and Songs 1978, Collected Poems 1978–1985 1987, Notes on Post-Modernism 1990, Letters (five vols) 1994–2001, Notes on Imagination 1995, Selected Notebooks Vol. 1 2000, Vol. 2 2001, The Hidden Plot: Notes on Theatre and the State 2000. *Honours:* City of Lyon Medal 2007; Hon. DLitt (Yale) 1977; George Devine Award 1968, John Whiting Award 1968, Obie Award 1976. *Literary Agent:* c/o Casarotto Ramsay, Waverley House, 7–12 Noel Street, London, W1F 8GQ, England. *Telephone:* (20) 7287-4450. *Fax:* (20) 7287-9128. *E-mail:* tom@casarotto.uk.com. *Website:* www.casarotto.uk.com.

BOND, Nancy Barbara, BA; American librarian and writer; b. 8 Jan. 1945, Bethesda, Md. *Education:* Mount Holyoke Coll., Coll. of Librarianship, Wales. *Career:* Instructor (part-time), Simmons Coll., Centre for the Study of Children's Literature 1979–2001. *Publications include:* A String in the Harp (Newbery Honour) 1976, The Best of Enemies 1978, Country of Broken Stone 1980, The Voyage Begun (Boston Globe-Horn Book Award) 1981, A Place to Come Back To 1984, Another Shore 1988, Truth to Tell 1994, The Love of Friends 1997, Career Ideas for Kids Who Like Art 1998, Career Ideas for Kids Who Like Sports 1998. *Honours:* Int. Reading Asscn Award 1976, Welsh Arts Council Tir na n-Og Award 1976. *Address:* 109 The Valley Road, Concord, MA 01742-4900, USA (home).

BOND, Ruskin; Indian writer; b. 19 May 1934, Kasauli, Himachal Pradesh; s. of Aubrey Alexander Bond. *Publications include:* over 100 short stories and 30 books for children including The India I Love, Rain in the Mountains, The Parrot Who Wouldn't Talk, Angry River 1992, Leopard On The Mountain 1998, Season of Ghosts 2000, Night Train at Deoli 2000, When Darkness Falls And Other Stories 2001, A Long Walk for Bina 2002, Hanuman to the Rescue 2004, Face In The Dark And Other Hauntings 2004, Roads to Mussoorie 2005, Funny Side Up 2006, Rendezvous with Horror 2007, Potpourri 2007, All Roads Lead to Ganga 2007, Susanna's Seven Husbands, Escape From Java and Other Tales of Danger 2010, Crazy Times With Uncle Ken 2011; poetry: A Little Night Music 2004, Ruskin Bond's Book of Verse 2007; collections: Ruskin Bond's Book of Humour 2008, Classic Ruskin Bond 2010; novels: The Room on the Roof (John Llewellyn Rhys Prize) 1957, Delhi is not Far 1994, Rain In The Mountains 2000, Friends in Small Places 2003, Vagrants in the Valley 2003, Hidden Pool 2004, A Flight of Pigeons, The Sensualist, A Handful of Nuts; non-fiction: Lamp is Lit 2000, Landour Days: A Writer's Journal 2002, Tales of the Open Road 2005, A Town Called Dehra 2008, Notes From a Small Room 2009. *Honours:* Sahitya Akademi Award 1992, Padma Shri 1999. *Address:* Marketing and Promotions Department, Penguin Books India Private Limited 11, Community Centre, Panchsheel Park, New Delhi 110 017, India. *Telephone:* (11) 26494401. *Fax:* (11) 26494403. *E-mail:* publicity@in.penguingroup.com. *Website:* www.penguinbooksindia.com.

BOND, (Thomas) Michael, OBE; British author; b. 13 Jan. 1926, Newbury, Berks.; m. 1st Brenda Mary Johnson 1950 (divorced 1981); one d. one s.; m. 2nd Susan Marfrey Rogers 1981. *Education:* Presentation Coll. *Career:* served in RAF, Middlesex Regiment of British Army during World War II; also worked as cameraman for BBC. *Publications include:* for children: A Bear Called Paddington 1958, More About Paddington 1959, Paddington Helps Out 1960, Paddington Abroad 1961, Paddington at Large 1962, Paddington Marches On 1964, Paddington at Work 1966, Here Comes Thursday 1966, Thursday Rides Again 1968, Paddington Goes to Town 1968, Thursday Ahoy 1969, Parsley's Tail 1969, Parsley's Good Deed 1969, Parsley's Problem Present 1970, Parsley's Last Stand 1970, Paddington Takes the Air 1970, Thursday in Paris 1971, Michael Bond's Book of Bears 1971, Michael Bond's Book of Mice 1971, The Day the Animals Went on Strike 1972, Paddington Bear 1972, Paddington's Garden 1972, Parsley Parade 1972, The Tales of Olga de Polga 1971, Olga Meets her Match 1973, Paddington's Blue Peter Story Book 1973, Paddington at the Circus 1973, Paddington Goes Shopping 1973, Paddington at the Seaside 1974, Paddington at the Tower 1974, Paddington on Top 1974, Windmill 1975, How to Make Flying Things 1975, Eight Olga Readers 1975, Olga Carries On 1976, Paddington Takes the Test 1979, Paddington's Cartoon Book 1979, J. D. Polson and the Liberty Head Dime 1980, J. D. Polson and the Dillogate Affair 1981, Paddington on Screen 1981, Olga Takes Charge 1982, The Caravan Puppets 1983, Paddington at the Zoo 1984, Paddington's Painting Exhibition 1985, Oliver the Greedy Elephant 1985, Paddington Minds the House 1986, Paddington at the Palace 1986, Paddington's Busy Day 1987, Paddington and the Magical Maze 1987, Paddington: A Classic Collection 1997, Paddington and the Christmas Surprise 1997, Paddington at the Carnival 1998, Paddington and the Tutti Frutti Rainbow 1998, Paddington – My Scrapbook 1999, Paddington's Party Tricks 2000, Paddington in Hot Water 2000, Paddington Goes to Hospital 2001, Paddington Treasury 2001, Olga Moves House 2001, Olga Follows her Nose 2002, Paddington and the Grand Tour 2003, Paddington Rules the Waves 2008, Paddington: My Book of Marmalade 2008, Paddington Here and Now 2008, The Paddington Treasury for the Very Young 2010, Paddington's London Treasury 2011, Paddington's Guide to London 2011, Paddington's Cookery Book 2011, Paddington Goes for Gold 2012, Paddington Races Ahead 2012; for adults: Monsieur Pamplemousse 1983, Monsieur Pamplemousse and the Secret Mission 1984, Monsieur Pamplemousse on the Spot 1986, Monsieur Pamplemousse Takes the Cure 1987, The Pleasures of Paris, Guide Book 1987, Monsieur Pamplemousse Aloft 1989, Monsieur Pamplemousse Investigates 1990, Monsieur Pamplemousse Rests his Case 1991, Monsieur Pamplemousse Stands Firm 1992, Monsieur Pamplemousse on Location 1992, Monsieur Pamplemousse Takes the Train 1993, Bears and Forebears (autobiog.) 1996, Monsieur Pamplemousse Afloat 1998, Monsieur Pamplemousse on Probation 2000, Monsieur Pamplemousse on Vacation 2002, Monsieur Pamplemousse Hits the Headlines 2003, Monsieur Pamplemousse and the Militant Midwives 2006, Monsieur Pamplemousse and the French Solution 2007, Monsieur Pamplemousse and the Carbon Footprint 2010. *Honours:* Hon. DLitt (Univ. of Reading) 2007. *Literary Agent:* c/o The Agency, 24 Pottery Lane, Holland Park, London, W11 4LZ, England. *Telephone:* (20) 7727-1346. *E-mail:* info@theagency.co.uk. *Website:* www.paddingtonbear.com.

BONDAREV, Yuriy Vasiliyevich; Russian writer; *Chairman, International Committee, Mikhail Sholokhov Prize;* b. 15 March 1924, Orsk; s. of the late Vasili Vasilevich Bondarev and the late Claudia Iosifovna Bondareva; m. Valentina Nikitichna Mosina 1950; two d. *Education:* Gor'kiy Inst., Moscow 1951. *Career:* writer 1949–; mem. CPSU 1944–91; First Deputy Chair. of RSFSR Writers' Union, Chair. of Bd 1990–93; Pres. Yedineniye (Unity) Asscn 1995–; served in Soviet Army 1941–45; Deputy to Supreme Soviet 1975–80 and Deputy Chair.; Chair., Int. Cttee, Mikhail Sholokhov Prize; Chair. Union of Writers 1990–94; Co-Chair., Int. Community of Writers' Unions 1991–999; Deputy Chair. Council of Nationalities of the Supreme Soviet of the USSR 1984–89; mem. Int. Slavian Acad., Acad. of Literature, Peter the Great Acad., Russian Acad.; mem. Editorial Bd Literary Gazette 1959–63; Ed.-in-Chief Asscn of Writers and Filmmakers 1961–66. *Film:* screenplay for epic film Liberation 1964–70. *Play:* The Turnover 1994. *Publications include:* novels: On the Big River 1953, Young Commanders 1956, Fire for the Battalions 1957, Last Salute 1959, Silence 1962, Relatives 1965, Hot Snow 1969, The Shore 1975, A Choice 1980, The Game 1984, Temptation 1991, Instants (essays) 1981–87 and 1987–94, 2001, Collected Works (eight vols) 1993–94, Non-Resistance to Evil 1994, The Bermuda Triangle 2000, Without Mercy 2004. *Honours:* Hon. Citizen of Volgograd, Hon. Prof. of Moscow State Teachers, Univ. of Mikhail Sholokhov, Hon. mem. Pushkin Acad.; Order of Honour of Transdniestrian Repub.; Hero of Socialist Labour 1984, two State prizes, Lenin Prize, RSFSR Prize, Tolstoy Prize 1993, Sholokhov Prize 1994, Vladimir Dal Prize 2002, Alexander Nevsky Prize. *Address:* Lomonosovsky Prospekt N19, Apt 148, 117311 Moscow, Russia. *Telephone:* (495) 334-59-92.

BONDER, Nilton, BS, MA, PhD; Brazilian rabbi and writer; *Rabbi of the Jewish Congregation of Brazil;* b. 27 Dec. 1957, Porte Alegre; m. Esther Bonder 1991; one s. two d. *Education:* Catholic Univ. of Rio de Janeiro, Jewish Theological Seminary, New York City. *Career:* Rabbi, Associacao Religiosa Israelita, Jewish Congregation of Brazil; Pres., Inst. for Religious Studies (ISER), Midrash Cultural Center. *Plays:* The Immoral Soul (voted Play of the Year, Veja magazine 2007), Heaven's Criminal Code 2010. *Publications include:* A Tractade on Impunity 1993, The Art of Saving Yourself 1994, The Jewish Way of Problem Solving 1995, Secret Portals 1996, The Kabbalah of Money 1996, The Kabbalah of Envy 1997, The Kabbalah of Food 1998, The Immoral Soul 2001, Boundaries of Intelligence 2002, The Kabbalah of Time 2003, Heaven's Criminal Code 2004, To Have or Not to Have 2005, The Sacred 2007, Taking off Your Shoes 2008, The Jews Were Internauts 2010, Xpiritual 2010. *Literary Agent:* c/o Karen Schindler, PO Box 19051, 04599-970 São Paulo, SP, Brazil. *Telephone:* (21) 2492-1260 (office). *Fax:* (21) 2493-5735 (office). *E-mail:* nbonder@globo.com. *Website:* www.cjb.org.br (office); www.midrash.org.br (office); www.niltonbonder.org.

BONNEFOY, Yves Jean, LèsL; French writer and poet; b. 24 June 1923, Tours; s. of Elie Bonnefoy and Hélène Maury; m. Lucille Vines 1968; one d. *Education:* Lycée Descartes, Tours, Faculté des Sciences, Poitiers and Faculté des Lettres, Paris. *Career:* Prof., Collège de France 1981; contrib. to Mercure de France, Critique, Encounter, L'Ephémère, La Nouvelle Revue Française etc.; has travelled in Europe, Asia and N America; lectures or seminars at Brandeis, Johns Hopkins, Princeton, Williams Coll., Calif., Geneva, Nice, Yale, CUNY, New York and other univs. *Publications:* poems: Du mouvement et de l'immobilité de Douve 1953 (English 1968), Hier régnant désert 1958, Pierre écrite 1964 (English 1976), Selected Poems 1968, Dans le leurre du seuil 1975, Poèmes (1947–1975) 1978, Ce qui fut sans lumière 1987, Entretiens sur la Poésie 1990, Début et fin de la neige 1991, Les planches courbes 2001, Raturer outre 2010; essays: L'Improbable 1959, Arthur Rimbaud 1961 (English trans. 1973), Un rêve fait à Mantoue 1967, Le nuage rouge 1977, Rue traversière 1977; on art: Peintures murales de la France Gothique 1954, Miró 1963, Rome 1630 1969, L'Arrière-Pays 1972, Entretiens sur la poésie 1981, La Présence et l'Image 1983, Récits en rêve 1987, La Vérité de Parole 1988, Alberto Giacometti 1991, La vie errante 1993, Remarques sur le dessin 1993, Dessin, couleur et lumière 1995, Théâtre et poésie: Shakespeare et Yeats, l'Encore aveugle 1998, Zao-Wou-ki (jtly) 1998, Lieux et destins de l'image 1999, La Communauté des traducteurs 2000, Baudelaire: La Tentation de l'oubli 2000, Keats et Léopardi 2000, Sous l'Horizon du Langage 2001, Remarques sur le regard 2001, Breton à l'avant de soi 2001, Poésie et architecture 2001, L'Enseignement de Léopardi 2001, Le poète et le flot mouvant des multitudes 2003, Le sommeil de personne 2004, La stratégie de l'énigme 2006, L'imaginaire métaphysique 2006, Goya: les peintures noires 2006, Dans un débris de miroir 2006, L'alliance de la poésie et de la musique 2007, Ce qui alarma Paul Celan 2007, La Poésie à voix haute 2007, Le Grand Espace 2008, Notre besoin de Rimbaud 2009, Deux Scènes et notes conjointes 2009, La beauté dès le premier jour 2010, La communauté des critiques 2010, Le siècle où la parole a été victime 2010, L'inachevable 2010, L'heure présente 2011, Sous le signe de Baudelaire 2011; co-ed. L'Ephémère, trans. of Shakespeare, W. B. Yeats, Keats, Léopardi, Petrarque. *Honours:* Commdr des Arts et des Lettres; Hon. DHumLitt (American Coll., Paris, Univ. of Chicago, Univ. of Neuchâtel, Trinity Coll., Dublin, Rome, Edin., Siena, Oxford, Naples); Prix Montaigne 1980, Grand Prix de poésie (Acad. Française) 1981, Prix Florence Gould 1987, Grand Prix national 1993, Prix de la Fondation Cino-del-Duca 1995, Prix Balzan 1995, Prix Prince Louis de Polignac 1998, American Acad. of Arts and Letters Award, Franz Kafka Prize 2007, Prix Mario Luzi 2010, Prix Viareggio 2011, Griffin Trust for Excellence in Poetry's Lifetime Recognition Award 2011, and numerous other prizes. *Address:* Collège de France, 11 place Marcelin Berthelot, 75005 Paris, France (office). *E-mail:* yves.bonnefoy@college-de-france.fr (office).

BONNER, Gerald, MA, FSA; British academic (retd); *Reader Emeritus, Durham University*; b. 18 June 1926, London; s. of Frederick J. Bonner and Constance E. Hatch; m. Priscilla J. Hodgson 1967; one s. one d. *Education:* The Stationers' Co.'s School, London and Wadham Coll., Oxford. *Career:* mil. service 1944–48; Asst Keeper, Dept of Manuscripts, British Museum 1953–64; Lecturer in Theology, Durham Univ. 1964, promoted to personal Readership 1969, Reader Emer. 1989–; Convener and Sec., Bedan Conf., Durham 1973; Distinguished Prof. of Early Christian Studies, Catholic Univ. of America 1991–94; delivered Cathedral Lecture, Durham 1970, Augustine Lecture, Villanova Univ. Pa, 1970, Otts Lectures, Davidson Coll., NC 1992; Visiting Prof. in Augustinian Studies, Villanova Univ. 1999. *Publications:* The Warfare of Christ 1962, St Augustine of Hippo: Life and Controversies 1963, Famulus Christi: Essays in Commemoration of the Thirteenth Centenary of the Venerable Bede (ed.) 1976, God's Decree and Man's Destiny 1987, St Cuthbert, His Cult and His Community (co-ed. with D. Rollason and C. Stancliffe), Church and Faith in the Patristic Tradition: Augustine, Pelagianism and Early Christian Northumbria 1996, Augustine of Hippo: The Monastic Rules 2004, Freedom and Necessity: St Augustine's Teaching on Divine Power and Human Freedom 2007, A Last Apology for Pelagianism? 2010; articles in the Augustinus-Lexikon (Basle) 1986– and other learned journals including Journal of Ecclesiastical History, Journal of Theological Studies. *Honours:* Johannes Quasten Medal 1994. *Address:* 7 Victoria Terrace, Durham, DH1 4RW, England (home). *Telephone:* (191) 386-3407 (home).

BONNER, Terry Nelson (see KRAUZER, Steven Mark)

BONNETT VELÉZ, Piedad, BA; Colombian poet, playwright, novelist and academic; *Professor in Literature, Universidad de los Andes*; b. 1951, Amalfi, Antioquia. *Education:* Universidad de los Andes, Escuela de Investigación Linguística y Literaria, Madrid, Universidad Nacional de Colombia. *Career:* Prof. in Literature, Universidad de los Andes 1981–. *Publications include:* poetry: De circulo y ceniza 1989, Nadie en casa 1994, El hilo de los días 1995, Ese animal triste 1996, Todos los amantes son guerreros 1997, No es más que la vida 1998, Demás es silencio 2003, Tretas del débil 2004, Los privilegios del olvido 2008, Las herencias 2008; novels: Después de todo 2001, Para otros es el cielo 2004, Siempre fue invierno 2007, El prestigio de la belleza 2010; plays: Gato por liebre 1991, Se arrienda pieza, Sanseacabó; essays: Que muerde el aire afuera 1997, Imaginación y oficio 2003. *Honours:* Premio Nacional de Poesía, Instituto Colombiano de Cultura 1994. *Address:* Universidade de los Andes, Cra 1 Nº 18A–12, Bogotá, Colombia (office). *Telephone:* (1) 339-4949 (office); (1) 339-4999 (office). *E-mail:* pbonnet@uniandes.edu.co (office); info@piedadbonnett.com. *Website:* ww.uniandes.edu.co (office); www.piedadbonnett.com.

BONTLY, Thomas John, BA, PhD; American writer and academic; *Professor Emeritus, Department of English, University of Wisconsin-Milwaukee*; b. 25 Aug. 1939, Madison, Wis.; m. Marilyn R. Mackie 1962; one s. *Education:* Univ. of Wisconsin at Madison, Corpus Christi Coll., Cambridge, UK, Stanford Univ. *Career:* Asst Prof., Univ. of Wisconsin-Milwaukee 1966–71, Assoc. Prof. 1971–76, Co-ordinator of Creative Writing 1975–77, 1987–90, 1995–97, and Chair. 1979–82, Prof., Dept of English 1976, now Prof. Emer.; Fulbright Sr Lectureship, West Germany 1984; mem. Council for Wisconsin Writers (mem. Bd of Dirs 1991–). *Publications include:* fiction: The Competitor 1966, The Adventures of a Young Outlaw 1974, Celestial Chess 1979, The Giant's Shadow 1989; contribs to anthologies and many periodicals, essays and reviews. *Honours:* Wallace Stegner Creative Writing Fellowship 1965–66, Maxwell Perkins Commemorative Award 1966, First Prizes for Short Fiction, Council for Wisconsin Writers 1975, 1989, 1997, Wisconsin Arts Board New Work Award 1990. *Address:* Department of English, University of Wisconsin-Milwaukee, PO Box 413, Milwaukee, WI 53201, USA. *Telephone:* (414) 229-4511. *Fax:* (414) 229-2643. *Website:* www4.uwm.edu/letsci/english/index.cfm.

BOOKER, Christopher John Penrice; British journalist and writer; b. 7 Oct. 1937, Eastbourne, Sussex, England; m. Valerie Patrick 1979; two s. *Education:* Corpus Christi Coll., Cambridge. *Career:* contrib., Daily Telegraph 1959–97, jazz critic 1961, Way of the World column 1987–90, columnist, Sunday Telegraph 1990–; Ed. Private Eye 1961–63, regular contributor 1965–; scriptwriter, That Was the Week That Was (TV show) 1962–63; contrib. to Spectator 1962–. *Publications include:* The Neophiliacs: A Study of the Revolution in English Life in the 50s and 60s 1969, Goodbye London (with Candida Lycett-Green) 1973, The Booker Quiz 1976, The Seventies 1980, The Games War: A Moscow Journal 1981, The Repatriations from Austria in 1945 1990, The Mad Officials: How the Bureaucrats are Strangling Britain (with Richard North) 1994, The Castle of Lies: Why Britain Must Get Out of Europe (with Richard North) 1996, A Looking Glass Tragedy: The Controversy Over the Repatriations from Austria in 1945 1997, The Great Deception: The Secret History of the European Union (with Richard North) 2003, The Seven Basic Plots: Why We Tell Stories 2004, Scared to Death (co-author) 2007, The Real Global Warming Disaster 2009, Climategate to Cancun: The Real Global Warming Disaster Continues (co-author) 2011. *Honours:* Jt Winner, Campaigning Journalist of the Year 1973, Aims of Industry Free Enterprise Award 1992. *Address:* The Old Rectory, Litton, Bath, BA3 4PW, England (office). *Telephone:* (1761) 241263 (office). *Fax:* (1761) 241260 (office). *E-mail:* cblitton@aol.com (home).

BOOS, Jürgen, BEcons; German publisher; *Director, Frankfurt Book Fair*; b. 9 May 1961, Lörrach. *Education:* Univ. of Mannheim. *Career:* Sales Man. Droemer (publisher) 1991, Carl Hanser 1992; Man. Lange & Springer scientific book shop, Berlin 1993; Head of Int. Sales Julius Springer 1996; mem. Exec. Bd Wiley-VCH 1997–2005; Dir Frankfurt Book Fair 2005–. *Address:* Ausstellungs- und Messe GmbH, Frankfurt Book Fair, Reineckstr. 3, 60313 Frankfurt am Main, Germany (office). *E-mail:* info@book-fair.com (office). *Website:* www.frankfurt-book-fair.com (office).

BOOTH, Geoffrey Thornton, (Edward Booth O. P.), BA, MA, PhD; British writer, priest and academic; b. 16 Aug. 1928, Evesham, Worcs. *Education:* Univ. of Cambridge. *Career:* entered English province, Order of Dominicans 1952, ordained, RC priest 1958; Lecturer, Pontifical Beda Coll. 1978–80, Pontifical Univ. of St Thomas, Rome 1980–88. *Publications include:* Aristotelian Aporetic Ontology in Islamic and Christian Thinkers 1983, Saint Augustine and the Western Tradition of Self Knowing: The Saint Augustine Lecture 1986 1989; contribs to The New Grove Dictionary of Music and Musicians 1980, La Production du livre universitaire au moyen age: Exemplar et Pecia 1988, Kategorie und Kategorialität, Historisch-Systematische Untersuchungen zum Begriff der Kategorie im philosophischen Denken, Festschrift für Klaus Hartmann 1990, Gott und sein Bild–Augustins De Trinitate im Spiegel der neueren Forschung 2000; also many articles and book reviews in journals. *E-mail:* edward.booth@english.op.org (office).

BOOTH, Rosemary, (Frances Murray), DipEd, MA; British teacher and author; b. 10 Feb. 1928, Glasgow, Scotland; m. Robert Edward Booth 1950; three d. *Education:* Univ. of Glasgow, Univ. of St Andrews, Dundee Coll. of Educ. *Career:* history teacher. *Publications include:* Ponies on the Heather 1966, The Dear Colleague 1972, The Burning Lamp 1973, The Heroine's Sister 1975, Ponies and Parachutes 1975, Red Rowan Berry 1976, Castaway 1978, White Hope 1978, Payment for the Piper (US edn as Brave Kingdom) 1983, The Belchamber Scandal 1985, Shadow Over the Islands 1986, The British Open 2000, So Who Will Inherit the Lobster? 2006, Voices From the Margins 2007, Summer in the Hebrides 2009.

BOOTH, Stephen, BA; British journalist and novelist; b. 30 June 1952, Burnley, Lancs., England; m. Gail Lesley Bowker. *Education:* Birmingham Polytechnic (now Birmingham City Univ.). *Career:* fmrly sports reporter and journalist on local newspapers, night shift sub-ed. on Scottish Daily Express, production ed. on Farming Guardian. *Publications include:* novels: Black Dog 2000, Dancing with the Virgins 2001, Blood on the Tongue 2002, Blind to the Bones 2003, One Last Breath 2004, The Dead Place 2005, Scared to Live 2006, Dying to Sin 2007, The Kill Call 2009, Lost River 2010, The Devil's Edge 2011, Dead and Buried 2012. *Honours:* Lichfield Prize, Lichfield Int. Arts Festival 1999, Barry Award for Best British Crime Novel 2000, 2001, Crime Writers Asscn Dagger in the Library 2003. *Literary Agent:* c/o Teresa Chris Literary Agency, 43 Musard Road, London, W6 8NR, England. *Telephone:* (20) 7386-0633. *Fax:* (20) 7386-0955. *E-mail:* teresachris@litagency.co.uk. *Website:* www.teresachrisliteraryagency.co.uk. *Address:* Little, Brown Book Group, 100 Victoria Embankment, London, EC4Y 0DY, England. *Telephone:* (20) 7911-

8000 (office). *Fax:* (20) 7911-8100 (office). *E-mail:* info@littlebrown.co.uk (office). *Website:* www.stephen-booth.com (home).

BORCHERS-CARLÉ, Elisabeth; German writer; b. 27 Feb. 1926, Homberg; d. of Rudolf Sarbin and Claire Sarbin (née Beck); m. Claus Carlé 1998; two s. *Career:* worked as interpreter 1945–54; Ed. Luchterhand 1960–71, Suhrkamp Verlag and Insel Verlag 1971–98; mem. PEN, Acad. of Sciences and Literature, Mainz 1969, Acad. of Language and Poetry, Darmstadt 1989, Erich Fried Int. Soc. for Literature and Language, Vienna, Académie Européenne de Poésie, Luxembourg. *Publications include:* Gedichte 1961, Nacht aus Eis, Szenen und Spiele 1965, Der Tisch an dem wir sitzen (prose) 1967, Eine glückliche Familie und andere Prosa 1970, Von der Grammatik des heutigen Tages 1992, Was ist die Antwort 1998, Alles redet, schweigt und ruft 2001, Eine Geschichte auf Erden 2002, Marie Luise Kaschnitz Liebesgeschichten (ed) 2003, Das ist die Nachtigall, sie singt (ed) 2004. *Honours:* Order of Merit of First Class (Germany) 1996; Erzahlerpreis Suddeutscher Rundfunk, German Industry Culture Prize, Roswitha-Gedenk-Medaille 1976, Friedrich-Hölderlin-Preis 1986. *Address:* Arndtstrasse 17, 60325 Frankfurt, Germany (home). *Telephone:* (69) 746391 (home). *Fax:* (69) 74093909 (home).

BORDELOIS, Ivonne Aline, PhD; Argentine linguist, poet and academic; b. 5 Nov. 1934, Alberdi, Prov. of Buenos Aires; d. of Gastón Bordelois and Felisa S. Bordelois. *Education:* Univ. of Buenos Aires, Univ. of Paris, Sorbonne, Massachusetts Inst. of Tech. (with Noam Chomsky), USA. *Career:* Prof. of Linguistics, Utrecht Univ., Netherlands 1975–88; returned to Argentina, freelance writer 1994–; collaborator with La Nación. *Publications include:* El Alegre Apocalipsis 1995, Correspondencia Pizarnik 1998, Un triángulo crucial: Borges, Lugones y Güiraldes 1999, La palabra amenazada 2003, El País que nos Habla (Premio Sudamericana) 2005, Etimología de la pasiones 2006, A la escucha del cuerpo 2009, Del silencio como porvenir 2010. *Honours:* Guggenheim Fellowship 1983, French Embassy Fellowship, Premio Municipal 2000, Premio Konex 2004, Premio Sudamericana-La Nación 2005, Premio Esteban Echeverría 2008. *Address:* Leopoldo Kulesz, Libros del Zorzal, Tucumán 3350, 1°, Of. N, Buenos Aires, Argentina. *Telephone:* (11) 4864-4150. *E-mail:* info@delzorzal.com.ar. *Website:* delzorzal.com.ar.

BORDEN, Anthony, BA; American journalist; *Executive Director, Institute for War and Peace Reporting. Education:* Yale Univ. *Career:* freelance and staff reporter, New York 1983–88; Staff Reporter, American Lawyer (magazine), New York 1988–90; Launch Ed. Transitions, Inst. for Journalism, London and Prague 1998; Ed. War Report, London 1991–98; Consultant, Dept for Int. Devt, UK 1999–2002; Founder and Exec. Dir Inst. for War and Peace Reporting 1991–; Assoc. Gov. New End Primary School, London, mem. Exec. Cttee New End Second Century Campaign. *Publications include:* Breakdown: War and Reconstruction in Yugoslavia (co-ed.) 1992, An Elections Handbook for Bosnian Journalists (co-ed.) 1996, Reporting Macedonia: The New Accommodation (co-ed.) 1998, Out of Time: Draskovic, Djindjic and Serbian Opposition Against Milosevic (co-ed.) 2000; numerous contribs to newpapers and journals. *Honours:* One World Media Awards, New Media Award 2004. *Address:* Institute for War and Peace Reporting, 48 Gray's Inn Road, London, WC1X 8LT, England (office). *Telephone:* (20) 7831-1030 (office). *Fax:* (20) 7831-1050 (office). *E-mail:* tony@iwpr.net (office). *Website:* www.iwpr.net (office).

BORDEN, Louise Walker, BA; American writer; b. 30 Oct. 1949, Cincinnati, OH; d. of William Lee Walker and Louise Walker (née Crutcher); m. Peter A. Borden 1971; one s. two d. *Education:* Denison Univ. *Career:* Teaching Asst, Meadowbrook School, Weston 1971–73; pre-primary teacher, Cincinnati Country Day School, Cincinnati 1973–74; Co-owner The Bookshelf (bookstore in Cincinnati) 1988–91; mem. Soc. of Children's Book Writers and Illustrators, Authors' Guild, Ohio Council of Teachers of Language Arts. *Publications include:* Caps, Hats, Socks and Mittens 1989, The Neighborhood Trucker 1990, The Watching Game 1991, Albie the Lifeguard 1993, Just in Time for Christmas 1994, Paperboy 1996, The Little Ships (Parents' Choice Award, Reading Magic Award, Notable Book in the Field of Social Studies 1998) 1997, Thanksgiving Is... 1997, Good-bye, Charles Lindbergh 1998, Good Luck, Mrs K! (Christopher Award 2000) 1999, A. Lincoln and Me (Parents' Choice Award 2000) 1999, Sleds on Boston Common 2000, Fly High 2001, America Is... 2002, Touching the Sky – Flying Adventures of Wilbur and Orville Wright 2003, Sea Clocks – The Story of Longitude 2004, The A+ Custodian 2004, The Greatest Skating Race – A WW2 Story from the Netherlands (Ohioana Book Award for Juvenile Literature 2005) 2004, The Journey That Saved Curious George – The True Wartime Escape of Margret and H.A Rey 2005, The Last Day of School 2006, Across the Blue Pacific – A WW2 Story 2006, The John Hancock Club 2007, Cecily O. and the Nine Monkeys 2007, Off to First Grade 2008, Big Brothers Don't Take Naps 2011. *Honours:* Silver Gertie Award 1998, Goodall Award 2000, Ohioana Children's Literature Award 2002, Denison Univ. Alumni Citation Award 2002. *Address:* 70 West Street, Montgomery, OH 45242-7651 (home); Simon and Schuster Children's Division, 1230 Avenue of the Americas, 4th Floor, New York, NY 110020, USA. *Fax:* (513) 793-8932 (home). *Website:* www.louiseborden.com.

BORDIER, Roger; French writer; b. 5 March 1923, Blois; s. of Robert Bordier and Valentine Jeufraux; m. Jacqueline Bouchaud. *Education:* secondary school. *Career:* journalist in the provinces, later in Paris; contrib. to Nouvelles Littéraires and Aujourd'hui; radio and TV writer. *Publications:* poems: Les épicentres 1951; novels: La cinquième saison 1959, Les blés 1961, Le mime 1963, L'entracte 1965, Un âge d'or 1967, Le tour de ville 1969, Les éventails 1971, L'océan 1974, Meeting 1976, Demain l'été 1977; plays: Les somnambules 1963, Les visiteurs 1972; essays: L'objet contre l'art 1972, Le progrès: Pour qui? 1973, L'art moderne et l'objet 1978, A la recherche de Paris 2004; novels: La grande vie 1981, Les temps heureux 1983, La longue file 1984, 36 La fête 1985, La belle de mai 1986, Les saltimbanques de la Révolution 1989, Vel d'hib 1989, Les fusils du 1er Mai 1991, Chroniques de la Cité Joyeuse 1995, Le Zouave du Pont de l'Alma 2001; other: L'interrogatoire, dialogue 1998. *Honours:* Officier, Ordre des Arts et des Lettres; Prix Renaudot 1961. *Address:* Editions Albin Michel, 22 rue Huyghens, 75014 Paris (office); 8 rue Geoffroy St Hilaire, 75005 Paris, France (home).

BORDO, Susan Rebecca, BA, PhD; American writer and academic; *Otis A. Singletary Professor, University of Kentucky;* b. (Susan Rebecca Klein), 24 Jan. 1947, Newark, NJ; d. of Julius Alexander Klein and Regina Siegel Klein; m. 1st 1968 (divorced 1971); m. 2nd 1998. *Education:* Carleton Univ., SUNY at Stony Brook. *Career:* Assoc. Prof. of Philosophy, Le Moyne Coll., Syracuse, New York 1987–93, Joseph C. Georg Prof. 1991–94; Visiting Scholar in Women's Studies, Douglass Coll., Rutgers Univ. 1985; Rockefeller Humanist-in-Residence, Duke Univ. and Univ. of North Carolina Center for Research on Women 1987–88; Visiting Assoc. Prof., Duke Univ. 1989; Otis A Singletary Prof., Univ. of Kentucky, Lexington 1994–, currently also Prof. of English and Gender and Women's Studies; mem. American Philosophical Asscn, Soc. for Phenomenology and Existential Philosophy, Soc. for Women in Philosophy, American Studies Asscn. *Publications include:* The Flight to Objectivity: Essays on Cartesianism and Culture 1987, Gender-Body-Knowledge: Feminist Reconstructions of Being and Knowing (co-ed.) 1989, Unbearable Weight: Feminism, Western Culture, and the Body 1993, Twilight Zones: The Hidden Life of Cultural Images from Plato to O. J. 1997, Feminist Interpretation of Descartes (ed.) 1999, The Male Body: A New Look at Men in Public and in Private 1999. *Honours:* ACLS-Ford Foundation Fellowship 1988, Scholar of the Year Award, Le Moyne Coll. 1990, Notable Book of the Year, New York Times 1993, Distinguished Publication Award, Asscn for Women in Psychology 1994. *Address:* Department of Gender and Women's Studies, University of Kentucky, 111 Breckinridge Hall, Lexington, KY 40506-0027, USA (office). *Telephone:* (859) 257-1895 (office). *Fax:* (859) 257-1895 (office). *E-mail:* bordo@uky.edu (office). *Website:* www.as.uky.edu (office).

BORIS, Martin, BA, MA; American writer; b. 7 Aug. 1930, New York, NY; m. Gloria Shanf 1952; one s. two d. *Education:* New York Univ., Long Island Univ., Brooklyn Coll. of Pharmacy. *Publications include:* Two and Two 1979, Woodridge 1946 1980, Brief Candle 1990. *Address:* 1019 Northfield Avenue, Woodmere, NY 11598, USA (home). *Telephone:* (516) 374-2058 (home).

BORNHOLDT, Jenny, BA; New Zealand poet; b. 1 Nov. 1960, Lower Hutt; m. Gregory O'Brien. *Education:* Victoria Univ. *Career:* Te Mata Estate New Zealand Poet Laureate 2005–07; Writers' Fellow, Victoria Univ. 2009; Creative Writer-in-Residence, New Zealand Victoria Univ. 2010. *Publications include:* This Big Face 1988, Moving House 1989, Waiting Shelter 1991, How We Met 1995, My Heart Goes Swimming (ed. with Gregory O'Brien) 1996, Miss New Zealand: Selected Poems 1997, An Anthology of New Zealand Poetry in English (ed. with Gregory O'Brien and Mark Williams) (Montana New Zealand Book Award for Poetry) 1997, These Days 2000, My Heart Goes Swimming: New Zealand Love Poems (co-ed) 2000, Summer 2004, The Colour of Distance: New Zealand Writers in France, French Writers in New Zealand (ed. with Gregory O'Brien) 2005, Mrs Winter's Jump 2007, The Rocky Shore (Montana New Zealand Book Award for Poetry 2009) 2008, The Hill of Wool 2011. *Honours:* Meridian Energy Katherine Mansfield Fellowship 2002, Laureate Award, Arts Foundation of New Zealand 2003. *Address:* Victoria University Press, PO Box 600, Wellington, New Zealand. *Telephone:* (4) 463-6580. *Fax:* (4) 463-6581. *E-mail:* victoria-press@vuw.ac.nz. *Website:* www.victoria.ac.nz/vup.

BORSON, Ruth (Roo) Elizabeth, BA, MFA; Canadian/American poet and essayist; b. 20 Jan. 1952, Berkeley, Calif.; pnr Kim Maltman. *Education:* Univ. of California, Santa Barbara, Goddard Coll., Univ. of British Columbia. *Career:* Writer-in-Residence, Univ. of Western Ontario 1987–88, Concordia Univ. 1993, Massey Coll., Univ. of Toronto 1998, Green Coll., Univ. of British Columbia 2000; Writer-in-Residence, Univ. of Guelph 2005; Founder-mem. Pain Not Bread; mem. Int. PEN, Writers' Union of Canada. *Publications include:* Landfall 1977, Rain 1980, In the Smoky Light of the Fields 1980, A Sad Device 1982, The Whole Night, Coming Home 1984, The Transparence of November/Snow (with Kim Maltman) 1985, Intent, or the Weight of the World 1989, Night Walk: Selected Poems 1994, Water Memory 1996, Introduction to the Introduction to Wang Wei (with Kim Maltman and Andy Patton) 2000, Short Journey Upriver Toward Oishida (Gov. Gen. Literary Award 2004, Griffin Canadian Poetry Prize 2005, Pat Lowther Award 2005) 2004, Personal History 2008 (essays); contribs to many anthologies and periodicals. *Honours:* Univ. of British Columbia MacMillan Prize for Poetry 1977, CBC First Prize for Poetry 1982, CBC Third Prize for Poetry 1989, CBC Third Prize for Personal Essay 1990, Malahat Long Poem Prize 1993. *Address:* McClelland and Stewart Ltd, 75 Sherbourne Street, Fifth Floor, Toronto, ON M5A 2P9, Canada. *Telephone:* (416) 598-1114. *Fax:* (416) 598-7764. *E-mail:* editorial@mcclelland.com. *Website:* www.mcclelland.com.

BORTNIK, Aida; Argentine scriptwriter; b. 16 July 1941, Buenos Aires. *Screenplays include:* Sebastián y su amigo el artista (TV) 1971, La Tregua (The Truce) 1974, Una mujer (A Woman) 1975, Crecer de golpe (Growing Up Suddenly) 1977, La isla (The Island) 1979, Hombres en pugna (TV mini-series)

1980, Un tiro al aire 1980, Volver (To Return) 1982, Ruggero (TV series) 1983, La historia oficial (The Official Story) (Acad. Award for Best Foreign Language Film (jtly) 1985) 1985, Pobre mariposa (Poor Butterfly) 1986, Old Gringo 1989, Tango feroz: la leyenda de Tanguito (aka Tanguito) 1993, Caballos salvajes (Wild Horses) 1995, Cenizas del paraíso (Ashes from Paradise) 1997, La soledad era ésto (This Was Solitude) 2002, Vientos de agua 2006, Azucena 2008, 375 días 2008.

BOSHER, John Francis, PhD, FRSC, FRHistS; Canadian historian and academic; b. 28 May 1929, Sidney, BC; s. of John Ernest Bosher and Grace Simister; m. Kathryn Cecil Berry 1968; one s. three d. *Education:* Univ. of British Columbia, Univ. of Paris, France, Univ. of London, UK. *Career:* Jr Admin. Asst and Personnel Selection Officer Civil Service Comm., Ottawa 1951–53; Asst Lecturer, King's Coll., London 1956–59; Asst Prof., Univ. of British Columbia 1959–67; Prof. of History, Cornell Univ. 1967–69, York Univ., Toronto 1969–96; Visiting Fellow, All Souls Coll., Oxford, UK 1991–92. *Publications include:* The Single Duty Project: A Study of the Movement for a French Customs Union in the 18th Century 1964, French Finances 1775–1795: From Business to Bureaucracy 1970, French Society and Government: Essays in Honour of Alfred Cobban (ed.) 1973, The Canada Merchants 1713–1763 1987, The French Revolution 1988, Men and Ships in the Canada Trade 1660–1760: A Biographical Dictionary 1992, Business and Religion in the Age of New France 1600–1760 1994, The Gaullist Attack on Canada 1998, Imperial Vancouver Island: Who Was Who 1850–1950 2010; numerous articles on France. *Address:* 280 Chapel Street, Ottawa, ON K1N 7Y9, Canada (home). *Telephone:* (613) 565-6724 (home). *E-mail:* jfbosher@primus.ca.

BOSLEY, Keith Anthony, BA; British poet and translator; b. 16 Sept. 1937, Bourne End, Bucks.; m. Satu Salo 1982; three s. *Education:* Univ. of Reading, Univs of Paris and Caen, France. *Career:* mem. of staff, BBC 1961–93; Visiting Lecturer, BBC and British Council, Middle East 1981; Corresponding mem. Finnish Literature Soc., Helsinki. *Publications include:* The Possibility of Angels 1969, And I Dance 1972, Dark Summer 1976, Mallarmé: The Poems (trans.) 1977, Eino Leino: Whitsongs (trans.) 1978, Stations 1979, The Elek Book of Oriental Verse 1979, From the Theorems of Master Jean de La Ceppède (trans.) 1983, A Chiltern Hundred 1987, The Kalevala (trans.) 1989, I Will Sing of What I Know (trans.) 1990, Luis de Camões: Epic and Lyric (trans.) 1990, The Kanteletar (trans.) 1992, The Great Bear (trans.) 1993, Aleksis Kivi: Odes (trans.) 1994, André Frénaud: Rome the Sorceress (trans.) 1996, Eve Blossom has Wheels: German Love Poetry 1997, Skating on the Sea: Poetry from Finland 1997, An Upton Hymnal 1999; contribs to many newspapers, reviews, magazines and journals. *Honours:* Knight, First Class, Order of the White Rose (Finland) 1991; Finnish State Prize for Translation 1978, First Prize, British Comparative Literature Asscn Translation Competition 1980, First Prize, Goethe Soc. Translation Competition 1982, Pension, Royal Literary Fund 2001. *Address:* 108 Upton Road, Upton-cum-Chalvey, Slough, SL1 2AW, England (home). *Telephone:* (1753) 525249 (home). *Fax:* (1753) 525249 (home). *E-mail:* bosleykssg@msn.com (home).

BOTSFORD, Keith, (I. I. Magdalen, Eleni Magdalen, Liam Brady, Nick Matchwell), AM; American writer, editor, journalist and academic; *Editor and Publisher, The Republic of Letters;* b. 29 March 1928, Brussels, Belgium; s. of Willard Hudson Botsford and Carolina Rangoni-Machiavelli-Publicola-Santacroce; nine c. *Education:* Yale Univ., Univ. of Iowa, Columbia Univ., Manhattan School of Music, Holborn Coll. of Law. *Career:* Prof. of Journalism, History and Int. Relations, Boston Univ., now Prof. Emer.; Prof., Bard Coll., Univ. of Puerto Rico, Univ. of Texas, Bogazici Univ.; journalist, ed, publr, sports writer, food writer and US correspondent for numerous newspapers and journals, including The Sunday Times, The Independent, La Stampa; Dir Nat. Translation Center; Deputy Int. Sec., Int. PEN; currently Ed. and Publr The Republic of Letters; Ed. Yale Poetry Review, Poetry New York, Kolokol, Delos, The Noble Savage, ANON, Grand Prix Int.; Asst Producer, CBS TV, Stratford Shakespeare Festival. *Publications include:* as Keith Botsford: fiction: Master Race 1955, The Eighth Best-Dressed Man in the World 1958, Benvenuto 1961, The March-man 1965, Dominguin 1972, The Mothers 2001, Out of Nowhere 2002, Collaboration 2008, Death & the Maiden 2009; non-fiction: Driving Ambition (with Alan Jones) 1981, Keke (with Keke Rosberg) 1985, The Champions of Formula 1 1988, The Republic of Letters (with Saul Bellow) 1999, The Editors: The Best from Five Decades (with Saul Bellow) 2001, Josef Czapski 2009, Fragments I 2009, Fragments II 2010, Fragments I–III 2011, Collaboration 2011; as I. I. Magdalen: fiction: The Search for Anderson 1982, Ana P. 1983, Lennie and Vance and Benji 2002, Emma H. 2003. *Address:* The Republic of Letters, Apartado 29, Cahuita 70403, Costa Rica (office). *Telephone:* 2755-0123 (office); 2955-0100 (office). *E-mail:* nickmatchwell@gmail.com (office). *Website:* mag.trolbooks.com (office); www.keithbotsford.com.

BOTTING, Douglas Scott, MA, FRGS; British writer; b. 22 Feb. 1934, London; m. 1964; two d. *Education:* St Edmund Hall, Oxford. *Career:* mem. King's African Rifles, East Africa; exploration filmmaker, BBC TV; Special Corresp., BBC, Geographical Magazine, Time-Life and other periodicals; mem. Royal Inst. of Int. Affairs, Soc. of Authors, Biographers' Club, NCICA, Friends of Soqotra. *Publications include:* Island of the Dragon's Blood 1958, The Knights of Bornu 1961, One Chilly Siberian Morning 1965, Humboldt and the Cosmos 1973, Wilderness Europe 1976, Rio de Janeiro 1977, The Pirates 1978, The Second Front 1978, The U-Boats 1979, The Giant Airships 1980, The Aftermath in Europe 1945, Nazi Gold 1984, The Story of the World's Greatest Robbery 1984, In the Ruins of the Reich 1985, Wild Britain 1988, Hitler's Last General: The Case Against Wilhelm Mohnke 1989, America's Secret Army 1989, Gavin Maxwell: A Life 1993, Sex Appeal: The Art and Science of Sexual Attraction (with Kate Botting) 1995, Gerald Durrell: The Authorised Biography 1999, The Saga of Ring of Bright Water 2000, Dr Eckener's Dream Machine: The Historic Saga of the Round-the-World Zeppelin 2001, Hitler and Women – the Love Life of Adolf Hitler 2004, My Darling Enemy 2007, Lost Horizons, Forgotten Worlds: An Autobiography of Travels and Explorations around the World 2008; contribs to Oxford Dictionary of National Biography, BBC TV and radio, various periodicals. *Literary Agent:* Andrew Hewson, Johnson & Alcock Ltd, Clerkenwell House, 45–47 Clerkenwell Green, London, EC1R 0HT, England. *Telephone:* (20) 7251-0125. *Fax:* (20) 7251-2172. *E-mail:* info@johnsonandalcock.co.uk. *Address:* 2 The Old School House, 1 Dinton Road, Kingston upon Thames, Surrey, KT2 5JT, England (home). *E-mail:* douglasbotting@compuserve.com. *Website:* www.douglasbotting.co.uk.

BOUBLIL, Alain Albert; French writer and dramatist; b. 5 March 1941, Tunis; four s. *Career:* wrote libretto and lyrics for: La Révolution Française 1973, Les Misérables 1980, Abbacadabra 1984, Miss Saigon 1989, Martin Guerre 1996, The Pirate Queen 2006, Marguerite 2008; Le Journal d'Adam et Eve (play) 1994. *Honours:* two Tony Awards, Two Grammy Awards, two Victoire de la Musique Awards, Molière Award (all for Les Misérables), Evening Standard Drama Award (for Miss Saigon), Laurence Olivier Award (for Martin Guerre).

BOUCHARDEAU, Huguette; French politician, writer and editor; b. 1 June 1935, St-Etienne; d. of Marius Briaut and Rose Briaut (née Noël); m. Marc Bouchardeau 1955; one s. two d. *Career:* teacher of philosophy, Lycée Honoré d'Urfé 1961–70; Lecturer in Educ. Sciences, Univ. of Lyon 1970; Sec.-Gen. Parti Socialiste unifié 1979–83; unsuccessful presidential cand. 1981; Sec. of State for Environment and Quality of Life 1983–84; Minister for the Environment 1984–86; Founder Ed. H.B. Editions 1995–2008; Mayor Aigues-Vives 1995–2001. *Publications include:* Pas d'histoire, les femmes 1977, Hélène Brion: La voie feministe 1978, Un coin dans leur monde 1980, Le ministère du possible 1986, Choses dites de profil 1988, George Sand, La lune et les sabots 1990, Rose Noël 1990, La grande verrière 1991, Carnets de Prague 1992, Le Déjeuner 1993, La Famille Renoir 1994, Simone Weil 1995, Les Roches rouges 1996, Faute de regard 1997, Agatha Christie 1999, Voyage autour de ma bibliothèque 2000, Elsa Triolet 2001, Mes Nuits avec Descartes 2002, Nathalie Sarraute 2003, Differents receuils de textes choisis de G. Saud 2003–04, Simone de Beauvoir 2007. *Honours:* Chevalier, Légion d'honneur.

BOUCHÈNE, Abderrahmane; Algerian publisher; b. 1941, Algiers; m.; four c. *Education:* Algeria and Lausanne Univs. *Career:* worked in family clothing shop; admin. posts at Société nat. d'édition et de diffusion, Entreprise nat. du livre and Ministry of Culture; f. Editions Bouchène publishing house, Kouba, in late 1980s; by 1990 owner of two bookshops in Algiers, one in Riad-El-Feth; forced to flee Algeria and close business 1994; exile in Tunisia 1994–96; moved to Paris and set up new co. specializing in Algerian historical texts and historical anthropology of Maghreb socs. *Address:* Editions Bouchène, 113–115 rue Danielle Casanova, 93200 Saint-Denis, Paris, France (office). *Telephone:* 1-48-20-93-75 (office). *Fax:* 1-48-20-20-78 (office). *E-mail:* edbouchene@wanadoo.fr (office). *Website:* www.bouchene.com (office).

BOUCHER, David Ewart George, BA, MSc, PhD, FRHistS; British writer, editor and academic; *Head of School of European Studies, Cardiff University;* b. 15 Oct. 1951, Ebbw Vale, Monmouthshire, Wales; s. of Richard George Boucher and Irene Davies; m. Clare Mary French Mullen 1979; two d. *Education:* Univ. Coll., Swansea, London School of Econs, Univ. of Liverpool. *Career:* Tutorial Fellow, Univ. Coll., Cardiff 1980–83, Temporary Lecturer in Politics 1983–84; Lecturer, La Trobe Univ., Melbourne, Australia 1985–88, Sr Lecturer in Politics 1988–89; Research Fellow, ANU, Canberra 1989–90, Lecturer 1990, Sr Lecturer in Politics 1991; Reader, Univ. of Wales, Swansea 1995–98, Prof. of Political Theory and Govt 1998–2000; Professorial Fellow, Cardiff Univ. 2000–, Dir Grad. School in Humanities 2004–07, Head, School of European Studies 2008–, also currently Deputy Pro Vice-Chancellor for Staffing and Diversity and Chair. of Political Philosophy and Int. Relations; Visiting Fellow, Inst. for Cultural and Social Anthropology, Oxford Oct.-Dec. 2001; Visiting Professorial Fellow, Dept of Politics and Nat. Centre for Study of Europe, Univ. of Canterbury, New Zealand March–June 2003; Sr Research Fellow, Centre Study of Scottish Philosophy, Aberdeen Univ. 2005; Dir Collingwood and British Idealism Centre, Cardiff Univ. 1993–; Chair. Bd of Trustees, Collingwood Soc. 1993–; mem. Political Studies Asscn; mem. Editorial Bd, Australian Journal of Political Science 1990–92, Contemporary Political Theory 2002–. *Publications include:* Texts in Context: Revisionist Methods for Studying the History of Ideas 1985, The Social and Political Thought of R. G. Collingwood 1989, A Radical Hegelian: The Political Thought of Henry Jones (with Andrew Vincent) 1994, Political Theories of International Relations: From Thucydides to the Present 1998, Steel Skill and Survival 2000, British Idealism and Political Theory (with Andrew Vincent) 2000, Politics, Poetry and Protest: Bob Dylan and Leonard Cohen 2003, The Limits of Ethics in International Relations: Natural Law, Natural Rights and Human Rights in Transition 2009, British Idealism: A Guide for the Perplexed (with Andrew Vincent) 2011; Ed.: Essays in Political Philosophy, by R. G. Collingwood 1989, The New Leviathan, revised edn, by R. G. Collingwood 1992, The Social Contract from Hobbes to Rawls (with Paul Kelly) 1994, Philosophy, Politics and Civilization (with T. Modood and J. Connelly) 1995,

The British Idealists 1997, Social Justice: From Hume to Walzer (with Paul Kelly) 1998, Political Thinkers (with Paul Kelly) 2003, revised 2009, The Political Art of Bob Dylan (with Gary Browning) 2004, The Scottish Idealists 2004, R.G. Collingwood, The Philosophy of Enchantment (with Wendy James and Phillip Smallwood) 2005, An Autobiography, by R. G. Collingwood 2011; contribs to scholarly journals. *Honours:* Edwin Drew Prize, Univ. Coll., Swansea 1975, Leverhulme Fellowship 2007, numerous other grants. *Address:* School of European Studies, University of Wales, Cardiff, CF10 3YS, Wales (office). *Telephone:* (29) 2087-4862 (office). *Fax:* (29) 2087-4946 (office). *E-mail:* BoucherDE@cardiff.ac.uk (office). *Website:* www.cardiff.ac.uk (office).

BOUČKOVÁ, Tereza; Czech writer; b. 24 May 1957, Prague; d. of Pavel Kohout and Anna Cornová; m. Jiří Bouček; one s. two adopted s. *Career:* mem. Int. PEN. *Films:* screenplays: Smradi 2002, Zemský ráj to na pohled 2009. *Plays:* adaptations: La Strada 2007, Sodoma Komora 2009. *Publications include:* Indiánský běh 1991, Křepelice 1993, Když milujete muže 1995, Krákorám 1998, Indiánský běh 1999, Jen si tak trochu schnít 2004, Rok kohouta 2008, Boží a jiná muka - fejetony o lásce ke kolu 2010, Čin čin 2010. *Honours:* Jiří Orten Prize 1990. *Address:* Na Výsluní 100, 267 11 Vráž, Czech Republic (home). *Telephone:* 728659360 (mobile). *E-mail:* tereza.bouckova@seznam.cz; tereza.bouckova@klikni.cz. *Website:* www.terezabouckova.cz.

BOUDJEDRA, Rachid, BPhil; Algerian novelist, essayist and poet; b. 5 Sept. 1941, Aïn Beïda, Constantinois; m. *Education:* Univ. of Paris (Sorbonne). *Career:* lived in France 1969–72, Morocco 1972–75; worked in Ministry of Information and Culture 1977; columnist, Révolution africaine (weekly magazine); Reader, SNED, Lecturer IEP Algiers 1981; Founding mem. Ligue Algérienne pour la Défense des droits de l'homme. *Film screenplays:* Chronique des années de braise 1975, Ali aux pays des mirages. *Publications include:* poetry: Pour Ne Plus Rêver 1965, Greffe 1984; novels: La Répudiation 1969, L'Insolation 1972, Topographie idéale pour une agression caractérisée 1975, L'Escargot entêté 1977, Les 1001 Années de la nostalgie 1979, Le Vainqueur de coupe 1981, Le Démantèlement (in trans.) 1982, La Macération (in trans.) 1985, La Pluie (in trans.) 1987, La Prise de Gibraltar (in trans.) 1987, Le Désordre des choses (in trans.) 1991, Philippe Djian 1992, Barbès-Palace 1993, Timimoun 1994, La Vie à l'endroit 1997, Fascination 2000, Le Directeur des promenades 2002, Cinq Fragments du désert 2001, Les Funérailles 2003, La Passion de l'Intertexte 2003, Les Figuiers de Barbarie 2010, Hôtel St Georges 2011; other: Le FIS de la haine (non-fiction) 1994, Mines de rien (play) 1995, Lettres algériennes (non-fiction) 1995, Rachid Boudjedra: Une poétique de la subversion (auto-biog.) 1999, Peindre l'Orient (non-fiction) 2003, Nouvelles d'Algérie (short stories, co-author) 2009; numerous essays. *Honours:* Prix Les Enfants Terribles 1969, Prix des Libraires 2007.

BOULANGER, Daniel; French writer; b. 24 Jan. 1922, Compiègne, Oise; s. of Michel Boulanger and Hélène Bayart; m. 2nd Clémence Dufour; four s. three d. *Education:* Petit Séminaire Saint-Charles, Chauny. *Career:* sub-ed., Affaires économiques 1946–48; writer 1948–; has written scripts or screenplays for over 100 films, including Cartouche 1962, L'Homme de Rio 1963, Les Tribulations d'un Chinois en Chine 1965, La Vie de Château 1966, Le Voleur 1967, Le Diable par la Queue 1968, Le Roi de Coeur (Prix Louis-Delluc) 1969, Les Maries de l'An II 1971, L'Affaire Dominici 1973, Police Python 1975, Une femme fidèle 1976, La Menace 1976, Cheval d'Orgueil 1980, Chouans 1988, La Révolution Française 1989; numerous plays; mem. Acad. Goncourt 1983–2008. *Publications include:* novellas: Les Noces du Merle (Prix de la Nouvelle) 1963, L'été des Femmes 1964, Fête Ste Beuve 1966, Le Chemin des Caracoles 1966, Le jardin d'Armide 1969, Mémoire de la Ville 1970, Vessies et Lanternes (Prix de l'Académie française) 1971, Fouette Cocher (Prix Goncourt de la Nouvelle) 1974; novels: La Confession d'Omer 1991, Ursacq 1992, Le Retable Wasserfall 1994, Caporal Supérieur 1994, Le Miroittier 1995, Tombeau d'Héraldine 1997, Talbard 1998, Images mes catins 1999, Le Ciel de Bargetal 1999, Clémence et Auguste 2000, Les Mouches et l'âne 2001, Cache-Cache 2002, Du temps qu'on plaisantait 2003, La Poste de Nuit 2004, Le ciel est aux petits porteurs 2006; poems: Tchadiennes 1969, Retouches (Prix Max Jacob 1970) 1969, Jules Bouc 1987, Un Eté à la diable 1992, A la courte paille 1993, Etiquettes 1994, Taciturnes 1995, Fenêtre mon navire 2008. *Honours:* Officier, Légion d'honneur, Ordre nat. du Mérite, Commdr, des Arts et des Lettres; Prix Pierre de Monaco for complete body of work 1979, Prix Kléber Haedens 1983. *Address:* 22 rue du Heaume, 60300 Senlis, France (home).

BOULARÈS, Mohamed Habib; Tunisian politician, writer and journalist; b. 29 July 1933, Tunis; s. of Sadok Ben Mohamed and Zoubeida Bent Abdelkader Aziz; m. Line Poinsignon 1966; one d. *Education:* Collège Sadiki, Tunis. *Career:* mem. staff exec. office, Parti Destourien 1955; Deputy Ed. daily Essabah 1956; in charge of publications, Ministry of Information 1957; Ed. Nat. Radio news service 1958; Ed. Al Amal (Parti Destourien daily newspaper) 1960; first Man. Dir Tunis Afrique Presse news agency 1961; Dir Radio Télévision Tunisienne, Dir of Information, Ministry of Cultural Affairs and Information 1962; mem. Econ. and Social Council 1964–70; Minister of Cultural Affairs and Information 1970; Dir Ecole Internationale de Bordeaux, France 1972–73; teacher, Institut de Langues Orientales, Paris for four years; mem. Parl. 1981–86, 1989–94, re-elected 1994; Amb. to Egypt 1988; Minister of Culture 1988–89, of Culture and Information 1989–90, of Foreign Affairs 1990–91, of Nat. Defence Feb.–Oct. 1991; Special Adviser to Pres. of Repub. 1990; Pres. Chamber of Deputies 1991–97; Sec.-Gen., Arab Maghreb Union 2002–06. *Publications:* La Tunisie 1978, Islam: the Fear and the Hope 1990, Hannibal 2000; several other non-fiction works and plays. *Honours:* Grand Officier Ordre de l'Indépendence, Grand Cordon Ordre de la République, Commdr Ordre du 7 Novembre, numerous foreign decorations. *Address:* c/o L'Union du Maghreb Arabe, 14, rue Zelagh Agdal, Rabat, Morocco.

BOULLOSA, Carmen; Mexican novelist, poet, playwright and academic; *Distinguished Lecturer, Department of Foreign Languages, City College, City University of New York*; b. (María del Carmen Boullosa Velázquez), 4 Sept. 1954, Mexico City; m. 2nd Mike Wallace; two c. (from previous m.). *Education:* Univ. Iberoamericana, Univ. Nacional Autónoma de México. *Career:* Visiting Prof. and Andrés Bello Chair, NYU 2002–03; Visiting Prof., Columbia Univ. 2003–04; Distinguished Lecturer, Dept of Foreign Languages, City Coll., CUNY 2004–; co-f. (with Salman Rushdie) Mexico City House for Persecuted Writers; co-f. Café Nueva York 2007; Fellow, Centre for Scholars and Writers, New York Public Library 2001; Fellow, Cullman Center; DAAD Visiting Writer, Berlin; has held visiting appts at San Diego State Univ., Georgetown Univ., La Sorbonne (France); lectured at Brown Univ., Princeton Univ., Univ. of California, Irvine, UCLA and insts in England, Germany, Austria, France, Spain, Argentina, Ecuador, Venezuela, Colombia. *Plays:* Cocinar hombres 1985, Los Totoles (Mexico City Critics Play of the Year) 1995, Roja Doméstica (Foro del Museo Tamayo) 1998. *Radio play:* Pesca de Piratas (Radio Educación, México) 1998. *Television:* Nueva York (CUNY-TV) 2003–10. *Publications include:* novels: Mejor desaparece 1987, Antes 1989, Son vacas, somos puercos 1991, El médico de los piratas 1992, Llanto 1992, La milagrosa 1993, Duerme 1994, Quiza 1995, Cielos de la tierra 1997, Treinta años 1999, De un salto descabalga la reina 2002, La otra mano de Lepanto 2005, La Novela Perfecta 2006, El Velázquez de Paris 2007, La virgen y el violín 2008, El complot de los románticos 2009, Las paredes hablan 2010; juvenile: La midas 1986, Sólo para muchachos 1997; plays: Teatro herético 1997; Los Totoles 2000; essays: Papeles irresponsables 1989, Cuando me volví mortal 2010; poems: La memoria vacía 1978, El hilo olvida 1979, Ingobernable 1979, Lealtad 1981, Abierta 1983, La salvaja 1988, Soledumbre 1992, Envenenada: antología personal 1993, Niebla 1997, La delirios 1998, Jardín Elíseo 1999, La bebida 2002, Salto de mantarraya (y otros dos) 2002; Todos los amores (ed.) 2000; art books, ed. of other books; contrib. to anthologies and publications. *Honours:* Guggenheim Fellow; Premio Xavier Villaurrutia, Liberatur Preis, Anna Seghers Prize, Premio de Novela Café Gijón. *Literary Agent:* Elaine Markson Literary Agency, 44 Greenwich Avenue, New York, NY 10011, USA. *Telephone:* (212) 243-8480. *E-mail:* julia@marksonagency.com. *E-mail:* carmenboullosa@gmail.com. *Website:* www.carmenboullosa.net.

BOULTON, Adam, BA, MA; British broadcast journalist; *Political Editor, Sky News*; b. 15 Feb. 1959, Reading, Berks.; m. Angela Hunter 2006; three d. *Education:* Westminster School, Christ Church, Oxford and School of Advanced Int. Studies, Washington, DC. *Career:* jr staff mem., BBC External Services 1982; Political Ed. TV-am 1983; Founder-mem. and Political Ed. Sky News 1989–; presenter, Sunday with Adam Boulton (Plain English Campaign Nat. Programme Award 2001) 1994–, Tonight 1995–98, Forum, Answer the Question, The Boulton Factor; contribs to numerous publications, including The Times, The Independent, The Business, Scotland on Sunday. *Publications include:* Tony's Ten Years 2008, Hung Together: The 2010 Election and the Coalition Government (co-author) 2010. *Address:* BSkyB, Grant Way, Isleworth, TW7 5QD, England (office). *E-mail:* news@sky.com (office). *Website:* www.sky.com/skynews (office).

BOULTON, James Thompson, BA, BLitt, PhD, FRSL, FBA; British writer and academic; b. 17 Feb. 1924, Pickering, Yorks., England; s. of the late Harry Boulton and Annie Mary Penty Thompson; m. Margaret Helen Leary 1949; one s. one d. *Education:* Univ. Coll., Durham, Lincoln Coll., Oxford, Univ. of Nottingham. *Career:* served as pilot in RAF 1943–46; Lecturer, Univ. of Nottingham, becoming Sr Lecturer, Reader in English Literature 1951–63, Prof. 1964–75, Dean, Faculty of Arts 1970–73; Prof. of English Studies and Head of Dept, Univ. of Birmingham 1975–88, Prof. Emer. 1989–, Dean, Faculty of Arts 1981–84, Public Orator 1984–88, Dir, Inst. for Advanced Research in Arts and Social Sciences 1987–99, Deputy Dir 1999–2007, Dir Emer. 2007–. *Publications include:* Edmund Burke – Sublime and Beautiful (ed.) 1958, The Language of Politics in the Age of Wilkes and Burke 1963, Samuel Johnson – The Critical Heritage 1971, Defoe – Memoirs of a Cavalier (ed.) 1972, The Letters of D.H Lawrence (ed.) (eight vols) 1979–2000, Selected Letters of D.H Lawrence (ed.) 1997, The Writings and Speeches of Edmund Burke, Vol. One (co-ed.) 1997, D.H Lawrence – Late Essays and Articles (ed.) 2004, James Boswell – An Account of Corsica (co-ed.) 2006. *Honours:* Hon. Prof., Bangor Univ.; Hon. DLitt (Durham) 1991, (Nottingham) 1993; Harry T. Moore Distinguished Scholar Award 1990. *Address:* Tyn y Ffynnon Cottage, Nant Peris, Caernarfon, Gwynedd, LL55 4UH, Wales (office). *Telephone:* (1286) 872057 (office).

BOURAOUI, Hédi, LèsL, MA, PhD; Canadian poet, writer and academic; *Writer-in-Residence, Stong College, York University*; b. 16 July 1932, Sfax, Tunisia. *Education:* Université de Toulouse, France, Indiana Univ., USA, Cornell Univ., Ithaca, USA. *Career:* Master, Stong Coll., York Univ. 1978–88, now Univ. Prof. Emer., Writer-in-Residence 2005–; Jt Ed.-in-Chief poetry review, Envol; Jt Ed.-in-Chief, LittéRéalité; Deputy Gov. to Bd of Govs, American Biographical Inst. Research Asscn 1995; mem. Royal Soc. of Canada (Acad. des Lettres et Sciences Humaines). *Publications include:* poetry: Musocktail 1966, Tremblé 1969, Eclate-Module 1972, Vésuviade 1976, Haïtuvois, suivi de Antillades 1980, Vers et l'Envers 1982, Ignescent 1982, Echosmos 1986, Arc-en-Terre 1991, Emigressence 1992, Nomadaime 1995,

Illuminations Autistes (Pensées-Eclairs) 2003, Struga, suivi de Margelle d'un Festival 2003, Sfaxitude 2005, Livr'Errance 2005, Visages du Dedans 2008, Adamesques 2009; novels: L'Icônaison 1985, Bangkok Blues 1994, Retour à Thyna 1996, La Pharaone 1998, Ainsi parle la Tour CN 1999, La Composée 2001, La Femme d'entre les lignes 2002, Sept Portes pour une Brûlance 2005, Puglia à bras ouverts 2007, Cap Nord 2008, Les Aléas d'une Odyssée 2009, Méditerranée à voile toute 2010; numerous essays and works of criticism. *Honours:* Officier, Ordre des Palmes Académiques 2004; Grand Prix du Salon du livre de Toronto 1998, Prix du Nouvel Ontario 1999, Salon du livre de Toronto Prix Christine Dumitriu van Saanen 2000, Prix Int. de Poésie Emmanuel Roblès 2004, APFUCC Prix du Meilleur Ouvrage d'Érudition 2006. *Address:* 332 Stong College, York University, 4700 Keele Street, Toronto, ON M3J 1P3, Canada (office). *Telephone:* (416) 736-2100 ext. 77323 (office). *E-mail:* bouraoui@yorku.ca (office). *Website:* www.arts.yorku.ca/french/cmc (office); www.hedibouraoui.com.

BOURAOUI, Nina; French writer; b. 31 July 1967, Rennes; d. of Rachid Bouraoui and Maryvonne Henry-Bouraoui. *Education:* Lycée Français, Algiers, Algeria and Zurich, Switzerland, Inst. Catholique, Paris and Univ. of Paris II (Panthéon-Assas). *Career:* moved to Algiers with her family 1967, stayed until aged 15, family then lived in Switzerland and UAE, moved to Paris to pursue univ. studies. *Music:* wrote two songs for Celine Dion, Immensité and Les paradis 2007. *Publications include:* La voyeuse interdite (Prix du Livre Inter) 1991, Poing mort 1992, Le bal des murènes 1996, L'âge blessé 1998, Garçon manqué 2000, Le jour du séisme 2001, La vie heureuse 2002, Poupée Bella 2004, Mes mauvaises Pensées (Prix Renaudot) 2005, Avant Les Hommes 2007, Tomboy 2007, Appelez-moi par mon prénom 2008, Nos baisers sont des adieux 2010. *Honours:* Chevalier des Arts et des Lettres. *Address:* 31 rue de Fleuris, 75006 Paris, France (home). *Telephone:* 1-43-37-54-31 (home).

BOURKE, Joanna, MA, PhD; New Zealand/British historian, writer and academic; *Professor of History, Department of History, Classics and Archaeology, Birkbeck College, London;* b. 1963. *Education:* Auckland Univ., Australian Nat. Univ. *Career:* brought up by missionary parents in Zambia, Solomon Islands and Haiti; has held academic posts in Australia, New Zealand and Cambridge, England; Prof., Dept of History, Classics and Archaeology, Birkbeck Coll., London 1992–; Treaty of Utrecht Chair 2011. *Publications include:* Husbandry to Housewifery: Women, Economic Change and Housework in Ireland, 1890–1914 (Ronald Tress Prize) 1993, Working-Class Cultures in Britain 1890–1960 1996, Dismembering the Male: Men's Bodies, Britain and the Great War 1999, An Intimate History of Killing (Fraenkel Prize in Contemporary History 1998, Wolfson Prize for Historical Writing 2000) 1999, The Second World War: A People's History 2001, The Misfit Soldier: Edward Casey's War Story 1914–32 (ed.) 2001, Fear: A Cultural History of the Twentieth Century 2004, Rape: A History from 1860 to the present 2007, Are Women Animals?: Historical Reflections on What It Means To Be Human, 1791 to the Present 2011; contribs to scholarly books and journals, on Irish history, British social history and the history of warfare; currently writing a book on the history of bodily pain. *Honours:* Fraenkel Prize in Contemporary History,Wolfson Prize for Historical Writing. *Address:* Department of History, Classics and Archaeology, Birkbeck College, Room B12, 28 Russell Square, Bloomsbury, London, WC1B 5DQ, England (office). *Telephone:* (20) 7631-6269 (office). *E-mail:* j.bourke@bbk.ac.uk (office). *Website:* www.bbk.ac.uk/history/jb (office).

BOURNE, Stephen Robert Richard, MA, FCA, FRSA; British publisher; *President, Cambridge University Press;* b. 20 March 1952, Kampala, Uganda; s. of Colyn M. Bourne and Kathleen Bourne; m. Stephanie Ann Bickford 1978; one s. one d. *Education:* Berkhamsted School, Univ. of Edinburgh. *Career:* with Deloitte Haskins and Sells, London and Hong Kong 1974–80; with Exxon Chemical Asia-Pacific, Hong Kong 1980–86; Financial Dir Asia, Dow Jones Telerate, London and Hong Kong 1986–89, Gen. Man. Northern Europe 1989–94; Man. Dir, Financial Printing Div., St Ives PLC, London 1994–96; Devt Dir, Cambridge Univ. Press 1997–2000, Chair. of Printing Div. 2000–, CEO 2002–12, Pres. 2012–; Bd mem. Britten Sinfonia, The Wine Soc., CBI East, Univ. of the Arts London; mem. Publishing Studies Advisory Bd, Univ. Coll. London, City Univ., London Coll. of Communication; Fellow, Clare Hall, Cambridge, Inst. of Printing; Liveryman and Chair. Trade and Industry Forum, The Stationers' Co. *Address:* Cambridge University Press, UPH, Shaftesbury Road, Cambridge, CB2 8BS (office); Falmouth Lodge, Snailwell Road, Newmarket, CB8 7DN, England (home). *Telephone:* (1223) 358331 (office). *E-mail:* sbourne@cambridge.org (office). *Website:* www.cambridge.org (office).

BOUVARD, Marguerite Anne Guzman, BA, MA, MFA, PhD; American writer, poet and academic; *Resident Scholar, Women's Studies Research Center, Brandeis University;* b. 10 Jan. 1937, Trieste, Italy; George Galembert and Valeria Guzman Schlegel Von Gottlieben; m. Jacques Bouvard 1959; one s. one d. *Education:* Northwestern Univ., Radcliffe Coll., Harvard Univ., Boston Univ. *Career:* Prof. of Political Science and English, Regis Coll.; currently Resident Scholar, Women's Studies Research Center, Brandeis Univ.; Ed.-in-Chief Healing Ministry magazine; Founding ed. All Sides of Ourselves (series); mem. New England Poetry Club, PEN, Poetry Soc. of America. *Publications include:* The Search for Community 1975, Journeys Over Water 1982, Landscape and Exile (ed.) 1985, Voices From An Island 1985, Of Light and Silence 1990, With the Mothers of the Plaza de Mayo 1993, Revolutionizing Motherhood 1994, Women Reshaping Human Rights 1996, The Body's Burning Fields 1997, The Path through Grief 1998, Grandmothers: Granddaughters Remember 1998, Wind, Fire and Frost 2001, Prayers for Comfort in Difficult Times 2004, Healing: A Life with Chronic Illness 2007, Mothers in All But Name: Grandmothers, Aunts, Sisters, Friends, Strangers, Nannie 2009, The Unpredictability of Light (MassBook Award for Poetry 2010) 2009; contribs to Ploughshares, Partisan Review, Ohio Journal, Mid-West Quarterly, West Branch, Southern Humanities Review, Sojourner, Yarrow, Radcliffe Quarterly, Literary Review, The Redcoast Review, Centennial Review, Caesura, San Jose Studies, Christian Science Monitor, Tiferet, Healing Ministry, Raving Dove, Women's Voices for Change. *Honours:* Scholarship in Poetry, Bread Loaf Writers' Conf. 1976, Residencies at MacDowell Colony, Leighton Arts Colony, Banff, Yaddo, Virginia Centre for Creative Arts, Djerassi Foundation, Villa Montalvo, Cottages at Hedgebrook 1978–2009. *Address:* 6 Brookfield Circle, Wellesley, MA 02181, USA (home). *Telephone:* (781) 237-1340 (home). *Fax:* (781) 235-8560 (home). *E-mail:* marguerite@bouvard.us; bouvard@brandeis.edu. *Website:* www.brandeis.edu/centers/wsrc (office).

BOUZFOUR, Ahmed; Moroccan author; b. 1940, Taza. *Education:* Univ. of Al Qaraouiyine, Mohammed V Univ. *Career:* fmr Prof. of pre-Islamic poetry, Univ. of Rabat; fmr Prof. of Arabic literature, Univ. of Casablanca. *Publications:* short stories: Yas'alounaka âni al-qatl 1971, An-nadar fi al-wajh al-âaziz 1983, Al-Ġābir Al-Dāhir 1987, Sayyād al-Naâam 1993, La flautista azul: diez cuentos de Ahmed Bouzfour 2010; Ta'abbata shiâran, Dīwān as-sindibād, Az-zarāfa al-mushtaâila; contrib. to Aljamía, Banipal. *Address:* c/o Union des écrivains du Maroc, Rabat, Morocco.

BOVA, Benjamin (Ben) William, BA, MA; American writer, editor and lecturer; b. 8 Nov. 1932, Philadelphia, PA. *Education:* Temple Univ., SUNY at Albany. *Career:* Editorial Dir, Omni Magazine; Ed., Analog Magazine; Lecturer; Fellow British Interplanetary Soc.; mem. Nat. Space Soc. (pres. emeritus), PEN, SFWA. *Publications include:* fiction: The Star Conquerors 1959, Star Watchman 1964, The Weathermakers 1967, Out of the Sun 1968, The Dueling Machine 1969, Escape! 1969, Exiled from Earth 1971, THX1138 (with George Lucas) 1971, Flight of Exiles 1972, As on a Darkling Plain 1972, When the Sky Burned 1972, Forward in Time 1973, Gremlins, Go Home! 1974, End of Exile 1975, The Starcrossed 1975, City of Darkness 1976, Millennium 1976, The Multiple Man 1976, Colony 1978, Maxwell's Demons 1978, Kinsman 1979, Voyagers 1981, Test of Fire 1982, The Winds of Altair 1983, Orion 1984, The Astral Mirror 1985, Privateers 1985, Prometheans 1986, Voyagers II: The Alien Within 1986, Battle Station 1987, The Kinsman Saga 1987, Vengeance of Orion 1988, Peacekeepers 1988, Cyberbooks 1989, Voyagers III: Star Brothers 1990, Future Crime 1990, Cyborgs in the Dying Time 1990, The Trikon Deception 1992, Mars 1992, To Save the Sun 1992, Triumph 1993, Challenges 1993, Empire Builders 1993, Sam Gunn Unlimited 1993, Orion and the Conqueror 1994, To Fear the Light 1994, Death Dream 1994, Orion Among the Stars 1995, Brothers 1996, Moonrise 1996, Twice Seven 1998, Sam Gunn Forever 1998, Moonwar 1998, Return to Mars 1999, Venus 2000, Jupiter 2001, The Precipice 2001, The Rock Rats 2002, Saturn 2003, Tales of the Grand Tour 2004, The Silent War 2004, Powersat 2005, Mercury 2005, Titan 2006, Mars Life 2008, The Return 2009, Able One 2010; non-fiction: The Milky Way Galaxy 1961, Giants of the Animal World 1962, Reptiles Since the World Began 1964, The Uses of Space 1965, In Quest of Quasars 1970, Planets, Life & LGM 1970, The Fourth State of Matter 1971, The Amazing Laser 1972, The New Astronomies 1972, Starflight and Other Improbabilities 1973, Man Changes the Weather 1973, Survival Guide for the Suddenly Single (with Barbara Berson) 1974, The Weather Changes Man 1974, Workshops in Space 1974, Through Eyes of Wonder 1975, Science: Who Needs it? 1975, Notes to a Science Fiction Writer 1975, Closeup: New Worlds (with Trudy E. Bell) 1977, Viewpoint 1977, The Seeds of Tomorrow 1977, The High Road 1981, Vision of the Future: The Art of Robert McCall 1982, Assured Survival 1984, Star Peace 1986, Welcome to Moonbase! 1987, Interactions (with Sheldon Glashow) 1988, The Beauty of Light 1988, First Contact (ed. and contrib.) 1990, The Craft of Writing Science Fiction that Sells 1994, Space Travel 1997, Immortality 1998, The Story of Light 2001, Faint Echoes, Distant Stars 2004. *Honours:* Distinguished Alumnus Temple Univ. 1981, Alumni Fellow 1982, Robert A. Heinlein Award 2008. *Address:* c/o Hodder, 338 Euston Road, London, NW1 3BH, England. *Website:* www.benbova.net.

BOWDEN, Jim (see Spence, William John Duncan)

BOWDEN, Roland Heywood; British poet and dramatist; b. 19 Dec. 1916, Lincoln, England; m. 1946; one s. one d. *Education:* School of Architecture, Liverpool Univ. 1934–39. *Career:* mem. Nat. Poetry Secretariat. *Publications:* Poems From Italy 1970, Every Season is Another 1986; plays: Death of Paolini 1980, After Neruda 1984, The Fence 1985; contrib.: Arts Review: London Magazine, Panurge, Words International. *Honours:* Arts Council Drama Bursary 1978, Cheltenham Festival Poetry Prize 1982, First Prize, All-Sussex Poets 1983.

BOWEN, Kevin, PhD; American poet and translator; m.; two c. *Education:* Univ. of Massachusetts, Boston, State Univ. of New York, Buffalo. *Career:* served with US Army, Viet Nam 1968–69; Co-Dir William Joiner Centre for the Study of War and its Social Consequences, Univ. of Massachusetts Boston 1983–94, apptd Dir 1993. *Publications:* Playing Basketball with the Viet-Cong 1994, Writing Between the Lines: An Anthology on War and Its Social Consequences 1997, Not on the Map (with Bruce Weigl) 1997, Forms of Prayer at the Hotel Edison: Poems by Kevin Bowen 1998, Mountain River:

Vietnamese Poetry from the Wars 1948–93 (co-ed.) 1998, Wil's Bones 2000, Six Vietnamese Poets (with Nguyen Ba Chung) 2001, Two Rivers: New Vietnamese Writing from America and Viet Nam (Manoa) (co-ed.) 2002, Eight True Maps of the West 2003, The Third Funeral 2003, Thai Binh 2009; contrib. to Distant Road 1999. *Address:* c/o William Joiner Center for the Study of War and Social Consequences, University of Massachusetts Boston, 100 Morrissey Boulevard, Boston, MA 02125-3393, USA.

BOWEN, Lynne, BSc, MA; Canadian writer; *Co-Chair of Creative Non-Fiction Writing, Rogers Communications*; b. 22 Aug. 1940, Indian Head, SK; d. of Desmond and Isobel Crossley; m. Richard Allen Bowen; two s. one d. *Education:* Univ. of Alberta, Univ. of Victoria. *Career:* Co-Chair. of Creative Non-Fiction Writing, Rogers Communications 1992–; Co-Chair., Creative Writing Program, Univ. of BC 2000–02; mem. Writers' Union of Canada, PEN Int. *Publications:* Boss Whistle: The Coal Miners of Vancouver Island Remember 1982, Three Dollar Dreams 1987, Muddling Through: The Remarkable Story of the Barr Colonists 1992, Those Lake People: Stories of Cowichan Lake 1995, Robert Dunsmuir, Laird of the Mines 1999. *Honours:* Canadian Historical Asscn Regional Certificates of Merit 1984, 1993, Lieutenant Gov.'s Medal 1987, Hubert Evans Non-Fiction Prize 1993, City of Nanaimo Excellence in Culture Award 1999, Concordia Univ. Coll. of Alberta Distinguished Alumni Award 2000. *Address:* 4982 Fillinger Crescent, Nanaimo, BC V9V 1J1, Canada (office). *E-mail:* lynne@island.net (home).

BOWEN, William Gordon, BS, PhD; American academic; *President Emeritus, Princeton University*; b. 6 Oct. 1933, Cincinnati, Ohio; s. of Albert A. Bowen and Bernice Pomert; m. Mary Ellen Maxwell 1956; one s. one d. *Education:* Denison and Princeton Univs. *Career:* Asst Prof. of Econs, Princeton Univ. 1958–61, Assoc. Prof. 1961–65, Prof. 1965–87, Dir of Grad. Studies, Woodrow Wilson School of Public and Int. Affairs 1964–66, Provost Princeton Univ. 1967–72, Pres. 1972–88, Pres. Emer. 1988–; Lecturer, Univ. of Oxford , UK 2000; Regent Smithsonian Inst. 1980, now Regent Emer.; Pres. Andrew W. Mellon Foundation, New York 1988–2006; Co-Chair. Research Alliance for New York City Public Schools 2009–12; Dir NCR Corpn 1975–91; mem. Bd of Overseers, Teachers Insurance and Annuity Asscn and College Retirement Equities Fund 1995–2010; Trustee, Denison Univ. 1966–75, 1992–2000, Center for Advanced Study in the Behavioral Sciences 1973–84, 1986–92, Reader's Digest 1985–97, American Express 1988–2006, ISTOR 1995–, Merck and Co. 1986–2009, Ithaka Harbors, Inc. *Publications:* The Wage-Price Issue: A Theoretical Analysis 1960, Performing Arts: The Economic Dilemma (with W. J. Baumol) 1966, The Economics of Labor Force Participation (with T. A. Finegan) 1969, Ever the Teacher 1987, Prospects for Faculty in the Arts and Sciences (with J. A. Sosa) 1989, In Pursuit of the PhD (with Neil L. Rudenstine) 1992, Inside the Boardroom: Governance by Directors and Trustees (with T. Nygren, S. Turner and E. Duffy) 1994, The Charitable Nonprofits 1994, Universities and Their Leaderships (ed. Harold Shapiro) 1998, The Shape of the River: Long-Term Consequences of Considering Race in College and University Admissions (with Derek Bok) 1998, The Game of Life: College Sports and Educational Values 2001, At a Slight Angle to the Universe (also Romanes Lecture, Univ. of Oxford) 2001, Reclaiming the Game: College Sports and Educational Values (with Sarah A. Levin) 2003, Equity and Excellence in Higher Education 2005, Crossing the Finish Line: Completing College at America's Public Universities 2009, The Board Book 2009, Lesson Learned 2010. *Honours:* Woodrow Wilson Fellow, Ford Foundation Fellow, Social Science Research Council Faculty Research Fellow, Ford Foundation Faculty Research Fellow, James Madison Medal, Princeton Univ., Joseph Henry Medal, Smithsonian Inst., Grawemeyer Award in Educ., Rolex Achievement Award, Asscn for the Study of Higher Educ., Phyllis Franklin Award, Modern Language Asscn, Teachers' Coll. Distinguished Service Award, Pierre Boudreau Leadership Award, José Vasconcelos World Award of Educ., Clark Kerr Award for Distinguished Leadership in Higher Educ. *Address:* c/o Andrew W. Mellon Foundation, 151 East 61st Street, New York, NY 10065, USA (office). *Telephone:* (212) 826-8114 (office).

BOWERING, George Harry, OC, MA; Canadian writer, poet and academic; *Professor Emeritus, Simon Fraser University*; b. 1 Dec. 1936, Penticton, BC; s. of Ewart Bowering and Pearl Bowering (née Brinson); m. 1st Angela Luoma 1962 (died 1999); one d.; m. 2nd Jean Baird 2006. *Education:* Victoria Coll., Univ. of British Columbia, Univ. of Western Ontario. *Career:* served as Royal Canadian Air Force photographer 1954–57; Lecturer, Univ. of Calgary 1963–66; Writer-in-Residence, Sir George Williams Univ., Montreal 1967–68, Lecturer 1968–71; Prof., Simon Fraser Univ., Burnaby, BC 1972–2001, Prof. Emer. 2001–. *Exhibition:* portraits of fire fighters of Oliver, BC 1952. *Play:* The Home for Heroes 1962. *Radio plays:* George Vancouver (CBC) 1972, Sitting in Mexico (CBC) 1973, Music in the Park (CBC) 1986, The Great Grandchildren of Bill Bissett's Mice (CBC) 1989. *Television play:* What Does Eddie Williams Want? (CBC) 1966. *Publications include:* poetry collections: Sticks & Stones 1963, Points on the Grid 1964, The Man in Yellow Boots/El hombre de las botas amarillas 1965, Rocky Mountain Foot 1969, The Gangs of Kosmos 1969, Touch: Selected Poems 1960–1969 1971, In the Flesh 1974, The Catch 1976, Poem & Other Baseballs 1976, The Concrete Island 1977, Another Mouth 1979, West Window: Selected Poetry 1982, Smoking Mirrow 1982, Seventy-One Poems for People 1985, Delayed Mercy & Other Poems 1986, George Bowering Selected: Poems 1961–1992 1993; chapbooks: How I Hear Howl 1967, Two Police Poems 1969, The Sensible 1972, Layers 1–13 1973, In Answer 1977, Uncle Louis 1980, Spencer & Groulx 1985, Quarters 1991, Do Sink 1992, A, You're Adorable 1998, 6 Little Poems in Alphabetical Order 2000, Joining the Lost Generation 2002; long poems: Sitting in Mexico 1965, George,Vancouver 1970, Geneve 1971, Autobiology 1972, Curious 1973, At War With the US 1974, Allophanes 1976, Kerrisdale Elegies 1984, His Life: A Poem 2000, Baseball: A poem in the magic number 9 2003, Changing on the Fly 2004, Vermeer's Light 2006, Fulgencio 2008, A Little Black Strap 2009, My Darling Nelly Grey 2010; novels: Mirror on the Floor 1967, A Short Sad Book 1977, Burning Water 1980, En eaux troubles 1982, Caprice 1987, Harry's Fragments 1990, Shoot! 1994, Parents from Space 1994, Piccolo Mondo 1998, Diamondback Dog 1998; short story collections: Flycatcher & Other Stories 1974, Concentric Circles 1977, Protective Footwear 1978, A Place to Die 1983, Standing on Richards 2004, The Box 2009; non-fiction: Al Purdy 1970, Three Vancouver Writers 1979, The Mask in Place 1983, Craft Slices 1985, Imaginary Hand 1988, Bowering's B.C. 1996, Egotists and Autocrats – The Prime Ministers of Canada 1999, A Magpie Life (memoir) 2001, Cars (memoir) 2002, Stone Country (history) 2003, Left Hook (criticism) 2005, Baseball Love (memoirs) 2006, Horizontal Surfaces (chapbook) 2010, The Diamond Alphabet 2011, How I Wrote Certain of My Books (essays) 2011. *Honours:* First Parl. Poet Laureate 2002–04; Order of BC 2005; Hon. DLit (British Columbia) 1997, (Western Ontario) 2003; Gov.-Gen.'s Award for poetry 1967, for fiction 1980, bpNichol Chapbook Awards for Poetry 1991, 1992, Canadian Authors' Asscn Award for Poetry 1993, Lt-Gov.'s Award for Literary Excellence 2011, Alumni Award of Distinction, Univ. of British Columbia 2011. *Address:* 4403 West 11th Avenue, Vancouver, BC V6R 2M2, Canada (home). *Telephone:* (604) 224-4898 (home). *E-mail:* bowering@sfu.ca.

BOWERING, Marilyn, MA; Canadian novelist and poet; *University-College Professor, Vancouver Island University*. *Education:* Univs of Victoria, British Columbia and New Brunswick. *Career:* Instructor in Continuing Educ., Univ. of British Columbia 1977; Ed., writer, Gregson/Graham Marketing and Communications 1978–80; Ed., Noel Collins and Blackwells, Edinburgh, UK 1980–82; Visiting Lecturer, Dept of Creative Writing, Univ. of Victoria 1978–80, Lecturer 1982–86, 1989, Visiting Assoc. Prof. 1993–98; Writer-in-Residence, Memorial Univ. of Newfoundland 1995; Univ.-Coll. Prof., Malaspina Univ. Coll./Vanouver Island Univ. 1998–; mem. Writers' Union of Canada, PEN, League of Canadian Poets. *Plays:* Hajimari-No-Hajimari – Four Myths of the Pacific Rim 1986, Anyone Can See I Love You 1988, Temple of the Stars 1996. *Film script:* Divine Fate (Heart of the Festival Award, Earth Peace Int. Film Festival 1994, UNICEF Award for Animation, Int. Animation Festival 1994) 1993. *Radio includes:* Grandfather Was a Soldier 1983, Anyone Can See I Love You 1986, Laika and Folchakov – A Journey in Time and Space 1987, A Cold Departure 1989. *Publications:* poetry: The Liberation of Newfoundland 1973, One Who Became Lost 1976, Many Voices: An Anthology of Contemporary Canadian Indian Poetry (co-ed. with David A. Day) 1977, The Killing Room 1977, Third/Child Zian 1978, The Book of Glass 1978, Sleeping with Lambs 1980, Giving Back Diamonds 1982, The Sunday Before Winter – New and Selected Poetry 1984, Anyone Can See I Love You 1987, Grandfather was a Soldier 1987, Calling All the World – Laika and Folchakov 1989, Love As It Is 1993, Interior Castle 1994, Autobiography 1996, Human Bodies: New and Collected Poems, 1987–1999 1999, The Alchemy of Happiness 2003; fiction: The Visitors Have All Returned 1979, To All Appearances a Lady (New York Times Notable Book) 1990, Visible Worlds (Ethel Wilson Fiction Prize) 1997, Cat's Pilgrimage 2004, What It Takes To Be Human 2006, Green 2007; non-fiction: Guide to the Labor Code of British Columbia (ed.) 1980; contribs to anthologies and journals. *Honours:* Du Maurier Award for Poetry (Gold) 1977, Nat. Magazine Awards for Poetry 1978, 1988, Malahat Review Long Poem Prize 1994, Pat Lowther Award 1997, Fulbright Award 2008. *Literary Agent:* c/o Jackie Kaiser, Westwood Creative Artists Ltd, 94 Harbord Street, Toronto, ON M5S 1G6, Canada. *Telephone:* (416) 964-3302. *Fax:* (416) 975-9209. *E-mail:* jackie@wcaltd.com. *Address:* Department of Creative Writing, Vancouver Island University, 900 Fifth Street, Nanaimo, BC V9R 5S5, Canada (office). *E-mail:* marilyn.bowering@viu.ca (office). *Website:* www.marilynbowering.com.

BOWKER, Gordon, MA, PhD; British writer and journalist; b. 19 March 1934, Birmingham. *Education:* Univ. of Nottingham, Univ. of London. *Career:* teacher, Goldsmiths Coll., London 1966–91; mem. PEN, Soc. of Authors, Writers' Guild. *Publications:* Under Twenty (ed.) 1966, Freedom: Reason or Revolution (ed.) 1970, Malcolm Lowry Remembered (ed.) 1985, Malcolm Lowry: Under the Volcano (ed.) 1988, Apparently Incongruous Parts: The Worlds of Malcolm Lowry (co-ed.) 1990, Pursued by Furies: A Life of Malcolm Lowry 1993, Through the Dark Labyrinth 1996, George Orwell (aka Inside George Orwell) 2003, Perseguido Por los Demonios: Vida de Malcolm Lowry 2008, James Joyce: A Biography 2011, Slightly Foxed 2011; contrib. to London Magazine, The Independent, The Independent on Sunday, Times Literary Supplement, New York Times. *Literary Agent:* David Higham Associates, 5–8 Lower John Street, Golden Square, London, W1F 9HA, England.

BOWKER, John Westerdale, MA; British academic and writer; b. 30 July 1935, London. *Education:* Univ. of Oxford. *Career:* Fellow, Corpus Christi Coll., Cambridge 1962–74; Lecturer, Univ. of Cambridge 1965–74; Prof. of Religious Studies, Univ. of Lancaster 1974–85; Fellow, Dean, Trinity Coll., Cambridge 1984–93; Hon. Canon, Canterbury Cathedral 1985–; Gresham Prof. 1992–97, Fellow 1997–, Gresham Coll., London. *Publications:* The Targums and Rabbinic Literature 1969, Problems of Suffering in Religions of the World 1970, Jesus and the Pharisees 1973, The Sense of God: Sociological, Anthropological and Psychological Approaches to the Origin of the Sense of

God 1973, Uncle Bolpenny Tries Things Out 1973, The Religious Imagination and the Sense of God 1978, Worlds of Faith 1983, Violence and Aggression (ed.) 1984, Licensed Insanities 1987, The Meanings of Death 1991, A Year to Live 1991, Hallowed Ground 1993, Is God a Virus? Genes, Culture and Religion 1995, The Oxford Dictionary of World Religions 1997, World Religions 1997, The Complete Bible Handbook 1998, What Muslims Believe 1998, God: A Brief History 2002, The Sacred Neuron: Extraordinary New Discoveries Linking Science and Religion 2005, Beliefs That Changed the World 2007, The Aerial Atlas of the Holy Land 2008, Conflict and Reconciliation: The Contribution of Religions 2008, Knowing the Unknowable: Science and Religions on God and the Universe 2008, An Alphabet of Animals 2009. *Honours:* Harper Collins Biennial Prize 1993, Benjamin Franklin Award 1999. *Address:* 14 Bowers Croft, Cambridge, CB1 8RP, England (home).

BOWLER, Peter John, BA, MSc, PhD, FBA, MRIA; British academic and writer; *Professor Emeritus of History of Science, Queen's University, Belfast;* b. 8 Oct. 1944, Leicester, Leics., England; m. Sheila Mary Holt 1966; one s. one d. *Education:* Univs of Cambridge and Sussex, Univ. of Toronto, Canada. *Career:* Asst Prof., Univ. of Toronto 1971–72; Lecturer, Science Univ. of Malaysia, Penang 1972–75; Asst Prof., Univ. of Winnipeg, Canada 1975–79; Lecturer, Queen's Univ., Belfast 1979–87, Reader 1987–92, apptd Prof. of History of Science 1992, now Emer.; mem. British Soc. for the History of Science, History of Science Soc. *Publications:* Fossils and Progress: Paleontology and the Idea of Progressive Evolution in the Nineteenth Century 1976, The Eclipse of Darwinism: Anti-Darwinian Evolution Theories in the Decades Around 1900 1983, Evolution: The History of an Idea 1984, Theories of Human Evolution: A Century of Debate 1844–1944 1986, The Non-Darwinian Revolution: Reinterpreting a Historical Myth 1988, The Mendelian Revolution: The Emergence of Hereditarian Concepts in Modern Science and Society 1989, The Invention of Progress: The Victorians and the Past 1990, Darwin: L'origine delle specie 1990, Charles Darwin: The Man and his Influence 1990, The Fontana History of the Environmental Sciences 1992 (US edn as The Norton History of the Environmental Sciences 1993), Biology and Social Thought 1850–1914, 5 lectures 1993, Darwinism 1993, E. Ray Lankester and the Making of Modern British Biology (ed. and co-author with J. Lester) 1995, Life's Splendid Drama: Evolutionary Biology and the Reconstruction of Life's Ancestry 1860–1940 1996, Reconciling Science and Religion: The Debate in Early Twentieth-Century Britain 2001, Monkey Trials and Gorilla Sermons 2007; contrib. to journals. *Address:* c/o School of History and Anthropology, Queen's University of Belfast, Belfast, BT7 1NN, Northern Ireland (office). *E-mail:* p.bowler@qub.ac.uk (office).

BOWLT, John Ellis, BA, MA, PhD; American (b. British) academic and writer; *Professor, Department of Slavic Languages and Literatures, University of Southern California;* b. 6 Dec. 1943, London, England; m. Nicoletta Misler 1981. *Education:* Univ. of Birmingham, Univ. of St Andrews. *Career:* Lecturer, Univ. of St Andrews 1968–79, Univ. of Birmingham 1970; Asst Prof., Univ. of Kansas, USA 1970–71; Asst to Assoc. Prof., Univ. of Texas 1971–81, Assoc. Prof. to Prof. 1981–88; Visiting Prof., Univ. of Otago, NZ 1982, Hebrew Univ., Jerusalem, Israel 1985; Prof., Dept of Slavic Languages and Literatures, Univ. of Southern California 1988–; mem. American Asscn for the Advancement of Slavic Studies, Coll. Art Asscn, New York; Sr Fellow, Wolfsonian Foundation, Miami 1995; Gen. Ed. Experiment 1990–. *Publications:* Russian Formalism (co-ed. with Stephen Bann) 1973, The Russian Avant-Garde: Theory and Criticism 1902–1934 1976, The Silver Age: Russian Art of the Early Twentieth Century 1979, The Life of Vasilii Kandinsky in Russian Art (with Rose Carol Washton-Long) 1980, Pavel Filonov: A Hero and his Fate (with Nicoletta Misler) 1984, Mikalojus Konstantinas Ciurlionis: Music of the Spheres (with Alfred Senn and Danute Staskevicius) 1986, Russian Samizdat Art (co-author) 1986, Gustav Kluzis 1988, Aus Vollem Halse: Russische Buchillustration und Typographie 1900–1930 (with B. Hernad) 1993, Russian and East European Paintings in the Thyssen-Bornemisza Collection (with Nicoletta Misler) 1993, The Salon Album of Vera Sudeikin-Stravinsky 1995, Painting Revolution 1999, Spheres of Light, Stations of Darkness: The Art of Solomon Nikritin 2004, The One and a Half-Eyed Archer (trans.) 2004, Moscow and St. Petersburg 1900–1920. Art, Life and Culture of the Russian Silver Age 2008 (simultaneous edns in French and German), Nikolai Kalmakov i labirint dekadentsva (Nikolai Kalmakov and the Labyrinth of Decadence) (in Russian, with Yuliia Balybina) 2008, Etonnemoi! Serge Diaghilev et Les Ballets Russes (co-ed.) 2009 (English trans. as A Feast of Wonders); contribs to books, scholarly journals, periodicals and exhbn catalogues. *Honours:* Order of Friendship (Russia) 2009; British Council Scholarship 1966–68, Woodrow Wilson Nat. Fellowship 1971, Yale Univ. Nat. Humanities Inst. Fellow 1977–78, Fulbright-Hays Award, Paris 1981, ACLS Award, Italy 1984, Int. Research and Exchanges Bd (IREX) Award, Moscow 1986, 1988, 1991, 1994, Casden Inst. for Jewish Studies Faculty Research Grant 2003, IREX IARO Grantee 2004, IREX Fellow 2005, Borchard Award for study of Ferris collection 2007–08, Fulbright Award for study of the work of Leon Bakst in Russia 2007–08. *Address:* Department of Slavic Languages and Literatures, University of Southern California, Box 4353, Los Angeles, CA 90095-4353, USA (office). *Telephone:* (213) 740-2735 (office). *Fax:* (213) 740-8550 (office). *Website:* dornsife.usc.edu/sll (office).

BOYCOTT, Rosie; British journalist and author; b. 13 May 1951, d. of Charles Boycott and Betty Boycott; m. 1st David Leitch (divorced); one d.; m. 2nd Charles Howard 1999. *Education:* Cheltenham Ladies Coll., Kent Univ. *Career:* f. Spare Rib 1972; est. Virago Books 1973; worked on Village Voice (magazine), New York; subsequently edited Arabic women's magazine in Kuwait; Features Ed. Honey; Deputy Ed. Daily Mail's Male and Femail pages; Ed. Discount Traveller; Commissioning Ed. The Sunday Telegraph; Deputy Ed. Harpers & Queen 1989; Deputy Ed. and Features Ed. (British) Esquire 1991, Ed. 1992–96, of Ind. on Sunday 1996–98, of the Ind. 1998, of the Express 1998–2001, of the Express on Sunday 1998–2001; Chair., Panel of Judges, Orange Prize for Fiction 2001; Chair. London Food 2008–; mem. Exec. Cttee English PEN. *Publications:* A Nice Girl Like Me (autobiog.) 1983, All For Love 1985, Our Farm: A Year in the Life of a Smallholding 2007. *Address:* c/o London Food, London Development Agency, Palestra, 197 Blackfriars Road, London, SE1 8AA, England (office).

BOYD, William Andrew Murray, CBE, MA, FRSL; British writer; b. 7 March 1952, Ghana; s. of Dr Alexander Murray Boyd and Evelyn Boyd; m. Susan Anne Boyd (née Wilson) 1975. *Education:* Gordonstoun School, Glasgow Univ., Jesus Coll., Oxford. *Career:* lecturer in English, St Hilda's Coll., Oxford 1980–83; TV critic, New Statesman 1981–83. *Film appearance:* Rabbit Fever 2006. *Publications include:* A Good Man in Africa (Whitbread Prize 1981, Somerset Maugham Award 1982) 1981 (screenplay 1994), On the Yankee Station 1981, An Ice-Cream War (John Llewellyn Rhys Prize) 1982, Stars and Bars 1984 (screenplay 1988), School Ties 1985, The New Confessions 1987, Scoop (screenplay) 1987, Brazzaville Beach (McVities Prize and James Tait Black Memorial Prize) 1990, Aunt Julia and the Scriptwriter (screenplay) 1990, Mr Johnson (screenplay) 1990, Chaplin (screenplay) 1992, The Blue Afternoon (novel) 1993, A Good Man in Africa (screenplay) 1994, The Destiny of Nathalie 'X' 1995, Armadillo 1998 (screenplay 2001), Nat Tate: An American Artist 1998, The Trench (screenplay, also dir) 1999, Sword of Honour (screenplay) 2001, Any Human Heart 2002, Fascination 2004, Bamboo (collection of literary reviews) 2005, A Waste of Shame (screenplay) 2005, Restless (novel) (Costa Book Award for Novel of the Year, Yorkshire Post Book of the Year 2007) 2006, Granta 100 (Ed.) 2008, The Dream Lover (short stories) 2008, Ordinary Thunderstorms (novel) 2009. *Honours:* Officier, Ordre des Arts et des Lettres; Hon. DLitt (St Andrews), (Glasgow), (Stirling). *Literary Agent:* The Agency, 24 Pottery Lane, Holland Park, London, W11 4LZ, England.

BOYDEN, Joseph, MFA; Canadian writer; b. 1968, s. of the late Raymond Wilfrid Boyden; m. Amanda Boyden; one s. *Education:* York Univ., Univ. of New Orleans, USA. *Career:* taught at Northern Coll., Moosonee, Ont.; currently lecturer in Canadian literature and creative writing, Univ. of New Orleans. *Publications:* Born with a Tooth (short stories) 2001, Three-Day Road (novel) (Rogers Writers' Trust Fiction Prize, CBA Libris Fiction Book of the Year, Amazon.ca/Books in Canada First Novel Award, McNally Robinson Aboriginal Book of the Year) 2005, Through Black Spruce (novel) (Scotiabank Giller Prize) 2008. *Address:* c/o Nicole Winstanley, Hamish Hamilton Canada, 90 Eglinton Avenue East, Suite 700, Toronto, Ontario, M4P 2Y3, Canada (office). *E-mail:* info@penguin.ca (office). *Website:* www.penguin.ca (office); www.josephboyden.com.

BOYLE, Thomas Coraghessan (T. C.), BA, MFA, PhD; American academic and writer; *Professor, Department of English, University of Southern California;* b. 2 Dec. 1948, Peekskill, NY; m. Karen Kvashay 1974; two s. one d. *Education:* SUNY at Potsdam, Univ. of Iowa. *Career:* Founder-Dir, Creative Writing Program 1978–86, Asst Prof. of English 1978–82, Assoc. Prof. of English 1982–86, Prof. of English 1986–, Univ. of Southern California; mem. Nat. Endowment of the Arts literature panel 1986–87; Nat. Endowment for the Arts grants 1977, 1983; Guggenheim Fellowship 1988, mem. American Acad. of Arts and Letters 2009–. *Publications:* Descent of Man 1979, Water Music 1982, Budding Prospects 1984, Greasy Lake 1985, World's End 1987, If the River was Whiskey 1989, East is East 1990, The Road to Wellville 1993, Without a Hero 1994, The Tortilla Curtain 1995, Riven Rock 1998, T.C. Boyle Stories 1998, A Friend of the Earth 2000, After the Plague 2001, Drop City 2003, The Inner Circle 2004, Tooth and Claw 2006, Talk Talk 2006, The Women 2009, Wild Child 2010; contrib. to numerous anthologies and periodicals. *Honours:* Hon. DHumLitt (SUNY) 1991; PEN/Faulkner Award 1988, Commonwealth Club of California Gold Medal for Literature 1988, O. Henry Short Story Awards 1988, 1989, Prix Passion Publishers' Prize, France 1989, Eds' Choice, New York Times Book Review 1989, Harold D. Vursell Memorial Award, American Acad. of Arts and Letters 1993, Prix Médicis Étranger 1997. *Address:* Department of English, University of Southern California, Los Angeles, CA 90089, USA (office). *Telephone:* (213) 740-3734 (office). *E-mail:* tcb@tcboyle.com (office). *Website:* www.tcboyle.com.

BOYNE, John, BA, MA; Irish novelist; b. 30 April 1971, Dublin. *Education:* Trinity Coll., Dublin and Univ. of East Anglia. *Career:* fmr creative writing teacher, Irish Writers' Centre; Univ. of East Anglia Writing Fellowship 2005. *Publications:* novels: The Thief of Time 2000, The Congress of Rough Riders 2001, Crippen 2004, The Boy in the Striped Pyjamas (juvenile) 2006, Next of Kin 2006, Mutiny on the Bounty 2008, The House of Special Purpose 2009, Noah Barleywater Runs Away (juvenile) 2010. *Honours:* Curtis Brown Prize, two Irish Book Awards, Bisto Book of the Year, Que Leer Award. *Address:* 5 The Dell, Marley Grange, Rathfarnham, Dublin 16, Ireland. *Website:* www.johnboyne.com.

BRABCOVÁ, Zuzana; Czech novelist; b. 23 March 1959, Prague; d. of Jiří Brabec and Zina Trochová; m.; one d. *Career:* fmr librarian and cleaner; Ed. at publisher, Český spisovatel (Czech Writer) 1995–. *Publications:* Daleko od stromu (Far from the Tree) 1984, Zlodějina (Thievery) 1995, Rok perel 2000.

Honours: Jiří Orten Prize. *Address:* c/o Czech PEN Centre, Vodièkova str. 32, 110 00 Prague 1, Czech Republic (office).

BRACKENBURY, Alison, BA; British poet and writer; b. 20 May 1953, Gainsborough, Lincs., England. *Education:* St Hugh's Coll., Oxford. *Radio play:* The Country of Afternoon 1985. *Publications:* Journey to a Cornish Wedding 1977, Two Poems 1979, Dreams of Power and Other Poems 1981, Breaking Ground and Other Poems 1984, Christmas Roses and Other Poems 1988, Selected Poems 1991, 1829 1994, After Beethoven 2000, The Story of Sigurd 2003, Bricks and Ballads 2004, Singing in the Dark 2008, Shadow 2009; contrib. to journals, including PN Review. *Honours:* Eric Gregory Award 1982, Cholmondeley Award 1997. *Address:* c/o Carcanet Press, Fourth Floor, Alliance House, 30 Cross Street, Manchester, M2 7AQ, England. *Website:* www.alisonbrackenbury.co.uk.

BRADBURY, Edward P. (see Moorcock, Michael John)

BRADBY, Tom, MA; British journalist and writer; *Political Editor, ITV News*; b. 1967, Malta; m.; three c. *Education:* Sherborne School, Univ. of Edinburgh. *Career:* editorial trainee ITN 1990, Producer, for political Ed. ITV News 1992–93, NI Correspondent 1993–96, Political Correspondent 1996–98, Asia Correspondent, based in Hong Kong 1998–2001, Royal Correspondent, then UK Ed. 2001–05, Political Ed. 2005–. *Publications:* novels: Shadow Dancer 1998, The Sleep of the Dead 2001, The Master of Rain 2002, The White Russian 2003, The God of Chaos 2004, Blood Money 2009. *Address:* ITN, 200 Gray's Inn Road, London, WC1X 8XZ, England (office). *E-mail:* tom.bradby@itn.co.uk (office). *Website:* www.itn.co.uk (office).

BRADFORD, Barbara Taylor, OBE; British writer and journalist; b. Leeds, England; d. of Winston Taylor and Freda Walker; m. Robert Bradford 1963. *Career:* reporter, Yorkshire Evening Post 1949–51, Women's Ed. 1951–53; Fashion Ed. Woman's Own 1953–54; columnist, London Evening News 1955–57; Exec. Ed. London American 1959–62; Ed. Nat. Design Center Magazine 1965–69; syndicated columnist, Newsday Specials, Long Island 1968–70; nat. syndicated columnist, Chicago Tribune-New York (News Syndicate), New York 1970–75, Los Angeles Times Syndicate 1975–81; Dir Library of Congress, DL; mem. Bd American Heritage Dictionary, Police Athletic League, Author's Guild Foundation 1989–; Girls Inc. *Television:* ten novels adapted into TV mini-series. *Publications:* Complete Encyclopaedia of Homemaking Ideas 1968, A Garland of Children's Verse 1968, How to be the Perfect Wife 1969, Easy Steps to Successful Decorating 1971, How to Solve your Decorating Problems 1976, Decorating Ideas for Casual Living 1977, Making Space Grow 1979, A Woman of Substance (novel) 1979, Luxury Designs for Apartment Living 1981, Voice of the Heart 1983, Hold the Dream 1985, Act of Will (novel) 1986, To Be The Best 1988, The Women in his Life (novel) 1990, Remember (novel) 1991, Angel (novel) 1993, Everything to Gain (novel) 1994, Dangerous to Know (novel) 1995, Love in Another Town (novel) 1995, Her Own Rules 1996, A Secret Affair 1996, Power of a Woman 1997, A Sudden Change of Heart 1998, Where You Belong 2000, The Triumph of Katie Byrne 2001, Three Weeks in Paris 2002, Emma's Secret 2003, Unexpected Blessings 2004, Just Rewards 2006, The Ravenscar Dynasty 2007, Heirs of Ravenscar 2007, Being Elizabeth 2008, Breaking the Rules 2009, Playing the Game 2011. *Honours:* Hon. DLit (Leeds) 1990, (Bradford) 1995; Hon. DHumLit (Teikyo Post Univ.) 1996; numerous awards and prizes. *Address:* Bradford Enterprises, 450 Park Avenue, New York, NY 10022, USA (office). *Telephone:* (212) 308-7390 (office). *Fax:* (212) 935-1636 (office). *E-mail:* btbweb@barbarataylorbradford.com (office). *Website:* www.barbarataylorbradford.com.

BRADFORD, Karleen, BA; Canadian writer; b. 16 Dec. 1936, Toronto, ON; m. James Creighton Bradford 1959, two s. one d. *Education:* University of Toronto. *Career:* Chair., Public Lending Right Commission of Canada 1998–2000; mem. PEN, IBBY, Writers' Union of Canada. *Publications:* A Year for Growing 1977, The Other Elizabeth 1982, Wrong Again, Robbie 1983, I Wish There Were Unicorns 1983, The Stone in the Meadow 1984, The Haunting at Cliff House 1985, The Nine Days Queen 1986, Write Now! 1988, Windward Island 1989, There Will be Wolves 1992, Thirteenth Child 1994, Animal Heroes 1995, Shadows on a Sword 1996, More Animal Heroes 1996, Dragonfire 1997, A Different Kind of Champion 1998, Lionhearts Scribe 1999, Whisperings of Magic 2001, With Nothing But Our Courage 2002, You Can't Rush a Cat 2003, Angeline 2004, The Scarlet Cross 2007, Dragonmaster 2009. *Honours:* Canadian Library Asscn Young Adult Novel Award 1993. *Address:* RR No. 2, Owen Sound, ON N4K 5N4, Canada (home). *Fax:* (705) 484-1596 (office). *E-mail:* karleenbradford@cottagecountry.net (office). *Website:* www.karleenbradford.com.

BRADFORD, S. W. (see Battin, B. W.)

BRADFORD, Sarah Mary Malet, (Viscountess Bangor); British biographer, historian and broadcaster; b. 3 Sept. 1938, Bournemouth; d. of the late Brig. Hilary Anthony Hayes and Mary Beatrice de Carteret Malet; m. 1st Anthony John Bradford 1959; one s. one d.; m. 2nd Viscount Bangor 1976. *Education:* St Mary's Convent, Shaftesbury and Lady Margaret Hall, Oxford. *Career:* manuscript expert at Christie's 1975–78. *Publications:* Portugal and Madeira 1969, Portugal 1973, Cesare Borgia 1976, The Englishman's Wine 1969, re-published as The Story of Port 1978, Disraeli 1982, Princess Grace 1984, King George VI 1989, Sacheverell Sitwell 1993, Elizabeth – A Biography of Her Majesty The Queen 1996, America's Queen – The Life of Jacqueline Kennedy Onassis 2000, Lucrezia Borgia – Life, Love and Death in Renaissance Italy 2004, Diana 2006, Queen Elizabeth II – Her Life in Our Times 2012; contribs to periodicals. *Literary Agent:* c/o Aitken Alexander Associates Ltd, 18–21 Cavaye Place, London, SW10 9PT, England. *Telephone:* (20) 7373-8672. *Fax:* (20) 7373-6002. *E-mail:* reception@aitkenalexander.co.uk. *Website:* www.aitkenalexander.co.uk; www.sarahbradford.co.uk (home).

BRADHURST, Jane, BA, MSc, DipEd; Australian artist, writer, dramatist and poet; b. 28 Oct. 1926, Sydney, NSW; d. of Frank Bradhurst and Winifred Bradhurst; m. Colin Russell-Jones (deceased); two s. one d. *Education:* Univ. of Sydney, Univ. of Canberra, Goulburn CAE. *Career:* eight solo exhbns; works in main lobby of Australian Embassy, Washington, DC, USA to celebrate opening of Nat. Museum of Australia; 20 works acquired by Nat. Gallery of Australia 2005; mem. ACT Writers' Centre, Australian Writers' Guild. *Art Exhibitions:* Mood Kimberley, Canberra Museum and Gallery 2002–03, Kimberley Retrospective and New Works, Megalo Gallery 2007. *Publications:* five novels and two vols of plays, including The Flowers of the Snowy Mountains 1977, Document of Our Day: Women of the Pre-Pill Generation 1986, Three One-Act Plays 1987, Duet String Trio Quartet 1987, Australis 1788 (musical) 1988, Animalia in Australia 1992, 100 Poems 1993, The BD II 1995, Love in a Hot Climate 1996, Three Festival Plays 1998, Summertime (musical) 1998, There is no Mystery (anthology) 1999, Mystery in Manhattan 2000, Always on Call: Tales of an Outback Doctor 2002, Outback Lives and Border Fence Brides – More Tales of an Outback Doctor 2004, A Dangerous Beauty 2006. *Honours:* Jt Winner, Best Play, Int. Women's Year 1975, Best Play, Fed. of Australian Drama 1975, Jt Winner, Everyman 1979. *Address:* PO Box 9009, Deakin, ACT 2600 (office); 50 Beauchamp Street, Deakin, ACT 2600, Australia (home). *Telephone:* (2) 62814633 (home).

BRADLEE, Benjamin Crowninshield, AB; American newspaper editor; *Vice-President at Large, Washington Post*; b. 26 Aug. 1921, Boston; s. of Frederick Bradlee and Josephine de Gersdorff; m. 1st Jean Saltonstall 1942; one s.; m. 2nd Antoinette Pinchot 1956; one s. one d.; m. 3rd Sally Quinn 1978; one s. *Education:* Harvard Univ. *Career:* reporter, New Hampshire Sunday News, Manchester 1946–48, Washington Post 1948–51; Press Attaché, Embassy in Paris 1951–53; European corresp. Newsweek, Paris 1953–57; reporter, Washington Bureau, Newsweek 1957–61, Sr Ed. and Chief of Bureau 1961–65; Man. Ed. Washington Post 1965–68, Vice-Pres. and Exec. Ed. 1968–91, Vice-Pres. at Large 1991–; Chair. History of St Mary's City Comm. 1992–. *Publications:* That Special Grace 1964, Conversations with Kennedy 1975, A Good Life: Newspapering and Other Adventures (autobiography) 1995, A Life's Work: Fathers and Sons 2012. *Honours:* Dr hc (Georgetown Univ.) 2006; Burton Benjamin Award 1995. *Address:* 1150 15th Street, NW, Washington, DC 20071-0001, USA (home). *Telephone:* (202) 334-7510 (home).

BRADLEY, Clive, CBE, MA (Cantab.); British publishing and media executive and barrister; *Convenor, Confederation of Information Communication Industries*; b. 25 July 1934, London, England; s. of Alfred Bradley and Annie Kathleen Bradley. *Education:* Felsted School, Essex, Clare Coll., Cambridge, Yale Univ., USA. *Career:* barrister (Middle Temple); with BBC 1961–63; Broadcasting Officer, Labour Party 1963–65; Political Ed., The Statist 1965–67; Group Labour Adviser, Int. Publishing Corpn and Deputy Gen. Man. Mirror Group Newspapers 1967–73; Dir The Observer 1973–75; Chief Exec. The Publishers Asscn 1976–97; Convenor Confed. of Information Communication Industries 1984–; Chair. Central London Valuation Tribunal 1972–2006, Age Concern Richmond upon Thames 1999–2003, Richmond upon Thames Arts Council 2003–09, BookPower 2008–11; Gov. Felsted School 1972–2009. *Publications:* many articles and broadcasts on politics, econs, industrial relations, industry media and current affairs. *Address:* 8 Northumberland Place, Richmond upon Thames, Surrey, TW10 6TS, England (home). *Telephone:* (20) 8940-7172 (home). *E-mail:* bradley_clive@btopenworld.com (home).

BRADLEY, George, BA; American writer and poet; b. 22 Jan. 1953, Roslyn, New York; m. Spencer Boyd 1984; one d. *Education:* Yale Univ., Univ. of Virginia. *Publications:* Terms to Be Met 1986, Of the Knowledge of Good and Evil 1991, The Fire Fetched Down 1996, The Yale Younger Poets Anthology (Ed.) 1998, Some Assembly Required 2001; contribs to periodicals. *Honours:* Acad. of American Poets Prize 1978, Yale Younger Poets Prize 1985, Lavan Younger Poets Award 1990, Witter Bynner Prize 1992. *Address:* 82 W Main Street, Chester, CT 06412, USA (office). *Telephone:* (860) 526-3900 (office). *E-mail:* georgecbradley@sbcglobal.net (office).

BRADLEY, John, BA, MA, MFA; American teacher, writer and poet; b. 26 Sept. 1950, New York, NY; m. Jana Brubaker 1988; one s. *Education:* Univ. of Minnesota, Colorado State Univ., Bowling Green State Univ. *Career:* Instructor in English, Bowling Green State Univ. 1989–91, Northern Illinois Univ. 1992–. *Publications:* Love in Idleness: The Poetry of Roberto Zingarello 1989, Atomic Ghost: Poets Respond to the Nuclear Age 1995, Learning to Glow: A Nuclear Reader 2000, Terrestrial Music 2006; contribs to Ironwood, Rolling Stone, Poetry East.

BRADLEY, John Edmund, Jr, BA; American writer; b. 12 Aug. 1958, Opelousas, LA. *Education:* Louisiana State University. *Career:* Staff Writer, Washington Post 1983–87, Contributing Writer 1988–89. *Publications:* Tupelo Nights 1988, The Best There Ever Was 1990, Love & Obits 1992, Smoke 1994, My Juliet 2000, It Never Rains in Tiger Stadium 2007; contributions: Esquire, Sports Illustrated and other periodicals. *Address:*

2035 Delmas Street, Opelousas, LA 70570-4715, USA (home). *Telephone:* (337) 942-5285 (home).

BRADY, Conor, BA, MA; Irish journalist and academic; b. 24 April 1949, Dublin; s. of Conor Brady and Amy MacCarthy; m. Ann Byron 1971; two s. *Education:* Mount St Joseph Cistercian Abbey, Univ. Coll. Dublin. *Career:* reporter Irish Times 1969–73, Asst Ed. 1977–81, Dir and Deputy Ed. 1984–86, Ed. and Group Editorial Dir 1986–2002, Ed. Emer. 2002–; Ed. Garda Review 1973–74; Tutor, Dept of Politics, Univ. Coll. Dublin 1973–74 Presenter/Reporter RTE News At One and This Week 1974–75; Ed. The Sunday Tribune 1981–82; Chair. Bd of Counsellors, European Journalism Centre, Maastricht 1993–98; Pres. World Eds' Forum, Paris 1995–2000; mem. Bd of Dirs World Press Freedom Cttee, Federation International des Editeurs de Journeaux 1995–2000; Commr, Garda Síochána Ombudsman Comm. 2006–11; fmr Chair. British-Irish Asscn; Visiting Prof., John Jay Coll., CUNY; Sr Teaching Fellow, Michael Smurfit Grad. School of Business, Univ. Coll. Dublin; Cttee Mem. UNESCO Int. Press Freedom. *Publications:* Guardian of the Peace 1974, Up With The Times 2005, Cead Bliain Faoi Rath: The Story of Cistercian College Roscrea 1905–2005 (co-ed.) 2005, A June of Ordinary Murders 2012. *Honours:* Award for Outstanding Work in Irish Journalism 1979. *Address:* c/o Garda Síochána Ombudsman Commission, 150 Abbey Street Upper, Dublin 1, Ireland.

BRADY, Joan, BS; American/British writer; b. 4 Dec. 1939, San Francisco, Calif.; m. Dexter Masters 1963; one s. *Education:* Columbia Univ., Open Univ. *Publications:* The Imposter (novel) 1979, The Unmaking of a Dancer (autobiog.) 1982, Theory of War (novel) (Costa/Whitbread Novel of the Year and Book of the Year 1993, Prix du Meilleur Livre Étranger 1995) 1992, Prologue (autobiog.) 1994, Death Comes for Peter Pan (novel) 1996, The Emigré (novel) 1999, Bleedout (novel) 2005, Venom (novel) 2010, The Blue Death (novel) 2012; contribs to Harpers, London Times, Sunday Times, Telegraph, Independent, Guardian. *Honours:* NEA grant 1986. *E-mail:* joan@joanbrady.co.uk (office). *Website:* www.joanbrady.co.uk.

BRADY, Nicholas (see Levinson, Leonard)

BRADY, Terence Joseph, BA; British dramatist, writer and actor; b. 13 March 1939, London, England; m. Charlotte Mary Therese Bingham, one s. one d. *Education:* Trinity College, Dublin. *Career:* actor in films, radio and television; mem. Point-to-Point Owners Asscn; Society of Authors. *Television:* as writer: Upstairs Downstairs, Take Three Girls, Thomas and Sarah, Nanny, Forever Green, Making the Play, Such as Small World, One of the Family, Father Matthew's Daughter, Pig in the Middle, Magic Moments, Love with a Perfect Stranger, I Wish I Wish, The Shell Seekers, Lost, Below Stairs, Adam and Eve. *Publications:* Rehearsal 1972, Victoria (with Charlotte Bingham) 1972, Rose's Story (with Charlotte Bingham) 1973, Victoria and Company (with Charlotte Bingham) 1974, The Fight Against Slavery 1976, Yes-Honestly 1977, Point-to-Point (with Michael Felton) 1990; contributions: stage, radio, television series and periodicals. *Honours:* BBC Radio Writers' Guild Award 1972. *Literary Agent:* c/o Annabel Merullo, PFD, Drury House, 34–43 Russell Street, London WC2B 5HA, England. *Telephone:* (20) 7344-1000. *Fax:* (20) 7836-9543. *E-mail:* info@pfd.co.uk. *Website:* www.pfd.co.uk.

BRAGG, Baron (Life Peer), cr. 1998, of Wigton in the County of Cumbria; **Melvyn Bragg,** MA, FRS, FRSL, FRTS; British author and television presenter; b. 6 Oct. 1939, Carlisle; s. of Stanley Bragg and Mary E. Park; m. 1st Marie-Elisabeth Roche 1961 (deceased); one d.; m. 2nd Catherine M. Haste 1973; one s. one d. *Education:* Nelson-Thomlinson Grammar School, Wigton and Wadham Coll., Oxford. *Career:* BBC Radio and TV Producer 1961–67; TV Presenter and Ed. The South Bank Show for ITV 1978–2010; Head of Arts, London Weekend TV 1982–90, Controller of Arts and Features 1990–2010; Deputy Chair. Border TV 1985–90, Chair. 1990–96; novelist 1965–; writer and broadcaster 1967–, writer and presenter of BBC Radio Four's Start the Week 1988–98, In Our Time 1998–, Routes of English 1999–, The Adventure of English 2001; mem. Arts Council and Chair. Literature Panel of Arts Council 1977–80; Pres. Cumbrians for Peace 1982–, Northern Arts 1983–87, Nat. Campaign for the Arts 1986–; Gov. LSE 1997–; Chancellor Univ. of Leeds 1999–; mem. Bd Really Useful Co. 1989–90; Pres. Nat. Acad. of Writing –2009, MIND; Appeal Chair. Royal Nat. Inst. for the Blind Talking Books Appeal 1998–2005. *Plays:* Mardi Gras 1976, Orion 1977, The Hired Man 1985, King Lear in New York 1992. *Screenplays:* Isadora, The Music Lovers, Jesus Christ Superstar, A Time to Dance. *Publications:* novels: For Want of a Nail 1965, The Second Inheritance 1966, Without a City Wall 1968, The Hired Man 1969, A Place in England 1970, The Nerve 1971, The Hunt 1972, Josh Lawton 1972, The Silken Net 1974, A Christmas Child 1976, Autumn Manoeuvres 1978, Kingdom Come 1980, Love and Glory 1983, The Cumbrian Trilogy 1984, The Maid of Buttermere 1987, A Time to Dance (televised 1992) 1990, Crystal Rooms 1992, Credo 1996, The Sword and the Miracle 1997, The Soldier's Return 1999, A Son of War 2001, Remember Me 2008; non-fiction: Speak for England 1976, Land of the Lakes 1983, Laurence Olivier 1984, Rich, The Life of Richard Burton 1988, The Seventh Seal: A Study on Ingmar Bergman 1993, On Giants' Shoulders 1998, The Adventure of English 2003, Crossing the Lines 2005, Twelve British Books That Changed the World 2006, The South Bank Show: Final Cut 2010, In Our Time (ed.) 2010. *Honours:* Hon. Fellow, Lancashire Polytechnic 1987, The Library Asscn 1994, Wadham Coll. Oxford 1995, Univ. of Wales, Cardiff 1996, Domus Fellow, St Catherine's Coll., Oxford 1990; Hon. DLitt (Liverpool) 1986, (CNAA) 1990, (Lancaster) 1990, (South Bank) 1997, (Leeds) 2000, (Bradford) 2000, Hon. DUniv (Open Univ.) 1988, Hon. DCL (Northumbria) 1994, Hon. DSc (UMIST) 1998, (Brunel) 2000, Dr hc (St Andrews) 1993, (Sunderland) 2001; John Llewellyn Rhys Memorial Award 1968, PEN Award for Fiction 1970, Richard Dimbleby Award for Outstanding Contribution to TV 1987, Ivor Novello Award for Best Musical 1985, VLV Award 2000, WHSmith Literary Award 2000, four Prix Italia Awards, various BAFTA Awards including Acad. Fellowship 2010, South Bank Show Life Achievement Award. *Address:* 12 Hampstead Hill Gardens, London, NW3 2PL, England (office). *Telephone:* (20) 7261-3128 (office). *Fax:* (20) 7261-3299 (office).

BRAINARD, Cecilia Manguerra; American (b. Philippine) writer; b. (Cecilia Cuenco Manguerra), 21 Nov. 1947, Cebu, Philippines; d. of Mariano Manguerra and Concepcion Manguerra; m. Lauren R. Brainard; three s. *Education:* St Theresa's Coll., Cebu and Maryknoll Coll., Quezon City, UCLA. *Career:* worked in communications and as documentary scriptwriter and asst dir of development 1969–81; freelance writer 1981–; Adjunct Prof., Animation Dept, Univ. of Southern California; creative writing teacher, UCLA-Extension Writers' Programme; gives lectures worldwide. *Publications include:* Woman with Horns and Other Stories 1988, When the Rainbow Goddess Wept (novel, aka Song of Yvonne) 1991, Philippine Woman in America (essays) 1991, Seven Stories from Seven Sisters (ed.) 1992, Fiction by Filipinos in America (ed.) 1993, The Beginning and Other Asian Folktales (ed.) 1995, Acapulco at Sunset and Other Stories 1995, Journey of 100 Years: Reflections on the Centennial of Philippine Independence (ed.), Growing Up Filipino: Stories for Young Adults (ed.), Contemporary Fiction by Filipinos in America (ed.) 1998, Magdalena (novel) 2002, Cecilia's Diary 1962–1968 2003, Behind the Walls: Life of Convent Girls (co-ed.) 2005, A la Carte Food and Fiction (ed.) 2007, Finding God: True Stories of Spiritual Encounters (co-ed.) 2009, Fundamentals of Creative Writing 2009. *Honours:* Fortner Prize (for short story, The Balete Tree) 1985, California Arts Council Fellowship in Fiction 1989–90, City of Los Angeles cultural grant 1990–91, Brody Arts Fund Fellowship 1991, Los Angeles Board of Education Special Recognition Award 1991, Filipino Women's Network Literature Award 1992, Makati Rotarian Award 1994, Outstanding Individual Award from the City of Cebu, Philippines 1998, Filipinas Magazine Achievement Award for Arts and Culture 2001. *Address:* PO Box 5099, Santa Monica, CA 90409, USA (home). *E-mail:* CBrainard@aol.com (home). *Website:* www.ceciliabrainard.com; cbrainard.blogspot.com.

BRAINE, David, BA, BPhil; British academic and writer; *Honorary Research Fellow, University of Aberdeen;* b. 2 Sept. 1940, Devon. *Education:* Magdalen Coll., Oxford. *Career:* Lecturer, Univ. of Aberdeen 1965–89, Hon. Lecturer 1989–2002, Hon. Research Fellow 2002–; mem. American Catholic Philosophical Asscn, Aristotelian Soc. *Publications:* Medical Ethics and Human Life 1982, The Reality of Time and the Existence of God 1988, Ethics, Technology and Medicine (ed. and contributor, with Harry Lesser) 1988, The Human Person: Animal and Spirit 1992, Language and Human Understanding, 2012; contrib. to scholarly books and professional journals on philosophy and theology. *Honours:* Demyship, Magdalen Coll., Oxford 1958–62, Gifford Fellow Univ. of Aberdeen 1981–87. *Address:* 104–106 High Street, Old Aberdeen, AB24 3HE, Scotland (home).

BRAITHWAITE, Eustace, MSc; Guyanese writer and diplomatist; b. 27 June 1922. *Education:* New York Univ. and Cambridge Univ. *Career:* RAF, Second World War; schoolteacher, London 1950–57; Welfare Officer, London Co. Council 1958–60; Human Rights Officer, World Veterans Foundation, Paris 1960–63; Lecturer and Educ. Consultant, UNESCO, Paris 1963–66; Perm. Rep. of Guyana to UN 1967–68; Amb. to Venezuela 1968–69. *Publications:* To Sir, With Love 1959, A Kind of Homecoming 1961, Paid Servant 1962, A Choice of Straws 1965, Reluctant Neighbours 1972, Honorary White 1976. *Honours:* Franklin Prize, Ainsfield Wolff Literary Award for To Sir, With Love.

BRAITHWAITE, Sir Rodric Quentin, GCMG; British fmr diplomatist; b. 17 May 1932, London; s. of Henry Warwick Braithwaite and Lorna Constance Davies; m. Gillian Mary Robinson 1961; four s. (one deceased) one d. *Education:* Bedales School, Christ's Coll., Cambridge. *Career:* mil. service 1950–52; joined Foreign Service 1955; Third Sec., Jakarta 1957–58; Second Sec., Warsaw 1959–61; Foreign Office 1961–63; First Sec. (Commercial), Moscow 1963–66; First Sec., Rome 1966–69; FCO 1969–72, Head of European Integration Dept (External) 1973–75, Head of Planning Staff 1979–80, Asst Under-Sec. of State 1981, Deputy Under-Sec. of State 1984–88; Head of Chancery, Office of Perm. Rep. to EEC, Brussels 1975–78; Minister, Commercial, Washington 1982–84; Amb. to Soviet Union 1988–92; Foreign Policy Adviser to Prime Minister 1992–93; Chair. Jt Intelligence Cttee 1992–93; currently Sr Consultant in Global Investment Banking, Deutsche Bank AG, London; Chair. Britain Russia Centre 1994–2000, Moscow School of Political Studies 1998–; mem. European Strategy Bd ICL 1994–2000, Supervisory Bd Deutsche Bank Moscow 1998–99, Bd Ural Mash Zavody (Moscow and Ekaterinburg) 1998–99; mem. Advisory Bd Sirocco Aerospace 2000–; mem. RAM 1993–2002 (Chair. of Govs 1998–2002); Visiting Fellow All Souls Coll. Oxford 1972–73. *Publications:* Engaging Russia (with Blackwill and Tanaka) 1995, Russia in Europe 1999, NATO at Fifty: Perspectives of the Future of the Atlantic Alliance (jtly) 1999, Across the Moscow River 2002, Moscow 1941 2006. *Honours:* Hon. Fellow Christ's Coll. Cambridge; Hon. FRAM; Hon. Prof. (Birmingham) 2000; Dr hc (Birmingham) 1998. *E-mail:* info@rodricbraithwaite.co.uk (office). *Website:* www.rodricbraithwaite.co.uk.

BRAMLY, Serge; French writer, essayist and photographer; b. 31 Jan. 1941, Tunis, Tunisia; m. Bettina Rheims (divorced); one s. *Education:* Lycée Janson-de-Sailly, Univ. of Paris-Nanterre. *Publications:* novels: L'Itinéraire du fou (Del Duca Prize for a First Novel) 1978, Un piège à lumière 1979, La danse du loup (Prix des Libraires) 1982, Madame Satan 1992, Un poisson muet, surgi de la mer 1993, La terreur dans le boudoir 1993, Le réseau Melchior 1996, Anonym 2000, Ragots 2001, Le voyage de Shangai 2005, Le premier principe, le second principe (Prix Interallié) 2008; essays: Terre Wakan: l'univers sacré des indiens d'Amérique du Nord 1974, Macumba: the teachings of Maria-José, mother of the gods 1981; other: Man Ray 1980, Leonardo: Discovering the Life of Leonardo da Vinci (biog.) (Vasari Prize) 1988, Leonardo: The Artist and the Man 1995, Mona Lisa: The Enigma 2005; with Bettina Rheims: Chambre Close 1992, I.N.R.I 1999. *Address:* c/o Éditions J.C. Lattès, 17 rue Jacob, 75006 Paris, France (office). *Website:* www.editions-jclattes.fr (office).

BRAMPTON, Sally; British editor and novelist; m.; one d. *Career:* began career at Vogue; fmr Fashion Ed., Observer; Ed., British Elle magazine 1985–90; Ed., Red magazine 2000; currently Visiting Prof., Central St Martins College of Art and Design; currently Advice Columnist, The Times (London). *Publications:* Good Grief 1992, Lovesick 1995, Concerning Lily 1998, Love, Always 2000, Shoot the Damn Dog: A Memoir of Depression 2008. *Literary Agent:* United Agents, 12–26 Lexington Street, London, W1F 0LE, England. *Telephone:* (20) 3214-0800. *Fax:* (20) 3214-0801. *E-mail:* info@unitedagents.co.uk. *Website:* unitedagents.co.uk. *E-mail:* sallybrampton@hotmail.com (home).

BRANCH, Taylor, AB; American writer; b. 14 Jan. 1947, Atlanta, GA; m. Christina Macy; one s. one d. *Education:* Univ. of North Carolina at Chapel Hill, Princeton Univ. *Career:* staff, The Washington Monthly magazine, Washington, DC 1971–73, Harper's magazine, New York 1973–75, Esquire magazine, New York 1975–76. *Publications:* Blowing the Whistle: Dissent in the Public Interest (with Charles Peters) 1972, Second Wind: The Memoirs of an Opinionated Man (with Bill Russell) 1979, The Empire Blues 1981, Labyrinth (with Eugene M. Propper) 1982, Parting the Waters: America in the King Years 1954–63 (Nat. Book Critics Circle Award for General Non-fiction 1988, Pulitzer Prize in History 1989) 1988, Pillar of Fire: America in the King Years 1963–65 1998, At Canaan's Edge 2006, The Clinton Tapes: Wrestling History with the President 2009; contrib. articles to magazines and journals, including The Washington Monthly. *Honours:* Christopher Award 1988; Nat. Humanities Medal 1999, Dayton Literary Peace Prize for Lifetime Achievement 2008. *Address:* 1806 South Road, Baltimore, MD 21209, USA (office). *E-mail:* info@taylorbranch.com (office). *Website:* www.taylorbranch.com.

BRAND, Alice Glarden, BA, MEd, DEd; American poet, writer and professor of English; b. 8 Sept. 1938, New York, NY; m. Ira Brand 1960; three c. *Education:* Univ. of Rochester, City Coll., City Univ. of New York, Rutgers Univ. *Career:* Asst Prof. 1980–86, Assoc. Prof. of English, 1987, Univ. of Missouri-St Louis; Visiting Scholar, Univ. of California, Berkeley, 1982–83; Assoc. Prof. of English and Dir of Writing, Clarion Univ. of Pennsylvania 1987–89; Assoc. Prof. of English, Coll. at Brockport, State Univ. of New York 1989–91, Dir of Composition 1989–93, Prof. of English 1992–99; many workshops, lectures and readings; mem. Acad. of American Poets; mem. Nat. Council of Teachers of English, Poetry Soc. of America; Poets and Writers. *Publications:* poetry: As it Happens 1983, Studies on Zone 1989; others: Therapy in Writing: A Psycho-Educational Enterprise 1980, The Psychology of Writing: The Affective Experience 1989, Presence of Mind: Writing and the Domain Beyond the Cognitive (ed. with Richard L. Graves) 1994, Court of Common Pleas 1996, Writing in the Majors: A Guide to Disciplinary Faculty 1998; contrib. to numerous anthologies and periodicals. *Honours:* Wildwood Poetry Prize 1988. *Address:* c/o Department of English, College at Brockport, State University of New York, 211 Hartwell Hall, 350 New Campus Drive, Brockport, NY 14420-2968.

BRAND, Dionne, BA, MA; Canadian poet, novelist, essayist, film-maker and academic; *Professor of English and University Research Chair, University of Guelph*; b. 7 Jan. 1953, Guayaguayare, Trinidad. *Education:* Univ. of Toronto, Ontario Inst. for Studies in Education. *Career:* f. mem., ed., Our Lives newspaper; extensive community work; f. mem., fmr Chair., Women's Issues Committee of the Ontario Coalition of Black Trade Unionists; fmr writer-in-residence, Halifax City Regional Library; fmr teacher of poetry, West Coast Women and Words Society Summer School and Retreat; Writer-in-Residence, Univ. of Toronto 1990–91; Asst Prof. of English, Univ. of Guelph 1992–94, Writer-in-Residence 2003, currently Prof. of English and Univ. Research Chair.; Ruth Wynn Woodward Prof. in Women's Studies, Simon Fraser Univ. 2000–02; Distinguished Visiting Scholar and Writer-in-Residence, St Lawrence Univ. 2004–05; Distinguished Poet for the Ralph Gustafson Poetry Chair., Vancouver Island Univ. 2006; mem. Program faculty, Writing Studio, Banff Centre 2007–08; Poet Laureate of Toronto 2009–. *Films:* documentaries: Older, Stronger, Wiser (assoc. dir) 1989, Sisters in the Struggle (co-dir) 1991, Long Time Comin' (co-dir) 1993, Listening for Something: Adrienne Rich and Dionne Brand in Conversation (dir) 1996, Beyond Borders: Arab Feminists Talk about their Lives (narrator) 1999, Under One Sky: Arab Women in North America Talk about the Hijab (narrator) 1999, Borderless: A Docu-Drama about the Lives of Undocumented Workers (narrator) 2006. *Publications include:* poetry: 'Fore Day Morning: Poems 1978, Earth Magic 1978, Primitive Offensive 1982, Winter Epigrams and Epigrams to Ernesto Cardenal in Defense of Claudia 1983, Chronicles of the Hostile Sun 1984, No Language is Neutral 1990, Land to Light On (Gov.-Gen.'s Award for Poetry, Trillium Award) 1997, Thirsty 2002, Inventory 2006, Ossuaries 2010; fiction: Sans Souci (short stories) 1988, In Another Place, Not Here (novel) 1996, At the Full Change of the Moon 1999, What We All Long For 2005; other: Rivers Have Sources, Trees Have Roots: Speaking of Racism (with Krisantha Sri Bhaggiydatta) 1986, Sight Specific: Lesbians and Representation 1988, No Burden to Carry: Narratives of Black Working Women in Ontario 1920s to 1950s (with Lois de Shield) 1991, We're Rooted Here and They Can't Pull Us Up: Essays in African Canadian Women's History (co-author) 1994, Bread Out of Stone: Recollections Sex, Recognitions Race, Dreaming Politics 1994, A Kind of Perfect Speech 2008. *Honours:* Harbourfront Festival Prize for contrib. to literature 2006. *Address:* School of English and Theatre Studies, Mackinnon Building, Room 435, University of Guelph, Guelph, ON N1G 2W1, Canada (office). *Telephone:* (519) 824-4120 (office). *E-mail:* dbrand@uoguelph.ca (office). *Website:* arts.uoguelph.ca/creativewritingmfa/faculty (office).

BRAND, Stewart, BS; American editor, writer and publisher; *President, The Long Now Foundation*; b. 14 Dec. 1938, Rockford, Ill.; m. 1st Lois Jennings 1966 (divorced 1972); m. 2nd Ryan Phelan 1983; one s. from a previous relationship. *Education:* Phillips Exeter Acad., Stanford Univ. *Career:* served in US Army 1960–62; fmrly with Merry Pranksters; consultant to Gov. of Calif. 1976–78; research scientist Media Lab., MIT 1986; Visiting Scholar Royal Dutch/Shell 1986; f. America Needs Indians, Whole Earth Review 1985, Point Foundation, Hacker's Conf.; co-f. The Well (Whole Earth 'Lectronic Link—internet bulletin bd) 1985–, Global Business Network consultancy 1988–, The Long Now Foundation 1996– (also Pres.), All Species project 2000–; Trustee, Santa Fe Inst. 1989–. *Television:* How Buildings Learn (writer and presenter) 1997. *Publications:* Two Cybernetic Frontiers 1974, The Media Lab: Inventing the Future at MIT 1987, How Buildings Learn 1994, The Clock of the Long Now 2000, Whole Earth Discipline: An Ecopragmatist Manifesto 2009; ed. (or co-ed.) and publr: The Last Whole Earth Catalog 1968–72 (Nat. Book Award), Whole Earth Epilog 1974, Whole Earth Epilog: Access to Tools 1974, The Co-Evolution Quarterly 1974–85, The Next Whole Earth Catalog 1980–81, The (Updated) Last Whole Earth Catalog: Access to Tools (16th edn) 1975, Space Colonies, Whole Earth Catalog 1977, Soft-Tech 1978, The Next Whole Earth Catalog: Access to Tools 1980, (revised 2nd edn) 1981, Whole Earth Software Catalog (Ed.-in-Chief) 1983–85, Whole Earth Software Catalog for 1986, '2.0 edition' of above title (Ed.-in-Chief) 1985, News That Stayed News 1974–1984: Ten Years of CoEvolution Quarterly 1986. *Address:* 3E Gate 5 Road, Sausalito, CA 94965 (home); The Long Now Foundation, Fort Mason Center, Landmark Building A, San Francisco, CA 94123, USA (office). *Telephone:* (415) 561-6582 (office). *Fax:* (415) 561-6297 (office). *E-mail:* sb@gbn.org (home). *Website:* www.longnow.org (office); web.me.com/stewartbrand.

BRANDT, Diana (Di) Ruth, BTh, BA, MA, PhD; Canadian poet and writer; *Canada Research Chair in English and Creative Writing, Brandon University*; b. 31 Jan. 1952, Winkler, Manitoba; m. Les Brandt 1971 (divorced 1990); two d. *Education:* Canadian Mennonite Bible College, University of Manitoba, University of Toronto. *Career:* Faculty, University of Winnipeg 1986–95; Writer-in-Residence, University of Alberta 1995–96; Research Fellow, University of Alberta 1996–97; Assoc. Prof. of English and Creative Writing, University of Windsor 1997–2005; Canada Research Chair in English and Creative Writing, Brandon Univ. 2005–; mem. Canadian PEN, League of Canadian Poets, Manitoba Writers' Guild, Writers' Union of Canada. *Publications:* poetry: questions i asked my mother 1987, Agnes in the sky 1990, mother, not mother 1992, Jerusalem, beloved 1995, Bouquet for St Mary 2003, Now You Care 2003, Speaking of Power: The Poetry of Di Brandt 2006; other: Wild Mother Dancing: Maternal Narrative in Canadian Literature 1993, Dancing Naked: Narrative Strategies for Writing Across Centuries 1996, So this is the world and here I am in it 2007; contributions: various publications. *Honours:* Gerald Lampert Award for Best First Book of Poetry in Canada 1987, McNally Robinson Award for Manitoba Book of the Year 1990, Silver National Magazine Award 1995, Canadian Authors' Asscn National Poetry Award 1996. *Address:* Department of English, Brandon University, Brandon, Manitoba R7A 6A9, Canada (office). *Telephone:* (204) 571-8548 (office). *Fax:* (204) 726-0473 (office). *E-mail:* brandtd@brandonu.ca (office). *Website:* www.brandonu.ca/di_brandt (office).

BRANDT, Per Aage, MA, PhD; Danish writer and academic; *Emile B. Sauzé Professor of Modern Languages, Case Western Reserve University*; b. 26 April 1944, Buenos Aires, Argentina; m. Mette Brudevold 1966 (divorced 1983); one d. *Education:* Univ. of Copenhagen, Sorbonne Univ. I, France. *Career:* Lecturer, Roskilde Universitetscenter, Denmark 1972–75; Lecturer, Univ. of Århus, 1975–88, apptd Prof. (docentur) 1988; Co-Founder and Teacher, School of Writers, Copenhagen 1987, Research Prof. 1996–98, Prof. 1998–2005; Emile B. Sauzé Prof. of Modern Languages and Literatures and Cognitive Science, Case Western Reserve Univ., Cleveland, USA 2005–, also Dir Center for Culture and Cognition, Lab. of Applied Research in Cognitive Semiotics. *Publications include:* more than 28 volumes of poetry including: Poesi I, II 1969, Pamplona 1971, Wie die Zeit vergeht 1973, Dødshjælp 1977, Beskyttelse 1978, Indsigt i det nodvendige 1979, Det skulle ikke være sådan 1982, Ondskab 1982, Livet i himlen 1985, Fraværsmusik 1986, Credo 1988, Ostinato 1989, Ingen kan vaagne 1990, Rubato 1991, Physis 1992, Largo 1994, Ups and downs 1996, Fisk 1997, Night and Day 1999, Om noget og hoad deraf følger 2001, These Hands 2011; others: 12 academic books, numerous trans. of Borges, Jabès, Roubaud, Bataille, Sade, Lorca, Calderón, Molière, Koltès; contribs: periodicals, including: Action Poétique, Poesie, Banana Split. *Honours:* Officier, Order des Arts et des Lettres 2002, Cross, Order of the

Dannebrog 2004; Danish Ministry of Culture Prizes 1971, 1994, Emil Aarestrup Medal 1993, Grand Prix de Philosophie, l'Académie Française 2002. *Address:* Department of Cognitive Sciences, Case Western Reserve University, 10900 Euclid Avenue, Cleveland, OH 44106, USA (office). *Telephone:* (216) 368-2725 (office). *E-mail:* peraage.brandt@case.edu (office). *Website:* www.case.edu/artsci/dmll (office); www.case.edu/artsci/cogs/CenterforCognitionandCulture.html (office).

BRANFIELD, John Charles, MA, MEd; British writer and teacher; b. 19 Jan. 1931, Burrow Bridge, Somerset, England; m. Kathleen Elizabeth Peplow; two s. two d. *Education:* Queens' Coll., Cambridge, Univ. of Exeter. *Publications:* A Flag in the Map 1960, Look the Other Way 1963, In the Country 1966, Nancekuke 1972, Sugar Mouse 1973, The Fox in Winter 1980, Thin Ice 1983, The Falklands Summer 1987, The Day I Shot My Dad 1989, Lanhydrock Days 1991, A Breath of Fresh Air 2001, Ella and Charles Naper, Art and Life at Lamorna 2003, Charles Simpson, Painter of Animals and Birds, Coastline and Moorland 2005, Geoffrey and Jill Garnier, A Marriage of the Arts 2010. *Address:* Mingoose Villa, Mingoose, Mount Hawke, Truro, Cornwall, TR4 8BX, England (home).

BRANIGAN, Keith, BA, PhD; British academic and writer; *Professor of Prehistory and Archaeology, University of Sheffield*; b. 15 April 1940, Bucks.; m. Kuabrat Sivadith 1965; one s. two d. *Education:* Univ. of Birmingham. *Career:* Research Fellow, Univ. of Birmingham 1965–66; Lecturer, Univ. of Bristol 1966–67; Prof. of Prehistory and Archaeology, Univ. of Sheffield 1976–; mem. Prehistory Soc. (vice-pres. 1984–86); Dir Sheffield Centre for Aegean Archaeology 1997–2003; Fellow, Soc. of Antiquaries 1970–. *Publications:* Copper and Bronzeworking in Early Bronze Age Crete 1968, The Foundations of Palatial Crete: A Survey of Crete in the Early Bronze Age 1970, The Tombs of Mesara: A Study of Funerary Architecture and Ritual in Southern Crete, 2800–1700 B.C. 1970, Latimer: Belgic, Roman, Dark Age, and Early Modern Farm 1971, Town and Country: The Archaeology of Verulamium and the Roman Chilterns 1973, Reconstructing the Past: A Basic Introduction to Archaeology 1974, Aegean Metalwork of the Early and Middle Bronze Ages 1974, Atlas of Ancient Civilizations 1976, Prehistoric Britain: An Illustrated Survey 1976, The Roman West Country: Classical Culture and Celtic Society (ed. with P. J. Fowler) 1976, The Roman Villa in South-West England 1977, Gatcombe: The Excavation and Study of a Romano-British Villa Estate, 1967–1976 1978, Rome and the Brigantes: The Impact of Rome on Northern England (ed.) 1980, Roman Britain: Life in an Imperial Province 1980, Hellas: The Civilizations of Ancient Greece (with Michael Vickers) 1980, Atlas of Archaeology 1982, Prehistory 1984, The Catuvellauni 1986, Archaeology Explained 1988, Romano-British Cavemen (with M. J. Dearne) 1992, Dancing with Death: Life and Death in Southern Crete c.3000–2000 B.C. 1993, Lexicon of the Greek and Roman Cities and Place Names in Antiquity, c.1500 B.C.–A.D. 500 (ed. with others) 1993, The Archaeology of the Chilterns (ed.) 1994, Barra: Archaeological Research on Ben Tangaval (with P. Foster) 1995, Cemetery and Society in the Aegean Bronze Age (ed.) 1998, From Barra to Berneray (with P. Foster) 2000, Barra and the Bishop's Isles (with P. Foster) 2002, Urbanism in the Aegean Bronze Age (ed.) 2002, The Roman Chilterns (with R. Niblett) 2004, From Clan to Clearance 2005, Ancient Barra: Exploring the Archaeology of the Outer Hebrides 2007, The Last of the Clan 2010, Moni Odigitria: A Prepalatial Cemetery in the Asterousia, Southern Crete (with Andonis Vasilakis) 2010; contribs to professional journals. *Honours:* Gold Medal for Distinguished Service to Aegean Prehistory, Inst. for Aegean Prehistory 2010. *Address:* Department of Prehistory and Archaeology, University of Sheffield, Sheffield, S10 2TN, England (office). *Telephone:* (114) 222-2910 (office); (114) 258-1523 (home). *E-mail:* archaelogy@sheffield.ac.uk (office).

BRANTENBERG, Gerd, cand. philol.; Norwegian novelist; b. 27 Oct. 1941, Oslo. *Education:* Fredrikstad Grammar School, Royal High Commercial Inst., Edinburgh, Scotland, Univ. of Oslo. *Career:* high school teacher 1971–82; full-time writer 1982–; reading tours in Scandinavia, England, Germany, USA, Canada; monthly columnist Fredriksstad Blad and Blikk; feminist activist; initiated Refugee Centre for battered wives and rape victims, Oslo; f. Women's High School, Denmark, Lesbian Movements, Copenhagen and Oslo; co-organizer Int. Feminist Book Fairs, London 1984, Oslo 1986, Barcelona 1990, Amsterdam 1992; co-f. Literary Women's Forum 1978; bd mem. Union of 1948, Denmark and Norway; mem. Norwegian Writers' Union (bd mem. 1981–83). *Publications:* Opp alle jordens homofile (novel, trans. as What Comes Naturally 1986) 1973, Egalias døtre (novel, trans. as The Daughters of Egalia 1985) 1977, Ja, vi slutter (novel) 1978, Sangen om St. Croix (novel) 1979, Favntak (novel) 1983, Ved fergestedet (novel) 1985, På sporet av den tapte lyst (co-author, literary criticism) 1986, For alle vinder (novel, trans. as The Four Winds 1996) 1989, Eremitt og entertainer (essays) 1991, Ompadorastedet (juvenile) 1992; contrib. numerous short stories and articles. *Address:* c/o Seal Press, Avalon Publishing Group, 1400 65th Street, Suite 250, Emeryville, CA 94608, USA (office).

BRANTLINGER, Patrick Morgan, BA, MA, PhD; American academic and writer; *James Rudy and College Alumni Association Distinguished Professor Emeritus of English, Indiana University*; b. 20 March 1941, Indianapolis, IN; m. Ellen Anderson 1963, two s. one d. *Education:* Antioch Coll., Harvard Univ. *Career:* Asst Prof. of English, Indiana Univ. 1968–74, Assoc. Prof. of English 1974–79, James Rudy and Coll. Alumni Asscn Distinguished Prof. Emer. of English 1979–, Chair Dept of English 1990–94; Ed. Victorian Studies, also Dir Victorian Studies Graduate Program 1980–90; Vice-Pres. and Pres., Midwest Victorian Studies Asscn 1991–93; MLA Victorian Literature Cttee 1988–93. *Publications:* The Spirit of Reform: British Literature and Politics 1832–1867 1977, Bread and Circuses: Theories of Mass Culture and Social Decay 1983, Rule of Darkness: British Literature of Imperialism 1830–1914 1986, Crusoe's Footprints: Cultural Studies in Britain and America 1990, Fictions of State: Culture and Credit in Britain 1694–1994 1996, The Reading Lesson: Mass Literacy as Threat in Nineteenth Century British Fiction 1998, Who Killed Shakespeare? What's Happened to English Since the Radical Sixties 2000, The Blackwell Companion to the Victorian Novel (co-ed.) 2002, Dark Vanishings: Discourse on the Extinction of Primitive Races 1800–1930 2003, Victorian Literature and Postcolonial Studies 2010, Taming Cannibals: Race and the Victorians 2011; contrib. to scholarly books and journals. *Honours:* Guggenheim Fellowship 1978–79, Nat. Endowment for the Humanities Fellowship 1983,. *Address:* c/o Department of English, Indiana University, 107 S. Indiana Avenue, Bloomington, IN 47405, USA.

BRATA, Sasthi; Indian writer and poet; b. (Sasthibrata Chakravarti), 16 July 1939, Kolkata; m. Pamela Joyce Radcliffe (divorced). *Education:* Presidency Coll., Kolkata, Univ. of Calcutta. *Career:* London columnist, Statesman 1977–80. *Publications:* Eleven Poems 1960, My God Died Young 1968, Confessions of an Indian Woman Eater 1971, She and He 1973, A Search for Home 1975, Astride Two Worlds: Traitor to India 1976, Encounter (short stories) 1978, The Sensuous Guru: The Making of a Mystic President 1980, Labyrinths in the Lotus Land 1985, India: The Perpetual Paradox 1986. *Address:* c/o Penguin Books India Pvt. Ltd, 11 Community Centre, Panchsheel Park, New Delhi 110 017, India (office).

BRATHWAITE, Edward Kamau, BA, CertEd, DPhil; Barbadian academic, poet, writer and editor; *Professor of Comparative Literature, New York University*; b. 11 May 1930, Bridgetown; m. Doris Monica Welcome 1960; one s. *Education:* Harrison Coll., Barbados, Pembroke Coll., Cambridge and Univ. of Sussex. *Career:* education officer Ministry of Education, Ghana 1955–62; tutor Extramural Dept, Univ. of the West Indies, St Lucia 1962–63; Lecturer 1963–76, Reader 1976–82, Prof. of Social and Cultural History from 1982, Univ. of the West Indies, Kingston; founding Sec. Caribbean Artists Movement 1966; Ed. Savacou magazine 1970–; Visiting Fellow Harvard Univ. 1987; currently Prof. of Comparative Literature, New York Univ.; several visiting professorships. *Publications include:* poetry: Rights of Passage 1967, Masks 1968, Islands 1969, Penguin Modern Poets 15 (with Alan Bold and Edwin Morgan) 1969, Panda No. 349 1969, The Arrivants: A New World Trilogy 1973, Days and Nights 1975, Other Exiles 1975, Poetry '75 International 1975, Black + Blues 1976, Mother Poem 1977, Soweto 1979, Word Making Man: A Poem for Nicolas Guillen 1979, Sun Poem 1982, Third World Poems 1983, X-Self 1987, Sappho Sakyi's Meditations 1989, Shar 1990; other: Folk Culture of the Slaves in Jamaica 1970, The Development of Creole Society in Jamaica, 1770–1820 1971, Caribbean Man in Space and Time 1974, Contradictory Omens: Cultural Diversity and Integration in the Caribbean 1974, Our Ancestral Heritage: A Bibliography of the Roots of Culture in the English-Speaking Caribbean 1976, Wars of Respect: Nanny, Sam Sharpe, and the Struggle for People's Liberation 1977, Jamaica Poetry: A Checklist 1686–1978 1979, Barbados Poetry: A Checklist, Slavery to the Present 1979, Kumina 1982, Gods of the Middle East 1982, National Language Poetry 1982, The Colonial Encounter: Language 1984, History of the Voice: The Development of a National Language in Anglophone Caribbean Poetry 1984, Jah Music 1986, Roots 1986; editor: Iouanaloa: Recent Writing from St Lucia 1963, New Poets from Jamaica 1979, Dream Rock 1987. *Honours:* Arts Council of Great Britain Bursary 1967, Camden Arts Festival Prize 1967, Cholmondeley Award 1970, Guggenheim Fellowship 1972, Bussa Award 1973, Casa de las Américas Prize, Cuba 1976, Fulbright Fellowships 1982–83, 1987–88, Inst. of Jamaica Musgrave Medal 1983. *Address:* Department of Comparative Literature, New York University, 13–19 University Place, 3rd Floor, New York, NY 10003-4556, USA (office). *Telephone:* (212) 998-3845 (office). *E-mail:* kb5@nyu.edu (office). *Website:* www.nyu.edu/fas/dept/complit (office).

BRAUCHLI, Marcus, BA; American journalist; *Executive Editor, The Washington Post*; b. 19 June 1961, Boulder, Colo; s. of Christopher R. Brauchli and Margot L. Brauchli; m. Maggie Farley. *Education:* Columbia Univ. *Career:* began career as copyreader for AP-Dow Jones 1984; foreign correspondent in Hong Kong, Dow Jones Newswires 1984–87, in Scandinavia 1987–88, in Japan 1988–95, Head, China Bureau 1995–99; News Ed. Wall Street Journal 1999–2000, Nat. News Ed. 2000–03, Global News Ed. 2003–05, Deputy Man. Ed. 2005–07, Man. Ed. 2007–08 (resgnd); Exec. Ed., The Washington Post 2008–. *Address:* The Washington Post, 1150 15 St. NW, Washington, DC 20071, USA (office). *Telephone:* (202) 334-6000 (office). *E-mail:* letters@washpost.com (office). *Website:* www.washingtonpost.com (office).

BRAULT, Jacques, MA; Canadian poet, writer, critic and teacher; b. 29 March 1933, Montréal, QC. *Education:* Univ. of Montréal, Univ. of Paris, Univ. of Poitiers. *Career:* teacher, Institut des Sciences Médiévales; Faculty of Letters, Univ. of Montréal. *Publications:* poetry: La poésie et nous (with others) 1958, Mémoire 1965, La poésie ce matin 1971, L'en dessous, l'admirable (trans. as Within the Mystery) 1972, Poèmes des quartre côtés 1975, Trois fois passera 1981, Moments fragiles 1981, Poèmes 1986, Il n'y a plus de chemin (trans. as On the Road No More) 1990, Au petit matin (with Robert Melancon) 1993, Au bras de ombres 1997; prose: Nouvelles (short stories) 1963, Alain Grandbois 1968, Miron le magnifique 1969, Trois partitions (plays) 1972, Chemin faisant 1975, Agonie (novel, trans. as

Death-watch) 1984, La poussière de chemin 1989, Ô saison, ô châteaux 1991, Que la vie est quotidienne 1993, Au fonds du jardin 1996. *Honours:* Prix France-Canada 1968, Gov.-Gen.'s Literary Award 1971, Prix Duvernay 1979, Prix du Athanse-David 1986.

BRAUN, Volker; German poet and playwright; b. 7 May 1939, Dresden. *Education:* Univ. of Leipzig. *Career:* Asst Dir Deutsches Theater, Berlin 1972–77, Berlin Ensemble 1979–90; Brother Grimm Prof., Univ. of Kassel 1999–2000; mem. Akad. der Künste, Berlin, Deutsche Akademie für Sprache und Dichtung, Sächsischen Akademie der Künste. *Plays:* Die Kipper 1965, Grosser Frieden 1979, Dmitri 1982, Die Ubergangsgesellschaft 1987, Lenins Tod 1988, Transit Europa: Der Ausflug der Toten 1988, Böhmen am Meer 1992. *Publications:* Provokation für mich 1965, Vorläufiges 1966, KriegsErklärung 1967, Wir und nicht sie 1970, Gedichte 1972, Gegen die symmetrische Welt 1974, Es genügt nicht die einfache Wahrheit 1975, Unvollendete Geschichte 1977, Training des aufrechten Gangs 1979, Hinze-Kunze-Roman 1985, Langsamer knirschender Morgen 1987, Verheerende Folgen magnelnden Anscheins innerbetrieblicher Demokratie (essays) 1988, Der Stoff zum Leben 1990, Bodenloser Satz 1990, Der Wendehals: Eine Enterhaltung 1995, Lustgarten Preussen 1996, Wir befinden uns soweit wohl. Wir sind erst einmal am Ende 1998, Tumulus 1999, Das Wirklichgewollte 2000, Das unbesetzte Gebiet 2004, Auf die schönen Possen 2005, Das Mittagsmahl (Ver.di-Literature Prize) 2007, Machwerk oder Das Schichtbuch des Flick von Lauchhammer 2008, Die hellen Haufen 2011. *Honours:* Heinrich Mann Prize 1980, Bremen Literature Prize 1986, Nat. Prize, First Class 1988, Berlin Prize 1989, Schiller Commemorative Prize 1992, Deutschen Kritikerpreis 1996, Erwin Schrittmatter Prize 1998, Georg Büchner Prize 2000. *Address:* Wolfshagenerstrasse 68, 13187 Berlin, Germany (home).

BRAVERMAN, Melanie; American writer; b. 9 Oct. 1960, Iowa City, IA. *Education:* Evergreen State College. *Career:* currently Lecturer in Creative Writing, Brandeis Univ. *Publications:* East Justice (novel) 1996, Red (poetry) 2002. *Honours:* Fellow in Poetry and Fiction, Massachusetts Cultural Council 1996. *Address:* 633 Commercial Street, Apartment 5, Provincetown, MA 02657-1731, USA (home). *Telephone:* (508) 487-2349 (home). *E-mail:* braver@brandeis.edu (office).

BRAX, Najwa Salam, BA, MA; Lebanese poet, writer and academic; *Professor of Arabic, The New School*; b. 3 Sept. 1948, Aley; m. Ghazi Brax 1981. *Education:* Lebanese Univ., Queens Coll., CUNY. *Career:* teacher of Arabic literature 1972–86; Prof. of Arabic Language, Columbia Univ., New York 2003, The New School 2005–. *Publications:* in English: Dr Dahesh: A Great Writer and his Literary Works 1981, Halim Dammous and Spirituality in his Writings 1984, Dahesh As I Knew Him, Wings 1993, Zephyrus Wings 1994, Daring Wings 1996, Growing Wings 1998, Ethereal Wings 1999; contribs to more than 150 US, Canadian, Italian, Indian and British publs. *Honours:* more than 160 poetry awards 1990–. *Address:* 150-16 60th Avenue, Flushing, NY 11355, USA (home).

BRAYFIELD, Celia Frances; British author and journalist; *Senior Lecturer in Creative Writing, Brunel University, London*; b. 21 Aug. 1945, Wembley Park; d. of the late Felix Brayfield and Ada Ellen Brayfield (née Jakeman); one d. *Education:* St. Paul's Girls' School, Universitaire de Grenoble. *Career:* feature writer, Daily Mail 1969–71, TV critic, Evening Standard 1974–82, The Times 1983–88; columnist, Sunday Telegraph 1989–90, The Times 1998–; contrib. to numerous other media; Dir Nat. Acad. of Writing 1999–2003; Sr Lecturer in Creative Writing, Brunel Univ., London 2005–; Trustee One Parent Families 1988–; mem. Soc. of Authors. *Publications:* The Body Show Book 1981, Glitter: The Truth About Fame 1985, Pearls 1987, The Prince 1990, White Ice 1993, Harvest 1995, Bestseller 1996, Getting Home 1998, Sunset 1999, Heartswap 2000, Mr Fabulous and Friends 2003, Wild Weekend 2004, Deep France 2004; contrib. various journals, magazines and newspapers. *Literary Agent:* Curtis Brown Ltd, Haymarket House, 28–29 Haymarket, London, SW1Y 4SP, England. *Telephone:* (20) 7393-4400. *Fax:* (20) 7393-4401. *Website:* www.curtisbrown.co.uk. *E-mail:* celia@celiabrayfield.com (office). *Website:* www.celiabrayfield.com.

BRECHER, Michael, PhD, FRSC; Canadian political scientist and academic; *R. B. Angus Professor of Political Science, McGill University*; b. 14 March 1925, Montreal; s. of Nathan Brecher and Gisela Hopmeyer; m. Eva Danon 1950; three d. *Education:* McGill and Yale Univs. *Career:* mem. Faculty, McGill Univ. 1952–, R. B. Angus Prof. of Political Science 1993–; Pres. Int. Studies Asscn 1999–2000; Visiting Prof., Univ. of Chicago 1963, Hebrew Univ., Jerusalem 1970–75, Univ. of Calif., Berkeley 1979, Stanford Univ. 1980; Nuffield Fellow 1955–56; Rockefeller Fellow 1964–65; Guggenheim Fellow 1965–66; f. Shashtri Indo-Canadian Inst. 1968 (Pres. 1969–71). *Publications:* The Struggle for Kashmir 1953, Nehru: A Political Biography 1959, The New States of Asia 1963, Succession in India 1966, India and World Politics 1968, Political Leadership in India 1969, The Foreign Policy System of Israel 1972, Israel, the Korean War and China 1974, Decisions in Israel's Foreign Policy 1975, Studies in Crisis Behavior 1979, Decisions in Crisis 1980, Crisis and Change in World Politics 1986, Crises in the 20th Century (Vols I, II) 1988, Crisis, Conflict and Instability 1989, Crises in World Politics 1993, A Study of Crisis 1997, 2000, Millennial Reflections on International Studies (Vols 1–5) 2002, International Political Earthquakes 2008; over 85 articles in journals. *Honours:* Watumull Prize (American Hist. Asscn) 1960, Killam Awards (Canada Council) 1970–74, 1976–79, Woodrow Wilson Award (American Political Science Asscn) 1973, Fieldhouse Award for Distinguished Teaching (McGill Univ.) 1986, Distinguished Scholar Award (Int. Studies Asscn) 1995, Léon-Gérin Quebec Prize 2000, Award for High Distinction in Research, McGill Univ. 2000, Lifetime Achievement Award 2009. *Address:* Department of Political Science, McGill University, 855 Sherbrooke Street West, Montreal, PQ H3A 2T7, Canada (office); PO Box 4438, Jerusalem 91043, Israel (home). *Telephone:* (514) 398-4816 (office). *Fax:* (514) 398-1770 (office). *E-mail:* michael.brecher@mcgill.ca (office). *Website:* www.mcgill.ca/politicalscience (office).

BREE, Marlin, BA; American author and publisher; b. 16 May 1933, Norfolk, Neb.; m. Loris Gutzmer 1963; one s. *Education:* Univ. of Nebraska, Lincoln. *Career:* Ed.'s Reporter, Stars and Stripes Newspaper, 1956; Ed., Sunday Magazine, Minneapolis Star-Tribune, 1968–72; Columnist, Corporate Report Magazine, 1973–77; Editorial Dir, Marlor Press, 1983–; mem. Minnesota Press Club, Pres. 1963; Chair. Midwest Book Awards 1992; Judge, Boating Writers Int. Writing Contest 2008–. *Publications:* Alone Against the Atlantic (co-author) 1981, In the Teeth of the Northeaster 1988, Call of the North Wind 1996, Kid's Travel Fun Book (co-author and illustrator) 2000, Wake of the Green Storm: A Survivor's Tale 2001, Broken Seas: True Tales of Extraordinary Seafaring Adventures 2005, The Dangerous Book for Boaters 2009, Amazing Gulls 2011. *Honours:* Golden Web Award 2004, Boating Writers' Int. Grand Prize 2004, 2008, BWI First Place Award 2009, Bronze Award, Int. Regional Magazine Asscn 2009. *Address:* 4304 Brigadoon Drive, St Paul, MN 55126, USA (home). *E-mail:* marlin.marlor@minn.net (home). *Website:* www.marlinbree.com.

BREEZE, Jean 'Binta', MBE; Jamaican dub poet, writer and film director; b. 1956; m. 1st (divorced 1978); three c. *Education:* Jamaica School of Drama, Kingston. *Career:* Jt Ed. Critical Quarterly. *Film screenplays include:* Hallelujah Anyhow 1990. *Recordings include:* Tracks 1991, Hearsay 1994, Riding on de Riddym 1996. *Publications:* poetry: Riddym Ravings and other poems 1988, Spring Cleaning 1992, On the Edge of an Island 1997, Song Lines 1997, The Arrival of Brighteye and other poems 2000, The Fifth Figure 2006. *Honours:* Nat. Endowment of Science Tech. and Arts Award 2004. *Literary Agent:* c/o 57 Productions, 57 Effingham Green, Lea Green, London, SE12 8NT, England. *Telephone:* (20) 8463-0866. *Fax:* (20) 8463-0866. *E-mail:* paul@57productions.com. *Website:* www.57productions.com. *Address:* Bloodaxe Books Ltd, Highgreen, Tarset, Northumberland, NE48 1RP, England (office). *Website:* www.bloodaxebooks.com (office).

BRÉGOU, Christian Robert; French publisher; b. 19 Nov. 1941, Neuilly-sur-Seine, Hauts-de-Seine. *Education:* Ecole Supérieure des Sciences Économiques et Commerciales. *Career:* apptd Financial Dir Havas Group 1971; Dir-Gen. CEP Communication 1975, Pres. 1979–97; Pres. Dir-Gen. Groupe de la Cité 1988, Groupe Expansion 1994, l'Express 1995–97; adviser Socpresse SA 1997; Pres. media group DI (Desfossés International—part of LVMH Group) 2001–03.

BREILLAT, Catherine; French film director, screenwriter and novelist; *Professor of Auteur Cinema, European Graduate School*; b. 13 July 1948, Bressuire. *Career:* currently Prof. of Auteur Cinema, European Grad. School, Switzerland. *Film roles include:* Last Tango in Paris 1972, Dracula Père et Fils 1977. *Films directed include:* Une vraie jeune fille (A Real Young Girl) 1975 (released 2000), Tapage nocturne (Nocturnal Uproar) 1979, 36 Fillette (Virgin) 1988, Sale comme un ange (Dirty Like an Angel) 1990, Parfait Amour (Perfect Love, jtly) 1996, Romance 1999, À ma soeur! (Fat Girl) 2001, Brève traversée (Brief Crossing) 2001, Scènes intimes 2002, Sex is Comedy 2002, Anatomie de l'enfer 2004, Une Vieille Maîtresse (The Last Mistress) 2007, Barbe bleue 2009, La Belle Endormie 2010, Bad Love 2011; screenplays: Catherine et Cie (Catherine & Co., jtly) 1975, Bilitis 1977, La peau (The Skin) 1981, Et la nave va (And the Ship Sails On) 1983, L'araignée de satin (The Satin Spider) 1984, Police 1985, Milan noir (Black Milan, jtly) 1987, Zanzibar (jtly) 1988, La nuit de l'océan (The Night of the Ocean, jtly) 1988, Aventure de Catherine C. (The Adventure of Catherine C., jtly) 1990, Le diable au corps 1990, La Thune (Money, jtly) 1991, Couples et amants (Couples and Lovers, jtly) 1994, Viens jouer dans la cour des grands (TV) 1997, Selon Matthieu 2000. *Publications include:* L'homme facile (novel), Tapage nocturne 1979, Romance 1999, Le livre du plaisir 1999, Une vraie jeune fille 2000, À ma soeur! 2001, Pornocratie 2001, Ein Mädchen 2001, Abus de faiblesse 2009. *Address:* European Graduate School, Alter Kehr 20, Ringacker, 3953 Leuk-Stadt, Switzerland (office). *Telephone:* 274749917 (office). *Fax:* 274749969 (office). *Website:* www.egs.edu (office).

BRENDEL, Alfred; Austrian pianist and writer; b. 5 Jan. 1931, Wiesenberg; s. of Ing. Albert and Ida Brendel (née Wieltschnig); m. 1st Iris Heymann-Gonzala 1960 (divorced 1972); one d.; m. 2nd Irene Semler 1975; one s. two d. *Career:* studied piano under Sofija Deželić (Zagreb), Ludovika v. Kaan (Graz), Edwin Fischer (Lucerne), Paul Baumgartner (Basel), Edward Steuermann (Salzburg); studied composition under A. Michl (Graz) and harmony under Franjo Dugan (Zagreb); first piano recital Musikverein Graz 1948; concert tours through Europe, Latin America, North America 1963–2008; Australia 1963, 1966, 1969, 1976; has appeared at many music festivals, including Salzburg 1960–2008, Vienna, Edinburgh, Aldeburgh, Athens, Granada, Lucerne, Puerto Rico, London Proms and has performed with most of the major orchestras of Europe and USA, etc.; mem. American Acad. of Arts and Sciences. *Recordings:* extensive repertoire; Beethoven's Complete Piano Works, Beethoven Sonatas, three sets of Beethoven Concertos (with Vienna Philharmonic Orchestra and Simon Rattle) 1998. *Publications:* essays on music and musicians in Phono, Fono Forum, Österreichische Musikzeitschrift, Music and Musicians, Hi-Fi Stereophonie, New York Review of Books, Die Zeit, Frankfurter Allgemeine Zeitung, Musical Thoughts and Afterthoughts 1976, Nachdenken über Musik 1977, Music Sounded Out (essays) 1990, Musik beim Wort genommen 1992, Fingerzeig 1996, Störendes Lachen während des Jaworts 1997, One Finger Too Many 1998, Kleine Teufel 1999, Collected Essays on Music 2001, Augerechnet Ich (aka The Veil of Order: In Conversation with Martin Meyer) 2001, Spiegelbild und Schwarzer Spuk (poems) 2003, Cursing Bagels (poems) 2004, Alfred Brendel über Musik 2005. *Honours:* Hon. RAM; Hon. RCM; Hon. Fellow, Exeter Coll. Oxford 1987; Commdr, Ordre des Arts et des Lettres 1985, Hon. KBE 1989, Ordre pour le Mérite (Germany) 1991; Hon. DMus (London) 1978, (Oxford) 1983, (Warwick) 1991, (Yale) 1992, (Exeter) 1998, (Southampton) 2002, Hon. DLitt (Sussex) 1981, Dr hc (Cologne) 1995; Premio Città de Bolzano, Concorso Busoni 1949, Grand Prix du Disque 1965, Edison Prize (five times 1973–87), Grand Prix des Disquaires de France 1975, Deutscher Schallplattenpreis (four times 1976–84, 1992), Wiener Flötenuhr (six times 1976–87), Gramophone Award (six times 1977–83), Japanese Record Acad. Award (five times 1977–84, with Scottish Symphony Orchestra/Sir Charles Mackerras 2002), Japanese Grand Prix 1978, Franz Liszt Prize (four times 1979–83), Frankfurt Music Prize 1984, Diapason D'Or Award 1992, Heidsieck Award for Writing on Music 1990, Hans von Bülow-Medaille, Kameradschaft der Berliner Philharmoniker eV, 1992, Cannes Classical Award 1998, Ehrenmitgliedschaft der Wiener Philharmoniker 1998, Léonie Sonnings Musikpris, Denmark 2002, Ernst von Siemens Musikpreis 2004, Prix Venezia 2007, Praemium Imperiale 2009, Gramophone Lifetime Achievement Award 2010. *Address:* c/o Ingpen & Williams, 7 St George's Court, 131 Putney Bridge Road, London, SW15 2PA, England (office). *Telephone:* (20) 8874-3222 (office). *Fax:* (20) 8877-3113 (office). *E-mail:* info@ingpen.co.uk (office).

BRENDON, Piers George Rundle, MA, PhD, FRSL; British writer and broadcaster; b. 21 Dec. 1940, Stratton, Cornwall, England; m. Vyvyen Davis 1968; two s. *Education:* Magdalene Coll., Cambridge. *Career:* Lecturer in History, Cambridgeshire Coll. of Arts and Tech. 1966–79, Head, Dept of History 1977–79; Keeper of the Archives Centre, Churchill Coll., Cambridge 1995–2001, Fellow 1995–. *Publications:* Reading They've Liked (co-ed. with William Shaw) 1967, Reading Matters (co-ed. with William Shaw) 1969, By What Authority? (co-ed. with William Shaw) 1972, Hurrell Froude and the Oxford Movement 1974, Hawker of Morwenstow: Portrait of a Victorian Eccentric 1975, Eminent Edwardians 1979, The Life and Death of the Press Barons 1982, Winston Churchill: A Brief Life 1984, Ike: The Life and Times of Dwight D. Eisenhower 1986, Our Own Dear Queen 1986, Thomas Cook: 150 Years of Popular Tourism 1991, The Windsors: A Dynasty Revealed 1995, The Motoring Century: The Story of the Royal Automobile Club 1997, The Dark Valley: A Panorama of the 1930s 2000, The Decline and Fall of the British Empire: 1781–1997 2007; contrib. to periodicals, including The Guardian, The Independent, The Oldie. *Address:* 4B Millington Road, Cambridge, CB3 9HP, England (home). *Telephone:* (1223) 351886 (home). *Fax:* (1223) 329729 (home). *E-mail:* pb204@cam.ac.uk (home).

BRENON, Anne; French archivist, historian and writer; b. 14 Nov. 1945, Mâcon; d. of Georges Brenon and Jeanne Brenon (née Charpigny); m. 1st Alain Jolliot 1968 (divorced 1974); m. 2nd Michel Rion 1976 (divorced 1983); two s. one d. *Education:* Lycées de Pont de Vaux and Henri IV, Paris, Ecole Nat. des Chartes and Ecole des Hautes Etudes en Sciences Religieuses, Paris. *Career:* Curator, Departmental Archive Services 1970–82; Curator seconded to the Centre Nat. d'Etudes Cathares 1982–98; Founder and Editorial Sec., Heresis (journal); Lecturer in Medieval History, Univ. of Montpellier; Hon. Curator, Archives de France; mem. Société des Historiens Médiévistes. *Publications include:* Les fils du malheur, Les cités sarrasines, Le vrai visage du Catharisme 1988, Les Archipels Cathares Vol. 1 – Dissidence Chrétienne dans l'Europe Médiévale, Les femmes Cathares 1992, Le dico des Cathares, Les prénoms occitans au temps du Catharisme 1992, Ecritures cathares 1995, Les Cathares: Pauvres du Christ ou Apôtres de Satan? 1997, Jordane: Petite fille cathare de Fanjeaux 1999, L'impénitente 2001, Autour de Montaillou – un village occitan 2001, Joan, petit berger de Montaillou 2002, Inquisition à Montaillou 2004, Les Femmes Cathares 2005, Le Choix Hérétique 2006, Les Cathares 2007, Cathares: La Contre-Enquête 2008. *Honours:* Chevalier des Palmes académiques 1991; Prix Notre Histoire 1990. *Address:* c/o Albin Michel, 22 rue Huyghens, 75014 Paris, France (office).

BRENTON, Howard, BA; British playwright; b. 13 Dec. 1942, Portsmouth, Hants., England; s. of Donald Henry Brenton and Rose Lilian Brenton (née Lewis); m. Jane Fry 1970; two s. *Education:* Chichester High School for Boys and St Catharine's Coll., Cambridge. *Career:* resident writer, Royal Court Theatre, London 1972–73; Writer-in-Residence, Univ. of Warwick 1978–79; Granada Artist in Residence, Univ. of California, Davis 1997; Arts and Humanities Research Bd Fellowship, Univ. of Birmingham 2000. *Publications:* Revenge (play) 1969, Christie in Love 1969, Scott of the Antarctic (or What God Didn't See) 1970, Lay By (co-author) 1972, Plays for Public Places 1972, Hitler Dances 1972, Magnificence 1973, Brassneck (with David Hare) 1973, The Churchill Play 1974, Government Property 1975, The Saliva Milkshake 1975, Weapons of Happiness 1976, The Paradise Run (TV play) 1976, Sore Throats 1979, Plays for the Poor Theatre 1980, The Romans in Britain 1980, Thirteenth Night 1981, The Genius 1983, Desert of Lies (TV play) 1983, Sleeping Policemen (with Tunde Ikoli) 1983, Bloody Poetry 1984, Pravda (with David Hare) 1985, Dead Head 1986, Greenland 1988, Diving for Pearls (novel) 1989, Iranian Nights (with Tariq Ali) 1989, Hess is Dead 1990, Moscow Gold (with Tariq Ali) 1990, Berlin Bertie 1992, Hot Irons (Essays and Diaries) 1995, Playing Away (opera) 1994, Goethe's Faust, Parts I and II (adaptation) 1995, Plays I 1996, Plays II 1996, In Extremis 1997, Ugly Rumours (with Tariq Ali) 1998, Collateral Damage (with Tariq Ali and Andy de la Tour), Nasser's Eden (play for radio) 1999, Snogging Ken (with Tariq Ali and Andy de la Tour) 2000, Kit's Play 2000, Spooks (TV series) 2002–05, Paul (play) 2005, In Extremis (play) 2006, Never So Good (play) 2008, Anne Boleyn (play) 2010, Danton's Death (version) 2010, The Ragged Trousered Philanthropists (adaptation) 2010. *Honours:* Hon. Dr of Arts (North London) 1996, (Westminster), (Portsmouth); John Whiting Award 1970, Standard Best Play of the Year Award 1976, Standard Best Play of the Year (with David Hare) 1985. *Literary Agent:* c/o Casarotto Ramsay Ltd, Waverley House, 7–12 Noel Street, London, W1F 8GQ, England. *Telephone:* (20) 7287-4450. *Fax:* (20) 7287-9128. *E-mail:* info@casarotto.co.uk. *Website:* www.casarotto.co.uk.

BRETT, Simon Anthony Lee, BA; British writer; b. 28 Oct. 1945, Surrey, England; m. Lucy Victoria McLaren 1971, two s. one d. *Education:* Wadham Coll., Oxford. *Career:* mem. CWA (chair. 1986–87), Detection Club, PEN, Soc. of Authors (chair. 1995–97). *Publications include:* 17 Charles Paris crime novels 1975–97; A Shock to the System 1984; Dead Romantic 1985; six Mrs Pargeter crime novels 1986–99; The Booker Book 1989, How to be a Little Sod 1992, Singled Out 1995, The Body on the Beach 2000, The Hanging in the Hotel 2003, The Stabbing in the Stables 2006, Death Under the Dryer 2007, Blood at the Bookies 2008, A Small Family Murder 2008, The Poisoning at the Pub 2009, Blotto, Twinks and the Ex-King's Daughter 2009, A Healthy Grave 2010, The Shooting in the Shop 2010, Blotto, Twinks and the Dead Dowager Duchess 2010; editor: The Detection Collection (short stories) 2005 and several Faber books; other: After Henry (radio and television series), 1985–92, On Second Thoughts 2006. *Honours:* Writers' Guild Best Radio Feature 1973, Broadcasting Press Guild Outstanding Radio Programme 1987. *Address:* Frith House, Burpham, Arundel, West Sussex BN18 9RR, England (home). *Website:* www.simonbrett.com.

BRETTON, Barbara; American writer; b. 15 June 1950, New York, NY; m. Roy Bretton 1968. *Education:* Queens Coll., City Univ. of New York. *Career:* mem. Romance Writers of America. *Publications include:* Love Changes 1983, The Sweetest of Debts 1984, No Safe Place 1985, Starfire 1985, The Edge of Forever 1986, Promises in the Night 1986, Shooting Star 1986, Somewhere in Time 1992, One and Only 1994, The Invisible Groom 1994, Tomorrow and Always 1994, Destiny's Child 1995, Maybe This Time 1996, Guilty Pleasure 1996, Operation: Baby 1997, Sleeping Alone 1997, The Perfect Wife 1997, Always 1998, Operation: Family 1998, Laced with Magic 2009; contribs: anthologies and periodicals. *Address:* c/o The Axelrod Agency, 55 Main Street, Chatham, NY 12037, USA. *Website:* www.barbarabretton.com.

BREWSTER, Elizabeth Winifred, BLS, MA, PhD; Canadian academic and writer; *Professor Emerita of English, University of Saskatchewan*; b. 26 Aug. 1922, Chipman, NB; d. of Frederick Brewster and Ethel Brewster (née Day). *Education:* Univ. of New Brunswick, Radcliffe Coll., King's Coll., London, Univs of Toronto and Indiana, USA. *Career:* Faculty mem. Univ. of Saskatchewan 1972–, Prof. of English 1980–90, Prof. Emer. 1990–; staff mem. numerous libraries; mem. League of Canadian Poets, Writers' Union of Canada, Asscn of Canadian Univ. Teachers of English, Canadian Asscn of Commonwealth Literature and Language Studies, PEN Club Int. *Publications include:* poetry: East Coast 1951, Lillooet 1954, Roads 1957, Passage of Summer 1969, Sunrise North 1972, In Search of Eros 1974, Sometimes I Think of Moving 1977, It's Easy to Fall on the Ice 1977, The Way Home 1982, Digging In 1982, Selected Poems of Elizabeth Brewster 1944–84 1985, Entertaining Angels 1988, Spring Again 1990, The Invention of Truth 1991, Wheel of Change 1993, Footnotes to the Book of Job 1995, Away From Home (autobiog.) 1995, Garden of Sculpture 1998, Burning Bush 2000, Jacob's Dream 2002, Collected Poems Vol. 1 2003, Bright Centre 2005; novels: The Sisters 1974, Junction 1982; short stories: A House Full of Women 1983, Visitations 1987. *Honours:* mem. Order of Canada 2001; Hon. DLitt (New Brunswick) 1982; Canada Council Sr Artists Awards for Poetry 1971–72, 1976, 1978–79, 1985–86, Pres.'s Medal for Poetry, Univ. of Western Ontario 1980, Literary Award, Canadian Broadcasting Corp. 1991, Saskatoon Arts Bd Award for Lifetime Excellence in the Arts 1995, Saskatchewan Book Award for Poetry 2003. *Address:* Department of English, 320 Arts Tower, 9 Campus Drive, University of Saskatchewan, Saskatoon, SK S7N 5A5 (office); 206 Colony Square, 910 9th Street E, Saskatoon, SK S7H 0N1, Canada (home). *Telephone:* (306) 966-5486 (office); (306) 343-7695 (home). *Fax:* (306) 966-5951 (office). *Website:* www.usask.ca/english (office).

BREYTENBACH, Breyten; South African/French poet and writer; b. 16 Sept. 1939, Bonnievale; m. Yolande Ngo Thi Hoang Lien 1962. *Education:* Univ. of Cape Town. *Career:* Visiting Prof., Univ. of Cape Town 2000–02, also Univ. of Natal, Princeton Univ. *Publications:* poetry: The Iron Cow Must Sweat (A.P.B. prize 1965) 1964, The House of the Deaf 1967, Gangrene 1969, Lotus 1970, The Remains 1970, Scrit: Painting Blue a Sinking Ship 1972, In Other Words 1973, Foot Writing 1976, Sinking Ship Blues 1977, And Death White as Words. An Anthology 1978, In Africa Even the Flies Are H 1978, Flower Writing 1979, Eclipse 1983, YK 1983, Buffalo Bill 1984, Living Death 1985, Judas Eye 1989, As Like 1990, Nine Landscapes of our Times Bequeathed to a Beloved 1993, The Handful of Feathers 1995, The Remains. An Elegy 1997, Paper Flower 1998, Lady One 2000, Iron Cow Blues 2001, Lady One: Of Love and other Poems 2002, The Undanced Dance: Prison

Poetry 1975–1983 2005, The Windcatcher 2007, Voice Over: A Nomadic Conversation with Mahmoud Darwish (Max Jacob Prize, Mahmoud Darwish Literature Prize 2010) 2009; prose: Catastrophes (A.P.B. Prize 1965) 1964, The Tree Behind the Moon 1974, The Anthill Bloats ... 1980, A Season in Paradise 1980, Mouroir: Mirror Notes of a Novel 1983, Mirror Death 1984, End Papers 1985, The True Confessions of an Albino Terrorist 1985, Memory of Snow and of Dust 1987, All One Horse. Fiction and Images 1989, Sweet Heart 1991, Return to Paradise. An African Journal (Alan Paton Award) 1992, The True Confessions of an Albino Terrorist 1994, The Memory of Birds in Times of Revolution 1996, Dog Heart: A Travel Memoir 1998, Word Work 1999, A Veil of Footsteps 2008, All One Horse 2008, Mouroir: Mirror Notes of a Novel 2008, Intimate Stranger 2009, Notes From The Middle World: Essays 2009, Notes from the Middle World 2009. *Honours:* Dr hc (Univ. of Cape Town), (Univ. of Natal, Durban); Hertzog Prize 1984, 1999, Rapport Prize 1986, Alan Paton Award 1994, CNA Prize, Jan Campert Foundation Special Prize, Van der Hoogt Prize.

BREZHNEV, Dennis (see Barnett, Paul Le Page)

BRIANÇON, Pierre, LLM; French journalist; b. 3 Aug. 1954, Tunis, Tunisia; s. of Claude Briançon and Geneviève Pochard; three c. *Education:* Université Paris II, Institut d'Etudes Politiques, Paris. *Career:* journalist, Forum International 1979; Econs and Business Ed. Libération 1981–88, Moscow Corresp. 1988–91, USA Bureau Chief, Washington 1992–95, Ed.-in-Chief 1996–98; contrib. France Inter radio 1982–86; Asst Editorial Dir L'expansion 1998–2000; Chief Dow Jones Newswire Paris Bureau 2003–06; Paris corresp. Breaking-Views.com 2006–; Dir Startup Avenue (econ. information site) 2000–; fmr CEO and Chair. B to B Avenue.com. *Publications:* A Droite en sortant de la gauche? 1986, Héritiers du désastre 1992, Messier Story 2002. *Address:* c/o Breaking Views Ltd, 80 rue Taitbout, 75009 Paris, France (office). *Telephone:* 1-53-20-99-27 (office). *Fax:* 1-53-20-99-27 (office). *E-mail:* pierre .briancon@breakingviews.com (office). *Website:* www.breakingviews.com.

BRIDGEMAN, Rt-Hon. The Viscountess Victoria Harriet Lucy, (Harriet Bridgeman), MA, FRSA; British fine arts specialist, picture library executive, art historian and editor; *Executive Chairman, The Bridgeman Art Library*; b. (Victoria Harriet Lucy Turton), 30 March 1942, Co. Durham; d. of Ralph Meredyth Turton and Mary Blanche Turton (née Chetwynd Stapylton); m. Viscount Bridgeman 1966; four s. (one deceased). *Education:* St Mary's School, Wantage, Trinity Coll., Dublin. *Career:* worked as editorial trainee with The Lady magazine; Exec. Ed. The Masters 1965–69; Ed. Discovering Antiques 1970–72; est. own co. producing books and articles on fine and decorative arts; Founder and Exec. Chair. The Bridgeman Art Library 1971–; Cttee mem. British Asscn of Picture Libraries and Agencies; Founder Artists' Collecting Soc. 2006. *Publications:* Encyclopaedia of Victoriana, Needlework: An Illustrated History, The British Eccentric 1975, Society Scandals 1977, Beside the Seaside 1977, Guide to the Gardens of Europe 1980, The Last Word 1982 (all jtly with Elizabeth Drury), eight titles in Connoisseur's Library series. *Honours:* European Woman of the Year (Arts Section) Award 1997, Int. Business Woman of the Year 2005. *Address:* The Bridgeman Art Library, 17–19 Garway Road, London, W2 4PH (office); 19 Chepstow Road, London, W2 5BP (home); Watley House, Sparsholt, Winchester, Hants., SO21 2LU, England (home). *Telephone:* (20) 7727-4065 (London) (office); (20) 7727-5400 (London) (home); (1962) 776297 (Winchester) (home). *Fax:* (20) 7792-8509 (London) (office); (20) 7792-9178 (London) (home); (1962) 776297 (Winchester) (home). *E-mail:* harriet.bridgeman@bridgemanart.co.uk (office). *Website:* www.bridgemanart.com (office).

BRIERLEY, David, BA; British author; b. 30 July 1936, Durban, South Africa; m. (separated); one d. *Education:* Univ. of Oxford. *Publications:* Cold War 1979, Blood Group O 1980, Big Bear, Little Bear 1981, Shooting Star 1983, Czechmate 1984, Skorpion's Death 1985, Snowline 1986, One Lives, One Dies 1987, On Leaving a Prague Window 1995, The Horizontal Woman 1996, The Cloak-and-Dagger Girl 1998, Death & Co 1999.

BRIGGS, Baron (Life Peer), cr. 1976, of Lewes in the County of Sussex; **Asa Briggs,** BSc, MA, FBA; British historian; b. 7 May 1921, Keighley, Yorks., England; s. of William Walker Briggs and Jane Briggs; m. Susan Anne Banwell 1955; two s. two d. *Education:* Keighley Grammar School and Sidney Sussex Coll., Cambridge. *Career:* Cryptographer, Bletchley Park 1942–45; Fellow, Worcester Coll., Oxford 1945–55, Reader in Recent Social and Econ. History, Univ. of Oxford 1950–55; Prof. of Modern History, Univ. of Leeds 1955–61; Prof. of History, Univ. of Sussex 1961–76, Dean of Social Studies 1961–65, Pro-Vice-Chancellor 1961–67, Vice-Chancellor 1967–76; Provost Worcester Coll., Oxford 1976–91; Chancellor, Open Univ. 1979–94; Pres. Workers Educational Asscn 1958–67; Chair. Appts Comm. Press Council 1972–88; mem. Univ. Grants Cttee 1959–67; Trustee, Int. Broadcast Inst. 1968–86, Hon. Trustee 1990–; Gov. British Film Inst. 1970–76; Chair. European Inst. of Educ. 1974–84; mem. Council of UN Univ. 1974–80; Chair. Cttee on Nursing 1970–72, Heritage Educ. Group 1976–86, Commonwealth of Learning 1988–93; Pres. Social History Soc. 1976–, Ephemera Soc. 1984–, Victorian Soc. 1983–; Vice-Pres. Historical Asscn 1986–; Vice-Chair. of Council, UN Univ. 1974–80. *Publications:* Patterns of Peacemaking (with D. Thomson and E. Meyer) 1945, History of Birmingham, 1865–1938 1952, Victorian People 1954, Friends of the People 1956, The Age of Improvement 1959 (revised edn 2000), Ed. Chartist Studies 1959, History of Broadcasting in the United Kingdom, Vol. I 1961, Vol. II 1965, Vol. III 1970, Vol. IV 1979, Vol. V 1995, Victorian Cities 1963, The Nineteenth Century (ed.) 1970, Cap and Bell (with Susan Briggs) 1972, Essays in the History of Publishing (ed.) 1974, Essays in Labour History 1918–1939 1977, Governing the BBC 1979, From Coalbrookdale to the Crystal Palace 1980, The Power of Steam 1982, Marx in London 1982, A Social History of England 1983, The BBC—The First Fifty Years 1985, The Collected Essays of Asa Briggs, (Vol. 1, 2, 3), The Franchise Affair (with Joanna Spicer) 1986, Victorian Things 1988, The Longman Encyclopedia (ed.) 1989, Haut-Brion: An Illustrious Lineage 1994, The Channel Islands: Occupation and Liberation 1940–45 1995, Fins de Siècle (co-ed.) 1996; co-author Modern Europe 1789–1989 1996, The History of Bethlem 1997, Chartism 1998, Go to It! War: Working for Victory on the Home Front, 1939–45 2000, Michael Young: Social Entrepreneur 2000, A Social History of the Media (with Peter Burke) 2002, A History of Longmans and Their Books, 1724–1990: Longevity in Publishing 2008. *Honours:* Hon. mem. American Acad. of Arts and Sciences 1970–; Hon. LLD, Hon. DLitt, Hon. DSc; Marconi Medal for Services to Study of Broadcasting 1975, Medal of French Acad. for Architecture 1982, Wolfson History Prize 2001. *Address:* The Caprons, Keere Street, Lewes, Sussex, BN7 1TY, England (home). *Telephone:* (1273) 474704 (home). *Fax:* (1273) 474704 (home). *E-mail:* pat.spencer@ ukgateway.net (office).

BRIGGS, Raymond Redvers, NDD, DFA, FSCD, FRSL; British writer, illustrator and cartoonist; b. 18 Jan. 1934, Wimbledon, London; s. of Ernest R. Briggs and Ethel Bowyer; m. Jean Taprell Clark 1963 (died 1973). *Education:* Rutlish School, Merton, Wimbledon School of Art and Slade School of Fine Art, London. *Career:* freelance illustrator 1957–; part-time lecturer in illustration, Brighton School of Art 1961–87; children's author 1961–; mem. Soc. of Authors. *Radio play:* When the Wind Blows, The Man. *Publications:* The Strange House 1961, Midnight Adventure 1961, Ring-a-Ring o' Roses 1962, Sledges to the Rescue 1963, The White Land 1963, Fee Fi Fo Fum 1964, The Mother Goose Treasury 1966, Jim and the Beanstalk 1970, The Fairy Tale Treasury 1972, Father Christmas 1973 (also film version), Father Christmas Goes on Holiday 1975, Fungus the Bogeyman 1977, The Snowman 1978 (also film version), Gentleman Jim 1980 (also stage version), When the Wind Blows 1982 (stage and radio versions 1983, animated film version 1987), The Tinpot Foreign General and the Old Iron Woman 1984, The Snowman Pop-Up 1986, Unlucky Wally 1987, Unlucky Wally Twenty Years On 1989, The Man 1992, The Bear 1994 (also film version), Ethel and Ernest 1998, UG 2001, Blooming Books (with Nicolette Jones) 2003, The Puddleman 2004. *Honours:* Hon. Fellow, Univ. of the Arts London; awards include Kate Greenaway Medal 1966, 1973, BAFTA Award, Francis Williams Illustration Award, Victoria & Albert Museum 1982, Broadcasting Press Guild Radio Award 1983, Children's Author of the Year 1992, Kurt Maschler Award 1992, Illustrated Book of the Year Award 1998, Smarties Silver Award 2001, Lifetime Achievement Award, Cartoon Art Museum. *Address:* Weston, Underhill Lane, Westmeston, nr Hassocks, Sussex, BN6 8XG, England (home).

BRIJS, Stefan; Belgian writer; b. 29 Dec. 1969, Genk. *Publications:* De verwording (novel) 1997, Kruistochten (essays) 1998, Arend (novel) 2000, Twee levens (short story) 2001, Villa Keetje Tippel (biog.) 2001, De engelenmaker (novel) (Gouden Uil Prijs van de Lezer, De Vijfjaarlijkse Prijs voor Proza van de Koninklijke Academie voor Nederlandse Taal- en Letterkunde 2006) 2005, Korrels in Gods grote zandbak (essays) 2006. *Address:* c/o Uitgeverij Atlas, Herengracht 481, 1017 BT Amsterdam, The Netherlands (office). *Telephone:* (20) 5249800 (office). *Fax:* (20) 6276851 (office). *E-mail:* mail@stefanbrijs.be; atlas@uitgeverijatlas.nl (office). *Website:* www .stefanbrijs.be; www.uitgeverijatlas.nl (office).

BRINDLEY, Dame Lynne Janie, DBE, MA, FLA, FRSA, CCMI; British librarian; b. 2 July 1950, London; d. of Ivan Blowers and Janie Blowers (née Williams); adopted d. of Ronald Williams and Elaine Williams (née Chapman); m. Timothy Stuart Brindley 1972. *Education:* Truro High School, Univ. of Reading, Univ. Coll. London. *Career:* Head of Marketing and of Chief Exec.'s Office, British Library 1979–85, Chief Exec. British Library 2000–12; Dir of Library and Information Services, also Pro-Vice Chancellor, Univ. of Aston 1985–90; Prin. Consultant, KPMG 1990–92; Librarian and Dir of Information Services, LSE 1992–97; Librarian and Pro-Vice Chancellor, Univ. of Leeds 1997–2000, Visiting Prof. of Knowledge Man., 2000–; Visiting Prof. of Information Man., Leeds Metropolitan Univ. 2000–03; mem. Int. Cttee on Social Science Information, UNESCO 1992–97, Lord Chancellor's Advisory Cttee on Public Records 1992–98, Stanford Univ. Advisory Council for Libraries and Information Resources 1999–, Resource Bd 2002–, Eng and Physical Sciences Research Council User Panel 2002–04, Ithaka Bd; Trustee, Thackray Medical Museum, Leeds 1999–2001. *Publications:* numerous articles on electronic libraries and information man. *Honours:* Freeman, City of London 1989, Liveryman, Goldsmiths' Co. 1993, Hon. Fellow, Univ. Coll. London 2002, Univ. of Wales 2007; Hon. DLitt (Nottingham Trent) 2001, (Oxford) 2002, (Leicester) 2002, (Sheffield) 2004, (Reading) 2004, (Leeds) 2006, (Aston) 2008, Hon. DPhil (London Guildhall) 2002, Hon. DSc (City) 2005. *Address:* c/o The British Library, 96 Euston Road, London, NW1 2DB, England (office). *Telephone:* (20) 7412-7273 (office). *Fax:* (20) 7412-7093 (office). *E-mail:* chief-executive@bl.uk (office). *Website:* www.bl.uk (office).

BRINES, Francisco; Spanish poet; b. 1932, Oliva, Valencia. *Education:* Univ. of Deusto, Univ. of Valencia, Univ. of Salamanca. *Career:* fmr Reader of Spanish Literature, Univ. of Cambridge, UK; fmr Prof. of Spanish Literature, Univ. of Oxford, UK; mem. Royal Spanish Acad. 2001– (replaced playwright Antonio Buero upon his death). *Publications:* Las brasas (Premio Adonais

1959) 1960, El santo inocente 1965, Palabras a la oscuridad (Premio de la Crítica 1967) 1966, Aún no 1971, Ensayo de una despedida 1960–71 1974, Insistencias en Luzbel 1977, Poesía. 1960–81 1984, Poemas excluidos 1985, El otoño de las rosas (Premio Nacional de Literatura 1987) 1986, La rosa de las noches 1986, Poemas a DK 1986, Espejo Ciego 1993, La última costa (Fastenrath Prize 1998) 1995, Breve antología personal 1997, Selección de poemas 1997, Poesía completa (1960–97) 1997, Antología poética 1998, Ensayo de una despedida 1998, La Iluminada Rosa Negra 2003, Amada vida mía 2004. *Honours:* Valencian Literature Award 1967, Nat. Award for Spanish Literature 1999, Creativity Award 'Ricardo Marin' 2004, IV Poetry Prize Federico García Lorca 2007, Queen Sofia Award for Poetry 2010. *Address:* Royal Spanish Acad., 4 Felipe IV, 28014 Madrid, Spain (office). *Telephone:* (91) 4201478 (office). *Fax:* (91) 4200079 (office). *E-mail:* prorae@rae.es (office). *Website:* www.rae.es (office).

BRINGHURST, Robert, BA, MFA, DLitt; Canadian/American poet, writer and translator; b. 16 Oct. 1946, Los Angeles, Calif., USA; m. Jan Zwicky. *Education:* Massachusetts Inst. of Tech., Univ. of Utah, Defense Language Inst., Indiana Univ., Univ. of British Columbia. *Career:* Gen. Ed. Kanchenjunga Poetry Series 1973–79; Reviews Ed., Canadian Fiction Magazine 1974–75; Visiting Lecturer, Univ. of British Columbia 1975–77, Lecturer 1979–80; Poet-in-Residence, Banff School of Fine Arts 1983, Ojibway and Cree Cultural Centre Writers' Workshops 1985–86, Univ. of Western Ontario 1998–99; Contributing Ed., Fine Print: A Review for the Arts of the Book 1985–90; Writer-in-Residence Univ. of Edinburgh 1989–90; Ashley Fellow, Trent Univ. 1994, Adjunct Prof., Frost Centre for Native Studies and Canadian Studies 1998–2010; Philips Fund Research Fellow, American Philosophical Soc. 2000; Adjunct Prof., Centre for Studies in Publishing, Simon Fraser Univ. 2000–12; Ralph Gustafson Chair in Poetry, Malaspina Univ. Coll. (now Vancouver Island Univ.) 2003; Visiting Lecturer, Univ. of Alberta 2005, Cátedra Atwood-Roy en la literatura canadiense, Univ. Autónoma de México 2008; Distinguished Writer-in-Residence, Univ. of Wyoming 2010. *Exhibition:* The Poetry & Typography of Robert Bringhurst, Clark Library, UCLA, Los Angeles 1993. *Dance:* Jacob Singing, choreography by Liz Gorrie, Kaleidoscope Theatre 1977, Ursa Major: A Polyphonic Masque for Speakers and Dancers, choreography by Robin Poitras, New Dance Horizons 2002. *Radio:* Blue Roofs of Japan. directed by Don Mowatt, CBC Radio 1986. *Television:* The Spirit of Haida Gwaii, film directed by Alan Clapp (CBC) 1992. *Publications:* The Shipwright's Log 1972, Cadastre 1973, Eight Objects 1975, Bergschrund 1975, Jacob Singing 1977, The Stonecutter's Horses 1979, Tzuhalem's Mountain 1982, The Beauty of the Weapons: Selected Poems 1972–82 1982, Visions: Contemporary Art in Canada 1983, The Raven Steals the Light 1984, Ocean, Paper, Stone 1984, Tending the Fire 1985, The Blue Roofs of Japan 1986, Pieces of Map, Pieces of Music 1986, Conversations with Toad 1987, The Black Canoe 1991, The Elements of Typographic Style 1992 (third edn 2004), The Calling: Selected Poems 1970–95 1995, Elements 1995, Boats is Saintlier than Captains 1997, Native American Oral Literatures and the Unity of the Humanities 1998, A Story as Sharp as a Knife: The Classical Haida Mythtellers and Their World 1999 (second edn 2011), A Short History of the Printed Word 1999, The Book of Silences 2001, Ursa Major 2003 (second edn 2009), Prosodies of Meaning 2003, Carving the Elements: A Companion to the Fragments of Parmenides 2004, The Solid Form of Language 2004, The Old in Their Knowing 2005, New World Suite No. 3 2006, Wild Language 2006, The Tree of Meaning 2006, Everywhere Being Is Dancing 2007, The Surface of Meaning 2008, Selected Poems (Canada) 2009, Selected Poems (UK) 2010; translations: Nine Visits to the Mythworld (by Ghandl of the Qayahl Llaanas) 2000, Being in Being: The Collected Works of Skaay of the Qquuna Qiighawaay 2001, The Fragments of Parmenides 2003, Floating Overhead (by Skaay of the Qquuna Qiighawaay) 2007; editor: Visions: Contemporary Art in Canada 1983, Solitary Raven 2000 (second edn 2009); contrib. to many anthologies. *Honours:* Hon. DLitt (Fraser Valley) 2006; Macmillan Prize 1975, Alcuin Soc. Design Awards 1984, 1985, Canadian Broadcasting Corporation Poetry Prize 1985, Guggenheim Fellowship 1987–88, Canada Council & Scottish Arts Council Canada/Scotland Exchange Fellow 1989–90, Charles Watts Award for outstanding endeavour in the polity of poetry 1999, Edward Sapir Prize 2004, Lt-Gov.'s Award for Literary Excellence 2005, Hubert Evans Prize for Literary Nonfiction 2008, American Printing History Asscn annual laureate 2009, Witter Bynner Fellow in Poetry, Library of Congress 2011. *Address:* Box 51, Heriot Bay, BC V0P 1H0, Canada (office). *Fax:* (250) 285-2670 (home).

BRINK, André Philippus, MA; South African writer and academic; *Honorary Professor, Department of English Language and Literature, University of Cape Town*; b. 29 May 1935, Vrede; s. of Daniel Brink and Aletta Brink (née Wolmarans); three s. one d. *Education:* Lydenburg High School, Potchefstroom Univ., Sorbonne, Paris. *Career:* began writing at an early age; first novel (Afrikaans) published 1958; on return from Paris became mem. and spokesman of young Afrikaans writers' group Sestigers; returned to Paris 1968; went back to South Africa to resist apartheid through writing; novel Kennis van die Aand banned 1973 (first Afrikaans novel to be banned); began to write in English as well; Dir several plays, but abandoned theatre owing to censorship; resumed playwriting 1996; Founder-mem. Afrikaans Writers' Guild; Prof. of Afrikaans and Dutch Literature, Rhodes Univ. (previously lecturer) 1980–89; Prof. of English, Univ. of Cape Town 1991–2000, now Hon. Prof. *Publications include:* File on a Diplomat 1966, Looking on Darkness (novel) 1974, An Instant in the Wind (novel) 1976, Rumours of Rain (novel) 1978, A Dry White Season (novel) 1979, A Chain of Voices (novel) 1982, Mapmakers (essays) 1983, The Wall of the Plague (novel) 1984, The Ambassador (novel) 1985, A Land Apart (co-ed with J M Coetzee) 1986, States of Emergency (novel) 1988, An Act of Terror (novel) 1991, The First Life of Adamastor (novel) 1993, On the Contrary (novel) 1993, Imaginings of Sand (novel) 1996, Reinventing a Continent (essays) 1996, Devil's Valley (novel) 1998, The Rights of Desire (novel) 2000, The Other Side of Silence (novel) 2002, Before I Forget (novel) 2004, Praying Mantis 2004, Other Lives: A Novel in Three Parts 2008, A Fork in the Sand (auto-biog.) 2009; several plays 1965–75, The Jogger 1997. *Honours:* Chevalier Légion d'honneur 1983, Commdr Ordre des Arts et des Lettres 1992; Hon. DLitt (Witwatersrand) 1985, (Univ. of Free State) 1997, (Montpellier) 1998, (Rhodes) 2001, (Pretoria) 2003; Reina Prinsen Geerlings Prize 1964, CNA Award for Literature, South Africa 1965, 1978 and 1982, Martin Luther King Memorial Prize 1979, Prix Médicis Etranger, France 1979, Biannual Freedom of Speech Prize by Monismanien Foundation, Univ. of Uppsala 1991, Premio Mondello (Italy) 1997, Commonwealth Prize for Literature (Africa) 2003, Sunday Times Fiction Award 2004. *Address:* Department of English Language and Literature, University of Cape Town, Rondebosch 7701, South Africa (office). *Fax:* (21) 685-3945 (home). *Website:* web.uct.ac.za/depts/english.

BRINKLEY, Alan, BA, PhD; American historian and academic; *Provost and Allan Nevins Professor of History, Columbia University*; b. 2 June 1949, Washington, DC; s. of the late David Brinkley; m. Evangeline Morphos 1989; one d. *Education:* Princeton and Harvard Univs. *Career:* Asst Prof. of History, MIT 1978–82; visiting position, Harvard Univ. 1980, Dunwalke Assoc. Prof. of American History 1982–88; Prof. of History, Grad. School and Univ. Center, CUNY 1988–91; visiting positions, Princeton Univ. 1991, Univ. of Turin 1992, New York Univ. 1993, École des Hautes Études en Sciences Sociales, Paris 1996; Prof. of History, Columbia Univ. 1991–98, Allan Nevins Prof. of History 1998–, Provost 2003–08; Harmsworth Prof. of American History, Univ. of Oxford 1998–99; Fellow, Soc. of American Historians 1984– (Exec. Bd mem. 1989–); mem. American Historical Asscn, Org. of American Historians (Exec. Bd mem. 1990–93), Century Foundation (Trustee 1995–, Chair. 1999–), Nat. Humanities Center (Trustee 2004–), American Acad. of Arts and Sciences. *Publications:* Voices of Protest: Huey Long, Father Coughlin, and the Great Depression 1982, American History: A Survey 1983, The Unfinished Nation: A Concise History of the American People 1993, The End of Reform: New Deal Liberalism in Recession and War 1995, Eyes of the Nation: A Visual History of the United States (with others) 1997, New Federalist Papers (with Kathleen Sullivan and Nelson Polsby) 1997, Liberalism and Its Discontents 1998, The Chicago Handbook for Teachers (co-ed.) 1999, The Reader's Companion to the American Presidency (co-ed.) 2000, Franklin Delano Roosevelt 2009, The Publisher: Henry Luce and His American Century 2010, Memories of the Bush Administration 2011; contribs to scholarly books and journals. *Honours:* Nat. Endowment for the Humanities Fellowship 1972–73, American Council of Learned Socs Fellowship 1981, Robert L. Brown Prize, Louisiana Historical Asscn 1982, Nat. Book Award for History 1983, Guggenheim Fellowship 1984–85, Woodrow Wilson Center for Int. Scholars Fellowship 1985, Joseph R. Levenson Memorial Teaching Prize, Harvard Univ. 1987, Nat. Humanities Center Fellowship 1988–89, Media Studies Center Fellowship 1993–94, Russell Sage Foundation Fellowship 1996–97, Great Teacher Award, Columbia Univ. 2003. *Address:* Office of the Provost, 205 Low Library, Columbia University, New York, NY 10027, USA (office). *Telephone:* (212) 854-2403 (office). *E-mail:* ab65@columbia.edu (office). *Website:* www.columbia.edu/cu/history (office).

BRINKLEY, Douglas Gregg, BA, MA, PhD; American academic and writer; *Professor of History and Fellow, James A. Baker III Institute for Public Policy, Rice University*; b. 14 Dec. 1960, Atlanta, GA; m.; two c. *Education:* Ohio State Univ. and Georgetown Univ. *Career:* Instructor, US Naval Acad. 1987; Visiting Research Fellow, Woodrow Wilson School of Public Policy and Int. Affairs 1987–88; Lecturer, Princeton Univ. 1988; Asst Prof. of History, Hofstra Univ. 1989–93; Visiting Assoc. Dir 1993–94, Dir from 1994, Eisenhower Center for American Studies, Assoc. Prof. of History 1993–96; Stephen E. Ambrose Prof. of American History, Univ. of New Orleans 1997–2005; Prof. of History, Tulane Univ. 2005–07; Prof. of History and Fellow, James A. Baker III Institute for Public Policy, Rice Univ. 2007–; Contributing Ed., LA Times, American History; mem. Council on Foreign Relations, Theodore Roosevelt Asscn, Franklin and Eleanor Roosevelt Inst., Century Asscn, National D-Day Museum. *Publications:* Jean Monnet: The Path of European Unity (ed. with Clifford Hackett) 1991, The Atlantic Charter (ed. with D. Facey-Crowther) 1992, Dean Acheson: The Cold War Years, 1953–1971 1992, Driven Patriot: The Life and Times of James Forrestal (with Townsend Hoopes) 1992, Dean Acheson and the Making of US Foreign Policy (ed.) 1993, Theodore Roosevelt: The Many-Sided American (ed. with Gable and Naylor) 1993, The Majic Bus: An American Odyssey 1993, Franklin Roosevelt and the Creation of the United Nations (with Townsend Hoopes) 1997, John F. Kennedy and Europe (ed.) 1997, Hunter S. Thompson: The Proud Highway Saga of a Desperate Southern Gentleman 1955–1967 (ed.) 1997, American Heritage: History of the United States (Benjamin Franklin Award) 1998, The Unfinished Presidency: Jimmy Carter's Journey Beyond The White House 1998, Rosa Parks: A Biography 2000, Hunter S. Thompson: Fear and Loathing in America (ed.) 2001, Wheels for the World: Henry Ford, his Company and a Century of Progress 2004, Tour of Duty: John Kerry and the Vietnam War 2004, The Boys of Pointe Du Hoc: Ronald Reagan, D-Day and the US Army 2nd Ranger Battalion 2005, Parish Priest (with Julie M. Fenster) 2006, The Great Deluge (Robert F. Kennedy Book Award 2007) 2006, The Reagan Diaries (Ed.) 2007,

The Wilderness Warrior: Theodore Roosevelt and the Crusade for America 2009; contrib. to books, popular magazines and scholarly journals. *Honours:* Hon. DH (Trinity Coll., CT) 1997; New York Times Notable Book of the Year Citations 1993, 1998, Hofstra Univ. Stessin Award for Distinguished Scholarship 1993, Theodore and Franklin Roosevelt Naval History Prize 1993, Bernath Lecture Prize 1996. *Address:* James A. Baker III Institute for Public Policy, Rice University MS-40, 6100 Main Street, PO Box 1892, Houston, TX 77251-1892, USA (office). *Telephone:* (713) 348-4683 (office). *Fax:* (713) 348-5993 (office). *E-mail:* douglas.brinkley@rice.edu (office). *Website:* www.bakerinstitute.org (office).

BRINTON, Alexander (see Battin, B. W.)

BRISTOW, Robert O'Neil, BA, MA; American author; b. 17 Nov. 1926, St Louis, Mo.; m. 1st Gaylon Walker 1950 (divorced); two s. two d; m. 2nd Gail Hamiter Rosen 2003. *Education:* Univ. of Oklahoma. *Career:* Writer-in-Residence, Winthrop Coll., SC 1961–87. *Publications:* Time for Glory 1968, Night Season 1970, A Faraway Drummer 1973, Laughter in Darkness 1974; more than 200 short stories published in magazines and journals. *Honours:* Award for Literary Excellence 1969, Friends of American Writer's Award 1974. *Address:* 613 1/2 Charlotte Avenue, Rock Hill, SC 29730-3629, USA (home). *E-mail:* bobbristow@comporium.net (home).

BRISVILLE, Jean-Claude Gabriel; French writer and playwright; b. 28 May 1922, Bois-Colombes/Hauts-de-Seine; s. of Maurice Brisville and Geneviève Gineste; m. 2nd Irène Kalaschnikowa 1963; one s. one d. by first m. *Education:* Lycée Jacques Decour, Paris. *Career:* literary journalist 1946–; Reader, Hachette 1951–58; Sec. to Albert Camus 1957–59; Deputy Literary Dir Juilliard 1959–64, Literary Dir 1964–70; Head of Drama Video Section, ORTF 1971–75; Literary Dir Livre de poche 1976–81. *Plays:* Le Fauteuil à bascule (Prix Ibsen, Prix de la meilleure création dramatique) 1982, Le Bonheur à Romorantin, L'entretien de M. Descartes avec M. Pascal le jeune, La Villa bleue, Les Liaisons dangereuses (adaptation), Le Souper (Prix du Théâtre, Acad. Française) 1990, L'Officier de la Garde 1990, L'Antichambre 1991, Contre-jour 1993, Dernière Salve 1995, Sept comédies en quête d'acteurs 2007. *Publications include:* narrative works: Prologue 1948, D'un amour (Prix Sainte-Beuve) 1954, La Fuite au Danemark 1962, La petite Marie 1972, La Zone d'ombre 1976, La révélation d'une voix et d'un nom 1982, Vive Henri IV 2002; essays; stories for children. *Honours:* Chevalier, Légion d'honneur, Chevalier, Ordre des Arts et des Lettres; Prix du Théâtre de la Société des Auteurs et Compositeurs Dramatiques (SACD). *Address:* 85 rue Republique, 59172 Roeulx, France (home). *Telephone:* 3-27-43-27-75 (home).

BRITTAN, Sir Samuel, Kt, MA; British writer and journalist; *Columnist, Financial Times*; b. 29 Dec. 1933, London; brother of Lord Brittan of Spennithorne. *Education:* Kilburn Grammar School, Jesus Coll., Cambridge. *Career:* journalist on The Financial Times 1955–61, prin. economic commentator 1966–, Asst Ed. 1978–95; Econs Ed. The Observer 1961–64; Adviser, Dept of Econ. Affairs 1965; Research Fellow, Nuffield Coll., Oxford 1973–74, Visiting Fellow 1974–82; Visiting Prof., Chicago Law School, USA 1978; mem. Peacock Cttee on Finance of the BBC 1985–86. *Publications:* Steering the Economy (3rd edn 1970), Left or Right: The Bogus Dilemma 1968, The Price of Economic Freedom: A Guide to Flexible Rates 1970, Is There an Economic Consensus? 1973, Capitalism and the Permissive Society 1973 (new edn A Restatement of Economic Liberalism 1988), The Delusion of Incomes Policy (with Peter Lilley) 1977, The Economic Consequences of Democracy 1977, How to End the 'Monetarist' Controversy 1981, Role and Limits of Government: Essays in Political Economy 1983, There Is No Such Thing As Society 1993, Capitalism with a Human Face 1995, Essays, Moral, Political and Economic 1998, Against the Flow 2005. *Honours:* Hon. Prof. of Politics Univ. of Warwick 1987–92; Hon. Fellow Jesus Coll., Cambridge 1988; Chevalier, Légion d'honneur 1993; Hon. DLitt (Heriot-Watt) 1985; Hon. DUniv (Essex) 1995; first winner Sr Harold Wincott Award for financial journalists 1971, George Orwell Prize for political journalism 1980, Ludwig Erhard Prize 1987. *Address:* The Financial Times, Number 1 Southwark Bridge, London, SE1 9HL, England (office). *Telephone:* (20) 7873-3000 (office). *Fax:* (20) 7873-4343 (office). *E-mail:* samuel.brittan@ft.com (office). *Website:* www.samuelbrittan.co.uk.

BROBST, Richard Alan, BA; American teacher, poet, writer and editor; b. 13 May 1958, Sarasota, FL; m. Pamela Millace 1986; two s. one d. *Education:* University of Florida. *Career:* Co-founder and Ed., Albatross Poetry Journal 1986–99; Resident Poet, Charlotte County Schools 1989–. *Publications:* Inherited Roles 1997, Dancing With Archetypes 1998, Songs From the Lost Oaks 1999, The Cody Star 2000; contributions: anthologies and periodicals. *Honours:* winner Duanne Locke Chapbook Series 1997. *Address:* 17145 Urban Avenue, Port Charlotte, FL 33954, USA (home). *E-mail:* aliasd13@aol.com (home).

BROCK, William Ranulf, MA, PhD, FBA, FRHistS; British historian; *Professor Emeritus of Modern History, University of Glasgow*; b. 16 May 1916, Farnham, Surrey; s. of Stewart E. Brock and Katherine Temple Roberts; m. Constance H. Brown 1950 (died 2000); one s. one d. *Education:* Christ's Hosp., Horsham and Trinity Coll., Cambridge. *Career:* Fellow, Selwyn Coll., Cambridge 1947–, Life Fellow 1967; Prof. of Modern History, Univ. of Glasgow 1967–81, Prof. Emer. 1981–. *Publications:* Lord Liverpool and Liberal Toryism 1941, Character of American History 1960, An American Crisis 1865–67 1963, Conflict and Transformations, USA 1844–77 1973, USA 1789–1890: Sources of History 1975, Parties and Political Conscience 1979, Scotus Americanus 1981, Investigation and Responsibility 1984, Welfare, Democracy and the New Deal 1988, Selwyn College: a History (with P. H. M. Cooper) 1994. *Honours:* Hon. LittD (Keele) 1998. *Address:* 49 Barton Road, Cambridge, CB3 9LG, England (home). *Telephone:* (1223) 529655 (home). *E-mail:* wrb20@cam.ac.uk (home).

BROCKMAN, John, MBA; American editor, publisher and literary agent; *Chief Executive Officer, Brockman Inc.*; b. 16 Feb. 1941, Boston, MA; m. Katinka Matson; one s. *Education:* Babson Inst. of Business Admin, Columbia Univ., NY. *Career:* multimedia artist 1965–69; f. and CEO Brockman Inc. literary and software agency 1973–; f. and Pres. Edge Foundation, Ed. and Publisher Edge website 1988–; co-f. and Chair. Content.com Inc. (web-based digital publishing co.); agent and co-f. The Reality Club; co-f. rightscenter.com. *Publications:* By the Late John Brockman 1969, Doing Science: The Reality Club (ed.) 1988, The Third Culture: Beyond the Scientific Revolution 1995, Digerati: Encounters with the Cyber Elite 1996, The Greatest Inventions in the Past Two Thousand Years (ed.) 2000, The Next Fifty Years: Science in the First Half of the Twenty-First Century (ed.) 2003, The New Humanists: Science at the Edge (ed.) 2004, What is Your Dangerous Idea? 2006, What Are You Optimistic About? 2007. *Address:* Brockman Inc., 5 E 59th Street, New York, NY 10022, USA (office). *E-mail:* editor@edge.org (office). *Website:* www.brockman.com; www.edge.org.

BRODBER, Erna, MSc, PhD; Jamaican novelist and sociologist; b. 21 April 1940, Woodside, St Mary. *Education:* Univ. Coll. of the W Indies (now UWI), Kingston. *Career:* fmr civil servant, teacher, sociology lecturer; fmr Fellow/staff mem. Inst. for Social and Econ. Research (ISER), Mona; fmr Lecturer Univ. of the W Indies, Mona; Whichard Distinguished Prof. in Women's Studies E Carolina Univ. Thomas Harriot Coll. of Arts and Sciences 2003. *Publications:* fiction: Jane and Louisa Will Soon Come Home 1980, Myal (Commonwealth Regional Prize for Literature) 1988, Louisiana 1997, Rainmaker's Mistake 2007; non-fiction: People of my Jamaican Village 1999, Standing Tall etc. 2003, The Continent of Black Consciousness 2003, The Second Generation of Freemen in Jamaica, Woodside Pear Tree Grove; contribs to ISER and UNESCO. *Honours:* Order of Distinction, Jamaica; Musgrave Gold Award for Literature and Orature, Prince Claus Laureate 2006. *Address:* Woodside, Pear Tree Grove, St. Mary/ St Catherine, Jamaica (home). *Telephone:* 819-7721 (home); 410-8737 (home). *E-mail:* ernabrodber_1@yahoo.com (home).

BRODERICK, Damien Francis, BA, PhD; Australian writer; b. 22 April 1944, Melbourne, Vic. *Education:* Monash Univ., Deakin Univ. *Career:* Writer-in-Residence, Deakin Univ. 1986; Sr Fellow, Univ. of Melbourne; Science Fiction Ed., Cosmos: The Science of Everything. *Publications:* A Man Returned (short stories) 1965, The Zeitgeist Machine (ed.) 1977, The Dreaming Dragons 1980, The Judas Mandala 1982, Valencies (with Rory Barnes) 1983, Transmitters 1984, Strange Attractors (ed.) 1985, The Black Grail 1986, Striped Holes 1988, Matilda at the Speed of Light (ed.) 1988, The Dark Between the Stars (short stories) 1991, The Lotto Effect 1992, The Sea's Furthest End 1993, The Architecture of Babel: Discourses of Literature and Science 1994, Reading by Starlight: Postmodern Science Fiction 1995, The White Abacus 1997, Zones (with Rory Barnes) 1997, Theory and its Discontents 1997, The Spike 1997, Not the Only Planet (ed.) 1998, Centaurus (co-ed. with David G. Hartwell) 1999, The Last Mortal Generation 1999, Stuck in Fast Forward (with Rory Barnes) 1999, The Book of Revelation (with Rory Barnes) 1999, Transrealist Fiction 2000, The Game of Stars and Souls 2000, Earth is But a Star (ed.) 2001, Transcension 2002, Jack and the Aliens 2002, Jack and the Skyhook 2003, The Hunger of Time (with Rory Barnes) 2004, x, y, z, t: Dimensions of Science Fiction 2004, Ferocious Minds 2005, Godplayers 2005, K-Machines 2006, I Suppose a Root's Out of the Question? (with Rory Barnes) 2007, Outside the Gates of Science 2007, Post Mortal Syndrome (with Barbara Lamarr) 2007, Year Million: Science at the Far Edge of Knowledge (ed.) 2008, I'm Dying Here: A Comedy of Bad Manners (with Rory Barnes) 2009; contributions: periodicals. *Honours:* several writing fellowships, Australian Council 1980–, Ditmar Award (Australian Science Fiction Achievement Award) 1981, 1985, 1989, 1998, 2002, Aurealis Award 1997, 2002, 2006. *Address:* c/o Wildside Press, 9710 Traville Gateway Dr #234, Rockville, MD 20850, USA (office). *Website:* www.wildsidepress.com (office).

BRODEUR, Hélène, BA; Canadian writer; b. 13 July 1923, Val Racine, QC; m. Robert L. Nantais 1947; three s. two d. *Education:* Teacher's Certificate, Ottawa University Normal School; Ottawa University, Canadian Government College. *Career:* Writer-in-Residence, Visiting Prof., French Creative Writing, Ottawa University; mem. Ontario Authors Asscn, Union des écrivains, PEN International, Press Club. *Publications:* Chroniques du Nouvel-Ontario, Vol. 1, La quête d'Alexandre 1981, Vol. 2, Entre l'aube et le jour 1983, Vol. 3, Les routes incertaines 1986, Vol. 4 L'Ermitage 1996, Alexander 1983, Rose-Delima 1987, The Honourable Donald 1990; contributions: Extension magazine. *Honours:* Champlain Award 1981, Le Droit Award 1983, Prix du Nouvel-Ontario 1984.

BRODEUR, Paul Adrian, Jr, BA; American writer; b. 16 May 1931, Boston; m. (divorced); one s. one d. *Education:* Harvard Coll. *Career:* staff writer, The New Yorker magazine 1958–96; Lecturer, Columbia Univ. Graduate School of Journalism 1969–80, Boston Univ. School of Public Communications 1978–79, Univ. of California, San Diego 1989. *Publications include:* The Sick Fox 1963, The Stunt Man 1970, Downstream 1972, Expendable Americans 1974, The Zapping of America 1977, Outrageous Misconduct 1985, Restitution 1985, Currents of Death 1989, The Great Power-Line Coverup 1993, Secrets 1997;

contrib. to The New Yorker. *Honours:* Sidney Hillman Prize 1973, Columbia Univ. Nat. Magazine Award 1973, American Asscn for the Advancement of Science Award 1976, Guggenheim Fellowship 1976–77, Alicia Patterson Foundation Fellowship 1978, American Bar Asscn Certificate of Merit 1983, UNEP Global 500 Honor Roll 1989, American Soc. of Professional Journalists Public Service Award 1990. *Address:* POB 793, North Truro, MA 02652, USA (office).

BRODY, Jane Ellen, MS; American journalist and author; *Personal Health Columnist, New York Times*; b. 19 May 1941, Brooklyn, New York; d. of Sidney Brody and Lillian Kellner; m. Richard Engquist 1966; twin s. *Education:* New York State Coll. of Agric., Cornell Univ., Univ. of Wisconsin. *Career:* reporter, Minneapolis Tribune 1963–65; science writer, personal health columnist, New York Times 1965–; mem. Advisory Council, New York State Coll. of Agric. 1971–77. *Publications:* Secrets of Good Health (with R. Engquist) 1970, You Can Fight Cancer and Win (with A. Holleb) 1977, Jane Brody's Nutrition Book 1981, Jane Brody's New York Times Guide to Personal Health 1982, Jane Brody's Good Food Book 1985, Jane Brody's Good Food Gourmet 1990, Jane Brody's Good Seafood Book (with Richard Flaste) 1994, Jane Brody's Cold and Flu Fighter 1995, Jane Brody's Allergy Fighter 1997, The New York Times Book of Health 1997, The New York Times Book of Women's Health 2000, The New York Times Book of Alternative Medicine 2001, Jane Brody's Guide to the Great Beyond 2009. *Honours:* Dr hc (Princeton Univ., Hamline Univ., Univ. of Minnesota School of Public Health, State Univ. of New York School of Public Health); Howard Blakeslee Award, American Heart Asscn 1971, Science Writers' Award, ADA 1978, J.C. Penney Univ. of Missouri Journalism Award 1978, Lifeline Award, American Health Foundation 1978. *Address:* New York Times, 620 Eighth Avenue, New York, NY 10018, USA (office). *E-mail:* engquist@nytimes.com (office). *Website:* www.nytimes.com (office); janebrody.net (home).

BRØGGER, Suzanne; Danish writer, poet and dramatist; b. 18 Nov. 1944, Copenhagen; m. Keld Zeruneith 1991. *Education:* Univ. of Copenhagen. *Career:* mem. Danish Acad., Rungstedlund-The Karen Blixen Museum. *Publications include:* Fri os fra kærlighed (Deliver Us From Love) 1973, Kærlighedens veje og vildveje (Love's Paths and Pitfalls) 1975, Creme Fraiche (Crème Fraîche) 1978, Ja (Yes) 1984, Efter Orgiet (play, After the Orgy) 1991, Transparence (Transparency) 1993, Mørk (play, Dark) 1994, En gris der har været oppe at slås kan man ikke stege (A Fighting Pig is Too Tough to Eat) 1979, Tone (epic poem) 1981, Vølvens spådom (Völuspá, adaptation) 1994, The Jade Cat (novel, in trans.) 1997, Jadekatten 1999, Sejd 2001, Smuler fra kaerlighedens bord 2004, Et Frit og muntert lig 2005, Blå biografi 2006, Sølve 2007, Sløret 2008, Jeg har set den gamle verden forsvinde-hvor er mine øreringe? 2010. *Honours:* Kt of the Dannebrog; Dr hc (Copenhagen); numerous Danish awards. *Address:* Gyldendal, Klareboderne 3, 1001 Copenhagen K, Denmark (office). *E-mail:* gyldendal@gyldendal.dk (office). *Website:* www.gyldendal.dk (office).

BROKAW, Thomas (Tom) John, BA; American broadcast journalist and writer; b. 6 Feb. 1940, Webster, S Dakota; s. of Anthony O. Brokaw and Eugenia Conley; m. Meredith Lynn Auld 1962; three d. *Education:* Univ. of South Dakota. *Career:* morning news KMTV, Omaha 1962–65; news ed., anchorman, WSB-TV, Atlanta 1965–66; reporter, corresp., anchorman KNBC-TV, Los Angeles 1966–73; White House corresp. NBC, Washington, DC 1973–76; anchorman, Saturday Night News, New York 1973–76; host, Today Show, New York 1976–82; anchor and Man. Ed., NBC Nightly News 1982–2004 (retd), Special Corresp. NBC News 2005–; mem. Bd of Dirs Council on Foreign Relations, Cttee to Protect Journalists, Int. Rescue Cttee; mem. advisory cttee Reporters Cttee for Freedom of Press, Gannett Journalism Center, Columbia Univ.; Trustee, Norton Simon Museum of Art, Pasadena, Calif.; mem. American Acad. of Arts and Sciences. *Publications:* The Greatest Generation 1998, The Greatest Generation Speaks 1999, An Album of Memories 2001, A Long Way from Home 2002, Boom! Voices of the Sixties 2007, The Time of Our Lives: A Conversation about America 2011. *Honours:* Dr hc (Univ. of South Dakota), (Washington Univ., St. Louis), (Syracuse Univ.), (Hofstra Univ.), (Boston Coll.), (Emerson Coll.), (Simpson Coll.), (Duke Univ.) 1991, (Notre Dame Univ.) 1993; Hon. DHL (Dartmouth Coll.) 2005; two Dupont Awards, Peabody Award, Alfred I. duPont-Columbia Univ. Award for Excellence in Broadcast Journalism 1997, ten Emmy Awards including Emmy for Outstanding Interview 2003, Records of Achievement Award, Foundation for the Nat. Archives 2005, George Catlett Marshall Medal, Asscn of the US Army 2005, Edward R. Murrow Award for Lifetime Achievement in Broadcasting, Wash. State Univ. 2006, Sylvanus Thayer Award, US Military Acad. at West Point 2006, Walter Cronkite Award for Journalism Excellence, Ariz. State Univ. 2006; elected to TV Hall of Fame 1997. *Address:* c/o Board of Directors, Council on Foreign Relations, The Harold Pratt House, 58 East 68th Street, New York, NY 10021, USA (office).

BROCKOVICH-ELLIS, Erin L. E.; American legal clerk, environmental activist and television host; *President, Brockovich Research & Consulting*; b. 28 June 1960, Lawrence, Kan.; d. of Frank Pattee and Betty Jo O'Neal-Pattee; m. 1st Shawn Brown 1982 (divorced 1987); one s. one d.; m. 2nd Steven Brockovich 1989 (divorced 1990); one d.; m. 3rd Eric L. Ellis 1999. *Education:* Lawrence High School, Wades Business Coll., Kansas State Univ., Manhattan, Kan. *Career:* worked as man. trainee for K-Mart, Southern Calif. 1981, then at Fluor Engineers and Constructor, Southern Calif., then sec. at local brokerage, Kan. 1989; host, Challenge America with Erin Brockovich on ABC 2001, Final Justice on Lifetime 2003; has participated with Edward L. Masry in other anti-pollution lawsuits; currently consultant for Weitz & Luxenberg (law firm), New York. *Achievements include:* helped construct case against Pacific Gas & Electric Co. of California 1993 which alleged contamination of drinking water with chromium (VI), in southern California town of Hinkley, case settled for US$333 million (largest settlement ever paid in a direct action lawsuit in US history) 1996;. *Publications:* Rock Bottom (with C. J. Lyons) 2011, Hot Water (with C. J. Lyons) 2011. *Honours:* Hon. DHumLitt (Loyola Marymount Univ., Los Angeles) 2007; Miss Pacific Coast 1981; Award, Harvard School of Public Health 2005, Commencement Speaker, Loyola Marymount Univ. 2007. *Literary Agent:* c/o William Morris Agency, One William Morris Place, Beverly Hills, CA 90212, USA. *Telephone:* (310) 859-4000. *Fax:* (310) 859-4462. *Website:* www.wma.com. *E-mail:* erin@brockovich.com (office). *Website:* www.brockovich.com (office); www.brockovichblog.com (office); myspace.com/erin_brockovich.

BROKS, Paul, DPhil; British neuropsychologist. *Education:* Univs of Sheffield and Oxford. *Career:* practising neuropsychologist, Leeds and Sheffield; academic posts at Birmingham and Sheffield; Sr Clinical Lecturer, Univ. of Plymouth 2000; columnist Prospect Magazine. *Publications:* Into the Silent Land: Travels in Neuropsychology 2003; contrib. to Schitzotypy: Implications for Illness and Health 1997, numerous journals. *Address:* School of Psychology, University of Plymouth, A202, Portland Square, Drake Circus, Plymouth, Devon, PL4 8AA, England (office). *Telephone:* (1752) 233826 (office). *E-mail:* p.broks@plymouth.ac.uk (office). *Website:* www.psy.plymouth.ac.uk (office).

BROMBERT, Victor Henri, BA, MA, PhD; American writer and academic; *Professor Emeritus of Romance and Comparative Literatures, Princeton University*; b. 11 Nov. 1923, Germany; m. Beth Anne Archer 1950; one s. one d. *Education:* Yale Univ., Univ. of Rome, Italy. *Career:* Faculty, Yale Univ. 1951–75, Assoc. Prof. 1958–61, Prof. 1961–75, Benjamin F. Barge Prof. of Romance Literatures 1969–75; Henry Putnam Univ. Prof. of Romance and Comparative Literatures, Princeton Univ. 1975–99, Prof. Emer. of Romance and Comparative Literatures 1999–; many visiting lectureships and professorships; mem. American Comparative Literature Asscn, American Asscn of Teachers of French, American Philosophical Soc., Modern Language Asscn (Pres. 1989), Soc. des Études Françaises, Soc. des Études Romantiques; Fellow, American Acad. of Arts and Sciences. *Publications:* The Criticism of T. S. Eliot 1949, Stendhal et la Voie Oblique 1954, The Intellectual Hero 1961, Stendhal: A Collection of Critical Essays (ed.) 1962, The Novels of Flaubert 1966, Stendhal: Fiction and the Themes of Freedom 1968, Flaubert par lui-même 1971, La Prison romantique 1976, The Romantic Prison: The French Tradition 1978, Victor Hugo and the Visionary Novel 1984, The Hidden Reader 1988, In Praise of Antiheroes 1999, Trains of Thought 2002, Les trains du souvenir 2005, Stendhal: Roman et liberté 2007; contribs to many books, journals and periodicals. *Honours:* Commdr, Ordre des Palmes académiques, Chevalier, Légion d'Honneur 2008; Hon. LHD (Chicago) 1981; Hon. HLD (Toronto) 1997; Fulbright Fellowship 1950–51, Guggenheim Fellowships 1954–55, 1970, Nat. Endowment for the Humanities Sr Fellow 1973–74, Rockefeller Foundation Resident Fellow, Bellagio, Italy 1975, 1990, Harry Levin Prize for Comparative Literature 1978, Médaille Vermeil de la Ville de Paris 1985. *Address:* 49 Constitution Hill W, Princeton, NJ 08540, USA (home).

BRONNER, Leila Leah, BA, MA, LittD; American academic and writer; b. 22 April 1930, Czechoslovakia; m. Joseph Bronner 1950; three c. *Education:* Beth Jacob Teachers Seminary of America, Hebrew University, Jerusalem, University of the Witwatersand, University of Pretoria. *Career:* Assoc. Prof., University of the Witwatersrand 1960–84; Senior Lecturer, Hebrew Teachers College 1966–78; Visiting Fellow, Harvard University 1984; Visiting Prof., Yeshiva University 1985–87; Visiting Scholar, University of Southern California at Los Angeles 1986–87; Adjunct Assoc. Prof., University of Judaism 1987–90; Prof., Institute of Bible and Jewish Studies 1991–; mem. American Society for Religion;, Asscn of Jewish Studies, National Asscn of Profs of Hebrew, Ou Testamentiese Werkgemeenskap in Suid Africa, Society for Biblical Literature, World Union of Jewish Studies, Jerusalem. *Publications:* Sects and Separatism During the Second Jewish Commonwealth 1967, The Stories of Elijah and Elisha 1968, Biblical Personalities and Archaeology 1974, From Eve to Esther: The Rabbinic Reconstruction of Biblical Woman 1994, Stories of Biblical Mothers: Maternal Power in the Hebrew Bible 2004; contributions: numerous books and journals. *Honours:* Leila Bronner School, Johannesburg, named after her. *Address:* 180 N Las Palmas Avenue, Los Angeles, CA 90004-1048, USA (home). *Telephone:* (323) 933-8476 (home). *Website:* www.bibleandjewishstudies.com.

BRØNNUM, Jakob, MA (Theol); Danish author and poet; *Editor, Præsteforeningens Blad*; b. 16 April 1959, Copenhagen; m. Rúna í Baianstovu 2009; one s. one d. *Career:* Ed., Præsteforeningens Blad 1997–; Chair. Baltic Writers' Council 1999–2002; mem. Danish Writers' Asscn; mem. Council of Innovation, HUMUS Acad., Univ. of Örebro 2008–11. *Publications:* Skyggedage (prose) 1989, Europadigte (poems) 1991, Den Lange Søndag (novel) 1994, Mørke (novel) 1996, Sjaelen og Landskaberne (poems) 1997, Kulturhistoriske Årstal (reference) 2001, Kun sig selv (novel) 2004, Vejen ud og vejen hjem (poems) 2004, Forfølgeren (novel) 2007, Pinballmesterens Drøm (short story) 2010, Månen i din hånd 2010; contrib. among other books to: Sproget i litteraturen, Gyldendals sprogbøger (short story) 2007, Rockprofeter (essay) 2008; contrib. to Literaturnaja Gazetta (Russia), Parnasso (Finland), Lyrikvännen (Sweden). *Honours:* Grant Statens Kunstfond (Denmark) 2005, 2008. *Website:* sites.google.com/site/jakobbronnum.

BROOKE, Christopher Nugent Lawrence, CBE, MA, LittD, FBA, FRHistS, FSA; British historian and academic; *Professor Emeritus, University of Cambridge*; b. 23 June 1927, Cambridge, England; s. of Zachary Nugent Brooke and Rosa Grace Brooke (née Stanton); m. Rosalind Beckford Clark 1951; three s. (one deceased). *Education:* Winchester Coll., Gonville and Caius Coll., Cambridge. *Career:* Fellow, Gonville and Caius Coll., Cambridge 1949–56, 1977–, Asst Lecturer, Univ. of Cambridge 1953–54, Lecturer 1954–56, Dixie Prof. of Ecclesiastical History 1977–94, Prof. Emer. 1994–; Prof. of Medieval History, Univ. of Liverpool 1956–67; Prof. of History, Westfield Coll., London 1967–77; Pres. Soc. of Antiquaries 1981–84; mem. Royal Comm. on Historical Monuments 1977–83, Reviewing Comm. on Export of Works of Art 1979–82; Corresp. mem. Monumenta Germaniae Historica, Bavarian Acad. of Sciences; Corresp. Fellow, Medieval Acad. of America; Fellow, Società Internazionale di Studi Francescani. *Publications include:* The Letters of John of Salisbury Vol. I (ed.) 1955, From Alfred to Henry III 1961, The Saxon and Norman Kings 1963, Europe in the Central Middle Ages 1964, Gilbert Foliot and his Letters (with A. Morey) 1965, Time the Archsatirist 1968, The Twelfth Century Renaissance 1969, Structure of Medieval Society 1971, London 800–1216 (with G. Keir) 1975, Marriage in Christian History 1977, The Letters of John of Salisbury vol. II (ed.) 1979, Oxford (fmrly Nelson's) Medieval Texts (gen. ed.) 1979–87, Nelson's History of England (gen. ed.), Councils and Synods Vol. I (co-ed. with D. Whitelock and M. Brett) 1981, Popular Religion in the Middle Ages, 1000–1300 (with Rosalind Brooke) 1984, A History of Gonville and Caius College 1985, Oxford and Cambridge (with Roger Highfield and Wim Swaan) 1988, A History of the University of Cambridge (four vols) 1988–2004, The Medieval Idea of Marriage 1989, Churches and Churchmen in Medieval Europe (with R. B. Brooke) 1999, Jane Austen: Illusion and Reality 1999, The Age of the Cloister 2001; contribs: articles and reviews to professional journals. *Honours:* Hon. DUniv (York) 1984; Lord Mayor's Midsummer Prize City of London 1981. *Address:* Gonville and Caius College, Cambridge, CB2 1TA, England (home).

BROOKE, Robert Taliaferro (Tal), BA, MA; American author and lecturer; b. 21 Jan. 1945, Washington, DC. *Education:* Univ. of Virginia, Princeton Univ. *Career:* Vice-Pres. of Public Relations, Telecom Inc 1982–83; Pres. and Chair., Spiritual Counterfeits Project Inc, Conservative think-tank, Berkeley, CA 1989–; founder End Run Publ. 1999–; lecturer on Eastern thought and the occult at colls, univs, conventions and seminars in the USA and abroad; many radio and television appearances; mem. Int. Platform Asscn, Authors' Guild, Soc. of the Cincinnati. *Publications:* Lord of the Air 1976, 1990, The Other Side of Death 1979, Riders of the Cosmic Circuit 1986, Millennium Edition 2002, Avatar of Night 1987, Harvest (with Chuck Smith) 1988, When the World Will Be As One 1989, Virtual Gods 1997, Conspiracy to Silence the Son 1998, One World 2000, The Mystery of Death 2001. *Honours:* Spring Arbor Nat. Bestseller 1989, first place Critical Review Category, Nat. EPA Awards 1991. *Address:* SCP Inc, PO Box 4308, Berkeley, CA 94704, USA (office). *Telephone:* (510) 540-0300 (office). *Website:* www.scp-inc.org (office); www.endrunpublishing.com (office).

BROOKENS, Diane, BEd, MA; British/American teacher, poet and writer; *Founder and Director, Naturama School of Drama*; b. 29 May 1952, Raleigh, NC, USA; d. of the late Floyd Brigham Brookens and Marjorie Brookens (née Snape). *Education:* Univ. of London, Hertfordshire Univ. *Career:* Founder-Dir, Naturama School of Drama 1985– (devised own form of drama, Naturama, exploring nature and human nature through drama); appearances on radio and TV, including poetry readings on BBC Radio Lancashire 1997–2004; poetry performances at 125th Anniversary of The Winter Gardens, Blackpool 2003; mem. Asscn of Lamda Teachers, Writers' Guild of GB, Actors' Equity. *Publications:* The Artistic Value of the American Musical 1977, Timothy Earle and Other Poems for Children 1986, Poems from a Chrysalis 1997, A Linguistic Analysis of Past Life Regression 1998, Across the Atlantic: Memories of America 2000, Back to Blackpool: The Lancashire Poems 2001; contrib. to poetry magazines and reviews. *Honours:* first prize for self-publishing poetry, David Thomas Charitable Trust, Writers News and Writing Magazine 1998. *Address:* 41 Park Lane, Little Ratton, Eastbourne, East Sussex, BN21 2UY, England (home). *E-mail:* dbrookens1@talktalk.net (home). *Website:* www.dianebrookens.com; www.naturama.info.

BROOKNER, Anita, CBE, BA, PhD, FRSL; British academic, writer and art historian; b. 16 July 1928, London; d. of Newson Brookner and Maude Brookner. *Education:* James Allen's Girls' School, King's Coll., London, Courtauld Inst. and Paris. *Career:* Visiting Lecturer in Art History, Univ. of Reading 1959–64; Lecturer, Courtauld Inst. of Art 1964–77, Reader in Art History 1977–87; Slade Prof., Univ. of Cambridge 1967–68; Fellow, New Hall Cambridge, King's Coll. London. *Publications:* fiction: A Start in Life 1981, Providence 1982, Look at Me 1983, Hôtel du Lac (Booker Prize) 1984, Family and Friends 1985, A Misalliance 1986, A Friend from England 1987, Latecomers 1988, Lewis Percy 1989, Brief Lives 1990, A Closed Eye 1991, Fraud 1992, A Family Romance 1993, A Private View 1994, Incidents in the rue Laugier 1995, Altered States 1996, Soundings 1997, Visitors 1997, Falling Slowly 1998, Undue Influence 1999, The Bay of Angels 2000, The Next Big Thing 2002, The Rules of Engagement 2003, Leaving Home 2005, Strangers 2009; non-fiction: An Iconography of Cecil Rhodes 1956, J. A. Dominique Ingres 1965, Watteau 1968, The Genius of the Future: Studies in French Art Criticism 1971, Greuze: The Rise and Fall of an Eighteenth-Century Phenomenon 1972, Jacques-Louis David, a Personal Interpretation: Lecture on Aspects of Art 1974, Jacques-Louis David 1980; editor: The Stories of Edith Wharton (two vols) 1988; contrib. to books and periodicals, including Burlington Magazine. *Honours:* Commdr, Ordre des Arts et Lettres 2002; Hon. DLitt (Loughborough Univ. of Tech.) 1990; Dr hc (Smith Coll., USA). *Address:* 68 Elm Park Gardens, London, SW10 9PB, England (home). *Telephone:* (20) 7352-6894 (home).

BROOKS, George Edward, MA, PhD; American academic, historian and writer; *Professor Emeritus, Indiana University*; b. 20 April 1933, Lynn, MA; m. 1st Mary C. Crowley 1957; two s.; m. 2nd Elaine Claire Rivron 1985; two d. *Education:* Dartmouth Coll., Boston Univ. *Career:* instructor, Boston Univ. 1960, 1962; Asst Prof., Indiana Univ. 1962–68, Assoc. Prof. 1968–75, Prof. 1975–2007, Prof. Emer. 2007–; Visiting Assoc. Prof., Tufts Univ. 1969; Visiting Fulbright Prof., Univ. of Zimbabwe 1984; Visiting Prof., Shandong Univ., People's Repub. of China 1985; mem. Liberian Studies Asscn, MANSA/Mande Studies Asscn, World History Asscn (mem. Exec. Council 1990–93); Fellow, African Studies Asscn. *Publications:* New England Merchants in Africa: A History Through Documents 1802–1865 (co-ed. with Norman R. Bennett) 1965, Yankee Traders, Old Coasters and African Middlemen: A History of American Legitimate Trade with West Africa in the Nineteenth Century 1970, The Kru Mariner in the Nineteenth Century: An Historical Compendium 1972, Themes in African and World History 1973, Perspectives on Luso-African Commerce and Settlement in The Gambia and Guinea-Bissau Region, 16th–19th Centuries 1980, Kola Trade and State-Building: Upper Guinea Coast and Senegambia, 15th–17th Centuries 1980, Western Africa to c. 1860 A.D.: A Provisional Historical Schema Based on Climate Periods 1985, Landlords and Strangers: Ecology, Society, and Trade in Western Africa, 1000–1630 1993, The Aspen World History Handbook: An Organizational Framework, Lessons, and Book Reviews for Non-Centric World History (co-ed. with Dik A. Daso, Marilynn Hitchens, and Heidi Roupp) 1994, Getting Along Together: World History Perspectives for the 21st Century 1999, Eurafricans in Western Africa: Commerce, Social Status, Gender and Religious Observance from the Sixteenth to the Eighteenth Century 2003; contrib. to many scholarly books and journals. *Honours:* Ford Foundation Training Fellowship 1960–62, Social Science Research Council grant 1971–72, Nat. Endowment for the Humanities grant 1976–77, Indiana Univ. Pres.'s Council on Int. Programs Award 1978, American Council of Learned Socs grant 1990, Visiting Fellowship, Africa: Precolonial Achievement Conf., Humanities Research Centre, ANU 1995. *Telephone:* (812) 855-7581 (office). *Website:* www.indiana.edu (office).

BROOKS, Geraldine; Australian writer and journalist; b. 1955, Sydney; m. Tony Horwitz 1984; two c. *Education:* Bethlehem Coll., Ashfield, Univ. of Sydney, Columbia Univ., USA. *Career:* began her career as reporter, Sydney Morning Herald; worked for The Wall Street Journal, New York, covering crises in the Middle East, Africa, the Balkans. *Publications:* novels: Year of Wonders 2001, March (Pulitzer Prize in Fiction 2006) 2005, People of the Book 2008; non-fiction: Nine Parts of Desire: The Hidden World of Islamic Women 1994, Foreign Correspondence 1997. *Honours:* Greg Shackleton Australian News Correspondents Scholarship 1982, Dayton Literary Peace Prize for Lifetime Achievement 2010. *Address:* c/o Louise Braverman, Viking Penguin Publicity, Penguin Group USA, 375 Hudson Street, 4th Floor, New York, NY 10014, USA (office). *E-mail:* louise.braverman@us.penguingroup.com (office). *Website:* www.geraldinebrooks.com.

BROOKS, Mel; American actor, writer, producer and director; b. (Melvin Kaminsky Brooks), 28 June 1926, Brooklyn, New York, NY; m. 1st Florence Baum; two s. one d.; m. 2nd Anne Bancroft 1964 (died 2005); one s. *Career:* script writer for TV series Your Show of Shows 1950–54, Caesar's Hour 1954–57, Get Smart 1965; set up feature film production co. Brooksfilms. *Television:* Get Smart (writer) 1965–70, The Nutt House (writer) 1989, Mad About You (Emmy Award for Outstanding Guest Actor in a Comedy Series 1997, 1998, 1999). *Films include:* The Critic (writer, cartoon) (Academy Award 1964) 1963, The Producers (writer, dir) (Acad. Award for Best Screenplay) 1968, The Twelve Chairs (writer, dir, actor) 1970, Shinbone Alley (writer) 1971, Blazing Saddles (writer, dir, actor) 1974, Young Frankenstein (writer, dir) 1974, Silent Movie (writer, dir, actor) 1976, High Anxiety (writer, dir, actor, producer) 1977, The Muppet Movie (actor) 1979, The Elephant Man (exec. producer) 1980, History of the World Part I (writer, dir, actor, producer) 1981, My Favourite Year 1982, To Be or Not to Be (actor, producer) 1983, The Doctor and the Devils (exec. producer) 1985, Solarbabies (exec. producer) 1986, Fly I 1986, Spaceballs (writer, dir, actor, producer) 1987, 84 Charing Cross Road (exec. producer) 1987, Fly II 1989, Life Stinks (writer, dir, actor, producer) 1991, The Vagrant (exec. producer) 1992, Robin Hood: Men in Tights (writer, dir, actor, producer) 1993, The Little Rascals (actor) 1994, Dracula: Dead and Loving It (writer, dir, actor, producer) 1995, Svitati (actor) 1999, The Producers: The Movie Musical 2005. *Musical:* The Producers (producer, co-writer, composer) (Tony Awards for Best Book, Best Score, Best Musical 2001, Evening Standard Award for Best Musical 2004, Critics Circle Theatre Award for Best Musical 2005) 2001, Young Frankenstein 2007. *Honours:* Kennedy Center Honor 2009. *Address:* c/o The Culver Studios, 9336 W Washington Boulevard, Culver City, CA 90232, USA (office).

BROSMAN, Catharine Savage, BA, MA, PhD; American academic, poet and writer; *Professor Emerita of French, Tulane University*; b. (Catharine Hill), 7 June 1934, Denver, Colo; d. of Paul Victor Hill and Della Hill (née Stanforth); m. 1st Patric Savage 1955 (divorced 1964, re-m. 2008); m. 2nd Paul W.

Brosman, Jr 1970 (divorced 1993); one d. *Education:* Rice Univ. *Career:* Instructor, Rice Univ. 1960–62; Asst Prof. of French, Sweet Briar Coll. 1962–63, Univ. of Florida 1963–66; Assoc. Prof. of French, Mary Baldwin Coll. 1966–68; Assoc. Prof. of French, Tulane Univ. 1968–72, Prof. of French 1972–92, Andrew W. Mellon Prof. of Humanities 1990, Kathryn B. Gore Prof. of French 1992–96, Prof. Emerita 1997–; De Velling and Willis Visiting Prof., Univ. of Sheffield, UK 1996; Poetry Ed., Chronicles: A Magazine of American Culture, 2007–. *Publications:* poetry (with prose): Watering 1972, Abiding Winter 1983, Journeying from Canyon de Chelly 1990, The Shimmering Maya and Other Essays 1994, Passages 1996, The Swimmer and Other Poems 2000, Places in Mind 2000, Finding Higher Ground: A Life of Travels 2003, Petroglyphs: Poems and Prose 2003, The Muscled Truce 2003, Range of Light 2007, Breakwater 2009, Trees in a Park 2010, Under the Pergola 2011; non-fiction: André Gide: l'évolution de sa pensée religieuse 1962, Malraux, Sartre, and Aragon as Political Novelists 1964, Roger Martin du Gard 1968, Jean-Paul Sartre 1983, Jules Roy 1988, Art as Testimony: The Work of Jules Roy 1989, An Annotated Bibliography of Criticism on André Gide, 1973–1988 1990, Simone de Beauvoir Revisited 1991, Visions of War in France: Fiction, Art, Ideology 1999, Existential Fiction 2000, Albert Camus 2000; editor: French Novelists, 1900–1930 1988, French Novelists, 1930–1960 1988, French Novelists since 1960 1989, Nineteenth-Century French Fiction Writers, 1800–1860: Romantics and Realists 1992, Nineteenth-Century French Fiction Writers, 1860–1900: Naturalists and Beyond 1992, Twentieth-Century French Culture, 1900–1975 1995, Retour aux 'Nourritures terrestres': Le Centenaire d'un bréviaire (with David H. Walker) 1997; contrib. to Southern Review, Sewanee Review, Southwest Review, New England Review, Georgia Review, Shenandoah, Critical Quarterly, Interim, American Scholar, South Carolina Review, Europe (Paris), Nouvelle Revue Française. *Honours:* Third Place Award, Best Poems of 1973, Distinguished Alumna Award, Rice Univ. 2000. *Address:* 2001 Holcombe Boulevard, Suite 1705, Houston, TX 77030 (home); 417 East Kiowa Street, Suite 406, Colorado Springs, CO 80903, USA (summer) (home). *Telephone:* (281) 814-1758 (home); (719) 227-1368 (summer) (home). *E-mail:* cbrosman@tulane.edu (home).

BROSSARD, Nicole, OC, LèsL; Canadian poet and novelist; b. 1943, Montréal, Québec; one d. *Education:* Université de Montréal, Université du Québec, Montréal. *Career:* mem. Acad. des Lettres du Québec 1993–, Soc. Royale du Canada 2006–; named to Assemblée parlementaire de la francophonie. *Publications:* poetry: Mécanique jongleuse (trans. as Daydream Mechanics) 1973, Le centre blanc 1978, The Story So Far 6 (ed.) 1978, Amantes (trans. as Lovhers) 1980, Double Impression 1984, Mauve 1984, Journal intime (trans. as Intimate Journal) 1984, Character/Jeu de lettres 1986, Sous la langue/Under Tongue (bilingual edn) 1987, A tout regard 1989, Installations (trans. as Installations) 1989, Langues obscures 1991, Anthologie de la poésie des femmes au Québec (ed.) 1991, La Nuit verte du parc labyrinthe (trilingual edn) 1992, Vertige de l'avant-scène 1997, Musée de l'os et de l'eau (trans. as Museum of Bone and Water) 1999, Au présent des veines 1999, Poèmes à dire la francophonie 2002, Cahier de roses et de civilisation (trans. as Notebook of Roses and Civilization) 2003, Je m'en vais à Trieste 2003, Mobility of Light 2008, Ardeur 2008, D'aube et de civilisation 2008, Selections: the Poetry of Nicole Brossard 2009, Lointaines 2010; fiction: Un livre (trans. as A Book) 1970, Sold-Out (trans. as Turn of a Pang) 1973, French Kiss (trans.) 1974, L'amèr (trans. as These Our Mothers, or, The Disintegrating Chapter) 1977, Le Sens apparent (trans. as Surfaces of Sense) 1980, Picture Theory (trans.) 1982, Le Désert mauve (trans. as Mauve Desert) 1987, Baroque d'aube (trans. as Baroque at Dawn) 1995, Hier (trans. as Yesterday, at the Hotel Clarendon) 2001, The Blue Books 2003, La Capture du Sombre (trans. as Fences in Breathing) 2007; essays: La Lettre aérienne (trans. as The Aerial Letter) 1985; contrib. to numerous anthologies. *Honours:* Chevalier, Ordre de la Pléiade 2006; Dr hc (Western Ontario) 1991, (Sherbrooke) 1997; Gov.-Gen. Prizes 1974, 1984, Therafields Foundation Chapbook Award 1986, Foundation Les Forges Grand Prix de Poésie 1989, 1999, Prix Athanase-David 1991, Prix W.O. Mitchell 2003, Molson Prize, Canada Council of Arts 2006. *Address:* 34 avenue Robert, Outrement, QC H3S 2P2, Canada (home). *E-mail:* nicolebrossard60@hotmail.com (home).

BROTTON, Jerry, BA, MA, PhD; British historian, academic and writer; *Professor of Renaissance Studies, Queen Mary, University of London. Education:* Univs of Sussex, Essex and London. *Career:* Prof. of Renaissance Studies, School of English and Drama, Queen Mary, Univ. of London; Sr Visiting Fellow, Centre for Editing Lives and Letters; Visiting Research Fellow, The Globe theatre, London; Trustee, J. B. Harley Trust. *Television:* Leonardo (contrib., BBC 1), Medici (series consultant and contrib., Channel 4), Newsnight Review (BBC 2). *Publications:* Trading Territories: Mapping the Early Modern World 1997, Global Interests: Renaissance Art between East and West (with Lisa Jardine) 2000, The Renaissance Bazaar: From the Silk Road to Michelangelo 2002, The Renaissance: A Very Short Introduction 2006, The Sale of the Late King's Goods: Charles I and his Art Collection 2006; contrib. of articles and reviews to Literary Review, BBC History Magazine, The New Statesman. *Honours:* Leverhulme Research Fellow 2002, Arts and Humanities Research Council Research Leave Scheme 2006–07, 2010–11. *Address:* School of English and Drama, Queen Mary, University of London, Mile End Road, London, E1 4NS, England (office). *E-mail:* j.r.brotton@qmul.ac.uk (office).

BROUMAS, Olga, BA, MFA; Greek poet and translator; *Co-Director of Creative Writing, Brandeis University*; b. 6 May 1949, Hermoupolis; m. Stephen Edward Bangs 1973 (divorced 1979). *Education:* Univ. of Pennsylvania, Univ. of Oregon at Eugene. *Career:* Instructor, Univ. of Oregon 1972–76; Visiting Assoc. Prof., Univ. of Idaho 1978; Poet-in-Residence, Goddard Coll., Plainfield, Vt 1979–81, Women Writers' Center, Cazenovia, New York 1981–82; Founder-Assoc. Faculty, Freehand Women Writers' and Photographers' Community, Provincetown, Mass 1982–87; Visiting Assoc. Prof., Boston Univ. 1988–90; Fanny Hurst Poet-in-Residence 1990, Co-Dir of Creative Writing 1995–, Brandeis Univ. *Publications:* Restlessness 1967, Caritas 1976, Beginning with O 1977, Soie Sauvage 1980, Pastoral Jazz 1983, Black Holes Black Stockings 1985, Perpetua 1989, Sappho's Gymnasium 1994, Rave: Poems 1975–1999 1999; translations of poems and essays of Greek Nobel Laureate, Odysseas Elytis: What I Love 1986, The Little Mariner 1988, Open Papers, Selected Essays 1995, Eros, Eros, Eros: Poems, Selected and Last 1997, Rave: Poems 1975–1999 1999. *Honours:* Yale Younger Poets Award 1977, Nat. Endowment for the Arts Grant 1978, Guggenheim Fellowship 1981–82. *Address:* Department of English and American Literature, Brandeis University, MS 023, PO Box 549110, Waltham, MA 02454-9110 (office); 162 Mill Pond Drive, Brewster, MA 02631, USA (home). *Telephone:* (781) 736-2157 (office). *E-mail:* broumas@brandeis.edu (office). *Website:* www.brandeis.edu/departments/english (office).

BROVINA, Flora, PhD; Albanian poet, pediatrician and activist; b. 30 Sept. 1949, Skënderaj, Kosovo; m.; two s. *Education:* Medical School of Prishtina Univ., Medical School of Univ. of Zagreb. *Career:* newspaper journalist, Rilindja, Prishtina 1973–81; pediatrician –1989; founder, League of Albanian Women of Kosova 1992; est. Center for the Rehabilitation of Women and Children 1998, imprisoned by Serbian Paramilitary 1999, released 2000; subsequently est. centre for war orphans; fmr editorial bd mem. Kosovarja and Teuta magazines; unsuccessful presidential cand. in Kosovo elections 2001. *Publications:* Verma emrin tim (Call Me by My Name) 1973, Bimë e zë (Plant and Voice) 1979, Snowball Flower 1988, Mat e çmat (With the Tape it Measures) 1995. *Honours:* Swedish PEN Club Tucholsky Award 1999, honoured by AAAS 2001, UNIFEM and Int. Alert UN Millennium Peace Prize for Women 2001, American PEN Center Barbara Goldsmith Freedom to Write Award 2000, Dutch PEN Award 2000, Foundation of Child and Family/UNESCO Woman of the Balkans Award 2000, Jonathan Mann Award for Health and Human Rights 2000, (jtly) 2004, La Ferthe Award 2000, Heinrich Böll Foundation Human Rights Award, Berlin 2000.

BROWN, Andrew; British writer. *Career:* Scandinavia correspondent and reporter, The Spectator 1980s; Religious Affairs correspondent, writer, Independent 1986–96; currently writes for the Guardian, writes and presents analysis programmes for BBC Radio 4. *Publications:* Watching the Detectives 1988, The Darwin Wars: The Scientific Battle for the Soul of Man 2002, In the Beginning was the Worm: Finding the Secrets of Life in a Tiny Hermaphrodite 2003, Fishing in Utopia: Sweden and the Future that Disappeared (Orwell Prize for Political Writing 2009) 2008; contrib. to News of the World, Vogue, New York Review of Books, Guardian, Times, Sunday Telegraph, Daily Mail, Daily Express, Church Times, New Statesman, Salon, Waterlog. *Honours:* Templeton Prize 1995. *Address:* c/o The Guardian, Kings Place, 90 York Way, London N1 9GU, England (office). *E-mail:* andrew.brown@guardian.co.uk (office); blog_comments@thewormbook.com (office). *Website:* www.guardian.co.uk (office); www.thewormbook.com (office).

BROWN, Archibald Haworth, CMG, BSc, MA, FBA; British academic and writer; *Professor Emeritus of Politics, University of Oxford*; b. 10 May 1938, Annan, Scotland; m. Patricia Susan Cornwell 1963; one s. one d. *Education:* London School of Econs, Univ. of Oxford. *Career:* Lecturer in Politics, Univ. of Glasgow 1964–71; British Council Exchange Scholar, Moscow Univ., USSR 1967–68; Lecturer in Soviet Institutions, Univ. of Oxford 1971–89, Prof. of Politics 1989–2005, Prof. Emer. 2005–; Visiting Prof. and Henry L. Stimson Lecturer, Yale Univ., USA 1980; Visiting Prof., Univ. of Connecticut 1980, Columbia Univ. 1985, Univ. of Texas, Austin 1990–91; Distinguished Visiting Fellow, Kellogg Inst. for Int. Studies, Univ. of Notre Dame, USA 1998; mem. American Asscn for the Advancement of Slavic Studies, American Political Science Asscn, British Nat. Asscn for Slavonic and East European Studies, Political Studies Asscn of the UK, Acad. of Learned Socs for the Social Sciences. *Publications:* Soviet Politics and Political Science 1974, The Soviet Union since the Fall of Khrushchev (co-ed. with Michael Kaser) 1975, Political Culture and Political Change in Communist States (co-ed. with Jack Gray) 1977, Authority, Power, and Policy in the USSR: Essays Dedicated to Leonard Schapiro (co-ed. with T. H. Rigby and Peter Reddaway) 1980, The Cambridge Encyclopedia of Russia and the Soviet Union (co-ed. with John Fennell, Michael Kaser, and Harry T. Willetts) 1982, Soviet Policy for the 1980s (ed.) 1982, Political Culture and Communist Studies (ed.) 1984, Political Leadership in the Soviet Union (ed.) 1989, The Soviet Union: A Biographical Dictionary (ed.) 1990, New Thinking in Soviet Politics (ed.) 1992, The Cambridge Encyclopedia of Russia and the Former Soviet Union (co-ed. with Michael Kaser and Gerald S. Smith) 1994, The Gorbachev Factor 1996, The British Study of Politics in the Twentieth Century (co-ed. with Jack Hayward and Brian Barry) 1999, Contemporary Russian Politics: A Reader 2001, Gorbachev, Yeltsin and Putin: Political Leadership in Russia's Transition (co-ed. with Lilia Shevtsova) 2001, The Demise of Marxism-Leninism in Russia (ed.) 2004, Seven Years that Changed the World: Perestroika in Perspective 2007, The Rise and Fall of Communism 2009; contribs to scholarly journals and symposia. *Honours:* Foreign Hon. mem. American Acad. of Arts and

Sciences 2003; Nove Prize 1997, W.J.M. Mackenzie Prize 1998, 2010. *Address:* St Antony's College, University of Oxford, Oxford, OX2 6JF, England (office).

BROWN, Craig Edward Moncrieff; British journalist and writer; b. 23 May 1957, England; m. Frances Welch 1987; one s. one d. *Education:* Eton, Univ. of Bristol. *Career:* columnist (as Wallace Arnold), The Spectator 1987–, The Times 1988, Private Eye 1989–, Independent on Sunday 1991, The Evening Standard 1993–, The Guardian (as Bel Littlejohn) 1995–, The Telegraph, The Mail on Sunday; restaurant columnist, Sunday Times 1988–93. *Radio:* This is Craig Brown (BBC Radio 4) 2003. *Publications:* The Marsh Marlowe Letters 1983, A Year Inside 1988, The Agreeable World of Wallace Arnold 1990, Rear Columns 1992, Welcome to My Worlds 1993, Craig Brown's Greatest Hits 1993, The Hounding of John Thenos 1994, The Private Eye Book of Craig Brown Parodies 1995, This is Craig Brown 2003, 1966 and All That 2005, The Tony Years 2007. *Address:* c/o Ebury Press Publicity, Random House Group, 20 Vauxhall Bridge Road, London, SW1V 2SA, England (office). *Website:* www.eburypublishing.co.uk (office).

BROWN, Dan; American writer; b. 1965, Exeter, NH; m. Blythe Newlon 1997. *Education:* Phillips Exeter Acad., Amherst Coll. *Career:* English teacher 1986–1996. *Publications:* 187 Men to Avoid (as Danielle Brown) 1995, Digital Fortress 1998, Angels and Demons 2001, Deception Point 2002, The Da Vinci Code (British Book Award for Book of the Year 2005) 2003, The Lost Symbol 2009. *Literary Agent:* Heide Lange, Sandford J. Greenburger Associates Inc., 55 Fifth Avenue, New York, NY 10003, USA. *Telephone:* (212) 206-5600. *Fax:* (212) 463-8718. *E-mail:* queryHL@sjga.com. *Website:* www.greenburger.com; www.danbrown.com.

BROWN, Diana, AA, BA, MLS, MA; American research librarian and author; b. 8 Aug. 1928, Twickenham, England; d. of Antranik Magarian and Violet Muriel Florence Maynard; m. Ralph Herman Brown 1964 (deceased); two d. *Education:* San Jose City Coll., San Jose State Univ. *Career:* Librarian, Signetics Corpn, Sunnyvale, Calif. 1978–79, NASA/Ames Research Center, Moffett Field 1979–80; Academic Information Specialist, Univ. of Phoenix, San Jose Div. 1984–86; Research Librarian, San Jose Public Library from 1988; mem. Authors' Guild, Jane Austen Soc., Special Libraries Asscn. *Publications:* The Emerald Necklace 1980, Come Be My Love 1981, A Debt of Honour 1981, St Martin's Summer 1981, The Sandalwood Fan 1983, The Hand of a Woman 1984, The Blue Dragon 1988. *Honours:* American Library Asscn Booklist for Outstanding Adult Novel 1984. *Address:* PO Box 2846, Carmel-by-the-Sea, CA 93921-2846, USA. *E-mail:* anab_8@comcast.net.

BROWN, Eleanor; British poet and writer; b. 1969; m.; one s. one d. *Education:* Univ. of York. *Career:* Writing Fellow, Univ. of Strathclyde, Univ. of Glasgow. *Plays:* Philoctetes by Sophocles (adaptation) 1997, Franziska by Frank Wedekind (adaptation) 1998. *Publications:* poetry: Maiden Speech 1996. *Address:* c/o Bloodaxe Books Ltd, Highgreen, Tarset, Northumberland, NE48 1RP, England (office). *Website:* www.bloodaxebooks.com (office).

BROWN, Ian James Morris, MA, DipEd, MLitt, PhD, FRSA; British academic and playwright; b. 28 Feb. 1945, Barnet, England; m. 1st Judith Sidaway 1969 (divorced 1997); m. 2nd Nicola Axford 1997; one s. one d. *Education:* University of Edinburgh, Crewe and Alsager College. *Career:* Lecturer in Drama, Dunfermline College, Edinburgh 1971–76; Senior Principal Lecturer, Crewe and Alsager College 1978–86; Drama Dir, Arts Council of Great Britain 1986–94; Reader in Drama, Queen Margaret University College, Edinburgh 1994–95, Head of Drama 1995–99, Prof. of Drama 1999–2002, Dean of Arts 1999–2002; Dir, Scottish Centre for Cultural Management and Policy 1996–2002; currently External Prof., Centre for the Study of Media and Culture in Small Nations, Univ. of Glamorgan; mem. Scottish Society of Playwrights, chair., 1973–75, 1984–87, 1997–99; BTI, chair., 1985–87. *Plays:* Mother Earth 1970, The Bacchae 1972, Carnegie 1973, The Knife 1973, Rabelais 1973, The Fork 1976, New Reekie 1977, Mary 1977, Runners 1978, Mary Queen and the Lock Tower 1979, Pottersville 1982, Joker in the Pack 1983, Beatrice 1989, First Strike 1990, The Scotch Play 1991, Wasting Reality 1992, Margaret 2000, A Great Reckoning 2000; poetry: Poems for Joan 2001. *Publications include:* The Edinburgh History of Scottish Literature (ed.) 2007. *Address:* Centre for the Study of Media and Culture in Small Nations, University of Glamorgan, Pontypridd CF37 1DL, Wales (office). *Website:* culture.research.glam.ac.uk (office).

BROWN, John Russell, BA, BLitt, PhD; British academic, theatre director and writer; Honorary Visiting Professor, University College London; b. 15 Sept. 1923, Bristol, England; s. of Russell Alan Brown and Olive Helen (Nellie) Brown (née Golding); m. Hilary Sue Baker 1961; one s. two d. *Education:* Univs of Oxford and Birmingham. *Career:* Fellow, Shakespeare Inst., Stratford-upon-Avon 1951–53; Faculty, Univ. of Birmingham 1955–63, Head, Dept of Drama and Theatre Arts 1964–71; Prof. of English, Univ. of Sussex 1971–82; Assoc. Dir and Head of Script Dept, Nat. Theatre, London 1973–88; Prof. of Theatre Arts, State Univ. of NY at Stony Brook, USA 1982–85; Artistic Dir, Project Theatre 1985–89; Prof. of Theatre, Univ. of Michigan 1985–97; consultant 1994–2000; Hon. Visiting Prof., Middlesex Univ. 2000–07, Univ. Coll., London 2007–; dir of various theatre productions in Europe and N America; Visiting Lecturer or Prof. in Europe, N America and NZ; mem. Theatre Museum (Advisory Council 1974–83, Chair. 1979–83), Arts Council of GB (Chair. Drama Panel 1980–83). *Publications include:* Shakespeare and his Comedies 1957, Shakespeare: The Tragedy of Macbeth 1963, Shakespeare's Plays in Performance 1966, Effective Theatre 1969, Shakespeare's The Tempest 1969, Shakespeare's Dramatic Style 1970, Theatre Language 1972, Free Shakespeare 1974, Discovering Shakespeare 1981, Shakespeare and His Theatre 1982, A Short Guide to Modern British Drama 1983, Shakescenes 1993, William Shakespeare: Writing for Performance 1996, What is Theatre?: An Introduction and Exploration 1997, New Sites for Shakespeare 1999, William Shakespeare: The Tragedies 2001, Shakespeare and the Theatrical Event 2002, Shakespeare Dancing 2005, Directors' Shakespeare 2008, Studying Shakespeare in Performance 2011, Actors' Shakespeare 2011; General Ed. Stratford-upon-Avon Studies 1960–67, Stratford-upon-Avon Library 1964–69, Theatre Production Studies 1981–2002, Theatre Concepts 1992–2001, Theatres of the World 2001–, Oxford Illustrated History of Theatre 1995; ed.: various plays of Shakespeare; contribs to scholarly journals. *Address:* Court Lodge, Hooe, Battle, East Sussex, TN33 9HJ, England (home). *Telephone:* (1424) 844493 (home). *E-mail:* johnrussellbrown@googlemail.com (office).

BROWN, Malcolm Carey, BA, MA; British historian; b. 7 May 1930, Bradford, West Yorkshire, England; m. Beatrice Elsie Rose Light 1953, two s. one d. *Education:* St John's College, Oxford. *Career:* general trainee, BBC 1955; Production Asst, BBC TV 1958–60; Television Documentary Producer, BBC 1960–86; Freelance Historian, Imperial War Museum 1989–; Hon. Research Fellow, Centre for First World War Studies, University of Birmingham 2002–. *Publications:* Scapa Flow (co-author) 1968, Tommy Goes to War 1978, Christmas Truce (co-author) 1984, A Touch of Genius (co-author) 1988, The Letters of T. E. Lawrence (ed.) 1988, The Imperial War Museum Book of the First World War 1991, The Imperial War Museum Book of the Western Front 1993, The Imperial War Museum Book of the Somme 1996, The Imperial War Museum Book of 1918: Year of Victory 1998, Verdun 1916 1999, Spitfire Summer 2000, T.E. Lawrence 2003, The Imperial War Museum Book of 1914 2004, Lawrence of Arabia: The Selected Letters (ed.) 2005, Lawrence of Arabia: The Life, The Legend 2005. *Address:* Centre for First World War Studies, Departments of Medieval and Modern History, Arts Building, University of Birmingham, Edgbaston, Birmingham B15 2TT, England (office). *E-mail:* mcbrown@freenetname.co.uk (home). *Website:* www.firstworldwar.bham.ac.uk (office).

BROWN, Marc, BFA; American children's writer, illustrator and television producer; b. 25 Nov. 1946, Erie, PA; m. Laurie Krasny Brown; three c. *Education:* Cleveland Art Inst. *Career:* worked on fmr First Lady, Barbara Bush's literacy initiative 1992, 2003, 2004, 2005; featured author and speaker at Library of Congress Nat. Book Festival 2001, 2004; represented USA at Children's Book Festival, Moscow, Russia 2003; Hon. Co-Chair. Nat. Braille Press 'Readbooks! Because Braille Matters' programme 2003; speaker at 'Celebration of Reading' 2003; mem. bd of dirs Cleveland Inst. of Art 2000–; mem. bd of overseers Boston Museum of Fine Arts 2003–; mem. advisory council Harvard Center for Soc. and Health, Harvard School of Public Health 2003–. *Publications include:* juvenile: Arthur Accused, Arthur Babysits, Arthur Chapter Books 1–6, Arthur Goes to Camp, Arthur Helps Out, Arthur Loses his Marbles, Arthur Lost and Found, Arthur Makes the Team, Arthur Meets the President, Arthur Plays the Blues, Arthur Rocks with Binky, Arthur Tells a Story, Arthur Writes a Story, Arthur and the 1,001 Dads, Arthur and the Bad-Luck Brain, Arthur and the Best Coach Ever, Arthur and the Big Blow-Up, Arthur and the Comet Crisis, Arthur and the Cootie-Catcher, Arthur and the Crunch Cereal Contest, Arthur and the Dog Show, Arthur and the Double Dare, Arthur and the Goalie Ghost, Arthur and the Lost Diary, Arthur and the Nerves of Steal, Arthur and the No-Brainer, Arthur and the Pen Pal Playoff, Arthur and the Perfect Brother, Arthur and the Poetry Contest, Arthur and the Popularity Test, Arthur and the Race to Read, Arthur and the Recess Rookie, Arthur and the Scare-Your-Pants-Off-Club, Arthur and the Seventh-Inning Stretcher, Arthur and the True Francine, Arthur and the World Record, Arthur's April Fool, Arthur's Baby, Arthur's Birthday, Arthur's Chicken Pox, Arthur's Christmas, Arthur's Computer Disaster, Arthur's Eyes, Arthur's Family Vacation, Arthur's First Sleepover, Arthur's Halloween, Arthur's Heart Mix-Up, Arthur's Homework, Arthur's Jelly Beans, Arthur's Mystery Babysitter, Arthur's Mystery Envelope, Arthur's New Puppy, Arthur's Nose, Arthur's Off to School, Arthur's Perfect Christmas, Arthur's Pet Business, Arthur's TV Trouble, Arthur's Teacher Moves In, Arthur's Teacher Trouble, Arthur's Thanksgiving, Arthur's Tooth, Arthur's Underwear, Arthur's Valentine, Arthur, It's Only Rock 'N' Roll, BINKY Rules, Buster Baxter, Cat Saver, Buster Makes the Grade, Buster's Dino Dilemma, Buster's New Friend, D.W. Go To Your Room!, D.W. Thinks Big, D.W.'s Guide to Preschool, D.W.'s Library Card, D.W.'s Lost Blankie, D.W. All Wet, D.W. Flips, D.W. Rides Again, D.W. The Big Boss, D.W. the Picky Eater, D.W.'s Perfect Present, Francine the Superstar, Francine, Believe It or Not, Good Night, D.W., King Arthur, Locked in the Library!, Muffy's Secret Admirer, Scared Silly, The Mystery of the Stolen Bike, What's the Big Secret?, When Dinosaurs Die, Who's in Love with Arthur?; Postcards from Buster series: Buster Changes his Luck, Buster Hits the Trail, Buster on the Farm, Buster on the Town, Buster Plays Along, Buster and the Dance Contest, Buster and the Giant Pumpkin, Buster's Sugartime, Buster Catches a Wave, Buster Climbs the Walls, Buster Hunts for Dinosaurs, Buster and the Great Swamp; Dino Life Guides for Families series: Dinosaurs Beware (American Library Asscn Notable Book 1982), Dinosaurs to the Rescue!: A Guide to Protecting Our Planet, Dinosaurs Travel: A Guide for Families on the Go, Dinosaurs Alive and Well!: A Guide to Good Health, Dinosaurs Divorce: A Guide for Changing Families, How To Be A Friend. *Honours:* New York Festival Bronze Medal for Best Writing 1997, Silver Medal for Best Writing 1998, Gold Medal for Best Animation 1998,

Silver Medal for Children's Programs (age 2–6) 1999, Gold Medal for Children's Programs (age 2–6) 2000, 2003, Grand Award for Best Children's Youth Program 2003; Weekly Reader Children's Book Club Award (for Arthur's Nose) 1992, Atlantic Film Festival Award 1997, Alliance for Children and Television Awards of Excellence for Best Animated Program 1997, 1998, US Int. Film and Video Festival Awards 1997, 1998, 1999, 2000, 2001, 2002, Parents' Choice Award 1997, 2001, 2002, Worldfest Houston Award for TV Series for Family/Children 1997, 1998, 1999, 2000, 2001, 2002, Worldfest Flagstaff Award for TV Series for Family/Children 1999, Daytime Emmy Award for Outstanding Children's Animated Program 1997, 1998, 1999, 2001, Parenting Magazine Video Magic Award 1998, Prix Jeunesse Int. 1998, Parent's Guide to Children's Media Inc. Award for Outstanding Achievement in Classic Television Programs 1999, 2000, 2001, 2002, Unda-USA Gabriel Award for Outstanding Achievement in Children's Programs 1999, 2002, Clarion Award for Children's Educational Television Program 1999, 2000, 2001, Director's Choice Award 2000, Print Magazine Award of Design Excellence 2000, George Foster Peabody Award for Excellence in Broadcasting and Cable Television 2001, Environmental Protection Agency Nat. Environmental Asthma Educator Award (for Buster's Breathless) 2002, American Council for the Blind Vernon Henley Award 2002, Humanitas Award 2002, 2004, 2005; Hon. DArts (Cleveland Inst. of Art) 2000. *Address:* PO Box 873, West Tilbury, MA 02575 (home); c/o Author Mail, Little, Brown and Company, 237 Park Avenue, New York, NY 10017, USA (office). *Telephone:* (508) 696-5888 (office). *Fax:* (508) 693-6540 (office). *E-mail:* j.hartnett@arthurworldwide.com. *Website:* www.marcbrownstudios.com.

BROWN, Patricia Ann Fortini, MA, PhD; American academic and art historian; *Professor, Princeton University*; b. 16 Nov. 1936, Oakland, CA; m. 1st Peter Claus Meyer 1957 (divorced 1978); two s.; m. 2nd Peter Robert Lamont Brown 1980 (divorced 1989). *Education:* Univ. of California at Berkeley. *Career:* Asst Prof., Princeton Univ. 1983–89, Assoc. Prof. 1989–91, Andrew W. Mellon Prof. 1991–95, Prof. 1997–, Chair. Dept of Art and Archaeology 1999–; Slade Prof. of Fine Arts, Univ. of Cambridge 2001; mem. Renaissance Soc. of America, American Acad. in Rome, Coll. Art Asscn. *Publications:* Venetian Narrative Painting in the Age of Carpaccio 1988, Venice and Antiquity: The Venetian Sense of the Past 1996, The Renaissance in Venice: A World Apart 1997, Private Lives in Renaissance Venice 2004, Art Architecture and the Family 2004; contrib. to Art History, Christian Science Monitor, Monitor Book Review, Burlington Magazine, Renaissance Quarterly, Biography, Journal of the Society of Architectural Historians. *Honours:* Premio Salotto Veneto (Italy), Phyllis Goodhart Gordan Book Prize 1998. *Address:* Department of Art and Archaeology, Princeton University, 309 McCormick Hall, Princeton, NJ 08544, USA (office). *Telephone:* (609) 258-3798 (office). *E-mail:* pbrown@prineton.edu (office). *Website:* www.princeton.edu/artandarchaeology/faculty/brown (office).

BROWN, Paul, BSc, MScSoc, PhD; Australian playwright and lecturer. *Education:* Univ. of New South Wales. *Career:* fmrly documentary maker for television, Campaign Man. for Greenpeace Australia; founder, Death Defying Theatre (now Urban Theatre Projects) 1981; Lecturer in History and Philosophy of Science. *Plays:* Aftershcoks 1993, Room 207 Nikola Tesla 2003, Maralinga 2006. *Literary Agent:* RGM Associates, PO Box 128, Surry Hills, NSW 2010, Australia. *Telephone:* (2) 9281-3911. *Fax:* (2) 9281-4705. *E-mail:* info@rgm.com.au. *Website:* www.rgm.com.au.

BROWN, Peter Robert Lamont, BA, MA, PhD; British professor of history and writer; *Philip and Beulah Rollins Professor Emeritus of History, Princeton University*; b. 26 July 1935, Dublin, Ireland; m. 1st Friedl Esther 1959; two d.; m. 2nd Patricia Ann Fortini 1980; m. 3rd Elizabeth Gilliam 1989. *Education:* New Coll., Oxford. *Career:* Harmsworth Sr Scholar, Merton Coll., Oxford 1956, Lecturer in Medieval History 1970–75; Special Lecturer in Late Roman and Early Byzantine History, Univ. of Oxford 1970–73, Reader 1973–75; Prof. of History, Royal Holloway Coll., London 1975–78; Prof. of History and Classics, Univ. of California at Berkeley 1978–86; Visiting Prof., Princeton Univ. 1983–86, apptd Philip and Beulah Rollins Prof. of History 1986, currently Philip and Beulah Rollins Prof. Emer. of History; Fellow, All Souls Coll., Oxford 1956–75, American Acad. of Arts and Sciences 1978–, British Acad., Royal Historical Soc., American Soc. of Arts and Sciences, American Philosophical Soc., Medieval Acad. of America, Royal Netherlands Acad., Academia de Bones Artes, Barcelona. *Publications:* Augustine of Hippo: A Biography 1967, The World of Late Antiquity 1971, Religion and Society in the Age of St Augustine 1971, The Making of Late Antiquity 1978, The Cult of the Saints: Its Rise and Function in Latin Christianity 1980, Society and the Holy in Late Antiquity 1982, The Body and Society: Men, Women and Sexual Renunciation in Early Christianity 1989, Power and Persuasion in Late Antiquity: Towards a Christian Empire 1992, Authority and the Sacred: Aspects of the Christianization of the Roman World 1995, The Rise of Western Christendom: Triumph and Diversity, AD 200–1000 1996, Poverty and Leadership in the Later Roman Empire 2002; contrib. to scholarly journals. *Honours:* Chevalier de l'Ordre des Lettres et des Arts 1996; Dr hc (Univ. of Chicago) 1978, (Trinity Coll., Dublin) 1990, (Wesleyan Univ.) 1993, (Columbia Univ.) 2001, (Harvard Univ.) 2002, (Southern Methodist Univ.) 2004, (Cambridge Univ.) 2004, (Central European Univ.) 2005, (Yale Univ.) 2006, (Univ. of Oxford) 2006, (Notre Dame Univ.) 2008, (King's Coll., (Univ. of London) 2008; Arts Council of Great Britain Award 1967, MacArthur Fellowship 1982, Guggenheim Fellowship 1989, Ralph Waldo Emerson Award, 1989, Vursell Award 1990, Heineken Prize 1994, Award for Distinguished Teaching, Princeton Univ. 2000, Mellon Foundation Distinguished Achievement Award 2001, John W. Kluge Prize, Library of Congress 2008. *Address:* Department of History, 135 Dickinson Hall, Princeton University, Princeton, NJ 08544-1017, USA (office). *Telephone:* (609) 258-4154 (office). *Fax:* (609) 258-5326 (office). *E-mail:* prbrown@princeton.edu (office). *Website:* www.princeton.edu/history (office).

BROWN, Rebecca, BA, MFA; American writer, journalist and teacher; *MFA Faculty Member, Godard College, Vermont*; b. 27 March 1956, San Diego, CA; d. of Vergil Neal Brown, Jr and Barbara Ann Wildman Brown; pnr Christine Galloway. *Education:* George Washington Univ., Univ. of Virginia. *Career:* fmr Creative Dir, Port Townsend Writers' Conference; fmr visiting writer, Brown Univ., Northwestern Univ., Univ. of Texas, Univ. of Alaska, Wesleyan Univ., Eastern Michigan Univ., Evergreen State Coll., Univ. of Washington at Bothell; currently Faculty Advisor, MFA in Creative Writing, Goddard Coll. *Dance:* The Onion Twins (libretto for dance opera) (Better Biscuit Dance), Pro Re Nata (text) (Launch Dance Co.), The Tragedy (Better Biscuit Dance). *Play:* The Toaster (New City Theater). *Publications:* Evolution of Darkness and Other Stories 1984, The Haunted House 1986, The Children's Crusade 1989, The Terrible Girls 1990, Annie Oakley's Girl 1993, The Gifts of the Body 1994, What Keeps Me Here: A Book of Stories 1996, The Dogs: A Modern Bestiary 1997, The End of Youth 2003, Excerpts from a Family Medical Dictionary 2003, Woman In Ill Fitting Wig 2003, The Last Time I Saw You 2005, American Romances 2009. *Honours:* Lambda Literary Award, Boston Book Review Award, Washington State Governor's Award, Pacific Northwest Bookseller's Award, Hugo House Founders' Award, Breneman Jaech Foundation Award, Stranger Genius Award. *Address:* Department of English, Goddard College, 123 Pitkin Road, Plainfield, VT 05667, USA (office). *E-mail:* rebeccabrown@qwest.net (office); rebecca.brown@goddard.edu (office). *Website:* www.goddard.edu/rebeccabrown (office).

BROWN, Rita Mae, PhD; American writer and scriptwriter; b. 28 Nov. 1944, Hanover, PA; d. of Ralph and Julia Brown. *Education:* Broward Jr Coll., Univ. of New York, School of Visual Arts and Inst. of Policy Studies. *Career:* Lecturer, Fed. City Coll. 1970–71; mem. Faculty Goddard Coll. 1973–; Pres. American Artists Inc., VA 1980–; mem. Bd of Dirs Human Rights Campaign Fund, New York 1986. *TV includes:* I Love Liberty 1982, The Long Hot Summer 1985, My Two Loves 1986, The Mists of Avalon 1986, The Girls of Summer 1989, Rich Men, Single Women 1989, Southern Exposure 1990, The Thirty Nine Year Itch 1990, The Woman Who Loved Elvis 1992, A Family Again 1994, Cat on the Scent 1999, Loose Lips 1999, Out Foxed 2000, Pawing Through the Past 2000. *Publications include:* The Hand that Rocks the Cradle 1971, Rubyfruit Jungle 1973, A Plain Brown Rapper 1976, Six of One 1978, Southern Discomfort 1982, Sudden Death 1983, High Hearts 1986, Starting From Scratch: A Different Kind of Writer's Manual 1988, Bingo 1988, Wish You Were Here 1990, Rest in Pieces 1991, Dolley 1992, Murder at Monticello 1992, Venus Envy 1994, Pay Dirt 1995, Riding Shotgun 1996, Murder, She Meowed 1996, Murder on the Prowl 1998, Cat on the Scent 1999, Sneaky Pie's Cookbook for Mystery Lovers 1999, Pawing Through the Past 2000, Catch as Cat Can 2002, Outfoxed 2002, Hotspur 2002, Full Cry 2003, The Tail of the Tip-Off 2003, Whisker of Evil 2004, The Hunt Ball 2005, Cat's Eyewitness 2006, Sour Puss 2006, The Hounds and the Fury 2007, Puss 'n Cahoots 2008, The Tell-Tale Horse 2008, Santa Clawed 2008, Hounded to Death 2009, Purrfect Murder 2009, Animal Magnetism (auto-biog.) 2009, Cat of the Century 2010, A Nose for Justice 2010, Murder Unleashed 2011. *Honours:* Award for Best Variety Show, TV Writers' Guild of America 1982. *Address:* c/o Ballantine/Bantam Books, Random House, 1745 Broadway, New York, NY 10019, USA (office). *Website:* www.ritamaebrown.com.

BROWN, Rosellen, BA, MA; American writer, poet and professor of creative writing; b. 12 May 1939, Philadelphia, PA; m. Marvin Hoffman 1963; two d. *Education:* Barnard Coll., Brandeis Univ. *Career:* Instructor, Tougaloo Coll., Mississippi 1965–67; Staff, Bread Loaf Writer's Conf., Middlebury 1974, 1991, 1992; Instructor, Goddard Coll., Plainfield 1976; Visiting Prof. of Creative Writing, Boston Univ. 1977–78; Assoc. Prof. in Creative Writing, Univ. of Houston 1982–85, 1989–; currently teaches in MFA in Writing Program, School of Art Inst. of Chicago; Fellow, Woodrow Wilson Nat. Fellowship Foundation 1960, Radcliffe Inst. 1973–75. *Publications:* Some Deaths in the Delta and Other Poems 1970, The Whole World Catalog: Creative Writing Ideas for Elementary and Secondary Schools (with others) 1972, Street Games: A Neighborhood (short stories) 1974, The Autobiography of My Mother (novel) 1976, Cora Fry (poems) 1977, Banquet: Five Short Stories 1978, Tender Mercies (novel) 1978, Civil Wars: A Novel (Janet Kafka Prize) 1984, A Rosellen Brown Reader: Selected Poetry and Prose 1992, Before and After (novel) 1992, Cora Fry's Pillow Book (poems) 1994, Half a Heart 2000; contrib. books, anthologies and periodicals. *Honours:* Great Lakes Colleges New Writers Award 1976, Guggenheim Fellowship 1976–77, American Acad. and Inst. of Arts and Letters Award 1988, Ingram Merrill Grant 1989–90. *E-mail:* rosellen@rosellenbrown.com.

BROWN, Sandra; American writer; b. 1948, Waco, Tex.; m. Michael Brown 1968; one s. one d. *Education:* Texas Christian Univ. *Career:* fmr model, Dallas Apparel Mart, and in TV, including weathercasting for WFAA-TV in Dallas; feature reporter, PM Magazine; has written 65 novels since 1981; has had 20 books on New York Times bestseller list since 1990; attended numerous Roman Writers of America confs; mem. Authors' Guild, Mystery Writers of America, Int. Asscn of Crime Writers, Novelists, Inc., Literacy Partners. *Publications include:* 70 novels including Love's Encore (as Rachel Ryan),

Love Beyond Reason, Slow Heat in Heaven 1988, Best Kept Secrets 1989, Mirror Image 1990, Breath of Scandal 1991, French Silk 1992 (also ABC-TV film), Where There's Smoke 1993, Charade 1994, The Witness, Exclusive 1996, Long Time Coming 1997, Fat Tuesday 1997, Unspeakable 1998, The Alibi 1999, The Switch 2000, Words of Silk 2001, Seduction by Design 2001, Envy 2001, The Crush 2002, A Kiss Remembered 2002, Standoff 2003, Hello, Darkness 2003, White Hot 2004, Led Astray 2005, Chill Factor 2005, Ricochet 2006, Play Dirty 2007, Smoke Screen 2008, Smash Cut 2009, Rainwater 2009, Tough Customer 2010. *Honours:* Distinguished Circle of Success, American Business Women's Asscn, B'nai B'rith Distinguished Literary Achievement Award, A.C. Greene Award, Lifetime Achievement Award, Romance Writers of America, Texas Medal of Arts Award for Literature 2007. *Address:* c/o Simon & Schuster, Inc., 1230 Avenue of the Americas, New York, NY 10020, USA (office). *E-mail:* sandrab@sandrabrown.net (office). *Website:* www .sandrabrown.net.

BROWN, Stewart, MA, PhD; British academic, poet and artist; *Director, Centre of West African Studies, University of Birmingham*; b. 14 March 1951, Lymington, Hants., England; m. Priscilla Margaret Brant 1976; one s. one d. *Education:* Nottingham Coll. of Educ., Falmouth School of Art, Univ. of Sussex, Univ. of Wales. *Career:* Lecturer in English, Bayero Univ., Kano, Nigeria 1980–83; Reader in African and Caribbean Literature, Univ. of Birmingham 1988–, Dir Centre of West African Studies 2004–; Visiting Prof., Univ. of the West Indies, Barbados 2007; mem. Welsh Acad. *Composition:* Splashes from the Cauldron: a cantata for Ceridwen (performed with Paul Shallcross, Brecon Jazz Festival) 1986. *Art exhibition:* BABEL: beautiful, unsayable, meaningless, profound (Errol Barrow Centre for Creative Imagination, Univ. of the West Indies, Barbados) 2007, Tanzania Publishing House, Dar es Salaam 2009, Drum Arts Centre, Birmingham 2010, Castellani House, Nat. Gallery of Guyana, Georgetown 2011. *Publications:* Mekin Foolishness (poems) 1981, Caribbean Poetry Now 1984, Zinder (poems) 1986, Lugard's Bridge (poems) 1989, Voiceprint: An Anthology of Oral and Related Poetry from the Caribbean (co-ed. with Mervyn Morris and Gordon Rohler) 1989, Writers from Africa: A Readers' Guide 1989, New Wave: The Contemporary Caribbean Short Story 1990, The Art of Derek Walcott: A Collection of Critical Essays 1991, The Heinemann Book of Caribbean Poetry (with Ian McDonald) 1992, The Art of Kamau Brathwaite: A Collection of Critical Essays 1995, The Pressures of the Text: Orality, Texts and the Telling of Tales 1995, Caribbean New Voices I 1996, The Oxford Book of Caribbean Short Stories (with John Wickham) 1998, African New Voices 1999, Elsewhere: New and Selected Poems 1999, All are Involved: The Art of Martin Carter 2000, Kiss and Quarrel: Youba/English, Strategies of Mediation 2000, The Oxford Book of Caribbean Verse (with Mark McWatt) 2005, Martin Carter: Poems (with Ian McDonald) 2006, Tourist, Traveller, Troublemaker: essays on poetry 2007, The Bowling was Superfine: West Indian Writers on West Indian Cricket (with Ian McDonald) 2012; contribs to anthologies and periodicals. *Honours:* Hon. Fellow, Centre for Caribbean Studies, Univ. of Warwick 1990–; Eric Gregory Award 1976, Southwest Arts Literature Award 1978. *Address:* Centre of West African Studies, University of Birmingham, Edgbaston, Birmingham, B15 2TT, England (office). *Telephone:* (121) 414-5128 (office). *Fax:* (121) 414-3228 (office). *E-mail:* s.brown@bham.ac.uk (office). *Website:* www.catalystpress.co.uk.

BROWN, Terence, MA, PhD; Irish academic, writer and editor; *Fellow Emeritus, Trinity College, Dublin*; b. 17 Jan. 1944, Loping, China; m. Suzanne Marie Krochalis 1969; one s. one d. *Education:* Trinity Coll., Dublin. *Career:* Lecturer, Trinity Coll., Dublin 1968–82, Dir of Modern English 1976–83, Fellow 1976–86, Registrar 1980–81, Assoc. Prof. of English 1982–93, Prof. of Anglo-Irish Literature 1993–2009, now Fellow Emer.; mem. Royal Irish Acad., Academia Europaea, Int. Asscn of Prof. of English. *Publications:* Time Was Away: The World of Louis MacNeice (co-ed. with Alec Reid) 1974, Louis MacNeice: Sceptical Vision 1975, Northern Voices: Poets from Northern Ulster 1975, The Irish Short Story (co-ed. with Patrick Rafroidi) 1979, Ireland: A Social and Cultural History, 1922–1979 1981, revised edn as Ireland: A Social and Cultural History, 1922 to the Present 1985, The Whole Protestant Community: The Making of a Historical Myth 1985, Hermathena (co-ed. with N. Grene) 1986, Samuel Ferguson: A Centenary Tribute (co-ed. with B. Hayley) 1987, Ireland's Literature: Selected Essays 1988, Traditions and Influence in Anglo-Irish Literature (co-ed. with N. Grene) 1989, The Field Day Anthology of Irish Writing (contributing ed.) 1991, James Joyce: Dubliners (ed.) 1992, Celticism (ed.) 1996, Journalism: Derek Mahon, Selected Prose (ed.) 1996, The Life of W. B. Yeats: A Critical Biography 1999 2001; contributing ed., The Encyclopaedia of Ireland 2003. *Honours:* Hon. Fellow, the English Asscn; Hon. Companion of St Michael and St George 2002. *Address:* Department of English, Trinity College, Dublin 2, Ireland (office). *Telephone:* (1) 8961400 (office). *Fax:* (1) 6717114 (office). *E-mail:* tbrown@tcd .ie (office). *Website:* www.tcd.ie/English/staffandresearch/brown.php (office).

BROWN, Wayne; Trinidad and Tobago poet and writer; b. 1944, Woodbrook. *Career:* teacher, Univ. of the West Indies; columnist, Trinidad Express. *Publications:* poetry: On the Coast (Commonwealth Prize for Poetry) 1972, Derek Walcott: Selected Poetry (ed.) 1981, Voyages 1989, Jullia Rypinski: The Light and the Dark – Selected Poems (ed.) 2003, M. G. Smith: In the Kingdom of Light – Collected Poems (ed.) 2003; short stories: Child of the Sea 1990, Landscape with Heron 2000; non-fiction: Edna Manley: The Private Years 1900–38 1976.

BROWNE, Anthony; British writer, artist and illustrator; b. 1946, Sheffield; m.; two c. *Education:* Leeds Coll. of Art. *Career:* fmr medical illustrator, Leeds Royal Infirmary; fmr greetings card illustrator; Illustrator-in-Residence, Tate Britain 2001–02; Children's Laureate 2009–11. *Publications:* Through the Magic Mirror 1976, A Walk in the Park 1977, Bear Hunt 1979, Look What I've Got! 1980, Hansel and Gretel 1981, Bear Goes to Town 1982, Gorilla (Kate Greenaway Medal, Kurt Maschler Emil Award) 1983, The Visitors Who Came to Stay 1984, Willy the Wimp 1985, Knock, Knock, Who's There 1985, Willy the Champ 1985, Piggybook 1986, Kirsty Knows Best 1988, Alice's Adventures in Wonderland (Kurt Maschler Emil Award) 1988, Little Bear Book 1988, I Like Books 1988, Things I Like 1989, A Bear-y Tale 1989, The Tunnel 1990, Trail of Stones 1990, Changes 1990, Willy and Hugh 1991, The Night Shimmy 1991, Zoo (Kate Greenaway Medal) 1992, The Big Baby 1993, The Topiary Garden 1993, The Daydreamer 1994, King Kong 1994, Willy the Wizard 1995, Willy the Dreamer 1997, Voices in the Park (Kurt Maschler Emil Award) 1998, My Dad 2000, Willy's Pictures 2000, The Animal Fair 2002, The Shape Game (Honor Book, Boston Globe-Horn Book Awards) 2003, Into the Forest 2004, My Mum 2008, Silly Billy 2006, My Brother 2007, Little Beauty 2008. *Honours:* Hon. D.Ed (Kingston Univ.) 2005; Boston Globe Book Award, Hans Christian Andersen Award 2000. *Address:* c/o Walker Books, 87 Vauxhall Walk, London, SE11 5HJ, England (office). *E-mail:* childrenslaureate@ booktrust.org.uk (office). *Website:* www.walker.co.uk (office); www .childrenslaureate.org.uk (office).

BROWNE, Michael Dennis, BA, MA; American academic, writer, librettist and poet; *Emeritus Professor, University of Minnesota*; b. 28 May 1940, Walton-on-Thames, England; s. of Edgar Dennis Browne and Winifred Margaret Denne; m. Lisa Furlong McLean 1981; one s. two d. *Education:* Hull Univ., Univ. of Oxford, Univ. of Iowa. *Career:* Visiting Lecturer, Univ. of Iowa 1967–68; Instructor, Columbia Univ. 1967, 1968, Visiting Adjunct Asst Prof. 1968; Faculty, Bennington Coll., Vermont 1969–71; Visiting Asst Prof., Univ. of Minnesota 1971–72, Asst Prof. 1972–75, Assoc. Prof. 1975–83, Prof. 1983–2010, fmr Morse-Alumni Distinguished Teaching Prof., Prof. Emer. 2010–; mem. The Loft, Poetry Soc. of America. *Music:* many texts for music by Stephen Paulus, John Foley S.J., Carolyn Jennings, Juliana Hall and David Lord, including To Be Certain of the Dawn (post-Holocaust oratorio) 2006. *Publications:* The Wife of Winter 1970, Sun Exercises 1976, The Sun Fetcher 1978, Smoke From the Fires 1985, You Won't Remember This 1992, Selected Poems 1965–1995 1997, Give her the River 2004, Things I Can't Tell You 2005, What the Poem Wants 2008, contributions: numerous anthologies and journals. *Honours:* Fulbright Scholarship 1965–67, Borestone Poetry Prize 1974, Nat. Endowment for the Arts Fellowships 1977, 1978, Bush Fellowship 1981, Loft-McKnight Writers' Award 1986, Minnesota Book Award for Poetry 1993, 1998. *Address:* 2111 E. 22nd St, Minneapolis, MN 55404, USA (office). *E-mail:* mdb@umn.edu (office). *Website:* english.cla.umn.edu/faculty/browne/ (office).

BROWNE, Nichola; British journalist; *Editor, Kerrang!*. *Career:* began career as staff writer, J-17 magazine; News Ed., Kerrang!, later Features Ed. 2002–09, Ed. 2009–. *Address:* Kerrang!, Emap Metro, Mappin House, 4 Winsley Street, London W1R 7AR, England (office). *Telephone:* (20) 7436-1515 (office). *Fax:* (20) 7312-8910 (office). *E-mail:* kerrang@emap.com (office). *Website:* www.kerrang.com (office).

BROWNJOHN, Alan Charles, MA, FRSL; British poet, novelist and critic; b. 28 July 1931, London. *Education:* Merton Coll., Oxford. *Career:* Lecturer, Battersea Coll. of Educ. 1965–76, Polytechnic of the South Bank 1976–79; Visiting Lecturer, London Metropolitan Univ. 2001–03; poetry critic, New Statesman 1968–76, Encounter 1978–82, Sunday Times 1990–; mem. Arts Council of Great Britain (literature panel 1968–72), Poetry Soc. (chair. 1982–88), Writers' Guild of Great Britain, Soc. of Authors. *Publications:* poetry: Travellers Alone 1954, The Railings 1961, The Lions' Mouths 1967, Sandgrains on a Tray 1969, Penguin Modern Poets 14 1969, First I Say This: A Selection of Poems for Reading Aloud 1969, Brownjohn's Beasts 1970, Warrior's Career 1972, A Song of Good Life 1975, A Night in the Gazebo 1980, Collected Poems 1982, The Old Flea-Pit 1987, The Observation Car 1990, In the Cruel Arcade 1994, The Cat Without E-Mail 2001, The Men Around her Bed 2004, Collected Poems 2006, Ludbrooke & Others 2010; fiction: To Clear the River 1964, The Way You Tell Them 1990, The Long Shadows 1997, A Funny Old Year 2001, Windows on the Moon 2009; non-fiction: Philip Larkin 1975, Meet and Write 1985–87, The Gregory Anthology 1990; translations: Torquato Tasso (play, Goethe) 1985, Horace (play), Corneille (play) 1996. *Honours:* Writers' Guild Books Cttee Special Award 2007. *Address:* 2 Belsize Park, London, NW3 4ET, England (home). *Telephone:* (20) 7794-2479 (also fax) (home).

BROWNLOW, Kevin; British film historian and television director; b. 2 June 1938, Crowborough, Sussex; s. of Robert Thomas Brownlow and Niña Fortnum; m. Virginia Keane 1969; one d. *Education:* Univ. Coll. School, Hampstead. *Career:* joined World Wide Pictures 1955; became film ed., then co-dir 1964; with Thames TV 1975–90. *Films include:* It Happened Here 1964, Winstanley 1975 (both with Andrew Mollo). *Television includes:* 13-part series Hollywood 1980, three-part Unknown Chaplin 1983, three-part British Cinema 1986, three-part Buster Keaton: A Hard Act to Follow 1987, two-part Harold Lloyd 1988, three-part D.W. Griffith 1993, six-part Cinema Europe: The Other Hollywood 1995 (all with David Gill), Universal Horror 1998, Lon Chaney: A Thousand Faces 2000, The Tramp and the Dictator (with Michael Kloft) 2002, Cecil B. De Mille: American Epic 2003; with Christopher

Bird: Buster Keaton: So Funny It Hurt 2004, Garbo 2005, I'm King Kong: The Exploits of Merion C. Cooper 2005. *Publications:* Parade's Gone By 1968, The War, the West and the Wilderness 1978, Napoleon (Abel Gance's Classic Film) 1983, Behind the Mask of Innocence 1990, David Lean: A Biography 1996, Mary Pickford Rediscovered 1999, Winstanley: Warts and All 2009, The Search for Charlie Chaplin 2010. *Honours:* Hon. Acad. Award, Acad. of Motion Picture Arts and Sciences 2010. *Address:* c/o Photoplay Productions, 21 Princess Road, London, NW1 8JR, England (office). *Telephone:* (20) 7722-2500 (office).

BROYLES, William Dodson, Jr, MA; American journalist; b. 8 Oct. 1944, Houston; s. of William Dodson and Elizabeth (née Bills) Broyles; m. 1st Sybil Ann Newman 1973; one s. one d.; m. 2nd Linda Purl 1988 (divorced 1992); m. 3rd Andrea Bettina Berndt; three c. *Education:* Rice Univ., Houston, Oxford Univ. *Career:* Marine Corps Reserve 1969–71; teacher Philosophy Naval Acad. 1970–71; Asst Supt Houston Public Schools 1971–72; Ed.-in-Chief Texas Monthly 1972–82; Ed.-in-Chief California Magazine 1980–82; Ed.-in-Chief Newsweek Magazine 1982–84; Columnist, US News and World Report 1986; mem. Advisory Council, Harry Ransom Center, Univ. of Texas at Austin. *Television:* China Beach (co-producer, exec. consultant) 1988–91. *Films:* screewriter: Apollo 13 (with Al Reinert) 1995, Entrapment 1999, Cast Away 2000, Planet of the Apes 2001, Unfaithful 2002, The Polar Express 2004, Jarhead 2005, Flags of Our Fathers 2006. *Publications:* Brothers in Arms: A Journey from War to Peace 1986, Cast Away: The Shooting Script 2001, All Aboard the Polar Express (Ed.) 2004. *Honours:* Bronze Star, inducted into Texas Film Hall of Fame 2002. *Address:* Harry Ransom Center, University of Texas at Austin, PO Drawer 7219, Austin, TX 78713-7219, USA (office). *Fax:* (512) 471-9646 (office). *Website:* www.hrc.utexas.edu (office).

BRUCE, (William) Harry, BA; Canadian journalist, editor and writer; b. 8 July 1934, Toronto, ON; m. Penny Meadows 1955; two s. one d. *Education:* Mount Allison University, Massey College, University of Toronto. *Career:* Reporter, Ottawa Journal 1955–59, Globe and Mail 1959–61; Asst Ed., Maclean's 1961–64, Columnist 1970–71; Managing Ed., Saturday Night 1964–65, Canadian Magazine 1965–66; Assoc. Ed. and Columnist, Star Weekly 1967–68; Columnist, Toronto Daily Star 1968–69; Talk-show Host, CBC-TV, Halifax, NS 1972; Ed. Atlantic Insight 1979–80, Exec. Ed. 1981; Ed., Atlantic Salmon Journal 1991–. *Publications:* The Short Happy Walks of Max MacPherson 1968, Nova Scotia 1975, Lifeline 1977, R.A.: The Story of R. A. Jodrey, Entrepreneur 1979, A Basket of Apples: Recollections of Historic Nova Scotia 1982, The Gulf of St Lawrence 1984, Each Moment as it Flies 1984, Movin' East: The Further Writings of Harry Bruce 1985, The Man and the Empire: Frank Sobey 1985, Down Home: Notes of a Maritime Son 1988, Maud: The Life of L. M. Montgomery 1992, Corporate Navigator 1995; contributions: various anthologies and periodicals. *Honours:* Evelyn Richardson Memorial Literary Award 1978, Brascan Award for Culture, National Magazine Awards 1981, Top Prize for Magazine Writing, Atlantic Journalism Awards 1983, 1984, 1986, 1993, City of Dartmouth Book Award 1989, Booksellers' Choice Award, Atlantic Provinces Booksellers' Asscn 1989.

BRUCE-LOCKHART, Robin, MSI; British writer; b. 13 April 1920, London; s. of Robert Bruce-LockhartKCMG; m. 1st Margaret Crookdake 1941 (divorced 1953); one d.; m. 2nd Eila McLean 1987. *Education:* Royal Naval Coll., Dartmouth, Univ. of Cambridge. *Career:* Foreign Man., Financial Times 1946–53; General Man., Beaverbrook Newspapers, Daily Express, Sunday Express, Evening Standard 1953–60; mem. London Stock Exchange 1960; mem. Sussex Author Asscn (chair. 1970–78). *Publications:* Half Way to Heaven: The Secret Life of the Carthusians 1965, Reilly: Ace of Spies 1967, Reilly: The First Man 1987, Listening to Silence 1997, O Bonitas 2000. *Address:* 11–12 Dover Street, London, W1S, England (office).

BRUCHAC, Joseph, AB, MA, PhD; American author, poet, publisher and editor; b. 16 Oct. 1942, Saratoga Springs, NY; m. Carol Worthen 1964; two s. *Education:* Cornell Univ., Syracuse Univ., State Univ. of New York at Albany. *Career:* Co-founder and Dir Greenfield Review Press 1969–; Ed. Greenfield Review literary magazine, 1971–90; Visiting Scholar and Writer-in-Residence at various insts; mem. Dawnland Singers 1993–; mem. Nat. Asscn for the Preservation and Perpetuation of Storytelling, PEN, Poetry Soc. of America. *Publications:* Indian Mountain and Other Poems 1971, Turkey Brother and Other Iroquois Folk Tales 1976, The Dreams of Jesse Brown (novel) 1977, Stone Giants and Flying Heads: More Iroquois Folk Tales 1978, Breaking Silence: An Anthology of Contemporary Asian American Poets (American Book Award) 1983, The Wind Eagle and Other Abenaki Stories 1984, Iroquois Stories 1985, Walking With My Sons and Other Poems 1986, Survival This Way: Interviews with Native American Poets 1987, Near the Mountains: New and Selected Poems 1987, Keepers of the Earth (short stories) 1988, The Faithful Hunter: Abenaki Stories 1988, Long Memory and Other Poems 1989, Return of the Sun: Native American Tales from the Northeast Woodlands 1989, Hoop Snakes, Hide-Behinds and Side-Hill Winders: Tall Tales from the Adirondacks 1991, Keepers of the Animals (with Michael Caduto) (short stories) 1991, Thirteen Moons on Turtle's Back (with Jonathan London) (poems and stories) 1992, Dawn Land (novel) 1993, The First Strawberries 1993, The Native American Sweat Lodge: History and Legends, 1993, Flying With the Eagle, Racing the Great Bear (short stories) 1993, The Girl Who Married the Moon (with Gayle Ross) (short stories) 1994, A Boy Called Slow 1995, The Boy Who Lived With Bears (short stories) (Horn Book Honor, Boston Globe Book Award 1996) 1995, Dog People (short stories) 1995, Long River (novel) 1995, The Story of the Milky Way (with Gayle Ross) (Scientific American Children's Book Award) 1995, Beneath Earth and Sky 1996, Children of the Long House (novel) 1996, Four Ancestors: Stories, Songs and Poems from Native North America 1996, Roots of Survival: Native American Storytelling and the Sacred 1996, Heart of a Chief (Jane Addams Children's Book Award 1999) 1998, Crazy Horse's Vision (Parents Choice Gold Award) 2000, Skeleton Man (Parents Guide to Childrens' Media Award) 2003, Code Talker: A Novel About the Navajo Marines of World War Two 2006, Wabi: A Hero's Tale 2006, The Return of Skeleton Man 2006, Bearwalker 2007, March Toward the Thunder 2008, Night Wings 2009, My Father Is Taller than a Tree 2010, Dragon Castle 2011, Wolf Mark 2011; edited over 15 books; contribs to many anthologies, books and periodicals. *Honours:* Nat. Endowment for the Arts Fellowship 1974, Rockefeller Foundation Humanities Fellowship 1982–83, Notable Children's Book in the Language Arts Award 1993, Scientific American Young Readers Book Award 1995, Parents Choice Award 1995, American Library Asscn Notable Book Award 1996, Knickerbocker Award for Juvenile Literature, New York Library Asscn 1996, Lifetime Achievement Award, Native Writers Circle of the Americas 1999, Virginia Hamilton Literary Award 2005, Writer of the Year Award, Native Writers Circle of the Americas 1998, Storyteller of the Year Award, Native Writers Circle of the Americas 1998, Cherokee Nation Prose Award, Hope S. Dean Award for Notable Achievement in Children's Literature. *Address:* Greenfield Review Press, PO Box 308, Greenfield Center, Greenfield, NY 12833, USA (office). *Telephone:* (518) 584-1728 (office). *Fax:* (518) 583-9741 (office). *E-mail:* nudatlog@earthlink.net (office). *Website:* www.josephbruchac.com.

BRUCKNER, Pascal, DèsSc, PhD; French writer and lecturer; b. 15 Dec. 1948, Paris; s. of René Bruckner and Monique Bruckner; m. Violaine Barret 1970 (divorced 1973); one s.; also one d. by Caroline Thompson. *Education:* Lycée Henri IV, Univs de Paris I (Sorbonne), Paris VII (Jussieu). *Career:* annual travels in Asia 1977–90; Lecturer, Inst. d'Etudes Politiques, Paris 1990–94; Visiting Prof., Univ. of San Diego and New York Univ. 1986–95; mem. Bd of Dirs Action contre la faim 1983–88; mem. Cercle de l'Oratoire (French think tank) 2001–. *Theatre:* many of his books have been played on stage throughout Europe and in India. *Publications:* Le Nouveau Désordre Amoureux 1977, Lune de Fiel 1982 (adapted for screen by Roman Polanski under the title Bitter Moon 1992), Le sanglot de l'homme blanc 1983, Le palais des claques 1986, Le Divin Enfant 1992, La Tentation de l'Innocence (Prix Médicis) 1995, Les Voleurs de Beauté (Prix Renaudot) 1997, Les ogres anonymes 1998, L' Euphorie perpétuelle, essai sur Le devöir de bonheur 2000, Misère de la prospérité. La religion marchande et ses ennemis (Sénat Prix du Livre d'économie) 2002, Au secours, le Père Noël revient 2003, L'amour du prochain 2006, La Tyrannie de la pénitence: Essai sur le masochisme en Occident 2006; translations in 25 countries. *Honours:* Chevalier des Arts et des Lettres, Légion d'honneur 2002. *Address:* 8 rue Marie Stuart, 75002 Paris, (home); c/o Editions Denoel, 9 Rue de Cherche-Midi, 75248 Paris, France (office). *Telephone:* 1-40-26-68-79 (home). *Fax:* 1-40-56-34-37 (home). *E-mail:* bruckner@wanadoo.fr (home); contact@lemeilleurdesmondes.org (office). *Website:* www.lemeilleurdesmondes.org (office).

BRULOTTE, Gaëtan, BA, MA, PhD; Canadian academic and writer; *Professor of French and Francophone Literature, University of South Florida, Tampa*; b. 8 April 1945, Lévis, Québec. *Education:* Laval Univ., École des Hautes Études en Sciences Sociales, Univ. Paris VII. *Career:* instructor, Laval Univ. 1969; Prof. of French, Trois-Rivières Coll. 1970–83; Visiting Prof., Université du Québec à Trois-Rivières 1973, 1980, 1981, 1989, 1990, Univ. of New Mexico 1981, 1982, 1983, 1984, 1993, 1994, Univ. of California, Santa Barbara 1982, Brevard Community Coll. 1983–84, Université Stendhal 1993, Sorbonne, Paris 1994; Distinguished Visiting Prof., New Mexico State Univ. 1988; Visiting Prof., Univ. of South Florida, Tampa 1984–88, Prof. of French and Francophone Literature 1988–, Distinguished Univ. Prof. 2005–; mem. Int. Council on Francophone Studies, MLA, PEN Club, UNEQ, CEAD, Montreal, SACD Paris, EAT (Ecrivains Associés du Théâtre), Paris. *Plays:* Le Client (stage production by La Patience, France; Dir Charles Tordjman, cr. in residence at Théâtre de La Mure, France) 2001, La Liquidation 2007, Univ. of Grenoble 2007. *Radio:* Seuils (The Threshold of the Imagination; director and producer of 15 half-hour radio programmes, CFCQ FM, Trois-Rivières) 1979, Le Surveillant (Radio-Canada FM) 1979, Le Balayeur (Radio-Canada FM) 1979, Les Ecrivains (director and producer of 31 half-hour radio programmes on the craft of writing, CFCQ FM, Trois-Rivières) 1980–81, L'Indication (Radio-Canada FM) 1980, Histoire d'Albert (Radio-Canada FM) 1980, En voiture (Radio-Canada FM) 1981, Les Cadenas (Radio-Canada FM) 1981, Le Client (radio drama; First Prize, XIth Concours d'oeuvres dramatiques radiophoniques de Radio-Canada) 1983, La Contravention, Monsieur Desfossés (Radio-Canada FM) 1986, Le Bail, L'Exclusion de Hoper (Radio-Canada FM) 1987, La fulgurante ascension de Bou (Radio-Canada FM) 1994. *Television:* L'Emprise (TV script with Jean Sarrazin), Les Beaux Dimanches (part of series Les Chemins de l'imaginaire, CBC) 1980. *Publications:* L'Emprise (novel, trans. as Double Exposure) 1979, Écrivains de la Mauricie (ed.) 1981, Le Surveillant (short stories, trans. as The Secret Voice) 1982, Ce qui nous tient 1988, L'Univers du peintre Jean Paul Lemieux (critical essay) 1996, Oeuvres de Chair: Figures du discours érotique 1996, Les cahiers de Limentinus: Lectures fin de Siècle (essays) 1998, Epreuves (short stories) 1999, Le Client (play) 2001, La Vie de Biais (short stories) 2002, La chambre des lucidités (essay) 2003, Encyclopedia of Erotic Literature (2 vols) 2006, La nouvelle québécoise 2010; contribs to books, anthologies, textbooks, scholarly journals and periodicals. *Honours:* Robert-Cliche Award 1979, Adrienne-Choquette Award 1981, France-Québec Award 1983, First Prize, XIth CBC

Radio Drama Contest 1983, Trois-Rivières Literary Grand Prize 1989, John-Glassco Trans. Award 1990, Laureate, Journées de Lyon des auteurs de Théâtre 1996, Artist/Scholar of the Year (Phi Kappa Phi) 1998, Theodore and Venette Ashkounes-Ashford Distinguished Scholar Award 1999, Odyssée Award, Quebec 2002, Presidential Award for Faculty Excellence 2003, Outstanding Research Achievement 2004. *Address:* World Languages, University of South Florida, 4202 East Fowler Avenue, CPR 424, Tampa, FL 33620, USA (office). *Telephone:* (813) 974-2782 (office). *Fax:* (813) 974-3265 (office). *E-mail:* brulotte@usf.edu (office). *Website:* www.gbrulotte.com.

BRUMMER, Alexander, BSc, MBA; British journalist; *City Editor, Daily Mail*; b. 25 May 1949, Hove, England; m. Tricia Brummer; two s. *Education:* University of Southampton, University of Bradford Management Center. *Career:* worked for J. Walter Thomson and Haymarket Publishing 1970–72; Financial Corresp., The Guardian 1972–78, US Financial and Washington Corresp., then Foreign Ed., Financial Ed., Assoc. Ed. 1978–98; Consultant Ed., Financial Mail on Sunday 1999–2000; City Ed., Daily Mail 2000–; regular contrib. to the Jewish Chronicle, New Statesman. *Publications:* American Destiny 1986, Hanson: A Biography 1994, Weinstock: A Biography 1998, The Crunch: The Scandal of Northern Rock and the Escalating Credit Crisis 2008, The Great Pensions Robbery 2010. *Honours:* Overseas Press Club Award 1989, Financial Journalist of the Year, British Press Awards 2000, Best City Journalist, Media Awards 2000. *Address:* Daily Mail, Northcliffe House, 2 Derry Street, London W8 5TT, England (office). *Telephone:* (20) 7938-6000 (office). *Fax:* (20) 7937-7374 (office). *E-mail:* city@dailymail.co.uk (office). *Website:* www.dailymail.co.uk (office).

BRUNA, Hendrik (Dick); Dutch writer and illustrator; b. 23 Aug. 1927, Utrecht; s. of Albert Bruna; m. Irene de Jongh 1953; two s. one d. *Career:* creator, numerous illustrated children's book characters, including Miffy 1955–. *Publications (in translation):* Miffy series: Miffy, Miffy at the Zoo, Miffy in the Snow, Miffy at the Seaside, Miffy Goes Flying, Miffy's Birthday, Miffy at the Playground, Miffy in Hospital, Miffy's Dream, Miffy's Bicycle, Miffy at School, Miffy Goes to Stay, Grandpa and Grandma Bunny, Miffy is Crying, Miffy's House, Auntie Alice's Party, Miffy in the Tent (De Zilveren Penseel 1996), Dear Grandma Bunny (De Zilveren Griffel 1997), Miffy at the Gallery, Miffy and Melanie, Miffy the Ghost, Miffy the Fairy, Miffy Dances, Miffy's Letter, The New Baby, Miffy's Garden, Miffy in Lolly Land, A Flute for Miffy, Flopear, Queen Miffy, Miffy Wanted, Miffy Loves New York City!; Poppy Pig series: Poppy Pig, Poppy Pig's Garden, Poppy Pig's Birthday, Poppy Pig is Sick, Poppy Pig Goes on Holiday, Poppy Pig's Shop, A Song for Poppy Pig; Snuffy series: Snuffy, Snuffy and the Fire, Snuffy's Puppies, Snuffy is Lost; Boris and Barbara series: Boris Bear (De Gouden Penseel 1990), Boris and Barbara, Boris on the Mountain, Boris in the Snow, Boris, Barbara and Benny, Boris Bear's Boat, Boris and the Umbrella, Boris the Pilot, Barbara's Clothes Chest, Boris the Champion, Boris Does the Shopping; other titles: The Apple, The Bird, Kitty Nell, Tilly and Tessa, The Egg, The King, Circus, The Fish, The Sailor, B is for Bear, A Book Without Words, My Vest is White, Animal Book, Flower Book, I Can Read, I Can Read More, I Can Read Much More, I Can Read Difficult Words, I Can Do Sums, Christmas, Farmer John, The Rescue, The Orchestra, Spring, Summer, Autumn and Winter, Stop at the Kerb!. *Honours:* many prizes for illustration on posters; Companion of the Order of Oranje-Nassau 1993. *Address:* c/o Marja Kerkhof, Mercis, Johannes Vermeerplein 3, 1071 Amsterdam, Netherlands. *E-mail:* info@mercis.nl. *Website:* www.miffy.com.

BRUNNER, Eva; Swiss playwright, translator and photographer; b. 26 Nov. 1952, Lucerne. *Education:* American Coll. of Rome, Univ. of Charleston, W Va, Ostkreuzschule für Fotografie, Berlin, Masterclass Arno Fischer. *Career:* Artist in Residence, Swiss Cultural Foundation Landy & Gyr, Stadtmühle Willisau, Acad. of the Arts, Wewelsfleth; mem. Swiss Writers' Asscn. *Art exhibitions:* solo: Festival Voies Off, Arles, France, exp12, exposure twelve Gallery, Berlin, Galerie Das Ding, Lucerne, Switzerland, Casa de Cultura Les Bernardes Salt, Girona, Spain, Buchhandlung Hirslanden, Zurich, Switzerland, Fenster61, Berlin, El Local, Figueres, Spain, Can Ginebreda, Spain, Stadtmühle Willisau, Switzerland; group exhbns: exp12 Gallery, Berlin, Germany, ORi Galerie, Berlin, A Book About Death, Emily Harvey Foundation Gallery, New York, USA, Museu Brasileiro da Escultura, São Paolo, Brazil, Alpineum, Lucerne, Ostkreuzschule für Fotografie, Berlin. *Plays:* Kalt 1984, Granit 1985, Von Wegen Abwege 1988, Alles Wird Gut 1994, Die Strick-Trilogie 1997, Sutters Salut 1998, Intimi.Date 2003. *Radio plays:* Geist trug die Steine, Ich trag' sie alleine 1988, Herrscher und Herrscherin 1989, Der Schweiz den Rückenkehren? 1991, Frieda Flachmann (Hörspiel morgen Förderpreis 1997) 1997, Im Paradies der Plauderer 1999, Blauensee (Prix Suisse for Best Swiss Radio Drama 2008) 2007. *Television:* Der Krösus von Luzern. *Address:* Erich-Weinert-Str. 64, 10439 Berlin, Germany. *E-mail:* mail@evabrunner.com (office). *Website:* www.evabrunner.com.

BRUNSKILL, Ronald William, OBE, MA, PhD, FSA; British architect (retd), lecturer and writer; b. 3 Jan. 1929, Lowton; m. Miriam Allsopp 1960; two d. *Education:* Univ. of Manchester. *Career:* Commonwealth Fund Fellow in Architecture and Town Planning, MIT 1956–57; Architect, Williams Deacon's Bank 1957–60; Lecturer 1960–73, Senior Lecturer 1973–84, Reader in Architecture 1984–89, Hon. Fellow, School of Architecture 1989–95, University of Manchester; Partner 1966–69, Consultant 1969–73, Carter, Brunskill & Assocs, architects; Visiting Prof., University of Florida at Gainesville 1969–70; Pres., Vernacular Architect Group 1974–77; Hon. Visiting Prof. 1994–95, Prof., School of the Built Environment 1995–2001, De Montfort University; mem. Cumberland and Westmorland Antiquarian and Archaeological Society, vice-pres. 1975–90, pres. 1990–93; Historic Buildings Council for England 1978–84; Cathedrals Advisory Committee for England 1981–91; Cathedrals Fabric Commission 1991–96; Ancient Monuments Society, hon. architect 1983–88, vice-chair. 1988–90, chair. 1990–2000, pres. 2004–09; Royal Commission on the Ancient and Historical Monuments for Wales 1983–97, vice-chair. 1993–97; British Historic Buildings Trust, trustee 1985–92; Historic Buildings and Monuments Commission 1989–95; Fabrics Advisory Cttee, Chester Cathedral 1989–95, 2004–09; Friends of Friendless Churches, Chair. 1990–98, Pres. 1999–2009. *Publications:* Illustrated Handbook of Vernacular Architecture 1971, Vernacular Architecture of the Lake Counties 1974, English Brickwork (with Alec Clifton-Taylor) 1977, Traditional Buildings of Britain 1981, Traditional Farm Buildings of Britain 1982, Timber Building in Britain 1985, Brick Building in Britain 1990, Houses and Cottages of Britain 1997, Traditional Farm Buildings of Britain and Their Conservation 1999, Vernacular Architecture: An Illustrated Handbook 2000, Traditional Buildings of Cumbria 2002, Clay and Brick Building in Britain 2009; contribs to scholarly journals. *Honours:* Hon. Doctor of Art, De Montfort Univ.; Pres.'s Award, Manchester Soc. of Architects 1977, Henry H. Glassie Award, Vernacular Architecture Forum, USA 2009. *Address:* 8 Overhill Road, Wilmslow, SK9 2BE, England (home). *Telephone:* (1625) 522099 (home).

BRUSSIG, Thomas; German writer, poet and playwright; b. 1965, Berlin. *Publications:* Wasserfarben (poems) 1991, Helden wie wir (trans. as Heroes Like Us) 1995, Am kürzeren Ende der Sonnenallee (Drehbuchpreis der Bundesregierung, with Leander Haußmann) 1999, Heimsuchung (play) 2000, Leben bis Männer 2001, Wie es leuchtet 2004, Berliner Orgie 2007, Schiedsrichter Fertig, Eine Litanei 2008; contrib. to Die Welt, Die Welt am Sonntag, FAZ, Tageszeitung, Süddeutsche Zeitung, Max, Wir sind nostalgisch, weil wir Menschen sind (essay in Sehnsucht nach dem Kommunismus) 2001. *Honours:* Hans-Fallada-Preis der Stadt Neumünster 2000. *Address:* c/o Piper Verlag GmbH, Georgenstrasse 4, 80799 Munich, Germany (office). *Website:* www.piper-verlag.de (office); www.thomasbrussig.de.

BRUTON, Eric, (Eric Moore); British author and business executive; b. 1915, London, England. *Career:* Managing Dir, NAG Press Ltd, Colchester 1963–93, Diamond Boutique Ltd 1965–80; Chair., Things & Ideas Ltd 1970–78; mem. British Horological Institute 1955–62, CWA 1959–62, Gemmological Asscn of Great Britain, council mem. 1972–91, pres., 1994–95, National Asscn of Goldsmiths, pres. 1983–85. *Publications:* True Book about Clocks 1957, Death in Ten Point Bold 1957, Die Darling Die 1959, Violent Brothers 1960, True Book about Diamonds 1961, The Hold Out 1961, King Diamond 1961, The Devil's Pawn 1962, Automation 1962, Dictionary of Clocks and Watches 1962, The Laughing Policeman 1963, The Longcase Clock 1964, The Finsbury Mob 1964, The Smithfield Slayer 1964, The Wicked Saint 1965, The Fire Bug 1967, Clocks and Watches 1400–1900 1967, Clocks and Watches 1968, Diamonds 1970, Antique Clocks and Clock Collecting 1974, The History of Clocks 1978, The Wetherby Collection of Clocks 1980, Legendary Gems 1984, Collector's Dictionary of Clocks and Watches 1999, History of Clocks and Watches Handbook 2003.

BRYANT, Dorothy Mae, BA, MA; American writer, dramatist, teacher and publisher; b. 8 Feb. 1930, San Francisco, CA; d. of Joseph Calvetti and Judith Chiarle Calvetti; m. 1st 1949 (divorced 1964); one s. one d.; m. 2nd Robert Bryant 1968; one step-s. one step-d. *Education:* San Francisco State Univ. *Career:* high school teacher 1953–64; teacher, San Francisco State Univ., San Francisco Mission Adult School, Golden Gate Coll. 1961–64, Contra Costa Coll. 1964–76; Publr Ata Books 1978–. *Plays:* Dear Master 1991, Tea with Mrs Hardy 1992, The Panel 1996, The Trial of Cornelia Connelly 1996, Posing for Gauguin 1998. *Publications:* fiction: Ella Price's Journal 1972, The Kin of Ata Are Waiting for You 1976, Miss Giardino 1978, The Garden of Eros 1979, Prisoners 1980, Killing Wonder 1981, A Day in San Francisco 1983, Confessions of Madame Psyche 1986, The Test 1991, Anita, Anita 1993, The Berkeley Pit 2007; non-fiction: Writing a Novel 1979, Myths to Lie By: Essays and Stories 1984, Literary Lynching 2002. *Honours:* American Book Award 1987, Bay Area Theatre Critics Circle Award for Best Script 1991. *E-mail:* dorbob@sbcglobal.net (office). *Website:* dorothybryantwriter.com.

BRYANT, John; British journalist; *Chairman, Press Association Trust*. *Career:* trainee journalist The Scotsman; fmr Exec. Ed. The Daily Mail; fmr Managing Ed. The Times 1986, then Deputy Ed.; fmr Ed. The Sunday Correspondent 1990, The European; Consulting Ed. The Daily Mail –2005; Ed.-in-Chief Telegraph Newspapers 2005–, acting Ed. The Daily Telegraph 2005; Chair. Press Asscn Trust 2008–; Chair. Editorial Bd, London Evening Standard 2009–. *Publications:* non-fiction: 3:59.4 2005, The London Marathon 2006. *Address:* London Evening Standard, Northcliffe House, 2 Derry Street, London, W8 5TT, England (office). *Website:* www.standard.co.uk (office).

BRYANT, Joseph Allen, Jr, AB, MA, PhD; American academic and writer; b. 26 Nov. 1919, Glasgow, KY; m. 1st Mary Virginia Woodruff 1946; two s.; m. 2nd Sara C. Bryant 1993. *Education:* Western Kentucky Univ., Vanderbilt Univ., Yale Univ. *Career:* Instructor to Assoc. Prof., Vanderbilt Univ. 1945–56; Assoc. Prof., Univ. of the South at Sewanee 1956–59, Duke Univ. 1959–61; Prof., Univ. of North Carolina, Greensboro 1961–68, Syracuse Univ. 1968–71, Univ. of Kentucky 1973–90; mem. MLA. *Publications:* Hippolyta's View: Some Christian Aspects of Shakespeare's Plays 1961, The Compassionate Satirist: Ben Jonson and His Imperfect World 1972, Understanding Randall Jarrell

1986, Shakespeare and the Uses of Comedy 1986, Twentieth Century Southern Literature 1997. *Honours:* Hon. DLitt (Univ. of the South) 1993.

BRYCE ECHENIQUE, Alfredo; Peruvian writer; b. 19 Feb. 1939, Lima. *Publications:* Huerto cerrado (short stories) 1968, Un mundo para Julius (novel) 1970, La felicidad ja ja (short stories) 1974, Tantas veces Pedro (novel) 1977, A vuelo de buen cubero y otras crónicas (non-fiction) 1977, La vida exagerada de Martín Romaña (novel) 1981, El hombre que hablaba de Octavia de Cádiz 1984, Magdalena peruana y otros cuentos (short stories) 1986, Crónicas personales 1986, La última mudanza de Felipe Carrillo (novel) 1988, Dos señoras conversan (novella) 1990, Permiso para vivir (Antimemorias) (memoir) 1993, No me esperen en abril (novel) 1995, A trancas y barrancas (articles) 1997, Reo de nocturnidad (novel) 1997, Guía triste de París (short stories) 1999, La amigdalitis de Tarzán (novel) 1999, El huerto de mi amada 2002, Doce cartas a dos amigos 2003, Entrevistas escogidas 2004, Entre la soledad y el amor 2005, Las obras infames de Pancho Marambio 2007. *Honours:* Premio Nacional de Literatura de Perú 1972, Premio Passion, France 1983, Encomienda de Isabel la Católica, Spain 1993, Premio Nacional de Narrativa, Spain 1998, Encomienda de Alfonso X El Sabio, Spain 2000, Premio Grinzane Cavour, Piemonte, Italy 2002, Premio Planeta, Spain 2002; Commdr, Ordre des Arts et des Lettres 2000. *Website:* www.bryce-echenique .com.

BRYSON, Bill; American writer; b. 1951, Des Moines, Ia; m.; four c. *Education:* Drake Univ. *Career:* travelled to UK and worked as orderly in mental hosp. 1973; worked as journalist for The Times and the Independent; returned with his family to USA 1993; apptd to selection panel, Book of the Month Club 2001; Commr for English Heritage; Chancellor Durham Univ. 2005–11; Pres. Campaign to Protect Rural England 2007–. *Publications:* Penguin Dictionary of Troublesome Words (re-printed as Bryson's Dictionary of Troublesome Words) 1985, The Lost Continent 1987, The Mother Tongue: English and How It Got That Way, Made in America 1994, Neither Here Nor There: Travels in Europe 1995, Notes From a Small Island 1995, A Walk in the Woods 1998, I'm a Stranger Here Myself (essays, aka Notes From a Big Country) 1999, In a Sunburned Country (aka Down Under) 2000, The Best American Travel Writing (ed.), African Diary 2002, A Short History of Nearly Everything (Aventis Prize 2004, Descartes Science Communication Prize 2005) 2003, The Life and Times of the Thunderbolt Kid (memoirs) 2006, Shakespeare: A Short Life (biog.) 2007, Bryson's Dictionary for Writers and Editors 2008, At Home: A Short History of Private Life 2011. *Honours:* Hon. DCL (Durham) 2004, Hon. OBE 2006. *Literary Agent:* The Marsh Agency, 50 Ablemarle Street, London, W1S 4BD, England. *Telephone:* (20) 7493-4361. *Fax:* (20) 7495-8961. *Website:* www.marsh-agency.co.uk. *Address:* c/o Publicity Department, Transworld Publishers, 61–63 Uxbridge Road, London, W5 5SA, England. *Website:* www.cpre.org.uk; www.randomhouse.com/features/ billbryson.

BRZEZINSKI, Zbigniew Kazimierz, PhD; American academic and fmr government official; *Counsellor, Center for Strategic and International Studies*; b. 28 March 1928, Warsaw, Poland; s. of Tadeusz Brzezinski and Leonia Roman; m. Emilie Anna (Muska) Benes 1955; two s. one d. *Education:* McGill and Harvard Univs. *Career:* settled in N America 1938; Instructor in Govt and Research Fellow, Russian Research Center, Harvard Univ. 1953–56; Asst Prof. of Govt, Research Assoc. of Russian Research Center and of Center for Int. Affairs, Harvard Univ. 1956–60; Assoc. Prof. of Public Law and Govt, Columbia Univ. 1960–62, Prof. 1962–89 (on leave 1966–68, 1977–81) and Dir Research Inst. on Communist Affairs 1961–77 (on leave 1966–68); mem. Policy Planning Council, Dept of State 1966–68; mem. Hon. Steering Cttee, Young Citizens for Johnson 1964; Dir Foreign Policy Task Force for Vice-Pres. Humphrey 1968; Asst to the Pres. for Nat. Security Affairs 1977–81; mem. Nat. Security Council 1977–81; Counsellor, Center for Strategic and Int. Studies, Washington, DC 1981–; Robert E. Osgood Prof. of American Foreign Policy, Paul Nitze School of Advanced Int. Studies, Johns Hopkins Univ. 1989–; Fellow, American Acad. of Arts and Sciences 1969–; mem. Council on Foreign Relations, New York, Bd of Trustees, Freedom House; Guggenheim Fellowship 1960, Ford Fellowship 1970. *Publications include:* Political Controls in the Soviet Army 1954, The Permanent Purge–Politics in Soviet Totalitarianism 1956, Totalitarian Dictatorship and Autocracy (with Carl Joachim Friedrich) 1957, The Soviet Bloc–Unity and Conflict 1960, Ideology and Power in Soviet Politics 1962, Africa and the Communist World (ed. and contrib.) 1963, Political Power: USA/USSR (with Samuel P. Huntington) 1964, Alternative to Partition: For a Broader Conception of America's Role in Europe 1965, Dilemmas of Change in Soviet Politics (ed. and contrib.) 1969, Between Two Ages: America's Role in the Technetronic Era 1970, The Fragile Blossom: Crisis and Change in Japan 1972, The Relevance of Liberalism 1977, Power and Principle: Memoirs of the National Security Adviser 1977–1981 1983, Game Plan: A Geostrategic Framework for the Conduct of the US-Soviet Contest 1986, In Quest of National Security 1988, The Grand Failure: The Birth and Death of Communism in the 20th Century 1989, Out of Control: Global Turmoil on the Eve of the Twenty-First Century 1993, The Grand Chessboard: American Primacy and its Geostrategic Imperatives 1996, The Geostrategic Triad: Living with China, Europe, and Russia 2000, The Choice: Global Domination or Global Leadership 2004, Second Chance: Three Presidents and the Crisis of American Superpower 2007, America and the World: Conversations on the Future of American Foreign Policy (with Brent Scowcroft) 2008; contrib. to many publications, journals and periodicals. *Honours:* Order of White Eagle (Poland) 1995, Order of Merit (Ukraine) 1996, Masaryk Order 1998, Gedymim Order 1998; Dr hc (Alliance Coll.) 1966, (Coll. of the Holy Cross) 1971, (Fordham Univ.) 1979, (Williams Coll.) 1986, (Georgetown Univ.) 1987, (Catholic Univ. of Lublin) 1990, (Warsaw Univ.) 1991; Presidential Medal of Freedom 1981. *Address:* Center for Strategic and International Studies, 1800 K Street NW, Washington, DC 20006, USA (office). *Telephone:* (202) 833-2408 (office). *Fax:* (202) 833-2409 (office). *E-mail:* zb@csis.org (office). *Website:* www.csis.org (office).

BUARQUE, Chico; Brazilian singer, songwriter, musician (guitar), writer and poet; b. (Francisco Buarque de Hollanda), 19 June 1944, Rio de Janeiro; s. of Sérgio Buarque de Hollanda and Maria Amélia Cesário de Hollanda; brother of vocalist Miucha, uncle of Bebel Gilberto. *Career:* left Univ, of São Paulo to absorb local Bossa Nova scene and began writing songs; came to prominence when compositions recorded by singer Nara Leao. *Recordings include:* albums: Pedro Pedriero 1965, Chico Buarque de Hollanda 1966, Morte e Vida Severina 1966, Umas e outras 1969, Chico Buarque na Itália 1969, Apesar de você 1970, Per un pugno di samba 1970, Construção 1971, Quando o carnaval chegar 1972, Caetano e Chico juntos e ao vivo 1972, Chico canta 1973, Sinal fechado 1974, Chico Buarque & Maria Bethânia ao vivo 1975, Meus caros amigos 1976, Cio da Terra 1977, Os saltimbancos 1977, Gota d'água 1977, Chico Buarque 1978, Ópera do malandro 1979, Vida 1980, Show 1° de Maio 1980, Almanaque 1981, Saltimbancos trapalhões 1981, Chico Buarque en espanhol 1982, Para viver um grande amor 1983, O grande circo místico 1983, Chico Buarque 1984, O Corsário do rei 1985, Ópera do malandro 1985, Malandro 1985, Melhores momentos de Chico & Caetano 1986, Francisco 1987, Dança do meia-lua 1988, Chico Buarque ao vivo Paris Le Zenith 1990, Paratodos 1993, Uma palavra 1995, Terra 1997, As Cidades 1998, Chico ao Vivo 1999, Cambaio 2001, Chico Buarque Duetos 2002, Carioca 2006, Carioca ao Vivo 2007. *Film music:* Anjo assassino 1966, Garota de Ipanema 1967, Roda Vida (play, also score) 1968, Quando o carnaval chegar 1972, Os saltimbancos trapalhões 1981, Ópera do malandro 1986, Ed Mort 1996, O mandarim 1995. *Publications:* A Banda (songbook) 1966, Fazenda modelo (novel) 1974, Chapeuzinho Amarelo (poems) 1979, A bordo do Rui Barbosa 1981, Estorvo (novel) 1991, Benjamim (novel) 1995, Budapeste 2003, Leite Derramado 2009. *Address:* c/o Discmedi SA, Ronda Guinardó, 59 Bis, Baixos, 08024 Barcelona, Spain. *Website:* www.chicobuarque.com.br.

BUCHANAN, Mark; American writer. *Publications:* Ubiquity: The Science of History, or Why the World is Simpler Than We Think 2000, Nexus: Small Worlds and the Groundbreaking Science of Networks 2002, Small World: Uncovering Nature's Hidden Networks 2002, The Social Atom 2007. *E-mail:* buchanan.mark@gmail.com (office). *Website:* pagesperso-orange.fr/mark .buchanan/indexMB.html.

BUCHANAN, Patrick (Pat) Joseph, MS; American journalist and fmr government official; b. 2 Nov. 1938, Washington; s. of William Buchanan and Catherine Crum; m. Shelley A. Scarney 1971. *Education:* Georgetown and Columbia Univs. *Career:* editorial writer, St Louis Globe Democrat 1962–64, asst editorial writer 1964–66; Exec. Asst to Richard Nixon 1966–69; Special Asst to Pres. Nixon 1969–73; consultant to Pres. Nixon and Pres. Ford 1973–74; Asst to Pres., Dir of Communications, White House, Washington, DC 1985–87; syndicated columnist, political commentator, New York Times special features 1975–78, Chicago Tribune-New York News Syndicate 1978–85, Tribune Media Services 1987–91, 1993–95; commentator, NBC Radio Network 1978–82; co-host Crossfire (TV Show) Cable News Network 1982–85, 1987–91, 1993–95, 1997; appeared as host and panellist in TV shows 1978–; Ed.-in-Chief PJB—From the Right (newsletter) 1990–91; moderator, Capital Gang TV show CNN 1988–92; Chair. The American Cause 1993–95, 1997–, Pat Buchanan & Co., Mutual Broadcasting System 1993–95; unsuccessful cand. for Republican Presidential nomination 1992, 1996; Republican. *Publications:* The New Majority 1973, Conservative Votes, Liberal Victories 1975, Right from the Beginning 1988, Barry Goldwater, The Conscience of A Conservative 1990, The Great Betrayal 1998, A Republic, not an Empire 2000, State of Emergency 2006, Day of Reckoning 2008. *Address:* The American Cause, 501 Church Street, Suite 315, Vienna, VA 22180 (office); 1017 Savile Lane, McLean, VA 22101, USA (home). *Telephone:* (703) 255-2632 (office). *Fax:* (703) 255-2219 (office). *E-mail:* americancause@gmail.com (office). *Website:* www.theamericancause.org (office).

BUCHER, Werner; Swiss poet, writer, journalist and editor; b. 19 Aug. 1938, Zürich; m. Josiane Fidanza 1968. *Career:* mem. Swiss Writers' Union. *Publications:* Nicht Solche Aengste, du... (poetry) 1974, Zeitzünder 3: Dank an den Engel 1987, Was ist mit Lazarus? 1989, Einst & Jetzt & Morgen (poems) 1989, Ein anderes Leben: Versuch, sich einem Unbekannten anzunahern, De Wand: Roman; Eigentlich wunderbar, das Leben...: Tagtag-Gedichte und Nachtnacht-Nachrichten; Das bessere Ende: Gedichte, Mouchette (poem) 1995, Wegschleudern die Brillen, die Lügen (poetry) 1995, Unruhen 1997, Wenn der zechpreller gewinnt (poetry) 1997, Urwaldhus, Tierhag, Ochsenhutte & Co, Die Schonsten Ostschweizer Beizen 1997, Im Schatten des Campanile 2000, Weitere Stürme sind angesagt (poetry) 2002, Den Fröschen zuhrören, den toten Vätem 2005, Du mit deinem leisen Lächeln 2007, Die schlasfende Santa Maria von Vezio und andere Geschichten 2007; contributions: Entwürfe, Tobel und Hoger, Literarisches aus dem Appenzellerland 2001. *Address:* Wirtschaft Rütegg, 9413 Oberegg, Switzerland (office). *Telephone:* 718881556 (office). *E-mail:* info@wernerbucher.ch (office). *Website:* www.wernerbucher.ch.

BUCHOLZ, Arden, MA, PhD; American historian; *Distinguished Teaching Professor of History, State University of New York College at Brockport*; b. 14 May 1936, Chicago, Ill.; m. Sue Tally 1962; two c. *Education:* Dartmouth Coll., Univ. of Vienna, Austria, Univ. of Chicago. *Career:* teacher of English, Amerikan Orta Okulu, Talas-Kayseri, Turkey 1958–60; served to Lt, US Army, including Counterintelligence in Germany 1961–64; teacher of History, Latin School of Chicago 1965–70; Distinguished Teaching Prof. of History, State Univ. of New York Coll. at Brockport 1970–; Programme Co-Dir, Brunel Univ., Uxbridge, UK 1987–88. *Publications:* Hans Delbruck and the German Military Establishment 1985, Moltke, Schlieffen, and Prussian War Planning 1991, Delbruck's Modern Military History 1997, Moltke and The German Wars, 1864–1871 2001. *Honours:* Outstanding Book in Mil. History Citation, Int. Comm. on Mil. History 1991. *Address:* 306 Main Street, Brockport, NY 14420, USA (home). *Telephone:* (585) 637-3099 (home). *E-mail:* abucholz@brockport.edu.

BUCHT, Gunnar, PhD; Swedish composer and writer; b. 5 Aug. 1927, Stocksund; m. Bergljot Krohn 1958. *Education:* studied composition with Karl Birger-Blomdahl, Carl Orff, Goffredo Petrassi, Max Deutsch, piano with Yngve Flyckt. *Career:* debut as composer and pianist 1949; Chair. Soc. of Swedish Composers 1963–69; teacher, Stockholm Univ. 1965–69; Vice-Pres. Int. Soc. for Contemporary Music 1969–72; Cultural Attaché, Embassy in Bonn 1970–73; Prof. of Composition, Royal Coll. of Music 1975–85, Dir 1987–93; mem. Royal Acad. of Music. *Compositions include:* 12 symphonies 1952–97, two cello concertos 1955–90, three string quartets 1951, 1959, 1997, String Quintet 1950, Sonata for piano and percussion 1955, La fine della diaspora for tenor, chorus and orchestra (Quasimodo) 1957, The Pretenders (opera, after Ibsen) 1966, Symphonie pour la musique libérée for tape 1969, Lutheran Mass 1973, Journées oubliées 1975, Au delà 1977, Violin Concerto 1978, The Big Bang – and After 1979, Georgica 1980, En Clairobscur for chamber orchestra 1981, One Day I Went Out Into The World, novel for orchestra 1983–84, Blad från mitt gulsippeänge for clarinet and piano 1985, Fresques mobiles 1986, Unter Vollem Einsatz for organ and five percussionists 1987, Tönend bewegte Formen for orchestra 1987, Piano Concerto 1994, Coup sur Coup for percussion 1995, Concerto de Marle for viola and orchestra 1996, Movements in Space for orchestra 1996, Panta Rei for soli, chorus and orchestra 1998–99, Alienus' Dream for orchestra 1999, Partita for two violins 2001, Den starkare (Strindberg) monodram for mezzo-soprano and orchestra 2001, Superstrings for orchestra 2002, Tre per due for two violins 2004, Notenbüchlein für Duo Gelland for two violins 2008, Wie die Zeit vergeht (Quasi una sinfonia) for orchestra 2009. *Recordings:* Symphony 7, Violin Concerto, Piano Concerto, Georgica, Cantata, Quatre pièces pour le pianiste, Coup sur Coup, Sections of One Day I Went Out Into the World, Odysseia (Kazantzakis) half-scenic oratorio for soli, chorus and orchestra, part one 2000–03, The Infinite Melody for orchestra 2004. *Publications:* Electronic Music in Sweden 1977, Europe in Music 1996, Född på Krigsstigen (autobiog.) 1997, Rum, rörelse, tid 1999, Pythagoras' String 2005, Rum, Människa, Musik 2009, Quid est tonus 2009; contrib. to Swedish Journal of Musicology, Nordic Journal of Aesthetics. *Honours:* Royal Medal Litteris et artibus, Royal Acad. of Music Medal for För tonkonstens främjande. *Address:* Rådmansgatan 74, 11360 Stockholm, Sweden (home). *Telephone:* (8) 736-60-31 (home). *E-mail:* gb.bucht@telia.com (home). *Website:* www.gunnarbucht.com.

BUCHWALD, Christoph; German publishing executive; *Publisher, Uitgeverij Cossee*; b. 30 Nov. 1951, Tübingen. *Education:* Freie Universität, Berlin, Technische Universität, Berlin. *Career:* fmrly Ed. Hanser, Munich; fmrly Publr Luchterhand Literaturverlag; fmrly with Suhrkamp Verlag KG, Frankfurt; Co-founder and Publr Uitgeverij Cossee, Amsterdam. *Honours:* Kt, Orde van Oranje-Nassau (Netherlands) 2011. *Address:* Uitgeverij Cossee, Kerkstraat 361, 1017 HW Amsterdam, Netherlands (office). *Telephone:* (20) 5289911 (office). *Fax:* (20) 5289912 (office). *E-mail:* buchwald@cossee.com (home). *Website:* www.uitgeverijcossee.nl (office).

BUCK, Joan Juliet; American writer and magazine editor; b. Los Angeles; m. John Heilpern (divorced). *Career:* raised in Paris and London; fmr journalist with numerous magazines including Interview, WWD (as London and Italian Corresp.), The Observer Magazine, Condé Nast, Vogue USA, The New Yorker; Ed.-in-Chief French Vogue 1994–2000; TV critic Vogue Magazine, New York; co-f. wowowow.com website 2008–; mem. PEN Newsletter Cttee. *Film appearance:* Greyfriars Bobby: The True Story of a Dog 1961. *Television appearance:* as herself in Fashion Victim: The Killing of Gianni Versace (TV) 2001. *Publications include:* The Only Place To Be 1982, Daughter of the Swan 1989; contrib. to numerous magazines. *E-mail:* info@wowowow.com (office). *Website:* www.wowowow.com (office).

BUCKLEY, Christine; American journalist and author; b. New York. *Career:* contrib., LA Weekly, OC Weekly, Lonely Planet, New York Times. *Radio:* many contribs to Weekend Edition (NPR). *Publications:* Slave Hunter: One Man's Quest to Free Victims of Human Trafficking (with Aaron Cohen) 2008. *Honours:* Associated Press Award. *Address:* c/o Simon & Schuster, 1230 Avenue of the Americas, 11th Floor, New York, NY 10020, USA (office). *Telephone:* (212) 698-7148 (office). *Website:* authors.simonandschuster.com/Christine-Buckley/60107631 (office).

BUCKLEY, William K., MA, PhD; American academic, writer and poet; *Professor, Indiana University Northwest*; b. 14 Nov. 1946, San Diego, Calif.; m. Mary Patricia 1969; one s. *Education:* Univ. of San Diego, California State Univ. at San Diego, Miami Univ., Oxford, OH. *Career:* instructor, San Diego Community Colls 1972–74; Co-founder and Co-Ed. Recovering Literature 1972–85; Dir Learning Skills Center, California State Univ. at San Diego 1974–75; Teaching Fellow, Miami Univ., Oxford, OH 1975–79; Visiting Asst Prof., Hanover Coll. 1979–82; Visiting Asst Prof., Indiana Univ. Northwest, Gary, Ind. 1982–84, Prof. 1985–; Ed. Plath Profiles (online Int., peer-reviewed journal of Plath studies) 2008–; mem. Acad. of American Poets. *Publications:* A Half-Century of Céline (co-author) 1983, Critical Essays on Louis-Ferdinand Céline (ed.) 1989, Senses' Tender: Recovering the Novel for the Reader 1989, New Perspectives on the Closing of the American Mind (co-ed.) 1992, Lady Chatterley's Lover: Loss and Hope 1993; poetry: By the Horses Before the Rains (Modern Poetry journal Best Chapbook of the Year 1997) 1996, Heart Maps 1997, 81 Mygrations 1998, Athena in Steeltown 1999, Sylvia's Bells 2002, Lost Heartlands Found 2004, On Heartland Soils 2005. *Address:* Department of English, Indiana University Northwest, 3400 Broadway, Gary, IN 46408, USA (office). *Telephone:* (219) 980-6570 (office). *E-mail:* wbuckley@iun.edu (office).

BUDBILL, David, BA, MDiv; American writer, poet and dramatist; b. 13 June 1940, Cleveland, OH; m. Lois Eby; two c. *Education:* Muskingum Coll., New Concord, OH, Columbia Univ., Union Theological Seminary, New York. *Career:* Poet-in-Residence, Niagara Erie Writers, Buffalo, NY 1984, Jamestown Community Coll., Jamestown, New York 1986, 1987; mem. PEN, Dramatists' Guild. *Plays:* Thingy World!, Little Acts of Kindness, Two for Christmas 1996, Judevine. *Publications:* poetry: Barking Dog 1968, The Chain Saw Dance 1977, Pulp Cutters' Nativity 1981, From Down to the Village 1981, Why I Came to Judevine 1987, Judevine: The Complete Poems 1991, Moment to Moment: Poems of a Mountain Recluse 1999, While We've Still Got Feet 2005; children's fiction: Christmas Tree Farm 1974; other: Danvis Tales: Selected Stories by Rowland Robinson (ed.) 1995; contributions: many anthologies and periodicals. *Honours:* Hon. DHumLitt (New England Coll.) 2009; Williamstown Repertory Theatre Playwright's Fellowship 1965, Publication Grant, American Studies Inst. 1967, Poetry Fellowships, Vermont Council on the Arts 1973, 1977, 1979, Kirkus Reviews Best Books 1974, 1976, Guggenheim Fellowship 1982–83, Playwriting Fellowship, Nat. Endowment for the Arts 1991, San Francisco Bay Area Critics' Circle Award 1991. *Literary Agent:* Susan Schulman Literary Agency, 454 West 44th Street, New York, NY 10036, USA. *Telephone:* (212) 713-1633. *Fax:* (212) 581-8830. *E-mail:* schulman@aol.com. *E-mail:* budbill@sover.net (office). *Website:* www.davidbudbill.com.

BUDD, Holly (see Judd, Alan)

BUECHNER, (Carl) Frederick, AB, BD; American writer and minister; b. 11 July 1926, New York, NY; m. Judith Friedrike Merck 1956; three c. *Education:* Princeton Univ., Union Theological Seminary. *Career:* Teacher of Creative Writing, New York Univ., summers 1954, 1955; Ordained Minister, United Presbyterian Church 1958; Chair., Dept of Religion 1958–67, Minister 1960–67, Phillips Exeter Acad.; William Belden Noble Lecturer, Harvard Univ. 1969; Russell Lecturer, Tufts Univ. 1971; Lyman Beecher Lecturer, Yale Univ. 1977; Harris Lector, Bangor Seminary 1979; Smyth Lecturer, Columbia Seminary 1981; Lecturer, Trinity Inst. 1990; mem. Council on Religion in Independent Schools, regional chair. 1958–63; Nat. Council of Churches, cttee on literature 1954–57; Presbytery of Northern New England. *Publications:* A Long Day's Dying 1950, The Season's Difference 1952, The Return of Ansel Gibbs 1958, The Final Beast 1965, The Magnificent Defeat 1966, The Hungering Dark 1969, The Alphabet of Grace 1970, The Entrance to Porlock 1970, Lion Country 1971, Open Heart 1972, Wishful Thinking 1973, The Faces of Jesus 1974, Love Feast 1974, Telling the Truth 1977, Treasure Hunt 1977, The Book of Bebb 1979, Peculiar Treasures 1979, Godric 1980, The Sacred Journey 1982, Now and Then 1983, A Room Called Remember 1984, Brendan 1987, Whistling in the Dark 1988, The Wizard's Tide 1990, Telling Secrets 1991, The Clown in the Belfry 1992, Listening to Your Life 1992, The Son of Laughter 1993, The Longing for Home 1996, On the Road with the Archangel 1997, The Storm 1998, The Eyes of the Heart 1999, Speak What We Feel 2001, Secrets in the Dark 2007. *Honours:* O'Henry Prize 1955, Richard and Hinda Rosenthal Award 1958. *Address:* 3572 State Route 315, Pawlet, VT 05761, USA (home).

BUICAN, Denis, DèsScNat, DèsL et ScHum; Romanian/French academic, biologist and philosopher of biology; *Honorary Professor, Université de Paris X Nanterre*; b. 21 Dec. 1934, Bucharest; s. of Dumitru Peligrad and Elena Buican. *Education:* Bucharest Univ., Faculté des Sciences de Paris, Univ. de Paris I-Sorbonne. *Career:* teaching asst, Bucharest Univ. 1956–57, Prin. Scientific Researcher 1957–60, Course Leader Gen. Biology and Genetics with History of Science course 1960–69, Invited Prof. 1990–; Invited Prof. First Class, History of Sciences, Faculté des Sciences, Univ. de Paris 1969–70, Univ. de Paris-Sorbonne 1970–74, Assoc. Prof., History and Philosophy of Science 1970–74; Assoc. Prof., History and Philosophy of Science, Univ. of Dijon 1974–80; Assoc. Prof., History of Sciences, Univ. of Paris I Panthéon-Sorbonne 1980–83; Assoc. Prof. First Class, History of Sciences, Univ. of Paris X 1983–86; Invited Prof. Collège de France 1984, 1993; Prof. First Class, Univ. of Paris X Nanterre 1986–2003, Hon. Prof. 2003–. *Achievements include:* developed new synergetic theory of evolution and Biognoseology theory of knowledge. *Publications include:* Histoire de la génétique et de l'évolutionnisme en France 1984, La Génétique et l'évolution 1986, Génétique et pensée évolutionniste 1987, Darwin et le darwinisme 1987, Lyssenko et le lyssenkisme 1988, L'Evolution et les évolutionnismes 1989, La Révolution de l'évolution 1989, L'Explosion biologique, du néant au Sur-être 1991,

Dracula et ses avatars de Vlad l'Empaleur à Staline et Ceausescu 1991, Charles Darwin 1992, Mendel et la génétique d'hier et d'aujourd'hui 1993, Les Métamorphoses de Dracula 1993, Biognoséologie: Evolution et révolution de la connaissance 1993, Jean Rostand 1994, Histoire de la Biologie 1994, Evolution de la pensée biologique 1995, L'Evolution aujourd'hui 1995, L'Evolution: la grande aventure de la vie 1995, Ethologie comparée 1996, Dictionnaire de Biologie 1997, L'Evolution et les théories évolutionnistes 1997, L'Epopée du vivant, L'Evolution de la biosphère et les avatars de l'Homme 2003, Le Darwinisme et les évolutionnismes 2005, Memorii 2007, L'Odyssée de l'Evolution 2008, Darwin dans l'histoire de la pensée biologique 2008, Mendel dans l'histoire de la génétique 2008, Mosaïque profane 2010, Biologie, Histoire et Philosophie 2010, Darwin et l'épopée de l'évolutionnisme 2012; poetry books: Arbre seul 1974, Lumière aveugle 1976, Mamura 1993, Spice (poèmes anciens et nouveaux) 2006, Margaritare negre (Perles noires) 2008, Roue de torture-Roue de lumière 2009. *Honours:* Hon. Citizen of Saliste (Romania) 2003; Grand Prix, Acad. Française 1989. *Address:* 15 rue Poliveau, 75005 Paris, France (home). *Telephone:* 1-43-36-33-97 (home).

BUIDA, Yuri; Russian author; b. 1954, USSR. *Publications:* Don Domino (novel), Yermo (novel), Boris and Gleb (novel), The Prussian Bride (short stories) 1998, Zero Train (novel) 2001; contrib. to Glas, Novy Mir, Znamya, Oktyabr, Volga. *Address:* c/o Dedalus Ltd, Langford Lodge, St Judith's Lane, Sawtry, Cambridgeshire PE28 5XE, England (office). *E-mail:* info@dedalusbooks.com (office). *Website:* www.dedalusbooks.com (office).

BUISSERET, David Joseph, PhD, FRHistS; British/American writer, historian and academic; *Senior Research Fellow, Newberry Library*; b. 18 Dec. 1934, Totland Bay, Isle of Wight, England; m. Patricia Connolly 1961; three s. two d. *Education:* Corpus Christi Coll., Cambridge. *Career:* Research Fellow, Corpus Christi Coll., Cambridge 1961–64; Lecturer then Sr Lecturer, Univ. of the West Indies 1964–72, Reader 1972–75, Prof. of History 1975–80; Ed. The Jamaican Historical Review 1968–80, Terrae Incognitae 1982–2007; Dir Hermon Dunlap Smith Center for the History of Cartography, Newberry Library, Chicago 1980–95, currently Sr Research Fellow; Jenkins and Virginia Garrett Prof. in Southwestern Studies and the History of Cartography, Univ. of Texas, Arlington 1995–2006. *Publications include:* Sully and the Growth of Centralized Government in France, 1598–1610 1969, The Wars of Religion (Vol. 10, Hamlyn History of the World) 1969, Historic Jamaica from the Air (with J. S. Tyndale-Biscoe) 1969, Les Oeconomies Royales de Sully (co-ed. with Bernard Barbiche) Vol. I 1970, Vol. II 1988, The Fortifications of Kingston, 1660–1900 1971, Huguenots and Papists 1972, A Popular History of the Port of Kingston 1973, Port Royal, Jamaica (with Michael Pawson) 1975, Historic Architecture of the Caribbean 1980, Henry IV 1984, Histoire de l'Architecture dans la Caraibe 1984, Skokie: A Community History using Old Maps (with Gerald Danzer) 1985, From Sea Charts to Satellite Images: Interpreting North American History through Maps (ed.) 1990, Historic Illinois from the Air 1990, A Guidebook to Resources for Teachers of the Columbian Encounter (co-ed. with Tina Reithmaier) 1992, Monarchs, Ministers and Maps: The Emergence of Cartography as a Tool of Government in Early Modern Europe (ed.) 1992, Elk Grove: A Community History in Maps (with James Issel) 1996, Rural Images: The Estate Map in the Old and New Worlds (ed.) 1996, Envisioning the City 1998, France in America (ed.) 1998, Creolization in the Americas (with Steven Reinhardt) 2000, Ingénieurs et Fortifications avant Vauban: l'Organisation d'un service royal aux XVIe-XVIIe Siècles 2001, The Mapmaker's Quest: Depicting New Worlds in Renaissance Europe 2003, A Cartographic History of Arlington and the Dallas-Fort Worth Area 2006, Jamaica in 1687 (ed.) 2009, Historic Texas from the Air 2009; contrib. to scholarly books and journals. *Honours:* Chevalier, Ordre des Palmes académiques 1993; Inst. of Jamaica Centennial Medal 1979. *Address:* 5126 Lunt Avenue, Skokie, IL 60077, USA (home). *Telephone:* (847) 679-2885 (home). *E-mail:* buisser@uta.edu (office).

BUKHT, Baidar, MA; Pakistani journalist; *Editor/Chairman of Editorial Committee, Daily Jang, Lahore*; b. 20 Dec. 1957, Lahore; s. of Muhammad Siddique and Ameer Siddique; one s. one d. *Education:* Punjab Univ., Lahore. *Career:* Sub-Ed., Daily Jang 1982, later Chief News Ed., currently Ed./Chair. of Editorial Cttee; involved in setting up Daily Pakistan and Daily Khabrain newspapers. *Honours:* President's Pride of Performance Award (Journalism) 2005. *Address:* Daily Jang, 13 Davis Road, Lahore, Pakistan (office). *Telephone:* (4) 26367480 (office). *Fax:* (4) 26309757 (office). *E-mail:* baidar.bakht@lhr.janggroup.com.pk (office). *Website:* www.jang.com.pk (office).

BULARD, Martine, LèsL; French newspaper editor; b. 12 June 1952. *Career:* apptd Chief Econ. Columnist on L'Humanité newspaper (organ of French Communist Party) 1980, fmr Ed.-in-Chief L'Humanité Dimanche; columnist, Le Monde diplomatique, currently Deputy Ed. *Publication:* Chine, Inde: La Course du dragon et de l'éléphant 2008. *Address:* Le Monde diplomatique, 1 avenue Stephen-Pichon, 75013 Paris, France (office). *Telephone:* 1-53-94-96-26 (office). *Fax:* 1-53-94-96-01 (office). *Website:* mondediplo.com (office).

BULAWAYO, NoViolet Mhka, BA, MA, MFA; Zimbabwean writer and academic; *Truman Capote Fellow and Lecturer in English, Cornell Univesity*; b. (Elizabeth Tshele), Tsholotsho. *Education:* Texas A&M Univ., Southern Methodist Univ., Cornell Univ., USA. *Career:* spent her childhood and youth in Gwanda and Bulawayo; Truman Capote Fellow and Lecturer in English, Cornell Univ. 2011–; Caine Prize/Georgetown Univ. Writer-in-Residence, Georgetown Univ., Washington, DC 2011. *Publications:* poetry and short stories published in Boston Review, The Warwick Review, Callaloo and in anthologies in Zimbabwe, South Africa and UK. *Honours:* Caine Prize for African Writing (for story Hitting Budapest) 2011. *Address:* Department of English, 347 Goldwin Smith Hall, Cornell University, Ithaca, NY 14853-3201, USA (office). *Telephone:* (607) 255-6800 (office). *Fax:* (607) 255-6661 (office). *E-mail:* ezt4@cornell.edu (office). *Website:* www.arts.cornell.edu/english (office).

BUNCH, Richard Alan, AA, BA, MA, MDiv, DD, JD; American teacher, poet and writer; *Instructor, Solano College and Napa Valley College*; b. 1 June 1945, Honolulu, HI; s. of Thornton Carlisle Bunch and DeLores Virginia Veal Bunch; m. Rita Anne Glazar 1990; one s. one d. *Education:* Napa Valley Coll., Stanford Univ., Univ. of Arizona, Vanderbilt Univ., Temple Univ., Univ. of Memphis, Sonoma State Univ. *Career:* staff mem., Nashville Human Rights Forum, Vanderbilt Univ. 1974–75; law clerk, Circuit Court, Memphis 1979–81; Attorney, Horne and Peppel, Memphis 1981–83; law clerk, Tennessee Court of Appeals, Memphis 1983; Assoc. News Ed. and features writer, Napa Valley Times 1985–86; teaching asst in philosophy, Vanderbilt Univ. 1973–74; instructor in history, philosophy, Belmont Univ. 1973–74, Chapman Univ. 1986–87; instructor in law, Univ. of Memphis 1982–83; instructor in history and humanities, Napa Valley Coll. 1985–, Diablo Valley Coll. 1991–94, 1997, Solano Coll. 1988–; instructor in law 1986–87, in Philosophy 1990–91, Sonoma State Univ.; Lecturer, Univ. of California, Berkeley 1995; judge, Davis Poetry Contest for Teens 2002, 2004; mem., Ina Coolbrith Poetry Circle. *Publications:* poetry: Summer Hawk 1991, Wading the Russian River 1993, A Foggy Morning 1996, Santa Rosa Plums 1996, South by Southwest 1997, Rivers of the Sea 1998, Sacred Space 1998, Greatest Hits: 1970–2000 2001, Running for Daybreak 2004; plays: The Russian River Returns 1999, Smokescreens, A Crude Awakening; prose: Night Blooms 1992, Hawking Moves: Plays, Poems and Stories 2007; contrib. poems to Oregon Review, Orbis, Hawaii Review, California Quarterly, short stories to The Plaza 2000, Goose River Anthologies 2003, 2004, 2005, 2006, 2007, Poetry Nottingham, Poetry New Zealand. *Honours:* grand prize Ina Coolbirth Nat. Poetry Day Contest 1989, Jessamyn West Prize 1990. *Address:* 248 Sandpiper Drive, Davis, CA 965616, USA (home).

BURCHILL, Julie; British journalist and writer; b. 3 July 1959, Bristol; m. 1st Tony Parsons (divorced); m. 2nd Cosmo Landesman (divorced); m. 3rd Daniel Raven. *Career:* journalist NME (New Musical Express) 1976–79, The Face 1980–84, Mail on Sunday 1984–93, Sunday Times 1993–94, Guardian 1998–2003, The Times 2003–06, The Independent 2010–; freelance journalist Sunday Express; co-founder Modern Review. *TV includes:* Prince (film), several plays. *Publications:* The Boy Looked at Johnny 1979, Love It or Shove It 1983, Girls on Film 1986, Damaged Goods 1987, Ambition 1989, Sex and Sensibility 1992, No Exit 1993, I Knew I Was Right (autobiog.) 1998, Diana 1998, Married Alive 1998, On Beckham 2002, Sugar Rush 2004, Made in Brighton (with Daniel Raven) 2007, Sweet 2007, Not in My Name: A Compendium of Modern Hypocrisy (with Chas Newkey-Burden) 2008. *Literary Agent:* c/o Robert Caskie, PFD, Drury House, 34–43 Russell Street, London, WC2B 5HA, England. *Telephone:* (20) 7344-1000. *Fax:* (20) 7836-9539. *E-mail:* info@pfd.co.uk. *Website:* www.pfd.co.uk.

BURDA, Hubert, DPhil; German publisher and author; *CEO, Hubert Burda Media*; b. 9 Feb. 1940, Heidelberg; s. of Franz Burda and Aenne Lemminger; m. Maria Furtwängler. *Education:* Univ. of Munich. *Career:* Man. Bild & Funk 1966–74; partner, Burda GmbH 1974, currently CEO and Acting Partner, Hubert Burda Media; Co-Publr Elle-Verlag GmbH, Munich; Founder Hubert Burda Centre for Innovative Communications, Ben-Gurion Univ. in Beer Sheva, Israel; Co-founder Europe Online SA, Luxembourg, European Publishers Council; currently Pres. Asscn of German Magazine Publishers; currently also Chair. of the Council, Munich Ludwig-Maximilians Univ.; est. Felix Burda Foundation 2001; f. Petrarca Prize (for poetry), Bambi (Media-Prize), Corp. Art Prize 1997; Publr Anna, Bunte, Burda Moden, Das Haus, Elle, Elle Bistro, Elle Deco, Elle TopModel, Focus, Focus Online, Focus TV, Freundin, Freizeit Revue, Futurekids, Glücks Revue, Haus + Garten, Lisa, Lisa Kochen & Backen, Lisa Wohnen & Dekorieren, Mein schöner Garten, Meine Familie & ich, Norddeutsche Neueste Nachrichten, Schweriner Volkszeitung, Starwatch Navigation, Super Illu, Super TV, TraXXX, Verena; Bd mem. German School of Journalism, Munich. *Honours:* Great Cross of Merit (Germany); Interfaith Gold Medallion, Council of Christians and Jews 1999, European Print Media Prize, Gold Medal Freedom of Speech, European Asscn of Communications Agencies, Leo Baeck Prize, Cen. Council of Jews in Germany 2006. *Address:* Hubert Burda Media, Arabellastrasse 23, 81925 Munich, Germany (office). *E-mail:* info@hubert-burda-media.com (office). *Website:* www.hubert-burda-media.com (office); www.hubert-burda.de (office).

BUREAU, Jérôme, DHist; French journalist; *Director of Communications, Métropole Télévision 6 (M6)*; b. 19 April 1956, Paris; m. Fabienne Pauly 1999; two c. (and two from previous marriage). *Career:* journalist with Libération 1978–81; Sr Reporter L'Équipe Magazine 1981–87, Ed.-in-Chief 1989–93; Ed.-in-Chief Le Sport 1987–88; Editorial Dir L'Équipe, L'Équipe-TV 1997–2003, L'Équipe Magazine, Vélo, XL, Tennis de France 1993–2003, lequipe.fr 1999–2003; TV and Radio Producer, Sport FM 2004; Dir of Communications, Métropole Télévision 6 (M6) 2004–. *Publications:* L'Amour-Foot 1986, Les Géants du football 1996, L'année du football 2004, Euro 2004: la grande fête du football 2004, Les champions d'Athènes 2004, Braaasil: Les magiciens du football 2005. *Address:* Métropole Télévision 6 (M6), 89 avenue Charles de Gaulle, 92575 Neuilly sur Seine cedex (office); 20 avenue Pernety, 75014

Paris, France (home). *E-mail:* jerome.bureau6@wanadoo.fr (home). *Website:* www.m6.fr (office).

BURENGA, Kenneth L.; American publishing executive; b. 30 May 1944, Somerville, NJ; s. of Nicholas Burenga and Louanna Chamberlin; m. Jean Case 1964; one s. one d. *Education:* Rider Coll. *Career:* budget accountant, Dow Jones & Co., S Brunswick, NJ 1966–67, Asst Man. data processing control 1968–69, staff asst for systems devt 1970–71, Man. systems devt and control 1972–76, circulation marketing Man. 1977–78, circulation sales dir 1979–80, Vice-Pres. circulation and circulation dir 1980–86; Chief Financial Officer and Admin. Officer, Dow Jones & Co., New York 1986–88, Exec. Vice-Pres., Gen. Man. 1989–91, Pres. COO 1991, Pres. and CEO –1998 (retd); fmr Gen. Man. Wall Street Journal 1989; mem. Bd of Dirs Dow Jones Courier. *Address:* 1076 Grona Schandua Road, Fredericksburg, TX 78624-7624, USA (home). *Telephone:* (830) 997-9944 (home).

BURGIN, Richard Weston, MA, MPhil; American academic, writer and editor; *Professor of Communication and English, St Louis University*; b. 30 June 1947, Boston, MA; m. Linda K. Harris 1991; one s. one step-d. *Education:* Brandeis Univ., Columbia Univ. *Career:* instructor, Tufts Univ., Mass 1970–74; Critic-at-Large, Boston Globe Magazine 1973–74; Founding Ed. and Dir New York Arts Journal 1976–83; Visiting Lecturer, Univ. of California at Santa Barbara 1981–84; Assoc. Prof. of Humanities, Drexel Univ., Phila 1984–96; Founder-Ed. Boulevard literary journal 1985–; Prof. of Communication and English, St Louis Univ., Mo. 1996–; mem. Nat. Book Critics Circle 1988–. *Recordings:* (music and lyrics) In All Of The World 2000, House Of Sun 2001, Doll Of Dreams 2002, Don't Go There 2005, Cold Ocean 2005, The Trouble With Love 2008. *Publications:* Conversations with Jorge Luis Borges 1969, The Man with Missing Parts (novella) 1974, Conversations with Isaac Bashevis Singer 1985, Man Without Memory (short stories) 1989, Private Fame (short stories) 1991, Fear of Blue Skies (short stories) 1998, Jorge Luis Borges: Conversations (ed.) 1998, Ghost Quartet (novel) 1999, The Spirit Returns (short stories) 2001, Stories and Dreamboxes (short stories, with illustrations by Gloria Vanderbilt) 2002, The Identity Club: New and Selected Stories (accompanied by CD, Don't Go There) (one of The Times Literary Supplement's Best Books of 2006) 2005, The Conference on Beautiful Moments (short stories) 2007, Rivers Last Longer 2010; contribs to numerous anthologies, reviews, journals and newspapers. *Honours:* Pushcart Prizes 1983, 1986, 1999, 2002, 2007, Best American Mystery Stories 2005. *Address:* 7507 Byron Place, First Floor, St Louis, MO 63105, USA (office). *Telephone:* (314) 862-2643 (office). *Fax:* (314) 862-2982 (office). *E-mail:* richardburgin@att.net (office). *Website:* www.richardburgin.net.

BURGIN, Victor, ARCA, MFA; British artist, writer and academic; *Millard Professor of Fine Art, Goldsmiths College, London*; b. 24 July 1941, Sheffield; s. of Samuel Burgin and Gwendolyne A. Crowder; m. 1st Hazel P. Rowbotham 1964 (divorced 1975); m. 2nd Francette Pacteau 1988; two s. *Education:* Firth Park Grammar School, Sheffield, Sheffield Coll. of Art, Royal Coll. of Art, London and Yale Univ., USA. *Career:* Sr Lecturer, Trent Polytechnic, Nottingham 1967–73; Prof. of History and Theory of Visual Arts, Faculty of Communication, Polytechnic of Cen. London 1973–; Prof. of Art History, Univ. of Calif., Santa Cruz 1988–95, Prof. of History of Consciousness 1995–2001, Prof. Emer. of History of Consciousness 2001–; Millard Prof. of Fine Art Goldsmiths Coll., Univ. of London 2001–; Deutscher Akademischer Austauschdienst Fellowship 1978–79; Picker Professorship, Colgate Univ., Hamilton, New York 1980; mem. arts advisory panel, Arts Council of Great Britain 1971–76, 1980–81; numerous mixed and solo exhbns at galleries around the world from 1965. *Publications:* Work and Commentary 1973, Thinking Photography 1982, The End of Art Theory 1986, Between 1986, Passages 1991, In/Different Spaces 1996, Some Cities 1996, Venice 1997, Shadowed 2000, The Remembered Film 2005; contrib. to exhbn catalogues. *Honours:* Hon. DUniv (Sheffield Hallam). *Address:* c/o Goldsmiths College, New Cross, London, SE14 6NW, England (office). *Telephone:* (20) 7919-7671 (office). *Fax:* (20) 7919-7673 (office). *E-mail:* v.burgin@gold.ac.uk (office). *Website:* www.goldsmiths.ac.uk/departments/visual-arts (office).

BURKE, Gregory; British playwright; b. 1969, Dunfermline, Scotland. *Career:* writer-in-residence at the Nat. Theatre Studio. *Plays:* Gagarin Way 2001, The Straits 2003, On Tour 2005, Black Watch 2006, Hoors 2009. *Honours:* Pearson Television Bursary 2002. *Address:* c/o Faber & Faber Ltd, Bloomsbury House, 74–77 Great Russell Street, London, WC1B 3DA, England (office). *Website:* www.faber.co.uk (office).

BURKE, James Lee, BA, MA; American writer; b. 5 Dec. 1936, Houston, Tex.; m. Pearl Pai 1960; one s. three d. *Education:* Univ. of Southwest Louisiana, Univ. of Missouri. *Career:* mem. Amnesty Int. *Publications:* Half of Paradise 1965, To the Bright and Shining Sun 1970, Lay Down My Sword and Shield 1971, Two for Texas 1983, The Convict and Other Stories 1985, The Lost Get-Back Boogie 1986, The Neon Rain 1987, Heaven's Prisoners 1988, Black Cherry Blues 1989, A Morning for Flamingos 1990, A Stained White Radiance 1992, Texas City, Nineteen Forty-Seven 1992, In the Electric Mist with Confederate Dead 1993, Dixie City Jam 1994, Burning Angel 1995, Heartwood 1999, Purple Cane Road 2000, Bitterroot 2001, Jolie Blon's Bounce 2002, White Doves at Morning 2002, Last Car to Elysian Fields 2003, In the Moon of Red Ponies 2004, Crusader's Cross 2005, Pegasus Descending 2006, The Tin Roof Blowdown 2007, Jesus Out to Sea (short stories) 2008, Swan Peak 2008, Rain Gods 2009, The Glass Rainbow 2010; contrib. to periodicals. *Honours:* Bread Loaf Fellow 1970, Southern Federation of State Arts Agencies grant 1977, Guggenheim Fellowship 1989, MWA Edgar Allan Poe Awards 1989, 1998, named Grand Master, Mystery Writers of America 2009. *Address:* c/o Orion Publishing Group Ltd, Orion House, 5 Upper St Martin's Lane, London, WC2H 9EA, England.

BURKE, (Ulick) Peter, MA, FRHistS, FBA; British historian and academic; *Professor Emeritus of Cultural History, University of Cambridge*; b. 16 Aug. 1937, Stanmore, London, England; s. of John Burke and Jenny Burke (née Colin); m. 1st Susan Patricia Dell 1972 (divorced 1983); m. 2nd Maria Lucía García Pallares 1989. *Education:* St Ignatius' Coll., Stamford Hill, St John's Coll., Oxford, St Antony's Coll., Oxford. *Career:* Asst Lecturer, then Lecturer, then Reader in History (later Intellectual History), School of European Studies, Univ. of Sussex 1962–78; Lecturer in History, Univ. of Cambridge 1979–88, Reader in Cultural History 1988–96, Prof. of Cultural History 1996–2004, Prof. Emer. 2004–; Fellow, Emmanuel Coll. Cambridge 1979–; Visiting Prof., Univ. of São Paulo, Brazil 1986, 1987, Nijmegen Univ. 1992–93 and Groningen Univ. 1998–99, The Netherlands, Heidelberg Univ., Germany 2002; Fellow, Wissenschaftskolleg, Berlin 1989–90, Netherlands Inst. for Advanced Study 2005. *Publications include:* The Renaissance Sense of the Past 1969, Culture and Society in Renaissance Italy 1972, Venice and Amsterdam 1974, Popular Culture in Early Modern Europe 1978, Sociology and History 1980, Montaigne 1981, Vico 1985, Historical Anthropology of Early Modern Italy 1987, The Renaissance 1987, The French Historical Revolution: The Annales School 1929–1989 1990, The Fabrication of Louis XIV 1992, History and Social Theory 1992, Antwerp: A Metropolis in Europe 1993, The Art of Conversation 1993, The Fortunes of the Courtier 1995, Varieties of Cultural History 1997, The European Renaissance 1998, A Social History of Knowledge 2000, Eyewitnessing 2001, (co-author) A Social History of the Media 2002, Languages and Communities in Early Modern Europe 2004. *Honours:* Erasmus Prize, Academia Europaea 1999. *Address:* Emmanuel College, Cambridge, CB2 3AP (office); 14 Warkworth Street, Cambridge, CB1 1EG, England (home). *Telephone:* (1223) 334272 (home). *Fax:* (1223) 334426 (office). *E-mail:* upb1000@cam.ac.uk (office). *Website:* www.hist.cam.ac.uk (office).

BURLATSKY, Fedor Mikhailovich, DPhil; Russian journalist, writer and politician; b. 4 Jan. 1927, Kiev; s. of Mikhail Burlatsky and Sofia Burlatsky; m. 1st Seraphyma Burlatsky 1952 (divorced 1974); two s.; m. 2nd Kyra Burlatsky 1974; one d. *Education:* Tashkent Law Inst. *Career:* journalist Tashkent 1948–50; post grad. at Inst. of State Law, USSR Acad. of Sciences 1950–53; journalist with Kommunist 1953–59; head of section in Cen. Cttee Dept for Liaison with Communist and Workers' Parties of Socialist Countries 1959–65; political observer with Pravda 1965–67; Deputy Dir of USSR Inst. of Sociological studies 1968–72; head of section, USSR Inst. of State and Law (later Chief Scientific Researcher 1990–) and Head of Philosophy Dept, Inst. of Social Science, Cen. Cttee of CPSU 1975–88; Vice-Pres. Soviet Assoc. of Political Science 1976, currently Pres.; USSR People's Deputy 1989–91; Chair. Sub cttee on Humanitarian, Scientific and Cultural Co-operation, Cttee on Foreign Affairs 1989–91; political observer Literaturnaya Gazeta 1983–90, Ed.-in-Chief 1990–91; Chair. of Public Comm. for Int. Co-operation on Humanitarian Problems and Human Rights 1987–90; Dir Public Consultative Council to Chair. of State Duma 1993–96; Chief Scientific Researcher Inst. of State and Law 1992–; Visiting Prof. Heidelberg Univ. 1988, Harvard Univ. 1992, Oxford Univ. 1993; Pres. Euro-Asian Fund for Humanitarian Co-operation 1996–, Int. League for Defence of Culture; Chair., Scientific Council on Politology, Pres. Russian Acad. of Sciences 1995–; Pres. Fund 'International Cultural Co-operation' 2003–, Fund 'Euro-Atlantic State Co-operation' 2003–; mem. Acad. of National Sciences 1993, Acad. of Socio-Political Sciences 1996. *Publications include:* Mao Zedong (biography) 1976, The Modern State and Politics 1978, The Legend of Machiavelli 1987, New Thinking 1988, Leaders and Advisers 1990, Khrushchev and the First Russian Spring 1992, The End of the Red Empire 1993, Russian Sovereigns–Age of the Reformation 1996. *Honours:* Italian Senate Prize 1988. *Address:* Institute of State and Law, Znamenka str. 10, 119841 Moscow, Russia (office); Novovagankovsky per. 22, Apt 90, 123022 Moscow, Russia (home). *Telephone:* (495) 291-88-16 (office); (495) 291-85-06 (home). *Fax:* (495) 291-87-56 (office). *E-mail:* isl-ran@rinet.ru (office).

BURLEIGH, Michael Christopher Bennet, BA, PhD, FRHistS; British historian, journalist and academic; *Research Professor, University of Buckingham*; b. 3 April 1955, London, England; m. Linden Mary Brownbridge 1990. *Education:* Univ. Coll. London, Bedford Coll., London. *Career:* Weston Jr Research Fellow, New Coll., Oxford 1984–87; British Acad. Postdoctoral Fellow, Queen Mary Coll. 1987–88; Lecturer, LSE 1988–93, Reader in Int. History 1993–95; Distinguished Research Prof. in Modern European History, Univ. of Cardiff 1995–2000; Raoul Wallenburg Visiting Prof. of Human Rights, Rutgers Univ. 1999–2000; William R. Kenan Prof. of History, Washington and Lee Univ. 2000, Distinguished Visiting Prof., Stanford Univ. 2004; Distinguished Visiting Fellow, Hoover Inst., Stanford 2006; Research Prof., Univ. of Buckingham 2010–. *Television:* writer and presenter, Dark Enlightenment (More 4), writer, Selling Murder (Channel 4), Hell Herbie (Channel 4). *Publications:* Prussian Society and the German Order 1984, Germany Turns Eastwards: A Study of 'Ostforschung' in the Third Reich 1988, The Racial State: Germany 1933–1945 1991, Death and Deliverance: 'Euthanasia' in Germany 1994, Confronting the Nazi Past: New Debates on Modern German History (ed.) 1996, Ethics and Extermination: Reflections on Nazi Genocide 1997, The Third Reich: A New History 2000,

Earthly Powers: The Conflict Between Religion and Politics from the French Revolution to the Great War 2005, Sacred Causes: Politics and Religion from the European Dictators to Al-Qaeda 2006, Blood and Rage: A Cultural History of Terrorism 2008, Moral Combat: A History of World War II 2010. *Honours:* BFI Award for Archival Achievement 1992, New York Film and TV Festival Bronze Medal 1993, Samuel Johnson Prize for Non-Fiction 2001. *Address:* c/o The Wylie Agency, 17 Bedford Square, London, WC1B 3JA, England; c/o The Wylie Agency, 250 West 57th Street, Suite 2114, New York, NY 10107, USA. *Telephone:* (20) 7908-5900 (London) (office); (212) 246-0069 (New York). *Fax:* (20) 7908-5901 (London); (212) 586-8953 (New York). *E-mail:* mail@wylieagency.co.uk; mail@wylieagency.com.

BURNHAM, Sophy, BA; American writer and dramatist; b. 12 Dec. 1936, Baltimore, MD; m. David Bright Burnham 1960 (divorced 1984); two d. *Education:* Smith Coll. *Career:* Acquisitions Ed., David McKay Inc 1971–73; Contributing Ed., Town & Country 1975–80, New Art Examiner 1985–86; ind. consultant to various organizations 1975–88; Adjunct Lecturer, George Mason Univ., 1982–83; Staff Writer, New Woman magazine 1984–92; Staff Writer and Columnist, Museum & Arts/Washington 1987–96; Exec. Dir, Fund for New American Plays, John F. Kennedy Center for the Performing Arts, Washington, DC 1992–96; mem. Authors' Guild, Authors League of America, Cosmos Club. *Publications:* The Exhibits Speak 1964, The Art Crowd 1973, The Threat to Licensed Nuclear Facilities (ed.) 1975, Buccaneer (novel) 1977, The Landed Gentry 1978, The Dogwalker (novel) 1979, A Book of Angels 1990, Angel Letters 1991, Revelations (novel) 1992, The President's Angel (novel) 1993, For Writers Only 1994, The Ecstatic Journey: Walking the Mystical Path in Everyday Life 1997, The Treasure of Montségur (novel) 2002, The Path of Prayer 2002; plays: Penelope 1976, The Witch's Tale 1978, The Study 1979, revised edn as Snowstorms 1993, Beauty and the Beast 1979, The Nightingale 1980, The Meaning of Life 2001, Prometheus 2002; contributions: essays and articles in many periodicals; seminars, talks, workshops. *Honours:* Daughter of Mark Twain, Mark Twain Society 1974, First Prize, Women's Theatre Award, Seattle 1981, Helene Wurlitzer Foundation Grants 1981, 1983, 1991, Virginia Duvall Mann Award 1993. *E-mail:* sophyb@verizon.net (office). *Website:* www.sophyburnham.com.

BURNS, Alan; British writer, dramatist and academic; b. 29 Dec. 1929, London, England; m. 1st Carol Lynn 1954; m. 2nd Jean Illien 1980; one s. two d. *Education:* Merchant Taylors' School, London. *Career:* C. Day-Lewis Writing Fellow, Woodberry Down School 1973, Prof. of English, University of Minnesota 1977–90, Writer-in-Residence, Associated Colleges of the Twin Cities, Minneapolis-St Paul 1980; Writing Fellow, Bush Foundation of Minnesota 1984–85; Lecturer, Lancaster University 1993–96. *Publications:* Buster 1961, Europe After the Rain 1965, Celebrations 1967, Babel 1969, Dreamerika 1972, The Angry Brigade 1973, The Day Daddy Died 1981, Revolutions of the Night 1986, Art by Accident 1997; plays: Palach 1970, To Deprave and Corrupt 1972, The Imagination on Trial 1981; contributions: journals and periodicals. *Honours:* Arts Council Maintenance Grant 1967 and Bursaries 1969, 1973.

BURNS, James MacGregor, BA, MA, PhD; American political scientist, historian, academic and writer; b. 3 Aug. 1918, Melrose, Massachusetts; m. 1st Janet Rose Dismorr Thompson 1942 (divorced 1968); two s. two d.; m. 2nd Joan Simpson Meyers 1969 (divorced 1991). *Education:* Williams College, National Institute of Public Affairs, Harvard University, Postdoctoral Studies, LSE. *Career:* Faculty, Williams College 1941–47, Asst Prof. 1947–50, Assoc. Prof. 1950–53, Prof. of Political Science 1953–88, Prof. Emeritus 1988–; Senior Scholar, Jepson School of Leadership, University of Richmond 1990–93; Scholar-in-Residence, Center for Political Leadership and Participation, University of Maryland at College Park 1993–; mem. American Civil Liberties Union; American Historical Assn, American Legion, American Philosophical Assn, American Political Science Assn, pres., 1975–76, International Society of Political Psychology, pres., 1982–83, New England Political Science Assn, pres., 1960–61. *Publications:* Okinawa: The Last Battle (co-author) 1947, Congress on Trial: The Legislative Process and the Administrative State 1949, Government by the People: The Dynamics of American National Government and Local Government (with Jack Walter Peltason and Thomas E. Cronin) 1952, Roosevelt: The Lion and the Fox 1956, Functions and Policies of American Government (with Jack Walter Peltason) 1958, John Kennedy: A Political Profile 1960, The Deadlock of Democracy: Four-Party Politics in America 1963, Presidential Government: The Crucible of Leadership 1966, Roosevelt: The Soldier of Freedom 1970, Uncommon Sense 1972, Edward Kennedy and the Camelot Legacy 1976, State and Local Politics: Government by the People 1976, Leadership 1978, The American Experiment: Vol. I, The Vineyard of Liberty 1982, Vol. II, The Workshop of Democracy 1985, Vol. III, The Crosswinds of Freedom 1989, The Power to Lead: The Crisis of the American Presidency 1984, Cobblestone Leadership: Majority Rule, Minority Power (with L. Marvin Overby) 1990, A People's Charter: The Pursuit of Rights in America (with Stewart Burns) 1991, Dead Centre: Clinton-Gore Leadership and the Perils of Moderation (with Georgia Sorenson) 2000, The 3 Roosevelts: Patrician Leaders Who Transformed America 2001, Running Alone: Presidential Leadership JFK to Bush II (with Susan Dunn) 2006, Packing the Court: The Rise of Judicial Power and the Coming Crisis of the Supreme Court 2009. *Honours:* Tamiment Institute Award for Best Biography 1956, Woodrow Wilson Prize 1957, Pulitzer Prize in History 1971, National Book Award 1971, Francis Parkman Prize, Society of American Historians 1971, Sarah Josepha Hale Award 1979, Christopher Awards 1983, 1990, Harold D. Lassell Award 1984, Robert F. Kennedy Book Award 1990, Rollo May Award in Humanistic Services 1994, Arthur M. Schlesinger Jr Award, Soc. of American Historians 2010. *Address:* Highgate Barn, High Mowing, 604 Bee Hill Road, Williamstown, MA 01267-2714, USA (home). *Telephone:* (413) 458-8607 (home).

BURNS, Jim, BA; British writer and poet; b. 19 Feb. 1936, Preston, Lancs. *Education:* Bolton Inst. of Tech. *Career:* Ed. Move 1964–68, Palantir 1976–83; Jazz Ed. Beat Scene 1990–. *Publications:* A Single Flower 1972, The Goldfish Speaks from Beyond the Grave 1976, Fred Engels in Woolworths 1977, Internal Memorandum 1982, Out of the Past: Selected Poems 1961–1986 1987, Confessions of an Old Believer 1996, The Five Senses 1999, As Good a Reason as Any 1999, Beats, Bohemians and Intellectuals 2000, Take it Easy 2003, Short Statements 2006, Laying Something Down 2007, What I Said 2008, Cool Kerouac 2008, Streetsinger 2010; contrib. to London Magazine, Stand, Ambit, Jazz Journal, Critical Survey, The Guardian, New Statesman, Tribune, New Society, Penniless Press, Prop, Verse. *Address:* 11 Gatley Green, Gatley, Cheadle, Cheshire, SK8 4NF, England (home). *Telephone:* (161) 428-7996 (home).

BURNS, John Fisher; British journalist; *Chief of Bureau for London, New York Times;* b. 4 Oct. 1944, Nottingham, England; s. of Air Cdre R. J. B. Burns and Dorothy Burns (née Fisher); m. 1st Jane Pequegnat 1972 (divorced); m. 2nd Jane Scott-Long 1991; two s. one d. *Education:* Stowe School, McGill Univ., Canada and Harvard Univ., USA. *Career:* China correspondent, Globe and Mail, Toronto, Canada; Foreign Corresp. New York Times 1975–80, Soviet Union 1981–84, China 1984–86, Canada 1987–88, Afghanistan 1989–90, Persian Gulf 1990, Balkans 1991–94, India 1994–98, Special Corresp. for Islamic Affairs 1999–2002, Chief of Bureau for Baghdad 2002–07; Chief of Bureau for London 2007–; Chief of Bureau for Pakistan and Afghanistan, Washington Post 2002. *Honours:* Pulitzer Prize for Int. Reporting 1993 (co-winner for reporting from Bosnia), 1997 (for coverage of the Taliban regime in Afghanistan); George Polk Prize for Foreign Correspondence 1978, 1997. *Address:* The New York Times, London Bureau, 66 Buckingham Gate, London SW1E 6AU, England (office). *Telephone:* (20) 7799-5050 (office). *Website:* www.nytimes.com (office).

BURNS, Ralph, MFA; American poet, editor and academic; *Professor of English, University of Arkansas at Little Rock;* b. 8 June 1949, Norman, OK; m. Candace Wilson Calhoun 1974; one s. *Education:* Univ. of Montana. *Career:* Prof. of English, Univ. of Arkansas at Little Rock 1985–; Ed., Crazyhorse magazine. *Publications:* Us 1983, Windy Tuesday Nights 1984, Any Given Day 1985, Mozart's Starling 1990, Swamp Candles 1996, Ghost Notes 2001. *Honours:* two National Endowment for the Arts Fellowships, Iowa Poetry Prize 1996. *Address:* Department of English, University of Arkansas at Little Rock, 501–T Stabler Hall, 2801 South University Avenue, AR 72204, USA (office). *Telephone:* (501) 569-8314 (office). *E-mail:* rmburns@ualr.edu (office). *Website:* ualr.edu/english/index.php/home/faculty/burns (office).

BURNS, Rex Sehler, (Tom Sehler), AB, MA, PhD; American academic and writer; *Professor Emeritus of English, University of Colorado at Denver;* b. 13 June 1935, San Diego, CA; m. Terry Fostvedt 1987 (divorced 1996); three s. one d. *Education:* Stanford Univ., Univ. of Minnesota. *Career:* Asst Prof., Central Missouri State Coll. 1965–68; Assoc. Prof., Univ. of Colorado at Denver 1968–75, Prof. of English 1975–2000, Chair Dept of English 1996–99, Prof. Emer. of English 2000–; Fulbright Lecturer, Aristotle Univ., Thessaloniki 1969–70, Universidad Católica, Buenos Aires 1974; book reviewer, Rocky Mountain News 1982–92; Sr Lecturer, Univ. of Kent, Canterbury 1992–93; mem. Int. Asscn of Crime Writers, MWA. *Publications:* fiction: The Alvarez Journal (Edgar Allan Poe Award 1976) 1975, The Farnsworth Score 1977, Speak for the Dead 1978, Angle of Attack 1979, The Avenging Angel 1983, Strip Search 1984, Ground Money 1986, Suicide Season 1987, The Killing Zone 1988, Parts Unknown 1990, When Reason Sleeps 1991, Body Guard 1991, Endangered Species 1993, Blood Line 1995, The Leaning Land 1997; non-fiction: Success in America: The Yeoman Dream and the Industrial Revolution 1976, Crime Classics: The Mystery Story from Poe to the Present (ed with Mary Rose Sullivan) 1990; contrib. to periodicals and anthologies, Starz Encore Mystery Channel. *Honours:* Colorado Authors League Awards 1978, 1979, 1980, Univ. of Colorado System Pres.'s Teaching Scholar (lifetime title) 1990, Univ. Service Award. *E-mail:* rexburns@comcast.net. *Website:* www.rexburns.com.

BURNSIDE, John; Scottish writer and poet; *Professor of English, University of St Andrews;* b. 19 March 1955, Dunfermline, Fife. *Career:* fmr Writer-in-Residence, Dundee Univ.; currently Prof. of English, Univ. of St Andrews. *Publications:* fiction and memoir: The Dumb House 1997, The Mercy Boys 1999, Burning Elvis 2000, The Locust Room 2001, A Lie About My Father 2006, The Devil's Footprints 2007, Glister 2008, Waking Up in Toytown 2010; poetry: The Hoop 1988, Common Knowledge 1991, Feast Days 1992, The Myth of the Twin 1994, Swimming in the Flood 1995, A Normal Skin 1997, The Asylum Dance 2000, The Light Trap 2002, The Good Neighbour 2005, Selected Poems 2006, Gift Songs 2007, The Hunt in the Forest 2009, Black Cat Bone (Forward Prize for Best Collection 2011, TS Eliot Prize for Poetry 2012) 2011; as ed.: Love for Love 2000, Wild Reckoning 2004; contrib. to newspapers, journals and periodicals. *Honours:* Scottish Arts Council Book Awards 1988, 1991, Geoffrey Faber Memorial Prize 1994, Whitbread Prize for Poetry 2000, Cholmondeley Award 2008, Prix Zepter 2009. *Literary Agent:* c/o Rogers,

Coleridge and White, 20 Powis Mews, London, W11 1JN, England. *Telephone:* (20) 7221-3717. *Website:* www.rcwlitagency.com.

BURRINGTON, Ernest; British newspaper executive; b. 13 Dec. 1926, s. of the late Harold Burrington and of Laura Burrington; m. Nancy Crossley 1950; one s. one d. *Career:* reporter, Oldham Chronicle 1941–44, reporter and sub-ed. 1947–49; mil. service 1945–47; sub-ed. Bristol Evening World 1950; sub-ed. Daily Herald, Manchester 1950, night ed. 1955, London night 1957; night ed. IPC Sun 1964, Asst ed. 1965; Asst ed. and night News Int. Sun 1969; deputy night ed. Daily Mirror 1970; Deputy Ed. Sunday People 1971, Assoc. Ed. 1972; Ed. The People 1985–88, 1989–90; Dir Mirror Group Newspapers 1985–92, Deputy Chair. and Asst Publr 1988–91, Man. Dir 1989–91, Chair. 1991–92; Chair. Syndication Int. 1989–92; Deputy Chair. Mirror Publishing Co. 1989–91; Dir Mirror Group Magazine and Newsday Ltd 1989–92, Legionstyle Ltd 1991–92, Mirror Colour Print Ltd 1991–92; Dir (non-exec.) Sunday Correspondent 1990, The European 1990–91, IQ Newsgraphics 1990–92, Sygma Picture Agency, Paris 1990–91; Deputy Publr Globe Communications, Montreal, Canada 1993–95, Exec. Vice-Pres. and Assoc. Publr 1995–96; Pres. Atlantic Media 1996–98; Consultant Head of Marketing Harveys PLC, UK 1998–2000; mem. Council Nat. Press Asscn 1988–92, Int. Press Inst. British Exec. 1988–92; Trustee Int. Centre for Child Studies 1986–90; Life mem. NUJ 1960–. *Honours:* Hon. Life mem. NUJ 1996; Hon. Red Devil (Manchester United Football Club) 1985. *Address:* 17499 Tiffany Trace Drive, Boca Raton, FL 33487, USA (home); South Hall, Dene Park, Shipbourne Road, Tonbridge, TN11 9NS, England (home). *Telephone:* (561) 995-9897 (USA) (home); (1732) 368517 (England) (home). *Fax:* (561) 995-9897 (USA) (home); (1732) 368517 (England) (home). *E-mail:* burringtone@aol.com (home).

BURROW, John Anthony, MA, FBA; British academic and writer; b. 1932, Loughton. *Education:* Christ Church, Oxford. *Career:* Fellow, Jesus Coll., Oxford 1961–75; Winterstoke Prof., Univ. of Bristol 1976–98, Emer. Prof. and Research Fellow 1998–. *Publications:* A Reading of Sir Gawain and the Green Knight 1965, Geoffrey Chaucer: A Critical Anthology 1969, Ricardian Poetry: Chaucer, Gower Langland and the Gawain Poet 1971, Sir Gawain and the Green Knight (ed.) 1972, English Verse 1300–1500 1977, Medieval Writers and Their Work 1982, Essays on Medieval Literature 1984, The Ages of Man 1986, A Book of Middle English 1992, Langlands Fictions 1993, Thomas Hoccleve 1994, Thomas Hoccleve's Complaint and Dialogue 1999, The Gawain-Poet 2001, Gestures and Looks in Medieval Narrative 2002, The Poetry of Praise 2008. *Address:* 9 The Polygon, Clifton, Bristol, BS8 4PW, England (home).

BURROWAY, Janet Gay, BA, MA; American academic, writer and poet; *Robert O. Lawson Distinguished Professor Emerita, Florida State University*; b. 21 Sept. 1936, Tucson, Ariz.; d. of Paul M. Burroway and Alma May Burroway (née Milner); m. 1st Walter Eysselinck 1961 (divorced 1973); two s.; m. 2nd William Dean Humphries 1978 (divorced 1981); m. 3rd Peter Ruppert 1993; one step-d. *Education:* Univ. of Arizona, Barnard Coll., Univ. of Cambridge, UK, Yale School of Drama. *Career:* Instructor, Harpur Coll., Binghamton, New York, 1961–62; Lecturer, Univ. of Sussex, UK 1965–70; Assoc. Prof., Florida State Univ. 1972–77, Prof. 1977–, MacKenzie Prof. of English 1989–95, Robert O. Lawson Distinguished Prof. 1995–2002, Robert O. Lawson Distinguished Prof. Emer. 2002–; Visiting Prof. of Creative Writing, Northwestern Univ. 2009–10; fiction reviewer, Philadelphia Enquirer 1986–90; reviewer, New York Times Book Review 1991–; essay-columnist, New Letters: A Magazine of Writing and Art 1994–; mem. Associated Writing Programs, Authors' Guild, Dramatists' Guild, Chicago Dramatists, Midwest New Musicals. *Dance:* texts for dance: Dadadata, Text/tiles, The Empty Dress, Quiltings (all Florida State Univ.) 1995–2000. *Plays:* Medea With Child 1997, Sweepstakes 1999, Parts of Speech 2004, Morality Play (musical adaptation of Barry Unsworth novel) 2012. *Radio:* adaptation of Opening Nights for NPR 1996. *Television:* The Beauty Operators (Thames Television) 1970, Hoddinott Veiling (ATV Network TV; UK entry in the 1970 Monte Carlo Festival) 1970. *Publications:* fiction: Descend Again 1960, The Dancer From the Dance 1965, Eyes 1966, The Buzzards 1969, The Truck on the Track 1970, The Giant Jam Sandwich 1972, Raw Silk 1977, Opening Nights 1985, Cutting Stone 1992, Bridge of Sand 2009; poetry: But to the Season 1961, Material Goods 1980; other: Writing Fiction: A Guide to Narrative Craft 1982 (eighth edn 2010), Embalming Mom (essays) 2002, Imaginative Writing: The Elements of Craft 2002 (third edn 2010), From Where You Dream: The Process of Writing Fiction (ed.) 2005; contribs to numerous journals and periodicals. *Honours:* Nat. Endowment for the Arts Fellowship 1976, Yaddo Residency Fellowships 1985, 1987, Lila Wallace-Reader's Digest Fellow 1993–94, Carolyn Benton Cockefaire Distinguished Writer-in-Residence, Univ. of Missouri 1995, Woodrow Wilson Visiting Fellow, Furman Univ., Greenville, S Carolina 1995, Visiting Writer, Erskine Coll., Due West, S Carolina 1997, Drury Coll., Springfield, Ill. 1999, Narrative Magazine Fiction Prize 2009, Silver Medal, Florida Book Awards 2009. *Literary Agent:* c/o Emma Sweeney Agency, 245 East 80th Street, New York, NY 10021, USA. *Telephone:* (646) 827-4381. *E-mail:* info@emmasweeneyagency.com. *Address:* 240 De Soto Street, Tallahassee, FL 32303 (home); N2484 Elgin Club Drive, Lake Geneva, WI 53147 (home); 6 North Michigan, Chicago, IL 60602, USA (home). *Telephone:* (850) 222-8272 (Tallahassee) (home); (262) 245-5462 (Lake Geneva) (home). *Fax:* (850) 222-8272 (Tallahassee) (home). *E-mail:* jburroway@fsu.edu (office). *Website:* www.janetburroway.com.

BURTON, Anthony George Graham; British writer and broadcaster; b. 24 Dec. 1934, Thornaby; m. 1959; two s. one d. *Career:* mem. Outdoor Writers' Guild. *Publications:* A Programmed Guide to Office Warfare 1969, The Jones Report 1970, The Canal Builders 1972, The Reluctant Musketeer 1973, Canals in Colour 1974, Remains of a Revolution 1975, The Master Idol 1975, The Miners 1976, The Navigators 1976, Josiah Wedgwood 1976, Canal 1976, Back Door Britain 1977, A Place to Stand 1977, Industrial Archaeological Sites of Britain 1977, The Green Bag Travellers 1978, The Past At Work 1980, The Rainhill Story 1980, The Past Afloat 1982, The Changing River 1982, The Shell Book of Curious Britain 1982, The National Trust Guide to Our Industrial Past 1983, The Waterways of Britain 1983, The Rise and Fall of King Cotton 1984, Walking the Line 1985, Wilderness Britain 1985, Britain's Light Railways 1985, The Shell Book of Undiscovered Britain and Ireland 1986, Britain Revisited 1986, Landscape Detective 1986, Opening Time 1987, Steaming Through Britain 1987, Walk the South Downs 1988, Walking Through History 1988, The Great Days of the Canals 1989, Cityscapes 1990, Astonishing Britain 1990, Slow Roads 1991, The Railway Builders 1992, Canal Mania 1993, The Grand Union Canal Walk 1993, The Railway Empire 1994, The Rise and Fall of British Shipbuilding 1994, The Cotswold Way 1995, The Dales Way 1995, The West Highland Way 1996, The Southern Upland Way 1997, William Cobbett: Englishman 1997, The Wye Valley Walk 1998, The Caledonian Canal 1998, Best Foot Forward 1998, The Cumbria Way 1999, The Wessex Ridgeway 1999, Thomas Telford 1999, Weekend Walks: Dartmoor and Exmoor 2000, Weekend Walks: The Yorkshire Dales 2000, Traction Engines 2000, Richard Trevithick 2000, The Orient Express 2001, Weekend Walks: The Peak District 2001, The Anatomy of Canals: The Early Years 2001, The Daily Telegraph Guide to Britain's Working Past 2002, The Anatomy of Canals: The Mania Years 2002, Daily Telegraph Guide to Britain's Maritime Past 2003, Hadrian's Wall Path 2003, The Anatomy of Canals: Decline & Renewal 2003, On the Rails 2004, The Ridgeway 2005. *Literary Agent:* Sara Menguc, 4 Hatch Place, Kingston upon Thames, KT2 5NB, England. *Address:* 31 Lansdown, Stroud, Gloucestershire, GL5 1BG, England (home). *Fax:* (1453) 751541 (office). *E-mail:* tony.pip@btinternet.com (office).

BURTON, Gabrielle, BA, MFA; American writer; b. (Gabrielle Baker), 21 Feb. 1939, Lansing, MI; m. Roger V. Burton 1962; five d. *Education:* Marygrove Coll., Michigan, American Film Inst., Los Angeles. *Career:* teacher, Fiction in the Schools, Writers in Educ. Project, New York 1985; various prose readings and workshops; Equinoxe Fellow, Bordeaux, France 2000; mem Usage Panel, American Heritage Dictionary 1990–. *Publications:* I'm Running Away From Home But I'm Not Allowed to Cross the Street 1972, Heartbreak Hotel 1986, Manna From Heaven (screenplay, filmed, DVD 2005) 2000, Searching for Tamsen Donner (memoir) 2009, Impatient with Desire: the Lost Journal of Tamsen Donner (Western Heritage Award for Outstanding Novel 2011) 2010; contribs to numerous publs. *Honours:* MacDowell Colony Fellowships 1982, 1987, 1989, Yaddo Fellowship 1983, Maxwell Perkins Prize 1986, Great Lakes Colleges Asscn Award 1987, Bernard De Voto Fellow in Non-Fiction, Bread Loaf Writers' Conf. 1994, Mary Pickford Foundation Award for First Year Screenwriter 1996, First Prize, Austin Film Festival Screenwriting Contest 2000, Nicholl Fellow 2000. *Address:* 29 Paloma Avenue, Venice, CA 90291, USA (home). *Telephone:* (310) 399-1398 (home). *Website:* www.gabrielleburton.com.

BURTON, Tim; American film director and screenwriter; b. 25 Aug. 1958, Burbank, Calif.; pnr Helena Bonham Carter; one s. one d. *Education:* California Arts Inst. *Career:* began career as animator, Walt Disney Studios (projects included The Fox and the Hound and The Black Cauldron). *Films as director:* Vincent (also animator) 1982, Luau 1982, Hansel and Gretel (TV) 1982, Frankenweenie (short, for Disney) 1984, Pee-Wee's Big Adventure 1985, Alfred Hitchcock Presents (TV episode, The Jar) 1985, Beetlejuice 1988, Batman 1989, Edward Scissorhands (also prod.) 1991, Batman Returns (also prod.) 1992, Ed Wood (also prod.) 1994, Mars Attacks! (also prod.) 1996, Sleepy Hollow 1999, Planet of the Apes 2001, Big Fish 2003, Charlie and the Chocolate Factory 2005, Corpse Bride (also prod.) 2005, Sweeney Todd: The Demon Barber of Fleet Street (Best Dir, Nat. Bd of Review 2007, Golden Globe for Best Musical or Comedy 2008) 2007, Alice in Wonderland (also producer) 2010, Dark Shadows 2012, Frankenweenie (also producer) 2012. *Films as producer:* Beetlejuice (TV series) 1993, Family Dog (TV series) 1993, The Nightmare Before Christmas 1993, Cabin Boy 1994, Batman Forever 1996, James and the Giant Peach 1996, Lost in Oz (TV series) 2000, 9 2009, Abraham Lincoln: Vampire Hunter 2012. *Film screenplays:* The Island of Doctor Agor 1971, Stalk of the Celery 1979, Vincent 1982, Luau 1982, Beetlejuice (story) 1988, (TV series creator) 1989, Edward Scissorhands (story) 1990, The Nightmare Before Christmas (story) 1993, Lost in Oz (TV pilot episode story) 2000, Point Blank (TV series) 2002. *Film appearance:* Men in Black III. *Publications:* My Art and Films 1993, The Melancholy Death of Oyster Boy and Other Stories 1997, Burton on Burton 2000; various film tie-in books. *Honours:* Chevalier, Ordre des Arts et des Lettres 2010; short-length film awards include two from Chicago Film Festival, Golden Lion Lifetime Achievement Award, Venice Int. Film Festival 2007. *Literary Agent:* Chapman, Bird & Grey, 1990 South Bundy Drive, Suite 200, Los Angeles, CA 90025, USA. *Website:* www.timburton.com.

BURUMA, Ian; Dutch author and academic; *Henry R. Luce Professor of Human Rights and Journalism, Bard College*; b. 28 Dec. 1951, The Hague. *Education:* Leiden Univ., Nihon Univ., Tokyo. *Career:* actor and performer in Tokyo 1970s; documentary filmmaker and photographer, Tokyo 1977–80;

journalist and reporter in 1980s; Cultural Ed. Far Eastern Economic Review, Hong Kong 1983–86; Foreign Ed. The Spectator, London 1990–91; numerous articles and essays for New York Review of Books, Los Angeles Times, The New Yorker, New York Times Magazine, Project Syndicate; Henry R. Luce Prof. of Human Rights and Journalism, Bard Coll. 2003–; Fellow, Wissenschaftskolleg, Berlin 1991–92, Woodrow Wilson Center, Washington DC 1998–99, St Antony's Coll., Univ. of Oxford 1999–2000, New York Public Library Cullman Center 2011–12; Chair. of Humanities Centre, Cen. European Univ., Budapest 2000–04; mem. of Bd Einstein Forum, Potsdam 2005–, Human Rights in China, New York 2006–. *Publications:* The Japanese Tattoo (co-author) 1980, Behind the Mask: On Sexual Demons, Sacred Mothers, Transvestites, Gangsters, Drifters and Other Japanese Cultural Heroes 1983, Tokyo: Form and Spirit (co-author) 1986, God's Dust: A Modern Asian Journey 1989, Great Cities of the World: Hong Kong 1991, The Wages of Guilt: Memories of War in Germany and in Japan 1994, Voltaire's Coconuts (aka Anglomania in Europe/Anglomania: A European Love Affair) 1998, The Missionary and the Libertine: Love and War in East and West 2000, Conversations with John Schlesinger 2000, Inventing Japan: From Empire to Economic Miracle 1853–1964 2003, Occidentalism: The West in the Eyes of its Enemies (co-author) 2004, Murder in Amsterdam: The Death of Theo Van Gogh and the Limits of Tolerance (LA Times Book Prize for Best Current Interest Book 2006) 2006, Taming the Gods: Religion and Democracy on Three Continents 2010; novels: Playing the Game 1991, The China Lover 2008. *Honours:* Int. Erasmus Prize 2008, Shorenstein Journalism Award 2008, Abraham Kuyper Prize, Princeton Theological Seminary 2012. *Address:* c/o Bard College, PO Box 5000, Annandale-on-Hudson, NY 12504-5000, USA (office). *Telephone:* (845) 758-7535 (office). *E-mail:* buruma@bard.edu (office). *Website:* www.bard.edu (office); www.ianburuma.com.

BUSBY, Roger Charles; British writer and public relations officer; b. 24 July 1941, Leicester, England. *Education:* Univ. of Aston, Birmingham. *Career:* Journalist, Caters News Agency, Birmingham 1959–66; Journalist, Birmingham Evening Mail 1966–73; Head of Public Relations, Devon & Cornwall Police 1973; mem. CWA, Institute of Public Relations, National Union of Journalists. *Publications:* Main Line Kill 1968, Robbery Blue 1969, The Frighteners 1970, Deadlock 1971, A Reasonable Man 1972, Pattern of Violence 1973, New Face in Hell 1976, Garvey's Code 1978, Fading Blue 1984, The Hunter 1986, Snow Man 1987, Crackhot 1990, High Jump 1992.

BUSH, Duncan Eric, BA, DPhil; British poet, writer and teacher; *Editor, The Amsterdam Review*; b. 6 April 1946, Cardiff, Wales; m. Annette Jane Weaver 1981; two s. *Education:* Univ. of Warwick, Duke Univ., USA, Wadham Coll., Oxford. *Career:* European Ed. The Kansas Quarterly and Arkansas Review; writing tutor with various insts; Co-founder and Ed. The Amsterdam Review 2004–; mem. Welsh Acad., Soc. of Authors. *Publications:* Aquarium 1983, Salt 1985, On Censorship (ed.) 1985, Black Faces, Red Mouths 1986, The Genre of Silence 1987, Glass Shot 1991, Masks 1994, The Hook 1997, Midway 1998, The Last Coming, The Rage; contrib. to BBC and periodicals. *Honours:* Eric Gregory Award for Poetry 1978, Barbara Campion Memorial Award for Poetry 1982, Welsh Arts Council Prizes for Poetry, Arts Council of Wales Book of the Year 1995. *Address:* Godre Waun Oleu, Brecon Road, Ynyswen, Penycae, Powys, SA9 1YY, Wales (office). *Telephone:* (1639) 730652 (office). *E-mail:* dcolophon@excite.com (office). *Website:* duncanbush.com.

BUSH, Ronald, BA, MA, PhD; American academic and writer; *Drue Heinz Professor of American Literature, University of Oxford*; b. 16 June 1946, Philadelphia, Pa; s. of Raymond Bush and Esther Bush; m. Marilyn Wolin 1969; one s. *Education:* Univ. of Pennsylvania, Univ. of Cambridge, UK, Princeton Univ. *Career:* Asst to Assoc. Prof., Harvard Univ. 1974–82; Assoc. Prof., California Inst. of Tech. 1982–85, Prof. 1985–97; Visiting Fellow, Exeter Coll. Oxford, UK 1994–95; Drue Heinz Prof. of American Literature, Univ. of Oxford, 1997–; Visiting Fellow, Program in American Civilization, Harvard Univ. 2004. *Publications:* The Genesis of Ezra Pound's Cantos 1976, T. S. Eliot: A Study in Character and Style 1983, T. S. Eliot: The Modernist in History (ed.) 1991, Prehistories of the Future: The Primitivist Project and the Culture of Modernism (co-ed. with Elazar Barkan) 1995, Claiming the Stones/Naming the Bones: Cultural Property and the Negotiation of National and Ethnic Identity (co-ed. with Elazar Barkan) 2003; contribs to scholarly books and journals. *Honours:* Nat. Endowment for the Humanities Fellowships 1977–78, 1992–93, AHRB Research Award 2003–04. *Address:* St John's College, Oxford, OX1 3JP, England (office). *Telephone:* (1865) 277300 (home). *E-mail:* ron.bush@ell.ox.ac.uk (office).

BUSHNELL, Candace; American writer; b. 1959, Glastonbury, CT; m. Charles Askegard 2002. *Education:* Rice Univ., TX and New York Univ. *Career:* wrote 'Sex and the City' column, New York Observer 1994–96 (made into TV series); host, TV programme Sex, Lives and Video Clips (VH-1) 1997. *Publications:* novels: Sex and the City 1997, Four Blondes 2000, Trading Up 2003, Lipstick Jungle 2005, One Fifth Avenue 2008, The Carrie Diaries (teen novel) 2010. *Address:* c/o Hyperion Editorial Department, 77 W 66th Street, 11th Floor, New York, NY 10023, USA. *E-mail:* beth.dickey@abc.com. *Website:* www.candacebushnell.com.

BUTALA, Sharon Annette, OC, BA, BEd; Canadian writer; b. 24 Aug. 1940, Nipawin, Sask.; d. of Achille Antoine Le Blanc and Margaret Amy Graham; m. Peter Butala 1976 (died 2007); one s. *Education:* Univ. of Saskatchewan. *Career:* mem. PEN Canada, Saskatchewan Writers' Guild, Writers' Union of Canada. *Plays:* Sweet Time, Natural Disasters, A Killing Frost, The Element of Fire, Rodeo Life, Billy Bock: An Entertainment. *Publications:* fiction: Country of the Heart (novel) 1984, Queen of the Headaches (short stories) 1985, The Gates of the Sun (novel) 1986, Luna (novel) 1988, Fever (short stories) 1990, Upstream: Le Pays d'en Haut (autobiographical novel) 1991, The Fourth Archangel (novel) 1992, The Garden of Eden 1998, Real Life 2002; non-fiction: Harvest 1992, The Perfection of the Morning (autobiog.) 1994, Coyote's Morning Cry 1995, Wild Stone Heart 2000, Old Man on his Back 2002, Lilac Moon: Dreaming of the Real West (Saskatchewan Book Award) 2005, The Girl in Saskatoon: A Meditation on Friendship, Memory and Murder 2008; contrib. to periodicals. *Honours:* Saskatchewan Order of Merit (2009); Hon. LLD (Univ. of Regina) 2000, Hon. DLitt (Univ. of Saskatchewan) 2004; Canada 125 Commemorative Medal 1993, Saskatchewan Book Award for Non-Fiction 1994, 2005, Marian Engel Award 1998, Queen's Golden Jubliee Medal 2002, Gov. Gen.'s Award 2002, Saskatchewan Centennial Medal 2005. *Address:* Box 428, Eastend, Sask. S0N 0T0, Canada (home). *Telephone:* (306) 295-3810 (home). *E-mail:* sharon@sharonbutala.com.

BUTALIA, Urvashi, BA, MA; Indian publisher and writer; *Director, Zubaan Books*; b. 1952, Ambala, Punjab. *Education:* Univ. of Delhi, Univ. of London. *Career:* began career in publishing at Oxford Univ. Press, then Zed Books, London 1982–84; Co-founder and Dir Kali for Women (first women's publishing house in India) 1984; Founder and Dir Zubaan Books 2003–; Lecturer for professional publishing course, Univ. of Delhi, also Reader, Coll. of Vocational Studies; consultant, Oxfam India. *Publications include:* In Other Words: New Writing by Indian Women (co-edited) 1994, Making a Difference: Feminist Publishing in the South (co-author) 1995, Women and Right Wing Movements (co-author) 1995, The Other Side of Silence: Voices from the Partition of India (Oral History Book Association Award 2001) 1998, Speaking Peace: Women's Voices from Kashmir 2002; contribs to The Guardian, Times of India, Granta, Outlook, The New Internationalist, India Today, Lettre International. *Honours:* Chevalier, Ordre des Arts et des Lettres; Pandora Women in Publishing Award 2000, Nikkei Asia Award for Culture 2003. *Address:* Zubaan Books, 128B First Floor, Shahpur Jat, New Delhi 110 019, India (office). *Telephone:* (11) 26494617 (office). *E-mail:* contact@zubaanbooks.com (office). *Website:* www.zubaanbooks.com (office).

BUTLER, Gwendoline Williams, (Jennie Melville), MA; British author; b. 19 Aug. 1922, London, England; m. Lionel Butler 1949 (deceased), one d. *Education:* Lady Margaret Hall, Oxford. *Career:* historical crime critic, Crime Time Magazine 1999–2002; mem. CWA panel, Reform Club, Detection Club (hon. sec. 1992–95), MWA. *Publications include:* Receipt for Murder 1956, Dead in a Row 1957, The Dull Dead 1958, The Murdering Kind 1958, The Interloper 1959, Death Lives Next Door, US edn as Dine and Be Dead 1960, Make Me a Murderer 1961, Coffin on the Water 1962, Coffin in Oxford 1962, Coffin for Baby 1963, Coffin Waiting 1963, Coffin in Malta 1964, A Nameless Coffin 1966, Coffin Following 1968, Coffin's Dark Number 1969, A Coffin form the Past 1970, A Coffin for Pandora 1973, US edn as Olivia 1974, A Coffin for the Canary, US edn as Sarsen Place 1974, The Vesey Inheritance 1975, Brides of Friedberg, US edn as Meadowsweet 1977, The Red Staircase 1979, Albion Walk 1982, Coffin in Fashion 1987, Coffin Underground 1988, Coffin in the Black Museum 1989, Coffin and the Paper Man 1990, Coffin the Museum of Crime 1990, Coffin on Murder Street 1992, Cracking Open a Coffin 1992, A Coffin for Charley 1993, The Coffin Tree 1994, A Dark Coffin 1995, A Double Coffin 1996, Butterfly 1996, Let There Be Love 1997, Coffin's Game 1997, A Grave Coffin 1998, Coffin's Ghost 1999, The King Cried Murder 2000, A Cold Coffin 2000, Coffin Knows the Answer 2002; as Jennie Melville: Come Home and Be Killed 1962, Burning Is a Substitute for Loving 1963, Murderers' Houses 1964, There Lies Your Love 1965, Nell Alone 1966, A Different Kind of Summer 1967, The Hunter in the Shadows 1969, A New Kind of Killer, An Old Kind of Death 1970, US edn as A New Kind of Killer 1971, Ironwood 1972, Nun's Castle 1973, Raven's Forge 1975, Dragon's Eye 1976, Axwater, US edn as Tarot's Tower 1978, Murder Has a Pretty Face 1981, The Painted Castle 1982, The Hand of Glass 1983, Listen to the Children 1986, Death in the Garden 1987, Windsor Red 1988, A Cure for Dying 1989, Witching Murder 1990, Footsteps in the Blood 1990, Dead Set 1992, Whoever Has the Heart 1993, Baby Drop 1994, The Morbid Kitchen 1995, The Woman Who Was Not There 1996, Revengeful Death 1997, Stone Dead 1998, Dead Again 1999. *Honours:* Silver Dagger, CWA 1973, Silver Rose Bowl, Romantic Novelists Asscn 1981, Ellery Queen Short Story Award, Judge Ellis Peters Memorial Historical Crime Fiction Contest 2000, FRSA.

BUTLER, Judith, BA, PhD; American philosopher, academic and author; *Maxine Elliot Professor, Departments of Rhetoric and Comparative Literature, University of California, Berkeley*; b. 24 Feb. 1956. *Education:* Bennington Coll., Yale Univ. *Career:* has taught at Wesleyan and Johns Hopkins univs; currently Maxine Elliot Prof., Dept of Rhetoric and Comparative Literature, Univ. of Calif., Berkeley; currently also Hannah Arendt Prof. of Philosophy, European Graduate School, Saas-Fee, Switzerland; mem. American Philosophical Soc. 2007. *Publications:* Subjects of Desire: Hegelian Reflections in Twentieth-Century France 1987, Gender Trouble: Feminism and the Subversion of Identity 1990, Bodies That Matter: On the Discursive Limits of 'Sex' 1993, The Psychic Life of Power: Theories of Subjection 1997, Excitable Speech 1997, Antigone's Claim: Kinship Between Life and Death 2000, Hegemony, Contingency, Universality (with Ernesto Laclau and Slavoj Zizek) 2000, Women and Social Transformation (with Elisabeth Beck-Gernsheim and Lidia Puigvert) 2003, Precarious Life: Powers of Violence and Mourning 2004, The Judith Butler Reader 2004, Undoing Gender (essays) 2004, Giving an Account of Oneself 2005, Who Sings the Nation-State?: Language, Politics, Belonging (with Gayatri Spivak) 2007, Frames of War: When is Life Grievable? 2009; contribs: numerous chapters in books on cultural and literary theory, philosophy, psychoanalysis, feminism and sexual politics, numerous articles in academic journals. *Honours:* Brudner Prize, Yale Univ. 2004. *Address:* Rhetoric Department, 7408 Dwinelle Hall, University of California, Berkeley, CA 94720, USA (office). *Telephone:* (510) 642-2392 (office). *E-mail:* jpbutler@berkeley.edu (office). *Website:* rhetoric.berkeley.edu/faculty_bios/judith_butler.html (office).

BUTLER, Leo; British playwright; b. 1975, S Yorks., England. *Plays:* Made of Stone 2000, Redundant 2001, Devotion 2002, Lucky Dog 2004, The Early Bird 2006, Heroes 2007, Airbag 2007, I'll Be the Devil 2008, Faces in the Crowd 2008. *Film:* Self-Made (dir Gillian Wearing) 2010. *Honours:* George Devine Award 2001. *Literary Agent:* c/o Judy Daish Associates, 2 St Charles Place, London, W10 6EG, England. *Telephone:* (20) 8964-8811. *Fax:* (20) 8964-8966. *E-mail:* howard@judydaish.com.

BUTLER, Marilyn Speers, DPhil, FRSL, FRSA; British academic; b. (Marilyn S. Evans), 11 Feb. 1937, Kingston-upon-Thames, Surrey; d. of Trevor Evans and Margaret Evans (née Gribbin); m. David Edgeworth Butler 1962; three s. *Education:* Wimbledon High School, St Hilda's Coll. Oxford. *Career:* BBC trainee and producer 1960–62; Jr Research Fellow, St Hilda's Coll. Oxford 1970–73; Fellow and Tutor, St Hugh's Coll. Oxford 1973–86; King Edward VII Prof. of English Literature, Cambridge Univ. 1986–93; Fellow King's Coll. Cambridge 1987–93; Rector Exeter Coll., Oxford 1993–; Titular Prof. of English Language and Literature, Univ. of Oxford 1998–; British Acad. Reader 1982–85; Foreign mem. US Acad. of Arts and Sciences 1999; Hon. Fellow, St Hilda's Coll. Oxford, St Hugh's Coll. Oxford, King's Coll. Cambridge. *Publications:* Maria Edgeworth: A Literary Biography 1972, Jane Austen and the War of Ideas 1975, Peacock Displayed 1979, Romantics, Rebels and Reactionaries 1981, Burke, Paine, Godwin and the Revolution Controversy (ed.) 1984, Collected Works of Wollstonecraft (Ed. with J. Todd) 1989, Edgeworth's Castle Rackrent and Ennui (ed.) 1992, Mary Shelley's Frankenstein (ed.) 1993, Jane Austen's Northanger Abbey (ed.) 1995, Collected Works of Edgeworth (ed. with M. Myers), 12 Vols, 1999. *Honours:* Hon. LittD (Leicester) 1992, (Birmingham) 1993, (Oxford Brookes) 1994, (Williams Coll., Mass) 1995, (Lancaster, Warwick, Surrey) 1997, (Kingston) 1998, (Open) 2000, (Roehampton) 2000. *Address:* 151 Woodstock Road, Oxford, OX2 7NA, England (home). *Telephone:* (1865) 558323 (home). *E-mail:* marilyn.butler@exeter.ox.ac.uk (home).

BUTLER, Robert Olen, BS, MA; American writer, screenwriter and academic; *Frances Eppes Distinguished Professor of English, Florida State University*; b. 20 Jan. 1945, Granite City, IL; m. 1st Carol Supplee 1968 (divorced 1972); m. 2nd Marylin Geller 1972 (divorced 1987); two s.; m. 3rd Maureen Donlan 1987 (divorced 1995); m. 4th Elizabeth Dewberry 1995 (divorced 2007). *Education:* Northwestern Univ., Univ. of Iowa, New School for Social Research, New York. *Career:* Ed.-in-Chief, Energy User News 1975–85; Prof., Master of Fine Arts in Creative Writing Program, McNeese State Univ. 1985–2000; Frances Eppes Distinguished Prof. of English, Florida State Univ. 2000–; faculty, various summer writing conferences; mem. Writers Guild of America West. *Publications:* The Alleys of Eden 1981, Sun Dogs 1982, Countrymen of Bones 1983, On Distant Ground 1985, Wabash 1987, The Deuce 1989, A Good Scent from a Strange Mountain (Pulitzer Prize in Fiction 1993) 1992, They Whisper 1994, Tabloid Dreams 1996, The Deep Green Sea 1998, Mr Spaceman 2000, Fair Warning 2002, Had a Good Time: Stories from American Postcards 2004, From Where You Dream 2005, Severance 2006, Intercourse 2008, Hell 2009; other: several screenplays; contrib. to anthologies, newspapers, and journals. *Honours:* Hon. DHumLitt (McNeese State Univ.) 1993, Hon. DLitt (State Univ. of NY) 2009; Charter Recipient, Tu Do Chinh Kien Award, Vietnam Veterans of America 1987, Emily Clark Balch Award, Virginia Quarterly Review 1991, Southern Review/Louisiana State Univ. Prize for Short Fiction 1992, Notable Book Citation, American Library Asscn 1993, Richard and Hinda Rosenthal Foundation Award, American Acad. of Arts and Letters 1993, Guggenheim Fellowship 1993, Nat. Endowment for the Arts Fellowship 1994, Lotos Club Award of Merit 1996, William Peden Prize, Missouri Review 1997, Author of the Year Award, Illinois Asscn of Teachers of English 1997, National Magazine Award for Fiction 2001, 2005. *Literary Agent:* Warren Frazier, John Hawkins Agency, Suite 1600, 71 West 23rd Street, New York, NY 10010, USA. *Telephone:* (212) 807-7040. *E-mail:* frazier@jhalit.com. *Website:* www.jhalit.com. *Address:* Department of English, Florida State University, 411 Williams Building, Tallahassee, FL 32306-1580, USA (office). *Telephone:* (850) 644-0238 (office). *E-mail:* rbutler@fsu.edu (office). *Website:* www.robertolenbutler.com.

BUTLIN, Martin Richard Fletcher, CBE, MA, DLit, FBA; British museum curator and art historian; b. 7 June 1929, Birmingham; s. of K.R. Butlin and Helen M. Butlin (née Fletcher); m. Frances C. Chodzko 1969. *Education:* Trinity Coll., Cambridge and Courtauld Inst. of Art., Univ. of London. *Career:* Asst Keeper, Tate Gallery, London 1955–67, Keeper of the Historic British Collection 1967–89. *Publications:* A Catalogue of the Works of William Blake in the Tate Gallery 1957, 1971, 1990, Samuel Palmer's Sketchbook of 1824, 1962, 2005, Turner Watercolours 1962, Turner (with Sir John Rothenstein) 1964, Tate Gallery Catalogues: The Modern British Paintings, Drawings and Sculpture (with Mary Chamot and Dennis Farr) 1964, The Later Works of J.M.W. Turner 1965, William Blake 1966, The Blake-Varley Sketchbook of 1819 1969, The Paintings of J.M.W. Turner (with E. Joll) 1977, 1984, The Paintings and Drawings of William Blake 1981, Aspects of British Painting 1550–1800 1988, Turner at Petworth (with Mollie Luther and Ian Warrell) 1989, The Oxford Companion to J.M.W. Turner (co-ed. with Evelyn Joll and Luke Herrmann) 2001, William Blake's Watercolour Inventions in Illustration of The Grave by Robert Blair 2010; catalogues, articles, reviews etc. *Honours:* Mitchell Prize (jtly) 1978. *Address:* 74C Eccleston Square, London, SW1V 1PJ, England (home).

BUTLIN, Ron, MA, DipCDAE; British novelist, poet, playwright, critic and opera librettist; *Poet Laureate, City of Edinburgh*; b. (Ronald Young Butlin), 17 Nov. 1949, Edinburgh, Scotland; m. Regula Staub 1993. *Education:* Univ. of Edinburgh. *Career:* Writer-in-Residence, Univ. of Edinburgh 1983, 1985, Midlothian Region 1990–91, Univ. of Stirling 1993 (Examiner in Creative Writing 1997–), Craigmillar Literary Trust 1997–98, Univ. of St Andrews 1998–; Poet Laureate (Makar), City of Edinburgh 2008–; mem. Scottish Arts Council (mem. Literature Cttee 1995–96); apptd, with Ian Rankin, first-ever Hon. Writing Fellow, Univ. of Edinburgh 2009, Royal Literary Fund Fellow and Lecturer, Office of Lifelong Learning 2010, cr. and delivered 'Symphonies for All' course; Specialist Advisor to Creative Scotland 2010–11. *Libretti:* Faraway Pictures (children's opera, commissioned by composer Ken Dempster for Creative Scotland Award) 2000, The Voice Inside (concerto, BBC Radio 3 comm.) 2001, Good Angel, Bad Angel (opera, with Lyell Cresswell), Edward Harper's Voice of a City (Scottish Chamber Orchestra (SCO) comm.) 2006, Edward Harper's 2nd Symphony (SCO comm.) 2006, The Perfect Woman (opera with Lyell Cresswell for Scottish Opera) 2008, text for Edward Harper's Third Symphony 2009 (SCO comm.), The Money Man (opera with Lyell Cresswell commissioned by Scottish Opera) 2010. *Plays:* numerous plays for BBC Radio over many years; The Sound of My Voice (Citizens Theatre, Glasgow, with Jeremy Raison) 2008, Vivaldi and the Number 3 (with jazzers!) 2011, The Magicians of Edinburgh (jazzers again!) 2012, Sweet Dreams (Oran Mor) 2012. *Radio:* numerous poems, stories etc. on BBC World Service, BBC Radio 3, BBC Radio 4 and BBC Radio Scotland, many also broadcast abroad, occasional essays for BBC Radio 4's Today programme, twice selected for BBC Radio 4's Pick of the Week. *Television:* Making of The Perfect Woman (opera, BBC 2), numerous appearances on BBC and STV, discussion programmes etc.. *Publications:* Creature Tamed by Cruelty (poems) 1979, The Exquisite Instrument (poems) 1982, The Tilting Room (stories) 1984, Ragtime in Unfamiliar Bars 1985, The Sound of My Voice 1987, Faber Book of Twentieth Century Scottish Poetry 1992, Histories of Desire 1995, Night Visits 1997, When We Jump We Jump High! (ed.) 1998, Our Piece of Good Fortune (selected poetry, Spanish bilingual) 2002, Panther Book of Scottish Short Stories 2002, Vivaldi and the Number 3 (short stories) 2003, Without a Backward Glance: Selected Poems 2005, Belonging (novel) 2006, No More Angels (stories) 2007, The Magicians of Edinburgh (poems) 2012; contrib. to numerous reviews, periodicals, anthologies and journals both in UK and abroad. *Honours:* Writing Bursaries 1977, 1987, 1990, 1994, 2002, 2007, Scottish Arts Council Book Awards 1982, 1984, 1985, Scottish-Canadian Writing Fellow 1984, Poetry Book Soc. Recommendation 1985, Prix Mille Pages for Best Foreign Novel 2004, Prix Lucioles for Best Foreign Novel 2005. *Literary Agent:* c/o Lucy Luck Associates, 18–21 Cavaye Place, London, SW10 9PT, England. *Telephone:* (20) 7373-8672. *E-mail:* lucy@lucyluck.com. *Website:* www.lucyluck.com. *E-mail:* ronbutlin@blueyonder.co.uk (home). *Website:* www.ronbutlin.co.uk.

BUTOR, Michel; French writer and lecturer; b. 14 Sept. 1926, Mons-en-Baroeul, Nord; s. of Emile Butor and Anne Brajeux; m. Marie-Josephe Mas 1958; four d. *Education:* Univ. of Paris. *Career:* teacher at Sens, France 1950, Minieh, Egypt 1950–51, Manchester, UK 1951–53, Salonica, Greece 1954–55, Geneva, Switzerland 1956–57; Visiting Prof., Bryn Mawr and Middlebury, USA 1960, Buffalo, USA 1962, Evanston, USA 1965, Albuquerque, USA 1969–70, 1973–74, Nice and Geneva 1974–75; Assoc. Prof., Vincennes 1969, Nice 1970–73; Prof. of Modern French Literature, Geneva 1975–91; Reader, Éditions Gallimard 1958–. *Publications:* novels: Passage de Milan 1954, L'emploi du temps 1956, La modification 1957, Degrés 1960, Intervalle 1973; essays: Le Génie du lieu 1958, Répertoire 1960, Histoire extraordinaire 1961, Mobile 1962, Réseau aérien 1963, Description de San Marco 1963, Les oeuvres d'art imaginaires chez Proust 1964, Répertoire II 1964, Portrait de l'artiste en jeune singe 1967, Répertoire III 1968, Essais sur les essais 1968, Les mots dans la peinture 1969, La rose des vents 1970, Le génie du lieu II 1971, Dialogue avec 33 variations de L. van Beethoven 1971, Répertoire IV 1974, Matière de rêves 1975, Second sous-sol 1976, Troisième dessous 1977, Boomerang 1978, Quadruple Fond 1981, Répertoire V 1982; poetry: Illustrations 1964, 6,801.000 litres d'eau par second 1965, Illustrations II 1969, Travaux d'approche 1972, Illustrations III 1973, Illustrations IV 1976, Envois 1980, Brassée d'Avril 1982, Exprès 1983, Herbier Lunaire 1984, Mille et un plis 1985, Le Retour du Boomerang 1988, Improvisations sur Flaubert 1991, Patience, Collation 1991, Transit A, Transit B 1993, Improvisations sur Michael Butor 1994, L'Utilité Poétique 1995, Le Japon depuis la France, un rêve à l'ancre 1995, Curriculum Vitae 1996 (jtly), Gyroscope 1996, Ici et là 1997, Improvisations sur Balzac 1998, Entretiens 1999, M. Butor par M. Butor 2003, Anthologie nomade 2004, L'Horticulteur itinérant 2004, Octogénaire 2006, Seize Lustres 2006, Oeuvres complètes I–IV 2006, V–VI 2007, VII–VIII 2008, IX–X 2009, XI–XII 2010. *Honours:* Chevalier, Ordre nat. du Mérite, Ordre des Arts et des Lettres; Hon. PhD (Univ. of Mainz) 1995, (Univ. of Massachusetts) 1999, (Univ. of Thessaloniki) 2001; Prix Felix Féneon 1957, Prix Renaudot 1957, Grand prix de la critique littéraire 1960. *Address:* à l'Ecart, 216 Place de l'Eglise, 74380 Lucinges, France (office).

BUTTERWORTH, Jeremy (Jez); British writer, playwright and film director; b. 4 March 1969, London; m. Gilly Richardson. *Education:* Verulam School, St Albans, Univ. of Cambridge. *Television:* Night of the Golden Brain 1993, Christmas 1996. *Films:* as dir: Mojo (also writer) 1997, Birthday Girl (also writer) 2001; as writer: The Last Legion 2007, Huge 2009, Fair Game (also producer) (co-winner Paul Selvin Award, Writers Guild of America West 2011) 2010. *Publications:* I Believe In Love 1992, Huge 1993, Mojo 1995, The Winterling 1996, Birthday Girl (with Tom Butterworth) 2001, The Night Heron 2002, Parlour Song 2008, Jerusalem 2008, Jez Butterworth Plays: One 2011, Mojo and Other Plays 2012. *Honours:* George Dence Award for Most Promising Playwright 1995, Writers' Guild New Writer of the Year Award 1995, Evening Standard Award for Most Promising Playwright 1995, Olivier Award for Britain's Best Comedy 1995, E.M. Forster Award 2007. *Literary Agent:* Creative Artists Agency, 4th Floor, Space One, 1 Beadon Road, London, W6 0EA, England. *Telephone:* (20) 8846-3000. *Fax:* (20) 8846-3090. *Website:* www.caa.com.

BUTTERWORTH, (David) Neil, BA, MA; British fmr composer, conductor, writer and broadcaster; b. 4 Sept. 1934, London; m. Anne Mary Barnes 1960; three d. *Education:* Univ. of London, Guildhall School of Music, London, Univ. of Nottingham. *Career:* Lecturer, Kingston Coll. of Tech. 1960–68; Head of Music Dept, Napier Coll., Edinburgh 1968–87; conductor Edinburgh Schools Choir 1968–72, Glasgow Orchestral Soc. 1975–83, 1989–2002, Edinburgh Chamber Orchestra 1983–85; music critic, Times Educational Supplement 1983–97; Winston Churchill Travelling Fellowship 1975; mem. Inc. Soc. of Musicians, Performing Right Soc., Scottish Soc. of Composers. *Compositions include:* two horn concertos, Overture Budapest, A Scott Cantata, Dunblane, In Memory of Auschwitz, Partita, Dances for Dalkeith, Count Dracula (opera), many songs and instrumental works. *Publications:* Haydn 1970, 400 Aural Training Exercises 1970, A Musical Quiz Book 1974, Dvořák 1978, A Dictionary of American Composers 1983, revised edn 2005, Aaron Copland 1984, 20th Century Sight-singing Exercises 1984, Sight-singing Exercises from the Masters 1984, Vaughan Williams 1989, Neglected Music 1991, The American Symphony 1998; contrib. to periodicals, including Classic CD, Classical Music, Musical Opinion, The Scotsman, The Herald, The Sunday Times. *Honours:* Hon. FLCM; Guildhall School of Music and Drama Conducting Prize 1961. *Address:* The Lodge, 42 E High Street, Greenlaw, Berwickshire, TD10 6UF, Scotland (home). *Telephone:* (1361) 810408 (home).

BUTTERWORTH, Nick; British children's writer and illustrator; b. 1946, Kingsbury, London, England; m.; two c. *Career:* worked as a typographic designer, printing dept, Nat. Children's Home; fmr graphic designer, Frank Overton Design Assocs and Pentagram, London, later freelance; fmr TV presenter Rub-a-Dub-Tub (TV-AM); Co-founder and Dir, Snapper Productions LLP; currently full-time children's writer and illustrator; numerous collaborations with illustrator, Mick Inkpen. *Publications include:* B.B. Blaksheep and Company 1981, Windy Day at Upney Junction 1983, Monster at Upney Junction 1983, Invasion at Upney Junction 1983, Treasure Trove at Upney Junction 1983, The Gravedigger File 1983, The Nativity Play 1985, The House on the Rock 1986, The Lost Sheep 1986, The Precious Pearl 1986, The Two Sons 1986, Who Made Me?... 1987–, Nice and Nasty 1987, I Wonder... (series with Mick Inkpen) 1987–, Sports Day! 1988, The Fox's Story: Jesus is Born 1988, The Mouse's Story: Jesus and the Storm 1988, The Magpie's Story: Jesus and Zacchaeus 1988, The Cat's Story: Jesus at the Wedding 1988, Just Like Jasper 1989, The Ten Silver Coins 1989, The Good Stranger 1989, The Little Gate 1989, The Rich Farmer 1989, One Snowy Night 1989, My Dad is Brilliant 1989, My Mum is Fantastic 1989, The School Trip 1990, Wonderful Earth 1990, Amanda's Butterfly 1991, Field Day 1991, Jasper's Beanstalk 1992, My Dad is Awesome 1992, My Grandma is Wonderful 1992, After the Sun 1992, Rescue Party 1993, Making Faces 1993, The Secret Path 1994, My Mom is Excellent 1994, The Fox's Hiccups 1995, A Year in Percy's Park 1995, All Together Now! 1995, Jake 1995, The Badger's Bath 1996, The Hedgehog's Balloon 1996, Jill the Farmer and her Friends 1996, Jack the Carpenter and his Friends 1996, The Cross Rabbit 1996, Treasure Hunt 1996, Thud! 1997, The Owl's Lesson 1997, One Warm Fox 1997, Four Feathers in Percy's Park 1998, Jake in Trouble 1998, Learn with Percy: A-B-C 1998, Learn with Percy: 1-2-3 1998, Jingle Bells 1998, Percy's Bumpy Ride 1999, The Lost Acorns 2000, Q Pootle 5 2000, Owl Takes Charge 2000, Percy the Park Keeper and his Friends (series) 2001–, My Family 2002, Make a Wish 2002, Albert Le Blanc 2002, Q Pootle 5 in Space 2004, The Whisperer (Nestle Children's Gold Award) 2004, Tiger 2006, Tiger in the Snow 2006, Animal Tales 2006, Tiger 2008, Tiger in the Snow 2008, Albert Le Blanc to the Rescue 2008, One Snowy Night 2009, Trixie the Witch's Cat 2009. *Address:* c/o HarperCollins Childrens Books, 77–85 Fulham Palace Road, Hammersmith, London, W6 8JB, England. *Website:* www.harpercollins.co.uk.

BUTTROSE, Ita Clare, AO, OBE; Australian editor, broadcaster, author and publishing executive; *Managing Director, IB Specialist Publishing;* b. 17 Jan. 1942, Sydney; d. of Charles Oswald Buttrose and Mary Clare Buttrose (née Rodgers); m. 1st Alasdair MacDonald 1963 (divorced); m. 2nd Peter Sawyer 1979 (divorced); one s. one d. *Education:* Sacred Heart Convent, Rose Bay, Sydney and Dover Heights High School, Sydney. *Career:* joined Australian Consolidated Press Pty Ltd 1958, Dir 1974–81, Publr Women's Div. 1977–80; Founding Ed. Cleo 1972–75; Ed. Australian Women's Weekly 1975–76, Ed.-in-Chief 1976–77, columnist and feature writer 1998–; Sub-Ed. Woman's Own, UK 1967–69; Ed.-in-Chief The Daily Telegraph and The Sunday Telegraph, Sydney 1981–84; Dir News Ltd Australia 1981–84; Ed.-in-Chief The Sun-Herald 1988; Publishing Consultant, Woman's Day and Portfolio magazines 1983–88; Ed. Ita Magazine 1989–94; CEO Capricorn Publishing Pty Ltd 1988–94; Broadcaster Radio 2KY, 2UE, Sydney 1984–87, Radio 3UZ, Melbourne 1988–90; TV personality Beauty & the Beast Foxtel and Network TEN 1996; Man. Dir. The Good Life Publishing Co., Ed.-in-Chief bark! magazine –2007; Ed.-at-Large OK! Magazine; Man. Dir IB Specialist Publishing; Dir TV and Telecasters Pty Ltd 1991–93, Prudential Corpn Australia Ltd 1990–96; Dir Hope Town Special School Wyong Ltd 1990–; Chair. Nat. Advisory Cttee on AIDS (NACAIDS) 1984–88, Chair. AIDS Trust of Australia 1990–94; Convenor First Nat. Family Summit, Canberra; Communications Strategist, World Vision Australia 1995–97; Chair. Australian Services Nurses Nat. Memorial Fund Cttee 1997–99; Nat. Spokesperson Arthritis Foundation of Australia 1997–99, 2001–, Pres. 2003–06; Dir Sydney Symphony Council 1996, The Smith Family 1997, Prostate Cancer Foundation 2002; Fellow, Australian Inst. of Co. Dirs, Autralian Inst. of Man.; Assoc. Fellow Professional Marketing Asscn; mem. Council Australian Nat. Art Gallery 1989–, Australian Soc. of Authors, Chief Exec. Women; mem. Program Reference Group 2001, Australian Govt's Women Speak Conf.; Amb. Melbourne Museum 2001–; Patron Active Ageing Week 2004. *Publications include:* A Guide to Modern Etiquette 1985, Early Edition: My First Forty Years 1985, A Passionate Life 1998, A Word to the Wise 1999, What is Love? 2000, How Much is Enough? (co-author) 2003, Motherguilt (co-author) 2005, Get in Shape (co-author) 2007, Eating for Eye Health (co-author) 2009, A Guide to Australian Etiquette 2011. *Honours:* honoured by UN for convening Australia's first Nat. Family Summit 1992, RSA Hartnett Medal (first woman recipient) 1992, Centenary Medal for service to Australian society in business leadership 2003, twice voted Australia's Most Admired Woman. *Literary Agent:* ICMI Melbourne, PO Box 2311, Prahran, Vic. 3181, Australia. *Telephone:* (3) 9529-3711. *Fax:* (3) 9529-4573. *E-mail:* icmi@icmi.com.au. *Website:* www.icmi.com.au.

BUTTS, Anthony, BA, MA, MFA, PhD; American writer, poet, professor of English and professor of creative writing; b. 28 July 1969, Detroit, MI; m. Leah Samuel 2004. *Education:* Wayne State Univ., Western Michigan Univ., Univ. of Missouri at Columbia. *Career:* faculty mem., English Dept, Carnegie Mellon Univ.; Prof. of English and Creative Writing, Univ. of Dayton, Ohio; Assoc. Prof. of Creative Writing, Carnegie Mellon Univ., Pittsburgh; Assoc. Poetry Ed. Carnegie Mellon Univ. Press; Poetry Ed. Paper Street 2006–; Co-host, Different Voices interview show (KOPN-FM Radio); mem. Conf. on Christianity and Literature; Assoc. mem. Acad. of American Poets. *Publications:* Fifth Season 1997, Evolution 1998, The Next Generation 2000, Little Low Heaven (William Carlos William Prize 2004) 2003, Male Hysteria 2007, The Golden Underground 2009. *Honours:* William Carlos Williams Award 2004. *Address:* c/o Department of English, Carnegie Mellon University, Baker Hall 259, 5000 Forbes Avenue, Pittsburgh, PA 15213, USA.

BUZAN, Barry, BA, PhD, FBA, ACSS; British/Canadian academic, writer and editor; *Professor of International Relations, London School of Economics;* b. 28 April 1946, London, England; m. Deborah Skinner 1973. *Education:* Univ. of British Columbia, London School of Econs. *Career:* Research Fellow, Inst. of Int. Relations, Univ. of British Columbia 1973–75; Lecturer, Univ. of Warwick 1976–83, Sr Lecturer 1983–88, Reader, Dept of Int. Studies 1988–89, Prof., Dept of Politics and Int. Studies 1990–95; Dir Project on European Security, Copenhagen Peace Research Inst. 1988–2003; Ed. European Journal of International Relations 2004–; Research Prof. of Int. Studies, Univ. of Westminster 1995–2002; Olof Palme Visiting Prof., Sweden 1997–98; Prof. of Int. Relations, LSE 2002–. *Publications include:* Seabed Politics 1976, Change and the Study of International Relations: The Evaded Dimension (co-ed. with R. J. Barry Jones) 1981, People, States, and Fear: The National Security Problem in International Relations 1983, second edn as An Agenda for International Security Studies in the Post-Cold War Era 1991, South Asian Insecurity and the Great Powers (co-author) 1986, An Introduction to Strategic Studies: Military Technology and International Relations 1987, The International Politics of Deterrence (ed.) 1987, The European Security Order Recast: Scenarios for the Post-Cold War Era (co-author) 1990, The Logic of Anarchy: Neorealism to Structural Realism (co-author) 1993, Identity, Migration and the New Security Agenda in Europe (co-author) 1993, The Mind Map Book (with T. Buzan) 1993, Security: A New Framework for Analysis (co-author) 1998, Anticipating the Future: Twenty Millennia of Human Progress (with G. Segal) 1998, The Arms Dynamic in World Politics (with E. Herring) 1998, International Systems in World History: Remaking the Study of International Relations (with R. Little) 2000, Regions and Powers: The Structure of International Security (with O. Waever) 2003, From International to World Society 2004, The United States and the Great Powers 2004, International Society and the Middle East (co-ed. with A. Gonzalez-Pelaez 2009, The Evolution of International Security Studies (with L. Hansen) 2009; contrib. to many scholarly publs. *Honours:* Hon. Prof., Jilin Univ. 2003–, Univ. of Copenhagen 2005–; Francis Deak Prize, American Journal of International Law 1982. *Address:* Department of International Relations, London School of Economics, Houghton Street, London, WC2A 2AE (office); Garden Flat, 17 Lambolle Road, London, NW3 4HS, England (home). *E-mail:* b.g.buzan@lse.ac.uk (office).

BYAM SHAW, Nicholas Glencairn; British publisher; b. 28 March 1934, London; s. of the late David Byam Shaw and Clarita Pamela Clarke; m. 1st Joan Elliott 1956 (divorced 1973); two s. one d.; m. 2nd Suzanne Filer (née Rastello) 1974; m. 3rd Constance Mary Wilson (née Clarke) 1987. *Education:*

Royal Naval Coll., Dartmouth. *Career:* served RN, retiring with rank of Lt 1951–56; on staff of Collins (printers and publrs), Sales Man. 1956–64; joined Macmillan Publrs Ltd as Sales Man. 1964, Deputy Man. Dir 1968, Man. Dir 1970–90, Chair. 1990–97, Deputy Chair. 1998–99; Dir St Martin's Press 1980–99 (Deputy Chair. 1997–99), Pan Books Ltd 1983–99 (Chair. 1986–99), Gruppe Georg von Hotzbrinck, Stuttgart, Germany 1996–99; mem. British Council Publrs' Advisory Cttee, Byam Shaw School Council. *Address:* 9 Kensington Park Gardens, London, W11 3HB, England (home). *Telephone:* (20) 7221-4547 (home).

BYATT, Dame Antonia Susan (A.S.), (Dame Antonia Duffy), DBE, BA, FRSL; British writer; b. 24 Aug. 1936, Sheffield, Yorkshire; d. of His Honour John F. Drabble, QC and the late Kathleen M. Bloor; sister of Margaret Drabble; m. 1st Ian Charles Rayner Byatt 1959 (divorced 1969); one s. (deceased) one d.; m. 2nd Peter John Duffy 1969; two d. *Education:* Sheffield High School, The Mount School, York, Newnham Coll., Cambridge, Bryn Mawr Coll., PA, USA and Somerville Coll., Oxford. *Career:* Extra-Mural Lecturer, Univ. of London 1962–71; Lecturer in Literature, Cen. School of Art and Design 1965–69; Lecturer in English, Univ. Coll., London 1972–81, Sr Lecturer 1981–83; Assoc. Newnham Coll., Cambridge 1977–82; mem. BBC Social Effects of TV Advisory Group 1974–77; mem. Bd of Creative and Performing Arts 1985–87, Bd of British Council 1993–98; Kingman Cttee on English Language 1987–88; Man. Cttee Soc. of Authors 1984–88 (Chair. 1986–88); mem. Literature Advisory Panel of the British Council 1990–98; broadcaster, reviewer and judge of literary prizes; Fellow English Asscn. *Radio:* dramatisation of quartet of novels (BBC Radio) 2002. *Television:* profile on Scribbling (series, BBC 2) 2002, interview with Mark Lawson (BBC 4) 2010. *Films:* Angels and Insects 1996, Possession 2002. *Publications:* fiction: The Shadow of the Sun 1964, The Game 1967, The Virgin in the Garden 1978, Still Life (PEN/Macmillan Silver Pen for Fiction 1986) 1985, Sugar and Other Stories 1987, Possession: A Romance (Booker Prize 1990, Irish Times-Aer Lingus Int. Fiction Prize 1990, Eurasian Regional Award of the Commonwealth Writers' Prize 1991) 1990 filmed 2002, Angels and Insects (novellas) 1992 filmed 1996, The Matisse Stories 1993, The Djinn in the Nightingale's Eye (Mythopoeic Fantasy Award 1998) 1994, Babel Tower 1996, Elementals, Stories of Fire and Ice 1998, The Biographer's Tale 2000, A Whistling Woman 2002, Little Black Book of Stories 2003, The Children's Book (James Tait Black Memorial Prize 2010) 2009, Ragnarok: the End of the Gods 2012; non-fiction: Degrees of Freedom: The Novels of Iris Murdoch (revised edn as Degrees of Freedom: The Early Novels of Iris Murdoch) 1965, Wordsworth and Coleridge in Their Time (revised edn as Unruly Times: Wordsworth and Coleridge in Their Time) 1970, Iris Murdoch 1976, Passions of the Mind (selected essays) 1991, Imagining Characters: Conversations About Women Writers (with Ignês Sodré) 1995, New Writing 4 (ed. with Alan Hollinghurst) 1995, New Writing 6 (co-ed.) 1997, The Oxford Book of English Short Stories (ed.) 1998, On Histories and Stories (essays) 2000, Portraits in Fiction 2001, Bird Hand Book (with V. Schrager) 2001, Memory (ed., anthology, with Harriet Harvey Wood) 2008; ed. and introduction to numerous works by other writers. *Honours:* Hon. Fellow, Newnham Coll. Cambridge 1999, London Inst. 2000, Univ. Coll. London 2004, Somerville Coll. Oxford 2005; Chevalier, Ordre des Arts et Lettres 2003; Hon. DLitt (Bradford) 1987, (Durham, York) 1991, (Nottingham) 1992, (Liverpool) 1993, (Portsmouth) 1994, (London) 1995, (Cambridge) 1999, (Sheffield) 2000, (Kent at Canterbury) 2004, (Oxford) 2007, (Winchester) 2007, (Leiden, Holland) 2010; Premio Malaparte Award, Capri 1995, Toepfer Foundation Shakespeare Prize, Hamburg 2002, Grand Prix littéraire du Metropolis Bleu (Canada) 2009. *Literary Agent:* c/o Rogers, Coleridge & White, 20 Powis Mews, London, W11 1JN, England. *Telephone:* (20) 7221-3717 (office). *Fax:* (20) 7229-9084 (office). *Website:* www.asbyatt.com.

BYKOV, Dmitry; Russian writer, editor and poet; *Editor, Sobesednik;* b. 20 Dec. 1967, Moscow; m. Irina Lukyanova; two c. *Education:* Moscow State Univ. *Career:* Ed. Sobesednik newspaper; other editorial work for Profil and Moulin Rouge magazines; hosts weekly radio show; columnist, Novaya Gazeta, and Ogonyok; teacher and lecturer. *Television:* Maxim Gorky (film, St Petersburg TV) 2008. *Publications include:* novels: Orthography 2003, Acquittal 2001, Evakuator (The Evacuator) 2005, Pravda (jtly), Zh.D 2006; other: Boris Pasternak (biog.) (Big Book Prize 2006) 2005, Enlisted 2008, Ostromov 2009, Bulat Okudjava (biog.) 2009; also eight collections of poetry; contrib. articles, reviews and essays to numerous publs. *Honours:* ABC Prizes 2003, 2005, 2007. *Address:* Sobesednik Gazeta, 101484 Moscow, Novoslobodskaya 73, POB 4, Russia (office). *Telephone:* (495) 685-16-50 (office). *E-mail:* bykov@sobesednik.ru (office). *Website:* www.sobesednik.ru (office).

BYNG, Jamie, BA; British publishing director; *Managing Director, Canongate Books;* b. 1969, Winchester; s. of the Earl of Strafford; m. 1st (divorced); one s. one d.; m. 2nd Elizabeth Sheinkman 2005. *Education:* Edinburgh Univ. *Career:* joined Canongate Books as unpaid worker 1992, bought the co. 1994, Man. Dir 1994–, books published include Yann Martel's Life of Pi (winner of Man Booker Prize, over two million copies sold) 2002. *Honours:* Canongate named Publisher of the Year 2003. *Address:* Canongate Books, 14 High Street, Edinburgh, EH1 1TE, Scotland (office); Canongate Books, Basement, 151 Chesterton Road, London, W10 6ET, England (office). *Telephone:* (131) 557-5111 (office); (20) 8969-6011 (office). *Fax:* (131) 557-5211 (office); (20) 8969-8462 (office). *E-mail:* info@canongate.co.uk (office). *Website:* www.canongate .co.uk (office).

BYNUM, Sarah Shun-lien, MFA; American writer and academic; *Professor of Writing, Otis College of Art and Design;* b. 14 Feb. 1972, Houston, Tex. *Education:* Brown Univ., Univ. of Iowa Writer's Workshop. *Career:* fmr high school teacher, New York; fmr Prof. of Writing, Univ. of California, San Diego; Prof. of Writing, Otis Coll. of Art and Design. *Publications:* novels: Madeleine is Sleeping (Kafka Prize) 2004, Ms. Hempel Chronicles 2008; contribs to The New Yorker, Tin House, The Georgia Review, The Best American Short Stories. *Honours:* Whiting Writers' Award, Nat. Endowment for the Arts Fellowship. *Address:* Graduate Writing, Otis College of Art and Design, 9045 Lincoln Blvd, Los Angeles, CA 90045, USA (office). *E-mail:* sbynum@otis.edu (office). *Website:* mshempelchronicles.com.

BYRD, Harry Flood, Jr; American newspaper executive and politician; b. 20 Dec. 1914, s. of Harry Flood Byrd, Sr; m. Gretchen B. Thomson 1941 (died 1989); two s. one d. *Education:* John Marshall High School, Richmond, Virginia Mil. Inst. and Univ. of Virginia. *Career:* Ed. and writer, Winchester Evening Star 1935, Ed. and Publr 1935–81, Ed. and Publr Harrisonburg Daily News-Record 1937–2000; also active in firm of H. F. Byrd, Inc., apple growers; mem. Va State Senate 1947–65; mem. Democratic State Cen. Cttee 1940–70; served in USNR 1941–46; Dir Associated Press 1950–66; US Senator from Virginia (succeeding his father) 1965–83; Ind. *Address:* Rockingham Publishing Co. Inc., 2 North Kent Street, Winchester, VA 22601 (office); 411 Tennyson Avenue, Winchester, VA 22601, USA (home). *Telephone:* (540) 662-7745 (office). *Fax:* (540) 667-6729 (office).

C

CABOT, Meggin (Meg) Patricia, (Patricia Cabot, Jenny Carroll), BFA; American writer; b. 1 Feb. 1967, Bloomington, IN; d. of A. Victor Cabot and Barbara Cabot; m. Benjamin D. Egnatz. *Education:* Indiana Univ. *Career:* fmrly illustrator, Asst Man. of undergraduate dormitory, New York Univ., mem. Authors Guild, Authors League of America, Soc. of Children's Book Authors and Illustrators, Romance Writers of America. *Publications include:* as Patricia Cabot, adult fiction: Where Roses Grow Wild 1998, Portrait of my Heart 1999, An Improper Proposal (Reviewers Choice Award, Romantic Times) 1999, A Little Scandal 2000, Lady of Skye 2000, Educating Caroline 2001, Kiss the Bride 2002; as Meg Cabot, juvenile fiction: The Princess Diaries 2000, The Princess Diaries, Vol. II: Princess in the Spotlight 2001, The Princess Diaries, Vol. III: Princess in Love 2002, Nicola and the Viscount 2002, All-American Girl 2002, The Boy Next Door 2002, She Went All the Way 2002, Victoria and the Rogue 2003, The Princess Diaries, Vol. IV: Princess in Waiting 2003, Princess Lessons: A Princess Diaries Book 2003, The Princess Diaries, Vol. IV and a Half: Project Princess 2003, Boy Meets Girl 2004, The Princess Diaries, Vol. V: Princess in Pink 2004, Perfect Princess: A Princess Diaries Book 2004, Teen Idol 2004, The Princess Diaries: Sixsational 2005, All American Girl: Ready or Not 2005, Avalon High 2005, The Princess Diaries: Seventh Heaven 2006, How to be Popular When You're a Social Reject Like Me, Steph L! 2007, Jinx 2007, Missing You 2007, Moving Day 2008, The New Girl 2008, Best Friends and Drama Queens 2009, The Mediator 2010, Abandon 2011, Insatiable 2011, Overbite 2011, Underworld 2012; as Jenny Carroll, juvenile fiction: The Mediator: Shadowland 2000, 1-800-WHERE-R-YOU: When Lightning Strikes 2001, The Mediator: Ninth Key 2001, The Mediator: Reunion 2001, 1-800-WHERE-R-YOU: Code Name Cassandra 2001, The Mediator: Darkest Hour 2001, 1-800-WHERE-R-YOU: Safe House 2002, 1-800-WHERE-R-YOU: Sanctuary 2002, Haunted: A Tale of the Mediator 2003, 1-800-WHERE-R-YOU: Missing You 2006. *Literary Agent:* c/o 275 President Street, Suite 3, Brooklyn, NY 11231, USA. *Address:* PO Box 4904, Key West, FL 33041-4904 (office); 532 La Guardia Place, No. 359, New York, NY 10012, USA (office). *Website:* www.megcabot.com.

CADE, Robin (see Nicole, Christopher Robin)

CAFFREY, Idris; British writer; b. 16 Nov. 1949, Rhayader, Powys, Wales; m.; four c. *Education:* Swansea Coll. of Education. *Career:* mem. Academi 2009–. *Publications include:* Pacing Backwards 1996, Pathways 1997, Other Places 1998, Warm Rain 2000, Touch the Earth 2001, Departures and Returns 2002, Relatively Unscathed 2007, Selected Poems 2009.

CAHILL, Mike (see Nolan, William Francis)

CAIPÍN, Áine an (see Wilton-Jones, Anni)

CAIRNCROSS, Frances Anne, BA, MA; British journalist and academic; *Rector, Exeter College, Oxford;* b. 30 Aug. 1944, Otley, Yorks.; d. of Alexander Kirkland Cairncross and Mary Frances Cairncross; m. Hamish McRae 1971; two d. *Education:* St Anne's Coll., Oxford and Brown Univ., Providence, RI, USA. *Career:* staff mem. The Times 1967–69, The Banker 1969, The Observer 1969–71; Econs Corresp., The Guardian 1973–81, Women's Ed. 1981–84; Britain Ed., The Economist 1984–89, Public Policy Ed. 1997–2000, Man. Ed. 2000–04; Chair., Econ. and Social Research Council 2001–07; High Sheriff of London 2004–05; Rector, Exeter Coll., Oxford 2004–; Pres. BAAS 2005–06; Sr Fellow, School of Public Policy, UCLA; Visiting Fellow, Nuffield Coll. *Publications:* Capital City (with Hamish McRae) 1971, The Second Great Crash 1973, The Guardian Guide to the Economy 1981, Changing Perceptions of Economic Policy 1981, Second Guardian Guide to the Economy 1983, Guide to the Economy 1987, Costing the Earth 1991, Green, Inc. 1995, The Death of Distance 1997, The Company of the Future 2002. *Honours:* Hon. Fellow, St Anne's Coll., Oxford, St Peter's Coll., Oxford; Dr hc (Univs of Glasgow, Birmingham, City, Loughborough, Trinity Coll. Dublin, East Anglia). *Address:* Exeter College, Oxford, OX1 3DP, England (office). *Telephone:* (1865) 279647 (office). *Website:* www.exeter.ox.ac.uk (office).

CAIRNS, David Adam, CBE, MA; British journalist and musicologist; b. 8 June 1926, Loughton, Essex; s. of Sir Hugh William Bell Cairns and Barbara Cairns (née Smith); m. Rosemary Goodwin 1959; three s. *Education:* Dragon School, Winchester Coll., Oxford, Princeton Univ. Graduate Coll., USA. *Career:* Library Clerk, House of Commons 1951–53; critic, Record News 1954–56; mem. editorial staff, Times Educational Supplement 1955–58; music critic, Spectator 1958–63, Evening Standard 1958–63; asst music critic, Financial Times 1963–67; music critic, New Statesman 1967–70; mem. staff, Philips Records, London 1968–70, Classic Programme Co-ordinator 1970–73; asst music critic, Sunday Times 1975–84, music critic 1985–92; Leverhulme Research Fellow 1972–74; Distinguished Visiting Prof., Univ. of California, Davis 1985; Distinguished Visiting Scholar, Getty Center for the History of Art and Humanities 1992; Visiting Resident Fellow, Merton Coll., Oxford 1993. *Publications:* The Memoirs of Hector Berlioz (ed. and trans.) 1969, Responses: Musical Essays and Reviews 1973, The Magic Flute (co-author, ENO Opera Guide) 1980, Falstaff (co-author, ENO Opera Guide) 1982, Berlioz: The Making of an Artist 1803–1832 (ASCAP Deems Taylor Award 2001) 1989, Berlioz: Servitude and Greatness 1832–1869 (Whitbread Biog. of the Year 2000, Samuel Johnson Non-Fiction Prize 2000, Prix de l'Académie Charles Croz 2003) 1999, Mozart and his Operas 2006; contrib. to articles on Beethoven and Berlioz, in Viking Opera Guide 1993. *Honours:* Officier, Ordre des Arts et des Lettres 1991; Hon. DLitt (Southampton) 2001; British Acad. Derek Allen Memorial Prize 1990, Royal Philharmonic Soc. Award 1990, 1999, Yorkshire Post Prize 1990. *Address:* 49 Amerland Road, London, SW18 1QA, England (office). *Telephone:* (20) 8870-4931 (office). *E-mail:* d03.cairns@zen.co.uk (office).

CALCAGNO, Anne, BA, MFA; American academic and fiction and travel writer; *Lecturer, School of the Art Institute of Chicago;* b. 14 Nov. 1957, San Diego, Calif.; m. Leo 1986; one s. one d. *Education:* Williams Coll., Univ. of Montana. *Career:* part-time Lecturer, North Park Coll. and American Conservatory of Music, Chicago 1989–91; Teacher and Lecturer, School of the Art Inst. of Chicago 1990–93, 2004–; Artist-in-Educ., Illinois Arts Council 1992–93; Lecturer, DePaul Univ. 1992–93, Assoc. Prof. of English 1993–2004; mem. Associated Writing Programs, Authors' Guild, Poets and Writers. *Publications include:* Pray for Yourself (short stories) 1993, Travelers Tales, Italy (ed.) (Foreward's Silver Medal 1999) 1998; novel: Love Like a Dog 2010; anthologies fiction: Fiction of the Eighties 1991, American Fiction (Vol. 2) 1991, Don't Tell Mama: The Penguin Book of Italian American Writing 2002, The Milk of Almonds: Italian American Women Writers 2002; non-fiction anthologies: Whose Panties Are These? 2004, Thirty Days in Italy 2006. *Honours:* Nat. Endowment for the Arts Creative Writing Fellowship 1989, Illinois Arts Council Artists Fellowship 1993, James D. Phelan Literary Award, San Francisco Foundation 1993, Ed.'s Choice Award, Journey Woman 1999, Illinois Arts Council Literary Award 2003. *Literary Agent:* c/o Representation for Artists, 63 Carmine Street, #3D, New York, NY 10014, USA. *Telephone:* (212) 924-1894. *Fax:* (212) 924-6467. *Address:* 37 South Wabash, Chicago, IL 60603-3122, USA (office). *Telephone:* (312) 301-3122 (office). *E-mail:* acalcagno1@artic.edu (office). *Website:* www.annecalcagno.com; www.lovelikeadog.net.

CALDECOTT, Moyra, MA; British author; b. 1 June 1927, Pretoria, SA; m. Oliver Zerffi Stratford Caldecott 1951; two s. one d. *Education:* Univ. of Natal, SA. *Publications include:* The Weapons of the Wolfhound 1976, Guardians of the Tall Stones, Vol. I, The Tall Stones 1977, Vol. II, The Temple of the Sun 1977, Vol. III, Shadow on the Stones 1978, Adventures by Leaf Light 1978, The Lily and the Bull 1979, Child of the Dark Star 1980, The King of Shadows: A Glastonbury Story 1981, The Twins of the Tylwyth Teg 1983, Taliesin and Avagddu 1983, Bran, Son of Llyr 1985, The Tower and the Emerald 1985, Guardians of the Tall Stones 1986, The Son of the Sun 1986, The Silver Vortex 1987, Etheldreda 1987, Women in Celtic Myth 1988, Hatshepsut: Daughter of Amun 1989, The Green Lady and the King of Shadows 1989, Tutankhamun and the Daughter of Ra 1990, The Crystal Legends 1990, Myths of the Sacred Tree 1993, The Winged Man 1993, Mythical Journeys: Legendary Quests 1996, The Waters of Sul 1997, Aquae Sulis 1997, The Eye of Callanish 2001, The Ghost of Akhenaten 2001, Multi-Dimensional Life (auto-biog.) 2007, The Breathless Pause (poems) 2007, Three Celtic Tales 2007, Adventures by Leaflight and Other Stories 2007; contrib. to anthologies and periodicals. *Electronic publications include:* The Eye of Callanish 2002, Three Celtic Tales 2002, Hatshepsut: Daughter of Amun 2003, Akhenaten: Son of the Sun 2003, Tutankhamun and the Daughter of Ra 2003, The Ghost of Akhenaten 2003, Weapons of the Wolfhound 2003, The Lily and the Bull 2003, The Tower and the Emerald 2003, Child of the Dark Star 2003, The Silver Vortex 2004, Crystal Legends 2005, Etheldreda 2005, The Winged Man 2006, The Waters of Sul 2006, The Tall Stones 2006, The Temple of the Sun 2006, Shadow on the Stones 2006, The Green Lady and the King of Shadows 2007, Adventures by Leaflight and Other Stories 2007, Multi-Dimensional Life 2007, The Breathless Pause 2007, The Green Lady and the King of Shadows 2007, Mythical Journeys Legendary Quests 2007. *Address:* c/o Mushroom Publishing, 156 Southlands Weston, Bath, BA1 4EB, England. *Telephone:* (1225) 484063. *Fax:* (871) 242-6853. *E-mail:* moyrac@mushroompublishing.com. *Website:* www.moyracaldecott.co.uk.

CALDER, Elisabeth (Liz) Nicole, BA; British publisher; b. 20 Jan. 1938, New Zealand; d. of Ivor George Baber and Florence Mary Baber; m. 1st Richard Henry Calder 1958 (divorced 1972); one s. one d.; m. 2nd Louis Baum 2000. *Education:* Palmerston North Girls' High School, NZ and Univ. of Canterbury, NZ. *Career:* catwalk model in Brazil 1965–68; reader Metro-Goldwyn-Mayer Story Dept 1969–70; Publicity Man. Victor Gollancz 1971–74, Editorial Dir 1975–78; Editorial Dir (fiction), Jonathan Cape 1979–86; Founding Publishing Dir Book Div., Bloomsbury Publishing 1986–2008, Ed. 2008–09; co-f. Full Circle Editions 2009–; co-f. Women in Publishing 1979; co-f. Groucho Club, London 1984; f. Parati Int. Literary Festival, Brazil 2003–; Chair. Royal Court Theatre 2001–05, Vice-Chair. 2005–. *Honours:* Order of Merit for services to culture, Brazil 2004. *Address:* c/o Bloomsbury Publishing plc, 38 Soho Square, London, W1V 5DF, England (office). *Website:* www.bloomsbury.com (office).

CALDER, John Mackenzie; British publisher, critic, playwright and theatre administrator; *Managing Director, Calder Publishers Ltd;* b. 25 Jan. 1927; m. 1st Mary A. Simmonds 1949; one d.; m. 2nd Bettina Jonic 1960 (divorced 1975); one d. *Education:* Gilling Castle, Yorks., Bishops Coll. School, Canada, McGill Univ., Montreal, Sir George Williams Coll. and Univ. of Zürich, Switzerland. *Career:* Founder and Man. Dir John Calder (Publishers)

Ltd 1950–91, Calder Publishers Ltd 1991–, Calder and Boyars Ltd 1964–75, f. Calder Bookshop; expanded to Edin. 1971; organized literature confs, Edin. Festival 1962, 1963, Harrogate Festival 1969; f. Ledlanet Nights (music and opera festival) Kinross-shire 1963–74; Pres. Riverrun Press Inc., New York 1978–; Prof. of Literature and Philosophy, Ecole Active Bilingue, Paris 1994–96; Lecturer in History, Univ. of Paris-Nanterre 1995; acquired bookselling business of Better Books, London 1969; Chair. North American Book Clubs 1982–89, Fed. of Scottish Theatres 1972–74; Co-founder Defence of Literature and the Arts Soc.; Dir of other cos associated with opera, publishing etc.; f. Godot Company, Waterloo, London; Theatre Admin. Godot Co. *Plays include:* Lorca, The Voice, The Trust. *Publications:* A Samuel Beckett Reader, The Burroughs Reader 1981, New Beckett Reader 1983, Henry Miller Reader 1985, Nouveau Roman Reader 1986, The Defence of Literature 1991, The Garden of Eros 1992, The Philosophy of Samuel Beckett 1998, What's Wrong, What's Right (poetry) 1999, Pursuit (autobiography) 2001, Solo (poems); contribs to anthologies. *Honours:* Chevalier des Arts et des Lettres; Officier, Ordre nat. du Mérite; Dr hc (Edinburgh, Zurich, Napier) 2008. *Address:* Calder Publications Ltd, 51 The Cut, London, SE1 8LF, England (office); 9 rue de Romainville, 93100 Montreuil, France (home). *Telephone:* (20) 7633-0599 (UK) (home); 1-49-88-75-12 (France). *E-mail:* info@calderpublications.com (office). *Website:* www.calderpublications.com (office).

CALDER, Nigel David Ritchie, MA; British writer; b. 2 Dec. 1931, London; s. of Lord Peter Ritchie-Calder and Lady Mabel Ritchie-Calder; m. Elisabeth Palmer 1954; two s. three d. *Education:* Sidney Sussex Coll., Cambridge. *Career:* Research Physicist, Mullard Research Laboratories, Redhill, Surrey 1954–56; staff writer, New Scientist 1956–60, Science Ed. 1960–62, Ed. 1962–66; Science Corresp., New Statesman 1959–62, 1966–71; ind. author and scriptwriter 1966–; mem. Asscn of British Science Writers, Royal Astronomical Soc. *Television includes:* scripts for 31 science documentaries. *Publications include:* The Environment Game (aka Eden Was No Garden: an Inquiry into the Environment of Man) 1967, Technopolis: Social Control of the Uses of Science 1969, Violent Universe: An Eyewitness Account of the New Astronomy 1970, The Mind of Man: An Investigation into Current Research on the Brain and Human Nature 1970, Restless Earth: A Report on the New Geology 1972, The Life Game: Evolution and the New Biology 1974, The Weather Machine: How Our Weather Works and Why it is Changing 1975, The Human Conspiracy: The New Science of Social Behavior 1976, The Key to the Universe: A Report on the New Physics 1977, Spaceships of the Mind 1978, Einstein's Universe 1979 (updated 2005), Nuclear Nightmares: An Investigation into Possible Wars 1980, The Comet is Coming!: The Feverish Legacy of Mr Halley 1981, Timescale: An Atlas of the Fourth Dimension 1984, 1984 and Beyond: Nigel Calder Talks to his Computer About the Future 1984, The English Channel 1986, The Green Machines 1986, Future Earth: Exploring the Frontiers of Science (co-ed. with John Newell) 1989, Scientific Europe (ed.) 1990, Spaceship Earth 1991, Giotto to the Comets 1992, Beyond This World 1995, The Manic Sun: Weather Theories Confounded 1997, Magic Universe: The Oxford Guide to Modern Science 2003, Albert Einstein: Relativity (introduction) 2006, The Chilling Stars: A New Theory of Climate Change (with Henrik Svensmark) 2007 (updated 2008); contribs to radio and TV documentaries, numerous periodicals. *Honours:* Hon. Fellow, AAAS 1986; UNESCO Kalinga Prize for the Popularization of Science 1972. *Literary Agent:* c/o Liz Calder, 26 Boundary Road, Crawley, West Sussex, RH10 8BT, England. *Telephone:* (1293) 549969. *E-mail:* lizcalder@talktalk.net. *Address:* 26 Boundary Road, Northgate, Crawley, West Sussex, RH10 8BT, England (office). *Telephone:* (1293) 549969 (office). *E-mail:* nc@windstream.demon.co.uk (office). *Website:* calderup.wordpress.com.

CALDERWOOD, James Lee, BA, PhD; American academic and writer; *Professor Emeritus, University of California, Irvine*; b. 7 April 1930, Corvallis, Ore.; m. Cleo Xeniades Calderwood 1955; two s. *Education:* Univ. of Oregon, Univ. of Washington. *Career:* Instructor, Michigan State Univ. 1961–63; Asst Prof., Univ. of California, Irvine 1963–66, 1966–68, Assoc. Prof. 1968–71, Prof. 1971–94, Assoc. Dean of Humanities 1974–94, Prof. Emer. 1994–. *Publications include:* Shakespearean Metadrama 1971, Metadrama in Shakespeare's Henriad 1979, To Be and Not to Be: Negation and Metadrama in Hamlet 1983, If It Were Done: Tragic Action in Macbeth 1986, Shakespeare and the Denial of Death 1987, The Properties of Othello 1989, A Midsummer Night's Dream 1992; editor: Forms of Poetry (with H. E. Toliver) 1968, Perspectives on Drama (with H. E. Toliver) 1968, Perspectives on Poetry (with H. E. Toliver) 1968, Perspectives on Fiction (with H. E. Toliver) 1968, Forms of Drama (with H. E. Toliver) 1969, Essays in Shakespearean Criticism (with H. E. Toliver) 1969, Shakespeare's Love's Labour's Lost 1970, Forms of Prose Fiction (with H. E. Toliver) 1972, Forms of Tragedy (with H. E. Toliver) 1972; contribs to scholarly journals. *Honours:* Alumni Achievement Award, Univ. of Oregon 1991. *Address:* 1323 Terrace Way, Laguna Beach, CA 92651-2829, USA (home). *Telephone:* (949) 494-0359 (home).

CALDWELL, Grant, BComm, MA, PhD; Australian writer, poet and teacher; *Lecturer, University of Melbourne*; b. 6 March 1947, Melbourne, Vic. *Education:* Univ. of Melbourne. *Career:* Ed.-Publr MEUSE art and literature magazine 1980–82; teacher, Victoria Coll. of the Arts, Univ. of Melbourne 1995–2000, Lecturer in Creative Writing, Univ. of Melbourne 1995–; mem. of Australian Poetry Centre, Melbourne Poets Union, Overload Poetry Festival, Steering Cttee for the Melbourne UNESCO City of Literature Bid, Wheeler Centre; judge, FAW Colin Thiele Poetry Award 2004–, 24 Hour Poetry Fix Play, Wheeler Centre 2010; judge and Chair. Val Vallis (Queensland Writers Centre) 2007–10, C.J. Dennis Prize for Poetry: Victorian Premier's Literary Awards 2010; Guest Poetry Ed., Going Down Swinging literary magazine 2010; Man. Ed. Blue Dog, the Poetry Journal of the Australian Poetry Centre 2007–10. *Publications include:* poetry: The Screaming Frog That Ralph Ate 1979, The Bells of Mr Whippy 1982, The Nun Wore Sunglasses 1984, Einstein, Buddhism & My Stiff Neck 1990, The Life of a Pet Dog 1993, You Know What I Mean 1996, Dreaming of Robert de Niro 2003, Glass Clouds 2010; other: The Revolt of the Coats (short stories) 1988, Malabata (novel) 1991; contribs: anthologies, journals, newspapers and magazines. *Honours:* Australia Council Established Writers Fellowship (category B) 1992, Australia Council Established Writers Fellowship (category A) 1994, VicArts Grant 1993 and 1994, Writer's Residence Award, Heinrich Boll Cottage, C. Mayo, Ireland 2007, Australia Council for the Arts Self-Organised Residence Funding Grant 2007. *Address:* Room 227, East Tower John Meldey Building, University of Melbourne, Melbourne, Vic. 3010, Australia (office). *Telephone:* (3) 8344-8727 (office). *Fax:* (3) 8344-5494 (office). *E-mail:* cal@unimelb.edu.au (office).

CALDWELL-MOORE, Sir Patrick Alfred, (R. T. Fishall), Kt, CBE, FRS; English astronomer and writer; b. 4 March 1923, Pinner, Middx; s. of the late Capt. Caldwell-Moore, MC and Gertrude Lilian Moore (née White). *Education:* privately. *Career:* Officer, Bomber Command, RAF 1940–45; Ed. Year Book of Astronomy 1962–; Dir Armagh Planetarium 1965–68; freelance 1968–; Pres. British Astronomical Asscn 1982–84, then Life Hon. Vice-Pres.; mem. Royal Astronomical Soc. of Canada, Royal Astronomical Soc. of NZ. *Play:* Quintet (Chichester) 2002. *Television includes:* The Sky at Night (BBC) 1957–. *Radio:* frequent broadcaster on radio. *Compositions:* Perseus (opera) 1975, Theseus 1982, Galileo 2003. *Publications include:* The Amateur Astronomer 1970, Atlas of the Universe 1970, Guide to the Planets 1976, Guide to the Moon 1976, Guide to the Stars 1977, Guide to Mars 1977, Out of the Darkness: The Planet Pluto (jtly) 1980, The Unfolding Universe 1982, Travellers in Space and Time 1983, History of Astronomy 1983, The Return of Halley's Comet (with Heather Couper) 1984, The Story of the Earth (with Peter Cattermole) 1985, Patrick Moore's Armchair Astronomy 1985, Stargazing 1985, Exploring the Night Sky with Binoculars 1986, The A–Z of Astronomy 1986, TV Astronomer 1987, Astronomy for the Under Tens 1987, Astronomers' Stars 1987, The Planet Uranus (jtly) 1988, Space Travel for the Under Tens 1988, The Planet Neptune 1989, Mission to the Planets 1990, The Universe for the Under Tens 1990, A Passion for Astronomy 1991, Fireside Astronomy 1992, The Starry Sky 1994, The Great Astronomical Revolution 1994, Stars of the Southern Skies 1994, Guinness Book of Astronomy 1995, Passion for Astronomy 1995, Teach Yourself Astronomy 1995, Eyes on the Universe 1997, Brilliant Stars 1998, Patrick Moore on Mars 1999, Yearbook of Astronomy AD 1000 (with Allan Chapman) 1999, Astronomy Data Book 2000, Eighty Not Out 2003, Stars of Destiny 2004, Venus 2004, Patrick Moore The Autobiography 2004, Patrick Moore on the Moon 2005, Bang! The Complete History of the Universe (with Brian May and Chris Lintott) 2006, Moore on Mercury 2007, Space: The First 50 Years (with HJP Arnold) 2007. *Honours:* Hon. DSc (Lancaster) 1974, (Hatfield Polytechnic) 1989, (Birmingham) 1990, (Leicester) 1996, (Portsmouth) 1997; Dr hc (Keele) 1994; Lorimer Gold Medal 1962, Goodacre Medal (British Astronomical Asscn) 1968, Jackson Gwilt Gold Medal (Royal Astronomical Soc.) 1977, Roberts-Klumpke Medal (Astronomical Soc. of the Pacific) 1979, Royal Astronomical Soc. Millennium Award 2000, BAFTA Special Award 2002, Minor Planet No. 2602 is named in his honour; Royal TV Soc. Baird Medal 2007. *Address:* Farthings, 39 West Street, Selsey, Sussex, PO20 9AD, England (office). *Telephone:* (1243) 603668 (office). *Fax:* (1243) 607237 (office); (1243) 607237 (home).

CALHOUN, Craig Jackson, BA, MA, PhD; American academic, writer and editor; *Professor of Sociology, New York University*; b. 16 June 1952, Watseka, Ill.; m. Pamela F. DeLargy; two c. *Education:* Univ. of Southern California, Columbia Univ., New York, Univ. of Manchester and St Antony's Coll., Oxford, UK. *Career:* Instructor, Univ. of North Carolina, Chapel Hill 1977–80, Asst Prof. 1980–85, Assoc. Prof. 1985–89, Prof. of Sociology and History 1989–96, Dir Univ. Center for Int. Studies 1993–96; Ed. Comparative Social Research 1988–93, Sociological Theory 1994–99; Visiting Lecturer, Univ. of Oslo 1991, Prof. (part-time) 1993–; Prof. of Sociology and Chair. Dept of Sociology, New York Univ. 1996–; Howard W. Beers Lecturer, Univ. of Kentucky 1997; Benjamin J. Meaker Distinguished Visiting Prof., Univ. of Bristol 2000; Hans Speier Distinguished Lecturer, New School for Social Research 2001; Pitirim Sorokin Lecturer, Univ. of Saskatchewan 2004; Pres. Social Science Research Council 1999–; Consulting Ed. McGraw-Hill Publrs 1990–2000; mem. Editorial Bds Thesis Eleven, European Journal of Social Theory, Ethnicities, British Journal of Sociology, Irish Journal of Sociology, Journal of Civil Society; mem. American Anthropological Asscn, American Historical Asscn, American Sociological Asscn, Int. Sociological Asscn, Int. Studies Asscn, Royal Anthropological Inst., Social Science History Asscn, Soc. for the Study of Social Problems, Sociological Research Asscn. *Publications include:* The Question of Class Struggle: Social Foundations of Popular Radicalism During the Industrial Revolution 1982, Sociology (with Donald Light and Suzanne Keller) 1989, Neither Gods Nor Emperors: Students and the Struggle for Democracy in China 1995, Critical Social Theory: Culture, History and the Challenge of Difference 1995, Nationalism 1997, Nations Matter: Citizenship, Solidarity, and the Cosmopolitan Dream 2007; ed.: The Anthropological Study of Education (with F. A. J. Ianni) 1976, Structures of Power and Constraint: Essays in Honor of Peter M. Blau (with W. R. Scott and M. Meyer) 1990, Habermas and the Public Sphere 1992, Contradictions: Perspectives in Theory and Culture (series ed., 17 vols) 1992–, Bourdieu:

Critical Perspectives (with E. LiPuma and M. Postone) 1993, Social Theory and the Politics of Identity 1994, Hannah Arendt and the Meaning of Politics (co-ed.) 1997, Dictionary of the Social Sciences 2002, The Classical Social Theory Reader (with J. Gerteis, J. Moody et al.) 2002, Understanding September 11: Perspectives from the Social Sciences (with P. Price and A. Timmer) 2002, Lessons of Empire: Imperial Histories and American Power (with Frederick Cooper and Kevin W. Moore) 2005, Sociology in America: The ASA Centennial History 2007, Practicing Culture 2007; contrib. of articles and chapters in books and scholarly journals, reviews, translations. *Honours:* Hon. mem. Order of the Golden Fleece 1988, Hon. Research Fellow, Inst. of Sociology, Chinese Acad. of Social Sciences 2000; Dr hc (La Trobe Univ.) 2005; W.K. Kellogg Nat. Fellowship 1982–85, R. J. Reynolds Fund Award 1985, W.R. Kenan Fellowship 1988–89, P. and R. Hettleman Faculty Fellowship 1991, American Sociological Asscn Distinguished Contrib. to Scholarship Award (Section on Political Sociology) 1995, Distinguished Book Award 2007, American Asscn for the Advancement of Science 2008. *Address:* Institute for Public Knowledge, New York University, 29 Cooper Square, New York, NY 10012 (office); Social Science Research Council, One Pierrepont Plaza, 15th Floor, Brooklyn, New York, NY 11201, USA (office). *Telephone:* (212) 377-2700 (office). *Fax:* (212) 377-2727 (office). *E-mail:* craig.calhoun@nyu.edu (office); calhoun@ssrc.org (office). *Website:* www.ssrc.org/calhoun (office).

CALLAGHAN, Barry, BA, MA; Canadian writer, poet, editor, publisher and translator and academic; *Distinguished Scholar and Professor Emeritus, York University;* b. 5 July 1937, Toronto, Ont.; one s. *Education:* St Michael's Coll., Univ. of Toronto. *Career:* teacher, Atkinson Coll., York Univ., Toronto, 1965–2003, Distinguished Scholar and Prof. Emer. 2003–; Literary Ed., Telegram, Toronto 1966–71; Host and Documentary Producer, Weekend, CBC-TV 1969–72; Founder-Publr Exile 1972–; Exile Editions 1976–; Writer-in-Residence, Univ. of Rome 1987, Nat. Univ. of Mexico, Mexico City 2004. *Publications include:* poetry: The Hogg Poems and Drawings 1978, As Close As We Came 1982, Stone Blind Love 1987, Hogg: The Poems and Drawings 1997, Hogg: Seven Last Words 2001; fiction: The Black Queen Stories 1982, The Way the Angel Spreads Her Wings 1989, When Things Get Worst 1993, A Kiss is Still a Kiss 1995, Between Trains 2007, Beside Still Waters 2009; non-fiction: Barrelhouse Kings 1998, Raise You Five 1964–2004 Vol. I (essays) 2005, Raise You Ten 1964–2004 Vol. II (essays) 2006; editor: various anthologies and books. *Honours:* Hon. DLitt (State Univ. of NY) 1999, Hon. LLD (Guelph Univ.) 2001; many Nat. Magazine Awards, Pres.'s Medal for Excellence in Magazine Articles, Univ. of Western Ont. 1979, 1983, Nat. Canadian Travel Writing Award 1983, Canada Council Award for Translation 1978, 1979, 1985, Award for TV Host of the Year, Alliance of Canadian Cinema, Television and Radio Artists 1984, CBC Award for Fiction 1985, Co-winner, Int. Authors Festival Award, Toronto 1986, Pushcart Prize for Prose (USA) 1989, Toronto Arts Award 1993, Salute to the City 1997, Inaugural Winner W.O. Mitchell Prize for Fiction and Editorial Mentoring 1998. *Address:* 20 Dale Avenue, Toronto, ON M4W 1K4, Canada (home). *Telephone:* (416) 922-8221 (home). *Fax:* (416) 969-9556 (home). *E-mail:* exile2@eol.ca (home).

CALLICOTT, John Baird, BA, MA, PhD; American academic and writer; *University Distinguished Research Professor, University of North Texas;* b. 9 May 1941, Memphis, Tenn.; s. of Burton H. Callicott and Evelyne E. Baird; m. 1st Ann Nelson Archer 1963 (divorced 1985); one s.; m. 2nd Frances Moore Lappe 1985 (divorced 1990). *Education:* Rhodes Coll., Syracuse Univ. *Career:* Woodrow Wilson Fellow 1963–64; Lecturer, Syracuse Univ. 1965–66; Instructor, Univ. of Memphis 1966–69; Asst Prof., Univ. of Wisconsin at Stevens Point 1969–74, Assoc. Prof. 1974–82, Dir of Environmental Studies Program 1980–86, Prof. of Philosophy 1982–95, Prof. of Natural Resources 1984–95; Visiting Prof., Univ. of Florida 1983; Knight Visiting Scholar, Presbyterian Coll. 1995; Prof. of Philosophy, Univ. of North Texas 1995–2006, Regents Prof., Dept of Philosophy and Religion Studies 2006–10, Chair. Dept of Philosophy and Religion Studies 2008–10, Univ. Distinguished Research Prof. 2010–; Visiting Prof., Yale Univ. 2004–05; Pres. Int. Soc. for Environmental Ethics 1997–2000; mem. American Philosophical Asscn, AAAS, American Soc. for Environmental History, Int. Soc. for Ecosystem Health, Int. Devt Ethics Asscn, Soc. for Asian and Comparative Philosophy, Soc. for Conservation Biology. *Publications include:* Plato's Aesthetics: An Introduction to the Theory of Forms 1972, Clothed-in-Fur and Other Tales: An Introduction to An Ojibwa World View 1982, In Defense of the Land Ethic: Essays in Environmental Philosophy 1989, Earth's Insights: A Survey of Ecological Ethics from the Mediterranean Basin to the Australian Outback 1994, Beyond the Land Ethic: More Essays in Environmental Philosophy 1999; ed.: several books; contribs to numerous books and journals. *Honours:* Univ. Scholar Award, Univ. of Wisconsin at Stevens Point 1995. *Address:* Department of Philosophy and Religion Studies, College of Arts and Sciences, University of North Texas, 1155 Union Circle, PO Box 310920, Denton, TX 76203-5017, USA (office). *Telephone:* (940) 565-2266 (office). *Fax:* (940) 565-4448 (office). *E-mail:* callicott@unt.edu (office). *Website:* www.phil.unt.edu (office).

CALLIL, Carmen Thérèse, BA, FRSA, FRSL; Australian/British publisher and writer; b. 15 July 1938, Melbourne, Vic.; d. of Frederick Alfred Louis Callil and Lorraine Claire Allen Callil. *Education:* Star of the Sea Convent, Loreto Convent, Melbourne and Melbourne Univ. *Career:* settled in UK 1960; Buyer's Asst, Marks and Spencer 1963–65; Editorial Asst, Hutchinson Publishing Co. 1965–66, B.T. Batsford 1966–67, Publicity Man., Granada Publishing 1967–70, André Deutsch 1971–72; f. Carmen Callil Ltd, Book Publicity Co. and Virago Press 1972, Chair. and Man. Dir Virago 1972–83, Chair. 1982–95, Man. Dir Chatto and Windus, The Hogarth Press 1983–93; Publr-at-Large, Random House, UK 1993–94; Ed.-at-Large, Knopf, New York 1993–94; mem. Bd Channel 4 1985–91, Random Century 1989–94; Chair. Booker Prize for Fiction 1996. *Publications:* The Modern Library: The 200 Best Novels in England Since 1950, (co-author) 1999, Bad Faith: A Forgotten History of Family and Fatherland 2006. *Honours:* Hon. DLitt (Sheffield) 1994, (Oxford Brookes Univ.) 1995; Hon. DUniv (York) 1995, (Open) 1997; Int. Women's Writing Guild Distinguished Service Award. *Literary Agent:* c/o Rogers, Coleridge & White Literary Agency, 20 Powis Mews, London, W11 1JN, England. *Telephone:* (20) 7221-3717. *Fax:* (20) 7229-9084. *E-mail:* info@rcwlitagency.co.uk. *Website:* www.rcwlitagency.co.uk.

CALLISON, Brian Richard; British writer; b. 13 July 1934, Manchester, England; m. Phyllis Joyce Jobson 1958; two s. *Education:* Dundee Coll. of Art. *Career:* Royal Literary Fund Fellow, Univ. of Dundee 2005–08; currently literary consultant and career adviser; mem. Royal Inst. of Navigation, Soc. of Authors, The Authors' Licensing and Collecting Soc. *Publications include:* A Flock of Ships 1970, A Plague of Sailors 1971, Dawn Attack 1972, A Web of Salvage 1973, Trapp's War 1974, A Ship is Dying 1976, A Frenzy of Merchantmen 1977, The Judas Ship 1978, Trapp's Peace 1979, The Auriga Madness 1980, The Sextant 1981, Spearfish 1982, Bone Collectors 1984, Thunder of Crude 1986, Trapp and World War Three 1988, The Trojan Hearse 1990, Crocodile Trapp 1993, Ferry Down 1998, The Stollenberg Legacy 2000, Redcap 2006, Trapp's Secret of War 2008. *Address:* Iffies End, West Bankhead, By Kellas, Angus, DD5 3QG, Scotland (office). *Telephone:* (1382) 350353 (office). *E-mail:* brian.callison@writermentoring.co.uk (office). *Website:* www.writermentoring.co.uk (office).

CALLOW, Simon Philip Hugh, CBE; British actor, director and writer; b. 15 June 1949, London, England; s. of Neil Callow and Yvonne Mary Callow. *Education:* London Oratory Grammar School, Queen's Univ., Belfast, Drama Centre. *Career:* debut Edinburgh Festival 1973; repertory seasons, Lincoln and Traverse Theatre, Edin.; work at the fringe theatre, the Bush, London; joined Joint Stock Theatre Group 1977, Nat. Theatre 1979; regular book reviewer The Guardian. *Stage appearances include:* Passing By 1975, Plumbers Progress 1975, Arturo Ui 1978, Titus Andronicus 1978, Mary Barnes 1978, As You Like It 1979, Amadeus 1979, Sisterly Feeling 1979, Total Eclipse 1982, Restoration 1982, The Beastly Beatitudes of Balthazar B 1982, The Relapse 1983, On The Spot 1984, Melancholy Jacques 1984, Kiss of the Spider Woman 1985, Faust 1988, Single Spies 1988, 1989, The Destiny of Me 1993, The Alchemist 1996, The Importance of Being Oscar 1997, Chimes at Midnight 1997, The Mystery of Charles Dickens 2000–02, Through the Leaves 2003, The Holy Terror 2004, The Woman in White (Palace Theatre, London) 2005, Aladdin (Richmond Theatre, London) 2005, Present Laughter (tour) 2006, Equus (tour) 2008, Dr Marigold and Mr Chops (Edinburgh Assembly Rooms and Riverside Studios) 2008–09, Peter Pan (Richmond) 2008, There Reigns Love (Stratford, Ontario) 2008, Waiting for Godot (Theatre Royal, Haymarket) 2009, The Man from Stratford (tour) 2010, Twelfth Night (Nat. Theatre) 2011, Being Shakespeare (Trafalgar Studios) 2011, Tuesday at Tesco's (Assembly Hall, Edinburgh) 2011, Dr Marigold and Mr Chops (tour) 2011, A Christmas Carol (Arts Theatre, London) 2011, , Being Shakespeare 2012. *Directed:* Loving Reno 1983, Passport 1985, Nicolson Fights Croydon 1986, Amadeus 1986, The Infernal Machine 1986, Così Fan Tutte 1987, Jacques and His Master 1987, Shirley Valentine (theatre production) 1988/89, Die Fledermaus 1989/90, Facades 1988, Single Spies 1988/89, Stevie Wants to Play the Blues 1990, The Ballad of the Sad Café (film) 1991, Carmen Jones (Evening Standard Olivier Award) 1991, My Fair Lady 1992, Shades 1992, The Destiny of Me 1993, Carmen Jones 1994, Il Trittico 1995, Les Enfants du Paradis (RSC) 1996, Stephen Oliver Trilogy 1996, La Calisto 1996, Il Turco in Italia 1997, HRH 1997, The Pajama Game 1999, The Consul 1999, Tomorrow Week (play for radio) 1999, Le Roi Malgré Lui 2003, Everyman 2003, Jus' Like That 2004, The Magic Flute 2008. *Films include:* Amadeus 1983, A Room with a View 1984, The Good Father 1985, Maurice 1986, Manifesto 1987, Mr and Mrs Bridge 1991, Postcards from the Edge 1991, Soft Top Hard Shoulder 1992, Four Weddings and A Funeral 1994, Jefferson in Paris 1994, Victory 1994, Le Passager Clandestin 1995, England, My England 1995, Ace Ventura: When Nature Calls 1995, James and the Giant Peach (voice) 1996, The Scarlet Tunic 1996, Woman In White 1997, Bedrooms and Hallways 1997, Shakespeare in Love 1997, No Man's Land 2000, Thunderpants 2001, A Christmas Carol 2001, George and the Dragon 2004, The Phantom of the Opera 2004, Rag Tale 2005, The Civilization of Maxwell Bright 2005, Bob The Butler 2005, Ripley Under Ground 2005, The Best Man 2005, Some Break (short) 2006, Surveillance 2007, Arn: The Knight Templar 2007, Chemical Wedding 2008, Natural Selection (short) 2010, The Mr. Men Movie (voice, UK version) 2010, Late Bloomers 2011, Save Our Bacon (short) 2011, No Ordinary Trifle 2011, Love's Kitchen 2011 Miss in Her Teens 2012, Acts of Godfrey 2012. *Television includes:* Wings of Song 1977, Instant Enlightenment inc. VAT 1979, La Ronde 1980, Man of Destiny 1982, Chance in a Million 1982–86, Deadhead 1984, Handel 1985, David Copperfield 1986, Cariani and the Courtesan 1987, Old Flames 1989, Patriot Witness 1989, Trial of Oz 1991, Bye Bye Columbus 1992, Femme Fatale 1993, Little Napoleons 1994, An Audience with Charles Dickens 1996, A Christmas Dickens 1997, The Woman in White 1998, Trial-Retribution 1999, 2000, Galileo's Daughter, The Mystery of Charles Dickens 2002, Angels in America (mini-series) 2003, Hans Christian Andersen: My Life as a Fairy Tale (film) 2003, Shoebox Zoo (series) 2004, Agatha Christie's

Marple (film) 2004, Doctor Who (series) 2005, 2011, Rome (series) 2005, Midsomer Murders 2006, The Curse of King Tut's Tomb (film) 2007, The Roman Mysteries (series) 2007, The Company (mini-series) 2007, What's on Theatre (series) 2008, Anatomy of Hope (film) 2009, Lewis (series) 2009, The Sarah Jane Adventures (series) 2009, Ice (series) 2011, Comic Relief: Uptown Downstairs Abbey (film) 2011, This Is Jinsy (series) 2011. *Publications:* Being An Actor 1984 (expanded edn 2004), A Difficult Actor: Charles Laughton 1987, Shooting the Actor, or the Choreography of Confusion (with Dusan Makevejev) 1990 (expanded edn 2004), Acting in Restoration Comedy 1991, Orson Welles: The Road to Xanadu 1995, Les Enfants du Paradis 1996, Snowdon – On Stage 1996, The National 1997, Love is Where it Falls 1999, Shakespeare on Love 2000, Charles Laughton's the Night of the Hunter 2000, Oscar Wilde and His Circle 2000, The Nights of the Hunter 2001, Henry IV Part 1 2002, Henry IV Part 2 2003, Dicken's Christmas 2003, Orson Welles: Hello Americans 2006, My Life in Pieces: An Alternative Autobiography 2010, Charles Dickens and the Great Theatre of the World 2012; translations of works of Cocteau, Kundera, Prévert, Chabrier; weekly column in Sunday Express, Independent, Country Life; contrib. to The Times, The Sunday Times, The Guardian, The Observer, Evening Standard, etc. *Honours:* Hon. Fellow, Univ. of the Arts, London; Hon. DLitt (Queen's Univ., Belfast) 1999, (Birmingham) 2000, (Open Univ.) 2010; Evening Standard Patricia Rothermere Award 1999. *Address:* c/o Brebners, The Quadrangle, 180 Wardour Street, London, W1F 8LB, England. *Telephone:* (20) 7413-0869 (office). *Fax:* (20) 7413-0870 (office). *E-mail:* simon.callow@yahoo.co.uk (office).

CALVERT, Peter Anthony Richard, BA, MA, PhD, FRHistS; British political scientist, writer and academic; *Professor Emeritus of Comparative and International Politics, School of Social Sciences, University of Southampton*; b. 19 Nov. 1936, Islandmagee, Co. Antrim, NI; s. of the late Raymond Calvert and Irene Calvert; m. Susan Ann Milbank 1987; two s. *Education:* Campbell Coll., Belfast, Queens' Coll., Cambridge, Univ. of Michigan, Ann Arbor, USA. *Career:* Lecturer, Univ. of Southampton 1964–71, Sr Lecturer 1971–74, Reader 1974–83, Prof. of Comparative and Int. Politics 1984–2002, Prof. Emer. 2002–; Research Fellow, Charles Warren Center, Harvard Univ. 1969–70; Visiting Lecturer/Prof., Birkbeck Coll., London, 1983–84; Co-Ed. Democratization (journal) 1996–2007. *Publications include:* The Mexican Revolution 1910–1914 1968, 2008, A Study of Revolution 1970, The Falklands Crisis 1982, The Concept of Class 1982, The Foreign Policy of New States 1986, Argentina: Political Culture and Instability (with Susan Calvert) 1989, Revolution and Counter Revolution 1990, Latin America in the 20th Century (with Susan Calvert) 1990, 1993, International Politics of Latin America 1994, Politics and Society in the Third World (with Susan Calvert) 1995, The South, the North and the Environment (with Susan Calvert) 1999, Comparative Politics: An Introduction 2002, A Political and Economic Dictionary of Latin America 2004, Politics and Society in the Developing World (with Susan Calvert) 2007, Terrorism, Civil War, and Revolution 2010; editor: The Process of Political Succession 1987, The Central American Security System 1988, 2008, Political and Economic Encyclopedia of South America and the Caribbean 1991, The Resilience of Democracy (with Peter Burnell) 1999, Civil Society in Democratization (with Peter Burnell) 2004, Border and Territorial Disputes of the World (fourth edn) 2004. *Honours:* Fulbright Scholar 1960, 1969, Ford Foundation grantee 1984–88. *E-mail:* pcpol@soton.ac.uk (office). *Website:* www.soton.ac.uk (office).

CAMDESSUS, Michel Jean; French international civil servant; *Honorary Governor, Banque de France*; b. 1 May 1933, Bayonne; s. of Alfred Camdessus and Madeleine Cassembon; m. Brigitte d'Arcy 1957; two s. four d. *Education:* Notre Dame Coll., Betharram, Inst. of Political Studies, Paris, Nat. School of Admin. *Career:* civil servant, Treasury, Ministry of Finance 1960–66; Chief, Bureau of Industrial Affairs, Treasury, Ministry of Econ. and Finance 1969–70; Chair. 'Investissements' Sub-cttee of Treasury 1971; Deputy Dir of Treasury 1974–82, Dir 1982–84; Financial Attaché, Perm. Representation, EEC, Brussels 1966–69; mem. Monetary Cttee, EEC 1978, Pres. 1982; Sec. Conseil de Direction du Fonds de Développement Economique et Social 1971; Asst Dir 'Épargne et Crédit' Sub-cttee 1972; Deputy Gov. Banque de France 1984, Gov. 1984–87, Hon. Gov. 1987–; Man. Dir IMF 1987–2000; Pres. Club de Paris 1978–84; Chair. Centre d'études prospectives et d'informations internationales 2000–04, Semaines Sociales de France 2001–07; UN Sec.-Gen. Special Envoy to the Monterrey Conf. 2002; Dir Banque Européenne d'Investissements, Banque Cen. des États de l'Afrique de l'Ouest, Air France, Soc. Nat. des Chemins de fer Français, Crédit Lyonnais (all 1978); Personal Rep. to Africa for French Govt and G8 Heads of State 2002. *Publications:* Notre foi dans ce siècle (with M. Albert, J. Boissonnat), Eau (with Bertrand Badré, Ivan Chéret, Pierre-Frédéric Tenière-Buchot) 2004, Le Sursaut: Vers une nouvelle croissance pour la France 2004, Lettre ouverte aux candidats à l'élection présidentielle 2006, Rapport de la mission sur la modernisation de la distribution du livret A et des circuits de financement du logement social 2007, Réaliser l'objectif constitutionnel d'équilibre des finances publiques 2010, Contrôle des Rémunérations des professionnels de marché 2011, Reform of the International Monetary System (Palais-Royal Initiative) 2011. *Honours:* Commdr, Légion d'honneur; Chevalier, Ordre nat. du Mérite; Croix de la Valeur militaire. *Address:* Banque de France, 09–1060, 75049 Paris Cedex 01 (office); 27 rue de Valois, 75001 Paris, France (home). *Telephone:* 1-42-97-73-38 (office). *Fax:* 1-42-97-76-42 (office). *E-mail:* lyliane.huot@banque-france.fr.

CAMERON, Dame Averil Millicent, DBE, MA, PhD, DLitt, FBA, FSA; British historian of late antiquity and Byzantine studies and writer; b. 8 Feb. 1940, Leek, Staffs.; d. of Tom Roy Sutton and Millicent Drew; m. Alan Douglas Edward Cameron 1962 (divorced 1980); one s. one d. *Education:* Somerville Coll., Oxford, Univ. Coll., London. *Career:* Asst Lecturer in Classics, King's Coll., London 1965, Lecturer 1968, Reader in Ancient History 1970, Prof. 1978–88, Prof. of Late Antique and Byzantine Studies 1988–94, Dir Centre for Hellenic Studies 1989–94, Fellow 1987–; Warden of Keble Coll., Oxford 1994–2010, Prof. of Late Antique and Byzantine History, Univ. of Oxford 1997–; Pro-Vice-Chancellor, Univ. of Oxford 2001–; Visiting Prof., Columbia Univ., New York 1967–68; Visiting mem. Inst. for Advanced Study, Princeton, NJ 1977–78, Distinguished Visitor 1992; Summer Fellow, Dumbarton Oaks 1980; Sather Prof. of Classical Literature, Univ. of California, Berkeley 1985–86; Visiting Prof., Coll. de France 1987, Lansdowne Lecturer, Victoria, BC 1992; Ed. Journal of Roman Studies 1985–90; Pres. Soc. for the Promotion of Roman Studies 1995–98, Ecclesiastical History Soc. 2005–06, Council for British Research in the Levant 2005–, Fédération internationale des asscns d'études classiques (FIEC) 2009–; Chair. Cathedrals Fabric Comm. for England 1999–2005, Review Group on the Royal Peculiars 1999–2000; Corresp. mem. Akad. der Wissenschaften zu Göttingen 2006. *Publications:* Procopius 1967, Agathias 1970, Corippus, In laudem Iustini minoris 1976, Images of Women in Antiquity (ed.) 1983, Continuity and Change in Sixth-Century Byzantium 1981, Constantinople in the Eighth Century (ed.) 1984, Procopius and the Sixth Century 1985, 1996, History as Text (ed.) 1989, The Greek Renaissance in the Roman Empire (ed.) 1990, Christianity and the Rhetoric of Empire 1991, The Byzantine and Early Islamic Near East I (ed.) 1992, II (ed.) 1994, III (ed.) 1995, The Later Roman Empire 1993, The Mediterranean World in Late Antiquity A.D. 395–600 1993 (second edn 2011), Changing Cultures in Early Byzantium (ed.) 1996, Cambridge Ancient History Vol. XIII. The Late Empire (ed.) 1998, Eusebius, Life of Constantine (ed. and trans.) 1999, Cambridge Ancient History Vol. XIV. Late Antiquity: Empire and Successors (ed.) 2000, Fifty Years of Prosopography (ed.) 2003, Cambridge Ancient History Vol. XII. The Crisis of Empire (ed.) 2005, The Byzantines 2006, Doctrine and Debate in the East Christian World (ed.) 2011. *Honours:* Hon. Fellow, Somerville Coll., Oxford; Hon. DLitt (Warwick, St Andrews, Queen's, Belfast, Aberdeen, London); Hon. DTheol (Lund). *Address:* Keble College, Oxford, OX1 3PG, England (office). *E-mail:* averil.cameron@keble.ox.ac.uk (office).

CAMERON, Charla (see Skinner, Gloria Dale)

CAMERON, Deborah; British academic and author; *Rupert Murdoch Professor of Language and Communication, University of Oxford*. *Career:* Lecturer in English Language, Roehampton Inst. of Higher Educ. 1983–88; Asst Prof. of English, William and Mary Coll., Va, USA 1988–90; Sr Lecturer in Literary Linguistics, Univ. of Strathclyde 1991–96, Prof. of English 1996–99; Prof. of Languages in Educ., Inst. of Educ., London Univ. 1999–2004; Rupert Murdoch Prof. of Language and Communication, Univ. of Oxford 2004–; visiting appointments have included Univ. of Gothenburg, New York Univ.; Contributing Ed. Critical Quarterly; Consulting Ed., Cambridge Encyclopaedia of the Language Sciences. *Publications include:* Analysing Conversation: Rules and Units in the Structure of Talk (with T. J. Taylor) 1987, The Lust To Kill: A Feminist Investigation of Sexual Murder (with E. Frazer) 1987, Women in their Speech Communities: New Perspectives on Language and Sex (co-ed.) 1988, Researching Language: Issues of Power and Method (co-author) 1992, Feminism and Linguistic Theory 1992, Verbal Hygiene 1995, The Feminist Critique of Language: A Reader 1998, Good To Talk? Living and Working in a Communication Culture 2000, Working with Spoken Discourse 2001, The Words Between the Spaces: Buildings and Language (with T. Markus) 2002, Globalization and Language Teaching (co-ed.) 2002, Language and Sexuality (with D. Kulick) 2003, The Language and Sexuality Reader (co-ed.) 2006, On Language and Sexual Politics 2006, The Myth of Mars and Venus: Do Men and Women Really Speak Different Languages? 2007; contribs: numerous chapters in books, including The Handbook of Language and Gender 2003, New Media Discourse 2003, Language, Communication and the Economy 2005, Speaking Out: The Female Voice in Public Contexts 2006; numerous articles in academic journals including Intercultural Pragmatics, Applied Linguistics, Feminism & Psychology, Contemporary Feminist Theories, and many others. *Address:* Worcester College, Oxford, OX1 2HB, England (office). *Telephone:* (1865) 278300. *Fax:* (1865) 278369. *E-mail:* deborah.cameron@ell.ox.ac.uk (office). *Website:* www.english.ox.ac.uk (office).

CAMERON, Donald Allan, (Silver Donald Cameron), BA, MA, PhD; Canadian author; *Host and Executive Producer, www.TheGreenInterview.com*; b. 21 June 1937, Toronto, Ont.; s. of Dr Maxwell A Cameron and Hazel Robertson Cameron; m. 1st Catherine Ann Cahoon 1959; three s. one d.; m. 2nd Lulu Terrio 1980 (died 1996); one s.; m. 3rd Marjorie L. Simmins 1998. *Education:* Univ. of British Columbia, Univ. of California, USA, Univ. of London, UK. *Career:* teacher, Lucerne Jr Sr High School, New Denver, BC 1957–58, Prin. Beaverdell Superior School, Beaverdell, BC 1958–59, Lecturer, Univ. of British Columbia 1962–64, Killam Postdoctoral Fellow, Dalhousie Univ. 1967–68, Assoc. Prof. of English, Univ. of New Brunswick 1968–71; Writer-in-Residence, Univ. Coll. of Cape Breton, NS 1978–80, Dean, School of Community Studies 1994–96, Special Asst to the Pres. 1997–99; Writer-in-Residence, Univ. of Prince Edward Island 1985–86, Nova Scotia Coll. of Art and Design 1987–88; columnist, Halifax Sunday Herald, NS 1998–2011; Host and Exec. Producer www.TheGreenInterview.com 2010–; mem. Writers Fed. of NS, Writers Union of Canada, Writers Guild of Canada. *Play:* The Prophet at Tantramar (Ship's Company Theatre) 1988. *Radio:* numerous radio dramas, commentaries and documentaries. *Television:* numerous documentaries and commentaries. *Publications include:* novels: Faces of Leacock 1967, Conversations with Canadian Novelists 1973, Dragon Lady 1980, The Baitchopper 1982; nonfiction books: The Education of Everett Richardson 1977, Seasons in the Rain 1978, Schooner: Bluenose and Bluenose II 1984, Outhouses of the West 1988, Wind, Whales and Whisky: A Cape Breton Voyage (City of Dartmouth Book Award 1992, Atlantic Provinces Booksellers Award 1992) 1991, Lifetime: A Book of Uncommon Wisdoms (coauthor) 1992, Iceboats to Superferries: An Illustrated History of Marine Atlantic (coauthor) 1992, Once Upon A Schooner: A Foreign Voyage in Bluenose II 1992, Sniffing the Coast: An Acadian Voyage 1993, Sterling Silver: Rants, Raves and Revelations 1994, An Island Parish (coauthor) 1995, The Living Beach (Evelyn Richardson Award) 1998, Sailing Away from Winter 2007, A Million Futures: The Remarkable Legacy of the Canada Millennium Scholarship Foundation; other: numerous articles, radio dramas, short stories, TV scripts and stage plays. *Honours:* Hon. DCL (King's Coll., Halifax) 2004; Hon. DLitt (Cape Breton Univ.) 2007; four Nat. Magazine Awards, Best Short Film, Canadian Film Celebration, Moonsnail Award, Canada Council Nonfiction Grants, Canada Council Explorations Grants, Province of Nova Scotia Established Writers Grants, Banff Centre Fellowship. *Address:* 24 Armshore Drive, Halifax, NS B3N 1M5, Canada. *Telephone:* (902) 446-5577. *Fax:* (902) 446-6099. *E-mail:* sdc@thegreeninterview.com; sdc@silverdonaldcameron.ca. *Website:* www.silverdonaldcameron.ca; www.thegreeninterview.com.

CAMERON, Matt; Australian playwright and screenwriter; b. 1969. *Plays:* Mr Melancholy (ANPC New Dramatists' Award) 1995, Footprints on Water (British Council Int. New Playwriting Award) 1997, Tear From a Glass Eye (Wal Cherry Play of the Year Award) 1998, The Eskimo Calling 2000, Whispering Death 2000, Man the Balloon 2001, Ruby Moon 2003, Hinterland 2004, Poor Boy 2009. *Television writing:* Sea Change 1998, Small Tales and True 1998, Introducing Gary Petty (also co-creator and dir) 2000. *Honours:* Centenary Medal for Service to Australian Soc. and Literature, AWGIE Award for Best Television Comedy. *Address:* Currency Press, PO Box 2287, Strawberry Hills, NSW 2012, Australia (office). *Telephone:* (2) 9319-5877 (office). *E-mail:* sian@currency.com.au (office). *Website:* www.currency.com.au (office).

CAMERON WATT, Donald, MA, DLitt, FBA, FRHistS; British historian and academic; *Professor Emeritus of International History, London School of Economics;* b. 17 May 1928, Rugby; s. of Robert Cameron Watt and Barbara Bidwell; m. 1st Marianne R. Grau 1951 (died 1962); m. 2nd Felicia Cobb Stanley 1962 (died 1997); one s., one step-d. *Education:* Rugby School and Oriel Coll., Oxford. *Career:* Asst Ed. (Foreign Office Research Dept), Documents on German Foreign Policy 1918–1945, 1951–54, 1951–59; Asst Lecturer in Political History, LSE 1954–56, Lecturer in International History 1957–63, Sr Lecturer 1964–65; Reader in International History, Univ. of London 1966–72, Prof. in International History 1972–82, Stevenson Prof. of International History 1982–93, Prof. Emer. 1993–; Ed. Survey of Int. Affairs, Royal Inst. of International Affairs 1962–71; Historian, Cabinet Office Historical Section 1977–94; Rockefeller Fellow in Social Sciences 1960–61; Fellow, Polish Acad. of Arts and Sciences, Kraków; fmr FRSA; Sec. Comm. for History of International Relations 1982–95, Vice Pres. 1995–. *Publications:* Oxford Poetry 1950 (ed.) 1951, Britain and the Suez Canal 1956, Documents on the Suez Crisis 1957, Britain Looks to Germany 1965, Personalities and Policies 1965, A History of the World in the 20th Century 1967, Contemporary History in Europe 1969, Hitler's Mein Kampf (ed.) 1969, 1992, Current British Foreign Policy 1970–72, Too Serious a Business 1975, 1992, Succeeding John Bull, America in Britain's Place 1900–1975 1983, Documents on British Foreign Affairs 1867–1939 1985–97, How War Came 1989, Argentina Between the Great Powers 1990, Defence Organisation Since the War 2008. *Honours:* Hon. Fellow, Oriel Coll., Oxford 1998; Wolfson Prize for History 1990.

CAMILLERI, Andrea; Italian novelist; b. 6 Sept. 1925, Porto Empedocle, nr Agrigento; m.; three c. *Career:* dir and scriptwriter since World War II; especially known for crime TV productions featuring Lt Sheridan and Insp. Maigret; as novelist created Insp. Montalbano. *Publications include:* Il corso delle cose 1978, Un filo di fumo 1980, La stagione della caccia 1992, La bolla di componenda 1993, La forma dell'acqua (trans. as The Shape of Water) 1994, Il birraio di Preston 1995, Il gioco della mosca 1995, Il cane di terracotta (trans. as The Terracotta Dog) 1996, Il ladro di merendine (trans. as The Snack Thief) 1996, La voce del violino (trans. as The Voice of the Violin) 1997, La strage dimenticata 1997, La concessione del telefono 1998, La Gita a Tindari (trans. as Excursion to Tindari) 2000, Un mese con Montalbano 1998, Gli arancini di Montalbano 1999, La mossa del cavallo 1999, Biografia di un figlio cambiato 2000, Favole del tramonto 2000, La scomparsa di Patò: romanzo 2000, Gocce di Sicilia 2001, Le parole raccontate 2001, L'odore della notte (trans. as The Scent of the Night) 2001, Racconti quotidiani 2001, Il re di Girgenti 2001, La paura di Montalbano 2002, L'ombrello di Noe 2002, Le inchieste del commissario Collura 2002, La linea della palma 2002, Montalbano a viva voce 2002, Storie di Montalbano 2002, Il Giro di Boa (trans. as Rounding the Mark) 2003, La presa di Macallè 2003, Teatro 2003, La Pazienza del Ragno (trans. as The Patience of the Spider) 2004, Romanzi storici e civili 2004, La prima indagine di Montalbano 2004, Privo di titolo 2005, La Luna di Carta (trans. as The Paper Moon) 2005, Il diavolo: tentatore, innamorato 2005, Il medaglione 2005, La Vampa d'Agosto 2006, Le Ali della Sfinge 2006, La Pensione Eva 2006, La Pista di Sabbia 2007, Il colore del sole 2007, Le pecore ed il pastore 2007, La novella di Antonello da Palermo 2007, Voi non sapete 2007, Maruzza Musumeci 2007, Il Campo del Vasaio 2008, Il Tailleur Grigio 2008, L'età del dubbio 2008, Le Prime Indagini 2009, La Danza del gabbiano 2009. *Honours:* Dr hc (Univ. of Pisa) 2005; numerous literary awards. *Address:* c/o Mondadori, Via Durazzo 4, 20134 Milan, Italy. *Telephone:* (02) 75421. *Fax:* (07) 5423047. *E-mail:* stampalibri@mondadori.it. *Website:* www.andreacamilleri.net.

CAMPBELL, Donald; British fmr poet and dramatist; b. 25 Feb. 1940, Caithness, Scotland; m. Jean Fairgrieve 1966; one s. *Career:* Writer-in-Residence, Edinburgh Educ. Dept 1974–77, Royal Lyceum Theatre 1981–82; Fellow in Creative Writing, Univ. of Dundee 1987–89; Writer-in-Residence, Dumfries and Galloway Arts Asscn; William Soutar Fellow, Perth Libraries 1991–93; Royal Literary Fund Fellow, Napier Univ. 2000–02. *Publications:* poetry: Poems 1971, Rhymes 'n' Reasons 1972, Murals: Poems in Scots 1975, Blether: A Collection of Poems 1979, A Brighter Sunshine 1983, Selected Poems 1870–90 1990, Playing for Scotland 1996, Edinburgh: A cultural and literary history 2003, Homage to Rob Donn 2007; plays for stage, radio and TV including The Widows of Clyth 2007, Nancy Sleekit/Howard's Revenge 2007, Till All the Seas Run Dry 2007. *Honours:* Hon. Fellow, Asscn of Scottish Literary Studies 2010. *Address:* 85 Spottiswoode Street, Edinburgh, EH9 1BZ, Scotland (home). *Telephone:* (131) 447-2305 (home). *E-mail:* d.campbell123@btinternet.com (home).

CAMPBELL, Ewing, BBA, MA, PhD; American writer and academic; b. 26 Dec. 1940, Alice, Tex. *Education:* North Texas State Univ., Univ. of Southern Mississippi, Oklahoma State Univ. *Career:* Lecturer, Univ. of Texas at Austin 1981–82, Oklahoma State Univ. 1982–83, Wharton Community Coll. 1983–84; Asst Prof., Texas A&M Univ. 1984–90, Assoc. Prof. 1990–99, apptd Prof. 1999; mem. Texas Inst. of Letters; lives in Mexico. *Publications include:* fiction: Weave It Like Nightfall 1977, The Way of Sequestered Places 1982, The Rincón Triptych 1984, The Tex-Mex Express 1993, Madonna, Maleva 1996, Afoot in the Garden of Enchantments 2007; short fiction: Piranesi's Dream 1986; criticism: Raymond Carver: A Study of the Short Fiction 1992; contribs: stories and articles to numerous periodicals. *Honours:* Fulbright Scholar, Nat. Univ. of Córdoba, Argentina 1989, Univ. of La Laguna, Tenerife, Spain 1997, Nat. Endowments for the Arts Fellowship for Fiction 1990, Dobie-Paisano Ralph A. Johnston Award 1992, Chris O'Malley Fiction Prize 1998, two US Information Agency Grants to represent the USA in Russia 1998, and Croatia 1999, American Literary Fiction Prize 2002.

CAMPBELL, Ian McDonald, MA, PhD; British academic and writer; *Professor Emeritus, Department of English, University of Edinburgh;* b. 25 Aug. 1942, Lausanne, Switzerland. *Education:* Univs of Aberdeen and Edinburgh. *Career:* Reader in English, Univ. of Edinburgh 1967–92, Prof. of Scottish and Victorian Literature 1992–2009, Prof. Emer. 2009–; British Council appointments in France, Germany; mem. Carlyle Soc. (Pres.), Scottish Asscn for the Speaking of Verse, Asscn for Scottish Literary Studies (Council mem.). *Publications include:* Thomas Carlyle Letters (33 vols) 1970–2005, Carlyle 1974, Nineteenth Century Scottish Fiction: Critical Essays 1978, Thomas and Jane 1980, Kailyard 1981, Lewis Grassic Gibbon 1986, Spartacus 1987, Gibbon's Complete Works (ed.); contrib. to numerous papers to learned journals. *Honours:* British Acad. Research Fellowship 1980. *Address:* Department of English Literature, University of Edinburgh, David Hume Tower, George Square, Edinburgh, EH8 9JX, Scotland (office). *E-mail:* ian.campbell@ed.ac.uk (office).

CAMPBELL, John Malcolm, MA, PhD; British writer; b. 2 Sept. 1947, London, England; m. Alison McCracken 1972 (divorced 2008); one s. one d. *Education:* Charterhouse, Univ. of Edinburgh. *Career:* mem. Soc. of Authors. *Publications include:* Lloyd George: The Goat in the Wilderness 1977, F. E. Smith, First Earl of Birkenhead 1983, Roy Jenkins: A Biography 1983, Nye Bevan and the Mirage of British Socialism 1987, The Experience of World War II (ed.) 1989, Makers of the Twentieth Century (ed.) 1990–92, Edward Heath (NCR Book Award for Non-Fiction 1994) 1993, Margaret Thatcher: Vol. I: The Grocer's Daughter 2000, Vol. II: The Iron Lady 2003, If Love Were All...: the Story of Frances Stevenson and David Lloyd George 2006, Pistols at Dawn: Two Hundred Years of Political Rivalry from Pitt and Fox to Blair and Brown 2009; contrib. of book reviews to The Times, TLS, The Independent, Sunday Telegraph, others. *Honours:* Yorkshire Post Best First Book Award 1977. *Address:* 2 Lansdowne Crescent, London, W11 2NH, England (home). *Telephone:* (20) 7727-1920 (home). *E-mail:* johncampbell_@hotmail.com (home).

CAMPBELL, Judith (see Pares, Marion)

CAMPBELL, Philip Henry Montgomery, PhD, FInstP, FRAS; British journalist and academic; *Editor-in-Chief, Nature;* b. 19 April 1951, s. of Hugh Campbell and Mary Montgomery Campbell; m. Judie Yelton 1980 (died 1992); two s. *Education:* Shrewsbury School, Univ. of Bristol, Queen Mary Coll., London, Univ. of Leicester. *Career:* postdoctoral research asst, Dept of Physics, Univ. of Leicester 1977–79; Asst Ed. Nature journal 1979–82, Physical Sciences Ed. 1982–88, Ed., Nature journal and Ed.-in-Chief Nature journal and Nature publications 1995–, Dir Nature Publishing Group 1997–; Founding Ed. Physics World magazine 1988–95; Trustee Cancer Research UK. *Radio:* broadcasts on BBC World Service. *Publications:* numerous papers and articles in journals, magazines and newspapers. *Honours:* Hon. DSc (Leicester) 1999. *Address:* c/o Nature Publishing Group, The Macmillan Building, 4 Crinan Street, London, N1 9XW, England (office). *Telephone:* (20)

7833-4000 (office). *Fax:* (20) 7843-4596 (office). *E-mail:* exec@nature.com (office). *Website:* www.nature.com (office).

CAMPBELL, Ramsey; British writer and film critic; b. 4 Jan. 1946, Liverpool, England; m. Jenny Chandler 1971; one s. one d. *Career:* film reviewer, BBC Radio Merseyside 1969–2007; full-time writer 1973–; mem. British Fantasy Soc. (currently Pres.), Soc. of Fantastic Films (currently Pres.). *Publications include:* fiction: The Doll Who Ate His Mother 1976, The Face That Must Die 1979, The Parasite (British Fantasy Award for Best Novel) 1980, The Nameless 1981, Incarnate (British Fantasy Award for Best Novel 1985) 1983, The Claw 1983 (US edn as Night of the Claw), Obsession 1985, The Hungry Moon (British Fantasy Award for best Novel 1988) 1986, The Influence (British Fantasy Award for Best Novel 1989, Premios Gigamesh 1994) 1988, Ancient Images (Children of the Night Award, Bram Stoker Award) 1989, Midnight Sun (British Fantasy Award 1991) 1990, The Count of Eleven 1991, The Long Lost (British Fantasy Award for Best Novel 1994) 1993, The One Safe Place 1995, The House on Nazareth Hill (Best Novel, Int. Horror Guild 1998) 1996, The Last Voice They Hear 1998, No End of Fun 2000, Silent Children 2000, The Darkest Part of the Woods 2002, The Overnight 2003, Secret Story 2005, The Grin of the Dark (British Fantasy Award for Best Novel) 2007, Thieving Fear 2008, Creatures of the Pool 2009, The Seven Days of Cain 2010; short stories: The Inhabitant of the Lake and Less Welcome Tenants 1964, Demons by Daylight 1973, The Height of the Scream 1976, Dark Companions 1982, Cold Print 1985, Black Wine (with Charles L. Grant) 1986, Night Visions 3 (with Clive Barker and Lisa Tuttle) 1986, Scared Stiff 1987, Dark Feasts: The World of Ramsey Campbell 1987, Waking Nightmares 1991, Alone With the Horrors (World Fantasy Award and Stoker Award for Best Collection 1994) 1993, Strange Things and Stranger Places 1993, Ghosts and Grisly Things (British Fantasy Award for Best Collection 1999) 1998, Told by the Dead (British Fantasy Award for Best Collection) 2003, Inconsequential Tales 2008, Just Behind You 2009; novella: Needing Ghosts 1990; other: Ramsey Campbell, Probably (collected non-fiction) (Best Non-Fiction, International Horror Guild, Stoker Award of the Horror Writers of America, Superior Achievement in Non-Fiction and British Fantasy Award for Best Collection) 2002. *Honours:* Liverpool Daily Post and Echo Award for Literature 1993, , Grand Master, World Horror Convention 1999, Lifetime Achievement Award, Horror Writers' Asscn 1999. *Address:* 31 Penkett Road, Wallasey, Merseyside, CH45 7QF, England (home). *E-mail:* errolundercliffe@aol.com (office). *Website:* www.ramseycampbell.com.

CAMPION, Daniel Ray, AB, MA, PhD; American editor, poet and literary critic; *Manager of Editorial Quality Assurance, ACT, Inc.;* b. 23 Aug. 1949, Oak Park, Ill.; s. of Raymond E. Campion and Wilma F. Campion; m. JoAnn E. Castagna. *Education:* Univ. of Chicago, Univ. of Illinois, Chicago, Univ. of Iowa. *Career:* Production Ed. Encyclopaedia Britannica Inc., Chicago, Ill. 1972–74; Children's Book Ed., Follett Publishing Co., Chicago 1977–78; Teaching and Research Asst, Univ. of Iowa 1978–84; Test Specialist Sr Ed. and Man. Editorial Quality Assurance, ACT Inc. 1984–; mem. Authors' Guild, Modern Language Asscn (MLA), Midwest MLA, Nat. Council of Teachers of English, Soc. for the Study of Midwestern Literature. *Publications include:* Walt Whitman: The Measure of his Song (co-ed.) 1981, Calypso (poems) 1981, Peter De Vries and Surrealism 1995; contrib. of poetry and articles to periodicals, including College English, Literary Magazine Review, The Writer's Chronicle, Hispanic Journal, Rolling Stone, Chicago Tribune, Chicago Reader, Ascent, Poet Lore, English Journal, Poetry, The North American Review. *Honours:* Univ. of Chicago Festival of the Arts Poetry Award 1967, Triton Coll. All-Nations Poetry Contest Award, River Grove, Ill. 1975, Illinois Arts Council Poetry Award 1979, Harold Witt Memorial Award 2007, 2010. *Address:* 1700 Rochester Avenue, Iowa City, IA 52245-6035, USA (home). *E-mail:* dan.campion@act.org (office).

CAMROSE, 4th Viscount (cr. 2001), of Hackwood Park, Southampton; **Adrian Michael Berry,** MA, FRGS, FRAS; British writer and journalist; b. 15 June 1937, London, England; m. Marina Beatrice Sulzberger 1967; one s. one d. *Education:* Eton Coll., Christ Church, Oxford. *Career:* Corresp., Time Magazine, New York 1965–67; Science Corresp., Daily Telegraph, London 1977–96, Consulting Ed. (Science) 1996–; Fellow, British Interplanetary Soc. 1986–. *Publications include:* The Next Ten Thousand Years: A Vision of Man's Future in the Universe 1974, The Iron Sun: Crossing the Universe Through Black Holes 1977, From Apes to Astronauts 1981, The Super Intelligent Machine 1983, High Skies and Yellow Rain 1983, Koyama's Diamond (fiction) 1984, Labyrinth of Lies (fiction) 1985, Ice With Your Evolution 1986, Computer Software: The Kings and Queens of England 1985, Harrap's Book of Scientific Anecdotes 1989, The Next 500 Years 1995, Galileo and the Dolphins 1996, The Giant Leap 1999. *Address:* Apartment 3, 81 Holland Park, London, W11 3RZ, England (home). *Telephone:* (20) 7792-2982 (home). *E-mail:* adrianberry@safe-mail.net. *Website:* www.adrianberry.net.

CANIN, Ethan, BA, MFA, MD; American writer; b. 19 July 1960, Ann Arbor, Mich. *Education:* Stanford Univ., Univ. of Iowa, Harvard Univ. *Career:* Faculty mem. Iowa Writers' Workshop, Univ. of Iowa; Co-founder San Francisco Writers' Grotto; Houghton Mifflin Literary Fellowship 1986; Nat. Endowment for the Arts Fellowship 1987,1996; Guggenheim Fellowship 2010. *Publications include:* Emperor of the Air 1988, Blue River 1991, The Palace Thief 1993, For Kings and Planets 1998, Carry Me Across the Water 2001, America America 2008; contribs to anthologies and periodicals. *Honours:* Henfield/Transatlantic Review Prize 1987, The California Book Award/Gold Medal in Literature 1994, The Lyndhurst Prize 1994, 1995, 1996. *Address:* c/o Random House Publicity, 1745 Broadway, New York, NY 10019, USA. *E-mail:* ecanin@ethancanin.com. *Website:* www.randomhouse.com.

CANNADINE, Sir David Nicholas, Kt, DPhil, LittD, FRHistS, FBA, FRSA, FRSL; British historian and academic; *Whitney J. Oates Senior Research Scholar, Princeton University;* b. 7 Sept. 1950, s. of Sydney Douglas Cannadine and Dorothy Mary Hughes; m. Linda Jane Colley (q.v.) 1982; one d. (deceased). *Education:* King Edward's Five Ways School, Birmingham, Clare Coll., Cambridge, St John's Coll., Oxford, Princeton Univ., USA. *Career:* Resident Fellow, St John's Coll. Cambridge 1975–77, Asst Lecturer in History 1976–80, Lecturer 1980–88; Fellow, Christ's Coll. Cambridge 1977–88, Dir of Studies in History 1977–83, Tutor 1979–81; Prof. of History, Columbia Univ., New York 1988–92, Moore Collegiate Prof. 1992–98; Dir Inst. of Historical Research Univ. of London 1998–2003, Prof. 1998–2003, Queen Elizabeth the Queen Mother Prof. of British History 2003–08, Hon. Fellow 2005–, Consultant, History in Educ. 2008–; Visiting mem., Inst. for Advanced Study, Princeton, NJ 1980–81; Visiting Fellow, Council of the Humanities 2003–05, Whitney J. Oates Sr Research Scholar 2008–; Visiting Prof., Birkbeck Coll., London 1995–97; Visiting Fellow, Whitney Humanities Center, Yale Univ. 1995–96; Visiting Scholar, Pembroke Coll., Cambridge 1997; Pres. Worcs. Historical Soc. 1999–; Vice-Pres. British Records Soc. 1998–, Royal Historical Soc. 1998–2002; Chair. IHR Trust 1999–2003; mem. Advisory Bd Centre for Study of Soc. and Politics, Kingston Univ. 1998–2003, ICBH 1998–2003, Advisory Council Warburg Inst. 1998–2003, Inst. of US Studies 1999–2004, Public Record Office 1999–2004, Inst. of English Studies 2000–03, Inst. of Latin American Studies 2000–04, Kennedy Memorial Trust 2000–, Nat. Trust Eastern Regional Cttee 2000–, Royal Mint Advisory Cttee 2004–, Editorial Bd History of Parliament 2004–, Advisory Council Inst. for the Study of the Americas 2004–; Gov. Ipswich School 1982–88; Fellow, Berkeley Coll., Yale Univ. 1985, J. P. Morgan Library, New York 1992–98; American Council of Learned Socs Fellowship 1990–91; regular radio and TV broadcaster; Ed.-in-Chief Journal of Maritime History 1999–; Gen. Ed. Studies in Modern History 1979–2002, Penguin History of Britain 1989–, Penguin History of Europe 1991–, Historical Research 1998–2003; Trustee Kennedy Memorial Scholarship Fund 1999–, Nat. Portrait Gallery 2000– (Chair. of Trustees 2005–), British Empire and Commonwealth Museum 2003–, Commr English Heritage 2001–; Visiting Fellow, ANU, Canberra 2005 (Adjunct Prof. 2006), Nat. Humanities Center, North Carolina 2006; Chair. Blue Plaques Panel, English Heritage. *Radio:* A Point of View (BBC Radio 4) 2005–06. *Publications include:* Lords and Landlords: The Aristocracy and the Towns 1774–1967 1980, Patricians, Power and Politics in Nineteenth-Century Towns (ed. and contrib.) 1982, H. J. Dyos, Exploring the Urban Past (co-ed. and contrib.) 1982, Rituals of Royalty: Power and Ceremonial in Traditional Societies (co-ed. and contrib.) 1987, The Pleasures of the Past 1989, The Decline and Fall of the British Aristocracy (Lionel Trilling Prize) 1990, G. M. Trevelyan: A Life in History 1992, Aspects of Aristocracy: Grandeur and Decline in Modern Britain 1994, Class in Britain 1998, History in Our Time 1998, Making History Now 1999, Ornamentalism: How the British Saw Their Empire 2001, In Churchill's Shadow: Confronting the Past in Modern Britain 2002, What is History Now? (ed.) 2002, History and the Media (ed.) 2004, Winston Churchill in the 21st Century (co-ed. and contrib.) 2004, Admiral Lord Nelson, his context and legacy (ed.) 2005, Trafalgar: A Battle and its Afterlife (ed.) 2006, National Portrait Gallery: A Brief History 2007, Empire, the Sea and Global History: Britain's Maritime World c. 1763–1840 (ed.) 2007, History and Philanthropy: Past Present Future (co-ed. and contrib.) 2008, Making History Now and Then: Discoveries, Controversies and Explanations 2008; numerous contribs to other books and learned journals. *Honours:* Hon. Fellow, Christ's Coll. Cambridge 2005; Hon. Prof., Univ. of London 2008; Hon. DLitt (East Anglia, South Bank) 2001, (Birmingham) 2002; T. S. Ashton Prize, Econ. History Soc. 1977, Silver Jubilee Prize, Agric. History Soc. 1977, Lionel Trilling Prize 1991, Governors' Award 1991, Dean's Distinguished Award in the Humanities, Columbia Univ. 1996. *Address:* Institute of Historical Research, Senate House, Malet Street, London, WC1E 7HU, England (office). *Fax:* (20) 7862-8754 (office). *E-mail:* jennifer.wallis@sas.ac.uk (office). *Website:* www.history.ac.uk (office).

CANNON, Steve, BA; American writer, dramatist, educator and publisher; b. 10 April 1935, New Orleans, La; one s. (deceased). *Education:* Univ. of Nebraska. *Career:* Prof. of Humanities, Medgar Evers Coll., CUNY 1971–92; Founder A Gathering of Tribes (arts org.); mem. PEN, New York Chapter. *Publications include:* Groove, Bang and Jive Around 1969, Introduction to Rouzing the Rubble 1991, Reminicin' in C 1995; plays: The Set Up 1991, Chump Change 1992, Nothing to Lose 1993, Now What, What Now? 1994, En Vogue 1994, Top of the World 1995, Marvellous 1996. *Address:* 285 East Third Street, New York, NY 10009-7813, USA (office). *Telephone:* (212) 674-3778 (office). *Fax:* (212) 674-5776. *Website:* www.tribes.org (office).

CANOBBIO, Andrea; Italian writer and publisher; *Head of Foreign Fiction, Einaudi Publishing;* b. 1962, Turin. *Career:* with Bompiani publrs 1989–91; joined Einaudi Publishing 1991, Head of Foreign Fiction 1995–. *Publications include:* novels: Vasi cinesi 1989, Traslochi 1992, Padri di padri 1997, Indivisibili 2000, Il naturale disordine delle cose (trans. as The Natural Disorder of Things) 2004, Der Garten 2005, Presentimento (novella) 2008. *Address:* Giulio Einaudi Editore, Uff. proposte editoriali, Via Biancamano 2, 10121 Turin, Italy (office). *Telephone:* (011) 56561 (office). *Fax:* (011) 542903 (office). *E-mail:* canobbio@einaudi.it (office). *Website:* www.einaudi.it (office).

CANSINO, Eliacer; Spanish writer and academic; *Professor of Philosophy, I.E.S. Mateo Alemán;* b. 1954, Sevilla. *Career:* Prof. of Philosophy, I.E.S. Mateo Alemán 1980– , also Head of Dept. *Publications:* El maravillloso señor Plot 1987, Paisaje de las sombras 1988, Los ojos de Ícaro 1991, Retrato de opositores 1991, Tras los ojos de la garza 1992, Yo, Robinsón Sánchez, habiendo naufragado (International Prize Infanta Elena) 1992, Tras los ojos de la garza 1993, Un viajante, una ciudad 1995, El misterio Velázquez 1997, La metamorfosis de Avellaneda 1998, El misterio Velázquez (Lazarillo Prize 1997) 1998, Nube y los niños 2004, La apuesta de Pascal 2004, El paraguas poético 2004, El lápiz que encontró su nombre 2005, Una película desastrosa 2005, El gigante que leía Don Quijote 2005, Stalwart de acero 2005, un poco Diablo de una reunión 2007, Leyendas de Bécquer contadas por Eliacer Cansino 2008, Mis primeras leyendas de Bécquer 2008, Julián tiene miedo 2009, Una habitación en Babel (Anaya Award 2009 and Premio Nacional de Literature Infantil y Juvenil 2010) 2009, OK, señor Foster 2009, El lazarillo de Amberes 2009. *Address:* I.E.S. Mateo Alemán, C/ Juan Ramón Jiménez, 41920 San Juan de Aznalfarache, Spain (office). *Telephone:* (95) 5622723 (office). *Fax:* (95) 5622724 (office). *E-mail:* filosofiamateoaleman@gmail.com. *Website:* www.juntadeandalucia.es/averroes/iesmateoaleman (office).

CANTALUPO, Charles, BA, MA, PhD; American academic, poet and writer; *Professor of English, Comparative Literature and African Studies, Pennsylvania State University;* b. 17 Oct. 1951, Orange, NJ; m. 1st Catherine Musello 1976 (died 1983); one s. (deceased); m. 2nd Barbara Dorosh 1988; one s. three d. *Education:* Univ. of Kent at Canterbury, Washington Univ., St Louis, Rutgers Univ. *Career:* Teaching Asst, Rutgers Univ. 1973–76, Instructor 1977–79; Instructor, Pennsylvania State Univ. 1980–81, Asst Prof. 1981–89, Assoc. Prof. 1989–96, Prof. of English 1996–99, Prof. of English and Comparative Literature 1999–2001, Prof. of English, Comparative Literature and African Studies 2002–. *Publications include:* The Art of Hope (poetry) 1983, A Literary Leviathan: Thomas Hobbe's Masterpiece of Language 1991, The World of Ngugi wa Thiong'o (ed.) 1995, Poetry, Mysticism, and Feminism: From th' Nave to the Chops 1995, Ngugi wa Thiong'o: Text and Contexts (ed.) 1995, Anima/l Wo/man and Other Spirits (poetry) 1996, We Have Our Voice: Selected Poems of Reesom Haile (trans.) 2000, We Invented the Wheel: Poems by Reesom Haile (trans.) 2002, Light the Lights (poetry) 2004, Who Needs a Story? 2006, War and Peace in Contemporary Eritrean Poetry 2009; contribs to books, anthologies, scholarly journals, periodicals, newspapers and websites. *Honours:* American Acad. of Poets Prize 1976, Penn State Schuylkill, Faculty Organization Teaching Award 1986, Penn State Schuylkill, Student Government Association Teaching Award 1987, Penn State Schuylkill, Faculty Organization Research Award 1991, 1996, 2008, African Students Association, Penn State University, Faculty Achievement Award 2001. *Address:* Department of English, Penn State University, 117 Burrowes Building, University Park, PA 16802, USA (office). *Telephone:* (570) 385-6055 (office). *E-mail:* cxc8@psu.edu (office). *Website:* english.la.psu.edu (office).

CANTSIN, Monty (see Home, Stewart Ramsay)

CANTWELL, Aston (see Platt, Charles Michael)

CAPIE, Forrest Hunter, BA, MSc, PhD, FRSA; British academic; *Official Historian, Bank of England;* b. 1 Dec. 1940, Glasgow, Scotland; m. Dianna Dix 1967. *Education:* Univ. of Auckland, New Zealand, Univ. of London. *Career:* Econs Tutor, LSE 1970–72; Lecturer, Univ. of Warwick 1972–74, Univ. of Leeds 1974–79; Visiting Lecturer, City Univ., London 1978–79, Lecturer 1979–82, Sr Lecturer 1982–83, Reader 1983–86, Prof. of Econ. History 1986–; various guest lectureships; Ed. Econ. History Review 1993–; Official Historian, Bank of England 2004–; currently Special Prof. of Accounting and Finance Div., Business School, Univ. of Nottingham; mem. Asscn of Business Historians, Cliometrics Soc., Econ. History Asscn, Econ. History Soc., Royal Econ. Soc., Western Econs Asscn. *Publications include:* The British Economy Between the Wars (with M. Collins) 1983, Depression and Protectionism: Britain Between the Wars 1983, A Monetary History of the United Kingdom, 1870–1982: Data Sources and Methods (with A. Webber) 1985, Financial Crises and the World Banking System (co-ed. with G. E. Wood) 1986, Monetary Economics in the 1980s: Some Themes from Henry Thornton (co-ed. with G. E. Wood) 1989, A Directory of Economic Institutions (ed.) 1990, Unregulated Banking: Chaos or Order? (co-ed. with G. E. Wood) 1991, Major Inflations in History (ed.) 1991, Protectionism in the World Economy (ed.) 1992, Did the Banks Fail British Industry? (with M. Collins) 1992, Monetary Regimes in Transition (co-ed. with M. Bordo) 1993, A History of Banking (ed., 10 vols) 1993, Tariffs and Growth 1994, The Future of Central Banking (with Charles Goodhart, Stanley Fischer and Norbert Schnadt) 1994, Monetary Economics in the 1990s (co-ed. with G. E. Wood) 1996, Asset Prices and the Real Economy (co-ed. with G. E. Wood) 1997, Policy Makers on Policy (co-ed. with G. E. Wood) 2001, World Economic Liberalization in Historical Perspective 2001, Capital Controls: A Cure Worse Than the Disease 2002; contrib. to scholarly books and journals. *Honours:* several grants and fellowships. *Address:* Bank of England, Threadneedle Street, London, EC2R 8AH, England (office). *Telephone:* (20) 7601-3680 (office). *E-mail:* forrest.capie@bankofengland.co.uk (office).

CAPUTO, Philip Joseph, BA; American writer and screenwriter; b. 10 June 1941, Chicago, Ill.; m. 1st Jill Esther Ongemach 1969 (divorced 1982); two s.; m. 2nd Marcelle Lynn Besse 1982 (divorced 1985); m. 3rd Leslie Blanchard Ware 1988. *Education:* Purdue Univ., Loyola Univ. *Career:* fmr US Marine in Viet Nam 1965–66; staff, Chicago Tribune 1969–72, Foreign Corresp. 1972–77; freelance writer 1977–; screenwriter, Mercury-Douglas Productions, Paramount Pictures 1987–; mem. Authors' Guild. *Publications include:* A Rumor of War (memoir) 1977, Horn of Africa (novel) 1980, Del Corso's Gallery (novel) 1983, Indian Country: A Novel 1987, Means of Escape (memoir) 1991, Equation for Evil (novel) 1996, Exiles (three novellas) 1997, The Voyage (novel) 1999, Acts of Faith 2005, Ten Thousand Days of Thunder 2005, 13 Seconds: A Look Back at the Kent State Shootings 2005, Crossers 2009; contrib. to various periodicals. *Honours:* Pulitzer Prize for Reporting (with George Bliss) 1973, George Polk Award 1973, Overseas Press Club Award, Sidney Hillman Award. *Literary Agent:* c/o Aaron M. Priest Literary Agency, 708 Third Avenue, 23rd Floor, New York, NY 10017-4201, USA. *Telephone:* (212) 818-0344. *E-mail:* info@aaronpriest.com. *Website:* www.aaronpriest.com.

CARD, Orson Scott, (Brian Green, Byron Walley), BA, MA; American writer; b. 24 Aug. 1951, Richland, Wash.; m. Kristine Allen 1977; two s. three d. *Education:* Brigham Young Univ., Univ. of Utah. *Career:* Distinguished Prof. of English, Southern Virginia Univ. 2005–; mem. Authors' Guild, Science Fiction and Fantasy Writers of America. *Publications include:* Capitol 1978, Hot Sleep: The Worthing Chronicle 1978, A Planet Called Treason 1979, revised edn as Treason 1988, Songmaster 1980, Unaccompanied Sonata and Other Stories 1980, Saintspeak: The Mormon Dictionary 1981, Ainge 1982, Hart's Hope 1983, A Woman of Destiny 1983, revised edn as Saints 1988, The Worthing Chronicle 1983, Ender's Game 1985, Speaker for the Dead 1986, Cardography 1987, Free Lancers (with others) 1987, Seventh Son 1987, Wyrms 1987, Characters and Viewpoint 1988, Red Prophet 1988, Folk of the Fringe 1989, The Abyss 1989, Prentice Alvin 1989, How to Write Science Fiction and Fantasy 1990, Eye for Eye–The Tunesmith (with Lloyd Biggle) 1990, Maps in a Mirror: The Short Fiction of Orson Scott Card 1990, Worthing Saga 1990, Xenocide 1991, The Changed Man 1992, Cruel Miracles 1992, Flux 1992, The Memory of Earth 1992, Lost Boys 1992, The Call of the Earth 1993, Monkey Sonatas 1993, The Ships of Earth 1993, Lovelock (with Kathryn H. Kidd) 1994, Earthfall 1994, Turning Hearts: Short Stories on Family Life (co-ed. with David C. Dollahite) 1994, Alvin Journeyman 1995, Earthborn 1995, Children of the Mind 1996, Pastwatch: The Redemption of Christopher Columbus 1996, Treasure Box 1996, Stone Tables 1997, Heartfire 1998, Homebody 1998, Enchantment 1999, Ender's Shadow 1999, Magic Mirror 1999, Sarah 2000, Shadow of the Hegemon 2001, Rebekah, 2001, Shadow of the Hegemon, 2001, Shadow Puppets 2002, The Crystal City 2003, Rachel and Leah 2004, Zanna's Gift 2004, Shadow of the Giant 2005, Magic Street 2005, Empire 2006, Invasive Procedures (with Aaron Johnston) 2007, War of Gifts 2007, Keeper of Dreams 2008, Ender in Exile 2008, Hidden Empire 2010, The Lost Gate 2010; contributions: periodicals. *Honours:* John W. Campbell Award, World Science Fiction Convention 1978, Utah State Inst. of Fine Arts Prize 1980, Hamilton-Brackett Awards 1981, 1986, Nebula Awards 1985, 1986, Hugo Awards 1986, 1987, Locus Awards 1987, 1988, 1989, Mythopoeic Fantasy Award, Mythopoeic Soc. 1988. *Address:* 401 Willoughby Boulevard, Greensboro, NC 27408-3135, USA (home). *Telephone:* (336) 282-9848 (home). *Website:* www.hatrack.com.

CARDENAL, Ernesto; Nicaraguan poet, priest and government official; b. 20 Jan. 1925, Granada; s. of Rodolfo Cardenal and Esmerelda Cardenal (née Martinez). *Education:* Univ. of Mexico, Columbia Univ., New York. *Career:* ordained RC priest 1965–; Minister of Culture 1979–90; Co-founder and Hon. Pres. Casa de los Tres Mundos (literary org.). *Publications:* Proclama del conquistador 1947, Gethsemani Ky 1960, Hora 0 1960, Epigramas 1961, Poemas 1961, Salmos 1964, Oración por Marilyn Monroe y otros poemas 1965, La voz de un monje en la era nuclear 1965, El estrecho dudoso 1966, Homenaje a los Indios Americanos 1969, Mayapán 1970, Vida en el amor 1971, La hora cero y otros poemas 1971, Canto nacional al F.S.L.N. 1972, Oráculo sobre Managua 1973, El evangelio en solentiname 1975, La santidad de la revolución 1976, Cátulo marcial 1978, Nueva antología poética 1978, Viaje a New York 1980, Nostalgia del futuro 1982, Crónica de un reencuentro 1982, Waslala 1983, Vuelos de victoria 1984, With Walker in Nicaragua and other early poems 1949–54 1984, Quetzalcoatl 1985, Nuevo cielo y tierra nueva 1985, From Nicaragua with Love: Poems 1976–1986 1986, Cántico cósmico 1989, La noche iluminada de palabras 1991, Los ovnis de oro 1991, El telescopio en la noche oscura 1993, Del monasterio al mundo: correspondencia entre Ernesto Cardenal y Thomas Merton 1998, Vida perdida 1999, Los años de Granada 2002, Las ínsulas extrañas 2002, La revolución perdida 2003, Thomas Merton—Ernesto Cardenal: Correspondencia (1959–1968) 2004, Versos del pluriverso 2005. *Honours:* Premio de la Paz 1980. *E-mail:* escritor@ibw.com.ni (office). *Website:* www.ernestocardenal.org.

CARDOSO, Dulce Maria; Portuguese writer; b. 1964, Trás-os-Montes; two c. *Education:* Universidade de Lisboa. *Publications include:* Campo de Sangue (Grande Prémio Aconteca de Romance) 2002, Os Meus Sentimentos (EU Prize for Literature 2009) 2005, Coeurs arrachés 2005, Les anges, Violeta 2006, Até Nós 2008, O Chão dos Pardais 2009. *Address:* c/o Edições Asa, Rua Cidade de Córdova 2, 2610-038 Alfragide, Portugal (office). *Telephone:* (21) 4272200. *Fax:* (21) 4272201. *Website:* www.asa.pt (office).

CAREW, Jan Rynveld; Guyanese academic, writer and poet; b. 24 Sept. 1920, Agricola. *Education:* Howard Univ., Western Reserve Univ., USA, Charles Univ., Prague, Czechoslovakia, Univ. of the Sorbonne, Paris, France. *Career:* Lecturer in Race Relations, Extra-Mural Dept, Univ. of London, UK 1953–57; Writer and Ed., BBC Overseas Service, London 1954–65; Ed. African Review, Ghana 1965–66; CBC Broadcaster, Toronto 1966–69; Sr Fellow,

Council of Humanities and Lecturer, Dept of Afro-American Studies, Princeton Univ., USA 1969–72; Prof., Dept of African-American Studies, Northwestern Univ., USA 1972–87; Visiting Clarence J. Robinson Prof. of Caribbean Literature and History, George Mason Univ., USA 1989–91; Visiting Prof. of International Studies, Illinois Wesleyan Univ., USA 1992–93; Dir Center for the Comparative Study of the Humanities, Lincoln Univ., Pa, USA 1993–95; Visiting Liberal Studies Prof., Dept of Pan-African Studies, Univ. of Louisville, USA 2000; Perm. Advisor to Univ. of Namibia, Windhoek, St Petersburg Univ., Russia. *Publications include:* Streets of Eternity 1952, Black Midas 1958 (US edn as A Touch of Midas 1958), The Wild Coast 1958, The Last Barbarian 1961, Moscow is Not My Mecca 1964, Green Winter 1964, University of Hunger 1966, The Third Gift 1975, Children of the Sun 1980, Sea Drums in My Blood 1981, Grenada: The Hour Will Strike Again 1985, Fulcrums of Change 1987, Ghosts in our Blood: with Malcolm X in Africa, England and the Caribbean 1994, The Sisters and Manco's Stories 2002, Rape of Paradise: Columbus and the Birth of Racism in the Americas 2006, The Guyanese Wanderer 2007, Black Midas 2009, The Wild Coast 2009. *Address:* 1360 South First Street, Louisville, KY 40208-2302, USA (home). *Telephone:* (502) 635-1969 (home). *E-mail:* jancarew@aol.com (home).

CAREY, John, MA, DPhil, FRSL, FBA; British literary critic and academic; *Merton Professor Emeritus of English Literature, University of Oxford*; b. 5 April 1934, London, England; s. of Charles William and Winifred Ethel Carey (née Cook); m. Gillian Mary Florence Booth 1960; two s. *Education:* Richmond and East Sheen County Grammar School, St John's Coll., Oxford. *Career:* served in East Surrey Regt 1953–54; Harmsworth Sr Scholar, Merton Coll., Oxford 1957–58; Lecturer, Christ Church, Oxford 1958–59; Andrew Bradley Jr Research Fellow, Balliol Coll., Oxford 1959–60; Tutorial Fellow, Keble Coll., Oxford 1960–64, St John's Coll. 1964–75; Merton Prof. of English Literature, Univ. of Oxford 1976–2001, Prof. Emer. 2001–; Chief Book Reviewer, Sunday Times (London) 1976–; T.S. Eliot Memorial Lecturer, Univ. of Kent 1989; Northcliffe Lecturer, Univ. Coll., London 2004; Chair. Booker Prize Judges 1982, 2003, Int. Booker Prize Judges 2005; Judge, WH Smith Prize 1989–95. *Publications:* The Poems of John Milton (co-ed. with Alastair Fowler) 1968, Milton 1969, The Violent Effigy: A Study of Dickens' Imagination 1973, Thackeray: Prodigal Genius 1977, John Donne: Life, Mind and Art 1981, The Private Memoirs and Confessions of a Justified Sinner, by James Hogg (ed.), William Golding: The Man and His Books (ed.) 1986, Original Copy: Selected Reviews and Journalism 1987, The Faber Book of Reportage (ed.) 1987, John Donne (Oxford Authors) (ed.) 1990, The Intellectuals and the Masses 1992, The Faber Book of Science (ed.) 1995, The Faber Book of Utopias (ed.) 1999, Pure Pleasure 2000, What Good are the Arts? 2005, William Golding: The Man Who Wrote Lord of the Flies (James Tait Black Memorial Prize 2010) 2009; articles in Review of English Studies, Modern Language Review etc. *Honours:* Hon. Fellow, St John's Coll. Oxford 1991, Balliol Coll. Oxford 1992; Hon. Prof. Univ. of Liverpool 2004–. *Address:* Brasenose Cottage, Lyneham, Oxon., OX7 6QL (home); 57 Stapleton Road, Headington, Oxford, England (home). *Telephone:* (1865) 764304 (home). *E-mail:* john.carey123@btinternet.com (home).

CAREY, Peter Philip, FRSL; Australian/American writer and academic; *Executive Director, Creative Writing Program, Hunter College, City University of New York*; b. 7 May 1943, Bacchus Marsh, Vic., Australia; s.; of Percival Stanley Carey and Helen Jean Warriner; m. 2nd Alison Summers 1985 (divorced); two s.; m. 3rd Frances Rachel Coady 2007. *Education:* Geelong Grammar School and Monash Univ. *Career:* fmr Teacher of Creative Writing, New York Univ., New School, New York, Columbia Univ., Princeton Univ., Barnard Univ.; currently Exec. Dir Creative Writing Program, Hunter Coll., CUNY. *Screenplay:* Bliss (co-author), Until the End of the World (co-author). *Publications:* The Fat Man in History (short stories, aka Exotic Pleasures 1981) 1974, War Crimes (short stories) (NSW Premier's Award) 1979, Bliss (novel) (Miles Franklin Award, Nat. Book Council Award, NSW Premier's Award) 1981, Illywhacker (novel) (Age Book of the Year Award, Nat. Book Council Award, Victorian Premier's Award) 1985, Oscar and Lucinda (Booker Prize for Fiction 1988, Miles Franklin Award, Nat. Book Council Award, Adelaide Festival Award, Foundation for Australian Literary Studies Award) 1988, Until the End of the World 1990, The Tax Inspector (novel) 1991, The Unusual Life of Tristan Smith (novel) (Age Book of the Year Award) 1994, Collected Stories 1995, The Big Bazoohley (children's novel) 1995, Jack Maggs 1997, The True History of the Kelly Gang (Booker Prize 2001) 2000, 30 Days in Sydney: A Wildly Distorted Account 2001, My Life as a Fake 2003, Wrong About Japan 2005, Theft: A Love Story 2006, His Illegal Self 2008, Parrot and Olivier in America 2009, The Chemistry of Tears 2012. *Honours:* Hon. LittD (Queensland); Hon. DLit (Monash), (New School, NY, USA). *Literary Agent:* c/o Amanda Urban, ICM, 825 Eighth Avenue, New York, NY 10019, USA. *Telephone:* (212) 556-5764. *E-mail:* aurban@icmtalent.com. *Website:* www.hunter.cuny.edu/creativewriting (office); petercareybooks.com.

CARFAX, Catherine (see Fairburn, Eleanor M.)

ČARIJA, Jelena; Croatian novelist; b. 1980, Split. *Education:* Zagreb Drama and Film Acad. *Career:* won award in 2002 for then unpublished novel Klonirana, orig. written as filmscript; currently studying production. *Publications:* Klonirana (novel) 2003. *Address:* c/o Rende, Hadži Đerina 7, II sprat, stan br. 8, 11000 Belgrade, Serbia (office). *E-mail:* rende@sbb.co.yu (office).

CARKEET, David Corydon, AB, MA, PhD; American academic and writer; b. 15 Nov. 1946, Sonora, Calif.; m. Barbara Lubin 1975; three d. *Education:* Univ. of California, Davis, Univ. of Wisconsin, Indiana Univ. *Career:* Asst Prof., Univ. of Missouri 1973–79, Assoc. Prof. 1979–87, Prof. 1987–. *Publications include:* fiction: Double Negative 1980, The Greatest Slump of All Time 1984, I Been There Before 1985, The Full Catastrophe 1990, The Error of Our Ways 1997, Campus Sexpot: A Memoir 2005, From Away 2010, Double Carkeet 2010; young adult fiction: The Silent Treatment 1988, Quiver River 1991; contribs to scholarly journals, short stories and popular essays in periodicals. *Honours:* James D. Phelan Award in Literature, San Francisco Foundation 1976, Notable Books of the Year, New York Times Book Review 1981, 1990, 1997, O. Henry Award 1982, National Endowment for the Arts Fellowship 1983. *Address:* Department of English, University of Missouri, 1 University Building, Saint Louis, MO 63121-4400 (office); 418 Macey Road, North Middlesex, VT 05682, USA (home). *Telephone:* (902) 229-9496 (home). *E-mail:* davidcarkeet@hotmail.com (home). *Website:* www.davidcarkeet.com.

CARLE, Eric; American children's writer and illustrator; b. 1929, Syracuse, NY; m. Barbara; one s. one d. *Education:* Akad. der bildenden Künste, Stuttgart, Germany. *Career:* fmrly graphic designer promotion Dept, New York Times; fmr art dir of an advertising agency; co-f. Eric Carle Museum of Picture Book Art, Amherst, Mass 2002. *Publications include:* 1, 2, 3 to the Zoo 1968, The Very Hungry Caterpillar 1969, Pancakes, Pancakes! 1970, The Tiny Seed 1970, Do You Want to Be My Friend? 1971, Rooster's Off to See the World 1972, The Very Long Tail 1972, The Very Long Train 1972, The Secret Birthday Message 1972, Walter the Baker 1972, Have You Seen My Cat? 1973, I See a Song 1973, My Very First Book of Numbers 1974, My Very First Book of Colors 1974, My Very First Book of Shapes 1974, My Very First Book of Words 1974, All About Arthur 1974, The Mixed-Up Chameleon 1975, Eric Carle's Storybook, Seven Tales by the Brothers Grimm 1976, The Grouchy Ladybug 1977, Watch Out! A Giant! 1978, Seven Stories by Hans Christian Andersen 1978, Twelve Tales from Aesop 1980, The Honeybee and the Robber 1981, Catch the Ball! 1982, Let's Paint A Rainbow 1982, What's For Lunch? 1982, The Very Busy Spider 1984, All Around Us 1986, Papa, Please Get the Moon for Me 1986, My Very First Book of Sounds 1986, My Very First Book of Food 1986, My Very First Book of Tools 1986, My Very First Book of Touch 1986, My Very First Book of Motion 1986, My Very First Book of Growth 1986, My Very First Book of Homes 1986, My Very First Book of Heads 1986, All in a Day (with others) 1986, A House for Hermit Crab 1987, Eric Carle's Treasury of Classic Stories for Children 1988, The Very Quiet Cricket 1990, Draw Me a Star 1992, Today is Monday 1993, My Apron 1994, The Very Lonely Firefly 1995, Little Cloud 1996, The Art of Eric Carle 1996, From Head to Toe 1997, Flora and Tiger: 19 very short stories from my life 1997, Hello, Red Fox 1998, You Can Make a Collage: A Very Simple How-to Book 1998, The Very Clumsy Click Beetle 1999, Does A Kangaroo Have A Mother, Too? 2000, Dream Snow 2000, "Slowly, Slowly, Slowly," said the Sloth 2002, Where Are You Going? To See My Friend! (with Kazuo Iwamura) 2003, Mister Seahorse 2004, 10 Little Rubber Ducks 2005, Baby Bear, Baby Bear, What Do You See? 2007; many books illustrated for other authors. *Honours:* Officer's Cross of the Order of Merit (Germany) 2001; Hon. PhD (Coll. of Our Lady the Elms, Chicopee, Mass) 2001, (Niagara Univ., Niagara, NY) 2002, (Bates Coll., Lewiston, Me) 2007; Silver Medal, Milan, Italy 1989, David McCord Children's Literature Citation, Framingham State Coll. and Nobscot Reading Council of the Int. Reading Asscn 1995, Univ. of Southern Mississippi Medallion from DeGrummond Collection 1997, Catholic Library Asscn Regina Medal 1999, Pittsburgh Children's Museum Outstanding Friend of Children 1999, Mainichi Newspaper Japan Picture Book Award for Lifetime Achievement 2000, American Library Asscn Laura Ingalls Wilder Award 2003, John P. McGovern Award in Behavioral Sciences, Smithsonian Inst. 2006, NEA Foundation Award for Outstanding Service to Public Educ. 2007, Kurt Vonnegut Jr Literature Award, Indianapolis-Marion County Public Library 2008. *Address:* PO Box 485, Northampton, MA 01060, USA (home). *Website:* www.carlemuseum.org (office); www.eric-carle.com.

CARLILE, Henry David, BA, MA; American academic, poet and writer; *Professor Emeritus of English, Portland State University*; b. 6 May 1934, San Francisco, Calif.; one d. *Education:* Grays Harbor Coll., Univ. of Washington. *Career:* instructor, Portland State Univ. 1967–69, Asst Prof. 1969–72, Assoc. Prof. 1972–78, Prof. of English 1980–2003, Prof. Emer. 2003–; Visiting Lecturer, Writers Workshop, Univ. of Iowa 1978–80. *Publications include:* The Rough-Hewn Table (Devins Award) 1971, Running Lights 1981, Rain 1994, Oregon 2013; contribs to numerous anthologies, reviews and journals. *Honours:* Nat. Endowment for the Arts Discovery Grant 1970, Nat. Endowment for the Arts Fellowship in Poetry 1976, PEN Syndicated Fiction Awards 1983, 1986, Ingram Merrill Poetry Fellowship 1985, Helen Foundation Award 1986, Pushcart Prizes 1986, 1992, Poetry Award, Crazyhorse 1988, Oregon Arts Comm. Literary Fellowship 1994. *Address:* 7349 SE 30th Avenue, Portland, OR 07202-8836, USA (home). *Telephone:* (503) 774-0944 (home).

CARMICHAEL, Jack Blake, BA, PhD; American writer, poet and editor; *President, Dynamics Press*; b. 31 Jan. 1938, Ravenswood, W Va; m. Julie Ann Carmichael 1981; four d. *Education:* Ohio Wesleyan Univ., Michigan State Univ., Univ. of Oregon. *Career:* Ed., Pres. and Publr Dynamics Press 1990–; Fellow, American Int. Coll.; mem. Acad. of American Poets; fmrly in charge of UNIDO environmental programme 1973–89. *Art exhibitions include:* Wheaton Gallery 2008, Turner Dodge Mansion 2008. *Publications include:* fiction: A New Slain Knight 1991, Black Knight 1991, Tales of the Cousin 1992, Memoirs of the Great Gorgeous 1992, The Humpty Boys in Michigan 1996, Hear Me America, with other poems and short stories 1999; other: Industrial

Water Use and Treatment Practices (with Kenneth M. Strzepek) 1987; contrib. of poems to anthologies and journals. *Honours:* Hon. Co-Chair. Business Advisory Council; Outstanding Achievement Award, American Poetry Asscn 1990, Poet of the Year, Materials Dynamics 2003, Nat. Republican Congressional Cttee Leadership Award 2004, Artistic Merit Award, Dynamics Press 2007. *Address:* c/o Dynamics Press, 519 S Rogers Street, Mason, MI 48854, USA (office). *Telephone:* (517) 676-5211 (office); (517) 282-5821 (mobile). *Fax:* (517) 676-5211 (office). *E-mail:* jackbcarmi@prodigy.net (office).

CARNERO, Guillermo, BEcons, PhD; Spanish poet, writer and academic; b. 7 May 1947, Valencia; one s. *Education:* Universitat de Barcelona, Universitat de València. *Career:* Visiting Prof., Univs of Virginia, Berkeley and Harvard, USA, and Universidad Menéndez Pelayo; currently Prof., Universidad de Alicante; fmr Co-Dir of Clásicos Taurus collection; Ed., (Vols 6–8) Historia de la Literatura Española (f. by R. Menéndez Pidal); mem. Editorial Bd Castilla, Dieciocho, Hispanic Review, Ínsula, La Nueva Literatura Hispánica, Studi Ispanici, Voz y Letra literary magazines, and Dir Anales de Literatura Española literary journal; mem. Bd March Foundation, Sociedad Estatal de Conmemoraciones Culturales for centenary of Rafael Alberti, Tres mitos españoles: Don Quijote, Don Juan Tenorio y La Celestina (exhibition at Museo del Prado and Centro Cultural Conde Duque); mem. Real Academia de Cultura Valenciana 2005. *Publications include:* poetry: Dibujo de la muerte 1967, El sueño de Escipión 1971, Variaciones y figuras sobre un tema de La Bruyère 1974, El azar objetivo 1975, Ensayo de una teoría de la visión (Poesía 1966–1977) 1979, Música para fuegos de artificio 1989, Divisibilidad indefinida 1990, Dibujo de la muerte. Obra poética completa 1998, Verano inglés (Premio Nacional de Literatura 2000, Premio Nacional de la Crítica 2000, Premio Fastenrath de la Real Academia Española 2002) 1999, Ut pictura poesis (anthology) 2001, Sepulcros y jardines 2001, Espejo de gran niebla 2002, Poemas arqueológicos 2003, Pensil de nobles doncellas 2005, Fuente de Médicis 2006, Cuatro noches romanas 2009; prose: El grupo 'Cántico' de Córdoba. Un episodio clave en la historia de la poesía española de posguerra 1976 (second enlarged edn 2009), Los orígenes del Romanticismo reaccionario español. El matrimonio Böhl de Faber 1978, La cara oscura del Siglo de las luces 1983, Las armas abisinias. Ensayos sobre literatura y arte del siglo XX 1989, Estudios sobre el teatro español del Siglo XVIII 1997, Espronceda 1999, Poética y poesía 2004, Salvador Dalí y otros estudios sobre arte y vanguardia 2007, Poéticas y entrevistas (1970–2007) 2008, Estudios sobre narrativa y otros temas dieciochescos 2009. *Honours:* Premio de la Crítica Valenciana 2000, 2003, Premio Internacional de Poesía Loewe 2005, Premio de las Letras Valencianas 2008. *Address:* Universidad de Alicante, Dpto de Filología Española, Linguística General y Teoría de la Literatura, Campus de San Vicente del Raspeig, 03690 San Vicente del Raspeig, Alicante, Spain (office). *Telephone:* (96) 5909452 (office). *E-mail:* guillermo.carnero@ua.es (office).

CAROFIGLIO, Giovanni Enrico (Gianrico); Italian novelist, prosecutor and senator; *Senator, Italian Parliament*; b. 30 May 1961, Bari. *Career:* judge in Prato, N Italy; prosecutor in Foggia, S Italy; anti-Mafia prosecutor, Bari; adviser to Anti-Mafia Parl. Cttee; Senator, Italian Parl. *Publications include:* Testimone inconsapevole (trans. as Involuntary Witness) (Marisa Rusconi Prize, Rhegium Julii Award, Città di Cuneo Award, Città di Chiavari Award, Fortunato Seminara Award) 2002, Ad occhi chiusi (trans. as A Walk in the Dark) (Lido di Camaiore Award, Biblioteche di Roma Award) 2003, Il passato è una terra straniera (trans. as The Past is a Foreign Country) (Bancarella Award 2005) 2004, Ragionevoli dubbi (trans. as Reasonable Doubts) (Fregene Award and Viadana Award 2007, Tropea Award 2008) 2006, Cacciatori nelle tenebre 2007, L'arte del dubbio 2007, Né qui né altrove (Bremen Prize Grinzane Cavour Noir Award) 2008, Il paradosso del poliziotto 2009, Le perfezioni provvisorie 2010, Non esiste saggezza (short stories) 2010, La manomissione delle parole (essay) 2010. *Address:* c/o Bitter Lemon Press, 37 Arundel Gardens, London, W11 2LW, England. *E-mail:* books@bitterlemonpress.com.

CARON, Louis; Canadian author, poet and dramatist; b. 1942, Sorel, QC. *Career:* Pres. Union des Écrivains du Québec, mem. Acad. des lettres de Québec 1995–. *Publications include:* L'illusionniste 1973, Le guetteur 1973, L'emmitouflé (Prix Québec, Paris) 1977, (trans. as The Draft-Dodger) 1980, Le Bonhomme sept-heures 1978, Le canard de bois 1981, La corne de brume (Prix Jean, Hamelin) 1982, Racontages 1983, Le Vrai voyage de Jacques Cartier 1984, Marco-Polo-Le nouveau livre des merveilles 1985, La Vie d'artiste 1987, Au fond des mers 1987, Le coup de poing 1990, La tuque et le béret 1992, Le bouleau et l'epinette 1993, Les Chemins du Nord 1995, Terre des Inuit 1997, L'outarde et la palombe (Prix littéraire des professionnels de la documentation 2000) 1999, Le Corps collectionneur 2000, Il n'y a plus d'Amérique 2002, Tête heureuse 2005; other: numerous radio and TV plays. *Honours:* Prix Hermes, France 1977, Prix France-Canada 1977, Prix Ludger-Duvernay 1984, Société Saint-Jean-Baptiste, Montréal 1984.

CARPENTER, Bogdana Maria Magdalena, MA, PhD; American (b. Polish) academic, writer and translator; *Professor Emerita of Slavic Languages and Literatures, University of Michigan, Ann Arbor*; b. 2 June 1941, Czestochowa, Poland; d. of Jozef Chetkowski and Maria Gordon-Chetkowska; m. John Randell Carpenter 1963; one s. one d. *Education:* Univ. of Warsaw, Poland, Univ. of California, Berkeley. *Career:* Acting Asst Prof., Univ. of California, Berkeley 1971–73, Lecturer 1973–74; Asst Prof., Univ. of Washington, Seattle 1974–83; staff reviewer, World Literature Today 1977–; Asst Prof., Univ. of Michigan, Ann Arbor 1983–85, Assoc. Prof. 1985–91, Prof. of Slavic Languages and Literatures 1991–2008, Prof. Emer. 2008–, Chair. Dept of Slavic Languages and Literatures 1991–95, 1998–99, 2006–; Dir Copernicus Foundation 1991–95; mem. Academic Advisory Council, Woodrow Wilson Center, East European Program 1985–90; mem. The Polish Review (Advisory Bd 1993–2007). *Publications include:* The Poetic Avant-Garde in Poland, 1918–1939 1983, Cross Currents: A Yearbook of Central European Culture (assoc. ed.) 1987–93, Monumenta Polonica: The First Four Centuries of Polish Poetry 1989, Czeslaw Milosz' To Begin Where I Am (essays, ed. with Madeleine Levine) 2001; translator: Works by Zbigniew Herbert (with John Carpenter): Selected Poems of Zbigniew Herbert 1977, Report from the Besieged City and Other Poems 1987, Still Life with a Bridle 1991, Mr Cogito 1993, Elegy for Departure and Other Poems 1999, The King of Ants 1999, In Praise of the Unfinished 2008; contrib. to books, scholarly journals and general periodicals. *Honours:* Golden Cross of Merit (Poland) 1999; IREX and Fulbright-Hays Grants for Faculty 1976–77, Poetry Soc. of America Witter Bynner Poetry Trans. Prize 1977, IREX Grant for Sr scholars 1986, Nat. Endowment for the Humanities Trans. grant 1987–88, ACLS Fellowship 1990–91, First Prize, American Council for Polish Culture Clubs 1991, Columbia Univ. Trans. Center Merit Award 1992, Nat. Endowment for the Arts Trans. grant 2006–07. *Address:* Department of Slavic Languages and Literatures, 3040 Modern Languages Building, University of Michigan, Ann Arbor, MI 48109-1275 (office); 1606 Granger, Ann Arbor, MI 48104, USA (home). *Telephone:* (764) 763-5715 (office). *E-mail:* bogdana@umich.edu (office). *Website:* www.lsa.umich.edu/slavic (office).

CARPENTER, Lucas, BS, MA, PhD; American academic, writer, poet and editor; *Charles Howard Candler Professor of English, Oxford College of Emory University*; b. 23 April 1947, Elberton, Ga; m. Judith Leidner 1972; one d. *Education:* Coll. of Charleston, Univ. of North Carolina, Chapel Hill, State Univ. of NY (SUNY), Stony Brook. *Career:* Instructor, SUNY, Stony Brook 1973–78; Instructor, Suffolk Community Coll. 1978–80, Assoc. Prof. of English 1980–85; Assoc. Prof. of English, Oxford Coll. of Emory Univ. 1985–94, Prof. of English 1994–, Charles Howard Candler Prof. of English 2000–, Chair. Humanities Div.; Editorial Consultant, Prentice-Hall Inc. 1981–; Resident Fellow in Poetry and Fiction Writing, Hambidge Center for the Creative Arts 1991; mem. Nat. Council of Teachers of English, Poetry Atlanta, Poetry Soc. of America, Southeast Modern Language Asscn, Poets and Writers. *Publications include:* A Year for the Spider (poems) (UNC Pitcher Poetry Award 1973) 1972, The Selected Poems of John Gould Fletcher (co-ed. with E. Leighton Rudolph) 1988, The Selected Essays of John Gould Fletcher (ed.) 1989, John Gould Fletcher and Southern Modernism 1990, The Selected Correspondence of John Gould Fletcher (co-ed. with E. Leighton Rudolph) 1996, Perils of the Affect (poems) 2002; contrib. to anthologies, scholarly journals and periodicals. *Honours:* Oxford Coll. Prof. of the Year Awards 1994, 1996, 2003, Fulbright Distinguished Scholar, Belgium 1999–2000, Scholar-Teacher of the Year, Emory Univ. 2004. *Address:* Department of English, Oxford College of Emory University, 100 Hamill Street, Oxford, GA 30054, USA (office).

CARR, Sir (Albert) Raymond Maillard, Kt, MA, DLitt, FRSL, FRHistS, FBA; British historian; b. 11 April 1919, Bath, England; s. of Reginald Henry Maillard Carr and Ethel Gertrude Marion Carr; m. Sara Ann Mary Strickland 1950; three s. one d. *Education:* Brockenhurst School and Christ Church, Oxford. *Career:* Gladstone Research Exhibitioner, Christ Church 1941; Fellow, All Souls Coll., Oxford 1946–53, New Coll. 1953–64, St Antony's Coll. 1964–; Dir Latin American Centre 1964–68, Chair. Soc. for Latin American Studies 1966–68; Prof. of History of Latin America, Univ. of Oxford 1967–68, Warden St Antony's Coll. 1968–87; mem. Nat. Theatre Bd 1980; Corresp. mem. Royal Acad. of History, Madrid 1968. *Publications:* Spain 1808–1939 1966, Latin American Affairs (ed.) 1969, The Republic and the Civil War in Spain (ed.) 1971, English Fox Hunting 1976, The Spanish Tragedy: The Civil War in Perspective 1977, Spain: Dictatorship to Democracy (co-author) 1979, Modern Spain 1980, Fox-Hunting (with Sara Carr) 1982, Puerto Rico: A Colonial Experiment 1984, The Spanish Civil War (ed.) 1986, The Chances of Death: A Diary of the Spanish Civil War (ed.) 1995, Visiones de fin de siglo 1999, Spain: A History (ed.) 2001; contrib. to scholarly books and journals. *Honours:* Hon. Fellow, Christ Church Coll., St Antony's Coll., Oxford; Grand Cross of the Order of Alfonso El Sabio (for services to Spanish history) 1983; Hon. DLitt (Madrid); Prince of Asturias Award in Social Sciences 1999. *Address:* 58 Fitzgeorge Avenue, London, W14 0SW, England (home). *Telephone:* (20) 7603-6975 (home).

CARR, Caleb, BA; American writer and historian; b. 2 Aug. 1955, New York, NY. *Education:* Kenyon Coll., New York Univ. *Career:* Visiting Prof. of History, Bard Coll.; Ed. MHQ: The Quarterly Journal of Military History 2005–. *Publications include:* Casing the Promised Land 1980, America Invulnerable: The Quest for Absolute Security, from 1812 to Star Wars (with James Chace) 1988, The Devil Soldier: The Story of Frederick Townsend Ward 1991, The Alienist 1994, The Angel of Darkness 1997, Killing Time 2000, The Mysterious Island 2001, The Lessons of Terror 2002, The Italian Secretary 2005, The Cold War: A Military History (with Stephen E Ambrose, Thomas Fleming and Victor Hanson) 2006; contribs to professional journals, newspapers and periodicals. *Address:* Department of Historical Studies, Bard College, PO Box 5000, Annandale-on-Huston, NY 12504-5000, USA (office). *Telephone:* (845) 758-7296 (office). *E-mail:* carr@bard.edu (office). *Website:* www.bard.edu (office).

CARR, Margaret, (Martin Carroll, Carole Kerr, Belle Jackson); British writer; b. 25 Nov. 1935, Salford, England. *Publications include:* Begotten Murder 1967, Spring into Love 1967, Blood Vengeance 1968, Goodbye is Forever 1968, Too Beautiful to Die 1969, Hear No Evil 1971, Tread Warily at Midnight 1971, Sitting Duck 1972, Who's the Target? 1974, Not for Sale 1975, Shadow of the Hunter 1975, A Time to Surrender 1975, Out of the Past 1976, Love All Start 1977, Twin Tragedy 1977, Lamb to the Slaughter 1978, The Witch of Wykham 1978, Daggers Drawn 1980, Stolen Heart 1981, Sharendel 1987, Blindman's Bluff 1987, Too Close for Comfort 1988, In the Dark of the Day 1988, Valdez's Lady 1989, Innocent Abroad 1989, Wait for the Wake 1989, Deadly Pursuit 1991, Dark Intruder 1991, Learning and Teaching Stories 2000, Assessment in Early Childhood Settings 2001, Heat Of The Moment 2007, Italian Inheritance 2007, Beloved Enemy 2008, A Dark Gentleman 2008, Waiting Time 2009, House in the Pines 2009, A Caring Heart 2011. *Address:* Waverly, Wavering Lane, Gillingham, Dorset, SP8 4NR, England.

CARR, Nicholas George, MA; American writer; b. 1959. *Education:* Dartmouth Coll., Harvard Univ. *Career:* fmr Exec. Ed., Harvard Business Review; fmr columnist, The Guardian; fmr Writer-in-Residence, Univ. of California, Berkeley; writer, Rough Type (blog); mem. Editorial Bd of Advisers, Encyclopaedia Britannica; mem. Steering Bd World Econ. Forum's cloud computing project. *Publications include:* Does IT Matter? Information Technology and the Corrosion of Competitive Advantage 2004, The Big Switch: Rewiring the World, from Edison to Google 2008, The Shallows: What the Internet Is Doing to Our Brains 2010; contrib. articles and essays to The Atlantic, New York Times, Wall Street Journal, Wired, The New Republic, The Times, Financial Times, Die Zeit. *Address:* c/o W. W. Norton & Company, Inc., 500 Fifth Avenue, New York, NY 10110, USA. *Website:* www.nicholasgcarr.com.

CARR, Pat Moore, BA, MA, PhD; American writer and academic; b. 13 March 1932, Grass Creek, Wyo.; d. of Stanley Moore and Bee Moore; m. 1st Jack Esslinger 1955 (divorced 1970); m. 2nd Duane Carr 1971; one s. three d. *Education:* Rice Univ., Tulane Univ. *Career:* teacher, Texas Southern Univ. 1956–58, Univ. of New Orleans 1961, 1965–69, 1987–88, Univ. of Texas at El Paso 1969–79, Univ. of Arkansas at Little Rock 1983, 1986–87, Western Kentucky Univ. 1988–96; mem. Int. Women's Writing Guild (Bd mem. 1996–), Texas Inst. of Letters 1991, PEN, Authors' Guild 2004. *Publications include:* fiction: The Grass Creek Chronicle 1976, Bluebirds 1993, Beneath the Hill 1999, If We Must Die 2002, Border Ransom 2006; short story collections: From Beneath the Hill of the Three Crosses (South and West Fiction Chapbook Award) 1969, The Women in the Mirror (Iowa Short Fiction Award) 1977, Night of the Luminarias (Austin Council for the Arts Award) 1986, Sonahchi 1988, Death of a Confederate Colonel 2007; criticism: Bernard Shaw 1976, Mimbres Mythology 1979, In Fine Spirits (Arkansas Endowment Award) 1986, Writing Fiction with Pat Carr 2010, One Page at a time: On a Writing Life 2010; contrib. of articles and short stories to numerous publs, including The Southern Review, Best American Short Stories. *Honours:* Library of Congress Marc IV Award for Short Fiction 1970, Nat. Endowment for the Humanities Award 1973, Texas Inst. of Letters Short Story Award 1978, Arkansas Endowment for the Humanities Award 1985, Green Mountain Short Fiction Award 1986, First Stage Drama Award 1990, Al Smith Fellowship in Fiction 1995, Chateau de Lavigny Writing Fellowship 1999, Judy and A.C. Greene Literary Award 2000, Texas Council of the Arts Literary Award 2000, PEN Southwest Fiction Award 2007, John Estes Cook Fiction Award 2007. *Address:* 10695 Venice Road, Elkins, AR 72727, USA (home). *Telephone:* (479) 643-3647 (home). *E-mail:* patcarr313@aol.com (home).

CARR, Roberta (see Roberts, Irene)

CARRÈRE, Emmanuel; French writer, screenwriter and director; b. 9 Dec. 1957, Paris; s. of Hélène Carrère d'Encausse; m.; two c. *Television:* Léon Morin prêtre (adaptation) 1991, Monsieur Ripois (adaptation) 1993, Le Blanc à lunettes (adaptation) 1995, Pêcheur d'Islande (adaptation) 1996, Les Clients d'Avrenos (adaptation) 1996, Denis (with others) 1998, Désiré Landru (story) 2005. *Films:* La Classe de neige (screenplay, with Claude Miller) (Prix spécial du jury, Cannes Film Festival) 1998, Retour à Kotelnitch (screenplay, also dir) 2003, La Moustache (screenplay, also dir) 2005. *Publications include:* Werner Herzog (essay) 1982, L'Amie du jaguar 1983, Bravoure 1984, La Moustache 1986, Le Détroit de Behring 1986, Hors d'atteinte? 1988, Je suis vivant et vous êtes morts (biog.) 1993, La Class de neige (Prix Fémina) 1995, L'Adversaire 2000, Facciamo un gioco 2004, Un Roman Russe 2007, D'autres vies que la mienne 2009, Limonov (Prix Renaudot 2011) 2011. *Address:* c/o P.O.L. Editeur, 33 rue Saint-André-des-Arts, 75006 Paris, France (office).

CARRÈRE D'ENCAUSSE, Hélène, DèsSc; French political scientist; *Secretary for Life, Académie Française*; b. 6 July 1929, Paris; d. of Georges Zourabichvili and Nathalie von Pelken; m. Louis Carrère 1952; one s. two d. *Education:* Univ. of Paris, Sorbonne. *Career:* fmr Prof., Univ. of Paris (Sorbonne); currently Prof., Inst. d'Etudes Politiques, Paris and Dir of Research, Fondation Nationale des Sciences Politiques; Pres. Radio Sorbonne-Radio France 1984–87; Advisor on Reconstruction and Devt, European Bank 1992; fmr mem. Bd of Dirs East-West Inst. for Security Studies; Visiting Prof. at numerous univs in USA; mem. Acad. Française, Sec. for Life 2000–; Foreign mem. Russian Acad. of Sciences 2003–, Acad. of Georgia; Assoc. mem. Acad. Royale de Belgique; mem. European Parl. 1994–99; fmr Vice-Pres. Comm. on Foreign Affairs and Defence, on French Diplomatic Archives; mem. Nat. Council for New Devts in Human and Social Sciences 1998; Pres. Statistical Observatory on Immigration and Integration 2004. *Publications include:* Le marxisme et l'Asie 1965, Réforme et révolution chez les musulmans de l'Empire russe 1966, L'URSS et la Chine devant les révolutions dans les sociétés pré-industrielles 1970, L'Empire éclaté (Prix Aujourd'hui) 1978, Lénine: la révolution et le pouvoir 1979, Staline: l'ordre par la terreur 1979, Le pouvoir confisqué 1982, Le Grand Frère 1983, La déstalinisation commence 1984, Ni paix ni guerre 1986, Le Grand Défi: bolcheviks et nations 1917–30 1987, Le Malheur russe 1988, La Gloire des nations ou la fin de l'Empire soviétique 1991, Victorieuse Russie 1992, Nicholas II: la transition interrompue (Prix des Ambassadeurs) 1996, Lénine 1998, La Russie inachevée 2000, Catherine II 2002, L'Impératrice et l'abbé un duel littéraire ivédit 2003, L'Empire d'Eurasie 2005, La Deuxième Mort de Staline 2006. *Honours:* Hon. mem. Acad. of Georgia; Grand-Croix de la Légion d'honneur 2011, Officier, Ordre nat. du Mérite; Dr hc (Montréal, Louvain); Prix de la Fondation Louis-Weiss 1986, Prix Comenius 1992. *Address:* Académie Française, 23 quai Conti, 75270 Paris Cedex 06 – CS 90618, France (office). *Telephone:* 1-44-41-43-00 (office). *Fax:* 1-43-29-47-45 (office). *E-mail:* contact@academie-francaise.fr (office). *Website:* www.academie-francaise.fr (office).

CARRIER, Roch, OC, BA, MA; Canadian author, dramatist and poet; b. 13 May 1937, Sainte-Justine-de-Dorchester, QC; m. Diane Gosselin 1959, two d. *Education:* Collège Saint-Louis, Univ. of Montréal, Sorbonne, Univ. of Paris. *Career:* teacher, Collège Militaire, St-Jean 1964–70, Dir French Dept 1973–80; teacher, Université de Montréal 1970–71; Sec.-Gen., Théatre du Nouveau Monde, Montréal 1971–73; Dir, Canada Council 1994–97; Nat. Librarian of Canada 1997. *Publications include:* poetry: Les Jeux incompris 1956, Cherche tes mots, cherche tes pas 1958; fiction: Jolis deuils (Prix Littéraire de la Province de Québec 1965) 1964, La guerre, yes sir! 1968, Floralie, ou es-tu? (trans. Floralie, Where Are You?) 1969, Il est par la le soleil (trans. Is it the Sun, Philibert?) 1970, Le deux-millième é'tage (trans. They Won't Demolish Me!) 1973, Le jardin des délices (trans. The Garden of Delights) 1975, Les enfants du bonhomme dans la lune (trans. The Hockey Sweater and Other Stories) 1979, Il n'y a pas de pays sans grand-père (trans. No Country Without Grandfathers) 1979, Les fleurs vivent-elles ailleurs que sur la terre 1980, La dame qui avait des chaines aux cheville 1981, De l'amour dans la feraille (trans. Heartbreaks Along the Road) 1984, La fleur et autres personnages 1985, Prières d'un enfant très très sage (Stephen Leacock Memorial Medal for Humour 1992) 1988, L'homme dans le placard 1991, Une Bonne et heureuse annee 1991, Fin 1992, The Longest Home Run 1993, Petit homme tornade 1996, Une chaise 1999, Our Life with the Rocket 2001, Les moines dans la tour 2004; plays: La celeste bicyclette (trans. The Celestial Bycycle) 1980, Le cirque noir 1982, L'ours et le kangourou 1986; other: various poems. *Honours:* Grand Prix Littéraire de la Ville de Montréal 1980, Québec Writer of the Year 1981.

CARRIER, Warren Pendleton, AB, MA, PhD; American academic, writer and poet; b. 3 July 1918, Cheviot, Ohio; m. 1st Marjorie Jane Regan 1947 (deceased); one s.; m. 2nd Judy Lynn Hall 1973; one s. *Education:* Wabash Coll., Miami Univ., Oxford, OH, Harvard Univ., Occidental Coll. *Career:* instructor in Romance languages, Univ. of North Carolina 1942–44; Founder-Ed. Quarterly Review of Literature 1943–44; Assoc. Ed., Western Review 1949–51; instructor, Boston Univ. 1945–49; Asst Prof., Univ. of Iowa 1949–52; Assoc. Prof., Bard Coll. 1953–57; Faculty mem., Bennington Coll. 1955–58; Visiting Prof., Sweet Briar Coll. 1958–60; Prof., Deep Springs Coll., Calif. 1960–62, Portland State Univ., Ore. 1962–64; Prof. and Chair. Dept of English, Univ. of Montana 1964–68; Assoc. Dean, Prof. of English and Comparative Literature and Chair. Dept of Comparative Literature, Livingston Coll., Rutgers Univ. 1968–69; Dean Coll. of Arts and Letters, San Diego State Univ. 1969–72; Vice-Pres. Academic Affairs, Univ. of Bridgeport, Conn. 1972–75; Chancellor Univ. of Wisconsin, Platteville 1975–82, Chancellor Emer. 1982–. *Publications include:* Desire for Death 1942, City Stopped in Time 1949, The Hunt 1952, The Cost of Love 1953, Reading Modern Poetry (co-ed.) 1955, Bay of the Damned 1957, Toward Montebello 1966, Leave Your Sugar for the Cold Morning 1977, Guide to World Literature (ed.) 1980, Literature from the World (co-ed.) 1981, The Diver 1986, Death of a Chancellor 1986, An Honorable Spy 1992, Murder at the Strawberry Festival 1993, An Ordinary Man 1997, Death of a Poet 1999, Risking the Wind 2000, Justice at Christmas 2000, Coming to Terms 2004; contrib. to periodicals. *Honours:* Nat. Foundation for the Arts Award for Poetry 1971, Collady Prize for Poetry 1986. *Address:* 69 Colony Park Circle, Galveston, TX 77551, USA (home).

CARRIÈRE, Jean-Claude; French writer and screenwriter; b. 19 Sept. 1931, Colombières-sur-Orb, Hérault, Languedoc-Roussillon; s. of Felix Carrière and Alice Carrière; m. Nicole Carrière 1952; one c . *Film screenplays:* Rupture 1961, Le Soupirant 1962, Le Journal d'une femme de chambre 1964, Le Bestiaire d'amour 1965, Yoyo 1965, Viva María! 1965, Miss Muerte 1966, Tant qu'on a la santé 1966, Cartes sur table 1966, Hotel Paradiso 1966, Le Voleur 1967, Belle de jour 1967, Pour un amour lointain 1968, La Pince à ongles 1969, La Voie lactée 1969, Le Grand amour 1969, Borsalino 1970, L'Alliance 1971, Taking Off 1971, Le Droit d'aimer 1972, Le Charme discret de la bourgeoisie 1972, Un homme est mort 1972, Le Moine 1973, Dorotheas Rache 1974, France société anonyme 1974, Le Fantôme de la liberté 1974, La Femme aux bottes rouges 1974, Sérieux comme le plaisir 1975, La Chair de l'orchidée 1975, Der Dritte Grad 1975, Leonor 1975, Les Oeufs brouillés 1976, Le Diable dans la boîte 1977, Le Gang 1977, Julie pot de colle 1977, Cet obscur objet du désir 1977, Le Franc-tireur 1978, Un papillon sur l'épaule 1978, Photo-souvenir 1978, Chaussette surprise 1978, Slachtvee 1979, L'Homme en colère 1979, Retour à la bien-aimée 1979, Die Blechtrommel 1979, L'Associé 1979, Sauve qui peut (la vie) 1980, Lundi 1980, Le Bouffon 1981, Black Mirror 1981, Die Fälschung 1981, La Double vie de Théophraste Longuet 1981, Je tue il 1982, L'Accompagnateur 1982, Le Retour de Martin Guerre 1982, L'Indiscrétion 1982, Antonieta 1982, Credo 1983, Danton 1983, Itinéraire bis 1983, Le Jardinier récalcitrant 1983, Il Generale dell'armata morte 1983, La Joven y la tentación 1984, L'Aide-mémoire 1984, Un amour de Swann 1984, Les Étonnements d'un couple moderne 1985, Auto défense 1985, Les Exploits d'un jeune Don Juan 1987, La Nuit Bengali 1988, The Unbearable Lightness of Being 1988, Une femme tranquille 1989, J'écris dans l'espace 1989, Bouvard et Pecuchet 1989, Valmont 1989, Milou en mai 1990, Es ist nicht leicht ein Gott zu sein 1990, Cyrano de Bergerac 1990, At Play in the Fields of the Lord 1991, La Controverse de Valladolid 1992, Le Retour de Casanova 1992, The Night and the Moment 1995, Le Hussard sur le toit 1995, Une femme explosive 1996, Golden Boy 1996, Der Unhold 1996, L'Associé 1996, Les Paradoxes de Buñuel 1997, Chinese Box 1997, Clarissa 1998, La Guerre dans le Haut Pays 1999, Salsa 2000, Rien, voilà l'ordre 2003, Birth 2004, Galilée ou L'amour de Dieu 2005, Marie-Antoinette 2006, Goya's Ghosts 2006, Ulzhan 2007. *Television writing:* Robinson Crusoé (series) 1964, The Mahabharata (mini-series) 1989, Associations de bienfaiteurs (mini-series) 1995, Ruy Blas (play) 2002, Les Thibault (mini-series) 2003, Marie-Antoinette 2006. *Film and television appearances:* Insomnie 1963, Le Journal d'une femme de chambre 1964, Les cocardiers 1967, La Voie lactée 1969, L'Alliance 1971, Un peu de soleil dans l'eau froide 1971, La chute d'un corps 1973, Serieux comme le plaisir 1974, Le Jardin des supplices 1976, Le Jeu du solitaire 1976, Julie pot de colle 1977, Photo-souvenir 1978, Chaussette surprise 1978, Ils sont grands, ces petits 1979, L'Amour nu 1981, La Double vie de Théophraste Longuet 1981, L'Écarteur 1982, L'Homme de la nuit (TV series) 1983, Vive les femmes! 1984, Sueurs froides (episode of À la mémoire d'un ange) 1988, Bouvard et Pecuchet (voice) 1989, Eugénie Grandet (voice) 1994, The Night and the Moment 1995, Le Parfum de Jeannette (voice) 1996, Jaya Ganga 1998, Buñuel y la mesa del rey Salomón 2001, Madame de … 2001, Les Thibault (TV series) 2003, Tajnata kniga 2003, Avida 2006. *Films:* Heureux anniversaire (producer) 1962, La Pince à ongles (dir) 1969, L'Unique (dir) 1986. *Publications include:* novels: Le lezard 1957, Monsieur Hulot's Holiday 1959, L'Alliance 1971, Le clou brulant 1972, Le pari 1973, Mon Oncle 1974, Harold et Maude 1974, Le carnaval et la politique 1979, Please Mr Einstein (with John Brownjohn) 2006; plays: The Mahabharata 1989, Milou in May 1990, Chinese Box and a Film-maker's Diary 1998, The Little Black Book 2003, The Controversy of Valladolid 2005; non-fiction: The Secret Language of Film 1994, Violence and Compassion (with The Dalai Lama) 2001. *Address:* 190 rue Grenelle, 75007 Paris, France (home). *Telephone:* 1-44-18-93-27 (home).

CARRINGTON, Ruth (see James, Michael Leonard)

CARROLL, Jenny (see Cabot, Meggin (Meg) Patricia)

CARROLL, Martin (see Carr, Margaret)

CARROLL, Steven Kenneth, BA; Australian author; b. 20 Nov. 1949, Melbourne, Vic.; s. of William Francis Carroll and Jean Irene Carroll (née Williams); pnr Fiona Capp; one s. *Education:* La Trobe Univ. *Career:* fmr English teacher in secondary schools; fmr rock musician; fmr Lecturer, RMIT Univ., Melbourne; fmr Drama Critic, The Age newspaper. *Publications include:* novels: Remember Me, Jimmy James 1992, Momoko 1994, The Love Song of Lucy McBride 1998, The Art of the Engine Driver 2001, The Gift Of Speed 2004, The Time We Have Taken (Commonwealth Writers' Prize 2008, Miles Franklin Literary Award 2008) 2007, Lovers' Room 2007, Twilight in Venice 2008, The Lost Life 2009. *Literary Agent:* Sheil Land Associates Ltd, 52 Doughty Street, London, WC1N 2LS, England. *Telephone:* (20) 7405-9351. *Fax:* (20) 7831-2127. *E-mail:* info@sheilland.co.uk. *Address:* HarperCollins Publicity, PO Box 321, Pymble, NSW 2073, Australia. *Telephone:* (2) 9952-5000. *Fax:* (2) 9952-5555. *Website:* www.harpercollins.com.au.

CARRUTHERS, Peter Michael, MPhil, DPhil; British philosopher, academic and writer; *Professor of Philosophy, University of Maryland*; b. 16 June 1952, Manila, Philippines; m. Susan Levi 1978; two s. *Education:* Univ. of Leeds, Balliol Coll., Oxford. *Career:* Lecturer, Univ. of St Andrews 1979–81, Queens Univ., Belfast 1981–83, Univ. of Essex 1985–91; Visiting Assoc. Prof., Univ. of Michigan, USA 1989–90; Sr Lecturer, Univ. of Sheffield 1991–92, Prof. 1992–2001, Founder and fmr Dir Hang Seng Centre for Cognitive Studies; Prof. of Philosophy, Univ. of Maryland 2001–, Chair., Dept of Philosophy 2001–08; mem. Aristotelian Soc., Cognitive Science Colloquium, Univ. of Maryland. *Publications include:* The Metaphysics of the Tractatus 1990, Introducing Persons: Theories and Arguments in the Philosophy of Mind 1991, Human Knowledge and Human Nature: A New Introduction to the Ancient Debate 1992, The Animals Issue: Moral Theory in Practice 1992, Language, Thought and Consciousness 1996, Phenomenal Consciousness 2000, The Nature of the Mind 2004, Consciousness 2005, The Architecture of the Mind 2006; contribs to journals. *Address:* Department of Philosophy, University of Maryland, 1125 Skinner, College Park, MD 20742, USA (office). *Telephone:* (301) 270-5107 (office). *Fax:* (301) 405-5705 (office). *E-mail:* pcarruth@umd.edu (office). *Website:* www.philosophy.umd.edu/Faculty/pcarruthers (office).

CARSON, Anne, BA, MA, PhD; Canadian academic, poet and writer; *Professor, Department of English, University of Michigan*; b. 21 June 1950, Toronto, Ont. *Education:* St Michael's Coll., Univ. of Toronto, Univ. of St Andrews, Scotland. *Career:* Prof. of Classics, Univ. of Calgary 1979–80, Princeton Univ. 1980–87, Emory Univ. 1987–88; fmr John MacNaughton Prof. of Classics, McGill Univ. and Dir of Grad. Studies, Classics; currently Prof., Dept of English, Univ. of Michigan; Guggenheim Fellowship 1999; John D. and Catherine T. MacArthur Foundation Fellowship 2001; Anna-Maria Kellen Fellow, American Acad., Berlin, Germany 2007. *Publications include:* Eros the Bittersweet: An Essay 1986, Short Talks 1992, Plainwater 1995, Glass, Irony and God 1995, Autobiography of Red 1998, Economy of the Unlost 1999, Men in the Off Hours (Griffin Poetry Prize 2001) 2000, The Beauty of the Husband (Poetry Book Soc. T. S. Eliot Prize 2001) 2001, Sophocles' Electra 2001, If Not, Winter: Fragments of Sappho (trans.) 2002, Decreation 2005, Grief Lessons: Four Plays by Euripides (trans.) 2006, An Oresteia (trans.) (PEN Award for Poetry in Translation 2010) 2009, Nox 2010, Antigonick 2012; contribs to anthologies and journals. *Honours:* Lannan Literary Award 1996, Pushcart Prize for Poetry 1997. *Address:* Department of English, University of Michigan, 435 South State Street, 3143 Angell Hall, Ann Arbor, MI 48109, USA (office); 5900 Esplanade Avenue, Montréal, PQ H2T 3A3, Canada (home). *Telephone:* (734) 763-2265 (office). *E-mail:* carsona@umich.edu (office); decreation@hotmail.com (home). *Website:* www.lsa.umich.edu/english (office).

CARSON, Ciaran, BA; Northern Irish poet; *Director, Seamus Heaney Centre for Poetry and Professor of Poetry, Queen's University Belfast*; b. 9 Oct. 1948, Belfast; m. Deidre Shannon 1982; two s. one d. *Education:* Queen's Univ., Belfast. *Career:* Traditional Arts Officer, Arts Council of Northern Ireland 1975–98; Prof. of Poetry, Dir, Seamus Heaney Centre for Poetry, Queen's Univ., Belfast. *Publications include:* poetry: The New Estate 1976, The Lost Explorer 1978, Irish Traditional Music 1986, The Irish For No (Alice Hunt Bartlett Award) 1987, Belfast Confetti (Irish Times Irish Literature Prize for Poetry) 1990, First Language: Poems (T. S. Eliot Prize) 1993, Belfast Frescoes (with John Kindness) 1995, Letters from the Alphabet 1995, Opera Et Cetera 1996, The Alexandrine Plan (adaptations of other poets' sonnets) 1998, The Ballad of HMS Belfast: A Compendium of Belfast Poems 1999, The Twelfth of Never 1999, Breaking News (Forward Poetry Prize for best poetry collection) 2003, The Midnight Court: A New Translation of Cúirt An Mheán Oíche by Brian Merriman 2005, The Táin: Translated from the Old Irish Epic Táin Bó Cúailnge 2007, For All I Know 2008, Collected Poems 2009, Until Before After 2010; prose: Last Night's Fun: About Time, Food and Music 1996, The Star Factory (Yorkshire Post Book Award for Book of the Year) 1997, Fishing for Amber 1999, Shamrock Tea (novel) 2001, The Inferno of Dante Alighieri (Trans.) 2002, The Pen Friend 2009; contrib. to TLS, New Yorker, Irish Review, Honest Ulsterman, London Review of Books. *Honours:* Eric Gregory Award 1978, Cholmondeley Award 2003. *Address:* Seamus Heaney Centre for Poetry, Queen's University, Belfast, BT7 1NN, NI (office). *Telephone:* (28) 9097-1074. *E-mail:* c.carson@qub.ac.uk (office). *Website:* www.qub.ac.uk/schools/SeamusHeaneyCentreforPoetry (office).

CARSON, Paul, BA, MB, BChir, BAO; Northern Irish doctor and novelist; *Medical Director, Slievemore Clinic*; b. 1949, Belfast, Co. Down. *Education:* Garron Tower School, Trinity Coll., Dublin. *Career:* Medical Dir, Slievemore Clinic, Dublin 1984–. *Publications include:* novels: Scalpel 1997, Cold Steel 1999, Final Duty 2000, Ambush 2004, Betrayal 2005; also five health books, two children's books, and numerous medical publications. *Address:* c/o William Heinemann, Random House UK Ltd, 20 Vauxhall Bridge Road, London, SW1V 2SA, England. *Website:* www.randomhouse.co.uk (office); www.paul.carson.net.

CARTANO, Tony, LèsL, DipES; French author and editor; b. 27 July 1944, Bayonne; m. Françoise Perrin 1966; one s. one d. *Education:* Univ. of Paris. *Career:* Dir Foreign Dept, Éditions Albin Michel, Paris. *Publications include:* Le Single Hurteur 1978, Malcolm Lowry (essay) 1979, Blackbird 1980, La Sourde Oreille 1982, Bocanegra 1985, Stockholm 1987, Schmutz 1987, Le Bel Arturo 1989, Le soufflé de Satan 1991, American Boulevard (travel book) 1992, Mister Sax 1999, Un dernier soir avant la fin du monde 2000, Milonga 2004. *Honours:* Chevalier, Ordre des Arts et des Lettres. *Address:* Éditions Albin Michel, 22 rue Huyghens, 75014 Paris, France (office). *Telephone:* 1-42-79-10-00 (office). *Fax:* 1-43-27-21-58 (office). *Website:* www.albin-michel.fr (office).

CĂRTĂRESCU, Mircea, PhD; Romanian poet and novelist; b. 1 June 1956, Bucharest; m. Ioana Nicolaie. *Education:* Dimitrie Cantemir High School, Univ. of Bucharest. *Career:* teacher of Romanian language and literature, Bucharest 1980–89; fmr Ed. Contrapunct literary journal; Assoc. Prof. of Romanian Literature, Univ. of Bucharest 1991–; Visiting Prof., Univ. of Amsterdam, Netherlands 1994–95; mem. Romanian Writers' Union, PEN Romania, ASPRO. *Publications include:* poetry: Faruri, vitrine, fotografii (Romanian Writers' Union Literary Debut Prize) 1980, Aer cu diamante 1982, Poeme de amor 1983, Totul 1985, Levantul (Romanian Writers' Union Prize) 1990, Dragostea 1994, Double CD 1998; fiction: Desant '83 1983, Visul (Romanian Acad. Prize) 1989, Travesti (Romanian Writers' Union Prize, ASPRO) 1994, Orbitor (ASPRO Prize) 1996, Corpul 2002, Enciclopedia zmeilor 2002, De ce iubim femeile 2004, Aripa dreapta 2007; essay: Visul chimeric 1992, Postmodernismul romanesc 1999; other: Antologia poeziei gene 1995, Generatia '80 1999. *Honours:* Flacara Prize 1990, Ateneu Prize 1996, Medicis Prize 1992, Prize of the Best Foreign Book 1992, Prize of the Union 1992, LatineCuvântul prize 1997. *Address:* Department of Romanian

Literature, Faculty of Letters, University of Bucharest, Str Edgar Quinet nr 5–7, Sector 1, Bucharest, Romania (office). *E-mail:* info@unibuc.ro (office).

CARTER, (Edward) Graydon; Canadian magazine editor; *Editor-in-Chief, Vanity Fair;* b. 14 July 1949, s. of E.P. Carter and Margaret Ellen Carter; m. 2nd Cynthia Williamson 1982 (divorced 2000); four c.; m. Anna Scott 2005; one d. *Education:* Carleton Univ., Univ. of Ottawa. *Career:* Ed. Canadian Review 1973–77; writer, Time 1978–83, Life 1983–86; Founder, Ed. Spy 1986–91; Ed. New York Observer 1991–92; Ed.-in-Chief, Vanity Fair 1992–; Co-owner Waverly Inn, Monkey Bar. *Television as executive producer:* 9/11 (CBS) (Emmy Award, Peabody Award) 2002. *Film as producer:* The Kid Stays in the Picture 2002. *Publications:* Vanity Fair's Hollywood (ed.) 2000, Tom Ford: Ten Years (co-author) 2004, What We"e Lost 2004, Oscar Night: 75 Years of Hollywood Parties (ed.) 2004, Spy - The Funny Years (co-author, ed.) 2006, Vanity Fair Portraits (ed.) 2008, Vintage Postcards from Vanity Fair: One Hundred Classic Covers, 1913-1936 2011. *Honours:* Hon. Ed. Harvard Lampoon 1989; Advertising Age Editor of the Year 1996, Nat. Magazine Award for Gen. Excellence 1997, 1999, Nat. Magazine Award for Photography 2000, 2002, Nat. Magazine Award for Reviews and Criticism 2003. *Address:* Vanity Fair, Condé Nast Building, 4 Times Square, New York, NY 10036-6522, USA (office). *E-mail:* letters@vf.com (office). *Website:* www.vanityfair.com (office).

CARTER, James (Jimmy) Earl, Jr, BSc; American politician, international political consultant, farmer and fmr head of state; *Chairman, Carter Center;* b. 1 Oct. 1924, Plains, Ga; s. of the late James Earl Carter, Sr and Lillian Gordy; m. Eleanor Rosalynn Smith 1946; three s. one d. *Education:* Plains High School, Georgia Southwestern Coll., Georgia Inst. of Tech., US Naval Acad., Annapolis, Md, Union Coll., New York State. *Career:* served in USN 1946–53, attained rank of Lt (submarine service); peanut farmer, warehouseman 1953–77, businesses include Carter Farms, Carter Warehouses, Plains, Ga; State Senator, Ga 1962–66; Gov. of Georgia 1971–74; Pres. of USA 1977–81; Distinguished Prof., Emory Univ., Atlanta 1982–; leader of int. observer teams Panama 1989, Nicaragua 1990, Dominican Repub. 1990, Haiti 1990; hosted peace negotiations in Ethiopia 1989; visited Democratic People's Repub. of Korea (in pvt. capacity) June 1994; negotiator in Haitian crisis Sept. 1994; visit to Bosnia Dec. 1994; f. Carter Presidential Center 1982; est. Jimmy and Rosalynn Carter Work Project for Habitat for Humanity International 1984; Chair. Bd of Trustees, Carter Center Inc. 1986–, Carter-Menil Human Rights Foundation 1986–, Global 2000 Inc. 1986–, Council of Freely Elected Heads of Govt 1986–, Council of Int. Negotiation Network 1991–; mem. Sumter Co., Ga, School Bd 1955–62 (Chair. 1960–62), Americus and Sumter Co. Hosp. Authority 1956–70, Sumter Co. Library Bd 1961; Pres. Plains Devt Corpn 1963; Georgia Planning Asscn 1968; Dir Ga Crop Improvement Asscn 1957–63 (Pres. 1961); Chair. West Cen. Ga Area Planning and Devt Comm. 1964; State Chair. March of Dimes 1968–70; Dist Gov. Lions Club 1968–69; Chair. Congressional Campaign Cttee, Democratic Nat. Cttee 1974; Democrat. *Publications:* Why Not the Best? 1975, A Government as Good as Its People 1977, Keeping Faith: Memoirs of a President 1982, The Blood of Abraham: Insights into the Middle East 1985, Everything to Gain: Making the Most of the Rest of Your Life 1987, An Outdoor Journal 1988, Turning Point: A Candidate, a State and a Nation Come of Age 1992, Always a Reckoning (poems) 1995, Sources of Strength 1997, The Virtues of Ageing 1998, An Hour Before Daylight 2001, The Hornet's Nest (novel) 2003, Our Endangered Values 2005, Palestine: Peace Not Apartheid 2006, We Can Have Peace in the Holy Land: A Plan that Will Work 2009, White House Diary 2010. *Honours:* several hon. degrees; Ansel Adams Conservation Award, Wilderness Society 1982, World Methodist Peace Award 1984, Albert Schweitzer Prize for Humanitarianism 1987, Onassis Foundation Award 1991, Notre Dame Univ. Award 1992, Matsunaga Medal of Peace 1993, J. William Fulbright Prize for Int. Understanding 1994, shared Houphouët Boigny Peace Prize, UNESCO 1995, UNICEF Int. Child Survival Award (jtly with Rosalynn Carter) 1999, Presidential Medal of Freedom 1999, Eisenhower Medallion 2000, Nobel Peace Prize 2002. *Address:* The Carter Center, 453 Freedom Parkway, 1 Copenhill Avenue NE, Atlanta, GA 30307, USA (office). *Telephone:* (404) 420-5100 (office). *Fax:* (404) 420-5196 (office). *E-mail:* carterweb@emory.edu (office). *Website:* www.cartercenter.org (office).

CARTER, Robert Ayres, AB; American writer and lecturer; b. 16 Sept. 1923, Omaha, Neb.; m. Reade Johnson 1983; two s. *Education:* New School for Social Research, New York. *Career:* mem. Poets and Writers, Mystery Writers of America, Int. Asscn of Crime Writers; Life mem. The Players. *Publications include:* Manhattan Primitive 1972, Written in Blood (aka Casual Slaughters) 1992, Final Edit 1994, Buffalo Bill Cody: The Man Behind the Legend 2002, The Language of Stones 2004, Flying to Calcutta 2005, The Giants' Dance 2005, Sunday's Child 2005, Whitemantle 2006, September Song 2007, Nobody Yet Knows Who I Am 2007, Tell Me The Truth About Love 2008, Somewhere I Have Never Traveled: Memories of A Writer's Life 1969–1976 2010; three textbooks; contrib. to Publishers Weekly, International Journal of Book Publishing. *Honours:* Fulbright Scholar 1949.

CARTER, Stephen Lisle, BA, JD; American academic and lawyer; *William Nelson Cromwell Professor of Law, Yale University;* b. 1954, Washington, DC; m.; c. *Education:* Stanford and Yale Univs. *Career:* fmr Note Ed. Yale Law Journal; admitted to Bar, Washington, DC 1981; law clerk, Judge Spottswood W. Robinson III, US Court of Appeal, Washington, DC 1979–80; law clerk, Justice Thurgood Marshall, US Supreme Court 1980–81; Assoc. Shea & Gardner, Washington, DC 1981–82; Asst Prof. of Law, Yale Univ. 1982–84, Assoc. Prof. 1984–85, Prof. 1986–91, William Nelson Cromwell Prof. of Law 1991–; Official Adviser to US Pres. Bill Clinton 1993. *Publications include:* Reflections of an Affirmative Action Baby 1991, The Culture of Disbelief 1993, The Confirmation Mess 1994, Integrity 1996, The Dissent of the Governed 1998, Civility 1998, God's Name in Vain 2000, The Emperor of Ocean Park 2002, New England White 2007, Palace Council 2008, Jericho's Fall 2009, The Impeachment of Abraham Lincoln 2012. *Honours:* Hon. LLD (Univ. of Notre Dame) 1996. *Address:* c/o Gabrielle Brooks, Knopf Publishing (Author Mail), 1745 Broadway, New York, NY 10019 (office); Yale Law School, POB 208215, New Haven, CT 06520, USA (office). *E-mail:* stephen.carter@yale.edu (office). *Website:* www.law.yale.edu/outside/html/home/index.htm (office); www.stephencarterbooks.com.

CARTWRIGHT, Justin, (Suzy Crispin, Penny Sutton), MBE; British writer; b. 1933, South Africa; m. Penny Cartwright; two s. *Education:* Univ. of Oxford. *Career:* started career as copywriter 1972; directed several TV commercials and documentaries. *Publications include:* Fighting Men 1977, The Revenge 1978, The Horse of Darius 1980, Freedom for the Wolves 1983, Interior 1988, Look at it This Way 1990, Masai Dreaming 1993, In Every Face I Meet (Commonwealth Writers Prize) 1995, Not Yet Home 1996, Leading the Cheers (Whitbread Novel of the Year) 1998, Half in Love 2002, White Lightning 2002, The Promise of Happiness (Hawthornden Prize 2005, Sunday Times Fiction Award, South Africa 2005) 2004, The Song Before It Is Sung 2007, This Secret Garden: Oxford Revisited 2008, To Heaven by Water 2009, Other People's Money 2011. *Literary Agent:* c/o James Gill, United Agents, 12–26 Lexington Street, London, W1F 0LE, England. *Telephone:* (20) 3214-0887. *E-mail:* jgill@unitedagents.co.uk; lhughesyoung@unitedagents.co.uk. *Website:* www.unitedagents.co.uk.

CARVALHO, Bernardo; Brazilian writer and journalist; b. 1960, Rio de Janeiro. *Career:* fmr Ed. Folhetim (newspaper supplement); fmr Paris and New York Corresp., Folha de São Paulo. *Publications include:* novels: Onze 1995, Os Bêbados e os Sonâmbulos 1996, Teatro 1998, As Iniciais 1999, Medo de Sade 2000, Nove Noites 2002, Mongólia 2003, O Sol se Põe em São Paulo 2007, O Filho da Mãe 2009; short stories: Aberração 1993. *Literary Agent:* c/o Laurence Laluyaux, Rogers, Coleridge and White, 20 Powis Mews, London, W11 1JN, England. *Telephone:* (20) 7221-3717. *Fax:* (20) 7229-9084. *E-mail:* info@rcwlitagency.com. *Website:* www.rcwlitagency.com.

CARWARDINE, Richard John, BA, MA, DPhil, FBA, FRHistS; British historian, academic and writer; *President, Corpus Christi College, Oxford;* b. 12 Jan. 1947, Cardiff, Wales; s. of John Francis Carwardine and Beryl Carwardine; m. Linda Margaret Kirk 1975. *Education:* Univ. of Oxford. *Career:* Lecturer, Univ. of Sheffield, later Sr Lecturer, Reader, Prof. 1971–2002; Visiting Prof., Syracuse Univ. NY, USA 1974–75; Visiting Fellow, Univ. of North Carolina, Chapel Hill 1989; Rhodes Prof. of American History, Univ. of Oxford 2002–09; Pres. Corpus Christi Coll. 2010–, Fellow, St Catherine's Coll. 2002–09; Founding Fellow, Learned Soc. of Wales 2010. *Publications include:* Transatlantic Revivalism: Popular Evangelicalism in Britain and America 1790–1865 1978, Evangelicals and Politics in Antebellum America 1993, Lincoln 2003, Lincoln: A Life of Purpose and Power 2006, The Global Lincoln 2010. *Honours:* ACLS-Fulbright Research Fellowship 1989, Leverhulme Research Fellowship 2001–03, Lincoln Prize Laureate 2004. *Address:* Corpus Christi College, Oxford, OX1 4JF, England (office). *Telephone:* (1865) 276740 (office). *E-mail:* president@ccc.ox.ac.uk (office). *Website:* www.ccc.ox.ac.uk (office).

CARY, Lorene Emily, BA, MA; American writer; *Senior Lecturer, University of Pennsylvania;* b. 29 Nov. 1956, Philadelphia, Pa; d. of John Cary and Carole Cary; m. R. C. Smith 1983; two d. one step-s. *Education:* Univ. of Pennsylvania, Univ. of Sussex, UK. *Career:* reporter and writer for TIME magazine 1980; Assoc. Ed., TV Guide 1980–82; Contributing Ed., Newsweek Magazine 1991; Lecturer, Univ. of Pennsylvania 1995–, currently Sr Lecturer; mem. PEN, Authors' Guild. *Publications include:* Black Ice 1991, The Price of a Child 1995, Pride 1998, If Sons, Then Heirs 2011; children's fiction: Free! 2006. *Honours:* Hon. DLitt (Colby Coll., Me) 1992, (Keene State Coll., NH, Chestnut Hill Coll., Philadelphia, Muhlenberg Coll., Allentown, Pa, Arcadia Univ., Glenside, Pa); Philadelphia Award 2003. *Address:* 1801 West Diamond Street, Philadelphia, PA 19121, USA (home). *E-mail:* lcary@mail.artsanctuary.org (office). *Website:* www.lorenecary.org.

CASAS, Fabián Andres; Argentine poet, writer and journalist; b. 7 April 1965, Boedo, Buenos Aires. *Career:* participated in Iowa Int. Writers Workshop 1998; Ed., literary and cultural supplements, Clarín newspaper, perfil.com. *Publications include:* poetry: Publicó Otoño, poemas de desintoxicación y tristeza 1985, Tuca 1990, El Salmón 1996, Pogo 2000, Bueno, eso es todo 2000, Oda 2004, El spleen de Boedo 2004, El bosque pulenta 2004; novels: Ocio 2000, Los Lemmings y otros 2005. *Honours:* Antorchas Scholarship 2003, Guggenheim Fellowship, Anna Seghers Award 2007. *Address:* c/o Santiago Arcos Editor, José Bonifacio 1402, Buenos Aires, Argentina. *E-mail:* santiagoarcosprensa@yahoo.com.ar.

CASEY, John Dudley, BA, LLB, MFA; American writer and academic; b. 18 Jan. 1939, Worcester, Mass; m. Rosamond Pinchot Pittman 1982; four d. *Education:* Harvard Coll., Harvard Law School, Univ. of Iowa. *Career:* Prof., Univ. of Virginia, later Henry Hoyns Prof. of English 1972–92, 1999–; Guggenheim Foundation Fellowship 1979–80, Nat. Endowment for the Arts Fellowship 1983, Ingram Merrill Foundation Fellowship 1990; residency, American Acad. in Rome 1990–91; mem. PEN. *Publications include:* An

American Romance (novel) 1977, Testimony and Demeanor (short stories) 1979, Spartina (novel) (Nat. Book Award) 1989, Avid (short story) (O. Henry Award) 1989, Supper at the Black Pearl 1996, The Half-Life of Happiness (novel) 1998, Compass Rose 2010; as trans.: You're an Animal, Viskovitz, Enchantments; contrib. of stories, articles and reviews in newspapers and magazines, including The New Yorker, The New York Times Magazine, Esquire, Harper's. *Honours:* Friends of American Writers Award 1980, American Acad. of Arts and Letters Strauss Living Award 1991–97, Rome Prize 1991. *Address:* Department of English, University of Virginia, 219 Bryan Hall, PO Box 400121, Charlottesville, VA 22904-4121 (office); 1326 Rugby Road, Charlottesville, VA 22903, USA (home). *E-mail:* jdc@cms.mail.virginia.edu (office).

CASO, Ángeles; Spanish writer and art historian; b. 1959, Gijón. *Career:* has worked at numerous cultural orgs including Fundación Príncipe de Asturias and Instituto Feijoo de Estudios del Siglo XVIII, Universidad de Oviedo; presenter, Telediario news programme (TVE) 1985–87. *Publications include:* Asturias desde la noche 1988, Elisabeth, emperatriz de Austria-Hungria 1993, El Peso de las Sombras 1994, El Immortal 1996, El Mundo Visto desde el Cielo 1997, El Resto de la Vida 1998, El Verano de Lucky 1999, La Trompa de los monos 1999, La Alegría de Vivir 1999, Un Largo Silencio (Premio Fernando Lara) 2000, Giuseppe Verdi, la intensa vida de un genio 2001, Las Olvidadas 2005, Contra el Viento (Premio Planeta) 2009. *Address:* c/o Editorial Planeta, Avenida Diagonal 662–664, 08034 Barcelona, Spain. *Website:* www.planeta.es; blogs.publico.es/desdelejos.

CASS, Sir Geoffrey Arthur, Kt, MA, CCMI; British publishing executive and arts and lawn tennis administrator; b. 11 Aug. 1932, Bishop Auckland; s. of the late Arthur Cass and Jessie Cass (née Simpson); m. Olwen Mary Richards, JP, DL 1957; four d. *Education:* Queen Elizabeth Grammar School, Darlington and Jesus Coll., Oxford. *Career:* Nuffield Coll., Oxford 1957–58; RAF 1958–60; ed. Automation 1960–61; Consultant, PA Man. Consultants Ltd 1960–65; Pvt. Man. Consultant, British Communications Corpn and Controls and Communications Ltd 1965; Dir Controls and Communications Ltd 1966–69; Dir George Allen & Unwin 1965–67, Man. Dir 1967–71; Dir Weidenfeld Publrs. 1972–74, Univ. of Chicago Press, UK 1971–86; Chief Exec. Cambridge Univ. Press 1972–92, Consultant 1992–; Sec. Press Syndicate, Univ. of Cambridge 1974–92; Univ. Printer 1982–83, 1991–92; Fellow, Clare Hall, Cambridge 1979–; Trustee Shakespeare Birthplace Trust 1982–94 (Life Trustee 1994–); Chair. Royal Shakespeare Co. 1985–2000 (Deputy Pres. 2000–), Royal Shakespeare Theatre Trust 1983–, British Int. Tennis and Nat. Training 1985–90, Nat. Ranking Cttee; mem. Bd of Man., Lawn Tennis Asscn of GB 1985–90, 1993–2000, Deputy Pres. 1994–96, Pres. 1997–99; Chair. Tennis Foundation 2003–07, Pres. 2007–; mem. Cttee of Man., Wimbledon Championships 1990–2002; Pres., Chair. or mem. numerous other trusts, bds, cttees, charitable appeals and advisory bodies particularly in connection with theatre, sport and medicine; Oxford tennis Blue and badminton; played in Wimbledon Tennis Championships 1954, 1955, 1956, 1959; British Veterans Singles Champion, Wimbledon 1978. *Publications:* articles in professional journals. *Honours:* Hon. Fellow, Jesus Coll., Oxford 1998; Chevalier, Ordre des Arts et Lettres. *Address:* Middlefield, Huntingdon Road, Cambridge, CB3 0LH, England (home). *Website:* www.tennisfoundation.org.uk.

CASSELLS, Cyrus Curtis, BA; American poet, academic, translator and actor; b. 16 May 1957, Dover, Del.; s. of Cyrus Cassells, Jr and Mary Isabel Williston. *Education:* Stanford Univ. *Career:* currently Prof. of Creative Writing, Texas State Univ. –San Marcos; mem. PEN, Poetry Soc. of America. *Films:* as actor: Code Name: Wolverine 1996; Through the Glass Prison 2010; Differences Between Men and Women; as writer: Dreaming-Out Loud Days 2010. *Publications include:* The Mud Actor 1982, Soul Make a Path Through Shouting 1994, Beautiful Signor 1997, More than Peace and Cypresses 2004, The Crossed-Out Swastika 2012; contribs to Southern Review, Callaloo, Translation, Seneca Review, Quilt, Sequoia. *Honours:* Acad. of American Poets Prize 1979, Nat. Poetry Series Winner 1982, Callaloo Creative Writing Award 1983, Massachusetts Artists Foundation Fellowship 1985, Nat. Endowment for the Arts Fellowships 1986 and 2005, Lavan Younger Poets Award 1992, Lannan Literary Award 1993, William Carlos Williams Award 1994, Pushcart Prize 1995, Lambda Literary Award for Gay Men's Poetry 1998, Sister Circle Book Award 1998, Dean's Award for Scholarly/ Creative Activity 2006, Texas State Univ. Rising Star 2010. *Address:* Department of English, Texas State University, 601 University Drive, FH M14, San Marcos, TX 78666, USA (office). *Telephone:* (512) 245-3799 (office). *E-mail:* cc37@txstate.edu (office). *Website:* www.english.txstate.edu (office).

CASSIDY, Anne; British children's writer; b. 1952, London, England; m.; one s. *Career:* full-time writer 2000–. *Publications include:* Big Girl's Shoes 1990, In Real Life 1993, Driven to Death 1994, Talking to Strangers 1994, A Family Affair 1995, Accidental Death 1996, No Through Road 1996, The End of the Line 1996, The Hidden Child 1997, Brotherly Love 1997, Death by Drowning 1999, Killing Time 1999, Dead Quiet 2000, Tough Love 2001, Missing Judy 2002, Blood Money 2003, Love Letters 2003, Looking for JJ (Booktrust Teenage Book of the Year, Staffordshire YTF Book Award 2005) 2004, Birthday Blues 2005, Witness 2005, Innocent 2006, The Story of my Life 2006, Careless 2007, The Bone Room 2007, Forget Me Not (Angus Book Award 2009) 2008, Just Jealous 2009, The Dead House 2009, Wizard Wizzle – Wizard Prince 2011, Heart Burn 2011. *Address:* c/o Scholastic UK, 24 Eversholt Street, London, NW1 1DB, England (office). *Telephone:* (20) 7756-7756. *Website:* www.annecassidy.com.

CASTEL, Albert Edward, BA, MA, PhD; American historian and academic; b. 11 Nov. 1928, Wichita, Kan.; m. GeorgeAnn Bennett 1959; one s. one d. *Education:* Wichita State Univ., Univ. of Chicago. *Career:* Instructor, Univ. of California, Los Angeles 1957–58; Asst Prof., Waynesburg Coll., Pa 1958–60; Asst Prof., Western Michigan Univ. 1960–63, Assoc. Prof. 1963–67, Prof. 1967–91. *Publications include:* A Frontier State of War 1958, William Clarke Quantrill 1962, Sterling Price and the Civil War in the West 1968, The Guerrilla War 1974, The Yeas and Nays: Key Congressional Votes (co-author) 1975, Fort Sumter: 1861 1976, The Presidency of Andrew Johnson 1979, A Frontier State at War: Kansas, 1861–1865 1979, Decision in the West: The Atlanta Campaign of 1864 1992, Winning and Losing in the Civil War: Essays and Stories 1996, Bloody Bill Anderson (co-author) 1998, Tom Taylor's Civil War 2000, Articles of War 2001; contrib. to many scholarly journals. *Honours:* American Historical Asscn Albert J. Beveridge Award 1957, Civil War Times Illustrated Best Author Award 1979, Eastern Nat. Park and Monument Asscn Peterson Award 1989, Atlanta Civil War Round Table Harwell Award 1993, Gettysburg Coll. Lincoln Prize 1993, Civil War Round Table of Kansas City Truman Award 1994. *Address:* c/o Mayfair Village Retirement Community, 3011 Hayden Road, Columbus, OH 43235, USA (home).

CASTEL-BLOOM, Orly; Israeli novelist; b. 1960, Tel-Aviv; m.; two c. *Education:* Tel-Aviv Univ. *Career:* fmr Lecturer, Harvard Univ., UCLA, Univ. of California, Berkeley, New York Univ., Univs of Oxford and Cambridge, UK; currently teaches creative writing at Tel-Aviv Univ. *Publications include:* novels: Heichan Ani Nimtzet (trans. as Where Am I?) 1990, Dolly City 1992, Ha-Mina Lisa (trans. as The Mina Lisa) 1995, Taking the Trend 1998, Human Parts (Wizo Prize 2005) 2002, Textile 2006, Winter Life 2010; short story collections: Not Far from the Centre of Town 1987, Hostile Surroundings 1989, Unbidden Stories 1993, Free Radicals 2000, Selected Stories 1987–2004 2004, You Don't Argue with Rice 2004; juvenile: Let's Behave Ourselves 1997. *Honours:* Tel-Aviv Prize for Literature 1990, Alterman Prize 1993, Prime Minister's Prize 1994, 2001, Newman Prize 2003, Leah Goldberg Prize 2007. *Address:* Institute for the Tranlsation of Hebrew Literature, PO Box 10051, Raman Gat, 52001, Israel (office). *E-mail:* litscene@ithl.org.il (office). *Website:* www.ithl.org.il (office).

CASTELL, Megan (see Williams, Jeanne)

CASTELLET, Josep María, BL; Spanish poet and academic; b. 15 Dec. 1926, Barcelona; m. *Education:* Univ. of Barcelona. *Career:* fmr Prof. of Philosophy and Law, Univ. of Barcelona; Pres. Asscn of Catalan Language Writers 1978–83, currently mem. Advisory Bd; Dir of Seminars, Menénez Pelayo Int. Univ. 1981–87; fmr mem. Asscn Internationale des critiques littéraires, Paris; fmr mem. Bd of Trustees, Univ. of Barcelona; fmr mem. Advisory Council, Culture of the Generalitat of Catalonia; fmr mem. Steering Cttee, PEN Club, Barcelona, European degli Scrittori, Rome; mem. Bd of Dirs Literary Peninsula Edition, Edicions 62 1964–97; Chair. Man. Grup 62 2000, currently Hon. mem. Advisory Cttee; Dean Inst. of Catalan Letters 2006–10. *Publications:* Notas sobre literatura española contemporánea 1955, La hora del lector 1957, La evolución espiritual de E. Hemingway 1958, Veinte años de poesía española 1960, Poesia Catalana del segle XX (co-author Joaquim Molas) 1963, Poesia, realisme, història 1965, Lectura de Marcuse 1969, Ocho siglos de poesía catalana 1969, Nueve novísimos poetas españoles 1970, Iniciació a la poesia de Salvador Espriu 1971, Qüestions de literatura, política i societat 1975, Literatura, ideología y política 1976, Maria Girona. Una pintura en llibertat (co-author A.M. Moix) 1977, i Josep Pla o la raó narrativa 1978, Per un debat sobre la cultura a Catalunya 1983, La cultura y las culturas 1985, L'hora del lector. Seguido de Poesia, realisme, història 1987, Els escenaris de la memòria 1988, Nueve novísimos 2001, Vuit segles de poesia catalana (co-author Joaquim Molas), 2005, Dietari de 1973 2007, Seductors, il·lustrats i visionaris 2009. *Honours:* Creu de Sant Jordi de la Generalitat de Cataluna 1983, Medalla Procultura hungàrica de la República d'Hongria 1987, Officier, Ordre nat. du Mérite 1988, Medalla de oro de las Bellas artes del Ministerio de Cultura 1992, Medalla d'or al mèrit artístic de l'Ajuntament de Barcelona 1993, Medalla d'or de la Generalitat de Catalunya 2003; Taurus d'assaig 1970, Gaziel de periodisme 1977, Josep Pla de prosa 1977, Creu de Sant Jordi de la Generalitat de Catalunya 1983, Joanot Martorell de narrativa 1987, Medal Procultura Hungarian 1987, Crítica Serra d'Or 1988, Nacional de la literatura catalana 1989, Lletra d'Or 1989, Gold Medal of the Generalitat of Catalonia 2002, Nacional de cultura a la Trajectòria Professional i Artística 2009, Premi Nacional de Cultura 2009, Nat. Prize for Spanish Literature 2010, Crítica Serra d'Or 2010. *Address:* Edicions 62, 4 Foot of the Cross, 08001 Barcelona, Spain (office). *Telephone:* (93) 4437100 (office). *Fax:* (93) 4437130 (office). *E-mail:* info@edicions62.cat (office). *Website:* www.edicions62.cat (office).

CASTER, Sylvie; French journalist and writer; b. 1952. *Education:* in Bordeaux. *Career:* fmr Ed. at Canard enchaîné. *Publications include:* Les Chênes verts 1980, La France fout la camp 1982, Nel est mort 1985, Bel-Air 1991, H. B., la bombe humaine 1994, La petite Sibérie 1995, Dormir (Prix Jean Freustié 2003, Prix Charles Exbrayat 2003) 2002, Ici-bas 2010. *Address:* c/o Editions Pauvert, Fayard, 13 rue du Montparnasse, 75006 Paris, France. *E-mail:* presse@editions-fayard.fr. *Website:* www.fayard.fr.

CASTILLO, Michel Xavier Janicot del, LèsL, LenP; French writer; b. 2 Aug. 1933, Madrid, Spain; s. of Michel Janicot and Isabelle del Castillo. *Education:* Coll. des jésuites d'Ubeba, Spain, Lycée Janson-de-Sailly, Paris. *Career:* mem. Soc. des gens de lettres, PEN. *Publications:* Tanguy 1956 (Prix des Neufs), La Guitare 1957, Le Colleur d'affiches 1958, Le Manège espagnol 1960, Tara

1962, Gerardo Laïn 1967, Le Vent de la nuit 1972, Le Silence des pierres 1975, Le Sortilège espagnol 1977, Les Cyprès meurent en Italie 1979, Les Louves de l'Escurial 1980, La nuit du décret 1981, La Gloire de Dina 1984, La Halte et Le Chemin 1985, Nos Andalousies 1985, Le Démon de l'oubli 1987, Mort d'un poète 1989, Une Femme en Soi 1991, Andalousie 1991, Le Crime des Pères 1993, Carlos Pradal 1993, Rue des Archives 1994, Mon frère l'idiot 1995 (Prix de l'Ecrit Intime), Le Sortilege Espagnol: Les Officiants De La Mort 1996, La Tunique d'infamie 1997, De père français 1998, Colette, une certaine France (Prix Femina 1999), L'Adieu au siècle 2000, Droit d'auteur 2000, Les Etoiles Froides 2001, Colette En Voyage 2002, Algerie, L'Extase Et Le Sang 2002, Les Portes Du Sang 2003, Le Jour Du Destin 2003, Sortie Des Artistes 2004, Le Dictionnaire Amoureux De L'Espagne (Prix Méditerranée) 2005. *Honours:* Chevalier Légion d'honneur; Commdr des Arts et Lettres; Prix des Magots 1973, Grand Prix des libraires 1973, Prix Chateaubriand 1975, Prix Renaudot 1981, Prix Maurice Genevoix 1994. *Address:* Editions Stock, 27 rue Cassette, 75006 Paris (office); Le Colombier, 7 avenue Camille Martin, 30190 La Calmette, France (home). *E-mail:* webmaster@micheldelcastillo.com (office). *Website:* www.micheldelcastillo.com.

CASTLEDEN, Rodney, DipEd, MA, MSc; British geomorphologist, writer, archaeologist and composer; b. 23 March 1945, Worthing, Sussex, England; s. of Dennis Castleden and Gwendoline Dennett; m. Sarah Dee 1987. *Education:* Hertford Coll., Oxford. *Career:* freelance writer, researcher; mem. Soc. of Authors, Sussex Archaeological Soc.; Head of Geography Dept, Roedean School 1979–90, Head of Humanities Faculty 1990–2001, Head of Social Science Faculty 2001–04; writer 2004–. *Compositions include:* Cuckmere Suite (for string orchestra) 1999, Winfrith (chamber opera) 2000, revised 2003, String Sextet 2007. *Publications include:* Classic Landforms of the Sussex Coast 1982, The Wilmington Giant: The Quest for a Lost Myth 1983, Classic Landforms Series (ed.) 1983–99, The Stonehenge People: An Exploration of Life in Neolithic Britain 1987, The Knossos Labyrinth 1989, Minoans: Life in Bronze Age Crete 1990, Book of British Dates 1991, Neolithic Britain 1992, The Making of Stonehenge 1993, World History: A Chronological Dictionary of Dates 1994, British History: A Chronological Dictionary of Dates 1994, The Cerne Giant 1996, Knossos, Temple of the Goddess 1996, Atlantis Destroyed 1998, Out in the Cold 1998, The English Lake District 1998, The Search for King Arthur 1999, Ancient British Hill Figures 2000, History of World Events 2003, Britain 3000 BC 2003, Infamous Murderers 2004, Serial Killers 2004, The World's Most Evil People 2005, Mycenaeans 2005, People Who Changed the World 2005, Events that Changed the World 2005, The Attack on Troy 2006, English Castles 2006, Castles of the Celtic Lands 2006, The Book of Saints 2006, Assassinations and Conspiracies 2006, Natural Disasters That Changed the World 2007, Inventions that Changed the World 2007, Great Unsolved Crimes 2007, Conflicts that Changed the World 2008, Discoveries that Changed the World 2008, Witness to History 2008, Encounters that Changed the World 2009; contribs: 100 articles published in various journals and magazines. *Address:* Rookery Cottage, Blatchington Hill, Seaford, East Sussex, BN25 2AJ, England (home). *Telephone:* (1323) 873985 (office). *E-mail:* rodney@castleden.fsnet.co.uk (home).

CASTRO, Brian Albert, MA; Australian writer and teacher; b. 16 Jan. 1950, Kowloon, Hong Kong; m. Josephine Mary Gardiner 1976. *Education:* Univ. of Sydney. *Career:* journalist, Asiaweek, Hong Kong 1983–87, All-Asia Review of Books, Hong Kong 1989–; Writer-in-Residence, Mitchell Coll., NSW 1985; Visiting Fellow, Nepean Coll., Kingswood, NSW 1988; fmr Tutor in Literary Studies, Univ. of Western Australia; currently, Prof. of Creative Writing, Univ. of Melbourne. *Publications include:* novels: Birds of Passage 1982, Pomeroy 1991, Double-Wolf 1991, After China 1992, Drift 1994, Stepper 1998, Shanghai Dancing 2003, The Garden Book (Queensland Premier Award for Fiction 2006) 2005, The Bath Fugues 2009; non-fiction: Writing Asia: Two Lectures 1995, Looking for Estrellita: Essays on Culture and Writing 1999; contribs to anthologies and periodicals. *Honours:* Book of the Year Award 1992. *Address:* School of Culture and Communication, Room 245, East Tower, John Medley Building, University of Melbourne, Melbourne, Vic. 3010, Australia (office). *E-mail:* bcastro@unimelb.edu.au (office); heat@giramondopublishing.com. *Website:* www.culture-communication.unimelb.edu.au (office); www.giramondopublishing.com.

CASTRO, Jan Garden, BA, MAT, MA; American writer, poet, academic, editor and arts consultant; b. 8 June 1945, St Louis, Mo. *Education:* Univ. of Wisconsin, Radcliffe Coll., Washington Univ., St Louis. *Career:* Dir Big River Asscn, St Louis 1975–85; Ed. River Styx magazine 1975–86; Lecturer, Lindenwood Coll., St Charles, Missouri 1980, later Sr Lecturer in Humanities –2004; Founder and Dir River Styx PM Series, St Louis 1981–83; Arts Consultant, Harris-Stowe State Coll. 1986–87; Contributing Ed. Sculpture Magazine; Fellow, Nat. Endowment for the Humanities 1988, 1990, Camargo Foundation 1996; Founder mem. Margaret Atwood Soc., mem. Modern Language Asscn, PEN American Center. *Publications include:* Mandala of the Five Senses (poems) 1975, The Art and Life of George O'Keeffe 1985, Margaret Atwood: Vision and Forms (co-ed.) 1988, Seeking St Louis: Voices from a River City 1670–2000 (co-ed.) 2000, The Last Frontier (poems) 2001; contribs: various reviews and television. *Honours:* Arts and Letters Award, St Louis Magazine 1985, Co-ordinating Council of Literary Magazines Award 1986, Leadership Award, Young Women's Christian Asscn, St Louis, 1988. *E-mail:* jancastro1@gmail.com. *Website:* jancastro.com.

CAULO, Ralph Daniel, MA; American publishing executive; b. 7 Jan. 1935; two s. one d. *Education:* Univ. of Redlands. *Career:* SW Regional Man. Schools Dept Harcourt Brace Jovanovich Inc. 1974–75, Man. Gen. Sales 1975–78, Deputy Dir 1978–79, Vice-Pres. 1979–81, Sr Vice-Pres. 1981–83, Exec. Vice-Pres. 1983–88, Pres. and COO 1988–89, Pres. and CEO 1989–91; Exec. Vice-Pres., later Pres. Simon & Schuster 1991–98; consultant to Ripplewood Holdings LLC 1998–; fmr Dir, Weekly Reader and CompassLearning, a subsidiary of WRC Media Inc.; Group Pres., curriculum, Assessment, and Educational Tech. Group, a subsidiary of WRC Media Inc. 2002–; Dir and Vice-Chair. WRC Media Inc. 1999– (interim CEO 2005–). *Address:* 778 Lower Elgin Road, Elgin, TX 78621-5519, USA (home). *Telephone:* (512) 281-0551 (home).

CAUTE, (John) David, (John Salisbury), MA, DPhil, JP, FRSL; British writer; b. 16 Dec. 1936; m. 1st Catherine Shuckburgh 1961 (divorced 1970); two s.; m. 2nd Martha Bates 1973; two d. *Education:* Edinburgh Acad., Wellington, Wadham Coll., Oxford. *Career:* St Antony's Coll., Oxford 1959; army service in Gold Coast 1955–56; Henry Fellow, Harvard Univ. 1960–61; Fellow, All Souls Coll., Oxford 1959–65; Visiting Prof., New York Univ. and Columbia Univ. 1966–67; Reader in Social and Political Theory, Brunel Univ. 1967–70; Regents' Lecturer, Univ. of California 1974, Visiting Prof. Univ. of Bristol 1985; Literary Ed. New Statesman 1979–80; Co-Chair. Writers' Guild 1982. *Plays:* Songs for an Autumn Rifle 1961, The Demonstration 1969, The Fourth World 1973, Brecht and Company (BBC TV) 1979. *Radio plays:* The Demonstration 1971, Fallout 1972, The Zimbabwe Tapes (BBC Radio) 1983, Henry and the Dogs (BBC Radio) 1986, Sanctions (BBC Radio) 1988, Animal Fun Park (BBC Radio) 1995. *Publications include:* At Fever Pitch (novel) (Authors' Club Award 1960, John Llewellyn Rhys Award 1960) 1959, Comrade Jacob (novel) 1961, Communism and the French Intellectuals 1914–1960 1964, The Left in Europe Since 1789 1966, The Decline of the West (novel) 1966, Essential Writings of Karl Marx (ed.) 1967, The Confrontation: A Trilogy, The Demonstration (play), The Occupation (novel), The Illusion 1971, The Fellow-Travellers 1973, Collisions: Essays and Reviews 1974, The Great Fear: The Anti-Communist Purge Under Truman and Eisenhower 1978, Under the Skin: The Death of White Rhodesia 1983, The Baby-Sitters (novel, as John Salisbury) 1978, Moscow Gold (novel, as John Salisbury) 1980, The K-Factor (novel) 1983, The Espionage of the Saints 1986, Sixty Eight: The Year of the Barricades 1988, Veronica or the Two Nations (novel) 1989, The Women's Hour (novel) 1991, Joseph Losey: A Revenge on Life 1994, Dr Orwell and Mr Blair (novel) 1994, Fatima's Scarf (novel) 1998, The Dancer Defects: The Struggle for Cultural Supremacy During the Cold War 2003, Marechera and the Colonel 2009, Politics and the Novel During the Cold War 2010. *Address:* 41 Westcroft Square, London, W6 0TA, England (home).

CEBRIÁN ECHARRI, Juan Luis, BS; Spanish writer and journalist; *CEO, El País*; b. 30 Oct. 1944, Madrid; s. of Vicente Cebrián and Carmen Echarri; m. 1st María Gema Torallas 1966 (divorced); two s. two d.; m. 2nd Teresa Aranda 1988; one s. one d. *Education:* Univ. of Madrid. *Career:* Sr Ed. newspapers Pueblo, Madrid 1962–67, Informaciones, Madrid 1967–69; Founder-mem. of magazine Cuadernos para el Diálogo, Madrid 1963; Deputy Ed.-in-Chief, Informaciones 1969–74, 1974–76; apptd Dir News Programming, Spanish TV 1974; Founding Ed.-in-Chief newspaper El País, Madrid 1976–88, CEO El País 1988–; Vice-Pres. International Press Inst. 1982–86, Chair. 1986–88, later mem.; CEO Grupo PRISA 1988–, Canal Plus 1989–, Estructura 1989–; Non-Exec. and Proprietary Dir Sogecable SA 1989–; Vice-Pres. SER 1990–; Pres., Asscn of Spanish Newspaper Eds 2003–04; Dir (non-exec.) Media Capital S.G.P.S 2005–; Pres. and CEO Liberty Acquisition Holdings Virginia Inc. 2010–; mem. Royal Acad. of the Spanish Language 1996. *Publications:* La Prensa y la Calle 1980, La España que bosteza 1980, ¿Qué pasa en el mundo? 1981, Crónicas de mi país 1985, La rusa Alfaguara 1986, El Tamaño del elefante 1987, Red Doll 1987, La isla del viento 1990, El tamaño del elefante 1993, El siglo de las sombras 1994, Cartas a un joven periodista 1997, Exaltación del vino, y de la alegria 1998, La red 1998, La agonía del dragón 2000, El futuro no es lo que era 2001, Francomomribundia 2003, El Fundamentalismo Democrático 2004. *Honours:* Hon. Prof., (Universidad Iberoamericana de Santo Domingo) Dominican Republic; Chevalier, Ordre des Arts et des Lettres; Dr hc (Iberoamericana Univ., Santo Domingo) 1988, (La Plata Univ.) Argentina 2003; Control Prize for Outstanding Newspaper Ed. 1976, 1977, 1978, 1979, Víctor de la Serna Prize for Journalism, Press Asscn Fed. 1977, Outstanding Ed. of the Year (World Press Review, New York) 1980, Spanish Nat. Journalism Prize 1983, Freedom of Expression Medal, F. D. Roosevelt Four Freedoms Foundation 1986, Medal of Honor, Univ. of Miss. 1986, Trento Int. Prize for Journalism and Communication 1987, Gold Medal, Spanish Inst. New York 1988, Medal for Merit, Univ. of Veracruz, Mexico. *Address:* El País, Miguel Yuste 40, 28037 Madrid, Spain (office). *Telephone:* (91) 3378200 (office). *Fax:* (91) 3048766 (office). *Website:* www.elpais.com (office).

CELATI, Gianni, PhD; Italian novelist, editor and translator; b. 1937, Sondrio, Ferrara. *Education:* Univ. of Bologna. *Career:* Lecturer in Anglo-American Literature, Univ. of Bologna; fmr teacher at Caen Univ., France, Cornell Univ. and Brown Univ., USA. *Publications include:* Comiche 1971, Le avventure di Guizzardi 1971, Il chiodo in testa 1975, Finzioni occidentali 1975, La banda dei sospiri 1976, La bottega dei mimi 1977, Lunario del paradiso 1978, Narratori delle pianure 1985, Quattro novelle sulle apparenze 1987, Verso la foce 1989, Parlamenti buffi 1989, Profili delle nuvole 1989, Avventure in Africa (New York Univ. Prize for Italian Fiction 1999) 1998, Cinema Naturale 2001, Fata Morgana 2005, Vite di Pascolanti (Premio Viareggio Repaci) 2006, Costumi degli italiani: 1 2008, Sonetti del Badalucco nell'Italia odierna 2010. *Honours:* Mondello Prize 1990. *Address:* Giangiacomo Feltrinelli Editore, via Andegari 6, 20121 Milan, Italy. *Telephone:* (02) 725721. *Fax:* (02) 72572500.

CERCAS, Javier; Spanish novelist; *Lecturer in Spanish Literature, University of Girona*; b. 6 April 1962, s. of José Cercas and Blanca Cercas; m. Mercè Mas; one s. *Education:* Univ. Autónoma, Barcelona. *Career:* teacher, Univ. of Illinois, USA 1987–89; Lecturer in Spanish Literature, Univ. of Girona 1989–. *Publications include:* El móvil (trans. as The Motive) 1987, El inquilino (trans. as The Tenant) 1989, La obra literaria de Gonzalo Suárez 1993, El vientre de la ballena (trans. as The Belly of the Whale) 1997, Una buena temporada 1998, Relatos reales (trans. as True Tales) 2000, Soldados de Salamina (trans. as Soldiers of Salamis) (Independent Foreign Fiction Prize 2004) 2001, Der Mieter 2003, La velocidad de la luz (trans. as The Speed of Light) 2005, Anatomía de un instante (trans. as The Anatomy of a Moment) 2009; contrib. to El País. *Honours:* Premio Libreter 2001, Premio Ciutat de Barcelona 2002, Premio de la Crítica de Chile 2002, Premio Salambó 2002, Premio Qué Leer 2002, Premio Extremadura 2002, Premio Cálamo 2002, Premio Grinzane-Cavour 2003. *Address:* Facultat de Lletres, Universitat de Girona, Plaça Ferrater Mora 1, 17071 Girona, Spain (office). *Website:* www.udg.edu (office).

ČERNIAUSKAITĖ, Laura Sintija; Lithuanian writer and playwright; b. 8 Dec. 1976, Vilnius; m. Regimantas Tamošaitis; one s. one d. *Education:* Vilnius Univ. *Career:* freelance publicist for Malonumas magazine 1998–99; language ed. Genys (children's magazine) 2000; journalist, Tavo vaikas 2001–02; mem. Lithuanian Writers' Union. *Plays:* Išlaisvinkit auksinį kumeliuką 2001, Liučė Skates (First Prize, Theatertreffen festival, Berlin) 2005. *Publications include:* Trys paros prie mylimosios slenksčio (short stories) (Lithuanian Writers' Union Best First Book) 1994, Kambarys jazmino krūme, Liučė čiuožia (short stories & plays) 2003, Artumo jausmas (short stories & plays) 2005, Kvėpavimas į marmurą (novel) (EU Prize for Literature 2009) 2006, Benedikto slenksčiai (novel) 2008. *Telephone:* (85) 262 89 45 (office)*Address:* c/o Alma Littera, Ulonų str. 2, 08245 Vilnius, Lithuania (office). *E-mail:* vadovas@rsleidykla.lt. *Website:* www.rsleidykla.lt.

CERONETTI, Guido; Italian writer, philosopher, poet and translator; b. 1927, Turin. *Publications include:* Libro di Giobbe 1972, Cantico del Cantici 1975, Poesie, frammenti, poesie separate 1968, Peosie per vivere e per non vivere 1979, I Salmi 1967, Libro del Profeta Isaia 1981, La Vita Apparente 1982, Viaggio in Italia 1983, La Iena di Sa Giorgio 1984, Albergo Italia 1985, Libro dei Salmi 1985, Come un Talismano 1986, Compassioni e disperazioni 1987, Aquilegia 1988, Qohelet o l'Ecclesiaste 1990, La Pazienza dell'arrostito 1990, Scavi e segnali 1991, Viaggi a, viaggia 1992, D.D. Deliri Disarmati 1993, Tra pensieri 1994, Il Silenzio del Corpo 1994, Pensieri del tè 1994, La Distanza 1996, Cara Incertezza 1997, L'occhiate malinconico 1998, Briciole di colonna 1999, Lo scittore inesistente 1999, La carta è stanca 2000, La fragilità del pensare 2000, La vera storia di Rosa Vercesi e della sua amica Vittoria 2000, N.U.E.D.D. 2001, Messia 2002, Qohélet 2002, Piccolo inferno torinese 2003, l teatro dei sensibili 2004, Oltre Chiasso 2004, La Lanterna del filosofo 2005, Centoventuro pensieri del Filosofo Ignoto 2006, Marziale, Epigrammi 2007, Due Cuori una Vigna 2007, Trafitture di tenerezza. Poesia tradotta 1963–2008 2008, Giovenale, Le satire 2008, Le ballate dell'angelo ferito 2009, Insetti senza frontiere 2009. *Address:* c/o La Finestra Editrice, Piazza Grazioli 12, 38015 Lavis, Trento, Italy (office). *E-mail:* info@la-finestra.com (office). *Website:* www.la-finestra.com (office).

CERVANTES, Lorna Dee; American poet and academic; b. 1954, San Jose, Calif. *Career:* fmr Assoc. Prof. of English and Dir Creative Writing Program, Univ. of Colorado, Boulder; Founding Ed. and Publr Mango (literary magazine), Red Dirt (poetry journal); Visiting Scholar, Mexican American Studies Program, Univ. of Houston 1994–95. *Publications include:* Emplumada (American Book Award 1982) 1981, From the Cables of Genocide: Poems on Love and Hunger (Paterson Prize for Best Book of Poetry 1991, Latino Literature Award) 1991. *Honours:* Nat. Endowment for the Arts Fellowships 1978, 1993, Nat. Asscn of Chicano Scholars Outstanding Chicana Scholar 1993, Pushcart Prize 1980, Lila-Wallace Reader's Digest Fund Writers' Award 1995. *Website:* lornadice.blogspot.com.

CHA, Louis, (Jin Yong), GBM, OBE, BLaw, MA, PhD; Chinese/Hong Kong novelist and essayist; b. 6 Feb. 1924, Haining, Zhejiang, China; m. three times; two s. (one deceased) two d. from 2nd m. *Education:* Hangzhou High School, Jiaxing High School, Zhejiang Prov., Faculty of Foreign Languages, Central Univ., Chongqing, Faculty of Law, Dongwu Univ., Soochow Univ., St John's Coll., Cambridge, UK. *Career:* joined newspaper agency Ta Kung Pao in Shanghai as a journalist 1947, posted to Hong Kong div. as a copy editor 1948, transferred to Hsin Wan Pao as Deputy Ed.; began writing first serialized martial arts novel, The Book and the Sword following his meeting with Chen Wentong 1955; worked as a scenarist-dir and scriptwriter at Great Wall Movie Enterprises Ltd and Phoenix Film Co. 1957–59; co-f., with Shen Baoxin, Ming Pao (Hong Kong daily) 1959, first Ed.-in-Chief; writes fiction in wuxia genre (martial arts and chivalry), widespread following in Chinese-speaking regions, including mainland China, Hong Kong, Taiwan, SE Asia and USA; numerous adaptations of his works into films, TV series, manhua (comics) and video games; mem. Hong Kong Basic Law drafting cttee (resgnd following Tiananmen Square massacre 1989); mem. Preparatory Cttee set up by Chinese Govt to supervise Hong Kong's transition 1996. *Publications include:* The Book and the Sword 1955–56, Sword Stained with Royal Blood 1956, The Legend of the Condor Heroes 1957–59, Fox Volant of the Snowy Mountain 1959, The Return of the Condor Heroes 1959–61, Other Tales of the Flying Fox 1960–61, Swordswoman Riding West on White Horse 1961, Blade-dance of the Two Lovers 1961, Heaven Sword and Dragon Sabre 1961, A Deadly Secret 1963, Demi-Gods and Semi-Devils 1963–66, Ode to Gallantry 1966–67, The Smiling Proud Wanderer 1967–69, The Deer and the Cauldron 1969–72, Sword of the Yue Maiden 1970. *Honours:* Hon. Prof., Peking Univ., Zhejiang Univ., Nankai Univ., Soochow Univ., Huaqiao Univ., Nat. Tsing Hua Univ., Hong Kong Univ. (Dept of Chinese Studies), Univ. of British Columbia, Sichuan Univ.; Hon. Fellow, St Antony's Coll., Oxford, Robinson Coll., Cambridge; Wynflete Fellow, Magdalen Coll., Oxford; Grand Bauhinia Medal; Chevalier, Légion d'honneur 1992, Commdr, Ordre des Arts et des Lettres 2004; Dr hc (Hong Kong Univ.), (Hong Kong Polytechnic Univ.), (Open Univ. of Hong Kong), Univ. of British Columbia), (Soka Univ.), (Univ. of Cambridge) 2004; Asteroid 10930 Jinyong (1998 CR2) named after him. *E-mail:* info@jinyong.com. *Website:* www.jinyong.com.

CHABON, Michael, MFA; American writer; b. 1964, Columbia, Md; m. Ayelet Waldman; two s. two d. *Education:* Univ. of Pittsburgh, Univ. of Calif., Irvine. *Career:* Fellow, American Acad. of Arts and Sciences 2009–. *Publications:* The Mysteries of Pittsburgh 1988, A Model World (short stories) 1991, The Wonder Boys 1995, Werewolves in Their Youth (short stories) 1995, The Amazing Adventures of Kavalier & Clay (Pulitzer Prize for fiction 2001) 2000, The Final Solution 2005, The Yiddish Policemen's Union (novel) (Nebula Award for Best Novel 2008, Hugo Award for Best Novel 2008) 2007, Gentlemen of the Road 2007, Maps and Legends: Reading and Writing along the Borderlands 2008, Manhood for Amateurs: The Pleasures and Regrets of a Husband, Father, and Son 2009; contrib. short stories to several magazines. *Honours:* Publishers Weekly Best Book 1995, New York Times Notable Book 1995, O. Henry Award 1999. *Literary Agent:* Steven Barclay Agency, 12 Western Avenue, Petaluma, CA 94952, USA. *Telephone:* (707) 773-0654. *Fax:* (707) 778-1868. *Website:* www.barclayagency.com.

CHADWICK, Cydney; American writer and editor; b. 12 July 1959, Oakland, Calif. *Education:* Sonoma State Univ., Kootenay School of Writing. *Career:* Regional Sales Man., Chadwick Marketing, Penngrove, Calif. 1984–92; Exec. Dir Syntax Projects for the Arts; freelance typesetter, designer, ed. and manuscript consultant; Fellow, California Arts Council 1997; mem. PEN West. *Publications include:* Enemy Clothing (stories) 1993, Dracontic Nodes (chapbook) 1993, Persistent Disturbances (stories, chapbook) 1994, Oeuvres (story, chapbook) 1994, The Gift Horse's Mouth (story, chapbook) 1995, Interims (stories, chapbook) 1997, Inside the Hours (fiction) 1998, Benched (novella) 2000, Flesh and Bone (Ind. Publr Book Award 2002) 2001, Under the Sun 2003, Cut and Run 2005. *Honours:* Gertrude Stein Award in Innovative Writing 1995, New American Writing Award in Fiction 1998, Nat. Endowment for the Arts Creative Writing Fellowship 2001. *Address:* PO Box 1059, Penngrove, CA 94951, USA (home). *Telephone:* (707) 793-2114 (office). *Fax:* (707) 769-0880 (office). *E-mail:* aveclivres@yahoo.com. *Website:* www.avecbooks.org.

CHADWICK, Geoffrey (see Wall, Geoffrey)

CHADWICK, Whitney, BA, MA, PhD; American art historian and academic; *Professor Emeritus of Art and Art History, San Francisco State University*; b. 28 July 1943, New York; d. of Cecil Chadwick and Helen Reichert; m. Robert A. Bechtle 1982. *Education:* Middlebury Coll. and Pennsylvania State Univ. *Career:* teacher at MIT 1972–78, Univ. of California, Berkeley 1977, Stanford Univ. 1990; Prof. of Art and Art History, San Francisco State Univ. 1978–2008, now Emer.; mem. Bd of Dirs, Coll. Art Asscn 1989–92; Nat. Endowment for the Humanities Fellow 1981; Sr Fellow, American Council of Learned Socs 1988; Trustee, San Francisco Art Inst. 2008–. *Publications include:* Myth in Surrealist Painting 1929–1939: Dali, Ernst, Masson 1980, Women Artists and the Surrealist Movement 1985, Women, Art and Society 1990, Significant Others: Creativity and Intimate Partnership (co-ed) 1993, Leonora Carrington: La Realidad de la Imaginación 1994, Confessions of the Guerrilla Girls 1995, More Than Minimal: Feminism and Abstraction in the '70's 1996, Mirror Images: Women, Surrealism, and Self-Representation 1998, American Dreamer: The Art of Philip C. Curtis 1999 (co-author), Amazons in the Drawing Room: The Art of Romaine Brooks (co-author) 2000, Framed 2000, Bent: Gender and Sexuality in Contemporary Scandinavian Art 2006. *Honours:* Dr hc (Gothenburg) 2003. *Address:* Art Department, San Francisco State University, FA 268, 1600 Holloway Avenue, San Francisco, CA 94132 (office); 871 DeHaro Street, San Francisco, CA 94107, USA (home). *Telephone:* (415) 338-6524 (office). *Fax:* (415) 338-6537 (office). *E-mail:* wchad@sfsu.edu (office). *Website:* creativearts.sfsu.edu/art (office).

CHADWICK, Sir (William) Owen, Kt, OM, KBE, FBA, FRSE; British historian and academic; b. 20 May 1916, Bromley, Kent, England; s. of John Chadwick and Edith Chadwick (née Horrocks); m. Ruth Hallward 1949; two s. two d. *Education:* St John's Coll., Cambridge. *Career:* Fellow, Trinity Hall, Cambridge 1947–56, Master of Selwyn Coll., Cambridge 1956–83, Fellow 1983–, Dixie Prof. of Ecclesiastical History, Univ. of Cambridge 1958–68, Regius Prof. of Modern History 1968–83; Vice-Chancellor Univ. of Cambridge 1969–71; Pres. British Acad. 1981–85; Chancellor Univ. of East Anglia 1985–94; Chair. of Trustees Nat. Portrait Gallery 1988–94. *Publications:* From Bossuet to Newman 1957, The Victorian Church (two vols) 1966–70, John Cassian (2nd edn) 1968, The Reformation (20th edn) 1986, The Secularization of the European Mind 1976, The Popes and European Revolution 1981, Britain and the Vatican during the Second World War 1987, Michael Ramsey: A Life 1990,

The Christian Church in the Cold War 1992, A History of Christianity 1995, A History of the Popes 1830–1914 1998, The Early Reformation on the Continent 2001; numerous articles and reviews in learned journals. *Honours:* Hon. mem. American Acad. of Arts and Sciences; Hon. DD (St Andrews) 1960, (Oxford) 1973, (Wales) 1993: Hon. DLitt (Kent) 1970, (Columbia Univ.) 1977, (East Anglia) 1977, (Bristol) 1977, (London) 1983, (Leeds) 1986, (Cambridge) 1987; Hon. LLD (Aberdeen) 1986; Wolfson Literary Award 1981. *Address:* 67 Grantchester Street, Cambridge, CB3 9HZ, England (home). *Telephone:* (1223) 314000 (home). *E-mail:* oc207@cam.ac.uk (office).

CHAFE, Robert; Canadian playwright; b. St John's, Nfld. *Career:* Artistic Assoc., Artistic Fraud of Newfoundland theatre company and Magnetic North Theatre Festival; has taught at Sir Wilfred Grenfell Coll., Corner Brook, Newfoundland and Nat. Theatre School of Canada, Montreal; author of 15 plays and co-author of 10 more. *Plays include:* Vive La Rose (Stephenville Theatre Festival), Under Wraps, Emptygirl, Signals, Place of First Light, Charismatic Death Scenes, Lemons, Isle des Demons (Gros Morne Theatre Festival), Tempting Providence (Theatre Newfoundland Labrador), One Foot Wet (Theatre Newfoundland Labrador/Gros Morne Theatre Festival 2007), AfterImage (Artistic Fraud/HarbourFront Centre's World Stage Festival 2009). *Publications:* Robert Chafe: Two Plays. Butler's Marsh, Tempting Providence 2004, Afterimage (Gov.-Gen.'s Award for Drama) 2010. *Literary Agent:* Catalyst TCM Inc., #310, 100 Broadview Avenue, Toronto, ON M4M 3H3, Canada. *Telephone:* (416) 645-0935. *Fax:* (416) 645-0936. *E-mail:* ian@catalysttcm.com. *Website:* www.catalysttcm.com. *Address:* c/o Theatre Newfoundland and Labrador, PO Box 655, Corner Brook, NL A2H 6G1, Canada (office). *E-mail:* tnl@theatrenewfoundland.com (office). *Website:* www.theatrenewfoundland.com.

CHAGALL, David, BA; American writer and journalist; b. 22 Nov. 1930, Philadelphia, Pa; m. Juneau Joan Alsin 1957. *Education:* Swarthmore Coll., Pennsylvania State Univ., Univ. of Paris (Sorbonne), France. *Career:* Assoc. Ed., IEE 1960–61; Investigative Reporter, Nation Magazine 1975–; Ed., Publr, Inside Campaigning 1982–86; fmr Chair., Elder Bd, Agoura Bible Fellowship, southern California 1984; Contributing Ed., Los Angeles Magazine 1986–89; Host, TV series, The Last Hour 1994–; Chair. Selective Service Bd 1999–; currently Dir Chosen Prophetic Ministries, California; mem. Authors' Guild, American Acad. of Political Science. *Publications include:* The Century God Slept 1963, Diary of a Deaf Mute 1971, The Spieler for the Holy Spirit 1972, The New Kingmakers 1981, Television Today 1981, The Sunshine Road 1988, The World's Greatest Comebacks 1989, Surviving the Media Jungle 1996, Media and Morality 1999, Target: Special Victims of the Holocaust 2000; contribs to periodicals. *Honours:* Hon. mem. Mark Twain Soc.; Carnegie Award 1964, Nat. Book Award 1972, Health Journalism Award 1980, Presidential Achievement Award 1982. *Address:* PO Box 85, Agoura Hills, CA 91376, USA (home). *Telephone:* (760) 200-1029 (office). *Fax:* (800) 373-0545 (office). *E-mail:* dchagall@aol.com (home). *Website:* www.lasthour.org.

CHAKRABORTI, Rajorshi, PhD; Indian writer; b. 1977, Calcutta (now Kolkata). *Education:* Univs of Hull and Edinburgh, UK. *Career:* teacher of literature and creative writing, Univ. of Edinburgh; regular tutor in creative writing at Scottish univ. int. summer school; contrib. to Edinburgh Review. *Publications include:* Or the Day Seizes You 2006, Derangements 2008, Shadow Play 2010, Balloonists 2010. *Honours:* Philip Larkin Prize. *Address:* Department of English, 12 Buccleuch Place, Room 2.02, Second Floor, Edinburgh, EH8 9JX, Scotland (office). *Telephone:* (131) 650-3620 (office). *Fax:* (131) 650-6898 (office). *E-mail:* rchakrab@staffmail.ed.ac.uk (office). english.literature@ed.ac.uk (office). *Website:* www.ed.ac.uk/schools-departments/literatures-languages-cultures/english-literature (office).

CHAKRAVARTI, Sudeep; Indian writer and journalist. *Education:* Mayo Coll., Rajasthan, St Stephen's Coll., Univ. of Delhi. *Career:* began career at South Asia Bureau, Asian Wall Street Journal 1985; Business Ed., Sunday magazine 1988–91; Business Ed., India Today, later, Sr Ed., Deputy Ed., Exec. Ed. 1991–2002; Dir India Today Conclave; Consultant Ed., Hindustan Times 2003–04; Dir Hindustan Times Leadership Initiative; Visiting Faculty mem., Manipal Inst. of Communications, Univ. of Manipal; Ed.-at-Large, Rolling Stone magazine, India; Professional mem. World Future Soc. *Publications include:* The Other India (ed.) 2000, The India Today Book of Cartoons (co-ed.) 2000, The Peace Dividend: Progress for India and South Asia 2004, Tin Fish 2005, Red Sun: Travels in Naxalite Country 2008, Once Upon a Time in Aparanta 2008, Millennium Series for India Today. *Address:* c/o Penguin Books India Pvt., 11 Community Centre, Panchsheel Park, New Delhi 110 017, India (office). *E-mail:* sudeep.chakravarti@gmail.com (home). *Website:* www.penguinbooksindia.com (office); schakravarti.blogspot.com.

CHAKRAVARTY, Radha; Indian author, editor, translator and teacher; *Associate Professor of English Literature, Gargi College, University of Delhi*; b. 23 March 1957. *Career:* Assoc. Prof. of English Literature, Gargi Coll., Univ. of Delhi 1988–. *Publications:* Feminism and Contemporary Women Writers 2008, Tagore and the Modern Novel 2011; as ed. and compiler: Bodymaps: Stories by South Asian Women 2007; as co-ed.: Writing Freedom: South Asian Voices 2010, The Essential Tagore 2011; as translator: numerous works by Rabindranath Tagore, Bankimchandra Chatterjee, Mahasweta Devi; contrib. to several anthologies. *Address:* Gargi College, University of Delhi, Siri Fort Road, Delhi, 110049, India (office). *Telephone:* 26494544 (office). *Fax:* 2649421 (office). *E-mail:* gargifaculty@gmail.com (office); radha.chakravarty@gmail.com (home). *Website:* www.gargicollege.in (office); sites.google.com/site/radhachakravarty (home).

CHALFONT, Baron (Life Peer), cr. 1964, of Llantarnam in the County of Monmouthshire; **(Arthur) Alun Gwynne Jones,** PC, OBE, MC, FRSA; British politician and writer; b. 5 Dec. 1919, Llantarnam, Wales; s. of Arthur Gwynne Jones and Eliza Alice Hardman; m. Dr Mona Mitchell 1948; one d. (deceased). *Education:* West Monmouth School. *Career:* commissioned into S. Wales Borderers (24th Foot) 1940; served in Burma 1941–44, Malaya 1955–57, Cyprus 1958–59; resgnd comm. 1961; Defence Corresp. The Times, London 1961–64; consultant on foreign affairs to BBC TV, London 1961–64; Minister of State for Foreign Affairs 1964–70, Minister for Disarmament 1964–67, 1969–70, in charge of day-to-day negotiations for Britain's entry into Common Market 1967–69; Perm. Rep. to WEU 1969–70; Foreign Ed. New Statesman 1970–71; Chair. All-Party Defence Group House of Lords 1980–96, Pres. 1996–; Chair. Industrial Cleaning Papers 1979–86, Peter Hamilton Security Consultants Ltd 1984–86, UK Cttee for Free World 1981–89, European Atlantic Group 1983–, VSEL Consortium PLC 1987–93, Marlborough Stirling Group 1994–99; Deputy Chair. IBA 1989–90; Chair. Radio Authority 1991–94; Pres. Hispanic and Luso Brazilian Council 1975–80, Royal Nat. Inst. for Deaf 1980–87, Llangollen Int. Music Festival 1979–90; Chair. Abington Corpn (Consultants) Ltd 1981–, Nottingham Building Soc. 1983–90, Southern Mining Corpn 1997–99; Dir W. S. Atkins Int. 1979–83, IBM UK Ltd 1973–90 (mem. IBM Europe Advisory Council 1973–90), Lazard Brothers and Co. Ltd 1983–90, Shandwick PLC 1985–95, Triangle Holdings 1986–90, TV Corpn PLC 1996–2001; Pres. Freedom in Sport Int.; mem. IISS, Royal Inst.; Hon. Fellow, Univ. Coll. Wales, Aberystwyth 1974. *Publications:* The Sword and the Spirit 1963, The Great Commanders (ed.) 1973, Montgomery of Alamein 1976, Waterloo: Battle of Three Armies (ed.) 1979, Star Wars: Suicide or Survival 1985, Defence of the Realm 1987, By God's Will: A Portrait of the Sultan of Brunei 1989, The Shadow of My Hand (autobiog.) 2000; contrib. to The Times and nat. and professional journals. *Address:* House of Lords, London, SW1A 0PW, England (office).

CHALIDZE, Valery Nikolayevich; Russian writer, physicist and publisher; b. 1938, Moscow; m. Lisa Leah Barnhardt 1981. *Education:* Moscow Univ., then Faculty of Physics, Tbilisi Univ. 1965. *Career:* head of research unit in Plastics Research Inst., Moscow 1965–70; Founding mem. of Moscow Human Rights Cttee; dissident activity 1969–, when started samizdat journal Obshchestvennyye problemy (Problems of Society), trip to USA to lecture on human rights in USSR, subsequently deprived of Soviet citizenship 1972; f. Chalidze Publications, New York City, USA; MacArthur Fellow 1985–90. *Publications include:* numerous samizdat articles and books and Ugolovnaya Rossiya (Crime in Russia) 1977, USSR – The Workers' Movement 1978. A Foreigner in the Soviet Union. A Juridical Memoir 1980, Communism Vanquished (Stalin) 1981, The Responsibility of a Generation 1982, National Problems and Perestroika 1988, The Dawn of the Legal Reform 1990, Responsibility of the Generation 1991, A Hierarchical Man 1991, Entropy Demystified: Potential Order, Life and Money 2000, Mass and Electric Charge in the Vortex Theory of Matter 2001, Infinity or Not? 2005. *Address:* Editorial and Administrative Offices, Universal Publishers, Inc., 23331 Water Circle, Boca Raton, FL 33486-8540, USA. *Fax:* (561) 750-6797. *Website:* www.universal-publishers.com.

CHAMBERLAIN, Lesley, BA, MLitt; British writer; b. 26 Sept. 1951, Rochford, Essex, England; one d.; m. Pavel Seifter 1999. *Education:* Univ. of Exeter, Wolfson Coll., Oxford. *Career:* Lecturer, Portsmouth Polytechnic 1977–86; corresp. and Sr Sub-Ed. Reuters, Moscow 1978–79; freelance writer and teacher 1986–, regular contrib. to The TLS, Los Angeles Times Book Review, The Independent and other nat. publs; Russian columnist, Open Democracy; author and broadcaster on radio and TV. *Publications include:* The Food and Cooking of Russia 1982, The Food and Cooking of Eastern Europe 1989, F.T. Marinetti's The Futurist Cookbook (ed.) 1989, In the Communist Mirror 1990, Volga, Volga A Journey Down the Great River 1994, Nietzsche in Turin 1996, In a Place Like That 1998, The Secret Artist – A Close Reading of Sigmund Freud 2000, Girl in a Garden (novel) 2003, Motherland: A Philosophical History of Russia 2004, The Philosophy Steamer: Lenin and the Exile of the Intelligentsia 2006. *Literary Agent:* c/o Anthony Sheil, Aitken Alexander Associates, 18-21 Cavaye Place, London, SW10 9PT, England. *Telephone:* (20) 7373-6002. *E-mail:* leah@aitkenalexander.co.uk. *Address:* c/o Atlantic Books, Ormond House, 26–27 Boswell Street, London, WC1N 3JZ, England. *Website:* www.lesleychamberlain.co.uk.

CHAMBERLAND, Paul, BPhil; Canadian poet and essayist; *Associate Professor, Université du Québec à Montréal*; b. 16 May 1939, Longueuil, Québec. *Education:* Collège Saint-Laurent, Univ. of Québec, Montréal, Univ. of Paris (Sorbonne), France. *Career:* co-f. literary journal Parti pris 1963; Assoc. Prof., Département d'Études Littéraires, Université du Québec, Montréal 1985–; mem. Union des écrivaines et des écrivains québécois, Acad. des lettres du Québec. *Publications include:* poetry: Genèses 1962, Le Pays 1963, Terre Québec (Prix Du Maurier) 1964, L'Afficheur hurle 1964, L'Inavouable 1967, Éclats de la pierre noire d'où rejaillit ma vie: poèmes suivis d'une révélation 1966–1969 1972, Demain les dieux naîtront 1974, Le Prince de sexamour 1976, Extrême survivance, extrême poésie 1978, Terre souveraine 1979, L'Enfant doré: 1974–1977 1980, Émergence de l'adultenfant (poems and essays) 1981, Fidèles d'amour 1981, Le Courage de la poésie: fragments d'art total 1981, Du côté hiéroglyphe de ce qu'on appelle le réel: suivi de Devant le temple de Louxor le 31 juillet 1980 1982, Aléatoire instantané 1983, Le recommencement du monde: méditations sur le processus apocalyptique 1983, Compagnons chercheurs 1984, Phoenix intégral: poèmes 1975–1987 1988, Intarsia 1990, Le Multiple évènement terrestre: géogrammes 1 1979–1985 1991, L'Assaut contre les vivants: géogrammes 2 1986–1991 1994, Témoin nomade: carnets I 1975–1981 1995, Dans la proximité des choses 1996, Le Froid coupant du dehors: géogrammes 3 1992–1996 1997, Intime faiblesse des mortels (Estuaire Prix de Poésie Terrasses Saint-Sulpice) 1999, Au seuil d'une autre Terre 2003; non-fiction: En nouvelle barbarie (essay) (Spirale Prix de l'essai 2000), Une politique de la douleur (essay) (Prix Victor-Barbeau 2005) 2004, Résister ou disparaître, un manifeste 2007, Cœur creuset. Carnets 1997–2004 2008, Comme une seule chair 2009; Contrib. to Estuaire, Forces, Hobo-Québec, La Barre du jour, Liberté, Mainmise, Possibles. *Honours:* Prix David 1964, Prix de la Province de Québec 1964, Prix Édouard J. Maunick 1991, Prix Athanase-David 2007, Prix du Québec 2007. *Address:* Département d'Études Littéraires, Université du Québec à Montréal, Case Postale 8888, succursale Centre-ville, Montréal QC H3C 3P8, Canada (office). *E-mail:* etudes.litteraires@uqam.ca (office).

CHAMBERLIN, Ann; American writer and dramatist; b. 28 March 1954, Salt Lake City, UT; d. of Richard E. Chamberlin and Francis E. Maude; m. Curt F. Setzer 1978, two s. *Education:* Brigham Young Univ., Univ. of Utah, Univ. of Tel-Aviv, Israel. *Publications include:* The Virgin and the Tower 1979, Tamar 1994, Sofia 1996, Jihad (Play) (Best new play 1996, Oober Award 1998) 1996, The Sultan's Daughter (Critic's Choice Award 1998) 1997, The Reign of the Favored Women 1999, Leaving Eden 1999, The Merlin of St Gilles' Well 1999, The Merlin of the Oak Wood 2001, Gloria: The Merlin and the Saint 2005, A History of Women's Seclusion in the Middle East: The Veil in the Looking Glass 2006. *Address:* PO Box 71114, Salt Lake City, UT 84171, USA (home). *E-mail:* setzers@msn.com (home); ann@annchmberlin.com. *Website:* www.annchamberlin.com.

CHAMBERS, Aidan, FRSL; British writer, publisher and teacher; b. 27 Dec. 1934, Chester-le-Street, Co. Durham, England; m. Nancy Harris Lockwood 1968. *Education:* Borough Road Coll., Isleworth, Univ. of London. *Career:* co-f. Thimble Press 1969; mem. Soc. of Authors, School Library Asscn (Pres. 2003–06). *Publications include:* Johnny Salter 1966, Cycle Smash 1967, Marle 1968, The Chicken Run 1968, The Reluctant Reader 1969, Introducing Books to Children 1973, Snake River 1975, Breaktime 1978, Seal Secret (Dutch Silver Pencil 1985) 1980, The Dream Cage 1981, Dance on My Grave 1982, The Present Takers (Dutch Silver Pencil 1986) 1983, Booktalk 1985, Now I Know 1987, The Reading Environment 1991, The Toll Bridge (Dutch Silver Pencil 1994) 1992, Tell Me: Children, Reading and Talk 1993, Only Once 1998, Postcards From No Man's Land (Carnegie Medal 1999, Italian Andersen Award 2000, Stockport School Book Award K4 2000, Michael L. Printz Award, J. Hunt Award 2002) 1999, Reading Talk 2001, Favourite Ghost Stories 2002, This is All: The Pillow Book of Cordelia Kenn 2005, The Kissing Game (short stories) 2011; contrib. to numerous magazines and journals. *Honours:* Dr hc (Umeå Univ., Sweden) 2003, Hon. DLitt (Gloucestershire) 2008, Hon. DLetters (Oxford Brookes) 2011; Children's Literature Award for Outstanding Criticism 1979, Eleanor Farjeon Award 1982, Hans Christian Andersen Award 2002, Lifetime Achievement Award, Nat. Asscn for Teaching of English 2010. *Address:* Lockwood, Station Road, Woodchester, Stroud, Glos., GL5 5EQ, England (home). *Telephone:* (1453) 872208 (home). *E-mail:* aidan@chambersmail.co.uk. *Website:* www.aidanchambers.co.uk.

CHAMLING, Pawan Kumar; Indian politician, poet and writer; *Chief Minister of Sikkim*; b. 22 Sept. 1950, Yangang Busty, South Sikkim; s. of Shri Ash Bahadur Chamling and Smt. Asharani Chamling; m. Tika Maya Chamling; four s. four d. *Career:* began career as ind. farmer; entered politics in 1973; Vice-Pres. Dist Youth Congress 1975; Pres. Sikkim Handicapped Persons Welfare Mission 1976–77; Ed. Nava Jyoti 1976–77, Founder Nirman Prakashan 1977, Ed. Nirman (quarterly literary magazine) 1977–; Gen. Sec. and Vice-Pres. Sikkim Prajatantra Congress 1978–84; Pres., Yangang Gram Panchayat 1982; mem. Sikkim Legis. Ass. 1985–; Minister for Industries, Printing and Information and Public Relations 1989–92; formed Sikkim Democratic Front Party 1993, Leader 1993–; Chief Minister of Sikkim 1994–; Chair. Sikkim Distilleries Ltd 1985–. *Publications include:* Veer koh Parichaya (poem) 1967, Antahin Sapana Meroh Bipana 1985, Perennial Dreams and My Reality, Prarambhek Kabitaharu 1991, Pratiwad 1992, Damthang Heejah ra Aajah 1992, Ma koh Hun 1992, Sikkim ra Narikon Maryadha 1994, Crucified Prashna Aur Anya Kabitaye 1996, Sikkim ra Prajatantra 1996, Democracy Redeemed 1997, Prajatantra koh Mirmireymah 1997, Meroh Sapana Ko Sikkim 2002, Perspectives and Vision 2002. *Honours:* Hon. PhD (Manipal Univ.) 2003; numerous awards including Chinton Puraskar 1987, Bharat Shiromani 1996, Man of the Year 1998, The Greenest Chief Minister of India 1998, Man of Dedication 1999, Secular India Harmony Award 1998, Manav Sewa Puraskar 1999, Pride of India Gold Award 1999, Best Citizen of India 1999, Poets' Foundation Award 2001, Nat. Citizens of India Award 2002. *Address:* CM Secretariat, Tashiling, Gangtok, Sikkim 737 101 (office); Ghurpisay, Namchi, South Sikkim 737 126, India (home). *Telephone:* (3592) 222263 (office); (3592) 228200 (office); (3592) 222536 (home); (3595) 263748 (home). *Fax:* (3592) 222245 (office); (3592) 224710 (home). *E-mail:* cm-skm@nic.in (office). *Website:* sikkim.nic.in (office).

CHAMOISEAU, Patrick, LèsDP; French writer; b. 3 Dec. 1953, Fort de France, Martinique; m. Ghislaine Chamoiseau 1975, one c. *Education:* Univ. of Martinique, Univ. of Sceaux, France. *Publications include:* Manman Dlo contre la fée Carabosse, Chronique des sept misères 1986, Solibo Magnifique (Trans. as Solibo Magnificent) 1988, Martinique 1988, Eloge de la créolité (co-author) 1989, Lettres créoles: Traces antillaises et continentales de la littérature (co-author) 1991, Texaco (Prix Goncourt) 1992, Antan d'enfance (Prix Garbet de la Caraibe) 1993, Au temps de l'antan (Trans. as Creole Folktales) 1994, Guyane: Traces-mémoires du bagne 1994, Chemin-d'école (Trans. as School Days) 1994, Biblique des derniers gestes (Prix spécial du jury RFO 2002) 2001, Les bois sacrés d'Hélénon (co-author) 2002, Le commandeur d'une pluie (co-author) 2002, Livret des villes du deuxième monde 2002, Une enfance créole 2005, Un dimanche au cachot 2007, Les Neuf consciences du Malfini 2009. *Address:* 31 Favorite, 97232 Larentin, Martinique (home). *E-mail:* chamoiseau@cgit.com (home).

CHAMORRO BARRIOS, Cristiana, BA; Nicaraguan foundation director and editor; *Director, Fundación Violeta Barrios de Chamorro*; d. of Pedro Joaquin Chamorro Cardenal and Violeta Barrios de Chamorro. *Career:* Dir Diario La Prensa 1986–90, Chair. 1991–93, currently mem. Bd of Dirs and mem. Editorial Advisory Bd; Vice-Pres. Comm. for the Freedom of Expression 1987–93; Adviser to Pres. of Nicaragua Violeta Barrios de Chamorro 1990–97; Ed. Servicio Especial de Mujeres (SEM), Costa Rica; Founder-Dir Fundación Violeta Barrios de Chamorro (non-profit org. for peace, democracy and freedom of expression) 1990–. *Publications:* Anchorman: Editorial on Freedom of Expression and the Republic Of Paper In Nicaragua 1948–1977. *Honours:* Excellence in Journalism Award, Inter-American Press Soc., Int. Press Asscn . *Address:* Fundación Violeta Barrios de Chamorro, CC. Plaza España, Edificio Málaga Módulo B-17, Managua, Nicaragua (office). *Telephone:* (505) 2268-6500 (office). *Fax:* (505) 2268-6502 (office). *E-mail:* cristiana@cablenet.com.ni (office); cristiana.chamorro@ibw.com.ni (office). *Website:* www.violetachamorro.org.ni (office).

CHAMPION DE CRESPIGNY, (Richard) Rafe, (Rafe de Crespigny), BA, MA, PhD, FAHA; Australian historian and writer; *Adjunct Professor of Asian Studies, Australian National University*; b. 16 March 1936, Adelaide, SA; s. of (Richard) Geoffrey Champion de Crespigny and Kathleen Cavenagh Champion de Crespigny (née Cudmore); m. Christa Charlotte Boltz; one s. one d. *Education:* Univ. of Cambridge, UK, Univ. of Melbourne, Australian Nat. Univ. *Career:* Lecturer, ANU, Canberra 1964–70, Sr Lecturer 1970–73, Reader in Chinese 1973–99, Master Univ. House 1991–2001, Adjunct Prof. of Asian Studies 1998–; Visiting Prof., Asian Studies Program, Univ. of Hawaii, USA 1978; Guest Prof., Coll. of Chinese Culture, Taiwan 1978; Pres. Chinese Studies Asscn of Australia 1999–2001; Visiting Fellow, Clare Hall, Cambridge 1971–72, Sinologisch Instituut, Univ. of Leiden, The Netherlands 1986; mem. Australian Inst. of Int. Affairs, Asian Studies Asscn of Australia, Historical Asscn (UK), Royal Geographical Soc. of Australasia, Int. Congress for Asian and North African Studies; Fellow, Oriental Soc. of Australasia. *Publications include:* The Biography of Sun Chien 1966, Official Titles of the Former Han Dynasty (with H. H. Dubs) 1967, The Last of the Han 1969, The Records of the Three Kingdoms 1970, China: The Land and its People 1971, China This Century: A History of Modern China 1975, Portents of Protest 1976, Northern Frontier 1984, Emperor Huan and Emperor Ling 1989, Generals of the South 1990, To Establish Peace 1996, A Biographical Dictionary of Later Han to the Three Kingdoms 2007, Imperial Warlord: A Biography of Cao Cao 155–220 (Stanislas Julien Prize, French Acad. of Inscriptions and Belles-Lettres 2011) 2010. *Honours:* Australian Centenary Medal 2003. *Address:* School of Culture, History and Language, Australian National University, Canberra, ACT 0200, Australia (office). *E-mail:* rafe.decrespigny@anu.edu.au (office). *Website:* asiapacific.anu.edu.au/people/personal/decrespigny_rafe.php (office).

CHAN, Stephen, OBE, MA, PhD; New Zealand/British academic, writer and poet; *Professor of International Relations, School of Oriental and African Studies*; b. 11 May 1949, Auckland; m. *Education:* Univ. of Auckland, King's Coll., London, Univ. of Kent, Canterbury. *Career:* Int. Civil Servant, Commonwealth Secretariat 1977–83; Lecturer in Int. Relations, Univ. of Zambia 1983–85; Visiting Lecturer, Univ. of Wellington; Faculty, Univ. of Kent 1987–96; adviser to Commonwealth Scholarship Comm. 1995–2001; Prof. in Int. Relations and Ethics, Head of Int. Studies, Dean of Humanities, Nottingham Trent Univ. 1996–2002; Founding Dir Kwok Meil Wah Foundation, Foundation Dean of Law and Social Sciences 2002–07, Interim Dean of Law and Social Sciences 2011–12; Prof. of Int. Relations, SOAS 2002–; Visiting Prof., Wenzao Ursuline Coll., Kaohsiung, Taiwan 2008, 2010; mem. Univ. of London Senate 2003–07, Africa-China-US Trilateral Dialogue 2006–07, Brenthurst Foundation Group 2009–10, Exec. Cttee David Davies Memorial Inst. of Int. Studies, Chair. Editorial Bd of Inst.'s journal, International Relations; visiting fellowships; Trustee, Street Action. *Publications include:* The Commonwealth Observer Group in Zimbabwe: A Personal Memoir 1985, Issues in International Relations: A View from Africa 1987, The Commonwealth in World Politics: A Study of International Action, 1965–85 1988, Exporting Apartheid: Foreign Policies in Southern Africa, 1978–1988 1990, Social Development in Africa Today: Some Radical Proposals 1991, Kaunda and Southern Africa: Image and Reality in Foreign Policy 1991, Twelve Years of Commonwealth Diplomatic History: Commonwealth Summit Meetings, 1979–1991 1992, Mediation in South Africa (co-ed. with Vivienne Jabri) 1993, Renegade States: The Foreign Policies of Revolutionary States (co-ed. with Andrew Williams) 1994, Towards a Multicultural Roshamon Paradigm in International Relations 1996, Portuguese Foreign Policy in Southern Africa (with M. Venancio) 1996, Theorists and Theorising in International Relations (co-ed. with Jarrold Wiener) 1997, War and Peace in Mozambique (with M. Vanancio) 1998, Giving Thought: Currents in International Relations (co-ed. with Jarrold Wiener) 1998, Twentieth Century International History (co-ed. with Jarrold Wiener) 1998, Zambia and the Decline of Kaunda 1984–1998 2000, Security and Development in Southern Africa 2001, Robert Mugabe: A Life of Power and Violence 2003, Out of Evil: New International Politics and Old Doctrines of War 2004, Citizen of Africa: Conversations with Morgan Tsvangirai 2006, Grasping Africa: A Tale of Achievement and Tragedy 2007, The End of Certainty: Towards a New Internationalism 2009, Bonded for the future 2009, Arabic translation, Cairo: The Egypt Council 2010, Southern Africa: Old Treacheries and New Deceits 2011; poetry: Postcards from Paradise (with Rupert Glover and Merlene Young) 1971, Arden's Summer 1975, Songs of the Maori King 1986, Crimson Rain 1991. *Honours:* Hon. Prof., Univ. of Zambia 1993–95, Univ. of Johannesburg 2010–(13); Hon. LittD, WAAC, Istanbul; Eminent Scholar in Global Development award, Int. Studies Asscn 2010. *Address:* School of Oriental and African Studies, University of London, Thornhaugh Street, Russell Square, London, WC1H 0XG, England (office). *E-mail:* sc5@soas.ac.uk (office). *Website:* www.stephen-chan.com.

CHANCE, Jane Marie, BA, AM, PhD; American academic, writer, poet and editor; *Andrew W. Mellon Distinguished Chair in English, Rice University*; b. 26 Oct. 1945, Neosho, Mo.; d. of Donald William Chance and Julia Mile; m. 1st Dennis Carl Nitzsche 1966 (divorced 1967); one d.; m. 2nd Paolo Passaro 1981 (divorced 2002); two s. *Education:* Purdue Univ., Univ. of Illinois. *Career:* Lecturer, Univ. of Saskatchewan 1971–72, Asst Prof. of English 1972–73; Asst Prof., Rice Univ. 1973–77, Assoc. Prof. 1977–80, Prof. of English 1980–2008, Andrew W. Mellon Distinguished Chair in English 2008–; Founder and first Pres. TEAMS (Consortium for the Teaching of the Middle Ages, Inc.) 1987–92; Founder and Dir Rice Univ. Medieval Studies Program 2005–08; Dir NEH Summer Seminar for Coll. Teachers on Chaucer and Mythography 1985, Dir NEH Summer Inst. for Coll. Teachers on the Literary Traditions of Medieval Women 1997, Founding mem. and Acting Dir Scientia: Inst. for the Study of Knowledge, mem. and Sec. AAUP, Rice Univ. chapter; mem. Editorial Bd Rice Univ. Press 1981–88; Gen. Ed. Library of Medieval Women 1988–; Series Ed. Greenwood Guides to Historic Events in the Medieval World 2001–05, Praeger Series on the Middle Ages 2003–; Visiting Research Fellow, Inst. for Advanced Studies in the Humanities, Univ. of Edinburgh 1994; Eccles Research Fellow, Univ. of Utah, Humanities Centre 1994–95; mem. Inst. for Advanced Study, Princeton, NJ 1988–89; mem. Exec. Cttee and Vice-Pres. Texas Faculty Asscn 1995–2000; mem. Int. Christine de Pizan Soc., Medieval Acad. of America, Modern Language Asscn (MLA), South Central MLA (SCMLA); mem. and Chair., MLA Roth/Scaglione Prize for Best Trans. of a Literary Work 2006–09; mem. Advisory Bd, Publications of the Modern Language Association (literary journal) 2009–12. *Publications include:* The Genius Figure in Antiquity and the Middle Ages 1975, Tolkien's Art: A 'Mythology for England' 1979, Woman as Hero in Old English Literature 1986, Tolkien's Lord of the Rings: The Mythology of Power 1992, Medieval Mythography (two vols) 1994, 2000, The Mythographic Chaucer: The Fabulation of Sexual Politics 1995; editor: Christine de Pizan, Letter of Othea to Hector 1990, Gender and Text in the Later Middle Ages 1996, The Assembly of Gods 1999, Tolkien the Medievalist 2003, Tolkien and the Invertion of Myth 2004, Tolkien's Modern Middle Ages 2005, Women Medievalists and the Academy 2005, The Literary Subversions of Medieval Women (SCMLA Best Book Prize 2008) 2007; contrib. to scholarly books and journals. *Honours:* Hon. Research Fellow, Univ. Coll. London 1977–78; Nat. Endowment for the Humanities Fellowship 1977–78, Guggenheim Fellowship 1980–81, Rockefeller Foundation residency, Bellagio, Italy 1988, South Central MLA Best Book Award 1994, 1995, 2008, IMPACT Award for Outstanding Rice Faculty Woman for Empowerment of Women, Rice University Women's Resource Center 1998, Soc. for Medieval Feminist Scholarship Best Essay Prize 2005. *Address:* Department of English MS-30, Rice University, PO Box 1892, Houston, TX 77251-1892 (office). *Telephone:* (713) 348-2625 (office). *Fax:* (713) 348-5991 (office). *E-mail:* jchance@rice.edu (office). *Website:* www.english.rice.edu (office).

CHANCE, Megan, BA; American writer; b. 31 Dec. 1959, Columbus, Ohio; m. Kany Levine 1995; two d. *Education:* Western Washington Univ. *Career:* fmr TV news photographer; mem. Romance Writers of America. *Publications include:* A Candle in the Dark 1993, After the Frost 1994, The Portrait 1995, A Heart Divided 1996, Fall from Grace 1977, The Way Home 1997, The Gentleman Caller 1998, A Season in Eden 1999, Susannah Morrow 2002, An Inconvenient Wife 2006, The Spiritualist 2008, Prima Donna 2010, City of Ash 2011. *Honours:* Reviewer's Choice Award for Best First Historical Romance Novel, Romantic Times 1993, RITA Award for Excellence in Romantic Fiction 1994, Puget Sound Romance Readers' Sunrise award, for most promising new author 1994, Romantic Times Reviewer's Choice Certificate of Excellence for Historical Romance 1994, 1995, Romantic Times Reviewer's Choice nomination for Best Victorian Romance 1996, Emerald City Keeper Award for Best Historical Romance 1997. *E-mail:* meganchance@meganchance.com (office). *Website:* www.meganchance.com.

CHANCELLOR, Alexander Surtees, CBE, BA; British journalist; b. 4 Jan. 1940, Ware, Herts., England; s. of Sir Christopher Chancellor, CMG and Sylvia Mary Chancellor (née Paget); m. Susanna Elizabeth Debenham 1964; two d. *Education:* Eton Coll., Trinity Hall, Cambridge. *Career:* with Reuters News Agency 1964–74, Chief Corresp. in Italy 1968–73; with ITV News 1974–75; Ed. The Spectator 1975–84; Ed. Time and Tide 1984–86; Deputy Ed. Sunday Telegraph 1986; Washington Ed. The Independent 1986–88; Ed. The Independent Magazine 1988–92; The New Yorker (Ed. The Talk of the Town) 1992–93; columnist, The Times 1992–93, The Guardian 1996–2012, Slate 1997, The Daily Telegraph 1998–2004, Saga Magazine 2002–. *Publication:* Some Times in America 1999. *Address:* The Court House, Stoke Park, Stoke Bruerne, Towcester, Northants., NN12 7RZ, England. *Telephone:* (1604) 862329. *E-mail:* chancellor@dial.pipex.com.

CHANDLER, Frank (see Harknett, Terry)

CHANDLER, Kenneth A.; British journalist and consultant; b. 2 Aug. 1947, Westcliff-on-Sea, Essex; s. of Leonard Gordon Chandler and Beatrix Marie Chandler (née McKenzie); m. Erika Schwartz; five c. *Career:* Man. Ed. The New York Post 1978–86, 1993–99, Ed.-in-Chief, then Publr 1999–2002; Ed. Boston Herald 1986–93, Editorial Dir 2004–06; f. ChandlerMedia (media consulting firm), New York 2006, now Chandler Regan Strategies; Exec. Producer Fox TV's A Current Affair 1993; CEO Natural Energy Solutions Corpn 2002–03; mem. Bd of Dirs The Bridge Fund. *Telephone:* (914) 310-0876 (office). *E-mail:* ken@kchandler.com (office). *Website:* chandlermedia.com (office).

CHANDRA, Vikram, BA, MA, MFA; Indian writer and academic; *Senior Lecturer, University of California, Berkeley*; b. 23 July 1961, New Delhi; s. s. of Navin Chandra and Kamna Chandra; m. Melanie Abrams; one d. *Education:* Mayo Coll., St Xavier's Coll., Mumbai, Pomona Coll., Johns Hopkins Univ. and Univ. of Houston, USA. *Career:* Adjunct Prof., Univ. of Houston 1987–93; Visiting Writer, George Washington Univ. 1994–95, Assoc. Prof. 1995–2005; Sr Lecturer, Univ. of California, Berkeley 2005–. *Publications include:* Red Earth and Pouring Rain (David Higham Prize 1995, Commonwealth Writers Prize for Best First Published Book 1996) 1995, Love and Longing in Bombay (Eurasia Region Commonwealth Writers Prize for Best Book 1998) 1997, Sacred Games (Hutch Crossword Award for English Fiction 2006, Salon Book Awards 2007) 2006; contribs to several periodicals. *Honours:* Discovery Prize, Paris Review 1994. *Literary Agent:* c/o Janklow & Nesbit Associates, 445 Park Avenue, New York, NY 10022-2606, USA. *Telephone:* (212) 421-1700. *Fax:* (212) 980-3671. *E-mail:* info@janklow.com. *E-mail:* vikram@vikramchandra.com (office). *Website:* www.vikramchandra.com.

CHANDRAKANTA, MA; Indian author and poet; b. 3 Dec. 1938, Srinagar. *Education:* Rajasthan Univ. *Publications include:* Ailana Gali Zinda Hai 1984, Poshnool Ki Vapasi Tatha Anya Kahaniyan 1988, Yahan Vitasta Behti Hai 1992, Kothe Par Kaga 1993, Apne Apne Konark 1995, Katha Satisar (Vyas Samman Prize 2005) 2001, Sreshtha ancalika kahaniyam 2005, Antim Sakshya aur Arthantar 2006, Abbu Ne Kaha Tha 2006, Badalte Haalat Mein, Suraj Ugne Tak, Kali Baraf, O Sonkisri, Baki Sab Khariyat Hai, Salakhon Ke Peeche, Galat Logon Ke Beech, Katha Nagar, Prem Kahaniyan, Charchit Kahaniyan, Tanti Bai, Dahleez Per Niyay, Yaheen Kahin Aas Paas (poetry), Hashiye Kee Ibaratein (memoir). *Address:* c/o Remadhav Publications, C-22, 3rd Floor, RDC Raj Nagar, Ghaziabad, UP, 201 002, India (office). *Telephone:* (12) 4185000 (office). *Fax:* (12) 4185005 (office). *E-mail:* contact@remadhav.com (office). *Website:* www.remadhav.com (office).

CHANDRASEKARAN, Rajiv; American journalist and writer; *National Editor, The Washington Post*; b. San Francisco, Calif.; m. *Education:* Stanford Univ. *Career:* fmr Ed.-in-Chief, The Stanford Daily, Stanford Univ.; joined The Washington Post as Metropolitan staff reporter 1994, later nat. tech. corresp., and corresp. in Afghanistan, Indonesia, Egypt, bureau chief in Baghdad 2003–04, Asst Man. Ed. and Head, Continuous News 2004, Nat. Ed. 2006–; Journalist-in-Residence, Int. Reporting Project, Johns Hopkins School for Advanced Int. Studies 2005; Public Policy Scholar, Woodrow Wilson Int. Center 2005; frequent appearances as commentator on TV and radio include CNN, MSNBC, NPR. *Play:* Green Zone 2009. *Publication:* Imperial Life in the Emerald City (Overseas Press Club Book Award, Ron Ridenhour Prize, BBC Four Samuel Johnson Prize for Non-Fiction 2007) 2006. *Literary Agent:* c/o Random House Speakers Bureau, MD 24–4, 1745 Broadway, New York, NY 10019, USA. *Telephone:* (212) 572-2013. *E-mail:* rhspeakers@randomhouse.com. *Website:* www.rhspeakers.com. *Address:* c/o Knopf Publicity, Random House Inc., 1745 Broadway, New York, NY 10019, USA. *Telephone:* (212) 572-2013 (office). *Website:* www.rajivc.com.

CHANEY, Edward Paul de Gruyter, BA, MPhil, PhD, FSA, FRHistS; British academic and writer; *Professor of Fine and Decorative Arts, Southampton Solent University*; b. 11 April 1951, Hayes, Middx, England; m. Lisa Maria Jacka 1973 (divorced); two d. *Education:* Univ. of Reading, Warburg Inst., London Univ., European Univ. Inst., Florence, Italy. *Career:* Lecturer, Univ. of Pisa, Italy 1979–85; Adjunct Asst Prof., Charles A. Strong Center, Georgetown Univ. Florence Program, Villa Le Balze, Florence 1982, 1983; Assoc., Harvard Univ. Center for Italian Renaissance Studies, Villa I Tatti, Florence 1984–85; Shuffrey Research Fellow in Architectural History, Lincoln Coll., Oxford 1985–90; part-time History of Art Lecturer, Oxford Polytechnic 1991, Oxford Brookes Univ. 1993–; historian, London Div., English Heritage 1991–93; currently Prof. of Fine and Decorative Arts and Chair of History of Collecting Research Centre, Southampton Solent Univ.; Leverhulme Major Research Fellow 2010–12; mem. Exec. Cttee or Editorial Bd, Wyndham Lewis Soc., Walpole Soc., Catholic Record Soc., British Art Journal, British-Italian Soc., The Court Historian. *Publications include:* Oxford, China and Italy: Writings in Honour of Sir Harold Acton on his Eightieth Birthday (co-ed. with N. Ritchie) 1984, The Grand Tour and the Great Rebellion: Richard Lassels and 'The Voyage of Italy' in the Seventeenth Century 1985, Florence: A Travellers' Companion (with Harold Acton) 1986, England and the Continental Renaissance: Essays in Honour of J. B. Trapp (co-ed. with Peter Mack)

1990, English Architecture: Public and Private: Essays for Kerry Downes (co-ed. with John Bold) 1993, The Evolution of the Grand Tour: Anglo-Italian cultural relations since the Renaissance 1998, The Stuart Portrait: Status and Legacy (with G. Worsdale) 2001, Richard Eurich (1903–1992): Visionary Artist (with C. Clearkin) 2003, The Evolution of English Collecting: Receptions of Italian Art in the Tudor and Stuart Periods 2003, Inigo Jones's Roman Sketchbook 2006, William Rose: Tradition and an Individual Talent 2009; contrib. to reference works, books, scholarly journals, periodicals, newspapers, TV and radio. *Honours:* Hon. Life mem. British Inst. of Florence 1984; Hon. Assoc., Soc. of Fine Art Auctioneers; Commendatore of the Italian Repub. 2003; Hon. Dottore di Laurea in Lingue e Letterature Straniere (Univ. of Pisa) 1983;. *Address:* Southampton Solent University, East Park Terrace, Southampton, Hants., SO14 0RF, England (office). *Telephone:* (23) 8031-9478 (office). *E-mail:* edward.chaney@solent.ac.uk (office).

CHANG, Jung, PhD; British writer; b. 25 March 1952, Yibin, Sichuan Prov., China; d. of Chang Shou-Yu and Xia De-Hong; m. Jon Halliday 1991. *Education:* Sichuan Univ., Univ. of York. *Career:* fmrly worked as a peasant, a 'barefoot doctor', a steelworker and an electrician; Asst Lecturer, Sichuan Univ.; moved to UK to study linguistics 1978; now full-time writer. *Publications:* Madame Sun Yat-sen (with Jon Halliday) 1986, Wild Swans: Three Daughters of China (NCR Book Award 1992, UK Writers' Guild Best Non-Fiction Book 1992, Fawcett Soc. Book Award 1992, Book of the Year 1993, Golden Bookmark Award, Belgium 1993, 1994, Best Book Award, Humo, Belgium 1993) 1991, Mao: the Unknown Story (with Jon Halliday) 2005. *Honours:* Dr hc (Buckingham) 1996, (Warwick, York) 1997, (Open Univ.) 1998, (Bowdoin Coll., USA) 2005; Bjørnsonordenen, Den Norske Orden for Literature, Norway 1995.

CHANG, Lan Samantha, MFA, MPA, BA; Chinese/American writer; b. 1965, Appleton, Wis.; m. *Education:* Yale Univ., Harvard Univ., Stanford Univ. and Univ. of Iowa. *Career:* Wallace Stegner and Truman Capote fellowships, Stanford Univ. 1993; Briggs-Copeland Lecturer in Creative Writing, Harvard Univ.; Dir Iowa Writers' Workshop 2005–. *Publications include:* Hunger: A Novella and Stories 1998, Inheritance 2004, All is Forgotten, Nothing is Lost 2010; contribs to Atlantic Monthly, Ploughshares, Best American Short Stories. *Honours:* Henfield/Transatlantic Review Award, Guggenheim Fellowship 2008. *Address:* c/o W.W. Norton & Co. Inc., 500 Fifth Avenue, New York, NY 10110, USA (office).

CHANNER, Colin; Jamaican novelist; *Assistant Professor of English, Medgar Evans College*; b. 1963, Kingston; two c. *Career:* currently Asst Prof. of English, Medgar Evans Coll., NY; bass player for reggae band Pipecock Jaxxon; Founder and Artistic Dir Calabash Int. Literary Festival 2001. *Publications include:* novels: Waiting in Vain 1998, I'm Still Waiting (novella, featured in anthology Got to be Real) 2001, Satisfy My Soul 2002, Passing Through 2004, Iron Balloons (ed.) 2006, The Girl with the Golden Shoes 2007, Lover's Rock 2011. *E-mail:* colin@colinchanner.com (office); colinchanner@hotmail.com. *Website:* www.colinchanner.com.

CHAO, Patricia, BA, MA; American novelist and poet; b. 1955, Monterey, Calif. *Education:* Brown Univ., New York Univ. *Career:* Creative Writing Teacher, Sarah Lawrence Coll., Bronxville, NY; reviewer for Global Rhythm magazine; Ed. Global City Review special issue 1996; New York Foundation of the Arts Fellowship 2002; Japan-US Creative Arts Fellowship 2009. *Publications include:* novels: Monkey King 1997, Mambo Peligroso 2005; contribs to periodicals and books. *Honours:* Rose Low Memorial Poetry Prize, Brown Univ. 1978, Fellowship, New York Univ. Master's Programme in Creative Writing 1990–92, Dean's Fiction Prize, New York Univ. 1992, New Voice Award for Poetry, The Writer's Voice 1996.

CHAPLIN, Jenny Telfer, (Tracie Telfer, Wendy Wentworth), DCE, FSA Scot; Scottish editor, publisher, novelist, poet and public speaker; b. 22 Dec. 1928, Glasgow; m. J. McDonald Chaplin 1951 (died 2008); one d. *Education:* Govan High School, Jordanhill Coll. of Educ., Glasgow. *Career:* fmr teacher, Rothesay Primary School, Bute 1950; Headmistress and Owner, Middle-Farm School, Bota, Cameroon, W Africa 1950s; teacher, Edgbaston High School for Girls, Birmingham, Jordanmill Coll. School, Glasgow 1970s; Founder, Ed. and Publr International: The Writers Rostrum 1984–93; public speaker 2004–. *Play:* Ah'm Awa Tae Ardyne 1979. *Publications include:* Tales of a Glasgow Childhood 1994, Alone in a Garden 1994, Happy Days in Rothesay 1995, From Scotland's Past 1996, Childhood Days in Glasgow 1996, Thoughts on Writing (with Fay Goldie and V. Cuthbert) 1996, An Emigrant's Farewell, in A Scottish Childhood Vol. II, anthology of memoirs from famous Scottish people 1998, We Belonged to Glasgow 2001; novels as Jenny Telfer Chaplin: The Kinnon Trilogy (aka The Candleriggs Trilogy): The Kinnons of Candleriggs 2004, The Widow of Candleriggs 2005, The Ashes of Candleriggs 2006, A Life to Live in Glasgow 2008, We Came Frae Govan 2009, Beyond the Bridge of Time 2010; contrib. to The Scots Magazine, The Highlander Magazine, Scottish Memories, The Scottish Banner, The Friendship Book of Francis Gay, anthologies. *Honours:* Proclaimed Champion Poet of Largs, Ayrshire 2000. *Address:* Tigh na Mara Cottage, 14 Ardbeg Road, Rothesay, Bute, PA20 0NJ, Scotland (home). *Telephone:* (1700) 502737 (home).

CHAPLINA, Nataliya; Russian newspaper editor; *CEO and Editor-in-Chief, RosBalt News Agency*; b. 15 Feb. 1957, Leningrad (now St Petersburg); m 2nd Viktor Cherkesov 1996; two d. *Education:* St Petersburg State Univ. *Career:* journalist 1975–; Founder and Ed.-in-Chief Chas Pik (first ind. newspaper in Russian Fed.) 1990–2003, fmr Chair.; Project Dir RosBalt news agency 2003–, currently CEO and Ed.-in-Chief. *Publications:* several books. *Honours:* USSR Journalists' Union Award 1991, Russian Journalists' Union Award 1994. *Address:* Rosbalt News Agency, 190000 St Petersburg, 7 Konnogvardeisky Boulevard, Russia (office). *Telephone:* (812) 320-50-30 (office). *Fax:* (812) 320-50-31 (office). *E-mail:* rosbalt@rosbalt.ru (office). *Website:* www.rosbalt.ru (office).

CHAPMAN, (Francis) Ian, CBE, CBIM, FRSA, FFCS; British publisher; b. 26 Oct. 1925, St Fergus, Aberdeenshire, Scotland; s. of Rev. Peter Chapman and Frances Burdett; m. Marjory Stewart Swinton 1953; one s. one d. *Education:* Shawlands Acad., Ommer School of Music, Glasgow. *Career:* served in RAF 1943–44; miner (nat. service) 1945–47; with William Collins Sons & Co. Ltd (fmrly W.M. Collins Holdings PLC, now Harper Collins) 1947, man. trainee, New York br. 1950–51, Sales Man., London br. 1955; mem. main operating Bd, Group Sales Dir 1959, Jt Man. Dir 1967–76, Deputy Chair. 1976–81, Chair. CEO 1981–89; Deputy Chair. Orion Publishing Group 1993–94, Dir William Collins overseas cos 1968–89: Canada 1968–89, USA 1974–89, South Africa 1978–89, NZ 1978–89, William Collins Int. Ltd 1975–89; Chair. Scottish Radio Holdings PLC (fmrly Radio Clyde) 1972–96 (Hon. Pres. 1996–2000), Harvill Press 1976–89, Hatchards Ltd 1976–89, William Collins Publrs Ltd 1979–81, The Listener Publs PLC 1988–93, RadioTrust PLC 1997–2001, Guinness Publrs Ltd 1991–98; Dir Pan Books Ltd 1962–84 (Chair. 1973–76), Book Tokens Ltd 1981–94, Ind. Radio News 1984–85, Stanley Botes Ltd 1986–89, Guinness PLC (non-exec.) 1986–91; Pres.-Dir Gen. Guinness Media SAS, Paris 1996–99; f. Chapmans Publrs, Chair. and Man. Dir 1989–94; Trustee, Book Trade Benevolent Soc. 1982–2003, The Publishers Asscn 1989–97; mem. Gov. Council SCOTBIC; mem. Council Publishers Asscn 1962–77, Vice-Pres. 1978, Pres. 1979–81; Chair. Nat. Acad. of Writing 2000–03, Vice-Pres. 2003; mem. Bd Book Devt Council 1967, Ancient House Bookshop 1972–89, Scottish Opera, Theatre Royal Ltd 1974–79, IRN Ltd 1983–85; Chair. Advisory Bd Strathclyde Univ. Business School 1985–88. *Honours:* Hon. DLitt (Strathclyde) 1990; Scottish Free Enterprise Award 1985. *Address:* Kenmore, 46 The Avenue, Cheam, Surrey, SM2 7QE, England (home). *Telephone:* (20) 8642-1820 (home). *E-mail:* fichapman@25googlemail.com (home).

CHAPMAN, Jean, BA (Hons); British writer; b. 30 Oct. 1929, England; m. Lionel Alan Chapman 1961; one s. two d. *Education:* Open Univ. *Career:* tutored on-line for Nottingham Trent Univ.; fmr reviewer, appraiser and creative writing tutor for East Midlands arts, Readers' Digest and community colls; fmr Pres. Leicester Writer's Club; Chair., Romantic Novelists Asscn 2001–03; mem. Society of Authors, Crime Writers Asscn. *Publications include:* The Unreasoning Earth 1981, Tangled Dynasty 1984, Forbidden Path 1986, Savage Legacy 1987, The Bellmakers 1990, Fortune's Woman 1992, A World Apart 1993, The Red Pavilion 1995, The Soldier's Girl 1997, This Time Last Year 1999, A New Beginning 2001, And a Golden Pear 2002, Danced Over the Sea 2004, Both Sides of the Fence 2009, A Watery Grave March 2011; many short stories. *Address:* 3 Arnesby Lane, Peatling Magna, Leicester, LE8 5UN, England (home). *E-mail:* jean.chapman1@btinternet.com.

CHAPMAN, Stanley David, BSc, MA, PhD; British writer and fmr academic; b. 31 Jan. 1935, Nottingham, England; m.; two s. *Education:* London School of Econs, Univs of Nottingham and Manchester. *Career:* Lecturer, Univ. of Nottingham 1968–73, Pasold Reader in Business History 1973–, Prof. 1993–97, Prof. Emer. 1998–; Ed. Textile History Bi Annual 1984–2002. *Publications include:* The Early Factory Masters 1967, The Beginnings of Industrial Britain 1970, The History of Working Class Housing 1971, The Cotton Industry in the Industrial Revolution 1972, Jesse Boot of Boots the Chemists 1974, The Devon Cloth Industry in the 18th Century 1978, European Textile Printers in the 18th Century (with S. Chassagne) 1981, Stanton and Staveley 1981, The Rise of Merchant Banking 1984, Merchant Enterprise in Britain from the Industrial Revolution to World War I 1992, Hosiery and Knitwear: Four Centuries of Small-Scale Industry in Britain 1589–2000 2002, Southwell Town and People (co-ed. with D. Walker) 2006, Minster People (co-ed. with D. Walker) 2009. *Address:* Rochester House, Halam Road, Southwell, Notts., NG25 0AD, England (home).

CHAPPELL, Fred Davis, BA, MA; American poet, writer and fmr teacher; b. 28 May 1936, Canton, NC; m. Susan Nicholls 1959; one s. *Education:* Duke Univ. *Career:* teacher, Univ. of North Carolina, Greensboro 1964–2004; Burlington Industries Prof. of English 1988; Poet Laureate, NC 1997–2003. *Publications include:* poetry: The World Between the Eyes 1971, River 1975, The Man Twice Married to Fire 1977, Bloodfire 1978, Awakening to Music 1979, Wind Mountain 1979, Earthsleep 1980, Driftlake: A Lieder Cycle 1981, Midquest 1981, Castle Tzingal 1984, Source 1985, First and Last Words 1989, C: 100 Poems 1993, Spring Garden: New and Selected Poems 1995, Poetry Collection: Family Gathering 2000, Backsass 2004, Shadow Box 2009; fiction: It is Time, Lord 1963, The Inkling 1965, Dagon 1968, The Gaudy Place 1972, Moments of Light (short story) 1980, I Am One of You Forever 1985, Brighten the Corner Where You Are 1989, More Shapes Than One (short story) 1991, The Somewhere Doors (short story) (World Fantasy Award) 1992, The Lodger (short story) (World Fantasy Award) 1994, Farewell, I'm Bound to Leave You 1996, Look Back All the Green Valley 1999, Ancestors and Others (short stories) 2009; other: Plow Naked: Selected Writings on Poetry 1993, A Way of Happening: Observations of Contemporary Poetry 1998. *Honours:* Rockefeller Grant 1967–68, Nat. Inst. of Arts and Letters Award 1968, Académie Française Prix de Meilleur des Livres Étrangers 1972, Sir Walter Raleigh Prize 1972, Roanoke-Chowan Poetry Prizes 1972, 1975, 1979, 1980, 1985, 1989, North Carolina Award in Literature 1980, Bollingen Prize in Poetry

1985, O. Max Gardner Award 1987, Ingersoll Foundation T. S. Eliot Prize 1993, Aiken Taylor Award in Poetry 1996, Thomas Wolfe Prize 2006, Caroliniana Award 2007, John Tyler Caldwell Award 2010, William Walker Lifetime Achievement Award 2012. *Address:* 305 Kensington Road, Greensboro, NC 27403, USA. *Telephone:* (336) 275-8851.

CHAPPLE, John Alfred Victor, MA; British academic and writer; *Professor Emeritus, Hull University*; b. 25 April 1928, Barnstaple, Devon, England. *Education:* Univ. Coll., London. *Career:* Research Asst, Univ. Coll., London 1953–55, Yale Univ., USA 1955–58; Asst Lecturer, Univ. of Aberdeen 1958–59; Asst Lecturer, Univ. of Manchester 1959–61, Lecturer 1961–67, Sr Lecturer 1967–71; Prof., Univ. of Hull 1971–92, Prof. Emer. 1992–; Visiting Fellow, Corpus Christi Coll., Cambridge 1991–92; mem. Gaskell Soc. (Pres. 1992–2006), Int. Asscn of Univ. Profs of English, Johnson Soc., Friends of Erasmus, Darwin House. *Publications include:* The Letters of Mrs Gaskell 1966, Documentary and Imaginative Literature 1880–1920 1970, Elizabeth Gaskell: A Portrait in Letters 1980, Science and Literature in the 19th Century 1986, Private Voices: The Diaries of Elizabeth Gaskell and Sophia Holland 1996, Elizabeth Gaskell: The Early Years 1997, Further Letters of Mrs Gaskell 2000, 2003, Life of Dryden in Samuel Johnson, The Lives of the Poets 2010. *Address:* 8 Lomax Close, Lichfield, Staffs., WS13 7EY, England (home).

CHARBONNEAU, Eileen, BA; American writer and performer; b. 11 April 1951, Long Island, NY; d. of Vincent Charbonneau and Catherine Zorovich; m. Edward Gullo 1972; two d. one s. *Education:* State Univ. of NY, Fredonia, River Arts Film School, Woodstock, NY, New School for Social Research. *Career:* fmr freelance writer for The New York Times, Lady's Circle, Romantic Interludes, and Mothering Magazine; mem. Sisters in Story, Historical Novel Soc., Novelists Inc. *Plays:* Manituwak, Place of the Spirits, Genie (with James Green), Hats Off to Our 50 States. *Films:* Endowment for the Planet (Ed Gullo) 1990, Racing Daylight 2007, Divine Sparks 2008. *Publications include:* The Ghosts of Stony Clove 1988, In the Time of the Wolves 1994, The Mound Builders' Secret 1994, Disappearance at Harmony Festival 1994, Honor to the Hills 1996, Waltzing in Ragtime 1996, The Randolph Legacy (Reviewer's Choice Award) 1997, Rachel LeMoyne 1998, The Connor Emerald 2000; contribs to periodicals. *Honours:* Romance Writers of America Golden Medallion Award 1989, American Library Asscn Best Books Citations 1994, Council of Books for Children Best Books Citation 1996, Washington Post Book World 1998, Christopher Columbus Screenwriting Award 1999, Washington Romance Writers of America Lifetime Achievement Award 2004, Phyllis A. Whitney Writing Award. *Address:* PO Box 20, Cold Spring, NY 10516-0020, USA (home). *E-mail:* aponteliterary@gmail.com (office); eileencharbonneau@gmail.com (home). *Website:* eileencharbonneau.googlepages.com.

CHARBONNEAU-TISSOT, Claudette (see Aude)

CHARKIN, Richard Denis Paul, MA; British publishing executive; *Executive Director, Bloomsbury PLC*; b. 17 June 1949, London; s. of Frank Charkin and Mabel Doreen Charkin (née Rosen); m. Susan Mary Poole 1972; one s. two d. *Education:* Haileybury, Imperial Service Coll., Univ. of Cambridge and Harvard Business School. *Career:* Science Ed. Harrap & Co. 1972; Sr Publishing Man. Pergamon Press 1973; Medical Ed. Oxford Univ. Press 1974, Head of Science and Medicine 1976, Head of Reference 1980; Man. Dir Academic and Gen. 1984; joined Octopus Publishing Group (Reed Int. Books) 1988; Chief Exec. Reed Consumer Books 1989–94, Exec. Dir Reed Books Int. 1988–96, Chief Exec. 1994–96; CEO Current Science Group 1996–97; CEO Macmillan Ltd 1998–2007; Exec. Dir Bloomsbury PLC 2007–; Non-Exec. Dir, Inst. of Physics Publishing 2009–; Visiting Prof., Univ. of Arts, London 2004–; Visiting Fellow, Green Coll., Oxford 1987; Chair. Common Purpose 1998–2008; mem. man. cttee John Wisden; mem. Publishers Asscn (Vice-Pres. 2004–05, Pres. 2005–06). *Publications:* Charkin Blog: The Archive 2008. *Address:* Bloomsbury Publishing PLC, 36 Soho Square, London, W1D 3QY, England (office). *Telephone:* (20) 7494-2111 (office). *Fax:* (20) 7434-0151 (office). *Website:* www.bloomsbury.com (office).

CHARLES-ROUX, Edmonde; French writer; *President, Académie Goncourt*; b. 17 April 1920, Neuilly-sur-Seine; d. of François Charles-Roux and Sabine Gounelle; m. Gaston Defferre 1973 (deceased). *Education:* Italy. *Career:* served as nurse, then in Resistance Movt, during Second World War, in which she was twice wounded; reporter, magazine Elle 1947–49; Features Ed., French edn of Vogue 1949–54, Ed.-in-Chief 1954–66; mem. Académie Goncourt 1983–, Pres. 2002–. *Dance:* collaboration with La Compagnie nationale des Ballets de Roland Petit, Marseille. *Publications:* Oublier Palerme 1966, Elle Adrienne 1971, L'irrégulière ou mon itinéraire Chanel 1974, Le temps Chanel 1979, Stèle pour un bâtard, Don Juan d'Autriche 1980, Une enfance sicilienne 1981, Un désir d'Orient: La jeunesse d'Isabelle Eberhardt 1988, Nomade j'étais: Les années africaines d'Isabelle Eberhardt 1995, L'homme de Marseille 2001. *Honours:* Croix de guerre 1940–45, Commdr, Légion d'honneur 2010, Caporal d'honneur, Légion Etrangère 2007; Prix Goncourt 1966, Grand Prix Littéraire de Provence 1977. *Address:* c/o Editions Grasset, 61 rue des Saints-Pères, Paris 75006, France (office). *Website:* www.academie-goncourt.fr.

CHARNAS, Suzy McKee, (Rebecca Brand), BA, MA; American writer and teacher; b. (Suzy McKee) 22 Oct. 1939, New York, NY; d. of Robinson McKee and Maxine Szanton; m. Stephen Charnas 1968; one step-s. one step-d. *Education:* Barnard Coll., New York Univ. *Career:* Instructor, Clarion West Writers Workshop, Seattle 1984, 1986, 1997, Taos Writers School 1993–96, Clarion Writers Workshop, Michigan 1987, 2000, 2004, Univ. of New Mexico 1993, 2005; Chair. Archive Project Cttee, Nat. Council of Returned Peace Corps Volunteers 1986–88; mem. Authors' Guild, Science Fiction and Fantasy Writers of America, Dramatists Guild. *Play:* Vampire Dreams 1990. *Publications include:* Walk to the End of the World (Tiptree Award 1996) 1974, Motherlines (Tiptree Award 1996) 1978, The Vampire Tapestry 1980, The Bronze King 1985, Dorothea Dreams 1986 (revised 2010), The Silver Glove 1988, The Golden Thread 1989, The Kingdom of Kevin Malone (Aslan Award 1994) 1993, Vampire Dreams (play) 1990, The Furies 1994, The Ruby Tear 1997, The Conqueror's Child (Tiptree Award) 1999, Strange Seas 2001, My Father's Ghost 2002, Stagestruck Vampires 2004, Late Bloomer 2011; short fiction: Unicorn Tapestry (Nebula Award 1980, Gigamesh Award 1990), The Ancient Mind at Work (Gigamesh Award 1990), Boobs (Hugo Award for Best Short Story 1990), Listening to Brahms, Beauty and the Opera, or the Phantom Beast, Lowland Sea, Evil Thoughts, etc. *Honours:* Gaylactic Spectrum Hall of Fame Award 2003. *Address:* 212 High Street NE, Albuquerque, NM 87102, USA (home). *E-mail:* pagemail@swcp.com (home). *Website:* www.suzymckeecharnas.com.

CHARRY, Brinda S., MA, PhD; Indian writer and academic; *Assistant Professor of English, Keene State College*; b. Bangalore, Karnataka. *Education:* Mount Carmel Coll. and Syracuse Univ., USA. *Career:* fmrly taught at Syracuse Univ., New York; Asst Prof. of English, Keene State Coll., USA 2005–. *Publications include:* The Hottest Day of the Year (novel) 2001, Shadow (short story) 2003, Naked in the Wind (Golden Quill Award 2008) 2007, First Love 2009, Emissaries in Early Modern Literature and Culture (co-ed with Gitanjali Shahani) 2009; contrib. to First Love and Other Stories 2009, to Indian periodicals. *Honours:* Katha Award 1997, 2003, Winner, Asian Age Short Story Competition, Hindu-Picador Short Story Competition, Commonwealth Broadcasting Asscn Short Story Competition. *Address:* Department of English, Keene State College, 229 Main Street, Keene, NH 03435, USA (office). *Telephone:* (603) 358-2727 (office). *E-mail:* bcharry@keene.edu (office). *Website:* www.keene.edu (office).

CHARTERIS, Richard, BA, MA, PhD, FAHA, FRHistS; New Zealand/Australian musicologist, academic, writer and editor; *Professor Emeritus in Historical Musicology, University of Sydney*; b. 24 June 1948, Chatham Islands, NZ. *Education:* Victoria Univ., Wellington and Univ. of Canterbury, NZ, Univ. of London, UK. *Career:* Research Fellow, Univ. of Sydney, Australia 1976–78, 1981–1990, Sr Research Fellow (Reader) 1991–94, Prof. in Historical Musicology, Music Dept 1995–2008, Prof. Emer. in Historical Musicology 2009–, Dir Centre of Early Venetian Music; Research Fellow, Univ. of Queensland, Australia 1979–80; Australian Acad. of Humanities Travelling Fellow 1979–80; mem. American Musicological Soc., Australian Acad. of the Humanities, Dolmetsch Foundation of GB, Inst. of Historical Research, London, Int. Musicological Soc., Musicological Soc. of Australia, Nat. Early Music Asscn of GB, Royal Historical Soc., London, Royal Musical Asscn of GB, Viola da Gamba Soc. of America, Viola da Gamba Soc. of GB. *Publications include:* more than 200 books, journal articles and critical and performing edns devoted to the music of Johann Christian Bach, Giovanni Bassano, John Coprario, Alfonso Ferrabosco the Elder, Domenico Maria Ferrabosco, Andrea and Giovanni Gabrieli, Hans Leo Hassler, John Hingeston, Thomas Lupo, Claudio Monteverdi, Daniel Purcell and others, mostly in the series Corpus Mensurabilis Musicae, Musica Britannica, Recent Researches in the Music of the Baroque Era, Fretwork Editions, Baroque and Classical Music Series, Viol Consort Series, Boethius Editions and King's Music Editions; books on composers, music, collectors and early sources in the series Boethius Editions, Thematic Catalogues Series, Annotated Reference Tools in Music, Detroit Studies in Music Bibliography, Musicological Studies and Documents and Altro Polo. *Honours:* Sr Scholar 1970–71, Mary Duncan Scholar 1975, Louise Dyer Award, Royal Musical Asscn 1975, Top Award, Australian Hi Fi FM Classical Music Section 1988, Australian Centenary Medal 2003. *Address:* Arts Music Unit, Seymour Theatre Centre J09, University of Sydney, Sydney, NSW 2006, Australia (office). *Website:* www-personal.arts.usyd.edu.au/charteris (office).

CHARYN, Jerome, BA; American writer and educator; *Professor of Film Studies, American University of Paris*; b. 13 May 1937, New York, NY. *Education:* Manhattan's High School of Music and Art, Columbia Univ. *Career:* English teacher, Manhattan's High School of Music and Art, School of Performing Arts, New York City 1962–64; Lecturer in English, City Coll. of New York 1965; Asst Prof., Stanford Univ. 1966–68; Prof., Lehman Coll., CUNY 1968–80; Founding Ed. The Dutton Review 1970; Visiting Prof., Rice Univ. 1979, City Coll. of New York 1988–89; Lecturer, Princeton Univ. 1980–86; Prof. of Film Studies, American Univ. of Paris 1995–2008, Prof. Emer. 2008–; mem. PEN, Authors' Guild, Writers Guild of America, Int. Asscn of Crime Writers. *Publications include:* fiction: Once Upon a Droshky 1964, On the Darkening Green 1965, The Man Who Grew Younger 1967, Going to Jerusalem 1967, American Scrapbook 1969, The Single Voice: An Anthology of Contemporary Fiction 1969, The Troubled Vision 1970, Eisenhower, My Eisenhower 1971, The Tar Baby 1973, Blue Eyes 1975, Marilyn the Wild 1976, The Education of Patrick Silver 1976, The Franklin Scare 1977, Secret Isaac 1978, The Seventh Babe 1979, The Catfish Man 1980, Darlin' Bill 1980, Panna Maria 1982, Pinocchio's Nose 1983, The Isaac Quartet 1984, War Cries Over Avenue C 1985, Paradise Man 1987, The Good Policeman 1990, Elsinore 1991, Maria's Girls 1992, Back to Bataan 1993, Montezuma's Man 1993, Little

Angel Street 1995, El Bronx 1997, Death of a Tango King 1998, Citizen Sidel 1999, Captain Kidd 1999, Hurricane Lady 2001, The Isaac Quartet 2002, The Green Lantern 2004, Johnny One-Eye 2008, The Secret Life of Emily Dickinson 2010; non-fiction: Metropolis: New York as Myth, Marketplace and Magical Land 1986, Movieland: Hollywood and the Great American Dream Culture 1989, The Dark Lady from Belorusse 1997, The Black Swan 2000, Sizzling Chops and Devilish Spins 2001, Bronx Boy 2002, Gangsters & Gold Diggers 2003, Savage Shorthand: The Life and Death of Isaac Babel 2005, Inside the Hornet's Head: an anthology of Jewish American Writing 2005, Raised by Wolves: The Turbulent Art and Times of Quentin Tarantino 2005, Marilyn: The Last Goddess 2008, Joe DiMaggio: The Long Vigil 2011. *Honours:* Commdr, Ordre des Arts et des Lettres 2002. *Address:* 302 West 12th Street, Apt 10C, New York, NY 10014, USA (home). *E-mail:* jeromecharyn@aol.com (home). *Website:* www.jeromecharyn.com.

CHASE, Elaine Raco; American writer; b. 31 Aug. 1949, Schenectady, NY; d. of Ernest Salvatore Raco and Helen Nancy Scavia; m. Gary Dale Chase 1969; one s. one d. *Education:* Albany Business Coll., Union Coll., State Univ. of New York. *Career:* mem. Romance Writers of America, Sisters in Crime (Nat. Pres. 1995–96). *Publications include:* Rules of the Game 1980, Tender Yearnings 1981, A Dream Come True 1982, Double Occupancy 1982, Designing Woman 1982, No Easy Way Out 1983, Video Vixen 1983, Best Laid Plans 1983, Special Delivery 1984, Lady Be Bad 1984, Dare the Devil 1987, Dangerous Places 1987, Dark Corners 1988, Partners in Crime 1994, Amateur Detective (non-fiction) 1996, Calculated Risk 1999; contribs to several publs. *Honours:* Walden Book Award 1985, Top Romantic Supsense Series Award 1987–88. *Address:* 22575 Leanne Terrace 213, Ashburn, VA 20148, USA (home). *Telephone:* (703) 726-0948 (home). *E-mail:* elainerc@juno.com (office).

CHASE BRENES, Alfonso; Costa Rican writer, poet and academic; b. 19 Oct. 1944, Cartago. *Career:* fmr Dir of Publications, Ministry of Culture; Faculty mem., Universidad Nacional, Heredia 1974–, currently Prof. of Literature; fmr Scholar-in-Residence, Arkansas Univ., USA; Founder Asociación de Escritores de América Central 1993, Costa Rica PEN 1955; mem. Costa Rican chapter of the Int. Bd on Books for Young People (IBBY), Phi Beta Delta Honor Soc. for Int. Scholars, USA; Foreign mem. of Honor, Popular Culture Asscn, USA. *Publications include:* poetry: Los reinos de mi mundo 1966, El árbol del tiempo 1967, Para escribir sobre el agua 1970, Cuerpos 1972, Max Jiménez 1973, El libro de la patria 1975, Los pies sobre la tierra 1978, Obra en marcha 1982, El tigre luminoso 1982, Entre el ojo y la noche 1990, Jardines de asfalto (Premio Nacional Aquileo J. Echeverría) 1995, El pavo real y la mariposa 1996; prose: Los juegos furtivos 1968, Las puertas de la noche 1974, Mirar con inocencia 1975, Días y territorios 1980, La pajarita de papel 1988, Ella usaba bikini 1991, El hombre que se quedó adentro del sueño 1994, Nuestra Señora de los Ángeles 1995, Los herederos de la promesa 1997, El Pavo Real y la Mariposa 1998, Cara de santo, uñas de gato 1999; also essays, children's books.

CHASE-RIBOUD, Barbara Dewayne, BFA, MFA, PhD; American/French sculptor and writer; b. 26 June 1939, Philadelphia, Pa; d. of Charles Edward Chase and Vivian May Braithwaite West Chase; m. 1st Marc Eugene Riboud 1961 (divorced 1981); m. 2nd S. G. Tosi 1981; two s. *Education:* Temple Univ., Yale Univ. *Career:* rep. in perm. collections in USA and France; Fellow, John Hay Whitney Foundation 1958, Nat. Endowment for Arts 1973. *Exhibitions include:* solo: Berkeley Museum, CA 1973, MIT 1973, Museum of Modern Art, Paris 1974, Kunstmuseum, Düsseldorf, Germany 1974, Bronx Museum, New York 1979, Pasadena Coll., CA 1990, Metropolitan Museum of Art, New York 1999, Walters Museum Washington, DC 2000, Philadelphia Art Museum 2005–06, Shanghai Museum of Contemporary Art 2005–06, Muscarelle Museum of Art, Virginia 2009; numerous group exhbns in Italy, France, USA, Germany, Australia, UK, China. *Publications include:* From Memphis and Peking, Poems 1974, Sally Hemings, A Novel 1979, Valide 1986, Portrait of a Nude Woman as Cleopatra 1987, Amistad: Echo of Lions 1989, The President's Daughter 1995, Roman Egyptian 1995, The Sculpture of Barbara Chase-Riboud, Selz, Jansen A. Abrams 2001, Hottentot Venus 2003, Love Perfecting, Collected Poems 1974–2007 2008, Central Park 2009. *Honours:* Kt of French Repub. 1996, Chevalier, Ordre des Arts et des Lettres; Hon. PhD (Temple Univ., Univ. of Connecticut, Mullenberg Coll., Dillard Univ.) 2005; Kafka Prize 1979, Acad. of Italy Gold Medal 1979, Carl Sandburg Poetry Prize 1988, US Gen. Services Design Award for Best Public Sculpture 1998, American Library Asscn Black Caucus Prize for Best Fiction 2004, Coll. Art Asscn Lifetime Achievement Award 2005, American Coll. Bd Lifetime Achievement Award 2007, Detroit Art Inst. Lifetime Achievement Award 2007. *Literary Agent:* c/o Sandra Dijkstra Agency, PMB515, 1155 Camino de Mar, Del Mar, CA 92014, USA. *Telephone:* (858) 755-3115. *Fax:* (858) 794-2822. *E-mail:* sdla@dijkstraagency.com. *Website:* www.dijkstraagency.com. *Address:* 3 rue Auguste Comte, 75006 Paris, France (home); Palazzo Ricci, 146 via Guilia, 00186 Rome, Italy (home). *Telephone:* 1-43-29-69-63 (Paris) (home). *Fax:* 1-43-29-47-53 (Paris) (home). *E-mail:* bchaseriboud@hotmail.com (office).

CHÂTELET, Noëlle, PhD; French academic, actress and writer; b. 16 Oct. 1944, Meudon, Seine; d. of Robert Jospin and Mireille Jospin (née Dandieu); m. François Châtelet (deceased); one s. *Education:* Lycée mixte de Meaux, Lycée Hélène Boucher, Paris, Univs of Sorbonne and Paris VIII—Vincennes Saint-Denis. *Career:* Asst Lecturer then Lecturer of Communication Studies, Univ. of Paris XI—Sud Orsay 1970–89; Dir French Inst. of Florence, Italy 1989–91; Head Dept of Culture, Univ. of Versailles—Saint-Quentin 1991–93; apptd Lecturer, Univ. of Paris V—René Descartes 1993, now Prof.; Co-Chair. Maison des écrivains 1995–; mem. Cttee Soc. des gens de lettres 1996–; jury mem. for various literary awards in France; mem. support cttee for Lionel Jospin, her brother, during French presidential election 2002; Deputy Pres. Soc. des Gens de Lettres 2003–. *Films include:* Les Autres 1972, Vera Baxter 1977, La Banquière 1980. *Television includes:* Les Buddenbrooks 1978–79, La Vie de Berlioz 1982, A coeur battant 2009, Passion grand-mère 2012. *Publications include:* Le corps à corps culinaire (essay) 1972, Histoires de bouches (Prix Goncourt de la nouvelle) 1987, A contre-sens 1989, La Courte échelle (Rene Fallet Prize, Francophone Schools and Univs Prize) 1991, A Table 1992, Trompe l'oeil (essay) 1993, La dame en bleu (Anna de Noailles Prize, Acad. française) 1996, La femme coquelicot 1997, Corps sur mesure (essay) 1998, Corps à corps culinaire 1998, La petite aux tournesois 1999, La tête en bas 2002, La dernière leçon 2004, À table 2007, Le Baiser d'Isabelle 2007, Au pays des vermeilles 2009. *Honours:* Chevalier, Ordre nat. du Mérite, Légion d'honneur. *Address:* 7 ter, rue Clauzel, 75009 Paris, France (home). *Telephone:* 1-48-78-57-84 (home).

CHATTERJEE, Debjani, MBE, BA, MA, PhD, PGCE; British writer, poet, editor, storyteller and translator; b. 21 Nov. 1952, Delhi, India; d. of Sanat Kumar Chatterjee and Tara Chatterjee; m. Brian D'Arcy 1983. *Education:* American Univ., Cairo, Egypt, Univ. of Kent, Canterbury, Univ. of Lancaster, Sheffield City Polytechnic (now Sheffield Hallam Univ.). *Career:* Assoc. Ed., Tadeeb Int., Pratibha India; Literary Ed., The Colour of Health; Mentor for Survivors Poetry; Founder and Dir Sahitya Press 1985–; Chair. Nat. Asscn of Writers in Education; Chair. Arts Council Translation Panel 1997–2000; Jt Chair. Hyphen-21 2008–; Vice-Chair. Sheffield Cancer Voices 2010–; Founder-mem. and Chair. Bengali Women's Support Group 2000–; Founder-mem. Sheffield Inter-faith; Founder-mem. The Healing Word 2011–; Patron of Survivors' Poetry 2003–; Life mem. Poetry Soc. (India, UK); mem. Arts Council of England, Literature Advisory Group 1996–99, Mini Mushaira 1996–, Tai Chi for Breast Cancer Group 2009–11, Macmillan Cancer Voices 2009–, Adult Cancer Survivorship Project 2009–10, Sheffield Carers Centre 1992–. *Publications include:* Peaces, Poems for Peace 1987, Whistling Still: Bloody Lyres 1989, I Was That Woman 1989, Northern Poetry, Vol. II 1991, The Sun Rises in the North 1993, A Little Bridge 1997, Albino Gecko 1998, Songs in Exile (trans.) 1999, Cette femme-là... 2000, The Redbeck Anthology of British South Asian Poetry 2000, Animal Antics 2000, My Birth Was Not in Vain: Selected Poems by Seven Bengali Women 2001, Jade Horse Torso: Poems and Translations 2003, Rainbow World: Poems from Many Cultures 2003, Generations of Ghazals: Ghazals by Nasir Kazmi & Basir Sultan Kazmi 2003, Daughters of a Riverine Land 2003; other: The Role of Religion in A Passage to India 1984, The Elephant-Headed God and Other Hindu Tales 1989, Barbed Lines 1990, Sweet and Sour 1993, The Parrot's Training (trans.) 1993, The Monkey God and Other Hindu Tales 1993, Sufi Stories from Around the World 1994, Nyamia and the Bag of Gold 1994, Home to Home 1995, The Most Beautiful Child 1996, Album (trans.) 1997, The Message of Thunder and Other Plays 1999, The Snake Prize and Other Folk Tales from Bengal 1999, Who Cares? Reminiscences of Yemeni Carers in Sheffield 2001, Namaskar: New & Selected Poems 2004, A Slice of Sheffield 2005, The Song of the Scythe 2005, A Special Assembly 2007, Raising their Voices 2008, Words Spit & Splinter 2009, A Tasty Garland 2010, Journeys & Places 2010, Let's Celebrate: Festival Poems from around the World 2011. *Honours:* Hon. Adviser of Word Masala; Hon. Life mem. Nasir Kazmi Soc. (Pakistan) 2006; Hon. DPhil (Sheffield Hallam Univ.) 2002; Shankars Int. Children's Competition Poetry Prize, Lancaster LitFest Poems Competition Winner, Peterloo Poets Open Poetry Competition, Artrage Annual Literature Award, Raymond Williams Community Publishing Prize 1990, Yorkshire and Humberside Arts Writer's Award 1995, Royal Literary Fund Fellow 2006–09, Muse India Poetry in Translation Prize 2008, Lesley Pearse Women of Courage Award Finalist 2010. *Address:* 11 Donnington Road, Sheffield, S2 2RF, England (home). *Website:* www.debjanichatterjee.moonfruit.com (office).

CHATTERJEE, Margaret, PhD; Indian (b. British) philosopher, writer and academic; b. 13 Sept. 1925, London, England; d. of Norman Herbert and Edith Gantzer; m. Nripendranath Chatterjee 1946; one s. two d. *Education:* Parkstone Grammar School, Somerville Coll., Oxford, UK and Univ. of Delhi. *Career:* moved to India 1946; teacher, later Prof. of Philosophy, Univ. of Delhi 1956–90; Prof. of Comparative Religion, Visva-Bharati, Santiniketan 1976–77; Visiting Prof., Drew Univ., NJ, USA 1983; Prof., Westminster Coll., Oxford 1992–98; Dir Indian Inst. of Advanced Study, Simla 1986–89, Visiting Scholar 2004; Visiting Fellow, Woodbrooke, Birmingham, UK 1990; Spalding Visiting Fellow in Indian Philosophy, Wolfson Coll., Oxford 1991; Commonwealth Visiting Fellow, Univ. of Calgary, Canada 1991; Pres. Int. Soc. for Metaphysics 1985–90. *Publications include:* Our Knowledge of Other Selves 1963, Philosophical Enquiries 1968, The Existentialist Outlook 1974, The Language of Philosophy 1981, Gandhi's Religious Thought 1983, The Religious Spectrum 1984, The Concept of Spirituality 1989, The Philosophy of Nikunja Vihari Banerjee 1990, Gandhi and his Jewish Friends 1992, Studies in Modern Jewish and Hindu Thought 1997, Contemporary Indian Philosophy 1998, Hinterlands and Horizons 2002, Lifeworlds, Philosophy and India Today 2005, Gandhi and the Challenge of Religious Diversity 2005, Gandhi's Diagnostic Approach Rethought 2007, Lifeworlds and Ethics 2007, Inter-religious Communication: A Gandhi Perspective 2009, Sketches from Memory Vols I and II 2009, Circumstance and Dharma 2009, Modalities of Otherness 2010, Sketches & Conversations Recalled 2011, Visiting Old Friends 2012, A Cluster of Perspectives 2012; poetry: The Spring and the Spectacle 1967, Towards the Sun 1970, The Sandalwood Tree 1972, The Sound of Wings 1978,

The Rimless World 1987, Poems 2010; short stories: At the Homeopath's 1975. *Address:* 49 Kala Kunj, A/0 Shalimar Bagh, Delhi 110 088, India (home). *Telephone:* (11) 27477054 (home).

CHATTERJEE, Upamanyu; Indian civil servant and writer; b. 1959, Patna, Bihar; m.; two d. *Education:* St Xavier's School, St Stephen's Coll., Univ. of Delhi. *Career:* joined Indian Civil Service 1983; Dir of Languages, Ministry of Human Resource Devt 1998; Writer-in-Residence, Univ. of Kent, UK 1990. *Publications include:* English, August: An Indian Story 1988, The Last Burden 1993, Mammaries of the Welfare State (Sahitya Akademi Award) 2000, Weight Loss 2006, Way to Go 2010. *Honours:* Officier, Ordre des Arts et des Lettres 2008. *Address:* c/o Marketing and Promotions Department, Penguin Books India Pvt., 11 Community Centre, Panchsheel Park, New Delhi 110 017, India (office). *E-mail:* publicity@in.penguingroup.com (office). *Website:* www.penguinbooksindia.com (office).

CHATTERTON-NEWMAN, Roger; British author; *Associate Editor, Polo Magazine;* b. 17 March 1949, Haslemere, Surrey, England. *Career:* editorial staff, Haymarket Publishing 1970–89; Archivist, Cowdray Park Polo Club 1990–2000; Deputy Ed. Polo Quarterly International, later Ed. 1997–2007; currently Assoc. Ed. Polo Magazine. *Publications include:* A Hampshire Parish 1976, Brian Boru, King of Ireland 1983, Murtagh and the Vikings 1986, Betwixt Petersfield and Midhurst 1991, Edward Bruce: A Medieval Tragedy 1992, Polo at Cowdray 1992, Murtagh the Warrior 1996, Great Polo Clubs of the World 2009; contribs to Hampshire Magazine, Horse and Hound, Polo Quarterly International, West Sussex History, Downs Country, International Polo Review, The Ring Fort Annual. *Address:* Polo Magazine, Regency House, 19 Suffolk Road, Cheltenham, Glos., GL50 2AF, England (office). *Telephone:* (1242) 222055 (office). *E-mail:* info@thepolomagazine.com (office). *Website:* www.thepolomagazine.com (office).

CHAUDHURI, Amit, BA, DPhil, FRSL; Indian writer and academic; *Professor of Contemporary Literature, University of East Anglia;* b. 15 May 1962, Calcutta (now Kolkata); m. Rinka Khastgir 1991; one d. *Education:* Univ. of London and Balliol Coll., Oxford. UK. *Career:* Creative Arts Fellow, Wolfson Coll., Oxford 1992–95; Leverhulme Fellow in English, Univ. of Cambridge 1997–99; Visiting Prof., Columbia Univ., USA 2002; Samuel Fischer Guest Prof., Freie Univ., Berlin, Germany 2005; currently Prof. of Contemporary Literature, Univ. of East Anglia. *Compositions include:* This is Not Fusion 2004, Found Music 2010. *Publications include:* A Strange and Sublime Address (Betty Trask Award 1991, Guardian Fiction Prize 1991, Commonwealth Writers Prize for Best First Book 1992) 1991, Afternoon Raag (Southern Arts Literature Prize 1993, Encore Award 1994) 1993, Freedom Song (Los Angeles Times Book Award for Fiction 2000) 1998, A New World (Sahitya Akademi Award 2002) 2000, Picador Book of Modern Indian Literature (ed.) 2001, Real Time: Stories and a Reminiscence 2002, D. H. Lawrence and 'Difference': Postcoloniality and the Poetry of the Present 2003, St Cyril Road and Other Poems 2005, Clearing a Space 2008, The Immortals 2009; contribs to anthologies and periodicals, including London Review of Books. *Honours:* K. Blundell Trust Award 1993, Arts Council of GB Writers' Award 1993–94. *Address:* School of Literature and Creative Writing, Faculty of Arts and Humanities, University of East Anglia, Norwich, Norfolk, NR4 7TJ, England (office). *Telephone:* (1603) 592294 (office). *E-mail:* a.chaudhuri@uea.ac.uk (office). *Website:* www.uea.ac.uk/lit (office); www.amitchaudhuri.com.

CHAUDHURI, Supriya, MA, DPhil; Indian academic, writer and translator; b. 30 June 1953. *Education:* Univ. of Oxford, UK. *Career:* currently Prof. of English, Jadavpur Univ., Kolkata, Head of English Dept 1995–97, Co-ordinator of Advanced Study 2001–; Visiting Fellow, Centre for Research in Arts, Univ. of Cambridge, UK 2009; mem. Int. Karate Asscn (Japan), Soc. for Renaissance Studies, London, Shakespeare Soc. of India; mem. Advisory Bd Electronic Journal of Indian Culture and Society, Visva Bharati Quarterly. *Publications include:* Lucius, thou art translated: Adlington's Apuleius 2008, Literature and Gender (co-ed with Sajni Mukherji); trans.: Relationships (Rabindranath Tagore's novel) 2005, Jogajog, Selected Short Stories, numerous modern Bengali poems. *Address:* Department of English, Jadavpur University, Kolkata 700 032, India (office). *Telephone:* (33) 23372516 (office). *E-mail:* prantik@cal3.vsnl.net.in (office). *Website:* www.jadavpur.edu (office).

CHAUHAN, Anuja; Indian writer and advertising executive; b. 17 Sept. 1970, Meerut, UP; m. Niret Alva; one s. two d. *Education:* Miranda House, Delhi, Royal Melbourne Inst. of Tech., Australia. *Career:* Exec. Creative Dir and Vice-Pres. J. Walter Thompson Advertising, Delhi 1993–2010; has created campaigns for brands including Pepsi, Nokia and Nestle. *Publications include:* The Zoya Factor (Cosmopolitan Magazine, Fun Fearless Female Award 2008, India Today Woman Award 2009) 2008, Battle For Bittora 2010. *Address:* c/o HarperCollins Publishers India, A 53, Sector 57, Noida, India (office). *E-mail:* contact@harpercollins.co.in (office). *Website:* www.harpercollins.co.in (office).

CHÁVEZ CASTAÑEDA, Ricardo, BA, MA; Mexican writer, psychologist and academic; *Visiting Professor, Middlebury College;* b. 1961, Mexico City. *Education:* Universidad Nacional Autonoma de Mexico, New Mexico State Univ., USA. *Career:* currently teaches creative writing at Middlebury Coll., Vt, USA. *Publications:* novels: La Generación Fría 1992, Para una evolución de la víctima negra en el cine 1994, El día del hurón 1997, Estación de la Vergüenza (Honorable Mention Fiction Contest Casa de las Americas) 1999, El final de las nubes 2001, La conspiración idiota 2003, El fin de la pornografía 2005, El libro del silencio (Premio de Novela Ciudad de la Paz 2005) 2006; stories: La guerra enana del jardín 1993 and 2008, Amores como naufragio, cajones y muertos 1993, Y sobrevivir con las manos abiertas. Una historia de todos los fines del mundo 2001; essays: La generación de los enterradores 2000, La generación de los enterradores II 2003, Crack, instrucciones de uso 2004; juvenile literature: Miedo, el mundo de a lado (XX Latin American Short Story Competition Edmundo Valadés) 1994 and 2006, La Valla 2000, Fernanda y los mundos secretos 2004, Mañanario 2006, Las peregrinas del fuisoyeseré 2007, Fababela y el diablo 2009, El país de los muchos suelos (Young Mercosur pageant) 2009, El cadáver más bello del mundo 2010, Severiana 2010; children's literature: Los Ensebados 1993, El secreto de Gorco (Novel Award for Youth International Book Fair for Children and Youth 1992) 1994 and 2006, Las montañas azules 1998, La niña que tenía el mar adentro 2001, El beso más largo del mundo (International Children's Literature Biennial Rid-July Coba) 2003 and 2004, Las mil ciento trece capas del copo de nieve 2006, Salvavidas 2006, Rigoberto y los lobos 2006, El laberinto de las pesadillas (Premio Literario Casa de las Américas 2009) 2007, El séptimo hermanito 2009; anthologies: Cuarenta y nueve escritores mexicanos 1994, Ni cuento que los aguante (La ficción en México) 1997, Dispersión Multitudinaria 1997, Cuentos mexicanos 1997, Páginas Amarillas: antología de nuevos narradores latinoamericanos 1999, Se habla español 2000, El sabueso de los Baskerville 2001, Cuentos Villa de Bilbao 2002, Historias para sentir 2004, El cuento Jíbaro. Antología del microrrelato mexicano 2006, Cuentos eróticos 2007, Cuentos para siempre 2007, A cincuenta años del descubrimiento de Everest 2007, Sube a la alcoba por la ventana, Munhakdongne 2008, El libro rojo 2008. *Honours:* Premio Borges de cuento 1987, Ecological Univ. Short Story Competition 1989, Short Story Competition Salvador Gallardo Story Award 1991, San Luis Potosi 1991, Premio Latinoamericano de cuento 1994, Accesit Premio Aresti de cuento 2000, 2003. *Address:* Middlebury Language Schools, Sunderland Language Center, Middlebury College, Middlebury, VT 05753, USA (office). *Telephone:* (802) 443-5020 (office). *Fax:* (802) 443-2075 (office). *E-mail:* rchavez@middlebury.edu (office); richaneda@yahoo.es. *Website:* ricardochavezcastaneda.com.

CHEETHAM, Anthony John Valerian, BA; British publisher; *Associate Publisher, Atlantic Books;* b. 12 April 1943, s. of Sir Nicolas John Alexander Cheetham; m. 1st Julia Rollason 1969 (divorced); two s. one d.; m. 2nd Rosemary de Courcy 1979 (divorced); two d.; m. 3rd Georgina Capel 1997. *Education:* Eton Coll., Balliol Coll., Oxford. *Career:* Editorial Dir Sphere Books 1968; Man. Dir Futura Publs 1973, Macdonald Futura 1979; Chair. Century Publishing 1982–85; Man. Dir Century Hutchinson 1985; Chair. and CEO Random Century Group 1989–91; Founder and CEO Orion Publishing Group (fmrly Orion Books) 1991–2003; Exec. Chair. Quercus Publishing plc 2005–08, Chair. (non-exec.) 2008–09; Assoc. Publisher, Atlantic Books 2009–. *Publication:* Richard III 1972. *Address:* Atlantic Books, Ormond House, 26–27 Boswell Street, London, WC1N 3JZ, England (office). *Telephone:* (20) 7269-1610 (office). *E-mail:* enquiries@groveatlantic.co.uk (office). *Website:* www.atlantic-books.co.uk (office).

CHELES, Luciano, BA, MPhil, PhD; Italian academic; *Professor of Italian Studies, University of Poitiers;* b. 7 Sept. 1948, Cairo, Egypt. *Education:* Univs of Reading and Essex and Lancaster Univ., UK. *Career:* Sr Lecturer in Italian Studies, Lancaster Univ. 1994–2000; Visiting Lecturer, Univ. of Lyons II, France 1994–95, 1996; Prof. of Italian Studies, Univ. of Poitiers, France 2000–; Terra Foundation for American Art Senior Scholar Fellowship 2006–07; mem. Asscn for the Study of Modern Italy, Istituto di Studi Rinascimentali, Soc. for Renaissance Studies, Groupe d'Etudes et de Recherches sur la Culture Italienne. *Publications include:* The Studiolo di Urbino: An Iconographic Investigation (revised Italian edn as Lo Studiolo di Urbino: Iconografia di un microcosmo principesco) 1986, Neo-Fascism in Europe (co-ed. with R. G. Ferguson and M. Vaughan, revised edn as The Far Right in Western and Eastern Europe) 1991, Grafica Utile: L'affiche d'utilité publique en Italie, 1975–1995 1995, The Art of Persuasion: Political Communication in Italy, from 1945 to the 1990s (co-ed. with L. Sponza) 2001; contrib. to scholarly books and journals. *Honours:* Frontino-Montefeltro Prize 1992. *Address:* Département d'Études Italiennes, Université de Poitiers, 86000 Poitiers, France (office). *Telephone:* (5) 49-45-32-80 (office). *E-mail:* luciano.cheles@laposte.net (office); luciano.cheles@univ-poitiers.fr (office).

CHEN, Jiangong; Chinese writer; b. Nov. 1949, Beihai, Guangxi Prov. *Education:* Peking Univ. *Career:* started career as coal miner in Jingxi Mine; joined Beijing Writers' Asscn 1981; Sec. of Secr., Chinese Writers' Asscn 1995–2001, 2003–, Vice-Chair. 2001–; currently Curator Nat. Museum of Modern Chinese Literature, Beijing; mem. exec. council, China Overseas Friendship Asscn. *Television:* dramas: Haung Cheng Gen Er, Song of Youth, When We Were Still Young. *Publications:* The Meandering Stream 1980, the Fluttering Flowered Scarf 1981, A Girl with the Eyes of a Red Phoenix 1981, Selected Novels by Chen Jiangong, No. 9 Huluba Alley, Letting Go, Curly Hair, Previous Offence, Phoenix Eyes, Manic Starry Sky, At the Foot of Imperial City, The Selection of Chen Jiangong, Imperial City Wall (co-author) (Excellence Saga Novel Award), Sun Stone (Best Novella Award), Confusion Star Sky, Frizzle (Literature Award), Criminal Record, Slim Eyes (Nat. Award for Best Short Story), Colorful Turban Along with Wind (Nat. Award for Best Short Story), Free Captive Animals (Excellence Novella Award); essays: Be honest to Me, The Flavor of Beijing, Essay Selection of Chen Jiangong, Fess Up. *Address:* c/o Beijing Writers' Association, Beijing, People's Republic of China.

CHEN, Jo-Hsi, BA, MA; Taiwanese novelist; b. 15 Nov. 1938, Taiwan; m. Tuan Shiyao; two s. *Education:* Taiwan Nat. Univ., Johns Hopkins Univ., USA. *Career:* has lived and worked in Taiwan, USA, China, Hong Kong, Canada; Lecturer, Univ. of California, Berkeley 1983. *Publications include:* fiction: Mayor Yin 1976, Selected Works by Jo-Hsi Chen 1976, The Old Man 1978, Repatriation 1978, The Execution of Mayor Yin, and Other Stories from the Great Proletarian Cultural Revolution 1978, Inside and Outside the Wall 1981, Tu Wei 1983, Selected Short Stories by Jo-Hsi Chen 1983, Foresight 1984, The Two Hus 1985, Paper Marriage 1986, The Old Man and Other Stories 1986, Woman from Guizhou 1989, Wangzhou's Sorrows 1995, Home of Daughters 1998, Create a Paradise 1998; other: Reminiscences of the Cultural Revolution 1979, Random Notes 1981, Democracy Wall and the Unofficial Journals 1982, Read to Kill Time 1983, Flower Grown Naturally 1987, Trip to Tibet 1988, Trip to Inner Mongolia 1988. *Honours:* Wu Zhuoliu Prize 1978.

CHEN, Li; Taiwanese poet, essayist and translator; b. 1954, Hualien; m. Chang Fen-ling. *Education:* Nat. Taiwan Normal Univ. *Career:* started writing poetry early 1970s; secondary school teacher 1975–; Guest Lecturer, Nat. Dong Hwa Univ.; also trans. of poetry of Szymborska, Plath, Heaney, Neruda, Paz into Chinese. *Publications include:* In Front of the Temple 1975, Animal Lullaby 1980, The Love Song of Buffet the Clown 1990, Traveling in the Family 1993, Microcosmos 1993, The Edge of the Island 1995, Intimate Letters: Selected Poems of Chen Li (with English trans. by Chang Fen-ling) 1997, The Cat at the Mirror 1999. *Address:* c/o Council for Cultural Affairs, 102 Ai Kuo East Road, Taipei, Taiwan.

CHEN, Zhongshi; Chinese novelist; *Chairman, Shaanxi Provincial Writers' Association*; b. 1942, Xian, Shanxi Prov. *Career:* Chair. Shaanxi Prov. Writers' Asscn 1993–; Vice-Chair. Chinese Writers' Asscn 2001; Hon. Dean, Dept of Humanities, Shiyou Univ. 2004; took part as torchbearer in Olympic Flame Relay, Xian 2008. *Publications:* Bai Lu Yuan (White Deer Plain) (Mao Dun Prize for Literature 1997) 1993, Early Summer, Mr. Blue Gown, The Cellar 1994, numerous novellas and short stories. *Address:* Shanxi Provincial Writers' Association, Xian, People's Republic of China (office).

CHENEY-COKER, Syl; Sierra Leonean academic and poet; b. 28 June 1945, Freetown; m. *Education:* Univs of Oregon, California and Wisconsin, USA. *Career:* Prof. of English, Univ. of the Philippines, Quezon City 1975–77; Sr Lecturer, Univ. of Maiduguri, Nigeria 1977–88; Writer-in-Residence, Univ. of Iowa, USA 1988; Ed. of newspaper, Vanguard, Freetown –1997; writer in the City of Asylum programme, Las Vegas, USA. *Publications include:* poetry: The Road to Jamaica 1969, Concerto for an Exile 1973, The Graveyard Also Has Teeth 1980, The Blood in the Desert's Eyes 1990, Stone Child and Other Poems 2008; novel: The Last Harmattan of Alusine Dunbar (Commonwealth Writers Prize, African region) 1990. *Address:* c/o HEBN Publishers, 1 Ighodaro Road, Jericho, P.M.B. 5205, Ibadan, Nigeria. *Telephone:* (2) 2410747. *Fax:* (2) 2411089. *E-mail:* info@hebnpublishers.com. *Website:* www.hebnpublishers.com.

CHENG, Naishan; Chinese writer; b. 14 June 1946, Shanghai; d. of Cheng Xueqiao and Pan Zuojun; m. Yan Erchun 1969; one d. *Education:* Shanghai Educational Inst. *Career:* family left China 1949, returned 1956; teacher 1965–85; writer 1985–; invited to speak in Germany, USA and Philippines 1986–; moved to Hong Kong 1990s. *Publications include:* The Blue House 1983, The Clove Villa 1984, The Poor Street 1984, Daughters' Tribulations 1985, Qian zheng 1988, Ni hao, Pake 1989, The Bankers 1989, The Piano Tuner 1989, Jin rong jia 1990, Lao Xianggang: Dong fang zhi zhu 2000, Shanghai Tango 2002, When a Baby is Born 2009.

CHERKOVSKI, Neeli, (Neeli Cherry), BA; American writer, poet and editor; b. 1945, Santa Monica, Calif.; partner Jesse Guinto Cabrera 1983. *Education:* San Bernardino Community Coll., California State Univ., Hebrew Union Coll. Jewish Inst. of Religion. *Career:* fmr Writer-in-Residence, New Coll. of California; currently teaches at Floating Univ. *Publications include:* Anthology of Los Angeles Poets (co-ed.) 1972, Don't Make a Move 1974, Public Notice 1975, The Waters Reborn 1975, Ferlinghetti: A Life 1979, Love Proof 1980, Juggler Within 1983, Clear Wind 1984, Whitman's Wild Children 1989, Hank: The Life of Charles Bukowski 1991, Ways in the Wood 1993, Animal 1996, Elegy for Bob Kaufman 1996, Leaning Against Time 2004, Naming the Nameless 2004, A Packet of Love Poems 2007, From the Canyon Outward 2009, Bukowski: A Life and Ferlinghetti: A Biography. *Honours:* Friends of the SF Public Library Literary Laureate, Pen Oakland-Josephine Miles Literary Award 2005. *Address:* c/o R.L. Crow Publications, PO Box 262, Penn Valley, CA 95946, USA. *Telephone:* (530) 432-8195. *E-mail:* info@rlcrow.com. *Website:* www.rlcrow.com.

CHERNOW, Ron, BA, MA; American writer; b. 3 March 1949, New York, NY; m. Valerie Stearn 1979 (died 2006). *Education:* Yale Coll., Pembroke Coll., Cambridge. *Career:* fmr freelance journalist; Dir of Financial Policy Studies Twentieth Century Fund (think tank) 1982; book reviewer, essayist, TV and radio commentator; mem. PEN American Center (fmr Sec., Pres. 2006–07), Authors' Guild; contrib. to New York Times, Wall Street Journal. *Publications:* The House of Morgan: An American Banking Dynasty and the Rise of Modern Finance (Nat. Book Award for Nonfiction 1990) 1990, The Warburgs: The Twentieth-Century Odyssey of a Remarkable Jewish Family (George S. Eccles Prize for the best business book 1993) 1993, The Death of the Banker: The Decline and Fall of the Great Financial Dynasties and the Triumph of the Small Investor (essays) 1997, Titan: The Life of John D. Rockefeller Sr 1998, Alexander Hamilton (George Washington Book Prize 2005) 2004, Washington: A Life (Pulitzer Prize for Biography 2011) 2010. *Honours:* United Steelworkers of America Jack London Award 1980, English-Speaking Union of the USA Amb. Book Award 1990. *Address:* c/o Penguin Group (USA) Inc., c/o The Penguin Press Publicity, 375 Hudson Street, New York, NY 10014, USA (office).

CHERRY, Carolyn Janice, (C. J. Cherryh), BA, MA; American writer; b. 1 Sept. 1942, St Louis, MO. *Education:* Univ. of Oklahoma, Johns Hopkins Univ. *Career:* taught Latin and ancient history in Oklahoma City Public Schools 1965–77; fmr Artist-in-Residence, Univ. of Central Oklahoma, Edmond 1980–81; mem. Nat. Space Soc., Science Fiction and Fantasy Writers of America. *Publications include:* Gate of Ivrel 1976, Brothers of Earth 1976, The Faded Sun 1978, Downbelow Station (Hugo Award 1982) 1981, Sunfall 1981, The Pride of Chanur 1982, Chanur's Venture 1984, Forty Thousand in Gehenna 1984, Cuckoo's Egg 1985, Chanur's Homecoming 1986, Visible Light 1986, Angel with the Sword 1987, Glass and Amber 1987, Cyteen (Locus Award 1988, Hugo Award 1989) 1988, The Paladin 1988, Rusalka 1989, Sunfall 1990, Rimrunners 1990, Chernevog 1991, Heavy Time 1991, Chanur's Legacy 1992, The Goblin Mirror 1993, Hellburner 1993, Finity's End 1994, Foreigner 1994, Faery in Shadow 1994, Tripoint 1994, Fortress in the Eye of Time 1995, Invader 1995, Rider at the Gate 1995, Cloud's Rider 1996, Lois and Clark 1996, Inheritor 1996, Fortress of Eagles 1998, Precursor 1999, Fortress of Owls 1999, Fortress of Dragons 2000, Explorer 2002, Hammerfall 2002, At the Edge of Space 2003, Foreigner 2004, Forge of Heaven 2005, Chanur's Endgame 2007, Fortress of Ice 2007, Pretender 2007, Deliverer 2008, Regenesis 2009, Conspirator 2009, Deceiver 2010, Betrayer 2011, Intruder 2012. *Honours:* John Campbell Award 1977, Hugo Award 1979, Edward E. Smith Memorial Award 1988, Oklahoma Professional Writers Hall of Fame 1991, Arrell Gibson Lifetime Achievement Award 2005. *Address:* 162 S Coeur Dalene Street, Apartment B303, Spokane, WA 99201-6439, USA. *E-mail:* cj@cherryh.com. *Website:* www.cherryh.com.

CHERRY, Neeli (see Cherkovski, Neeli)

CHERRYH, C. J. (see Cherry, Carolyn Janice)

CHEUNG, Angelica, BA, MBA; Chinese journalist; *Editorial Director, Vogue China*; m.; one d. *Education:* Peking Univ., Univ. of Southern Australia. *Career:* fmrly journalist for newspapers and magazines in Hong Kong, then Ed.-in-Chief, Marie Claire (Hong Kong), Editorial Dir, Elle China; Editorial Dir, Vogue China 2005–. *Address:* Vogue China, Room 505, Tower C1, Beijing Oriental Plaza, 1 East Changan Avenue, Beijing 100738, China (office). *Telephone:* (10) 85187700 (office). *Fax:* (10) 85189686 (office). *E-mail:* voguechina@condenast.com.cn (office). *Website:* www.vogue.com.cn (office).

CHEUSE, Alan, BA, PhD; American author, critic and teacher; b. 23 Jan. 1940, Perth Amboy, NJ; m. 1st Mary Agan 1964 (divorced 1974), one s.; m. 2nd Marjorie Pryse 1974, two d.; m. 3rd Kristin M. O'Shee 1991. *Education:* Perth Amboy High School, Lafayette Coll., Rutgers Univ. *Career:* Faculty mem., Bennington Coll. 1970–78, George Mason Univ. 1987–; Co-Dir Bennington Summer Writing Workshops 1978–85, Acting Dir 1986–87; Visiting Lecturer, Univ. of Tennessee 1980–83, Univ. of Virginia 1987; Visiting Fellow, Univ. of the South 1984; Writing Program, Univ. of Michigan 1984–86; Visiting Writer, Univ. of Houston 1991–92; mem. Nat. Book Critics Circle, PEN. *Radio:* book commentator All Things Considered (Nat. Public Radio) 1983–, producer and host The Sound of Writing (Center for the Book/Nat. Public Radio) 1988–99. *Publications include:* fiction: Candace & Other Stories 1980, The Bohemians 1982, The Grandmothers' Club 1986, The Tennessee Waltz and Other Stories 1990, The Light Possessed 1990, Lost and Old Rivers 1999, The Fires 2007, To Catch the Lightning (Grub Street Nat. Prize for Fiction 2009) 2008, Song of Slaves in the Desert 2011; other: Fall Out of Heaven 1987, The Sound of Writing: Stories from the Radio (co-ed. with Caroline Marshall) 1991, Listening to Ourselves: More Stories from the Sound of Writing (co-ed. with Caroline Marshall) 1994, Talking Horse: Bernard Malamud on Life and Work (co-ed. with Nicholas Delbanco) 1996, Listening to the Page: Adventures in Reading and Writing 2001, Writer's Workshop in a Book (co-ed. with Lisa Alvarez) 2007, Seeing Ourselves: Great American Short Fiction (ed.) 2007, A Trance after Breakfast 2009, Craft and Voice (three vols) (with Nicholas Delbanco) 2010; contribs to anthologies, reference books, reviews, journals and newspapers. *Honours:* Nat. Endowment for the Arts Creative Writing Fellowship 1979–80, New York Times Notable Book of the Year citation 1982, Antioch Review Prize for Distinguished Non-Fiction 2001. *Address:* 3611 35th Street NW, Washington, DC 20016, USA (home). *Website:* www.alancheuse.com.

CHEVALIER, Tracy, MA, FRSL; American writer; b. Oct. 1962, Washington, DC; m.; one s. *Education:* Oberlin Coll., Univ. of East Anglia, UK. *Career:* moved to London, England 1984; fmr reference book ed. –1993; mem. Council, Soc. of Authors. *Publications:* novels: The Virgin Blue 1997, Girl with a Pearl Earring 1999, Falling Angels 2001, The Lady and the Unicorn 2003, Burning Bright 2007, Remarkable Creatures 2009. *Honours:* Barnes & Noble Discover Award 2000. *Literary Agent:* c/o Jonny Geller, Curtis Brown, Haymarket House, 28–29 Haymarket, London, SW1Y 4SP, England. *Telephone:* (20) 7393-4400 (office). *E-mail:* hello@tchevalier.com (home). *Website:* www.tchevalier.com.

CHÍAS, Edgar; Mexican playwright, actor and academic; b. 1973, Mexico City. *Education:* Universidad Nacional Autónoma de México. *Career:* fmr programmer and project coordinator, Hellenic Cultural Center Theatre,

Mexico City; Fellow, Fundación Carolina, Spain 2003; mem. Sistema Nacional de Creadores de Arte FONCA 2009–; currently teaches dramatic composition at Coll. of Dramatic Literature and Theatre, Universidad Nacional Autónoma de México; Young Artists Fellowship, Nat. Fund for Culture and the Arts 2001–02, 2005–06. *Publications:* books: ¿Último round? 2002, Telefonemas (Mención de Honor, Premio Nacional de Dramaturgia Manuel Herrera 2002) 2003, Cada quien su Clitemnestra 2005, On Insomnia and Midnight (Premio Óscar Liera de la AMCT) 2007, Crack, o de las cosas sin nombre (Premio Óscar Liera de la AMCT, Premio Nacional de Literatura José Fuentes Mares 2009) 2007, Le Ciel dans la Peau 2008, On Crack, o delle cose senze nome 2008, De insomnio y medianoche (Premio Nacional de Literatura José Fuentes Mares 2009) 2008, Heaven on Foot 2009, Cólico miserere 2009, El cielo en la piel 2010, Rapsodias para la escena 2010, Güera es la patria 2010, Una merienda de negros 2010, Fronteras 2010; theatre: ¿Último round? 2000, Circo para bobos 2001, Cuando quiero llorar no lloro 2002, La mirada del sord o 2002, Comedia de los errores 2002, Vestido de novia 2003 and 2004, El cielo en la piel 2004, Telefonemas 2005, On Insomnia and Midnight 2006, En las montañas azules (Premio Nacional de Dramaturgia Manuel Herrera and Premio tripartita 2005) 2006, Crack, o de las cosas sin nombre 2006, Cuento oblongo 2007, Historias de una hiena vacía 2007, De insomnio y medianoche 2007, Benito antes de Juárez 2007 and 2008, Güera es la patria 2008, Serial 2008. *Address:* c/o El Fenix Producciones México DF, Mexico (office).

CHIASSON, Dan, PhD; American poet, literary critic and academic; b. Burlington, Vt. *Education:* Amherst Coll., Harvard Univ. *Career:* teacher at Amherst Coll. and Wellesley Coll.; fmr Asst Prof. Dept of English, State Univ. of New York, Stony Brook, also Dir Poetry Center; Poetry Ed., Paris Review 2008–. *Publications include:* poetry: The Afterlife of Objects 2002, Natural History 2005, Where's the Moon, There's the Moon 2010; criticism: One Kind of Everything: Poem and Person in Contemporary America 2006; contrib. of articles to New York Times, The Threepenny Review, Poetry, Slate. *Honours:* Pushcart Prize, Whiting Writers' Award 2004, Guggenheim Fellowship 2008. *Address:* English Department, Wellesley College, Founders Hall 101, 106 Central Street, Wellesley, MA 02481, USA (office). *Telephone:* (781) 283-2544 (office). *E-mail:* dchiasso@wellesley.edu (office). *Website:* www.wellesley.edu/english (office).

CHIASSON, Herménégilde, BA, BFA, MA, MFA; Canadian writer, artist, academic and fmr politician; b. 7 April 1946, Saint-Simon, New Brunswick; m. Marcia Chiasson; one d. *Education:* Université de Moncton, Mount Allison Univ., Université de Paris 1, France, State Univ. of New York, USA Univ. of Paris (Sorbonne). *Career:* Dir Galerie d'art de l'Université de Moncton 1974; Pres. Galerie Sans Nom 1980; Founding Pres. Éditions Perce-Neige (publishing house) 1984; Pres. Asscn acadienne des artistes professionnels du Nouveau Brunswick 1993–95; Founding Pres. Productions du Phare-Est 1998; invited curator, Anecdotes and Enigmas: The Marion McCain Atlantic Art Exhbn, Beaverbrook Art Gallery 1994; Lt-Gov. of New Brunswick 2003–09; Artist-in-Residence, Univ. of Ottawa 2003, Université de Moncton and Mount Allison Univ. 2009–10; mem. RSC. *Exhibitions:* has participated in more than 100 exhibitions, including 18 solo exhibitions, including La Frise des Archers 1983 and Mythologies 1996; group exhibitions include Quoifaire? Quoi dire? 1986. *Films:* has directed 17 films, including Toutes les photos finissent par se ressembler 1985, Le Grand Jack 1987, Robichaud 1989, Taxi Cormier 1990, Épopée 1996. *Publications include:* numerous books, including Mourir à Scoudouc 1974, Claude Roussel/Sculpteur/Sculptor 1985 (in collaboration with Patrick Condon Laurette), Vous (France-Acadie Prize 1992) 1991, Climats 1996, Conversations (Gov.-Gen.'s Literary Award) 1999; and 15 poetry collections; has written 25 plays, including Pierre, Hélène et Michael 1990, L'exil d'Alexa 1993, Aliénor 1997. *Honours:* Chevalier, Ordre des Arts et des Lettres 1990, Ordre des francophones d'Amérique 1993, Kt of the Order of la Pléiade; Dr hc (Université de Moncton) 1999; Prix France-Acadie 1986, 1992, Grand Prix de la francophonie canadienne 1999, Prix quinquennal Antonine-Maillet-Acadie Vie 2003, Prix Montfort 2004, Molson Prize 2011. *Address:* c/o Éditions Prise de parole, 109 Elm Street, Suite 205, Sudbury, ON P3C 1T4, Canada.

CHICHETTO, James William, BA, MA; American writer, ecclesiastic, poet, academic and editor; *Professor of Writing and Communications, Stonehill College;* b. 5 June 1941, Boston, Mass; s. of Frank A. Chichetto and Christina Chichetto (née McInnis). *Education:* Stonehill Coll., Holy Cross Coll., Wesleyan Univ., Chicago Univ., Catholic Univ. *Career:* ordained priest, Congregation of Holy Cross 1968; educator and missionary, Peru 1968–72; Assoc. Ed. Gargoyle Magazine 1974–80; Ed., The Connecticut Poetry Review 1982–87, Artist 1990–; Prof. of Writing and Communications, Stonehill Coll., North Easton, Mass 1982–; art work for The Connecticut Poetry Review 1995–2005 (in archives at John Hay Library, Brown Univ., Providence, RI); mem. Connecticut Literary Forum, Nat. Asscn of Scholars, Directory of American Scholars, Massachusetts Foundation for Humanities Scholars, Asscn of Literary Scholars and Critics; Fellow, Contemporary Authors Series, Nat. Asscn for Humanities Educ., World Literary Acad. *Publications include:* Poems 1975, Dialogue: Emily Dickinson and Christopher Cauldwell 1978, Stones: A Litany 1980, Gilgamesh and Other Poems 1983, Victims 1987, Homage to Father Edward Sorin 1992, Dream of Norumbega 2000, Reckoning Genocide 2002, Dream of Norumbega Book I, II, III (An Epic Poem on the United States of America) 2002, 2005, 2008; play: The Bakers' Wind; contrib. to Boston Phoenix, Colorado Review, Boston Globe, The Manhattan Review, The Patterson Review, The Connecticut Poetry Review, America, Harpers, East West Literary Journal, London Tablet, National Catholic Reporter, etc.; to anthologies, books: Perversions of Justice, Indigenous Peoples of Anglo-American Law 2003, Blood To Remember: American Poets on the Holocaust 1991, And What the Rough Beast 2000, Mr Cogito (trans.), Hitler's Priests, Catholic Clergy in National Socialism (rendered poetic trans.) 2007, and others. *Honours:* book grants, Nat. Endowment for the Arts 1980, 1983, Nat. Endowment for the Humanities 1992, 1993, 1994, Sri Chinmoy Poetry Award 1984, Stonehill Alumni Service Award 1997, Connecticut Literary Forum Award 2003, CPR Talent Award 2005, Stonehill Devt Grant 2007. *Address:* Stonehill College, North Easton, MA 02357, USA (office). *Telephone:* (508) 565-1271 (office). *E-mail:* jchichetto@stonehill.edu (office).

CHILD, Lee; British writer; b. (Jim Grant), 1954, Coventry, West Midlands, England; m. Jane; one d. *Education:* Univ. of Sheffield. *Career:* Presentation Dir, Granada TV, Manchester 1977–95; full-time crime writer 1997–; Pres. Mystery Writers of America 2009–10. *Publications include:* Killing Floor (Barry Award, Anthony Award 1998) 1997, Die Trying (WH Smith Thumping Good Read Award) 1998, Tripwire 1999, Running Blind (UK edition: The Visitor) 2000, Echo Burning 2001, Without Fail 2002, Persuader 2003, The Enemy 2004, One Shot 2005, The Hard Way 2006, Bad Luck and Trouble 2007, Nothing to Lose 2008, Gone Tomorrow 2009, 61 Hours 2010, Worth Dying For 2010, The Affair 2011. *Honours:* Dr hc (Sheffield) 2009; Bob Kellogg Good Citizen Award 2005. *Literary Agent:* c/o Madeleine Buston, Darley Anderson Literary Agency, Estelle House, 11 Eustace Road, London, SW6 1JB, England. *Telephone:* (20) 7385-6652. *E-mail:* madeleine@darleyanderson.com. *Website:* darleyanderson.com. *E-mail:* www@leechild.com (office). *Website:* www.leechild.com.

CHILDISH, Billy; British singer, songwriter, musician (guitar), writer and poet and painter; b. (Stephen Hamper), 1 Dec. 1959, Chatham, Kent, England; m. Julie Childish; one c. *Career:* mem. various bands, including Pop Rivets, the Milkshakes, Thee Mighty Caesars, the Delmonas, Thee Headcoats, the Natural Born Lovers, The Buff Medways, The Musicians of the British Empire. *Recordings include:* albums: I Remember, I've Got Everything Indeed, Laughing Gravy, Plump Prizes and Little Gems, The 1982 Cassettes, Which Dead Donkey Daddy?, Talkin' Bout Milkshakes, Acropolis Now, In Tweed We Trust, Ypres 1917 Overture 1987, Play: Capt'n Calypso's Hoodoo Party 1988, Poems of Laughter and Violence 1988, Long Legged Baby 1989, I Am the Billy Childish 1991, The Original Chatham Jack 1992, At the Bridge 1993, Live in the Netherlands 1993, Hunger at the Moon 1994, Live 1994, Devil in the Flesh 1998, The Cheeky Cheese 1999, In Blood 1999, I Am the Object of Your Desire 2000, Steady the Buffs 2002, Here Come the Fleece 2002, Medways 2003, Medway Wheelers 2005, Heavens Journey (with The Chatham Singers) 2005, Punk Rock at the British Legion Hall 2007, Thatcher's Children 2008, Juju Claudius 2009, Archive From 1959 – The Billy Childish Story 2009, Poets of England 2010. *Publications include:* Poems from the Barrier Block 1984, Monks Without God 1986, Companions in a Death Boat 1987, To the Quick 1988, Girl in the Tree 1988, Maverick Verse 1988, Admissions to Strangers 1989, Death of a Wood 1989, The Silence of Words (short stories) 1989, The Deathly Flight of Angels 1990, Like a God I Love All Things 1990, Child's Death Letter 1990, The Hart Rises 1991, Poems of Laughter and Violence: Selected Poetry 1981–86 1992, Poems to Break the Harts of Impossible Princesses 1994, Days With a Hart Like a Dog 1994, Big Hart and Balls 1995, Messerschmitt Pilot's Severed Hand 1996, My Fault (novel) 1996, Billy Childish and his Famous Headcoat 1997, Notebooks of a Naked Youth (novel) 1997, I'd Rather You Lied: Selected Poems 1980–1998 1999, Chatham Town Welcomes Desperate Men (poems) 2001, Chathams Burning 2004, Knite of the Sad Face 2004, Sex Crimes of the Futcher 2005, My Fault 2005, The Idiocy of Idears 2007, Bombs, Buggery and Buddhism or Diaries of a Mock Human (Part one) 2010. *Address:* c/o Hangman Books, 11 Boundary Road, Chatham, Kent, ME4 6TS, England. *Website:* www.billychildish.com.

CHILTON, Rev. Bruce, AB, MDiv, PhD, DD; American academic and writer; *Bernard Iddings Professor of Religion, Bard College;* b. 27 Sept. 1949, Roslyn, NY; s. of Bruce D. Chilton and Virginia M. Chilton; m. Odile Sevault 1982, two s. *Education:* Bard Coll., Gen. Theological Seminary, St John's Coll., Cambridge. *Career:* Ed.-in-Chief Bulletin for Biblical Research; Founding Ed. Journal for the Study of the New Testament, Studying the Historical Jesus series; Lecturer in Biblical Studies, Univ. of Sheffield, UK 1976–85; Lillian Claus Prof. of the New Testament, Yale Univ. 1985–87; Bernard Iddings Prof. of Religion, Bard Coll., Annandale, NY 1987–; Rector Church of St John the Evangelist 1987–; Bishop Henry Martin Memorial Lecturer, Univ. Coll. of Emmanuel and St Chad; mem. Studiorum Novi Testamenti Societas, Soc. of Biblical Literature; Heinrich Hertz Scholar, Germany, Asher Edelman Fellow, Bard Coll., Evangelical Fellow, Pew Charitable Trust. *Publications include:* The Glory of Israel: The Theology and Provinence of the Isaiah Targum 1983, The Kingdom of God in the Teaching of Jesus (ed.) 1984, A Galilean Rabbi and his Bible: Jesus' Own Interpretation of Isaiah 1984, Targumic Approaches to the Gospels: Essays in the Mutual Definition of Judaism and Christianity 1986, The Isaiah Targum (trans.) 1987, Beginning New Testament Study 1986, Jesus and the Ethics of the Kingdom (co-author) 1988, Profiles of a Rabbi: Synoptic Opportunities in Reading about Jesus 1989, The Temple of Jesus: His Sacrificial Program within a Cultural History of Sacrifice 1992, A Feast of Meanings: Eucharistic Theologies from Jesus through Johannine Circles 1994, Studying the Historical Jesus: Evaluations of the State of Current Research (co-ed.) 1994, Judaic Approaches to the

Gospel 1994, Judaism in the New Testament: Practices and Beliefs (co-author) 1995, Revelation: The Torah and the Bible (co-author) 1995, Pure Kingdom: Jesus' Vision of God 1996, The Body of Faith: Israel and the Church (co-author) 1996, Trading Places: The Intersecting Histories of Judaism and Christianity (co-author) 1996, The Intellectual Foundations of Christian and Jewish Discourse: The Philosophy of Religious Argument (co-author) 1997, Jesus' Prayer and Jesus' Eucharist: His Personal Practice of Spirituality 1997, Trading Places Sourcebook: Readings in the Intersecting Histories of Judaism and Christianity 1997, Rabbi Jesus: An Intimate Biography 2000, Rabbi Paul: An Intellectual Biography 2004, Mary Magdalene: A Biography 2005, The Cambridge Companion to the Bible 2007, Abraham's Curse 2008, Starting New Testament Study 2009, The Way of Jesus: To Repair and Renew the World 2010. *Address:* Faculty of Religion, Bard College, Annandale, NY 12504, USA (office). *Telephone:* (845) 758-7335 (office). *Fax:* (845) 758-7826 (office). *E-mail:* chilton@bard.edu (office). *Website:* www.bard.edu (office).

CHIMOMBO, Steve, DEd; Malawi poet, writer, playwright and literary critic; *Professor of English, University of Malawi*; b. 1945, Zomba; s. of Bernard Miles Chimombo and Rhoda Botha; m. Moira Primula Foort; two s. one d. *Education:* Univ. of Malawi, Columbia Univ., Univ. of Iowa, USA, Univ. of Wales. *Career:* Prof. of English, Univ. of Malawi; Ed. Wasi Writer journal. *Plays include:* The Rainmaker 1978, Wachiona Ndani? 1983, Sister! Sister! 1995. *Publications include:* poetry: Vipya 1966, Napolo Poems 1987, Python!, Python! 1992, Breaking the Beadstrings 1995, Epic of the Forest Creatures 2005, The Hyena wears Darkness 2006, Napalo and Other Poems 2009; novels: The Basket Girl 1990, The Wrath of Napolo 2000; short stories: Of Life, Love and Death 2009; criticism: Oral Literature in Malawi 1860–1986 1987, Malawian Oral Literature: The Aesthetics of Indigenous Arts 1988, The Culture of Democracy 1996, AIDS, Artist and Authors 2007. *Honours:* Hon. Fellow, Univ. of Iowa 1984. *Address:* PO Box 317, Zomba, Malawi (home). *Telephone:* 1525289 (office); 293636 (home). *E-mail:* wasc.sbmc@yahoo.com (office).

CHINODYA, Shimmer, (B. Chirasha), BA, MA; Zimbabwean novelist and writer; b. 1957, Gweru; m. *Education:* Univ. of Zimbabwe, Univ. of Iowa, USA. *Career:* Distinguished Visiting Prof. in Creative Writing, St Lawrence Univ., New York 1995–97; also curriculum developer, materials designer, ed. and screenwriter. *Film script:* Everyone's Child 1994. *Radio:* serializations: Dew in the Morning, Harvest of Thorns. *Publications:* Dew in the Morning 1982, Farai's Girls 1984, Child of War (as B. Chirasha) 1985, Harvest of Thorns (Commonwealth Writers Prize for African Literature) 1990, Can We Talk and Other Stories 1998, Tale of Tamari 2004, Chairman of Fools 2005, Strife (Noma Award, Nat. Arts Merit Award 2007) 2006, Tindos Quest 2009, Chioniso and Other Stories 2012; several children's books as B. Chirasha. *Honours:* Ragdale Fellowship, Lake Forest 1993. *Address:* 39 Lorraine Drive, Bluff Hill, PO Westgate, Harare, Zimbabwe (home). *Telephone:* (4) 331877 (home). *E-mail:* shimmerchi2000@yahoo.com.

CHIPASULA, Frank Mkalawile, BA, MA, PhD; Malawi poet and academic; *Associate Professor of Black American Studies, Southern Illinois University*; b. 1949, Likoma Island, Lake Malawi. *Education:* Chancellor Coll., Univ. of Malawi, Univ. of Zambia, and Brown and Yale Univs, USA. *Career:* fmr teacher, Brown and Yale Univs, St Olaf Coll., Northfield, MN; fmr Assoc. Prof. of Black Studies, Univ. of Nebraska at Omaha, USA; currently Assoc. Prof. of Black American Studies, Southern Illinois Univ. Carbondale, USA. *Publications include:* poetry: Visions and Reflections 1972, O Earth, Wait for Me 1984, When My Brothers Come Home: Poems from Central and Southern Africa (ed.) 1985, Nightwatcher, Nightsong 1986, Whispers in the Wings 1991, In a Dark Season (novel), The Heinemann Book of African Women's Poetry (co-ed.) 1995, Whispers in the Wings: New and Selected Poems 2001, Bending the Bow: An Anthology of African Love Poetry 2009. *Honours:* hon. mention, Noma Award for Publishing in Africa 1985, BBC Poetry Prize 1989. *Address:* Department of Black American Studies, Southern Illinois University, Mailcode 2438, Carbondale, IL 62901, USA (office). *Telephone:* (618) 453-7147 (office). *E-mail:* fchipasu@siu.edu (office). *Website:* www.siuc.edu (office).

CHIRASHA, B. (see Chinodya, Shimmer)

CHISHOLM, Anne, FRSL; British biographer and reviewer; m. Michael Davie. *Career:* fmr staff mem., Time Magazine, New York, Observer; regular reviewer, Sunday Telegraph; fmr reader and occasional ed., Jonathan Cape and Bloomsbury; Visiting Fellow, Univ. of Texas, USA 2003; Fellow, Oxford Brookes Univ. 2005–07; Fellow, RSL, mem. of Council 2003–08, Chair. 2008–. *Publications include:* non-fiction: Philosophers of the Earth 1972, Nancy Cunard: A Biography (Silver PEN Award) 1979, Faces of Hiroshima: A Report 1985, Beaverbrook: A Life (with Michael Davie) 1992, Rumer Godden: A Storyteller's Life 1998, Frances Partridge: The Biography 2009; contrib. to The Spectator. *Address:* c/o Enquiries, The Orion Publishing Group, Orion House, 5 Upper Saint Martin's Lane, London, WC2H 9EA, England. *Website:* www.orionbooks.co.uk.

CHITHAM, Edward Harry Gordon, PGCE, MA, PhD, FRSA; British education consultant and writer; b. 16 May 1932, Harborne, Birmingham, England; m. Mary Patricia Tilley 1962; one s. two d. *Education:* Jesus Coll., Cambridge, Univs of Birmingham, Warwick and Sheffield. *Career:* mem. Asscn of Classics Teachers, Gaskell Soc., Brontë Soc. *Publications include:* The Black Country 1972, Ghost in the Water 1973, The Poems of Anne Brontë 1979, Brontë Facts and Brontë Problems (with T. J. Winnifrith) 1983, Selected Brontë Poems (with T. J. Winnifrith) 1985, The Brontës' Irish Background 1986, A Life of Emily Brontë 1987, Charlotte and Emily Brontë (with T. J. Winnifrith) 1989, A Life of Anne Brontë 1991, A Bright Start 1995, The Poems of Emily Brontë (with Derek Roper) 1996, The Birth of Wuthering Heights: Emily Brontë at Work 1998, A Brontë Family Chronology 2003, Harborne: A History 2004, Rowley Regis: A History 2006, West Bromwich: A History 2009; contrib. to Byron Journal, Gaskell Society Journal, ISIS Magazine, Brontë Society Transactions. *Address:* 25 Fugelmere Close, Harborne, Birmingham, B17 8SE, England (home). *Telephone:* (121) 420-1249 (home).

CHITTICK, William C., BA, PhD; American writer and academic; *Professor of Religious Studies, State University of New York, Stony Brook*; b. 29 June 1943, Milford, Conn.; s. of Oliver B. Chittick and Margaret Clark Chittick; m. Sachiko Murata. *Education:* Coll. of Wooster, OH, Univ. of Tehran, Iran. *Career:* Asst Prof., Center for the Humanities, Aryamehr Tech. Univ., Tehran 1974–78; Asst Prof., Imperial Iranian Acad. of Philosophy, Tehran 1978–79; Asst Ed., Encyclopaedia Iranica, Columbia Univ. 1981–84; Asst Prof. of Religious Studies, Dept of Asian and Asian American Studies, State Univ. of New York, Stony Brook 1983–91, Prof. of Religious Studies 1991–; Visiting Prof. of Arabic Literature, Harvard Univ. 1996; Directeur d'études, L'École des Hautes Études en Sciences Sociales, Paris 2004. *Publications include:* A Shi'ite Anthology 1981, The Sufi Path of Love 1983, The Psalms of Islam 1988, The Sufi Path of Knowledge 1989, Faith and Practice of Islam 1992, Imaginal Worlds 1994, The Vision of Islam (co-author) 1996, The Self-Disclosure of God 1998, Sufism: A Short Introduction 2000, The Heart of Islamic Philosophy 2001, Me & Rumi: The Autobiography of Shams-i Tabrizi 2004, The Elixir of the Gnostics 2005, The Sufi Doctrine of Rumi: Illustrated Edition 2005, Science of the Cosmos, Science of the Soul 2007, The Inner Journey: Views from the Islamic Tradition 2007, The Sage Learning of Liu Zhi: Islamic Thought in Confucian Terms (co-author) 2009, In Search of the Lost Heart: Explorations in Islamic Thought 2012. *Honours:* Fellowship for Ind. Study and Research, Nat. Endowment for the Humanities 1986–87, Fellowship for Univ. Profs, Nat. Endowment for the Humanities 1993–94, World Prize for the Book of the Year in Iranian Studies within the American Countries (Iran) 2005, Mevlâna Arastirmalari Özel Ödülü, Kombassan Foundation (Konya Turkey) 2000, Anjoman-e Athar va Mafakhir Melli Award (Iran) 2008; Farabi Int. Award (Iran) 2008, Fellowship, Nat. Endowment for the Humanities 2010–11. *Address:* Department of Asian and Asian American Studies, State University of New York, Stony Brook, NY 11794-5343, USA (office). *Telephone:* (631) 632-7690 (office). *E-mail:* wchittick@notes.cc.sunysb.edu (office).

CHITTY, Susan Elspeth; British writer, journalist and lecturer; b. 18 Aug. 1929, London, England; m. Sir Thomas Willes Chitty 1951; one s. three d. *Education:* Somerville Coll., Oxford. *Publications include:* fiction: The Diary of a Fashion Model 1958, White Huntress 1963, My Life and Horses 1966; non-fiction: The Woman Who Wrote Black Beauty 1972, The Beast and the Monk 1975, Charles Kingsley and North Devon 1976, On Next to Nothing (with Thomas Willes Chitty) 1976, The Great Donkey Walk (with Thomas Willes Chitty) 1977, The Young Rider 1979, Gwen John 1876–1939 1981, Now to My Mother 1985, That Singular Person Called Lear 1988; editor: The Intelligent Woman's Guide to Good Taste 1958, The Puffin Book of Horses (with Anne Parry) 1975, Antonia White: Diaries 1926–1957 (two vols) 1991–92, Playing the Game: Biography of Henry Newbolt 1997. *Address:* Bow Cottage, West Hoathly, Sussex, RH19 4QF, England (home).

CHITTY, Sir Thomas Willes, (Thomas Hinde), Bt; British writer; b. 2 March 1926, Felixstowe, Suffolk, England; s. of Sir (Thomas) Henry Willes Chitty and the late Ethel Constance; m. Susan Elspeth Chitty (née Hopkinson) 1951; one s. three d. *Education:* Winchester Coll. and Univ. Coll., Oxford. *Career:* served in RN 1944–47; with Shell Group 1953–60; Granada Arts Fellow, Univ. of York 1964–65; Visiting Lecturer, Univ. of Ill., USA 1965–67; Visiting Prof., Boston Univ. 1969–70; currently freelance writer. *Achievements include:* expedition on foot and donkey with wife and two young daughters, Santiago to Salonika 1975–76. *Publications include:* fiction: Mr Nicholas 1952, Happy As Larry 1957, For the Good of the Company 1961, A Place Like Home 1962, The Cage 1962, Ninety Double Martinis 1963, The Day the Call Came 1964, Games of Chance 1965, The Village 1966, High 1968, Bird 1970, Generally a Virgin 1972, Agent 1974, Our Father 1975, Daymare 1980; non-fiction: Spain 1963, On Next to Nothing (with Susan Elspeth Chitty) 1976, The Great Donkey Walk (with Susan Elspeth Chitty) 1977, The Cottage Book 1979, Sir Henry and Sons (autobiog.) 1980, Stately Gardens of Britain 1983, A Field Guide to the English Country Parson 1983, Forests of Britain 1984, The Domesday Book: England's Heritage, Then and Now 1986, Courtiers: 900 Years of Court Life 1986, Tales from the Pump Room: An Informal History of Bath 1988, Capability Brown 1986, Imps of Promise: A History of the King's School Canterbury 1990, Looking-Glass Letters (ed.) (letters of Lewis Carroll) 1991, Paths of Progress, A History of Marlborough College 1992, A History of Highgate School 1993, A History of King's College School 1994, Carpenter's Children: A History of the City of London School 1995, An Illustrated History of the University of Greenwich 1996, The Martlet and the Griffen: A History of Abingdon School 1997, In Time of Plague 2006. *Address:* c/o Andrew Hewson, John Johnson, 45–47 Clerkenwell Green, London, EC1R 0HT (office); Bow Cottage, West Hoathly, Sussex, RH19 4QF, England (home). *Telephone:* (20) 7251-0125 (office); (1342) 810269 (home). *E-mail:* thomas.chitty@ukgateway.net (home).

CHIZIANE, Paulina; Mozambican author; b. 4 June 1955, Manjacaze. *Education:* Eduardo Mondlane Univ., Maputo. *Career:* worked for Int. Red

Cross during civil war; first woman novelist to be published in Mozambique. *Publications include:* novels: Balada de Amor ao Vento 1990, Ventos do Apocalipse 1996, O Setimo Juramento 2000, Niketche: Uma História de Poligamia (José Craveirinha Prize 2003) 2002, O Alegre Canto da Perdiz 2008, Niketche: A Story of Polygamy 2010. *Address:* c/o Editorial Caminho, SA, Estrada de Paço de Arcos, 66, 66-A, 2735-336 Cacém, Portugal. *E-mail:* info@editorial-caminho.pt. *Website:* www.editorial-caminho.pt.

CHO, Ramaswamy, BSc, BL; Indian journalist, playwright, actor, lawyer and political commentator; b. 5 Oct. 1934, Madras (now Chennai); s. of R. Srinivasan and Rajammal Srinivasan; m. 1966; one s. one d. *Education:* P.S. High School, Loyola Coll., Vivekananda Coll., Madras and Madras Law Coll., Madras Univ. *Career:* practiced as lawyer, Madras High Court 1957; Legal Adviser to T.T.K. Group of Cos 1961–; film scriptwriter and actor 1966–; theatre dir, actor and playwright 1958–; Ed. Thuglak (Tamil political fortnightly) 1970–; Pres. People's Union of Civil Liberties, Tamilnadu 1980–82; nominated mem. of Rajya Sabha (Parl.); has acted in 180 films, written 14 film scripts, directed four films; written, directed and acted in four TV series and 23 plays in Tamil. *Publications:* 23 plays and 10 novels in Tamil; numerous articles on politics, in English and Tamil. *Honours:* Haldi Gati Award, Maharana of Mewar, for nat. service through journalism 1985, Veerakesari Award for investigative journalism 1986, B. D. Goenka Award for Excellence in Journalism, Panchajanya Award for promotion of nationalism 1998. *Address:* 46 Greenways Road, Chennai 600 028; 35 Meena Bagh, New Delhi 110 011, India. *Telephone:* (44) 4936913 (Chennai); (11) 3792520 (New Delhi). *Fax:* (44) 24936915. *Website:* www.thuglak.com.

CHOI, Susan, MFA; American novelist; b. 1969, South Bend, Ind.; m. Pete Wells; two s. *Education:* Yale Univ., Cornell Univ. *Career:* fmr fact checker, The New Yorker; Provincetown Fine Arts Work Center Fellow 1997–98. *Publications include:* The Foreign Student (Asian American Literary Award for Fiction) 1998, Wonderful Town: New York Stories from the New Yorker (co-ed) 2001, American Woman 2003, A Person of Interest 2008. *Honours:* fellowships from Nat. Endowment for the Arts and Guggenheim Foundation, PEN/W.G. Sebald Award for a Fiction Writer in Mid-Career 2010. *Address:* c/o Yen Cheong, Viking and Penguin Books, 375 Hudson Street, Fourth Floor, New York, NY 10014, USA. *Telephone:* (212) 366-2275. *E-mail:* Yen.Cheong@us.penguingroup.com (office). *Website:* www.susanchoi.com.

CHOMSKY, (Avram) Noam, MA, PhD; American theoretical linguist and writer; *Professor Emeritus, Department of Linguistics, Massachusetts Institute of Technology*; b. 7 Dec. 1928, Philadelphia; s. of William Chomsky and Elsie Simonofsky; m. Carol Schatz 1949 (died 2008); one s. two d. *Education:* Univ. of Pennsylvania. *Career:* Asst Prof., MIT 1955–58, Assoc. Prof. 1958–61, Prof. of Modern Languages 1961–66, Ferrari P. Ward Prof. of Modern Languages and Linguistics 1966–76, Inst. Prof. 1976–; Visiting Prof., Columbia Univ. 1957–58; NSF Fellow, Inst. for Advanced Study, Princeton, NJ 1958–59; American Council of Learned Socs Fellow, Center for Cognitive Studies, Harvard Univ. 1964–65; Linguistics Soc. of America Prof., UCLA 1966; Beckman Prof., Univ. of California, Berkeley 1966–67; John Locke Lecturer, Univ. of Oxford 1969; Shearman Lecturer, Univ. Coll., London 1969; Bertrand Russell Memorial Lecturer, Univ. of Cambridge 1971; Nehru Memorial Lecturer, Univ. of Delhi 1972; Whidden Lecturer, McMaster Univ. 1975; Huizinga Memorial Lecturer, Univ. of Leiden 1977; Woodbridge Lecturer, Columbia Univ. 1978; Kant Lecturer, Stanford Univ. 1979; Jeanette K. Watson Distinguished Visiting Prof., Syracuse Univ. 1982; Pauling Memorial Lecturer, Oregon State Univ. 1995; mem. American Acad. of Arts and Sciences, Linguistic Soc. of America, American Philosophical Asscn, American Acad. of Political and Social Science, NAS, Bertrand Russell Peace Foundation, Deutsche Akademie der Naturforscher Leopoldina, Nat. Acad. of Sciences, Royal Anthropological Inst., Utrecht Soc. of Arts and Sciences; Fellow, AAAS; Corresp. Fellow, British Acad. *Publications include:* Syntactic Structures 1957, Current Issues in Linguistic Theory 1964, Aspects of the Theory of Syntax 1965, Cartesian Linguistics 1966, Topics in the Theory of Generative Grammar 1966, Language and Mind 1968, The Sound Pattern of English (with Morris Halle) 1968, American Power and the New Mandarins 1969, At War with Asia 1970, Problems of Knowledge and Freedom 1971, Studies on Semantics in Generative Grammar 1972, For Reasons of State 1973, The Backroom Boys 1973, Counter-revolutionary Violence (with Edward Herman) 1973, Peace in the Middle East? 1974, Reflections on Language 1975, The Logical Structure of Linguistic Theory 1975, Essays on Form and Interpretation 1977, Human Rights and American Foreign Policy 1978, Language and Responsibility 1979, The Political Economy of Human Rights (two vols, with Edward Herman) 1979, Rules and Representations 1980, Lectures on Government and Binding 1981, Radical Priorities 1981, Towards a New Cold War 1982, Concepts and Consequences of the Theory of Government and Binding 1982, Fateful Triangle: The United States, Israel and the Palestinians 1983, Modular Approaches to the Study of the Mind 1984, Turning the Tide 1985, Knowledge of Language: Its Nature, Origins and Use 1986, Barriers 1986, Pirates and Emperors 1986, Generative Grammar: Its Basis, Development and Prospects 1987, On Power and Ideology 1987, Language and Problems of Knowledge 1987, Language in a Psychological Setting 1987, The Chomsky Reader 1987, The Culture of Terrorism 1988, Manufacturing Consent (with Edward Herman) 1988, Language and Politics 1988, Necessary Illusions 1989, Deterring Democracy 1991, What Uncle Sam Really Wants 1992, Chronicles of Dissent 1992, Year 501: The Conquest Continues 1993, Rethinking Camelot: JFK, the Vietnam War and US Political Culture 1993, Letters from Lexington: Reflections on Propaganda 1993, The Prosperous Few and the Restless Many 1993, Language and Thought 1994, World Orders, Old and New 1994, The Minimalist Program 1995, Powers and Prospects 1996, Class Warfare 1996, The Common Good 1998, Profit over People 1998, The New Military Humanism 1999, New Horizons in the Study of Language and Mind 2000, Rogue States: The Rule of Force in World Affairs 2000, A New Generation Draws the Line 2000, Architecture of Language 2000, Propaganda and the Public Mind 2001, 9-11 2001, Understanding Power 2002, On Nature and Language 2002, Middle East Illusions 2003, Hegemony or Survival: America's Quest for Global Dominance 2003, Failed States: America 2006, Interventions 2007, What We Say Goes 2008, Perilous Power (with Gilbert Achcar) 2008, Hopes and Prospects 2010, Gaza in Crisis: Reflections on Israel's War Against the Palestinians (with Ilan Pappé) 2010; numerous lectures, contribs to scholarly journals. *Honours:* Hon. Fellow, British Psychological Soc. 1985, Royal Anthropological Inst.; Hon. DHL (Chicago) 1967, (Loyola Univ., Swarthmore Coll.) 1970, (Bard Coll.) 1971, (Massachusetts) 1973, (Maine, Gettysburg Coll.) 1992, (Amherst Coll.) 1995, (Buenos Aires) 1996; Hon. DLitt (London) 1967, (Delhi) 1972, Visva-Bharati (West Bengal) 1980, (Pennsylvania) 1984, (Cambridge) 1995; Dr hc (Tarragona) 1998, (Guelph) 1999, (Columbia) 1999, (Connecticut) 1999, (Pisa) 1999, (Harvard) 2000, (Toronto) 2000, (Western Ontario) 2000, (Kolkata) 2001; George Orwell Award, Nat. Council of Teachers of English 1987, Kyoto Prize in Basic Sciences 1988, James Killian Award, MIT 1992, Helmholtz Medal, Berlin Brandenburgische Akad. Wissenschaften 1996, Benjamin Franklin Medal, Franklin Inst., Philadelphia 1999, Rabindranath Tagore Centenary Award, Asiatic Soc. 2000, Peace Award, Turkish Publrs Asscn 2002. *Address:* Department of Linguistics and Philosophy, Massachusetts Institute of Technology, 77 Massachusetts Avenue, Bldg. 32-D808, Cambridge, MA 02139 (office); 15 Suzanne Road, Lexington, MA 02420, USA (home). *Telephone:* (617) 253-7819 (office); (781) 862-6160 (home). *Fax:* (617) 253-9425 (office). *E-mail:* chomsky@mit.edu (office). *Website:* web.mit.edu/linguistics/www (office).

CHORLTON, David; British writer, poet and artist; b. 15 Feb. 1948, Spittal-an-der-Drau, Austria; m. Roberta Elliott 1976. *Education:* Stockport Coll. *Career:* earlier worked as graphic designer; co-ed The Signal (magazine) with Joan Silva. *Publications include:* Corn dance 1978, Sonoran Journal 1980, Kino's Dream 1981, Allegiance to the Fire 1984, Without Shoes 1987, Honest Citizens 1988, Purgatory 1988, The Village Painters 1990, Measuring Time 1990, Forget the Country You Came From 1992, Haydn's Skull Returning 1992, Outposts 1994, Assimilation 2000, Common Sightings 2001, A Normal Day Amazes Us 2003, Return to Waking Life 2004, Another Word 2005, Waiting for the Quetzal 2006, Places You Can't Reach 2006, The Porous Desert 2007, The Lost River (Ronald Wardall Award) 2008, The Epistemological Question Mark 2008, A Venetian sequence 2008, From the Age of Miracles (Slipstream Poetry Chapbook Award) 2009; contrib. to numerous reviews and journals. *Address:* 118 West Palm Lane, Phoenix, AZ 85003, USA (home). *Telephone:* (602) 253-5055 (home). *E-mail:* rdchorlton@netzero.com (office). *Website:* www.davidchorlton.mysite.com (office).

CHOUAKI, Aziz, DipLit; French (b. Algerian) writer, playwright, poet and musician; b. 1951, Algiers. *Education:* Univ. of Algiers. *Career:* guitarist in rock groups 1975; writer 1982–; Artistic Dir Triangle jazz club, Algiers; moved to France 1991. *Plays include:* Poussières d'Ange (Théâtre Jean Vilar, Vitry sur Seine), Fruits de Mer (24 radio plays, for Radio Suisse Romande) 1993, Brisants de mémoire (five short dramas) 1995, Les Oranges (TILF, La Villette) 1997, Boudin-purée (Gare au Théâtre, Vitry sur Seine) 1998, Bazar (La Laiterie, Strasbourg) 1999, Le Père indigne (Gare au Théâtre, Vitry) 1999, El Maestro (ARC, Creusot) 2000, Le Trésor (Théâtre SaulCy, Metz) 2000, Le Portefeuille (La Laiterie, Strasbourg) 2001, L'Arrêt de bus 2003, Une Virée (Théâtre des Amandiers, Nanterre) 2005, Le tampon vert (lectures, Théâtre des Amandiers, Nanterre) 2007, Dom Juan 2009, Les Coloniaux 2009, Chez Mimi 2010. *Publications include:* Argo (poems and novellas) 1982, Baya (novel) 1989, L'Etoile d'Alger (novel, trans. as The Star of Algiers) 1998, Aigle (novel) 2000, Une enfance outremer 2001, Avoir 20 ans à Alger (fiction) 2001, La stella d'Algeri 2003, Arobase (novel) 2004, Nadia Ferroukhi: Photographe 2005, Brûleur (with Thomas Chable) 2006. *E-mail:* aziz.chouaki@mac.com (office). *Website:* www.azizchouaki.com.

CHOUDHURY, Chandrahas; Indian author and critic; b. Orissa. *Education:* Delhi Univ., Univ. of Cambridge, UK. *Career:* currently fiction and poetry ed., The Caravan (Indian magazine on politics and the arts); contrib., New York Times, Observer, Wall Street Journal, Sunday Telegraph, San Francisco Chronicle, Mint Lounge. *Publications:* Arzee the Dwarf (novel) 2009; as ed.: India: A Traveler's Literary Companion 2010. *Address:* c/o The Caravan magazine, Delhi Press Building, E-3 Jhandewalan, Rani Jhansi Road, New Delhi 110 055 (office); c/o HarperCollins Publishers India, A 53, Sector 57, Noida, Uttar Pradesh, India (office). *Telephone:* 41398888 (office); 23529557 (office); 0120-4044800 (office). *Fax:* 23625020 (office). *E-mail:* thecaravan@delhipress.in (office); contact@harpercollins-india.com (office); hashblog@gmail.com (home). *Website:* www.caravanmagazine.in (office); www.harpercollins.co.in (office); middlestage.blogspot.co.uk (home).

CHOYCE, Lesley, BA, MA; Canadian academic, writer, poet and editor; b. 21 March 1951, Riverside, NJ, USA; m. Terry Paul 1974; two d. *Education:* Rutgers Univ., Montclair State Coll., City Univ. of New York. *Career:* Ed. Pottersfield Press 1979–; Prof., Dalhousie Univ. 1986–. *Recordings include:* Long Lost Planet 1996, Sea Level 1998. *Publications include:* adult fiction:

Eastern Sure 1981, Billy Botzweiler's Last Dance 1984, Downwind 1984, Conventional Emotions 1985, The Dream Auditor 1986, Coming Up for Air 1988, The Second Season of Jonas MacPherson 1989, Magnificent Obsessions 1991, Ecstasy Conspiracy 1992, Margin of Error 1992, The Republic of Nothing 1994, The Trap Door to Heaven 1996, Beautiful Sadness 1997, Dance the Rocks Ashore 1997, World Enough 1998, The Summer of Apartment X 1999, Cold Clear Morning 2001, Reaction 2010, Raising Orion 2011; young adult fiction: Skateboard Shakedown 1989, Hungry Lizards 1990, Wavewatch 1990, Some Kind of Hero 1991, Wrong Time, Wrong Place, 1991, Clearcut Danger 1992, Full Tilt 1993, Good Idea Gone Bad 1993, Dark End of Dream Street 1994, Big Burn 1995, Falling Through the Cracks 1996, Couleurs Troubles 1997, Roid Rage 1999, Refuge Cove 2002, Shoulder the Sky 2002, Smoke and Mirrors 2004, Thunderbowl 2004, Sudden Impact 2005, Deconstructing Dylan 2006, Wave Warrior 2007, The End of the World as We Know It 2007, Hell's Hotel 2008, Skate Freak 2008, The Book of Michael 2008, Running the Risk 2009, Reckless 2010; poetry: Re-Inventing the Wheel 1980, Fast Living 1982, The End of Ice 1985, The Top of the Heart 1986, The Man Who Borrowed the Bay of Fundy 1988, The Coastline of Forgetting 1995, Beautiful Sadness 1998, Caution to the Wind 2000, Typographical Eras 2003; non-fiction: An Avalanche of Ocean 1987, December Six: The Halifax Solution 1988, Transcendental Anarchy (autobiog.) 1993, Nova Scotia: Shaped by the Sea 1996, The Coasts of Canada 2002, Sea of Tranquility 2003, Revenge of the Optimist 2004, Driving Minnie's Piano 2006, Skunks for Breakfast 2006, Nova Scotia: A Traveller's Companion 2006, Seven Ravens: Two Summers in a Life by the Sea 2009, Living Outside the Lines 2010, How to Fix Your Head 2011; editor: Chezzetcook 1977, The Pottersfield Portfolio (seven vols) 1979–85, Visions from the Edge (with John Bell) 1981, The Cape Breton Collection 1984, Ark of Ice: Canadian Futurefiction 1992. *Honours:* Event Magazine's Creative Nonfiction Competition Winner 1990, Dartmouth Book Awards 1990, 1995, Ann Connor Brimer Award for Children's Literature 1994, Authors Award, Foundation for the Advancement of Canadian Letters 1995, Landmar East Literacy Award 2000, Poet Laureate Peter Gzowski Invitational Golf Tournament 2000. *Address:* 83 Leslie Road, East Lawrencetown, NS B2Z 1P8, Canada.

CHRISTENSEN, Lars Saabye; Norwegian poet, writer and playwright; b. 21 Sept. 1953, Oslo. *Career:* Ed., Signaler 1986–90. *Plays:* Columbus' ankomst 1981, Kvitt eller dobbelt 1984, Jokeren 1987, Til pengene tar slutt, Al 1988, Lyset på yttersida 2001, Mekka 1994, Chet baker spiller ikke her 2010. *Publications:* Historien om Gly 1976, Amatøren 1977, Kamelen i mitt hjerte 1978, Jaktmarker 1979, Billettene 1980, Jokeren 1981, Paraply 1982, Beatles 1984, Blodets bånd 1985, Åsteder 1986, Sneglene 1987, Herman 1988, Stempler 1989, Versterålen 1989, Bly 1990, Gutten som ville være en av gutta 1992, Ingens 1992, Den akustiske skyggen 1993, Jubel 1995, Den andre siden av blått 1996, Den misunnelige frisøren 1997, Noen som elsker hverandre 1999, Falleferdig himmel 1999, Pasninger 1999, Kongen som ville ha mer enn en krone 1999, Under en sort paraply 1999, Pinnsvinsol 2000, Mann for sin katt 2000, Halvbroren 2001, Maskeblomstfamilien 2003, Sanger og steiner 2003, SATS 2003, Oscar Wildes heis 2004, Modellen 2005, Norske omveier i blues og bilder 2005, Saabyes sirkus 2006, Den arktiske drømmen 2007, Ordiord 2007, Bisettelsen 2008, Visning 2009, Men buicken står der fremdeles 2009, Bernhard Hvals forsnakkelser 2010, Mitt danske album 2010. *Honours:* Commdr, Order of St Olaf 2006, Chevalier, Ordre des Arts et des Lettres 2008; Tarjei Vesaas debutantpris 1976, Cappelenprisen 1984, Rivertonprisen 1987, Kritikerprisen 1988, Sarpsborgprisen 1988, Bokhandlerprisen 1990, Amandaprisen 1991, Doblougprisen 1993, Riksmålsforbundets litteraturpris 1997, Sarpsborgprisen 1999, Aamot-statuetten 2001, Bokhandlerprisen 2001, Brageprisen 2001, Den norske leserprisen 2001, Natt & Dags bokpris 2001, Nordisk Råds Litteraturpris 2002. *Literary Agent:* c/o Cappelen Damm AS, 0055 Oslo, Norway. *Telephone:* 22-61-65-00. *E-mail:* rights@cappelendamm.no. *Website:* www.cappelendamm.no.

CHRISTIAN, Beatrix; Australian playwright and screenwriter. *Education:* Nat. Inst. of Drama. *Career:* affiliate writer and Writer-in-Residence, Sydney Theatre Co. 1993–94, Writer-in-Residence 2002. *Plays include:* Inside Dry Water 1993, Blue Murder 1994, The Governor's Family 1997, Faust's House, Fred, Old Masters, The Promised Land, Spumante Romantica, Ten Things Not to Do on a First Date, Then the Mountain Comes; adaptations: A Doll's House (Ibsen), Life is a Dream (Calderón de la Barca); adaptations with Benedict Andrews: Three Sisters (Chekhov). *Film screenplay:* Jindabyne 2005. *Television writing:* White Colour Blue. *Honours:* Sydney Critics' Circle Award for Best Australian Play, New York New Dramatists' Award 1997, Queensland Premier's Literary Award 2002. *Literary Agent:* Shanahan Management, Level 3, Berman House, 92 Campbell Street, Surry Hills, NSW 2010, Australia. *Telephone:* (2) 8202-1800. *Fax:* (2) 8202-1801. *E-mail:* nellief@shanahan.com.au.

CHRISTIAN, John (see Dixon, Roger)

CHRISTOPHER, Nicholas, AB; American poet and writer; b. 28 Feb. 1951, New York, NY; m. Constance Barbara Davidson 1980. *Education:* Harvard Coll. *Career:* previously taught at Yale Univ., New York Univ., Barnard Coll.; currently Prof., School of the Arts, Columbia Univ. *Publications include:* novels: The Soloist 1986, Veronica 1996, A Trip to the Stars 2000, Franklin Flyer 2002, The Bestiary 2007; poetry: On Tour with Rita 1982, A Short History of the Island of Butterflies 1986, Desperate Characters 1988, In the Year of the Comet 1992, 5 Degrees and Other Poems 1994, Walk and Other Poems 1995, The Creation of the Night Sky 1998, Atomic Field: Two Poems 2000, Crossing the Equator: New and Selected Poems 1972–2004 2004; nonfiction: Somewhere in the Night: Film Noir and the American City 1997; others: Under 35: The New Generation of American Poets (ed.) 1989, Walk on the Wild Side: Urban American Poetry Since 1975 (ed.) 1994; contribs to anthologies and periodicals. *Honours:* New York Foundation for the Arts Fellowship 1986, National Endowment for the Arts Fellowship 1987, Peter I. B. Lavan Award, Acad. of American Poets 1991, Guggenheim Fellowship 1993, Melville Cane Award 1994. *Literary Agent:* c/o Janklow & Nesbit Associates, 445 Park Avenue, New York, NY 10022, USA. *Telephone:* (212) 421-1700. *Address:* 415 Dodge Hall, Columbia University, New York, NY 10027, USA (office). *Telephone:* (212) 854-4391 (office). *E-mail:* nic@nicholaschristopher.com (office). *Website:* www.nicholaschristopher.com.

CHROBÁKOVÁ REPAR, Stanislava, PhD; Slovak/Slovenian poet, writer, translator and editor; *Editor, Društvo Apokalipsa, Ljubljana*; b. (Stanislava Kvapilová), 5 May 1960, Bratislava, Czechoslovakia; d. of Stanislav Kvapil and Terézia Kvapilová; m. Primoz Repar; one s. *Education:* Comenius Univ., Bratislava, Inst. of Slovak Literature, Slovak Acad. of Sciences, Bratislava, Univ. in Nova Gorica, Slovenia. *Career:* researcher, Dept of Aesthetics, Culturology and Art Sciences, Comenius Univ., Bratislava 1984–1991; journalist, Kultúrny Zivot 1990–91; researcher in contemporary Slovak literature, Slovak Acad. of Sciences 1991–2003; Ed., Romboid (literary magazine published by Asscn of Slovak Writers' Orgs) 1996–2003; Ed., Publishing House Apokalipsa, Ljubljana 2001–; Co-founder Review within Review project 2002–; Research Fellow, Mirovni Inštitut, Ljubljana 2007–08. *Publications include:* fiction: Krutokradma (trans. as Cruelstealth) 1997, Anjelské utópie (trans. as Angelic Utopias) 2001, Slovenka na kvadrat – razglednice iz Slovenije (trans. as Slovak/Slovene Squared – Postcards from Slovenia) 2009; poetry: Zo spoločnej zimy (trans. as From a Shared Winter) 1994, Na hranici jazyka (trans. as On the Boundary of Language) 1997, Iz skupne zime (trans. as From a Shared Winter) 2006, Nahá v tŕní (trans. as Naked in Thorns) 2006, Dotakniti se prazne sredine (trans. as Touching Empty Centre) 2010; non-fiction: Mila Haugová 2002, Ohnisko reči alebo mlčanlivá hlbka horizontu (trans. as Speech Focus, or Silent Depth of Horizon) 2007; ed.: Sto let slovaške knjizevnosti – One Hundred Years of Slovak Literature 2000, series FRAKTAL (29 books) 2003–, special gender-issues of literature review Apokalipsa 2003–, Antología de la poesía eslovaca contemporánea 2008, special "Review within Review" issues of literature reviews in Romboid (SK) and Apokalipsa (SLO). *Honours:* Alexander Matuška Award 1995, Slovak Writers' Soc. Award 2003. *Address:* Kuklovská 5, 841 04 Bratislava, Slovakia (home); Lili Novy 25, 1000 Ljubljana, Slovenia (home). *Telephone:* (1) 2562250 (Ljubljana) (home). *Fax:* (1) 2562250 (Ljubljana) (home). *E-mail:* stanislava.repar@t-2.net (home). *Website:* www.litcentrum.sk/39968 (office).

CHUA, Amy, AB, JD; American lawyer and professor of law; *John M. Duff, Jr Professor of Law, Yale University*; b. 1962, d. of Leon Chua; m. Jed Rubenfeld; two d. *Education:* El Cerrito High School, Harvard Coll., Harvard Univ. *Career:* law clerk to Chief Judge Patricia M. Wald, US Court of Appeals for the DC Circuit, Washington, DC 1987–88; Corp. Law Assoc., Cleary, Gottlieb, Steen & Hamilton, New York (worked on privatization of Teléfonos de México and numerous int. transactions throughout Asia, Europe and Latin America) 1988–93; Assoc. Prof. of Law, Duke Univ. 1994–99, Prof. of Law 1999–2001; Visiting Prof. of Law, Columbia Univ. Autumn 1999, Stanford Univ. Spring 2000, New York Univ. School of Law Autumn 2000; Prof. of Law, Yale Univ. 2001–05, John M. Duff, Jr Prof. of Law 2005–; Exec. Ed. Harvard Law Review; mem. New York State Bar 1990. *Publications include:* World on Fire: How Exporting Free Market Democracy Breeds Ethnic Hatred and Global Instability 2003, Day of Empire: How Hyperpowers Rise to Global Dominance – And Why They Fall 2007, Battle Hymn of the Tiger Mother 2011; book chapters and articles on int. business transactions, law and devt, ethnic conflict, and globalization and the law. *Honours:* Nat. Merit Scholar 1980, John Harvard Scholar and Elizabeth Cary Agassiz Scholar, Harvard Coll., Int. Affairs Fellowship, Council on Foreign Relations 1998–99, Distinguished Teaching Award, Yale Law School 2002–03. *Address:* Yale Law School, PO Box 208215, New Haven, CT 06520, USA (office). *Telephone:* (203) 432-4992 (office). *E-mail:* amy.chua@yale.edu (office). *Website:* www.law.yale.edu (office).

CHUNN, Louise; New Zealand magazine editor; *Editor, Psychologies;* m. 2nd Andrew Anthony 2001; one s. two d. *Education:* Auckland Univ. *Career:* ed. trade magazines, Auckland; writer, Auckland Star evening newspaper; moved to USA, Asst Ed. Cornell Univ. alumni magazine; moved to London, UK as news reporter, Fashion Weekly 1982–83; Features Ed., then Deputy Ed. Just 17 magazine 1983–85, Ed. 1985–86; Deputy Ed. Elle 1986–89; Women, Parents and Style Pages Ed., Guardian newspaper 1989–95; Features Ed., Features Dir, then Deputy Ed., Vogue 1995–98; Ed. ES magazine 1998–2000; Deputy Ed. In Style 2000–02, Ed. 2002–06; Ed. Good Housekeeping 2006–08; Ed. Psychologies 2009–. *Honours:* PPA Consumer Magazine of the Year 2004, EMAP Writer of the Year 1984. *Address:* Psychologies, Hachette Filipacchi (UK) Ltd, 64 North Row, London, W1K 7LL, England (office). *Telephone:* (20) 7150-7000 (office). *E-mail:* psychologies@hf-uk.com (office); louise.chunn@hf-uk.com (office); louisechunn49@yahoo.co.uk (home). *Website:* www.psychologies.co.uk (office).

CHURCH, Robert; British author; b. 20 July 1932, London, England; m. Dorothy June Bourton 1953; two d. *Education:* Beaufoy Coll., London. *Career:* served in British Army 1950–52; Metropolitan Police 1952–78; Probation

Service 1978–88. *Publications include:* Murder in East Anglia 1987, Accidents of Murder 1989, More Murder in East Anglia 1990, Murder in East Anglia 1993, Anglian Blood (co-ed.) 1995, Well Done Boys 1996; contrib. to miscellaneous journals. *Honours:* Salaman Prize for Non-Fiction 1997. *Address:* Woodside, 7 Crome Walk, Gunton Park, Lowestoft, Suffolk, NR32 4NF, England (home). *Telephone:* (1502) 518072 (home).

CHURCHILL, Caryl, BA; British playwright; b. 3 Sept. 1938, London; d. of Robert Churchill and Jan Churchill (née Brown); m. David Harter 1961; three s. *Education:* Trafalgar School, Montréal, Canada, Lady Margaret Hall, Oxford. *Career:* first play, Downstairs, performed at Nat. Union of Students Drama Festival 1958; writes mainly for theatre but has also written numerous radio plays and several TV plays. *Stage plays include:* Having a Wonderful Time (Oxford Players, 1960), Owners (Royal Court, London) 1972, Objections to Sex and Violence (Royal Court) 1975, Vinegar Tom (Monstrous Regiment toured 1976), Light Shining in Buckinghamshire (performed by Joint Stock Co., Edinburgh Festival 1976, then Royal Court), Traps (Royal Court) 1977, Cloud Nine (Joint Stock Co., Royal Court) 1979, 1980, Lucille Lortel Theater, New York 1981–83, Top Girls (Royal Court) 1982, 1983, Public Theater, New York 1983, Fen (Joint Stock Co., Almeida Theatre, London 1983, Royal Court 1983, Public Theater, New York 1983), Softcops (RSC 1984), A Mouthful of Birds (Joint Stock, Royal Court and tour 1986), Serious Money (Royal Court 1987, Wyndham Theatre 1987, Public Theater New York 1988), Icecream (Royal Court 1989, Public Theater New York 1990), Mad Forest (Cen. School of Drama, Nat. Theatre Bucharest, Royal Court 1990), Lives of the Great Poisoners (Second Stride Co. Riverside Studios, London and tour 1991), The Skriker (Nat. Theatre 1994), Thyestes (by Seneca, translation; Royal Court Theatre Upstairs 1994); Hotel (Second Stride Co., The Place) 1997, This Is A Chair (Royal Court) 1997, Blue Heart (Out of Joint, Royal Court) 1997, Far Away (Royal Court) 2000, (Albery) 2001, A Number (Royal Court) 2002, Drunk Enough to Say I Love You? (Royal Court) 2006, Seven Jewish Children (Royal Court) 2009. *Radio:* The Ants, Not . . Not . . not . . not enough Oxygen, Abortive, Schreiber's Nervous Illness, Identical Twins, Perfect Happiness, Henry's Past. *Television:* The Judge's Wife, The After Dinner Joke, The Legion Hall Bombing, Fugue (jtly). *Publications:* Owners 1973, Light Shining 1976, Traps 1977, Vinegar Tom 1978, Cloud Nine 1979, Top Girls 1982, Fen 1983, Fen and Softcops 1984, A Mouthful of Birds 1986, Serious Money 1987, Plays I 1985, Plays II 1988, Objections to Sex and Violence in Plays by Women Vol. 4 1985, Ice Cream 1989, Mad Forest 1990, Lives of the Great Poisoners 1992, The Striker 1994, Thyestes 1994, Blue Heart 1997, This is a Chair 1999, Far Away 2000, A Number 2002, Drunk Enough to Say I Love You? 2006; anthologies. *Literary Agent:* c/o Casarotto Ramsay Ltd, National House, 60–66 Wardour Street, London, W1V 3HP, England. *Telephone:* (20) 7287-4450. *Fax:* (20) 7734-9293.

CHUTE, Robert Maurice, ScD; American poet, biologist and academic (retd); *Professor Emeritus of Biology, Bates College*; b. 13 Feb. 1926, Bridgton, Me; s. of James Cleveland and Elizabeth Davis Chute; m. Virginia Hinds 1946; one s. one d. *Education:* Fryeburg Acad., Univ. of Maine, Johns Hopkins Univ. School of Hygiene and Public Health. *Career:* Instructor and Asst Prof., Middlebury Coll. 1953–59; Asst Prof. Northridge State Coll. 1959–61; Assoc. Prof. and Chair. of Biology, Lincoln Univ. 1961; Prof. and Chair. of Biology, then Dana Prof. of Biology, Bates Coll. 1962–93, Prof. Emer. 1993–; Fellow, AAAS. *Publications:* Environmental Insight 1971, Introduction to Biology 1976, Sweeping the Sky: Soviet Women Flyers in Combat 1999; poetry: Quiet Thunder 1975, Uncle George 1977, Voices Great and Small 1977, Thirteen Moons/Treize Lunes 1982, Samuel Sewell Sails for Home 1986, When Grandmother Decides to Die 1989, Woodshed on the Moon: Thoreau Poems, Barely Time to Study Jesus 1996, Androscoggin Too 1997, Bent Offerings 2003, Reading Nature 2006, Cat Tales, Constellations: Collected Story Poems; novel: Coming Home, Return to Sender; trans.: Thirteen Moons into Micmac Maliseet (native American) 2002; contribs to Kansas Quarterly, Beloit Poetry Review, Bitterroot, South Florida Poetry Review, North Dakota Review, Cape Rock, Fiddlehead, Greenfield Review, Literary Review, Poet Pore, Sow's Ear Poetry Review. *Honours:* Maine Arts and Humanities Award 1978, Chad Walsh Award (Beloit Poetry Journal) 1997, Maine Writers and Publrs Alliance Poetry Competition 2001, Maine Writers and Publrs Lifetime Distinguished Achievement Award 2011. *Address:* 68 Schellinger Road, Poland Spring, ME 04274, USA (home). *Telephone:* (207) 998-1073 (home). *E-mail:* vrchute@gmail.com.

ÇIÇEKOĞLU, Feride, PhD; Turkish writer; b. 27 Jan. 1951, Ankara; d. of Hasan and Nihal Çiçekoğlu; m. Zafer Aldemir 1986; one d. *Education:* Middle East Tech. Univ. and Univ. of Pennsylvania, USA. *Career:* teacher 1977–80; political prisoner 1980–84; Ed., writer and Film Consultant 1984–92; apptd Sec-Gen. Cultural Foundation for Audiovisual and Cinema, Istanbul 1991; Ed.-in-Chief, Istanbul (journal) 1995–99. *Films:* Ucurtmayi Vurmasinlar (Golden Orange Award for Best Screenplay, Prix du Public Rencontres Internationales) 1989, Journey of Hope (Acad. Award for Best Foreign Film) 1991, Suyun Ote Yani 1992. *Publications include:* Uçurtmayi Vurmasinlar (trans. as Don't let Them Shoot the Kite) (novel) 1986, Suyun Ote Yani (trans. as The Other Side of the Water) (novella) 1990, Did Your Father Ever Die 1990, New York-Istanbul 2003, Vesikai Şehir 2007. *Address:* c/o Metis Publishing, Ipek Sokak No.5, 34433 Beyoglu, Istanbul, Turkey (office). *Website:* www.metiskitap.com (office).

CIFERRI, Elvio, DLitt; Italian writer, historian and academic; *Professor of Italian Literature and History, Leopoldo and Alice Franchetti Institute*; b. 1 April 1965, Città di Castello; s. of Luigi Ciferri and Elena Massimina Radicchi del Citerna. *Education:* Perugia Univ. *Career:* Prof. of History and Italian Literature, Perugia 1992; Prof. of Italian Literature and History, Leopoldo and Alice Franchetti Inst., Città di Castello 1999–. *Publications include:* non-fiction: Editti e notificazioni di mons. Giovanni Muzi vescovo di Città di Castello 1989, Luigi Piccardini e il suo tempo 1993, Tifernati illustri (three vols) 2000–03, Serafina Brunelli: vita visioni e profezie della mistica di Montone 2007; contrib. to numerous journals, Bibliotheca Sanctorum 2000, Encyclopedia of the Romantic Era 2004, Encyclopedia of World Geography 2005, Encyclopedia of the French Revolutionary and Napoleonic Wars 2006, Greenwood Encyclopedia of Love, Courtship and Sexuality through History 2007, Encyclopedia of the Cold War 2008, Dizionario Biografico degli Italiani 2008–10, The International Encyclopedia of Revolution and Protest 2009, Encyclopedia of Medieval Pilgrimage 2009. *Honours:* Gold Medal Atheste Prize for historical research 2002, S. Valentino Prize 2010. *Address:* Via Toscana 51, 06012 Lerchi, Italy (home). *Telephone:* (075) 8554902 (home). *E-mail:* elcif@tiscali.it (home). *Website:* www.elviociferri.it; www.serafinabrunelli.it.

CIRESI, Rita, BA, MA, MFA; American writer and academic; b. 29 Sept. 1960, New Haven, Conn. *Education:* New Coll., Univ. of Iowa, Pennsylvania State Univ. *Career:* Asst Prof. of English, Hollins Coll. 1992–95; Asst Prof., Univ. of South Florida 1995, Assoc. Prof. 1995–; mem. American Italian Historical Asscn, Associated Writing Programs, Italian American Writers' Asscn; Teaching Fellow, Wesleyan Writers' Conf. 1995. *Publications include:* Mother Rocket (Flannery O'Connor Award 2002) 1993, Blue Italian 1996, Pink Slip (Pirate's Alley Faulkner Prize) 1999, Sometimes I Dream in Italian 2000, Remind Me Again Why I Married You 2003, Teacher of the Year; contribs to anthologies, reviews and quarterlies. *Honours:* Master Fellowship, Pennsylvania Council on the Arts 1989. *Address:* Department of English, University of South Florida, 4202 East Fowler Avenue, CPR-107, Tampa, FL 33620-5550, USA (office). *Telephone:* (813) 974-9570 (office). *E-mail:* rciresi@hotmail.com (office); rciresi@usf.edu (office). *Website:* www.ritaciresi.com.

CISNEROS, Sandra, BA, MFA; American writer and poet; b. 20 Dec. 1954, Chicago, Ill. *Education:* Loyola Univ., Univ. of Iowa. *Career:* fmr teacher and counsellor to high school dropouts, Latino Youth Alternative High School, Chicago; fmr coll. recruiter and arts admin.; Visiting Writer, Univ. of California, Univ. of Michigan; fmr Roberta Holloway Lectureship, Univ. of California 1988; Writer-in-Residence, Our Lady of the Lake Univ., San Antonio; Founder and Pres. Macondo Foundation, Alfredo Cisneros Del Moral Foundation. *Publications include:* Bad Boys 1980, The House on Mango Street (Before Columbus Foundation's American Book Award 1985) 1983, The Rodrigo Poems 1985, My Wicked, Wicked Ways 1987, Woman Hollering Creek and Other Stories (PEN Center West Award, Quality Paperback Book Club New Voices Award, Anisfield-Wolf Book Award, Lannan Foundation Literary Award) 1991, Hairs-Pelitos 1994, Loose Women (Mountains & Plains Booksellers' Award) 1994, Caramelo (Premio Napoli 2005) 2002, Vintage Cisneros 2003; contrib. to periodicals. *Honours:* Hon. DLitt (State Univ. of New York, Purchase) 1993, Hon. HLD (Loyola Univ., Chicago) 2002; Texas Inst. of Letters Dobie-Paisano Fellowship 1984, Illinois Artists Grant 1984, Chicano Short Story Award, Univ. of Arizona 1986, Nat. Endowment for the Arts Fellowships 1982, 1988, John D. and Catherine T. MacArthur Foundation Fellowship 1995, Texas Medal of the Arts 2003. *Literary Agent:* Susan Bergholz Literary Services, 17 West 10th Street, Suite 5, New York, NY 10011, USA. *Telephone:* (212) 387-0545. *Fax:* (212) 387-0546. *E-mail:* susan@susanbergholz.com. *Website:* www.sandracisneros.com.

CIXOUS, Hélène, DèsSc; French academic and author; b. 5 June 1937, Oran, Algeria; d. of Georges Cixous and Eve Klein; one s. one d. *Education:* Lycée d'Alger, Lycée de Sceaux, Sorbonne. *Career:* mem. staff. Univ. of Bordeaux 1962–65; Asst Lecturer, Sorbonne 1965–67; Lecturer, Univ. of Paris X (Nanterre) 1967–68; helped found Univ. of Paris VIII (Vincennes) 1968, Chair. and Prof. of Literature 1968–, Founder and Dir Centre d'Etudes Féminines 1974–; Co-Founder of journal Poétique 1969. *Theatre:* Portrait de Dora 1976, Le nom d'Oedipe 1978, La prise de l'école de Madhubaï 1984, L'Histoire terrible mais inachevée de Norodom Sihanouk, roi du Cambodge 1985, L'Indiade ou l'Inde de leurs rêves 1987, On ne part pas on ne revient pas 1991, Voile noire voile blanche 1994, L'Histoire qu'on ne connaîtra jamais 1994, La Ville Parjure ou le Réveil des Erinyes 1994, Tambours sur la digue 1999 (Molière Award 2000), Rouen la trentième nuit de mai 31 2001. *Publications include:* Le Prénom de Dieu 1967, Dedans 1969, Le Troisième corps, Les Commencements 1970, Un vrai jardin 1971, Neutre 1972, Tombe, Portrait du Soleil 1973, Révolutions pour plus d'un Faust 1975, Souffles 1975, La 1976, Partie 1976, Angst 1977, Préparatifs de noces au-delà de l'abîme 1978, Vivre l'orange 1979, Anankè 1979, Illa 1980, With ou l'art de l'innocence 1981, Limonade tout était si infini 1982, Le Livre de Promethea 1983, Manne 1988, Jours de l'An 1990, L'Ange au secret 1991, Déluge 1992, Beethoven à jamais 1993, La fiancée juive 1995, Messie 1996, Or, les lettres de mon père 1997, Osnabrück 1999, Les Rêveries de la femme sauvage 2000, Le Jour où je n'étais pas là 2000, Portrait de Jacques Derrida en jeune saint juif 2001, Benjamin à Montaigne, il ne faut pas le dire 2001, Manhattan. Lettres de la Préhistoire 2002; essays: L'exil de James Joyce 1969, Prénoms de personne 1974, La Jeune née 1975, La venue à l'écriture 1977, Entre l'écriture 1986, L'heure de Clarice Lispector 1989, Reading with Clarice Lispector 1990, Readings, the Poetics of Blanchot, Joyce, Kafka, Lispector, Tsvetaeva 1992, Three Steps on the Ladder of Writing 1993, Photos de racines 1994, Stigmata

1998, Escaping Texts 1998. *Honours:* Southern Cross of Brazil 1989; Chevalier de la Légion d'honneur 1994; Officier Ordre nat. du Mérite 1998; Dr hc (Queen's Univ., Kingston, Canada) 1991, (Edmonton, Canada) 1992, (York, UK) 1993, (Georgetown, Washington, DC, USA) 1995, (Northwestern, Chicago, USA) 1996; Prix Médicis 1969, Prix des critiques for best theatrical work of the year 1994, 2000, Amb. of Star Awards, Pakistan 1997. *Address:* Éditions Galilée, 9 rue Linné, 75005 Paris (office); Centre d'études féminines, Université Paris VIII, 2 rue de la Liberté, 93526 Saint-Denis cedex 2, France.

ČIŽOVA, Elena; Russian writer; b. 1957, St Petersburg; m.; two c. *Career:* Dir Russian PEN Club. *Publications:* Vremja ženshin (Russian Booker Prize 2009). *Honours:* Severnaya palmira 2001, Znamya Award 2001. *Literary Agent:* c/o Natasha Banke, Okno Literary Agency, Solid Entertainment AB, Ostra Varvsgatan 3, 211 19 Malmo, Sweden. *Telephone:* (702) 40-50-55. *E-mail:* banke@okno-agency.com. *Website:* www.okno-agency.com.

CLANCY, Joseph Patrick Thomas, BA, MA, PhD; American teacher, writer, poet and translator; b. 8 March 1928, New York, NY; m. Gertrude Wiegand 1948; four s. four d. *Education:* Fordham Univ. *Career:* Faculty mem., Marymount Manhattan Coll. 1948, Prof. 1962, now Prof. Emer.; mem. American Literary Translators' Asscn, Dramatists' Guild, Yr Academi Gymreig, Eastern States Celtic Asscn, St Davids Soc. of New York. *Publications include:* poetry: The Significance of Flesh: Poems 1950–1983 1984, Here & There 1994, Ordinary Time 1999, Passing Through 2008; non-fiction: Pendragon: King Arthur and His Britain 1971, Other Words: Essays on Poetry and Translation 1999; short story: The Retired Life (as P. G. Thomas) 1997; novel: Death is a Pilgrim: A Canterbury Tale 1993; Trans.: The Odes and Epodes of Horace 1960, Medieval Welsh Lyrics 1965, The Earliest Welsh Poetry 1970, Twentieth Century Welsh Poems 1982, Living a Life: Selected Poems by Gwyn Thomas 1982, The Plays of Saunders Lewis 1985, Bobi Jones: Selected Poems 1987, The World of Kate Roberts 1991, Saunders Lewis: Selected Poems 1993, Where There's Love: Welsh Folk Poems of Love and Marriage 1995, The Light in the Gloom: Poems and Prose by Alun Llywellyn Williams 1998, Medieval Welsh Poems 2002; Contribs: Poetry Wales, Planet, Anglo Welsh Review, Book News from Wales, Epoch, College English, America. *Honours:* Hon. Fellow, Aberystwyth Univ.; Hon. DLitt (Univ. of Wales); American Philosophical Society Fellowships 1963, 1968, Nat. Trans. Centre Fellowship 1968, Welsh Arts Council, Literature Award 1971, Major Bursary 1972, Nat. Endowment for the Arts Trans. Fellowship 1983, St Davids Soc. of New York Annual Award 1986. *Address:* Marymount Manhattan College, 221 East 71st Street, New York NY 10021, USA (office). *Telephone:* (212) 517-0400 (office).

CLANCY, Laurence James, BA, MA; Australian academic and writer; b. 2 Dec. 1942, Melbourne, Vic.; m. (divorced); two s. *Education:* Christian Brothers Coll., Melbourne Univ. *Career:* Lecturer, La Trobe Univ. 1967–96; mem. PEN International. *Publications include:* A Collapsible Man (Co-Winner, National Book Council Award) 1975, The Wife Specialist 1978, Xavier Herber 1981, Perfect Love (FAW ANA Literature Award) 1983, The Novels of Vladimir Nabokov 1984, City to City 1989, A Reader's Guide to Australian Fiction 1992, The Wild Life Reserve 1994, Night Parking 1999, Culture and customs of Australia 2004, Loyalties 2007; contribs to newspapers and journals. *Honours:* Co-winner FAW John Morrison Short Story Award 1974, Australian Natives Asscn Award 1983. *Address:* 227 Westgarth Street, Northcote, Vic. 3070, Australia (home).

CLANCY, Thomas (Tom) Leo, Jr, BA; American writer; b. 12 March 1947, Baltimore, Md; m. 1st Wanda Thomas 1969 (divorced 1998); one s. three d.; m. 2nd Alexandra Marie Llewellyn 1999. *Education:* Loyola Coll. *Career:* fmr insurance broker; Co-founder Red Storm Entertainment (computer game developer) 1996; part-owner of the Baltimore Orioles professional baseball team. *Publications:* The Hunt for Red October 1984, Red Storm Rising 1986, Patriot Games 1987, Cardinal of the Kremlin 1988, Clear and Present Danger 1989, The Sum of all Fears 1991, Without Remorse 1992, Submarine 1993, Debt of Honour 1994, Tom Clancy's Op Centre (with Steve Pieczenik) 1994, Reality Check 1995, Games of State: Op Centre 03 (with Steve Pieczenik) 1996, Tom Clancy's Op Centre II (with Steve Pieczenik) 1996, Executive Orders 1996, Into the Storm (with Fred Franks Jr) 1997, Politika (with Martin Greenberg) 1997, Rainbow Six 1998, Ruthless.com (with Martin Greenberg) 1998, Carrier 1999, Shadow Watch (with Martin Greenberg) 1999, Bio-Strike (with Martin Greenberg) 2000, The Bear and the Dragon 2000, Cold War (with Martin Greenberg) 2001, Red Rabbit 2002, Cutting Edge (with Martin Greenberg) 2002, The Teeth of the Tiger 2003, Zero Hour (with Martin Greenberg) 2003, Wild Card (with Martin Greenberg) 2004, Tom Clancy's Splinter Cell (with David Michaels) 2004, Operation Barracuda (with David Michaels) 2005, Checkmate (with David Michaels) 2006, Fallout (with David Michaels) 2007, The Archimedes Effect 2007, Against All Enemies 2012. *Honours:* Hon. DHumLitt (Rensselaer Polytechnic Inst.) 1992. *Address:* 111 West 40th Street, New York, NY 10018-2506, USA (office).

CLARE, Ellen (see Sinclair, Olga Ellen)

CLARK, Anne (see Amor, Anne Clark)

CLARK, Brian Robert, BA, FRSL; British dramatist; b. 3 June 1932, Bournemouth, Dorset, England; m. 1st Margaret Paling 1961; two s.; m. 2nd Anita Modak 1983; one step-s. one step-d.; m. 3rd Cherry Potter 1990. *Education:* Redland Coll. of Educ., Bristol, Central School of Speech and Drama, London, Univ. of Nottingham. *Career:* Staff Tutor in Drama, Univ. of Hull 1966–70; Founder Amber Lane Press 1978. *Television plays:* more than 30 since 1971. *Publications include:* plays: Lay By 1971, England's Ireland 1972, Truth or Dare? 1972, Whose Life Is It Anyway? 1972, Post Mortem 1975, Campion's Interview 1976, Can You Hear Me at the Back? 1979, Switching in the Afternoon or, As the Screw Turns 1980, Kipling 1984, All Change at the Wells (with Stephen Clark) 1985, The Petition 1986, Hopping to Byzantium (with Kathy Levin) 1990, In Pursuit of Eve – A Dramatic Sonnet Sequence 2001; screenplay: Whose Life is it Anyway? 1981; other: Group Theatre 1971, Out of Bounds (with Jim Hawkins) 1979. *Honours:* Soc. of West Theatre Award for Best Play 1977. *Literary Agent:* c/o Judy Daish Associates, 2 St Charles Place, London, W10 6EG, England. *Telephone:* (20) 8964-8811. *Fax:* (20) 8964-8966. *E-mail:* judy@judydaish.com. *Website:* www.judydaish.com.

CLARK, Candida; British writer; b. 1970; m. George Tapps-Gervis-Meyrick; one d. *Education:* Univ. of Cambridge. *Career:* worked as film scriptwriter, TV arts presenter; Lecturer in Creative Writing, Birkbeck Univ. of London; Arts and Cultures Ed. online current affairs magazine, openDemocracy.net; Mentor, Arvon Foundation's post-MA masterclass series; West Midlands Arts Fellow Warwick Writing Programme 2001. *Publications include:* novels: The Last Look 1998, The Constant Eye 2000, The Mariner's Star 2002, Ghost Music 2003, A House of Light 2005, The Chase 2006; contrib. reviews to The Observer, The Daily Telegraph, poetry and short fiction in various anthologies, newspapers and magazines. *Address:* c/o Headline Publishing Group, 338 Euston Road, London, NW1 3BH, England. *Telephone:* (20) 7873-6000.

CLARK, David Ridgley, BA, MA, PhD; American academic and writer; b. 17 Sept. 1920, Seymour, Conn.; m. Mary Adele Matthieu 1948; two s. two d. *Education:* Wesleyan Univ., Yale Univ. *Career:* instructor, Univ. of Massachusetts 1951–57, Asst Prof. 1957–58, Assoc. Prof. 1958–65, Prof. 1965–85, Prof. Emer.; Visiting Prof., St Mary's Coll., Notre Dame, Ind. 1985–87, Williams Coll., Williamstown, Mass 1989–91; mem. American Conf. for Irish Studies, Int. Asscn for the Support of Anglo-Irish Literature, Modern Language Asscn of America. *Publications include:* A Curious Quire (with G. S. Koehler, L. O. Barron and R. G. Tucker) 1962, W. B. Yeats and the Theatre of Desolate Reality 1965, Irish Renaissance 1965, Dry Tree 1966, Reading Poetry (with Fred B. Millett and Arthur Hoffman 1970, Riders to the Sea 1970, A Tower of Polished Black Stones: Early Versions of the Shadowy Waters 1971, Twentieth Century Interpretations of Murder in the Cathedral 1971, Druid Craft 1971, Lyric Resonance 1972, That Black Day: The Manuscripts of Crazy Jane on the Day of Judgement 1980, Yeats at Songs and Choruses 1983, W. B. Yeats: The Writing of Sophocles' King Oedipus (with James McGuire) 1989, W. B. Yeats: The Winding Stair (1929): Manuscript Materials 1995, W. B. Yeats: Words for Music Perhaps and Other Poems (1932): Manuscript Materials 1999, The Collected Works of W. B. Yeats, Vol. II, The Plays 2001, Parnell's Funeral and Other Poems, from A Full Moon in March: Manuscript Materials 2003. *Honours:* W.B. Yeats Soc. of New York M.L. Rosenthal Award 2004. *Address:* 481 Holgerson Road, Sequim, WA 98382-7326, USA (home). *Telephone:* (360) 681-7565 (home).

CLARK, Eric; British author and journalist; b. 29 July 1937, Birmingham, England; s. of Horace Clark and Hilda Milchley; m. Frances Robina Grant 1958 (divorced 1971); m. 2nd Marcelle Bernstein 1972; one s. two d. *Education:* Handsworth Grammar School, Birmingham. *Career:* staff of various newspapers including Daily Mail, The Guardian, The Observer 1962–72; full-time writer 1972–; mem. Soc. of Authors, Authors' Guild, PEN International UK Centre (Fellow), Nat. Union of Journalists, Int. Fed. of Journalists, Mystery Writers of America. *Publications include:* Len Deighton's London Dossier (co-author) 1967, Everybody's Guide to Survival 1969, Corps Diplomatique (US edn as Diplomat) 1973, Black Gambit 1978, The Sleeper 1979, Send in the Lions 1981, Chinese Burn (US edn as China Run) 1984, The Want Makers (Inside the Hidden World of Advertising) 1988, Hide and Seek 1994, The Real Toy Story 2007; contribs: Observer, Sunday Times, Daily Mail, Daily Telegraph, Washington Post, Los Angeles Times, Melbourne Age. *Honours:* Authors' Foundation Award 2003, 2010. *Literary Agent:* c/o Bill Hamilton, A. M. Heath Agency, 6 Warwick Court, London, WC1R 5DJ, England.

CLARK, Johnson (John) Pepper, BA; Nigerian poet, dramatist and academic; b. 3 April 1935, Kiagbodo; s. of Fuludu Bekederemo Clark; m. Ebunoluwa Bolajoko Odutola; one s. three d. *Education:* Govt Coll. Ughelli, Univ. Coll. Ibadan, Princeton Univ., USA. *Career:* Ed. The Horn (Ibadan) 1958; Head of Features and editorial writer, Express Group of Newspapers, Lagos 1961–62; Research Fellow, Inst. of African Studies, Univ. of Lagos 1963–64, Lecturer, Dept of English 1965–69, Sr Lecturer 1969–72, Prof. of English 1972–80; consultant to UNESCO 1965–67; Ed. Black Orpheus (journal) 1965–78; Visiting Distinguished Fellow, Center for Humanities, Wesleyan Univ., Conn., USA 1975–76; Visiting Research Prof., Inst. of African Studies, Univ. of Ibadan 1979–80; Distinguished Visiting Prof. of English and Writer in Residence, Lincoln Univ., Pa 1989; Visiting Prof. of English, Yale Univ. 1990; Trustee and mem. Petroleum (Special) Trust Fund and Man. Bd, Abuja 1995–; mem. Nat. Council of Laureates (Nigeria) 1992; Foundation Fellow, Nigerian Acad. of Letters 1996. *Drama includes:* Song of a Goat 1961, Three Plays 1964, Ozidi 1968, The Bikoroa Plays 1985, The Wives' Revolt. *Poetry published includes:* Poems 1962, A Reed in the Tide 1965, Casualties 1970, A Decade of Tongues 1981, State of the Union 1985, Mandela and Other Poems 1988, A Lot From Paradise 1997. *Other publications:* America, Their America 1964, The Example of Shakespeare 1970, Transcription and Translation from the Oral Tradition of the Izon of the Niger Delta; The Ozidi Saga (trans.) 1977, The Hero as a Villain 1978. *Honours:* Nigerian Nat. Order of Merit; Nigerian Nat. Merit Award. *Address:* 23 Oduduwa Crescent, GRA, Ikeja, Lagos; Okemeji Place, Funama, Kiagbodo, Burutu Local Government Area, Delta State, Nigeria. *Telephone:* (1) 497-8436 (Lagos). *Fax:* (1) 497-8463 (Lagos).

CLARK, Jonathan Charles Douglas, PhD, FRHistS; British historian and academic; *Joyce and Elizabeth Hall Distinguished Professor of British History, University of Kansas*; b. 28 Feb. 1951, London, England; s. of Ronald James Clark and Dorothy Margaret Clark; m. Katherine Redwood Penovich 1996. *Education:* Univ. of Cambridge. *Career:* Research Fellow, Peterhouse, Cambridge 1977–81; Research Fellow, The Leverhulme Trust; Fellow, All Souls Coll., Oxford 1986–95, Sr Research Fellow 1995; Joyce and Elizabeth Hall Distinguished Prof. of British History, Univ. of Kansas, USA 1995–; Visiting Prof., Cttee on Social Thought, Univ. of Chicago 1993; Visiting Prof., Forschungszentrum Europäische Aufklärung, Potsdam 2000, Univ. of Northumbria 2001–03, Oxford Brookes Univ. 2009–; Visiting Distinguished Lecturer, Univ. of Manitoba 1999; mem. Ecclesiastical History Soc., Church of England Record Soc., N American Conf. on British Studies, British Soc. for Eighteenth Century Studies. *Publications:* The Dynamics of Change 1982, English Society 1688–1832 1985, Revolution and Rebellion 1986; The Memoirs and Speeches of James, 2nd Earl Waldegrave (ed.) 1988, Ideas and Politics in Modern Britain (ed.) 1990, The Language of Liberty 1660–1832 1993, Samuel Johnson 1994, Edmund Burke's Reflections on the Revolution in France (ed.) 2001, English Society 1660–1832 (revised edn) 2000, Samuel Johnson in Historical Context (co-ed.) 2002, Our Shadowed Present 2003, A World by Itself: A History of the British Isles (ed.) 2010, The Politics of Samuel Johnson (co-ed.) 2012, The Interpretation of Samuel Johnson (co-ed.) 2012; articles on British and American history. *Address:* Department of History, University of Kansas, 1445 Jayhawk Boulevard, Lawrence, KS 66045-7590, USA (office). *Telephone:* (785) 864-3569 (office). *Fax:* (785) 864-5046 (office). *E-mail:* jcdclark@ku.edu (office). *Website:* www.history.ku.edu (office).

CLARK, Mary Higgins, BA; American writer and business executive; b. 24 Dec. 1931, New York; d. of Luke Higgins and Nora Durkin; m. Warren Clark 1949 (died 1964); two s. three d. *Education:* Fordham Univ. *Career:* advertising asst Remington Rand 1946; stewardess, Pan Am 1949–50; radio scriptwriter, producer Robert G. Jennings 1965–70; Vice-Pres., Pnr, Creative Dir, Producer Radio Programming, Aerial Communications, New York 1970–80; Chair. and Creative Dir D.J. Clark Enterprises, New York 1980–; mem. American Acad. of Arts and Sciences, Mystery Writers of America, Authors League. *Publications:* Aspire to the Heavens, A Biography of George Washington 1969, Where Are the Children? 1976, A Stranger is Watching 1978, The Cradle Will Fall 1980, A Cry in the Night 1982, Stillwatch 1984, Weep No More, My Lady 1987, While My Pretty One Sleeps 1989, The Anastasia Syndrome 1989, Loves Music, Loves to Dance 1991, All Around the Town 1992, I'll Be Seeing You 1993, Remember Me 1994, The Lottery Winner 1994, Bad Behavior 1995, Let Me Call You Sweetheart 1995, Silent Night 1996, Moonlight Becomes You 1996, My Gal Sunday 1996, Pretend You Don't See Her 1997, The Plot Thickens 1997, You Belong to Me 1998, All Through the Night 1998, We'll Meet Again 1999, Before I Say Good-Bye 2000, Deck the Halls (with Carol Higgins Clark) 2000, Daddy's Little Girl 2002, On the Street Where You Live 2002, Mount Vernon Love Story: A Novel of George and Martha Washington 2002, The Second Time Around 2003, Nighttime is My Time 2004, No Place Like Home 2005, Little Girls in Blue 2006, Santa Cruise 2006, Ghost Ship: A Cape Cod Story 2007, I Heard that Song Before 2007, Where Are You Now? 2008, Just Take my Heart 2009, The Shadow of Your Smile 2010, The Lost Years 2012. *Honours:* several hon. degrees; Grand Prix de Littérature Policière, France 1980. *Address:* c/o Simon and Schuster, Inc., 1230 Avenue of the Americas, New York, NY 10020, USA (office). *Website:* www.simonsays.com (office).

CLARK, Patricia Denise, (Claire Lorrimer, Patricia Robins, Susan Patrick); British writer and poet; b. 1 Feb. 1921, Hove, Sussex, England; d. of Arthur Robins and Denise Robins; m. D. C. Clark (divorced 1948); two s., one d. *Career:* sub-ed., Writer Woman's Illustrated, London, 1938–40; served in mil. radar filter room, Women's Auxiliary Air Force, RAF 1940–45; mem. Soc. of Authors, Romantic Novelists' Asscn. *Publications include:* as Claire Lorrimer: A Voice in the Dark 1967, The Shadow Falls 1974, Relentless Storm 1975, The Secret of Quarry House 1976, Mavreen 1976, Tamarisk 1978, Chantal 1980, The Garden (a cameo) 1980, The Chatelaine 1981, The Wilderling 1982, Last Year's Nightingale 1984, Frost in the Sun 1986, House of Tomorrow (biog.) 1987, Ortolans 1990, The Spinning Wheel 1991, Variations (short stories) 1991, The Silver Link 1993, Fool's Curtain 1994, Beneath the Sun 1996, Connie's Daughter 1997, The Reunion 1997, The Woven Thread 1998, The Reckoning 1998, Second Chance 1998, An Open Door 1999, Never Say Goodbye 2000, Search for Love 2000, For Always 2001, The Faithful Heart 2002, Deception 2003, Over My Dead Body 2003, Troubled Waters 2004, Dead Centre 2005, Infatuation 2007, You Never Know (autobiog.) 2007, Truth to Tell 2008, Emotions (short stories) 2008, Dead Reckoning 2009; as Patricia Robins: To the Stars 1944, See No Evil 1945, Three Loves 1949, Awake My Heart 1950, Beneath the Moon 1951, Leave My Heart Alone 1951, The Fair Deal 1952, Heart's Desire 1953, So This is Love 1953, Heaven in Our Hearts 1954, One Who Cares 1954, Love Cannot Die 1955, The Foolish Heart 1956, Give All to Love 1956, Where Duty Lies 1957, He Is Mine 1957, Love Must Wait 1958, Lonely Quest 1959, Lady Chatterley's Daughter 1961, The Last Chance 1961, The Long Wait 1962, The Runaways 1962, Seven Loves 1962, With All My Love 1963, The Constant Heart 1964, Second Love 1964, The Night is Thine 1964, There Is But One 1965, No More Loving 1965, Topaz Island 1965, Love Me Tomorrow 1966, The Uncertain Joy 1966, The Man Behind the Mask 1967, Forbidden 1967, Sapphire in the Sand 1968, Return to Love 1968, Laugh on Friday 1969, No Stone Unturned 1969, Cinnabar House 1970, Under the Sky 1970, The Crimson Tapestry 1972, Play Fair with Love 1972, None But He 1973, Fulfilment 1993, Forsaken 1993, Forever 1993, The Legend 1997. *Address:* Chiswell Barn, Marsh Green, Edenbridge, Kent, TN8 5PR, England. *Website:* www.clairelorrimer.com.

CLARKE, Austin, OC; Canadian writer; b. 26 July 1934, St James, Barbados. *Education:* Univ. of Toronto. *Career:* fmrly journalist and broadcaster; teacher of creative writing and cultural attaché, Barbados Embassy in Washington, DC, USA;. *Publications include:* novels: Survivors of the Crossing 1964, Among Thistles and Thorns 1965, The Meeting Place 1967, Storm of Fortune 1971, The Bigger Light 1975, The Prime Minister 1977, Proud Empires 1988, The Origin of Waves 1997, The Question (W. O. Mitchell Prize) 1999, The Polished Hoe (Giller Prize 2002, Commonwealth Writers' Prize 2003) 2002. More (Toronto Book Award 2009) 2008; short story collections: When He Was Free and Young and He Used to Wear Silks 1971, When Women Rule 1985, Nine Men Who Laughed 1986, In This City 1992, There are No Elders 1993, Choosing His Coffin 2003; memoirs: Growing Up Stupid Under the Union Jack 1980, Public Enemies: Police Violence and Black Youth 1992, A Passage Back Home: A Personal Reminiscence of Samuel Selvon 1994, Pigtails 'n' Breadfruit 1999. *Literary Agent:* c/o The Bukowski Agency, 14 Prince Arthur Avenue, Suite 202, Toronto, ON M5R 1A9, Canada. *Telephone:* (416) 928-6728. *Fax:* (416) 963-9978. *E-mail:* info@thebukowskiagency.com. *Website:* www.thebukowskiagency.com.

CLARKE, Brenda Margaret Lilian, (Brenda Honeyman, Kate Sedley); British writer; b. 30 July 1926, Bristol, England; m. Ronald John Clarke 1955; one s. one d. *Publications include:* The Glass Island 1978, The Lofty Banners 1980, The Far Morning 1982, All Through the Day 1983, A Rose in May 1984, Three Women 1985, Winter Landscape 1986, Under Heaven 1988, An Equal Chance (aka Riches of the Heart) 1989, Sisters and Lovers 1990, Beyond the World 1991, A Durable Fire 1993, Sweet Auburn 1995, Richard Plantagenet 1997, Last of the Barons 1998, The Warrior King 1998, A Royal Alliance 1999; as Brenda Honeyman: Richard by Grace of God 1968, The Kingmaker 1969, Richmond and Elizabeth 1970, Harry the King 1971, Brother Bedford 1972, Good Duke Humphrey 1973, The King's Minions 1974, The Queen and Mortimer 1974, Edward the Warrior 1975, All the King's Sons 1976, The Golden Griffin 1976, At the King's Court 1977, A King's Tale 1977, Macbeth, King of Scots 1977, Emma, the Queen 1978, Harold of the English 1979; as Kate Sedley: Death and the Chapman 1991, The Plymouth Cloak 1992, The Hanged Man 1993, The Holy Innocents 1994, The Eve of St Hyacinth 1995, The Wicked Winter 1996, The Brothers of Glastonbury 1997, The Weaver's Inheritance 1998, The Saint John's Fern 1999, The Goldsmith's Daughter 2001, The Lammas Feast 2002, Nine Men Dancing 2003, The Midsummer Rose 2004, The Burgundian's Tale 2005, The Prodigal Son 2006, The Three Kings of Cologne 2007, The Green Man 2008, The Dance of Death 2009, Wheel of Fate 2010, The Midsummer Crown 2011. *Literary Agent:* c/o David Grossman Literary Agency Ltd, 118B Holland Park Avenue, London, W11 4UA, England. *Address:* 25 Torridge Road, Keynsham, Bristol, BS31 1QQ, England.

CLARKE, George Elliott, OC, BA, MA, PhD; Canadian poet, playwright and writer; *E.J. Pratt Professor of Canadian Literature, University of Toronto*; b. 12 Feb. 1960, Windsor, NS; s. of William Clarke and Geraldine Clarke. *Education:* Univ. of Waterloo, Dalhousie Univ., Queen's Univ. *Career:* parliamentary researcher, Toronto 1982–83, parliamentary aide, Ottawa 1987–91; fmr newspaper ed. in Halifax and Waterloo, social worker in Halifax; columnist, Halifax Herald; Lecturer in English and Canadian Studies, Duke Univ. 1994–99; Visiting Seagrams Chair in Canadian Studies, McGill Univ. 1998–99; Prof. of English, Univ. of Toronto 1999–2003, E.J. Pratt Prof. of Canadian Literature 2003–. *Plays include:* Beatrice Chancy 1999, Whylah Falls: The Play 1999, Quebecite: A Jazz Fantasia in three cantos 2003, Trudeau: Long March/Shining Path 2007. *Publications include:* novel: George and Rue 2005; poetry: Saltwater Spirituals and Deeper Blues 1983, Whylah Falls 1990, Provençal Songs 1993, Lush Dreams, Blue Exile: Fugitive Poems 1978–93 1993, Provençal Songs II 1997, Gold Indigoes 2000, Execution Poems (Gov.-Gen.'s Literary Award for Poetry) 2001, Blue 2001, Illuminated Verses 2005, Black 2006, I & I 2009; libretti: Beatrice Chancy 1998, Québécité: A Jazz Fantasia 2003, Trudeau: Long March/Shining Path 2006; novel: George and Rue 2005; essays: Odysseys Home: Mapping African-Canadian Literature 2002; editor: Fire on the Water: An Anthology of Black Nova Scotian Writing 1991–92, Eyeing the North Star: Directions in African–Canadian Literature 1997. *Honours:* Hon. Fellow, Haliburton Literary Soc., Univ. of King's Coll. 2008; Order of Nova Scotia; Hon. LLD (Dalhousie) 1999, Hon. DLitt (New Brunswick) 2000, Hon. DLitt (Alberta) 2005, (Waterloo) 2006; Archibald Lampman Award for Poetry 1991, Nova Scotia Arts Council Portia White Prize for Artistic Achievement 1998, Bellagio Center Fellowship 1998, Outstanding Writer in Film and TV 2000, Martin Luther King Jr Award 2004, Pierre Elliott Trudeau Fellows' Prize, Montréal 2005, Univ. of Toronto Distinguished Teaching Award 2005, Univ. of Toronto Black Alumni Asscn Faculty Achievement Award 2005, Univ. of Toronto Undergraduate Teaching Award 2005, Planet Africa TV Renaissance Award 2005, Dartmouth Book Award for Fiction 2006, Premiul Poesis 2006, William P. Hubbard Award

2009. *Literary Agent:* c/o The Bukowski Agency, 14 Prince Arthur Avenue, Suite 202, Toronto, ON M5R 1A9, Canada. *E-mail:* assistant@thebukowskiagency.com. *Website:* www.thebukowskiagency.com. *Address:* Department of English, University of Toronto, 170 St George Street, Toronto, ON M5R 2MB, Canada (office). *Telephone:* (416) 946-3143 (office).

CLARKE, Gillian, BA; British poet, writer, editor, translator and academic; *Tutor of Writing, University of Glamorgan*; b. 8 June 1937, Cardiff, Glamorgan, Wales; d. of Penri Williams and Ceinwen Evans; m. 2nd David Thomas; one d. two s. (from previous m.). *Education:* Univ. Coll., Cardiff. *Career:* Lecturer, Gwent Coll. of Art and Design, Newport 1975–82; Ed. Anglo-Welsh Review 1976–84; Pres. Ty Newydd (Welsh creative writers' house) Gwynedd 1993–; Tutor in Writing, Univ. of Glamorgan 1993–; apptd Capital Poet of Cardiff, funded by Cardiff City and Co. Council, to commemorate Cardiff's 2005 celebrations 2005–; Fellow, Univ. of Wales, Cardiff 1984; Nat. Poet of Wales 2007–; mem. Welsh Acad. (Chair. 1988–93). *Publications include:* poetry: Snow on the Mountain 1971, The Sundial 1978, Letter From a Far Country 1982, Selected Poems 1985, Letting in the Rumour 1989, The King of Britain's Daughter 1993, Collected Poems 1997, Five Fields 1998, The Animal Wall 1999, Nine Green Gardens 2000, Owain Glyndŵr 2000, Making the Beds for the Dead 2004, At the Source 2008, A Recipe for Water 2009; children books: One Moonlit Night 1991, I Can Move the Sea 1996, The Whispering Room 1996, The Animal Wall 1999; prose: A Local Habitation and a Name 1998; ed.: The Poetry Book Society Anthology 1987–88 1987; also translations. *Honours:* Hon. Fellow, Univ. of Wales, Aberystwyth 1995, Swansea 1996, Lampeter 2002; Hon. MA (Univ. of Wales) 2002; Cholmondeley Award for Poetry 1997, Owain Glyndwr Award for Outstanding Contribution to Arts in Wales 1999, Queen's Gold Medal for Poetry 2010. *Address:* Blaen Cwrt, Talgarreg, , Llandysul, Ceredigion, SA44 4EU, Wales (home). *Website:* www.gillianclarke.co.uk.

CLARKE, Mary; British editor and writer; *Editor Emerita, Dancing Times*; b. 23 Aug. 1923, London, England. *Education:* Mary Datchelor Girls' School, London. *Career:* London Corresp., Dance Magazine, New York 1943–55; Asst Ed. and Contrib., Ballet Annual 1952–63; Asst Ed. Dancing Times 1954–63, Ed. 1963–2008, Ed. Emer. 2008–; London Ed., Dance News, New York 1955–70; Dance Critic, The Guardian 1977–94 (retd). *Publications include:* The Sadler's Wells Ballet: A History and Appreciation 1955, Six Great Dancers 1957, Dancers of Mercury: The Story of Ballet Rambert 1962, Ballet: An Illustrated History (with Clement Crisp) 1973, Making a Ballet (with Clement Crisp) 1974, Introducing Ballet (with Clement Crisp) 1976, Encyclopedia of Dance and Ballet (ed. with David Vaughan) 1977, Design for Ballet (with Clement Crisp) 1978, Ballet in Art (with Clement Crisp) 1978, The History of Dance (with Clement Crisp) 1981, Dancer: Men in Dance (with Clement Crisp) 1984, Ballerina (with Clement Crisp) 1987, Diana: Once Upon a Time 1994; contrib. to Encyclopaedia Britannica, New Dictionary of National Biography, newspapers and magazines. *Honours:* Kt, Order of Dannebrog (Denmark) 1992; Second Prize, Cafe Royal Literary Prize for Best Book on the Theatre 1955, Royal Acad. of Dancing Queen Elizabeth II Coronation Award 1990, Polish Ministry of Culture Nijinsky Medal 1995. *Address:* 45–47 Clerkenwell Green, London, EC1R 0EB (office); 54 Ripplevale Grove, London, N1 1HT, England (home). *Telephone:* (20) 7250-3006 (office).

CLARKE, Robert (see Platt, Charles Michael)

CLARKE, Susanna; British writer; b. 1 Nov. 1959, Nottingham, England; partner Colin Greenland. *Education:* St Hilda's Coll., Oxford. *Career:* fmrly worked in non-fiction publishing and as teacher of English; Ed., Simon and Schuster 1993–2003. *Publications include:* short stories: The Ladies of Grace Adieu, in Starlight 1 (World Fantasy Award 1997) 1996, Stopp't-Clock Yard, in Sandman: Book of Dreams 1996, On Lickerish Hill, in Black Swan, White Raven 1997, Mrs Mabb, in Starlight 2 1998, The Duke of Wellington Misplaces his Horse, in A Fall of Stardust 1999, Mr Simonelli, or the Fairy Widower, in Black Heart, Ivory Bones 2000, Tom Brightwind, or How the Fairy Bridge was Built at Thoresby, in Starlight 3 2001, Antickes and Frets (New York Times) 31 Oct. 2004, The Ladies of Grace Adieu and Other Stories 2006; novel: Jonathan Strange & Mr Norrell (Time's Best Novel of the Year 2004, British Book Award for Newcomer of the Year Award 2005, Locus Award 2005, Mythopoeic Award 2005, World Fantasy Award 2005, Hugo Award 2005) 2004, The Ladies of Grace Adieu and Other Stories 2006, The Dweller in High Places 2007. *Address:* c/o Bloomsbury Publishing PLC, 38 Soho Square, London, W1D 3HB, England (office). *Website:* www.jonathanstrange.com.

CLARKE, (Victor) Lindsay, BA; British writer; b. 14 Aug. 1939, Halifax, West Yorks., England; m. Phoebe Clare Mackmin 1980; one d. *Education:* King's Coll., Cambridge. *Career:* Co-ordinator of Liberal Studies, Norwich City Coll.; Co-Dir, European Centre, Friends World Coll.; Writer-in-Residence and Assoc. Lecturer in Creative Writing, Univ. of Wales, Cardiff; Creative Consultant to the Pushkin Trust. *Publications include:* Sunday Whiteman 1987, The Chymical Wedding (Whitbread Fiction Award 1989) 1989, Alice's Masque 1994, Essential Celtic Mythology 1997, Parzival and the Stone from Heaven 2001, The War at Troy 2004, Return from Troy 2005, Stoker (poetry) 2006, The Water Theatre 2010. *Literary Agent:* c/o United Agents, 12–26 Lexington Street, London, W1F 0LE, England. *Telephone:* (20) 3214-0800. *Fax:* (20) 3214-0801. *E-mail:* info@unitedagents.co.uk. *Website:* unitedagents.co.uk.

CLARKSON, Stephen, CM, BA, FRSC; Canadian academic and writer; *Professor of Political Economy Emeritus, University of Toronto*; b. 21 Oct. 1937, London, England; m. Christina McCall 1978 (divorced); three d. *Education:* Upper Canada Coll., Sorbonne, Univ. of Paris, Univ. of Toronto, Univ. of Oxford. *Career:* Lecturer, Univ. of Toronto 1964–65, Asst Prof. 1965–67, Assoc. Prof. 1967–80, Prof. of Political Economy 1980–, now Emer.; Sr Fellow, Columbia Univ. 1967–68; Policy Chair., Liberal Party, Ontario 1969–73; Dir, Maison Française de Toronto 1972; Jean Monnet Fellow, European Univ. Inst. 1995–96; Killam Research Fellow 1999–2001; Woodrow Wilson Fellow 2000–01; Sr Fellow, Centre for Int. Governance Innovation 2006; mem. Canadian Inst. of Int. Affairs, Canadian Political Science Asscn, Int. Political Science Asscn, Univ. League for Social Reform (pres.). *Publications include:* An Independent Foreign Policy for Canada? (ed.) 1968, L'Analyse Soviétique des problèmes indiens de sous-développement 1970, Visions 2020: Fifty Canadians in Search of a Future (ed.) 1970, City Lib: Parties and Reform in Toronto 1972, The Soviet Theory of Development: India and the Third World in Marxist-Leninist Scholarship 1978, Canada and the Reagan Challenge: Crisis in the Canadian-American Relationship 1982, Trudeau and Our Times, Vol. 1: The Magnificent Obsession (co-author) 1990, Vol. 2: The Heroic Delusion (co-author) 1994, Uncle Sam and Us: Globalization, Neoconservatism and the Canadian State 2002, The Big Red Machine: How the Liberal Party Dominates Canadian Politics 2005, Patriot's Reward 2007, Does North America Exist? Governing the Continent after NAFTA and 9/11 2008, A Perilous Imbalance: The Globalization of Canadian Law and Governance (with Stepan Wood) 2010; contrib. to scholarly books and professional journals. *Honours:* Rhodes Scholar 1959, Woodrow Wilson Fellow 1961, John Porter Prize 1984, Governor-General's Award for Non-Fiction 1990. *Address:* University College, 15 King's College Circle, Toronto, ON M5S 3H7, Canada (office).

CLAUDEL, Philippe; French writer, screenwriter and film director; b. 2 Feb. 1962, Dombasle-sur-Meurthe; m. Dominique Kucharzewski; one d. *Education:* Univ. of Nancy. *Career:* Prof. of Literature, Univ. of Nancy. *Films include:* Sur le bout des doigts (screenplay) 2002, Les Âmes grises (screenplay) 2005, I've Loved You So Long (screenplay and dir) (BAFTA Award for Film not in the English Language (jtly) 2009) 2008. *Publications include:* novels: J'abandonne (Prix France Télévision) 2000, Meuse l'oubli (Premier Roman) 2000, Quelques-uns des cent regrets (Prix Marcel Pagnol) 2000, Au revoir Monsieur Friant 2001, Le Bruit des trousseaux 2002, Mirhaela 2002, Barrio Flores 2002, Le Café de l'Excelsior 2002, Les Petites mécaniques (Prix Goncourt de la Nouvelle) 2003, Les Âmes grises (Prix Renaudot 2003, Martin Beck Award 2003, Prix des lectrices de Elle Roman 2004) 2003, Trois petites histoires de jouets 2004, La Petite fille de Monsieur Linh 2005, An meine Tochter 2006, By a Slow River 2007, Le Rapport de Brodeck (Prix Goncourt des Lycéens, Ind. Foreign Fiction Prize 2010) 2009; other: La Mort dans le paysage (with Nicolas Matula) 2002. *Honours:* Prix du Public, Berlin Film Festival 2008, Prix du Jury oecuménique, Berlin Film Festival 2008, Prix du Public, Vancouver Film Festival 2008, César Award for First Film 2009. *Literary Agent:* c/o Artmédia, 20 avenue Rapp, 75007 Paris, France; c/o Bob Bookman, CAA, 2000 Avenue of the Stars, Los Angeles, CA 90067, USA. *Telephone:* 1-43-17-33-00 (Paris); (424) 288-2000 (Los Angeles). *Fax:* (424) 288-2900 (Los Angeles). *E-mail:* info@artmedia.fr. *Website:* www.artmedia.fr; www.caa.com. *Address:* c/o Editions Stock, 31 rue de Fleurus, 75006 Paris, France. *E-mail:* plpclaudel@orange.fr (office). *Website:* www.editions-stock.fr.

CLAYTON, John Jacob, AB, MA, PhD; American writer and academic; *Professor Emeritus of English, University of Massachusetts at Amherst*; b. 5 Jan. 1935, New York, NY; m. 1st Marilyn Hirsch 1956 (divorced 1974); one s. one d.; m. 2nd Marlynn Krebs (divorced 1983); one s.; m. 3rd Sharon Dunn 1984; one s. *Education:* Columbia Univ., New York Univ., Indiana Univ. *Career:* instructor, Univ. of Victoria, BC 1962–63; Lecturer, Overseas Div., Univ. of Maryland 1963–64; Asst Prof. of Humanities, Boston Univ. 1964–69; Assoc. Prof., Univ. of Massachusetts at Amherst 1969–75, Prof. (now Emer.) of English 1975–. *Publications include:* Saul Bellow: In Defense of Man 1968, What Are Friends For? (novel) 1979, Bodies of the Rich (short stories) 1984, Gestures of Healing: Anxiety and the Modern Novel 1991, Radiance (collection of stories) (Ohio State Univ. Award) 1998, The Man I Never Wanted To Be (novel) 1998, Kuperman's Fire (novel) 2007, Wrestling with Angels (stories) 2007, The Mitzvah Man (novel) 2011; ed.: The D. C. Heath Introduction to Fiction; contribs to anthologies and periodicals. *Honours:* Pushcart Prize 1998, 2006, O. Henry Short Story Award, Nat. Endowment for the Arts Fellowship. *Address:* 12 Lawton Road, Leverett, MA 01054, USA (home). *Telephone:* (413) 548-9645 (home). *E-mail:* jclayton@english.umass.edu (office). *Website:* www.johnjclayton.com.

CLAYTON, Martin David, BA, MA; British art historian and writer; *Deputy Curator of the Print Room, Royal Library, Windsor Castle*; b. 1967, Harrogate, North Yorks., England. *Education:* Christ's Coll., Cambridge. *Career:* currently Deputy Curator of the Print Room, Royal Library, Windsor Castle. *Publications include:* Leonardo da Vinci: The Anatomy of Man 1992, Seven Florentine Heads 1993, Poussin: Works on Paper 1995, Leonardo da Vinci: A Curious Vision 1996, Raphael and his Circle 1999, Leonardo da Vinci, The Divine and the Grotesque 2002, Holbein to Hockney 2004, Canaletto in Venice 2005, Amazing Rare Things 2007, The Aztec Herbal 2009. *Address:* Royal Library, Windsor Castle, Berks., SL4 1NJ, England (office). *E-mail:* martinclayton@royalcollection.org.uk (office). *Website:* www.royalcollection.org.uk (office).

CLEMENS, Kate (see Mackey, Mary)

CLÉMENT, Paul (see Amette, Jacques-Pierre)

CLOSETS, François de; French writer, journalist and producer; b. 25 Dec. 1933, Enghien-les-Bains; s. of Louis-Xavier de Closets and Marie-Antoinette Masson; m. 1st Danièle Lebrun; one s.; m. 2nd Janick Jossin 1970; one s. one d. *Education:* Lycée d'Enghien, Faculté de Droit de Paris and Inst. d'Etudes Politiques, Paris. *Career:* Ed. then special envoy of Agence France-Presse in Algeria 1961–65; scientific journalist, Sciences et Avenir 1964–, Acualités Télévisées 1965–68; contrib. L'Express 1968–69; Head of Scientific Service, TV Channel 1 1969–72; Head of Scientific and Tech. Service of TV Channel 2 1972; contrib. to Channel 1 1974; Asst Ed.-in-Chief TF1; Co-producer l'Enjeu (econ. magazine) 1978–88; Dir of Econ. Affairs, TFI 1987; Co-producer, Médiations magazine 1987–93; Producer, illustrator "Savoir Plus" for France 2 1992–2000, "Les Grandes Enigmes de la Science" for France 2 1992–2003. *Publications:* L'Espace, terre des hommes, La lune est à vendre 1969, En danger de progrès 1970, Le Bonheur en plus 1974, La France et ses mensonges 1977, Scénarios du futur (Vol. I) 1978, Le monde de l'an 2000 (Vol. II) 1979, Le Système EPM 1980, Toujours plus 1982, Tous ensemble pour en finir avec la syndicatrie 1985, La Grande Manip 1990, Tant et Plus 1992, Le Bonheur d'apprendre, et comment on l'assassine 1996, Le compte à Rebours 1998, L'Imposture informatique 2000, La dernière liberté 2001, Ne dites pas à Dieu ce qu'il doit faire 2004, Plus encore 2006, Le divorce français 2008, Zéro Faute: L'orthographe, une passion française 2009. *Honours:* Grand Prix du reportage du Syndicat des journalistes et écrivains 1966, Prix Cazes 1974, 7 d'or du meilleur journaliste 1985, Prix Aujourd'hui 1985, Roland Dorgelès Prize 1997. *Address:* c/o Editions Fayard, 13 rue de la Montparnasse, 75006 Paris, France (office). *E-mail:* fclosets@noos.fr (home).

CLOUDSLEY, Timothy, MA; British academic, poet and writer; b. (Timothy Cloudsley-Thompson), 18 Sept. 1948, Cambridge, England; s. of John Cloudsley-Thompson and Anne Cloudsley-Thompson; two s. *Education:* Univ. of Cambridge, Durham Univ. *Career:* Lecturer in Sociology, Newcastle Univ. 1972–74, Napier Univ., Edinburgh 1974–76, Heriot-Watt Univ., Edinburgh 1976–77, Glasgow Caledonian Univ. 1977–97, Univ. Industrial de Santander, Bucaramanga, Colombia 2005–07; mem. of arts and literature org., Open Circle, Glasgow (literary sec. 1990–96); currently lives in Colombia. *Publications include:* Poems to Light (Through Love and Blood) 1980, Mair Licht (anthology) 1988, The Construction of Nature (social philosophy) 1994, Coincidence (anthology) 1995, Incantations to Streams of Fire 1997, Poems 1998, Shamanism and the Sublime 2000, Dreams of Paradise (Sueños de Paraiso) 2005, Dos Ensayos sobre la Colombia Indígena 2007, Short Stories/ Cuentos Cortos 2008; contrib. to Northlight Poetry Review, Understanding Magazine, Interactions, Romantic Heir, The People's Poetry, Cadmium Blue Literary Journal, Le Journal des Poètes, Dandelion Magazine, Consciousness, Literature and the Arts, The European Legacy, Shadow, Indigenous Affairs; to electronic literary journals www.raunchland.co.uk, www.aber.ac.uk/tfts/journal. *Address:* Cra 17, No. 68-17, La Victoria, Bucaramanga, Colombia (home). *Telephone:* (76) 647-0354 (home). *Website:* www.timcloudsley.com.

CLOUGH, Brenda Wang, BA; American writer; b. 13 Nov. 1955, Washington, DC; m. Lawrence A. Clough 1977; one d. *Education:* American School of Vientiane, Laos, Carnegie Mellon Univ. *Career:* teacher at Writer's Center, Bethesda, Md. *Publications include:* The Crystal Crown 1984, The Dragon of Mishbil 1985, The Realm Beneath 1986, The Name of the Sun 1988, An Impossible Summer 1992, How Like a God 1997, Doors of Death and Life 2000, Alanta Nights 2005, Revise the World 2008; contribs: short stories in anthologies and periodicals. *Address:* 1941 Barton Hill Road, Reston, VA 20191-5009, USA (home). *E-mail:* brenda@sff.net; clough@erols.com. *Website:* www.sff.net/people/Brenda.

CLOUTIER, Cécile, BA, LèsL, MA, PhD; Canadian poet, writer and academic; b. 13 June 1930, Québec; m. Jerzy Wojciechowski 1966; two d. *Education:* Collège de Sillery, Université Laval, Université de Paris, McMaster Univ., Univ. of Toronto, Université de Tours. *Career:* Prof. of French and Québec Literature, Univ. of Ottawa 1958–64; Prof. of Aesthetics and French and Québec Literature, Univ. of Toronto 1964–95, Prof. Emer. 1995–; mem. Asscn des Écrivains de Langue française, PEN Club de France, Soc. des Écrivains, Soc. des Gens de Lettres de Paris, Union des écrivaines et des écrivains québécois. *Publications include:* Mains de sable 1960, Cuivre et soies 1964, Cannelles et craies 1969, Paupières 1970, Câblogrammes 1972, Chaleuils 1979, Springtime of Spoken Words 1979, Près 1983, Opuscula Aesthetica Nostra: Essais sur l'Esthétique 1984, La Girafe 1984, L'Échangeur 1985, L'Écouté (Gov.-Gen.'s Award for Poetry) 1986, Solitude Rompue 1986, Lampées 1990, Périhélie 1990, La Poésie de l'Hexagone 1990, Ancres d'Encre 1993, Ostraka 1995, Bagues (prix du Club Richelieu Bernard-Monpetit) 1996, Le Poaimier 1996; contrib. to various publs. *Honours:* Soc. des Écrivains de France medal 1960, Centennial Medal, Canada 1967, Soc. des Poètes français medal 1994. *Address:* La Chacunière, 44 Farm Greenway, Don Mills, ON M2A 3M2 (home); Department of French Studies, University of Toronto, 50 rue Saint-Joseph, Toronto, ON M5S 1J4, Canada (office). *Telephone:* (416) 445-6287 (home); (416) 978-7165 (office).

CLUYSENAAR, Anne, (Alice Andrée), BA; Irish academic, poet, songwriter, librettist and painter; b. 15 March 1936, Brussels, Belgium; d. of John Cluysenaar and Sybil Fitzgerald Hewat; m. Walter Freeman Jackson 1976; three step-c. *Education:* Trinity Coll., Dublin, Univ. of Edinburgh. *Career:* Asst Lecturer, Univ. of Manchester 1957–58; reader to (blind) critic and novelist, Percy Lubbock 1959; Librarian, Chester Beatty Library of Oriental Manuscripts, Dublin; Lecturer, King's Coll., Aberdeen, UK 1963–65, Lancaster Univ. 1965–71, Huddersfield Polytechnic 1972, Univ. of Birmingham 1973–76, Sheffield City Polytechnic 1976–89; part-time Lecturer, Univ. of Wales, Cardiff 1990–2002; Founder-Ed. Sheaf 1979; Founder-Dir Verbal Arts Asscn 1983–86; Co-founder and Sec. Usk Valley Vaughan Asscn 1995–; Founding Gen. Ed., now Poetry Ed., U.V.V.A. journal Scintilla 1997–; Fellow, Welsh Acad. 2001. *Publications include:* A Fan of Shadows 1967, Nodes 1971, Introduction to Literary Stylistics 1976, Selected Poems of James Burns Singers (ed.) 1977, Double Helix 1982, Timeslips: New and Selected Poems 1997, Henry Vaughan Selected Poems (ed.) 2004, The Hare That Hides Within (co-ed.) 2004, Batu-Angas 2008, Water to Breath 2009, Migrations 2011; other: contrib. of poems to New Poets of Ireland 1963, English Poetry since 1960 1972, Poetry Introduction 4 1978, Virago Book of Love Poetry 1990, The Virago Book of Love Poetry 1990, Hepworth 1992, The White Page/An Phileog Bhan – Twentieth Century Irish Women Poets 1999, Private People 1999, Poetry in the Parks 2000, The White Page 2000, Scintilla (co-ed.) 2000, Parents 2000, Blodeuedd 2001, Birdsong 2002, Making Worlds 2003, Agenda 2004, The Hare That Hides Within: Poems About St. Melangell (co-ed.) 2004, Is a Religious Poem Possible in the Early 21st Century? (co-ed.) 2004; essays in British Poetry Since 1960 1972, The Life of Metrical and Free Verse in Twentieth-Century Poetry 1997, Poets on Poets 1997; contribs to Stand, Planet, New Welsh Review, Poetry Wales and others. *Honours:* Vice-Chancellor's Prize for Poetry, Trinity Coll., Dublin. *Address:* Little Wentwood Farm, Llantrisant, Usk, Gwent, NP15 1ND, Wales (home). *Telephone:* (1291) 673797 (home). *E-mail:* anne.cluysenaar@virgin.net (home).

COASE, Ronald Harry, BCom, DScEcon; British economist and academic; *Clifton R. Musser Professor Emeritus of Economics, The Law School, University of Chicago*; b. 29 Dec. 1910, London; s. of Henry Coase and Rosalie Coase; m. Marian Hartung 1937. *Education:* London School of Econs. *Career:* Asst Lecturer, Dundee School of Econs 1932–34; Asst Lecturer, Univ. of Liverpool 1934–35; Asst Lecturer to Reader, LSE, 1935–40, 1946–51; Head, Statistical Division, Forestry Comm. 1940–41; Statistician, later Chief Statistician, Cen. Statistical Office, Offices of War Cabinet, 1941–46; Prof., Univ. of Buffalo 1951–58; Prof., Univ. of Virginia 1958–64; Ed. Journal of Law and Economics 1964–92; Clifford R. Musser Prof. of Econs, Univ. of Chicago 1964–82, Prof. Emer. and Sr Fellow in Law and Econs 1982–; Fellow, American Acad. of Arts and Sciences; Distinguished Fellow, American Econ Asscn; Rockefeller Fellow 1948; Sr Research Fellow, Hoover Inst., Stanford Univ. 1977; Corresponding Fellow, British Acad., European Acad. *Publications:* British Broadcasting: a study in Monopoly 1950, The Firm, the Market and the Law 1988, Essays on Economics and Economists 1994. *Honours:* Hon. Fellow, LSE, Royal Econ. Soc.; numerous hon. degrees; Nobel Prize for Economic Science 1991. *Address:* University of Chicago Law School, 1111 East 60th Street, Chicago, IL 60637 (office); The Hallmark, Apt 1100, 2960 North Lake Shore Drive, Chicago, IL 60657, USA (home). *Telephone:* (773) 702-7342 (office). *Website:* www.law.uchicago.edu (office).

COBEN, Harlan, BA; American writer; b. 4 Jan. 1962, Newark, NJ; m. Anne Armstrong 1988; two s. two d. *Education:* Amherst Coll. *Career:* mem. MWA (pres. 2008–09), Sisters in Crime. *Publications:* novels: Play Dead 1990, Miracle Cure 1991, Deal Breaker (World Mystery Conference Anthony Award for Best Paperback Original Novel 1996) 1995, Drop Shot 1996, Fade Away (MWA Edgar Award for Best Paperback Original Mystery Novel, Shamus Award for Best Paperback Original Novel, Private Eye Writers of America 1997) 1996, Back Spin 1997, One False Move (WH Smith Fresh Talent Award) 1997, The Final Detail 1999, Darkest Fear 2000, Tell No One 2001, Gone For Good (WH Smith Thumping Good Read Award) 2002, No Second Chance 2003, Just One Look 2004, The Innocent 2005, Promise Me 2006, The Woods 2007, Hold Tight 2008, Long Lost 2009, Caught 2010, Shelter 2011; short stories: A Simple Philosophy 1999, The Key to My Father 2003. *Literary Agent:* Aaron Priest Literary Agency, 708 Third Avenue, New York, NY 10017, USA. *E-mail:* me@harlancoben.com (office). *Website:* www.harlancoben.com.

COBURN, Andrew; American writer; b. 1 May 1932, Exeter, NH; m. Bernardine Casey Coburn; four d. *Education:* Suffolk Univ., Boston. *Publications include:* fiction: The Trespassers 1974, The Babysitter 1979, Off Duty 1980, Company Secrets 1982, Widow's Walk 1984, Sweetheart 1985, Love Nest 1987, Goldilocks 1989, No Way Home 1992, Voices in the Dark 1994, Birthright 1997, On the Loose 2006, My Father's Daughter 2007; non-fiction: Plum Island 2007, Updike of Ipswich 2009; contribs: Transatlantic Magazine, Massachusetts Review, Rio Grande Review, Consequence Magazine, Fifth Wednesday Journal, J Journal, Contrary Magazine, North Atlantic Review, Harpur Palate. *Honours:* Hon. DLitt (Merrimack Coll.) 1986; Eugene Saxton Memorial fellowship (Harper and Row) 1965. *Address:* 3 Farrwood Drive, Andover, MA 01810, USA (home). *Telephone:* (508) 475-8701 (home). *E-mail:* coburnand@aol.com (home).

COBURN, Donald Lee; American dramatist; b. 4 Aug. 1938, Baltimore, Md; m. 1st Nazlee Joyce French 1964 (divorced 1971); one s. one d.; m. 2nd Marsha Woodruff Maher 1975. *Education:* public schools in Baltimore. *Career:* mem. Authors League of America, Dramatists Guild of America, Soc. des Auteurs et Compositeurs Dramatiques, Texas Inst. of Letters, Writers' Guild of America. *Plays include:* The Gin Game (Pulitzer Prize 1978) 1977, Bluewater Cottage 1979, The Corporation Man 1981, Currents Turned Awry 1982, Guy 1983, Noble Adjustment 1985, Anna-Weston 1988, Return to Blue Fin 1991, Fear of Darkness 1995, Firebrand 1997, The Cause 1998. *Screenplays include:* Flights of Angels 1987, A Virgin Year 1991, Legal Access 1994. *Honours:* Golden

Apple 1978. *Literary Agent:* c/o Abrams Artists Agency, 275 Seventh Avenue, 26th Floor, New York, NY 10001, USA. *Telephone:* (646) 486-4600. *E-mail:* info@abramsart.com. *E-mail:* dlcbusiness@earthlink.net (home). *Website:* www.thegingame.com (office).

COCKE, Ulla, BA; Swedish magazine editor; *Editor-in-Chief, Matmagasinet*; b. 14 April 1947, d. of Gert Ljungstrom and Lisa Ljungstrom; m. Thomas Cocke 1974; one d. *Education:* Stockholm Univ. *Career:* journalist 1980–; Ed.-in-Chief Min Värld 1984, Hemmets Veckotidning weekly magazine 1985; currently Ed.-in-Chief Matmagasinet. *Address:* Landskronavägen 23, 251 85 Helsingborg, Sweden (office). *Telephone:* (42) 17-35-00 (office). *Fax:* (42) 17-37-56 (office). *E-mail:* matmagasinet@aller.se (office). *Website:* matmagasinet.se (office).

CODRESCU, Andrei; American (b. Romanian) academic, writer, poet, editor and radio commentator and film maker; *MacCurdy Distinguished Professor Emeritus of English, Louisiana State University*; b. 20 Dec. 1946, Sibiu, Romania; m. Alice Henderson 1969 (divorced 1998); two s.; m. Laura Cole 2000. *Education:* Colegiul Naţional 'Gheorghe Lazăr', Sibiu. *Career:* MacCurdy Distinguished Prof. of English and Comparative Literature, Louisiana State Univ. 1984–2009, Emer. 2009–; author, Ed. Exquisite Corpse (literary journal) 1983–2011; mem. Jury, Neustadt Prize, Nat. Book Award. *Compositions include:* The Valley of Christmas (musical play) 2000, Into the Maelstorm, lyrics by Andreo Codrescu, performed by the New Orleans Klezmer-All Stars with Ivan Neville. *Radio:* commentator, All Things Considered, Nat. Public Radio. *Film:* Road Scholar (for PBS) (George Foster Peabody Award 1995) 1994. *Publications include:* fiction: Monsieur Teste in America and Other Instances of Realism (stories) 1987, The Repentance of Lorraine 1994, The Blood Countess 1995, Messiah 1999, Casanova in Bohemia 2002, Wakefield 2004; poetry: License to Carry a Gun (Big Table Poetry Award) 1970, A Serious Morning 1973, The Marriage of Insult & Injury 1974, For the Love of a Coat 1975, The Lady Painter 1979, Necrocorrida 1982, Comrade Past and Mister Present 1991, Belligerence 1993, Alien Candor: Selected Poems, 1970–1995 1996, It Was Today: New Poems Minneapolis 2003, Instrumental Negru: Poezii 1966–2004 2004, It Was Today 2006, Submarinul Iertat (with Ruxandra Cesereanu) (Romania Radio Cultural Award 2008) 2007, Jealous Witness 2008; essays: Raised by Puppets Only to be Killed by Research 1987, Craving for Swan 1988, The Disappearance of the Outside: A Manifesto for Escape 1990, The Hole in the Flag: A Romanian Exile's Story of Return and Revolution 1991, Road Scholar: Coast to Coast Late in the Century 1993, The Muse is Always Half-Dressed in New Orleans 1995, Zombification: Essays from NPR 1995, The Dog With the Chip in his Neck: Essays from NPR & Elsewhere 1996, Ay, Cuba! A Socio-Erotic Journey 1999, New Orleans, Mon Amour 2006, The Posthuman Dada Guide: Tzara and Lenin Play Chess 2009, The Poetry Lesson 2010, Whatever Gets You through the Night: A Story of Sheherezade and the Arabian Nights 2011; ed.: American Poetry Since 1970: Up Late 1988, The Stiffest of the Corpse: An Exquisite Corpse Reader, 1983–1990 1990, American Poets Say Goodbye to the 20th Century 1996, The Exquisite Corpse Annual 2008–09; numerous syndicated radio and newspaper contribs. *Honours:* Star of Romania, Commdr rank; Dr hc (Boston Coll. of Art, Univ. of Pennsylvania, Univ. of Bucharest); Nat. Endowment for the Arts Poetry Award 1974, American Civil Liberties Union Freedom of Speech Award 1995, Romanian Cultural Foundation Literature Prize 1996, Ovidius Prize 2005, Pushcart Prize, Peabody Award. *E-mail:* acodrescu@gmail.com (office). *Website:* www.codrescu.com (home).

CODY, James (see Rohrbach, Peter Thomas)

COE, Jonathan, BA, MA, PhD; British writer; b. 19 Aug. 1961, Birmingham, England; m. Janine McKeown 1989; two d. *Education:* Trinity Coll., Cambridge, Univ. of Warwick. *Career:* fmr legal proofreader. *Publications:* The Accidental Woman 1987, A Touch of Love 1989, The Dwarves of Death 1990, Humphrey Bogart: Take It and Like It 1991, James Stewart: Leading Man 1994, What A Carve Up! (John Llewellyn Rhys Prize 1995, Prix du Meilleur Livre Étranger 1996) 1994, The House of Sleep (Writers' Guild Best Fiction Award 1997, Prix Médicis Étranger 1998) 1997, The Rotters' Club (Bollinger Everyman Wodehouse Prize 2001, Premio Arcebispo Juan de San Clemente 2004) 2001, The Closed Circle 2004, Like a Fiery Elephant: The Story of B. S. Johnson (BBC Four Samuel Johnson Prize for non-fiction 2005) 2004, The Rain Before It Falls (Prix de l'Europe de la médiatheque de Bussy Saint-Georges 2010) 2007, The Terrible Privacy of Maxwell Sim 2010; contrib. to periodicals. *Honours:* Chevalier, Ordre des Arts et des Lettres 2004. *Literary Agent:* c/o Peake Associates, 14 Grafton Crescent, London, NW1 8SL, England.

COELHO, Paulo; Brazilian writer; b. 24 Aug. 1947, Rio de Janeiro; m. Christina Oiticica. *Education:* law school. *Career:* fmr playwright, theatre dir and popular songwriter; imprisoned for alleged subversive activities against Brazilian Govt 1974; regular columnist for O Globo (newspaper) 2007–; elected mem. Brazilian Acad. of Arts 2002–, UN Messenger of Peace 2007–. *Publications:* Arquivos do inferno 1982, O Diário de um mago (trans. as The Pilgrimage, aka The Diary of a Magus: The Road to Santiago) 1987, O Alquimista (trans. as The Alchemist) 1988, Brida 1990, O Dom Supremo (trans. as The Gift) 1991, As Valkírias (trans. as The Valkyries) 1992, Maktub 1994, Na margem do rio Piedra eu sentei e chorei (trans. as By the River Piedra I Sat Down and Wept) 1994, Frases 1995, O Monte Cinco (trans. as The Fifth Mountain) 1996, Cartas de Amor do Profeta (trans. as Love Letters from a Prophet) 1997, Manual do guerreiro da luz (trans. as Manual of the Warrior of Light) 1997, Veronika decide morrer (trans. as Veronika Decides to Die) 1998, Palavras essenciais (trans. as The Confessions of a Pilgrim) 1999, O demônio e a Srta Prym (trans. as The Devil and Miss Prym) 2000, Histórias para pais, filhos e netos (trans. as Fathers, Sons and Grandsons) 2001, Onze minutos (trans. as Eleven Minutes) 2003, O Gênio e as Rosas (trans. as The Genie and the Roses, juvenile) 2004, O Zahir (trans. as The Zahir) (Kiklop Literary Award, Croatia 2006, Austrian Booksellers' Platin Book Award 2006) 2005, Like the Flowing River (thoughts and short stories) 2006, A Bruxa do Portobello (trans. as The Witch of Portobello) (EMPiK's Ace Award) 2006, O Vencedor está Só (trans. as The Winner Stands Alone) 2008, O Aleph (trans. as The Aleph) 2010. *Honours:* Chevalier, Ordre des Arts et des Lettres 1996, Comendador de Ordem do Rio Branco 1998, Chevalier, Légion d'honneur 2000, Order of St Sophia (Ukraine) 2004, Cruz do Mérito do Empreendedor Juscelino Kubitschek 2006; numerous awards including Prix Lectrices d'Elle, France 1995, Golden Book Awards, Yugoslavia 1995, 1996, 1997, 1998, 1999, 2000, Flaiano Int. Award, Italy 1996, Super Grinzane Cavour Book Award, Italy 1996, Golden Medal of Galicia, Spain 1999, Crystal Mirror Award, Poland 2000, XXIII Premio Internazionale Fregene, Italy 2001, Bambi Award, Germany 2001, Budapest Prize, Hungary 2005, Goldene Feder Award, Germany 2005, Religion Communicators Council Wilbur Award, USA 2006, Premio Álava en el Corazón, Spain 2006, Asscn of Mexican Booksellers Pergolas Prize 2006, Distinction of Honour from the City of Odense (Hans Christian Andersen Award), Denmark 2007, best selling foreign book in Poland 2007, Best Int. Writer Award, ELLE Awards, Spain 2008. *Literary Agent:* c/o Sant Jordi Asociados Agencia Literaria SL, Paseo García Faria, 73–75, 08019 Barcelona, Spain. *Telephone:* (93) 2240107. *Fax:* (93) 3562696. *E-mail:* readers@santjordi-asociados.com. *Website:* www.santjordi-asociados.com. *E-mail:* paulo@paulocoelho.com (office). *Website:* www.paulocoelho.com (home).

COETZEE, J(ohn) M(axwell), MA, PhD; South African/Australian writer and academic; b. 9 Feb. 1940, Cape Town; one s. one d. *Education:* Univ. of Cape Town, Univ. of Texas. *Career:* Asst Prof. of English, State Univ. of NY (SUNY), Buffalo 1968–71; Lecturer, Univ. of Cape Town 1972–76, Sr Lecturer 1977–80, Assoc. Prof. 1981–83, Prof. of Gen. Literature 1984–2001; Visiting Prof. of Humanities, Univ. of Adelaide, Australia 2002–; Prof. of Social Thought, Univ. of Chicago, USA 1995–2000, Distinguished Service Prof. 2001–03. *Publications:* Dusklands 1974, In the Heart of the Country 1977, Waiting for the Barbarians 1980, Life and Times of Michael K (Booker-McConnell Prize 1983, Prix Femina Etranger 1985) 1983, Foe 1986, White Writing 1988, Age of Iron (Sunday Express Book of the Year Prize 1990) 1990, Doubling the Point: Essays and Interviews (ed. by David Atwell) 1992, The Master of Petersburg (Premio Mondello 1994, Irish Times Int. Fiction Prize 1995) 1994, Giving Offence: Essays on Censorship 1996, Boyhood 1997, The Lives of Animals (lecture) 1999, Disgrace (Booker Prize 1999, Commonwealth Writers Prize 2000) 1999, The Humanities in Africa 2001, Stranger Shores: Essays 1986–1999 2001, Youth 2002, Elizabeth Costello: Eight Lessons 2003, Slow Man (novel) 2005, Inner Workings (essays) 2007, Diary of a Bad Year (novel) 2007, Summertime (fiction) 2009, Scenes from Provincial Life 2011. *Honours:* Chevalier, Ordre des Arts et des Lettres, Ridder van de Orde van de Leeuw (Netherlands), Order of Mapungubwe (South Africa); Dr hc (Strathclyde) 1985, (State Univ. of New York) 1989, (Cape Town) 1995, (Oxford) 2002; CNA Literary Award 1977, 1980, 1983, Nobel Prize for Literature 2003. *Address:* PO Box 3045, Newton, SA 5074, Australia (office). *E-mail:* john.coetzee@adelaide.edu.au (home).

COFFEY, Brian (see Koontz, Dean Ray)

COFFEY, Marilyn June, BA, MFA; American writer, poet and academic; b. 22 July 1937, Alma, Neb.; m. 1961 (divorced); one s. *Education:* Univ. of Nebraska, Brooklyn Coll., City Univ. of New York. *Career:* Faculty mem., Pratt Inst., New York 1966–69, 1973–90; Adjunct Communication Instructor, St Mary's Coll., Lincoln, Neb. 1990–92; Assoc. Prof. of Creative Writing, Fort Hays State Univ. 1992–; mem. E.A. Burnett Soc., Charter mem. Poets and Writers. *Publications include:* Marcella (novel) 1973, Pricksong (Pushcart Prize 1976) 1975, Great Plains Patchwork (non-fiction) 1989, A Cretan Cycle: Fragments Unearthed From Knossos (poems) 1991, Creating the Classic Short Story: A Workbook 1995, Delicate Footsteps: Poems About Real Women 1995, Mail-Order Kid 2010; contribs to anthologies, journals, reviews, and newspapers. *Honours:* Master Alumnus, Univ. of Nebraska 1977, winner, Newark Public Library Competitions, NJ 1985, 1987–88, several grants. *Address:* Department of English, Fort Hays State University, Hays, KS 67601, USA.

COFFEY, Shelby, III; American journalist; *Vice-Chairman, Newseum*; m. Mary Lee Coffey. *Education:* Univ. of Virginia. *Career:* with Washington Post 1968–85, later Asst Man. Ed. for nat. news and Deputy Man. Ed. for features; Ed. US News and World Report 1985–86; fmr Sr Vice-Pres. and Ed. Dallas Times Herald; Deputy Assoc. Ed. Los Angeles Times 1986–88, Exec. Ed. 1988–89, Ed. and Exec. Vice-Pres. 1989–97; Pres. CNN Business News and CNNfn 1999–2001; fmr Exec. Vice-Pres. ABC News; apptd Sr Fellow, Freedom Forum Foundation 2001, currently Vice-Chair. Newseum; Bd mem. Pacific Council on International Policy; mem. Council on Foreign Relations, International Press Inst. *Publications:* The Art of Leadership in News Organizations. *Honours:* Nat. Press Foundation Ed. of the Year 1994, Ida B. Wells Award 1995. *Address:* Newseum, 555 Pennsylvania Avenue, NW, Washington, DC 20001, USA (office). *Telephone:* (888) 639-7386 (office). *E-mail:* info@newseum.org (office). *Website:* www.newseum.org (office).

COHAN, Tony, BA; American writer; b. (Anthony Robert Cohan), 28 Dec. 1939, New York, NY; s. of Philip Cohan and Mary Helen Foster; m. 1974; two d. *Education:* Univ. of California. *Career:* mem. Authors' Guild, PEN. *Publications include:* Nine Ships 1975, Outlaw Visions 1977, Canary 1981, The Flame 1983, Opium 1984, Agents of Desire 1997, Mexicolor 1997, On Mexican Time 2001, Native State 2003, Mexican Days 2007, Valparaiso 2012. *Honours:* Notable Book of the Year 1981. *Address:* PO Box 870, Venice, CA 90294, USA (home). *E-mail:* tobo101@cs.com (home); tony@tonycohan.com. *Website:* tonycohan.com.

COHEN, Leonard, CC, BA; Canadian singer, songwriter and poet; b. 21 Sept. 1934, Montreal; s. of Nathan B. Cohen and Masha Klinitsky; two c. *Education:* McGill Univ. *Career:* f. country-and-western band, The Buckskin Boys 1951; initially wrote poetry; moved to New York early 1960s; as a songwriter, over 2,000 renditions of his songs have been recorded; limited edition artwork first displayed to public 2005, lithograph prints have achieved widespread critical acclaim and nearly 600 limited edition prints had been sold by 2010. *Recordings include:* albums: The Songs of Leonard Cohen 1968, Songs From A Room 1969, Songs of Love and Hate 1971, Live Songs 1973, New Skin For the Old Ceremony 1974, Greatest Hits 1975, The Best of Leonard Cohen 1976, Death of a Ladies' Man 1977, Recent Songs 1979, Various Positions 1985, I'm Your Man 1988, The Future 1992, Cohen Live 1994, More Best Of 1997, Live Songs 1998, Ten New Songs 2001, Field Commander Cohen 2001, The Essential Leonard Cohen 2002, Dear Heather 2004, Old Ideas 2012. *Film:* Leonard Cohen I'm Your Man 2006. *Publications include:* poetry: Let Us Compare Mythologies (McGill Literary Award) 1956, The Spice-Box of Earth 1961, Flowers for Hitler 1964, Beautiful Losers 1966, Parasites of Heaven 1966, Selected Poems 1956–1968 1968, The Energy of Slaves 1972, Death of a Ladies' Man 1978, Book of Mercy (Canadian Authors' Asscn Literary Award) 1984, Stranger Music: Selected Poems and Songs 1993, Book of Longing 2006; other: The Favourite Game (novel) (Quebec Literary Prize) 1963. *Honours:* Dr hc (Dalhousie Univ.) 1970, (McGill Univ.) 1992; Grand Officer, Nat. Order of Quebec 2008; numerous awards including William Harold Moon Award (Recording Rights Org. of Canada) 1984, Juno Hall of Fame 1991, Gov. Gen.'s Performing Arts Award 1993, Canadian Songwriters' Hall of Fame 2006, Rock and Roll Hall of Fame 2008, Grammy Award for Album of the Year on Herbie Hancock's River: the Joni Letters 2008, Grammy Lifetime Achievement Award 2010, Prince of Asturias Award 2011, Glenn Gould Prize 2011, PEN New England Excellence in Lyrics Award 2012. *Literary Agent:* 9300 Wilshire Boulevard, Suite 200, Beverly Hills, CA 90212, USA.

COHEN, Marcel; French writer and journalist; b. 9 Oct. 1937, Asnières. *Education:* École Supérieure de Journalisme and École du Louvre, Paris. *Career:* journalist 1958–; mil. corresp. 1960–61. *Publications include:* Galpa 1969, Malestroit: Chroniques du Silence 1973, Voyage à Waizata 1976, Murs 1979, Du désert au livre: Entretiens avec Edmond Jabès (trans. as From the Desert to the Book) 1981, Miroirs (trans. as Mirrors) 1981, Je ne sais pas le nom 1986, Le grand paon-de-nuit (trans. as The Peacock Emperor Moth) 1990, Lettre à Antonio Saura (trans. as In Search of a Lost Ladino: Letter to Antonio Saura) 1997, Assassinat d'un garde 1998, Faits 2002, Faits II 2007, Walls (Anamneses) 2009; contrib. to anthologies, journals and magazines.

COHEN, Michael Joseph, BA, PhD; Israeli/British academic and writer; *Professor Emeritus, Bar-Ilan University*; b. 29 April 1940, London, England; s. of Simon Cohen and Kate Cohen; one s. one d. *Education:* Univ. of London, London School of Econs and Political Science. *Career:* Lecturer, Bar Ilan Univ. 1972–77, Sr Lecturer 1977–81, Assoc. Prof. 1981–86, Prof. (now Emer.) 1986–, Lazarus Philips Chair of History 1990–2008; Visiting Prof., Stanford Univ., USA 1977, 1981, Hebrew Univ., Jerusalem 1978–80, 1981–83, Duke Univ. and Univ. of North Carolina, Chapel Hill, USA 1980–81, Univ. of British Columbia, Canada 1985–86; Bernard and Audre Rapaport Fellow, American Jewish Archives, Cincinnati 1988–89; Meyerhoff Visiting Prof. of Israel Studies, Univ. of Maryland, College Park 1992–98; mem. Inst. of Advanced Studies, Princeton, NJ, USA 1998; Visiting Fellow 1999; Visiting Prof., San Diego State Univ. 1999, Centre for Int. Studies, LSE 2002–03. *Publications include:* Palestine: Retreat From the Mandate, 1936–45 1978, Palestine and the Great Powers 1945–48 1982, Churchill and the Jews 1985 (revised 2004), The Origins of the Arab-Zionist Conflict, 1914–1948 1987, Palestine to Israel: From Mandate to Independence 1988, Truman and Israel 1990, Fighting World War Three from the Middle East: Allied Contingency Plans, 1945–1954 1997, Strategy and Politics in the Middle East 1954–1960: Defending the Northern Tier 2004; ed.: The Weizmann Letters, Vols XX, XXI, 1936–1945 1979, The History of the Founding of Israel, Part III, The Struggle for the State of Israel, 1939–1948 (ten vols) 1988, Bar-Ilan Studies in Modern History 1991, British Security Problems in the Middle East During the 1930s: The Conquest of Abyssinia to World War Two (with Martin Kolinsky) 1992, The Demise of Empire: Britain's Responses to Nationalist Movements in the Middle East, 1943–1955 (with Martin Kolinsky) 1998; contrib. to scholarly journals. *Address:* c/o General History Department, Bar-Ilan University, 52900 Ramat-Gan, Israel.

COHEN, Morton Norton, (John Moreton), AB, MA, PhD, FRSL; American academic and writer; *Professor Emeritus, City University of New York*; b. 27 Feb. 1921, Calgary, Alberta, Canada. *Education:* Tufts Univ., Mass and Columbia Univ., New York, USA. *Career:* Tutor to Prof., City Coll., CUNY 1952–81, mem. Doctoral Faculty, CUNY 1964–81, Deputy Exec. Officer, PhD Programme in English 1976–78, 1979–80, Prof. Emer. 1981–; mem. Lewis Carroll Soc., Lewis Carroll Soc. of North America, Lewis Carroll Soc. of Japan, Century Asscn, New York. *Publications include:* Rider Haggard: His Life and Works 1960, A Brief Guide to Better Writing (co-author) 1960, Rudyard Kipling to Rider Haggard: The Record of a Friendship 1965, Lewis Carroll's Photographs of Nude Children (aka Lewis Carroll, Photographer of Children: Four Nude Studies) 1978, The Russian Journal II 1979, The Letters of Lewis Carroll (ed., two vols) 1979, Lewis Carroll and the Kitchins 1980, Lewis Carroll and Alice 1832–1882 1982, The Selected Letters of Lewis Carroll 1982, Lewis Carroll and the House of Macmillan (co-ed.) 1987, Lewis Carroll: A Biography 1995, Reflections in a Looking Glass (A Celebration of Lewis Carroll's Photographs) 1998, Lewis Carroll and his Illustrators 2003; contrib. to many magazines, journals, papers and books. *Honours:* Fulbright Fellow 1954–55, 1974–75, Guggenheim Fellowship 1966–67, Nat. Endowment for the Humanities research grant 1974–75, Guggenheim Foundation publication grant 1979. *Address:* 55 East Ninth Street, Apt 10-D, New York, NY 10003, USA.

COHEN, Stephen Frand, BA, MA, PhD; American academic and writer; *Professor of Russian Studies and History, New York University*; b. 25 Nov. 1938, Indianapolis, Ind.; m. 1st Lynn Blair 1962 (divorced); one s. one d.; m. 2nd Katrina vanden Heuvel 1988; one d. *Education:* Indiana Univ., Columbia Univ., New York. *Career:* Instructor, Columbia Coll. 1965–68; Jr Fellow, Columbia Univ. 1965–68, Sr Fellow 1971–73, 1976–77, 1985, Assoc. 1972–85, Visiting Prof. 1973–84, Visiting Scholar 1980–81; Asst Prof., Princeton Univ. 1968–73, Assoc. Prof. 1973–80, Prof. 1980–98, Prof. of Politics Emer. 1998–; Prof. of Russian Studies and History, New York Univ. 1998–; Contributing Ed., The Nation; mem. American Asscn for the Advancement of Slavic Studies, American Historical Asscn, American Political Science Asscn, Council on Foreign Relations. *Documentary films:* (with Rosemarie Reed): Conversations with Gorbachev 1994, Russia Betrayed? 1995, Widow of the Revolution 2000. *Publications include:* The Great Purge Trial (co-ed.) 1965, Bukharin and the Bolshevik Revolution: A Political Biography, 1888–1938 1973, The Soviet Union Since Stalin (co-ed.) 1980, An End to Silence: Uncensored Opinion in the Soviet Union (ed.) 1982, Rethinking the Soviet Experience: Politics and History Since 1917 1985, Voices of Glasnost: Interviews with Gorbachev's Reformers (co-author and co-ed.) 1989, Failed Crusade: America and the Tragedy of Post-Communist Russia 2000, (revised and expanded edn) 2001, The Question of Questions: Why Did the Soviet Union? (in Russian) 2007, The Long Return: Gulag Survivors after Stalin (in Russian) 2009, Soviet Fates and Lost Alternatives: From Stalinism to the New Cold War 2009, The Victims Return: Survivors of the Gulag After Stalin 2010; contrib. to books, scholarly journals and periodicals. *Honours:* Russian Presidential Order of Friendship 2008; Hon. Prof., Moscow State Econs and Trade Univ. 2008; Guggenheim Fellowships 1976–77, 1989, Rockefeller Foundation Humanities Fellowship 1980–81, Nat. Endowment for the Humanities Fellowship 1984–85, Page One Award for Column Writing 1985, Fulbright-Hays Faculty Research Abroad Fellowship 1988–89, Indiana Univ. Distinguished Alumni Award 1998, New York Univ. Award for Excellence in Teaching 2001, Columbia Univ. Harriman (Russian) Inst. Alumnus of the Year 2002. *Address:* Department of Russian Studies, New York University, 19 University Place, New York, NY 10003-4556, USA (office). *Telephone:* (212) 998-8289 (office). *Fax:* (212) 995-4604 (office). *E-mail:* sfc1@nyu.edu (office).

COHN, Samuel Kline, Jr, BA, MA, PhD; American academic and writer; *Professor of Medieval History, University of Glasgow*; b. 13 April 1949, Birmingham, Ala; m. Genevieve A. Warwick 1994, two s. *Education:* Union Coll., Univ. of Wisconsin at Madison, Univ. degli Studi di Firenze, Italy, Harvard Univ. *Career:* Asst Prof., Wesleyan Univ. 1978–79; Asst Prof., Brandeis Univ. 1979–85, Assoc. Prof. 1986–89, Prof. of History 1989–95; Visiting Prof., Brown Univ. 1990–91; Prof. of Medieval History, Univ. of Glasgow, UK 1995–; Distinguished Visiting Prof. in Medieval Studies, Univ. of California, Berkeley 2008; mem. American Historical Asscn, Soc. for Italian Historical Studies; Fellow, Center for European Studies, Harvard Univ. 1977–; Guest Fellow, Villa I Tatti, Settignano, Italy 1988–89. *Publications include:* The Laboring Classes in Renaissance Florence 1980, Death and Property in Siena 1205–1800: Strategies for the Afterlife 1988, The Cult of Remembrance and the Black Death: Six Renaissance Cities in Central Italy 1992, Portraits of Medieval and Renaissance Living: Essays in Memory of David Herlihy (ed.) 1996, Women in the Streets: Essays on Sex and Power in the Italian Renaissance 1996, The Black Death and the Transformation of the West (with David Herlihy) 1996, Creating the Florentine State: Peasants and Rebellion 1348–1434 1999, Popular Protest in Late Medieval Europe 2004, Lust for Liberty 2006, Cultures of Plague: Medical Thinking at the End of the Renaissance 2009; contrib. to scholarly books and journals including Economic History Review, Past & Present, English Historical Review, Journal of Interdisciplinary History; American Historical Review. *Honours:* Hon. FRHistS; Hon. Krupp Foundation Fellowship 1976, Fulbright-Hays Fellowship, Italy 1977, Nat. Endowment for the Humanities Research Fellowship 1982–83, Howard R. Marraro Prize, American Catholic Historical Asscn 1989, Outstanding Academic Book Selection, Choice magazine 1993, Villa I Tatti Fellowship 1993–94, Guggenheim Fellowship 1994–95, Wellcome Trust grant, Econ. and Social Research Council grant. *Address:* Department of History (Medieval), University of Glasgow, 10 University Gardens, Glasgow, G12 8QQ, Scotland (office). *Telephone:* (141) 330-4369 (office). *Fax:* (141) 330-2348 (office). *E-mail:* s.cohn@history.arts.gla.ac.uk (office); samuel.cohn@glasgow.ac.uk.

COKER, Christopher; British academic and writer; *Professor of International Relations, London School of Economics. Career:* NATO Fellow 1981–; currently Prof. of Int. Relations, LSE; adviser to several UK Conservative Party think tanks including Inst. for European Defence and Strategic Studies and Centre for Policy Studies; visiting lecturer, Jt Staff Coll., Royal Coll. of Defence Studies, London, NATO Coll., Rome, Centre for Int. Security, Geneva, Nat. Inst. for Defence Studies, Tokyo; mem. Washington Strategy Seminar, Inst. for Foreign Policy Analysis, Cambridge, Mass, Black Sea Univ. Foundation, Moscow School of Politics; fmr Ed. Atlantic Quarterly; fmr mem. Council of Royal United Services Inst. *Publications include:* A Nation in Retreat 1991, Britain's Defence Policy in the 1990s: An Intelligent Person's Guide to the Defence Debate 1992, War and the Twentieth Century 1994, Twilight of the West 1997, War and the Illiberal Conscience 1998, Humane Warfare 2001, Waging War without Warriors 2002, The Future of War: the Re-enchantment of War in the Early 21st Century 2004, The Warrior Ethos: Military Culture and the War on Terror 2007, Ethics and War in the 21st Century 2008, War in an Age of Risk 2009; numerous contribs to books, newspapers and journals, including Wall Street Journal, The Times, Independent, The Spectator, The Times Literary Supplement. *Address:* Room CLM. D511, Department of International Relations, London School of Economics, Houghton Street, London, WC2A 2AE, England (office). *Telephone:* (20) 7955-7387 (office). *E-mail:* c.coker@lse.ac.uk (office). *Website:* www2.lse.ac.uk/internationalRelations (office).

COLE, Babette, BA; British writer and illustrator; *Consultant, Authors Bookshop Limited*; b. 10 Sept. 1949, Jersey, Channel Islands; d. of Frederick Cole and Iris Cole (née Horseford). *Education:* Convent FCJ, St Helier and Canterbury Coll. of Art. *Career:* mem. staff, BBC, Children's TV; lived in Okavango Swamps, Botswana 1976; writer of children's books; consultant, Authors Bookshop Ltd; owns stud farm in UK and breeds and rides show hunters; Fellow, Kent Inst. of Art and Design, British Book Awards Acad. *Achievement:* Nat. Champion, Side Saddle Working Hunter 2008, 2009. *Art Exhibition:* Illustration Cupboard 2011. *Television:* Prince Cinders, Princess Smartypants, Dr Dog. *Publications include:* Promise Solves the Problem 1976, Nungu and the Hippo 1978, Nungu and the Elephant 1980, Promise and the Monster 1981, Don't Go Out Tonight 1981, Beware of the Vet 1982, Nungu and the Crocodile 1983, The Trouble with Mum 1983, The Hairy Book 1984, The Trouble with Dad 1985, The Slimey Book 1985, Princess Smartypants (Kate Greenaway Prize, BLA Annabell Fargeon Award) 1986, Prince Cinders (Kate Greenaway Prize) 1987, The Trouble with Gran 1987, The Trouble with Grandad 1988, King Changealot 1988, The Silly Book 1989, Cupid 1989, Three Cheers for Errol 1989, Beastly Birthday Book 1991, The Trouble with Uncle 1992, Supermoo! 1992, Bible Beasties 1992, Mummy Laid an Egg (sold one million copies) (Best Illustrated Children's Book of the Year) 1993, Dr Dog (Kurt Maschler Award) 1994, Winni Allfours 1995, Drop Dead (Kurt Mascher Award) 1996, four mini-novelties: My Dog, My Cat, My Fish, My Horse 1997, The Bad Good Manners Book 1997, Two of Everything 1997, four more mini-novelties: My Aunt etc. 1997, Hair in Funny Places 1999, Lady Lupin's Book of Etiquette 2001, True Love 2001, Animals Scare Me Stiff 2002, Mummy Never Told Me 2003, The Wind in the Willows Pop-Up Book, The Hairy Book 2003, That's Why 2006, Another Dose of Dr Dog 2007, Princess Smartypants Breaks the Rules 2009, If I Were You (Early Learning Award) 2009, Fetlocks Hall: Unicorn Princess 2010, Fetlocks Hall: The Ghostly Blinkers 2010; other: applications for iPhone and iPad, Mummy Laid an Egg 2011, The Curse of the Pony Vampires (Fetlocks Hall) 2011, The Enchanted Ponies (Fetlocks Hall) 2011. *Honours:* Smarties Prize 1987. *Literary Agent:* c/o Rosemary Sandberg Ltd, 6 Bayley Street, London, WC1B 3HB, England. *Telephone:* (20) 7304-4110. *E-mail:* babette@babette-cole.com (office). *Website:* www.babette-cole.com; www.authorsbookshop.co.uk; www.holnestparkstud.co.uk.

COLE, Barry; British writer and poet; b. 13 Nov. 1936, Woking, Surrey, England; m. Rita Linihan 1959; three d. *Career:* Northern Arts Fellow in Literature, Univs of Durham and Newcastle upon Tyne 1970–72. *Publications include:* Blood Ties 1967, Ulysses in the Town of Coloured Glass 1968, A Run Across the Island 1968, Moonsearch 1968, Joseph Winter's Patronage 1969, The Search for Rita 1970, The Visitors 1970, The Giver 1971, Vanessa in the City 1971, Pathetic Fallacies 1973, Dedications 1977, The Edge of the Common 1989, Inside Outside: New and Selected Poems 1997, Lola and the Train 1999, Ghosts Are People Too 2003, Joseph Winter's Patronage 2008; contribs to The Oxford Book of Twentieth Century Verse, British Poetry Since 1945 (anthology). *Address:* 68 Myddelton Square, London, EC1R 1XP, England (home). *Telephone:* (20) 278-2837 (home). *E-mail:* poetbarrycole@btinternet.com (home).

COLE, John Morrison; Northern Irish journalist, broadcaster and writer; b. 23 Nov. 1927, Belfast, Northern Ireland; m. Margaret Isobel Williamson 1956; four s. *Education:* Belfast Royal Acad., Univ. of London. *Career:* Political Ed., BBC 1981–92; mem. Athenaeum Club. *Publications include:* The Poor of the Earth 1976, The Thatcher Years 1987, As It Seemed to Me: Political Memoirs 1995, A Clouded Peace 2001; contribs to The Guardian, New Statesman. *Honours:* Dr hc (Open Univ.) 1992, (Queen's Univ., Belfast) 1992, (Univ. of Ulster) 1992, (Univ. of St Andrews) 1993; Granada TV Newspaper Award 1960, Broadcast Journalist of the Year Award, Royal Television Soc. 1990, BAFTA Richard Dimbleby Award 1992.

COLE, Martina; British novelist; b. 1959, Essex, England. *Publications include:* Dangerous Lady 1992, The Ladykiller 1993, Goodnight Lady 1994, The Jump 1995, The Runaway 1997, Two Women 1999, Broken 2000, Faceless 2001, Maura's Game 2002, The Know 2003, The Graft 2004, The Take (British Book Awards Worldbooks Crime Thriller of the Year 2006) 2005, Close 2006, Faces 2007, The Business 2008, Hard Girls 2009, The Family 2010. *Address:* c/o Hodder Headline, 338 Euston Road, London, NW1 3BH, England. *Website:* www.martinacole.co.uk.

COLE, Peter, BA; American poet and translator; b. 1957, Paterson, NJ; m. Adina Hoffman. *Education:* Hampshire Coll. *Career:* Visiting Prof. and Writer, Wesleyan Univ., Middlebury Coll., Yale Univ.; mem. Editorial Bd, Ibis Editions. *Publications include:* poetry: Rift 1989, Hymns and Qualms 1997, What Is Doubled: Poems 1981–1998 2005, The Dream of the Poem: Hebrew Poetry from Muslim and Christian Spain 2007, Things on Which I've Stumbled 2008, Sacred Trash: The Lost and Found World of the Cairo Geniza (with Adina Hoffman) 2011; numerous books of translations from Hebrew and Arabic poetry and prose by Taha Muhammad Ali, Aharon Shabtai, Yoel Hoffman, and others, Hebrew Writers on Writing (ed.). *Honours:* Nat. Jewish Book Award, PEN Trans. Prize for Poetry, MLA Scaglione Trans. Prize, Times Literary Supplement Trans. Prize, Nat. Endowment for the Humanities Fellowship, Nat. Endowment for the Arts Fellowship, Franke Fellowship in the Humanities, Yale Univ. 2006, John Simon Guggenheim Foundation Fellowship, Macarthur Fellowship 2007, G.E. Younger Writers' Award, Asscn of American Publishers' Hawkins Award, American Acad. of Arts and Letters Award 2010. *Address:* PO Box 32340, Jerusalem, Israel (office). *E-mail:* ibis@netvision.net.il (office). *Website:* www.ibiseditions.com (office).

COLE, Teju, BA, MA, MPhil; Nigerian/American author; *Distinguished Writer-in-Residence, Bard College*; b. (Obayemi Babajide Adetokunbo), 27 June 1975, USA. *Education:* Kalamazoo Coll., School of Oriental Studies, Univ. of London, UK, Columbia Univ. *Career:* raised in Nigeria; has taught at Hofstra, Columbia and New York Univs; Chinua Achebe Fellow, Bard Coll. 2011, Distinguished Writer-in-Residence, Bard Coll. 2011–; Andrew W. Mellon Fellow in the Humanities 2001–02. *Publications include:* Every Day is for the Thief (novella) 2007, Open City (novel) (New York City Book Award for Fiction 2012, Hemingway Foundation/PEN Award 2012, American Acad. of Arts and Letters Rosenthal Award 2012) 2011; contrib. to New York Times, New Yorker, Transition, Tin House, A Public Space. *Literary Agent:* c/o The Lavin Agency, 1123 Broadway, Suite 1107, New York, NY 10010, USA. *Telephone:* (212) 242-1212. *E-mail:* info@thelavinagency.com. *Website:* www.thelavinagency.com. *Address:* Bard College, PO Box 5000, Annandale-on-Hudson, NY 12504-5000, USA (office). *Telephone:* (845) 758-7231 (office). *E-mail:* tcole@bard.edu (office). *Website:* www.bard.edu (office); www.tejucole.com.

COLEGATE, Isabel, FRSL; British writer; b. 10 Sept. 1931, Lincs.; d. of Arthur Colegate and Winifred Colegate; m. Michael Briggs 1953; two s. one d. *Education:* Runton Hill School, Norfolk. *Career:* literary agent, Anthony Blond Ltd, London 1952–57. *Publications include:* The Blackmailer 1958, A Man of Power 1960, The Great Occasion 1962, Statues in a Garden 1964, The Orlando Trilogy 1968–72, News From the City of the Sun 1979, The Shooting Party (WH Smith Literary Award 1981, filmed 1985) 1980, Three Novels 1984, A Glimpse of Sion's Glory 1985, Deceits of Time 1988, The Summer of the Royal Visit 1991, Winter Journey 1995, A Pelican in the Wilderness – Hermits Solitaries and Recluses 2002. *Honours:* Hon. MA (Univ. of Bath) 1988. *Address:* c/o Penguin Books, 80 Strand, London, WC2R 0RL, England.

COLEMAN, Jane Candia, BA; American writer and poet; *Fiction Mentor, MFA Program, Carlow University, Pittsburgh*; b. 1 Jan. 1939, Pittsburgh, Pa; m. 1st Bernard Coleman 1965 (divorced 1989); two s.; m. 2nd Glenn Boyer 1989. *Education:* Univ. of Pittsburgh. *Career:* fmr fiction mentor, MFA Program, Carlow Univ., Pittsburgh; Co-founder and fmr Dir Carlow Coll. Woman's Creative Writing Center; mem. Authors' Guild, Women Writing the West, Western Writers of America. *Publications include:* No Roof But Sky (poems) (Western Heritage Award 1991) 1990, Stories From Mesa Country (Western Heritage Award 1992) 1991, Discovering Eve (short stories) 1993, Shadows in My Hands (memoir) 1993, The Red Drum (poems) 1994, Doc Holliday's Woman (novel) 1995, Moving On (short stories) 1997, I, Pearl Hart (novel) 1998, The O'Keefe Empire (novel) 1999, Doc Holliday's Gone (novel) 1999, Borderlands (short stories) 2000, Desperate Acts (novel) 2001, The Italian Quartet (novel) 2001, Mountain Time (memoir) 2001, Country Music (short stories) 2002, Wives and Lovers (short stories) 2002, Matchless (novel) 2003, Tombstone Travesty (novel) (Willa Award) 2004, The White Dove (poems) 2007, The Silver Queen 2008, Tumbleweed: Allie Earp Remembers 2008, Bandit Queen 2009; contribs to periodicals. *Honours:* Western Heritage Award 1994, Spur Awards for short fiction Western Writers of America 1993, 1995, Arizona Comm. on the Arts Poetry Grant 1993. *Address:* 1702 East Lind Road, Tucson, AZ 85719, USA (home). *Telephone:* (520) 795-5588 (home). *E-mail:* elcisco@candiasystems.com.

COLEMAN, Terence (Terry) Francis Frank, LLB, FRSA; British journalist and writer; b. 13 Feb. 1931, s. of Jack Coleman and D. I. B. Coleman; m. 1st Lesley Fox-Strangeways Vane 1954 (divorced); two d.; m. 2nd Vivien Rosemary Lumsdaine Wallace 1981; one s. one d. *Education:* 14 schools, latterly Poole Grammar School, Univ. of London. *Career:* fmr reporter, Poole Herald; fmr Ed. Savoir Faire; fmr Sub-Ed. Sunday Mercury, Birmingham Post; Reporter then Arts Corresp. The Guardian 1961–70, Chief Feature Writer 1970–74, 1976–79, New York Corresp. 1981, Special Corresp. 1982–89; Special Writer with Daily Mail 1974–76; Assoc. Ed. The Independent 1989–91; columnist, The Guardian 1992–. *Publications include:* The Railway Navvies

(Yorkshire Post Prize for Best First Book of the Year) 1965, A Girl for the Afternoons 1965, Providence and Mr Hardy (with Lois Deacon) 1966, The Only True History: Collected Journalism 1969, Passage to America 1972, An Indiscretion in the Life of an Heiress (Hardy's first novel) (ed.) 1976, The Liners 1976, The Scented Brawl: Collected Journalism 1978, Southern Cross 1979, Thanksgiving 1981, Movers and Shakers: Collected Interviews 1987, Thatcher's Britain 1987, Empire 1994, W. G. Grace: A Biography 1997, Nelson: The Man and the Legend (biog.) 2001, Olivier: The Authorised Biography 2005, Great Interviews of the 20th Century 2008. *Honours:* Feature Writer of the Year, British Press Awards 1982, Journalist of the Year (What the Papers Say Award) 1988. *Literary Agent:* c/o PFD, Drury House, 34–43 Russell Street, London, WC2B 5HA, England. *Telephone:* (20) 7344-1000. *Fax:* (20) 7836-9543. *Website:* www.pfd.co.uk. *Telephone:* (20) 7720-2651 (home).

COLEMAN, Wanda; American poet and writer; b. 13 Nov. 1946, Los Angeles, Calif. *Career:* fmr edical sec., magazine ed., journalist and scriptwriter; Literary Fellow, City of Los Angeles Dept of Cultural Affairs 2003–04. *Publications include:* Mad Dog Black Lady 1979, Imagoes 1983, Heavy Daughter Blues: Poems and Stories, 1968–1986 1987, A War of Eyes and Other Stories 1988, Women for All Seasons: Poetry and Prose About the Transitions in Women's Lives (ed. with Joanne Leedom-Ackerman) 1988, Dicksboro Hotel and Other Travels 1989, African Sleeping Sickness: Stories and Poems 1990, Hand Dance 1993, Native in a Strange Land: Trials & Tremors 1996, Bathwater Wine (Lenore Marshall Poetry Prize, Acad. of American Poets 1999) 1998, Mambo Hips & Make Believe: A Novel 1999, Mercurochrome: New Poems 2001, Ostinato Vamps 2003, The Riot Inside Me: More Trials and Tremors 2005, Jazz and Twelve O'Clock Tales 2008; contribs to anthologies and periodicals. *Honours:* Fellowships from Simon Guggenheim Foundation, Nat. Endowment for the Arts, California Arts Council. *Address:* c/o David R. Godine, Black Sparrow Books, 9 Hamilton Place, Boston, MA 01208-4715, USA. *Website:* www.blacksparrowbooks.com.

COLERIDGE, Geraldine Margaret (Gill); British literary agent; *Partner, Rogers, Coleridge & White*; b. 26 May 1948, d. of Antony Duke Coleridge and June Marian Caswell; m. David Roger Leeming 1974; two s. *Education:* Queen Anne's School, Caversham and Marlborough Secretarial Coll., Oxford. *Career:* mem. staff, BPC Partworks, Sidgwick & Jackson, Bedford Square Book Bang 1968–71; Publicity Man. Chatto & Windus 1971–72; Dir and Literary Agent, Anthony Sheil Assocs 1971–87; Partner, Rogers, Coleridge & White, Literary Agents 1987–; Pres. Assoc. of Authors' Agents 1988–91; mem. British Library Publishing Bd 1993–2003; mem. Public Lending Right Bd 2000–07, Cttee Royal Literary Fund 2008–. *Address:* c/o Rogers, Coleridge & White, 20 Powis Mews, London, W11 1JN, England (office). *Telephone:* (20) 7221-3717 (office). *Fax:* (20) 7229-9084 (office). *Website:* www.rcwlitagency.com (office).

COLERIDGE, Nicholas David, CBE; British publisher, journalist and author; *Vice-President, Condé Nast International*; b. 4 March 1957, s. of David Ean Coleridge and Susan Coleridge (née Senior); m. Georgia Metcalfe 1989; three s. one d. *Education:* Eton, Trinity Coll., Cambridge. *Career:* Assoc. Ed. Tatler 1979–81; columnist Evening Standard 1981–84; Features Ed. Harpers and Queen 1985–86, Ed. 1986–89; Editorial Dir Condé Nast Publs 1989–91, Man. Dir Condé Nast UK 1992–, Vice-Pres. Condé Nast Int. 1999–, Dir Condé Nast France, Condé Nast India; Chair. British Fashion Council 2000–03, Fashion Rocks for The Prince's Trust 2003, Periodical Publrs Asscn 2004–07; mem. Council RCA 1995–2000. *Publications:* Tunnel Vision 1982, Around the World in 78 Days 1984, Shooting Stars 1984, The Fashion Conspiracy 1988, How I Met My Wife and Other Stories 1991, Paper Tigers 1993, With Friends Like These 1997, Streetsmart 1999, Godchildren 2002, A Much Married Man 2006, Deadly Sins 2009. *Honours:* Young Journalist of the Year, British Press Awards 1983, Mark Boxer Award for Editorial Excellence 2001. *Address:* Condé Nast, Vogue House, Hanover Square, London, W1S 1JU (office); 29 Royal Avenue, London, SW3 4QE (home); Wolverton Hall, Nr. Pershore, Worcs., WR10 2AU, England (home). *Telephone:* (20) 7499-9080 (office). *Website:* www.condenast.co.uk (office).

COLES, Donald Langdon, BA, MA; Canadian academic and poet; b. 12 April 1928, Woodstock, Ont.; m. 1958; one s. one d. *Education:* Victoria Coll., Univ. of Toronto, Univ. Cambridge, UK. *Career:* Fiction Ed., The Canadian Forum 1975–76; Dir Creative Writing Programme, York Univ. 1979–85; Poetry Ed., May Studio, Banff Centre for the Fine Arts 1984–93; mem. PEN International. *Publications include:* Sometimes All Over 1975, Anniversaries 1979, The Prinzhorn Collection 1982, Landslides 1986, K in Love 1987, Little Bird 1991, Forests of the Medieval World 1993, Someone Has Stayed in Stockholm: Selected and New Poems 1994, Kurgan 2000, Essential Don Coles 2009, Where We Might Have Been 2011; contribs to Saturday Night, Canadian Forum, London Review of Books, Poetry (Chicago), Globe and Mail, Arc, Ariel. *Honours:* Ont. Confed. of Univ. Faculty Asscns Teaching Award c. 1975, CBC Literary Competition 1980, Gold Medal for Poetry, Nat. Magazine Awards 1986, Gov.-Gen.'s Award for Poetry 1993, Trillium Prize 2000. *Address:* 122 Glenview Avenue, Toronto, ON M4R 1P8, Canada (home). *Telephone:* (416) 485-9252 (home).

COLES, Robert Martin, AB, MD; American child psychiatrist; b. 12 Oct. 1929, Boston, Mass.; s. of Philip W. Coles and Sandra Coles (née Young); m. Jane Hallowell 1960; three s. *Education:* Harvard Coll. and Columbia Univ. *Career:* Intern, Univ. of Chicago clinics 1954–55; Resident in Psychiatry, Mass. Gen. Hosp., Boston 1955–56, McLean Hosp., Belmont 1956–57; Resident in Child Psychiatry, Judge Baker Guidance Center, Children's Hosp., Roxbury, Mass. 1957–58, Fellow 1960–61; mem. psychiatric staff, Mass. Gen. Hosp. 1960–62; Clinical Asst in Psychiatry, Harvard Univ. Medical School 1960–62; Research Psychiatrist in Health Services, Harvard Univ. 1963–, Lecturer in Gen. Educ. 1966–, Prof. of Psychiatry and Medical Humanities, Harvard Univ. Medical School 1977–; mem. American Psychiatric Asscn; Fellow, American Acad. of Arts and Sciences. *Publications:* Harvard Diary 1988, Times of Surrender: Selected Essays 1989, The Spiritual Life of Children, Handing One Another Along: Literature and Social Reflection 2010; numerous books and articles in professional journals. *Honours:* awards include Pulitzer Prize for vols II and III of Children of Crisis 1973, Sara Josepha Hale Award 1986. *Address:* POB 674, Concord, MA 01742-0674; 81 Carr Road, Concord, MA 01742, USA (home). *Telephone:* (617) 495-3736 (office); (617) 369-6498 (home).

COLFER, Eoin; Irish children's writer; b. 14 May 1965, Wexford; m. Jackie; two s. *Career:* fmr teacher; invited to write new novel in Hitchhiker's Guide to the Galaxy series 2008. *Publications:* juvenile: Benny and Omar 1998, Benny and Babe 1999, The Wish List 2000, Artemis Fowl 2001, Artemis Fowl: The Arctic Incident 2002, Artemis Fowl: The Eternity Code 2003, The Seventh Dwarf (novella) 2004, The Legend of Spud Murphy 2004, The Supernaturalist 2004, The Artemis Fowl Files 2004, Artemis Fowl: The Opal Deception 2005, Artemis Fowl and the Lost Colony 2006, Half Moon Investigations 2006, Airman 2008, Artemis Fowl and the Atlantis Complex 2010; for younger children: Going Potty 1999, Ed's Funny Feet 2000, Ed's Bed 2001; has also written plays; other: And Another Thing ... Douglas Adams' Hitchhiker's Guide to the Galaxy: Part Six of Three 2009. *Honours:* British Book Awards WH Smith Children's Book of the Year 2001, WH Smith Book Award 2002, German Children's Book Award 2004. *Address:* 1 Priory Hall, Spawell Road, Wexford, Ireland (office); Brookes Batchellor LLP, 102–108 Clerkenwell Road, London, EC1M 5SA, England. *Website:* www.eoincolfer.com.

COLL, Steve; American editor and journalist; *President, New America Foundation*. *Education:* Thomas S. Wootton High School, Occidental Coll. *Career:* joined The Washington Post 1985, Financial Corresp., Investigative Corresp., South Asia Corresp. 1989–92, Man. Ed. 1998–2004, Assoc. Ed. 2004–05; staff writer, The New Yorker 2005–; Pres. New America Foundation 2007–. *Publications include:* The Deal of the Century: The Break Up of AT&T 1986, The Taking of Getty Oil: The Full Story of the Most Spectacular – and Catastrophic – Takeover of All Time 1989, Eagle on the Street (with David A. Vise) 1991, On the Grand Trunk Road: A Journey into South Asia 1993, Ghost Wars: The Secret History of the CIA, Afghanistan and bin Laden, from the Soviet Invasion to September 10, 2001 (Pulitzer Prize 2005) 2004, The Bin Ladens: An Arabian Family in the American Century (Nat. Book Critics' Circle Award) 2008. *Honours:* Pulitzer Prize 1990, SAJA Journalism Leader Award 2002. *Address:* New America Foundation, 1630 Connecticut Avenue NW, 7th Floor, Washington, DC 20009, USA England (office). *Telephone:* (202) 986-2700 (office). *Fax:* (202) 986-3696 (office). *E-mail:* president@newamerica .net (office). *Website:* www.newamerica.net (office).

COLLEY, Linda Jane, CBE, PhD, FRSL, FBA; British academic and writer; *Shelby M.C. Davis 1958 Professor of History, Princeton University*; b. 13 Sept. 1949, Chester, England; d. of Roy Colley and the late Marjorie Colley (née Hughes); m. David Nicholas Cannadine (q.v.) 1982; one d. (deceased). *Education:* Univs of Bristol and Cambridge. *Career:* Eugenie Strong Research Fellow, Girton Coll., Cambridge 1975–78, Fellow, Newnham Coll., Cambridge 1978–79, Christ's Coll., Cambridge 1979–81; Asst Prof. of History, Yale Univ., USA 1982–85, Assoc. Prof. 1985–90, Prof. of History 1990–92, Richard M. Colgate Prof. of History 1992–98, Dir Lewis Walpole Library 1982–96; Prof., School of History, LSE 1998–2003, Leverhulme Personal Research Prof., European Inst. 1998–2003; Shelby M.C. Davis 1958 Prof. of History, Princeton Univ., USA 2003–; mem. Bd British Library 1999–2003, Princeton University Press 2007–; mem. Advisory Bd Tate Britain 1999–2003, Paul Mellon Centre for British Art 1999–2003; Visiting Fellowship, Humanities Research Centre, ANU, Canberra 2005; Glaxo-Smith-Kline Sr Fellowship Nat. Humanities Center, NC 2006; Fletcher Jones Distinguished Fellowship, Huntington Library, Calif. 2010. *Exhibitions:* guest-curated "Taking Liberties" exhbn, British Library 2008–09. *Publications:* In Defiance of Oligarchy: The Tory Party 1714–60 1982, Namier 1989, Crown Pictorial: Art and the British Monarchy 1990, Britons: Forging the Nation 1707–1837 (Wolfson Prize 1993) 1992, Captives: Britain, Empire and the World 1600–1850 2002, The Ordeal of Elizabeth Marsh: A Woman in World History 2007 (rated one of the ten best books of the year by The New York Times 2007), Taking Stock of Taking Liberties (catalogue of British Library exhbn) 2008; numerous articles and reviews in UK and American learned journals. *Honours:* Hon. Fellow, Christ's Coll., Cambridge 2005; Dr hc (South Bank, London) 1999, (Essex) 2004, (East Anglia) 2005, (Bristol) 2006, (Hull) 2012; Wolfson Prize 1993, Anstey Lecturer, Univ. of Kent 1994, William Church Memorial Lecturer, Brown Univ. 1994, Distinguished Lecturer in British History, Univ. of Texas 1995, Trevelyan Lecturer, Univ. of Cambridge 1997, Wiles Lecturer, Queen's Univ. Belfast 1997, Prime Minister's Millennium Lecture 2000, Raleigh Lecturer, British Acad. 2002, Nehru Lecturer 2002, Bateson Lecturer, Oxford 2003, Chancellor Dunning Trust Lecturer, Queen's Univ., Ont. 2004, Byrn Lecturer, Vanderbilt Univ. 2005, Annual Lecture in Int. History, LSE 2006, C.P. Snow Lecture, Cambridge 2007, Pres's Lecture, Princeton Univ. 2007, Political Science Quarterly Lecture 2007, Gordon B. Hinkley Lecturer 2010, Univ. of Utah, Bosley-Warnock Lecturer, Univ. of Delaware 2010, Annual ISEHR Lecturer,

Delhi 2011, Keyser Lecturer, George Washington Univ. 2011. *Literary Agent:* c/o Gill Coleridge, Rogers, Coleridge & White Ltd, 20 Powis Mews, London, W11 1JN, England. *Address:* Department of History, Princeton University, 129 Dickinson Hall, Princeton, NJ 08544-1017, USA (office). *Telephone:* (609) 258-8076 (office). *E-mail:* lcolley@princeton.edu (office). *Website:* his.princeton.edu (office).

COLLIER, Catrin (see Watkins, Karen Christna)

COLLIER, Michael Robert, BA, MFA; American academic, poet, writer and editor; *Professor of English, University of Maryland at College Park*; b. 25 May 1953, Phoenix, Ariz.; m. Katherine A. Branch 1981; two s. *Education:* Connecticut Coll., Univ. of Arizona. *Career:* Lecturer in English, George Mason Univ. 1982, Trinity Coll., Washington, DC 1982–83; Writing Staff, The Writer's Center, Bethesda, MD 1982–85; Visiting Lecturer 1984–85, Adjunct Instructor 1985–86, Asst Prof. of English 1986–90, Prof. of English 1995–, Univ. of Maryland at Coll. Park; Visiting Lecturer, Johns Hopkins Univ. 1986–89, Yale Univ. 1990, 1992; Teacher, Warren Wilson Coll. 1991–93, 1996; Assoc. Staff 1992–94, Dir 1994–, Bread Loaf Writers' Conf., Middlebury Coll.; mem. Acad. of American Poets; Poetry Soc. of America; Writing Fellow, Fine Arts Work Center, Provincetown 1979–80; Theodore Morrison Fellow in Poetry 1986, Fellow, Timothy Dwight Coll., Yale Univ. 1992–96. *Publications include:* prose: The Book of Life 2007, Secret of the Ages 2008, The Life Magnet 2010; poetry: The Clasp and Other Poems 1986, The Folded Heart 1989, The Neighbor 1995, The Ledge 2000, Dark Wild Realm 2006; ed.: The Wesleyan Tradition: Four Decades of American Poetry 1993, The New Bread Loaf Anthology of Contemporary American Poetry (with Stanley Plumly) 1999, The New American Poets: A Bread Loaf Anthology 2000; contribs to anthologies, journals and magazines. *Honours:* 'Discovery' The Nation Award 1981, Margaret Bridgeman Scholar in Poetry 1981, Bread Loaf Writers' Conference; Nat. Endowment for the Arts Creative Writing Fellowships, 1984, 1994, Alice Faye di Castagnola Award, Poetry Soc. of America 1988, Guggenheim Fellowship 1995–96, Maryland Arts Council Grant, 2000, Poet Laureate of Maryland 2001. *E-mail:* collierm@umd.edu (office).

COLLINS, Billy, PhD; American poet and academic; *Distinguished Professor, Lehman College, City University of New York*; b. 22 March 1941, New York; m. Diane Collins 1979. *Education:* Holy Cross Coll., Univ. of California at Riverside. *Career:* Prof. of English Lehman Coll., City Univ. of New York 1969–2001, Distinguished Prof. 2001–; Visiting Writer Poets House, N Ireland 1993–96, Lenoir-Rhyne Coll. 1994, Ohio State Univ. 1998; Resident Poet Burren Coll. of Art, Ireland 1996, Sarah Lawrence Coll. 1998–2000; Adjunct Prof. Columbia Univ. 2000–01; conducts summer poetry workshops at Univ. Coll. Galway, Ireland; Library of Congress's Poet Laureate Consultant in Poetry 2001, US Poet Laureate 2001–03; Fellow, New York Foundation for the Arts, Nat. Endowment for the Arts, Guggenheim Foundation; NEA Fellowship 1993; Guggenheim Fellowship 1995. *Publications include:* Pokerface 1977, Video Poems 1980, The Apple that Astonished Paris 1988, Questions About Angels 1991, The Art of Drowning 1995, Picnic, Lightning 1998, Taking Off Emily Dickinson's Clothes 2000, Sailing Alone Around the Room: New and Selected Poems 2001, Nine Horses 2002, The Trouble with Poetry 2005, She Was Just Seventeen 2006, Ballistics 2008, Horoscopes for the Dead 2010; editor: Poetry 180: A Turning Back to Poetry, 180 More: Extraordinary Poems for Everyday Life; poems in many anthologies, including The Best American Poetry 1992, 1993, 1997 and periodicals, including Poetry, American Poetry, Review, American Scholar, Harper's, Paris Review and The New Yorker. *Honours:* New York Foundation for the Arts Poetry Fellowship 1986, Nat. Endowment for the Arts Creative Writing Fellowship 1988, Nat. Poetry Series Competition Winner 1990, Bess Hokin Prize 1991, Literary Lion, New York Public Library 1992, Frederick Bock Prize 1992, Guggenheim Fellowship 1993, Levinson Prize 1995, Paterson Poetry Prize 1999, J. Howard and Barbara M. J. Wood Prize 1999, Pushcart Prize 2002, Poet Laureate of New York State 2004–06. *Literary Agent:* Steven Barclay Agency, 12 Western Avenue, Petaluma, CA 94952, USA. *Telephone:* (718) 960-8550. *Website:* www.barclayagency.com. *Address:* c/o Lehman College, 250 Bedford Park Boulevard West, Business Office, Shuster Hall Building, Bronx, New York, NY 10468, USA (office); 185 Route 202, Somers, NY 10589 (home). *Website:* www.lehman.cuny.edu (office); www.bigsnap.com (home).

COLLINS, Gail, BA, MA; American writer, editor and columnist; b. 25 Nov. 1945, Cincinnati, Ohio; m. Dan Collins. *Education:* Marquette Univ., Univ. of Massachusetts, Columbia Univ. *Career:* early career writing for newspapers in Milwaukee and Conn.; f. Conn. State News Bureau 1970s; columnist, United Press Int., New York Daily News 1985–91, New York Newsday 1991–95; mem. Editorial Bd, New York Times 1995–, later Op-Ed. columnist, Editorial Page Ed. (first woman) 2001–07, columnist 2007–. *Publications include:* The Millennium Book (with Dan Collins), Scorpion Tongues: The Irresistible History of Gossip in American Politics 1998, America's Women: Four Hundred Years of Dolls, Drudges, Helpmates and Heroines 2003, When Everything Changed: The Amazing Journey of American Women from 1960 to the Present 2009. *Address:* New York Times, 620 Eighth Avenue, New York, NY 10018, USA (office). *Telephone:* (212) 556-1234 (office). *Website:* www.nytimes.com (office).

COLLINS, Jackie; British novelist; b. 4 Oct. 1937, sister of Joan Collins (q.v.); *TV mini-series include:* Hollywood Wives (ABC TV), Lucky Chances (NBC TV), Lady Boss (NBC TV). *Screenplays include:* Yesterday's Hero, The World is Full of Married Men, The Stud. *Publications include:* The World is Full of Married Men 1968, The Stud 1969, Sunday Simmons and Charlie Brick 1971, Lovehead 1974, The World is Full of Divorced Women 1975, Lovers and Gamblers 1977, The Bitch 1979, Chances 1981, Hollywood Wives 1983, Lucky 1985, Hollywood Husbands 1986, Rock Star 1988, Lady Boss 1990, American Star 1993, Hollywood Kids 1994, Vendetta – Lucky's Revenge 1996, Thrill 1998, LA Connections (four-part serial novel) 1998, Dangerous Kiss 1999, Hollywood Wives: The New Generation 2001, Lethal Seduction 2001, Deadly Embrace 2002, Hollywood Divorces 2003, Lovers and Players 2006, Drop Dead Beautiful 2007, Married Lovers 2008, Poor Little Bitch Girl 2010, Goddess of Vengeance 2011. *Honours:* Galaxy Nat. Book Award for Outstanding Achievement 2011. *Address:* Steve Troha, St Martin's Press, 175 Fifth Avenue, New York, NY 10010, USA. *Telephone:* (646) 307-5569. *E-mail:* steve.troha@stmartins.com. *Website:* www.jackiecollins.com.

COLLINS, James (Jim) Lee; American author and editor; b. 30 Dec. 1945, Beloit, Wis.; m. Joan Hertel 1974; two s. *Career:* mem. Colorado Authors League, Nat. Writers Club, Western Writers of America. *Publications include:* Comanche Trail 1984, Gone to Texas 1984, War Clouds 1984, Campaigning 1985, Orphans Preferred 1985, Riding Shotgun 1985, Mister Henry 1986, The Brass Boy 1987, Spencer's Revenge 1987, Western Writers Handbook 1987, Teaching and Learning Language Collaboratively 1991, Restructuring the English Classroom 1992, Settling the American West 1993, Strategies for Struggling Writers 1998; contribs to The Blue and the Gray, Writers Digest Magazine.

COLLINS, Joan Henrietta, OBE; British actress and author; b. 23 May 1933, London; d. of Joseph William Collins and Elsa Collins (née Bessant); sister of Jackie Collins (q.v.); m. 1st Maxwell Reed 1954 (divorced 1957); m. 2nd George Anthony Newley 1963 (divorced 1970); one s. one d.; m. 3rd Ronald S. Kass 1972 (divorced 1983); one d.; m. 4th Peter Holm 1985 (divorced 1987); m. 5th Percy Gibson 2002. *Education:* RADA. *Career:* actress in numerous stage, film, and TV productions, producer and author. *Plays include:* The Last of Mrs Cheyne, London 1979–80, Private Lives London 1990, Broadway 1991, Love Letters, USA tour 2000, Over the Moon, London 2001, Full Circle (UK tour) 2004. *Films include:* I Believe in You 1952, Our Girl Friday 1953, The Good Die Young 1954, Land of the Pharaohs 1955, The Virgin Queen 1955, The Girl in the Red Velvet Swing 1955, The Opposite Sex 1956, Island in the Sun 1957, Sea Wife 1957, The Bravados 1958, Seven Thieves 1960, Road to Hong Kong 1962, Warning Shot 1966, The Executioner 1969, Quest for Love 1971, Revenge 1971, Alfie Darling 1974, The Stud 1979, The Bitch 1980, The Big Sleep, Tales of the Unexpected, Neck 1983, Georgy Porgy 1983, Nutcracker 1984, Decadence 1994, In the Bleak Midwinter 1995, Hart to Hart 1995, Annie: A Royal Adventure 1995, The Clandestine Marriage 1998, Joseph and the Amazing Technicolor Dreamcoat 1999, The Flintstones – Viva Rock Vegas 2000, These Old Broads 2000, Clandestine Marriage 2001, Ozzie 2001. *Television appearances include:* Dynasty (series) 1981–89, Cartier Affair 1985, Sins 1986, Monte Carlo 1986, Tonight at 8.30 1991, Pacific Palisades (series) 1997, Will and Grace 2000, Guiding Light 2002, Hotel Babylon 2006, Footballers Wives 2006. *Publications include:* Past Imperfect 1978, The Joan Collins Beauty Book 1980, Katy, A Fight for Life 1982, Prime Time 1988, Love and Desire and Hate 1990, My Secrets 1994, Too Damn Famous 1995, Second Act 1996, My Friends' Secrets 1999, Star Quality 2002, Joan's Way 2002, Misfortune's Daughters 2004. *Honours:* Best TV Actress, Golden Globe, 1982; Favourite TV Performer, People's Choice 1985. *Address:* c/o Paul Keylock, 16 Bulbecks Walk, South Woodham Ferrers, Essex, CM3 5ZN, England (office). *Telephone:* (1245) 328367 (office). *Fax:* (1245) 328625 (office). *E-mail:* pkeylock@aol.com (office). *Website:* www.joancollins.net (office).

COLLINS, Merle, BA, MA, PhD; Grenadian poet and novelist; *Professor of Comparative Literature, University of Maryland*; b. 29 Sept. 1950, d. of John Collins and Helena Collins. *Education:* Univ. of the West Indies, Georgetown Univ., USA and London School of Econs, UK. *Career:* fmr high school teacher in Grenada and Saint Lucia; research co-ordinator for govt 1981; Writer-in-Residence, London Borough of Waltham Forest, UK 1987; Lecturer in Caribbean Studies, Univ. of North London 1990–95; Prof. of Creative Writing and Caribbean Literature, Univ. of Maryland, USA 1995, Faculty Dir Maryland in Mexico Programme 1997, currently Prof. of Comparative Literature; mem. African Dawn music and poetry group 1985–; numerous appearances on TV and radio programmes; reviewer for Ariel, Journal of the Asscn of Caribbean Women Writers. *Publications include:* Because the Dawn Breaks (poems) 1985, Angel (novel) 1987, Rain Darling (short stories) 1990, Rotten Pomerack (poems) 1992, The Colour of Forgetting (novel) 1995, Lady in a Boat (poems) 2003, The Ladies are Upstairs (novel) 2011; contribs to Callaloo: A Grenada Anthology 1984, Watchers and Seekers: Creative Writing by Black Women in Britain 1987, Facing the Sea: An Anthology of Writing from the Caribbean 1990, Penguin Modern Poets Vol. 8 1996, The Oxford Book of Caribbean Short Stories 1999. *Honours:* Guggenheim Fellowship 2003–04. *Address:* Department of English, University of Maryland, Room 4145, Susquehanna Hall, College Park, MD 20742-8825, USA (office). *Telephone:* (301) 405-3775 (office). *E-mail:* collinsm@umd.edu (office). *Website:* www.english.umd.edu (office).

COLLINS, Michael, PhD; Irish writer and athlete; b. 1964, Limerick. *Education:* Univ. of Notre Dame, USA. *Career:* taught at various colls, including Art Inst. of Chicago, Western Washington Univ., Univ. of Notre Dame; worked for Microsoft, USA; as an 'extreme' athlete, has won The Last Marathon, Antarctica (co-winner) 1997, Redwoods Marathon 1997, The

Himalayan 100 Mile Stage Race 1999, The Everest Challenge Marathon 1999, The North Pole Marathon 2006; also completed The Sahara Half Marathon 2005, Bronze Medal at World 100km (62 Miles) Championship in Gibraltar 2010 (also captain of the Irish team). *Publications include:* novels: The Meat Eaters 1993, The Life and Times of a Teaboy 1995, Emerald Underground 1999, The Keepers of Truth (Kerry Ingredients Irish Novel of the Year) 2000, The Resurrectionists (PNBA Novel of the Year 2003) 2002, Exodus 2004, Lost Souls (USA Today Editor's Choice) 2005, The Secret Life of E. Robert Pendleton (The Breakout Novel of the Year in France 2008) 2006, Of Uncertain Significance 2011; short stories: The Man Who Dreamt of Lobsters 1993, The Feminists Go Swimming 2003, Write to Work 2010. *Honours:* Hennessy/Sunday Tribune Award, Ireland, Pushcart Prize for short stories, Univ. of Notre Dame Graduate School Alumni of the Year 2008. *Address:* c/o Weidenfeld & Nicolson, Orion House, 5 Upper St Martin's Lane, London, WC2H 9EA, England. *E-mail:* michaelcollinsauthor@michaelcollinsauthor.net (office). *Website:* www.michaelcollinsauthor.net.

COLLINS, Suzanne, BA; American author and screenwriter; b. 10 Aug. 1962, Hartford, Conn.; m.; two c. *Education:* Alabama School of Fine Arts, Indiana Univ. *Career:* television writer for children's series; wrote five books in the Underland Chronicles series for young readers 2003–07; wrote The Hunger Games trilogy 2008–10. *Television:* as writer: Clarissa Explains It All 1993, Little Bear 1995, The Mystery Files of Shelby Woo (also story editor) 1996–98, Generation O! (also series co-creator) 2000–01, Santa Baby 2001 (TV film), Wow! Wow! Wubbzy! 2008–09. *Film:* The Hunger Games (screenplay) 2012. *Publications include:* children's fiction: The Underland Chronicles: Gregor the Overlander 2003, Gregor and the Prophecy of Bane 2004, When Charlie McButton Lost Power 2005, Gregor and the Curse of the Warmbloods 2005, Gregor and the Marks of Secret 2006, Gregor and the Code of Claw 2007, When Charlie McButton Gained Power 2009; fiction: The Hunger Games 2008, Catching Fire 2009, Mockingjay 2010. *Honours:* NAIBA Children's Novel Award 2004, KIRKUS Best Young Adult Book 2008, CYBIL Award for Fantasy and Science Fiction 2008, Georgia Peach Book Awards for Teen Readers 2010, California Young Reader Medal 2011. *Address:* c/o Scholastic Publishing Inc., 557 Broadway, New York, NY 10012, USA (office). *Telephone:* (212) 343-6100 (office). *Fax:* (212) 343-6930 (office). *Website:* www.scholastic.com (office); www.suzannecollinsbooks.com.

COLLIS, Louise Edith, BA; British writer; b. 29 Jan. 1925, Arakan, Burma; d. of the late Maurice Collis and Eleanor Collis. *Education:* Univ. of Reading. *Career:* mem. Soc. of Authors, Int. Asscn of Art Critics. *Publications include:* Without a Voice 1951, A Year Passed 1952, After the Holiday 1954, The Angel's Name 1955, Seven in the Tower 1958, The Apprentice Saint 1964, Soldier in Paradise 1965, The Great Flood 1966, A Private View of Stanley Spencer 1972, Maurice Collis Diaries (ed.) 1976, Impetuous Heart: The Story of Ethel Smyth 1984, Memoirs of a Medieval Woman 1991; contrib. to Books and Bookmen, Connoisseur, Art and Artists, Arts Review, Collectors Guide, Art and Antiques. *Address:* 65 Cornwall Gardens, London, SW7 4BD, England (home). *Telephone:* (20) 7937-1950 (home).

COLOMBANI, Jean-Marie; French journalist; b. 7 July 1948, Dakar, Senegal; m. Catherine Sénès 1976; five c. *Education:* Lycée Hoche, Versailles, Lycée La Pérouse, Nouméa, New Caledonia, Univ. of Paris II-Assas, Univ. of Paris I Panthéon-Sorbonne, Inst. d'Etudes Politiques, Paris and Inst. d'Etudes Supérieures de Droit Public. *Career:* journalist, ORTF, later Office of FR3, Nouméa 1973; Ed. Political Service, Le Monde 1977, Head of Political Service 1983, Ed.-in-Chief 1990, Deputy Editorial Dir 1991; Man. Dir S.A.–Le Monde March–Dec. 1994, Chair. of Bd and Dir of Publs 1994–2007, mem. Bd of Dirs 2007–08; Co-founder online magazine in France based on Slate.com 2009; Chair. Advisory Council, Midi-Libre Group 2000–. *Publications:* Contradictions: entretiens avec Anicet Le Pors 1984, L'utopie calédonienne 1985, Portrait du président ou le monarque imaginaire 1985, Le mariage blanc (co-author) 1986, Questions de confiance: entretiens avec Raymond Barre 1987, Les héritiers (co-author), La France sans Mitterrand 1992, La gauche survivra-t-elle aux socialistes? 1994, Le Double Septennat de François Mitterrand, Dernier Inventaire (jtly) 1995, De la France en général et de ses dirigeants en particulier 1996, Le Résident de la République 1998, La Cinquième ou la République des phratries (co-author) 1999, Les infortunes de la Republique 2000, Tous Américains? 2002. *Address:* 12, rue d' Athènes, 75009, Paris (office); 5 rue Joseph Bara, 75006 Paris, France (home). *Telephone:* 1-79-85-81-14 (office). *E-mail:* jmc@jmcmedia.fr (office). *Website:* www.slate.fr.

COLOMBO, John Robert, CM, BA, DLitt; Canadian editor, author and consultant; b. 24 March 1936, Kitchener, Ont.; m. Ruth F. Brown 1959; two s. one d. *Education:* Kitchener-Waterloo Collegiate Inst., Waterloo Coll. and Univ. Coll., Univ. of Toronto. *Career:* editorial asst, Univ. of Toronto Press 1957–59; Asst Ed. The Ryerson Press 1960–63; Instructor, York Univ., Downsview, Ont. 1963–65; Consulting Ed. McClelland & Stewart 1963–70, Ed.-at-Large 1963–; Gen. Ed. The Canadian Global Almanac 1992–2000; Writer-in-residence, Mohawk Coll., Hamilton, Ont. 1979–80; Consultant, American Man. Asscn/Canadian Man. Centre; Assoc. Northrop Frye Centre, Victoria Coll., Univ. of Toronto. *Television:* Presenter: Colombo Quotes (series), CBC-TV 1978, Unexplained Canada (series), Space Network 2006. *Publications include:* over 200 books of poetry, prose, reference, science fiction anthologies and translations including Colombo's Canadian Quotations 1974, Colombo's Canadian References 1976, Colombo's Book of Canada 1978, Canadian Literary Landmarks 1984, 1,001 Questions about Canada 1986, Colombo's New Canadian Quotations 1987, Mysterious Canada 1988, Songs of the Great Land 1989, Mysterious Encounters 1990, The Dictionary of Canadian Quotations 1991, UFOs over Canada 1991, Worlds in Small 1992, The Mystery of the Shaking Tent 1993, Walt Whitman's Canada 1993, Voices of Rama 1994, 1995, Close Encounters of the Canadian Kind 1995, Ghost Stories of Ontario 1995, Haunted Toronto 1996, The New Consciousness 1997, Weird Stories 1999, Ghosts in our Past 2000, 1000 Questions about Canada 2001, The Penguin Book of Canadian Jokes 2002, The Penguin Treasury of Popular Canadian Poems and Songs 2002, The Penguin Book of More Canadian Jokes 2003, O Rare Denis Saurat 2003, True Canadian Ghost Stories 2003, The Midnight Hour 2004, The Denis Saurat Reader 2004, The Monster Book of Canadian Monsters 2004, Early Earth 2006, All the Poems 2006, All the Aphorisms 2006, Autumn in August 2006, Miniatures 2006, The Penguin Dictionary of Popular Canadian Quotations 2006, Terrors of the Night 2007, The Big Book of Canadian Ghost Stories 2008, Whistle While You Work 2008, A Far Cry 2009, The Big Book of Canadian Hauntings 2009, Indifferences 2009. *Honours:* Order of Cyril and Methodius 1979; Esteemed Kt of Mark Twain 1979; Hon. DLitt (York Univ., Toronto) 1998; Centennial Medal 1967, Harbour Front Literary Prize 1985. *Address:* 42 Dell Park Avenue, Toronto, ON M6B 2T6, Canada (home). *Telephone:* (416) 782-6853 (home). *Fax:* (416) 782-0285 (home). *E-mail:* jrc@ca.inter.net (office). *Website:* www.colombo-plus.ca (home).

COMAN, Otilia Valeria, (Ana Blandiana), BA; Romanian writer and poet; *President, Academia Civica Foundation and Romanian PEN Centre*; b. 25 March 1942, Timişoara; d. of Gheorghe Coman and Otilia Coman; m. Romulus Rusan 1960. *Education:* Univ. of Cluj. *Career:* columnist, Romania (literary magazine) 1974–88; has given numerous lectures on cultural and civic issues in Italy, Spain, UK, France, Netherlands, Norway, Austria and Germany; participated in int. seminars on human rights and multiculturalism in Canada, France, Greece, Germany, USA, Norway and Russian Fed., confs at Univ. of Rome 1991, The German Rectors' Conf., Bonn 1992, Free Univ. of Berlin 1992, Univ. of Paris, Sorbonne 1993, Univ. of Vienna 1994, Univ. of Prague 1994, Univ. of Heidelberg, Austria 1995, INALCO, Paris 1996, and poetry festivals in Finland, Paris, Romania, USA, Italy, UK, France, Austria and Norway; Pres. Academia Civica Foundation, Romanian PEN Centre; Founder and Leader, Civic Alliance Foundation 1994; mem. European Acad. of Poetry, Acad. of Poetry Stéphane Mallarmé, Writers' Union of Romania. *Publications include:* poetry: The Third Sacrament 1960, First Person in the Plural 1964, The Vulnerable Heel 1966, 50 Poems 1970, Poems 1974, The Sleep in the Sleep 1977, Events in my Garden 1980, The Eye of the Cricket 1981, October, November, December 1982, The Sand Hour 1984, The Prey Star 1986, Other Events in my Garden 1987, Events on my Street 1988, Poems 1988, The Architecture of the Waves 1990, 100 Poems 1991, The Ebb of the Senses 2004; essays: The Witness Quality 1970, I Write, You Write, He/She Writes 1975, The Most Beautiful of the Possible Worlds 1978, Passage of Mirrors 1983, Self-portrait with Palimpsest 1985, City of Syllables 1987, To Be Or To See 2005; short stories: Four Seasons 1977, Projects of the Past 1982, Imitation of a Nightmare 1995, The Melted Town and Other Fantastical Stories 2004; novels: The Drawer with Applause 1992, The Sun After the Death 2002. *Honours:* Romanian Writers' Union Poetry Prize 1969, 2000, Romanian Acad. Poetry Prize 1970, Asscn of Writers in Bucharest Poetry Prize 1980, Int. Herder Prize, Austria 1982, Opera Omnia Prize 2002, Int. Vilenica Prize, Slovenia 2002, Premio Int. per la poesia, Camaiore, Italy 2004, Premio Acerbi per la Poesia, Italy 2004, European Poetry Prize, KOV, Serbia 2009. *Address:* Academia Civica, Piata Amzei 13 et 2, CP 22-216, Bucharest, Romania (office). *Telephone:* (21) 3129852 (office). *Fax:* (21) 3125854 (office). *E-mail:* acivica@memorialsighet.ro (office). *Website:* www.anablandiana.eu.

COMAROFF, John Lionel, BA, PhD; American writer; *Harold H. Swift Distinguished Service Professor of Anthropology and Social Sciences, University of Chicago*; b. 1 Jan. 1945, Cape Town, South Africa; m. Jean Rakoff 1967; one s. one d. *Education:* Univ. of Cape Town, London School of Econs, UK. *Career:* Lecturer in Social Anthropology, Univ. Coll. of Swansea, UK 1971–72, Univ. of Manchester, UK 1972–78; Visiting Asst Prof. of Anthropology, Univ. of Chicago 1978, Assoc. Prof. of Anthropology and Sociology 1981–87, Prof. of Anthropology and Social Sciences 1987–96, Harold H. Swift Distinguished Service Prof. of Anthropology and Social Sciences 1996–; Directeur d'Études, École des Hautes Études en Sciences Sociales, Paris, France 1988, Directeur d'Études Associé 1995; Visiting Scholar, Centre for Modern Oriental Studies, Berlin, Germany 1998; Visiting Research Assoc., Univ. of the North West, SA 1999–2000; Visiting Prof., Tel-Aviv Univ., Israel 2000, Univ. of Basel, Switzerland 2005; mem. Royal Anthropological Inst., African Studies Asscn, Int. African Inst., Asscn of Social Anthroplogists, American Anthropological Asscn, Asscn of Political and Legal Anthropology (Pres. 1995–96); Fellow, Radcliffe Inst. for Advanced Study, Harvard Univ. 2003; Faculty Fellow and Co-founder Chicago Center for Contemporary Theory 2004–. *Publications include:* The Structure of Agricultural Transformation in Barolong 1977, Rules and Processes: The Cultural Logic of Dispute in an African Context (with S. A. Roberts) 1981, Of Revelation and Revolution: Christianity and Colonialism in South Africa (with Jean Comaroff) 1991, Ethnography and the Historical Imagination (with Jean Comaroff) 1992, Modernity and its Malcontents: Ritual and Power in Africa (co-ed. with Jean Comaroff) 1993, Perspectives on Nationalism and War (co-ed. with Paul C. Stern) 1993, Millennial Capitalism and the Culture of Neoliberalism (co-ed. with Jean Comaroff) 2001, Perspectives on African Modernities 2002, Law and Disorder in the Postcolony (co-ed. with Jean Comaroff) 2006, Ethnicity, Inc. (co-ed. with

Jean Comaroff) 2009, Vital Matters: Religious Movements, Emergent Socialities and the Post-Nation 2010, American Anthropologist 2010; contribs to scholarly books and journals. *Honours:* Hon. Prof., Univ. of Cape Town 2004–; Nat. Endowment for the Humanities grants 1984–85, 1986–87, NSF Grants 1986–87, 1993, Spencer Foundation Grant 1991, Laing Prize, Univ. of Chicago 1993, American Acad. of Arts and Sciences 1995, Spencer Foundation Mentor Award 1996. *Address:* Department of Anthropology, University of Chicago, 1126 East 59th Street, Chicago, IL 60637, USA (office). *Telephone:* (773) 702-7768 (office). *E-mail:* jcomarof@uchicago.edu (office). *Website:* anthropology.uchicago.edu (office).

COMINI, Alessandra, BA, MA, PhD; American art historian, musicologist, academic, author and lecturer; *University Distinguished Professor Emerita of Art History, Southern Methodist University, Dallas*; b. 24 Nov. 1934, Winona, Minn.; d. of Raiberto Comini and Megan Laird. *Education:* Barnard Coll., Univ. of California, Berkeley, Columbia Univ., New York. *Career:* Instructor, Columbia Univ. 1968–69, Asst Prof. 1970–74; Assoc. Prof., Southern Methodist Univ. 1974–75, Prof. 1975–83, Univ. Distinguished Prof. of Art History 1983–2005, now Emer.; Alfred Hodder Fellow, Princeton Univ. 1972–73; Visiting Asst Prof., Yale Univ. 1973; Assoc. Ed. Arts Magazine 1977–88; Lansdown Prof., Univ. of Victoria, BC 1981; Visiting Distinguished Prof., California State Univ., Chico 1990; Distinguished Visiting Fellow, European Humanities Research Centre, Univ. of Oxford 1996; mem. Coll. Art Asscn of America, Texas Inst. of Letters, Women's Caucus for Art. *Publications include:* Schiele in Prison 1973, Egon Schiele's Portraits 1974, Gustav Klimt 1975, Egon Schiele 1976, The Fantastic Art of Vienna 1978, The Changing Image of Beethoven: A Study in Mythmaking 1987, Egon Schiele's Nudes 1994, In Passionate Pursuit: A Memoir 2004; contrib. to books, journals, magazines and exhbn catalogues. *Honours:* Grand Decoration of Honor for Services to the Austrian Repub. 1990; Charles Rufus More Book Award, Coll. Art Asscn of America 1976, Lifetime Achievement Award, Women's Caucus for Art 1995, Teacher of the Year Award 1996, Laurence Perrine Prize for Teaching and Scholarship 2003, annual Comini Lecture Series est. in her honour, Southern Methodist Univ. 2005, Distinguished Alumna Award, Barnard Coll. 2011. *Address:* 2900 McFarlin, Dallas, TX 75205, USA (home). *Telephone:* (214) 369-8523 (home). *Fax:* (214) 369-8523 (home). *E-mail:* acomini@smu.edu (office). *Website:* www.alessandracomini.com.

COMPAGNON, Antoine Marcel Thomas; French academic and writer; *Blanche W. Knopf Professor of French and Comparative Literature, Columbia University*; b. 20 July 1950, Brussels, Belgium; s. of Gen. Jean Compagnon and Jacqueline Terlinden. *Education:* Lycée Condorcet, Paris, The Maret School, Washington, DC, USA, Prytanée Militaire, La Flèche, Ecole Polytechnique, Paris, Ecole Nat. des Ponts et Chaussées, Paris, Univ. of Paris VII. *Career:* with Fondation Thiers and Research Attaché, CNRS 1975–78; Asst Lecturer, Univ. of Paris VII 1975–80; Asst Lecturer, Ecole des Hautes Etudes en Sciences Sociales, Paris 1977–79; Lecturer, Ecole Polytechnique, Paris 1978–85; teacher at French Inst., London 1980–81; Lecturer, Univ. of Rouen 1981–85; Prof. of French, Columbia Univ., New York 1985–91, Blanche W. Knopf Prof. of French and Comparative Literature 1991–; Visiting Prof., Univ. of Pennsylvania 1986, 1990; Prof., Univ. of Le Mans 1989–90; Prof., Univ. of Paris IV-Sorbonne 1994–2006, Collège de France 2006–; Sec. Gen. Int. Asscn of French Studies 1998–2008; Guggenheim Fellow 1988; Visiting Fellow, All Souls Coll., Oxford 1994; Fellow, American Acad. of Arts and Sciences 1997, Academia Europaea 2006; Corresp. Fellow, British Acad. 2009. *Publications:* La Seconde Main ou le travail de la citation 1979, Le Deuil antérieur 1979, Nous, Michel de Montaigne 1980, La Troisième République des lettres, de Flaubert à Proust 1983, Ferragosto 1985, critical edn of Marcel Proust, Sodome et Gomorrhe 1988, Proust entre deux siècles 1989, Les Cinq Paradoxes de la modernité 1990, Chat en poche: Montaigne et l'allégorie 1993, Connaissez-vous Brunetière? 1997, Le Démon de la théorie 1998, Baudelaire devant l'innombrable 2003, Les Antimodernes 2005, Le Cas Bernard Faÿ 2009; numerous articles on French literature and culture. *Honours:* Commdr des Palmes académiques, Chevalier de la Légion d'honneur; Dr hc (King's Coll., London) 2010; Prix Claude Lévi-Strauss 2011. *Address:* Columbia University, Department of French and Romance Philology, 513 Philosophy Hall, 1150 Amsterdam Avenue, New York, NY 10027, USA (office); Collège de France, 11 place Marcelin-Berthelot, 75005 Paris, France (office). *Telephone:* (212) 854-2500 (New York) (office); 1-44-27-10-79 (Paris) (office). *Fax:* (212) 854-5863 (New York) (office). *E-mail:* amc6@columbia.edu (office); antoine.compagnon@college-de-france.fr (office). *Website:* www.columbia.edu/cu/french (office).

COMPTON, David Guy, (Guy Compton, Frances Lynch); British writer; b. 19 Aug. 1930, London, England. *Education:* Cheltenham Coll., Gloucester. *Career:* Ed. Reader's Digest Condensed Books, London, 1969–81; moved to USA 1981. *Publications include:* Too Many Murderers 1962, Medium for Murder 1963, Dead on Cue 1964, Disguise for a Dead Gentleman 1964, High Tide for Hanging 1965, The Quality of Mercy 1965, Farewell Earth's Bliss 1966, The Silent Multitude 1966, And Murder Came Too 1966, Synthajoy 1968, The Palace 1969, The Electric Crocodile 1970, Hot Wireless Sets, Aspirin Tablets, the Sandpaper Sides of Used Matchboxes and Something that Might Have Been Castor Oil 1971, The Missionaries 1972, The Continuous Katherine Mortenhoe 1974, Twice Ten Thousand Miles 1974, The Fine and Handsome Captain 1975, Stranger at the Wedding 1977, A Dangerous Magic 1978, A Usual Lunacy 1978, Windows 1979, In the House of Dark Music 1979, Ascendancies 1980, Scudder's Game 1985, Ragnarok (with John Gribbin) 1991, Nomansland 1992, Stammering 1993, Justice City 1994, Back of Town Blues 1996, In Which Avu Giddy Tries to Stop Dancing 2001. *Honours:* named Author Emer., Science Ficton and Fantasy Writers of America 2007.

CONDÉ, Maryse, PhD; French/American author, dramatist and academic; *Professor Emerita, Columbia University*; b. (Maryse Boucolon), 11 Feb. 1937, Pointe-à-Pitre; m. 1st Mamadou Condé 1958 (divorced 1981); three c.; m. 2nd Richard Philcox 1982. *Education:* Sorbonne, Univ. of Paris. *Career:* Programme Prod., French Services, BBC, London 1968–70, France Culture, Radio France Internationale, Paris 1980–85; Asst, Jussieu campus, Univ. of Paris 1970–72, Lecturer, Nanterre campus 1973–80, Chargé de cours, Sorbonne 1980–85; Prof. of French, Univ. of California at Berkeley 1989–92, Univ. of Maryland at Coll. Park 1992–95, Columbia Univ. 1995– (now Emer.); Visiting Prof., California Inst. of Tech. 1989, Univ. of Virginia 1993–95, Harvard Univ. 1995; many visiting lectureships; Pres. Comité pour la Mémoire de l'Esclavage 2002–05. *Publications include:* fiction: Heremakhonon 1976, Une Saison à Rihata (A Season in Rihata) 1981, Ségou: Les murailles de terre (Segu) 1984, Ségou II: La terre en miettes (The Children of Segu) 1985, Pays Melé, suivi de Nanna-ya (Land of Many Colors, and Nanny-ya) 1985, Moi, Tituba, sorcière noire (I, Tituba, Black Witch of Salem) 1986, La Vie scélérate (Tree of Life) 1987, A Novel of the Caribbean, 1992, Traversée de la mangrove (Crossing the Mangrove) 1990, Les derniers rois mages (The Last of the African Kings) 1992, La colonie du nouveau monde 1993, La migration des coeurs (Windward Heights) 1995, Desirada, 1997, Le Coeur à Rire et à Pleurer: Contes vrais de mon enfance (Tales from the Heart) 1998, Celanire cou-coupé: Roman fantastique (Who Slashed Celanire's Throat?) 2000, La Belle Créole 2001, Histoire de la femme cannibale (The Story of the Cannibal Woman) 2004, Victoire, les saveurs et les mots (Victoire, My Mother's Mother) 2006, Les Belles Ténébreuses 2008, En Attendant la Montee Des Eaux 2010; plays: Dieu nous l'a donné 1972, Mort d'Oluwemi d'Ajumako 1973 Le Morne de Massabielle (The Hills of Massabielle) 1974, Pension les Alizes (The Tropical Breeze Hotel) 1988, Antan Révolysion 1989, Comédie d'amour 1993, Comme deux frères 2007, La Faute à La Vie 2008; children's books: Hugo Le Terrible 1991, La Planète Orbis 2002, Rêves Amers 2005, A La Courbe du Joliba 2006, Chiens Fous dans la Brousse 2008, Savannah Blues 2009, Conte Cruel 2009; other: Anthologie de la littérature africaine d'expression française (ed) 1966, La Poésie antillaise (ed) 1977, Le Roman antillais (ed) 1977, La Civilisation du bossale 1978, Le profil d'une oeuvre: Cahier d'un retour au pays natal 1978, La Parole des femmes: Essai sur des romancières des Antilles de langue française 1979, Bouquet de voix pour Guy Tirolien (ed) 1990, L'héritage de Caliban (co-ed) 1992, Penser la créolite (with Madeleine Cottenet-Hage) 1995, Conversations with Maryse Condé (with Françoise Pfaff) 1996, Nouvelles d'Amérique (co-ed with Lise Gauvin) 1998; contrib. to anthologies and journals. *Honours:* Commdr, Ordre des Arts et des Lettres 2001; Chevalier, Légion d'honneur 2004; Chevalier, Ordre nat. du Mérite 2007, Grand Officier 2011; Dr hc (Occidental Coll.) 1986, (Lehman Coll., CUNY) 1994, (Univ. of the West Indies, Barbados) 2005; Fulbright Scholar 1985–86, Prix littéraire de la Femme (Prix Alain Boucheron) 1986, Guggenheim Fellowship 1987–88, Académie Française Prize 1988, Prix Carbet de la Caraïbe 1997, Marguerite Yourcenar Prize 1999, Lifetime Achievement Award, New York Univ. 1999, Hurston/Wright Legacy Award 2006, Prix Tropiques 2007, Trophées des Arts Afro-Caribéens 2008, 2009, Grand Prix du Livre Metis 2010. *Address:* 456 Riverside Drive, Apt 6B, New York, NY 10027, USA (home); 4 rue Chapon, 75003 Paris, France (home). *E-mail:* mc363@columbia.edu (home).

CONKIN, Paul Keith, BA, MA, PhD; American historian and writer; *Distinguished Research Professor, Vanderbilt University*; b. 25 Oct. 1929, Chuckey, Tenn.; m. Dorothy L. Tharp 1954; one s. two d. *Education:* Milligan Coll., Vanderbilt Univ. *Career:* Asst Prof. of Philosophy and History, Univ. of Southwestern Louisiana 1957–59; Asst Prof., Univ. of Maryland, College Park 1959–61, Assoc. Prof. 1961–66, Prof. of History 1966–67; Prof. of History, Univ. of Wisconsin, Madison 1967–76, Merle Curti Prof. of History 1976–79; Distinguished Prof. of History, Vanderbilt Univ. 1979–2000, Distinguished Research Prof. 2000–; mem. American Historical Asscn, Org. of American Historians, Southern Historical Asscn (Pres. 1996–97). *Publications include:* Tomorrow a New World: The New Deal Community Program 1959, Two Paths to Utopia: The Hutterites and the Llano Colony 1964, F. D. R. and the Origins of the Welfare State 1967, also published as The New Deal 1967, Puritans and Pragmatists: Eight Eminent American Thinkers 1968, The Heritage and Challenge of History (with Roland N. Stromberg) 1971, Self-evident Truths 1974, A History of Recent America (with David Burner) 1974, New Directions in American Intellectual History (co-ed. with John Higham) 1979, Prophets of Prosperity: America's First Political Economists 1980, TVA: Fifty Years of Grass-Roots Bureaucracy (co-ed. with Erwin C. Hargrove) 1983, Gone with the Ivy: A Biography of Vanderbilt University (with Henry Lee Swint and Patricia S. Miletich) 1985, Big Daddy from the Padernales: Lyndon Baines Johnson 1986, The Southern Agrarians 1988, Heritage and Challenge: The History and Theory of History (with Roland N. Stromberg) 1989, Cane Ridge, America's Pentecost 1990, The Four Foundations of American Government: Consent, Limits, Balance, and Participation 1994, The Uneasy Center: Reformed Christianity in Antebellum America 1995, American Originals: Homemade Varieties of Christianity 1997, When All Gods Trembled: Darwinism, Scopes, and American Intellectuals 1998, A Requiem for the American Village 2000, Peabody College 2002, The State of the Earth 2007, A Revolution Down on the Farm 2008; contribs to scholarly books and journals. *Honours:* Albert J. Beveridge Award in American History 1958, Guggenheim Fellowship 1966–67, Nat. Endowment for the Humanities Sr Fellowship

1972–73, Univ. Fellowship 1990. *Address:* 1003 Tyne Blvd, Nashville, TN 37220-1026, USA (home).

CONLEY, Robert Jackson, BA, MA; American writer and poet; *Sequoyah Distinguished Professor in Cherokee Studies, Western Carolina University*; b. 29 Dec. 1940, Cushing, Okla; s. of Robert Parris Conley and Peggy Marie Jackson Conley; m. Evelyn Snell 1978; two c. *Education:* Midwestern State Univ. *Career:* Instructor in English, Northern Illinois Univ. 1968–71, Southwest Missouri State Univ. 1971–74; Co-ordinator of Indian Culture, Eastern Montana Coll. 1975–77; Dir of Indian Studies, Bacone Coll. 1979–80, Morningside Coll. 1979–86, Assoc. Prof. of English 1986–90; Sequoyah Distinguished Prof. in Cherokee Studies, Western Carolina Univ. 2008–; Pres. Western Writers of America; mem. Int. Poetry Soc. *Play:* Mountain Windsong. *Publications include:* Twenty-One Poems 1975, Adawosgi: Swimmer Wesley Snell, A Cherokee Memorial 1980, Echoes of Our Being (ed.) 1982, The Rattlesnake Band and Other Poems 1984, Back to Malachi 1986, The Actor 1987, Killing Time 1988, Wilder and Wilder 1988, Yellow Bird (Spur Award) 1988, The Witch of Goingsnake and Other Stories 1988, Colfax 1989, The Saga of Henry Starr 1989, Quitting Time 1989, Go-ahead Rider 1990, Ned Christie's War 1990, Strange Company 1991, Mountain Windsong: A Novel of the Trail of Tears 1992, The Way of the Priests 1992, Nickajack (Spur Award) 1992, Border Line 1993, The Dark Way 1993, The Long Trail North 1993, The White Path 1993, The Long Way Home 1994, Geronimo: An American Legend (with John Milius and Larry Gross) 1994, To Make a Killing 1994, Crazy Snake 1994, The Way South 1994, Zeke Proctor: Cherokee Outlaw 1994, The Dark Island (Spur Award) 1995, Captain Dutch 1995, Outside the Law 1995, The War Trail North 1995, War Woman: A Novel of the Real People 1997, The Meade Solution 1998, The Peace Chief: A Novel of the Real People 1998, Incident at Buffalo Crossing 1998, Brass 1999, Cherokee Dragon: A Novel of the Real People 2000, Barjack 2000, Fugitive's Trail 2000, Broke Loose 2000, The Gunfighter 2001, A Cold Hard Trail 2001, Spanish Jack: A Novel of the Real People 2001, Cherokee Medicine Man 2007, A Cherokee Encyclopedia 2008, No Need for a Gunfighter 2008; contribs to anthologies and periodicals. *Honours:* Oklahoma Writer of the Year, Univ. of Oklahoma Professional Writing Program 1999, Cherokee Medal of Honor, Cherokee Honor Soc. 2000, Wordcraft Circle of Native Writers Writer of the Year, Native Writers Circle of the Americas, Lifetime Achievement Award, Arrel M. Gibson Lifetime Achievement Award. *Address:* Department of Cherokee Studies, College of Arts and Sciences, McKee Building, Western Carolina University, Cullowhee, NC 28723, USA (office). *Telephone:* (828) 227-2306 (office). *E-mail:* rconley@email.wcu.edu (office). *Website:* www.wcu.edu (office).

CONLEY, Tom Clark, BA, MA, PhD; American academic and writer; *Professor of French, Harvard University*; b. 7 Dec. 1943, New Haven, Conn.; m. Verena Conley; one s. one d. *Education:* Lawrence Univ. of Wisconsin, Columbia Univ., Sorbonne, Univ. of Paris, France, Univ. of Wisconsin, Madison. *Career:* Asst Prof., Assoc. Prof., Prof. of French, Univ. of Minnesota, Twin Cities 1971–95, Head of Dept of French and Italian 1983–88; Prof. of French, Harvard Univ. 1995–; several visiting positions; mem. Int. Asscn of Philosophy and Literature, Modern Language Asscn (MLA) of America, Midwest MLA, Soc. Française des Seiziémistes; Fellow, Inst. for Research in the Humanities, Univ. of Wisconsin, Madison 1990–91. *Publications include:* Su realismo: Lectura de Buñuel 1988, Film Hieroglyphics: Ruptures in Classical Cinema 1991, The Graphic Unconscious in Early Modern French Writing 1992, The Self-Made Map: Cartographic Writing in Early Modern France 1996, L'Inconscient graphique 2000, Cartographies of Cinema 2006, Cartographic Cinema 2007, Casablanca: Movies and Memory (with Marc Augé) 2009, An Errant Eye: Poetry and Topography in Early Modern France 2011; also translations of seven vols, contrib. to books and numerous articles and reviews to periodicals. *Honours:* Woodrow Wilson Fellow 1965–66, Fulbright Fellow 1968–69, American Council of Learned Socs Fellow 1975–76, Nat. Endowment for the Humanities grants 1975, and Summer Fellow 1988, Newberry Library Quintennial Fellow 1988–89, Ville de Tours Medal of Honour 1990, Newberry Library Hermon Dunlap Smith Fellow 1992, Guggenheim Fellow 2003–04. *Address:* 85 Dunster Street, Cambridge, MA 02138, USA (home). *E-mail:* tconley@fas.harvard.edu (office). *Website:* www.rll.fas.harvard.edu/icb/icb.do (office).

CONLON, Kathleen (see Lloyd, Kathleen Annie)

CONN, Stewart; Scottish poet and playwright; b. 5 Nov. 1936, Glasgow. *Career:* radio producer, BBC, Glasgow 1962–77, Head of Radio Drama, Edinburgh 1977–92; literary adviser, Royal Lyceum Theatre, Edinburgh 1972–75; appointed to Edinburgh's poet laureateship, the Edinburgh Makar 2002–05; mem. Knight of Mark Twain, Shore Poets (Pres.), Scottish Soc. of Playwrights; Fellow, Royal Scottish Acad. of Music and Drama. *Publications include:* poetry: Thunder in the Air 1967, The Chinese Tower 1967, Stoats in the Sunlight (aka Ambush and Other Poems) 1968, An Ear to the Ground 1972, PEN New Poems 1973–74 (ed.) 1974, Under the Ice 1978, In the Kibble Palace: New and Selected Poems 1987, The Luncheon of the Boating Party 1992, In the Blood 1995, At the Aviary 1995, The Ice Horses (ed.) 1996, Stolen Light: Selected Poems 1999, The Loving-Cup 2007, 100 Favourite Scottish Love Poems 2008; plays: The Aquarium and Other Plays 1976, Thistlewood 1979, The Burning in Scots Plays of the 70s 2000, Herman 2007; prose and poetry: Distances 2001, Ghosts at Cockcrow 2005, The Breakfast Room 2010; contrib. to anthologies, journals, radio. *Honours:* Hon. Fellow, Asscn for Scottish Literary Studies; E.C. Gregory Award 1964, Scottish Arts Council Awards and Poetry Prize 1968, 1978, 1992, English-Speaking Union Travel Scholarship 1984, Scottish Arts Council Playwrights Bursary 1995, Soc. of Authors Travel Bursary 1996. *Literary Agent:* c/o Lemon Unna & Durbridge Ltd, 24 Pottery Lane, Holland Park, London, W11 4LZ, England. *Address:* 1 Fettes Row, Edinburgh, EH3 6SF, Scotland. *E-mail:* stewart@jsconn.freeserve.co.uk (home).

CONNELL, Evan Shelby, Jr, BA; American author and poet; b. 17 Aug. 1924, Kansas City, Mo. *Education:* Dartmouth Coll., Univ. of Kansas, Stanford Univ., Columbia Univ., San Francisco State Coll. *Career:* Ed. Contact magazine 1960–65; mem. American Acad. of Arts and Letters. *Publications include:* fiction: The Anatomy Lesson and Other Stories 1957, Mrs Bridge 1959, The Patriot 1960, At the Crossroads: Stories 1965, The Diary of a Rapist 1966, Mr Bridge 1969, The Connoisseur 1974, Double Honeymoon 1976, St Augustine's Pigeon 1980, The Alchymist's Journal 1991, The Collected Stories of Evan S. Connell 1995, Deus Lo Volt!: Chronicle of the Crusades 2000, Lost in Uttar Pradesh 2008; poetry: Notes From a Bottle Found on the Beach at Carmel 1963, Points for a Compass Rose 1973; nonfiction: A Long Desire 1979, The White Lantern 1980, Son of the Morning Star: Custer and the Little Bighorn 1984, Mesa Verde 1992, The Aztec Treasure House 2001, Francisco Goya: A Life 2004; contribs to periodicals. *Honours:* Eugene F. Saxton Fellow 1953, Guggenheim Fellowship 1963, Rockefeller Foundation Grant 1967, California Literature Silver Medal 1974, Los Angeles Times Book Award 1985, American Acad. of Arts and Letters Award 1987, Lannan Foundation Lifetime Achievement Award 2000, Robert Kirsch Award for Lifetime Achievement 2009. *Address:* 320 Artist Road, Sante Fe, NM 87501-2079, USA. *Telephone:* (505) 986-1261.

CONNELLY, Karen Marie; Canadian poet and writer; b. 12 March 1969, Calgary, Alberta; m.; one s. *Career:* has lived and worked in Thailand, Spain, France, Greece; teacher, Humber Coll.; mem. PEN Canada, Free Burma Movt. *Publications include:* poetry: The Small Words in My Body (Pat Lowther Award 1991) 1990, This Brighter Prison: A Book of Journeys 1993, The Disorder of Love 1997, The Border Surrounds Us 2000, Grace and Poison (reprint of The Small Words in My Body and The Disorder of Love with new preface) 2001; novel: The Lizard Cage (Orange Broadband Prize for New Writers 2007) 2005; other: Touch the Dragon: A Thai Journal (Gov.-Gen.'s Award for non-fiction) 1992, One Room in a Castle 1995, Burmese Lessons: A Love Story 2010. *Literary Agent:* Westwood Creative Artists, 94 Harbord Street, Toronto, ON M5S 1G6, Canada. *Telephone:* (416) 964-3302. *Fax:* (416) 975-9209. *E-mail:* jackie@wcatld.com. *Website:* www.wcaltd.com; www.karenconnelly.ca.

CONNELLY, Mark, BA, MA, PhD; American writer and teacher; b. 8 July 1951, Philadelphia, Pa. *Education:* Carroll Coll., Univ. of Wisconsin, Milwaukee. *Career:* Instructor, Milwaukee Area Tech. Coll. 1986–; Prof. and Dir of Admissions, Univ. of Kent, UK; mem. Irish Cultural and Heritage Center of Wisconsin, Vice-Pres.; mem. Modern Language Asscn. *Publications include:* The Diminished Self: Orwell and the Loss of Freedom 1987, The Sundance Reader 1997, Orwell and Gissing 1997, The Sundance Writer 2000, Deadly Closets: The Fiction of Charles Jackson 2001, Fifteen Minutes 2004, The Red Shoes 2005, Steady the Buffs! A Regiment, a Region and the Great War 2006, Get Writing: Sentences and Paragraphs 2009, The Last Decision You'll Ever Make: A Groom's Survival Guide 2011; contribs: short stories in Milwaukee Magazine, Wisconsin Review, Indiana Review. *Honours:* Milwaukee Magazine Fiction Award 1982. *Address:* Room No. N4.W6, School of History, Rutherford College, University of Kent, Canterbury, Kent, CT2 7NX England (office). *Telephone:* (1227) 823424 (office). *E-mail:* M.L.Connelly@kent.ac.uk (office). *Website:* www.kent.ac.uk/history/staff/profiles/connelly (office).

CONNELLY, Michael; American novelist; b. 1956, Philadelphia, Pa. *Education:* Univ. of Florida. *Career:* crime reporter for newspapers based in Daytona Beach and Fort Lauderdale, Fla and for the Los Angeles Times; Pres. Mystery Writers of America Org. 2003, 2004. *Television writing:* Level 9 (co-creator, writer and producer) 2000. *Publications include:* novels: The Black Echo (Edgar Award for Best First Novel) 1992, The Black Ice 1992, The Concrete Blonde 1994, The Last Coyote 1995, The Poet 1996, Trunk Music 1997, Angels Flight 1998, Blood Work 1998, Void Moon 1999, A Darkness More Than Night 2001, City of Bones 2002, Chasing the Dime 2002, Lost Light 2003, The Narrows 2004, The Closers 2005, The Lincoln Lawyer 2005, Echo Park (Los Angeles Times Book Prize for Mystery/Thriller) 2006, The Overlook 2007, The Brass Verdict 2008, The Scarecrow 2009, Nine Dragons 2009, The Reversal 2010, The Fifth Witness 2011, The Drop 2011, The Black Box 2012; other: Crime Beat (collected journalism) 2006; ed.: The Best American Mystery Stories 2003. *Honours:* Anthony Award, Macavity Award, Nero Award, Barry Award, Ridley Award, Shamus Award, Dilys Award, Audie Award, Maltese Falcon Award (Japan), .38 Caliber Award (France), Grand Prix (France), Pepe Carvalho award (Spain), Premio Bancarella Award (Italy). *Address:* c/o Orion Publishing Group Ltd, Orion House, 5 Upper St Martin's Lane, London, WC2H 9EA, England (office). *Website:* www.michaelconnelly.com.

CONNOLLY, Ray; British writer; b. (John Raymond Connolly), 4 Dec. 1940, St Helens, Lancs., England; s. of John Connolly and Anne Connolly; m. Elaine Balmforth 1966; two s. one d. *Education:* London School of Econs and Political Science. *Career:* columnist, London Evening Standard 1967–73, 1983–84, The Times 1989–90; regular contrib., Daily Mail 1998–2010, Sunday Times, Daily Telegraph, Observer; has also written films, TV series, documentaries, short stories, radio plays. *Film screenplays include:* That'll Be the Day 1973, Stardust (Best Original British Screenplay, Writers' Guild of GB) 1974, James Dean: The First American Teenager (documentary) 1975, Forever Young 1984. *Compositions include:* lyrics for Forever Young, Americana Stray Cat Blues, Dea Sancta. *Radio includes:* God Bless Our Love, Unimaginable, An Easy Game to Play (play) 1982, A Day To Remember (documentary) 1994, Lost Fortnight (play) 1996, Tim Merryman's Days of Clover (drama series) 2003, Unimaginable (play) 2005, I Saw Her Standing There (story) 2008, God Bless Our Love (play) 2010. *Television includes:* as writer: Honky Tonk Heroes (series) 1980, Lytton's Diary 1985, Perfect Scoundrels 1989, The Rhythm of Life (documentary series) 1997. *Publications include:* A Girl Who Came to Stay 1973, That'll Be the Day (novel) 1973, Stardust (novel) 1974, Trick or Treat? 1975, Newsdeath 1978, A Sunday Kind of Woman 1980, John Lennon 1940–1980 1981, The Sun Place 1981, Stardust Memories (anthology) 1983, Forever Young (novel) 1984, Lytton's Diary 1985, Defrosting the Fridge 1988, Perfect Scoundrels 1989, Sunday Morning 1992, Shadows on a Wall 1994, In the Sixties (anthology) 1995, Love Out of Season 2007, Kill for Love (e-book) 2010, The Ray Connolly Beatles Archive (e-book) 2011, Let Nothing You Dismay (Christmas short story) 2011. *Literary Agent:* c/o United Agents, 12–26 Lexington Street, London, W1F 0LE, England. *Telephone:* (20) 3214-0800. *Fax:* (20) 3214-0801. *E-mail:* info@unitedagents.co.uk. *Website:* unitedagents.co.uk. *E-mail:* mail@rayconnolly.co.uk (office). *Website:* www.rayconnolly.co.uk.

CONNOR, Joan, BA, MA, MFA; American writer, poet and educator; *Professor of English, Ohio University*; b. 21 Jan. 1954, Holyoke, Mass; m. Nils Wessell (separated); one s. *Education:* Mount Holyoke Coll., Middlebury Coll., Vermont Coll. *Career:* Assoc. Fiction Ed., Chelsea 1994–96; Visiting Prof., Ohio Univ., Athens 1995–96, Prof. of English 1996–, Dir Creative Writing 2003–08; Prof., Univ. of Southern Maine, Low Residency MFA Program, 2002–, Interim Co-Dir 2009; mem. Associated Writing Programs (AWP), Young Writers' Inst.; Fellow, Vermont Studio Colony 1990, MacDowell Colony 1992, Virginia Center for the Creative Arts 1993, Yaddo Colony 1993, Fairfield Univ. 2009–11. *Publications include:* Here on Old Route 7 1997, We Who Live Apart 2000, History Lessons 2003, The World Before Mirrors 2006, How to Stop Loving Someone 2011; contribs: anthologies and periodicals. *Honours:* AWP Award, Pushcart Prize, John Gilgun Award, Headlands Fellowship, First Alternate 1999, Leapfrog Press Award in Adult Fiction, River Teeth Award in Non-fiction. *Address:* 328 Carroll Road, Athens, OH 45701, USA (home). *Telephone:* (740) 594-3059 (office). *E-mail:* connor@oak.cats.ohiou.edu (office); connor@ohio.edu.

CONQUEST, (George) Robert (Acworth), (J. E. M. Arden, Victor Grey, Ted Pauker), CMG, OBE, MA, DLitt, FBA, FRSL; British/American writer, academic and fmr diplomatist; *Senior Research Fellow, Hoover Institution, Stanford University*; b. 15 July 1917, Malvern, Worcs., England; s. of Robert Folger W. Conquest and Rosamund A. Acworth; m. 1st Joan Watkins 1942 (divorced 1948); two s.; m. 2nd Tatiana Milhailova 1948 (divorced 1962); m. 3rd Caroleen Macfarlane 1964 (divorced 1978); m. 4th Elizabeth Neece 1979. *Education:* Winchester Coll., Univ. of Grenoble and Magdalen Coll., Oxford. *Career:* mil. service 1939–46; HM Foreign Service 1946–56; Sydney and Beatrice Webb Research Fellow, LSE 1956–58; Visiting Poet, Univ. of Buffalo 1959–60; Literary Ed. The Spectator 1962–63; Sr Fellow, Russian Inst., Columbia Univ. 1964–65; Fellow, Woodrow Wilson Int. Center, Washington, DC 1976–77; Sr Research Fellow, Hoover Inst., Stanford Univ. 1977–79, 1981–; Distinguished Visiting Fellow, Heritage Foundation 1980–81; Fellow, British Interplanetary Soc., American Acad. of Arts and Sciences; mem. Soc. for the Promotion of Roman Studies. *Television:* presenter, Red Empire (Granada TV) 1991. *Publications:* A World of Difference 1955, Poems 1955, Common Sense About Russia 1960, Power and Policy in the USSR 1961, Soviet Deportation of Nationalities 1960, Courage of Genius: The Pasternak Affair 1961, Between Mars and Venus 1962, Russia after Khrushchev 1965, The Egyptologists (with Kingsley Amis) 1965, The Great Terror: Stalin's Purge of the Thirties 1968, Arias from a Love Opera 1969, The Nation Killers 1970, Where Marx Went Wrong 1970, V.I. Lenin 1972, Kolyma: The Arctic Death Camps 1978, Present Danger 1979, Forays 1979, The Abomination of Moab 1979, Coming Across 1979, We and They: Civic and Despotic Cultures 1980, What To Do When the Russians Come (with Jon Manchip White) 1984, Inside Stalin's Secret Police: NKVD Politics 1936–1939 1985, The Harvest of Sorrow: Soviet Collectivization and the Terror-Famine 1986, New and Collected Poems 1988, Tyrants and Typewriters: Communiqués in the Struggle for Truth 1989, Stalin and the Kirov Murder 1989, The Great Terror: A Reassessment 1990, Stalin: Breaker of Nations 1991, History, Humanity, and Truth 1993, Demons Don't 1999, Reflections on a Ravaged Century 1999, The Dragons of Expectation: Reality and Delusion in the Course of History 2005, The Great Terror: 40th Anniversary 2008, Penultimata 2009, Blokesongs and Blokelore 2012. *Honours:* Order of Yaroslav Mudryi (Ukraine) 2006, Order of Merit (Estonia) 2008, Order of Merit (Poland) 2009; Alexis de Tocqueville Award 1992, Jefferson Lectureship 1993, Michael Braude Award for Light Verse, American Acad. of Arts and Letters 1997, Richard Weaver Award for Scholarly Letters 1999, Peter Shaw Memorial Award, Nat. Asscn of Scholars 2001, Nagrody Przegladu Wschodniego (Warsaw) 2003, Fondazione Liberal Career Award 2004. *Address:* Hoover Institution, Stanford University, Stanford, CA 94305-6010 (office); 52 Peter Coutts Circle, Stanford, CA 94305-2506, USA (home). *Telephone:* (650) 723-1647 (office). *Fax:* (650) 723-1687 (office). *E-mail:* conquest@stanford.edu (office). *Website:* www.hoover.org/fellows/9765 (office).

CONRAN, Shirley Ida, OBE; British designer and author; b. 21 Sept. 1932, d. of W. Thirlbey Pearce and Ida Pearce; m. 1st Sir Terence Conran (divorced 1962); two s.; m. 2nd; m. 3rd. *Education:* St Paul's Girls' School and Portsmouth Art Coll. *Career:* Press Officer, Asprey Suchy (jewellers) 1953–54; Publicity Adviser to Conran Group cos 1955; organized and designed several kitchen and design exhbns; ran Conran Fabrics Ltd 1957; started Textile Design Studio 1958; Home Ed., Daily Mail 1962, Women's Ed. 1968; Women's Ed. The Observer Colour Magazine and contrib. to Woman's Own 1964; Fashion Ed. The Observer 1967, columnist and feature writer 1969–70; columnist, Vanity Fair 1970–71, Over 21 1972; numerous TV and radio appearances. *Publications include:* Superwoman 1974, Superwoman Yearbook 1975, Superwoman in Action 1977, Futures 1979, Lace 1982, The Magic Garden 1983, Lace 2 1984, Savages (novel) 1987, Down with Superwoman 1990, The Amazing Umbrella Shop 1990, Crimson 1991, Tiger Eyes 1994, The Revenge of Mimi Quinn 1998, Lace 2007.

CONRAN, Anthony (Tony), BA, MA; Welsh poet, dramatist, translator and critic; b. 7 April 1931, Kharghpur, India. *Education:* Univ. of Wales. *Career:* Research Asst, Univ. of Wales, Bangor 1957–66, Research Fellow and Tutor in English 1966–80; mem. Welsh Acad. 1970, British Pteridological Soc., English Folk Dance and Song Soc., SIEF Ballad commission, Welsh Union of Writers, Asscn for the Study of Welsh Writers in English. *Publications include:* Formal Poems 1960, Metamorphoses 1961, Stalae 1966, Poems 1951–67 (four vols) 1965–67 (combined edn) 1974, The Penguin Book of Welsh Verse 1967, Claim, Claim, Claim 1969, Spirit Level 1974, Life Fund 1979, The Cost of Strangeness: Essays on the English Poets of Wales 1982, Welsh Verse 1987, Bloddeuwedd and Other Poems 1989, Castles 1993, The Angry Summer by Idris Davies (ed.) 1993, All Hallows: A Symphony in Three Movements 1995, Visions and Praying Mantids: The Angelogical Notebooks 1997, The Peacemakers, by Waldo Williams (trans.) 1997, Frontiers in Anglo Welsh Poetry 1997, A Theatre of Flowers: Collected Pastorals 1998, Eros Proposes a Toast 1998, A Gwynedd Symphony 1999, Ragbag for Folkies: Poems and Songs 2001, Branwen and Other Dance Dramas and Plays 2003, Shape of My Country 2004, The Red Sap of Love 2006, What Brings You Here So Late? 2008; contribs to numerous magazines and journals. *Honours:* Hon. Fellow, Welsh Acad. 1995; Hon. DLitt (Univ. of Wales) 1997; Welsh Arts Council Prize 1960, 1989, Second Prize, BBC Wales Writer of the Year Award 1993, Welsh Union of Writers, Tony Conran Festival, Bangor 1995. *Address:* Min Menai, Siliwen Road, Bangor, Gwynedd, LL57 2BS, Wales (home). *Telephone:* (1248) 379161 (home).

CONROY, (Donald) Patrick (Pat), BA; American writer; b. 26 Oct. 1945, Atlanta, GA; s. of Col Donald Conroy and Frances (Peg) Dorothy Conroy; m. 1st Barbara Bolling 1969 (divorced 1977); m. 2nd Lenore Gurewitz 1981 (divorced 1995); one s. five d. *Education:* The Citadel. *Career:* mem. Authors' Guild of America, PEN, Writers Guild. *Film screenplays:* Invictus 1988, The Prince of Tides (with Becky Johnson) 1991, Beach Music 1997. *Publications:* non-fiction: The Boo 1970, The Water is Wide 1972, My Reading Life 2010; novels: The Great Santini 1976, The Lords of Discipline 1980, The Prince of Tides 1986, Beach Music 1995, My Losing Season 2002, The Pat Conroy Cookbook 2004, South of Broad 2009. *Honours:* Ford Foundation Leadership Devt Grant 1971, Nat. Endowment for the Arts Award for Achievement in Educ. 1974, SC Hall of Fame, Acad. of Authors 1988, Golden Plate Award, American Acad. of Achievement 1992, Ga Comm. on the Holocaust Humanitarian Award 1996, Lotos Medal of Merit for Outstanding Literary Achievement 1996 and many others. *Literary Agent:* Marly Rusoff and Associates, PO Box 524, Bronxville, NY 10708, USA. *Telephone:* (914) 961-7939. *E-mail:* mra_queries@rusoffagency.com. *Website:* www.rusoffagency.com; www.patconroy.com.

CONSARNAU, Joan Margarit i, BArch; Spanish architect and poet; b. 11 May 1938, Sanaüja, Segarra; s. of Joan Margarit i Serradell and Trinitat Consarnau i Sabaté; m. Mariona Ribalta; one s. three d. *Education:* Institut Ausiàs March, Collegi Major Sant Jordi. *Career:* fmr Prof. of Structural Calculations, l'Escola Tècnica Superior d'Arquitectura de Barcelona. *Architectural works include:* Mercado de Vitoria 1977, Rehabilitación de la Fábrica Aymerich de Tarrasa como Museo de la Ciencia y de la Técnica de Cataluña, Reforma del Monumento a Cristóbal Colón 1982–84, Estadio y anillo olímpico de Montjuïc 1989, Forma parte del equipo que dirige las obras de la Sagrada Familia. *Publications:* Nuevas cartas a un joven poeta 2009; poetry: Cantos para la coral de un hombre solo 1963, Crónica 1975, Predicación para un bárbaro 1979, L'ombra de l'altre mar 1981, Vell malentès (Premio de la Crítica 1981, Premio Vicent Andrés Estellés de poesía 1982) 1981, El passat i la joia 1982, Cants d'Hekatònim de Tifundis (Premi Miquel de Palol 1981, Premi de la Crítica Serra d'Or 1982) 1982, Raquel: la fosca melangia de Robinson Crusoe 1983, L'ordre del temps 1985, Mar d'hivern (Premi Carles Riba 1985) 1986, Cantata de Sant Just 1987, La dona del navegant (Premi de la Crítica Serra d'Or) 1987, Llum de plua. Barcelona: Península, 1987, Poema per a un fris 1987, Edat roja 1990, Els motius del llop 1993, Aiguaforts 1995, Remolcadors entre la boira 1995, Estació de França 1999, Poesía amorosa completa (1980–2000) 2001, Joana 2002, El primer frío. Poesía 1975–95 (Premis Literaris de Cadaqués 2006) 2004, Cálculo de estructuras (Premi de la Crítica Serra d'Or 2006) 2005, Arquitecturas de la memoria 2006, Casa de misericordia (Premi Cavall Verd de poesia 2008, Premio de la Crítica 2008, Premio Nacional de Poesía 2008) 2007, Tugs in the fog (English translation by Anna Crowe) (Poetry Book Society recommended Translation) 2007, Barcelona amor final 2007, Misteriosamente feliz 2009, Intemperie. Antología 2010.

CONSTANT, Paule, DèsSc; French author; b. 25 Jan. 1944, Gan; d. of Yves Constant and Jeanne Tauzin; m. Auguste Bourgeade 1968; one s. one d. *Education:* Univ. of Bordeaux and Univ. of Paris (Sorbonne). *Career:* Asst Lecturer in French Literature, Univ. of Abidjan 1968–75; Maître-assistant, then Maître de Conférences in French Literature and Civilization, Univ. of Aix-Marseille III 1975–90, Inst. of French Studies for Foreign Students 1986–95; Prof. Université Aix–Marseille III 1995–; diarist, Revue des Deux Mondes, Paris 1990–92; Founder and Pres. Centre des Ecrivains du Sud - Jean Giono. *Television includes:* L'Education des Jeunes Filles de la Légion d'Honneur 1992, Mon héros préféré: La Princesse de Clèves 1996, Les grands fleuves racontés par des écrivains: L'Amazone 1997, Galilée: Paule Constant sur les traces de Jean Giono 2001. *Publications:* novels: Ouregano 1980 (Prix Valery Larbaud), Propriété privée 1981, Balta 1983, White Spirit 1989 (Prix François Mauriac, Prix Lutèce, Prix du Sud Jean-Baumel, Grand Prix du Roman, Acad. Française), Le Grand Ghâpal 1991, La Fille du Gobernator 1994, Confidence pour confidence 1998 (Prix du roman France-Télévision, Prix Goncourt Un monde à l'usage des demoiselles (essay) 1987 (Grand Prix de l'Essai, Acad. Française 1987), Sucre et Secret 2003 (Prix du roman, Amnesty international), La Bête à Chagrin 2007. *Honours:* Chevalier, Légion d'honneur, Ordre de l'Educ. Nat. de Côte d'Ivoire. *Address:* Institut d'études françaises pour étudiants étrangers, 23 rue Gaston de Saporta, 13100 Aix-en-Provence (office); 29 rue Cardinale, 13100 Aix-en-Provence, France. *Telephone:* 4-42-38-45-08 (office). *Fax:* 4-42-23-02-64 (office). *Website:* www.pauleconstant.com.

CONSTANTINE, David John, BA, PhD, FRSL; British poet, writer and translator; *Co-Editor, Modern Poetry in Translation*; b. 4 March 1944, Salford, Lancs.; m. Helen Frances Best 1966; one s. one d. *Education:* Wadham Coll., Oxford. *Career:* Lecturer in Sr Lecturer in German, Univ. of Durham 1969–81; Fellow in German, The Queen's Coll., Oxford 1981–2000; Co-Ed. (with Bernard O'Donoghue) Oxford Poets anthologies 2000–11, (with Helen Constantine) Modern Poetry in Translation magazine 2004–; mem. Poetry Soc., Soc. of Authors. *Publications:* poetry: A Brightness to Cast Shadows 1980, Watching for Dolphins 1983, Mappi Mundi 1984, Madder 1987, Selected Poems 1991, Caspar Hauser 1994, Sleeper 1995, The Pelt of Wasps 1998, Something for the Ghosts 2002, Collected Poems 2004, A Poetry Primer 2004, Nine Fathom Deep 2009; fiction: Davies 1985, Back at the Spike 1994, Under the Dam (short stories) 2005, The Shieling (short stories) 2009, Tea at Midland (short story) (BBC Nat. Short Story Prize 2010); non-fiction: The Significance of Locality in the Poetry of Friedrich Hölderlin 1979, Early Greek Travellers and the Hellenic Ideal 1984, Hölderlin 1988, Friedrich Hölderlin 1992, Fields of Fire: A Life of Sir William Hamilton 2001, A Living Language 2004; translator: Hölderlin: Selected Poems 1996, Henri Michaux: Spaced, Displaced (with Helen Constantine) 1992, Philippe Jaccottet: Under Clouded Skies/Beauregard (with Mark Treharne) 1994, Goethe: Elective Affinities 1994, Kleist: Selected Writings 1998, Hölderlin's Sophocles 2001, Hans Magnus Enzensberger: Lighter Than Air 2002, Goethe: Faust 2005, 2009; ed.: German Short Stories 2 1972, Goethe: Werther. *Honours:* Hon. DLitt (Durham) 2009; Alice Hunt Bartlett Prize 1984, Runciman Prize 1985, Southern Arts Literature Prize 1987, European Poetry Trans. Prize 1998, BBC Nat. Short Story Award 2010. *Address:* Modern Poetry in Translation, The Queen's College, Oxford, OX1 4AW (office); 1 Hill Top Road, Oxford, OX4 1PB, England (home). *Telephone:* (1865) 244701 (office). *E-mail:* david.constantine@queens.ox.ac.uk (office). *Website:* www.mptmagazine.com (office).

CONSTANTINE, Helen Frances, MA, MLitt; British translator; *Co-Editor, Modern Poetry in Translation*; b. 29 Jan. 1943, Launceston, Cornwall, England; d. of Richard Stanley Best and Florence Elizabeth Best; m. David Constantine 1966; one s. one d. *Education:* Lady Margaret Hall, Oxford, Newcastle Univ. *Career:* fmr Head of Languages at Bartholomew School, Eynsham; Co-Ed. (with David Constantine) Modern Poetry in Translation magazine 2004–. *Publications include:* trans.: Henri Michaux: Spaced, Displaced (with David Constantine) 1992, Paris Tales: A Literary Tour of the City 2004, Théophile Gautier: Mademoiselle de Maupin 2005, Choderlos de Laclos: Dangerous Liaisons 2007, French Tales 2008, Modern Poetry in Translation: e.g. Frontiers (with David Constantine) 2009, Paris Metro Tales 2011; ed.: Berlin Tales 2009, Rome Tales 2011, Balzac The Wild Ass's Skin 2012, Madrid Tales 2012. *Address:* Modern Poetry in Translation, The Queen's College, Oxford, OX1 4AW (office); 1 Hill Top Road, Oxford, OX4 1PB, England (home). *Telephone:* (1865) 244701 (home). *E-mail:* helenconstantine@btinternet.com (home). *Website:* www.mptmagazine.com (office).

CONSTANTINE, Storm; British writer; b. 12 Oct. 1956, England. *Career:* Man. Dir and Commissioning Ed., Immanion Press 2003–. *Publications include:* The Enchantments of Flesh and Spirit 1987, The Bewitchments of Love and Hate 1988, The Fulfillments of Fate and Desire 1989, The Monstrous Regiment 1989, Hermetech 1991, Aleph 1991, Burying the Shadow 1992, Sign for the Sacred 1993, Wraeththu 1993, Calenture 1994, Stalking Tender Prey 1995, Scenting Hallowed Blood 1996, Stealing Sacred Fire 1997, Thin Air 1999, The Thorn Boy 1999, Sea Dragon Heir 1999, The Crown of Silence 2000, Silverheart 2000, The Way of Light 2001, The Wraiths of Will and Pleasure 2003, The Shades of Time and Memory 2004, The Hienama 2004, The Ghosts of Blood and Innocence 2005, The Wraeththu Chronicles 2005, Student of Kyme 2008, Sekhem Heka 2008, Mythangelus 2009, Mytholumina 2010, Grimoire Dehara: Kaimana 2011. *Address:* 8 Rowley Court, Stafford, Staffs., ST17 9BJ, England. *Website:* www.stormconstantine.com.

CONTE, Steven, PhD; Australian writer; *Writer-in-Residence, Trinity College, University of Melbourne*; b. 1966, Sydney, NSW. *Education:* Univ. of Canberra, Defence Force Acad., Univ. of Melbourne. *Career:* worked as life model, taxi driver, public servant and book reviewer; Writer-in-Residence, Trinity Coll., Univ. of Melbourne. *Publication:* The Zookeeper's War (Australian Prime Minister's Literary Award 2008) 2007. *Literary Agent:* c/o Jenny Darling & Associates Pty Ltd, PO Box 413, Toorak, Vic. 3142, Australia. *Telephone:* (3) 9827-3883. *Fax:* (3) 9827-1270. *E-mail:* jda@jd-associates.com.au. *Website:* www.jd-associates.com.au; www.stevenconte.com.

COOK, Christopher Paul, BA, MA; British artist, poet and academic; *Reader in Painting, University of Plymouth*; b. 24 Jan. 1959, Great Ayton, N Yorks., England; s. of E. P. Cook and J. Leyland; m. Jennifer Jane Mellings 1982; two s. *Education:* Univ. of Exeter, Royal Coll. of Art, Accademia di Belle Arti, Bologna, Italy. *Career:* Italian Govt Scholar, Accad. di Belle Arti, Bologna 1986–89; Fellow in Painting, Exeter Coll. of Art 1989–90; guest artist, Stadelschule, Frankfurt 1991; Visiting Fellow, Ruskin School, Univ. of Oxford 1992–93; Distinguished Visiting Artist, Calif. State Univ., Long Beach 1994; Visiting Artist to Banaras Hindu Univ., Varanasi, India 1994, 1996; Reader in Painting, Univ. of Plymouth 1997–; Artist in Residence, Eden Project, Cornwall 2001–03; Resident Artist, Univ. of Memphis 2004; Yokohama Museum residency, Japan 2005; Artist-in-Residence, Savannah Coll. of Art and Design, Atlanta, USA 2009; Resident Artist, Langgeng Foundation, Jogjakarta, Indonesia 2011. *Solo exhibitions include:* Camden Arts Centre 1985, Cleveland Gallery, Middlesbrough 1989, Museum van Rhoon, Rotterdam 1992, Northern Centre for Contemporary Art 1993, Helmut Pabst Gallery, Frankfurt 1995, Haugesund Kunstforening, Norway 1997, De Beyerd Museum, Breda 1999, Heidelberger Kunstverein 1999, Bundanon Trust, NSW 2000, Hirschl Contemporary Art, London 2000, Koraalberg Gallery, Antwerp 2002, Europaïsche Zentral Galerie, Frankfurt 2003, Dibou Gallery, New Orleans 2004, Art Museum, Memphis 2004, California State Univ., Long Beach 2005, Yokohama Museum, Japan 2005, Mary Ryan Gallery, New York 2007, 2010, Today Art Museum, Beijing 2007, Fine Art Soc., London 2009, Peninsula Arts Gallery, Plymouth 2009, ICA, Singapore 2011. *Film:* Journey 2007. *Publications:* Dust on the Mirror 1997, For and Against Nature 2000, A Thoroughbred Golden Calf 2003, Notes to the Graphites 2009. *Honours:* Prizewinner, John Moores Univ., Liverpool XXI 1999, Arts Council of England Award 2000, British Council Award to Artists 2003, Daiwa Award 2005, AHRC Award 2005, British Council Award, Beijing 2006, 2007, Phillips Award, British School at Rome 2009. *Address:* c/o Mary Ryan Gallery, Inc., 24 West 57th Street, 2nd Floor, New York, NY 10019, USA (office). *Telephone:* (212) 397-0669 (home). *Fax:* (212) 397-0766 (office). *E-mail:* c1cook@plymouth.ac.uk (home). *Website:* www.cookgraphites.com (office).

COOK, Christopher Piers, BA, MA, DPhil, FRHistS; British writer and historian; b. 20 June 1945, Leicester, England. *Education:* Univs of Cambridge and Oxford. *Career:* Ed. Pears Cyclopedia 1976–. *Publications include:* Sources in British Political History (six vols) 1975–84, The Slump (with John Stevenson) 1976, Dictionary of Historical Terms (second edn) 1989, World Political Almanac 1989, Longman Handbook of World History Since 1914 1991, Britain Since 1945 (with John Stevenson) 1995, What Happened Where (with Diccon Bewes) 1996, Longman Handbook of Modern American History 1763–1996 (with David Waller) 1997, Longman Handbook of Modern European History 1763–1999 1998, Longman Handbook of the Modern World (with John Stevenson) 1998, European Political Facts of the Twentieth Century (with John Paxton) (fifth edn) 2001, Longman Handbook of Modern British History 1714–2001 2002, Longman Handbook of Twentieth Century Europe (with John Stevenson) 2003, The Routledge Companion to Britain in the Nineteenth Century, 1815–1914 2005, The Routledge Companion to World History since 1914 (with John Stevenson) 2005, The Routledge Guide to British Political Archives 2006, The Routledge Companion to Early Modern Europe 1453–1763 (with Philip Broadhead) 2006, A Short History of the Liberal Party: The Road Back To Power 2010; contrib. to Guardian, TLS, THES. *Address:* Pears Cyclopedia, Penguin Press, Penguin Books, 80 Strand, London, WC2R 0RL, England (office).

COOK, David Kenneth; British actor and writer; b. 21 Sept. 1940, Preston, Lancs., England. *Education:* Royal Coll. of Dramatic Art, London. *Career:* professional actor 1961–; Writer-in-Residence, St Martin's Coll., Lancaster 1982–83; mem. Soc. of Authors, Writers Guild, PEN. *Screenplays include:* Walter 1982, Second Best 1994. *Radio:* Walter Now 2010. *Television includes:* Willy 1973, Why Here 1976, A Place Like Home, Jenny Can't Work any Faster 1975, Mary's Wife 1980, Walter and June 1983, Singles Weekend 1984, Love Match 1986, Missing Persons 1990, Closing Numbers 1993, Second Best 1994, Hetty Wainthrop Investigates 1996–98. *Publications include:* Albert's Memorial 1972, Happy Endings (E.M. Forster Award 1977) 1974, Walter (Hawthornden Prize) 1978, Winter Doves 1979, Sunrising (Southern Arts Fiction Prize 1984) 1983, Missing Persons 1986, Crying Out Loud 1988, Walter and June 1989, Second Best (Odd Fellows Social Concern Award 1992) 1991. *Honours:* Writers Guild Award 1977, Arthur Welton Scholarship 1991, BAFTA Award. *Literary Agent:* c/o Deborah Rogers, 20 Powis Mews, London,

W11 1JN, England. *Address:* Flat 17, Ockham Court, 24 Bardwell Road, Oxford, OX2 6SR, England (home).

COOK, Glen Charles, (Greg Stevens); American writer; b. (Glen Charles Keltch), 9 July 1944, New York, NY; s. of Charles Glen Keltch and Lowella Mable Handy Keltch; m. Carol Ann Fritz 1971; three s. *Education:* Univ. of Missouri. *Career:* worked at General Motors (retd). *Publications include:* The Heirs of Babylon 1972, Shadow of All Night Falling 1979, October's Baby 1980, All Darkness Met 1980, Shadowline 1982, Starfishers 1982, Stars' End 1982, The Swordbearer 1982, The Black Company 1984, The Fire in His Hands 1984, Shadows Linger 1984, Doomstalker 1985, A Matter of Time 1985, Passage at Arms 1985, Warlock 1985, The White Rose 1985, With Mercy Toward None 1985, Ceremony 1986, Reap the East Wind 1987, Sweet Silver Blues 1987, All Ill Fate Marshalling 1988, Bitter Gold Hearts 1988, Cold Copper Tears 1988, The Dragon Never Sleeps 1988, Old Tin Sorrows 1989, Shadow Games 1989, The Silver Spike 1989, The Tower of Fear 1989, Dread Brass Shadows 1990, Dreams of Steel 1990, Sung in Blood 1990, Red Iron Nights 1991, Deadly Quicksilver Lies 1993, Bleak Seasons 1996, Petty Pewter Gods 1996, She is the Darkness 1997, Water Sleeps 1999, Faded Steel Heat 2000, Soldiers Live 2000, Angry Lead Skies 2002, Whispering Nickel Idols 2005, The Tyranny of the Night 2005, Lord of the Silent Kingdom 2006, A Cruel Wind 2006, A Fortress in the Shadow 2006, Chronicles of the Black Company 2006, Cruel Zinc Melodies 2007, Surrender to the Will of the Night 2009, Gilded Latten Bones 2010; contrib. to anthologies and periodicals. *Literary Agent:* c/o Scovil, Chichak, Galen Literary Agency, Inc., 276 Fifth Avenue, Suite 708, New York, NY 10001, USA. *Telephone:* (212) 679-8686. *Address:* 4106 Flora Place, St Louis, MO 63110, USA (home). *E-mail:* gcookwrite@sbcglobal.net (home).

COOK, Lila (see Africano, Lillian)

COOK, Paul, BA, MA, PhD; American academic, science fiction writer and classical music critic; *Principal Lecturer, Department of English, Arizona State University*; b. 12 Nov. 1950, Tucson, Ariz.; s. of Harlin Maurice Cook and Patricia Cochran Cook; m. Cecily Ring Cook. *Education:* Northern Arizona Univ., Arizona State Univ., Univ. of Utah. *Career:* Lecturer in English, Arizona State Univ., Tempe 1982–, currently Prin. Lecturer; classical music critic, American Record Guide, ClassicsToday.com, Classical Pulse!. *Publications include:* Tintagel 1981, The Alejandra Variations 1984, Duende Meadow 1985, Halo 1986, On the Rim of the Mandala 1987, Fortress on the Sun 1997, The Engines of Dawn 1999, Karma Kommandos 2008. *Address:* Department of English, Arizona State University, PO Box 870302, Tempe, AZ 85287-0302, USA (office). *Telephone:* (480) 965-7294 (office). *E-mail:* paul.cook@asu.edu (office). *Website:* english.clas.asu.edu (office); www.paulcook-sci-fi.com.

COOK, Petronelle Marguerite Mary, (Margot Arnold), BA, DipArch, MA; British/American writer and teacher; b. 16 May 1925, Plymouth, Devon, England; m. Philip R. Cook 1949 (divorced 1979); two s. one d. *Education:* Univ. of Oxford. *Career:* mem. New England Historic and Genealogical Soc., Cornwall Family History Soc., Univ. of Oxford Archaeological Soc. (Pres. 1945). *Publications include:* The Officers' Woman 1972, The Villa on the Palatine 1975, Marie 1979, Exit Actors, Dying 1980, The Cape Cod Caper 1980, Death of a Voodoo Doll 1981, Zadok's Treasurer 1981, Affairs of State 1981, Love Among the Allies 1982, Lament for a Lady Laird 1982, Death on the Dragon's Tongue 1982, Desperate Measures 1983, Sinister Purposes 1985, The Menehune Murders 1989, Toby's Folly 1990, The Catacomb Conspiracy 1991, The Cape Cod Conundrum 1992, Dirge for a Dorset Druid 1994, The Midas Murders 1995, Survivors and Non-Survivors 2002, The Well Man Trilogy 2003–04, Murder, with Supporting Cast 2005; as Petronelle Cook: The Queen Consorts of England 1993; contribs: numerous short stories to magazines. *Honours:* Nat. Writers Club Fiction Prize 1983. *Address:* 11 High School Road, Hyannis, MA 02601-3901, USA (home). *Telephone:* (508) 790-9468 (home). *E-mail:* margot@verizon.net (home).

COOK, Robin, BA, MD; American physician and writer; b. 4 May 1940, New York, NY; m. Barbara Ellen Mougin 1979. *Education:* Wesleyan Univ., Columbia Univ., Harvard Univ. *Career:* fmr Lt Commdr in the Navy; Resident in General Surgery, Queen's Hospital, Honolulu 1966–68; Resident in Ophthalmology 1971–75, staff 1975–, Massachusetts Eye and Ear Infirmary, Boston; teaches at Harvard Medical School. *Publications include:* fiction: The Year of the Intern 1972, Coma 1977, Sphinx 1979, Brain 1981, Harmful Intent 1982, Fever 1982, Godplayer 1983, Mindbend 1985, Outbreak 1987, Mortal Fear 1988, Mutation 1989, Vital Signs 1991, Blindsight 1992, Fatal Cure 1993, Terminal 1993, Acceptable Risk 1995, Contagion 1996, Chromosome Six 1997, Invasion 1997, Toxin 1998, Vector 1999, Shock 2001, Abduction 2002, Seizure 2003, Marker 2005, Critical 2007, Foreign Body 2008, Intervention 2009, Cure 2010. *Honours:* Author of Vision, RP Int. Org. 2002. *Address:* Penguin Group (USA) Inc., c/o Putnam Publicity, 375 Hudson Street, New York, NY 10014, USA (office). *Website:* us.penguingroup.com (office).

COOK, Stanley, BA; British lecturer (retd) and poet; b. 12 April 1922, Austerfield, Yorks., England; m. Kathleen Mary Daly; one s. two d. *Education:* Christ Church, Oxford. *Career:* Lecturer, Huddersfield Polytechnic 1969–81; Ed. Poetry Nottingham 1981–85. *Publications include:* Form Photograph 1971, Sign of Life 1972, Staff Photograph 1976, Alphabet 1976, Woods Beyond a Cornfield 1981, Concrete Poems 1984, Barnsdale 1986, Selected Poems 1972–86 1986, The Northern Seasons 1988, Squirrel in Town and Other Nature Poems 1988, The Dragon on the Wall and Other Poems 1989, The Poem Box 1991; other: Children's poems. *Honours:* Cheltenham Festival Competition Prize 1972.

COOK, Stanton R., BS; American newspaper publisher; b. 3 July 1925, Chicago, Ill.; s. of Rufus M. Cook and Thelma M. Borgerson; m. Barbara Wilson 1950 (died 1994). *Education:* Northwestern Univ. *Career:* Dist sales rep. Shell Oil Co. 1949–51; Production Eng Chicago Tribune Co. 1951–60, Asst Production Man. 1960–65, Production Man. 1965–67, Production Dir 1967–70, Dir Operations 1970, Gen. Man. 1970–72, Publr 1973–90, Pres. 1972–74, Chief Officer 1974–76, Chair. 1974–81; Dir Tribune Co. Chicago 1972–96, Pres. and CEO 1974–88, Chair. 1989–91; Chair. Chicago Nat. League Ball Club (Chicago Cubs) 1990–94; Dir A.P. 1975–84; Deputy Chair. and Dir Fed. Reserve Bank of Chicago 1980–83, Chair. 1984–85; mem. Bd of Dirs Robert R. McCormick Tribune Foundation 1990–; numerous trusteeships. *Address:* 224 Raleigh Road, Kenilworth, IL 60043-1209, USA (home).

COOK, Thomas H., BA, MA, MPhil; American writer; b. 19 Sept. 1947, Fort Payne, Ala; m. Susan Terner 1978; one d. *Education:* Georgia State Coll., Hunter Coll., City Univ. of New York, Columbia Univ. *Career:* teacher of English and history, Dekalb Community Coll., Clarkston, Ga 1978–81; Contributing Ed. and Book Review Ed., Atlanta magazine 1978–82; mem. Authors' Guild, Authors' League. *Publications include:* fiction: Blood Innocents 1980, The Orchids 1982, Tabernacle 1983, Elena 1986, Sacrificial Ground 1988, Flesh and Blood 1989, Streets of Fire 1989, Night Secrets 1990, The City When It Rains 1991, Evidence of Blood 1991, Mortal Memory 1993, Breakheart Hill 1995, The Chatham School Affair 1996, Instruments of Night 1998, Places in the Dark 2000, The Interrogation 2002, Red Leaves 2006, The Murmur of Stones 2006, The Cloud of Unknowing 2007, Master of the Delta 2008, The Fate of Katherine Carr 2009, The Last Talk with Lola Faye 2010, The Quest for Anna Klein: An Otto Penzler Book 2011; non-fiction: Early Graves: The Shocking True-Crime Story of the Youngest Woman Ever Sentenced to Death Row 1990, Blood Echoes: The True Story of an Infamous Mass Murder and its Aftermath 1992. *Honours:* Edgar Allan Poe Awards 1981, 1988, Int. Asscn of Crime Writers Hammett Prize 1995, Mystery Writers of America Award 1996. *Address:* c/o Houghton Mifflin Company, Trade Division, Adult Editorial, 8th Floor, 222 Berkeley Street, Boston, MA 02116-3764, USA. *Website:* www.houghtonmifflinbooks.com.

COOKE, John Peyton; American editor and writer; b. 7 March 1967, Amarillo, Tex.; m. *Education:* Univ. of Wisconsin, Madison. *Career:* Assoc. Ed., Scientific American Medicine periodical, New York 1994; mem. Mystery Writers of America. *Publications include:* The Lake 1989, Out for Blood 1991, Torsos 1993, The Chimney Sweeper 1994, Haven 1996, The Rape of Ganymede 1998, After You've Gone 2002, Serostatus 2004, The Fall of Lucifer 2008; contribs to anthologies and periodicals. *Honours:* First Place, Wyoming Young Author Competition 1982. *E-mail:* jpcooke@sympatico.ca (office); johnpeytoncooke@gmail.com. *Website:* www.johnpeytoncooke.com.

COOLIDGE, Clark; American poet; b. 26 Feb. 1939, Providence, RI; m. Susan Hopkins; one d. *Education:* Brown Univ. *Publications include:* Flag Flutter and US Electric 1966, Poems 1967, Ing 1969, Space 1970, The So 1971, Moroccan Variations 1971, Suite V 1973, The Maintains 1974, Polaroid 1975, Quartz Hearts 1978, Own Face 1978, Smithsonian Depositions, and Subjects to a Film 1980, American Ones 1981, A Geology 1981, Research 1982, Mine: The One That Enters the Stories 1982, Solution Passage: Poems, 1978–1981 1986, The Crystal Text 1986, Mesh 1988, At Egypt 1988, Sound as Thought: Poems, 1982–1984 1990, The Book of During 1991, Odes of Roba 1991, Baffling Means 1991, On the Slates 1992, Lowell Connector: Lines and Shots from Kerouac's Town 1993, Own Face 1994, Registers: (People in All) 1994, The ROVA Improvisations 1994, Heart of the Breath: Poems 1979–1992 1996, Now It's Jazz (writing on music) 1999, On the Nameways 2000, Alien Tatters 2000, Bomb (anthology, with Keith Waldrop) 2001, On the Nameways 2001, On the Slates 2002, Calmer or mer 2005, Counting on Planet Zero 2007, The Cave (with Bernadette Mayer) 2008, The Act of Providence 2010, This Time We Are Both 2010. *Honours:* Nat. Endowment for the Arts grant 1966, New York Poets Foundation Award 1968. *Address:* 108 Prospect Street, Petaluma, CA 94952-2926, USA (home). *Telephone:* (707) 781-9149 (home).

COONEY, Raymond George Alfred, OBE; British actor, dramatist and director; b. 30 May 1932, London, England; m. Linda Dixon 1962; two s. *Career:* mem. Dramatists' Club. *Publications include:* plays, both solo and in collaboration with others: One for the Pot 1961, Chase Me, Comrade 1964, Charlie Girl 1965, Bang Bang Beirut 1966, Not Now, Darling 1967, My Giddy Aunt 1968, Move Over Mrs Markham 1969, Why Not Stay for Breakfast? 1970, There Goes the Bride 1974, Run For Your Wife 1984, Two Into One 1985, Wife Begins at Forty 1986, It Runs in the Family 1987, Out of Order 1990, Funny Money 1994, Caught in the Net 2000, Tom, Dick and Harry: A Comedy 2005, Twice in a Lifetime 2010, London Girls. *Address:* Ray Cooney Plays, Everglades, 29 Salmons Road, Chessington, Surrey, KT9 2JE, England (office). *Telephone:* (20) 8397-0021 (office). *Fax:* (20) 8397-0070 (office). *E-mail:* alan@raycooneyplays.co.uk (office). *Website:* www.raycooneyplays.co.uk.

COOPER, Jilly, OBE; British writer; b. 21 Feb. 1937, Hornchurch, Essex; d. of Brig. W. B. Sallitt, OBE and Mary Elaine Whincup; m. Leo Cooper 1961; one s. one d. *Education:* Godolphin School, Salisbury. *Career:* reporter, Middx Independent 1957–59; account exec.; copy writer; publr's reader; various temporary roles 1959–69; columnist, The Sunday Times 1969–82, Mail on Sunday 1982–87. *Publications:* How to Stay Married 1969, How to Survive from Nine to Five 1970, Jolly Super 1971, Men and Super Men 1972, Jolly

Super Too 1973, Women and Super Women 1974, Jolly Superlative 1975, Emily 1975, Super Men and Super Women 1976, Bella 1976, Harriet 1976, Octavia 1977, Work and Wedlock 1977, Superjilly 1977, Imogen 1978, Prudence 1978, Class 1979, Intelligent and Loyal 1980, Supercooper 1980, Violets and Vinegar (co-ed with Tom Hartman) 1980, The British in Love (ed) 1980, Love and Other Heartaches 1981, Jolly Marsupial 1982, Animals in War 1983, Leo and Jilly Cooper on Rugby 1984, The Common Years 1984, Riders 1985, Hotfoot to Zabriskie Point 1985, How to Survive Christmas 1986, 1996, Turn Right at the Spotted Dog 1987, Rivals 1988, Angels Rush In 1990, Polo 1991, The Man Who Made Husbands Jealous 1993, Araminta's Wedding 1993, Apassionata 1996, Score! 1999, Pandora 2002, Wicked! 2006, Jump! 2010. *Honours:* British Book Awards Lifetime Achievement Award 1998; Hon. DLitt (Univ. of Gloucester) 2009; Dr hc (Anglia Ruskin Univ.) 2011. *Literary Agent:* c/o Vivienne Schuster, Curtis Brown Ltd, Fourth Floor, Haymarket House, 28–29 Haymarket, London, SW1Y 4SP, England. *Telephone:* (20) 7393-4400. *Fax:* (20) 7393-4401. *E-mail:* cb@curtisbrown.co.uk. *Website:* www.curtisbrown.co.uk.

COOPER, Richard Newell, PhD; American economist, academic and fmr public official; *Maurits C. Boas Professor of International Economics, Harvard University;* b. 14 June 1934, Seattle, Wash.; s. of Richard W. Cooper and Lucile Newell; m. 1st Carolyn Cahalan 1956 (divorced 1980); m. 2nd Ann Lorraine Hollick 1982 (divorced 1994); m. 3rd Jin Chen 2000; two s. two d. *Education:* Oberlin Coll., London School of Econs, UK, Harvard Univ. *Career:* Sr Staff Economist, Council of Econ. Advisers, The White House 1961–63; Deputy Asst Sec. of State for Monetary Affairs, US State Dept, Washington, DC 1965–66; Prof. of Econs, Yale Univ. 1966–77, Provost 1972–74; Under-Sec. of State for Econ. Affairs, 1977–81; Maurits C. Boas Prof. of Int. Econs, Harvard Univ. 1981–; Chair. Nat. Intelligence Council 1995–97; mem. Bd of Dirs Fed. Reserve Bank of Boston 1987–92, Chair. 1990–92; mem. Bd of Dirs Rockefeller Brothers Fund 1975–77, Schroders Bank and Trust Co. 1975–77, Warburg-Pincus Funds 1986–98, Center for Naval Analysis 1992–95, Phoenix Cos 1983–2005, Circuit City Stores 1983–2004, CNA Corpn 1997–, Inst. for Int. Econs 1983–; consultant to US Treasury, Nat. Security Council, World Bank, IMF, USN; Marshall Scholarship (UK) 1956–58; Fellow, American Acad. of Sciences 1974. *Publications:* The Economics of Interdependence 1968, Economic Policy in an Interdependent World 1986, The International Monetary System 1987, Stabilization and Debt in Developing Countries 1992, Boom, Crisis and Adjustment (co-author) 1993, Environment and Resource Policies for the World Economy 1994, Trade Growth in Transition Economies (ed.) 1997, What The Future Holds (ed.) 2002; more than 300 articles. *Honours:* Hon. LLD (Oberlin Coll.) 1958; Dr hc (Paris II) 2000; Nat. Intelligence Distinguished Service Medal 1996. *Address:* Center for International Affairs, Harvard University, 1737 Cambridge Street, Cambridge, MA 02138 (office); 33 Washington Avenue, Cambridge, MA 02140, USA (home). *Telephone:* (617) 495-5076 (office). *Fax:* (617) 495-7730 (office). *E-mail:* rcooper@harvard.edu (office). *Website:* www.economics.harvard.edu (office).

COOPER, Susan Mary, MA; British writer; b. 23 May 1935, Burnham, Bucks., England; m. 1st Nicholas J. Grant 1963 (divorced 1982); one s. one d.; m. 2nd Hume Cronyn 1996 (died 2003). *Education:* Somerville Coll., Oxford. *Career:* fmr reporter, Sunday Times; mem. Authors' Guild, Soc. of Authors, Writers' Guild of America, Nat. Children's Book and Literacy Alliance, Dramatists Guild of America. *Publications include:* Mandrake 1964, Behind the Golden Curtain: A View of the USA 1965, Essays of Five Decades by J. B. Priestley (ed.) 1968, J. B. Priestley: Portrait of an Author 1970, Foxfire (play with Hume Cronyn) 1982, Dreams and Wishes: Essays on Writing for Children 1996, The Magic Maker: A Portrait of John Langstaff, Creator of The Christmas Revels 2011; children's fiction: Over Sea, Under Stone 1965, Dawn of Fear 1970, The Dark is Rising (Newbery Honor Book 1974) 1973, Greenwitch 1973, The Grey King (Newbery Medal 1976, Tir na nÓg Award 1976) 1975, Silver on the Tree (Tir na nÓg Award 1977) 1975, Jethro and the Jumbie 1979, Seaward (Janusz Korczak Literary Prize) 1983, The Selkie Girl 1986, The Silver Cow: A Welsh Tale 1983, Matthew's Dragon 1991, Tam Lin 1991, Danny and the Kings 1993, The Boggart 1993, The Boggart and the Monster 1997, King of Shadows 1999, Frog 2002, Green Boy 2002, The Magician's Boy 2005, Victory 2006; TV screenplays; contrib. to periodicals and anthologies. *Honours:* Horn Book Fanfares 1967, 1971, 1974, 1976, 1987, 1994, 2000, Newbery Honor 1974, Newbery Medal 1976, Boston Globe-Horn Book Awards 1974, 1999, Silver Hugo Award 1984, Writers' Guild of America Awards 1984, 1985, Christopher Award 1985, Judy Lopez Memorial Award for Children's Literature 1993, Children's Book Award, Scottish Arts Council 1999, five ALA Notable Children's Books, two Carnegie Medal Honor Books, Humanitas Prize. *E-mail:* sixsigns@comcast.net (office). *Website:* thelostland.com.

COOVER, Robert Lowell, BA, MA; American writer, dramatist and teacher; *Professor of Literary Arts, Brown University;* b. 4 Feb. 1932, Charles City, Ia; m. Maria del Pilar Sans-Mallafré 1959; one s. two d. *Education:* Southern Illinois Univ., Indiana Univ., Univ. of Chicago. *Career:* Teacher, Bard Coll. 1966–67, Univ. of Iowa 1967–69, Princeton Univ. 1972–73, Brown Univ. 1980–, Prof. of Literary Arts 1989–; various guest lectureships and professorships; mem. American Acad. and Inst. of Arts and Letters, American Acad. of Arts & Sciences, PEN Int., Bd of Dirs The Electronic Literature Org., numerous advisory bds. *Film:* On a Confrontation in Iowa City. *Plays include:* The Kid, Love Scene, Rip Awake, A Theological Position, Charlie in the House of Rue. *Radio includes:* Pratt Falls Again, Between the Acts. *Publications include:* The Origin of the Brunists 1966, The Universal Baseball Asscn, J. Henry Waugh, Prop. 1968, Pricksongs & Descants (short fictions) 1969, A Theological Position (plays) 1972, The Public Burning 1977, A Political Fable (The Cat in the Hat for President) 1980, Spanking the Maid 1982, In Bed One Night & Other Brief Encounters (short fictions) 1983, Gerald's Party 1986, A Night at the Movies 1987, Whatever Happened to Gloomy Gus of the Chicago Bears? 1987, Pinocchio in Venice 1991, John's Wife 1996, Briar Rose 1997, Ghost Town 1998, The Grand Hotels (of Joseph Cornell) 2002, The Adventures of Lucky Pierre 2002, Stepmother 2004, A Child Again 2005, Noir 2010, The Universal Baseball Association 2011; contribs: plays, poems, fiction, trans, essays and criticism in numerous publications and anthologies. *Honours:* William Faulkner Award for Best First Novel 1966, Rockefeller Foundation Grant 1969, Guggenheim Fellowships 1971, 1974, Obie Awards 1972–73, American Acad. of Arts and Letters Award 1976, Nat. Endowment of the Humanities Grant 1985, Rhode Island Gov.'s Arts Award 1988, Deutscher Akademischer Austauschdienst Fellowship, Berlin 1990, Rhode Island Pell Award 1999, Lannan Foundation Fellowship 2000, Mercantile Library Clifton Award 2006. *Address:* Program in Literary Arts, Brown University, Providence, RI 02912, USA (office). *Telephone:* (401) 863-1152 (office). *E-mail:* robert_coover@brown.edu (office). *Website:* www.brown.edu (office).

COPE, Wendy Mary, OBE, MA, FRSL; British writer; b. 21 July 1945, Erith, Kent, England; d. of Fred Stanley Cope and Alice Mary Cope (née Hand); partner Lachlan Mackinnon. *Education:* Farringtons School, St Hilda's Coll., Oxford, Westminster Coll. of Educ., Oxford. *Career:* primary school teacher, London 1967–86; freelance writer 1986–; mem. Soc. of Authors (mem. Man. Cttee 1992–95). *Publications include:* Across the City 1980, Hope and the 42 1984, Making Cocoa for Kingsley Amis 1986, Poem from a Colour Chart of House Paints 1986, Men and Their Boring Arguments 1988, Does She Like Wordgames? 1988, Twiddling Your Thumbs 1988, The River Girl 1990, Serious Concerns 1992, If I Don't Know 2001; editor: Is That the New Moon? – Poems by Women Poets 1989, The Orchard Book of Funny Poems 1993, The Funny Side 1998, The Faber Book of Bedtime Stories 2000, Heaven on Earth – 101 Happy Poems 2001, George Herbert: Verse and Prose (a selection) 2002, Two Cures for Love: Selected Poems 2008, Family Values 2011; contribs to newspapers and reviews. *Honours:* Hon. DLitt (Winchester) 2000, (Oxford Brookes) 2003; Cholmondeley Award for Poetry 1987, Michael Braude Award for Light Verse, American Acad. of Arts and Letters 1995. *Literary Agent:* c/o Faber and Faber, Bloomsbury House, 74–77 Great Russell Street, London, WC1B 3DA, England. *Telephone:* (20) 7927-3800. *Website:* www.faber.co.uk.

COPELAND, Ann (see Furtwängler, Virginia Walsh)

COPLEY, Paul; British actor and writer; b. 25 Nov. 1944, Denby Dale, Yorks., England; m. Natasha Pyne 1972. *Education:* Northern Counties Coll. of Education (Teacher's Certificate ADB). *Career:* fmrly taught English and Drama in Walthamstow; mem. Writers' Guild. *Stage performances:* John Wilson's For King and Country (Mermaid Theatre) (Plays and Players Most Promising Actor, Laurence Olivier Award for Actor of the Year) 1976, The Servant (Birmingham Rep) (Martini/TMA Award for Best Actor in a Supporting Role) 1995, Kent in King Lear (Globe Theatre, London) 2008. *Stage plays as writer:* Pillion (Bush Theatre, London) 1977, Viaduct (Bush Theatre, London) 1979, Tapster (Stephen Joseph Theatre, Scarborough) 1981, Fire-Eaters (Tricycle Theatre, London) 1984, Calling (Stephen Joseph Theatre, Scarborough) 1986. *Plays broadcast:* On May-Day (BBC Radio 4 Sunday Play) 1986, Tipperary Smith (BBC Radio 4) 1994, Words Alive (BBC Education Radio) 1996–2003. *Films include:* Alfie Darling 1974, A Bridge Too Far 1976, On a Paving Stone Mounted 1978, Zulu Dawn 1979, The Remains of the Day 1993, Jude 1996, Blow Dry 2000, The Day My Nan Died (short) 2012. *Radio includes:* played Mr Farthing in Kes by Barry Hines 1971, numerous plays and readings including King Street Junior by Jim Eldridge (more than 100 episodes playing Mr Long, BBC Radio 4) 1985–98, The Fool to Corin Redgrave's King Lear, readings for Words and Music (BBC Radio 3) 2010. *Television includes:* Days of Hope (dir Ken Loach) 1975, Trinity Tales by Alan Plater 1975, Ben Gunn in Treasure Island (BBC) 1977, David Edgar's Destiny (dir Mike Newell) 1978, Death of a Princess (dir Antony Thomas) 1980, Oedipus at Colonus (BBC) 1986, Cracker 1993–95, The Bill 1994, 2003, 2008, 2010, This Life 1996–97, The Lakes 1997–98, Hornblower 1998–2003, Queer as Folk (Channel 4) 1998, The Worst Witch 1999, How Clean is Your House (narrator) 2003–09, Shameless 2005, Life on Mars 2005, Coronation Street 2007, Torchwood – Children of Earth 2009, George Gently 2009, Casualty 2010, Downton Abbey (Series 2) 2011, White Heat 2012. *Publications include:* plays: Odysseus and the Cyclops 1998, Chaucer's The Pardoner's Tale (adaptation) 1999, Jennifer Jenks and Her Excellent Day Out 2000, Loki the Mischief Maker 2000. *Literary Agent:* c/o Amanda Howard, AHA, 21 Berwick Street, London, W1F 0PZ, England. *Telephone:* (20) 7287-9277. *E-mail:* amanda@amandahowardassociates.co.uk. *Website:* www.amandahowardassociates.co.uk. *Literary Agent:* c/o Casarotto Ramsay Ltd, 60 Wardour Street, London, W1V 4ND, England. *E-mail:* t_clark_2001@yahoo.com (office). *Website:* www.paulcopley.com.

CORBIN, Alain, BA, MA, PhD; French academic and writer; b. 12 Jan. 1936, Courtomer; m. Annie Lagorce 1963; two s. *Education:* Univ. of Caen. *Career:* Asst Lecturer, Univ. of Limoges 1968–69; Sr Lecturer, Univ. of Tours 1969–72, Asst Prof. 1973–85, Prof. of History 1985–86; Prof. of History, Univ. of Paris 1987–. *Publications include:* (in English trans.) The Foul and the Fragrant: Odor and the French Social Imagination 1986, A History of Private Life, Vol. 4, From the Fires of Revolution to the Great War (with Michelle Perrot) 1990,

The Village of Cannibals: Rage and Murder in France, 1870 1991, Women for Hire: Prostitution and Sexuality in France After 1850 1992, The Lure of the Sea 1994, Time, Desire, and Horror 1996, Village Bells: Sound and Meaning in the Nineteenth-Century Countryside 1998, Archaism and Modernity in the Nineteenth Century Limousin, 1845–1880 1999, The life of an unknown 2001, Social History of Odors 2006, History of Christianity 2007, 1515 and the Key Dates in the History of France 2008, The Harmony of Pleasures 2008; contribs to scholarly books and journals.

CORK, Richard Graham, MA, PhD; British art critic, writer, broadcaster, exhibition organizer and curator; b. 25 March 1947, Eastbourne; m. Vena Jackson 1970; two s. two d. *Education:* Trinity Hall, Cambridge. *Career:* art critic, Evening Standard 1969–77, 1980–83, The Listener 1984–90; Ed., Studio International 1975–79; Durning-Lawrence Lecturer, Univ. Coll. London 1987; Slade Prof. of Fine Art, Cambridge 1989–90; Chief Art Critic, The Times 1991–2002; Art Critic, The New Statesman 2003–06; Henry Moore Foundation Sr Fellow, Courtauld Inst. of Art, London 1992–95; mem. Arts Council Visual Arts Panel (Chair.), British Council Visual Arts Advisory Cttee, Contemporary Art Soc., South Bank Bd Visual Art Advisory Panel, Syndic of Fitzwilliam Museum, Cambridge, Paul Mellon Centre Advisory Council; Trustee, Wyndham Lewis Memorial Trust, Maggie's Arts Group; Curator, Vorticism and its Allies, Hayward Gallery 1974, Beyond Painting and Sculpture 1974, David Bomberg, Tate Gallery 1988, A Bitter Truth: Avant-Garde Art and the Great War, Barbican Art Gallery 1994, British Art Show 1995, A Life of Their Own, Lismore Castle 2008, Wild Thing: Jacob Epstein, Henri Gaudier-Brzeska and Eric Gill, Royal Acad. 2009–10. *Publications include:* Vorticism and Abstract Art in the First Machine Age (two vols) 1975–76, The Social Role of Art 1979, Art Beyond the Gallery in Early Twentieth Century England 1985, David Bomberg 1987, Architect's Choice 1992, A Bitter Truth: Avant-Garde Art and the Great War 1994, Bottle of Notes: Claes Oldenburg and Coosje van Bruggen 1997, Jacob Epstein 1999, Everything Seemed Possible: Art in the 1970s 2003, New Spirit, New Sculpture, New Money: Art in the 1980s 2003, Breaking Down the Barriers: Art in the 1990s 2003, Annus Mirabilis? Art in the Year 2000 2003, Michael Craig-Martin 2006, The Healing Presence of Art: A History of Western Art in Hospitals 2011; numerous essays for catalogues and contribs to art magazines and periodicals. *Honours:* John Llewelyn Rhys Memorial Prize 1976, Sir Banister Fletcher Award 1986, Nat. Art Fund Award 1995. *Address:* 24 Milman Road, London, NW6 6EG, England (home).

CORKHILL, Annette Robyn, BA, DipEd, MA, PhD, NAATI 3; Australian writer, poet and translator; b. (Annette Robyn Vernon), 10 Sept. 1955, Brisbane, Qld; d. of Donald Vernon and Mavis Vernon; m. Alan Corkhill 1977; two s. one d. *Education:* Kangaroo Point State School, Somerville House, Univ. of Queensland. *Career:* teacher of foreign languages; self-employed trans. from German 1993–. *Publications include:* The Jogger: Anthology of Australian Poetry 1987, Destination, Outrider 1987, Mangoes Encounter – Queensland Summer 1987, Age 1, LINQ 1987, Two Soldiers of Tiananmen, Earth Against Heaven 1990, Australian Writing: Ethnic Writers 1945–1991 1994, The Immigrant Experience in Australian Literature 1995; contrib. to Outrider, Australian Literary Studies. *Honours:* Hon. Mention, The Creativity Centre, Harold Kesteven Poetry Prize 1987; Dux of the School, Karl and Frieda Reber Memorial Prize, Mary Alison Miles Munro Scholarship. *Address:* 5 Wattletree Place, The Gap, Qld 4061, Australia. *Telephone:* (7) 3300-4634. *Fax:* (7) 3300-4878. *E-mail:* annettecorkhill@gmail.com; annette.germantranslation@gmail.com. *Website:* www.germantranslation.com.au (home).

CORMAN, Avery, BS; American novelist; b. 28 Nov. 1935, New York, NY; m. Judith Lishinsky 1967, two s. *Education:* New York Univ. *Career:* mem. Bd of Dirs City Parks Foundation; mem. PEN American Center, Writers Guild of America. *Publications include:* Oh God! 1971, Kramer vs. Kramer 1977, The Bust-Out King 1977, The Old Neighborhood 1980, Fifty 1987, Prized Possessions 1991, The Big Hype 1992, A Perfect Divorce 2004, The Boyfriend from Hell 2006. *Address:* 141 East 88th Street, New York, NY 10128-2248, USA (home).

CORN, Alfred, BA, MA; American poet, writer, critic and translator; b. 14 Aug. 1943, Bainbridge, Ga; m. Ann Jones 1967 (divorced 1971). *Education:* Emory Univ., Columbia Univ. *Career:* Poet-in-Residence, George Mason Univ. 1980, Blaffer Foundation, New Harmony, IN 1989, James Thurber House 1990; Humanities Lecturer, New School for Social Research, New York City 1988; Ellison Chair in Poetry, Univ. of Cincinnati 1989; Bell Distinguished Visiting Prof., Univ. of Tulsa 1992; Hurst Residency in Poetry, Washington Univ., St Louis 1994; numerous coll. and univ. seminars and workshops; many poetry readings; mem. Nat. Book Critics Circle, PEN, Poetry Soc. of America; Woodrow Wilson Fellow 1965–66, Fulbright Fellow, Paris 1967–68. *Publications include:* poetry: All Roads at Once 1976, A Call in the Midst of the Crowd 1978, The Various Light 1980, Tongues on Trees 1980, The New Life 1983, Notes from a Child of Paradise 1984, An Xmas Murder 1987, The West Door 1988, Autobiographies 1992, Present 1997, Contradictions 2002; novel: Part of His Story 1997; criticism: The Metamorphoses of Metaphor 1987, Incarnation: Contemporary Writers on the New Testament (ed.) 1990, The Pith Helmet 1992, A Manual of Prosody 1997, Atlas: Selected Essays 1989–2007 2009; contribs: books, anthologies, scholarly journals, and periodicals. *Honours:* Ingram Merrill Fellowships 1974, 1981, Nat. Endowment for the Arts Fellowships for Poetry 1980, 1991, Gustav Davidson Prize, Poetry Soc. of America 1983, American Acad. and Institute of Arts and Letters Award 1983, New York Foundation for the Arts Fellowships 1986, 1995, Guggenheim Fellowship 1986–87, Acad. of American Poets Prize 1987, Yaddo Corporation Fellowship in Poetry 1989, Djerassi Foundation Fellowship in Poetry 1990, Rockefeller Foundation Fellowship in Poetry, Bellagio, Italy 1992, MacDowell Colony Fellowships in Poetry 1994, 1996. *Website:* alfredcornsweblog.blogspot.com.

CORNWELL, Bernard, (Susannah Kells), BA; British writer; b. 23 Feb. 1944, London; m. Judy Acker 1980. *Education:* Univ. of London. *Publications include:* Redcoat 1987, Wildtrack 1988, Sea Lord (aka Killer's Wake) 1989, Crackdown (aka Murder Cay) 1990, Stormchild 1991, Scoundrel 1992, Stonehenge 2000 BC 1999, The Archer's Tale 2001, The Last Kingdom 2004, The Pale Horseman 2005, Lords of the North Country 2006, Agincourt 2008, The Burning Land 2009, The Fort 2010; Starbuck Chronicles series: Rebel 1993, Copperhead 1994, Battle Flag 1995, The Bloody Ground 1996; Arthur series: The Winter King 1995, Enemy of God 1996, Excalibur 1997; Sharpe series: Sharpe's Eagle 1981, Sharpe's Gold 1981, Sharpe's Company 1982, Sharpe's Sword 1983, Sharpe's Enemy 1984, Sharpe's Honour 1985, Sharpe's Regiment 1986, Sharpe's Siege 1987, Sharpe's Rifles 1988, Sharpe's Revenge 1989, Sharpe's Waterloo 1990, Sharpe's Devil 1992, Sharpe's Battle 1995, Sharpe's Tiger 1997, Sharpe's Triumph 1998, Sharpe's Fortress 1999, Sharpe's Trafalgar 2000, Sharpe's Prey 2001, Sharpe's Skirmish (short story) 2002, Sharpe's Havoc 2003, Sharpe's Escape 2004, Sharpe's Fury 2006; Grail Quest series: Harlequin 2000, Heretic 2003; as Susannah Kells: A Crowning Mercy 1983, The Fallen Angels 1984, Coat of Arms 1986, The Aristocrats 1987. *Literary Agent:* Toby Eady Associates Ltd, Third Floor, 9 Orme Court, London, W2 4RL, England. *Telephone:* (20) 7792-0092. *Fax:* (20) 7792-0879. *E-mail:* toby@tobyeady.demon.co.uk. *Website:* www.tobyeadyassociates.co.uk; www.bernardcornwell.net (home).

CORNWELL, David John Moore, (John le Carré), BA; British writer; b. 19 Oct. 1931, Poole, Dorset, England; s. of Ronald Thomas Archibald Cornwell and Olive Glassy; m. 1st Alison Ann Veronica Sharp 1954 (divorced 1971); three s.; m. 2nd Valerie Jane Eustace 1972; one s. *Education:* St Andrew's Preparatory School, Pangbourne, Sherborne School, Berne Univ., Switzerland and Lincoln Coll., Oxford. *Career:* teacher, Eton Coll. 1956–58; in Foreign Service (Second Sec., Bonn, then Political Consul Hamburg) 1959–64. *Publications:* Call for the Dead 1961, Murder of Quality 1962, The Spy Who Came in from the Cold 1963, The Looking Glass War 1965, A Small Town in Germany 1968, The Naive and Sentimental Lover 1971, Tinker, Tailor, Soldier, Spy 1974, The Honourable Schoolboy 1977, Smiley's People 1979, The Quest for Karla (collected edn of previous three titles) 1982, The Little Drummer Girl 1983, A Perfect Spy 1986, The Russia House 1989, The Secret Pilgrim 1991, The Night Manager 1993, Our Game 1995, The Tailor of Panama 1996, Single and Single 1999, The Constant Gardener (British Book Awards Play.com TV & Film Book of the Year 2006) 2000, Absolute Friends 2004, The Mission Song 2006, A Most Wanted Man 2008, Our Kind of Traitor 2010. *Honours:* Hon. Fellow, Lincoln Coll., Oxford 1984–; Commdr des Arts et des Lettres 2005; Hon. DLitt (Exeter) 1990, (St Andrews) 1996, (Southampton) 1997, (Bath) 1998, (Berne Univ., Switzerland) 2008, (Oxford) 2012; Somerset Maugham Award 1963, MWA Edgar Allan Poe Award 1965, James Tait Black Award 1977, CWA Gold Dagger 1978, MWA 'Grand Master Award' 1986, Premio Malaparte 1987, CWA Diamond Dagger 1988, Nikos Kazantzakis Prize 1991, CWA 'Dagger of Daggers' 2005, Sunday Times Award for Literary Excellence 2010, Goethe Medal (Germany) 2011. *Literary Agent:* c/o Curtis Brown, 28–29 Haymarket, London, SW1Y 4SP, England. *Telephone:* (20) 7393-4400. *Fax:* (20) 7393-4401. *Website:* www.johnlecarre.com.

CORNWELL, Patricia Daniels, BA; American writer; b. 9 June 1957, Miami, FL. *Education:* Davidson Coll. (NC). *Career:* police reporter, Charlotte Observer, NC 1979–81; computer analyst, Office of the Chief Medical Examiner, Richmond, Va 1985–91; mem. Authors' Guild, Int. Asscn of Identification, Int. Crime Writers Asscn, Nat. Asscn of Medical Examiners. *Publications include:* non-fiction: A Time of Remembering: The Story of Ruth Bell Graham 1983 (re-issued as Ruth: a Portrait 1997); fiction: Postmortem (John Creasey Award, British Crime Writers' Asscn 1991, Anthony Award, Boucheron Award, World Mystery Convention, MacAvity Award, Mystery Readers Int) 1990, Body of Evidence 1991, All That Remains 1992, Cruel and Unusual 1993, The Body Farm 1994, From Potter's Field 1995, Cause of Death 1996, Hornet's Nest 1996, Unnatural Exposure 1997, Point of Origin 1998, Southern Cross 1999, Black Notice 1999, The Last Precinct 2001, Isle of Dogs 2001, Portrait of a Killer: Jack the Ripper 2002, Blow Fly 2003, Trace 2004, Predator 2005, At Risk 2006, Book of the Dead (British Book Award for Best Crime Thriller 2008) 2007, Scarpetta 2008, The Front 2008, The Scarpetta Factor 2009, Port Mortuary 2010, Red Mist (RBA Int. Thriller Prize) 2011. *Honours:* Investigative Reporting Award, North Carolina Press Asscn 1980, Gold Medallion Book Award, Evangelical Christian Publishers Asscn 1985, Edgar Award 1990, Prix du Roman d'Aventure 1991, Gold Dagger Award 1993, Sherlock Holmes Award 1999. *Address:* c/o Don Congdon Associates Inc., 156 5th Avenue, Suite 625, New York, NY 10010-7002, USA. *Website:* www.patriciacornwell.com.

CORONEL, Sheila S., BA, MA; Philippine journalist and academic; *Toni Stabile Professor of Professional Practice in Investigative Journalism, Columbia University*; b. 1958, Manila. *Education:* Univ. of the Philippines, London School of Econs, UK. *Career:* began as cub reporter for Philippine Panorama 1983; reporter for The Manila Times, Manila Chronicle; Co-founder and Exec. Dir Philippine Center for Investigative Journalism 1989–2006; Dir, Toni Stabile Center for Investigative Journalism, Columbia Univ., currently

Toni Stabile Prof. of Professional Practice in Investigative Journalism. *Publications:* more than 12 books, including Coups, Cults and Cannibals, The Rulemakers, Pork and Other Perks. *Honours:* Ramón Magsaysay Award for Journalism 2003, Presidential Teaching Award, Columbia Univ. 2011. *Address:* Toni Stabile Center for Investigative Journalism, School of Journalism, Columbia University, 2950 Broadway, New York, NY 10027, USA (office). *Telephone:* (212) 854-5748 (office). *E-mail:* ssc2136@columbia.edu (office). *Website:* www.stabilecenter.org (office).

ĆOSIĆ, Dobrica; Serbian writer and politician; b. 29 Dec. 1921, Velika Drenova; m. Božica Ćosić; one d. *Education:* Belgrade Univ., Higher Party School. *Career:* war service 1941–45; worked as journalist, then as freelance writer; corresp. mem. Serbian Acad. of Arts and Sciences 1970, mem. 1976; left League of Communists of Yugoslavia (LCY), prosecuted; resumed active political activity 1980s; Pres. of Repub. of Yugoslavia 1992–93. *Publications:* The Sun is Far 1951, Roots 1954, Sections 1961, Fairy Tale 1965, The Time of Death (Vols 1–4) 1972–79, The Time of Evil: Sinner (Vols 1–4) 1985, Apostate 1986, Believer 1990, The Time of Power 1995, Kosovo; studies and essays: Hope and Fear 2001, Real and Possible 2001, Serbian Question (Vols 1–4) 2002, Writer's Notes (Vols 1–4) 2002. *Address:* Serbian Academy of Sciences and Arts, Knez Mikhailova Str. 35, Belgrade (office); Branka Djonovića 6, Belgrade, Serbia (home). *Telephone:* (11) 3342400 (office); (11) 663437 (home). *E-mail:* sasapres@bib.sanu.ac.yu (office).

COSMOS, Jean; French playwright; b. (Jean Louis Gaudrat), 14 June 1923, Paris; s. of Albert Gaudrat and Maria Maillebuau; m. Alice Jarrousse 1948; one s. two d. *Education:* Inst. St Nicholas, Igny, Coll. Jean-Baptiste Say, Paris. *Career:* songwriter 1945–50, writer for radio 1952–60, for TV 1964–; mem. Comm. Soc. des auteurs dramatiques 1971–; co-librettist Goya 1996 (opera). *Plays:* author or adapter of numerous plays for the theatre including la Fille du roi 1952, Au jour le jour 1952, les Grenadiers de la reine 1957, Macbeth 1959, 1965, le Manteau 1963, la Vie et la Mort du roi Jean 1964, Arden de Faversham 1964, Monsieur Alexandre 1965, la Bataille de Lobositz 1969, Major Barbara 1970, le Marchand de Venise 1971, Sainte Jeanne des Abattoirs 1972, Ce sacré Bonheur 1987; author of numerous TV plays including les Oranges (Albert Ollivier prize) 1964, le Pacte 1966, Un homme, un cheval 1968, la Pomme oubliée (after Jean Anglade), l'Ingénu (after Voltaire), Bonsoir Léon, la Tête à l'envers, le Trêve, le Coup Monté, Aide-toi, Julien Fontanes, magistrat (TV Series 1980–89), La Dictée 1984; with Jean Chatenêt: 16 à Kerbriant, Ardéchois coeur fidèle (Critics' choice) 1975, Les Yeux Bleus, la Lumière des Justes (after Henri Troyat); with Gilles Perrault: le Secret des dieux, la Filière, Fabien de la Drôme, seven-part serial of Julien Fontanes, Magistrat, regular contrib. to les Cinq dernières minutes. *Films include:* Bonjour toubib 1959 La vie et rien d'autre 1989, Le Colonel Chabert 1994, La fille de d'Artagnan 1994, Capitaine Conan 1996, Le bossu 1997, Laissez-passer 2002, Effroyables jardins 2003, Fanfan la tulipe 2003, Agents secrets 2004, Aurore 2006, Le Grand Meaulnes 2006, Michou d'Auber 2007, Dialogue avec mon jardinier 2007. *Honours:* Chevalier, Légion d'honneur, Officier des Arts et des Lettres; Soc. des auteurs et compositeurs prizes 1970. *Address:* c/o Artmédia, 20 avenue Rapp, 75007 Paris (office); 57 rue de Versailles, 92410 Ville d'Avray, France (home). *Telephone:* 1-43-17-33-00 (office). *E-mail:* info@artmedia.fr (office).

COTTA, Michèle, LèsL; French journalist; b. 15 June 1937, Nice; d. of Jacques Cotta and Helène Scoffier; m. 1st Claude Tchou (divorced); one s. (deceased) one d.; m. 2nd Phillipe Barret 1992. *Education:* Lycée de Nice, Faculté de Lettres de Nice and Inst. d'études politiques de Paris. *Career:* journalist with L'Express 1963–69, 1971–76; Europ I 1970–71, 1986; political diarist, France-Inter 1976–80; Head of political service, Le Point 1977–80, Reporter 1986; Chief Political Ed. RTL 1980–81; Pres. Dir-Gen. Radio France 1981–82; Pres. Haute Autorité de la Communication Audiovisuelle 1982–86; Producer Faits de Soc. on TF1 1987, Dir of Information 1987–92, Pres. Sofica Images Investissements 1987; producer and presenter La Revue de presse, France 2 1993–95; political ed. Nouvel Economiste 1993–96; producer and presenter Polémiques, France 2 1995–99, Dir-Gen. France 2 1999–2002 (retd); apptd Dir-Gen. JLA Groupe 2002; editorial writer, RTL 1996–99; mem. Conseil économique et social. *Publications:* La collaboration 1940–1944, 1964, Les elections présidentielles 1966, Prague, l'été des Tanks 1968, La Vième République 1974, Les miroirs de Jupiter 1986, La Sixième République 1992, Les Secrets d'une Victoire 1999, Politic Circus 2004, Cahiers secrets of the Fifth Republic (Vol. 1) 1965–1977 2007, Cahiers secrets of the Fifth Republic (Vol. 2) 1977–1986 2008, Cahiers secrets of the Fifth Republic (Vol. 3) 1986–1997 2009, Cahiers secrets of the Fifth Republic (Vol. 4) 1997–2007 2010. *Honours:* Chevalier, Légion d'honneur, Officier, Ordre nat. du mérite. *Address:* 70 boulevard Port Royal, 75005 Paris, France (home). *E-mail:* mcotta@noos.fr.

COTTRELL BOYCE, Frank, (Martin Hardy), BA, PhD; British screenwriter and author; *Professor of Reading and Communication, Liverpool Hope University*; b. 23 Sept. 1959, Liverpool; m.; seven c. *Education:* Keble Coll., Univ. of Oxford. *Career:* fmr television critic, Living Marxism mid-1980s; writer for TV serials 1986–96; screenwriter for films 1990–; author 2004–; Prof. of Reading and Communication, Liverpool Hope Univ. 2012–. *Films include:* as screenwriter: Forget About Me (TV) 1990, Butterfly Kiss 1995, New York Crossing 1996, Saint-Ex 1996, Welcome to Sarajevo 1997, Hilary and Jackie 1998, Pandaemonium 2000, The Claim 2000, 24 Hour Party People 2002, The Revengers Tragedy 2002, Code 46 (Best Screenplay, Catalonian Int. Film Festival 2004) 2003, Millions (British Ind. Best Film Award 2005) 2004, A Cock and Bull Story (as Martin Hardy) (Chlotrudis Award for Best Adapted Screenplay 2007) 2006, Grow Your Own 2007, Framed 2009. *Television:* as scriptwriter: Brookside 1986–89, Damon and Debbie 1987, Coronation Street 1991–96 , A Woman's Guide to Adultery 1993, God on Trial 2008. *Plays:* Proper Clever, Liverpool Playhouse 2008. *Publications:* Millions (Carnegie Medal 2004) 2004, Framed 2005, Cosmic 2008, Desirable 2008, The Unforgotten Coat 2011, Chitty Chitty Bang Bang Flies Again 2011. *Address:* Liverpool Hope University, Hope Park, Liverpool, L16 9JD (office); c/o Walker Books, 87 Vauxhall Walk, London, SE11 5HJ (office); c/o Northern Soul Film Productions Limited, 31 Sandhurst Street, Aigburth, Liverpool, Merseyside, L17 7BT, England (office). *Telephone:* (151) 291-3000 (Hope Univ.) (office); (20) 7793-0909 (Walker Books) (office). *E-mail:* enquiry@hope.ac.uk (office); editorial@walker.co.uk (office); info@northernsoulfp.com (office). *Website:* www.hope.ac.uk (office); www.walker.co.uk (office); www.northernsoulfp.com (office).

COULOMBE, Charles Aquila; American writer; b. 8 Nov. 1960, New York, NY; s. of the late Guy Coulombe and of Patricia Coulombe. *Education:* New Mexico Mil. Inst., Roswell. *Career:* fmr Contributing Ed., Nat. Catholic Register; mem. Authors' Guild, Catholic Writers' Guild of GB. *Publications include:* Everyman Today Call Rome 1987, The White Cockade 1990, Puritan's Progress 1996, The Muse in the Bottle 2002, Classic Horror Tales 2003, Vicars of Christ 2003, Rum 2004, Haunted Places in America 2004, Haunted Castles Around the World 2005, The Pope's Legion: The Multinational Fighting Force that Defended the Vatican 2008, Puritan's Empire 2008, Desire & Deception 2009; contrib. to periodicals. *Honours:* Christian Law Inst.'s Christ the King Award 1992, Knight Commdr of St Sylvester. *Literary Agent:* Wieser & Elwell, 80 Fifth Avenue, Suite 1101, New York, NY 10011, USA. *Address:* PO Box 660771, Arcadia, CA 91066, USA (office). *Telephone:* (626) 357-7236 (office). *E-mail:* ccoulomb@charlesacoulombe.com (office).

COUPER, Heather Anita, CBE, BSc, PhD, CPhys, FInstP, FRAS; British science broadcaster and writer; b. 2 June 1949, d. of George Couper and the late Anita Couper (née Taylor). *Education:* St Mary's Grammar School (Northwood) and Univs of Leicester and Oxford. *Career:* man. trainee, Peter Robinson Ltd 1967–69; Research Asst, Cambridge Observatories 1969–70; Lecturer, Greenwich Planetarium, Old Royal Observatory 1977–83; Gresham Prof. of Astronomy 1993–96; mem. Millennium Comm. 1994–; Co-founder and Dir Pioneer Productions 1988–99; Pres. British Astronomy Asscn 1984–86; presenter numerous TV and radio programmes; columnist, The Independent. *Television includes:* Heavens Above 1981, Spacewatch 1983, The Planets (series, Channel 4) 1985, The Stars (series, Channel 4) 1988, The Neptune Encounter (ITV) 1989, A Close Encounter of the Second Kind (BBC, Horizon) 1992, ET – Please Call Earth (Channel 4) 1992, Space Shuttle Discovery (Channel 4) 1993, Arthur C. Clarke: Visionary (Discovery Channel Europe) 1995, Electric Skies (Channel 4) 1996, The Science Behind Science Fiction (series, Channel 4) 1996, On Jupiter 1996, Black Holes 1997, Raging Planet (series, Channel 4) 1997–98, The Caspian Sea Monster (Channel 4) 1998, Killer Earth (series, Channel 4) 1998, Stormforce (series, Channel 4) 1999, Stephen Hawking: A Profile (BBC) 2002, Space Shuttle: Human Time Bomb? (Channel 4) 2003. *Radio includes:* Science Now 1983, Cosmic Pursuits 1985, Seeing Stars 1991–2001, ET on Trial 1993, Starwatch (series, BBC Radio 4) 1996, Sun Science 1999, The Essential Guide to the 21st Century (series, BBC World Service) 2000, Worlds Beyond (series, BBC Radio 4), Red Planet (series, BBC Radio 4), Naming the Universe (series, BBC Radio 4), The Modern Magi (BBC Radio 4), Down Your Way (BBC Radio 4), With Great Pleasure (BBC Radio 4); numerous guest broadcasts, interviews, etc. *Publications include:* Exploring Space 1980, Heavens Above (with Terence Murtagh) 1981, Journey into Space 1984, Starfinder (co-author) 1984, The Halley's Comet Pop-Up Book (with Patrick Moore) 1985, The Universe: A 3-Dimensional study (with David Pelham) 1985, Space Scientist (series) 1985–87, Comets and Meteors: The Planets, The Stars, The Sun (co-author), The Moon (co-author), Galaxies and Quasars (co-author), Satellites and Spaceprobes (co-author), Telescopes and Observatories (co-author), The Space Atlas (with Nigel Henbest) 1992, The Guide to the Galaxy (with Nigel Henbest) 1994, How the Universe Works (with Nigel Henbest) 1994, Black Holes (co-author) 1996, Big Bang (co-author) 1997, Is Anybody Out There? (co-author) 1998, To the Ends of the Universe (with Nigel Henbest) 1998, Space Encyclopedia (with Nigel Henbest) 1999, Universe (with Nigel Henbest) 1999, Mars: The Inside Story of the Red Planet (co-author) 2001, Extreme Universe (with Nigel Henbest) 2001, Mars: The Inside Story of the Red Planet (with Nigel Henbest) 2001, Philip's Stargazing 2005 (with Nigel Henbest) 2004, Universe: Stunning Satellite Imagery from Outer Space 2007, History of Astronomy 2007. *Honours:* Hon. DLitt (Loughborough) 1991, Hon. DSc (Hertfordshire) 1994, (Leicester) 1994; Times Educational Supplement Sr Information Book Award 1987, New York TV Awards Gold Medal 1994, 1996, Banff Rockie Award 1995, New York Festivals Grand Award 1997 and Gold Medal 1998. *Literary Agent:* c/o Anthony Goff, David Higham Associates, 5–8 Lower John Street, Golden Square London W1R 4HA, England. *Telephone:* (20) 7434-5900. *Fax:* (20) 7437-1072. *Website:* www.davidhigham.co.uk. *E-mail:* heather@hencoup.com (office). *Website:* www.hencoup.com/en/heather.

COUPLAND, Douglas Campbell; Canadian writer and artist; b. 30 Dec. 1961, Baden-Solingen, Germany. *Education:* Emily Carr Inst. for Art and Design, Vancouver, also studied in Japan and Italy. *Publications include:* Generation X: Tales for an Accelerated Culture 1991, Shampoo Planet 1992, Life After God 1994, Microserfs 1995, Polaroids from the Dead (non-fiction)

1996, Girlfriend in a Coma 1997, Miss Wyoming 1999, City of Glass (non-fiction) 2000, God Hates Japan 2001, All Families are Psychotic 2001, Souvenir of Canada (non-fiction) 2002, School Spirit (non-fiction) 2002, Hey Nostradamus! 2003, September 10 (play) 2004, Souvenir of Canada 2 (non-fiction) 2004, Eleanor Rigby 2004, JPod 2006, The Gum Thief 2007, Microserfs: A Novel (P.S.) 2008, Generation A 2009, Player One 2010, Marshall McLuhan: You Know Nothing of My Work! 2010, Darwin's Bastards: Astounding Tales from Tomorrow (co-author) 2010; contrib. to Art Forum, New Republic, New York Times, Wired. *Address:* c/o Bloomsbury Publishing Plc, 36 Soho Square, London, W1D 3QY, England. *Telephone:* (20) 7494-2111. *Fax:* (20) 7434-0151. *Website:* www.bloomsbury.com; www.coupland.com.

COUR, Ajeet, MEcons; Indian writer; *Chairman, Academy of Fine Arts and Literature*; b. 16 Nov. 1934, Lahore, Pakistan; d. of M. S. Bajaj and Jaswant Kaur; m. Rajinder Singh 1953 (deceased); one d. (Arpana Cour). *Education:* Univ. of Delhi. *Career:* writer 1961–, accredited journalist 1963–; Chief Ed. Rupee Trade 1963–; Chair. Acad. of Fine Arts and Literature 1975–; Vice-Chair. Indian Council of Poverty Alleviation 1991; Founder and Pres. Foundation of SAARC Writers and Literature 1987–; Writer-Del. Int. Women's Congress (Moscow, Russian Fed.) 1987; numerous works have been made into TV films, including Doosra Kewal (13 episodes). *Publications include:* Directory of Indian Women Today (ed.), Directory of Trade Between India and East European Countries; short stories: Gul Bano 1962, Mahik Di Maut, But Shikan, Faltu Aurat, Saviyan Chirian, Maut Ali Babe Dee, Na Maaro, Guari; Novellas: Dhupp Wala Shehar, Post Mortem, Pebbles in a Tin Drum 1997, Kulwant Singh Virk Diyan Chonvian Kahaniyan 1998, Kannū 2009; autobiog.: Khaana Badosh (Sahitya Akademi Award 1986); translations and adaptations: Portrait of a Lady (Henry James), Return of the Red Rose (K. A. Abbas), The Scarlet Letter (Hawthorne), The Sikhs (Khushwant Singh). *Honours:* numerous awards, including Shiromani Sahitkar of the Year 1979, Punjabi Sahitya Samikhta Bd 1979, one of Nine Distinguished Punjabi Writers and Artists, Punjab Govt 1979, Int. IATA Award 1984, Sahitya Akademi Award 1985, Bharatiya Bhasha Parishad (Calcutta) Award 1989, Punjabi Sahitya Sabha Award 1989, Dhaliwal Award 1990, Padma Shri 2006. *Address:* Academy of Fine Arts and Literature, 4/6 Siri Fort Road, Industrial Area, New Delhi 110 049 (office); 166 SFS Flats, Mount Kallash, opp Delhi Public School, New Delhi 110 065, India (home). *Telephone:* (11) 6438070.

COURTENAY, Bryce; Australian author; b. 14 Aug. 1933, Johannesburg, South Africa; m. Benita Courtenay; three s. *Career:* brought up in Limpopo Prov., SA, studied journalism in London, UK, emigrated to Australia; fmr advertising copywriter and creative dir of McCann Erickson, J. Walter Thompson & George Patterson Advertising. *Publications include:* novels: The Power of One 1989, Tandia 1992, April Fool's Day 1993, Recipe for Dreaming 1994, The Power of One to One 1995, The Potato Factory 1995, Tommo & Hawk 1997, The Family Frying Pan 1997, The Stranger Inside: An Erotic Adventure 1997, Yowie Series 1997, Jessica 1998, The Night Country 1998, The Power of One: Young Reader's Edn 1999, Solomon's Song 1999, Four Fires 2001, Smoky Joe's Cafe 2001, Matthew Flinders' Cat 2002, Brother Fish 2004, Whitethorn 2005, Sylvia 2006, The Persimmon Tree 2007, Fishing For Stars 2009, The Story of Danny Dunn 2010, Fortune Cookie 2010. *Address:* c/o Authors, Penguin Group (Australia), PO Box 701, Hawthorn, Vic. 3122, Australia. *E-mail:* marketing@au.penguingroup.com. *Website:* www.penguin.com.au; www.brycecourtenay.com.

COURTER, Gay, AB; American writer and film-maker; b. 1 Oct. 1944, Pittsburgh, Pa; m. Philip Courter 1968; two s. one d. *Education:* Antioch Coll., OH. *Career:* mem. Authors' Guild, Writers Guild of America East, Guardian Ad Litem, Int. Childbirth Asscn. *Publications include:* The Bean Sprout Book 1974, The Midwife 1981, River of Dreams 1984, Code Ezra 1986, Flowers in the Blood 1990, The Midwife's Advice 1992, I Speak for This Child 1995, How to Survive Your Husband's Midlife Crisis 2003; contribs: Parents, Women's Day, Publishers Weekly. *Telephone:* (352) 795-2156 (office). *Fax:* (352) 795-6144 (office). *E-mail:* gay@gaycourter.com (office). *Website:* gaycourter.com.

COURTNEY, Dayle (see Goldsmith, Howard)

COURTNEY, Nicholas Piers, MRICS, MRAC; British author; b. 20 Dec. 1944, Berks., England; m. Vanessa Hardwicke 1980. *Education:* Nautical Coll., Berks., Royal Agricultural Coll., Cirencester. *Career:* mil. service 1964–66; Estate Man. to Col C. G. Lancaster, Kelmarsh Hall, Northampton1966–69; Gen. Man. Island of Mustique, St Vincent, West Indies 1970–77; writer 1980–; mem. Royal Inst. of Chartered Surveyors, Brook's. *Publications include:* Shopping and Cooking in Europe 1980, The Tiger: Symbol of Freedom 1981, Diana: Princess of Wales 1982, Royal Children 1982, Prince Andrew 1983, Sporting Royals 1983, Diana, Princess of Fashion 1984, Queen Elizabeth, The Queen Mother 1984, The Very Best of British 1985, In Society: The Brideshead Years 1986, Princess Anne 1986, Luxury Shopping in London 1987, Sisters in Law 1988, A Stratford Kinshall 1989, The Mall 1990, Windsor Castle 1991, A Little History of Antiques 1995, Gale Force 10: The Life and Legacy of Admiral Beaufort 2002, The Queen's Stamps 2004, Still Getting Away With It 2005, A Cut Above the Rest 2005; contribs to The Times, Redbook, Spectator, Independent, House and Garden. *Address:* 9 Kempson Road, London, SW6 4PX, England (home).

COUSINEAU, Philip Robert, BA; American writer; b. 26 Nov. 1952, Columbia, SC; m. Jo Beaton; one s. *Education:* Univ. of Detroit. *Television:* host, Global Spirit (LINK TV). *Publications include:* The Hero's Journey: Joseph Campbell on His Life and Work 1990, The Soul of the World 1991, Deadlines: A Rhapsody on a Theme of Famous Last Words 1991, Soul: An Archaeology: Readings from Socrates to Ray Charles 1994, Prayers at 3am 1995, Design Outlaws (with Christopher Zelov) 1996, Soul Moments: Stories from the Marvelous World of Synchronicity 1997, The Art of Pilgrimage: A Seeker's Guide to Making Travel Sacred 1998, The Soul Aflame: A Modern Book of Hours 1999, Riddle Me This: A World Treasury of Riddles 1999, Once the Book of Roads: Travel Stories from Michigan to Marrakesh 2000, Once and Future Myths: The Power of Ancient Stories in Modern Times 2001, The Blue Museum: Poems 2003, The Olympic Odyssey: Rekindling the Flame of the Great Games 2004, The Way Things Are: Huston Smith on the Spiritual Life 2005, A Seat at the Table 2006, Angkor Wat: The Marvelous Enigma 2007, Night Train: New Poems 2007, The Jaguar People 2007, Stoking the Creative Fires 2008, Fungoes and Fastballs: Great Moments in Baseball Haiku 2008, The Meaning of Tea (with Scott Chamberlin Hoyt) 2009, The Oldest Story in the World: A Mosaic of Meditations 2009, Wordcatcher: One Man's Odyssey into the Weird and Wonderful World of Words 2010, Beyond Forgiveness 2011; contribs to Parabola Magazine, Paris Magazine, Utne Reader, Hollwood Scriptwriter, Indian Country Today, Beatitude, Hungry Mind Review, The Scream. *Honours:* Fallot Literary Award 1991. *Literary Agent:* c/o Amy Rennert Literary Agency, 98 Main Street #302, Tiburon, CA 94920, USA. *E-mail:* amyrennert@amyrennertagency.com. *Address:* c/o Sisyphus Press, PO Box 330098, San Francisco, CA 94133, USA. *E-mail:* pilgrimage@earthlink.net (home). *Website:* www.philcousineau.net.

COUSINS, Lucy, BA; British children's writer and illustrator; b. 1964; m.; four c. *Education:* Canterbury Coll., Royal Coll. of Art. *Publications include:* Maisy the Mouse series: Maisy's House (Bologna Ragazzi Prize 1997) 1995, Where is Maisy? 1999, Where Does Maisy Live? 2000, At Home with Maisy 2002, Maisy's Year 2002, 1, 2, 3, What is Maisy Doing? 2003, Go Maisy Go 2003, How Will You Get There, Maisy? 2004, Maisy by the Sea 2004, Maisy Goes Camping 2004, Good Night Maisy 2004, Maisy, Charley and the Wobbly Tooth 2006, Maisy's Amazing Big Book of Words 2007, Maisy's Christmas Day 2008, Maisy Goes to the Playground 2008, Maisy's Snowy Christmas Eve 2009, Maisy Goes to Preschool 2010, Where Are Maisy's Friends? 2010, Maisy Goes to the City 2011, Maisy's First Clock 2011; other books: Around the House 1992, Around the Farm 1992, Noah's Ark 1995, Katy Cat and Beaky Boo 2001, Jazzy in the Jungle (Smarties Book Prize) 2002, Za-za's Baby Brother 2003, Farm Animals 2004, What Can Rabbit Hear? 2005, Hooray for Fish! 2005, Yummy 2009, I'm the Best 2010. *Address:* c/o Walker Books, 87 Vauxhall Walk, London, SE11 5HJ, England. *Website:* www.walkerbooks.co.uk; www.maisyfunclub.com.

COUSINS, Mark; British writer on film, producer and director; *Director, 4Way Pictures*; b. 3 May 1965, Coventry. *Education:* Univ. of Stirling. *Career:* programmer, then Dir Edinburgh Film Festival 1991–96; has presented Moviedrome (BBC 2); f. 4Way Pictures film co. (with Antonia Bird and Robert Carlyle) 1998–; currently staff mem. for MSc in Film Studies, Univ. of Edinburgh; f. charity Scottish Kids Are Making Movies, now Chair. *Television:* creator, presenter, dir Scene by Scene (BBC), The Story of Film: An Odyssey 2011. *Films include:* Dear Mr Gorbachev (assoc. dir), The First Movie 2009. *Publications include:* Imagining Reality: Faber Book of the Documentary (ed., with Kevin Macdonald) 1997, Scene by Scene 2002, The Story of Film 2004, Widescreen: Watching Real People Elsewhere 2008; contrib. to newspapers and magazines, including Prospect, The Times, Evening Standard, Scotland on Sunday, Sight and Sound, The Scotsman. *Honours:* Hon. Lecturer, Univ. of Stirling. *Literary Agent:* c/o PBJ and JBJ Management, 7 Soho Street, London, W1D 3DQ, England. *Telephone:* (20) 7287-1112. *Fax:* (20) 7287-1191. *E-mail:* general@pbjmgt.co.uk. *Website:* www.pbjmgt.co.uk. *Address:* School of Literatures, Languages and Cultures, University of Edinburgh, 12.16 David Hume Tower, George Square, Edinburgh, EH8 9JX, Scotland (office). *Telephone:* (131) 650-3030 (office). *Fax:* (131) 650-3029 (office). *Website:* www.filmstudies.llc.ed.ac.uk (office).

COUTO, Mia; Mozambican biologist, writer and journalist; b. (António Emílio Leite Couto), 5 July 1955, Beira. *Career:* fmr Dir Mozambique Information Agency; columnist, Notícias daily newspaper, Tempo magazine; currently works as environmental biologist at Limpopo Transfrontier Park. *Publications include:* Raiz d'orvalho (poems) 1983, Vozes Anoitecidas (trans. as Voices Made Night) 1986, Cada homem e uma raca 1991 (trans. as Every Man is a Race 1994), Terra Sonambula 1992, Under the Frangipani 2001, Um Rio Chamado Tempo, Uma Casa Chamada Terra 2002, Vozes Anoitecidas 2002, Contos do Nascer da Terra 2002, The Last Flight of the Flamingo 2004, O fio das missangas 2002, A chuva pasmada 2004, Pensatempos 2005, O outro pé da Sereia 2006, Sleepwalking Land 2006, A River Called Time 2008 and collections of short stories. *Honours:* Nat. Award for Literature, Mozambican Nat. Journalistic Asscn 1991, "Best of 1995" Award, Sao Paulo Art Critics Asscn 1996, Prémio Vergílio Ferreira 1999, Latin Union Prize for Literature 2007. *Address:* c/o Serpent's Tail, 3A Exmouth House, Pine Street, London, EC1R 0JH, England (office).

COUZYN, Jeni, BA; Canadian poet, psychotherapist, lecturer and broadcaster; b. 26 July 1942, Johannesburg, South Africa. *Education:* Univ. of Natal. *Career:* Writer-in-Residence, Univ. of Victoria, BC 1976; Founder and Dir Bethesda Arts Centre, Nieu Bethesda, SA 1999–; mem. Guild of Psychotherapists, Poetry Soc. (Gen. Council 1968–75). *Publications include:* Flying 1970, Monkeys' Wedding 1972, Christmas in Africa 1975, House of Changes 1978, The Happiness Bird 1978, Life by Drowning 1983, In the Skin House 1993, Homecoming 1998, A Time to Be Born 1999, Selected Poems

2000, Psycho and Eros 2000; ed.: Bloodaxe Book of Contemporary Women Poets 1985, Singing Down the Bones 1989; other: children's books and edns of poetry. *Honours:* Arts Council of GB grants 1971, 1974, Canada Council grants 1977, 1983. *Address:* Firelizard, PO Box 26327, London, N8 8WU, England (office). *E-mail:* info@firelizard.co.uk (office). *Website:* www.firelizard.co.uk (office).

COVARRUBIAS ORTIZ, Miguel Alejandro, LicenLet, MLit; Mexican writer, poet and academic; *Director de la Revista 'Armas y Letras', Universidad Autónoma de Nuevo León;* b. 27 Feb. 1940, Monterrey; m. Silvia Mijares 1967; two d. *Education:* Universidad Autónoma de Nuevo León, Monterrey. *Career:* Dir Postgraduate Studies Div., Universidad Autónoma de Nuevo León, Monterrey 1973–76, Dir Centre for Literary and Linguistic Research 1976–79, Dir Inst. of Fine Arts 1976–79, Co-ordinator Creative Writing Workshop 1981–2001, 2006–07, Dean of the Faculty of Philosophy and Letters 2000–01, currently Dir de la Revista 'Armas y Letras'; mem. Deslinde cultural review (Dir 1985–2000), Sociedad General de Escritores de México. *Publications include:* fiction: La raíz ausente 1962, Custodia de silencios 1965, 1982, Minusculario 1966; poetry: El poeta 1969, El segundo poeta 1977, 1981, 1988, Pandora 1987, Sombra de pantera 1999, 2011, Antología o tiranía 2003; essays: Papelería 1970, Olavide o Sade 1975, Nueva papelería 1978, Papelería en trámite 1997, Papelorio 2006; translations: El traidor (French and German contemporary poetry) 1993, 2008, Poemas de familia de Martin Pouliot 2001, Poemas de Schwitters/Cendrars 2003, Archivo de traducciones 2006; conversations: Junto a una taza de café 1994, El rojo caballo de tu sonrisa 1997; contribs to various pubs and anthologies, including Antología de autores contemporáneos (fiction) 1972, Antología de autores contemporáneos (drama) 1980, Desde el Cerro de la Silla (Arts & Literature of Nuevo Léon) 1992, Homenaje a Miguel Covarrubias 2010. *Honours:* Xalapa Arts Festival Second Place for Story 1962, Universidad Autónoma de Nuevo León Arts Prize for Literature 1989, Gobierno del Estado du Nuevo León Medal of Civic Merit in Literature and Arts 1993, Nat. Inst. of Fine Arts Poetry Translation Prize 1994. *Address:* Kant 2801, Contry/La Silla, Guadalupe, NL 67173 (home); Casa Universitaria del Libro, Universidad Autónoma de Nuevo León, Avenida Universidad s/n, Cd. Universitaria, San Nicolás de los Garza, NL, Mexico. *Telephone:* (81) 8357-4189 (office); (81) 8329-4111 (office). *E-mail:* covas@prodigy.net.mx (home). *Website:* publicaciones@uanl.mx (office).

COVINGTON, Vicki, BA, MSW; American writer; b. (Vicki Marsh), 22 Oct. 1952, Birmingham, Ala; m. Dennis Covington 1977; two d. *Education:* Univ. of Alabama. *Career:* fmr teacher of creative writing, Univ. of Alabama, Birmingham. *Publications include:* Gathering Home 1988, Bird of Paradise 1990, Night Ride Home 1992, The Last Hotel for Women 1996, Cleaving: The Story of a Marriage (with Dennis Covington) 1999, Women in a Man's World, Crying: Essays 2002. *Honours:* Nat. Endowment for the Arts Fellowship 1988.

COWASJEE, Saros, MA, PhD; Canadian (b. Indian) academic, writer and editor; *Professor Emeritus, University of Regina;* b. 12 July 1931, Secundrabad, India. *Education:* St John's Coll., Agra, Agra Univ. and Univ. of Leeds, UK. *Career:* Asst Ed. Times of India Press, Mumbai 1961–63; teacher, Univ. of Regina, Canada 1963–71, Prof. of English 1971–95, Prof. Emer. 1995–; Gen. Ed. Literature of the Raj series, Arnold Publrs, New Delhi 1984–2000; mem. Cambridge Soc., Asscn of Commonwealth Literature and Language Studies. *Publications include:* Sean O'Casey: The Man Behind the Plays 1963, Sean O'Casey 1966, Stories and Sketches 1970, Goodbye to Elsa (novel) 1974, Coolie: An Assessment (criticism) 1976, So Many Freedoms: A Study of the Major Fiction of Mulk Raj Anand 1977, Nude Therapy (short stories) 1978, The Last of the Maharajas (screenplay) 1980, Studies in Indian and Anglo-Indian Fiction 1993, The Assistant Professor (novel) 1996, Strange Meeting and Other Stories (short stories) 2006; editor: fiction anthologies, including Stories from the Raj 1982, More Stories from the Raj and After 1986, Women Writers of the Raj 1990, The Best Short Stories of Flora Annie Steel 1995, Orphans of the Storm: Stories on the Partition of India 1995, The Oxford Anthology of Raj Stories 1998, The Mulk Raj Anand Omnibus 2004, A Raj Collection 2005, Selected Short Stories of Mulk Raj Anand 2006, The Lasting Legacies of Mulk Raj Anand 2008, Conversations in Bloomsbury by Mulk Raj Anand 2011; contrib. to reviews and journals. *Honours:* four Canada Council and SSHRC Leave Fellowships, J.N. Tata Scholarship to research PhD at Univ. of Leeds. *Address:* Suite 308, 3520 Hillside Street, Regina, SK S4S 5Z5, Canada (home). *Telephone:* (306) 586-3896 (home). *E-mail:* saros.cowasjee@uregina.ca (home).

COWELL, Stephanie; American writer; b. 25 July 1943, New York, NY; m. Russell O'Neal Clay 1995, two s. *Career:* mem. Authors' Guild. *Publications include:* Nicholas Cooke (actor, soldier, physician, priest) 1993, The Physician of London 1995, The Players: Shakespeare 1997, Marrying Mozart 2004, Claude and Camille 2010. *Honours:* American Book Award 1996. *Literary Agent:* c/o Emma Sweeney Agency, 245 East 80th Street, Suite 7E, New York, NY 10075-0506, USA. *E-mail:* info@emmasweeneyagency.com. *Website:* emmasweeneyagency.com. *Address:* 585 West End Avenue, New York, NY 10024, USA (home). *E-mail:* StephanieCowell@nyc.rr.com. *Website:* www.stephaniecowell.com.

COX, Richard, (R. W. Heber), TD, MA (Oxon.); British writer; b. (Richard Hubert Francis Cox), 8 March 1931, Winchester, Hants., England; m. 1963 (divorced); two s. one d. *Education:* St Catherine's Coll., Oxford, King's Coll., London. *Career:* staff corresp., Daily Telegraph 1966–72; mem. States of Alderney 2001–07, Guernsey States 2003–06, Guernsey Overseas Aid Comm. 2004–08, CARE Int. Council of Patrons 2006–. *Publications include:* Operation Sealion 1974, Sam7 1976, Auction 1978, KGB Directive 1981, Ground Zero 1985, The Columbus Option 1986, An Agent of Influence 1988, Park Plaza 1991, Eclipse 1996, Murder at Wittenham Park (as R. W. Heber) 1998, How to Meet a Puffin (juvenile) 2004, Island of Ghosts 2008, A pure Merino (biography) 2012; contrib. to periodicals. *Honours:* Territorial Decoration; Gen. Service Medal. *Address:* The Mews, Salisbury Road, Coombe Bissett, Wilts., SP5 4JT, England. *Telephone:* (1722) 718505 (office). *E-mail:* richardcox@cwgsy.net (office).

COX-JOHNSON, Ann (see SAUNDERS, Ann Loreille)

COYLE, Harold, BA; American writer; b. 6 Feb. 1952, New Brunswick, NJ; m. Patricia A. Bannon 1974; two s. one d. *Education:* Virginia Mil. Inst. *Career:* Commissioned Officer, US Army 1974–91; mem. Asscn of Civil War Sites, Reserve Officers Asscn. *Publications include:* Team Yankee 1987, Sword Point 1988, Bright Star 1991, Trial by Fire 1992, The Ten Thousand 1993, Code of Honor 1994, Look Away 1995, Until the End 1996, Savage Wilderness 1997, God's Children 2000, Dead Hand 2001, Against all Enemies 2002, More than Courage 2003, They Are Soldiers 2004, Cat and Mouse 2005, Pandora's Legion 2007, Prometheus's Child 2007, Vulcan's Fire 2008, Rapiers and Goose Quills 2009, No Warriors, No Glory 2009. *Address:* 22421 Wagner Road, Easton, KS 66020-7262, USA (home). *Telephone:* (913) 773-8230 (home).

COZ, Steve; American editor and publishing executive; b. 26 March 1957, Grafton, Mass.; s. of Henry Coz and Mary Coz; m. Valerie Virga 1987. *Education:* Harvard Univ. *Career:* freelance writer for various US publs 1979–82; reporter, Nat. Enquirer, Fla 1982–95, Ed.-in-Chief 1995, then Editorial Dir and Exec. Vice-Pres. American Media Inc.; Founder and Pres. Coz Media Group LLC; Co-founder and Man. Pnr, MyReforma 2007–; American celebrity analyst BBC Radio 1995–96. *Honours:* Edgar Hoover Memorial Award for Distinguished Public Service 1996; Haven House Award of Excellence for Outstanding Reporting on Domestic Violence Issues 1996. *Address:* Coz Media Group LLC, 2 Osprey Court, Boynton Beach, FL 33435-7033 (office); MyReforma, 1122 East Atlantic Ave, #4, Delray Beach, FL 33483, USA. *Telephone:* (561) 736-9159 (office). *Website:* www.myreforma.com.

COZARINSKY, Edgardo; Argentine film director and writer; b. 13 Jan. 1939, Buenos Aires. *Career:* founder of film magazine, Flashback; film critic 1960s–70s; exiled in Paris, France 1974. *Films include:* ... (Puntos suspensivos) (dir) 1970, Les apprentis-sorciers (dir) 1977, La memoire courte (writer) 1979, Not in Vain (dir) 1980, La guerre d'un seul homme (dir-ed.) 1981, Memoire: Marie MacCarthy (TV, dir) 1982, Autoportrait d'un inconnu: Jean Cocteau (dir) 1983, Haute Mer (dir) 1984, Sarah (dir) 1988, Guerriers et captives (writer, co-dir) 1989, Boulevard des crépuscules (dir) 1992, Citizen Langlois (dir) 1994, Tango deseo (writer, dir) 2002, La quimera de los héroes (writer) 2003, Ronda nocturna (writer, dir) 2004, Nocturnos (dir) 2010. *Publications include:* El laberinto de la apariencia (essay) 1964, Borges y el cine (ed, collection of Borges' criticism, trans. as Borges in/and/on Film) 1970, El relato indefendible (essay) (La Nación essay prize) 1979, Vudú Urbano (short stories, trans. as Urban Voodoo) 1985, El pase del testigo (essays, trans. as The Witness' Pass) 2001, La novia de Odessa (novel, trans. as The Bride from Odessa) 2001, El Rufián Moldavo 2004, Museo del Chisme 2005, Tres Fronteras 2006, Palacios Plebeyos 2006, Maniobras Nocturnas 2007, Milongas 2007, Lejos de donde 2009, Burundanga 2009, La tercera manana (Coleccion Andanzas) 2011. *Address:* Tusquets Editores SA, Cesare Cantù 8, 08023 Barcelona, Spain. *Telephone:* (93) 2530400. *Fax:* (93) 4176703.

CRACE, Jim, BA; British writer and dramatist; b. 1 March 1946, Brocket Hall, Lemsford, Hertfordshire; m. Pamela Ann Turton 1975; one s. one d. *Education:* Birmingham Coll. of Commerce, Univ. of London. *Career:* freelance writer and journalist 1976–87; Distinguished Writer in Residence, James Michener Center, Univ. of Texas, Austin 2008. *Publications:* Continent 1986, The Gift of Stones 1988, Arcadia 1992, Signals of Distress 1994, The Slow Digestions of the Night 1995, Quarantine 1997, Being Dead 1999, The Devil's Larder 2001, Genes 2001, Six 2003, Genesis 2003, The Pesthouse 2007, All That Follows 2010; short stories: Refugees 1977, Annie, California Plates 1977, Helter Skelter, Hang Sorrow, Care'll Kill a Cat 1977, Seven Ages 1980; other: radio plays. *Honours:* Dr hc (Univ. of Central England) 2000; David Higham Award 1986, Guardian Prize for Fiction 1986, Whitbread Awards 1986, 1997, Antico Fattore Prize, Italy 1988, GAP Int. Prize for Literature 1989, Soc. of Authors Travel Award 1992, RSL Winifred Holtby Memorial Prize 1995, E. M. Forster Award 1996, Nat. Critics' Circle Award, USA 2001. *Literary Agent:* c/o David Godwin Associates, 55 Monmouth Street, London, WC2H 9DG, England. *Website:* www.davidgodwinassociates.co.uk.

CRAFT, Robert Lawson, BA; American conductor and writer on music; b. 20 Oct. 1923, Kingston, NY. *Education:* Juilliard School of Music, New York, Berkshire Music Center, Tanglewood, studied conducting with Pierre Monteux. *Career:* Conductor Evenings-on-the-Roof and Monday Evening Concerts, Los Angeles 1950–68; asst to, later close assoc. of Igor Stravinsky 1948–71; numerous collaborations with Stravinsky; conducted first performances of various later works by Stravinsky; conducted works ranging from Monteverdi to Boulez; US premiere of Berg's Lulu (two-act version) Santa Fe 1963; conducted most of world's major orchestras in USA and Europe. *Recordings include:* works of Stravinsky, Webern and Schoenberg. *Publications include:* Conversations with Igor Stravinsky 1959, Memories and Commentaries 1960, Expositions and Developments 1962, Dialogues and a

Diary 1963, Themes and Episodes 1967, Retrospections and Conclusions 1969, Chronicle of a Friendship 1972, Prejudices in Disguise 1974, Stravinsky in Photographs and Documents (with Vera Stravinsky) 1976, Current Convictions: Views and Reviews 1977, Present Perspectives 1984, Stravinsky's Selected Correspondence (trans. and ed. two vols) 1982, 1984, Stravinsky: Glimpses of a Life 1992, The Moment of Existence: Music, Literature and the Arts 1996, An Improbable Life 2003, Down a Path of Wonder (memoirs) 2006; contrib. to various journals and other publs. *Address:* 1390 South Ocean Blvd, Pompano Beach, FL 33062, USA (home). *E-mail:* tony@generation-media.com (office). *Website:* www.robertcraft.net.

CRAGGS, Stewart Roger, MCLIP, FCLIP, MA, PhD; British academic librarian, writer and researcher; b. 27 July 1943, Ilkley, West Yorks., England; m. Valerie J. Gibson 28 Sept. 1968; one s. one d. *Education:* Leeds Polytechnic, Univ. of Strathclyde. *Career:* Teesside Polytechnic 1968–69; JA Jobling 1970–72; Sunderland Polytechnic, later Univ. 1973–95; Prof. of Music Bibliography, Univ. of Sunderland 1993; consultant, William Walton Edn, Oxford University Press 1995–; mem. Chartered Inst. of Library and Information Professionals (Fellow). *Publications include:* William Walton: A Thematic Catalogue 1977, Arthur Bliss: A Bio-Bibliography 1988, William Walton: A Catalogue 1990, Richard Rodney Bennett: A Bio-Bibliography 1990, John McCabe: A Bio-Bibliography 1991, William Walton: A Source Book 1993, John Ireland: A Catalogue, Discography and Bibliography 1993, Alun Hoddinott: A Bio-Bibliography 1993, Edward Elgar: A Source Book 1995, William Mathias: A Bio-Bibliography 1995, Arthur Bliss: A Source Book 1996, Soundtracks: An International Dictionary of Composers for Films 1998, Malcolm Arnold: A Bio-Bibliography 1998, William Walton: Music and Literature 1999, Lennox Berkeley: A Source Book 2000, Benjamin Britten: A Bio-Bibliography 2001, Arthur Bliss: Music and Literature 2002, Peter Maxwell Davies: A Source Book 2002, Alan Bush: A Source Book 2007, Alun Hoddinott: A Source Book 2007. *Honours:* Library Asscn McColvin Medal for Best Reference Book 1990. *Address:* 106 Mount Road, High Barnes, Sunderland, SR4 7NN, England (home). *E-mail:* stewartr.craggs@btinternet.com (home).

CRAIG, Amanda Pauline; British novelist and journalist; b. 22 Sept. 1959, South Africa; m. Robin John Cohen 1988; one s. one d. *Education:* Clare Coll., Cambridge. *Career:* mem. Soc. of Authors (Man. Cttee 2000). *Publications include:* Foreign Bodies 1990, A Private Place 1991, A Vicious Circle 1996, In a Dark Wood 2000, Love in Idleness 2003, Hearts and Minds 2009; contribs to periodicals. *Honours:* Young Journalist of the Year 1996, Catherine Pakenham Award 1998. *Literary Agent:* c/o Curtis Brown Ltd, Haymarket House, 28–29 Haymarket, London, SW1Y 4SP, England. *Telephone:* (20) 7393-4400. *Fax:* (20) 7393-4401. *E-mail:* info@curtisbrown.co.uk. *Website:* www.curtisbrown.co.uk; www.amandacraig.com.

CRAIG, George; American publishing executive. *Career:* Dir Production, Honeywell Computers Scotland 1965–74; Vice-Chair. and Group Man. Dir William Collins, UK 1974–87; Pres. and CEO Harper & Row Publrs Inc. (now HarperCollins Publrs), New York 1987–96; mem. Bd of Dirs The News Corpn Ltd; mem. Editorial Advisory Bd Publrs Weekly Int.

CRAIK, Elizabeth Mary, MA, MLitt, DLitt; British academic, writer and editor; *Visiting Professor, Newcastle University*; b. 25 Jan. 1939, Portmoak, Scotland; m. Alexander Craik 1964; one s. one d. *Education:* Univ. of St Andrews, Girton Coll., Cambridge. *Career:* Research Fellow in Greek, Univ. of Birmingham 1963–64; Asst Lecturer to Sr Lecturer in Greek, Univ. of St Andrews 1964–97; Prof. of Classics, Kyoto Univ., Japan 1997–2002; Leverhulme Emer. Fellowship, Newcastle Univ. 2003–05; Visiting Prof. 2003–; mem. Classical Soc. of Japan, Cambridge Philological Soc., Hellenic Soc. *Publications include:* The Dorian Aegean 1980, Marriage and Property (ed.) 1984, Euripides: Phoenician Women 1988, Owls to Athens (ed.) 1990, Hippocrates: Places in Man 1998, Stobaeus: The Seven Deadly Sins 1998, Hippocrates: On Sight and On Anatomy 2006, Hippocrates: On Glands 2009; contribs to scholarly journals. *Honours:* Hon. Prof., Univ. of St Andrews; British Acad. Awards 1981, 1986, Carnegie Trust Award 1986. *Address:* School of Historical Studies, Faculty of Humanities, Arts and Social Sciences, Newcastle University, Newcastle upon Tyne, NE1 7RU, England (office). *Telephone:* (191) 222-7844 (office). *E-mail:* e.m.craik@ncl.ac.uk (office). *Website:* www.ncl.ac.uk/historical/staff/profile/27678 (office).

CRAIK, Thomas Wallace, BA, MA, PhD; British academic, writer and editor; *Professor Emeritus, Durham University*; b. 17 April 1927, Warrington, Cheshire, England; m. 1st Wendy Ann Sowter 1955 (divorced 1975); one s.; m. 2nd Stella McNichol 2006. *Education:* Christ's Coll., Cambridge. *Career:* Asst Lecturer, Univ. of Leicester 1953, Lecturer 1954–65; Lecturer, Univ. of Aberdeen 1965–67; Sr Lecturer 1967–73; Prof. of English 1973–77; Prof. of English, Durham Univ. 1977–89; Prof. Emer. 1989–; mem. Int. Shakespeare Asscn. *Publications include:* The Tudor Interlude 1958, The Comic Tales of Chaucer 1964; Ed.: Marlowe: The Jew of Malta 1966, Shakespeare: Twelfth Night 1975, Beaumont and Fletcher: The Maid's Tragedy 1988, Shakespeare: The Merry Wives of Windsor 1989, Shakespeare: King Henry V 1995; contrib. to scholarly journals and British Acad. Shakespeare Lecture 1979. *Address:* 8 Little Dene, Lodore Road, Newcastle upon Tyne, NE2 3NZ, England (home).

CRAIS, Robert; American crime novelist and screenwriter; b. 20 June 1953, Independence, La; m. Pat Crais; one d. *Education:* Louisiana State Univ. *Career:* screenwriter for several television series 1977–85; created series of Elvis Cole and Joe Pike detective novels 1985–. *Television includes:* screenwriter for several series including: Baretta 1977–78, Quincy M.E. 1978–79, Riker 1981, Hill Street Blues 1981, Cassie & Co. 1982, Cagney & Lacey 1982, The Mississippi 1983, The Twilight Zone 1986, Miami Vice 1986–88, The Equalizer 1988, LA Law 1992. *Films include:* as screenwriter: The Monkey Mission (TV) 1981, In Self Defense (TV) 1987, Cross of Fire (TV) 1989, The Invisible Man (TV) 1998. *Publications:* Elvis Cole/Joe Pike novel series: The Monkey's Raincoat (Anthony Award 1987, Macavity Award 1987) 1987, Stalking the Angel 1989, Lullaby Town 1992, Free Fall 1993, Voodoo River 1995, Sunset Express (Shamus Award 1996) 1996, Indigo Slam 1997, L.A. Requiem (Dilys Award 1999) 1999, The Last Detective 2003, The Forgotten Man 2005, The Watchman (Barry Award for Best Thriller 2007, Mystery Ink Gumshoe Award for Best Thriller 2007) 2007, Chasing Darkness 2008, The First Rule 2010, The Sentry 2011, Taken 2012; other novels: Demolition Angel 2000, Hostage 2001, The Two-Minute Rule (London Evening Standard Best Crime Novel of the Year 2006) 2006. *Honours:* Ross Macdonald Literary Award 2006. *Literary Agent:* c/o Aaron Priest, The Aaron M. Priest Literary Agency Inc., 708 Third Avenue, 23rd Floor, New York, NY 10017-4201, USA. *Telephone:* (212) 818-0344. *E-mail:* info@aaronpriest.com. *Website:* www.aaronpriest.com. *E-mail:* robert@robertcrais.com. *Website:* www.robertcrais.com.

CRAMER, Richard Ben, BA, MS; American journalist and writer; b. 12 June 1950, Rochester, NY. *Education:* Johns Hopkins Univ., Columbia Univ. *Publications include:* Ted Williams: The Season of the Kid 1991, What It Takes: The Way to the White House 1992, Joe DiMaggio: The Hero's Life 2000, How Israel Lost: The Four Questions 2004, What Do You Think of Ted Williams Now?: A Remembrance 2011; Contrib. to periodicals. *Honours:* journalism awards. *Address:* c/o Simon and Schuster Publicity Department, Simon and Schuster Inc., 1230 Avenue of the Americas, New York, NY 10020, USA. *Website:* www.simonandschuster.com.

CRANE, Hamilton (see Mason, Sarah J.)

CRANE, Richard Arthur, BA, MA; British writer and playwright; b. 4 Dec. 1944, York, England; s. of Rev. Robert Crane and Nowell Crane; m. Faynia Williams 1975; two s. two step-d. *Education:* Jesus Coll., Cambridge. *Career:* Fellow in Theatre, Univ. of Bradford 1972–74; Resident Dramatist, Nat. Theatre 1974–75; Fellow in Creative Writing, Univ. of Leicester 1976; Literary Man., Royal Court Theatre 1978–79; Assoc. Dir, Brighton Theatre 1980–85; Dramaturg, Tron Theatre, Glasgow 1983–84; Visiting Writers Fellowship, Univ. of East Anglia 1988; writer-in-residence, Birmingham Polytechnic 1990–91, HM Prison Bedford 1993; Lecturer in Creative Writing, Univ. of Sussex 1994–2007. *Stage plays include:* Three Ugly Women 1967, The Tenant 1971, Crippen 1971, Tom Brown 1971, Decent Things 1972, The Blood Stream 1972, Mutiny on the Bounty 1972, David King of the Jews 1973, Thunder 1973, Secrets 1973, The Pied Piper 1973, Bleak Midwinter 1973, The Quest 1974, Route of All Evil 1974, Humbug 1974, Mean Time 1975, Clownmaker 1975, Venus and Superkid 1975, Bloody Neighbours 1975, Gunslinger 1976, Nero and the Golden House 1976, Ten Years On 1976, Satan's Ball 1977, Gogol 1978, Vanity 1980, Sand 1981, Brothers Karamazov 1981, The Possessed (with Yuri Lyubimov) 1985, Mutiny! (with David Essex) 1985, Soldier Soldier (with Tony Parker) 1986, Envy (with Donald Swann) 1986, Pushkin 1987, Red Magic 1988, Rolling the Stone 1989, Phaedra (with Michael Glenny) 1990, Baggage and Bombshells 1991, Under the Stars 1993, The Quiz 2003, Fool in the Night 2007, Circus Maximus 2008, Dancing With Demons 2009. *Television plays include:* Rottingdean 1980, The Possessed 1985. *Radio includes:* Gogol 1980, Decent Things 1984, Optimistic Tragedy 1986, Anna and Marina 1991, Understudies 1992, Vlad the Impaler 1992, The Sea The Sea (classic serial) 1993, Plutopia (with Donald Swann) 1994, Eugene Onegin 1999. *Publications include:* Thunder 1976, Gunslinger 1979, Crippen 1993, Under the Stars 1994; ed.: Poems from the Waiting Room 1993, The Last Minute Book 1995, Pandora's Books 1997; contrib. to Edinburgh Fringe, Guardian, Independent, Stage, Index on Censorship, TLS. *Honours:* Edinburgh Fringe First Awards 1973, 1974, 1975, 1977, 1980, 1986, 1987, 1988, 1989. *Literary Agent:* c/o Micheline Steinberg, Fourth Floor, 104 Great Portland Street, London, W1W 6PE, England. *Telephone:* (20) 7631-1310. *E-mail:* micheline@steinplays.com.

CRAWFORD, John William, AA, BA, BSE, MSE, DEd; American poet, writer and academic; *Professor Emeritus of English, Henderson State University*; b. 2 Sept. 1936, Ashdown, Ariz.; m. Kathryn Bizzell 1962; one s. one d. *Education:* Texarkana Coll., Ouachita Baptist Coll., Drake Univ., Oklahoma State Univ. *Career:* Instructor in English, Clinton Community Coll. 1962–66; Asst Prof., Henderson State Univ. 1967–68, Assoc. Prof. 1968–73, Prof. of English 1973–97, Chair Dept of English 1977–86, Prof. Emer. 1997–; mem. Arkansas Philological Asscn, Coll. English Asscn, Poets' Roundtable of Arkansas, South Central MLA. *Publications include:* poetry: Making the Connection 1989, I Have Become Acquainted with the Rain 1997; non-fiction: Shakespeare's Comedies: A Guide 1968, Shakespeare's Tragedies: A Guide 1968, Steps to Success: A Study Skills Handbook 1976, Discourse: Essays on English and American Literature 1978, Romantic Criticism of Shakespearean Drama 1978, Early Shakespearian Actresses 1984, The Learning, Wit and Wisdom of Shakespeare's Renaissance Women 1997, Life in Honeysuckle Valley: The Adventures of a Dog Named Kirby 2006; contribs to anthologies, reviews, quarterlies, journals, etc. *Honours:* Sybil Nash Abrams Prizes 1982, 1995, Poets' Roundtable of Arkansas Merit Award 1988, Arkansas Haiku Soc. Award 1998, Grand Prize, Int. Soc. of Poetry 2007. *Address:* 1813 Walnut,

Arkadelphia, AR 71923, USA (home). *Telephone:* (501) 767-1328 (office). *E-mail:* jwcraw@cablelynx.com (home).

CRAWFORD, Robert, MA, DPhil, FRSE; British poet, writer and academic; *Professor of Modern Scottish Literature, University of St Andrews;* b. 23 Feb. 1959, Bellshill, Scotland; m. Alice Wales 1988; one s. one d. *Education:* Univ. of Glasgow, Univ. of Oxford. *Career:* Elizabeth Wordsworth Jr Research Fellow, Oxford 1984–87; British Acad. Postdoctoral Fellow, Univ. of Glasgow 1987–89; Lecturer in Modern Scottish Literature, Univ. of St Andrews 1989–95, Prof. of Modern Scottish Literature 1995–; Founding Ed. Verse poetry magazine 1984–95; gave Smithies Lectures, Balliol Coll., Oxford 2004; mem. English Asscn, Royal Soc. of Edinburgh. *Publications include:* poetry: A Scottish Assembly 1990, Sharawaggi (with W. N. Herbert) 1990, Talkies 1992, Masculinity 1996, Penguin Modern Poets 9 (with John Burnside and Kathleen Jamie) 1996, Spirit Machines 1999, The Tip of My Tongue 2003, Selected Poems 2005, Apollos of the North 2006, Full Volume 2008; prose: The Savage and the City in the Work of T. S. Eliot 1987, Devolving English Literature 1992, Identifying Poets: Self and Territory in Twentieth-Century Poetry 1993, Literature in Twentieth-Century Scotland: A Select Bibliography 1995, The Modern Poet 2001, Scotland's Books: The Penguin History of Scottish Literature (Saltire Soc./Nat. Library of Scotland Research Book of the Year Award) 2007, The Bard: Robert Burns, a Biography (Saltire Soc. Scottish Book of the Year Award) 2009; ed.: Other Tongues: Young Scottish Poets in English, Scots, and Gaelic 1990, About Edwin Morgan (with Hamish Whyte) 1990, The Arts of Alasdair Gray (with Thom Nairn) 1991, Reading Douglas Dunn (with David Kinloch) 1992, Liz Lochhead's Voices (with Anne Varty) 1994, Talking Verse: Interviews with Poets (with Henry Hart, David Kinloch, Richard Price) 1995, Robert Burns and Cultural Authority 1997, Launch-site for English Studies: Three Centuries of Literary Studies at the University of St Andrews 1997, The Penguin Book of Poetry from Britain and Ireland since 1945 (with Simon Armitage) 1998, The Scottish Invention of English Literature 1998, The New Penguin Book of Scottish Verse (with Mick Imlah) 2000, Scottish Religious Poetry (with Meg Bateman and James McGonigal) 2000, Heaven-Taught Fergusson: Robert Burns's Favourite Scottish Poet 2003, The Book of St Andrews 2005, Contemporary Poetry and Contemporary Science 2006, New Poems Chiefly in the Scottish Dialect 2009, The Best Laid Schemes: Selected Poetry and Prose of Robert Burns (with Christopher MacLachlan) 2009, The Ayrshire Wreath, a Collection of Prose and Verse Relating to Ayrshire 2010. *Honours:* Eric Gregory Award 1988, selected for Arts Council of GB New Generation Poets 1994, two Scottish Arts Council Book Awards. *Address:* School of English, Castle House, University of St Andrews, St Andrews, Fife, KY16 9AL, Scotland (office). *Telephone:* (1334) 462666 (office). *Fax:* (1334) 462655 (office). *E-mail:* robert.crawford@st-and.ac.uk (office); rc4@st-andrews.ac.uk (office). *Website:* www.st-andrews.ac.uk/english/people/academicstaff/crawford (office).

CRAWFORD, Robert (see Rae, Hugh Craufurd)

CRAWFORD, Thomas, MA; British academic and writer; b. 6 July 1920, Dundee, Scotland; m. Jean Rennie McBride 1946, one s. one d. *Education:* Univ. of Edinburgh, Univ. of Auckland. *Career:* Lecturer, Univ. of Auckland 1953–60, Senior Lecturer 1961–62, Assoc. Prof. of English 1962–65; Lecturer in English, Univ. of Edinburgh 1965; Commonwealth Research Fellow, McMaster Univ., Hamilton, Ont., Canada 1966–67; Reader in English, Univ. of Aberdeen 1967–85, Hon. Reader in English 1985–; Ed. Scottish Literary Journal 1974–84; mem. Asscn for Scottish Literary Studies (Pres. 1984–88), Saltire Soc., Scots Language Soc., Scottish Text Soc. *Publications include:* Burns: A Study of the Poems 1960, Scott 1965, Sir Walter Scott: Selected Poems (ed.) 1972, Love, Labour, and Liberty 1976, Society and the Lyric 1979, Longer Scottish Poems 1650–1830 1987, Boswell, Burns and the French Revolution 1989, The Correspondence of James Boswell and William Johnson Temple 1756–1795: Vol. I, 1756–1777 (ed.) 1997; contribs to scholarly journals. *Address:* School of Language & Literature, English Department, Taylor Building, University of Aberdeen, Old Aberdeen, AB24 3UB, Scotland (office). *Telephone:* (1224) 272625 (office). *Fax:* (1224) 272624 (office). *E-mail:* english.dept@abdn.ac.uk (office).

CRAY, Robert (see Emerson, Ru)

CRECY, Jeanne (see Williams, Jeanne)

CREECH, Sharon, BA, MA; American children's writer; b. 29 July 1945, Cleveland, Ohio; m. Lyle Rigg; one s. one d. *Education:* Hiram Coll., George Mason Univ. *Career:* fmr teacher, editorial Asst, indexer, researcher. *Publications include:* Absolutely Normal Chaos 1990, Walk Two Moons 1994, Pleasing the Ghost 1995, The Ghost of Uncle Arvie 1996, Chasing Redbird 1997, Bloomability 1998, The Wanderer 2000, Fishing in the Air 2000, A Fine Fine School 2001, Love That Dog 2001, Granny Torrelli Makes Soup 2003, Ruby Holler (Carnegie Medal) 2002, Heartbeat 2004, Who's that Baby 2005, Replay 2005, The Castle Corona 2007, Hate That Cat 2008, The Unfinished Angel 2009. *Honours:* US Newbery Medal 1995, 2001, Claudia Lewis Poetry Award 2002, Christopher Award 2002, Mitten Award 2002. *Address:* c/o Harper Collin's Children's Cooks, Author Mail, 1350 Avenue of the Americas, New York, NY 10019, USA (office). *Website:* www.sharoncreech.com.

CREGIER, Don Mesick, BA, MA, PhD; American historian and writer; b. 28 March 1930, Schenectady, NY; s. of Harry M. Cregier and Marion Louella Cregier; m. Sharon Kathleen Ellis 1965. *Education:* Union Coll., New York, Univ. of Michigan, Columbia Pacific Univ. *Career:* Asst Instructor, Clark Univ., Worcester, Mass 1952–54; Instructor, Univ. of Tennessee, Martin 1956–57; Asst Prof., Baker Univ., Baldwin, Kan. 1958–61; Asst Prof., Keuka Coll., Keuka Park, NY 1962–64; Visiting Asst Prof., St John's Univ., Collegeville, Minn. 1964–65; Sr Fellow and Tutor, Mark Hopkins Coll., Brattleboro, Vt 1965–66; Assoc. Prof., St Dunstan's Univ., Charlottetown, PEI 1966–69; Assoc. Prof., Univ. of Prince Edward Island 1969–85, Prof. of History 1985–96, Adjunct Prof. 1996–2002; Abstractor, ABC/Clio Information Services 1978–2009; Foreign Book Review Ed., Canadian Review of Studies in Nationalism 1996–98; mem. Historical Soc., American Historical Asscn, Soc. for Academic Freedom and Scholarship, Canadian Asscn of Univ. Teachers, Mark Twain Soc., North American Conf. on British Studies, Int. Churchill Soc., Lloyd George Soc.; Mark Hopkins Fellow 1965, Canada Council Fellow 1972, Research Grant, Social Sciences and Humanities Research Council of Canada 1984–86. *Publications include:* Bounder from Wales: Lloyd George's Career Before the First World War 1976, Novel Exposures: Victorian Studies Featuring Contemporary Novels 1979, Chiefs Without Indians: Asquith, Lloyd George, and the Liberal Remnant, 1916–1935 1982, The Decline of the British Liberal Party: Why and How? 1985, Freedom and Order: The Growth of British Liberalism Before 1868 1988, The Rise of the Global Village (co-author) 1988; contribs to reference works and professional journals. *Address:* PO Box 1100, Montague, PEI C0A 1R0, Canada (home). *E-mail:* dcregier@upei.ca (home). *Website:* www.cheironscourt.ca (office).

CREMISI, Teresa Emiliana Jacqueline, DipLit; Italian publisher; *President and CEO, Flammarion Press;* b. 7 Oct. 1945, Alexandria, Egypt; d. of Vittorio Cremisi and Gabrielle Helou; m. Giovanni Pinna 1967; two c. *Education:* Notre-Dame de Sion, Alexandria, Lycée Marcelline and Univ. of Bocconi, Milan, Italy. *Career:* moved to Italy 1956; lexicographer, Garzanti Press, Milan 1963–66, Head of Educ. Dept 1966–72, Dir of Production 1972–79, Literary Dir 1979–85, Co-Dir-Gen. 1985–89; contrib. to radio and TV Co., RAI 1972–80, to cultural pages of l'Espresso and la Stampa 1979–89; Editorial Dir, Gallimard 1989–96, Publishing Dir 1996–2005; Pres. and CEO Flammarion Press (part of Rizzoli-Corriere della Sera—RCS MediaGroup) 2005–, and Dir in charge of European strategy for RCS Libri 2005–10, Vice-Pres. RCS Libri 2010–; Vice-Pres. Action Against Hunger 2003–06. *Honours:* Officier, Ordre des Arts et des Lettres 1994, Chevalier, Légion d'honneur 2004. *Address:* Flammarion, 87 quai Panhard et Levasson, Paris 75013, France (office). *Website:* www.flammarion.com (office).

CREMONA, Hon. John Joseph, KM, LLD, DLitt, PhD, DJur; Maltese jurist, historian and writer; b. 6 Jan. 1918, Gozo; s. of Dr Antonio Cremona and Anne Camilleri; m. Beatrice Barbaro Marchioness of St George 1949; one s. two d. *Education:* Malta, Rome, London, Cambridge and Trieste Univs. *Career:* Crown Counsel 1947; Lecturer in Constitutional Law, Royal Univ. of Malta 1947–65; Attorney Gen. 1957–64; Prof. of Criminal Law, Univ. of Malta 1959–65; Prof. Emer. 1965–; Pres. of Council 1972–75; Crown Advocate-Gen. 1964–65; Vice Pres. Constitutional Court and Court of Appeal 1965–71; Judge, European Court of Human Rights 1965–92, Vice-Pres. 1986–92; Pro-Chancellor, Univ. of Malta 1971–74; Chief Justice of Malta, Pres. of the Constitutional Court, the Court of Appeal and the Court of Criminal Appeal 1971–81; mem. UN Cttee on Elimination of Racial Discrimination 1984–88, Chair. 1986–88; Judge, European Tribunal in Matters of State Immunity 1986–92, Vice-Pres. 1986–92; fmr Acting Gov.-Gen., Acting Pres. of Malta; Chair. Human Rights Section, World Asscn of Lawyers; Chair. Public Broadcasting Services Ltd 1996–98; Pres. Malta Human Rights Asscn; Vice-Pres. Int. Inst. of Studies Documentation and Information for the Protection of the Environment 1980–; mem. Int. Inst. of Human Rights 1992; mem. Editorial Bd several human rights journals in Europe and America; Fellow, Royal Historical Soc.; Hon. Fellow LSE; Hon. mem. Real Academia de Jurisprudencia y Legislación, Madrid. *Publications include:* The Treatment of Young Offenders in Malta 1956, The Malta Constitution of 1835 1959, The Legal Consequences of a Conviction in the Criminal Law of Malta 1962, The Constitutional Development of Malta 1963, From the Declaration of Rights to Independence 1965, Human Rights Documentation in Malta 1966, Selected Papers (1946–89) 1990, The Maltese Constitution and Constitutional History 1994, Malta and Britain: The Early Constitutions 1996; three volumes of poetry; articles in French, Italian, German, Portuguese and American law reviews. *Honours:* Kt of Magisterial Grace, Sovereign Mil. Order of Malta; Kt Grand Cross Order of Merit (Italy); Kt Grand Cross, Constantine St George; Kt Order of St Gregory the Great; Kt Most Venerable Order of St John of Jerusalem; Companion of the Nat. Order of Merit (Malta); Chevalier, Légion d'honneur. *Address:* Villa Barbaro, Main Street, Attard, Malta (home). *Telephone:* 440818 (home).

CRESSWELL, Jasmine Rosemary, BA, MA; American writer; b. 14 Jan. 1941, Dolgelly, Wales; m. Malcolm Candlish 1963; one s. three d. *Education:* Univ. of Melbourne, Macquarie Univ., Case Western Reserve Univ. *Career:* mem. Authors' Guild, Colorado Authors' League, Novelists Inc. (Founder and Past Pres.), Rocky Mountain Fiction Writers. *Publications include:* Nowhere to Hide 1992, Keeping Secrets 1993, Eternity 1994, Desires and Deceptions 1995, No Sin Too Great 1996, Secret Sins 1997, The Daughter 1998, The Disappearance 1999, The Conspiracy 2001, The Third Wife 2002, Dead Ringer 2002, Decoy 2003, Full Pursuit 2004, Final Justice 2005, Payback 2007, Suspect 2007, Missing 2007. *Honours:* Colorado Romance Writer of the Year Awards 1986, 1989. *Literary Agent:* c/o Dominick Abel Literary Agency Inc., 146 West 82nd Street, No. 1B, New York, NY 10024, USA. *E-mail:* jasmine@jasminecresswell.com (office). *Website:* www.jasminecresswell.com.

CREWS, Frederick Campbell, BA, PhD; American academic and writer; *Professor Emeritus, University of California at Berkeley*; b. 20 Feb. 1933, Philadelphia, Pa; m. Elizabeth Peterson 1959; two d. *Education:* Yale Univ., Princeton Univ. *Career:* Instructor, Univ. of California, Berkeley 1958–60, Asst Prof. 1960–62, Assoc. Prof. 1962–66, Prof. of English 1966–94, Prof. Emer. 1994–; Fulbright Lecturer, Turin 1961–62; Ward-Phillips Lecturer, Univ. of Notre Dame 1974–75; Dorothy T. Burstein Lecturer, UCLA 1984; Frederick Ives Carpenter Visiting Prof., Univ. of Chicago 1985; Nina Mae Kellogg Lecturer, Portland State Univ., Oregon 1989; David L. Kubal Memorial Lecturer, California State Univ., Los Angeles 1994; Fellow, American Acad. of Arts and Sciences; mem. Cttee for Scientific Inquiry (Advisory Bd); ACLS Fellow 1965–66; Fellow, Center for Advanced Study in the Behavioral Sciences 1965–66. *Publications include:* The Tragedy of Manners 1957, E. M. Forster: The Perils of Humanism 1962, The Pooh Perplex 1963, The Sins of the Fathers 1966, Starting Over (ed.) 1970, Psychoanalysis and Literary Process (ed.) 1970, The Random House Handbook 1974, The Random House Reader (ed.) 1981, Out of My System 1975, The Borzoi Handbook for Writers (co-author) 1985, Skeptical Engagements 1986, The Critics Bear it Away 1992, The Memory Wars (co-author) 1995, Unauthorized Freud (ed.) 1998, Postmodern Pooh 2001, Follies of the Wise 2006; contrib. to scholarly journals and to magazines. *Honours:* Guggenheim Fellowship 1970–71, Univ. of California at Berkeley Distinguished Teaching Award 1985, Spielvogel Diamonstein PEN Prize 1992. *Address:* 636 Vincente Avenue, Berkeley, CA 94707-1524, USA (home).

CRICK, Donald Herbert; Australian writer; b. 16 July 1916, Sydney, NSW; m. 1943; one d. *Career:* mem. Australian Soc. of Authors (Bd of Man.). *Screenplays include:* The Veronica 1983, A Different Drummer 1985, The Moon to Play With 1987. *Publications include:* fiction: Bikini Girl 1963, Martin Place 1964, Period of Adjustment 1966, A Different Drummer 1972, The Moon to Play With 1981; contrib. to Sydney Morning Herald, The Australian, Overland, The Australian Author. *Honours:* Mary Gilmore Centenary Award for Novel 1966, Rigby Anniversary Award for Novel 1980, Awgie Screenplay Award 1983–85. *Address:* 1/1 Elamang Avenue, Kirribilli, NSW 2061, Australia (home).

CRISCUOLO, Anthony Thomas, (Tony Crisp); British writer, journalist, broadcaster, psychotherapist and fmr teacher; *Director, DreamHawk.com*; b. (Tony Criscuolo), 10 May 1937, Amersham, Bucks., England; s. of Alfred Criscuolo and Elizabeth Banning; m. 1st Brenda Crisp (divorced 1978); m. 2nd Hyone Criscuolo 1982; four s. one d.; partner Ros Lynes. *Education:* London Polytechnic, Ruskin Coll., Oxford. *Career:* left school aged 15 without qualifications to work in Fleet Street as a photographer; started own business as freelance photo-journalist 1953; Nat. Service, RAF 1955–57; trained as male nurse; worked as photographer 1958–68; Dir, Landseer Studios and Photo Repro Co.; ran The Arcane Library in spare time, specializing in popular psychology, meditation, dreams, spiritual philosophy, sold to Helios Books 1969; began the study of dreams 1962; taught relaxation, yoga, meditation classes throughout Bucks. and at London Dance Centre; Founding mem. The British Wheel of Yoga; worked at Tyringham Naturopathic Clinic, Bucks.; moved to Devon and helped his wife run a vegetarian wholefood guest-house 1970–71; started Ashram, Combe Martin, Devon (one of the first growth centres in UK) 1972–80; worked as dream corresp. for The Daily Mail and She magazine 1982–83; regularly worked as teacher and sometimes Dir, Atsitsa holistic holiday community on the Greek island of Skyros and at Skyros Inst. 1983–; dream interpreter, LBC, London 1984–91; taught dream work and self-regulation in Montreal, Canada and in Iceland; worked as dream interpreter with Teletext, UK 1993–95; lived in Melbourne, Australia 1995; worked for New Zealand Teletext producing a dream page 1995; currently living in Ystragynlais, Wales, running a website, www.dreamhawk.com; currently publishing Dream Dictionaries and eBooks on mobile phone and iPhone. *Publications include:* Yoga and Relaxation 1970, Do You Dream? 1971, Yield 1974, Yoga and Childbirth 1975, The Instant Dream Book 1984, Mind and Movement 1987, Dream Dictionary 1990, Liberating the Body 1992, The New Dream Dictionary 1994, The Hand Book 1994, Super Minds 1998, Dreams and Dreaming 1999, Coincidences 2000, Dream Power 2003, Your Dream Interpreter 2004, Lucid Dreaming 2005, The Eye of Dreams 2008; eBooks: Sexercises 2010, Surviving Love and Relationships 2010, Africa Sky Stories 2010, I Ching – The Chinese Oracle 2010, Using Your Intuition 2010, The Chakras 2010, Core Experience, Death and Beyond 2010, Face to Face with the Future 2010, Another Kind of Beauty 2011, Exploring Inner Space 2011, Prayer and Dream Interpretation 2011, House of the Ancestors 2011, Enlightenment 2011, Dream Yoga 2011, Every 7 Years You Change 2011, Interview with a Sex Worker 2011, Meetings With Christ 2011, No More Back Labor 2011, Poems from the Lodge 2011, Possession and Dreams 2011, Prophetic Dream of the Coming Years 2011, The Hidden Bible – The Hidden Meaning of Genesis 2011, The Story of a Premature Baby 2011, This is the Time of the Quickening 2011, Yield 2011, Your Guru the Dream 2011, The Sacred Tree - In Dreams and Myth 2012; contrib. to newspapers, journals, radio and TV. *Address:* 1 Troedyrhiw, Caerlan, Abercrave, Swansea, SA9 1SX, Wales. *Telephone:* (1639) 731091; 7765-014270 (mobile). *E-mail:* tonycrisp@yahoo.com. *Website:* www.dreamhawk.com.

CRISP, Clement Andrew, OBE, BA; British dance critic; b. 21 Sept. 1931, s. of Charles Evelyn Gifford Crisp and Bertha Dorothy Dean. *Education:* Oxted School, Univ. of Oxford. *Career:* Dance Critic, The Financial Times 1970–, The Spectator; Assoc. Prof. Univ. of Notre Dame, London campus 1993. *Publications include:* Making a Ballet 1975, Ballerina: Portraits and Impressions of Nadia Nerina (ed.) 1975, Fifty Years of the Ballet Rambert, 1926–76 (ed.) 1976, The Colourful World of Ballet 1977, Lynn Seymour (co-author) 1980, Ballet Rambert: 50 Years and On 1981, Rambert: A Celebration – A Survey of the Company's First Seventy Years (jtly) 1996; with Mary Clarke: Understanding Ballet 1976, Ballet in Art 1978, Introducing Ballet 1978, Ballet Art: From the Renaissance to the Present 1978, Design for Ballet 1978, Ballet Goer's Guide 1981, The History of Dance 1983, Dancer: Men in Dance 1986, How to Enjoy Ballet 1987, Ballerina: The Art of Women in Classical Ballet 1989, London Contemporary Dance Theatre: The First 21 Years 1989, Ballet: An Illustrated History 1992; with Peter Brinson: Ballet for All 1972, Ballet and Dance: A Guide to the Repertory 1981. *Honours:* Kt, Order of Dannebrog (Denmark) 1992; Queen Elizabeth II Award Royal Acad. of Dancing 1992. *Address:* c/o The Financial Times, One Southwark Bridge, London, SE1 9HL, England (office). *Website:* news.ft.com/arts (office).

CRISP, Tony (see Criscuolo, Anthony Thomas)

CRISPIN, Suzy (see Cartwright, Justin)

CRITCHLOW, Donald T., BA, MA, PhD; American historian, writer and editor; *Professor of History, Saint Louis University*; b. 18 May 1948, Pasadena, Calif.; m. Patricia Critchlow 1978; two d. *Education:* San Francisco State Univ., Univ. of California at Berkeley. *Career:* Teaching Asst, Univ. of California at Berkeley 1974, Research Asst, Inst. of Industrial Relations 1975, Acting Instructor in Environmental Studies 1977; Acting Instructor in History, San Francisco State Univ. 1976; Asst Prof. of History, North Central Coll., Napierville, Ill. 1978–81, Univ. of Dayton 1981–83; Asst Prof., then Assoc. Prof. of History, Univ. of Notre Dame 1983–91; currently Prof. of History, Saint Louis University; Ed., Journal of Policy History; Series Ed., Critical Issues in European and American History. *Publications include:* The Brookings Institution, 1916–1952: Expertise and the Public Interest in a Democratic Society 1985, Socialism in the Heartland: The Midwestern Experience, 1890–1920 (ed.) 1986, Federal Social Policy: The Historical Dimension (co-ed.) 1989, Poverty and Public Policy in Modern America (co-ed.) 1989, America! A Concise History (co-author) 1995, Studebaker: The Life and Death of an American Corporation 1996, The Politics of Abortion and Birth Control in Historical Perspective (ed.) 1996, The Serpentine Way: Family Planning Policy in Postwar America: Elites, Agendas, and Political Mobilization 1997, Intended Consequences: Birth Control, Abortion and the Federal Government in Modern America 1999, America's Promise: A Concise History of the United States (co-author) 2004, Phyllis Schlafly and Grassroots Conservatism: A Woman's Crusade 2005, The Conservative Ascendancy: How the GOP Right Made Political History 2007, Debating the American Conservative Movement: 1945–present (co-author) 2009. *Address:* Department of History, College of Arts and Sciences, Saint Louis University, 3800 Lindell Boulevard, Saint Louis, MO 63108, USA (office). *Telephone:* (314) 977-2910 (office). *Fax:* (314) 977-1603 (office). *E-mail:* dcritchlow@sbcglobal.net (office). *Website:* www.slu.edu (office).

CROCETTI, Nicola; Greek editor, journalist and translator; *Editor, Poesia magazine*; b. 1940, Patrasso. *Career:* lives in Italy; Founder Crocetti Editore poetry publr 1981–; Ed. and Dir Poesia magazine 1988–. *Honours:* Albo d'Oro 1999. *Address:* Crocetti Editore Srl, Via E. Falck 53, 20151 Milan, Italy (office). *Telephone:* (02) 3538277 (office). *E-mail:* info@crocettieditore.it (office). *Website:* www.crocettieditore.com.

CROFT, Andy, BA, PhD; British poet and writer; b. 13 June 1956, Handforth, Cheshire, England; m. Nikki Wray; four s. two d. *Education:* Univ. of Nottingham. *Career:* full-time Lecturer, Univ. of Leeds 1983–96; freelance 1996–; Writer-in-Residence, Great North Run 2000, HM Prison Holme House 2000–04. *Publications include:* Red Letter Days 1990, Out of the Old Earth 1994, Nowhere Special 1996, Gaps Between Hills 1996, A Weapon in the Struggle 1998, Selected Poems of Randall Swingler 2000, Just as Blue 2001, Great North 2001, Headland 2001, Comrade Heart 2003, Comrade Laughter 2004, Ghost Writer 2007, Sticky 2009. *Address:* c/o Five Leaves Publications, PO Box 8786, Nottingham, NG1 9AW, England. *Telephone:* (115) 969-3597. *E-mail:* info@fiveleaves.co.uk. *Website:* www.fiveleaves.co.uk.

CROFT, Julian Charles Basset, BA, MA; Australian academic and writer; *Professor Emeritus, University of New England, Armidale*; b. 31 May 1941, Newcastle, NSW; m. 1st Loretta De Plevitz 1967; one s.; m. 2nd Caroline Ruming 1987; one s. *Education:* Univ. of New South Wales, Univ. of Newcastle, NSW. *Career:* Lecturer, Univ. of Sierra Leone 1968–70; Assoc. Prof., Univ. of New England, Armidale 1970–94, Prof. 1994–, now Emer.; mem. Asscn for the Study of Australian Literature. *Publications include:* T. H. Jones 1975, The Collected Poems of T. Harri James (ed. with Don Dale-Jones) 1976, Breakfasts in Shanghai (poems) 1984, Their Solitary Way (novel) 1985, The Portable Robert D. FitzGerald (ed.) 1987, Confessions of a Corinthian 1991, The Life and Opinions of Tom Collins 1991, After a War (Any War) 2002, Ocean Island 2006. *Address:* School of Arts, University of New England, Armidale 2351, Australia (office). *E-mail:* jcroft5@une.edu.au (office).

CROGGON, Alison; Australian poet, novelist and dramatist; b. 1962, South Africa; m. Daniel Keene. *Career:* theatre critic, The Bulletin, Melbourne 1989–92; Poetry Ed., Overland Extra 1992, Modern Writing 1992–94, Voices 1996; founder Ed. of online arts journals, Masthead and Theatre Notes; Australia Council Writer-in-Residence, Univ. of Cambridge, UK 2000; Australian co-ordinator, Poets Against the War 2003; mem. Artistic Council,

Malthouse Theatre. *Plays include:* Lenz 1996, Samarkand 1997, The Famine 1998, Blue 2001, Monologues for an Apocalypse (radio text) 2001; music theatre: Confidentially Yours 1998, The White Army. *Libretti:* The Burrow 1995, Gauguin 2000. *Publications include:* poetry: This is the Stone (Anne Elder Prize, Dame Mary Gilmore Prize) 1991, The Blue Gate 1997, Mnemosyne (chapbook) 2001, Attempts at Being 2002, The Common Flesh 2003, November Burning 2004, Ash 2007, Theatre 2008; novels: The Gift (aka The Naming) 2002, The Riddle 2004, The Crow 2006, The Singing 2008. *Honours:* four Australia Council Fellowships. *Literary Agent:* c/o Jenny Darling and Associates, PO Box 413, Toorak, Vic. 3142, Australia. *Telephone:* (3) 9827-3883. *Fax:* (3) 9827-1270. *Website:* www.jd-associates.com.au. *E-mail:* ajcroggon@bigpond.com (office). *Website:* www.alisoncroggon.com.

CRONENBERG, David, OC, FRSC; Canadian film director, producer and screenwriter; b. 15 March 1943, Toronto. *Education:* Univ. of Toronto. *Career:* fmr cinematographer and film editor; has directed fillers and short dramas for TV. *Plays:* Opera version of The Fly, Théâtre du Châtelet, Paris 2008. *Films:* Transfer (writer, dir, producer) 1966, From the Drain (writer, dir) 1967, Stereo (writer, dir, producer) 1969, Crimes of the Future (writer, dir, producer) 1970, The Victim (dir) 1974, Shivers (writer, dir) 1974, Rabid (writer, dir) 1976, Fast Company (writer, dir) 1979, The Brood (writer, dir) 1979, Scanners (writer, dir) 1980, Videodrome (writer, dir) 1982, The Dead Zone (dir) 1983, Into the Night (actor) 1985, The Fly (writer, dir, actor) 1986, Dead Ringers (writer, dir, producer) 1988, Nightbreed (actor) 1990, Naked Lunch (writer, dir) 1991, Blue (actor) 1992, M. Butterfly (dir) 1993, Henry & Verlin (actor) 1994, Boozecan (actor) 1994, Trial by Jury (actor) 1994, To Die For (actor) 1995, Blood & Donuts (actor) 1995, Crash (writer, dir, producer) (Cannes Jury Special Prize 1997) 1996, The Stupids (actor) 1996, Extreme Measures (actor) 1996, I'm Losing You (exec. producer) 1998, Last Night (actor) 1998, Resurrection (actor) 1999, eXistenZ (writer, dir, producer) (Silver Berlin Bear 1999) 1998, Camera (writer, dir) 2000, Jason X (actor) 2001, Spider (dir, producer) 2002, A History of Violence (dir, producer) 2005, Chacun son cinéma (dir, segment) 2007, Eastern Promises (People's Choice Award, Toronto Int. Film Festival 2007) 2007, Drone (producer) 2008, A Dangerous Method (dir) 2011, Cosmopolis 2012. *Television:* Programme X (dir episode: Secret Weapons) 1970, Tourettes (film dir, writer) 1971, Letter from Michelangelo (film dir, writer) 1971, Jim Ritchie Sculptor (film dir, writer, prod.) 1971, Winter Garden (film dir, writer) 1972, Scarborough Bluffs (film dir, writer) 1972, Lakeshore (film dir, writer) 1972, In the Dirt (film dir, writer) 1972, Fort York (film dir, writer) 1972, Don Valley (film dir, writer) 1972, Peep Show (dir episodes: The Lie Chair, The Victim) 1975, Teleplay (writer, dir episode: The Italian Machine) 1976, Friday the 13th (dir episode: Faith Healer) 1987, Scales of Justice (dir episode: Regina vs Horvath) 1990, Moonshine Highway (actor) 1996, The Judge (actor) 2001. *Publications:* Crash 1996, Cronenberg on Cronenberg 1996. *Honours:* Hon. Patron, Univ. Philosophical Soc., Trinity Coll., Dublin 2010; Chevalier, Légion d'honneur 2009. *Address:* David Cronenberg Productions Ltd, 217 Avenue Road, Toronto, ON M5R 2J3, Canada (office); c/o John Burnham, William Morris Agency, 151 South El Camino Drive, Beverly Hills, CA 90212, USA (office).

CRONIN, Anthony; Irish author; b. 23 Dec. 1928, Co. Wexford; s. of John Cronin and Hannah Barron; m. 1st Thérèse Campbell 1955; two d.; m. 2nd Anne Haverty 2003. *Education:* Blackrock Coll., Univ. Coll., Dublin and Kings Inns, Dublin. *Career:* Assoc. Ed. The Bell 1952–54; Literary Ed. Time and Tide 1956–58; Visiting Lecturer in English, Univ. of Montana, USA 1966–68; Writer-in-Residence, Drake Univ., Ia 1968–70; columnist, Irish Times 1973–80; cultural and artistic adviser to the Prime Minister of Ireland 1980–83, 1987–92; Founding mem. Aosdána (arts asscn), elected Saoi 2003. *Publications:* Poems 1958, The Life of Riley 1964, A Question of Modernity 1966, Dead as Doornails 1976, Identity Papers 1980, New and Selected Poems 1982, Heritage Now 1982, An Irish Eye 1985, No Laughing Matter, The Life and Times of Flann O'Brien 1989, The End of the Modern World 1989, Relationships 1994, Samuel Beckett: The Last Modernist 1996, The Minotaur and Other Poems 1999, Anthony Cronin's Personal Anthology 2000, Collected Poems 2004, The Fall 2009. *Honours:* Hon. DLitt (Trinity Coll., Dublin, Univ. of Ulster, Nat. Univ. of Ireland); Martin Toonder Award for contrib. to Irish literature 1983. *Address:* 30 Oakley Road, Dublin 6, Ireland (home). *Telephone:* (1) 4970490 (home). *Fax:* (1) 4970490 (home).

CRONIN, Jeremy, MA; South African poet and politician; *Deputy Minister of Transport*; b. 12 Sept. 1949, Durban; s. of Denis Cronin and Freda Kemp; m. Gemma Paine; one s. one d. *Education:* Univ. of Cape Town and Sorbonne, Univ. of Paris. *Career:* Lecturer in Philosophy and Political Science, Univ. of Cape Town 1974–76; imprisoned for seven years for his involvement with the African Nat. Congress (ANC) 1976; fmr Educ. Officer, United Democratic Front; spent time in exile in England and Zambia; Ed. African Communist, Umsebenzi; Deputy Minister of Transport 2009–; mem. cen. cttee South African Communist Party 1989–, Deputy Sec.-Gen. 1995–; mem. Nat. Exec. Cttee, ANC 1991–; mem. Parl. 1999–, Chair. Standing Cttee on Transport. *Publications include:* poetry: Inside (Ingrid Jonker Prize) 1983, Even the Dead 1997, Inside and Out 1999, More Than a Casual Contact 2006; non-fiction: Ideologies of Politics (co-ed.) 1976, 30 Years of the Freedom Charter (with R. Suttner) 1986, 50 Years of Freedom Charter (with R. Suttner) 2006. *Address:* Ministry of Transport, Private Bag X193, Pretoria 0001 (office); PO Box 1027, 2000 Johannesburg, South Africa (office). *Telephone:* (12) 3093000 (office). *Fax:* (12) 3285926 (office).

CRONON, William John, BA, MA, MPhil, DPhil, PhD; American academic and writer; *Frederick Jackson Turner and Vilas Research Professor of History, Geography and Environmental Studies, University of Wisconsin-Madison*; b. 11 Sept. 1954, New Haven, Conn.; s. of E. David Cronon and Mary Jean Cronon (née Hotmar); m. Nancy Elizabeth Fey 1977; one s. one d. *Education:* Univ. of Wisconsin-Madison, Univ. of Oxford, UK, Yale Univ. *Career:* writer and dir of educational slide sets and films at Local Materials Center, Madison, Wis. 1971–73; worked at Univ. Bookstore, Madison 1973–76; Asst American Sec. to Rhodes Scholarship Trust 1978–80; Calhoun Coll. Seminar Coordinator, Yale Univ. 1979–80, Asst Prof. of History, Yale Univ. 1981–86, Assoc. Prof. of History 1986–91 (tenured 1988), Prof. of History 1991–92; Frederick Jackson Turner Prof. of History, Geography and Environmental Studies, Univ. of Wisconsin-Madison 1992–2003, Frederick Jackson Turner and Vilas Research Prof. of History, Geography and Environmental Studies 2003–; mem. Agricultural History Soc., American Anthropological Asscn, American Antiquarian Soc., American Historical Asscn, American Soc. for Environmental History, American Soc. for Ethnohistory, American Studies Asscn, Asscn of American Geographers, Ecological Soc. of America, Economic History Asscn, Forest History Soc., Org. of American Historians, Soc. of American Historians, Urban History Asscn. *Publications include:* Changes in the Land: Indians, Colonists, and the Ecology of New England 1983, Nature's Metropolis: Chicago and the Great West 1991, Under an Open Sky: Rethinking America's Western Past (co-ed. with George Miles and Jay Gitlin) 1992, Uncommon Ground: Toward Reinventing Nature (ed.) 1995, The Rhine: An Eco-biography, 1815–2000 (with Mark Cioc) 2002, Remembering Ahanagran: A History of Stories (with Richard White) 2003, The Fishermen's Frontier: People and Salmon in Southeast Alaska (with David F. Arnold) 2008, A Storied Wilderness: Rewilding the Apostle Islands (with James W. Feldman) 2011; contrib. to books and scholarly journals. *Honours:* Rhodes Scholarship 1976–78, Francis Parkman Prize 1984, MacArthur Fellowship 1985–90, Bancroft Prize 1992, George Perkins Marsh Prize, American Soc. for Environmental History 1992, Charles A. Weyerhaeuser Award, Forest History Soc. 1993, Guggenheim Fellowship 1995. *Address:* Department of History, 3211 Humanities Building, 455 North Park Street, University of Wisconsin, Madison, WI 53706, USA (office). *Telephone:* (608) 265-6023 (office). *E-mail:* wcronon@wisc.edu (office). *Website:* www.williamcronon.net.

CROOK, Joseph Mordaunt, CBE, BA, MA, DPhil, FBA, FSA; British academic and writer; *Supernumerary Fellow, Brasenose College, Oxford*; b. 27 Feb. 1937, London, England; m. 1st Margaret Mullholland 1964; m. 2nd Susan Mayor 1975. *Education:* Wimbledon Coll., Univ. of Oxford. *Career:* Asst Lecturer, Univ. of Leicester 1963–65; Lecturer, Bedford Coll., London 1965–75, Reader in Architectural History 1975–81; Ed. Architectural History 1967–75; Slade Prof. of Fine Art, Univ. of Oxford 1979–80; Visiting Fellow, Brasenose Coll., Oxford 1979–80, Humanities Research Centre, ANU, Canberra, Australia 1985, Gonville and Caius Coll., Cambridge 1986; Prof. of Architectural History, Royal Holloway and Bedford New Coll. 1981–99, Prof. Emer. 1999–, Dir Victorian Studies Centre 1990–99; Waynflete Lecturer and Visiting Fellow, Magdalen Coll., Oxford 1984–85; Public Orator, Univ. of London 1988–90; Humanities Fellow, Princeton Univ., USA 1990; Supernumerary Fellow, Brasenose Coll., Oxford 2002–10, Hon. Fellow 2010–; Vice-Chair. Westminster Abbey Fabric Comm. 2001–10; mem. Council of the British Acad. 1989–92, Historic Buildings Council for England 1974–80, Soc. of Architectural Historians of Great Britain (Exec. Cttee 1964–77, Pres. 1980–84), Victorian Soc. (Exec. Cttee 1970–77, Council 1978–88). *Publications include:* The Greek Revival 1968, Victorian Architecture: A Visual Anthology 1971, The British Museum 1972, The Greek Revival: Neo-Classical Attitudes in British Architecture 1760–1870 1973, The Reform Club 1973, The History of the King's Works (co-author), Vol. VI 1973, Vol. V 1976, William Burges and the High Victorian Dream 1981, Axel Haig and the Victorian Vision of the Middle Ages (co-author) 1984, revised edn 2012, The Dilemma of Style: Architectural Ideas from the Picturesque to the Post-Modern 1987, John Carter and the Mind of the Gothic Revival 1995, The Rise of the Nouveaux Riches: Style and Status in Victorian and Edwardian Architecture 1999, The Architect's Secret: Victorian Critics and the Image of Gravity 2003, Brasenose: The Biography of an Oxford College 2008; ed.: Eastlake: A History of the Gothic Revival 1970, Emmett: Six Essays 1972, Kerr: The Gentleman's House 1972, The Strange Genius of William Burges 1981, Clark: The Gothic Revival 1995; contrib. to books and scholarly journals. *Honours:* Freeman, Worshipful Co. of Goldsmiths 1979, Liveryman 1984; Hon. DLit (London) 2004; Hitchcock Medallion 1974. *Address:* 55 Gloucester Avenue, London, NW1 7BA, England (home).

CROOKER, Barbara Poti, BA, MS; American educator, reviewer, essayist, translator and poet; b. 21 Nov. 1945, Cold Spring, NY; d. of Emil Vincent Poti and Isabelle Smith Poti; m. Richard McMaster Crooker 1975; one s. three d. *Education:* Douglass Coll., Rutgers Univ., Elmira Coll. *Career:* instructor, County Coll. of Morris 1978–79, Women's Center, Cedar Crest Coll. 1982–85, Lehigh Community Coll. 1993, Cedar Crest Coll. 1999–; Asst Prof., Northampton Co. Area Community Coll. 1980–82; Artist-in-Educ. (poet in the schools) 1989–93; mem. Poetry Soc. of America, Acad. of American Poets; 14 residencies at Virginia Center for the Creative Arts. *Publications include:* Writing Home 1983, Starting from Zero 1987, Looking for the Comet Halley 1987, The Lost Children 1989, Obbligato 1992, Moving Poems, In the Late Summer Garden 1998, Ordinary Life 2001, The White Poems 2001, Paris 2002, Greatest Hits 1980–2000 2003, Impressionism 2004, Radiance 2005, Line Dance 2008, More 2010; contrib. to anthologies, reviews, quarterlies, journals and magazines. *Honours:* three Pennsylvania Council on the Arts Fellowships, Karamu Poetry Contest winner, New Millennium Writings Y2K Prize, Byline Chapbook Competition, April is the Cruelest Month competition (Poets & Writers), Thomas Merton Poetry of the Sacred Award, Grayson Books Chapbook Competition, W.B. Yeats Soc. of New York Poetry Prize, Pennsylvania Center for the Book Poster Competition, TallGrass Writers' Guild Poetry Prize, Word Press First Book Award, Rosebud Ekphrastic Poetry Prize, Pen and Brush Poetry Prize, Paterson Award for Literary Excellence. *Address:* 7928 Woodsbluff Run, Fogelsville, PA 18051, USA (office). *Telephone:* (610) 395-5845 (office). *E-mail:* bcrooker@ix.netcom.com (office). *Website:* www.barbaracrooker.com.

CROSBIE, Lynn, BA, MA, PhD; Canadian poet, novelist, critic and academic; *Artist Instructor, Ontario College of Art;* b. 7 Aug. 1963, Montreal, PQ; d. of Douglas Crosbie and Heather Crosbie; m. Tony Burgess. *Education:* York Univ., Univ. of Toronto. *Career:* fmrly taught at Univ. of Guelph, York Univ.; currently Artist Instructor, Ont. Coll. of Art; currently teaches at Univ. of Toronto; columnist for Globe and Mail; Contributing Ed. Fashion. *Publications include:* Miss Pamela's Mercy 1992, Villainelle 1994, Pearl 1995, Paul's Case: The Kingston Letters 1997, Queen Rat: New and Selected Poems 1998, Dorothy L'Amour 1999, Phoebe 2002: An Essay in Verse (co-author) 2003, Missing Children 2003, Liar 2006, Life is About Losing Everything 2012; as ed.: The Girl Wants To: Women's Representations of Sex and the Body 1993, Click: Becoming Feminists 1997. *Honours:* Winner, Nat. Magazine Award 2001. *Address:* c/o House of Anansi Press, 110 Spadina Avenue, Suite 801, Toronto, ON M5V 2K4 (office); c/o Art Gallery of Ontario (AGO), 317 Dundas Street West, Toronto, ON M5T 1G4, Canada (office). *Telephone:* (416) 363-4343 (House of Anansi) (office); (416) 979-6648 (AGO) (office). *Fax:* (416) 363-1017 (House of Anansi) (office). *E-mail:* publicity@houseofanansi.com (office). *Website:* www.houseofanansi.com (office); www.ago.net (office).

CROSLAND, Margaret McQueen, BA; British writer and translator; b. 17 June 1920, Bridgnorth, Shropshire, England; d. of Leonard Crosland and Beatrice Crosland (née Wainwright); m. Max Denis (divorced); one s. *Education:* Royal Holloway Coll., London. *Career:* temp. civil servant and researcher, then worked in antiquarian book trade; now writer and trans. *Publications include:* Madame Colette 1953, Jean Cocteau 1955, Louise of Stolberg 1962, Colette, The Difficulty of Loving 1973, Women of Iron and Velvet 1976, Beyond the Lighthouse 1981, Piaf 1985, Simone de Beauvoir 1992, The Enigma of Giorgio de Chirico 1999, Madame de Pompadour 2000, The Marquis de Sade Reader: The Passionate Philosopher (ed.) 2001, Meeting & Parting (poems) 2004, The Life and Legend of Jane Shore 2006, A Cry From the Heart: The Biography of Edith Piaf 2008. *Honours:* Prix de Bourgogne (France) 1973–74, Enid McLeod Literary Prize 1993. *Address:* 25 Thornton Meadow, Wisborough Green, Billingshurst, West Sussex, RH14 0BW, England (home). *Telephone:* (1403) 700652 (home). *Fax:* (1403) 700652 (home). *E-mail:* crosland.denis@virgin.net (home).

CROSS, Anthony Glenn, BA, MA, PhD, AM, LittD, DLitt, FBA; British academic, writer and editor; *Professor Emeritus of Slavonic Studies, University of Cambridge;* b. 21 Oct. 1936, Nottingham, England; m. Margaret Elson 1960; two d. *Education:* Trinity Hall, Cambridge, Harvard Univ., USA, Univ. of East Anglia, Fitzwilliam Coll., Cambridge. *Career:* Lecturer, Univ. of East Anglia 1964–69, Sr Lecturer 1969–72, Reader in Russian 1972–81; Visiting Fellow, Univ. of Illinois, USA 1969–70, All Souls Coll., Oxford 1977–78; Reviews Ed. Journal of European Studies 1971–; Ed. Study Group on Eighteenth-Century Russia Newsletter 1973–2009; Roberts Prof. of Russian, Univ. of Leeds 1981–85; Chair. British Academic Cttee for Liaison with Soviet Archives 1983–95, Academia Rossica 2000–05; Prof. of Slavonic Studies, Univ. of Cambridge 1985–2004, Fellow, Fitzwilliam Coll. 1986–2004, retired Professorial Fellow 2004–, Prof. Emer. of Slavonic Studies 2004–; Frank Knox Fellow, Harvard Univ. 1960–61; Leverhulme Emer. Fellow 2008; mem. British Univs Asscn of Slavists (Pres. 1982–84). *Publications include:* N. M. Karamzin 1971, Russia Under Western Eyes 1517–1825 1971, Russian Literature in the Age of Catherine the Great (ed.) 1976, Anglo-Russian Relations in the Eighteenth Century 1977, Great Britain and Russia in the Eighteenth Century (ed.) 1979, By the Banks of the Thames 1980, Russia and the West in the Eighteenth Century (ed.) 1981, The Tale of the Russian Daughter and her Suffocated Lover 1982, Eighteenth Century Russian Literature, Culture and Thought: A Bibliography (co-ed.) 1984, The Russian Theme in English Literature 1985, Russia and the World of the Eighteenth Century (co-ed.) 1988, An English Lady at the Court of Catherine the Great (ed.) 1989, Anglophilia on the Throne: The British and the Russians in the Age of Catherine II 1992, Engraved in the Memory: James Walker, Engraver to Catherine the Great and his Russian Anecdotes (ed.) 1993, Anglo-Russica: Aspects of Anglo-Russian Cultural Relations in the Eighteenth and Early Nineteenth Centuries 1993, Literature, Lives and Legality in Catherine's Russia (co-ed.) 1994, By the Banks of the Neva: Chapters From the Lives of the British in Eighteenth-Century Russia 1996, Russia in the Reign of Peter the Great: Old and New Perspectives (ed.) 1998, Britain and Russia in the Age of Peter the Great: Historical Documents (co-ed.) 1998, Peter the Great through British Eyes: Perceptions and Representations of the Tsar since 1698 2000, Catherine the Great and the British: A Pot-Pourri of Essays 2001, St Petersburg 1703–1825 (ed.) 2003, Anglo-Russian Cultural Encounters and Collisions (ed.) 2005, Days from the Reigns of Eighteenth Century Russian Rulers (ed.), St Petersburg and the British 2008; contrib. to scholarly journals. *Honours:* Academician, Russian Acad. of the Humanities 1995; Dr hc (Inst. of Russian Literature, St Petersburg) 2008; Antsiferov Prize, St Petersburg 1998, Nove Prize 1998, Dashkova Medal, Moscow 2003. *Address:* Fitzwilliam College, Storey's Way, Cambridge, CB3 0DG, England (office). *Telephone:* (1223) 472121 (office). *E-mail:* agc28@cam.ac.uk (office).

CROSS, Gillian, MA, DPhil; British children's writer; b. 24 Dec. 1945, London, England; m. Martin Cross 1967; two s. two d. *Education:* Univs of Oxford and Sussex. *Publications include:* The Runaway 1979, The Iron Way 1979, Revolt at Ratcliff's Rags 1980, Save Our School 1981, A Whisper of Lace 1981, The Dark Behind the Curtain 1982, The Demon Headmaster 1982, The Mintyglo Kid 1983, Born of the Sun 1983, On the Edge 1984, The Prime Minister's Brain 1985, Swimathon! 1986, Chartbreak 1986, Roscoe's Leap 1987, A Map of Nowhere 1988, Rescuing Gloria 1989, Twin and Super-Twin 1990, Wolf 1990, The Monster from Underground 1990, Gobbo the Great 1991, Rent-A-Genius 1991, New World 1992, The Great Elephant Chase (aka The Great American Elephant Chase) 1992, Beware Olga 1993, The Tree House 1993, The Furry Maccaloo 1993, The Revenge of the Demon Headmaster 1994, What Will Emily Do? 1994, The Crazy Shoe Shuffle 1995, Posh Watson 1995, The Roman Beanfeast 1996, Pictures in the Dark 1996, The Demon Headmaster Strikes Again 1996, The Demon Headmaster Takes Over 1997, The Goose Girl 1998, Tightrope 1999, Down With the Dirty Danes 2000, Calling a Dead Man (aka Phoning a Dead Man) 2001, The Treasure in the Mud 2001, Facing the Demon Headmaster 2002, Beware of the Demon Headmaster 2002, The Dark Ground 2004, The Black Room 2005, The Nightmare Game 2006, Brother Aelred's Feet 2007, Where I Belong 2010, Cave Wars 2011. *Honours:* Hon. DLitt (Glamorgan); Library Asscn Carnegie Medal 1990, Whitbread Children's Novel Award 1992, Smarties Prize 1992. *Address:* c/o Oxford Children's Books, Oxford University Press, Great Clarendon Street, Oxford, OX2 6DP, England. *Website:* www.gillian-cross.co.uk.

CROSSAN, John Dominic, DD; Irish/American theologian, writer and academic; *Professor Emeritus of Religious Studies, DePaul University;* b. 17 Feb. 1934, Nenagh, Co. Tipperary, Ireland; m. Sarah Crossan. *Education:* Stonebridge Priory, Lake Bluff, Ill., Maynooth Coll., Kildare, Ireland, Pontifical Biblical Inst., Rome, Ecole Biblique, Jerusalem. *Career:* ordained RC priest 1957–69; Asst Prof. of Biblical Studies, Stonebridge Priory 1961–65, Mundelein Seminary, Ill. 1967–68, Catholic Theological Union, Chicago, Ill. 1968–69; Assoc. Prof., DePaul Univ., Chicago 1969–73, Prof. of Religious Studies 1973–95, Prof. Emer. 1995–; Croghan Bicentennial Visiting Prof. of Religion, Williams Coll., Williamstown, Mass 1996; Distinguished Prof. of Religious Studies, Univ. of Central Florida, Orlando; Chair. Parables Seminar 1972–75; Ed. Semeia: An Experimental Journal for Biblical Criticism 1980–86; Co-Chair. Jesus Seminar 1985–96; mem. Servites religious order 1950–69, American Acad. of Religion, Catholic Biblical Asscn, Chicago Soc. of Biblical Research (Pres. 1978–79), Soc. of Biblical Literature, Studiorum Novi Testamenti Societas. *Publications include:* Scanning the Sunday Gospel 1966, The Gospel of Eternal Life 1967, In Parables: The Challenge of the Historical Jesus 1973, The Dark Interval: Towards a Theology of Story 1975, Raid on the Articulate: Comic Eschatology in Jesus and Borges 1976, Finding Is the First Act: Trove Folktales and Jesus' Treasure Parable 1979, Cliffs of Fall: Paradox and Polyvalence in the Parables of Jesus 1980, A Fragile Craft: The Work of Amos Niven Wilder 1981, In Fragments: The Aphorisms of Jesus 1983, Four Other Gospels: Shadows on the Contours of Canon 1985, Sayings Parallels: A Workbook for the Jesus Tradition 1986, The Cross that Spoke: The Origins of the Passion Narrative 1988, The Historical Jesus: The Life of a Mediterranean Jewish Peasant 1991, Jesus: A Revolutionary Biography 1994, The Essential Jesus: Original Sayings and Earliest Images 1994, Who Killed Jesus?: Exposing the Roots of Anti-Semitism in the Gospel Story of the Death of Jesus 1995, Who is Jesus?: Answers to Your Questions about the Historical Jesus 1996, The Birth of Christianity 1998, In Search of Paul (with Jonathan L. Reed) 2005, The Last Week 2006, God and Empire 2007, The First Christmas 2007, The First Paul (with Marcus J. Borg) 2009, The Greatest Prayer: Rediscovering the Revolutionary Message of The Lord's Prayer 2010, Parables: How Jesus with Parables became Christ in Parables 2011; contrib. to many scholarly books and journals. *Honours:* Hon. Dr of Humanities (Stetson Univ.) 2003; American Acad. of Religion Award for Excellence in Religious Studies 1989, Ninth Annual Rev. William T. Cortelyou-Martin J. Lowery Award 1991, DePaul Univ. Via Sapientiae Award 1995, Albert Schweitzer Memorial Award 2007. *Address:* c/o HarperCollins, 1350 Avenue of the Americas, New York, NY 10019, USA. *E-mail:* harperonepublicity@harpercollins.com. *Website:* www.johndominiccrossan.com.

CROSSLEY-HOLLAND, Kevin John William, MA, FRSL; British poet, writer, editor, translator and librettist and academic; b. 7 Feb. 1941, Mursley, Bucks., England; s. of Peter Charles Crossley-Holland and Joan Mary Crossley-Holland (née Cowper); m. 1st Caroline Fendall Thompson 1963; two s.; m. 2nd Ruth Marris 1972; m. 3rd Gillian Paula Cook 1982; two d.; m. 4th Linda Marie Waslien 1999. *Education:* St Edmund Hall, Oxford. *Career:* Fiction and Poetry Ed., Macmillan & Co. 1962–69; Lecturer in English, Tufts-in-London Programme 1967–78; Gregory Fellow in Poetry, Univ. of Leeds 1969–71; Talks Producer, BBC 1972; Editorial Dir, Victor Gollancz 1972–77; Lecturer in English Language and Literature, Univ. of Regensburg 1979–80; Editorial Consultant, Boydell and Brewer 1983–89; Arts Council Fellow in Writing, Winchester School of Art 1983, 1984; Visiting Prof. of English and Fulbright Scholar-in-Residence, St Olaf Coll., Minn., USA 1987–89; Endowed Chair in Humanities and Fine Arts, Univ. of St Thomas, St Paul, Minn. 1991–95; Dir Minnesota Composers' Forum 1993–97; mem. Steering Cttee

King's Lynn Festival 1997; Co-founder and Chair. Poetry-next-to-the-Sea 1997–2006; Patron, Thomas Lovell Beddoes Soc. 2000, Soc. of Storytelling 2003, Publishing House Me 2008, European Storytelling Archive 2009. *Music:* song cycles, songs and carols with Sir Arthur Bliss, William Mathias, Stephen Paulus, Steve Heitzeg, Bob Chilcott, Giles Swayne, Lynne Plowman, Tom Smail, Bernard Hughes and others. *Opera:* with Nicola LeFanu: The Green Children, The Wildman; with Rupert Bawden: The Sailor's Tale. *Drama:* The Wuffings (with Ivan Cutting). *Radio:* many talks, features and participation in discussion programmes. *Publications include:* poetry: The Rain-Giver 1972, The Dream-House 1976, Between My Father and My Son 1982, Time's Oriel 1983, Waterslain 1986, The Painting-Room 1988, East Anglian Poems 1989, New and Selected Poems 1991, The Language of Yes 1996, Poems from East Anglia 1997, Selected Poems 2001, Moored Man (with Norman Ackroyd) 2006, The Mountains of Norfolk: New and Selected Poems 2011; children's fiction: Havelok the Dane 1964, King Horn 1965, The Green Children 1966, The Callow Pit Coffer 1968, Wordhoard (with Jill Paton Walsh) 1969, The Pedlar of Swaffham 1971, The Sea Stranger 1973, Green Blades Rising 1974, The Fire-Brother 1974, The Earth-Father 1976, The Wildman 1976, The Dead Moon 1982, Beowulf 1982, The Mabinogion (with Gwyn Thomas) 1984, Axe-Age, Wolf-Age 1985, Storm 1985, The Fox and the Cat: Animal Tales from Grimm (with Susanne Lugert) 1985, British Folk Tales 1987, The Quest for the Olwen (with Gwyn Thomas) 1988, Boo!: Ghosts and Graveyards 1988, Dathera Dad: Fairy Tales 1988, Small Tooth Dog: Wonder Tales 1988, Piper and Pooka: Boggarts and Bogles 1988, Wulf 1988, Under the Sun and Over the Moon 1989, Sleeping Nanna 1989, Sea Tongue 1991, Tales from Europe 1991, Long Tom and the Dead Hand 1992, The Tale of Taliesin (with Gwyn Thomas) 1992, The Labours of Herakles 1993, The Old Stories: Tales From East Anglia and the Fen Country 1997, Short! 1998, The King Who Was and Will Be 1998, Arthur: The Seeing Stone 2000, Enchantment 2000, The Ugly Duckling 2001, Arthur: At the Crossing Places 2001, Viking! 2002, Arthur: King of the Middle March 2003, How Many Miles to Bethlehem? 2004, King Arthur's World 2004, Outsiders 2005, Gatty's Tale 2006, Waterslain Angels 2008, Short Too! 2011, Bracelet of Bones 2011; non-fiction: Pieces of Land: A Journey to Eight Islands 1972, The Norse Myths 1980, The Stones Remain (with Andrew Rafferty) 1989; editor: Running to Paradise 1967, Winter's Tales for Children 3 1967, Winter's Tales 14 1968, New Poetry 2 (with Patricia Beer) 1976, The Faber Book of Northern Legends 1977, The Faber Book of Northern Folk-Tales 1980, The Riddle Book 1982, Folk-Tales of the British Isles 1985, The Oxford Book of Travel Verse 1986, Northern Lights 1987, Medieval Lovers 1988, Medieval Gardens 1990, Peter Grimes by George Crabbe 1990, The Young Oxford Book of Folk-Tales 1998, The New Exeter Book of Riddles (with Lawrence Sail) 1999, Light Unlocked (with Lawrence Sail) 2006, Crossing To Paradise 2008, The Hidden Roads: A Memoir of Childhood 2010; drama: The Wuffings (with Ivan Cutting) 1997; individual poems, translations from Old English, opera libretti, programmes for television and radio; contribs to numerous journals and magazines. *Honours:* Hon. Fellow, St Edmund Hall, Oxford 2001; Hon. DLitt; Arts Council Award for Best Book for Young Children 1966–68, Poetry Book Soc. Choice 1976, and Recommendation 1986, Carnegie Medal 1986, Nestlé Smarties Prize Bronze Medal 2000, Guardian Children's Fiction Award 2001, Tír na n-Óg Award 2001, Spoken Awards Silver Medal 2001. *Literary Agent:* c/o Rogers, Coleridge & White Literary Agency, 20 Powis Mews, London, W11 1JN, England. *Telephone:* (20) 7221-3717. *Fax:* (20) 7229-9084. *E-mail:* info@rcwlitagency.co.uk. *Website:* www.rcwlitagency.co.uk. *Address:* Chalk Hill, Ringstead Road, Burnham Market, Norfolk PE31 8JR, England (home). *Telephone:* (1328) 730167 (office). *E-mail:* kevin@crossley-holland.com (office).

CROWE, Thomas Rain, BA; American author, poet, editor, publisher and translator; *Publisher, New Native Press;* b. 23 Aug. 1949, Chicago, Ill.; partner Nan Watkins; one s. *Education:* Furman Univ., Greenville, SC. *Career:* Ed. Beatitude magazine and Press, San Francisco, Calif. 1974–78; Founder-Dir San Francisco Int. Poetry Festival 1976; Founder-Ed. Katuah Journal, Asheville, NC 1983–87; Publr, New Native Press, Cullowhee, NC 1988–; masterclass instructor, South Carolina Gov.'s School for the Arts 1989, 1990; Ed.-at-Large, Asheville Poetry Review 1994–2001; Founder-Prod., Fern Hill Records 1994–; Founder-Performer, Thomas Rain Crowe & The Boatrockers 1996; mem. Amnesty International, Foundation for Global Sustainability and other environmental orgs and groups. *Opera:* The Eyes of the Butterfly (writer and dir of full-length multi-media theatre performance piece) 1987. *Recordings:* with Thomas Rain Crowe & The Boatrockers: The Perfect Work 2000, Live at Lipinsky 2007, The Thief of Words 2011. *Radio:* numerous appearances on various talk shows and performances with poetry and music band. *Television:* feature segments on local TV in San Francisco and Asheville, NC. *Publications include:* Learning to Dance (poems) 1985, Poems of Che Guevara's Dream 1991, The Sound of Light (poems and music) 1991, Deep Language 1992, The Personified Street 1993, Night Sun (poems, three vols) 1993, Water from the Moon 1995, The Laugharne Poems 1997, Writing the Wind: A Celtic Resurgence (co-ed. and trans.) 1997, In Wineseller's Street: Poems of Hafiz (trans.) 1998, Drunk on the Wine of the Beloved: 100 Poems of Hafiz (trans.) 2001, Zoro's Field: My Life in the Appalachian Woods (memoir) 2005, The Baby Beats and the Second San Francisco Renaissance (ed., anthology) 2005, 10,000 Dawns: Love Poems of Yvan & Claire Goll (trans.) 2004, Radiogenesis (Selected Poems 1989–2006) 2007, A House of Girls (autobiographical fiction) 2007, The Book of Rocks (poems) 2007, Rare Birds: Conversations with Music Legends (interviews) 2008, The End of Eden (essays) 2008, The Blue Rose of Venice (poems), The Sacred Land (poems), Crack Light (poems) 2011, The Wake Up Man (children's book) 2011, A House of Girls (French trans.) 2011, The Thief of Words (spoken word CD) 2011; many magazine translations from the French 1991–2010. *Honours:* Thomas E. McDill Poetry Prize 1980, Atlanta Review Int. Merit Award 1996, Appalachian Writers Asscn Publrs' Book of the Year Award 1997, Ragan Old North State Award Cup for Non-fiction, NC Literary & Historical Asscn 2005, Phillip D. Reed Memorial Award for Outstanding Writing on the Southern Environment, Southern Environmental Law Center 2006, Ind. Publr Book Awards 2006. *Literary Agent:* c/o 407 Canada Road, Tuckasegee, NC 28723, USA. *Telephone:* (828) 293-9237. *Address:* New Native Press, PO Box 661, Cullowhee, NC 28723, USA (office). *Telephone:* (828) 293-9237 (office). *E-mail:* newnativepress@hotmail.com (office). *Website:* www .newnativepress.com (office).

CROWLEY, John, BA; American writer; b. 1 Dec. 1942, Presque Isle, Me. *Education:* Indiana Univ. *Publications include:* fiction: The Deep 1975, Beasts 1976, Engine Summer 1979, Little, Big 1981, Ægypt 1987, Love & Sleep 1994, Dæmonomania 2000, The Translator 2002, Lord Byron's Novel 2005, Endless Things 2007, The Solitudes (The Aegypt Cycle) 2007, Four Freedoms 2009, The Businessman: A Tale of Terror (Supernatural Minnesota) (with Thomas M. Disch) 2010; short stories: Antiquities 1977, Where the Spirits Gat Them Home 1978, The Reason for the Visit 1980, The Green Child 1981, Novelty 1983, Snow 1985, The Nightingale sings at Night 1989, In Blue 1989, Missolonghi 1824 1990, Great Work of Time 1991, Exogamy 1993, Gone 1996, Lost and Abandoned 1997, An Earthly Mother Sits and Sings 2000, The War Between the Objects and the Subjects 2002, Little Yeses, Little Nos 2005; other: film scripts, television scripts, including America Lost and Found, The World of Tomorrow, and No Place to Hide; contribs to periodicals. *Honours:* World Fantasy Award 1982, American Film Festival Award 1982, American Acad. and Institute of Arts and Letters Award in Literature 1992. *Website:* crowleycrow.livejournal.com.

CROWTHER, Kitty; Belgian writer and illustrator; b. 1970, Brussels. *Publications include:* more than 35 books for children including Mon Ami Jim 1996, Moi et rien 2000, Scritch scratch dip clapote 2002, L'anniversaire de l'écureuil et autres fêtes des animaux 2002, L'enfant racine 2003, Petits meurtres et autres tendresses 2004, Le grand Désordre 2005, La visite de Petite Mort 2005, Poka et Mine (series) 2006, Alors? 2006, Annie du lac 2009, Petits poèmes pour passer le temps (co-author) 2009, Petit homme et Dieu 2010. *Honours:* Astrid Lindgren Memorial Award 2010. *Address:* L'École des Loisirs en Belgique, 79 Blvd Louis Schmidt, 1040 Brussels, Belgium (office). *Telephone:* (2) 736-44-62 (office). *E-mail:* edl@ecoleloisirs.be (office); c.k@ euphonynet.be. *Website:* www.ecoledesloisirs.com (office).

CROZIER, Brian Rossiter, (John Rossiter); British writer and journalist; b. 4 Aug. 1918, Kuridala, Queensland, Australia; s. of R. H. Crozier and Elsa Crozier (née McGillivray); m. 1st Mary Lillian Samuel 1940 (died 1993); one s. three d.; m. 2nd Jacqueline Marie Mitchell 1999. *Education:* Lycée, Montpellier, Peterborough Coll., Harrow, Trinity Coll. of Music, London. *Career:* music and art critic, London 1936–39; reporter and sub-ed., Stoke-on-Trent, Stockport, London 1940–41; aeronautical inspection 1941–43; sub-ed., Reuters 1943–44, News Chronicle 1944–48, sub-ed. and writer Sydney Morning Herald, Australia 1948–51; corresp., Reuters-AAP 1951–52; Features Ed., Straits Times, Singapore 1952–53; leader writer and corresp., The Economist 1954–64; BBC commentator, English, French and Spanish overseas services 1954–66, Chair. Forum World Features 1965–74; Ed., Conflict Studies 1970–75; Co-founder and Dir Inst. for the Study of Conflict 1970–79, Consultant 1979–; Columnist, Now!, London 1980–81, Nat. Review, New York 1978–90 (contributing ed. 1982–), The Times 1982–84, The Free Nation, London 1982–89; Adjunct Scholar, The Heritage Foundation 1983–95; Distinguished Visiting Fellow, Hoover Inst., Stanford, Calif., USA 1996–2001. *Art Exhibitions:* London 1948, Sydney 1949–50. *Publications:* The Rebels 1960, The Morning After 1963, Neo-Colonialism 1964, South-East Asia in Turmoil 1965, The Struggle for the Third World 1966, Franco 1967, The Masters of Power 1969, The Future of Communist Power (in USA: Since Stalin) 1970, De Gaulle (vol. I) 1973, (vol. II) 1974, A Theory of Conflict 1974, The Man Who Lost China (Chiang Kai-shek) 1977, Strategy of Survival 1978, The Minimum State 1979, Franco: Crepúsculo de un hombre 1980, The Price of Peace 1980, Socialism Explained (co-author) 1984, This War Called Peace (co-author) 1984, The Andropov Deception (novel) (under pseudonym John Rossiter) 1984, The Grenada Documents (ed.) 1987, Socialism: Dream and Reality 1987, The Gorbachev Phenomenon 1990, Communism: Why Prolong its Death Throes? 1990, Free Agent: The Unseen War 1993, The KGB Lawsuits 1995, Le Phénix rouge (co-author) 1995, The Rise and Fall of the Soviet Empire 1999 and contribs to journals in numerous countries. *Address:* 18 Wickliffe Avenue, Finchley, London, N3 3EJ, England (home). *Telephone:* (20) 8346-8124 (home). *Fax:* (20) 8346-4599 (home). *E-mail:* b-crozier@ ntlworld.com (home).

CROZIER, Lorna, MA; Canadian poet and academic; *Distinguished Professor of Poetry, University of Victoria;* b. 24 May 1948, Swift Current, Sask.; d. of Emerson Crozier and Peggy Crozier (née Ford); m. Patrick Lane 1978. *Education:* Univs of Saskatchewan, Regina and Alberta. *Career:* English teacher 1966–73; Special Lecturer, Univ. of Saskatchewan 1986–91; Writer-in-Residence, Univ. of Toronto, Ont. 1989–90; apptd Assoc. Prof. Dept of Writing, Univ. of Victoria, BC 1991, now Distinguished Prof. of Poetry and Chair Dept of Writing; guest at int. poetry festivals in Faenza, Italy, Cheltenham, UK, Toronto and Vancouver; mem. Saskatchewan Writers'

Guild. *Publications include:* Inside is the Sky 1976, Crow's Black Joy 1978, No Longer Two People (with Patrick Lane) 1979, Animals of Fall 1979, Humans and Other Beasts 1980, The Weather 1981, The Garden Going On Without Us 1983, Angels of Flesh, Angels of Silence 1988, Inventing the Hawk (Gov.-Gen.'s Award for Poetry 1992, Canadian Authors' Asscn 1992, Pat Lowther Award for Poetry 1992) 1992, Everything Arrives at the Light (Pat Lowther Award for Poetry) 1995, A Saving Grace: The Collected Poems of Mrs Bentley 1996, The Transparency of Grief: 5 New Poems 1996, What the Living Won't Let Go (poetry) 1999, Apocrypha of Light 2002, Bones in Their Wings 2003, Whetstone 2005, Before the First Word 2005, The Blue Hour of the Day 2007, Small Beneath the Sky: A Prairie Memoir 2009, The Best Canadian Poetry in English (with Molly Peacock) 2010, Small Mechanics 2011; ed.: A Sudden Radiance 1987, Breathing Fire: The New Generation of Canadian Poets (with Patrick Lane) 1995, Desire in Seven Voices (essays) 1999, Addicted: Notes from the Belly of the Beast (essays) (with Patrick Lane) 2001, Bones in their Wings: Ghazals 2004, Whetstone (poetry) 2005, Breathing Fire 2 (with Patrick Lane) 2005. *Honours:* Hon. DJur (Univ. of Regina) 2004; Prize of CBC Literary Competition 1987, Nat. Magazine Award Gold Medal 1996, Distinguished Prof. Award, Univ. of Victoria 2004, Dorothy Livesay Poetry Prize, Monday Magazine Award for Best Book of Poetry 2006, Hubert Evans Non-Fiction Prize 2010. *Literary Agent:* c/o McClelland & Stewart Inc., 481 University Avenue, Suite 900, Toronto, ON M5G 2E9, Canada. *Address:* Department of Writing, University of Victoria, PO Box 1700, STN CSC, Victoria, BC V8W 2Y2 (office); 1886 Cuttra Avenue, Saanichton, BC V8M 1L7, Canada (home). *Telephone:* (250) 721-7306 (office); (604) 652-3956 (home). *Fax:* (604) 652-1430 (home). *E-mail:* lcrozier@finearts.uvic.ca (office). *Website:* www.finearts.uvic.ca/~lcrozier (office); www.lornacrozier.ca.

CRUMEY, Andrew David William Bernard, BSc, PhD; British writer; b. 12 Oct. 1961, Glasgow, Scotland; m.; two c. *Education:* Imperial Coll., London, St Andrews Univ. *Career:* care worker 1987–88; Research Assoc., Imperial Coll. and Univ. of Leeds 1989–92; school teacher, Newcastle upon Tyne 1992–96; writer 1996–; Literary Ed., Scotland on Sunday 2000–06; currently Lecturer in Creative Writing, Newcastle Univ. *Publications include:* novels: Music in a Foreign Language 1994, Pfitz 1995, D'Alembert's Principle 1996, Mr Mee 2000, Mobius Dick 2004, Sputnik Caledonia (Northern Rock Writer's Award 2006) 2008. *Honours:* Saltire Soc. Award for Best First Book 1994, Arts Council Writer's Award, Scottish Arts Council Book Award. *Literary Agent:* c/o A. M. Heath & Co Ltd, 6 Warwick Court, London, WC1R 5DJ, England. *Telephone:* (20) 7242-2811. *Fax:* (20) 7242-2711. *Website:* www.amheath.com. *E-mail:* acrumey@yahoo.co.uk (office). *Website:* www.crumey.toucansurf.com.

CRUMMEY, Michael, BA, MA; Canadian poet and writer; b. 18 Nov. 1965, Buchans, Newfoundland; s. of Arthur Crummey and Mazie Crummey. *Education:* Memorial Univ., St John's, Queen's Univ., Kingston. *Publications include:* poetry: Arguments With Gravity (Writer's Alliance of Newfoundland and Labrador Book Award for Poetry) 1996, Hard Light 1998, Emergency Roadside Assistance 2001, Salvage 2002, Went With 2007; fiction: Flesh and Blood (short stories) 1998, River Thieves (novel) (Thomas Head Raddall Award, Winterset Award for Excellence in Newfoundland Writing, Atlantic Ind. Booksellers' Choice Award) 2001, The Wreckage (novel) 2005, Galore (novel) (Commonwealth Writers' Prize for Best Book, Caribbean and Canada Region 2010) 2009; non-fiction: Newfoundland: Journey Into a Lost Nation (with photographer Greg Locke) 2004; other: Afterimage (play, with Robert Chafe); contrib. to magazines and anthologies, including League of Canadian Poets' annual contest anthology. *Honours:* Gregory J. Power Poetry Contest, Memorial Univ. 1986, Bronwen Wallace Memorial Award 1994. *Address:* c/o Anchor Canada Publicity, 1 Toronto Street, Suite 300, Toronto, ON M5C 2V6, Canada (office). *E-mail:* mcrummey@yahoo.com (home). *Website:* www.randomhouse.ca (office); www.library.utoronto.ca/canpoetry/crummey/index.htm.

CRYSTAL, David, OBE, BA, PhD, FRCST, FBA; British writer and editor; b. 6 July 1941, Lisburn, Co. Antrim, Northern Ireland; s. of Samuel Cyril Crystal and Mary Agnes Morris; m. 1st Molly Stack 1964 (died 1976); two s. two d.; m. 2nd Hilary Norman 1976; one s. *Education:* Univ. Coll., London. *Career:* Asst Lecturer, Univ. Coll. of North Wales 1963–65; Lecturer and Reader, Univ. of Reading 1965–76, Prof. of Linguistic Science 1976–85; Ed. Child Language Teaching and Therapy 1985–96, Linguistics Abstracts 1985–96; Consultant Ed., English Today 1986–94; radio and TV presenter. *Play:* Living On 1998. *Publications include:* Linguistics, Language and Religion 1965, What Is Linguistics? (third edn) 1974, The English Tone of Voice 1975, Child Language, Learning and Linguistics 1976, Working with LARSP 1979, Eric Partridge: In His Own Words 1980, A Dictionary of Linguistics and Phonetics 1980, Introduction to Language Pathology 1980, Clinical Linguistics 1981, Directions in Applied Linguistics 1981, Linguistic Controversies 1981, Profiling Linguistic Disability 1982, Linguistic Encounters with Language Handicap 1984, Language Handicap in Children 1984, Who Cares About English Usage? 1984, Listen to Your Child 1986, The English Language 1988, Cambridge Encyclopedia of Language 1987 (third edn 2010), Rediscover Grammar 1988 (third edn 2004), The Cambridge Encyclopedia 1990 (fourth edn 2000), Language A–Z 1991, Nineties Knowledge 1992, An Encyclopedic Dictionary of Language and Languages 1992, The Cambridge Factfinder 1993 (fourth edn 2000), The Cambridge Biographical Encyclopaedia 1994 (second edn 1998), The Cambridge Encyclopedia of the English Language 1995 (second edn 2003), Discover Grammar 1996, English as a Global Language 1997 (second edn 2003), Language Play 1998, Words on Words (with Hilary Crystal) 2000, Language Death 2000, John Bradburne's Mutemwa 2000, Language and the Internet 2001 (second edn 2006), Shakespeare's Words (with Ben Crystal) 2002, The New Penguin Encyclopedia (third edn 2006) 2002, The New Penguin Factfinder 2003 (third edn 2007), The Penguin Concise Encyclopedia 2003 (third edn 2007), The Stories of English 2004, The Language Revolution 2004, Making Sense of English Grammar 2004, A Glossary of Textspeak and Netspeak 2004, Pronouncing Shakespeare 2005, The Shakespeare Miscellany (with Ben Crystal) 2005, Dr Johnson's Dictionary 2005, How Language Works 2006, Words, Words, Words 2006, The Fight for English 2006, By Hook or By Crook: A Journey in Search of English 2007, Think On My Words 2008, Txting: the gr8 db8 2008, Just a Phrase I'm Going Through 2009, Fowler's Dictionary of Modern English Usage 2009, John Bradburne on Love 2009, A Little Book of Language 2010, Begat: The King James Bible and the English Language 2010, Evolving English 2010, Internet Linguistics 2011, The Story of English in 100 Words 2011; also children's non-fiction books and educational DVDs. *DVDs:* A Comprehensive Framework for Language Study (Devon County Council Curriculum Services) 2003, A-level Primers I: 1 English – the global language; 2 Accents and dialects; 3 Playing with language; 4 Being pragmatic about pragmatics; 5 Language and ICT (Devon County Council Curriculum Services) 2003, A-level Primers II: 1 The importance of grammar; 2 Tone of voice; 3 Language and literature; 4 Child language acquisition; 5 The death of languages (Devon County Council Curriculum Services) 2003, The Future of Language, three lectures with accompanying book 2009, David Crystal's Introduction to Language 2011. *Honours:* Hon. Prof., Univ. of Wales, Bangor 1985–; Wheatley Medal 2001. *Address:* Akaroa, Gors Avenue, Holyhead, Anglesey, LL65 1PB, Wales. *E-mail:* davidcrystal2@gmail.com. *Website:* www.davidcrystal.com; david-crystal.blogspot.com.

CSOÓRI, Sándor; Hungarian poet and writer; b. 3 Feb. 1930, Zámoly, Co. Fejér. *Education:* Lenin Inst., Budapest. *Career:* contrib. to Irodalmi Újság (monthly) 1954–55, Új hang (monthly) 1955–56; drama critic Mafilm Studio 1968; joined opposition movt 1980; participated in political discussions of Monor 1985 and Lakitelek 1987; Founding mem. Hungarian Democratic Forum 1987, presidium mem. 1988–92; Chair. Illyés Gyula Foundation 1990–94; Pres. World Fed. of Hungarians 1991–2000. *Films:* scriptwriter: Tízezer nap (Ten thousand days), Földobott kő (The thrown-up stone), 80 huszár (Eighty Hussars), Tüske a köröm alatt (A Thorn under the Fingernail), Hószakadás (Snow-Storm), Nincs idö (No Time Left). *Publications:* selected poems: Fölröppen a madár (The Bird Takes Wing) 1954, Ördögpille (Demon Butterfly) 1957, Menekülés a magányból (Escape from Loneliness) 1962, Elmaradt lázálom (Postponed Nightmare) 1980, Knives and Nails 1981, Hóemléke (Memory of Snow) 1983, Várakozás a tavaszban (Waiting in the Spring) 1983, Hattyúkkal ágyútűzben (In Cannon Fire with Swans) 1995, Ha volna életem (If I Had a Life) 1996, Quiet Vertigo 2001, Before and After the Fall 2004; sociographies: Tudósítás a toronyból (Report From the Tower) 1963, Kubai utinapló (Cuban Travel Diary) 1965; essay volumes: Faltól falig (From Wall to Wall) 1968, Nomád napló (Nomadic Diary) 1979, Félig bevallott élet (Half Confessed Life) 1984, Készülődés a számadásra (Preparation for Final Reckoning) 1987, Nappali hold (Daytime Moon) 1991, Tenger és diólevél I. II. (The Sea and Nut Leaves) 1994, Száll a alá poklokra (Descent into Hell) 1997. *Honours:* Order of Merit (Hungary) 2000; Attila József Prize 1954, Cannes Film Festival Prize 1964, 1968, Herder Prize 1981, Istvan Bibo Prize 1984, Tibor Déry Prize 1987, Joseph Fitz Award 1989, Kossuth Prize 1990, Radnóti Biennial Poetry Prize 1990, Eeva Joenpelto Prize 1995, The Hungarian Book of the Year Award 1995, Karoli Gaspar Award 1995, Hungarian Heritage Award 1997, 2005, Hungarian Art Prize 2004, Balint Balassi Memorial Sword Award 2006, Prima Primissima Award 2008. *Address:* Benczúr u. 15, 1068 Budapest, Hungary.

CUCURTO, Washington; Argentine writer, poet and publisher; b. (Santiago Vega), 1973, Quilmes. *Career:* works at Evaristo Carriego library, Buenos Aires; Founder and Dir, Eloísa Cartonera publishing house 2003–. *Publications include:* poetry: Zelarayán 1998, La Máquina de hacer paraguayitos 2000, La fotocopiadora y otros poemas 2002, 20 pungas contra un pasajero 2003; novels: Fer 2003, Cosa de Negros 2003, Panambí 2004, Las aventuras del Sr Maíz 2005, El curandero del amor 2006, 1810 2008. *Address:* Eloísa Cartonera, Brandsen 647, Barrio de la Boca, Buenos Aires, Argentina (office). *Telephone:* (15) 5502-1590 (office). *Fax:* (15) 5105-1326 (office). *E-mail:* cucurto@yahoo.com.ar (home). *Website:* www.eloisacartonera.com.ar (office).

CUECO, Henri Aguilella; French artist and writer; b. 19 Oct. 1929, Uzerche, Corrèze; s. of Vincent Aguilella Cueco and Jeanne Aguilella Cueco (née Lagrange); m. Andrée Laval 1956; two s. *Education:* Coll. Moderne d'Uzerche. *Career:* f. mem. Coopérative des Malassis; teacher Faculté de Vincennes and Paris I; Prof. Ecole Nat. Supérieure des Beaux-Arts, Paris; numerous radio and TV broadcasts. *Art exhibitions:* Musée d'Art moderne Arc 1, Paris 1970, Arc 2 1982, Ecole Nat. Supérieure des Beaux Arts 1993; also in Japan; numerous group exhbns in France and Italy. *Major works:* Les Hommes rouges 1968–70, Le Grand méchoui 1972, Onze variations sur le thème du Radeau de la Méduse 1974, Les Chiens 1975, Murs et Claustras 1975–76, Les Herbes 1977–87, Les Chiens de Saqqarah 1990, Sols d'Afrique 1992, Les Pommes de terre 1987–93, Peintures d'après Poussin et Philippe de Champaigne 1995–97, murals and mosaics; theatre sets for Comédie française, Karlsrühe Opera. *Publications include:* Le Journal d'une pomme de terre 1993, Le Collectionneur de collections 1995, Cueco (monograph) 1997, Le Volcan 1998, Le Troubadour à plumes 1999, Dialogue avec mon jardinier (trans. as Conversations with my Gardener) 2000, La Petite peinture 2001, Mésanges 2002, Dialogue avec mon jardinier 2004, Le collectionneur de collections 2005, Ingres-Cueco 2010. *Honours:* Prix de la Fondation Félix Fénéon, Prix du Salon de la Jeune Peinture. *Address:* 88 rue Carnot, 95360 Montmagny (office); Le Pouget, 19410 Vigeois, France (home).

CULP, Marguerite (see Kearns, Marguerite)

CUMMING, Peter E., BA, DipEd, MA; Canadian writer, dramatist and teacher; b. 23 March 1951, Brampton, Ont.; m. Mary Shelleen Nelson 1970. *Career:* Resident Artist in Drama, Wilfrid Laurier Univ 1972–73; Exec. Dir, Atlantic Publishers Asscn 1984–85; currently Assoc. Prof. of Children's Studies and Dir of Undergraduate Studies, Div. of Humanities, York Univ; Contributing Ed., Quill and Quire 1982–84; mem. Playwrights Union of Canada, Writers Union of Canada, Canadian Soc. of Children's Authors, Illustrators, and Performers, Asscn of Canadian Coll. and Univ Teachers of English. *Publications include:* Snowdreams 1982, Ti-Jean 1983, A Horse Called Farmer 1984, Mogul and Me 1989, Out on the Ice in the Middle of the Bay 1993. *Honours:* First Prize, Children's Prose 1980, First Prize, Adult Fiction 1981, Writers Fed. of Nova Scotia; Toronto Bd of Educ. Canada Day Playwriting Competition 1981, Our Choice, Children's Book Centre 1984, 1989, 1993, Hilroy Award for Innovative Teaching 1990, George Wicken Prize in Canadian Literature 1994, Tiny Torgi Award 1995. *Address:* 212 Vanier College, York University, 4700 Keele Street, Toronto, ON M3J 1P3, Canada (office). *Telephone:* (416) 736-2100 (office). *Fax:* (416) 736-5460 (office). *E-mail:* cummingp@yorku.ca (office). *Website:* www.arts.yorku.ca/huma/cummingp (office).

CUMMINGS, David Alexander; British musician (guitar) and screenwriter; b. 26 Nov. 1958. *Education:* Univ. of East Anglia. *Career:* mem. The Higsons 1980–81, Lloyd Cole & The Commotions 1987, Del Amitri 1987–95; writer for TV and film comedy 1994–, collaborators include Harry Enfield, Paul Whitehouse and Alexei Sayle. *Recordings include:* with Del Amitri: albums: Waking Hours 1989, Change Everything 1992, Twisted 1995, Hatful Of Rain: The Best Of 1998; singles: Always The Last To Know 1992, Be My Downfall 1992, Just Like A Man 1992, When You Were Young 1993, Here And Now 1995, Driving With The Brakes On 1995, Roll To Me 1995, Tell Her This 1995. *Writing for film:* The Last Seduction II 1999, Kevin and Perry Go Large 2000. *Radio:* Rockton Manor Studios (BBC) 2009. *Writing for television:* The Fast Show (BBC) 1994–2000, Harry Enfield & Chums (Tiger Aspect/BBC) (jt winner, Writers' Guild of GB Award 1997) 1994–98, Alexei Sayle's Merry-Go-Round (BBC) 1998, Happiness (BBC) 2001–03, Spine Chillers: Goths (BBC) 2003, Death Metal Chronicles (BBC) 2005, Parents of the Band (BBC) 2009. *Publication includes:* The Fast Show Book (with Paul Whitehouse and Charlie Higson) 1996. *Literary Agent:* c/o Cathy King, Independent Talent Group, 76 Oxford Street, London, W1D 1BS, England. *Telephone:* (20) 7636-6565. *E-mail:* cathyking@independenttalent.com (office). *Website:* www.independenttalent.com.

CUMMINS, Walter Merrill, BA, MA, MFA, PhD; American academic, writer, editor and publisher; *Professor Emeritus, Farleigh Dickinson University*; b. 6 Feb. 1936, Long Branch, NJ; m. 1st Judith Gruenberg 1957 (divorced 1981); m. 2nd Alison Cunningham 1981; two d. *Education:* Rutgers Univ., Univ. of Iowa. *Career:* Instructor, Univ. of Iowa 1962–65; Asst Prof., Fairleigh Dickinson Univ. 1965–69, Assoc. Prof. 1969–74, Prof. of English 1974–2002, Prof. Emer. 2002–; Assoc. Ed., The Literary Review 1978–83, Ed.-in-Chief 1983–2002, Ed. Emer. 2002–; Distinguished Retiring Ed., Council of Editors of Learned Journals 2002; mem. core faculty, Fairleigh Dickinson Univ. MFA in Creative Writing; Co-Publr Serving House Book. *Publications include:* A Stranger to the Deed (novel) 1968, Into Temptation (novel) 1968, The Other Sides of Reality: Myths, Visions and Fantasies (co-ed.) 1972, Witness (short stories) 1975, Managing Management Climate (with George G. Gordon) 1979, Where We Live (short stories) 1983, Shifting Borders: East European Poetry of the Eighties (ed.) 1993, The Literary Traveler 2005, Programming Our Lives: Television and the Change in American Identity 2006, Local Music (short stories) 2007, The End of the Circle (short stories) 2010, Florham: The Lives of an American Estate (with Carol Bere and Samuel Convissor) 2011; contrib. stories, articles and reviews to many publs. *Honours:* New Jersey State Council on the Arts Fellowship 1982–83, Nat. Endowment for the Arts grants for The Literary Review 1987–88, 1990–91. *Address:* 6 Hanover Road, Florham Park, NJ 07932, USA. *E-mail:* walter.cummins@gmail.com. *Website:* www.waltercummins.com.

CUMPER, Patricia (Pat), MA; British playwright; *Artistic Director, Talawa Theatre Company*; b. 1955, Jamaica. *Education:* Univ. of Cambridge. *Career:* currently Artistic Dir Talawa Theatre Co. *Plays include:* Fallen Angel and the Devil Concubine 1989, The Key Game 2002; musicals: Fabula Urbis (with Simon Deacon) 2002, Elysium. *Radio contributions:* Another Country (BBC Radio 3), A Caribbean Blue (BBC Radio 4), Home Truths (BBC Radio 4), Something Understood (BBC Radio 4). *Television plays:* Doctors (BBC 1). *Publication includes:* One Bright Child (novel) 2004. *Literary Agent:* c/o Bill McLean Personal Management Ltd, 23B Deodar Road, London, SW15 2NP, England. *Telephone:* (20) 8789-8191. *Address:* Talawa Theatre Company, 53–55 East Road, London, N1 6AH, England (office). *Telephone:* (20) 7251-6644 (office). *Fax:* (20) 7251-6644 (office). *E-mail:* patricia@talawa.com (office). *Website:* www.talawa.com (office).

CUNILLÉ, Lluïsa; Spanish playwright; b. 28 Oct. 1961, Badalona. *Education:* Sala Beckett, Barcelona. *Career:* co-founder (with Paco and Lola Lopez Zarzoso) Companyia Hongaresa de Teatre 1995. *Publications:* Rodeo (Calderon de la Barca) 1992, Moi novembro 1993, A festa 1994, Joker 1994, Auga, terra, lume e ar 1995, Accident (Institute of Catalan Letters theater) 1996, El mercat de las delícies 1996, As prazas 1996, La venda 1997, Dedina, alí fora 1997, Privado 1998, Dotze treballs 1998, Paula.doc: El instante 1998, Apocalypse 1998, La cita 1999, L'afer (Premio Ciudad de Alcoy) 1999, O Caso 1999, O testimone 1999, A cita 1999, L'aniversari 2000, Passatge Gutenberg 2000, Ultramarins 2000, Vacants 2000, Libración 2001, Privado 2001, Máis de Paraíso Extraño 2001, Vou che dicir a verdade 2002, O aniversario de matrimonio 2002, Calquera aire infinito 2003, Barcelona, mapa d'ombres 2004, Il·lusionistes 2004, Occisió 2005, PPP 2005, La cantant calba al Mc Donald's 2006, Après moi, le déluge 2007, El dúo de La Africana 2007, Assajant Pitarra 2007. *Honours:* Winner of Alcoy 1995, City of Barcelona Prize for Drama 2004, Best Spanish Author 2007, Nat. Prize of Arts of the Generalitat of Catalonia 2007, Gold Award Letter 2008. *Address:* c/o Free Art, 4 Ramon Llull, 08950 Esplugues de Llobregat, Spain (office). *Telephone:* (93) 4738669 (office). *Fax:* (93) 3725948 (office). *E-mail:* welcome@freeart.es (office).

CUNLIFFE, Sir Barrington (Barry) Windsor, Kt, CBE, BA, MA, PhD, LittD, FBA, FSA; British archaeologist, academic and writer; *Professor Emeritus of European Archaeology, Keble College, Oxford*; b. 10 Dec. 1939, Portsmouth, Hants., England; m. Margaret Herdman 1979; one s. one d. *Education:* St John's Coll., Cambridge. *Career:* Lecturer in Classics, Univ. of Bristol 1963–66; Prof. of Archaeology, Univ. of Southampton 1966–72; Prof. of European Archaeology and Fellow, Keble Coll., Oxford 1972–2007, Prof. Emer. 2007–; Commr, Historic Buildings and Monuments Comm. for England 1987–95, 2006–; Gov., Museum of London 1995–97; mem. Medieval Soc., Prehistoric Soc., Royal Archaeological Inst., Soc. of Antiquaries (Vice-Pres. 1982–86, Pres. 1994–95); Trustee, British Museum 2000–09. *Publications include:* Excavations at Richborough, Vol. 5 1968, Roman Bath (ed.) 1969, Excavations at Fishbourne 1961–69 (two vols) 1971, Fishbourne: A Roman Palace and its Gardens 1971, Roman Baths Discovered 1971, Guide to the Roman Remains of Bath 1971, The Cradle of England 1972, The Making of the English 1973, The Regni 1974, Iron Age Communities in Britain: An Account of England, Scotland, and Wales from the Seventh Century BC until the Roman Conquest 1974, Excavations at Porchester Castle, Hants (five vols) 1975, 1976, 1977, 1985, 1994, Rome and the Barbarians 1975, Oppida: The Beginnings of Urbanisation in Barbarian Europe (with Trevor Rowley) 1976, Hengistbury Head 1978, Rome and her Empire 1978, The Celtic World 1979, Excavating Bath 1950–75 (ed.) 1979, Coinage and Society in Britain and Gaul: Some Current Problems (ed.) 1981, Antiquity and Man (ed.) 1982, Danebury: Anatomy of an Iron Age Hillfort 1983, Aspects of the Iron Age in Central Southern Britain (co-ed. with David Miles) 1984, Danebury: An Iron Age Hillfort in Hampshire, Vols 1 and 2 1984, Vols 4 and 5 1991, Vol. 6 1995, Heywood Sumner's Wessex 1985, Temple of Sulis Minerva at Bath Vol. I (with Peter Davenport) 1985, The City of Bath 1986, Hengistbury Head, Darcet, Vol. I 1987, Origins: The Roots of European Civilisation (ed.) 1987, Mount Batten, Plymouth: A Prehistoric and Roman Port 1988, Greeks, Romans & Barbarians: Spheres of Interaction 1988, Wessex to AD 1000 1993, The Oxford Illustrated Prehistory of Europe (ed.) 1994, Social Complexity and the Development of Towns in Iberia (co-ed. with S. Keay) 1995, The Ancient Celts 1997, Science and Stonehenge (co-ed. with C. Renfrew) 1997, The Guadajoz Project, Andalucia in the First Millennium BC (with M.-C. Fernandez Castro) 1999, The Danebury Environs Programme, Vols 1 and 2 2000, Facing the Ocean: The Atlantic and Its People (Wolfson Foundation History Prize) 2001, The Extraordinary Voyage of Pytheas the Greek 2001, The Celts 2003, Mediterranean Urbanization 800–600 BC (ed with R. Osborne), England's Landscape: The West (ed.) 2006, Europe Between the Oceans 9000 BC–AD 1000 2008, Druids 2010, Celts from the West (co-ed. with J. T. Koch) 2010; contribs to periodicals and archaeological journals. *Honours:* Dr hc (Sussex, Bath, Open, Southampton, Kent); American Historical Asscn James Henry Breasted Prize 2001, Wolfson History Prize 2001, Grahame Clark Medal 2004, Gold Medal of the Soc. of Antiquaries. *Address:* Institute of Archaeology, University of Oxford, 36 Beaumont Street, Oxford, OX1 2PG, England (office). *Telephone:* (1865) 278240 (office). *Fax:* (1865) 278254 (office). *E-mail:* barry.cunliffe@arch.ox.ac.uk (office). *Website:* www.arch.ox.ac.uk (office).

CUNLIFFE, John; British children's writer and poet. *Career:* worked as a teacher and librarian before becoming a full-time writer; creator of the popular characters, Postman Pat, and Rosie and Jim. *Publications include:* Farmer Barnes series: numerous publs 1964–; Riddles and Rhymes and Rigmaroles 1971, The Giant Who Stole the World 1971, Giant Kippernose and Other Stories 1972, The King's Birthday Cake 1973, The Great Dragon Competition and Other Stories 1973, Small Monkey Tales 1974, Giant Brog and the Motorway 1976, Mr Gosling and the Runaway Chair 1978, Mr Gosling and the Great Art Robbery 1979, Our Sam: The Daftest Dog in the World 1980, Sara's Giant and the Upside-down House 1981, Fog Lane School and the Great Racing Car Disaster 1989, The Minister's Cat 1989, Big Jim and Little Jim 1990; Postman Pat series: numerous publs 1981–, including Postman Pat's Treasure Hunt, Postman Pat and the Mystery Thief, Postman Pat's Secret, Postman Pat's Rainy Day, Postman Pat's Foggy Day, Postman Pat's Difficult Day, Postman Pat's Tractor Express, Postman Pat Takes a Message, Postman Pat's Thirsty Day, Postman Pat's Letters on Ice, Postman Pat's A.B.C. Story, Postman Pat's 1, 2, 3 Story, Postman Pat to the Rescue, Postman Pat Plays for Greendale, Postman Pat's Safari, Postman Pat's Winter Storybook, Postman

Pat and the Christmas Puddings, Postman Pat and the Greendale Ghost, Postman Pat Goes to Town, Postman Pat and the Toy Soldiers, Postman Pat's House, Postman Pat Gets a Pet, Postman Pat's Three Wishes, Postman Pat Gets Fat, Postman Pat and the Suit of Armour, Postman Pat's Christmas, Postman Pat Goes Football Crazy, Postman Pat and the Ice Cream Machine, Postman Pat and the Job Well Done; Rosie and Jim series: numerous publs 1991–, including Rosie and Jim and the Water Wizard, Rosie and Jim and the Rainbow, Rosie and Jim and the Man in the Wind, Rosie and Jim and the Drink of Milk, A Family for Duck, Jim Gets Lost, Rosie and Jim at the Seaside; poetry: Dare You Go 1992, Fizzy Whizzy Poetry Book 1995. *Literary Agent:* c/o Anthony Goff, David Higham Associates, 5–8 Lower John Street, Golden Square, London, W1F 9HA, England. *Telephone:* (20) 7434-5900. *Fax:* (20) 7437-1072. *E-mail:* anthonygoff@davidhigham.co.uk. *Website:* www.davidhigham.co.uk. *E-mail:* john.cunliffe@metronet.co.uk (home).

CUNNINGHAM, Michael, MA, MFA; American novelist and screenwriter; b. 6 Nov. 1952, Cincinnati. *Education:* Stanford Univ., Univ. of Iowa. *Career:* fmr bartender; joined Univ. of Iowa Writers' Workshop 1978; writer for Carnegie Corpn; fmr Adjunct Asst Prof., Columbia Univ.; Donald I. Fine Prof. in Creative Writing, Brooklyn Coll. 2001, Distinguished Prof. of English 2001, also head of MFA Writing Program, now Visiting Prof.; Guggenheim Fellowship 1993. *Screenplays include:* A Home at the End of the World 2004, Evening 2007. *Publications:* Golden States 1984, A Home at the End of the World 1990, Flesh and Blood 1995, The Hours (Pulitzer Prize, PEN/Faulkner Award for Fiction 1999) 1998, Specimen Days 2005, By Nightfall 2010. *Honours:* Lambda Literary Award for Gay Men's Fiction 1995. *Literary Agent:* Steven Barclay Agency, 12 Western Avenue, Petaluma, CA 94952, USA. *Website:* www.barclayagency.com/cunningham.html. *Address:* English Department, 2308 Boylan Hall, Brooklyn College, 2900 Bedford Avenue, Brooklyn, NY 11210, USA (office). *Telephone:* (718) 951-5195 (office). *Website:* academic.brooklyn.cuny.edu/english (office).

CUOMO, Mario Matthew, LLB; American fmr state governor and lawyer; *Of Counsel, Corporate and Financial Services Department and Litigation Department, Wilkie Farr & Gallagher LLP;* b. 15 June 1932, Queen's County, NY; s. of Andrea and Immaculata Cuomo; m. Matilda Raffa 1954; two s. (including Andrew Cuomo) three d. *Education:* St John's Coll. and St John's Univ. *Career:* admitted to New York Bar 1956, Supreme Court Bar 1960; Confidential Legal Asst to Hon. Adrian P. Burke, New York State Court of Appeals 1956–58; Assoc., Corner, Weisbrod, Froeb and Charles, Brooklyn 1958–63, Partner 1963–75; Sec. of State, New York 1975–79; Lt-Gov. of New York State 1979–82, Gov. 1983–95; Partner, Wilkie Farr and Gallagher LLP 1995, currently Of Counsel, Corporate and Financial Services Dept and Litigation Dept; Adjunct Prof., St John's Univ. Law School 1963–75; counsel to community groups 1966–72; mem. Bd of Eds, New York Law Journal; fmr Co-Chairman and mem. Bd of Dirs Partnership for a Drug-Free America; Democrat. *Publications:* Forest Hills Diary: The Crisis of Low-Income Housing 1974, Maya 1984, Lincoln on Democracy (jtly) 1990, The New York Idea 1994, Common Sense 1995, Reason to Believe 1995, The Blue Spruce 1999, Why Lincoln Matters Today More Than Ever 2004, Lincoln Lessons: Reflections on America's Greatest Leader (contrib.) 2009. *Honours:* New York Rapallo Award, Columbia Lawyers' Asscn 1976, Dante Medal, Italian Govt./American Asscn of Italian Teachers 1976, Silver Medallion, Columbia Coalition 1976, Public Admin. Award, C.W. Post Coll. 1977, American Acad. of Arts and Letters Medal 1999, Federal Bar Council's Emory Buckner Medal 2007. *Address:* Wilkie, Farr and Gallagher LLP, 787 7th Avenue, New York, NY 10019-6099 (office); 50 Sutton Place South, New York, NY 10022, USA. *Telephone:* (212) 728-8260 (office). *Fax:* (212) 728-9260 (office). *E-mail:* mcuomo@willkie.com (office). *Website:* www.willkie.com (office).

CUPITT, Rev. Don, MA; British ecclesiastic and university lecturer; b. 22 May 1934, Oldham; s. of Robert Cupitt and Norah Cupitt; m. Susan Marianne Day 1963; one s. two d. *Education:* Charterhouse, Trinity Hall, Cambridge, Westcott House, Cambridge. *Career:* ordained 1959; Curate, St Philip's Church, Salford 1959–62; Vice-Prin. Westcott House, Cambridge 1962–65; Fellow, Emmanuel Coll., Cambridge 1965–96, Dean 1966–91, Life Fellow 1996–; Asst Lecturer, Univ. of Cambridge 1968–73, Lecturer in Divinity 1973–96; Fellow of the Jesus Seminar, Westar Inst., Ore., USA 2001. *Television documentaries:* Who Was Jesus? 1977, The Sea of Faith (series) 1984. *Publications:* Christ and the Hiddenness of God 1971, Crisis of Moral Authority 1972, The Leap of Reason 1976, The Worlds of Science and Religion 1976, Who Was Jesus? (with Peter Armstrong) 1977, The Nature of Man 1979, Explorations in Theology 1979, The Debate about Christ 1979, Jesus and the Gospel of God 1979, Taking Leave of God 1980, The World to Come 1982, The Sea of Faith 1984, Only Human 1985, Life Lines 1986, The Long-Legged Fly 1987, The New Christian Ethics 1988, Radicals and the Future of the Church 1989, Creation out of Nothing 1990, What is a Story? 1991, The Time Being 1992, After All 1994, The Last Philosophy 1995, Solar Ethics 1995, After God: The Future of Religion 1997, Mysticism after Modernity 1997, The Religion of Being 1998, The Revelation of Being 1998, The New Religion of Life in Everyday Speech 1999, The Meaning of It All in Everyday Speech 1999, Kingdom Come in Everyday Speech 2000, Philosophy's Own Religion 2000, Reforming Christianity 2001, Emptiness and Brightness 2001, Is Nothing Sacred? 2002, Life, Life 2003, The Way to Happiness: A Theory of Religion 2005, The Great Questions of Life 2006, The Old Creed and the New 2006, Radical Theology 2006, Impossible Loves 2007, Above Us It's Only Sky 2008, The Meaning of the West 2008, A New Method of Religious Enquiry 2008, Jesus and Philosophy 2009, Theology's Strange Return 2010, A New Great Story 2010, The Fountain 2010, Turns of Phrase 2011, The Last Testament 2012. *Honours:* Hon. DLitt (Bristol) 1985. *Address:* Emmanuel College, Cambridge, CB2 3AP, England (office). *Telephone:* (1223) 334200 (office). *Fax:* (1223) 334426 (office). *E-mail:* susan.cupitt@gmail.com (home). *Website:* www.doncupitt.com.

CURIOL, Céline; French journalist and writer; b. 1975, Lyon. *Career:* journalist for various French media, including Libération, France-Inter, Radio France, and BBC Afrique; has lived in New York City, London and Buenos Aires. *Publications include:* novels: Voces En El Laberinto 2000, Voix sans issue (trans. as Voice Over) 2005, Permission 2007, Von Liebe sprechen 2007, Exil intermédiaire 2009; other: Route rouge (travel journal). *Address:* c/o Éditions Actes Sud, BP 90038, 13633 Arles Cedex, France. *Website:* www.actes-sud.fr.

CURREY, Richard; American writer; b. 19 Oct. 1949, Parkersburg, W Va. *Education:* West Virginia Univ., Howard Univ. *Career:* writer 1972–; Visiting Prof., Univ. of New Mexico 1993; Distinguished Writer-in-Residence, Wichita State Univ. 1993; mem. Writers Film Project, Chesterfield Film Co. 1996–97. *Publications include:* Fatal Light 1988, The Wars of Heaven 1990, Crossing Over: The Vietnam Stories 1993, Lost Highway 1997. *Honours:* D.H. Lawrence Fellow in Literature 1981, Fellow, Nat. Endowment for the Arts 1982, 1987, Short Fiction Prize, Associated Writing Programs 1984, O. Henry Award 1988, Special Citation, Hemingway Foundation 1989, Excellence in the Arts Award, Vietnam Veterans of America 1989, Pushcart Prize 1990, Fellow, Western States Arts Federation 1993, Writer-in-Residence, State of West Virginia 1994, Daugherty Award in the Humanities 1997. *E-mail:* admin@sfwp.com (office). *Website:* www.richardcurrey.com.

CURRIE JONES, Edwina, MA, MSc; British writer, broadcaster and politician; b. 13 Oct. 1946, Liverpool, England; d. of the late Simon Cohen; m. 1st Raymond F. Currie 1972 (divorced 2001); two d.; m. 2nd John Jones 2001. *Education:* Liverpool Inst. for Girls, St Anne's Coll., Oxford, London School of Econs. *Career:* teacher and lecturer in econs, econ. history and business studies 1972–81; mem. Birmingham City Council 1975–86; Conservative MP for Derbyshire S 1983–97; Parl. Pvt. Sec. to Sec. of State for Educ. and Science 1985–86; Parl. Under-Sec. of State for Health 1986–88; mem. Parl. Select Cttee on Social Services 1983–86; Jt Chair. Conservative Group for Europe 1995–97; Vice-Chair. European Movt 1995–99; Jt Chair. Future of Europe Trust 1995–97; Trustee, Marie Curie Cancer Care 1992–94, Patients Asscn 2005–09; Patron, Reigate and Banstead Women's Aid 2005–, MRSA Action UK 2008–; contrib. to radio and TV including Winner Celebrity Mastermind 2004. *Radio presenter:* Late Night Currie (BBC) 1998–2003. *Publications include:* Life Lines 1989, What Women Want 1990, Three Line Quips 1992, A Parliamentary Affair (novel) 1994, A Woman's Place (novel) 1996, She's Leaving Home (novel) 1997, The Ambassador (novel) 1998, Chasing Men (novel) 2000, This Honourable House (novel) 2001, Diaries 1987–92 2002. *Honours:* Speaker of the Year, Asscn of Speakers' Clubs 1990, 1994 Campaigner of the Year, The Spectator/Highland Park Parliamentarian of the Year Awards. *Address:* c/o Currie Jones Associates Ltd, 3 The Maltings, Coopers Hill Road, Redhill, RH1 5PD, England. *Telephone:* 7802-741494 (mobile). *Website:* edwina.currie.co.uk.

CURTEIS, Ian Bayley, FSA; British dramatist; b. 1 May 1935, London; m. 1st Dorothy Joan Armstrong 1964 (died 2009); two s.; m. 2nd Joanna Trollope (q.v.) 1985; two step-d.; m. 3rd Lady Deirdre Grantley; two step-s. *Education:* Univ. of London. *Career:* dir and actor in theatres throughout UK and BBC TV script reader 1956–63; BBC and ATV staff dir (drama) 1963–67; Chair. Cttee on Censorship, Writers' Guild of Great Britain 1981–85, Pres. of Guild 1998–2001. *Plays for TV:* Beethoven, Sir Alexander Fleming (BBC entry, Prague Festival 1973), Mr. Rolls and Mr. Royce, Long Voyage Out of War (trilogy), The Folly, The Haunting, Second Time Round, A Distinct Chill, The Portland Millions, Philby, Burgess and Maclean (British entry, Monte Carlo Festival 1978), Hess, The Atom Spies, Churchill and the Generals (Grand Prize for Best Programme of 1981, New York Int. Film and TV Festival), Suez 1956, Miss Morrison's Ghosts (British entry Monte Carlo Festival), BB and Lord D.; writer of numerous TV series; screenplays: La Condition humaine (André Malraux), Lost Empires (adapted from J.B. Priestley), Eureka, Graham Greene's The Man Within (TV) 1983, The Nightmare Years (TV) 1989, The Zimmerman Telegram 1990, Yalta 1991, The Choir (BBC 1), The Falklands Play 2002, More Love 2003, Yet More Love 2004, Miss Morrison's Ghosts 2004, The Bargain 2007, Boscobel 2008, The Last Tsar 2009; numerous articles and speeches on the ethics and politics of broadcasting. *Plays for radio:* Eroica 2000, Love 2001, After the Break, The Falklands Play 2002. *Publications:* Long Voyage Out of War (trilogy) 1971, Churchill and the Generals 1980, Suez 1956, 1980, The Falklands Play 1987. *Address:* Markenfield Hall, North Yorks., HG4 3AD; 2 Warwick Square, London, SW1V 2AA, England. *Telephone:* (1765) 603411 (office); (20) 7821-8606 (home). *Fax:* (1765) 607195 (office).

CURTIS, Anthony Samuel, BA, MA, FRSA, FRSL; British journalist, editor and writer; b. 12 March 1926, London, England; m. Sarah Curtis 1960; three s. *Education:* Merton Coll., Oxford. *Career:* Deputy Ed., TLS 1959–60; Literary Ed., Sunday Telegraph 1960–70, Financial Times 1970–90; mem. Royal Literary Fund (Treas. 1975–98), Soc. of Authors (Pension Fund Trustee), Literary Soc. *Publications include:* The Pattern of Maugham 1974, Somerset Maugham: The Critical Heritage (with John Whitehead) 1987, Lit Ed: On

Reviews and Reviewing 1998, Before Bloomsbury: The 1890s Diaries of Three Kensington Ladies 2002, Virginia Woolf: Bloomsbury and Beyond 2006, Golden Opportunities (play adaptation) 2006; contrib. to periodicals and radio. *Honours:* Harkness Fellowship in Journalism (USA) 1958–59. *Address:* 9 Essex Villas, London, W8 7BP, England (home). *E-mail:* anticurtis@aol.com (home).

CURTIS, Jamie Lee, Lady Haden-Guest; American actress and author; b. 22 Nov. 1958, Los Angeles, Calif.; d. of the late Tony Curtis and Janet Leigh; m. Christopher Guest; one s. one d. *Education:* Choate School, Conn., Univ. of the Pacific, Calif. *Films include:* Halloween, The Fog, Terror Train, Halloween II, Road Games, Prom Night, Love Letters, Trading Places, The Adventures of Buckaroo Banzai: Across the 8th Dimension, Grandview, USA, Perfect, 8 Million Ways to Die, Mother's Boys, Drowning Mona, Amazing Grace and Chuck, A Man in Love, Dominick and Eugene, A Fish Called Wanda, Blue Steel, My Girl, Forever Young, My Girl 2, True Lies 1994 (Golden Globe Award for Best Actress in a musical or comedy), House Arrest 1996, Fierce Creatures 1996, Halloween H20 1998, Virus 1999, The Tailor of Panama 2000, Daddy and Them 2001, Halloween: Resurrection 2002, True Lies 2 2003, Freaky Friday 2003, Christmas with the Cranks 2004, Beverly Hills Chihuahua 2008, You Again 2010, Little Engine That Could (voice) 2011. *Television includes:* She's In The Army Now, Dorothy Stratten: Death of a Centrefold, Operation Petticoat, The Love Boat, Columbo, Quincy, Charlie's Angels, Anything but Love (dir), Money on the Side, As Summers Die, Anything but Love, Actor, The Heidi Chronicles, Nicholas' Gift. *Publications:* When I Was Little, A Four-Year-Old's Memoir of her Youth 1993, Tell Me Again About the Night I Was Born 1996, Today I Feel Silly and Other Moods That Make My Day 1999, Where Do Balloons Go? An Uplifting Mystery 2000, I'm Gonna Like Me Letting Off a Little Self-Esteem 2002, It's Hard To Be Five, Learning How To Work My Control Panel 2004, Is There Really a Human Race? 2006. *Address:* c/o Rick Kurtzman, CAA, 2000 Avenue of the Stars, Los Angeles, CA 90067, USA (office).

CURTIS, Richard Whalley Anthony, CBE, BA; British screenwriter, film director and film producer; b. 8 Nov. 1956, New Zealand; s. of Anthony J. Curtis and Glynness S. Curtis; two s. one d. by Emma Vallencey Freud. *Education:* Harrow School, Christ Church, Oxford. *Career:* Co-founder and Producer Comic Relief 1985–2000. *Films:* Dead On Time 1983, The Tall Guy (writer) 1988, Four Weddings and a Funeral (writer, exec. producer) 1994, Bean (writer, exec. producer) 1997, Notting Hill (writer, exec. producer) 1999, Bridget Jones's Diary (screenplay) 2001, Love Actually (writer, dir) 2003, Bridget Jones: The Edge of Reason (screenplay) 2004, The Boat that Rocked (writer) 2009. *Television:* Not the Nine O'Clock News (series writer) 1979–82, The Black Adder (series writer) 1983, Spitting Image (series writer) 1984, Blackadder II (series writer) 1986, Blackadder the Third (series writer) 1987, Blackadder's Christmas Carol (writer) 1988, Blackadder: The Cavalier Years (writer) 1988, Blackadder Goes Forth (series writer) 1989, The Robbie Coltrane Special (contrib.) 1989, Mr Bean (series writer) 1989–95, Bernard and the Genie (writer) 1991, Merry Christmas Mr Bean (writer) 1992, Rowan Atkinson Live (contrib.) 1992, The Vicar of Dibley (series writer, exec. producer) 1994–2007, Hooves of Fire (writer) 1999, French & Saunders Live (contrib.) 2000, Legend of the Lost Tribe (exec. producer) 2002, The Girl in the Café (writer and exec. producer) (Humanitas Prize 2006) 2005, The No.1 Ladies' Detective Agency 2008. *Honours:* BAFTA Fellowship 2007. *Literary Agent:* United Agents, 12–26 Lexington Street, London, W1F 0LE, England. *Telephone:* (20) 3214-0800. *Fax:* (20) 3214-0801. *E-mail:* info@unitedagents.co.uk. *Website:* unitedagents.co.uk. *Address:* Portobello Studios, 138 Portobello Road, London W11 2DZ, England (office).

CURTIS, Tony, BA, MFA, DLitt, FRSL; British academic and poet; *Professor of Poetry, University of Glamorgan*; b. 26 Dec. 1946, Carmarthen, Wales; m. Margaret Blundell 1970; one s. one d. *Education:* Univ. Coll. of Swansea, Goddard Coll., Vermont, Univ. of Glamorgan. *Career:* fmr schoolmaster, coll. lecturer, univ. lecturer, currently Emer. Prof. of Poetry, Univ. of Glamorgan. *Publications include:* poetry: Walk Down a Welsh Wind 1972, Home Movies 1973, Album 1974, The Deerslayers 1978, Carnival 1978, Preparations: Poems 1974–79 1980, Letting Go 1983, Selected Poems 1970–85 1986, The Last Candles 1989, Taken for Pearls 1993, Heaven's Gate 2001, Crossing Over 2007; other: Islands (radio play) 1975, Out of the Dark Wood: Prose Poems, Stories 1977, Dannie Abse 1985, The Art of Seamus Heaney (ed.) 1986, The Poetry of Snowdonia 1989, The Poetry of Pembrokeshire (ed.) 1989, How to Study Modern Poetry 1990, Love from Wales 1993, How Poets Work (ed.) 1996, Welsh Painters Talking (ed.) 1996, Coal 1997, Welsh Artists Talking (ed.) 2001, After the First Death (ed.) 2007, Wales at War (ed.) 2007, Following Petra (ed.) 2008, The Meaning of Apricot Sponge – Selected Writing of John Tripp (ed.) 2010, Real South Pembrokeshire 2011, Tokens for the Foundlings (ed.) 2012. *Honours:* Eric Gregory Award 1972, Arts Council of Wales Young Writers Prize 1974, Nat. Poetry Competition Winner 1984, Dylan Thomas Prize 1993, Cholmondeley Award 1997. *Address:* Pentwyn, 55 Colcot Road, Barry, Vale of Glamorgan, CF62 8DL, Wales (home). *Telephone:* (1443) 482570 (office). *E-mail:* t.curtis@glam.ac.uk (office).

CURTIS, Wade (see Pournelle, Jerry Eugene)

CUSK, Rachel, BA; British writer; b. 8 Feb. 1967, Canada; d. of Peter Cusk and Carolyn Cusk; m. Adrian Clarke; two d. *Education:* St Mary's Convent, Cambridge and New Coll., Oxford. *Career:* writer 1992–. *Publications include:* novels: Saving Agnes (Whitbread First Novel Award 1993) 1992, The Temporary 1995, The Country Life (Somerset Maugham Award) 1997, The Lucky Ones 2003, In the Fold 2005, Arlington Park 2006, The Bradshaw Variations 2009, Bienvenue à Egypt Farm 2010, The Rainbow (Vintage Classics) (with D. H. Lawrence) 2011; non-fiction: A Life's Work 2001, The Last Supper: A Summer in Italy 2009. *Literary Agent:* c/o The Wylie Agency, 17 Bedford Square, London, WC1B 3JA, England. *Telephone:* (20) 7908-5900. *Fax:* (20) 7908-5901. *E-mail:* mail@wylieagency.co.uk. *Website:* www.wylieagency.co.uk.

CUSSLER, Clive Eric, PhD; American novelist; b. 15 July 1931, Aurora, Ill.; s. of Eric Cussler and Amy Hunnewell; m. Barbara Knight 1955; three c. *Education:* Pasadena City Coll., Orange Coast Coll., California State Univ. *Career:* Owner, Bestgen & Cussler Advertising, Newport Beach, Calif. 1961–65; Copy Dir Darcy Advertising, Hollywood, Calif. and Instructor in Advertising Communications, Orange Coast Coll. 1965–67; Advertising Dir Aquatic Marine Corpn, Newport Beach, Calif. 1967–79; Vice-Pres. and Creative Dir of Broadcast, Meffon, Wolff and Weir Advertising, Denver, Colo 1970–73; Chair. Nat. Underwater and Marine Agency; Fellow, New York Explorers Club, Royal Geographical Soc. *Publications include:* The Mediterranean Caper 1973, Iceberg 1975, Raise the Titanic 1976, Vixen O-Three 1978, Night Probe 1981, Pacific Vortex 1982, Deep Six 1984, Cyclops 1986, Treasure 1988, Dragon 1990, Sahara 1992, Inca Gold 1994, Shock Wave 1995, Sea Hunters 1996, Flood Tide 1997, Clive Cussler and Dirk Pitt Revealed 1997, Serpent 1998, Atlantis Found 1999, Blue Gold 2000, Valhalla Rising 2001, Fire Ice (with Paul Kemprecos) 2002, Sea Hunters II 2002, The Golden Buddha (with Craig Dirgo) 2003, White Death 2003, Trojan Odyssey 2003, Black Wind (with Dirk Cussler) 2004, Sacred Stone 2005, Lost City (with Paul Kemprecos) 2006, Skeleton Coast 2006, Treasure of Khan (with Dirk Cussler) 2006, Dark Watch (with Jack Du Brul) 2007, The Chase 2007, Polar Shift 2007, Plague Ship 2008, Arctic Drift 2008, Corsair (with Jack du Brul) 2009, Medusa (with Paul Kemprecos) 2009, Spartan Gold (with Grant Blackwood) 2009, The Wrecker (with Justin Scott) 2009, The Silent Sea (with Jack du Brul) 2010, The Adventures of Hotsy Totsy 2010, The Spy (with Justin Scott) 2010, Lost Empire (with Grant Blackwood) 2010, Crescent Dawn (with Dirk Cussler) 2010, The Race (with Justin Scott) 2011, Devil's Gate (with Graham Brown) 2011, The Kingdom (with Grant Blackwood) 2011, The Jungle (with Jack Du Brul) 2011, Serpent (with Paul Kemprecos) 2011. *Honours:* Lowel Thomas Award, New York Explorers Club. *Address:* c/o Penguin Group (USA) Inc., Putnam Publicity, 375 Hudson Street, New York, NY 10014, USA. *Website:* www.penguin.com.

CUTHBERT, Valerie; British writer, journalist and poet; b. 30 Oct. 1923, London; m. 1965. *Career:* mem. Writers Asscn of Kenya. *Publications include:* The Great Siege of Fort Jesus 1970, Yusuf Bin Hasan 1972, Jomo Kenyatta: The Burning Spear 1982, Dust and the Shadow 1988, Thoughts on Writing 1990, Beneath the Rainbow: A Collection of Children's Stories and Poems from Kenya 1993, Escape from Somalia 1999, Wings of the Wind (Jomo Kenyatta Prize for Literature 2005) 2004; contribs: various anthologies and other publications. *Honours:* Second Prize, Short Story Competition, Writers Asscn of Kenya 1993. *Address:* PO Box 82727, Mombasa, Kenya.

CUTTS, Simon; British artist, poet and publisher; *Director, Coracle Press*; b. 30 Dec. 1944, Derby; s. of George Tom Cutts and Elizabeth Purdy; m. 1st Annira Uusi-Illikainen (divorced 1973); one s.; m. 2nd Margot Hapgood (died 1985). *Education:* Herbert Strutt Grammar School, Belper, Derbyshire, Nottingham Coll. of Art, Trent Polytechnic. *Career:* travel and miscellaneous employment including the Trent Bookshop, Nottingham 1962–69; Jt Ed. Tarasque Press 1964–72; publishing, lecturing and writing 1972–74; Dir and Co-Partner Coracle Press Books (now Coracle Press) 1975–87, 1996–, Dir, Coracle Press Gallery 1983–86; Dir Victoria Miro Gallery 1985–; org. of exhbns in Europe and New York. *Publications:* Quelques Pianos 1976, Pianostool Footnotes 1983, Petits-Airs for Margot 1986, Seepages 1988, The Rubber Stamp Mini Printer 1993, 1995, After Frank O'Hara and Morton Feldman (with Erica van Horn) 1996, The A. Goldsworthy Questionnaires 1997, A Smell of Printing 2000, Eclogues 2004, A English Dictionary of French Place Names 2004, Ceillets des Poètes 2005, Some Forms of Availability 2006, As If It Is At All 2007, Some More Notes on Writing & Drinking 2010, The Manifestation of the Poem 2011, 8 Old Irish Potatoes 2011, Six Jugs (co-author) 2011, Affinity 2011. *E-mail:* books@coracle.ie (office); coraclepress@eircom.net (office). *Website:* www.coracle.ie (office).

CZERNEDA, Julie Elizabeth, BSc; Canadian writer and editor; b. 11 April 1955, Exeter, Ont.; m. Roger Henry Czerneda 1976; one s. one d. *Education:* Univ. of Waterloo, Univ. of Saskatchewan, Queen's Univ., Kingston, Ont. *Career:* Pres. Czerneda Publishing Inc. 1991–98. *Publications include:* fiction: A Thousand Words for Stranger 1997, Beholder's Eye 1998, Ties of Power 1999, Changing Vision 2000, Hidden in Sight 2002, In the Company of Others 2002, Survival 2004, Migration 2005, Regeneration 2006, Reap the Wild Wind 2007, Misspelled 2008, Riders of the Storm 2009, Rift in the Sky 2009, A Turn of Light 2011; other: numerous non-fiction books 1986–; contribs to anthologies. *E-mail:* julie.czerneda@sff.net (office). *Website:* www.czerneda.com.

D

DABYDEEN, Cyril, BA, MA, MPA; Guyanese/Canadian poet, author, editor and essayist; *Lecturer in English, University of Ottawa*; b. 15 Oct. 1945, Guyana; s. of the late Abel Dabydeen and of Hilda Persaud (née Oudit); previously married. *Education:* Lakehead Univ., Thunder Bay, Queen's Univ., Kingston. *Career:* juror, Neustadt Int. Prize for Literature 2000, Gov.-Gen.'s Award for Literature 2000, 2006; speaker, reader across Canada, USA, UK, Europe, India, Cuba, Caribbean and South America; currently Lecturer in English, Univ. of Ottawa; mem. US Asscn of Commonwealth Language and Literature Studies, Int. PEN. *Publications include:* poetry: Distances 1977, Goatsong 1977, Heart's Frame 1979, This Planet Earth 1980, Islands Lovelier Than a Vision 1988, Coastland: New and Selected Poems 1989, Dark Swirl 1989, Stoning the Wind 1994, Born in Amazonia 1996, Discussing Columbus 1997, Hemisphere of Love 2003, Imaginary Origins: Selected Poems 2004, Uncharted Heart 2008, Unanimous Night 2009; fiction: Still Close to the Island 1980, To Monkey Jungle 1986, The Wizard Swami 1989, Dark Swirl 1989, Jogging in Havana 1992, Sometimes Hard 1994, Berbice Crossing (short stories) 1996, Black Jesus and Other Stories 1997, My Brahmin Days and Other Stories 2000, North of the Equator (short stories) 2001, Play a Song, Somebody (short stories) 2004, Drums of my Flesh 2005; Ed. A Shapely Fire: Changing the Literary Landscape 1987, Another Way to Dance: Contemporary Asian Poetry from Canada and the US 1996; contribs to Canadian Forum, Canadian Fiction Magazine, Fiddlehead, Dalhousie Review, Antigonish Review, World Literature Today, Atlanta Review, The Critical Quarterly, Wascana Review, Literary Review, Globe and Mail, Caribbean Quarterly, Kunapipi, Planet International: Wales. *Honours:* Sandbach Parker Gold Medal, A. J. Seymour Lyric Poetry Prize, Poet Laureate of Ottawa, Okanagan Fiction Award, recipient Canada Council, Ontario Arts Council, Ottawa-Carleton Region Literary Awards, Best Book of Fiction, Guyana Prize for Literature 2006, Certificate of Merit for the Arts, honoured for work in race relations by City of Ottawa and the Fed. of Canadian Municipalities, Dean of Arts Award 2007, Lifetime Achievement Award, Guyana Council of Canadians 2010. *Address:* 295 Somerset Street E, Ottawa, ON K1N 6V9, Canada (home). *Telephone:* (613) 230-7854 (office). *E-mail:* cdabydeen@ncf.ca.

DABYDEEN, David, BA, PhD, FRSL; Guyanese/British diplomatist, poet, writer and academic; *Ambassador to People's Republic of China*; b. 9 Dec. 1955, Guyana. *Education:* Univs of Cambridge and London. *Career:* Jr Research Fellow, Univ. of Oxford 1983–84; Lecturer in Caribbean Studies, Univ. of Warwick 1984–97, Prof. of Literature, Centre for Trans. and Comparative Cultural Studies 1997–; Guyana's Amb. to UNESCO 1997; Amb. to People's Repub. of China 2010–; mem. Arts Council of GB, literature panel 1985–89. *Publications include:* Slave Song 1984, Coolie Odyssey 1988, The Intended 1991, Black Writers in Britain, 1780–1890 1991, Disappearance 1993, Turner 1994, The Counting House 1996, Across the Dark Waters: Indian Identity in the Caribbean 1996, Slavery, Abolition and Emancipation: Black Writers 1999, A Harlot's Progress 1999, Our Lady of Demerara 2004, Slave Song 2005, Molly and the Muslim Stick 2008; ed.: Lutchmee & Dilloo: A Study of West Indian Life 2003, Oxford Companion to Black British History 2007; contrib. to various periodicals. *Honours:* Commonwealth Poetry Prize 1984, Guyana Literature Prize 1992, Raja Rao Award 2004, Hind Rattan Award 2007, Anthony Sabga Prize 2008. *Address:* Embassy of Guyana, 1 Xiu Shui Dong Jie, Jian Guo Men Wai, Beijing 100600, People's Republic of China (office); Yesu Persaud Centre for Caribbean Studies, Humanities Building, Room H106, University of Warwick, Coventry, CV4 7AL, England (office). *Telephone:* (10) 65321601 (Beijing) (office); (24) 7652-3467 (Coventry) (office). *Fax:* (10) 65325741 (Beijing) (office). *E-mail:* guyemb@public3.bta.net.cn (office); d.dabydeen@warwick.ac.uk (office). *Website:* www.warwick.ac.uk/fac/arts/ccs/staff/dabydeen (office).

DACEY, Philip, BA, MA, MFA; American poet and fmr teacher; b. 9 May 1939, St Louis, Mo.; m. Florence Chard 1963 (divorced 1986); two s. one d. *Education:* St Louis Univ., Stanford Univ., Univ. of Iowa. *Career:* Instructor in English, Univ. of Missouri at St Louis 1967–68; Faculty, Dept of English, Southwest State Univ., Marshall, Minn. 1970–2005; Distinguished Writer-in-Residence, Wichita State Univ. 1985. *Publications include:* poetry: The Beast with Two Backs 1969, Fist, Sweet Giraffe, The Lion, Snake, and Owl 1970, Four Nudes 1971, How I Escaped from the Labyrinth and Other Poems 1977, The Boy Under the Bed 1979, The Condom Poems 1979, Gerard Manley Hopkins Meets Walt Whitman in Heaven and Other Poems 1982, Fives 1984, The Man with Red Suspenders 1986, The Condom Poems II 1989, Night Shift at the Crucifix Factory 1991, What's Empty Weighs the Most 1997, The Deathbed Playboy 1999, The Paramour of Moving Air 1999, The Adventures of Alixa Doom and other Love Poems 2003, The Mystery of Max Schmitt: Poems on the Life and Work of Thomas Eakins 2004, Master Five-by-Five 2005, Three Shades of Green: Poems of Fatherhood 2006, The New York Postcard Sonnets: A Midwesterner Moves to Manhattan 2007, Vertebrae Rosaries 2009, Mosquito Operas 2010; ed.: I Love You All Day: It is That Simple (with Gerald M. Knoll) 1970, Strong Measures: Contemporary American Poetry in Traditional Forms (with David Jaus) 1986. *Honours:* Woodrow Wilson Fellowship 1961, New York YM-YWHA Discovery Award 1974, Nat. Endowment for the Arts Fellowships 1975, 1980, Minnesota State Arts Board Fellowships 1975, 1983, Bush Foundation Fellowship 1977, Loft-McKnight Fellowship 1984, Fulbright Lecturer 1988, First Prize, The Ledge Magazine Poetry Awards 2009. *Address:* 102 West 76th Street, Apartment 2R, New York, NY 10023, USA (office). *E-mail:* philipdacey@gmail.com (office). *Website:* www.philipdacey.com.

DACRE, Paul Michael, BA, FRSA; British newspaper editor; *Editor-in-Chief, Associated Newspapers*; b. 14 Nov. 1948, London, England; s. of Peter Dacre and Joan Dacre (née Hill); m. Kathleen Thomson 1973; two s. *Education:* Univ. Coll. School, London, Univ. of Leeds. *Career:* reporter, feature writer, Assoc. Features Ed., Daily Express 1970–76, Washington and New York Corresp. 1976–79; New York Bureau Chief, Daily Mail 1980, News Ed., London 1981–85, Asst Ed. (News and Foreign) 1986, Asst Ed. (Features) 1987, Exec. Ed. 1988, Assoc. Ed. 1989–91, Ed. Daily Mail 1992–, Ed.-in-Chief Assoc. Newspapers 1998–; Ed. Evening Standard 1991–92; Dir Associated Newspaper Holdings 1991–, Daily Mail & General Trust PLC 1998–, Teletext Holdings Ltd 2000–02; Chair. Editors' Code of Practice Cttee 2008–; mem. Press Complaints Comm. 1998–2008, Press Bd of Finance 2001–, Govt Review into 30 Year Rule 2008; Amb. for Alzheimer's Soc. 2007. *Honours:* Hon. mem. Nat. Soc. for the Prevention of Cruelty to Children 2009; Cudlipp Lecturer, London Coll. of Commerce 2007. *Address:* Daily Mail, Northcliffe House, 2 Derry Street, London, W8 5TT, England (office). *Telephone:* (20) 7938-6000 (office). *Fax:* (20) 7937-7977 (office). *E-mail:* news@dailymail.co.uk (office). *Website:* www.dailymail.co.uk (office).

DAENINCKX, Didier; French novelist and essayist; b. 27 April 1949, Saint-Denis; m. Jocelyne Cardin. *Career:* has worked as a printer 1966–77, cultural leader 1977–79, local journalist 1979–82; currently full-time writer. *Dance:* Heroïnes 1997. *Screenplay:* Lumière Noire 1994, La repentie 2000. *Television writing:* Meurtres pour mémoire (TF1/Hamster) 1985, La Rançon de la gloire (FR3/Vamp) 1988, La Cicatrice (INA/La Sept/Coup d'œil) 1989, Novacek (France 2/Tanaïs) 1994, Le Premier qui dit non (France 2/VF Prod.) 1997, Chacun son Tour (France 2/Tanaïs) 1997, La Mort n'oublie Personne (France 2) 2008, On achève bien les disc-jockeys (France 2) 2009. *Publications include:* novels: Meurtres pour mémoire (Prix Paul Vaillant Couturier 1984, Grand Prix de Littérature Policière 1985) 1984, Le Géant inachevé (Prix du Roman Noir 1985) 1984, Le Der des ders 1985, Métropolice 1985, Play-Back (Prix Mystère de la Critique 1987) 1986, Le Bourreau et son double 1986, Lumière Noire 1987, La Mort n'oublie personne 1989, Le Facteur fatal (Prix Populiste 1990) 1990, À louer sans commission 1991, Hors-limites 1992, Zapping (Prix Louis Guilloux 1993) 1992, Autres lieux 1993, Main courante 1994, En Marge 1994, Un Château en Bohême 1994, Les Figurants 1995, Nazis dans le métro 1996, À nous la vie 1996, Le Goût de la vérité 1997, Mort au premier tour 1997, Écrire en contre 1997, La Couleur du noir 1998, Passages d'enfer 1998, Cannibale 1998, Belleville Ménilmontant 1998, Banlieue nord 1999, La Repentie 1999, Éthique en toc 2000, Le Dernier Guérillero 2000, 12, rue Meckert 2001, Ceinture rouge 2001, La mort en dédicace 2001, Corvée de bois 2002, Le Retour d'Ataï 2002, Les Corps râlent 2003, Raconteur d'histoires 2003, La Route du rom 2003, Je tue il 2003, Le Crime de Sainte-Adresse 2004, Cités perdues 2005, Itinéraire d'un Salaud Ordinaire 2005, Histoire et faux-semblants 2007, Camarades de classe 2008, Missak 2009, L'affranchie du périphérique 2009, Galadio 2010; children's books: La Fêtes des mères 1986, Le Chat de Tigali (Prix Polar Jeunes 1988) 1988, Le Papillon de toutes les couleurs (Premier Prix Goncourt du Livre de Jeunesse) 1998, La Péniche aux enfants 1999, Il faut désobéir 2002, Un Violon dans la nuit 2003, Viva la liberté 2004, L'Enfant du zoo 2004; essays: Jirinovski, le Russe qui fait trembler le monde (with Pierre Drachline) 1994, Négationnistes, les chiffonniers de l'Histoire 1997, Paroles à la bouche du présent 1997, Le jeune poulpe contre la Vieille Taupe 1997, Au nom de la loi (with Valère Staraselski) 1998. *Honours:* Soc. des Gens de Lettres Prix Paul Féval de Littérature Populaire 1994. *Address:* c/o Éditions Verdier, 17–19 rue Houdart, 75020 Paris, France. *E-mail:* didier.daeninckx@orange.fr. *Website:* www.editions-verdier.fr.

D'AGUIAR, Fred, BA, RMN; British poet, novelist, dramatist, essayist and academic; *Gloria D. Smith Professor of Africana Studies and Professor of English, Virginia Polytechnic Institute and State University*; b. 2 Feb. 1960, London, England. *Education:* Maudsley Hosp., Univ. of Kent. *Career:* Writer-in-Residence, London Borough of Lewisham 1986–87, Birmingham Polytechnic 1988–89; instructor in writing, Arvon Foundation 1986–; Judith Wilson Visiting Fellow, Univ. of Cambridge 1989–90; Northern Arts Literary Fellow, Newcastle and Durham Univs 1990–92; Visiting Writer, Amherst Coll., Massachusetts 1992–94; Asst Prof. of English, Bates Coll., Lewiston, Me 1994–95; Prof. of English, Univ. of Miami 1995–2003; Prof. and Dir Creative Writing, Virginia Polytechnic Inst. and State Univ. 2003–06, Gloria D. Smith Prof. of Africana Studies and Prof. of English 2006–. *Play:* A Jamaican Airman Foresees his Death 1995. *Radio:* play: Days and Nights in Bedlam 2006. *Television:* Sweet Thames 1992, Rwanda Stories 1995, The Longest Memory 1998. *Publications:* poetry: Mama Dot 1985, Airy Hall 1989, British Subjects 1993, Bill of Rights 1998, Bloodlines (verse novel) 2000, An English Sampler, New and Selected Poems 2001, Continental Shelf 2009; fiction: The Longest Memory 1994, Dear Future 1996, Feeding the Ghosts 1998, Bethany Bettany 2003; co-ed.: The New British Poetry 1989; selected essays in The Age of Anxiety 1996, Black British Culture and Society 1999, Best American Essays 2000, Bomb magazine, Fulcrum magazine. *Honours:* Hon. Fellow, Goldsmiths

Coll., London 2012; Hon. PhD (Kent) 2009; Guyana Poetry Award 1987, BBC Race in the Media Award 1992, BFI Most Innovative Film Award 1993, Whitbread First Novel Award 1995, David Higham First Novel Award 1995, Guyana Fiction Award 1996. *Literary Agent:* c/o David Higham Associates Ltd, 5–8 Lower John Street, Golden Square, London, W1F 9HA, England. *Telephone:* (20) 7434-5900. *Fax:* (20) 7437-1072. *Website:* www.davidhigham.co.uk. *Address:* Department of English, Virginia Polytechnic Institute and State University, Blacksburg, VA 24061, USA (office). *Telephone:* (540) 231-7759 (office). *Fax:* (540) 231-5692 (office). *E-mail:* fredd@vt.edu (office). *Website:* www.poetryarchive.org/poetryarchive/singlePoet.do?poetId=137.

DAHL, Sophie; British fmr model and author; b. 1978, granddaughter of the late Patricia Neal and the late Roald Dahl; m. Jamie Cullum 2010. *Career:* began career as a model; gave up modelling to concentrate on writing career 2007; fmr long-term Contributing Ed. at Men's Vogue, currently a regular contrib. to both US and UK edns of Vogue, and to Waitrose Food Illustrated magazine; has also contributed to, amongst others, The Observer, The Guardian, The Saturday Times Magazine; wrote book chronicling her misadventures with food, Miss Dahl's Voluptuous Delights 2009; wrote and presented BBC 2 TV cookery programme, The Delicious Miss Dahl 2010; currently working on a documentary film project with Keo Films. *Publications:* The Man with the Dancing Eyes (illustrated novella) (Times bestselling book) 2003, Playing with the Grown Ups 2007, Miss Dahl's Voluptuous Delights 2009, From Season to Season 2011. *Literary Agent:* c/o Angela Becker, Becker Brown Management, 11 Knightsbridge, 3rd Floor, London, SW1X 7LY, England. *E-mail:* info@beckerbrown.com.

DAHLEN, Beverly Jean, BA; American poet and teacher; b. 7 Nov. 1934, Portland, Ore.; m. Richard Pervier 1957 (divorced 1966). *Education:* California State Univ., Humboldt, California State Univ. at San Francisco. *Career:* Asst Sec., Poetry Center, California State Univ., San Francisco, 1967–73; Creative Writing Teacher, California Poetry-in-the-Schools Project 1970–74; Creative Writing Teacher, East Bay Community Arts Project 1974–80; Adult Learning Center, City Coll. of San Francisco 1980–; Creative Writing Teacher, Coll. of Marin, San Francisco State Univ.; teacher, summer writing workshops, Foothill Coll., Los Altos, Calif., Lake Placid Art Center, Lake Placid, NY, Naropa Inst., Boulder, Colo; Founder HOWever. *Publications include:* poetry: Out of the Third 1974, A Letter at Easter: To George Stanley 1976, The Egyptian Poems 1983, A Reading, 1–7 1985, A Reading, 11–17 1989, A Reading, 8–10 1992, A Reading Spicer and Eighteen Sonnets 2004, A Reading, 18–20 2006, A Reading: Birds 2011; contribs: periodicals including: Shocks Magazine, Room, Bed, Isthmus, Transfer, Feminist Studies, Ironwood, Poetics Journal, Sagetrieb, Conjunctions, Acts, Hambone, HOW(-ever). *Honours:* Residency, Briarcombe, Bolinas, Calif. 1983, Residency, Djerrasi Foundation, Woodside, Calif. 1984. *Address:* 15 1/2 Mirabel Avenue, San Francisco, CA 94110-4614, USA (home). *Telephone:* (415) 824-6649 (home).

DAIF, Rachid al-, PhD, DEA; Lebanese writer; *Professor of Creative Writing, Lebanese American University*; b. 1945, s. of Boulos Daif and Yasmine Daif; one s. *Education:* Univ. of Paris, Université Libanaise. *Career:* teacher of Arabic language, Univ. of Paris 1972–74; Prof. of Arabic, Université Libanaise 1974–2008; Visiting Prof., Univ. of Toulouse 1999; Prof. of Creative Writing, Lebanese American Univ. 2008–. *Publications include:* (in translation) Dear Mr Kawabata (novel) 1998, Learning English 1998, Passage to Dusk 2001, This Side of Innocence 2001, Forget About The Car 2002, Maabad Makes It In Baghdad 2005, The German Returns To His Senses 2005. *Address:* PO Box 13-5991, Chourane, Beirut, Lebanon (office). *Telephone:* (1) 807769 (home). *E-mail:* daifrachid@gmail.com (office). *Website:* www.rachideldaif.com.

DALAI LAMA, The, former temporal and spiritual head of Tibet; Fourteenth Incarnation (Tenzin Gyatso); Tibetan; b. 6 July 1935, Taktser, Amdo Prov., NE Tibet; s. of Chujon Tsering and Tsering Dekyi. *Career:* born of Tibetan peasant family in Amdo Prov.; enthroned at Lhasa 1940; rights exercised by regency 1934–50; assumed political power 1950; fled to Chumbi in S Tibet after abortive resistance to Chinese State 1950; negotiated agreement with China 1951; Vice-Chair. Standing Cttee CPPCC, mem. Nat. Cttee 1951–59; Hon. Chair. Chinese Buddhist Asscn 1953–59; Del. to Nat. People's Congress 1954–59; Chair. Preparatory Cttee for the 'Autonomous Region of Tibet' 1955–59; fled Tibet to India after suppression of Tibetan national uprising 1959; Dr of Buddhist Philosophy (Monasteries of Sera, Drepung and Gaden, Lhasa) 1959; Supreme Head of all Buddhist sects in Tibet (Xizang); announced his retirement from active participation in Tibetan political affairs March 2011. *Publications include:* My Land and People 1962, The Opening of the Wisdom Eye 1963, The Buddhism of Tibet and the Key to the Middle Way 1975, Universal Responsibility and the Good Heart 1977, Deity Yoga (with Jeffrey Hopkins) 1981, Four Essential Buddhist Commentaries 1982, Collected Statements, Interviews & Articles 1982, Advice from Buddha Shakyamuni 1982, Kindness, Clarity and Insight 1984, A Human Approach to World Peace 1984, Opening the Mind and Generating a Good Heart 1985, Opening of the Eye of New Awareness (translated by Donald S. Lopez with Jeffrey Hopkins) 1985, Kalachakra Tantra – Rite of Initiation (with Jeffrey Hopkins) 1985, Tantra in Tibet (with Jeffrey Hopkins) 1987, The Union of Bliss & Emptiness (translated by Dr Thupten Jinpa) 1988, Transcendent Wisdom (translated, edited and annotated by B. Alan Wallace) 1988, The Dalai Lama at Harvard (translated and edited by Jeffrey Hopkins) 1988, The Bodhgaya Interviews (edited by Jose Ignacio Cabezon) 1988, Ocean of Wisdom 1989, Policy of Kindness (compiled and edited by Sidney Piburn) 1990, The Nobel Peace Prize and the Dalai Lama (compiled and edited by Sidney Piburn) 1990, My Tibet (with Galen Rowell) 1990, The Global Community & the Need for Universal Responsibility 1990, Freedom in Exile (autobiog.) 1991, Path to Bliss 1991, Mind Science – An East-West Dialogue (with Herbert Benson, Robert A. Thurman, Howard E. Gardner and Daniel Goleman) 1991, Cultivating a Daily Meditation 1991, Gentle Bridges – Conversations with the Dalai Lama on the Sciences of the Mind (with Jeremy Hayward and Francisco Verela) 1992, Worlds in Harmony (with conf. participants) 1992, Generous Wisdom – Commentaries on the Jatakamala 1993, Words of Truth 1993, A Flash of Lightning in the Dark of Night 1994, The World of Tibetan Buddhism (translated, edited and annotated by Dr Thupten Jinpa) 1995, The Way to Freedom (edited by John Avedon and Donald S. Lopez) 1995, The Spirit of Tibet: Universal Heritage – Selected Speeches and Writings (edited by A. A. Shiromany) 1995, The Power of Compassion 1995, The Path to Enlightenment (translated and edited by Glenn H. Mullin) 1995, His Holiness the Dalai Lama Speeches Statements Articles Interviews from 1987 to June 1995 1995, Dimensions of Spirituality 1995, Dialogues on Universal Responsibility and Education 1995, Commentary on the Thirty Seven Practices of a Bodhisattva (translated by Acharya Nyima Tsering, edited by Vyvyan Cayley and Mike Gilmore) 1995, Awakening the Mind, Lightening the Heart (edited by John Avedon and Donald S. Lopez) 1995, The Good Heart – A Buddhist Perspective on the Teachings of Jesus 1996, Beyond Dogma 1996, Buddha Nature 1997, Sleeping, Dreaming and Dying (edited and narrated by Francisco Varela) 1997, Love, Kindness and Universal Responsibility 1997, The Joy of Living and Dying in Peace (edited by John Avedon & Donald S. Lopez) 1997, The Heart of Compassion 1997, Healing Anger – The Power of Patience from a Buddhist Perspective (translated by Dr Thupten Jinpa) 1997, The Gelug/Kagyu Tradition of Mahamudra (with Alexander Berzin) 1997, Spiritual Advice for Buddhists and Christians 1998, The Political Philosophy of His Holiness the Dalai Lama – Selected Speeches and Writings (edited by A. A. Shiromany) 1998, The Path to Tranquillity – Daily Meditations (compiled and edited by Renuka Singh) 1998, The Four Noble Truths (translated by Dr Thupten Jinpa, edited by Dominique Side and Dr Thupten Jinpa) 1998, The Art of Happiness (with Howard C. Cutler) 1998, Ethics for the New Millennium 1998, Violence and Compassion 1998, The Power of Buddhism (with Jean-Claude Carriere) 1999, Imagine All the People – The Dalai Lama on Money, Politics and Life as It Could Be (with Fabian Quaki) 1999, Introduction to Buddhism 1999, Training the Mind 1999, The Little Book of Buddhism (compiled and edited by Renuka Singh) 1999, The Heart of the Buddha's Path (translated by Dr Thupten Jinpa, edited by Dominique Side and Dr Thupten Jinpa) 1999, Consciousness at the Crossroads – Conversations with the Dalai Lama on Brain Science and Buddhism 1999, Ancient Wisdom, Modern World – Ethics for a New Millennium 1999, Essential Teachings 1999, The Path to Tranquility: Daily Wisdom 1999, Buddha Heart, Buddha Mind – Living the Four Noble Truths 2000, Dalai Lama's Book of Wisdom (edited by Matthew Bunson) 2000, Transforming the Mind: Eight Verses on Generating Compassion and Transforming Your Life (translated by Dr Thupten Jinpa, edited by Dominique Side and Dr Thupten Jinpa) 2000, The Little Book of Wisdom 2000, A Simple Path: Basic Buddhist Teachings by His Holiness the Dalai Lama 2000, The Meaning of Life – Bhuddhist Perspectives on Cause and Effect (translated and edited by Jeffrey Hopkins) 2000, The Art of Living: A Guide to Contentment, Joy and Fulfillment 2001, The Transformed Mind – Reflections on Truth, Love and Happiness 2001, Stages of Meditation: Training the Mind for Wisdom (translated by Geshe Lobsang Jordhen, Lobsang Choephel Ganchenpa and Jeremy Russell) 2001, An Open Heart (edited by Nicholas Vreeland) 2001, Pocket Dalai Lama (compiled and edited by Mary Craig) 2002, Compassionate Life 2001, His Holiness the Dalai Lama: In My Own Words 2001, Illuminating the Path to Enlightenment 2002, Essence of the Heart Sutra 2002, How to Practice (translated and edited by Jeffrey Hopkins) 2002, The Spirit of Peace 2002, Advice on Dying (translated and edited by Jeffrey Hopkins) 2002, Healing Emotions – Conversation with the Dalai Lama on Emotions and Health 2003, Heart of Compassion 2003, 365 – Dalai Lama Daily Advice from the Heart (edited by Mathieu Ricard) 2003, Warm Heart Open Mind 2003, The Compassionate Life 2003, Destructive Emotions (with Daniel Goleman) 2004, Practicing Wisdom – The Perfection of Shantideva's Bodhisattva Way (translated by Geshe Tubten Jinpa) 2004, New Physics and Cosmology – Dialogues with the Dalai Lama (with Arthur Zajonc and Zara Houshmand) 2004, Dzogchen: Heart Essence of the Great Perfection 2004, The Wisdom of Forgiveness (with Victor Chan) 2004, Many Ways to Nirvana 2004, Path of Wisdom, Path of Peace – A Personal Conversation (with Felizitas Von Schoenborn) 2005, Lighting the Path, Teachings on Wisdom and Compassion (translated by Geshe Tubten Jinpa) 2005, Art of Happiness at Work (with and Howard C. Cutler) 2005, Widening the Circle of Love (translated and edited by Jeffrey Hopkins) 2005, The Universe in a Single Atom – The Convergence of Science and Spirituality 2005, Yoga Tantra – Paths to Magical Seats (with Dzong-ka-ba and Jeffrey Hopkins) 2005, Teachings on Je Tsong Khapa's Three Principal Aspects of the Path (translated by Ven. Lhakdor and edited by Jeremy Russell) 2006, Activating Bodhichitta and a Meditation on Compassion 2006, Mind in Comfort and Ease – The Vision of Enlightenment in the Great Perfection 2007, How to See Yourself as You Really Are 2007, Dalai Lama at MIT (edited by Anne Harrington and Arthur Zajonc) 2008, In My Own Words – An Introduction to My Teachings and Philosophy (edited by Rajiv Mehrotra) 2008, Becoming Enlightened (translated and edited by Jeffrey Hopkins) 2009, Emotional Awareness (with Paul Ekman) 2009, Art of Happiness in a Troubled World (with Howard C. Cutler) 2009, All You Ever

Wanted to Know about Happiness, Life and Living (compiled by Rajiv Mehrotra) 2009, Leaders's Way – Business, Buddhism and Happiness in an Interconnected World (with Laurens van den Muyzenberg) 2009, The Middle Way – Faith Grounded in Reason (translated by Thubten Jinpa) 2009, Toward a True Kinship of Faiths 2010, My Spiritual Journey (with Sofia Stril-rever) 2010. *Honours:* Presidential Distinguished Prof., Emory Univ., USA 2007–; Hon. Citizen of Paris 2008; Memory Prize 1989, Congressional Human Rights Award 1989, Nobel Peace Prize 1989, Freedom Award (USA) 1991, Presidential Congressional Gold Medal (USA) 2007, ranked by Forbes magazine amongst The World's Most Powerful People (39th) 2009–10, (51st) 2011, Templeton Prize 2012. *Address:* The Office of His Holiness the Dalai Lama Thekchen Choeling, PO McLeod Ganj, Dharamsala 176219, Himachal Pradesh, India (office). *Telephone:* (1892) 221343 (office); (1892) 221879 (office). *Fax:* (1892) 221813 (office). *E-mail:* ohhdl@dalailama.com (office). *Website:* www.dalailama.com (office).

DALE, Peter John, BA (Hons); British poet, writer and translator; b. 21 Aug. 1938, Addlestone, Surrey, England; m. Pauline Strouvelle 1963; one s. one d. *Education:* St Peter's Coll., Oxford. *Career:* secondary school teacher 1963–93; Co-Ed. Agenda 1972–96; Editorial Dir Between the Lines 1997–; Poetry Ed. Oxford Today 1999–2010; mem. Soc. of Authors, Translation Asscn, Welsh Acad. *Publications include:* poetry: Walk from the House 1962, The Storms 1968, Mortal Fire 1976, One Another (sonnet sequence) 1978, Too Much of Water 1983, A Set of Darts (epigrams with W. S. Milne and Robert Richardson) 1990, Earth Light: New Poems 1991, Edge to Edge: Selected Poems 1996, Da Capo (poem sequence) 1997, Under the Breath 2002, Eight by Five 2007, Local Habitation: A Sequence of Poems 2009, Diffractions: New and Collected Poems 2012; prose: Michael Hamburger in Conversation with Peter Dale 1998, An Introduction to Rhyme 1998, Anthony Thwaite in Conversation with Peter Dale and Ian Hamilton 1999, Richard Wilbur in Conversation with Peter Dale 2000, Peter Dale in Conversation with Cynthia Haven 2003; translator: Selected Poems of François Villon 1978, Poems of Jules Laforgue 1986, The Divine Comedy, terza rima version 1996, Poems of Jules Laforgue 2001, Poems of François Villon 2001, Tristan Corbière: Wry-Blue Loves and Other Poems (Les Amours jaunes) 2005, Charms and Other Pieces, Paul Valery 2007; contrib. to journals and periodicals. *Honours:* Arts Council bursary 1970. *Address:* 11 Heol y Gors, Whitchurch, Cardiff, CF14 1HF, Wales (home). *E-mail:* btluk@aol.com (office). *Website:* www.interviews-with-poets.com; www.poetryarchive.org; www.anvilpress.com; www.literaturewales.org.

DALLEK, Robert, BA, MA, PhD; American writer, biographer and academic; *Professor Emeritus of History, University of California, Los Angeles*; b. 16 May 1934, New York, NY; m. 1st Ilse F. Shatzkin 1959 (died 1962); m. 2nd Geraldine R. Kronmal 1965; one s. one d. *Education:* Univ. of Illinois, Columbia Univ. *Career:* Instructor in History, Columbia Univ. 1960–64; Asst Prof. to Prof. of History, UCLA 1964–94, Prof. Emer. 1994–; Assoc., Southern California Psychoanalytic Inst. 1981–85; Commonwealth Fund Lecturer, Univ. Coll. London, UK 1984; Thompson Lecturer, Univ. of Wyoming 1986; Charles Griffin Lecturer, Vassar Coll. 1987; Visiting Prof., California Inst. of Tech. 1993, LBJ School of Public Affairs, Univ. of Texas 1996; Harmsworth Visiting Prof., Univ. of Oxford, UK 1994–95; Prof. of History, Boston Univ. 1996; Marjorie Harris Weiss Lecturer, Brown Univ. 1998; Herbert Marcuse Lecturer, Brandeis Univ. 1999; Harry Seigle Lecturer, Washington Univ., St Louis 2001; Charles Grant Lecturer, Middlebury Coll. 2001; George Bancroft Lecturer, US Naval Acad. 2001; Montgomery Fellow and Visiting Prof., Dartmouth Coll. 2004–05; Visiting Prof., Stanford Univ. in Washington 2006–09; Fellow, American Acad. of Arts and Sciences, Soc. of American Historians (Pres. 2004–05), American Council of Learned Socs 1984–85; mem. American Psychoanalytic Asscn, Soc. of Historians of American Foreign Relations (Pres. 1995). *Publications include:* Democrat and Diplomat: The Life of William E. Dodd 1968, Western Europe: Vol. I of The Dynamics of World Power: A Documentary History of United States Foreign Policy 1945–1973 (ed.) 1973, Franklin D. Roosevelt and American Foreign Policy 1932–1945 1979, The American Style of Foreign Policy: Cultural Politics and Foreign Affairs 1983, Ronald Reagan: The Politics of Symbolism 1984, The Great Republic: A History of the American People (co-author) third edn 1985, Lone Star Rising: Lyndon Johnson and his Times 1908–1960 1991, The Encyclopedia of 20th-Century American History (assoc. ed. with others, four vols) 1995, Hail to the Chief: The Making and Unmaking of American Presidents 1996, Flawed Giant: Lyndon Johnson and his Times 1961–1973 1998, John F. Kennedy: An Unfinished Life 1917–1963 2003, Nixon and Kissinger: Partners in Power 2007, Harry S. Truman 2008, The Lost Peace: Leadership in a Time of Horror and Hop: 1945–1953 2010; contrib. to scholarly books and journals. *Honours:* Guggenheim Fellowship 1973–74, Sr Fellow, Nat. Endowment for the Humanities 1976–77, Bancroft Prize 1980, Rockefeller Foundation Humanities Fellow 1981–82, New York Times Book Review Notable Book Citations 1983, 1991, 1998, Lyndon B. Johnson Foundation research grants 1984–85, 1988–89. *Address:* 2138 Cathedral Avenue NW, Washington, DC 20008, USA (home). *Telephone:* (202) 588-8963 (home); (202) 302-0699 (home). *Fax:* (202) 588-8964 (home). *E-mail:* rdallek@aol.com.

DALMAS, John, BSc, PhD; American writer; b. (John Robert Jones), 3 Sept. 1926, Chicago, Ill.; s. of John Robert Jones II and Harriett Evelyn Engstrom; m. Gail Hill 1954; one s. one d. *Education:* Michigan State Coll., Univ. of Minnesota, Colorado State Univ. *Career:* mem. Science Fiction and Fantasy Writers of America, Vasa Order of America. *Publications include:* The Yngling 1969, The Varkaus Conspiracy 1983, Touch the Stars: Emergence (with Carl Martin) 1983, Homecoming 1984, Fanglith 1985, Aspen: Its Ecology and Management in the Western United States (sr author) 1985, The Reality Matrix 1986, The Walkaway Clause 1986, The Regiment 1987, The Playmasters (with Rodney Martin) 1987, Return to Fanglith 1987, The General's President 1988, The Lizard War 1989, The White Regiment 1990, The Kalif's War 1991, The Yngling and the Circle of Power 1992, The Orc Wars (collection) 1992, The Regiment's War 1993, The Yngling in Yamato 1994, The Lion of Farside 1995, The Bavarian Gate 1997, The Three Cornered War 1999, The Lion Returns 1999, Soldiers 2001, The Puppet Master 2001, Otherwhens, Otherwheres (collection) 2003, The Second Coming 2004, The Regiment: A Trilogy (collection) 2004; contrib. to professional journals, fiction magazines and themed anthologies. *Address:* 7308 Country Meadow Lane, Plain City, OH 43064, USA (home). *Telephone:* (614) 873-5862 (home). *E-mail:* dalmas@earthlink.net. *Website:* www.sfwa.org/members/dalmas (home); www.johndalmas.com (home).

DALRYMPLE, Theodore; British physician, psychiatrist and essayist; b. (Anthony Daniels), 11 Oct. 1949, London, England. *Career:* fmrly worked in a British prison; Contributing Ed., City Journal, New York; columnist, The Spectator, London; Dietrich Weismann Fellow, Manhattan Inst. *Publications include:* Life at the Bottom: The Worldview that Makes the Underclass 2003, Our Culture – What's Left Of It (essays) 2005, Junk Medicine: Doctors, Lies and the Addiction Bureaucracy 2007, Not with a Bang But a Whimper 2008, Second Opinion 2009, The New Vichy Syndrome 2010, Spoilt Rotten! The Toxic Cult of Sentimentality 2010; contrib. to The Spectator, The Times, The Daily Telegraph, New Statesman, New Criterion, National Review, Wall Street Journal. *Honours:* Freedom Prize 2011. *Address:* City Journal, Manhattan Institute for Policy Research, 52 Vanderbilt Avenue, New York, NY 10017, USA (office). *Telephone:* (212) 599-7000 (office). *Fax:* (212) 599-0371 (office). *Website:* www.city-journal.org (office).

DALRYMPLE, William Benedict Hamilton, MA, DLit, FRSL, FRGS, FRAS; British writer and historian; b. 20 March 1965, Edinburgh, Scotland; s. of Sir Hew Hamilton-Dalrymple and Lady Anne-Louise Hamilton-Dalrymple; m. Olivia Fraser; two s. one d. *Education:* Ampleforth Coll., Trinity Coll., Cambridge. *Career:* Founder and Co-Dir Jaipur Literature Festival. *Radio:* Three Miles an Hour 2002, The Long Quest 2002. *Television:* Stones of the Raj 1997, Indian Journeys 1998, Sufi Soul 2005. *Publications include:* In Xanadu 1989, City of Djinns 1993, From the Holy Mountain 1997, The Age of Kali (Prix de l'Astrobale-Etonnants voyageurs, France 2005) 1998, White Mughals: Love and Betrayal in Eighteenth-Century India 2002, Begums, Thugs and White Moghuls 2003, The Last Mughal (Duff Cooper Prize 2007, Vodafone Crossword Book Award 2007) 2006, Nine Lives: In Search of the Sacred in Modern India (Asia House Award 2010) 2009; contrib. to TLS, Guardian, New York Times, New York Review of Books, New Statesman. *Honours:* Dr hc (Univ. of Lucknow) 2007; Yorkshire Post Best First Work Award 1990, Scottish Arts Council Award 1990, Thomas Cook Travel Book Award 1994, Sunday Times Young British Writer of the Year 1994, Scottish Arts Council Autumn Book Award 1997, BAFTA Grierson Award for Best Documentary 2002 Mungo Park Medal, Royal Scottish Geographical Soc. 2002, Stanford St Martin Religious Broadcasting Prize 2002, Wolfson History Prize 2003, Scottish Book of the Year 2003, Prix d'Astrolabe 2005, RSAA Percy Sykes Award 2005, FPA Media Award for Print Artist of the Year 2005, James Todd Memorial Prize 2008, Media Citizen Puraskar 2010. *Literary Agent:* c/o David Godwin Associates, 55 Monmouth Street, London, WC2H 9DG, England. *Telephone:* (20) 7240-9992. *Fax:* (20) 7395-6110. *E-mail:* sophie@davidgodwinassociates.co.uk. *Website:* www.davidgodwinassociates.co.uk. *Address:* 1 Pages' Yard, Church Street, London, W4 2PA, England (home). *E-mail:* wdalrymple1@aol.com. *Website:* www.williamdalrymple.com.

DALTON, Amanda, BA, MA; British writer; b. 1957, Coventry, Warwicks., England. *Education:* Univ. of Leeds, Durham Univ., Univ. of Glamorgan. *Career:* teacher; fmr Centre Dir Arvon Foundation in Lumb Bank; Educ. Dir Royal Exchange Theatre, Manchester. *Radio:* original dramas broadcast on BBC Radio 3 and 4 include: No Harm 2004, Strike 2006. *Play:* Powder Monkey 2010. *Theatre:* works include: Mulgrave (Wilson Wilson Co.), Strawgirl, Secret Heart (Royal Exchange Theatre), Dog Boy (Royal Exchange, Manchester), Mapping the Edge (Sheffield Theatres/Wilson Wilson Co.). *Publications include:* The Dad Baby 1994, Room of Leaves (adapted for BBC Radio 4 1998) 1996, How to Disappear 1999; contrib. to Comma: Anthology of Short Stories 2002; numerous poetry anthologies and journals. *Honours:* PBS/Guardian Next Generation Poet 2004. *Address:* c/o Bloodaxe Books Ltd, Highgreen, Tarset, Northumberland, NE48 1RP, England. *Telephone:* (1422) 844442 (home). *E-mail:* amandadalton@tiscali.co.uk. *Website:* www.bloodaxebooks.com.

DAMLUJI, Maysoon Salem ad-, RIBA; Iraqi government official and architect; b. 1962, Baghdad. *Career:* worked as architect, London 1984, various positions internationally, including architectural designer and site architect; Mem. of Parliament; Sr Deputy Minister of Culture 2003–06; f. Iraqi Artists Asscn, UK (mem. exec. cttee); Founder-Pres. Iraqi Ind. Women's Group 2003–; mem. Council of Reps 2006–; Ed.-in-Chief of monthly magazine for women published in Iraq, NOON; Founding mem. Studio of the Actor, London, UK 1994–; mem. Asscn of Iraqi Ind. Democrats 2003–; Official Spokesman for Iraqiya 2010–. *E-mail:* aldamluji@aol.com (office).

D'AMOUR, Lisa, MFA; American playwright, performer and teacher. *Education:* Millsaps Coll., Jackson, Univ. of Texas, Austin. *Career:* mem. New Dramatists 1999–2006; writes plays for theatre and collaborates on interdisciplinary art installations, often in non-traditional sites; plays produced by theatres in New York, Austin, Houston, San Francisco and Minneapolis; theatre commissions from Playwrights' Horizons, Children's Theater Company, Guthrie Theater and The Talking Band, and Steppenwolf Theater; commissions for art installations from the Whitney Museum of Art, The Mitchell Center for the Arts in Houston and Brookfield Properties in New York; presentations by HERE Arts Center, The Walker Arts Center in Minneapolis, ArtSpot Productions in New Orleans, and the Fuse Box Festival in Austin. *Plays include:* 16 Spells to Charm the Beast, Tales of a West Texas Marsupial Girl, Red Death, Anna Bella Eema (New Georges Theater, New York 2003), The Cataract, Hide Town (Infernal Bridegroom Productions, Houston 2006), Night Sky, Detroit (Steppenwolf Theater, Chicago 2010, Broadway 2011). *Interdisciplinary art projects include:* The Grove, Landmark: 24 Hours on the Stone Arch Bridge (producer/performer), Slabber, Limo (writer/director), Nita and Zita (writer/director, ArtSpot Productions, New Orleans 2002) (Village Voice OBIE Award 2003), Stanley (writer/director), Swimming Cities of the Switchback Sea (also director), Nest, Terrible Things (dance theatre, director/co-creator), How to Build a Forest (visual art installation/theatre) 2011. *Publications:* My California 2001, Frostbite 2002, Red Death 2003, Anna Bella Eema 2007. *Honours:* numerous awards, grants, residencies and fellowships including MacDowell Colony Fellowship 1999, Alpert Award for the Arts 2008, Creative Capital Grant (jtly) 2009. *Literary Agent:* c/o Antje Oegel, AO International. *Telephone:* (773) 754-7628. *E-mail:* aoegel@aoegelinternational.com. *E-mail:* ljdamour@mac.com (office). *Website:* www.lisadamour.com.

DAN, Zeng; Chinese politician, journalist and writer; *Vice-General Manager, Chinese Centre for Tibet Research;* b. 1946, Tibet. *Education:* Fudan Univ., Shanghai. *Career:* began publishing career 1980; reporter, Tibet Daily, later Assoc. Chief Ed.; Dir Bureau of Culture, Tibet Autonomous Region, Vice-Sec. CCP Tibet Autonomous Region Cttee; Vice-Chair. China Fed. of Literary and Arts Circles, Vice-Chair. Chinese Writers' Asscn; Alt. mem. 12th CCP Cen. Cttee. 1982–87, 13th CCP Cen. Cttee. 1987–92, 14th CCP Cen. Cttee. 1992–97, 15th CCP Cen. Cttee. 1997–2002; currently Vice-Gen. Man. Chinese Centre for Tibet Research. *Publications include:* Report from the Roof of the World, The Blessing of the Deity. *Honours:* Tibet Autonomous Region Newspaper of the Year Award 1979, Tibet Autonomous Region Best Short Story Award 1980. *Address:* c/o Chinese Communist Party Tibetan Autonomous Region Committee, Lhasa, Tibet, People's Republic of China.

D'ANCONA, Matthew; British journalist and writer; b. 1968, London; m. Sarah Schaefer; two s. *Education:* St Dunstan's Coll., Magdalen Coll., Oxford. *Career:* fmrly worked for human rights magazine, Index on Censorship; trainee, news reporter, education correspondent The Times 1991–94, Asst Ed. 1994–95; Deputy Ed. comment section and political columnist The Sunday Telegraph 1996–98, Deputy Ed. 1998–2006; Ed. The Spectator 2006–09; political columnist GQ magazine 2006–; mem. Millennium Commission 2001–; Fellow All Souls, Oxford 1989–96. *Publications:* The Jesus Papyrus (non-fiction, with Carsten Peter Thiede) 1997, The Quest for the True Cross (non-fiction, with Carsten Peter Thiede) 2002, Going East (novel) 2004, Tabatha's Code (novel) 2006, Nothing to Fear 2008. *Honours:* British Press Award for Political Journalist of the Year 2004. *Address:* c/o The Spectator, 22 Old Queen Street, London, SW1H 9HP, England (office). *Website:* www.spectator.co.uk (office).

DANGAREMBGA, Tsitsi; Zimbabwean novelist, playwright, film-maker and politician; b. 1959, Mutoko, Southern Rhodesia. *Education:* Univ. of Cambridge, UK, Univ. of Harare, Deutsche Film and Fernseh Akad., Berlin, Germany. *Career:* Founder Nyerai Films (production co.); mem. MDC-M Party, currently Sec. for Educ. *Films:* Neria 1992, Everyone's Child 1996, Mother's Day 2006, Nyami-Nyami 2010. *Publications include:* The Lost of the Soil (play) 1983, The Letter (short story) 1985, She No Longer Weeps (play) 1987, Nervous Conditions (novel) (Commonwealth Writers' Prize, Africa region 1989) 1988, The Book of Not 2006. *Address:* Nyerai Films, PO Box 1520, Borrowdale, Harare, Zimbabwe (office). *Telephone:* (4) 862355 (office). *E-mail:* tsitsi@nyeraifilms.com (office). *Website:* www.nyeraifilms.com (office).

DANGOR, Achmat, BA; South African foundation executive, poet and novelist; *CEO, Nelson Mandela Foundation;* b. 2 Oct. 1948, Newclare, Johannesburg; m. Audrey Dangor. *Education:* Rhodes Univ. *Career:* mem. Black Thoughts 1970s, Congress of South African Writers (COSAW) 1980s; banned from publication 1973–79; Founding Exec. Dir Kagiso Trust 1986–91; fmr Sr Exec., Revlon Inc., S Africa; fmr Chief Exec. Nelson Mandela's Children's Fund; Dir of Advocacy, Communications and Leadership, Jt UN Programme on HIV/AIDS (UNAIDS) 2004–07; CEO Nelson Mandela Foundation 2007–. *Play:* Majiet 1986. *Publications include:* poetry: Bulldozer 1983, Private Voices 1992; fiction: Waiting for Leila 1978, The Z Town Trilogy (novel) 1989, Kafka's Curse: A Novella and Three Other Stories 1997, Bitter Fruit (novel) 2003; co-ed.: Voices from Within: Black Poetry from South Africa 1986; contrib. to The Return of the Amasi Bird 1982, Modern South African Poetry 1984, New Nation, Staffrider. *Honours:* Mofolo-Plomer Prize, BBC Prize for African Poetry. *Address:* Nelson Mandela Foundation, Mandela House, Private Bag X70000, Houghton 2041, South Africa (office). *Telephone:* (11) 5475600 (office). *Fax:* (11) 7281111 (office). *E-mail:* nmf@nelsonmandela.org (office). *Website:* www.nelsonmandela.org (office).

DANIEL, Colin (see WINDSOR, Patricia)

DANIEL, Wayne Wendell, BSEd, MPH, PhD; American academic and writer; *Professor Emeritus, Georgia State University;* b. 14 Feb. 1929, Tallapoosa, Ga; m. Mary Yarbrough 1956; one s. two d. *Education:* Univ. of Georgia, Univ. of North Carolina, Univ. of Oklahoma. *Career:* Statistical Research Asst, Georgia Dept of Public Health 1957–58, Research Statistician 1959–60, Biostatistical Analyst 1960–63, Chief, Mental Health Statistics Section, Biostatistics Service 1965–67, Dir Biostatistics Service 1967–68, Chief Statistician 1968; Asst Prof. to Prof. of Decision Sciences, Georgia State Univ. 1968–91, Prof. Emer. 1991–; mem. American Public Health Asscn (Fellow). *Publications include:* Biostatistics: A Foundation for Analysis in the Health Sciences 1974, Business Statistics for Management and Economics (with James C. Terrell) 1975, Introductory Statistics with Applications 1977, Applied Nonparametric Statistics 1978, Essentials of Business Statistics 1984, Pickin' on Peachtree: A History of Country Music in Atlanta 1990; contrib. to numerous journals and periodicals. *Address:* 2943 Appling Drive, Chamblee, GA 30341-5113, USA (home).

DANIELS, Max (see GELLIS, Roberta Leah)

DANIELS, Olga (see SINCLAIR, Olga Ellen)

DANIS, Daniel; Canadian playwright; b. 1962, Hawkesbury, Ont. *Career:* Assoc. Playwright, Théâtre de la Colline, Paris 2003–04; plays performed in Québec, Toronto, Vancouver, Calgary, Edmonton and in Scotland, Ireland, Belgium, France and Germany. *Plays include:* Celle-là (Théâtre Ouvert) 1993 (Prix de la Critique de Montréal, Prix du Gouverneur-général de Toronto 1993, Prix de la meilleure création en langue française, Syndicat Professionnel de la Critique Dramatique et Musicale 1995), Cendres de cailloux (Théâtre Espace Go, Montréal) 1993 (Prix du meilleur texte original Soirée des Masques, Premier Prix Concours Int. de Manuscrits Festival de Maubeuge, Prix Radio France Int.), Le chant du dire-dire (Théâtre Espace Go) 1998 (Théâtre Nat. de la Colline, Paris) 1999 (Prix de la meilleure création en langue française, Syndicat Professionnel de la Critique Dramatique et Musicale, Prix littéraire du Gouverneur-général 2007), Le Langue-à-langue des chiens de roche (Théâtre de la Colline, Paris) 1999 (Prix littéraire du Gouverneur-général 2002) 2005, E, Roman dit (Grand Prix de littérature dramatique 2006) 2005, La Trilogie des flous mille anonymes ayiti te frajil ou l'Ile saline 2004; for young people: Le pont de pierres et la peau d'images 1992, Sous un ciel de chamaille 2007, Kiwi (Prix Louise-Lahaye, Remis Par Cead Diffusion, Deutscher Jugendtheaterpreis, Prix Littéraire Abitibibowater Théâtre) 2007, Bled 2008. *Honours:* Chevalier, Ordre des Arts et des Lettres 2000. *Address:* c/o L'Arche Editeur, 86 rue Bonaparte, 75006 Paris, France. *E-mail:* info@danieldanis.org (office). *Website:* compagniedanieldanis.blogspot.com (office).

DANN, Colin Michael; British writer; b. 10 March 1943, Richmond, Surrey, England; m. 1st Janet Elizabeth Stratton 1977 (died 2004); m. 2nd Susanne Elizabeth Stanbury 2009. *Career:* mem. Soc. of Authors. *Publications include:* The Animals of Farthing Wood 1979, In the Grip of Winter 1981, Fox's Feud 1982, The Fox Cub Bold 1983, The Siege of White Deer Park 1985, The Ram of Sweetriver 1986, King of the Vagabonds 1987, The Beach Dogs 1988, The Flight from Farthing Wood 1988, Just Nuffin 1989, In the Path of the Storm 1989, A Great Escape 1990, A Legacy of Ghosts 1991, The City Cats 1991, Battle for the Park 1992, The Adventure Begins 1994, Copycat 1998, Nobody's Dog 1999, Journey to Freedom 1999, Lion Country 2000, Pride of the Plains 2002. *Honours:* Arts Council Nat. Award for Children's Literature 1980. *Address:* Castle Oast, Ewhurst Green, East Sussex, England. *Telephone:* (1580) 830325.

DANN, Jack, BA; American writer, lecturer and editor; b. 15 Feb. 1945, Johnson City, NY; s. of Murray I. Dann and Edith Nash; m. 1st Jeanne Van Buren 1983 (divorced 1994); one step-s. one d.; m. 2nd Janeen Suzanne Webb 1995. *Education:* State Univ. of NY at Binghamton, St John's Law School. *Career:* Man. Ed. SFWA Bulletin 1970–75; Instructor of Writing, Science Fiction, Broome Community Coll., Binghamton 1972, 1990, 1991; Asst Prof., Cornell Univ., Ithaca, NY 1973; mem. Bd Dirs Nat. Home Life Assurance Co., New York; Prin. Partner, Aultman Robertson & Assocs (advertising and public relations firm), Alverson & Dann (advertising and public relations firm); mem. SFWA. *Play:* Marilyn or the Monster (with Brian Smith) (Seeing Ear Theater/Scifi.Com). *Publications include:* Starhiker: A Novel 1977, Christs and Other Poems 1978, Timetipping (short stories) 1980, Junction 1981, The Man Who Melted 1984, Slow Dancing In Time (short stories with Gardner Dozois, Michael Swanwick, Susan Casper, Jack C. Haldeman II) 1990, Echoes of Thunder (short novel, with Jack C. Haldeman II) 1991, High Steel (with Jack C. Haldeman II) 1993, The Memory Cathedral: A Secret History of Leonardo da Vinci 1995, The Silent 1998, Jubilee: The Essential Jack Dann 2001, Da Vinci Rising 2001, Counting Coup 2001, The Rebel: An Imagined Life of James Dean 2004, The Fiction Factory (short stories with Susan Casper, Gardner Dozois, Gregory Frost, Jack C. Haldeman II et al.) 2005, Promised Land: Stories Of Another America 2007, The Economy of Light; editor or co-editor: Wandering Stars: An Anthology of Jewish Fantasy and Science Fiction 1974, Faster Than Light: An Anthology of Stories about Interstellar Travel (with George Zenrowski) 1976, Immortal 1977, More Wandering Stars 1981, In the Field of Fire (with Jeanne Van Buren Dann) 1987, Three in Time: White Wolf Rediscovery Trio, Vol. 1 (with Pamela Sargent and George Zebroeski) 1998, Avram Davidson's Everybody has Somebody in Heaven: Essential Jewish Tales of the Spirit (with Grania Davis)

2000, Dreaming Down-Under (with Janeen Webb) 2001, Gathering the Bones (with Ramsey Campbell and Dennis Etchinson) 2003, Nebula Awards Showcase 2005, Dreaming Again: Thirty-five New Stories Celebrating the Wild Side of Australian Fantasy Writing 2008; co-editor with Gardner Dozois: Future Power 1976, Aliens! 1980, Unicorns! 1982, Magicats! 1984, Bestiary! 1985, Mermaids! 1985, Sorcerers! 1986, In the Field of Fire 1987, Demons! 1987, Dogtails!, Seaserpents! 1989, Dinosaurs! 1990, Little People 1991, Magicats II 1991, Unicorns II 1992, Dragons 1993, Invaders 1993, Horses! 1994, Angels 1995, Dinosaurs II 1995, Hackers 1996, Timegates 1997, Clones 1998, Nanotech 1998, Future War 1999, Armageddons 1999, Aliens Among Us 2000, Space Soldiers 2001, Genometry 2001, Future Sports 2002, Beyond Flesh 2002, Future Crimes 2003, AIs 2004, Robots 2005, Beyond Singularity 2005, Escape From Earth: New Adventures in Space (young adult volume) 2006, Futures Past 2006, Wizards (publ. as Dark Alchemy in UK) 2007, The Dragon Book 2009; contrib. to New Dimensions, Orbit, New Worlds, Asimov's Science Fiction Magazines, Fiction Writers' Handbook, Arbor House Treasury of Horror and the Supernatural, Playboy, Writer's Digest, Omni, SciFi.Com, Washington Post, Penthouse, Polyphony, Postscripts. *Honours:* Esteemed Kt, Mark Twain Soc. 1975–, Co-winner, Gilgamesh Award 1986, Nebula Award for Best Novella 1996, Co-Winner, Aurealis Award for Best Science Fiction Story 1997, Ditmar Awards for Best Science Fiction Story 1997, for Best Anthology 1999, for Best Short Fiction 2002, Co-Winner, World Fantasy Award for Best Anthology 1999, Peter McNamara Achievement Award 2004, Darrell Award for Best MidSouth Novel 2005, Peter McNamara Convenors' Award 2009, Ditmar Award for Best Collected Work 2009. *Literary Agent:* Writers House Inc., 21 W 26th Street, New York, NY 10010, USA. *Telephone:* (212) 685-2400 (office). *Fax:* (212) 685-1781 (office). *Address:* PO Box 101, Foster, Vic. 3960, Australia (office). *E-mail:* jackdann@jackdann.com (office). *Website:* www.jackdann.com.

DANTICAT, Edwidge, BA, MFA; American writer; b. 19 Jan. 1969, Port-au-Prince, Haiti; m. Faidherbe Boyer 2002. *Education:* Clara Barton High School, New York, Barnard Coll., New York and Brown Univ., Rhode Island. *Career:* documentary film work with Jonathan Demme 1993–95; teacher at univs in Miami, New York and Texas. Films as associate producer: Courage and Pain 1996, The Agronomist 2003. *Publications:* fiction: Breath, Eyes, Memory 1994, Krik? Krak! (short stories) 1995, The Farming of Bones 1998, Behind the Mountain 2002, The Dew Breaker 2004, Anacaona: Golden Flower, Haiti, 1490 2005; non-fiction: Odillon Pierre, Artist of Haiti (with Jonathan Demme) 1999, The Beacon Best of 2000: Great Writing by Women and Men of All Colors and Cultures (ed.) 2000, The Butterfly's Way: Voices from the Haitian Dyaspora in the United States (ed.) 2001, After the Dance 2002, Brother, I'm Dying (Nat. Book Critics' Circle Award for Autobiography 2007) 2007, Create Dangerously: The Immigrant Artist at Work 2010. *Honours:* Pushcart Short Story Prize 1995, Granta's Best of American Novelists Citation 1996, American Book Award 1998, MacArthur Fellowship 2009. *Address:* c/o Soho Press, 853 Broadway, No. 1903, New York, NY 10003, USA (office).

DANTO, Arthur Coleman, BA, MA, PhD; American academic, writer and editor; *Professor Emeritus, Columbia University*; b. 1 Jan. 1924, Ann Arbor, Mich.; m. 1st Shirley Rovetch 1946 (died 1978); two d.; m. 2nd Barbara Westman 1980. *Education:* Wayne State Univ., Columbia Univ., Univ. of Paris, France. *Career:* teacher 1952–72, Johnsonian Prof. of Philosophy 1972–92, Chair Philosophy Dept 1979–87, Prof. Emer. 1992–, Columbia Univ.; Ed., Journal of Philosophy 1975–; Distinguished Fulbright Prof. to Yugoslavia 1976; art critic, The Nation 1984–2009. *Publications include:* Analytical Philosophy of History 1965, Nietzsche as Philosopher 1965, Analytical Philosophy of Knowledge 1968, What Philosophy Is 1968, Mysticism and Morality 1972, Analytical Philosophy of Action 1973, Jean-Paul Sartre 1975, The Transfiguration of the Commonplace 1981, Narration and Knowledge 1985, The Philosophical Disenfranchisement of Art 1986, The State of the Art 1987, Connections to the World 1989, Encounters and Reflections 1990, Beyond the Brillo Box 1992, Embodied Meaning 1994, Playing with the Edge 1995, After the End of Art 1996, The Madonna of the Future 2000, The Abuse of Beauty 2003, Unnatural Wonders 2005, Andy Warhol 2009, Shirin Neshat (co-author) 2010; contrib.: articles and reviews in many publs. *Honours:* Fulbright Scholarship 1949–50, Guggenheim Fellowships 1969, 1982, Lionel Trilling Book Prize 1982, George S. Polk Award for Criticism 1985, Nat. Book Critics' Circle Award in Criticism 1990, New York Public Library Literary Lion 1993, Frank Jewett Mather Prize in Criticism, Coll. Art Asscn 1996, Prix Philosophie 2003. *Address:* 420 Riverside Drive, Apartment 1C, New York, NY 10025-7751, USA (home). *Telephone:* (212) 666-3588 (office). *Fax:* (212) 666-1016 (office). *E-mail:* acd1@columbia.edu (office).

DAOUD, Hassan; Lebanese writer and journalist; b. (Hassan Zebib), 1950. *Education:* Beirut Univ. *Career:* reporter, then Cultural Ed., Assafir newspaper 1979–89; Cultural Ed. Al-Hayat newspaper 1989–99; Chief Ed. of Nawafez cultural supplement of al-Mustaqbal daily newspaper 1999–. *Publications include:* fiction: Tahta Urfat n 1984, Rau al-ayt al mazn 1985, Nuzhat al-malk 1992, Sanat al-tmtk 1996, L'immeuble Mathilde 1998, Aiym zida 2000, Des jours en trop 2001, In al-barq 2003, Makiage khafif lihazihi Allailah 2003, Year of the Revolutionary New Bread Machine 2007, 180 Sunsets 2008, Borrowed Time 2009. *Address:* c/o Al-Mustaqbal, POB 14-5426, Beirut, Lebanon. *Website:* www.almustaqbal.com.lb.

DAOUST, Jean-Paul, MA; Canadian writer, poet, teacher and editor; b. 30 Jan. 1946, Valleyfield, PQ. *Education:* Univ. of Montréal. *Career:* Prof., Cegep Edouard-Montpetit, Québec; mem. Editorial Bd, Estuaire magazine; mem. Union des écrivaines et des écrivains québécois. *Publications include:* poetry: Oui, cher: Récit 1976, Chaises longues 1977, Portrait d'intérieur 1981, Poèmes de Babylone 1982, Taxi 1984, Dimanche après-midi 1985, La peau du coeur et son opéra 1985, Les garçons magiques 1986, Suite contemporaine 1987, Les Centres bleues 1990, Rituels d'Amérique 1990, Les Poses de la lumière 1991, Du Dandysme 1991, L'Amérique 1993, Poèmes faxés (co-author) 1994, 111, Wooster Street 1996, Taxi pour Babylone 1996, Les Chambres de la Mer 1991, Les Saisons de L'Ange, Tome I 1997, Tome II 1999, Le Poème déshabillé 2000, Les versets amoureux 2001, Lèvres ouvertes 2001, Roses labyrinthes 2002, Cobra et Colibri 2006, Cinéma Gris 2006, Fleurs Lascives 2007, Poèmes de Babylone 2007, Élégie Nocturne 2008, Elsewhere-Episode I: Charleville-Mezieres 2008, Le Vitrail Brisé 2009, Carnets de Moncton 2010, Libellules, couleuvres et autres merveilles 2011; other: Soleils d'acajou (novel) 1983, Le Désert Rose (novel) 2000. *Honours:* Gov.-Gen.'s Literary Award in Poetry 1990, Grand Prize of Quebecor Int. Festival of Poetry 2009. *Address:* 8213 Saint-André Street, Montréal, PQ H2P 1Y4, Canada (home). *Telephone:* (514) 279-8741 (home).

DARBY, John, OBE, BA, DipEd, DPhil; Northern Irish academic and writer; *Professor of Comparative Ethnic Studies, the Joan B. Kroc Institute for Professor of International Peace Studies, University of Notre Dame*; b. 18 Nov. 1940, Belfast, Northern Ireland; s. of Patrick Darby and Sadie Darby; m. Marie Darby 1966; two s. *Education:* Queen's Univ., Belfast, St Joseph's Coll. of Education, Belfast, Univ. of Ulster. *Career:* teacher of history, St Malachy's Univ., Belfast 1963–71; Research and Publs Officer, NI Community Relations Comm., Belfast 1971–74; Lecturer in Social Admin, New Univ. of Ulster 1974–85; Assoc. in Educ., Grad. School of Educ., Harvard Univ., USA 1980; Dir Centre for the Study of Conflict, Univ. of Ulster 1985–91, Prof. of Ethnic Studies 1985–98; Visiting Prof., Center for Int. Studies, Duke Univ., USA 1988; Dir Ethnic Studies Network 1991–, INCORE (Initiative on Conflict Resolution and Ethnicity), Univ. of Ulster and UN Univ., Japan 1992–97; Visiting Prof., Univ. of Notre Dame, Ind. 1999–2001, Prof. of Comparative Ethnic Studies, the Joan B. Kroc Inst. for Prof. of Int. Peace Studies 2000–, Dir RIREC (Research Initiative for the Resolution of Conflict) 2002–06, Co-Dir PRIME (the Peace Process Implementation Effort) 2006–08; Dir Peace Accords Matrix 2008–. *Publications include:* Conflict in Northern Ireland 1976, Northern Ireland: Background to the Conflict (ed.) 1983, Dressed to Kill: Cartoonists and the Northern Irish Conflict 1983, Intimidation and the Control of Conflict in Northern Ireland 1986, Political Violence (co-ed. with N. Dodge and A. C. Hepburn) 1990, Scorpions in a Bottle 1997, The Management of Peace Processes (co-ed. with R. MacGinty) 2000, The Effects of Violence on Peace Processes 2001, Guns and Government: The Management of the Northern Ireland Peace Process 2002, Contemporary Peacekeeping (co-ed. with Roger MacGinty) 2003, 2008, Violence and Reconstruction 2005, Peacebuilding after Peace Accords (with Tristan Anne Borer and Siobhan McEvoy Levy) 2006; contrib. to many books and journals. *Honours:* Outstanding Academic Book Citation, Choice 1977, Visiting Scholar, Rockefeller Centre, Bellagio, Italy 1990, Guest Fellow, Woodrow Wilson Center, Washington, DC 1992, Hon. Prof., Univ. of Sunderland 1997, Jennings Randolph Sr Fellow, US Inst. of Peace, Washington, DC 1998, Fellow, Fulbright New Century Scholars Program 2003, NSF Award 2009–12. *Address:* 61 Strand Road, Portstewart, BT55 7LU, Northern Ireland (home). *Telephone:* (28) 7083-3098 (home). *E-mail:* john.darby.3@nd.edu (office).

D'ARCY, Margaretta Ruth; Irish playwright, writer, broadcaster and film maker; b. 14 June 1934, London, England; m. John Arden 1957; five s. (one deceased). *Career:* Artistic Dir Corrandulla Arts and Entertainment Club 1973, Galway Women's Entertainment 1982, Galway Women's Sceal Radio, Radio Pirate-Woman 1986, Women in Media and Entertainment 1987; mem. Aosdána 1982. *Exhibition:* 24 Hours in the Life of a Woman. *Plays produced:* The Happy Haven 1961, Business of Good Government 1962, Ars Longa Vita Brevis 1964, The Royal Pardon 1966, Friday's Hiding 1967, The Hero Rises Up 1969, The Island of the Mighty 1974, The Non-Stop Connolly Show 1975, Vandaleur's Folly 1978, The Little Gray Home in the West 1978, The Making of Muswell Hill 1979 (all with John Arden), A Pinprick of History 1977. *Films:* Circus Exposé 1987, Big Plane Small Axe (The Mis-Trials of Mary Kelly) 2005, Shell Hell 2005, Yellow Gate Women, Breda Lewis – A Portrait. *Radio includes:* Keep Those People Moving 1972, The Manchester Enthusiasts 1984, Whose Is the Kingdom? 1988, A Suburban Suicide 1994 (all with John Arden). *Television documentary:* Profile of Sean O'Casey (with John Arden) 1973. *Publications:* Tell Them Everything (Prison Memoirs) 1981, Awkward Corners (with John Arden) 1988, Galway's Pirate Women, a Global Trawl 1996, Loose Theatre (Memoirs of a Guerrilla Theatre Activist) 2005. *Honours:* Arts Council Playwriting Award (with John Arden) 1972, Women's Int. Newsgathering Service, Katherine Davenport Journalist of the Year Award 1998, Documentary Award, Galway Film Fleadh 2005. *Literary Agent:* c/o Casarotto Ramsay, 60–66 Wardour Street, London, W1V 3HP, England. *Telephone:* (91) 565430 (home). *Website:* www.margarettadarcy.com.

D'ARGY SMITH, Marcelle; British journalist and magazine editor; b. 1947. *Career:* writer, Cosmopolitan magazine 1983–89, Ed. 1989–95; freelance journalist and broadcaster 1995–97; Ed. Woman's Journal 1997–99; stood as Pro Euro Conservative cand. in European elections 1999; Visiting Tutor, City Univ. *Publication:* The Lovers' Guide: What Women Really Want 2002; contribs to The Daily Mail, The Times, The Guardian, New Statesman. *Honours:* Women's Magazine Ed. of the Year 1991. *E-mail:* marcelle@dargysmith.com.

DARKO, Amma, BA; Ghanaian novelist and civil servant; b. 26 June 1956, Tamale; m.; three c. *Education:* Univ. of Science and Tech., Kumasi. *Career:* lived and worked in Germany during 1980s; currently working as a tax inspector, Accra; Fellow, Cambridge Seminar, IWP-Iowa, Akad. Solilitude Germany. *Publications include:* Der verkaufte Traum (Beyond the Horizon) 1991, Spinnweben 1996, Verirrtes Herz 2000, Die Gesichtslosen (Faceless) 2003, Das Lächeln der Nemesis (Not without Flowers) 2006. *Honours:* Ghana Book Award 1999. *Address:* c/o Sub-Saharan Publishers, PO Box 358, Legon, Accra, Ghana. *Telephone:* (21) 404954 (home). *E-mail:* mmafoko@yahoo.com (home); mail@ammadarko.de. *Website:* www.ammadarko.de.

DARNTON, Robert Choate, DPhil; American historian and academic; *Carl H. Pforzheimer Professor and Director of the University Library, Harvard University*; b. 10 May 1939, New York; s. of the late Byron Darnton and Eleanor Darnton; m. Susan Lee Glover 1963; one s. two d. *Education:* Harvard Univ., Oxford Univ., UK. *Career:* reporter, The New York Times 1964–65; Jr Fellow, Harvard Univ., 1965–68; Asst Prof., subsequently Assoc. Prof., Prof., Princeton Univ. 1968–, Shelby Cullom Davis Prof. of European History 1984–2007, Dir Program in European Cultural Studies 1987–95; Carl H. Pforzheimer Prof. and Dir of Univ. Library, Harvard Univ. 2007–; fellowships and visiting professorships include Ecole des Hautes Etudes en Sciences Sociales, Paris 1971, 1981, 1985, Netherlands Inst. for Advanced Study 1976–77, Inst. for Advanced Study, Princeton 1977–81, Oxford Univ. (George Eastman Visiting Prof.) 1986–87, Collège de France, Wissenschafts-Kolleg zu Berlin 1989–90, 1993–94; Pres. Int. Soc. for Eighteenth-Century Studies 1987–91, American Historical Asscn 1999–2000; mem. Bd of Dirs, Voltaire Foundation, Oxford, Social Science Research Council 1988–91; mem. Bd of Trustees Center for Advanced Study in the Behavioral Sciences 1992–96, Oxford Univ. Press, USA 1993–, The New York Public Library 1994–; mem. various editorial bds; Fellow, American Acad. of Arts and Sciences, American Philosophical Soc., American Antiquarian Soc.; Adviser, Wissenschafts-Kolleg zu Berlin 1994–; Foreign mem. Academia Europaea, Acad. Royale de Langue et de Littérature Françaises de Belgique; Guggenheim Fellow 1970; Corresp. Fellow, British Acad. 2001. *Television series:* Démocratie (co-ed.), France 1999. *Publications:* Mesmerism and the End of the Enlightenment in France 1968, The Business of Enlightenment 1979, The Literary Underground of the Old Regime 1982, The Great Cat Massacre 1984, The Kiss of Lamourette 1989, Revolution in Print (co-ed.) 1989, Edition et sédition 1991, Berlin Journal, 1989–1900 1991, Gens de lettres, gens du livre 1992, The Forbidden Best-Sellers of Pre-Revolutionary France 1995, The Corpus of Clandestine Literature 1769–1789 1995, Démocratie (co-ed.) 1998, J.-P. Brissot: His Career and Correspondence 1779–1787 2001, Poesie und Polizei 2002, Pour les Lumières 2002, George Washington's False Teeth: An Unconventional Guide to the 18th Century 2003, The Case for Books: Past, Present, and Future 2009. *Honours:* Officier Ordre des Arts et des Lettres 1995, Chevalier Légion d'Honneur 2000; Dr hc (Neuchâtel) 1986, (Lafayette Coll.) 1989, (Univ. of Bristol) 1991, (Univ. of Warwick) 2001, (Univ. of Bordeaux) 2005; Leo Gershoy Prize, American Historical Asscn 1979, MacArthur Prize 1982, Los Angeles Times Book Prize 1984, Prix Médicis 1991, Prix Chateaubriand 1991, Nat. Book Critics Circle Award 1996, Gutenberg Prize 2004. *Address:* Office of the Director, Harvard University Library, Wadsworth House, 1341 Massachusetts Avenue, Cambridge, MA 02138, USA (office). *Telephone:* (617) 495-3650 (office); (609) 924-6905 (home). *Fax:* (617) 495-0370 (office). *E-mail:* administration@hulmail.harvard.edu (office). *Website:* hul.harvard.edu (office).

DARRIEUSSECQ, Marie; French writer; b. 3 Jan. 1969, Bayonne; m. *Education:* Ecole normale supérieure, Paris. *Career:* fmr teacher, Lille Univ. *Publications include:* Truismes (novel, trans. as Pig Tales) 1996, Naissance des fantômes (novel, trans. as My Phantom Husband) 1998, Le Mal de mer (novel, trans. as Undercurrents, aka Breathing Underwater) 1999, Précisions sur les vagues (novel) 1999, Bref séjour chez les vivants (novel, trans. as A Brief Stay With the Living) 2001, Le Bébé (non-fiction) 2002, White (novel) 2003, Le Pays 2005, Zoo 2006, Tom est Mort 2007. *Address:* c/o Editions P.O.L 2000, 33, rue Saint-André-des-Arts, 75006 Paris, France. *Website:* www.pol-editeur.fr.

DARUWALLA, Keki Nasserwanji, MA; Indian poet, writer and fmr government official; *Member, National Commission for Minorities*; b. 24 Jan. 1937, Lahore, Pakistan (then part of British India); s. of N. C. Daruwalla; m. Khorshed Keki Daruwalla 1965 (died 2000); two d. *Education:* Univ. of the Punjab. *Career:* joined Indian Police Service 1958; Special Asst to Prime Minister 1979; Chair. Jt Intelligence Cttee –1995; Visiting Fellow, Queen Elizabeth House, Oxford, UK 1980–81; served at Indian High Comm. in London; Pres. Poetry Soc. of India; mem. Sahitya Akademi (Advisory Bd for English 1983–87, Convenor 2003–08), Nat. Comm. for Minorities 2011–. *Publications include:* poetry: Under Orion 1970, Apparition in April (UP State Award 1972) 1971, Crossing of Rivers 1976, Winter Poems 1980, The Keeper of the Dead 1982, Landscapes 1987, Night River 2000, The Map Maker 2002, The Scarecrow and the Ghost (children's verse) 2004, Collected Poems 1975–2005 2006; fiction: Sword and Abyss 1979, A House in Ranikhet (short stories) 2003, For Pepper and Christ (novel) 2009; ed.: Two Decades of Indian Poetry, 1960–80 1981, The Minister for Permanent Unrest 1996; contribs to anthologies, journals and periodicals. *Honours:* Indian Police Medal 1975, Sahitya Akademi Award 1984, Pres.'s Police Medal 1985, Commonwealth Poetry Award (Asia Region) 1987. *Address:* National Commission for Minorities, Government of India, 5th Floor, Lok Nayak Bhawan, Khan Market, New Delhi 110 003 (office); 79 Mount Kailash, Pocket-A, SFS Apartments, New Delhi 110 065, India (home). *Telephone:* (11) 24621177 (office); (11) 26441574 (home). *Fax:* (11) 24693302 (office). *E-mail:* keki.75@nic.in (office); kekikhurshid@gmail.com (home). *Website:* www.ncm.nic.in (office).

DARVILL, Timothy Charles, OBE, BA, PhD, DSc, FSA, FSA (Scot); British archaeologist and academic; *Professor of Archaeology, University of Bournemouth*; b. 22 Dec. 1957, Cheltenham, Glos., England. *Education:* Univ. of Southampton. *Career:* Dir Timothy Darvill Archaeological Consultants 1985–91; Prof. of Archaeology, Univ. of Bournemouth 1991–; mem. Cotswold Archaeological Trust (Chair. 1992–), Council for British Archaeology, Inst. of Field Archaeologists (Chair. 1989–91), Council of the Nat. Trust 1988–97, Register of Professional Archaeologists; Co-ordinator Neolithic Studies Group 1983–; Chair. Subject Cttee for Archeaology 2000–03. *Publications include:* Megalithic Chambered Tombs of the Cotswold-Severn Region 1982, The Archaeology of the Uplands 1986, Prehistoric Britain 1987, Ancient Monuments in the Countryside 1987, Prehistoric Gloucestershire 1987, Neolithic Houses in Northwest Europe and Beyond (co-ed. with Julian Thomas) 1996, Prehistoric Britain from the Air 1996, The Concise Oxford Dictionary of Archaeology 2002, Long Barrows of the Cotswolds 2004, Stonehenge: the biography of a landscape 2006, Round Mounds and Monumentality in the British Neolithic and Beyond (co-author) 2010; contribs to scholarly books and journals. *Honours:* Nat. Award 2006. *Address:* School of Applied Sciences, University of Bournemouth, Poole House, Talbot Campus, Fern Barrow, Poole, Dorset, BH12 5BB, England (office). *Telephone:* (1202) 965536 (office). *E-mail:* tdarvill@bournemouth.ac.uk (office). *Website:* www.bournemouth.ac.uk/conservation (office).

DAS, Gurcharan; Indian author and fmr business executive; b. 3 Oct. 1943; m.; two c. *Education:* Harvard Univ., Harvard Business School. *Career:* Chair. and Man. Dir Richardson Hindustan Ltd 1981–85; CEO Procter & Gamble India, Vice-Pres. Procter & Gamble Far East 1985–92, Vice-Pres. and Man. Dir Procter & Gamble Worldwide (Strategic Planning) 1992–94; regular columnist, Times of India 1995–2010; contrib. Time, Newsweek, Wall Street Journal, Financial Times, Foreign Affairs. *Publications:* A Fine Family (novel) 1991, India Unbound 2001, The Elephant Paradigm 2002, The Difficulty of Being Good: On the Subtle Art of Dharma 2009; anthology of plays: Three English Plays 2003. *Address:* c/o Penguin Books India Pvt Limited, 11 Community Centre, Panchsheel Park, New Delhi 110017, India (office). *E-mail:* business@in.penguingroup.com (office). *Website:* www.penguinbooksindia.com (office); gurcharandas.org; gurcharandas.blogspot.co.uk.

DASGUPTA, Rana, BA, MA; British writer; b. 5 Nov. 1971, Canterbury, Kent, England; s. of Ashish Brata Dasgupta and Barbara Ann Dasgupta; m. Monica Narula; one d. *Education:* Univ. of Oxford, Univ. of Wisconsin-Madison, USA. *Career:* fmr Marketing Consultant, London and New York; currently lives in New Delhi, India. *Publications include:* novels: Tokyo Cancelled 2005, Solo (Commonwealth Writers' Prizes for Best Book, South Asia and Europe Region and for Best Overall Book 2010) 2009. *Honours:* Fulbright Scholarship 1995, Univ. of Wisconsin Alumni Research Foundation Fellow 1995. *Literary Agent:* c/o Sarah Chalfant, The Wylie Agency, 17 Bedford Square, London, WC1B 3JA, England. *Telephone:* (20) 7908-5900. *E-mail:* schalfant@wylieagency.co.uk. *Website:* www.wylieagency.com. *E-mail:* rana@ranadasgupta.com (office). *Website:* www.ranadasgupta.com.

DASHKOVA, Polina Victorovna; Russian writer; b. (Tatyana Polyachenko), 14 July 1960, Moscow; d. of Vitaly Vassiliyevich Polyachenko and Tatyana Leonidovna Polyachenko; m. Alexei Vitalyevich Shishov; two d. *Education:* Moscow Literary Inst. *Career:* freelance writer, began career as poet and trans. 1976–; journalist, Selskaya Molodezh magazine 1980–88; Head, Div. of Literature, Russian-American magazine Russian Courier 1988–93. *Publications include:* Blood of the Unborn 1996, Chechen Puppet 1996, Light Steps of Craziness 1997, No One Will Cry 1997, A Place Under the Sun 1998, Image of the Enemy, Golden Sand 1999, Time on Air 1999, Nursery 2000, Cherub 2001, Russian Orchid. *Address:* Maly Tishinsky pe 11/12, Apt 10, 123056 Moscow, Russia. *Telephone:* (495) 253-17-39.

DAUGHARTY, Janice; American writer; b. 24 Oct. 1944, Valdosta, Ga; m. Seward Daugharty 1963; one s. two d. *Education:* Valdosta State Univ. *Career:* Writer-in-Residence, Valdosta State Univ. *Publications include:* Dark of the Moon 1994, Going through the Change 1994, Necessary Lies 1995, Pawpaw Patch 1996, Earl in the Yellow Shirt 1997, Whistle 1998, Like a Sister 1999, Just Doll 2004, Staten Bay 2, Staten Bay 3, Troublesome Creek, The Little Known 2010, Heir to the Everlasting 2011. *Website:* www.janicedaugharty.com.

DAUNTON, Martin James, BA, PhD, LittD, FBA; British college principal, economic historian and academic; *Master of Trinity Hall and Professor of Economic History, University of Cambridge*; b. 7 Feb. 1949, Cardiff, Wales; s. of Ronald Daunton and Dorothy Daunton; m. Claire Gobbi 1984. *Education:* Univs of Nottingham, Kent and Cambridge. *Career:* Lecturer, Durham Univ. 1973–79; Lecturer, Univ. Coll. London 1979–85, Reader 1985–89, Prof. of History 1989–97; Convenor Studies in History series, Royal Historical Soc. 1995–2000; Prof. of Economic History, Univ. of Cambridge 1997–, Chair. Faculty of History 2001–03, Chair. School of the Humanities and Social Sciences 2003–05, Head of the School 2012–, Master of Trinity Hall 2004–; Chair. Fitzwilliam Museum Syndicate 2008–; mem. Royal Historical Soc. (Pres. 2004–08); mem. Academic Advisory Bd, Leverhulme Trust 2009–;

Trustee, Nat. Maritime Museum 2002–10, Baring Archives 2006–. *Publications include:* Coal Metropolis: Cardiff, House and Home in the Victorian City 1850–1914, Royal Mail: The Post Office Since 1840, A Property Owning Democracy?, Progress and Poverty, Trusting Leviathan, Just Taxes; contrib. to Economic History Review, Past & Present, Business History, Historical Research, Journal of Urban History, Charity, Self-Interest and Welfare in the English Past, English Historical Review, Twentieth Century British History, Empire, Organisation of Knowledge in Victorian Britain 2005, Wealth and Empire 2007, State and Market in Victorian Britain 2008. *Honours:* Hon. LitD (London); Hon. DLitt (Nottingham, Kent). *Address:* Trinity Hall, Trinity Lane, Cambridge, CB2 1TJ, England (office). *Telephone:* (1223) 332540 (office). *E-mail:* mjd42@cam.ac.uk (office). *Website:* www.trinhall.cam.ac.uk (office).

DAVEY, Frankland Wilmot, BA, MA, PhD; Canadian writer, poet and editor; *Carl F. Klinck Professor Emeritus of Canadian Literature, University of Western Ontario;* b. 19 April 1940, Vancouver, BC; m. 1st Helen Simmons 1962 (divorced 1969); m. 2nd Linda McCartney 1969; one s. one d. *Education:* Univ. of British Columbia, Vancouver, Univ. of Southern California at Los Angeles. *Career:* Lecturer, Royal Roads Military Coll., Victoria, BC 1963–67; Asst Prof. 1967–69; Writer-in-Residence, Sir George Williams Univ., Montreal 1969–70; Asst Prof., York Univ., Toronto 1970–72, Assoc. Prof. 1972–80, Prof. of English 1980–90, Chair. Dept of English 1985–88, 1989–90; Carl F. Klinck Prof. of Canadian Literature, Univ. of Western Ontario, London 1990–, now Emer.; mem. Asscn of Canadian Coll. and Univ. Teachers of English, Pres., 1994–96. *Publications include:* poetry: D-Day and After 1962, City of the Gulls and Sea 1964, Bridge Force 1965, The Scarred Hill 1966, Four Myths for Sam Perry 1970, Weeds 1970, Griffon 1972, King of Swords 1972, L'An Trentiesme: Selected Poems 1961–70 1972, Arcana 1973, The Clallam 1973, War Poems 1979, The Arches: Selected Poems 1981, Capitalistic Affection! 1982, Edward and Patricia 1984, The Louis Riel Organ and Piano Company 1985, The Abbotsford Guide to India 1986, Postcard Translations 1988, Popular Narratives 1991, Cultural Mischief: A Practical Guide to Multiculturalism 1996, Dog 2002, Back to the War 2005, Risky Propositions 2005, Lack On! 2009, How We Won the War in Iraq 2009, Bardy Google 2010, Afghanistan War: True, False or Not 2010; criticism: Five Readings of Olson's 'Maximus' 1970, Earle Birney 1971, From There to Here: A Guide to English-Canadian Literature Since 1960 1974, Louis Dudek and Raymond Souster 1981, The Contemporary Canadian Long Poem 1983, Surviving the Paraphrase: 11 Essays on Canadian Literature 1983, Margaret Atwood: A Feminist Poetics 1984, Reading Canadian Reading 1988, Post-National Arguments: The Politics of the Anglophone-Canadian Novel Since 1967 1993, Reading 'KIM' Right 1993, Canadian Literary Power: Essays on Anglophone-Canadian Literary Conflict 1994, Karla's Web: A Cultural Examination of the Mahaffy-French Murders 1994; other: How Linda Died 2002, Mr & Mrs G.G 2003, When TISH Happens 2011; contribs: books and journals. *Honours:* Macmillan Prize 1962, Dept of Defence Arts Research Grants 1965, 1966, 1968, Canada Council Fellowships 1966, 1974, Humanities Research Council of Canada Grants 1974, 1981, Canadian Fed. for the Humanities Grants 1979, 1992, Social Sciences and Humanities Research Council Fellowship 1981. *Address:* Department of English, University of Western Ontario, University College, Room 173, London, ON N6A 3K7, Canada (office). *E-mail:* fdavey@uwo.ca (office). *Website:* publish.uwo.ca/~fdavey/homenew.html (office).

DAVEY, William; American poet and writer; b. 20 March 1913, New York, NY; s. of Randall Davey and Florence Sittenham Davey; m. 7th Susan Steenrod 1965. *Education:* Princeton Univ., NJ, Univ. of California, Berkeley, New York Univ., Univ. of Paris (Sorbonne), France. *Career:* Commando, First Special Service Force, Canadian-American Elite Unit, World War II; Contributing and Foreign Language Ed. The Long Story magazine 1991–2011; mem. Poetry Soc. of America, Poetry Soc. of Virginia, World Congress of Poets, US Chess Asscn, Royal Astronomical Soc. of Canada, US Polo Asscn. *Publications include:* Dawn Breaks the Heart (novel) 1932, Arms, Angels, Epitaphs, and Bones (poems) 1935, The Angry Dust (novel, in Chinese) 1995, (in English) 2006, The Trial of Pythagoras and Other Poems 1996, (in Greek 1998), Lost Adulteries and Other Stories 1998, Bitter Rainbow and Other Poems 1999, (in Greek) 2003, Brother of Cloud in the Water (novel) 2008, Splendor from Darkness (novel) 2011; contrib. to anthologies, periodicals and magazines world-wide. *Address:* PO Box 129, Keene, VA 22946, USA (office). *E-mail:* daveywdsd@aol.com. *Website:* www.williamdavey.com.

DAVID, Esther; Indian author and illustrator; b. 17 March 1945, Ahmedabad, Gujarat; d. of Reuben David and Sarah David; one s., one d. *Education:* Maharaja Sayajirao Univ., Vadodara. *Career:* trained as artist and sculptor; writes on Indian Jewish life; teacher CEPT Univ. and NIFT, Ahmedabad; art critic, Times of India 1979–92, columnist 1996–2005; fmr columnist, Femina; Writer-in-Residence, Villa Mont Noir, France 1999–2000, St. Nazaire, France 2001–02. *Publications:* The Walled City 1997, By the Sabarmati 1999, Book of Esther 2002, Book of Rachel (Prix Eugene Brazier 2009, Sahitya Akademi Award 2010) 2006, My Father's Zoo 2007, Shalom India Housing Society 2007, The Man with Enormous Wings 2010; as coauthor: India's Jewish Heritage: Ritual, Art and Life Cycle 2002. *Address:* c/o Penguin Books India Pvt Limited, 11 Community Centre, Panchsheel Park, New Delhi 110017, India (office). *E-mail:* business@in.penguingroup.com (office). *Website:* www.penguinbooksindia.com (office); www.estherdavid.com.

DAVIDAR, David, BSc, Diploma in Publishing; Indian novelist and publisher; b. 27 Sept. 1958, Kanyakumari district, Tamil Nadu; m. Rachna Singh 1997. *Education:* Sainik School, Amaravathinagar, Madras Christian Coll., Harvard Univ., USA. *Career:* journalist for magazines including Himmat, Keynote, Gentleman; Publr and CEO Penguin India 1985–2004; Publr and CEO Penguin Canada, Toronto 2004–10; Co-founder Aleph Book Co., India 2011–. *Publications:* novels: The House of Blue Mangoes 2002, The Solitude of Emperors 2007, Ithaca 2011. *Address:* Aleph Book Company, 161 B4 Ground Floor, Gulmohar House, Yusuf Sarai Community Centre, New Delhi 110 049, India (office). *Telephone:* (11) 49226666 (office). *E-mail:* info@alephbookcompany.com (office). *Website:* www.alephbookcompany.com (office).

DAVIDSON, Michael, BA, PhD; American academic, poet and writer; *Distinguished Professor of American Literature, University of California, San Diego;* b. 18 Dec. 1944, Oakland, Calif.; m. 1st Carol Wikarska 1970 (divorced 1974); m. 2nd Lois Chamberlain 1988, two c. *Education:* San Francisco State Univ., State Univ. of NY, Buffalo, Univ. of California, Berkeley. *Career:* Visiting Lecturer, San Diego State Univ. 1973–76; Curator, Archive for New Poetry 1975–85, Prof. of Literature, Univ. of California, San Diego 1977–, now Distinguished Prof. of American Literature. *Publications include:* poetry: Exchanges 1972, Two Views of Pears 1973, The Mutabilities, and the Foul Papers 1976, Summer Letters 1976, Grillwork 1980, Discovering Motion 1980, The Prose of Fact 1981, The Landing of Rochambeau 1985, Analogy of the Ion 1988, Post Hoc 1990, The Arcades 1998, Concerto for the Left Hand: Disability and the Defamiliar Body 2008, Outskirts of Form: Practicing Cultural Poetics 2011; other: The San Francisco Renaissance: Poetics and Community at Mid-Century 1989, Ghostlier Demarcations: Modern Poetry and the Material World 1997, Guys Like Us: Citing Masculinity in Cold War Poetics 2003; contribs to periodicals. *Honours:* Nat. Endowment for the Arts Grant 1976. *Address:* University of California, 9500 Gilman Drive, Literature Department 0410, La Jolla, CA 92093-0410, USA (office). *Telephone:* (858) 534-2101 (office). *E-mail:* mdavidson@ucsd.edu (office). *Website:* literature.ucsd.edu (office).

DAVIES, Andrew Wynford, BA; British screenwriter; b. 20 Sept. 1936, Rhiwbina, Cardiff, Wales; m. Diana Huntley 1960; one s. one d. *Education:* Whitchurch Grammar School, Cardiff, Univ. Coll., London. *Career:* teacher, St Clement Danes Grammar School, London 1958–61, Woodberry Down Comprehensive School, London 1961–63; Lecturer, Coventry Coll. of Educ. 1963–71, Univ. of Warwick, Coventry 1971–87; full-time writer 1987–, also adapting numerous classics for TV and film. *Television series:* Look and Read (episode 'Badgergirl') 1967, Bedtime Stories 1974, To Serve Them All My Days 1980, Educating Marmalade 1981, Danger: Marmalade at Work 1984, Badger Girl 1984, A Very Peculiar Practice 1986, Mother Love 1989, Alfonso Bonzo 1990, House of Cards 1990, The Old Devils 1992, To Play the King 1993, Middlemarch 1994, Game On (with Bernadette Davis) 1995, Pride and Prejudice 1995, Vanity Fair 1998, Wives and Daughters 1999, The Way We Live Now 2001, Doctor Zhivago 2002, He Knew He Was Right 2004, Bleak House 2005, Fanny Hill 2007, Sense and Sensibility 2008, Little Dorrit 2008. *Television plays:* Who's Going to Take Me On? 1967, Is That Your Body Boy? 1970, No Good Unless It Hurts 1973, The Water Maiden 1974, Grace 1975, The Imp of the Perverse 1975, The Signalman 1976, A Martyr to the System 1976, Eleanor Marx 1977, Happy in War 1977, Velvet Glove 1977, Fearless Frank 1978, Renoir My Father 1978, The Legend of King Arthur 1979, Bavarian Night 1981, Heartattack Hotel 1983, Diana 1984, Pythons on the Mountain 1985, Inappropriate Behaviour 1987, Lucky Sunil 1988, Baby, I Love You 1988, Ball-Trap on the Cote Sauvage 1989, A Private Life 1989, Filipina Dreamers 1991, The Old Devils 1992, Harnessing Peacocks 1992, Anglo-Saxon Attitudes 1992, A Very Polish Practice 1992, Anna Lee 1993, A Few Short Journeys of the Heart 1994, The Final Cut 1995, Wilderness 1996, The Fortunes and Misfortunes of Moll Flanders 1996, Emma 1996, Getting Hurt 1998, A Rather English Marriage 1998, Take a Girl Like You 2000, Othello 2001, Tipping the Velvet 2002, The Way We Live Now 2002, Daniel Deronda 2002, He Knew He Was Right 2004, Falling 2005, The Chatterley Affair 2006, The Line of Beauty 2006, Northanger Abbey 2007, The Diary of A Nobody 2007, A Room With A View 2007, Fanny Hill 2007, Affinity 2008, Sleep with Me 2009, South Riding 2011. *Radio plays:* The Hospitalization of Samuel Pellett 1964, Getting the Smell of It 1967, A Day in Bed 1967, Come on then, Astonish Me! 1970, Steph and the Man of Some Distinction 1971, The Innocent Eye 1971, The Shortsighted Bear 1972, Steph and the Simple Life 1972, Steph and the Zero Structure Lifestyle 1976, Accentuate the Positive 1980, Campus Blues 1984, The Purple Hand 2011. *Films:* Time After Time 1985, Consuming Passions 1988, Circle of Friends 1995, The Tailor of Panama (screenplay) 2001, Bridget Jones's Diary (screenplay) 2001, Boudica 2003, Bridget Jones: The Edge of Reason (screenplay) 2004, Brideshead Revisited (screenplay) 2006, 3 Musketeers 2011. *Stage productions:* Can Anyone Smell the Gas? 1972, The Shortsighted Bear 1972, Filthy Fryer and the Woman of Mature Years 1974, What Are Little Girls Made Of? 1975, Rohan and Julie 1975, Randy Robinson's Unsuitable Relationship 1976, Teacher's Gone Mad 1977, Going Bust 1977, Fearless Frank 1978, Brainstorming with the Boys 1978, Battery 1979, Diary of a Desperate Woman 1979, Rose 1980, Prin 1990. *Publications include:* The Fantastic Feats of Doctor Boox 1972, Conrad's War 1978, Marmalade and Rufus 1980, Poonam's Pets (with Diana Davies) 1990, Getting Hurt 1990, B. Monkey 1992. *Honours:* Dr hc (Cardiff, Coventry, De Montfort, Open Univ., Warwick, Univ. Coll. London); Guardian Children's Fiction Award 1979, Boston Globe-Horn Book Award 1980, Broadcast Press Guild Award 1980, 1990, Pye Colour TV Award 1981, Royal TV Soc. Award 1987, 2006, BAFTA Award 1989, 1993, 2002, 2006, BAFTA Fellowship 2002,

Writers' Guild Award 1991, 1992, Emmy Award 1991, 2009. *Literary Agent:* c/o Lemon, Unna and Durbridge, 24 Pottery Lane, London, W11 4LZ, England. *Telephone:* (20) 7727-1346.

DAVIES, (Edward) Hunter, BA, DipEd; British writer; b. 7 Jan. 1936, Renfrew, Scotland; m. Margaret Forster 1960; one s. two d. *Education:* Univ. Coll., Durham. *Publications include:* Here We Go Round the Mulberry Bush 1965, The Beatles 1968, The Glory Game 1972, A Walk Along the Wall 1974, A Walk Around the Lakes 1979, In Search of Columbus 1991, Wainwright: The Biography 1998, The Eddie Stobart Story 2001, Gazza: My Story 2004, Being Gazza: My Journey to Hell and Back 2006, The Beatles, Football and Me (auto-biog.) 2006, My Story So Far (with Wayne Rooney) 2006, The Bumper Book of Football 2007, Cold Meat and How to Disguise It 2009, Confessions of a Collector 2009, Postcards from the Edge of Football: A Social History of a British Game 2010; contrib. to Sunday Times 1960–84, Punch 1979–89, Independent (London) 1990–2000, New Statesman 1998–. *Address:* New Statesman, 1st Floor, Boundary House, 91–93 Charterhouse Street, London, EC1M 6HR, England (office). *Telephone:* (20) 7730-3444 (office). *E-mail:* info@newstatesman.co.uk (office). *Website:* www.newstatesman.com (office).

DAVIES, (Ivor) Norman Richard, CMG, MA, PhD, FBA, FRHistS; British academic and writer; *Visiting Fellow, St Antony's College, Oxford;* b. 8 June 1939, Bolton, England; m. 1st Maria Zielińska 1966; one s.; m. 2nd Maria Korzeniewicz 1984; one s. *Education:* Univ. of Grenoble, Magdalen Coll., Oxford, Univ. of Sussex, Jagiellonian Univ. *Career:* Alistair Horne Research Fellow, St Antony's Coll., Oxford 1969–71; Lecturer 1971–84, Reader 1984–85, Prof. of Polish History 1985–96, Prof. Emer. 1996–, Univ. of London; Visiting Prof., Columbia Univ. 1974, McGill Univ. 1977–78, Hokkaido Univ. 1982–83, Stanford Univ. 1985–86, Harvard Univ. 1991, ANU 1998–99; Sr Research Assoc., Univ. of Oxford 1997–; Supernumerary Fellow, Wolfson Coll. 1999–2006; Eleminasator Principalis, UNESCO Chair. Jagiellonian Univ. 2003–; Visiting Research Fellow, Clare Hall, Cambridge 2006–; Visiting Fellow, St Antony's Coll., Oxford 2007–. *Publications include:* White Eagle, Red Star: The Polish–Soviet War of 1919–1920 1972, God's Playground: A History of Poland (two vols) 1981, Heart of Europe: A Short History of Poland 1984, Europe: A History 1996, The Isles: A History 1999, Microcosm: Portrait of a Central European City (with Roger Moorehouse) 2002, Rising '44: The Battle for Warsaw 2004, Europe at War 1939–1945: No Simple Victory 2006, Europe East and West 2006, Vanished Kingdoms: The Lives and Afterlives of Europe's Lost Realms 2010; contrib. to scholarly books and journals. *Honours:* Dr hc (UMCS) 1993, (Gdańsk) 1997, (Kraków) 2004, (Sussex) 2006, (Warsaw) 2007; Kt's Cross, Order of Polonia Restituta 1984, Commdr's Cross, Order of Merit (Poland) 1992, Grand Cross, Order of Merit (Poland) 1999, Repub. Order of the Cross of St Mary's Land (Estonia) 2008. *Literary Agent:* c/o DGA, 55 Monmouth Street, London, WC2, England. *Telephone:* (20) 7240-9992. *Website:* www.normandavies.com.

DAVIES, Paul Charles William, BSc, PhD; British theoretical physicist, cosmologist, writer and broadcaster; *College Professor and Head, Centre for Fundamental Concepts in Science, Arizona State University;* b. 22 April 1946, London, England. *Education:* Univ. Coll., London, Univ. of Cambridge. *Career:* fmrly at Univ. of Cambridge, Imperial Coll. London, Univ. of Newcastle upon Tyne; fmr Visiting Prof., Univ. of Queensland, Brisbane, Australia; moved to Australia 1990; fmrly at Univ. of Adelaide; currently Prof. of Natural Philosophy, Australian Centre for Astrobiology, Macquarie Univ.; took up Chair of SETI: Post-Detection Science and Tech. Taskgroup, Int. Acad. of Astronautics 2005–; Coll. Prof. and Head of Centre for Fundamental Concepts in Science, Arizona State Univ., USA 2006–; mem. Editorial Advisory Bd Cosmos Magazine 2006–. *Television includes:* The Big Questions (six-part series for Australian SBS TV) 1995, More Big Questions (series for SBS TV) 1998, The Cradle of Life (BBC documentary) 2002. *Radio includes:* documentary on the wire telegraph for BBC Radio 4, series of 45-minute documentaries (including Desperately Seeking Superstrings) for BBC Radio 3, series of 30-minute documentaries for BBC World Service, The Genesis Factor (three-part BBC Radio 4 series on the origin of life) 2000. *Publications include:* The Physics of Time Asymmetry 1974, Space and Time in the Modern Universe 1977, The Runaway Universe 1978, The Forces of Nature 1979, Other Worlds 1980, The Search for Gravity Waves 1980, The Edge of Infinity 1981, The Accidental Universe 1982, Quantum Fields in Curved Space (with N. D. Birrell) 1982, God and the New Physics 1983, Superforce 1984, Quantum Mechanics 1984, The Ghost in the Atom (with J. R. Brown) 1986, Fireball 1987, The Cosmic Blueprint 1987, Superstrings: A Theory of Everything? (with J. R. Brown) 1988, The New Physics (ed.) 1989, The Matter Myth (with J. Gribbin) 1991, The Mind of God 1992, The Last Three Minutes 1994, About Time: Einstein's Unfinished Revolution 1995, Are We Alone? The Philosophical Basis of the Search for Extraterrestrial Life 1995, The Big Questions (with Phillip Adams) 1996, One Universe or Many Universes? 1998, More Big Questions (with Phillip Adams) 1998, The Fifth Miracle: The Search for the Origin of Life (aka The Origin of Life) 1998, How to Build a Time Machine 2001, Science and Ultimate Reality (co-ed. with John D. Barrow & Charles Harper) 2004, The Goldilocks Enigma: Why is the Universe Just Right for Life? 2006, Quantum Aspects of Life (with Derek Abbott and Arun Pati) 2008, The Eerie Silence: Renewing our Search for Alien Intelligence 2010, Information and the Nature of Reality: From Physics to Metaphysics 2010; contrib. numerous articles to journals, newspapers and other publs, including The Economist, The Guardian, The New York Times, The Australian, The Sydney Morning Herald, The Age, The Bulletin, New Scientist. *Honours:* Glaxo Science Writers Fellowship, Templeton Prize 1995, the asteroid 1992 OG was officially named (6870) Pauldavies in his honour 1999, Kelvin Medal and Prize, Inst. of Physics (UK) 2001, Royal Soc. Michael Faraday Prize 2002, Advance Australia Award, two Eureka Prizes. *Address:* Center for Fundamental Concepts in Science, Arizona State University, PO Box 871504, Tempe, AZ 85287-1504, USA (office). *Telephone:* (480) 965-9011 (office). *E-mail:* deepthought@asu.edu (office). *Website:* cosmos.asu.edu (office); beyond.asu.edu (office).

DAVIES, Peter Ho, BS, BA, MA; British writer; b. 30 Aug. 1966, Coventry, England; m. *Education:* Manchester Univ., Univ. of Cambridge, Boston Univ., USA. *Career:* Business Man., Varsity magazine; Dir of MFA Program in Creative Writing, Univ. of Michigan, Ann Arbor, USA. *Publications include:* The Ugliest House in the World (short stories) (John Llewellyn Rhys Prize, PEN Macmillan Prize 1999) 1998, Equal Love (short stories) 2000, The Welsh Girl (novel) 2007; contribs: short stories to Atlantic, Granta, Best American Short Stories 1995, 1996, 2001. *Honours:* H.L. Davis Oregon Book Award 1997, O. Henry Award 1998, New York Times Notable Book of the Year 2000. *Literary Agent:* c/o Abner Stein Agency, 10 Roland Gardens, London, SW7 3PH, England. *Telephone:* (20) 7373-0456. *E-mail:* abner@abnerstein.co.uk. *Website:* www.peterhodavies.com.

DAVIES, Peter Joseph, MB, MD, MRCP, FRACP; Australian physician and writer; b. 15 May 1937, Terang, Vic.; m. Clare Loughnan 1960; one d. *Career:* mem. Gastro-Enterological Soc. of Australia, Royal Musical Asscn, American Musicological Soc., Friends of Mozart (New York), Friends Int. Stiftung Mozareum (Salzburg). *Publications include:* Mozart in Person: His Character and Health 1989, Mozart's Health, Illnesses and Death 1993, The Cause of Beethoven's Deafness 1996, Beethoven in Person: His Deafness, Illnesses and Death 2001, The Character of a Genius: Beethoven in Perspective 2002; contrib. to Journal of Medical Biography 1995. *Address:* 14 Hamilton Street, East Kew, Vic. 3102, Australia (home).

DAVIES, Piers Anthony David, LLB; New Zealand barrister, solicitor, screenwriter and poet; b. 15 June 1941, Sydney, NSW, Australia; m. Margaret Elaine Haswell 1973; one d. *Education:* Univ. of Auckland, City of London Coll., UK. *Career:* barrister and solicitor, Wackrow, Williams & Davies Ltd, Auckland; Chair., Short Film Fund, New Zealand Film Comm. 1987–91; mem. Int. Law Asscn (Cultural Heritage Law Cttee 1997–, Convenor, Auckland Sub-br. 1997–). *Writing for film:* screenplays: The Life and Flight of Rev Buck Shotte (with Peter Weir) 1969, Homesdale (with Peter Weir) 1971, The Cars That Ate Paris (with Peter Weir) 1973, Skin Deep 1978, The Lamb of God 1985, A Fair Hearing 1995; documentaries: R. v. Huckleberry Finn 1979, Olaf's Coast 1982. *Publications include:* East and Other Gong Songs 1967, Day Trip from Mount Meru 1969, Diaspora 1974, Bourgeois Homage to Dada 1974, Central Almanac (ed.) 1974, Jetsam 1984; contribs to anthologies and periodicals, chapters in Law Stories 2003, The Protection of the Underwater Cultural Heritage 2006, Encyclopaedia of New Zealand Forms and Precedents (ongoing), The Magic Giraffe 2011. *Honours:* Officer, New Zealand Order of Merit. *Address:* 16 Crocus Place, Remuera, Auckland 1050, New Zealand (home). *Telephone:* (9) 379-5026 (office); (9) 524-6927 (home). *E-mail:* piers@wwandd.co.nz (office).

DAVIES, Stephanie (Stevie), BA, MA, PhD, FRSL; Welsh writer and lecturer; *Director of Creative Writing, University of Wales, Swansea;* b. 2 Dec. 1946, Swansea; three c. *Education:* Univ. of Manchester. *Career:* Lecturer in English Literature, Victoria Univ. of Manchester 1971–84, Univ. of Salford 1989–90; Sr Research Fellow in English Literature, Univ. of Surrey 1994–2001; Royal Literary Fund Writing Fellow, Univ. of Wales, Swansea 2001–03, Dir of Creative Writing 2004–; Fellow, Welsh Acad. *Publications include:* fiction: Boy Blue 1987, Primavera 1990, Arms and the Girl 1992, Closing the Book 1994, Four Dreamers and Emily 1996, The Web of Belonging 1997, Impassioned Clay 1999, The Element of Water 2001, Kith and Kin 2004, The Eyrie 2007, Into Suez 2010, Egos and Greed 2010; non-fiction: Renaissance Views of Man 1978, Images of Kingship in 'Paradise Lost': Milton's Politics and Christian Liberty 1983, Emily Brontë: The Artist as a Free Woman 1983, The Idea of Woman in Renaissance Literature: The Feminine Reclaimed 1987, Emily Brontë 1988, Virginia Woolf's 'To the Lighthouse' 1989, John Milton 1991, Shakespeare's 'Twelfth Night' 1993, Emily Brontë: Heretic 1994, John Donne 1994, Henry Vaughan 1995, Shakespeare's 'The Taming of the Shrew' 1995, Emily Brontë 1998, Unbridled Spirits: Women of the English Revolution 1640–1660 1998, A Century of Troubles: England 1600–1700 2001; contrib. to reference books, anthologies, quarterlies, reviews and journals. *Honours:* Fawcett Soc. Book Prize 1989, Arts Council of Wales Book of the Year 2002, Soc. of Authors Travel Grant 1999. *Address:* 9 Oystermouth Court, Castle Road, Mumbles, Swansea, SA3 5TD, Wales (home). *E-mail:* contact@steviedavies.com. *Website:* www.steviedavies.com.

DAVIS, Albert Joseph, Jr, (Albert Belisle Davis), BA, MA, PhD; American academic, writer and poet; *Dean, University College, Nicholls State University;* b. 23 June 1947, Houma, La; m. 1st Carol Anne Campbell 1968 (divorced 1992); one s.; m. 2nd Mary Archer Freet 1994; one d. *Education:* Nicholls State Univ., Colorado State Univ., Univ. of Louisiana at Lafayette. *Career:* Novelist-in-Residence, Nicholls State Univ. 1991–, Distinguished Service Prof. of Languages and Literature 1994–, Assoc. Dean, Coll. of Arts and Sciences 1999–2001, Alcee Fortier Distinguished Prof. 2003–, Dean, Univ. Coll. 2005–; mem. Acad. of American Poets, Associated Writing Programs, Louisiana Asscn of Educators, Louisiana Div. of the Arts (literary panel 1995–97), Nat.

Educ. Asscn, PEN American Center, Gov.'s Comm. on Remedial Educ. 2011. *Publications include:* What They Wrote on the Bathhouse Walls (poems) 1989, Leechtime (novel) 1989, Marquis at Bay (novel) 1992, Virginia Patout's Parish (poems) 1999; contrib. to anthologies and literary journals. *Honours:* Ione Burden Award for the Novel 1983, John Z. Bennet Award for Poetry 1984, Louisiana Div. of the Arts Creative Writing Fellowship 1989. *Address:* University College, Nicholls State University, PO Box 2008, Thibodaux, LA 70310, USA (office). *Telephone:* (985) 448-4090 (home). *E-mail:* albert.davis@nicholls.edu (office). *Website:* www.nicholls.edu (office).

DAVIS, David Brion, AB, AM, PhD; American academic and writer; *Sterling Professor Emeritus of History, Yale University*; b. 16 Feb. 1927, Denver, Colo; m. 1st; one s. two d.; m. 2nd Toni Hahn Davis 1971; two s. *Education:* Dartmouth Coll., Harvard Univ. *Career:* Instructor, Dartmouth Coll. 1953–54; Asst Prof., Cornell Univ. 1955–58, Assoc. Prof. 1958–63, Prof. and Ernest I. White Prof. of History 1963–69; Fulbright Sr Lecturer, American Studies Research Centre, Hyderabad, India 1967; Harmsworth Prof., Univ. of Oxford, UK 1969–70; Prof. and Farnam Prof. of History, Yale Univ. 1969–78, Sterling Prof. of History 1978–2001, Sterling Prof. Emer. of History 2004–; Fellow, Center for Advanced Study in the Behavioral Sciences, Stanford 1972–73; Fulbright Lecturer, Univs of Guyana and the West Indies 1974; French-American Foundation Chair in American Civilization, École des Hautes Études en Sciences Sociales, Paris 1980–81; Gilder-Lehrman Inaugural Fellow 1996–97; Dir The Gilder-Lehrman Center at Yale for the Study of Slavery, Resistance and Abolition 1998–2004; Corresp. Fellow, British Acad.; mem. American Acad. of Arts and Sciences, American Antiquarian Soc., American Philosophical Soc., Inst. of Early American History and Culture, Org. of American Historians (Pres. 1988–89). *Publications include:* Homicide in American Fiction, 1798–1860: A Study in Social Values 1957, The Problem of Slavery in Western Culture (Pulitzer Prize in General Non-Fiction 1967, Anisfield Wolf Award in Race Relations 1967) 1966, Ante-Bellum Reform (ed.) 1967, The Slave Power Conspiracy and the Paranoid Style 1969, Was Thomas Jefferson an Authentic Enemy of Slavery? 1970, The Fear of Conspiracy: Images of un-American Subversion from the Revolution to the Present (ed.) 1971, The Problem of Slavery in the Age of Revolution, 1770–1823 (Nat. Book Award for History and Biography 1976, American Historical Asscn Albert J. Beveridge Award 1975, Bancroft Prize 1976) 1975, The Great Republic (co-author) 1977, Antebellum American Culture: An Interpretive Anthology 1979, The Emancipation Moment 1984, Slavery and Human Progress 1984, Slavery in the Colonial Chesapeake 1986, From Homicide to Slavery: Studies in American Culture 1986, Revolutions: Reflections on American Equality and Foreign Liberations 1990, The Antislavery Debate: Capitalism and Abolitionism as a Problem in Historical Interpretation (with Thomas Bender) 1992, Challenging the Boundaries of Slavery 1993, The Boisterous Sea of Liberty: A Documentary History of America from Discovery Through the Civil War (with Steven Mintz) 1998, In the Image of God: Religion, Moral Values, and Our Heritage of Slavery 2001, Challenging the Boundaries of Slavery 2003, Inhuman Bondage: The Rise and Fall of Slavery in the New World (Connecticut Book Award for Nonfiction 2007, Asscn of American Publrs Award for Excellence in History and American Studies 2007, Phi Beta Kappa Soc. Ralph Waldo Emerson Award 2007) 2006. *Honours:* Hon. LittD (Dartmouth Coll.) 1977, (Columbia Univ.) 1999, Hon. LHD (Univ. of New Haven) 1986; Mass Media Award, NCCJ 1967, Guggenheim Fellowship 1958–59, Dartmouth Coll. Presidential Medal for Outstanding Leadership and Achievement 1991, Soc. of American Historians Bruce Catton Award for Lifetime Achievement 2004, New England History Teachers Asscn Kidger Award 2004, American Historical Asscn Award for Scholarly Distinction 2006, Harvard Univ. Millennial Medal 2009, Phi Beta Kappa DeVane Award for Teaching and Scholarship, Yale Univ. 2011. *Address:* 733 Lambert Road, Orange, CT 06477, USA. *E-mail:* david.b.davis@yale.edu (office).

DAVIS, Richard (Dick), BA, MA, PhD, FRSL; British academic and poet; *Professor of Persian, Ohio State University*; b. 18 April 1945, Portsmouth, Hants., England; m. Afkham Darbandi 1974; two d. *Education:* King's Coll., Cambridge, Univ. of Manchester. *Career:* fmrly teacher in Greece, Italy and Iran; teacher, Univs of Tehran, Iran 1970–78, Durham, Newcastle, California at Santa Barbara, USA; freelance writer, translator and reviewer 1978–84; poetry critic, The Listener 1980–86; Contributing Ed., PN Review 1983–89; Asst Prof., Dept of Near Eastern Languages and Cultures, Ohio State Univ. 1988–93, Assoc. Prof. of Persian 1993, currently Prof. of Persian and Chair. *Publications include:* Shade Mariners (poems, chapbook) 1970, In the Distance (poems) 1975, Seeing the World (poems) (Heinemann Award 1981) 1980, Selected Writings of Thomas Traherne (ed.) 1980, Visitations (poems, chapbook) 1983, Wisdom and Wilderness: The Achievement of Yvor Winters (criticism) 1983, What the Mind Wants (poems, chapbook) 1984, The Conference of the Birds (trans. from the Persian of Attar, with Afkham Darbandi) (American Inst. of Iranian Studies Trans. Prize 2001) 1984, The Covenant (poems) 1984, The Little Virtues (trans. of Le Piccole Virtu by Natalia Ginzburg) 1985, The City and The House (trans. of La Citta e la Casa by Natalia Ginzburg) 1986, Lares (poems, chapbook) 1986, The Rubaiyat of Omar Khayyam, trans. by Edward Fitzgerald (ed.) 1989, Devices and Desires: New and Selected Poems (The Times and The Daily Telegraph Book of the Year) 1989, A Kind of Love: New & Selected Poems (Ingram Merrill Award 1993) 1991, The Legend of Seyavash (trans. of part of The Shahnameh by Ferdowsi) 1992, Epic and Sedition: the Case of Ferdowsi's Shahnameh (Persian Heritage Foundation Award) 1993, My Unce Napoleon (trans. of Dai Jan Napoleon by Iraj Pezeshkzad) (American Inst. of Iranian Studies Trans. Prize 2000) 1996, Touchwood: Poems 1991–1995 1996, Medieval Persian Epigrams (trans.) (Poetry Soc. of Great Britain recommendation) 1996, The Lion and the Throne: Stories from the Shahnameh of Ferdowsi (vol. one) 1998, Fathers and Sons: Stories from the Shahnameh of Ferdowsi (vol. two) 2000, Belonging (poems) (Economist Book of the Year) 2002, Panthea's Children: Hellenistic Novels and Medieval Persian Romances 2002, Sunset of Empire: Stories from the Shahnameh of Ferdowsi (Vol. III) 2004, The Shahnameh: the Persian Book of Kings 2006, The Trick of Sunlight (poems) 2006, Vis and Ramin (trans.) 2008; contrib. of poems to numerous magazines and journals, including TLS, The Listener, The Spectator, Critical Quarterly, Poetry Review, Poetry Nation Review, Paris Review, Southern Review, Sequoia, Spectrum, The Hudson Review, Drastic Measures, Numbers, Helix, Other Poetry, Rialto, Agenda, Poetry Durham, TriQuarterly, Cambridge Review, Sewanee Review, Threepenny Review, Yale Review, New Criterion, Hellas, The Epigrammatist, la fontana, Dark Horse; contrib. articles and reviews to TLS, Journal of American Oriental Studies, International Journal of Middle Eastern Studies, Iranian Studies, Encyclopaedia Iranica, Encyclopaedia of Islam, Threepenny Review, New York Review of Books. *Honours:* Arts Council of Great Britain Writers' Award 1979, British Inst. of Persian Studies Award 1981, Fulbright Travel Award 1987, Guggenheim Fellow 1999–2000, Nat. Endowment for the Humanities Fellow 2001, Encyclopaedia Iranica Ferdowsi Award for Services to Persian Poetry 2001, Ohio State Univ. Distinguished Scholar Award 2002. *Address:* Department of Near Eastern Languages and Cultures, Ohio State University, 207E Jennings Hall, 1735 Neil Avenue, Columbus, OH 43210, USA (office). *Telephone:* (614) 292-5643 (office). *Fax:* (614) 292-1262 (office). *E-mail:* davis.77@osu.edu (office). *Website:* nelc.osu.edu/people (office).

DAVIS, Dorothy Salisbury, AB; American writer; b. 26 April 1916, Chicago, Ill.; m. Harry Davis 1946. *Education:* Barat Coll., Lake Forest, Ill. *Career:* mem. Mystery Writers of American, Crime Writers Asscn, Authors' Guild. *Publications include:* A Gentle Murderer 1951, The Clay Hand 1952, A Town of Masks 1952, Men of No Property 1956, Death of an Old Sinner 1957, A Gentleman Called 1968, Old Sinners Never Die 1959, The Evening of the Good Samaritan 1961, Black Sheep, White Lamb 1964, The Pale Betrayer 1965, Enemy and Brother 1967, Where the Dark Streets Go 1969, Crime Without Murder 1972, The Little Brothers 1974, Shock Wave 1974, A Death in the Life 1976, Scarlet Night 1980, Lullaby of Murder 1984, Tales for a Stormy Night 1985, The Habit of Fear 1987, A Gentleman Called 1989, Old Sinners Never Die 1991, In the Still of the Night 2001; contribs: New Republic. *Honours:* MWA Grand Master's Award 1985, Bouchereon XX Lifetime Achievement Award 1989.

DAVIS, J(ames) Madison, Jr, BA, MA, PhD; American writer and academic; *Gaylord Family Endowed Professor of Journalism and Mass Communication, University of Oklahoma*; b. 10 Feb. 1951, Charlottesville, Va; s. of James Madison Davis and Alma Luci; m. 1st Simonne Evelyn Eck 1977 (divorced); two s.; m. 2nd Melissa Anne Haymes 1997; one s. *Education:* George Washington Univ., Franklin and Marshall Coll., Univ. of Maryland at College Park, Johns Hopkins Univ., Univ. of Southern Mississippi. *Career:* Instructor of English and journalism, Allegany Community Coll., Cumberland, Md 1975–77; instructor, part-time instructor and teaching asst, Univ. of Southern Mississippi 1977–79; Asst Prof. of English Composition, Pennsylvania State Univ., Erie 1979–84, Assoc. Prof. of English 1984–90, Prof. of English 1990–91; Writer-in-Residence, Mercyhurst Coll. 1989, 1990; Prof. on the Professional Writing Program, Gaylord Coll. of Journalism and Mass Communication, Univ. of Oklahoma, Norman 1991–2008, Gaylord Family Endowed Prof. of Journalism and Mass Communication 2008–; mem. Int. Asscn of Crime Writers N America Br. (Pres. 1993–97, Sec. 1997–2001). *Publications include:* fiction: The Murder of Frau Schütz 1988, White Rook 1990, Bloody Marko 1991, Red Knight 1992, And the Angels Sing 1996; non-fiction: Intro 14 (co-ed.) 1984, Critical Essays on Edward Albee (with Philip C. Kolin) 1986, Dick Francis 1989, Conversations with Robertson Davies 1989, Stanislaw Lem 1990, The Shakespeare Name Dictionary (with A. Daniel Frankforter, aka The Shakespeare Name and Place Dictionary) 1995, Murderous Schemes (contributing co-ed. with Donald Westlake) 1996, The Novelist's Essential Guide to Creating Plot 2000, Alfred Hitchcock in the Vertigo Murders 2000, Law and Order: Deadline 2004, The Van Gogh Conspiracy 2005; contrib. to books, newspapers, reviews, quarterlies and journals. *Honours:* Resident Fellow in Prose 1974, Resident Fellow in Fiction 1981, Fellowship 1988, Virginia Center for the Creative Arts, Contemporary Best Fiction Prize 1978, Resident Fellow in Fiction, Ragdale Foundation 1982, Hambridge Center for Creative Arts and Sciences 1982, Pennsylvania Council of the Arts Fellowship in Fiction 1984, MWA Edgar Allan Poe Scroll Award 1988. *Literary Agent:* c/o Peter Rubie Literary Agency, 240 W 35th Street, Suite 500, New York, NY 10001, USA. *Telephone:* (212) 279-1776. *Fax:* (212) 279-0927. *E-mail:* prubie@prlit.com. *Website:* www.prlit.com. *Address:* 1713 Asbury Court, Norman, OK 73071, USA (home). *Telephone:* (405) 325-4171 (office); (405) 321-5033 (home). *E-mail:* jmadisondavis@ou.edu (office). *Website:* www.ou.edu/content/gaylord (office).

DAVIS, Jon Edward, BA, MFA; American poet, writer and academic; *Professor of Creative Writing and Literature, Institute of American Indian Arts*; b. 28 Oct. 1952, New Haven, Conn.; m. 2nd Teresa White; one d. three step-c. *Education:* Univ. of Bridgeport, Univ. of Montana. *Career:* Ed. CutBank 1982–85; Managing Ed. Shankpainter 1986–87; Fellow, Fine Arts Work Center, Provincetown, Mass 1986–87, Co-ordinator Writing Program

1987–88; Visiting Asst Prof., Salisbury State Univ., Md 1988–90; Prof. of Creative Writing and Literature, Inst. of American Indian Arts, Santa Fe, NM 1990–; Co-Ed. Countermeasures 1993–2000; screenwriting instructor, ABC/ Disney TV and film workshops 2004–07. *Films:* as screenwriter: The Burden Carriers, The Hand Drum, CIA News. *Publications include:* poetry: West of New England 1983, Dangerous Amusements 1987, The Hawk, The Road, The Sunlight After Clouds 1995, Local Color 1995, Scrimmage of Appetite 1995, Preliminary Report 2010, With: A Collaborative Chapbook 2012; contribs to anthologies, reviews, quarterlies and journals. *Honours:* Connecticut Poetry Circuit Competition winner 1980, Acad. of American Poets Prize 1985, INTRO Award for Fiction 1985, Nat. Endowment for the Arts Fellowship 1986, Richard Hugo Memorial Award, CutBank 1988, Maryland Arts Council Fellowship 1990, Owl Creek Press Chapbook Contest Winner 1994, Palanquin Press Chapbook Contest Winner 1995, Lannan Literary Award 1998, Nat. Endowment for the Arts Fellowship 2005, Lannan Foundation Residency 2012. *Address:* Chair of Creative Writing, Institute of American Indian Arts, 83A Van Nu Po Road, Santa Fe, NM, USA (office). *Telephone:* (505) 424-2365 (office). *Fax:* (505) 424-3030 (office). *E-mail:* jdavis@iaia.edu (office). *Website:* www.voydofcourse.blogspot.com (office).

DAVIS, Margaret Thomson; Scottish writer; b. 24 May 1926, Bathgate, West Lothian; m. (divorced); one s. *Education:* Albert Secondary Modern School, Glasgow. *Career:* mem. PEN, Scottish Labour History Soc., Soc. of Authors. *Publications include:* The Breadmakers 1972, A Baby Might Be Crying 1973, A Sort of Peace 1973, The Prisoner 1974, The Prince and the Tobacco Lords 1976, Roots of Bondage 1977, Scorpion in the Fire 1977, The Dark Side of Pleasure 1981, The Making of a Novelist 1982, A Very Civilized Man 1982, Light and Dark 1984, Rag Woman, Rich Woman 1987, Mothers and Daughters 1988, Wounds of War 1989, A Woman of Property 1991, A Sense of Belonging 1993, Hold Me Forever 1994, Kiss Me No More 1995, A Kind of Immortality 1996, Burning Ambition 1997, Gallaghers 1998, The Glasgow Belle 1998, A Tangled Web 1999, The Clydesiders 2000, The Gourlay Girls 2001, Strangers in a Strange Land 2001, The Clydesiders at War 2002, A Darkening of the Heart 2004, A Deadly Deception 2005, Write from the Heart (autobiog.) 2006, Goodmans of Glassford Street 2007, Red Alert 2008, Double Danger 2009, The Kellys of Kelvingrove 2010; contrib. of some 200 short stories to various periodicals. *Literary Agent:* c/o Heather Jeeves Literary Agency, 9 Kingsfield Crescent, Witney, Oxon., OX28 2JB, England.

DAVIS, William Virgil, AB, MA, MDiv, PhD; American literary scholar, academic and poet; *Professor of English and Writer-in-Residence, Baylor University;* b. 26 May 1940, Canton, Ohio; s. of Virgil Sanor Davis and Anna Bertha Davis (née Orth); m. Carol Ann Demske 1971; one s. *Education:* Ohio Univ., Pittsburgh Theological Seminary. *Career:* Teaching Fellow, Ohio Univ. 1965–67, Asst Prof. of English 1967–68, Consultant, Creative Writing Program 1992–98; Asst Prof. of English, Central Connecticut State Univ. 1968–72, Univ. of Illinois, Chicago 1972–77; Assoc. Prof. of English, Baylor Univ., Tex. 1977–79, Prof. of English and Writer-in-Residence 1979–, Centennial Prof. 2002–03; Guest Prof., Univ. of Vienna, Austria 1979–80, 1989–90, 1997, Univ. of Copenhagen, Denmark 1984; Visiting Scholar-Guest Prof., Univ. of Wales, Swansea, UK 1983; Writer-in-Residence, Univ. of Montana 1983; Adjunct MFA Faculty, Southwest Texas State Univ. 1990–98; Adjunct mem. Grad. Faculty, Texas Christian Univ. 1992–96; mem. Acad. of American Poets, Int. Asscn of Univ. Profs of English, Modern Language Asscn, Pacific Ancient and Modern Language Asscn, South Cen. Modern Language Asscn, Poetry Soc. of America, Poets and Writers, Texas Asscn of Creative Writing Teachers; Councillor, Texas Inst. of Letters 1993–97, Pres. 2008–10; Ordained Minister, Presbyterian Church in the USA 1971. *Publications include:* George Whitefield's Journals, 1737–1741 (ed.) 1969, Theodore Roethke: A Bibliography (contributing ed.) 1973, One Way to Reconstruct the Scene (Yale Series of Younger Poets Prize) 1980, The Dark Hours (Calliope Press Chapbook Prize) 1984, Understanding Robert Bly 1988, Winter Light 1990, Critical Essays on Robert Bly (ed.) 1992, Miraculous Simplicity: Essays on R. S. Thomas (ed.) 1993, Robert Bly: The Poet and His Critics 1994, R. S. Thomas: Poetry and Theology 2007, Landscape and Journey (New Criterion Poetry Prize 2009, Helen C. Smith Memorial Award in Poetry 2010) 2009; contrib. of articles to scholarly journals and poems in numerous anthologies and other publs; four books of poetry and more than 1,200 poems in periodicals. *Honours:* Scholar in Poetry 1970, John Atherton Fellow in Poetry 1980, Bread Loaf Writers' Conf., Lilly Foundation Grant 1979–80, James Sims Prize in American Literature 2002, Fellowship in Creative Writing, Poetry, Writers' League of Texas 2002, Distinguished Alumnus Award, The Pittsburgh Theological Seminary 2012. *Address:* 2633 Lake Oaks Road, Waco, TX 76710, USA (home). *Telephone:* (254) 772-3198 (office). *Fax:* (254) 710-6878 (office). *E-mail:* william_davis@baylor.edu (office).

DAVIS-GARDNER, Angela, BA, MFA; American writer and academic; *Professor Emeritus, North Carolina State University;* b. 21 April 1942, Charlotte, NC; one s. *Education:* Duke Univ., Univ. of North Carolina at Greensboro. *Career:* taught at Meredith Coll., Guilford Coll.; fmr William Blackburn Writer-in-Residence, Duke Univ.; currently Prof. Emer. North Carolina State Univ.; mem. Authors' Guild, Poets and Writers. *Publications include:* Felice 1982, Forms of Shelter 1991, Plum Wine 2006, Butterfly's Child 2011; contribs: short stories in: Kansas Quarterly, Carolina Quarterly, Crescent Review, Greensboro Review, other literary quarterlies. *Honours:* Artists Fellowship, North Carolina Arts Council 1981–82, Sir Walter Raleigh Award 1991, Best Novel by North Carolinian. *Address:* Department of English, North Carolina State University, Box 8105, Raleigh, NC 27695, USA (office). *Website:* www.angeladavisgardner.com (home).

DAVIS-GOFF, Annabel Claire; Irish writer; b. 19 Feb. 1942, Dublin; one s. one d. *Career:* teacher of Literature, Bennington Coll., Vermont. *Publications include:* Walled Gardens 1989, The Literary Companions to Gambling 1996, The Dower House 1998, This Cold Country 2002, The Fox's Walk 2003. *E-mail:* adg@annabeldavisgoff.com (office). *Website:* www.annabeldavisgoff .com.

DAVISON, Geoffrey Joseph, TD, FRICS; British writer; b. 10 Aug. 1927, Newcastle upon Tyne, England; m. Marlene Margaret Wilson 1956; two s. *Career:* mem. Pen and Palette Club. *Publications include:* The Spy Who Swapped Shoes 1967, Nest of Spies 1968, The Chessboard Spies 1969, The Fallen Eagles 1970, The Honorable Assassins 1971, Spy Puppets 1973, The Berlin Spy Trap 1974, No Names on Their Graves 1978, The Bloody Legionnaires 1981, The Last Waltz (Vienna May 1945) 2001, The Colombian Contract 2001, The Dead Island 2001. *Address:* 95 Cheviot View, Ponteland, Newcastle upon Tyne, NE20 9BH, England (home). *Telephone:* (1661) 822347 (home). *E-mail:* davipont@onetel.com (home).

DAVISON, Liam, BA; Australian writer and educator; b. 29 July 1957, Melbourne, Vic.; m. Francesca White 1983; one s. one d. *Education:* St Bede's Coll., Melbourne State Coll. *Career:* Instructor in Creative Writing, Peninsular Coll. of Tech. and Further Educ.; freelance writer 1988–. *Publications include:* novels: The Velodrome 1988, Soundings (Banjo Award, Nat. Book Council) 1993, The White Woman 1994, The Betrayal 2001; short stories: The Shipwreck Party 1989, Collected Stories 2001; other: The Spirit of Rural Australia. *Honours:* Australia Council-Literature Board Fellowships 1989, 1991, Marten Bequest Travelling Scholarship for Prose 1992, Nat. Book Council Banjo Award for Fiction 1993. *Literary Agent:* c/o Curtis Brown Australia Pty Ltd, PO Box 19, Paddington, NSW 2021, Australia. *Telephone:* (2) 9331-5301. *Fax:* (2) 9360-3935. *E-mail:* info@curtisbrown.com.au. *Website:* www.curtisbrown.com.au.

DAWE, Donald Bruce, AO, MLitt, PhD; Australian writer; b. 15 Feb. 1930, Geelong; s. of Alfred James Dawe and Mary Ann Matilda Dawe; m. Gloria Desley Dawe (née Blain) 1964 (died 1997); two s. two d. *Education:* Northcote High School, Univs of Melbourne, New England and Queensland. *Career:* Educ. Section, RAAF 1959–68; teacher, Downlands Sacred Heart Coll., Toowoomba, Queensland 1969–71; Lecturer, Sr Lecturer, Assoc. Prof., Faculty of Arts, Univ. of Southern Queensland 1971–93. *Publications:* poetry: No Fixed Address 1962, A Need of a Similar Name (Ampol Arts Award 1966) 1964, An Eye for a Tooth 1968, Beyond the Subdivisions 1969, Condolences of the Season: Selected Poems 1971, Over Here, Hark! and Other Stories 1983, Speaking in Parables 1987, The Side of Silence: Poems 1987–90 1990, Mortal Instruments: Poems 1990–95 1995, Sometimes Gladness: Collected Poems 1954–97 1997, A Poet's People 1999, Towards a War 2003; non-fiction: Essays and Opinions 1990; children's fiction: No Cat – and That's That 2002, The Chewing Gum Kid 2002, Luke and Lulu 2004, Smarty-Cat 2007. *Honours:* Hon. Prof. (Univ. of Southern Queensland) 1995; Hon. DLitt (Univ. of Southern Queensland) 1995, (Univ. of NSW) 1997; Myer Poetry Prize 1965, 1968, Patrick White Award 1980, Christopher Brennan Award 1984, Paul Harris Fellowship, Rotary Int. 1990, Philip Hodgins Memorial Medal for Literary Excellence 1997, Australia Council for the Arts Emer. Writers Award 2001, Centenary Medal 2003. *Address:* Authors, c/o Penguin Group (Australia), PO Box 701, Hawthorn 3122, Vic., Australia (office). *Website:* www .penguin.com.au (office).

DAWE, Gerald Chartres, BA, MA, FTCD, FEA; Irish poet and lecturer; *Director, Oscar Wilde Centre for Irish Writing, School of English, Trinity College, Dublin;* b. 22 April 1952, Belfast, Northern Ireland; s. of Gordon Aubrey Dawe and Norma Fitzgerald Bradshaw; m. Dorothea Melvin 1979; one s. one d. *Education:* Univ. of Ulster, Univ. Coll., Galway. *Career:* Tutor in English, Asst Lecturer, Univ. Coll., Galway 1978–87; Lecturer, Trinity Coll. Dublin 1987–2007, Sr Lecturer 2007–, Dir MPhil in Creative Writing 1997–, Lecturer in English and Dir of the Oscar Wilde Centre for Irish Writing 1999–, Fellow, Trinity Coll. Dublin 2004–; Burns Visiting Prof., Boston Coll., USA 2005; Heimbold Chair, Villanova Univ., Philadelphia, USA 2009; mem. Int. Asscn for the Study of Irish Literature, Poetry Ireland; readings and lectures in many parts of the world; Fellow, English Asscn 2003. *Radio:* Presenter, The Poetry Programme (RTE) 2008–09. *Publications:* poetry: Sheltering Places 1978, The Lundys Letter 1985, Sunday School 1991, Heart of Hearts 1995, The Morning Train 1999, Lake Geneva 2003, The Visible World: Selected Poems 1973–2003, Points West 2008, The Night Fountain: Selected Early Poems by Salvatore Quasimodo (with Marco Sonzogni) 2008, Country Music: Uncollected Poems 1974–1989 2009; criticism: Across a Roaring Hill: The Protestant Imagination in Modern Ireland, with Edna Longley 1985, How's the Poetry Going?: Literary Politics and Ireland Today 1991, The Poet's Place, with John Wilson Foster 1991, Against Piety: Essays in Irish Poetry 1995, The Rest is History 1998, Stray Dogs and Dark Horses (selected essays) 2000; editor: The Younger Irish Poets 1982, 1991, Krino (anthology with Jonathan Williams) 1986–96, The Ogham Stone (anthology with Michael Mulreany) 2001, The Writer Fellow (anthology with Terence Brown) 2004, The Proper Word: Collected Criticism 2007, My Mother-City and Bit Parts 2007, High Pop: The Irish Times Column of Stewart Parker (with Maria Johnston) 2008, Dramatis Personae and other writings by Stewart Parker (with Maria Johnston and Clare Wallace) 2008, The World as Province: Selected Prose 1980–2008 2009,

Conversations: Poets & Poetry 2011; contrib. to scholarly journals, newspapers, reviews and radio. *Honours:* Hon. MA (Dublin) 2005; Major State Award 1974–77, Arts Council Bursary for Poetry 1980, 2005, Macaulay Fellowship in Literature 1984, Hawthornden Int. Writers' Fellowship 1988, Ledwig-Rowholt Fellowship 1999, Ulster Titanic Soc. Lifetime Achievement Award 2002, Arts Council Bursary for Poetry 2005. *Address:* School of English, Arts Building, Trinity College, Dublin 2, Ireland (office). *Telephone:* (1) 8962897 (office). *Fax:* (1) 8962886 (office). *E-mail:* gdawe@tcd.ie (office). *Website:* www.tcd.ie/oscarwildecentre (office); www.gallerypress.com; www.gerald-dawe.net.

DAWES, Kwame Senu Neville, BA, PhD; American/Ghanaian/Jamaican poet, playwright, critic and novelist; *Distinguished Poet-in-Residence and Louise Frye Scudder Professor of Humanities, University of South Carolina*; b. 28 July 1962, Accra, Ghana; s. of Neville Agustus Dawes and Sophia Dawes (née Tevi); m. Lorna Marie; three c. *Education:* Univ. of the West Indies, Univ. of New Brunswick. *Career:* moved to Jamaica 1971; Chair. of the Division of Arts and Letters 1993–96; Asst Prof. in English, Univ. of S Carolina (USC) at Sumter 1992–96, Guest Lecturer, USC at Columbia 1994, Assoc. Prof. of English, USC 1996–2001, Prof. of English 2002–, currently Distinguished Poet-in-Residence and Louise Frye Scudder Prof. of Humanities, Dir MFA/Creative Writing program 2001–03; Series Ed. Caribbean Play Series, Peepal Tree Books, UK 1999–, Assoc. Poetry Ed. Peepal Tree Books 2006–; Criticism Ed. Obsidian II literary journal, Raleigh, NC 2000–05; programmer of annual Calabash Int. Literary Festival, Jamaica 2000–; Dir USC English Dept Spring Writers Festival 2002–03, S Carolina Poetry Initiative (founder) 2003–; Exec. Dir USC Arts Inst. 2005–; Faculty Mem., Pacific Univ. MFA program; mem. Nat. Book Critics' Circle, S Carolina Humanities Council (Bd mem.) 2000–07, S Carolina Book Festival (mem. Advisory Bd); Assoc. Fellow, Univ. of Warwick 1996. *Plays:* In the Warmth of the Cold, And the Gods Fell, In Chains of Freedom, The System, The Martyr, It Burns and it Stings, Charity's Come, Even Unto Death, Friends and Almost Lovers, Dear Pastor, Confessions, Brown Leaf, Coming in from the Cold, Song of an Injured Stone (musical), In My Garden, Charades, Passages, A Celebration of Struggle, Stump of the Terebinth, Valley Prince, One Love 2001. *Writing for radio:* Salut Haiti (poem/drama), Samaritans (play), New World A-Comin' (play). *Publications:* poetry: Progeny of Air 1994, Resisting the Anomie 1995, Prophets 1995, Jacko Jacobus 1996, Requiem 1996, Shook Foil 1998, Wheel and Come Again: Reggae Anthology (ed.) 1998, Mapmaker (chapbook) 2000, Midland 2001, Selected Poems 2002, Bruised Totems 2004, Wisteria: Twilight Songs from The Swamp Country 2005, Brimming 2006, Gomer's Song 2007, Impossible Flying 2007; fiction: A Place to Hide (short stories) 2002, She's Gone (novel) 2007; non-fiction: Natural Mysticism: Towards a New Reggae Aesthetic (literary criticism) 1998, Talk Yuh Talk: Interviews with Caribbean Poets 2000, Bob Marley: Lyrical Genius 2002, A Far Cry from Plymouth Rock (memoir) 2007; contrib. to numerous journals and periodicals, including Beat Magazine, Black Issues, Black Warrior Review, Bristol Evening Post, Calabash, Caribbean Writer, Dagens Nyheter (Sweden), Globe and Mail, Impact, Library Journal, Lines, Morning Star, Poetry London Newsletter, Poetry Review, Publishers Weekly, The Atlanta Journal/Constitution, The Brunswickan, The Courier, The Daily Gleaner, The Daily News, The English Review, The Guardian, The Herald, The London Times, The Observer, The State, The Sumter Item, The Telegraph Journal, The Voice, Time Out London, Venue, Wasafiri, Western Daily Press, World Literature Today, World Literature Written in English, Granta. *Honours:* Hon. Fellow Univ. of Iowa Int. Writing Program 1986; Forward Poetry Prize for Best First Collection 1994, S Carolina Arts Comm. Individual Artist Fellowship 1996, Winner Poetry Business Chapbook Competition 2000, Ohio Univ. Press Hollis Summers Poetry Prize 2000, Pushcart Prize 2001, Hurston Wright Legacy Award for Fiction. *Address:* English Department, University of South Carolina, Columbia, SC 29208 (office); Alison Granucci, Blue Flower Arts LLC, PO Box 1361, Millbrook NY 12545, USA (office). *Telephone:* (803) 777-2096 (office). *Fax:* (803) 777-9064 (office). *E-mail:* alison@blueflowerarts.com (office); dawesk@mailbox.sc.edu (office). *Website:* www.kwamedawes.com (home); www.blueflowerarts.com (office).

DAWKINS, (Clinton) Richard, MA, DSc, FRS, FRSL; British biologist, academic and author; *Professorial Fellow, New College, University of Oxford*; b. 26 March 1941, Nairobi, Kenya; s. of Clinton John Dawkins and Jean Mary Vyvyan Dawkins (née Ladner); m. 1st Marian Stamp 1967 (divorced 1984); m. 2nd Eve Barham 1984 (died 1999); one d.; m. 3rd Hon. Lalla Ward 1992. *Education:* Balliol Coll., Oxford. *Career:* Asst Prof. of Zoology, Univ. of California, Berkeley, USA 1967–69; Lecturer, Univ. of Oxford 1970–89, Reader in Zoology 1989–96, Charles Simonyi Reader in the Public Understanding of Science 1995–96, Charles Simonyi Prof. 1996–2008 (retd), Professorial Fellow, New Coll., Oxford 1970–; Ed. Animal Behaviour 1974–78, Oxford Surveys in Evolutionary Biology 1983–86; Gifford Lecturer, Univ. of Glasgow 1988, Sidgwick Memorial Lecturer, Newnham Coll., Cambridge 1988; Kovler Visiting Fellow, Univ. of Chicago 1990; Nelson Lecturer, Univ. of California, Davis 1990; f. Richard Dawkins Foundation for Reason and Science 2006. *Television includes:* Nice Guys Finish First (BBC) 1985, The Blind Watchmaker (BBC) 1986, Break the Science Barrier (Channel 4) 1994, Royal Institution Christmas Lectures (BBC) 1992, Big Ideas in Science (Channel 5) 2004, The Root of All Evil? (Channel 4) 2006, The Enemies of Reason (Channel 4) 2007, The Genius of Charles Darwin (Channel 4) (Best TV Documentary Series, British Broadcast Awards 2008) 2008, Doctor Who: The Stolen Earth (as himself) 2008, Expelled: No Intelligence Allowed (as himself) 2008, The Purpose of Purpose – Lecture tour among American universities 2009, Faith School Menace? (More4) 2010, Beautiful Minds (BBC 4 documentary) 2012. *Publications include:* The Selfish Gene 1976, The Extended Phenotype 1982, The Blind Watchmaker (RSL Prize 1987, LA Times Literature Prize 1987) 1986, The Tinbergen Legacy (ed with M. Dawkins and T. R. Halliday) 1991, River Out of Eden 1995, Climbing Mount Improbable 1996, Unweaving the Rainbow: Science, Delusion and the Appetite for Wonder 1998, A Devil's Chaplain (essays) 2003, The Ancestor's Tale: A Pilgrimage to the Dawn of Life 2004, The God Delusion 2006, The Oxford Book of Modern Science Writing (ed) 2008, The Greatest Show on Earth: The Evidence for Evolution 2009, The Magic of Reality: How We Know What's Really True 2011; numerous articles in scientific journals. *Honours:* Hon. Fellow, Regent's Coll., London 1988, Balliol Coll. 2004, Hon. Patron, Philosophical Soc., Trinity Coll. Dublin 2004; mem. Freedom From Religion Foundation's Hon. Bd of distinguished achievers 2010; Hon. DLitt (St Andrews) 1995, (ANU Canberra) 1996; Hon. DSc (Westminster) 1997, (Hull) 2001, (Sussex) 2005, (Durham) 2005, (Brussels) 2005; Hon. DUniv (Open Univ.) 2003; numerous awards including Silver Medal, Zoological Soc. 1989, Michael Faraday Award, Royal Soc. 1990, Nakayama Prize 1994, Int. Cosmos Prize 1997, Kistler Prize 2001, Bicentennial Kelvin Medal, Royal Soc. of Glasgow 2002, Richard Dawkins Award given annually by Atheist Alliance International to the atheist whose work has done most to raise public awareness of atheism 2003–, Shakespeare Prize for contribution to British Culture, Hamburg 2005, British Book Award for Author of the Year 2007, e Nierenberg Prize for Science in the Public Interest 2009. *Address:* New College, Holywell Street, Oxford, OX1 3BN (office); Richard Dawkins Foundation for Reason and Science, Suite 184, 266 Banbury Road, Oxford, OX2 7DL, England (office). *E-mail:* contact@richarddawkins.net (office). *Website:* richarddawkins.net; www.richarddawkinsfoundation.org.

DAWNAY, Caroline Margaret; British literary agent; *Joint Head of Books, United Agents*; b. 22 Jan. 1950, Reading, Berks., England; d. of Oliver Dawnay and Margaret Boyle; one s. *Education:* St Mary's School, Wantage, Oxon., Univ. per Stranieri, Florence, Italy and Alliance Française, Paris. *Career:* with Noel Gay Artists 1968–70, Michael Joseph publrs, London 1971–77; Dir, A.D. Peters & Co. Ltd 1977–88, Peters Fraser & Dunlop Group Ltd (PFD) 1988–2007; Jt Head of Books, United Agents 2007–; Dir, June Hall Literary Agency; Treas. Asscn of Authors' Agents 1991–94, Pres. 1994–97. *Publication:* An Alphabet of Aunts (with Mungo McCosh) 2007. *Address:* United Agents, 12–26 Lexington Street, London, W1F 0LE, England (office). *Telephone:* (20) 3214-0800 (office). *Fax:* (20) 3214-0801 (office). *E-mail:* cdawnay@unitedagents.co.uk (office). *Website:* www.unitedagents.co.uk (office).

DAWSON, Clay (see LEVINSON, Leonard)

DAWSON, Janet, BS, MA; American writer and fmr journalist; b. 31 Oct. 1949, Purcell, Okla. *Education:* Univ. of Colorado, Boulder, California State Univ., Hayward. *Career:* mem. Mystery Writers of America, Sisters in Crime, Private Eye Writers of America, American Crime Writers League, Authors' Guild, Mystery Readers International. *Publications include:* Kindred Crimes 1991, Till the Old Men Die 1992, Take a Number 1993, Don't Turn Your Back on the Ocean 1994, Nobody's Child 1995, A Credible Threat 1996, Witness to Evil 1997, Where the Bodies are Buried 1998, A Killing at the Track 2000, Scam and Eggs 2002, Bit Player 2011; short stories: By the Book, Little Red Corvette, Invisible Time, Witchcraft, Mrs Lincoln's Dilemma, What the Cat Dragged In. *Honours:* Award for Best First Private Eye Novel, St Martin's Press-Private Eye Writers Asscn 1990. *E-mail:* catbird555@yahoo.com. *Website:* www.janetdawson.com.

DAWSON, Jill Dianne, BA, MA; British writer, poet, editor and teacher; b. 1962, Durham, England; pnr Meredith Bowles; two s. *Education:* Univ. of Nottingham, Sheffield Hallam Univ. *Career:* mem. Nat. Asscn of Writers in Education, Soc. of Authors. *Publications:* School Tales (ed.) 1990, How Do I Look? (non-fiction) 1991, Virago Book of Wicked Verse (ed.) 1992, Virago Book of Love Letters (ed.) 1994, Wild Ways (ed. with Margo Daly), White Fish with Painted Nails (poems) 1994, Trick of the Light (novel) 1996, Magpie (novel) 1998, Fred and Edie (novel) 2001, Gas & Air (ed. with Margo Daly), Wild Boy (novel) 2003, Watch Me Disappear 2006, The Great Lover 2009; contrib. to anthologies and periodicals. *Honours:* Eric Gregory Award 1992, second prize, London Writers Short Story Competition 1994, Blue Nose Poet of the Year 1995, London Arts Board New Writers 1998. *Literary Agent:* United Agents, 12–26 Lexington Street, London, W1F 0LE, England. *Telephone:* (20) 3214-0800. *Fax:* (20) 3214-0801. *E-mail:* info@unitedagents.co.uk. *Website:* unitedagents.co.uk; www.jilldawson.co.uk.

DAYAN, Yael; Israeli politician, writer and journalist; *Chairperson, Council of Tel-Aviv–Jaffa*; b. 12 Feb. 1939, Nahalal; d. of the late Gen. Moshe Dayan and of Ruth Dayan; m. Dov Sion; one s. one d. *Education:* Hebrew Univ. of Jerusalem, Open Univ. of Israel. *Career:* Capt. in Israeli Defense Forces Spokesman's Office; mem. (Labour Party) Knesset (Parl.) 1992–2003, Founder and Chair. Cttee for the Advancement of the Status of Women, Chair. Sub-cttee for Admin of the Occupied Territories; fmr mem. Cttee for Defence and Foreign Affairs, Cttee for Constitution, Law and Justice, Sub-cttee for Gay and Lesbian Rights; mem. Sub-cttee for Violence Against Women 2003–08; currently Ind. Chair. Council of Tel-Aviv–Jaffa (Mezet Party). *Publications include:* fiction: New Face in the Mirror 1959, Envy the Frightened 1961, Dust 1963, Death Had Two Sons 1967, Three Weeks in the Fall 1979; non-fiction: The Promised Land – Memoirs of Shmuel Dayan (ed.) 1961, A Soldier's Diary

1967, My Father, His Daughter 1985; political commentaries for Hebrew and foreign press. *Honours:* Bruno Kreisky Human Rights Award 1991, Olof Palme Award for Peace 1998, selected by L'Express magazine as one of 100 Women Who Make the World Move 1995, State of the World Forum's Women Redefining Leadership Award 1997, Peace Awards in Austria and Spain. *Address:* Office of the Deputy Mayor, Rabin Square, Municipality of Tel-Aviv–Jaffa, Tel-Aviv (office); 10 Rupin Street, Tel-Aviv, Israel. *Telephone:* (3) 5218250 (office); (3) 5272611 (home). *Fax:* (3) 5216052 (office); (3) 5232004 (home). *E-mail:* yaeld@tel-aviv.gov.il (office); yael.d@banak.net.il.

DAYIOĞLU, Gülten; Turkish writer; b. 15 May 1935, Emet, Kütahya; d. of Lüftü and Emine Uyan; m. Ceudet Dayioğlu 1958; two s. *Education:* Atatürk Girls' School, Istanbul and Istanbul Univ. *Career:* primary school teacher 1962–77; journalist, Cumhuriyet 1965–67, Milliyet 1967; writer from 1977, has written TV and radio plays, novels, short stories, travel books for children, series of children's books and research works on Turkish educ. system. *Publications include:* (titles in trans.) adult fiction: Offspring (short stories, Yunus Nadi Story Award 1964–65), Those Left Behind (short stories), Back Home, Green Cherry (novel), Green Cherry II, The Eight Colour, Mo's Secret, Flowers of the Doomsday, Birds of the Twilight, Mystical Powers of Yada; children's books: Fadiş, Brothers and Sisters, Suna's Sparrows, When I Grow Up, Smart Fleas, Children of the Radiation Era, The Immortal Queen, A Bird flew Over the Danube, Purple Clouds in the Sky, Ganga, If Only the World Belonged to Children, They Were Four Siblings, The Stork in the Snow (Children's Literature Story Award, Arkin Bookstore 1974–75), The Beautiful Lady (Children's Literature Tale Award, Arkin Bookstore 1974–75), Gül The Bride (Story Award, Turkish Family Planning Foundation) 1987, Journey to the Back of the Mountain Kaf (Children's Literature Award, Ministry of Culture and Tourism) 1988, Mystery of the Parbat Mountain (İzmir Metropolitan Municipality Children's Novel Award) 1989, Trip to a Totally Different World: America 1990, Trip to The Country of Legends; China 1990, A Trip to the World of Kangaroos: Australia, The Eyes of the Midos Eagle (Altin Kitap Odülü Golden Books Award) 1991. *Address:* Nişantaşi Ihlamuryolu 45, Çatalkaya Apt Daire 9, 80200 Nişantaşi, Istanbul, Turkey (home). *Telephone:* (1) 1483087 (home). *Fax:* (1) 1483087 (home). *E-mail:* gulten@gultendayioglu.com. *Website:* www.gultendayioglu.com.

DÉ, Shobhaa; Indian writer, journalist and editor; b. (Shobha Rajadhyaksha), 7 Jan. 1948, Satara, Maharashtra; m. 1st (divorced); m. 2nd Dilip Dé 1984; two s. four d. *Education:* Queen Mary's School, St Xavier's Coll., Mumbai. *Career:* fmr model; later copywriter; launched India's first gossip magazine Stardust; also launched magazines Society, Celebrity and TV soap-opera Swabhimaan 1995; columnist, Times of India, Statesman, Sunday Observer; Publisher, Shobha Dé Books, Penguin India 2010–. *Publications include:* Socialite Evenings 1989, Sisters 1992, Strange Obsessions 1993, Uncertain Liaisons 1993, Shooting From the Hip: Selected Writings 1994, Sultry Days 1994, Snapshots 1995, Small Betrayals (short stories) 1995, Second Thoughts 1996, Surviving Men 1998, Selective Memory: Stories From My Life 1998, Speedpost 1999, Socialite Evenings 2005, Sisters 2005, Starry Nights 2005, Spouse: The Truth about Marriage 2005, Superstar India 2008, Sandhya's Secret 2009, articles and columns in newspapers and magazines. *Honours:* Kelvinator GR8! Women Awards 2007. *Address:* c/o Marketing and Promotions Department, Penguin Books India Pvt. Ltd, 11 Community Centre, Panchsheel, Park, New Delhi 110 017, India (office). *E-mail:* publicity@in.penguingroup.com (office). *Website:* www.penguinbooksindia.com; shobhaade.blogspot.com.

DE ARAUGO, Sarah Therese (Tess); Australian writer; b. 26 May 1930, Lismore, Vic.; d. of Ivor O'Mullane and Rose Ryan; m. Maurice De Araugo 1950; two s. two d. *Education:* Notre Dame de Sion Coll., Warragal, Vic., Stotts Business Coll., Melbourne. *Career:* proprietor various businesses 1954–2002; Publisher, Rose Publishing House 1993–2002; mem. Australian Soc. of Authors, Genealogical Soc. of Vic. *Radio:* participated in radio serials, 3UL Warragul, Gippsland, Vic.. *Publications include:* You Are What You Make Yourself To Be 1980, The Kurnai of Gippsland 1985, Boonorong on the Mornington Peninsula 1993, Dear Feathers 2000, Short Stories 1997–2005; contrib. to encyclopaedias and periodicals. *Honours:* New South Wales Premier's Award for Australian Literature 1985, Nat. Book Council Banjo Award in Australian Literature 1985, Australian Literature Bd Fellowship 1987, Writer's Grant 1989, PEN Int. Short Story Award, Australia 1991, Red Cross Award for Essay Red Cross in Wartime. *Address:* 161 Sixth Avenue, Rosebud, Vic. 3939, Australia (home). *Telephone:* (59) 865632 (home).

DE BELOT, Jean Marie Louis, MA; French journalist and editor; b. 15 Dec. 1958, Neuilly-sur-Seine; s. of Philippe de Belot and Claude de Belot (née Vimal-Dessaignes); m. Frédérique Brunet 1983; two s. three d. *Education:* Univ. of Paris II-Panthéon Assas. *Career:* journalist, La Tribune de l'economie 1984; journalist then Chief Econ. Reporter, Le Figaro 1985, Chief Reporter, Expansion Group 1987, Chief of Financial Services 1990, Editorial Dir 2000–04; Jt Chief Ed. Les Echos 1992, Chief Econ. Ed. 1998; Vice-Pres. and Partner Euro RSCG 2005–07; f. Aria Partners (public relations co.) 2007. *Publications:* La chute d'un agent de change: L'affaire Baudouin 1989. *Address:* Aria Partners, 3, Avenue Hoche , 75008 Paris, France. *Website:* www.aria-partners.com.

DE BENOIST, Alain, (Fabrice Laroche, Robert de Herte); French journalist, essayist, philosopher and lecturer; b. 11 Dec. 1943, Saint-Symphorien; s. of Alain de Benoist and Germaine de Benoist (née Langouet); m. Doris M. Christians 1972; two s. *Education:* Lycées Montaigne et Louis-le-Grand, Paris, Sorbonne, Paris. *Career:* Ed.-in-Chief, L'Observateur européen 1964–68, Nouvelle Ecole 1969–, Midi-France 1970–71; journalist, L'Echo de la presse et de la publicité 1968, Courrier de Paul Dehème 1969–76; critic, Valeurs actuelles and Spectacle du monde 1970–2012, Figaro-Magazine 1977–92; Dir, Krisis 1988–; mem. several socs, research groups, etc. *Publications include:* Les Indo-Européens 1966, L'Empirisme logique et la Philosophie du Cercle de Vienne 1970, Avec ou sans Dieu 1970, Morale et Politique de Nietzsche 1974, Vu de droite: Anthologie critique des idées contemporaines 1977, Les Idées à l'endroit 1979, Guide pratique des prénoms 1980, Comment peut-on être paien? 1981, Feter Noël 1982, Orientations pour des années décisives 1982, Traditions d'Europe 1983, Démocratie: Le problème 1985, Europe, Tiers monde, même combat 1986, Le Grain de sable 1994, La Ligne de mire 1995, L'Empire intérieur 1995, Céline et l'Allemagne 1996, Famille et société 1996, Ernst Jünger 1997, L'écume et les galets 2000, Dernière année 2002, Critiques-Théoriques 2003, Au-delà des droits de l'homme 2004, Bibliographie Carl Schmitt 2004, Bibliographie générale des droites françaises 2004–05, Nous et les autres 2006, C'est-à-dire 2006, Jésus et ses frères 2006, Carl Schmitt actuel, Demain la décroissance 2007, Dictionnaire des prénoms 2009, Au temps des idéologies à la mode 2009, International Carl-Schmitt-Bibliographie 2010, Cartouches 2010, Des animaux et des hommes 2011, Au bord du gouffre 2011; contribs to various publs. *Honours:* Grand prix de l'essai de l' Acad. française 1978. *Address:* 5 rue Carrière-Mainguet, 75011 Paris, France (office). *Telephone:* 1-40-24-25-11 (office). *E-mail:* alain.de.benoist@free.fr (office). *Website:* www.alaindebenoist.com.

DE BERNIÈRES, Louis, BA, MA, PGCE; British writer; b. (Louis Henry Piers de Bernière-Smart), 8 Dec. 1954, London; s. of Maj. Reginald Piers Alexander de Bernière-Smart. *Education:* Bradfield Coll., Berkshire, Univ. of Manchester, Leicester Polytechnic, Inst. of Educ., Univ. of London. *Career:* landscape gardener 1972–73; teacher and rancher, Colombia 1974; philosophy tutor 1977–79; car mechanic 1980; English teacher 1981–84; bookshop asst 1985–86; supply teacher 1986–93; mem. Antonius Players 2003–; mem. PEN. *Publications:* The War of Don Emmanuel's Nether Parts 1990, Señor Vivo and the Coca Lord 1991, The Troublesome Offspring of Cardinal Guzman 1992, Captain Corelli's Mandolin 1994, Labels 1997, The Book of Job 1999, Gunter Weber's Confession 2001, Sunday Morning at the Centre of the World 2001, Red Dog 2001, Birds Without Wings 2004, A Partisan's Daughter 2008, Notwithstanding 2009; contrib. to Second Thoughts, Granta. *Honours:* Hon. Fellow, Trinity Coll. of Music; Dr hc (Univ. of East Anglia, Deree Univ. of Athens, Univ. of Aberdeen, Inst. of Educ., London); Granta Best of Young British Novelists 1994, Author of the Year Award 1997, Whittaker Platinum Award, Millepages Prize for Best Foreign Novel (France) 2006. *Literary Agent:* Lavinia Trevor Agency, 29 Addison Place, London W11 4RJ, England. *Telephone:* (1986) 788665.

DE BONO, Edward Francis Charles Publius, DPhil, PhD; British author and academic; b. 19 May 1933, s. of the late Prof. Joseph de Bono and of Josephine de Bono (née O'Byrne); m. Josephine Hall-White 1971; two s. *Education:* St Edward's Coll., Malta, Royal Univ. of Malta and Christ Church, Oxford. *Career:* Research Asst, Univ. of Oxford 1958–60, Jr Lecturer in Medicine 1960–61; Asst Dir of Research, Dept of Investigative Medicine, Univ. of Cambridge 1963–76, Lecturer in Medicine 1976–83; Dir Cognitive Research Trust, Cambridge 1971–; Sec.-Gen. Supranational Independent Thinking Org. 1983–; f. Edward de Bono Nonprofit Foundation; Chair. Council, Young Enterprise Europe 1998–; creator of two TV series: The Greatest Thinkers 1981, de Bono's Thinking Course 1982; apptd EU Amb. for Thinking for the Year of Creativity 2009. *Publications:* The Use of Lateral Thinking 1967, The Five-Day Course in Thinking 1968, The Mechanism of Mind 1969, Lateral Thinking: A Textbook of Creativity 1970, The Dog Exercising Machine 1970, Technology Today 1971, Practical Thinking 1971, Lateral Thinking for Management 1971, Children Solve Problems 1972, Po: Beyond Yes and No 1972, Think Tank 1973, Eureka: A History of Inventions 1974, Teaching Thinking 1976, The Greatest Thinkers 1976, Wordpower 1977, The Happiness Purpose 1977, The Case of the Disappearing Elephant 1977, Opportunities: A Handbook of Business Opportunity Search 1978, Future Positive 1979, Atlas of Management Thinking 1981, de Bono's Thinking Course 1982, Conflicts: A Better Way to Resolve Them 1985, Six Thinking Hats 1985, Letter to Thinkers 1987, I Am Right You Are Wrong 1990, Positive Revolution for Brazil 1990, Six Action Shoes 1991, Serious Creativity 1992, Teach Your Child to Think 1992, Water Logic 1993, Parallel Thinking 1994, Teach Yourself to Think 1995, Mind Pack 1995, Edward de Bono's Textbook of Wisdom 1996, How to be More Interesting 1997, Simplicity 1998, New Thinking for the New Millennium 1999, Why I Want to be King of Australia 1999, The Book of Wisdom 2000, The de Bono Code 2000, H+ (Plus) A New Religion 2006, Tactics: The Art and Science of Success 2007, How to Have Creative Ideas 2007, Six Frames for Looking at Information, Think–Before it is too late 2009, Reversed Quotations; numerous publs in Nature, Lancet, Clinical Science, American Journal of Physiology. *Honours:* Hon. Registrar St Thomas' Hosp. Medical School, Harvard Medical School; Hon. Consultant Boston City Hosp. 1965–66; planet DE73 named edebono after him. *Address:* Cranmer Hall, Fakenham, Norfolk, NR21 9HX, England (home); L2 Albany, Piccadilly, London, W1V 9RR (office). *Website:* www.edwarddebono.com.

DE BORTOLI, Ferruccio; Italian journalist; *Editor-in-Chief, Corriere della Sera, RCS MediaGroup*; b. 20 May 1953, Milan; s. of Giovanni De Bortoli and

Giancarla Soresini; m. Elisabetta Cordani 1982; one s. one d. *Education:* Univ. of Milan. *Career:* journalist 1973–; mem. editorial staff, Corriere d'Informazione 1975–78; Econs Corresp. Corriere della Sera, RCS MediaGroup 1978–85, Ed.-in-Chief, Econs Section 1987–93, Deputy Ed. 1993–96, Ed. 1997–2003, Ed.-in-Chief 2009–; Ed.-in-Chief, L'Europeo (magazine) 1985–86; apptd CEO RCS Libri 2003; apptd Pres. Flammarion 2003; Dir Il Sole 24 Ore 2005–09. *Honours:* Renato Fabrizi Benedict Award 2012. *Address:* RCS MediaGroup, Via Angelo Rizzoli 8, 20132 Milan (office); Via Donatello 36, 20131 Milan, Italy (home). *Telephone:* (02) 25841 (office). *Website:* www.rcsmediagroup.it (office).

DE BOTTON, Alain; Swiss writer; b. 20 Dec. 1969, Zürich. *Education:* Gonville and Caius Coll., Cambridge. *Publications:* Essays in Love (aka On Love) 1993, The Romantic Movement: Sex, Shopping, and the Novel 1994, Kiss and Tell 1995, How Proust Can Change Your Life: Not a Novel 1997, The Consolations of Philosophy 2000, The Art of Travel (Charles Veillon European Essay Prize, Switzerland 2003) 2002, Status Anxiety 2004; The Architecture of Happiness 2006, The Pleasures and Sorrows of Work 2009, A Week at the Airport: A Heathrow Diary 2009; contrib. articles, book and television reviews to various periodicals. *Honours:* Chevalier, Ordre des Arts et des Lettres 2003. *Literary Agent:* United Agents, 12–26 Lexington Street, London, W1F 0LE, England. *Telephone:* (20) 3214-0800. *Fax:* (20) 3214-0801. *E-mail:* info@unitedagents.co.uk. *Website:* unitedagents.co.uk.

DE BRUYN, Günter; German writer; b. 1 Nov. 1926, Berlin; one s. *Education:* studied in Berlin. *Career:* mem. Akad. der Künste, Berlin, Deutsche Akad. für Sprache und Dichtung e. v., Darmstadt. *Publications include:* Der Hohlweg 1963, Buridans Esel 1968, Preisverleihung 1972, Das Leben des Jean Paul Richter 1975, Tristan und Isolde 1975, Märkische Forschungen: Erzählung für Freunde der Literaturgeschichte 1978, Im Querschnitt 1979, Babylon 1980, Neue Herlichkeit 1984, Rahels erste Liebe: Rahel Levin und Karl Graf von Finckenstein in ihren Briefen 1985, Frauendienst 1986, Lesefreuden: Uber Bücher und Menschen 1986, Jubelschreie, Trauergesänge: Deutsche Befindlichkeiten 1991, Zwischenbilanz: Eine Jugen in Berlin 1992, Vierzig Jahre: Ein Lebensbericht 1996, Mein Brandenburg 1997, Die Finckensteins 1999, Preußens Luise 2000, Unter den Linden 2003, Abseits 2005, Als Poesie gut 2006. *Honours:* two hon. doctorates; Heinrich Mann Prize 1965, Lion Feuchtwanger Prize 1980, Thomas Mann Prize 1990, Heinrich Böll Prize 1990, Grant Cross of Merit, Federal Republic of Germany 1994, Konrad Adenauer Foundation Prize for Literature 1996, Jacob Grimm German Language Prize 2006, Gleim Literary Prize 2007, Hanns Martin Schleyer Prize 2007, Hoffmann von Fallersleben Prize 2008. *Address:* Blabber 1, 15848 Tauche, Germany (home). *E-mail:* gdebruyn@web.de.

DE CATALDO, Giancarlo; Italian writer and judge; b. 1956, Taranto. *Career:* judge, Criminal Court, Rome. *Play:* Acido fenico 2001. *Publications include:* novels: Nero come il cuore 1989, Contessa 1993, Il padre e lo straniero 1997, Storie di matricidi 1998, Teneri assassini 2000, Romanzo criminale (Premio Scerbanenco) 2002, Fuoco! 2006, Nelle Mani Giuste 2007, Milano, Edizioni Ambiente 2007, L'india, l'elefante e me 2008, Trilogia criminale 2009, Romanzo Criminale 2010, I traditori 2010, La forma della paura 2010; ed: Crimini. *Address:* c/o Einaudi, Via Umberto Biancamento 2, 10121 Turin, Italy. *Website:* www.einaudi.it.

DE CUENCA Y CUENCA, Luis Alberto; Spanish philologist, poet, translator and writer; b. 1950, Madrid. *Education:* Universidad Autónoma de Madrid. *Career:* Prof. of Philology Inst. of Council for Scientific Research, then Publs Dir; literary critic for several publs including El País; Dir Biblioteca Nacional (Nat. Library) 1996–2000; Sec. of State for Culture 2000–04; Academician, Academia de Buenas Letras de Granada 2009–, Real Academia de la Historia 2010–. *Publications include:* Los Retratos 1971, Elsinore 1972, scholia 1978, Necrofilia 1983, Breviora 1984, La Caja de Plata 1985, Seis poemas por amor 1986, El otro sueño 1987, Poesía 1970–89 1990, Nausícaa 1991, El héroe y sus máscaras 1991, 77 Poemas 1992, Willendorf 1992, El hacha y la rosa 1993, El desayuno y otros poemas 1993, Los gigantes de hielo 1994, Animales domésticos 1995, Tres poemas 1996, Por fuertes y fronteras 1996, El bosque y otros poemas 1997, En el país de las maravillas 1997, Los mundos y los días 1998, Alicia 1999, Insomnios 2000, Mitologías 2001, Vamos a ser felices y otros poemas de humor y deshumor 2003, El enemigo oculto 2003, El puente de la espada: poemas inéditos 2003, Diez poemas y cinco prosas 2004, Ahora y siempre 2004, Su nombre era el de todas las mujeres y otros poemas de amor y desamor 2005, La vida en llamas 2006, Poesía 1979–1996 2006, A quemarropa 2006, Manantial 2007, Los mundos y los días : poesía 1970-2002 2007, Héroes y villanos del cómic 2007, En la cama con la muerte 25 poemas fúnebres 2011, Nombres propios 2011. *Honours:* Gran Cruz de Isabel la Católica 2004; Premio de Cultura (Literatura), Madrid 2007. *Address:* c/o Biblioteca Nacional, Paseo de Recoletos 22, 28001 Madrid, Spain.

DE GRASSE TYSON, Neil, BA, PhD; American astrophysicist and writer; *Director, Hayden Planetarium, American Museum of Natural History*; b. 5 Oct. 1958, New York, NY; m.; two c. *Education:* Bronx High School of Science, Univ. of Harvard, Columbia Univ. *Career:* full-time research scientist at Princeton Univ., NJ; essayist for Natural History magazine 1995–; part of cttee studying the future of the US Aerospace Industry 2001, and the Implementation of the US Space Exploration Policy 2004; currently Dir of Hayden Planetarium, American Museum of Natural History, NY; astrophysicist at American Museum of Natural History. *Publications include:* non-fiction: Merlin's Tour of the Universe 1989, Universe Down to Earth 1994, Just Visiting This Planet 1998, The Sky is Not the Limit: Adventures of an Urban Astrophysicist 2000, One Universe: at Home in the Cosmos 2000, Cosmic Horizons: Astronomy at the Cutting Edge (ed.) 2001, City of Stars 2002, My Favorite Universe 2003, Origins: Fourteen Billion Yars of Csmic Eolution (with Donald Goldsmith) 2005, Death by Black Hole 2007, The Pluto Files 2009. *Honours:* Dr hc (York Coll., Univ. of New York) 1997, (Ramapo Coll.) 2000, (Pace Univ.) 2006, (Univ. of Pennsylvania) 2008, (Univ. of Alabama) 2010, (Gettysburg Coll.) 2011; Medal of Excellence, Columbia Univ., New York City, NASA Distinguished Public Service Medal, Klopsteg Memorial Award 2007, Douglas S. Morrow Public Outreach Award 2009, Isaac Asimov Award 2009. *Address:* Department of Astrophysics, American Museum of Natural History, Central Park West at 79th Street, New York, NY 10024, USA (office). *Telephone:* (212) 769-5912 (office). *Fax:* (212) 769-5934 (office). *E-mail:* tyson@amnh.org (office). *Website:* www.haydenplanetarium.org/tyson.

DE GROEN, Alma; New Zealand playwright and screenwriter; b. 1941, Foxton Beach; d. of Archibald Mathers and Eileen Mathers; m. Geoffrey De Groen (divorced); one d. *Career:* moved to Australia 1964; became playwright 1970; Writer-in-Residence, West Australia Inst. of Tech. 1986, Queensland Univ. 1989, Rollins Coll., Fla, USA 1989; dramaturg, Griffin Theatre Co. 1987. *Plays include:* The Joss Adams Show 1970, Perfectly All Right (aka Sweatproof Boy) 1972, The After-Life of Arthur Cravan 1973, Chidley 1977, Going Home 1976, Vocations (also screenplay) 1981, The Rivers of China 1986, The Girl Who Saw Everything 1991, The Woman in the Window 1999, Wicked Sisters 2003. *Television writing:* Man of Letters 1985, Singles, After Marcuse, Rafferty's Rules: The Women 1988. *Radio writing:* Available Light 1991, Stories in the Dark (with Ian D. MacKenzie). *Honours:* Australian Writers' Guild Award for Best TV Adaptation 1985, for Best Stage Play 1993, Premier's Literary Award for Drama in New South Wales and Victoria 1988, Patrick White Literary Award 1998. *Literary Agent:* RGM Associates, PO Box 128, Surry Hills, NSW 2010, Australia. *Telephone:* (2) 9281-3911. *Fax:* (2) 9281-4705. *E-mail:* info@rgm.com.au. *Website:* www.rgm.com.au.

DE GROOT, Albert; Dutch publisher; b. 3 May 1945, Rotterdam; s. of Albertus A. De Groot and Cornelia A. Hess; m. Janetta C. Pasman 1964; one s. one d. *Career:* no formal educ.; Production Man. Rotterdam Univ. Press 1963, Sales Man. 1967; Ed., Elsevier Nederland 1969, Ed.-in-Chief 1972, Vice-Man. 1974; Man. Dir Veen, Luitingh-Sijthoff, Kosmos, Contact 1979, Uitgeverij L. J. Veen BV; Dir Veen Uitgevers Groep. *Address:* Veen Uitgevers Groep, 2160 Wommelgem, Belgium.

DE GRUCHY, John Wesley, BA, BD, MTh, DTh, DSocSci; South African academic, writer and editor; *Professor Emeritus of Christian Studies, University of Cape Town*; b. 18 March 1939, Pretoria; m. Isobel Dunstan; two s. one d. *Education:* Rhodes Univ., Chicago Theological Seminary, Univ. of S Africa, Univ. of Cape Town. *Career:* ordained Minister, United Congregational Church 1961; Pastor, Durban, 1961–68, Johannesburg 1968–73; Dir S African Council of Churches, 1968–73; Lecturer, Univ. of Cape Town 1973–75, Sr Lecturer 1975–80, Assoc. Prof. 1980–86, Robert Selby Taylor Prof. of Christian Studies 1986–2004, Prof. Emer. 2004–, Dir Grad. School in Humanities 2000–03, Sr Research Scholar 2003–; Founder-Ed. Journal of Theology for Southern Africa 1973–; Pres. United Congregational Church 1980–81. *Publications include:* The Church Struggle in South Africa 1979, Apartheid is a Heresy (co-ed. with Charles Villa-Vicencio) 1983, Bonhoeffer and South Africa 1985, Resistance and Hope: South African Essays in Honour of Beyers Naude (co-ed. with Charles Villa-Vicencio) 1985, Cry Justice! Prayers, Meditations, and Readings from South Africa 1986, Theology and Ministry in Context and Crisis: A South African Perspective 1987, Dietrich Bonhoeffer: Witness to Jesus Christ 1987, Reinhold Niebuhr (co-ed. with Larry Rasmussen) 1988, Karl Barth: Theologian of Freedom (co-ed. with Clifford Green) 1989, Karl Rahner: Theologian of the Graced Search for Meaning (co-ed. with Geoffrey Kelly) 1989, Adolf von Harnack: Liberal Theology at Its Height (co-ed. with H. Martin Rumscheidt) 1989, A Southern African Guide to World Religions (co-ed. with Martin Prozesky) 1991, In Word and in Deed: Towards a Practical Theology of Social Transformation: A Framework for Reflection and Training (with Jim Cochrane and Robin Petersen) 1991, Liberating Reformed Theology: A South African Contribution to an Ecumenical Debate 1991, Doing Ethics in Context: South African Perspectives (co-ed. with Charles Villa-Vicencio) 1994, Religion and the Reconstuction of Civil Society (co-ed. with Stephen Martin) 1995, Living Faiths in South Africa (co-ed. with Martin Prozesky) 1995, Christianity and Democracy 1995, Bonhoeffer for a New Day: Theology in a Time of Transition (co-ed.) 1997, The Cambridge Companion to Dietrich Bonhoeffer 1999, Facing the Truth: South African Faith Communities and the Truth and Reconciliation Commission (co-ed. with Jim Cochrane and Stephen Martin) 1999, The London Missionary Society in Southern Africa: Historical Essays in Celebration of the Bicentenary of the LMS in Southern Africa, 1799–1999 (co-ed.) 2000, Christianity, Art, and Transformation 2001, Reconciliation (monograph) 2002, Confessions of a Christian Humanist 2006, On Being Human 2007, Christianity and the Modernisation of South Africa 2009; contribs to scholarly journals. *Honours:* Hon. DLitt (Chicago Theological Seminary) 2002, (Rhodes Univ.) 2004. *Address:* Research Office, University of Cape Town, Post Bag Rondebosch 7701, Cape Town (office); PO Box 130, Hermanus 7200, South

Africa (home). *Telephone:* (28) 3130844 (home). *Fax:* (28) 3130844 (home). *E-mail:* jwdeg@global.co.za.

DE KRETSER, Michelle, MA; Australian writer; b. Colombo, Sri Lanka. *Education:* Melbourne Univ., Univ. of the Sorbonne, Paris, France. *Career:* moved to Australia aged 14; fmrly teacher in Montpellier, ed. for Lonely Planet, freelance ed. *Publications include:* fiction: The Rose Grower 1999, The Hamilton Case (Commonwealth Writers Prize, SE Asia and South Pacific Region 2004) 2003, The Lost Dog 2007 (New South Wales Premier's Literary Award 2008); ed.: Brief Encounters: Stories of Love, Sex and Travel 1998. *Address:* c/o Allen and Unwin, PO Box 8500, St Leonards, NSW 1590, Australia. *Website:* www.allenandunwin.com.

DE LA BILLIÈRE, Gen. Sir Peter (Edgar de la Cour), Kt, KCB, KBE, DSO, MC, DL; British army officer (retd) and banker (retd); b. 29 April 1934, Plymouth; s. of Surgeon Lt-Commdr Claude Dennis Delacour de Labillière and Frances Christing Wright Lawley; m. Bridget Constance Muriel Goode 1965; one s. two d. *Education:* Harrow School, Staff Coll., Royal Coll. of Defence Studies. *Career:* joined King's Shropshire Light Infantry 1952; commissioned, Durham Light Infantry; served Japan, Korea, Malaya (despatches 1959), Jordan, Borneo, Egypt, Aden, Gulf States, Sudan, Oman, Falkland Islands; Commdg Officer, 22 Special Air Service (SAS) Regt 1972–74; Gen. Staff Officer 1 (Directing Staff), Staff Coll. 1974–77; Commdr British Army Training Team, Sudan 1977–78; Dir SAS and Commdr SAS Group 1978–83; Commdr British Forces, Falkland Islands and Mil. Commr 1984–85; Gen. Officer Commdg Wales 1985–87; Col Comdt. Light Div. 1986–90; Lt-Gen. Officer commanding SE Dist 1987–90; Commdr British Forces in Middle East Oct. 1990–91; rank of Gen. 1991 after Gulf War, Ministry of Defence Adviser on Middle East 1991–92; retd from army June 1992; Pres. SAS Asscn 1991–96, Army Cadet Force 1992–99; mem. Council Royal United Services Inst. 1975–77; Chair. Jt Services Hang Gliding 1986–88; Cdre Army Sailing Asscn 1989–90; Commr Duke of York's School 1988–90; Freeman City of London 1991; Hon. Freeman Fishmongers' Co. 1991; Pres. Harrow School Asscn 2002–; Trustee Imperial War Museum 1992–99; Dir (non-exec.), Middle East and Defence Adviser, Robert Fleming Holdings 1992–99; Chair. Meadowland Meats 1994–2002; Jt Chair. Dirs FARM Africa 1995–2001 (mem. Bd 1992–2001); DL Hereford and Worcester 1993; Trustee Naval and Mil. Club 1999–2003, mem. Bd 1999–2003; Pres. Friends of Imperial War Museum 2003; Pres. Harrow Asscn 2002–. *Television:* Discovery: Clash of the Generals 2004. *Publications:* Storm Command: a personal story of the Gulf War 1992, Looking for Trouble (autobiog.) 1994, Supreme Courage: Heroic Stories from 150 Years of the Victoria Cross 2004. *Honours:* Hon. DSc (Cranfield) 1992; Hon. DCL (Durham) 1993; Legion of Merit Chief Commdr (USA), Order of Abdul Aziz 2nd Class (Saudi Arabia), Meritorious Service Cross (Canada), Kuwait Decoration of the First Class, Order of Qatar Sash of Merit.

DE LA MARTINIÈRE, Hervé; French publisher; *President and CEO, Groupe La Martinière.* *Career:* fmrly in sales, Hachette; fmr Ed., Hachette Littérature, Hachette-Réalités, Nathan; f. Editions La Martinière 1992–, currently Pres. and CEO Groupe La Martinière; CEO Editions du Seuil 2005–06. *Address:* Groupe La Martinière, 2 rue Christine, 75006 Paris, France (office). *Telephone:* 1-40-51-52-00 (office). *Fax:* 1-40-51-52-05 (office). *Website:* www.lamartinieregroupe.com (office).

DE LANGE, Nicholas Robert Michael, DPhil, PhD, DD; British scholar and translator; *Professor of Hebrew and Jewish Studies, University of Cambridge;* b. 7 Aug. 1944, Nottingham, Notts., England. *Education:* Christ Church, Oxford, Univ. of Cambridge. *Career:* Prof. of Hebrew and Jewish Studies, Univ. of Cambridge, Fellow, Wolfson Coll.; mem. British Asscn of Jewish Studies, European Asscn of Jewish Studies, Soc. of Authors, Translation Asscn. *Publications include:* Apocrypha 1978, Atlas of the Jewish World 1984, Judaism 1986, Illustrated History of the Jewish People 1997, An Introduction to Judaism 2000, Ignaz Maybaum: A Reader 2001, Penguin Dictionary of Judaism 2008; numerous trans.; contrib. to Tel-Aviv Review, Jerusalem Review. *Honours:* George Webber Prize for Trans. 1990, TLS/Porjes Prize for Trans. 2001, 2004, Risa Domb/Porjes Prize for Translation from Hebrew 2007. *Address:* Faculty of Divinity, West Road, Cambridge, CB3 9BS, England (office). *Telephone:* (1223) 763019 (office). *E-mail:* nrml1@cam.ac.uk (office).

DE LINT, Charles Henri Diederick Hoefsmit, (Samuel M. Key); Canadian writer, musician and artist; b. 22 Dec. 1951, Bussum, The Netherlands; m. MaryAnn Harris 1980. *Career:* owner and Ed., Triskell Press; Writer-in-Residence, Ottawa and Gloucester Public Libraries 1995; mem. Science Fiction and Fantasy Writers of America, Science Fiction Writers of Canada. *Publications include:* De Grijze Roos 1983, The Riddle of the Wren 1984, Moonheart: A Romance 1984, The Harp of the Grey Rose 1985, Mulengro: A Romany Tale 1985, Yarrow: An Autumn Tale 1986, Ascian in Rose 1987, Jack the Giant-Killer (Canadian SF/Fantasy Award for Best Work in English 1988) 1987, Greenmantle 1988, Wolf Moon 1988, Svaha 1989, The Valley of Thunder (Philip José Farmer's The Dungeon Vol. 3) 1989, Berlin 1989, Westlin Wind 1989, The Hidden City (Philip José Farmer's The Dungeon Vol. 5) 1990, The Fair in Emain Macha 1990, Drink Down the Moon 1990, Ghostwood 1990, Angel of Darkness (as Samuel M. Key) 1990, The Dreaming Place 1990, The Little Country (New York Public Library's Best Books for the Teen Age 1992, Homer Award for Best Fantasy Novel 1992) 1991, Uncle Dobbin's Parrot Fair 1991, Ghosts of Wind and Shadow 1991, Death Leaves an Echo 1991, Hedgework and Guessery 1991, Our Lady of the Harbour 1991, Paperjack 1991, Spiritwalk 1992, Merlin Dreams in the Mondream Wood 1992, From a Whisper to a Scream (as Samuel M. Key) 1992, I'll Be Watching You (as Samuel M. Key) 1992, Dreams Underfoot 1993, The Wishing Well 1993, Into the Green 1993, The Wild Wood 1994, Memory & Dream 1994, The Ivory and the Horn 1995, Jack of Kinrowan (YALSA Popular Paperbacks for Young Adults 2003) 1997, Trader (YALSA Best Books for Young Adults 1999) 1997, Someplace to be Flying 1998, Moonlight and Vines (World Fantasy Award for Best Collection 2000) 1999, The Newford Stories 1999, The Buffalo Man 1999, Forests of the Heart 2000, Triskell Tales 2000, The Road to Lisdoonvarna 2001, The Onion Girl 2001, Seven Wild Sisters (YALSA Best Books for Young Adults 2003) 2002, Waifs and Strays 2002, Tapping the Dream Tree 2002, A Circle of Cats 2003, A Handful of Coppers 2003, Spirits in the Wires 2003, Refinerytown 2003, Medicine Road 2004, The Blue Girl (YALSA Best Books for Young Adults 2005, Ontario Library Asscn White Pine Award for Best Canadian young adult fiction 2006, Great Lakes Great Books Award 2007) 2004, Quicksilver & Shadow 2005, The Hour Before Dawn 2005, Make A Joyful Noise 2006, Triskell Tales 2 2006, Widdershins 2006, Promises to Keep 2007, Old Man Crow 2007, Little (Grrl) Lost 2007, Dingo 2008, What the Mouse Found 2008, Yellow Dog 2008, Woods and Waters Wild 2009, The Onion Girl 2009, The Mystery of Grace 2009, Medicine Road 2009, Eyes Like Leaves 2009, Muse and Reverie 2009, The Very Best of Charles de Lint 2010, The Painted Boy 2010. *Honours:* Small Press and Artists Org. Award for Fiction 1982, Int. Asscn for the Fantastic in the Arts William L. Crawford Award for Best New Fantasy Author 1984, Readercon Small Press Award for Best Short Work 1989, Reality 1 Commendations Best Fantasy Author Award (for The Drowned Man's Reel) 1991, Prix Ozone for Best Foreign Fantasy Short Story (for Timeskip) 1997. *Address:* PO Box 9480, Ottawa, ON K1G 3V2, Canada (office). *Fax:* (613) 521-1221 (office). *E-mail:* cdl@charlesdelint.com (office). *Website:* www.charlesdelint.com.

DE LUCA, Erri; Italian writer and journalist; b. 1950, Naples. *Career:* self-taught ancient Hebrew, has translated several sections of the Bible. *Publications include:* Non ora, non qui 1989, Variazioni sopra una nota sola – Lettere a Francesca 1990, Una nuvola come tappeto 1991, Aceto, arcobaleno 1993, In alto a sinistra 1994, Pianoterra 1995, Ora prima 1997, Alzaia 1997, Tu, mio 1999, L'urgenza della libertà 1999, Cattività 1999, Tre cavalli 2000, Un papavero rosso all'occhiello senza coglierne il fiore 2000, Elogio del massimo timore 2000, Altre prove di risposta 2000, Montedidio (Prix Femina étranger 2003) 2001, Lettere da una città bruciata 2002, Opera sull'acqua e altre poesie (poetry) 2002, Nocciolo d'oliva 2002, L'ultimo viaggio di Sindbad 2003, Il contrario di uno 2003, Immanifestazione 2003, Mestieri all'aria aperta 2004, Morso di luna nuova (written in Neapolitan dialect) 2004, Precipitazioni 2004, Solo andata. Righe che vanno troppo spesso a capo (poetry) 2005, Chisciottimista 2005, Sulla traccia di Nives 2005, In nome della madre 2006, Napolide 2006, Chisciotte e gli invincibili 2007, Sottosopra 2007, Lettere fratterne 2007, Pianoterra 2008, L'isola è una conchiglia 2008, Senza sapere invece 2008, Almerno 5 2008, Il cielo in una stalla 2008, L'ospite incallito (poetry) 2008, Il giorno primo della felicità 2009, Il peso della farfalla 2009, Tu non c'eri 2010, E disse 2011. *Address:* c/o Giangiacomo Feltrinelli Editore s.r.l., via Andegari 6, 20121 Milan, Italy. *E-mail:* scrivimi@feltrinelli.it. *Website:* www.feltrinellieditore.it.

DE MADARIAGA, Isabel, PhD, FBA, FRHistS; British historian, academic and writer; *Professor Emerita of Russian Studies, School of Slavonic and East European Studies, University of London;* b. 27 Aug. 1919, Glasgow, Scotland; d. of Salvador de Madariaga and Constance Archibald; m. Leonard B. Schapiro 1943 (divorced 1976). *Education:* Ecole Internationale, Geneva, Switzerland, Headington School for Girls, Oxford, Instituto Escuela, Madrid, Univ. of London. *Career:* with BBC Monitoring Service 1940–43; with Cen. Office of Information London 1943–47, Econ. Information Unit, Treasury 1947–48; Editorial Asst, Slavonic and East European Review 1951–64; Part-time Lecturer in History, LSE 1953–66; Lecturer in History, Univ. of Sussex 1966–68; Sr Lecturer in Russian History, Univ. of Lancaster 1968–71; Reader in Russian Studies, School of Slavonic and East European Studies, Univ. of London 1971–81, Prof. 1981–84, Prof. Emer. 1984–; Corresp. mem. Royal Spanish Acad. of History. *Publications:* Britain, Russia and the Armed Neutrality of 1780 1963, Opposition (with G. Ionescu) 1965, Russia in the Age of Catherine the Great 1981, Catherine II: A Short History 1990, Politics and Culture in Eighteenth-Century Russia 1998, Ivan the Terrible 2005; books translated into many languages including Turkish and Russian; many scholarly articles. *Address:* 25 Southwood Lawn Road, London, N6 5SD, England (home). *Telephone:* (20) 8341-0862 (home).

DE MOOR, Margriet; Dutch novelist; b. 21 Nov. 1941. *Career:* fmr singer; started writing 1988. *Publications include:* Op de rug gezien (short stories, trans. as Seen From Behind) 1988, Dubbelportret (short stories, trans. as Double Portrait) 1989, Eerst grijs dan wit dan blauw (novel, trans. as First Grey Then White Then Blue) (Ako Literature Prize) 1991, De virtuoos (novel, trans. as The Virtuoso) 1993, Ik droom dus (short stories) 1995, Hertog van Egypte (novel, trans. as The Duke of Egypt) 1996, Zee-Binnen (novel, trans. as Sea Island) 1999, Verzamelde verhalen (collection) 2000, Kreutzersonate (novel, trans. as The Kreutzer Sonata) 2001, De Verdronkene (novel) 2005, De Virtuosos en Kreutzersonate 2005, De Kegelwerper (novel) 2006, Als een hond een blinde baas (essays) 2007, De schilder en het meisje (novel) 2010. *Honours:* Lucy B. and C. W. van der Hoogt Prize 1990. *Address:* c/o Uitgeverij Contact, Keizersgracht 205, 1016 Amsterdam, The Netherlands. *Website:* www.uitgeverijcontact.nl; www.margrietdemoor.nl.

DE NAPOLI, Francesco, DScS; Italian writer, poet and librarian; b. 15 June 1954, Potenza; m. Assunta Cardile 1987; two d. *Career:* Dir Istituto 'A. Labriola', Cassino; Pres. Giuria Premio Letterario Internazionale 'Succisa Virescit'. *Publications include:* poetry: Noùmeno e realtà 1979, Fernfahrplan 1980, La dinamica degli eventi 1983, L'attesa 1987, Il pane di Siviglia 1989, Urna d'amore 1992, Dialogo serale 1993, Poesie per Urbino 1996, Nel tempo, a Zenja 1998, Carte da gioco 1999, La Casa del Porto 2002, La dimensione del noùmeno 2003; essays: Contagi 1990, Giogo/forza 2000, Welfare all'Italiana 2011; contrib. to anthologies: Dossier Poesia 1993, Poeti di Paideia 1994, Ciò che non siamo. Omaggio a Eugenio Montale nel centenario della nascita 1996, Il Fiore del deserto 1998, Ritmo Cassinese 2000, Rocco Scotellaro oltre il Sud 2003; prose: Banalità 1994, Animatore d'ombre 1996; essay collections: La letteratura di protesta del Novecento in Europa e in America 1990, Breve Profilo della Poesia Italiana del secondo Novecento 1993, Del mito, del simbolo e d'altro. Cesare Pavese e il suo tempo 2000, Graffiti poetici 2000, Evgenij Evtushenko cantore dei mali del mondo 2002, Per una cultura del libro 2003; contrib. to various publs. *Honours:* Hon. Prof. of Italian Literature, Brussels 1993; Hon. PhD (Paris) 1994, (Massachusetts) 1995; Premio Città di Valletta, Premio David, Premio Albatros, Premio Cultura della Presidenza del Consiglio dei Ministri 1982, Premio Monferrato 1982, Premio Firenze Capitale Europea della Cultura 1986, Premio Casentino 1990, Premio Goffredo Parise 1998, Premio Luci de Ciociaria 1998, Premio Eugenio Montale 1998. *Address:* Via Belvedere 21, Località Foresta, 03044 Cervaro, Frosinone, Italy (home). *E-mail:* fdenapoli@libero.it. *Website:* www.francescodenapoli.it.

DE PALCHI, Alfredo; Italian poet and editor; b. 13 Dec. 1926, Verona; m. 1st Sonia Raiziss 1952 (deceased); one d.; m. 2nd Rita Di Pace 1988. *Career:* fmr Ed. Chelsea Publications Inc.; Trustee, Sonia Raiziss Giop Charitable Foundation. *Publications include:* Modern European Poetry, Italian section (co-ed.) 1966, Sessioni con l'analista (poems) 1967, in English as Sessions with My Analyst 1970, Mutazioni (poems) 1988, The Scorpion's Dark Dance (poems) 1993, Costellazione Anonima (poems) 1998, in English as Anonymous Constellation 1997, The Metaphysical Streetcar Conductor: Sixty Poems by Luciano Erba 1998, Addictive Aversions (poems) 1999, Paradigma (poems) 2001, Paradigma, Tutte le poesie: 1947–2005 (poems) 2006. *Honours:* Premio Nazionale di Poesia, Città di S. Vito al Tagliamento 1988. *Address:* 33 Union Square West, New York, NY 10003, USA.

DE POSADAS, Carmen; Uruguayan writer; b. 13 Aug. 1953, Montevideo; d. of Luis de Posadas and Sara de Posadas; m. 1st (divorced); two d.; m. 2nd Mariano Rubio (died 1979). *Education:* British Schools in Uruguay and Madrid, Spain and St Julian's Convent, Oxford, UK. *Publications include:* Mr North Wind (Ministry of Culture Prize) 1984, Cinco moscas azules 1996, Liliana Broja 1997 (Special Mention, Bologna Fook Fair), Nada es lo que parece 1997, Pequeñas Infamias (Planeta Prize) 1998, Un verano llamado amor 1999, La Belle Oltero (biog.), The Good Servant (novel); 20 works for children, two screenplays; works translated into 22 languages including Japanese, Chinese. *Address:* c/o Editorial Planeta, Jovellanos No. 5, 280141 Madrid, Spain. *Telephone:* (91) 5213860. *Fax:* (91) 5217190. *E-mail:* visiortega@hotmail.com.

DE RIVOYRE, Christine Berthe Claude Denis, LèsL; French writer and journalist; b. 29 Nov. 1921, Tarbes, Hautes-Pyrénées; d. of François de Rivoyre and Madeleine Ballande. *Education:* Instituts du Sacré-Coeur of Bordeaux and Poitiers, Faculté des Lettres de Paris and School of Journalism, Syracuse Univ., NY, USA. *Career:* journalist with Le Monde 1950–55; Literary Ed. of Marie-Claire 1955–65; mem. Haut comité de la langue française 1969–, Jury of Prix Médicis 1970–. *Publications include:* L'alouette au miroir 1956, La mandarine 1957, La tête en fleurs 1960, La glace à l'ananas 1962, Les sultans 1964, Le petit matin (Prix Interallié 1968) 1968, Le seigneur des chevaux (with Alexander Kalda) 1969, Fleur d'agonie 1970, Boy (Prix des Trois Couronnes 1973) 1973, Le voyage à l'envers 1977, Belle alliance 1982, Reine-mère 1985, Crépuscule taille unique 1989, Racontez-moi les flamboyants 1995, Archaka 2007. *Honours:* Officier, Légion d'honneur; Officier, Ordre des Arts et des Lettres; Grand Prix de la ville de Bordeaux 1973, Grand Prix littéraire Prince Rainier de Monaco 1982, Prix Paul Morand 1984. *Address:* c/o Editions Grasset, 61 rue des Saints-Pères, 75006 Paris, France; 101 rue Las Yaougues, Onesse et Laharie 40110, France (home).

DE SOUZA, Carl; Mauritian writer; b. 4 March 1949, Rose Hill. *Education:* Royal Coll., Port Louis, Royal Coll., Curepipe and Univ. of London. *Career:* teacher, St Esprit Coll. –1995; Rector St Mary's Coll., Rose Hill 1995–; played badminton for nat. team, later becoming man. of nat. team; fmr Pres. Mauritius Badminton Fed. and Sec.-Gen. African Badminton Fed. *Publications include:* novels: Le Sang de l'Anglais (Prix de l'ACCT) 1993, La Maison qui marchait vers la large (Prix des Mascareignes) 1996, Les Jours Kaya 2000, Ceux qu'on jette à la mer 2001; short stories: La Comète de Halley (Prix Pierre Renaud) 1986, Le Raccourci 1993. *Honours:* Chevalier, Ordre des Arts et des Lettres. *Address:* c/o Editions de l'Olivier, 27 rue Jacob, Paris 75006, France.

DE SOUZA, Eunice, BA, MA, PhD; Indian poet and writer; b. 1 Aug. 1940, Poona. *Education:* Univ. of Mumbai, Marquette Univ., USA. *Career:* Reader in English 1969, Head of Dept of English 1990–2000, St Xavier's Coll., Mumbai. *Publications include:* Folk Tales from Gujarat 1975, Statements (co-ed) 1976, Himalayan Tales 1978, Fix 1979, Women in Dutch Painting 1988, Ways of Belonging: Selected Poems (Poetry Book Soc. Recommendation) 1990, Selected and New Poems 1994, Nine Indian Women Poets (ed.) 1997, Talking Poems 1999, Dangerlok (novel) 2001, Women's Voices (co-ed with Lindsay Pereira) 2002, Dev & Simran: A Novel 2003, 101 Folktales From India (ed) 2004, Purdah: An Anthology (ed) 2004, Early Indian Poetry in English: An Anthology 1829-1947, (ed) 2005, The Satthianadhan Family Album (Sahitya Akademi 2005); has also written several children's books; contrib. to Mumbai Mirror, numerous anthologies. *Address:* c/o Department of English, St Xavier's College, Mumbai 400 001, India.

DE VIGAN, Delphine; French writer; b. March 1966. *Career:* fmr Dir of Studies. *Publications include:* Jours sans Faim (as Lou Delvig) 2001, Les Jolis Garçons 2005, Un Soir de Décembre (Prix Saint–Valentin) 2006, No et Moi (Priz des Libraires 2008) 2007, Sous le manteau 2008, Les Heures souterraines (Prize of Novel Enterprise 2009) 2009. *Address:* c/o Éditions JC Lattès, 17 rue Jacob, 75006 Paris, France. *Telephone:* 1-44-41-74-00. *Fax:* 1-43-25-30-47. *Website:* www.editions-jclattes.fr.

DE WAAL, Edmund, OBE, BA, FRSA; British ceramic artist, potter and writer; b. 1964, Nottingham; s. of Victor de Waal. *Education:* Trinity Hall, Cambridge. *Career:* apprenticed as a potter in Canterbury, Kent 1981–83; studied in Japan; works in 30 int. museum collections; has cr. major installations for Victoria & Albert Museum and Tate Britain; writes on art and ceramics; Sr Research Fellow in Ceramics, Univ. of Westminster, London 2000, 2002, Prof. of Ceramics 2004–. *Exhibitions include:* solo: Galerie Heller, Heidelberg, Germany 1996, Scottish Gallery, Edinburgh, Scotland 1997, Garth Clark Gallery, New York, USA 1997, High Cross House, Dartington Hall Modern Home 1998, Geffrye Museum, London 2001, 2002, Galery Noerby, Copenhagen, Denmark, Blackwell House, Cumbria, Kunstindustri Museum, Copenhagen, Denmark 2004, Millgate Museum, Newark, Nat. Museums and Galleries of Wales, Cardiff 2005, Kettle's Yard, Cambridge, MIMA, Middlesbrough 2007, Cheltenham Art Gallery and Museum, V & A Ceramics Gallery, London 2009, New Art Centre, Roche Court, Wiltshire, Leamington Spa Art Gallery and Museum, Alan Cristea Gallery, London 2010; group exhbns in UK, USA, Denmark Brazil, Netherlands, Germany, France, Japan, Canada, Italy, Korea, Australia and Switzerland 1996–2010. *Publications include:* The Hare with Amber Eyes (Costa Award for Biography) 2010, The Pot Book 2011. *Honours:* Hon. Fellow, Trinity Hall, Cambridge; London Arts Bd Individual Artists Award 1996, British Council Award 1998, Leverhulme Special Research Fellowship 2000, 2002, Ondaatje Prize 2011. *Address:* 6 Parade Mews, Tulse Hill, London, SE27 9AX, England (office). *Telephone:* (20) 8674-1122 (office). *E-mail:* warburtonbland@randomhouse.co.uk (office); studio@edmunddewaal.com (office). *Website:* www.edmunddewaal.com.

DE WAARD, Elly; Dutch poet; b. 8 Sept. 1940, Bergen, North Holland; m. M. Weijters. *Education:* Murmellius Gymnasium, Alkmaar and Univ. of Amsterdam. *Career:* teacher of poetry, Amazone 1983–; Founder-mem., Anna Bijns Foundation and Anna Bijns Prijs (prize for women writers) 1985, De Nieuwe Wilden (The New Wild Ones, group of young female poets) 1988. *Publications include:* Afstand (Distance) 1978, Luwte (Shelter) 1979, Furie (Fury) 1981, Strofen 1983, Een wildernis van verbindingen 1986, Onvoltooiing 1988, Eenzang 1992, Anderling 1998, Zestig 2000, Van cadmium lekken de bossen 2002, De Hemel van Toulouse 2004, Proeven van Moord 2005, In het Halogeen 2009. *Honours:* one of three writers of Best Poem of the Year 2002. *E-mail:* e.de.waard13@kpnplanet.nl (office). *Address:* c/o Uitge-verij De Harmonie, Postbus 3547, 1001 Amsterdam, The Netherlands. *E-mail:* info@ellydewaard.nl (home); e.de.waard13@kpnplanet.nl (office). *Website:* www.ellydewaard.nl.

DE WEESE, Thomas Eugene (Gene), (Jean DeWeese, Thomas Stratton, Victoria Thomas); American writer; b. 31 Jan. 1934, Rochester, IN; m. Beverly Amers 1955. *Education:* Valparaiso Technical Inst., Indiana Univ., Kokomo, Univ. of Wisconsin, Milwaukee, Marquette Univ. *Publications include:* fiction: Jeremy Case 1976, The Wanting Factor 1980, A Different Darkness 1982, Something Answered 1983, Chain of Attack 1987, The Peacekeepers 1988, The Final Nexus 1988, Renegade 1991, Into the Nebula 1995, King of the Dead 1996, Lord of the Necropolis 1997; with Robert Coulson: The Invisibility Affair 1967, The Mind-Twisters Affair 1967, Gates of the Universe 1975 Now You See It/Him/Them… 1976, Charles Fort Never Mentioned Wombats 1977, Nightmare Universe 1985; as Jean DeWeese: The Reimann Curse 1975, The Moonstone Spirit 1975, The Carnelian Cat 1975, Cave of the Moaning Wind 1976, Web of Guilt 1976, The Doll With Opal Eyes 1976, Nightmare in Pewter 1978, Hour of the Cat 1980, The Backhoe Gothic 1981; as Victoria Thomas: Ginger's Wish (with Connie Kugi) 1987; other: Black Suits From Outer Space; several other science fiction novels for children; non-fiction: Fundamentals of Space Navigation 1968, Fundamentals of Digital Computers 1972, Fundamentals of Integrated Circuits 1972, Making American Folk Art Dolls (with Gini Rogowski) 1975, Computers in Entertainment and the Arts 1984; contribs: anthologies and magazines. *Honours:* Best Novel Awards 1976, 1982, Best Juvenile Book Award 1979, Council for Wisconsin Writers, Notable Science Book of the Year, NSTA 1984. *Address:* 2718 North Prospect Avenue, Milwaukee, WI 53211-3768, USA (home). *Telephone:* (414) 332-7306 (home).

DEAMBROSIS, Mercedes; Spanish/Greek novelist; b. 1 Oct. 1955, Madrid, Spain. *Publications include:* Un Après-midi avec Rock Hudson 2001, Milagrosa 2002, Suite et Fin au grand Condé 2002, La Promenade des Délices 2003, La Plieuse de parachutes 2006, Candelaria ne viendra pas 2008, Juste pour le Plaisir 2009, Rien de bien grave 2009. *Address:* c/o Buchet Chastel, 7 rue des Canettes, 75006 Paris, France. *Website:* www.editions-libella.com.

DEAN, Winton Basil, MA, FBA; British musicologist and author; b. 18 March 1916, Birkenhead, Merseyside; s. of Basil Dean and Esther Dean (née Van Gruisen); m. Hon. Thalia Mary Shaw 1939 (died 2000); one s. (two d. deceased) one adopted d. *Education:* Harrow, King's Coll., Cambridge. *Career:* mem. Music Panel, Arts Council of GB 1957–60; Ernest Bloch Prof. of Music, Univ. of California, Berkeley, USA 1965–66, Regent's Lecturer 1977; mem. Council, Royal Musical Asscn 1965–98 (Vice-Pres. 1970–98, Hon. mem. 1998–); mem. Vorstand, GF Händel-Gesellschaft, Halle 1980– (Vice-Pres. 1991–99, Hon. mem. 1999), Kuratorium, Göttinger Händel-Gesellschaft 1982–97, Hon. mem. 1997–; Corresp. mem. American Musicological Soc. *Publications:* Bizet 1948, Carmen 1949, Handel's Dramatic Oratorios and Masques 1959, Shakespeare and Opera 1964, Georges Bizet, His Life and Work 1965, Handel and the Opera Seria 1969 (Japanese trans., revised 2005), The New Grove Handel 1982, Handel's Operas 1704–1726 (with J. M. Knapp) 1987, Essays on Opera 1990, (co-ed.) Handel's Opera Giulio Cesare in Egitto 1999, Handel's Operas 1726–1741 2006; major contribs to New Oxford History of Music, Vol. VIII 1982 and Grove's Dictionary of Music and Musicians, fifth and sixth edns 1954 1980. *Honours:* Hon. RAM; Hon. MusDoc (Cambridge) 1996; City of Halle Handel Prize 1995. *Address:* Hambledon Hurst, Hambledon, Godalming, Surrey, GU8 4HF, England (home). *Telephone:* (1428) 682644 (home). *E-mail:* deans84@aol.com (home).

DEANE, John F.; Irish poet, writer and translator; b. 1943, Achill Island, Co. Mayo. *Education:* Mungret and Univ. Coll. Dublin. *Career:* teacher; re-founded Poetry Ireland and Poetry Ireland Review 1979; Visiting Scholar, Boston Coll., USA 2008; Ed., The Dedalus Press –2005. *Publications include:* poetry: Stalking After Time 1977, High Sacrifice 1981, Winter in Meath 1984, Road with Cypress and Star 1988, The Stylized City: Selected and New Poems 1991, Walking on Water 1994, Toccata and Fugue 2001, Manhandling the Deity 2003, The Instruments of Art 2005, A Little Book of Hours 2008; novels: One Man's Place 1994, Flightlines 1996, Undertow 2002; short story collections: Free Range 1994, The Coffin Master and Other Stories 2000, The Heather Fields and other stories 2007, Where No Storms Come 2010; non-fiction: In Dogged Loyalty 2006, The Eye of the Hare 2011; trans. of works by Marin Sorescu, Tomas Tranströmer and Jacques Rancourt. *Honours:* Chevalier, Ordre des Arts et des Lettres 2007; Robert Penn Warren Prize 2000, Howard Nemerov Sonnet Award 2001, Firman Houghton Award 2002, Robert Frost Award 2002, New Criterion Poetry Prize 2004. *E-mail:* johnfmdeane@gmail.com (home). *Website:* www.johnfdeane.com.

DEANE, Seamus Francis, BA, MA, PhD, MRIA; Irish academic, poet and novelist; *Donald and Marilyn Keough Professor Emeritus of Irish Studies, University of Notre Dame, Indiana;* b. 9 Feb. 1940, s. of Winifred Deane and Frank Deane; m. 1st Marion Treacy 1963; three s. one d.; m. 2nd Emer Nolan; one d. *Education:* Queen's Univ., Belfast, Univ. of Cambridge. *Career:* Fulbright and Woodrow Wilson Scholar, Visiting Lecturer, Reed Coll., Portland, Ore. 1966–67; Visiting Lecturer, Univ. of California, Berkeley 1967–68, Visiting Prof. 1978; Lecturer, Univ. Coll., Dublin 1968–77, Sr Lecturer 1978–80, Prof. of English and American Literature 1980–93; Visiting Prof., Univ. of Notre Dame, Indiana, USA 1977, Donald and Marilyn Keough Prof. of Irish Studies 1993–2005, Prof. Emer. 2005–; Walker Ames Prof., Univ. of Washington, Seattle 1987, Jules Benedict Distinguished Visiting Prof., Carleton Coll., Minn. 1988; Dir Field Day Theatre Co. 1980–; Ed. Field Day Review 2005–. *Publications:* Gradual Wars (AE Memorial Award for Literature 1972) 1972, Celtic Revivals 1985, Short History of Irish Literature 1986, Selected Poems 1988, The French Revolution and Enlightenment in England 1789–1832 1988, Field Day Anthology of Irish Writing 550–1990 1991, Reading in the Dark (Guardian Fiction Prize 1996, Irish Times Int. Fiction Prize 1997, Irish Times Irish Literature Prize 1997, Ruffino Antico Fattore Int. Literary Award 1998) 1996, Strange Country 1997, Foreign Affections: Essays on Edmund Burke 2005. *Honours:* Hon. DLitt (Ulster) 1999; Ireland/ America Fund Literary Award 1988, South Bank Award for Literature 1997. *Address:* Field Day Publications, c/o Newman House, 86 St Stephen's Green, Dublin 2, Ireland (office). *E-mail:* deane.4@nd.edu (office).

DEAR, Nick, BA; British playwright; b. 11 June 1955, Portsmouth, Hants., England; m. Penny Downie; two s. *Education:* Univ. of Essex. *Career:* Playwright-in-Residence, Univ. of Essex 1985, Royal Exchange Theatre 1987–88; mem. Writer's Guild of GB, Soc. of Authors. *Film screenplays:* The Monkey Parade 1983, The Ranter 1988, Persuasion 1995, The Gambler 1997, The Turn of the Screw 1999, Cinderella 2000, Byron 2003, Eroica 2003, The Hollow 2004, Cards on the Table 2006, Three Act Tragedy 2009. *Television screenplays:* Mrs McGinty's Dead 2008. *Opera libretti:* A Family Affair 1993, Siren Song 1994, The Palace in the Sky 2000. *Publications include:* Temptation 1984, The Art of Success 1986, Food of Love 1988, A Family Affair (after Ostrovsky) 1988, In the Ruins 1989, The Last Days of Don Juan (after Tirso) 1990, Le Bourgeois Gentilhomme (after Molière) 1992, Pure Science 1994, Zenobia 1995, Summerfolk (after Gorky) 1999, The Villains' Opera 2000, The Promise (after Arbuzov) 2002, Power 2003, Lunch in Venice 2005, The Turn of the Screw (after James) 2005, Frankenstein 2011; several radio plays. *Honours:* John Whiting Award 1987, BAFTA Award 1996, Broadcasting Press Guild Award 1996, South Bank Show Theatre Award 1999, Prix Italia 2004. *Address:* c/o Rosica Colin Ltd, 1 Clareville Grove Mews, London, SW7 5AH, England.

DEARDEN, James Shackley; British writer, editor and book collector; b. 9 Aug. 1931, Barrow-in-Furness, Cumbria, England. *Education:* Bembridge School. *Career:* Curator Ruskin Galleries, Bembridge School, Isle of Wight and Brantwood Coniston 1957–96; mem. Ruskin Soc., Turner Soc., Companion of the Guild of St George (fmr Master), Old Bembridgians Asscn (Past Pres.), Isle of Wight Foot Beagles (fmr Master and Pres.), Friends of Ruskin's Brantwood (Hon. Life mem. and Vice-Pres.). *Publications include:* The Professor: Arthur Severn's Memoir of Ruskin 1967, A Short History of Brantwood 1967, Iteriad by John Ruskin (ed.) 1969, Facets of Ruskin 1970, Ruskin and Coniston (with K. G. Thorne) 1971, John Ruskin 1973 (revised edn 2004), Turner's Isle of Wight Sketch Book 1979, John Ruskin e Les Alpi 1989, John Ruskin's Camberwell 1990, A Tour to the Lakes in Cumberland: John Ruskin's Diary for 1830 (ed.) 1990, John Ruskin and Victorian Art 1993, Ruskin, Bembridge and Brantwood 1994, Hare Hunting on the Isle of Wight 1996, John Ruskin, A Life in Pictures 1999, King of the Golden River by John Ruskin (ed.) 1999, John Ruskin, An Illustrated Life 2004, Brantwood: The Story of John Ruskin's Coniston Home 2009, Further Facets of Ruskin 2009, John Ruskin's Guild of St George 2010; contrib. to Book Collector, Connoisseur, Apollo, Burlington, Bulletin of John Rylands Library, Country Life, Ruskin Newsletter (ed.), Ruskin Research Series (gen. ed.), Journal of Pre-Raphaelite Studies (editorial advisory bd), Whitehouse Edition of Ruskin's Works (jt gen. ed.), Friends of Ruskin's Brantwood Newsletter, Ruskin Review and Bulletin. *Honours:* Hon. DLitt (Lancaster) 1998. *Address:* 4 Woodlands, Foreland Road, Bembridge, Isle of Wight, PO35 5RX, England (home).

DEAVER, Jeffery Wilds, DJur; American fmr journalist and novelist; b. 6 May 1950, Chicago, Ill.; s. of Danny Deaver and Dee Deaver. *Education:* Univ. of Missouri, Fordham Law School. *Career:* magazine journalist, lawyer, full-time writer 1990–; charged with writing new James Bond novels. *Television:* As the World Turns (cameo role). *Publications include:* fiction: Voodoo 1987, Manhattan is My Beat 1988, Death of a Blue Movie Star 1990, Hard News 1991, Shallow Graves 1992, Mistress of Justice 1992, Bloody River Blues 1993, The Lesson of her Death 1993, Praying for Sleep 1994, A Maiden's Grave 1995, The Bone Collector 1997, The Coffin Dancer 1998, The Devil's Teardrop 1999, The Empty Chair (WHSmith Thumping Good Read Award 2001) 2000, Speaking in Tongues 2000, Hell's Kitchen 2001, The Blue Nowhere 2001, The Stone Monkey 2002, The Vanished Man 2003, Twisted 2004, Garden of Beasts 2004, The Cold Moon 2006, More Twisted 2007, The Sleeping Doll 2007, The Broken Window 2008, The Bodies Left Behind 2008, Roadside Crosses 2009, The Burning Wire 2010, Edge 2010, Carte Blanche 2012; ed.: A Century of Great Suspense Stories 2001, A Hot and Sultry Night for Crime 2003; non-fiction: The Complete Law School Companion 1992; contrib. to Crimes of the Heart 1995, The Best of the Best 1997, Irreconcilable Differences 1999, The World's Finest Mystery and Crime Stories Vols 1, 3 and 4 2000–03, A Confederacy of Crime 2000, Opening Shots 2 2001, Much Ado About Murder 2002, Men from Boys 2003. *Honours:* two British Crime Writers' Asscn Awards, three Ellery Queen Reader's Awards for Best Short Story of the Year. *Address:* c/o Hodder & Stoughton, 338 Euston Road, London, NW1 3BH, England. *E-mail:* info@jefferydeaver.com. *Website:* www.jefferydeaver.com.

DEBELJAK, Aleš, PhD; Slovenian poet, writer, translator and academic; *Senior Research Fellow, Centre for Cultural and Religious Studies, University of Ljubljana;* b. 25 Dec. 1961, Ljubljana; s. of Pavel Debeljak and Mija Debeljak; m. Erica Johnson; three c. *Education:* Univ. of Ljubljana and Syracuse Univ., USA. *Career:* joined Univ. of Ljubljana 1985, Assistant Prof. 1992–99, Sr Research Fellow, Centre for Cultural and Religious Studies 1995–99, Assoc. Prof. 1999–2005, Prof. 2005–; Recurring Visiting Prof. in European Advanced Interdisciplinary Studies, Coll. d'Europe, Natolin-Warsaw 2005–; Roberta Buffett Visiting Prof. in Int. Studies, Northwestern Univ., USA 2006–07; Gen. Ed. Terra Incognita: Writings from Central Europe book series; Contributing Ed., Trafika: An International Literary Review; Ed. Sarajevo Notebooks magazine; Fellow, Inst. of Advanced Study, Collegium Budapest 1996, Sr Fulbright Fellow, Univ. of California, Berkeley 1997; mem. Advisory Bd Cultural Sociology journal; mem. European Council on Foreign Relations. *Publications include:* poetry: Zamenjave, zamenjave 1982, Imena smrti 1985, Slovar tišine (Dictionary of Silence) 1987, Minute strahu (Anxious Moments) 1992, Mesto in otrok (The City and the Child) 1996, Medokončane hvalnice 2000, Pod gladino 2004, Tihotapci 2009, Without Anesthesia: New and Selected Poems 2011; contrib. numerous poems to anthologies and journals; non-fiction in English trans.: Twilight of the Idols: Recollections of a Lost Yugoslavia 1994, Reluctant Modernity: The Institution of Art and its Historical Forms 1998, The Hidden Handshake: National Identity and Europe in the Post Communist World 2004; ed.: Ameriška metafikcija 1988, Shifting Borders: East European Poetries in the Eighties 1993, Prisoners of Freedom: Contemporary Slovenian Poetry 1994, Selected Poems of Edvard Kocbek 1995, The Imagination of Terra Incognita: Slovenian Writing 1945–95 1997. *Honours:* Slovenian Amb. of Science 2001; Hayden Carruth Poetry Prize 1989, Kristal Vilenica Poetry Award 1990, Preseren Foundation Prize 1990, Miriam Lindberg Israel Poetry for Peace Prize, Tel-Aviv 1996, Chiqyu Poetry Prize, Tokyo 2000, Jenko Poetry Prize 1989, 2009. *Address:* Department of Cultural Studies, School of Social Sciences, University of Ljubljana, Kardeljeva pl. 5, Ljubljana 1000 (office); Zvezna 41, Ljubljana 1000, Slovenia (home). *Telephone:* (1) 5805280 (office). *Fax:* (1) 5805101 (office). *E-mail:* ales.debeljak@fdv.uni-lj.si (office); ales.debeljak@guest.arnes.si. *Website:* www.fdv.uni-lj.si (office); www.fdv-kulturologija.si (office).

DEBRAY, (Jules) Régis; French writer and government official; b. 2 Sept. 1940, Paris; s. of Georges Debray and Janine Alexandre; m. Elisabeth Burgos 1968; one d. *Education:* Ecole normale supérieure de la rue d'Ulm. *Career:* colleague of Che Guevara, imprisoned in Bolivia 1967–70; Co-ed. Comité d'études sur les libertés 1975; adviser on foreign affairs to François Mitterrand; responsible for Third World Affairs, Secr.-Gen. of Presidency of Repub. 1981–84; Office of Pres. of Repub. 1984–85, 1987–88; Maître des requêtes, Conseil d'Etat 1985–93; Sec.-Gen. Conseil du Pacifique Sud 1984–85; Pres. Conseil scientifique de l'École nationale supérieure des sciences de l'information 1998–2002, Institut Européen en Sciences en Religions 2002–04. *Publications:* La Critique des armes 1973, La Guerilla du Che 1974, Entretiens avec Allende 1971, Les Epreuves du fer 1974, L'Indésirable 1975, La Neige brûle (Prix Fémina) 1977, Lettre aux communistes français et á quelques autres 1978, Le Pouvoir intellectuel en France 1979, Le Scribe 1980, Critique de la raison politique 1981, La Puissance et les rêves 1984, Les Empires contre l'Europe 1985, Comète, ma comète 1986, Eloges 1986, Les Masques, une éducation amoreuse 1988, Que vive la République 1988, A demain de Gaulle 1990, Cours de médiologie générale 1991, Christophe Colomb, le visiteur de l'aube: les traités de Tordesillas 1992, Vie et mort de l'image: une histoire du regard en Occident 1992, Contretemps: Eloge des idéaux perdus 1992, Ledannois 1992, L'Etat séducteur 1993, L'Oeil naïf 1994, Manifestes médiologiques 1994, Loués soient les seigneurs 1996, Par amour de l'art 1998, L'Abus monumental 1999, Croire, voir, faire 1999, L'Emprise 2000, i.f. suite et fin 2000, Introduction à la médiologie 2000, L'Enseignement du fait religieux dans l'école laïque 2002, L'Edit de Caracalla ou plaidoyer pour les Etats-Unis d'occident 2002, L'Ancien Testament à travers 100 chefs-d'œuvre de la peinture 2003, Le Nouveau Testament à travers 100 chefs-d'œuvre de la peinture 2003, Dieu, un itinéraire 2003, Haïti et la France: Rapport à Dominique de Villepin, ministre des Affaires étrangères 2004, Le siecle et la règle 2004, Ce que nous voile le voile 2004, La Mythologie gréco-latine à travers 100 chefs-d'oeuvres de la peinture 2004, L'Histoire ancienne à travers 100 chefs-d'oeuvres de la peinture 2004, Chroniques de l'idiotie triomphante 2004, Journal D'Un Petit Bourgeois Entre Deux Feux Et Quatre Murs 2004, Le Plan Vermeil 2004, Le Feu Sacré 2005, Julien Le Fidèle Ou Le Banquet Des Démons 2005, Sur le pont d'Avignon 2005, Aveuglantes Lumières 2006, Supplique Aux Nouveaux Progressistes Du Xxie Siècle 2006. *Address:* c/o Editions Gallimard, 5 rue Sébastien Bottin, 75007 Paris, France (office). *Website:* www.regisdebray.com.

DECAUX, Alain; French historian and television producer; b. 23 July 1925, Lille; s. of Francis Decaux and Louise Tiprez; m. 1st Madeleine Parisy 1957; one d.; m. 2nd Micheline Pelletier 1983; one s. one d. *Education:* Lycée Faidherbe, Lille, Lycée Janson-de-Sailly, Paris and Univ. of Paris. *Career:* journalist 1944–; historian 1947–; cr. radio programme La tribune de l'histoire with André Castelot, Colin-Simard and later Jean-François Chiappe 1951; cr. TV programmes: La caméra explore le temps, with Stellio Lorenzi and André Castelot 1956, Alain Decaux raconte 1969, L'histoire en question 1981, Le dossier d'Alain Decaux 1985; f. magazine L'histoire pour tous 1960; Pres. Groupement syndical des auteurs de télévision 1964–66, 1971–72; Vice-Chair. Société des auteurs et compositeurs dramatiques 1965–67, 1969–71, Chair. 1973–75; Dir Société Técipress 1967–91; Vice-Chair. Syndicat nat. des auteurs et compositeurs 1968–73; Admin. Librairie Plon 1969–72; Dir Historia Magazine 1969–71; worked on various periodicals, including Les nouvelles littéraires, Le Figaro littéraire, Historia, Histoire pour tous, Miroir de l'histoire, Lecture pour tous; Chair. Centre d'animation culturelle des Halles et du Marais (Carré Thorigny) 1971–73; mem. Conseil supérieur des lettres 1974; mem. Man. Cttee, Centre nat. des lettres 1974–75; Minister of Francophone Affairs 1988–91; Policy Co-ordinator, French Overseas TV 1989; elected to Académie Française 1979; Chair. Centre d'action culturelle de Paris 1981–; Chair. Société des amis d'Alexandre Dumas 1971; Pres. Coll. des conservateurs du Château de Chantilly 1998–2009. *Publications:* Louis XVII 1947, Letizia, mère de l'empereur 1949, La conspiration du général Malet 1952, La Castiglione, dame de cœur de l'Europe 1953, La belle histoire de Versailles 1954, De l'Atlantide à Mayerling 1954, Le prince impérial 1957, Offenbach, roi de Second Empire 1958, Amours Second Empire 1958, L'énigme Anastasia 1960, Les heures brillantes de la Côte d'Azur, Les grands mystères du passé 1964, Les dossiers secrets de l'histoire 1966, Grands secrets, grandes énigmes 1966, Nouveaux dossiers secrets 1967, Les Rosenberg ne doivent pas mourir (play) 1968, Grandes aventures de l'histoire 1968, Histoire des Françaises (two vols) 1972, Histoire de la France et des Français (with André Castelot, 13 vols) 1970–74, Le cuirassé Potemkine (co-writer, play) 1975, Blanqui 1976, Les face à face de l'histoire 1977, Alain Decaux raconte (four vols) 1978, 1979, 1980, 1981, L'Histoire en question (two vols) 1982–83, Notre-Dame de Paris (co-writer, play) 1978, Danton et Robespierre (co-writer, play) 1979, Un homme nommé Jésus (co-writer, play) 1983, Victor Hugo (biog.) 1984, Les Assassins 1986, Le Pape pèlerin 1986, Destins fabuleux 1987, Alain Decaux raconte l'Histoire de France aux enfants 1987, L'Affaire du Courrier de Lyon 1987, Alain Decaux raconte la Révolution Française aux enfants 1988, La Liberté ou la mort (co-writer) 1988, La Révolution racontée aux enfants 1988, Alain Decaux raconte Jésus aux enfants 1991, Jésus était son nom (play) 1991, Le Tapis rouge 1992, Je m'appelais Marie-Antoinette (co-writer, play) 1993, Histoires Extraordinaires 1993, Nouvelles histoires extraordinaires 1994, L'abdication 1995, C'était le XXe siècle 1996, Alain Decaux raconte la Bible aux enfants 1996, Monaco et ses princes 1997, La course à l'abîme 1997, La Guerre absolue 1998, De Staline à Kennedy 1999, De Gaulle, celui qui a dit non (co-writer) 1999, Morts pour Vichy 2000, L'Avorton de Dieu: une vie de Saint Paul 2003, Tous les personnages sont vrais (Prix Saint-Simon 2005) 2004, La Révolution de la Croix – Néron et les Chrétiens 2007, Coup d'Etat à l'Elysée 2008, Dictionnaire amoureux d'Alexandre Dumas 2010. *Honours:* Grand Officier, Légion d'honneur, Grand Croix, Ordre nat. du Mérite, Commdr des Arts et des Lettres; Prix d'histoire, Acad. française 1950, Grande médaille d'or, Ville de Versailles 1954, Grand prix du disque for Révolution française 1963, Prix Plaisir de lire 1968, Oscar de la télévision et de la radio 1968, 1973, Prix de la Critique de Télévision 1972, Médaille de vermeil de la Ville de Paris 1973, Prix littéraire de la Paulée de Meursault 1973. *Address:* 86 boulevard Flandrin, 75116 Paris, France (office). *Telephone:* 1-44-05-90-95 (office).

DECLEMENTS, Barthe, BA, MEd; American writer; b. 8 Oct. 1920, Seattle, Wash.; m. 1st Don Macri (divorced); m. 2nd Gordon Greimes (divorced); four c. *Education:* Western Washington Coll., Univ. of Washington, Seattle. *Career:* school teacher 1944–46, 1961–78; high school counselor 1978–83. *Publications include:* Nothing's Fair in Fifth Grade 1981, How Do You Lose Those Ninth Grade Blues? 1983, Seventeen and In-Between 1984, Sixth Grade Can Really Kill You 1985, I Never Asked You to Understand Me 1986, Double Trouble (with Christopher Greimes) 1987, No Place For Me 1987, The Fourth Grade Wizards 1988, Five-Finger Discount 1989, Monkey See, Monkey Do 1990, Wake Me at Midnight 1991, Breaking Out 1991, The Bite of the Gold Bug 1992, The Pickle Song 1993, Tough Loser 1994, Spoiled Rotten 1996, Liar, Liar 1998; contribs: periodicals. *Honours:* more than 25 awards. *Address:* 1511 Russell Road, Snohomish, WA 98290-5624, USA (home).

DEE, Jonathan; American novelist and writer; b. 1962, New York City; m. Denise Shannon; one d. *Education:* Yale Univ. *Career:* fmr Ed. The Paris Review; contributing writer, The New York Times Magazine; teaches in grad. writing programmes at Columbia Univ. and The New School. *Publications:* novels: The Lover of History 1990, St Famous 2002, Palladio 2003, The Liberty Campaign 2004, The Privileges 2010; contrib. to Harper's Magazine. *Address:* c/o The New York Times, 620 Eighth Avenue, New York, NY 10018, USA (office); c/o Curtis Brown, 5th Floor, Haymarket House, 28-29 Haymarket, London SW1Y 4SP, England. *Website:* www.nytimes.com/pages/magazine/index.html.

DEFORD, Frank, BA; American writer and commentator; b. 16 Dec. 1938, Baltimore, Md; m. Carol Penner 1965; one s. two d. *Education:* Princeton Univ. *Career:* Contributing Ed., Sports Illustrated 1962–69, 1998–, Vanity Fair 1993–96; writer and commentator, Cable News Network 1980–86, Nat. Public Radio 1980–89, 1991–, NBC 1986–89, ESPN 1992–96, Real Sports With Bryant Gumbel (HBO) 1996–; Ed.-in-Chief, The National 1989–91; writer, Newsweek Magazine 1991–93, 1996–98. *Film screenplays:* Trading Hearts 1986, Four Minutes 2005. *Publications include:* Five Strides on the Banked Track 1969, Cut 'N' Run 1971, There She Is 1972, The Owner 1974, Big Bill Tilden: The Triumphs and the Tragedy 1977, Everyone's All-American 1981, Alex: The Life of a Child 1982, Spy in the Deuce Court 1987, World's Tallest Midget 1988, Casey on the Loose 1989, Love and Infamy 1993, The Best of Frank Deford 1999, The Other Adonis 2001, An American Summer 2002, The Old Ball Game 2005, The Entitled 2007, Bliss, Remembered 2010, Over Time: My Life as a Sportswriter 2012; contrib. to numerous magazines. *Honours:* Nat. Asscn of Sportswriters and Sportscasters Sportswriter of the Year 1982–88, Emmy Award 1988, Cable Ace 1996, Peabody Award 1999. *Literary Agent:* Sterling Lord Literistic Inc., 65 Bleecker Street, New York, NY 10012, USA.

DEFORGES, Régine Marie Léone, Princess Wiazemsky; French writer and publisher; b. 15 Aug. 1935, Montmorillon (Vienne); d. of Clément Deforges and Bernadette Deforges (née Peyon); one s. one d.; m. 2nd Pierre Wiazemsky 1984; one d. *Education:* Inst St-Martial, Montmorillon. *Career:* bookseller 1960–76; Founder and Chair. Editions l'Or du Temps 1968 (Editions Régine Deforges from 1984); Rep. to Ministry of Culture 1982–83; mem. Comité consultatif de la langue française, PEN-Club; mem. judging panel Prix Femina 1984–; Chair. Soc. des Gens de Lettres de France 1988–, Éditions Ramsay & Régine Deforges 1989–92. *Publications include:* O m'a dit 1975, Blanche et Lucie 1977, Le cahier volé 1978, Contes pervers, Lola et quelques autres 1979, La révolte des nonnes 1981, La bicyclette bleue (three vols) 1982–86, Les enfants de Blanche 1983, Léa aux pays des dragons 1983, 101 avenue Henri Martin 1984, Le diable en rit encore 1985, L'Apocalypse 1985, Pour l'amour de Marie Salat 1986, Le livre du point de croix 1986, Sous le ciel de Novgorod 1988, Ma cuisine 1989, Juliette Gréco 1990, Noir Tango 1990, Rue de la Soie 1994, Roger Stéphane ou la passion d'admirer 1995, La dernière colline 1996, L'orage 1996, Pêle-mêle. Chroniques de l'Humanité 1998, 1999, 2000, Paris Chansons 1998, Cuba libre! 1999, Camilo 1999, Alger, ville blanche 2003, Journal de l'année 2003, Les Généraux du Crepuscule 2004, Le collier de perles 2004, Les poètes et les putains 2004, La hire ou la colère de Jehanne 2005, Deborah, la femme adultère 2011, et quand viendra la fin du voyage 2011, Paris de mes amours 2011, Toutes les femmes s'appellent Marie 2012. *Honours:* Officier, Légion d'honneur 1992, Ordre nat. du Mérite, Commdr, Ordre des Arts et des Lettres 2006; Maisons de la Presse Award 1981. *Address:* 58 rue St André des Arts, 75006 Paris, France (home). *Telephone:* 1-43-25-13-47 (home). *Fax:* 1-43-54-39-16 (home). *E-mail:* rdeforgessec@netcourrier.com.

DEGUY, Michel; French poet, writer and editor; *Professor Emeritus, Université de Paris;* b. 23 May 1930, Paris. *Education:* studied in Paris. *Career:* Ed. Poésie 1972–; Univ. Prof., Paris; currently Prof. Emer., Université de Paris; fmr Pres. Collège Int. de Philosophie, Paris; Prof. European Grad. School; Ed. Les Temps Modernes. *Publications include:* Les Meurtrières 1959, Fragments du cadastre 1960, Poèmes de la presqu'île 1961, Approche de Hölderlin 1962, Le Monde de Thomas Mann 1963, Biefs 1964, Actes 1966, Oui-dire 1966, Histoire des rechutes 1968, Figurations 1969, Tombeau de Du Bellay 1973, Poèmes 1960–1970 1973, Reliefs 1975, Jumelages suivi de Made in U.S.A. 1978, Donnant, donnant 1981, La Machine matrimoniale ou Marivaux 1982, René Girard et le problème du mal (with J.-P. Dupuy) 1982, Gisants 1985, Poèmes II 1970–1980 1986, Brevets 1986, Choses de la poésie et affaire culturelle 1986, Le Comité: Confessions d'un lecteur de grande maison 1988, La Poésie n'est pas seule: Court traité de Poétique 1988, Arrets fréquents 1990, Aux heures d'affluence 1993, A ce qui n'en finit pas 1995, L'Energie du Desespoir 1998, La Raison Poétique 2000, L'Impair 2000, Spleen de Paris 2001, Poèmes en pensée 2001, Sans Retour 2004, Au Jugé 2004, Desolatio 2007, La Fin dans le Monde 2009, L'Etat de la désunion: Que dire à l'Unesco? 2010. *Honours:* Officier, Ordre nat. du Mérite, Commdr, Ordre des Arts et des Lettres, Chevalier, Légion d'honneur; Grand Prix nat. de la poésie 1989, Grand Prix de Poésie de l' Acad. française 2004. *Address:* 8 rue Abbé de l'Epée, Paris 75005, France (home). *Fax:* 1-47-05-70-37 (office). *E-mail:* micheldeguy@noos.fr; redactron@pourpesie.net (office).

DEIGHTON, Len; British writer; b. 1929, London, England. *Publications:* The Ipcress File 1962 (also film), Horse under Water 1963, Funeral in Berlin 1964 (also film), Où est le Garlic 1965, Action Cook Book 1965, Cookstrip Cook Book (USA) 1966, Billion Dollar Brain 1966 (also film), An Expensive Place to Die 1967, Len Deighton's London Dossier (guide book) 1967, The Assassination of President Kennedy (co-author) 1967, Only When I Larf 1968 (also film), Bomber 1970 (also radio dramatization), Declarations of War (short stories) 1971, Close-Up 1972, Spy Story 1974 (also film), Yesterday's Spy 1975, Twinkle, Twinkle, Little Spy 1976, Fighter: The True Story of the Battle of Britain 1977, SS-GB 1978, Airshipwreck (co-author) 1978, Blitzkrieg 1979, Battle of Britain (co-author) 1980, XPD 1981, Goodbye Mickey Mouse 1982, Berlin Game 1983, Mexico Set 1984, London Match 1985, Winter: A Berlin Family 1899–1945 1987, Spy Hook 1988, ABC of French Food 1989, Spy Line 1989, Spy Sinker 1990, Basic French Cookery Course 1990, Mamista 1991, City of Gold 1992, Violent Ward 1993, Blood, Tears and Folly 1993, Faith 1994, Hope 1995, Charity 1996. *Literary Agent:* c/o Jonathan Clowes Ltd, 10 Iron Bridge House, Bridge Approach, London, NW1 8BD, England. *Telephone:* (20) 7722-7674. *Fax:* 871-528-3647. *E-mail:* admin@jonathanclowes.co.uk. *Website:* www.jonathanclowes.co.uk.

DEL GIUDICE, Daniele; Italian writer, essayist and literary critic; b. 1949, Rome. *Career:* teacher of drama, Univ. Inst. of Architecture, Venice. *Play:* I Tigi, canto per Ustica 2001. *Publications include:* Lo stadio di Wimbledon (novel, also film) (Premio Viareggio) 1983, Atlante Occidentale (novel) (Premio Bergamo) 1985, Nel museo di Reims 1988, Taccuino Australe (travel journal), Staccando l'ombra da terra (short stories) (Premio Bagutta) 1994, Mania (short stories) 1997, Orizzonte mobile 2009; essays on Italo Svevo, Sigmund Freud, Thomas Bernhard, Stefan Zweig, R.L. Stevenson, Primo Levi; articles in various newspapers. *Honours:* Premio Feltrinelli, Accad. dei Lincei 2002, European Union Prize for Literature 2009. *Address:* c/o Einaudi Editore, Att.ne Ufficio comunicazione, Via Biancamano 2, 10121 Turin, Italy. *Website:* www.einaudi.it (office).

DEL PASO, Fernando; Mexican writer, poet and artist; b. 1 April 1935, Mexico City. *Education:* Universidad Nacional Autónoma de México. *Career:* fmrly worked on Int. Writing Program, Univ. of Iowa, USA for two years, worked for BBC in London, England for 14 years, worked for Radio France Internationale, then as Consul Gen. Mexico, both in France for eight years; mem. El Colegio Nacional. *Art exhibitions include:* works exhibited in Museo de Arte Moderno and Museo Carrillo Gil in Mexico City, Hospicio Cabañas in Guadalajara, and in the UK, USA, Spain and France. *Publications include:* Sonetos del amor y de lo diario (poems) 1958, De la A a la Z por un poeta (poems for children), Paleta de diez colores (poems for children), José Trigo (novel) 1966, Palinuro de México (novel) (Premio Novela México 1976, Premio Internacional Rómulo Gallegos 1982, Premio a la Mejor Novela Publicada en Francia 1985) 1976, Noticias del imperio (novel) 1986, Linda 67: Historia de un crimen (novel) 1995, La muerte se va a Granada (play) 1998, Memoria y olvido. Vida de Juan José Arreola (non-fiction) 2003. *Honours:* Premio Xavier Villaurrutia 1966, Premio Nacional de Letras y Artes 1991, Premio Juan Rulfo 2007. *Address:* El Colegio Nacional, Luis González Obregón 23, Centro Histórico, Mexico City 06020 DF, Mexico (office).

DELANEY, Francis (Frank) James Joseph; Irish writer and broadcaster; b. 24 Oct. 1942, Tipperary; s. of Edward Delaney and Josephine Delaney; m. Diane Meier. *Career:* TV and radio broadcaster, journalist and reporter, RTE News Dublin, BBC Northern Ireland, BBC TV and BBC Radio 4; mem. Athenaeum, Chelsea Arts. *Publications include:* James Joyce's Odyssey 1981, Betjeman Country 1983, The Celts 1986, A Walk in the Dark Ages 1988, My Dark Rosaleen (novella) 1989, Legends of the Celts 1989, The Sins of the Mothers 1992, A Walk to the Western Isles 1993, Telling the Pictures 1993, A Stranger in Their Midst 1995, The Amethysts 1997, Desire and Pursuit 1998, Pearl 1999, At Ruby's 2001, Jim Hawkins and the Curse of Treasure Island (as Francis Bryan) 2001, Ireland (novel) 2004, Simple Courage 2006, Tipperary (novel) 2007, Shannon (novel) 2009, Venetia Kelly's Traveling Show 2010, The Matchmaker of Kenmare 2011. *Literary Agent:* c/o Meier, 907 Broadway, New York, NY 10010, USA. *Telephone:* (212) 460-5655. *Fax:* (212) 460-5957. *Website:* www.meierbrand.com. *E-mail:* frankdelaney@frankdelaney.com. *Website:* www.frankdelaney.com.

DELANEY, Lawrence (Larry); Canadian newspaper editor and publisher; *Editor, Country Music News;* b. 30 Aug. 1942, Eastview, Ont.; m. Joanne Bonell 1964; one s. one d. *Career:* Co-founder, Ed. and Publr Country Music News, Canada's nat. music newspaper 1980–, providing int. exposure and profile for Canadian country music artists and industry; mem. Canadian Country Music Asscn, CMA, CPPA. *Honours:* received CCMA Country Music Person of the Year citation 11 times, inducted into Canadian Country Music Hall of Fame 1989, Ottawa Valley Country Music Hall of Fame 1993, CCMA Hall of Honour 1996. *Address:* Country Music News, PO Box 7323, Vanier Terminal, Ottawa, ON K1L 8E4, Canada (office). *E-mail:* larry@countrymusicnews.ca (office). *Website:* www.countrymusicnews.ca (office).

DELANY, Samuel Ray; American writer and academic; *Professor of Creative Writing, Temple University;* b. 1 April 1942, New York, NY; m. 1961 (divorced 1980); one s. one d. *Education:* City Coll., City Univ. of New York. *Career:* Ed. Wuark 1970–71; Sr Fellow, Center for 20th Century Studies, Univ. of Wisconsin, Milwaukee, Wis. 1977, Soc. for the Humanities, Cornell Univ. 1987; Prof. of Comparative Literature, Univ. of Massachusetts, Amherst 1988–2001; Prof. of Creative Writing, Temple Univ. 2001–. *Publications include:* The Jewels of Aptor 1962, The Fall of the Towers, Vol. 1, Captives of the Flames 1963, as Out of the Dead City 1968, Vol. 2, The Towers of Toron 1964, Vol. 3, City of a Thousand Suns 1965, The Ballad of Beta-2 1965, Empire Star 1966, Babel-17 1966, The Einstein Intersection 1967, Nova 1968, Driftglass: Ten Tales of Speculative Fiction 1971, Dhalgren 1975, Triton 1976, The Jewel-Hinged Jaw: Notes on the Language of Science Fiction 1977, The American Shore 1978, Empire 1978, Nebula Award Winners 13 (ed.) 1979, Distant Stars 1981, Stars in My Pocket Like Grains of Sand 1984, Starboard Wine: More Notes on the Language of Science Fiction 1984, The Splendour and Misery of Bodies 1985, Flight from Neveryon 1985, They Fly at Ciron 1992, Neveryon 1993, Tales of Neveryon 1993, The Mad Man 1994, Hogg 1995, Aye, and Gomorrah 2003, Phallos 2004, Dark Reflections (Stonewall Book Award 2008) 2007, Through the Valley of the Nest of Spiders 2011. *Address:* Creative Writing Program, Department of English, Temple University, 1114 West Berks Street, Philadelphia, PA 19122-6090, USA (office). *Telephone:* (215) 204-7344 (office). *E-mail:* sdelany@temple.edu (office). *Website:* www.temple.edu/creativewriting (office).

DELAY, Florence; French writer and university lecturer; b. 19 March 1941, Paris; d. of the late Jean Delay and of Marie Madeleine Delay (née Carrez). *Education:* Lycée Jean de la Fontaine, Paris, Sorbonne. *Career:* Lecturer in Gen. and Comparative Literature, Univ. of Paris III 1972–; Theatre Critic Nouvelle Revue française 1978–85; mem. Editorial Bd Critique magazine 1978–96, Reading Cttee Gallimard publrs 1979–86; mem. Acad. française 2000–. *Film:* Procès de Jeanne d'Arc 1962, Le Jouet criminel 1969, Mort de Raymond Roussel 1975, Écoute voir 1979. *Publications:* Minuit sur les jeux 1973, Le Aïe aïe de la corne de brume 1975, L'Insuccès de la fête 1980, Riche et légère (Prix Femina) 1983, Course d'amour pendant le deuil 1986, Petites formes en prose après Edison (essays) 1987, Les Dames de Fontainebleau (essays) 1987, Partition rouge 1989 (jtly), Hexaméron 1989, Etxemendi (Prix François Mauriac) 1990, Semaines de Suzanne 1991, Catalina 1994, La Fin des temps ordinaires 1996, La Séduction brève (essays) 1997, Dit Nerval 1999, L'Evangile de Jean (trans. of Gospel of John) 2001, Trois désobéissances 2004, Graal Theatre 2005, Mon Espagne or et ciel (essays) 2008, Mes Cendriers 2010; several trans of Spanish dramatists including Fernando de Rojas, Pedro Calderón, Lope de Vega. *Honours:* Commdr des Arts et des Lettres; Chevalier Légion d'honneur; Chevalier Ordre nat. du Mérite; Grand prix du roman de la Ville de Paris 1999. *Address:* c/o Gallimard, 5 rue Sébastien Bottin, 75007 Paris, France (office).

DELBANCO, Andrew Henry, AB, AM, PhD; American academic and writer; *Julian Clarence Levi Professor in the Humanities, Columbia University;* b. 20 Feb. 1952, White Plains, NY; m. Dawn Ho Delbanco 1973; one s. one d. *Education:* Harvard Univ. *Career:* Asst Prof., Harvard Univ. 1981–85; Assoc. Prof., Columbia Univ. 1985–87, Prof. 1987–, Julian Clarence Levi Prof. in the Humanities 1995–, currently also Dir of American Studies; Adjunct Prof., Yale Univ. 1989; mem. Soc. of American Historians. *Publications include:* William Ellery Channing: An Essay on the Liberal Spirit in America 1981, The Puritan Ordeal 1989, The Death of Satan: How Americans Have Lost the Sense of Evil 1995, Required Reading: Why Our American Classics Matter Now 1997, The Real American Dream 1999, Melville: His World and Work (Lionel Trilling Award) 2005, His Own Best Straight Man 2010; ed.: The Puritans in America: A Narrative Anthology (with Alan Heimert) 1985, The Sermons of Ralph Waldo Emerson, Vol. II (with Teresa Toulouse) 1990, The Portable Abraham Lincoln 1992, Writing New England 2001; contribs: New York Review of Books, The New Republic, professional journals and to general periodicals. *Honours:* Guggenheim Fellowship, ACLS Fellowship, Nat. Endowment for the Humanities Fellowship, Nat. Humanities Center Fellowship, New York State Scholar, New York Council for the Humanities 2003. *Address:* Department of American Studies, Columbia University, 418 Hamilton Hall, MC 2810, 1130 Amsterdam Avenue, New York, NY 10027, USA (office). *Telephone:* (212) 854-6698 (office). *Fax:* (212) 854-1618 (office). *E-mail:* ad19@columbia.edu (office). *Website:* www.columbia.edu/cu/amstudies (office).

DELBANCO, Nicholas Franklin, BA, MA; American writer and academic; *Professor, University of Michigan;* b. 27 Aug. 1942, London, England; m. Elena Carter Greenhouse 1970; two d. *Education:* Harvard Univ., Columbia Univ. *Career:* Faculty, Language and Literature Div., Bennington Coll. 1966–85, Founder-Dir, Bennington Coll. Writing Workshops 1977–85; Visiting Lecturer, Iowa Writers Program, Univ. of Iowa 1979; Adjunct Prof., School of the Arts, Columbia Univ. 1979, 1996, 1997; Visiting Writer-in-Residence, Trinity

Coll. 1980; M. Scott Bundy Visiting Prof. of English, Williams Coll. 1982, 1985; staff, Bread Loaf Writers' Conf. 1984–94; Prof. of English, Skidmore Coll. 1984–85; Prof., Univ. of Michigan, Ann Arbor 1985–, Robert Frost Distinguished Univ. Professorship 2006–; mem. Associated Writing Programs, Authors' League, Authors' Guild, Signet Soc., New York State Writers' Inst., PEN. *Publications include:* The Martlet's Tale (novel) 1966, Grasse 3/23/66 (novel) 1968, Consider Sappho Burning (novel) 1969, News (novel) 1970, In the Middle Distance (novel) 1971, Fathering (novel) 1973, Small Rain (novel) 1975, Possession (novel) 1977, Sherbrookes (novel) 1978, Stillness (novel) 1980, Group Portrait: Conrad, Crane, Ford, James, and Wells 1982, About My Table and Other Stories 1983, The Beaux Arts Trio: A Portrait 1985, Running in Place: Scenes from the South of France 1989, The Writers' Trade, and Other Stories 1990, Speaking of Writing: Selected Hopwood Lectures (ed.) 1990, Writers and Their Craft: Short Stories and Essays on the Narrative (co-ed. with Laurence Goldstein) 1991, In the Name of Mercy (novel) 1995, Talking Horse: Bernard Malamud on Life and Art (co-ed. with Alan Cheuse) 1996, Old Scores (novel) 1997, The Lost Suitcase: Reflections on the Literary Life 2000, What Remains (novel) 2000, The Writing Life: Further Hopwood Lectures (ed.) 2000, The Countess of Stanlein Restored: A History of the Paganini Stradivarius Violoncello of 1707 2002, The Vagabonds (novel) 2004, Anywhere Out of The World (essays) 2005, Spring and Fall (novel) 2006, The Count of Concord (novel) 2008, Lastingness: The Art of Old Age (non-fiction) 2011; contribs to periodicals, anthologies, quarterlies, reviews and journals. *Honours:* Nat. Endowment for the Arts Creative Writing Fellowships 1973, 1982, Guggenheim Fellowship 1980, Nat. Endowment for the Arts/PEN Syndicated Fiction Awards 1983, 1985, 1989, MacDowell Colony Fellowship 1985, Yaddo Fellowships 1987, 1989, 1994, Robert Frost Collegiate Professorship, Univ. of Michigan 1998, Michigan Author of the Year 2002. *Literary Agent:* c/o Brandt & Hochman Literary Agents Inc., 1501 Broadway, New York, NY 10036, USA. *Address:* The Hopwood Room, 1186 Angell Hall, University of Michigan, Ann Arbor, MI 48109, USA (office). *Telephone:* (734) 764-6296 (office).

DELEHANTY, Randolph Stephen, BA, MA, PhD; American author, lecturer and exhibition curator; *Historian, Presidio Trust, San Francisco*; b. 5 July 1944, Memphis, Tenn. *Education:* Georgetown Univ., Univ. of Chicago and Harvard Univ. *Career:* author of historical and architectural books; curator of major art, nature and history exhbns; Founding Dir Ogden Museum of Southern Art, Univ. of New Orleans 1995–99; Historian for Presidio Trust, Golden Gate Nat. Parks, San Francisco, Calif. 2000–; mem. American Asscn of Museums Press Editorial Advisory Bd. *Exhibitions:* Japan at the Dawn of the Modern Age Woodblock Prints from Meiji Era 2002, Birds of the Pacific Slope 2004, From Above – A Robert Cameron Aerial Photography Retrospective 2005, Plants + Insects/Art + Science 2006, War & Dissent The U.S. in the Philippines 1898–1915, exhibited in San Francisco and Manila 2009, exhibit in progress, Crown Jewels: Six Great Nat. Parks around the World and the Challenges They Face. *Publications include:* San Francisco: Walks and Tours in the Golden Gate City 1980, California: A Guidebook 1984, Preserving the West 1985, In the Victorian Style 1991, New Orleans: Elegance and Decadence 1993, San Francisco: The Ultimate Guide 1995, Classic Natchez 1996, Art in the American South 1996, Randolph Delehanty's Ultimate Guide to New Orleans 1998, San Francisco Victorians 2000, A Guide to San Francisco Recreation and Parks 2000, Treasure Houses: Louisiana Museums for a New Millennium 2000, New Guardians for the Golden Gate: How America got a Great National Park (with Amy Meyer) 2006; contrib. to The Companion to Southern Literature 2002, work in progress on art, religion, sex, love, politics and crime in Italy. *Address:* 2004 Gough Street, San Francisco, CA 94109-3418, USA (home). *E-mail:* randolph_delehanty@post.harvard.edu. *Website:* www.presidio.gov/teachers/exhibit/waranddissent (office).

DeLILLO, Don, BA; American writer; b. 20 Nov. 1936, New York, NY; m. Barbara Bennett 1975. *Education:* Cardinal Hayes High School, Fordham Coll., New York. *Career:* fmr advertising copywriter Ogilvy, Benson & Mather. *Plays:* The Day Room 1987, Valparaiso 1999. *Publications:* Americana 1971, End Zone 1972, Great Jones Street 1973, Ratner's Star 1976, Players 1977, Running Dog 1978, The Names 1982, White Noise 1985 (Nat. Book Award 1985), Libra 1988 (Irish Times Fiction Prize 1989), Mao II 1991 (PEN/Faulkner Award 1992), Underworld 1997, The Body Artist 2000, Cosmopolis 2003, Falling Man 2007, Point Omega 2010, The Angel Esmeralda: Nine Stories 2011. *Honours:* American Acad. of Arts and Letters Award in Literature 1984, Jerusalem Prize for the Freedom of the Individual in Soc. 1999, William Dean Howells Medal 2000, PEN/Saul Bellow Award for Achievement in American Fiction 2010. *Literary Agent:* Wallace Literary Agency, 301 East 79th Street, 14-J, New York, NY 10075, USA. *Telephone:* (212) 570-9090 (office). *Fax:* (212) 772-8979 (office).

DELIUS, Friedrich Christian; German author; b. 13 Feb. 1943, Rome, Italy. *Education:* Free Univ., Technical Univ. *Career:* literary ed., Klaus Wagenbach and Rotbuch publishing houses 1970–78; freelance writer 1978–. *Publications:* Kerbholz 1965, Wir Unternehmer (co-author) 1966, Wenn wir, bei Rot 1969, Der Held und sein Wetter 1971, Unsere Siemens-Welt 1972, Rezepte für Friedenszeiten (co-author) 1973, Ein Bankier auf der Flucht 1975, Ein Held der inneren Sicherheit 1981, Die unsichtbaren Blitze 1981, Adenauerplatz 1984, Einige Argumente zur Verteidigung der Gemüseesser 1985, Mogadischu Fensterplatz 1987, Japanische Rolltreppen 1989, Die Birnen von Ribbeck 1991, Himmelfahrt eines Staatsfeindes 1992, Selbstporträt mit Luftbrücke 1993, Der Sonntag, an dem ich Weltmeister wurde 1994, Der Spaziergang von Rostock nach Syrakus 1995, Die Zukunft der Wörter 1995, Die Verlockungen der Wörter oder Warum ich immer noch kein Zyniker bin 1996, Amerikahaus und der Tanz um die Frauen 1997, Die Flatterzunge 1999, Transit Westberlin (co-author) 1999, Der Königsmacher 2001, Warum ich schon immer Recht hatte – und andere Irrtümer 2003, Mein Jahr als Mörder 2004, Die Minute mit Paul McCartney 2005, Bildnis der Mutter als junge Frau (Evangelischer Buchpreis 2009) 2006, Die Frau, für die ich den Computer erfand 2009, Der Held und sein Wetter 2011, Als die Bücher noch geholfen haben 2012. *Honours:* Preis Junge Generation zum Kunstpreis Berlin 1967, Villa-Massimo Stipendium 1971, Gerrit-Engelke Preis 1989, Aufenthaltsstipendium Schloss Wiepersdorf 1996, Mainzer Stadtschreiber 1997, Daimler-Chrysler-Stipendium der Casa di Goethe 2001, Samuel-Bogumil-Linde Preis 2002, Walter-Hasenclever-Literaturpreis 2004, Fontane-Preis für Literatur der Stadt Neuruppin 2004, Schubart-Literaturpreis 2007, Deutscher Kritikerpreis 2007, Joseph-Breitbach-Preis 2007, Stadtschreiber von Bergen 2008–09, Georg-Büchner-Preis 2011, Gerty-Spies-Literaturpreis 2012. *Address:* c/o Rowohlt Berlin Verlag, Kreuzbergstr. 30, 10965 Berlin, Germany (office). *Telephone:* (30) 2853840 (office). *E-mail:* info@rowohlt.de (office); graf@agenturgraf.de (office). *Website:* www.rowohlt.de (office); www.fcdelius.de (home).

DEMARIA, Robert, BA, MA, PhD; American academic, writer and poet; *Professor Emeritus of English, Dowling College*; b. 28 Sept. 1928, New York, NY; m. 1st Maddalena Buzeo; m. 2nd Ellen Hope Meyer; three s. one d. *Education:* Columbia Univ., New York. *Career:* instructor, Univ. of Oregon 1949–52; Asst Prof., Hofstra Univ. 1952–61; Assoc. Dean, New School for Social Research, New York 1961–64; Prof. of English, Dowling Coll. 1965–97; Prof. Emer. 1997–; Ed. and Publr, The Mediterranean Review 1969–73; Publr, The Vineyard Press 1999–. *Publications include:* fiction: Carnival of Angels 1961, Clodia 1965, Don Juan in Lourdes 1966, The Satyr 1972, The Decline and Fall of America 1973, To Be a King 1976, Outbreak 1978, Blowout 1979, The Empress 1980, Secret Places 1981, A Passion for Power 1983, Sons and Brothers (two vols) 1985, Stone of Destiny 1986, That Kennedy Girl 1999, The White Road 2000, Blood of the Hunter 2006, Shadow World 2007, Hello Bones! (poetry) 2007; My Secret Childhood: Growing Up in New York (memoir) 2005; non-fiction (textbooks): The College Handbook of Creative Writing 1991, A Contemporary Reader for Creative Writing 1995; contrib. of fiction, poetry and articles in numerous publs. *Address:* 106 Vineyard Place, Port Jefferson, NY 11777, USA (home). *Telephone:* (631) 928-3460 (home). *E-mail:* debobaria@optonline.net. *Website:* www.thevineyardpress.com.

DEMERS, Patricia, BA, MA, PhD; Canadian academic; *University Professor, Department of English and Film Studies, University of Alberta*. *Education:* McMaster Univ. and Univ. of Ottawa. *Career:* currently Univ. Prof., Dept of English and Film Studies, Univ. of Alberta, Chair of Dept 1995–98; Vice-Pres. Social Sciences and Humanities Research Council 1998–2002; inducted into RSC 2000, Hon. Ed., Exec. mem., Pres. (first woman) 2005–07. *Publications include:* From Instruction to Delight: Children's Literature to 1850 (ed.) (second edn 2004), A Garland from the Golden Age, Women's Writing in English 2005; contrib. numerous articles in professional journals including Mosaic, English Studies in Canada, Semeia, Sixteenth Century Journal, Huntington Library Quarterly, Renaissance and Reformation, Bunyan Studies, Literature and Theology and Topia. *Honours:* Univ. Cup, Univ. of Alberta 2005. *Address:* Department of English and Film Studies, University of Alberta, 3–5 Humanities Centre, Edmonton, Alberta, T6G 2E5, Canada (office). *Telephone:* (780) 492-3258 (office). *Fax:* (780) 492-8142 (office). *E-mail:* patricia.demers@ualberta.ca (office). *Website:* www.ualberta.ca (office).

DEMETILLO, Ricaredo, AB, MFA; Philippine academic, poet and writer; b. 2 June 1920, Dumangas. *Education:* Diliman Univ., Univ. of Iowa, USA. *Career:* Asst Prof., Univ. of the Philippines 1959–70, Chair., Dept of Humanities 1961–62, Assoc. Prof. 1970–75, Prof. of Humanities 1975–86. *Publications include:* poetry: No Certain Weather 1956, La Via: A Spiritual Journey 1958, Daedalus and Other Poems 1961, Barter in Panay 1961, Masks and Signature 1968, The Scare-Crow Christ 1973, The City and the Thread of Light 1974, Lazarus, Troubadour 1974, Sun, Silhouettes and Shadow 1975, First and Last Fruits 1989; novel: The Genesis of a Troubled Vision 1976; play: The Heart of Emptiness is Black 1973; non-fiction: The Authentic Voice of Poetry 1962, Major and Minor Keys 1986.

DEMICK, Barbara; American journalist and writer. *Career:* Corresp. for Philadelphia Inquirer newspaper in Eastern Europe 1993–97, in Middle East 1997–2001; Bureau Chief in Seoul, South Korea, Los Angeles Times 2001–07, moved to Beijing Bureau 2007, Bureau Chief 2009–; Visiting Prof., Princeton Univ. 2006–07. *Publications include:* Logavina Street: Life and Death in a Sarajevo Neighborhood 1996, Nothing to Envy: Ordinary Lives in North Korea (BBC Samuel Johnson Prize for Non-Fiction 2010) 2009. *Honours:* Robert F. Kennedy Journalism Award 1994, George Polk Award 1994, Arthur Ross Award for Distinguished Reporting and Analysis on Foreign Affairs, American Acad. of Diplomacy 2005, Print Journalist of the Year, Los Angeles Press Club 2006, Osborn Elliott Prize for Excellence in Asian Journalism, Asia Soc. 2006, Joe and Laurie Dine Award for Human Rights Reporting, Overseas Press Club 2006. *Address:* Los Angeles Times, 202 West 1st Street, Los Angeles, CA 90012, USA (office). *E-mail:* barbara.demick@latimes.com (office). *Website:* www.latimes.com (office).

DEMOS, John Putnam, BA, MA; American academic and writer; *Samuel Knight Professor Emeritus of History, Yale University*; b. 2 May 1937, Cambridge, Mass; m. Elaine Virginia Damis 1963; two c. *Education:* Harvard

Univ., Univ. of Oxford, UK, Univ. of California, Berkeley. *Career:* Teaching Fellow, Harvard Univ. 1966–68; Asst Prof., Brandeis Univ. 1968–72, Prof. of History 1972–86; fmr Prof. of History, Yale Univ., Samuel Knight Prof. of History –2008, Emer. 2008–; mem. American Historical Asscn. *Publications include:* A Little Commonwealth: Family Life in Plymouth Colony 1970, Remarkable Providences, 1600–1760 (ed.) 1972, Turning Points: Historical and Sociological Essays on the Family (co-ed. with Sarane Boocock) 1978, Entertaining Satan: Witchcraft and the Culture of Early New England 1982, Past, Present, and Personal: The Family and the Life Course 1986, The Unredeemed Captive 1994, Circles and Lines: The Shape of Life in Early America 2004, The Enemy Within: 2,000 Years of Witch-Hunting in the Western World 2008; contribs: scholarly journals and other publs. *Honours:* Bancroft Prize in American History, Columbia Univ. 1983, Francis Parkman Prize 1995, Ray Allen Billington Prize 1995. *Address:* Department of History, Yale University, PO Box 208324, New Haven, CT 06520-8324, USA (office). *Telephone:* (203) 432-1366 (office). *E-mail:* john.demos@yale.edu (office). *Website:* www.yale.edu/history/faculty/demos (office).

DEMPSEY, Gaylene Katharan; Katharan editor; b. 1 Aug. 1960, Winnipeg, Man.; m. David Sherman 1993. *Career:* Ed. monthly entertainment paper, Circuit 1989–; Ed.-in-Chief monthly entertainment paper, The Insider 1990–; Ed. Jazz Winnipeg Festival Programme 1990–; volunteer, Winnipeg Folk Festival 1990–; Exec. Dir Manitoba Audio Recording Industry Asscn 1991–; represents the Manitoba Music Industry from songwriters to labels; freelance work; mem. FACTOR Nat. Advisory Bd, Artspace (Exec. mem.). *Publications include:* contributed several articles to SOCAN Words and Music, Grafitti Magazine. *Address:* 242 Spence Street, Winnipeg, MB R3C 1Y4, Canada (home). *Telephone:* (204) 786-2191 (home).

DENBY, Joolz; British writer and performance artist. *Career:* has performed at numerous UK arts festivals, including five Edinburgh Fringe Festivals, two Edinburgh Book Festivals, 20 Glastonbury Festivals, also in Canada, the Netherlands, Germany, Norway, Israel, Poland, Slovakia; readings and seminars world-wide; mem. Red Sky Coven cult performance group; regular broadcasts on radio and TV. *Recordings:* War of Attrition (poems, with music) 1983, The Kiss (poems, with music) 1984, Never Never Land (spoken word) 1984, Love Is Sweet Romance (poems, with music) 1985, Mad, Bad, & Dangerous to Know (poems, with music) 1986, Hex (poems, with music) 1990, Weird Sister (poems, with music) 1991, Joolz 1983–85, True North (poems, with music) 1997. *Publications include:* fiction: The Quick & the Dead 2 (short story), Trouble (short story), Stone Baby (novel) (The Crime Writers' Asscn New Crime Writer of the Year Award) 2000, Corazon (novel) 2001, Billie Morgan (novel) (Orange Prize for Fiction) 2005, Borrowed Light 2006, The Curious Mystery of Miss Lydia Larkin & The Widow Marvell 2011; poetry: Mad, Bad, & Dangerous to Know 1986, Emotional Terrorism 1990, The Pride of Lions 1994, Errors of the Spirit 2000, Pray for Us Sinners 2005. *Address:* Castle Dragonbat, PO Box 162, Bradford, BD3 8PY, England (office). *Fax:* (1274) 667974 (office). *E-mail:* joolz@joolz.net (office). *Website:* www.joolz-denby.co.uk.

DENEZHKINA, Irina; Russian writer; b. 3 Oct. 1984. *Publications include:* Give Me (Songs for Lovers) (short stories, in trans.) (Nat. Bestseller Award, Russia) 2002. *Honours:* Ovid Festival Prize 2008. *Address:* c/o Chatto & Windus, Random House, 20 Vauxhall Bridge Road, London, SW1V 2SA, England.

DENG, Xiaohua, (Can Xue); Chinese writer; b. 30 May 1953, Changsha, Hunan; d. of Deng Jun Hong and Li Ying; m. Lu Rong 1979; one s. *Career:* parents were condemned as ultra-rightists in 1957, forced to leave school aged 13; factory worker 1970–80; tailor 1980–85; professional writer 1985–. *Publications include:* Soap Bubbles on Dirty Water, Dialogues in Paradise (short stories) 1989, Yellow Mud Street, Dating, Old Floating Cloud (novella) 1989, Apple Tree in the Corridor, The Instant when the Cuckoo Sings 1991, The Embroidered Shoes (short stories) 1997, Castle of the Soul (essays on Kafka) 1999, Blue Light in the Sky, Five Spice Street (novel); works on Borges and Shakespeare. *Honours:* Hon. mem. Int. Writing Program, Univ. of Iowa, USA . *Address:* c/o 3-3 Building, No. 904, He Xi, Changsha, Hunan, People's Republic of China.

DENGLER, Sandy, BS, MS, PhD; American writer; b. 8 June 1939, Newark, Ohio; m. William F. Dengler 1963; two d. *Education:* Bowling Green State Univ., OH, Arizona State Univ., Univ. of Oklahoma. *Career:* mem. Mystery Writers of American, Soc. of Vertebrate Palaeontologists, Writers' Guild. *Publications include:* non-fiction: Fanny Crosby 1985, John Bunyan 1986, D. L. Moody 1987, Susanna Wesley 1987, Florence Nightingale 1988; fiction: Barn Social 1978, Yosemite's Marvellous Creatures 1979, Summer of the Wild Pig 1979, Melon Hound 1980, The Horse Who Loved Picnics 1980, Mystery at McGehan Ranch 1982, Chain Five Mystery 1984, Summer Snow 1984, Winterspring 1985, This Rolling Land 1986, Jungle Gold 1987, Code of Honor 1988, Power of Pinjarra 1989, Taste of Victory 1989, East of Outback 1990, Death Valley 1993, Cat Killer 1993, Dublin Crossing 1993, Mouse Trapped 1993, Gila Monster 1994, Last Dinosaur 1994, Murder on the Mount 1994, Shamrock Shore 1994, Emerald Sea 1994, The Quick and the Dead 1995, King of the Stars 1995, Hyaenas 1996, African Adventure 2003, The Comatose Cat 2004, The Wicked Step-Twister 2005; contrib. to journals and magazines. *Honours:* Warm Beach Writer of the Year 1986, Romance Writers of America Golden Medallion 1987. *Address:* 2563 Highland Loop, Port Townsend, WA 98368, USA (home). *E-mail:* sdengler@aol.com.

DENNETT, Daniel Clement, BA, DPhil; American philosopher, academic and author; *University Professor, Austin B. Fletcher Professor of Philosophy and Co-Director, Center for Cognitive Studies, Tufts University*; b. 28 March 1942, Boston, Mass; s. of Daniel C. Dennett, Jr and Ruth M. Leck; m. Susan Bell 1962; one s. one d. *Education:* Phillips Exeter Acad., Wesleyan Univ., Harvard Univ., Univ. of Oxford. *Career:* Asst Prof. of Philosophy, Univ. of California, Irvine 1965–70, Assoc. Prof. 1971; Assoc. Prof., Tufts Univ. 1971–75, Prof. 1975–85, Distinguished Arts and Sciences Prof. 1985–2000, Co-Dir Center for Cognitive Studies 1985–, Univ. Prof. 2000–, also Austin B. Fletcher Prof. of Philosophy; Visiting Prof., Harvard 1973–74, Pittsburgh 1975, Oxford 1979, Ecole Normale Supérieure, Paris 1985, Dept of Philosophy, Auburn Univ. 2011; Visiting Fellow, All Souls Coll., Oxford 1979; Writer-in-Residence, Bellagio Study and Conf. Centre, Italy 1990, 2001; Fellow, Center for Advanced Study in Behavioral Sciences 1979, American Acad. of Arts and Sciences 1987, Zentrum für Interdisziplinäre Forschung, Bielefeld, Germany 1990; Visiting Erskine Fellow, Univ. of Canterbury, Christchurch, NZ 1995; Distinguished Fellow, Centre for the Mind, Inst. for Advanced Study, ANU, Canberra 1998, Collegium Budapest, Hungary 2002; Fellow, SAGE Center, Univ. of California, Santa Barbara 2008; William Miller Fellow, Santa Fe Inst., NM 2010; Fellow, AAAS 2009. *Publications:* Content and Consciousness 1969, Brainstorms 1978, The Mind's I (with Douglas Hofstadter) 1981, Elbow Room 1984, The Intentional Stance 1987, Consciousness Explained 1991, Darwin's Dangerous Idea 1995, Kinds of Minds 1996, Brainchildren 1998, Freedom Evolves 2003, Breaking the Spell: Religion as a Natural Phenomenon 2006, Dove nascono le idée (translated by Francesca Garofoli) 2006, Science and Religion: Are They Compatible? (with Alvin Plantinga) 2011, Inside Jokes: Using Humor to Reverse-Engineer the Mind (with Matthew Hurley and Reginald B. Adams, Jr) 2011; numerous articles in professional journals. *Honours:* Hon. DHumLitt (Connecticut) 2003; Hon. DLitt (Edinburgh) 2007; Hon. DSc (McGill) 2007; Dr hc (Amsterdam) 2012; Woodrow Wilson Fellow 1963, Guggenheim Fellow 1973, 1986, Santayana Fellowship, Harvard Univ. (hon.) 1974, Nat. Endowment for the Humanities Younger Humanist Fellowship 1974, Fulbright Fellow 1978, John Locke Lecturer, Oxford 1983, Gavin David Young Lecturer, Adelaide, Australia 1984, Jean Nicod Lecturer, Institut Nicod, Paris 2001, Daewoo Lecturer, Seoul, S Korea 2002, Petrus Hispanus Lecturer, Faculdade de Letras de Lisboa, Lisbon 2004, Patten Lecturer, Indiana Univ. 2006, Distinguished Fellow Award, Cognitive Science Soc. 2009, Erasmus Prize 2012. *Address:* Center for Cognitive Studies, Tufts University, Medford, MA 02155-7059, USA (office). *Telephone:* (617) 627-3297 (office). *Fax:* (617) 627-3952 (office). *E-mail:* daniel.dennett@tufts.edu (office). *Website:* ase.tufts.edu/cogstud/incbios/dennettd/dennettdcv.htm (office).

DENNIS, Carl, BA, PhD; American poet and writer; b. 17 Sept. 1939, St Louis, Mo. *Education:* Oberlin Coll., Univ. of Chicago, Univ. of Minnesota, Univ. of California, Berkeley. *Career:* Prof. of English, SUNY at Buffalo 1966–2002; mem. PEN. *Publications include:* poetry: A House of My Own 1974, Climbing Down 1976, Signs and Wonders 1979, The Near World 1985, The Outskirts of Troy 1988, Meetings with Time 1992, Ranking the Wishes 1997, Practical Gods 2001, New and Selected Poems 1974–2004 2004, Unknown Friends 2007, Callings 2010; other: Poetry as Persuasion 2001; contribs: many anthologies, quarterlies, reviews and journals. *Honours:* Guggenheim Fellowship, Nat. Endowment for the Arts Fellowship, Fellow, Rockefeller Study Center, Bellagio, Italy, Ruth Lilly Prize 2000, Pulitzer Prize in Poetry 2002. *Address:* 49 Ashland Avenue, Buffalo, NY 14222, USA (home). *E-mail:* cedennis@buffalo.edu.

DENNIS, Everette Eugene, Jr, BS, MA, PhD; American foundation executive, academic, author and university administrator; *Dean, Northwestern University in Qatar*; b. 15 Aug. 1942, Seattle, Wash.; m. Emily T. Smith 1988. *Education:* Univ. of Oregon, Syracuse Univ., Univ. of Minnesota. *Career:* Asst Prof., Journalism, Mass Communication, Kansas State Univ., Manhattan 1968–72; Instructor, Asst Prof., Assoc. Prof., School of Journalism and Mass Communication, Univ. of Minnesota 1972–81; Visiting Prof., Medill School of Journalism, Northwestern Univ. 1976–77; Dean and Prof., School of Journalism, Univ. of Oregon 1981–84; Exec. Dir The Freedom Forum Media Studies Center, Columbia Univ. 1984–96; Felix E. Larkin Distinguished Prof. and Dir, Center for Communications, Graduate School of Business, Fordham Univ. 1997–2011; Dean, Northwestern Univ. in Qatar 2011–; Founding Pres. American Acad. in Berlin 1996–2000; Sr Vice-Pres. The Freedom Forum, Arlington, Va; mem. Int. Communication Asscn, Eastman House Int. Museum of Photographs, American Antiquarian Soc., Asscn for Education in Journalism and Mass Communication, Int. Press Inst., Soc. of Professional Journalists. *Publications include:* Other Voices: The New Journalism in America 1973, The Media Society 1978, The Economics of Libel 1986, Understanding Mass Communication (ed.) 1988, Demystifying Media Technology 1993, America's Schools and the Mass Media 1993, The Culture of Crime 1995, Radio, The Forgotten Medium 1995, American Communication Research 1996, Understanding Media in the Digital Age 2010; contribs: hundreds of articles to popular, professional and scholarly periodicals. *Honours:* Harvard Univ. Fellowships 1978–79, 1980, 1981, other fellowships, various writing prizes and awards. *Address:* Office of the Dean, Northwestern University in Qatar, PO Box 34102, Doha, Qatar (office). *Telephone:* 44545000 (home). *Fax:* 44545180 (office). *Website:* www.qatar.northwestern.edu (office).

DENNY, Neill; British journalist; *Editor-in-Chief, The Bookseller*; b. 1966, London, England; s. of Alfred Christoper Denny and Alison Mary Denny (née

McLellan); m.; three c. *Education:* Dulwich Coll., Hounslow Borough Coll. *Career:* worked at Haymarket and Centaur on magazines including Marketing, Marketing Direct and Precision Marketing; Ed., Marketing Direct 1995–98, Retail Week 1999–2004; Ed.-in-Chief, The Bookseller 2004–. *Honours:* Freeman of the City of London. *Address:* The Bookseller, Fifth Floor, Endeavour House, Shaftesbury Avenue, London, WC2H 8TJ, England (office). *Telephone:* (20) 3358-0362 (office). *E-mail:* neill.denny@bookseller.co.uk (office). *Website:* www.thebookseller.com (office).

DEPESTRE, René; French poet and writer; b. 29 Aug. 1926, Jacmel, Haiti; m. Nelly Campano 1962. *Education:* Sorbonne, Univ. of Paris. *Career:* Attaché, Office of Culture, UNESCO, Paris 1978–86, mem. Cabinet of Dir-Gen. 1978–82, Section de la Création Artistique 1982–86. *Publications include:* poetry: Etincelles 1945, Gerbe de sang 1946, Minerai noir 1956, Un arc-en-ciel pour l'occident chrétien 1967, Journal d'un animal marin (selected poems, 1956–90) 1990, Au matin de la négritude 1990, Anthologie personnelle 1993, Rage de Vivre (Robert Ganzo Poetry Award 2007) 2007; fiction: Alléluia pour une femme jardin 1973, Le Mat de cocagne 1979, Hadriana dans tous mes rêves 1988, Eros dans un train chinois: Neuf histories d'amour et un conte sorcier 1990, L'oeillet ensorcelé 2006; non-fiction: Pour la révolution, pour la poésie 1969, Bonjour et adieu a la négritude 1980, Le Métier à métisser 1998, Encore une mer á traverser 2004, Non-assistance à poètes en danger 2005. *Honours:* Prix Goncourt 1982, Prix Renaudot 1988, Prix Antigone, Montpellier, Prix de la Société des Gens de Lettres, Prix du Roman de l'Académie royale de langue et de littérature françaises de Belgique, Prix Grisane, Italy. *Address:* 31 bis, Route de Roubia, 11200 Lezignan-Corbières, France (home). *Telephone:* 4-68-27-54-84 (home). *Fax:* 4-68-27-53-57 (home).

D'ERASMO, Stacey, BA, MA; American author, literary critic and academic; *Assistant Professor of Writing, Columbia University*; b. 1961. *Education:* Barnard Coll., New York Univ. *Career:* fmr teacher, Yale Univ., Barnard Coll., Sarah Lawrence Coll., Warren Wilson Coll.; Sr Ed. Voice Literary Supplement 1988–95; Stegner Fellow in Fiction, Stanford Univ. 1995–97; creator and developerof Bookforum (fiction review) 1997–98; Writer-in-Residence, Eugene Lang Coll., New School Univ. 2005–06; mem. Faculty, Breadloaf Writers Conf. 2007, 2008, Warren Wilson Coll. 2008–; currently Assistant Prof. of Writing, Columbia Univ.; Sovern/Columbia Affiliated Fellow, American Acad. in Rome 2010–11. *Publications include:* novels: Tea 2000, A Seahorse Year (Ferro-Grumley Award 2004, Lambda Literary Award 2012) 2004, The Sky Below 2009; contrib. numerous articles and podcasts, New York Times Book Review, New York Times Magazine, Ploughshares, Los Angeles Times. *Honours:* Guggenheim Fellowship in Fiction 2009. *Literary Agent:* c/o Bill Clegg, William Morris Endeavor Entertainment, 1325 Avenue of the Americas, New York, NY 10019, USA. *E-mail:* BC@WMEEntertainment.com. *Website:* www.wmeentertainment.com. *Address:* Undergraduate Creative Writing Program, Columbia University, 415 Dodge Hall, New York, NY 10027, USA (office). *Telephone:* (212) 854-4391 (office). *E-mail:* smd2121@columbia.edu (office); stacey@staceyderasmo.com. *Website:* arts.columbia.edu/writing/stacey-derasmo (office); www.staceyderasmo.com.

DERFLER, (Arnold) Leslie, BA, MA, PhD; American academic and writer; *Professor of History, Florida Atlantic University*; b. 11 Jan. 1933, New York, NY; m. Gunilla Derfler 1962; four d. *Education:* City Coll., City Univ. of New York, Univ. of Chicago, Univ. of Paris, France, Columbia Univ., New York. *Career:* Faculty mem. City Coll., CUNY 1959–62, Carnegie Mellon Univ. 1962–68, Univ. of Massachusetts, Amherst 1968–69; Prof. of History, Florida Atlantic Univ. 1969–; Visiting Prof., London Center, Florida State Univ. 1985. *Publications include:* The Dreyfus Affair: Tragedy of Errors 1963, The Third French Republic, 1870–1940 1966, Socialism Since Marx 1973, Alexandre Millerand: The Socialist Years 1977, President and Parliament: A Short History of the French Presidency 1984, An Age of Conflict: Readings in 20th Century European History 1990, Paul Lafargue and the Founding of French Marxism, 1842–1882 1991, Paul Lafargue and the Flowering of French Socialism, 1882–1911 1998, The Dreyfuys Affair 2002, The Fall and Rise of Political Leaders: Olof Palme, Olusegun Obasanjo, Indira Gandhi 2011. *Honours:* American Philosophical Soc. Grants 1967, 1976, 1981, 1991, Distinguished Scholar Award, Florida Atlantic Univ. 1982, Nat. Endowment for the Humanities Fellowship 1984–85. *Address:* Department of History, Florida Atlantic University, Boca Raton, FL 33431, USA (office).

DERR, Mark, AB, MA; American writer; b. (Mark Burgess Derr), 20 Jan. 1950, Baltimore, Md; m. Gina L. Maranto 1982. *Education:* Johns Hopkins Univ., Baltimore. *Publications include:* Some Kind of Paradise: A Chronicle of Man and the Land in Florida 1989, Over Florida 1992, The Frontiersman: The Real Life and the Many Legends of Davy Crockett 1993, Dog's Best Friend: Annals of the Dog–Human Relationship 1997, A Dog's History of America: How Our Best Friend Explored, Conquered and Settled A Continent 2004, How the Dog Became the Dog: From Wolves to Our Best Friends 2011; contrib. to The Atlantic, Audubon Society, Natural History, Wall Street Journal, New York Times. *Address:* 4245 Sheridan Avenue, Miami Beach, FL 33140, USA (home). *Telephone:* (305) 534-2604 (office). *E-mail:* m.derr@markderr.com (office). *Website:* mbdog.markderr.com; www.markderr.com.

DERSHOWITZ, Alan Morton, LLB; American lawyer and academic; *Felix Frankfurter Professor of Law, Harvard University*; b. 1 Sept. 1938, New York, NY; s. of Harry Dershowitz and Claire Ringel; m. Carolyn Cohen; two s. one d. *Education:* Brooklyn Coll. and Yale Univ. *Career:* admitted to DC Bar 1963, Mass Bar 1968, US Supreme Court 1968; law clerk to Chief Judge David Bazelon, US Court of Appeal 1962–63, to Justice Arthur Goldberg, US Supreme Court 1963–64; mem. Faculty, Harvard Coll. 1964–, Prof. of Law 1967–, Felix Frankfurter Prof. of Law 1993–; Fellow, Center for Advanced Study of Behavioral Sciences 1971–72; consultant to Dir Nat. Inst. for Mental Health 1967–69, Pres.'s Comm. on Civil Disorders 1967, Pres.'s Comm. on Causes of Violence 1968, Nat. Asscn for Advancement of Colored People Legal Defense Fund 1967–68, Pres.'s Comm. on Marijuana and Drug Abuse 1972–73, Ford Foundation Study on Law and Justice 1973–76; rapporteur, Twentieth Century Fund Study on Sentencing 1975–76; Guggenheim Fellow 1978–79; mem. Comm. on Law and Social Action, American Jewish Congress 1978; Dir American Civil Liberties Union 1968–71, 1972–75, Asscn of Behavioral and Social Sciences, NAS 1973–76; Chair. Civil Rights Comm. New England Region, Anti-Defamation League, B'nai B'rith 1980. *Publications:* Psychoanalysis, Psychiatry and the Law (with others) 1967, Criminal Law: Theory and Process 1974, The Best Defense 1982, Reversal of Fortune: Inside the von Bülow Case 1986, Taking Liberties: A Decade of Hard Cases, Bad Laws and Bum Raps 1988, Chutzpah 1991, Contrary to Popular Opinion 1992, The Abuse Excuse 1994, The Advocate's Devil 1994, Reasonable Doubt 1996, The Vanishing American Jew 1997, Sexual McCarthyism 1998, Just Revenge 1999, The Genesis of Justice 2000, Letters to a Young Lawyer 2001, Shouting Fire: Civil Liberties in a Turbulent Age 2002, Why Terrorism Works 2002, Supreme Injustice: How the High Court Hijacked Election 2000 2002, America Declares Independence 2003, America on Trial 2004, Letters to a Young Lawyer 2005, The Case for Israel 2005, Rights from Wrongs: A Secular Theory of the Origins of Rights 2005, The Case for Peace: How the Arab-Israeli Conflict Can be Resolved 2006, Preemption: A Knife That Cuts Both Ways 2007, What Israel Means to Me 2007, Blasphemy 2008, The Case against Israel's Enemies 2008, Finding, Framing, and Hanging Jefferson 2009, The Case for Moral Clarity 2009, The Trials of Zion 2010, Israel on Trial 2011; contrib. articles to legal journals. *Honours:* Hon. MA (Harvard Coll.) 1967; Hon. LLD (Yeshiva) 1989. *Address:* Harvard University Law School, Hauser Hall 520, 1575 Massachusetts Avenue, Cambridge, MA 02138-2801, USA (office). *Telephone:* (617) 495-4617 (office). *Fax:* (617) 495-7855 (office). *E-mail:* dersh@law.harvard.edu (office). *Website:* www.law.harvard.edu (office); www.alandershowitz.com.

DESAI, Anita, BA, FRSL; Indian writer and academic; *John E. Burchard Professor Emerita of Humanities, Massachusetts Institute of Technology*; b. 24 June 1937, Mussoorie; d. of Toni Nimé and D. N. Mazumdar; m. Ashvin Desai 1958; two s. two d. *Education:* Queen Mary's School, Delhi and Miranda House, Univ. of Delhi. *Career:* Elizabeth Drew Visiting Prof., Smith Coll., Mass, USA 1987–88; Purington Prof. of English, Mount Holyoke Coll. 1988–92; John E. Burchard Prof. of Humanities, MIT, Cambridge, Mass 1993–2002, now Prof. Emer.; Gildersleeves Prof., Barnard Coll.; Visiting Scholar, Rockefeller Foundation, Bellagio, Italy; Sidney Harman Visiting Prof. and Writer-in-Residence, Baruch Coll. 2003; mem. American Acad. of Arts and Letters, PEN, Sahitya Akademi, India. *Film screenplay:* In Custody 1994. *Television:* The Village By The Sea (BBC) 1994. *Publications:* Cry, The Peacock 1963, Voices in the City 1965, Bye-Bye, Blackbird 1971, Where Shall We Go This Summer? 1973, Fire on the Mountain 1978, Games at Twilight 1979, Clear Light of Day 1980, The Village by the Sea 1983, In Custody 1984, Baumgartner's Bombay 1988, Journey to Ithaca 1995, Fasting, Feasting 1999, Diamond Dust and Other Stories 2000, The Zigzag Way 2004, The Artist of Disappearance 2011; children's books: The Peacock Garden, Cat on a Houseboat. *Honours:* Hon. Fellow, Girton Coll., Cambridge 1988, Clare Hall, Cambridge 1991, Hon. mem. American Acad. of Arts and Letters; Royal Soc. of Literature Winifred Holtby Prize 1978, Sahitya Acad. Prize 1978, Fed. of Indian Publishers Award 1978, Guardian Prize for Children's Fiction 1983, Hadassah Prize, New York 1988, Padma Sri 1989, Literary Lion, New York Public Library 1993, Scottish Arts Council Neil Gunn Award for Int. Writing 1994, Alberto Moravia Prize for Literature, Italy 1999. *Literary Agent:* Rogers, Coleridge & White Ltd, 20 Powis Mews, London, W11 1JN, England. *Telephone:* (20) 7221-3717. *Fax:* (20) 7229-9084. *Website:* www.rcwlitagency.com.

DESAI, Kiran; Indian novelist; b. 3 Sept. 1971, New Delhi, India; d. of Anita Desai and Ashvin Desai; pnr Orhan Pamuk. *Education:* Bennington Coll., Hollins Univ. and Columbia Univ., USA. *Publications include:* novels: Hullabaloo in the Guava Orchard (Betty Trask Award) 1998, The Inheritance of Loss (Man Booker Prize, Nat. Book Critics Circle Fiction Award) 2006; Aids Sutra: Untold Stories from India 2008. *Literary Agent:* InkWell Management, 521 Fifth Avenue, 26th Floor, New York, NY 10175, USA. *Telephone:* (212) 922-3500. *Fax:* (212) 922-0535. *E-mail:* info@inkwellmanagement.com. *Website:* www.inkwellmanagement.com.

DESAI, Baron (Life Peer), cr. 1991, of St Clement Danes in the City of Westminster; **Meghnad Jagdishchandra Desai,** PhD; British economist and academic; *Professor Emeritus of Economics, London School of Economics*; b. 10 July 1940, Baroda, India; s. of Jagdishchandra Desai and Mandakini Desai (née Majmundar); m. 1st Gail Wilson 1970 (divorced 2004); one s. two d.; m. 2nd Kishwar Rosha 2004. *Education:* Univ. of Bombay, Univ. of Pennsylvania, USA. *Career:* Assoc. Specialist, Dept of Agricultural Econs, Univ. of Calif., Berkeley, USA 1963–65; Lecturer, LSE 1965–77, Sr Lecturer 1977–80, Reader 1980–83, Prof. of Econs 1983–, now Prof. Emer., Head Devt Studies Inst. 1990–95, Dir Centre for the Study of Global Governance 1992–2003, Chair. Econ. Research Div. 1983–95; consultant at various times to FAO, UNCTAD, Int. Coffee Org., World Bank, UNIDO, Ministries of

Industrial Devt and Educ., Algeria, British Airports Authority and other bodies; Co-Ed. Journal of Applied Econometrics 1984–; mem. Editorial Bds Int. Review of Applied Econs and several other journals; mem. Council, Royal Econ. Soc. 1988; mem. Exec. Cttee Asscn of Univ. Teachers in Econs 1987– (Pres. 1987–90); mem. Univ. of London Senate representing LSE 1981–89; mem. Nat. Exec. of Council for Academic Freedom and Democracy 1972–83, Speaker's Comm. on Citizenship 1989–, Berndt Carlson Trust; mem. or fmr mem. Governing Body of Courtauld Inst., British Inst. in Paris, Cen. School of Arts, Polytechnic of N London; Chair. Holloway Ward (Islington Cen.) Labour Party 1977–80; Chair. Islington S and Finsbury Labour Party 1986–92, Pres. 1992–. *Films:* Life Goes On (cameo) 2009. *Publications:* Marxian Economic Theory 1974 (trans. in several languages), Applied Econometrics 1976, Marxian Economics 1979, Testing Monetarism 1981, Marx's Revenge 2001, Global Governance and Financial Crises 2003, Nehru's Hero: Dilip Kumar in the Life of India 2004, Development and Nationhood 2004, Development and Nationhood 2005, The Route of All Evil: Political Economy of Ezra Pound 2006, Rethinking Islamism 2006, Dead on Time (novel) 2009, The Rediscovery of India 2009; ed. several books; numerous papers and contribs to books and journals. *Honours:* Dr hc (Kingston Univ.) 1992; Hon. DSc (Econs) (E London) 1994; Hon. DPhil (London Guildhall) 1996; Hon. LLD (Monash Univ.) 2005; Pravasi Phraskar (Distinguished Diaspora Indian Award) 2004, Distinguished Alumnus Award, Martin School of Finance 2004. *Address:* House of Lords, London, SW1A 0AA (office); 3 Deepdene Road, London, SE5 8EG, England (home). *Telephone:* (20) 7219-5066 (office); (20) 7274-5561 (home). *Fax:* (20) 7219-5979 (office). *E-mail:* desaim@parliament.uk (office); lord.mdesai@gmail.com (home). *Website:* www.lse.ac.uk/Depts/global (office).

DESCÔTEAUX, Bernard; Canadian journalist and publisher; *Chief Editor, Le Devoir;* b. 16 Sept. 1947, Sainte-Monique, Quebéc; two c. *Education:* Univ. of Toronto, Univ. of Montréal in Québec (UQAM), Univ. of Montréal. *Career:* journalist La Voix de l'est (The Voice of the East) 1969–70; information officer, Canadian Industries Ltd 1970–71; travel co-ordinator, Tourbec Inc. 1972–73; information officer, Information Canada 1973–74; Municipal Chronicler, Le Devoir newspaper 1974–76, Parl. Corresp. to French Nat. Ass. 1976–83, 1987–90, Parl. Corresp. to Fed. Govt, Ottawa 1983–87, Chief Ed. and Dir of Information 1990–92, Chief Ed. 1992–. *Address:* Le Devoir, 2050 rue de Bleury, Ninth Floor, Montréal, PQ H3A 3M9, Canada (office). *Telephone:* (514) 985-3333 (office). *Fax:* (514) 985-3360 (office). *E-mail:* redaction@ledevoir.com (office). *Website:* www.ledevoir.com (office).

DESHPANDE, Shashi, BA, MA, BL; Indian writer; b. 19 Aug. 1938, Dharwad, Karnataka; d. of Adya Rangacharya and Sharada Adya; m. D. H. Deshpande 1962; two s. *Education:* Univs of Mumbai and Bangalore. *Career:* fmrly worked for a law journal and magazine; full-time writer 1970–; mem. Sahitya Akademi Bd for English 1989–94. *Film script:* Drishti 1990. *Publications include:* The Dark Holds No Terrors (Nanjangud Thirumalamba Award) 1980, If I Die Today 1982, Come Up and Be Dead 1982, Roots and Shadows 1983, That Long Silence (Sahitya Akademi Award 1990) 1988, The Binding Vine 1993, A Matter of Time 1999, Small Remedies 2000, Moving On 2004, In the Country of Deceit 2008; short stories: The Legacy and Other Stories 1978, It Was Dark 1986, The Miracle and Other Stories 1986, It Was the Nightingale 1986, The Intrusion and Other Stories 1994, The Stone Women 2000, Collected Stories, Vol. I 2003, Vol. II 2004; non-fiction: Writing from the Margin and other essays 2003, Opening Scenes (trans. from Kannada of memoirs and a play), Deliverance (novel translated from Marathi). *Honours:* Thirumathi Rangammal Prize 1984, Padma Shri 2009. *E-mail:* shashideshpande04@gmail.com. *Literary Agent:* c/o Alison M. Bond Agency, 155 West 72nd Street, New York, NY 10023, USA. *Telephone:* (212) 874-2850 (office). *E-mail:* alison@bondlit.com. *Address:* 409 41st Cross, Jayanagar V Block, Bangalore 560 041, India (home). *Telephone:* (80) 26636228 (home). *Fax:* (80) 26641137 (home). *E-mail:* shashideshpande04@gmail.com (home).

DESMÉE, Gilbert Georges, Dip; French writer, editor and educator; b. 29 Jan. 1951, Suresnes; m. Maria Desmée 1952. *Education:* Univ. of Cachan, Univ. of Versailles. *Career:* Dir, Sapriphage literary review 1988–2002; mem. ELVIR. *Publications include:* Le Schiste Métamorphique 1990, L'Infini pour respirer in Histoire de livres d'artistes 1991, Un Magdalénien Contemporain in Robert Pérot 1994, En écho des corps d'écriture 1995, Je m'en dit tu 1996, Seul le geste serait fécond 1997; contribs: anthologies, including: Le Bel Aujourd'hui; Boris Lejeune, journals, including: Encres Vives, Sapriphage, Agone, Contre-Vox, L'Estracelle, Textuerre, Présage, L'Arbre à Paroles, Le Cri d'Os. *Telephone:* (6) 98-51-13-34 (office). *E-mail:* gilbert.desmee@wanadoo.fr (office). *Website:* gilbert.desmee.20six.fr.

DESMOND, Richard Clive; British publishing and media executive; *Chairman, Northern & Shell PLC;* b. 8 Dec. 1951, s. of Cyril Desmond and Millie Desmond; m. Janet Robertson 1983 (divorced 2010); one s. *Career:* Advertisement Exec. Thomson Newspapers 1967–68; Group Advertisement Man. Beat Publs Ltd 1968–74; f. Northern & Shell Network 1974 (later Northern & Shell PLC) Chair. 1974–; launched Int. Musician (magazine) 1974; Demonde Advertising 1976–89; Publr Next, Fitness, Cook's Weekly, Venture, Penthouse, Bicycle, Stamps, Electric Blue, Rock CD, Guitar, For Woman, Attitude, Arsenal, Liverpool; f. Fantasy Channel 1995, OK! Magazine 1993–, OK! TV 1999–; owner Express Newspapers 2000–. *Address:* Northern & Shell PLC, 10 Lower Thames Street, London, EC3R 6EN, England (office). *Telephone:* (871) 434-1010 (office). *Website:* www.northernandshell.co.uk (office).

DESOLA, David; Spanish writer. *Career:* fmr film critic, Temps Moderns. *Films:* Tiles (Public Award in FIKE Int. Short Film Festival Vâvora, Portugal, First Prize, Int. Film Festival Islantilla 2002 and Nat. Short Film Competition Video from Medina Countryside 2002) 1999, La duda del rey negro (scriptwriter), Ojos clandestinos (scriptwriter), Lucio en el Estado del bienestar (scriptwriter) (Official Selection of young filmmakers Granada Festival 1999, Best Short Film and Best Screenplay Mollet Ficció 1998, Best Short Film and Best Screenplay Calella Film Festival 1999), Senderillos de gloria (screenwriter and director), Micro Obert (screenwriter and director), Maldito corazón (screenwriter and director) (Best Video "argument/Ficció", Festival of Calella 1999). *Plays:* Baldosas (First Prize Bradomin Marquis 1999), Working Class, El Horno Judas. *Publications:* Assassinas (co-author) 1999, Monoloco (co-author) 1999, The twin tube 1999, Stored (Brothers Award Machado) 2002, Twentieth century which art in heaven 2006, La charca inútil (Premio Lope de Vega) 2007, Epoxy. *Address:* Secretariat of the Sample of Spanish Theatre of Contemporary Authors, 18 Pintor Velázquez, mezzanine, 03004 Alicante, Spain. *Telephone:* (96) 5123856. *Fax:* (96) 5980123. *E-mail:* info@muestrateatro.com. *Website:* www.muestrateatro.com.

DeSOTO, Lewis, MFA; South African writer and artist; b. 1952, Bloemfontein; m. Gunilla Josephson. *Education:* Univ. of British Columbia. *Career:* moved to Canada 1967; fmr Ed., Literary Review of Canada. *Exhibitions:* paintings in public and private galleries across Canada. *Publications include:* A Blade of Grass 2004; contrib. to numerous literary journals. *Honours:* Books in Canada/Writers' Trust Short Prose Award. *Address:* c/o The Maia Press Ltd, 82 Forest Road, London, E8 3BH, England.

DETHERIDGE, Andrew John, BA, MA, PGCE; British writer, poet and lecturer; b. 11 April 1969, Stourport, Worcestershire; s. of Colin Detheridge and Barbara Norris; m. Alexandra Jayne Cope; two d. *Education:* Univ. of Nottingham, Univ. of Wolverhampton. *Career:* English/History Teacher, St Peter's School 1994–95; English Teacher, George Dixon School 1995–96, Castle High School 1996–99; Lecturer and Poet-in-Residence, Sandwell Coll., West Midlands 1999–2004, Castle High School 2005–; mem. Equity. *Publications include:* Naked 1999, In the Light of Dreams 2000, Ocean's Spray 2001, In Character 2001, The City of the Dead 2002, The World Spins Darkly 2002, Vast Skies 2002, Travelling Through Life 2003, Snow Falls from the Branch 2005, The Break-dancing Spider 2005, Away with Words 2006, contrib. poetry, short stories, haiku, senryu to numerous magazines and anthologies. *Honours:* Forward Press one of the top 100 poets of the year 1999, 2003, Partners in Poetry Open Competition winner 1999, jt first prize East Barnet Festival Competition 2001, two haiku in Museum of Haiku Literature, award winner Hoshi-to-Mori Int. Tanka Contest 2004. *Address:* Haden House, 188b Cradley Road, Netherton, Dudley, West Midlands, DY2 9TE, England (home). *Telephone:* (1384) 416988 (home). *E-mail:* adetheridge@castle.dudley.gov.uk (office).

DEV SEN, Nabaneeta, BA, MA, AM, PhD; Indian writer and academic; b. 1938, d. of Narendra Dev and Radharani Devi; m. Amartya Sen (divorced); three d. *Education:* Calcutta (now Kolkata) Univ., Jadavpur Univ., Harvard Univ., Indiana Univ., USA. *Career:* Bengali writer; Researcher, Newnham Coll., Cambridge 1961–64; Asst Prof. of Comparative Literature, Jadavpur Univ. 1970–72, Assoc. Prof. 1972–83, Prof. 1983–2002, Chair., Dept of Comparative Literature 1987–89; Maytag Prof. of Comparative Literature, Univ. of Colorado, USA 1988–89; Visiting Fellow, St Antony's Coll., Oxford 1997; Radhakrishnan Memorial Lecturer, Oxford Univ. 1996–97; Founder and Pres. West Bengal Women Writers' Asscn; Vice-Pres. Indian Nat. Comparative Literature Asscn; mem. Bharatiya Jnanpith Award Language Advisory Cttee 1975–90, Advisory Bd Bengali, Sahitya Akademi 1978–82. *Publications include:* fiction: Ami Anupan 1978, Prabaase Doibera Bashe 1985, Swabhumi 1986, Sheet Saahasik Hemanta lok 1988, Ekti Dupur 1996, Baamaa Bodhini 1997, Deshaantar 1998, Thhikaanaa 1999, Maayaa Roye Gelo 2000, Shani-Rabi 2001, Paari 2002, Ural 2003, Dashti Upanyas 2003, Titli 2004, Albatross 2004, Ekati Iitibachak Premkahini 2005, Dwiragaman 2006, Ramdhan Mittir Lane 2006; juvenile fiction: Samudrer Sannyasini 1979, Icchamati 1995, Kayak 1996, Palachpurer Picnic 1997, Buddhi Bechaar Saudagar 1999, Chakum-chukum 2000, Saat Kanyer Desh 2000, Monkemoner Galpa 2002, Chhotoder Galpasangra 2005, Rankineer Rajyapat 2005, Sandesher Galpa 2006, Ek Dazan Roopkatha 2006; non-fiction: Karuna tomaar Kon Path Diye 1978, Ishwarer Pratidwandwi o Anyanya Prabandha 1978, Truckbahoney MacMahoney 1983, Hey Purna Taba Charaner Kachhe 1984, Birashaiba Santakabi ebang Birashaiba Sadhana 1987, Tin Bhubaner Parey 1990, Bhraamer Nabaneeta 2006; poetry: Pratham Pratyay 1959, Swaagata Debdut 1974, Shreshthha Kabita 1989. *Honours:* Kavi Prize for Poetry 1976, Pratisuti Award for Literary Criticism 1979, Prasad Prize for Poetry 1985, Sisir Kumar Prize 1986, Kalkut Prize 1988, Celli Award 1993, Sanskritiki Award 1994, Saratchandra Award 1994, Archana Choudhury Memorial Prize 1998, Marwari Mitra Samsad Samman for Literature 1998, Harmony Award 1998, Shatabir Kanya Award 1999, Sahitya Akademi Award 1999, Bishwa Banga Sammelan Award 2000, Rajiv Gandhi Memorial Millennium Gold Medal 2000, Bharat Nirman Award 2000, Padma Shri 2000, Bimal Mitra Memorial Award 2001, Mahadevi Verma Memorial Award 2001, Shreyasi Samman for Literature 2001, Lifetime Achievement Award, Bangla Acad. 2003, Pratima Mitra Memorial Prize 2004, Narayan Gangopadhyay Smarak Puraskar 2006, Saratchandra Smriti Puraskar 2007, Bharatiya Bhasha Parishad Award, Gouridevi Memorial Award, Prasad Puraskar. *Address:* 72

Hindustan Park, Kolkata 700 029, India (home). *Telephone:* (33) 24641603 (home).

DEVANE, Terry (see Healy, Jeremiah)

DEVENNE, François, PhD; French writer; b. 1964, Nantes. *Career:* wrote student thesis on geography and agriculture of Kilimanjaro; fmr course co-ordinator Univ. d'Artois; worked at Inst. Français de Recherche en Afrique (IFRA), Nairobi, Kenya; now lives in Paris. *Publications include:* Kilimandjaro montagne, mémoire, modernité (co-ed., essays and photographs) 2003, Trois rêves au Mont Mérou (novel) 2003, La Traversée des contes (novel) 2006, Tilorète et le roi qui pète (with Agnès Devenne and Juliette Boulard) 2010. *Address:* c/o Actes Sud, BP 90038, 13633 Arles, France. *Website:* www.actes-sud.fr.

DEVEREAUX, Emily (see Lewis-Smith, Anne Elizabeth)

DEVERELL, Rex Johnson, BA, BD, STM; Canadian playwright; b. 17 July 1941, Toronto, ON; m. Rita Joyce Shelton 1967; one s. *Education:* McMaster Univ., Union Theological Seminary. *Career:* Resident Playwright, Globe Theatre, Regina 1975–91; Pres., Playwrights Union of Canada 1991–93; mem. Saskatchewan Writers Guild, Playwrights Union of Canada, Saskatchewan Playwrights Centre, Amnesty International. *Plays include:* The Brothers 1970, Sam and the Tigers 1971, Shortshrift 1972, Soup 1972, Sarah's Play 1973, The Copetown City Kite Crisis 1973, The Underground Lake 1974, Harry Oddstack and the Case of the Missing King 1975, Power Trip 1975, The Shinbone General Store Caper 1975, Next Town: Nine Miles 1976, Boiler Room Suite 1977, Superwheel 1977, The Up-Hill Revival 1977, In Short Supply 1978, For Lands Sake 1978, The Gadget 1979, Drift 1980, Medicare 1980, Black Powder 1981, Righteousness 1983, Fallout 1985, Beyond Batoche 1985, The Riel Commission 1985, Switching Places 1986, Quartet for Three Actors 1987, The Afternoon of the Big Game 1988, Weird Kid 1988, Mandarin Oranges II 1989, Video Wars 1991, Belonging 1994, Brooks! 1997. *Publications include:* contribs: Canadian Theatre Review, Canadian Children's Literature, Canadian Drama, Prairie Fire, Grain. *Honours:* McMaster Univ. Honour Soc. 1963, Ohio State Award 1974, Canadian Authors Asscn Medal 1978, Major Armstrong Award 1986. *Website:* deverell.blogspot.com.

DEVERELL, William Herbert, BA, DJuris; Canadian writer; b. 4 March 1937, Regina, Sask.; m. Tekla Melnyk; one s. one d. *Education:* Univ. of Saskatchewan. *Career:* on staff, Saskatoon Star-Phoenix 1956–60, Canadian Press, Montréal 1960–62, Vancouver Sun, 1963; partner in law firm, Vancouver 1964–79; writer 1979–; mem. British Columbia Civil Liberties Asscn (Hon. Dir), Crime Writers' Asscn, Crime Writers of Canada, Writers Union of Canada (Chair. 1994–95), Canadian Writers Guild. *Television:* cr. Street Legal series (CBC). *Publications include:* fiction: Needles 1979, High Crimes 1979, Mecca 1983, Dance of Shiva 1984, Platinum Blues 1988, Mindfield 1989, Kill All the Lawyers 1994, Street Legal – The Betrayal 1995, Trial of Passion 1997, Slander 1999, Laughing Falcon 2001, Mind Games 2003, April Food 2005, Kill all the Judges 2008, Snow Job 2009; non-fiction: Fatal Cruise: The Trial of Robert Frisbee 1991. *Honours:* Hon. DLitt (Simon Fraser Univ.); Seal First Novel Award 1979, Book of the Year Award, Periodical Distributors Asscn of Canada 1980, Arthur Ellis Award for Best Canadian crime novel 1998, 2006, Dashiel Hammett Award for literary merit in crime fiction in North America 1998, Lifetime Achievement Award, Canadian Crime Writers. *Address:* 6641 Razor Point Road, North Pender Island, BC V0N 2M1, Canada (home). *E-mail:* william@deverell.com (office). *Website:* www.deverell.com.

DEVEREUX, Eve (see Barnett, Paul Le Page)

DEVI, Ananda, PhD; Mauritian novelist; b. 23 March 1957, Trois-Boutiques. *Career:* currently living in France. *Publications include:* novels: Rue la Poudrière 1989, Le Voile de Draupadi 1993, L'Arbre fouet 1997, Moi, l'interdite 2000, Pagli 2001, Soupir 2002, Le Long désir 2003, La Vie de Joséphin le Fou 2003, Ève de ses Décombres (Prix des Cinq Continents de la Frncophonie) 2006, Indian Tango 2007, Le sari vert (Prix Louis-Guilloux 2010) 2009; short stories: Solstices 1977, Le Poids des êtres 1987. *Honours:* Chevalier des Arts et des Lettres 2010. *Address:* c/o Éditions Gallimard, 5 rue Sébastien-Bottin, Paris 75328, France. *Website:* www.gallimard.fr.

DEVI, Mahasweta, BA, MA; Indian writer; b. 14 Jan. 1926, Dacca, East Bengal (now Bangladesh); d. of Manish Chandra Ghatak and Dharitri Devi; m. Bijon Bhattacharya 1946 (divorced 1962); one s. *Education:* Vishvabharati Univ., Calcutta (now Kolkata) Univ. *Career:* Lecturer, Bijougarh Jyotish Roy Coll., Kolkata 1964–84; f. Bortika magazine 1980; reporter, Jugantar newspaper 1964, Bartaman 1984–91. *Publications include:* almost 100 novels and twenty short story collections including, Jhansir Rani (trans. as The Queen of Jhansi) 1956, Nati 1957, Madhurey Madhur 1958, Yamuna Teer 1958, Etotuku Asha 1959, Premtara 1959, Amrita Sanchay 1964, Bioscoper Baksho 1964, Kavi Bandyoghoti Gayiner Jivan i Mrityu 1966, Andhanmalik 1967, Aranyer Adhikar (Sahitya Akademi Award 1979) 1975, Hajar Churashir Ma 1975, Swaha 1977, Agnigarbha 1978, Chotti Munda o Tar Tir 1980, Subhaga Basanta 1980, Sidhu Kanhur Daakay 1981, Daulati 1984, Srinkhalito 1985, Bish-Ekush 1986, Iter Parey It 1987, Prothorn Paath 1988, Bashai Tudu 1993, Rudali 1993, Paschim Banga Kheria Sabar Kalyan Samiti 1994, Dakatey Kahini 1998. *Honours:* Dr hc (Indira Gandhi Nat. Open Univ.) 1999; Padma Shri 1986, Jnanpith Award 1996, Ramon Magsaysay Award 1997, Padma Vibhushan 2006, Yashwantrao Chavan Nat. Award 2010. *Address:* c/o Seagull Books, 26 Circus Avenue, Kolkata 700 017, India. *Telephone:* (33) 22873737; (33) 22877942. *E-mail:* books@seagullindia.com. *Website:* www.seagullindia.com.

DEVLIN, Polly, OBE; Irish writer, journalist, broadcaster, film-maker and art critic; b. Co. Tyrone; m. Adrian Garnett; three d. *Education:* Nat. Film School. *Career:* Features Ed. Vogue magazine; columnist, New Statesman, London Evening Standard; journalist with Vogue (American edn), Sunday Times, the Observer; hosted series of talks and interviews on TV for BBC Northern Ireland 1980s, has broadcast numerous talks and has written a radio play for BBC, London, mem. Northern Ireland team, Round Britain Quiz, BBC Radio 4; art critic for The International Herald Tribune 1990–91; currently Adjunct Prof. of Creative Writing, Barnard Coll.; mem. judging panel Booker Prize, UK, Irish Times-Aer Lingus Irish Literature Prizes 1992. *Film:* The Daisy Chain (documentary, also writer and dir. *Publications include:* Vogue Book of Fashion Photography 1979, The Far Side of the Lough 1983, All of Us There 1983, Dora or the Shifts of the Heart 1990, Mitchell Beazley Guide Book to Dublin, Only Sometimes Looking Sideways (essays) 1998, The Rising Tide 2006, A Year in the Life of an English Meadow 2007. *Honours:* winner Vogue talent competition 1964. *Address:* Department of English, Barnard College, 417 Barnard Hall, 3009 Broadway, New York, NY 10027-6598, USA (office). *E-mail:* english@barnard.edu (office). *Website:* www.barnard.edu/english (office); www.pollydevlin.co.uk.

DEW, Robb (Reavill) Forman; American writer; b. 26 Oct. 1946, Mount Vernon, OH; d. of Oliver Duane Forman and Helen Ransom Forman; m. Charles Burgess Dew 1968, two s. *Education:* Louisiana State Univ. *Career:* Fellow, Iowa Writers' Workshop 1984. *Publications include:* Dale Loves Sophie to Death (Nat. Book Award) 1982, The Time of Her Life 1984, Fortunate Lives 1991, A Southern Thanksgiving: Recipes and Musings for a Manageable Feast 1992, The Family Heart: A Memoir of When Our Son Came Out 1994, The Evidence Against Her 2001, The Truth of the Matter 2005, Being Polite to Hitler 2010. *Honours:* Guggenheim Grant 1983. *Literary Agent:* Miriam Altshuler Literary Agency, 53 Old Post Road North, Red Hook, NY 12571, USA. *Telephone:* (845) 758-9408. *Fax:* (845) 758-3118. *E-mail:* malalit@ulster.net. *Address:* 218 Buckley Street, Williamstown, MA 01267, USA (home). *Telephone:* (413) 458-3477 (home). *Fax:* (413) 458-5171 (home). *E-mail:* robbdew@me.com; robbformandew@aol.com.

DEWDNEY, Christopher; Canadian poet and writer; b. 9 May 1951, London, Ont.; m. 1st Suzanne Dennison 1971 (divorced 1975); one d.; m. 2nd Lise Downe 1977 (divorced 1990); one s.; m. 3rd Barbara Gowdy. *Education:* South and Westminster Collegiate Institutes, London, Ont., H.B. Beal Art Annex, London, Ont. *Career:* mem. Editorial Bd Coach House Publishing 1986–, Poetry Chair 1988, mem. Bd of Dirs 1988–; Academic Adviser, Calumet Coll., York Univ., Toronto 1997–01, Hiring Cttee mem. Schulich School of Business 1997–2001, Chair. Masters' Council of Academic Advisors 2000–, Fellow 1998–; mem. Bd of Dirs Toronto Arts Council 2000–, Literary Chair 2000–; Fellow, McLuhan Program in Culture and Tech., Univ. of Toronto 1993. *Publications include:* Poetry: A Palaeozoic Geology of London, Ontario 1973, Fovea Centralis 1975, Spring Trances in the Control Emerald Night 1978, Alter Sublime 1980, The Cenozoic Asylum 1982, Predators of the Adoration 1983, Radiant Inventory 1988, Demon Pond 1994, Signal Fires 2000, The Natural History 2002, Children of the Outer Dark 2007; Poetry Monographs: Golders Green 1972, The Cenozoic Asylum 1983, Concordat Proviso Ascendant 1991, Demon Spawn 2002; Non-Fiction: The Immaculate Perception, 1986, The Secular Grail 1993. Last Flesh 1998, Acquainted with the Night 2004, Soul of the World 2008. *Honours:* Design Canada Award 1974, CBC Prize 1986, Harbour Front Festival Prize 2007.

DEWEESE, Jean (see De Weese, Thomas Eugene (Gene))

DEWHIRST, Ian, MBE, BA; British librarian (retd), writer and poet; b. 17 Oct. 1936, Keighley, Yorkshire; s. of Harold Dewhirst and Mary E. Dewhirst. *Education:* Victoria Univ. of Manchester. *Career:* staff, Keighley Public Library 1960–91; mem. Yorkshire Dialect Soc., Edward Thomas Fellowship. *Publications include:* The Handloom Weaver and Other Poems 1965, Scar Top and Other Poems 1968, Gleanings from Victorian Yorkshire 1972, A History of Keighley 1974, Yorkshire Through the Years 1975, Gleanings from Edwardian Yorkshire 1975, The Story of a Nobody 1980, You Don't Remember Bananas 1985, Keighley in Old Picture Postcards 1987, In the Reign of the Peacemaker 1993, Down Memory Lane 1993, Images of Keighley 1996, A Century of Yorkshire Dialect (co-ed.) 1997, Keighley in the Second World War 2005, Nah Then! A Treasury of Yorkshire Dialect Quotations (compiler) 2010; contrib. to Yorkshire Ridings Magazine, Lancashire Magazine, Dalesman, Cumbria, Pennine Magazine, Transactions of the Yorkshire Dialect Society, Yorkshire Journal, Down Your Way, Northern Life. *Honours:* Hon. DLitt (Bradford) 1997. *Address:* 14 Raglan Avenue, Fell Lane, Keighley, West Yorkshire, BD22 6BJ, England (home). *Telephone:* (1535) 662268 (home).

DEWHURST, Eileen Mary, MA (Oxon.); British writer; b. 27 May 1929, Liverpool; m. (divorced). *Education:* St Anne's Coll., Oxford. *Career:* mem. CWA, Soc. of Authors. *Publications:* crime novels: Death Came Smiling 1975, After the Ball 1976, Curtain Fall 1977, Drink This 1980, Trio in Three Flats 1981, Whoever I Am 1982, The House That Jack Built 1983, There Was a Little Girl 1984, Playing Safe 1985, A Private Prosecution 1986, A Nice Little Business 1987, The Sleeper 1988, Dear Mr Right 1990, The Innocence of Guilt 1991, Death in Candie Gardens 1992, Now You See Her 1995, The Verdict on Winter 1996, Alias the Enemy 1997, Roundabout 1998, Death of a Stranger 1999, Double Act 2000, Closing Stages 2001, No Love Lost 2001, Easeful

Death 2003, Naked Witness 2003; contrib. to Ellery Queen's Mystery Magazine, CWA Annual Anthologies. *Literary Agent:* c/o Gregory and Co., 3 Barb Mews, London, W6 7PA, England.

DEWHURST, Keith, BA; British writer; b. 24 Dec. 1931, Oldham, England; m. 1st Eve Pearce 1958 (divorced 1980); one s. two d.; m. 2nd Alexandra Cann 1980. *Education:* Peterhouse, Cambridge. *Career:* sports writer, Evening Chronicle, Manchester 1955–59; presenter, Granada TV 1968–69, BBC2 TV, London 1972; arts columnist, The Guardian, London 1969–72; writer-in-residence, Western Australia APA, Perth 1984. *Publications include:* Lark Rise to Candleford (two plays) 1980, Captain of the Sands (novel) 1981, Don Quixote (play) 1982, McSullivan's Beach (novel) 1986, Black Snow (play) 1992, War Plays (plays) 1997, Philoctetes (trans. of play) 2000, King Arthur (play) 2006, Impossible Plays (co-author) 2006, When You Put On a Red Shirt 2009. *Address:* c/o Yellow Jersey Press, Random House, 20 Vauxhall Bridge Road, London, SW1V 2SA, England.

DeWITT, Patrick; Canadian author; b. 1975, Vancouver Island, BC; m.; one s. *Publications include:* Ablutions 2009, The Sisters Brothers (Rogers Writers' Trust Fiction Prize 2011, Governor General's Award for English Language Fiction 2011) 2011. *Literary Agent:* Foundry Literary + Media, 33 West 17th Street, PH, New York, NY 10011, USA. *Telephone:* (212) 929-5064. *Fax:* (212) 929-5471. *Website:* www.foundrymedia.com; www.patrickdewitt.net.

DEXTER, (Norman) Colin, OBE, MA (Cantab.), MA (Oxon.); British author; b. 29 Sept. 1930, Stamford, Lincs., England; s. of Alfred Dexter and Dorothy Dexter (née Towns); m. Dorothy Cooper 1956; one s. one d. *Education:* Stamford School, Christ's Coll., Cambridge. *Career:* nat. service (Royal Signals) 1948–50; taught Classics 1954–66; Sr Asst Sec. Oxford Delegacy of Local Examinations 1966–88; Fellow, St Cross Coll., Oxford. *Publications:* Last Bus to Woodstock 1975, Last Seen Wearing 1977, The Silent World of Nicholas Quinn 1977, Service of All the Dead 1979, The Dead of Jericho 1981, The Riddle of the Third Mile 1983, The Secret of Annexe 3 1986, The Wench is Dead 1989, The Jewel That Was Ours 1991, The Way through the Woods 1992, Morse's Greatest Mystery and Other Stories 1993, The Daughters of Cain 1994, Death is Now My Neighbour 1996, The Remorseful Day 1999, Book of 'Morse' Crosswords 2006, Cracking Cryptic Crosswords 2009. *Honours:* Freedom of the City of Oxford 2001; Gold Dagger, Crime Writers' Asscn (twice), Silver Dagger (twice), Cartier Diamond Dagger, ITV 3 Writer's Award for Classic TV Drama 2008. *Address:* 456 Banbury Road, Oxford, OX2 7RG, England.

DEXTER, Peter (Pete) Whittemore, BA; American columnist and writer; b. 22 July 1943, Pontiac, MI; m. Dian McDonough; one c. *Education:* Univ. of South Dakota. *Career:* columnist, Philadelphia Daily News 1976–86, Esquire magazine 1985–86, Sacramento Bee 1986–90s. *Film screenplays:* Rush 1991, Mulholland Falls 1996, Michael 1996, Shortcut to Happiness 2003. *Publications include:* God's Pocket 1983, Deadwood (also screenplay, as Wild Bill) 1986, Paris Trout (also screenplay) (Nat. Book Award) 1988, Brotherly Love 1991, The Paperboy 1994, Train 2003, Paper Trails 2007, Spooner 2009. *Honours:* Associated Press (California-Nevada) Mark Twain Award 1987, Penn West Award, Los Angeles 1988, Bay Area Book Reviewers Award 1988. *Address:* c/o Author Mail, Grand Central Publishing, 237 Park Avenue, New York, NY 10017, USA. *Website:* www.hachettebookgroup.com.

DHALIWAL, Daljit, MA; British journalist; b. London; m. Lee Patrick Sullivan (divorced). *Education:* Univ. of East London, Univ. of London. *Career:* reporter for BBC, London 1990, NI Corresp. and Anchor, BBC World – 1995; reporter ITN, London 1995, Anchor, World News for Public TV, Channel 4 News and World Focus –2001; Anchor, Your World Today and World Report CNN (Cable Network News) Int., Atlanta, Ga USA 2002–04; Anchor, Wide Angle (Public Broadcasting System), New York, 2002, 2006–07, Anchor, Global Watch 2008, host, Foreign Exchange with Daljit Dhaliwal 2008–; moderator and host, UN confs in New York and The Hague; Judge, Amnesty Int. Media Awards, BAFTA Awards. *Honours:* Dr hc (Univ. of East London). *Address:* c/o Thirteen/WNET, 450 West 33rd Street, New York, NY 10001, USA (office). *E-mail:* info@foreignexchange.tv (office). *Website:* foreignexchange.tv (office).

DHASAL, Namdeo Laxman; Indian poet and writer; b. 15 Feb. 1949, Pur-Kanersar, near Pune, Maharashtra; m. Malika Amar Sheikh. *Career:* Marathi writer; f. Dalit Panther militant movt 1972. *Publications include:* poetry: Golpitha (Soviet Land Nehru Award 1974) 1972, Moorkha Mhatayane Dongar Halavile 1975, Priyadarshini 1976, Tuhi Iyatta Kanchi 1981, Ambedkari Chalwal 1981, Khel 1983, Gandu Bagicha 1986, Ya Sattet Jeev Ramat Nahi 1995, Andhale Shatak 1997, Mee Marale Sooryachya Rathache Ghode Saat 2005, Tujhe Bot Dharoon Chalalo Ahe Mee 2006; prose: Ambedkari Chalwal 1981, Andhale Shatak 1997, Hadki Hadavala, Ujedaachi Kali Dunia, Sarva Kahi Samashtisathi, Buddha Dharma: Kahi Shesh Prashna. *Honours:* Maharashtra State Award 1973, 1974, 1982, 1983, Padma Shree 1999, Lifetime Achievement Award, Sahitya Akademi 2004. *Address:* c/o Navayana Publishing, 155, Second Floor, Shahpur Jat, New Delhi 110 049, India. *Telephone:* (11) 26494795. *E-mail:* navayana@gmail.com. *Website:* www.navayana.org.

DI BLASI, Debra, BFA; American educator, writer and publisher; b. (Debra Lynn Pickens), 27 May 1957, Kirksville, MO; m. 1st Carlos Roberto di Blasi 1984 (divorced 1989); m. 2nd Mark Shapiro 2000. *Education:* Univ. of Missouri at Columbia, Kansas City Art Inst., San Francisco State Univ. *Career:* Advertising Man., Robert Half of Northern California, San Francisco 1986–89; Asst to the Exec. Dir, Accessible Arts Inc, Kansas City, MO 1990–92; Sr Sec., Int. Network Design and Engineering Dept, Sprint Communications, Kansas City, MO 1992–95; Tutor, Kansas City Art Inst., Kansas City, MO 1995–2003; Pres., Jaded Ibis Productions 2000–; freelance lecturer on writing and experimental literary forms 2003–; Assoc. Guest Ed., SOMA; lectures, readings from her works; mem. Nat. Geographic Soc., Writers Place, Kansas City Art Inst. Alumni Circle. *Publications include:* The Season's Condition (screenplay) 1993, Drought (screenplay) 1997, Drought and Say What You Like (novellas) 1997, Prayers of an Accidental Nature (novellas) 1999, The Jiri Chronicles and Other Fictions (short stories) 2007, What the Body Requires (novel) 2009, Skin of the Sun 2010; contribs: short stories in anthologies, include: Lovers: Writings by Women 1992, Exposures: Essays by Missouri Women 1997; short stories in periodicals, include: Moondance, Cottonwood, Potpourri, New Letters, Sou'wester, New Delta Review, AENE, Colorado-North Review, Transfer, Essays, articles and reviews to periodicals, include: SOMA, New Art Examiner. *Honours:* Eyster Prize for Fiction, for short story An Interview with My Husband, New Delta Review 1991, Cinovation Screenwriting Award 1998, Thorpe Menn Book Award 1998, James C. McCormick Fellowship in Fiction 2003, Inspiration Award, Kansas City Metropolitan Arts Council 2008, Diagram Innovative Writing Award 2008. *Telephone:* (816) 204-1467 (office). *E-mail:* debra@debradiblasi.com (office). *Website:* www.debradiblasi.com.

DI CICCO, Pier Giorgio, BA, BEd, MDiv, BSTheol; Canadian poet and priest; b. 5 July 1949, Arezzo, Italy. *Education:* Univ. of Toronto, St Paul's Univ. *Career:* founder and Poetry Ed., Poetry Toronto Newsletter, 1976–77; Assoc. Ed., Books in Canada, 1976–79; Co-Ed., 1976–79, Poetry Ed., 1980–82, Waves; Ordained Roman Catholic Priest and Assoc. Pastor, St Anne's Church, Brampton, Ontario, 1993–; Poet Laureate of Toronto 2007–. *Publications include:* We Are the Light Turning 1975, The Sad Facts 1977, The Circular Dark 1977, Dancing in the House of Cards 1977, A Burning Patience 1978, Roman Candles: An Anthology of 17 Italo-Canadian Poets (ed.) 1978, Dolce-Amaro 1979, The Tough Romance 1979, A Straw Hat for Everything 1981, Flying Deeper into the Century 1982, Dark to Light: Reasons for Humanness: Poems 1976–1979 1983, Women We Never See Again 1984, Twenty Poems, 1984, Post-Sixties Nocturne 1985, Virgin Science: Hunting Holistic Paradigms 1986, The City of Hurried Dreams 1993, The Honeymoon Wilderness 2002, The Dark Time of Angels 2003, Dead Men of the Fifties 2004, The Visible World 2006. *Honours:* Canada Council Awards 1974, 1976, 1980, Carleton Univ. Italo-Canadian Literature Award 1979.

DI MICHELE, Mary, MA; Canadian poet, writer and academic; b. 6 Aug. 1949, Lanciano, Italy; m. (divorced); one d. *Education:* Univ. of Windsor. *Career:* Poetry Ed., Toronto Life 1980–81, Poetry Toronto 1982–84; Writer-in-Residence, Univ. of Toronto 1985–86, Metro Reference Library, Toronto 1986, Regina Public Library 1987–88; Writer-in-Residence Concordia Univ., 1990, then Assoc. Prof., Prof. Creative Writing Programme; mem. Italian-Canadian Writers Asscn; Writers Union. *Publications include:* poetry: Tree of August 1978, Bread and Chocolate 1980, Mimosa and Other Poems 1981, Necessary Sugar 1984, Immune to Gravity 1986, Luminous Emergencies 1990, Stranger in You: Selected Poems & New 1995, Debriefing the Rose 1998; novels: Under My Skin 1994, Tenor of Love 2005; ed.: Anything is Possible 1984; contribs: anthologies and periodicals. *Honours:* First Prize for Poetry, CBC Literary Competition 1980, Silver Medal, DuMaurier Poetry Award 1982, Air Canada Writing Award 1983. *Address:* Department of English, Concordia University, Office LB 683-5, 1455 de Maisonneuve Blvd West, Montreal, PQ H3G 1M8, Canada. *Telephone:* (514) 848-2424 (office). *Website:* english.concordia.ca/MDiMichele.html (office).

DI PRIMA, Diane; American poet, writer, dramatist, translator and publisher and artist; b. 6 Aug. 1934, New York, NY; m. 1st Alan S. Marlowe 1962 (divorced 1969); m. 2nd Grant Fisher 1972 (divorced 1975); two s. three d. *Education:* Swarthmore Coll. *Career:* co-founder, New York Poets Theater, 1961–65; Co-Ed. (with LeRoi Jones), 1961–63, Ed., 1963–69, Floating Bear magazine; Publisher, Poets Press, 1964–69, Eidolon Editions, 1974–; Faculty, Naropa Institute, 1974–97, New College of California, San Francisco, 1980–87; Co-Founder, San Francisco Institute of Magical and Healing Arts, 1983–91; Sr Lecturer, California College of Arts and Crafts, Oakland, 1990–92; Visiting Faculty, San Francisco Art Institute, 1992; Adjunct Faculty, California Institute of Integral Studies 1994–95; Master Poet-in-Residence Columbia College Chicago 2000. *Publications include:* This Kind of Bird Flies Backward 1958; Ed. Various Fables from Various Places 1960, Dinners and Nightmares 1961, The New Handbook of Heaven 1962; Trans. The Man Condemned to Death 1963, Poets Vaudeville 1964, Seven Love Poems from the Middle Latin 1965, Haiku 1966, New Mexico Poem 1967, Earthsong 1968, Hotel Albert 1968; Ed. War Poems 1968, Memoirs of a Beatnik 1969, LA Odyssey 1969, The Book of Hours 1970, Kerhonkson Journal 1966, Revolutionary Letters 1971, The Calculus of Variation 1972, Loba, Part 1 1973; Ed. The Floating Bear: a Newsletter 1973, Freddie Poems 1974, Brass Furnace Going Out 1975, Selected Poems 1956–1975, 1975, Loba, Part 2 1976, Loba as Eve 1977, Loba, Parts 1–8 1978, Wyoming Series 1988, The Mysteries of Vision 1988, Pieces of a Song: Selected Poems 1990, Seminary Poems 1991, The Mask is the Path of the Star 1993, Loba, Parts 9–16 1998, Recollections of My Life as a Woman 2001, Fun with Forms 2001, Towers Down (with Clive Matson) 2002, The Ones I Used to Laugh With 2003; work trans. into over 20 languages. contribs: Over 300 literary and popular magazines and newspapers; Work appeared in over 100 anthologies. *Honours:* Hon. DLitt (St Lawrence Univ., Canton, New York) 1999; Nat. Endowment for the Arts 1966, 1973, Co-ordinating Council of Little Magazines Grants 1967, 1970, Lapis Foundation Awards 1978, 1979, Inst. for Aesthetic Devt Award 1986, Lifetime Service Award, Nat. Poetry Asscn 1993. *Address:* 78 Niagara Avenue, San Francisco, CA 94112, USA.

DI ROSA, Antonio, BSc; Italian journalist; b. 17 April 1951, Messina; s. of Calogero Rossetti and Anna Rossetti; partner; one s. two d. *Career:* began career at Giornale di Calabria 1974–78; moved to Gazzetta del Popolo 1978, Deputy Head Home News 1979–81, Head 1981–84; joined La Stampa 1984, Head Home News April–July 1988; Deputy Cen. Ed.-in-Chief Corriere della Sera 1988–93, Cen. Ed.-in-Chief 1993–96, Deputy Ed. 1996–2000; Ed. Il Secolo XIX 2000; Ed. La Gazzetta dello Sport 2004–06. *Honours:* Premio Senigallia 1983. *Address:* Via G. Morelli 1, Milan, Italy (home).

DIAMOND, Jared Mason, BA, PhD; American biologist, physiologist, academic and writer; *Professor of Geography and Physiology, David Geffen School of Medicine, University of California, Los Angeles*; b. 10 Sept. 1937, Boston, Mass; s. of Louis K. Diamond and Flora K. Diamond; m. Marie Nabel Cohen 1982; two s. *Education:* Harvard Coll., Univ. of Cambridge, UK. *Career:* Fellow, Trinity Coll., Cambridge 1961–65, Jr Fellow, Soc. of Fellows, Harvard Univ. 1962–65; Assoc. in Biophysics, Harvard Medical School 1965–66; Assoc. Prof. of Physiology, David Geffen School of Medicine, Univ. of California Medical School, Los Angeles 1966–68, Prof. of Geography, UCLA 1968–; Research Assoc., Dept of Ornithology American Museum of Natural History 1973–; US Regional Dir World Wide Fund for Nature; mem. Editorial Bd Skeptic Magazine; mem. NAS; Fellow, American Acad. of Arts and Sciences, American Physiological Soc., Biophysics Soc., American Philosophical Soc., American Soc. of Naturalists, American Ornithologists Union 1978. *Television:* Guns, Germs and Steel (three-part PBS documentary) 2005. *Publications:* The Avifauna of the Eastern Highlands of New Guinea 1972, Ecology and Evolution of Communities (co-ed.) 1975, Birds of Karkar and Bagabab Islands, New Guinea (co-author) 1979, The Avifaunas of Rennell and Bellona Islands. The Natural History of Rennell Islands, British Solomon Islands 1984, Community Ecology (co-author) 1985, Birds of New Guinea (co-author) 1986, The Third Chimpanzee: The Evolution and Future of the Human Animal 1992, 2006, Why is Sex Fun? – The Evolution of Human Sexuality 1997, Guns, Germs, and Steel: The Fates of Human Societies (Pulitzer Prize 1998, Cosmos Prize 1998) 1998, The Birds of Northern Melanesia: Speciation, Ecology, & Biogeography (co-author) 2001, Guns, Germs, and Steel Reader's Companion 2003, Collapse: How Societies Choose to Fail or Succeed 2004; several hundred research papers on physiology, ecology and ornithology; contribs to Discover, Natural History, Nature. *Honours:* Hon. DLitt (Sejong Univ., S Korea) 1995; Hon. PhD (Katholieke Universiteit Leuven, Belgium) 2008; Prize Fellowship in Physiology, Trinity Coll., Cambridge 1961–65, Lederle Medical Faculty Award 1968–71, Distinguished Teaching Award, UCLA Medical Class 1972, 1973, Distinguished Achievement Award, American Gastroenterological Asscn 1975, Kaiser Permanente/Golden Apple Teaching Award 1976, Nathaniel Bowditch Prize, American Physiological Soc. 1976, Franklin L. Burr Award, Nat. Geographic Soc. 1979, MacArthur Foundation 'Genius' Grant 1985, Archie Carr Medal 1989, MacArthur Foundation Fellow 1990, Tanner Lecturer, Univ. of Utah (and many other endowed lectureships) 1992, Royal Soc. Prizes for Science Books (Rhone-Poulenc Prize) 1992, 1998, Science Book Prize, New Scientist London 1992, Los Angeles Times Science Book Prize 1992, Zoological Soc. of San Diego Conservation Medal 1993, Randi Award, Skeptics Soc. 1994, Faculty Research Lecturer, UCLA 1996, Phi Beta Kappa Science Book Prize 1997, Elliott Coues Award, American Ornithologists' Union 1998, Gold Medal in nonfiction, California Book Awards 1998, Nat. Medal of Sciences 1999, Lannan Literary Award for Nonfiction 1999, Tyler Prize for Environmental Achievement 2001, Lewis Thomas Prize for Writing about Science 2002, Dickson Prize in Science 2006. *Address:* 1251A Bunche Hall, University of California at Los Angeles, Los Angeles, CA 90095-1524, USA (office). *Telephone:* (310) 825-6177 (office). *Fax:* (310) 206-5976 (office). *E-mail:* jdiamond@geog.ucla.edu (office). *Website:* 149.142.237.180/faculty/diamond.htm (office); www.geog.ucla.edu (office).

DÍAZ, Junot, BA, MFA; Dominican/American writer; *Professor, Massachusetts Institute of Technology*; b. 31 Dec. 1968, Santo Domingo, Dominican Repub.; s. of Rafael Díaz and Virtudes Sánchez; m. Elizabeth de León. *Education:* Rutgers Univ., Cornell Univ. *Career:* moved to USA aged six; currently Prof., Program in Writing and Humanistic Studies, MIT; Millet Writing Fellow, Wesleyan Univ.; Fiction Ed., Boston Review. *Publications include:* Drown (short stories) 1996, Negocios 1997, The Brief Wondrous Life of Oscar Wao (novel; Nat. Book Critics Circle Award for Fiction 2007, John Sargent Sr First Novel Prize 2007, Pulitzer Prize for Fiction 2008) 2007, Wildwood 2007, Alma 2007, The Pura Principle 2010; contrib. to New Yorker, Paris Review, African Verse, anthologies. *Honours:* Rome Fellowship, American Acad. of Arts and Letters 2007, John Simon Guggenheim Memorial Foundation Fellowship. *Address:* c/o Riverhead Books, Penguin Group (USA), 375 Hudson Street, New York, NY 10014, USA. *E-mail:* junot@mit.edu. *Website:* www.junotdiaz.com.

DiCHRISTINA, Mariette, BS; American editor; *Editor-in-Chief, Scientific American*; b. 16 April 1964, North Tarrytown, NY; m. Carl John Gerosa 1989; two d. *Education:* Boston Univ. *Career:* reporter, Gannett-Westchester newspapers 1986–87; joined Popular Science magazine as copy ed., later becoming Assoc. Ed., Sr Ed. and Exec. Ed. 1987–2001; Exec. Ed. Scientific American 2001–09, Ed.-in-Chief 2009–; Adjunct Prof. in Science Writing, New York Univ.; Pres. Nat. Asscn of Science Writers 2009–10; adviser, Citizen Science Alliance, Origins Inst. at Arizona State Univ., Bulletin of Atomic Scientists; Fellow, AAAS 2011. *Honours:* Douglas S. Morrow Public Outreach Award 2001, Scientific American Nat. Magazine Award for General Excellence 2011. *Address:* Scientific American, Nature America, 75 Varick Street, 9th Floor, New York, NY 10013-1917, USA (office). *Telephone:* (212) 451-8200 (office). *E-mail:* mdichristina@sciam.com (office). *Website:* www.scientificamerican.com (office).

DICKEY, Christopher, BA, MS; American writer, foreign correspondent and editor; *Paris Bureau Chief and Middle East Regional Editor, Newsweek*; b. 31 Aug. 1951, Nashville, TN; m. 1st Susan Tuckerman 1969 (divorced 1979); one s.; m. 2nd Carol Salvatore 1980. *Education:* Univ. of Virginia, Boston Univ. *Career:* staff, Washington Post, 1974–86, Cairo Bureau Chief, Newsweek 1986–88, Paris Bureau Chief 1988–93, 1995–, Middle East Regional Ed. 1993–; mem. Council on Foreign Relations. *Publications include:* With the Contras: A Reporter in the Wilds of Nicaragua 1986, Expats: Travels in Arabia, from Tripoli to Teheran 1990, Innocent Blood (novel) 1997, Summer of Deliverance: A Memoir of Father and Son 1998, The Sleeper (novel) 2004, Securing the City: Inside America's Best Counterterror Force – the NYPD 2009; contrib. to periodicals. *Honours:* Interamerican Press Asscn Award 1980, Mary Hemingway Award, Overseas Press Club 1983, Edward Weintal Award for Diplomatic Reporting, Georgetown Univ. 1998. *Address:* Newsweek, 395 Hudson Street, New York, NY 10014, USA (office). *E-mail:* chris@christopherdickey.com. *Website:* www.christopherdickey.com.

DICKINSON, Donald Percy, BA, MFA; Canadian writer and teacher; b. 28 Dec. 1947, Prince Albert, Sask.; s. of Jack Dickinson and Grace Dickinson (née Green); m. Chellie Eaton 1970; two s. one d. *Education:* Univs of Saskatchewan and British Columbia. *Career:* Fiction Ed., Prism International 1977–79; teacher of English, Lillooet Secondary School 1981–2003; currently Sessional Instructor, Thompson Rivers Univ., Kamloops. *Publications include:* novels: The Crew 1993, Robbiestime 2000; short stories: Third Impressions 1982, Fighting the Upstream 1987, Blue Husbands 1991; contrib. to Best Canadian Short Fiction 1984, Words We Call Home 1990, The New Writers 1992, The Porcupine Quill Reader 1996. *Honours:* Bankson Award 1979, Ethel Wilson Fiction Prize 1991. *Address:* 554 Victoria Street, Lillooet, BC V0K 1V0, Canada (home). *Telephone:* (250) 256-7916 (home). *Fax:* (250) 256-7917 (office). *E-mail:* dondickinson@shaw.ca (office).

DICKINSON, Margaret (see Muggeson, Margaret Elizabeth)

DICKINSON, Peter, MA, DMus, FRCO, LRAM, ARCM; British composer, writer and pianist; *Professor Emeritus, Keele University* and *University of London*; b. 15 Nov. 1934, Lytham St Annes, Lancs., England; s. of Frank Dickinson and Muriel Dickinson (née Porter); m. Bridget Jane Tomkinson; two s. *Education:* Queens' Coll., Cambridge, Juilliard School of Music, New York, USA. *Career:* various teaching posts in New York, London and Birmingham; First Prof. of Music, Keele Univ. 1974–84, Prof. Emer. 1984–; Prof., Goldsmiths Coll., London 1991–97, Prof. Emer. 1997–; Head of Music, Inst. of US Studies, Univ. of London 1997–2004; performances, broadcasts and recordings as pianist, mostly with sister, mezzo-soprano Meriel Dickinson; Chair. Bernarr Rainbow Trust. *Compositions include:* Transformations of Satie for orchestra 1970, Organ Concerto 1971, Piano Concerto 1984, Merseyside Echoes for orchestra 1985, Violin Concerto 1986, chamber music, choral works, songs, keyboard music, church music. *Recordings include:* vocal works to poems of Auden, Dylan Thomas, E. E. Cummings, John Heath-Stubbs, Lord Berners, Philip Larkin, Burns, Gregory Corso, Lord Byron, Stevie Smith, Blake, Clare and Hardy; numerous recordings of own music, including as pianist. *Television:* subject of South Bank Show 1987. *Publications include:* 20 British Composers (ed.) 1975, The Complete Songs and The Complete Piano Music of Lord Berners (two vols, ed.) 1982, Collected Works for Solo Piano of Lennox Berkeley (ed.) 1989, Marigold: The Music of Billy Mayerl 1999, Copland Connotations: Studies and Interviews 2002, The Music of Lennox Berkeley 2003, Cage Talk: Dialogues With and About John Cage 2006, Lord Berners: Composer, Writer, Painter 2008, Samuel Barber Remembered 2010, Complete Piano Duets of Lord Berners 2010, Lennox Berkeley and His Friends 2012; contrib. to various books, journals and dictionaries. *Honours:* Hon. FTCL; Hon. DMus (Keele Univ.) 1999; Rotary Foundation Fellowship 1958–59. *Address:* c/o Novello & Co., 14–15 Berners Street, London, W1T 3LJ, England. *Website:* www.foxborough.co.uk.

DICKSON, Peter George Muir, DLitt, FBA; British historian and academic; *Professor Emeritus, University of Oxford*; b. 26 April 1929, London; s. of William Muir Dickson and Regina Dowdall-Nicolls; m. Ariane Flore Faye 1964; one d. *Education:* St Paul's School, London, Worcester Coll., Oxford. *Career:* Fellow Nuffield Coll., Oxford 1954–56; Tutor, St Catherine's Soc., Oxford 1956–60, Fellow St Catherine's Coll. 1960–96, Emer. Fellow 1996–, Univ. Reader in Modern History 1978–89, Prof. of Early Modern History 1989–96, Emer. Prof. 1996–. *Publications include:* The Sun Insurance Office 1710–1960 1960, The Financial Revolution in England 1688–1756 1967, Finance and Government under Maria Theresia 1740–1780 1987. *Address:* St Catherine's College, Oxford, OX1 3UJ (office); Field House, Iffley, Oxford, OX4 4EG, England (home). *Telephone:* (1865) 271768 (office); (1865) 779599 (home).

DIDION, Joan, BA; American writer; b. 5 Dec. 1934, Sacramento, Calif.; d. of Frank Reese Didion and Eduene Didion (née Jerrett); m. John Gregory Dunne

1964 (died 2003); one d. (died 2005). *Education:* Univ. of Calif., Berkeley. *Career:* Assoc. Features Ed. Vogue magazine 1956–63; fmr columnist Esquire, Life, Saturday Evening Post, fmr contributor Nat. Review; freelance writer 1963–; mem. American Acad. of Arts and Letters, American Acad. of Arts and Sciences, Council on Foreign Relations. *Screenplays:* The Panic in Needle Park 1971, Play It as It Lays 1972, A Star is Born 1976, True Confessions 1981, Hills Like White Elephants 1991, Broken Trust 1995, Up Close and Personal 1996. *Publications include:* novels: Run River 1963, Play It as It Lays 1970, A Book of Common Prayer 1977, Telling Stories 1978, Democracy 1984, The Last Thing He Wanted 1996; essays: Slouching Towards Bethlehem 1969, The White Album 1978, After Henry 1992; non-fiction: Salvador 1983, Miami 1987, After Henry 1992, Political Fictions 2001, Where I Was From: A Memoir 2003, The Year of Magical Thinking (Nat. Book Award for Non-fiction; also screenplay) 2005, Blue Nights 2011. *Honours:* First Prize Vogue's Prix de Paris 1956, American Acad. of Arts and Letters Morton Dauwen Zabel Prize 1978, Edward McDowell Medal 1996, George Polk Award 2001, American Acad. of Arts and Letter Gold Medal for Belles Lettres 2005, Medal for Distinguished Contrib. to American Letters, Nat. Book Foundation 2007. *Literary Agent:* Janklow & Nesbit, 445 Park Avenue, New York, NY 10022-2606, USA.

DIEKMANN, Kai; German newspaper executive; *Editorial Director, Bild Group*; b. 27 June 1964, Ravensburg. *Career:* Parl. Corresp., Bild and Bild am Sonntag, Bonn 1987; Chief Reporter Bunte magazine, Munich 1989–91; Deputy Ed. B.Z., Berlin 1991–92, Deputy Ed. and Chief Political Corresp. Bild, Hamburg 1992–97; Chief Ed. Welt am Sonntag, Berlin 1998–2000, Ed.-in-Chief Bild and Publr Bild and Bild am Sonntag, Hamburg 2001–, Content Exec. bild.de 2007–; Editorial Dir Bild Group 2007–; Head, Bild hilft e.V. – Ein Herz für Kinder (charity org.) 2001–; External Bd mem. Hürriyet 2004–; non-Exec. Bd mem. Times Newspaper Holdings Ltd 2011–. *Publications include:* Rita Süssmuth im Gespräch (co-author) 1994, Die neue Bundespräsident im Gespräch (co-author) 1994, Helmut Kohl. Ich wollte Deutschlands Einheit (co-author) 1996, Der große Selbstbetrug 2007. *Honours:* Goldene Feder 2000, 2005, World Media Award 2002, German Media Exec. of the Year 2009. *Address:* Bild, Axel Springer AG, Axel-Springer-Straße 65, 10888 Berlin, Germany (office). *Telephone:* (30) 2591-0 (office). *Fax:* (30) 2591-76009 (office). *Website:* www.bild.de (office).

DIESCHO, Joseph, PhD; Namibian author and political analyst; b. 10 April 1955, Andara, Southwest Africa. *Education:* Fort Hare Univ., SA, Hamburg Univ., Germany, Columbia Univ., USA. *Career:* imprisoned as a student for opposing SA's apartheid regime; helped establish worker's union while working at a diamond mine; moved to New York, USA 1984; fmr Prof. of Int. Law, City Univ., New York; Head of Public Relations and Devt, Univ. of South Africa (Unisa) 1994–99; Public Affairs Dir, Uthingo Management, official operator of SA's nat. lottery 1999–2001; Dir of Public Affairs for org. of UN World Summit on Sustainable Devt, Johannesburg 2002; Consultant to Eskom public utility co. on the African Leadership Devt Project 2003–; SA facilitator, Interactive Pan-African Leadership Training Programme 2004–; currently visiting lecturer, Centre for African Renaissance Studies, Unisa; mem. Bd of Dirs, Namibia Inst. for Democracy. *Television:* presenter, South Africa Now, New York public tv 1988–91, The Big Picture (SABC 2), SA 1997–98. *Publications include:* novels: Born of the Sun 1988, Troubled Waters 1993; non-fiction: The Namibian Constitution in Perspective 1994, Government and opposition in post-independence Namibia: perceptions and performance 1996, Understanding the New Partnership for Africa's Development 2002. *Address:* c/o Gamsberg Macmillan Publishers Ltd, POB 22830, 19 Faraday Street, Windhoek, Namibia. *E-mail:* publishing@gamsberg.com.na. *Website:* www.gamsberg.com.na.

DIEZ, Rolo; Argentine novelist, screenwriter and journalist; b. (Rolando Aurelio Diez Suárez), 1940, Junín. *Career:* lived in Mexico 1980–. *Publications include:* Los compañeros 1987, Vladimir Ilich contra los uniformados 1989, Paso de Tigre 1991, Gatos de azotea 1992, Mato y voy 1992, Una baldosa en el valle de la muerte 1992, Luna de Escarlata 1994, Gambito de dama y La Vida que me doy (Flauta Magica) 2001, Papel Picado 2003, Tequila Blue 2004, La carabina de Zapata 2004. *Honours:* Dashiell Hammett Award 1995, Premio José Rubén Romero 1999. *E-mail:* atencion@edicionesurano.com (office). *Website:* www.umbrieleditores.com.

DIFORIO, Robert George, BA; American publishing executive; *Principal, D4EO Literary Agency*; b. 19 March 1940, Mamaroneck, NY; s. of Richard John Diforio, Sr and Mildred Kuntz; m. Birgit Rasmussen 1983; one s. one d. *Education:* Williams Coll., Williamstown, Mass and Harvard Business School's Advanced Man. Program. *Career:* Vice-Pres. Kable News Co. 1970; Vice-Pres. and Sales Man. New American Library (NAL) 1972, Sr Vice-Pres. and Marketing Dir 1976, Pres. and Publr 1980–82, CEO and Chair. Bd NAL/E. P. Dutton 1983–89; Prin. D4EO Literary Agency 1991–; helped launch paperback writing careers of Erica Jong, Stephen King, Robin Cook and Ken Follett. *Address:* 7 Indian Valley Road, Weston, CT 06883, USA (office). *Telephone:* (203) 544-7180 (office); (203) 544-7182 (home). *Fax:* (203) 544-7160 (office). *E-mail:* bob@d4eo.com (office). *Website:* www.d4eo.com (office); www.d4eoliteraryagency.com (office).

DILKS, David Neville, BA, FRSL, FCGI; British historian, academic and university administrator; b. 17 March 1938, Coventry; s. of Neville Ernest and Phyllis Dilks; m. Jill Medlicott 1963; one s. *Education:* Royal Grammar School, Worcester, Hertford Coll. and St Antony's Coll., Oxford. *Career:* Asst Lecturer, then Lecturer LSE 1962–70; Prof. of Int. History, Univ. of Leeds 1970–91, Chair. School of History 1974–79, Dean Faculty of Arts 1975–77; Vice-Chancellor Univ. of Hull 1991–99; Visiting Fellow, All Souls Coll., Oxford 1973; Chair. and Founder Commonwealth Youth Exchange Council 1968–73; mem. Advisory Council on Public Records 1977–85, Univs Funding Council 1988–91; Trustee Edward Boyle Memorial Trust 1982–96, Imperial War Museum 1983–91, Lennox-Boyd Trust 1984–91, Royal Commonwealth Soc. Library Trust 1987–91; Pres. Int. Cttee for the History of the Second World War 1992–2000; Freeman, Goldsmiths' Co. 1979, Liveryman 1984; Fellow, City and Guilds of London Inst. *Television:* historical adviser, The Gathering Storm (HBO/BBC) 2002, Winston Churchill at War (HBO/BBC) 2009. *Publications:* Curzon in India (Vols 1 & 2) 1969, 1970, The Diaries of Sir Alexander Cadogan (ed.) 1971, Retreat from Power (two vols, ed.) 1981, The Missing Dimension: Government and Intelligence Communities in the Twentieth Century (ed.) 1984, Neville Chamberlain: Pioneering & Reform, 1869–1929 1984, Barbarossa 1941, The Axis, The Allies and World War: Retrospect, Recollection, Revision (co-ed.) 1994, Grossbritannien und der deutsche Widerstand (co-ed.) 1994, The Great Dominion: Winston Churchill in Canada 1900–1954 2005, Churchill and Company 2012; and numerous articles in learned journals. *Honours:* Dr hc (Russian Acad. of Sciences) 1996; Curzon Prize, Univ. of Oxford 1960, Prix du rayonnement de la langue française 1994, Médaille de Vermeil, Acad. Française 1994. *Address:* Wits End, Long Causeway, Leeds, LS16 8EX, West Yorks., England (home). *Telephone:* (113) 267-3466 (home).

DILLARD, Annie, MA; American author; b. 30 April 1945, Pittsburgh, Pa; d. of Frank Doak and Gloria Lambert; m. 1st R. H. W. Dillard 1965; m. 2nd Gary Clevidence 1979 (divorced); m. 3rd Robert D. Richardson, Jr 1988; one d. two step-d. *Education:* Hollins Coll. *Career:* Contributing Ed. Harper's Magazine 1974–85; Distinguished Visiting Prof., Wesleyan Univ. 1979–83, Adjunct Prof. 1983–, Writer in Residence 1987–; mem. Bd of Dirs Writers' Conf. 1984– (Chair. 1991–); mem. Nat. Cttee on US –China Relations 1982–. *Publications:* Tickets for a Prayer Wheel (poetry), Pilgrim at Tinker Creek (Pulitzer Prize 1975) 1974, Holy the Firm 1978, Living by Fiction 1982, Teaching a Stone to Talk 1982, Encounters with Chinese Writers 1984, An American Childhood 1987, The Writing Life 1989, The Living (novel) 1992, The Annie Dillard Reader 1994, Mornings Like This (poetry) 1995, For the Time Being 1999, The Maytrees (prose) 2007. *Honours:* Nat. Endowment for the Arts (Literature) Grant 1981, John Simon Guggenheim Memorial Grant 1985, Gov. of Connecticut's Award 1993, Campion Award 1994, Milton Prize 1994, American Arts and Letters Award in Literature 1998. *Address:* c/o Timothy Seldes, Russell and Volkening, 50 W 29th New York, NY 10001-4227, USA.

DILLARD, Richard Henry Wilde, BA, MA, PhD; American academic, writer, poet and editor; *Professor of English, Hollins University*; b. 11 Oct. 1937, Roanoke, Virginia; m. 1st Annie Doak 1965 (divorced 1972); m. 2nd Cathy Hankla 1979. *Education:* Roanoke Coll., Univ. of Virginia. *Career:* Instructor, Roanoke Coll. 1961, Univ. of Virginia 1961–64; Asst Prof., Hollins Univ., Virginia 1964–68, Assoc. Prof. 1968–74, Prof. of English 1974–; Contributing Ed., Hollins Critic 1966–77; Ed.-in-Chief, Children's Literature 1992–. *Publications include:* fiction: The Book of Changes 1974, The First Man on the Sun 1983, Omniphobia 1995, Sallies 2001; poetry: The Day I Stopped Dreaming About Barbara Steele and Other Poems 1966, News of the Nile 1971, After Borges 1972, The Greeting: New and Selected Poems 1981, Just Here, Just Now 1994; non-fiction: Horror Films 1976, Understanding George Garrett 1988; ed.: The Experience of America: A Book of Readings (with Louis D. Rubin Jr) 1969, The Sounder Few: Essays from 'The Hollins Critic' (with George Garrett and John Rees Moore) 1971; contrib.: periodicals. *Honours:* Acad. of American Poets Prize 1961. Ford Foundation Grant 1972, O. B. Hardison Jr Poetry Award, Folger Shakespeare Library, Washington, DC 1994, Assen of Writer/George Garrett Award for Outstanding Community Service in Literature 2007. *Address:* Department of English, Hollins University, PO Box 9677, Roanoke, VA 24020, USA (office). *Telephone:* (540) 362-6316 (office). *E-mail:* rdillard@hollins.edu (office). *Website:* www.hollins.edu (office).

DILLINGHAM, William Byron, BA, MA, PhD; American academic and writer; *Charles Howard Candler Professor Emeritus, Emory University*; b. 7 March 1930, Atlanta, Ga; s. of Cornelius Howard Dillingham and Emerald Storey; m. Elizabeth Joiner 1952; one s. two d. *Education:* Emory Univ., Univ. Pennsylvania. *Career:* Instructor, Emory Univ. 1956–58, Asst Prof., Assoc. Prof., Prof., Charles Howard Candler Prof. of American Literature 1959–96, Prof. Emer. 1996–; mem. Advisory Bds Nineteenth-Century Literature, South Atlantic Bulletin. *Publications include:* Humor of the Old Southwest 1965, Frank Norris: Instinct and Art 1969, An Artist in the Rigging: The Early Work of Herman Melville 1972, Melville's Short Fiction, 1853–1856 1977, Melville's Later Novels 1986, Practical English Handbook (10th edn) 1996, Melville and his Circle: The Last Years 1996, Rudyard Kipling: Hell and Heroism 2005, Being Kipling 2008; contrib. numerous articles and reviews to scholarly journals. *Honours:* Guggenheim Fellow, NEH Fellowship, Fulbright Teaching Fellowship (Norway), Emory Univ. Scholar/Teacher of the Year 1984, Emory Univ. Award of Distinction 2000, Distinguished Emer. Award 2004, numerous other awards. *Address:* 1416 Vista Leaf Drive, Decatur, GA 30033, USA (home). *Telephone:* (404) 636-4486 (home). *E-mail:* wdillin@emory.edu (office).

DILLON, Millicent Gerson, BA, MA; American writer; b. (Millicent Gerson), 24 May 1925, New York, NY; d. of Ephraim Gerson and Claire Gerson; m. 1st Murray Lesser 1948 (divorced 1959); two d.; m. 2nd David Dillon (divorced

1964). *Education:* Hunter Coll., City Univ. of New York, San Francisco State Univ. *Career:* Guggenheim Fellowship, two Nat. Endowment for the Humanities Fellowships; mem. PEN, Authors' Guild. *Plays:* She is in Tangier, Prisoners of Ordinary Need. *Radio:* plays: Inside, By The Water. *Publications include:* Baby Perpetua and Other Stories 1971, The One in the Back is Medea (novel) 1973, A Little Original Sin: The Life and Work of Jane Bowles 1981, Out in the World: The Selected Letters of Jane Bowles (ed.) 1985; After Egypt 1990, The Dance of the Mothers (novel) 1991, The Portable Paul and Jane Bowles (ed.) 1994, You Are Not I: A Portrait of Paul Bowles 1998, Harry Gold: A Novel 2000, A Version of Love 2003; contribs to Southwest Review, Witness, Threepenny Review, The New Yorker, Raritan, The Believer. *Honours:* Five O. Henry Short Story Awards, Best American Short Stories 1992, McGinnis-Richie Award for Fiction 2002. *Address:* 1850 Sand Hill Road, Apt 54, Palo Alto, CA 94304, USA (home). *E-mail:* millicentdillon@gmail.com. *Website:* millicentdillon.com.

DILSAVER, Paul, BA, BS, MA, MFA; American poet, writer and editor; b. 8 Dec. 1949, Colorado. *Education:* Univ. of Southern Colorado, Colorado State Univ., Bowling Green State Univ., Ohio, SUNY. *Career:* Instructor, Laramie County Community Coll., Cheyenne, WY 1973–74, Casper Coll., WY 1974–77, Western Illinois Univ., Macomb 1979–81; Poetry Ed., Rocky Mountain Creative Arts Journal and Chapbook Series 1974–78; Poet-in-Residence, Wyoming Arts Council 1977–78; Ed., Blue Light Books 1979–, Blue Light Review 1983–91; Asst Prof. of English, Carroll Coll., Helena, Montana 1981–84; Lecturer in English, Univ. of Southern Colorado 1986–91; Visiting Instructor of English, Anoka-Ramsey Coll., Coon Rapids, Minnesota 1991–92. *Publications include:* Malignant Blues (poetry) 1976, Words Wyoming (anthology) 1976, A Brutal Blacksmith: An Anvil of Bruised Tissue (poetry) 1979, Encounters with the Antichrist (prose poetry) 1982, Character Scatology (poetry) 1984, Stories of the Strange (fiction) 1985, Nurtz! Nurtz! (novel) 1989, A Cure for Optimism (poetry) 1993, The Toilet Papers (anthology) 1994, Medi-Phoria 1999, Hardcore Haiku 2000; contribs.: various anthologies and periodicals.

DIMARCO, Cris, BA, MAT; American editor and writer; b. (Cris Newport), 14 July 1960, Melrose Park, IL; m.; two c. *Education:* Univ. of Massachusetts at Boston, Tufts Univ. *Career:* Asst Prof. of English 1991, Assoc. Prof. of English 1994, New Hampshire Technical Institute; Sr Ed., Windstorm Creative 1997–. *Publications include:* Sparks Might Fly 1994, The White Bones of Truth 1994, Queen's Champion: The Legend of Lancelot Retold 1997, 1001 Nights: Exotica 1 1999, Exotica 2 2002, Kresh: The Golton Box 2004; contrib. to periodicals. *Address:* PO Box 28, Port Orchard, WA 98366, USA.

DIMBLEBY, David, MA; British broadcaster and journalist; b. 28 Oct. 1938, Surrey, England; s. of the late Richard Dimbleby and Dilys Thomas; m. 1st Josceline Gaskell 1967 (divorced 2000); one s. two d.; m. 2nd Belinda Giles 2000; one s. *Education:* Univs of Oxford, Paris and Perugia. *Career:* presenter and interviewer, BBC Bristol 1960–61; Chair. Dimbleby and Sons Ltd 1986–2001, apptd Man. Dir 1967; currently commentator and presenter BBC; also Pres. Inst. for Citizenship. *Television:* Quest (religious programme), What's New? (children's science), People and Power 1982–83, General Election Results Programmes 1979, 1983, 1987, 2001, various programmes for the Budget, by-elections, local elections etc.; Presenter, Question Time (BBC) 1994–, A Picture of Britain (BBC) 2005–, How We Built Britain (also writer) 2007–, Seven Ages of Britain (BBC 1) 2010–. *Films:* documentaries: Ku-Klux-Klan, The Forgotten Million, Cyprus: The Thin Blue Line 1964–65, South Africa: The White Tribe (Royal TV Soc. Supreme Documentary Award) 1979, The Struggle for South Africa (US Emmy Award, Monte Carlo Golden Nymph) 1990, US –UK Relations: An Ocean Apart 1988, David Dimbleby's India 1997; live commentary on many public occasions including: State Opening of Parliament, Trooping the Colour, Wedding of HRH Prince Andrew and Sarah Ferguson, HM The Queen Mother's 90th Birthday Parade (Royal TV Soc. Outstanding Documentary Award), Funeral of Diana, Princess of Wales 1997, memorial services including Lord Olivier (Royal TV Soc. Outstanding Documentary Award). *Publications:* An Ocean Apart (with David Reynolds) 1988, A Picture of Britain 2005, How We Built Britain 2007, Seven Ages of Britain 2010. *Honours:* Dr hc (Univ. of Essex) 2005; Richard Dimbleby Award, BAFTA 1998. *Literary Agent:* c/o Rosemary Scoular, United Agents, 12–26 Lexington Street, London, W1F 0LE, England. *Telephone:* (20) 3214-0894. *Fax:* (20) 3214-0801. *E-mail:* wmillyard@unitedagents.co.uk. *Website:* www.unitedagents.co.uk.

DIMBLEBY, Jonathan, BA; British broadcaster, journalist and writer; b. 31 July 1944, Aylesbury, Bucks.; s. of the late Richard Dimbleby and Dilys Thomas; m. 1st Bel Mooney 1968 (divorced); one s. one d.; m. 2nd Jessica Ray 2007; two d. *Education:* Univ. Coll. London. *Career:* reporter BBC Bristol 1969–70, World at One (BBC Radio) 1970–71, This Week (Thames TV) 1972–78, 1986–88, TV Eye 1979, Jonathan Dimbleby in Evidence series (Yorkshire TV) 1980–84; Assoc. Ed./Presenter First Tuesday 1982–86; Presenter/Ed. Jonathan Dimbleby on Sunday (TV-am) 1985–86, On the Record (BBC TV) 1988–93, Charles: the Private Man, the Public Role (Central TV) 1994, weekly political programme Jonathan Dimbleby (ITV) 1995–2006; presenter Any Questions? and Any Answers? (both BBC Radio 4) 1987–; main presenter of Gen. Election coverage (ITV); Chair. Index on Censorship 2009–; Pres. Voluntary Service Overseas 1999–, Soil Asscn 1997–2009, Royal Soc. for the Protection of Birds 2001–04, Bath Festivals Trust 2003–06; Vice-Pres. Campaign for Protection of Rural England 1997–; Trustee Dimbleby Cancer Care. *Publications:* Richard Dimbleby 1975, The Palestinians 1979, The Prince of Wales: A Biography 1994, The Last Governor 1997, Russia: A Journey to the Heart of a Land and its People 2008. *Honours:* Richard Dimbleby Award 1974. *Literary Agent:* David Higham Associates, Ltd, 5 Lower John Street, Golden Square, London, W1R 4HA, England. *Telephone:* (20) 7437-7888 (office).

DINNERSTEIN, Leonard, BA, MA, PhD; American academic and writer; *Professor Emeritus of American History, University of Arizona, Tucson;* b. 5 May 1934, New York, NY; s. of Abraham Dinnerstein and Lillian Kubrik; m. Myra Anne Rosenberg 1961; one s. one d. *Education:* City Coll., City Univ. of New York, Columbia Univ. *Career:* Instructor, New York Inst. of Tech. 1960–65; Asst Prof., Fairleigh Dickinson Univ. 1967–70; Assoc. Prof., Univ. of Arizona, Tucson 1970–72, Prof. of American History 1972–2003, Prof. Emer. 2003–. *Publications include:* The Leo Frank Case (Anisfield Wolf Award 1969) 1968, The Aliens (with F. C. Jaher, aka Uncertain Americans) 1970, American Vistas (with K. T. Jackson) 1971, Antisemitism in the United States 1971, Jews in the South (with M. D. Palsson) 1973, Decisions and Revisions (with J. Christie) 1975, Ethnic Americans: A History of Immigration and Assimilation (with D. M. Reimers) 1975, Natives and Strangers (with R. L. Nichols and D. M. Reimers) 1979, America and the Survivors of the Holocaust 1982, Uneasy at Home 1987, Antisemitism in America (Jewish Book Prize) 1994. *Address:* 1981 Miraval Cuarto, Tucson, AZ 85718, USA (home). *Telephone:* (520) 615-8585 (home). *Fax:* (520) 615-8586 (home). *E-mail:* dinnerst@u.arizona.edu.

DIONNE, Joseph Lewis, BA, MS; American publisher; b. 29 June 1933, Montgomery, Ala; s. of Antonio Ernest Joseph Dionne and Myrtle Mae (Armstrong) Dionne; m. Joan F. Durand 1954; two s. one d. *Education:* Hofstra Univ., Columbia Univ. *Career:* Guidance Counsellor, LI public schools 1956–61; Asst Prof., Hofstra Univ., Hempstead, NY 1962–63; Dir of Instruction, Project Dir Ford Foundation School Improvement, Brentwood, NY public schools 1963–66; Vice-Pres. (Research and Devt) Educational Devt Labs, Huntington, NY 1966–68; Vice-Pres. and Gen. Man. CTB/McGraw-Hill, Monterey, Calif. 1968–73, Sr Vice-Pres. (Corp. Planning) McGraw-Hill Inc., New York 1973–77, Pres. McGraw-Hill Information Systems Co., New York 1977–79, Exec. Vice-Pres. (Operations) McGraw Hill Inc. 1979–81, Pres. 1981–93, CEO 1983–98, Chair. 1988–98; mem. Bd of Dirs, Equitable Life Insurance Co. of America, United Telecommunications Inc.; Trustee, Harris Corpn, Teachers' Coll., Columbia Univ., Hofstra Univ.

DIRIE, Waris; Somali writer and model; b. 1964. *Career:* emigrated to London 1978; maid to Somalian amb., janitor McDonald's, model; f. Desert Dawn; UNFPA Special Amb. for Women's Rights in Africa 1997–; Founder Waris Dirie Foundation (to campaign against Female Genital Mutilation). *Publications:* Desert Flower 1998, Desert Dawn 2002, Desert Children 2005. *Honours:* Hon. mem. Club of Budapest. *Address:* Waris Dirie Foundation, Verein zur Förderung von Hilfsaktionen für Afrika, Lerchenfelderstr. 88–90/28, 1080 Vienna, Austria (office). *Telephone:* (1) 4027916 (office). *Fax:* (1) 402791655 (office). *E-mail:* waris@utanet.at (office). *Website:* www.waris-dirie-foundation.com (office).

DISANAYAKA, Jayaratna Banda, PhD; Sri Lankan diplomatist and academic; *Ambassador to Thailand;* b. 16 April 1937; m. Kusum R. Disanayaka. *Education:* Dharmaraja Coll., Ananda Coll., Univs of Ceylon, Colombo. *Career:* Lecturer, later Head of Dept of Sinhala, Univ. of Colombo, now Prof. Emer.; Amb. to Thailand 2007–; received Fulbright scholarship to Univ. of Calif., Berkeley. *Publications include:* Aspects of Sinhala Folklore 1984, Say It in Sinhala 1985, Mihintale, cradle of Sinhala Buddhist civilization 1987, Simhala vehera vihara 1988, Nutana Simhala lekhana vyakaranaya 1990, Studies in Sinhala Literacy 1990, Simhala budu samaya 1991, Water in Culture 1992, The Monk and the Peasant 1993, Samakalina Simhala lekhana vyakaranaya 1995, Simhala bhasave nava muhunuvara 1996, Gamaka suvanda siv siya gavu aseya 1996, Banda vata pada rata 1996, Siyalanga ru soba 1998, Understanding the Sinhalese 1998, Kalani Vihare situvam 2000, Udarata Simhalaya 2002, Paintings of Kelani Vihara 2004, Lanka, the Land of Kings 2007. *Address:* Sri Lankan Embassy, Ocean Tower II, 13th Floor, 75/6–7 Sukhumvit, Soi 19, Klongtoey, Wattana, Bangkok 10110, Thailand (office). *Telephone:* (2) 261-1934 (office). *Fax:* (2) 261-1936 (office). *E-mail:* slemb@ksc.th.com (office).

DISKI, Jenny, FRSL; British writer; b. (Jennifer Simmonds), 8 July 1947, London, England; d. of James Simmonds and Rene Rayner; pnr Ian Patterson; one d. *Education:* Univ. Coll., London. *Career:* teacher 1970s–early 1980s. *Television writing:* A Fair and Easy Passage, The Ultimate Object of Desire, Murder in Mind. *Publications:* novels: Nothing Natural 1986, Rainforest 1987, Then Again 1990, Happily Ever After 1991, Monkey's Uncle 1994, The Dream Mistress 1996, Only Human: A Comedy 2000, After These Things 2004, Apology for the Woman Writing 2008; short stories: The Vanishing Princess 1995; essay collections: Don't 1998, A View from the Bed 2001; travel writing: Stranger on a Train: Daydreaming and Smoking Around America with Interruptions 2002, On Trying to Keep Still 2006; non-fiction: The Sixties 2009, What I Don't Know About Animals 2010; autobiog.: Skating to Antarctica 1997; contrib. to The Observer, The Guardian, The Telegraph, The Independent, LRB, New Yorker, Harper's Magazine, New York Times Magazine. *Honours:* Mind Prize 1997, Thomas Cook Travel Book Award 2003, J. R. Ackerley Prize for Autobiography 2003. *Literary Agent:* c/o Peter Straus, Rogers, Coleridge & White Literary Agency, 20 Powis Mews, London, W11 1JN, England. *Telephone:* (20) 7221-3717. *Fax:* (20) 7229-9084. *E-mail:* info@

rcwlitagency.co.uk. *Website:* www.rcwlitagency.co.uk. *E-mail:* info@jennydiski.co.uk (office). *Website:* www.jennydiski.co.uk.

DIVINE, Robert Alexander, BA, MA, PhD; American academic and writer; *Professor Emeritus of American History, University of Texas at Austin*; b. 10 May 1929, New York, NY; m. 1st Barbara Christine Renick 1955; three s. one d. (died 1993); m. 2nd Darlene S. Harris 1996 (died 2003); m. 3rd Joan G. Burdick 2007. *Education:* Yale Univ. *Career:* Instructor, Univ. of Texas at Austin 1954–57, Asst Prof. 1957–61, Assoc. Prof. 1961–63, Prof. 1963–80, George W. Littlefield Prof. of American History 1981–96, Prof. Emer. 1996–; Fellow, Center for Advanced Study in the Behavioural Sciences, Stanford 1962–63; Albert Shaw Lecturer, Johns Hopkins Univ. 1968; mem. Soc. for Historians of American Foreign Relations. *Publications:* American Immigration Policy 1924–1952 1957, The Illusion of Neutrality 1962, The Reluctant Belligerent: American Entry into World War II 1965, Second Chance: The Triumph of Internationalism in America During World War II 1967, Roosevelt and World War II 1969, Foreign Policy and US Presidential Elections 1940–1960 (two vols) 1974, Since 1945: Politics and Diplomacy in Recent American History 1975, Blowing on the Wind 1978, Eisenhower and the Cold War 1981, America: Past and Present (with T. H. Breen, George Fredrickson and R. Hal Williams) 1984, The Sputnik Challenge 1993, Perpetual War for Perpetual Peace 2000; editor: American Foreign Policy 1960, The Age of Insecurity: America 1920–1945 1968, Twentieth-Century America: Contemporary Documents and Opinions (with John A. Garraty) 1968, American Foreign Policy Since 1945 1969, Causes and Consequences of World War II 1969, The Cuban Missile Crisis 1971, Exploring the Johnson Years 1981, The Johnson Years: Vol. Two, Vietnam, the Environment and Science 1987, The Johnson Years: Vol. Three, LBJ at Home and Abroad 1994; contrib. to scholarly books and journals. *Honours:* Rockefeller Humanities Fellowship 1976–77, Univ. of Texas Grad. Teaching Award 1986, Eugene E. Emme Astronautical Literature Award 1993. *Address:* 10617 Sans Souci Place, Austin, TX 78759, USA (home). *E-mail:* rdivine@austin.rr.com (home).

DIXON, Roger, (John Christian, Charles Lewis); British author and playwright; b. 6 Jan. 1930, Portsmouth, England; m. Carolyn Anne Shepheard 1966; two s. four d. *Publications:* Noah II 1970, Christ on Trial 1973, The Messiah 1974, Going to Jerusalem 1977, Georgiana 1984, Return to Nebo 1991, Edward Burne-Jones: The Hidden Humorist 2011; as John Christian: Five Gates to Armageddon 1975, Symbolists And Decadents 1978, The Last Romantics: The Romantic Tradition in British Art: Burne-Jones to Stanley Spencer 1989; as Charles Lewis: The Cain Factor 1975; musical: The Commander of New York (with Phil Medley and Basil Bova) 1987; other: over 50 radio plays and series.

DIXON, Stephen, BA; American writer and university teacher (retd); b. 6 June 1936, New York, NY, USA; m. Anne Frydman 1982, two d. *Education:* City College, CUNY 1958. *Career:* Prof., Johns Hopkins Univ. 1980–2008. *Publications:* No Relief 1976, Work 1977, Too Late 1978, Quite Contrary 1979, 14 Stories 1980, Movies 1983, Time to Go 1984, Fall and Rise 1985, Garbage 1988, Love and Will 1989, The Play and Other Stories 1989, All Gone 1990, Friends 1990, Frog 1991, Long Made Short 1993, The Stories of Stephen Dixon 1994, Interstate 1995, Man on Stage 1996, Gould 1997, Sleep 1999, 30 1999, Tisch 2000, I. 2002, Old Friends 2004, Phone Rings 2005, End of I. 2006, Meyer (novel) 2007, What Is All This: Uncollected Stories 2010; contrib. to anthologies and periodicals. *Honours:* Stegner Fiction Fellowship, Stanford Univ. 1964–65; National Endowment of the Arts Grants 1974–75, 1990–91; American Acad. and Institute of Arts and Letters Award 1983; John Train Prize, Paris Review 1984; Guggenheim Fellowship 1985–86, two Pushcart Prizes, three Bestamerican Prizes, three O'Henry Prizes, Best Story from the South. *Address:* 1315 Boyce Ave, Baltimore, MD 21204, USA (home). *Telephone:* (410) 825-8038 (home). *E-mail:* anne_fdixon@yahoo.com (home).

DJEBAR, Assia; Algerian novelist, poet, dramatist, filmmaker and academic; *Silver Chair Professor of Francophone Literature and Civilization, New York University*; b. (Fatima-Zohra Imalhayène), 30 June 1936, Cherchell; d. of the late Tahar Imalhayène and Bahia Sahraoui; m. 1st Ahmed Ould-Rouïs 1958 (divorced 1975); m. 2nd Malek Alloula 1981 (divorced 2005); one d. *Education:* Lycée Fénélon, Paris and École Normale Supérieure de Sèvres, France. *Career:* taught history at Univ. of Algiers 1962–65, 1974–84; Foundation Distinguished Prof. and Dir Center for French and Francophone Studies, Louisiana State Univ., USA 1995–2001; Silver Chair Prof. of Francophone Literature and Civilization, New York Univ. 2002–; mem. Acad. Royale de Langue Française de Belgique 2000–, Acad. Française 2005–. *Films:* La Nouba des femmes du Mont Chenoua 1979, La Zerda ou les chants d'oubli 1982. *Publications:* La Soif (trans. as The Mischief) 1957, Les Impatients 1958, Women of Islam 1961, Les Enfants du nouveau monde 1962, Les Alouettes naïves 1967, Poèmes pour l'Algérie heureuse 1969, Rouge l'aube (with Walid Garn) 1969, La Nouba des femmes du Mont Chenoua 1969, Femmes d'Alger dans leur appartement (trans. as Women of Algiers in their Apartment) 1980 (new edn 2002), L'Amour la fantasia (trans. as Fantasia: An Algerian Cavalcade) 1985, Ombre sultane (trans. as A Sister to Scheherazade) 1987, Loin de Médine (trans. as Far from Medina) 1991, Chronique d'un été algérien 1993, Le Blanc de l'Algérie (trans. as Algerian White) 1995, Vaste est la prison (trans. as So Vast the Prison) 1995, Oran, langue morte 1997, Les Nuits de Strasbourg 1997, Ces voix qui m'assiègent 1999, Filles d'Ismaël dans le vent et la tempête (musical drama in five acts) 2002, La Femme sans sepulture 2002, La Disparation de la langue française 2004, Nulle part dans la maison de mon père (ed Fayard) 2007. *Honours:* Dr hc (Concordia Univ., Montréal) 2002, (Osnabrück Univ.) 2005; Venice Film Festival Int. Critics' Prize 1979, Prix Maurice Maeterlinck 1995, Neustadt Int. Prize for Literature (USA) 1996, Yourcenar Prize 1997, Friedenspreis des Deutschen Buchhandels, Frankfurt 2000, Pablo Neruda Prize, Italy 2005, Grinzane Cavour Prize, Italy 2006. *Address:* Department of French, New York University, 13 University Place, Office 621, New York, NY 10003-4556, USA (office). *Telephone:* (212) 992-9509 (office). *E-mail:* assia.djebar@nyu.edu (office). *Website:* french.as.nyu.edu/object/assiadjebar.html (office); www.assiadjebar.net (home).

DJEDIDI, Hafedh; Tunisian poet, novelist and journalist; b. 1954. *Career:* fmr Dir, Institut Supérieur des Beaux Arts de Sousse. *Publications:* Rien que le fruit pour toute bouche (poems) (Prix de l'ACTT, Paris) 1985, Chassés/croisés (novel, with Guy Coissard) 1986, Intempéries 1987, Le Cimeterre ou le Souffle du Vénérable (Prix de l'ACTT, Paris) 1987, Les sept grains du chapelet 2003, Les vents de la nostalgie 2003, Fièvres dans Hach-Médine 2003. *Address:* c/o Institut Supérieur des Beaux Arts de Sousse, Place de la Gare, 4000 Sousse, Tunisia.

DJEMAÏ, Abdelkader; Algerian novelist, journalist and dramatist; b. 16 Nov. 1948, Oran. *Career:* exiled in France 1993–; freelance journalist for publs, including La République, Algérie-Presse-Service, El Moudjahid, Algérie Actualité, Le Matin, Ruptures, Le Monde Diplomatique, Les Temps Modernes, Machrek-Maghreb, Qantara, France Culture; mem. Soc. des Gens de Lettres. *Plays:* L'affaire R.D., Paroles de quartier, Histoires parallèles. *Publications:* Saison de pierres 1986, Mémoires de nègre 1991, Camus à Oran 1995, Un Été en cendres (Prix Découverte Albert Camus, Prix Tropiques) 1995, Sable rouge 1996, Histoire d'un amour 1997, 31 rue de l'aigle 2000, Camping (Prix Amerigo Vespucci) 2002, Gare du Nord 2003, Le Nez sur la vitre (Lauréat du Prix littéraire de la Ville d'Ambronay 2005) 2004, Le Caire qui bat 2006, Pain, adour et fantaisies 2006, Un taxi vers la mer 2007, Un moment d'oubli 2009, Zorah sur la terrasse 2010, La dernière nuit de l'Emir 2012; contrib. to Petites agonies urbaines 2006. *Honours:* Chevalier, Ordre des Arts et des Lettres; Price Tropics 1995, Amerigo Vespucci-Price 2002.

DJERASSI, Carl, AB, PhD; American/Austrian chemist, academic and author; *Professor Emeritus of Chemistry, Stanford University*; b. 29 Oct. 1923, Vienna, Austria; s. of Dr Samuel Djerassi and Dr Alice Friedmann; m. 1st Virginia Jeremiah (divorced 1950); m. 2nd Norma Lundholm (divorced 1976); one s. one d. (deceased); m. 3rd Diane W. Middlebrook 1985 (died 2007). *Education:* Kenyon Coll., Univ. of Wisconsin. *Career:* Research Chemist, Ciba Pharmaceutical Co., Summit, NJ 1942–43, 1945–49; Assoc. Dir of Research, Syntex, SA, Mexico City 1949–51, Research Vice-Pres. 1957–60, Pres. Syntex Research 1968–72; Assoc. Prof. of Chem., Wayne State Univ., Detroit 1952–54, Prof. 1954–59; Prof. of Chem., Stanford Univ. 1959–2002, Prof. Emer. 2002–; Pres. Bd Zoecon Corpn (renamed Sandoz Crop Protection Corpn) 1968–83, Chair. 1968–88; f. Djerassi Foundation Resident Artists Program; mem. Editorial Bd Journal of the American Chemical Society 1968–76, Journal of Organic Chemistry 1955–58, Tetrahedron 1958–92, Steroids 1963–2002, Proceedings of NAS 1964–70; mem. NAS Bd on Science and Tech. for Int. Devt 1967–76, Chair. 1972–76; mem. American Pugwash Cttee 1967–81; mem. NAS, NAS Inst. of Medicine, Brazilian Acad. of Sciences, American Acad. of Arts and Sciences; Foreign mem. German Acad. of Science (Leopoldina), Royal Soc. (London), Royal Swedish Acad. of Sciences 1973, Bulgarian Acad. of Sciences 1979, Royal Swedish Acad. of Eng Sciences 1984, Academia Europaea. *Plays:* An Immaculate Misconception 1998, Oxygen (with Roald Hoffmann) 2000, Calculus 2003, EGO 2003, Three on a Couch 2004, Phallacy 2005, Taboos 2006, Verrechnet (with Isabella Gregor) 2009, Foreplay 2011. *Radio:* five radio plays, BBC World Service, West German Radio (WDR), Austrian Radio (ORF), NPR (USA), Swedish Radio, Radio Prague; numerous broadcasts. *Publications:* (author or co-author) Optical Rotatory Dispersion 1960, Steroid Reactions 1963, Interpretation of Mass Spectra of Organic Compounds 1964, Structure Elucidation of Natural Products by Mass Spectrometry (two vols) 1964, Mass Spectrometry of Organic Compounds 1967, The Politics of Contraception 1979, 1981, The Futurist and Other Stories (fiction) 1988, Cantor's Dilemma (novel) 1989, Steroids Made It Possible (autobiog.) 1990, The Clock Runs Backward (poetry) 1991, The Pill, Pygmy Chimps and Degas' Horse (autobiog.) 1992, Bourbaki Gambit (novel) 1994, From the Lab into the World (collected essays) 1994, Marx, deceased (novel) 1996, Menachem's Seed (novel) 1997, NO (novel) 1998, This Man's Pill (memoir) 2001, Newton's Darkness: Two Dramatic Views (with David Pinner) 2003, Sex in an Age of Technological Reproduction 2008, Four Jews on Parnassus: A Conversation 2008, Foreplay 2011, Insufficiency 2011; numerous scientific articles, also poems, memoirs and short stories. *Honours:* Hon. Fellow, Royal Chemical Soc. 1968, American Acad. of Pharmaceutical Science; Austrian Cross for Culture and Science 1999, Grosse Goldene Ehrenzeichen für Verdienste um das Bundenland Niederösterreich 2002, Ehrenmedaille der Bundeshauptstadt Wien in Gold 2002, Great Merit Cross of Germany 2003, Great Merit Cross for Services to Austria 2008, Gold Honour Ring of Austrian Acad. of Sciences 2008; 26 hon. doctorates; Award in Pure Chem. 1958, Baekeland Medal 1959, Fritzsche Medal 1960, Royal Chemical Soc. Centenary Lecturer 1964, Royal Swedish Acad. of Eng Sciences 13th Chemical Lecturer 1969, Intra-Science Research Award 1969, Freedman Foundation Patent Award 1971, Swedish Pharmaceutical Soc. Scheele Lecturer 1972, Creative Invention Award 1973, Chemical Pioneer Award 1973, American Inst. of Chemists; Nat. Medal of Science 1973 (for synthesis of first oral contraceptive), Perkin Medal 1975, Wolf Prize in Chem. 1978, Bard

Award in Medicine and Science 1983, Award in the Chem. of Contemporary Technological Problems 1983, Roussel Prize (Paris) 1988, Esselen Award for Chem. in the Public Interest, ACS 1989, NAS Award for the Industrial Application of Science 1990, Nat. Medal of Tech. 1991, Priestley Medal, ACS 1992, Nevada Medal 1992, Thomson Gold Medal, Int. Mass Spectrometry Soc. 1994, Prince Mahidol Award (Thailand) 1996, Willard Gibbs Medal 1997, Othmer Gold Medal, Chem. Heritage Foundation 2000, Erasmus Medal, Academia Europaea 2003, Gold Medal, American Inst. of Chemists 2004, on postage stamp, Austrian Post Office 2005, Serono Prize for Fiction, Rome 2005, Lichtenberg Medal, Göttingen Acad. of Sciences 2005, Edinburgh Medal 2011. *Address:* Department of Chemistry, Stanford University, Stanford, CA 94305-5080, USA (office). *Telephone:* (650) 723-2783 (office). *E-mail:* djerassi@stanford.edu (office). *Website:* www.djerassi.com (office).

DJØRUP, Adda, BA; Danish writer; b. 1972; one c. *Opera libretto:* Korus' Cabaret (Aarhus Summer Opera 2011). *Publications include:* Monsieur's Monologues (poems) 2005, If One Were To Begin To Ask Oneself (short stories) (Danish Arts Council Award) 2007, Den mindste modstand (novel) (The Least Resistance) (EU Prize for Literature 2010) 2009, Korus' Cabaret (libretto) 2010; contrib. poems and stories to anthologies and journals. *Address:* c/o Samleren, Rosinante & Co., Købmagergade 62, 4. sal, PO Box 2252, 1019 Copenhagen K, Denmark (office). *Telephone:* 33411800 (office). *Fax:* 3411800 (office). *E-mail:* info@rosinante-co.dk (office); adda@addadjorup.com (home). *Website:* www.addadjorup.com.

DJWA, Sandra Ann, BEd, PhD, FRSC; Canadian academic, biographer, critic and literary historian; b. 16 April 1939, St John's, Newfoundland; d. of Walter William Drodge and Dora Beatrice Drodge; m. 1st Peter Djing Kioe Djwa 1958 (divorced 1987); one s.; m. 2nd Lalit Srivastava 1991. *Education:* Univ. of British Columbia. *Career:* Asst Prof. of English, Simon Fraser Univ., BC 1968–73, Assoc. Prof. 1973–80, Prof. 1981–2002, Woodsworth Resident Scholar, Humanities 2002–04, Chair. Dept of English 1986–94; Co-founder Asscn for Study of Canadian and Québec Literatures 1973; Ed. Annual Review of Poetry, Letters in Canada, Univ. of Toronto Quarterly 1979–84; Sr Killam Family Fellow 1981–82; mem. Asscn of Canadian Univ. Teachers of English. *Publications include:* E. J. Pratt: The Evolutionary Vision 1974, Saul and Selected Poetry of Charles Heavysege 1976, On F. R. Scott: Essays on his Contributions to Law, Literature and Politics (co-ed.) 1983, The Politics of the Imagination: A Life of F. R. Scott 1987, E. J. Pratt: Complete Poems (co-ed.), Giving Canada a Literary History: A Memoire (ed.) by Carl F. Klinck 1991, Selected Poems of E. J. Pratt (co-ed.) 2000, Professing English: A Life of Roy Daniells (Lorne Pierce Gold Medal for Literature, RSC 2002) 2002. *Honours:* Hon. DLitt (Memorial Univ. of Newfoundland) 2002; Garnett Sedgewick Memorial Lecturer (first woman), Univ. of British Columbia 1999. *Address:* Department of English, Simon Fraser University, 8888 University Drive, AQ 6117, Burnaby, BC V5A 1S6 (office); 2947 Marine Drive W, Vancouver, BC V7V 1M3, Canada. *Telephone:* (604) 291-5436 (office). *E-mail:* djwa@sfu.ca (office). *Website:* www.sfu.ca/~djwa (office).

DOBAI, Péter, DipEd; Hungarian writer, poet, screenwriter and translator; b. 12 Aug. 1944, Budapest; m. 1st Donatella Failoni 1972; m. 2nd Maria Mate 1992. *Education:* Univ. of Budapest. *Career:* mem. Hungarian Acad. of Artists, Hungarian Writers' Asscn (mem. Exec. Bd), PEN Club, Hungary. *Publications:* fiction: Csontmolnárok 1974, Tartozó élet 1975, Lavina 1980, Vadon 1982, Háromszögtan 1983, A birodalom ezredese 1985, Iv 1988, Lendkerék 1989; short story collections: Játék a szobákkal 1976, Sakktábla két figurával 1978, Párbaj tükörben 2000; poetry: Kilovaglás egy öszi erödböl 1973, Egy arc módosulásai 1976, Hanyatt 1978, Az éden vermei 1985, Válogatott versek 1989, Vitorlák emléke 1994, Önmúltszázad 1996, Versek egy elnémult klavírra 2002, Ma könnyebb. Holnap messzebb 2004, Barth hadapród, becsületszavamra, visszatér a nyár 2005, Emlékek jövöidöben 2008, Latin lélegzet 2010; essays: Angyali agresszió (P.P.Pasolini) 2002; 15 screenplays 1971–95. *Honours:* József Attila Prize 1976, several awards, Hungarian Literary Foundation and Minister of Culture, various screenplay awards, including Cannes Film Festival 1981, Agrigento-Cinema Narrativa 1982. *Address:* Közraktár u 12/B, 1093 Budapest, Hungary (home).

DOBBS, Baron (Life Peer), cr. 2010, of Wylye in the County of Wiltshire; **Michael John Dobbs,** PhD, MALD, MA; British author, politician and broadcaster; b. Nov. 1948, Herts., England; m. Rachel Dobbs; four s. *Education:* Christ Church, Oxford and Fletcher School of Law and Diplomacy, USA. *Career:* UK Govt Special Adviser 1981–87; Chief of Staff, UK Conservative Party 1986–87, Jt Deputy Chair. 1994–95; Deputy Chair. Saatchi & Saatchi 1983–91; BBC TV and radio presenter 1999–2009; mem. (Conservative) House of Lords 2010–. *Publications:* House of Cards 1989, Wall Games 1990, Last Man to Die 1991, To Play the King 1992, The Touch of Innocents 1994, The Final Cut 1995, Goodfellowe MP 1997, The Buddha of Brewer Street 1998, Whispers of Betrayal 2000, Winston's War 2002, Never Surrender 2003, Churchill's Hour 2004, Churchill's Triumph 2005, First Lady 2006, The Lords' Day 2007, The Edge of Madness 2008, The Reluctant Hero 2010, A Sentimental Traitor 2011. *Address:* House of Lords, Westminster, London, SW1A 0PW (office); Newton House, Wylye, Wilts. BA12 0QS, England (home). *E-mail:* michael@michaeldobbs.com (office); dobbsm@parliament.uk (office). *Website:* www.michaeldobbs.com.

DOBSON, Andrew Nicholas Howard, BA, DPhil; British political scientist, writer and academic; *Professor of Politics, Research Institute for Law, Politics and Justice, Keele University*; b. 15 April 1957, Doncaster, England. *Education:* Univs of Reading and Oxford. *Career:* founding Co-Ed. and Chair. Editorial Bd Environmental Politics 1991–; mem. Editorial Bd Environmental Values 1991–2004, Anarchist Studies 1991–2000, Cambridge Quarterly of Healthcare Ethics, Global Environmental Politics, Philosophy and Geography and Social Movement Studies; Lecturer in Politics, Research Inst. for Law, Politics and Justice, Keele Univ. 1987–93, Prof. of Politics and Chair. Dept of Politics 1993–2001, 2006–, Dir Grad. School of Social Sciences 1999–2001, 2006–, Acting Dean of Postgraduate Affairs 2001; Prof. of Politics, Open Univ. 2002–06; Visiting Prof. of Politics, Luleå Univ. of Technology, Sweden 1997–2002; unsuccessful Green Party cand. in UK Gen. Election 2005, also ran in local elections contesting Keele Ward 2006. *Publications include:* monographs: An Introduction to the Politics and Philosophy of José Ortega y Gasset 1989, Green Political Thought 1990, 2007, Jean-Paul Sartre and the Politics of Reason: A Theory of History 1993, Justice and the Environment: Conceptions of Environmental Sustainability and Dimensions of Social Justice 1998, Citizenship and the Environment 2003; edited books: The Green Reader (ed.) 1991, The Politics of Nature: Exploration in Green Political Theory (co-ed. with Paul Lucardie) 1993, Contemporary Political Studies, Vols 1 and 2 (co-ed.) 1998, Fairness and Futurity: Essays on Environmental Sustainability and Social Justice (ed.) 1999, Environmental Citizenship (co-ed. with Derek Bell) 2005, Citizenship, Environment, Economy (co-ed. with Angel Valencia) 2005, Political Theory and the Ecological Challenge (co-ed. with Robyn Eckerlsey) 2006, The Politics of Protection: Sites of Insecurity and Political Agency (co-ed.) 2006; works have been translated into Spanish, Chinese, Japanese and Korean; numerous book chapters and articles in professional journals; book reviews for Times Literary Supplement, Times Higher Education Supplement, Political Studies, Environmental Politics, Environmental Values, Modern Languages Review, Sociological Review, Sociology, Radical Philosophy, Tribune, Anarchist Studies, International Affairs, APSR. *Honours:* Spanish Govt Scholar 1983–84, Econ. and Social Science Research Council Postdoctoral Research Fellow at St John's Coll. Oxford 1984–87, Keele Univ. Research Fellowship 1991, Harrison Prize for best article published in 2006 in Political Studies 2007. *Address:* Room CBB2.024, Humanities and Social Sciences: Politics, International Relations and Philosophy (SPIRE), Chancellor's Building, Keele University, Newcastle-under-Lyme, Staffs., ST5 5BG, England (office). *Telephone:* (1908) 652022 (office); (1782) 583591 (office). *Fax:* (1782) 584592 (office). *E-mail:* a.n.h.dobson@keele.ac.uk (office); a.n.h.dobson@pol.keele.ac.uk (office); andy@andrewdobson.com. *Website:* www.keele.ac.uk/research/lpj; www.andrewdobson.com; www.tandf.co.uk/journals/titles/09644016.asp.

DOBSON, Joanne, BA, MA, PhD; American writer and academic; b. 27 March 1942, New York, NY; m. David Eugene Dobson 1963; one s. two d. *Education:* King's Coll., New York, SUNY at Albany, Univ. of Massachusetts at Amherst. *Career:* founding mem., Legacy: Journal of American Women Writers 1983–93, mem., Editorial Board 1993–96; General Co-ed., American Women Writers reprint series, Rutgers University Press 1984–92; Visiting Prof. of English and American Studies, Amherst Coll., Amherst, Massachusetts 1985–86; Visiting Asst Prof. of English, Tufts Univ., Medford, Massachusetts 1986–87; Asst Prof., Fordham Univ., Bronx, New York 1987–92, Assoc. Prof. of English 1992–; mem., Editorial Board, American Literature 1995–97; mem., Emily Dickinson International Society, Mem., Board of Dirs 1988–91. *Publications:* The Hidden Hand (ed.) 1988, Dickinson and the Strategies of Reticence: The Woman Writer in Nineteenth-Century America 1989, Quieter than Sleep (novel) 1997, The Northbury Papers (novel) 1998, The Raven and the Nightingale (novel) 1999, Cold and Pure and Very Dead (novel) 2000, The Maltese Manuscript (novel) 2003, Death Without Tenure 2010; contributions: periodicals including American Quarterly. *Literary Agent:* Deborah Schneider, Gelfman Schneider, 250 W 57th Street, New York, NY 10107, USA. *E-mail:* jadobson@aol.com (office). *Website:* www.joannedobson.com.

DOBSON, Rosemary, AO; Australian writer, poet and editor; b. 18 June 1920, Sydney, NSW; d. of Austin A. G. Dobson and Marjorie Dobson (née Caldwell); m. Alexander Thorley Bolton 1951; two s. one d. *Education:* Frensham School, Mittagong, NSW and Univ. of Sydney. *Career:* teacher of art; mem. Editorial Dept Angus and Robertson Publrs, Sydney; freelance writer 1951–; mem. Australian Soc. of Authors. *Publications include:* In a Convex Mirror 1944, The Ship of Ice and Other Poems (Sydney Morning Herald Award for Poetry) 1948, Child with a Cockatoo and Other Poems 1955, Australian Poets: Rosemary Dobson 1963, Cock Crow 1965, Songs for all Seasons 1968, Focus on Ray Crooke (prose) 1971, Selected Poems 1973, Moscow Trefoil (co-author) 1975, Greek Coins: A Sequence of Poems 1977, Australian Voices (ed.) 1978, Over the Frontier 1978, Seven Russian Poets (co-author) 1979, Selected Poems 1980, The Three Fates and Other Poems (Grace Leven Prize for Poetry 1984, Victoria Premier's Literary Awards for Poetry (jtly) 1985) 1984, Summer Press 1987, Collected Poems 1991, Untold Lives: A Sequence of Poems 1992, Untold Lives and Later Poems 2000. *Honours:* Hon. Life mem. Asscn for the Study of Australian Literature 1985; Hon. DLit (Sydney) 1996; FAW Christopher Brennan Award 1978, Robert Frost Prize 1979, Sr Literary Fellowship, Australia Council 1980, Patrick White Award for Literature 1984, Emer. Fellowship, Literature Bd of Australia Council 1996, Age Book of the Year Award 2000, NSW Premier's Literary Award Special Award 2006, NSW Soc. of Women Writers Alice Award 2006. *Literary Agent:* Curtis Brown Pty Ltd, POB 19, Paddington, NSW 2021, Australia. *E-mail:* rdobsonbolton@gmail.com (home).

DOBSON, Sue, BA; British travel writer, media consultant and fmr magazine editor; b. Maidstone, Kent; m. Michael Dobson 1966 (divorced 1974). *Education:* convent schools in Kent and Polytechnic of North-East London. *Career:* Ed., Small Trader, London 1964; Fashion, Cookery and Beauty Ed., Femina, SA 1965–69; Contributing Ed., Fair Lady, SA 1969–71; Ed., S Africa Inst. of Race Relations 1972–74, Wedding Day and First Home, London 1978–81, Successful Slimming, London 1981–82, Woman and Home, London 1982–94; Ed.-in-Chief, Choice magazine 1994–2002; freelance writer. *Publication:* The Wedding Day Book (2nd edn) 1989, Travellers Cape Verde 2008, Travellers Namibia 2008. *Honours:* Travel Writing Award 2001, 2004, 2006. *E-mail:* dobsonsue@btinternet.com (office).

DOBYNS, Stephen, BA, MFA; American academic, poet and writer; b. 19 Feb. 1941, Orange, NJ; m.; three c. *Education:* Shimer Coll., Mount Carroll, Ill., Wayne State Univ., Univ. of Iowa. *Career:* Instructor, SUNY at Brockport 1968–69; Reporter, Detroit News 1969–71; Visiting Writer, Univ. of New Hampshire 1973–75, Univ. of Iowa 1977–79, Boston Univ. 1978–79, 1980–81, Syracuse Univ. 1986; Faculty, Goddard Coll., Plainfield, Vermont 1978–80, Warren Wilson Coll., Swannanoa, NC 1982–87; Prof. of Creative Writing, Syracuse Univ., New York 1987–. *Publications:* poetry: Concurring Beasts 1972, Griffon 1976, Heat Death 1980, The Balthus Poems 1982, Black Dog, Red Dog 1984, Cemetery Nights 1987, Body Traffic 1991, Velocities: New and Selected Poems, 1966–1992 1994, Common Carnage 1996, Pallbearers Envying the One Who Rides 1999, Do They Have a Reason? 2000, The Porcupine's Kisses 2002, Mystery, So Long 2005, Winter's Journey 2010; fiction: A Man of Little Evils 1973, Saratoga Longshot 1976, Saratoga Swimmer 1981, Dancer with One Leg 1983, Saratoga Headhunter 1985, Cold Dog Soup 1985, Saratoga Snapper 1986, A Boat Off the Coast 1987, The Two Deaths of Señora Puccini 1988, Saratoga Bestiary 1988, The House of Alexandrina 1989, Saratoga Hexameter 1990, After Shocks/Near Escapes 1991, Saratoga Haunting 1993, The Wrestler's Cruel Study 1993, Saratoga Backtalk 1994, Saratoga Fleshpot 1995, Saratoga Trifecta 1995, The Church of Dead Girls 1997, Saratoga Strongbox 1998, Boy in the Water 1999, Eating Naked 2000. *Honours:* Lamont Poetry Selection Award 1971, MacDowell Colony Fellowships 1972, 1976, Yaddo Fellowships 1972, 1973, 1977, 1981, 1982, National Endowment for the Arts Grants 1974, 1981, Guggenheim Fellowship 1983, National Poetry Series Prize 1984. *Address:* 22 Mount Auburn Street, Watertown, MA 02472-3992, USA (home).

DOCHERTY, David, BA, PhD; British broadcasting executive and writer; *CEO, CSC Media Group*; b. 10 Dec. 1956, Scotland; s. of David Docherty and Anna Docherty; m. Kate Stuart-Smith 1992; two d. *Education:* Univ. of Strathclyde, London School of Econs. *Career:* Research Fellow, Broadcasting Research Unit, London 1984–88; Dir of Research Broadcasting Standards Council 1988–89; Head of Broadcasting Analysis, BBC TV 1990–92, Head of TV Planning and Strategy, BBC Network TV 1992–96, Dir of Strategy and Channel Devt, BBC Broadcast 1996–97, Deputy Dir of TV BBC Broadcasting 1997, Dir New Services, BBC Bd of Man. 1999; Man. Dir of Broadband Content, Telewest Communications 2000–02; CEO iPublic div., YooMedia PLC's 2003–04; Group Chief Exec. YooMedia PLC 2004–05; CEO CSC Media Group 2005–; Chair. Living Health; Chair. Bd of Govs and Pro Vice-Chancellor, Univ. of Luton 2001–06; fmr mem. Bd BBC America UKTV; columnist, The Guardian. *Publications:* The Last Picture Show?: Britain's Changing Film Audience 1987, Keeping Faith?: Channel 4 and Its Audience 1988, Running the Show: 21 Years of London Weekend Television 1990, Violence in Television Fiction 1991, The Spirit Death 2000, The Killing Jar 2002, The Fifth Season 2003, Fear Less 2005. *Honours:* Hon. Fellow, Leeds Univ. *Address:* c/o Julian Friedmann, Blake Friedmann, 122 Arlington Road, London, NW1 7HP; Serge Hill, Abbots Langley, Herts., WD5 0RY, England (home). *Telephone:* (20) 7284-0408. *Fax:* (20) 7284-0442. *E-mail:* info@blakefriedmann.co.uk.

DOCHERTY, John (see Sills-Docherty, Jonathan John)

DOCTOROW, Edgar Lawrence (E.L.), AB; American novelist, essayist, dramatist and academic; *Lewis and Loretta Gluckman Professor of American and English Letters, New York University*; b. 6 Jan. 1931, New York; s. of David Richard and Rose Doctorow (née Levine); m. Helen Esther Setzer 1954; one s. two d. *Education:* Kenyon Coll., Gambier, Ohio, Columbia Univ. *Career:* served with US army 1953–55; script reader, Columbia Pictures 1956–59; Ed. New American Library, New York 1960–64; Ed.-in-Chief Dial Press., New York 1964–69, Publr 1969; Writer-in-Residence, Univ. of Calif., Irvine 1969–70; mem. faculty, Sarah Lawrence Coll., Bronxville, NY 1971–78; Creative Writing Fellow, Yale School of Drama 1974–75; Creative Artists Program Service Fellow 1973–74; Visiting Sr Fellow, Council on Humanities, Princeton Univ. 1980–81; Adjunct Prof. of English, New York Univ. 1982–87; Lewis and Loretta Gluckman Prof. of American and English Letters 1987–; mem. Authors Guild, American PEN, Writers Guild of America East, Century Asscn, American Acad. of Arts and Letters, American Acad. of Arts and Sciences, American Philosophical Soc., Guggenheim Fellow 1973. *Publications:* Welcome to Hard Times 1960, Big as Life 1966, The Book of Daniel 1971, Ragtime 1975, Drinks before Dinner (play) 1978, Loon Lake 1980, Lives of the Poets: Six Stories and a Novella 1984, World's Fair 1985, Billy Bathgate 1989, Jack London, Hemingway and the Constitution: Selected Essays 1977–92 1993, The Waterworks 1994, The Best American Short Stories (ed. with Katrina Kenison) 2000, City of God 2000, Sweet Land Stories 2004, Reporting the Universe (lectures) 2004, The March 2006, Creationists: Selected Essays 1993–2006, Homer & Langley 2009, All the Time in the World: New and Selected Stories 2011. *Honours:* Hon. LHD (Kenyon Coll.) 1976, (Hobart Coll.) 1979, Hon. DLitt (William Smith Coll.) 1979, Hon. DHL (Brandeis Univ.) 1989; Arts and Letters Award (American Acad. and Nat. Inst. of Art) 1976, Nat. Book Critics Circle Award 1976, 1990, 2005, Guggenheim Fellow 1973, Nat. Book Award 1986, William Dean Howells Medal, American Acad. of Arts and Letters 1990, PEN/Faulkner Prize 1990, 2005, Nat. Humanities Medal 1998, Commonwealth Award 2000. *Literary Agent:* c/o Amanda Urban, International Creative Management, 825 8th Avenue, New York, NY 10019, USA. *Telephone:* (212) 556-5764 (office). *E-mail:* AUrban@icmtalent.com (office). *Address:* English Department, New York University, 58 West 10th St, New York, NY 10011 (office); c/o Random House Publishers, 1745 Broadway, New York, NY 10019, USA (office). *Telephone:* (212) 998-8833 (office); (212) 572-2764 (office). *E-mail:* JyMartin@randomhouse.com (office). *Website:* www.E.L.Doctorow.com (office).

DODD, Wayne Donald, BA, MA, PhD; American poet, writer, editor and academic; *Distinguished Professor Emeritus, Ohio University*; b. 23 Sept. 1930, Clarita, Okla; m. 1st Betty Coshow 1958 (divorced 1980); m. 2nd Joyce Barlow 1981; two c. *Education:* Univ. of Oklahoma. *Career:* Instructor 1960–64, Univ. of Colorado at Boulder, Asst Prof. of English 1964–68; Fellow, Center for Advanced Studies, Wesleyan Univ. 1964; Assoc. Prof., Ohio Univ. 1968–73, Prof. of English 1973–94, Edwin and Ruth Kennedy Distinguished Prof. of Poetry 1994–2001, Distinguished Prof. Emer. 2001–; Ed., Ohio Review 1971–2001; mem. Associated Writing Programs. *Publications:* poetry: We Will Wear White Roses 1974, Made in America 1975, The Names You Gave It 1980, The General Mule Poems 1981, Sometimes Music Rises 1986, Echoes of the Unspoken 1990, Of Desire and Disorder 1994, The Blue Salvages 1998, Is 2003; fiction: A Time of Hunting 1975; other: Poets on the Line (ed.) 1987, Toward the End of the Century: Essays into Poetry 1992, Art and Nature: Essays by Contemporary Writers (ed.) 1993, Mentors (ed.) 1994; contrib. to anthologies, reviews, quarterlies and journals. *Honours:* ACLS Fellowship 1964–65, Ohio Arts Council Fellowships 1980, 1989, 1998, NEA Fellowship in Poetry 1982, Ohioana Library Foundation Krout Award for Lifetime Achievement in Poetry 1991, Rockefeller Foundation Fellowship 1995, Fellowship, Bellagio, Italy 1995, Ohio Gov.'s Award for the Arts 2001. *Address:* 11292 Peach Ridge Road, Athens, OH 45701, USA (home). *E-mail:* doddw@ohio.edu (office). *Website:* www.waynedodd.com.

DOHERTY, Berlie, BA; British writer, dramatist and poet; b. 6 Nov. 1943, Liverpool, England; m. Gerard Doherty 1966 (divorced 1996); one s. two d. *Education:* Durham Univ., Liverpool Univ., Sheffield Univ. *Career:* mem. Arvon Foundation, Lumb Bank (Chair. 1988–93). *Plays:* Home 1982, A Case for Probation 1986, Morgan's Field 1995, Dear Nobody 1996, Street Child 2000, Lorna Doone 2001, Granny was a Buffer Girl 2003, The Snake-Stone 2005. *Radio:* The Drowned Village 1980, Requiem 1982: Sacrifice 1985, There's a Valley in Spain 1990, Dear Nobody 1993, The Snow Queen 1994, Heidi 1996, The Water Babies (Talkies Award) 1999. *Television:* White Peak Farm (Film and Television awards) 1988, Children of Winter 1994, Zzaap and the Word Master 1991. *Opera:* The Magician's Cat, Wildcat: Daughter of the Sea. *Publications:* juvenile: How Green You Are 1982, The Making of Fingers Finnigan 1983, White Peak Farm 1984, Tilly Mint Tales 1984, Children of Winter 1985, Granny Was a Buffer Girl (Carnegie Medal, Burnley Children's Book of the Year Award 1987) 1986, Tilly Mint and the Dodo 1988, Paddiwak and Cosy 1988, Tough Luck 1988, Spellhorn 1989, Requiem (short story, also play) 1991, Dear Nobody (Carnegie Medal, Sankei Award (Japan), Writer's Guild of Great Britain Award 1992) 1991, Snowy (Children's Book Award) 1993, Big, Bulgy, Fat Black Slug 1993, Old Father Christmas 1993, Street Child 1993, Walking on Air (poems) 1993, Willa and Old Miss Annie 1994, The Vinegar Jar 1994, The Snake-Stone 1995, The Golden Bird (Nasen Award) 1995, The Magical Bicycle (Oppenheim Gold Seal Award) 1995, Our Field 1996, Daughter of the Sea (Writers Guild of Great Britain Award 1997) 1996, Bella's Den 1997, Running on Ice 1997, Tales of Wonder and Magic 1997, The Midnight Man 1998, The Forsaken Merman 1998, The Snow Queen 1998, The Sailing Ship Tree 1998, The Famous Adventures of Jack 2000, Fairy Tales 2000, Zzaap and the Wordmaster 2000, Holly Starcross 2001, Lorna Doone (play) 2001, Deep Secret 2003, Blue John 2003, Coconut Comes to School 2003, Tricky Nelly's Birthday Treat 2003, The Starburster 2004, Jeannie of White Peak Farm (Phoenix Award) 2004, Jinnie Ghost 2005, The Humming Machine 2006, Abela 2007, The Windspinner 2008; other: Requiem (adult novel) 1991, The Oxford Book of Bible Studies 2007, A Beautiful Place For a Murder 2008; contrib. to periodicals and literary journals. *Honours:* Hon. doctorate (Derby) 2002; Boston Globe-Horn Book Award 1987. *Literary Agent:* c/o Veronique Baxter, David Higham Associates, 5-8 Lower John Street, Golden Square, London W1R 4HA, England. *E-mail:* veroniquebaxter@davidhigham.co.uk. *Website:* www.berliedoherty.com.

DOHLE, Markus; German business executive; *Chairman and CEO, Random House*; b. 28 June 1968, Arnsberg. *Education:* Univ. of Karlsruhe. *Career:* with Bertelsmann AG 1994–, asst to Man. Dir, Bertelsmann Distribution 1994–95, Vice-Pres. Bertelsmann Service Group 1998–2002; Vice-Pres. Vereinigte Verlagsauslieferung 1995–98, CEO 1998–2002; Man. Dir Medienvertrieb und Logistk GmbH 2000–02; apptd Man. Dir Verlegerdienst München GmbH 2002; CEO Mohn Media Group 2002–08; Chair. and CEO Random House 2008–; mem. Exec. Bd Arvato 2006–08, Bertelsmann AG 2008–. *Address:* Random House, Inc., 1745 Broadway, New York, NY 10019, USA (office). *Telephone:* (212) 782-9000 (office). *Website:* www.randomhouse.com (office).

DOLIS, John, BA, MA, PhD; American scholar, critic and poet; *Professor of English and American Studies, Pennsylvania State University*; b. 25 April 1945, St Louis, Mo. *Education:* St Louis Univ., Loyola Univ., Chicago. *Career:* Teaching Asst Loyola Univ., Chicago 1967–69, 1970–73, Lecturer 1974–75, 1978–80, Instructor, Columbia Coll. 1970–71, Northeastern Illinois Univ. 1978–80, Univ. of Kansas 1981–85; Fulbright Lecturer, Univ. of Turin, Italy 1980–81; Asst Prof., Pennsylvania State Univ., Scranton 1985–92, Assoc. Prof. 1992–2005, Prof. of English and American Studies 2005–; Sr Fulbright Lecturer, Univ. of Bucharest, Romania 1989–90; Visiting Prof. of American Culture and Literature, Bilkent Univ., Ankara 1995–96; mem. Editorial Bd Antemnae, Arizona Quarterly, Journal of American Culture, Nathaniel Hawthorne Review; mem. American Culture Asscn, American Literature Asscn, American Philosophical Asscn, Asscn for Applied Psychoanalysis, Int. Asscn for Philosophy and Literature, Int. Husserl and Phenomenological Research Soc., Int. Soc. for Phenomenology and the Human Sciences, Int. Soc. for Phemomenology and Literature, Modern Language Asscn, Nathaniel Hawthorne Soc., Nat. Social Science Asscn, Soc. for the Advancement of American Philosophy, Soc. for Phenomenology and Existential Philosophy, Soc. for Philosophy and Psychiatry, Soc. for Romanian Studies, Thoreau Soc., World Phenomenology Inst. *Publications:* The Style of Hawthorne's Gaze: Regarding Subjectivity 1993, Bl( )nk Space 1993, Time Flies: Butterflies 1999, Tracking Thoreau: Double-Crossing Nature and Technology 2005, Enlightenment 2008, Picture Perfect 2009, (P)ear 2009; contrib. of articles in scholarly journals, poems in anthologies and magazines. *Honours:* Nat. Endowment for the Humanities Fellowships 1979, 1988, Pharmakon Research Int. Award for Excellence in Scholarly Activities, Pennsylvania State Univ. 1991, various grants. *Address:* 711 Summit Pointe, Scranton, PA 18508, USA (home). *Telephone:* (570) 961-9787 (office). *E-mail:* jjd3@psu.edu (office). *Website:* www.ws.psu.edu/courses/jjd3 (office).

DOLL, Mary Aswell, BA, MA, PhD; American academic; b. 4 June 1940, New York, NY; m. William Elder Doll Jr 1966 (divorced 1994); one s. *Education:* Connecticut Coll., New London, Johns Hopkins Univ., Syracuse Univ. *Career:* Asst Prof., SUNY at Oswego 1978–84; Lecturer, Univ. of Redlands, CA 1985–88; Asst Prof., Loyola Univ. 1988; Visiting Asst Prof., Tulane Univ. 1988; Assoc. Prof. Our Lady of Holy Cross Coll. 1989–93, Prof. 1993–99; Prof., Savannah Coll. of Art and Design 2000–; mem. MLA, Thomas Wolfe Society. *Publications:* Rites of Story: The Old Man at Play 1987, Beckett and Myth: An Archetypal Approach 1988, In the Shadow of the Giant: Thomas Wolfe 1988, Walking and Rocking 1989, Joseph Campbell and the Power of the Wilderness 1992, Stoppard's Theatre of Unknowing 1993, To the Lighthouse and Back 1996, Like Letters in Running Water: A Mythopoetics of Curriculum 2000, Triple Takes On Curricular Worlds 2006; contribs to periodicals. *Honours:* Outstanding Book Citation Choice 1989, Sears-Roebuck Teaching Excellence Award. *Address:* 527 E 56th Street, Savannah, GA 31405-3523, USA (home). *E-mail:* MDoll4444@aol.com (home).

DOLLIMORE, Jonathan, BA, PhD; British academic and writer; b. 31 July 1948, Leighton Buzzard. *Education:* Keele Univ., Univ. of London. *Career:* Lecturer, School of English and American Studies, Univ. of Sussex 1976–89, Senior Lecturer 1989–90, Reader 1990–93, Prof. of English, Graduate Research Centre for the Humanities 1993–95, Prof. 1995–99; Visiting Fellow, Humanities Research Centre, Canberra 1988, Human Sciences Research Council of South Africa 1996; Mellon Fellow, National Humanities Center, NC 1988–89; Scholar-in-Residence, Centre for Renaissance and Baroque Studies, Univ. of Maryland 1991–92; Cecil and Ida Green Visiting Prof., Univ. of British Columbia 1997; Prof. of English, Univ. of York 1999; Visiting Prof., LeHigh Univ., Univ. of Oregon and Univ. of Tel-Aviv, 2002; currently Hon. Prof., Univ. of Sussex. *Publications:* The Selected Plays of John Webster (ed. with Alan Sinfield) 1983, Radical Tragedy: Religion, Ideology and Power in the Drama of Shakespeare and his Contemporaries 1984, Political Shakespeare: New Essays in Cultural Materialism (ed. with Alan Sinfield) 1985, Sexual Dissidence: Augustine to Wilde, Freud to Foucault 1991, Death, Desire and Loss in Western Culture 1998, Sex, Literature and Censorship 2001; contributions: many scholarly books and journals. *Address:* c/o Department of English, University of Sussex, Arts Building B274, Falmer, Brighton BN1 9QN, England. *E-mail:* skodajag@aol.com (office).

DOMÍNGUEZ, Carlos María; Argentine writer, journalist and literary critic; b. 1955, Buenos Aires. *Career:* has lived in Montevideo, Uruguay 1989–. *Publications:* fiction: Pozo de Vargas 1985, Mares baldíos (short stories), Bicicletas negras 1991, La Mujer Hablada (Bartolomé Hidalgo Prize) 1998, La Casa de papel (trans. as The Paper House) (Premio de la Fundación Lolita Rubial, Vienna's Jury of Young Readers Prize) 2001, Tres Muescas en mi carabina (Juan Carlos Onetti Prize) 2003; non-fiction: Construcción de la noche: la vida de Juan Carlos Onetti (biog., with María Esther Gilio) 1993, El Bastardo: la vida de Roberto de las Carreras y su madre Clara (biog.) 1997, Delitos de amores crueles: las mujeres uruguayas frente a la justicia 1865–1911 2001, Tola Invernizzi: la rebelión de la ternura (biog.) 2001, La Rebelión de la ternura 2001, Historia de un dictador (biog.), Escritos en el agua (Premio del Ministerio de Educación y Cultura de Uruguay) 2002, El norte profundo 2004, El compás de oro (collected articles), Historias del polvo y el camino (collected articles), La Puertas de la Tierra 2007; plays: La incapaz, Polski (with Jorge Boccanera). *Address:* c/o Alfaguara, Grupo Santillana Argentina, Avenida L.N. Alem 720, 1001 Buenos Aires, Argentina (office). *E-mail:* info@alfaguara.com.ar (office). *Website:* www.alfaguara.com.ar (office).

DOMMISSE, Ebbe, BA, MA; South African newspaper editor; b. 14 July 1940, Riversdal; s. of Jan Dommisse and Anna Dommisse; m. Daléne Laubscher 1963; two s. one d. *Education:* Univ. of Stellenbosch, Grad. School of Journalism, Columbia Univ., USA. *Career:* reporter, Die Burger, Cape Town 1961, Chief Sub-Ed. 1968, News Ed. 1971; Asst Ed. and Political Commentator, Beeld, Johannesburg (Founder-mem. of new Johannesburg daily) 1974; Asst Ed. Die Burger 1979, Sr Asst Ed. 1984, Ed. 1990–2000; Exec. mem. Nasionale Koerante; Trustee, Helpmekaarfonds; mem. Akad. vir Wetenskap en Kuns. *Publications:* with Alf Ries: Broedertwis 1982, Leierstryd 1990, Anton Rupert 2005. *Address:* c/o NB Publishers, PO Box 879, Cape Town 8000, South Africa.

DONALDSON, (Charles) Ian Edward, BA, MA; Australian/British academic and writer; *Honorary Professorial Fellow, University of Melbourne*; b. 6 May 1935, Melbourne, Vic.; s. of Dr William Edward Donaldson and Mary Claudia Elizabeth Donaldson; m. 1st Tamsin Jane Procter 1962 (divorced 1990); one s. one d.; m. 2nd Grazia Maria Therese Gunn 1991. *Education:* Univ. of Melbourne, Magdalen Coll., Oxford. *Career:* Sr Tutor in English, Univ. of Melbourne 1958, Visiting appointment 1991; Harmsworth Sr Scholar, Merton Coll., Oxford, UK 1960–62; Fellow and Lecturer in English, Wadham Coll., Oxford 1962–69; CUF Lecturer in English, Univ. of Oxford 1963–69; visiting appointments, Univ. of California, Santa Barbara, USA 1967–68, Gonville and Caius Coll., Cambridge, UK 1985, Cornell Univ., USA 1988, Folger Shakespeare Library, Washington, DC, USA 1988; Prof. of English, ANU, Canberra 1969–91, Foundation Dir, Humanities Research Centre 1974–90, Interim Dir 2004–07, Prof. Emer. 2007–; Regius Prof. of Rhetoric and English Literature, Univ. of Edinburgh, UK 1991–95; Grace I Prof. of English, King's Coll., Cambridge 1995–2002, Dir Centre for Research in the Arts, Social Sciences and Humanities, Univ. of Cambridge 2001–03; Pres. Australian Acad. of the Humanities 2007–09; Pres. Nat. Acads Forum (Australia) 2009. *Publications:* The World Upside Down: Comedy From Jonson to Fielding 1970, Ben Jonson: Poems (ed.) 1975, The Rapes of Lucretia: A Myth and its Transformations 1982, Jonson and Shakespeare (ed.) 1983, Transformations in Modern European Drama (ed.) 1983, Seeing the First Australians (co-ed. with Tamsin Donaldson) 1985, Ben Jonson 1985, Shaping Lives: Reflections on Biography (co-ed.) 1992, Jonson's Walk to Scotland 1993, The Death of the Author and the Life of the Poet 1995, Ben Jonson: Selected Poems (ed.) 1995, Jonson's Magic Houses 1997, Ben Jonson: A Life 2011, The Cambridge Edition of the Works of Ben Jonson (seven vols, ed.) 2012; contribs to scholarly journals. *Honours:* Hon. Professorial Fellow, Univ. of Melbourne; Fellow Australian Acad. of the Humanities 1975, Fellow British Acad. 1993 (Corresponding Fellow 1987), Fellow Royal Society of Edinburgh 1993. *E-mail:* ido@unimelb.edu.au (office).

DONALDSON, Julia Catherine, MBE; British children's writer and teacher; *Children's Laureate*; b. 1948, London, England; m. Malcolm Donaldson. *Education:* Univ. of Bristol. *Career:* children's songwriter for BBC TV and radio; Children's Laureate 2011–; Patron Artlink Central; lives in Glasgow. *Plays:* All Aboard 1995, Problem Page 2000, High Impact 2000, Bombs and Blackberries 2003. *Publications:* juvenile fiction: A Squash and a Squeeze 1993, The Magic Twig 1995, Mr Snow 1996, Spacegirl Sue 1996, Storyworlds 1997, Books and Crooks 1998, Waiter! Waiter! 1998, The Brownie King 1998, The Gruffalo 1999, Rabbit's Nap 2000, Hide and Seek Pig 2000, Fox's Socks 2000, Monkey Puzzle 2000, Postman Bear 2000, Blue Banana 2002, Night Monkey Day Monkey 2002, Room on the Broom 2002, Spinderella 2002, The Dinosaur's Diary 2002, Princess Mirror-Belle 2003, The Smartest Giant in Town 2003, The Spiffiest Giant in Town 2003, Chameleons: Brick-a-Breck 2003, Conjuror Cow 2003, The Magic Paintbrush 2003, The Snail and the Whale 2003, The Wrong Kind of Bark 2004, One Ted Falls Out of Bed 2004, Crazy Mayonnaisy Mum 2004, Sharing a Shell 2004, The Gruffalo's Child (British Book Award for Children's Book of the Year 2005) 2004, Wriggle and Roar!: Rhymes to Join in With 2004, Rose's Hat 2005, Princess Mirror-Belle 2 2005, Chocolate Mousse for Greedy Goose 2005, Hippo Has a Hat 2005, Charlie Cook's Favourite Book 2005, Follow the Swallow 2007, Tyrannosaurus Drip 2007, Tiddler (with Alex Scheffler) 2007, One Mole Digging a Hole 2008, Stick Man (with Alex Scheffler) 2008, Running on the Cracks (Nasen Inclusive Children's Book Award) 2009, What the Ladybird Heard (with Lydia Monks) 2009, Toddle Waddle (with Nick Sharratt) 2009, The Troll (with David Roberts) 2009, Tabby McTat (with Axel Scheffler) 2009, Cave Baby 2010, Zog 2010. *Address:* c/o Pan Macmillan Publishers, 20 New Wharf Road, London, N1 9RR, England. *Website:* www.juliadonaldson.co.uk; www.childrenslaureate.org.uk.

DONALDSON, Stephen Reeder, (Reed Stephens), BA, MA; American writer; b. 13 May 1947, Cleveland, OH; m. 1st (divorced); m. 2nd Stephanie 1980; one s. one d. *Education:* Coll. of Wooster, Kent State Univ. *Career:* Assoc. Instructor, Ghost Ranch Writers' Workshops 1973–77; Contributing Ed., Journal of the Fantastic in the Arts; mem. Int. Asscn for the Fantastic in the Arts. *Publications:* Thomas Covenant series: The Chronicles of Thomas Covenant the Unbeliever, Vol. I Lord Foul's Bane 1977, Vol. 2 The Illearth War 1977, Vol. 3 The Power that Preserves 1977; The Second Chronicles of Thomas Covenant, Vol. 1 The Wounded Land 1980, Vol. 2 The One Tree 1982, Vol. 3 White Gold Wielder 1983; The Last Chronicles of Thomas Covenant: The Runes of the Earth 2004, Fatal Revenant 2007, Against All Things Ending 2010; Mordant's Need, Vol. 1 The Mirror of Her Dreams 1986, Vol. 2 A Man Rides Through 1987; the Gap sequence: The Gap Into Conflict: The Real Story 1991, The Gap Into Vision: Forbidden Knowledge 1991, The Gap Into Power: A

Dark and Hungry God Arises 1992, The Gap Into Madness: Chaos and Order 1994, The Gap Into Ruin: This Day All Gods Die 1996; other novels: Gilden-Fire 1982, Daughter of Regals and Other Tales 1984, Reave the Just and Other Tales 1999, The Man Who Fought Alone 2001; as Reed Stephens: The Man Who Killed His Brother 1980, The Man Who Risked His Partner 1984, The Man Who Tried to Get Away 1990; editor: Strange Dreams: Unforgettable Fantasy Stories 1993; contrib. to magazines. *Honours:* Hon. DLitt (Coll. of Wooster) 1993; British Fantasy Soc. Best Novel Award 1978, World Science Fiction Convention John W. Campbell Award 1979, Balrog Awards 1981, 1983, 1985, Saturn Award 1983. *Literary Agent:* Howard Morhaim Literary Agency, 841 Broadway, Suite 604, New York, NY 10003, USA. *Telephone:* (718) 222-8400. *E-mail:* howard@morhaimliterary.com. *Website:* www.stephendonaldson.com.

DONALDSON, William, MA, PhD; British teacher and writer; *Visiting Lecturer, Massachusetts Institute of Technology;* b. 19 July 1944, Ellon, Scotland; two s. one d. *Education:* Univ. of Aberdeen. *Career:* Registrar of the North East Survey; teacher of English; Assoc. Lecturer, Open Univ.; currently Visiting Lecturer, MIT. *Publications:* Popular Literature in Victorian Scotland 1986, The Jacobite Song 1988, The Language of the People 1989, The Highland Pipe and Scottish Society 2000, Pipers: A Guide to the Players and Music of the Highland Bagpipe 2005. *Honours:* Blackwell Prize 1988, Scottish Arts Council Book Award 1989, Piper & Drummer Online Award 2000. *Address:* 77 Massachusetts Avenue, Literature Section, Building 14N, Room 407, Cambridge, MA 02139, Scotland (office).

DONGLI JIEFU (see Zhang Changxin)

DONLEAVY, James Patrick; Irish author; b. 23 April 1926, New York City; s. of Patrick Donleavy and Margaret Donleavy; m. 1st Valerie Heron (divorced 1969); one s. one d.; m. 2nd Mary Wilson Price (divorced 1989); one s. one d. *Education:* Preparatory School, New York and Trinity Coll., Dublin. *Career:* served in USN during World War II. *Publications:* (novels) The Ginger Man 1955, A Singular Man 1963, The Beastly Beatitudes of Balthazar B 1968, The Onion Eaters 1971, A Fairy Tale of New York 1973, The Destinies of Darcy Dancer, Gentleman 1977, Schultz 1979, Leila 1983, Wrong Information is Being Given Out at Princeton 1998; (short stories and sketches) Meet My Maker the Mad Molecule 1964, An Author and His Image 1997; (novella) The Saddest Summer of Samuel S. 1966; also: The Unexpurgated Code: A Complete Manual of Survival and Manners 1975, De Alfonce Tennis, The Superlative Game of Eccentric Champions: Its History, Accoutrements, Rules, Conduct and Regimen, A Legend 1984, J. P. Donleavy's Ireland: In All Her Sins and in Some of Her Graces 1986, A Singular Country 1989, The History of the Ginger Man 1993, The Lady Who Liked Clean Rest Rooms 1995; (plays) The Ginger Man 1959, Fairy Tales of New York 1960, A Singular Man 1964, The Saddest Summer of Samuel S. 1968, The Plays of J. P. Donleavy 1972, The Beastly Beatitudes of Balthazar B. 1981, Are You Listening Rabbi Löw? 1987, That Darcy, That Dancer, That Gentlemen 1990. *Honours:* Evening Standard Drama Award 1960, Brandeis Univ. Creative Arts Award 1961–62, Citation, American Acad. and Nat. Inst. of Arts and Letters 1975, Worldfest Houston Gold Award 1992, Cine Golden Eagle Writer and Narrator 1993. *Address:* Levington Park, Mullingar, Co. Westmeath, Ireland (home). *Telephone:* (44) 9348903 (home). *Fax:* (44) 9348351 (home).

DONNELLY, Jennifer, BA; American writer; b. Port Chester, NY; m. *Education:* Univ. of Rochester. *Career:* fmr antiques dealer, reporter, copywriter. *Publications:* fiction: The Tea Rose 2002, The Winter Rose 2006; juvenile: Humble Pie 2002, A Gathering Light (aka A Northern Light) (Carnegie Medal 2004) 2003, Revolution 2010. *Honours:* Michael Printz Honor, Borders Original Voices Young Adult Prize, Los Angeles Times Book Prize. *Address:* c/o Bloomsbury Publishing PLC, 38 Soho Square, London, W1D 3HB, England. *E-mail:* jen@jenniferdonnelly.com (office). *Website:* www.jenniferdonnelly.com.

DONNER, Jörn Johan, BA; Finnish film director, writer, politician and diplomatist; b. 5 Feb. 1933, Helsinki; s. of Dr Kai Donner and Greta von Bonsdorff; m. 1st Inga-Britt Wik 1954 (divorced 1962); m. 2nd Jeanette Bonnier 1974 (divorced 1988); m. 3rd Bitte Westerlund 1995; five s. one d. *Education:* Univ. of Helsinki. *Career:* worked as writer and film dir in Finland and Sweden, writing own film scripts; contrib. and critic to various Scandinavian and int. journals; CEO Jörn Donner Productions 1966–; Dir Swedish Film Inst., Stockholm 1972–75, Exec. Producer 1975–78, Man. Dir 1978–82; Chair. Bd Finnish Film Foundation 1981–83, 1986–89, 1992–95; mem. Bd Marimekko Textiles and other cos; mem. Helsinki City Council 1969–1972, 1984–92; mem. Parl. 1987–95, Vice-Chair. Foreign Affairs Cttee 1991–95, Chair. Finnish EFTA Parliamentarians 1991–95; Consul-Gen. of Finland, Los Angeles, USA 1995–96; mem. European Parl. 1996–99. *Films include:* as dir: A Sunday in September (Venice Film Festival Best First Film 1963) 1963, To Love 1964, Adventure Starts Here 1965, Rooftree 1967, Black on White 1968, Sixty-nine 1969, Portraits of Women 1970, Anna 1970, Images of Finland 1971, Tenderness 1972, Three Scenes with Ingmar Bergman 1976, The Bergman File 1975–77, Men Can't Be Raped 1978, Dirty Story 1984, Letters from Sweden 1987, Ingmar Bergman, a Conversation 1998, The President 2000, The Interrogation 2009; numerous films as producer including: Fanny och Alexander (Fanny and Alexander) (Acad. Award for Producer of Best Foreign Language Film 1984) 1982, The Faceless Man 1995, Abandoned Houses, Empty Homes 2000, Raja 1918 2007, Yksinteoin 2 2011. *Television:* host of talk show (Sweden and Finland) 1974–95. *Publications:* 52 books including: Father and Son (Finlandia Prize 1985), Report from Berlin 1958, The Personal Vision of Ingmar Bergman 1962. *Address:* PO Box 214, 00171 Helsinki (office); Pohjoisranta 12, 00170 Helsinki, Finland (home). *Telephone:* (9) 1356060 (home); 400-205606 (mobile) (office). *Fax:* (9) 137568 (office). *E-mail:* j.donner@surfnet.fi (home).

DONOGHUE, Denis, PhD; Irish literary critic and academic; *Henry James Professor of English and American Letters, New York University;* b. 1 Dec. 1928, Tullow, Co. Carlow; m. Frances Donoghue; three s. five d. *Education:* Univ. Coll., Dublin. *Career:* Admin. Office, Irish Dept of Finance 1951–54; Asst Lecturer, Univ. Coll., Dublin 1954–57, Coll. Lecturer 1957–62, 1963–64, Prof. of Modern English and American Literature 1965–79; Visiting Scholar, Univ. of Pennsylvania 1962–63; Univ. Lecturer, Univ. of Cambridge and Fellow, King's Coll. 1964–65; Henry James Prof. of English and American Letters, New York Univ., USA 1979–; mem. Int. Cttee of Asscn of Univ. Profs of English. *Publications:* The Third Voice 1959, Connoisseurs of Chaos 1965, The Ordinary Universe 1968, Emily Dickinson 1968, Jonathan Swift 1969, Yeats 1971, Thieves of Fire 1974, Sovereign Ghost: Studies in Imagination 1978, Ferocious Alphabets 1981, The Arts Without Mystery 1983, We Irish: Essays on Irish Literature and Society 1987, Walter Pater: Lover of Strange Souls 1995, The Practice of Reading 1998, Words Alone: The Poet T. S. Eliot 2000, Adam's Curse: Reflections on Literature and Religion 2001, Speaking of Beauty 2003, The American Classics: A Personal Essay 2005; contribs to reviews and journals and ed. of three vols. *Honours:* Hon. DLitt; BBC Reith Lecturer 1982. *Address:* English Department, New York University, 726 Broadway (7th Floor), New York, NY 10003, USA (office); Gaybrook, North Avenue, Mount Merrion, Dublin, Ireland (home). *Telephone:* (212) 998-3954 (office). *E-mail:* dd1@nyu.edu (office).

DONOGHUE, Emma, BA, PhD; Irish/Canadian writer and dramatist; b. 1969, Dublin, Ireland; d. of Denis and Frances Donoghue; partner, Christine Roulston; one s., one d. *Education:* Univ. Coll., Dublin, Univ. of Cambridge, UK. *Career:* mem. Authors' Soc., Writers' Union of Canada. *Plays:* I Know My Own Heart (Dublin) 1993, Ladies and Gentlemen (Dublin) 1993, Kissing the Witch (San Francisco) 2000. *Radio:* plays: Trespasses (RTE) 1996, Don't Die Wondering (BBC Radio 4) 2000, Mix (BBC Radio 3) 2003; series: Exes (BBC Radio 4) 2001, Humans and Other Animals (BBC Radio 4) 2003. *Publications:* Passions Between Women 1993, Stir-Fry (novel) 1994, Hood (novel) 1995, Kissing the Witch (short stories) 1997, What Sappho Would Have Said (aka Poems Between Women, anthology) 1997, We Are Michael Field (biog.) 1998, Ladies and Gentlemen (play) 1998, The Mammoth Book of Lesbian Short Stories (anthology) 1999, Slammerkin (novel) 2000, The Woman Who Gave Birth to Rabbits (short stories) 2002, Life Mask (novel) 2004, Touchy Subjects (short stories) 2006, Landing (novel) 2007, The Sealed Letter (novel) 2008, Inseparable: Desire between Women in Literature (non-fiction) 2010, Room (novel) (Rogers Writers' Trust Award for Fiction, Galaxy Nat. Book Award for Paperback of the Year 2011) 2010. *Honours:* Gay, Lesbian and Bisexual Book Award, American Library Asscn 1997, Ferro-Grumley Fiction Award 2002, Golden Crown Literary Award 2008, Lambda Literary Award (Lesbian Fiction) 2009, Hughes & Hughes Irish Novel of the Year, Bord Gáis Energy Irish Book Awards 2010, Rogers Writers' Trust Fiction Prize 2010, Stonewall Book Award-Israel Fishman Non-Fiction Award, American Library Asscn 2011. *Literary Agent:* c/o Caroline Davidson Literary Agency, 5 Queen Anne's Gardens, London, W4 1TU, England. *Telephone:* (20) 8995-5768. *Fax:* (20) 8994-2770. *E-mail:* cdla@ukgateway.net. *E-mail:* emma@emmadonoghue.com (office). *Website:* www.emmadonoghue.com.

DONOVAN, Anne; Scottish writer. *Publications:* Hieroglyphics and Other Stories 2001, Buddha Da (novel) 2003, Being Emily 2008. *Honours:* Macallan/Scotland on Sunday Short Story Competition 1997, Canongate Prize 2000, Scottish Arts Council Award 2004, Le Prince Maurice Award (Mauritius) 2004. *Address:* c/o Canongate Books, 14 High Street, Edinburgh, EH1 1TE, Scotland (office). *E-mail:* info@canongate.co.uk (office). *Website:* www.canongate.co.uk (office).

DONOVAN, Gerard; Irish poet and novelist; b. Wexford. *Education:* Johns Hopkins Univ. *Career:* frmly taught at Johns Hopkins Univ., Univ. of Arkansas; currently Adjunct Assoc. Prof. of English, Southampton Coll., New York, USA. *Publications:* Columbus Rides Again (poems) 1992, Kings and Bicycles (poems) 1995, The Lighthouse (poems) 2000, Schopenhauer's Telescope (novel) 2003, Doctor Salt (novel) 2005, Julius Winsome (novel) 2006, Sunless (novel) 2007, Country of the Grand (short stories) 2008; short stories; contrib. to The Sewanee Review, New Statesman, Stand, Irish Times, Poetry Ireland Review, The Salmon, Writing in the West, Paris Review. *Address:* c/o Faber and Faber Ltd, Bloomsbury House, 74–77 Great Russell Street, London WC1B 3DA, England (office). *Website:* www.faber.co.uk (office).

DONOVAN, Paul James Kingsley, MA; British writer and journalist; b. (Vivian Donovan), 8 April 1949, Sheffield, Yorks., England; m. Hazel Case 1979, one s. two d. *Education:* Oriel Coll., Oxford. *Career:* reporter and TV Critic, Daily Mail 1978–85; Showbusiness Ed. and Critic, Today 1986–88; radio columnist, Sunday Times 1988–. *Publications:* Roger Moore 1983, Dudley 1988, The Radio Companion 1991, All Our Todays 1997; contribs to The Times, Sunday Times, Observer, Guardian, The Author; several articles to Oxford Dictionary of National Biography. *Address:* Homelea, The Square, Dolton, EX19 8QF, Devon, England (home). *Telephone:* (1805) 804523 (home). *Fax:* (20) 8747-4850 (home). *E-mail:* pauldon@scribbler.freeserve.co.uk (home).

DOODY, Margaret Anne, BA, MA, PhD; Canadian academic and writer; *John and Barbara Glynn Family Professor of Literature, University of Notre Dame*; b. 21 Sept. 1939, St John, NB; d. of Rev. Hubert Doody and Anne Ruth Cornwall. *Education:* Centreville Regional High School, NB, Dalhousie Univ., Halifax, Lady Margaret Hall, Oxford, UK. *Career:* Instructor in English 1962–64; Asst Prof., English Dept, Vic. Univ. 1968–69; Lecturer, Univ. Coll. of Swansea, UK 1969–77; Visiting Assoc. Prof. of English, Univ. of California, Berkeley 1976–77, Assoc. Prof. 1977–80; Prof. of English, Princeton Univ., NJ 1980–89, Stanley Kelley Jr Visiting Prof. for Distinguished Teaching 2008–09; Andrew W. Mellon Prof. of Humanities and Prof. of English, Vanderbilt Univ., Nashville, Tenn. 1989–99, Dir Comparative Literature 1992–99; John and Barbara Glynn Family Prof. of Literature, Univ. of Notre Dame, Ind. 2000–, Dir PhD Program in Literature 2001–07; Commonwealth Fellowship 1960–62, Canada Council Fellowship 1964–65, Imperial Oil Fellowship 1965–68, Guggenheim Foundation Fellowship 1978, Nat. Endowment for the Humanities Fellowship 2007. *Play:* Clarissa (co-writer), New York 1984. *Publications:* non-fiction: A Natural Passion: A Study of the Novels of Samuel Richardson 1974, The Daring Muse 1985, Frances Burney: The Life in the Works 1988, Samuel Richardson: Tercentenary Essays (ed. with Peter Sabor) 1989, The True Story of the Novel 1996, Anne of Green Gables (co-ed. with Wendy Barry and Mary Doody Jones) 1997, Tropic of Venice 2007; Aristotle detective series: Aristotle Detective 1978, Aristotle and the Fatal Javelin (short story) 1980, Aristotle and Poetic Justice 2002, Aristotle and the Secrets of Life 2003, Poison in Athens (novel) 2004, Mysteries of Eleusis (novel) 2005, Annello di Bronzo (novella); other fiction: The Alchemists (novel) 1980. *Honours:* Hon. LLD (Dalhousie) 1985; Rose Mary Crawshay Prize 1986. *E-mail:* info@maassagency.com. *Website:* www.maassagency.com*Address:* English Department, 356 O'Shaughnessy Hall, University of Notre Dame, Notre Dame, IN 46556 (office); 435 Edgewater Drive, Mishawaka, IN 46545, USA (home). *Telephone:* (574) 257-7927 (home). *E-mail:* mdoody@nd.edu (office); margaret.doody.1@nd.edu (office). *Website:* www.nd.edu/~mdoody (office).

DÖPFNER, Mathias, MA, PhD; German publishing executive; *CEO and Chairman, Axel Springer AG*; b. 15 Jan. 1963, Bonn; m. *Career:* journalist, Frankfurter Allgemeine Zeitung 1982; dir public relations agency 1988–90; fmr Asst to CEO, Gruner & Jahr, Hamburg; Ed.-in-Chief Wochenpost, Berlin 1994–96, Hamburger Morgenpost 1996–98; joined Axel Springer AG 1998, Ed.-in-Chief Die Welt 1998–2000, mem. Man. Bd, Multimedia Div. 2000–, Head of Newspapers Div. 2000–02, Chair. and CEO 2002–; mem. Bd of Dirs Time Warner 2006–, RHJ Int. 2008–. *Publications:* Neue Deutsche Welle: Kunst oder Mode 1983, Erotik in der Musik 1986, Musikkritik in Deutschland seit 1945 1991, Brüssel: das Insider-Lexikon 1992, Axel Springer: Neue Blicke auf den Verleger (ed.) 2005, Ernst Cramer: Ich habe es erlebt (ed.) 2008. *Honours:* Axel Springer Prize for Young Journalists 1992, Golden Pen Award, Bauer Verlagsgruppe 2000, Journalism Award of German medium-sized businesses 2000, World Econ. Forum Global Leader of Tomorrow 2001, Berlin Order of Merit 2007, Leo Baeck Medal 2007, Jerusalem Award 2008, Global Leadership Award, American Inst. for Contemporary German Studies, New York 2008. *Address:* Axel Springer AG, Axel-Springer-Straße 65, 10888 Berlin, Germany (office). *Telephone:* (30) 2591-0 (office). *Website:* www.axelspringer.com (office).

DOR, Moshe, BA; Israeli poet, journalist and editor; b. 9 Dec. 1932, Tel-Aviv; m. Ziona Dor 1955; two s. *Education:* Hebrew Univ. of Jerusalem, Univ. of Tel-Aviv. *Career:* Counsellor for Cultural Affairs, Embassy of Israel, London 1975–77; apptd Distinguished Writer-in-Residence, American Univ., Washington, DC 1987; mem. Asscn of Hebrew Writers, Israel, Nat. Fed. of Israel Journalists, Israel PEN Centre (Pres. 1988–90). *Publications:* White Cypresses 1954, The Chocolate Boat 1968, Amir's Castle 1970, Who Wants to Be a Magician? 1975, From the Outset 1984, On Top of the Cliff 1986, One Day and Another Day 1986, The Owl's Party 1987, Crossing the River 1989, From the Outset 1989, Crossing the River 1989, Love and Other Calamities 1993, Khamsin 1994, The Silence of the Builder 1996, Why the Whale Smoked a Pipe 1996, No Man's Land: Selected Poems 2004, Sorched by the Sun 2011; co-ed. English anthologies of Israeli Hebrew poetry: The Burning Bush 1977, The Stones Remember 1991, After the First Rain 1997, books of poetry, children's verse, literary essays, interviews with writers, trans. of poetry and literature from English into Hebrew. *Honours:* Holon Prize for Literature 1981, Bialik Prize for Literature 1987, Prime Minister's Award for Literature 2008. *Address:* c/o Word Works, PO Box 42164, Washington, DC 20015, USA.

DORESKI, William, BA, MA, PhD; American academic, writer and poet; *Professor of English, Keene State College*; b. 10 Jan. 1946, Stafford, Conn.; m. Carole Doreski 1981. *Education:* Goddard Coll., Boston Univ., Princeton Univ., Dartmouth Coll. *Career:* Writer-in-Residence, Emerson Coll. 1973–75; Instructor in Humanities, Goddard Coll. 1975–80; Asst Prof., Keene State Coll., NH 1982–87, Assoc. Prof. 1988–91, Prof. of English 1992–; mem. American Studies Asscn, Associated Writing Programs, Asscn of Scholars and Critics, Modern Language Asscn, New Hampshire Writers' Project, Robert Frost Soc., Wallace Stevens Soc. *Publications:* The Testament of Israel Potter 1976, Half of the Map 1980, Earth That Sings: The Poetry of Andrew Glaze 1985, How to Read and Interpret Poetry 1988, The Years of Our Friendship: Robert Lowell and Allen Tate 1990, Ghost Train 1991, The Modern Voice in American Poetry 1995, Sublime of the North and Other Poems 1997, Pianos in the Woods 1998, Shifting Colors: The Public and the Private in the Poetry of Robert Lowell 1999, My Shadow Instead of Myself 2004, Sacra Via 2005, Another Ice Age 2007, Waiting for the Angel 2009; contrib. to books, journals, reviews, quarterlies and magazines. *Honours:* Poet Lore Trans. Prize 1975, Black Warrior Prize 1979, Nat. Endowment for the Humanities grants 1987, 1995, Whiting Foundation Fellowship 1988, Clay Potato Fiction Prize 1997, Frith Press Poetry Award 1997, Keene State Coll. Award for Faculty Distinction in Research and Scholarship 2002, Aesthetica Poetry Award 2010. *Address:* Department of English, Keene State College, Keene, NH 03435, USA (office). *Telephone:* (603) 358-2698 (office); (603) 924-7987 (home). *Fax:* (603) 358-2773 (office). *E-mail:* wdoreski@keene.edu (office).

DORET, Michel, BA, BS, MA, MPhil, PhD; American architect, artist, writer and poet; b. 5 Jan. 1938, Petion-Ville, Haiti; m. Liselotte Bencze 1970. *Education:* Pace Univ., New York Univ., State Univ. of NY, George Washington Univ. *Career:* Founder and Dir, Les Editions Amon Ra 1982–97; Founder-Producer, Michel's Video Studios New York 2000–; three art collections displayed in more than 30 group and solo exhbns in Europe, USA and on Internet; festivals; mem. several literary orgs. *Exhibitions:* Museum of the Americas, Doral, Fla, Institut français, Haiti. *Videos as producer:* 150 films in three series, 30 shown on Channel 20 Public Access Long Island Broadcasting Station. *Publications:* Isolement 1979, La Poésie francophone (eight vols) 1980, Panorama de la poésie feminine Suisse Romande 1982, Aliénation dans la poésie d'Haiti du XXème siecle 1982, Panorama de la poésie féminine francophone 1984, La negritude dans la poésie haïtienne 1985, Poétesses Genevoises francophones 1985, Haiti en Poésie 1990, Les Mamelles de Lutèce 1991, Lyrisme du Moi 1992, The History of the Architecture of Ayiti (two vols) 1995, Frédéric Doret (1866–1935) 2008, Leksik Kreyol-franse 2010, André Rigaud. La vraie silhouette 2011; contrib. to numerous books, journals, reviews and other publs. *Honours:* various medals, diplomas, and hon. mentions. *Address:* CP 15.558, Petion-Ville, Haiti (office). *E-mail:* mdor26@aol.com (home).

DORFMAN, (Vladimiro) Ariel; Chilean/American writer and academic; *Walter Hines Page Distinguished Professor of Literature and Latin American Studies, Duke University*; b. 6 May 1942, Buenos Aires, Argentina; s. of Adolfo Dorfman; m. Angélica Dorfman 1966; two s. *Education:* Univ. of Chile, Santiago. *Career:* Teaching Asst, Univ. of Chile 1963–65, Asst Prof. of Spanish Literature and Journalism 1965–68, Assoc. Prof. 1968–70, Prof. 1970–73; exiled after Chilean coup 1973; Maître des Conférences Spanish-American Literature, Sorbonne Paris IV 1975–76; Head Scientific Research, Spanns Seminarium, Univ. of Amsterdam 1976–80; Visiting Prof., Univ. of Maryland 1983; Post-Doctoral Fellow and Consultant Latin American Council, Duke Univ., NC 1984, Visiting Prof. of Literature and Latin American Studies 1985–89, Research Prof. of Literature and Latin American Studies, 1989–96, Walter Hines Page Distinguished Prof. of Literature and Latin American Studies, Center for Int. Studies and Romance Studies 1996–; Research Scholar Univ. of Calif., Berkeley 1968–69; Friedrich Ebert Stiftung Research Fellow 1974–76; Fellowship at Woodrow Wilson Int. Center for Scholars 1980–81; Visiting Fellow, Inst. for Policy Studies 1981–84; Fellow, American Acad. of Arts and Sciences. *Plays:* Widows (Kennedy Center New American Plays Award) 1988, Death and the Maiden (Olivier Award for Best Play, London 1992) 1991, Reader (Kennedy Center Roger L. Stevens Award) 1992, Who's Who (with Rodrigo Dorfman) 1998, Speak Truth to Power: Voices from Beyond the Dark 2000, Manifesto from Another World: Voices from Beyond the Dark 2004, Purgatorio 2005, Picasso's Closet 2006, The Other Side 2006, Dancing Shadows (with Eric Woolfson) 2007. *Film screenplays:* Death and the Maiden 1994, Prisoners in Time 1995, My House is on Fire 1997, A Promise to the Dead: The Exile Journey of Ariel Dorfman (Insight Award for Excellence in Writing, Nat. Asscn of Film and Digital Media Artists 2008) 2007. *Publications:* fiction: Hard Rain 1973, My House is On Fire 1979, Widows 1983, Dorando la pildora 1985, Travesía 1986, The Last Song of Manuel Sendero 1987, Máscara 1988, Konfidenz 1995, The Nanny and the Iceberg 1999, Blake's Therapy 2001, The Rabbit's Rebellion 2001, The Burning City (with Joaquin Dorfman) 2003, Americanos: Los Pasos de Murieta 2009; poetry: Missing 1982, Last Waltz in Santiago and Other Poems of Exile and Disappearance 1988, In Case of Fire in a Foreign Land: New and Collected Poems from Two Languages 2002; non-fiction: How to Read Donald Duck (with Armand Mattelart) 1971, The Empire's Old Clothes 1983, Some Write to the Future 1991, Heading South, Looking North: A Bilingual Journey 1998, Exorcising Terror: The Incredible Ongoing Trial of General Augusto Pinochet 2002, Desert Memories: Journeys Through the Chilean North 2004, Other Septembers, Many Americas: Selected Provocations, 1980–2004 2004. *Honours:* Dr hc (Ill. Wesleyan Univ.) 1989, (Wooster Coll.) 1991, (Bradford Coll.) 1993, (American Univ.) 2001; Time Out Award 1991, New York Public Library Literary Lion 1992, Dora Mavor Award 1994, Int. Poetry Forum Charity Randall Citation 1995, Writers' Guild of Great Britain Best Film for Television 1995, ALOA Prize, Denmark 2002, Lowell Thomas Silver Award for Travel Book 2004, O. Henry Award 2006, North American Congress on Latin America (NACLA) Award for Peace and Justice 2008. *Address:* c/o Center for International Studies, Duke University, PO Box 90404, Durham, NC 27708, USA. *Fax:* (919) 684-8749 (office). *E-mail:* adorfman@duke.edu (office). *Website:* www.adorfman.duke.edu (office).

DORIN, Françoise Andrée Renée; French actress, novelist, playwright and songwriter; b. 23 Jan. 1928, Paris; d. of late René Dorin and of Yvonne Guilbert; m. Jean Poiret (b. Poiré) (divorced); one d. *Career:* at Théâtre des Deux-Ânes, then du Quartier Latin (Les Aveux les plus doux 1957), then La Bruyère (Le Chinois 1958); Presenter TV programme Paris-Club 1969; playwright and author 1967–. *Songs include:* Que c'est triste Venise 1965,

La danse de Zorba 1965, Qu'est-ce que vous voulez que j'en fasse 1965, La bourse et la vie 1966, C'est ton nom 1966, C'est pas croyable 1966, Au coin de mes rêves 1966, Dieu que ça lui ressemble 1966, Une chanson comme on n'en fait plus 1967, Mais mon coeur est vide 1968, Il n'y a en que pour la rose 1968, Il a fallu 1968, Depuis le temps 1968, Quand on a notre âge 1968, Le reconnais-tu? 1968, Pourquoi je t'aime 1968, Les souvenirs que l'on a pas eus, Les filles et les roses, Mourir de soif, Pourquoi pas nous, Téléphoner à Sylvie, Les Fans de Mozart, Tout était pareil, Dis-moi, Oh non, ce n'est pas toi 1976, Tous les chemins mènent à l'homme, Le tournant, L'humour ensemble, Ma dernière chanson, N'avoue jamais, Faisons l'humour ensemble, Les miroirs truqués 1982, Et s'il n'en restait qu'une, je serai celle-là 2006, On s'est aimé à cause 2006. *Plays include:* Comme au théâtre 1967, La Facture 1968, Un sale égoiste, Les Bonshommes 1970, Le Tournant 1973, Le Tube 1974, L'Autre Valse 1975, Si t'es beau, t'es con 1976, Le Tout pour Le tout 1978, L'Intoxe 1980, La valise en carton 1986, Les Cahiers Tango 1987, Et s'il n'en restait qu'un 1992; lyrics for Vos gueules les mouettes 1971, Monsieur Pompadour 1972, L'Etiquette 1983, Les jupes-culottes 1984, La valise en carton (musical comedy) 1986, L'âge en question 1986, La Retour en Toupaine 1993, Monsieur de Saint-Futile (Vaudeville) 1996, Soins intensifs 2001. *Publications:* novels include Virginie et Paul, La Seconde dans Rome, Va voir Maman, Papa travaille 1976, Les lits à une place 1980, Les miroirs truqués 1982, Les jupes-culottes 1984, Les corbeaux et les renardes 1988, Nini patte-en-l'air 1990, Au nom du père et de la fille 1992, Pique et Coeur 1993, La Mouflette 1994, Les Vendanges tardives 1997, La Courte paille 1999, Les Julottes 2001, La mouflette 2001, Le rêve party 2002, Tout est toujours possible 2004, Et puis...après 2005, En avant toutes 2007. *Honours:* Chevalier, Légion d'honneur, Officier, Ordre nat. du Mérite, Arts et Lettres; trophée Dussane 1973, Grand Prix du théâtre (for L'Etiquette) 1981. *Address:* c/o Artmédia, 20 avenue Rapp, 75007 Paris, France (office).

DORMANN, Geneviève; French writer and journalist; b. 24 Sept. 1933, Paris; d. of Maurice Dormann and Alice Dormann; m. 1st Philippe Lejeune (divorced); three d.; m. 2nd Jean-Loup Dabadie (divorced); one d. *Career:* writer and journalist, Le Figaro newspaper. *Screenplays:* Der Fangschuß (Coup de grâce) 1976, Mont-Oriol (TV adaptation) 1980, Quatre femmes, quatre vies: Des chandails pour l'hiver 1981. *Television:* Mont-Oriol 1980, Quatre femmes, quatre vies: Des chandails pour l'hiver 1981. *Publications:* novels: La Fanfaronne 1959, Le chemin des dames 1964, La passion selon saint Jules 1967, Je t'apporterai des orages (Prix des Quatre Jurys) 1971, Le bateau du courrier (Prix des Deux Magots 1975) 1974, Mickey, l'ange 1977, Fleur de péché 1980, Le roman de Sophie Trébuchet (Prix Kleber Haedens, Prix de la Ville de Nantes) 1982, Amoureuse Colette 1984, Le livre du point de croix 1986, Le bal du Dodo (Grand Prix du Roman, Acad. française) 1989, Paris est une ville pleine de lions 1991, La petite main 1993, La gourmandise de Guillaume Apollinaire 1994, Adieu phénomène (Prix Genevois) 1999; short stories: La première pierre 1957. *Honours:* Prix des Quatre-Jurys 1971, le Prix des Deux Magots 1974, le Grand Prix de la ville de Paris 1980, Grand Prix du Roman, Ville de Paris 1981. *Address:* 9 rue de Poitiers, 75007 Paris, France.

DORMER, Richard; Irish actor and playwright; b. 11 Nov. 1969, Armagh; m. Rachel O'Riordan. *Education:* RADA, London. *Career:* co-founder and writer-in-residence, Ransom Productions 2002–. *Plays:* Hurricane 2002, The Half 2005, This Piece of Earth 2007, The Gentlemen's Tea-Drinking Society 2009. *Films:* Middletown 2006, My Boy Jack 2007, Five Minutes of Heaven 2009, Pumpgirl 2009. *Honours:* The Stage Best Actor Award, BBC Stewart Parker Award. *Address:* Ransom Productions, 15 Church Street, Belfast, BT1 1PG (office); 22 Rossmore Avenue, Belfast, BT7 3HB, Northern Ireland (home). *Telephone:* (28) 9096-4320 (home). *E-mail:* ransomproduction@btconnect.com (office). *Website:* www.ransomproductions.co.uk (office).

DORNER, Majorie, BA, MA, PhD; American academic and writer; b. 21 Jan. 1942, Luxembourg, WI; two d. *Education:* St Norbert Coll., Marquette Univ., Purdue Univ. *Career:* Prof. of English Literature, Winona State Univ., Minnesota 1971–2002. *Publications:* Nightmare 1987, Family Closets 1989, Freeze Frame 1990, Winter Roads, Summer Fields 1992, Blood Kin 1992, Seasons of Sun and Rain 1999; contributions: various publications. *Honours:* Minnesota Book Awards 1991, 1993.

DORR, James Suhrer, BS, MA; American writer and poet; b. 12 Aug. 1941, Pensacola, Fla; s. of Frank J. Dorr and Betty S. Dorr; m. Ruth Michelle Clark 1975 (divorced 1982). *Education:* Massachusetts Inst. of Tech., Indiana Univ. *Career:* tech. writer, Ed., Wrubel Computing Center, Bloomington, Ind. 1969–81; writer, Marketing Consultant, The Stackworks 1982; Assoc. Ed., Bloomington Area Magazine 1983–86; freelance writer 1982–; mem. Science Fiction and Fantasy Writers of America, Horror Writers Asscn, Science Fiction Poetry Asscn, Short Mystery Fiction Soc. *Publications:* Towers of Darkness (chapbook, poems) 1990, Strange Mistresses (short fiction) 2001, Darker Loves (short fiction) 2007, The Garden (novella) 2009, Vamps (poems) 2011, Vanitas (chapbook, fiction) 2011; contrib. to Borderlands II 1991, Grails 1992, Dark Destiny I and II 1994–95, Dante's Disciples 1996, Darkside: Horror for the Next Millennium 1996, Dark Tyrants 1997, Gothic Ghosts 1997, Asylums and Labyrinths 1997, The Best of Cemetery Dance 1998, New Mythos Legends 1999, Children of Cthulhu 2002, The Darker Side: Generations of Horror 2002, Spooks! 2004, Love and Sacrifice 2007, Escape Clause 2009, Rapunzel's Daughters 2011, In Poe's Shadow 2011; also to anthologies, periodicals, journals, reviews, magazines, quarterlies and newspapers in USA, Canada, UK, Australia, France, Brazil, The Netherlands. *Honours:* Rhysling Hon. Mention 1993, 1995, 1996, 1997, 2001. *Telephone:* (812) 332-6668. *Address:* 1404 East Atwater Avenue, Bloomington, IN 47401, USA (home). *E-mail:* edgarc@rocketmail.com (home). *Website:* jamesdorrwriter.wordpress.com.

DORSETT, Danielle (see Daniels, Dorothy)

DORSEY, Candas Jane, BA, BSW; Canadian writer, poet and editor; b. 16 Nov. 1952, Edmonton, AB. *Education:* Univ. of Alberta, Univ. of Calgary. *Career:* freelance writer and ed., Edmonton Bullet, Edmonton, AB 1980; has also worked in theatre and as social worker. *Publications:* This Is for You (poems) 1973, Orion Rising (poems) 1974, Results of the Ring Toss (poems) 1976, Hardwired Angel (novel, co-author) 1987, Machine Sex and Other Stories 1988, Tesseracts Three: Canadian Science Fiction (co-ed.) 1990, Leaving Marks (poems) 1992, Dark Earth Dreams (novel, co-author) 1995, Black Wine 1997, Vanilla and Other Stories 2000, A Paradigm of Earth 2001; contributions: short fiction to books including: Getting Here, Tesseracts. *Honours:* first prize, shared with co-author, for Hardwired Angel, Ninth Annual Pulp Press International 3-Day Novel Competition 1987. *Address:* 9346 105 Avenue West, Edmonton, AB T5H 0J6, Canada (home). *Telephone:* (780) 431-0562 (home).

DORST, Tankred; German writer; b. 19 Dec. 1925, Sonneberg; s. of Max Dorst and Elisabeth Dorst; m. Ursula Ehler-Dorst. *Education:* Universität München. *Career:* dir production of Wagner's Ring, Bayreuth Festival 2006; mem. German PEN Centre, Bayerische Akad. der schönen Künste, Deutsche Akad. der darstellenden Künste, Deutsche Akad. für Sprache und Dichtung. *Film as director and screenwriter:* Eisenhans. *Plays:* around 40 plays including Toller, Eiszeit, Merlin oder das wüste Land, Herr Paul, Was sollen wir tun, Fernando Krapp hat mir diesen Brief geschrieben, Ich Feuerbach, Die Legende vom Armen Heinrich, Karlos, Korbes, Ich bin nur vorübergehend hier 2007, Künstler 2008, Ich soll den eingebildet Kranken spielen 2009; several opera libretti; five plays for children; several plays in collaboration with Ursula Ehler. *TV films (writer and director):* Klaras Mutter, Mosch, Eisenhaus. *Publications:* Plays (Vols 1–8), Merlins Zauber, Die Reise nach Stettin, Der schöne Ort, Sich im Ordischen zü uben, Glûck ist ein Vorübergehender Schwächezustand, Plays (Vol 8) 2008. *Honours:* several prizes including Gerhart Hauptmann Prize, Georg-Büchner Prize 1990, Schiller Prize 2010. *Address:* Suhrkamp Verlag, Pappelallee 78–79, 1043 Berlin; Karl Theodor Strasse 102, 80796 Munich, Germany (home). *Telephone:* (30) 7407440 (office). *Fax:* (89) 3073256 (home).

DOSHI, Tishani, MA; Indian/British poet, writer and dancer; b. 1975, Madras. *Education:* Queens Coll., Charlotte, North Carolina, Johns Hopkins Univ., USA. *Career:* worked in advertising dept, Harper's & Queen magazine, London 1999–2001; moved back to India 2001; began dance career working with the choreographer, Chandralekha 2001–06; writes cricket blog about the Indian Premier League. *Publications:* poetry: Countries of the Body (Forward Prize for Best First Collection) 2006; fiction: The Pleasure Seekers 2010. *Honours:* Eric Gregory Award 2001, British Council All India Poetry Prize (for The Day We Went to the Sea) 2005. *Literary Agent:* David Godwin Associates Ltd, 55 Monmouth Street, London, WC2H 9DG, England. *Telephone:* (20) 7240-9992. *Fax:* (20) 7395-6110. *Website:* www.davidgodwinassociates.co.uk. *E-mail:* tishani@tishanidoshi.com (office). *Website:* www.tishanidoshi.com.

DOTTO, Lydia; Canadian science writer and photographer; d. of August Dotto and Assunta Dotto. *Education:* Carleton Univ., Ont. *Career:* joined Edmonton Journal 1969, Toronto Star 1970, 1971; science writer, Toronto Globe and Mail 1972–78; has covered space missions 1972–; freelance writer 1978–; Exec. Ed. Canadian Science News Service 1982–92; freelance photographer 2007–; two dives under Arctic ice, Resolute Bay, NWT 1974; participant zero-gravity training flight, Johnson Space Center, Houston, Tex., USA 1983; Co-Dir SpaceNet Canada 1995–99; currently Lecturer, Trent Univ. *Publications include:* The Ozone War (co-author) 1978, Thinking the Unthinkable: Civilization and Rapid Climate Change 1988, Canada in Space 1987, Planet Earth in Jeopardy: The Environmental Consequences of Nuclear War 1986, Asleep in the Fast Lane: The Impact of Sleep on Work 1990, Asleep in the Fast Lane – How Your Sleeping Habits Affect Your Life 1990, Losing Sleep: How Your Sleeping Habits Affect Your Life 1990, Blue Planet – A Portrait of Earth 1991, Ethical Choices and Global Greenhouse Warming 1993, The Astronauts: Canada's Voyageurs in Space 1993, Storm Warning – Gambling with the Climate of our Planet 1999. *Honours:* Canadian Science Writers' Awards for newspaper and magazine articles 1974, 1981, 1984, 1994, Canadian Meteorological Soc. Award 1975, Stanford Fleming Medal, Royal Canadian Inst. 1982–83. *E-mail:* lydiadotto@trentu.ca (office). *Website:* www.imageinnovationphotography.com (office).

DOTY, Mark, BA, MFA; American poet and academic; *Professor of English, Rutgers University*; b. 10 Aug. 1953, Maryville, TN. *Education:* Drake Univ., Goddard Coll. *Career:* faculty, MFA Writing Program, Vermont Coll. 1981–94, Writing and Literature, Goddard Coll. 1985–90; guest faculty, Sarah Lawrence Coll. 1990–94, 1996; Fannie Hurst Visiting Prof., Brandeis Univ. 1994; visiting faculty, Univ. of Iowa 1995, 1996, Columbia Univ. 1996; Prof., Creative Writing Program, Univ. of Utah 1997–98; John and Rebecca Moores Prof. of English, Univ. of Houston –2009; Prof. of English, Rutgers Univ. 2009–. *Publications:* Turtle, Swan 1987, Bethlehem in Broad Daylight 1991, My Alexandria 1993, Atlantis 1995, Heaven's Coast (memoir) 1996, Firebird (memoir) 1999, Source 2001, School of Arts (poetry) 2005, Dog Years 2008, Theories and Apparitions (poetry) 2008, Fire to Fire (poetry) (Nat. Book Award for Poetry) 2008, The Art of Description: World into Word 2010;

contrib. to many anthologies and journals. *Honours:* Theodore Roethke Prize 1986, NEA Fellowships in Poetry 1987, 1995, Pushcart Prizes 1987, 1989, Los Angeles Times Book Prize 1993, Ingram Merrill Foundation Award 1994, National Book Critics Circle Award 1994, Guggenheim Fellowship 1994, Whiting Writers Award 1994, Rockefeller Foundation Fellowship, Bellagio, Italy 1995, New York Times Notable Book of the Year citations 1995, 1996, American Library Asscn Notable Book of the Year 1995, T. S. Eliot Prize 1996, Bingham Poetry Prize 1996, Ambassador Book Award 1996, Lambda Literary Award 1996, Lila Wallace-Reader's Digest Writers' Award 2000. *Address:* Department of English, Rutgers University, Murray Hall, Room 040A, College Avenue Campus, New Brunswick, NJ 08901, USA (office). *E-mail:* markdoty@rci.rutgers.edu (office); markdoty@aol.com (office). *Website:* english.rutgers.edu (office); www.markdoty.org.

DOUAIHY, Jabbour, PhD; Lebanese novelist and university professor; *Professor of French Literature, Lebanese University, Tripoli;* b. 5 Jan. 1949, Zghorta; m. Therese Dahdah. *Education:* Univ. of Paris III, France. *Career:* currently Prof. of French Literature, Lebanese Univ., Tripoli. *Publications:* Al maout bayn al 'ahli nou'as (short stories; trans. as Death Among Sleeping Parents) 1990, Autumn Equinox (novel) 2001, Spirit of the Jungle (children's short story; San Exupery prize, France) 2001, Ayn Warda (novel; trans. as Rose Fountain) 2002, Matar Hzayran (novel; trans. as June Rain) 2006. *Literary Agent:* c/o Raya Agency. *E-mail:* info@rayaagency.org. *Website:* www.rayaagency.org. *Address:* c/o Editions Dar an-Nahar SAL, BP 11-226, 36 rue Andraos, Immeuble Media Centre, Beirut, Lebanon (office). *Telephone:* (1) 561687 (office). *Fax:* (1) 561693 (office). *E-mail:* darannahar@darannahar.com (office); lettres3@ul.edu.lb (office). *Website:* www.darannahar.com (office).

DOUGHTY, Louise, BA, MA; British novelist, playwright and commentator; b. 4 Sept. 1963, Melton Mowbray, England. *Education:* Leeds Univ., Univ. of East Anglia. *Career:* Theatre Critic, Mail on Sunday 1993–95; Columnist, Express on Sunday 1996, Daily Telegraph 2006–07; Chair of judges, Orange Award for New Writers 2006, John Llewellyn Rhys Prize 2009; judge, Man Booker Prize 2008; mem. Society of Authors 1998–. *Radio:* plays: Maybe 1991, The Koala Bear Joke 1994, Nightworkers 1998, Geronimo! 2004, The Withered Arm 2006; as presenter: A Good Read (BBC Radio 4) 1998–2001. *Publications:* fiction: Crazy Paving 1995, Dance With Me 1996, Honey-Dew 1998, Fires in the Dark 2003, Stone Cradle 2006, Whatever You Love 2010; non-fiction: A Novel in a Year 2007. *Honours:* Radio Times Drama Award 1991, Ian St James Award 1991, K. Blundell Trust Award 1999, Arts Council Writers Award 2001. *Literary Agent:* c/o Antony Harwood Ltd, 103 Walton Street, Oxford OX2 6EB, England. *Telephone:* (1865) 559615. *Fax:* (1865) 310660. *E-mail:* ant@antonyharwood.com. *Website:* www.antonyharwood.com; www.louisedoughty.com.

DOUGLAS, Garry (see Kilworth, Garry Douglas)

DOUTINÉ, Heike, PhD; German writer; b. 1946, Hamburg. *Education:* Univ. of Hamburg/Cologne. *Career:* numerous novels, short stories and poems; Guest Prof. Univ. of Los Angeles and Ford Foundation, USA. *Publications include:* novels: Wanke nicht, mein Vaterland, Berta, Wir Zwei, Die Meute, Der Hit, Im Lichte Venedigs (jtly) 1987, Blutiger Mund – Die Tage des Mondes 1991, A London Diary 2009; poetry: In tiefer Trauer, Das Herz auf dem Lanze, Blumen begießen, bevor es anfängt zu regnen (also short stories) 1986, Lieder und Canones 1995, Roses and Other Songs 2001, The Blue Land Poetry Zyklus 2007, Murnau 2007; short stories: Deutscher Alltag – Meldungen über Menschen; librettos for Peace Cantata by Norbert Linke 1996, Desire by Ali Sadé 2003, Concerto for soprano by Ali Sadé 2004, Peace Oratorio by Linke, Oratorio of the Roses. *Honours:* Prize for Novel, Neue Literarische Gesellschaft, Villa Massimo Prize, Italy 1973–74, Prix de Rome.

DOVE, Rita Frances, BA, MFA; American writer, poet and academic; *Commonwealth Professor of English, University of Virginia;* b. 28 Aug. 1952, Akron, Ohio; d. of Ray Dove and Elvira Dove (née Hord); m. Fred Viebahn 1979; one d. *Education:* Miami Univ., Ohio, Univ. of Tübingen, Germany and Univ. of Iowa. *Career:* Asst Prof., Ariz. State Univ., Tempe 1981–84, Assoc. Prof. 1984–87, Prof. of English 1987–89; Prof., Univ. of Virginia, Charlottesville 1989–93, Commonwealth Prof. of English 1993–; Poet Laureate of the USA 1993–95, of the Commonwealth of Virginia 2004–06; Consultant in Poetry, Library of Congress 1993–95; Special Consultant in Poetry, Library of Congress Bicentennial 1999–2000; Assoc. Ed., Callaloo 1986–98, adviser and Contributing Ed. 1998–; adviser and Contributing Ed. Gettysburg Review 1987–, TriQuarterly 1988–, Meridian 1989–, Ploughshares 1992–, Georgia Review 1994–, Bellingham Review 1996–, Poetry Int. 1996–, Int. Quarterly 1997–, Mid-American Review 1998–, Hunger Mountain 2003–, American Poetry Review 2005–; Writer-in-Residence, Tuskegee Inst., Ala 1982; poetry panellist, Nat. Endowment for Arts, Washington, DC 1984–86 (Chair. 1985); judge, Pulitzer Prize in Poetry 1991 (Chair. of Jury 1997); mem. Bd of Dirs Associated Writing Programs 1985–88, Pres. 1986–87; mem. jury Anisfield-Wolf Book Awards; Chancellor The Acad. of American Poets 2006–; mem. Acad. of American Poets, Associated Writing Programs, Poetry Soc. of America, Poets and Writers; Fulbright Fellow 1974–75, Nat. Endowment for the Arts grants 1978, 1989, Portia Pittman Fellow, Tuskegee Inst. 1982, Guggenheim Fellowship 1984, Rockefeller Foundation Residency in Bellagio, Italy 1988, Mellon Fellow, Nat. Humanities Center 1989, Fellow, Center for Advanced Studies, Univ. of Virginia 1989–92. *Publications:* poetry: Ten Poems 1977, The Only Dark Spot in the Sky 1980, The Yellow House on the Corner 1980, Mandolin 1982, Museum 1983, Thomas and Beulah (Pulitzer Prize in Poetry 1987) 1986, The Other Side of the House 1988, Grace Notes 1989, Selected Poems 1993, Lady Freedom Among Us 1994, Mother Love 1995, Evening Primrose 1998, On the Bus with Rosa Parks 1999, Best American Poetry (ed.) 2000, American Smooth 2004, Sonata Mulattica 2009; prose: Fifth Sunday (short stories) 1985, Through the Ivory Gate (novel) 1992, The Darker Face of Earth (verse play) 1994, The Poet's World (essays) 1995. *Honours:* 22 hon. degrees; numerous awards, including Acad. of American Poets Peter I. B. Lavan Younger Poets Award 1986, Callaloo Award 1986, Gen. Electric Foundation Award for Younger Writers 1987, Ohio Gov.'s Award 1988, Ohioana Library Book Awards 1990, 2000, NY Public Library Literary Lion Awards 1990, 1996, 2000, Nat. Book Award in Poetry 1991, NAACP Great American Artist Award 1993, American Acad. of Achievement Golden Plate Award 1994, Folger Shakespeare Library Renaissance Forum Award 1994, Charles Frankel Prize/Nat. Humanities Medal 1996, Heinz Award in the Arts and Humanities 1996, Barnes and Noble Writers Award 1997, Levinson Prize 1998, Duke Ellington Lifetime Achievement Award in the Literary Arts, Ellington Fund in Washington, DC 2001, Commonwealth Award of Distinguished Service 2006, Library of Virginia Lifetime Achievement Award 2008, Fulbright Asscn Lifetime Achievement Medal 2009, Hurston/Wright Foundation Award for Poetry 2010, Amb.'s Award from Oklahoma Center for Poets and Writers 2010, Ohioana Book Award for Poetry 2010, Celebrating Black History Now: 40 Firsts In 40 Years, Essence Magazine 2010, 40th Anniversary Portfolio: Our 40 Favorite Poets, Essence Magazine 2010. *Address:* 219 Bryan Hall, University of Virginia, PO Box 400121, Charlottesville, VA 22904-4121, USA (office). *Telephone:* (434) 924-6618 (office). *Fax:* (434) 924-1478 (office). *E-mail:* rfd4b@virginia.edu (office). *Website:* www.people.virginia.edu/~rfd4b (office).

DOVEY, Ceridwen, MA; Australian/South African novelist; b. 11 Nov. 1980, Pietermaritzburg, S Africa; d. of Ken Dovey and Teresa Dovey; m. Blake Munting. *Education:* Harvard Univ., USA Univ. of Cape Town, S Africa, New York Univ., USA. *Career:* grew up in South Africa and Australia, now lives in Sydney; wrote her first novel in Cape Town. *Publications:* Blood Kin (novel) (Univ. of Johannesburg Award 2007, South Africa Times Fiction Prize 2008) 2007 (published in 15 languages), Civil Twilight (novel) forthcoming. *Honours:* selected as one of Nat. Book Foundation's '5 Under 35' (a recognition of five talented authors under the age of 35). *Address:* c/o Penguin South Africa, 24 Sturdee Avenue, Rosebank, Johannesburg, 2169 South Africa. *E-mail:* info@za.penguingroup.com. *Website:* www.penguinbooks.co.za; www.ceridwendovey.com.

DOW, Unity; Botswana author, judge and human rights activist; *Judge, High Court of Botswana;* b. 1959. *Education:* univs of Botswana and Swaziland, Univ. of Edin., UK. *Career:* fmrly pnr in Botswana's first all female private law practice; worked as prosecutor, Attorney-Gen.'s office; f. Metlhaetsile Women's Information Centre 1990, Dir 1994–98; acted as plaintiff in legal case that led to a change in Botswana's nationality law enabling women to pass on nationality to their children; High Court Judge (first woman) 1998–; fmr co-ordinator Women and Law in Southern Africa Research Project; mem. Int. Comm. of Jurists 2004–; Exec. Cttee 2006–. *Publications:* fiction: Far and Beyon' 2000, The Screaming of the Innocent 2002, Juggling Truths 2003, The Heavens May Fall 2006. *Honours:* Hon. LLD (Kenyon College, Ohio, USA); William Brennan Human Rights Award. *Address:* High Court of Botswana, Private Bag 1, Lobatse, Botswana (office); c/o Spinifex Press, PO Box 212, 504 Queensberry Street, North Melbourne, Vic. 3051, Australia (office). *Telephone:* 5330396 (Botswana) (office). *Fax:* 5332317 (Botswana) (office). *E-mail:* women@spinifexpress.com.au (office). *Website:* www.spinifexpress.com.au (office).

DOWLING, Vincent; American (b. Irish) actor, director, producer and playwright; *Founding Director and President-for-Life, Miniature Theatre of Chester;* b. 7 Sept. 1929, Dublin; s. of Mai Kelly Dowling and William Dowling; m. 1st Brenda Doyle 1952 (deceased); m. 2nd Olwen Patricia O'Herlihy 1975; one s. four d. *Education:* St Mary's Coll., Rathmines, Dublin, Rathmines School of Commerce, Brendan Smith Acad. of Acting. *Career:* with Standard Life Insurance Co., Dublin 1946–50; Brendan Smith Productions, Dublin 1950–51; Roche-David Theatre Productions 1951–53; actor, Dir, Deputy Artistic Dir, Lifetime Assoc., Abbey Theatre, Dublin 1953–76, Artistic Dir 1987–89; Producing Dir Great Lakes Shakespeare Festival, Cleveland, Ohio 1976–84; Artistic and Producing Dir Solvang Theaterfest 1984–86; Prof. of Theatre, Coll. of Wooster, Ohio 1986–87; Producing Dir, Abbey Theatre 1989–90; Founding Dir and Pres.-for-Life, Miniature Theatre of Chester 1990–; residency Tyrone Guthrie Arts Centre, Annamackerrig, Ireland 2005; host Shooting from the Hip WXOT Northampton Valley Free Radio 2005–06; Co-Founder, Jacob's Ladder Trail Business Asscn; Founder, Vincent Dowling Theatre Co.; several distinguished visiting professorships at univs in USA. *Film appearances:* My Wife's Lodger 1953, Boyds Shop 1959, Johnny Nobody 1963, Young Cassidy 1965. *Original plays:* The Fit-Ups 1978, Acting is Murder 1986, A Day in the Life of an Abbey Actor 1990, Wilde About Oscar, Another Actor at the White House (one-man show), The Upstart Crow (A Two-Person Play about Will Shakespeare) 1995, 4 P's (one-man autobiographical), The Miraculous Revenge (adapted; played, produced and co-directed) 2004. *Plays:* as producer: Arthur Miller's The Price 2005, Solomon 2005. *Radio:* role of Christy Kennedy (for 17 years) in The Kennedys of Castlerosse, Radio Éireann; writer, narrator Festival Scrapbook, Radio WCLV, Cleveland, Ohio 1980–84. *Television:* dir and producer The Playboy of the Western World (Emmy Award) Public Broadcasting Service, USA 1983, One Day at a Time,

ABC Television 1998. *Publication:* Astride the Moon (autobiog.) 2000, My Abbey (Theatre), articles for Irish Echo Newspaper, 75th Anniversary Issue, Irish Sunday Independent Magazine. *Honours:* Hon. DFA (Westfield State Coll., Mass. John Carroll Univ., Cleveland, Ohio, Coll. of Wooster, Ohio 1999), DHumLitt (Kent State Univ.) 2003; European Artist's Prize, Loyola Univ. 1969; Outstanding Producer, Cleveland Critics Circle Award 1982 for The Life and Adventures of Nicholas Nickelby; Irishman of the Year 1982; Wild Geese Award 1988, Loyola Mellon Humanitarian Award 1989, Walks of Life Award, Irish American Archives Soc. of Cleveland 2000, Amb. (of Ireland to USA) Award 2005. *Address:* 322 East River Road, Huntington, MA 01050-9645, USA (home). *Telephone:* (413) 667-3906 (home). *Fax:* (413) 667-3906 (home). *E-mail:* newlo@compuserve.com (home). *Website:* vincentdowling.com.

DOWNES, David Anthony, (David Anton), BA, MA, PhD; American academic and writer; *Professor of English Emeritus, California State University, Chico*; b. 17 Aug. 1927, Victor, CO; m. Audrey Romaine Ernst 1949; one s. three d. *Education:* Regis Univ., Marquette Univ., Univ. of Washington. *Career:* Asst Prof., Prof. and Chair of Dept, Univ. of Seattle 1953–68; Prof. of English and Dean of Humanities and Fine Arts, California State Univ., Chico 1968–72, Dir of Educational Development Projects 1972–73, Dir of Humanities Programme 1973–74, Dir of Graduate English Studies 1975–78, Chair of Dept 1978–84, Prof. Emeritus 1991; Consultant, Cowles Rare Book Library, Gonzaga Univ. 1997. *Publications:* Gerard Manley Hopkins: A Study of his Ignatian Spirit 1959, Victorian Portraits: Hopkins and Pater 1965, Pater, Kingsley and Newman 1972, The Great Sacrifice: Studies in Hopkins 1983, Ruskin's Landscape of Beatitude 1984, Hopkins' Sanctifying Imagination 1985, The Ignatian Personality of Gerard Manley Hopkins 1990, The Belle of Cripple Creek (novel) 2001, Hopkins' Achieved Self 2002, The Hopkins' Society: The Making of a World-Class Poet 2005, The Angel in Wax (novel) 2005, Sailing: Inside Passages (novel) 2006, The Mysterious Furies of the God in a Tent (novel) 2009; contrib. scholarly books and journals. *Honours:* Hon. DJur (Gonzaga Univ.) 1997; Exceptional Merit Awards for Scholarship 1984, 1988, 1990, 1992. *Address:* 1076 San Ramon Drive, Chico, CA 95973-1027, USA (office). *Telephone:* (530) 345-2297 (office). *E-mail:* ddownes@csuchico.edu (office).

DOWNIE, Leonard, Jr, MA; American newspaper executive and academic; b. 1 May 1942, Cleveland, OH; s. of Leonard Downie, Sr and Pearl Evenheimer; m. 1st Barbara Lindsey 1960 (divorced 1971); two s.; m. 2nd Geraldine Rebach 1971 (divorced 1997); one s. one d.; m. 3rd Janice Galin 1997. *Education:* Ohio State Univ. *Career:* joined The Washington Post 1964, became investigative reporter in Washington, specializing in crime, housing and urban affairs, helped to supervise coverage of Watergate affair, Asst Man. Ed. Metropolitan News 1974–79, London Corresp. 1979–82, Nat. Ed. 1982–84, Man. Ed. 1984–91, Exec. Ed. 1991–2008, Vice-Pres. at Large, The Washington Post Co. 2008–, Dir Los Angeles Times–Washington Post News Service 1991–2008, International Herald Tribune 1996–2002; Weil Family Prof. of Journalism, Walter Cronkite School of Journalism and Mass Communication, Arizona State Univ. 2009–; Founder and Bd mem. Investigative Reporters and Editors Inc.; Chair. Bd of Advisors, Kaiser Health News 2009–; mem. Bd of Dirs Investigative Reporters and Editors, Inc. Missouri School of Journalism 2009–, Center for Investigative Reporting 2009–, Fellow, Alicia Patterson Foundation 1971–72. *Publications:* Justice Denied 1971, Mortgage on America 1974, The New Muckrakers 1976, The News About the News (with Robert G. Kaiser) 2002, The Rules of the Game (novel) 2009. *Honours:* Hon. LLD, Ohio State Univ.; two Washington-Baltimore Newspaper Guild Front Page Awards, American Bar Asscn Gavel Award for legal reporting, John Hancock Award for business and financial writing, Ben Bradlee Editor of the Year Award, National Press Foundation 2008, Award for Editorial Leadership, American Society of News Editors 2009. *Address:* Room 389, Walter Cronkite School of Journalism, Arizona State University, 555 North Central Avenue, Phoenix, AZ 85004, USA. *Telephone:* (602) 496-7973 (office). *E-mail:* leonard.downie@asu.edu (office). *Website:* cronkite.asu.edu (office).

DOWNIE, Mary Alice Dawe, BA; Canadian writer and editor; b. 12 Feb. 1934, Alton, Ill., USA; d. of Robert Grant Hunter and Doris Mary Rogers; m. John Downie 1959; three d. *Education:* Trinity Coll., Univ. of Toronto. *Career:* Editorial Asst, Canadian Medical Assn Journal 1956–57; Publicity Manager, Oxford University Press, Toronto 1958–59; Book Review Ed., Kingston Whig-Standard 1973–78; mem. Writers' Union of Canada, PEN. *Plays:* (with M.-A. Thompson, music by Mark Sirett) The Kingdom of The Saguenay: A Musical Fable, The Winter Children: A Musical Vignette. *Publications:* The Wind Has Wings: Poems from Canada (with Barbara Robertson) 1968, Honor Bound (with John Downie) 1971, Scared Sarah 1974, The Magical Adventures of Pierre 1974, Dragon on Parade 1974, The Witch of the North: Folktales from French Canada 1975, The King's Loon 1979, And Some Brought Flowers: Plants in a New World (with Mary Hamilton) 1980, The Last Ship 1980, Jenny Greenteeth 1981, Seeds and Weeds: A Book of Country Crafts (with Jillian Gilliland) 1981, A Proper Acadian (with George Rawlyk) 1982, The Wicked Fairy-Wife 1983, Alison's Ghost (with John Downie) 1984, Stones and Cones (with Jillian Gilliland) 1984, The New Wind Has Wings: Poems from Canada (with Barbara Robertson) 1984, The Window of Dreams: New Canadian Writing for Children 1986, The Well-Filled Cupboard (with Barbara Robertson) 1987, How the Devil Got his Cat 1988, The Buffalo Boy and the Weaver Girl (with Mann Hwa Huang-Hsu) 1989, Doctor Dwarf and Other Poems for Children, by A. M. Klein (with Barbara Robertson) 1990, Cathal the Giant-Killer and the Dun Shaggy Filly 1991, Written in Stone: A Kingston Reader (with M. A. Thompson) 1993, The Cat Park 1993, Snow Paws 1996, Bright Paddles 1999, Danger in Disguise (with John Downie) 2000, A Song for Acadia/Une Chanson pour l'Acadie 2004, A Pioneer ABC 2005, Early Voices (with Barbara Robertson); contrib. to Hornbook Magazine, Pittsburgh Press, Kingston Whig-Standard, Ottawa Citizen, Globe and Mail, Montréal Gazette, Toronto Star and others. *Honours:* Univ. of Toronto Board of Fame 1990, assorted Canada Council and Ontario Arts Council Awards and grants. *Address:* 190 Union Street, Kingston, ON K7L 2P6, Canada (home). *Telephone:* (613) 542-3464 (home). *Fax:* (613) 542-3464 (home). *E-mail:* downiej@queensu.ca (office).

DOWNING, Michael Bernard, AB; American writer, academic, playwright and editor; *Lecturer in English, Tufts University*; b. 8 May 1958, Pittsfield, Mass; partner Michael Bryant. *Education:* Harvard Univ. *Career:* Sr Ed., Oceanus periodical, Woods Hole, Mass 1983–84, FMR periodical, Milan, Italy 1984–86; Instructor in English, Bentley Coll., Waltham, Mass 1987–88; Instructor, Wheelock Coll., Boston, Mass 1988–91, Asst Prof. of Humanities, Dir of Writing Programme 1992; currently Lecturer in English, Tufts Univ.; mem. PEN, Authors' Guild, Authors' League of America, Share Our Strength (Writers' Cttee). *Publications:* A Narrow Time (novel) 1987, Mother of God (novel) 1990, The Last Shaker (play, produced 1995), Perfect Agreement (novel) 1997, Breakfast with Scot (novel) 1999, Shoes Outside the Door 2001, Spring Forward: The Annual Madness of Daylight Saving Time 2005, Life with Sudden Death 2009; contribs to anthologies including Louder than Words, Stories; poems, essays and reviews to periodicals including New York Times, Wall Street Journal, Washington Post, Toronto Globe and Mail, Boston Globe, America, Commonweal, Harvard. *Honours:* Harvard-Shrewsbury Fellow, Shropshire, UK 1980–81, Best Book Citation, Newsday 1997, Best Book Citation, Amazon.com 1997, 1999, Best Book Citation, American Library Asscn . *Address:* Department of English, Tufts University, 314 East Hall, Medford, MA 02155, USA (office). *Telephone:* (617) 627-3459 (office). *E-mail:* michael.downing@tufts.edu (office). *Website:* michaeldowningbooks.com.

DOWNING, Warwick (Wick), BA, LLB; American writer and lawyer; b. (Warwick Miller Downing II), 3 Jan. 1931, Denver, CO; s. of Richard Downing and Dorothy Mae Downing; pnr Shirley Schley; three s. *Education:* Univ. of Wyoming, Univ. of Denver, San Francisco State Coll. *Publications:* The Player 1973, The Mountains West of Town 1974, The Gambler, The Minstrel, and the Dance Hall Queen 1975, Kid Curry's Last Ride 1989, A Clear Case of Murder 1990, The Water Cure 1992, A Lingering Doubt 1993, Choice of Evils 1994, Leonardo's Hand 2001, The Trials of Kate Hope 2008. *Honours:* three Colorado Author's League Top Hand Awards, Colorado Center for the Book. *Address:* 2121 Osceola Street, Denver, CO 80220, USA (office). *Telephone:* (303) 782-5042 (office). *E-mail:* wickdowning@comcast.net (office). *Website:* www.wickdowning.com.

DOWRICK, Rev. Stephanie Barbara; Australian fmr publishing executive, writer, psychotherapist and minister; b. 2 June 1947, Wellington, New Zealand; d. of Harold Dowrick and Mary Dowrick (née Brisco); one s. one d. *Education:* Sacred Heart Coll., Lower Hutt and Univ. of Wellington, New Seminary, New York, USA, Univ. of Western Sydney, Australia. *Career:* Co-Founder The Women's Press, London 1977, Man. Dir 1977–82, Chair. 1991–2002; moved to Sydney, Australia 1983; Fiction Publr, Allen and Unwin, NSW 1991–92; columnist, Good Weekend magazine 2001–; ordained Interfaith Minister 2005; Amb., Breast Cancer Network Australia, Petrea King's Quest for Life Centre, The Ted Noff's Foundation; regular guest on ABC Radio; gives talks and conducts retreats and workshops on various spiritual, psychological and ethical issues. *Publications include:* non-fiction: Land of Zeus 1975, Why Children? (co-ed.) 1982, Intimacy and Solitude 1991, The Intimacy & Solitude Workbook, The Intimacy & Solitude Self-Therapy Book, Speaking With the Sun (co-ed.) 1991, After the Gulf War: For Peace in the Middle East 1991, The Intimacy and Solitude Workbook 1993, Forgiveness and Other Acts of Love 1997, Daily Acts of Love 1998, The Universal Heart 2000, Every Day a New Beginning 2001, Free Thinking 2004; audio: Accepting Yourself & Loving Others (two CDs), Guided Meditations: Grace & Courage, The Art of Acceptance – Living in an Imperfect world, Living with Change, The Humane Virtues; fiction: Running Backwards Over Sand 1985, Tasting Salt 1997, Katherine Rose Says NO (children's fiction). *Address:* c/o Andrew Hawkins, Allen and Unwin Pty Ltd, 83 Alexander Street, Crows Nest, NSW 2065, Australia (office). *Telephone:* (2) 9810-3277 (office). *E-mail:* kristyr@allenandunwin.com (office); stephanie@stephaniedowrick.com (office). *Website:* www.stephaniedowrick.com.

DOYLE, Charles Desmond, (Mike Doyle), DipEd, BA, MA, PhD; Canadian academic, writer and poet; *Professor Emeritus, University of Victoria*; b. 18 Oct. 1928, Birmingham, England; m. 1st Helen Merlyn Lopdell 1952 (deceased); m. 2nd Doran Ross Smithells 1959 (divorced); three s. one d. *Education:* Univ. of New Zealand, Univ. of Auckland. *Career:* Lecturer, Univ. of Auckland 1961–66, Sr Lecturer 1966–68; Assoc. Prof., Univ. of Victoria, BC 1968–76, Prof. of English 1976–93, Prof. Emeritus 1993–; mem. New Canterbury Literary Soc., Writers' Union of Canada, PEN Canada. *Publications:* A Splinter of Glass 1956, The Night Shift: Poems on Aspects of Love (with others) 1957, Distances 1963, Messages for Herod 1965, A Sense of Place 1965, Quorum-Noah 1970, Abandoned Sofa 1971, Earth Meditations 1971, Earthshot 1972, Preparing for the Ark 1973, Pines (with P. K. Irwin) 1975, Stonedancer 1976, A Month Away from Home 1980, A Steady Hand 1982, The Urge to Raise Hats 1989, Separate Fidelities 1991, Intimate Absences: Selected Poems 1954–1992 1993, Trout Spawning at the Lardeau River 1997,

Living Ginger 2004, Paper Trombones 2007; non-fiction: R. A. K. Mason 1970, James K. Baxter 1976, William Carlos Williams and the American Poem 1982, William Carlos Williams: The Critical Heritage (ed.) 1982, The New Reality (co-ed.) 1984, Wallace Stevens: The Critical Heritage (ed.) 1985, After Bennett (co-ed.) 1986, Richard Aldington: A Biography 1989, Richard Aldington: Reappraisals (ed.) 1990; contrib. to journals, reviews and periodicals. *Honours:* UNESCO Creative Arts Fellowship 1958–59, ACLS Fellowship 1967–68. *Address:* 641 Oliver Street, Victoria, BC V8S 4W2, Canada (home). *Telephone:* (250) 595-5006 (home). *E-mail:* doylec@uvic.ca (home).

DOYLE, Roddy; Irish writer and playwright; b. 1958, Dublin; m. Belinda Doyle; two s. *Career:* lecturer at universities. *Play:* Brown Bread 1992, USA 1992. *Publications:* The Commitments 1987, screenplay (with Dick Clement and Ian La Frenais) 1991, The Snapper 1990, screenplay 1992, The Van 1991, Paddy Clarke Ha Ha Ha (Booker Prize) 1993, The Woman Who Walked into Doors 1996, A Star Called Henry 1999, The Giggler Treatment 2000, Rory and Ita 2002, Oh, Play That Thing 2004, Paula Spencer 2006, Wilderness 2007, The Deportees (short stories) 2007, The Dead Republic 2010. *Address:* c/o Publicity Department, Jonathan Cape, Random House, 20 Vauxhall Bridge Road, London SW1V 2SA, England (office).

DRAAISMA, Douwe; Dutch psychologist and writer; *Professor of History of Psychology, University of Gröningen;* b. 1953. *Education:* Univ. of Gröningen. *Career:* currently Prof. of History of Psychology Univ. of Gröningen; mem. Heymans Inst. for Fundamental Psychological Research, Research School Science, Technology and Modern Culture, European Soc. for the History of the Human Sciences. *Publications:* Het verborgen raderwerk: Over tijd, machines en bewustzijn 1990, De metaforenmachine: Een geschiedenis van het geheugen 1993, Een droevige zaak: Damasio over Descartes, Hersenen en Emoties, The Age of Precision: F.C.Donders and the Measurement of Mind 2002, Waarom het leven sneller gaat als je ouder wordt: Over het autobiografisch geheugen 2002, Ontregelde Geesten 2006, De heimweefabriek 2008, Vergeetboek 2010; contrib. chapters to books and articles to journals, including Feit en Fictie, History of the Human Sciences, Nature, Annals of Science, Arts, lettres et cultures de Flandres et des Pays-Bas, Psychological Medicine. *Honours:* Heymans Award, Dutch Psychological Asscn 1990, four nat. prizes. *Address:* University of Groningen, PO Box 72, 9700 AB, Gröningen, The Netherlands (office). *Telephone:* (50) 3639111 (office). *Fax:* (50) 3635380 (office). *E-mail:* communicatie@rug.nl (office); draaisma@douwedraaisma.nl. *Website:* www.rug.nl (office); www.douwedraaisma.nl.

DRABBLE, Dame Margaret, DBE, FRSL, BA; British author; b. 5 June 1939, Sheffield; d. of the late J. F. Drabble and Kathleen Drabble (née Bloor); sister of A. S. Byatt; m. 1st Clive Swift 1960 (divorced 1975); two s. one d.; m. 2nd Michael Holroyd (q.v.) 1982. *Education:* Newnham Coll., Cambridge. *Career:* Chair., Nat. Book League 1980–82; Ed. The Oxford Companion to English Literature 1979–2000; Chair., Soc. of Authors 2008–09. *Publications:* fiction: A Summer Bird-Cage 1963, The Garrick Year 1964, The Millstone (John Llewelyn Rhys Memorial Prize 1966) 1965, Jerusalem the Golden 1967, The Waterfall 1969, The Needle's Eye 1972, The Realms of Gold 1975, The Ice Age 1977, The Middle Ground 1980, The Radiant Way 1987, A Natural Curiosity 1989, The Gates of Ivory 1991, The Witch of Exmoor 1996, The Peppered Moth 2001, The Seven Sisters 2002, The Red Queen 2004, The Sea Lady 2006; plays: Laura 1964, Isadora 1968, Thank You All Very Much 1969, Bird of Paradise 1969; non-fiction: Wordsworth 1966, Arnold Bennett: A Biography 1974, The Genius of Thomas Hardy (ed.) 1976, For Queen and Country: Britain in the Victorian Age 1978, A Writer's Britain 1979, The Oxford Companion to English Literature (co-ed.) 1985, 2000, The Concise Oxford Companion to English Literature (co-ed. with Jenny Stringer) 1987, Angus Wilson: A Biography 1995, The Pattern in the Carpet: A Personal History with Jigsaws (memoirs) 2009, A Day in the Life of a Smiling Woman: Complete Short Stories 2011. *Honours:* Hon. Foreign mem. American Acad. of Arts and Letters 2002; Hon. Fellow, Sheffield City Polytechnic 1989; Hon. DLitt (Sheffield) 1976, (Bradford) 1988, (Hull) 1992; Dr hc (Manchester) 1987, (Keele) 1988, (East Anglia) 1994, (York) 1995, (Cambridge) 2006; James Tait Black Memorial Prize 1968, Book of the Year Award, Yorkshire Post 1972, E. M. Forster Award, American Acad. of Arts and Letters 1973, St Louis Literary Award 2003, Golden PEN Award 2011. *Address:* c/o Viking Publicity, Penguin, 80 Strand, London, WC2R 0RL, England (office). *Website:* www.penguin.co.uk (office).

DRAGOMÁN, György, BA, PhD; Hungarian novelist and translator; b. 10 Sept. 1973, Marosvásárhely, Romania; m. Anna T. Szabó; two c. *Education:* Eötvös Loránd Univ. (ELTE), Budapest. *Career:* moved to Hungary 1988; has translated numerous writers' work into Hungarian including Samuel Beckett, James Joyce, Ian McEwan. *Play:* Nihil 2003. *Publications include:* novels: A pusztítás könyve (The Book of Destruction aka Genesis Undone) (Brody Prize for Best First Novel 2003) 2002, A fehér király (The White King) (Déry Tibor Prize 2005) 2005. *Honours:* Soros Scholarship 2002, Mozgó Világ Special Prize 2002, Hungarian Ministry of Defense Special Prize for Best War-Themed Short Story 2002, Sándor Márai Prize 2006, Artisjus Prize 2006, Attila József Prize 2007, Márciusi Ifjak Prize 2008, Cultural Prize of Romanian Cultural Centre, Budapest 2008. *Literary Agent:* c/o Chris Parris-Lamb, The Gernert Company, 136 East 57th Street, New York, NY 10022, USA. *Telephone:* (212) 838-7777. *Fax:* (212) 838-6020. *E-mail:* dragoman.gy@gmail.com. *Website:* www.thegernertco.com. *E-mail:* dragoman.gy@gmail.com (home). *Website:* gyorgydragoman.com.

DRAKE, Barbara Ann, BA, MFA; American academic, poet and writer; *Professor of English Emerita, Linfield College;* b. 13 April 1939, Abilene, KS; of J. Ward Robertson and Monica C. Robertson; m. 1st Albert Drake 1960 (divorced 1985); one s. two d.; m. 2nd William Beckman 1986. *Education:* Univ. of Oregon. *Career:* Instructor, Michigan State Univ. 1974–83; Prof. of English, Linfield Coll. 1983–2007, Prof. Emer. 2007–. *Publications:* poetry: Narcissa Notebook 1973, Field Poems 1975, Love at the Egyptian Theatre 1978, Life in a Gothic Novel 1981, What We Say to Strangers 1986, Bees in Wet Weather 1992, Space Before A 1996, Small Favors 2003; textbook: Writing Poetry 1983; prose: Peace at Heart: An Oregon Country Life (memoir) 1998; contrib. to many books, anthologies, reviews, quarterlies and journals. *Honours:* Northwest Arts Foundation grant 1985, Nat. Endowment for the Arts Fellowship 1986, Linfield Coll. Edith Green Distinguished Prof. Award 1993. *Address:* 6104 NW Lilac Hill Road, Yamhill, OR 97148, USA (home). *Telephone:* (503) 662-3373 (office). *E-mail:* bdrake@linfield.edu (office); bdrake1@verizon.net (home).

DRAKE, Nick; British poet, novelist and screenwriter; b. 1961. *Education:* Magdalene Coll., Cambridge. *Play produced:* To Walk the Clouds, Nottingham Playhouse 2006. *Screenplay:* Romulus My Father, directed by Richard Roxburgh 2007 (Four Australian Film Awards, including Best Film). *Radio:* Mr Sweet Talk (writer) 2006. *Publications:* poetry: Chocolate and Salt (pamphlet) 1990, The Man in the White Suit (Forward Prize for Best First Collection) 1999, From the Word Go 2007; fiction: Nefertiti: The Book of the Dead 2006; non-fiction: The Poetry of W. B. Yeats 1991; translator: Peribañez and Comendador of Ocaña, by Lope de Vega 1998. *Honours:* Eric Gregory Award 1990. *Literary Agent:* c/o Julia Kreitman, The Agency, 24 Pottery Lane, Holland Park, London, W11 4LZ, England. *Telephone:* (20) 7727-1346. *Fax:* (20) 7727-9037. *E-mail:* info@theagency.co.uk. *Website:* www.theagency.co.uk. *E-mail:* nickfdrake@hotmail.com.

DRAKULIĆ, Slavenka; Croatian journalist and writer; b. 4 July 1949. *Education:* Univ. in Zagreb. *Career:* staff writer Start (bi-weekly newspaper), Danas (weekly newspaper) 1982–92; currently Contributing Ed. The Nation magazine. *Publications include:* How We Survived Communism and Even Laughed 1991, Holograms of Fear 1992, Balkan Express 1993, Marble Skin 1993, Café Europa 1996, The Taste of a Man 1997, S: A Novel About the Balkans 1999, They Would Never Hurt a Fly 2004, Tijelo njenog tijela 2006, Frida's Bed 2008, Two Underdogs and a Cat 2009, A Guided Tour Through the Museum of Communism: Fables from a Mouse, a Parrot, a Bear, a Cat, a Mole, a Pig, a Dog and a Raven 2011; contribs to newspapers and magazines, including The Nation, The New Republic, La Stampa, Dagens Nyheter, Frankfurter Rundechau and The Observer. *Honours:* Leipzig Book-FairAward 2004. *Literary Agent:* c/o Anneli Høier Leonhardt & Høier Literary Agency A/S, Studiestræde 3,5, 1455 Copenhagen K, Denmark. *Telephone:* 33-13-25-23. *Fax:* 33-13-49-92. *E-mail:* anneli@leonhardt-hoier.dk. *Website:* www.leonhardt-hoier.dk. *E-mail:* info@slavenkadrakulic.com. *Website:* www.slavenkadrakulic.com.

DRAPER, Hastings (see Jeffries, Roderic Graeme)

DRAPER, Ronald Philip, BA, PhD; British academic (retd) and writer; *Professor Emeritus, University of Aberdeen;* b. 3 Oct. 1928, Nottingham, England; m. Irene Margaret Aldridge 1950; three d. *Education:* Univ. of Nottingham. *Career:* Lecturer in English, Univ. of Adelaide, Australia 1955–56; Lecturer, Univ. of Leicester 1957–68, Sr Lecturer 1968–73; Prof., Univ. of Aberdeen 1973–86, Regius Chalmers Prof. of English 1986–94, Prof. Emer. 1994–. *Publications:* D. H. Lawrence 1964, D. H. Lawrence: The Critical Heritage (ed.) 1970, Hardy: The Tragic Novels (ed.) 1975, George Eliot, The Mill on the Floss and Silas Marner (ed.) 1977, Tragedy, Developments in Criticism (ed.) 1980, Lyric Tragedy 1985, The Winter's Tale: Text and Performance 1985, Hardy: Three Pastoral Novels (ed.) 1987, The Literature of Region and Nation (ed.) 1989, An Annotated Critical Bibliography of Thomas Hardy (with Martin Ray) 1989, The Epic: Developments in Criticism (ed.) 1990, A Spacious Vision: Essays on Hardy (co-ed.) 1994, An Introduction to Twentieth-Century Poetry in English 1999, Shakespeare: The Comedies 2000; contrib. to books and scholarly journals. *Address:* Maynestay, Chipping Campden, Glos., GL55 6DJ, England (home). *Telephone:* (1386) 840796 (home). *E-mail:* rpdraper@tiscali.co.uk (home).

DRAŠKOVIĆ, Vuk; Serbian politician, journalist and writer; *President, Serbian Renewal Movement;* b. 29 Nov. 1946, Međa, Žitište municipality, Central Banat Region, Vojvodina; s. of Vidak Drašković and Stoja Drašković; m. Danica Bošković 1974. *Education:* Univ. of Belgrade. *Career:* moved to Herzegovina; as student took part in demonstrations 1968; mem. staff Telegraph Agency of Yugoslavia TANJUG 1969–78, worked in Lusaka, Zambia; dismissed from post of corresp. for disinformation 1978; Adviser Council of Trade Unions of Yugoslavia 1978–80; Ed. Rad (newspaper) 1980–85; freelance journalist and writer 1985–; Founder and Pres. Serbian Renewal Movt 1990–; cand. for presidency of SFR Yugoslavia 1990, 1992, of Serbia 1997; mem. Nat. Ass.; detained, released from detention July 1993; leader of mass protests against Pres. Milošević from Nov. 1996; Deputy Prime Minister of Yugoslavia 1998–99 (resgnd); Minister of Foreign Affairs of Serbia and Montenegro 2004–06. *Publications include:* novels: Judge, Knife, Prayer 1, Prayer 2, Russian Consul, Night of the General, Target, Polemics, Answers; numerous articles and collections of articles. *Address:* Serbian Renewal Movement (Srpski pokret obnove), 11000 Belgrade, Kneza Mihailova 48, Serbia (office). *Telephone:* (11) 2635281 (office); (11) 2626031 (office); (11)

3283620 (office). *Fax:* (11) 2628170 (office). *E-mail:* vuk@spo.rs (office). *Website:* www.spo.rs (office).

DRAZEN, Jeffrey M., BS, MD; American writer; *Editor-in-Chief, New England Journal of Medicine*; b. 19 May 1946, St Louis, Mo.; m.; two s. *Education:* Tufts Univ. *Career:* currently Prof. of Physiology, Harvard School of Public Health and Prof., Dept of Environmental Health, also Distinguished Parker B. Francis Prof. of Medicine, Harvard Medical School; currently also Sr Physician Brigham and Women's Hospital; Ed.-in-Chief, New England Journal of Medicine 2000–; fmr Assoc. Ed. Journal of Clinical Investigation, American Review of Respiratory Disease. *Publications:* Five Lipoxygenase Products in Asthma (ed.) 1998; contribs to Genomic Medicine: Articles from the New England Journal of Medicine 2001. *Honours:* Dr hc (Univ. of Ferrara, Italy), (Nat. and Kapodistrian Univ. of Athens, Greece). *Address:* New England Journal of Medicine, 10 Shattuck Street, Boston, MA 02115-6094, USA (office). *Telephone:* (617) 734-9800 (office). *Fax:* (617) 739-9864 (office). *E-mail:* jdrazen@nejm.org (office). *Website:* www.nejm.org (office).

DREW, Bettina, BA, MA,; American writer, poet and teacher; b. 23 April 1956, New York, NY. *Education:* Univ. of California, Berkeley, City Coll., CUNY, Yale Univ. *Career:* Lecturer in English, Coll. of New York; Lecturer in Humanities, New York Univ. 1990–93; Part-time Acting Instructor, Yale Univ. 1995–97; Asst Prof. of English and Creative Writing, Univ. of Missouri 2003–04; mem. PEN American Center, Biography Seminar, New York Univ. *Publications:* Nelson Algren: A Life on the Wild Side 1989, The Texas Stories of Nelson Algren (ed.) 1995, Crossing the Expendable Landscape 1997, Master Andrew Jackson 2005; contributions: Boulevard, The Writer, Chicago Tribune, Threepenny Review, Washington Post Book World, Chicago Tribune Book World, Ms; Black American Literature Forum, Michigan Quarterly Review, poems to various magazines. *Honours:* Fellowship, New York Foundation for the Arts.

DREWE, Robert Duncan; Australian writer and dramatist; b. 9 Jan. 1943, Melbourne; m. 3rd Candida Baker; four s. two d. *Education:* Hale School, Perth. *Career:* Literary Ed. The Australian 1972–75; Writer-in-Residence, Univ. of Western Australia, Nedlands 1979, La Trobe Univ., Bundoora 1986, South Bank Centre, Royal Festival Hall, London, England, Brixton Prison, London, England; columnist, Mode, Sydney, and Sydney City Monthly 1981–83; mem. Man. Cttee Australian Soc. of Authors, Sydney Writers' Festival, Byron Bay Writers' Festival; Film Critic, Sydney Morning Herald. *Publications:* The Savage Crows 1976, A Cry in the Jungle Bar 1979, Fortune 1986, Our Sunshine 1991, The Drowner (novel) 1996, Our Sunshine 2001, Grace 2005; non-fiction: Walking Ella 1998, The Shark Net: Memories and Murder 2000, Perth (co-author) 2005, Mangrove Point 2007, Sand (co-author) 2010; short stories: The Bodysurfers 1983, The Bay of Contented Men 1989, The Rip 2008; plays: The Bodysurfers: The Play 1989, South American Barbecue 1991; Ed.: The Picador Book of the Beach 1993, The Penguin Book of the City 1997, The Best Australian Stories 2006, Best Australian Stories 2007, Best Australian Essays 2010; contribs to The Bulletin, The Australian, TLS, Granta. *Honours:* Hon. DLitt (Univ. of Queensland) 1997, (Univ. of Western Australia); Nat. Book Council Award 1987, Commonwealth Writers' Prize 1990, Australian Creative Artists' Fellowship 1993–96, New South Wales, Victoria, West Australia and South Australia Premiers' literary prizes 1997, Book of the Year 1997, Adelaide Festival Prize for Literature 1998. *Address:* c/o Curtis Brown Group Ltd, Haymarket House, 28-29 Haymarket, London, SW1Y 4SP, England.

DREYER, Inge, Rektorin i.R.; German poet; b. 12 June 1933, Berlin; d. of Curt Ganswindt and Katharina Ganswindt. *Education:* Univ. of Berlin Coll. of Educ. *Career:* teacher, Fritz-Karsen-Schule, Berlin 1956–68; Headmistress Walt-Disney-Schule, Berlin 1968–78; retd from teaching 1978; professional writer 1978–; works with Project Märchen zaubern Brot für Kinder in co-operation with Berliner Märchentage, SOS Kinderdörfer, UNICEF, others 2003–. *Publications:* Achtung Stolperstelle 1982, Schule mit Dachschaden 1985, Tönende Stille 1985, Die Streuner von Pangkor 1987, Die Blütenkrone 2002, Der Schatz des goldenen Bären 2002, Der Federfächer 2002, Die Schattenschwingen 2002, Die Himmelsschlange 2003, Die goldene Heuschrecke 2003, Muckepuck und Klitzerlitzchen 2003, Märchen für einen kleinen Wolf 2003, Die klingende Krone 2003, Das Weihnachtsgespenst 2003, Das stille Licht 2003, Die Nikolausvögel 2003, Die Tochter des Berggeistes 2003, Der Mondschein-Bubu 2004, König Brummelmax 2004, Die hölzernen Flügel 2004, Das Diamantenherz 2004, Der goldene Käfig 2004, Die Zaubertrommel 2004; contribs to several anthologies and literary journals; poems, fairy-tales, stories on website. *Honours:* Hon. Prof. of Literature, Univ. of Paris 1992–; Hon. DLitt (London) 1992; Golden Crown World Poets' Award 1990, Int. Cultural Diploma of Honour 1995, ABI Woman of the Year 1997, SOS Kinderdörfer Spenderin des Monats 2005. *Address:* Winkler Str. 4A, 14193 Berlin, Germany (home). *Telephone:* (30) 8915783 (home). *Website:* www.inge-dreyer.de (home).

DRISCOLL, F. Paul; American opera director and writer; *Editor-in-Chief, Opera News*; b. 23 Aug. 1954, New York, NY. *Education:* Regis High School, Manhattan and Coll. of the Holy Cross. *Career:* fmr actor, Foothills Theater, Worcester; freelance dir and designer for theatre; worked at departmental store, Lord & Taylor in various roles 1978–85; Product Development Man., Metropolitan Opera Guild retail programme 1985–90; freelance writer and dir 1990–, contributing reviews, stories and essays to publs, including Chamber Music, Musical America, Opera News, Stagebill; Picture Ed., Opera News, apptd Man. Ed. 1998, later Exec. Ed., Ed.-in-Chief 2003–; Dir of some 20 musicals and operettas, Coll. Light Opera Co., Falmouth –1998; Artistic Dir, Scarsdale Summer Music Theater; Dir Washington Chamber Symphony, Kennedy Center; Dramatic Dir Blue Hill Troupe 1998–2004. *Television:* host, Opera New York (WNYE) 2002–04. *Publications:* 25 Years at Highfield: A History of the College Light Opera Company 1992, Fantastic Opera (with artist, John Martinez) 1997. *Address:* Opera News, 70 Lincoln Center Plaza, 6th Floor, New York, NY 10023-6593, USA (office). *Telephone:* (212) 769-7080 (office). *Fax:* (212) 769-8500 (office). *E-mail:* info@operanews.com (office). *Website:* www.operanews.com (office).

DRIVER, Charles Jonathan (Jonty), BA, BEd, MPhil, FRSA; British writer and poet; b. 19 Aug. 1939, Cape Town, South Africa; s. of Rev. K. E. Driver and P. E. M. Driver (née Gould); m. Ann Elizabeth Hoogewerf 1967; two s. one d. *Education:* Univ. of Cape Town, Trinity Coll., Oxford. *Career:* Pres. Nat. Union of South African Students 1963–64; Housemaster, Int. Sixth Form Centre, Sevenoaks School 1968–73; Dir of Sixth Form, Matthew Humberstone Comprehensive School 1973–78; Research Fellow, Univ. of York 1976; Principal, Island School, Hong Kong 1978–83; Headmaster, Berkhamsted School 1983–89; The Master, Wellington Coll., Crowthorne, Berks. 1989–2000; Ed. Conference and Common Room 1993–2000. *Publications:* novels: Elegy for a Revolutionary 1968, Send War in Our Time, O Lord 1970, Death of Fathers 1972, A Messiah of the Last Days 1974, Shades of Darkness 2004; poetry: I Live Here Now 1979, Occasional Light (with Jack Cope) 1979, Hong Kong Portraits 1985, In the Water-Margins 1994, Holiday Haiku 1996, Requiem 1998, So Far: Selected Poems 1960–2004 2004; non-fiction: Patrick Duncan (biog.) 1980; contribs to numerous magazines and journals. *Address:* Apple Yard Cottage, Mill Lane, Northiam, nr Rye, East Sussex, TN31 6JU, England (home). *Telephone:* (1797) 253289 (home). *E-mail:* jontydriver@hotmail.com (home). *Website:* www.jontydriver.co.uk.

DRIVER, Paul William, MA; British music critic and writer; b. 14 Aug. 1954, Manchester, England. *Education:* Univ. of Oxford. *Career:* music critic, The Boston Globe 1983–84, Sunday Times 1985–; mem. Editorial Bd Contemporary Music Review; mem. Critics Circle; Patron, Manchester Musical Heritage Trust. *Radio:* Ear to the Ground (series of conversations with composers, BBC Radio 4) 2004. *Publications:* A Diversity of Creatures (ed.) 1987, Music and Text (ed.) 1989, Manchester Pieces 1996, Penguin English Verse (ed., Vols 1–6) 1995, Penguin Popular Poetry (ed., Vols 1–6) 1996, Four Elegies (poems) 2009, A Metropolitan Recluse (novel) 2010; contrib. to Sunday Times, Financial Times, Tempo, London Review of Books, Opera, New York Times, Gramophone, TLS and numerous others. *Address:* Louise Greenberg Books Ltd, The End House, Church Crescent, London, N3 1BG, England (office). *Telephone:* (20) 7624-4501 (office). *E-mail:* paul@driver4044.freeserve.co.uk (home).

DRUMMOND, June, BA; South African author; b. 15 Nov. 1923, Durban. *Education:* University of Cape Town. *Career:* mem. Soroptimist International, Writers Circle of South Africa. *Publications:* The Black Unicorn 1959, Northern Miner 1959, Thursday's Child 1961, A Time to Speak 1962, Welcome, Proud Lady 1964, A Cage of Humming Birds 1964, Cable-car 1965, The Saboteurs 1967, The Gantry Episode 1968, People in Glass Houses 1969, Farewell Party 1971, Bang! Bang! You're Dead! 1973, Boon Companions 1974, Slowly the Poison 1975, Funeral Urn 1976, The Patriots 1979, I Saw Him Die 1979, Such a Nice Family 1980, The Trojan Mule 1982, The Bluestocking 1985, Junta 1989, The Unsuitable Miss Pelham 1990, Burden of Guilt 1991, The Impostor 1992, Hidden Agenda 1993, Loose Cannon 2003, The Meddlers 2004, Old Bones Buried Underneath 2006, Countdown Murder 2008.

DRYSDALE, Andrew; South African journalist and author; b. 19 Oct. 1935, Duiwelskloof, Transvaal; s. of Andrew Patarson Drysdale. *Education:* Parktown High School. *Career:* fmr Ed. The Argus; Fellow, Harvard Univ., USA. *Publications include:* My Neighbour Madiba and Others 2007. *Address:* PO Box 56, Cape Town 8000, South Africa.

DRYSDALE, Helena Claire, MA, FRSL; British writer; *Royal Literary Fund Fellow, Exeter University*; b. 6 May 1960, London; m. Richard Pomeroy 1987, two d. *Education:* Trinity Coll., Cambridge. *Career:* mem. RGS, Soc. of Authors, London Library, Pro Patrimonio. *Television:* Dancing with the Dead (Granada/WNET). *Publications:* Alone Through China and Tibet 1986, Dancing with the Dead 1991, Looking for Gheorghe: Love and Death in Romania (aka Looking for George) 1995, Mother Tongues: Travels Through Tribal Europe 2002, Strangerland 2006; contrib. to Vogue, Marie Claire, Independent, Independent on Sunday, Sunday Times, Daily Telegraph, Harpers and Queen, Cosmopolitan, World, New Statesman. *Honours:* exhibitioner Trinity Coll., PEN/J. R. Ackerley Award for Autobiography 1995, Esquire/Waterstones/Apple Award for Autobiography 1995. *Literary Agent:* AP Watt Ltd, 20 John Street, London, WC1N 2DR, England. *E-mail:* info@helenadrysdale.com (office). *Website:* www.helenadrysdale.com.

DU, Daozheng, Chinese journalist; *Publisher, Yanhuang Chunqiu*; b. Nov. 1923, Dingxiang Co., Shanxi Prov.; s. of Du Xixiang and Qi Luaying; m. Xu Zhixian 1950; one s. four d. *Education:* Middle School, Dingxiang, Shanxi and Beijing Marx-Lenin Coll. *Career:* joined CCP 1937; Chief of Hebei and Guangdong Bureau, Xinhua News Agency 1949–56; Ed.-in-Chief Yangchen Wanbao 1956–69; Dir Home News Dept, Xinhua News Agency 1977–82; Ed.-in-Chief Guangming Daily 1982; Dir Media and Publs Office 1987–88; Deputy 7th NPC 1988–92; Dir State Press and Publs Admin. 1988–89; Founder and Publisher, Yanhuang Chunqiu (journal) 1991–. *Publications:* Explore Japan (co-author), Interviews with Famous Chinese Journalists. *Honours:* Hon. Pres. Newspaper Operation and Man. Asscn 1988; Nat. News Prize 1979. *Address:* Yanhuang Chunqiu, Xicheng District, Yue Tan South Street No. 69, Beijing 100045, People's Republic of China (office). *Telephone:* (10) 68532048 (office). *Fax:* (10) 68532569 (office). *E-mail:* yhcqw01@126.com (office). *Website:* www.yhcqw.com (office).

DUBÉ, Marcel, BA; Canadian dramatist, author, poet and translator; b. 3 Jan. 1930, Montréal, QC; m. Nicole Fontaine 1956. *Education:* Collège Sainte-Marie, Univ. of Montréal, theatre schools in Paris. *Career:* mem. Académie canadienne-française, fellow; Federation of Canadian Authors and Artists, pres., 1959; Royal Society of Canada, fellow. *Publications:* over 30 plays, including: Zone 1955, Un simple soldat 1958, Le temps des lilas (trans. as Time of the Lilacs) 1958, Florence 1958, Bilan 1968, Les beaux dimanches 1968, Au retour des oies blanches (trans. as The White Geese) 1969, Hold-up! (with Louis-George Carrier) 1969, Un matin comme les autres 1971, Le naufrage 1971, De l'autre côté du mur 1973, L'impromptu de Québec, ou Le testament 1974, L'été s'appelle Julie 1975, Le réformiste, ou L'honneur des hommes 1977, Le trou 1986, L'Amérique à sec 1986; other: television series. poetry: Poèmes de sable 1974; non-fiction: Textes et documents 1968, La tragédie est un acte de foi 1973, Jean-Paul Lemieux et le livre 1988, Andrée Lachapelle: Entre ciel et terre 1995. *Honours:* Prix Victor-Morin, Saint-Jean-Baptiste Society 1966, Prix David, Québec 1973, Molson Prize, Canada Council 1984, Académie Canadienne-Française Medal 1987, Gov.-Gen's Performing Arts Award for Lifetime Artistic Achievement 2005.

DUBERMAN, Martin, BA, MA, PhD; American academic and writer; b. 6 Aug. 1930, New York, NY. *Education:* Yale Univ., Harvard Univ. *Career:* Teaching Fellow, Harvard Univ. 1955–57; Instructor, Yale Univ. 1957–61, Morse Fellow 1961–62; Bicentennial Preceptor and Asst Prof., Princeton Univ. 1962–65, Assoc. Prof. 1965–67, Prof. 1967–71; Distinguished Prof. of History, Lehman Coll. and Graduate School and Univ. Center, CUNY 1972–, now Prof. Emeritus; founder-Dir, Center for Lesbian and Gay Studies, Graduate School and Univ. Center, CUNY 1986–96; Visiting Randolph Distinguished Prof., Vassar Coll. 1992. *Publications:* Charles Francis Adams, 1807–1886 1960, In White America 1964, The Antislavery Vanguard: New Essays on the Abolitionists (ed.) 1965, James Russell Lowell 1966, The Uncompleted Past 1969, The Memory Bank 1970, Black Mountain: An Exploration in Community 1972, Male Armor: Selected Plays, 1968–1974 1975, Visions of Kerouac 1977, About Time: Exloring the Gay Past 1986, Hidden from History: Reclaiming the Gay and Lesbian Past (co-ed.) 1989, Paul Robeson 1989, Cures: A Gay Man's Odyssey 1991, Mother Earth: An Epic Play on the Life of Emma Goldman 1991, Stonewall 1993, Midlife Queer 1996, A Queer World: The Center for Lesbian and Gay Studies Reader (ed.) 1997, Queer Representations: Reading Lives, Reading Cultures (ed.) 1997, Left Out: The Politics of Exclusion (essays) 1999, The Worlds of Lincoln Kirstein 2007, Radical Acts 2008, Waiting to Land 2009, A Saving Remnant 2011; contrib. to journals and newspapers. *Honours:* Bancroft Prize 1961, Vernon Rice/Drama Desk Award 1965, Borough of Manhattan Pres.'s Gold Medal in Literature 1988, two Lambda Book Awards 1990, Asscn of Gay and Lesbian Psychiatrists Distinguished Service Award 1996, Key to the City of Cambridge, MA 1994, Legal Public Service Award 1995, NOMAS Men's Studies Award 1998, GALA Award 1998. *Address:* 475 West 22nd Street, Apartment 2, New York, NY 10011-2549, USA (home). *Telephone:* (212) 929-2639 (home). *E-mail:* martinduberman@aol.com (home).

DUBERSTEIN, Larry, BA, MA; American writer and cabinet maker; b. 18 May 1944, New York, NY; three d. *Education:* Wesleyan Univ., Harvard Univ. *Publications:* Nobody's Jaw 1979, The Marriage Hearse 1983, Carnovsky's Retreat 1988, Postcards from Pinsk 1991, Eccentric Circles 1992, The Alibi Breakfast 1995, The Handsome Sailor 1998, The Mt Monadnock Blues 2003, The Day The Bozarts Died 2007, The Twoweeks 2011; contribs include articles, essays, poems, reviews in Saturday Review, Boston Review, The National, The Phoenix, New York Times Book Review, Boston Globe. *Honours:* New York Times New and Noteworthy 1987, New American Writing Awards 1987, 1991, New York Times Notable Book 1998, Book Sense Notable Book 2007. *Address:* Brimstone Corner Road, Hancock, NH 03449, USA.

DUBIE, Norman Evans, Jr, BA, MFA; American academic, writer and poet; *Professor of English, Arizona State University;* b. 10 April 1945, Barre, Vt. *Education:* Goddard Coll., Univ. of Iowa. *Career:* teaching asst, Goddard Coll. 1967–69; teaching asst, Univ. of Iowa 1969–70, Writing Fellow 1970–71, Distinguished Lecturer and mem. of the Graduate Faculty 1971–74; Poetry Ed., Iowa Review 1971–72, Now Magazine 1973–74; Asst Prof., Ohio Univ. 1974–75; Lecturer, Arizona State Univ. 1975–76, Dir, Creative Writing 1976–77, Assoc. Prof. 1978–81, Prof. of English 1982–. *Publications:* The Horsehair Sofa 1969, Alehouse Sonnets 1971, Indian Summer 1973, The Prayers of the North American Martyrs 1975, Popham of the New Song 1975, In the Dead of Night 1975, The Illustrations 1977, A Thousand Little Things 1977, Odalisque in White 1978, The City of the Olesha Fruit 1979, Comes Winter, the Sea Hunting 1979, The Everlastings 1980, The Window in the Field 1982, Selected and New Poems 1983, The Springhouse 1986, Groom Falconer 1989, Radio Sky 1991, The Clouds of Magellan 1992, The Choirs of June and January 1993, The Mercy Seat: Collected and New Poems 1967–2001 2001, Ordinary Mornings of a Coliseum 2004; contributions: anthologies and periodicals. *Honours:* Bess Hokin Prize 1976, Guggenheim Fellowship 1977–78, Pushcart Prize 1978–79, National Endowment for the Arts grant 1986, Ingram Merrill Grant 1987. *Address:* Department of English, Arizona State University, PO Box 870302, Tempe, AZ 85287-0302, USA (office). *Telephone:* (480) 965-2407 (office). *E-mail:* n.dubie@asu.edu (office). *Website:* www.english.clas.asu.edu (office).

DUBNER, Stephen J., MFA; American journalist and writer; b. New York City; m. Ellen Binder; two c. *Education:* Appalachian State Univ., Columbia Univ. *Career:* fmr mem. of a rock band, signed a recording contract with Arista Records; mem. editorial staff New York Magazine 1990–94, New York Times Magazine 1994–99; fmr tv corresp. Public Broadcasting Service. *Television:* contrib. to ABC News, Good Morning America, World News Tonight. *Publications:* Turbulent Souls 1998 (re-published as Choosing My Religion 2006), Confessions of a Hero-Worshiper 2003, Freakonomics: A Rogue Economist Explores the Hidden Side of Everything (with Steven D. Levitt) (Booksense Ind. Booksellers Nonfiction Book of the Year, Quill Award for Best Business Book of the Year) 2005, The Boy With Two Belly Buttons (children's fiction) 2007, Superfreakonimics: Global Cooling, Patriotic Prostitutes and Why Suicide Bombers Should Buy Life Insurance 2009; contrib. to New York Times, New York Times Magazine, Time, The New Yorker. *Literary Agent:* Suzanne Gluck, William Morris Agency, 1325 Avenue of the Americas, New York, NY 10019, USA. *Telephone:* (212) 903-1169. *Fax:* (212) 246-3583. *E-mail:* sg@wma.com (office). *Website:* www.wma.com. *E-mail:* sjd@stephenjdubner.com (office). *Website:* stephenjdubner.com; www.freakonomics.com.

DUBOIS, Frédéric, (Julien Dunilac); Swiss fmr diplomatist, writer and poet; b. 24 Sept. 1923, Neuchâtel; m. Lydia Induni 1947; one s. two d. *Education:* Neuchâtel and Paris. *Career:* mem. Société Ecrivains neuchâtelois et jurassiens, Autrices et Auteurs de Suisse, Société Suisse des Auteurs, Pro Litteris. *Publications:* poetry: La Vue Courte 1952, La Part du Feu 1954, Corps et Biens 1957, Passager clandestin 1962, Futur mémorable 1970, L'Un 1974, La Passion selon Belle 1985, Plein ciel 1985, Mythologiques 1987, Précaire Victoire 1991, Hôtel le Soleil 1995, Chroniques, suivi de fragments d'une île 2003, Territoires de l'esil 2003, Cassandre, suivi de poèmes du temps ordinaire 2004, Chanson du Feu 2007, Rapaces 2009, Le présomptif été 2010; novels: Les Mauvaises Têtes 1958, L'Habit et le moine 1996, Le Coup de grâce 1998, Garden-party 2000, Le dos au mur 2001, La Méduse 2002, Le Funiculaire 2004, Heloïse au miroir 2006, Le garde forestier 2006, La Voisine des Vieux 2007, Lettre du Placard 2008, L'Érangère 2009, La Dernière Tonte avant L'Hiver 2009, L'arnaque; non-fiction: Georges Sand sous la loupe 1978, François Mitterrand sous la loupe 1981, Le Conseil fédéral sous la loupe 1991, Jean-Jacques Rousseau ou le deuil éclatant du bonheur 2011; contribs to various publications and radio. *Honours:* Prix Ondas, Barcelona 1987. *Address:* Rue des Parcs 5, 2000 Neuchâtel, Switzerland (home). *Telephone:* (32) 724-4828 (home). *Fax:* (32) 724-4828 (home). *E-mail:* frederic.dubois@net2000.ch (home).

DUBOIS, Jean-Paul; French writer; b. 1950, Toulouse. *Career:* journalist, Le Nouvel Observateur. *Publications:* Tous les matins je me lève (novel) 1988, La vie me fait peur (novel) 1994, Kennedy et moi (novel) (Prix France Télévision) 1996, L'Amérique m'inquiète 1996, Prends soin de moi 1997, Je pense à autre chose 1997, Si ce livre pouvait me rapprocher de toi 1999, Les poissons me regardent 2001, Jusque-là tout allait bien en Amérique 2002, Une vie française (trans. as A French Life 2007) (Prix du Roman FNAC, Prix Femina) 2004, Vous plaisantez, monsieur Tanner 2006, Maria est morte 2006, Vous aurez de mes nouvelles 2006, Parfois je rus tout seul 2007, Nouvelles Mythologies 2007, Eloge de gaucher 2008, Les Accommodements Raisonnables 2008, Hommes entre eux 2008. *Address:* c/o Le Nouvel Observateur, 10–12 place de la Bourse, 75002 Paris, France (office). *Website:* hebdo.nouvelobs.com (office).

DUBUS, Andre, III; American writer and academic; b. 1959, s. of Andre Dubus; m. Fontaine Dollas Dubus; three c. *Education:* Univ. of Texas. *Career:* began writing fiction at age 22; fmr teacher, Harvard Univ., Tufts Univ., Emerson Coll.; currently Asst Prof. of English, Univ. of Massachusetts, Lowell, Jack Kerouac Writer-in-Residence 1997; mem. PEN American Center; jury mem., Nat. Book Foundation, Nat. Endowment for the Arts. *Publications:* The Cage Keeper and Other Stories 1989, Bluesman 1993, House of Sand and Fog 1999, The Garden of Last Days 2008, Townie: A Memoir 2011. *Honours:* Guggenheim Fellowship, Nat. Magazine Award for Fiction 1985, Pushcart Prize 1999. *Literary Agent:* Philip G. Spitzer Literary Agency, 50 Talmage Farm Lane, East Hampton, NY 11937, USA. *Telephone:* (631) 329-3650 (office). *E-mail:* spitzer516@aol.com (office). *Address:* O'Leary Library 407, 61 Wilder St., Lowell, MA 01854, USA. *Telephone:* (978) 934-4193. *E-mail:* Andre_Dubus@uml.edu. *Website:* andredubus.com.

DUCHARME, Réjean; Canadian novelist, dramatist, screenwriter, sculptor and painter; b. 12 Aug. 1941, Saint-Félix-de-Valois, QC. *Education:* Ecole Polytechnique, Montréal. *Publications:* fiction: L'avalée des avalés (trans. as The Swallower Swallowed) 1966, Le nez qui voque 1967, L'océantume 1968, La fille de Christophe Colomb 1969, L'huver de force 1973, Les enfantomes 1976, Dévadé 1990, Va savoir 1994, Gros Mots 1990; plays: Le Cid maghané 1968, Le marquis qui perdit 1970, Inès Pérée et Inat Tendu 1976, HA! ha!... 1982; screenplays: Les bons débarras (with Francis Manckiewicz) 1979, Les beaux souvenirs (with Francis Manckiewicz) 1981. *Honours:* Governor-General's Awards for Fiction 1966, Drama 1982. *Address:* 10678 Saint-Vital Boulevard, Montreal, QC H1H 4T3, Canada (home). *Telephone:* (514) 321-5337 (home).

DUCKWORTH, Marilyn, OBE; New Zealand writer; b. (Marilyn Rose Adcock), 10 Nov. 1935, Auckland; d. of Cyril John Adcock and Irene Robinson;

sister of Fleur Adcock (q.v.); m. 1st Harry Duckworth 1955 (divorced 1964); m. 2nd Ian Macfarlane 1964 (divorced 1972); m. 3rd Daniel Donovan 1974 (died 1978); m. 4th John Batstone 1985; four d. *Education:* Queen Margaret Coll., Wellington and Victoria Univ., Wellington. *Career:* ten writing fellowships 1961–96 including Katherine Mansfield Fellowship, Menton 1980, Fulbright Visiting Writer's Fellowship, USA 1987, Victoria Univ. Writing Fellowship 1990, Hawthornden Writing Fellowship, Scotland 1994, 2001, Sargeson Writing Fellowship, Auckland 1995, Auckland Univ. Literary Fellowship 1996. *Plays:* Home to Mother, Feet First. *Television:* Close to Home (series). *Publications:* 15 novels, including A Gap in the Spectrum 1959, The Matchbox House 1960, A Barbarous Tongue 1963, Over the Fence Is Out 1969, Disorderly Conduct 1984, Married Alive 1985, Pulling Faces 1987, A Message from Harpo 1989, Unlawful Entry 1992, Seeing Red 1993, Leather Wings 1995, Studmuffin 1997, Swallowing Diamonds 2003, Playing Friends 2007; short stories: Explosions on the Sun 1989; poems: Other Lovers' Children 1975; memoir: Camping on the Faultline 2000. *Honours:* NZ Literary Fund Award for Achievement 1963, NZ Book Award for Fiction 1985. *Address:* 41 Queen Street, Mt Victoria, Wellington 6011, New Zealand (home). *Telephone:* (4) 384-9990 (home). *Fax:* (4) 384-9990 (home). *E-mail:* marilynduckworth@paradise.net.nz (home).

DUCORNET, Erica (Rikki) Lynn, BA; American/French writer, artist and teacher; b. 19 April 1943, New York; d. of Gerard De Gré and Muriel Harris; m. Jonathan Cohen; one s. *Career:* apptd Novelist-in-Residence, Univ. of Denver 1988; has taught writing at Writers at Work, Bard Coll., Brown Univ., Naropa Univ., Vermont Studio Center, Centrum Writer's Workshop, Univ. of Trento; Writer-in-Residence Univ. of Louisiana, Lafayette 2007–09; mem. PEN. *Publications:* novels: The Stain 1984, Entering Fire 1986, The Fountains of Neptune 1989, Eben Demarst 1990, The Jade Cabinet 1993, The Butcher's Tales 1994, Phosphor in Dreamland 1995, The Word 'Desire' 1997, The Fan Maker's Inquisition (Los Angeles Times Book of the Year) 2000, Gazelle 2004, Netsuke 2011; short fiction: The Complete Butcher's Tales 1994, The Word 'Desire' 1997, The One Marvelous Thing 2008; poetry: From The Star Chamber 1974, Wild Geraniums 1975, Bouche a Bouche 1975, Weird Sisters 1976, Knife Notebook 1977, The Illustrated Universe (1979, The Cult of Seizure 1989; essay: The Monstrous and the Marvelous 1999. *Honours:* Lannan Literary Award in Fiction 1993, 2004, Critics Choice Award 1995, Charles Flint Kellogg Award in Arts and Letters 1998, Lannon Literary Fellowship 1998, Academy Award, American Acad. of Arts and Letters 2008. *Address:* c/o Coffee House Press, 79 Thirteenth Avenue NE, Suite 110, Minneapolis, MN 55413, USA (office). *E-mail:* rikki@rikkiducornet.com. *Website:* www.rikkiducornet.com (office).

DUDA, Virgil; Romanian novelist; b. 25 Feb. 1939, Barlad. *Education:* Coll. of Juridicial Sciences, Bucharest. *Career:* emigrated to Israel 1988; fmr Ed. Ultima ora newspaper; fmr vice-pres. Asscn of Israeli Writers in the Romanian Language. *Publications:* novels: Povestiri din provincie 1967, Catedrala 1969, Anchetatorul penal 1972, Deruta 1973, Al doilea pasaj 1976, Cora 1977, Mastile 1979, Razboiul amintirilor 1981, Hartuiala 1984, Oglinda salvata 1986, Alvis si destinul 1993, Romania, sfarsit de Decembrie 1994, A trai in pacat 1996, Viata cu efect intirziat 1999, Sase femei 2002, Evreul ca simbol 2004, Despartirea de Ierusalim 2005, Ultimele iubin 2008; short stories: Anchetatorul apatic. *Honours:* Arcadia Literature Prize 1992, Sion Prize 2001.

DUDEN, Anne; German writer; b. 1 Jan. 1942, Oldenburg. *Education:* West Berlin. *Career:* trained as bookseller, studied literature and sociology, had various jobs, then worked in publishing; co-founder Rotbuch Verlag (Publrs), Berlin 1973, mem. staff 1973–78; freelance writer, London 1978–. *Publications include:* Übergang (short stories) 1982, Das Judasschaf 1985, Steinschlag (poems) 1993, Wimpertier (mixed prose pieces and poems) 1995, Der wunde Punkt im Alphabet (essays, sketches and commentaries on painting) 1995, Hingegend (poems) 2001, Heimaten 2001. *Honours:* Krahichsteiner Literaturpreis 1986, Heinrich Böll Literaturpreis 2003.

DUDLEY, Helen (see Hope-Simpson, Jacynth Ann)

DUEMER, Joseph, BA, MFA; American academic, poet and writer; *Professor of Humanities, Clarkson University;* b. 31 May 1951, San Diego, Calif.; m. Carole A. Mathery 1987. *Education:* Univ. of Washington, Univ. of Iowa. *Career:* Lecturer, Western Washington Univ. 1981–83, San Diego State Univ. 1983–87; Assoc. Prof. of Humanities, Clarkson Univ. 1987–2002, Prof. 2002–; Poet-in-Residence, St Lawrence Univ. 1990; Fulbright Sr Research Fellow, Viet Nam 2000–01; mem. Associated Writing Programs (mem. Bd of Dirs 1998–2002). *Publications:* poetry: Fool's Paradise 1980, The Light of Common Day 1985, Customs 1987, Static 1996, Primitive Alphabets 1998, Magical Thinking 2001; editor: Dog Music (with Jan Simmerman) 1996; contrib. to reference books, anthologies, reviews, journals, magazines and radio. *Honours:* NEA Creative Writing Fellowships 1984, 1992, Nat. Endowment for the Humanities grants 1985, 1995. *Address:* Department of Humanities and Social Sciences, Clarkson University, 273 Bertrand H/ Snell Hall, Potsdam, NY 13699, USA (office). *Telephone:* (315) 268-3967 (office). *E-mail:* duemer@clarkson.edu (office). *Website:* www.sharpsand.net.

DUFF, Alan; New Zealand columnist and writer; b. 26 Oct. 1950, Rotorua; m. Joanna Robin Harper 1990. *Career:* syndicated newspaper columnist 1971–. *Publications:* Once Were Warriors 1994, State Ward 1994, One Night Out Stealing 1995, What Becomes of the Broken Hearted? 1996, Out of the Mist and Steam 1999, Szabad 2001, Jake's Long Shadow 2002.

DUFF-WARE, Freddie (see Barnett, Paul Le Page)

DUFFY, Carol Ann, CBE, BA, FRSL; British poet and dramatist; *Poet Laureate;* b. 23 Dec. 1955, Glasgow, Scotland; d. of Frank Duffy and May Black; one d. *Education:* St Joseph's Convent, Stafford and Univ. of Liverpool. *Career:* Poetry Ed. Ambit 1983–; Lecturer in Creative Writing, then Prof. of Contemporary Poetry, Manchester Metropolitan Univ. 1996–; Poet Laureate 2009–; mem. Poetry Soc. (Vice-Pres.). *Plays:* Take My Husband 1984, Cavern Dreams 1986, Grimm Tales 1994, More Grimm Tales 1997. *Publications include:* poetry: Fleshweathercock 1973, Standing Female Nude (Scottish Arts Council Award) 1985, Selling Manhattan (Scottish Arts Council Award, Somerset Maugham Award 1988) 1987, Home and Away 1988, The Other Country (Dylan Thomas Award) 1990, Mean Time (Whitbread Poetry Award, Forward Poetry Prize, Scottish Arts Council Book Award) 1993, Selected Poems 1994, The Pamphlet 1998, The World's Wife 1999, Time's Tidings 1999, Feminine Gospels 2001, Underwater Farmyard 2002, Out of Fashion (ed.) 2004, Rapture (T. S. Eliot Prize 2006) 2005, Another Night Before Christmas 2005, Selected Poems 2006, The Lost Happy Endings (with Jane Ray) 2006, The Hat (for children) 2007, Answering Back (ed.) 2008, New and Collected Poems for Children 2009, Another Night Before Christmas 2010, The Bees (Costa Book Award for Poetry 2011) 2011. *Honours:* C. Day-Lewis Fellowships 1982–84, Eric Gregory Award 1985, Cholmondeley Award 1992, Lannan Award (USA) 1995, Signal Poetry Award 1997, PEN Pinter Prize 2012. *Literary Agent:* Rogers, Coleridge and White, 20 Powis Mews, London W11 1JN, England. *Telephone:* (20) 7221-3717. *Fax:* (20) 7229-9084. *E-mail:* info@rcwlitagency.com. *Website:* www.rcwlitagency.co.uk. *Address:* c/o Pan Macmillan Ltd, 20 New Wharf Road, London, N1 9RR, England (office).

DUFFY, Eamon, PhD, DD, FBA, FSA; Irish writer and academic; *Professor of the History of Christianity, University of Cambridge;* b. 1947, Dundalk; m. Jennifer Elizabeth Browning; one s. two d. *Education:* Hull Univ., Selwyn Coll., Cambridge. *Career:* Prof. of the History of Christianity, Univ. of Cambridge. *Publications:* Challoner and his Church: Catholic Bishop in Georgian England 1981, What Catholics Believe About Mary 1989, The Stripping of the Altars: Traditional Religion in England 1400–1580 1992, The Creed in the Catechism: The Life of God for Us 1996, Saints and Sinners: A History of the Popes 1997, The Voices of Morebath: Reformation and Rebellion in an English Village 2001, Faith of our Fathers 2004, Marking the Hours: English People and Their Prayers 1240–1570 2006, Walking to Emmaus 2006, Fires of Faith: Catholic England Under Mary Tudor 2009; contrib. to New York Review of Books. *Honours:* Hon. DD (Hull) 2004, Hon. DLitt (King's Coll., London) 2009; Hon. Fellowship, St Mary's Coll., Strawberry Hill 2004; Longman's History Today prize 1994, Hawthornden Prize 2002. *Address:* c/o Yale University Press London, 47 Bedford Square, London, WC1B 3DP, England (office). *Telephone:* (1223) 332144 (office).

DUFFY, Maureen Patricia, BA, FRSL, FKC; British writer and poet; b. 21 Oct. 1933, Worthing, Sussex; d. of Grace Rose Wright. *Education:* Trowbridge High School for Girls, Sarah Bonnell High School for Girls, King's Coll., London. *Career:* staged pop art exhbn with Brigid Brophy 1969; Chair. Greater London Arts Literature Panel 1979–81, Authors Lending and Copyright Soc. 1982–94, Copyright Licensing Agency 1996–99 (Vice-Chair. 1994–96); Pres. Writers' Guild of GB 1985–88 (Jt Chair. 1977–78); Co-founder Writers' Action Group 1972–79; Vice-Pres. European Writers Congress 1992–2003 (Pres. 2003–05), Beauty without Cruelty 1975–, British Copyright Council 1998–2003 (Vice-Chair. 1981–86, Chair. 1989–98, Hon. Pres. 2003); Fellow, King's Coll., London 2002. *Radio:* The Passionate Shepherdess, Only Goodnight. *Television:* Upstairs Downstairs (Episode 11). *Plays:* Pearson (London Playwrights' Award), Rites (Nat. Theatre) 1969, A Nightingale in Bloomsbury Square (Hampstead Theatre) 1974, The Masque of Henry Purcell (Southwark Theatre) 1995. *Publications:* That's How It Was 1962, The Single Eye 1964, The Microcosm 1966, The Paradox Players 1967, Lyrics for the Dog Hour (poems) 1968, Wounds 1969, Love Child 1971, The Venus Touch 1971, The Erotic World of Faery 1972, I Want to Go to Moscow 1973, Capital 1975, Evesong (poems) 1975, The Passionate Shepherdess 1977, Housespy 1978, Memorials of the Quick and the Dead (poems) 1979, Inherit the Earth 1980, Gorsaga 1981, Londoners: An Elegy 1983, Men and Beasts 1984, Collected Poems 1949–84 1985, Change 1987, A Thousand Capricious Chances: Methuen 1889–1989 1989, Illuminations 1991, Occam's Razor 1992, Henry Purcell (biog.) 1994, Restitution 1998, England: The Making of a Myth from Stonehenge to Albert Square 2001, Alchemy 2004, Family Values 2008, The Orpheus Trail 2009. *Honours:* Hon. Pres. Authors Lending and Copyright Soc. 2002; CISAC Gold Medal for Literature 2002, Benson Medal RSL 2004. *Address:* 18 Fabian Road, London, SW6 7TZ, England (office). *Telephone:* (20) 7385-3598 (office). *Fax:* (20) 7385-2468 (office). *E-mail:* 113714.1610@compuserve.com (office). *Website:* www.maureenduffy.co.uk.

DUFFY, Stella, BA; British/New Zealand writer, performer and theatre director; b. 1963, London; pnr Shelley Silas. *Education:* Victoria Univ., Wellington. *Career:* raised in NZ, returned to England 1986. *Plays:* The Tedious Predictability of Falling in Love (Oval House) 1990, The Hand (Bristol Old Vic and tour) 1995, Close to You (Hen and Chickens Theatre) 1996, Crocodiles and Bears (BAC) 1999, Immaculate Conceit (Lyric Hammersmith) 2003, Breaststrokes (BAC) 2004, Cell Sell (Nat. Youth Theatre, Soho Theatre) 2005, Prime Resident (Nat. Youth Theatre, Soho Theatre) 2006, Medea (adaptation) (Steam Industry, The Scoop) 2009. *Radio:* The Vocation of Antonia Bright 2002, Old Dogs, New Tricks 2002, From the River's Mouth 2008, The Inter-Not 2008. *Publications:* novels: Calendar Girl 1994,

Wavewalker 1996, Beneath the Blonde 1997, Singling Out the Couples 1998, Fresh Flesh 1999, Eating Cake 1999, Immaculate Conceit 2000, Tart Noir (co-ed with Lauren Henderson) 2001, State of Happiness 2004, Parallel Lies 2005, Mouths of Babes 2005, The Room of Lost Things 2008, Theodora: Actress, Empress, Whore 2010. *Honours:* Crime Writers Asscn Short Story Dagger 2002, Stonewall Writer of the Year 2008, 2010. *Literary Agent:* Stephanie Cabot, The Gernert Company, 136 East 57th Street, New York, NY 10022, USA. *Address:* Virago Press, Little Brown Book Group, 100 Victoria Embankment, London, EC4Y 0DY, England (office). *E-mail:* virago.press@littlebrown.co.uk (office). *Website:* www.stelladuffy.wordpress.com.

DUFOSSÉ, Christophe; French writer; b. 24 Oct. 1963, Paris. *Career:* literature teacher. *Publications:* novels: L'Heure de la sortie (trans. as School's Out) (Prix du Premier Roman 2002) 2002, La Diffamation 2004, Dévotion 2006. *Address:* c/o Éditions Denoël, 9 rue du Cherche-Midi, 75278 Paris cédex 06, France (office). *E-mail:* dchris2410@aol.com (office). *Website:* www.denoel.fr (office).

DUGGAN, Christopher, BA; British academic and writer; *Professor of Italian History, University of Reading;* b. 11 April 1957, London, England; m. Jennifer Virginia Mundy 1987. *Education:* Merton Coll., Oxford. *Career:* Jr Research Fellow, Wolfson Coll., Oxford 1983–85; Lecturer, Univ. of Reading 1987–94, Reader in Italian History 1994–02, Prof. of Modern Italian History 2002–, Dir of Centre for the Advanced Study of Italian Soc. 1987–, Head, School of Languages and European Studies 2008–, currently also Dir of the Centre for Modern Italian History; Fellow, All Souls Coll., Oxford 1985–97. *Publications:* A History of Sicily (co-author) 1986, Fascism and the Mafia 1989, A Concise History of Italy 1994, Francesco Crispi 2003, The Force of Destiny 2007; contributions: articles and reviews to various journals and newspapers. *Honours:* Commendatore, Ordine della Stella della Solidarietà Italiana 2008. *Address:* Department of Italian Studies, University of Reading, Whiteknights, PO Box 217, Reading, RG6 6AA, England (office). *Telephone:* (118) 378-8403 (office). *E-mail:* c.j.h.duggan@reading.ac.uk (office). *Website:* www.reading.ac.uk/italian/about/staff/duggan (office).

DUGGAN, Laurence (Laurie), BA, PhD; Australian poet and teacher; b. 1949, Melbourne. *Education:* Monash Univ. and Melbourne Univ. *Career:* media studies teacher, Swinburne 1976, Canberra Coll. 1983; taught at Victoria Univ. of Tech. 1994, Univ. of Western Sydney 1999; film scriptwriter 1978–83; Poetry Ed. Meanjin 1994–97; poetry reviewer, Times on Sunday 1986; columnist, Australian Book Review 1992–94; Hon. Research Adviser, Australian Studies Centre, Univ. of Queensland 2002–06; Sr Lecturer and Writer-in-Residence, Griffith Univ. –2006; freelance 2006–. *Publications:* poetry: The Ash Range (Victorian Premier New Writing Award) 1987, The Epigrams of Martial (Wesley Michael Wright Award), Mangroves (Age Poetry Book of the Year 2003, ASAL Gold Medal 2004) 2003, Compared to What: Selected Poems 1971–2003 2005, Let's Get Lost (with Pam Brown and Ken Bolton) 2005, The Passenger 2006; non-fiction: Ghost Nation: Imagined Space and Australian Visual Culture 1901–39 2001; contrib. of numerous poems to anthologies and journals. *E-mail:* laurieduggan@btinternet.com (home). *Website:* graveneymarsh.blogspot.com.

DUKAJ, Jacek; Polish science fiction writer; b. 30 July 1974, Tarnów. *Education:* Jagiellonian Univ. *Publications:* Złota Galera (trans. as The Golden Galley) (short story) 1990, Ruch Generała (novella) 2000, Katedra (novella) 2000, Czarne oceany (novel) 2001, Aguerre w świcie (novel) 2001, Inne pieśni (novel) 2003, Perfekcyjna niedoskonałość (novel) 2004, Lód (EU Prize for Literature 2009) 2007. *E-mail:* jacduk@mail.zetosa.com.pl (home). *Website:* www.dukaj.pl.

DUKE, Elizabeth (see Wallington, Vivienne Elizabeth)

DUKORE, Bernard Frank, BA, MA, PhD; American writer, theatre director and academic; *University Distinguished Professor Emeritus of Theatre Arts and Humanities, Virginia Polytechnic Institute and State University;* b. New York, NY; one s. two d. *Education:* Brooklyn Coll., Ohio State Univ., Univ. of Illinois, Champagn-Urbana. *Career:* Instructor, Hunter Coll. in the Bronx 1957–60; Asst Prof., Univ. of Southern California, Los Angeles 1960–62; Asst then Assoc. Prof., California State Univ., Los Angeles 1962–66; Assoc. Prof. then Prof. of Theatre, CUNY 1966–72; Prof. of Drama and Theatre, Univ. of Hawaii 1972–86; Univ. Distinguished Prof. of Theatre Arts and Humanities, Virginia Polytechnic Inst. and State Univ., Blacksburg 1986–97, Univ. Distinguished Prof. Emer. 1997–; Hoffman Eminent Scholar Chair in Theatre, Florida State Univ. 1997; Fellow, American Theatre Asscn; mem. Pinter Soc., Int. Shaw Soc., Shaw Soc. UK. *Plays directed include:* The Beelzebub Sonata by Stanislaw Ignacy Witkiewicz 1974, Arms and the Man by George Bernard Shaw 2001. *Publications:* Bernard Shaw, Director 1971, Bernard Shaw, Playwright 1973, Dramatic Theory and Criticism 1974, Where Laughter Stops: Pinter's Tragicomedy 1976, Collected Screenplays of Bernard Shaw 1980, Money and Politics in Ibsen, Shaw and Brecht 1980, The Theatre of Peter Barnes 1981, Harold Pinter 1982, Alan Ayckbourn: A Casebook 1991, The Drama Observed (ed. and annotator, four vols) 1992–93, Shaw and the Last Hundred Years (ed.) 1994, Barnestorm: The Plays of Peter Barnes 1995, Bernard Shaw and Gabriel Pascal 1996, Not Bloody Likely: The Columbia Book of Bernard Shaw Quotations 1997, Shaw on Cinema (ed. and annotator) 1997, Sam Peckinpah's Feature Films 1999, Shaw's Theatre 2000. *Honours:* Guggenheim Fellowship 1969–70, Nat. Endowment for the Humanities Fellowships 1976–77, 1984–85, 1990, Visiting Fellowship, Humanities Research Centre of Australian Nat. Univ. 1979, Fulbright Research Scholarship, UK and Ireland 1991–92. *Address:* Department of Theatre and Cinema, Virginia Polytechnic Institute and State University, Blacksburg, VA 24061-0141 (office); 2510 Plymouth Street, Blacksburg, VA 24060, USA (home). *Telephone:* (540) 961-6999 (home). *E-mail:* bdukore@vt.edu (office). *Website:* www.theatre.vt.edu (office).

DUMONT, André, BA, BEd; Canadian writer; b. 12 April 1929, Campbellton, NB; m. Germaine Richard 1958; two s. two d. *Publications:* Français Renouvele I 1964, II 1966, Le Parti Acadien (co-author) 1972, Jeunesse Mouvementée 1979, Quand Je Serai Grand 1989, Pour un Français Moderne 1990, Avancez en Arrière 1996; contributions: over 100 articles on different topics, mostly political.

DUNANT, Peter (see Dunant, Sarah)

DUNANT, Sarah, (Peter Dunant), BA; British broadcaster and writer; b. 8 Aug. 1950, London; d. of David and Estelle (née Joseph) Dunant; pnr Ian David Willox; two d. *Education:* Godolphin and Latymer School and Newnham Coll., Cambridge. *Career:* actress 1972–73; teacher (Japan) 1973–74; travelling (Asia) 1973–74, (S and Cen. America) 1976–77; Producer BBC Radio 1974–76; freelance journalist, novelist, scriptwriter, radio and TV presenter 1977–; sometime Presenter Woman's Hour, BBC Radio Four 1986–, The Late Show BBC 2 TV 1989–95, Night Waves BBC Radio 3 1997–. *Publications:* as Sarah Dunant: Snow Storms in a Hot Climate 1988, Birth Marks 1991, Fatlands (CWA Silver Dagger Award) 1993, The War of the Words: Essays on Political Correctness (ed.) 1994, Under My Skin 1995, The Age of Anxiety (ed.) 1996, Transgressions 1997, The Age of Anxiety (ed.) 1998, Mapping the Edge 1999, The Birth of Venus 2002, In the Company of the Courtesan 2006, Sacred Hearts 2009; as Peter Dunant: Exterminating Angels (co-author) 1983, Intensive Care (co-author) 1986; contrib. to various London magazines, Listener, Guardian. *Literary Agent:* Aitken Alexander Associates Ltd, 18–21 Cavaye Place, London, SW10 9PT, England. *Telephone:* (20) 7373-8672. *Fax:* (20) 7373-6002. *E-mail:* reception@aitkenalexander.co.uk. *Website:* www.aitkenalexander.co.uk. *Address:* 1A Highwood Road, London, N19 4PN, England (home). *Telephone:* (20) 7281-1555 (home). *Fax:* (20) 7272-4147 (home). *Website:* www.sarahdunant.co.uk.

DUNCAN, Lois, BA; American writer; b. 28 April 1934, Philadelphia, PA; m. Donald W. Arquette 1965; two s. three d. *Education:* Duke Univ., Univ. of New Mexico. *Publications:* Debutante Hill 1957, The Littlest One in the Family 1959, The Middle Sister 1960, Game of Danger 1962, Giving Away Suzanne 1962, Season of the Two-Heart 1965, Point of Violence 1966, Ransom 1966, They Never Came Home 1968, Major Andre, Brave Enemy 1969, Peggy 1970, Hotel for Dogs 1971, A Gift of Magic 1971, I Know What You Did Last Summer 1973, When the Bough Breaks 1974, Down a Dark Hall 1974, Summer of Fear 1976, Killing Mr Griffin 1978, Daughters of Eve 1979, Stranger With My Face 1981, My Growth as a Writer 1982, The Third Eye 1984, Locked in Time 1985, Horses of Dreamland 1986, The Twisted Window 1987, Wonder Kid Meets the Evil Lunch Snatcher 1988, Songs From Dreamland 1989, The Birthday Moon 1989, Don't Look Behind You 1989, Who Killed My Daughter? 1992, The Circus Comes Home 1993, Psychic Connections: A Journey into the Mysterious World of Psi (co-author William Roll) 1995, The Magic of Spider Woman 1996, Gallows Hill 1997, Night Terrors (edited anthology) 1997, Trapped (edited anthology) 1998, The Longest Hair in the World 1999, I Walk at Night 2000, Song of the Circus 2002, Seasons of the Heart 2007, News for Dogs 2009. *E-mail:* loisduncan123@arquettes.com (home). *Website:* www.loisduncan.arquettes.com.

DUNCAN-JONES, Katherine Dorothea, BLitt, MA, FRSL; British editor and academic; *Senior Research Fellow, Somerville College, Oxford;* b. 13 May 1941, Chichester, Sussex; d. of Austin Ernest Duncan-Jones and Elise Elizabeth Duncan-Jones; m. Andrew N. Wilson 1971 (divorced 1990); two d. *Education:* King Edward VI High School for Girls, Birmingham and St Hilda's Coll., Oxford. *Career:* Mary Ewart Research Fellow, Somerville Coll., Oxford 1963–65, Fellow, New Hall, Cambridge 1965–66, Fellow and Tutor in English Literature, Somerville Coll., Oxford 1966–, Sr Research Fellow 2001–, Prof. of English Literature, Univ. of Oxford 1998–2001. *Publications include:* biography: Sir Philip Sidney: Courtier Poet 1991, Ungentle Shakespeare 2001, Shakespeare: Upstart Crow to Sweet Swan 1592-1623 2011; editor: Miscellaneous Prose of Sir Philip Sidney 1977, Sir Philip Sidney 1989, Shakespeare's Sonnets 1997, Shakespeare's Poems (with H.R.Woudhuysen) 2007; contrib. to Review of English Studies, TLS and other journals. *Honours:* Hon. Research Fellow, Univ. Coll., London 2000; Ben Jonson Discoveries Prize 1996. *Address:* Somerville College, Oxford, OX2 6HD, England (office). *Telephone:* (1865) 281267 (office). *E-mail:* katherine.duncan-jones@some.ox.ac.uk (office).

DUNCKER, Patricia, MA, DPhil; British writer; *Professor of Modern Literature, University of Manchester;* b. 29 June 1951, Kingston, Jamaica. *Education:* Univ. of Cambridge, Univ. of Oxford. *Career:* Lecturer, Roehampton Inst. 1978–80, Oxford Polytechnic 1980–86, Univ. of Poitiers, France 1987–91, Univ. of Wales, Aberystwyth 1991–2002; Prof. of Creative Writing, Univ. of East Anglia 2002–07; Prof. of Modern Literature, Univ. of Manchester 2007–; mem. Soc. of Authors, Yr Academi Gymreig (The Welsh Acad.), PEN, RSA. *Publications:* Sisters and Strangers: An Introduction to Contemporary Feminist Fiction 1992, Hallucinating Foucault 1996, Cancer Through the Eyes of Ten Women 1996, Monsieur Shoushana's Lemon Trees 1997, James Miranda Barry (aka The Doctor) 1999, The Deadly Space Between 2002, Writing on the Wall 2002, Seven Tales of Sex and Death 2003, Miss Webster and Chérif 2006, The Strange Case of the Composer and His Judge 2010;

contrib. to Critical Quarterly, Stand Magazine, Women: A Cultural Review. *Honours:* Dillons First Fiction Award, McKitterick Prize. *Literary Agent:* ICM, 4–6 Soho Square, London, W1D 3PZ, England. *Telephone:* (20) 7432-0800. *E-mail:* books@icmtalent.com. *Address:* Department of English and American Studies, University of Manchester, Samuel Alexander Building-W106, Oxford Road, Manchester, M13 9PL, England (office). *Telephone:* (161) 306-1250 (office). *E-mail:* patricia.duncker@manchester.ac.uk (office). *Website:* www.arts.manchester.ac.uk (office).

DUNHAM, William Wade, BS, MS, PhD; American academic and writer; *Truman Koehler Professor of Mathematics, Muhlenberg College*; b. 8 Dec. 1947, Pittsburgh, PA; m. Penelope Higgins 1970; two s. *Education:* Univ. of Pittsburgh, Ohio State Univ. *Career:* Truman Koehler Prof. of Mathematics, Muhlenberg Coll. 1992–; Visiting Prof. of Mathematics, Harvard Univ. 2008; mem. Mathematical Asscn of America, Nat. Council of Teachers of Mathematics. *Publications:* Journey Through Genius: The Great Theorems of Mathematics 1990, The Mathematical Universe 1994, Euler: The Master of Us All 1999, The Calculus Gallery 2005, The Genius of Euler (ed.) 2007; contrib. to American Mathematical Monthly, Mathematics Magazine, College Mathematics Journal, Mathematics Teacher. *Honours:* Univ. of Pittsburgh M. M. Culver Award 1969, Hanover Coll. Master Teacher Award 1981, Nat. Endowment for the Humanities Summer Seminars on Great Theorems 1988–96, Indiana Humanities Council Humanities Achievement Award for Scholarship 1991, Mathematical Asscn of America George Pólya Award 1993, Mathematical Asscn of America Trevor Evans Award 1997, Muhlenberg Coll. Lindback Teaching Award 2001, Mathematical Asscn of America Lester R. Ford Award 2006, Mathematical Asscn of America Beckenbach Prize 2008, Mathematical Asscn of America Trevor Evans Award 2008. *Address:* Department of Mathematics, Muhlenberg College, Allentown, PA 18104, USA (office).

DUNKERLEY, James, BA, BPhil, PhD; British academic and writer; *Professor in Politics and History, Queen Mary and Westfield College, London*; b. 15 Aug. 1953, Wokingham. *Education:* Univ. of York, Hertford Coll., Oxford, Nuffield Coll., Oxford. *Career:* researcher, Latin America Bureau, London 1979–80, 1983–84; Research Fellow, Inst. for Latin American Studies, Univ. of London 1981–82, Dir 1998–; Research Fellow, Centre for Latin American Studies, Univ. of Liverpool 1982–83; Fellow, Kellogg Inst., Univ. of Notre Dame, IN 1985; Reader in Politics, Queen Mary and Westfield Coll., London 1986–, Prof. in Politics and History 1990–; Dir Inst. for the Study of the Americas 2004–. *Publications:* Unity is Strength: Trade Unions in Latin America (with C. Whitehouse), 1980; Bolivia: Coup d'Etat, 1980; The Long War: Dictatorship and Revolution in El Salvador, 1982; Rebellion in the Veins: Political Struggle in Bolivia, 1952–1982, 1984; Granada: Whose Freedom? (with F. Amburseley), 1984; Origenes del poder militar en Bolivia 1879–1935, 1987; Power in the Isthmus: A Political History of Central America, 1988; Political Suicide in Latin America and Other Essays, 1992; The Pacification of Central America, 1994, Warriors and Scribes 2000; Americana, The Americas in the World, around 1850 2000. Contributions: scholarly journals, newspapers, and magazines. *Address:* Institute for the Study of the Americas, Senate House, Malet Street, London, WC1E 7HU, England (office). *Telephone:* (20) 7862-8870 (office). *Fax:* (20) 7862-8886 (office). *E-mail:* americas@sas.ac.uk (office). *Website:* www.americas.ac.uk (office).

DUNLAP, Susan, BA, MAT; American writer; b. 20 June 1943, Kew Gardens, NY; m. Newell Dunlap 1970. *Education:* Bucknell University, University of North Carolina. *Career:* founding mem., Sisters in Crime (pres. 1990–91). *Publications:* An Equal Opportunity Death 1984, Karma 1984, As a Favor 1984, Not Exactly a Brahmin 1985, The Bohermian Connection 1986, The Last Annual Slugfest 1986, Too Close to the Edge 1987, A Dinner to Die For 1987, Pious Deception 1989, Diamond in the Buff 1990, Rogue Wave 1991, Death and Taxes 1993, Time Expired 1993, High Fall 1994, Sudden Exposure 1995, Cop Out 1997, No Immunity 1998, Fast Friends 2004, A Single Eye 2006, Hungry Ghosts 2008, Civil Twilight 2009, Power Slide 2010; other: Deadly Allies II: Private Eye Writers of America and Sisters in Crime Collaborative Anthology (co-ed.) 1994; contributions: numerous short stories to periodicals including Ellery Queen's Mystery Magazine, Alfred Hitchcock's Mystery Magazine. *Address:* c/o Counterpoint Press, 2117 Fourth Street, Suite D, Berkeley, CA 94710, USA (office). *Website:* www.counterpointpress.com (office).

DUNMORE, Helen, BA; British poet and novelist; b. 1952, Yorkshire; m.; one s. one d. one step-s. *Education:* York Univ. *Career:* cttee mem. Soc. of Authors (Chair. 2005–). *Publications include:* poetry: The Apple Fall 1983, The Sea Skater (Poetry Soc. Alice Hunt Bartlett Award) 1986, The Raw Garden (Poetry Book Soc. Choice) 1988, Short Days, Long Nights: New & Selected Poems 1991, Secrets (Signal Poetry Award 1995) 1994, Recovering a Body 1994, Bestiary 1997, Out of the Blue: New and Selected Poems 2001, Glad of These Times 2007; fiction: Going to Egypt 1992, Zennor in Darkness (McKitterick Prize 1994) 1993, In the Money 1993, Burning Bright 1994, A Spell of Winter (Orange Prize for Women Writers of Fiction 1996) 1995, Talking to the Dead 1996, Your Blue-Eyed Boy 1998, With Your Crooked Heart 1999, The Siege 2001, The Silver Bead 2003, Ingo 2005, House of Orphans 2006, The Tide Knot 2006, The Deep 2007, Counting the Stars 2008, The Betrayal 2011; short stories: Love of Fat Men 1997, Ice Cream 2000, Mourning Ruby 2003. *Honours:* Hon. FRSL; winner, Nat. Poetry Competition (for The Malarkey) 2009. *Literary Agent:* Caradoc King, A. P. Watt Ltd, 20 John Street, London, WC1N 2DR, England. *Telephone:* (20) 7405-6774. *Fax:* (20) 7831-2154. *Website:* www.apwatt.co.uk; www.helendunmore.com.

DUNMORE, John, BA, PhD; New Zealand academic and writer; *Professor Emeritus, Massey University*; b. 6 Aug. 1923, Trouville, France; m. Joyce Megan Langley 1946; one s. one d. *Education:* Univ. of London, UK, Univ. of New Zealand. *Career:* Lecturer, Massey Univ., then Sr Lecturer, Prof., Dean 1961–83, Prof. Emer. 1984–; est. Dunmore Press 1969, Heritage Press 1985; mem. Australasian Language and Literature Asscn (Pres. 1980–82). *Publications:* French Explorers in the Pacific 1966–69, The Fateful Voyage of the St Jean Baptiste (Wattie Book of the Year Award 1970) 1969, Norman Kirk: A Portrait 1972, Pacific Explorer 1985, New Zealand and the French 1990, The French and the Maoris 1992, Who's Who in Pacific Navigation 1992, The Journal of La Perouse 1994–95, I Remember Tomorrow 1998, Monsieur Baret: First Woman Around the World 2002, The Pacific Journal of Bougainville 2003, Storms and Dreams 2005, Where Fate Beckons 2006, Wild Cards 2006, Mrs Cook's Book of Recipes: For Mariners in Distant Seas 2006, From Venus to Antarctica: The Life of Dumont D'Urville 2007, Catalogus Librorum in Quavis Lingua & Facultate Insignium Instructissimarum Bibliothecarum Tum Clarissimi Doctissimique Viri D. Doctoris Benjaminis Wo 2010; contrib. to numerous learned journals and periodicals. *Honours:* Chevalier de la Légion d'honneur 1976, Officier 2007, New Zealand Commemoration Medal 1990, Companion New Zealand Order of Merit 2001; Hon. DLitt (Massey Univ.) 2006; New Zealand Book of the Year 1970, Academic Palms 1986, Massey Medal 1993.

DUNN, Douglas Eaglesham, OBE, BA, FRSL; Scottish poet and academic; *Professor of Creative Writing, University of St Andrews*; b. 23 Oct. 1942, Inchinnan; s. of William D. Dunn and Margaret McGowan; m. 1st Lesley B. Wallace 1964 (died 1981); m. 2nd Lesley Jane Bathgate 1985; one s. one d. *Education:* Univ. of Hull. *Career:* full-time writer 1971–91; Writer-in-Residence, Duncan of Jordanstone Coll. of Art and Dundee Dist Libraries 1986–88; Fellow in Creative Writing, Univ. of St Andrews 1989–91, Prof. 1991–, Head School of English 1994–99; Dir St Andrews Scottish Studies Inst. 1992–; Hon. Visiting Prof., Dundee Univ. 1987–89; mem. Scottish PEN. *Publications:* Terry Street (Somerset Maugham Award 1972) 1969, The Happier Life 1972, New Poems 1972–73 (ed.) 1973, Love or Nothing (Faber Memorial Prize 1976) 1974, A Choice of Byron's Verse (ed.) 1974, Two Decades of Irish Writing (criticism) 1975, The Poetry of Scotland (ed.) 1979, Barbarians 1979, St Kilda's Parliament (Hawthornden Prize 1982) 1981, Europa's Lover 1982, A Rumoured City: New Poets from Hull (ed.) 1982, To Build a Bridge: A Celebration of Humberside in Verse (ed.) 1982, Elegies (Whitbread Poetry Award and Whitbread Book of the Year 1986) 1985, Secret Villages (short stories) 1985, Selected Poems 1986, Northlight 1988, New and Selected Poems 1989, Poll Tax: The Fiscal Fake 1990, Andromache 1990, The Essential Browning (ed.) 1990, Scotland. An Anthology (ed.) 1991, Faber Book of Twentieth Century Scottish Poetry (ed.) 1992, Dante's Drum-Kit 1993, Boyfriends and Girlfriends (short stories) 1995, Oxford Book of Scottish Short Stories (ed.) 1995, The Donkey's Ears, The Year's Afternoon 2000, 20th Century Scottish Poems (ed.) 2000, The Faber Browning 2004. *Honours:* Hon. Fellow, Humberside Coll. 1987; Hon. LLD (Dundee) 1987; Hon. DLitt (Hull) 1995; Cholmondeley Award 1989. *Address:* School of English, The University of St Andrews, St Andrews, Fife, KY16 9AL, Scotland (office). *Telephone:* (1334) 462666 (office). *Fax:* (1334) 462655 (office). *E-mail:* ded@st-andrews.ac.uk (office). *Website:* www.st-andrews.ac.uk/~www_se (office).

DUNN, John Montfort, BA, FBA, FSA, AcSS; British political theorist; *Professor of Political Theory Emeritus, University of Cambridge*; b. 9 Sept. 1940, Fulmer; s. of Brig. Henry G. M. Dunn and Catherine M. Kinloch; m. 1st Susan D. Fyvel 1965; m. 2nd Judith F. Bernal 1971; m. 3rd Ruth Ginette Scurr 1997; two s. (one deceased) two d. *Education:* Winchester Coll., Millfield School, King's Coll., Cambridge and Harvard Univ., USA. *Career:* Grad. School of Arts and Sciences; Official Fellow in History, Jesus Coll., Cambridge 1965–66; Fellow, King's Coll., Cambridge 1966–, Coll. Lecturer, Dir of Studies in History 1966–72; Lecturer in Political Science, Univ. of Cambridge 1972–77, Reader in Politics 1977–87, Prof. of Political Theory 1987–2007, Emer. 2007–; Visiting Lecturer, Univ. of Ghana 1968–69; Chair. Section P. (Political Studies), British Acad. 1994–97, Bd of Consultants, Kim Dae-Jung Peace Foundation for the Asia-Pacific Region 1994–; Distinguished Visiting Prof., Univs of Tulane, Minnesota, Yale; mem. Council of British Acad. 2004–07. *Publications:* The Political Thought of John Locke 1969, Modern Revolutions 1972, Dependence and Opportunity (with A. F. Robertson) 1973, Western Political Theory in the Face of the Future 1979, Political Obligation in its Historical Context 1980, Locke 1984, The Politics of Socialism 1984, Rethinking Modern Political Theory 1985, The Economic Limits to Modern Politics (ed.) 1990, Interpreting Political Responsibility 1990, Storia delle dottrine politiche 1992, Democracy: The Unfinished Journey (ed.) 1992, Contemporary Crisis of the Nation State? (ed.) 1994, The History of Political Theory 1995, Great Political Thinkers (21 vols, co-ed.) 1997, The Cunning of Unreason 2000, Pensare la Politica 2002, Locke: A Very Short Introduction 2003, Setting the People Free: The Story of Democracy 2005, Exploring Utopian Futures of Politics (with Inwon Choue and John Ikenberry) 2008. *Honours:* hon. foreign mem. American Acad. of Arts and Sciences 1991. *Address:* King's College, Cambridge, CB2 1ST (office); The Merchant's House, 31 Station Road, Swavesey, Cambridge, CB4 5QJ, England (home). *Telephone:* (1223) 331258 (office); (1954) 231451 (home). *Fax:* (1223) 331315 (office). *E-mail:* jmd24@cam.ac.uk (office).

DUNN, Stephen, BA, MA; American poet and writer; *Distinguished Professor of Creative Writing, Richard Stockton College of New Jersey*; b. 24 June 1939, New York, NY; m. 1st Lois Kelly 1964 (divorced); two d.; m. 2nd Barbara Hurd 2003. *Education:* Hofstra Univ., New School for Social Research, New York, Syracuse Univ. *Career:* Asst Prof., Southwest Minnesota State Coll., Marshall 1970–73; Visiting Poet, Syracuse Univ. 1973–74, Univ. of Washington at Seattle 1980; Assoc. Prof. to Prof. Richard Stockton Coll. of NJ 1974–90, Distinguished Prof. of Creative Writing 1990–; Adjunct Prof. of Poetry, Columbia Univ. 1983–87. *Publications:* poetry: Five Impersonations 1971, Looking for Holes in the Ceiling 1974, Full of Lust and Good Usage 1976, A Circus of Needs 1978, Work and Love 1981, Not Dancing 1984, Local Time 1986, Between Angels 1989, Landscape at the End of the Century 1991, New and Selected Poems, 1974–1994 1994, Loosestrife 1996, Riffs and Reciprocities 1998, Different Hours 2000, Local Visitations 2003, Everything Else in the World 2006, What Goes On: Selected and New Poems, 1995–2009 2009; other: Walking Light: Essays and Memoirs 1993; contributions: periodicals. *Honours:* Acad. of American Poets Prize 1970, National Endowment for the Arts Fellowships 1973, 1982, 1989, Bread Loaf Writers Conference Robert Frost Fellowship 1975, Theodore Roethke Prize 1977, New Jersey Arts Council Fellowships 1979, 1983, Helen Bullis Prize 1982, Guggenheim Fellowship 1984, Levinson Prize 1988, Oscar Blumenthal Prize 1991, James Wright Prize 1993, American Acad. of Arts and Letters Award 1995, Pulitzer Prize in Poetry 2001. *Address:* Richard Stockton College of New Jersey, PO Box 195, Pomona, NJ 08240, USA (office). *Telephone:* (609) 652-1776 (office). *E-mail:* webmaster@stockton.edu (office). *Website:* www.stockton.edu (office).

DuNOUR, Shlomo; Israeli writer and teacher; b. 1921, Łodz, Poland; m. Mirian DuNour (deceased). *Career:* moved to Palestine 1938; fmr leader of the Aliyat Ha Noar Movement; fmr teacher, Dept of History, Hebrew Univ., Univ. of Haifa. *Publications include:* novels: Yet Another (Newman Prize) 1978, Adiel (co-author) (Jerusalem Literary Prize) 2001. *Honours:* Newman Prize 1978, Jerusalem Prize for Literature 1999.

DUONG, Thu Huong; Vietnamese writer and screenwriter; b. 3 Jan. 1947, Thai Binh Prov.; m. 1968 (divorced 1981); one s. one d. *Education:* Ecole de Théorie Professionnelle, Ministry of Culture and Ecole de Formation Littéraire Nguyen Du. *Career:* volunteer, Cultural Activities, Binh Tri Thien 1968–77; film studio work, North Viet Nam 1977–; first female combatant/war corresp. at front when China attacked Viet Nam in 1979; mem. Exec. Cttee Asscn des Cinéastes 1989; books banned in Viet Nam; expelled from Vietnamese CP 1989, imprisoned without trial for speech advocating political reform April 1991, accused by Vietnamese Govt of collaborating with "reactionary organizations" and smuggling "secret documents" out of the country; recognized by PEN Writers' Club, Amnesty International and other human rights orgs as a political prisoner; her arrest and imprisonment sparked int. protest; released from prison 1991; currently lives in France. *Publications in translation:* Beyond Illusions 1987 (trans. 2002), Paradise of the Blind 1988 (trans. 1991), Fragments of a Life 1989, Novel Without a Name (trans. 1995), Memories of a Pure Spring (trans. 2000), No Man's Land 2005, Dinh Cao Choi Loi (translated into French as Au zénith) 2009; four scripts, one children's novel, ten collections of stories. *Honours:* Chevalier, Ordre des Arts et des Lettres 1994; First Prize, Concours de récit 1979, Gold Medal, two Silver Medals, Vietnamese Film Festivals for feature films scripted, Prince Claus Foundation Award 1999, Premio Grinzane Cavour 2005. *Literary Agent:* c/o Susanna Lea Associates, 28 rue Bonaparte, Paris 75006, France. *Telephone:* 1-53-10-28-40. *Fax:* 1-53-10-28-49. *E-mail:* postmaster@susannalea.com. *Website:* www.susannaleaassociates.com.

DUQUESNE, Jacques Henri Louis, LenD; French journalist and writer; b. 18 March 1930, Dunkerque; s. of Louis Duquesne and Madeleine Chevalier; m. Edith Dubois 1954; one s. one d. *Education:* Coll. Jean-Bart, Dunkirk, Faculté de Droit, Paris, Institut d'Études Politiques, Paris. *Career:* reporter, La Croix 1957–64; Deputy Dir Panorama Chrétien 1964–70, head of investigations 1967; Asst Ed.-in-Chief, L'Express 1970–71; Co-founder and Asst Ed.-in-Chief, Le Point 1972–74, Ed.-in-Chief 1974–77, Pres.-Dir-Gen. 1985–90; Dir-Gen. La Vie Catholique group of publs 1977–79; news reporter, Europe No. 1 1969–97, La Croix 1983–, Midi Libre 1997–; Chair. Bd L'Express 1997–2005; mem. Jury, Prix Interallié 1986–. *Publications:* L'Algérie ou la guerre des mythes 1959, Les 16–24 ans 1964, Les prêtres 1965, Les catholiques français sous l'occupation 1966, Demain une Eglise sans prêtres 1968, Dieu pour l'homme d'aujourd'hui 1970, La gauche du Christ 1972, Les 13–62 ans 1974, La grande triche 1977, Une voix, la nuit 1979, La rumeur de la ville 1981, Maria Vadamme 1983, Alice Van Meulen 1985, Saint-Eloi 1986, Au début d'un bel été 1988, les Vents du Nord m'ont dit 1989, Catherine Courage 1990, Jean Bart 1992, Laura C. 1994, Jésus 1994, Théo et Marie 1996, les Années Jean-Paul II 1996 (jtly), Le Dieu de Jésus 1997, Le Bonheur en 36 vertus, Romans du Nord 1999, Les Héritières 2000, Pour comprendre la guerre d'Algérie 2001, Et pourtant nous étions heureux 2003, Marie 2004, Dieu malgré tout 2005, Judas, le deuxieme jour 2007, Le mal d'Algérie 2011. *Honours:* Chevalier, Légion d'honneur. *Address:* 13 rue de Poissy, 75005 Paris, France (home). *Telephone:* 1-43-54-32-41 (home).

DURAN COHEN, Ilan, MFA; French film director, screenwriter and novelist; b. 1963. *Education:* New York Univ. Film School, USA. *Career:* lives and works in Paris, France. *Television:* Les Amants du Flore (movie) 2006. *Films:* Lola Zipper (writer, dir) 1991, La confusion des genres (writer, dir, producer) 2000, Les petits fils (writer, dir, producer) 2004, Les amants du Flore (dir) 2006, Le Plaisir de Chanter (writer, dir, assoc. producer) 2008, Face Aux Masses: Roman 2008. *Radio:* Reality Zoo (France Culture). *Publications:* novels: Chronique alicienne 1997, Le Fils de la sardine 1999, Mon cas personnel 2002. *Honours:* Horizon Prize, Venice Film Festival 2004. *Address:* Fugitive Productions, 9 rue Charles Lecocq, 75015 Paris, France (office). *Telephone:* 1-53-53-07-55 (office). *Fax:* 1-45-61-27-97 (office). *E-mail:* fugitiveprod@wanadoo.fr (office).

DURAND, Claude; French publisher; *Chairman and CEO, Librairie Arthème Fayard*; b. 9 Nov. 1938, Livry-Gargan (Seine-et-Oise); s. of Félix Durand and Suzanne Durand (née Thuret); m. Carmen Perea 1965; two s. *Education:* Ecole normale d'instituteurs de Versailles. *Career:* fmr schoolteacher; Literary Dir Editions du Seuil 1965–78; Gen. Man. Editions Grasset 1978–80; Chair. and CEO Librairie Arthème Fayard 1980–, Librairie Stock 1991–98; Chair. Bd of Dirs Inst. Mémoire de l'édition contemporaine 1990–93, Deputy Chair. 1993–; Pres. Pre-Production Revenues Comm., Centre National de la Cinématographie 2005–. *Publication:* La Nuit zoologique (novel, Prix Médicis) 1979. *Honours:* Officier, Légion d'honneur, Chevalier, Ordre nat. du Mérite, Commdr des Arts et des Lettres. *Address:* Librairie Fayard, 13 rue du Montparnasse, 75006 Paris (office); 46 rue de Naples, 75008 Paris, France (home). *Telephone:* 1-45-49-82-00 (office). *E-mail:* presse@editions-fayard.fr (office). *Website:* www.fayard.fr (office).

DURBAN, (Rosa) Pam, BA, MFA; American academic and writer; *Doris Betts Distinguished Professor of Creative Writing, Department of English and Comparative Literature, University of North Carolina at Chapel Hill*; b. 4 March 1947, Aiken, South Carolina; m. Frank H. Hunter 1983. *Education:* Univ. of North Carolina, Greensboro, Univ. of Iowa. *Career:* Ed. Atlanta Gazette 1974–75; Visiting Asst Prof. of Creative Writing, State Univ. of New York, Geneseo 1979–80; Asst Prof. of Creative Writing, Murray State Univ. 1980–81; Assoc. Prof. of Creative Writing, Ohio Univ. 1981–86; Prof. of English and Creative Writing, Georgia State Univ. 1986–2001; Doris Betts Distinguished Prof. of Creative Writing, Dept of English and Comparative Literature, Univ. of North Carolina at Chapel Hill 2000–; contribs to Atlanta Gazette 1974–75; Founding Co-ed. Five Points. *Publications:* All Set About with Fever Trees and Other Stories 1985, The Laughing Place 1993, So Far Back (Lillian Smith Book Award 2001) 2000; contribs to anthologies and periodicals. *Honours:* Rinehart Award in Fiction, Rinehart Foundation 1984, Whiting Writer's Award 1987, Townsend Prize for Fiction 1994. *Address:* Department of English and Comparative Literature, University of North Carolina at Chapel Hill, Greenlaw Hall, CB 3520, Chapel Hill, NC 27599-3520, USA (office). *Telephone:* (919) 962-4006 (office). *E-mail:* durban@email.unc.edu (office). *Website:* englishcomplit.unc.edu/people/durbanp (office).

DURBEN, Maria-Magdalena; German writer; b. 8 July 1935, d. of Bernhard Block and Eva Block (née Klein); m. 2nd Wolfgang Durben 1967. *Education:* studied in Erfurt and Berlin. *Career:* writes in collaboration with Wolfgang Durben. *Publications:* Ein Stückchen von Gott, Gruß an Taiwan, Wenn der Schnee fällt, Da schrie der Schatten fürchterlich, Schaukle am blauen Stern, Unterm Glasnadelzelt: Gedichte 1976, Roter Rausch und weiße Haut, Wenn das Feuer fällt, Wenn die Asche fällt 1977, Lichtrunne, Zwischen Knoblauch und Chrysanthemen 1979, Haiku mit Stäbchen: Japan-Abenteuer, Reise auf einer Teewolke 1980. *Honours:* Dr hc (Gdańsk, Poland) 1977, (New York); Hon. DLitt (Karachi) 1978, (World Acad. of Languages and Literature, São Paulo, Brazil) 1978, (World Acad. of Arts and Culture, Taipei) 1979; numerous awards. *Address:* Schulstr. 8–10, 66701 Beckingen, Germany.

DURKIN, Barbara Rae Wernecke, AA, BS; American writer; b. 13 Jan. 1944, Baltimore, MD; m. William J. Durkin 1973, two s. *Education:* Essex Community College, Towson State College, Morgan State College, John Hopkins University. *Career:* mem. American PEN Women, International Women's Writing Guild. *Publications:* Oh, You Dundalk Girls, Can't You Dance the Polka? 1984, Visions and Viewpoints (ed.) 1993. *Honours:* American Library Asscn Best of 1984 List 1984.

DURRANI, Tehmina; Pakistani writer; b. 18 Feb. 1953, d. of S. U. Durrani; m. 1st Anees; m. 2nd Ghulam Mustafa Khar (divorced); two d.; m. 3rd Mian Shahbaz Sharif 2005. *Career:* currently associated with Ana Hadjra Labaek (NGO that works for the rehabilitation of battered wives). *Publications:* My Feudal Lord (autobiography), Mirror to the Blind 1996, Blasphemy 1998. *Address:* c/o Ana Hadjra Labaek, Lahore, Pakistan.

DÜRRSON, Werner, PhD; German poet, writer, dramatist and translator; b. 12 Sept. 1932, Schwenningen am Neckar. *Education:* Trossingen, Tübingen, Munich. *Career:* has taught at several univs in France and Germany; mem. Asscn Internationale des Critiques littéraires, Paris, Asscn of German Writers, PEN. *Publications:* Dreizehn Gedichte (poems) 1965; Schatten=geschlecht (poems) 1966; Drei Dichtungen (poems) 1970; Schubart (play) 1980, Stehend bewegt (poem) 1980, Der Luftkünstler (prose) 1983, Wie ich lese? (essay) 1986, Ausleben (selection of poems) 1988, Abbreviaturen (aphorisms) 1989, Werke (poetry and prose, four vols) 1992, Ausgewählte Gedichte (poems) 1995, The Kattenhorn Silence (trans. by Michael Hamburger) 1995, Stimmen aus der Gutenberg-Galaxis (literary essays) 1997, Der verkaufte Schatten 1997, Wasserspiele (poems) 1999, Pariser Spitzen (poems) 2001, Aufgehobene Zeit 2002, Schillerknochen (poem) 2005; several works in co-operation with painters, including Klaus Staeck, Erich Heckel, HAP Grieshaber, Jonny Friedlaender, and musicians, including Klaus Fessmann; trans of authors, including Guillaume d'Aquitaine, Marguerite de Navarre, Stéphane Mallarmé, Arthur Rimbaud, Yvan Goll, René Char and Henri Michaux; contrib. to anthologies and radio. *Honours:* South West German Press Lyric Poetry Prize

1953, German Awards for Short Stories 1973, 1983, Literary Prize, Stuttgart 1978, Literary Prize, Überlingen 1985, Bundesverdienstkreuz 1993, Prize of the Schiller Foundation, Weimar 1997, Eichendorff Literary Prize 2001, Villa Massimo, Rome 2004. *Address:* Schloss Neufra, 88499 Riedlingen/Donau, Germany (home). *Telephone:* 73714242 (home). *E-mail:* wernerdurrson@aol.com (home).

DWORKIN, Ronald Myles, FBA; American legal scholar, philosopher and writer; *Professor of Law, New York University*; b. 11 Dec. 1931, s. of David Dworkin and Madeline Talamo; m. Betsy Celia Ross 1958 (died 2000); one s. one d. *Education:* Harvard Coll., Oxford Univ., UK, Harvard Law School. *Career:* Legal Sec. to Judge Learned Hand 1957–58; Assoc., Sullivan & Cromwell, New York 1958–62; Assoc. Prof. of Law, Yale Law School 1962–65, Prof. 1965–68, Wesley N. Hohfeld Prof. of Jurisprudence 1968–69; Prof. of Jurisprudence, Oxford Univ. 1969–98, now Emer., Fellow, Univ. Coll. 1969–98, now Emer.; Quain Prof. of Jurisprudence, Univ. Coll., London 1998–2004, Bentham Prof. of Law and Philosophy 2004–; Visiting Prof. of Philosophy, Princeton Univ. 1974–75; Prof. of Law, New York Univ. Law School 1975–; Prof.-at-Large, Cornell Univ. 1976–80; Visiting Prof. of Philosophy and Law, Harvard Univ. 1977, of Philosophy 1979–82; mem. Council, Writers and Scholars Educational Trust 1982–, Programme Cttee, Ditchley Foundation 1982–; Co-Chair. US Democratic Party Abroad 1972–76; Fellow, American Acad. of Arts and Sciences 1979. *Publications:* Taking Rights Seriously 1977, The Philosophy of Law (Ed.) 1977, A Matter of Principle 1985, Law's Empire 1986, Philosophical Issues in Senile Dementia 1987, A Bill of Rights for Britain 1990, Life's Dominion 1993, Freedom's Law 1996, Sovereign Virtue 2000, Justice in Robes 2006; articles in legal and philosophical journals. *Honours:* Hon. Queen's Counsel; Hon. LLD (Williams Coll.) 1981, (John Jay Coll. of Criminal Justice) 1983, (Claremont Coll.) 1987, (Kalamazoo Coll.) 1987; Holberg Int. Memorial Prize 2007. *Address:* New York University School of Law, 4111 Vanderbilt Hall, 40 Washington Square South, New York, NY 10012, USA (office); 17 Chester Row, London, SW1W 9JF, England (home). *Telephone:* (212) 998-6248 (office). *Fax:* (212) 995-4526 (office). *E-mail:* ronald.dworkin@nyu.edu (office). *Website:* its.law.nyu.edu/facultyprofiles (office).

DWYER, Deanna (see Koontz, Dean Ray)

DWYER, K. R. (see Koontz, Dean Ray)

DYBEK, Stuart, BS, MA, MFA; American poet, writer and academic; *Distinguished Writer-in-Residence, Northwestern University*; b. 10 April 1942, Chicago, Ill.; m. Caren Bassett 1966; one s. one d. *Education:* Loyola Univ., Univ. of Iowa. *Career:* teaching asst, Univ. of Iowa 1970–72, Teaching and Writing Fellow 1972–73; Prof. of English, Western Michigan Univ. 1974–2006; Guest Writer and Teacher, Michigan Council for the Arts' Writer in the Schools Program 1973–92; Faculty, Warren Wilson MFA Program in Creative Writing 1985–89; Visiting Prof. of Creative Writing, Princeton Univ. 1990, Univ. of California, Irvine 1995; Univ. of Iowa Writers' Workshop 1998; currently Distinguished Writer-in-Residence, Northwestern Univ.; numerous readings, lectures and workshops. *Publications:* Brass Knuckles (poems) 1979, Childhood and Other Neighbourhoods (short stories) 1980, The Coast of Chicago (short stories) 1990, The Story of Mist (short stories and prose poems) 1994, I Sailed with Magellan (novel) 2003, Streets in Their Own Ink (poems); contrib. to many anthologies and magazines. *Honours:* Soc. of Midwest Authors Award for Fiction 1981, 2004, Friends of American Literature Cliffdwellers Award for Fiction 1981, special citation PEN/Hemingway Prize Cttee 1981, Michigan Council for the Arts grants 1981, 1992, Guggenheim Fellowship 1982, Nat. Endowment for the Arts Fellowships 1982, 1994, Pushcart Prize 1985, O. Henry Prize 1985, Nelson Algren Prize 1985, Whiting Writers Award 1985, Arts Foundation of Michigan Arts Award 1986, American Acad. of Arts and Letters Award for Fiction 1994, PEN/Malamud Award 1995, Rockefeller Residency, Bellagio, Italy 1996, Lannan Writers Award 1998, Soc. of Midland Authors Award in Fiction 2003, REA Award for the Short Story 2007, MacArthur Fellowship 2007. *Address:* 320 Monroe, Kalamazoo, MI 49006, USA (home). *E-mail:* sdybek@earthlink.net (home).

DYER, Charles; British playwright, actor and director; b. 17 July 1928, Shrewsbury; m. Fiona 1960; three s. *Career:* acted in 250 plays. *Plays as writer:* Time, Murderer, Please 1956, Wanted – One Body! 1956, Prelude to Fury 1959, Red Cabbage and Kings 1960, Rattle of a Simple Man (Garrick, London, Booth Theatre, Broadway) 1962, Staircase (RSC, Aldwych, London, Biltmore Theatre, Broadway) 1966, Mother Adam (also dir, Royal Shakespeare Theatre, Stratford-upon-Avon, Arts Theatre, London) 1971, A Hot Godly Wind 1973, Futility Rites 1980, Lovers Dancing (Albery Theatre, London) 1982. *Film appearances:* The Loneliness of the Long-Distance Runner 1962, Rattle of a Simple Man 1964, The Knack 1965, How I Won the War 1967. *Film screenplays:* Rattle of a Simple Man 1964, Staircase 1969. *Publications:* Turtle in the Soup 1948, Who On Earth 1950, Poison in Jest 1952, Jovial Parasite 1955, Red Cabbage and Kings 1958, Rattle of a Simple Man (novel, play) 1962, Staircase (novel, play) 1966, Mother Adam 1970, Lovers Dancing 1982, Those Old Trombones (autobiographical novel) 2006, The Lonely Trilogy 2011. *Address:* Old Wob, Gerrards Cross, Bucks., SL9 8SF, England (home).

DYER, Geoff, FRSL; British writer; b. 5 June 1958, Cheltenham, England. *Education:* Corpus Christi Coll., Oxford. *Publications:* Ways of Telling (criticism) 1986, The Colour of Memory (novel) 1989, But Beautiful (novel) 1991, The Search (novel) 1993, The Missing of the Somme (non-fiction) 1994, Out of Sheer Rage (literary essay) 1997, Paris Trance (novel) 1998, Anglo-English Attitudes (essays) 1999, Yoga for People Who Can't be Bothered to Do It (non-fiction) 2003, The Ongoing Moment (non-fiction) 2005, Jeff in Venice, Death in Varanasi (Bollinger Everyman Wodehouse Award for Comic Fiction) 2009, Working the Room: Essays and Reviews 1999–2010 2010. Otherwise Known as the Human Condition: Slected Essays and Reviews 2011; contrib. to New York Times Book Revew, The American Scholar, LA Times, Granta, LA Weekly, Nerve, The Observer. *Honours:* Somerset Maugham Prize 1992, Lannan Literary Fellowship 2003, E.M. Forster Award, American Acad. of Arts and Letters 2006, ICP Infinity Award for Writing on Photography 2006. *Address:* c/o Little, Brown, Brettenham House, Lancaster Place, London, WC2E 7EN, England (office).

DYER, James Frederick, MA; British writer; b. 23 Feb. 1934, Luton, Beds., England. *Education:* Univ. of Leicester. *Career:* writer on archaeology and local history; Ed. Shire Archaeology 1974–2010; mem. Soc. of Authors, Royal Archaeological Inst., Soc. of Antiquaries, Beds. Historical Records Soc. *Publications:* Southern England: An Archaeological Guide 1973, Penguin Guide to Prehistoric England and Wales 1981, Discovering Archaeology in England and Wales 1985, Discovering Prehistoric England 1993, Ancient Britain 1995, The Stopsley Book 1998, The Stopsley Picture Book 1999, Rhubarb and Custard: The History of Luton Modern School 2004, Hillforts of England and Wales 2010. *Honours:* Hon. DArts (Luton) 1999, (Bedfordshire) 2010. *Address:* 6 Rogate Road, Luton, Beds., LU2 8HR, England (home). *Telephone:* (1582) 724808 (home). *E-mail:* fjdyer77@btinternet.com (office).

DYSON, Freeman John, FRS; American physicist and academic; *Professor Emeritus of Physics, Institute for Advanced Study*; b. 15 Dec. 1923, Crowthorne, England; s. of late Sir George Dyson and Lady Mildred (Atkey) Dyson; m. 1st Verena Huber 1950 (divorced 1958); one s. one d.; m. 2nd Imme Jung 1958; four d. *Education:* Cambridge and Cornell Univs. *Career:* Fellow of Trinity Coll., Cambridge 1946; Warren Research Fellow, Birmingham Univ. 1949; Prof. of Physics, Cornell Univ. 1951–53; Prof., Inst. for Advanced Study, Princeton 1953–94, Prof. Emer. 1994–; Chair. Fed. of American Scientists 1962; mem. NAS 1964–; Foreign Assoc. Acad. des Sciences, Paris 1989. *Publications:* Disturbing the Universe 1979, Weapons and Hope 1984, Origins of Life 1986, Infinite in All Directions 1988, From Eros to Gaia 1992, Imagined Worlds 1997, The Sun, The Genome and the Internet 1999, The Scientist as Rebel 2006, A Many-colored Glass 2007; papers in The Physical Review, Journal of Mathematical Physics, etc. *Honours:* Hon. DSc (City Univ., UK) 1981, (Oxford) 1997; Gifford Lecturer, Aberdeen 1985, Heineman Prize, American Inst. of Physics 1965, Lorentz Medal, Royal Netherlands Acad. 1966, Hughes Medal, Royal Soc. 1968, Max Planck Medal, German Physical Soc. 1969, Harvey Prize, Israel Inst. of Tech. 1977, Wolf Prize (Israel) 1981, Matteucci Medal, Rome 1990, Fermi Award (USA) 1994, Templeton Prize 2000. *Address:* Institute for Advanced Study, Princeton, NJ 08540 (office); 105 Battle Road Circle, Princeton, NJ 08540, USA (home). *Telephone:* (609) 734-8055 (office). *Fax:* (609) 951-4489 (office). *E-mail:* dyson@ias.edu (office). *Website:* www.sns.ias.edu/~dyson (office).

DZHAGAROV, Georgi; Bulgarian poet, playwright and politician; b. 1925, Byala, Sliven. *Education:* Maxim Gorky Literary Inst., Moscow. *Career:* Vice-Pres. State Council 1971–89; mem. Union of Bulgarian Writers (chair. 1966–72). *Plays include:* Prokurorat (The Public Prosecutor) 1964, Slanchev udar 1977. *Publications:* Moite Pesni (My Songs) 1954, Lirika (Lyrics) 1956, V minuti na mulchanie (During Moments of Silence) 1958, Stikhotvoreniya (Poems) 1969, Izpoved (Confession) 1984, Ptitsi sreshtu vyatura (Birds Against the Wind) 1985. *Honours:* Académie Française special prize for world poetry 1982. *Address:* c/o Sajuz na Balgarskite Pisateli, ul. A. Kancev 5, 1040 Sofia, Bulgaria.

DZIUBA, Ivan Mykhailovych; Ukrainian literary critic and academic; b. 26 July 1931, Mykolaivka, Ukraine; s. of Mykhailo Dzyuba and Olga Dzyuba; m. Marta Lenets 1963; one d. *Education:* Donetsk Pedagogical Inst. *Career:* ed. various journals and publs published by Ukrainian State Publishing House; published An Ordinary Man or a Petit Bourgeois as well as numerous samizdat articles in 1960s; expelled from Writers' Union 1972 after publication of Internationalism or Russification? (numerous edns); arrested 1972, sentenced to 5 years' imprisonment 1973; recanted and released Nov. 1973; Writers' Union membership restored 1980s; Academician, Nat. Acad. of Sciences of Ukraine 1992–, mem. Presidium 1997–; Academician-Sec. Dept of Literature, Language and Arts 1996–2004; Minister of Culture Dec. 1992–94; Sr Researcher, T. Shevchenko Inst. of Literature 1994–; Ed.-in-Chief Suchasnist (magazine) 1991–2003, Encyclopaedia of Modern Ukraine 1998–; Head of Cttee Tazas Shevchenko Nat. Ukrainian Award; freelance literary corresp. 1982–. *Publications:* 25 books including Between Politics and Literature 1998, Thirst 2001, Trap 2003; numerous articles on history and devt of Ukrainian literature and reform of former USSR. *Honours:* Order of Rising Sun (Japan) 2006; O. Biletski Prize 1987, Laureate, Shevchenko's Award 1991, Int. Antonovich Prize 1992, V. Zhabotinsky Prize 1996, Vernadsky Prize 2001. *Address:* Presidium of the National Academy of Sciences of Ukraine, 01601 Kyiv 30, Vladimirskaya St., 54 (office); Shevchenko Institute of Literature, 01601 Kyiv 1, vul.M.Hrushevskoho, 4 (office); Antonova str. 7, Apt 60, Kiev 03186, Ukraine (home). *Telephone:* (44) 235-09-81 (office); (44) 229-10-84 (office); (44) 248-41-77 (home). *Website:* www.nas.gov.ua (office).

E

EAGLETON, Terence (Terry) Francis, PhD, FBA; British academic; *Distinguished Professor of English Literature, Lancaster University*; b. 22 Feb. 1943, Salford, Lancs.; s. of Francis Paul Eagleton and Rosaleen Riley; m. 1st Elizabeth Rosemary Galpin 1966 (divorced 1976); two s.; m. 2nd Willa Murphy 1996; one s. one d. *Education:* Trinity Coll., Cambridge. *Career:* Fellow in English, Jesus Coll., Cambridge 1964–69; Tutorial Fellow, Wadham Coll., Oxford 1969–89; Lecturer in Critical Theory and Fellow of Linacre Coll., Oxford 1989–92; Thomas Warton Prof. of English Literature and Fellow of St Catherine's Coll., Oxford 1992–2001; fmr Prof. of Cultural Theory, Univ. of Manchester, John Edward Taylor Prof. of English Literature 2001–08; Distinguished Prof. of English Literature, Lancaster Univ. 2008–. *Film:* screenplay for Wittgenstein. *Plays:* St Oscar 1989, Disappearances 1998. *Publications:* Criticism and Ideology 1976, Marxism and Literary Criticism 1976, Literary Theory: an Introduction 1983, The Function of Criticism 1984, The Rape of Clarissa 1985, Against the Grain 1986, William Shakespeare 1986, The Ideology of the Aesthetic 1990, Ideology: An Introduction 1993, The Crisis of Contemporary Culture 1993, Heathcliff and the Great Hunger 1995, The Illusions of Postmodernism 1996, Literary Theory 1996, Crazy John and the Bishop and Other Essays on Irish Culture 1998, Scholars and Rebels in Ireland 1999, The Idea of Culture 2000, The Gatekeeper (autobiog.) 2001, Sweet Violence: The Idea of the Tragic 2002, Figures of Dissent (essays) 2003, After Theory 2003, The English Novel: An Introduction 2004, Holy Terror 2005, The Meaning of Life 2007, Trouble with Strangers: A Study of Ethics 2008, How to Read a Poem 2008, Reason, Faith and Revolution: Reflections on the God Debate 2009, On Evil 2010, Why Marx Was Right 2011; contribs to periodicals incl. London Review of Books. *Honours:* Hon. DLitt (Salford) 1994; Dr hc (Nat. Univ. of Ireland) 1995, (Santiago di Compostela) 1997; Irish Sunday Tribune Arts Award 1990. *Address:* Department of English and Creative Writing, County College, Lancaster University, Lancaster, LA1 4YD, England (office). *Website:* www.lancs.ac.uk/fass/english (office).

EARLEY, Tony, BA, MFA; American writer; *Samuel Milton Fleming Chair in English, Vanderbilt University*; b. 1961, San Antonio, TX; m. Sarah Earley. *Education:* Warren Wilson Coll., Univ. of Alabama at Tuscaloosa. *Career:* fmrly reporter, The Thermal Belt News Journal, Columbus, Sports Ed. and features writer, The Daily Courier, Forest City; fmr instructor, Carnegie-Mellon Univ., Univ. of Alabama; Asst Prof., Vanderbilt Univ. 1997–, now Samuel Milton Fleming Chair in English. *Publications include:* Charlotte (short story, in Harper's) 1992, The Prophet from Jupiter (short story, in Harper's) 1993, Here We Are in Paradise (short story collection) 1994, Jim the Boy (novel) 2000, Somehow Form a Family: Stories That are Mostly True (essays) 2001, The Blue Star (novel) 2008; contrib. to journals, including The New Yorker, Harper's, Esquire, and anthologies, including Best American Short Stories. *Honours:* PEN Syndicated Fiction Award 1993, Granta Best of Young American Novelists citation 1996. *Address:* English Department, 413 Benson Hall, Vanderbilt University, Nashville, TN 37235, USA (office). *Telephone:* (615) 322-2334 (office). *Fax:* (615) 343-8028 (office). *E-mail:* tony.l.earley@vanderbilt.edu (office). *Website:* www.vanderbilt.edu/english/tony_earley (office).

EARLS, Nick, MBBS; Australian writer, editor and physician; b. 8 Oct. 1963, Newtownards, Northern Ireland, UK; m. Sarah Garvey 1991. *Education:* Univ. of Queensland. *Career:* medical practitioner, Brisbane, Qld, Australia 1987–94; freelance writer 1988–; continuing Medical Education Ed., Medical Observer, Qld 1994–. *Publications include:* Passion (short stories) 1992, After January (young adult novel) (3M Talking Book of the Year Award, Young People's Category 1996, CBE-International Youth Library Notable Book, Munich 1997) 1996, Zigzag Street (novel) (Betty Trask Award 1998) 1996, Bachelor Kisses 1998, 48 Shades of Brown (young adult novel) 2000, Making Law for Clouds (young adult novel) 2002, Perfect Skin 2003, Solid Gold, World of Chickens, Monica Bloom (young adult novel) 2006, The Thompdon Gunner 2006, Joel and Cat Set the Story Straight (with Rebecca Sparrow) (young adult novel) 2007, The True Story of Butterfish 2009, The Fix 2011; contrib. of short fiction to anthologies, including Nightmares in Paradise. *Honours:* Queensland Writers Centre Centenary Medal 2003, Univ. of Queensland Alumnus of the Year 2006. *E-mail:* nickearls@optusnet.com.au (office). *Website:* www.nickearls.com.

EARLY, Gerald, BA, MA, PhD; American academic, writer and poet; *Merle Kling Professor of Modern Letters, Washington University in St Louis*; b. 21 April 1952, Philadelphia, Pa; m. Ida Haynes 1977; two d. *Education:* Univ. of Pennsylvania, Cornell Univ. *Career:* Instructor in Black Studies, Washington Univ. in St Louis 1982, Asst Prof. of Black Studies 1982–84, Asst Prof. of English and African and Afro-American Studies 1984–88, Assoc. Prof. 1988–90, Prof. 1990–, Dir, American Culture Studies Program 1990–96, Dir, African and Afro-American Studies Program 1992–99, Merle Kling Prof. of Modern Letters 1996–, Co-Dir, American Culture Studies Inst. 2000–02, Dir, Int. Writers Center 2001–03, Dir Center for Humanities 2003–; mem. Bd of Advisory Eds, American Quarterly, Journal of the American Studies Asscn 1993–96, American Studies, Univ. of Kansas 1993–, Nine: A Journal of Baseball History and Social Policy Perspectives 1994–, Journal of Sport History 1996–, The Oxford Companion to African-American Literature; mem. Advisory Bd, The Antioch Review 1994–, Gateway Heritage, the magazine of the Missouri Historical Soc. 1995–2002; mem. American Studies Asscn Council 1996–99; mem. Bd of Govs, Negro Leagues Baseball Museum, Kansas City 2002–; mem. Bd of Trustees, Negro Leagues Baseball Museum, Kansas City 1999–2002, Missouri Historical Soc. 2000–; mem. Jazz Study Group, Columbia Univ., organized by Robert O'Meally 1993–2002. *Publications include:* Tuxedo Junction: Essays on American Culture 1990, My Soul's High Song 1991, Lure and Loathing 1993, Daughters: One Family and Fatherhood 1994, The Culture of Bruising 1994, One Nation Under a Groove: Motown and American Culture 1994, How the War in the Streets is Won 1995, This is Where I Came In: Black America in the 1960s 2003, Best African American Fiction 2010 (co-ed.) 2009; contribs: essays, reviews and poetry to many journals including American Poetry Review, Northwest Review, Tar River Poetry, Raccoon, Seneca Review, Obsidian, Black American Literature Forum. *Honours:* Whiting Foundation Writers' Award 1988, CCLM-General Electric Foundation Award for Younger Writers 1988, Washington University's Arthur Holly Compton Faculty Award 1997, Phi Beta Kappa Evelyn and William Jaffe Medal for Distinguished Service to the Humanities 2006, Distinguished Service to Education Award 2007, Excellence in the Arts Award 2008; several fellowships. *Address:* Department of English, Washington University, Campus Box 1122, One Brookings Drive, St Louis, MO 63130 (office); 53 Jefferson Road, Webster Groves, MO 63119, USA (home). *Telephone:* (314) 935-5576 (office); (314) 963-0267 (home). *E-mail:* glearly@artsci.wustl.edu (office). *Website:* english.artsci.wustl.edu (office).

EASTAUGH, Kenneth; British critic and writer; b. 30 Jan. 1929, Preston, Lancs., England. *Career:* TV Critic, Daily Mirror 1965–67, show business writer 1967–70; Chief Show Business Writer, The Sun 1970–73; TV Columnist, The Times 1977; Film Critic, Prima Magazine 1976; Music Critic, Classical Music Weekly 1976; Chief Show Business Exec., Daily Star, London 1978–83. *Publications include:* The Event (TV play) 1968, Better Than a Man (TV play) 1970, Dapple Downs (radio serial) 1973–74, Awkward Cuss (play) 1976, Havergal Brian: The Making of a Composer (biog.) 1976, Coronation Street (TV series) 1977–78, The Carry On Book (cinema) 1978, Havergal Who? (TV documentary) 1980, Mr Love (novel, screenplay) 1986, Dallas (TV serial) 1989, Embers (play) 1998, The New Carry On Book 1998.

EATWELL, Baron (Life Peer), cr. 1992, of Stratton St Margaret in the County of Wiltshire; **John Leonard Eatwell,** PhD; British academic; *President, Queens' College, Cambridge*; b. 2 Feb. 1945, s. of Harold Jack Eatwell and Mary Eatwell; m. 1st Hélène Seppain 1970 (divorced); two s. one d.; m. 2nd Susan Elizabeth Digby 2006. *Education:* Headlands Grammar School, Swindon, Queens' Coll. Cambridge, Harvard Univ., USA. *Career:* Teaching Fellow, Grad. School of Arts and Sciences, Harvard Univ. 1968–69; Research Fellow, Queens' Coll. Cambridge 1969–70; Fellow, Trinity Coll. Cambridge 1970–96, Asst Lecturer, Faculty of Econs and Politics, Cambridge Univ. 1975–77, Lecturer 1977, currently Prof. of Financial Policy, Pres. Queens' Coll. 1997–; Visiting Prof. of Econs, New School for Social Research, New York 1982–96; Econ. Adviser to Neil Kinnock, Leader of Labour Party 1985–92; Opposition Spokesman on Treasury Affairs and on Trade and Industry, House of Lords 1992–93, Prin. Opposition Spokesman on Treasury and Econ. Affairs 1993–97; Trustee Inst. for Public Policy Research 1988–95, Sec. 1988–97, Chair. 1997–; Dir (non-exec.) Anglia TV Group 1994–2001, Cambridge Econometrics Ltd 1996–2007; Chair. Extemporary Dance Theatre 1990, Crusaid 1993–98, British Screen Finance Ltd 1997–2000 and assoc. cos; Gov. Contemporary Dance Trust 1991–95; Dir Arts Theatre Trust, Cambridge 1991–98, Bd, Securities and Futures Authority 1997–2001; mem. Bd Royal Opera House 1998–2006; Chair. Royal Ballet 1998–2001, Commercial Radio Cos Asscn 2000–04, British Library Bd 2001–06, Royal Opera House Pension Scheme 2007–, Consumer Panel, Classic FM 2007–; mem. Regulatory Decisions Cttee, FSA 2001–05, Econ. Affairs Cttee, House of Lords 2009–; Dir Cambridge Endowment for Research in Finance 2002–; Gov. Royal Ballet School 2003–06, Artsworks Ltd 2007–, SAV Credit Ltd 2008–. *Publications:* An Introduction to Modern Economics (with Joan Robinson) 1973, Whatever Happened to Britain? 1982, Keynes's Economics and the Theory of Value and Distribution (ed. with Murray Milgate) 1983, The New Palgrave: A Dictionary of Economics, 4 Vols 1987, The New Palgrave Dictionary of Money and Finance, 3 Vols 1992 (both with Murray Milgate and Peter Newman), Transformation and Integration: Shaping the Future of Central and Eastern Europe (jtly) 1995, Global Unemployment: Loss of Jobs in the '90s (ed.) 1996, Not "Just Another Accession": The Political Economy of EU Enlargement to the East (jtly) 1997, Global Finance at Risk: The Case for International Regulation (with L. Taylor) 2000, Hard Budgets, Soft States 2000, Social Policy Choices in Central and Eastern Europe 2002, International Capital Markets (with L. Taylor) 2002; articles in scientific journals. *Address:* The President's Lodge, Queens' College, Cambridge, CB3 9ET, England (home). *Telephone:* (1223) 335556 (home). *Fax:* (1223) 335555 (home). *E-mail:* president@queens.cam.ac.uk (office).

EAVES, Will; British writer, editor and teacher; *Assistant Professor, University of Warwick*; b. 1967, Bath. *Education:* King's Coll., Cambridge. *Career:* Arts Ed., The Times Literary Supplement 1995–2011; Asst Prof., Univ. of Warwick 2011–; Publr Brockwell Press. *Publications include:* The Oversight (novel) 2001, Nothing To Be Afraid Of (novel) 2005, Small Hours (poems) 2006, Sound Houses (poems) 2011, This Is Paradise (novel) 2012. *Address:* Department of English, University of Warwick, Warwick, CV4 7AL, England (office). *Website:* www.warwick.ac.uk (office).

EBADI, Shirin, JD; Iranian lawyer, human rights activist and academic; b. 1947, Hamadan; d. of Mohammad Ali Ebadi; m.; two d. *Education:* Univ. of Tehran. *Career:* apptd Judge (first and only woman) and Pres. of Tehran City Court 1974, forced to step down from bench after 1979 revolution, retd 1984; currently runs own law practice specializing in human rights; arrested on charges of "disturbing public opinion" 2000, received suspended sentence Sept. 2000; mem. Cttee for the Defence of Rights of the Victims of Serial Murders; Founder Soc. for Protecting the Rights of the Child, Centre for Defence of Human Rights; Lecturer in Law, Univ. of Tehran; Founding mem. Nobel Women's Initiative 2006. *Publications include:* The Rights of the Child: A Study of Legal Aspects of Children's Rights in Iran 1994, History and Documentation of Human Rights in Iran 2000, Iran Awakening 2006, Refugee Rights in Iran 2008; numerous other books and journal articles. *Honours:* Hon. LLD (Brown Univ.) 2004, (Univ. of British Columbia) 2004; Dr hc (Univ. of Maryland, College Park) 2004, (Univ. of Toronto) 2004, (Simon Fraser Univ.) 2004, (Univ. of Akureyri) 2004, (Australian Catholic Univ.) 2005, (Univ. of San Francisco) 2005, (Concordia Univ.) 2005, (Univ. of York) 2005, (Université Jean Moulin, Lyon) 2005, (Loyola Univ., Chicago) 2007, (New School Univ.) 2007; Human Rights Watch Award 1996, Rafto Prize 2001, Nobel Peace Prize (first Iranian and first Muslim woman) 2003, International Democracy Award 2004, Lawyer of the Year Award 2004, ranked 99th by Forbes magazine amongst 100 Most Powerful Women 2004, UCI Citizen Peacebuilding Award 2005, The Golden Plate Award, Acad. of Achievement 2005. *Address:* Society for Protecting the Rights of the Child, 26 Tenth Street, Nobakht Street, Tehran, Iran (office). *Website:* www.irsprc.org (office).

EBERT, Alan, BA, MA; American author; b. 14 Sept. 1935, New York, NY. *Education:* Brooklyn Coll., City Univ. of New York, Fordham Univ. *Career:* mem. American Soc. of Journalists and Authors. *Publications include:* The Homosexuals 1977, Every Body is Beautiful (with Ron Fletcher) 1978, Intimacies 1979, Traditions (novel) 1981, The Long Way Home (novel) 1984, Marriages (novel) 1987; contribs to Family Circle, Essence, Look, Us, Good Housekeeping.

EBERT, Roger Joseph, BS; American film critic, writer and lecturer; b. 18 June 1942, Urbana, Ill.; m. Chaz Hammelsmith 1992. *Education:* Univ. of Illinois, Univ. of Cape Town, SA, Univ. of Chicago. *Career:* reporter, News Gazette, Champaign-Urbana, I 1958–66; Instructor, Chicago City Coll. 1967–68; film Critic, Chicago Sun-Times 1967–, US Magazine 1978–79, WMAQ-TV, Chicago 1980–83, WLS-TV, Chicago 1984–, New York Post 1986–88, New York Daily News 1988–92, Compu Serve 1991–, Microsoft Cinemania 1994–97; Lecturer, Univ. of Chicago 1969–; Co-host, Sneak Previews, WTTW-TV, Chicago 1977–82; At the Movies, syndicated TV programme 1982–86; Siskel and Ebert, syndicated TV programme 1986–99; Ebert and Roeper and the Movies, syndicated TV programme 1999–; mem. Acad. of London, American Newspaper Guild, Nat. Soc. of Film Critics, Writers' Guild of America. *Publications include:* An Illini Century 1967, A Kiss is Still a Kiss 1984, Roger Ebert's Movie Home Companion (annual vols) 1986–93, subsequently Roger Ebert's Video Companion 1994–98, The Perfect London Walk (with Daniel Curley) 1986, Two Weeks in the Midday Sun: A Cannes Notebook 1987, The Future of the Movies: Interviews with Martin Scorsese, Steven Spielberg, and George Lucas (with Gene Siskel) 1991, Behind the Phantom's Mask 1993, Ebert's Little Movie Glossary 1994, The Future of the Movies: The Computer Insectiary (co-author) 1994, Roger Ebert's Book of Film 1996, Questions for the Movie Answer Man 1997, Roger Ebert's Movie Yearbook 1998–, Ebert's Bigger Little Movie Glossary 1999, I Hated, Hated, Hated This Movie 2000, The Great Movies 2003, The Great Movies II 2006, Your Movie Sucks 2007, Roger Ebert's Four-Star Reviews 1967–2007 2008, The Great Movies III 2010, Life Itself: A Memoir 2011; contribs to newspapers and magazines. *Honours:* Dr hc (Univ. of Colorado) 1993; Overseas Press Club Award 1963, Rotary Fellow 1965, Pulitzer Prize for Criticism 1975, Chicago Emmy Award 1979, Kluge Fellow in Film Studies, Univ. of Virginia 1995–96. *Address:* Chicago Sun Times, 350 North Orleans Street, 10th Floor, Chicago, IL 60654, USA (office). *E-mail:* feedback@rogerebert.com (office). *Website:* rogerebert.suntimes.com.

ÉBERT, Tibor, BA; Hungarian writer, poet and dramatist; b. 14 Oct. 1926, Bratislava, Czechoslovakia; m. Eva Gati 1968; one d. *Education:* Ferenc Liszt Acad. of Music, Eötvös Lóránd Univ., Budapest. *Career:* Dramaturg József Attila Theatre, Budapest 1984–85; Ed.-in-Chief Agora Publrs, Budapest 1989–92; Ed. Hirvivo Literary Magazine 1990–92; mem. PEN Club, Asscn of Hungarian Writers, Literary Asscn Berzsenyi. *Plays:* Les Escaliers, Musique de Chambre, Demosthenes, Esterhaźy, Bartók, Attila, Le Rout Casimir et Olivier, Le Tableau. *Publications:* Mikrodrámák 1971, Rosarium 1987, Kobayashi 1989, Legenda egy fúvószenekarról 1990, Jób könyve 1991, Fagyott Orpheusz (poems) 1993, Esö 1996, Egy város glóriája 1997, Bartók 1997, Eredök 1998, Éltem 1998, Drámák 2000, Bolyongás 2001, Vecseruye 2001, Kaleidoszkóp 2002, Álmomban 2002, Feljegyzcsék 2004, Tüzfalau 2006, Vár 2006, Örvényben 2011; contrib. numerous short stories, poems, dramas and essays to several leading Hungarian literary journals and magazines. *Honours:* Hon. mem. Franco-Hungarian Soc. 1980–; Order of Hungarian Repub. 1996; Bartók Prize 1987, Commemorative Medal, City of Pozsony-Pressburg-Bratislava 1991, Esterházy Prize 1993. *Address:* Csévi u 15c, 1025 Budapest, Hungary (home).

ECHENOZ, Jean Maurice Emmanuel; French writer; b. 26 Dec. 1947, Orange, Vaucluse; s. of Marc Echenoz and Annie Languin; one s. *Education:* Univ. of Aix-en-Provence, Sorbonne and Univ. of Paris. *Career:* professional writer 1979–. *Film:* Le Rose et le blanc (dir Robert Pansard-Besson) (co-script writer) (Prix Georges Sadoul) 1979. *Publications:* Le Méridien de Greenwich (Prix Fénéon 1980) 1979, Cherokee (Prix Médicis) 1983, L'Equipée malaise (trans. as Double Jeopardy) 1986, L'Occupation des sols 1988, Lac (Grand Prix du Roman de la Société des Gens de Lettres 1990, European Literature Prize, Glasgow 1990) 1989, Nous trois 1992, Les Grandes blondes (trans. as Big Blondes) (Prix Novembre) 1995, Un An 1997, Je m'en vais (trans. as I'm Gone) (Prix Goncourt) 1999, Jérôme Lindon 2001, Josué, Samuel, Daniel, Maccabées (trans. of Bible, jtly) 2001, Au piano (trans. as Piano) 2003, Ravel 2006, Courir (trans. as Running) 2008, Des éclairs (trans. as Lightning) 2010. *Honours:* Grand Prix du roman de la Ville de Paris 1997, Grand Prix de littérature Paul Morand de l' Acad. française 2007. *Address:* c/o Editions de Minuit, 7 rue Bernard-Palissy, 75006 Paris, France. *Website:* www.leseditionsdeminuit.com.

ECO, Umberto, PhD; Italian writer and academic; *Professor, University of Bologna*; b. 5 Jan. 1932, Alessandria, Piedmont; s. of Giulio Eco and Giovanna Bisio; m. Renate Ramge 1962; one s. one d. *Education:* Liceo Plana, Alessandria, Univ. degli Studi, Turin. *Career:* cultural ed. Italian TV (RAI), Milan 1954–59; mil. service 1958–59; Sr Non-fiction Ed., Bompiani, Milan 1959–75; Asst Lecturer in Aesthetics, Univ. of Turin 1956–63, Lecturer 1963–64; Lecturer, Faculty of Architecture, Univ. of Milan 1964–65; Prof. of Visual Communications, Univ. of Florence 1966–69; Prof. of Semiotics, Milan Polytechnic 1970–71; Assoc. Prof. of Semiotics, Univ. of Bologna 1971–75, Prof. 1975–, Dir Inst. of Communications Disciplines 1993–, Pres. Scuola Superiore di Studi Umanistici, f. School of Arts 2000; Visiting Prof. New York Univ. 1969–70, 1976, Northwestern Univ. 1972, Yale Univ. 1977, 1980, 1981, Columbia Univ. 1978, 1984; Columnist on L'Espresso 1965; Ed. VS 1971–; mem. Academia Europaea 1998–, Accademia dei Lincei 2010–. *Publications:* Il Problema Estetico in San Tommaso (trans. as The Aesthetics of Thomas Aquinas) 1956, Sviluppo dell'Estetica Medioevale (trans. as Art and Beauty in the Middle Ages) 1959, Opera Aperta 1962, Diario Minimo 1963, Apocalittici e Integrati 1964, L'Oeuvre Ouverte 1965, La Struttura Assente 1968, Il Costume di Casa 1973, Trattato di Semiotica Generale 1975, A Theory of Semiotics 1976, The Role of the Reader 1979, Il Nome della Rosa (novel, trans. as The Name of the Rose) 1981, Semiotics and the Philosophy of Language 1984, Sette anni di desiderio 1977–83 1984, Faith in Fakes 1986, Il pendolo di Foucault 1988, The Open Work 1989, The Limits of Interpretation 1990, Misreadings 1993, How to Travel with a Salmon and Other Essays 1994, L'isola del giorno prima (novel, trans. as The Island of the Day Before) 1995, The Search for the Perfect Language 1995, Serendipities 1997, Kant and the Platypus 1999, Baudolino (novel) 2000, Experiences in Translation 2000, Five Moral Pieces 2001, Mouse or Rat?: Translation as Negotiation 2003, On Beauty: A History of a Western Idea (ed.) 2004, The Mysterious Flame of Queen Loana 2005, Turning Back the Clock: Hot Wars and Media Populism (essays) 2007, On Ugliness 2007, An Infinity of Lists: From Homer to Pynchon 2009, The Prague Cemetery 2011. *Honours:* Hon. Fellow, Kellogg Coll., Univ. of Oxford; Chevalier de la Légion d'honneur, Ordre pour le Mérite, Cavaliere di Gran Croce (Italy); Hon. DLitt (Glasgow) 1990, (Kent) 1992 and numerous other hon. academic degrees; Medici Prize 1982, McLuhan Teleglobe Prize 1985, Crystal Award (World Econ. Forum) 2000, Prince of Asturias Prize for Communication and the Humanities 2000, UCLA Medal 2005, Manzoni Prize 2008. *Address:* Scuola Superiore Studi Umanistici, Via Marsala 26, Bologna, Italy (office). *Telephone:* (051) 2917111 (office). *E-mail:* sssub@dsc.unibo.it (office).

EDGAR, David Burman, BA; British writer; b. 26 Feb. 1948, Birmingham; s. of Barrie Edgar and Joan Edgar (née Burman); m. Eve Brook 1979 (died 1998); two step-s.; pnr Stephanie Dale. *Education:* Oundle School, Manchester Univ. *Career:* Fellow in Creative Writing, Leeds Polytechnic 1972–74; Resident Playwright, Birmingham Repertory Theatre 1974–75, Bd mem. 1985–; Lecturer in Playwriting, Univ. of Birmingham 1975–78, Dir of Playwriting Studies 1989–, Prof. 1995–99; Founder Writers' Union 1970s; UK/US Bicentennial Arts Fellow resident in USA 1978–79; Literary Consultant, RSC 1984–88; Fellow Birmingham Polytechnic 1991, Judith E. Wilson Fellow, Clare Hall, Cambridge 1996. *Plays:* Two Kinds of Angel 1970, Rent or Caught in the Act 1972, State of Emergency 1972, The Dunkirk Spirit 1974, Dick Deterred 1974, O Fair Jerusalem 1975, Saigon Rose 1976, Blood Sports 1976, Destiny (for RSC) 1976, Wreckers 1977, The Jail Diary of Albie Sachs (for RSC) 1978, Mary Barnes 1978–79, Teendreams 1979, The Adventures of Nicholas Nickleby (adaptation for RSC) 1980, Maydays (for RSC) 1983, Entertaining Strangers 1985, That Summer 1987, The Shape of the Table 1990, Dr Jekyll and Mr Hyde (adaptation for RSC) 1991, Pentecost 1994, Other Place 1994, Young Vic 1995, Albert Speer (adaptation for Nat. Theatre) 2000, The Prisoner's Dilemma 2001, Continental Divide 2003, Playing with Fire (Nat. Theatre, London) 2005, A Time to Keep 2007, Testing the Echo 2008. *TV Plays:* I Know What I Meant 1974, Baby Love 1974, Vote for Them 1989, Buying a Landslide 1992, Citizen Locke 1994. *Radio:* Ecclesiastes 1977, A Movie Starring Me 1991. *Film:* Lady Jane 1986. *Publications:* Destiny 1976, Wreckers 1977, Teendreams 1979, Maydays 1983, Plays One 1987, The Second Time as Farce 1988, Heartlanders 1989, Plays Two 1990, Plays Three 1991, Pentecost 1995, State of Play (ed.) 1999, Albert Speer 2000, The Prisoner's Dilemma 2001, Continental Divide 2004, Playing With Fire 2005. *Honours:* Hon. Sr Research Fellow, Univ. of Birmingham 1988–92, Hon. Prof.

1992–; Hon. MA (Bradford) 1986; DUniv (Surrey) 1993, (Birmingham) 2002; Soc. of West End Theatres Best Play Award 1980, Tony Award for Best Play 1981, Plays and Players Award for Best Play 1983, Evening Standard Award for Best Play 1995. *Literary Agent:* Alan Brodie Representation, 211 Piccadilly, London, W1J 9HF, England. *Telephone:* (20) 7917-2871. *Fax:* (20) 7917-2872. *E-mail:* info@alanbrodie.com. *Website:* www.alanbrodie.com.

EDGECOMBE, Jean Marjorie, AM, BA; Australian writer; b. 28 Feb. 1914, Bathurst, NSW; d. of Edwin Ray and Katie Helen Ray (née Hazlewood); m. Gordon Henry Edgecombe 1945; two d. two s. *Education:* Sydney Univ., Metropolitan Secretarial Coll., Sydney. *Career:* worked at Metropolitan Secretarial Coll., Sydney; joined Women's Australian Air Force 1943, served as Acting Flight Officer, Melbourne; mem. Australian Conservation Foundation, The Australian Museum Soc., Australian Soc. of Authors, Hornsby Shire Historical Soc., Nat. Trust of Australia (NSW), State Library of NSW Foundation, Wildlife Preservation Soc. Queensland, The Coast and Mountain Walkers of NSW. *Publications include:* Discovering Lord Howe Island (with Isobel Bennett) 1978, Discovering Norfolk Island (with Isobel Bennett) 1983, Flinders Island, the Furneaux Group 1985, Flinders Island and Eastern Bass Strait 1986, Lord Howe Island, World Heritage Area 1987, Phillip Island and Western Port 1989, Norfolk Island, South Pacific: Island of History and Many Delights 1991, Discovering Flinders Island 1992, Discovering King Island, Western Bass Strait 1993; contrib. of articles and poems to various publs. *Address:* 7 Oakleigh Avenue, Thornleigh, NSW 2120, Australia.

EDRIC, Robert (see Armitage, Gary Edric)

EDSON, Russell; American poet and writer; b. 9 April 1935; m. Frances Edson. *Education:* Art Students' League, New York, The New School, New York, Columbia Univ., Black Mountain Coll., NC. *Publications include:* poetry: Appearances: Fables and Drawings 1961, A Stone is Nobody's: Fables and Drawings 1964, The Boundary 1964, The Very Thing That Happens: Fables and Drawings 1964, The Brain Kitchen: Writings and Woodcuts 1965, What a Man Can See 1969, The Childhood of an Equestrian 1973, The Calm Theatre 1973, A Roof with Some Clouds Behind It 1975, The Intuitive Journey and Other Works 1976, The Reason Why the Closet-Man is Never Sad 1977, Edson's Mentality 1977, The Traffic 1978, The Wounded Breakfast: Ten Poems 1978, With Sincerest Regrets 1981, Wuck Wuck Wuck! 1984, The Wounded Breakfast 1985, Tick Tock 1992, The Tunnel: Selected Poems 1994, The Tormented Minor 2001, The Rooster's Wife 2005, See Jack 2009; fiction: Gulping's Recital 1984, The Song of Percival Peacock 1992. *Honours:* Guggenheim Fellowship 1974, Nat. Endowment for the Arts Grant 1976, and Fellowship 1982, Whiting Foundation Award 1989. *Address:* 29 Ridgeley Street, Darien, CT 06820-4110, USA (home). *Telephone:* (203) 655-1575 (home).

EDUGYAN, Esi; Canadian author; b. 1977, Calgary, Alberta; m. Steven Price. *Education:* Univ. of Victoria, Johns Hopkins Univ. *Publications include:* The Second Life of Samuel Tyne 2004, Half-Blood Blues (Scotiabank Giller Prize 2011, Ethel Wilson Fiction Prize 2012, Anisfield-Wolf Book Award 2012) 2011; also features in: Best New American Voices 2003, Revival: An Anthology of Black Canadian Writing 2006. *Literary Agent:* c/o Peter Straus, Rogers, Coleridge & White Ltd., 20 Powis Mews, London, W11 1JN, England. *Telephone:* (20) 7221-3717. *Fax:* (20) 7229-9084. *E-mail:* info@rcwlitagency .com. *Website:* www.rcwlitagency.com. *E-mail:* edugyan@gmail.com. *Website:* www.esiedugyan.com.

EDWARDS, Anne; American writer; b. (Anne Josephson), 20 Aug. 1927, Porchester, NY; d. of Milton Josephson and Marion Fistt Josephson; m. Stephen Citron; one s. one d. *Education:* Univ. of California, Los Angeles, Southern Methodist Univ. *Career:* Pres. Authors' Guild of America 1982–86; mem. Bd Emerita Authors' Guild 1986–2005. *Films:* Haunted Summer. *Plays:* One More Song (with Stephen Citron). *Publications include:* A Child's Bible (adaptation) 1967, The Survivors 1968, Miklos Alexandrovitch is Missing 1969, Shadow of a Lion 1970, The Hesitant Heart 1974, Judy Garland: A Biography 1974, Haunted Summer 1974, The Inn and Us (with Stephen Citron) 1975, Child of Night 1975, P. T. Barnum 1976, The Great Houdini 1977, Vivien Leigh: A Biography 1977, Sonya: The Life of the Countess Tolstoy 1981, The Road to Tara: The Life of Margaret Mitchell 1983, Matriarch: Queen Mary and the House of Windsor 1984, A Remarkable Woman: Katherine Hepburn 1985, Early Reagan: The Rise to Power 1986, The Demilles: An American Dynasty 1987, American Princess: A Biography of Shirley Temple 1988, Royal Sisters: Queen Elizabeth and Princess Margaret 1990, Wallis: The Novel 1991, The Grimaldis of Monaco: Centuries of Scandals, Years of Grace 1992, La Divina 1994, Throne of Gold: The Lives of the Aga Khans 1995, Streisand: It Only Happens Once 1996, Diana: The Life She Led 1999, Maria Callas: Her Life, Her Loves, Her Music 2001, The Reagans: Portrait of a Marriage 2003, Being an Expert Professional Practitioner: The Relational Turn in Expertise 2010; contrib. to Architectural Digest magazine. *Honours:* Birmingham Coll. Woman of Achievement Award, Birmingham, Ala 2002. *Literary Agent:* Curtis Brown Ltd, 10 Astor Place, New York, NY 10003, USA. *Telephone:* (212) 473-5400. *E-mail:* ejj@cbltd.com. *Website:* www.curtisbrown .com.

EDWARDS, F. E. (see Nolan, William Francis)

EDWARDS, (James) Griffith, CBE, DM, BSc, FRCP, FRCPsych, FMedSci; British psychiatrist and academic; *Emeritus Professor of Addiction Behaviour, Institute of Psychiatry, King's College, University of London;* b. 3 Oct. 1928, India; s. of the late J. T. Edwards and Constance Amy Edwards (née McFadyean); m. 1st 1969 Evelyn Morrison (divorced 1981); one s. two d. (one deceased); m. 2nd Frances Susan Stables 1981. *Education:* Andover Grammar School, Balliol Coll., Univ. of Oxford. *Career:* served RA 2nd Lt 1948–49; jr hosp. appointments, King George Ilford, St Bartholomew's, the Maudsley Hosp. 1956–62; worker, Inst. of Psychiatry 1962, Lecturer 1966, Sr Lecturer 1967; Dir Addiction Research Unit 1967–94; fmrly Chair. Nat. Addiction Centre; Prof. of Addiction Behaviour, Inst. of Psychiatry, King's Coll., Univ. of London 1979–94, Emer. Prof. 1994–; Ed. Addiction (formerly British Journal of Addiction) 1978–96, Ed.-in-Chief 1996–2004; Series Ed. Int. Monographs on the Addictions 1995–;. *Publications:* Alcohol: the Ambiguous Molecule 2000, Matters of Substance: Drugs and Why We Use Them 2004; papers on scientific and clinical aspects of addiction. *Honours:* Hon. Prof. Univ. of Chile 1992–; Jellinek Memorial Prize (int. award for alcohol research) 1981, Nathan B. Eddy Gold Medal (int. award for drug misuse research) 1996, Auguste Forrell Prize (European award for alcohol research) 1998. *Address:* c/o National Addiction Centre, Institute of Psychiatry, King's College London, De Crespigny Park, London, SE5 8AF (office); 32 Crooms Hill, London, SE10 8ER, England (home). *Telephone:* (20) 8858-5631 (home). *E-mail:* grifsu@crooms .freeserve.co.uk (home).

EDWARDS, Jorge; Chilean writer and diplomatist; b. 29 July 1931, Santiago. *Education:* Univ. of Chile, Princeton Univ., USA. *Career:* diplomatist 1957–73, Amb. to Cuba 1970, Advisory Minister in Paris 1971–73. *Publications:* (novels) El patio 1952, Gente de la ciudad 1962, Las máscaras 1967, Temas y variaciones 1969, Fantasmas de carne y hueso 1992, El peso de la noche 1965, Las máscaras 1967, Temas y variaciones 1969, Persona non grata 1973, Desde la cola del dragón 1977, Los convidados de piedra 1978, El museo de cera 1981, La mujer imaginaria 1985, El anfitrión 1988, Cuentos completos 1990, Adiós poeta 1990, El regalo 1991, Fantasmas de carne y hueso 1993, El whisky de los poetas 1994, El origen del mundo 1996, El sueño de la Historia 2000, Diálogos en un tejado 2003, El inútil de la familia 2005, La casa de Dostoievsky (Premio Iberoamericano Planeta–Casa de América de Narrativa) 2008. *Honours:* Literary Prize of the City of Santiago 1961, 1991, Atenea Prize of Univ. of Concepción (Chile), Essay Prize of the City of Santiago 1991, Cervantes Prize 1999. *Address:* c/o Alfaguara, Torrelaguna 60, 28043 Madrid, Spain.

EDWARDS, Josh (see Levinson, Leonard)

EDWARDS, Philip Walter, PhD, FBA; British academic; b. 7 Feb. 1923, Barrow-in-Furness; s. of the late R. H. Edwards and B. Edwards; m. 1st Hazel Valentine 1947 (died 1950); m. 2nd Sheila Wilkes 1952; three s. one d. *Education:* King Edward's High School, Birmingham, Univ. of Birmingham. *Career:* Lecturer in English, Univ. of Birmingham 1946–60; Prof. of English Literature, Trinity Coll. Dublin 1960–66; Visiting Prof., Univ. of Mich. 1964–65; Prof. of Literature, Univ. of Essex 1966–74; Visiting Prof., Williams Coll., Mass. 1969; Visiting Fellow, All Souls Coll., Oxford 1970–71; King Alfred Prof. of English Literature, Univ. of Liverpool 1974–90; Visiting Prof., Univ. of Otago, New Zealand 1980, Int. Christian Univ., Tokyo 1989. *Publications:* Sir Walter Raleigh 1953, The Spanish Tragedy (ed.) 1959, Shakespeare and the Confines of Art 1968, Massinger, Plays and Poems (ed. with C. Gibson) 1976, Pericles Prince of Tyre (ed.) 1976, Threshold of a Nation 1979, Hamlet Prince of Denmark (ed.) 1985, Shakespeare: A Writer's Progress 1986, Last Voyages 1988, The Story of the Voyage 1994, Sea-Mark: The Metaphorical Voyage, Spenser to Milton 1997, The Journals of Captain Cook (ed.) 1999, Pilgrimage and Literary Tradition 2005. *Address:* High Gillingrove, Gillinggate, Kendal, Cumbria, LA9 4JB, England (home). *Telephone:* (1539) 721298 (home).

EDWARDS, Robert John, CBE; British journalist; b. 26 Oct. 1925, Farnham, Surrey; s. of Gordon Edwards and Margaret Edwards (née Grain); m. 1st Laura Ellwood 1952 (dissolved 1972); two s. two d.; m. 2nd Brigid Segrave 1977. *Education:* Ranelagh School. *Career:* Ed. Tribune 1951–55; Deputy Ed. Sunday Express 1957–59; Ed. Daily Express 1961–62, 1963–65; Ed. Evening Citizen (Glasgow) 1962–63; Ed. Sunday People (fmrly The People) 1966–72; Ed. Sunday Mirror 1972–84; Dir Mirror Group Newspapers 1976–86, Sr Group Ed. 1984–85, Deputy Chair. (non-exec.) 1985–86; Chair. London Press Club Scoop of the Year Awards Panel 1990–2003; Ombudsman to Today newspaper 1990–95. *Publication:* Goodbye Fleet Street 1988. *Address:* Tregeseal House, Nancherrow, St Just, Penzance, TR19 7PW, England (home). *Telephone:* (1736) 787060 (home). *Fax:* (1736) 786617 (home). *E-mail:* edwardsrj@aol.com (home).

EGAN, Gregory Mark, BSc; Australian writer; b. 20 Aug. 1961, Perth, WA. *Education:* Univ. of Western Australia. *Publications include:* fiction: An Unusual Angle 1983, Quarantine 1992, Permutation City (John W. Campbell Memorial Award 1995) 1994, Distress 1995, Diaspora 1997, Teranesia 1999, Schild's Ladder 2002, Incandescence 2008, Zendegi 2010, The Clockwork Rocket 2011; short stories: Axiomatic 1995, Luminous 1998, Oceanic and other stories 2000, Reasons to be Cheerful and other stories 2003, Singleton 2006, Dark Integers 2008, Crystal Nights and other stories 2009; contribs to Interzone Magazine, Asimov's Science Fiction Magazine. *Honours:* Hugo Award 1999. *Address:* c/o Enquiries, Gollancz, Orion Publishing Group, Orion House, 5 Upper Martin's Lane, London, WC2H 9EA, England. *Website:* www .orionbooks.co.uk; www.gregegan.net.

EGAN, Jennifer; American novelist and writer; b. 1962, Chicago, m.; two s. *Publications include:* fiction: Look at Me 2001, The Invisible Circus (also film) 2007, The Keep 2008, Emerald City (short stories), A Visit from the Goon

Squad (Nat. Book Critics Circle Award 2011, Los Angeles Times Book Prize, Pulitzer Prize for Fiction 2011, Galaxy Nat. Book Award for Int. Author of the Year 2011) 2010; contrib. stories to The New Yorker, Harper's Magazine, GQ, Zoetrope, All-Story and Ploughshares, and non-fiction to The New York Times Magazine. *Honours:* Guggenheim Fellowship, Nat. Endowment for the Arts Fellowship, Dorothy and Lewis B. Cullman Fellowship at the New York Public Library, Carroll Kowal Journalism Award 2002, Nat. Alliance on Mental Illness Outstanding Media Award for Science and Health Reporting 2009. *Literary Agent:* Amanda Urban, International Creative Management, 825 Eighth Avenue, New York, NY 10019, USA. *Telephone:* (212) 556-5600 (office). *E-mail:* pholtzman@icmtalent.com (office). *Website:* www.icmtalent.com; jenniferegan.com.

EGGERS, Dave; American writer; m. Vendela Vida 2003. *Career:* Ed. Might magazine 1994–97, Timothy McSweeney's Quarterly Concern, or 'McSweeney's', journal and publishers 1998–. *Publications:* A Heartbreaking Work of Staggering Genius (memoir) 2000, You Shall Know Our Velocity (novel) 2003, The Future Dictionary of America (with Jonathan Safran Foer and Nicole Krauss) 2004, The Best of McSweeney's: Volume 1 (ed.) 2004, Volume 2 (ed.) 2005, How We Are Hungry 2005, What is the What: The Autobiography of Valentino Achak Deng: A Novel (Prix Médicis Étranger 2009) 2006, Zeitoun (LA Times Book Prize, Dayton Literary Peace Prize for Non-Fiction 2010) 2009, The Wild Things 2009, A Hologram for the King 2012; contrib. to periodicals. *Honours:* LA Times Innovators Award 2009. *Address:* McSweeney's, 849 Valencia Street, San Francisco, CA 94110, USA (office). *E-mail:* letters@mcsweeneys.net (office). *Website:* www.mcsweeneys.net (office).

EGLETON, Clive Frederick William; British writer and army officer (retd) and civil servant (retd); b. 25 Nov. 1927; m. Joan Evelyn Lane 1949 (died 1996); two s. *Education:* Staff Coll., Camberley. *Career:* mem. Crime Writers Asscn, Soc. of Authors. *Publications include:* A Piece of Resistance 1970, Last Post for a Partisan 1971, The Judas Mandate 1972, Seven Days to a Killing 1973, The October Plot 1974, Skirmish 1975, State Visit 1976, The Mills Bomb 1978, Backfire 1979, The Winter Touch 1981, A Falcon for the Hawks 1982, The Russian Enigma 1982, A Conflict of Interests 1983, Troika 1984, A Different Drummer 1985, Picture of the Year 1987, Gone Missing 1988, Death of a Sahib 1989, In the Red 1990, Last Act 1991, A Double Deception 1992, Hostile Intent 1993, A Killing in Moscow 1994, Death Throes 1994, A Lethal Involvement 1995, Warning Shot 1996, Blood Money 1997, Dead Reckoning 1999, The Honey Trap 2000, One Man Running 2001, Cry Havoc 2002, Assassination Day 2003, The Renegades 2005, The Sleeper 2005, The Loner 2006, The Presidential Affair 2006, Pandora's Box (Charles Winter) 2008. *Address:* Dolphin House, Beach House Lane, Bembridge, PO35 5TA, Isle of Wight (office). *Telephone:* (1983) 873893 (office). *Fax:* (1983) 872151 (office).

EGNER, Eugen; German writer, draughtsman and musician (electric guitar); b. 10 Oct. 1951, Ingelfingen. *Career:* contributed cartoons to Titanic and Der Rabe, Frankfurter Allgemeine Zeitung, Die Zeit, short stories to Der Rabe, Frankfurter Rundschau, taz, Berliner Zeitung; occasional activities in improvised music. *Radio:* plays for Westdeutscher Rundfunk; contributed music to Die Beseitigung (play for WDR Radio) with Band TseTse!. *Publications include:* Als die Erlkönige sich Freiheiten herausnahmen 1986, Aus dem Tagebuch eines Trinkers (trans. as From the Diary of an Alcoholic) 1991, Glücklich ist, wer vergißt, daß er nicht zu retten ist 1991, Das Blöken der Blumen 1992, Als der Weihnachtsmann eine Frau war und andere erstaunliche Geschichten 1992, Der künstliche Mann (trans. as The Artificial Man) 1992, Meisterwerke der grauen Periode 1992, Der Universums-Stulp 1993, Phrenesie-Album 1994, Wir brauchen Motoren, wir bauen sie selbst 1994, Getaufte Hausschuhe und Katzen mit Blumenmuster 1996, Was geschah mit der Pygmac-Expedition? 1996, Die Tagebücher des W. A. Mozart (trans. as The Diaries of W. A. Mozart) 1998, Androiden auf Milchbasis (trans. as Androids from Milk) 1999, Der Notfall erfordert alles 2000, Aus der Welt der Menschen 2001, Die Eisenberg-Konstante 2001, Die Durchführung des Luftraums 2002, Gift Gottes 2003, Darwins Lücke 2004, Als der Weihnachtsmann eine Frau war 2005, Das Schattenfräulein 2006, Was macht eigentlich Harry Absolut 2006, Nach Hause 2007, Schmutz 2008, Shuk 2008, Olga La Fong 2009, Die Traumdüse 2009. *Honours:* Kasseler Literaturpreis für Grotesken Humor 2003. *Address:* c/o Edition Phantasia, Joachim Körber, Wünschelstrasse 18, 76756 Bellheim, Germany. *E-mail:* mail@edition-phantasia.de. *Website:* www.edition-phantasia.de; www.eugenegner.com.

EHLE, John Marsden, Jr, BA, MA; American writer; b. 13 Dec. 1925, Asheville, NC; m. 1st Gail Oliver 1952 (divorced 1967); m. 2nd Rosemary Harris 1967; one d. *Education:* Univ. of North Carolina, Chapel Hill. *Career:* mem. Faculty, Univ. of North Carolina, Chapel Hill 1951–63; Special Asst to NC Gov. Terry Sanford 1963–64; Programme Officer, Ford Foundation, New York 1964–65; mem. White House Group for Domestic Affairs, Washington, DC 1964–66; Special Consultant, Duke Univ. 1976–80; mem. Authors' League, PEN, State of North Carolina Awards Comm. 1982–93. *Publications include:* fiction: Move Over, Mountain 1957, Kingstree Island 1959, Lion on the Hearth 1961, The Land Breakers 1964, The Road 1967, Time of Drums 1970, The Journey of August King 1971, The Changing of the Guard 1975, The Winter People 1981, Last One Home 1983, The Widows Trial 1989; non-fiction: The Free Men 1965, The Survivor 1968, Trail of Tears: The Rise and Fall of the Cherokee Nation 1988, Dr Frank: Living with Frank Porter Graham 1993; screenplay: The Journey of August King 1995. *Honours:* Hon. DLitt 1999; Walter Raleigh Prizes for Fiction, North Carolina Dept of Cultural Affairs 1964, 1967, 1970, 1975, 1984, Mayflower Soc. Cup 1965, State of North Carolina Award for Literature 1972, North Carolina Gov.'s Award for Distinguished Meritorious Service 1978, Lillian Smith Prize, Southern Regional Council 1982, Distinguished Alumnus Award, Univ. of North Carolina at Chapel Hill 1984, Thomas Wolfe Memorial Award, Western North Carolina Historical Asscn 1984, W.D. Weatherford Award, Berea Coll. 1985, Caldwell Award, North Carolina Humanities Council 1995. *Address:* 125 Westview Drive NW, Winston-Salem, NC 27104, USA (home).

EHRENREICH, Barbara, PhD; American writer; b. 26 Aug. 1941. *Education:* Reed Coll., Rockefeller Univ., New York. *Career:* columnist, TIME magazine 1991–97, The Progressive; teacher of essay-writing, Grad. School of Journalism, Univ. of California, Berkeley 1998, 2000; guest columnist, New York Times 2004; currently contributing writer Time magazine; f. United Professionals (non-profit org.) 2006; mem. Bd of Dirs Nat. Org. for the Reform of Marijuana Laws. *Publications include:* non-fiction: The American Health Empire: Power, Profits and Politics (with John Ehrenreich) 1971, Witches, Midwives and Nurses: A History of Women Healers (with Deirdre English) 1972, For Her Own Good: 150 Years of the Experts' Advice to Women (with Deirdre English) 1978, The Hearts of Men: American Dreams and the Flight from Commitment 1983, Re-Making Love: The Feminization of Sex (with Elizabeth Hess and Gloria Jacobs) 1986, The Mean Season: The Attack on Social Welfare (with Frances Fox Piven, Richard Cloward and Fred Block) 1987, Fear of Falling: The Inner Life of the Middle Class 1989, The Worst Years of Our Lives: Irreverent Notes from a Decade of Greed (essays) 1990, Complaints and Disorders: The Sexual Politics of Sickness (with Deirdre English) 1991, Blood Rites: Origins and History of the Passions of War 1991, The Snarling Citizen 1995, Nickel and Dimed (Sydney Hillman Award for Journalism 1999, Brill's Content Hon. Mention 1999 for chapter that appeared in Harper's Jan. 1999) 2002, Global Woman: Nannies, Maids and Sex Workers in the New Economy (essays, co-ed. with Arlie Russell Hochschild) 2002, Bait and Switch: The Futile Pursuit of the Corporate Dream 2006, Dancing in the Streets: A History of Collective Joy 2007, This Land is Their Land: Reports from a Divided Nation 2008, Bright-sided: How the Relentless Promotion of Positive Thinking has Undermined America 2009; fiction: Kipper's Game 1993; contrib.: essays to Maid to Order, Harper's 2000 and Welcome to Cancerland 2003, articles to magazines, including Ms., Harper's, The Nation, The Progressive, The New Republic, The Atlantic Monthly and the New York Times Magazine. *Honours:* Hon. Co-Chair. Democratic Socialists of America; Dr hc (Reed Coll., State Univ. of New York at Old Westbury, Coll. of Wooster in Ohio, John Jay Coll., Univ. of Massachsuetts-Lowell, La Trobe Univ., Melbourne, Australia); Nat. Magazine Award for Excellence in Reporting (co-recipient) 1980, Ford Foundation Award for Humanistic Perspectives on Contemporary Soc. 1982, Guggenheim Fellowship 1987–88, John D. and Catherine T. MacArthur Foundation grant for research and writing 1995, Award in Literature, American Acad. of Arts and Letters 2007. *E-mail:* up@unitedprofessionals.org (office). *Website:* www.unitedprofessionals.org (office); www.barbaraehrenreich.com.

EHRET, Terry, BA, MA; American poet and lecturer; b. 12 Nov. 1955, San Francisco, Calif.; m. Donald Nicholas Moe 1979; three c. *Education:* Stanford Univ., Chapman Coll., San Francisco State Univ. *Career:* Instructor in English, Santa Rosa Junior Coll. 1991–; Lecturer in Poetry, Sonoma State Univ. 1994–, San Francisco State Univ. 1995–99; Founding Ed. Sixteen Rivers Press 1999–; Poet Laureate, Sonoma Co. 2004–06; numerous poetry readings and lectures; mem. Acad. of American Poets, Associated Writing Programs, California Poets in the Schools, Poets and Writers. *Publications include:* Suspensions (with Steve Gilmartin and Susan Herron Sibbet) 1990, Lost Body 1993, Travel/How We Go on Living 1995, Translations from the Human Language 2001, Lucky Break 2008; contribs to reviews and journals. *Honours:* Nat. Poetry Series Award 1992, California Commonwealth Club Book Award for Poetry 1994, Pablo Neruda Poetry Prize, Nimrod magazine 1995. *Address:* 924 Sunnyslope Road, Petaluma, CA 93952, USA (home). *Telephone:* (707) 762-2689 (home). *E-mail:* terry@terryehret.com (home). *Website:* www.terryehret.com.

EHRLICH, Paul Ralph, MA, PhD; American entomologist, population biologist and academic; *Bing Professor of Population Studies and President, Center for Conservation Biology, Stanford University;* b. 29 May 1932, Philadelphia, Pa; s. of William Ehrlich and Ruth Ehrlich (née Rosenberg); m. Anne Fitzhugh Howland 1954; one d. *Education:* Univs of Pennsylvania and Kansas. *Career:* Field Officer, Northern Insect Survey (Canadian Arctic and Sub-arctic) summers of 1951 and 1952; Research Asst, DDT Resistance Project, Dept of Entomology, Univ. of Kansas 1952–54, Kansas Univ. Fellow 1954–66, NSF Pre-Doctoral Fellow 1955–57, Assoc. Investigator, USAF research project, Alaska and Univ. of Kansas 1956–57, Research Assoc., Chicago Acad. of Sciences and Univ. of Kansas Dept of Entomology 1957–59; Asst Prof. of Biological Sciences, Stanford Univ. 1959–62, Assoc. Prof. of Biological Sciences 1962–66, Prof. of Biological Studies 1966–, Dir Grad. Studies, Dept of Biological Sciences 1966–69, 1974–76, Bing Prof. of Population Studies 1977–, Pres. Center for Conservation Biology 1988–; NSF Sr Post-Doctoral Fellow, Univ. of Sydney 1965–66; Assoc., Center for the Study of Democratic Insts, Santa Barbara, Calif. 1969–72; Sec. Lepidopterists' Soc. 1957–63, mem. Exec. Council 1968; Corresp. NBC News 1989–92; Pres. Zero Population Growth 1969–70 (Hon. Pres. 1970–), Zero Population Growth Fund 1972–73, The Conservation Soc. 1972–73, American Inst. of Biological Sciences 1989, Asscn for Tropical Lepidoptera 2001; Vice-Pres. Soc. for the Study of Evolution 1970; Co-Chair. Research Cttee, Rocky Mountain

Biological Lab. 1973–75, Trustee 1971–86; Mem.-at-Large, Governing Bd American Inst. of Biological Sciences 1969–70; mem. Advisory Council, Friends of the Earth 1970–, Scientific Advisory Cttee, Sierra Club 1972–, Council, Soc. for the Study of Evolution 1974–76; mem. and Active Cttee mem., Int. Asscn for the Study of Ecology 1969–70; mem. Bd Dirs Common Cause 1972; mem. Bd of Consultants, Lizard Island Research Station 1975–78; mem. Bd of Govs Soc. for Conservation Biology 1986–88; mem. Editorial Bd Systematic Zoology 1964–67, International Journal of Environmental Sciences 1969–71, American Naturalist 1974–76, Oecologia 1981–85, 1991–, Revista de Biologia Tropical, Universidad de Costa Rica 1996–; Sr Assoc. Ed. American Naturalist 1984; Advisory Ed. Human Nature 1977–79; mem. NAS 1985, American Philosophical Soc. 1990, European Acad. of Sciences and Arts 1992; Elective mem. American Ornithologists' Union 1989; Foreign mem. Russian Acad. of Natural Sciences 1997–; Fellow, California Acad. of Sciences 1961, AAAS 1978, American Acad. of Arts and Sciences 1982, Entomological Soc. of America 1987. *Publications include:* How to Know the Butterflies 1960, Process of Evolution 1963, The Population Bomb 1968, 1971, Population Resources, Environment: Issues in Human Ecology (with A. H. Ehrlich) 1970, 1972, How to Be a Survivor (with R. L. Harriman) 1971, The Race Bomb (with S. Feldman) 1977, Extinction: The Causes and Consequences of the Disappearance of Species (with A. H. Ehrlich) 1981, The Golden Door: International Migration, Mexico and the United States (with D. L. Bilderback and A. H. Ehrlich) 1981, The Cold and the Dark: The World After Nuclear War (with Carl Sagan, Donald Kennedy and Walter Orr Roberts) 1984, Earth (with A. H. Ehrlich) 1987, Science of Ecology (with Joan Roughgarden) 1987, New World, New Mind (with R. Ornstein) 1988, The Birder's Handbook: A Field Guide to the Natural History of North American Birds (with David S. Dobkin and Darryl Wheye) 1988, The Cassandra Conference: Resources and the Human Predicament 1988, The Population Explosion (with A. H. Ehrlich) 1990, Healing the Planet: Strategies for Resolving the Environmental Crisis (with A. H. Ehrlich) 1991, Birds in Jeopardy: The Imperiled and Extinct Birds of the United States and Canada, Including Hawaii and Puerto Rico (with David S. Dobkin and Darryl Wheye) 1992, The Stork and the Plow (with A. H. Ehrlich and G. C. Daily) 1995, A World of Wounds: Ecologists and the Human Dilemma 1997, Betrayal of Science and Reason: How Anti-Environment Rhetoric Threatens Our Future (with A. H. Ehrlich) 1998, Human Natures: Genes, Cultures, and the Human Prospect 2002, One With Nineveh: Politics, Consumption and the Human Future (with A. H. Ehrlich) 2004, The Dominant Animal: Human Evolution and the Environment (with A. H. Ehrlich) 2008; co-ed.: Man and the Ecosphere: Readings from Scientific American (with J. P. Holdren and R. W. Holm) 1971, Global Ecology (with J. P. Holdren) 1971, Human Ecology: Problems and Solutions (with A. H. Ehrlich and J. P. Holdren) 1973, Introductory Biology 1973, Ark II (with D. Pirages) 1974, The Process of Evolution (with R. W. Holm and D. R. Parnell) 1974, The End of Affluence (with A. H. Ehrlich) 1974, Biology and Society (with R. W. Holm and I. Brown) 1976, Ecoscience: Population, Resources, Environment (with A. H. Ehrlich and J. P. Holdren) 1977, Introduction to Insect Biology and Diversity (with H. V. Daly and J. T. Doyen) 1978, Machinery of Nature 1986, Wild Solutions 2001, Butterflies: Ecology and Evolution taking Flight (with Carol Boggs and Ward Watt) 2003, On the Wings of Checkerspots: A Model System for Population Biology (with Ilkka Hanski) 2004; more than 950 scientific and popular articles. *Honours:* Hon. Life mem. American Humanist Asscn 1989, British Ecological Soc. 1989, Int. Soc. for Philosophical Enquiry 1991; Sigma Xi-Resa Grant-in-Aid of Research done in Alaska and NW Canada 1955, First Prize, Mitchell Foundation 1979, John Muir Award, Sierra Club 1980, Humanist Distinguished Service Award, American Humanist Asscn 1985, First Distinguished Achievement Award, Soc. for Conservation Biology 1987, Gold Medal, World Wildlife Fund Int. 1987, AAAS/Scientific American Gerard Piel Award for Service to Science in the Cause of Humankind 1989, UN Global 500 Roll of Honour 1989, Crafoord Prize in Population Biology and the Conservation of Biological Diversity, Royal Swedish Acad. of Sciences 1990, Distinguished Service Citation, Univ. of Kansas 1991, MacArthur Prize Fellowship 1990–95, Major Achievement Award, New York City Audubon Soc. 1991, Volvo Environment Prize 1993, World Ecology Medal, Int. Center for Tropical Ecology 1993, UNEP Sasakawa Environment Prize 1994, Heinz Award for the Environment 1995, Distinguished Peace Leader, Nuclear Age Peace Foundation 1996, Tyler Prize for Environmental Achievement 1998, Dr A.H. Heineken Prize for Environmental Sciences 1998, Nat. Audubon Soc., One Hundred Champions of Conservation 1998, Blue Planet Prize, Asahi Glass Foundation (Japan) 1999, Distinguished Scientist Award, American Inst. of Biological Sciences 2001, Eminent Ecologist Award, Ecological Soc. of America 2001. *Address:* Department of Biology, HERRIN 409, Stanford University, Stanford, CA 94305-5020, USA (office). *Telephone:* (650) 723-3171 (office). *Fax:* (650) 723-5920 (office). *Website:* www.stanford.edu/group/CCB/Staff/Ehrlich.html (office).

EISEN, Cliff, BA, MA, PhD; Canadian musicologist and academic; *Reader in Historical Musicology, King's College London*. *Education:* Univ. of Toronto, Cornell Univ. *Career:* Assoc. Ed., New Köchel Catalogue; Gen. Ed., Oxford Companion to Mozart; Reader in Historical Musicology, King's Coll., London 1997–; served as musicological adviser to Robert Levin, Christopher Hogwood and Acad. of Ancient Music for recordings of the Mozart's piano concertos. *Publications include:* Mozart Studies (ed. and contrib.) 1991, New Mozart Documents 1991, Wolfgang Amadeus Mozart, Symphony K. 425 ('Linz') 1992, Mozarts Streichquintette: Beiträge zum musikalischen Satz, zum Gattungskontext und zu Quellenfragen (co-ed. with W. D. Seiffert, also contrib.) 1994, Orchestral Music in Salzburg, 1750–1780 (co-author) 1994, Mozart Studies 2 (ed. and contrib.) 1997, Four Viennese String Quintets 1998, A Companion to Mozart's Piano Concertos (with Arthur Hutchings) 1998, The New Grove Mozart (with Stanley Sadie) 2000, W. A. Mozart: Piano Concerto in E-flat, KV 271 (with Robert Levin) 2000, Mozart: A Life in Letters (with Stewart Spencer) 2006, The Cambridge Mozart Encyclopedia (with Simon P. Keefe) 2006, Coll' Astuzia, Col Giudizio: Essays in Honor of Neal Zaslaw 2009; contribs to Journal of the Royal Musical Asscn, Early Music, numerous chapters in academic works. *Address:* Department of Music, King's College London, Strand, London, WC2R 2LS, England (office). *Telephone:* (20) 7848-2307 (office). *Fax:* (20) 7848-2326 (office). *E-mail:* cliff.eisen@kcl.ac.uk (office). *Website:* www.kcl.ac.uk/artshums/depts/music (office).

EISENBERG, Deborah, BA; American writer; b. 20 Nov. 1945, Chicago, Ill.; partner Wallace Shawn. *Education:* Marlboro Coll., Vt, New School Coll., New School for Social Research. *Career:* teacher, MFA Creative Writing Program, Univ. of Virginia. *Plays:* Pastorale (play) 1982. *Publications include:* Transactions in a Foreign Currency (short stories) 1986, Under the 82nd Airborne (short stories) 1992, Air, 24 Hours: Jennifer Bartlett (monograph) 1994, The Stories (So Far) of Deborah Eisenberg 1996, All Around Atlantis 1997, Twilight of the Superheroes (short stories) 2006, The Collected Stories of Deborah Eisenberg (short stories) 2010. *Honours:* O. Henry Awards 1986, 1995, 1997, 2002, Whiting Writer's Award 1987, Guggenheim Fellowship 1987, Deutscher Akademischer Austauschdienst Fellowship, Berlin 1991, Friends of American Writers Award 1993, Ingram Merrill Foundation Award 1993, American Acad. of Arts and Letters Award for Literature 1993, Smart Foundation Prize for Best Story in Yale Review 1996, The Rea Award for the Short Story 2000, Lannan Foundation Fellowship 2003, MacArthur Fellowship 2009. *Address:* Department of English, University of Virginia, 405 Bryan Hall, PO Box 400121, Charlottesville, VA 22904-4121, USA (office). *Telephone:* (434) 924-6621 (office). *Fax:* (434) 924-1478 (office). *E-mail:* de2b@virginia.edu (office). *Website:* www.engl.virginia.edu (office).

EKINS, Paul Whitfield, BSc, MSc, MPhil, PhD; British economist and writer; *Professor of Energy and Environment Policy, UCL Energy Institute, University College, London*; b. 24 July 1950, Jakarta, Indonesia; m. Susan Anne Lofthouse 1979; one s. *Education:* Imperial Coll., London, Birkbeck Coll., London, Univ. of Bradford. *Career:* Research Fellow, School of Peace Studies, Univ. of Bradford 1987–90; Research Assoc., Dept of Applied Econs, Univ. of Cambridge 1991–98; Sr Lecturer, School of Politics, Int. Relations and the Environment, Keele Univ. 1996–98, Reader 1998–2000, Prof. 2000–02; Prof. of Sustainable Devt, Univ. of Westminster 2002–07, Head Environment Group Policy Studies Inst. 2002–07; Prof. of Energy and Environment Policy, King's Coll., London 2008–09; Prof. of Energy and Environment Policy, Univ. Coll., London 2009–; mem. Royal Comm. on Environmental Pollution 2002–08; mem. Global 500 Forum, Int. Soc. for Ecological Econs; Fellow, Energy Inst. *Publications include:* The Living Economy: A New Economics in the Making (ed.) 1986, A New World Order: Grassroots Movements for Global Change 1992, Wealth Beyond Measure: An Atlas of New Economics (with Mayer Hillman and Robert Hutchison) 1992, Real Wealth: Green Economics in the Classroom (with Ken Webster) 1994, Global Warming and Energy Demand (co-ed. with Terry Barker and Nick Johnstone) 1995, Economic Growth and Environmental Sustainability: The Prospects for Green Growth 2000, Understanding the Costs of Environmental Regulation (co-ed.) 2009, Trade, Globalization, and Sustainability Impact Assessment: A Critical Look at Methods and Outcomes (co-ed.) 2009, Carbon-Energy Taxation: Lessons from Europe (co-ed.) 2009, Hydrogen Energy: Economic and Social Challenges (ed.) 2010, Energy 2050 (co-ed.) 2010, Environmental Tax Reform (ETR): A Policy for Green Growth (with Stefan Speck) 2011; contrib. to books, journals, reviews and newspapers. *Honours:* Hon. Fellow, Centre for Social and Environmental Accounting Research, Univ. of Dundee 1992–; UNEP Global 500 Award for Environmental Achievement 1994, cited in a special survey by Environment Agency (England and Wales) as among 'the 100 greatest eco-heroes of all time' 2006, placed by Independent on Sunday in its Green List of Britain's Top 100 Environmentalists 2008. *Address:* UCL Energy Institute, Central House, University College, 14 Upper Woburn Place, London, WC1H 0HY, England (office). *Telephone:* (20) 3108-5990 (office). *Fax:* (20) 3108-5986 (office). *E-mail:* p.ekins@ucl.ac.uk (office). *Website:* www.ucl.ac.uk/energy (office).

EKLUND, Gordon Stewart; American writer; b. 24 July 1945, Seattle, Wash.; one d. *Education:* Contra Costra Coll. *Career:* mem. Science Fiction and Fantasy Writers of America. *Publications include:* The Eclipse of Dawn 1971, A Trace of Dreams 1972, Beyond the Resurrection 1973, All Times Possible 1974, Serving in Time 1975, Falling Toward Forever 1975, If the Stars are Gods 1976, The Dance of the Apocalypse 1976, The Grayspace Beast 1976, Starless World (Star Trek Adventures) 1978, Devil World (Star Trek Adventures) 1979, Find the Changeling 1980, The Garden of Winter 1980, Thunder on Neptune 1989, Find the Changeling (with Gregory Benford) 2010; contribs to Analog, Galaxy, If Science Fiction, Fantasy and Science Fiction, Universe, New Dimensions, Amazing Stories, Fantastic. *Honours:* Nebula Award 1975.

ELDER, Karl, BS, MS, MFA; American poet, writer, editor and academic; *Jacob and Lucile Fessler Professor of Creative Writing and Poet-in-Residence, Lakeland College*; b. 7 July 1948, Beloit, Wis.; m. Brenda Kay Olson 1969; two s. *Education:* Northern Illinois Univ., Wichita State Univ. *Career:* instructor,

Southwest Missouri State Univ. 1977–79; Faculty mem., Lakeland Coll. 1979–89, Jacob and Lucile Fessler Prof. of Creative Writing and Poet-in-Residence 1990–. *Publications include:* poetry: Can't Dance an' it's Too Wet to Plow 1975, The Celibate 1982, Phobophobia 1987, What Is the Future of Poetry? (ed.) 1991, A Man in Pieces 1994, The Geocryptogrammatist's Pocket Compendium of the United States 2001, Mead: Twenty-six Abecedariums 2005, The Minimalist's How-to Handbook 2005, Gilgamesh at the Bellagio 2007, The Houdini Monologues 2010; contrib. to numerous anthologies, reviews, quarterlies and journals. *Honours:* Lucien Stryk Award for Poetry 1974, Illinois Arts Council Award 1975, and grant 1977, Lakeland Coll. Outstanding Teacher Award 1987, Robert Schuricht Endowment 1993, Pushcart Prize 2000, Mikrokosmos Prize for Poetry 2002, Lorine Neidecker Award for Poetry 2004, Chad Walsh Award for Poetry 2005, Posner Book Award Honorable Mention 2006, Nat. Poetry Review Book Award 2007. *Address:* Creative Arts Division, Lakeland College, PO Box 359, Sheboygan, WI 53082-0359, USA (office). *Telephone:* (920) 565-1276 (office). *E-mail:* karlelder1@wi.rr.com (home). *Website:* www.lakeland.edu (office); www.greatlakeswritersfestival.org (office); www.karlelder.com.

ELDERKIN, Susan, MA; British novelist, journalist and teacher; b. 1968, Crawley, Surrey, England; m.; one s. *Education:* Univ. of Cambridge, Univ. of East Anglia. *Career:* creative writing teacher; travel writer and critic (mainly for Financial Times); bibliotherapist for The School of Life, London. *Publications include:* Sunset over Chocolate Mountains 2000, The Voices 2003. *Honours:* Betty Trask Award 2000, one of Granta's 20 Best Young British Novelists of the Decade 2003. *Literary Agent:* c/o Aitken Alexander Associates, 18–21 Cavaye Place, London, SW10 9PT, England. *Telephone:* (20) 7373-8672. *Fax:* (20) 7373-6002. *E-mail:* clare@aitkenalexander.co.uk. *Website:* www.aitkenalexander.co.uk; www.susanelderkin.com.

ELDRED-GRIGG, Stevan Treleaven, MA, PhD; New Zealand writer and historian; b. 5 Oct. 1952, Grey Valley; s. of Gilbert Eldred-Grigg and Valerie Rita Forbes; m. Lauree Arlene Hunter 1976 (divorced 1994); three s. *Education:* Univ. of Canterbury, Australian Nat. Univ. *Career:* Judge, New Zealand Book Awards 1984; Arts Council of NZ Scholar-in-Letters 1991; Prof. of Literature Shanghai Int. Studies Univ., China 2003–04; Wellington Branch Pres. NZ Soc. of Authors 1995–98, Nat. Vice-Pres. 1998–99; mem. PEN New Zealand Centre, Canterbury Provincial Committee; Trustee Christchurch Book Festival Trust 1996–2000; Postdoctoral Fellow, Univ. of Canterbury, Christchurch 1981; Writing Fellow, Victoria Univ. 1986; New Zealand Writing Fellow, Iowa Univ., USA;. *Publications include:* fiction: Oracles and Miracles 1987, adapted as radio play 1989, stage play 1990, The Siren Celia 1989, The Shining City 1991, Gardens of Fire 1993, My History, I Think 1994, Mum 1995, Blue Blood 1997, Kaput! 2001, Sheng Xian Qi Ji 2002, Shanghai Boy 2006; non-fiction: A Southern Gentry: New Zealanders Who Inherited the Earth 1980, A New History of Canterbury 1982, Pleasures of the Flesh 1984, New Zealand Working People 1890–1990 1990, The Rich 1996, Diggers, Hatters and Whores: The Story of the New Zealand Gold Rushes 2008, The Great Wrong War 2010; contribs short stories to periodicals, including Island, Landfall, New Zealand Listener; historical essays to periodicals, including New Zealand Journal of History, Journal of the Royal Australian Historical Society, New Zealand Geographic; literary and critical essays to Landfall, Sites, Island, Ming Dao Literature and Arts, New Zealand Books. *Honours:* A.W. Reed Memorial Book Award 1984, Second Prize, Goodman Fielder Wattie Award, Book Publishers Asscn of New Zealand 1988, Commonwealth Writers Prize for South-East Asia and the South Pacific 1988, Trust Bank Canterbury Community Trust Arts Excellence Award 1996, Writer's Award, CLL New Zealand 2006, New Zealand History Research Trust Fund Award in History 2009. *Address:* 10/381 Adelaide Road, Wellington 6021, New Zealand (office). *Telephone:* (4) 3800352 (home). *E-mail:* scibblnz@yahoo.co.uk (office). *Website:* www.eldred-grigg.com.

ELDRIDGE, Colin Clifford, BA, PhD, FRHistS; British academic and writer; *Professor of History, University of Wales Trinity Saint David*; b. 16 May 1942, Walthamstow, England; m. Ruth Margaret Evans 1970 (died 2003); one d. *Education:* Univ. of Nottingham. *Career:* Postdoctoral Fellow in the Arts and Social Sciences, Univ. of Edinburgh 1966–68; Lecturer, Univ. of Wales, Lampeter (now Univ. of Wales Trinity Saint David) 1968–75, Sr Lecturer in History 1975–92, Reader 1992–98, Prof. of History 1998–; mem. Historical Asscn, Asscn of History Teachers in Wales, British Asscn of Canadian Studies, British Australian Studies Asscn. *Publications include:* England's Mission: The Imperial Idea in the Age of Gladstone and Disraeli 1973, Victorian Imperialism 1978, Essays in Honour of C. D. Chandaman 1980, British Imperialism in the 19th Century 1984, Empire, Politics and Popular Culture 1989, From Rebellion to Patriation: Canada and Britain in the Nineteenth and Twentieth Centuries 1989, Disraeli and the Rise of a New Imperialism 1996, The Imperial Experience: From Carlyle to Forster 1996, The Zulu War, 1879 1996, Kith and Kin: Canada, Britain and the United States form the Revolution to the Cold War 1997; contrib. to various learned journals. *Address:* School of Archaeology, History and Anthropology, University of Wales Trinity Saint David, Lampeter, Ceredigion, SA48 7ED (office); Tanerdy, Ciliau Aeron, Lampeter, Ceredigion, SA48 8DL, Wales (home). *Telephone:* (1570) 424744 (office); (1570) 470667 (home). *E-mail:* c.eldridge@tsd.ac.uk (office). *Website:* www.tsd.ac.uk/history (office).

ELDRIDGE, David; British playwright; b. 1974. *Education:* Univ. of Exeter. *Plays include:* Serving it Up 1996, A Week with Tony 1996, Summer Begins 1997, Thanks Mum 1998, Falling 1999, Under the Blue Sky 2001, Festen (adaptation) 2004, M.A.D. 2004, Incomplete and Random Acts of Kindness 2005, The Wild Duck (adaptation) 2005, Market Boy 2006, John Gabriel Borkman (adaptation) 2007, The List 2009. *Television:* Our Hidden Lives 2005. *Literary Agent:* c/o Methuen Drama, A & C Black Publisher Ltd, 36 Soho Square, London, W1D 3QY, England. *Telephone:* (20) 7758-0200. *Website:* www.acblack.com.

ELEGANT, Robert Sampson, BA, MA, MS; British author and journalist; b. 7 March 1928, New York, NY, USA; m. 1st Moira Clarissa Brady 1956 (died 1999); one s. one d.; m. 2nd Ursula Rosemary Righter (née Douglas) 2003. *Education:* Univ. of Pennsylvania, US Army Language School, Yale Univ., Columbia Univ. *Career:* War, Southeast Asia Corresp., various agencies 1951–61; Cen. European Bureau, Newsweek 1962–64; Los Angeles Times, Washington Post 1965–70; Foreign Affairs Columnist 1970–76; Visiting Prof., Univ. of South Carolina 1976, Boston Univ. 1994–95; Fellow, American Enterprise Inst. for Public Policy Research, Washington, DC 1976–78; Sr Fellow, Inst. for Advanced Study, Berlin 1993–94; mem. Authors' League of America; Hong Kong Foreign Correspondents' Club (Pres. 1960). *Publications include:* China's Red Masters 1951, The Dragon's Seed 1959, The Centre of the World 1961, Mao v Chiang: The Battle for China 1972, The Great Cities, Hong Kong 1977, Pacific Destiny 1990; fiction: A Kind of Treason 1966, The Seeking 1969, Dynasty 1977, Manchu 1980, Mandarin 1983, White Sun, Red Star 1987 (published in US as From a Far Land 1988), Bianca 1992, The Everlasting Sorrow 1994, Last Year in Hong Kong 1997, The Big Brown Bears 1998, Bianca 2000, Cry Peace 2005; contribs to newspapers and periodicals. *Honours:* Viet Nam, Korea, Matuya Service Medals (USA and UK), World War II; Pulitzer Fellow 1951–52, Ford Foundation Fellowship 1954–55, Overseas Press Club Awards 1963, 1966, 1967, 1972, Sigma Delta Chi Award 1966, Edgar Allan Poe Award 1967. *Literary Agent:* c/o Christopher Sinclair-Stevenson, 3 South Terrace, London, SW7 2TB, England. *Address:* 10 Quick Street, London, N1 8HL, England (office). *Telephone:* (20) 7837-1009 (office). *Fax:* (20) 7837-1009 (office). *E-mail:* relegant@yahoo.com (home).

ELFYN, Menna, BA; British poet; *Director of Creative Writing, Trinity College, Camarthen*; b. 1951, S Wales; d. of Rev. T. Elfyn Jones and Rachel Maria Jones; m. Wynfford James 1974; two c. *Education:* Univs of Swansea and Aberystwyth. *Career:* Lecturer, St David's Coll., Lampeter 1979–86, Writing Fellow 1984; Lecturer in Educ., Univ. of Swansea 1989–92; Co-Dir of Creative Writing, Trinity Coll., Carmarthen 1997, Dir 1998–, later Fellow; Royal Literary Fund Fellow, Univ. of Aberystwyth 2002–06; columnist, Western Mail 1996–; Royal Literary Fellow, Swansea Univ. 2007–; Artist-in-Residence at various schools, colls and hosps, UK and USA; readings worldwide at festivals and for British Council in Sri Lanka, Philippines, Zimbabwe, Macedonia, Estonia, Poland, Romania; work translated into 15 languages; has presented TV documentaries; mem. Gorsedd of Bards 1993. *Plays:* seven stage plays, two for TV; four plays for BBC Radio 2002–06. *Music:* co-writer choral symphony Garden of Light for New York Philharmonic Orchestra. *Publications include:* Aderyn Bach Mewn Llaw (Welsh Arts Council Prize) 1990, Eucalyptus: Detholiad o Gerddi 1995, Cell Angel 1996, Cusan Dyn Dall/Blind Man's Kiss 2000, Modern Welsh Poetry (co-ed. with John Rowlands) 2003, Perffaith Nam (Perfect Flaw) 2005, Perffaith Nam/Perfect Blemish: New and Selected Poems 1995–2007 2007, Er dy fod 2007, Sunflowers in Your Eyes (short stories) (ed.) 2010, Merch Perygl: Cerddi Menna Elfyn 1976–2011 (co-author) 2011; other vols of poetry; two novels for teenagers; various works for music, produced as librettist for four US composers. *Honours:* many poetry prizes including Best Vol. of Eisteddfod 1977, Welsh Arts Council Best Book of the Year 1990–2003, Poet Laureate for the Children of Wales 2002–03. *Address:* Cysgod y Craig, Stryd y Gwynt, Llandysul, Ceredigion, Wales (home); c/o Bloodaxe Books Ltd, Highgreen, Tarset, Northumberland, NE48 1RP, England. *Telephone:* (1559) 362122 (home). *E-mail:* m.elfyn@trinity-cm.ac.uk (office); menna@elfyn.fsnet.co.uk (home). *Website:* www.mennaelfyn.co.uk.

ELÍASSON, Gyrðir; Icelandic author and poet; b. 4 April 1961, Reykjavik; m.; three c. *Career:* short story writer, novelist and poet, also translates many prestigious works into Icelandic. *Publications include:* The Wandering Squirrel (novel) (Gangandi ikorni) 1987, Sandárbókin (novel) (The Book of Sandá River), The Yellow House (Gula húsid) (Icelandic Literature Prize 2000, Halldor Laxnes Prize for Literature 2000) 2000, Steintré (trans as Stone Tree 2009) 2003, Milli trjánna (Among the Trees) (Nordic Council Literature Prize 2011) 2011, Nookur almenn orð um kulnun sólar (A Few General Remarks on the Cooling of the Sun) (poetry) 2011. *Address:* c/o Ra Page, Comma Press, MadLab, 36–40 Edge Street, Manchester, M4 1HN, England (office). *E-mail:* ra.page@commapress.co.uk (office). *Website:* www.commapress.co.uk (office).

ELIOT, Karen (see Home, Stewart Ramsay)

ELISHA, Ron, MB, BS; Australian medical practitioner and playwright; b. 19 Dec. 1951, Jerusalem, Israel; m. Bertha Rita Rubin 1981; one s. one d. *Education:* Univ. of Melbourne. *Career:* self-employed gen. practitioner; mem. Australian Writers' Guild. *Publications include:* In Duty Bound 1983, Two 1985, Einstein 1986, The Levine Comedy 1987, Pax Americana 1988, Safe House 1989, Esterhaz 1990, Impropriety 1993, Choice 1994, Pigtales 1994, Unknown Soldier 1996, Too Big 1997, The Goldberg Variations 2000, A Tree, Falling 2003, Ladies & Gentlemen 2005, Wrongful Life 2005, Controlled Crying 2006, Renaissance (Mitch Mathews Award) 2006, Ten Minutes 2007, The Schelling Point 2010, Carbon Dating 2011; contribs to Business Review

Weekly, The Age, Vogue Australia, Generation Magazine, Australian Book Review, Centre Stage Magazine, Melbourne Jewish Chronicle, The Westerly, Medical Observer. *Honours:* Best Stage Play 1982, 1984, Major Award 1982, Gold Award, Best Screenplay, Houston Int. Film Festival 1990, Best TV Feature, Australian Writers' Guild Award 1992. *Literary Agent:* Marea Jablonski, BGM, 39A Newry Street, Prahran, Vic. 3181, Australia. *Telephone:* (3) 9525-1755. *E-mail:* marea@bgmagebcy.com.au. *Website:* www.bgmagency.com.au. *Address:* 2 Malonga Court, North Caulfield, Vic. 3161, Australia (home). *Telephone:* (3) 9571-9933 (office). *Fax:* (3) 9571-3604 (office). *E-mail:* relisha@bigpond.net.au (home).

ELKINS, Aaron, BA, MA, EdD; American writer; b. 24 July 1935, New York, NY; s. of Irving Elkins and Jennie Elkins; m. 1st Toby Siev 1959 (divorced 1972); two s.; m. 2nd Charlotte Trangmar 1972. *Education:* Hunter Coll., City Univ. of New York, Univ. of Wisconsin, Madison, Univ. of Arizona, California State Univ., Los Angeles, Univ. of California, Berkeley. *Career:* various admin. positions, fed. and local govt; held various teaching positions, Univ. of Maryland, Golden Gate Univ., California State Univ. 1960–83; author 1982–. *Publications include:* Fellowship of Fear 1982, The Dark Place 1983, Murder in the Queen's Armes 1985, A Deceptive Clarity 1987, Old Bones (MWA Edgar Allan Poe Award 1988) 1987, Curses 1989, Icy Clutches 1990, A Glancing Light 1991, Make No Bones 1991, Old Scores 1993, Dead Men's Hearts 1994, Twenty Blue Devils 1997, Loot 1999, Skeleton Dance 2000, Turncoat 2002, Good Blood 2004, Where There's A Will 2005, Unnatural Selection 2006, Little Tiny Teeth 2007, Uneasy Relations 2008, Skull Duggery 2009, The Worst Thing 2011; with Charlotte Elkins: A Wicked Slice 1989, Rotten Lies 1995, Nasty Breaks 1998, Where Have All the Birdies Gone? 2004, On the Fringe 2005. *Honours:* Agatha Award (co-recipient) 1992, Nero Wolfe Award 1994. *Literary Agent:* c/o Lisa Erbach Vance, The Aaron Priest Agency Inc., 708 Third Avenue, 23rd Floor, New York, NY 10017, USA. *Telephone:* (212) 818-0344. *Fax:* (212) 573-9417. *E-mail:* levance@aaronpriest.com. *E-mail:* acelkins@olypen.com (office). *Website:* www.aaronelkins.com.

ELKINS, Caroline, PhD; American academic and author; *Hugo K. Foster Associate Professor of African Studies, Harvard University*; b. 1969. *Education:* Princeton Univ., Harvard Univ. *Career:* Hugo K. Foster Assoc. Prof. of African Studies and Policy Fellow, Kennedy School of Govt in the Carr Centre for Human Rights Policy, Harvard Univ.; has travelled and worked in rural Africa; speaks Swahili and some Kikuyu. *TV and radio broadcasts include:* All Things Considered (NPR), The World (BBC), Charlie Rose (PBS). *Publications include:* Imperial Reckoning: The Untold Story of Britain's Gulag in Kenya (Pulitzer Prize in General Non-Fiction) 2005, Settler Colonialists in the 20th Century: Projects, Practices, Legacies (co-ed. with Susan Pedersen) 2005; contrib. to The New York Times Book Review, The Atlantic, The New Republic and to academic journals. *Address:* Department of History, Harvard University, Robinson Hall, 35 Quincy Street, Cambridge, MA 02138, USA (office). *Telephone:* (617) 495-2568 (office). *E-mail:* elkins@fas.harvard.edu (office).

ELLIOT, Alistair, BA, MA; British poet, translator, editor and fmr librarian; b. 13 Oct. 1932, Liverpool; m. 1956; two s. *Education:* Fettes Coll., Edinburgh, Christ Church, Oxford. *Career:* Librarian, Kensington Public Library, London 1959–61, Keele Univ. 1961–65, Pahlavi Univ., Iran 1965–67, Newcastle Univ. 1967–82. *Publications include:* Air in the Wrong Place 1968, Contentions 1977, Kisses 1978, Talking to Bede 1982, Talking Back 1982, On the Appian Way 1984, My Country: Collected Poems 1989, Turning the Stones 1993, Facing Things 1997, The Real Poems 2008; ed.: Poems by James I and Others 1970, Virgil, The Georgics with John Dryden's Translation 1981; ed. and trans.: French Love Poems (bilingual) 1991, Italian Landscape Poems (bilingual) 1993, Roman Food Poems 2003; trans.: Alcestis, by Euripides 1965, Peace, by Aristophanes 1965, Femmes Hombres, by Paul Verlaine 1979, The Lazarus Poems, by Heinrich Heine 1979, Medea, by Euripides 1993, La Jeune Parque, by Paul Valéry 1997, Phaethon, by Euripides (a reconstruction) 2008; contrib. to numerous journals, reviews and magazines. *Honours:* Arts Council of GB grant 1979, Ingram Merrill Foundation Fellowships 1983, 1989, Prudence Farmer Awards, New Statesman 1983, 1991, Djerassi Foundation Fellowship 1984, Cholmondeley Award, Soc. of Authors 2000. *Address:* 27 Hawthorn Road, Newcastle upon Tyne, NE3 4DE, England (home). *E-mail:* alistair.elliot@btinternet.com.

ELLIOT, Bruce (see FIELD, Edward)

ELLIOTT, Sir John Huxtable, Kt, FBA; British historian and academic; b. 23 June 1930, Reading, Berks.; s. of Thomas Charles Elliott and Janet Mary Payne; m. Oonah Sophia Butler 1958. *Education:* Eton Coll. and Trinity Coll., Cambridge. *Career:* Asst Lecturer in History, Univ. of Cambridge 1957–62, Lecturer 1962–67; Prof. of History, King's Coll., Univ. of London 1968–73; Prof., School of Historical Studies, Inst. for Advanced Study, Princeton, NJ 1973–90; Regius Prof. of Modern History, Univ. of Oxford and Fellow, Oriel Coll., Oxford 1990–97; Fellow, Trinity Coll., Cambridge 1954–67; mem. Scientific Cttee, Prado Museum 1996; Fellow, Royal Acad. of History, Madrid, American Acad. of Arts and Sciences, American Philosophical Soc., King's Coll., Univ. of London 1998, Accad. Naz. dei Lincei 2003, Accad. delle Scienze di Torino 2009, Académico de honor, Real Academia de Buenas Letras de Sevilla 2009. *Publications:* Imperial Spain, 1469–1716 1963, The Revolt of the Catalans 1963, Europe Divided, 1559–1598 1968, The Old World and the New, 1492–1650 1970, The Diversity of History (co-ed. with H. G. Koenigsberger) 1970, A Palace for a King (with J. Brown) 1980 (revised edn 2003), Memoriales y Cartas del Conde Duque de Olivares 1978–80, Richelieu and Olivares 1984, The Count-Duke of Olivares 1986, Spain and Its World 1500–1700 1989, The Hispanic World (ed.) 1991, The World of the Favourite (co-ed.) 1999, The Sale of the Century (with J. Brown) 2002, Empires of the Atlantic World (Francis Parkman Prize 2007) 2006, Spain, Europe and the Wider World 1500–1800 2009. *Honours:* Hon. Fellow, Trinity Coll. Cambridge 1991, Oriel Coll. Oxford 1997; Commdr, Order of Alfonso X El Sabio 1984, Commdr, Order of Isabel la Católica 1987, Grand Cross of Order of Alfonso X, El Sabio 1988, Grand Cross of Order of Isabel la Católica 1996, Cross of Sant Jordi (Catalonia) 1999; Dr hc (Universidad Autónoma de Madrid) 1983, (Genoa) 1992, (Portsmouth) 1993, (Barcelona) 1994, (Warwick) 1995, (Brown) 1996, (Valencia) 1998, (Lleida) 1999, (Madrid Complutense) 2003, (Coll. of William and Mary) 2005, (London) 2007, (Carlos III, Madrid) 2008; Visitante Ilustre of Madrid 1983, Leo Gershoy Award, American Historical Asscn 1985, Wolfson Literary Award for History and Biography 1986, Medal of Honour, Universidad Int. Menéndez y Pelayo 1987, Gold Medal for Fine Arts (Spain) 1991, Eloy Antonio de Nebrija Prize (Univ. of Salamanca) 1993, Prince of Asturias Prize in Social Sciences 1996, Gold Medal, Spanish Inst., New York 1997, Balzan Prize for History 1500–1800 1999. *E-mail:* john.elliott@history.ox.ac.uk (office). *Address:* 122 Church Way, Iffley, Oxford, OX4 4EG, England. *Telephone:* (1865) 716703.

ELLIOTT, Sir Roger James, Kt, MA, DPhil, FRS; British physicist and publisher; b. 8 Dec. 1928, Chesterfield, Derbyshire; s. of James Elliott and Gladys Elliott (née Hill); m. Olga Lucy Atkinson 1952; one s. two d. *Education:* Swanwick Hall School, Derbyshire, New Coll., Oxford. *Career:* Research Assoc., Univ. of California, Berkeley, USA 1952–53; Research Fellow, Atomic Energy Research Establishment, Harwell 1953–55; Lecturer, Univ. of Reading 1955–57; Lecturer, Univ. of Oxford 1957–65, Reader 1965–74, Fellow, St John's Coll. 1957–74 (now Hon. Fellow), New Coll. 1974–96 (now Hon. Fellow), Wykeham Prof. of Physics 1974–89, Prof. of Physics 1989–96, Prof. Emer. 1996–; Del., Oxford University Press 1971–88, Sec. to Dels and Chief Exec. 1988–93, Chair. Computer Bd 1983–87; mem. Bd Blackwell Ltd 1996–, Chair. 1999–2002; Visiting Prof., Univ. of California, Berkeley 1960–61; Miller Visiting Prof., Univ. of Illinois, Urbana, USA 1966; Visiting Distinguished Prof., Florida State Univ. 1981, Michigan State Univ. 1997–2000; Physical Sec. and Vice-Pres. Royal Soc. (London) 1984–88; Treas. Publrs Asscn 1990–92, Pres. 1992–93; Chair. ICSU Press 1997–2002, Disability Information Trust 1998–2001; mem. Bd (part-time) UKAEA 1988–94, British Council 1990–98, Mexican Acad. of Science 2003; Fellow, Inst. of Physics; Treas. ICSU 2002. *Publications:* Magnetic Properties of Rare Earth Metals 1972, Solid State Physics and its Applications 1973; articles in academic journals. *Honours:* Hon. DSc (Paris) 1983, (Bath) 1991, (Essex) 1993; Maxwell Medal (Physical Soc.) 1968, Guthrie Medal 1989. *Address:* 11 Crick Road, Oxford, OX2 6QL, England (home). *Telephone:* (1865) 273997 (office). *Fax:* (1865) 273947 (office). *E-mail:* r.elliott1@physics.ox.ac.uk (office).

ELLIS, Bret Easton, BA; American writer; b. 7 March 1964, Los Angeles. *Education:* Bennington Coll. *Career:* mem. Authors' Guild. *Publications:* Less Than Zero 1985, The Rules of Attraction 1987, American Psycho 1989, The Informers 1994, Glamorama 1998, Lunar Park 2005, Imperial Bedrooms 2010; contrib. to Rolling Stone, Vanity Fair, Elle, Wall Street Journal, Bennington Review. *Literary Agent:* c/o Amanda Urban, International Creative Management, 825 Eighth Avenue, New York, NY 10019, USA. *Telephone:* (212) 556-5600. *Website:* www.icmtalent.com.

ELLIS, David George, MA, PhD; British academic, writer and translator; *Professor Emeritus of English and American Literature, University of Kent at Canterbury*; b. 23 June 1939, Swinton, Lancs., England; m. 1966; two d. *Education:* Univ. of Cambridge. *Career:* Lecturer, La Trobe Univ., Melbourne, Vic., Australia, 1968–72; Lecturer, Sr Lecturer, Prof., Univ. of Kent at Canterbury 1972–, now Prof. Emer. of English and American Literature. *Publications include:* Stendhal, Memoirs of an Egotist (trans.) 1975, Wordsworth, Freud and the Spots of Time: Interpretation in 'The Prelude' 1985, D. H. Lawrence's Non-Fiction: Art, Thought and Genre (with Howard Mills) 1988, Imitating Art: Essays in Biography (ed.) 1993, Dying Game, Vol. 3, New Cambridge Biography of D. H. Lawrence 1998, Literary Lives: Biography and the Search for Understanding 2000, That Man Shakespeare 2005, Shakespeare's Practical Jokes: An Introduction to the Comic in his Work 2007, Death and the Author: How D. H. Lawrence Died, and Was Remembered 2008, Byron in Geneva: That Summer of 1816 2011, The Truth about William Shakespeare: Fact, Fiction and Modern Biographies 2012. *Address:* English School, University of Kent at Canterbury, Canterbury, CT2 7NX, England (office).

ELLIS, Gavin Peter; New Zealand journalist; b. 6 March 1947, Auckland; s. of Peter Fisher Dundass Ellis and Catherine Ellis (née Gray); m. 1st Janine Laurette Sinclair 1969; m. 2nd Jennifer Ann Lynch 1991; one s. *Education:* Mount Roskill Grammar School and Auckland Univ. *Career:* on staff of Auckland Star paper 1965–70; public relations consultant 1970–71; joined New Zealand Herald 1972, Asst Ed. 1987–96, Ed. 1996–99, Ed.-in-Chief 1999–2006; Harry Brittain Memorial Fellow 1980; Chair. NZ Section, Commonwealth Press Union; mem. New Zealand Knowledge Wave Trust; mem. NZ Council for Security Co-operation Asia-Pacific. *Honours:* Commonwealth Astor Prize for Press Freedom 2005. *E-mail:* gavin.ellis@xtra.co.nz (home).

ELLIS, John Martin, BA, PhD; American academic; *Professor Emeritus of German Literature, University of California, Santa Cruz*; b. 31 May 1936, London, England; s. of John Albert Ellis and Emily Ellis; m. Barbara Rhoades

1978; two s. two d. one step-d. *Education:* City of London School and Univ. Coll., London. *Career:* Royal Artillery 1954–56; Tutorial Asst in German, Univ. of Wales, Aberystwyth 1959–60; Asst Lecturer in German, Univ. of Leicester 1960–63; Asst Prof. of German, Univ. of Alberta, Canada 1963–66; Assoc. Prof. of German Literature, Univ. of Calif., Santa Cruz 1966–70, Prof. 1970–94, Prof. Emer. 1994–, Dean Graduate Div. 1977–86; Literary Ed. Heterodoxy 1992–2000; Sec.-Treas. Asscn of Literary Scholars and Critics 1994–2001; Pres. Calif. Asscn of Scholars 2007–; Guggenheim Fellowship, Nat. Endowment for the Humanities Sr Fellowship. *Publications include:* Narration in the German Novelle 1974, The Theory of Literary Criticism: A Logical Analysis 1974, Heinrich von Kleist 1979, One Fairy Story Too Many: The Brothers Grimm and Their Tales 1983, Against Deconstruction 1989, Language, Thought and Logic 1993, Literature Lost: Social Agendas and the Corruption of the Humanities 1997. *Honours:* Nat. Asscn of Scholars' Peter Shaw Memorial Award (for Literature Lost). *Address:* 144 Bay Heights, Soquel, CA 95073, USA (home). *Telephone:* (831) 476-1144 (home). *Fax:* (831) 476-1188 (home). *E-mail:* johnellis2608@att.net (office).

ELLIS, Peter Berresford, (Peter MacAlan, Peter Tremayne), FRHistS; British writer; b. 10 March 1943, Coventry, Warwicks., England; m. Dorothea Cheesmur 1966. *Education:* Brighton Coll. of Art, Univ. of East London. *Career:* mem. Celtic League, Int. Chair. 1988–90, Crime Writers' Asscn, Irish Literary Soc., London Asscn for Celtic Educ. (Chair. 1989–90, Vice-Pres. 1990–96), Soc. of Authors; Fellow, Royal Soc. of Antiquaries of Ireland. *Publications include:* Wales – A Nation Again!: The Nationalist Struggle for Freedom 1968, The Creed of the Celtic Revolution 1969, The Scottish Insurrection of 1820 (with Seumas Mac a'Ghobhainn) 1970, The Problem of Language Revival (with Seumas Mac a'Ghobhainn) 1971, A History of the Irish Working Class 1972, The Cornish Language and Its Literature 1974, Hell or Connaught!: The Cromwellian Colonisation of Ireland, 1652–1660 1975, The Boyne Water: The Battle of the Boyne, 1690 1976, The Great Fire of London: An Illustrated Account 1976, Caesar's Invasion of Britain 1978, A Voice From the Infinite: The Life of Sir Henry Rider Haggard, 1856–1925 1978, MacBeth: High King of Scotland, 1040–57 AD 1979, By Jove, Biggles!: The Life of Captain W. E. Johns (with Piers Williams) 1981, The Liberty Tree 1982, The Last Adventurer: The Life of Talbot Mundy, 1879–1940 1984, Celtic Inheritance 1985, The Celtic Revolution: A Study in Anti-Imperialism 1985, The Rising of the Moon: A Novel of the Fenian Invasion of Canada 1987, A Dictionary of Irish Mythology 1987, The Celtic Empire: The First Millennium of Celtic History, c. 1000 BC–51 AD 1990, A Guide to Early Celtic Remains in Britain 1991, A Dictionary of Celtic Mythology 1992, Celt and Saxon: The Struggle for Britain AD 410–937 1993, The Celtic Dawn: A History of Pan Celticism 1993, The Book of Deer 1994, The Druids 1994, Celtic Women: Women in Celtic Society and Literature 1996, Celt and Greek: Celts in the Hellenic World 1997, Celt and Roman: The Celts of Italy 1998, The Chronicles of the Celts: New Tellings of Their Myths and Legends 1999, Erin's Blood Royal: The Gaelic Noble Dynasties of Ireland 2001, Eyewitness to Irish History 2004; as Peter MacAlan: The Judas Battalion 1983, Airship 1984, The Confession 1985, Kitchener's Gold 1986, The Valkyrie Directive 1987, The Doomsday Decree 1988, Fireball 1991, The Windsor Protocol 1993; as Peter Tremayne: The Hound of Frankenstein 1977, Dracula Unborn 1977, The Vengeance of She 1978, The Revenge of Dracula 1978, The Fires of Lan-Kern 1978, The Ants 1979, The Curse of Loch Ness 1979, Dracula, My Love 1980, Zombie! 1981, The Return of Raffles 1981, The Morgow Rises! 1982, The Destroyers of Lan-Kern 1982, The Buccaneers of Lan-Kern 1983, Snowbeast! 1983, Raven of Destiny 1984, Kiss of the Cobra 1984, Swamp! 1985, Angelus! 1985, My Lady of Hy-Brasil and Other Stories 1987, Nicor! 1987, Trollnight! 1987, Ravenmoon 1988, Island of Shadows 1991, Aisling and Other Irish Tales of Terror 1992, Murder by Absolution 1994, Shroud for the Archbishop 1995, Suffer Little Children 1995, The Subtle Serpent 1996, The Spider's Web 1997, The Un-Dead: The Legend of Bram Stoker and Dracula (with Peter Haining) 1997, Valley of the Shadow 1998, The Monk Who Vanished 1999, Act of Mercy 1999, Hemlock at Vespers 2000, Our Lady of Darkness 2000, Smoke in the Wind 2001, The Haunted Abbot 2002, Badger's Book 2003, The Leper's Bell 2004, Whispers of the Dead 2004, Master of Souls 2005, A Prayer for the Damned 2006, Dancing with Demons 2007, The Council of the Cursed 2009, The Dove of Death 2010; contribs to anthologies, newspapers and magazines. *Honours:* Bard of the Cornish Gorsedd 1987, Irish Post Award 1988. *Address:* c/o Headline Publishing Group, 338 Euston Road, London, NW1 3BH, England. *Website:* www.hachettelivre.co.uk.

ELLIS, Richard J., BA, MA, PhD; British academic and writer; *Mark O. Hatfield Professor of Politics, Willamette University*; b. 27 Nov. 1960, Leicester, England; m. Juli Takenaka 1987. *Education:* Univ. of California, Santa Cruz, Univ. of California at Berkeley. *Career:* Asst Prof., Willamette Univ., Salem, Ore. 1990–95, Assoc. Prof. 1995–99, Mark O. Hatfield Prof. of Politics 1999–; mem. American Political Science Asscn, Org. of American Historians. *Publications include:* Dilemmas of Presidential Leadership (co-author) 1989, Cultural Theory (co-author) 1990, American Political Cultures 1993, Presidential Lightning Rods: The Politics of Blame Avoidance 1994, Politics, Policy and Culture (co-ed.) 1994, Culture Matters: Essays in Honor of Aaron Wildavsky (co-ed.) 1997, The Dark Side of the Left: Illiberal Egalitarianism in America 1997, Speaking to the People: The Rhetorical Presidency in Historical Perspective 1998, The Founding of the American Presidency 1999, Democratic Delusions; The Initiative Process in America 2002, To The Flag: The Unlikely History of the Pledge of Allegiance 2005, Presidential Travel: The Journey from George Washington to George W. Bush 2008, Judging Executive Power: Sixteen Supreme Court Cases That Have Shaped the American Presidency 2009, Debating the Presidency: Conflicting Perspectives on the American Executive (co-ed.) 2010, Debating Reform: Conflicting Perspectives on How to Fix the American Political System (co-ed.) 2010; contrib. to Comparative Studies in Society and History; Journal of Behavioural Economics; Presidential Studies Quarterly; Journal of Theoretical Politics: Studies in American Political Development; Review of Politics; Polity; Western Political Quarterly; Critical Review; American Political Science Review. *Honours:* Regents Fellowship, Univ. of California 1983–85, I. G. S. Harris Fellowship 1986–88, Summer Stipend, Nat. Endowment for the Humanities 1991, 2003, Fellowship, George and Eliza Howard Foundation 1993–94, Oregon Council for the Humanities Research Grant 1994, 2003, Arnold L. and Lois S. Graves Award in the Humanities 1998, Lawrence D. Cress Award for Excellence in Faculty Scholarship 2003, Langum Prize in Legal History 2005, Outstanding Scientist Prize, Oregon Acad. of Science 2007, Oregon Prof. of the Year, Carnegie Foundation for Advancement of Teaching 2008. *Address:* Willamette University, Salem, OR 97301, USA (office). *Telephone:* (503) 370-6081 (office). *E-mail:* rellis@willamette.edu (office). *Website:* www.willamette.edu/cla/politics/faculty/ellis (office).

ELLIS, (Christopher) Royston (George), (Richard Tresillian, Raynard Devine, Rachel Delauney, Bianca Perera, Shirley Prince); British writer and poet; b. 10 Feb. 1941, Pinner, Middx, England; one s. *Education:* Harrow County and Harrow Weald schools. *Career:* Asst Ed., Jersey News and Features Agency 1961–63; Assoc. Ed., Canary Islands Sun, Las Palmas 1963–66; Ed., The Educator, Dir, Dominica Broadcasting Services and Reuters, Cana Corresp. 1974–76; Man. Ed., Wordsman Features Agency 1977–86; Editorial Consultant, Explore Sri Lanka 1990–2005; Travel and Colonial Property Corresp., Sunday Times, Colombo 1991–; Warden, Southern Prov., Sri Lanka, British High Comm.; mem. Inst. of Rail Transport (India), Royal Commonwealth Soc. *Publications include:* Jiving to Gyp 1959, Rave 1960, The Big Beat Scene 1961, The Rainbow Walking Stick 1961, Rebel 1962, Burn Up 1963, The Mattress Flowers 1963, The Flesh Merchants 1966, The Rush at the End 1967, The Bondmaster Series (seven books) 1977–83, The Fleshtrader Series (three books) 1984–85, The Bloodheart Series (three books) 1985–87, Giselle 1987, Guide to Mauritius 1988–98, India By Rail 1989–97, Sri Lanka By Rail 1994, Bradt Guide to the Maldives 1995–2008, A Maldives Celebration (with Gemunu Amarasinghe) 1997, A Man For All Islands 1998, Festivals of the World: Madagascar, Trinidad 1999, A Hero In Time 2001, Bradt Guide to Sri Lanka 2002–08, The Big Beat Scene 2010, Gone Man Squared 2010, Sri Lanka: Step By Step 2010; contribs to newspapers and magazines. *Honours:* Duke de Gypino y Tintinabulation de Redonda 1961; Dominica Nat. Poetry Awards 1967, 1971. *Address:* Horizon Cottage, Kaikawala Road, Induruwa, Sri Lanka (home). *Telephone:* (34) 2271556 (home). *E-mail:* royston@roystonellis.com (office). *Website:* www.roystonellis.com.

ELLISON, Harlan Jay; American author and screenwriter; b. 27 May 1934, Cleveland, OH; s. of Louis Laverne Ellison and Serita (née Rosenthal) Ellison; m. 1st Charlotte Stein 1956 (divorced 1959); m. 2nd Billie Joyce Sanders 1961 (divorced 1962); m. 3rd Lory Patrick 1965 (divorced 1965); m. 4th Lori Horwitz 1976 (divorced 1977); m. 5th Susan Toth 1986. *Education:* Ohio State Univ. *Career:* part-time actor, Cleveland Playhouse 1944–49; f. Cleveland Science-Fiction Soc. 1950 and Science-Fantasy Bulletin; served US Army 1957–59; ed. Rogue magazine, Chicago 1959-60, Regency Books, Chicago 1960–61; lecturer at colls and univs; voice-overs for animated cartoons; book critic, LA Times 1969–82; Editorial Commentator Canadian Broadcasting Co. 1972–78; Instructor Clarion Writers Workshop, Michigan State Univ. 1969–77; Pres. The Kilimanjaro Corpn 1979–; TV writer for Alfred Hitchcock Hour, Outer Limits, The Man from U.N.C.L.E., Burke's Law; film writer for The Dream Merchants, The Oscar, Nick the Greek, Best By Far, Harlan Ellison's Movie; scenarist: I, Robot 1978, Bug Jack Barron 1982–83; creative consultant, writer and dir The Twilight Zone 1984–85; conceptual consultant, Babylon 5 1993–98; mem. American Writers' Guild and American Science Fiction Writers. *Publications include:* Web of the City 1958, The Deadly Streets 1958, Sex Gang 1959, A Touch of Infinity 1960, The Sound of a Scythe 1960, Spider Kiss 1961, Children of the Streets 1961, Gentleman Jackie 1961, Ellison Wonderland 1962, Paingod 1965, I Have No Mouth and I Must Scream 1967, From the Land of Fear 1967, Dangerous Visions (ed.) 1967, Doomsman 1967, Love ain't Nothing but Sex Mispelled 1968, The Beast that Shouted Love at the Heart of the World 1969, Over the Edge 1970, The Glass Teat 1970, De Helden van de Highway 1973, Approaching Oblivion 1974, Deathbird Stories 1975, No Doors, No Windows 1975, The Other Glass Teat 1975, A Boy and His Dog 1975, Strange Wine 1978, Shatterday 1980, Stalking the Nightmare 1982, An Edge in My Voice 1985, Demon with a Glass Hand 1986, Night and the Enemy 1987, The Essential Ellison 1987, Angry Candy 1988, Harlan Ellison's Watching 1989, Vic and Blood 1989, The Harlan Ellison Hornbook 1990, Harlan Ellison's Movie 1990, All the Lies that are my Life 1991, Run for the Stars 1991, Mefisto in Onyx 1993, Mind Fields (33 stories inspired by the art of Jacek Yerka) 1994, Robot: The Illustrated Screenplay 1994, City on the Edge of Forever (screenplay) 1995, Jokes without Punchlines 1995, Slippage 1996, Harlan Ellison's Dream Corridor 1996, Edgeworks: The Collected Ellison (four vols) 1996–97, Repent, Harlequin 1997, Troublemakers 2001. *Honours:* Hugo Awards 1967, 1968, 1973, 1974, 1975, 1977, 1986, Special Achievement Awards 1968–72, Certificate of Merit, Trieste Film Festival 1970, Edgar Allan Poe Award, Mystery Writers 1974, 1988, American Mystery Award 1988, Bram Stoker Award, Horror Writers Asscn 1988, 1990, 1994; World Fantasy

Award 1989, Georges Méliès Award for cinematic achievement 1972, 1973, PEN Award for journalism 1982; Americana Annual American Literature: Major Works 1988, World Fantasy 1993 Life Achievement Award, two Audie Awards, Audio Publishers Asscn 1999 and numerous other awards. *Address:* c/o The Harlan Ellison Recording Collection, PO Box 55548, Sherman Oaks, CA 91413-0548, USA (office). *Website:* harlanellison.com.

ELLMANN, Lucy, MA; American/British writer, screenwriter and critic; b. 18 Oct. 1956, Evanston, Ill.; d. of Richard Ellmann and Mary Ellmann (née Donahue); m. Todd McEwen; one d. *Education:* Falmouth School of Art, Cornwall, Univ. of Essex and Courtauld Inst., London, UK. *Career:* mem. judging panel, Irish Times-Aer Lingus Int. Fiction Prize 1992, Hawthornden Fellow 1992, Royal Literary Fund Fellow 2005. *Publications include:* novels: Sweet Desserts (Guardian Fiction Prize) 1988, Varying Degrees of Hopelessness 1991, Man or Mango 1998, Dot in the Universe 2003, Doctors & Nurses 2006; contrib. to various periodicals and newspapers, including New Statesman, TLS, Guardian, Independent on Sunday, Observer, Washington Post, New York Times Book Review. *Literary Agent:* c/o David Godwin Associates, 55 Monmouth Street, London, WC2H 9DG, England. *Telephone:* (20) 7240-9992. *Fax:* (20) 7395-6110. *E-mail:* assistant@davidgodwinassociates.co.uk. *Website:* www.davidgodwinassociates.co.uk. *Address:* c/o Bloomsbury Publishing, 36 Soho Square, London, W1D 3QY, England.

ELLROY, James; American writer; b. (Lee Earle Ellroy), 4 March 1948, Los Angeles, Calif.; m. 1st Mary Doherty 1988 (divorced 1991); m. 2nd Helen Knode 1991. *Education:* John Burroughs Junior High School and Fairfax High School, Los Angeles. *Films include:* Dark Blue 2002, Street Kings (screenplay and story) 2008. *Publications:* Brown's Requiem 1981, Clandestine 1982, Blood on the Moon (Lloyd Hopkins series) 1983, Because the Night (Lloyd Hopkins series) 1984, Killer on the Road 1986, Silent Terror 1986, Suicide Hill (Lloyd Hopkins series) 1986, The Black Dahlia (LA series) 1987, The Big Nowhere (LA series) 1988, LA Confidential (LA series) 1990, White Jazz (LA series) 1992, Hollywood Nocturnes (essays and stories) 1994, American Tabloid (Underworld USA series) (Time Magazine Novel of the Year) 1995, My Dark Places (memoir) (Salon.com Book of the Year) 1996, LA Noir 1998, Crime Wave (essays and stories) 1999, The Cold Six Thousand (Underworld USA series) 2001, Destination: Morgue (essays and stories) 2003, Blood's a Rover 2009, The Hilliker Curse: My Pursuit of Women 2010. *Literary Agent:* Sobel Weber Associates Inc, 146 East 19th Street, New York, NY 10003-2404, USA. *Telephone:* (212) 420-8585. *Website:* www.sobelweber.com.

ELMSLIE, Kenward Gray, (Lavinia Sanchez), BA; American poet, librettist, writer and performance artist; b. 27 April 1929, New York, NY. *Education:* Harvard Univ. *Career:* mem. American Soc. of Composers, Authors and Publrs. *Publications include:* poetry: The Champ 1968, Album 1969, Circus Nerves 1971, Motor Disturbance 1971, Tropicalism 1976, The Alphabet Work 1977, Communications Equipment 1979, Moving Right Along 1980, Sung Sex 1989, Pay Dirt (with Joe Brainard) 1992, Champ Dust 1994, Girl Machine, White Attic, Routine Disruptions: Selected Poems and Lyrics 1998, Cyberspace (with Trevor Winkfield) 2000, Blast from the Past 2000, Nite Soil 2000, Snippets 2002, Agenda Melt 2004; musical theatre: Lizzie Borden 1966, Miss Julie 1966, The Sweet Bye and Bye 1973, The Seagull 1974, Washington Square 1976, Three Sisters 1986; musical plays: The Grass Harp 1971, Lola 1982, Postcards on Parade 1993; fiction: The Orchid Stories 1972, Bimbo Dirt 1981, 26 Bars 1986; other: City Junket (play) 1987, Bare Bones (memoir) 1995, LingoLand (musical revue) 2005; contrib. to numerous anthologies, reviews and journals. *Honours:* Frank O'Hara Poetry Award 1971. *Address:* PO Box 38, Calais, VT 05648, USA (office). *Fax:* (802) 456-8123 (office). *Website:* www.kenwardelmslie.com.

ELSOM, John Edward, BA, PhD; British dramatist, journalist, broadcaster and lecturer; *Director, AI (Arts Interlink) Management Consultants Limited*; b. 31 Oct. 1934, Leigh on Sea, Essex, England; s. of Ernest Leonard Elsom and Marjorie Louise Elsom (née Dines); m. Sally Mays 1956, two s. *Education:* Magdalene Coll., Cambridge, City Univ., London. *Career:* script adviser, Paramount Pictures 1960–68; theatre critic, London Magazine 1963–68, The Listener 1972–82; corresp., Contemporary Review 1978–88; Lecturer and Course Leader in Arts Criticism, City Univ., London 1986–96; Contributing Ed., The World and I 1986–2003; consultant, South Bank Univ. 1996–97; School for Oriental and African Studies, Univ. of London 1997; Dir, AI (Arts Interlink) Management Consultants Ltd 2000–; Visiting Prof. in Theatre, Univ. of Pomerania 2008–09; Visiting Prof., Univ. of Bedfordshire 2009–10; Dir, The Shaping of Experience (Arts Management Seminars), Moeller Centre, Churchill Coll., Cambridge 2008–09; mem. Liberal Party Art and Broadcasting Cttee (chair. and convenor 1978–88); Pres. Int. Asscn of Theatre Critics 1985–92, Hon. mem. 1992–. *Plays include:* Peacemaker 1956, Maui, How I Coped trilogy (One More Bull, The Well-Intentioned Builder, How I Coped) 1969, The Man of the Future is Dead 2001, Second Time Round 2007, Old Boy 2009. *Publications include:* Theatre Outside London 1969, Erotic Theatre 1974, Post-War British Theatre 1976, The History of the National Theatre 1978, Change and Choice 1978, Post-War British Theatre Criticism (ed.) 1981, Is Shakespeare Still Our Contemporary? (ed.) 1989, Cold War Theatre 1992, Missing the Point 1998; also plays; contrib. to Observer, Mail on Sunday, Encounter, TLS, The World and I, Sunday Telegraph, Plays International, Plays & Players, San Diego Union and others. *Honours:* Companion and Order of Merit (Romania) 2003; China Creative Industries Top Int. Award 2008. *Address:* 14 Homersham Road, Kingston-upon-Thames, Surrey KT1 3PN, England (office). *Telephone:* (20) 8541-1448 (office); (20) 8541-1448 (office). *E-mail:* johnelsom@aol.com (office).

ELTIS, Walter Alfred, MA, DLitt; British economist; *Fellow Emeritus, Exeter College, Oxford*; b. 23 May 1933, Warnsdorf, Czechoslovakia; s. of Rev. Martin Eltis and Mary Schnitzer; m. Shelagh M. Owen 1959; one s. two d. *Education:* Wycliffe Coll., Emmanuel Coll. Cambridge and Nuffield Coll. Oxford. *Career:* Research Fellow in Econs, Exeter Coll., Oxford 1958–60; Lecturer in Econs, Univ. of Oxford 1961–88; Fellow and Tutor in Econs, Exeter Coll. Oxford 1963–88, Fellow Emer. 1988–; Econ. Dir Nat. Econ. Devt Office 1986–88, Dir-Gen. 1988–92; Chief Econ. Adviser to the Pres. of Bd of Trade 1992–95; Visiting Reader in Econs, Univ. of Western Australia 1970–71; Visiting Prof., Univ. of Toronto 1976–77, European Univ. Florence 1979, Univ. of Reading 1992–2004; Gresham Prof. of Commerce, Gresham Coll. London 1993–96; mem. Reform Club (Chair. 1994–95), Political Economy Club, European Soc. for the History of Econ. Thought (Vice-Pres. 2000–04). *Publications:* Growth and Distribution 1973, Britain's Economic Problem: Too Few Producers (with R. Bacon) 1976, The Classical Theory of Economic Growth 1984, Keynes and Economic Policy (with P. Sinclair) 1988, Classical Economics, Public Expenditure and Growth 1993, Britain's Economic Problem Revisited 1996, Condillac: Commerce and Government (co-ed. with S. M. Eltis) 1998, Britain, Europe and EMU 2000. *Address:* Danesway, Jarn Way, Boars Hill, Oxford, OX1 5JF, England (home). *Telephone:* (1865) 735440 (home).

ELTON, Benjamin (Ben) Charles, BA; British writer and performer; b. 3 May 1959, s. of Prof. Lewis Richard Benjamin Elton and Mary Elton (née Foster); m. Sophie Gare 1994. *Education:* Godalming Grammar School, S Warwicks. Coll. of Further Educ., Univ. of Manchester. *Career:* first professional appearance Comic Strip Club 1981; numerous tours as stand-up comic 1986–. *Film:* Much Ado About Nothing (actor) 1993, Maybe Baby (writer and dir) 2000. *Television:* writer: Alfresco 1982–83, The Young Ones (jtly) 1982–84, Happy Families 1985, Filthy Rich and Catflap 1986, Blackadder II (jtly) 1986, Blackadder the Third (jtly) 1987, Blackadder Goes Forth (jtly) 1989, The Thin Blue Line (jtly) 1995–96; writer and performer: South of Watford (jtly, documentary series) 1984–85, Saturday Live 1985–87, Friday Night Live 1988, Ben Elton Live 1989, 1993, 1997, The Man from Auntie 1990, 1994, Stark 1993, The Ben Elton Show (jtly) 1998. *Theatre:* Gasping 1990, Silly Cow 1991, Popcorn 1996, Blast from the Past 1998, The Beautiful Game (musical, book and lyrics) 2000, We Will Rock You (story to musical) 2002, Tonight's the Night (story to musical) 2003. *Recordings:* albums: Motormouth 1987, Motorvation 1989. *Publications:* novels: Bachelor Boys 1984, Stark 1989, Gridlock 1992, This Other Eden 1993, Popcorn 1996, Blast from the Past 1998, Inconceivable 1999, Dead Famous 2001, High Society 2002, Past Mortem 2004, The First Casualty 2005, Chart Throb 2006, Blind Faith 2007, Meltdown 2009. *Honours:* British Acad. Best Comedy Show Awards 1984, 1987, Best New Comedy Laurence Olivier Award 1998. *Literary Agent:* c/o Phil McIntyre Promotions, Second Floor, 35 Soho Square, London, W1D 3QX, England. *Telephone:* (20) 7439-2270 (office).

ELVIN, Jo; Australian journalist and editor; *Editor, Glamour*; b. 21 Feb. 1970; m.; one d. *Career:* began career at Dolly magazine, Australia; moved to UK; Deputy Ed., Smash Hits; Ed. Sugar 1994–96; Founder and Ed. B Magazine 1996–97; Ed. New Woman 1999–2000; Ed. Glamour 2000–. *Honours:* five British Soc. of Magazine Editors Awards. *Literary Agent:* c/o Jo Carlton, Talent4 Media Ltd, Studio LG16, Shepherds Building Central, Charecroft Way, London, W14 0EH, England. *Telephone:* (20) 7183-4330. *Fax:* (20) 7183-4331. *E-mail:* jo@talent4media.com. *Website:* www.talent4media.com. *Address:* Glamour, 6–8 Old Bond Street, London, W1S 4PH, England (office). *Telephone:* (20) 7499-9080 (office). *E-mail:* glamoureditorialmagazine@condenast.co.uk (office). *Website:* www.glamourmagazine.co.uk (office).

EMECHETA, (Florence Onye) Buchi, BSc; Nigerian/British writer and lecturer; b. 21 July 1944, Lagos, Nigeria; d. of Jeremy Nwabudike Emecheta and Alice Okwuekwu Emecheta; m. Sylvester Onwordi 1960; two s. three d. *Education:* Methodist Girls' High School, Lagos and Univ. of London. *Career:* fmr librarian and community worker; Sr Research Fellow, Visiting Prof. of English, Univ. of Calabar 1980–81; Lecturer, Yale Univ., USA 1982, Univ. of London 1982; numerous visiting professorships at univs in USA; Propr Ogwugwn Afo Publishing Co.; mem. Home Sec.'s Advisory Council on Race 1979, Arts Council 1982–83, PEN International. *Publications include:* In the Ditch 1972, Second Class Citizen 1975, The Bride Price 1976, The Slave Girl (New Statesman Jock Campbell Award for Commonwealth Writers 1979) 1977, The Joys of Motherhood 1979, Naira Power 1981, On Our Freedom 1981, Destination Biafra 1982, Double Yoke 1982, Adah's Story 1983, A Land of Marriage 1983, The Rape of Shavi 1983, Head Above Water (autobiog.) 1984, Family Bargain 1987, Gwendolen 1990, Kehinde 1994, The New Tribe 2000; children's books: Titch the Cat 1979, Nowhere to Play 1980, The Moonlight Bride 1980, The Wrestling Match 1980; contrib. to newspapers and periodicals, including New Statesman, New Society, New International, Sunday Times Magazine, Times Literary Supplement, Guardian. *Honours:* Hon. OBE 2005; Jack Campbell Award, New Statesman 1979, one of Best Young British Writers 1983.

EMERSON, Ru, (Robert Cray), LLB; American writer; b. 15 Dec. 1944, Monterey, CA. *Education:* Univ. of Montana, Louisiana Co. Bar Asscn. *Career:* mem. Science Fiction and Fantasy Writers of America. *Publications include:* Princess of Flames 1986, To the Haunted Mountains 1987, In the Caves of

Exile 1988, On the Seas of Destiny 1989, SpellBound 1990, Beauty and the Beast 1990, Trilogy: Night Threads (The Calling of the Three 1990, The Two in Hiding 1991, One Land, One Duke 1993), The Bard's Tale: Fortress of Frost and Fire (with Mercedes Lackey) 1993, The Sword and the Lion 1993, Trilogy: Night Threads (The Craft of Light 1993, The Art of the Sword 1994, The Science of Power 1995), Xena: Warrior Princess The Empty Throne 1996, Xena: Warrior Princess The Huntress and the Sphynx 1997, Xena: Warrior Princess The Thief of Hermes 1997, Voices of Chaos (with A. C. Crispin) 1998, Against the Giants 1999, Trilogy: Xena: Warrior Princess (Go Quest, Young Man 1999, Questward Ho! 2000, How the Quest Was Won 2000), Keep on the Borderlands 2001; contrib. to anthologies and magazines. *Address:* 2600 Reuben Boise Road, Dallas, OR 97338-9681, USA (home). *Telephone:* (503) 623-3203 (home). *E-mail:* ruemerson@aol.com (home).

EMMETT, Nicholas; Irish writer and translator; b. 22 July 1935, Dublin; m. Anne Brit Emmett 1965. *Education:* Univ. of Oslo, Norway, Univ. of Galway. *Career:* left school at 14 to work in tobacco factory; taxi-owner and driver six years; interpreter-trans., Indian Embassy, Oslo 1973; Founding Co-Ed., Ragtime, English cultural magazine, Norway; mem. The Irish Writers' Union, Soc. of Authors. *Publications include:* The Cave (novel) 1987, The Red Mist and Other Stories 1988; short stories include Brains on the Dump 1991, An Empty Glass House, A Pale Green Moon; contrib. of 87 short stories and articles in newspapers, anthologies and magazines, UK, USA, Ireland, Norway 1970–2004; 23 stories broadcast on BBC and RTE Radio. *Honours:* Irish Arts Council writing grant 1976. *Address:* Rathcoffey North, Donadea, Co. Kildare, Ireland (home). *Telephone:* (86) 366-8426 (home).

EMMOTT, William (Bill) John, BA; British journalist; b. 6 Aug. 1956, Hammersmith, London; s. of Richard Emmott and Audrey Emmott; m. 1st Charlotte Crowther 1982 (divorced); m. 2nd Carol Barbara Mawer 1992. *Education:* Latymer Upper School, Hammersmith and Magdalen and Nuffield Colls, Oxford. *Career:* Brussels Corresp., The Economist 1980–82, Econs Corresp. 1982–83, Tokyo Corresp. 1983–86, Finance Ed. 1986–89, Business Affairs Ed. 1989–93, Ed.-in-Chief 1993–2006, Editorial Dir Economist Intelligence Unit May–Dec. 1992; Chair., London Library 2009–, PeerIndex 2010–; Trustee, IISS 2010–. *Publications:* The Pocket Economist (with R. Pennant-Rea) 1983, The Sun Also Sets 1989, Japanophobia 1993, Kanryo no Taizai 1996, 20:21 Vision: The Lessons of the 20th Century for the 21st 2003, Hiwa Mata Noboru 2006, Japan's New Golden Age - of the next ten years 2006, Nihon no sentaku 2007, Sekai Choryu no Yomikata 2008, Rivals: How the Power Struggle between China, India and Japan will Shape our Next Decade 2008, Forza, Italia: Come Ripartire dopo Berlusconi 2010. *Honours:* Hon. Fellow, Magdalen Coll. Oxford 2002; Hon. LLD (Warwick) 1999, (Northwestern) 2009; Hon. DLitt (City) 2001. *Address:* PO Box 23, Dulverton, TA22 9WW, England (office). *E-mail:* bill@billemmott.com (office). *Website:* www.billemmott.com.

ENDICOTT, Marina; Canadian writer, editor and director; b. Golden, BC. *Career:* fmr Dramaturge, Saskatchewan Playwrights Centre, Banff Centre Playwrights Colony; currently Lecturer in Creative Writing, Univ. of Alberta. *Publications include:* Open Arms 2001, Good to a Fault (Commonwealth Writers Prize, Canada and the Caribbean Region 2009) 2008, The Little Shadows 2011. *Address:* Department of Creative Writing, University of Alberta, Augustana Campus, N28 North Hall, Edmonton, AB T4V 2R3, Canada (office). *Telephone:* (780) 679-1100 (office). *E-mail:* marina.endicott@ualberta.ca (office). *Website:* www.arts.ualberta.ca (office).

ENG, Stephen Richard, BA, MS; American biographer, poet and literary journalist; b. 31 Oct. 1940, San Diego, Calif.; m. Anne Jeanne Kangas 1969; two s. two d. *Education:* George Washington Univ., Washington, DC, Portland State Univ., Oregon. *Career:* Poetry Ed., The Diversifier 1977–78; Assoc. Ed., Triads 1985; Dir and Ed., Nashville House 1991–; Staff Book Reviewer, Nashville Banner 1993–98; mem. Broadcast Music Inc. 1972–, Syndic, F. Marion Crawford Memorial Soc. 1978–, Country Music Assen 1990–, Science-Fiction Poetry Asscn 1990–. *Publications include:* Elusive Butterfly and Other Lyrics (ed.) 1971, The Face of Fear and Other Poems (ed.) 1984, The Hunter of Time: Gnomic Verses (ed.) 1984, Toreros: Poems (ed.) 1990, Poets of the Fantastic (co-ed.) 1992, A Satisfied Mind: The Country Music Life of Porter Wagoner 1992, Jimmy Buffett: The Man From Margaritaville Revealed 1996, Yellow Rider and Other Lyrics 2000, The Defrauding of the Worms: Thirty years of Poetry 2007; contribs to Lyric, Night Cry, Journal of Country Music, Tennessee Historical Quarterly, Bookpage, Nashville Banner, Music City Blues, Space & Time. *Honours:* American Poets' Fellowship Soc. Certificate of Merit 1973, Co-winner Rhysling Award, Science Fiction Poetry Asscn 1979, Best Writer 1979, 1983, Special Achievement 1985, Small Press Writers and Artists Org.

ENGEL, Howard, OC, BA; Canadian writer; b. 2 April 1931, Toronto, Ont.; m. 1st Marian Ruth Passmore 1962 (divorced); one s. one d.; m. 2nd Janet Evelyn Hamilton 1978 (deceased); one s. *Education:* St Catharine's Collegiate Inst., McMaster Univ., Ontario Coll. of Educ. *Career:* Barker Fairley Distinguished Visitor in Canadian Culture, Univ. Coll., Univ. of Toronto 1995–96; mem. Crime Writers of Canada (Chair. 1986–87), Int. Asscn of Crime Writers, Mystery Writers of America, Writers' Guild of Canada. *Publications include:* The Suicide Murders 1980, The Ransom Game 1981, Murder on Location 1982, Murder Sees the Light 1984, A City Called July 1986, A Victim Must Be Found 1988, Dead and Buried 1990, Murder in Montparnasse 1992, Criminal Shorts: Mysteries by Canadian Crime Writers (co-ed. with Eric Wright) 1992, There was an Old Woman 1993, Getting Away With Murder 1995, Lord High Executioner: An Unashamed Look at Hangmen, Headsmen, and Their Kind 1996, Mr Doyle and Dr Bell 1997, A Child's Christmas in Scarborough 1997, The Cooperman Variations 2001, Memory Book 2005, The Man Who Forgot How To Read (memoir) 2007, East of Suez 2008; contrib. to radio and TV. *Honours:* Hon. LLD (Brock) 1994, Hon. DLit (McMaster); Arthur Ellis Award for Crime Fiction 1984, Harbourfront Festival Prize 1990, Crime Writers of Canada Derrick Murdoch Award for Contrib. to the Genre 1998, Grant Allen Award for pioneering work in Canadian 2004, Matt Cohen Literary Award for a body of work 2005. *Literary Agent:* c/o Beverley Slopen Literary Agency, 131 Bloor Street W, Suite 711, Toronto, ON M5S 1S3, Canada. *Telephone:* (416) 964-9598. *E-mail:* beverley@slopenagency.ca. *Website:* www.slopenagency.ca. *Address:* 281 Major Street, Toronto, ON M5S 2L5, Canada (home).

ENGEL, Johannes K.; German journalist and editor; b. 29 April 1927, Berlin; s. of Karl and Anna (née Helke) Engel; m. Ruth Moter 1951; one s. one d. *Career:* journalist, Int. News Service and Der Spiegel magazine 1946–, office man., Frankfurt am Main 1948, Dept Head 1951, Ed.-in-Chief, Hamburg 1961, co-Ed.-in-Chief Der Spiegel (with Erich Böhme) 1973–86. *Address:* Kirchenredder 7, 22339 Hamburg, Germany (office). *Telephone:* 30071 (office).

ENGELL, Hans; Danish politician, columnist, author and newspaper editor; b. 8 Oct. 1948, Copenhagen; s. of Knud Engell Andersen; m. Pernille Kongsoe. *Education:* Coll. of Journalism. *Career:* journalist for Berlingske newspaper consortium 1968–78; Head of Press Service of Conservative People's Party 1978–82; mem. Parl. 1984–2000; Minister for Defence 1982–87, of Justice 1989–93; Chair. Conservative Parl. Group 1987–89; Leader Conservative People's Party 1995–97; Ed.-in-Chief Ekstra Bladet 2000–07. *Honours:* Commdr, Order of Dannebrog, Grand Commdr Order of Benemerencia p.p. *Address:* Puggaardsgade 13, 1573 Copenhagen, Denmark (home). *Telephone:* 33-13-09-13 (office). *E-mail:* hans.engell@eb.dk (office).

ENGLADE, Kenneth (Ken) Francis, BA; American writer and fmr journalist; b. 7 Oct. 1938, Memphis, Tenn.; m. 1st Sharon Flynn 1960 (divorced); two s. one d.; m. 2nd Sara Elizabeth Crewe 1980 (divorced 1991); m. 3rd Heidi Hizel 1997. *Education:* Louisiana State Univ. *Career:* mem. American Soc. of Journalists and Authors, Authors' Guild, Southwest Writers. *Publications include:* non-fiction: Cellar of Horror 1989, Murder in Boston 1990, Beyond Reason: The True Story of a Shocking Double Murder, a Brilliant and Beautiful Virginia Socialite, and a Deadly Psychotic Obsession 1990, Deadly Lessons 1991, A Family Business 1992, To Hatred Turned: A True Story of Love and Death in Texas 1992, Blood Sister 1994, Hot Blood: The Millionairess, the Money, and the Horse Murders 1996; fiction: People of the Plains 1996, The Tribes 1996, The Soldiers 1996, Battle Cry 1996. *Address:* 3228 Renaissance Drive SE, Rio Rancho, NM 87124-7634, USA (home). *Telephone:* (505) 994-4901 (home).

ENGLANDER, Nathan, BA, MA; American writer; b. 1970, New York; s. of Herbert Englander and Merle Englander. *Education:* Binghampton Univ., Univ. of Iowa. *Career:* lived in Jerusalem, Israel 1996–2001; Fellow, Cullman Center for Scholars and Writers, New York Public Library 2004. *Publications include:* For the Relief of Unbearable Urges (PEN/Faulkner Malamud Award 2000, Sue Kaufman Prize for First Fiction, American Acad. of Arts and Letters) 1999, The Ministry of Special Cases 2008, What We Talk About When We Talk About Anne Frank (short stories) 2012; contribs to The Atlantic Monthly, The New Yorker. *Honours:* Bard Fiction Prize, Guggenheim Fellowship 2003, Pushcart Prize. *Address:* c/o Random House, Publicity Department, 1745 Broadway, New York, NY 10019, USA. *E-mail:* scrosley@randomhouse.com. *Website:* www.nathanenglander.com.

ENGLE, Margarita, BS, MS; American novelist and poet; b. 2 Sept. 1951, Pasadena, Calif.; m. Curtis Engle 1978; one s. one d. *Education:* California Polytechnic Univ., Iowa State Univ. *Career:* mem. PEN USA West. *Publications include:* Singing to Cuba 1993, Skywriting 1995, The Poet Slave of Cuba, A Biography of Juan Francisco Manzano 2006, The Surrender Tree 2008, Tropical Secrets 2009; The Firefly Letters: A Suffragette's Journey to Cuba 2010, Hurricane Dancers: The First Caribbean Pirate Shipwreck 2011. *Honours:* Cintas Fellowship, San Diego Book Award, Pura Belpré Author Award 2009. *Address:* 9433 North Fowler Avenue, Clovis, CA 93619-8683, USA (home).

ENQUIST, Anna; Dutch writer, poet, psychoanalyst and musician; b. 19 July 1945, Amsterdam; m. B. E. Widlund; two c. *Education:* Univ. of Leiden, The Hague Conservatory. *Career:* pianist, psychology teacher, school psychologist; staff, Netherlands Psychoanalytical Inst. 1987–2000. *Publications include:* poetry: Soldatenliederen (C. Buddingh' Prize 1992) 1991, Jachtscènes 1992, Een nieuw afscheid 1994, Klaarlichte dag 1996, De tweede helft 2000, Hier was vuur (The Fire Was Here) 2003, De tussentijd (Poetry Prize) 2004, Alle gedichten 2005, Kerstmis in februari: de vroege gedichten 2007, Drie gedichten 2007; novels: Het meesterstuk (Debuut Prize) (The Masterpiece) 1994, Het geheim (The Secret) (Trouw Publiekprize) 1997, De ijsdragers (The Ice Carriers) 2002, De thuiskomst (Prix de Livres Corderie Royale-Hermione 2007) 2005, Letzte Reise 2006, Mei 2007, Kontrapunkt 2008, Die Erbschaft des Herrn de Leon 2008, A Leap 2009, Nieuws van nergens 2010; short stories: De kwetium (The Injury) 1999, Twaalf keer tucht 2011; monologues: De sprong 2003. *Honours:* Lucy B. and C.W. van der Hoogt Prize 1993,. *Address:* De Arbeiderspers, Herengracht 370–372, Amsterdam, The Netherlands (office). *Telephone:* 20-5247500 (office). *Fax:* 20-6224937 (office). *E-mail:* info@arbeiderspers.nl (office). *Website:* www.arbeiderspers.nl (office).

ENQUIST, Lynn W., BS, PhD; American biologist, editor and writer; *Henry L. Hillman Professor and Chair, Department of Molecular Biology, Princeton University. Education:* South Dakota State Univ., Medical Coll. of Virginia. *Career:* Staff Fellow, Nat. Inst. of Health 1973–77, Staff Scientist 1977–81, mem. Experimental Virology Section 1987–92; Research Dir, Molecular Genetics Inc., Minnesota 1981–84; Instructor, Advances Bacterial Genetics Course, Cold Spring Harbor 1981–85; Research Leader, Viral Diseases Group, E.I. DuPont de Nemours and Co. 1984–90; Sr Research Fellow, DuPont Merck Pharmaceutical Co. 1991–93; Prof. of Molecular Biology, Princeton Univ. 1993–2007, Assoc. Chair., Dept of Molecular Biology 2003–04, Chair. 2004–, Henry L. Hillman Prof. 2007–; mem. Editorial Bd, Journal of Virology 1992–94, Ed. 1994–2002, Ed.-in-Chief 2002–; mem. American Soc. for Microbiology, Div. Chair. DNA Viruses 1990–94, Pres. 2003–05. *Publications include:* contrib. to Experiments with Gene Fusions 1984, Principles of Virology: Molecular Biology, Pathogenesis and Control 1999; numerous articles on molecular biology. *Address:* Enquist Laboratory, Princeton University, 301 Schultz Laboratory, Princeton, NJ 08544, USA (office). *Telephone:* (609) 258-4990 (office). *Fax:* (609) 258-1035 (office). *E-mail:* lenquist@princeton.edu (office). *Website:* www.princeton.edu (office); jvi.asm.org (office).

ENQUIST, Per Olov, MA; Swedish novelist, playwright, journalist and poet; b. 1934, Hjoggböle; m. 2nd Lone Bastholm. *Education:* Univ. of Uppsala. *Career:* Visiting Prof. UCLA 1973. *Publications:* Kristallögat 1961, Färdvägen 1963, Magnetisörens Femte Vinter 1964, Bröderna Casey 1964, Hess 1966, Sextiotalskritik 1966, Legionärerna 1968, Sekonden 1971, Katedralen i München 1972, Berättelser Från de Inställda Upprorens Tid (short stories) 1974, Tribadernas Natt 1975, Chez Nous (with Anders Ehnmark) 1976, Musikanternas Uttåg 1978, Mannen På Trottoaren 1979, Till Fedra 1980, Från Regnormarnas Liv 1981, En Triptyk 1981, Doktor Mabuses Nya Testamente (with Anders Ehnmark) 1982, Strindberg Ett Liv 1984, Nedstörtad Ängel 1985, Två Reportage om Idrott 1986, I Lodjurets Timma 1988, Kapten Nemos Bibliotek 1991, Hamsun (screenplay) 1996, Bildmakarna (play) 1998, Livläkarens Besök (The Visit of the Ryal Physician) 1999, Systrarna (play) 2000, Lewis Resa (Lewi's Journey) 2001, Boken om Blanche och Marie (The Story of Blanche and Marie) 2004, Et Annat Liv 2008; contrib. to literary criticism in newspapers, including Uppsala Nya Tidning, Svenska Dagbladet, Expressen. *Honours:* Nordic Council literary prize 1968, August Award 1999, Independent Foreign Fiction Prize 2003, Augustpriset 2008. *Address:* c/o Norstedts, Tryckerigatan 4, Box 2052, 103 12 Stockholm, Sweden (office). *Website:* www.panorstedt.se (office).

ENRIGHT, Anne, BA, MA, FRSL; Irish author; b. 11 Oct. 1962, Dublin; m. Martin Murphy; two c. *Education:* Lester Pearson United World Coll. of the Pacific, Victoria, BC, Canada, Trinity Coll. Dublin, Univ. of East Anglia, UK. *Career:* fmr TV producer for RTÉ, worked on programmes including Nighthawks; full-time writer 1993–. *Publications include:* fiction: The Portable Virgin (short stories; Rooney Prize for Irish Literature) 1991, The Wig My Father Wore (novel) 1995, What Are You Like? (novel; Royal Soc. of Authors Encore Prize) 2000, The Pleasure of Eliza Lynch (novel) 2002, The Gathering (novel; Man Booker Prize, Irish Novel of the Year) 2007, Taking Pictures (short stories) 2008, Yesterday's Weather (short stories) 2008, The Forgotten Waltz 2011; other: Making Babies: Stumbling into Motherhood (essays) 2004, The Granta Book of the Irish Short Story (ed.) 2010; contrib. of short stories to The New Yorker, The Paris Review, Granta. *Honours:* Davy Byrne Irish Writing Award 2004. *Literary Agent:* c/o Gill Coleridge, Rogers, Coleridge & White Ltd, 20 Powis Mews, London, W11 1JN, England. *Telephone:* (20) 7221-3717. *Fax:* (20) 7229-9084. *E-mail:* info@rcwlitagency.com. *Website:* www.rcwlitagency.com. *Address:* c/o Jonathan Cape, Random House, 20 Vauxhall Bridge Road, London, SW1V 2SA, England. *Telephone:* (20) 7840-8579. *Fax:* (20) 7932-0077. *E-mail:* clewis@randomhouse.co.uk. *Website:* www.randomhouse.co.uk.

ENSLER, Eve; American playwright; b. 25 May 1953, New York City; m. Richard McDermott (divorced). *Education:* Middlebury Coll. *Career:* best known for play The Vagina Monologues, translated into nearly 50 languages and performed in over 140 countries; toured 20 North American cities with play The Good Body 2005–06; regular contrib. to Glamour Magazine, The Guardian, Marie Claire, Huffington Post, Washington Post, Utne Reader, O Magazine; Co-founder and Artistic Dir V-Day (global activist movt to stop violence against women and girls) 1998. *Films include:* The Vagina Monologues 2002, What I Want My Words to Do to You: Voices From Inside a Women's Maximum Security Prison 2003, Until the Violence Stops 2004. *Publications:* Plays: Conviction, Lemonade, The Depot, Floating Rhoda and the Glue Man, Extraordinary Measures, The Vagina Monologues (Obie Award for Best New Play 1996) 1996, The Good Body, Necessary Targets, The Treatment, Here 2010; Books: Vagina Warriors 2005, A Memory, A Monologue, A Rant and A Prayer 2006, Insecure at Last: Losing It in Our Security Obsessed World 2006, The Good Body, Necessary Targets, I Am An Emotional Creature 2010. *Honours:* Hon. DLit (Middlebury Coll.) 2003; Hon. DHumLitt (Manhattanville Coll.) 2005; Hon. Dr of Communications (Simmons Coll.) 2006; numerous awards including Guggenheim Fellowship Award in Playwriting 1999, Amnesty International Media Spotlight Award for Leadership 2002. *E-mail:* tech@vday.org (office). *Website:* www.vday.org (office).

ENZENSBERGER, Hans Magnus, (Andreas Thalmayr), DPhil; German poet and writer; *Artistic Director, Renaissance Theatre Berlin;* b. 11 Nov. 1929, Kaufbeuren; m. 1st Dagrun Averaa Christensen; one d.; m. 2nd Maria Alexandrowna Makarowa 1986; m. 3rd Katharina Bonitz; one d. *Education:* Univs of Erlangen, Freiburg im Breisgau, Hamburg and Paris. *Career:* Third Programme Ed., Stuttgart Radio 1955–57; Lecturer, Hochschule für Gestaltung, Ulm 1956–57; Literary Consultant to Suhrkamp's (publrs), Frankfurt 1960–; mem. 'Group 47', Ed. Kursbuch (review) 1965–75, Publr 1970–90; Ed. TransAtlantik (monthly magazine) 1980–82; Publr and Ed., Die Andere Bibliothek 1985–2005; Artistic Dir Renaissance Theatre Berlin 1995–. *Publications:* poetry: Verteidigung der Wölfe 1957, Landessprache 1960, Blindenschrift 1964, Poems for People Who Don't Read Poems (English edn) 1968, Gedichte 1955–1970 1971, Mausoleum 1975, Gedichte 1950-2005 2006; essays: Clemens Brentanos Poetik 1961, Einzelheiten 1962, Politik und Verbrechen 1964; also: Deutschland, Deutschland unter Anderen 1967, Das Verhör von Habana (play) 1970, Freisprüche 1970, Der kurze Sommer der Anarchie (novel) 1972, Gespräche mit Marx und Engels 1973, Palaver 1974; Ed. Museum der Modernen Poesie 1960, Allerleirauh 1961, Andreas Gryphius Gedichte 1962, Edward Lears kompletter Nonsense (trans.) 1977, Raids and Reconstruction (essays, English edn), Der Untergang der Titanic (epic poem) 1978, Die Furie des Verschwindens 1980, Politische Brosamen 1982, Critical Essays 1982, Der Menschenfreund 1984, Ach Europa! 1987, Mittelmass und Wahn 1988, Requiem für eine romantische Frau 1988, Der Fliegende Robert 1989, Zukunftsmusik (poems) 1991, Die grosse Wanderung 1992, Aussichten auf den Bürgerkrieg 1993, Diderots Schatten 1994, The Palace (libretto) 1994, Civil War (English edn) 1994, Selected Poems (English edn) 1994, Kiosk (poems) 1995 (English edn 1997), Voltaires Neffe (play) 1996, Der Zahlenteufel 1997, The Number Devil (English edn) 1998, Zickzack 1997, Wo warst du, Robert? (novel) 1998, Where were you, Robert? (English edn) 2000, Leichter als Luft (poems) 1999 (English edn 2001), Mediocrity and Delusion (English edn) 1992, Die Elixiere der Wissenschaft (essays and poems) 2002, Nomaden im regal (essays) 2003, Die Geschichte der Wolken (poems) 2003, Dialoge (prose) 2005, Hammerstein oder der Eigensinn 2008; as Andreas Thalmayr: Heraus mit der Sprache 2005. *Honours:* Ordre pour le Mérite 2000; Hugo Jacobi Prize 1956, Kritiker Prize 1962, Georg Büchner Prize 1963, Premio Pasolini 1982, Heinrich Böll Prize 1985, Kultureller Ehrenpreis der Stadt München 1994, Heinrich Heine Prize, Düsseldorf 1997, Príncipe de Asturias 2002, Griffin Trust for Excellence in Poetry's Lifetime Recognition Award 2009, and others. *Address:* c/o Suhrkamp-Verlag, Lindenstr. 29, 60325 Frankfurt am Main, Germany (home).

EPHRON, Delia; American author, scriptwriter and producer; b. 1945, Beverly Hills, Calif.; d. of the late Henry Ephron and of Phoebe Ephron (née Wolkind); sister of Nora Ephron; m. Jerome Kass. *Career:* began career as journalist, New York Magazine and New York Times; co-writer of screenplays and plays with sister, Nora Ephron. *Screenplays include:* This is My Life 1992, Sleepless in Seattle (assoc. producer) 1993, Mixed Nuts (also exec. producer) 1994, Michael (also exec. producer and composer of song, Lips Like a Blowfish) 1996, You've Got Mail (also exec. producer) 1998, Lucky Numbers 1999, Hanging Up (also exec. producer) 2000, The Sisterhood of the Traveling Pants 2005, Bewitched 2005. *Plays:* Love, Loss, and What I Wore 2009. *Publications include:* How to Eat Like A Child 1979, Teenage Romance or How to Die of Embarrassment 1981, Funny Sauce 1986, Hanging Up 1995, Big City Eyes 2000; children's books: My Life and Nobody Else's, The Girl Who Changed the World, Santa and Alex, Frannie in Pieces 2007, The Girl with the Mermaid Hair 2010. *E-mail:* frannieinpieces@aol.com (office). *Website:* www.deliaephron.com.

EPSTEIN, Joseph, BA; American editor, writer and lecturer; b. 9 Jan. 1937, Chicago, Ill.; m. Barbara Maher 1976; one s. *Education:* Univ. of Chicago. *Career:* Assoc. Ed., The New Leader 1962–63; Sr Ed., Encyclopaedia Britannica 1965–69, Quadrangle/New York Times Books 1969–70; Lecturer, Northwestern Univ. 1974–; Ed. The American Scholar from 1975. *Publications include:* Divorced in America 1975, Ambition 1979, Familiar Territory 1980, The Middle of My Tether 1983, Plausible Prejudices 1985, Once More Around the Block 1987, Partial Payments 1989, A Line Out for a Walk 1991, The Golden Boys: Stories 1991, Pertinent Players 1993, With My Trousers Rolled 1995, Life Sentences 1997, Narcissus Leaves the Pool 1999, Snobbery: The American Version 2002, Fabulous Small Jews 2003, Friendship: An Exposé 2006, Alexis de Tocqueville: Democracy's Guide 2007, Fred Astaire 2008, The Love Song of A. Jerome Minkoff: And Other Stories 2010, Gossip: The Untrivial Pursuit 2011; ed.: Masters: Portraits of Teachers 1980, Best American Essays 1993, Norton Book of Personal Essays 1997; contrib. to books, and to journals, including Atlantic Monthly, Harper's Magazine, The New Yorker. *Address:* c/o Houghton Mifflin Company, Trade Division, Adult Editorial, Eighth Floor, 222 Berkeley Street, Boston, MA 02116-3764, USA.

EPSTEIN, Leslie, MA, DFA; American writer and teacher; *Director, Creative Writing Program, Boston University;* b. 1938, Los Angeles, Calif.; s. of Philip G. Epstein and Lillian Epstein (née Targan); m. Ilene Epstein; two s., one d. *Education:* Yale, Merton Coll., Oxford, UK, Univ. of California, Los Angeles, Yale Drama School. *Career:* Dir of Creative Writing Program, Boston Univ.; Ed. Tikkun; Writer-in-Residence and Fellow, Rockefeller Inst., Bellagio, Italy. *Plays:* King of the Jews (Boston Playwrights Theater, Olney Theater). *Publications include:* P. D. Kimerakov 1975, The Steinway Quintet Plus Four 1976, King of the Jews 1978, The Elder 1979, Regina 1982, Goldkorn Tales 1986, Pinto and Sons 1990, Pandaemonium 1997, Ice Fire Water: A Leib Goldkorn Cocktail, San Remo Drive: a Novel from Memory 2003, The Eighth Wonder of the World 2006, Liebestod: Opera Buffa with Leib Goldkorn 2012;

contrib. to numerous magazines and newspapers. *Honours:* Rhodes Scholar 1960–72, Fulbright Scholar, Nat. Endowment for the Arts Fellow 1972, 1981–82, Guggenheim Fellow 1977–78, Award for Distinction in Literature, American Acad. and Inst. of Arts and Letters. *Address:* Creative Writing Program, Department of English, Boston University, 236 Bay State Road, Boston, MA 02215, USA (office). *Telephone:* (617) 353-2510 (office). *E-mail:* leslieep@bu.edu (office). *Website:* www.bu.edu/writing (office).

EPSTEIN, Seymour (Sy); American writer and academic; b. 2 Dec. 1917, New York, NY; m. Miriam Kligman 1956; two s. *Education:* City Coll., New York Univ. *Career:* served in USAAF during World War II; taught creative writing at the New School for Social Research; fmr Prof., Univ. of Denver, Colo; mem. Authors' Guild, PEN. *Publications include:* Pillar of Salt 1960, The successor 1962, Leah (Edward Lewis Wallant Memorial Award 1965) 1964, A Penny for Charity Stories 1965, Caught in That Music 1967, The Dream Museum 1971, Looking for Fred Schmidt 1973, Love Affair 1979, A Special Destiny 1986, September Faces 1987, Light 1989; contribs to periodicals. *Honours:* Guggenheim Fellowship 1965.

ERBA, Luciano, PhD; Italian poet, translator, writer and academic (retd); b. 18 Sept. 1922, Milan. *Education:* Catholic Univ., Milan. *Career:* Prof. of Comparative Literature, Rutgers Univ., NJ, USA 1964–65; Prof. of Italian and French Literature, Univ. of Washington, Seattle, USA 1965–66; Prof. of French Literature, Univ. of Padua 1973–82, Univ. of Verona 1982–87, Catholic Univ., Milan 1987–97. *Publications include:* Linea K 1951, Il bel paese 1956, Il prete di Ratanà 1959, Il male minore 1960, Il prato più verde 1977, Il nastro di Moebius 1980, Il cerchio aperto 1983, L'ippopotamo 1989, L'ipotesi circensi 1995, Negli spazi intermedi 1998, Nella terra di mezzo 2000, Poesie: 1951–2001 2002, Si passano le stgioni 2003, Un po' di repubblica 2005, Remi in barca 2006; other: Françoise (novel) 1982, radio plays, translations. *Honours:* Viareggio Prize 1980, Bagutta Prize 1988, Librex-Guggenheim Eugenio Montale Prize 1989, Italian PEN Club Prize 1995. *Address:* Via del Maino Giasone 16, 20146 Milan, Italy (home).

ERBSEN, Claude Ernest, BA; American journalist; *Senior Consultant, Innovation International Media Consultancy Group;* b. 10 March 1938, Trieste, Italy; s. of Henry M. Erbsen and Laura Erbsen; m. 1st Jill J. Prosky 1959; m. 2nd Hedy M. Cohn 1970; two s. one d. *Education:* Amherst Coll. Mass. *Career:* reporter and printer, Amherst Journal Record 1955–57; staff reporter, El Tiempo, Bogotá 1960; with Associated Press (AP) in New York and Miami 1960–65; reporter to Chief of Bureau, AP Brazil 1965–69; Exec. Rep. for Latin America, AP 1969–70; Business Man. and Admin. Dir AP-Dow Jones Econ. Report, London 1970–75; Deputy Dir AP World Services, New York 1975–80, Vice-Pres., Dir 1987–2003; Vice-Pres., Dir AP-Dow Jones News Services 1980–87; fmr Dir, Innovation Int. Media Consultancy Group, currently Sr Consultant; mem. Bd of Dirs World Press Inst. St Paul; mem. Int. Press Inst., Council on Foreign Relations. *Publications:* Her Job: Planning Meals for 200! 1963. *Honours:* San Giusto d'Oro Award, City of Trieste 1995. *Address:* Innnovation, 27 Stratton Road, Scarsdale, NY 10583-7556, USA (office). *Telephone:* (914) 725-1809 (office). *E-mail:* erbsen@innovation-mediaconsulting.com (office); headquarters@innovation-mediaconsulting.com (office). *Website:* www.innovation-mediaconsulting.com (office).

ERDRICH, (Karen) Louise, MA; American writer and poet; b. 7 June 1954, Little Falls, MN; d. of Ralph Louis Erdrich and Rita Joanne (Gourneau) Erdrich; m. Michael Anthony Dorris 1981 (died 1997); six c. (one s. deceased). *Education:* Dartmouth Coll., Johns Hopkins Univ. *Career:* Visiting Poetry Teacher, ND State Arts Council 1977–78; Teacher of Writing, Johns Hopkins Univ., Baltimore 1978–79; Communications Dir, Ed., Circle-Boston Indian Council 1979–80; Textbook Writer Charles Merrill Co. 1980; mem. PEN (mem. Exec. Bd 1985–90); Guggenheim Fellow 1985–86. *Publications include:* fiction: Love Medicine (Nat. Book Critics' Circle Award for best work of fiction) 1984, The Beet Queen 1986, Tracks 1988, The Crown of Columbus (with Michael Anthony Dorris) 1991, The Bingo Palace 1994, The Bluejay's Dance 1995, Tales of Burning Love 1996, The Antelope Wife 1998, The Birchbark House 1999, The Last Report on the Miracles at Little No Horse 2001, The Master Butcher's Singing Club 2003, Four Souls 2004, The Painted Drum 2005, The Plague of Doves 2008, The Red Convertible: Selected and New Stories 1978–2008 2009, Shadow Tag 2010; poetry: Jacklight 1984, Baptism of Desire 1989; non-fiction: Imagination (textbook) 1980; contrib. short stories, children's stories, essays and poems to anthologies and journals, including American Indian Quarterly, Atlantic, Frontiers, Kenyon Review, Ms, New England Review, New York Times Book Review, New Yorker, North American Review, Redbook. *Honours:* Nelson Algren Award 1982, Pushcart Prize 1983, Nat. Magazine Fiction Award 1983, 1987, First Prize O. Henry Awards 1987. *Literary Agent:* The Wylie Agency, 250 West 57th Street, Suite 2114, New York, NY 10107, USA. *Telephone:* (212) 246-0069. *Fax:* (212) 586-8953. *E-mail:* mail@wylieagency.com. *Website:* www.wylieagency.com.

ERENUS, Bilgesu, BA; Turkish playwright; b. 13 Aug. 1943, Bilecik; d. of Avni Duru and Aliye Duru; m. M. Erenus 1967 (divorced 1990); one s. *Education:* Kadiköy High School for Girls, Istanbul, Istanbul Conservatory of Music and Univ. of Istanbul. *Career:* scriptwriter, Türkiye Radyo Televizyon Kurumu (TRT—Turkish Radio-Television Corpn) 1965–73; playwright 1973–, 13 plays performed in Turkey, six published, several translated into French and German, one performed in Paris; social activist under mil. regime 1980–83, prosecuted by martial courts and held in solitary confinement. *Films include:* as scriptwriter: Bir Tren Yolculuğu 1988, İkili Oyun 1989, Devlerin Ölümü 1990. *Plays include:* Red Black Tree 2003. *Publications include:* Güneyli Bayan Lillian Hellman 1984, İnsan Aklını Koruma Enstitüsü 1994, Dokumacılar 1994, Kırmızı Karaağaç 1996, Gece 1996, Göz 1997, Kazi 1997, Halide 2000, Aydinlik Zindan (co-author) 2002, Böyle Bir Dünya 2002, Samur Kürk Uzayan Yolculuk 2004, Misafir 2004, Çağrı 2004. *Honours:* First Prize, World Children's Year Play Competition 1976, named Best Playwright in Turkey 1978. *Address:* Ayazpaşa Cami Sok, Saray Apt 10/12, Taksim, Istanbul, Turkey (home). *Telephone:* (1) 1432112 (home). *Website:* bilgesuerenus.com.

ERICKSON, Stephen (Steve) Michael, BA, MA; American novelist; b. 20 April 1950, Santa Monica, Calif.; m. Lori Precious; one s. one d. *Education:* Univ. of California, Los Angeles. *Career:* Arts Ed., LA Weekly 1989–91, Film Ed. 1992–93; Political Corresp., Rolling Stone 1995–96; Film Critic, Los Angeles magazine 2001–; Ed.-in-Chief Black Clock 2004–; Instructor, Calif. Inst. of the Arts 2001–. *Publications include:* Days Between Stations 1985, Rubicon Beach 1986, Tours of the Black Clock 1989, Leap Year 1989, Arc d'X 1993, Amnesiascope 1996, American Nomad 1997, The Sea Came in at Midnight 1999, Our Ecstatic Days 2005, Zeroville 2007; contrib. to New York Times, Esquire, Rolling Stone, Details, Elle, Los Angeles Times, Los Angeles Magazine, LA Weekly, LA Style, San Francisco Magazine, Salon, Conjunctions. *Honours:* Samuel Goldwyn Award 1972, Nat. Endowment for the Arts Fellowship 1987, John Simon Guggenheim Foundation Fellowship 2007. *Literary Agent:* c/o Melanie Jackson Agency, 41 West 72nd Street, Suite 3F, New York, NY 10023, USA. *Telephone:* (212) 873-3373. *E-mail:* m.jackson@mjalit.com. *Website:* www.steveerickson.org.

ERNAUX, Annie; French writer; b. (Annie Duchesne), 1 Sept. 1940, Lillebonne, Seine-Maritime; d. of the late Alphonse Duchesne and Blanche Dumenil; m. Philippe Ernaux 1964 (divorced); two s. *Education:* Lycée Jeanne-d'Arc, Rouen, Univs of Rouen, Bordeaux and Grenoble. *Career:* lived in Yvetot, Normandy as a child; turned from fiction to concentrate on autobiography early in her career; teacher of literature 1966–2000. *Publications:* Les armoires vides 1974, Ce qu'ils disent ou rien 1977, La femme gelée 1981, La place (Prix Renaudot 1984) 1984, Une femme 1989, Passion simple 1991, Journal du dehors 1993, La honte 1997, Je ne suis pas sortie de ma nuit 1997, La Vie Extérieure: 1993–1999 2000, L'événement 2000, Se perdre 2001, L'occupation 2002, L'écriture comme un couteau 2003, L'usage de la photo 2005, Les Années 2008, L'autre fille 2011, L'atelier noir 2011, Écrire la vie 2011. *Address:* 23 rue des Lozères, 95000 Cergy, France (home). *E-mail:* annie.ernaux@tiscali.fr (home).

ERPENBECK, Jenny; German author; b. 1967, Berlin; d. of John Erpenbeck and Doris Kilias; one s. *Career:* has worked on opera and theatre productions; currently freelance writer. *Plays:* Katzen Haben Sieben Leben (trans. as Cats Have Nine Lives) 2000. *Music:* operas directed: Cats Have Nine Lives, Graz 2000, Erwartung by Schoenberg and Bluebeard's Castle by Bartók, Opera House, Graz, Austria 2001, Acis and Galathea by Handel, States Opera Berlin 2003. *Publications include:* Geschichte vom alten Kind (trans. as The Old Child) 1999, Tand (short stories) 2001, Wörterbuch (trans. as The Book of Words) 2005, Heimsuchung (trans. as Visitation) 2008, Dinge, die verschwinden 2009, Le Bois de Klara 2009. *Honours:* Jury Prize, Ingeborg Bachmann Competition 2001, Solothurn Literature Prize, Switzerland 2008, Doderer Prize, Germany 2008. *Address:* c/o Eichborn AG, Kaiserstraße 66, Frankfurt am Main 60329, Germany. *Telephone:* (69) 256003-0. *Fax:* (69) 256003-30. *Website:* www.eichborn.de.

ERSKINE, Barbara, MA; British writer; b. 10 Aug. 1944, Nottingham, England; m.; two s. *Education:* Univ. of Edinburgh. *Career:* mem. Soc. of Authors, Scientific and Medical Network, Welsh Acad. *Publications include:* Lady of Hay 1986, Kingdom of Shadows 1988, Encounters 1990, Child of the Phoenix 1992, Midnight is a Lonely Place 1994, House of Echoes 1996, Distant Voices 1996, On the Edge of Darkness 1998, Whispers in the Sand 2000, Hiding from the Light 2002, Sands of Time 2003, Daughters of Fire 2006, The Warrior's Princess 2008, Time's Legacy 2010; contrib. of numerous short stories to magazines and journals. *Literary Agent:* c/o Blake Friedmann, 122 Arlington Road, London, NW1 7HP, England. *Telephone:* (20) 7284-0408. *Fax:* (20) 7284-0442. *Website:* www.blakefriedmann.co.uk.

ESCANDELL, Noemi, BLitt, BA, MA, PhD; Cuban academic and poet; b. (Noemi Escandell Santana), 27 Sept. 1936, Havana; d. of Luis Escandell and Ada Santana; m. Peter Knapp 1957 (divorced 1972); two s. two d. *Education:* Instituto de la Vibora, Queens Coll., City Univ. of New York, Harvard Univ. *Career:* Asst Prof., Bard Coll. 1976–83; Language Programme Dir, Nuevo Instituto de Centroamerica, Esteli, Nicaragua 1987–88; Prof. of Spanish, Westfield State Coll. 1983–93; Dir Afterschool Programme, Ross School, Washington, DC 1995–96; Poet-in-Residence, Millay Colony for the Arts, Austerlitz, New York 1983, 1991; mem. Academia Iberoamericana de Poesía (Washington, DC chapter). *Publications include:* Cuadros 1982, Ciclos 1982, Palabras/Words 1986; contrib. to anthologies and periodicals. *Honours:* First Prize in Poetry, Certamen Literario Int. Odon Betanzos Palacio 1996. *Address:* 1205 Mariposa Avenue, Apartment 426, Coral Gables, FL 33146, USA (home). *Telephone:* (305) 666-4075 (home). *E-mail:* noemiescandell@gmail.com (home).

ESENOV, Rahim; Turkmenistani journalist and writer. *Career:* freelance reporter for Radio Free Europe/Radio Liberty. *Publications include:* Ventsenosny Skitalets (The Crowned Wanderer, novel) 2003, Teni 'Zheltogo dominiona' 2009. *Honours:* PEN/Barbara Goldsmith Freedom to Write Award

(USA). *Address:* Radio Free Europe/Radio Liberty, Vinohradska 1, 110 00 Prague 1, Czech Republic (office). *E-mail:* rausovaa@rferl.org.

ESHLEMAN, (Ira) Clayton, BA, MAT; American poet, writer, translator, editor and academic; *Professor Emeritus, Eastern Michigan University*; b. 1 June 1935, Indianapolis, Ind.; s. of Ira Clayton and Gladys Maine Eshleman; m. 1st Barbara Novak 1961 (divorced 1967); one s.; m. 2nd Caryl Reiter 1970. *Education:* Indiana Univ. *Career:* Ed. Folio (three issues) 1959–60, Quena (one issue) 1966; Instructor in English, Univ. of Maryland Eastern Overseas Div. 1961–62; English Language Instructor, Matsushita Electric Corpn, Kobe, Japan 1962–64; Instructor, New York Univ. American Language Inst. 1966–68; Publr Caterpillar Books 1966–68; Founder-Ed. and Publr Caterpillar magazine 1967–73; Faculty mem. School of Critical Studies, California Inst. of the Arts, Valencia 1970–72; teacher of American poetry, American Coll., Paris, France 1973–74; Dreyfuss Poet-in-Residence and Lecturer in Creative Writing, California Inst. of Tech., Pasadena 1979–84; Visiting Lecturer in Creative Writing, Univ. of California at San Diego, Los Angeles, Santa Barbara and Riverside 1979–86; reviewer, Los Angeles Times Book Review 1979–86; Founder-Ed. Sulfur magazine 1981–2000; Prof. of English, Eastern Michigan Univ., Ypsilanti 1986–2003, Prof. Emer. 2003–; Regents Lecturer, UCLA 2007, Visiting Prof. 2008; numerous residencies, lecture programmes, workshops, readings across USA and abroad. *Publications include:* poetry and prose: Mexico & North 1962, The Chavin Illumination 1965, Lachrymae Mateo: Three Poems for Christmas 1966, Walks 1967, The Crocus Bud 1967, Cantaloups and Splendour 1968, Brother Stones 1968, T'ai 1969, Indiana 1969, The House of Ibuki 1969, The House of Okumura 1969, The Yellow River Record 1969, A Pitch-blende 1969, A Caterpillar Anthology: A Selection of Poetry and Prose from Caterpillar Magazine (ed.) 1971, Altars 1971, The Wand 1971, Bearings 1971, The Sanjo Bridge 1972, The Last Judgment: For Caryl on her Thirty-first Birthday, for the End of her Pain 1973, Coils 1973, Human Wedding 1973, Realignment 1974, Aux Morts 1974, Grotesca 1975, Portrait of Francis Bacon 1975, The Gull Wall 1975, The Woman Who Saw through Paradise 1976, Cogollo 1976, The Name Encanyoned River 1977, On Mules Sent from Chavin: A Journal and Poems 1977, Core Meander 1977, What She Means 1978, Nights We Put the Rock Together 1980, Hades in Manganese 1981, Fracture 1983, The Name Encanyoned River: Selected Poems 1960–85 1986, The Parallel Voyages (co-ed.) 1987, Hotel-Cro-Magnon 1989, Novices: A Study of Poetic Apprenticeship 1989, Antiphonal Swing: Selected Prose 1962–87 1989, Under World Arrest 1994, Nora's Roar 1996, From Scratch 1998, Erratics 2000, A Cosmogonic Collage: Sections I, II and V 2000, Jisei 2000, Companion Spider (essays) 2002, Sweetheart 2002, Everwhat 2002, Juniper Fuse: Upper Paleolithic Imagination & the Construction of the Underworld 2003, My Devotion 2004, Reciprocal Distillations 2006, A Shade of Paden 2006, An Alchemist with One Eye on Fire 2006, Deep Thermal (with Mary Heebner) 2006, Archaic Design 2007, The Grindstone of Rapport/A Clayton Eshleman Reader 2008, Anticline 2010, An Anatomy of the Night 2011; translations: Pablo Neruda, Residence on Earth 1962, César Vallejo, The Complete Posthumous Poetry (with Jose Rubia Barcia) 1978, Aimé Césaire, The Collected Poetry (with Annette Smith) 1983, Michel Deguy, Given Giving 1984, Bernard Bador, Sea Urchin Harakiri 1986, Conductors of the Pit: Major Works by Rimbaud, Vallejo, Césaire, Artaud & Holan 1988 and 2005, Aimé Césaire, Lyric & Narrative Poetry 1946–1983 (with Annette Smith) 1990, César Vallejo, Trilce (American Acad. of Poets Landon Trans. Prize) 1992, Antonin Artaud, Watchfiends & Rack Screams (with Bernard Bador) 1995, Aimé Césaire, Notebook of a Return of the Native Land (with Annette Smith) 2001, César Vallejo, The Complete Poetry (American Acad. of Poets Landon Trans. Prize) 2007, Solar Throat Slashed: The Unexpurgated 1948 Edition. Aimé Césaire (with A. James Arnold) 2011, Endure: Poems by Bei Dao 2011, Curdled Skulls: Poems by Bernard Bador 2011; contrib. of poems, essays, reviews and translations to periodicals, including Agni, American Poetry Review, Antaeus, Big Table, Boxkite (Australia), Brooklyn Rail, Chicago Review, Conjunctions, Denver Quarterly, Evergreen Review, Exquisite Corpse, Facture, Fence, Grand Street, Harper's, House Organ, Hunger, Kenyon Review, Los Angeles Times Book Review, Mandorla (Mexico City), Montemora, New American Writing, New Directions Annual, New York Times Sunday Book Review, Origin, Paris Review, Parnassus, Partisan Review, PoeSie (Paris), Poetry (Chicago), Rehauts (Paris), Sugar Mule, Tri-Quarterly, Ur Vox, Verse; numerous contribs to anthologies 1963–2005. *Honours:* Hon. DLitt (State Univ. of NY) 2000; Organization of American States grant 1964–65, Nat. Trans. Center Award (for trans. of Poemas Humanos) 1967, Poetry magazine award (for Five Poems) 1968, Nat. Trans. Center grants 1968, 1969, Co-ordinating Council of Literary Magazines grants (for Caterpillar) 1968–70, Fels Non-fiction Award 1975, Carnegie Author's Fund Award 1977, PEN Trans. Prize 1977, California Arts Council grants 1977–78, Guggenheim Fellowship (for research on Upper Paleolithic cave art) 1978, Nat. Book Award in Trans. 1979, Nat. Endowment for the Arts Poetry Fellowship 1979, grant 1983–96, and Trans. Fellowship 1988, Nat. Endowment for the Humanities grant (for research on Upper Paleolithic cave art) 1980, and Trans. Fellowship 1981, Witter Bynner trans. grant 1981, Soros Foundation travel grant to Hungary 1986, Cooper Fellow Swarthmore Coll. 1987, Michigan Arts Council grant 1988, USIA Mexican Trans. Project academic specialist grant 1992, Arts Foundation of Michigan Artists Award 1992, Council of Literary Magazines and Presses editorial fellowship (for Sulfur) 1992, Eastern Michigan Univ. Distinguished Faculty Research/Creativity Award 1989, research grants 1997, 1999, 2001, Research Fellowship 2002, and scholarship recognition (for Companion Spider) 2002, San Diego State Univ. Alfonse X. Sabio Award for Excellence in Literary Trans. 2002, residency Rockefeller Study Center, Bellagio, Italy 2004, Int. César Vallejo Conference 2007. *Address:* 210 Washtenaw Avenue, Ypsilanti, MI 48197, USA. *Telephone:* (734) 483-9787. *E-mail:* spidermind@comcast.net. *Website:* www.claytoneshleman.com.

ESLER, Gavin William James, BA, MA, FRSA; British broadcaster and writer; *Presenter, Newsnight*; b. 27 Feb. 1953, Glasgow, Scotland; m. Patricia Warner; one s. one d. *Education:* Univs of Kent and Leeds. *Career:* Presenter on BBC TV News and Radio (including Newsnight BBC 2, Dateline London BBC World, Four Corners BBC Radio 4); newspaper columnist. *Publications include:* fiction: Loyalties 1990, Deep Blue 1992, The Blood Brother 1995, A Scandalous Man 2008, Power Play 2010; non-fiction: The United States of Anger 1997; contrib. to anthologies, journals, periodicals, quarterlies, newspapers and magazines. *Honours:* Hon. MA (Univ. of Kent); Hon. DCL 2006; Royal Television Soc. Award, Sony Gold Award 2007. *Literary Agent:* c/o Toby Eady Associates, 9 Orme Court, London, W2 4RL, England. *Telephone:* (20) 7792-0092. *E-mail:* toby@tobyeady.demon.co.uk. *Website:* www.tobyeadyassociates.co.uk. *Address:* BBC Newsnight, Room G680, BBC TV Centre, Wood Lane, London, W12 7RJ, England (office). *E-mail:* gavin.esler@bbc.co.uk (office). *Website:* news.bbc.co.uk/1/hi/programmes/newsnight (office).

ESMENARD, Francis; French publisher; b. 8 Dec. 1936, Paris; s. of Robert Esmenard and Andrée Michel; one s. *Career:* Pres. and Dir-Gen. Editions Albin Michel 1982–, Paris; Vice-Pres. Nat. Publishing Syndicat 1979–; Prés. du Directoire 1999–. *Address:* Editions Albin Michel, 22 rue Huyghens, 75014 Paris, France (office). *Telephone:* 1-42-79-10-00 (office). *Fax:* 1-43-27-21-58 (office). *E-mail:* virginie.caminade@albin-michel.fr (office). *Website:* www.albin-michel.fr (office).

ESPADA, Martin, BA, JD; American poet and educator; *Professor of English, University of Massachusetts, Amherst*; b. 1957, Brooklyn, NY; m.; one s. *Education:* Univ. of Wisconsin, Northeastern Univ., Boston, Mass. *Career:* Prof. of English, Univ. of Massachusetts, Amherst; Poet Laureate of Northampton, Mass. *Publications include:* poetry: Trumpets From the Islands of their Eviction 1987, Rebellion is the Circle of a Lover's Hands 1990, City of Coughing and Dead Radiators 1993, Imagine the Angels of Bread 1996, A Mayan Astronomer in Hell's Kitchen 2000, Alabanza: New and Selected Poems 1982–2002 2003, The Republic of Poetry 2006, Crucifixion in the Plaza De Armas 2008, The Lover of a Subversive Is Also a Subversive 2010, The Trouble Ball: Poems 2011; ed.: El Coro: A Chorus of Latino and Latina Poets 1997, Poetry Like Bread: Poets of the Political Imagination 2000; other: Zapata's Disciple: Essays 1998; contrib. to publs, including New York Times Book Review, Harpers, The Nation, The Best American Poetry. *Honours:* American Book Award, PEN/Voelker Award for Poetry, Paterson Poetry Prize, Ind. Publr Book Award, Nat. Endowment for the Arts Fellowships, PEN/Revson Fellowship, Massachusetts Artists Foundation Fellowship. *Address:* Department of English, University of Massachusetts, 251 Bartlett Hall, Amherst, MA 01003, USA (office). *Telephone:* (413) 545-6594 (office). *Fax:* (413) 545-3880 (office). *E-mail:* mespada@english.umass.edu (office); martin@martinespada.net (office). *Website:* www.umass.edu/english (office); www.martinespada.net.

ESPOSITO, Nancy Giller, BA, MA; American poet, writer, editor and academic; *Senior Lecturer, Bentley College*; b. 1 Jan. 1942, Dallas, Tex. *Education:* Univ. of Wisconsin, New York Univ. *Career:* Assoc. Prof., Illinois Central Coll., East Peoria 1968–70; Instructor, Harvard Univ. 1976–80, 1981–84, Wellesley Coll. 1980; Lecturer, Tufts Univ. 1986–93, Boston Coll. 1994; Sr Lecturer, Bentley Coll. 1986–; CIEE Seminar, Viet Nam 2002; Virginia Center for the Creative Arts Fellow 1979–81, 1990, 2003–04, Yaddo Fellow 1981, MacDowell Colony Fellow 1986–87, Ragdale Foundation Fellow 1990; mem. Acad. of American Poets, Associated Writing Programs, Poetry Soc. of America, Poets and Writers, PEN. *Publications include:* Changing Hands 1984, Mêm' Rain 2002, Greatest Hits 1978–2001 2003; contrib. to anthologies, including Two Decades of New Poets 1984, Ixok-Amar-Go 1987, Quarterly Review of Literature 50th Anniversary Anthology 1993, Poetry from Sojourner 2004, and to reviews, journals and periodicals. *Honours:* Discovery/The Nation Award 1979, Colladay Award 1984, Gordon Barber Memorial Award, Poetry Soc. of America 1987, Fulbright-Hays Grant, Egypt 1988, Publishing Award 1988, Faculty Devt Fund Grants, Bentley Coll. 1997, 1999, 2003, Bentley Coll. Faculty Grant (Viet Nam) 2002, (Argentina) 2003, Bentley Coll. Faculty Affairs Cttee Grant 2010. *Address:* Department of English, Bentley College, 175 Forest Street, Waltham, MA 02452 (office); 21 Hurd Road, Belmont, MA 02478-3549, USA (home). *Telephone:* (781) 891-3103 (home). *E-mail:* nesposito@bentley.edu (office). *Website:* www.bentley.edu/english (office).

ESQUIVEL, Laura; Mexican novelist; b. 30 Sept. 1950, México, DF; m. 1st Alfonso Arau (divorced); m. 2nd Javier Valdez. *Publications include:* Como agua para chocolate (trans. as Like Water for Chocolate, novel) 1990, La ley del amor (The Law of Love) 1996, Íntimas suculencias (Trans. as Between Two Fires: Intimate Writings on Life, Love, Food and Flavour) 1998, Estrellita Marinera 1999, El libro de las emociones: son de la razón sin corazón 2000, Tan veloz como el deseo (Swift as Desire) 2001, Malinche 2006, La Voce dell'acqua 2006, Bittersüße Schokolade 2007, Schnell wie die Sehnsucht 2008. *Honours:* American Booksellers Asscn ABBY Award 1994.

ESSOP, Ahmed, BA; South African/Indian writer; b. 1 Sept. 1931, Dabhel, India; m. 1960; one s. three d. *Education:* Univ. of South Africa. *Career:* teacher, secondary school Johannesburg 1980–85. *Publications include:* The Hajii and Other Stories (Olive Schreiner Award, English Acad. of Southern Africa 1979) 1978, The Visitation 1980, The Emperor 1984, Noorjehan and Other Stories 1990, The King of Hearts and Other Stories 1997, Narcissus and Other Stories 2002, Suleiman M. Nana: A Biographical and Historical Record of His Life and Times 2002, The Third Prophecy 2004, History and Satire in Salman Rushdie's The Satanic Verses 2009, Exile (poetry) 2010, A Commentary on the Ruba'iyat of Omar Khayyam 2010, The Universe and Other Essays 2010, The Moors in the Plays of Shakespeare 2011, The Garden of Shahrazad and Other Poems 2011. *Honours:* Literary Lifetime Achievement Award, Ministry of Arts and Culture 2007. *Address:* PO Box 1747, Lenasia 1820, Johannesburg, South Africa (home). *Telephone:* (11) 854-4267 (home). *E-mail:* kadera@telkomsa.net (home).

ESTERER-WANDSCHNEIDER, Ingeborg Charlotte Martha Katharina, DrPhil; German journalist; b. 18 Feb. 1926, Mainz; d. of Jakob-Ernst Günther and Charlotte Günther; m. 1st Rainer Esterer 1951; m. 2nd Hajo Wandschneider 1972; one s. one d. *Education:* high schools in Mainz and Berlin and Univs of Berlin and Hamburg. *Career:* freelance journalist 1948–51, 1990–; Sec. Inst. français, Hamburg 1951–53; Ed. Kristall (entertainment and science magazine) 1954–60; freelance radio journalist and trans. of French and English books 1960–70; Public Relations Officer, Amnesty International (German Section) 1968–70; Leading Ed. Vital (health and fitness magazine) 1970–83, Für Sie (women's magazine) 1983–90. *Honours:* First Prize (Medical Journalism—Ophthalmology) 1989. *Address:* Cranachstrasse 39, 2000 Hamburg 52, Germany. *Telephone:* (40) 893154.

ESTERHÁZY, Péter; Hungarian writer and essayist; b. 14 April 1950, s. of Mátyás Esterházy and Lili Mányoky; m. Gitta Reén; two s. two d. *Education:* Budapest Univ. *Career:* worked as a system supervisor; full-time writer 1978–. *Publications:* short stories: Fancsikó és Pinta 1976, Pápai vizeken ne kalózkodj! 1977, Utazás a 16-os mélyére 2006; novels: Termelési regény 1979, Függő 1981, Ki szavatol a lady biztonságáért? 1982, Fuharosok 1983, Kis magyar pornográfia (trans. as A Little Hungarian Pornography) 1984, A sziv segédigéi 1985, Bevezetés a szépirodalomba 1986, Tizenhét hattyúk (trans. as Csokonai Lili) 1987, Hrabal könyve (trans. as The Book of Hrabal) 1990, Hahn-Hahn grófnő pillantása (trans. as The Glance of Countess Hahn-Hahn Down the Danube) 1991, Egy nő (trans. as She Loves Me) 1995, Harmonia caelistis (trans. as Celestial Harmonies) 2000, Semmi művészet (trans. as Not Art) 2008; essays: A kitömött hattyú 1988, Az elefántcsonttoronyból 1991, A halacska csodálatos élete 1991, Egy kékharisnya följegyzéseiből 1994, Egy kék haris 1996, A szabadság nehéz mámora 2003. *Honours:* Füst Milán, Déry, Kossuth Prize 1996, József Attila, Krúdy, Aszu, Márai, Magyar Irodalini Díj, Vilenica awards, Österreichische Staatspreis für europäische Literatur, Grinzane Cavour Prize 2004, Frankfurt Book Fair Peace Prize 2004, Pro Europa Prize 2004, Premio Letterario Internazionale Pablo Neruda 2006, Angelus Prize 2008. *Address:* Emöd utca 20, 1031 Budapest, Hungary. *E-mail:* esterhazypeter@irolap.hu (office). *Website:* esterhazy.irolap.hu.

ESTES, Angie, PhD; American poet. *Education:* Univ. of Oregon. *Career:* fmr Prof. of American Literature and Creative Writing, California Polytechnic State Univ., San Luis Obispo; taught creative writing at Oberlin Coll., Univ. of Illinois, Urbana-Champaign, and Ohio State Univ.; mem. faculty, Ashland Univ. MFA program; mem. Oklahoma State Univ. MFA, PhD Program. *Publications include:* poetry collections: The Uses of Passion (Peregrine Smith Poetry Prize) 1995, Voice-Over (Field Poetry Prize 2001, Poetry Soc. of America Alice Fay di Castagnola Prize 2001) 2002, Chez Nous 2005, Tryst 2009; contrib. poems to numerous anthologies and literary magazines including TriQuarterly, The Paris Review, Ploughshares, Boston Review and Slate. *Honours:* fellowships, grants and residencies from Nat. Endowment for the Humanities, Nat. Endowment for the Arts, Woodrow Wilson Foundation, American Acad. in Rome, Calif. Arts Council, MacDowell Colony, Ohio Arts Council; Pushcart Prize, Poetry Soc. of America Cecil Hemley Memorial Award, Guggenheim Fellowship 2010. *Address:* c/o Oberlin College Press, 50 North Professor Street, Oberlin, OH 44074-1095, USA. *E-mail:* chezestes@yahoo.com. *Website:* www.angieestes.com.

ESTÉVEZ, Abilio, BLit, DPhil; Cuban writer; b. 7 Jan. 1954, Havana. *Education:* Havana Univ. *Career:* Ed. literary journal, El Caimán Barbudo 1987–88; Ed.-in-Chief literary journal, Conjunto (in Drama Dept, Casa de las Américas) 1988; Visiting Prof. of Hispanoamerican Literature, Sassari Univ., Italy 1989; Prof. of Drama, Escuela Nacional de Teatro Alvaro de Rosson, Venezuela 1991; Prof., Casa de las Américas, Havana 1992; Head of Drama Dept, Ollantay Org., New York, USA 1993; fmr Arts Ed., literary journals, Quimera de España, Dialog de Polonia, Casa de las Américas, Unión, Tablas, Revolución y Cultura; mem. Editorial Bd of literary journal, La Gaceta de Cuba. *Plays include:* La verdadera culpa de Juan Clemente Zenea (Premio de la Crítica 1987, Festival de Teatro de La Habana Premio Santiago Pita 1991) 1987, Yo tuve un sueño feliz (Premio de la Crítica 1991) 1989, Perla marina 1993, La Noche (Instituto de Cooperación Iberoamericana Premio Teatral Tirso de Molina, Madrid 1994) 1994, Santa Cecilia 1995. *Publications include:* Juego con Gloria (short stories) 1982, Manual de tentaciones (poems) (Premio Luis Cernuda, Spain 1989, Premio de Crítica Cubana 1989) 1989, Regreso a Cyterea (short story) 1993, Muerte y transfiguración (poem) 1995, Tuyo es el reino (novel, trans. as Thine Is the Kingdom) (Premio de la Crítica Cubana 1999) 1997, El horizonte y otros regresos (short stories) 1998, Los palacios distantes (novel, trans. as Distant Palaces) (Premio Internacional de Novela Rómulo Gallegos 2003) 2002, Ceremonias para actores desesperados 2004, Inventario secreto de La Habana 2005, El Navegante Dormido 2008, Le navigateur endormi 2010. *Honours:* Unión de Escritores y Artistas de Cuba Premio José Antonio Ramos 1984. *Address:* c/o Tusquets Editores, Cesare Cantù 8, 08023 Barcelona, Spain. *Website:* www.tusquetseditores.com.

ESTLEMAN, Loren Daniel, BA; American writer; b. 15 Sept. 1952, Ann Arbor, Mich.; s. of Leauvett C. Estleman and Louise A. Estleman; m. Deborah Ann Green 1993; one step-s. one step-d. *Education:* Eastern Mich., Univ. *Career:* police reporter, Ypsilanti Press 1972–73; Ed.-in-Chief, Community Foto News 1975–76; Special Writer, Ann Arbor News 1976; staff writer, Dexter Leader 1977–80; full-time novelist 1980–; Vice-Pres. Western Writers of America 1998–2000, Pres. 2000–02. *Publications:* novels: The Oklahoma Punk 1976, The Hider, Sherlock Holmes vs. Dracula 1978, The High Rocks 1979, Dr. Jekyll and Mr. Holmes, Stamping Ground, Motor City Blue 1980, Aces and Eights, Angel Eyes, The Wolfer 1981, Murdock's Law, The Midnight Man 1982, Mister St John, The Glass Highway 1983, This Old Bill, Sugartown, Kill Zone, The Stranglers 1984, Every Brilliant Eye, Roses Are Dead, Gun Man 1985, Any Man's Death 1986, Lady Yesterday 1987, Bloody Season, Downriver 1988, Silent Thunder, Peeper 1989, Sweet Women Lie, Whiskey River 1990, Sudden Country, Motown 1991, King of the Corner 1992, City of Widows 1994, Edsel 1995, Stress 1996, Never Street, Billy Gashade 1997, The Witchfinder, Journey of the Dead, Jitterbug 1998, The Rocky Mountain Moving Picture Association 1999, The Hours of the Virgin 1999, White Desert 2000, The Master Executioner 2001, Sinister Heights 2002, Something Borrowed, Something Black 2002, Black Powder, White Smoke 2002, Poison Blonde 2003, Port Hazard 2004, Retro 2004, Little Black Dress 2005, The Undertaker's Wife 2005, Nicotine Kiss 2006, The Adventures of Johnny Vermillion, 2006, American Detective 2007, Amos Walker's Detroit 2007, Frames 2008, Gas City 2008, The Branch and the Scaffold 2009, Alone 2009, The Book of Murdock 2010, Amos Walker: The Complete Story Collection 2010, The Left-Handed Dollar 2010, Infernal Angels 2011; non-fiction: The Wister Trace 1987, Writing the Popular Novel 2004; collections: General Murders 1988, The Best Western Stories of Loren D. Estleman 1989, People Who Kill 1993; anthologies: P.I. Files 1990, Deals with the Devil 1994, American West 2001. *Honours:* Western Writers of America Spur Award, Best Historical Novel 1981, Spur Award, Best Short Fiction 1986, 1996, Private Eye Writers of America Shamus Award, Best Novel 1984, Shamus Award, Best Short Story 1985, 1988, Mich. Foundation of the Arts Award for Literature 1987, Mich. Library Asscn Authors Award 1997, Spur Award, Best Western Novel 1999, Western Heritage Award, Outstanding Western Novel 1998, 2001, Western Heritage Award, Outstanding Short Story 2000, Western Heritage Award for Outstanding Western Novel 2001, Shamus Award for Best Short Story 2003; Dr hc of Humane Letters, Eastern Mich. Univ. 2002. *Address:* c/o Tor/Forge Books, 175 Fifth Avenue, New York, NY 10010 (office); 5552 Walsh Road, Whitmore Lake, MI 48189, USA (home). *Website:* www.lorenestleman.com.

ESZTERHAS, Joseph (Joe) A.; American scriptwriter; b. 23 Nov. 1944, Csakanydoroszlo, Hungary; s. of Stephen Eszterhas and Maria Biro; m. 1st Geraldine Javer 1972 (divorced 1994); one s. one d.; m. 2nd Naomi Baka 1994; one s. *Education:* Ohio State Univ. *Career:* reporter, Plain Dealer, Cleveland; staff writer, Man. Ed. Rolling Stone, San Francisco 1971–75; screenwriter 1975–; writer and producer, Checking Out 1980, Betrayed 1989. *Film screenplays:* FIST 1978, Flashdance 1983, Jagged Edge 1985, Big Shots 1987, Betrayed 1988, Checking Out 1989, Music Box 1990, Hearts of Fire 1990, Basic Instinct 1992, Nowhere to Run 1993, Sliver 1993, Showgirls 1995, Jade 1995, Telling Lies in America 1997, An Alan Smithee Film: Burn Hollywood Burn 1997, Basic Instinct 2 2006, Szabadság, szerelem 2006. *Publications:* novels: Thirteen Seconds: Confrontation at Kent State 1970, Charlie Simpson's Apocalypse 1974, Nark! 1974, Fist 1977; non-fiction: Hollywood Animal: A Memoir 2004, The Devil's Guide to Hollywood: The Screenwriter as God! 2006, Crossbearer: A Memoir of Faith 2008. *Honours:* recipient of various awards. *Address:* c/o St Martin's Press, 175 Fifth Avenue, New York, NY 10010, USA (office). *Website:* www.joeeszterhas.com.

ETCHEMENDY, Nancy Howell, BA; American writer and poet; b. 1952, Reno, Nev.; m. John W. Etchemendy 1973; one s. *Education:* Univ. of Nevada, Reno. *Career:* mem. Horror Writers' Asscn, Treas. 1996–97, Trustee 1997–98; mem. Soc. of Children's Book Writers, Science Fiction and Fantasy Writers of America (SFWA), Clarion Foundation Treas. 2006–. *Publications include:* The Watchers of Space 1980, Stranger from the Stars 1983, The Crystal City 1985, The Power of UN 2000, Cat in Glass 2002; contribs: numerous short stories, essays and individual poems to magazines and journals. *Honours:* Bram Stoker Award 1998, 2002, 2004, Georgia Children's Book Award, Golden Duck Award, Int. Horror Guild Award. *Literary Agent:* c/o Virginia Knowlton, Curtis Brown Ltd, 10 Astor Place, New York, NY 10003, USA. *Telephone:* (212) 473-5400 (office). *Website:* www.curtisbrown.com (office). *E-mail:* nancy@etchemendy.com. *Website:* etchemendy.com (office).

ETTER, David (Dave) Pearson, BA; American fmr poet, writer and editor; b. 18 March 1928, Huntington Park, Calif.; m. Margaret A. Cochran 1959; one s. one d. *Education:* Univ. of Iowa. *Career:* Promotion Dept, Indiana Univ. Press 1959–60; Rand McNally Publishing Co. 1960–61; Ed., Northwestern Univ. Press 1962–63; Asst Ed., Encyclopaedia Britannica, Chicago 1964–73; Ed., Northern Illinois Univ. Press 1974–80; freelance writer, poet and ed. 1981–87; teacher of creative writing and other jobs 1988–97. *Publications* include: Go Read the River 1966, The Last Train to Prophetstown 1968, Well You Needn't 1975, Central Standard Time 1978, Open to the Wind 1978, Riding the Rock Island Through Kansas 1979, Cornfields 1980, West of Chicago 1981, Boondocks 1982, Alliance, IL 1983, Home State 1985, Live at the Silver Dollar 1986, Selected Poems 1987, Midlanders 1988, Electric Avenue 1988, Carnival 1990, Sunflower County 1994, How High the Moon 1996, The Essential Dave Etter 2001, Greatest Hits 1960–2000 2002, Looking for Sheena Easton 2004, The Liontamer's Daughter: Poems of Humor and Satire 2008, Dandelions 2010; contrib. to Poetry, Nation, Chicago Review, Kansas Quarterly, Prairie Schooner, Poetry Northwest, TriQuarterly, Massachusetts Review, North American Review, Ohio Review, New Letters, Shenandoah, Beloit Poetry Journal, El Corno Emplumado, San Francisco Review, New Mexico Quarterly, Mark Twain Journal, Slow Dancer (England), among others. Honours: Soc. of Midland Authors Poetry Prize 1967, Friends of Literature Poetry Prize 1967, Bread Loaf Writers' Conference Fellowship in Poetry 1967, Illinois Sesquicentennial Poetry Prize 1968, Theodore Roethke Poetry Prize 1971, Carl Sandburg Poetry Prize 1982. Address: 628 East Locust Street, Lanark, IL 61046, USA (home). Telephone: (815) 493-4017 (home).

ETXEBARRIA, Lucía; Spanish writer; b. 7 Dec. 1966, Valencia. Career: Writer-in-Residence, Univ. of Aberdeen 2000; fmr journalist on Route 66; fmr promoter in New Media; fmr communication officer in Fnac Callao. Publications: La historia de Kurt y Courtney 1996, Amor prozac curiosidad y la duda 1997, Beatriz y los cuerpos celestes (LIV Ganador del Premio Nadal) 1998, Nosotras Que No Somos Como Las demas 1999, La Eva Futura, La letra Futura 2000, Ser único. En: Ser mujer. Freixas, Laura 2000, Estación de infierno 2001, De Todo Lo Lo visible y no invisible (V Premio de novela ganadora la primavera) 2001, En Brazos de la Mujer fetiche 2002, Una historia de amor como otra cualquiera 2003, Courtney y yo 2004, Actos de placer y de amor (Ganador del Premio Barcarola XX) 2004, Un milagro en Equilibrio (Ganador del Premio Planeta LIII) 2004; screenplay: Edge 1999, La mujer de mi vida 2001, Amor curiosidad prozac y dudas 2001, Te amo bebé 2001. Honours: Spring Prize Novel 2001. Address: Destino, 4 Peu de la Creu, 08001 Barcelona, Spain. Telephone: (49) 3437100. Fax: (49) 5057059. E-mail: edicionesedestino@edestino.es. Website: www.planetadelibros.com/editorial-ediciones-destino-7.html.

ETZIONI, Amitai, BA, MA, PhD; American sociologist, academic and writer; *Professor, George Washington University*; b. 4 Jan. 1929, Cologne, Germany; m. 1st Minerva Morales 1965 (died 1985); five s.; m. 2nd Patricia Kellogg 1992. Education: Hebrew Univ., Jerusalem, Israel, Univ. of California, Berkeley. Career: Faculty, Columbia Univ. 1958–67, Prof. of Sociology 1967–78, Chair. Dept of Sociology 1969–78; Founder-Dir Center for Policy Research 1968–; Guest Scholar, Brookings Inst. 1978–79; Sr Adviser, The White House, Washington, DC 1979–80; Prof., George Washington Univ. 1980–, Dir Center for Communitarian Studies 1995–; Thomas Henry Carroll Ford Foundation Visiting Prof., Grad. School of Business, Harvard Univ. 1987–89; Ed. The Responsive Community: Rights and Responsibilities quarterly 1990–; Founder-Dir The Communitarian Network 1993–; Fellow, Center for Advanced Study in the Behavioral Sciences 1965–66; mem. American Sociological Asscn (Pres. 1995), Soc. for the Advancement of Socio-Economics (Founder-Pres. 1989–90, Hon. Fellow). Publications include: A Comparative Analysis of Complex Organizations 1961, Modern Organizations 1964, Political Unification: A Comparative Study of Leaders and Forces 1965, Studies in Social Change 1966, The Active Society 1968, Genetic Fix 1973, Social Problems 1975, An Immodest Agenda 1982, Capital Corruption 1984, The Moral Dimension 1988, The Spirit of Community: Rights, Responsibilities and the Communitarian Agenda 1993, The New Golden Rule: Community and Morality in a Democratic Society 1996, The Limits of Privacy 1999, My Brother's Keeper 2004, The Common Good 2004, From Empire to Community: A New Approach to International Relations 2004, How Patriotic is the Patriot Act? Freedom versus Security in the Age of Terrorism 2004, Security First: For a Muscular, Moral Foreign Policy 2007, New Common Ground: A New America, A New World 2009, Essays in Socio-Economics (Ethical Economy) 2010, Law in a New Key: Essays on Law and Society 2011; contrib. to scholarly journals, newspapers, periodicals and TV. Honours: several hon. doctorates; Social Science Research Council Fellowship 1960–61, Guggenheim Fellowship 1968–69, American Revolution Bicentennial Comm. Certificate of Appreciation 1976, Simon Wiesenthal Center Tolerance Book Award 1997, Meister Eckhart Prize 2009. Address: Institute for Communication Policy Studies, George Washington University, Suite 703, 2130 H Street NW, Washington, DC 20052, USA (office). Telephone: (202) 994-8190 (office). Fax: (202) 994-1606 (office). E-mail: etzioni@gwv.edu (office). Website: www.communitariannetwork.org (office); www.amitaietzioni.org.

EUGENIDES, Jeffrey, BA, MA; American novelist; b. 8 March 1960, Detroit, Mich.; m.; one d. Education: Brown Univ., Stanford Univ. Career: Fellow, Berliner Künstlerprogramm 2002; Guggenheim Foundation Fellowship, Nat. Foundation for the Arts Fellowship, American Acad. in Berlin Prize Fellowship 2000–01; teacher in Creative Writing Program, Princeton Univ. 1999–2000, Prof. of Creative Writing, Peter B. Lewis Center for the Arts 2007–. Publications: The Virgin Suicides 1993, Middlesex (Pulitzer Prize for Fiction 2003, WELT-Literaturpreis, Great Lakes Book Award) 2002, Air Mail 2005, My Mistress's Sparrow is Dead (Ed.) 2008, The Marriage Plot 2011); contrib. to The New Yorker, The Paris Review, The Yale Review, The Gettysburg Review, Best American Short Stories, Granta's Best of Young American Novelists. Honours: Whiting Writers' Award, American Acad. of Arts and Letters Harold D. Vursell Memorial Award. Address: New South Building, Floor 6, Princeton University, 185 Nassau Street, Princeton, NJ 08544, USA (office). Telephone: (609) 258-8561 (office). Fax: (609) 258-2230 (office). E-mail: jeugenid@princeton.edu (office). Website: www.princeton.edu/~visarts/cwr (office).

EULO, Ken; American playwright, stage director and novelist; b. 17 Nov. 1939, Newark, NJ; m.; one s. Education: Univ. of Heidelberg, Germany. Career: Artistic Dir Courtyard Playhouse, New York; staff writer, Paramount; f. Brownstone Author Publr Services, Orlando, Fla; mem. Dramatists' Guild, Italian Playwrights of America, Writers' Guild of America. Publications include: plays: Bang? 1969, Zarf, I Love You 1969, SRO 1970, Puritan Night 1971, Billy Hofer and the Quarterback Sneak 1971, Black Jesus 1972, The Elevator 1972, 48 Spring Street 1973, Final Exams 1975, The Frankenstein Affair 1979, Say Hello to Daddy 1979; fiction: Bloodstone 1982, The Brownstone 1982, The Deathstone 1982, Nocturnal 1983, The Ghost of Veronica 1985, House of Caine 1988, Manhattan Heat 1991, Claw 1994; other: TV scripts; contribs to magazines and newspapers. Address: Brownstone Author Publisher Services, PO Box 999, Orlando, FL 32888, USA. Telephone: (407) 345-1615 (office). E-mail: info@brownstoneaps.com (office). Website: www.brownstoneaps.com.

EVANS, Aled Lewis, BA, BTh; Welsh poet, writer, tutor, lay preacher and broadcaster; b. 9 Aug. 1961, Machynlleth, Powys; s. of Lewis Evans and Iola Ann Atkinson. Education: Univ. Coll. of North Wales, Bangor and Univ. of Wales, Aberystwyth. Career: fmr teacher of Welsh, English and Head of Media, Ysgol Morgan Llwyd, Wrexham; teacher bilingual creative writing classes, Wrexham Library, Mold Library, Yale Coll., Wrexham; fmr producer and presenter, Marcher Sound radio; frequent contrib. to BBC Radio Cymru; judge at several Eisteddfodau, Wales Book of the Year 2010; mem. Gorsedd of Bards, Chester Poets, Literature Wales; Chair. Literature Cttee, Wrexham Nat. Eisteddfod 2011. Theatre includes: The Cafe, Wrexham Festival 2004, Mari'r Golau (to commemorate Welsh religious revival), Deufor Gyfarfod (to commemorate Welsh hymn-writer, Ann Griffiths), Ffenestri (pageant based on Glyn Ceiriog village hall windows) 2011. Music includes: translated worldwide hit You Raise Me Up into Welsh (subsequently recorded by Fron Choir, Rhydian Roberts, Ysgol Glanaethwy, Craig Ryder and others). Recordings include: original songs recorded on various CDs, including Deimli Di y Rhin and Ein Can featured in Can i Gymru Song for Wales 1999, also hymn Pan y gweli wyrth y cread; co-wrote Y Band Undyn with Daniel Lloyd (featured on BBC). Television: featured in S4C documentary Pobl y Ffin (People of the Border) 2011. Publications include: Tonnau 1989, Ga i ddarn o awyr las heddiw? 1991, Sglefrfyrddio 1994, Wavelengths (in trans.) 1995, Bro Maelor 1996, Mendio Gondola 1997, Llyfr Erchwyn Gwely 1998, Troeon 1998, Mixing the Colours (in trans.) 1999; fiction: Rhwng Dau Lanw Medi (Between Two September Tides) 1994, Y Caffi (The Cafe) 2002, Aur yn y Gwallt (short stories) 2004, Dim angen creu teledu yma 2007, Adlais 2007, Driftwood (short stories in English) (Wrexham County's Big Read Award 2010) 2010, Amheus O Angylion (Welsh edn) 2011, Something Someone (poetry collection) 2012; contrib. to Barn, Golwg, Y Traethodydd, Poetry Wales and other Welsh periodicals; to anthologies, including A White Afternoon 1998, The Bloodaxe Book of Modern Welsh Poetry 2003, several Welsh language anthologies. Honours: Nat. Eisteddfod of Wales literary awards 1991, 1998, 1999, Bursary, Academi Welsh Arts Council 2006. Address: 28 Jubilee Road, Pentrefelin, Wrexham, Wrexham Co., LL13 7NN, Wales (home). Telephone: (1978) 354164 (office). E-mail: aledlewisevans@yahoo.co.uk (office).

EVANS, C. Stephen, BA, PhD; American philosopher and writer; *University Professor of Philosophy and the Humanities, Baylor University*; b. 26 May 1948, Atlanta, Ga; m. Jan Walter Evans 1969, one s. two d. Education: Wheaton Coll., Yale Univ. Career: Asst Prof., Wheaton Coll., Ill. 1974–78, Assoc. Prof. 1978–82, Prof. 1982–84; Prof. of Philosophy and Psychology, Kierkegaard Library Curator, St Olaf Coll., Northfield, Minn. 1986–94, Division Chair 1991–93; Prof. of Philosophy, Calvin Coll., Grand Rapids, Mich. 1994–2001, William Spoelhof Teacher-Scholar 1994–96; Univ. Prof. of Philosophy and the Humanities, Baylor Univ. 2001–; Lectures; George C. Marshall Fellow 1977–78, Fellow, Center for Faith Development, Emory Univ. 1988–89; mem. American Philosophical Asscn, Kierkegaard Soc., Pres., 1991, Soc. of Christian Philosophers. Publications include: Despair: A Moment or a Way of Life? 1971, Preserving the Person: A Look at the Human Sciences 1977, Subjectivity and Religious Belief: An Historical Critical Study 1978, Kierkegaard's Fragments, and Postscripts: The Religious Philosophy of Johannes Climacus 1983, Contours of Christian Philosophy, Vol. IV: Philosophy of Religion: Thinking about Faith 1985, The Quest for Faith: Reason and Mystery as Pointers to God 1986, Wisdom and Humanness in Psychology 1989, Søren Kierkegaard's Christian Psychology 1990, Passionate Reason: Making Sense of Kierkegaard's Philosophical Fragments 1992, Foundation of Kierkegaard's Vision of Community: Religion, Ethics, and Politics in Kierkegaard 1992, The Historical Christ and the Jesus of Faith: The Incarnational Narrative as History 1996, Faith Beyond Reason 1998, Pocket Dictionary of Philosophy of Religion and Apologetics 2002, Kierkegaard's Ethic of Love: Divine Commands and Moral Requirements 2004, Kierkegaard on Faith and the Self: Collected Essays 2006, Kierkegaard: An Introduction 2009, Natural Signs and Knowledge of God: A New Look at Theistic Arguments 2010; contribs: articles and reviews to journals. Honours: Nat. Endowment for the Humanities Fellowships 1988–89, 2000–01, Pew Evangelical Senior Scholar 1991–94. Address: Department of Philosophy, Baylor

University, Morrison Hall 210, One Bear Place #97273, Waco, TX 76798-7273, USA (office). *Telephone:* (254) 710-7333 (office). *E-mail:* c_stephen_evans@baylor.edu (office). *Website:* www.baylor.edu/philosophy (office).

EVANS, George, BA, MA; American writer, poet, translator and editor; b. Pittsburgh, Pa. *Education:* Johns Hopkins Univ., Carnegie-Mellon Univ. *Career:* medical corpsman and sergeant in USAF 1967–70; Founder-Ed. Streetfare Journal project. *Publications include:* poetry: Nightvision 1983, Wrecking 1988, Eye Blade 1989, Sudden Dreams: New & Selected Poems 1991; ed.: Charles Olson and Cid Corman: Complete Correspondence 1950–64. *Honours:* Lanann Foundation Fellowship, Nat. Endowment of the Arts Fellowship, California Arts Fellowship, Monbusho Fellowship from Japanese Ministry of Educ. *Address:* c/o Curbstone Press, 321 Jackson Street, Willimantic, Conn. 06226-1738, USA. *E-mail:* info@curbstone.org.

EVANS, Sir Harold Matthew, Kt, KBE, MA; American (b. British) author, publisher and fmr newspaper editor and author; b. 28 June 1928, Manchester, England; s. of the late Frederick and Mary Evans; m. 1st Enid Parker 1953 (divorced 1978); one s. two d.; m. 2nd Tina Brown 1982; one s. one d. *Education:* St .Mary's Road Central School, Loreburn Coll., Manchester, Durham Univ. *Career:* Commonwealth Fund Fellow, Univ. of Chicago 1956–57; Lecturer, Workers' Education Asscn 1959; Ed. Sunday Times, London 1967–81, The Times 1981–82; mem. Bd Times Newspapers Ltd, Dir 1978–82; Int. Press Inst. 1974–80; Dir Goldcrest Films and Television 1982–85; Visiting Prof., Duke Univ. 1983; Ed.-in-Chief Atlantic Monthly 1984–86, Contributing Ed. 1986–, Editorial Dir and Vice-Chair. 1998–; Ed. Dir U.S. News and World Report 1984–86, Contributing Ed. 1986–, Editorial Dir and Vice-Chair. 1998, currently Editor at Large, The Week; Vice-Pres. and Sr Ed. Weidenfeld and Nicolson 1986–87; Adviser to Chair. Condé Nast Publications 1986–; Founding Ed.-in-Chief, Condé Nast Traveler 1986–90; Pres. and Publr Random House Adult Trade Group 1990–97; Editorial Dir Mortimer Zuckerman's media properties 1997–; Editorial Dir and Vice-Chair. New York Daily News Inc. 1998–99, Fast Co. 1998–; Poynter Fellow, Yale Univ.; author, Little, Brown and Co., NY 2000–; writer and presenter A Point of View (BBC Radio 4) 2005–; Fellow, Soc. Industrial Artists, Inst. of Journalists. *Radio:* Point of View BBC; Breakfast at Barneys literary conversations. *Television:* They Made America (four-part series, WGBH), Shots in the America (four-part series, WGBH), Mayor of America (BBC), What the Papers Say. *Publications:* Active Newsroom 1964, Editing and Design, Newsman's English 1970, Newspaper Design 1971, Newspaper Headlines 1973, Newspaper Text 1973, We Learned to Ski (co-author) 1974, Freedom of the Press 1974, Pictures on a Page 1978, Suffer the Children (co-author), How We Learned to Ski 1983, Good Times, Bad Times 1983, Front Page History 1984, The American Century 1998, They Made America 2004, We the People 2007, My Paper Chase 2009. *Honours:* Hon. Visiting Prof., Journalism City Univ. 1978; Dr hc (Stirling) 1982, (Teesside, London Inst.), Hon. DCL (Durham) 1998; Journalist of the Year Prize 1973, Int. Ed. of the Year Award 1975, Inst. of Journalists Gold Medal Award 1979; Design and Art Dir, Pres.'s Award 1981, Ed. of Year Award, Granada 1982, Hood Medal, Royal Photographic Soc. 1981, Press Photographers of GB Award 1986; Gold Award for Achievement, British Press Awards 2000, World Press Freedom Hero, Int. Press Inst. 2000. *Address:* Little, Brown and Co., 1271 Avenue of the Americas, New York, NY 10020, USA (office). *Telephone:* (646) 717-9543 (office); (212) 371-1193 (home). *Fax:* (212) 302-9671 (office); (212) 754-4273 (home). *E-mail:* cindyquillinan@gmail.com (office); harold371@aol.com. *Website:* sirharoldevans.com (office).

EVANS, Jonathan (see Freemantle, Brian Harry)

EVANS, Joni; American publishing executive. *Career:* Publr Linden Press, Simon & Schuster 1979–85, Pres. Simon & Schuster Trade Div. 1985–87; Publr Random House imprint 1987–90, Pres., Publr own imprint, apptd Exec. Vice-Pres. Random House Inc. 1990; Sr Vice-Pres. William Morris Agency Literary Dept 1993–2006; Co-founder and CEO wowowow.com website 2008–; Dir Dreyfus Foundation. *Honours:* named as one of the 101 Most Powerful People in Entertainment, Entertainment Weekly 1990. *E-mail:* info@wowowow.com (office). *Website:* www.wowowow.com (office).

EVANS, Max; American writer and painter; b. 29 Aug. 1925. *Publications include:* Southwest Wind (short stories) 1958, Long John Dunn of Taos 1959, The Rounders 1960, The Hi Lo Country 1961, Three Short Novels: The Great Wedding, The One-Eyed Sky, My Pardner 1963, The Mountain of Gold 1965, Shadow of Thunder 1969, Three West: Conversations with Vardis Fisher, Max Evans, Michael Straight 1970, Sam Peckinpah, Master of Violence 1972, Bobby Jack Smith, You Dirty Coward! 1974, The White Shadow 1977, The Mountain of Gold 1983, The Great Wedding 1983, Xavier's Folly and Other Stories 1984, Super Bull and Other True Escapades 1985, Bluefeather Fellini 1993, This Chosen Place 1997, Faraway Blue 1999, Albuquerque: Spirit of the West 2000, Madam Millie: Bordellos from Silver City to Ketchikan 2002, Now and Forever: A Novel of Love and Betrayal Incarnate 2003, Hi-Lo Country: Under the One-Eyed Sky 2004, Making a Hand: Growing Up a Cowboy in New Mexico 2005, For the Love of a Horse 2007, War and Music: A Medley of Love 2010.

EVANS, Nicholas, BA; British author; b. Bromsgrove, Worcs.; m. 2nd Charlotte Gordon Cumming; three s. one d. *Education:* Univ. of Oxford. *Career:* previously journalist for Evening Chronicle, Newcastle upon Tyne and producer documentaries for London Weekend TV, writer and producer films for TV and cinema; now novelist. *Publications:* The Horse Whisperer 1995, The Loop 1998, The Smoke Jumper 2001, The Divide 2005, The Brave 2010. *Literary Agent:* c/o AP Watt Ltd, 20 John Street, London, WC1N 2DR, England. *Telephone:* (20) 7405-6774. *Fax:* (20) 7831-2154. *E-mail:* apw@apwatt.co.uk. *Website:* www.apwatt.co.uk. *E-mail:* nicholas@nicholasevans.com (office). *Website:* www.nicholasevans.com.

EVANS, Sir Richard John, Kt, MA, DPhil, LittD, FBA, FRSL, FRHistS; British historian and academic; *Regius Professor of History and President, Wolfson College, University of Cambridge;* b. 29 Sept. 1947, Woodford, Essex; s. of the late Ieuan Trefor Evans and of Evelyn Evans (née Jones); m. 1st Elín Hjaltadóttir 1976 (divorced 1993); m. 2nd Christine L. Corton 2004; two s. *Education:* Forest School, London, Jesus Coll., Oxford, St Antony's Coll., Oxford. *Career:* Lecturer in History, Stirling Univ. 1972–76; Lecturer in European History, Univ. of East Anglia 1976–83, Prof. 1983–89; Prof. of History, Birkbeck Coll., London 1989–98, Vice-Master 1993–98, Acting Master 1997; Prof. of Modern History, Univ. of Cambridge 1998–, Regius Prof. of Modern History 2008–10, Regius Prof. of History 2010–, Chair. Faculty of History 2008–10, Fellow, Gonville and Caius Coll., Cambridge 1998–2010; Visiting Assoc. Prof. of European History, Columbia Univ., New York 1980; Fellow, Alexander von Humboldt Foundation, Free Univ. of Berlin 1981, Humanities Research Centre, ANU, Canberra, Australia 1986; Gresham Prof. of Rhetoric, Gresham Coll. 2009–; Pres. Wolfson Coll., Cambridge 2010–. *Publications:* The Feminist Movement in Germany 1894–1933 1976, The Feminists 1977, Society and Politics in Wilhemine Germany (ed.) 1978, Sozialdemokratie und Frauenemanzipation im deutschen Kaiserreich 1979, The German Family (co-ed.) 1981, The German Working Class (co-ed.) 1982, The German Peasantry (co-ed.) 1986, The German Unemployed (co-ed.) 1987, Death in Hamburg 1987, Comrades and Sisters 1987, Rethinking German History 1987, In Hitler's Shadow 1989, Kneipengespräche im Kaiserreich 1989, Proletarians and Politics 1990, Rituals of Retribution 1996, Rereading German History 1997, In Defence of History 1997, Tales from the German Underworld 1998, Lying about Hitler 2001, The Coming of the Third Reich 2003, The Third Reich in Power 2005, The Third Reich at War 2008, Cosmopolitan Islanders 2009; contrib. to scholarly journals, newspapers, magazines, radio and TV. *Honours:* Hon. Fellow, Jesus Coll., Oxford 1998, Birkbeck Coll. 1999; Stanhope Historical Essay Prize 1969, Wolfson Literary Award for History 1987, William H. Welch Medal, American Asscn for the History of Medicine 1988, Hamburg Civic Medal for Arts and Sciences 1993, Fraenkel Prize in Contemporary History 1994. *Address:* The President's Lodge, Wolfson College, Barton Road, Cambridge, CB3 9BB, England (office). *Telephone:* (1223) 335345 (office). *E-mail:* rje36@cam.ac.uk (office). *Website:* www.richardjevans.com.

EVANS, Robert John Weston, PhD, FBA; British historian and academic; *Regius Professor Emeritus of History, University of Oxford;* b. 7 Oct. 1943, Leicester; s. of T. F. Evans and M. Evans; m. Kati Robert 1969; one s. one d. (deceased). *Education:* Dean Close School, Cheltenham and Jesus Coll., Cambridge. *Career:* Research Fellow, Brasenose Coll., Oxford 1968–97, Univ. Lecturer in Modern History of East-Central Europe, Univ. of Oxford 1969–90, Reader 1990–92, Prof. of European History 1992–97, Regius Prof. of History 1997–2011, Emer. 2011–; Ed. English Historical Review 1985–95; Fellow, Hungarian Acad. of Sciences 1995, Austrian Acad. of Sciences 1997, Learned Soc. of Czech Repub. 2004. *Publications:* Rudolf II and His World 1973, The Wechel Presses 1975, The Making of the Habsburg Monarchy 1979, The Coming of the First World War (co-ed) 1988, Crown, Church and Estates (co-ed) 1991, The Revolutions in Europe 1848–9 (ed.) 2000, Austria, Hungary, and the Habsburgs, c. 1683–1867 2006, Curiosity and Wonder from the Renaissance to the Enlightenment (co-ed) 2007, Czechoslovakia in a Nationalist and Fascist Europe 1918-48 (co-ed) 2007, Wales and the Wider World (co-ed) 2010, The Uses of the Middle Ages in Modern European States (co-ed) 2011, The Holy Roman Empire, 1495–1806 (co-ed) 2011. *Honours:* Ehrenkreuz für Kunst und Wissenschaft (Austria) 2010, Wolfson Literary Award for History 1980, Anton Gindely-Preis (Austria) 1986, František Palacký Medal (Czechoslovakia) 1991. *Address:* Rowan Cottage, 45 Sunningwell, Abingdon, Oxon., OX13 6RD, England (home). *Telephone:* (1865) 736973 (office). *E-mail:* robert.evans@history.ox.ac.uk (office).

EVANS OF TEMPLE GUITING, Baron (Life Peer), cr. 2000, in the County of Gloucestershire; **Matthew Evans,** CBE, BSc Econs, FRSA; British publishing executive; b. 7 Aug. 1941, s. of the late George Ewart Evans and Florence Ellen Evans; m. 1st Elizabeth Amanda Mead 1966 (divorced 1991); two s., one d. 2nd Caroline Michel 1991; two s. one d. *Education:* Friends' School, Saffron Walden and LSE. *Career:* bookselling 1963–64; with Faber & Faber 1964–, Man. Dir 1972–93, Chair. 1981; Chair. Nat. Book League 1982–84, English Stage Co. 1984–90; mem. Council, Publishers' Asscn 1978–84; Gov. BFI 1982–97, Vice-Chair. 1996–97; Chair. Library and Information Comm. 1995–99; Govt Whip, House of Lords 2002–07; Govt Spokesperson for Office of the Deputy Prime Minister 2002–03, Justice/Lord Chancellor's Dept (Scotland and Wales) 2003–07, Trade and Industry 2003–04, Work and Pensions 2005–07, Treasury 2005–07, Cabinet Office 2007, Culture, Media and Sport 2007, Trade and Industry/Business, Enterprise and Regulatory Reform 2007, Environment, Food and Rural Affairs 2007, Opposition Spokesperson for Culture, Media and Sport 2010–; Chair. EFG Private Bank; Chair. Museums, Libraries and Archives Council 2000–02; Dir Which? Ltd 1997–; Vice-Pres. Hay Literary Festival, Philip Larkin Soc.; mem. Arts Council Nat. Lottery Advisory Panel 1997–99, Univ. for Industry Advisory Group 1997, Royal Opera House Working Group 1997, Arts and Humanities

Research Bd 1998–; mem. Franco-British Soc. 1981–; Founder mem. Groucho Club (Dir 1982–97). *Honours:* Hon. FRCA 1999; Hon. FLA 1999. *Address:* c/o House of Lords, London SW1A 0PW, England (office). *Telephone:* (20) 7219-6631 (office). *E-mail:* evansm@parliament.uk (office).

EVARISTO, Bernardine, MBE, FRSL, FRSA; British writer; b. 1959, London, England. *Career:* trained as an actor and worked in theatre; has also written for theatre, radio and print media; int. readings and teaching residencies, including Visiting Prof. Barnard Coll./Columbia Univ. 2002; writer-in-residence Univ. of the Western Cape, Cape Town 2000, Georgetown Univ. 2005, Virginia 2007; Writing Fellow Univ. of East Anglia 2000, and several British Council workshops; Dir Spread the Word Literature Devt Agency 1995–99; Special Adviser (Literature) Arts Council, London 2001–06; Literature Adviser British Council 2003–06; mem. Advisory Bd MA Creative Writing, City Univ. 2004–; mem. The Poetry Soc. (gen. council 2001–04, chair. 2003–04), Museum of London (advisory cttee 2004–). *Plays include:* Moving Through (Royal Court Theatre Upstairs, London), Mapping the Edge (co-writer, WilsonWilson Co. and Sheffield Crucible Theatre, and BBC Radio 3) 2002, Madame Bitterfly and The Stockwell Diva (BBC Radio 4) 2003, Cityscapes (multi-media collaboration with saxophonist Andy Sheppard and pianist Joanna MacGregor for City of London Festival) 2003. *Publications include:* Island of Abraham (poems) 1994, Lara (verse novel) (BT Ethnic and Multicultural Media Award for Best Book/Novel 1999) 1997, The Emperor's Babe (verse novel) 2001, Soul Tourists (verse novel) 2005, Blonde Roots (novel) 2008, Hello Mum 2009, Ten: New Poets Spread the Word (with Daljit Nagra) 2010. *Honours:* Emma Best Book Award 1999, Arts Council Writers' Award 2000, Nat. Endowment for Science, Technology and the Arts Award 2003, Orange Prize Youth Panel Award 2009, Big Red Read Award 2009. *Literary Agent:* c/o Karolina Sutton, Curtis Brown Agency, Haymarket House, 28–29 Haymarket, London, SW1Y 4SP, England. *E-mail:* karolina@curtisbrown.co.uk. *E-mail:* bernardine_evaristo@hotmail.com (office).

EVDOKIMOV, Aleksei; Latvian journalist; b. 1975. *Career:* journalist in Riga. *Publication:* Headcrusher (novel, in trans., with Alexander Garros) (Nat. Bestseller Prize, Russia) 2003. *Address:* c/o Chatto & Windus, Random House, 20 Vauxhall Bridge Road, London, SW1V 2SA, England.

EVENO, Bertrand; French publishing executive; b. 26 July 1944, Egletons; s. of Jean-Jacques Eveno and Suzanne Gavoille; m. 2nd Brigitte Pery 1984; five d. (three d. from previous m.). *Education:* Lycée Condorcet and Law Faculty, Paris. *Career:* Treasury Inspector 1973–77; Tech. Consultant to Health Minister 1977–78; Cabinet Dir for Minister of Culture and Communication 1978–81; mem. Atomic Energy Comm. Control Bd 1981–83; Deputy Gen. Man. André Shoe Co. 1984–86; Chair. Editions Fernand Nathan 1987–2000; Pres. Conseil d' admin., Fondation nationale de la photographie 1981–95, Gens d'Image 1986–2000; Chair. Larousse-Nathan Int. 1988–90, Le Robert dictionaries 1989–2000, Editions Masson 1995–98; Dir-Gen. Groupe de la Cité 1988–2000, Presses de la Cité 1991–95; Pres., Dir-Gen. Larousse-Bordas 1996–2000; Pres., Dir-Gen. Havas Educ. et Référence 1999–2000; Dir Anaya Groupe 1999–2000; Pres. Agence France Presse 2000–05; apptd Dir-Gen. Hachette Filipacchi Photos (includes agencies Gamma, Rapho, Hoa - Who, Keystone) (known as Eyedea 2007–10, taken over 2010) 2005; Pres. Literary Soc. of Friends of Emile Zola 2009–; Chair. Cttee on Cinema Arthouse, Nat. Centre for Cinematography 2009–. *Publication:* monograph on Willy Ronis in Les grands photographes 1983. *Address:* Committee on Cinema Arthouse, National Centre for Cinematography, 12 rue de Lubeck, 75116 Paris, France (office).

EVENSON, Brian, (Bjorn Verenson), BA, MA, PhD; American academic, writer and editor; *Chairman, Literary Arts Department, Brown University;* b. 12 Aug. 1966, Ames, Ia; m. 1st Connie Joyce Evenson 1989 (divorced 2001); two d.; partner Joanna Howard 2003–11; m. 2nd Kristen Tracy 2012. *Education:* Brigham Young Univ., Univ. of Washington. *Career:* Asst Prof. of English, Brigham Young Univ. 1994–96; Asst Prof. of English, Oklahoma State Univ. 1996–99; Dir of Creative Writing, Univ. of Denver 1999–2003; Prof. of Creative Writing, Brown Univ. 2003–, currently Chair. Literary Arts Dept; Fiction Ed., Cimarron Review 1996; Sr Ed. Conjunctions 1997–. *Publications include:* Altmann's Tongue 1994, The Din of Celestial Birds 1997, Prophets and Brothers 1997, Father of Lies 1998, Contagion 2000, Dark Property 2002, The Wavering Knife (IHG Award 2005) 2004, The Open Curtain 2006, Last Days (Best Horror Novel, RUSA Prize) 2009, Fugue State 2009, Baby Leg 2009. *Honours:* Nat. Endowment for the Arts Grant 1995, O. Henry Prize, Camargo Foundation Grant. *Literary Agent:* c/o Matt McGowan, Francis Goldin Literary Agency, 57 East 11th Street New York, NY 10003, USA. *Telephone:* (212) 777-0047. *Address:* Literary Arts Department, PO Box 1923, Brown University, Providence, RI 02912, USA (office). *Telephone:* (401) 863-9408 (office). *E-mail:* brian_evenson@brown.edu (office). *Website:* brown.edu/academics/literary-arts/home/literary-arts (office); www.brianevenson.com.

EVERDELL, William Romeyn, BA, MA, PhD; American educator and writer; *Dean of Humanities, Saint Ann's School;* b. 25 June 1941, New York, NY; s. of William Everdell and Eleanore Everdell; m. Barbara Scott 1966; two s. *Education:* Princeton Univ., Univ. of Paris, Harvard Univ., New York Univ. *Career:* Chair. of History Dept, Saint Ann's School 1972–73, Head of Upper School 1973–75, Co-Chair. of History Dept 1975–84, Dean of Humanities 1984–; Adjunct Instructor, New York Univ. 1984–89; mem. American Historical Asscn, Int. Soc. for Intellectual History, New York Acad. of Sciences, Soc. for Eighteenth-Century Studies, Soc. of French Historical Studies, Organization of History Teachers. *Publications include:* Rowboats to Rapid Transit (co-author) 1974, The End of Kings: A History of Republics and Republicans 1983 (revised 2000), Christian Apologetics in France, 1730–1790: The Roots of Romantic Religion 1987, The First Moderns: Profiles in the Origins of Twentieth-Century Thought 1997; contrib. to periodicals. *Honours:* Woodrow Wilson Fellowships 1964, 1970, Nat. Endowment for the Humanities Fellowships 1985, 1990, Nat. Endowment for the Humanities/Wallace Foundation Teacher-Scholar 1990–91, honoree New York Public Library Books to Remember 1998. *Address:* Saint Ann's School, 129 Pierrepont Street, New York, NY 11201, USA (office). *Telephone:* (718) 522-1660 (office). *Fax:* (718) 522-2599 (office). *E-mail:* weverdell@earthlink.net (home). *Website:* www.saintannsny.org/depart/history/histmain.htm (office).

EVERETT, Graham Lee, BA, MA, PhD; American academic, poet, writer, painter and producer; *Faculty Tutor in General Studies Program, Adelphi University;* b. 23 Dec. 1947, Oceanside, NY; s. of James Harvey Everett and Jacqueline Vaughan; m. Elyse Arnow 1981; one s. *Education:* Canisius Coll., State Univ. of NY, Stony Brook. *Career:* Ed. and Publr Street Press and Magazine 1972–; currently Faculty Tutor in Gen. Studies, Adelphi Univ.; producer Artist@Work series. *Exhibitions include:* Constructions 2006, Tragedy and Transformation 2007. *Films include:* Artist@Work Series (ongoing), Scopophilia 2003, Robert White, Sculptor: Sing the Body Electric 2010. *Music:* Multiverses by Middleclass Poetry Band. *Publications include:* Trees 1978, Strange Coast 1979, Paumanok Rising: An Anthology of Eastern Long Island Aesthetics (co-ed.) 1981, Sunlit Sidewalk 1985, Minus Green 1992, Minus Green Plus 1995, Corps Calleux 2000, Multiverses 2003, That Nod Toward Love 2006; contrib. to anthologies, reviews, quarterlies and journals. *Honours:* North Sea Poetry Scene Recognition Award 2006, Distinguished Faculty Excellence Award, Adelphi Univ. 2006. *Address:* PO Box 772, Sound Beach, NY 11789, USA (home). *Telephone:* (516) 877-3447 (office). *E-mail:* grahameverett@gmail.com (home).

EVERETT, Percival, BA, MA; American writer and academic; *Distinguished Professor of English, University of Southern California;* b. 22 Dec. 1956, Fort Gordon, Ga. *Education:* Univ. of Miami, Univ. of Oregon, Brown Univ. *Career:* Assoc. Prof., Univ. of Kentucky, Lexington 1985–89; Prof., Univ. of Notre Dame, Ind. 1988–91; Prof., Univ. of California, Riverside 1992–98, Prof., Univ. of Southern California 1999–, now Distinguished Prof. of English; mem. Modern Language Asscn, Writers' Guild of America. *Publications include:* Suder 1983, Walk Me to the Distance 1985, Cutting Lisa 1986, The Weather and Women Treat Me Fair 1989, Zulus 1989, For her Dark Skin 1989, The One That Got Away 1992, God's Country 1994, The Body of Martin Aguilera 1994, Big Picture 1996, Watershed 1996, Frenzy 1996, Glyph 1999, Erasure 2001, Damned If I Do 2005, American Desert 2005, re:f(gesture) 2006, Wounded 2007, The Water Cure 2008, I Am Not Sidney Poitier 2009, Swimming Swimmers Swimming 2011, Assumption: A Novel 2011; contrib. to anthologies and periodicals. *Address:* Department of English, University of Southern California, Taper Hall of Humanities, Room 402F, 3501 Trousdale Parkway, University Park, Los Angeles, CA 90089-0354, USA (office). *Telephone:* (213) 740-3743 (office). *E-mail:* peverett@usc.edu (office). *Website:* college.usc.edu/engl (office).

EYNON, Robert (Bob), BA; British academic and writer; b. 20 March 1941, Tynewydd, Rhondda, Wales. *Education:* Univ. of London. *Publications include:* Bitter Waters 1988, Texas Honour 1988, Johnny One Arm 1989, Gunfight at Simeons Ridge 1991, Gun Law Legacy 1991, Sunset Reckoning 1993, Anderton Justice 1997, Pecos Vengeance 1998, Brothers Till Death 1999, Dol Rhydian 1999, Lladd Akamuro 2000, Arizona Payback 2001, Poison Valley 2003, The Reluctant Lawman 2005; also Welsh novels and short stories for learners, including Perygl Yn Sbaen 1987, Yr Asiant Cudd 1997. *Address:* 5 Troedyrhiw Terrace, Treorchy, Rhondda, CF42 6PG, Wales (home).

F

FABEND, Firth Haring, (Firth Haring), BA, PhD; American writer and historian; b. 12 Aug. 1937, Tappan, NY; m. Carl Fabend 1966; two d. *Education:* Barnard Coll., New York Univ. *Career:* Fellow, Holland Soc. of New York 1993, New Netherland Project 1996. *Publications include:* as Firth Haring: The Best of Intentions 1968, Three Women 1972, A Perfect Stranger 1973, The Woman Who Went Away 1981, Greek Revival 1985; as Firth Haring Fabend: A Dutch Family in the Middle Colonies 1660–1800 2000, Zion on the Hudson: Dutch New York and New Jersey in the Age of Revivals 2000, A Catch of Grandmothers 2004, Land So Fair 2008, Only a Paper Life 2009; contribs to de Halve Maen, New York History. *Honours:* New York State Historical Asscn Ms Award 1989, Hendricks Prize 1989. *Address:* 54 Elston Road, Upper Montclair, NJ 07043-1956, USA (home). *Telephone:* (201) 746-5336 (home). *E-mail:* fhfabend@msn.com (home).

FABER, Michel; Dutch writer; b. 13 April 1960; m. 2nd Eva Youren; two step-s. *Education:* Melbourne Univ., Australia. *Career:* emigrated to Australia 1967; now lives in Scotland. *Publications include:* Fish (short story), Some Rain Must Fall (short stories) 1996, Under the Skin (novel) 1999, The 199 Steps (short story), The Courage Consort (short story), The Crimson Petal and the White (novel) 2002, The Fahrenheit Twins (short stories) 2005, The Apple (short stories) 2006, Vanilla Bright Like Eminem (short stories) 2007, The Fire Gospel 2008; contrib. to The Guardian. *Honours:* Macallan Short Story Award, Saltire First Book of the Year Award 1999. *Address:* c/o Canongate Books, 14 High Street, Edinburgh, EH1 1TE, Scotland. *Website:* www.canongate.net.

FADIMAN, Anne, BA; American writer, essayist, editor and academic; *Adjunct Professor of English and Francis Writer-in-Residence, Yale University*; b. 1953, New York, NY; d. of Clifton Fadiman and Annalee Whitmore Jacoby Fadiman; m. George Howe Colt; two c. *Education:* Harvard Univ. *Career:* Columnist (undergraduate), Harvard Magazine 1972; Instructor, Nat. Outdoor Leadership School, Wyoming 1975–76; Staff Writer, Life magazine 1979–88; Ed.-at-Large, Civilization magazine 1994–98; Visiting Lecturer, Smith Coll. 2000–02; Ed. The American Scholar 1997–2004; Adjunct Prof. of English and Francis Writer-in-Residence, Yale Univ. 2005–. *Publications include:* non-fiction: The Spirit Catches You and You Fall Down (Nat. Book Critics Circle Award, Salon Book Award, Los Angeles Times Book Prize, Boston Book Review Ann Rea Jewell Award) 1997, Ex Libris: Confessions of a Common Reader 1998, Best American Essays (ed.) 2003, Rereadings (ed.) 2005, At Large and At Small 2007; contrib. of numerous articles and essays to newspapers, magazines and journals, including Harper's, Lapham's Quarterly, Life, New Yorker, New York Times, Washington Post. *Honours:* Stanford Univ. John S. Knight Fellowship 1991–92, Nat. Magazine Award for Reporting, Nat. Magazine Award for Essays, New England Literary Light, MacDowell Fellowship. *Literary Agent:* c/o Robert Lescher (literary agent), Lescher & Lescher, 346 East 84th Street, New York, NY 10028; c/o Steven Barclay Agency (lecture agent), 12 Western Avenue, Petaluma, CA 94952, USA. *E-mail:* rl@lescherltd.com; steven@barclayagency.com. *Website:* www.barclayagency.com; english.yale.edu (office).

FAECKE, Peter; German journalist, writer and editor; b. 3 Nov. 1940, Grunwald, Silesia. *Education:* Univs of Göttingen, Berlin, Hamburg, Paris. *Career:* Lecturer, Univ. of Texas, Austin, USA; Dir Edition Köln , PEN-Centre Germany. *Publications:* Die Brandstifter (novel) 1962, Der Rote Milan (novel) 1965, Postversand-Roman (novel) (with Wolf Vostell) 1970, Gemeinsam gegen Abriss: Ein Lesebuch aus Arbeitersiedlungen 1974, Das Unaufhaltsame Glück der Kowalskis 1982, Flug ins Leben (novel) 1988, Der Mann mit den besonderen Eigenschaften (novel) 1993, Grabstein für Fritz (documentary film) 1993, Als Elizabeth Arden Neunzehn war (novel) 1994, Eine Liebe zum Land (film script) 1994, Ankunft eines Schüchternen im Himmel (novel) 2000, Das Kreuz des Südens (reports) 2001, Vom Überfliessen der Anden, Reportagen aus Peru 2001, Hochzeitsvorbereitungen auf dem Lande (novel) 2003, Die geheimen Videos des Herrn Vladimiro (novel) 2004, Lima die Schöne-Lima die Schreckliche (reports) 2005, Wenn bei uns ein Gratis stirbt ... (reports) 2005, Der Kardinal, ganz in Rot und frisch gebügelt (novel) 2007, Die Tango-Sängerin (novel) 2008, Dem alten Mann seine Kiste (novel) 2009. *Honours:* awards include stipend of Villa Massimo, Rome and literature prizes of Lower Saxony, North-Rhine-Westphalia and City of Cologne. *Address:* Pohlstadtsweg 414, 51109 Cologne, Germany (home). *Telephone:* (221) 726207 (home). *Fax:* (221) 1794149 (office). *E-mail:* edition.koeln@t-online.de (office); peterfaecke@t-online.de (home). *Website:* www.peterfaecke.de (home).

FAES, Urs, MA, Dr. phil. I; Swiss writer, poet and dramatist; b. 13 Feb. 1947, Aarau. *Education:* Univ. of Zurich. *Career:* journalist 1979–81, dramatist 1982–86, writer 1982–; mem. Auteurs de Suisse (AdS), PEN. *Publications include:* Eine Kerbe im Mittag (poems) 1975, Heidentum und Aberglaube (essay) 1979, Regenspur (poems) 1979, Webfehler (novel) 1983, Zugluft (play) 1983, Der Traum vom Leben (short stories) 1984, Kreuz im Feld (play) 1984, Bis ans Ende der Erinnerung (novel) 1986, Wartezimmer (play) 1986, Partenza (radio play) 1986, Sommerwende (novel) 1989, Alphabet des Abschieds 1991, Eine andere Geschichte (radio play) 1993, Augenblicke im Paradies (novel) 1994, Ombra (novel) 1997, Und Ruth (novel) 2001, Als hätte die Stille Türen (novel) 2005, Liebesarchiv 2007 (also translated into Chinese and Bulgarian), Paarbildung (novel) 2010. *Honours:* City of Zürich Prize 1986, Prize for Literature 1991, Kanton Solothurn Literary Prize 1999, Schiller Prize 2001, Werkjahrauszeichnung Kanton Zürich 2005, Werkpreis Stadt Zürich, Schiller Prize 2008, Werkpreis des Kantons Zürich 2011. *Literary Agent:* c/o Suhrkamp Verlag, Pappelallee 78–79, 10437, Berlin. *Telephone:* (30) 740744-0. *Address:* Lindenbachstrasse 17, 8006 Zurich, Switzerland (office). *Telephone:* 79-2613053 (mobile) (office); (43) 2449063 (home). *E-mail:* urs.faes@bluewin.ch (office). *Website:* www.ursfaes.ch.

FAGAN, Brian Murray, BA, MA, PhD; British academic and writer; b. 1 Aug. 1936, Birmingham, England; m. Lesley Ann Newhart 1985; two c. *Education:* Pembroke Coll., Cambridge. *Career:* Keeper of Prehistory, Livingstone Museum, Zambia 1959–65; Visiting Assoc. Prof., Univ. of Illinois 1966–67; Assoc. Prof., Univ. of California, Santa Barbara 1967–69, Prof. of Anthropology 1969–2003 (retd). *Publications include:* Victoria Falls Handbook 1964, Southern Africa During the Iron Age (ed.) 1966, Iron Age Cultures in Zambia (with S. G. H. Daniels and D. W. Phillipson), two vols 1967, 1969, A Short History of Zambia 1968, The Hunter-Gatherers of Gwisho (with F. Van Noten) 1971, In the Beginning 1972, People of the Earth 1974, The Rape of the Nile 1975, Elusive Treasure 1977, Quest for the Past, Archaeology: A Brief Introduction 1978, Return to Babylon 1979, The Aztecs, Clash of Cultures 1984, Adventures in Archaeology, Bareboating, Anchoring 1985, The Great Journey 1987, The Journey From Eden 1990, Ancient North America 1991, Kingdoms of Jade, Kingdoms of Gold 1991, Time Detectives 1995, Oxford Companion to Archaeology 1996, Into the Unknown 1997, From Black Land to Fifth Sun 1998, Floods, Famines and Emperors 2000, The Little Ice Age 2002, The Long Summer: How Climate Changed Civilisation 2004, Before California 2004, Writing Archaeology 2005, Fish on Friday: Feasting, Fasting and the Discovery of the New World 2006, World Prehistory: A Brief Introduction 2007, The Great Warming: Climate Change and the Rise and Fall of Civilizations 2009, The Complete Ice Age: How Climate Change Shaped the World (The Complete Series) 2009, Cro-Magnon: How the Ice Age Gave Birth to the First Modern Humans 2011, The First North Americans: An Archaeological Journey (Ancient Peoples and Places) 2011, Elixir: A History of Water and Humankind 2011. *E-mail:* brian@brianfagan.com (office). *Website:* www.brianfagan.com.

FAGUNDES TELLES, Lygia; Brazilian writer; b. 19 April 1923, São Paulo; d. of Durval de Azevedo Fagundes and Maria do Rosário Silva Jardim de Moura; m. Goffredo da Silva Telles Jr 1952 (divorced 1960); one s. *Education:* Univ. of São Paulo. *Career:* mem. Academia Paulista de Letras 1982, Academia Brasileira de Letras 1987. *Publications include:* short stories: Porão e sobrado 1938, Praia viva 1944, O cacto vermelho (Prêmio Afonso Arinos, da Academia Brasileira de Letras) 1946, Histórias do desencontro 1958, Histórias escolhidas 1964, O jardim selvagem 1965, Antes do baile verde 1970, Seminário de ratos 1977, Filhos pródigos 1978, A disciplina do amor 1980, Mistérios 1981, A noite escure e mais eu (Prêmio Jabuti) 1994, Invenção a Memória (Prêmio Jabuti) 2000, Durante aquele estranho chá: perdidos e achados 2002, Meus contos preferidos 2004, Histórias de mistério 2004, Meus contos esquecidos 2005; novels: Ciranda de pedra 1953, Verão no aquário 1963, As menínas (Prêmio Jabuti) 1973, As horas nuas 1989, La structure de la bulle de savon 2000. *Honours:* Ordem do Rio Branco 1985; Prêmio do Instituto Nacional do Livro 1958, Prêmio Guimarães Rosa 1972, Prêmio Coelho Neto, Academia Brasileira de Letras 1973, Prêmio Camões 2005. *Address:* c/o Editora Rocco Ltda, Avenida Presidente Wilson, 231, 8° andar, 20030-021 Rio de Janeiro, RJ, Brazil. *E-mail:* rocco@rocco.com.br. *Website:* www.rocco.com.br.

FAHRNER, Martin; Czech playwright, writer and poet; b. 1964, Jablonec nad Nisou. *Education:* DAMU Prague Theatre School. *Publications include:* Steiner aneb Co jsme delali (novel) 2001, Pošetilost doktora vinnetouologie (novel) 2004, Die Hand in der Luft 2006. *Literary Agent:* c/o Dana Blatná Literary Agency, Jináčovice 3, 66434 Kuřim, Czech Republic. *E-mail:* dblatna@volny.cz. *E-mail:* dramaturg@vcd.cz (office).

FAINLIGHT, Ruth, FRSL; American poet, writer, translator and librettist; b. 2 May 1931, New York, NY; m. Alan Sillitoe 1959; one s. one d. *Education:* Coll. of Arts and Crafts, Birmingham, Brighton, UK. *Career:* Poet-in-Residence, Vanderbilt Univ. 1985, 1990; Writing Tutor; libretti for Performing Arts Lab (Opera and Music Theatre) 1997–99; mem. PEN, Writers in Prison Cttee, Soc. of Authors. *Publications include:* poetry: Cages 1966, To See the Matter Clearly 1968, The Region's Violence 1973, Another Full Moon 1976, Sibyls and Others 1980, Climates 1983, Fifteen to Infinity 1983, Selected Poems 1987, The Knot 1990, Twelve Sibyls 1991, This Time of Year 1994, Selected Poems (expanded 2nd edn) 1995, Sugar-Paper Blue 1997, Burning Wire 2002, Moon Wheels 2006, New and Collected Poems 2010; translations: All Citizens Are Soldiers, from Lope de Vega (with Alan Sillitoe) 1969, Navigations 1983, Marine Rose: Selected Poems of Sophia de Mello Breyner 1988, The Theban Plays of Sophocles (with Robert J Littman) 2009; short stories: Daylife and Nightlife 1971, Dr Clock's Last Case 1994; libretti: The Dancer Hotoke 1991, The European Story 1993, Bedlam Britannica 1995; contrib. to Atlantic Monthly, Critical Quarterly, English, Hudson Review, Lettre Internationale, London Magazine, London Review of Books, New Yorker, Poetry Review, Threepenny Review, Times Literary Supplement. *Honours:* Cholmondeley Award for Poetry 1994, Hawthornden Award for

Poetry 1994. *Address:* 14 Ladbroke Terrace, London, W11 3PG, England (home). *E-mail:* ruth.fainlight@googlemail.com (office).

FAIRBAIRNS, Zoe Ann, MA; British writer; b. 20 Dec. 1948, England. *Education:* Univ. of St Andrews, Scotland. *Career:* Lecturer, City Lit Centre for Adult Learning, London 1977–82, 2004–; Writer-in-Residence, Deakin Univ., Australia 1983, Sunderland Polytechnic 1983–85; mem. Writer's Guild. *Radio:* The Belgian Nurse (BBC Radio 4) 2007. *Publications include:* Live as Family 1968, Down 1969, Benefits 1979, Stand We at Last 1983, Here Today 1984, Closing 1987, Daddy's Girls 1991, Other Names 1998, How Do You Pronounce Nulliparous? 2004; contribs to New Scientist, Guardian, Women's Studies International Quarterly, Spare Rib, Arts Express, The Independent, Newbooks, The Tablet. *Honours:* C. Day-Lewis Fellowship, Rutherford School, London 1977–78, Fawcett Book Prize 1985. *Website:* www.zoefairbairns.co.uk.

FAIRBURN, Eleanor M., (Catherine Carfax, Emma Gayle, Elena Lyons); Irish writer; b. 23 Feb. 1928; m. Brian Fairburn; one d. *Career:* tutor in practical writing, Univ. of Leeds Adult Educ. Centre (retd); mem. Middlesbrough Writers Group (Pres. 1988–90). *Publications include:* The Green Popinjays 1962, The White Seahorse 1964, The Golden Hive 1966, Crowned Ermine 1968, The Rose in Spring 1971, White Rose, Dark Summer 1972, The Rose at Harvest End 1975, Winter's Rose 1976, Edith Cavell (biog.) 1985, Mary Hornbeck Glyn (biog.) 1987, Grace Darling (biog.) 1988; as Catherine Carfax: A Silence with Voices 1969, The Semper Inheritance 1972, To Die a Little 1972, The Sleeping Salamander 1973, The Locked Tower 1974; as Emma Gayle: Cousin Caroline 1980, Frenchman's Harvest 1980; as Elena Lyons: The Haunting of Abbotsgarth 1980, A Scent of Lilacs 1982. *Literary Agent:* c/o S. Cashman, Wolfhound Press, Mountjoy Square, Dublin 1, Ireland. *Telephone:* (1642) 821550 (home). *E-mail:* eleanorfairburn@aol.com (home); eleanorfairburn@btinternet.com (home).

FAIRCLOUGH, Troy Andrew; British playwright; b. 1976, Brixton, London, England. *Plays include:* You Don't Kiss 2001, Justin Fashanu woz 'ere 2004, Homeward Bound 2006, Theatre Jihad: Inner Struggle 2007. *Honours:* Newham Writing Out Award 2001.

FAIRLEY, John Alexander, MA; British broadcasting executive and writer; b. 15 April 1939, Liverpool, England; three d. *Education:* Queen's Coll., Oxford. *Career:* journalist, Bristol Evening Post 1963, London Evening Standard 1964; Producer, BBC Radio 1965–68; Producer, Yorkshire TV 1968–78, Dir of Programmes 1984–92, Managing Dir 1992–95; Chair., ITV Broadcast Board 1995. *Publications include:* The Coup 1975, The Monocled Mutineer (with W. Allison) 1975, Arthur C. Clarke's Mysterious World 1980, Great Racehorses in Art 1984, Arthur C. Clarke's World of Strange Powers 1984, Chronicles of the Strange and Mysterious 1987, Racing in Art 1990, The Cabinet of Curiosities 1991, A Century of Mysteries 1993, The Art of the Horse 1995.

FAIRSTEIN, Linda; American lawyer and writer; b. 1947; m. Justin N. Feldman 1986. *Career:* lawyer, Office of the District Attorney, Manhattan, New York 1972, Head, Sex Crimes Unit 1974–2002; provided training for police, prosecution and medical staff, and rape counsellors; writer 1993–. *Publications include:* Sexual Violence: Our War Against Rape (non-fiction) 1993, Final Jeopardy 1996, Likely to Die 1997, Cold Hit 1999, The Deadhouse 2001, The Bonevault 2003, The Kills 2004, Entombed 2005, Death Dance 2006, Bad Blood 2007, Killer Heat 2007, Lethal Legacy 2009, The Prosecution Rests: New Stories about Courtrooms, Criminals and the Law (ed) 2009, Hell Gate 2010, Silent Mercy 2011. *Address:* c/o Dutton Books Publicity Department, Penguin Group, 375 Hudson Street, New York, NY 10014, USA (office). *Website:* www.lindafairstein.com.

FAKHOURY, Tamirace, BA, MA, PhD; Lebanese writer and poet; *Jean Monnet Fellow (Vincent Wright Fellowship in Comparative Politics), European University Institute*; b. 28 Nov. 1974, Beit Chabab. *Education:* Lebanese American Univ., Beirut, Univ. of Freiburg, Germany. *Career:* Asst, Hon. Consulate of Ghana, Lebanon 1995–96; teacher, Int. Coll., Beirut 1996–2002; Lecturer, American Univ. of Science and Tech., Beirut 1999–2002; scientific researcher, Arnold Bergstraesser Institut, Germany and Albert Ludwigs Universität, Freiburg, Germany 2003–07; freelance journalist, al-Anwar daily newspaper, Beirut; Jean Monnet Fellow (Vincent Wright Fellowship in Comparative Politics), European Univ. Inst. 2010–11; Visiting Fellowship, Univ. of California, Berkeley, USA 2011. *Publications include:* poetry books: Le pays de l'Empereur et de l'Enfant perdu 1984, Aubades 1996, Contre-Marées 2000, Poème absent 2004, Hémisphères 2008; non-fiction: Ethnic Conflict and the Methods of its Regulation (conf. report for UNESCO) 2004, International Relations in an Uncertain Hegemonial World System (conf. report for UNESCO) 2005, Power-sharing Systems: Exploratory Approaches and Case Studies 2007, Democracy and Power-Sharing in Stormy Weather: The Case of Lebanon 2009, Prophetenbeleidigung? Die Mohamad-Karikaturen und die Aktualität des religiösen Konfliktpotentials Freiburger Schriften für Entwicklung und Politik (co-author) 2009; contrib. to anthologies and books and of poems and articles to Lebanese, French, German and Canadian journals and magazines. *Honours:* Writing Award, Ministry of Culture, Lebanon 2000, Prix Belles Etrangères 2007. *Address:* European University Institute, Robert Schumann Centre for Advanced Studies, Via delle Fontanelle 19, 50014 San Domenico di Fiesole, Italy (office). *Telephone:* (055) 4685 (office). *Fax:* (055) 4685755. *E-mail:* tamy.fakhoury@gmail.com (home); tamirace.fakhoury@eui.eu (office). *Website:* www.eui.eu/DepartmentsAndCentres/RobertSchumanCentre/People/AcademicAssistants/Fakhoury.aspx (office).

FALCK, (Adrian) Colin, MA, PhD; British academic, writer and poet; b. 14 July 1934, London, England; two s. one d. *Education:* Univs of Oxford and London. *Career:* Lecturer in Sociology, LSE 1961–62; Assoc. Ed. The Review 1962–72; Lecturer in Literature, Chelsea Coll. 1964–84; Poetry Ed., The New Review 1974–78; Assoc. Prof., York Coll., Pa, USA 1989–99. *Publications include:* The Garden in the Evening 1964, Promises 1969, Backwards into the Smoke 1973, Poems Since 1900: An Anthology (co-ed. with Ian Hamilton) 1975, In This Dark Light 1978, Robinson Jeffers: Selected Poems (ed.) 1987, Myth, Truth and Literature 1989, Edna St Vincent Millay: Selected Poems (ed.) 1991, Memorabilia 1992, Post-Modern Love 1997, American and British Verse in the Twentieth Century 2004; contribs to professional journals and general periodicals. *Literary Agent:* c/o Johnson & Alcock Ltd, Clerkenwell House, 45–47 Clerkenwell Green, London, EC1R 0HT, England. *Address:* 40 Platt's Lane, London, NW3 7NT, England (home). *Telephone:* (20) 7435-6806 (home). *Fax:* (20) 7435-6806 (home).

FALCONER, Lee N. (see May, Julian)

FALCONES DE SIERRA, Idelfonso; Spanish writer and lawyer; b. 1959, Barcelona; m.; four c. *Career:* lawyer specializing in civil law. *Publications include:* La luna y el advenedizo 1998, La catedral del mar (Eskaudi de Plata Prize 2006, Premio Que Leer 2007, Premio Giovanni Boccaccio 2007) 2006, La Mano de Fátima 2009. *Address:* c/o Grijalbo, Random House Mondadori, Travessera de Grácia 47–49, 08021 Barcelona, Spain. *Telephone:* (93) 3660300. *Website:* www.megustaleer.com/Sellos/Division-1/Grijalbo.

FALK, Richard A., BS, LLB, SJD; American academic; *Professor Emeritus of International Law, Princeton University*; b. 13 Nov. 1930, New York, NY; s. of Edwin Albert Falk and Helene Pollak; m. Hilal Elver; three s. one d. *Education:* Wharton School, Univ. of Pennsylvania, Harvard Law School, Yale Law School. *Career:* Asst Prof., later Assoc. Prof., Coll. of Law, Ohio State Univ. 1955–61; Ford Foundation Fellow, Harvard Law School 1958–59; Visiting Assoc. Prof., Princeton Univ. 1961–62, Assoc. Prof. of Int. Law 1962–65, Albert G. Milbank Prof. of Int. Law and Practice 1965–2001, Sr Research Fellow 2002–, later Prof. Emer. of Int. Law, Acting Dir Center of Int. Studies 1975, 1982, Fellow, Center for Advanced Study in the Behavioral Sciences, Stanford, Calif. 1968–69, Research Prof., Global Studies 2002–; Visiting Prof. at numerous univs, including Stockholm, American Univ. in Cairo, Univ. of Wales, Univ. of California, Santa Barbara; Chair. Nuclear Age Peace Foundation; mem. Editorial Bd of numerous pubs, including The Nation, The Progressive, World Politics, Foreign Policy Magazine, Peace Forum; fmr mem. several int. panels of judges; participation in numerous int. and govt comms, including Ind. World Comm. on the Oceans 1995–2000, Ind. Int. Comm. on Kosovo 1999–2001; UN Special Rapporteur for Occupied Palestine, Human Rights Council 2008–. *Publications include:* Law, War and Morality in the Contemporary World 1963, Legal Order in a Violent World 1968, Crimes of War (co-ed.) 1971, A Global Approach to National Policy 1975, Human Rights and State Sovereignty 1981, Reviving the World Court 1986, Revitalizing International Law 1989, International Law and World Order (co-author) 1997, Human Rights Horizons 2001, Religion and Humane Global Governance 2002, Unlocking the Middle East 2002, The Great Terror War 2003, The Declining World Order: America's Imperial Geopolitics 2004, Achieving Human Rights 2008; numerous articles in learned journals. *Honours:* Hon. mem. Bd of Eds, American Journal of International Law; hon. degrees (Monmouth Coll.) 1987, (CUNY) 1999, (John Jay Coll., York Univ.) 2004. *Address:* 723 Alston Road, Santa Barbara, CA 93108, USA (home). *Telephone:* (805) 893-7860 (office). *Fax:* (805) 893-8003 (office). *E-mail:* falk@global.ucsb.edu (office).

FALLON, Ivan Gregory, FRSA; Irish journalist; *CEO, UK Group, Independent News and Media PLC*; b. 26 June 1944, s. of Padraic Fallon and Dorothea Maher; m. 1st Susan Mary Lurring 1967 (divorced 1997); one s. two d.; m. 2nd Elizabeth Rees-Jones 1997. *Education:* St Peter's Coll., Wexford, Trinity Coll. Dublin. *Career:* on staff of Irish Times 1964–66, Thomson Prov. Newspapers 1966–67, Daily Mirror 1967–68, Sunday Telegraph 1968–70; Deputy City Ed., Sunday Express 1970–71, Sunday Telegraph 1971–84, City Ed. 1979–84; Deputy Ed. Sunday Times 1984–94; Group Editorial Dir, Argus Group, SA 1994–; Chief Exec. Ind. Newspapers Holdings Ltd, South Africa 1997–2002; Exec. Chair. iTouch PLC 2000–05; CEO UK Group, Independent News and Media Group PLC 2002–; mem. Council, Univ. of Buckingham 1982–, Council of Govs, United Medical and Dental Schools of Guy's and St Thomas' Hosps 1985–94; Trustee Project Trust 1984–94, Generation Trust, Guy's Hosp. 1985–; Dir N. Brown Holdings 1994–. *Publications:* DeLorean: The Rise and Fall of a Dream-maker (with James L. Srodes) 1983, Takeovers 1987, The Brothers: The Rise of Saatchi and Saatchi 1988, Billionaire: The Life and Times of Sir James Goldsmith 1991, The Player: The Life of Tony O'Reilly 1994. *Address:* Independent News & Media PLC, Independent House, 2023 Bianconi Avenue, Citywest Business Campus, Naas Road, Dublin 24, Ireland (office). *Telephone:* (1) 4663200 (office). *Fax:* (1) 4663222 (office). *E-mail:* mail@inplc.com (office). *Website:* www.inmplc.com (office).

FALLON, Martin (see Patterson, Harry)

FALLON, Peter, BA, HDipEd, MA; Irish editor and poet; b. 26 Feb. 1951, Osnabrück, Germany; two c. *Education:* Trinity Coll., Dublin. *Career:* Founder-Ed. Gallery Press, Dublin 1970–; Poet-in-Residence, Deerfield

Acad., Mass, USA 1976–77, 1996–97; Int. Writer-in-Residence at various Indiana Schools 1979; Fiction Ed., O'Brien Press, Dublin 1980–85; Teacher, Contemporary Irish Poetry, School of Irish Studies, Dublin 1985–89; Writing Fellow, Poet-in-Residence, Trinity Coll., Dublin 1994; Heimbold Prof. of Irish Studies, Villanova Univ., Pa, USA 2000. *Publications include:* poetry: Among the Walls 1971, Co-incidence of Flesh 1972, The First Affair 1974, Finding the Dead 1978, The Speaking Stones 1978, Winter Work 1983, The News and Weather 1987, The Penguin Book of Contemporary Irish Poetry (ed. with Derek Mahon) 1990, Eye to Eye 1992, News of the World: Selected and New Poems 1993, The Georgics of Virgil (trans.) 2004, Morning Glory 2006, Airs and Angels 2007, The Company of Horses 2007; novel: Tarry Flynn 2004; contrib. to poetry anthologies, periodicals and journals. *Honours:* Dr hc (Villanova Univ.) 2000; Irish Arts Council Bursary 1981, Nat. Poetry Competition, England 1982, Meath Merit Award, Arts and Culture 1987, O'Shaughnessy Poetry Award 1993. *Address:* Gallery Press, Loughcrew, Oldcastle, Co. Meath, Ireland (office). *Telephone:* (40) 8541779 (office). *E-mail:* contactus@gallerypress.com (office). *Website:* www.gallerypress.com (office); www.peterfallon.com (home).

FALLOWELL, Duncan Richard; British writer; b. 26 Sept. 1948, London, England. *Education:* Magdalen Coll., Oxford. *Opera libretto:* Gormenghast 1998. *Publications include:* Drug Tales 1979, April Ashley's Odyssey 1982, Satyrday 1986, The Underbelly 1987, To Noto 1989, Twentieth Century Characters 1994, One Hot Summer in St Petersburg 1994, A History of Facelifting 2003, Going As Far As I Can 2008. *Address:* 44 Leamington Road Villas, London, W11 1HT, England (home). *Website:* www.duncanfallowell.com.

FALLOWS, David Nicholas, BA, MMus, PhD, FBA; British musicologist and academic; *Professor of Musicology, University of Manchester;* b. 20 Dec. 1945, Buxton, Derbyshire, England; m. Paulène Oliver 1976 (separated); one s. one d. *Education:* Jesus Coll., Cambridge, King's Coll., London, Univ. of California, Berkeley, USA. *Career:* Asst, Studio der Frühen Musik, Munich 1967–70; Lecturer in Music, Univ. of Wisconsin, Madison, USA 1973–74; Lecturer in Music, Univ. of Manchester 1976–82, Sr Lecturer 1982–92, Reader in Music 1992–97, Prof. of Musicology 1997–; Reviews Ed., Early Music 1976–95, 1999–2000; Visiting Assoc. Prof., Univ. of North Carolina, Chapel Hill, USA 1982–83; Founder and Gen. Ed. Royal Musical Asscn Monographs 1982–98; Visiting Prof. of Musicology, École Normale Supérieure, Paris, France 1993; Corresp. mem. American Musicological Soc. 1999–; mem. Int. Musicological Soc. (Vice-Pres. 1997–2002, Pres. 2002–07); Royal Musical Asscn (Vice-Pres. 2000–). *Publications include:* Dufay 1982, Chansonnier de Jean de Montchenu (co-author) 1991, Companion to Medieval and Renaissance Music (co-ed. with T. Knighton) 1992, The Songs of Guillaume Dufay 1995, Oxford Bodleian Library MS Canon Misc. 213: Late Medieval and Early Renaissance Music in Facsimile, Vol. 1 (ed.) 1995, Songs and Musicians in the Fifteenth Century 1996, The Songbook of Fridolin Sicher 1996, A Catalogue of Polyphonic Songs 1415–1480 1999, Josquin 2009, Composers and their Songs, 1400–1521 (Variorum Collected Studies Series) 2010; contrib. to reference works, scholarly books and professional journals, including Gramophone, The Guardian, Early Music, New Grove Dictionary of Music and Musicians 1980, 2001. *Honours:* Ingolf Dahl Prize in Musicology 1971, Dent Medal 1982; Chevalier, Ordre des Arts et des Lettres 1994. *Address:* 10 Chatham Road, Manchester, M16 0DR, England (home). *Telephone:* (161) 881-1188 (office). *E-mail:* david.fallows@manchester.ac.uk (home).

FALUDI, Susan C.; American journalist and writer; b. 18 April 1959, Yorktown Heights, NY. *Education:* Harvard Univ., Radcliffe Coll. *Career:* Man. Ed. Harvard Crimson student newspaper; copy clerk, New York Times 1981–86; reporter Miami Herald, Atlanta Constitution 1981–86, San José Mercury News 1986–88; reporter, San Francisco bureau, Wall Street Journal 1990–; contribs to Ms and Mother Jones magazines; mem. Advisory Bd Fairness and Accuracy in Reporting 1992–; mem. Nat. Writers Guild 1994–99. *Publications include:* Backlash: The Undeclared War Against American Women (Nat. Book Critics' Circle Award for Gen. Non-fiction 1992) 1991, Stiffed: The Betrayal of the American Man 2000, The Terror Dream 2007. *Honours:* Pulitzer Prize for Explanatory Journalism 1991 for a report on the leveraged buy-out of Safeway Stores, Inc.. *Literary Agent:* c/o Sandra Dijkstra Literary Agency, PMB 515, 1155 Camino del Mar, Del Mar, CA 92014, USA. *E-mail:* elise@dijkstraagency.com. *Website:* www.dijkstraagency.com. *Address:* c/o Metropolitan Books, 175 Fifth Avenue, New York, NY 10011, USA. *Website:* susanfaludi.com.

FAN, Jingyi; Chinese journalist; *President, China Society of News Photography;* b. 1931, Suzhou City, Jiangsu Prov. *Education:* St John's University, Shanghai. *Career:* joined CCP 1978; Ed., later Ed.-in-Chief, Deputy Dir, later Dir and mem. Editorial Bd Liaoning Daily 1979–84; Dir Foreign Languages Publ. and Distribution Bureau 1984–86; Ed.-in-Chief Economic Daily 1986–93, People's Daily 1993–98; Del., 13th CCP Nat. Congress 1987–92, 14th CCP Nat. Congress 1992–97; mem. 8th CPPCC Nat. Cttee 1993–98 (Vice-Chair. Economy Cttee); mem. Standing Cttee of 9th NPC 1998–2003 (Vice-Chair. Educ., Science, Culture and Public Health Cttee); Pres. China Soc. of News Photography 1995–; currently also Prof. of Journalism, Tsinghua Univ. *Honours:* Hon. Pres. Photo-Journalism Soc. 1994–; honoured as one of the excellent journalists of China 1991. *Address:* Omnicom Building, School of Journalism and Communication, Tsinghua University, Beijing 100084, People's Republic of China (office). *Telephone:* (10) 62781145 (office). *Fax:* (10) 62771410 (office). *E-mail:* tsjc@tsinghua.edu.cn (office). *Website:* www.tsjc.tsinghua.edu.cn (office).

FANTHORPE, Rev. Robert Lionel, BA (Hons), FRSA, FCMI; British ecclesiastic, author, broadcaster, management consultant and academic; *Partner, Fanthorpe Management Consultancy;* b. 9 Feb. 1935, Dereham, Norfolk, England; s. of Robert Fanthorpe and Greta Christine Fanthorpe (née Garbutt); m. Patricia Alice Tooke 1957; two d. *Education:* FCP, teaching certificate with advanced mains distinction, Anglican ordination certificate. *Career:* Headmaster, Glyn Derw High School, Cardiff 1979–89; consultant and Festival Co-ordinator, UK Year of Literature and Writing 1995; Dir of Media Studies, Cardiff Acad. 2002–10; guest celebrity poet, Margate Poetry Festival 2000; Chaplain to Blue Knights Police Motorcyclists Wales Chapter One; Partner, Fanthorpe Management Consultancy; Pres. Jumbo GB motorcyclists' charity, Asscn for the Scientific Study of Anomalous Phenomena 1999, British UFO Research Asscn (BUFORA) 2000; mem. MENSA, Equity, Soc. of Authors, Welsh Acad. *Film:* as actor: Bloodline 2008. *Radio includes:* Real Radio Reverend slot (Real Radio 105FM), Three Wise Men (BBC Radio Wales) 2000, Glastonbury Radio weekly show with Siobhan Peal 2010. *Television includes:* presenter, Fortean TV (Channel 4) 1997, The Real Nostradamus (Channel 4), Stranger than Fiction (Westcountry TV), Stations of the Cross (HTV), Holy Quiz (HTV) 2000, Talking Stones (series) 2002, 2003, role of Regression Detective, This Morning (Granada TV). *Publications include:* The Black Lion 1979 (revised 2009), The Holy Grail Revealed 1982, Life of St Francis 1988, God in All Things 1988, Thoughts and Prayers for Troubled Times 1989, Birds and Animals of the Bible 1990, Thoughts and Prayers for Lonely Times 1990, The First Christmas 1990, Rennes-le-Château 1992, The Oak Island Mystery 1995, Down the Badger Hole (anthology of prose), The Abbot's Kitchen 1995, The World's Greatest Unsolved Mysteries 1997, The World's Most Mysterious People 1998, The World's Most Mysterious Places 1998, Mysteries of the Bible 1999, Death, the Final Mystery 2000, Earth, Sea and Sky (poems) 2000, The World's Most Mysterious Objects 2002, The World's Most Mysterious Murders 2003, Unsolved Mysteries of the Sea 2004, The World's Most Mysterious Castles 2005, Mysteries and Secrets of the Templars 2005, Mysteries and Secrets of the Masons 2006, Mysteries and Secrets of Time 2007, Mysteries and Secrets of Voodoo 2008, Mysteries and Secrets of Undiscovered Treasure 2009, The Big Book of Mysteries 2010, Proverbs and Other Wisdom 2010, Satanism and Demonology 2011. *Honours:* Electrical Devt Asscn Diploma 1958, holder of seven World Championships for Professional Authors: Prose, Drama, Poetry and Autobiography, Grand Chaplain Gen. Knights Templar Priory of the Holy Lands 2002–04. *Address:* Rivendell, 48 Claude Road, Roath, Cardiff, CF24 3QA, Wales (home). *Telephone:* (2920) 498368 (office). *Fax:* (2920) 496832 (office). *E-mail:* fanthorpe@aol.com (home). *Website:* www.lionel-fanthorpe.com.

FAQIH, Ahmad Ibrahim al-, (Ahmed Fagih), PhD; Libyan author, playwright, short story writer and fmr diplomatist; b. 28 Dec. 1932, Mizda. *Education:* Univ. of Edinburgh, UK. *Career:* studied journalism in UNESCO programme in Egypt 1962, worked as journalist in Tripoli; studied theatre in London; apptd Dir Inst. of Music and Drama 1972, also apptd Head of Dept of Arts and Literature, Ministry of Information and Culture; est. Arab Cultural Trust, launched cultural quarterly magazine Azure, Ed.-in-Chief 1972; Press Counsellor, Embassy in London 1977, served in several diplomatic posts, including as Head of Mission in Greece and Romania; Founder, dir and actor, The New Theatre, Tripoli; f. Union of Libyan Writers, currently Sec.-Gen.; lives in Cairo and Rabat. *Plays:* John the Ripper, A Portrait of a Writer, Singing of the Stars, Evening Visitor, The Morning Paper, Harold, Gazelles (Shaw Theatre, London 1982), Muhammed Ali. *Publications include:* in Arabic: Maps of the Soul (historical saga in 12 vols – Bread of the Town, Sinful Joy, Naked Runs the Soul, The Powder of the Musk, Ululations for the Weddings of Death, Wolves Dancing in the Jungle, The Return to the Cities of Sand, The Locked Circles of love, Going into the Labyrinth, The Singing of the Jennies, I Said Farewell to the Storm, Fire in the Desert), Al-Bahr La Ma' Fib (There is No Water in the Sea) (short stories) (Royal Comm. of Fine Arts Award 1965), Sa Ahbiqa Madinatu Ukhra (I Shall Offer You Another City: part 1 of trilogy), Hadhihi Tukhum Mamlakati (The Borders of My Kingdom: part II), and Nafaq Tudiuhu Imra Wahida (A Tunnel Lit by One Woman: part III) (Award for Best Novel, Beirut Book Exhibition 1991); in trans.: Gardens of the Night (trilogy) 1995, Who's Afraid of Agatha Christie and Other Stories 2000, The Gazelles and Other Plays 2000, Valley of Ashes 2000, 30 Short Stories 2008, 5 Novels 2008, 8 Plays 2008, The Libyan Short Story 2008, Homeless Rats (novel) 2011; editor: Libyan Stories 2000. *Honours:* Grand al-Fatah Medal. *Address:* 9 Nablus Street, Muhandisien, Cairo, Egypt (home). *Telephone:* (2) 33020437 (home). *E-mail:* fagih@hotmail.com (home); fagih@yahoo.com (home). *Website:* www.fagih.org.

FARAH, Nuruddin; Somali writer; b. 24 Nov. 1945, Baidoa; s. of Farah Hassan and Fatuma Aleli; m. Amina Mama 1992 (divorced 2007); one s. one d. *Education:* Panjab Univ., Chandigarh, India, Univs of London and Essex, UK. *Career:* Lecturer, Nat. Univ. of Somalia, Mogadishu 1971–74; Assoc. Prof., Univ. of Jos, Nigeria 1981–83; Writer-in-Residence, Univ. of Minn. 1989, Brown Univ. 1991; Prof., Makerere Univ., Kampala 1990; Rhodes Scholar St Antony's Coll., Oxford 1996; Visiting Prof., Univ. of Texas at Austin 1997; now full-time writer; mem. Union of Writers of the African People, PEN Int., Somali-Speaking PEN Centre. *Plays include:* The Offering 1976, Yussuf and his Brothers 1982. *Publications:* From a Crooked Rib 1970, A Naked Needle 1976, Sweet and Sour Milk 1979, Sardines 1981, Close Sesame 1983, Maps

1986, Gifts 1992, Secrets 1998, Yesterday, Tomorrow: Voices from the Somali Diaspora 1999, Links 2004, Knots 2007; contrib. to Guardian, New African, Transition Magazine, New York Times, Observer, TLS, London Review of Books. *Honours:* Hon. DLitt (Univ. of Kent at Canterbury) 2000; English-speaking Union Literary Prize 1980, Tucholsky Award 1991, Premio Cavour Award 1992, Zimbabwe Annual Award 1993, Neustadt Int. Literary Prize 1998, Festival Étonnant Voyageur St Malo, France 1998. *Literary Agent:* c/o Deborah Rogers, Rogers, Coleridge & White, 20 Powis Mews, London, W11 1JN, England.

FARELY, Alison (see Poland, Dorothy Elizabeth Hayward)

FARHI, (Musa) Moris, MBE, BA, FRSL, FRGS; British (b. Turkish) novelist and poet; b. 5 July 1935, Ankara; s. of Hayim Daniel Farhi and Paloma Farhi (née Cuenca); m. Nina Ruth Gould 1978 (died 2009); one step-d. *Education:* Istanbul American Coll., Royal Acad. of Dramatic Art, London. *Career:* mem. Soc. of Authors, Writers' Guild, English PEN, International PEN (Vice-Pres.). *Television:* various scripts 1960–80. *Radio:* True Turk (story) 2010. *Publications include:* novels: The Pleasure of Death 1972, The Last of Days 1983, Journey Through the Wilderness 1989, Children of the Rainbow 1999, Young Turk 2004, A Designated Man 2009; poetry: Songs from Two Continents: Poems 2011; contrib. to Menard Press, Voices Within the Art: The Modern Jewish Poets, Men Cards, European Judaism, Modern Poetry in Translation, Frank, Jewish Quarterly, Steaua (Romania), Confrontation (USA), North Atlantic Review (USA), Reflections on the Universal Declaration of Human Rights. *Honours:* Associazione Thema Romano (Italy) 2002, Romani Acad. of Arts and Sciences Special Prize, Berlin 2003, Alberto Benveniste Prize for Literature, Paris 2007. *Address:* 17 Courtenay Gate, Courtenay Terrace, Hove, East Sussex, BN3 2WJ, England (home). *Telephone:* (1273) 729011 (office). *E-mail:* farhi@clara.net (home).

FARICY, Robert Leo, BS, PhL, MA, STL, STD; American academic and writer; *Professor Emeritus, Pontifical Gregorian University;* b. 29 Aug. 1926, St Paul, Minn.; s. of Roland Faricy and Claire Sullivan Faricy. *Education:* US Naval Acad., St Louis Univ., Lyon-Fourvière Seminaire des Missions, Catholic Univ. of America. *Career:* Asst Prof., Catholic Univ. of America 1965–71; Prof. of Spiritual Theology, Pontifical Gregorian Univ., Rome, Italy 1971–96, Prof. Emer. 1996–; Visiting Prof., Sogang Univ., Seoul, S Korea 1992–93, Pontifical Urbaniana Univ., Rome 2000–02, Regina Mundi Inst., Rome 2000–05, Milltown Inst., Nat. Univ. of Ireland, Dublin, Ireland 2008–09. *Publications include:* Seeking Jesus in Contemplation and Discernment 1983, Medjugorje Up Close: Mary Speaks to the World (with L. Rooney) 1985, Contemplating Jesus (with R. Wicks) 1986, The Contemplative Way of Prayer (with L. Rooney) 1986, The Healing of the Religious Life (with S. Blackborow) 1986, Lord, Teach Us to Pray (with L. Rooney) 1986, Wind and Sea Obey Him: Approaches to a Theology of Nature 1986, Medjugorje Journal (with L. Rooney) 1987, Lord Jesus, Teach Me to Pray (with L. Rooney) 1988, The Lord's Dealing 1988, Mary Among Us 1989, Medjugorje Retreat (with L. Rooney) 1989, Pilgrim's Journal 1990, Our Lady Comes to Scottsdale (with L. Rooney) 1991, Return to God (with L. Rooney) 1993, Knowing Jesus in the World (with L. Rooney) 1996, Your Wounds I Will Heal (with L. Rooney) 1998, Praying with Mary 2000, Gesu e lo Spirito 2006, Contemplazione e Discernimento 2008; contrib. to numerous theological and philosophical journals. *Address:* 1404 W Wisconsin Avenue, Milwaukee, WI 53233, USA (home). *Telephone:* (414) 550-4098 (office); (414) 288-5000 (home). *Fax:* (414) 288-1758 (home). *E-mail:* bobfaricy@yahoo.com (home). *Website:* www.robertfaricy.org.

FARKOUH, Elias, BA; Jordanian writer, translator and publisher; b. 14 March 1948, Amman. *Education:* Arab Univ. of Beirut. *Career:* cultural journalist 1977–79; worked in Al-Manarat publishing house –1990; set up Dar Al-Azmina publishing house 1992–; jury mem. Cairo Novel Prize; founding mem. Jordanian Publrs' Union. *Publications include:* novels: Kamat Az-Zubad (Essential Pillars) 1987, A'midat Al-Ghubar (Pillars of Dust) 1996, Ard al-Yambous (Land of Limbo) 2007; short story collections: Al-Safa (The Slap) 1978, Tuyour Amman Tuhalliq Munkhafida (Amman's Birds Fly Low) 1981, Ihda wa Eshrouna Talqa lil-Nabeyy (Twenty One Shots for the Prophet) (Jordanian Writers' Asscn Award) 1982, Huqoul Al-Zilal (Fields of Shadows) 2002; trans.: Other Fires (short stories) 1999. *Address:* PO Box 950252, Amman 11195, Jordan (home). *Telephone:* (79) 5620807 (mobile) (home). *Fax:* (6) 5522544 (home). *E-mail:* elias@farkouh.net (home). *Website:* elias.farkouh.net.

FARLEY, Carol, BA, MA; American children's writer; b. 20 Dec. 1936, Ludington, Mich.; m. 1954; one s. three d. *Education:* Western Michigan Univ., Michigan State Univ., Central Michigan Univ. *Career:* mem. Mystery Writers of America, Authors' Guild, Children's Book Guild, Soc. of Children's Book Writers, Chicago Children's Reading Round Table. *Publications include:* Mystery of the Fog Man 1974, The Garden is Doing Fine 1976, Mystery in the Ravine 1976, Mystery of the Melted Diamonds 1985, Case of the Vanishing Villain 1986, Case of the Lost Look Alike 1988, Korea, Land of the Morning Calm 1991, Mr Pak Buys a Story 1997, The King's Secret: The Legend of King Sejong 2001; contrib. to The Writer, Soc. of Children's Book Writer's Bulletin, Cricket, Disney Adventures, Challenge, Spider, Pockets, Appleseeds. *Honours:* Child Study Asscn Best Book of Year 1976, Friends of the Writer Best Juvenile Book by Mid-West Writer 1978, IRA/CBC Children's Choice Book 1987. *Address:* 7054 Fenway Avenue, Las Vegas, NV 89147-4739, USA (home). *Telephone:* (702) 330-5129 (home).

FARLEY, Paul; British poet and academic; *Professor of Poetry, Lancaster University;* b. 1965, Liverpool, England. *Education:* Chelsea School of Art. *Career:* fmr Writer-in-Residence with the Wordsworth Trust; Reader in Poetry, Lancaster Univ. 2006–07; Prof. of Poetry 2007–. *Publications include:* The Boy from the Chemist is Here to See You (Forward Prize for Best First Collection) 1998, The Ice Age: Poems (Whitbread Book Award for Best Poetry Collection 2003) 2002, Distant Voices, Still Lives 2006, Tramp in Flames 2006, Field Recordings 2009, The Atlantic Tunnel 2010, Edgelands 2011. *Honours:* Observer/Arvon Int. Poetry Prize 1996, Geoffrey Dearmer Memorial Prize 1997, Somerset Maugham Award 1998, Sunday Times Young Writer of the Year 1999, Royal Literary Fund Fellow, Liverpool Hope Univ. Coll. 2000–01, 2001–02, Forward Prize for the Best Single Poem (for Liverpool Disappears for a Billionth of a Second) 2005, E.M. Forster Award, American Acad. of Arts and Letters 2009, Jerwood Award for Non-Fiction, Royal Soc. of Literature 2009. *Literary Agent:* c/o Peter Straus, Rogers, Coleridge & White, 20 Powis Mews, London, W11 1JN, England. *Telephone:* (20) 7221-3717. *Address:* Department of English and Creative Writing, Lancaster University, Bailrigg, Lancaster, LA1 4YW, England (office). *E-mail:* p.j.farley@lancaster.ac.uk (office).

FARMER, Beverley Anne, BA; Australian writer; b. 7 Feb. 1941, Melbourne, Vic.; one s. *Education:* Univ. of Melbourne. *Publications include:* Alone 1980, Milk (NSW Premier's Prize for Fiction 1984) 1983, Home Time 1985, A Body of Water: A Year's Notebook 1990, Place of Birth 1990, The Seal Woman 1992, The House in the Light 1995, Collected Stories 1996, The Bone House 2005. *Honours:* Patrick White Award 2009.

FARMER, David Hugh, BLitt, FRHistS, FSA; British lecturer and writer; b. 30 Jan. 1923, Ealing, London, England; m. Pauline Ann Widgery 1966 (died 1999); two s. *Education:* Linacre Coll., Oxford. *Career:* Lecturer, Univ. of Reading 1967–77, Reader 1977–88; also lectured in Denmark and Italy. *Publications include:* Life of St Hugh of Lincoln 1961, The Monk of Farne 1962, The Rule of St Benedict 1968, The Oxford Dictionary of Saints 1978, Benedict's Disciples 1980, The Age of Bede 1983, St Hugh of Lincoln 1985, Bede's Ecclesiastical History 1990, Christ Crucified and Other Meditations 1994; contrib. to St Augustine's Abbey (English Heritage) 1997, Benedictines in Oxford 1997, The Story of Christian Spirituality 2001, Dictionnaire d'Histoire Ecclesiastique, New Catholic Encyclopedia, Bibliotheca Sanctorum, Lexikon der Christlichen Ikonographie, Studia Monastica, Studia Anselmiana, Journal of Ecclesiastical History, English Historical Review, The Tablet. *Address:* 23 Hartslock Court, Shooters Hill, Pangbourne, Berks., RG8 7BJ, England (home).

FARMER, Penelope Jane, BA, DipSoc; British writer; b. 14 June 1939, Westerham, Kent, England; m. 1st Michael John Mockridge 1962 (divorced 1977); one s. one d.; m. 2nd Simon Shorvon 1984 (divorced 1996). *Education:* St Anne's Coll., Oxford, Bedford Coll., London. *Career:* mem. PEN, Soc. of Authors. *Publications include:* fiction: Standing in the Shadow 1984, Eve: Her Story 1985, Away from Home 1987, Glasshouses 1988, Snakes and Ladders 1993; children's books: The China People 1960, The Summer Birds 1962, The Magic Stone 1964, The Saturday Shillings 1965, The Seagull 1965, Emma in Winter 1966, Charlotte Sometimes 1969, Dragonfly Summer 1971, A Castle of Bone 1972, William and Mary 1974, Heracles 1975, August the Fourth 1975, Year King 1977, The Coal Train 1977, Beginnings: Creation Myths of the World (ed.) 1979, The Runaway Train 1980, Thicker Than Water 1989, Stone Croc 1991, Penelope 1994, Twin Trouble 1996; other: Anthology: Two: The Book of Twins and Doubles 1996, Sisters 1998, Grandmothers 2000; short stories; radio and TV scripts; contribs to periodicals. *Honours:* American Library Asscn Notable Book 1962, Carnegie Medal Commendation 1963. *Website:* grannyp.blogspot.com.

FARNDALE, Nigel, MA; British author and journalist; b. 30 Sept. 1964, Ripon, N Yorks.; m.; three c. *Education:* Durham Univ. *Career:* feature writer and columnist, Sunday Telegraph, interview subjects have included Henry Kissinger, Mick Jagger, Woody Allen, the Dalai Lama, Prince Charles, Hillary Clinton, Paul McCartney, George Best and Stephen Hawking; radio appearances. *Publications:* A Sympathetic Hanging 2000, Last Action Hero of the British Empire: Cdr John Kerans 1915-1985 (biog.) 2001, Flirtation, Seduction, Betrayal: Interviews with Heroes and Villains 2002, Haw-Haw: The Tragedy of William and Margaret Joyce (biog.) 2006, The Blasphemer (novel) 2010. *Honours:* British Press Award. *Literary Agent:* c/o David Miller, Rogers, Coleridge & White, 20 Powis Mews, London, W11 1JN, England. *E-mail:* davidmiller@rcwlitagency.com. *Website:* www.nigelfarndale.com.

FAROOKI, Roopa; British author; b. 1974, Lahore, Pakistan; d. of the late Nasim Ahmed Farooki and Nilofar Farooki; m.; two s. two d. *Education:* New Coll., Univ. of Oxford. *Career:* raised in central London; graduate trainee accountant, Arthur Andersen; Advertising Account Dir, Saatchi & Saatchi and JWT –2004; full-time writer 2004–; teaches creative writing; Amb. for Family Counselling, Relate. *Publications include:* novels: Bitter Sweets 2007, Corner Shop 2008, The Way Things Look to Me 2009, Half Life 2011, The Flying Man 2012. *Literary Agent:* c/o Aitken Alexander Associates, 18–21 Cavaye Place, London, SW10 9PT, England. *Telephone:* (20) 7373-8672. *Fax:* (20) 7373-6002. *E-mail:* reception@aitkenalexander.co.uk. *Website:* www.aitkenalexander.co.uk; www.roopafarooki.com.

FARRINGTON, David Philip, OBE, MA, PhD, FBA, FMedSci; British psychologist, academic and criminologist; *Professor of Psychological Criminology, Institute of Criminology, University of Cambridge;* b. 7 March 1944, Ormskirk, Lancs.; s. of William Farrington and Gladys Holden Farrington; m. Sally

Chamberlain 1966; three d. *Education:* Univ. of Cambridge. *Career:* mem. staff, Inst. of Criminology, Univ. of Cambridge 1969–, Prof. of Psychological Criminology 1992–; Pres. European Asscn of Psychology and Law 1997–99; Visiting Fellow, US Nat. Inst. of Justice 1981; Chair. Div. of Criminological and Legal Psychology, British Psychological Soc. 1983–85; mem. Parole Bd for England and Wales 1984–87; Vice-Chair. US Nat. Acad. of Sciences Panel on Violence 1989–92; Visiting Fellow US Bureau of Justice Statistics 1995–98; Co-Chair. US Office of Juvenile Justice and Delinquency Prevention Study Group on Serious and Violent Juvenile Offenders 1995–97; Pres. British Soc. of Criminology 1990–93, Pres. American Soc. of Criminology 1998–99; Co-Chair. US Office of Juvenile Justice and Delinquency Prevention Study Group on Very Young Offenders 1998–2000; Chair. UK Dept of Health Advisory Cttee for the Nat. Programme on Forensic Mental Health 2000–03; mem. Bd of Dirs Int. Soc. of Criminology 2000–; Pres. Acad. of Experimental Criminology 2001–03; Co-Chair. Campbell Collaboration Crime and Justice Group 2000–. *Publications:* 27 books and over 420 articles on criminology and psychology. *Honours:* Sellin-Glueck Award of American Soc. of Criminology 1984, Sutherland Award of American Soc. of Criminology 2002, Joan McCord Award, Acad. of Experimental Criminology 2005, Beccaria Gold Medal, Criminology Soc. of German-Speaking Countries 2005. *Address:* Institute of Criminology, University of Cambridge, Sidgwick Avenue, Cambridge, CB3 9DA (office); 7 The Meadows, Haslingfield, Cambridge, CB3 7JD, England (home). *Telephone:* (1223) 335360 (office); (1223) 872555 (home). *Fax:* (1223) 335356 (office). *E-mail:* enquiries@crim.cam.ac.uk (office). *Website:* www.crim.cam.ac.uk (office).

FARROW, John (see Ferguson, Trevor)

FASQUELLE, Jean-Claude; French publisher; *Chairman of the Board, Éditions Grasset et Fasquelle;* b. 29 Nov. 1930, Paris; s. of Charles Fasquelle and Odette Cyprien-Fabre; m. 1st Solange de la Rochefoucauld; one d.; m. 2nd Nickla Jegher 1966. *Education:* Ecole des Roches, Verneuil-sur-Avre, Sorbonne and Faculté de Droit, Paris. *Career:* Pres.-Dir-Gen. Société des Editions Fasquelle 1953–60, Editions du Sagittaire 1958–; Admin.-Dir-Gen. Editions Grasset et Fasquelle 1960, Pres.-Dir-Gen. 1980–2000, Chair. of Bd 2000–; Dir Le Magazine littéraire (monthly) 1970–2004. *Address:* Éditions Grasset et Fasquelle, 61 rue des Saintes-Pères, 75006 Paris (office); 13 Square Vergennes, 75015 Paris, France (home). *Telephone:* 1-44-39-22-00 (office). *Fax:* 1-44-39-22-18 (office). *E-mail:* jcfasquelle@wanadoo.fr (home). *Website:* www.edition-grasset.fr (office).

FATCHEN, Maxwell Edgar, AM; Australian author and poet; b. 3 Aug. 1920, Adelaide, SA; m. Jean Wohlers 1942; two s. one d. *Career:* journalist and feature writer, Adelaide News 1946–55; special writer, The Advertiser 1955, 1981–84, Literary Ed. 1971–81; mem. Australian Soc. of Authors, Australian Fellowship of Writers, South Australian Writers' Centre, Media Alliance. *Publications include:* The River Kings 1966, Conquest of the River 1970, The Spirit Wind 1973, Chase Through the Night 1977, Closer to the Stars 1981, Wry Rhymes 1987, A Country Christmas 1990, Tea for Three 1994, Mostly Max: The Musings of Max Fatchen 1995, Life with Fatchen 1998, Songs for My Dog and Other Wry Rhymes 1999; contribs to Denver Post, Sydney Sun, Regional South Australian Histories, Adelaide Now. *Honours:* Advance Australia Award for Literature 1991, AMP-Walkley Award for Journalism 1996, South Australia Great Award for Literature 1999.

FAULKS, Sebastian, CBE, MA, FRSL; British writer; b. 20 April 1953, Newbury, Berks.; s. of Peter Faulks and Pamela Lawless; m. Veronica Youlten 1989; two s. one d. *Education:* Wellington Coll. and Emmanuel Coll., Cambridge. *Career:* reporter, Daily Telegraph newspaper 1979–83, feature writer, Sunday Telegraph 1983–86; Literary Ed. The Independent 1986–89, Deputy Ed. The Independent on Sunday 1989–90, Assoc. Ed. 1990–91; columnist, The Guardian 1992–97, Evening Standard 1997–99, Mail on Sunday 1999–2000; invited to write new James Bond 007 novel to celebrate centenary of Ian Fleming's birth 2008. *Radio:* Panelist, The Write Stuff, BBC Radio 4 1998–. *Television:* Churchill's Secret Army 2000, Faulks on Fiction 2011. *Publications:* A Trick of the Light 1984, The Girl at the Lion d'Or 1989, A Fool's Alphabet 1992, Birdsong 1993, The Fatal Englishman 1996, Charlotte Gray 1998, On Green Dolphin Street 2001, Human Traces 2005, Pistache 2006, Engleby 2007, Devil May Care (writing as Ian Fleming) (British Book Award for Popular Fiction 2009) 2008, A Week in December 2009, Faulks on Fiction 2011, A Possible Life 2012. *Honours:* Hon. Fellow, Emmanuel Coll., Cambridge 2007; Hon. DLitt (Tavistock Clinic, Univ. of East London). *Literary Agent:* c/o Aitken Alexander Associates Ltd, 18–21 Cavaye Place, London, SW10 9PT, England. *Telephone:* (20) 7373-8672. *Fax:* (20) 7373-6002. *E-mail:* reception@aitkenalexander.co.uk. *Website:* www.aitkenalexander.co.uk; www.sebastianfaulks.com.

FAURE, Roland; French journalist; b. 10 Oct. 1926, Montelimar; s. of Edmond Faure-Geors and Jeanne Gallet; m. Véra Hitzbleck 1956; three s. *Education:* Enclos Saint-François, Montpellier and Faculté de Droit, Aix-en-Provence. *Career:* journalist, Méridional-la France, Marseilles 1947; del. in America, Asscn de la presse latine d'Europe et d'Amerique 1951, Sec.-Gen. 1954–; Founder and Ed.-in-Chief, Journal français du Brésil, Rio de Janeiro 1952–53; Diplomatic Ed. L'Aurore 1954, Head of Diplomatic Service 1959, Ed.-in-Chief 1962, Dir and Ed.-in-Chief 1968–78; attached to Cabinet of Minister of Public Works 1957–58; Dir Toutes les nouvelles de Versailles 1954–86; mem. Admin. Bd Antenne 2 1975–79; Dir of Information, Radio-France 1979–81; Founder and Dir Radio CVS 1982; Pres. Dir-Gen. Société Nat. de programme Radio France 1986–89, Société Nat. de Radiodiffusion; Pres. Université radiophonique et télévisuelle int. (URTI) 1987–97, Communauté des radios publiques de langue française (CRPLF) 1987; Pres. Admin. Council Fondations Marguerite Long-Jacques Thibaud 1991–2007; Pres. Club DAB 1991–; mem. Conseil Supérieur de l'Audiovisuel (CSA) 1989–97, mem. numerous professional asscns. etc. *Publications:* Brésil dernière heure 1954; articles in newspapers and journals. *Honours:* Officier, Légion d'honneur, Officier, Ordre Nat. du Mérite, des Arts et des Lettres. *Address:* 94 boulevard de la Tour Maubourg, 75007 Paris, France (home). *Telephone:* 1-49-55-01-15 (office).

FAUSTINA, Bama, (Bama); Indian author and teacher; b. (Faustina Mary Fatima Rani), 1958, Puthupatti, Madras State. *Career:* served as nun for seven years; acclaimed Dalit fiction writer in Tamil; Founder and teacher of school for Dalit children, Uttiramerur, Tamil Nadu; participant in int. festivals in Paris, Singapore and Washington, DC. *Publications include:* Karukku (autobiographical novel) (Crossword Book Award 2000) 1992, Sangati 1994, Kusumbukkaran 1996, Vanmam 2002, Oru Tattvum Erumaiyum 2003. *Honours:* Kural Amaippu Award, Dalit Murasu Kalai Illakkiya Award, Amuthan Adigal Illakkiya Parisu Award. *Address:* c/o Oxford University Press India, 1st Floor, YMCA Library Building, 1 Jai Singh Road, Post Box 43, New Delhi 110 001, India (office). *Telephone:* (11) 43600300 (office). *Fax:* (11) 23360897 (office). *E-mail:* admin@oup.com (office). *Website:* www.oup.co.in (office).

FAWKES, Richard Brian, BA; British writer, dramatist and film director; b. 31 July 1944, Camberley, Surrey, England; m. Cherry Elizabeth Cole; two s. one d. *Education:* St David's Univ. Coll. *Career:* mem. Soc. of Authors, Soc. for Theatre Research. *Publications include:* The Last Corner of Arabia (with Michael Darlow) 1976, Fighting for a Laugh 1978, Dion Boucicault: A Biography 1979, Notes from a Low Singer (with Michael Langdon) 1982, Welsh National Opera 1986, Opera on Film 2000, The Classical Music Map of Britain 2010; other: plays for stage, radio, and TV, libretti, documentary film scripts; contribs to journals and magazines including, BBC Music Magazine, Opera Now, Classical Music and Daily Telegraph. *Honours:* West Midlands Arts Asscn Bursary 1978. *E-mail:* richard@richardfawkes.co.uk (office). *Website:* www.richardfawkes.co.uk.

FEDER, Kenneth, BA, MA, PhD; American archaeologist and writer; *Professor of Anthropology, Central Connecticut State University;* b. 1 Aug. 1952, New York, USA; m. Melissa Jean Kalogeros 1981; two s. *Education:* State Univ. of New York, Univ. of Connecticut. *Career:* Prof. of Anthropology, Central Connecticut State Univ. 1977–, Fellow, Cttee for the Scientific Investigation of Claims of the Paranormal, Excellence in Teaching. *Publications include:* Human Antiquity (with Michael Park) 1989, Frauds, Myths and Mysteries: Science and Pseudoscience in Archaeology 1990, A Village of Outcasts: Historical Archaeology and Documentary Research at the Lighthouse 1994, The Past In Perspective: An Introduction to Human Prehistory 1996, Field Methods in Archaeology (with Tom Hester and Harry Shafer) 1997, Lessons From the Past 1999, Dangerous Places: Health and Safety in Archaeology (co-ed. with David Poirier) 2001, Atlantis: Fact or Fiction, The Trojan War, Theseus and the Minotaur, Jason and the Argonauts (contribs to The Seventy Great Mysteries of the Ancient World, co-ed. by Brian Fagan) 2001, Linking to the Past 2004, Skeptics, Fencesitters and True Believers in Archaeological Fantasies 2005 (co-ed. Garrett Fagan), Encyclopedia of Dubious Archaeology: From Atlantis to the Walam Olum 2010; contrib. to Encyclopedia of Anthropology 2006. *Address:* Department of Anthropology, Central Connecticut State University, DiLoreto Hall, Room 110, New Britain, CT 06050, USA (office). *Telephone:* (860) 832-2615 (office). *E-mail:* feder@ccsu.edu (office). *Website:* www.anthropology.ccsu.edu/faculty/feder/Feder.html (office).

FEI MA (see Marr, William Wei-Yi)

FEIFFER, Jules Ralph; American cartoonist, writer and dramatist; b. 26 Jan. 1929, New York, NY; s. of David Feiffer and Rhoda Davis; m. 1st Judith Sheftel 1961 (divorced 1983); one d.; m. 2nd Jennifer Allen 1983; two c. *Education:* Art Students' League, Pratt Inst. *Career:* asst to syndicated cartoonist Will Eisner 1946–51; cartoonist, author, syndicated Sunday page, Clifford, engaged in various art jobs 1953–56; contributing cartoonist Village Voice, New York 1956–97; cartoons published weekly in The Observer (London) 1958–66, 1972–82, regularly in Playboy (magazine); sponsor Sane; US Army 1951–53; mem. Dramatists' Guild (council 1970); currently Adjunct Prof., Program in Writing and Literature, Stony Brook Southampton Coll.; fmr teacher Yale School of Drama, Northwestern Univ.; fmr Sr Fellow, Columbia Univ. Nat. Arts Journalism Program; mem. American Acad. of Arts and Letters 1995–. *Plays:* Crawling Arnold 1961, Little Murders 1966, God Bless 1968, The White House Murder Case 1970, Feiffer on Nixon: The Cartoon Presidency 1974, Knock Knock 1975, Grown Ups 1981, A Think Piece 1982, Carnal Knowledge 1988, Anthony Rose 1989, Feiffer The Collected Works (vols 1, 2, 3) 1990, A Bad Friend 2003. *Screenplays:* Little Murders 1971, Carnal Knowledge 1971, Popeye 1980, I Want to Go Home (Best Screenplay, Venice Film Festival) 1989, I Lost My Bear 1998, Bark, George 1999. *Publications:* Sick, Sick, Sick 1959, Passionella and Other Stories 1960, The Explainers 1961, Boy, Girl, Boy, Girl, 1962, Hold Me! 1962, Harry, The Rat With Women (novel) 1963, Feiffer's Album 1963, The Unexpurgated Memoirs of Bernard Mergendeiler 1965, The Great Comic Book Heroes 1967, Feiffer's Marriage Manual 1967, Pictures at a Prosecution 1971, Ackroyd (novel) 1978, Tantrum 1980, Jules Feiffer's America: From Eisenhower to

Reagan 1982, Marriage is an Invasion of Privacy 1984, Feiffer's Children 1986, Ronald Reagan in Movie America 1988, Elliott Loves (also play) 1990, The Man in the Ceiling (juvenile) 1993, A Barrel of Laughs, A Vale of Tears (juvenile) 1995, A Room with a Zoo (juvenile), The Daddy Mountain (juvenile), Explainers 2008, Backing into Forward: A Memoir 2010. *Honours:* Hon. Fellow, Inst. for Policy Studies 1987; Dr hc (Southampton Coll., Long Island Univ.) 1999; Acad. Award for Animated Cartoon (for Munro) 1961, Special George Polk Memorial Award 1962, Best Foreign Play, English Press (for Little Murders) 1967, Outer Critics Circle Award (Obie) 1969, (The White House Murder Case) 1970, Pulitzer Prize for Editorial Cartooning 1986, Writers Guild of America, East's Ian McLellan Hunter Award for Lifetime Achievement in Writing 2004, Nat. Cartoonist Soc. Milton Caniff Lifetime Achievement Award 2004, Benjamin Franklin Creativity Laureate Award 2006. *Literary Agent:* Royce Carlton Inc., 866 United Nations Plaza, New York, NY 10017, USA. *Telephone:* (212) 355-7700. *Fax:* (212) 888-8659. *E-mail:* info@roycecarlton.com. *Website:* www.roycecarlton.com. *E-mail:* info@julesfeiffer.com (office). *Website:* www.julesfeiffer.com.

FEINSTEIN, (Allan) David, BA, MA, PhD; American psychologist, administrator and writer; *CEO, Innersource*; b. 22 Dec. 1946, New York, NY; s. of Sol Feinstein and Edith Feinstein; m. Donna Eden 1984. *Education:* Whittier Coll., US Int. Univ., Union Inst. *Career:* Dir Energy Medicine Inst., Ashland, Ore.; has taught at Johns Hopkins Univ. School of Medicine, Antioch Coll., California School of Professional Psychology; CEO Innersource; mem. American Psychological Asscn. *Publications include:* Personal Mythology 1988, Rituals for Living and Dying 1990, The Mythic Path 1997, Energy Medicine 1999, Energy Psychology Interactive 2003, The Promise of Energy Psychology 2005, Ethics Handbook for Energy Healing Practitioners (with Donna Eden) 2011; contribs to The Futurist, Common Boundary, Psychotherapy, American Journal of Hypnosis, American Journal of Orthopsychiatry. *Honours:* William James Award, Whittier Coll., Outstanding Contribution Award, Asscn for Comprehensive Energy Psychology 2002, nine Nat. Book Awards, including US Book News Best Psychology/Mental Health Book of 2007. *Address:* Innersource, 777 East Main Street, Ashland, OR 97520, USA (office). *Telephone:* (541) 482-1800 (office). *Fax:* (541) 488-1739 (office). *E-mail:* energy@innersource.net (office). *Website:* www.innersource.net (office).

FEINSTEIN, Elaine Barbara, FRSL; British poet and writer; b. 24 Oct. 1930, Bootle, Lancs., England; three s. *Education:* Newnham Coll., Cambridge. *Career:* mem. editorial staff, Cambridge University Press 1960–62; Lecturer, Bishops Stortford Coll. 1963–66; Asst Lecturer, Univ. of Essex 1967–70. *Radio plays include:* Echoes 1980, A Late Spring 1981, A Day Off 1983, Marina Tsvetayeva: A Life 1985, If I Ever Get On My Feet Again 1987, The Man in her Life 1990, Foreign Girls, a trilogy 1993, A Winter Meeting 1994, Lady Chatterley's Confession (adaptation) 1996. *Television screenplays include:* Breath 1975, Lunch 1981, The Edwardian Country Gentlewoman's Diary 12-part series) 1984, A Brave Face 1985, The Chase (episode four) 1988, A Passionate Woman (six-part series on life of Marie Stopes) 1990, The Brecht Project (three parts of series). *Publications include:* poetry: In a Green Eye 1966, The Magic Apple Tree 1971, At the Edge 1972, The Celebrants and Other Poems 1973, Some Unease and Angels: Selected Poems 1977, Selected Poems 1977, The Feast of Eurydice 1980, Badlands 1987, City Music 1990, Selected Poems 1994, Daylight 1997, Gold 2000, Collected Poems and Translations 2002, Talking to the Dead 2007, Cities 2010; biographies: Bessie Smith 1985, A Captive Lion: The Life of Marina Tsvetayeva 1987, Lawrence's Women (aka Lawrence and the Women) 1993, Pushkin 1998, Ted Hughes: The Life of a Poet 2001, Anna of All the Russias: the Life of Anna Akhmatova 2005; novels: The Circle 1970, The Amberstone Exit 1972, The Glass Alembic (aka The Crystal Garden) 1973, Children of the Rose 1975, The Ecstasy of Dr Miriam Garner 1976, The Shadow Master 1978, The Survivors 1982, The Border 1984, Mother's Girl 1988, All You Need 1989, Loving Brecht 1992, Dreamers 1994, Lady Chatterley's Confession 1996, Dark Inheritance 2001, The Russian Jerusalem 2008; short stories: Matters of Chance 1972, The Silent Areas 1980. *Honours:* Hon. DLitt (Leicester) 1990; Arts Council Grant/Award for Trans. 1970, 1979, 1981, 2004, Daisy Miller Prize 1971, Chomondeley Award 1990. *Literary Agent:* c/o Rogers, Coleridge & White Ltd, 20 Powis Mews, London, W11 1JN, England. *Address:* c/o Carcanet Press, Fourth Floor, Alliance House, Cross Street, Manchester, M2 7AP, England (office).

FEIST, Raymond E., BA; American writer; b. 1945, Los Angeles, Calif.; m. Kathleen Starbuck; one c. *Education:* Univ. of California, San Diego. *Publications include:* novels: Magician 1982, Silverthorn 1985, A Darkness at Sethanon 1986, Magician's Apprentice 1986, Master 1986, Daughter of the Empire 1987, Faerie Tale 1988, Prince of the Blood 1989, Servant of the Empire 1990, Mistress of the Empire 1992, The King's Buccaneer 1992, Shadow of a Dark Queen 1994, Rise of a Merchant Prince 1995, Rage of a Demon King 1997, Shards of a Broken Crown 1998, The Betrayal 1998, The Assassins 1999, Tear of the Gods 2000, The Atlas of Midkemia 2000, Krondor 2001, Murder in Lamut 2002, Birthright: The Book of Man 2002, Honoured Enemy 2002, Talon of the Silver Hawk 2002, King of Foxes 2003, Jimmy the Hand 2003, Exile's Return 2004, Flight of the Nighthawks 2005, Into a Dark Realm 2006, Wrath of a Mad Dog 2008, Rides a Dread Legion 2009, At the Gates of Darkness 2010, A Kingdom Besieged: Book One of the Chaoswar Saga 2011. *Address:* c/o Voyager, Harper Collins Publishing, 10 East 53rd Street, New York, NY 10022, USA. *E-mail:* web3@crydee.com (office). *Website:* www.crydee.com.

FEKETE, John, BA, MA, PhD; Canadian academic and writer; *Distinguished Research Professor, Centre for Theory, Culture and Politics, Trent University*; b. 7 Aug. 1946, Budapest, Hungary; s. of Stephen Fekete and Lily Fekete; m. Victoria de Zwaan. *Education:* McGill Univ., Montreal, Univ. of Cambridge, UK. *Career:* Visiting Asst Prof. of English, McGill Univ. 1973–74; Assoc. Ed. Telos 1974–84; Visiting Asst Prof. of Humanities, York Univ., Toronto, Ont. 1975–76; Asst Prof., Trent Univ., Peterborough, Ont. 1976–78, Assoc. Prof. 1978–84, Prof. of English and Cultural Studies 1984–, Distinguished Research Prof. Centre for Theory, Culture and Politics 1990–; Chair. Cultural Studies Dept 1987–90; Dir, Cultural Studies PhD Program 2009–10. *Publications include:* The Critical Twilight: Explorations in the Ideology of Anglo-American Literary Theory from Eliot to McLuhan 1978, The Structural Allegory: Reconstructive Encounters With the New French Thought 1984, Life After Postmodernism: Essays on Culture and Value 1987, Moral Panic: Biopolitics Rising 1994; contrib. to Canadian Journal of Political and Social Theory, Canadian Journal of Communications, Science-Fiction Studies, Sexuality and Culture. *Honours:* Distinguished Research Award, Trent Univ. 1990. *Address:* Catharine Parr Traill College, Wallis Hall 111, Trent University, 310 London Street Ontario , Peterborough, ON K9H 7P4 (office); 1818 Cherryhill Road, Apt 406, Peterborough, ON K9K 1S6, Canada (home). *Telephone:* (705) 748-1771 (office). *E-mail:* jfekete@trentu.ca (office). *Website:* www.trentu.ca/culturalstudies (office); www.trentu.ca/english (office).

FELDMAN, Alan Grad, AB, MA, PhD; American writer, poet and teacher; b. 16 March 1945, New York, NY; m. Nanette Hass 1972; one s. one d. *Education:* Columbia Coll., Columbia Univ., State Univ. of NY, Buffalo. *Career:* fmr chair and Prof. Emer. of the English Dept of Framingham State Univ. *Publications include:* The Household 1966, The Happy Genius 1978, Frank O'Hara 1978, The Personals 1982, Lucy Mastermind 1985, Anniversary 1992, A Sail to Great Island 2004; contribs to The New Yorker, Atlantic, Kenyon Review, Mississippi Review, Ploughshares, North American Review, Threepenny Review, Boston Review, Tendril, College English. *Honours:* Award for Best Short Story in a Coll. Literary Magazine, Saturday Review-Nat. Student Asscn 1965, Elliston Book Award for Best Book of Poems by a Small Press in USA 1978, Felix Pollak Prize for Poetry 2004. *Address:* 399 Belknap Road, Framingham, MA 01701, USA (home).

FELDMAN, Irving Mordecai, BSSS, MA; American academic and poet; *Distinguished Professor, State University of New York, Buffalo*; b. 22 Sept. 1928, Brooklyn, NY; m. Carmen Alvarez del Olmo 1955; one s. *Education:* City Coll., City Univ. of New York, Columbia Univ. *Career:* teacher, Univ. of Puerto Rico, Rio Piedras 1954–56, Univ. of Lyons, France 1957–58, Kenyon Coll., Gambier, Ohio 1958–64; Prof. of English, State Univ. of NY, Buffalo 1964–, Distinguished Prof. 1991–. *Publications include:* poetry: Work and Days and Other Poems 1961, The Pripet Marshes and Other Poems 1965, Magic Papers and Other Poems 1970, Lost Originals 1972, Leaping Clear 1976, New and Selected Poems 1979, Teach Me, Dear Sister, and Other Poems 1983, All of us Here and Other Poems 1986, Beautiful False Things 2000, The Life and Letters 1994, Beautiful False Things 2000, Collected Poems 1954–2004 2004. *Honours:* Kovner Award, Jewish Book Council of America 1962, Ingram Merrill Foundation Grant 1963, 1981, 1982, American Acad. of Arts and Letters Grant 1973; Guggenheim Fellowship 1973, Creative Artists Public Service Grant 1980, Emily Clark Balch Poetry Prize (VQR) 1983, Acad. of American Poets Fellowship 1986, Nat. Endowment for the Arts Grant 1987, John D. and Catherine T. MacArthur Foundation Fellowship 1992, Smart Family Foundation Prize (Yale Review) 2000. *Address:* Department of English, State University of New York at Buffalo, Buffalo, NY 14260, USA (office). *Telephone:* (716) 885-4122 (office). *Fax:* (716) 885-4122 (office). *E-mail:* feldman@buffalo.edu (office).

FELDMAN, Paula R., BA, MA, PhD; American academic and writer; *C. Wallace Martin Professor of English and Louise Fry Scudder Professor of Liberal Arts, University of South Carolina, Columbia*; b. 4 July 1948, Washington, DC; d. of Samuel Feldman and Selma Leon Feldman; m. Peter Mugglestone; one c. *Education:* Bucknell Univ., Northwestern Univ. *Career:* Asst Prof. of English, Univ. of South Carolina, Columbia 1974–79, Assoc. Prof. 1979–89, Prof. of English 1989–, Dir Grad. Studies in English 1991–94, C. Wallace Martin Prof. of English 1999–, Louise Fry Scudder Prof. of Liberal Arts 2000–. *Publications include:* The Journals of Mary Shelley (co-ed. with Diana Scott-Kilvert, two vols) 1987, The Wordworthy Computer: Classroom and Research Applications in Language and Literature (with Buford Norman) 1987, Romantic Women Writers: Voices and Countervoices (co-ed. with Theresa Kelley) 1995, British Women Poets of the Romantic Era 1997, A Century of Sonnets: The Romantic Era Revival 1750–1850 (co-ed. with Daniel Robinson) 1999, Records of Woman (ed.) 1999, The Keepsake for 1829 (ed.) 2006; contrib. to Studies in English Literature 1980, Keats-Shelley Journal 1997, 2006, Papers of the Bibliographical Society of America 1978, ADE Bulletin 1995, New Literary History 2002, Approaches to Teaching Shelley's Frankenstein 1990, Blake: An Illustrated Quarterly 1994, Approaches to Teaching the Women Romantic Poets 1997, Romanticism and Women Poets 1997, Cambridge Guide to Women's Writing 1999, Women's Poetry, Late Romantic to Late Victorian: Gender and Genre 1999, Authorship, Commerce and the Public: Scenes of Writing 2002, Interdisciplinary Studies in Literature and Environment 2010. *Honours:* Distinguished Scholar, Keats-Shelley Asscn of America 2007. *Address:* Department of English, University of South Carolina, 1620 College Street, Columbia, SC 29208, USA (office). *Telephone:*

(803) 777-4204 (office). *Fax:* (803) 777-9064 (office). *E-mail:* feldmanp@mailbox.sc.edu (office). *Website:* www.paulafeldman.com.

FELL, Alison; Scottish writer and poet; *Royal Literary Fund Fellow, Courtauld Institute of Art*; b. 4 June 1944, Dumfries; m. Roger Coleman 1964 (divorced 1966); one s. *Education:* Edinburgh Coll. of Art, Univ. of London, Inst. of Educ., Nat. Film School. *Career:* Co-founder Welfare State Theatre Leeds-Bradford 1970, Women's Street Theatre London 1971; journalist, Underground Press 1971–75; Fiction Ed. Spare Rib 1975–79; C. Day-Lewis Fellow and Writer-in-Residence, London Borough of Brent 1978; Writer-in-Residence, London Borough of Walthamstow 1981–82, NSW Inst. of Tech., Australia 1986; Guest Writer, Female Eye Conf., Huddersfield, England 1996; Writing Fellow, Univ. of East Anglia 1998; British Council tours to Germany, Canada and USA 1996–97, 2000; Co-Judge and Presenter, New Blood Competition, Inst. of Contemporary Arts 1996; Royal Literary Fund Fellow, Univ. Coll. London 2002–03; Research Fellow, Middlesex Univ. 2003–06; Royal Literary Fund Fellow, Courtauld Inst. of Art 2006–; Lecturer in Creative Writing, Southampton Univ. 2008–; has led writing workshops; readings from her works; mem. Soc. of Authors, RSL. *Publications include:* fiction: The Grey Dancer 1981, Every Move You Make 1984, The Bad Box 1987, Mer de Glace 1991, The Pillow Boy of the Lady Onogoro 1994, The Mistress of Lilliput 1999, Tricks of the Light 2003; poetry: Kisses for Mayakovsky 1984, The Crystal Owl 1988, Dreams, like heretics 1997, Lightyear 2005; other: The Shining Mountain 1989, Dionysus Day (prose poem) 1992, The Weaver (feature film) 1993, Whispers in the Dark 1995, Medea: Mapping the Edge (play) 2001; contrib. to books and magazines. *Honours:* Alice Hunt Bartlett Prize, Nat. Poetry Soc. 1984, Boardman Tasker Award for Mountain Literature 1991. *Literary Agent:* c/o Peake Associates, 14 Grafton Crescent, London, NW1 8SL, England.

FELLOWES OF WEST STAFFORD, Baron (Life Peer), cr. 2011, of West Stafford in the County of Dorset; **Julian Alexander Kitchener-Fellowes,** BA, MA, DL; British novelist, screenwriter, actor, producer and director; b. 17 Aug. 1949, Cairo, Egypt; s. of the late Peregrine Edward Launcelot Fellowes and Olwen Mary Fellowes (née Stuart-Jones); m. Emma Joy Kitchener, LVO 1990; one s. *Education:* Ampleforth Coll., N Yorks., Magdalene Coll., Cambridge, Webber Douglas Acad. of Dramatic Art, London. *Career:* mem. Footlights, Univ. of Cambridge; numerous TV and film appearances; played part of Kilwillie in TV series Monarch of the Glen 2000–05; Chair. Royal Nat. Inst. for the Blind appeal for Talking Books; Vice-Pres. Weldmar Hospicecare Trust; mem. Appeal Council for Nat. Memorial Arboretum; Patron, South West br. of Age UK, Changing Faces, Living Paintings, Rainbow Trust, Breast Cancer Haven, Moviola (initiative to facilitate rural cinema screenings in West Country); Lord of the Manor of Tattershall, Lincs.; DL of Dorset 2009–; mem. (Conservative) House of Lords 2011–. *Plays include:* as actor: A Touch of Spring (by Samuel A. Taylor), Comedy Theatre, London 1975, Joking Apart (by Sir Alan Ayckbourn), Globe Theatre, London 1979, revival of Present Laughter (by Noel Coward); as writer: Mary Poppins (London 2004, Broadway 2006). *Films include:* as actor: Full Circle 1977, Priest of Love 1981, Baby: Secret of the Lost Legend 1985, Damage 1992, Shadowlands 1993, Sherwood's Travels 1994, Savage Hearts 1996, Jane Eyre 1996, Regeneration 1997, Tomorrow Never Dies 1997, Place Vendôme 1998, Shergar 1999; also Gosford Park (writer and exec. producer) (New York Film Critics' Circle Best Screenplay, Nat. Soc. of Film Critics Best Screenplay, Acad. Award for Best Original Screenplay, Walpole Medal of Excellence) 2001, Piccadilly Jim (screenplay) 2004, Two Brothers (English dialogue) 2004, Vanity Fair (writer) 2004, Separate Lies (writer and dir) (Nat. Bd of Review Best Directorial Debut) 2005, The Young Victoria (writer) 2009, From Time to Time (adaptation, also producer and dir) (Best Film, Chicago Children's Film Festival) 2009, The Tourist (screenplay) 2010. *Television includes:* as actor: Churchill's People (series) 1975, Victorian Scandals (series) 1976, Just William (series) 1977, The Duchess of Duke Street (series) 1977, BBC Play of the Month (series): Lord Neville 1978, The Old Crowd (film) 1979, My Son, My Son (mini-series) 1979, Tales of the Unexpected (series) 1980, The Bunker (film) 1981, Doctor's Daughters (series) 1981, Peter and Paul (film) 1981, Maybury (series) 1981, Hotline (film) 1982, The Scarlet Pimpernel (film) 1982, The Old Men at the Zoo (series) 1983, Rita Hayworth: The Love Goddess (film) 1983, Angels (series) 1983, Swallows and Amazons Forever!: Coot Club (film) 1984, Cold Warrior (series) 1984, Florence Nightingale (film) 1985, Dempsey and Makepeace (series) 1985, Seal Morning (series, uncredited) 1986, Lord Elgin and Some Stones of No Value (film) 1986, Knights of God (series) 1987, Sophia and Constance (series) 1988, Goldeneye (film) 1989, Casualty (series) 1989, Little Sir Nicholas (series short) 1990, The Treaty (film) 1991, Screen Two (series) 1991, For the Greater Good (film) 1991, Woof! (series) 1992, The Young Indiana Jones Chronicles (series) 1992, To Be the Best (film) 1992, Covington Cross (series) 1992, Rumpole of the Bailey (series) 1992, Sharpe's Rifles (film) 1993, A Very Open Prison (film) 1994, All Quiet on the Preston Front (series) 1994, Love Hurts (series) 1994, Pie in the Sky (series) 1994, Martin Chuzzlewit (mini-series) 1994, Killing Me Softly (film) 1995, Little Lord Fauntleroy (mini-series) 1995, The Governor (series) 1995, The Final Cut (series) 1995, Crossing the Floor (film) 1996, Our Friends in the North (mini-series) 1996, Sharpe's Regiment (film) 1996, Kavanagh QC (series) 1998, Aristocrats (mini-series) 1999, Monarch of the Glen 2000–05, Dirty Tricks (film) 2000, Heartbeat (series) 2001; also A Married Man (series, assoc. producer) 1983, Little Sir Nicholas (writer) 1990, Little Lord Fauntleroy (writer) (Int. Emmy Award) 1995, The Prince and the Pauper (writer and producer) 1996, The Children's Party at the Palace (TV special, script editor) 2006, Downton Abbey (ITV series, creator, writer and producer) (Emmy Award for Outstanding Writing for a Miniseries, Movie or a Dramatic Special 2011) 2010–, Titanic 2012; as writer and host: Julian Fellowes Investigates: A Most Mysterious Murder (films) 2004–05, Never Mind the Full Stops (BBC 4) 2006. *Publications include:* novel: Snobs: A Novel 2004, The Curious Adventures of the Abandoned Toys 2006, Past Imperfect 2008; other: A Viewer's Guide to Aristocrats 1999, Mary Poppins: The Musical; fiction as Rebecca Greville: Poison Presented 1975, Court in the Terror 1976; as Alexander Moraut: The Princess and the Parvenu. *Address:* House of Lords, Westminster, London, SW1A 0PW (office); c/o Weidenfield & Nicolson, Orion House, 5 Upper St Martin's Lane, London, WC2H 9EA, England. *Telephone:* (20) 7219-5353 (office). *Fax:* (20) 7219-5979 (office). *Website:* www.parliament.uk/biographies/julian-fellowes/90418.

FENBY, Jonathan Theodore Starmer, CBE; British writer and journalist; *Director, China Research, Trusted Sources*; b. 11 Nov. 1942, London; s. of the late Charles Fenby and June Fenby (née Head); m. Renée Wartski 1967; one s. one d. *Education:* King Edward's School, Birmingham, Westminster School and New Coll. Oxford. *Career:* corresp. and ed. Reuters World Service, Reuters Ltd 1963–77; corresp. (France and Germany), The Economist 1982–86; Home Ed. and Asst Ed. The Independent 1986–88; Deputy Ed. The Guardian 1988–93; Ed. The Observer 1993–95; Dir Guardian Newspapers 1990–95; Ed. South China Morning Post 1995–99; Ed. Netmedia Group; Assoc. Ed. Sunday Business 2000–01; Ed. Business Europe 2000–01; Ed. www.earlywarning.com 2004–06; currently Dir China Research, Trusted Sources; mem. Bd European Journalism Centre, Belgian–British Colloquium. *Radio:* broadcasts on BBC, CBC and French and Swiss radio. *Television:* broadcasts on BBC, CNN, CNBC, Channel Four, FR2, Sky, Bloomberg. *Publications:* The Fall of the House of Beaverbrook 1979, Piracy and the Public 1983, The International News Services 1986, On the Brink: The Trouble with France 1998 (new edn 2002), Comment peut-on être Français? 1999, Dealing With the Dragon: A Year in the New Hong Kong 2000, Generalissimo: Chiang Kai-shek and the China He Lost 2003, The Sinking of the Lancastria 2005, Alliance: The Inside Story of How Roosevelt, Stalin and Churchill Won One War and Began Another 2007, The Penguin History of Modern China: The Fall and Rise of a Great Power (1850–2008) 2008, The General: Charles De Gaulle and the France He Saved 2010; contrib. to newspapers and magazines in Europe, USA, Asia. *Honours:* Chevalier, Ordre du Mérite (France) 1992. *Address:* Trusted Sources, 48 Charlotte Street, London, W1T 2NS (office); 101 Ridgmount Gardens, Torrington Place, London, WC1E 7AZ, England (home). *Telephone:* (20) 3008-5764 (office). *E-mail:* jtfenby@hotmail.com (home). *Website:* www.trustedsources.co.uk (office).

FENDRICH, James Max, BA, MA, PhD; American sociologist and writer; b. 31 Oct. 1938, Salem, SDak; m. 1st Judith Curtin-Ausman 1963 (divorced 1983); m. 2nd Mary E. Bryant 1985; two s. two d. *Education:* Seattle Univ., Univ. of Notre Dame, Michigan State Univ. *Career:* Asst Prof., Florida State Univ., Tallahassee 1965–68, Assoc. Prof. 1968–74, Prof. of Sociology 1974–94; mem. American Sociological Asscn, Southern Sociological Asscn, Soc. for the Study of Social Problems. *Publications include:* Leadership in American Society: A Case Study of Black Leadership (co-author) 1969, Ideal Citizens: The Legacy of the Civil Rights Movement 1993. *Address:* 3595 Birdie Drive, Apartment 108, Lake Worth, FL 33467-2874, USA (home). *Telephone:* (561) 963-5674 (home).

FENNARIO, David; Canadian playwright; b. (David Wiper), 26 April 1947, Verdun, QC; m. Elizabeth Fennario 1976; one c. *Education:* Dawson Coll., Montréal. *Career:* Playwright-in-Residence, Centaur Theatre, Montreal 1973–; Co-founder Cultural Workers Asscn; mem. International Socialist. *Publications include:* plays: On the Job 1976, Nothing to Lose 1977, Toronto 1978, Without a Parachute 1978, Balconville 1980, Changes 1980, Moving 1983, The Murder of Catherine Parr 1986, Doctor Thomas Neill Cream 1988, The Death of René Lévesque 1990, Joe Beef 1991, Banana Roots 1994, Placeville Marie 1996, Fessenden's Follies 2006, Fennario's War 2009. *Honours:* Canada Council grant 1973, Chalmers Awards 1976, 1979, Prix Pauline Julien 1986.

FENNELLY, Antonia (Tony), BA; American author; b. 25 Nov. 1945, Orange, NJ; m. James Richard Catoire 1972. *Education:* Univ. of New Orleans. *Career:* mem. Mystery Writers of America (MWA), Authors' Guild, Int. Asscn of Crime Writers, Sisters in Crime. *Publications include:* The Glory Hole Murders 1985, The Closet Hanging 1987, Kiss Yourself Goodbye 1989, The Hippie in the Wall 1994, 1-900-D-E-A-D 1997, Don't Blame the Snake 2001, Home Dead For Christmas: A Margo Fortier Mystery 2009, The Bitch's Guide To Handling Men 2010. *Honours:* MWA Edgar Allan Poe Special Award 1986. *E-mail:* author@tonyfennelly.com (office). *Website:* www.tonyfennelly.com.

FENTON, James Martin, MA, FRSL, FRSA, FSA; British poet, writer and journalist; b. 25 April 1949, Lincoln; s. of Rev. Canon J. C. Fenton and Mary Hamilton Ingoldby. *Education:* Durham Choristers School, Repton School, Magdalen Coll., Oxford. *Career:* Asst Literary Ed., New Statesman 1971, Editorial Asst 1972, Political Columnist 1976–78; freelance corresp. in Indo-China 1973–75; German Corresp., The Guardian 1978–79; Theatre Critic, Sunday Times 1979–84; Chief Book Reviewer, The Times 1984–86; Far East Corresp. The Independent 1986–88, columnist 1993–95; Prof. of Poetry, Univ. of Oxford 1994–99, Trustee, Nat. Gallery London 2002, Visitor, Ashmolean Museum 2003. *Publications include:* Our Western Furniture 1968, Terminal

Moraine 1972, A Vacant Possession 1978, A German Requiem 1980, Dead Soldiers 1981, The Memory of War 1982, You Were Marvellous 1983, Children in Exile 1984, Poems 1968–83 1985, The Fall of Saigon (in Granta 15) 1985, The Snap Revolution (in Granta 18) 1986, Cambodian Witness: The Autobiography of Someth May (ed.) 1986, Partingtime Hall (poems, with John Fuller) 1987, All the Wrong Places: Adrift in the Politics of Asia 1989, Manila Envelope 1989, Underground in Japan, by Rey Ventura (ed.) 1992, Out of Danger (poems) 1993, Collected Stories by Ernest Hemingway (ed.), Leonardo's Nephew: Essays on Art and Artists 1998, The Strength of Poetry: Oxford Lectures, An Introduction to English Poetry 2002, A Garden from a Hundred Packets of Seed, The Love Bomb & Other Musical Pieces 2003, Selected Poems 2006; trans.: Verdi's Rigoletto 1982, Simon Boccanegra 1985, Tamar's Revenge 2004; libretti: Haroun and the Sea of Stories (composer Charles Wuorinen) 2004, Tsunami Song Cycle (composer Dominic Muldowney) 2009; theatre: Pictures from an Exhibition 2009. *Honours:* Hon. Fellow, Magdalen Coll., Oxford 1999; Antiquary to the RA 2002; Queen's Gold Medal for Poetry 2007. *Literary Agent:* United Agents, 12–26 Lexington Street, London, W1F 0LE, England. *Telephone:* (20) 3214-0800 (office). *Fax:* (20) 3214-0801 (office). *E-mail:* info@unitedagents.co.uk (office). *Website:* www.unitedagents.co.uk (office); www.jamesfenton.com (home).

FÉRAL, Josette, PhD; Canadian critic, theatre scholar and academic; *Professor, École Supérieure de Théâtre, Université du Québec. Education:* Université de Paris. *Career:* Prof., Univ. of Toronto 1978–81; Titular Prof., École Supérieure de Théâtre de l'Université du Québec 1981, Montréal, currently Dir; Vice-Pres. Int. Fed. for Theatre Research (FIRT) 1995–99, Pres. 1999–2003. *Publications include:* non-fiction: La Culture contre l'art 1990, Dresser un monument à l'éphémère 1995, Mise en scène et Jeu de l'acteur (two vols) 1997–98, Trajectoires du soleil 1998, Les Chemins de l'acteur, Acerca de la teatralidad 2004, Teatro, Teorica y practica: mas alla de las fronteras 2004, Os camiños do actor 2004, Režija in igra 2008; ed.: Théâtralité, écriture et mise en scène 1985, Substance 98/99 2002, L'école du jeu 2003, Ariane Mnouchkine und Das Théâtre du Soleil 2003; contribs. to numerous books and journals. *Honours:* Prix Jean Beraud 1989–90. *Address:* École Supérieure de Théâtre, Université du Québec à Montréal, CP 8888, succursale Centre-Ville, Montréal, QC H3C 3P8, Canada (office). *Telephone:* (514) 987-4116 (office). *Fax:* (514) 987-7881 (office). *E-mail:* feral.josette@uqam.ca (office). *Website:* www.josette-feral.org.

FERDINANDY, György (Georges), DèsL; American academic and writer; b. 11 Oct. 1935, Budapest, Hungary; m. 1st Colette Peyrethon 1958; m. 2nd Maria Teresa Reyes-Cortes 1981; three s. one d. *Education:* Univ. of Strasbourg, France. *Career:* freelance literary critic, Radio Free Europe, 1977–86; Prof., Univ. of Puerto Rico, Cayey, Puerto Rico 1964–2001; mem. Société des Gens de Lettres, France, Hungarian Writers' Asscn, Int. PEN. *Publications include:* in French: L'ile sous l'eau 1960, Famine au Paradis 1962, Le seul jour de l'annèe 1967, Itinéraires 1973, Chica, Claudine, Cali 1973, L'oeuvre hispanoaméricaine de Zs Remenyik 1975, Fantomes magnétiques 1979, Youri 1983, Hors jeu 1986, Mémoires d'un exil terminé 1992, Entre chien et loup 1996, Le roi des fous: récit 2008; in Hungarian: Latoszemueknek 1962, Tizenharom Töredék 1964, Futoszalagon 1965, Nemezio Gonzalex 1970, Valencianal a tenger 1975, Mammuttemetö 1982, A Mosoly Albuma 1982, Az elveszett gyermek 1984, A Vadak Utjan 1986, Szerecsenségem Története 1988, Furcsa, idegen szerelem 1990, Uzenöfüzet 1991, Szomorü Szigetek 1992, A Francia Völegény 1993, Ta'vlattan 1994, Az Amerikai telefon 1996, Magányos gerle 2005, A Pourtalés-kastély lakói 2005, Csak egy nap a világ 2008; in Spanish: Saldo a medio camino 1976, Hambre en el Paraiso 1998, Exilio 2000, Regreses 2004, Cielo vacios 2006; contribs to Le Monde, NRF, Europe, Elet és Irodalom, Kortars, Uj Hold, Magyar Naplo. *Honours:* Del Duca Prix 1961, St Exupéry Literary Award 1964, Book of the Year 1993, Prize Jòzsef Attila, Budapest 1995, Prize Ma'rai Sàndor, Budapest 1997, Prize Gyula Krudy 1999, PEN Club Int. Prize 2001, Alföld Prize 2004, MAOE Grand Prize 2006. *Address:* 1481 SW, 124th Court, Apartment 7-D, Miami, FL 33184-2611, USA (home). *Telephone:* (305) 485-5527 (home).

FERGUSON, Gillian K.; British poet and journalist; b. Edinburgh, Scotland. *Education:* Univ. of Edinburgh. *Career:* jewellery maker, artist; fmr columnist, The Scotsman; fmr TV critic, Scotland on Sunday; currently columnist, The Herald newspaper, Financial Times weekend magazine. *Publications include:* poetry: Air for Sleeping Fish 1997, Baby: Poems on Pregnancy, Birth and Babies 2001, Chemistries 2005, The Human Genome: Poems on the Book of Life 2008; contrib. to anthologies and journals. *Honours:* three Writers' Bursaries from the Scottish Arts Council; prizewinner Daily Telegraph Arvon Int. Poetry Competition, Creative Scotland Award 2006. *Website:* www.thehumangenome.co.uk; www.gilliankferguson.com.

FERGUSON, (John) Trevor, (John Farrow); Canadian novelist, playwright and screenwriter; *Teacher, Creative Writing, Concordia University*; b. 11 Nov. 1947, Seaforth, Ont.; s. of the late P. A. Ferguson and M. V. Joyce (Jo) Ferguson (née Sanderson); m. Lynne Hill. *Career:* honoured guest at book fairs in Montréal, Guadalajara, Paris; currently Teacher of Creative Writing, Concordia Univ.; mem. Writers' Union of Canada (Chair. 1990–91). *Plays produced include:* Long Long Short Long (Montréal) 2002, Beach House, Burnt Sienna (Hudson, QC) 2002, Barnacle Wood (Montreal) 2004, Zarathustra Said Some Things, No? (New York) 2006, (Montreal) 2008. *Film:* The Timekeeper 2009. *Publications include:* novels: High Water Chants 1977, Onyx John 1985, The Kinkajou 1989, The True Life Adventures of Sparrow Drinkwater 1993, The Fire Line 1995, The Timekeeper 1995; as John Farrow: City of Ice 1999, 2011, Ice Lake 2001, 2011, La dague de Cartier 2009, River City 2011. *Honours:* Hugh MacLennan Award for Fiction, Quebec Writers' Fed. 1996, Nat. Magazine Awards Foundation Gold Award. *Address:* c/o Lien De Nil, Westwood Creative Artists, 94 Harbord Street. Toronto, ON M5S 1G6, Canada. *Telephone:* (416) 964-3302. *Fax:* (416) 975-9209. *E-mail:* wca_office@wcaltd.com. *Website:* www.wcaltd.com.

FERGUSON, Niall Campbell Douglas, MA, DPhil; British historian, writer, academic and television presenter; *Laurence A. Tisch Professor of History, Harvard University*; b. 18 April 1964, Glasgow, Scotland; s. of James Campbell Ferguson and Molly Hamilton; m. Susan M. Douglas 1994; two s. one d. *Education:* Univ. of Oxford, Univ. of Hamburg. *Career:* Fellow, Christ's Coll., Cambridge 1989–90, Peterhouse, Cambridge 1990–92, Jesus Coll. Oxford 1992–; Houblon Norman Fellowship, Bank of England 1998–89; Prof. of Political and Financial History, Univ. of Oxford 2000–02, Herzog Prof. of Financial History, Stern School of Business, New York Univ. 2002–04; Laurence A. Tisch Prof. of History, Harvard Univ. 2004–; William Ziegler Prof. of Business Admin, Harvard Business School 2006–; Sr Fellow, Hoover Inst., Stanford Univ. 2003–; mem. Bd Dirs Chimerica Media Ltd 2006–; consultant, GLG Pnrs (hedge fund) 2007–; Sr Adviser, Morgan Stanley 2007–. *Television:* Empire: How Britain Made the Modern World 2003, American Colossus 2004, War of the World 2006, The Ascent of Money 2008. *Publications:* Paper and Iron: Hamburg Business and German Politics in the Era of Inflation 1897–1927 1995, (ed.) Virtual History: Alternatives and Counterfactuals 1997, The World's Banker: A History of the House of Rothschild, The Pity of War 1998, The Cash Nexus: Money and Power in the Modern World 1700–2000 2001, Empire: How Britain Made the Modern World 2003, Colossus: the Price of America's Empire 2004, The War of The World: History's Age of Hatred 2006, The Ascent of Money: A Financial History of the World 2008, High Fincancier: The Lives and Time of Siegmund Warburg 2010. *Honours:* Wadsworth Prize for Business History 1998. *Address:* Harvard University, Minda de Gunzberg Center for European Studies, Adolphus Busch Hall, 27 Kirkland Street, Cambridge, MA 02138, USA (office). *Telephone:* (617) 495-4303 (ext. 203) (office). *Fax:* (617) 496-9594 (office). *E-mail:* nfergus@fas.harvard.edu (office). *Website:* www.ces.fas.harvard.edu (office); www.niallferguson.org.

FERGUSON, Robert Thomas, BA (Hons); British writer and translator; b. 2 June 1948, Stoke on Trent, Staffs., England; m. 1987. *Education:* Univ. Coll., London. *Publications include:* Enigma: The Life of Knut Hamsun 1987, Henry Miller: A Life 1991, Henrik Ibsen: A New Biography 1996, Dr Ibsens Gjengangere (radio play, in Norwegian, trans. as Dr Ibsen's Ghosts) 1999, Siste Kjaerlighet (novel, in Norwegian, trans. as Last Love) 2002, The Short Sharp Life of T. E. Hulme 2002, Fleetwood (novel, in Norwegian) 2004, The Hammer and the Cross: A New History of the Vikings 2009; contrib. to Best Radio Drama 1984, Best Radio Drama 1986. *Honours:* BBC Methuen Giles Cooper Awards 1984, 1986, J. G. Robertson Prize 1985–87. *Address:* Trudvangvn 25, 0363 Oslo, Norway. *E-mail:* r-ferguson@hotmail.com. *Website:* www.robertferguson.org.

FERGUSON, William Rotch, PhD; American academic, writer and poet; b. 14 Feb. 1943, Fall River, Mass; m. Nancy King 1983. *Education:* Harvard Univ. *Career:* Instructor, Boston Univ. 1971–75, Asst Prof. 1975–77; Visiting Prof., 1977–79, Asst Prof., Clark Univ., Worcester, Mass 1979–83, Assoc. Prof. of Spanish 1983–, Adjunct Prof. of English 1989–, Chair., Foreign Languages 1990–98; Visiting Lecturer in Spanish Renaissance Literature, Univ. of Pennsylvania 1986–87; Assoc. Ed., Hispanic Review 1986–87; mem. American Asscn of Univ. Profs, Int. Inst. in Spain, Modern Language Asscn. *Publications include:* Dream Reader (poems) 1973, Light of Paradise (poems) 1973, La versificación imitativa en Fernando de Herrera 1981, Freedom and Other Fictions (short stories) 1984; contrib. to scholarly journals, anthologies, periodicals and magazines. *Address:* 1 Tahanto Road, Worcester, MA 01602, USA (home).

FERLINGHETTI, Lawrence, MA, PhD, DUniv; American writer and painter; b. 24 March 1920, Yonkers, New York; s. of Charles Ferlinghetti and Clemence Mendes-Monsanto; m. Selden Kirby-Smith 1951; one s. one d. *Education:* Columbia Univ., Univ. of Paris. *Career:* served as Lt Commdr in USNR in World War II; co-f. (with Peter D. Martin) the first all-paperback bookshop in USA, City Lights Bookstore, San Francisco 1953; f. City Lights publishing co. 1955; arrested on obscenity charges following publ. of Allan Ginsberg's 'Howl' 1956 (later acquitted); participant One World Poetry Festival, Amsterdam 1980, World Congress of Poets, Florence 1986; First Poet Laureate of San Francisco 1998–99; Ed. City Lights Books; mem. Nat. Acad. of Arts and Letters 2003. *Exhibitions:* solo: Ethel Guttman Gallery, San Francisco 1985, Peter Lembcke Gallery, San Francisco 1991, Butler Inst., Youngstown OH 1993, Retrospective Exhbn, Palazzo delle Esposizioni, Rome 1996, George Krevsky Fine Arts, San Francisco 2004, 2006, New Paintings, Yerba Buena Center for Arts, San Francisco 2008, Fluxist Underwear, Archivio Conz, Rome 2008. *Publications include:* Pictures of the Gone World (poems) 1955, Selections from Paroles by Jacques Prévert, A Coney Island of the Mind (poems) 1958, Berlin 1961, Her (novel), Starting from San Francisco (poems) 1961, Where is Vietnam? 1965, An Eye on the World 1967, After the Cries of the Birds 1967, Unfair Arguments with Existence (seven plays), Routines (plays), The Secret Meaning of Things (poems) 1969, Tyrannus Nix? (poem) 1969, The Mexican Night (travel journal) 1970, Back Roads to Far Places (poems) 1971, Open Eye, Open Heart (poems) 1973, Who Are We Now? 1976, Northwest Ecolog 1978, Landscapes of Living and Dying (poems) 1979,

Literary San Francisco: A Pictorial History from the Beginnings to the Present (with Nancy J. Peters) 1980, Leaves of Life: Drawings from the Model 1983, The Populist Manifestos 1983, Over All the Obscene Boundaries (poems) 1984, Endless Life: Selected Poems 1984, Seven Days in Nicaragua Libre 1984, Inside the Trojan Horse 1987, Love in the Days of Rage (novel) 1988, When I Look at Pictures (poems and paintings) 1990, These Are My Rivers: New and Selected Poems 1993, A Far Rockaway of the Heart 1997, How to Paint Sunlight: New Poems 2001, Americus (Book One) 2004, Poetry as Insurgent Art (prose and poetry) 2007, At Sea 2011. *Honours:* Commdr, French Acad. of Arts and Letters 2007; Poetry Prize, City of Rome 1993, Premio Internazionale Flaiano, Italy 1999, Premio Internazionale di Camaiore, Italy 1999, Premio Cavour, Italy 2000, Los Angeles Times Book Festival Lifetime Achievement Award 2001, Poetry Soc. of America Robert Frost Medal 2003, Nat. Book Foundation Literarian Award 2005, Douglas MacAgy Distinguished Achievement Award, San Francisco Art Inst. 2012. *Address:* City Lights Bookstore, 261 Columbus Avenue, San Francisco, CA 94133, USA (office). *Telephone:* (415) 362-8193 (office). *Fax:* (415) 362-4921 (office). *Website:* www.citylights.com (office).

FERLITA, Ernest Charles, BS, STL, DFA, SJ; American writer and priest; *Professor Emeritus of Drama, Loyola University*; b. 1 Dec. 1927, Tampa, Fla. *Education:* Spring Hill Coll., St Louis Univ., Yale Univ. *Career:* Jesuit priest; Prof. Emer. of Drama, Loyola Univ., New Orleans; mem. Dramatists Guild, Int. Hopkins Soc. *Publications include:* The Theatre of Pilgrimage 1971, Film Odyssey (co-author) 1976, The Way of the River 1977, The Parables of Lina Wertmuller (co-author) 1977, Religion in Film (contrib.) 1982, Gospel Journey 1983, The Mask of Hiroshima in Best Short Plays 1989, The Uttermost Mark 1990, The Paths of Life, Cycles A, B, C 1992, 1993, 1994, The Road to Bethlehem 1997, Two Cities 1999, In the Light of the Lord 2002, Come Home, Come Home 2003; play: Big Tom 2008. *Honours:* First Prize, Christian Theatre Artists Guild 1971, American Radio Scriptwriting Contest 1985, Miller Award 1986, Winner, Catholic Univ. One-Act Play Competition 2004, Hon. Mention, Catholic Univ. of America 2004. *Address:* 1575 Calhoun Street, New Orleans, LA 70118-6153, USA (home).

FERLOSIO, Rafael Sanchez; Spanish/Italian writer; b. 1927, Rome, Italy. *Career:* contribs to las revistas El Urogallo, Claves de Razón Práctica, Cuadernos Hispanoamericanos y Revista de Occidente, and in newspapers Arriba, ABC, El País and Diario 16. *Publications include:* El Jarama (Nadal Prize 1955, Spanish Nat. Critics' Prize 1957) 1955, Narraciones italianas 1961, Las semanas del jardin 1974, El huésped de las nieves 1983, El Escuto de Jotán 1983, Mientras no cambien los dioses, nada ha cambiado 1986, La homilía del ratón 1986, Campo de Marte 1986, El Ejército nacional 1986, El testimonio de yarfoz 1986, Ensayos y artículos 1992, Vendrán más años malos y nos harán más ciegos 1993, Esas Yndias equivocadas y malditas 1994, El alma y la vergünza 2000, La hija de la guerra y la madre de la patria 2002, Non olet 2003, Glosas castellanas y otros ensayos 2005, El geco 2005, Un escrito sobre la guerra 2005, La forja de un plumífero 2005, Sobre la guerra 2007, Apuntes de polemologia 2008, Guapo y sus isotopos 2009. *Honours:* Dr hc (Univ. La Sapienza of Rome, Autonomous Univ. of Madrid); Premio Cervantes 2004. *Address:* c/o Dedalus Ltd, Langford Lodge, St Judith's Lane, Sawtry, Cambs., PE28 5XE, England. *E-mail:* info@dedalusbooks.com. *Website:* www .dedalusbooks.com.

FERNANDEZ, Dominique, DèsSc; French writer; b. 25 Aug. 1929, Neuilly-sur-Seine; s. of Ramon Fernandez and Liliane Chomette; m. Diane Jacquin de Margerie (divorced); one s. one d. *Education:* Lycée Buffon, Paris and Ecole Normale Supérieure. *Career:* Prof. Inst. Français, Naples 1957–58; Prof. of Italian, Univ. de Haute-Bretagne 1966–89; literary critic, L'Express 1959–84, Le Nouvel Observateur 1985–; music critic, Diapason 1977–85, Opera International 1978, Classical Repertoire 2000–; elected mem. Académie française 2007; mem. Reading Cttee, Editions Bernard Grasset 1959–. *Publications:* Le roman italien et la crise de la conscience moderne 1958, L'écorce des pierres 1959, L'aube 1962, Mère Méditerranée 1965, Les Evènements de Palerme 1966, L'échec de Pavèse 1968, Lettre à Dora 1969, Les enfants de Gogol 1971, Il Mito dell'America 1969, L'arbre jusqu'aux racines 1972, Porporino 1974, Eisenstein 1975, La rose des Tudors 1976, Les Siciliens 1977, Amsterdam 1977, L'étoile rose 1978, Une fleur de jasmin à l'oreille 1980, Le promeneur amoureux 1980, Signor Giovanni 1981, Dans la main de l'ange 1982, Le volcan sous la ville 1983, Le banquet des anges 1984, L'amour 1986, La gloire du paria 1987, Le rapt de Perséphone (opera libretto) 1987, Le radeau de la Gorgone 1988, Le rapt de Ganymede 1989, L'Ecole du Sud 1991, Porfirio et Constance 1992, Séville 1992, L'Or des Tropiques 1993, Le Dernier des Médicis 1993, La Magie Blanche de Saint-Pétersbourg 1994, Prague et la Bohême (jtly) 1995, La Perle et le croissant 1995, Le Musée idéal de Stendhal 1995, Saint-Pétersbourg 1996, Tribunal d'honneur 1997, Le musée de Zola 1997, Le voyage d'ltalie 1998, Rhapsodie roumaine 1998, Palerme et la Sicile 1998, Le loup et le chien 1999, Les douze muses d'Alexandre Dumas 1999, Bolivie 1999, Nicolas 2000, Errances solaires 2000, L'amour qui ose dire son nom 2001, Syrie 2002, La Course à l'abîme 2003, Dictionnaire amoureux de la Russie 2004, Rome 2004, Sentiment indien 2005, Sicile 2006, Jérémie! Jérémie! 2006, l'Art de raconter 2007, Place rouge 2008, Ramon 2009, Avec Tolstoï 2010, Pise 1951 2011, Transsibérien 2012. *Honours:* Chevalier, Légion d'honneur, Commdr, Ordre nat. du Mérite, Cruzeiro do Sul (Brazil); Prix Médicis 1974, Prix Goncourt 1982, Grand Prix Charles Oulmont 1986, Prix Prince Pierre de Monaco 1986, Prix Méditerranée 1988, Prix Oscar Wilde 1988. *Address:* 14 rue de Douai, 75009 Paris (home); c/o Editions Bernard Grasset, 61 rue des Saints-Pères, 75006 Paris, France (office).

FERNÁNDEZ-ARMESTO, Felipe Fermín Ricardo, BA, MA, DPhil, FRHistS; British historian and academic; *Prince of Asturias Chair of Spanish Civilization, Tufts University, Boston*; b. 6 Dec. 1950, London, England; m. Lesley Patricia Hook 1977; two s. *Education:* Magdalen Coll., Oxford. *Career:* journalist, The Diplomatist 1972–74; Sr Visiting Fellow, John Carter Brown Library, Brown Univ., USA 1997–99; Professorial Fellow, Queen Mary Univ. of London 2000–; Prince of Asturias Chair. of Spanish Civilization, Tufts Univ., Boston 2005–; mem. Hakluyt Soc., Soc. of Authors, PEN, Athenaeum, Historical Asscn, Asscn of Hispanists, American Historical Asscn; Fellow, Soc. of Antiquaries, Netherlands Inst. *Publications include:* The Canary Islands after the Conquest 1982, Before Columbus 1987, The Spanish Armada 1988, Barcelona 1991, The Times Atlas of World Exploration (gen. ed.) 1991, Columbus 1991, Edward Gibbon's Atlas of the World 1992, Millennium 1995, The Times Guide to the People of Europe 1995, The Times Illustrated History of Europe 1995, Reformation (with Derek Wilson) 1996, Truth 1997, Religion 1997, Civilizations 2000, The Americas: A History of the Continents 2003, So You Think You're Human 2004, Pathfinders 2006, The World: A History 2006, Amerigo: The Man who gave his Name to America 2007, Ideas That Changed the World 2007, The Modern Scholar: Ideas that Shaped Mankind (audiobook) 2008, 1492: The Year the World Began 2010, Columbus on Himself 2010; contrib. to scholarly books, newspapers and periodicals. *Honours:* Hon. DLitt (La Trobe Univ., Australia) 1997; Arnold Modern History Prize 1971, Leverhulme Research Fellowship 1981, Library Asscn commendation 1992, Nat. Maritime Museum Caird Medal 1997, John Carter Brown Medal 1999. *Literary Agent:* c/o David Higham Associates, 5–8 Lower John Street, Golden Square, London, W1F 9HA, England. *Address:* Department of History, Tufts University, Upper Campus Road, East Hall, Room 08, Medford, MA 02155, USA (office). *Telephone:* (617) 627-3520 (office). *Fax:* (617) 627-3479 (office). *E-mail:* felipe.fernandez-armesto@tufts.edu (office). *Website:* www.tufts.edu (office).

FERNÁNDEZ RETAMAR, Roberto, Dr en Fil; Cuban writer; b. 9 June 1930, Havana; s. of José M. Fernández Roig and Obdulia Retamar; m. Adelaida de Juan 1952; two d. *Education:* Univ. de la Habana, Univ. de Paris à la Sorbonne and Univ. of London. *Career:* Prof., Univ. de la Habana 1955–; Visiting Prof., Yale Univ. 1957–58; Dir Nueva Revista Cubana 1959–60; Cultural Counsellor of Cuba in France 1960; Sec., Union of Writers and Artists of Cuba 1961–65; Ed. Casa de las Américas 1965–, now Pres.; Visiting Lecturer, Columbia Univ. 1957, Univ. of Prague 1965. *Publications:* poetry: Elegía como un Himno 1950, Patrias 1952, Alabanzas, Conversaciones 1955, Vuelta de la Antigua Esperanza 1959, Con las Mismas Manos 1962, Poesía Reunida 1948–1965 1966, Buena Suerte Viviendo 1967, Que veremos arder 1970, A quien pueda interesar 1970, Cuaderno paralelo 1973, Juana y otros temas personales 1981, Aquí 1995; studies: La Poesía contemporánea en Cuba 1954, Idea de la Estilística 1958, Papelería 1962, Ensayo de otro mundo 1967, Introducción a Cuba: la historia 1968, Caliban 1971, Lectura de Martí 1972, El son de Vuelo popular 1972, Introducción a Martí 1978. *Honours:* Felix Varela Order of first grade 1981, Orden de Mayo, Argentina 1998; Nat. Prize for Poetry, Cuba 1952, Rúben Dario Latin American Prize 1980, Int. Prize for Poetry Nikola Vaptsarov, Bulgaria 1989, Nat. Literary Award, Cuban Book Inst. 1989, Int. Prize for Poetry, Pérez Bonalde, Argentina 1989, Official Medal of Arts and Letters (France) 1998. *Address:* Casa de las Américas, 3ra y G Street, El Vedado, Havana, Cuba (office). *E-mail:* webmaster@casa.cult.cu (office). *Website:* www.casadelasamericas.com (office).

FERRANTI, Marie; French writer; b. 1964, Corsica. *Career:* fmr literature teacher before becoming full-time novelist. *Publications include:* Les Femmes de San Stefano (Prix François Mauriac) 1995, La Chambre des Défunts 1996, La Fuite aux Agriates 2000, La Princess de Mantoue (Grand Prix du Roman, Acad. française) 2002, Le Paradoxe de l'ordre (essay) 2002, La Chasse de nuit 2004, Lucie de Syracuse 2006, La Cadillac des Montadori 2008. *Address:* c/o Editions Gallimard, 5 rue Sébastian-Bottin, 75328 Paris Cedex 7, France.

FERRÉ, Rosario, MA, PhD; American writer; b. 28 July 1942, Ponce, Puerto Rico; m. Benigno Trigo 1960 (divorced); two s. one d. *Education:* Univ. of Puerto Rico, Univ. of Maryland. *Career:* Founder-Dir, Zona de carga y descarga, Puerto Rican literary journal; Contributing Ed., The San Juan Star (Puerto Rico's fmr English language newspaper); visiting Prof., Rutgers Univ. and Johns Hopkins Univ. *Publications include:* fiction: Papeles de Pandora 1976, El Medio Pollito 1981, Maldito Amor 1985, La Batalla de la Vigenes 1994, La Casa de la Lagina 1997, Vecindaros Excentricos 1999, El Vuelo del Cisne 2001, La extrana muerte del Capitancito Candelario 2002, Lazos de sangre 2010; other: El romántico en su observatorio 1992, Las Puertas Del Placer (essay) 2006; poetry: Fabulas de la Garza Desangrada 1982, Las dos Venecias 1992, Duelo del lenguaje 2002, Fisuras 2006; contribs to anthologies.

FERRIS, Joshua, BA, MFA; American writer; b. 8 Nov. 1974, Danville, Ill.; m.; one s. *Education:* Univ. of Iowa, Univ. of California, Irvine. *Career:* fmr advertising exec.; currently full-time writer. *Publications include:* novels: Then We Came to the End (Barnes and Noble Discover Award 2007, Hemingway Foundation/PEN Award 2008) 2007, Open Space 2007, The Unnamed 2010; contribs to The New Yorker, Granta, The Guardian, Tin House. *Literary Agent:* c/o Barer Literary LLC, 270 Lafayette Street, Suite 1504, New York, NY 10012, USA. *Telephone:* (212) 691-3513. *Fax:* (212) 691-

3540. E-mail: jbarer@barerliterary.com. Website: www.barerliterary.com. E-mail: hello@joshuaferris.com (office). Website: www.joshuaferris.com.

FERRIS, Paul Frederick; British writer and dramatist; b. 15 Feb. 1929, Swansea, Wales. *Television plays:* The Revivalist 1975, Dylan 1978, Nye 1982, The Extremist 1983, The Fasting Girl 1984. *Publications include:* A Changed Man 1958, The City 1960, Then We Fall 1960, The Church of England 1962, A Family Affair 1963, The Doctors 1965, The Destroyer 1965, The Nameless: Abortion in Britain Today 1966, The Dam 1967, Men and Money: Financial Europe Today 1968, The House of Northcliffe 1971, The New Militants 1972, The Detective 1976, Talk to Me about England 1979, Richard Burton 1981, A Distant Country 1983, Gentlemen of Fortune 1984, Children of Dust 1988, Sex and the British 1993, Caitlin 1993, The Divining Heart 1995, Dr Freud: A Life 1997, Dylan Thomas: The Biography 1999, Infidelity 1999, New Collected Letters of Dylan Thomas 2000, Cora Crane 2003, Gower in History: Myth, People, Landscape 2010, The Admiral's Wife 2011. *Literary Agent:* c/o Sinclair-Stevenson, 3 South Terrace, London, SW7 2TB, England. *Telephone:* (20) 7581-2550. *E-mail:* paul@paulferris.co.uk. *Website:* www.paulferris.co.uk.

FERRY, David Russell, PhD; American academic, poet, writer and translator; *Professor Emeritus of English, Wellesley College*; b. 5 March 1924, Orange, NJ; s. of Robert Edward Ferry and Elsie Ferry (née Russell); m. Anne Elizabeth Davidson 1958 (died 2006); one s. one d. *Education:* Harvard Univ. *Career:* Instructor, Wellesley Coll. 1952–55, Asst Prof. 1955–61, Assoc. Prof. 1961–67, Prof. of English 1967–71, Sophie Chantal Hart Prof. of English 1971–89, Prof. Emer. 1989–; Fannie Hurst Visiting Poet, Washington Univ., St Louis 1999; Fellow, Acad. of American Poets 1994, American Acad. of Arts and Sciences 1998. *Publications include:* The Limits of Mortality: An Essay on Wordsworth's Major Poems 1959, On the Way to the Island (poems) 1960, British Literature (co-ed., two vols) 1974, Strangers: A Book of Poems 1983, Gilgamesh: A New Rendering in English Verse 1992, Dwelling Places: Poems and Translations 1993, The Odes of Horace: A Translation 1997, The Eclogues of Virgil: A Translation 1999, Of No Country I Know: New and Selected Poems and Translations 1999, The Epistles of Horace: A Translation 2001; contribs to literary journals. *Honours:* Hon. Fellow, Acad. of American Poets 1995; Hon. DLitt (Amherst Coll.) 2006; Pushcart Prize 1988, Ingram Merrill Award for Poetry and Trans. 1993, Teasdale Prize for Poetry 1995, Guggenheim Fellowship 1996–97, William Arrowsmith Trans. Prize, AGNI 1999, Bingham Poetry Prize, Boston Book Review 2000, Lenore Marshall Poetry Prize 2000, Rebekah Johnson Bobbitt Nat. Prize for Poetry, Library of Congress 2000, American Acad. of Arts and Letters Award for Literature 2001, Harold Morton Landon Trans. Prize, Acad. of American Poets 2002, Golden Rose Award (New England Poetry Club) 2006, Ruth Lilly Poetry Prize 2011. *Address:* 49 Cypress Street #2, Brookline, MA 02138, USA (home). *Telephone:* (617) 232-5111 (office). *E-mail:* dferry@wellesley.edu (office); david_ferry@hotmail.com (home).

FERRY, Luc, Dr rer. pol; French philosopher, politician and academic; *President Delegate, Conseil d'Analyse de la Société*; b. 3 Jan. 1951, Colombes; s. of Pierre Ferry and Monique Faucher; m. Marie-Caroline Becq de Fouquières 1999; three d. (one from previous m.). *Education:* Lycée Saint-Exupéry, Centre nat. de télé-enseignement, Sorbonne, Univ. of Heidelberg. *Career:* Lecturer, Teacher Training Coll., Arras, Asst Lecturer, Univ. of Reims 1977–79; Asst Lecturer, Ecole Normale Supérieure, Paris 1977–79, 1980–82; Research Attaché Nat., CNRS 1980–82; Asst Lecturer, Univ. of Paris I-Panthéon Sorbonne and Paris X-Nanterre 1980–88; Prof. of Political Sciences, Inst. of Political Studies, Univ. of Lyon II–Lumière 1982–88; Prof. of Philosophy, Univ. of Caen 1989–97; Asst Lecturer, Paris I 1989; Prof. of Philosophy, Univ. of Paris VI-Jussieu 1996–; Founder-mem. and Sec. Gen. Coll. of Philosophy 1974–; responsible for Ideas section then Editorial Adviser, L'Express 1987–94; Pres. Nat. Curriculum Council (CNP) 1994–2002; Minister for Nat. Educ., Research and Tech. 1997–2002; Minister of Youth, Nat. Educ. and Research 2002–04; mem. Comm. for UNESCO 1997–2002; Pres. Conseil d'analyse de la société 2004–; Dir Editions Grasset collection of Coll. of Philosophy; fmr mem. Saint-Simon Foundation; columnist for Le Point 1995–. *Publications include:* Philosophie politique (three vols 1984–85), la Pensée 68, le Nouvel ordre écologique: l'arbre, l'animal et l'homme (Prix Jean-Jacques Rousseau) 1992, Homo aestheticus – L'Intervention du goût à l'âge démocratique 1990 (Prix Médicis 1992), l'Homme Dieu ou le sens de la vie (Prix Littéraire des Droits de l'Homme) 1996, La Sagesse des Modernes 1998, Le Sens du Beau 1998, Philosopher à dix-huit ans (co-author) 1999, Qu'est-ce que l'homme? (co-author) 2000, Qu'est-ce qu'-une vie réussie 2002, Lettres à tous ceux qui aiment l'école (co-author) 2003, Le Religieux après la religion 2004, Comment peut-on être ministre? 2005, Apprendre à vivre 2006, Vaincre les peurs 2006, Kant. Une lecture des trois Critiques 2006, Familles, je vous aime 2007, Kant. L'oeuvre philosophique expliquée 2008, Nietzsche. L'oeuvre philosophique expliquée 2008, La tentation du christianisme (co-author) 2009, Quel devenir pour le christianisme (co-author) 2009, Face à la crise 2009; numerous articles on philosophy. *Honours:* Chevalier, Légion d'honneur, Ordre des Arts et des Lettres. *Address:* Conseil d'analyse de la société, 113 rue de Grenelle, 75007 Paris, France (office). *Telephone:* 1-42-75-86-89 (office). *Fax:* 1-42-75-87-40 (office). *E-mail:* luc.ferry@yahoo.fr (office). *Website:* www.cas.gouv.fr (office); www.lucferry.fr.

FFORDE, Jasper; British novelist; b. 1961, London, England. *Education:* Dartington Hall School. *Career:* fmrly worked in the film industry. *Publications include:* The Eyre Affair 2001, Lost in a Good Book 2002, The Well of Lost Plots (Bollinger Everyman Wodehouse Prize for Comic Writing 2004) 2003, Something Rotten 2004, The Big Over Easy 2005, The Fourth Bear 2006, Thursday Next: First Among Sequels 2007, Shades of Grey 2009, The Last Dragonslayer 2010, One of Our Thursdays Is Missing: A Novel 2011, Dragonslayer 2: The Song of the Quarkbeast 2011. *Honours:* Sherlock Award for Best Comic Detective 2002. *Literary Agent:* c/o Janklow & Nesbit UK, 33 Drayson Mews, London, W8 4LY, England. *Website:* www.janklowandnesbit.co.uk. *E-mail:* jasper@jasperfforde.com (office). *Website:* www.jasperfforde.com.

FIDO, Martin Austin, BA, BLitt; British/American academic and writer; *Senior Lecturer, CAS Writing Program, Boston University*; b. 18 Oct. 1939, Penzance, Cornwall, England; s. of Austin Harry Fido and Enid May Fido (née Hobrough); m. 1st Judith Mary Spicer 1961 (divorced 1972); two d.; m. 2nd Norma Elaine Wilson 1972 (divorced 1984); one s.; m. 3rd Karen Lynn Sandel 1994. *Education:* Lincoln Coll., Oxford. *Career:* Andrew Bradley Jr Research Fellow, Balliol Coll., Oxford 1963–66; Lecturer in English, Univ. of Leeds 1966–72; Visiting Assoc. Prof., Michigan State Univ. 1971–72; Reader in English and Head, Dept of English and Linguistics, Univ. of the West Indies, Barbados 1973–83; Writing Instructor, Boston Univ. 2001–07, Lecturer in CAS Writing Program 2008–, currently Sr Lecturer; Actor, Hoevec Investors Ltd, Barbados 1981–83; Courier, Guide-Lecturer: Footprints Walks, City Walks, King Arthur Land Tours 1983–2001; broadcaster, LBC Radio 1987–2002, BBC Radio 2 1992. *Plays:* Let's Go Bajan! 1982. *Publications include:* Charles Dickens: An Authentic Account of His Life and Times 1970, Oscar Wilde 1973, Rudyard Kipling 1974, Shakespeare 1978, Murder Guide to London 1986, The Crimes, Detection and Death of Jack the Ripper 1987, Bodysnatchers: A History of the Resurrectionists, 1742–1832 1989, Murders after Midnight 1990, The Peasenhall Murder (co-author) 1990, The Jack the Ripper A to Z (co-author) 1991, The Chronicle of Crime: The Infamous Felons of Modern History and Their Hideous Crimes 1993, Deadly Jealousy 1993, Great Crimes and Trials of the Twentieth Century (co-author) 1994, Twentieth Century Murder 1995, The World's Worst Medical Mistakes (co-author) 1996, Our Family (co-author) 1997, The World of Charles Dickens 1997, The World of Sherlock Holmes 1998, The World of Agatha Christie 1999, The Official Encyclopedia of Scotland Yard (co-author) 1999, The Krays: Unfinished Business 2000, To Kill and Kill Again 2000 (reissued as A History of British Serial Killers 2001), The Complete Jack the Ripper A to Z (co-author) 2010; other: writer and reader of audiotapes dealing with criminals and true crime stories; contrib. of essays to journals including Criticism, Notes and Queries, English Language Studies, Modern Language Review, Dutch Opera Yearbook, Ripperologist, Ripperana, and reviews to periodicals including Times Educational Supplement, TLS, Oxford Review, Oxford Magazine. *Honours:* Ripperana Award 1999. *Literary Agent:* c/o Richard Jeffs, Communications Consultants, 52 Warwick Crescent, Edgbaston, Birmingham, B15 2LH, England. *Telephone:* (121) 455-8840. *Address:* 34 Streeter Hill Road, North Falmouth, MA 02556 (home); CAS Writing Center, Boston University, 730 Commonwealth Avenue, Boston, MA 02215, USA (office). *Telephone:* (617) 358-1513 (office). *E-mail:* fido@bu.edu (office).

FIELD, Edward, (Bruce Elliot); American writer and poet; b. 7 June 1924, Brooklyn, NY; partner Neil Derrick. *Education:* New York Univ. *Career:* Fellow, American Acad. of Rome. *Films:* wrote narration for To Be Alive (Acad. Award 1965) 1964. *Recordings:* Standing Up Together (with Ack Van Rooyen and Peter Tiehuis). *Publications include:* Stand Up, Friend, With Me 1963, Variety Photoplays 1967, Eskimo Songs and Stories 1973, A Full Heart 1977, A Geography of Poets (ed.) 1979, New and Selected Poems 1987, Counting Myself Lucky 1992, A Frieze for a Temple of Love 1998, Magic Words 1998, The Villagers 2000, The Man Who Would Marry Susan Sontag, and Other Intimate Literary Portraits of the Bohemian Era 2006, After the Fall, Poems Old and New 2007, Kabuli Days, Travels In Old Afghanistan 2008; contrib. to reviews, journals and periodicals. *Honours:* Lamont Award 1962, Guggenheim Fellowship 1963, Shelley Memorial Award 1974, Prix de Rome 1981, Lambda Award 1993, Bill Whitehead Lifetime Achievement Award 2005, W. H. Auden Award 2005. *Address:* 463 West Street, A323, New York, NY 10014, USA. *E-mail:* fieldinski2@yahoo.com. *Website:* www.edwardfield.com.

FIELDING, Helen; British author and journalist; b. 19 Feb. 1958, Morley, W Yorks.; partner Kevin Curran; one s. one d. *Education:* Univ. of Oxford. *Career:* began career working as producer for BBC; fmr columnist, The Independent. *Publications include:* Cause Celeb 1994, Bridget Jones's Diary 1996, Bridget Jones: The Edge of Reason 2000, Bridget Jones's Guide to Life (for Comic Relief charity) 2001, Olivia Joules and the Overactive Imagination 2004. *Honours:* Nielsen BookScan and The Times Platinum Book Award, British Book Awards 2002, listed in The Observer as one of the 50 funniest acts in British comedy 2003. *Address:* c/o Pan Macmillan Publishers, 20 New Wharf Road, London, N1 9RR, England. *Website:* www.panmacmillan.com.

FIENNES, Sir Ranulph Twisleton-Wykeham-, 3rd Bt, cr. 1916, OBE, DLitt; British travel writer, lecturer and explorer; b. 7 March 1944, Windsor; s. of Lt-Col Sir Ranulph Twisleton-Wykeham-Fiennes, DSO, 2nd Bt and Audrey Newson; m. 1st Virginia Pepper 1970 (died 2004); m. 2nd Louise Millington 2005; one d. *Education:* Eton. *Career:* Lt Royal Scots Greys 1966, Capt. 1968, retd 1970; attached 22 SAS Regt 1966, Sultan of Muscat's Armed Forces 1968; Leader, British Expeditions to White Nile 1969, Jostedalsbre Glacier 1970, Headless Valley, BC 1971, (Towards) North Pole 1977; Leader, Transglobe Expedition (first polar circumnavigation of world on its polar axis) 1979–82; led first unsupported crossing of Antarctic continent and longest unsupported polar journey in history Nov. 1992–Feb. 1993; first man to reach both poles on land; discovered lost city of Ubar in Oman 1993; ran seven marathons on seven continents in seven days 2003; climbed north face of Mount Eiger 2007; climbed Mount Everest 2009; Exec. Consultant to Chair. of Occidental Petroleum Corpn 1984–90. *Achievements include:* has raised £13.5 million for various charities. *Publications:* A Talent for Trouble 1970, Ice Fall in Norway 1972, The Headless Valley 1973, Where Soldiers Fear to Tread 1975, Hell on Ice 1979, To the Ends of the Earth 1983, Bothie – The Polar Dog (with Virginia Twisleton-Wykeham-Fiennes) 1984, Living Dangerously 1987, The Feather Men 1991, Atlantis of the Sands 1992, Mind over Matter 1993, The Sett 1996, Fit for Life 1998, Beyond the Limits 2000, The Secret Hunters 2001, Captain Scott 2003, Mad Bad and Dangerous to Know (auto-biog.) 2007, Mad Dogs And Englishmen 2009. *Honours:* Hon. mem. Royal Inst. of Navigation; Hon. DSc (Loughborough Coll.) 1986; Hon. DUniv (Univ. of Cen. England in Birmingham) 1995, (Univ. of Portsmouth) 2000, (Sheffield) 2005, (Univ. of Abertay, Dundee) 2007; Hon. DLitt (Glasgow Caledonian) 2002; Dhofar Campaign Medal 1969, Sultan's Bravery Medal 1970, Livingstone Medal, Royal Scottish Geographical Soc., Royal Inst. of Navigation 1977, Gold Medal of Explorers Club of NY 1983, Founders Medal Royal Geographical Soc. 1984, Polar Medal for Arctic and Antarctic, with Bars 1985, with clasp 1995, ITN Award for Int. Exploit of the Decade 1989, Explorers Club Millennium Award for Polar Exploration 2000, ITV1 Greatest Briton – Sportsman of the Year 2007. *Address:* Greenlands, Exford, Minehead, West Somerset, TA24 7NU, England (office). *Telephone:* (1643) 831350 (office).

FIFIELD, Christopher George, MusB, GRSM, ARCO, ARMCM; British conductor, music historian and lecturer; *Music Director, Lambeth Orchestra*; b. 4 Sept. 1945, Croydon, Surrey; m. 1st Judith Weyman 1972 (divorced); two c.; m. 2nd Anna Milton 2007; two c. *Education:* Univ. of Manchester, Royal Manchester Coll. of Music, Guildhall School, Cologne Musikhochschule, Germany, Univ. of Bristol. *Career:* fmrly Asst Dir of Music, Capetown Opera; music staff, Glyndebourne for 12 years; fmr Music Dir London Contemporary Dance Theatre; fmr Dir Northampton Symphony Orchestra, Central Festival Opera, Reigate and Redhill Choral Soc. and Jubilate Choir; fmr Conductor, Trinity Coll. of Music; Dir of Music, Univ. Coll. London 1980–90; fmr Chorus Master, Chelsea Opera Group; currently Music Dir and Conductor, Lambeth Orchestra; conducted British opera premieres of Verdi's Oberto 1982, Chabrier's Gwendoline 1983, Bruch's Die Loreley 1986, Smetana's The Devil's Wall 1987, world premiere of Diana Burrell's The Albatross, Spitalfields Festival, London 1997. *Publications include:* Max Bruch: his Life and Works 1988, 2005, Wagner in Performance 1992, True Artist and True Friend: A Biography of Hans Richter 1993, Letters and Diaries of Kathleen Ferrier 2003, 2011, Ibbs and Tillett: The Rise and Fall of a Musical Empire 2005; contrib. to reference books and journals, including Viking Opera Guide, International Opera Guide, New Grove Dictionary of Opera 1992, Grove 7, Dictionary of National Biography, Oxford Companion to Music. *Address:* 80 Wolfington Road, London, SE27 0RQ, England (home). *Telephone:* (20) 8761-3600 (home); 7752-273558 (mobile). *E-mail:* cgfifield@btinternet.com (home). *Website:* www.lambeth-orchestra.org.uk (office).

FIGES, Eva, BA; British writer; b. 15 April 1932, Berlin; d. of Emil Unger and Irma Unger; m. John Figes 1954 (divorced 1963); one s. one d. *Education:* Kingsbury Co. School, Queen Mary Coll., Univ. of London. *Publications include:* Winter Journey 1967, Patriarchal Attitudes 1970, B 1972, Nelly's Version 1977, Little Eden 1978, Waking 1981, Sex and Subterfuge 1982, Light 1983, The Seven Ages 1986, Ghosts 1988, The Tree of Knowledge 1990, The Tenancy 1993, The Knot 1996, Tales of Innocence and Experience 2003, Light 2007, Journey to Nowhere 2008. *Honours:* Guardian Fiction Prize 1967. *Literary Agent:* Rogers, Coleridge & White Ltd, 20 Powis Mews, London, W11 1JN, England. *Telephone:* (20) 7221-3717. *Fax:* (20) 7229-9084. *Website:* www.rcwlitagency.co.uk.

FIGES, Orlando, PhD; British historian, academic and writer; *Professor of History, Birkbeck College, London*; b. 20 Nov. 1959, s. of John Figes and Eva Figes (née Unger); m. Stephanie Palmer 1990; two d. *Education:* Gonville and Caius Coll., Cambridge, Trinity Coll., Cambridge. *Career:* Fellow Trinity Coll., Cambridge 1984–89, Dir of Studies in History 1988–98, Lecturer in History, Univ. of Cambridge 1987–99; Prof. of History, Birkbeck Coll., Univ. of London 1999–. *Publications include:* Peasant Russia, Civil War: the Volga Countryside in Revolution 1917–21 1989, A People's Tragedy: the Russian Revolution 1891–1924 (Wolfson History Prize, WHSmith Literary Award, NCR Book Award, Los Angeles Times Book Prize) 1996, Interpreting the Russian Revolution (co-author) 1999, Natasha's Dance: a Cultural History of Russia 2002, The Whisperers: Private Life in Stalin's Russia 2007, Crimea: The Last Crusade 2010; numerous review articles and contribs to other published books. *Address:* School of History, Classics and Archaeology, Birkbeck College, Malet Street, London, WC1E 7HX, England (office). *Telephone:* (20) 7631-6299 (office). *Fax:* (20) 7631-6552 (office). *E-mail:* o.figes@bbk.ac.uk (office). *Website:* www.bbk.ac.uk/hca/staff/orlandofiges (office); www.orlandofiges.com.

FILIMON, Valeria; Romanian journalist; b. 29 May 1949, Butimanu; d. of Ion Dumitrescu and Maria Dumitrescu; m. Vasile Filimon 1984. *Education:* Univ. of Bucharest. *Career:* freelance journalist for various Romanian dailies and literary magazines 1967–90; Assoc. Prof. 1970–90; journalist 1990–93; Ed.-in-Chief Femeia Moderna (magazine) 1993–98, Regala 1998–, Olimp 1999–; apptd Project Co-ordinator in Romania, International Fed. of Journalists 1996; Vice-Pres. Societatea Ziaristilor din Romania. *Publications:* Lyceum (collection of literary criticism in two vols) 1974. *Honours:* Romanian Writers' Union Prize. *Address:* Societatea Ziaristilor din Romania, Piata Presei Libere 1, Oficial Postal 33, 71341 Bucharest, Romania (office). *Telephone:* (21) 2228351 (office). *Fax:* (21) 2224266 (office).

FILIPACCHI, Daniel; French journalist and publisher; *Honorary President, Hachette Filipacchi Médias*; b. 12 Jan. 1928, Paris; s. of Henri Filipacchi and Edith Besnard. *Career:* typographer, Paris-Match 1944, photographer 1948, head of information and dir of photographic service 1953; fashion photographer, Marie-Claire 1957; producer of radio transmissions, Europe No. 1 1955, 1960; Owner and Dir Jazz Magazine 1955, Cahiers du cinéma 1961–70; Founder and Dir Salut les copains (became Salut 1976) 1961, Lui, Mlle Age tendre (became OK Age tendre 1976), Pariscope 1965, Photo 1967, Le Monde des Grands Musées 1968, Ski 1969, Union 1972, Playboy France 1973–84, Girls 1982; editorial adviser to Newlook 1982, Penthouse 1984; Pres.-Dir-Gen. WEA Filipacchi Music SA 1971–84, Cogedipresse; Owner and fmr Dir Paris-Match 1976; mem. editorial Cttee Elle 1981; Vice-Pres. Hachette 1981–93, Pres.-Dir-Gen. Hachette Magazines Inc. (USA) 1990; Pres.-Dir-Gen. Filipacchi Médias SA 1993–97; Jt Man. Cogédipresse 1994–97; Admin. and Hon. Pres. Hachette Filipacchi Médias 1997–. *Address:* Hachette Filipacchi Médias, 43, quai de Grenelle, 75905 Paris, France (office). *Website:* www.hachette.com (office).

FILIPPETTI, Aurélie; French politician and novelist; *Minister of Culture and Communication*; b. 17 June 1973, Villerupt (Meurthe-et-Moselle); of Italian descent, family originates from Gualdo, Umbria. *Education:* École normale supérieure de Fontenay–Saint-Cloud, agrégation in Classic Literature. *Career:* fmr mem. Les Verts (Green Party), now mem. Parti socialiste (PS—Socialist Party); Tech. Adviser for Minister of Environment, Yves Cochet 2001–02; mem. (PS) Assemblée nationale for the Eight Dist of the Moselle département 2007–; Minister of Culture and Communication 2012–. *Publications include:* Les derniers jours de la classe ouvrière (novel) 2003, wrote the script for theatre production Fragments d'humanité 2003, Un homme dans la poche 2006. *Address:* Ministry of Culture and Communication, 3 rue de Valois, 75001 Paris (office); Assemblée nationale, 126 rue de l'Université, 75355 Paris Cedex 07, France (office). *Telephone:* 1-40-15-80-00 (Ministry) (office); 1-40-63-60-00 (Assemblée nationale) (office). *Fax:* 1-40-15-81-72 (Ministry) (office); 1-45-55-75-23 (Assemblée nationale) (office). *E-mail:* point.culture@culture.fr (office); afilippetti@assemblee-nationale.fr (office). *Website:* www.culture.gouv.fr (office); www.assemblee-nationale.fr (office); aureliefilippetti.free.fr.

FILIPPINI, Serge; French writer and screenwriter; b. 29 Nov. 1950, Pontarlier; partner Jacqueline Goltman; one s. one d. *Publications include:* Angèle 1986, La Vie en double 1987, L'Aquarium 1989, L'Homme incendié (trans. as The Man in Flames) 1990, Comedia 1992, Haut mal 1993, Le Roi de Sicile 1998, L'Amant absolu 1999, Un Amour de Paul 2000, Érotique du mensonge 2003, On se retrouvera 2006, Deux Testaments 2008, Le Combat des Trente 2010, Viola d'amor 2011. *Address:* c/o Éditions Le Cercle, 14 rue Léonce Reynaud, 75116 Paris; c/o Grasset, 61 rue des Saints-Pères, 75006 Paris, France. *E-mail:* serge.filippini@orange.fr (home). *Website:* sergefilippini.org.

FINCH, Peter; British poet and writer; b. 6 March 1947, Cardiff, Wales; two s. one d. *Education:* Glamorgan Polytechnic. *Career:* Ed. Second Aeon 1966–75; ran Oriel Bookshop 1974–1998; Chief Exec. Academi, Welsh Nat. Literature Promotion Agency, Soc. for Writers, later Literature Wales, the nat. devt agency 1998–2011; Fellow, English Asscn; mem. Welsh Acad., Welsh Union of Writers. *Publications include:* Wanted 1967, Pieces of the Universe 1968, How to Learn Welsh 1977, Between 35 and 42 (short stories) 1982, Some Music and a Little War 1984, How to Publish Your Poetry 1985, Reds in the Bed 1986, Selected Poems 1987, How to Publish Yourself 1988, Make 1990, Poems for Ghosts 1991, Five Hundred Cobbings 1994, The Spe ell 1995, The Poetry Business 1995, Antibodies 1997, Useful 1997, Food 2001, Real Cardiff 2002, Vizet/Water 2003, Real Cardiff Two 2004, The Big Book of Cardiff (ed.) 2005, The Welsh Poems 2006, Selected Later Poems 2008, Real Wales 2009, Real Cardiff Three 2009, Zen Cymru 2010; Ed. the Real series; contrib. to magazines and journals. *Honours:* Hon. Fellow, Royal Soc. of Architects in Wales. *Address:* 19 Southminster Road, Roath, Cardiff, CF23 5AT, Wales (home). *E-mail:* peter@peterfinch.co.uk (office). *Website:* www.peterfinch.co.uk.

FINCKE, Gary William, BA, MA, PhD; American academic, poet, fiction writer and essayist; *Charles B. Degenstein Distinguished Professor of English and Creative Writing, Susquehanna University*; b. 7 July 1945, Pittsburgh, Pa; m. Elizabeth Locker 1968; two s. one d. *Education:* Thiel Coll., Miami Univ., Kent State Univ. *Career:* Instructor in English, Pennsylvania State Univ. of Monaca 1969–75; Chair. Dept of English, LeRoy Central School, New York 1975–80; Admin., Susquehanna Univ. 1980–93, Prof. of English and Dir of the Writers' Inst. 1993–, Charles B. Degenstein Distinguished Prof. of English and Creative Writing 2008–; Ed. The Apprentice Writer 1982–2011; syndicated columnist 1996–. *Publications include:* poetry: Breath 1984, The Coat in the Heart 1985, The Days of Uncertain Health 1988, Handing the Self Back 1990, Plant Voices 1991, The Public Talk of Death 1991, The Double Negatives of the Living 1992, Inventing Angels 1994, The Technology of Paradise 1998, The Almanac for Desire 2000; fiction: For Keepsies 1993, Emergency Calls 1996, The Inadvertent Scofflaw 1999, Blood Ties 2002, Writing Letters for the Blind 2003, The Stone Child 2003, Amp'd: A Father's Backstage Pass 2004, Sorry I Worried You 2004, Standing Around the Heart

2005, The Fire Landscape 2008, The Canals of Mars 2010, The History of Permanence 2011, Reviving the Dead 2011; contrib. to many anthologies, reviews, quarterlies, journals and magazines. *Honours:* CASE Prof. of the Year, Susquehanna Univ. 2005, 2006; various grants and fellowships; Beloit Fiction Journal Short Story Prize 1990, Bess Hokin Prize Poetry Magazine 1991, Book-of-the-Month Vietnam Veteran's Magazine 1993, Notable Fiction Book of the Year Dictionary of Literary Biography 1993, Pushcart Prize 1995, 2000, Rose Lefcowitz Prize Poet Lore 1997, Ohio State Univ. Press/The Journal Poetry Prize 2003, Flannery O'Connor Award for Short Fiction 2003, George Garrett Fiction Prize 2003, Davis Nonfiction Prize 2007, Press Poetry Book Prize, Stephen F. Austin Univ. *Address:* 3 Melody Lane, Selinsgrove, PA 17870, USA (home). *Telephone:* (570) 372-4164 (office). *E-mail:* gfincke@susqu.edu (office).

FINE, Anne, OBE, BA, FRSL; British writer; b. (Anne Laker), 7 Dec. 1947, Leicester; d. of Brian Laker and Mary Baker; m. Kit Fine 1968 (divorced 1991); two d. *Education:* Northampton High School for Girls and Univ. of Warwick. *Career:* Children's Laureate 2001–03; mem. Soc. of Authors. *Publications:* for older children: The Summer House Loon 1978, The Other Darker Ned 1978, The Stone Menagerie 1980, Round Behind the Icehouse 1981, The Granny Project 1983, Madame Doubtfire 1987, Goggle-Eyes (Guardian Children's Fiction Prize, Carnegie Medal 1990) 1989, The Book of the Banshee 1991, Flour Babies (Whitbread Children's Book of the Year, Carnegie Medal 1993) 1992, Step by Wicked Step 1995, The Tulip Touch (Whitbread Children's Book of the Year 1997) 1996, Very Different (short stories) 2001, Up on Cloud Nine 2002, Frozen Billy 2004, The Road of Bones 2006, The Devil Walks 2011; for younger children: Scaredy-Cat 1985, Anneli the Art Hater 1986, Crummy Mummy and Me 1988, A Pack of Liars 1988, Stranger Danger 1989, Bill's New Frock (Smarties Prize 1990) 1989, The Country Pancake 1989, A Sudden Puff of Glittering Smoke 1989, A Sudden Swirl of Icy Wind 1990, Only a Show 1990, Design-a-Pram 1991, A Sudden Glow of Gold 1991, The Worst Child I Ever Had 1991, The Angel of Nitshill Road 1991, Poor Monty (picture book) 1991, The Same Old Story Every Year 1992, The Chicken Gave It to Me 1992, The Haunting of Pip Parker 1992, The Diary of a Killer Cat 1994, The Return of the Killer Cat 2003, The Killer Cat Strikes Back 2006, The Killer Cat's Birthday Bash 2008, The Killer Cat's Christmas 2009, Press Play 1994, How to Write Really Badly 1996, Countdown 1996, Jennifer's Diary 1996, Care of Henry 1996, Loudmouth Louis 1998, Charm School 1999, Roll Over Roly 1999, Bad Dreams 2000, Ruggles (picture book) 2001, Notso Hotso 2001, The Jamie and Angus Stories 2002, Jamie and Angus Together 2008, Jamie and Angus Forever 2009, How to Cross the Road and Not Turn into a Pizza 2002, The More the Merrier 2003, Ivan the Terrible 2007, Eating Things on Sticks 2009, Trouble in Toadpool 2012; adult fiction: The Killjoy 1986, Taking the Devil's Advice 1990, In Cold Domain 1994, Telling Liddy 1998, All Bones and Lies 2001, Raking the Ashes 2005, Fly in the Ointment 2008, Our Precious Lulu 2009; non-fiction: Telling Tales: an Interview with Anne Fine 1999. *Honours:* Dr hc; Scottish Arts Council Writer's Bursary 1986, Scottish Arts Council Book Award 1986, Publishing News' British Book Awards Children's Author of the Year 1990, 1993, Nasen Special Educational Needs Book Award 1996, Prix Sorcière 1998, Prix Versele 1999, 2000, Boston Globe Horn Book Award 2003, Silver Medal, Nestlé Children's Book Prize 2007, Winner, Good Writing Award 2010. *Literary Agent:* c/o David Higham Associates, 5–8 Lower John Street, London, W1R 4HA, England. *Telephone:* (20) 7434-5900. *Fax:* (1833) 908127 (home). *Website:* www.annefine.co.uk.

FINK, Gerald R., BA, MS, PhD; American geneticist and professor of genetics; *American Cancer Society Professor of Genetics, Massachusetts Institute of Technology*; b. 1 July 1940, Brooklyn, NY; s. of Rebecca Fink and Benjamin Fink; m. Rosalie Lewis 1961; two d. *Education:* Amherst Coll., Yale Univ. *Career:* Postdoctoral Fellow, NIH 1965–66, 1966–67; Instructor, NIH Grad. Program 1966; Instructor, Cold Spring Harbor Summer Program 1970; Asst Prof. of Genetics, Cornell Univ. 1967–71, Assoc. Prof. 1971–76, Prof. 1976–79, Prof. of Biochemistry 1979–82; Prof. of Molecular Genetics, MIT 1982–; American Cancer Soc. Prof. of Genetics 1979–; Founding mem. Whitehead Inst. for Biomedical Research 1982–, Dir 1990–2001; Sec. Genetics Soc. of America 1977–80, Vice-Pres. 1986–87, Pres. 1988–89; Fellow, American Acad. of Arts and Sciences; mem. NAS, American Philosophical Soc., Inst. of Medicine 1996, American Acad. of Microbiology 1996. *Publications:* numerous scientific publs. *Honours:* Hon. DSc (Amherst Coll.) 1982, (Cold Spring Harbor) 1999; NAS-US Steel Prize in Molecular Biology 1981, Genetics Soc. of America Medal 1982, Yale Science and Eng Award 1984, Emil Christian Hansen Foundation Award for Microbiological Research 1986, Wilbur Lucius Cross Medal, Yale Univ. 1992, Bristol-Myers Squibb Infectious Disease Research Award 1993, Ellison Medical Foundation Sr Scholar Award 2001, George W. Beadle Award, Genetics Soc. of America 2001, Yeast Genetics and Molecular Biology Lifetime Achievement Award 2002, Genetics Prize, Peter and Patricia Gruber Foundation 2010. *Address:* Department of Biology, Massachusetts Institute of Technology, 77 Massachusetts Avenue 68-132, Cambridge, MA 02139, USA (office). *Telephone:* (617) 258-5215 (office). *E-mail:* gfink@wi.mit.edu (office). *Website:* www.biology.mit.edu (office).

FINLAY, Mary Louise, BA; Canadian journalist, broadcaster and writer; b. 29 March 1947, Ottawa, Ont.; d. of John Francis and Helen B. Finlay; one s. *Education:* Univ. of Ottawa and Harvard Univ., USA. *Career:* Historical Researcher, Trans. Canadian War Museum 1967–70; Current Affairs Interviewer, Producer 1970–75; Presenter Take 30 1975–77; Presenter, writer Finlay and Company 1976; contrib. As It Happens (radio) 1977–78, 90 Minutes Live 1977–78; Presenter, Producer Live It Up 1978–81; Co-Presenter Take 30 1975, Finlay and Company 1976–77, The National Driving Test 1980; Co-Presenter, Producer The Journal 1981–88; Presenter Sunday Morning 1988–94; Presenter Now The Details 1994–97; Co-Presenter As it Happens 1997–2005; Nieman Fellow, Harvard Univ. 1986; currently Fellow, Centre for the Study of Democracy, Queen's Univ.; mem. Canadian Civil Liberties Union. *TV documentaries scripted:* The Railroad Show 1974, The Mackenzie Valley Pipeline Inquiry 1976, All is Calm 1983, Timothy Findley's War 1983, Taking a Chance on Faro 1984, The Right to Die 1984, The Death of Clarence Warren 1985, Congress and the Contras 1985. *Publications:* The As It Happens Files: Radio That May Contain Nuts 2009. *Address:* Centre for the Study of Democracy, Queen's University, School of Policy Studies, Policy Studies Building, Room 335, 138 Union Street, Kingston, ON K7L 3N6, Canada (office). *Telephone:* (613) 533-6273 (office). *Fax:* (613) 533-2135 (office). *E-mail:* csd@queensu.ca (office). *Website:* www.queensu.ca/csd (office).

FINN, Pavel Konstantinovich; Russian scriptwriter; b. (Pavel Finn-Halfin), 28 June 1940, Moscow; m. Irina Chernova-Finn; one s. *Education:* All-Union State Inst. of Cinematography. *Career:* fmr journalist, documentary maker; freelance script writer 1968–; Head of Higher Workshop Course of Scriptwriters; Chair. Cinema Dramaturgy Council, Moscow Union of Cinematographers 2001; apptd Deputy Chair. Russian Union of Cinematographers 2001. *Films include:* Headless Horse Rider 1973, Armed and Very Dangerous 1977, 26 Days of Dostoyevsky's Life 1980, Icicle in a Warm Sea 1983, Witness 1985, Lady Macbeth of Mtsensk Region 1989, Accidental Waltz 1989, Sunset 1990, Myth about Leonid 1991, A Big Concert of Peoples 1991, Shylock 1993, Jester's Revenge 1994, For What 1995, Career of Arthur Whui 1996, Break Point, We Are Your Kids, Moscow, Eve's Gates, Death of Tairov or Princess Brambilla, Secrets of Court Coups: Film Two 2000, Miracles, or Pike in the Moscow Style 2001, Ravine 2007, The Gift to Stalin 2008, There Was Never a Better Brother 2011. *Honours:* Distinguished Artist of the Russian SFSR 1991. *Address:* 4th Rostovsky per. 2/1, Apartment 9, 119121 Moscow, Russia (home). *Telephone:* (495) 248-53-28 (home); (495) 334-59-34 (home). *E-mail:* pavelfinn@mtu-net.ru (home).

FINNIS, John Mitchell, LLB, DPhil, FBA; Australian/British academic and barrister; *Emeritus Professor of Law and Legal Philosophy, University of Oxford*; b. 28 July 1940, Adelaide, SA; s. of the late Maurice M. S. Finnis and of Margaret McKellar Stewart; m. Marie Carmel McNally 1964; three s. three d. *Education:* St Peter's Coll., Adelaide, St Mark's Coll., Univ. of Adelaide, Univ. Coll., Oxford. *Career:* Fellow and Praelector in Jurisprudence, Univ. Coll., Oxford 1966–2010, Stowell Civil Law Fellow 1973–2007, Vice-Master 2001–10; Lecturer in Law, Univ. of Oxford 1966–72, Rhodes Reader in the Laws of the Commonwealth and the United States 1972–89, Prof. of Law and Legal Philosophy 1989–2010, currently Prof. Emer., mem. Philosophy Sub-Faculty 1984–2010, Chair. Bd of Faculty of Law 1987–89; Prof. and Head of Dept of Law, Univ. of Malawi 1976–78; Biolchini Family Prof. of Law, Univ. of Notre Dame, Ind., USA 1995–, Adjunct Prof. of Philosophy 1999–; barrister, Gray's Inn 1970–; Gov., Plater Coll., Oxford 1972–92; Consultor, Pontifical Commission Iustitia et Pax 1977–89, mem. 1990–95; Special Adviser, Foreign Affairs Cttee, House of Commons, on role of UK Parl. in Canadian Constitution 1980–82; mem. Catholic Bishops' Jt Cttee on Bio-ethical Issues 1981–89, Int. Theological Comm. (Vatican) 1986–92; Gov. Linacre Centre for Medical Ethics 1981–96, 1998– (Vice-Chair. 1987–96, 1998–2008); Huber Distinguished Visiting Prof., Boston Coll. Law School 1993–94; mem. Pontifical Acad. Pro Vita 2001–. *Publications:* Halsbury's Laws of England (fourth edn) Vol. 6 (Commonwealth and Dependencies) 1974, 1990, 2003, (fifth edn) Vol. 13 (Commonwealth and Dependencies) 2009, Natural Law and Natural Rights 1980, Fundamentals of Ethics 1983, Nuclear Deterrence, Morality and Realism (with Joseph Boyle and Germain Grisez) 1987, Moral Absolutes 1991, Aquinas: Moral, Political and Legal Theory 1998; articles on constitutional law, legal philosophy, ethics, moral theology and late sixteenth-century history. *Address:* University College, Oxford, OX1 4BH, England (office); Notre Dame Law School, South Bend, IN 46556, USA (office). *Telephone:* (1865) 276641 (UK) (office); (574) 631-5989 (USA) (office); (1865) 558660 (UK) (home).

FINSCHER, Ludwig, PhD; German musicologist, lexicographer and academic (retd); b. 14 March 1930, Kassel. *Education:* Univ. of Göttingen. *Career:* Asst Lecturer, Univ. of Kiel 1960–65, Univ. of Saarbrücken 1965–68; Ed. Die Musikforschung 1961–68, Co-Ed. 1968–74; Prof. of Musicology, Univ. of Frankfurt am Main 1968–81, Univ. of Heidelberg 1981–95; mem. Akad. der Wissenschaften, Heidelberg, Akad. der Wissenschaften und der Literatur, Mainz, Academia Europaea; Corresp. mem. American Musicological Soc. *Publications:* Collected Works of Gaffurius (ed., two vols) 1955, 1960, Collected Works of Compère (ed., five vols) 1958–72, Loyset Compère (*c.* 1450–1518): Life and Works 1964, Geschichte der Evangelischen Kirchenmusik (co-ed., second edn) 1965, Studien zur Geschichte des Streichquartetts: I, Die Entstehung des klassischen Streichquartetts: Von den Vorformen zur Grundlegung durch Joseph Haydn 1974, Collected Works of Hindemith (co-ed. with K. von Fischer) 1976–, Renaissance-Studien: Helmuth Osthoff zum 80. Geburtstag (ed.) 1979, Quellenstudien zu Musik der Renaissance (ed., two vols) 1981, 1983, Ludwig van Beethoven (ed.) 1983, Claudio Monteverdi: Festschrift Reinhold Hammerstein zum 70. Geburtstag (ed.) 1986, Die Musik des 15. und 16. Jahrhunderts: Neues Handbuch der Musikwissenschaft (ed., Vol. 3/1–2) 1989–90, Die Mannheimer Hofkapelle im Zeitalter Carl Theodors (ed.) 1992, Die Musik in Geschichte und Gegenwart (ed., second edn, 26 vols)

1994–2007, Joseph Haydn 2000, Geschichte und Geschichten: Ausgewählte Aufsätze zur Musikhistorie 2003; contrib. editorially to the complete works of Mozart and Gluck, contrib. to scholarly books and journals. *Honours:* Hon. mem. Int. Musicological Soc., Gesellschaft für Musikforschung; Hon. Foreign mem. Royal Musical Asscn, London 1978; Ordre pour le Mérite 1994, Grand Order of Merit (Germany) 1997; Dr hc (Athens) 2002, (Zürich) 2003, (Saarbrücken) 2009; Akad. der Wissenschaften Prize, Göttingen 1968, Balzan Prize 2006. *Address:* Am Walde 1, 38302 Wolfenbüttel, Germany (home). *Telephone:* (5331) 32713 (home). *Fax:* (5331) 33276 (home).

FINSTAD, Suzanne, BA, JD; American author and attorney; b. 14 Sept. 1955, Minneapolis, Minn. *Education:* Univ. of Texas, Austin, Univ. of Houston, Univ. of Grenoble, France, Bates Coll. of Law, London School of Econs, UK. *Publications include:* Heir Not Apparent 1984, Ulterior Motives 1987, Sleeping with the Devil 1991, Child Bride: The Untold Story of Priscilla Beaulieu Presley 1997, Natasha: The Biography of Natalie Wood 2001, Warren Beatty: A Private Man 2005; contrib. to magazines. *Honours:* Order of the Barons 1980; American Jurisprudence Award in Criminal Law, Bancroft-Whitney Publishing Co 1979, Frank Wardlaw Award 1985.

FINZI, Sergio, BPhil; Italian psychoanalyst and writer; b. 15 May 1936, Brescia; m. Virginia Finzi Ghisi. *Education:* Univ. of Pavia, École Freudienne de Paris. *Publications include:* with Virgina Finzi: Un saggio in famiglia 1971, Il principe splendente 1973, Lavoro dell' inconscio e comunismo 1975, Nevrosi di guerra in tempo di pace 1989, Gli effetti dell' amore 1995, La scienza dei Vincoli 2000, Sul Monte della Preda 2004, L'Ombra del Grillo Parlante 2005, Tradimento e Fedelta 2008, La Cura Bastarda 2009; contribs to Il piccolo Hans 1974–95, Il Cefalopodo, Ambulatorio. *Address:* Via Rubens 9, 20148 Milan, Italy (office). *Telephone:* (02) 4046238 (office); (335) 5899367 (home). *Fax:* (02) 4046238 (office).

FIRER, Susan, BA, MA; American academic and poet; *Adjunct Associate Professor of English, University of Wisconsin at Milwaukee*; b. 14 Oct. 1948, Milwaukee, Wis.; one s. two d. *Education:* Univ. of Wisconsin, Milwaukee. *Career:* Teaching Asst, Univ. of Wisconsin, Milwaukee 1981–82, Lecturer 1982, Adjunct Assoc. Prof. of English 1988–; Poet Laureate of Milwaukee 2008–10. *Publications include:* My Life with the Tsar and Other Poems 1979, The Underground Communion Rail 1992, The Lives of the Saints and Everything 1993, The Laugh We Make When We Fall 2002, Milwaukee Does Strange Things to People: New and Selected Poems 1979–2007 2007; contribs to numerous anthologies, reviews, journals, and magazines. *Honours:* Wisconsin Arts Bd Fellowship 1979, Best American Poetry Selection 1992, Cleveland State Univ. Poetry Center Prize 1992, Wisconsin Council of Writers Posner Poetry Award 1993, Milwaukee County Artist Fellowship 1996, Backwaters Poetry Prize 2001, Lorine Niedecker Prize, Council for Wisconsin Writers 2009, Distinguished Alumnus, Univ. of Wisconsin, Milwaukee 2009. *Address:* Department of English, University of Wisconsin, PO Box 413, Milwaukee, WI 53201, USA (office). *Telephone:* (414) 229-6993 (office). *E-mail:* sfirer@uwm.edu (office). *Website:* www4.uwm.edu/letsci/english (office).

FIRST, Philip (see Williamson, Philip G.)

FISCHER, August A.; Swiss fmr publishing executive; b. 7 Feb. 1939, Zürich; m. Gillian Ann Fischer 1961; one s. one d. *Career:* various positions E.I. Du Pont De Nemours & Co. 1962–78; Man. Dir European subsidiary of Napp Systems Inc. 1978–81, Exec. Vice-Pres., then Pres. and COO Napp Systems Inc., San Diego 1981–89; Gen. Man. Devt, News International PLC 1989–90, Man. Dir 1990–95, mem. Bd and COO News Corpn Ltd 1991–95, Chief Exec. News International PLC (UK subsidiary of News Corpn) 1993–95; mem. Supervisory Bd Ringier AG, Zürich, consultant 1995–97; Chair. Bd and CEO Axel Springer Verlag AG 1998–2001; mem. Advisory Bd, RocSearch; mem. American Man. Asscn, The Pres.'s Asscn; Trustee, St Katharine and Shadwell Trust. *Address:* c/o RocSearch Ltd, 36–40 Rupert Street, London, W1D 6DW, England.

FISCHER, David Hackett, AB, PhD; American historian and academic; *Earl Warren Professor of History, Brandeis University*; b. 2 Dec. 1935, Baltimore, Md. *Education:* Princeton Univ., Johns Hopkins Univ. *Career:* Earl Warren Chair in American Constitutional 1971; Dir Nat. Endowment for the Humanities Summer Seminar 1979; currently Univ. Prof. and Earl Warren Prof. of History, Brandeis Univ.; Co-Ed. Pivotal Moments in American History series; Fellow, American Academy of Arts and Sciences 1995; Life mem., Bodleian Library 1993. *Publications include:* Albion's Seed: Four British Folkways in America (American Asscn of Univ. Presses Prize 1996) 1989, Paul Revere's Ride (Book of the Year 1995, Irving Medal for Literary Distinction, Old North Church Lantern Award, Boston Public Library Literary Light 1996) 1994, The Great Wave: Price Movements in Modern History 1996, Bound Away: Virginia and the Westward Movement 2000, Washington's Crossing (Pulitzer Prize for History 2005) 2004, Liberty and Freedom: A Visual History of America's Founding Ideas 2005, Champlain's Dream 2008. *Honours:* Hon. Life mem. Soc. of the Cincinnati 2006; Ordre des Arts et des Lettres 2009; Nat. Endowment for the Humanities Grant 1978, Fulbright Fellowship 1993, Ingersoll Foundation Prize for Scholarship 1996, Massachusetts Teachers Asscn Kidger Prize for Teaching 1997, Irving Kristol Prize 2006, Irving Kristol Prize 2006. *Address:* Department of History, Brandeis University, MS 036, PO Box 549110, Waltham, MA 02454-9110, USA (office). *Telephone:* (781) 736-2289 (office). *E-mail:* fischer@brandeis.edu (office). *Website:* www.brandeis.edu (office).

FISCHER, Tibor, FRSL; British journalist and novelist; b. 15 Nov. 1959, Stockport, Greater Manchester, England. *Education:* Univ. of Cambridge. *Publications include:* Under the Frog (aka Under the Frog: A Black Comedy) (Betty Trask Award) 1992, The Thought Gang 1994, The Collector Collector 1997, Don't Read This Book if You're Stupid (short stories, aka I Like Being Killed) 2000, Voyage to the End of the Room 2003, Good to be God 2008. *Honours:* one of Granta's Best of Young British Novelists 1993. *Literary Agent:* c/o Louise Greenberg, End House, Church Crescent, London, N3 1BH, England. *Telephone:* (20) 8349-1179. *E-mail:* louisegreenberg@msn.com.

FISCHEROVÁ, Sylva; Czech poet; b. 5 Nov. 1963, Prague; d. of Josef Ludvík and Jarmila Fischerová. *Education:* Olomouc Grammar School and Charles Univ. *Career:* teaching asst, Dept of Classical Studies, Charles Univ., Prague. *Publications include:* Zvláštní znamení (anthology) 1985, Chvění závodních koní 1986, Velká zrcadla 1990, V podsvětním městě 1994, Šance 1999, Zázrak 2005, Krvavý koleno 2005, Anděl na okně 2007, Cud 2008, The Swing in the Middle of Chaos 2010. *Address:* Dukelská 19, 772 00 Olomouc, Czech Republic (home). *Telephone:* (68) 259454 (home).

FISH, Joe (see Williamson, Philip G.)

FISH, Stanley Eugene, BA, MA, PhD; American academic and writer; *Davidson-Kahn Distinguished Professor of Law and Humanities, Florida International University*; b. 19 April 1938, Providence, RI; m. 1st Adrienne Aaron 1959 (divorced 1980); one d.; m. 2nd Jane Parry Tompkins 1982. *Education:* Univ. of Pennsylvania, Yale Univ. *Career:* Asst Prof. 1963–67, Assoc. Prof. of English 1967–69, Prof. of English 1969–74, Univ. of California at Berkeley; Visiting Asst Prof., Washington Univ., St Louis 1967; Visiting Prof., Sir George Williams Univ. 1969, Linguistics Inst., SUNY 1971, Columbia Univ. 1983–84; Visiting Prof. 1971, Prof. of English 1974–78, William Kenan Jr Prof. of English and Humanities 1978–85, Chair. Dept of English 1983–85, Johns Hopkins Univ.; Visiting Bing Prof. of English, Univ. of Southern California, Los Angeles 1973–74; Adjunct Prof., Univ. of Maryland Law School 1976–85; Arts and Sciences Prof. of English and Prof. of Law, Duke Univ. 1985–98; Exec. Dir, Duke Univ. Press 1993–98; Dean Coll. of Liberal Arts and Sciences, Univ. of Illinois, Chicago 1999–2005; Distinguished Visiting Prof., John Marshall Law School 2000–02; Fellow, Humanities Research Inst., Univ. of California, Irvine 1989; Davidson-Kahn Distinguished Prof. of Law and Humanities, Florida Int. Univ. 2005–; mem. American Acad. of Arts and Sciences, Milton Soc. of America (Pres. 1980). *Publications include:* John Skelton's Poetry 1965, Surprised by Sin: The Reader in Paradise Lost 1967, Seventeenth Century Prose: Modern Essays in Criticism (ed.) 1971, Self-Consuming Artifacts: The Experience of Seventeenth Century Literature 1972, The Living Temple: George Herbert and Catechizing 1978, Is There a Text in This Class?: The Authority of Interpretive Communities 1980, Doing What Comes Naturally: Change, Rhetoric, and the Practice of Theory in Literary and Legal Studies 1989, There's No Such Thing as Free Speech, and It's a Good Thing, Too 1994, Professional Correctness: Literary Studies and Political Change 1995, The Stanley Fish Reader (ed. by H. Aram Veeser) 1998, The Trouble with Principle 1999, How Milton Works 2001, Save the World on Your Own Time 2008, How to Write a Sentence 2010; contrib. to scholarly books and journals. *Honours:* ACLS Fellowship 1966, Univ. of California at Berkeley Humanities Research Professorship 1966, 1970, second place Explicator Prize 1968, Guggenheim Fellowship 1969–70, Milton Soc. of America Honored Scholar 1991, PEN/Spielvogel-Diamonstein Award 1994, Hanford Book Award 1998, Wilbur Cross Medal Recipient 2010. *Address:* Florida International University, College of Law, Rafael Diaz-Balart Hall 2070, 11200 SW Eighth Street, Miami, FL 33199, USA (office). *Telephone:* (305) 348-7820 (office). *E-mail:* fishs@fiu.edu (office).

FISHER, Allen, BA, MA; British painter, poet and art historian; *Professor Emeritus of Poetry and Art, Manchester Metropolitan University*; b. 1 Nov. 1944, Norbury, Surrey, England; s. of Thomas Henry Fisher and Doris May Fisher; m. Paige Mitchell. *Education:* Goldsmiths Coll., Univ. of London, Univ. of Essex. *Career:* fmr Prof. of Poetry and Art, Roehampton Univ.; fmr Head of Dept of Contemporary Arts and Prof. of Poetry and Art, Manchester Metropolitan Univ., now Emer. *Public collections:* Tate Gallery, London, King's Coll. Archive, Univ. of London, Hereford City Museum, Living Museum, Reykjavik, Iceland, King's Gallery, York. *Exhibitions include:* solo shows: Old Mayor's Parlour, Hereford 1991, King's Manor Gallery, York 1993, Lulham Gallery, London 1998, 2002, King's Archives London 2003; two-man retrospective exhbn: Hereford City Museum 1994. *Publications include:* Place Book One 1974, Brixton Fractals 1985, Unpolished Mirrors 1985, Stepping Out 1989, Future Exiles 1991, Fizz 1994, Civic Crime 1994, Breadboard 1994, Now's the Time 1995, The Topological Shovel (essays) 1999, Watusi 2000, Ring Shout 2001, Sojourns 2001, Gravity 2004, Entanglement 2004, Place 2005, Singularity Stereo 2006, Confidenc in Lack (essays) 2007, Leans 2007, Birds 2009, Proposals 2010; contrib. to various magazines and journals. *Honours:* Alice Hunt Bartlett Award (jtly) 1975. *Address:* Department of Contemporary Arts, Manchester Metropolitan University, Crewe Green Road, Crewe, CW1 5DU (office); 14 Hopton Road, Hereford, HR1 1BE, England (home). *E-mail:* allenfisherstudio@me.com (office). *Website:* www.allenfisher.co.uk.

FISHER, Carrie; American actress and author; b. 21 Oct. 1956, Beverly Hills; d. of Eddie Fisher and Debbie Reynolds; m. Paul Simon 1983 (divorced 1984); one d. *Education:* Beverly Hills High School and Cen. School of Speech and Drama, London. *Career:* appeared with her mother in nightclub act aged

13; appeared in chorus of Broadway production of Irene, starring Debbie Reynolds, aged 15; Broadway stage appearances in Censored Scenes from King Kong, Agnes of God; several TV credits; film début in Shampoo (Photoplay Award as Best Newcomer of the Year) 1974. *Films include:* Shampoo 1974, Star Wars 1977, The Empire Strikes Back 1980, The Blues Brothers 1980, Return of the Jedi 1983, Under the Rainbow, Garbo Talks, The Man With One Red Shoe 1985, Hannah and Her Sisters 1986, Amazing Women on the Moon 1987, Appointment With Death 1988, The 'Burbs 1989, Loverboy 1989, She's Back 1989, When Harry Met Sally... 1989, The Time Guardian 1990, Sibling Rivalry 1990, Drop Dead Fred 1991, Soapdish 1991, This is My Life 1992, Austin Powers: International Man of Mystery 2000, Scream 3 2000, Famous 2000, Heartbreakers 2001, Jay and Silent Bob Strike Back 2001, A Midsummer Night's Rave 2002. *Publications include:* Postcards From the Edge (novel and screenplay, PEN Award for first novel 1987) 1987, Surrender the Pink 1990, Delusions of Grandma 1994 (novels), The Best Awful There Is 2003, Wishful Drinking (memoir) 2009, Shockaholic 2011; short stories. *Literary Agent:* c/o William Morris Agency, 1 William Morris Place, Beverly Hills, CA 90212, USA.

FISHER, Leonard Everett, BFA, MFA; American painter, illustrator and writer; b. 24 June 1924, The Bronx, New York, NY; s. of Benjamin M. Fisher and Ray M. Fisher; m. Margery Meskin 1952; one s. two d. *Education:* Yale Univ. *Career:* served in US Army 1942–46; Grad. Asst, Yale Art School 1949–50; Dean, Whitney School of Art, New Haven, Conn. 1951–53; Academic Dean, Paier Coll. of Art, Hamden, Conn., now Dean Emer.; mem. Authors' Guild, Soc. of Illustrators, Soc. of Children's Book Authors and Illustrators; Life mem. Silvermine Guild of Artists, New Haven Paint and Clay Club; mem. Low Illustration Cttee, New Britain Museum of American Art. *Art:* illustrations and paintings in collections including Library of Congress, Smithsonian Inst., Union Coll., Schenectady, Mt Holyoke Coll., New Britain Museum of American Art, Butler Art Inst., New York Public Library, Mazza Museum, Ohio, Brandywine River Museum, Pa, Chicago Art Inst. and Univs of Minnesota, Southern Mississippi, Brown, Oregon, Connecticut. *Film:* Years in the Making: A Journey into Late Life Creativity (Fine Fettle Films; film by Martin West narrated by Keir Dullea) 2009. *Publications include:* non-fiction: Colonial Americans (19 vols) 1964–76, Ellis Island 1986, Look Around 1987, The Tower of London 1987, Galileo 1992, Tracks Across America 1992, Stars and Stripes 1993, Marie Curie 1994, Moses 1995, Gandhi 1995, Niagara Falls 1996, Anasazi 1997; fiction: Death of Evening Star 1972, Across the Sea from Galway 1975, Sailboat Lost 1991, Cyclops 1991, Kinderdike 1994, William Tell 1996, The Jetty Chronicles 1997, Gods and Goddesses of the Ancient Maya 1999, Sky, Sea, the Jetty and Me 2001, Gods and Goddesses of the Ancient Norse 2001; illustrator of around 260 books by other authors. *Honours:* American Service Medal, European-African-Middle Eastern Service Medal, Asiatic-Pacific Service Medal, Good Conduct Medal, World War II Victory Medal; hon. degree (Paier Coll. of Art); Winchester Fellowship, Yale Univ. 1949, Pulitzer Painting Scholarship, Columbia Univ. 1950, Premio Grafico Fiera di Bologno (Italy) 1968, Univ. of Southern Mississippi Medallion 1979, Christopher Medal 1980, Nat. Jewish Book Award for Children's Literature 1981, Children's Book Guild Washington Post Non-Fiction Award 1989, Catholic Library Asscn Regina Medal 1991, Univ. of Minnesota Kerlan Award 1991, American Library Asscn Arbuthnot Honour Lecture Citation 1994. *Literary Agent:* c/o William B. R. Reiss, John Hawkins and Associates, New York, NY 10010, USA. *Address:* 7 Twin Bridge Acres Road, Westport, CT 06880 (home); c/o Cavalier Galleries, 405 Greenwich Avenue, Greenwich, CT 06830, USA. *Telephone:* (203) 227-0133 (office). *Fax:* (203) 227-0133 (office). *E-mail:* l.e.fisher@sbcglobal.net (home).

FISHER, Marshall Jon, MA; American writer and author; b. 1963, Ithaca, NY; m.; two s. *Education:* Brandeis Univ., City Coll., New York. *Career:* worked as sportswriter in Miami and tennis pro in Munich; freelance writer and editor 1989–; regular contrib. to The Atlantic Monthly 1995–2002. *Publications:* The Ozone Layer (one of New York Public Library's Best Books for Teenagers) 1993, A Terrible Splendor (PEN/ESPN Award for Literary Sports Writing 2010) 2009; co-author (with father David E. Fisher): Tube: the Invention of Television 1996, Strangers in the Night: a Brief History of Life on Other Worlds (one of New York Public Library's 25 Books to Remember) 1998, Mysteries of Lost Empires 2000; contrib. of articles, essays and stories to Atlantic Monthly, Harper's, Discover, DoubleTake and others. *Literary Agent:* The Albert Lafarge Literary Agency, Boston, MA 02130, USA. *E-mail:* office@thelafargeagency.com. *E-mail:* marshalljonfisher@gmail.com (office). *Website:* marshalljonfisher.wordpress.com (office).

FISHER, Roy, BA, MA, FRSL; British poet and musician; b. 11 June 1930, Birmingham, England. *Education:* Univ. of Birmingham. *Career:* mem. Musicians' Union, Soc. of Authors. *Publications include:* City 1961, Interiors 1966, The Ship's Orchestra 1967, The Memorial Fountain 1968, Matrix 1971, The Cut Pages 1971, Metamorphoses 1971, The Thing About Joe Sullivan 1978, A Furnace 1986, The Left-Handed Punch 1987, Poems 1955–1987 1988, Birmingham River 1994, The Dow Low Drop: New and Selected Poems 1996, Interviews Through Time 2000, The Long and the Short of It: Poems 1955–2005 2005, Standard Midland 2010; contrib. to numerous journals and magazines. *Honours:* Hon. Poet of the City of Birmingham 2003; Hon. DLitt (Keele) 1999; Andrew Kelus Prize 1979, Cholmondeley Award 1981, Hamlyn Award 1997. *Address:* Four Ways, Earl Sterndale, Buxton, Derbyshire, SK17 0EP, England (home). *Telephone:* (1298) 83279 (home). *E-mail:* fourways.ear@virgin.net (home).

FISHKIN, Shelley Fisher, BA, MA, MPhil, PhD; American academic, writer and editor; *Professor of English, Stanford University*; b. 9 May 1950, New York, NY; m. James Steven Fishkin 1973; two s. *Education:* Swarthmore Coll., Yale Univ. *Career:* Visiting Lecturer, Yale Univ. 1981–84; Sr Lecturer, Univ. of Texas at Austin 1985–89, Assoc. Prof. 1989–92, Prof. of American Studies 1993–2003, Prof. of American Studies and English 1994–2003; Prof. of English, Stanford Univ. 2003–; Visiting Fellow, Clare Hall, Cambridge, UK 1992–93, Life mem. 1993–; Chair. First Book Prize Selection Comm. 2002–03; Assoc. Ed., American Nat. Biography 1989–; Founding Ed. Journal of Transnational American Studies 2009–; mem. Authors' Guild, Charlotte Perkins Gilman Soc., Co-founder and Exec. Dir 1990–, Modern Language Asscn, Nonfiction Prose Div., Exec. Council 1991–95, Int. Theodore Dreiser Soc., Mark Twain Circle of America (Pres. 1997–98), American Literature Asscn, American Studies Asscn (Pres. 2004–05); mem. Bd of Govs, Univ. of California Humanities Research Inst. 2008–. *Publications include:* From Fact to Fiction: Journalism and Imaginative Writing in America 1985, Was Huck Black?: Mark Twain and African-American Voices 1993, Listening to Silences: New Essays in Feminist Criticism (co-ed. with Elaine Hedges) 1994, The Oxford Mark Twain (ed.), 29 vols 1996, People of the Book: Thirty Scholars Reflect on Their Jewish Identity (ed.), Lighting Out for the Territory: Reflections on Mark Twain and American Culture 1997, Encyclopedia of Civil Rights in America (ed) 1997, Historical Guide to Mark Twain (ed) 2002, Is He Dead? (ed) 2003, Sport of the Gods and Other Essential Writings 2005, Anthology of American Literature (ed) 2006, Feminist Engagements: Forays into American Literature and Culture 2009, Mark Twain's Book of Animals (ed.) 2009, The Mark Twain Anthology: Great Writers on his Life and Works (ed) 2010; contrib. to books, journals, newspapers and periodicals. *Honours:* Mellon Fellow 1979, Rockefeller Humanist Fellow 1984, Aspen Inst., Frank Luther Mott-Kappa Tau Alpha Research Book Award, Nat. Journalism Scholarship Soc. 1986, ACLS Fellowship 1987–88, Humanities Scholar, Connecticut Humanities Council 1987, 1989–91, Outstanding Academic Book Citation, Choice 1994, 2009, Outstanding Reference Book Citation, New York Public Library 1998, Fulbright Distinguished Lecturer, Japan 1999, Harry H. Ransom Teaching Excellence Award 2000 , Lifetime Achievement Award in Literature, Town of Westport, Connecticut 2002, Callahan Award 2007–08, Mark Twain Circle Certificate of Merit 2009. *Address:* Department of English, Stanford University, Building 460, Margaret Jacks Hall, Stanford, CA 94305-2087, USA (office). *Telephone:* (650) 723-1804 (office). *E-mail:* sfishkin@stanford.edu (office). *Website:* english.stanford.edu (office).

FISHLOCK, Trevor; British journalist, broadcaster and writer; b. 21 Feb. 1941, Hereford, England; m. Penelope Symon 1978. *Career:* Portsmouth Evening News 1957–62; freelance news agency reporter 1962–68; staff corresp., Wales and West of England, The Times 1968–77, South Asia corresp. 1980–83, New York corresp. 1983–86; roving foreign corresp., Daily Telegraph 1986–89, 1993–96, Moscow Corresp. 1989–91; roving foreign corresp., Sunday Telegraph 1991–93; mem. Travellers' Club, Soc. of Authors, World Press Inst. *Television:* writer/presenter, Fishlock's Wild Tracks (ITV Wales) 1995–2008, Fishlock's Wales (ITV Wales) 2009–. *Publications include:* Wales and the Welsh 1972, Discovering Britain: Wales 1975, Talking of Wales 1975, Americans and Nothing Else 1980, India File 1983, The State of America 1986, Indira Gandhi (juvenile) 1986, Out of Red Darkness 1992, My Foreign Country 1997, Wild Tracks 1998, Cobra Road 1999, More Wild Tracks 2000, Fishlock's Sea Stories 2003, Conquerors of Time: Exploration and Invention in the Age of Daring 2004, More Fishlock's Sea Stories 2005, In This Place (centenary vol. of Nat. Library of Wales) 2007, Senedd: The National Assembly for Wales Building 2010, Pembrokeshire Journeys & Stories 2011. *Honours:* Hon. Fellow, Univ. of Wales, Lampeter 2008; Hon. MA (Univ. of Wales) 2008; David Holden Award for Foreign Reporting 1983, Int. Reporter of the Year 1986, British Press Awards. *Address:* 7 Teilo Street, Cardiff, CF11 9JN, Wales (home).

FISHMAN, Charles Monroe, (Charles Adés Fishman), BA, MA, DA; American academic, poet, writer and editor; *Distinguished Service Professor Emeritus, State University of New York, Albany*; b. 10 July 1942, Oceanside, NY; s. of Morris (Murray) Fishman and Naomi (Toby) Ades; m. Ellen Marcie Haselkorn 1967; two d. *Education:* Hofstra Univ., Stony Brook Univ., State Univ. of NY (SUNY) at Albany. *Career:* Founder-Dir Visiting Writers Program, at Farmingdale 1979–97, Distinguished Service Prof. 1989–, Prof. Emer. 1997–, Founder-Dir Distinguished Speakers Program 2001–07; Founder-Ed. Xanadu 1975–78; Poetry Ed. Gaia 1993–95, Cistercian Studies Quarterly 1998–99, Journal of Genocide Research 1999; Assoc. Ed. The Drunken Boat 1999–2005; Poetry Ed. New Works Review 2003–; Poetry Ed. PRISM: An Interdisciplinary Journal for Holocaust Educators 2008–; more than 400 readings in USA and abroad; past mem. Associated Writing Programs, Authors' Guild, Poetry Soc. of America, Poets and Writers; mem. Bd Walt Whitman Birthplace Asscn 2007–08. *Publications include:* An Index to Women's Magazines and Presses (ed.) 1977, Mortal Companions 1977, The Death Mazurka 1987, Zoom 1990, Catlives (by Sarah Kirsch; trans. with Marina Roscher) 1991, Blood to Remember: American Poets on the Holocaust (ed.) 1991, (revised edn) 2007, As the Sun Goes Down in Fire 1992, Nineteenth-Century Rain 1994, An Aztec Memory 1997, Time Travel Reports 2002, Country of Memory 2004, 5,000 Bells 2004, Chopin's Piano 2006, Water Under Water 2009, In the Language of Women 2011; contrib. to many anthologies and more than 350 periodicals. *Honours:* Pres.'s Award for Distinguished Doctoral Dissertation, Gertrude B. Claytor Memorial Award,

Poetry Soc. of America 1987, American Library Asscn Outstanding Academic Book of the Year 1989, Firman Houghton Poetry Award, New England Poetry Club 1995, New York Foundation for the Arts Fellowship in Poetry 1995, winner, Anabiosis Press Chapbook Competition 1996, Ann Stanford Poetry Prize, Southern California Anthology 1996, Eve of St Agnes Poetry Prize 1999, George M. Estabrook Award for Distinguished Service 2000, Walt Whitman Birthplace, Long Island Poet of the Year 2006, Paterson Award for Literary Excellence 2007, 2010. *Address:* 56 Wood Acres Road, East Patchogue, NY, USA (home). *Telephone:* (631) 805-5051 (mobile). *E-mail:* carolus@optonline.net (office); cfishman8@gmail.com (office). *Website:* www.charlesfishman.com.

FISK, Pauline; British writer; b. 27 Sept. 1948, London, England; m. David Davies 1972; two s. three d. *Publications include:* Midnight Blue 1990, Telling the Sea 1992, Tyger Pool 1994, Beast of Whixall Moss 1997, The Candle House 1999, Sabrina Fludde 2001, The Red Judge 2005, The Mrs Marridge Project 2005, Flying for Frankie 2009, In the Trees 2010; contribs to Homes and Gardens 1989 and anthologies, including Something to Do With Love 1996, Heading Out 2003, Hubble Bubble 2003, Love, Hate and My Best Mate 2004. *Honours:* Smarties Grand Prix Prize 1990. *Address:* c/o Faber and Faber, Bloomsbury House, 74–77 Great Russell Street, London, WC1B 3DA, England. *Website:* www.faber.co.uk.

FITZGERALD, Frances; American writer; b. 21 Oct. 1940, d. of Desmond Fitzgerald and Marietta Peabody Fitzgerald Tree; m. James Paul Sterba 1990. *Education:* Radcliffe Coll. *Career:* author of series of profiles for Herald Tribune magazine; freelance author of series of profiles, Vietnam 1966; frequent contrib. to The New Yorker; Vice-Pres. PEN International; mem. editorial bds The Nation, Foreign Policy. *Publications include:* Fire in the Lake – The Vietnamese and the Americans in Vietnam (Pulitzer Prize 1973, Nat. Book Award 1973) 1972, America Revised – History Schoolbooks in the Twentieth Century 1979, Cities on a Hill – A Journey Through Contemporary American Cultures 1986, Way Out There in the Blue – Reagan, Star Wars and the End of the Cold War (New York Times Ed.'s Choice, New York Public Library Helen Bernstein Award) 2000, Vietnam: Spirits of the Earth 2002, Our Cat Cookie 2011; contribs to The New York Review of Books, The New York Times Magazine, Esquire, Architectural Digest, Islands, Rolling Stone. *Honours:* Overseas Press Club Award 1967, Nat. Inst. of Arts and Letters Award 1973, Sydney Hillman Award 1973, George Polk Award 1973, Bancroft Award for History 1973. *Address:* 531 E 72nd Street, Apartment 3B, New York, NY 10021-4017, USA (home).

FITZGERALD, Judith Ariana, MA, PhD; Canadian poet, columnist and academic; b. 11 Nov. 1952, Toronto, Ont. *Education:* York Univ., Ont. and Univ. of Toronto. *Career:* teacher, Erindale Coll. 1978–81; Asst Prof., Laurentian Univ., Ont. 1981–83; Poetry Ed. Black Moss Press 1981–87; entertainment reporter, The Globe 1983–84; critic, The Toronto Star 1984–88, columnist 1987, 1992–93, 1997–99; Ed. Countrywave 1995–1996; creator and Sr Writer, Today's Country 1992–1998; numerous writer-in-residencies; juror, Gov.-Gen.'s Poetry Award 1998. *Publications include:* poetry: City Park 1972, Journal Entries 1975, Victory 1975, Lacerating Heartwood 1977, Easy Over: Poems 1981, Un Dozen: thirteen Canadian Poets (ed.) 1982, Split/Level 1983, Heart Attacks 1984, Beneath the Skin of Paradise: The Piaf Poems 1984, My Orange Gorange (juvenile) 1985, Given Names: New and Selected Poems, 1972–1985 (Writers' Choice Award 1986) 1985, Whale Waddleby (juvenile) 1986, SP/ELLES: Poetry by Canadian Women/Poésie de femmes canadiennes (ed.) 1986, Diary of Desire 1987, First Person Plural (ed.) 1987, Rapturous Chronicles 1991, Ultimate Midnight 1992, Habit of Blues: Rapturous Chronicles II 1993, Walkin' Wounded 1993, River 1995, AKA Paradise 1996, Building a Mystery: the Story of Sarah McLachlan and Lilith Fair 1997, Twenty-Six Ways Out of This World 1999, Sarah McLachlan: Building a Mystery 2000, Adagios 2000, Marshall McLuhan: Wise Guy 2001, Book One of the Adagios Quartet: Iphigenia's Song 2003, Book Two of the Adagios Quartet: Orestes' Lament 2004, The Spirit of Indian Women 2005, Adagios Quartet 2007; contribs: criticism and poetry in anthologies, journals and newspapers. *Honours:* Canada Council Arts Grant A 1988, 1990, 1991, 1993, Professional Writers' Grant 2000, Fiona Mee Award 1983, Silver Medal, New York Int. Radio Festival 1995, 1996, 1997, Gold 1998. *Address:* c/o Oberon Press, 205–145 Spruce Street, Ottawa, ON K1R 6PI, Canada. *E-mail:* oberon@sympatico.ca. *Website:* www.oberonpress.ca; www.judithfitzgerald.ca.

FITZGERALD, Niall, FRSA, BComm; Irish business executive; *Deputy Chairman, Thomson Reuters*; b. 13 Sept. 1945; m.; two s. two d. *Education:* Univ. Coll., Dublin. *Career:* joined Unilever 1967, various man. roles including CEO, Unilever Food Div., S Africa, early 1980s, later Treasurer, Unilever, London, Dir Unilever PLC and Unilever NV 1987–2004, Financial Dir 1987–89, Co-ordinator, Edible Fats and Dairy 1989–90, mem. Foods Exec. 1989–91, Co-ordinator, Detergents 1991–95, Vice-Pres. Unilever PLC 1994–96, Chair. 1996–2004, also becoming Vice-Chair. Unilever NV 1996–2004; Dir Reuters Group 2003–08, Chair. 2004–08, Deputy Chair. Thomson Reuters (following acquisition of Reuters) 2008–; Pres. Advertising Asscn, S Africa Int. Investment Advisory Council, Shanghai Major's Int. Business Leaders' Council; Vice-Chair. The Conf. Bd; mem. World Econ. Forum, Int. Advisory Bd, Council on Foreign Relations, Trilateral Comm., EU–China Cttee, US Business Council; Gov. Nat. Inst. of Econ. and Social Research; Trustee, Leverhulme Trust; fmr Dir Merck, Ericsson, Bank of Ireland, Prudential Corpn. *Honours:* Hon. KBE . *Address:* The Thomson Reuters Building, 30 South Colonnade, Canary Wharf, London, E14 5EP, England (office). *Telephone:* (20) 7250-1122 (office). *Fax:* (20) 7542-4064 (office). *Website:* www.thomsonreuters.com (office).

FITZMAURICE, Gabriel John; Irish teacher and poet; b. 7 Dec. 1952, Moyvane, Co. Kerry; m. Brenda Downey 1981; one s. one d. *Education:* St Michael's Coll., Listowel, Co. Kerry, Mary Immaculate Coll., Limerick. *Career:* Asst Teacher, Avoca Nat. School, Co. Wicklow 1972–74; Teacher, Christ the King Nat. School, Limerick City 1974–75; Prin. Teacher, Moyvane Nat. School, Co. Kerry 1975–2007; represented Ireland, Europees Poeziefestival, Leuven, Belgium 1987, 1991. *Publications include:* poetry in English: Rainsong 1984, Road to the Horizon 1987, Dancing Through 1990, The Father's Part 1992, The Space Between: New and Selected Poems 1984–92 1993, The Village Sings 1996, A Wrenboy's Carnival: Poems 1980–2000 2000, I and the Village 2002, The Boghole Boys 2005, Twenty One Sonnets 2007, The Essential Gabriel Fitzmaurice 2008, In Praise of Football 2009, Poems of Faith and Doubt 2011; poetry in Irish: Nocht 1989, Ag Síobshiúl Chun An Rince 1995, Giolla na nAmhrán: Dánta 1988–1998 1998; essays: Kerry on My Mind 1999, Beat the Goatskin Till the Goat Cries 2006; children's poetry in English: The Moving Stair 1989, But Dad! 1995, Puppy and the Sausage 1998, Dear Grandad 2001, A Giant Never Dies 2002, The Oopsy Kid 2003, Don't Squash Fluffy 2004, I'm Proud to Be Me 2005, Really Rotten Rhymes 2007, GF Woz Ere 2009; children's poetry in Irish: Nach Iontach Mar Ata 1994; children's poetry in English and Irish: Do Teachers Go to the Toilet?/An dTeann Muinteoiri go Tigh an Asail? 2010; trans.: The Purge, by Mícheál Ó hAirtnéide 1989, Poems I Wish I'd Written 1996, The Rhino's Specs/Speaclai an tSronbheannaigh (Selected Children's Poems of Gabriel Rosenstock) 2002, Poems from the Irish: Collected Translations 2004, Ventry Calling 2005, House, Don't Fall on Me 2007; ed.: The Flowering Tree 1991, Between the Hills and Sea: Songs and Ballads of Kerry 1991, Con Greaney: Traditional Singer 1991, Homecoming/An Bealach 'na Bhaile: Selected Poems of Cathal Ó Searcaigh (Cló lar-Chonnacnta 1993, Irish Poetry Now: Other Voices 1993, Kerry Through Its Writers 1993, The Listowel Literary Phenomenon: North Kerry Writers – A Critical Introduction 1994, Rusty Nails and Astronauts: A Wolfhound Poetry Anthology 1999, 'The Boro' and 'The Cross': The Parish of Moyvane-Knockanure (with Áine Cronin and John Looney) 2000, The Kerry Anthology 2000, Come all Good Men and True 2004, The World of Bryan MacMahon 2005; contribs to newspapers, reviews, and journals. *Honours:* Award Winner, Gerard Manley Hopkins Centenary Poetry Competition 1989. *Address:* Applegarth, Moyvane, Co. Kerry, Ireland (home). *E-mail:* gabren@eircom.net (office).

FITZSIMMONS, Thomas, BA, MA; American poet, writer, translator, editor and publisher and academic; *Professor Emeritus of English and Comparative Literature, Oakland University*; b. 21 Oct. 1926, Lowell, Mass; m. Karen Hargreaves; two s. *Education:* Fresno State Coll., Sorbonne and Institut de Sciences Politiques, Paris, Stanford Univ., Calif., Columbia Univ., New York. *Career:* writer and Ed., The New Republic magazine 1952–55; research team Chair., HRAF Press, Yale Univ. 1955–56, Dir of Research for Publ. 1956–58, Dir and Ed. 1958–59; Asst Prof., Oakland Univ., Rochester, Mich. 1959–61, Assoc. Prof. 1961–66, Prof. of English and Comparative Literature 1966–89, Prof. Emer. 1989–; Fulbright Lecturer, Tokyo Univ. of Educ. 1962–64, Tsuda Univ., Tokyo 1962–64, Univ. of Bucharest 1967–68, Univ. of Nice 1968; Visiting Lecturer, Japan Nat. Women's Univ., Tokyo 1973–75, Keio Univ., Tokyo 1973–75, Detroit Inst. of Arts 1986; Visiting Prof., Tokyo Univ. of Educ. 1973–75, Kyushu Nat. Univ., Fukuoka 1979; Visiting Poet and Scholar, Sophia Univ., Tokyo 1988–89; Ed.-Publr Katydid Books. *Publications include:* poetry: This Time This Place 1969, Mooning 1971, Meditation Seeds 1971, With the Water 1972, Playseeds 1973, The Big Huge 1975, The Nine Seas and the Eight Mountains 1981, Rocking Mirror Daybreak 1982, Water Ground Stone (poems and essays) 1994, The Dream Machine 1996, Fencing the Sky 1998, Iron Harp 1999, Build Me Ruins 2002, Is Two: Becomes One 2005, High Desert/High Country 2007, In the Cemetery There Are Lovers 2008, The Wonderful Wee & The Finger of God 2009; other: author, ed. or trans. of more than 60 vols 1955–2010; Ed. for Katydid Books/Univ. of Hawaii Press series: Asian Poetry in Translation: Japan (24 vols) and Reflections (five vols). *Honours:* Nat. Endowment for the Arts Fellowships 1967, 1982, 1989–90, and Grants 1984, 1986, Oakland Univ. Research Fellowship 1982, Japan-US Friendship Foundation Grant 1983, Michigan Council for the Arts Award 1986, Fulbright Research Fellowship, Japan 1988–89. *Address:* 1 Balsa Road, Santa Fe, NM 87508, USA (home). *Website:* www.katydidbooks.com.

FITZSIMONS, Sheila, BA, PGCE; British editor; *Executive Editor, The Guardian*. *Education:* Coloma Convent School, Somerville Coll., Oxford and Worcester Coll. of Higher Educ. *Career:* econs and business studies teacher 1984–90; Deputy Ed. of Educ., The Guardian 1990–92, Ed. of Educ. 1992–94, Asst News Ed. 1994–96; Business News Ed., The Observer 1996–98; Special Projects and Editorial Devt, The Guardian 1998–99, Exec. Ed. 1999–; mem. Bd, Guardian News and Media 2009–. *Address:* The Guardian, Kings Place, 90 York Way, London, N1 9GU, England (office). *Telephone:* (20) 3353-2000 (office). *E-mail:* sheila.fitzsimons@guardian.co.uk (office). *Website:* www.guardian.co.uk (office).

FLAGG, Fannie; American writer and actress; b. (Patricia Neal), 21 Sept. 1941, Birmingham, Ala. *Education:* Univ. of Alabama, Pittsburgh Playhouse, Town and Gown Theatre. *Career:* fmr TV news anchor; fmr co-host 'Candid Camera'. *Theatre includes:* Patio Porch, Come Back to the Five and Dime, Jimmy Dean, Jimmy Dean, The Best Little Whorehouse in Texas. *Films include:* Five Easy Pieces 1970, Some of My Best Friends Are 1971, Stay

Hungry 1976, Grease 1978, Rabbit Test 1978, My Best Friend is a Vampire 1988, Crazy in Alabama 1999. *Television appearances include:* The New Dick Van Dyke Show 1971–73, The New Original Wonder Woman 1975, Sex and the Married Woman 1977, Harper Valley P.T.A. 1981. *Publications include:* Daisy Fay and the Miracle Man, Coming Attractions: A Wonderful Novel 1981, Fried Green Tomatoes at the Whistle Stop Cafe (also screenplay, with Jon Avnet) 1987, Welcome to the World, Baby Girl! 1988, Standing in the Rainbow 2002, A Redbird Christmas 2004, Can't Wait to Get to Heaven 2006, I Still Dream About You 2010; contrib. to magazines and newspapers. *Address:* c/o Publicity Department, Random House Inc., 1745 Broadway, New York, NY 10019, USA. *Website:* www.randomhouse.com/features/fannieflagg.

FLAM, Jack Donald, BA, MA, PhD; American academic, foundation administrator and writer; *President, The Dedalus Foundation*; b. 2 April 1940, Paterson, NJ; m. Bonnie Burnham 1972 (divorced); one d. *Education:* Rutgers Univ., Columbia Univ., New York Univ. *Career:* Instructor in Art, Newark Coll. of Arts and Sciences, Rutgers Univ. 1962–66; Asst Prof. of Art, Univ. of Florida 1966–69, Assoc. Prof. of Art 1969–72; Assoc. Prof. of Art, Brooklyn Coll., CUNY 1975–79, Prof. of Art 1980–91, Distinguished Prof. of Art 1991–2010; Assoc. Prof. of Art History 1979–80, Prof. of Art History 1980–91, Distinguished Prof. of Art History 1991–2010, Grad. School and Univ. Center, CUNY, Distinguished Prof. Emer. 2010–; Pres. Dedalus Foundation 2002–; art critic, The Wall Street Journal 1984–92; mem. Int. Asscn of Art Critics, PEN. *Publications include:* Matisse on Art 1973, Zoltan Gorency 1974, Bread and Butter 1977, Henri Matisse Paper Cut-Outs (co-author) 1977, Robert Motherwell (co-author) 1983, Matisse: The Man and His Art 1869–1918 1986, Fernand Léger 1987, Matisse: A Retrospective 1988, Motherwell 1991, Richard Diebenkorn: Ocean Park 1992, Matisse: The Dance 1993, Western Artists/African Art 1994, The Paine Webber Art Collection (co-author) 1995, Robert Smithson: The Collected Writings (ed.) 1996, Judith Rothschild – An Artist's Search 1998, Les Peintures de Picasso: Un Théâtre Mentale 1998, The Modern Drawing 1999, Matisse and Picasso: The Story of Their Rivalry and Friendship 2003, Primitivism and Twentieth-Century Art: A Documentary History 2003, Matisse, his Art and his Textiles (co-author) 2004, Matisse–Derain, Collioure 1905, un été fauve (co-author) 2005, Matisse in Transition: Around Laurette 2006, Hungarian Fauves: From Paris to Nagybáná (co-author) 2006, Matisse, His Art and His Textiles: The Fabric of Dreams (co-author) 2004, Matisse-Derain, Collioure 1905, un été fauve (co-author) 2005, Traces du sacré (co-author) 2008, Pierre Bonnard: The Late Still Lifes and Interiors (co-author) 2009; contrib. to Apollo, Art in America, Art News, New York Review of Books. *Honours:* Guggenheim Fellowship 1979–80, Nat. Endowment for the Humanities Fellowship 1987–88. *Literary Agent:* c/o Georges Borchardt Inc., 136 East 57th Street, New York, NY 10022, USA.

FLAMMARION, Charles-Henri, LèsL, LèsLet, MBA; French publishing executive; b. 27 July 1946, Boulogne-Billancourt; s. of the late Henri Flammarion and of Pierrette Chenelot; m. Marie-Françoise Mariani 1968; one s. two d. *Education:* Lycée de Sèvres, Sorbonne, Paris, Institut d'Etudes Politiques, Paris and Columbia Univ., USA. *Career:* Asst Man., Editions Flammarion 1972–81, Gen. Man. 1981–85, Pres. Flammarion SA 1985–2003; Pres. Editions J'ai Lu 1982–2003, Audie-Fluide Glacial 1990–2003; mem. Bureau du Syndicat Nat. de l'Édition 1979–88, 1996–2003; Vice-Pres. Cercle de la Librairie 1988–94, Pres. 1994–2003; Pres. Casterman 1999–2003. *Address:* 15 rue des Barres, 75004 Paris, France (home). *E-mail:* flammarionch@gmail.com (home).

FLANAGAN, Mary, BA, MA; American novelist and critic; b. 20 May 1943, Rochester, NH. *Education:* Brandeis Univ., Waltham. *Career:* creative writing seminars (two terms), Univ. of East Anglia, UK, Arvon Foundation and Skyros Centre, Greece; Fellow, Univ. of Leicester 2001–02, Assoc. Fellow 2002–03; currently reviews books for The Independent; mem. PEN, Soc. of Authors. *Publications include:* Bad Girls 1984, Trust 1987, Rose Reason 1991, The Blue Woman 1994, Adèle 1997, Strength for Soul: Trust 2006.

FLANAGAN, Richard; Australian writer and film director; b. 1961, Tasmania. *Education:* Univ. of Oxford, UK. *Career:* fmr river guide; scriptwriter, author of history books, novelist. *Film:* The Sound of One Hand Clapping (dir). *Publications include:* non-fiction: A Terrible Beauty: A History of the Gordon River County, Codename Iago: The Story of John Friedrich, Parish-Fed Bastards: A History of the Politics of the Unemployed in Britain 1884–1939 1994; novels: Death of a River Guide (Victorian Premier's Award for Fiction) 1995, The Sound of One Hand Clapping 1998, Gould's Book of Fish (Commonwealth Writer's Prize) 2002, The Unknown Terrorist 2007, Wanting 2008. *Honours:* Rhodes Scholar. *Literary Agent:* Rogers, Coleridge and White, 20 Powis Mews, London, W11 1JN, England. *Telephone:* (20) 7221-3717. *Fax:* (20) 7229-9084. *E-mail:* info@rcwlitagency.com. *Website:* www.rcwlitagency.com.

FLANAGIN, Annette, RN, MA; American editor; *Managing Senior Editor, Journal of the American Medical Association*. *Education:* Georgetown Univ., Washington DC. *Career:* fmr Pres. Council of Science Eds; Man. Sr Ed. Journal of the American Medical Asscn; Distinguished Lecturer, Sigma Theta Tau International 1994–2001, Distinguished Writer 1998–2001, 2004–; Fellow, American Acad. of Nursing; mem. Council of Science Eds 1989–. *Publications include:* AMA Manual of Style (co-author) (ninth edn) 1998; more than 60 articles. *Honours:* Frances Larsen Memorial Award for Excellence in Medical Writing, American Medical Writers Asscn 1994. *Address:* Journal of the American Medical Assocation (JAMA), 515 North State Street, Chicago, IL 60610, USA (office). *Telephone:* (342) 464-2432 (office). *E-mail:* annette_flanagin@jama-archives.org (office). *Website:* jama.ama-assn.org (office).

FLEISCHMAN, Paul, BA; American children's writer and poet; b. 5 Sept. 1952, Monterey, Calif.; m. Becky Mojica 1978; two s. *Education:* Univ. of California, Berkeley, Univ. of New Mexico. *Career:* mem. Authors' Guild, Soc. of Children's Book Writers. *Publications include:* picture books: The Birthday Tree 1979, The Animal Hedge 1983, Rondo in C 1988, Shadow Play 1990, Time Train 1991, Weslandia 1999, Lost: A Story in String 2000, Sidewalk Circus 2004, Glass Slipper, Gold Sandal: A Worldwide Cinderella 2007, The Dunderheads (Horace Mann Upstanders Book Award 2010) 2009; young adult fiction: Graven Images 1982, Path of the Pale Horse 1983, Coming-and-Going Men 1985, Rear-View Mirrors 1986, Saturnalia 1990, The Borning Room 1991, A Fate Totally Worse than Death 1995, Bull Run 1995, Seedfolks 1997, Whirligig 1998, Breakout 2003; plays: Mind's Eye 1999, Seek 2001, ZAP 2005, Logomaniacs 2010; poetry: I Am Phoenix: Poems for Two Voices 1985, Joyful Noise: Poems for Two Voices 1989, Big Talk: Poems for Four Voices 2000; fiction: The Half-a-Moon Inn 1980, Finzel the Farsighted 1983, Phoebe Danger, Detective 1983; non-fiction: Townsend's Warbler 1992, Copier Creations 1993, Dateline: Troy 1996, Cannibal in the Mirror 2000. *Honours:* Silver Medal, Commonwealth Club of California 1980, Newbery Medals, American Library Asscn 1983, 1989, Parents Choice Award 1983, numerous citations by Soc. of Children's Book Writers, American Library Asscn, New York Times. *Address:* PO Box 646, Aromas, CA 95004, USA. *Website:* www.paulfleischman.net.

FLEISSNER, Robert F., (Archibald Harris), AB, MA, PhD; American academic and writer; b. 17 Oct. 1932, Auburn, NY; m. Judith Gerber 1966 (divorced 1967). *Education:* Hamilton Coll., Cornell Univ., Catholic Univ. of America, Middlebury Coll., Univ. of North Carolina, Chapel Hill, Ohio State Univ., New York Univ. *Career:* Instructor in English, Speech and Drama, Spring Hill Coll., Mobile, Ala 1958–59; Asst Instructor in English, Ohio State Univ. 1960–61; Lecturer in English, City Coll., CUNY 1962–64; Asst Prof. of English, Dominican Coll., Blauvelt, NY 1964–66; Instructor in English, Univ. of New Mexico, Albuquerque 1966–67; Asst Prof., then Assoc. Prof. of English, Central State Univ., Wilberforce, OH 1967–2005; mem. Modern Language Asscn of America, T.S. Eliot Soc., Shakespeare Asscn of America. *Plays:* some theatre work. *Publications include:* Dickens and Shakespeare: A Study in Histrionic Contrasts 1965, Resolved to Love: The 1592 Edition of Henry Constable's 'Diana' Critically Considered 1980, The Prince and the Professor: The Wittenberg Connection in Marlowe, Shakespeare, Goethe and Frost – A Hamlet-Faust(us) Analogy 1986, Ascending the Prufrockian Stair: Studies in a Dissociated Sensibility 1988, A Rose by Another Name: A Survey of Literary Flora from Shakespeare to Eco 1989, Shakespeare and the Matter of the Crux 1991, T. S. Eliot and the Heritage of Africa: The Magus and the Moor as Metaphor 1992, Frost's Road Taken 1996, Sources, Meaning, and Influences of Coleridge's 'Kubla Khan': Xanadu Re-Routed 2000, Names, Titles and Characters by Literary Writers: Shakespeare, 19th- and 20th-Century Authors 2001, The Master Sleuth on the Trail of 'Edwin Drood': Sherlock Holmes and the Jasper Syndrome (as Archibald W. Harris) 2002, Shakespearean and Other Literary Investigations with the Master Sleuth (and Conan Doyle): Homing in on Holmes 2003; Shakespeare and Africa: The Dark Lady of his Sonnets Revamped and Other Africa-Related Associations 2005, Shakespearean Puzzles: Essays on Textual, Dramatic and Biographical Epigrams in Some Plays by Shakespeare 2008, Shakespeare, Religion and Beyond 2010; contrib. to books and journals including The Sherlock Holmes Journal. *Address:* 367 East Cassilly Street, Springfield, OH 45503-3765, USA (home). *Telephone:* (937) 324-7533 (home).

FLEMING, Laurence William Howie; British author, artist and landscape designer; b. 8 Sept. 1929, Shillong, Assam, India. *Education:* The New School, Darjeeling, India, Repton School, Derbyshire, St Catharine's Coll., Cambridge. *Career:* RAF 1947–49; mem. International PEN, Writers Guild, Anglo-Brazilian Soc. *Publications include:* A Diet of Crumbs 1959, The English Garden 1979, The One Hour Garden 1985, Old English Villages 1986, Roberto Burle Marx: A Portrait 1996, Last Children of the Raj: British Childhoods in India, Vols I and II (ed.), On Torquemada's Sofa 2005; contribs to journals.

FLETCHER, John Walter James, (Jonathan Fune), BA, MA, MPhil, PhD; British academic, writer and translator; *Professor Emeritus, University of East Anglia*; b. 23 June 1937, Barking, Essex, England; s. of the late Roy Arthur Walter Fletcher MBE and Eileen Alice Fletcher (née Beane); m. Beryl Sibley Connop 1961; two s. one d. *Education:* Univ. of Cambridge, Univ. of Toulouse, France. *Career:* Exhibitioner, Trinity Hall, Cambridge 1956–59; Lector, Univ. of Toulouse 1961–64; Lecturer in French, Durham Univ. 1964–66; Lecturer in French, Univ. of East Anglia 1966–68, Reader in French 1968–69, Prof. of Comparative Literature 1969–89, Prof. of European Literature 1989–98, Prof. Emer. 1998–; Hon. Sr Research Fellow, Univ. of Kent at Canterbury 1997–; mem. Soc. of Authors, Translators' Asscn. *Publications include:* The Novels of Samuel Beckett 1964, Samuel Beckett's Art 1967, A Critical Commentary on Flaubert's Trois Contes 1968, New Directions in Literature: Critical Approaches to a Contemporary Phenomenon 1968, Samuel Beckett: Fin de Partie (co-ed. with Beryl S. Fletcher) 1970, Samuel Beckett: His Works and his Critics, An Essay in Bibliography (with Raymond Federman) 1970, Beckett: A Study of his Plays (with John Spurling) 1972, Claude Simon and Fiction Now 1975, Novel and Reader 1980, Alain Robbe-Grillet 1983, The Nouveau Roman Reader (co-ed. with John Calder)

1986, Iris Murdoch: A Primary and Secondary Bibliography (co-ed. with Cheryl Bove) 1994, Faber Critical Guide: Samuel Beckett 2000, About Beckett: The Playwright and the Work 2003; contrib. to scholarly journals, newspapers and periodicals. *Honours:* Scott Moncrieff Prize 1990. *Address:* University of Kent, Canterbury, CT2 7NF, England (office). *Telephone:* (1227) 827121 (office). *Fax:* (1227) 823641 (office). *E-mail:* jwjf@kent.ac.uk (office). *Website:* www.societyofauthors.net/profiles/writers/john-fletcher (office).

FLETCHER, Susan; British novelist; b. 1979, Birmingham, England. *Education:* Univ. of East Anglia. *Publications include:* Eve Green (novel) (Whitbread First Novel Award 2004, Betty Trask Prize 2005) 2004, Oystercatchers 2007, Corrag (also published as Witch Light 2011) 2010. *Literary Agent:* c/o Curtis Brown Group Ltd, Haymarket House, 28–29 Haymarket, London, SW1Y 4SP, England. *Telephone:* (20) 7393-4400. *Fax:* (20) 7393-4401. *E-mail:* info@curtisbrown.co.uk. *Website:* www.curtisbrown.co.uk.

FLETT, Kathryn Alexandra; British journalist; b. 1 April 1964, Herts., England; d. of Douglas J. Flett and Patricia Jenkins; two s. *Education:* Notting Hill and Ealing High School, Hammersmith and West London Coll., King's Coll., London. *Career:* staff writer, I-D magazine 1985–87; Fashion Ed., Features Ed. The Face magazine 1987–89; freelance contrib. to many int. publs including The Times, The Sunday Times, The Observer, The Guardian, The Face, Arena, Elle, Harpers Bazaar, etc. 1989–92; Contributing Ed., Arena Magazine 1991–92, Ed. 1992–95; Ed. Arena Homme Plus 1993–95; columnist and TV critic, The Observer 1994–2009, Assoc. Ed., Observer Life 1995–98; columnist She magazine 2010–11. *Publication:* The Heart-Shaped Bullet 1999. *Literary Agent:* c/o Jonny Geller, Curtis Brown Group Limited, Haymarket House, 28–29 Haymarket, London, SW1 4SP, England. *Telephone:* (20) 7393-4419. *E-mail:* gelleroffice@curtisbrown.co.uk. *Website:* www.curtisbrown.co.uk.

FLINT, James; British writer; b. 1968, Stratford-upon-Avon, Warwicks., England. *Education:* Univ. of East Anglia. *Career:* fmr Ed., Wired UK and mute magazines, journalist for Daily Telegraph; currently Ed., weekly world edn of The Telegraph newspaper and its online edn. *Publications include:* novels: The Nuclear Train (short story), Mute 2 1995, Habitus 1998, 52 Ways to Magic America (Amazon.co.uk Bursary Award 2000) 2002, The Book of Ash 2004, Soft Apocalypse: Twelve Tales from the Turn of the Millennium 2004; contrib. of short stories to collections, and to the Daily Telegraph and various magazines. *Website:* www.jamesflint.net.

FLINT, John (see Wells, Peter Frederick)

FLOOD, Josephine Mary, BA (Cantab.), MA, PhD, FRGS, FAHA; Australian (b. British) archaeologist and writer; *Adjunct Research Fellow, Centre for Archaeological Research, Australian National University*; b. (Josephine Mary Scarr), 25 July 1936, Yorks., England; d. of Philip Lowther and Mary Scarr; m. 1st Philip Flood 1964 (divorced); m. 2nd Nigel Peacock 1991; two s. one d. *Education:* Lowther Coll., Abergele, Girton Coll., Cambridge, UK and Australian Nat. Univ. *Career:* leader of first British women's Himalayan expedition 1961; Lecturer in Classical Archaeology, ANU 1963–64; Dir Aboriginal Heritage Section, Australian Heritage Comm. 1978–91; Prin. Investigator, Earthwatch (archaeology and rock art project in Qld and Northern Territory) 1981–82, 1988–92; researcher and writer 1991–; Adjunct Research Fellow, Centre for Archaeological Research, ANU 2011–. *Publications include:* Four Miles High 1966, The Moth Hunters 1980, Archaeology of the Dreamtime 1983 (seventh edn 2010), The Riches of Ancient Australia: An Indispensable Guide For Exploring Prehistoric Australia 1990, Rock Art of the Dreamtime 1997, The Original Australians 2006. *Honours:* Centenary Medal 2003. *Address:* 19 Chauvel Crescent, Tuross Head, NSW 2537, Australia (home). *E-mail:* josephinemflood@aol.com (home).

FLORA, Joseph Martin, BA, MA, PhD; American academic, writer and editor; *Atlanta Professor of Southern Culture, University of North Carolina*; b. 9 Feb. 1934, Toledo, Ohio; m. Glenda Christine Flora 1959; four s. *Education:* Univ. of Michigan. *Career:* Teaching Fellow to Instructor, Univ. of Michigan 1957–62; Instructor, Univ. of North Carolina, Chapel Hill 1962–64, Asst Prof. 1964–66, Assoc. Prof. 1966–77, Prof. 1977–2001, Atlanta Prof. of Southern Culture 2001–; Visiting Prof., Univ. of New Mexico 1976, 1996; Sr Ed. American Literature 1915–1945, Twayne Publrs 1989–; mem. American Literature Asscn, James Branch Cabell Soc., Hemingway Soc., Modern Language Asscn (MLA), Soc. for the Study of Southern Literature, South Atlantic MLA (Pres. 1998–99), Thomas Wolfe Soc. (Pres. 1995–97), Western Literature Asscn (Pres. 1992). *Publications include:* Vardis Fisher 1965, William Ernest Henley 1970, Frederick Manfred 1974, Southern Writers: A Biographical Dictionary (co-ed. with Robert Bain and Louis D. Rubin Jr) 1979, Hemingway's Nick Adams 1982, The English Short Story 1880–1945: A Critical History (ed.) 1985, Fifty Southern Writers after 1900 (co-ed. with Robert Bain) 1987, Fifty Southern Writers Before 1900 (co-ed. with Robert Bain) 1987, Ernest Hemingway: A Study of the Short Fiction 1989, Contemporary Fiction Writers of the South (co-ed. with Robert Bain) 1993, Contemporary Poets, Dramatists, Essayists, and Novelists of the South (co-ed. with Robert Bain) 1994, Rediscovering Vardis Fisher: Centennial Essays 2000, The Companion to Southern Literature (co-ed. with Lucinda MacKethan), Southern Writers (co-ed. with Amber Vogel) 2006, Reading Hemingway's Men Without Women 2008; contrib. to books and journals. *Honours:* Kenan Research Award 1978, Mayflower Award, North Carolina Literary and Historical Asscn 1982, Jules and Frances Landry Award 2006. *Address:* 505 Caswell Road, Chapel Hill, NC 27514, USA (home). *Telephone:* (919) 962-2503 (office); (919) 942-4902 (home). *Fax:* (919) 662-3520 (office). *E-mail:* jflora@email.unc.edu (office).

FLORENCE, Peter Kenrick, MBE, MA; British actor and festival director; *Director, Hay Festival*; b. 4 Oct. 1964, s. of Norman Florence; m. Becky Shaw; four s. *Education:* Ipswich School, Jesus Coll., Cambridge, Univ. of Paris IV, La Sorbonne. *Career:* Co-founder and Dir Hay Festivals Group, running events in Wales, Colombia, Mexico, USA, Spain, Canada, Ireland, Lebanon, India, Bangladesh, Kenya and the Maldives; Fellow, Hereford Coll. of Arts, Royal Welsh Coll. of Music and Drama, British-American Project; Creative Fellow, Univ. of Bangor. *Publications:* Oxtales (co-ed.) 2008, Oxtravels (co-ed.) 2010. *Honours:* Dr hc (Open Univ., Univ. of Glamorgan); Colombiano de Corazón, Pres. of Columbia. *Address:* Hay Festival, The Drill Hall, 25 Lion Street, Hay-on-Wye, HR3 5AD, England (office). *Telephone:* (1497) 822620 (office). *Fax:* (1497) 821066 (office). *E-mail:* peter@hayfestival.org (office). *Website:* www.hayfestival.org (office).

FLUSFEDER, David, BA, MA; American/British writer; b. 6 Nov. 1960, Summit, NJ; m. Susan Swift 1990; one s. one d. *Education:* Univs of Sussex and East Anglia. *Career:* fmr TV critic for The Times, poker columnist for the Sunday Telegraph; teacher of creative writing, Univ. of East Anglia, Brunel Univ., Univ. of East London, Pentonville Prison; currently lectures at Univ. of Kent. *Publications include:* novels: Man Kills Woman 1993, Like Plastic 1996, Morocco 2000, The Gift 2003, The Pagan House 2007, A Film by Spencer Ludwig 2010; contribs to short stories in anthologies, including New Writing 8, Fatherhood, The Agony and the Ecstasy; magazines and newspapers include Arena, Esquire, Jewish Quarterly, The Times, Guardian, TLS, GQ, Frankfurter Allgemeine Zeitung, Literaturen, Jewish Chronicle, Daily Telegraph. *Honours:* Encore Award 1997. *Address:* c/o Fourth Estate, Harper Collins Publishers, 77–85 Fulham Palace Road, London, W6 8JB, England. *Website:* www.davidflusfeder.co.uk.

FLYNN, Robert Lopez, MA; American academic and writer; b. 12 April 1932, Chillicothe, Tex.; m. Jean Sorrels 1953; two d. *Education:* Baylor Univ., Waco, Texas. *Career:* Asst Prof., Baylor Univ., Waco, Tex. 1959–63; Novelist-in-Residence, Trinity Univ., San Antonio, Tex. 1963–2001, Prof. Emer. *Plays:* dramatic adaptation of Faulkner's As I Lay Dying, also produced as Journey to Jefferson. *Publications include:* North to Yesterday 1967, In the House of the Lord 1969, The Sounds of Rescue, The Signs of Hope 1970, Seasonal Rain and Other Stories 1986, Wanderer Springs (Spur Award) 1987, A Personal War in Vietnam 1989, When I Was Just Your Age 1992, The Last Klick 1994, Living with the Hyenas 1996, The Devil's Tiger 2000, Tie-Fast Country 2001, Growing Up a Sullen Baptist, and Other Lies 2001, Paul Baker and the Integration of Abilities (co-ed.) 2003, Slouching Toward Zion and More Lies 2004, Burying the Farm: A Memoir of Chillicothe, Texas 2008, Echoes of Glory 2009, Jade: Outlaw 2010, Jade: The Law 2011. *Honours:* Distinguished Achievement Award 1998, Spur Award, Western Writers of America 2010. *Address:* 101 Cliffside Drive, San Antonio, TX 78231, USA (home). *Telephone:* (210) 492-1127 (home). *E-mail:* rlflynn@earthlink.net (home). *Website:* www.robert-flynn.net.

FO, Dario; Italian playwright, clown, actor and painter; b. 24 March 1926, San Giano; m. Franca Rame 1954; one c. *Education:* Acad. of Fine Arts, Milan. *Career:* comedian, Teatro di Rivista; co-founder theatre groups, Fo-Rame Co. 1957–68, Associazione Nuova Scena 1968–69, Collettivo Teatrale la Comune 1970–; cand. for Mayor of Milan 2006. *Film scripts:* Lo Svitato 1956, Musica per vecchi animali 1989. *Plays include:* Il dito nell'occhio (with Franco Parenti and Giustino Durano) 1953, I sani da legare (with Parenti and Durano) 1954, Ladri, manichini e donne nude 1957, Comica finale 1958, Gli arcangeli non giocano a flipper 1959, La storia vera di Piero d'Angera, che alla crociata non c'era 1960, Aveva due pistole con gli occhi bianchi e neri 1960, Chi ruba un piede è fortunato in amore 1961, Isabella, tre caravelle e un cacciaballe 1963, Settimo: ruba un po' meno 1964, La colpa è sempre del diavolo 1965, La signora è da buttare 1967, Grande pantomima per pupazzi piccoli, grandi e medi 1968, L'operaio conosce 300 parole, il padrone 1000, per questo lui è il padrone 1969, Legami pure, tanto spacco tutto lo stesso 1969, Il funeral e del padrone 1969, Mistero buffo 1969, Morte accidentale di un anarchico 1970, Fedayin 1971, Basta con i fascisti 1973, Ci ragiono e canto N.3 1973, Guerra di popolo in Cile 1973, Non si paga, non si paga! 1974, Fanfani rapito 1975, La marijuana della mamma è la più bella 1975, Tutta casa, letto e chiesa 1977, La tragedia di Aldo Moro 1979, Storia della tigre e altre storie 1979, Una madre (with Franca Rame) 1981, Clacson, trombette e pernacchi 1981, L'Opera dello sghignazzo 1982, Il fabulazzo osceno 1982, Coppia aperta 1982, Patapunfete 1983, Quasi per caso una donna: Elisabetta 1983, Dio li fa poi li accoppa 1983, Lisistrata romana 1983, Hellequin, Harlekin, Arlecchino 1985, Diario di Eva 1985, Parti femminili (with Franca Rame) 1986, Il ratto della Francesca 1986, La rava e la fava (aka La parte del leone) 1987, Lettera dalla Cina 1989, Il braccato 1989, Il papa e la strega 1989, Zitti! Stiamo precipitando! 1990, Johan Padan a la descoverta de le Americhe 1991, Parliamo di donne (two one-act pieces, L'Eroina and Grassa è bello) 1991, Settimo: ruba un po' meno! n. 2 1992, Dario Fo incontra Ruzzante 1993, Mamma! I sanculotti! 1993, Un palcoscenico per le donne 1994, Sesso? Grazie, tanto per gradire! 1994, Bibbia dei villani 1996, Il diavolo con le zinne 1996, Lu Santo Jullare Francesco 1999, My First Seven Years (Plus a Few More) (memoir) 2005, L'Anomalo Bicefalo (on the Premier Silvio Berlusconi) 2006. *Radio:* Poer Nano 1950, Chicchirichì, Cocoricò, Ragazzi in Gamba, Non si vive di solo pane 1951. *Television:* Canzonissima 1962, Il teatro di Dario Fo 1976, Buona sera con Franca Rame 1980, Trasmissione forzata 1987. *Honours:* Hon. DLitt (Westminster) 1997;

Dr hc (Univ. La Sapienza, Rome) 2006; Univ. of Copenhagen Sonning Prize 1981, Associazione Torre Nat. Award Against Violence and the Camorra 1986, Obie Prize 1986, Campione d'Italia Agro Dolce Prize 1987, Nobel Prize for Literature 1997. *Address:* C. So di Porta Romana 132, 20122 Milan, Italy (office). *Telephone:* (02) 58430506 (office). *E-mail:* francarame@iol.it (office). *Website:* www.francarame.it (office).

FOER, Jonathan Safran; American writer; b. 1977, Washington, DC; m. Nicole Krauss; two c. *Education:* Princeton Univ. *Career:* Visiting Prof. of Fiction, Yale Univ. 2008; currently Prof., Grad. Creative Writing Program, New York Univ. *Publications include:* A Convergence of Birds: Original Fiction and Poetry Inspired by the Work of Joseph Cornell (ed.) 2001, 2006, Everything is Illuminated (novel) (Nat. Jewish Book Award, Guardian First Book Award) 2002, Amelia Bedelia, Bookworm 2003, I'm OK 2004, The Future Dictionary of America (with Dave Eggers and Nicole Krauss) 2004, Extremely Loud and Incredibly Close 2005, Eating Animals (non-fiction) 2009, Tree of Codes 2010; contrib. to Paris Review, Conjunctions, New Yorker, New York Times. *Honours:* William Saroyan Int. Prize, Harold U. Ribalow Prize, Corine Int. Book Award, Prix Amphi, V&A Museum Illustration Award, Zoetrope: All Story Fiction Prize 2000, New York Public Library's Young Lions Fiction Award 2003. *Literary Agent:* Araqi Inc., 143 West 27th Street, New York, NY 10001, USA. *Telephone:* (212) 675-8353 (office). *E-mail:* queries@araqi.net (office).

FOERSTER, Richard Alfons, BA, MA; American editor, writer and poet; b. 29 Oct. 1949, New York, NY; s. of Alfons Foerster and Elizabeth Foerster; m. Valerie Elizabeth Malinowski 1972 (divorced 1985). *Education:* Fordham Univ., Univ. of Virginia, Manhattanville Coll. *Career:* Asst Ed., Clarence L. Barnhart Inc. 1973–75; Ed., Prentice Hall Inc. 1976–78; Assoc. Ed. 1978–94, Ed. 1994–2001, Chelsea Magazine; Hobart City Int. Writer-in-Residence 2002; Ed. Chautauqua Literary Journal 2003–07; mem. Acad. of American Poets, Maine Writers and Publrs Alliance, Poetry Soc. of America, Soc. for the Arts, Religion and Contemporary Culture, PEN, Poets' Prize Cttee, Book Critics' Circle. *Publications include:* Transfigured Nights 1990, Sudden Harbor 1992, Patterns of Descent 1993, Trillium 1998, Double Going 2002, The Burning of Troy 2006, Penetralia 2011; contrib. to Best American Poetry, Boulevard, Epoch, Kenyon Review, Nation, New Criterion, New Letters, Pleiades, Poetry, Shenandoah, Southern Review, Southwest Review, Texas Review, Tri-Quarterly. *Honours:* Discovery/The Nation Award 1985, Bess Hokin Prize 1992, Hawthornden Fellow 1993, Creative Writing Fellowship, Nat. Endowment for the Arts 1995, 2011, Individual Artist Fellowship, Maine Arts Comm. 1997, Amy Lowell Poetry Travelling Scholarship 2000–01, Maine Literary Book Award for Poetry 2007, 2011. *Address:* 31 River Road, Cape Neddick, ME 03902, USA (office).

FOGEL, Robert William, PhD, FAAS; American historian, academic, economist and biodemographer; *Charles R. Walgreen Distinguished Service Professor of American Institutions, Booth School of Business, University of Chicago*; b. 1 July 1926, New York, NY; s. of Harry Gregory and Elizabeth (Mitnik) Fogel; m. Enid Cassandra Morgan 1949 (deceased); two s. *Education:* Cornell, Columbia, Cambridge, Harvard and Johns Hopkins Univs. *Career:* Instructor, Johns Hopkins Univ. 1958–59; Asst Prof., Univ. of Rochester 1960–64; Assoc. Prof., Univ. of Chicago 1964–65, Prof. of Economics 1965–75, Prof. of Economics and History 1970–75; Prof., Harvard Univ. 1975–81; Charles R. Walgreen Distinguished Service Prof. of American Insts, Booth School of Business, Univ. of Chicago 1981–, Dir Center for Population Econs 1981–; Chair. History Advisory Cttee of the Math. Social Science Bd 1965–72; Pres. Econ. History Asscn 1977–78; Social Science History Asscn 1980–81; American Econ. Asscn 1998; Nat. Bureau of Econ. Research Assoc.; Fellow Econ. Soc., American Acad. of Arts and Sciences, NAS, Royal Historical Soc., AAAS, American Philosophical Soc. *Publications:* The Union Pacific Railroad: A Case in Premature Enterprise 1960, Railroads and American History (co-author) 1971, The Dimensions of Quantitative Research in History (co-author) 1972, Time on the Cross: The Economics of American Negro Slavery (with S. L. Engerman) 1974, Ten Lectures on the New Economic History 1977, Which Road to the Past?: Two Views of History (with G. R. Elton) 1983, Without Consent or Contract: The Rise and Fall of American Slavery (co-author), Vol. I 1989, Vols II–IV 1992, The Political Realignment of the 1850s: A Socio-economic Analysis 1996, The Fourth Great Awakening and the Future of Egalitarianism 2000, The Slavery Debates 1952–1990: a retrospective 2003, The Escape from Hunger and Premature Death 1700–2100: Europe, America and the Third World 2004, The Changing Body: Health, Nutrition, and Human Development in the Western World since 1700 (co-author) 2011; contribs to numerous books and scholarly journals. *Honours:* several hon. degrees; Arthur H. Cole Prize 1968, Schumpeter Prize 1971, Bancroft Prize in American History 1975, Gustavus Myers Prize 1990, Nobel Prize in Econs ((with Douglass North) 1993, Distinguished Alumni Award, Johns Hopkins Univ. 2000, Simon Kuznets Medal, Simon Kuznets Inst. for Development and Self-Organization 2011. *Address:* Booth School of Business, University of Chicago, 5807 South Woodlawn Avenue, Chicago, IL 60637 (office); 5321 S University Avenue, Chicago, IL 60615, USA (home). *Telephone:* (773) 702-7709 (office). *Fax:* (773) 702-2901 (office). *E-mail:* robert.fogel@chicagobooth.edu (office); rwf@cpe.uchicago.edu (office). *Website:* www.uchicago.edu (office).

FOIS, Marcello; Italian novelist and playwright; b. 1960, Nuoro, Sardinia; m.; two c. *Education:* Univ. of Bologna. *Plays include:* L'ascesa degli angeli ribelli, Di profilo, Stazione, Terra di nessuno, Cinque favole sui bambini. *Film screenplays include:* Ilaria Alpi – Il più crudele dei giorni 2002, Certi bambini 2004. *Television screenplays:* Distretto di Polizia (series) 2000–. *Publications include:* Ferro Recente 1992, Picta (Premio Calvino) 1992, Meglio Morti 1993, Falso gotico nuorese 1993, Il silenzio abitato delle case 1996, Gente del libro 1996, Sheol 1997, Nulla (Premio Dessi) 1997, Sempre caro (Premio Scerbanenco) 1998, Radiofavole 1998, Gap 1999, Sangue dal cielo 1999, Sola andata 1999, Cerimonia 2000, Compagnie Difficili 2000, Dura madre 2001, Piccole storie nere 2002, L'altro mondo 2002, Materiali 2002, Ilaria Alpi. Il più crudele dei giorni 2003, Tamburini. Cantata per voce sola 2004, Memoria del Vuoto (Premio Grinzane Cavour) 2006, L'ultima volta che sono rinato 2006, In Sardegna non c'è il mare 2008, Stirpe 2009. *Address:* c/o Giulio Einaudi Editore, via Biancamano 2, 10121 Turin, Italy. *Website:* www.einaudi.it.

FOLEY, John (Jack) Wayne Harold, BA, MA; American poet, writer, editor and broadcaster; b. 9 Aug. 1940, Neptune, NJ; m. Adelle Joan Abramowitz 1961; one s. *Education:* Cornell Univ., Univ. of California, Berkeley. *Career:* Host, Exec. Producer in charge of Poetry Programme, KPFA-FM, Berkeley, CA 1988–; Guest Ed., Poetry: San Francisco 1988–89; Ed.-in-Chief, Poetry USA, Oakland, CA 1990–95; Contributing Ed., Poetry Flash 1992–; Resident Artist, Djerassi Program 1994; performs poetry with wife; mem. Modern Language Asscn, Poets and Writers, Nat. Poetry Asscn, PEN, Oakland, Calif., Programme Dir 1990–97. *Publications include:* poetry: Letters/Lights – Words for Adelle 1987, Gershwin 1991, Adrift 1993, Exiles 1996, Bridget 1997, New Poetry from California: Dead/Requiem (with Ivan Argüelles) 1998, Some Songs by Georges Brassens (trans.) 2002, Greatest Hits 1974–2003 2004, Fennel in the Rain (with Adelle Foley) 2007; prose: Inciting Big Joy 1993, O Her Blackness Sparkles! – The Life and Times of the Batman Art Gallery, San Francisco, 1960–63 1995, O Powerful Western Star (criticism) 2000, Foley's Books (criticism) 2000, The 'Fallen Western Star' Wars (criticism, ed.) 2001, The Dancer & the Dance: A Book of Distinctions 2008; contribs to journals, including: Barque, Beloit Poetry Journal, Berkeley Poetry Review, Blue Beetle Press Magazine, Cafe Review, The Experioddicist, Exquisite Corpse, Galley Sail Review, Inkblot, MaLLife, Malthus, Meat Epoch, New York Quarterly, NRG, Outre, Talisman, Tight, Transmog, Wet Motorcycle, ELH, Heaven Bone, Konch, Linden Lane Magazine, Lower Limit Speech, Multicultural Review, Open Letter, Poetry Flash, Prosodia, Seattle Literary Quarterly, W'Orcs, Bright Lights, Journal of Popular Film, Artweek, East Bay Express, Poetry Flash; anthologies, including: Poly: New Speculative Writing, The Love Project, Online column (criticism) at The Alsop Review (www.alsopreview.com). *Honours:* Full Scholarship to Cornell Univ. 1958–63, Woodrow Wilson Fellowship, Univ. of California 1963–65, Yang Poetry Prize, Univ. of California, Berkeley 1971, Poetry Grantee, Oakland Arts Council 1992–95, The Artists Embassy Literary/Cultural Award 1998–2000. *Address:* 2569 Maxwell Avenue, Oakland, CA 94601-5521, USA (home). *Telephone:* (510) 532-3737 (home). *E-mail:* jasfoley@aol.com (home).

FOLEY, Johanna (Jo) Mary, BA; British magazine editor; b. 8 Dec. 1945, Co. Kerry, Ireland; d. of the late John Foley and Mary Foley; m. Desmond Francis Conor Quigley 1973. *Education:* St Joseph's Convent, Kenilworth and Manchester Univ. *Career:* reporter, Birmingham Post 1970; Beauty Ed., Woman's Own 1972–73, Sr Asst Ed. 1978; Launch Ed., Successful Slimming 1976; Woman's Ed., The Sun 1980; Ed. Woman 1982, Observer Magazine 1986, Options 1988–91; Exec. Ed. The Times 1984–85; freelance journalist and media consultant 1991–. *Honours:* Magazine Ed. of the Year 1983.

FOLEY, (Mary) Louise Munro, BA; American novelist; b. 22 Oct. 1933, Toronto, Ont., Canada; m. Donald J. Foley 1957; two s. *Education:* Univ. of Western Ontario, Ryerson Inst. of Tech., California State Univ., Sacramento. *Career:* columnist, News-Argus, Goldsboro, NC 1971–73; Ed. of Publications, Inst. for Human Service Man., California State Univ., Sacramento 1975–80; mem. Authors' Guild, California Writers Club, Nat. League of American Pen Women, Soc. of Children's Book Writers and Illustrators, Novelists Inc. *Publications include:* The Caper Club 1969, No Talking 1970, Sammy's Sister 1970, A Job for Joey 1970, Somebody Stole Second 1972, Stand Close to the Door (ed.) 1976, Tackle 22 1978, Women in Skilled Labor (ed.) 1980, The Train of Terror 1982, The Sinister Studies of KESP-TV 1983, The Lost Tribe 1983, The Mystery of the Highland Crest 1984, The Mystery of Echo Lodge 1985, Danger at Anchor Mine 1985, The Mardi Gras Mystery 1987, Mystery of the Sacred Stones 1988, Australia! Find the Flying Foxes 1988, The Cobra Connection 1990, Ghost Train 1991, Poison! Said the Cat 1992, Blood! Said the Cat 1992, Thief! Said the Cat 1992, In Search of the Hidden Statue 1993, Moving Target 1993, Stolen Affections 1995, Running Into Trouble 1996, The Vampire Cat Series: My Substitute Teacher's Gone Batty 1996, The Bird-Brained Fiasco 1996, The Phoney Baloney Professor 1996, The Cat-Nap Cat-Astrophe 1997. *Address:* 5010 Jennings Way, Sacramento, CA 95819-1522, USA (home).

FOLLETT, Kenneth (Ken) Martin, BA; British writer; b. 5 June 1949, Cardiff, Wales; s. of Martin D. Follett and Veenie Evans; m. 1st Mary Elson 1968 (divorced 1985); one s. one d.; m. 2nd Barbara Broer 1985; one step-s. two step-d. *Education:* Univ. Coll. London. *Career:* trainee reporter, South Wales Echo, Cardiff 1970–73; reporter, London Evening News 1973–74; Editorial Dir Everest Books, London 1974–76, Deputy Man. Dir 1976–77; full-time writer 1977–; Fellow, Univ. Coll. London 1994; Chair. Nat. Year of Reading 1998–99, Advisory Cttee, Reading is Fundamental UK 2003–07; Pres. Dyslexia Inst. 1998–2009; Vice-Pres. Stevenage Borough Football Club 2000–, Stevenage Community Trust 2002–; Chair. Govs, Roebuck Primary School and Nursery 2001–08; mem. Council, Nat. Literary Trust 1996–; Bd mem. Nat. Acad. of

Writing 2003–10; Dir, Stevenage Leisure Ltd 1999–2004; Patron, Stevenage Home-Start 2000–. *Publications:* The Shakeout 1975, The Bear Raid 1976, The Modigliani Scandal 1976, The Power Twins and the Worm Puzzle 1976, The Secret of Kellerman's Studio 1976, Paper Money 1977, Eye of the Needle (MWA Edgar Award 1979) 1978, Triple 1979, The Key to Rebecca 1980, The Man from St Petersburg 1982, On Wings of Eagles 1983, Lie Down with Lions 1986, The Pillars of the Earth 1989, Night Over Water 1991, A Dangerous Fortune 1993, A Place Called Freedom 1995, The Third Twin 1996, The Hammer of Eden 1998, Code to Zero 2000, Jackdaws (Corine Readers' Award, Germany 2003) 2001, Hornet Flight 2003, Whiteout 2004, World Without End 2007, Fall of Giants 2010; screenplays; contrib. to book reviews and essays. *Address:* Broadlands House, Primett Road, Stevenage, Herts., SG1 3EE, England (office). *Telephone:* (1438) 810400 (office). *Fax:* (1438) 810444 (office). *E-mail:* ken@ken-follett.com (office). *Website:* www.ken-follett.com.

FONER, Eric, BA, PhD; American academic and writer; *Professor of History, Columbia University*; b. 7 Feb. 1943, New York, NY; m. Lynn Garafola 1980; one d. *Education:* Columbia Coll., Oriel Coll., Oxford, UK, Columbia Univ., New York. *Career:* Prof., City Coll. and Grad. School and Univ. Center, CUNY 1973–82; Pitt Prof. of American History and Institutions, Univ. of Cambridge, UK 1980–81; Prof., Columbia Univ. 1982–88, DeWitt Clinton Prof. of History 1988–; Fulbright Prof. of American History, Moscow State Univ. 1990; Harmsworth Prof. of American History, Univ. of Oxford 1993–94; Corresp. Fellow, British Acad.; mem. American Acad. of Arts and Sciences, Org. of American Historians (Pres. 1993–94), American Historical Asscn (Pres. 2000), Soc. of American Historians (Pres. 2007). *Publications include:* Free Soil, Free Labor, Free Men: The Ideology of the Republican Party Before the Civil War 1970, Nat Turner 1971, Tom Paine and Revolutionary America 1976, Politics and Ideology in the Age of the Civil War 1980, Nothing But Freedom: Emancipation and its Legacy 1983, Reconstruction: America's Unfinished Revolution 1863–1877 1988, A Short History of Reconstruction 1990, A House Divided: America in the Age of Lincoln (with Olivia Mahoney) 1990, Freedom's Lawmakers: A Directory of Black Officeholders During Reconstruction 1993, Thomas Paine 1995, America's Reconstruction: People and Politics After the Civil War (with Olivia Mahoney) 1995, The Story of American Freedom 1998, Who Owns History? 2002, Give Me Liberty!: An American History 2004, Forever Free 2005, Our Lincoln 2008, The Fiery Trial: Abraham Lincoln and American Slavery (Pulitzer Prize for History 2011) 2010; contrib. to scholarly journals and periodicals. *Honours:* Order of Lincoln 2008; ACLS Fellowship 1972–73, Guggenheim Fellowship 1975–76, Nat. Endowment for the Humanities Sr Fellowships 1982–83, 1996–97, Los Angeles Times Book Award for History 1989, Bancroft Prize 1989, Parkman Prize 1989, Lionel Trilling Award 1989, Owsley Prize 1989, American Historical Asscn James Harvey Robinson Prize 1991, New York Public Library Literary Lion 1994, New York Council for the Humanities Scholar of the Year Award 1995. *Address:* 606 W 116th Street, New York, NY 10027, USA (office). *Telephone:* (212) 854-5253 (office). *Fax:* (212) 961-1903 (office). *E-mail:* ef17@columbia.edu (office). *Website:* www.ericfoner.com.

FONSECA, Rubem; Brazilian writer and screenwriter; b. 11 May 1925, Juiz de Fora, Minas Gerais; m. Théa Maud (deceased 1996); three c. *Education:* Escola de Policia, Rio de Janeiro, Fundação Getúlio Vargas, New York Univ. *Career:* started career as cop, apptd Police Commr São Cristóvão (RJ) 1952. *Television:* Mandrake 1983, 2005, Agosto 1993,. *Films:* Lúcia McCartney, Uma Garota de Programa 1971, Relatório de Um Homem Casado 1974, A Extorsão 1975, Stelinha 1990, A Grande Arte 1991, Bufo & Spallanzani 2001, The Man of the Year 2003, O Caso Morel 2006, El cobrador: In God We Trust 2006. *Publications:* Os prisioneiros 1963, A coleira do cão 1965, Lucía McCartney 1967, O caso Morel 1973, O homen de fevereiro ou março 1973, Feliz ano novo 1975, O cobrador (Prêmio Estácio de Sá) 1979, A grande arte (Prêmio Goethe, Prêmio Jabuti) 1983, Buffo & Spallanzani 1986, Vastas emoções e pensamentos imperfeitos (Prêmio Pedro Nava) 1988, Agosto 1990, Romance negro e outras histórias 1992, Contos reunidos 1994, O selvagem da ópera 1994, O buraco na parede (Prêmio Jabuti) 1995, Romance negro, Felis ano novo e outras histórias 1996, Histórias de amor 1997, E do meio do mundo prostitute só amores guardei ao meu charuto (Prêmio Machado de Assis) 1997, Confraria dos espadas (Prêmio Eça de Queiroz) 1998, O doente Molière (Prêmio de melhor romance do ano, Associação Paulista de Críticos de Arte) 2000, Secreções, excreções, desatinos 2001, Pequenas criaturas 2002, Diário de um fescenino 2003, 64 contos de Rubem Fonseca 2004, Ela e outras mulheres 2006, Los mejores relatos 2007, O Seminarista 2009, José 2011, Axilas e Outras Histórias Indecorosas 2011; contrib. to numerous anthologies. *Honours:* Premio Camões 2003, Premio Juan Rulfo 2003. *Address:* Companhia das Letras, Rua Bandeira Paulista 702 cj. 32, 04532-002 São Paulo, SP, Brazil. *Telephone:* (11) 3707-3500. *Fax:* (11) 3707-3501. *Website:* www.ciadasletras .com.br.

FONTAINE, André; French journalist; b. 30 March 1921, Paris; s. of Georges Fontaine and Blanche Rochon-Duvigneaud; m. Isabelle Cavaillé 1943; two s. one d. *Education:* Coll. Ste. Marie de Monceau, Paris, Sorbonne and Faculty of Law, Paris Univ. *Career:* journalist 1946–; joined Le Monde 1947, Foreign Ed. 1951–69, Chief Ed. 1969–85, Ed.-in-Chief and Dir 1985–91, Consultant to Dir 1991–; mem. Bd French Inst. of Int. Relations –1992, Bank Indosuez 1983–85; Chair. Group on Int. Strategy for the Ninth French Plan 1982; Vice-Chair. Franco-British Council (French section) 1999–2002. *Publications:* L'alliance atlantique à l'heure du dégel 1960, History of the Cold War (two vols) 1965, 1967, La guerre civile froide 1969, Le dernier quart du siècle 1976, La France au bois dormant 1978, Un seul lit pour deux rêves 1981, Sortir de l'hexagonie (with others) 1984, L'un sans l'autre 1991, Après eux le déluge 1995, La tache rouge 2004. *Honours:* Atlas Int. Ed. of the Year 1976. *Address:* Le Monde, 80 boulevard Auguste-Blanqui, 75707 Paris Cedex 13, France (office). *Telephone:* 1-57-28-20-00 (office). *Fax:* 1-57-28-21-21 (office). *E-mail:* a.fontaine@lemonde .fr (office). *Website:* www.lemonde.fr (office).

FONTENEAU, Pascale; Belgian writer; b. 1963, Fougères, Ille-et-Vilaine. *Education:* Université libre de Bruxelles. *Career:* broadcast first story Chronique des polars on campus radio, Université libre de Bruxelles; works for Passa Porta (literary asscn); contrib. to Le Monde newspaper, Paris 2003–. *Publications include:* Confidences sur l'escalier 1992, Etats de lame 1993, Les Fils perdus de Sylvie Derijke 1995, Les Damnés de l'artère 1996, Otto 1997, La Puissance du désordre 1997, Curieux Sentiments 2000, La Vanité des pions 2000, Où est passé René (with Didier Lange) 2003, Trop c'est Trop 2003, TGV 2003, Crois-moi 2005, Jour de gloire 2006, Contretemps 2007, 1275 Ares 2008, Propriétés privées 2010, Hasbeen 2010. *Address:* c/o Les Éditions du Masque, 17 rue Jacob, 75006 Paris, France.

FORAN, Charles William, BA, MA; Canadian writer; b. 2 Aug. 1960, North York, Ont.; m. Mary Foran; two d. *Education:* Univ. of Toronto, Univ. Coll., Dublin, Ireland. *Career:* librarian, bus driver, univ. lecturer; full-time author since 1990; currently Vice-Pres. PEN Canada. *Publications include:* Coming Attractions (five short stories) 1987, Sketches in Winter (non-fiction) 1992, Kitchen Music (novel) 1994, The Last House of Ulster (non-fiction) 1995, Butterfly Lovers (novel) 1996, The Story of My Life (So Far) (non-fiction) 1998, House on Fire (novel) 2001, Carolan's Farewell (novel) 2005, Join the Revolution, Comrade (essays) 2008, Mordecai: The Life and Times (biog.) 2010, Maurice Richard (biog.) 2011; contributing reviewer to Globe and Mail. *Honours:* QSpell Award, Fiction 1990, 1998, Non-Fiction 1995. *Address:* 298 Boswell Avenue, Peterborough, ON K9J 5G3, Canada (home). *E-mail:* charlie@charlesforan.com (office). *Website:* www.charlesforan.com.

FORBES, Bryan, CBE; British film industry executive, film director, screenwriter and novelist; b. 22 July 1926, Stratford, London; m. Nanette Newman 1955; two d. *Education:* West Ham Secondary School, RADA. *Career:* first stage appearance 1942; served in Intelligence Corps 1944–48; entered films as actor 1948; Head of Production, Assoc. British Picture Corpn 1969–71, subsequently named EMI Film Productions Ltd; mem. Gen. Advisory Council of BBC 1966–69, Experimental Film Bd of British Film Acad.; Govt Nominee BBC Schools Broadcasting Council 1972; mem. Beatrix Potter Soc. (Pres. 1982–96, now patron), Nat. Youth Theatre (Pres. 1984–2005), Writers Guild of GB (Pres. 1988–91); Founder and fmr Dir Capital Radio Ltd. *Films:* wrote and co-produced The Angry Silence (British Film Acad. Award) 1959; dir Whistle Down the Wind 1961; writer and dir The L-Shaped Room (UN Award) 1962, Seance on a Wet Afternoon (Best Screenplay Award) 1963, King Rat 1964; writer Only Two Can Play (Best Screenplay Award) 1964; producer and dir The Wrong Box 1965; writer, producer and dir The Whisperers 1966, Deadfall 1967, The Madwoman of Chaillot 1968, The Raging Moon (Long Ago Tomorrow in USA) 1970; dir Macbeth 1980, Killing Jessica 1986, Star Quality 1986, The Living Room 1987, One Helluva Life 2002; writer, producer and dir filmed biography of Dame Edith Evans for Yorkshire TV 1973; filmed documentary on lifestyle of Elton John for ATV 1974; wrote and dir The Slipper and the Rose 1975, Jessie (BBC) 1977, Ménage à trois (Better Late than Never in USA) 1981, The Endless Game 1989 (for Channel 4 TV); dir British segment of The Sunday Lovers 1980; dir The King in Yellow (for LWT TV) 1982, The Naked Face 1983; produced, wrote and dir International Velvet 1977. *Publications:* Truth Lies Sleeping (short stories) 1951, The Distant Laughter (novel) 1972, Notes for a Life (autobiography) 1974, The Slipper and the Rose 1976, Ned's Girl (biog. of Dame Edith Evans) 1977, International Velvet (novel) 1978, Familiar Strangers (novel, aka Stranger) 1979, That Despicable Race – A History of the British Acting Tradition 1980, The Rewrite Man (novel) 1983, The Endless Game (novel) 1986, A Song at Twilight (novel) 1989, A Divided Life (autobiography) 1992, The Twisted Playground (novel) 1993, Partly Cloudy (novel) 1995, Quicksand (novel) 1996, The Memory of All That 1999. *Honours:* Hon. DLitt (CNNA) 1987, (Sussex) 1999; many film festival prizes. *Literary Agent:* c/o Curtis Brown Ltd, Haymarket House, 28–29 Haymarket, London, SW1Y 4SP, England. *Telephone:* (20) 7393-4400. *Fax:* (20) 7393-4401. *E-mail:* info@curtisbrown.co.uk. *Website:* www .curtisbrown.co.uk.

FORBES, Calvin, MFA; American poet, writer and academic; *Professor, School of the Art Institute of Chicago*; b. 6 May 1945, Newark, NJ. *Education:* New School for Social Research, Rutgers Univ., Brown Univ. *Career:* Asst Prof. of English, Emerson Coll. 1969–73, Tufts Univ. 1973–74, 1975–77; Asst Prof. of Creative Writing, Washington Coll. 1988–89; Assoc. Prof., then Prof. and Chair. of Writing Program, School of the Art Inst. of Chicago 1991–; mem. Coll. Language Asscn, Modern Language Asscn of America. *Performance:* musical suite based on his poems, Rochester NY 2003. *Publications include:* poetry: Blue Monday 1974, From the Book of Shine 1979, The Shine Poems 2001; contrib. to many anthologies. *Honours:* Bread Loaf Writers' Conf. Fellowship 1973, Fulbright to teach at Univ. of Copenhagen, Denmark 1975–76, Yaddo Residency 1976–77, Nat. Endowment for the Arts Fellowship 1982–83, DC Comm. on the Arts Fellowship 1984, Illinois Arts Council Fellowship 1999. *Address:* School of the Art Institute of Chicago, 37 S Wabash Avenue, Chicago, IL 60603, USA (office). *E-mail:* cforbes777@msn.com (home).

FORBES, Leonie Evadne; Jamaican actress, broadcaster and playwright; b. 14 June 1937, Kingston; d. of Jonathan and Gladys Forbes; m. 1st Ludlow Galloway (divorced 1963); one s.; m. 2nd Keith Amil 1963 (divorced 1975); two d. one s.; m. 3rd Paul Harvey 1978 (divorced 1987). *Education:* Kingston Sr School, Excelsior High School, Durham Coll. and Royal Acad. of Dramatic Arts (London). *Career:* Sec. Extra Mural Dept, Univ. of West Indies 1955–60; studies and work in UK 1961–66; Announcer Jamaica Broadcasting Corpn 1960–61, Producer, Presenter Radio and TV 1966–68, Producer, Presenter TV 1970–72, Head FM Radio 2 1972–75, Dir of Broadcasting 1976–77, Head Dept of Theatre 1978–79; Librarian Radio and TV, Australian Broadcasting Corpn 1968–70. *Plays and films include:* Miss Unusual, Sea Mama, The Rope and The Cross, Old Story Time, Champagne and Sky Juice – Children of Babylon, I Marcus Garvey, Milk and Honey, Passion and Paradise, Whiplash. *TV appearances include:* I Is a Long Memoried Woman, Orchid House, Songs of Praise, South of the Border, Dixon of Dock Green, Hugh and I, Martin. *Publications include:* Moments by Myself 1988, Re-entry into Sound, Part IV (co-author) 1989; plays: Let's Say Grace, What's Good for the Goose, The Baby Born. *Honours:* Officer, Order of Distinction 1980; Bronze Musgrave Medal 1974, Silver 1987, Centenary Medal, Inst. of Jamaica 1991, Award of Excellence, Caribbean Acad. of Arts and Culture 1991.

FORBES, Malcolm Stevenson (Steve), Jr, LHD; American publishing executive; *President and CEO, Forbes Inc.*; b. 18 July 1947, Morristown, NJ; s. of Malcolm Forbes and Roberta Laidlaw; m. Sabina Beekman 1971. *Education:* Princeton Univ. and Lycoming Coll. Jacksonville Univ. *Career:* with Forbes Inc., New York 1970–, Pres. and COO 1980–90, Pres. and CEO 1990–; Deputy Ed.-in-Chief, Forbes magazine 1982–90, Ed.-in-Chief 1990–, Chair. 2008–; Chair. Forbes Newspapers 1989–; mem. Bd for International Broadcasting 1983–93, Chair. 1985–93; mem. Advisory Council, Dept of Econs Princeton Univ. 1985–; mem. Bd of Dirs FreedomWorks 2006–; mem. Bd of Trustees, Heritage Foundation. *Films:* Some Call It Greed (scriptwriter) 1977. *Publication:* Fact and Comment (ed.) 1974, A New Birth of Freedom 1999, Flat Tax Revolution: Using a Postcard to Abolish the IRS 2005, How Capitalism Will Save Us: Why Free People and Free Markets Are the Best Answer in Today's Economy (with Elizabeth Ames) 2009, Power Ambition Glory: The Stunning Parallels between Great Leaders of the Ancient World and Today... and the Lessons You Can Learn (with John Prevas) 2009. *Honours:* several hon. degrees. *Address:* Forbes Inc., 60 Fifth Avenue, New York, NY 10011, USA (office). *Website:* www.forbesinc.com (office).

FORD, David (see Harknett, Terry)

FORD, Kirk (see Spence, William John Duncan)

FORD, Peter; British author and editor; b. 3 June 1936, Harpenden, Herts., England; m. (divorced); two s. one d. *Education:* St George's School. *Career:* Ed., Cassell 1958–61; Sr Copy Ed., Penguin Books 1961–64; Sr Ed., Thomas Nelson 1964–70; mem. Soc. of Authors, New York Acad. of Sciences, Folklore Soc. *Publications include:* The Fool on the Hill 1975, Scientists and Inventors 1979, The True History of the Elephant Man 1980, Medical Mysteries 1985, The Picture Buyer's Handbook 1988, A Collector's Guide to Teddy Bears 1990, Rings and Curtains: Family and Personal Memoirs 1992, The Monkey's Paw and Other Stories by W. W. Jacobs 1994, A Willingness to Die: Memoirs of Brian Kingcome 1999.

FORD, Richard, BA, MFA; American writer and academic; *Professor, Trinity College, Dublin*; b. 16 Feb. 1944, Jackson, Miss.; m. Kristina Hensley Ford 1968. *Education:* Michigan State Univ., Univ. of California, Irvine. *Career:* Lecturer, Univ. of Michigan, Ann Arbor 1974–76; Asst Prof. of English, Williams Coll., Williamstown, Mass 1978–79; Lecturer, Princeton Univ. 1980–81; Prof., Trinity Coll., Dublin 2008–; Guggenheim Fellowship 1977–78; Nat. Endowment for the Arts Fellowships 1979–80, 1985–86; mem. American Acad. of Arts and Letters, PEN, Writers' Guild, American Acad. of Arts and Sciences. *Screenplays:* American Tropical 1983, Bright Angel 1991. *Publications:* A Piece of My Heart (novel) 1976, The Ultimate Good Luck (novel) 1981, The Sportswriter (novel) 1986, Rock Springs (short stories) 1987, My Mother in Memory (ed.) 1988, The Best American Short Stories (ed.) 1990, Wildlife (novel) 1990, The Granta Book of the American Short Story (ed.) 1992, Independence Day (novel, Pulitzer Prize for Fiction 1996, PEN/Faulkner Award for Fiction 1996) 1995, Women with Men (short stories) 1997, The Granta Book of the American Long Story (ed.) 1999, A Multitude of Sins (short stories) 2002, The Lay of the Land (novel) 2006, The New Granta Book of the American Short Story (ed.) 2007, The Bascombe Novels 2009, Canada (novel) 2012. *Honours:* Dr hc (Rennes, France, Michigan); Miss. Acad. of Arts and Letters Literature Award 1987, American Acad. and Inst. of Arts and Letters Award for Literature 1989, American Acad. of Arts and Letters Award in Merit for the Novel 1997, PEN-Malamud Award for Short Fiction 2001; Commdr, Ordre des Arts et des Lettres. *Literary Agent:* International Creative Management, 825 Eighth Avenue, New York, NY 10019, USA. *Telephone:* (212) 556-5764.

FOREMAN, Amanda, BA, PhD, FRSA; British historian, writer and journalist; b. 1968, London; d. of Carl Foreman; m.; one s. four d. *Education:* Sarah Lawrence Coll., Bronxville, NY, Columbia Univ., New York and Lady Margaret Hall, Oxford. *Career:* Henrietta Jex Blake Sr Scholarship, Univ. of Oxford 1998; TV and radio presenter 1998–. *Publications:* Georgiana: Duchess of Devonshire (Whitbread Award for Biography of the Year) 1998, Georgiana's World 2001, A World on Fire: An Epic History of Two Nations Divided 2010. *Honours:* Whitbread Prize 1999. *Literary Agent:* The Wylie Agency, 17 Bedford Square, London, WC1B 3JA, England. *E-mail:* mail@wylieagency.co.uk. *Website:* www.wylieagency.co.uk; www.amanda-foreman.com.

FOREMAN, Richard, BA, MFA; American dramatist, theatre director, designer and film director; b. 10 June 1937, New York, NY; s. of Albert Foreman and Claire Foreman; m. 1st Amy Taubin 1961 (divorced 1972); m. 2nd Kate Manhelm 1986. *Education:* Brown Univ., Yale Univ. *Career:* Artistic Dir Ontological-Hysteric Theatre, New York 1968–, Theatre O H, Paris 1973–85; Dir-in-Residence, New York Shakespeare Festival 1975–76; Dir Broadway and off-Broadway plays, Paris Opera, New York City Opera; mem. Dramatists Guild, PEN, Soc. of Stage Dirs. *Plays directed include:* Astronome 2009, Idiot Savant 2010. *Films include:* Strong Medicine 1976, The Ground Rules 2010. *Publications include:* Dr Selavy's Magic Theater 1972, Rhoda in Potatoland 1976, Theatre of Images 1977, Reverberation Machines 1985, Film is Evil: Radio is Good 1987, Unbalancing Acts: Foundations for a Theater 1992, My Head Was a Sledgehammer 1995, Paradise Hotel 2001, Bad Boy Nietzsche 2006, Plays and Manifestoes 2011. *Honours:* Hon. DArts (Brown) 1993, (Loughborough, UK) 2006; Officier, Ordre des Arts et des Lettres 2004; New York State Arts Council Creative Artists Public Service Fellow 1971, 1974, Guggenheim Fellowship 1972, Rockefeller Foundation Fellow 1974, Nat. Endowment for the Arts Lifetime Achievement Award 1990, American Acad. of Arts and Letters Prize in Literature 1992, John D. and Catherine T. MacArthur Foundation Fellow 1995–2000, PEN Master American Dramatist Award 2001. *Literary Agent:* c/o Performing Artservices, Inc., 260 West Broadway, New York, NY 10013, USA. *Telephone:* (212) 941-8911. *Fax:* (212) 334-5149. *E-mail:* contact@artservices.org. *Website:* www.artservices.org. *Address:* 152 Wooster Street, New York, NY 10012, USA (home). *Telephone:* (212) 260-3328 (office). *E-mail:* mmeedwarda@earthlink.net (home). *Website:* www.ontological.com.

FORKER, Charles Rush, AB, BA, MA, PhD; American academic and writer; *Professor Emeritus of English, Indiana University*; b. 11 March 1927, Pittsburgh, Pa; s. of Edson W. Forker and Mary Rush Forker; partner Lewis J. Overaker. *Education:* Bowdoin Coll., Merton Coll., Oxford, Harvard Univ. *Career:* Instructor, Univ. of Wisconsin 1957–59; Instructor, Indiana Univ. 1959–61, Asst Prof. 1961–65, Assoc. Prof. 1965–68, Prof. 1968–92, Prof. Emer. 1992–; Visiting Prof., Univ. of Michigan 1969–70, Dartmouth Coll. 1982–83, Concordia Univ., Montréal 1989, Colgate Univ. 2007–10; Folger Fellow 1963, Huntington Library Fellow 1969, Nat. Endowment for the Humanities Sr Research Fellow 1980–81; mem. American Asscn of Univ. Profs, Guild of Scholars of the Episcopal Church (pres. 1993–94), Int. Shakespeare Asscn, Malone Soc., Marlowe Soc., Modern Language Asscn, Renaissance Soc. of America, Shakespeare Soc. of America, Advisory Bd World Centre for Shakespeare Studies; fmr mem. Editorial Bd Hamlet Studies, Medieval and Renaissance Drama in England. *Publications include:* James Shirley: The Cardinal (ed.) 1964, William Shakespeare: Henry V (ed.) 1971, Edward Phillips's 'History of the Literature of England and Scotland': A Translation from the 'Compendiosa Enumeratio Poetarum' with an Introduction and Commentary (with Daniel G. Calder) 1973, Visions and Voices of the New Midwest (assoc. ed.) 1978, Henry V: An Annotated Bibliography (with Joseph Candido) 1983, Skull Beneath the Skin: The Achievement of John Webster 1986, Fancy's Images: Contexts, Settings, and Perspectives in Shakespeare and His Contemporaries 1990, Christopher Marlowe: Edward the Second (ed.) 1994, Richard II: The Critical Tradition 1998, William Shakespeare: Richard II (ed.) 2002; contrib. to scholarly books and journals. *Honours:* Fulbright Fellowship 1951–53. *Address:* 1219 East Maxwell Lane, Bloomington, IN 47401, USA (home). *Telephone:* (812) 332-6564 (home). *E-mail:* forker@indiana.edu (office). *Website:* www.guildofscholars.org/forker.html (office).

FORMAN, Robert Kraus Conrad, BA, MA, MPhil, PhD; American academic and writer; *CEO, The Forge Institute*; b. 3 Aug. 1947, Baltimore, Md; m. Yvonne Forman 1975; two c. *Education:* Univ. of Chicago, Columbia Univ., New York. *Career:* Adjunct Prof., New School for Social Research, New York City 1985–88; Instructor, Union Theological Seminary, New York City 1987; Visiting Asst Prof., Vassar Coll. 1989–90; Assoc. Prof. of Religion, Hunter Coll., CUNY 1990–2001; Sr Fellow, Columbia Univ. Writing Program 1993, Otto Friedrich Schoolhuset 2004–; Founder-Exec. Ed. Journal of Consciousness Studies: Controversies in Science and the Humanities 1991–; Co-Ed., Neuroscience, Consciousness, Spirituality Book Series; Founder CEO, The Forge Institute, The Forge Guild, GlobalSpiritualCitizenship.org project; mem. American Acad. of Religion, Asscn for Asian Studies, Asscn for Transpersonal Psychology, Inst. for Noetic Sciences, Sankat Mocan (Save the Ganges) Foundation. *Publications include:* The Problem of Pure Consciousness (ed.) 1990, Meister Eckhart: Mystic as Theologian: An Experiment in Methodology 1991, The Religions of Asia, third edn (gen. ed.) 1993, Religions of the World, third edn (gen. ed.) 1993, The Innate Capacity (ed.) 1997, Mysticism, Mind, Consciousness 2001, Grass Roots Spirituality: What It Is, Why It Is Here, Where It Is Going 2004, Enlightenment Ain't What It's Cracked up to Be 2011; contrib. to more than 30 scholarly books and journals. *Honours:* Dr hc (Lund); New World Foundation Grants 1992, 1993, 1994, 2005, CUNY Research Grant 1996, Fetzer Inst. Grants 1997, 2001, 2002, 2007, Bross Prize for Manuscript in Religion 2000, Inner Guidance Foundation Grant 2000, 2004, Jonas Foundation Grant, Jameson Grant, Angell Foundation Grant, Helsinki Univ. Medal, Finland. *Address:* 383 Broadway, Hastings-on-Hudson, NY 10706, USA (home). *Telephone:* (914) 478-7802 (office). *E-mail:* forman@theforge.org (office). *Website:* www.theforge.org (office).

FORNA, Aminatta, LLB; Sierra Leonean/British writer; b. 7 May 1964, Scotland; d. of Mohamed Sorie Forna and Maureen Christison; m. Simon Westcott 1994. *Education:* Univ. Coll., London. *Career:* BBC TV documentary producer and reporter 1989–99; writer 1999–; Chair. Rogbonko Village School Trust; Harkness Fellow, Univ. of California, Berkerley, USA 1996; mem. Advisory Cttee, Caine Prize for Africa, Advisory Cttee, Royal Literary Fund. *Publications include:* The Devil That Danced on the Water: A Daughter's Memoir 2002, Ancestor Stones 2006, The Memory of Love (Commonwealth Writers' Prize 2011) 2010, Haywards Heath (short story) 2010. *Honours:* Hurston Wright Legacy Award 2007, Liberaturpreis 2008, Aidoo-Snyder Book Prize 2010. *Literary Agent:* c/o DGA, 55 Monmouth Street, London, WC2H 9DG, England. *Telephone:* (20) 7240-9992. *Fax:* (20) 7395-6110. *E-mail:* assistant@davidgodwinassociates.co.uk. *Website:* www.davidgodwinassociates.co.uk.

FORNÉS, María Irene; Cuban/American playwright; b. 14 May 1930, Havana. *Career:* Man. Dir New York Theatre Strategy 1973–79; fmr TCG (Theatre Communications Group)/Pew Artist-in-Residence, Women's Project and Productions; contrib. to Performing Arts Journal and numerous anthologies. *Plays (many unpublished):* The Widow 1961, Tango Palace (aka There! You Died) 1963, The Office 1964, Promenade 1965, The Successful Life of 3 1965, The Annunciation 1967, A Vietnamese Wedding 1967, The Red Burning Light (aka Mission XQ3) 1968, Dr Kheal 1968, Molly's Dream 1968, Baboon!!! 1972, Aurora 1974, Cap-a-Pie 1975, Washing 1976, Fefu and Her Friends 1977, In Service 1978, Evelyn Brown 1979, Eyes on the Harem 1979, A Visit 1981, Sarita 1982, The Danube 1982, The Curse of the Langston House 1983, Mud 1983, Abingdon Square 1984, The Conduct of Life 1985, Drowning 1985, The Trial of Joan of Arc on a Matter of Faith 1986, Lovers and Keepers 1986, The Mothers 1986, Oscar and Bertha 1987, Hunger 1988, And What of the Night? 1989, Terra Incognita 1991, Springtime 1992, Enter the Night 1993, Ibsen and the Actress 1995, Manual for a Desperate Crossing 1996, The Summer in Gossensass 1997, The Audition 1998, Letters from Cuba 2000. *Honours:* nine Obie awards; NEA (National Endowment for the Arts) awards, including Distinguished Artists Award; Rockefeller Foundation grants; Guggenheim grant; American Acad. and Inst. of Arts and Letters Award; NY State Governor's Arts Award; PEN/Nabokov Award 2002. *Literary Agent:* c/o Morgan Jenness, Abrams Artists Agency, 275 Seventh Avenue, 26th Floor, New York, NY 10001, USA. *Telephone:* (646) 486-4600. *E-mail:* morgan.jenness@abramsartny.com. *Website:* www.abramsartists.com.

FORRESTER, Viviane; French writer and critic; b. 29 Sept. 1925, Paris; d. of Edgar Dreyfus and Yvonne Dreyfus (née Hirsch); m. 1st Simon Stoloff (divorced); two s.; m. 2nd; m. 3rd John Forrester 1967. *Career:* literary critic, La Quinzaine Littéraire 1974, Nouvel Observateur 1975, Le Monde 1994–; mem. Jury, Prix Fémina. *Radio:* cr. rôle of Anne-Marie Stretter, in India Song by Marguerite Duras. *Publications include:* Ainsi des Exilés 1970, Le Grand festin 1971, Virginia Woolf 1973, Le Corps entier de Marigda 1975, La violence du calme 1980, Les Allées cavalières 1982, Van Gogh ou l'enterrement dans les blés (Prix Fémina-Vacaresco de l'essai) 1983, L'Oeil de la nuit 1987, Ce soir, après la guerre (Prix de l' Acad. française) 1992, L'Horreur économique (Prix Médicis de l'essai) 1996, Une Étrange dictature 2000, Au Louvre avec Viviane Forrester: Leonardo da Vinci 2001, Le crime occidental 2004, Mes passions de toujours 2006, Virginia Woolf (Prix Goncourt de la Biographie) 2009. *Honours:* Chevalier, Légion d'honneur, Officier, Ordre nat. du Mérite, Commdr, Ordre des Arts et des Lettres. *Address:* 40 rue du Bac, 75007 Paris, France (home). *Telephone:* 1-42-22-65-36 (home).

FORSTER, Margaret, BA, FRSL; British writer; b. 25 May 1938, Carlisle; d. of Arthur Gordon Forster and Lilian Forster (née Hind); m. Edward Hunter Davies 1960; one s. two d. *Education:* Carlisle Co. High School and Somerville Coll., Oxford. *Career:* chief non-fiction reviewer, London Evening Standard 1977–80; mem. Arts Council Literary Panel 1978–81. *Publications:* non-fiction: The Rash Adventurer: The Rise and Fall of Charles Edward Stuart 1973, William Makepeace Thackeray: Memoirs of a Victorian Gentleman 1978, Significant Sisters: Grassroots of Active Feminism 1839–1939 1984, Elizabeth Barrett Browning: A Biography 1988, Elizabeth Barrett Browning: Selected Poems (ed.) 1988, Daphne du Maurier: The Authorised Biography 1993, Hidden Lives: A Family Memoir 1995, Rich Desserts and Captains Thin: A Family and Their Times 1831–1931 1997, Precious Lives (memoir) 1997, Good Wives?: Mary, Fanny, Jennie and Me 1845–2001 2001; novels: Dame's Delight 1964, Georgy Girl (filmscript with Peter Nichols 1966) 1963, The Bogeyman 1965, The Travels of Maudie Tipstaff 1967, The Park 1968, Miss Owen-Owen is at Home 1969, Fenella Phizackerley 1970, Mr Bone's Retreat 1971, The Seduction of Mrs Pendlebury 1974, Mother, Can You Hear Me? 1979, The Bride of Lowther Fell 1980, Marital Rites 1981, Private Papers 1986, Have the Men had Enough? 1989, Lady's Maid 1990, The Battle for Christabel 1991, Mothers' Boys 1994, Shadow Baby 1996, The Memory Box 1999, Diary of an Ordinary Woman 1914–1995 2003, Is There Anything You Want? 2005, Keeping the World Away 2006, Over 2007. *Honours:* RSL Award 1988, Fawcet Soc. Prize 1993. *Literary Agent:* The Sayle Literary Agency, Bickerton House, 25–27 Bickerton Road, London, N19 5JT, England. *Telephone:* (20) 7263-8681. *Fax:* (20) 7561-0529. *Address:* 11 Boscastle Road, London, NW5 1EE; Grasmoor House, Loweswater, nr Cockermouth, Cumbria, CA13 0RU, England. *Telephone:* (20) 7485-3785 (London); (1900) 85303 (Cumbria).

FORSYTH, Frederick, CBE; British writer; b. 25 Aug. 1938, Ashford, Kent; m. 1st Carole Cunningham 1973; two s.; m. 2nd Sandy Molloy. *Education:* Tonbridge School, Univ. of Granada, Spain. *Career:* with RAF 1956–58; reporter, Eastern Daily Press, Norfolk 1958–61; joined Reuters 1961, reporter, Paris 1962–63, Chief of Bureau, E Berlin 1963–64; radio and TV reporter, BBC 1965–66; Asst Diplomatic Corresp., BBC TV 1967–68; freelance journalist, Nigeria and Biafra 1968–69. *Television appearances include:* Soldiers (narrator) 1985, Frederick Forsyth Presents 1989. *Film appearance:* I Have Never Forgotten You: The Life and Legacy of Simon Wiesenthal 2006. *Publications:* fiction: The Day of the Jackal 1971, The Odessa File 1972, The Dogs of War 1974, The Shepherd 1975, The Devil's Alternative 1979, No Comebacks (short stories) 1982, The Fourth Protocol 1984, The Negotiator 1988, The Deceiver 1991, Great Flying Stories (ed.) 1991, The Fist of God 1993, Icon 1996, The Phantom of Manhattan 1999, Quintet 2000, The Veteran and Other Stories 2001, Avenger 2003, The Afghan 2006, The Cobra 2010; non-fiction: The Biafra Story 1969 (revised edn as The Making of an African Legend: The Biafra Story 1977), Emeka 1982, I Remember: Reflections on Fishing in Childhood 1995. *Honours:* MWA Edgar Allan Poe Award 1971. *Address:* c/o Penguin Group (USA) Inc., c/o Putnam Publicity, 375 Hudson Street, New York, NY 10014, USA (office). *Website:* us.penguingroup.com (office).

FORTE, Allen, BA, MA; American musician and writer; *Battell Professor Emeritus of the Theory of Music, Yale University*; b. 23 Dec. 1926, Portland, Ore.; s. of M. Palmer and Marion Eastman Forte. *Education:* Columbia Univ., New York. *Career:* Faculty mem., Teachers Coll., Columbia Univ. 1953–59, Manhattan School of Music 1957, Mannes Coll. of Music 1957–59; Instructor, Yale Univ. 1959–61, Asst Prof. 1961–64, Assoc. Prof. 1964–68, Prof. 1968–91, Battell Prof. of the Theory of Music from 1991, now Prof. Emer.; Ed. Journal of Music Theory 1960–67; Gen. Ed. Composers of the Twentieth Century 1980–; Fellow, American Acad. of Arts and Sciences 1995; mem. American Musicological Soc., Soc. for Music Theory (Pres. 1977–82). *Publications include:* Contemporary Tone-Structure 1955, Schenker's Conception of Musical Structure 1959, Bartók's 'Serial' Composition 1960, The Compositional Matrix 1961, Tonal Harmony in Concept and Practice 1962, A Theory of Set-complexes for Music 1964, A Program for the Analytical Reading of Scores 1966, Computer-implemented Analysis of Musical Structure 1966, Music and Computing: The Present Situation 1967, The Structure of Atonal Music 1970, The Harmonic Organization of The Rite of Spring 1978, Introduction to Schenkerian Analysis (with S. Gilbert) 1982, The American Popular Ballad of the Golden Era 1924–1950 1995, The Atonal Music of Anton Webern 1998, Olivier Messiaen as Serialist 2002, Listening to Classic American Popular Songs 2001, Toward a Theory of Intervallic Harmony 2004, Schoenberg's Opus 19, No. 4 2004, Songs of Yesterday for Today (pianist-arranger) 2005, Messiaen's Chords 2006, The Development of Diminutions in American Jazz 2006; contrib. to learned books and journals. *Honours:* Hon. PhD (Eastman School of Music) 1988; Sr Marshal Yale Univ. Commencement Ceremony 2004; WWII Victory Medal, Guggenheim Fellowship 1981, Festschrift published in his honour: Music Theory in Concept and Practice 1997. *Address:* Department of Music, PO Box 208310, Yale University, New Haven, CT 06520 (office); 10 Mulberry Hill, Hamden, CT 06517, USA (home). *Telephone:* (203) 288-8888 (home). *E-mail:* allen.forte@yale.edu (home). *Website:* www.allenforte.com.

FORTEY, Richard Alan, PhD, ScD, FRS, FRSL; British palaeontologist and writer; *Research Associate, Natural History Museum, London*; b. 15 Feb. 1946, London; s. of Frank Allen Fortey and Margaret Fortey (née Wilshin); m. 1st Bridget Elizabeth Thomas (divorced); one s.; m. 2nd Jacqueline Francis 1977; one. s. two d. *Education:* Ealing Grammar School for Boys, King's Coll. Cambridge. *Career:* Research Fellow, then Sr Scientific Officer, Natural History Museum, London 1970–77, Prin. Scientific Officer 1978–86, Sr Prin. Scientific Officer 1986–98, Merit Researcher 1998, currently Research Assoc.; Howley Visiting Prof., Memorial Univ. of Newfoundland, Canada 1977–78; Visiting Prof. of Palaeobiology, Univ. of Oxford 2000–; Collier Chair in Public Understanding of Science and Tech., Univ. of Bristol 2002–03; mem. Geological Soc. of London 1972– (Pres. 2007), British Mycological Soc. 1980–. *Publications:* The Roderick Masters Book of Money Making Schemes (as Roderick Masters) 1981, Fossils: The Key to the Past 1982, The Hidden Landscape 1993, Life: An Unauthorised Biography 1997, Trilobite! 2000, The Earth: An Intimate History 2004, Dry Store Room No. 1: The Secret Life of the Natural History Museum 2008. *Honours:* Hon. Fellow, BAAS 2008; Dr hc (St Andrews) 2007, (Open Univ.) 2007, (Birmingham) 2010; Natural World Book of the Year Award 1994, Lyell Medal, Geological Soc. of London 1996, Frink Medal, Zoological Soc. of London 2001, Lewis Thomas Prize, Rockefeller Univ. 2003, Linnean Medal for Zoology 2006, Michael Faraday Prize, Royal Soc. 2006, T.N. George Medal, Glasgow Geological Soc. 2007. *Address:* Department of Palaeontology, Natural History Museum, Cromwell Road, London, SW7 5BD, England (office). *Telephone:* (20) 7942-5493 (office). *Fax:* (20) 7942-5546 (office). *E-mail:* r.fortey@nhm.ac.uk (office). *Website:* www.nhm.ac.uk/palaeontology (office).

FOSSE, Jon, Cand. Philol; Norwegian writer, dramatist and poet; b. 29 Sept. 1959, Haugesund. *Education:* Univ. of Bergen. *Career:* teacher of creative writing, Acad. of Writing, Bergen 1987–93; professional writer 1993–. *Plays:* Og aldri skal vi skiljast 1994, Namnet 1995, Nokon kjem til å komme 1996, Barnet 1996, Mor og barn 1997, Sonen 1997, Natta syng sine songar 1997, Ein sommars dag 1999, Gitarmannen 199, Draum om hausten 1999, Besoek 2000, Vinter 2000, Ettermiddag 2000, Vakkert 2001, Doedsvariasjonar 2002, Jenta i sofaen 2003, Suzannah 2004, Sa ka la, 2004, Varmt 2005, Svevn 2005,

Rambuku 2006, Skuggar 2006, Eg er vinden 2007, Desse auga 2008, Jente i gul regnjakke 2009. *Publications:* fiction: Raudt, svart 1983, Stengd gitar 1985, Naustet 1989, Flaskesamlaren 1991, Bly og vatn 1992, Melancholia I 1995, Melancholia II 1996; shorter prose: Blod. Steinen er Forteljing 1987, To forteljingar 1993, Prosa frå ein oppvekst. Kortprosa 1994, Eldre kortare prosa 1997, Morgon og kveld 2000, Det er Ales 2004, Andvake 2007; poetry: Engel med vatn i augene 1986, Hundens bevegelsar 1990, Hund og engel 1992, Nye dikt 1997, Ange i vind 2003, Songar 2009; essays: Frå telling via showing til writing 1989, Gnostiske essays 1999; also books for children. *Honours:* Hon. mem. Norwegian Actors' Soc., Det Norske Samlaget, Norwegian Dramatists' Soc.; Chevalier, Ordre nat. du Mérite, Commdr, St Olavs Orden; Noregs Mållags Prize for Children's Books 1990, Andersson-Rysst Fondet 1992, Prize for Literature in New Norwegian 1993, 2003, Samlags Prize 1994, Ibsen Prize 1996, Sunnmoers Prize 1996, Melsom Prize 1997, Asshehoug Prize 1997, Dobloug Prize 1999, Gyldendal Prize 2000, Nordic Prize for Dramatists 2000, Nestroy Prize 2001, Scandinavian Nat. Theatre Prize 2002, Norwegian Council of Culture Prize of Honour 2003, Norwegian Theatre Prize of Honour (Hedda) 2003, UBU Prize for best foreign play, Italy 2004, Norwegian Prize for Literature of Honour (Brage) 2005, Anders Jahre Prize for Culture 2006, Nordic Prize, Swedish Acad. 2007, Deutscher Jugendliteraturpreis 2007, Bergen Prize for Artists 2009, Medal from Benedict XVI for participation in Meeting with the Artist in The Sistine Chapel 2009, Int. Ibsen Award 2010, given Grotten as hon. residence from Norwegian Govt 2011. *Literary Agent:* c/o Samlaget, Boks 4672, Sofienberg, 0506 Oslo, Norway; Colombine Teaterförlag, Gaffelgränd 1A, 111 30 Stockholm, Sweden.

FOSTER, Cecil Adolphus, BA, MA, PhD; Barbadian/Canadian writer, journalist and academic; *Associate Professor of Sociology and Anthropology, University of Guelph*; b. 26 Sept. 1954, Barbados; three s. *Education:* Univ. of the West Indies, York Univ., Toronto, Ont. *Career:* fmr columnist, reporter, ed. The Toronto Star, The Globe and Mail, Financial Post, CBC Radio, CBC TV, CTV; Prof. of Sociology and Anthropology, Univ. of Guelph; mem. PEN Canada, Writers' Union of Canada. *Publications include:* No Man in the House 1992, Sleep on Beloved 1994, Caribana: The Greatest Celebration 1995, A Place Called Heaven: The Meaning of Being Black 1996, Slammin' Tar 1998, Island Wing 1998, Dry Bones Memories 2001, Where Race Does Not Matter: The New Spirit of Modernity 2004, Blackness and Modernity: The Colour of Humanity and the Quest for Freedom (John Porter Tradition of Excellence Book Award 2008) 2007. *Honours:* Gordon Mantador Award 1997, African-Canadian Achievement Award 2006 John Porter Tradition of Excellence Book Prize, Canadian Sociological Asscn 2008. *Address:* Department of Sociology and Anthropology, University of Guelph, 6th Floor, Mackinnon Building, Guelph, ON N1G 2W1, Canada (office). *Telephone:* (519) 824-4120 (ext. 52511) (office). *E-mail:* cfoster@uoguelph.ca (office). *Website:* www.uoguelph.ca/socwww (office).

FOSTER, David Manning, BSc, PhD; Australian writer; b. 15 May 1944, Katoomba, NSW; m. 1st Robin Bowers 1964; one s. two d.; m. 2nd Gerda Busch 1975; one s. two d. *Education:* Univ. of Sydney, Australian Nat. Univ., Univ. of Pennsylvania. *Career:* professional fiction writer 1973–. *Publications:* novels: The Pure Land 1974, The Empathy Experiment 1977, Moonlite 1981, Plumbum 1983, Dog Rock: A Postal Pastoral 1985, The Adventures of Christian Rosy Cross 1986, Testostero 1987, The Pale Blue Crochet Coathanger Cover 1988, Mates of Mars 1991, The Glade Within the Grove 1996, The Ballad of Erinungarah 1997, In the New Country 1999, The Land Where Stories End 2001, Sons of the Rumour 2009. *Honours:* The Age Award 1974, Australian Nat. Book Council Award 1981, NSW Premier's Fellowship 1986, Keating Fellowship 1991–94, James Joyce Foundation Award 1996, Miles Franklin Award 1997, Courier Mail Award 1999, Patrick White Award 2010. *Address:* PO Box 57, Bundanoon, NSW 2578, Australia (office).

FOSTER, James Anthony (Tony); Canadian writer; b. 2 Aug. 1932, Winnipeg, Man.; m. 1964; one s. two d. *Education:* Univ. of Brunswick. *Career:* mem. Canadian Authors Asscn, PEN, Writers Guild of America, Writers' Union of Canada. *Publications include:* Zig Zag to Armageddon 1978, By-Pass 1982, The Money Burn 1984, A coeur ouvert 1985, Heart of Oak: A Pictorial History of the Royal Canadian Navy 1985, Meeting of Generals 1986, Sea Wings: A Pictorial History of Canada's Waterborne Defence Aircraft 1986, Muskets to Missiles 1987, Rue du Bac 1987, For Love and Glory 1989, The Bush Pilots: A Canadian Phenomena 1990, Ransom for a God 1990, The Sound and the Silence 1990, Coastguard Spirits 1992, Arid Lands 1995, Ice and Fire: Watercolour Diaries of Volcano Journeys 1998, The Museum Mystery 1999, Asleep on a Bicycle 2011.

FOSTER, Jeanne (see Williams, Jeanne)

FOSTER, Linda Nemec, BA, MFA; American poet, writer and teacher; *Founder and Member of Programming Committee, Contemporary Writers Series, Aquinas College*; b. 29 May 1950, Garfield Heights, Ohio; m. Anthony Jesse Foster 1974; one s. one d. *Education:* Aquinas Coll., Grand Rapids, Mich. and Goddard Coll., Plainfield, Vt. *Career:* teacher of creative writing and poetry, Mich. Council for the Arts 1980–2002; Instructor of English Composition, Ferris State Univ. 1983–84; Dir of Literature Programming, Urban Inst. for Contemporary Arts, Grand Rapids 1989–96; Founder and mem. of Programming Cttee, Contemporary Writers Series, Aquinas Coll. 1997–, Lecturer in Poetry 1999–; guest lecturer and speaker at various schools, colls and confs; first Poet Laureate of Grand Rapids, Mich. 2003; mem. Acad. of American Poets, Detroit Women Writers, Urban Inst. for Contemporary Arts, Poetry Soc. of America. *Recording:* Contemplating the Heavens (collaboration with Steve Talaga) 2007. *Plays:* poems used in production of Still Life with Conversation 1993. *Publications include:* A History of the Body 1987, A Modern Fairy Tale: The Baba Yaga Poems 1992, Trying to Balance the Heart 1993, Living in the Fire Nest 1996, Contemplating the Heavens 2001, Amber Necklace from Gdańsk 2001, Listen to the Landscape 2006, Ten Songs from Bulgaria 2008, Talking Diamonds 2009; contrib. to reviews, journals and magazines. *Honours:* Mich. Council for the Arts Creative Artist grants in poetry 1984, 1990, 1996, American Poetry Asscn Grand Prize 1986, hon. mention, Writers' Digest 1987, prizewinner McGuffin Poetry Contest 1987, 1994, Passages North Nat. Poetry Competition 1988, Poetry/Visual Art Selections, Sage Coll., New York 1994, 1995, Arts Foundation of Mich. Fellowship in Poetry 1996, Nat. Writer's Voice Project Fellowship 1999, Art Serve Mich. grant in poetry 2001, first runner-up Nat. Poetry Review Laureate Prize 2006, Creative Arts Award, Polish American Historical Asscn 2008. *Address:* 2024 Wilshire Drive SE, Grand Rapids, MI 49506, USA (home). *Website:* www.lindanemcfoster.com.

FOSTER, Paul, BA, LLB; American dramatist and screenwriter; b. 15 Oct. 1931, Pennsgrove, NJ. *Education:* Rutgers Univ., NJ, New York Univ. Law School. *Career:* mem. Dramatists Guild, Soc. of Composers and Dramatic Authors, France, Players Club, New York City. *Publications include:* 25 books of plays, including: Tom Paine 1971, Madonna in the Orchard 1971, Satyricon 1972, Elizabeth I 1972, Marcus Brutus 1976, Silver Queen Saloon 1976, Mellon and the National Art Gallery 1980, A Kiss is Just a Kiss 1984, 3 Mystery Comedies 1985, The Dark and Mr Stone 1985, Odon von Horvath's Faith, Hope and Charity, trans. 1987, Make Believe (with music by Solt Dome), musical book and lyrics 1994; films: Smile 1980, Cop and the Anthem 1982, When You're Smiling 1983, Cinderella 1984, Home Port 1984, Beckett and Zen 1989; contribs to Off-Off Broadway Book 1972, Best American Plays of the Modern Theatre 1975, New Stages magazine. *Honours:* Rockefeller Foundation Fellowship 1967, British Arts Council Award 1973, Guggenheim Fellowship 1974, Theater Heute Award 1977.

FOSTER, Robert Fitzroy (Roy), FBA; Irish historian, writer and academic; *Carroll Professor of Irish History, Hertford College, University of Oxford*; b. 16 Jan. 1949, Waterford. *Education:* Trinity Coll. Dublin. *Career:* Prof. of Modern British History, Birkbeck College, London 1989-91; Carroll Prof. of Irish History and Fellow, Hertford Coll., Oxford 1991–; visiting fellowships include St. Anthony's Coll., Oxford, Inst. for Advanced Study, Princeton, NJ, Princeton Univ.; Fellow, British Acad. 1989. *Publications:* biogs of Charles Stewart Parnell 1976 and Lord Randolph Churchill 1981, Modern Ireland 1600–1972 1988, The Oxford Illustrated History of Ireland 1989, Paddy and Mr Punch 1997, W. B. Yeats: A Life, Vol. I: The Apprentice Mage 1865–1914 2001, The Irish Story: Telling Tales and Making it Up in Ireland 2001 (Christian Gauss Award from Phi Beta Kappa 2003), W. B. Yeats: A Life, Vol. II: The Arch-Poet 1915–1939 2003, Conquering England: the Irish in Victorian London (with Fintan Cullen) 2005, Luck and the Irish 2007. *Honours:* Hon. DLitt (Aberdeen) 1997, (Queen's, Belfast) 1998, (Trinity Coll. Dublin) 2003, (Nat. Univ. of Ireland) 2004; Hon. Fellow, Birkbeck Coll., Univ. of London 2005. *Address:* Hertford College, Catte Street, Oxford, OX1 3BW, England (office). *Telephone:* (1865) 279400 (office). *E-mail:* roy.foster@hertford.ox.ac.uk (office). *Website:* www.hertford.ox.ac.uk (office).

FOTTORINO, Éric; French journalist and writer; b. 1960, Nice. *Career:* journalist, Le Monde 1986–, News Ed. 1998–2004, Ed.-in-Chief 2006–07, Dir June–Dec. 2007, Chair. Le Monde Group 2008–10. *Publications include:* Le Festin de la terre 1988, La Piste blanche 1991, Rochelle 1991, Besoin d'afrique 1992, Homme de terre 1993, La France en friche 1994, Mille et un soleils 1995, Aventures industrielles 1996, Coeur d'afrique 1997, Les Éphémères 1994, Voyage au centre du cerveau 1998, Un Territoire fragile (Prix Europe, Prix des Bibliothécaires) 2000, Nordeste 2001, Je pars demain 2001, C'est mon tour 2003, Caresse de rouge (Prix François-Mauriac) 2004, Korsakov (Prix Roman France Télévision 2004, Prix des libraires 2005, Prix Nice-Baie des Anges 2005) 2004, Baisers de cinéma 2007 (Prix Femina 2007), L'homme qui m'aimait tout bas 2009, Piccolo elogio della bicicletta 2009, Questions A Mon Pere 2010. *Address:* Le Monde, 80 boulevard Auguste Blanqui, 75707 Paris Cedex 13, France (office). *Telephone:* 1-42-17-20-00 (office). *Fax:* 1-42-17-21-21 (office). *E-mail:* lemonde@lemonde.fr (office). *Website:* www.lemonde.fr (office).

FOUDA, Yosri; Egyptian journalist; b. 1964. *Education:* American Univ. in Cairo. *Career:* taught mass communication and various media courses, Cairo Univ. 1986–92; producer Arabic-language TV Service, BBC, London, UK – 1996; reporter, Al Jazeera London Bureau, UK 1996–2009, Bureau Chief – 2009 (resgnd), also presenter, Top Secret TV programme; Ed. and Presenter, Last Word TV programme, ONTV 2009–. *Publication:* Masterminds of Terror: The Truth Behind the Most Devastating Attack The World Has Ever Seen (with Nick Fielding) 2003. *Honours:* Pan-Arab Cairo Radio and TV Production Festival award 1998, AUC's Outstanding Professional Performance Award (2000). *Website:* www.ontveg.com (office).

FOULDS, Adam, BA, MA; British writer and poet; b. 1974, London, England. *Education:* St Catherine's Coll., Oxford, Univ. of East Anglia. *Publications include:* fiction: The Truth About These Strange Times (Betty Trask Award 2007, Sunday Times Young Writer of the Year Award 2008) 2007, The Quickening Maze 2009; poetry: The Broken Word (Costa Book Award for Poetry 2008, Jerwood Aldeburgh Prize 2008, Somerset Maugham Award

2009) 2008. *Literary Agent:* c/o United Agents, 12–26 Lexington Street, London, W1F 0LE, England. *Telephone:* (20) 3214-0800. *Fax:* (20) 3214-0801. *E-mail:* info@unitedagents.co.uk. *Website:* unitedagents.co.uk.

FOULKE, Robert Dana, AB, MA, PhD; American academic, writer and travel writer; b. 25 April 1930, Minneapolis, Minn.; s. of Robert William Foulke and Bertha Peterson Foulke; m. Patricia Ann Nelson 1953; one s. two d. *Education:* Princeton Univ., Univ. of Minnesota. *Career:* Instructor in English, Univ. of Minnesota 1956–59, 1960–61; Asst Prof. of English, Trinity Coll., Hartford 1961–66, Assoc. Prof. 1966–70; Prof. of English, Skidmore Coll. 1970–92, Chair. Dept 1970–80; Visiting Assoc. and Life Mem. Clare Hall, Cambridge, UK 1976–77, 1990–91; Visiting Fellow, Dept of English, Princeton Univ. 1988; Literary Ed. The Oxford Encyclopedia of Maritime History 1999–2006; Fulbright Fellow, Univ. of London, UK 1959–60, Alexander O. Vietor Fellow, John Carter Brown Library, Brown Univ. 1993; mem. Coll. English Asscn, Modern Language Asscn, Joseph Conrad Soc., Melville Soc., American Soc. of Journalists and Authors, Soc. of American Travel Writers, Travel Journalists Guild (Co-Pres. 2004–06), Hakluyt Soc., Nat. Maritime Historical Soc., North American Soc. for Oceanic History (mem. Exec. Council 1995–), Soc. for Nautical Research. *Television:* Sailing with Confidence (three 30-minute programmes produced by WMHT, Troy, NY) 1990–. *Publications include:* An Anatomy of Literature (co-author and ed.) 1972, The Writer's Mind (co-ed.) 1983, The Sea Voyage Narrative 1997, 2002; travel guides: Europe Under Canvas 1980, Fielding's Motoring and Camping Europe 1986, Day Trips and Getaway Vacations in New England 1983, Day Trips and Getaway Vacations in Mid-Atlantic States 1986, Exploring Europe by Car 1991, Fielding's Great Sights of Europe 1994, Colonial America 1995, Romantic Weekends: New England 1998, Day Trips and Get Away Weekends: New England 1999, Day Trips and Get Away Weekends: Mid-Atlantic States 2000, Day Trips and Getaway Weekends: Connecticut, Rhode Island and Massachusetts 2002, Day Trips and Getaway Weekends: Vermont, New Hampshire and Maine 2002, An Adventure Guide to the Champlain and Hudson River Valleys 2003, A Visitor's Guide to Colonial and Revolutionary New England 2006, A Visitor's Guide to Colonial and Revolutionary Mid-Atlantic America 2007, A Visitor's Guide to the Colonial and Revolutionary South 2008, A Family of Friends: the First Hundred Years at the Lake George Club, 1909–2009 (co-ed.) 2009; contribs to numerous articles in scholarly journals and some 900 travel articles in magazines and newspapers. *Address:* 25 Dark Bay Lane, Lake George, NY 12845, USA (office). *Telephone:* (518) 668-2805 (office). *Fax:* (518) 668-2805 (office). *E-mail:* rfoulke@skidmore.edu (office); rfoulke@roadrunner.com (home).

FOUQUE, Antoinette, Dr rer. pol, DipLit; French psychoanalyst, feminist and publisher; b. 1 Oct. 1936, Marseilles; d. of Alexis Grugnardi and Vincente Grugnardi (née Bonavita); m. René Fouque; one d. *Education:* Univ. of Aix-Marseille and Ecole des Hautes Etudes, Paris. *Career:* teacher 1961; literary critic and trans. Cahiers du Sud, Quinzaine littéraire and Mercure de France 1964–68; Co-founder Mouvement de Libération des Femmes 1968; Organizer, Politique et Psychanalyse group 1968; Founder, Dir Editions Des Femmes publrs 1973, Founder three Des Femmes bookshops in Paris, Lyons and Marseilles 1974–99; Dir Le Quotidien des Femmes magazine 1974–76, Des Femmes en Mouvements magazine 1978–82; Founder Inst. de Recherche en Sciences des Femmes, Coll. de Féminiologie 1978; Founder talking book co. (books on cassette) 1980; Dir La Psychanalyste books 1983; Pres. Alliance française of San Diego, US 1986–88, Women Int. Centre, San Diego 1987–88; Founder and Pres. Alliance des Femmes pour la Démocratisation 1989; Rep. for the creation of a women's art museum to Sec. of State for the Rights of Women 1990; Ed. at Passages 1991; Founder and Hon. Pres. Parité 2000 club 1992; Founder mem. Women of Europe Cttee 1993; MEP (Energie Radicale list) 1994–99, Vice-Pres. Comm. on the Rights of Women 1994, mem. official del. to UN Int. Conf. on Women, Beijing 1995, French Del. to World Summit on Towns, Habitat II 1996; teacher Univ. of Paris I (Panthéon-Sorbonne) 1990, Paris VIII (St Denis) 1992 (Dir of Research 1994); Pres. Gynesis Women's Int. Foundation 2002; Founder Espace des Femmes publrs 2007; correspondent mem. European Acad. of Sciences, Arts and Letters. *Publications include:* Women in Movements, Yesterday, Today, Tomorrow 1992, Il y a deux sexes 1995, If It Is a Woman: Toward a New Human Contact 1999, Génération MLF: 1968–2008 2008. *Honours:* Commdr, Légion d'honneur, Officier, Ordre des Arts et des Lettres; Living Legacy Award, San Diego, CA 1986, Leading Women in Europe Award, Milan, Italy 1989, Susan B. Antony Award, USA 1990. *Address:* c/o Editions Des Femmes-Antoinette Fouque, 35 rue Jacob, 75006 Paris, France.

FOURNIER, Jean-Louis; French writer, comedian and television director; b. 19 Dec. 1938, Arras; s. of the late Paul Léandre Emile Fournier and Marie-Thérèse Françoise Camille Delcourt; m. Agnès Fournier (divorced); two s. (one deceased) one d. *Television includes:* as dir/scriptwriter: La Minute nécessaire de Monsieur Cyclopède (FR3) 1982–84, L'Or du diable (series) 1989, D'amoureuses histoires avec Ronny Coutteure (series) 1991, Un cercueil pour deux 1993, Arithmétique impertinente (documentary series) 1995, Je vais t'apprendre la politesse (mini-series) 1998, La Noiraude (cartoon series) 2006. *Publications include:* cartoon books for children (with Gilles Gay): La Noiraude, Encore La Noiraude, Pas folle la Noiraude; novels: Le Petit Meaulnes 2003, Satané Dieu! 2005, Où on va, papa? (Prix Femina) 2008, Les Mots des Riches 2009; numerous essays and narratives. *Address:* c/o Éditions Stock, 31 rue de Fleurus, 75278 Paris Cedex 06, France. *Website:* www.editions-stock.fr.

FOWLER, Alastair David Shaw, MA, DPhil, DLitt, FBA; British academic, writer and editor; *Regius Professor Emeritus, University of Edinburgh*; b. 17 Aug. 1930, Glasgow, Scotland; m. Jenny Catherine Simpson 1950; one s. one d. *Education:* Univ. of Edinburgh, Univ. of Oxford. *Career:* Jr Research Fellow, Queen's Coll., Oxford 1955–59; Instructor, Indiana Univ. 1957–58; Lecturer, Univ. Coll., Swansea 1959–61; Fellow and Tutor in English Literature, Brasenose Coll., Oxford 1962–71; Visiting Prof., Columbia Univ. 1964; mem. Inst. for Advanced Study, Princeton, NJ 1966, 1980; Visiting Prof., Univ. of Virginia 1969, 1979, 1985–90, Prof. of English 1990–98; Regius Prof. of Rhetoric and English Literature, Univ. of Edinburgh 1972–84, Prof. Emer. 1984–, Univ. Fellow 1985–87; Visiting Fellow, Council of the Humanities, Princeton Univ. 1974, Humanities Research Centre, Canberra 1980, All Souls Coll., Oxford 1984; General Ed. Longman Annotated Anthologies of English Verse 1977–80; mem. Editorial Bd New Literary History 1972–2003, English Literary Renaissance 1978–2003, Word and Image 1984–91, 1992–97, The Seventeenth Century 1986–2003, Connotations 1990–99, English Review 1990–, Translation and Literature 1990–; mem. Agder Akademi 2003. *Publications include:* De re poetica, by Richard Wills (ed. and trans.) 1958, Spenser and the Numbers of Time 1964, Spenser's Images of Life, by C. S. Lewis (ed.) 1967, The Poems of John Milton (co-ed. with John Carey) 1968, Triumphal Forms 1970, Silent Poetry (ed.) 1970, Topics in Criticism (co-ed. with Christopher Butler) 1971, Seventeen 1971, Conceitful Thought 1975, Catacomb Suburb 1976, Edmund Spenser 1977, From the Domain of Arnheim 1982, Kinds of Literature 1982, A History of English Literature 1987, The New Oxford Book of Seventeenth Century Verse (ed.) 1991, The Country House Poem 1994, Time's Purpled Masquers 1996, Milton: Paradise Lost (ed.) 1998, Renaissance Realism 2003, How to Write 2006; contrib. to scholarly books and journals. *Address:* 11 E Claremont Street, Edinburgh, EH7 4HT, Scotland (home). *Telephone:* (131) 556-0366 (home).

FOWLER, Don D., BA, PhD; American academic and writer; *Professor Emeritus of Historic Preservation and Anthropology, University of Nevada*; b. 24 April 1936, Torrey, Utah; m. Catherine Sweeney 1963. *Education:* Weber State Coll., Univ. of Utah, Univ. of Pittsburgh. *Career:* Instructor, Univ. of Nevada, Reno 1964–65, Asst Prof. 1965–67, Assoc. Prof. of Anthropology and Exec. Dir of Human Systems Center of the Desert Research Inst. 1968–71, Research Prof. and Exec. Dir of the Social Sciences Center of the Desert Research Inst. 1971–78, Mamie Kleberg Prof. of Historic Preservation and Anthropology 1978–, now Emer., Chair., Dept of Anthropology 1990–98; Visiting Postdoctoral Fellow, Smithsonian Inst., Washington, DC 1967–68, Research Assoc. 1970–; Fellow, American Anthropological Asscn, mem. Soc. for American Archaeology (pres. 1985–87). *Publications include:* Down the Colorado: John Wesley Powell's Diary of the First Trip Through the Grand Canyon (with Eliot Porter) 1969, The Anthropology of the Numa: John Wesley Powell's Manuscripts on Great Basin Indians, 1968–1980 (with C. S. Fowler) 1971, 'Photographed all the Best Scenery': Jack Hillers' Diary of the Powell Expedition, 1871–1875 (ed.) 1971, In Sacred Manner We Live: Edward S. Curtis' Indian Photographs 1972, Material Culture of the Numa: The John Wesley Powell Collection, 1867–1880 (with J. F. Matley) 1979, American Archaeology Past and Future: A Celebration of the Society for American Archaeology, 1935–1985 (co-ed. with D. J. Meltzer and J. A. Sabloff) 1986, Anthropology of the Desert West: Essays in Honor of Jesse D. Jennings (co-ed. with Carol J. Condie) 1986, The Western Photographs of Jack Hillers, 'Myself in the Water' 1989, Others Knowing Others: Perspectives on Ethnographic Careers (co-ed. with Donald L. Hardesty) 1994, A Laboratory for Anthopology: Science and Romanticism in the American Southwest, 1946–1930 2000, Philadelphia and the Development of Americanist Archaeology (co-ed. with D. R. Wilcox) 2003, Southwestern Archaeology in the Twentieth Century (co-ed. with L. Cordell) 2005, Anthropology Goes to the Fair (with Nancy J. Parezo) 2009, Laboratory for Anthropology 2010, The Glen Canyon Country: A Personal Memoir 2011; contrib. to many scholarly journals. *Honours:* many pvt. and govt grants, Distinguished Grad. Medal, Univ. of Pittsburgh 1986, Lifetime Achievement Award, Soc. for American Archaeology 2003, Outstanding Researcher, Univ. of Nevada, Reno 2003. *Address:* 1010 Foothill Road, Reno, NV 89511-9428, USA (home). *Telephone:* (775) 853-3471 (home).

FOWLER, Marian Elizabeth, BA, MA, PhD; Canadian writer; b. 15 Oct. 1929, Newmarket, Ont.; m. Dr Rodney Singleton Fowler 1953 (divorced 1977); one s. one d. *Education:* Univ. of Toronto. *Publications include:* The Embroidered Tent: Five Gentlewomen in Early Canada 1982, Redney: A Life of Sara Jeannette Duncan 1983, Below the Peacock Fan: First Ladies of the Raj 1987, Blenheim: Biography of a Palace 1989, In a Gilded Cage: From Heiress to Duchess 1993, The Way She Looks Tonight: Five Women of Style 1996, Hope: Adventures of a Diamond 2003; contrib. to English Studies in Canada, University of Toronto Quarterly, Dalhousie Review, Ontario History, Dictionary of Canadian Biography, Oxford Companion to Canadian Literature, New Canadian Encyclopaedia. *Honours:* Gov.-Gen.'s Gold Medal in English 1951, Canadian Biography Award 1979. *Address:* Apt 503, 77 St Clair Avenue East, Toronto, ON M4T 1M5, Canada (home).

FOWLER, Rebecca, BSc; British newspaper editor; b. 1958; m. Niall Ferguson; one s. one d. *Education:* Univ. of Southampton. *Career:* freelance journalist; Medical Corresp., Mail on Sunday, then Features Ed.; journalist Daily Mail; Assoc. Ed. Sunday Times 1991, then Deputy Ed.; fmr Ed. Sunday Express. *Address:* c/o Sunday Express, Ludgate House, 245 Blackfriars Road, London, SE1 9UX, England.

FOX, Hugh Bernard, (Connie Fox), BS, MA, PhD; American academic, writer, poet and dramatist; b. 12 Feb. 1932, Chicago, Ill.; m. 1st Lucia Alicia Ungaro 1957 (divorced 1969); one s. two d.; m. 2nd Nona W. Werner 1970; one s. two d.; m. 3rd Maria Bernadette Costa 1988. *Education:* Loyola Univ., Chicago, Univ. of Illinois, Urbana-Champaign. *Career:* Prof. of American Literature, Loyola Marymount Univ., Los Angeles 1958–68; Fulbright Prof., Mexico 1961, Venezuela 1964–66, Brazil 1978–80; Ed. Ghost Dance: The International Quarterly of Experimental Poetry 1968–95; Prof., Michigan State Univ. 1968–99, Prof. Emer.; Lecturer in Spain and Portugal 1975–76. *Publications include:* fiction: Honeymoon/Mom 1978, Leviathan 1980, Shaman 1993, The Last Summer 1995; poetry: The Face of Guy Lombardo 1975, Almazora 42 1982, Jamais Vu 1991, The Sacred Cave 1992, Once 1995, Techniques 1997; non-fiction: Henry James 1968, Charles Bukowski: A Critical and Bibliographical Study 1969, The Gods of the Cataclysm 1976, First Fire: Central and South American Indian Poetry 1978, Lyn Lifshin: A Critical Study 1985, The Mythological Foundations of the Epic Genre: The Solar Voyage as the Hero's Journey 1989, Stairway to the Sun 1996, Strata 1998, Back 1999, Slides 2000, The Angel of Death: O Ango da Morte 2001, Boston: A Long Poem 2002, Voices 2002, Hugh Fox: Greatest Hits 1968–2001 2003, The Book of Ancient Revelations 2004, The Home of the Gods 2005, Time and Other Poems 2005, Blood Cocoon: Selected Poetry (as Connie Fox) 2005, Collected Poetry 2006, Our Gang: The Last Act 2006, The Complete Poetry of Hugh Fox 1966–2007 2007; contrib. to many journals, reviews, quarterlies and periodicals. *Honours:* John Carter Brown Library Fellowship, Brown Univ. 1968, Organization of American States Grants, Argentina 1971, Chile 1986. *Address:* 333 Oxford Road, East Lansing, MI 48823-2628, USA (home). *Telephone:* (517) 337-2829 (home). *E-mail:* hughfox8@aol.com (home).

FOX, Merrion (Mem) Frances, AM, BA, BEd; Australian writer; b. 5 March 1946, Melbourne, Vic.; m. Malcolm 1969; one d. *Education:* Flinders Univ., Sturt Coll., Grad. Diploma, Underdale Coll. *Career:* mem. Australian Soc. of Authors, Australian Children's Book Council. *Publications include:* children's books: Possum Magic 1983, Wilfrid Gordon McDonald Partridge 1984, A Cat Called Kite 1985, Zoo-Looking 1986, Hattie and the Fox 1986, Sail Away 1986, Arabella 1986, Just Like That 1986, A Bedtime Story 1987, The Straight Line Wonder 1987, Goodnight Sleep Tight 1988, Guess What? 1988, Koala Lou 1988, Night Noises 1989, Shoes for Grandpa 1989, Feathers and Fools 1989, Sophie 1989, Memories 1992, Time for Bed 1993, Tough Boris 1994, Wombat Divine 1995, Boo to a Goose 1996, Whoever You Are 1998, Sleepy Bears 1999, Harriet, You'll Drive Me Wild! 2000, The Magic Hat 2002, Where is the Green Sheep? 2004, Hunwick's Egg 2005, A Particular Cow 2006, Where the Giant Sleeps 2007, Ten Little Fingers and Ten Little Toes 2008, Hello Baby! 2009, A Giraffe in the Bath 2010, Let's Count Goats! 2010; adult books: How to Teach Drama to Infants Without Really Crying 1984, Mem's the Word 1990, Dear Mem Fox, I Have Read All Your Books, Even the Pathetic Ones 1992, English Essentials 1993, Radical Reflectioons on Teaching, Learning and Living 1993, Reading Magic 2001; contribs to Language Arts, Horn Book, Australian Journal of Language and Literacy, Reading Teacher, Reading and Writing Quarterly, Dragon Lode. *Honours:* Dr hc (Univ. of Wollongong) 1996; NSW Premier's Literary Award, Best Children's Book 1984, KOALA First Prize 1987, Dromkeen Medal for Outstanding Services to Children's Literature 1990, Advance Australia Award 1990, Alice Award, Fellowship of Australian Women Writers 1994. *E-mail:* sfaxfox@bigpond.net.au (office). *Website:* www.memfox.com.

FOX, Paula; American writer; b. 22 April 1923, New York, NY; d. of Paul Hervey Fox and Elsoe de Sola; m. 1st Howard Bird 1940 (divorced); one d.; m. 2nd Richard Sigerson 1948 (divorced); two s.; m. 3rd Martin Greenberg 1962. *Education:* Columbia Univ. *Career:* mem. American Acad. of Arts and Letters. *Publications include:* novels: Poor George 1967, Desperate Characters 1970, The Western Coast 1972, The Widow's Children 1976, A Servant's Tale 1984, The God of Nightmares 1990; juvenile: Maurice's Room 1966, A Likely Place 1967, Dear Prosper 1968, The Stone-Faced Boy 1968, The King's Falcon 1969, Blowfish Live in the Sea 1970, The Slave Dancer 1973, The Little Swinehead and Other Tales 1978, A Place Apart 1980, One-Eyed Cat 1984, The Moonlight Man 1986, The Village by the Sea (aka In a Place of Danger) 1988, Monkey Island 1991, Western Wind 1993, The Eagle Kite (aka The Gathering Darkness) 1995, Amzat and His Brothers: Three Italian Tales 1999, Portrait of Ivan 2004, How Many Miles to Babylon? 2005, The Coldest Winter: A Stringer in Liberated Europe 2006; other: Borrowed Finery (memoir) 2001, News from the World: Stories & Essays 2011. *Honours:* Hans Christian Andersen Medal for Children's Literature, Newbery Medal 1974, Brandeis Fiction Award 1984, American Academy Arts and Letters Award of Merit 2002, Newbery Honor Award 1985, PEN Martha Albrand Award 2001, Deutschen Judenliteraturpreis 2008. *Address:* 306 Clinton Street, Brooklyn, NY 112011, USA (home). *E-mail:* foxgreenberg5@aol.com (home).

FRAILE, Medardo, PhD, DLitt; Spanish writer and academic; b. 21 March 1925, Madrid; m. Janet H. Gallagher; one d. *Education:* Univ. of Madrid. *Career:* mem. Gen. Soc. of Spanish Authors, Working Community of Book Writers, Asscn of Univ. Teachers. *Publications include:* Cuentos con algún amor 1954, A la luz cambian las cosas 1959, Cuentos de verdad 1964, Descubridor de nada y otros cuentos 1970, Con los días contados 1972, Samuel Ros hacia una generación sin crítica 1972, La penúltima Inglaterra 1973, Poesía y Teatro españoles contemporáneos 1974, Ejemplario 1979, Autobiografía (novella) 1986, Cuento español de Posguerra 1986, El gallo puesto en hora 1987, Entre paréntesis 1988, Santa Engracia, número dos o tres 1989, Teatro español en un acto 1989, El rey y el país con granos 1991, Cuentos completos 1991, Claudina y los cacos 1992, La familia irreal inglesa 1993, Los brazos invisibles 1994, Documento nacional 1997, Contrasombras 1998, Ladrones del Paraíso 1999, Cuentos de verdad (anthology) 2000, Descontar y contar (México) 2000, La letra con sangre 2001, Años de aprendizaje (Venezuela) 2001, Escritura y Verdad, Cuentos completos 2004, Palabra en el tiempo 2005, En Madrid también se vive en Oruro (Bolivia) 2007, Entradas de cine 2008, Autobiografia. Relevos de luz y sombra 2008; trans.: El Weir de Hermiston by R. L. Stevenson 1995; contrib. to many publs. *Honours:* Colegiado de Honor del Colegio Heráldico de España y de las Indias 1965, Comendador con Placa de la Orden Civil de Alfonso X El Sabio 1999, Orden venezolana de Don Balthasar de León de Primera Clase; Sésamo Award 1956, Literary Grant, Fundación Juan March 1960, Critics' Book of the Year 1965, La Estafeta Literaria Award 1970, Hucha de Oro 1971, Research Grant, Carnegie Trust for Univs of Scotland 1975. *Address:* 24 Etive Crescent, Bishopbriggs, Glasgow, G64 1ES, Scotland (home).

FRAIN, Irène Marie Anne; French writer and journalist; b. 22 May 1950, Lorient; d. of Jean Le Pohon and Simone Le Pohon (née Martelot); m. François Frain 1969; one d. *Education:* high schools in Lorient and Rennes and Univ. of Paris IV (Paris-Sorbonne). *Career:* teacher, secondary schools, then Univ. of Paris III (Sorbonne-Nouvelle) 1971–86; first book published 1979; journalist on Paris Match magazine 1984–. *Publications include:* Quand les Bretons peuplaient les mers 1979, Contes du cheval bleu les jours de grand vent 1980, Le Nabab (Prix des Maisons de la Presse) 1982, Modern Style 1984, Désirs (Prix des Ecrivains de l'Ouest) 1986, Secret de Famille (Prix Radio-Télé Luxembourg–RTL Grand Public) 1989, Histoire de Lou 1989, La guirlande de Julie 1991, Devi 1993, Quai des Indes 1993, Vive la mariée 1993, La vallée des hommes perdus 1994, L'homme fatal 1995, L'inimitable 1998, A jamais 1999, La maison de la source 2000, Pour que ne fleurisse le monde (with Jetsun Pema) 2002, Les Hommes, etc. 2003, Le Bonheru de faire l'amour dans sa cuisine et vice-versa 2004, Le Golfe et Vannes 2004, Les Couleurs de la mer 2005, Gandhi, la liberté en marche 2007, A la recherche du Royaume 2007, Au Royaume des Femmes 2007, Les naufragés de l'île Tromelin 2010, La Foret Des 29 2011. *Honours:* Officier, Ordre des Arts et Lettres 1989, Chevalier, Légion d'honneur 1998, Officier, Ordre nat. du Mérite 2002. *Address:* c/o Editions Fayard, 13 rue du Montparnasse, 75006 Paris, France. *Telephone:* 1-45-49-82-00. *Website:* www.irenefrain.com.

FRAJLICH, Anna, (Anna Frajlich-Zajac), MA, PhD; Polish poet and academic; Senior Lecturer, Columbia University; b. 10 March 1942, Katta Taldyk, Kyrgyzstan; m. Władysław Zajac 1965; one s. *Education:* Warsaw Univ., New York Univ. *Career:* Sr Lecturer, Dept of Slavic Languages, Columbia Univ. 1982–; mem. PEN, Center for Writers in Exile (USA), Asscn of Polish Writers, Polish PEN. *Publications include:* Aby Wiatr Namalowac (To Paint the Wind) 1976, Tylko Ziemia (Only the Earth) 1979, Indian Summer 1982, Który las 1986, Between Dawn and the Wind 1991, Ogrodem i ogrodzeniem (The Garden and the Fence) 1993, Jeszcze w drodze (Still on its Way) 1994, W słońcu listopada 2000, Znów szuka mnie wiatr 2001, Le Vent, Á Nouveau Me Cherche (bilingual collection) 2003, Between Dawn And The Wind 2006, The Legacy Of Ancient Rome in the Russian Silver Age 2007, Rodopi 2007, Laboratorium 2010, Czeslaw Milosz. Lekcje 2011; contribs to Terra Poetica, Artful Dodge, The Polish Review, Wisconsin Review, Mr Cogito, The Jewish Quarterly, Poésie Première, World Literature Today and Polish publs; chapters in several books, among them: Living in Translation (ed. Halina Stephan) 2003, Rethinking the Russo-Japanese War 1904–5 (ed. Rotem Kowner) 2007, Czeslaw Milosz: Conversations (ed. Cynthia L. Haven), An Invisible Rope (ed. Cynthia L. Haven). *Honours:* Hon. Amb. of Szczecin 2008; Kt's Cross of the Order of Merit (Poland) 2002; Koscielski Foundation Award, Switzerland 1981, Readers' Choice for Polish Book of the Month, Rzeczpospolita newspaper, Warsaw 2001, W. & N. Turzanski Foundation Literary Award, Canada 2003. *Address:* Department of Slavic Languages, Columbia University, New York, NY 10027, USA (office). *Telephone:* (212) 854-4850 (office). *Fax:* (212) 854-5009 (office). *E-mail:* af38@columbia.edu (office). *Website:* www.annafrajlich.com.

FRAME, Ronald William Sutherland, MA, MLitt; British author; b. 23 May 1953, Glasgow, Scotland; s. of the late Alexander D. Frame and Isobel D. Frame (née Sutherland). *Education:* The High School of Glasgow, Univ. of Glasgow, Jesus Coll. Oxford. *Career:* full-time author 1981–; many recent Scottish-set short stories published in UK, N America and Australia; regular weekly 'Carnbeg' short story in The Herald (Scotland) 2008, 'Carnbeg Days' in The Scotsman (Scotland) 2008–09, regular contrib. Scottish Review of Books (Sunday Herald). *TV screenplays:* Paris 1985, Out of Time 1987, Ghost City 1994, A Modern Man 1996, M R James: Four Ghost Stories for Christmas (adaptation) 2000, Darien: Disaster in Paradise 2003, Cromwell 2003, The Two Loves of Anthony Trollope (script contrib.) 2004. *Radio scripts include:* Winter Journey 1985, Twister 1986, Rendezvous 1987, Cara 1989, A Woman of Judah 1991, The Lantern Bearers 1997, The Hydro (serial) 1997–99, Havisham 1998, Maestro 1999, Pharos 2000, Don't Look Now (adaptation) 2001, Sunday at Sant' Agata 2001, Greyfriars 2002, The Servant (adaptation) 2005, The Razor's Edge (adaptation) 2005, A Tiger for Malgudi (adaptation) 2006, The Blue Room (adaptation) 2007, The Shell House 2008, Blue Wonder 2008, Monsieur Monde Vanishes (adaptation) 2009, Pinkerton 2010, Sunday (adaptation) 2010, Striptease (adaptation) 2010, The Other Simenon 1 (three adaptations) 2011, The Dreamer 2012, The Other Simenon 2 (three adaptations) 2012. *Publications include:* Winter Journey 1984, Watching Mrs.

Gordon 1985, A Long Weekend with Marcel Proust 1986, Sandmouth People 1987, Paris (TV play) 1987, A Woman of Judah 1987, Penelope's Hat 1989, Bluette 1990, Underwood and After 1991, Walking My Mistress in Deauville 1992, The Sun on the Wall 1994, The Lantern Bearers 1999, Permanent Violet 2002, Time in Carnbeg 2004, Unwritten Secrets 2010, A Carnbeg Affair, Carnbeg Piccalilli, Mysteries of Carnbeg (Kindle) 2011, Havisham 2012. *Honours:* Betty Trask Prize (jt first recipient) 1984, Samuel Beckett Prize 1986, TV Industries' Panel's Most Promising Writer New to TV Award 1986, Saltire Scottish Book of the Year 2000, American Library Asscn's Barbara Gittings Honor Prize for Fiction 2003. *Literary Agent:* c/o Sayle Screen Ltd, 11 Jubilee Place, London, SW3 3TD, England. *Telephone:* (20) 7823-3883. *Fax:* (20) 7823-3363. *E-mail:* info@saylescreen.com.

FRANÇA, José-Augusto, DèsLitt et Sc Hum, DHist; Portuguese writer, art historian and academic; *Professor Emeritus, Department of Art History, University of Lisbon*; b. 16 Nov. 1922, Tomar; s. of José M. França and Carmen R. França; m. 2nd Marie-Thérèse Mandroux; one d. (by previous m.). *Education:* Lisbon Univ., Ecole des Hautes Etudes and Univ. of Paris. *Career:* travels in Africa, Europe, Americas and Asia 1945–; Ed. Lisbon literary review Unicornio 1951–56, Co-Ed. Cadernos de Poesia 1951–53; Founder-Dir Galeria de Marco, Lisbon 1952–54; art critic 1946–; film critic 1948–; lexicographical publr 1948–58; Ed. Pintura & Näo 1969–70, Colóquio Artes 1970–96; Prof., Cultural History and History of Art, Dir Dept of Art History, New Univ. of Lisbon 1974–92, Prof. Emer. 1992–, Dir elect Faculty of Social Sciences 1982; Dir Fondation C. Gulbenkian, Centre Culturel Portugais, Paris 1983–89; Visiting Prof., Univ. of Paris III 1985–89; Vice-Pres. Int. Asscn of Art Critics 1970–73, Pres. 1985–87, Hon. Pres. 1987–; Vice-Pres. Acad. Européenne de Sciences, Arts et Lettres Paris 1985–2000, Hon. Pres. 2000–; City Councillor, Lisbon 1974–75; mem. of City Ass. Lisbon 1990–93; Pres. Inst. Cultura Portuguesa 1976–80, World Heritage Cttee, UNESCO 1999–2005, J-A F's art collection Museu of Tomar 2004; mem. Int. Asscn of Art Critics, Int. Cttee of Art History, PEN Club, Soc. Européenne de Culture, Soc. de l'Histoire de l'Art français, Acad. Nacional de Belas Artes (Pres. 1977–80), Acad. das Ciencias de Lisboa, Acad. Européenne de Sciences, Arts et Lettres, World Acad. of Arts and Science, Acad. Nat. Sciences, Arts et Lettres de Bordeaux, Ateneo Veneto, Real Acad. Bellas Artes San Fernando (Spain). *Publications:* Natureza Morta (novel) 1949, Charles Chaplin—the Self-Made Myth 1952, Amadeo de Souza-Cardoso 1957, Azazel (play) 1957, Despedida Breve (short stories) 1958, Situação da Pintura Ocidental 1959, Da Pintura Portuguesa 1960, Dez Anos de Cinema 1960, Une ville des lumières: La Lisbonne de Pombal 1963, A Arte em Portugal no Século XIX 1967, Oito Ensaios sobre Arte Contemporânea 1967, Le romantisme au Portugal 1972, Almada, o Português sem Mestre 1972, A Arte na Sociedade Portuguesa no Século XX 1972, Antonio Carneiro 1973, A Arte em Portugal no século XX 1974, Zé Povinho 1975, Manolo Millares 1977, Lisboa: Urbanismo e Arquitectura, O Retrato na Arte Portuguesa, Rafael Bordalo Pinheiro, o Português tal e qual 1980, Malhoa & Columbano, Historia da Arte Occidental 1780–1980 1987, Os Anos 20 em Portugal 1992, Bosch ou le visionnaire intégral, Thomar revisited 1994, Lisboa 1898, (In) definições de Cultura 1997, Memorias para o Ano 2000 2000, Monte Olivete, minha aldeia 2001, Buridan (novel) 2002, Regra de Três (novel), Cem Cenas, quadros e contos (short stories) 2003, A Bela Angevina (novel), Historia da Arte em Portugal 1750–2000 2004, José e os outros (novel), Exercícios de Passamento (short stories) 2005, Ricardo Coraçao de Leão (novel) 2007, João sem Terra (novel) 2008, Lisboa: história física e moral 2008, Guerra e Paz (novel) 2009, Ano X – Lisboa 1936 (essay) 2010, Mina e as coincidencias (novel) 2011, Ano XX — Lisboa 1946 (essay) 2012. *Honours:* Hon. mem. Union Journalistes Cinéma 2008, Ordem dos Arquitectos 2009; Officier, Ordre nat. du Mérite, Chevalier, Ordre des Arts et des Lettres, Commdr, Ordem Rio Branco (Brazil), Grand Cross Order of Public Instruction, Grand Cross Ordem Infante Dom Henrique, Officer, Ordem Santiago; Medal of Honour (Lisbon). *Address:* Av. Infante Santo, 17/8D, 1350-175 Lisbon, Portugal (home); 12 route de Beauvau, 49140 Jarzé, France (home). *Telephone:* (21) 3953512 (Lisbon) (home); 2-41-95-40-04 (Jarzé) (home). *Fax:* 2-41-95-40-04 (Jarzé) (home).

FRANCE, (Evelyn) Christine, BA; Australian art historian; b. 23 Dec. 1939, Sydney, NSW; m. Stephen Robert Bruce France 1962; one d. *Education:* Univ. of Sydney. *Publications include:* Justin O'Brien: Image and Icon 1987, Margaret Olley 1990, Marea Gazzard: Form and Clay 1994, Jean Appleton: A Lifetime with Art 1998; contribs: art and Australia; Australian newspapers.

FRANCIS, Clare Mary, MBE, BSc; British writer and fmr yachtswoman; b. 17 April 1946, Thames Ditton, Surrey, England; d. of Owen Francis; m. Jacques Robert Redon 1977 (divorced 1985); one s. *Education:* Royal Ballet School and Univ. Coll. London. *Career:* crossed Atlantic Ocean singlehanded in 37 days, Falmouth (UK) to Newport (USA) 1973; competed in Round Britain Race 1974, Azores Race 1975, L'Aurore Race 1975, 1976; women's record Observer Transatlantic Singlehanded Race (29 days) 1976; first woman skipper Whitbread Round the World Race 1977–78; full-time novelist 1981–; Fellow, Univ. Coll. London 1979; Pres. Action for ME (charity); Chair. Soc. of Authors 1997–99; Chair. Govt Advisory Cttee on Public Lending Right 2000–03. *TV series:* The Commanding Sea (co-writer and presenter) 1981. *Publications include:* non-fiction: Come Hell or High Water 1977, Come Wind or Weather 1978, The Commanding Sea 1981; novels: Night Sky 1983, Red Crystal 1985, Wolf Winter 1987, Requiem 1991, Deceit 1993 (televised 2000), Betrayal 1995, A Dark Devotion 1997, Keep Me Close 1999, A Death Divided 2001, Homeland 2004, Unforgotten 2008. *Honours:* Hon. Fellow, UMIST 1981. *Literary Agent:* c/o John Johnson Agency, 45–47 Clerkenwell Green, London, EC1R 0HT, England. *Website:* www.clarefrancis.com.

FRANCIS, Matthew, MA, PhD; British poet and novelist; *Lecturer in Creative Writing, University of Wales Aberystwyth*; b. 1956, Gosport, Hants., England; s. of Leslie Francis and Marian Mary Francis (née Rennie); m. Creina Burford-Bowden 1986. *Education:* Univs of Cambridge and Southampton. *Career:* fmrly Lecturer in Creative Writing, Univ. of Glamorgan, S Wales; Lecturer in Creative Writing, Univ. of Wales, Aberystwyth 2003–. *Publications include:* poetry: Blizzard 1996, Dragons 2001, Whereabouts 2006, Mandeville 2008, Ruskie: Beers, Bears & Babushkas 2009; novel: WHOM 1989; criticism: Where the People Are: Language and Community in the Poetry of W. S. Graham 2004; ed.: W. S. Graham, New Collected Poems 2004. *Honours:* Southern Arts Literature Prize 1997, Gathering Swallows Prize 1997, Hawthornden Fellowship 1998, MFCAP Prize 1999, TLS/Blackwells Prize 2000, Next Generation Poets List 2004. *Literary Agent:* c/o Faber and Faber Ltd, Bloomsbury House, 74–77 Great Russell Street, London, WC1B 3DA, England. *Telephone:* (1970) 622469 (office). *Fax:* (1970) 622530 (office). *E-mail:* mwf@aber.ac.uk (office). *Website:* www.aber.ac.uk (office); www.7greenhill .freeserve.co.uk.

FRANCK, Dan; French writer and screenwriter; b. 17 Oct. 1952, Paris; s. of Alain Franck and Marcelle Franck (née Refkolevsky); two s. *Education:* Lycée de la Celle-Saint-Cloud, Lycée de Rueil-Malmaison, Sorbonne Univ. *Films as writer:* Netchaïev est de retour 1991, Berlin Lady (TV) 1991, La Séparation 1994, Tykho Moon 1996, Les Parents modèles (TV) 1997, Jean Moulin (TV) 2002, Simon le juste (TV) 2003, Monsieur Max (TV) 2004, Les Enfants 2005, Plus tard 2008. *Film appearances:* Toujours seuls 1991, En compagnie d'Antonin Artaud 1993, Paddy 1999. *Publications include:* Les Calendes grecques (Prix du Premier Roman) 1980, Apolline 1982, La Dame du soir 1984, Les Adieux 1987, Le Cimetière des fous 1989, La Séparation (Prix Renaudot) 1991, Une jeune fille 1994, Tabac 1995, Nu couché 1998, Bohèmes 1998, Un siècle d'amour (with Enki Bilal) 1999, Libertad! 2004, Rondo noir 2008, Minuit 2010; with Jean Vautrin: Les Aventures de Boro, reporter-photographe: La Dame de Berlin 1988, Le Temps des cerises 1990, Les Noces de Guernica 1994, Mademoiselle Chat 1996, Boro s'en va en guerre 2000, Cher Boro 2002, Le Fête à Boro 2007, La Dame de Jérusalem 2009; essays: Les Têtes de l'art 1983, Le Petit livre de l'orchestre et de ses instruments 1993, Le Carnet de la Californie 1999. *Address:* c/o Grasset, 61 rue des Saints-Pères, 75006 Paris, France (office).

FRANCK, Julia; German writer and journalist; b. 20 Feb. 1970, Berlin; d. of Juergen Sehmisch and Anna Katharina Franck; two c. *Education:* Freie Universität Berlin. *Career:* has lived in USA and Cen. America; previous jobs included auxiliary nurse, waitress, typist, production asst for radio; freelance journalist for publs including Frankfurter Allgemeine Zeitung, Süddeutsche Zeitung, Cosmopolitan, Brigitte, Merian; currently Lecturer, Wiesbaden. *Publications include:* novels: Der neue Koch 1997, Liebediener 1999, Lagerfeuer (trans. as Campfire) 2003, Die Mittagsfrau (trans. as The Blind Side of the Heart) (Deutscher Buchpreis) 2007; short stories: Bauchlandung 2000, Mir nichts, dir nichts 2007. *Honours:* Alfred Döblin Scholarship, Acad. of Arts 1998, Scholarship of the Lower-Saxony Foundation 1999, 3sat Prize, Klagenfurt Literary Festival 2000, Marie-Luise-Kaschnitz Prize 2004, Roswitha Prize 2005, Villa Massimo Scholarship 2005, Wiesbad Poetry Prize 2006. *Address:* c/o S. Fischer Verlag GmbH, Postfach 700355, 60596 Frankfurt, Germany. *E-mail:* info@fischerverlage.de. *Website:* www .fischerverlage.de; www.juliafranck.de.

FRANCO, Tomaso, DJur; Italian poet and writer; b. 23 May 1933, Bologna; m. (divorced); two s. *Education:* studied classics, law and art. *Publications include:* poetry: Uno Scatto dell'Evoluzione 1984, Parole d'Archivio 1986, Il Libro dei Torti 1988, Casa di Frontiera 1990, Volavi Per Me 2000, In Un Luogo della Mente 2001, Nome Lontano 2004, plaguette, Esitante per Amore 2004; anthologies: Il Viaggiatore Indispensabile 2002; novels: Soldato dei Sogni 1995; short stories: I Muri della Casa 2005; essays: Sila-Torino 1961, Lettere a un Fuoruscito 1988, Antichità di Lavarone 2003; contrib. to various anthologies, newspapers, and journals. *Honours:* First Prize, Clemente Rèbora, Milan 1986, Gold Medal, City of Como 1990, First Prize (Nat.), Associazione Promozione Cultura in Toscana 1992. *Address:* Via San Domenico 2, 36100 Vicenza, Italy (home).

FRANCO ESTADELLA, Antonio; Spanish journalist; *Editor, El Periódico de Catalunya*; b. 21 Jan. 1947, Barcelona; s. of Alfonso Franco and Lolita Estadella; m. Marie-Hélène Bigatá; one s. one d. *Career:* Ed. Sports Section Diario Barcelona 1970, Ed.-in-Chief 1973, Asst Dir 1975; Dir Siete Días (TV programme) 1977; f. El Periódico de Catalunya 1977, Ed.-in-Chief 1987–2006; Jt Ed. El País 1982; apptd Asst Ed., Grupo Zeta 2006, currently Adviser to Pres. of Zeta Group; apptd Ed. Espai Public (TV programme, BTV) 2007; Pres. Asscn of Friends, Universitat Autònoma de Barcelona 2010–; mem. International Inst. for the Defense of Press Freedom. *Publications:* Deporte y sociedad 1975. *Honours:* Creu de Sant Jordi (Catalonian order) 2006; for journalism: Premio Ortega y Gasset, Premio Godó, Premio Luca de Tena, Premio Ciutat de Barcelona, Luca de Tena Journalism Award 2000, Antonio Asensio Prize 2007. *Address:* El Periódico de Catalunya, Consell de Cent 425–427, 08009 Barcelona, Spain (office). *Telephone:* (93) 2655353 (office). *Fax:* (93) 4846517 (office). *E-mail:* afranco@elperiodico.com (office); sac@ elperiodico.com (office). *Website:* www.elperiodico.es (office).

FRANCO RAMOS, Jorge; Colombian writer; b. 1964, Medellín. *Education:* London Int. Film School, UK, Pontificia Universidad Javeriana, Bogotá. *Publications include:* Maldito amor (short stories) (winner Concurso Nacional de Narrativa Pedro Gómez Valderrama) 1996, Mala noche (novel) (winner Concurso Nacional de Novela Ciudad de Pereira) 1997, Rosario Tijeras (novel) (Dashiell Hammett Prize 2000) 1999, Paraíso Travel (novel) 2001, Don Quijote de la Mancha en Medellin 2006, Melodrama 2006. *Honours:* Ministry of Culture nat. grant for novel 1999. *E-mail:* info@jorge-franco.com (office). *Website:* www.jorge-franco.com.

FRANK, Elizabeth, MA, PhD; American writer and academic; *Joseph E. Harry Professor of Modern Languages and Literature, Center for Curatorial Studies, Bard College;* b. 1945, Los Angeles, Calif. *Education:* Univ. of California, Berkeley. *Career:* Joseph E. Harry Prof. of Modern Languages and Literature, Center for Curatorial Studies, Bard Coll. 1982–. *Publications include:* Jackson Pollock (biog.) 1983, Louise Bogan: A Portrait (biog.) (Pulitzer Prize for Biog. 1986) 1985, Esteban Vicente (biog.) 1995, Cheat and Charmer (novel) 2004, Farewell, Shanghai (co-trans.) 2007, Isaac's Torah (co-trans.) 2008; contrib. numerous articles to New York Arts Journal, Art in America, Journal of Modern Literature, Twentieth-Century Literature, ARTnews, Bennington Review, The Nation, Salmagundi, New York Times Book Review, Partisan Review. *Honours:* Ford Foundation Fellowship 1967–72, Temple Univ. Fellowship 1977, The Newbery Library Fellowship 1977, American Council of Learned Socs Fellowship 1977, Nat. Endowment for the Humanities Fellowship. *Address:* Center for Curatorial Studies, Bard College, Annandale-on-Hudson, NY 12504-5000, USA (office). *E-mail:* frank@bard.edu (office).

FRANK, Joseph Nathaniel, PhD; American academic and writer; *Professor Emeritus of Comparative Literature and Slavic Languages and Literatures, Stanford University;* b. 6 Oct. 1918, New York, NY; m. Marguerite J. Straus 1953; two d. *Education:* New York Univ., Univ. of Wisconsin, Univ. of Paris, Univ. of Chicago. *Career:* Ed., Bureau of Nat. Affairs, Washington, DC 1942–50; Asst Prof., Dept of English, Univ. of Minnesota 1958–61; Assoc. Prof., Rutgers Univ. 1961–66; Prof. of Comparative Literature, Princeton Univ. 1966–85, Dir of Christian Gauss Seminars 1966–83; Visiting mem., Inst. for Advanced Study 1984–87; Prof. of Comparative Literature and Slavic Languages and Literatures, Stanford Univ. 1985–89, Prof. Emer. 1989–; mem. American Acad. of Arts and Sciences, fellow. *Publications include:* The Widening Gyre: Crisis and Mastery in Modern Literature 1963, Dostoevsky: The Seeds of Revolt, 1821–1849 1976, Dostoevsky: The Years of Ordeal, 1850–1859 1983, Dostoevsky: The Stir of Liberation, 1860–1865 1986, Selected Letters of Fyodor Dostoevsky (co-ed.) 1987, Through the Russian Prism 1989, The Idea of Spatial Form 1991, Dostoevsky: The Miraculous Years, 1865–1871 1995, Dostoevsky: The Mantle of the Prophet, 1871–1881 2003, Dostoevsky: A Writer in His Time 2009; contribs to Southern Review, Sewanee Review, Hudson Review, Partisan Review, Art News, Critique, Chicago Review, Minnesota Review, Russian Review, Le Contrat Social, Commentary, Encounter, New York Review. *Honours:* Fulbright Scholar 1950–51, Rockefeller Fellow 1952–53, 1953–54, Guggenheim Fellowships 1956–57, 1975–76, Award, Nat. Inst. of Arts and Letters 1958, Research Grants, ACLS 1964–65, 1967–68, 1970–71, James Russell Lowell Prize 1977, Christian Gauss Awards 1977, 1996, Rockefeller Foundation Fellowships 1979–80, 1983–84, Nat. Book Critics Circle Award 1984. *Address:* Department of Slavic Languages and Literatures, Stanford University, Stanford, CA 94305, USA (office).

FRANKE, William, BA, MA, PhD; American academic and poet; *Professor of Comparative Literature and Italian, Vanderbilt University;* b. 1 April 1956, Milwaukee, Wis.; m. Béatrice Machet. *Education:* Williams Coll., Oxford, UK, Univ. of California, Berkeley, Stanford Univ. *Career:* Adjunct Faculty mem. Columbia Coll. 1984–86; Faculty mem. Vanderbilt Univ., Nashville, Tenn. 1991–96, Prof. of Comparative Literature and Italian, and of Religious Studies 1996–; Lecturer, educational insts including Stanford Univ. 1991, Univ. of Tulsa 1992, Univ. of Reading, UK 1995; Visiting Assoc. Prof. of Comparative Literature, Univ. of Hong Kong 2005; Fulbright-Univ. of Salzburg Distinguished Chair., Intercultural Theology and Study of Religions 2007; Prof. of French-in-Residence, Vanderbilt-in-France, Aix-en-Provence 2008; mem. Dante Soc. Council, Dante Soc. of America. *Publications include:* Dante's Interpretative Journey 1996, On What Cannot Be Said 2007, Poetry and Apocalypse 2009, Dichtung und Apokalypse: Theologische Erschliesungen der dichterischen Sprache 2011; contribs to books including Through a Glass Darkly: Essays in the Religious Imagination, Dante: Contemporary Perspectives 1996; articles and poems to journals including SEAMS: Cultural Arts Journal, California State Poetry Quarterly, Italian Quarterly, Religion and Literature, Yeats-Eliot Review, Symploke: Journal for the Intermingling of Literary, Cultural, and Theoretical Scholarship. *Honours:* John E. Moody Scholar, Univ. of Oxford 1978–80, Scholarship to W. B. Yeats International Summer School, Sligo, Ireland 1979, Alexander von Humboldt Fellow, Germany 1994–95, Grants, Istituto Italiano per gli studi filosifici, Naples, Italy 1995, 1996, Robert Penn Warren Center for the Humanities Fellow 1995–96, Fellow, Camargo Foundation 1999, Fellow in Philosophy, Bogliasco Foundation 2006. *Address:* Department of French and Italian, Vanderbilt University, VU Station B #356312, 2301 Vanderbilt Place, Nashville, TN 37235-6312, USA (office). *E-mail:* william.p.franke@vanderbilt.edu (office). *Website:* sitemason.vanderbilt.edu/complit/franke (office).

FRANKEL, Max, MA; American journalist; b. 3 April 1930, Gera, Germany; s. of Jacob A. Frankel and Mary (Katz) Frankel; m. 1st. Tobia Brown 1956 (died 1987); two s. one d.; m. 2nd Joyce Purnick 1988. *Education:* Columbia Univ., New York. *Career:* mem. staff, The New York Times 1952, Chief Washington Corresp. 1968–72, Sunday Ed. 1973–76, Editorial Pages Ed. 1977–86, Exec. Ed. 1986–94, 1994–95, also columnist New York Times magazine 1995–2000. *Publication:* The Time of My Life and My Life with the Times 1999, High Noon in the Cold War: Kennedy, Khrushchev and the Cuban Missile Crisis 2004. *Honours:* Pulitzer Prize for Int. Reporting 1973. *Address:* c/o The New York Times Co., 15 West 67th Street, New York, NY 10023-6226, USA (office).

FRANKFURT, Harry Gordon, BA, MA, PhD; American writer and academic; *Professor Emeritus of Philosophy, Princeton University;* b. 29 May 1929, Langhorne, Pa; m. Joan Gilbert. *Education:* Johns Hopkins Univ., Cornell Univ. *Career:* instructor, Ohio State Univ. 1956–59, Asst Prof. 1959–62; Assoc. Prof., State Univ. of NY, Binghamton 1962–63; Research Assoc., Rockefeller Univ., New York 1963–64, Assoc. Prof. 1964–71, Prof. of Philosophy 1971–76; Visiting Fellow, All Souls Coll., Oxford, UK 1971–72; Visiting Prof., Vassar Coll. 1973–74, Univ. of Pittsburgh 1975–76, UCLA 1990; Prof. of Philosophy, Yale Univ. 1976–89, Chair. Dept of Philosophy 1978–87, John M. Schiff Prof. 1989; Prof. of Philosophy, Princeton Univ. 1990–2002, Prof. Emer. 2002–; Fellow, American Acad. of Arts and Sciences; mem. American Philosophical Asscn (Eastern Division) (Pres. 1991–92). *Publications include:* Demons, Dreamers, and Madmen: The Defense of Reason in Descartes's Meditations 1970, Leibniz: A Collection of Critical Essays (ed.) 1972, The Importance of What We Care About 1988, Necessity, Volition and Love 1999, The Reasons of Love 2004, On Bullshit 2005, On Truth 2006, Sich selbst ernst nehmen 2007. *Honours:* Nat. Endowment for the Humanities Fellowships 1981–82, 1994, Guggenheim Fellowship 1993. *Address:* c/o 110 University Press, Princeton University, Princeton, NJ 08544, USA (office). *Telephone:* (609) 258-8630 (office). *E-mail:* fraharg@princeton.edu (office). *Website:* philosophy.princeton.edu (office).

FRANKLAND, (Anthony) Noble, DFC, CBE, CB, MA, DPhil; British historian and writer; b. 4 July 1922, Ravenstonedale, Cumbria, England; m. 1st Diana Madeline Fovargue Tavernor 1944 (died 1981); one s. one d.; m. 2nd Sarah Katharine Davies 1982. *Education:* Trinity Coll., Oxford. *Career:* served in RAF 1941–45, Bomber Command 1943–45, Air Historical Br., Air Ministry 1948–50; Official British Mil. Historian, Cabinet Office 1951–58; Deputy Dir of Studies, Royal Inst. of Int. Affairs, London 1956–60; Dir Imperial War Museum 1960–82; Lees Knowles Lecturer, Trinity Coll., Cambridge 1963. *Television:* historical adviser to The World at War (series). *Publications include:* Documents on International Affairs 1958, 1959, 1960, Crown of Tragedy: Nicholas II 1960, The Strategic Air Offensive Against Germany 1939–45 (with Sir Charles Webster), four vols 1961, The Bombing Offensive Against Germany: Outlines and Perspectives 1965, Bomber Offensive: The Devastation of Europe 1970, The Politics and Strategy of the Second World War (co-ed.), eight vols 1974–78, Decisive Battles of the Twentieth Century: Land, Sea, Air (co-ed.) 1976, Prince Henry, Duke of Gloucester 1980, Encyclopedia of Twentieth Century Warfare (gen. ed. and contrib.) 1989, Witness of a Century: Prince Arthur, Duke of Connaught 1850–1942 1993, History at War: The Campaigns of an Historian 1998, The Unseen War (novel) 2007, Belling's War (novel) 2008; contribs to Encyclopaedia Britannica, TLS, The Times, Daily Telegraph, Spectator, Observer, military journals. *Address:* 26–27 Riverview Terrace, Abingdon, Oxon., OX14 5AE, England (home). *Telephone:* (1235) 521624 (home).

FRANKLIN, Dan; British publisher; *Publishing Director, Jonathan Cape.* *Career:* Publishing Dir, Jonathan Cape 1993–. *Address:* Jonathan Cape Ltd, Random House, 20 Vauxhall Bridge Road, London, SW1V 2SA, England (office). *E-mail:* dfranklin@randomhouse.co.uk (office). *Website:* www.randomhouse.co.uk (office).

FRANKLIN, Thomas G. (Tom), BA, MFA; American author and academic; *Professor in Creative Writing, MFA Program, University of Mississippi;* b. 1963, Dickinson, Ala; m. Beth Ann Fennelly; one s., one d. *Education:* Univ. of Southern Alabama, Univ. of Arkansas. *Career:* teacher, Univ. of Southern Alabama 1999; Phillip Roth Resident in Creative Writing, Bucknell Univ. 1999; Visiting Writer-in-Residence, Knox Coll. 2000; John and Renee Grisham Writer-in-Residence, Univ. of Mississippi 2000; taught at Sewannee Univ. 2002–03; currently Prof. in Creative Writing MFA Program, Univ. of Mississippi published in many periodicals and magazines including Chattahoochee Review, Brightleaf, Nebraska Review, Texas Review, Quarterly West, Smoke Magazine. *Publications include:* Poachers: stories (for title story: Edgar Allan Poe Award for Best Mystery Story 1999) 1999, Hell at the Breech 2003, Smonk: a Novel 2006, Crooked Letter, Crooked Letter (LA Times Book Prize for Best Mystery/Thriller 2011, Golden Dagger Award for Best Novel (UK) 2011, Willie Morris Award for Southern Fiction 2011) 2010; work appears in several anthologies. *Honours:* Writers at Work Literary Nonfiction Contest 1998, Arkansas Arts Council Grant for Short Story 1998, Guggenheim Fellowship 2001, Ala Library Award for Fiction. *Literary Agent:* c/o Sobel Weber Associates, Inc., 146 East 19th Street, New York, NY 10003-2404, USA. *Telephone:* (212) 420-8585. *Website:* www.sobelweber.com. *Address:* Department of English, University of Mississippi, W104 Bondurant Hall, PO Box 1848, University, MS 38677-1848, USA (office). *Telephone:* (662) 915-7914 (office). *E-mail:* tfrankli@olemiss.edu (office). *Website:* mfaenglish.olemiss.edu/?s=tom+franklin (office).

FRANZEN, Jonathan, BA; American writer; b. 17 Aug. 1959, Western Springs, IL. *Education:* Swarthmore Coll., Free Univ. of Berlin, Germany. *Career:* fmrly worked part-time in seismology lab., Harvard Univ. Dept of Earth and Planetary Sciences; currently full-time novelist, essayist, and journalist affiliated with The New Yorker. *Publications:* The Twenty-Seventh City (Whiting Award) 1988, Strong Motion 1991, The Corrections (Nat. Book Award for Fiction, New York Times Ed.'s Choice, James Tait Black Memorial Prize for Fiction 2003) 2001, How to be Alone (essays) 2002, The Discomfort Zone: A Personal History 2006, Spring Awakening (new trans. of Frank Wedekind play) 2007, Freedom 2010, Farther Away (essays) 2012. *Honours:* Hon. DHumLitt (Swarthmore Coll.) 2005; Whiting Award 1988, Guggenheim Fellowship, American Acad. Berlin Prize 2000, Granta Best Young American Novelist. *Literary Agent:* Steven Barclay Agency, 12 Western Avenue, Petaluma, CA 94952, USA. *Telephone:* (707) 773-0654 (office). *Fax:* (707) 778-1868 (office). *Website:* www.barclayagency.com (office). *Address:* c/o Susan Golomb Agency, 875 Sixth Avenue #2302, New York, NY 10001, USA (office). *Website:* www.jonathanfranzen.com.

FRASER, Lady Antonia Margaret Caroline, DBE, CBE, MA, FRSL; British historian and author; b. (Antonia Margaret Caroline Pakenham), 27 Aug. 1932, London; d. of the late 7th Earl and Countess of Longford; m. 1st Hugh Fraser 1956 (divorced 1977, died 1984); three s. three d.; m. 2nd Harold Pinter 1980 (died 2008); one step-s. *Education:* Dragon School, Oxford, St Mary's Convent, Ascot and Lady Margaret Hall, Oxford. *Career:* mem. Cttee English PEN 1979–88 (Pres. 1988–89, Vice-Pres. 1990–), Crimewriters Asscn 1980–86, Writers in Prison Cttee, Chair. 1985–88, 1990. *TV plays:* Charades 1977, Mister Clay 1985. *Publications:* King Arthur 1954, Robin Hood 1955, Dolls 1963, History of Toys 1966, Mary, Queen of Scots (James Tait Black Memorial Prize 1969) 1969, Cromwell: Our Chief of Men 1973, King James VI of Scotland and I of England 1974, Scottish Love Poems, A Personal Anthology 1974, Kings and Queens of England (ed.) 1975, Love Letters (anthology) 1976, King Charles II 1979, Heroes and Heroines (ed.) 1980, Oxford In Verse (ed.) 1982, The Weaker Vessel (Wolfson History Prize 1984) 1984, Boadicea's Chariot: The Warrior Queens 1988, The Six Wives of Henry VIII 1992, Charles II: His Life and Times 1993, The Gunpowder Plot (St Louis Literary Award 1996, CWA Non Fiction Gold Dagger 1996) 1996, The Lives of the Kings and Queens of England 1998, Marie Antoinette: The Journey (Enid McLeod Literary Prize, Franco-British Soc. 2001) 2001, Love and Louis XIV 2006, Must You Go? My Life with Harold Pinter 2010; Jemima Shore novels: Quiet as a Nun (TV adaptation 1978) 1977, The Wild Island 1978, A Splash of Red 1981, Cool Repentance 1982, Oxford Blood 1985, Jemima Shore's First Case 1986, Your Royal Hostage 1987, The Cavalier Case 1990, Jemima Shore at the Sunny Grave 1991, Political Death: A Jemima Shore Mystery 1994; anthologies (ed.): Scottish Love Poems 1975, Love Letters 1976; ed. The Pleasure of Reading 1992. *Honours:* Hon. DLitt (Hull) 1986, (Sussex) 1990, (Nottingham) 1993, (St Andrew's) 1994; Prix Caumont-La Force 1985, Norten Medlicott Medal, Historical Asscn 2000. *Literary Agent:* c/o Curtis Brown Group Ltd, Haymarket House, 28/29 Haymarket, London, SW1Y 4SP, England. *Telephone:* (20) 7396-6600. *Fax:* (20) 7396-0110.

FRASER, Sir David William, GCB, KCB, OBE; British author; b. 30 Dec. 1920, Camberley, Surrey, England; m. 1st Anne Balfour 1947 (divorced); one d.; m. 2nd Julia de la Hey 1957; two s. two d. *Education:* Christ Church, Oxford, British Army Staff Coll., Imperial Defence Coll. *Career:* Career Officer, British Army 1941–80, retiring with rank of Gen.; Vice-Lord Lt Hants. 1988–96. *Publications include:* Alanbrooke 1982, And We Shall Shock Them 1983, The Christian Watt Papers 1983, August 1988 1983, A Kiss for the Enemy 1985, The Killing Times 1986, The Dragon's Teeth 1987, The Seizure 1988, A Candle for Judas 1989, In Good Company 1990, Adam Hardrow 1990, Codename Mercury 1991, Adam in the Breach 1993, The Pain of Winning 1993, Knight's Cross: A Life of Field Marshal Erwin Rommel 1993, Will: A Portrait of William Douglas Home 1995, Frederick the Great 2000, Wars and Shadows 2002. *Literary Agent:* c/o PFD, Drury House, 34–43 Russell Street, London, WC2B 5HA, England. *Telephone:* (20) 7344-1000. *Fax:* (20) 7836-9543. *Website:* www.pfd.co.uk.

FRASER, Helen Jean Sutherland, CBE, MA; British publishing executive; *Managing Director, Penguin UK;* b. 8 June 1949, London, England; d. of the late G. S. and of Paddy Fraser; m. Grant James McIntyre 1982; two d. two step-d. *Education:* St Anne's Coll., Oxford. *Career:* Ed., Methuen Academic Ltd 1972–74, Open Books Ltd 1974–76; Ed., Fontana non-fiction, then Editorial Dir, William Collins 1977–87; Publr, William Heinemann 1987–91; Publr, Reed Trade Books 1991–96, Man. Dir 1996–97; Man. Dir Penguin Gen. Div. 1997–2001, Penguin UK 2001–09; CEO Girls' Day School Trust 2010–; Dir (non-exec.), Frances Lincoln Publrs 2010–. *Address:* Penguin Books Ltd, 80 Strand, London, WC2 0RL, England (office). *Telephone:* (20) 7010-3000 (office). *E-mail:* helen.fraser@uk.penguingroup.com (office). *Website:* www.penguin.co.uk (office).

FRASER, Jane (see Pilcher, Rosamunde)

FRASER, Kathleen Joy, BA; American academic, poet, publisher and editor; *Professor Emerita of Writing, San Francisco State University;* b. 22 March 1937, Tulsa, Okla; d. of James Ian Fraser and Marjorie Axtell; m. 1st Jack Marshall 1961 (divorced 1970); one s.; m. 2nd Arthur K. Bierman 1984. *Education:* Occidental Coll., Los Angeles, Columbia Univ., New School for Social Research, New York. *Career:* Visiting Prof., Univ. of Iowa 1969–71; Writer-in-Residence, Reed Coll., Portland, Ore. 1971–72; Dir, Poetry Center, San Francisco State Univ. 1972–75, Assoc. Prof. 1975–78, Prof. 1978–92, Prof. Emer. of Writing 1992–; Guest Writer, California Coll. of the Arts 2003–; Ed./Publr, How(ever); Publisher, HOW2; featured poet, Smerilliana (Italian trans.) 2006; Trans. of poetry of Andrea Raos; Dir and Founder The American Poetry Archive; trans. of many Italian poets; lectures on American poetry in univs in Italy; featured speaker, Centro Studi Americani grad. seminars. *Exhibitions include:* text/image collaborative works with painter Hermine Ford, Pratt Inst. of Architecture, Rome 2006; wall pieces from collaboration (ii ss) also at Melville House (Dumbo/Brooklyn) 2008. *Play:* Celeste & Sirius (produced for San Francisco Poets Theatre) 2003. *Publications include:* poetry: Change of Address and Other Poems 1966, In Defiance of the Rains 1969, Little Notes to You from Lucas Street 1972, What I Want 1974, Magritte Series 1978, New Shoes 1978, Each Next 1980, Something (Even Human Voices) in the Foreground, A Lake 1984, Notes Preceding Trust 1987, Boundayr 1988, Giotto, Arena 1991, When New Time Folds Up 1993, WING 1995, Il Cuore: The Heart, New and Selected Poems 1970–95, 1997, 20th Century 2000, hi dde violeth i dde violet 2003, Discrete Categories Forced Into Coupling 2004, WITNESS 2007, When I'm Gone 2009, movable TYYPE (sic) 2011; prose: Feminist Poetics: A Consideration of Female Construction of Language (ed.) 1984, Translating the Unspeakable, Poetry and the Innovative Necessity (essays) 1999. *Honours:* Dr hc (San Francisco State Univ.); YM-YWHA Discovery Award 1964, Nat. Endowment for the Arts grant 1969, Nat. Endowment for the Arts Poetry Fellowship 1978, Guggenheim Fellowship in Poetry 1981. *Address:* 1936 Leavenworth Street, San Francisco, CA 94133, USA (home). *E-mail:* kfraser@sfsu.edu (office).

FRASER, Sylvia Lois, BA; Canadian writer; b. 8 March 1935, Hamilton, Ont.; d. of the late George Meyers and Gladys Meyers; m. Russell James Fraser 1959 (divorced 1978). *Education:* Univ. of Western Ontario. *Career:* feature writer, The Toronto Star Weekly 1952–68; writer 1968–; Guest Lecturer, Banff Centre 1973–79, 1985, 1987, 1988; Writer-in-Residence, Univ. of Western Ontario 1980; Instructor, Huron Coll. Writers' Workshop 2003. *Publications include:* Pandora 1972, A Candy Factory 1975, A Casual Affair 1978, The Emperor's Virgin 1980, Berlin Solstice 1984, My Father's House (Canadian Authors' Asscn Non-Fiction Book Award) 1987, The Book of Strange (also published as The Quest for The Fourth Monkey, American Library Asscn Booklist Medal) 1992, The Ancestral Suitcase 1996, The Rope in the Water: a Pilgrimage to India 2001, The Green Labyrinth—Exploring the Mysteries of the Amazon 2003, Maggie and the Pedophiles 2011. *Honours:* Women's Press Club Medal 1967, 1968, Pres.'s Medal for Canadian Journalism 1968, Nat. Magazine Gold Medal 1994, 2004, 2005, Silver Medal 1996, 2002, Western Magazine Gold Medal 2006, Phoenix Women Rising Inaugural Award 2007. *Telephone:* (416) 703-7030 (home). *E-mail:* sylviafraser@sympatico.ca (home).

FRAYLING, Sir Christopher John, Kt, MA, PhD; British historian, arts administrator and broadcaster; *Rector, Department of Cultural History, Royal College of Art;* b. 26 Dec. 1946; m. Helen Anne Snowdon. *Education:* Repton School, Churchill Coll. Cambridge. *Career:* Lecturer, Univ. of Bath, Univ. of Exeter 1970s; Prof. of Cultural History, RCA 1979–, f. Dept of Cultural History, Rector 1996–; mem. Arts Council England 1987–2000, Chair. 2004–09; Chair. Design Council, Crafts Study Centre, Royal Mint Advisory Cttee, fmr Gov. BFI; mem. Arts & Humanities Research Bd; Trustee, Victoria & Albert Museum. *Television includes:* The Art of Persuasion (New York Film and Television Festival Gold Medal), The Face of Tutankhamun, Strange Landscape, Nightmare: The Birth of Horror 1996. *Radio includes:* The Rime of the Bounty (Sony Radio Award, Soc. of Authors Award). *Publications include:* Napoleon Wrote Fiction 1973, The Vampyre 1976, Spaghetti Westerns 1980, The Face of Tutankhamun 1992, Clint Eastwood: A Critical Biography 1993, Strange Landscape: A Journey through the Middle Ages 1995, Nightmare: The Birth of Horror 1996, Sergio Leone: Something to Do with Death 2000, Ken Adam: The Art of Production Design 2005, Mad, Bad and Dangerous? The Scientist and Cinema 2006. *Honours:* Hon. FRSA 2004, Hon. FRIBA 2005; six hon. doctorates. *Address:* Royal College of Art, Kensington Gore, London, SW7 2EU, England (office). *Telephone:* (20) 7590-4101 (office). *Fax:* (20) 7590-4100 (office). *Website:* www.rca.ac.uk (office).

FRAYN, Michael, BA, FRSL; British playwright and author; b. 8 Sept. 1933, London; s. of the late Thomas A. Frayn and Violet A. Lawson; m. 1st Gillian Palmer 1960 (divorced 1989); three d.; m. 2nd Claire Tomalin (q.v.) 1993. *Education:* Kingston Grammar School and Emmanuel Coll., Cambridge. *Career:* reporter, The Guardian 1957–59, columnist 1959–62; columnist, The Observer 1962–68; Cameron Mackintosh Prof. of Contemporary Theatre, Univ. of Oxford 2009–10. *Stage plays:* The Two of Us 1970, The Sandboy 1971, Alphabetical Order (Evening Standard Best Comedy of the Year 1975) 1975, Donkeys' Years (Laurence Olivier Award for Best Comedy 1976, Society of West End Theatre Comedy of the Year 1976) 1976, Clouds 1976, Balmoral 1978, Liberty Hall (new version of Balmoral) 1980, Make and Break 1980 (Evening Standard Best Comedy of the Year 1980), Noises Off (Evening Standard Best Comedy of the Year 1982, Laurence Olivier Award for Best Comedy 1982, Society of West End Theatre Comedy of the Year 1982) 1982, Benefactors (Laurence Olivier/BBC Award for Best New Play 1984) 1984, Look Look 1990, Here 1993, Now You Know 1995, Copenhagen (Evening Standard Award for Best Play of the Year 1998, West End Critics' Circle Best New Play Award 1998, Prix Molière Best New Play 1999, Tony Award for Best Play 2000) 1998, Alarms and Excursions 1998, Democracy (Evening Standard Theatre Award for Best Play, Critics' Circle Award for Best Play 2003) 2003,

Afterlife 2007. *TV includes:* plays: Jamie, on a Flying Visit (BBC) 1968, Birthday (BBC) 1969; documentary series: Second City Reports (with John Bird, Granada) 1964, Beyond a Joke (with John Bird and Eleanor Bron) 1972, Making Faces 1975; documentaries: One Pair of Eyes 1968, Laurence Sterne Lived Here 1973, Imagine a City Called Berlin 1975, Vienna: The Mask of Gold 1977, Three Streets in the Country 1979, The Long Straight (Great Railway Journeys of the World) 1980, Jerusalem 1984, Magic Lantern, Prague 1993, Budapest: Written in Water 1996 (all BBC documentaries); films: First and Last 1989, A Landing on the Sun 1994. *Cinema:* Clockwise 1986, Remember Me? 1997. *Plays translated include:* The Cherry Orchard, Three Sisters, The Seagull, Uncle Vanya, Wild Honey, The Sneeze (Chekhov), The Fruits of Enlightenment (Tolstoy), Exchange (Trifonov), Number One (Anouilh). *Publications:* novels: The Tin Men (Somerset Maugham Award 1966) 1965, The Russian Interpreter (Hawthornden Prize 1967) 1966, Towards the End of the Morning 1967, A Very Private Life 1968, Sweet Dreams 1973, The Trick of It 1989, A Landing on the Sun (Sunday Express Book of the Year) 1991, Now You Know 1992, Headlong 1999, Spies (Whitbread Award for Best Novel) 2002; non-fiction: Constructions (philosophy) 1974, Speak after the Beep 1995, Celia's Secret (with David Burke) 2000, The Human Touch: Our Part in the Creation of the Universe 2006, Stage Directions: Writing on Theatre 1970–2008 2008; Travels with a Typewriter 2009, My Father's Fortune: A Life 2010; several vols of collections of columns, plays and trans. *Honours:* Hon. Fellow, Emmanuel Coll., Cambridge, Hon. DLitt (Cambridge) 2001; Order of Merit (Germany) 2004; Heywood Hill Literary Prize 2002, Golden PEN Award 2003, Saint Louis Literary Award 2006, McGovern Award 2006, Companion of Literature 2007, Writers' Guild Lifetime Achievement Award 2010. *Literary Agent:* c/o Greene & Heaton Ltd, 37A Goldhawk Road, London, W12 8QQ, England.

FRAZIER, Charles, PhD; American writer; b. 4 Nov. 1950, Asheville, NC; m. Catherine Frazier; one d. *Education:* Univ. of North Carolina, Appalachian State Univ., Univ. of South Carolina. *Career:* fmr faculty mem., Univ. of Colo and North Carolina State Univ. *Publications:* Adventuring in the Andes: The Sierra Club Travel Guide to Ecuador, Peru, Bolivia, the Amazon Basin, and the Galapagos Islands (with Donald Secreast) 1985, Cold Mountain: Odyssey in North Carolina (novel, Nat. Book Award) 1997, Thirteen Moons (novel) 2006, Nightwoods 2012. *Literary Agent:* c/o Amanda Urban, International Creative Management, 825 Eighth Avenue, New York, NY 10019, USA. *Telephone:* (212) 556-5600. *Website:* www.icmtalent.com.

FRÈCHES, José Vincent, PhD; French writer and publisher; b. 25 June 1950, Dax, Landes; s. of Claude-Henri Frèches and Nicole Frèches (née Menguy); m. Claire Thory 1973; two d. one s. *Education:* lycées in Brazil, Italy, Portugal and France, Univs of Aix-en-Provence and Paris VII, Ecole nat. d' Admin. *Career:* Curator Musée des Beaux Arts, Grenoble, Guimet 1971–72; Maitre de Confs Ecole du Louvre, Insp. of Provincial Museums, Musées de France 1974–75; Auditeur Cour des Comptes 1978, Rapporteur Comm. des Marchés de bâtiment 1979–82, Chargé de mission Commissariat au Plan and Office of First Pres. Cour des Comptes 1980–82, Conseiller Cour des Comptes 1982; Chargé de mission to Dir-Gen. of Information and Exterior Relations, Ville de Paris 1982–83, Rapporteur Gen. Comm. du câble 1983–85, Asst Dir of Communication 1985, Dir Vidéothèque de Paris 1985, Admin. Bibliothèque publique d'information 1982–; Rapporteur Gen. Comm. Communication demain du RPR 1986; Conseiller in the cabinet of Prime Minister Jacques Chirac 1986–88; Dir Havas 1988, Visicable +; Dir-Gen. Groupe Fabre 1990–98, Admin. Pierre Fabre SA 1996–98; Admin. Midi Libre 1996–2000, Pres. 1998–2000; Pres. du conseil de surveillance des laboratoires Dolisos; mem. du conseil artistique de la Réunion des musées nat. 1988–; jury mem. Prix Méditerranée. *Publications include:* La Sinologie 1975, Les Musées de France 1980, L'ENA, voyage au centre de l'Etat 1981, La France socialiste 1983, Le Coût d'Etat permanent 1984, La Télévision par câble 1985, La Guerre des images 1985, Modernissimots 1987, Voyage au centre du pouvoir 1989, Le Poisson pourrit par la tête (co-author) 1992, Toulouse-Lautrec (co-author) 1991, Le Caravage, peintre et assassin 1995, Le Disque de Jade 2002, L'Imperatrice de la Soie 2003, Moi, Bouddha 2004, Art et Cie 2005, Il était une fois la Chine 2005, Le Centre d'Appel 2006, L'Empire des Larmes 2006, Die Handlerin 2008. *Honours:* Chevalier, Légion d'honneur. *Address:* Pierre Fabre SA, 45 place Abel Gance, 92100 Boulogne-Billancourt (office); 48 rue de Verneuil, 75007 Paris, France (home). *E-mail:* contact@josefreches.com (office). *Website:* www.josefreches.com.

FREEBORN, Richard Harry, BA, MA, DPhil; British academic, writer and translator; *Professor Emeritus of Russian Literature, University of London*; b. 19 Oct. 1926, Cardiff, Wales; m. Anne Davis 1954; one s. three d. *Education:* Univ. of Oxford. *Career:* Univ. Lecturer in Russian and Hulme Lecturer in Russian, Brasenose Coll., Oxford, 1954–64; Visiting Prof., UCLA 1964–65; Sir William Mather Chair of Russian Studies, Univ. of Manchester 1965–67; Prof. of Russian Literature, Univ. of London 1967–88, Prof. Emer. 1988–. *Publications include:* fiction: Two Ways of Life 1962, The Emigration of Sergey Ivanovich 1963, Russian Roulette 1979, The Russian Crucifix 1987; non-fiction: Turgenev: A Study 1960, A Short History of Modern Russia 1966, The Rise of the Russian Novel 1974 (reissued 2010), Russian Literary Attitudes from Pushkin to Solzhenitsyn (ed.) 1976, Russian and Slavic Literature to 1917, Vol. I (co-ed. with Charles Ward) 1976, The Russian Revolutionary Novel: Turgenev to Pasternak 1982, Ideology in Russian Literature (co-ed. with Jane Grayson) 1990, Furious Vissarion: Belinski's Struggle for Literature, Love and Ideas 2003, Dostoevsky 2003; trans.: Sketches from a Hunter's Album, by Turgenev 1967, Home of the Gentry, by Turgenev 1970, Rudin, by Turgenev 1974, Love and Death: Six Stories by Ivan Turgenev 1983, First Love and Other Stories, by Turgenev 1989, Fathers and Sons, by Turgenev 1991, A Month in the Country, by Turgenev 1991, An Accidental Family, by Dostoevsky 1994, Sketches from a Hunter's Album: The Complete Edition, by Turgenev 2006; editor: Anton Chekhov: The Steppe and Other Stories 1991, Ivan Goncharov: Oblomov 1992, Reference Guide to Russian Literature: Articles on the Classic Russian Novel, Gor'kii, Kuzmin, Pasternak *et al.* 1998, The Cambridge Companion to Tolstoy (contrib.) 2002, Solzhenitsyn (updated) – New Makers of Modern Culture 2007, Turgenev (contrib.) 2008; contribs to various publs. *Honours:* Hon. DLitt (London) 1984. *Address:* 24 Park Road, Surbiton, Surrey, KT5 8QD, England (home).

FREEDMAN, Sir Lawrence David, Kt, KCMG, CBE, DPhil, FRSA, FRHistS, FBA, FKC; British academic; *Professor of War Studies and Vice-Principal (Research), King's College London*; b. 7 Dec. 1948, Tynemouth; s. of the late Lt-Commdr Julius Freedman and Myra Robinson; m. Judith Hill 1974; one s. one d. *Education:* Whitley Bay Grammar School and Univs of Manchester, Oxford and York. *Career:* Research Assoc., IISS 1975–76; Research Fellow, Royal Inst. of Int. Affairs 1976–78, Head of Policy Studies 1978–82; Fellow, Head Dept of War Studies, King's Coll. London 1978–, Prof. 1982–, Head School of Social Science and Public Policy 2001–, Vice-Principal (Research); mem. Council, IISS 1984–92, 1993–, School of Slavonic and E European Studies 1993–97; Chair. Cttee on Int. Peace and Security, Social Science Research Council (USA) 1993–98; occasional newspaper columnist; Trustee Imperial War Museum 2001–09; cttee mem., The Iraq Inquiry 2009–. *Publications:* US Intelligence and Soviet Strategic Threat 1978, Britain and Nuclear Weapons 1980, The Evolution of Nuclear Strategy 1981, 1989, Nuclear War and Nuclear Peace (co-author) 1983, The Troubled Alliance (ed.) 1983, The Atlas of Global Strategy 1985, The Price of Peace 1986, Britain and the Falklands War 1988, US Nuclear Strategy (co-ed.) 1989, Signals of War (with V. Gamba) 1989, Europe Transformed (ed.) 1990, Military Power in Europe (essays, ed.) 1990, Britain in the World (co-ed.) 1991, Population Change and European Security (co-ed.) 1991, War, Strategy and International Politics (essays, co-ed.) 1992, The Gulf Conflict 1990–91, Diplomacy and War in the New World Order (with E. Karsh) 1993, War: A Reader 1994, Military Intervention in Europe (ed.) 1994, Strategic Coercion (ed.) 1998, The Revolution in Strategic Affairs 1998, The Politics of British Defence Policy 1979–1998 1999, Kennedy's Wars 2000, The Cold War 2001, Superterrorism (ed.) 2002, Deterrence 2004, The Official History of the Falklands Campaign 2005, A Choice of Enemies 2009; articles etc. *Honours:* Hon. Dir Centre for Defence Studies 1990–; Silver Medallist, Arthur Ross Prize, Council on Foreign Relations (USA) 2002, RUSI Chesney Gold Medal 2006, Lionel Gelber Prize 2009, Duke of Westminster Prize for Military History 2009. *Address:* King's College London, Office of the Principal, James Clerk Maxwell Building, 57 Waterloo Road, London, SE1 8WA, England (office). *Telephone:* (20) 7848-3984 (office); (20) 7848-3985 (office). *Fax:* (20) 7848-3668 (office). *E-mail:* lawrence.freedman@kcl.ac.uk (office); LFREED0712@aol.com (home).

FREELAND, Chrystia, MA; Canadian newspaper editor; *Global Editor-at-Large, Reuters*; b. 1969, Peace River, Alberta; m.; three c. *Education:* Harvard Univ., USA, St Anthony's Coll. Oxford, UK. *Career:* corresp. for Financial Times, The Economist and Washington Post in Kiev, Ukraine 1991–93; Eastern Europe Corresp. Financial Times (FT), London 1994–95, Moscow Bureau Chief 1995–96, UK News Ed. 1998–99, Ed. FT.com 2001–02, oversaw launch of subscription services 2002, Ed. FT Weekend (Saturday edn) 2002–03, Deputy Ed. FT 2003–08, US Man. Ed. 2008–10; Deputy Ed. The Globe & Mail, Toronto, Canada 1999–2001; Global Ed.-at-Large, Reuters 2010–; Sr Fellow, Int. Security Program, Belfer Center for Science and Int. Affairs, John F Kennedy School of Govt, Harvard Univ. *Publications include:* Sale of the Century: Russia's Wild Side from Communism to Capitalism 2000. *Honours:* Business Journalist of the Year Award for Best Energy Submission 2004. *Address:* Financial Times, 1330 Avenue of the Americas, New York, NY 10019, USA (office). *Telephone:* (212) 641-6503 (office). *Fax:* (212) 641-6504 (office). *E-mail:* chrystia.freeland@ft.com (office). *Website:* www.ft.com (office).

FREEMAN, Gillian, (Elisabeth von Stahlenberg), BA; British writer; b. 5 Dec. 1929, London, England; m. Edward Thorpe 1955, two d. *Education:* Univ. of Reading. *Career:* mem. Arts Council, Writers' Guild of GB. *Publications include:* The Liberty Man 1955, Fall of Innocence 1956, Jack Would be a Gentleman 1959, The Story of Albert Einstein 1960, The Leather Boys 1961, The Campaign 1963, The Leader 1965, The Undergrowth of Literature 1969, The Alabaster Egg 1970, The Marriage Machine 1975, The Schoolgirl Ethic: The Life and Work of Angela Brazil 1976, Nazi Lady: The Diaries of Elisabeth von Stahlenberg, 1938–48 1979, An Easter Egg Hunt 1981, Lovechild 1984, Life Before Man 1986, Ballet Genius (with Edward Thorpe) 1988, Termination Rock 1989, His Mistress's Voice 2000, But Nobody Lives in Bloomsbury 2006; other: screenplays and adaptations, ballet scenarios, contribs to periodicals.

FREEMAN, James Montague, BA, MA, PhD; American academic and writer; *Professor Emeritus, San Jose State University*; b. 1 Dec. 1936, Chicago, Ill.; m. Patricia Ann Freeman 1968; one s. *Education:* Northwestern Univ., Harvard Univ. *Career:* Asst Prof. to Prof. of Anthropology, San Jose State Univ. 1966–2000, Prof. Emer. 2000–; mem. Aid to Refugee Children Without Parents 1988–95, and its successor, Aid to Children Without Parents Inc. (Chair. 1995–99), Southwestern Anthropological Asscn (Pres. 1991–92), Friends of Hue Foundation (Chair.) 2000–06. *Film:* producer/writer/co-dir The Myth of the Buddha's Birthplace (documentary video) 2012. *Publications* include: Scarcity and Opportunity in an Indian Village 1977, Untouchable: An Indian Life History 1979, Hearts of Sorrow: Vietnamese-American Lives 1989, Changing Identities: Vietnamese Americans 1975–1995 1996, Voices from the Camps: Vietnamese Children Seeking Asylum (with Nguyen Dinh Huu) 2003, Busier than Ever!: Why American Families Can't Slow Down (with Charles N. Darrah and J.A. English-Lueck) 2007, Essays On Orissan Society 2009; contrib. to scholarly books and journals. *Honours:* American Inst. of Indian Studies Fellowship 1970–72, Social Science Research Council grant 1976–77, 1979–80, Fellow Center for Advanced Study in Behavioral Sciences, Stanford 1976–77, Choice Outstanding Academic Book 1979, Nat. Endowment for the Humanities Fellowship 1983–84, San Jose State Univ. Pres.'s Scholar 1984, San Jose State Univ. Outstanding Prof. 1986, Before Columbus Foundation American Book Award 1990, Asscn for Asian-American Studies Outstanding Book Award 1990, Austin D. Warburton Award for Outstanding Scholarship 1991, Nat. Science Foundation grant (jtly) 1998–99, Alfred P. Sloan Foundation grant (co-recipient) 1998–2000. *Address:* Department of Anthropology, San Jose State University, San Jose, CA 95192, USA (office). *E-mail:* jimfreeman36@gmail.com (office).

FREEMAN, John, BA; American editor and writer; *Editor, Granta;* b. Ohio. *Education:* Swarthmore Coll. *Career:* fmr freelance book critic; Pres. Nat. Book Critics Circle 2007–09; Acting Ed., Granta May–Oct. 2010, Ed. 2010–. *Publications include:* The Tyranny of E-Mail: The Four-Thousand-Year Journey to Your Inbox 2009. *Address:* Granta Publications, 12 Addison Avenue, London, W11 4QR, England (office). *Telephone:* (20) 7605-1360 (office). *Fax:* (20) 7605-1361 (office). *E-mail:* jfreeman@granta.com (office). *Website:* www.granta.com (office).

FREEMAN, Judith; American writer and critic; b. 1 Oct. 1946, Ogden, UT; m. Anthony Hernandez 1986; one s. *Career:* Lecturer, Professional Writing Program, Univ. of Southern California; contributing critic, Los Angeles Times Book Review; mem. PEN West. *Publications include:* Family Attractions 1988, The Chinchilla Farm 1989, Set for Life 1991, A Desert of Pure Feeling 1996, Red Water (Utah Book Award) 2002, The Long Embrace: Raymond Chandler and the Woman He Loved 2007. *Honours:* Western Heritage Award for Best Western Novel 1992, John Simon Guggenheim Fellowship 1997. *Telephone:* (213) 740-3252 (office). *E-mail:* jafreema@usc.edu (office); judith@judithfreeman.net (home). *Website:* www.judithfreeman.net.

FREEMANTLE, Brian Harry, (Harry Asher, Jonathan Evans, Richard Gant, Andrea Hart, John Maxwell, Jack Winchester); British writer; b. 10 June 1936, Southampton, Hants., England; m. Maureen Hazel Tipney 1957; three d. *Education:* secondary school, Southampton. *Career:* reporter, New Milton Advertiser 1953–58, Bristol Evening News 1958, Evening News, London 1959–61; reporter, Daily Express 1961–63, Asst Foreign Ed. 1963–69; Foreign Ed., Daily Sketch, London 1969–70, Daily Mail, London 1971–75; writer 1975–; mem. Mystery Writers of America. *Publications include:* fiction: The Touchables 1968, Goodbye to an Old Friend 1973, Face Me When You Walk Away 1974, The Man Who Wanted Tomorrow 1975, The November Man 1976, Hell's Kitchen 1977, The Iron Cage 1980, Deaken's War 1982, Rules of Engagement 1984, Vietnam Legacy 1984, The Lost American 1984, The Laundryman 1986, The Kremlin Kiss 1986, The Choice of Eddie Franks 1986, The Bearpit 1988, O'Farrell's Law 1990, The Factory 1990, Betrayals 1991, Little Grey Mice 1992, The Button Man 1993, No Time for Heroes 1995, Mindreader 1998, The Profiler 1998, At Any Price 1999, The Watchmen 2002, Ice Age 2002, Two Women 2003, The Holmes Inheritance 2004, Triple Cross 2004, Dead End 2005, The Holmes Factor 2005, Time To Kill 2006, The Namedropper 2007, Red Star Rising 2010; non-fiction: KGB 1982, CIA 1983, The Fix: Inside the World Drug Trade 1985, The Steal: Counterfeiting and Industrial Espionage 1987, The Octopus: Europe in the Grip of Organised Crime 1996; contrib. to periodicals. *Address:* c/o Ann Evans, Jonathan Clowes, 10 Iron Bridge House, Bridge Approach, London, NW1 8BD, England. *Website:* www.brianfreemantle.com.

FREI, Max; Russian writer. *Career:* pseudonym of Svetlana Martynchik and Igor Stepin, and also the protagonist of several novels. *Publications include:* fiction: The Labyrinths of Echo series; non-fiction: The ABCs of Contemporary Art, A Book of Indecencies, A Book of Fantasy Worlds, Russian Heterogeneous Fairy Tale. *Website:* www.frei.ru.

FREIBERG, Stanley Kenneth, BA, MA, PhD; American fmr teacher, poet and writer; b. 26 Aug. 1923, Wis.; m. Marjorie Ellen Speckhard 1947; one s. one d. *Education:* Univ. of Wisconsin. *Career:* Chair. English Dept, Cottey Coll., Nevada, Mo. 1954–58; Chair. Bd of Foreign Language Studies, Univ. of Baghdad, Iraq 1964–65. *Plays include:* Mad Blake at Felpham (Open Space Theatre, Victoria, BC 1987), Blake and Beethoven in The Tempest (Univ. of Victoria 1992), Bush, Blake and Job in the Garden of Eden (St Anne's Acad., Victoria 2005). *Music:* words and music for Seven Tone Poems, premiered at Victoria Conservatory of Music 2002–06. *Publications include:* The Baskets of Baghdad: Poems of the Middle East 1968, (reprinted with story and verse additions) 2006, Plumes of the Serpent: Poems of Mexico 1973, The Caplin-Crowded Seas: Poems of Newfoundland 1975, Nightmare Tales: Ten Stories of Nova Scotia 1980, Mad Blake at Felpham (play) 1987, The Hidden City: A Poem of Peru 1988, Blake and Beethoven in the Tempest (play) 1997, The Dignity of Dust: Poems from the Four Directions 1997, Sverre, King of Norway: Drama of 12th Century Norway 1999, Jahanara, Daughter of the Taj Mahal: Drama of the Mogul Empire 1631–1681 1999, Black Madonna of the Deluge: Drama of 17th Century Poland 2000, Anaho of the Southstars: Novella of Pyramid Lake, Nevada 2003, On Gravel Roads: Tales of Early Ontario 2004, Bush, Blake and Job in the Garden of Eden (play) 2005, Seven Tone Poems 2007, The Twin Towers of Baghdad and Troy: An Episodic Essay in Verse and Prose 2007, The Fourth Figure in the Furnace 2009; contrib. to Redlands Review, Christian Century, Dalhousie Review, Queen's Quarterly, Ariel, Parnassus of World Poets 1994. *Honours:* Canada Council Award 1978. *Address:* 202–268 Superior Street, Victoria, BC V8V 1T3, Canada (home). *Telephone:* (250) 382-9352 (home). *Website:* www.stanfreiberg.com.

FREIREICH, Valerie J., BA, JD; American lawyer and writer; b. 14 July 1952, Chicago, Ill.; m. Jordan L. Kaplan 1980; one s. *Education:* Univ. of Illinois, Champaign-Urbana. *Career:* lawyer, various law firms 1977–84; currently Partner, Chuhak & Tecson, Chicago; mem. ABA, Illinois State Bar Asscn, Science Fiction and Fantasy Writers of America, AAAS. *Publications include:* fiction: Becoming Human 1995, Testament 1995, The Beacon 1996, Sensations of the Mind (short story), Impostor 1997; contribs: short stories and novellas to periodicals including Aboriginal Science Fiction, Asimov's Science Fiction, Tomorrow Speculative Fiction. *Honours:* First Prize for short story, Writers of the Future Quarterly Prize 1990.

FREISINGER, Randall Roy, BJ, MA, PhD; American academic and poet; *Professor Emeritus of Rhetoric, Literature, and Creative Writing, Michigan Technological University;* b. 6 Feb. 1942, Kansas City, Mo.; m.; two s. *Education:* Univ. of Missouri. *Career:* Instructor, Jefferson Coll. 1964–68; Resident Lecturer, Univ. of Maryland Overseas Program 1968–69, 1975–76; Asst Prof., Columbia Coll. 1976–77; Asst, Assoc. Prof., Michigan Technological Univ. 1977–93, apptd Prof. of Rhetoric, Literature and Creative Writing 1993, now Prof. Emer.; Assoc. Ed., Laurel Review 1989–; mem. Associated Writing Programs, Nat. Council of Teachers of English. *Publications include:* Running Patterns 1985, Hand Shadows 1988, Plato's Breath 1997, Nostalgia's Thread 2009; contribs: anthologies, journals, reviews and quarterlies. *Honours:* Winner, Flume Press Nat. Chapbook Competition 1985, May Swenson Poetry Award 1996. *Address:* 1800 Robindale Drive, Houghton, MI 49931, USA (home). *Telephone:* (906) 482-8046 (office). *E-mail:* rfreisi@mtu.edu (office). *Website:* www.randallfreisinger.com.

FRENCH, Anne, MA; New Zealand poet, critic and publishing executive; b. 5 March 1956, Wellington; d. of Derek Lawrence and M. Olive French; one s. *Education:* Wellington Girls' Coll., Victoria Univ. of Wellington and Auckland Teachers' Coll. *Career:* Ed. Oxford Univ. Press (NZ br.) 1979, then Literary Ed., apptd Publr 1982; Sec. NZ PEN 1980, 1981; Councillor Book Publrs' Asscn of NZ 1984; Man. Ed. Museum of New Zealand Te Papa Tongarewa 1995–; mem. Council Local Publrs' Forum 1991, jury Montana New Zealand Book Awards 2004; Queen Elizabeth II Arts Council Writers' Bursary 1990; Inaugural Writing Fellow, Massey Univ. 1993–. *Publications include:* poetry: All Cretans are Liars 1987, The Male as Evader 1988, Cabin Fever 1990, Seven Days on Mykonos 1993, Boys' Night Out 1998, Wild 2004. *Honours:* PEN Young Writers' Award 1973, 1974, NZ Book Award for Poetry 1988, PEN Best First Book Award 1988. *Address:* 53 Ngatiawa Street, One Tree Hill, Auckland 5, New Zealand (home). *Telephone:* (9) 636-8910 (home). *Fax:* (9) 524-6723 (home).

FRENCH, Linda (see Mariz, Linda Catherine French)

FRENCH, Nicci (see French, Sean, and Gerrard, Nicci)

FRENCH, Patrick, BA; British historian and writer; b. 1966. *Education:* Univ. of Edinburgh. *Career:* fmr Dir (non-exec.), Free Tibet Campaign. *Publications include:* Younghusband: The Last Great Imperial Adventurer (Royal Soc. of Literature Heinemann Prize, Somerset Maugham Award) 1994, Liberty or Death: India's Journey to Independence and Division (Sunday Times Young Writer of the Year Award) 1997, Tibet, Tibet, A Personal History of a Lost Land 2003, The World Is What It Is: The Authorized Biography of V. S. Naipaul (Nat. Book Critics Circle Award for Biog. 2008, Hawthornden Prize 2009) 2008, India: A Portrait 2011. *Literary Agent:* c/o The Wylie Agency, 17 Bedford Square, London, WC1B 3JA, England. *Telephone:* (20) 7908-5900. *Fax:* (20) 7908-5901. *E-mail:* mail@wylieagency.co.uk. *Website:* www.wylieagency.com.

FRENCH, Philip Neville, BA; British writer, broadcaster and film critic; b. 28 Aug. 1933, Liverpool, England; m. Kersti Elisabet Molin 1957; three s. *Education:* Exeter Coll., Oxford, Indiana Univ., USA. *Career:* reporter, Bristol Evening Post 1958–59; Producer, North American Service 1959–61, Talks Producer 1961–67, Sr Producer 1968–90, BBC Radio; theatre critic 1967–68, arts columnist 1967–72, New Statesman; film critic, The Observer 1978–. *Publications include:* The Age of Austerity, 1945–51 (co-ed. with Michael Sissons) 1963, The Novelist as Innovator (ed.) 1966, The Movie Moguls 1969, Westerns: Aspects of a Movie Genre 1974, Three Honest Men: Portraits of Edmund Wilson, F. R. Leavis, Lionel Trilling 1980, The Third Dimension: Voices from Radio Three (ed.) 1983, The Press: Observed and Projected (co-ed. with Deac Rossell) 1991, Malle on Malle (ed.) 1992, The Faber Book of Movie Verse (co-ed. with Ken Wlaschin) 1993, Wild Strawberries (with Kersti French) 1995, Cult Movies (with Karl French) 1999, I Found It at the Movies 2011; contrib. to many anthologies and periodicals. *Honours:* Dr hc (Lancaster) 2006; Critic of the Year, Press Gazette Nat. Press Awards 2009. *Address:* 62 Dartmouth Park Road, London, NW5 1SN, England (home). *Telephone:* (20) 7485-1711 (home). *E-mail:* pn.french7@gmail.com (home).

FRENCH, Sean, (Nicci French), BA; British writer; b. 28 May 1959, Bristol, England; m. Nicci Gerrard 1990; two s. two d. *Education:* Univ. of Oxford.

Career: Theatre Critic Vogue magazine 1981–86; Deputy Literary Ed., Sunday Times, London 1984–86; Deputy Ed., New Society 1986–87; columnist, New Statesman and Society 1987–2000; fmr Film Critic Marie Claire; also writes with Nicci Gerrard, under joint pseudonym of Nicci French. *Publications include:* Fatherhood (ed.) 1992, The French Brothers' Wild and Crazy Film Quiz Book (with Karl and Patrick French) 1992, The Imaginary Monkey (novel) 1993, Patrick Hamilton: A Life (biog.) 1993, Bardot (biog.) 1994, Dreamer of Dreams (novel) 1995, The Terminator (criticism) 1996, Jane Fonda (biog.) 1997, The Faber Book of Writers on Writers (ed.) 1999, Start from Here (novel) 2004; as Nicci French: The Memory Game 1997, The Safe House 1998, Killing Me Softly 1999, Beneath the Skin 2000, The Red Room 2001, Land of the Living 2003, Secret Smile 2004, Things We Knew Were True 2004, Catch Me When I Fall 2005, Losing You 2007, Until It's Over 2008, What to do When Someone Dies 2008, Complicit 2009, The Other Side of the Door 2010, Blue Monday 2011. *Address:* Old Rectory, Elmsett, Ipswich, IP7 6NA, England (home). *E-mail:* seanicci@dircon.co.uk (home). *Website:* www.niccifrench.co.uk.

FRENCH, Tana; Irish author; b. 1973, Vt, USA; d. of David French and Elena Hvostoff-Lombardi; m.; one d. *Education:* Trinity Coll., Dublin. *Career:* fmr theatrical actress and voiceover artist. *Publications include:* novels: In the Woods (Edgar Award for Best First Novel 2008, Anthony Award for Best First Novel 2008, Macavity Award for Best First Mystery 2008, Barry Award for Best First Novel 2008) 2007, The Likeness 2008, Faithful Place 2010, Broken Harbor 2012. *Literary Agent:* c/o Darley Anderson Agency, Literary, TV and Film Agency, Estelle House, 11 Eustace Road, London, SW6 1JB, England. *Address:* Ben Petrone, Associate Director of Publicity, Viking/Penguin, Penguin Group USA, 375 Hudson Street, New York, NY 10014, USA (office). *Telephone:* (212) 366-2440 (office). *E-mail:* ben.petrone@us.penguingroup.com (office). *Website:* us.penguingroup.com (office); www.tanafrench.com.

FRENCH, Warren Graham, BA, MA, PhD; American academic and writer; b. 26 Jan. 1922, Philadelphia, Pa. *Education:* Univ. of Pennsylvania, Univ. of Texas. *Career:* mem. Int. John Steinbeck Soc., New Steinbeck Soc. of America, American Literature, Modern Language Assen of America, American Studies Asscn, Western American Literature Asscn. *Publications include:* John Steinbeck 1961, Frank Norris 1962, J. D. Salinger 1963, The Social Novel at the End of an Era 1966, Jack Kerouac 1986, J. D. Salinger, Revisited 1988, The San Francisco Poetry Renaissance, 1955–1960 1991; ed.: The Thirties 1967, The Forties 1969, The Fifties 1971, The Twenties 1975, The South and Film 1981; contribs to numerous American academic journals. *Honours:* Hon. DHL (Ohio) 1985.

FRESÁN, Rodrigo; Argentine writer and journalist; b. 1963, Buenos Aires. *Career:* journalist 1984–; moved to Barcelona, Spain 1999–. *Publications include:* Historia argentina (short stories) 1991, Vidas de santos (short stories) 1993, Trabajos manuales 1994, Esperanto (novel) 1995, La velocidad de las cosas (novel) 1998, Mantra 2001, Jardines de Kensington (novel, trans. as Kensington Gardens) 2004, El fondo del cielo 2009; contrib. to various publications, including Página 12. *Honours:* Premio Lateral de Narrativa 2004. *Address:* c/o Faber and Faber Ltd, Bloomsbury House, 74–77 Great Russell Street, London, WC1B 3DA, England. *Website:* www.faber.co.uk.

FREUD, Esther Lea; British writer; b. 2 May 1963, London, England; partner David Morrissey; two s. one d. *Education:* Drama Centre, London. *Career:* fmr actor; co-f. film production co., Tubedale Films. *Publications include:* Hideous Kinky (novel) 1991, Peerless Flats (short stories) 1993, Gaglow 1997, Summer at Gaglow 1998, The Wild 2000, The Sea House (novel) 2003, Love Falls 2007, Lucky Break: A Novel 2011. *Literary Agent:* c/o AP Watt Ltd, 20 John Street, London, WC1N 2DR, England. *Telephone:* (20) 7282-3106. *E-mail:* apw@apwatt.co.uk. *Website:* www.apwatt.co.uk.

FREUDENBERGER, Nell; American writer; b. 1975, New York, NY. *Career:* English teacher in Bangkok and New Delhi. *Publications include:* Lucky Girls (PEN/Malamud Award 2004) 2003, The Dissident 2006, The Newlyweds 2012; contrib. to The New Yorker, Granta. *Honours:* Whiting Writers' Award 2005. *Address:* c/o Ecco, Harper Collins Publishing, 10 East 53rd Street, New York, NY 10022, USA.

FREWER, Glyn Mervyn Louis, (Mervyn Lewis), MA; British writer and scriptwriter; b. 4 Sept. 1931, Oxford; m. Lorna Townsend 1956; two s. one d. *Education:* St Catherine's Coll., Oxford. *Career:* Student Officer, British Council, Oxford 1955; copywriter for various agencies 1955–64; Advertising Agency Assoc. Dir 1975–85; propr antiquarian/secondhand bookshop 1985–2001. *Scripts:* The Hitch-Hikers (BBC Radio play) 1957, also scripts for children's TV series, industrial films, etc.. *Publications include:* children's fiction: Adventure in Forgotten Valley (Jr Literary Guild of America Choice 1964) 1962, Adventure in the Barren Lands 1964, The Last of the Wispies 1965, The Token of Elkin 1970, Crossroad 1970, The Square Peg 1972, The Raid 1976, The Trackers 1976; adult fiction: Death of Gold (as Mervyn Lewis) 1970; wildlife fiction: Tyto: The Odyssey of an Owl 1978, Bryn of Brockle Hanger 1980, Fox 1984, The Call of the Raven 1987; poetry: Shout to the Sky 2007, Dance to the Music 2009; contrib. to various magazines and periodicals. *Honours:* Freeman of the City of Oxford 1967. *Address:* Ascott House, Wychwood Close, Charlbury, Oxford, OX7 3TB, England (home).

FRIDAY, Nancy; American feminist and writer; b. 27 Aug. 1937, Pittsburgh, Pa; m. 2nd Norman Pearlstine. *Education:* Wellesley Coll., Mass. *Career:* grew up in Charleston, SC; worked briefly as reporter for San Juan Island Times and as magazine ed. in New York, England, Italy and France before turning to full-time writing in 1963; has produced several books of 'pop psychology' since 1973. *Publications include:* My Secret Garden: Women's Sexual Fantasies 1973, Forbidden Flowers – More Women's Sexual Fantasies 1975, My Mother, My Self – The Daughter's Search for Identity 1977, Men in Love, Men's Sexual Fantasies – The Triumph of Love Over Rage 1980, Jealousy 1985, Women on Top – How Real Life Has Changed Women's Sexual Fantasies 1991, Self Exploration and Insatiable Lust 1991, The Power of Beauty 1996, To Be Seen 1996, The Mirrored Self 1997, Our Looks, Our Lives – Sex, Beauty, Power and the Need to Be Seen 1999, Beyond My Control: Forbidden Fantasies in an Uncensored Age 2009. *Address:* c/o Simon and Schuster Inc., Publicity Department, 1230 Avenue of the Americas, New York, NY 10020, USA. *Website:* www.simonandschuster.net.

FRIEDA, Leonie Harriet Elisabeth Natascha; Swedish historian and biographer; b. 1956, d. of Leo and Margareta Groth; m. Nigel Frieda 1986 (divorced 1998); one s. one d. *Education:* Moira House, Eastbourne, England, Rissen Gymnasium, Hamburg, Inst. of Linguists. *Career:* model, trans.; Propr MATRIX recording studios 1986–2001; also music business man. to various popstars, producers and engineers. *Publications:* Catherine de Medici: A Biography 2004, King Francis I of France 2008, The Deadly Sisterhood: Eight Princesses of the Italian Renaissance 2011. *Address:* c/o Weidenfeld & Nicholson, The Orion Publishing Group Ltd, Orion House, 5 Upper St Martin's Lane, London, WC2H 9EA, England (office). *Website:* www.leoniefrieda.com.

FRIEDLANDER, Saul P., PhD; Israeli academic and author; *Professor of History and 1939 Club Chair in Holocaust Studies, University of California, Los Angeles*; b. Prague, Czechoslovakia. *Education:* studied in Paris and at the Graduate Inst. of Int. Studies, Geneva. *Career:* survived the German Occupation as a Jewish child brought up in France; emigrated to Israel 1948; served as sec. to Nachum Goldman, Pres. of World Zionist Org. and World Jewish Congress; asst to Shimon Peres, Vice-Minister of Defence 1959; held teaching posts at Graduate Inst. of Int. Studies, Geneva, Hebrew Univ., Jerusalem, Tel-Aviv Univ. –1988; Prof. of History, UCLA 1988–, currently also 1939 Club Chair in Holocaust Studies. *Publications include:* Pius XII and the Third Reich 1965, Prelude to Downfall: Hitler and the United States 1939–1941 1967, Kurt Gerstein 1970, L'Antisémitisme nazi: histoire d'une psychose collective 1971, Arabs and Israelis: a Dialogue (with Mahmoud Hussein) 1975, Some aspects of the historical significance of the Holocaust 1977, History and Psychoanalysis: an Inquiry Into the Possibilities and Limits of Psychohistory 1979, When Memory Comes (memoir) 1979, Reflections of Nazism 1984, Visions of Apocalypse: End or Rebirth? 1985, Probing the Limits of Representation (ed.) 1992, Memory, History, and the Extermination of the Jews of Europe 1993, Nazi Germany and the Jews, Vol. 1: The Years of Persecution, 1933–1939 (Geschwister-Scholl-Preis 1998) 1997, Nazi Germany and the Jews, Vol. 2: The Years of Extermination 1939–1945 (Pulitzer Prize for General Non-Fiction 2008) 2007. *Honours:* MacArthur Foundation Grant 1999, German Book Trade Peace Prize 2007. *Address:* UCLA Department of History, 6265 Bunche Hall, Box 951473, Los Angeles, CA 90095-1473, USA (office). *Telephone:* (310) 825-3678 (office). *Fax:* (310) 206-9630 (office). *E-mail:* friedlan@history.ucla.edu (office). *Website:* www.history.ucla.edu (office).

FRIEDMAN, Alan Howard, BA, MA, PhD; American writer, critic and academic; *Professor Emeritus, University of Illinois*; b. 4 Jan. 1928, New York City, NY; s. of Harry M. Friedman and Mina Friedman; m. 1st Leonore Ann Helman 1950 (divorced); one s.; m. 2nd Kate Miller Gilbert 1977; one s. *Education:* Harvard Coll., Columbia Univ., Univ. of California, Berkeley. *Career:* mem. faculty, Columbia Univ., Swarthmore Coll., Queens Coll., CUNY; Prof. Emer., Univ. of Illinois. *Publications include:* The Turn of the Novel 1966, Hermaphrodeity (novel) 1972, The Cannibal Frames Herself 2011; contribs to Twentieth Century Mind 1900–1918, Far from the Madding Crowd (Norton edn), D. H. Lawrence's The Rainbow, Modern Critical Interpretations; contribs to New York Times Book Review, American Literary Anthology, Hudson Review, Mademoiselle, Partisan Review, New American Review, Paris Review, New York Times Book Review, Fiction International, Kansas Quarterly, Denver Quarterly, Raritan, Little Magazine, Formations. *Honours:* D.H. Lawrence Fellowship 1974, Nat. Endowment for the Arts Award 1975, Pen Syndicated Fiction Award 1987, Grand Prize, Nat. Library of Poetry 1998, Best Actor Award, Asscn of Community Theatres 2001. *Address:* 3530 Monte Real, Escondido, CA 92029, USA (home). *Telephone:* (760) 480-4486 (office). *E-mail:* alanfman@post.harvard.edu (office).

FRIEDMAN, Bruce Jay; BJ; American writer, dramatist and screenwriter; b. 26 April 1930, New York, NY; m. 1st Ginger Howard 1954 (divorced 1978); three s.; m. 2nd Patricia O'Donohue 1983; one d. *Education:* Univ. of Missouri. *Career:* Editorial Dir, Magazine Management Co., New York City 1953–64; mem. PEN. *Publications include:* Stern 1962, Far From the City of Class, and Other Stories 1963, A Mother's Kisses 1964, Black Humour (ed.) 1965, Black Angels 1966, Pardon Me, Sir, But Is My Eye Hurting Your Elbow? (with others) 1968, The Dick 1970, About Harry Towns 1974, The Lonely Guys Book of Life 1978, Let's Hear It for a Beautiful Guy, and Other Works of Short Fiction 1984, Tokyo Woes 1985, Violencia 1988, The Current Climate 1990, Collected Short Fiction of Bruce Jay Friedman 1995, The Slightly Older Guy 1995, A Father's Kisses 1996, Violencia! A Musical Novel 2002, Three Balconies 2008; other: plays and screenplays including Have You Spoken to Any Jews Lately 1995, A Father's Kisses 1996. *Address:* c/o Biblioasis, PO Box

92, Emeryville, Ont. N0R 1C0, Canada. *E-mail:* biblioasis@biblioasis.com. *Website:* www.biblioasis.com.

FRIEDMAN, Dennis, LRCP; British psychiatrist and writer; b. 23 Feb. 1924, London, England; m. Rosemary Tibber 1949; four d. *Education:* Royal Coll. of Physicians, London. *Career:* Fellow, Royal Coll. of Psychiatrists; mem. Royal Soc. of Medicine, Royal Coll. of Surgeons. *Publications include:* Inheritance: A Psychological History of the Royal Family 1993, Darling Georgie: The Enigma of King George V 1998, Ladies of the Bedchamber: The Role of the Royal Mistress 2003, An Unsolicited Gift: Why We Do What We Do 2010; contribs to books and other publs. *Address:* Apt 5, 3 Cambridge Gate, London, NW1 4JX, England (home). *Telephone:* (20) 7935-6252 (home). *Fax:* (20) 7486-2398 (home). *E-mail:* dennisfriedman@aol.com (home).

FRIEDMAN, (Eve) Rosemary, (Robert Tibber, Rosemary Tibber); British writer and playwright; b. (Rosemary Tibber), 5 Feb. 1929, London, England; d. of Maurice Tibber and Priscilla Tibber (née Deyong); m. Dennis Friedman 1949; four d. *Education:* Queen's Coll., London, Univ. Coll., London. *Career:* mem. judging panel, Authors' Club First Novel Award 1989, Betty Trask Fiction Award 1991, Jewish Quarterly Literary Prizes 1993, Macmillan Silver Pen Award 1996, 1997; mem. PEN, RSL, Soc. of Authors, Writers' Guild of Great Britain, BAFTA. *Plays include:* Home Truths 1997, Change of Heart 2004, An Eligible Man 2008. *Television:* Baby Blues (Doctors), Shrinks. *Publications include:* No White Coat 1957, Love on my List 1959, We All Fall Down 1960, Patients of a Saint 1961, The Fraternity 1963, The Commonplace Day 1964, Aristide 1966, The General Practice 1967, Practice Makes Perfect 1969, The Life Situation 1977, The Long Hot Summer 1980, Proofs of Affection 1982, A Loving Mistress 1983, Rose of Jericho 1984, A Second Wife 1986, Aristide in Paris 1987, To Live in Peace 1987, An Eligible Man 1989, Golden Boy 1994, Vintage 1996, The Writing Game 1999, Intensive Care 2001, Paris Summer 2004, A Writer's Commonplace Book 2006, Life is a Joke – A Writer's Memoir 2010; contribs to Confrontations with Judaism 1966, Reviewer, Sunday Times, TLS, Guardian, Sunday Times, Jewish Quarterly. *Address:* Apt 5, 3 Cambridge Gate, London, NW1 4JX, England (office). *Telephone:* (20) 7935-6252 (office). *Fax:* (20) 7486-2398 (office). *E-mail:* rosemaryfriedman@hotmail.com (office). *Website:* www.rosemaryfriedman.co.uk.

FRIEDMAN, Jane, BA; American publishing executive; *CEO, Open Road Integrated Media;* b. Sept. 1945, Brooklyn, NY. *Education:* New York Univ. *Career:* dictaphone typist, publicity dept Alfred A. Knopf, subsidiary co of Random House 1968, later Assoc. Publr Alfred A. Knopf; Pres. Random House Audio 1985; Publr Vintage Books 1990; Exec. Vice-Pres. Knopf Publishing Group, Random House Inc. 1992; fmr mem. Random House Exec. Cttee; Pres., HarperCollins Worldwide 1997–2007, CEO 1997–2008 (resgnd); co-founder and CEO, Open Road Integrated Media (digital publishing co.) 2009–. *Address:* Open Road Integrated Media, 233 Spring Street, 4th Floor, New York, NY 10013, USA (office). *Telephone:* (212) 691-0900 (office). *Fax:* (212) 691-0901 (office). *E-mail:* inquiries@openroadmedia.com (office). *Website:* www.openroadmedia.com.

FRIEDMAN, Lawrence J., BA, MA, PhD; American academic and writer; *Professor of History, Indiana University;* b. 8 Oct. 1940, Cleveland, Ohio. *Education:* Univ. of California, Riverside, Univ. of California, Los Angeles, Menninger Foundation Interdisciplinary Studies Program. *Career:* Asst Prof., Arizona State Univ. 1967–71; Assoc. Prof., Bowling Green State Univ. 1971–77, Prof. of History and American Studies 1977–91, Distinguished Univ. Prof. 1991–93; Visiting Scholar, Harvard Univ. 1991, 2004; Prof. of History, Indiana Univ. 1993–; Fulbright Distinguished Chair, Germany 2002–03; Visiting Prof. of History of Science, Harvard Univ. 2005; John Adams Fellow, Inst. of United States Studies, Univ. of London, UK; mem. American Asscn of Univ. Profs, American Historical Asscn, Cheiron, Org. of American Historians, Soc. of American Historians. *Publications include:* The White Savage: Racial Fantasies in the Postbellum South 1970, Inventors of the Promised Land 1975, Gregarious Saints: Self and Community in American Abolitionism 1830–1870 1982, Menninger: The Family and the Clinic 1990, Identity's Architect: A Biography of Erik Erikson 1999, Charity, Philanthropy and Civility in American History 2003; contribs to books and professional journals. *Honours:* Nat. Endowment for the Humanities Fellowships 1979–80, 1986–87, 1994–95, Ohioana Library Asscn Book Award in History 1983, Paul and Ruth Olscamp Distinguished Research Award 1989–92, Writer of the Year, Int. Biographical Center at Cambridge 2003, Independent Sector Research Prize 2003, Asscn of Fundraising Professionals Research Prize 2003. *Address:* 3709 Tamarron Drive, Bloomington, IN 47408 (home); Department of History, Indiana University, Bloomington, IN 47405, USA (office). *E-mail:* LJFriedm@indiana.edu (office).

FRIEDMAN, Lawrence Meir, AB, JD, MLL; American academic and writer; *Marion Rice Kirkwood Professor, School of Law, Stanford University;* b. 2 April 1930, Chicago, Ill.; s. of I. M. Friedman and Ethel Friedman; m. Leah Feigenbaum 1955; two d. *Education:* Univ. of Chicago. *Career:* Asst to Assoc. Prof. 1957–61, St Louis Univ., Childress Memorial Lecturer 1987; Assoc. Prof. to Prof. of Law, Univ. of Wisconsin, Madison 1961–68; Prof. of Law, Stanford Univ. 1968–76, Marion Rice Kirkwood Prof., School of Law 1976–; David Stouffer Memorial Lecturer, Rutgers Univ. 1969; Fellow, Center for Advanced Study in the Behavioral Sciences 1973–74, Inst. for Advanced Study, Berlin 1985; Sibley Lecturer, Univ. of Georgia 1976; Wayne Morse Lecturer, Univ. of Oregon 1985; Jefferson Lecture, Univ. of California, Berkeley 1995; Ruston Lecture, Cumberland School of Law 1997; Tucker Lecture, Washington and Lee Univ. 2000; Charter Lecture, Univ. of Georgia 2004; Childress Lecture, St Louis Univ. 2010; Pres. Research Cttee Sociology of Law 2003–06; mem. American Acad. of Arts and Sciences; mem. Law and Soc. Asscn (Pres. 1979–81, mem. Exec. Bd 2007–10), American Soc. for Legal History (Pres. 1990–91), Soc. of American Historians. *Publications include:* Contract Law in America 1965, Government and Slum Housing: A Century of Frustration 1968, Law and the Behavioral Sciences (with Stewart Macaulay) 1969, A History of American Law 1973, The Legal System: A Social Science Perspective 1975, Law and Society: An Introduction 1978, The Roots of Justice: Crime and Punishment in Alameda County, CA, 1870–1910 1981, Total Justice: What Americans Want from the Legal System and Why 1985, American Law and the Constitutional Order Historical Perspectives (co-ed. with Harry N. Schrieber) 1988, The Republic of Choice: Law, Authority and Culture 1990, Crime and Punishment in American History 1993, Law and Society: Readings on the Study of Law (co-ed.) 1995, Legal Culture and the Legal Profession (co-ed.) 1996, The Crime Conundrum (co-ed.) 1997, The Horizontal Society 1999, American Law in the 20th Century 2002, Law in America: A Short History 2002, Legal Culture in the Age of Globalization: Latin-America and Mediterranean Europe (co-ed.) 2003, Private Lives 2004, Guarding Life's Dark Secrets 2007, Dead Hands: A Social History of Wills, Trusts, and Inheritance Law 2009, Inside the Castle: Law and the Family in 20th Century (with Joanna Grossman) 2011, The Human Rights Culture 2011, Law in Many Societies (co-ed.) 2011. *Honours:* six hon. doctorates; Scribes Award 1974, Triennial Award Order of Coif 1976, Willard Hurst Prize 1982, Harry Kalven Prize 1992, Silver Gavel Award American Bar Asscn 1994. *Address:* School of Law, Stanford University, Stanford, CA 94305, USA (office). *Telephone:* (680) 723-3072 (office). *E-mail:* lmf@stanford.edu (office).

FRIEDMAN, Thomas Lauren, OBE, BA, MPhil; American journalist and writer; *Foreign Affairs Columnist, New York Times;* b. 20 July 1953, St Louis Park, Minneapolis, Minn.; m. Ann Bucksbaum; two d. *Education:* St Louis Park High School, Brandeis Univ., St Antony's Coll. Oxford, UK. *Career:* joined London bureau of United Press International, dispatched a year later to Beirut –1981; joined The New York Times 1981, Beirut Bureau Chief 1982–84, Israel Bureau Chief 1984–88, Washington Chief Diplomatic Corresp., Chief White House Corresp., Chief Econs Corresp., Foreign Affairs Columnist 1995–; fmr Visiting Prof., Harvard Univ. *Television:* documentaries: The Roots of 9/11 (New York Times TV), Straddling the Fence (Discovery Channel). *Publications include:* From Beirut to Jerusalem (Nat. Book Award for Non-Fiction, Overseas Press Club Award) 1989 (revised edn 1990), The Lexus and the Olive Tree: Understanding Globalization (Overseas Press Club Award for Best Non-Fiction Book on Foreign Policy 2000) 1999 (revised edn 2000), Longitudes and Latitudes: Exploring the World After September 11 2002 (reprinted as Longitudes and Attitudes: The World in the Age of Terrorism 2003), The World is Flat: A Brief History of the Twenty-first Century (Financial Times/Goldman Sachs Business Book Award) 2005 (expanded edn 2006, revised edn 2007), Hot, Flat and Crowded: Why We Need a Green Revolution – And How It Can Renew America 2008, That Used To Be Us (with Michael Mandelbaum) 2011. *Honours:* hon. degrees from several US univs; Pulitzer Prize for Int. Reporting 1983, 1988, for Distinguished Commentary 2002, Overseas Press Club Award for Lifetime Achievement 2004. *Address:* The New York Times, 1627 Eye Street, NW, Suite 700, Washington, DC 20006, USA (office). *Telephone:* (202) 862-0300 (office). *Fax:* (202) 862-0340 (office). *E-mail:* fsg.publicity@fsgbooks.com. *Website:* www .nytimes.com (office); www.thomaslfriedman.com.

FRIEDMANN, Patricia Ann, (Patty Friedmann), AB, MEd; American author; b. 29 Oct. 1946, New Orleans, La; d. of the late Werner Friedmann and Marjorie Cahn Friedmann; m. 1st Robert Skinner 1979 (divorced 1996); one s. one d.; m. 2nd Edward Muchmore 1999 (divorced 2011). *Education:* Smith Coll., Temple Univ., Univ. of Denver. *Career:* Managing Ed., Diplomat 1980–82; Ed., Jewish Times 1976–78; Adjunct Faculty, Loyola Univ. 1993–; Writer-in-Residence, Tulane Univ. 2001; mem. Authors' Guild, Int. Women Writers Guild, PEN America Center. *Publications include:* Too Smart to Be Rich 1988, The Exact Image of Mother 1991, The Accidental Jew (part of Native Tongues stage production) 1994, Eleanor Rushing 1998, Lovely Rita (part of Native Tongues stage production) 2000, Odds (novel) 2000, Secondhand Smoke (novel) 2002, Side Effects (novel) 2004, A Little Bit Ruined (novel) 2007, Taken Away (young-adult novel) 2010, Too Jewish (e-novel) 2010; contrib. of short stories, reviews and essays to anthologies and periodicals, including Publishers Weekly, Newsweek, Oxford American, Speakeasy, New Orleans Noir, My New Orleans, New Orleans Review, Horn Gallery, Intersections, Life in the Wake, Something in the Water. *Honours:* Discover Great New Writers, Original Voices, Book Sense 76 selection, one of 30 Most Underrated Southern Novels along with Gone with the Wind, Deliverance, and A Lesson Before Dying, Oxford American. *Address:* 8330 Sycamore Place, New Orleans, LA 70118, USA. *Telephone:* (504) 866-8888. *Fax:* (504) 866-6888. *E-mail:* afreelunch@aol.com. *Website:* www.pattyfriedmann.com.

FRIEDRICH, Paul William, BA, MA, PhD; American anthropologist, writer and poet; *Professor Emeritus, University of Chicago;* b. 22 Oct. 1927, Cambridge, Mass; m. 1st Lore Bucher 1950 (divorced 1966); one s. two d.; m. 2nd Margaret Hardin 1966 (divorced 1974); m. 3rd Deborah Joanna Gordon 1975 (divorced 1996); two d.; m. 4th Domnica Radulescu 1996 (divorced 2004); one s. *Education:* Williams Coll., Harvard Coll., Harvard Univ., Yale Univ. *Career:* Asst Prof., Harvard Univ. 1957–58; Jr Linguistic Scholar, Deccan Coll. India 1958–59; Asst Prof., Univ. of Pennsylvania

1959–62; Visiting Asst Prof., Univ. of Michigan 1960, 1961; Assoc. Prof., Univ. of Chicago 1962–67, Prof. of Anthropology, Linguistics, Social Thought 1967–96, Prof. Emer. 1996–; Visiting Prof., Indiana Univ. 1964, Georgetown Univ. 1998–2000, Washington and Lee Univ. 1999, Univ. of Virginia 2002; mem. Acad. of American Poets, American Acad. of Arts and Sciences, American Anthropological Asscn, American Asscn for Teachers of Slavic and East European Languages, Linguistic Soc. of America (Life mem.), Linguistic Soc. of India (Life mem.), Poetry Soc. of America. *Publications include:* Proto-Indo-European Trees 1970, The Tarascan Suffices of a Locative Space: Meaning and Morphotactics 1971, A Phonology of Tarascan 1973, On Aspect Theory and Homeric Aspect 1974, Proto-Indo-European Syntax: The Order of Meaningful Elements 1975, Neighboring Leaves Ride This Wind (poems) 1976, Agrarian Revolt in a Mexican Village 1977, The Meaning of Aphrodite 1978, Bastard Moons (poems) 1978, Language, Context, and the Imagination: Essays by Paul Friedrich (ed. by A. S. Dil) 1979, Redwing (poems) 1982, The Language Parallax: Linguistic Relativism and Poetic Indeterminacy 1986, The Princes of Naranja: An Essay in Anthrohistorical Method 1987, Sonata (poems) 1987, Russia and Eurasia: Encyclopedia of World Cultures, Vol. 6 (co-ed.) 1994, Music in Russian Poetry 1998, From Root to Flower: Selected Poems 2006, The Gita within Walden 2008, Harmony in Babel: Selected Poems and Translations 2008, Handholds (haiku poems) 2009, A Goldfinch Instant: Concord to India 2010; contribs to books, journals and anthologies. *Honours:* Ford Foundation Grant 1957, Social Science Research Council Grant 1966–67, Nat. Endowment for the Humanities Grant 1974–76, Guggenheim Fellowship 1982–83, Burlington Award for Excellence in Graduate Teaching 1999. *Address:* Committee on Social Thought, University of Chicago, 1130 East 59th Street, Chicago, IL 60637, USA (office). *Telephone:* (773) 702-7004 (office). *Fax:* (773) 702-4503 (office). *E-mail:* pfriedri@uchicago.edu (office).

FRIEL, Brian, FRSL; Irish writer; b. 9 Jan. 1929, Omagh, Co. Tyrone; s. of Patrick Friel and Christina MacLoone; m. Anne Morrison 1954; one s. four d. *Education:* St Columb's Coll., Derry, St Patrick's Coll., Maynooth, St Joseph's Training Coll., Belfast. *Career:* taught in various schools 1950–60; full-time writer 1960–; mem. Irish Acad. of Letters, Aosdána 1983–, American Acad. of Arts and Letters, RSL. *Plays:* Philadelphia, Here I Come! 1965, The Loves of Cass McGuire 1967, Lovers 1968, The Mundy Scheme 1969, Crystal and Fox 1970, The Gentle Island 1971, The Freedom of the City 1973, Volunteers 1975, Living Quarters 1976, Aristocrats 1979, Faith Healer 1979, Translations (Ewart-Biggs Memorial Prize, British Theatre Asscn Award) 1981, Three Sisters (trans.) 1981, The Communication Cord 1983, Fathers and Sons 1987, Making History (Best Foreign Play, New York Drama Critics Circle 1989) 1988, A Month in the Country 1990, Dancing at Lughnasa (Tony Award for Best Play 1992) 1990, The London Vertigo 1991, Wonderful Tennessee 1993, Selected Stories 1994, Molly Sweeney 1995, Give Me Your Answer, Do! 1997, Uncle Vanya (after Chekhov) 1998, The Yalta Game 2001, The Bear (trans.) 2002, Afterplay 2002, Performances 2003, The Home Place (Evening Standard Award for Best Play 2005) 2005, Hedda Gabler (trans.) 2008. *Publications:* The Last of the Name (ed.) 1988; collected stories: The Saucer of Larks 1962, The Gold in the Sea 1966. *Honours:* Hon. Fellow, Univ. Coll. Dublin; Hon. DLitt (Nat. Univ. of Ireland) 1983, (Queen's Univ., Belfast) 1992, (Georgetown Univ., Washington, DC, Dominican Coll., Chicago), (Trinity Coll., Dublin) 2004, (Glasgow); Ulysses Medal, Univ. Coll. Dublin; honoured with Brian Friel Theatre and Brian Friel Centre for Theatre Research, Queen's Univ., Belfast. *Address:* Drumaweir House, Greencastle, Co. Donegal, Ireland (home). *Telephone:* (74) 9381119 (home). *Fax:* (74) 9381408 (home).

FRIGGIERI, Oliver, BA, MA, PhD; Maltese academic, writer, poet and literary critic; *Professor of Maltese Literature, University of Malta*; b. 27 March 1947, Furjana, Malta; s. of Charles Friggieri and Mary Galea; m. Eileen Cassar; one d. *Education:* Univ. of Malta, Catholic Univ. of Milan. *Career:* Prof. of Maltese Literature, Univ. of Malta 1987–, Head of Dept of Maltese 1987–2004; Founder-mem. Academia Internationale Mihai Eminescu, Craiova 1995; mem. Asscn Int. des Critiques Littéraires, Paris; participant and guest speaker at 70 int. congresses throughout Europe; guest poet at numerous poetry recitals in major European cities; Co-founder Saghtar (nat. student magazine) 1971; Literary Ed. In-Nazzjon 1971–82. *Achievements:* author of first oratorio in Maltese: Pawlu ta' Malta 1985, first poetry album recording in Maltese 1997, various cantatas and religious hymns. *Radio:* weekly cultural programme presenter (Radio Malta). *Television:* regular appearances on Maltese and other networks. *Publications:* novels: Il-Gidba 1977, L-Istramb 1980, Fil-Parlament ma Jikbrux Fjuri 1986, Gizimin li Qatt ma Jiftah 1998, It-Tfal Jigu bil-Vapuri 2000, The Lie 2007; short stories: Stejjer ghal Qabel Jidlam Vol. I 1979, Vol. II 1983 (combined, enhanced edn) 1986, Fil-Gżira Taparsi jikbru l-Fjuri 1991, Koranta and Other Short Stories from Malta 1994, À Malte, histoires du crépuscule 2004; poetry: Mal-Fanal Hemm Harstek Tixghel 1988, Rewwixta (play-poem) 1990, Poeziji 1998, Il-Kliem li Tghidlek Qalbek 2001, Il-Poeziji Migbura 2002, A Poet's Creed 2006; literary criticism: Kittieba ta' Zmienna 1970, Ir-Ruh fil-Kelma 1973, Il-Kultura Taljana f'Dun Karm 1976, Fl-Gharbiel 1976, Storja tal-Letteratura Maltija 1979, Saggi Kritici 1979, Ellul Mercer f'Leli ta' Haz-Zghir Mir-Realta' ghall-Kuxjenza 1983, Gwann Mamo Il'Kittieb tar-Riforma Socjali 1984, Dizzjunarju ta' Termini Letterarji 1986, L'Idea tal'Letteratura 1986, Mekkanizmi Metaforici f'Dun Karm 1988, Dun Karm 'Il-Jien u Lil hinn Minnu' 1988, Il-Kuxjenza Nazzjonali Maltija 1995, L-Istudji Kritici Migbura 1995, L'Istorja tal-Poezija Maltija 2001; numerous works translated into various languages, poems in anthologies and articles in academic journals and newspapers. *Honours:* Nat. Order of Merit 1999; First Prize for Literary Criticism XIV Concorso Silarus 1982, Premio Internazionale Mediterraneo, Palermo 1988, Malta Govt Literary Award 1988, 1996, 1997, 1999, Premio Sampieri per la Poesia 1995, Premio Internazionale Trieste Poesia 2002, Gold Medal Award Malta Soc. of Arts, Manufactures and Commerce 2003, Premio Faber (Italy) 2004. *Address:* Faculty of Arts, University of Malta, Msida, Malta (office).

FRIMAN, Alice Ruth, BA, MA; American academic, poet and writer; *Poet-in-Residence, Georgia College and State University*; b. (Alice Ruth Pesner), 20 Oct. 1933, New York, NY; d. of Joseph Pesner and Helen Pesner; m. 1st Elmer Friman 1955; two s. one d.; m. 2nd Marshall Bruce Gentry 1989. *Education:* Brooklyn Coll., Indiana Univ. at Indianapolis, Butler Univ. *Career:* Lecturer in English, Indiana Univ.-Purdue Univ. of Indianapolis 1971–74; Faculty, Univ. of Indianapolis 1971–93, Prof. of English 1990–93, Prof. Emer. 1993–; Visiting Prof. of Creative Writing, Indiana State Univ. 1982, Ball State Univ. 1996; Writer-in-Residence, Curtin Univ., Perth, Australia 1989; Visiting Poet, Randolph Coll. 2009; Poet-in-Residence, Instructor of Creative Writing and Poetry, Georgia Coll. and State Univ., Milledgeville 2003–; Poetry Ed., Arts and Letters Journal of Contemporary Culture 2003–06; Editorial Asst, Georgia Review 2006; mem. Asscn of Writers and Writing Programs, Modern Language Asscn, Poetry Soc. of America, Writers' Center of Indiana (Bd mem. 1984–89, Hon. Life mem. 1993–). *Publications include:* A Question of Innocence 1978, Song to My Sister 1979, Loaves and Fishes: A Book of Indiana Women Poets (ed.) 1983, Reporting from Corinth 1984, Insomniac Heart 1990, Driving for Jimmy Wonderland 1992, Inverted Fire 1997, Zoo 1999, The Book of the Rotten Daughter 2006, Vinculum: Poems 2011; contrib. to several anthologies and numerous reviews, quarterlies and journals. *Honours:* Dr hc (Indianapolis) 2002; Virginia Center for the Creative Arts Fellowships 1983, 1984, 1993, 1996, 2000, Poetry Soc. of America Consuelo Ford Award 1988, Poetry Soc. of America Cecil Hemley Memorial Award 1990, Soc. for the Study of Midwestern Literature Midwest Poetry Award 1990, New England Poetry Club Erika Mumford Prize 1990, 2008, Millay Colony for the Arts Fellowship 1990, Yaddo Fellowship 1991, Poetry Soc. of America Lucille Medwick Memorial Award 1993, Univ. of Indianapolis Teacher of the Year Award 1993, First Prize, Abiko Quarterly Int. Poetry Contest 1994, New England Poetry Club Firman Houghton Award 1996, Indiana Arts Comm. Individual Artist Fellowship 1996–97, Truman State Univ. Ezra Pound Poetry Award 1998, Arts Council of Indianapolis Creative Renewal Fellowship 1999–2000, New England Poetry Club Sheila Margaret Motton Prize 2001, Georgia Poetry Circuit 2001–02, Shenandoah James Boatwright Prize for Poetry 2001, Bernheim Writing Fellowship 2003–04, MacDowell Fellowship 2004, Georgia Review/Bowers House Literary Center Fellow 2007. *Address:* Department of English, PO Box 44, Georgia College and State University, Milledgeville, GA 31061, USA (office). *Telephone:* (478) 414-1364 (home). *Fax:* (478) 445-5961 (office). *E-mail:* alicefriman@gmail.com (home). *Website:* alicefriman.com; al.gcsu.edu/askalice.php.

FRITZ, Walter Helmut; German writer; b. 26 Aug. 1929, Karlsruhe; s. of Karl T. Fritz and Hedwig Fritz. *Education:* Univ. of Heidelberg. *Career:* poetry teacher, Univ. of Mainz; has lectured in Europe, America and Africa; mem. Akad. der Wissenschaften und der Literatur, Mainz, Bayerische Akad. der Schönen Künste, Munich, Deutschen Akad. für Sprache und Dichtung, Darmstadt, PEN. *Publications:* poetry and prose, including: Achtsam sein 1956, Veranderte Jahre 1963, Umwege 1964, Zwischenbemerkungen 1965, Abweichung 1965, Die Verwechslung 1970, Aus der Nahe 1972, Die Beschaffenheit solcher Tage 1972, Bevor uns Horen und Sehen Vergeht 1975, Schwierige Uberfahrt 1976, Auch jetzt und morgen 1979, Gesammelte Gedichte 1979, Wunschtraum Alptraum (poems) 1981, Werkzeuge der Freiheit (poems) 1983, Cornelias Traum, Aufzeichnungen 1985, Immer einfacher immer schwieriger (poems) 1987, Zeit des Sehens (prose) 1989, Mit einer Feder aus den Flügen des Ikarus, Ausgewählte Gedichte, Mit einem Nachwort von Harald Hartung 1989, Die Schlüssel sind vertauscht (poems) 1992, Gesammelte Gedichte 1979–1994 1994, Das offene Fenster 1997, Zugelassen im Leben (poems) 1999, Maskenzug (poems) 2003, Mein Lesezeichen 2004; contrib. to journals and peiodicals. *Honours:* City of Karlsruhe Literature Prize 1960, Grosser Literaturpreis Bayerische Akad. der Schönen Künste Prize 1962, 1995, Heine-Taler Lyric Prize 1966, Fed. of German Industry Culture Circle Prize 1971, Stuttgarter Literaturpreis 1986, Villa Massimo-Stipendium, Georg-Trakl-Preis 1992. *Address:* Kolbergerstrasse 2A, 76139 Karlsruhe, Germany (home). *Telephone:* (721) 683346 (home).

FROMME, Friedrich Karl, DPhil; German journalist; b. 10 June 1930, Dresden; s. of Prof. Dr Albert Fromme and Dr Lenka Fromme; m. 1st Traute Kirsten 1961 (died 1992); m. 2nd Brigitte Burkert 1997. *Education:* studies in science, politics and public law. *Career:* teaching Asst, Univ. of Tübingen 1957–62; Ed. Süddeutscher Rundfunk 1962–64, Frankfurter Allgemeine Zeitung (FAZ) 1964–68; Bonn corresp. FAZ 1968–73; Ed. responsible for internal politics and co-ordination, FAZ 1974–97; freelance writer. *Publications:* Von der Weimarer Verfassung zum Bonner Grundgesetz 1962, Der Parlamentarier–ein Freier Beruf? 1978, Gesetzgebung im Widerstreit 1980. *Honours:* Grosses Bundesverdienstkreuz 1995, Theodor Wolff Prize 1997. *Address:* Welt am Sonntag, 20350, Hamburg (office); Mohrengarten 60, 40822 Mettmann, Germany (home). *Telephone:* (2104) 958768 (home).

FROST, Sir David Paradine, Kt, OBE, MA; British broadcast journalist and writer; b. 7 April 1939, Tenterden, Kent; s. of Rev. W. J. Paradine Frost; m. 1st Lynne Frederick 1981 (divorced 1982); m. 2nd Lady Carina Fitzalan Howard

1983; three s. *Education:* Gillingham and Wellingborough Grammar Schools, Gonville and Caius Coll., Cambridge. *Career:* appeared in BBC TV satire series That Was The Week That Was 1962–63, That Was The Year That Was 1962–63; other programmes with BBC included A Degree of Frost 1963, 1973, Not So Much A Programme More A Way Of Life 1964–65, The Frost Report 1966–67, Frost Over England 1967; appeared in The Frost Programme, ITA 1966–67, 1967–68, 1972; Chair. and CEO David Paradine Ltd 1966–; Jt Founder London Weekend Television 1967; Jt Deputy Chair. Equity Enterprises 1973–76 (Chair. 1972–73); Jt Founder and Dir TV-AM 1981–93, host of numerous programmes, including That Was The Week That Was (USA) 1964–65, Frost On Friday, Frost On Saturday, Frost On Sunday etc., David Frost Show (USA) 1969–72, David Frost Revue (USA) 1971–73, Frost Over Australia 1972–77, Frost Over New Zealand 1973–74, The Frost Interview 1974, We British 1975, The Sir Harold Wilson Interviews 1967–77, The Nixon Interviews 1976–77, The Crossroads of Civilisation 1977–78; David Frost Presents the Int. Guinness Book of World Records 1981–86, Frost over Canada 1982–83, The Spectacular World of Guinness Records 1987–88, Talking with David Frost 1991–97; Presenter Sunday Breakfast with Frost 1993–2005; The Frost Programme 1993–95; joined Al-Jazeera International 2005–, Host Frost Over the World; Pres. Lord's Taverners 1985, 1986; Companion TV and Radio Industries Club 1992. *Films produced:* The Rise and Rise of Michael Rimmer 1970, Charley One-Eye 1972, Leadbelly 1974, The Slipper and the Rose 1975, Dynasty 1975, The Ordeal of Patty Hearst 1978, The Remarkable Mrs Sanger 1979. *Publications:* That Was The Week That Was 1963, How to Live Under Labour 1964, Talking With Frost 1967, To England With Love (with Antony Jay) 1967, The Americans 1970, Whitlam and Frost 1974, I Gave Them a Sword 1978, I Could Have Kicked Myself 1982, Who Wants to Be a Millionaire? 1983, The Mid-Atlantic Companion (jtly) 1986, The Rich Tide (jtly) 1986, The World's Shortest Books 1987, David Frost An Autobiography: Part One 1993. *Honours:* Hon. Prof. Thames Valley Univ. 1994; Hon. DCL (Univ. of East Anglia) 2004; Golden Rose, Montreux (for Frost over England) 1967, Royal TV Soc.'s Award 1967, Richard Dimbleby Award 1967, Emmy Award 1970, 1971, Religious Heritage of America Award 1970, Albert Einstein Award (Communication Arts) 1971, BAFTA Fellowship 2005. *Address:* David Paradine Productions Ltd, The Penthouse, 346 Kensington High Street, London, W14 8NS, England (office); Al Jazeera English, POB 23127, Doha, Qatar (office). *Telephone:* 44897446 (office); (20) 7371-3111 (London) (office). *Fax:* 44897472 (office); (20) 7602-0411 (London) (office). *Website:* www.aljazeera.com.

FROST, Jason (see Obstfeld, Raymond)

FROST, Richard, BA, MA; American poet, writer and academic; b. 8 April 1929, Palo Alto, Calif.; m. 1st Frances Atkins 1951; one s. two d.; m. 2nd Carol Kydd 1969; two s. *Education:* San Jose State Coll. *Career:* Instructor in English, San Jose State Coll. 1956–57, Towson State Coll. 1957–59; Asst Prof., State Univ. of NY at Oneonta 1959–64, Assoc. Prof. 1964–71, Prof. of English 1971–, now Prof. Emer. *Publications include:* The Circus Villains 1965, Getting Drunk With the Birds 1971, Neighbor Blood 1996; contribs to magazines, reviews, quarterlies and journals. *Honours:* Danforth Fellow, Bread Loaf Writers' Conf. 1961, Resident Fellow, Yaddo 1979, 1981, 1983, Gustav Davidson Memorial Award, Poetry Soc. of America 1982, Creative Writing Fellowship, Nat. Endowment for the Arts 1992. *Address:* c/o Sarabande Books, 2234 Dundee Road, Suite 200, Louisville, KY 40205, USA. *Website:* www.sarabandebooks.org.

FROSTENSON, Katarina; Swedish poet, novelist and playwright; b. 5 March 1953, Brännkyrka. *Career:* Ed. Halifax (literary calendar) 1986–96; translated from French including Emanuel Bove, Marguerite Duras and Georges Bataille; mem. Swedish Acad. 1992, adjudication panel Nobel Prize for Literature. *Publications include:* verse collections: I mellan (Between) 1978, Rena land (Pure Countries) 1980, Den andra (The Other) 1982, I det gula (In the Yellow) 1985, Samtalet (The Conversation) 1987, Joner (Ions) 1991, Tankarna (The Thoughts) 1994, Korallen (The Choral) 1999; prose: Berättelser från dom (Tales From Them) 1992; drama: 4 monodramer (Four Monodramas) 1990, Traum (Dream) 1992, Sal P (Ward P) 1995, Staden (The City, libretto for opera by Sven-David Sandström) 1998, Kristallvägen (The Crystal Road) 2000, Safirgränd (Sapphire Lane) 2000, Skallarna 2001, Karkas 2004, Ordet 2006, Tal och regn 2008; Raymond Chandler och filmen (Raymond Chandler and film) (essay) 1978. *Honours:* Chevalier, Légion d'honneur 2003; Great Prize of Soc. of Nine 1989, Bellman Prize 1994, Swedish Radio Prize for Lyrical Poetry 1996. *Address:* Swedish Academy, PO Box 2118, 103 13 Stockholm, Sweden.

FRY, Stephen John, MA; British actor, writer and director; b. 24 Aug. 1957, s. of Alan John Fry and Marianne Eve Fry (née Newman). *Education:* Uppingham School, Queens' Coll. Cambridge. *Career:* columnist, The Listener 1988–89, Daily Telegraph 1990–; wrote first play Latin, performed at Edinburgh Festival 1980 and at Lyric Theatre, Hammersmith 1983; appeared with Cambridge Footlights in revue The Cellar Tapes, Edinburgh Festival 1981; re-wrote script Me and My Girl, London, Broadway, Sydney 1984; Chair. Criterion Theatre Trust 2010–; Pres. Friends for Life Terrence Higgins Trust; mem. Amnesty International, Comic Relief. *Plays:* Forty Years On, Chichester Festival and London 1984, The Common Pursuit, London 1988 (TV 1992). *Films include:* The Good Father, A Fish Called Wanda, A Handful of Dust, Peter's Friends 1992, IQ 1995, Wind in the Willows, Wilde 1997, Cold Comfort Farm 1997, A Civil Action 1997, Whatever Happened to Harold Smith? 2000, Relative Values 2000, Discovery of Heaven 2001, Gosford Park 2002, Bright Young Things (writer, dir, exec. producer) 2003, Mirrormask 2004, A Cock and Bull Story 2005, V for Vendetta 2005, Stormbreaker 2006, Little Claus and Big Claus 2006, Eichmann 2007, St Trinian's 2007, House of Boys 2009, Alice in Wonderland (voice) 2010, Sherlock Holmes: A Game of Shadows 2011, The Hobbit: There and Back Again 2012. *Radio:* Loose Ends 1986–87, Whose Line Is It Anyway? 1987, Saturday Night Fry 1987, 1998. *TV series:* There's Nothing to Worry About 1982, Alfresco 1983–84, The Young Ones 1984, Happy Families 1985, Blackadder II 1985, Saturday Live 1986–87, A Bit of Fry and Laurie 1987–95, Blackadder's Christmas Carol 1988, Blackadder Goes Forth 1989, Jeeves and Wooster 1990–93, Stalag Luft 1993, Laughter and Loathing 1995, Gormenghast 2000, Absolute Power 2003, QI 2003–, Kingdom 2007–09, Bones 2007–09, Stephen Fry in America 2008, Last Chance to See 2009, Fry's Planet Word 2011. *Publications:* Paperweight (collected essays) 1992, Stephen Fry Mixed Shrinkwrap 1993, X10 Hippopotamus Shrinkwrap 1993, The Liar (novel) 1993, The Hippopotamus 1994, A Bit of Fry and Laurie (with Hugh Laurie) 1994, 3 Bits of Fry and Laurie (with Hugh Laurie) 1994, Fry and Laurie 4 (with Hugh Laurie) 1994, Paperweight Vol. II (collected essays) 1995, Making History 1996, Moab is My Washpot (autobiog.) 1997, The Stars' Tennis Balls (novel) 2000, The Salmon of Doubt by Douglas Adams (ed.) 2002, Revenge (novel) 2002, Rescuing the Spectacled Bear (novel) 2002, Incomplete & Utter History of Classical Music (with Tim Lihoreau) 2005, The Ode Less Travelled: Unlocking the Poet Within 2005, Stephen Fry in America 2008, The Fry Chronicles: An Autobiography (Galaxy Nat. Book Awards Biography of the Year) 2010. *Honours:* Hon. LLD (Dundee) 1995, (East Anglia) 1999, Hon. DLit, Dr hc (Anglia Ruskin) 2005. *Literary Agent:* c/o Hamilton Hodell Ltd, Fifth Floor, 66–68 Margaret Street, London, W1W 8SR, England; c/o Toni Howard, ICM, 8942 Wilshire Blvd, Beverly Hills, CA 90211-1908, USA. *Telephone:* (20) 7636-1221 (London); (212) 556-5673 (Beverly Hills). *Fax:* (20) 7636-1226 (London). *Website:* www.stephenfry.com.

FRYER, Jonathan, (G. L. Morton), BA, MA; British writer, broadcaster and academic; b. 5 June 1950, Manchester, England. *Education:* Diplôme d'Etudes Françaises, Université de Poitiers, France, St Edmund Hall, Oxford. *Career:* journalist, Reuters, London and Brussels 1973–74; Visiting Lecturer, School of Journalism, Univ. of Nairobi, Kenya 1976; Subject Teacher, SOAS, Univ. of London 1993–; Chair. Liberal International British Group; mem. English PEN, RSL, Soc. of Authors. *Publications include:* The Great Wall of China 1975, Isherwood 1977, revised edn as Eye of the Camera 1993, Brussels as Seen by Naif Artists (with Rona Dobson) 1979, Food for Thought 1981, George Fox and the Children of the Light 1991, Dylan 1993, The Sitwells (with Sarah Bradford and John Pearson) 1994, André and Oscar 1997, Soho in the Fifties and Sixties 1998, Robbie Ross: Oscar Wilde's True Love 2000, Wilde 2005, In the Wake of the Pearl-Fishers 2006, Fuelling Kuwait's Development 2007, Kurdistan 2011; numerous political pamphlets, mainly on Third World themes; contribs to Economist, Tablet, Geographical Magazine, Guardian, London Magazine, Gay Times, Society Today, The Wildean, Liberator, The Liberal, and others. *Honours:* Chevalier, Ordre nat. du Mérite (Mauritania) 2000; Elizabeth Longford Historical Biography Award 2006. *Literary Agent:* Andrew Lownie, 38 Great Smith Street, London, SW1P 3BU, England. *Telephone:* (20) 7222-7574. *E-mail:* lownie@globalnet.co.uk. *Address:* 140 Bow Common Lane, London, E3 4BH, England (home). *Telephone:* (20) 8980-4382 (office). *E-mail:* jonathanfryer@hotmail.com (home).

FU, Tianlin; Chinese poet; b. 24 Jan. 1946, Zizhong Co., Sichuan Prov. *Education:* Chongqing Middle School, Electronic Tech. School. *Career:* worked in orchard Chongqing 1962–79; clerk, Beibei Cultural Centre 1980–82; Ed. Chongqing Publishing House 1982–. *Publications:* Green Musical Notes 1981, Between Children and the World 1983, Island of Music 1985, Red Strawberry 1986, Selected Poems of Seven Chinese Poets 1993. *Honours:* First Prize of Chinese Poetry 1983. *Address:* Chongqing Publishing House, 205 Changjiang 2 Road, Chongqing City 630050, Sichuan, People's Republic of China (office).

FUGARD, Athol; South African actor and playwright; b. 11 June 1932, s. of Harold David Fugard and Elizabeth Magdelene Potgiefer; m. Sheila Fugard 1956; one d. *Career:* leading role in Meetings with Remarkable Men (film) 1977, The Guest (BBC production) 1977; acted in and wrote script for Marigolds in August (film); currently Adjunct Prof. of Playwriting, Acting and Directing, Univ. of California at San Diego. *Plays:* The Blood Knot, Hello and Goodbye, People are Living Here, Boesman and Lena 1970, Sizwe Banzi is Dead 1973, The Island 1973, Statements After an Arrest Under the Immorality Act 1974, No Good Friday 1974, Nongogo 1974, Dimetos 1976, The Road to Mecca 1984, My Children, My Africa, The Guest (film script) 1977, A Lesson from Aloes 1979 (author and dir Broadway production 1980), Master Harold and the Boys 1981, A Place with the Pigs (actor and dir) 1988, Playland 1992, Sign of Hope 1992, Valley Song (actor and dir) 1996, The Captain's Tiger 1999, Sorrows and Rejoicings 2001, Exits and Entrances 2004, Victory 2007, Coming Home 2009, The Train Driver 2010. *Films include:* Marigolds in August 1981, The Guest 1984; acted in films Gandhi 1982, Road to Mecca 1991 (also co-dir). *Publications:* Notebooks 1960–77, Playland 1992; novel: Tsotsi 1980; plays: Road to Mecca 1985, A Place with the Pigs 1988, Cousins: A Memoir 1994. *Honours:* Hon. DLit (Natal and Rhodes Univs); Dr hc (Univ. of Cape Town, Georgetown Univ., Washington, DC, New York, Pennsylvania, City Univ. of New York); Hon. DFA (Yale Univ.) 1973; winner Silver Bear Award, Berlin Film Festival 1980, New York Critics Award for A Lesson From Aloes 1981, London Evening Standard Award for Master Harold and the Boys 1983, Commonwealth Award for Contrib. to American Theatre 1984. *Address:* Department of Theatre and Dance, University of California at

San Diego, 9500 Gilman Drice, La Jolla, CA 92093, USA (office). *Telephone:* (858) 534-3791 (office). *Website:* theatre.ucsd.edu/people/faculty/AtholFugard (office).

FUJINO, Chiya; Japanese novelist; b. 27 Feb. 1962, Fukuoka Pref., Kyushu. *Education:* Chiba Univ. *Career:* worked for a publishing co. –1995. *Publications include:* novels: Gogo no jikanwari (Afternoon Schedule) (Kaien Prize for New Writers) 1995, Shonen to shojo no poruka (Boy's and Girl's Polka) 1996, Oshaberi kaidan (A Chatty Ghost Story) (Noma Literary Prize) 1998, Natsu no yakusoku (Summer Promise) (Akutagawa Prize) 1999, Ruuto 225 (Route 225) 2002, Bejitaburu haitsu (Vegetable Apartment) 2005, Kanojo no heya (Her Room) 2006; contrib. of short stories to Tokyo Fragments 2004, Inside and Other Short Fiction 2006.

FUJISAWA, Shû; Japanese novelist. *Education:* Hôsei Univ. *Career:* Ed. Tosho Shimbun –1996;. *Publications include:* novels: Zonu o hidari ni magare (Turn Left at the Zone) 1993, Sotomawari, Saigon pikkuappu, Suna ti hikari, Shibō Yūgi, Satori, Solo et Saigon pikkuappu, Buenosu Airesu gozen reiji (Midnight in Buenos Aires) (Akutagawa Prize) 1998, Orenji ando tāru (Orange and Tar) 2000, Sadame 2000, Buyinuosiailisi wu ye ling dian 2000, Murasaki no ryobun 2002, Hakozaki Junction 2003, Yukiyami 2007. *Address:* Kawade Shobo Shinsha Publishers, 2-32-2 Sendagaya, Shibuya-ku, Tokyo 151-0051, Japan (office). *E-mail:* info@kawade.co.jp (office). *Website:* www.kawade.co.jp (office).

FUKUYAMA, Francis, PhD; American political scientist, writer and academic; *Olivier Nomellini Senior Fellow, Freeman Spogli Institute for International Studies, Stanford University*; b. 27 Oct. 1952, Chicago, Ill.; s. of Yoshio Fukuyama and Toshiko Fukuyama (née Kawata); m. Laura Holmgren; three c. *Education:* Cornell and Harvard Univs. *Career:* fmrly Sr Social Scientist, RAND Corpn, Washington, DC 1979–80, 1983–89, 1995–96; Deputy Dir US State Dept's Policy Planning Staff 1981–82, 1989; Hirst Prof. of Public Policy, George Mason Univ., Fairfax 1996–2000; Dean of Faculty, Paul H. Nitze School of Advanced Int. Studies, Johns Hopkins Univ. 2002–04, then Bernard L. Schwartz Prof. of Int. Political Economy –2010; Olivier Nomellini Sr Fellow, Freeman Spogli Inst. for Int. Studies, Stanford Univ. 2010–, also resident Center on Democracy, Development, and the Rule of Law; Chair. Editorial Bd The American Interest (magazine); Trustee, RAND Corpn; mem. Bd of Govs Pardee Rand Graduate School; mem. Pres.'s Council on Bioethics 2001–04; mem. advisory Bd Journal of Democracy, Inter-American Dialogue, New America Foundation; mem. American Political Science Asscn, Council on Foreign Relations; mem. US del. to Egyptian-Israeli talks on Palestinian autonomy 1981–82. *Publications:* The End of History and the Last Man 1992, Trust: The Social Virtues and the Creation of Prosperity 1996, The Great Disruption: Human Nature and the Reconstitution of the Social Order 1999, Our Posthuman Future 2002, State-Building: Governance and World Order in the 21st Century 2004, Nation-Building: Beyond Afghanistan and Iraq (ed.) 2005, After the Neocons 2006, America at the Crossroads: Democracy, Power, and the Neoconservative Legacy 2006, Falling Behind: Explaining the Development Gap between Latin American and the US 2008, The Origins of Political Order 2011. *Honours:* Dr hc (Connecticut Coll.), (Doane Coll.), (Doshisha Univ., Japan), (Kansai Univ., Japan), (Århus Univ., Denmark). *Address:* Freeman Spogli Institute for International Studies, Encina Hall, 616 Serra Street, Stanford, CA 94305, USA (office). *Telephone:* (650) 723-3214 (office). *Fax:* (650) 725-2592 (office). *E-mail:* f.fukuyama@stanford.edu (office). *Website:* fsi.stanford.edu (office); www.francisfukuyama.com.

FULFORD, Robert Marshall Blount, OC; Canadian journalist and writer; b. 13 Feb. 1932, Ottawa, Ont.; m. 1st Jocelyn Jean Dingman 1956 (divorced 1970); one s. one d.; m. 2nd Geraldine Patricia Sherman 1970; two d. *Education:* Malvern Collegiate, Toronto. *Career:* reporter, Globe and Mail 1950–53, 1956–57, columnist 1992–; Asst Ed. Canadian Homes and Gardens 1955, Mayfair 1956, Maclean's 1962–64; columnist, Toronto Star 1958–62, 1964–68, 1971–87; Ed. Saturday Night 1968–87; Barker Fairley Distinguished Visitor in Canadian Culture, Univ. Coll., Univ. of Toronto 1987–88; columnist and Contributing Ed., Financial Times 1988–92; Chair. Banff Centre Program in Arts Journalism 1989–91, Maclean Hunter Program in Communications Ethics, Ryerson Polytechnical Inst., Toronto 1989–93; mem. Canadian Civil Liberties Asscn. *Publications include:* This Was Expo 1968, Crisis at the Victory Burlesk 1968, Marshall Delaney at the Movies 1974, An Introduction to the Arts in Canada 1977, Canada: A Celebration 1983, Best Seat in the House: Memoirs of a Lucky Man 1988, Accidental City: The Transformation of Toronto 1995, Toronto Discovered 1998, The Triumph of Narrative: Storytelling in the Age of Mass Culture 1999. *Honours:* Dr hc (McMaster Univ.) 1986, (York Univ.) 1987, (Univ. of Western Ontario) 1988, (Univ. of Toronto) 1994; Prix d'Honneur, Canadian Conf. of the Arts 1981. *E-mail:* robert.fulford@utoronto.ca (office). *Website:* www.robertfulford.com.

FULLER, Alexandra, BA; American writer; b. 29 March 1969, England, UK; s. of Tim Fuller and Nicola Fuller; m. Charlie Ross; three c. *Education:* Acadia Univ., NS, Canada. *Career:* moved with her family to a farm in Rhodesia 1972, after outbreak of civil war moved to Malawi 1981, and later to Zambia; moved to USA with husband 1994. *Publications include:* Don't Let's Go to the Dogs Tonight (BookSense Best Non-Fiction Book, Winifred Holtby Memorial Prize 2002, New York Times' Notable Book) 2001, Scribbling the Cat: Travels with an African Soldier (Lettre Ulysses Award for the Art of Reportage 2006) 2004, The Legend of Colton H. Bryant 2008, Cocktail Hour Under the Tree of Forgetfulness 2011; contrib. of stories to Writing Still: New Stories from Zimbabwe 2003, National Geographic Magazine. *Honours:* Booksense Nonfiction Book of the Year, Ulysses Prize of Reportage. *Literary Agent:* c/o The Steven Barclay Agency, 12 Western Avenue, Petaluma, CA 94952, USA. *Telephone:* (707) 773-0654. *Fax:* (707) 778-1868. *E-mail:* eliza@barclayagency.com. *Website:* www.barclayagency.com; www.alexandrafuller.org.

FULLER, Charles; American dramatist; b. 5 March 1939, Philadelphia, Pa; m. Miriam A. Nesbitt 1962; two s. *Education:* Villanova Univ., LaSalle Coll. *Career:* Co-founder and Co-Dir Afro-American Arts Theatre, Philadelphia 1967–71; Writer and Dir, The Black Experience, WIP Radio, Philadelphia 1970–71; Prof. of African-American Studies, Temple Univ. –1993; mem. Dramatists Guild, PEN, Writers Guild of America. *Publications include:* plays: The Village: A Party 1968, revised version as The Perfect Party 1969, In My Names and Days 1972, Candidate 1974, In the Deepest Part of Sleep 1974, First Love 1974, The Rise 1974, The Lay Out Letter 1975, The Brownsville Raid 1976, Sparrow in Flight 1978, Zooman and the Sign (Obie Award) 1981, A Soldier's Play (Pulitzer Prize in Drama) 1982, We: Part I, Sally 1988, Part II, Prince, Part III, Jonquil 1989, Part IV, Burner's Frolic 1990, Eliot's Coming 1988, Jonquil 1990, Songs of the Same Lion 1991, What a New York Trooper Saw of the War 2010; other: screenplays and television series. *Honours:* Nat. Endowment for the Arts Grant 1976, Rockefeller Foundation Grant 1976, Guggenheim Fellowship 1977–78, New York Drama Critics Circle Award 1982, Edgar Allan Poe Mystery Award 1985. *Literary Agent:* c/o Creative Artists Agency, 2000 Avenue of the Stars, Los Angeles, CA 90067, USA. *Telephone:* (424) 288-2000. *Fax:* (424) 288-2900. *Website:* www.caa.com.

FULLER, Cynthia Dorothy, BA, PGCE, MLitt; British poet and adult education tutor; *Lecturer in Creative Writing, Newcastle University*; b. 13 Feb. 1948, Isle of Sheppey, Kent, England; m. (divorced); two s. *Education:* Univs of Sheffield, Oxford and Aberdeen. *Career:* teacher of English, Redborne School 1970–72; freelance in adult educ., Depts at Durham, Leeds and Newcastle Univs, also Open Univ. and Workers' Educ. Asscn; Lecturer in Creative Writing, Newcastle Univ. 2007–. *Publications include:* Moving Towards Light 1992, Instructions for the Desert 1996, Only a Small Boat 2001, Jack's Letters Home 2006, Background Music 2009; contrib. to various magazines, including Other Poetry, Iron, Poetry Durham, Literary Review. *Honours:* Northern Arts Financial Assistance.

FULLER, John Leopold, BA, BLitt, MA, FRSL; British poet and writer; *Emeritus Fellow, Magdalen College, Oxford*; b. 1 Jan. 1937, Ashford, Kent, England; s. of Roy Broadbent Fuller and Kathleen Smith; m. Cicely Prudence Martin 1960; three d. *Education:* New Coll., Oxford. *Career:* Fellow and Tutor, Magdalen Coll., Oxford, now Emer. Fellow. *Publications include:* Fairground Music 1961, The Tree That Walked 1967, Cannibals and Missionaries 1972, The Sonnet 1972, Epistles to Several Persons 1973, Penguin Modern Poets 22 1974, The Mountain in the Sea 1975, Lies and Secrets 1979, The Illusionists 1980, The Dramatic Works of John Gay (ed.) 1983, The Beautiful Inventions 1983, Flying to Nowhere 1983, The Adventures of Speedfall 1985, Selected Poems, 1954–82 1985, The Grey Among the Green 1988, Tell it Me Again 1988, The Burning Boys 1989, Partingtime Hall (with James Fenton) 1989, The Mechanical Body and Other Poems 1991, Look Twice 1991, The Worm and the Star 1993, The Chatto Book of Love Poetry 1994, Stones and Fires 1996, Collected Poems 1996, A Skin Diary 1997, W. H. Auden: A Commentary 1998, W. H. Auden: Poems Selected by John Fuller 2000, The Oxford Book of Sonnets (ed.) 2000, The Memoirs of Laetitia Horsepole 2001, Now and for a Time 2002, Ghosts 2004, Flawed Angel 2005, The Space of Joy 2006, Song & Dance 2008, Pebble and I 2010, Writing the Picture (with David Hurn) 2010, Who is Ozymandias?: And Other Puzzles in Poetry 2011; contrib. to periodicals, reviews and journals. *Honours:* Newdigate Prize 1960, Richard Hillary Award 1962, E. C. Gregory Award 1965, Geoffrey Faber Memorial Prize 1974, Southern Arts Prize 1980, Whitbread Prize 1983, Forward Prize 1996, Michael Braude Award 2006. *Address:* 4 Benson Place, Oxford, OX2 6QH, England (home).

FULLER, Lawrence Robert, BJ; American newspaper publisher; b. 9 Sept. 1941, Toledo; s. of Kenneth Fuller and Marjory Rairdon; m. Suzanne Hovik 1967; one s. one d. *Education:* Univ. of Missouri. *Career:* reporter, Globe Gazette, Mason City, Ia 1963–67; reporter, later City Ed. Minneapolis Star 1967–75; Exec. Ed. Messenger-Inquirer, Owensborough, Ky 1975–77; Exec. Ed. Argus Leader, Sioux Falls, South Dakota 1977–78, Pres., Publr 1974–84, 1986–99; Pres. Gannett News Media, Washington, DC 1984–85; Dir Corp. Communications, Gannett Co. Inc. Washington 1985–86; Vice-Pres. Gannett/West Regional Newspaper Group 1986–97, The Honolulu Advertisers 1986–97; mem. American Newspaper Publishers' Asscn, American Soc. of Newspaper Eds etc. *Address:* 1888 Halekoa Drive, Honolulu, HI 96821-1029, USA (home). *Telephone:* (808) 732-2800 (home).

FULLER, Steve William, MPhil, PhD, FRSA,; American philosopher, sociologist, writer and speaker; *Professor of Sociology, University of Warwick*; b. 12 July 1959, New York, NY; s. of Theodore Beardsley Fuller and Sylvia Malherbe Gonzalez; partner Dolores Marie Byrnes. *Education:* Regis High School, New York, Columbia Univ., New York, Univ. of Cambridge, UK, Univ. of Pittsburgh. *Career:* Teaching Fellow in History and Philosophy of Science, Univ. of Pittsburgh 1982–85; Asst Prof. of Philosophy, Univ. of Colorado, Boulder 1985–88; Asst to Assoc. Prof. of Science and Tech. Studies, Virginia Tech. 1988–94; Assoc. Prof. of Rhetoric and Communication, Univ. of Pittsburgh 1993–94; Prof. of Sociology and Social Policy, Durham Univ., UK 1994–99; Prof. of Sociology, Univ. of Warwick, UK 1999–; Visiting Prof.,

Netherlands, Germany, Sweden, Israel, Japan, USA, Denmark; Exec. Ed., Social Epistemology: A Journal of Knowledge, Culture and Policy 1987–97; Exec. Ed., Technoscience: The Newsletter of the Soc. for Social Studies of Science 1989–97; Pres. Acad. Bd, Knowledge Man. Consortium Int. 1999; Pres. for Sociology and Social Policy, British Asscn for the Advancement of Science 2008; Fellow, Economic and Social Research Council (ESRC), UK 2000; mem. numerous editorial bds and prize cttees; mem. American Philosophical Asscn, Philosophy of Science Asscn, Soc. for the Social Studies of Science (4S) (mem. Council 1998–), European Asscn for the Study of Science and Tech. (mem. council 1994–98), American Sociological Asscn, British Sociological Asscn, History of Science Soc., American Asscn for the Rhetoric of Science and Tech. (Founding Vice-Pres. 1993–94), Business Processes Resources Centre Warwick Univ. (mem. advisory bd 1999–); UK Partner, EU Sixth Framework Project on Knowledge Politics of Converging Technologies 2006–08; mem. Acad. Advisory Bd Zeppelin Univ., Germany 2010–. *Plays include:* Lincoln and Darwin: Live for One Night Only! 2008, Three Women after the Soul of William James 2009. *Publications include:* Social Epistemology 1988, Philosophy of Science and its Discontents 1989, Philosophy, Rhetoric and the End of Knowledge: The Coming of Science and Technology Studies (revised second edn subtitled A New Beginning for Science and Technology Studies, with James H. Collier) 1993, Science 1997, The Governance of Science: Ideology and the Future of the Open Society 2000, Thomas Kuhn: A Philosophical History for Our Times 2000, Knowledge Management Foundations 2002, Kuhn vs Popper: The Struggle for the Soul of Science (named Book of the Month by Popular Science magazine (USA) Feb. 2005) 2003, The Intellectual: The Positive Power of Negative Thinking (named Book of the Year by New Statesman magazine (UK)) 2005, The Philosophy of Science and Technology Studies 2006, The New Sociological Imagination 2006, New Frontiers in Science and Technology Studies 2007, The Knowledge Book: Key Concepts in Philosophy, Science and Culture 2007, Science vs Religion? Intelligent Design and the Problem of Evolution 2007, Dissent over Descent 2008, The Sociology of Intellectual Life 2009, Science – The Art of Living 2010, Humanity 2.0: What It Means to be Human – The Past, Present and Future 2011; ed.: The Cognitive Turn: Psychological and Sociological Perspectives on Science (with others) 1989, Controversial Science: From Content to Contention (with others) 1993, Social Psychology of Science (with William Shadish) 1994, Contemporary British and American Philosophy and Philosophers (with Ouyang Kang) 1998–2004; contrib. of numerous articles, book reviews, essays. *Honours:* NSF Post-Doctoral Fellowship in History and Philosophy of Science, Univ. of Iowa 1989, ESRC Fellow in Public Understanding of Science 1998; Hon. DLitt (Warwick) 2007; Kellett Fellowship, Clare Coll., Cambridge 1979–81, Andrew Mellon Pre-Doctoral Fellowship, Pittsburgh 1981–82, Apple Teaching Award 1985, Nat. Endowment for the Humanities Fellowship 1989, Ford Foundation Project grant 2002–03. *Address:* Department of Sociology, University of Warwick, 2.23 Ramphal Building, Gibbet Hill Road, Coventry, CV4 7AL, England (office). *Telephone:* (24) 7652-3940 (office). *Fax:* (24) 7652-3497 (office). *E-mail:* s.w.fuller@warwick.ac.uk (office). *Website:* www2.warwick.ac.uk/fac/soc/sociology/staff/academicstaff/sfuller/fullers_index (office).

FULTON, Alice, BA, MFA; American poet, writer and academic; *Ann S. Bowers Professor of English, Cornell University*; b. 25 Jan. 1952, Troy, NY; m. Hank De Leo 1980. *Education:* Empire State Coll., Albany, NY, Cornell Univ. *Career:* Asst Prof., Univ. of Michigan 1983–86, Willam Willhartz Prof. 1986–89, Assoc. Prof. 1989–92, Prof. of English 1992–2001; Visiting Prof. of Creative Writing, Vermont Coll. 1987, Univ. of California at Los Angeles 1991, also at Ohio State Univ., Univ. of North Carolina at Wilmington; Ann S. Bowers Prof. of English, Cornell Univ. 2001–; Holloway Poet, Univ. of California at Berkeley 2004. *Publications include:* Anchors of Light 1979, Dance Script with Electric Ballerina 1983, Palladium 1986, Powers of Congress 1990, Sensual Math 1995, Feeling as a Foreign Language: The Good Strangeness of Poetry 1999, Felt (Rebecca Johnson Bobbit Prize, Library of Congress 2002) 2001, Cascade Experiment: Selected Poems 2004, The Nightingales of Troy: Connected Stories 2008. *Honours:* Hon. DLit (State Univ. of NY); Macdowell Colony Fellowships 1978, 1979, Millay Colony Fellowship 1980, Emily Dickinson Award 1980, Acad. of American Poets Prize 1982, Provincetown Fine Arts Work Center Fellowship 1982–83, Michigan Soc. of Fellows Fellowship 1983–86, Consuelo Ford Award 1984, Rainer Maria Rilke Award 1984, Michigan Council for the Arts Grants 1986, 1991, Guggenheim Fellowship 1986–87, Yaddo Colony Fellowship 1987, Bess Hokin Prize 1989, Ingram Merrill Foundation Award 1990, John D. and Catherine T. MacArthur Foundation Fellowship 1991–96, Elizabeth Matchett Stover Award 1994, Henry Russel Award, Univ. of Michigan, Nat. Endowment for the Arts Fellowship 2005. *Literary Agent:* c/o Wendy Weil, The Wendy Weil Agency, 232 Madison Avenue, Suite 1300, New York, NY 10016-2901, USA. *Telephone:* (212) 685-0030. *E-mail:* info@wendyweil.com. *Website:* wendyweil.com. *Address:* Department of English, Cornell University, 239 Goldwin Smith Hall, Ithaca, NY 14853-3201, USA (office). *Telephone:* (607) 255-9307 (office). *E-mail:* af89@cornell.edu (office). *Website:* alicefulton.com.

FULTON, Len, BA; American writer and publisher; *Publisher, Dust Books*; b. 15 May 1934, Lowell, Mass; one s. one d. *Education:* Univ. of Wyoming. *Career:* mem. Literary Advisory Panel, Nat. Endowment for the Arts, 1976–78; mem. Advisory Bd, Center for the Book, Library of Congress, 1978–80; Publisher, Dust Books; mem. PEN. *Publications include:* The Grassman (novel) 1974, Dark Other Adam Dreaming (novel) 1976, (play) 1984, American Odyssey (travelogue) 1978, For the Love of Pete (play) 1988, Grandmother Dies (play) 1989, Headlines (play) 1990. *Address:* Dust Books, PO Box 100, Paradise, CA 95967, USA (office). *Telephone:* (530) 877-6110 (office). *Fax:* (530) 877-0222 (office). *E-mail:* info@dustbooks.com (office). *Website:* www.dustbooks.com (office).

FULTON, Robin, MA, PhD; Scottish poet, writer, translator and editor; b. 6 May 1937, Arran, Scotland. *Education:* Univ. of Edinburgh. *Career:* Sr Lecturer, Stavanger Univ., Norway 1973–2006. *Publications include:* poetry: Instances 1967, Inventories 1969, The Spaces Between the Stones 1971, The Man with the Surbahar 1971, Tree-Lines 1974, Following a Mirror 1980, Selected Poems 1963–78 1980, Fields of Focus 1982, Coming Down to Earth and Spring is Soon 1990, Scottish Poetry (supplement) 2003; criticism: Contemporary Scottish Poetry: Individuals and Contexts 1974, The Way the Words are Taken, Selected Essays 1989; ed.: Lines Review and assocd publs 1967–76, Iain Crichton Smith: Selected Poems 1955–80 1982, Robert Garioch: The Complete Poetical Works with Notes 1983, Robert Garioch: A Garioch Miscellany, Selected Prose and Letters 1986, Robert Garioch, Collected Poems 2004; translator: An Italian Quartet 1966, Five Swedish Poets 1972, Lars Gustafsson, Selected Poems 1972, Gunnar Harding: They Killed Sitting Bull and Other Poems 1973, Tomas Tranströmer: Selected Poems 1974, Östen Sjöstrand: The Hidden Music & Other Poems 1975, Toward the Solitary Star: Selected Poetry and Prose 1988, Werner Aspenström: 37 Poems 1976, Tomas Tranströmer: Baltics 1980, Werner Aspenström: The Blue Whale and Other Prose Pieces 1981, Kjell Espmark: Béla Bartók Against the Third Reich and Other Poems 1985, Olav Hauge: Don't Give Me the Whole Truth and Other Poems 1985, Tomas Tranströmer: Collected Poems 1987, Stig Dagerman: German Autumn 1988, Pär Lagervist: Guest of Reality 1989, Preparations for Flight, and other Swedish Stories 1990, Four Swedish Poets (Kjell Espmark, Lennart Sjögren, Eva Ström & Tomas Tranströmer) 1990, Olav Hauge: Selected Poems 1990, Hermann Starheimsaeter: Stone-Shadows 1991, Five Swedish Poets (Werner Aspenström, Kjell Espmark, Lennart Sjögren, Eva Ström, Staffan Söderblom) 1997, Tomas Tranströmer, New Collected Poems 1997, revised 2006, Henrik Nordbrandt, My Life, My Dream 2002, Olav Hauge, Leaf-Huts and Snow-Houses 2003, Chickweed Wintergreen: Selected Poems by Henry Martinson 2010. *Honours:* Gregory Award 1967, Writers Fellowship, Univ. of Edinburgh 1969, Scottish Arts Council Writers Bursary 1972, Arthur Lundquist Award for Trans. from Swedish 1977, Swedish Acad. Award 1978, 1998, 2007, 2010. *Address:* Mjughaug Terrasse 8, 4048 Hafrsfjord, Norway (home). *Telephone:* (51) 592346 (home). *E-mail:* robin37@getmail.no (office).

FUNDER, Anna, BA (Hons), LLB (Hons), MA; Australian writer; b. 1966, Melbourne, Vic.; d. of Prof. John Funder and the late Dr Kathleen Funder; m.; one s. two d. *Education:* Univ. of Melbourne, Free Univ. of Berlin, Germany, Univ. of Tech. *Career:* Co-Ed. Melbourne Univ. Law Review 1991; int. lawyer, Office of Int. Law, Attorney-Gen.'s Dept 1993–95; researcher and trans., Deutsche Welle TV, Berlin; Fellow, Rockefeller Foundation 2008; radio and TV producer, ABC, Australia; Writer-in-Residence, Australia Centre, Potsdam, Germany; has toured extensively internationally and spoken at many writers' festivals and special appearances; numerous radio and TV appearances. *Publications:* Stasiland: Stories from Behind the Berlin Wall (BBC 4 Samuel Johnson Prize 2004) 2002 (has been published in 20 countries and translated into 15 languages; chosen as BBC Book of the Week; has been adapted for radio and CD in Britain and Australia), All That I Am (novel) 2011. *Honours:* English Prize, Univ. of Melbourne, DAAD Scholarship, Australian-German Asscn Fellowship, Arts Victoria Literary Grant, Australia Council Literary Grant 2002, The Age Book of the Year Awards (non-fiction) 2002, Felix Meyer Creative Writing Award, Samuel Johnson Prize 2004, ASA Mander Jones Award 2008, NSW Writers Fellowship 2010. *Literary Agent:* c/o The Wylie Agency, 17 Bedford Square, London, WC1B 3JA, England.

FUNE, Jonathan (see Fletcher, John Walter James)

FUNKE, Cornelia Caroline; German children's writer; b. 1958, Dorsten, Westphalia; m. Rolf Funke (died 2006); one s. one d. *Education:* Hamburg Univ., Hamburg State Coll. of Design. *Career:* worked as designer of board games, illustrator of children's books; began writing/illustrating full-time aged 28; also works for ZDF state TV channel. *Publications:* Monstergeschichten 1993, Die Wilden Hühner 1993, Rittergeschichten 1994, Zwei wilde kleine Hexen 1994, Kein Keks für Kobolde 1994, Greta und Eule, Hundesitter 1995, Der Mondscheindrache 1996, Die Gespensterjäger auf eisiger Spur 1996, Die Wilden Hühner auf Klassenfahrt 1996, Hände weg von Mississippi 1997, Drachenreiter (trans. as Dragon Rider) (Sakura Medal 2006) 1997, Prinzessin Isabella (trans. as The Princess Knight) 1997, Tiergeschichten 1997, Das verzauberte Klassenzimmer 1997, Die Wilden Hühner Fuchsalarm 1998, Dachbodengeschichten 1998, Potilla und der Mützendieb 1998, Dicke Freundinnen 1998, Igraine Ohnefurcht (trans. as Igraine the Brave) 1998, Strandgeschichten 1999, Das Piratenschwein (trans. as Pirate Girl) 1999, Herr der Diebe (trans. as The Thief Lord) (Swiss Youth Literature Award, Zurich Children's Book Award, Venice House of Literature Book Award, Mildred L. Batchelder Award for the best trans. children's book of the year) 2000, Lilli und Flosse 2000, Mick und Mo im Wilden Westen (trans. as Mick and Mo in the Wild West) 2000, Die Wilden Hühner und das Glück der Erde 2000, Kleiner Werwolf 2001, Als der Weihnachtsmann vom Himmel fiel 2001, Dicke Freundinnen und der Pferdedieb 2001, Die Gespensterjäger im Feuerspuk 2001, Die Gespensterjäger in der Gruselburg 2001, Die Gespensterjäger in grosser Gefahr 2001, Der geheimnisvolle Ritter Namenlos 2001,

Die Wilden Hühner Bandenbuch 2001, Emma und der blaue Dschinn 2002, Die schönsten Erstlesegeschichten 2002, Die Glücksfee 2003, Hinter verzauberten Fenstern 2003, Käpten Knitterbart 2003, Tintenherz (trans. as Inkheart) 2003, Kribbel Krabbel Käferwetter 2003, Der wildeste Bruder der Welt 2003, Der verlorene Wackelzahn 2003, Die Wilden Hühner und die Liebe 2003, Die Wilden Hühner Tagebuch 2004, Tintenblut (trans. as Inkspell) 2005, When Santa Fell to Earth 2006, Tintentod (trans. as Inkdeath) 2008, Reckless 2010, Saving Mississippi 2010, Reckless 2 2012. *Honours:* numerous awards including Wildweibchenpreis for collected works 2000, Roswitha Prize 2008. *Literary Agent:* c/o Oliver Latsch Literary Agency & Translations, Dudelsackstraße 36, 67227 Frankenthal, Rheinland-Pfalz, Germany. *Telephone:* (6233) 549419. *Fax:* (6233) 62518. *E-mail:* info@oliverlatsch.com. *Website:* www.oliverlatsch.com; www.cornelia-funke.com.

FURST, Alan, BA, MA; American writer; b. 20 Feb. 1941, New York, NY. *Education:* Oberlin Coll., Pennsylvania State Univ. *Career:* fmr Fulbright Teaching Fellow, Faculté des Lettres, Univ. of Montpellier, France; worked for City of Seattle Arts Comm.; fmr columnist in France for International Herald Tribune. *Publications include:* Your Day in the Barrel 1976, The Paris Drop 1980, The Caribbean Account 1981, Shadow Trade 1983, Night Soldiers 1988, Dark Star 1991, The Polish Officer 1995, The World at Night 1996, Red Gold 1999, Kingdom of Shadows 2001, Blood of Victory 2002, Dark Voyage 2004, The Foreign Correspondent 2006, The Spies of Warsaw 2008, Spies of the Balkans 2010, Mission to Paris 2012 contrib. to periodicals. *Address:* c/o Random House Inc., 1745 Broadway, Third Floor, New York, NY 10019, USA. *E-mail:* alan@alanfurst.net (office). *Website:* www.alanfurst.net.

FURTWÄNGLER, Virginia Walsh, (Ann Copeland), BA, MA, PhD; American writer, teacher, pianist and accompanist; *Hallie Ford Chair Emeritus of English, Willamette University, Salem*; b. 16 Dec. 1932, Hartford, Conn.; m. Albert Furtwängler 1968; two s. *Education:* Coll. of New Rochelle, Catholic Univ. of America, Cornell Univ. *Career:* Lecturer in English, Coll. of New Rochelle; Writer-in-Residence, Coll. of Idaho 1980, Linfield Coll. 1980–81, Univ. of Idaho 1982, 1986, Wichita State Univ. 1988, Mt Allison Univ. 1990, St Mary's Univ. 1993; Hallie Ford Chair of English, Willamette Univ. 1996, currently Emer.; mem. Authors' Guild; has taught numerous writing workshops in USA and Canada. *Film:* Letter From Francis (winner of top TV Story Award for 1992). *Radio:* several stories read on CBC. *Publications include:* At Peace 1978, The Back Room 1979, Earthen Vessels 1984, The Golden Thread 1989, Strange Bodies on a Stranger Shore 1994, The ABC's of Writing Fiction 1996, Season of Apples 1996, Musicking – A Memoir of Musical Time (memoir); contribs to anthologies and magazines. *Honours:* Dr hc (Univ. of New Brunswick, St John); several Canada Council Awards, two Nat. Endowment for the Arts Writing Fellowships, Ingram Merrill Foundation Award, Province of New Brunswick Award. *Address:* 235 Oak Way NE, Salem, OR 97301, USA (home). *E-mail:* vfurtwan@willamette.edu (office). *Website:* members.authorsguild.net/acopeland.

FYFIELD, Frances (see HEGARTY, Frances)

G

GAARDER, Jostein; Norwegian writer; b. 1952, Oslo; m.; two s. *Education:* Univ. of Oslo. *Career:* fmr philosophy teacher. *Publications include:* Diagnosen og andre noveller (trans. as The Diagnosis and Other Stories) 1986, Barna fra Sukhavati (children's fiction; trans. as The Children from Sukhavati) 1987, Froskeslottet (children's fiction; trans. as The Frog Castle) 1988, Kabalmysteriet (trans. as The Solitaire Mystery) (Norwegian Ministry of Cultural Affairs award, The Critics' Prize 1991, Premi de Literatura Protagonista Jove, Spain 1996, Int. Bd on Books for Young People award, Poland) 1990, Sofies verden: Roman on filosofiens historie (trans. as Sophie's World: A Novel about the History of Philosophy) (Deutscher Jugendliteraturpreis, Die Zeit LUCHS 84 award, Germany, Sonja Hagemann Prize 1993, Le Prix des Libraires, Canada 1995, El Arcebispo Juan de San Clemente's Prize for Literature, Spain, Bancarella Award, Italy, Flaiano Award, Italy, La Vanguardia Award, Spain 2002) 1991, Julemysteriet (trans. as The Christmas Mystery) (Premio Internazionale Fregene, Italy) 1992, I et speil, i en gåte (trans. as Through a Glass, Darkly) (Buxtehuder Bulle, Jugendbuchpreis, Germany, Jugendbuchpreis, Jury der jungen Leser, Austria) 1993, Hallo? Er det noen her? (trans. as Hello? Is Anybody There?, children's book) 1996, Vita Brevis (trans. as That Same Flower, novella) 1996, Maya 1999, Sirkusdirektørens datter (trans. as The Ringmaster's Daughter) 2001, Appelsinpiken (trans. as The Orange Girl) (Norwegian Language Prize) 2004, Sjakk Matt' (trans. as Checkmate) 2006, De gule dvergene (trans. as The Yellow Dwarves) 2006, Slottet i Pyreneene (trans. as The Castle in the Pyrenees) 2008. *Honours:* Commdr, Royal Norwegian Order of St Olav 2005; Dr hc (Trinity Coll., Dublin) 2005; School Librarians' Union Literature Prize (three times), Fortuna bookstore's hon. award, Wettergren's Children's Book Acorn for authorship, Sweden 1997, Bergen Int. Festival Poet, elected 'Peer Gynt' of the Year by Norwegian Parl., Brage Hon. Prize for authorship 2003, Willy Brandt Prize. *Literary Agent:* c/o Aschehoug Agency, Sehesteds Gate 3, Postboks 363, Sentrum, 0102 Oslo, Norway. *Telephone:* 22-40-04-00. *E-mail:* eva.kuloy@aschehougagency.no. *Website:* www.aschehougagency.no.

GADDIS, John Lewis, PhD; American historian and academic; *Robert A. Lovett Professor of History, Yale University;* b. 1942; m. (divorced); two s.; m. 2nd Toni Dorfman 1997. *Education:* Univ. of Texas, Austin. *Career:* Lecturer and later Prof., Dept of History, Ohio Univ. 1969–94, f. Contemporary History Inst., Ohio 1987; Sr Fellow, Hoover Inst. 2000–02; Robert A. Lovett Prof. of History, Yale Univ. 1997–; fmr Lecturer, US Naval War Coll., Univ. of Helsinki, Finland, Princeton Univ., Univ. of Oxford, UK; George Eastman Visiting Prof., Balliol Coll., Oxford 2000–01; mem. Editorial Bd Foreign Affairs; mem. Advisory Bd Cold War Int. History Project; Fellow, American Acad. of Arts and Sciences 1995. *Publications include:* The United States and the Origins of the Cold War 1941–47 1972, Russia, The Soviet Union and the United States: An Interpretive History 1978, Strategies of Containment: A Critical Appraisal of Postwar American National Security Policy 1982, The Long Peace: Inquiries into the History of the Cold War 1987, The United States and the End of the Cold War: Reconsiderations, Implications, Provocations 1992, We Now Know: Rethinking Cold War History 1997, The Landscape of History: How Historians Map the Past 2002, Surprise, Security, and the American Experience 2004, The Cold War 2006, George F. Kennan: An American Life (Pulitzer Prize for Biography 2012) 2011. *Honours:* Nat. Humanities Medal 2005. *Address:* Department of History, Yale University, PO Box 208324, New Haven, CT 06520-8353, USA (office). *Telephone:* (203) 432-1374 (office). *Fax:* (203) 432-6520 (office). *E-mail:* john.gaddis@yale.edu (office). *Website:* www.yale.edu/history/faculty/gaddis.html (office).

GAEHTGENS, Thomas Wolfgang, DPhil; German art historian and academic; *Director, The Getty Research Institute;* b. 24 June 1940, Leipzig; m. Barbara Feiler 1969; two s. *Education:* Univs of Bonn and Freiburg and Univ. of Paris, France. *Career:* teacher, Univ. of Göttingen 1973, Prof. of Art History 1974–79, Technische Hochschule, Aachen 1979, Freie Univ. Berlin 1979–2007; Founder and Dir German Centre for the History of Art, Paris 1997–2007; Visiting Scholar, Inst. for Advanced Study, Princeton 1979–80; Visiting Scholar, The Getty Research Inst., Los Angeles, USA 1985–86, Dir 2007–; Pres. Comité International d'histoire de l'art 1992–96; mem. Akad. der Wissenschaften, Göttingen. *Publications:* Napoleon's Arc de Triomphe 1974, Versailles als Nationaldenkmal 1984, Joseph-Marie Vien 1988, Anton von Werner 1990, Die Berliner Museuminsel im Deutschen Kaiserreich 1992. *Honours:* Chevalier, Légion d'honneur; Dr hc (Courtauld Inst. of Art, UK) 2004; Grand Prix de la Francophonie 2009. *Address:* The Getty Research Institute, 1200 Getty Center Drive, Suite 1100, Los Angeles, CA 90049-1688, USA (office). *Telephone:* (310) 440-7335 (office). *E-mail:* griweb@getty.ed (office). *Website:* www.getty.edu/research (office).

GAGE, Elizabeth, BA; American writer; b. (Susan Libertson), 28 Dec. 1947, Chicago, Ill.; d. of the late Kenneth H. Rusch and of Alices Falces Rusch; m. Joseph Libertson 1969; one d. *Education:* West Sr High, Madison, Wis., Northwestern Univ., Evanston, Ill. *Career:* received largest ever advance to a first novelist (Simon & Schuster); Prof., Yale Univ. *Publications include:* Broken Pride 1978, A Glimpse of Stocking 1988, Pandora's Box 1990, The Master Stroke 1991, Taboo 1992, Intimate 1995, Confession 1998, Against All Odds 1998, The Hourglass 1999, The Rain Climber (awards from Writer's Digest Writing Contest and New York Book Festival) 2009. *Honours:* Hon. Mention Writer's Digest Writing Contest 2009, New York Book Festival Award 2010. *Address:* 11779 East Desert Vista Drive, Scottsdale, AZ 85255, USA (home). *Telephone:* (480) 502-0880 (home). *Fax:* (480) 502-0908 (home). *E-mail:* sliberts@cox.net (home).

GAGLIANO, Frank, BA, MFA; American playwright, screenwriter, novelist and academic; b. 18 Nov. 1931, New York, NY. *Education:* Queens Coll., City Univ. of New York, Univ. of Iowa, Columbia Univ. *Career:* Playwright-in-Residence, RSC, London 1967–69; Asst Prof. of Drama, Playwright-in-Residence, Dir of Contemporary Playwrights Center, Florida State Univ., Tallahassee 1969–73; Lecturer in Playwriting, Dir of Conkie Workshop for Playwrights, Univ. of Texas, Austin 1973–75; Distinguished Visiting Prof., Univ. of Rhode Island 1975; Benedum Prof. of Theatre, West Virginia Univ. 1976–; Artistic Dir, Carnegie Mellon, Showcase of New Plays 1986–99; Artistic Dir, Univ. of Michigan's Festival of New Works 2000–02. *Publications include:* The City Scene (two plays) 1966, Night of the Dunce 1967, Father Uxbridge Wants to Marry 1968, The Hide-and-Seek Odyssey of Madeleine Gimple 1970, Big Sur 1970, The Prince of Peasantmania 1970, The Private Eye of Hiram Bodoni (television play) 1971, Quasimodo (musical) 1971, Anywhere the Wind Blows (musical) 1972, In the Voodoo Parlour of Marie Laveau 1974, The Commedia World of Lafcadio Beau 1974, The Resurrection of Jackie Cramer (musical) 1974, Congo Square (musical) 1975, revised 1989, The Total Immersion of Madelaine Favorini 1981, San Ysidro (dramatic cantata) 1985, From the Bodoni County Songbook Anthology, Book I 1986, musical version 1989, Anton's Leap (novel) 1987, The Farewell Concert of Irene and Vernon Palazzo 1994, My Chekhov Light 1998. *E-mail:* sandrico@aol.com (office). *Website:* www.gaglianoriff.com.

GAGNON, Madeleine, BA, MA, PhD; Canadian writer and poet; b. 27 July 1938, Amqui, PQ; m. (divorced); two s. *Education:* Univ. Saint-Joseph du Nouveau-Brunswick, Univ. of Montréal, Univ. of Aix-en-Provence. *Career:* teacher of literature, Univ. of Québec at Montréal 1969–82; various guest professorships and writer-in-residencies; currently Writer-in-Residence, Univ. of Québec at Rimouski; mem. Union des écrivaines et des écrivains québécois, Acad. des Lettres du Québec, PEN Canada, Québec section. *Achievements include:* subject of conference, Le chant de la terre – Autour de Madeleine Gagnon, Univ. de Valenciennes (France) 2008. *Publications include:* Les Morts-vivants 1969, Pour les femmes et tous les autres 1974, Poélitique 1975, La Venue à l'écriture (with Hélène Cixous and Annie Leclerc) 1977, Retailles (with Denise Boucher) 1977, Antre 1978, Lueur: Roman archéologique 1979, Au coeur de la lettre 1981, Autographie 1 and 2: Fictions 1982, Les Fleurs du catalpa 1986, Toute écriture est amour 1989, Chant pour un Québec lointain 1991, La Terre est remplie de langage 1993, Les Cathédrales sauvages 1994, Le Vent majeur 1995, Le Deuil du soleil 1998, Rêve de Pierre 1999, Les Femmes et la guerre (trans. as Women in a World at War) 2000, My Name is Bosnia 2006, A l'ombre des mots, poèmes 1964–2006 2007; contrib. to numerous periodicals. *Honours:* Journal de Montréal Grand Prize 1986, Gov.-Gen.'s Award for Poetry 1991, Québec Grand Prize Athanase-David 2002, Prix Donald Gasparic for poetry, Romania 2007. *Address:* c/o Union des écrivaines et des écrivains québécois, La Maison des écrivains, 3492 avenue Laval, Montréal, PQ H2X 3C8, Canada (office).

GAILLARD, Frye, BA; American journalist and author; b. 23 Dec. 1946, Mobile, Ala; m. Nancy B. Gaillard; two d. *Education:* Vanderbilt Univ. *Career:* Writer-in-Residence, Univ. of Southern Alabama 2005–. *Publications include:* Watermelon Wine: The Spirit of Country Music 1978, Race, Rock and Religion 1982, The Catawba River 1983, The Unfinished Presidency: Essays on Jimmy Carter 1986, The Dream Long Deferred 1988, The Secret Diary of Mikhail Gorbachev 1990, Southern Voices 1991, Kyle at 200 MPH 1993, Lessons from the Big House 1994, The Way We See It 1995, If I Were a Carpenter: Twenty Years of Habitat for Humanity 1996, Mobile and the Eastern Shore 1997, As Long as the Waters Flow: Native Americans in the South and East 1998, The S21 All-Stars 1999, Cradle of Freedom: Alabama and the Movement that Changed America (Lilian Smith Award) 2005, Prophet from the Plains: Jimmy Carter and his Legacy 2007, In the Path of the Storms (co-ed.) 2008, With Music and Justice for All 2008, Alabama's Civil Rights Trail 2010; contribs to The Oxford American, Saturday Review, Parade, Southern Accents, Southern Magazine, New West. *Honours:* Gustavus Myers Award 1989, Small Press Award 1997, Library of Congress Legacies Recognition 1999. *Address:* Department of History, University of Southern Alabama, Humanities 344, Mobile, AL 36688-0002, USA (office). *E-mail:* history@jaguar1.usouthal.edu (office). *Website:* www.southalabama.edu/history (office).

GAIMAN, Neil Richard; British writer, journalist, screenwriter, producer and director; b. 10 Nov. 1960, Portchester, Hants., England; s. of the late David Gaiman and of Sheila Gaiman; three c. *Career:* creator and writer of Sandman comics (75 issues, collected in ten vols); collaborations with Dave McKean, Terry Pratchett; adult novelist and children's author; Fellow, Univ. of Liverpool; Patron Open Rights Group, The Science Fiction Foundation, The Bookend Trust (Tasmania). *Films include:* Princess Mononoke (writer of English version) 1997, A Short Film About John Bolton (writer, dir) 2003, MirrorMask (writer) 2004, Beowulf (writer of adaptation, exec. producer) 2007, Stardust (producer) 2007, Coraline (based on novel) 2009. *Play:* Wolves in the Walls 2006. *Radio:* Signal to Noise 1996, Mr Punch 2005. *Television writing:* Neverwhere (BBC) 1996, Babylon 5 (episode) 1997, Statuesque (writer, dir) 2009, Doctor Who (The Doctor's Wife) (BBC) 2010. *Publications include:* novels: Ghastly Beyond Belief 1985, Don't Panic 1987, Violent Cases 1987, Black Orchid 1988, Good Omens 1990, Miracleman – The Golden Age 1992, Signal to Noise 1992, Death – The High Cost of Living 1993, Neverwhere 1997, Stardust 1998, Sandman – The Dream Hunters 1999, American Gods (Hugo, Nebula, SFX Stoker and Locus Awards 2001) 2001, Sandman – Endless Nights 2003, Anansi Boys (Mythopoeic Award 2007) 2005; juvenile fiction: The Day I Swapped My Dad for Two Goldfish 1997, Coraline (also film) (Hugo, Nebula and Locus Awards 2003) 2002, Elizabeth Burr/Worzalla Award 2003) 2002, The Wolves in the Walls (with Dave McKean) (BSFA Best Short Fiction, Liber Award 2003, Andersen Award 2004) 2003, The Graveyard Book (John Newbery Medal 2009, Hugo Award for Best Novel 2009, Elizabeth Burr/ Worzalla Award 2009, Booktrust Teenage Prize 2009, Carnegie Medal 2010) 2008, Odd and the Frost Giants 2009; short stories: A Study in Emerald (Hugo Award for Best Short Story 2005) 2003, Fragile Things 2006; anthologies: Angels and Visitations 1993, Smoke and Mirrors – Short Fictions and Illusions 1998; other: The Absolute Sandman 2006; ed.: Now We Are Sick 1991, Stories: All-New Tales (co-ed.) 2010; contrib. to Time Out, The Sunday Times, Comic Relief, Punch, The Observer, The Face, BBC Radio 3, BBC Radio 4, NPR, New York Times, Washington Post, Wired. *Honours:* Int. Horror Critics' Guild Award for Best Collection, Eagle Award for Best Graphic Novel 1988, Best Writer of American Comics 1990, Will Eisner Comic Industry Award 1991–94, Diamond Distributors' Gem Award 1993, GLAAD Award for Best Comic 1996, Julia Verlanger Award (France) 1999, Bram Stoker Award 1999, 2002–03, 4-11 Award for Best Children's Illustrated Book 2003, Eagle Award 2004, World Fantasy Award for Best Short Story 1992, Mythopoeic Award for Best Adult Novel 1999, 2005, Audie Award 2002, Jim Henson Honours 2007, Galaxy Award (China) 2008, 2009, Newbery Medal (USA) 2008, Carnegie Medal (UK) 2009. *Literary Agent:* c/o Merrilee Heifetz, Writers House, 21 West 26th Street, New York, NY 10010, USA. *Telephone:* (212) 685-2400. *Website:* www.neilgaiman.com.

GAINES, Ernest James, BA; American writer and academic; *Professor of English, University of Louisiana, Lafayette*; b. 15 Jan. 1933, River Lake Plantation, Pointe Coupee Parish, La; m. Dianne Saulney. *Education:* San Francisco State Univ., Stanford Univ. *Career:* writer-in-residence, Denison Univ. 1971, Stanford Univ. 1981; Visiting Prof. 1983, writer-in-residence 1986, Whittier Coll.; Prof. of English and writer-in-residence, Univ. of La Lafayette (fmrly Univ. of Southwestern La) 1983–; Fellow American Acad. of Arts and Letters. *Publications:* Catherine Carmier 1964, Of Love and Dust 1967, Bloodline (short stories) 1968, The Autobiography of Miss Jane Pittman 1971, A Long Day in November 1971, In My Father's House 1978, A Gathering of Old Men 1983, A Lesson Before Dying (Nat. Book Critics Circle Award 1994, Southern Writers Conference Award 1994, La Library Asscn Award 1994) 1993. *Honours:* Fellow Stanford Univ. Creative Writing Program 1958, Nat. Endowment for the Arts grant 1967, Rockefeller Grant 1970, Guggenheim Fellowship 1971, John D. and Catherine T. MacArthur Foundation Fellowship 1993; Dr hc (Bard Coll.), (Brown Univ.), (Denison Univ.), (La State Univ.), (Loyola Univ.), (Savannah Coll. of Art and Design), (Tulane Univ.), (Univ. of Miami), (Univ. of the South, Sewanee), (Whittier Coll.); Black Acad. of Arts and Letters Award 1972, Commonwealth Club of Calif. Fiction gold medals 1972, 1984, American Acad. and Inst. of Arts and Letters Award 1987, La Humanist of the Year 1989, La Center for the Book Award 2000, Nat. Govs' Asscn Award for Distinguished Service in the Arts 2000, La Govs' Award for Lifetime Achievement 2000, La Writers' Award 2000, Nat. Humanities Medal 2000; Chevalier, Ordre des Arts et des Lettres 1996. *Literary Agent:* Tanya Bickley Enterprises Inc., PO Box 1656, New Canaan, CT 06840, USA. *Address:* c/o Department of English, University of Louisiana Lafayette, Griffin Hall, Room 221, Lafayette, LA 70504, USA (office).

GÁL, Róbert, BA; Slovak author and poet; b. 22 May 1968, Bratislava. *Education:* Charles Univ., Prague, New School Univ., New York, USA. *Career:* Founder mem. and singer Agnomia Quartet; Ed. GplusG Publishing 1997–2000; Ed. Prague Literary Review 2004–05; journalist, Literárni noviny (literary newspaper) 2009–10; work has appeared in Optimism, The Exquisite Corpse, Prague Post and numerous other journals. *Publications include:* Nihil sub sole novum 1995, Paradoxy a deštrukcie (Paradoxes & Destructions Vol. I) 1997, Epigraffiti 2001, Znaky a priznaky 2003, Signs and Symptoms 2003, Manipulzácie 2005, Krídlovanie 2006, Agnomia 2008. *Address:* c/o Twisted Spoon Press, PO Box 21, Preslova 12, 150 21 Prague 5, Czech Republic (office). *E-mail:* editor@twistedspoon.com (office); robogal@volny.cz. *Website:* www.twistedspoon.com/gal.html (office).

GALA, Antonio, LicenDer; Spanish writer; b. 2 Oct. 1930, Brazatortas, Ciudad Real; s. of Luis Gala and Adoración Velasco. *Education:* Univs of Seville and Madrid. *Career:* Founder-Pres., Fundación Antonio Gala. *Publications include:* plays: Los Verdes Campos del Edén, El caracol en el espejo 1964, El sol en el hormiguero 1966, Noviembre y un poco de hierba 1967, Canatr del Santiago para todos 1971, Los buenos días perdidos 1972, Suerte, campeón 1973, Anillos para una Dama 1973, Las cítaras colgadas de los árboles 1974, Por qué corres Ulises? 1975, Petra regalada 1980, Le vieja señorita del paraíso 1980, El Cementerio de los Pájaros 1982, Trilogia de la libertad 1983, Samarkanda 1985, El hotelito 1985, Séneca o el beneficio de la duda 1987, Carmen Carmen 1988, La Truhana 1992, Los Bellos Durmientes 1994, Café Cantante 1997, Las manzanas del viernes 2000; novels: El Manuscrito Carmesí (Planeta Prize) 1990, La Pasión Turca 1993, Más Allá del Jardín 1995, La Regla de Tres 1996, El Corazón Tardío 1998, Las Afuneras de Dios 1999, El imposible olvido 2001, Los invitados al jardin 2002, El dueño de la herida 2003, El pedestal de las estatuas 2007, Los papeles de agua 2008, Cosas nuestras 2008; poetry: Enemigo Intimo 1959, 11 Sonetos de la Zubia 1981, Poemas Cordobeses 1994, Testamento andaluz 1994, Poemas de amor 1997, El poema de Tobías desangelado 2005; essays: Charlas con Troylo, En Propia Mano, Cuaderno de la Dama de Otoño, Dedicado a Tobias. *Honours:* Dr hc (Univ. of Córdoba); Nat. Prize for Literature, Hidalgo Prize, Planeta Prize; many other literary and theatre awards. *Address:* Fundación Antonio Gala, Calle Ambrosio de Morales, 20, 14003 Córdoba, Spain (office). *Telephone:* (957) 487395 (office). *Fax:* (957) 487423 (office). *E-mail:* info@fundacionantoniogala.org (office). *Website:* www.fundacionantoniogala.org (office); www.antoniogala.es.

GALANAKI, Rhea, BA; Greek writer; b. 21 Nov. 1947, Irakleio, Crete; m. Prof. Elias Kouvelas; one d. *Education:* Nat. and Kapodistrian Univ. of Athens. *Career:* began as a poet, writing for magazines opposing dictatorship in Greece 1967–74; collaborated with film dir Theo Angelopoulos as script consultant on his last, unfinished film The Other Sea 2009–12; author of first Greek novel to be included in UNESCO's List of Representative Works (The Life of Ismail Ferik Pasha) 1994; mem. Athens Municipal Council 2010–11 (resgnd); Pres. City Radio Athens 9.84 2010–11 (resgnd); Founder-mem. Hellenic Authors' Soc.; works have been translated into 15 languages. *Publications:* novels: The Life of Ishmael Ferik Pasha 1989, 2008, I Shall Sign as Loui 1993, 2005, Eleni or Nobody (Greek State Prize 1999) 1998, 2004, The Century of Labyrinths (Greek Academy Prize 2003) 2002, Silent, Deep Sea (Nat. Book Centre Readers' Prize 2006) 2006, Judas' Fires and Oedipus Ashes 2009; short stories: Homocentric Stories 1986, An Almost Blue Hand (Greek State Prize 2005) 2004; essays: King or Soldier 1997, From Life to Literature 2011; poetry: Yet Joyful 1975, The Minerals 1979, The Cake 1980, Where Does the Wolf Live? 1982, Poems 2008; participation in collective works: Griechische Erzählungen 1991, Poetas Griegas Conteporáneas, 1930–1990 1992, Poesia Griega Contemporánea 1998, Modern Poetry in Translation No. 13 1998, Heat 7 1998, Das weiße Meer 1998, Näkymätön Ja Näkyvä 2000, Greek Writers Today, Vol. 1 2000, Conjunction: 38, Rejoicing – Revoicing 2002, Modern Greek Poetry, an Anthology 2003, Donne e Uomini di Grecia, a cura di Flora Molcho 2003, Jean Altamouras 2011, Modern Greek Writing, an Anthology in English Translation 2003, Antologia del Cuento Griego 2005, Patra, the Face of the City 2005, The Road to Omonia 2005, Literary Obsseesions 2007, Europa Erlesen, Kreta 2007, Greece, a traveller's literary companion 2007, Le lien, Desmos, No. 28 2008, Revue Svetovej, Literatúry, No. 2 2011. *Honours:* Nikos Kazantzakis Prize (Crete) 1987. *Telephone:* (210) 3822530. *E-mail:* info@kastaniotis.com (office). *Website:* www.kastaniotis.com.

GALASSI, Jonathan White, MA; American publishing executive; *President, Farrar, Straus & Giroux Inc.*; b. 4 Nov. 1949, Seattle, Wash.; s. of Gerard Goodwin Galassi and Dorothea Johnston Galassi (née White); m. Susan Grace Galassi 1975; two d. *Education:* Harvard Univ., Univ. of Cambridge, UK. *Career:* Ed. Houghton Mifflin Co., Boston, New York 1973–81; Sr Ed. Random House, Inc., New York 1981–86; Exec. Ed. and Vice-Pres. Farrar, Straus & Giroux Inc., New York 1986–87, Ed.-in-Chief and Sr Vice-Pres. 1988–93, Exec. Vice-Pres. 1993–99, Publr 1999–, Pres. 2002–; Poetry Ed. Paris Review 1978–88; Guggenheim Fellow 1989; mem. Acad. of American Poets (Dir 1990–2002, Pres. 1994–99, Chair. 1999–2002, Hon. Chair. 2002–); Fellow, American Acad. of Arts and Sciences 2002. *Publications:* Morning Run (poetry) 1988, The Second Life of Art: Selected Essays of Eugenio Montale (ed., trans.) 1982, Otherwise: Last and First Poems of Eugenio Montale (ed., trans.) 1986, Eugenio Montale, Collected Poems 1916–56 (ed., trans.) 1998 (revised edn 2012), North Street (poetry) 2000, Eugenio Montale, Posthumous Diary 2001, Giacomo Leopardi, Canti (ed, trans.) 2010, Left-handed (poetry) 2012. *Honours:* Roger Klein Award for Editing, PEN 1984, Award in Literature, American Acad. of Arts and Letters 2000. *Address:* Farrar, Straus & Giroux Inc., 18 W 18th Street, New York, NY 10011, USA (office). *Telephone:* (212) 741-6900 (office). *Website:* www.fsgbooks.com (office).

GALCHEN, Rivka, BA, MD, MFA; Canadian/American writer; *Lecturer in Creative Writing, Columbia University*; b. 19 April 1976, Toronto, Ont.; d. of Tzvi Galchen; m. *Education:* Princeton Univ., Mount Sinai School of Medicine, Columbia Univ. *Career:* currently Lecturer in Creative Writing, Columbia Univ.; Cullman Fellow, New York Public Library. *Publications:* novel: Atmospheric Disturbances 2008; short story and essay contribs to The New Yorker, The New York Times, The Believer, Harper's, Zoetrope, Scientific American. *Honours:* Rona Jaffe Foundation Writers' Award 2006. *Address:* c/o Farrar, Strauss & Giroux, 18 West 18th Street, New York, NY 10011, USA. *Website:* www.atmosphericdisturbances.com; www.galchen.net.

GALEANO, Eduardo Hughes; Uruguayan author and journalist; b. 3 Sept. 1940, Montevideo; m. 1st Silvia Brando 1959; one d.; m. 2nd Graciela Berro 1962, one s. one d.; m. 3rd Helena Villagra 1976. *Career:* Ed.-in-Chief, Marcha 1961–64, University Press 1965–73, Montevideo; Dir, Época, Montevideo 1964–66; Founder-Dir, Crisis, Buenos Aires 1973–76. *Publications include:* Los días siguientes 1963, China 1964, 1964, Guatamala: Clave de Latinoamerica (trans. as Guatemala: Occupied Country) 1967, Reportajes 1967, Los fantasmas del día del léon, y otros relatos 1967, Su majestad el fútbol 1968, Las venas abiertas de América Latina (trans. as The Open Veins of Latin America) 1971, Siete imágenes de Bolivia 1971, Crónicas latinoamericanas

1972, Vagamundo 1973, La cancion de nosotros 1975, Conversaciones con Ramón 1977, Días y noches de amor y de guerra (trans. as Days and Nights of Love and War) 1978, La piedra arde 1980, Voces de nuestro tiempo 1981, Memoria del fuego: Genesis (trans. as Memory of Fire: Genesis) 1982, Memoria del fuego: Las caras y las máscaras (trans. as Memory of Fire: Faces and Masks) 1984, Aventuras de los jóvenes dioses 1984, Ventana sobre Sandino 1985, Contraseña 1985, Memoria del fuego: El siglo del viento (trans. as Memory of Fire: Century of the Wind) 1986, El descubrimento de América que todavía no fue y otros escritos 1986, El tigre azul y otros artículos 1988, Entrevistas y artículos, 1962–1987 1988, El libro de los abrazos (trans. as The Book of Embraces) 1989, Nosostros decimos no (trans. as We Say No) 1989, América Latina para entenderte mejor 1990, Palabras: Antología personal 1990, An Uncertain Grace: Essays by Eduardo Galeano and Fred Ritchin 1990, Ser como ellos y otros artículos 1992, Amares 1993, Las palabras andantes (trans. as Walking Woods) 1993, Uselo y tírelo 1994, El fútbol a sol y sombra (trans. as Football in Sun and Shadow) 1995, Patas arriba: La escuela del mundo al revés (trans. as Upside Down: A Primer for the Looking-Glass World) 1998, Tejidos: antología 2001, Bocas del Tiempo 2004, Espejos: Una historia casi universal 2008. *Honours:* Premio Casa de las Américas 1975, 1978, American Book Award 1989.

GALGUT, Damon; South African playwright and novelist; b. 1963, Pretoria. *Education:* Univ. of Cape Town. *Plays:* Echoes of Anger, Party for Mother, Alive and Kicking, The Green's Keeper. *Publications:* novels: Echoes of Anger: And No.1 Utopia Lane 1983, A Sinless Season 1984, Small Circle of Beings 1988, The Beautiful Screaming of Pigs 1991, The Quarry 1995, The Good Doctor (Commonwealth Writers Prize for Best Book, Africa Region 2004) 2003, The Impostor 2008, In a Strange Room 2010. *Honours:* CNA Award 1992. *Literary Agent:* Peake Associates, 14 Grafton Crescent, London, NW1 8SL, England. *Telephone:* (20) 7482-0609. *Fax:* (870) 141-0447. *E-mail:* tony@tonypeake.com. *Website:* www.tonypeake.com.

GALIN, Alexander; Russian playwright, actor and film and theatre director; b. (Aleksandr Mikhailovich Pourer), 10 Sept. 1947, Rostovskya oblast, USSR; s. of Mikhail Pourer and Lubov Pourer; m. Galina Alekseyevna Pourer 1950; one s. *Education:* Inst. of Culture, Leningrad. *Career:* factory worker, later actor in puppet theatre; freelance writer 1978–. *Plays include:* The Wall 1971, Here Fly the Birds 1974, The Hole 1975, The Roof 1976, Retro 1979, The Eastern Tribune 1980, Stars in the Morning Sky 1982, The Toastmaster 1983, Jeanne 1986, Sorry 1990, The Title 1991, The Czech Photo 1993, The Clown and the Bandit 1996, The Anomaly 1996, Sirena and Victoria 1997, The Competition 1998; plays translated into several languages include Stars in the Morning Sky (selected plays translated into English) 1989, The Group 1995, Rendez-Vous in the Sea of Rain 2002, New Logic 2005, The Companions 2008, Dzinrikisya 2009, The Face 2010. *Film:* Casanova's Coat (The Delegation) (scriptwriter and dir), Photo (scriptwriter, actor and dir) 2003, My Last Will (screenplay) 2004, The Heathen (screenplay) 2005, The Casualty (scriptwriter and dir) 2009. *Publication:* Selected Plays 1989. *Honours:* Amb. of the Arts, Fla 1989. *Address:* Gorohowsky pereulok 15, Apt 11, 103064 Moscow, Russia (home). *Telephone:* (499) 267-70-21 (home). *Fax:* (499) 267-70-21 (home). *E-mail:* galinalexander@gmail.com (home). *Website:* www.webcenter.ru/~agalin.

GALINA, Maria, PhD; Russian writer and editor; *Chief Editor, Critical and Social Essays Department, Novy Mir magazine*; b. 10 Nov. 1958, Tver; m. Arkady Shtypel. *Education:* Odessa Univ. *Career:* qualified marine biologist; carried out environmental research, Bergen Univ., Norway; full-time writer, Moscow 1987–; first published in Yunost journal (Youth) 1991, has published fiction, poems, science fiction, translations; columnist, Literatunaya Gazeta (Literary Newspaper) 2000–01; Chief Ed., Drugaya Storona (The Other Side); Ed. and Vice-Pres. of Publicity, Novyi Mir magazine 2008–10, Chief Ed., Critical and Social Essays Dept 2010–; regular columnist, Znamya magazine (The Banner) 2006–08; participant, CEC ArtsLink's Open World Cultural Leaders Program 2007, Int. Writers Program, Univ. of Iowa 2007; Prof. of Modern Poetry in Russian, State Humanitarian Univ. 2010. *Publications include:* translated into English: The End of Summer (short story), Givi and Shenderovich (trans. as Iramifications) (Int. Portal Prize 2008, Academia Rossica Prize 2009) 2008, Malaya Glusha 2009; novels: Volchja zvezda (Wolf's Star) 2003, Makaya Glusha 2009, Medvedky (Mole Crickets) 2011; short story collections: Pokryvalodlya Abadonna (Avaddonn's Shroud) 2002, Ekspedicia (An Expedition) 2002 (translated into Polish), Bereg Nochju (The Night Shore) 2007, Krasnye volki, krasnye gusi (Red Wolves, Red Geese) 2010; poetry: Nezemlia 2005, Na dvuh nogah 2009; contrib. to anthologies: Amerika, Russian Women Poets (Modern Poetry in Translation) 2002, 2005, America – Russian Writers View the United States 2004, War and Peace: Contemporary Russian Prose 2006. *Honours:* 'Anthologia' Novyi Mir Award for Modern Russian Poetry Achievement 2005, Moskovski Schyot (Moscow Count) Prize for Best Poetry Book of the Year Published in Moscow 2006, Gratitude of Fed. Agency of Press and Mass Communications for input to devt and popularization of Russian literature 2010, numerous awards for science fiction and fantasy. *Address:* Novyi Mir (New World), 103806 Moscow, M. Putinkovskii per. 1/2, Russia (office). *Telephone:* (495) 650-57-02 (office). *E-mail:* marginala@gmail.com (office). *Website:* magazines.russ.ru/novyi_mi (office).

GALINDO, Rosario Arias de, (Doña Mami); Panamanian publishing executive; b. 4 Jan. 1920, Panamá; d. of Harmodio Arias (Pres. of Panama 1932–36) and Rosario Guardia de Arias; m. Gabriel Galindo V 1940; one s. two d. *Education:* Sacred Heart Convent, Santiago, Chile, schools in Brussels, Belgium and Paris, France and univ. studies in Geneva, Switzerland, Paris and Panamá. *Career:* mem. Bd Dirs Nat. Red Cross 1952–62, Cttee for Human Rights 1980–89, Nat. Ind. Union for Democratic Action 1981–89, Inter-American Press 1991; Pres. Editora Panamá América, SA 1962–2002; Publr El Panamá América and Crítica Libre daily newspapers –2002; mem. Bd of Trustees Isthmian Foundation for Econ. and Social Studies 1991, Foundation for the Advancement of Women 1991; mem. Latin American Inst. for Advanced Studies, Panamanian Art Inst., Nat. Concert Asscn. *Film:* Códigos de silencio (as herself) 1995. *Publications include:* articles on Human Rights, freedom of the press and democracy in Panamanian and American newspapers including Freedom House (New York) and La Prensa (Panamá). *Honours:* Keys to the City of Panamá 1991; Manuel Amador Guerrero decoration 1991, Lifetime Achievement Award, Centro Latinoamericano de Periodismo 2009. *Address:* PO Box B-4, Vía Fernández de Córdoba (Vista Hermosa), Panamá 9A, Panama (office). *Telephone:* (61) 2300 (office). *Fax:* (61) 3152 (office).

GALIOTO, Salvatore, BA, MA; American poet and academic (retd); b. 6 June 1925, Italy; m. Nancy Morris 1978; one s. *Education:* Univ. of New Mexico, Univ. of Denver, Yale Univ., Columbia Univ., Univ. of New Haven. *Career:* John Hay Fellow, Yale Univ.; Catskill Area Project Fellow, Columbia Univ., Asian Studies Fellow 1965–66; mem. Long Island Historians' Soc., Asian Soc., California State Poetry Soc., Poets and Writers of America, Int. Soc. of Poets. *Publications include:* The Humanities: Classical Athens, Renaissance Florence and Contemporary New York 1970, Bibliographic Materials on Indian Culture 1972, Let Us Be Modern (poems), English, Italian 1985, INAGO Newsletter (poems) 1988, Is Anybody Listening? (poems), English 1990, Flap Your Wings (poems) 1992, Rosebushes and the Poor (poems), Italian 1993, An Infantryman's Memoir of His Experiences in World War II 1997; contribs to anthologies and periodicals. *Honours:* Purple Heart, Bronze Star 1944; John Hay Fellowship 1958–59, First Prize, Chapbook Competition, The Poet 1985, 1986, Gold Medal Istituto Carlo Capodieci 1987, INAGO Newspaper Poet 1989.

GALL, Henderson Alexander (Sandy), CMG, CBE, MA; British television journalist; b. 1 Oct. 1927, Penang, Malaysia; m. 1958; one s. three d. *Education:* Univ. of Aberdeen. *Career:* Rector, Univ. of Aberdeen 1978–81; currently Chair. Sandy Gall's Afghanistan Appeal. *Publications include:* Gold Scoop 1977, Chasing the Dragon 1981, Don't Worry about the Money Now 1983, Behind Russian Lines: An Afghan Journal 1983, Afghanistan: Agony of a Nation 1988, Salang 1989, George Adamson: Lord of the Lions 1991, News From the Front: The Life of a Television Reporter 1994, The Bushmen of Southern Africa: Slaughter of the Innocent 2001. *Honours:* Hon. LLD (Aberdeen) 1981; Sitara-i-Pakistan 1986, Lawrence of Arabia Medal 1987. *Address:* PO Box 145, Tonbridge, Kent, TN11 8SA, England (office). *Telephone:* (1892) 870576 (office). *Fax:* (1892) 870977 (office). *E-mail:* sqaa@btinternet.com (office). *Website:* www.sandygallsafghanistanappeal.org (office).

GALLAGHER, Tess, BA, MA, MFA; American poet and writer; b. 21 July 1943, Port Angeles, Wash.; m. 1st Lawrence Gallagher 1963 (divorced 1968); m. 2nd Michael Burkard 1973 (divorced 1977); m. 3rd Raymond Carver (died 1988); pnr Josie Gray 1994. *Education:* Univ. of Washington, Seattle and Univ. of Iowa. *Career:* Instructor, St Lawrence Univ., Canton, New York 1974–75; Asst Prof., Kirkland Coll., Clinton, New York 1975–77; Visiting Lecturer, Univ. of Montana 1977–78; Asst Prof., Univ. of Arizona, Tucson 1979–80; Prof. of English, Syracuse Univ. 1980–89; Visiting Fellow, Williamette Univ. 1981; Lois and Willard Mackey Chair in Poetry, Beloit Coll. 1989, in Fiction 1990; Cockefair Chair and Writer-in-Residence, Univ. of Missouri, Kansas City 1994; Poet-in-Residence, Trinity Coll., Hartford, Conn. 1994; Edward F. Arnold Visiting Prof. of English, Whitman Coll., Walla Walla, Wash. 1996–97; Poet-in-Residence, Bucknell Univ. 1998, Peninsula Coll. 2003; mem. Writers Union, PEN, American Poetry Soc., Poets and Writers. *Films:* consultant: To Write and Keep Kind 1992, Short Cuts 1993, Luck, Trust & Ketchup 1993, I Stop Writing the Poem (writer) 2000, I Remember Theodore Roethke 2005. *Publications include:* poetry: Stepping Outside 1974, Instructions to the Double (Elliston Award) 1976, Under Stars 1978, Portable Kisses 1978, On Your Own 1978, Willingly 1984, Amplitude: New and Selected Poems 1987, Moon Crossing Bridge 1992, The Valentine Elegies 1993, Portable Kisses Expanded 1994, My Black Horse: New and Selected Poems 1995, Dear Ghosts 2006, Distant Rain: a conversation with a Buddhist nun (with Jakucho Setouchi) 2007, Midnight Lantern: New and Selected Poems 2011; short stories: The Lover of Horses 1986, At the Owl Woman Saloon 1997, Barnacle Soup and Other Stories (with Josie Gray), The Man from Kinvara (selection) 2009; non-fiction: Instead of Dying, A Concert of Tenses: Essays on Poetry 1986, Soul Barnacles: Ten More Years with Ray 2000; trans. (with Liliana Ursu and Adam Sorkin): The Sky Behind the Forest, by Liliana Ursu 1997, A New Path to the Ocean, by Liliana Ursu 2008; screenplay: Dostoevsky (with Raymond Carver) 1985, many introductions to the works of Raymond Carver 1988–2000, Introduction to Alfredo Arreguin, Patterns of Dreams and Nature, To Beyond Forgetting: Poetry and Prose about Alzheimer's Disease (Preface) 2008; contrib. to many anthologies. *Honours:* Hon. DHumLitt (Whitman Coll.), 1998, Hon. DLit (Univ. of Hartford) 2002; NEA grants 1977, 1981, 1987, Guggenheim Fellowship 1978, American Poetry Review Award 1981, Wash. State Governor's Awards 1984, 1986, 1987, 1993, New York State Arts grant 1988, Maxine Cushing Gray Foundation Award 1990, American Library Asscn Most Notable Book List 1993, Lyndhurst Prize 1993, Translation

Award 1997, Pryor Award for Literary Excellence 1999, Univ. of Wash. Alumna of the Year Award 2004, Wash. State Humanities Profs John Terry Award for Excellence 2004, Wash. State Poets Asscn Lifetime Achievement Award 2004. *Literary Agent:* c/o Andrew Wylie Agency Inc., 250 West 57th Street, Suite 2114, New York, NY 10107, USA. *Telephone:* (212) 246-0069. *Fax:* (212) 586-5953. *E-mail:* awylie@wylieagency.com.

GALLAHER, John Gerard, MA, PhD; American professor of history and writer; *Professor Emeritus of History, Southern Illinois University at Edwardsville;* b. 28 Dec. 1928, St Louis, MO; m. C. Maia Hofacker 1956; one s. two d. *Education:* Univ. of Paris and Univ. of Grenoble, France, Washington Univ., St Louis Univ. *Career:* Univ. Research Fellow, Southern Illinois Univ. at Edwardsville 1978–79, Prof. to Prof. Emer. of History; mem. Napoleonic Alliance, Pres. 2001–03. *Publications include:* The Iron Marshal: A Biography of Louis N. Davout 1976, The Students of Paris and the Revolution of 1848 1980, Napoleon's Irish Legion 1993, General Alexandre Dumas: Soldier of the French Revolution 1997, Napoleon's Enfant Terrible 2008; contribs to reference works, books and scholarly journals. *Honours:* Chevalier, Ordre des palmes académiques, Int. Napoleonic Soc. Legion of Merit; Fulbright Research Scholar, France 1959–60, Gold Medal, Renaissance Française. *Address:* 8461 SE 71st Street, Mercer Island, WA 98040, USA (home). *E-mail:* j_gallaher@msn.com (office).

GALLAIRE, Fatima; Algerian/French playwright, director, novelist and writer; b. (Fatima Bourega), 1944, El Harrouch; m.; two c. *Education:* Univ. of Algiers, Univ. of Paris VIII (Vincennes, St-Denis). *Career:* worked for Cinémathèque of Algiers and directed several documentary films; Cowles Visiting Author, Dept of French, Grinnell Coll., Ia, USA 2000; mem. Soc. des Auteurs et Compositeurs Dramatiques (France); lives and works in France. *Plays include:* Princesses (Soc. des Auteurs Award) 1987 (trans. You Have Come Back), Les Co-épouses 1990 (trans. House of Wives), Témoignage contre un homme stérile (trans. Madame Bertin's Testimony), La Fête virile 1992, Molly des sables 1994, Au cœur, la brûlure 1994, Les Richesses de l'hiver 1996, Le Secret des vieilles 1996, La Beauté de l'icône 2003, Théâtre I (collection) 2004; numerous short stories and novels for children. *Radio:* Des cailloux pour la soif (Pebbles for Your Thirst) (BBC Radio 4). *Honours:* Arletty Prize for Drama in French 1990, Acad. française AMIC Prize 1994. *Address:* 41 rue Dunois, Paris 75013, France (home). *E-mail:* fatima@gallaire.com (office). *Website:* www.gallaire.com.

GALLANT, Mavis Leslie, CC, OC, FRSL; Canadian writer and literary critic; b. 11 Aug. 1922, Montreal; m. John Gallant (divorced). *Education:* schools in Montreal and New York, USA. *Career:* worked with Nat. Film Bd of Canada; reporter Montreal Standard newspaper 1944–50; emigrated to France 1950; short stories published The New Yorker 1951–; has written reviews and essays for New York Review of Books, The New York Times Book Review; Writer-in-Residence, Univ. of Toronto 1983–84; Fellow, Royal Soc. of Literature. *Publications include:* short stories: The Other Paris 1956, My Heart is Broken 1964, The Pegnitz Junction 1973, The End of the World 1974, From the Fifteenth District 1978, Home Truths (Gov.-Gen. Award 1982) 1981, Overhead in a Balloon 1985, In Transit 1988, Across the Bridge 1993, Paris Notebooks 1997, Paris Stories 2002 Montreal Stories 2004, The Selected Stories of Mavis Gallant 2004, The Cost of Living 2009, Going Ashore 2009, Rencontres fortuites 2010; novels: Green Water, Green Sky 1969, A Fairly Good Time 1970; play: What is to Be Done? 1984; non-fiction: Paris Journals: Selected Reviews and Essays 1986. *Honours:* Foreign Hon. mem. American Acad. and Inst. of Arts and Letters 1989; hon. degree (Univ. Sainte Anne), Pointe de Eglise, NS 1984; Hon. LLD (Queen's) 1991; Canada-Australia Literary Prize 1984, Canada Council Molson Prize for the Arts 1997, Matt Cohen Prize 2000, Rea Award for the Short Story 2002, Special Achievement Award from Montreal's Blue Metropolis Literary Festival 2002; Tributee Int. Authors Festival, Harbourfront, Toronto 1993, Prix Athanase-David 2006. *Literary Agent:* c/o Bruce Hunter, David Higham Associates, 5–8 Lower John Street, Golden Square, London, W1F 9HA, England. *Telephone:* (20) 7434-5900. *Fax:* (20) 7437-1072. *E-mail:* brucehunter@davidhigham.co.uk. *Website:* www.davidhigham.co.uk.

GALLANT, Roy Arthur, BA, MS; American teacher and fmr author; b. 17 April 1924, Portland, Me; m. Kathryn Dale 1952, two s. *Education:* Bowdoin Coll., Columbia Univ. *Career:* Managing Ed. Scholastic Teachers Magazine 1954–57; Author-in-Residence, Doubleday 1957–59; Editorial Dir Aldus Books, London 1959–62; Ed.-in-Chief, The Natural History Press 1962–65; Consultant, The Edison Project, Israel Arts and Sciences Acad.; Dir Southworth Planetarium, Univ. Southern Maine 1980–2000, Prof. Emer. 2001–. *Publications include:* approximately 100 books, including: Our Universe 1986, Private Lives of the Stars 1986, Rainbows, Mirages and Sundogs 1987, Before the Sun Dies 1989, Ancient Indians 1989, The Peopling of Planet Earth 1990, Earth's Vanishing Forests 1991, A Young Person's Guide to Science 1993, The Day the Sky Split Apart 1995, Geysers 1997, Sand Dunes 1997, Limestone Caves 1998, Planet Earth 1998, When the Sun Dies 1998, Glaciers 1999, The Ever-Changing Atom 1999, Earth's Place in Space 1999, Early Humans 1999, Dance of the Continents 1999, The Origins of Life 2000, The Life Stories of Stars 2000, Stars 2000, Rocks 2000, Minerals 2000, Fossils 2000, Comets and Asteroids 2000, The Planets 2000, Water 2000, Space Station 2000, Meteorite Hunter 2002, Earth Structure 2003, Earth History 2003, Plate Tectonics 2003, Natural Resources 2003, Earth's Atmosphere 2003, Earth's Water 2003, Inheritance 2003, Biodiversity 2003. *Honours:* Thomas Alva Edison Foundation Mass Media Award 1955, Distinguished Achievement Award, Univ. of Southern Maine 1981, John Burroughs Award for Nature Writing 1995, Lifetime Achievement Award, Maine Library Asscn 2001. *Address:* PO Box 228, Beaver Mountain Lake, Rangeley, ME 04970, USA (home). *Telephone:* (207) 864-5135 (home).

GALLIMARD, Antoine; French publisher; *President and Director-General, Éditions Gallimard;* b. 1947, Paris. *Career:* fmr journalist; worked for family business, Éditions Gallimard 1972–81, Dir-Gen. 1981–, Pres. and Exec. Dir Gallimard 1988–. *Honours:* Officier, Légion d'Honneur 2009. *Address:* Éditions Gallimard, 5 rue Sébastien-Bottin, 75328 Paris cédex 07, France (office). *Website:* www.gallimard.fr (office).

GALLO, Max Louis, DenH, DèsSc; French politician, writer, historian and university teacher; b. 7 Jan. 1932, Nice; s. of Joseph Gallo and Mafalda Galeotti. *Education:* Univ. de Paris and Inst. d'Etudes Politiques. *Career:* early career in journalism; mem. CP –1956; teacher, Lycée de Nice 1960–65; Sr Lecturer, Univ. of Nice 1965–70; Gen. Ed. book series Ce Jour-là, l'Histoire que nous vivons, la Vie selon. . ., le Temps des révélations; contrib. to various newspapers; devised TV programme Destins du Siècle 1973; Deputy (Socialist) for Alpes-Maritimes 1981–83; jr minister and Govt spokesman 1983–84; Ed. Matin de Paris newspaper 1985–86; mem. European Parl. 1984–94; mem. Parti Socialiste 1974–, Nat. Sec. (Culture) Parti Socialiste 1988–90; mem. Acad. française (Seat 24) 2007. *Publications:* L'Italie de Mussolini 1964, La Grande Peur de 1989 (as Max Laugham) 1966, L'Affaire d'Ethiopie 1967, Maximilien Robespierre, Histoire d'une solitude 1968, Gauchisme, réformisme et révolution 1968, Histoire de l'Espagne franquiste 1969, Cinquième Colonne 1930–1940 1970, la Nuit des longs couteaux 1970, Tombeau pour la Commune, Histoire de l'Espagne franquiste 1971, Le Cortège des vainqueurs 1972, La Mafia, un pas vers la mer 1973, L'Affiche, miroir de l'Histoire (illustrated) 1973, L'Oiseau des origines 1974: La Baie des anges (Vol. I) 1975, Le Palais des fêtes (Vol. II) 1976, La Promenade des Anglais (Vol. III) 1976, Le Pouvoir à vif, Despotisme, démocratie et révolution, Que sont les siècles pour la mer 1977, Les hommes naissent tous le même jour: Aurore (Vol. I) 1978, Crépuscule (Vol. II) 1979, Une affaire intime 1979, L'Homme Robespierre: histoire d'une solitude 1978, Un crime très ordinaire 1982, Garibaldi 1982, La Demeure des puissants 1983, La Troisième alliance, pour un nouvel individualisme, Le Grand Jaurès 1984, Le Beau Rivage 1985, Lettre ouverte à Maximilien Robespierre sur les nouveaux Muscadins, Belle Epoque 1986, Que passe la justice du roi, la Route Napoléon 1987, Jules Vallès 1988, Une Affaire publique 1989, Les Clés de l'histoire contemporaine 1989, Manifeste pour une fin de siècle obscure 1989, La Gauche est morte, vive la gauche! 1990, Le Regard des femmes 1991, La Fontaine des innocents (Prix Carlton 1992), Une femme rebelle: Vie et mort de Rosa Luxembourg 1992, L'Amour au temps des solitudes 1993, Les Rois sans visage 1994, Le Condottiere 1994, Le Fils de Klara H. 1995, L'Ambitieuse 1995, La Part de Dieu 1996, Le Faiseur d'or 1996, La Femme derrière le miroir, Napoléon, Le chant du départ (biog., Vol. I) 1997, L'Immortel de Saint-Hélène (Vol. IV) 1997, De Gaulle: L'Appel du destin (Vol. I) 1998, La Solitude du combattant (Vol. II) 1998, Le Premier des Français (Vol. III) 1998, La Statue du Commandeur (Vol. IV) 1998, L'Amour de la France expliqué a mon fils, le Jardin des oliviers 1999, Bleu, blanc, rouge (three vols) 2000, Les Patriotes (four vols) 2000–01, Victor Hugo: Je suis une force qui va (Vol. I) 2001, Je serai celui-là (Vol. II) 2001, Les Chrétiens (three vols) 2002, Morts pour la France (three vols) 2003, César Imperator 2003, L'Empire (three vols) 2004, Les Fanatiques 2006, Fier d'être Français 2006, La croix de l'Occident (two vols) 2005, Les Romains (five vols) 2006, Louis XIV: Le Roi-Soleil (Vol. I) 2007, L'Hiver du grand roi (Vol. II) 2007, Révolution française: Le Peuple et le Roi (Vol. I) 2009, Aux armes, citoyens! (Vol. II) 2009. *Address:* c/o XO Editions, 33 avenue du Maine, BP 142, 75755 Paris, France. *E-mail:* vtaillefer@xoeditions.com (office). *Website:* www.maxgallo.com.

GALLOWAY, Janice, MA; British writer; b. 2 Dec. 1955, Ayrshire, Scotland; d. of the late James Galloway and Janet Clark McBride; one s. *Education:* Ardrossan Acad., Univ. of Glasgow, Hamilton Coll. of Educ., Glasgow Coll. of Building and Printing. *Career:* singing waitress 1972–74; welfare rights worker 1976; teacher of English 1980–90; Creative Writing Dept, Univ. of Glasgow 2002–06; mem. Soc. of Authors; Tutor, Faber Acad. 2010–. *Exhibition:* Roengarten (with Anne Bevan), Hunterian Gallery, Glasgow. *Play:* Fall 1998. *Music:* Monster (with Sally Beamish), Scottish Opera and Brighton Festival 2001. *Publications include:* The Trick is to Keep Breathing 1990, Blood 1991, Foreign Parts 1994, Where You Find It 1996, Pipelines (with sculptor Anne Bevan) 2000, Monster (opera libretto for composer Sally Beamish) 2002, Clara 2002, boy book see 2003, Rosengarten (with Anne Bevan) 2004, This Is Not About Me 2008, Collected Stories 2009, All Made Up 2011. *Honours:* MIND/Alan Lane Prize, Scottish Arts Council Award 1991, Scottish Arts Council Award 1994, McVitie's Prize 1994, American Acad. of Arts and Letters E. M. Forster Award 1994, Creative Scotland Award 2001, Saltire Book of the Year 2002, SMIT (Scottish Mortgage Investment Trust) Scottish Book of the Year (non-fiction) 2008. *Literary Agent:* c/o Derek Johns, AP Watt Ltd, 20 John Street, London, WC1N 2DR, England. *Telephone:* (20) 7405-6774. *Fax:* (20) 7831-2154. *E-mail:* djohns@apwatt.co.uk. *Website:* www.apwatt.co.uk (office); www.galloway.1to1.org.

GALVIN, Brendan, BS, MA, MFA, PhD; American academic and poet; b. 20 Oct. 1938, Everett, Mass; m. Ellen Baer 1968; one s. one d. *Education:* Boston Coll., Northeastern Univ., Univ. of Massachusetts. *Career:* Instructor, Northeastern Univ. 1964–65; Asst Prof., Slippery Rock State Coll., 1968–69; Asst Prof., Central Connecticut State Univ. 1969–74, Assoc. Prof. 1974–80, Prof. of English 1980–; Visiting Prof., Connecticut Coll., 1975–76; Ed. (with George

Garrett) Poultry: A Magazine of Voice, 1981–; Coal Royalty Chairholder in Creative Writing, Univ. of Alabama 1993. *Publications include:* The Narrow Land 1971, The Salt Farm 1972, No Time for Good Reasons 1974, The Minutes No One Owns 1977, Atlantic Flyway 1980, Winter Oysters 1983, A Birder's Dozen 1984, Seals in the Inner Harbour 1985, Wampanoag Traveler 1989, Raising Irish Walls 1989, Great Blue: New and Selected Poems 1990, Early Returns 1992, Saints in Their Ox-Hide Boat 1992, Islands 1993, Hotel Malabar 1998, Place Keepers: Poems 2003, Habitat: New And Selected Poems, 1965–2005 2005, Ocean Effects: Poems 2007, Whirl Is King: Poems from a Life List 2008. *Honours:* Nat. Endowment for the Arts Fellowships 1974, 1988, Connecticut Commission on the Arts Fellowships 1981, 1984, Guggenheim Fellowship 1988, Sotheby Prize, Arvon Int. Foundation 1988, Levinson Prize, Poetry magazine 1989, O.B. Hardison Jr Poetry Prize, Folger Shakespeare Library 1991, Charity Randall Citation, Int. Poetry Forum 1994. *Address:* c/o LSU Press, 3990 West Lakeshore Drive, Baton Rouge, LA 70808, USA.

GAMONEDA LOBÓN, Antonio; Spanish poet and writer; b. 30 May 1931, Oviedo; s. of Amelia Lobón; m. Maria Angeles Lanza 1960. *Career:* worked in finance 1945–69; Head of Cultural Services, León council 1969–77; Man. Dir Sierra-Pambley de León Foundation 1979–91; contrib. to Espadaña, Claraboya magazines. *Publications:* poetry: Sublevación inmóvil 1960, Descripción de la mentira 1977, León de la mirada 1979, Blues castellano 1982, Lápidas 1986, Edad (Poesía 1947–1986) (Premio Nacional de Poesía 1988) 1987, Libro del frío 1992, Sección de la memoria 1993, Mortal 1936 1994, El vigilante de la nieve 1995, Poemas 1996, Tu? 1988, Sólo luz 2000, Arden las pérdidas (Premio de la Crítica de Castilla y León 2004) 2003, El libro del frio 2003, Esta luz. Poesía reunida (1947–2004) 2004, Cecilia 2004, Reescritura 2004, Esta luz 2004, Silabas negras 2006, Antologia poética 2006, Extravío en la luz 2009; non-fiction: Echauz 1978, Barjola 1980, Zamora 1980, Silverio Rivas 1981, León, traza y memoria 1984, Encuentro en el territorio del frío 1995. *Honours:* Dr hc (Universidad de León) 2000; Castilla y León de las Letras 1985, Nat. Poetry Award 1988, Premio de Cultura de la Comunnidad de Madrid 2005, Prix Européen de Littérature 2006, Premio Reina Sofía de Poesía Iberamericana 2006, Premio Miguel de Cervantes 2006, Gold Medal of Bellas Artes 2006, Queen Sofia of Iberoamerican Poetry 2006. *Address:* c/o Fundación Sierra-Pambley, Calle Sierra Pambley 2, 24003 León, Spain.

GANDER, Forrest, BS, MA; American writer, editor and academic; *Professor of English and Comparative Literature, Brown University*; b. 21 Jan. 1956, Barstow, Calif.; m. C. D. Wright 1983; one s. *Education:* Coll. of William and Mary, San Francisco State Univ. *Career:* Prof. of English and Comparative Literature, Brown Univ.; mem. Associated Writing Programs, PEN, Center for Art in Translation, American Literary Translators Asscn, Boomerang Fund for Artists. *Publications include:* Rush to the Lake 1988, Eggplants and Lotus Root 1991, Lynchburg 1993, Mouth to Mouth: Poems by 12 Contemporary Mexican Women (ed.) 1993, Deeds of Utmost Kindness 1994, Science & Steepleflower 1998, Torn Awake 2001, Immanent Visitor: Selected Poems of Jaime Saenz (trans. with Kent Johnson) 2001, Eye Against Eye 2005, A Faithful Existence: Reading, Memory and Transcendence (trans. with K. Johnson) 2006, The Night, poem by Jaime Saenz (trans. with K. Johnson) 2007, Firefly under the Tongue, Selected Poems of Coral Bracho (trans.) 2008, As a Friend 2008, Core Samples from the World 2010, Watchword by Pura Lopez Colome (trans.) 2011. *Honours:* Nat. Endowment for the Arts Fellowships, Pushcart Prize 2000, Howard Foundation Fellowship 2005, Guggenheim Fellowship 2008, Rockefeller Fellowship, United States Artists 2008. *Literary Agent:* Blue Flower Arts. *Telephone:* (845) 677-8559. *E-mail:* alison@blueflowerarts.com. *Website:* www.blueflowerarts.com. *Address:* Literary Arts, PO Box 1923, Brown University, Providence, RI 02912, USA (office). *E-mail:* forthgone@brown.edu (office). *Website:* www.forrestgander.com (home).

GANGOPADHYAY, Sunil, MA; Indian writer and poet; *President, Sahitya Akademi;* b. 7 Sept. 1934, Madaripur, Bangladesh; s. of the late Kalipada Gangopadhyay and the late Mira Gangopadhyay; m. Swati Gangopadhyay; one s. *Education:* Surendranath Coll., Dumdum Mtozhil Coll., Univ. of Calcutta. *Career:* worked for Adult Educ. Scheme, UNESCO; Bengali writer; Founder-Ed. Krittibas magazine 1953; Vice-Pres. Sahitya Akademi 2003–08, Pres. 2008–. *Publications include:* over 200 books including Arjun, Pratidwandi, Ranu o Bhamu, Aatmaprakash, Arunyer Din-Raatri, Ekaa ebong Koyekjon, Sei Somoy (Sahitya Akademi Puroskar 1985), Pratham Alo, Rokto, Purush, Agniputro, Sorol Satya, Byaktigoto, Mohaprithibi, Roktomangsho, Bandhubandhab, Purba-Paschim, Jeeban je Rakam, Ardhek Manobi, Nihsanga Samrat, Hathat Nirar Janya, Kakababu Series. *Honours:* Ananda Puroskar 1972, 1989, named Nat. Poet 1979, Swarnakamal Prize 1980, Bankim Puroskar 1983, Sahitya Setu Puroskar, Annadashankar Puroskar 2003, Saraswati Samman 2005. *Address:* 24 Mandeville Gardens, Flat A2/9, Parijat, Kolkata 700 019, India (home). *E-mail:* secy@ndb.vsnl.net.in (office). *Website:* www.sunilgangopadhyay.com.

GANNON, Lucy, MBE; British writer; b. 1948; m. (deceased); one d. *Career:* fmrly nurse, residential social worker and military policewoman; has devised and written numerous TV series and dramas; writer-in-residence, Royal Shakespeare Co. 1987. *Television includes:* Keeping Tom Nice (Richard Burton Award 1987, John Whiting Award 1990), Wicked Old Nellie 1989, Testimony of a Child 1989, A Small Dance (Prix Europa 1991) 1991, Soldier, Soldier 1991, Peak Practice 1993, Tender Loving Care 1993, Bramwell 1995, Trip Trap 1996, Bramwell IV 1998, Bramwell – Our Brave Boys 1998, The Gift 1998, Big Cat 1998, Hope and Glory 1999, Pure Wickedness 1999, Plain Jane 2002, Servants 2003, Blue Dove 2003, Dad (BAFTA Cymru) 2005, Coronation Street 2007–, The Children 2008. *Publications:* Keeping Tom Nice (theatre play), Raping the Gold (theatre play). *Literary Agent:* The Agency (London) Ltd, 24 Pottery Lane, Holland Park, London, W11 4LZ, England. *Telephone:* (20) 7727-1346. *Fax:* (20) 7727-9037. *E-mail:* info@theagency.co.uk. *Website:* www.theagency.co.uk.

GANT, Richard (see Freemantle, Brian Harry)

GAO, Ertai, BA; Chinese writer, artist and philosopher; b. 1935, Jiangsu Province; s. of Gao Zhuyuan and Zheng Moxian; m. Gao Maya; two d. *Career:* sent to a labour camp after publication of essay, On Beauty 1957; sentenced to hard labour 1966–72 (exonerated 1978); imprisoned for writing 1989; exiled in the USA; fmrly worked in Dunhuang Research Inst., Chinese Acad. of Social Sciences, Lanzhou Univ., Sichuan Normal Univ., Nankai Univ., Nanjing Univ.; currently Fellow Int. Inst. of Modern Letters; currently Visiting Scholar Univ. of Nevada, USA; writer-in-residence, City of Asylum, Las Vegas 2003–06. *Art Exhibitions:* China Dream, Hong Kong Conference Hall, Hong Kong 1992, Buddhist Painting, Museum of Fo Guong Yuan, Taiwan 1996, Spirit of Ancient Buddhist Murals, The Nippon Gallery, New York 1997, Paintings and Calligraphy exhibits, Claremont McKenna Coll., Calif. 2010, also at Newark Museum, New Jersey, Mulvane Art Museum, Washburn Univ., Kansas, Int. Inst. of Modern Letters, Univ. of Nevada. *Publications:* The Awakening of Beauty, On Beauty, The Struggle of Beauty, Beauty, The Symbol of Freedom, In Search of My Homeland 2009; contrib. essays and articles to numerous journals and anthologies. *Honours:* Nat. Science Council State Expert with Distinguished Contributions 1986. *Address:* 3299 Fairview Lane, Las Vegas, NV 89121-5710, USA (home). *Telephone:* (702) 737-0733 (home). *E-mail:* dafengtong7@gmail.com (home).

GAO, Hongbo, (Xiang Chuan); Chinese poet; *Vice-President and Secretary of the Secretariat, Chinese Writers Association*; b. 1951, Kailu, Nei Monggol. *Education:* Peking Univ. *Career:* joined the PLA 1969; Vice-Chief News Section, Literature and Art Gazette; Vice-Dir Gen. Office of Chinese Writers' Asscn, later Assoc. Ed., Ed. Journal of Poetry, currently Vice-Pres. and Sec. Secr. of Chinese Writers' Asscn. *Publications:* Elephant Judge, Geese, Geese, Geese, The Crocodile that Eats Stones, The Secret of the Shouting Spring, I Love You, Fox, The Fox that Grows Grapes, The Maid and the Bubble Gum, Flying Dragon and Magic Pigeon, I Wonder, Whisper (Nat. Award for Best Children's Literature). *Address:* Chinese Writers' Association, No.25, East Tucheng Road, Chaoyang District, Beijing 100013, People's Republic of China (office). *Telephone:* (10) 64221865 (office). *Fax:* (10)64222240 (office).

GAO, Xingjian, BA; French (b. Chinese) writer and dramatist; b. 4 Jan. 1940, Ganzhou, Jiangxi Prov., People's Republic of China. *Education:* Dept of Foreign Languages, Beijing. *Career:* translator China Reconstructs (magazine), later for Chinese Writers Asscn.; spent five years in 're-education' during Cultural Revolution; Artistic Dir People's Art Theatre, Beijing 1981; left China 1987 after work banned in 1985, living in Paris 1988–, became French citizen 1998. *Publications include:* plays: Absolute Signal 1982, Bus Stop 1983, Wild Man 1990, The Other Shore 1999, Fugitives 1993, Tales of Mountains and Seas 1993, The Man Who Questions Death 2003; novels: Soul Mountain 1999, Return to Painting 2001, One Man's Bible 2002; other: Snow in August (opera) 2002, Buying a Fishing Rod for my Grandfather (short stories) 2004. *Honours:* Chevalier des Arts et des Lettres 1992; Prix Communauté française de Belgium 1994, Prix du Nouvel An Chinois 1997, Nobel Prize for Literature 2000; Légion d'honneur 2000. *Address:* c/o HarperCollins, 77-85 Fulham Palace Road, London, W6 8JB, England (office).

GAO, Ying; Chinese author and poet; b. 25 Dec. 1929, Jiaozuo, Henan; s. of Gao Weiya and Sha Peifen; m. Duan Chuanchen 1954; one s. two d. *Career:* Vice-Chair. Sichuan Br. and mem. Council, Chinese Writers' Asscn; Deputy Dir Ed. Bd, Sichuan Prov. Broadcasting Station 1983–; mem. Sichuan Political Consultative Conf. *Publications:* The Song of Ding Youjun, Lamplights around the Three Gorges, High Mountains and Distant Rivers, Cloudy Cliff (novel), Da Ji and her Fathers (novel and film script), The Orchid (novel), Loving-Kindness of the Bamboo Storey (collection of prose), Mother in my Heart (autobiographical novel), Songs of Da Liang Mountains (poems), Frozen Snowflakes (poems), Reminiscences, Xue Ma (novel), Gao Ying (short stories). *Address:* c/o Sichuan Branch of Chinese Association of Literary and Art Workers, Bu-hou-jie Street, Chengdu, Sichuan, People's Republic of China (office). *Telephone:* 66782836 (office).

GAPPAH, Petina, LLD; Zimbabwean writer and lawyer; one s. *Education:* Univ. of Zimbabwe, Univ. of Cambridge, UK, Karl-Franz Univ., Graz, Austria. *Career:* lawyer, Appellate Body Secr. of WTO 1999–2001; Counsel, Advisory Centre on WTO Law, Geneva 2002–. *Publications:* An Elegy for Easterly (short stories) (Guardian First Book Award) 2009. *Literary Agent:* c/o Claire Paterson, Janklow and Nesbit Ltd, 33 Drayson Mews, London W8 4LY, England. *Telephone:* (20) 7376-2733. *Fax:* (20) 7376-2915. *Website:* www.janklowandnesbit.co.uk. *E-mail:* petina.gappah@bluewin.ch (office). *Website:* www.petinagappah.com.

GARAFOLA, Lynn, AB, PhD; American dance critic, historian and teacher; *Professor of Dance, Barnard College*; b. 12 Dec. 1946, New York, NY; m. Eric Foner 1980; one d. *Education:* Barnard Coll., CUNY. *Career:* Ed., Studies in Dance History 1990–99; Adjunct Prof. Dept of Dance, Barnard Coll., New York 2003–; mem. Soc. of Dance History Scholars, Dance Critics Asscn; Fellow, American Acad. of Arts and Sciences. *Publications:* Diaghilev's Ballets Russes

1989, André Levinson on Dance: Writings from Paris in the Twenties (ed. with Joan Acocella) 1991, The Diaries of Marius Petipa (ed. and trans.) 1992, Jose Limon: An Unfinished Memoir (ed.) 1999, Dance for a City: Fifty Years of the New York City Ballet (ed.) 1999, The Ballets Russes and its World (ed.) 1999, Legacies of 20th-Century Dance 2005; contrib. to Dance Magazine, Dance Research, Ballet Review, Nation, Women's Review of Books, TLS, New York Times Book Review. *Honours:* Torre de los Buenos Prize 1989, CORD Award for Outstanding Publication 1999, Kurt Weill Prize 2001. *Address:* Department of Dance, Barnard College, New York, NY 10027, USA (office). *E-mail:* lgarafol@barnard.edu (office).

GARCÍA JAMBRINA, Luis, PhD; Spanish writer and academic; *Professor, Department of Spanish Literature, University of Salamanca*; b. 1960, Zamora; m.; one d. *Education:* Univ. of Salamanca. *Career:* currently Prof., Dept of Spanish Literature, Univ. of Salamanca; Dir Encuentros de Escritores y Críticos de las Letras Españolas. *Publications:* Oposiciones a la morgue y otros ajustes de cuentas 1995, De la ebriedad a la leyenda 1999, Claudio Rodríguez y la tradición literaria 1999, Muertos SA 2005, El manuscrito de piedra (Premio International de Novela Historica Ciudad de Zaragoza 2009) 2008, El manuscrito de nieve 2010. *Honours:* Fray Luis de Leon Prize 1999, Short Story Award, Fundacion Gaceta Regional 2006. *Address:* Department of Spanish Literature, University of Salamanca, Plaza de Anaya, 37008 Salamanca, Spain (office). *Telephone:* (92) 3294445 (office). *Fax:* (92) 3294585 (office). *E-mail:* jambrina@usal.es (office). *Website:* www.usal.es (office).

GARCÍA MÁRQUEZ, Gabriel (Gabo) José; Colombian writer; b. 6 March 1928, Aracataca; s. of Gabriel Eligio García and Luisa Santiaga Márquez; m. Mercedes Barch March 1958; two s. *Education:* secondary school and Universidad Nacional de Colombia, Universidad de Cartagena. *Career:* began writing books 1946; lived in Baranquilla; corresp. El Espectador in Rome, Paris; first novel published while living in Caracas, Venezuela 1957; est. bureau of Prensa Latina (Cuban press agency) in Bogotá; worked for Prensa Latina in Havana, Cuba, then as Deputy Head of New York Office 1961; lived in Spain, contributing to magazines Mundo Nuevo, Casa de las Américas; went to Mexico; founder-Pres., Fundación Habeas 1979–; invited back to Colombia by Pres. 1982; Hon. Fellow, American Acad. of Arts and Letters; Hon. Pres. Latin America Solidarity Action Foundation (Alas) 2006–. *Publications:* fiction: La hojarasca (trans. as Leaf Storm and Other Stories) 1955, El coronel no tiene quien le escriba (trans. as No One Writes to the Colonel and Other Stories) 1961, La mala hora (trans. as In Evil Hour) 1962, Los funerales de la Mamá Grande (trans. as Funerals of the Great Matriarch) 1962, Cien años de soledad (trans. as One Hundred Years of Solitude) 1967, Isabel viendo llover en Macondo 1967, La incredíble y triste historia de la cándida Eréndira y su abuela desalmada (trans. as Innocent Erendira and Other Stories) 1972, El negro que hizo esperar a los angeles 1972, Ojos de perro azul 1972, El otoño del patriarca (trans. as The Autumn of the Patriarch) 1975, Todos los cuentos de Gabriel García Márquez: 1947–1972 1975, Crónica de una muerte anunciada (trans. as Chronicle of a Death Foretold) 1981, El rastro de tu sangre en la nieve: El verano feliz de la señora Forbes 1982, María de mi corazón (screenplay, with J. H. Hermosillo) 1983, Collected Stories 1984, El amor en los Tiempos del cólera (trans. as Love in the Time of Cholera) 1984, El General en su laberinto (trans. as The General in his Labyrinth) 1989, Amores difíciles 1989, Doce cuentos peregrinos (trans. as Strange Pilgrims: Twelve Stories) 1992, Del amor y otros demonios (trans. as Of Love and Other Demons) 1994, La bendita manía de contar 1998, Memoria de mis putas tristes (trans. as Memories of my Melancholy Whores) 2004, Telling Tales (contrib. to charity anthology) 2004; non-fiction: La novela en América Latina: Diálogo (with Mario Vargas Llosa) 1968, Relato de un náufrago (trans. as The Story of a Shipwrecked Sailor) 1970, Cuando era feliz e indocumentado 1973, Crónicas y reportajes 1978, Periodismo militante 1978, De viaje por los países socialistas: 90 días en la 'cortina de hierro' 1978, Obra periodistica (four vols) 1981–83, El olor de la guayaba: Conversaciones con Plinio Apuleyo Mendoza (trans. as The Fragrance of Guava) 1982, Persecución y muerte de minorías: Dos perspectivas 1984, La aventura de Miguel Littín, clandestino en Chile: Un reportaje (trans. as Clandestine in Chile: The Adventures of Miguel Littín) 1986, Primeros reportajes 1990, Notas de prensa 1980–1984 1991, Elogio de la utopia: una entrevista de Nahuel Maciel 1992, Noticia de un secuestro (trans. as News of a Kidnapping) 1996, Vivir para contarla (memoir, vol. one, trans. as Living to Tell the Tale) 2002. *Honours:* Hon. LLD (Columbia Univ., New York) 1971; Colombian Asscn of Writers and Artists Award 1954, Premio Literario Esso (Colombia) 1961, Chianciano Award (Italy) 1969, Prix de Meilleur Livre Étranger (France) 1969, Books Abroad/Neustadt International Prize for Literature 1972, Rómulo Gallegos Prize (Venezuela) 1972, Nobel Prize for Literature 1982, Los Angeles Times Book Prize for Fiction 1988, Serfin Prize 1989, Premio Príncipe de Asturias 1999. *Literary Agent:* Agencia Literaria Carmen Balcells, Avenida Diagonal 580, 08021 Barcelona, Spain. *Telephone:* (93) 2008933. *Fax:* (93) 2007041. *E-mail:* ag-balcells@ag-balcells.com.

GARCIA-ROZA, Luiz Alfredo; Brazilian writer and academic; b. 1936, Rio de Janeiro. *Career:* Prof. of Philosophy, Universidade do Estado do Rio de Janeiro 1963–98. *Publications in translation:* The Silence of the Rain (Nestlé and Jabuti Prizes, Brazil) 1997, December Heat 2004, Southwesterly Wind 2005, A Window in Copacabana 2005, Pursuit 2006, Blackout 2009, Alone in the Crowd 2009. *Website:* www.garcia-roza.com.

GARCÍA SÁNCHEZ, Javier; Spanish writer and poet; b. 1955, Barcelona. *Publications:* Teoría de la eternidad 1984, Mutantes de invierno 1984, La Dama del Viento Sur 1985, El mecanógrafo 1989, Recuerda 1990, La hija del emperador 1990, E amor secreto de Luca Signorelli 1990, Crítica de la Razón Impura 1991, La historia más triste 1992, El alpe d'huez 1994, Continúa el misterio de los ojos verdes 1995, Óscar. La Aventura de correr 1997, Los Otros 1998, La mujer de ninguna parte 2000, Falta alma 2001, Dios se ha ido 2003, Ella Drácula 2005, K2 2006. *Address:* c/o Dedalus Ltd, Langford Lodge, St Judith's Lane, Sawtry, Cambridgeshire PE28 5XE, England (office).

GARDAM, Jane Mary, OBE, BA, FRSL; British novelist; b. 11 July 1928, Coatham; d. of William Pearson and Kathleen Pearson (née Helm); m. David Hill Gardam 1954; two s. one d. *Education:* Saltburn High School for Girls, Bedford Coll. for Women, Univ. of London. *Career:* co-ordinator UK Hosp. Libraries British Red Cross 1951–53; Literary Ed. Time and Tide 1952–54; mem. PEN. *Radio play:* The Tribute. *Publications:* juvenile fiction: A Long Way from Verona 1971, A Few Fair Days 1971, The Summer After the Funeral 1973, Bilgewater 1977; novels: God on the Rocks (Prix Baudelaire) 1978, The Hollow Land (Whitbread Literary Award 1983) 1981, Bridget and William 1981, Horse 1982, Kit 1983, Crusoe's Daughter 1985, Kit in Boots 1986, Swan 1987, Through the Doll's House Door 1987, The Queen of the Tambourine (Whitbread Novel Award) 1991, Faith Fox 1996, Tufty Bear 1996, The Green Man 1998, The Flight of the Maidens 2000, Old Filth 2004, The People of Privilege Hill 2007, The Man in the Wooden Hat 2009; short stories: Black Faces, White Faces (David Higham Award 1978, Winifred Holtby Award 1978) 1975, The Sidmouth Letters 1980, The Pangs of Love (Katherine Mansfield Award 1984) 1983, Showing the Flag 1989, Going into a Dark House 1994, Missing the Midnight 1997; non-fiction: The Iron Coast 1994. *Honours:* Hon. DLitt. *Address:* Haven House, Sandwich, Kent CT13 9ES (home); Throstlenest Farm, Crackpot, N Yorks; 34 Denmark Road, London, SW19 4PQ, England. *Telephone:* (1304) 612680 (home).

GARDEL, Louis; French publishing editor, novelist and screenwriter; b. 8 Sept. 1939, Algiers, Algeria; s. of Jacques Gardel and Janine Blasselle; m. 1st Béatrice Herr (deceased) 1963; m. 2nd Hélène Millerand 1990; two s. two d. *Education:* Lycée Bugeaud, Algiers, Lycée Louis-le-Grand, Paris and Institut d'Etudes Politiques, Paris. *Career:* Head of Dept Inst. des Hautes Etudes d'Outre-Mer 1962–64; Man. Soc. Rhône-Progil 1964–74; Head of Dept Conseil Nat. du Patronat 1974–80; Literary Consultant, Editions du Seuil 1980, Literary Ed. 1980–; mem. juries Prix Renaudot, Conseil Supérieur de la Langue Française. *Film screenplays:* Fort Saganne, Nocturne Indien, Indochine, La Marche de Radetzky 1996, Est.Ouest, Himalaya 1999, Princesse Marie 2005. *Publications:* L'Eté Fracassé 1973, Couteau de chaleur 1976, Fort Saganne 1980 (Grand Prix du Roman de l' Acad. française), Notre Homme 1986, Le Beau Rôle 1989, Darbaroud 1993. L'Aurore des Bien-Aimés 1997, Grand-Seigneur 1999, La Baie d'Alger 2007. *Honours:* Chevalier, Légion d'honneur. *Address:* 25 rue de la Cerisaie, 75004, Paris (home); Editions du Seuil, 27 rue Jacob, 75006 Paris, France (office). *Telephone:* 1-40-46-50-50 (office). *E-mail:* froumens@seuil.com (office).

GARDEN, Nancy, BFA, MA; American writer, editor and teacher; b. (Antoinette Elisabeth Garden), 15 May 1938, Boston, Mass; d. of Peter T. Garden and Elisabeth Yens Garden; partner Sandra Scott. *Education:* Columbia Univ. School of Dramatic Arts, Teachers Coll., Columbia Univ. *Career:* actress, Lighting Designer 1954–64; Teacher of Speech and Dramatics 1961–64; ed. of educational materials, textbooks 1964–76; teacher of Writing, Adult Educ. 1974, Correspondence School 1974–94; mem. Soc. of Children's Book Writers and Illustrators, Authors' Guild. *Publications include:* What Happened in Marston 1971, The Loners 1972, Maria's Mountain 1981, Fours Crossing 1981, Annie on My Mind 1982, Favourite Tales from Grimm 1982, Watersmeet 1983, Prisoner of Vampires 1984, Peace, O River 1986, The Door Between 1987, Lark in the Morning 1991, My Sister, the Vampire 1992, Dove and Sword 1995, My Brother, the Werewolf 1995, Good Moon Rising 1996, The Year They Burned the Books 1999, Holly's Secret 2000, Meeting Melanie 2002, Endgame 2006, Hear Us Out 2007; The Monster Hunter series: Case No. 1, Mystery of the Night Raiders 1987, Case No. 2: Mystery of the Midnight Menace 1988, Case No. 3: Mystery of the Secret Marks 1989, Case No. 4: Mystery of the Kidnapped Kidnapper 1994, Case No. 5: Mystery of the Watchful Witches 1995; non-fiction: Berlin: City Split in Two 1971, Vampires 1973, Werewolves 1973, Witches 1975, Devils and Demons 1976, Fun with Forecasting Weather 1977, The Kids' Code and Cipher Book 1981; contribs to Lambda Book Report. *Honours:* Robert B. Downs Award for Intellectual Freedom, Margaret Edwards Award for Lifetime Achievement, Katahden Award for Lifetime Achievement. *Address:* c/o McIntosh and Otis, Inc., 353 Lexington Avenue, New York, NY 10016, USA. *E-mail:* nancygarden@aol.com (office). *Website:* www.nancygarden.com.

GÄRDENFORS, Peter, PhD; Swedish philosopher and academic; *Professor of Cognitive Science, Lund University*; b. 21 Sept. 1949, Degeberga; s. of Torsten Gärdenfors and Ingemor Gärdenfors (née Jonsson); m. Annette Wald 1975 (divorced 2002); three s. one d. *Education:* Lund Univ., Princeton Univ., USA. *Career:* Lecturer in Philosophy, Lund Univ. 1974–80, Reader in Philosophy of Science 1975–77, Reader in Philosophy 1980–88, Prof. of Cognitive Science 1988–; Visiting Fellow, Princeton Univ., USA 1973–74, ANU, Australia 1986–87; Visiting Scholar, Stanford Univ., USA 1983–84; Visiting Prof., Univ. of Buenos Aires 1990; Ed. Theoria 1978–86, Journal of Logic, Language and Information 1991–96; mem. Royal Swedish Acad. of Letters, Academia Europaea, Deutsche Akad. für Naturforscher Leopoldina,

Royal Swedish Acad. of Science. *Publications:* Generalized Quantifiers (ed.) 1986, Knowledge in Flux 1988, Decision, Probability and Utility (with N.-E. Sahlin) 1988, Belief Revision (ed.) 1992, Blotta Tanken 1992, Fangslande Information 1996, Cognitive Semantics (with J. Allwood) 1998, Conceptual Spaces 2000, How Homo Became Sapiens 2003, The Dynamics of Thought 2005. *Honours:* Rausing Prize 1986. *Address:* Department of Philosophy, Lund University, Kungshuset, Lundagard, 222 22 Lund, Sweden (office). *Telephone:* (6) 222-48-17 (office). *Fax:* (6) 222-44-24 (office). *E-mail:* peter.gardenfors@lucs.lu.se (office). *Website:* www.lucs.lu.se/Peter.Gardenfors (office).

GARFINKEL, Patricia Gail, BA; American poet and writer; b. 15 Feb. 1938, New York, NY; divorced; two s. *Education:* New York Univ. *Career:* currently Head of Issues Policy Devt Group, Office of Legislative and Public Affairs, US Nat. Science Foundation; mem. Poets and Writers. *Publications:* Ram's Horn (poems) 1980, From the Red Eye of Jupiter (poems) 1990, Making the Skeleton Dance 2000; contrib. to numerous anthologies and other publications. *Honours:* Poetry in Public Places Award for New York State 1977, first prize Lip Service Poetry Competition 1990, Washington Writers Publishing House Book Competition 1990, winner Moving Words competition. *Address:* 900 N Stuart Street, Suite 1001, Arlington, VA 22203, USA (office). *Telephone:* (703) 292-7736 (office). *E-mail:* pgarfink@nsf.gov (office).

GARFITT, Roger, BA; British poet and writer; b. 12 April 1944, Melksham, Wiltshire, England; m. Frances Horovitz (deceased). *Education:* Merton Coll., Oxford. *Career:* Arts Council Creative Writing Fellow, Univ. Coll. of North Wales, Bangor 1975–77, and Poet-in-Residence, Sunderland Polytechnic 1978–80; Ed., Poetry Review 1977–82; Welsh Arts Council Poet-in-Residence, Ebbw Vale 1984; Poet-in-Residence, Pilgrim College, Boston 1986–87, Blyth Valley Disabled Forum 1992; Fellow, Swansea Univ. 2003–08; mem. National Asscn of Writers in Education: Poetry Society, Welsh Acad. *Publications:* Caught on Blue 1970, West of Elm 1974, The Broken Road 1982, Rowlstone Haiku (with Frances Horovitz) 1982, Given Ground 1989, Border Songs 1996, Travelling on Sunshine 1997, Selected Poems 2000; contributions: journals, reviews, and magazines. *Honours:* Guinness International Poetry Prize 1973, Gregory Award 1974. *E-mail:* r.garfitt@lineone.net (office).

GARG, Mridula, MA; Indian writer; b. 25 Oct. 1938, Calcutta (now Kolkata); d. of Birendra Prasad and Ravi Kanta Jain; m. Anand Garg 1963; two c. *Education:* Delhi School of Econs. *Career:* Lecturer in Econs 1960–63; Research Assoc., Centre for South Asian Studies, Univ. of California 1990; writer of short stories, novels and plays in Hindi, later English, contrib. to India Today. *Publications include:* fiction: Uske Hisse Ki Dhoop (M. P. Sahitya Acad. Award) 1975, A Touch of Sun 1977, Chittcobra 1979, Anitya 1980, Main Aur Main 1984, Daffodils on Fire (short stories) 1990, Kathgulab (Country of Goodbyes) (Vagdevi Sanman 2003, Vyas Sanman Award 2004, K. K. Birla Foundation 2005) 1996, The Colour of My Being 1996, Mere Desh Ki Mitti, Aha (short stories) 2001, Sangati-Visangti (short stories) 2004, Joote ka Jodh Gobhi ka Todh (short stories) 2006; plays include: Ek Aur Ajnabi (All India Radio Award) 1978, Jadoo-ka-Kalen (MP Sahitya Parishad Award 1993). *Honours:* Sahityakar Sanhan, Hindi Acad., Delhi 1988, Sahitya Bhushan, UP Hindi Sansthan 1999, Helamn-Hammett Grant, Human Rights Watch 2001, Vishna Hindi Sammelan San Man 2003, Katha Puraskar 2009. *Address:* E-118 Masjid Moth, Greater Kailash-3, New Delhi 110 048, India (home). *Telephone:* (98117) 66775 (office); (11) 29222140 (home). *Fax:* (11) 26673073 (office). *E-mail:* garg_anand@yahoo.com (office).

GARLAND, Alex, BA; British writer; b. 1970, London, England. *Education:* Univ. of Manchester. *Career:* occasionally works as an illustrator and a freelance journalist. *Publications:* The Beach (novel) 1996, The Tesseract (novel) 1999, 28 Days Later (screenplay) 2002, The Coma (novel) 2004, Sunshine (screenplay) 2007. *Address:* c/o Faber and Faber Ltd, Bloomsbury House, 74–77 Great Russell Street, London, WC1B 3DA, England (office). *Website:* www.faber.co.uk (office).

GARLICK, Raymond, BA, DLitt; British poet and lecturer (retd); b. 21 Sept. 1926, London; m. Elin Jane Hughes 1948; one s. one d. *Education:* Univ. Coll. of North Wales, Bangor, Central Univ., Pella, Ia, USA. *Career:* Principal Lecturer, Trinity Coll., Carmarthen 1972–86; Fellow, Welsh Acad. *Publications include:* poetry: Poems from the Mountain-House 1950, Requiem for a Poet 1954, Poems from Pembrokeshire 1954, The Welsh-Speaking Sea 1954, Blaenau Observed 1957, Landscapes and Figures: Selected Poems, 1949–63 1964, A Sense of Europe: Collected Poems, 1954–68 1968, A Sense of Time: Poems and Antipoems, 1969–72 1972, Incense: Poems, 1972–75 1975, Collected Poems, 1946–86 1987, Travel Notes: New Poems 1992, The Delphic Voyage 2003; other: An Introduction to Anglo-Welsh Literature 1970, Anglo-Welsh Poetry, 1480–1980 (ed.) 1982. *Honours:* Hon. Fellow, Trinity Coll., Carmarthen 1995, Univ. of Wales, Bangor 2006; Welsh Arts Council Prizes. *Address:* 26 Glannant House, College Road, Carmarthen, SA31 3EF, Wales (home). *Telephone:* (1267) 232587 (home).

GARNER, Alan, OBE; British writer; b. 17 Oct. 1934, Cheshire; s. of Colin Garner and Marjorie Garner (née Greenwood Stuart); m. 1st Ann Cook 1956 (divorced); one s. two d. m. 2nd Griselda Greaves 1972; one s. one d. *Education:* Manchester Grammar School, Magdalen Coll., Oxford. *Career:* mil. service with rank of Lt, RA; mem. Editorial Bd Detskaya Literatura Publrs, Moscow. *Plays:* Holly from the Bongs 1965, Lamaload 1978, Lurga Lom 1980, To Kill a King 1980, Sally Water 1982, The Keeper 1983, Pentecost 1997, The Echoing Waters 2000. *Dance drama:* The Green Mist 1970. *Libretti:* The Bellybag 1971, Potter Thompson 1972, Lord Flame 1996. *Screenplays:* The Owl Service 1969, Red Shift 1978, Places and Things 1978, Images 1981 (First Prize, Chicago Int. Film Festival), Strandloper 1992. *Publications:* The Weirdstone of Brisingamen 1960, The Moon of Gomrath 1963, Elidor 1965, Holly from the Bongs 1966, The Old Man of Mow 1967, The Owl Service (Library Asscn Carnegie Medal 1967, Guardian Award 1968) 1967, The Book of Goblins (ed.) 1969, Red Shift 1973, The Breadhorse 1975, The Guizer 1975, The Stone Book Quartet (Children's Book Asscn of USA Phoenix Award 1996) 1976–78, Tom Fobble's Day 1977, Granny Reardun 1977, The Aimer Gate 1978, Fairy Tales of Gold 1979, The Lad of the Gad 1980, A Book of British Fairy Tales (ed.) 1984, A Bag of Moonshine 1986, Jack and the Beanstalk 1992, Once Upon a Time 1993, Strandloper 1996, The Little Red Hen 1997, The Voice That Thunders 1997, The Well of the Wind 1998, Thursbitch 2003, Collected Folk Tales 2011, Boneland 2012. *Honours:* Hon. DLitt (Warwick), (Salford); Carnegie Medal 1968, Guardian Award 1968, Lewis Carroll Shelf Award, USA 1970, Chicago Int. Film Festival Gold Plaque 1981, Phoenix Award, Children's Literature Asscn of America 1996, Karl Edward Wagner Award 2003. *Literary Agent:* c/o Curtis Brown Ltd, 28–29 Haymarket, London, SW1Y 4SP, England. *Telephone:* (20) 7393-4400. *Fax:* (20) 7393-4401. *E-mail:* info@curtisbrown.co.uk. *Website:* www.curtisbrown.co.uk; alangarner.atspace.org.

GARNER, Helen, BA; Australian teacher, novelist and journalist; b. 7 Nov. 1942, Geelong, Vic.; d. of Bruce Ford and Gweneth Ford (née Gadsden); m. 3rd Murray Bail 1992 (divorced 1998); one d. *Education:* Univ. of Melbourne. *Publications:* Monkey Grip 1977, Honour, and Other People's Children 1980, The Children's Bach 1984, Postcards from Surfers 1985, Cosmo Cosmolino 1992, The Last Days of Chez Nous 1993, The First Stone 1995, True Stories 1996, The Feel of Steel 2001, Joe Cinque's Consolation 2004, The Spare Room 2008. *Honours:* Hon. DLitt (Newcastle) 2003, Hon. LLD (Melbourne) 2003. *Address:* c/o Barbara Mobbs, PO Box 126, Edgecliff, NSW 2027, Australia (office). *Telephone:* (2) 9363-5323 (office).

GARNETT, Richard Duncan Carey, BA, MA; British writer, publisher and translator; b. 8 Jan. 1923, London, England; m. (Mary Letitia) Jane Dickins 1954; two s. *Education:* King's Coll., Cambridge. *Career:* Production Man., Rupert Hart-Davis Ltd 1955–59, Dir 1957–66; Dir Adlard Coles Ltd 1963–66; Ed. Macmillan, London 1966–82, Dir 1972–82, Dir Macmillan Publishers 1982–87. *Publications:* Goldsmith: Selected Works (ed.) 1950, Robert Gruss: The Art of the Aqualung (trans.) 1955, The Silver Kingdom (aka The Undersea Treasure) 1956, Bernard Heuvelmans: On the Track of Unknown Animals (trans.) 1958, The White Dragon 1963, Jack of Dover 1966, Bernard Heuvelmans: In the Wake of the Sea-Serpents (trans.) 1968, Joyce (co-ed. with Reggie Grenfell) 1980, Constance Garnett: A Heroic Life 1991, Sylvia and David, The Townsend Warner/Garnett Letters (ed.) 1994, Rupert Hart-Davis Limited: A Brief History 2004. *Literary Agent:* c/o AP Watt Ltd, 20 John Street, London, WC1N 2DR, England. *Telephone:* (20) 7405-6774. *Fax:* (20) 7831-2154. *E-mail:* apw@apwatt.co.uk. *Website:* www.apwatt.co.uk. *Address:* 28 Albany Street, Salisbury, Wilts., SP1 3YH, England (home). *Telephone:* (1772) 416533 (home). *E-mail:* richardgarnett@waitrose.com (home).

GARRÉTA, Anne F., PhD; French writer and academic; *Research Professor (Literature), Duke University;* b. 1962, Paris. *Education:* Ecole Normale Supérieure, Fontenay, New York Univ., USA. *Career:* Assoc. Prof. of French Literature, Univ. of Rennes II – Haute Bretagne; Research Prof. (Literature), Duke Univ.; mem. L'Oulipo 2000–. *Publications include:* Sphinx 1986, Ciels liquides 1990, La Pyramide (short story) 1991, La Décomposition 1999, Pas un jour (Prix Médicis) 2002; articles in literary reviews. *Address:* Département Lettres, Université Rennes II – Haute Bretagne, Place Recteur Henri le Moal, CS 24307, 35043 Rennes, France (office). *Telephone:* 2-99-14-15-64 (office). *Fax:* 2-99-14-15-05 (office). *Website:* www.uhb.fr (office).

GARRISON, Deborah, BA, MA; American editor and poet; b. 12 Feb. 1965, Ann Arbor, Mich.; m. Matthew C. Garrison 1986; one s. two d. *Education:* Brown Univ., New York Univ. *Career:* mem. editorial staff, New Yorker magazine 1986–2000; Poetry Ed., Alfred A. Knopf 2000–; Sr Ed., Pantheon Books 2000–. *Publications include:* A Working Girl Can't Win and Other Poems 1998, The Second Child: Poems 2007; contribs to Slate, New York Times, New Yorker, Publisher's Weekly, Poets & Writers. *Address:* c/o Alfred A. Knopf, 1745 Broadway, New York, NY 10019-4305, USA (office).

GARROS, Alexander; Latvian journalist; b. 1975. *Career:* journalist in Riga. *Publication:* Headcrusher (novel, in trans., with Aleksei Evdokimov) (Nat. Bestseller Prize, Russia) 2003. *Address:* c/o Chatto & Windus, Random House, 20 Vauxhall Bridge Road, London, SW1V 2SA, England (office).

GARROW, David Jeffries, BA, MA, PhD; American writer and academic; *Senior Research Fellow, Homerton College, University of Cambridge;* b. 11 May 1953, New Bedford, Mass; m. Virginia Darleen Opfer 2003. *Education:* Wesleyan Univ., Duke Univ. *Career:* Senior Fellow, Twentieth Century Fund 1991–93; Visiting Distinguished Prof., Cooper Union 1992–93; James Pinckney Harrison Prof. of History, Coll. of William and Mary 1994–95; Distinguished Historian-in-Residence, American Univ., Washington, DC 1995–96; Presidential Distinguished Prof., Emory Univ. 1997–2005; Sr Research Fellow, Homerton Coll., Univ. of Cambridge 2011–. *Publications:* Protest at Selma 1978, The FBI and Martin Luther King Jr 1981, Bearing the Cross 1986, The Southern Christian Leadership Conference 1986, The Montgomery Bus Boycott and the Women Who Started It (ed.) 1987, The

Eyes on the Prize Civil Rights Reader (co-ed.) 1987, Liberty and Sexuality 1994, The Forgotten Memoir of John Knox (co-ed.) 2002; contrib. to New York Times, Washington Post, Newsweek, Dissent, Journal of American History, Constitutional Commentary. *Honours:* Pulitzer Prize in Biography 1987, Robert F. Kennedy Book Award 1987, Gustavus Myers Human Rights Book Award 1987. *Address:* Homerton College, Hills Road, Cambridge, CB2 8PH, England (office). *Telephone:* (1223) 507111 (office). *Fax:* (1223) 507120 (office). *E-mail:* djg52@cam.ac.uk (office). *Website:* www.davidgarrow.com.

GARTON ASH, Timothy John, CMG, MA, FRSA, FRHistS, FRSL; British writer and academic; *Professor of European Studies, University of Oxford*; b. 12 July 1955, London; m. Danuta Maria 1982; two s. *Education:* Exeter Coll., Oxford, St Antony's Coll., Oxford. *Career:* editorial writer The Times 1984–86; Foreign Ed. The Spectator 1984–90; Fellow Woodrow Wilson Int. Center for Scholars, Washington, DC 1986–87; Sr Assoc. mem., St Antony's Coll., Oxford 1987–89, Fellow and Sr Research Fellow in Contemporary European History 1990–, currently Prof. of European Studies, Isaiah Berlin Professorial Fellow, Univ. of Oxford; columnist The Independent 1988–90, The Guardian 2002–; Sr Fellow Hoover Inst., Stanford Univ. 2000–; Fellow Acad. of Sciences, Berlin-Brandenburg, European Acad. of Arts and Sciences; Corresp. Fellow Inst. for Human Sciences, Vienna; mem. PEN, Soc. of Authors. *Publications:* 'Und willst du nicht mein Bruder sein…': Die DDR heute 1981, The Polish Revolution: Solidarity 1983, The Uses of Adversity: Essays on the Fate of Central Europe 1989, We the People: The Revolution of '89 Witnessed in Warsaw, Budapest, Berlin and Prague 1990, In Europe's Name: Germany and the Divided Continent 1993, Freedom for Publishing for Freedom: The Central and East European Publishing Project (ed.) 1995, The File: A Personal History 1997, History of the Present 1999, Free World 2004, Facts are Subversive: Political Writing from a Decade Without a Name 2009; contribs to books, newspapers and magazines. *Honours:* Golden Insignia of the Order of Merit, Poland 1992, Kt's Cross of the Order of Merit, Germany 1995, Order of Merit, Czech Repub. 2000; Hon. DLitt (St Andrew's) 2004; Soc. of Authors Somerset Maugham Award 1984, Veillon Foundation Prix Européen de l'Essai 1989, David Watt Memorial Prize 1989, Granada Award for Commentator of the Year 1989, Friedrich Ebert Stiftung Prize 1991, Imre Nagy Memorial Plaque, Hungary 1995, Premio Napoli 1995, Orwell Prize for Journalism 2006, Ischia Prize for Int. Journalism 2008. *Address:* St Antony's College, Oxford, OX2 6JF, England (office). *Telephone:* (1865) 274470 (office). *Fax:* (1865) 274478 (office). *E-mail:* european.studies@sant.ox.ac.uk (office). *Website:* www.sant.ox.ac.uk (office); www.timothygartonash.com.

GARWOOD, Julie; American writer; b. 26 Dec. 1946, Kansas City, MO; m. Gerald Garwood 1967 (divorced); two s. one d. *Education:* Avila Coll. *Publications:* Gentle Warrior 1985, Rebellious Desire 1986, Honor's Splendor 1987, The Lion's Lady 1988, The Bride 1989, Guardian Angel 1990, The Gift 1990, The Prize 1991, The Secret 1992, Castles 1993, Saving Grace 1993, Prince Charming 1994, For the Roses 1995, The Wedding 1996, One Pink Rose 1997, One White Rose 1997, One Red Rose 1997, Come the Spring 1997, The Clayborne Brides 1998, Ransom 1999, Heartbreaker 2000, Shadow Dance 2007, Sizzle 2009. *Address:* PO Box 7574, Leawood, KS 66211, USA (office). *Website:* www.juliegarwood.com.

GASCOIGNE, John, FRHistS, BA, MA, PhD; British academic and writer; *Professor of History and Philosophy, University of New South Wales*; b. 20 Jan. 1951, Liverpool, England; m. Kathleen May Bock 1980; one s. one d. *Education:* Univ. of Sydney, Princeton Univ., Univ. of Cambridge. *Career:* Lecturer, St Paul's Teachers' Coll., Rabaul 1973, Univ. of Papua New Guinea, Port Moresby 1977–78; Tutor, Univ. of New South Wales 1980–84, Lecturer 1984–87, Senior Lecturer 1987–96, Assoc. Prof. of History 1997–2003, Prof. of History and Philosophy 2003–; Reviews Ed., Journal of Religious History 1996–. *Publications:* Cambridge in the Age of Enlightenment: Science, Religion and Politics from the Restoration to the French Revolution 1988, Joseph Banks and the English Enlightenment: Useful Knowledge and Polite Culture 1994, Science in the Service of Empire: Sir Joseph Banks and the British State in the Age of Revolution 1998, Science, Politics and Universities in Europe 1600–1800 1999, The Enlightenment and the Origins of European Australia 2002, Captain Cook: Voyager between Worlds 2007; contributions: scholarly books and journals. *Honours:* Hancock Prize, Australian Historical Society 1991, Fellow, Australian Acad. of the Humanities. *Address:* School of History and Philosophy, University of New South Wales, Level 3 - Morwen Brown Building, Faculty of Arts and Social Sciences, Sydney, NSW 2052, Australia (office). *Telephone:* (2) 9385-2341 (office). *E-mail:* j.gascoigne@unsw.edu.au (office). *Website:* hist-phil.arts.unsw.edu.au (office).

GASH, Jonathan (see Grant, John).

GASKELL, Jane; British writer; b. 7 July 1941, Lancashire, England. *Career:* staff mem., Daily Express 1961–65, Daily Sketch 1965–71, Daily Mail 1971–84. *Publications:* Strange Evil 1957, King's Daughter 1958, Attic Summer 1958, The Serpent 1963, The Shiny Narrow Grin 1964, The Fabulous Heroine 1965, Atlan 1965, The City 1966, All Neat in Black Stockings 1966, A Sweet Sweet Summer 1969, Summer Coming 1974, Some Summer Lands 1977, Sun Bubble 1990. *Honours:* Somerset Maugham Award 1970.

GASKIN, John Charles Addison, BLitt, MA, DLitt; British academic and writer; b. 4 April 1936, Hitchin, Herts.; m. Diana Dobbin 1972; one s. one d. *Education:* City of Oxford High School, St Peter's Coll., Oxford. *Career:* with Royal Bank of Scotland 1960–62; Lecturer, Trinity Coll., Dublin 1965–78, Fellow 1978–, Prof. of Philosophy 1982–97; Dir of Music, Paxton Trust and Festival; mem. Kildare St and Univ. Club, Dublin, Northern Counties Club, Newcastle upon Tyne. *Publications:* Hume's Philosophy of Religion 1978, The Quest for Eternity: An Outline of the Philosophy of Religion 1984, Varieties of Unbelief From Epicurus to Sartre 1989, David Hume: Dialogues Concerning Natural Religion and the Natural History of Religion (ed.) 1993, The Epicurean Philosophers (ed.) 1994, Thomas Hobbes: Human Nature and the De Corpore (ed.) 1994, Hobbes: Leviathan 1996, The Dark Companion: Ghost Stories 2001, The Long Retreating Day: Tales of Twilight and Borderlands 2005, Moments from a Life: Poems and Opinions 2008, The Traveller's Guide to Classical Philosophy 2011; contribs to scholarly journals, periodicals, reference books and anthologies of stories. *Honours:* Hon. Tutor and Cellarer, Hatfield Coll., Durham 1997–2010. *Address:* Crook Crossing, by Netherwitton, Morpeth, Northumberland, NE61 4PY, England (home). *Telephone:* (1669) 620249 (home).

GASS, William Howard, AB, PhD; American writer, critic and academic; *David May Distinguished University Professor Emeritus in the Humanities, Washington University in St Louis*; b. 30 July 1924, Fargo, ND; m. 1st Mary Pat O'Kelly 1952; two s. one d.; m. 2nd Mary Henderson 1969; two d. *Education:* Kenyon Coll., Cornell Univ. *Career:* Instructor in Philosophy, Coll. of Wooster 1950–54; Asst Prof., Purdue Univ. 1955–58, Assoc. Prof. 1960–65, Prof. of Philosophy 1966–69; Visiting Lecturer in English and Philosophy, Univ. of Illinois 1958–59; Prof. of Philosophy, Washington Univ. 1969–78, David May Distinguished Prof. in the Humanities 1979–2001, Prof. Emer. 2001–, Dir, International Writers Centre 1990–2001; mem. American Acad. of Arts and Letters, American Acad. of Arts and Sciences. *Publications:* fiction: Omensetter's Luck 1966, Willie Masters' Lonesome Wife 1968, The Tunnel (American Book Award) 1995; stories: In the Heart of the Heart of the Country 1968, Cartesian Sonata 1998; essays: Fiction and the Figures of Life 1971, On Being Blue 1976, The World Within the Word 1978, The Habitations of the Word (National Book Critics Circle Award for Criticism 1985) 1984, Finding a Form (National Book Critics Circle Award for Criticism 1997) 1996, Tests of Time (National Book Critics Circle Award for Criticism 2003) 2002, A Temple of Texts (Truman Capote Award for Literary Criticism) 2006, Life Sentences 2012; editor: The Writer in Politics (with Lorin Cuoco) 1996, The Writer and Religion (with Lorin Cuoco) 2000, Literary St Louis (with Lorin Cuoco) 2000; translator: Reading Rilke 1999; contributions: essays, criticism, poems, stories, and trans in various publications. *Honours:* Longview Foundation Prize for Fiction 1959, Rockefeller Foundation Grant 1965–66, Guggenheim Fellowship 1970–71, American Acad. and Institute of Arts and Letters Award 1975, and Medal of Merit 1979, Pushcart Prizes 1976, 1983, 1987, 1992, National Book Critics Circle Awards 1985, 1996, 2003, Getty Scholar 1991–92, Before Columbus Foundation 1996, Lannan Lifetime Achievement Award 1997, PEN-Nabokov Prize 2000, PEN Spielvogel Diamondstein Award 2003. *Address:* c/o Department of English, Washington University in St. Louis, Campus Box 1122, One Brookings Drive, St. Louis, MO 63130-4899 (office); 6304 Westminster Place, St. Louis, MO 63130, USA (home). *Telephone:* (314) 725-0317. *E-mail:* w.gass@sbcglobal.net.

GATENBY, Greg, BA; Canadian artistic director and poet; b. 5 May 1950, Toronto. *Education:* York Univ. *Career:* Ed., McClelland and Stewart, Toronto 1973–75; Artistic Dir, Harbourfront Reading Series and concomitant festivals 1975, Humber Coll. School of Creative Writing 1992–93, Int. Festival of Authors; mem. PEN Canadian Centre, Writers' Union of Canada. *Publications:* Imaginative Work: Rondeaus for Erica 1976, Adrienne's Blessing 1976, The Brown Stealer 1977, The Salmon Country 1978, Growing Still 1981; contrib. to anthologies, including 52 Pickup 1977, Whale Sound 1977, Whales: A Celebration 1983, The Definitive Notes 1991, The Wild is Always There 1993, Toronto Literary Guide 1999; translator: Selected Poems, by Giorgio Bassani 1980, The Wild Is Always There Vol. 2 1995, The Very Richness of that Past 1995. *Honours:* City of Toronto Arts Award for Literature 1989, hon. lifetime mem. League of Canadian Poets 1991, Jack Award for Lifetime Promotion of Canadian Books 1994, E. J. Pratt Lifetime Fellow 1995. *Address:* 243 Macdonell Avenue, Toronto, ON M6R 2A9, Canada (home). *Telephone:* (416) 588-3671 (home).

GATES, Henry Louis, Jr, MA, PhD; American academic, author and editor; *W. E. B. DuBois Professor of the Humanities and Director, W.E.B. DuBois Institute for African and African-American Research, Harvard University*; b. 16 Sept. 1950, Piedmont, W Va; s. of Henry-Louis Gates and Pauline Augusta Gates (née Coleman); m. Sharon Lynn Adams 1979; two d. *Education:* Yale Univ. and Clare Coll. Cambridge. *Career:* fmr European corresp. for Time magazine; lecturer in English, Yale Univ. 1976–79, Asst Prof. English and Afro-American Studies 1979–84, Assoc. Prof. 1984–85; Prof. of English, Comparative Literature and Africana Studies, Cornell Univ. 1985–90; John Spencer Bassett Prof. of English, Duke Univ. 1990–91; W. E. B. DuBois Prof. of the Humanities and Chair. Dept of African and African-American Studies, Harvard Univ. 1991–, also Dir W. E. B. DuBois Inst. for African and African-American Research; Pres. Afro-American Acad. 1984–; Co-founder AfricanDNA.com (genealogy website); Host African-American Lives (PBS); ed. African American Women's Writings (Macmillan reprint series), Encyclopedia Africana; columnist, New Yorker, New York Times; mem. Pulitzer Prize Bd. *Publications include:* Figures in Black (literary criticism) 1987, The Signifying Monkey 1988, Loose Canons (literary criticism) 1992, Colored People (short stories) 1994, The Future of the Race (with Cornel West) 1996, Thirteen Ways of Looking at a Black Man., Africana (jtly) (TV documentary), Wonders of the African World 1999, The Curitas Enthology of African – American Slave

Narratives, The African-American Century 2000; Co-Ed. Encarta Africana Encycloaedia 1999; Ed. The Bondswoman's Narrative 2002, America Behind the Color Line 2004, Faces of America: How 12 Extraordinary People Discovered their Pasts 2010, Tradition and the Black Atlantic: Critical Theory in the African Diaspora 2010. *Honours:* Hon. Citizenship of Benin 2001; numerous hon. degrees; American Book Award for The Signifying Monkey; McArthur Foundation Award, Nat. Humanities Medal 1998, Zora Neale Hurston Society Award for Cultural Scholarship, Tikkun National Ethics Award. *Address:* Department of African and African-American Studies, Barker Center, 2nd Floor, 12 Quincy Street, Cambridge, MA 02138, USA (office). *Telephone:* (617) 496-5468 (office). *Fax:* (617) 495-9490 (office). *Website:* www.fas.harvard.edu/~afroam (office); www.fas.harvard.edu/~du_bois (office).

GATHORNE-HARDY, Jonathan, BA; British writer; b. 17 May 1933, Edinburgh, Scotland; m. 1st Sabrina Tennant 1962; one s. one d.; m. 2nd Nicolette Sinclair Loutit 1985. *Education:* Trinity Coll., Cambridge. *Publications:* One Foot in the Clouds (novel) 1961, Chameleon (novel) 1967, The Office (novel) 1970, The Rise and Fall of the British Nanny 1972, The Public School Phenomenon 1977, Love, Sex, Marriage and Divorce 1981, Doctors 1983, The Centre of the Universe is 18 Baedeker Strasse (short stories) 1985, The City Beneath the Skin (novel) 1986, The Interior Castle: A Life of Gerald Brenan (biog.) 1992, Particle Theory (novel) 1996, Alfred C. Kinsey – Sex the Measure of All Things, A Biography 1998, Half an Arch (J.R. Ackerley Prize for Autobiography 2005); other: 11 novels for children; contrib. to numerous magazines and journals. *Address:* 31 Blacksmith's Yard, Binham, Fakenham, Norfolk, NR21 0AL, England (home). *Telephone:* (1328) 830400 (home). *Fax:* (1328) 830400 (home). *E-mail:* jonny@gathornehardy.com (home).

GATTEY, Charles Neilson; British author, playwright and lecturer; b. 3 Sept. 1921, London, England. *Education:* Univ. of London. *Career:* mem. Society of Civil Service Authors (pres. 1980–2005), The Garrick. *Publications:* The Incredible Mrs Van Der Eist 1972, They Saw Tomorrow 1977, Queens of Song 1979, The Elephant that Swallowed a Nightingale 1981, Peacocks on the Podium 1982, Foie Gras and Trumpets 1984, Excess in Food, Drink and Sex 1987, Prophecy and Prediction in the 20th Century 1989, Luisa Tetrazzini 1995, Crowning Glory: The Merits of the Monarchy 2003; other: television Play: The White Falcon 1955; film: The Love Lottery 1954.

GATTI, Armand; French playwright; b. (Dante Gatti), 26 Jan. 1924, Monaco; s. of Auguste Gatti and Letizia Luzona. *Education:* Seminary of Saint Paul, near Cannes. *Career:* fmr journalist, Libération, Paris-Match, l'Express, France-soir. *Films:* L'Enclos 1960, El Otro Cristobal 1962, Der Übergang über den Ebro 1969, Nous étions tous des noms d'arbres 1982. *Publications:* Le Poisson noir (Prix Fénéon 1959) 1958, La crapaud-buffle 1959, Le Voyage de Grand Chou 1960, Chant public devant deux chaises électriques 1966, V comme Vietnam 1967, Le Passion du général Franco 1968, Un homme seul 1969, Petit manuel de guérilla urbaine 1971, La colonne Durutti 1974, Die Hälfte des Himmels und wir 1975, Le labyrinthe 1982, Opéra avec titre long 1987, Oeuvres théâtrales, 3 tomes regroupant 44 pièces de 1958 à 1990 1991, Ces empereurs aux ombrelles trouées 1991, Le chant d'amour des alphabets d'Auschwitz 1992, Gatti à Marseille 1993, Adam quoi? 1993, La journée d'une infirmière 1995, Notre tranchée de chaque jour 1996, L'Inconnu no. 5 1996, Les personnages de théâtre meurent dans la rue 1997, La Parole errante 1999, L'anarchie comme un battement d'ailes (4 vols) 2001, 2003, Les 5 noms de Resistance de Georges Guingouin 2006, La Première lettre 2007, Le ciel est dans la rue: Cuba 1962–65 2007. *Honours:* Commdr Ordre des Arts et des Lettres 2004, Chevalier de la Légion d'honneur 2000; Prix Albert Londres 1954, Grand prix national du théâtre 1988, Médaille de vermeil Picasso UNESCO 1994, Prix théâtre du SACD 2005, Medaille Vermeil, Paris 2007. *Address:* La Parole Errante, 9 rue François-Debergue, 93100 Montreuil-sous-Bois, France (office). *Telephone:* 1-48-70-00-76 (office). *Fax:* 1-48-70-03-24 (office). *E-mail:* courrier@laparole-errente.fr (office).

GAUDÉ, Laurent; French novelist and playwright; b. 6 July 1972, Paris. *Plays include:* Combats de possédés 1999, Onysos le furieux 2000, Cendres sur les mains 2001, Pluie de cendres 2001, Le Tigre bleu de l'Euphrate 2002, Médéé Kali 2003, Salina 2003, Les Sacrifiées 2004, Sofia Douleur 2008, Sodome, ma douce 2009. *Publications include:* novels: Cris 2001, La Mort du roi Tsongor (Prix Goncourt, Prix des Libraires 2003) 2002, Le Soleil des Scorta (Prix Goncourt) 2004, Eldorado 2006, Dans la nuit Mozambique 2007, La Porte des Enfers 2008. *Address:* c/o Actes Sud, BP 38, 13633 Arles Cédex, France (office). *Website:* www.actes-sud.fr (office).

GAUNT, Graham (see Grant, John)

GAUTREAUX, Timothy (Tim) Martin, BA, PhD; American author and academic; *Writer-in-Residence and Professor Emeritus, Southeastern Louisiana University*; b. 19 Oct. 1947, Morgan City, La; s. of Minos Lee Gautreaux and Florence Ella Adoue Gautreaux; m. Winborne Howell Gautreaux; two s. *Education:* Nicholls State Univ., Thibodeaux, Univ. of South Carolina. *Career:* creative writing teacher, Southeastern Louisiana Univ. –2004, currently Writer-in-Residence and Prof. Emer.; work has appeared in The New Yorker, Atlantic, Harper's, GQ, Best American Short Stories. *Publications include:* novels: The Next Step in the Dance (Southeastern Booksellers Asscn Award 1999) 1999, The Clearing (Southern Ind. Booksellers Alliance Book Award 2003, Mid-South Ind. Booksellers Asscn Award 2003) 2003, The Missing 2009; short story collections: Same Place, Same Things 1997, Welding with Children 2009. *Honours:* John Dos Passos Prize 2005, Louisiana Writer Award 2009. *Address:* c/o Southeastern Louisiana University, Department of English, DVIC 335, Hammond, LA 70402, USA (office). *Telephone:* (985) 549-5788 (office). *E-mail:* tgautreaux@selu.edu (office). *Website:* www.selu.edu (office).

GAVALDA, Anna, MA; French writer and novelist; b. 9 Dec. 1970, Boulogne-Billancourt.; divorced; one s. one d. *Education:* Univ. of Paris-Sorbonne. *Career:* secondary school literature teacher, Melun 1993–2002; columnist, Elle magazine; mem. jury, Prix de la bande dessinée d'Angoulême. *Publications:* novels: La Plus Belle Lettre d'amour (Prix France Inter) 1992, L'Échappée belle 2001, Je l'aimais (trans. as Someone I Loved) 2003, Ensemble, c'est tout (trans. as Hunting and Gathering) 2004, À leurs bons cœurs 2005, La Consolante (trans. as Consolation) 2008; other: Je voudrais que quelqu'un m'attende quelque part (short stories) (trans. as I Wish Someone Were Waiting for Me Somewhere 2003) (Grand Prix RTL-Lire 2000) 1999, 35 kilos d'espoir (juvenile novel) 2002; contrib. short stories to anthologies and journals. *Address:* c/o Le Dilettante Editions, 19 rue Racine, 75006 Paris, France (office). *Website:* www.ledilettante.com (office).

GAVRAN, Miro; Croatian playwright and writer; b. 1961, Zagreb; m. Mladena Gavran; one s. *Education:* Zagreb Acad. for Theatre, Film and TV. *Career:* dramatist, Teater & TD 1986–89, Artistic Dir 1989–92; Ed. Plima literary magazine 1993–96; f. Epilogue Theatre, Zagreb 1995, resident dramatist 1995–2001; co-f. with wife Gavran Theatre 2002; f. GAVRANFest, annual theatre festival celebrating his works, Slovakia 2003–; first play Kreontova Antigona (Creon's Antigone) performed at Gavella Theatre 1983; premiere of Kraljevi i konjušari (Royalty and Rogues) performed at Eugene O'Neill Theater Center, USA 1999; plays performed world-wide and seen by over two million people in countries including Netherlands, Poland, Bulgaria, Hungary, Argentina, Greece, France, USA, India, Russia, Brazil, Slovakia, Czech Repub., Germany. *Plays:* Creon's Antigone 1983, Night of the Gods 1986, George Washington's Loves 1988, Chekhov Says Good-Bye to Tolstoy 1989, My Wife's Husband 1991, Shakespeare and Elizabeth 1994, Death of an Actor (Ministry of Culture's Marin Drić Prize) 1995, Dr Freud's Patient 1993, Forget Hollywood 1997, Royalty and Rogues 1999, All About Women 2000, How To Kill The President 2003, Laughing Forbidden (Ministry of Culture's Marin Drić Prize 2004), Nora in Our Time (Ministry of Culture's Marin Drić Prize) 2005, All About Men 2006, Parallel Worlds 2007, Greta Garbo's Secret 2008. *Publications:* novels: Forgotten Son 1989, How We Broke Our Legs 1995, Klara 1997, Margita, or A Journey into a Former Life 1999, Judith 2001, John the Baptist 2002, Pontius Pilates 2004; juvenile: All Sorts of Things in My Head (Ivana Brlic Mazuranic 1992) 1991, How Dad Won Mum 1994, Head Over Heels in Love 1994, Happy Days (Mato Lovrak award 1995) 1994, Try to Forget 1996, Farewell Letter 1994, The Teacher of My Dreams 2006, The Only Witness to Beauty 2009; other: Extraordinary Ordinary People (short stories) 1989. *Honours:* Cen. European Time Int. Literary Award 1999, European Circle Award 2003. *Address:* Dugi dol 58C, 10000 Zagreb, Croatia (home). *E-mail:* miro.gavran@zg.t-com.hr (home). *Website:* www.mgavran2.t-com.hr.

GAY, Marie-Louise; Canadian writer, illustrator, designer and playwright; b. 17 June 1952, Québec City, QC; d. of Bernard Roland and Colette Gay; m. David Toby Homel; two s. *Education:* Inst. des Arts Graphiques de Montréal, Montréal Museum of Fine Arts School, Acad. of Art Coll., San Francisco, USA. *Career:* Graphic Designer, Perspectives and Décormag magazines 1974–76; Art Dir, La Courte Echelle publrs 1980; Lecturer in Illustration, Univ. of Québec, Montréal 1981–1990, Ahuntsic Coll. 1984–85; author and/or illustrator of over 60 books for children; playwright and designer of three puppet plays; mem. Canadian Children's Book Centre, IBBY Canada, Communication-Jeunesse, PEN Canada. *Exhibitions:* solo and group exhbns world-wide. *Film:* as set designer: La Boîte, Nat. Film Bd of Canada animation 1989. *Children's puppet plays:* as writer and designer: Bonne Fête Willy 1989, Qui a peur de LouLou? 1993, Le jardin de Babel 1999. *Publications:* illustrator: Hou Ilva 1976, Dou Ilvien 1978, Hébert Luée 1980, Lizzy's Lion 1984, The Last Piece of Sky 1993, The Three Little Pigs 1994, When Vegetables Go Bad! 1994, The Fabulous Song 1996, Rumplestiltskin 1997, Dreams are More Real than Bathtubs 1998, The Christmas Orange 1998, How to Take Your Grandmother to the Museum 1998, Yuck, A Love Story 2000, Houndsley and Catina 2006, Houndsley and Catina and the Birthday Surprise 2006, Please Louise! 2007, Houndsley and Catina and the Quiet Time 2008, Houndsley and Catina, Plink and Plunk 2009; writer and illustrator: De Zéro à Minuit 1981, La Sœur de Robert 1983, La Drôle d'Ecole 1984, Moonbeam on a Cat's Ear 1986, Rainy Day Magic 1987, Angel and the Polar Bear 1988, Fat Charlie's Circus 1989, Willy Nilly 1990, Mademoiselle Moon 1992, Rabbit Blue 1993, Midnight Mimi 1994, Princess Pistache 1998, Stella, Star of the Sea 1999, Sur mon île 1999, Stella, Queen of the Snow 2000, Stella, Fairy of the Forest 2002, Good Morning Sam 2003, Good Night Sam 2003, Stella, Princess of the Sky 2004, Caramba 2005, What Are You Doing, Sam? 2006, Travels With My Family (co-written with David Homel) 2006, Les malheurs de Princesse Pistache 2007, On The Road Again! (co-written with David Homel) 2008, When Stella Was Very, Very Small 2009, Roslyn Rutabaga and The Biggest Hole on Earth! 2010, Caramba and Henry 2011. *Honours:* numerous awards include two Canadian Council prizes 1985, Gov.-Gen.'s Award 1988, 2000, Mr Christie's Book Award 1997–2000, CBA's Libris Award 2000, two Ruth Schwartz Awards 2000, 2006, Torgi, Print Braille Award 2001, Elisabeth Mrazik Cleaver Award 2001, Vicky Metcalfe Body of Work Award 2006, Marilyn Baillie Picture Book Award 2006, 2008. *E-mail:* marielouisegay@yahoo.ca (home). *Website:* www.marielouisegay.com.

GAY, Peter, PhD; American historian and academic; *Sterling Professor Emeritus of History, Yale University*; b. 20 June 1923, Berlin, Germany; s. of Morris Fröhlich and Helga Fröhlich; m. Ruth Slotkin 1959; three step-d. *Education:* Univ. of Denver and Columbia Univ. *Career:* left Germany 1939; Dept of Public Law and Govt, Columbia Univ. 1947–56, Dept of History 1956–69, Prof. of History 1962–69, William R. Shepherd Prof. 1967–69; Prof. of Comparative European Intellectual History, Yale Univ. 1969–, Durfee Prof. of History 1970–84, Sterling Prof. of History 1984–93, Sterling Prof. Emer. 1993–; Guggenheim Fellow 1967–68; Overseas Fellow, Churchill Coll., Cambridge, UK 1970–71; Visiting Fellow, Inst. for Advanced Study, Berlin 1984; Dir Center for Scholars and Writers, New York Public Library 1997–; mem. American Historical Asscn, French Historical Soc. *Publications:* The Dilemma of Democratic Socialism: Eduard Bernstein's Challenge to Marx 1951, Voltaire's Politics: The Poet as Realist 1959, Philosophical Dictionary 1962, The Party of Humanity: Essays in the French Enlightenment 1964, The Loss of Mastery: Puritan Historians in Colonial America 1966, The Enlightenment: An Interpretation, Vols I, II 1966, 1969, Weimar Culture: The Outsider as Insider 1969, The Bridge of Criticism: Dialogues on the Enlightenment 1970, The Question of Jean-Jacques Rousseau 1974, Modern Europe (with R. K. Webb) 1973, Style in History 1974, Art and Act: On Causes in History – Manet, Gropius, Mondrian 1976, Freud, Jews and Other Germans: Masters and Victims in Modernist Culture 1978, The Bourgeois Experience: Victoria to Freud, Vols I, II, III 1984, 1986, 1993, Freud for Historians 1985, Freud: A Life for Our Time 1988, A Freud Reader 1989, Reading Freud: Explorations and Entertainments 1990, The Cultivation of Hatred 1993, The Naked Heart 1995, Pleasure Wars 1998, My German Question: Growing Up in Nazi Berlin 1998, Mozart 1999, Schnitzler's Century 2001, Savage Reprisals 2002, Modernism 2007; also trans and anthologies. *Honours:* Hon. DHumLitt (Denver) 1970, (Maryland) 1979, (Hebrew Univ. Coll., Cincinnati) 1983, (Clark Univ., Worcester) 1985; Nat. Book Award 1967, Melcher Book Award 1967, Gold Medal for Historical Science, Amsterdam 1990, Geschwister Scholl Prize 1999. *Address:* 760 West End Avenue, Apt 15A, New York, NY 10025, USA (home). *Telephone:* (212) 930-9257 (office); (212) 865-0577 (home). *Fax:* (212) 930-0040 (office). *E-mail:* pgay@nypl.org (office).

GAYLE, Emma (see Fairburn, Eleanor M.)

GEBEYLI, Claire; Lebanese poet and journalist; b. 1935, Alexandria, Egypt; d. of Nicolas Dimitriou and Efy Sevastopoulo; m. Michel Gebeyli (deceased); two c. *Education:* Univ. of Alexandria, Egypt, Higher Inst. of Social Sciences, Greece. *Career:* Assoc. Ed. and columnist, L'Orient-le Jour newspaper 1967–; Lecturer, St Joseph's Univ., Beirut; mem. New York Acad. of Sciences 1995. *Publications:* poetry: Poésies latentes 1968, Mémorial d'exil 1975, Cantate pour l'oiseau mort (Albert Camus Prize) 1996; contrib. to La Corde Raide magazine, The Poetry of Arab Women: A Contemporary Anthology 2001. *Honours:* Nat. Order of Merit (Greece); Edgar Allen Poe Prize 1985, Int. Prize for Literature. *Address:* L'Orient-le Jour, Société Générale de Presse et d'Édition SAL, Damascus road, mounted Fiyaddiyé, 200m after Total petrol station, Beirut 11-2488, Lebanon (office). *Telephone:* (5) 956444 (office). *Fax:* (5) 957444 (office). *E-mail:* redaction@lorientlejour.com (office). *Website:* www .lorientlejour.com (office).

GÉBLER, Carlo, BA, PhD; Irish writer, filmmaker, prison teacher and academic; *Honorary Lecturer, Queen's University, Belfast*; b. 21 Aug. 1954, Dublin; s. of Ernest Gébler and Edna O'Brien; m. Tyga Thomason 1990; three s. two d. *Education:* Univ. of York, Nat. Film and Television School, Queen's University Belfast. *Career:* part-time teacher of creative writing, HM Prison Maze, Co. Antrim 1993–95; Writer-in-Residence, HM Prison Maghaberry, Co. Antrim 1997–; Temp. Lecturer in Creative Writing, Queen's Univ., Belfast 2006–07, Royal Literary Fund Fellow 2008–10, Hon. Lecturer 2010–; mem. Aosdána (Ireland) 1990; British Council Int. Writing Fellow, Trinity Coll., Dublin 2004, Arts Council Writing Fellow 2006, Visiting Fellow 2009, Visiting Lecturer 2010. *Television:* Put to the Test (Royal Television Soc. Best Regional Documentary Award 1999). *Publications:* The Eleventh Summer 1985, August in July 1986, Work & Play 1987, Driving Through Cuba 1988, Malachy and His Family 1990, The Glass Curtain: Inside an Ulster Community 1991, Life of a Drum 1991, The Witch That Wasn't 1991, The Cure 1994, W9 and Other Lives 1998 (revised reprint 2011), How to Murder a Man 1998, Frozen Out 1998, The Base 1999, Father & I 2000, Dance of Death 2000, Caught on a Train (Bisto Merit Award 2001) 2001, 10 Rounds 2002, August '44 2003, The Siege of Derry 2005, The Bull Raid 2005, Silhouette (short play, in How Long is Never? Darfur – a response) 2007, A Good Day for a Dog 2008, My Father's Watch (with Patrick Maguire) 2008, The Suicide Book 2009, Charles & Mary 2011, The Dead Eight 2011. *Literary Agent:* c/o Antony Harwood, 103 Walton Street, Oxford, OX2 6EB, England. *Telephone:* (1865) 559615; (1865) 513462. *Fax:* (1865) 310660. *E-mail:* ant@antonyharwood.com. *Website:* www.antonyharwood.com.

GEDDES, Gary Richard, BA, DipEd, MA, PhD; Canadian writer, poet and fmr academic; *Adjunct Professor in Creative Writing, University of British Columbia*; b. 9 June 1940, Vancouver, BC; s. of Laurie James Geddes and Hazel Lilian Irene Turner; m. 1st Norma Joan Fugler 1963 (divorced 1969); one d.; m. 2nd Jan Macht 1973 (divorced 1998); two d.; m. 3rd Ann Eriksson 2007; one step-s. one step-d. *Education:* Univ. of British Columbia, Univ. of Reading, Univ. of Toronto. *Career:* Lecturer, Carleton Univ., Ottawa, Ont. 1971–72, Univ. of Victoria, BC 1972–74; Writer-in-Residence, Univ. of Alberta, Edmonton 1976–77, Visiting Asst Prof. 1977–78; Assoc. Prof., Concordia Univ., Montreal 1978–79, Prof. of English 1979–98; Distinguished Prof. of Canadian Culture, Western Washington Univ. 1998–2001; Writer-in-Residence, Univ. of Ottawa 2004, Green Coll. 2005, Univ. of British Columbia 2005, Vancouver Public Library 2006, Vancouver Community Coll., Malaspina Coll.; currently Adjunct Prof. in Creative Writing, Univ. of British Columbia; mem. League of Canadian Poets, Writers' Union of Canada, Playwright's Guild of Canada, PEN Canada. *Publications:* poetry: Poems 1971, Rivers Inlet 1972, Snakeroot 1973, Letter of the Master of Horse 1973, War and Other Measures 1976, The Acid Test 1980, The Terracotta Army 1984, Changes of State 1986, Hong Kong 1987, No Easy Exit/Salida difícil 1989, Light of Burning Towers 1990, Girl By the Water 1994, Perfect Cold Warrior 1995, Active Trading: Selected Poems 1970–95, 1996, Flying Blind 1998, Skaldance 2004, Falsework 2007, Swimming Ginger 2010; short stories: The Unsettling of the West 1986; non-fiction: Letters from Managua: Meditations on Politics and Art 1990, Sailing Home: A Journey Through Time, Place and Memory 2001, Kingdom of Ten Thousand Things: An Impossible Journey from Kabul to Chiapas 2005, Drink the Bitter Root: A Writer's Search for Justice and Redemption in Africa 2011; play: Les Maudits Anglais 1984; criticism: Conrad's Later Novels 1980, Out of the Ordinary: Politics, Poetry & Narrative 2009; translation: I Didn't Notice the Mountain Growing Dark, by Li Bai and Du Fu (with George Liang) 1986; editor: 20th Century Poetry and Poetics 1969 and four subsequent edns, 15 Canadian Poets (with Phyllis Bruce) 1970 and three subsequent edns, Skookum Wawa: Writings of the Canadian Northwest 1975, Divided We Stand 1977, Chinada: Memoirs of the Gang of Seven 1983, The Inner Ear: An Anthology of New Canadian Poets 1983, Vancouver: Soul of a City 1986, Compañeros: Writings about Latin America (with Hugh Hazelton) 1990, The Art of Short Fiction: An International Anthology 1992. *Honours:* Hon. DJurs (Royal Roads Univ.) 2007; E.J. Pratt Medal, Canadian Authors Asscn Nat. Poetry Prize, Commonwealth Poetry Prize (Americas Region) 1985, Writers Choice Award, National Magazine Gold Award, Archibald Lampman Prize, Gabriela Mistral Prize 1996, Poetry Book Society Recommendation 1996, Lt-Gov.'s Award for Literary Excellence 2008. *Address:* Box 13-3, 81 Blue Heron Road, Thetis Island, BC V0R 2Y0, Canada (home). *Telephone:* (250) 246-8176 (office). *E-mail:* gedworks@islandnet.com (office).

GEDDES, John M., MA; American newspaper editor; *Managing Editor, The New York Times*; b. 1952. *Education:* Univs. of RI and Wis. *Career:* reporter Ansonia Evening Sentinel, Ansonia, Conn. 1976; reporter Associated Press-Dow Jones News Service, NY 1976–78, Bonn, Germany 1978–79; econs corresp. The Times, Bonn 1979–80; joined Wall Street Journal 1980, various positions including Bureau Chief, Bonn, Deputy Man. Ed. then Man. Ed. European Edn, News Ed., Asst Man. Ed., Sr Ed. and Nat. News Ed. –1993; fmr Prin. Friday Holdings; CEO BIS Strategic Decisions (market research co.) 1993–94; Business and Financial Ed. New York Times 1994–97, Deputy Man. Ed. 1997–2003, Man. Ed. for News Operations 2003–. *Address:* The New York Times, 620 Eighth Avenue, New York, NY 10018, USA (office). *Telephone:* (212) 556-1234 (office). *Website:* www.nytimes.com (office).

GEDGE, Pauline Alice; Canadian writer; b. 11 Dec. 1945, Auckland, New Zealand; m. Bernie Ramanauskas; two s. *Education:* Univ. of Manitoba. *Publications:* Child of the Morning 1977, The Eagle and the Raven 1978, Stargate 1982, The Twelfth Transforming 1984, Mirage 1990, The Covenant 1992, House of Dreams 1994, House of Illusions 1997, The Hippopotamus Marsh: Lords of the Two Lands (Vol. One) 1998, The Oasis: Lords of the Two Lands (Vol. Two) 1999, The Horus Road: Lords of the Two Lands(Vol. Three) 2000, The Twice Born 2007, Seer of Egypt 2008, The Kings Man 2011. *Honours:* Jeanne Boujassy Award, Société des Gens de Lettres, France 1978, Winner, New Novelist Competition, Alberta Culture 1978, Best Novel of the Year Award, Writers Guild of Alberta 1984. *Address:* c/o Bella Pomer, Bella Pomer Agency, 355 St. Clair Avenue West, Suite 801, Toronto, ON M5P 1N5, Canada. *Website:* www.paulinegedge.com.

GEE, Maggie Mary, OBE, MA, BLitt (Oxon.), PhD, FRSL; British author, journalist and lecturer; *Visiting Professor in Creative Writing, Sheffield Hallam University*; b. 2 Nov. 1948, Poole, Dorset, England; d. of V. V. Gee and Aileen Gee (née Church); m. Nicholas Rankin 1983; one d. *Education:* Horsham High School, Somerville Coll., Oxford, Wolverhampton Polytechnic. *Career:* Research Asst, Wolverhampton Polytechnic 1975–79; Eastern Arts Writing Fellow, Univ. of E Anglia 1982; Visiting Fellow, Sussex Univ. 1986–96, Teaching Fellow 1996–; Writer-in-Residence Northern Arts 1996; Visiting Lecturer, Northumbria Univ. 1999–; Writer-in-Residence, Kingston Univ. 2003–; Visiting Prof. in Creative Writing, Sheffield Hallam Univ. 2006–; regular reviews in Daily Telegraph, Sunday Times; judge Booker Prize 1989; Fellow, RSL (mem. Council 1999–, Chair. Council 2004–08, Vice-Pres. 2008–); Hawthornden Fellow 1989, 2002, 2009; mem. Soc. of Authors man. cttee 1991–94; mem. Cttee PLR 2000–07. *Publications:* fiction: Dying, in Other Words 1981, The Burning Book 1983, Light Years 1985, Grace 1988, Where Are the Snows? 1991, Christopher and Alexandra 1992, Lost Children 1994, The Ice People 1998, The White Family 2002, The Flood 2004, My Cleaner 2005, The Blue (short stories) 2006, My Driver 2009; non-fiction: Anthology of Writing Against War: For Life on Earth (ed.) 1982, How May I Speak in My Own Voice? Language and the Forbidden 1995, NW15: The Anthology of New Writing (co-ed. with Bernardine Evaristo) 2007, My Animal Life (memoir) 2010; contrib. to Diaspora City: The London New Writing Anthology 2003. *Honours:* Hon. Fellow, Univ. of Sussex 1986–; Best of Young British Novelists 1982. *Literary Agent:* c/o Karolina Sutton, Curtis Brown Ltd, 28–29 Haymarket, London, SW1Y 4SP, England. *Telephone:* (20) 7393-4400.

GEE, Maurice Gough, MA; New Zealand novelist; b. 22 Aug. 1931, Whakatane; m. Margaretha Garden 1970; one s. two d. *Education:* Avondale Coll., Auckland, Auckland Univ. *Career:* school teacher, librarian, other casual employment 1954–75; Robert Burns Fellow, Univ. of Otago 1964; Writing Fellow, Vic. Univ. of Wellington 1989; Katherine Mansfield Memorial Fellow, Menton, France 1992. *Publications include:* Plumb 1978, Meg 1981, Sole Survivor 1983, Collected Stories 1986, Prowlers 1987, The Burning Boy 1990, Going West 1992, Crime Story 1994, Loving Ways 1996, Live Bodies 1998, Ellie and the Shadow Man 2001, The Scornful Moon 2004, Blindsight (Deutz Medal for Fiction 2006, Montana New Zealand Book Award for Fiction 2006) 2005; juvenile fiction includes: Under the Mountain 1979, The O Trilogy 1982–85, The Fat Man 1994; also scripts for film and TV. *Honours:* Hon. DLitt (Victoria) 1987, (Auckland) 2004; NZ Fiction Award 1976, 1979, 1982, 1991, 1993, NZ Book of the Year Award (Wattle Award) 1979, 1993, James Tait Black Memorial Prize 1979, NZ Children's Book of the Year Award 1986, 1995, Prime Minister's Prize 2004. *Address:* 56 Nile Street, 7010 Nelson, New Zealand (home).

GEE, Shirley; British dramatist; b. 25 April 1932, London, England; m. Donald Gee 1965; two s. *Education:* Webber-Douglas Acad. of Music and Drama. *Career:* mem. Soc. of Authors, Writers Guild. *Publications:* Stones 1974, Moonshine 1977, Typhoid Mary 1979, Bedrock 1982, Never in My Lifetime (BBC Giles Cooper Award) 1983, Susan Smith Blackburn Prize 1985, Samuel Beckett Award) 1983, Flights 1984, Long Live the Babe 1985, Ask for the Moon 1986, Against the Wind 1988, Warrior 1989; other: stage adaptations, including The Forsyte Saga (co-adapter), children's poems, stories and songs. *Honours:* Radio Times Drama Bursary Award 1974, Pye Award 1979, Jury's Special Commendation Prix Italia 1979, Giles Cooper Awards 1979, 1983, Sony Award 1983, Samuel Beckett Award 1984 Susan Smith Blackburn Prize 1985.

GEHLHOFF-CLAES, Astrid Veronica, PhD; German writer; b. 6 Jan. 1928, Leverkusen; d. of Heinrich Claes and Wilma Claes; m. Joachim Gehlhoff 1957; two d. *Education:* Univ. of Cologne. *Career:* writer 1956–; Founder-Chair. Org. for writers working with prisoners 1975–88; Deutsche Literaturfonds Scholarship 1985; Guest, Villa Massimo 1991, 1992. *Publications include:* poetry: Der Mannequin 1956, Meine Stimme mein Schiff 1962, Gegen Abend ein Orangenbaum 1983, Nachruf auf einen Papagei 1989; play: Didos Tod 1964; short stories: Erdbeereis 1980; novel: Abschied von der Macht 1987, Juselu der Erinnerung 2002; publisher: Else Lasker-Schüler: Briefe an Karl Kraus 1959, 1960, Bis die Tür aufbricht: Literatur hinter Gittern (anthology) 1982, Einen Baum umarmen: Briefwechsel mit Felix Kamphausen 1976–91; trans. to German of books by Henry James; literary science: Der lyrische Sprachstil 2003. *Honours:* Bundesverdienstkreuz, First Class 1986, Verdienstorden des Landes Nordrhein-Westfalen 1990; Förderungspreis zum Gerhart-Hauptmann-Preis, Freie Volksbühne Berlin 1962, Förderungspreis zum Immermann-Preis, Düsseldorf 1965, Früde Drasbe Gabe, Düsseldorf 2003. *Address:* Rheinallee 133, 40545 Düsseldorf (home); c/o Grupello Verlag Bruno Kehrein, Schwerinstrasse 55, 40476 Düsseldorf, Germany (office). *Telephone:* (211) 555925 (home).

GEIER, Joan Austin, BS; American poet and writer; b. 6 March 1934, New York, NY; m. Walter Geier 1956; two s. one d. *Education:* Hunter Coll., CUNY. *Career:* mem. Brooklyn Poetry Circle, Poetry Soc. of America. *Publications:* Garbage Can Cat 1976, Mother of Tribes 1987, A Formal Feeling Comes 1994; contributions: Good Housekeeping, Christian Science Monitor, New York Newsday, Catholic Digest, Poetry Society of America Quarterly, SPSM&H, A Formal Feeling Comes, The Lyric, Poetpourri, Negative Capability, Hiram Poetry Review. *Honours:* Poetry Awards, World Order of Narrative Poets 1980, 1987, 1990, 1992, Gustav Davidson Award, Poetry Soc. of America 1982, John Masefield Award, World Order of Narrative Poets 1983, Amelia Special Award for Haiku 1985. *Address:* 39–91 48th Street, Sunnyside, NY 11104-1021, USA (home). *Telephone:* (718) 899-5919 (home). *Website:* joanaustingeier.wordpress.com.

GEIMAN, Leonid Mikhailovich, DrTechSci; Russian scientific publisher; b. 12 Aug. 1934, Moscow. *Education:* Moscow Ore Inst. *Career:* researcher, ore industry research orgs; Head of Div. Publrs' Sovietskaya Encyclopaedia 1963–88; Prof., Moscow Ore Inst.; researcher, All-Union Inst. of Foreign Geology; f. Ind. Encyclopaedic Ed. House (ETA); Pres. Encyclopaedic Creative Asscn; mem. Russian Acad. of Natural Sciences 1992, Academician-Sec. Dept of Encyclopaedia. *Publications:* Russian Encyclopaedia of Banks 1995, Russian National Electronic Encyclopaedia 1995, Encyclopaedia of Moscow Streets 1996, Encyclopaedia America 1997. *Address:* c/o Russian Academy of Natural Sciences, Varshavskoye shosse 8, 113105 Moscow, Russia.

GEISMAR, Ludwig Leo, MA, PhD; American academic (retd) and writer; b. 25 Feb. 1921, Mannheim, Germany; m. Shirley Ann Cooperman 1948; three d. *Education:* Univ. of Minnesota, Hebrew Univ., Jerusalem. *Career:* co-ordinator of Social Research, Ministry of Social Welfare, Israel, 1954–56; Research Dir, Family Centred Project, St Paul, Minnesota, USA, 1956–59; Assoc. Prof., 1959–62, Prof., Social Work and Sociology, Dir, Social Work Research Center, Grad. School of Social Work and Dept of Sociology, 1963–91, Rutgers Univ. *Publications:* Understanding the Multi-Problem Family: A Conceptual Analysis and Exploration in Early Identification (with M. A. LaSorte) 1964, The Forgotten Neighborhood: Site of an Early Skirmish in the War on Poverty (with J. Krisberg) 1967, Preventive Intervention in Social Work 1969, Family and Community Functioning 1971, Early Supports for Family Life 1972, 555 Families: A Social Psychological Study of Young Families in Transition 1973, Families in an Urban Mold (with S. Geismar) 1979, A Quarter Century of Social Work Education (ed. with M. Dinerman) 1984, Family and Delinquency: Resocializing the Young Offender (with K. Wood) 1986, Families at Risk (with K. Wood) 1989, The Family Functioning Scale: A Guide to Research and Practice (with M. Camasso) 1993, In the Shadow of the Holocaust 2005. *Honours:* Presidential Citation, Rutgers Univ. 1990. *Address:* 1050 George Street, Apt 9L, New Brunswick, NJ 08901-1016, USA (home).

GELLIS, Roberta Leah, (Max Daniels, Priscilla Hamilton, Leah Jacobs), BA, MS; American author; b. (Roberta Leah Jacobs), 27 Sept. 1927, New York, NY; d. of Morris Boris Jacobs and Margaret Segall; m. Charles Gellis 1947; one s. *Education:* Hunter Coll., City Univ. of New York, Brooklyn Polytechnic Inst. *Career:* chemist, Foster D. Snell Inc. 1947–53; copy ed., McGraw Hill Book Co. 1953–55; freelance ed. 1955–2000. *Publications include:* Knight's Honor 1964, Bond of Blood 1965, The Dragon and the Rose 1977, The Sword and the Swan 1977, The Space Guardian (as Max Daniels) 1978, The Roselynde Chronicles series: Roselynde 1978, Alinor 1978, Joanna 1979, Gilliane 1980, Rhiannon 1982, Sybelle 1983, Desiree 2005 (Romantic Times Bookclub Award); The Love Token (as Priscilla Hamilton) 1979; The Royal Dynasty series: Siren Song 1980, Winter Song 1982, Fire Song 1984, A Silver Mirror 1989; The Napoleonic Era series: The English Heiress 1980, The Cornish Heiress 1981, The Kent Heiress 1982, Fortune's Bride 1983, A Woman's Estate 1984; The Tales of Jernaeve series: Tapestry of Dreams 1985, Fires of Winter 1986; Irish Magic 1995, Shimmering Splendor 1995, Enchanted Fire 1996, Irish Magic II 1997; Dazzling Brightness 1994; Bull God 2000, Thrice Bound 2001, Overstars Mail Imperial Challenge 2004; A Mortal Bane 1999, A Personal Devil 2001, Bone of Contention 2002, Chains of Folly 2006, Lucrezia Borgia and the Mother of Poisons 2003; (with Mercedes Lackey) This Scepter'd Isle 2004, Ill Met by Moonlight (with Mercedes Lackey) 2005, By Slanderous Tongues (with Mercedes Lackey) 2007, And Less Than Kind (with Mercedes Lackey) 2008. *Honours:* Romance Writers of America Lifetime Achievement Award 1986, Romantic Times Award for Best Medieval Novel 1985, 1988, Romantic Times Lifetime Achievement Award for Historical Fantasy 1994–95. *Literary Agent:* c/o Lucienne Day, Knight Agency, 570 East Avenue, Madison, GA 30650, USA. *Telephone:* (813) 996-5901; (646) 872-3168 (mobile). *E-mail:* lucienne.diver@knightagency.net. *Fax:* (765) 471-2206 (home). *E-mail:* roberta.gellis@gmail.com (office). *Website:* www.robertagellis.com.

GELMAN, Aleksandr Isaakovich; Russian playwright and scriptwriter; b. 25 Oct. 1933, Moldavia; m. Tatyana Pavlovna Kaletskaya; two s. *Education:* Kishinev Univ. *Career:* mem. CPSU 1956–90; worked in factories 1956–67; corresp. for daily papers 1967–71; wrote scripts for series of documentary films 1971–74; worked with Moscow Art Theatre; People's Deputy of the USSR 1989–91. *Film scripts include:* Night Shift 1971, Consider me Grown Up 1974, Xenia, Fyodor's Favourite Wife 1974 (all with T. Kaletskaya), Prize 1975, Feedback (Best Script Writer, All-Union Film Festival 1978) 1977, Clumsy Man 1979, We, the Undersigned 1981, Zinulya 1984, We Met in a Strange Way 1990, Gorbachev: After the Empire 2001, Arie (with Roman Kachanov) 2004. *Theatre work includes:* Feedback 1976, We, the Undersigned 1979, The Bench 1983, Zinulya 1984, Misha's Party (co-author), Pretender 1999, The Most Recent Future 2010, Back, Connection,A Man with Connections, The Bonus. *Television documentary:* Gorbachev: After Empire 2001. *Publication:* Book of Plays 1985. *Honours:* USSR State Prize 1976. *Address:* Tverskoy, Blvd 3, Apartment 12, 103104 Moscow, Russia (home). *Telephone:* (495) 202-68-59 (home). *E-mail:* idcg@cityline.ru.

GELMAN, Juan; Argentine poet and writer; b. 1930, Buenos Aires. *Career:* Ed. Panorama 1969, Crisis 1973; Dir of literary supplement to La Opinión 1971; Bd mem. of newspaper, Noticias 1974; Correspondent Página 12; political exile in Europe 1976–89. *Publications:* Violín y otras cuestiones 1956, El juego en que andamos 1959, Velorio del solo 1961, Gotán 1956–1962 1962, Cólera Buey 1965, Los poemas de Sidney West 1969, Fábulas 1971, Relaciones 1973, Hechos 1974–1978 1978, Comentarios 1978–1979, Notas 1979, Citas 1979, Carta Abierta 1980, Si dulcemente 1980, Bajo la lluvia ajena 1980, Hacia el Sur 1982, Com/posiciones 1983–1984 1986, Exilio 1984, Eso 1983–1984, Dibaxu 1983–1985, La junta luz: Oratorio a las madres de Plaza de Mayo 1985, Com-posiciones 1986, Anunciaciones 1988, Interrupciones I 1988, Interrupciones II 1988, Carta a mi madre 1989, Salarios del impío 1984–1992 1993, La abierta oscuridad 1993, Sombra y vuelta y de ida 1997, Incompletamente 1997, Debí decir te amo 1997, Ni el flaco perdón de Diós/ Hijos de desaparecidos (with Mara La Madrid) 1997, Prosa de prensa 1997, Nueva prosa de prensa 1999, Tantear la noche 2000, Valer la pena 2002, Afganistán/Iraq: el imperio empantanado 2003, País que fue será 2004, Miradas 2005, Mundar 2007, De atrásalante en su porfía 2009, El emperrado corazón amora 2011; contribs to numerous anthologies. *Honours:* Hon. Prof., Univ. of Buenos Aires 2003, Cultural Amb. of the City of Buenos Aires 2006; Dr hc (Universidad Nacional General San Martín) 2001, (Universidad de Buenos Aires) 2003, (Universidad Nacional de Quilmes) 2006, (Causa de l'Université Lille, France) 2010; Nat. Poetry Prize 1997, Juan Rulfo Prize in Latin American and Caribbean Literature (Mexico) 2000, Pablo Neruda Prize (Chile) 2005, Queen Sofía Prize in Ibero-American Poetry (Spain) 2005,

Cervantes Prize (Spain) 2007, Premio Alfaguara 2008, Tibetan Antelope Award, Asscn of Chinese Poets 2009, Universal Gallego Writer Award (Spain) 2010, Cultural Award of Merit (Mexico) 2011, Latino Poets of the World Award (Mexico) 2011, Culture Award, Univ. of Cordoba 2011. *E-mail:* gelmaniana@juangelman.net. *Website:* www.juangelman.net.

GEN, Getsu; Japanese novelist; b. (Gen Minehide), 10 Feb. 1965, Osaka. *Publications:* novels: Ikyo no otoshigo (Born Out of Wedlock in a Foreign Land) 1998, Oppai (Breasts) 1998, Kage no sumika (A Dwelling in the Shade) (Akutagawa Prize) 1999.

GENET, Jacqueline Hélène Juliette Valentine, DèsL; French academic; *Professor Emerita, University of Caen;* b. 24 Feb. 1932, Evreux; d. of Jean Veyssié and Hélène Veyssié (née Delarue); m. Jean Genet 1961; two s. *Education:* Ecole Normale Supérieure de Sèvres, Univ. of Oxford, UK and Univ. of Paris-Sorbonne. *Career:* secondary school teacher 1957–66; Lecturer, later Sr Lecturer, Univ. of Limoges 1966–74; Sr Lecturer, Univ. of Caen 1974–77, Prof. 1977–92, Prof. Emer. 1992–, Pres. Univ. of Caen 1983–88; Pres. Soc. des Anglicistes de l'Enseignement Supérieur 1990–92; fmr Vice-Pres. Int. Asscn for the Study of Anglo-Irish Literature. *Publications:* W. B. Yeats: les fondements et l'évolution de la création poétique: Essai de psychologie littéraire 1976, La poétique de W. B. Yeats 1990, Le Théâtre de W. B. Yeats 1995, Words for Music Perhaps: Yeats's 'new art' 2010; numerous works of criticism, articles and translations. *Honours:* Chevalier, Ordre nat. du Mérite, Commdr des Palmes académiques; Dr hc (Nat. Univ. of Ireland) 1990, (Würzburg) 1995. *Address:* University of Caen, Esplanade de la Paix, 14032 Caen (office); 13 rue de Bretteville, 14000 Caen, France (home). *Telephone:* (2) 31-85-21-78 (home). *E-mail:* jacqueline.genet2@wanadoo.fr (home).

GENOVESE, Eugene Dominick, BA, MA, PhD; American academic and writer; b. 19 May 1930, New York City; m. Elizabeth Ann Fox 1969. *Education:* Brooklyn Coll., CUNY and Columbia Univ. *Career:* Asst Prof., Polytechnical Inst., Brooklyn 1958–63; Assoc. Prof., Rutgers Univ. 1963–67; Prof. of History, Sir George Williams Univ., Montréal 1967–69, Social Science Research Fellow 1968–69; Visiting Prof., Columbia Univ. 1967, Yale Univ. 1969; Prof. of History, Univ. of Rochester 1969–90, Distinguished Prof. of Arts and Sciences 1985–90; Pitt Prof. of American History and Insts, Univ. of Cambridge, England 1976–77; Sunderland Fellow and Visiting Prof. of Law, Univ. of Michigan 1979; Visiting Mellon Prof., Tulane Univ. 1986; Distinguished Scholar-in-Residence, Univ. Center, Ga 1990–95; Richard Watson Gilder Fellow, Columbia Univ. 1959, Center for Advanced Study in the Behavioral Sciences Fellow, Stanford, Calif. 1972–73, Nat. Humanities Center Fellow, Research Triangle Park, North California 1984–85, Mellon Fellow 1987–88, Guggenheim Fellowship 1987–88, Fellow, American Acad. of Arts and Sciences; mem. Historical Soc. (fmr Pres.), Nat. Asscn of Scholars. *Publications:* The Political Economy of Slavery 1965, The World the Slaveholders Made 1969, In Red and Black 1971, Roll, Jordan, Roll 1974, From Rebellion to Revolution 1979, Fruits of Merchant Capital (with Elizabeth Fox-Genovese) 1983, The Slaveholder's Dilemma 1991, The Southern Tradition 1994, The Southern Front 1995, A Consuming Fire 1998, The Mind of the Master Class (with Elizabeth Fox-Genovese) 2005, Slavery in Black and White (co-author) 2008, Miss Betsey: A Memoir of Marriage 2009; contrib. to scholarly journals. *Honours:* Bancroft Prize 1994. *Address:* 1487 Sheridan Walk NE, Atlanta, GA 30324, USA. *Telephone:* (404) 634-0596 (home).

GENTLE, Mary Rosalyn, (Roxanne Morgan), BA, MA; British writer; b. 29 March 1956, Sussex, England. *Publications:* A Hawk in Silver 1977, Golden Witchbreed 1983, The Harvest of Wolves 1983, Ancient Light 1987, Scholars and Soldiers 1989, Rats and Gargoyles 1990, The Architecture of Desire 1991, Grunts! 1992, Left to His Own Devices 1994, Human Waste 1994, Ash: A Secret History (British Science Fiction Asscn Award) 2000, White Crow 2003, 1610: A Sundial in a Grave 2003, Ilario: The Lion's Eye 2006, The Stone Golem 2007, The Black Opera 2012; as Roxanne Morgan: Dares 1995, Bets 1997, A Game of Masks 1999, Sinner Takes All 2000, Degrees of Desire 2001, Maximum Exposure 2004; Co-Ed.: The Weerde Book 1 1992, Villains! 1992, The Weerde Book 2, The Book of the Ancients 1993, A Secret History: The Book of Ash #1 1999, Carthage Ascendant: The Book of Ash #2, 2000, The Wild Machines, The Book of Ash #2 2000, Lost Burgundy, The Book of Ash #4 2000, Ash: A Secret History 2000; contrib. to reviews. *Honours:* BSFA Award for Best Novel 2000, Sidewise Award for Alternative History, Best Long Fiction Award 2000. *Address:* 29 Sish Lane, Stevenage, England.

GEORGE, (Susan) Elizabeth, MS; American author; b. 26 Feb. 1949, Warren, OH; d. of Robert George and Anne George; m. 1st Ira Toibin 1971 (divorced 1995); m. 2nd Thomas McCabe 2002. *Education:* Foothill Community Coll., Univ. of California and California State Univ. *Career:* teacher, El Toro High School, Calif. 1975–87, Coastline Community Coll., Fountainvalley, Calif. 1988–92; has lectured at Irvine Valley Coll., Irvine, Calif. 1989, Univ. of Calif. Extension 1990, Edinboro Univ. Summer School at Exeter Coll., Oxford, UK 1993, Univ. of British Columbia, Canada 1993, Univ. of Oklahoma 1995. *Television:* The Inspector Lynley Mysteries (BBC Productions). *Publications:* A Great Deliverance (Anthony Award, Bouchercon XXI 1989, Agatha Award, Malice Domestic 1989, Le Grand Prix de Literature Policière, Mystery Writers of France 1990) 1988, Payment in Blood 1989, Well-Schooled in Murder (MIMI Award 1991) 1990, Sisters in Crime, Vol. II – The Evidence Exposed 1990, A Suitable Vengeance 1991, For the Sake of Elena 1992, Missing Joseph 1993, A Novel by Any Other Name 1994, Playing for the Ashes 1994, In the Presence of the Enemy 1996, Women on the Case (ed.) 1996, Deception on His Mind 1998, In Pursuit of the Proper Sinner 1999, A Traitor to Memory 2001, I, Richard 2002, Crime From the Mind of a Woman (ed.) 2002, A Place of Hiding 2003, Write Away 2004, A Moment on the Edge (ed.) 2004, With No One as Witness 2005, What Came Before He Shot Her 2006, Careless in Red 2008, This Body of Death 2010. *Honours:* Hon. DHumLitt (Calif. State Univ.); numerous honours and awards including the establishment of The Elizabeth George Collection at Boston Univ. 1989, One of Forty Graduates Who Have Made a Difference, Univ. of California, Riverside 1994, Visions and Visionaries, Honoring Six Graduates from California State Univ., Fullerton. *Literary Agent:* Deborah Schneider, 250 West 57th Street, New York, NY 10107, USA. *Address:* 4111 Shorebreak Drive, Huntington Beach, CA 92649, USA (home). *Website:* www.elizabethgeorgeonline.com.

GEORGE, François, (Mathurin Maugarlonne); French writer and philosopher; b. 1947, Sceaux. *Career:* mem. editorial bd, Les Temps Modernes 1977–; founder mem., Asscn des amis d'Arsène Lupin. *Publications include:* Autopsie de Dieu 1965, Prof à T. 1974, Deux études sur Sartre 1976, La Loi et le phénomène 1978, Souvenirs de la maison Marx 1980, Staline à Paris 1982, Histoire personnelle de la France 1983, Alceste vous salue bien 1988, Plan de la nuit, De Bonaparte et de l'exception gaulliste, Arsène Lupin, gentilhomme-philospheur (with André Comte-Sponville) 1996, Traité de l'ombre 2000, Un Philosophe dans la résistance 2001, À la rencontre des disparus 2004, Le Concept d'existence: deux études sur Sartre 2005, Caverne cosmos 2006, Retour à Merleau-Ponty 2007. *Address:* c/o Éditions Grasset, 61 rue des Saints-Pères, 75006 Paris, France (office). *Website:* www.grasset.fr (office).

GEORGE, Kathleen Elizabeth, BA, MA, MFA, PhD; American academic, dramatist and writer; *Professor of Theatre, University of Pittsburgh;* b. 7 July 1943, Johnstown, PA; m. Hilary Thomas Masters 1994. *Education:* Univ. of Pittsburgh. *Career:* Asst Prof., Carlow College 1968–76; Asst Prof., Univ. of Pittsburgh 1976–81, Assoc. Prof. 1981–2001, Prof. of Theatre 2001–. *Publications:* Rhythm in Drama 1980, Playwriting: The First Workshop 1994, The Man in the Buick and Other Stories 1999, Taken 2002, Fallen 2004, Afterimage 2007, The Odds 2009; various short fiction; contrib. to reviews and journals. *Honours:* Virginia Center for the Arts Fellowships 1980–83, Pennsylvania Arts Council Grants 1982, 1987, MacDowell Colony Fellowships 1996, 2002, Mary Anderson Center Fellowship 1996. *E-mail:* kathy@kathleengeorgebooks.com (office). *Website:* www.kathleengeorge.net.

GERAS, Adèle Daphne, BA; British writer and poet; b. 15 March 1944, Jerusalem; m. Norman Geras 1967; two d. *Education:* St Hilda's Coll., Oxford. *Career:* mem. Soc. of Authors. *Publications include:* Facing the Light 2003, Other Echoes 2004, Ithaka 2005, Hester's Story 2005, Made in Heaven 2006, A Hidden Life 2007; contrib. to anthologies, reviews and journals. *Honours:* Winner, Smith-Doorstop Pamphlet Competition 1987, Jewish Quarterly Poetry Prize 1993, Arts Council Award 2000, A. E. Housman Poetry Award 2000. *Address:* 10 Danesmoor Road, Manchester, M20 3JS, England (home). *E-mail:* adele@adelegeras.com (office). *Website:* www.adelegeras.com.

GERDES, Eckhard, BA, MA, MFA; American novelist, playwright and educator; b. 17 Nov. 1959, Atlanta, Ga; m. Persis Alisa Wilhelm 1988; three s. *Education:* Univ. of Dubuque, Roosevelt Univ., Chicago, School of the Art Inst. of Chicago. *Career:* Ed., Journal of Experimental Fiction 1994–; Instructor, Macon State Coll. 1998–. *Publications:* Projections 1986, Truly Fine Citizen 1989, Ring in a River 1994, Truly Fine Citizen 1992, Cistern Tawdry 2002, Przewalski's Horse 2006, The Million-Year Centipede, or, Liquid Structures 2007, Nin and Nan 2008, My Landlady the Lobotomist 2008, The Unwelcome Guest 2010, Hugh Moore 2010, Three Psychedelic Novellas 2011; contrib. Rampike, Oyez Review, Coe Review, Tomorrow Magazine, Planet Roc, Strong Coffee, No Magazine, Random Weirdness. *Honours:* Richard Pike Bissell Creative Writing Awards 1987, 1988.

GERGELY, Ágnes, MA, PhD; Hungarian poet, novelist and translator; b. 1933, Endröd. *Education:* ELTE Univ. of Liberal Arts, Budapest. *Career:* fmrly secondary school teacher, radio producer, Ed. of publishing house, features ed. Nagyvilág (literary magazine); Lecturer in English, ELTE Univ. of Liberal Arts, Budapest 1992–2003; currently Sr Consultant, Hungarian Investment and Trade Devt Agency. *Publications include:* novels: A tolmács 1973, A chicagói változat 1976, Stációk 1983, Örizetlenek 2000, Die Unbehüteten 2002; poetry: Requiem for a Sunbird: Forty Poems 1997. *Honours:* Hon. Fellow, Int. Writing Program, Univ. of Iowa 1973–74; Attila József Prize 1977, 1987, Déry Prize 1985, 1996, Milán Füst Prize 1994, Getz Corporation Lifetime Achievement Award, USA 1996, Kossuth Prize 2000. *Address:* Hungarian Investment and Trade Development Agency, 1061 Budapest, Andrássy út 12, Hungary (office). *Telephone:* (1) 473-8206 (office). *Fax:* (1) 472-8180 (office). *E-mail:* agnes.gergely@itd.hu (office). *Website:* www.itd.hu (office).

GERHARDT, Renata; German publisher and translator; b. 14 April 1926, Berlin; m. Rainer M. Gerhardt 1948 (died 1954); two s. *Education:* Univs of Freiburg and Heidelberg. *Career:* Co-Founder, Publ. Verlag der Fragmente, Freiburg and Breisgau –1954; Co-Ed Fragmente Int. Revue für Moderne Dichtung –1954; Founder Gerhardt Verlag, Berlin 1962, publr of Surrealist art books and literature; trans. into German of modern and avant-garde writers, including Ezra Pound, Gertrude Stein, Henry Miller, Alfred Jarry, Antonin Artaud, Vladimir Nabokov, etc. *Address:* c/o Jenaerstrasse 7, 10717 Berlin, Germany.

GERMAIN, Sylvie, PhD; French writer; b. 1948, Châteauroux. *Education:* Sorbonne, Paris. *Career:* civil servant, attached to Ministry of Culture 1981–86, taught at L'École française, Prague 1986–93, full-time novelist 1994–. *Publications:* novels: Le Livre des nuits 1985, Nuit d'Ambre 1987, Jours de colère (Prix Femina) 1989, Opéra muet 1989, L'Enfant Méduse 1991, La Pleurante des rues de Prague 1992, Immensités 1993, Eclats de sel 1996, L'Encre du poulpe 1998, Tobie des marais 1998, La Chanson des mal-aimants 2002, Ateliers de lumière 2004, Magnus (Prix Goncourt des Lycéens) 2005, Frères 2006, L'inaperçu 2008, Hors Champ 2009; essays: Les Echos du silence 1996, Céphalophores 1996, Patience et songe de lumière: Vermeer 1996, Bohuslav Reyneck à Petrov: un nomade en sa demeure 1998, Etty Hillesum 1999, Mourir un peu 2000, La Grande nuit de Toussaint, Le Temps qu'il fait 2000, Cracovie à vol d'oiseau 2000, Célébration de la Paternité 2001, J'ai envie de rompre le silence (with René Vouland and Gérard Vouland) 2001, Songes du temps 2003, Les Personnages 2004, Les Echos du Silence 2006. *Address:* c/o Albin Michel, 22 rue Huyghens, 75014 Paris, France (office). *Website:* www.albin-michel.fr (office).

GEROVA, Darina Dimitrova; Bulgarian writer and journalist; b. 2 June 1934, Sofia; d. of Dimitar Guerov and Nevena Guerova; m. Vladimir Grancharov 1962 (died 1989); two s. *Education:* Univ. of Sofia. *Career:* ed. and journalist, Trud, Zhenata dnes (Women Today), Mladeg, Narodna Cultura, Septemvri etc.; freelance 2002–. *Publications include:* novels: Noon Rain 1967, Dusty Sun 1969, Hut on the Top 1972, Hello Sun! 1976, Post Festum 1981, Eve From the Third Floor 1982 (film adaptation 1987), We Have Sinned, O Lord! 1987, Icons For Non-Believers 1990, The Pain of Woman 1995, A Date at the Seaside 2004; travel book: America, America! 2012; numerous articles, reviews, essays and short stories on educ., youth, nat. culture and status of women. *Honours:* awards from Union of Bulgarian Journalists 1968, 1987, SS Cyril and Methodius Medal (First Grade) 1983. *Address:* 1618 Sofia, Buxton bl. 19 vh. E, Bulgaria (home). *Telephone:* (2) 856-18-69 (home).

GERRARD, Nicci, (Nicci French); British writer; m. 1st Colin Hughes (divorced 1989); one s. one d.; m. 2nd Sean French 1990; two s. two d. *Education:* Univ. of Oxford. *Career:* taught English Literature in Sheffield, London and Los Angeles; joined as Acting Literary Ed. The New Statesman 1989; later Deputy Literary Ed. The Observer, then Feature Writer and Exec. Ed.; also writes with Sean French, under joint pseudonym of Nicci French. *Publications:* Soham: a Story of Our Times 2004, Things We Knew Were True 2004, Solace 2005, The Middle Place 2008, The Winter House 2009, Missing Persons 2011; as Nicci French: The Memory Game 1997, The Safe House 1998, Killing Me Softly 1999, Beneath the Skin 2000, The Red Room 2001, Land of the Living 2003, Secret Smile 2004, Catch Me When I Fall 2005, Losing You 2007, Until it's Over 2008, What to do When Someone Dies 2008, Complicit 2009, Blue Monday 2011. *Address:* The Old Rectory, Elmsett, Ipswich IP7 6NA, England (home). *E-mail:* seanicci@dircon.co.uk (home). *Website:* www.niccifrench.co.uk.

GERRISH, Brian Albert, BA, MA, STM, PhD; British/American theologian and writer; *John Nuveen Professor Emeritus, University of Chicago*; b. 14 Aug. 1931, London, England; m. 1st; one s. one d.; m. 2nd Dawn Ann De Vries 1990; one d. *Education:* Queens' Coll., Cambridge, Union Theological Seminary, New York, Columbia Univ. *Career:* Asst Pastor, West End Presbyterian Church, New York 1956–58; Tutor, Philosophy of Religion, Union Theological Seminary, New York 1957–58; Instructor, McCormick Theological Seminary, Chicago 1958–59, Asst Prof. 1959–63, Assoc. Prof. 1963–65; Assoc. Prof., Divinity School, Univ. of Chicago 1965–68, Prof. 1968–85, John Nuveen Prof. 1985–96, John Nuveen Prof. Emer. 1996–; Distinguished Service Prof. of Theology, Union Theological Seminary, Va 1996–2002; Co-Ed. Journal of Religion 1972–85; Fellow, American Acad. of Arts and Sciences. *Publications:* Grace and Reason: A Study in the Theology of Luther 1962, Tradition and the Modern World: Reformed Theology in the Nineteenth Century 1978, The Old Protestantism and the New: Essays on the Reformation Heritage 1982, A Prince of the Church: Schleiermacher and the Beginnings of Modern Theology 1984, Grace and Gratitude: The Eucharistic Theology of John Calvin 1993, Continuing the Reformation: Essays on Modern Religious Thought 1993, Saving and Secular Faith: An Invitation to Systematic Theology 1999, The Pilgrim Road: Sermons on Christian Life 2000; editor: The Faith of Christendom: A Source Book of Creeds and Confessions 1963, Reformers in Profile 1967, Reformatio Perennis: Essays on Calvin and the Reformation in Honor of Ford Lewis Battles 1981, Reformed Theology for the Third Christian Millennium: The 2001 Sprunt Lectures 2003, Thinking with the Church: Essays in Historical Theology 2010. *Honours:* Dr hc (Univ. of St Andrews, Scotland) 1984; Guggenheim Fellowship, 1970. *Address:* 9142 Sycamore Hill Place, Mechanicsville, VA 23116, USA (home). *Telephone:* (804) 550-1377 (home).

GERRITSEN, Tess, MD; American writer; b. 12 June 1953, San Diego. *Education:* Stanford Univ., Univ. of California, San Francisco. *Career:* worked as a physician before becoming a full-time writer. *Television:* film screenplay: Adrift (CBS Movie of the Week) 1993. *Publications include:* novels: Call After Midnight 1987, Under the Knife 1990, Never Say Die 1992, Whistleblower 1992, Presumed Guilty 1993, In Their Footsteps 1994, Peggy Sue Got Murdered 1994, Thief of Hearts 1995, Keeper of the Bride 1996, Harvest 1996, Life Support 1997, Bloodstream 1998, Gravity 1999, The Surgeon 2001, The Apprentice 2002, The Sinner 2003, Body Double 2004, Vanish 2005, The Mephisto Club 2006, The Bone Garden 2007, The Keepsake (aka Keeping the Dead) 2008, Ice Cold (aka The Killing Place) 2010, The Silent Girl 2012. *E-mail:* tess@tessgerritsen.com (home). *Website:* www.tessgerritsen.com.

GERSTLER, Amy, BA, MFA; American poet and writer; b. 24 Oct. 1956, San Diego, CA. *Education:* Pitzer Coll., Bennington Coll. *Career:* has taught at Antioch Coll., Univ. of California at Irvine; currently teacher, Bennington Coll., Art Center Coll. of Design, Pasadena. *Publications:* poetry: Yonder 1981, Christy's Alpine Inn 1982, White Marriage/Recovery 1984, Early Heavens 1984, The True Bride 1986, Bitter Angel 1990, Nerve Storm 1995, Crown of Weeds 1997, Medicine 2000, Ghost Girl 2004, Dearest Creature 2009; fiction: Martine's Mouth 1985, Primitive Man 1987; other: Past Lives (with Alexis Smith) 1989; contributions: magazines. *Honours:* National Book Critics Circle Award 1991. *Address:* c/o Penguin Group (USA) Inc., Penguin Poets Publicity, 375 Hudson Street, New York, NY 10014, USA (office). *Website:* www.penguingroup.com (office).

GERVAIS, Charles Henry Martin (Marty), BA, MA; Canadian poet, writer, editor and publisher; *Publisher and Editor, Black Moss Press*; b. 20 Oct. 1946, Windsor; m. Donna Wright 1968; two s. one d. *Education:* Univ. of Guelph, Univ. of Windsor. *Career:* staff, Toronto Globe and Mail 1966, Canadian Press, Toronto 1967; Reporter, Daily Commercial News, Toronto 1967, Chatham Daily News, 1972–73; Teacher of Creative Writing, St Clair Coll., Windsor 1969–71; Publisher and Ed. Black Moss Press, Windsor 1969–; Ed. Sunday Standard, Windsor 1972; General News Reporter Windsor Star 1973–74, 1976–81, Bureau Chief 1974–76, Religion Ed. 1979–80, Book Ed. 1980, Entertainment Writer 1990; Poet Laureate of Windsor 2011–; Man. Ed. The Windsor Review magazine. *Publications:* Poetry: Sister Saint Anne 1968, Something 1969, Other Marriage Vows 1969, A Sympathy Orchestra 1970, Bittersweet 1972, Poems for American Daughters 1976, The Believable Body 1979, Up Country Lines 1979, Silence Comes with Lake Voices 1980, Into a Blue Morning: Selected Poems 1982, Public Fantasy: The Maggie T. Poems 1983, Letters From the Equator 1986, Autobiographies 1989, Playing God: New Poems 1994, To Be Now: Selected Poems (City of Windsor Mayor's Award for literature) 2003, Wait For Me 2006, Lucky Days: New Poems 2009; others: The Rumrunners: A Prohibition Scrapbook 1980, Voices Like Thunder 1984, The Border Police: One Hundred and Twenty-Five Years of Policing in Windsor 1992, Seeds in the Wilderness: Profiles of World Religious Leaders 1994, From America Sent: Letters to Henry Miller 1995, Tearing Into A Summer Day (Milton Acorn People's Poetry Award, City of Windsor Mayor's Award for literature) 1996, Reno 2005, Taking My Blood 2005, My Town: Faces of Windsor 2006, The Rumrunners: The Expanded Edition 2009, Afternoons With The Devil 2010; Ed.: The Writing Life: Historical and Critical Views of the Tish Movement 1976; children's books: How Bruises Lost His Secret 1975, Doctor Troyer and the Secret in the Moonstone 1976, If I Had a Birthday Everyday 1983. *Honours:* Dr hc (Assumption Univ.) 2010; Western Ontario Newspaper Awards 1983, 1984, 1987, Toronto's Harbourfront Festival Prize 1998. *Address:* Black Moss Press, 2450 Byng Road, Windsor, ON N8W 3E8, Canada (office). *Website:* www.blackmosspress.com (office).

GERVAIS, Ricky; British writer and comedian; b. 25 June 1961, Reading, Berks., England; partner Jane Fallon. *Education:* Ashmead School, Univ. of London. *Career:* mem. pop duo Seona Dancing 1983–84; fmr entertainment officer, Univ. of London; fmr man. Suede (pop band); Music Adviser, TV drama This Life (Island World/BBC 2) 1996–97. *Plays:* Animals 2002, Politics 2004. *Television:* The 11 O'Clock Show (TalkBack/Channel 4) 1999–2000, Bruiser (BBC 2) 2000, Meet Ricky Gervais (TalkBack/Channel 4) 2000, The Office (BBC 2) 2001–03, Extras (BBC 2) 2005–07, Life's Too Short (BBC 2) 2011, Derek (Channel 4) 2012. *Radio:* BBC Radio 1, XFM London. *Films include:* Dog Eat Dog 2001, Valiant (voice) 2005, For Your Consideration 2006, Night at the Museum 2006, Stardust 2007, Ghost Town 2008, Night at the Museum: Battle of the Smithsonian 2009, The Invention of Lying 2009. *Publications include:* The Office: Scripts Series 1 2002, The Office: Scripts Series 2 2003, Flanimals (juvenile) 2004, More Flanimals 2005, Flanimals: The Story so Far 2005, Flanimals of the Deep (British Book Award for Children's Book of the Year 2007) 2006, Flanimals: A Complete Natural History 2007, Flanimals: The Day of the Bletchling 2007. *Honours:* BAFTA Awards, including Best Comedy Performance 2007, British Comedy Awards, Golden Globes (USA), Emmy Awards (USA), Hon. Rose d'Or Award, Lucerne 2006. *Address:* c/o Faber and Faber Ltd, Bloomsbury House, 74–77 Great Russell Street, London, WC1B 3DA, England (office). *Website:* www.rickygervais.com.

GERY, John Roy Octavius, AB, MA; American academic, poet and critic; *Research Professor of English, University of New Orleans*; b. (John Roy Octavius Dougherty), 2 June 1953, Reading, Pa; s. of Malcolm Dougherty and Eugenie Gunesh Guran Gery, adopted s. of Addison Harbster Gery; m. Biljana D. Obradović; one s. *Education:* Princeton Univ., Univ. of Chicago, Stanford Univ. *Career:* Lecturer, Stanford Univ. and San Jose State Univ. 1977–79; Instructor, Univ. of New Orleans (UNO) 1979–84, Asst Prof. 1984–88, Assoc. Prof. 1988–95, Prof. of English 1995–2000, Research Prof. of English 2000–; Founding Dir Ezra Pound Center for Literature, Brunnenburg, Italy 1990–; Visiting Prof., Univ. of Iowa 1991–92; Visiting Research Fellow, Inst. for Advanced Study, Univ. of Minnesota 2006; Sec., Ezra Pound Int. Conf. 2005–; mem. Editorial Bd Twentieth Century Literature, New Orleans Review, New Orleans Poetry Journal Press; Series Ed., UNO Press; mem. Acad. of American Poets, Assoc. Writing Programs, MLA, Poets and Writers. *Publications:* Charlemagne: A Song of Gestures 1983, The Burning of New Orleans 1988, Three Poems 1989, The Enemies of Leisure 1995, Nuclear Annihilation and Contemporary American Poetry 1996, For the House of Torkom (co-trans.

with Vahe Baladouni) 1999, American Ghost: Selected Poems 1999, Davenport's Version 2003, In Venice and the Veneto with Ezra Pound (co-author) 2007, A Gallery of Ghosts 2008, Hmayeak Shems (with Vahe Baladouni) 2010, Ends and Beginnings: Essays on Ezra Pound (co-ed. with William Pratt) 2011; contribs to reviews and journals. *Honours:* Deep South Writers Poetry Award 1987, Charles William Duke Long Poem Award 1987, Wesleyan Writers' Conf. Poetry Fellowship 1989, UNO Alumni Assoc. Teaching Award 1990, Nat. Endowment for the Arts Fellowship 1992–93, Critics' Choice Award for Poetry 1996, European Award Circle Franz Kafka 2000, Louisiana Artist Fellowship 2002, Summer Poet-in-Residence, Bucknell Univ. 2001, 2003, 2006, Fulbright Fellowship, Belgrade Univ. 2007, Univ. of New Orleans Alumni Asscn Excellence in Teaching Award 1990, Seraphia D. Leyda Teaching Fellowship 2009–12. *Address:* Department of English, University of New Orleans, New Orleans, LA 70148-2315, USA (office). *Telephone:* (504) 280-6361 (office). *Fax:* (504) 280-7334 (office). *E-mail:* jgery@uno.edu (office). *Website:* english.uno.edu/faculty/gery.cfm (office); lowres.uno.edu/brunnenburg (office).

GEVE, Thomas, BSc; Israeli engineer and writer; b. 1929, Germany; m. 1963; one s. two d. *Publications:* Youth in Chains 1958, Guns and Barbed Wire 1987, There Are No Children Here 1997, Aufbrüche 2000, Il n'y a pas d'enfants ici 2009. *Address:* PO Box 4727, Haifa, Israel (home).

GEVIRTZ, Susan, BA, MA, PhD; American poet, writer and professor; *Professor, MFA in Poetry, Mills College, Oakland*; b. 27 Oct. 1955, Los Angeles; one d. *Education:* Evergreen State Coll., St John's Grad. Inst., Santa Fe, NM, Univ. of California, Santa Cruz. *Career:* Teaching Asst, Univ. of California at Santa Cruz 1983–87; teacher-poet, California Poets in the Schools, San Francisco 1984–86; teacher, Aegean Coll. of Fine Arts, Paros, Greece 1985; Assoc. Ed., HOW(ever) journal 1985–90; instructor, Univ. of San Francisco 1988–89, California Coll. of Arts and Crafts, Oakland 1989–91; Asst Prof., Hutchins School of Liberal Studies, Sonoma State Univ., Rohnert Park, CA 1989–98; Prof., MFA in Poetry Programs, Univ. of San Francisco and San Francisco State Univ. 2000–; Prof., MA in Visual Criticism Program, California Coll. of the Arts 2002–05; currently Prof., MFA in Poetry, Mills Coll., Oakland, Calif. 2008–; Prof., Hellenic Int. School of the Arts, Paros, Greece; Organiser (with Greek poets Siarita Korka and Liana Sakelliou), annual Paros Symposium of US and Greek poets, translators and scholars 2004–; collaboration with interdisciplinary artist Margaret Tedesco and British sound artist Robin Rimbaud aka Scanner. *Play:* Motion Picture Home, Poet's Theater 2002. *Publications:* poetry: Korean and Milkhouse 1991, Domino: Point of Entry 1992, Linen minus 1992, Taken Place 1993, Prosthesis: Caesarea 1994, Black Box Cutaway 1998, Spelt (with Myung Mi Kim) 2000, Hourglass Transcripts 2001, Thrall 2007, Aerodrome Orion 2008, Broadcast 2008; discursive books: Feminist Poetics: A Consideration of the 'Female' Construction of Language (assoc. ed.) 1984, Narrative's Journey: The Fiction and Film Writing of Dorothy Richardson 1995; contribs to anthologies, journals and magazines. *Honours:* awards, grants and fellowships, including New Langton Arts Bay Area Award in Literature 2000. *E-mail:* susangev@gmail.com (office).

GEYER, Georgie Anne, BSc, BA; American journalist; *Syndicated Columnist, Universal Press Syndicate*; b. 2 April 1935, Chicago, Ill.; d. of Robert George Geyer and Georgie Hazel Geyer. *Education:* Northwestern Univ. and Univ. of Vienna. *Career:* reporter, Southtown Economist, Chicago 1958; Society Reporter, Chicago Daily News 1959–60, Gen. Assignment Reporter 1960–64, Latin America Corresp. 1964–67, roving Foreign Corresp., columnist 1967–75; Syndicated Columnist, Los Angeles Times Syndicate 1975–80; columnist, Universal Press Syndicate 1980–; Lyle M. Spencer Prof. of Journalism, Syracuse Univ., NY 1976; int. lecture tours on American journalism sponsored by Int. Communication Agency, Nigeria, Somalia, Tanzania, Zambia 1979, Indonesia, Philippines 1981, Belgium, Iceland, Norway, Portugal 1982; regular TV and radio appearances; Sr Fellow, Annenberg Washington Program in Communications Policy Studies 1992–; Fellow, Soc. of Professional Journalists 1992–. *Publications:* The New Latins 1970, The New 100 Years War 1972, The Young Russians 1976, Buying the Night Flight (autobiog.) 1983, Guerilla Prince: The Untold Story of Fidel Castro 1991, Waiting for Winter to End: An Extraordinary Journey Through Soviet Central Asia 1994, Americans No More: The Death of Citizenship 1996, Tunisia: a Journey Through a Country That Works 2002, When Cats Reigned Like Kings 2004. *Honours:* 21 hon. degrees (Northwestern, Loyola, Univ. of S Carolina, and others); numerous awards include American Newspaper Guild First Prize 1962, Overseas Press Club Award for Best Writing on Latin America 1967, Weintal Prize Citation Georgetown Univ. 1984, Chicago Foundation for Literature Award 1984, Alumni Award, Northwestern Univ. 1991, Retired Intelligence Officers Award 2000, Soc. of Professional Journalists Hall of Fame 2001, Chicago Headline Club Lifetime Achievement Award 2003, Woman Extraordinaire Award Int. Women Assocs 2004. *Address:* The Plaza, 800 25th Street, NW, Washington, DC 20037, USA. *Telephone:* (202) 333-9176 (office). *Fax:* (202) 333-3198 (office). *E-mail:* gigi_geyer@juno.com (office). *Website:* www.uexpress.com (office); www.amuniversal.com/ups/features/georgie_geyer/bio.htm.

GHEORGHE, Ion; Romanian poet; b. 16 Aug. 1935, Florica, Buzău. *Education:* Bucharest Univ. *Career:* apptd Ed. Luceafărul magazine 1963; worked in Ministry of Culture 1992; cultural attaché, Romanian Embassy in China 1994–96. *Publications:* Pâine şi sare 1957, Căile pământului 1960, Ţara rândunelelor 1963, Cariatida 1964, Nopţi cu lună pe Oceanul Atlantic: Scrisori esenţiale 1966, Zoosophia 1967, Vine iarba 1968, Cavalerul trac 1969, Mai mult ca plânsul: Icoane pe sticlă 1970, Megalitice 1972, Avatara 1972, Poeme 1972, Cultul Zburătorului: Opiniile autorului despre lumea miturilor autohtone 1974, Noimele 1976, Dacia Feniks 1978, Proba logosului 1979, Cenuşile 1980, Joaca jocului 1984, Şi mai joaca jocului 1985, Condica în versuri 1987, Zalmoksiile 1988, Muzaios 2001, Elegii politice 2002, Cogaioanele: Munţii Marilor pontifi 2004, Mutul 2008, Sutrele ţăranului Iancu Arsene 2010, Concluziile senectuţii 2010, Epopeea Tapae 2011. *Website:* www.adioletea.ro.

GHEZALI, Salima; Algerian newspaper editor; *Editor-in-Chief, La Nation*; b. 1958, Bouira; m. (divorced); two c. *Career:* fmr schoolteacher, Mitidja Hills; Ed.-in-Chief La Nation weekly newspaper 1994–96, 2001–, newspaper suspended by Algerian authorities 1996–2001; f. Women of Europe and North Africa Asscn, Asscn for Women's Emancipation 1989; f. Nyssa magazine. *Publications:* Le Reve Algérien 1999, Los amantes de Sherezade 2000. *Honours:* Int. Press Club Award 1996, Sakharov Human Rights Prize 1997, Olof Palme Prize 1997. *Address:* La Nation, 33 rue Larbi Ben M'hidi, Algiers, Algeria (office). *Telephone:* (21) 43-21-76 (office).

GHITANI, Gamal al-; Egyptian journalist, novelist and short story writer; b. 1945, Sohag. *Career:* wrote his first story in 1959 at the age of 14; apprenticed to a carpet maker; imprisoned for six months for criticism of President Nasser; joined news desk of Akhbar el-Yawm newspaper in 1969, war corresp., then Cultural Ed. and columnist; Ed. Akhbar el-Adab (literary magazine) 1993–; co-f. Gallery 68 (literary magazine); mem. jury, Lettre Ulysses Award for Reportage 2006. *Publications:* short story collections: Awraq Shab 'Asha mundhu Alf 'Am 1969, Ard ... Ard 1972, Al-Hisar min Thalath Jihat 1975, Hikayat el-Gharib 1976, Dhikr ma Jara 1978, Ithaf aI-Zaman bi-Hikayat Jalbi al-Sultan 1985, Thimar al Waqt 1990, Min Daftar al-'Ishq wal-Ghurba 1993, Naftha Masdur 1993, Shatf al-Nar 1996; novels: Al- Zayni Barakat (trans. as Zayni Barakat 1988) 1974, Waqi'i' Harat al-Za'farani (trans. as The Zafarani Files) 1976, al-Rifai 1977, Risilat al-Basi'ir fi al-Masi'ir (trans. as Épître des destinées 1993) 1989, Shath al-Madina 1990, Risala min al-Sababa wal Wajd 1990, Ha-tif al-Maghib 1992, Mutun al-Ahram 1994, Pyramid Texts 2007; other: al-Zuwayl 1975, The Cairo of Naguib Mahfouz 2000; contrib. to Egyptian and Lebanese newspapers. *Honours:* Chevalier, Ordre des Arts et des Lettres 1987; State Prize for Fiction 1980. *Address:* c/o The American University in Cairo Press, 113 Kasr el Aini Street, POB 2511, Cairo 11511, Egypt (office). *Telephone:* (2) 2797-6926 (office). *Fax:* (2) 2794-1440 (office). *E-mail:* aucpress@aucegypt.edu (office). *Website:* www.akhbarelyom.org.eg (office).

GHOSE, Zulfikar, BA; British/American academic, poet and writer; *Professor Emeritus, University of Texas at Austin*; b. 13 March 1935, Sialkot, Pakistan; m. Helena de la Fontaine. *Education:* Keele Univ. *Career:* Prof. of English, Univ. of Texas at Austin 1969–2007, Prof. Emer. 2007–. *Publications:* poetry: The Loss of India 1964, Jets from Orange 1967, The Violent West 1972, A Memory of Asia 1984, Selected Poems 1991; fiction: The Contradictions 1966, The Murder of Aziz Khan 1967, The Incredible Brazilian the Native 1972, The Beautiful Empire 1975, Crump's Terms 1975, A Different World 1978, Hulme's Investigations into the Bogart Script 1981, A New History of Torments 1982, Don Bueno 1983, Figures of Enchantment 1986, The Triple Mirror of the Self 1992, Veronica and the Góngora Passion 1998; criticism: Hamlet, Prufrock and Language 1978, The Fiction of Reality 1983, The Art of Creating Fiction 1991, Shakespeare's Mortal Knowledge 1993, Beckett's Company 2009; autobiog.: Confessions of a Native-Alien 1965. *E-mail:* zulfji@gmail.com (home).

GHOSH, Amitav, BA, MA, DPhil; Indian writer and academic; b. 11 July 1956, Kolkata; m. Deborah Baker; two c. *Education:* St Stephen's Coll., Delhi Univ., Institut Bourguiba des Langues Vivantes, Tunis and Univ. of Oxford, UK. *Career:* Visiting Fellow, Centre for Social Sciences, Trivandrum, Kerala 1982–83; Research Assoc., Dept of Sociology, Delhi Univ. 1983–87, Lecturer, Dept of Sociology 1987; Visiting Prof., Depts of Literature and Anthropology, Univ. of Virginia, Charlottesville 1988; Visiting Prof., South Asia Centre, Columbia Univ. 1989; Visiting Prof., Dept of Anthropology, Univ. of Pennsylvania 1989; Fellow, Centre for Studies in Social Science, Kolkata 1990–92; Adjunct Prof., Dept of Anthropology, Columbia Univ. 1993, Visiting Prof. 1994–97; Distinguished Visiting Prof., American Univ. in Cairo 1994; fiction workshop Sarah Lawrence Coll., New York 1996; Distinguished Prof., Dept of Comparative Literature, Queens Coll., CUNY 1999–2003; Visiting Prof., Dept of English and American Literature and Language, Harvard Univ. 2004. *Publications include:* The Circle of Reason (New York Times Notable Book 1987, Prix Médicis Étranger 1990) 1986, The Shadow Lines (Sahitya Akademi Award, Ananda Puraskar 1990) 1988, In an Antique Land (non-fiction) (New York Times Notable Book of 1993) 1992, The Calcutta Chromosome (Arthur C. Clark Award 1997) 1996, Dancing in Cambodia and At Large in Burma (essays) 1998, Countdown 1999, The Glass Palace (Frankfurt International e-Book Awards Grand Prize for Fiction, New York Times Notable Book, Los Angeles Times Notable Book, Chicago Tribune Favourite Book 2001) 2000, The Imam and the Indian (essays) 2002, The Hungry Tide (Hutch Crossword Book Prize 2006) 2004, Sea of Poppies (Indiaplaza Golden Quill Awards for Best Book, Readers' Choice Award for Fiction, Vodafone Crossword Book Award 2009) 2008; contrib. to articles in Ethnology, Granta, The New Republic, New York Times, Public Culture, Subaltern Studies, Letra Internacional, Cultural Anthropology, Observer Magazine, Wilson Quarterly, The New Yorker, Civil Lines, American Journal of Archaeology, Kenyon Review, Desh. *Honours:* Best American Essays Award 1995, Padma Shri 2007, Pushcart Prize 1999, Grinzane Cavour Prize 2007, Dan David Prize 2010. *E-mail:* amitav@amitavghosh.com (office). *Website:* www.penguinbooksindia.com/amitavghosh; www.amitavghosh.com.

GIBBON, Gary, BA; British journalist; *Political Editor, Channel 4 News*; b. 15 March 1965, s. of Robert Gibbon and Elizabeth Gibbon; m. Laura Pulay 1993; two s. *Education:* Balliol Coll., Oxford. *Career:* fmr journalist, BBC; joined Channel 4 News 1990, Political Producer 1992–94, Political Corresp. 1994–2005, Political Ed. 2005–. *Honours:* RTS Home News Award 2006, Political Studies Asscn Political Broadcaster of the Year Award 2008. *Address:* Channel 4 News, ITN, 200 Gray's Inn Road, London, WC1X 8XZ, England (office). *Telephone:* (20) 7430-4996 (office). *E-mail:* gary.gibbon@itn.co.uk (office). *Website:* www.channel4.com/news (office).

GIBBONS, Kaye; American writer; b. 5 May 1960, Nash Co., North Carolina; m. Michael Gibbons 1984 (divorced); three d. *Education:* North Carolina State Univ., Univ. of North Carolina at Chapel Hill. *Publications:* Ellen Foster (Sue Kaufman Prize for First Fiction, American Acad. and Inst. of Arts and Letters 1988) 1987, A Virtuous Woman 1989, A Cure for Dreams 1991, Charms for the Easy Life 1993, Sights Unseen 1995, On the Occasion of My Last Afternoon 1998, Divining Women 2004, The Life All Around Me 2005. *Honours:* Nelson Algren Heartland Award for Fiction, Chicago Tribune 1991.

GIBBONS, (William) Reginald (Jr), AB, MA, PhD; American academic, poet, writer and translator; *Professor of English and Classics and Director, Center for the Writing Arts, Northwestern University*; b. 7 Jan. 1947, Houston, Tex.; m. Cornelia Maude Spelman 1983; one step-s. one step-d. *Education:* Princeton Univ., Stanford Univ. *Career:* Lecturer, Livingston Coll., Rutgers Univ. 1975–76, Princeton Univ. 1976–80, Columbia Univ. 1980–81; Ed., TriQuarterly magazine 1981–97; Prof. of English and Classics, Northwestern Univ. 1981–, Chair., Dept of English 2002–05, Dir Center for the Writing Arts 2006–12; Core Faculty, MFA Program for Writers, Warren Wilson Coll. 1989–; mem. The Guild Complex (co-founder), PEN American Center, Poetry Soc. of America, Texas Inst. of Letters. *Publications:* Roofs Voices Roads (poems) 1979, The Ruined Motel (poems) 1981, Criticism in the University (co-ed. with Gerald Graff) 1985, The Writer in Our World (ed.) 1986, Saints (poems) 1986, Writers from South Africa (ed.) 1988, William Goyen: A Study of the Short Fiction 1991, Thomas McGrath: Life and the Poem (ed. with Terrence Des Pres) 1991, Maybe It Was So (poems) 1991, Five Pears or Peaches (short stories) 1991, New Writings from Mexico (ed. and principal trans.) 1992, Sweetbitter (novel) 1994, Sparrow: New and Selected Poems 1997, Homage to Longshot O'Leary (poems) 1999, Selected Poems of Luis Cernuda (trans.) 2000, Euripides' Bakkhai (trans. with Charles Segal) 2001, It's Time (poems) 2002, Sophocles' Antigone (trans. with Charles Segal) 2003, In the Warhouse (poems) 2004, Fern-Texts (poems) 2005, William Goyen: Autobiographical Essays, Notebooks, Evocations, Interviews (ed.) 2007, Creatures of a Day (poems) 2008, Sophocles, Selected Poems (trans.) 2008, Slow Trains Overhead: Chicago Poems and Stories 2010; contrib. to many journals, reviews, quarterlies and magazines. *Honours:* Fulbright Fellowship, Spain 1971–72, co-winner, Denver Quarterly Trans. Award 1977, Guggenheim Fellowship 1984, Nat. Endowment for the Arts Fellowship 1984–85, Texas Inst. of Letters Short Story Award 1986, Illinois Arts Council Fellowship 1987, Poetry Soc. of America John Masefield Memorial Award 1991, Friends of the Chicago Public Library Carl Sandburg Award 1992, Anisfield-Wolf Book Award 1995, Texas Inst. of Letters Jesse Jones Award 1995, Pushcart Prize 1997, Shenandoah magazine Thomas H. Carter Prize 1998, Balcones Poetry Prize 1998, Folger Shakespeare Library O.B. Hardison Jr Poetry Prize 2004. *Address:* Department of English, 215 University Hall, 1897 Sheridan Road, Northwestern University, Evanston, IL 60208, USA (office). *Telephone:* (847) 491-7294 (office). *Fax:* (847) 467-1545 (office). *E-mail:* rgibbons@northwestern.edu (office). *Website:* www.english.northwestern.edu/people/gibbons.html (office).

GIBSON, Graeme, CM, BA; Canadian writer and conservationist; b. 9 Aug. 1934, London, Ont.; m. Margaret Atwood; two s. one d. *Education:* Univ. of Waterloo, Univ. of Edinburgh, UK, Univ. of Western Ontario. *Career:* currently Chair. Pelee Island Bird Observatory; mem. International PEN (Canadian Centre, Pres. 1987–89), Writers' Union of Canada (Chair. 1974–75). *Publications:* Five Legs 1969, Communion 1971, Eleven Canadian Novelists 1973, Perpetual Motion 1982, Gentleman Death 1993, A Bedside Book of Birds: An Avian Miscellany 2005, A Bedside Book of Beasts: A Wildlife Miscellany 2009. *Honours:* Hon. FRCGS; Jt Hon. Pres. (with Margaret Atwood) Birdlife International Rare Bird Club; Toronto Arts Award 1990, Harbourfront Festival Prize 1993, The Writers' Trust Award For Distinguished Contrib. 2008. *Address:* c/o Random House of Canada Ltd, One Toronto Street, Unit 300, Toronto, ON M5C 2V6, Canada.

GIBSON, Ian, BA; Irish historian and writer; b. 21 April 1939, Dublin. *Education:* Trinity Coll., Dublin. *Career:* Lecturer in Spanish, Queen's Univ., Belfast; Reader in Modern Spanish Literature, Univ. of London. *Publications:* La represión nacionalista de Granada en 1936 y la muerte de Federico García Lorca 1971, The Death of Lorca 1975, The English Vice: Beating, Sex and Shame in Victorian England and After 1979, The Assassination of Federico García Lorca 1983, Federico García Lorca: A Life 1989, Fire in the Blood 1992, Lorca's Granada: A Practical Guide 1992, Salvador Dalí: The Early Years (with others) 1995, The Shameful Life of Salvador Dalí 1997, Vida, Pasión y Muerte de Federico García Lorca 1998, Dalí-Lorca: La pasión que no pudo ser 1999, The Erotomaniac: The Secret Life of Henry Spencer Ashbee 2002, Viento del sur (novel) 2002, Yo, Rubén Darío: Memorias póstumas de un Rey de la Poesía (novel) 2002, Cela, el hombre que quiso ganar 2003, Dalí joven, Dalí genial 2004, Ligero de equipaje 2006, Cuatro poetas en guerra 2007, Lorca y el mundo gay 2009, Stuff of Legends 2010; contrib. to numerous magazines and newspapers. *Honours:* James Tait Black Memorial Prize 1989, Duff Cooper Memorial Prize, Premio Así Fue, Univ. of Barcelona. *E-mail:* iangibson@arrakis.es.

GIBSON, (George) Morgan, BA, MA, PhD; American fmr academic, poet, critic and writer; b. 6 June 1929, Cleveland, Ohio; s. of George Miles Gibson, Jr and Mary Elizabeth Gibson (née Leeper); m. 1st Barbara Gibson 1950 (divorced 1972); two d.; m. 2nd Keiko Matsui Gibson 1978; one s. *Education:* Oberlin Coll., Univ. of Iowa. *Career:* Instructor, Shimer Coll. 1953–54; Instructor, Wayne State Univ. 1954–58; Asst Prof., American Int. Coll. 1959–61; Asst, then Assoc. Prof. of English, Univ. of Wisconsin at Milwaukee 1961–72; Chair., Grad. Faculty, Goddard Coll., Vt 1972–75, Osaka Univ., Japan 1975–79; Visiting Prof., Michigan State Univ. 1979, Univ. of Illinois 1982, Knox Coll. 1989–91; Prof., Chukyo Univ., Japan 1987–89, Japan Women's Univ., Tokyo 1993–96, Kanda Univ. of Int. Studies 1997–2000; Lecturer, Pennsylvania State Univ. 1991–93; Lecturer, Shobi Univ., Saitama, Japan 2000–05; poetry readings in Japan and USA; fmr Poetry Ed., Arts in Society; fmr Columnist, Printed Matter; fmr Columnist and Contributing Ed., Kyoto Journal; Trustee, Yokohama Int. School 1999–2005. *Plays:* Madam CIA, Strongroom. *Film:* Signature of All Things (performing his poems). *Publications:* poetry: Stones Glow Like Lovers' Eyes 1970, Crystal Sunlake 1971, Dark Summer 1977, Wakeup 1978, Speaking of Light 1979, Kokoro: Heart-Mind 1979, The Great Brook Book 1981; criticism: Kenneth Rexroth 1972, Revolutionary Rexroth: Poet of East-West Wisdom (Outstanding Scholarly Book Award from Choice) 1986 (also online 2000), Among Buddhas in Japan 1988; contrib. to anthologies, books, journals, literary magazines and reviews. *Honours:* several awards and research grants. *Address:* 3-17-604 Sakashita-cho, Isogo-ku, Yokohama-shi 235-0003, Japan. *Telephone:* (45) 761-9223.

GIBSON, Walter Samuel, BFA, MA, PhD; American academic and writer; *Andrew W. Mellon Professor Emeritus of the Humanities, Case Western Reserve University*; b. 31 March 1932, Columbus, Ohio; s. of Walter Samuel Gibson and Grace B. Wheeler; m. Sarah Scott 1972. *Education:* Ohio State Univ., Harvard Univ. *Career:* Asst Prof., Case Western Reserve Univ. 1966–71, Assoc. Prof. 1971–78, Acting Chair. 1970–71, Chair. 1971–79, Dept of Art, Andrew W. Mellon Prof. of the Humanities 1978–97, Andrew W. Mellon Prof. Emer. of the Humanities 1997–; Murphy Lecturer, Univ. of Kansas and the Nelson-Atkins Museum of Art 1988; mem. American Asscn of Netherlandic Studies Coll. Art Asscn, Historians of Netherlandish Art, Midwest Art History Soc., Renaissance Soc. of America, Soc. for Emblem Studies; Fellow, Guggenheim Foundation 1978–79. *Publications:* Hieronymus Bosch 1973, The Paintings of Cornelis Engebrechtsz 1977, Bruegel 1977, Hieronymus Bosch: An Annotated Bibliography 1983, 'Mirror of the Earth': The World Landscape in Sixteenth-Century Flemish Painting 1989, Pieter Bruegel the Elder: Two Studies 1991, Pleasant Places: The Rustic Landscape from Bruegel to Ruisdael 2000, Peter Bruegel and the Art of Laughter 2006, Figures of Speech: Picturing Proverbs in Renaissance Netherlands 2010; contribs to scholarly books and journals. *Honours:* Fellow-in-Residence, Netherlands Inst. for Advanced Study, Wassenaar 1995–96. *Address:* 938 Mason Hill Road North, Pownal, VT 05261-9767, USA. *Telephone:* (802) 823-5861. *Fax:* (802) 823-0287.

GIBSON, William Ford, BA; American writer; b. 17 March 1948, Conway, SC; m. Deborah Thompson 1972; one s. one d. *Education:* Univ. of British Columbia. *Publications:* Neuromancer 1984, Count Zero 1986, Burning Chrome (short stories with John Shirley, Bruce Sterling, and Michael Swanwick) 1986, Mona Lisa Overdrive 1988, The Difference Engine (with Bruce Sterling) 1990, Agrippa: A Book of the Dead (with Dennis Ashbaugh and Keven Begos Jr) 1992, Virtual Light 1993, Pattern Recognition 2002, Spook Country 2007, Zero History 2010; other: Dream Jumbo (performance art text) 1989, Johnny Mnemonic (screenplay) 1995; contributions: anthologies and journals. *Honours:* Ditmar Award, Australian National Science Fiction Foundation 1984, Hugo Award, World Science Fiction Society 1984, Nebula Award, SFWA 1984, Porgie Award, West Coast Review of Books 1984. *Address:* c/o G.P. Putnam's Sons, Penguin Group (USA) Inc., 375 Hudson Street, New York, NY 10014, USA (office). *E-mail:* putnampublicity@us.penguingroup.com (office). *Website:* www.williamgibsonbooks.com.

GIDDENS, Baron (Life Peer), cr. 2004, of Southgate in the London Borough of Enfield; **Anthony Giddens,** PhD; British sociologist; *Chairman and Director, Polity Press Ltd*; b. 18 Jan. 1938, Edmonton; m. Jane Ellwood 1963; two d. *Education:* Minchenden School, Southgate, Univ. of Hull, London School of Economics, Univ. of Cambridge. *Career:* Lecturer in Sociology, Univ. of Leicester 1961–70; Visiting Asst Prof., Simon Fraser Univ., Vancouver 1967–68, Univ. of California, Los Angeles 1968–69; Lecturer in Sociology and Fellow, King's Coll., Cambridge 1970–84, Reader in Sociology 1984–86, Prof. of Sociology 1986–96; Dir LSE 1997–2003, Prof. Emer. 2004–; Chair. and Dir Polity Press Ltd 1985–; apptd Dir Blackwell-Polity Ltd 1985; Chair. and Dir Centre for Social Research 1989–; BBC Reith Lecturer 1999; numerous visiting professorships; Founder of 'The Third Way'; mem. Russian Acad. of Sciences, American Acad. of Science. *Publications:* Capitalism and Modern Social Theory 1971, Politics and Sociology in the Thought of Max Weber 1972, Emile Durkheim: selected writings (ed. and trans.) 1972, The Class Structure of the Advanced Societies 1973, New Rules of Sociological Method 1976,

Positivism and Sociology (ed.) 1973, Elites and Power in British Society (with P. H. Stanworth) 1974, Studies in Social and Political Theory 1977, Emile Durkheim 1978, Central Problems in Social Theory 1979, A Contemporary Critique of Historical Materialism 1981, Sociology: A Brief but Critical Introduction 1982, Classes, Conflict and Power (with D. Held) 1982, Classes and the Division of Labour (with G. G. N. Mackenzie) 1982, Profiles and Critiques in Social Theory 1983, The Constitution of Society: Outline of the Theory of Structuration 1984, The Nation-State and Violence 1985, Durkheim on Politics and the State 1986, Social Theory and Modern Sociology 1987, Social Theory Today (with Jon Turner) 1988, Sociology 1988, The Consequences of Modernity 1990, Modernity and Self-Identity 1991, Human Societies 1992, The Transformation of Intimacy 1992, Beyond Left and Right 1994, Reflexive Modernisation (with Ulrich Beck and Scott Lash) 1994, Politics, Sociology and Social Theory 1995, In Defence of Sociology 1996, Conversations with Anthony Giddens: Making Sense of Modernity (with Christopher Pierson) 1998, The Third Way: The Renewal of Social Democracy 1998, Runaway World: How Globalisation is Reshaping Our Lives 1999, The Third Way and its Critics 2000, On the Edge: Living with Global Capitalism (ed with Will Hutton) 2000, The Global Third Way Debate 2001, The Progressive Manifesto 2003, Essentials of Sociology 2006, Europe In The Global Age 2007, Over to You, Mr Brown - How Labour Can Win Again 2007, The Politics of Climate Change 2009; contrib. of articles, review articles and book reviews to professional journals and newspapers. *Honours:* Hon. Fellow, LSE 2004, Chilean Acad., Chinese Acad. of Social Sciences; Nat. Order of the Southern Cross (Brazil), Grand Cross, Order of the Infante Dom Henrique (Portugal); Hon. DLitt (Univ. of Anglia), (Open Univ.), (Univ. of Salford), (South Bank Univ.), (Univ. of Hull), (Univ. of Leicester), Hon. DScS (Univ. of Helsinki), Dr hc (Vesalius Coll., Vrije Univ. Brussels), (Univ. of Buenos Aires, Argentina), (Univ. of Twente, Netherlands); German British Forum Award 1999, Prince of Asturias Award (Spain) 2002, Gold Medal, Norwegian Acad. *Address:* Polity Press, 65 Bridge Street, Cambridge, CB2 1UR, England (office). *Telephone:* (1223) 324315 (office). *Fax:* (1223) 461385 (office). *E-mail:* editorial@politybooks.com (office). *Website:* www.polity.co.uk (office).

GIESBERT, Franz-Olivier; French journalist and writer; *Editor, Le Point*; b. 18 Jan. 1949, Wilmington, Del., USA; s. of Frederick Giesbert and Marie Allain; m. 1st Christine Fontaine (divorced); two s. one d.; m. 2nd Natalie Freund 2000; one s., one d. *Education:* Centre de Formation des Journalistes. *Career:* journalist at Le Nouvel Observateur 1971, Sr Corresp. in Washington, DC 1980, Political Ed. 1981, Ed.-in-Chief 1985–88; Ed.-in-Chief Le Figaro 1988–2000, Figaro Magazine 1997–2000, mem. Editorial Bd 1993–2000, Figaro Magazine 1997–2000; Ed. Le Point 2000–; Dir/presenter 'le Gai savoir' TV programme, Paris Première cable channel 1997–2001, Dir Culture et Dépendances France 3 TV channel 2001–; mem. jury Prix Théophraste Renaudot 1998–, Prix Louis Hachette, Prix Aujourd'hui; mem. Conseil Admin Musée du Louvre Paris 2000. *Publications:* François Mitterrand ou la tentation de l'Histoire (essay) 1977, Monsieur Adrien (novel) 1982, Jacques Chirac (biog.) 1987, Le Président 1990, L'Affreux (Grand Prix du Roman de l'Acad. Française) 1992, La Fin d'une Époque 1993, La Souille (William the Conqueror and Interallie Prize), Le Vieil homme et la Mort 1996, François Mitterrand, une vie 1996, Le Sieur Dieu (Prix Jean d'Heurs de Nice Baie des Anges) 1998, Mort d'un berger 2002, L'Abatteur 2003, L'Américain 2004, L'Immortel 2007, La Tragédie du président: scènes de la vie politique 2006, Le Huitième Prophète 2008, Le lessiveur 2009, Un très grand amour 2010, Dieu, ma mère et moi 2012. *Honours:* Aujourd'hui Best Essay Prize 1975, Prix Gutenberg 1987, Grand Prix du roman de l'Académie française 1992, Prix Interallié 1995, Prix Pierre de Monaco 1997, Prix Richelieu 1999, Prix Itheme for Best Talk Show 1999. *Address:* Le Point, 74 avenue du Maine, 75014 Paris Cedex, France (office). *Telephone:* 1-44-10-10-10 (office). *Fax:* 1-44-10-12-49 (office). *E-mail:* fogiesbert@lepoint.tm.fr (office). *Website:* www.lepoint.fr (office).

GIFFORD, Barry Colby; American writer; b. 18 Oct. 1946, Chicago, IL; m. Mary Lou Nelson 1970; one s. one d. *Education:* Univ. of Missouri, Univ. of Cambridge. *Films:* writer or co-writer: Wild at Heart 1990, Perdita Durango 1997, Lost Highway 1997, Ball Lightning 2002, City of Ghosts 2003, The Phantom Father 2011. *Opera:* libretto: Madrugada 2005. *Publications:* Jack's Book (co-author, biog.) 1978, Port Tropique 1980, Landscape with Traveler 1980, The Neighborhood of Baseball 1981, The Devil Thumbs a Ride 1988, Ghosts No Horse Can Carry 1989, Wild at Heart 1990, Sailor's Holiday 1991, New Mysteries of Paris 1991, A Good Man to Know 1992, Night People 1992, Arise and Walk 1994, Hotel Room Trilogy 1995, Baby Cat-Face 1995, The Phantom Father 1997, Lost Highway (co-author) 1997, Flaubert at Key West 1997, Perdita Durango 1997, The Sinaloa Story 1998, Bordertown 1998, The Wild Life of Sailor & Lula 1998, My Last Martini 1999, Southern Nights 1999, Wyoming 2000, Replies to Wang Wei 2001, American Falls 2002, The Rooster Trapped in the Reptile Room: A Barry Gifford Reader 2003, Brando Rides Alone 2003, Do the Blind Dream? 2004, The Stars Above Veracruz 2006, Memories from a Sinking Ship 2007, The Cavalry Charges 2007, The Imagination of the Heart 2009, Sad Stories of the Death of Kings 2010, Sailor & Lula: The Complete Novels 2010; contrib. to Punch, Esquire, Rolling Stone, La Nouvelle Revue Française. *Honours:* American Library Asscn Notable Book Awards 1978, 1988, 1991, NEA Fellowship 1982, Maxwell Perkins Award 1983, PEN Syndicated Fiction Award 1987, Premio Brancati, Italy 1993, Christopher Isherwood Foundation Prize for Fiction 2006, NEA Fiction Award 2010. *Literary Agent:* Curtis Brown Ltd, 10 Astor Place, New York, NY 10003, USA. *E-mail:* AskOscarAboutBarryGifford@gmail.com (office). *Website:* www.barrygifford.com.

GIGGAL, Kenneth, (Henry Marlin, Angus Ross); British writer; b. 19 March 1927, Dewsbury, Yorkshire, England. *Career:* mem. Savage Club, Arms and Armour Society. *Publications:* The Manchester Thing 1970, The Huddersfield Job 1971, The London Assignment 1972, The Dunfermline Affair 1973, The Bradford Business 1974, The Amsterdam Diversion 1974, The Leeds Fiasco 1975, The Edinburgh Exercise 1975, The Ampurias Exchange 1976, The Aberdeen Conundrum 1977, The Congleton Lark 1979, The Hamburg Switch 1980, A Bad April 1980, The Menwith Tangle 1982, The Darlington Jaunt 1983, The Luxembourg Run 1985, Doom Indigo 1986, The Tyneside Ultimatum 1988, Classic Sailing Ships 1988, The Greenham Plot 1989, The Leipzig Manuscript 1990, The Last One 1992, John Worsley's War 1992; other: television scripts and films; contributions: many magazines, national and international. *Honours:* Truth Prize for Fiction 1954.

GIGUERE, Diane Liliane; Canadian writer; b. 6 Dec. 1937, Montréal, QC. *Education:* Collège Marie de France, Conservatory of Dramatic Arts, Québec. *Career:* actress 1953–57; mem. Writers' Union, Québec, Asscn of French-Speaking Writers at Home and Overseas. *Publications:* Le Temps des Jeux 1961, L'Eau est Profonde 1965, Dans les Ailes du vent 1976, L'Abandon 1993, Un Dieu fantôme 2001, Chronique d'un temps Fixe 2005, La Petite Fleur de l'Hymalaya 2007. *Honours:* Prix du Cercle du Livre de France 1961, Guggenheim Fellowship 1969, France Québec Prize 1977. *Address:* 60 rue William Paul 304, Ile des Soeurs, QC H3E 1N5, Canada (home). *E-mail:* cali@info.internet.net (home).

GIKANDI, Simon; Kenyan/American writer and Nyeri; *Professor of English, Princeton University*. *Education:* Univ. of Nairobi, Univ. of Edinburgh, Northwestern Univ. *Career:* Robert Haydon Prof. of English Language and Literature, Univ. of Michigan; currently Robert Schirmer Prof. of English, Princeton Univ. *Publications include:* non-fiction: Reading the African Novel 1987, Reading Chinua Achebe: Language and Ideology in Fiction 1991, Writing in Limbo: Modernism and Caribbean Literature 1992, Maps of Englishness: Writing Identity in the Culture of Colonialism 1997, Cambridge Studies in African and Caribbean Literature: Ngugi wa Thiong'o 2000, The Cambridge History of African and Caribbean Literature (with F. Abiola Irele) 2004, The Columbia Guide to East African Literatures in English (with Evan Mwangi); editor: Uganda's Katakiro in England (Exploring Travel) by Ham Mukasa 1998, Death and the King's Horsemen by Wole Soyinka 2002, Encyclopedia of African Literature 2002. *Honours:* Fellow, John Simon Guggenheim Memorial Foundation. *Address:* Department of English, Princeton University, 45 McCosh Hall, Princeton, NJ 08544-1026, USA (office). *Telephone:* (609) 258-4072 (office). *E-mail:* sgikandi@princeton.edu (office). *Website:* english.princeton.edu/faculty (office).

GIL, David Georg, BA, MSW, DSW; American academic and writer; *Professor Emeritus of Social Policy, Brandeis University*; b. (Georg Engel), 16 March 1924, Vienna, Austria; s. of Oskar Engel and Helene Engel Weiss; m. Eva Breslauer 1947; two s. *Education:* Certificate in psychotherapy with children, Israeli Soc. for Child Psychiatry, diploma in social work, School of Social Work, Hebrew Univ., Jerusalem, Israel and Univ. of Pennsylvania. *Career:* agricultural work in Sweden and Palestine 1939–43; social work practice and research in Palestine, Israel and USA 1943–64; Prof. of Social Policy, Heller School for Social Policy and Management, Brandeis Univ. 1964–2010, Prof. Emer. 2010–; mem. Nat. Asscn of Social Workers, American Orthopsychiatric Asscn, Asscn of Humanist Sociology, Justice Studies Asscn, War Resisters Int. *Publications:* Violence Against Children 1970, Unravelling Social Policy 1973 (revised fifth edn 1992), The Challenge of Social Equality 1976, Beyond the Jungle 1979, Child Abuse and Violence (ed.) 1979, Toward Social and Economic Justice (co-ed. with Eva Gil) 1985, The Future of Work (co-ed. with Eva Gil) 1985, Confronting Injustice and Oppression 1998; contrib. of more than 50 articles to professional journals, book chapters, book reviews. *Honours:* UN Scholarship 1953–54, Brandeis Univ. Heller School Leadership in Human Services 1999, Nat. Asscn of Social Workers Massachusetts Social Worker of the Year 2000, Council on Social Work Educ. Presidential Award 2006, Justice Studies Asscn, Noam Chomsky Award 2008. *Address:* Heller School for Social Policy and Management, Brandeis University, Waltham, MA 02454-9110, USA (office). *Telephone:* (781) 736-3827 (office). *E-mail:* gil@brandeis.edu (office).

GILB, Dagoberto, BA, MA; American writer; b. 31 July 1950, Los Angeles; m. Rebeca Santos 1978; two s. *Education:* Univ. of California, Santa Barbara. *Career:* fmr construction worker, carpenter; Visiting Writer, Univ. of Texas 1988–89, Univ. of Arizona 1992–93, Univ. of Wyoming 1994; apptd teacher, MFA programme at Southwest Texas State Univ. (now Texas State Univ.) 1997; Writer-in-Residence, Univ. of Houston-Victoria 2009–, Exec. Dir of Centro Victoria: Center for Mexican American Literature and Culture; mem. Texas Inst. of Letters, PEN; Fellow, Guggenheim Foundation 1995. *Publications:* Winners on the Pass Line 1985, The Magic of Blood (PEN/Hemingway Award 1994, Jesse Jones Award 1994) 1993, The Last Known Residence of Mickey Acuña 1994, Woodcuts of Women (short stories) 2001, Gritos: Essays 2003, Hecho en Tejas; An Anthology of Texas Mexican Literature (ed) 2006, Flowers 2008, Before the End, After the Beginning 2011; contrib. of essays and fiction to periodicals, including The New Yorker, Harper's, The Best American Essays, Threepenny Review. *Honours:* James D. Phelan Award, San Francisco Foundation 1984, Whiting Writers' Award 1993, Texas Book

Festival Bookend Award 2007, PEN Southwest Book Award 2008. *Address:* University of Houston-Victoria, 3007 North Ben Wilson, Victoria, TX 77901, USA (office). *Telephone:* (361) 570-4848 (office). *Fax:* (361) 580-5507 (office). *E-mail:* gilbd@uhv.edu (office). *Website:* www.uhv.edu (office).

GILBERT, Daniel T., BA, PhD; American psychologist and writer; b. 1957. *Education:* Univ. of Colorado at Denver, Princeton Univ. *Career:* Asst Prof., Univ. of Texas at Austin 1985–90, Assoc. Prof. 1990–95, Prof. 1995–96; Prof., Harvard Univ. 1996–2005, Harvard Coll. Prof. 2005–10; gave Edward E. Jones Memorial Lectures, Princeton Univ. 2003; Ford Visiting Prof. of Behavioral Science, Univ. of Chicago School of Business 2003; gave Forry and Micken Lecture, Amherst Coll. 2005; Nat. Science Foundation Predoctoral Fellow 1981–84; Princeton Univ. Porter Ogden Jacobus Fellowship 1984–85; Univ. of Texas at Austin Raymond Dickson Centennial Endowed Teaching Fellowship 1987–88; Fellow Center for Advanced Study in the Behavioral Sciences 1991–92, Soc. for Personality and Social Psychology 1996, American Psychological Asscn 1997, Soc. of Experimental Social Psychology 1993, American Philosophical Soc. 1999, American Psychological Soc. 2003; John Simon Guggenheim Memorial Foundation Fellowship 1999. *Publications include:* The Handbook of Social Psychology (co-ed., fourth edition) 1998, The Selected Works of Edward E. Jones (ed.) 2003, Stumbling on Happiness (Royal Society Prize for Science Books 2007) 2006; contrib. science fiction stories to magazines; numerous articles to scientific journals. *Honours:* Univ. of Colorado at Denver Outstanding Graduate Award 1981, Univ. of Colorado at Denver Nell G. Fahrion Award for Excellence in Psychology 1981, Princeton Univ. Merit Prizes 1981, 1982, 1983, Univ. of Texas at Austin Pres.'s Assocs Teaching Excellence Award 1990–91, Nat. Inst. of Mental Health Research Scientist Development Award 1991–96, American Psychological Asscn Distinguished Scientific Award for an Early Career Contribution to Psychology 1992, James McKeen Cattell Award 1999, Harvard Univ. Phi Beta Kappa Teaching Prize 1999. *Address:* Department of Psychology, Harvard University, Cambridge, MA 02138, USA (office). *Telephone:* (617) 495-3892 (office). *E-mail:* gilbert@wjh.harvard.edu (office). *Website:* www.wjh.harvard.edu/~dtg/gilbert.htm (office).

GILBERT, Elizabeth; American writer and journalist; b. 1969, Waterbury, Conn.; m. Felipe 2007. *Education:* New York Univ. *Career:* journalist for magazines including Spin, GQ, The New York Times Magazine; full-time writer. *Publications:* Pilgrims (short stories) 1997, Stern Men (novel) 2000, The Last American Man (biog.) 2002, Eat, Pray, Love (travel memoir) 2006, Committed: A Skeptic Makes Peace With Marriage (memoir) 2010. *Literary Agent:* c/o Sarah Chalfant, The Wylie Agency, 250 West 57th Street, Suite 2114, New York, NY 10107, USA. *Telephone:* (212) 246-0069. *Fax:* (212) 586-8953. *E-mail:* mail@wylieagency.com. *Website:* www.wylieagency.com. *Address:* c/o Paul Slovak, Viking-Penguin, 375 Hudson Street, 4th Floor, New York, NY 10014, USA (office). *Website:* www.elizabethgilbert.com.

GILBERT, Harriett Sarah; British writer and broadcaster; b. 25 Aug. 1948, London, England; d. of Michael Gilbert. *Education:* Rose Bruford Coll. of Speech and Drama. *Career:* Co-Books Ed. City Limits magazine 1981–83; Deputy Literary Ed. New Statesman 1983–86, Literary Ed. 1986–88; Lecturer in Journalism, City Univ., London 1992–; mem. Writers Guild of Great Britain. *Television:* presenter: Meridian Books Programme (BBC World Service Radio 1991), World Book Club (BBC World Service), The Strand (BBC World Service), A Good Read (BBC Radio 4). *Publications:* I Know Where I've Been 1972, Hotels with Empty Rooms 1973, An Offence Against the Persons 1974, Tide Race 1977, Running Away 1979, The Riding Mistress 1983, A Women's History of Sex 1987, The Sexual Imagination (ed.) 1993, Writing for Journalists 1999; contrib. to Time Out, City Limits, New Statesman, Guardian, BBC, Australian Broadcasting Corpn, Washington Post, BBC World Service Radio. *Address:* BBC World Service, 1st Floor, Brock House, 19 Langham Street, London, W1A 1AA, England (office). *Website:* www.bbc.co.uk/worldservice.

GILBERT, Jack, BA, MA; American poet and writer; b. 17 Feb. 1925, Pittsburgh, Pa. *Education:* University of Pittsburgh, San Francisco State University. *Career:* taught at University of California, Berkeley 1958–59, San Francisco State University 1962–63, 1965–67, 1971, Syracuse University 1982–83, University of San Francisco 1985; Prof., Kyoto University, Tokyo 1974–75; Chair, Creative Writing, University of Alabama, Tuscaloosa 1986; Guggenheim Fellowship 1964; National Endowment for the Arts Award 1974. *Publications:* Poetry: Views of Jeopardy (Yale Younger Poet Award 1962) 1962, Monolithos (Stanley Kunitz Prize 1983, American Poetry Review Prize 1983, American Book Award 1983) 1982, The Great Fires: Poems 1982–1992 (Lannan Literary Award for Poetry 1995) 1994, Refusing Heaven (National Book Critics Circle Award 2005) 2005, Tough Heaven: Poems of Pittsburgh 2006, The Dance Most of All 2009, Collected Poems 2012; novels (co-author with Jean Maclean) My Mother Taught Me 1964, Forever Ecstasy 1968; contributions: various reviews, journals, and periodicals.

GILBERT, John Raphael, BA; British writer; b. 8 April 1926, London, England; m.; three s. *Education:* Columbia Univ., King's Coll., London. *Publications:* Modern World Book of Animals 1947, Cats, Cats, Cats 1961, Famous Jewish Lives 1970, Myths of Ancient Rome 1970, Pirates and Buccaneers 1971, Highwaymen and Outlaws 1971, Charting the Vast Pacific 1971, National Costumes of the World 1972, World of Wildlife 1972–74, Miracles of Nature 1975, Knights of the Crusades 1978;, Vikings 1978, Prehistoric Man 1978, Leonardo da Vinci 1978, La Scala 1979, Dinosaurs Discovered 1980, Macdonald Guide to Trees 1983, Macdonald Encyclopedia of House Plants 1986, Theory and Use of Colour 1986, Macdonald Encyclopedia of Roses 1987, Gardens of Britain 1987, Macdonald Encyclopedia of Butterflies and Moths 1988, Trekking in the USA 1989, Macdonald Encyclopedia of Orchids 1989, Macdonald Encyclopedia of Bulbs 1989, Trekking in Europe 1990, Macdonald Encyclopedia of Herbs and Spices 1990, Macdonald Encyclopedia of Bonsai 1990, Macdonald Encyclopedia of Amphibians and Reptiles 1990, Macdonald Encyclopedia of Saltwater Fishes 1992, Decorating Chinese Porcelain 1994.

GILBERT, The Rt Hon Sir Martin John, Kt, CBE, MA, DLitt, FRSL; British historian and academic; *Fellow, Merton College, Oxford;* b. 25 Oct. 1936, s. of Peter Gilbert and Miriam Gilbert; m. 1st Helen Robinson 1963; one d.; m. 2nd Susan Sacher; two s.; m. 3rd Esther Poznansky. *Education:* Highgate School and Magdalen Coll., Oxford. *Career:* Sr Research Fellow, St Antony's Coll., Oxford 1960–62, Fellow, Merton Coll., Oxford 1962–; Visiting Prof., Univ. of S Carolina 1965, Tel-Aviv Univ. 1979, Hebrew Univ. of Jerusalem 1980–; official biographer of Sir Winston Churchill 1968–; Gov. Hebrew Univ. of Jerusalem 1978–; Non-Governmental Rep., UN Comm. on Human Rights, Geneva 1987, 1988; mem. Prime Minister's del. to Israel, Gaza and Jordan 1995, to USA 1995, to Israel 2008; Cttee mem., The Iraq Inquiry 2009–11; Privy Councillor 2009; adviser to BBC and ITV for various documentaries; script designer and co-author, Genocide (Acad. Award for best documentary feature film) 1981; presenter, History Channel 1996–; Recent History Corresp. Sunday Times 1967. *Publications:* The Appeasers (with R. Gott) 1963, Britain and Germany between the Wars 1964, The European Powers 1900–1945 1965, Plough My Own Furrow: The Life of Lord Allen of Hurtwood 1965, Servant of India: A Study of Imperial Rule 1905–1910 1966, The Roots of Appeasement 1966, Recent History Atlas 1860–1960 1966, Winston Churchill 1966, British History Atlas 1968, American History Atlas 1968, Jewish History Atlas 1969, First World War Atlas 1970, Winston S. Churchill, Vol. III, 1914–16 1971, companion vol. 1973, Russian History Atlas 1972, Sir Horace Rumbold: Portrait of a Diplomat 1973, Churchill: A Photographic Portrait 1974, The Arab-Israeli Conflict: its history in maps 1974, Winston S. Churchill, Vol. IV, 1917–22 1975, companion vol. 1977, The Jews in Arab Lands: Their History in Maps 1975, Winston S. Churchill, Vol. V, 1922–39, 1976, companion Vols 1980, 1981, 1982, The Jews of Russia: Illustrated History Atlas 1976, Jerusalem Illustrated History Atlas 1977, Exile and Return: The Emergence of Jewish Statehood 1978, Children's Illustrated Bible Atlas 1979, Final Journey: The Fate of the Jews of Nazi Europe 1979, Auschwitz and the Allies 1981, Atlas of the Holocaust 1982, Winston S. Churchill, Vol. VI, 1939–41 1983, The Jews of Hope: A Study of the Crisis of Soviet Jewry 1984, Jerusalem: Rebirth of a City 1985, Shcharansky: Hero of our Time 1986, Winston S. Churchill, Vol. VII, 1941–45 1986, The Holocaust, The Jewish Tragedy 1986, Winston Churchill, Vol. VIII 1945–65 1988, Second World War 1989, Churchill, A Life 1991, The Churchill War Papers: At the Admiralty (ed.), Atlas of British Charities 1993, In Search of Churchill: A Historian's Journey 1994, The First World War: A Complete History 1994, The Churchill War Papers: Never Surrender (ed.) 1995, The Day the War Ended 1995, Jerusalem in the 20th Century 1996, The Boys, Triumph over Adversity 1996, A History of the World in the Twentieth Century (Vol. I 1900–1933) 1997, (Vol. II 1933–1951) 1998, (Vol. III 1952–1999) 1999, Holocaust Journey: Travelling in Search of the Past 1997, Israel, A History 1998, Winston Churchill and Emery Reeves; Correspondence 1998, Never Again: A History of the Holocaust 1999, The Jewish Century 2001, History of the Twentieth Century 2001, The Churchill War Papers: '1941, the Ever-Widening War' (ed.) 2001, Letters to Auntie Fori: 5,000 Years of Jewish History and Faith 2002, The Righteous: the Unsung Heroes of the Holocaust 2002, D-Day 2004, Churchill at War: His "Finest Hour" in Photographs, Churchill and America 2005, Kristallnacht: Prelude to Destruction 2006, Somme: The Heroism and Horror of War 2006, Will of the People: Churchill and Parliamentary Democracy 2006, Churchill and the Jews 2007, Routledge Atlas of the Second World War 2008, In Ishmael's House: A History of Jews in Muslim Lands 2010. *Honours:* Hon. Fellow, Univ. of Wales, Lampeter 1997; Hon. DLitt (Westminster Coll., Fulton, Mo.) 1981, (Univ. of Buckingham) 1992, (Univ. of Leicester) 2004. *Address:* Merton College, Oxford OX1 4JD, England (office). *Website:* www.martingilbert.com.

GILBERT, Robert Andrew, BA, PhD; British antiquarian bookseller, editor and writer; b. 6 Oct. 1942, Bristol, England; m. Patricia Kathleen Linnell 1970; three s. two d. *Education:* Univ. of Bristol, Univ. Coll., London. *Career:* Ed. Ars Quatuor Coronatorum 1994–2001, The Christian Parapsychologist 2008–; mem. Soc. of Authors. *Publications:* The Golden Dawn: Twilight of the Magicians 1983, A. E. Waite: A Bibliography 1983, The Golden Dawn Companion 1986, A. E. Waite: Magician of Many Parts 1987, The Treasure of Montsegur (with W. N. Birks) 1987, Elements of Mysticism 1991, World Freemasonry: An Illustrated History 1992, Freemasonry: A Celebration of the Craft (with J. M. Hamill) 1992, Casting the First Stone 1993, The Golden Dawn Scrapbook 1997; editor: The Oxford Book of English Ghost Stories (with M. A. Cox) 1986, Victorian Ghost Stories: An Oxford Anthology (with M. A. Cox) 1991, The Rise of Victorian Spiritualism (series ed.) 2000, The House of the Hidden Light 2003; contrib. to Ars Quatuor Coronatorum, Avallaunius, Christian Parapsychologist, Dictionary of Gnosis and Western Esotericism, Gnosis, Hermetic Journal, Cauda Pavonis, Yeats Annual, Dictionary of National Biography, Dictionary of Nineteenth Century British Scientists, Dictionary of British Philosophy, Encyclopaedia of New Religions. *Address:*

215 Clevedon Road, Tickenham, Clevedon, BS21 6RX, England (home). *Telephone:* (1275) 854486 (home). *E-mail:* sacregis42@hotmail.com (home).

GILBERT, Virginia, BA, MFA, PhD; American academic, poet and writer; b. 19 Dec. 1946, Elgin, Ill. *Education:* Iowa Wesleyan Coll., Univ. of Iowa, Univ. of Nebraska-Lincoln. *Career:* Peace Corps, Repub. of Korea 1971–73; Admin., Writers' Community, Acad. of American Poets 1976; ESL instructor, Iran 1976–79; Instructor, Coll. of Lake County, Ill. 1979; Teaching Asst, Univ. of Nebraska 1984–87; Asst Prof. of English and Creative Writing, Alabama A & M Univ. 1980–92, Assoc. Prof. 1992–2001, Prof. 2001–07, currently Prof. Emer.; Fulbright Fellow to China 1992; mem. Associated Writing Programs, Peace Corps Volunteer Asscn, Peace Corps Volunteer Readers and Writers Asscn, Poetry Soc. of America, Poets and Writers; Lecturer, Alabama Humanities Foundation's Speaker's Bureau 1997–98,. *Photography:* photographs in numerous exhbns. *Publications:* The Earth Above 1993, That Other Brightness 1996, Tripwire 2007, A Long Way From Home 2010; contrib. to anthologies, including Ordinary and Sacred as Blood, Claiming the Spirit Within: A Source Book of Women's Poetry; contrib. to journals, reviews and quarterlies. *Honours:* Best Pictures of the Year, Huntsville Photographic Soc. 1980–81, 1984, Special Merit Award Kodak International Newspaper Snapshot Awards 1986, Best Nebraska Entrant Seventh Annual Cornhusker International Exhbn of Photography 1987, Second Prize, Hackney Literary Awards 1990, First Place, Sakura Festival Haiku Contest 1992, First Place, Alabama State Poetry Soc. Poetry Slam 1998, Alabama Poet of the Year 2001, Univ. of Nebraska-Lincoln Alumni Achievement Award 2006. *Telephone:* (256) 464-9130 (home). *E-mail:* vgpoet@aol.com.

GILCHRIST, Ellen Louise, BA, PhD; American writer and poet; *Associate Professor, Department of English, University of Arkansas*; b. 20 Feb. 1935, Vicksburg, Miss.; d. of William Garth and Aurora Gilchrist; three s. *Education:* Millsaps Coll., Univ. of Arkansas. *Career:* freelance writer and journalist; commentator Nat. Public Radio news, Washington, DC 1984–85; fmr Writer-in-Residence, MA programme, Univ. of Arkansas, Fayetteville; apptd Writer-in-Residence and Andrew W. Mellon Fellow in the Humanities, Tulane Univ., New Orleans 2005; currently Assoc. Prof., Dept of English, Univ. of Arkansas; mem. Authors' Guild, Authors' League of America. *Publications:* The Land Surveyor's Daughter (poems) 1979, In the Land of Dreamy Dreams (short stories) 1981, The Annunciation (novel) 1983, Victory Over Japan: A Book of Stories (American Book Award) 1984, Drunk With Love (short stories) 1986, Riding Out the Tropical Depression (poems) 1986, Falling Through Space: The Journals of Ellen Gilchrist 1987, The Anna Papers (novel) 1988, Light Can be Both Wave and Particle: A Book of Stories 1989, I Cannot Get You Close Enough (three novellas) 1990, Net of Jewels (novel) 1992, Starcarbon: A Meditation on Love (Mississippi Acad. of Arts and Science Fiction Award 1994) 1992, Anabasis: A Journey to the Interior 1994, An Age of Miracles (short stories) 1995, The Courts of Love 1997, Rhoda: A Life in Stories 1995, Sarah Conley 1997, Collected Stories 2001, The Cabal and Other Stories 2002, I, Rhoda Manning, Go Hunting with My Daddy and Other Stories 2002, The Writing Life 2005, Nora Jane, A Life in Stories 2005, A Dangerous Age 2008; contrib. to many journals and periodicals. *Honours:* four hon. doctorates; Poetry Award Mississippi Arts Festival 1968, Univ. of Arkansas Poetry Award 1976, New York Quarterly Craft in Poetry Award 1978, Pushcart Prizes 1979–80, 1983, Prairie Schooner Fiction Award 1981, Mississippi Acad. of Arts and Science Fiction Award 1982, 1985, Saxifrage Award 1983, Univ. of Arkansas J. William Fulbright Prize 1985, Mississippi Inst. of Arts and Letters Literary Award 1985, Univ. of North Carolina, Chapel Hill Thomas Wolfe Award 2004. *Address:* Department of English, University of Arkansas, Kimpel Hall, 333, Fayetteville, AR 72701, USA (office). *Telephone:* (479) 575-4301 (office). *Fax:* (479) 575-5919 (office). *E-mail:* engl@uark.edu (office). *Website:* english.uark.edu/Faculty/Ellen_Gilchrist .php (office).

GILES, Frank Thomas Robertson, MA; British journalist (retd) and writer; b. 31 July 1919, London; m. Lady Katharine Sackville 1946 (died 2010); one s. two d. *Education:* Wellington Coll., Brasenose Coll., Oxford. *Career:* Asst Corresp., Paris Bureau, The Times newspaper 1947–50, Chief Corresp. Rome Bureau 1950–53, and Paris Bureau 1953–61, Foreign Ed., The Sunday Times 1961–77, Deputy Ed. 1967–81, Ed. 1981–83; Dir The Times Newspapers 1981–85. *Publications:* A Prince of Journalists: The Life and Times of Henri de Blowitz 1962, Sundry Times (autobiog.) 1986, Forty Years On (ed.) 1990, The Locust Years: History of the Fourth French Republic (Franco-British Soc. Prize) 1991, Corfu: The Garden Isle (ed.) 1994, Napoleon Bonaparte, England's Prisoner 2001; contrib. to books, newspapers and periodicals, including the Dictionary of National Biography. *Address:* 42 Blomfield Road, London, W9 2PF, England (home).

GILES, Molly, BA, MA; American academic and writer; *Professor, Department of English, University of Arkansas*; b. 12 March 1942, California; m. 1st Daniel Giles 1961 (divorced 1974); m. 2nd Richard King 1976 (divorced); three c. *Education:* Univ. of California at Berkeley, San Francisco State Univ. *Career:* Lecturer in Creative Writing, San Francisco State Univ. 1980–99; apptd Assoc. Prof., Dept of English, Univ. of Arkansas, Fayetteville 1999, currently Prof. *Publications:* Rough Translations (Flannery O'Connor Award) 1985, Creek Walk and Other Stories 1996, Iron Shoes 2000; contrib. to periodicals. *Honours:* Flannery O'Connor Award for Short Fiction 1986, Nat. Book Critics Circle Citation for Excellence in Book Reviewing 1991, Small Press Best Fiction/Short Story Award 1998. *Address:* Department of English, University of Arkansas, Kimpel Hall, 333, Fayetteville, AR 72701, USA (office). *Telephone:* (479) 575-4301 (office). *Fax:* (479) 575-5919 (office). *E-mail:* mollyg@uark.edu (office). *Website:* english.uark.edu/Faculty/Molly_Giles.php (office).

GILL, Anton, (Oliver Bowden, Ray Evans), BA, MA; British writer; b. 22 Oct. 1948, Ilford, Essex, England; m. Nicola Susan Browne 1982. *Education:* Clare Coll., Cambridge. *Career:* Asst Dir English Stage Co., Royal Court Theatre, London 1970–76; Drama Officer, Arts Council of Great Britain 1976–78; Script Ed. BBC Radio Drama 1976, Sr Drama Producer BBC. *Publications include:* The Journey Back From Hell, Berlin to Bucharest, City of the Horizon, City of Dreams, A Dance Between Flames, City of the Dead, An Honourable Defeat, The Devil's Mariner 1997, Peggy Guggenheim: The Life of an Art Addict 2001, The Great Escape 2002, The Egyptians: The Kingdom of the Pharaohs Brought to Life 2003, Empire's Children 2007, The Sacred Scroll 2012; Assassin's Creed series: Renaissance 2009, Brotherhood 2010, The Secret Crusade 2011, Revelations 2011. *Honours:* H. H. Wingate Award. *Literary Agent:* c/o Mark Lucas/Julian Alexander, L.A.W Writers' Agency, 14 Vernon Street, London, W14 0RJ, England. *Telephone:* (20) 7471-7900. *E-mail:* mark@lawagency.co.uk; julian@lawagency.co.uk. *Website:* www .antongill.com.

GILL, David Lawrence William, BA, PGCE; British poet, teacher and lecturer; b. 3 July 1934, Chislehurst, Kent; m. Irene Henry 1958; two s. one d. *Education:* Univ. Coll., London, Univ. of Birmingham, London External. *Career:* teacher, Bedales 1960–62, Nyakasura School, Uganda 1962–64, Magdalene Coll. School, Oxford 1965–71; Lecturer, Newland Park Coll. of Educ., later incorporated into Bucks Coll. of Higher Educ. 1971–79, Sr Lecturer 1979–87; EFL in Lisbon 1987–88, in Tokyo 1988–89; own micro-school with Irene Gill: Oxford Residential English 1992–2004. *Publications:* Men Without Evenings 1966, The Pagoda and Other Poems 1969, In the Eye of the Storm 1975, The Upkeep of the Castle 1978, Karel Klimsa (by Ondra Lysohorsky, trans.) 1984, One Potato, Two Potato (with Dorothy Clancy) 1985, Legends, Please 1986, The White Raven 1989, The New Hesperides 1991, The Cemetery of Pleasures 2003, A Little Collateral Damage 2003, Carp in the Wind 2004; contrib. to many journals, reviews and magazines. *Address:* 38 Yarnells Hill, Botley, Oxford, OX2 9BE, England (home). *Telephone:* (1865) 242919 (home). *E-mail:* irenedavidgill@btinternet.com (home).

GILL, Stephen Matthew, BA, MA; British poet, writer and editor; b. 25 June 1932, Sialkot, Pakistan; m. Sarala Gill 1970; one s. two d. *Education:* Punjab Univ., Meerut Coll., Agra Univ., India Univ. of Ottawa, Canada, Univ. of Oxford. *Career:* Ed. Canadian World Federalist 1971–73, 1977–79, Writer's Lifeline 1982–; Pres. Vesta Publications Ltd 1974–90; mem. Christian Cultural Asscn of South Asians (Vice-Pres.), Int. Acad. of Poets (Fellow), PEN International, World Acad. of Arts and Culture, World Federalists of Canada, Amnesty Int., Writers Union of Canada. *Publications:* Poetry: Reflections and Wounds 1978, Moans and Waves 1989, The Dove of Peace 1989, The Flowers of Thirst 1991, Songs for Harmony 1992, Flashes 1994, Aman Di Ghuggi 1994, Divergent Shades 1995, Shrine 1999; fiction: Life's Vagaries (short stories) 1974, Why 1976, The Loyalist City 1979, Immigrants 1982; non-fiction: Six Symbolist Plays of Yeats 1974, Discovery of Bangladesh 1975, Scientific Romances of H. G. Wells 1975, English Grammar for Beginners 1977, Political Convictions of G. B. Shaw 1980, Sketches of India 1980; ed.: various anthologies; contribs to more than 250 publs. *Honours:* Hon. DLitt (World Univ.) 1986; World Acad. of Arts and Culture 1990, Int. Eminent Poet, Int. Poets Acad., Chennai 1991, Pegasus Int. Poetry for Peace Award, Poetry in the Arts, Austin, Tex., USA 1991, Laureate Man of Letters, United Poets Laureate Int. 1992, Poet of Peace Award, Pakistan Asscn, Orleans, Ont. 1995, Mawaheb Culture Friendship Medal, Mawaheb Magazine 1997, Sahir Award of Honour 1999. *Address:* PO Box 32, Cornwall, Ont. K6H 5R9, Canada. *Telephone:* (613) 932-7735. *E-mail:* stephengillgazette@gmail.com. *Website:* www.stephengill.ca; www.stephengillcriticism.info.

GILLECE, Karen, LLB; Irish writer; b. (Karen Gillece Martin), 18 April 1974, Dublin; m. Conor Sweeney; one d. *Education:* Univ. Coll., Dublin. *Career:* full-time writer 2005–. *Radio:* short stories broadcast by BBC NI and RTÉ. *Publications:* Seven Nights in Zaragoza 2005, Longshore Drift (EU Prize for Literature 2009) 2006, My Glass Heart 2007, The Absent Wife 2008. *Honours:* EU Prize for Literature (Ireland) 2009. *Literary Agent:* c/o Faith O'Grady, The Lisa Richards Agency, 108 Upper Leeson Street, Dublin 4, Ireland. *Telephone:* (1) 6375000. *Fax:* (1) 6671256. *Website:* www.lisarichards.ie. *Address:* c/o Hachette Ireland, 8 Castlecourt, Castleknock, Dublin 15, Ireland. *E-mail:* karen@karengillece.com (office). *Website:* www.karengillece.com.

GILLIES, Valerie, MA, MLitt; British poet and writer; b. 4 June 1948, Edmonton, Canada; m. William Gillies 1972; one s. two d. *Education:* Univ. of Edinburgh, Univ. of Mysore, India. *Career:* Writer-in-Residence, Duncan of Jordanstone Coll. of Art, Dundee 1988–90, Univ. of Edinburgh 1995–98; fmr Commonwealth Scholar, Univ. of Mysore, India; Sr Hosp. Arts Worker, Artlink 1994–2002; Creative Writing Fellow, Univ. of Edinburgh 2002–05; Edinburgh Makar (poet laureate) 2005–08; Assoc., Faculty of Arts and Sciences, Harvard Univ., USA 2009–10; Fellow, Queen Margaret Univ. 2010–12, Soc. of Authors, Scotland; provided landmark poem inscriptions for sculptures: Source of the Tweed 1998, Galloway Forest Park 2001, Coldstream 2001, Leaderfoot 2001, City of Edinburgh 2007. *Publications:* Trio: New Poets from Edinburgh 1971, Each Bright Eye: Selected Poems 1977, Bed of Stone 1984, Leopardi: A Scottish Quair 1987, Tweed Journey 1989, The Chanter's Tune 1990, The Jordanstone Folio 1990, The Ringing Rock 1995, Men and

Beasts: Wild Men and Tame Animals of Scotland 2000, The Lightning Tree 2002, The Spring Teller 2008; contribs to radio, television, reviews, and journals. *Honours:* Scottish Arts Council Bursary 1976, Book Award 1996, Eric Gregory Award 1976, Creative Scotland Award 2005. *Address:* 67 Braid Avenue, Edinburgh, EH10 6ED, Scotland (home). *Telephone:* (131) 447-2876 (home). *E-mail:* valeriegillies@hotmail.com.

GILLON, Adam, MA, PhD; American academic, writer, filmmaker and poet; b. 17 July 1921, Poland; m. Isabella Zamojre 1946; one s. (deceased) one d. *Education:* Hebrew Univ. of Jerusalem, Columbia Univ., New York. *Career:* Prof. of English, Acadia Univ., NS 1957–62, Univ. of Haifa, 1979–84; Prof. of English and Comparative Literature, State Univ. of New York at New Paltz 1962–81, Prof. Emeritus 1981–; Founder and Pres. Joseph Conrad Soc. of America; Founding Ed. Joseph Conrad Today; mem. Haiku Soc. of America, MLA, Polish Inst. of Arts and Sciences. *Film:* The Bet – A Film by Adam Gillon (writer, dir and producer) 1993–96. *Publications:* poetry: Selected Poems and Translations 1962, In the Manner of Haiku: Seven Aspects of Man 1967, Daily New and Old: Poems in the Manner of Haiku 1971, Strange Mutations in the Manner of Haiku 1973, Summer Morn… Winter Weather: Poems 'Twixt Haiku and Senryu 1975, The Withered Leaf: A Medley of Haiku and Senryu 1982; fiction: A Cup of Fury 1962, Jared 1986; non-fiction: The Eternal Solitary: A Study of Joseph Conrad 1960, Joseph Conrad: Commemorative Essays (ed.) 1975, Conrad and Shakespeare and Other Essays 1976, Joseph Conrad 1982, Joseph Conrad: Comparative Essays 1994; other: trans., radio plays, and screenplays; contribs to journals, reviews, and periodicals. *Honours:* Alfred Jurzykowski Foundation Award 1967, Joseph Fels Foundation Award 1970, Nat. Endowment for the Humanities Grant 1985, Gold Award, Worldfest Int. Film Festival 1993, Adam Gillon Book Award for Conrad Criticism, Joseph Conrad Soc. of America 2004. *Address:* Lake Illyria, 490 Route 299 W, New Paltz, NY 12561, USA (home). *Telephone:* (845) 255-0616 (home). *E-mail:* conradfilm@aol.com (home).

GILMAN, George G. (see Harknett, Terry)

GILMAN, Rebecca, BA, MA, MFA; American playwright; b. Trussville, AL. *Education:* Birmingham-Southern Coll., Univ. of Virginia, Univ. of Iowa. *Career:* Featured Playwright, Eclipse Theatre Co. 2006; currently Assoc. Prof., Graduate Program in Writing for the Screen and Stage, Northwestern Univ. *Plays:* My Sin and Nothing More 1997, The Land of Little Horses 1998, The Glory of Living 1999, Spinning into Butter 2000, Boy Gets Girl 2000, Blue Surge 2002, The Sweetest Swing in Baseball 2004, Bill of (W)Rights 2004, The Crowd you're in With 2007, Dollhouse 2009, The True History of the Johnstown Flood 2010. *Honours:* Hon. DH (Birmingham-Southern Coll.) 2006; London Evening Standard Award for Most Promising Playwright 1999, American Theatre Critics' Asscn Osborn Award, Harper Lee Award 2008. *Address:* Department of Radio/Television/Fillm, Northwestern University, 1920 Campus Drice, Room 304, Evanston, IL 60201, USA (office). *Telephone:* (847) 491-7023 (office). *E-mail:* r-gilman@northwestern.edu (office). *Website:* www.communication.northwestern.edu (office).

GILMAN, Sander Lawrence, BA, PhD, FRSM; American academic and writer; *Distinguished Professor for the Liberal Arts and Sciences and Professor of Psychiatry, Emory University*; b. 21 Feb. 1944, Buffalo, NY; m. Marina von Eckardt 1969; two s. *Education:* Tulane Univ., Univ. of Munich and Free Univ. of Berlin, Germany. *Career:* Lecturer, St Mary's Dominican Coll., New Orleans 1963–64; Lecturer, Dillard Univ. 1967–68; Asst Prof., Case Western Reserve Univ. 1968–69; Asst Prof. of German, Cornell Univ. 1969–73, Assoc. Prof. of German 1976–95, Prof. of German 1974–81, 1983–84, 1987, Prof. of Psychiatry 1978–94, Prof. of Humane Studies 1983–87, Prof. of Near Eastern Studies 1984–91, Chair., Dept of German Studies 1986–90, Goldwin Prof. of Humane Studies 1987–95, Adjunct Prof. of Psychiatry 1994–; Henry R. Luce Prof. of the Liberal Arts in Human Biology, Prof. of German and Psychiatry, Univ. of Chicago 1994–2000, Chair. Dept of Germanic Studies 1997–2000, Distinguished Service Prof. 1998–2000; Distinguished Prof. of the Liberal Arts and Sciences and Medicine, Univ. of Illinois at Chicago 2000–05; Distinguished Prof. for the Liberal Arts and Sciences, Emory Univ. 2005–, Prof. of Psychiatry 2007–; Research Fellow, Section on the History of Psychiatry and the Behavioral Sciences, Cornell Medical Coll., New York, NY 1977–78; Visiting Prof. of German, Univ. of Paderborn 1980; Faculty Fellow, Soc. for the Humanities, Cornell Univ. 1981–82; Olive O'Connor Distinguished Prof. of the Humanities, Colgate Univ. 1982; Mellon Visiting Prof. of the Humanities, Tulane Univ., New Orleans, La 1988; Visiting Sr Fellow, Council of the Humanities and Old Dominion Foundation Fellow in English, Princeton Univ. 1988; (Spring) Northrop Frye Visiting Prof. of Literary Theory, Univ. of Toronto 1989; Visiting Prof. of Modern German Literature, Free Univ., Berlin 1989; Visiting Historical Scholar, Nat. Library of Medicine, NIH, Bethesda, Md 1990–91; B.G. Rudolf Visiting Prof. of Jewish Studies, Syracuse Univ. 1991; Mellon Foundation Visiting Prof., Univ. of the Witswatersrand, Johannesburg, SA 1994; Inaugural Distinguished Visitor, Dept of German, Ohio State Univ. 1994; Visiting Prof., Kaplan Centre for Jewish Studies, University of Cape Town, SA 1995; Visiting Prof., Univ. of Potsdam and Fellow, Moses Mendelssohn Center for Jewish Studies 1995; Fellow, Center for Advanced Studies in the Behavioral Sciences, Stanford, Calif. 1996–97; Visiting Fellow, The Humanities Center, Univ. of Michigan, Ann Arbor 1997; Visiting Prof. of Comparative Literature, Univ. of British Columbia 1997; Visiting Fellow, Getty Center for the Arts and Humanities 1998; Fellow, American Acad., Berlin 2000–01; Inaugural Drobny Lecturer in Jewish Studies, Univ. of Illinois, Chicago 1999; Faculty, Summer Inst. of Theory and Criticism, Cornell Univ., NY 2002; Nichols Visiting Professorship of the Humanities and the Public Sphere, Univ. of California, Irvine 2003; Canterbury Visiting Fellowship, Dept of Gender Studies, Univ. of Canterbury, Christchurch, NZ 2003; Weidenfeld Prof. of European Comparative Literature, Univ. of Oxford, UK 2004–05; Prof., Inst. in the Humanities, Birkbeck Coll. London, UK 2007–; Visiting Fellow, Inst. of Advanced Studies, Univ. of Warwick, UK 2008; Visiting Prof., Courtauld Inst. of Art, London, in the Mellon Foundation MA Special Option, Arts in Exile in Britain 1933–1945 2009; Cecil Green Visiting Prof., Green Coll., Univ. of British Columbia 2009; Distinguished Visitor, Ben Gurion Univ., Beersheva, Israel 2010; Visiting Research Prof., Univ. of Hong Kong 2010–(13); Fellow, Royal Soc. of Medicine, London 1982, Second Vice-Pres. 1993, First Vice-Pres. 1994, Pres. 1995; Corresp. mem. Inst. of Germanic Studies, Univ. of London 1994–. *Publications:* monographs: Form und Funktion: Eine strukturelle Untersuchung der Romane Klabunds 1971, The Parodic Sermon in European Perspective: Aspects of Liturgical Parody from the Middle Ages to the Twentieth Century 1974, Bertold Brecht's Berlin (with Wolf Von Eckardt) 1975, A Berlim de Bertolt Brecht: Um Album dos Anos 20 (trans. Alexandre Lissovsky) 1996, Nietzschean Parody: An Introduction to Reading Nietzsche 1976 (augmented edn 2001, The Face of Madness: Hugh W. Diamond and the Rise of Psychiatric Photography 1976, Wahnsinn, Text und Kontext: Die historischen Wechselbeziehungen der Literatur, Kunst und Psychiatrie. Literatur und Psychologie, 8 (ed. Wolfram Mauser) 1981, On Blackness without Blacks: Essays on the Image of the Black in Germany. Yale Afro-American Studies 1982, Seeing the Insane: A Cultural History of Psychiatric Illustration 1982, Difference and Pathology: Stereotypes of Sexuality, Race, and Madness 1985 (fourth paperback edn 1992), Jewish Self-Hatred: Anti-Semitism and the Hidden Language of the Jews 1986 (edited and revised German edn 1993), Excerpted in The Mind 1987, Oscar Wilde's London (Book of the Month Club 1989) 1987, Disease and Representation: Images of Illness from Madness to AIDS (with Wolf Von Eckardt and J. E. Chamberlin) 1988 (second edn 1991), Goethe's Touch: Touching, Seeing, and Sexuality. The Andrew W. Mellon Lecture for 1988, Tulane Univ. 1988, Sexuality: An Illustrated History 1989, Inscribing the Other 1991, The Jew's Body (selected by Choice magazine as one of the ten best academic books of 1992) 1991, Rasse, Sexualität, Seuche: Stereotype aus der Innenwelt der westlichen Kultur 1992, The Case of Sigmund Freud: Medicine and Identity at the Fin de Siècle 1993, The Visibility of the Jew in the Diaspora: Body Imagery and Its Cultural Context. The B.G. Rudolph Lecture for 1992 (Program in Jewish Studies, Syracuse Univ.) 1992, Freud, Race, and Gender (Austrian Studies Asscn Prize for the Best Book in Austrian Studies for 1995) 1993, Hysteria: A New History (with Helen King, Roy Porter, George Rousseau and Elaine Showalter) 1993, Jews in Today's German Culture: The Schwartz Lectures 1995, Jews in Today's German Culture (sound recording), Jewish Braille Inst. of America 1995, Health and Illness: Images of Difference 1995, Picturing Health and Illness: Images of Difference 1995, Franz Kafka: The Jewish Patient 1995, L'Autre et le Moi: Stéréotypes occidentaux de la race, de la sexualité et de la maladie 1996, Smart Jews: The Construction of the Idea of Jewish Superior Intelligence at the Other End of the Bell Curve (The Inaugural Abraham Lincoln Lectures) 1996, Love + Marriage = Death and Other Essays Representing Difference 1998, Creating Beauty to Cure the Soul: Race and Psychology in the Shaping of Aesthetic Surgery (Hon. Mention, Outstanding Book of 1998, Gustavus Meyer Center) 1998, Making the Body Beautiful: A Cultural History of Aesthetic Surgery 1999, How I Became a German: Jurek Becker's Life in Five Worlds. Occasional Paper No. 23, German Historical Inst., Washington, DC 1999, The Fortunes of the Humanities: Teaching the Humanities in the New Millennium 2000, Jurek Becker and Cultural Resistance in the German Democratic Republic. The Inaugural Heinz Bluhm Memorial Lecture, Boston Coll. 2001, Jurek Becker: Die Biographie 2002, Jewish Frontiers: Essays on Bodies, Histories, and Identities 2003, Jurek Becker – A Life in Five Worlds 2003, Fat Boys: A Slim Book 2004, Kann die jüdische Diasporaerfahrung als Modell für die heutige Muslimische Diaspora in Europa dienen? 2004, Franz Kafka 2005, Multiculturalism and the Jews 2006, Fat: A Cultural History of Obesity 2008, Diseases and Diagnoses: The Second Age of Biology 2010, Obesity: The Biography 2010; editions: Johannes Agricola, Die Sprichwörtersammlungen: Eine historisch-kritische Ausgabe (two vols) 1971, NS-Literaturtheorie: Eine Dokumentation 1971, The City and Sense of Community: A Symposium 1976, Friedrich Maximilian von Klinger, Werke (co-ed. 21-vol. edn and ed. of ten of Klinger's novels and his philosophical writings 1978ff, Vol. 11: Fausts Leben, Thaten und Höllenfahrt 1978, Vol. 18: Der Weltmann und der Dichter 1985, Vol. 12: Giafar der Barmeciden (with Thomas Salumets) 2004, Vol. 13: Raphael (with Thomas Salumets and Karl-Heinz Hartmann) 1990, Vol. 16: Geschichte eines Teutschen der neusten Zeit 2007, Robert Blum: Aus dem literarischen Nachlass (and reprint series of five vols of Blum's writings) (with Karl-Heinz Hartmann and Thomas Salumets) 1979, Begegnungen mit Nietzsche 1981 (third edn 1987), Introducing Psychoanalytic Theory 1982, J. P. Eckermann: Aphorismen 1984, Degeneration: The Dark Side of Progress 1985, Conversations with Nietzsche: A Life in the Words of his Contemporaries (with J. E. Chamberlin; translated by David Parent) (selected by Choice magazine as one of the ten best academic books of 1988) 1987, Friedrich Nietzsche on Rhetoric and Language: With the Full Text of His Lectures on Rhetoric Published for the First Time 1989, Mathemata retorikes (Greek trans.) (with Carole Blair and David Parent) 2004, "Zettelwirtschaft": Briefe Friedrich Gundolfs und Hermann Brochs an Gertrude von Eckardt-Lederer. Mit Briefen von Elisabeth Gundolf, Bertold Vallentin und Joachim Ringelnatz 1992, Anti-Semitism in Times of Crisis 1991, Heine and the Occident 1991,

Reading Freud's Reading (with Peter U. Hohendahl) 1993, Reemerging Jewish Culture in Germany: Life and Literature Since 1989 (with Jutta Birmele, Jay Geller and Valerie Greenberg) 1994, Freud (The German Library) (with Karen Remmler) 1995, Special Issue on "Germanité, judaïté, altérité", Revue Germanique Internationale 5 1996, Yale Companion to Jewish Writing and Thought in German Culture, 1006–1996 1997, Abgetrieben: Alexander Polzin (with texts by Sander L. Gilman, Thomas Brasch, Michael Hagner, Adolf Muschg, Doron Rabinovici, Moshe Zuckermann) (with Jack Zipes) 1997, Special Issue on "Ethnicity", PMLA 113, Jan. 1998, Special Issue on "New Illnesses – Old Problems; Old Illnesses – New Problems", Studies in 20th Century Literature 22, Winter 1998, Special Issue on "Medicine and Culture", Nineteenth Century Prose 25 Spring 1998, Der schejne Jid: Das Bild des "jüdischen Körpers" in Mythos und Ritual 1998, Jewries at the Frontier (with Robert Jütte) 1999, Gesichter der Weimarer Republik: eine physiognomische Kulturgeschichte (with Milton Shain) 2000, A New Germany in the New Europe (with Claudia Schmölders) 2000, Deutsch-jüdische Literatur der neunziger Jahre: Die Generation nach der Shoah (Beiheft zur Zeitschrift für deutsche Philologie 11) (with Todd Herzog) 2002, Special Issue on "The New Genetics and the Old Eugenics: The Ghost in the Machine", Patterns of Prejudice 36 (with Hartmut Steinecke) 2002, Special Issue on "Schönheit-Beauty", Formationen 2 2001, A Jew in the New Germany – Selected Writings of Henryk Broder (with Lilian Friedberg) 2003, Smoke: A Global History of Smoking (with Zhou Xun) 2004 (translated into several languages), Special Issue on "Body and the Mind in the History of Psychiatry", History of Psychiatry 17(1) 2006, Special Issue on "Race and Contemporary Medicine: Biological Facts and Fictions", Patterns of Prejudice 40 2006, Race and Contemporary Medicine: Biological Facts and Fictions 2008, Special Issue on "Beyond Klezmer: The Legacy of Eastern European Jewry Today", Shofar: An Interdisciplinary Journal of Jewish Studies 25 (with Elizabeth Loentz) 2006, Other Renaissances (with Brenda Schildgen and Zhou Gang) 2006, Diets and Dieting: A Cultural Encyclopedia 2007, B42 Special Issue on Psychoanalysis in the University: The Clinical Dimension, International Journal of Psychoanalysis 90: 5 Oct. 2009, Wagner and Cinema (with Jeongwon Joe) 2010. *Honours:* Hon. Prof., Depts of German and Comparative Literature, Free Univ. of Berlin 2000; Hon. mem. American Psychoanalytic Asscn 2007; Hon. LLD (Toronto) 1997; Outstanding Alumnus, Grad. School, Tulane Univ. 1979, Modern Language Asscn Distinguished Humanist Award, Melton Center for Jewish Studies, Ohio State Univ. 1994George Morgan Award for Creativity and Innovation in Interdisciplinary Education, Brown Univ. 1994, Mertes Prize, German Historical Inst., Washington, DC 1997, Alexander von Humboldt Research Prize, Humboldt Foundation, Bonn 1998, 2009, Berlin Prize, American Acad., Berlin 2000–01, Outstanding German Educator and Checkpoint Charlie Foundation Scholarship, American Asscn of Teachers of German 2002, Between Cultures: In Honor of Sander Gilman at 60: A Conference at the Einstein Forum, Potsdam 2005. *Address:* Graduate Institute of the Liberal Arts, Emory University, S415 Callaway Center, Atlanta, GA 30322-0660, USA (office). *Telephone:* (404) 712-4671 (office). *E-mail:* sander.gilman@emory.edu (office). *Website:* www.psp.emory.edu/sandergilman (office).

GILMOUR, Sir David, Kt, BA, FRSL; British writer; b. 14 Nov. 1952, London; m. Sarah Anne Bradstock 1975; one s. three d. *Education:* Balliol Coll., Oxford. *Career:* Deputy Ed. and Contributing Ed., Middle East International, London 1978–85; Research Fellow, St Antony's Coll., Oxford 1996–97. *Publications:* Dispossessed: The Ordeal of the Palestinians 1980, Lebanon: The Fractured Country 1983, The Transformation of Spain: From Franco to the Constitutional Monarchy 1985, The Last Leopard: A Life of Giuseppe di Lampedusa (Marsh Biography Award 1989) 1988, The Hungry Generations 1991, Cities of Spain 1992, Curzon (Duff Cooper Prize 1994) 1994, The French and Their Revolution (ed.) 1998, Paris and Elsewhere (ed.) 1998, The Long Recessional: The Imperial Life of Rudyard Kipling (Elizabeth Longford Prize for Historical Biography 2003) 2001, The Ruling Caste: Imperial Lives in the Victorian Raj 2005, The Last Leopard 2007; contrib. to periodicals, including New York Review of Books, the Spectator, Sunday Times. *Address:* The Barn House, Alkerton, Oxfordshire, OX15 6NL, England; 27 Ann Street, Edinburgh, EH4 1PL, Scotland (home).

GILROY, Frank Daniel, BA; American dramatist, screenwriter, writer, producer and director; b. 13 Oct. 1925, New York, NY; m. Ruth Dorothy Gaydos 1954; three s. *Education:* Dartmouth College, Yale School of Drama. *Career:* mem. Dirs Guild of America; Dramatists Guild (pres. 1969–71), Writers Guild of America. *Publications:* fiction: Private 1970, Little Ego (with Ruth Gilroy) 1970, Little Ego (with Ruth Gilroy) 1970, From Noon Till Three 1973; non-fiction: I Wake Up Screening: Everything You Need to Know About Making Independent Films Including a Thousand Reasons Not To 1993, Writing for Love And/Or Money 2007; other: plays: Who'll Save the Plowboy? 1957, The Subject was Roses 1962, That Summer, That Fall 1967, The Only Game in Town 1968, The Next Contestant 1978, Last Licks 1979, Real to Reel 1987, Match Point 1990, A Way with Words 1991, Give the Bishop My Faint Regards 1992, Any Given Day 1993, Contact with the Enemy 1999; films: The Fastest Gun Alive (with Russell House) 1956, Gallant Hours (with Beirne Lay Jr) 1960, Desperate Characters 1970, From Noon till Three 1977, Once in Paris 1978, The Gig 1985, The Luckiest Man in the World 1989. *Honours:* Obie Award 1962, Outer Circle Award 1964, Drama Critics Circle Award 1964, New York Theatre Club Award 1964–65, Tony Award 1965, Pulitzer Prize for Drama 1965, Best Screenplay Award, Berlin Film Festival 1970. *Address:* c/o Dramatists Guild, 1501 Broadway, New York, NY 10036, USA (office).

GIMFERRER, Pere; Spanish writer and literary manager; b. 22 June 1945, Barcelona; s. of the late Pere Gimferrer and Carmen Torrens; m. 1st María Rosa Caminals 1971 (died 2003); m. 2nd Cuca de Cominges 2006. *Education:* Univ. of Barcelona. *Career:* Head of Literary Dept, Editorial Seix Barral 1970, Literary Consultant 1973, Literary Man. 1981–; Academician, Real Acad. Española 1985–, Acad. Européenne de Poésie, Luxembourg, World Acad. of Poetry, Verona. *Publications:* Arde el Mar 1966, L'Espai Desert 1977, Dietari 1981, Fortuny 1983, El Vendaval 1988, La Llum 1991, The Roots of Miró 1993, Complete Catalan Work, Vol. I 1995, Vol. II 1995, Vol. III 1996, Vol. IV 1996, Vol. V 1997, Masquerade (poem) 1996, L'Agent Provocador 1998, Marea Solar, Marea Lunar 2000, El Diamant dins l'Aigua 2001, Interludio azul 2006, Amor en vilo 2006, Tornado 2008, Rapsodia (poem) 2011, Alma Verrs (poem) 2013. *Honours:* Nat. Prize for Poetry 1966, 1989, Critic's Prize 1983, 1989, Premio Nacional de las Letras Españolas 1998, Queen Sofía Prize for Iberoamerican Poetry 2000, Int. Octavio Paz Prize for Poetry and Essay 2006, Prize for Bullfighting 2010. *Address:* Editorial Seix Barral, Diagonal 662, Barcelona 08034 (office); Rambla de Catalunya 113, Barcelona 08008, Spain (home). *Telephone:* (93) 4967003 (office); (93) 2150242 (home). *Fax:* (93) 4967004 (office).

GINZBURG, Carlo, PhD; Italian historian and academic; b. 1939, Turin; s. of Leone Ginzburg and Natalia Levi; m. 1st (divorced); m. 2nd Luisa Ciammitti; two d. *Education:* Scuola Normale Superiore, Pisa, Warburg Inst., London, Univ. of Pisa. *Career:* fmr Asst in Modern Italian History, Univ. of Rome; apptd Prof. of Modern History, Univ. of Bologna 1970; Franklin D. Murphy Prof. of Italian Renaissance Studies, Univ. of California, Los Angeles 1988–2006; Visiting Prof., Princeton Univ.; currently teaches at Scuola Normale Superiore di Pisa; several visiting fellowships. *Publications:* I benandanti: Stregoneria e culti agrari tra Cinquecento e Seicento 1966, Il nicodemismo: Simulazione e dissimulazione religiosa nell'Europa del '500 1970, Giochi di pazienza: Un seminario sul Beneficio di Cristo (with Adriano Prosperi) 1975, Il formaggio e i vermi: Il cosmo di un mugnaio del '500 1976, Indagini su Piero: Il Battesimo, il Ciclo di Arezzo, la Flagellazione di Urbino 1981, Storia notturna: Una decifrazione del sabba 1989, Il giudice e lo storico: Considerazioni in margine al processo sofri 1991, Il registro: Carcere politico di Civitavecchia (ed. with Aldo Natoli and Vittorio Foa) 1994, Das Schwert und die Glühbirne 1999, No Island è un'isola 2000, Un dialogo 2003. *Honours:* Citta di Montesilvano 1989, Aby Warburg Prize 1992, Balzan Prize 2010. *Address:* Scuola Normale Superiore, Piazza dei Cavalieri, 7, 56126 Pisa, Italy (office). *Telephone:* (50) 509111 (office). *Fax:* (50) 563513 (office). *E-mail:* info@pec.sns.it (office). *Website:* www.sns.it (office).

GIOIA, (Michael) Dana, MA, MBA; American writer and poet; *Judge Widney Professor of Poetry and Public Culture, University of Southern California*; b. 24 Dec. 1950, Los Angeles, Calif.; s. of Michael Gioia and Dorothy Gioia (née Ortiz); m. Mary Hiecke 1980; three s. (one deceased). *Education:* Stanford and Harvard Univs. *Career:* fmr Visiting Writer, Colorado Coll., Johns Hopkins Univ., Wesleyan Univ.; Chair. Nat. Endowment for the Arts 2003–09; Dir Harman-Eisner Program in the Arts, Aspen Inst. 2009–11, Harman-Eisner Sr Fellow in the Arts 2011–; Judge Widney Prof. of Poetry and Public Culture, Univ. of Southern California 2011–; Chair. Nat. Endowment for the Arts 2003–09; mem. Bd and Vice-Pres. Poetry Soc. of America; mem. Wesleyan Univ. Writers' Conf., Citizens' Stamp Advisory Cttee (USA); regular contrib. to various journals, reviews and periodicals including San Francisco magazine (classical music critic). *Dance:* Counting the Children 1994. *Opera:* Nosferatu, Tony Caruso's Final Broadcast 2008. *Radio:* Nat. Endowment for the Arts Big Read radio shows (32 episodes). *Publications include:* The Ceremony and Other Stories 1984, Daily Horoscope 1986, Mottetti: Poems of Love (trans.) 1990, The Gods of Winter 1991, Can Poetry Matter? 1992, An Introduction to Poetry 1994, The Madness of Hercules (trans.) 1995, Interrogations at Noon (American Book Award 2002) 2001, Nosferatu (opera libretto with Alva Henderson) 2001, The Barrier of a Common Language (essays) 2003, Twentieth-century American Poetry 2004, Twentieth-century American Poetics 2004, 100 Great Poets of the English Language 2005, Literature for Life 2012, Pity the Beautiful 2012; also ed. of several works of literary criticism. *Honours:* ten hon. doctorates; Esquire Best of New Generation Award 1984, Frederick Bock Prize for Poetry 1985, American Book Award 2001, Nat. Civilian's Medal 2009, Laetare Medal 2010, John Carroll Medal 2011. *Address:* Taper Hall 355-K, University of Southern California, 3501 Trousdale Parkway, Los Angeles, CA 90089-0354 (office); 7190 Faught Road, Santa Rosa, CA 95403, USA (office). *Telephone:* (213) 740-2797 (office). *E-mail:* gioia@usc.edu (office). *Website:* www.danagioia.net.

GIORDANO, Paolo, BSc; Italian writer and physicist; b. 1982, Turin; s. of Bruno Giordano and Iside Giordano. *Education:* Univ. degli Studi di Torino. *Publication:* La solitudine dei numeri primi (Premio Campiello Opera Prima, Premio Fiesole Narrativa Under 40, Premio Strega) (trans. as The Solitude of Prime Numbers) 2008. *Address:* c/o Ufficio Stampa Mondadori, 5° Piano, via Mondadori 1, 20090 Segrate, Italy (office). *E-mail:* pgiordan@to.infn.it (office). *Website:* www.mondadori.it (office).

GIOSEFFI, Daniela, BA, MFA; Italian/Greek/Polish/American poet, novelist, literary critic, editor and teacher and performer (retd); b. (Dorothy Gioseffi), 12 Feb. 1941, Orange, NJ, USA; d. of Daniel Donato Gioseffi and Josephine Buzevski; m. 1st Richard J. Kearney 1965 (divorced 1982); one d.; m. 2nd Dr Lionel B. Luttinger 1986 (died 2007). *Education:* Montclair State Coll., Catholic Univ. of America, School of Arts and Sciences. *Career:* fmr actress and dancer; Prof. of World Literature and Intercultural Communication (retd); mem. Editorial Bd VIA, magazine of literature and culture at Calandra Inst., CUNY; fmr Pres. Skylands Writers' Asscn Inc.; Publr and Ed www.PoetsUSA.com; Ed.-in-Chief Electronic Magazine of Literature; Ed. literary websites: njpoets.com, italianamericanwriters.com, gioseffi.com; Founder/Admin. Bordighera Annual Poetry Prize 1998–; mem. PEN, Acad. of American Poets, Nat. Book Critics' Circle, Poetry Soc. of America, Poets' House, New York. *Radio broadcast:* interview and poetry reading on Library of Congress radio show The Poet and the Poem (Nat. Public Radio) 2006. *Theatre:* Care of the Body, The Sea Hag in the Cave of Sleep, The Birth Dance of Earth, The Brooklyn Bridge Poetry Walk. *Publications:* The Great American Belly Dance (novel) 1977, Eggs in the Lake (poems) 1979, Earth Dancing: Mother Nature's Oldest Rite 1980, Women on War 1990, On Prejudice: A Global Perspective 1993, Words, Wounds and Flowers 1995, Dust Disappears by Carilda Oliver Labra (trans.) 1995, In Bed With the Exotic Enemy: Stories and Novella 1997, Going On (poems) 2000, Symbiosis (poems) 2002, New & Selected Poems: Blood Autumn 2006, Wild Nights, Wild Nights: The Story of Emily Dickinson's Master, Lover of Science and Scientist in Dark Days of Republic (novel with non-fiction afterword) 2010; verse inscribed in marble on wall of Penn Station, NYC 2002; contrib. to Nation, Chelsea, Ambit, Poetry Review, Modern Poetry Studies, Anteus, The Paris Review, American Book Review, The Hungry Mind Review, Prairie Schooner, Independent publishers, Poetry East, The Cortland Review, Big City Lit, Mississippi Review, Pif magazine, Poet Lore, Rain Taxi, Chelsea Review, Rattupallax.com. *Honours:* New York State Council for the Arts Award Grants in Poetry 1972, 1977, American Book Award 1990, PEN American Centre Short Fiction Award 1990, World Peace Award 1993, Lifetime Achievement Award in Educ. and Creative Writing, American Asscn of Educators 2003, John Ciardi Award for Lifetime Achievement in Poetry 2007, NY State Literary Award, Order Sons of Italy in America 2008. *Address:* 57 Montague Street, Box 8G, Brooklyn Heights, New York, NY 11201, USA (home). *Telephone:* (718) 643-3837 (home). *Fax:* (718) 643-3837 (home). *E-mail:* daniela@garden.net (home). *Website:* www.gioseffi.com; www.poetsUSA.com.

GIOVANNI, Nikki, BA; American poet and academic; *University Distinguished Professor, Virginia Polytechnic Institute and State University*; b. (Yolande Cornelia Giovanni), 7 June 1943, Knoxville, Tenn.; d. of Jones Giovanni and Yolande Watson; one s. *Education:* Fisk Univ., Univ. of Cincinnati and Univ. of Pennsylvania. *Career:* Asst Prof. of Black Studies, City Coll. of New York 1968; Assoc. Prof. of English, Rutgers Univ. 1968–72; Prof. of Creative Writing, Coll. Mt. St Joseph on the Ohio 1985; Prof. of English, Va Polytechnic Inst. and State Univ. 1987–, Gloria D. Smith Prof. of Black Studies 1997–99, Univ. Distinguished Prof. 1999–; founder, Nixtom Ltd 1970; Visiting Prof. Ohio State Univ. 1984; recordings and TV appearances. *Publications include:* Black Feeling, Black Talk 1968, Black Judgement 1968, Re: Creation 1970, Poem of Angela Yvonne Davis 1970, Spin A Soft Black Song 1971, Gemini 1971, My House 1972, A Dialogue: James Baldwin and Nikki Giovanni 1973, Ego Tripping and Other Poems for Young Readers 1973, A Poetic Equation: Conversations Between Nikki Giovanni and Margaret Walker 1974, The Women and the Men 1975, Cotton Candy on a Rainy Day 1978, Vacationtime 1980, Those Who Ride the Night Winds 1983, Sacred Cows . . . and other Edibles 1988, Conversations with Nikki Giovanni 1992, Racism 101 1994, Grand Mothers 1994, Selected Poems of Nikki Giovanni 1996, Shimmy Shimmy Shimmy Like My Sister Kate 1996, Nikki in Philadelphia 1997, Love Poems 1997, Blues: For All the Changes 1999, Grand Fathers 1999, Quilting the Black-Eyed Pea: Poems and Not-Quite Poems 2002, The Collected Poetry of Nikki Giovanni 2003, The Prosaic Soul of Nikki Giovanni 2003, The Girls in the Circle 2004, Rosa 2005, Acolytes 2007, On My Journey Now 2007, The Grasshopper's Song 2008, Lincoln and Douglass: An American Friendship 2008, Hip Hop Speaks to Children 2008, Bicycles: Love Poems 2009, Best African American Fiction 2010 (co-ed.) 2009. *Honours:* recipient of numerous awards and 24 hon. degrees. *Address:* Department of English, Virginia Polytechnic Institute and State University, 323 Shanks Hall, Blacksburg, VA 24061, USA (office). *Telephone:* (540) 231-9453 (office). *E-mail:* info@nikki-giovanni.com (office). *Website:* www.english.vt.edu (office); www.nikki-giovanni.com.

GIRARD, Keith; American editor; *Editor and Publisher, The Improper. Career:* fmr reporter, The Washington Post, Regardie's, Washingtonian magazine; Ed.-in-Chief, The Daily Record 1992–99, Investment News 1999–2003, Billboard magazine 2003–04; Ed. and Publisher, The Improper Online magazine 2006–. *Address:* The Improper Online, 220 E. 60th Street, Suite 11C, New York, NY 10022, USA (office). *Telephone:* (646) 246-4477 (office). *E-mail:* kgirard@theimproper.com (office). *Website:* www.theimproper.com (office).

GIRARD, René Noël, PhD; French/American academic and writer; *Professor Emeritus, Stanford University*; b. 25 Dec. 1923, Avignon; s. of Joseph Girard and Thérèse Fabre; m. Martha Virginia McCullough 1951; two s. one d. *Education:* Lycée d'Avignon, Ecole des Chartes and Indiana Univ. *Career:* Instructor of French, Indiana Univ. 1947–51, Duke Univ. 1952–53; Asst Prof., Bryn Mawr Coll. 1953–57; Assoc. Prof., Johns Hopkins Univ 1957–61, Prof. 1961–68, Chair. Romance Languages 1965–68, James M. Beall Prof. of French and Humanities 1976–80; Prof. Inst. d'études françaises Bryn Mawr, Avignon 1961–68, Dir 1969; Distinguished Faculty Prof. of Arts and Letters, State Univ. of New York at Buffalo 1971–76; Andrew B. Hammond Prof. of French Language, Literature and Civilization, Stanford Univ. 1981–95, Courtesy Prof. of Religious Studies and Comparative Literature 1986–95, Dir Program of Interdisciplinary Research, Dept of French and Italian 1987–95, Prof. Emer. 1995–; mem. Center for Int. Security and Arms Control, 1990–95; Fellow, American Acad. of Arts and Sciences 1979, Guggenheim Fellow 1960, 1967; elected mem. Acad. Française 2005. *Publications include:* Mensonge romantique et vérité romanesque 1961, Dostoïevski: du double à l'unité 1963, La violence et le sacré 1972, Des choses cachées depuis la fondation du monde 1978, Le bouc émissaire 1982, La route antique des hommes pervers 1985, Shakespeare: Les feux de l'envie 1990, A Theatre of Envy. William Shakespeare 1991, Quand ces choses commenceront 1994, The Girard Reader 1996, Je vois Satan tomber comme l'éclair 1999, (in English) 2001, Celui par qui le scandale arrive 2001, La voix méconnue du réel 2002, Les Origines de la Culture 2004, Achever Clausewitz 2007, Battling to the End 2009. *Honours:* Hon. DLit (Vrije Univ.) 1985, Hon. DTheol (Innsbruck) 1988, (St Mary's Seminary, Baltimore) 2003, (Montreal) 2004, (London) 2005, Hon. DLit (Padua) 2001, Dr hc (Univ. of Antwerp) 1995, (Montreal) 2004, (St Andrews) 2008; Chevalier, Ordre Nat. de la Légion d'honneur 1984, Officier, Ordre des Arts et Lettres 1984; Acad. Française Prize 1973, Grand Prix de Philosophie 1996; Prix Médicis-Essai 1990, Premio Nonino (Percoto, Udine, Italy) 1998, Dr Leopold Lucas Prize, Tübingen 2006, Lifetime Achievement Award, Modern Language Asscn 2008.

GIRMAY, Aracelis, BA, MFA; American poet and academic; *Assistant Professor of Poetry, Hampshire College*; b. 1977, Santa Ana, Calif. *Education:* Connecticut Coll., New York Univ. *Career:* raised in Southern Calif.; fmrly taught at Queen's Coll.; teacher, Drew Univ. MFA Program; currently Asst Prof. of Poetry, Hampshire Coll. *Publications include:* poetry: Teeth 2007, Kingdom Animalia (Isabella Gardner Award 2011) 2011; other: changing, changing 2005. *Address:* c/o Mail Code IA, Hampshire College, 893 West Street, Amherst, MA 01002, USA (office). *Telephone:* (413) 549-4600 (Amherst) (office). *E-mail:* agIA@hampshire.edu (office). *Website:* www.hampshire.edu/faculty/agirmay.htm (office).

GISCOMBE, Cecil S., BA, MFA; American poet, writer and academic; *Professor, Department of English, University of California, Berkeley*; b. 30 Nov. 1950, Dayton, Ohio; m. Katharine Wright 1975; one d. *Education:* State Univ. of New York at Albany, Cornell Univ. *Career:* Faculty, Syracuse Univ. 1977, Cornell Univ. 1980–89; Prof. of English, Illinois State Univ. 1989–98, Pennsylvania State Univ.; Prof., Dept of English, Univ. of California, Berkeley 2010–; mem. Poets and Writers. *Publications:* poetry: Postcards 1977, Here 1994, Giscombe Road 1998, Inland 2001, Prairie Style 2008; non fiction: Into and Out of Dislocation 2000; contrib. to periodicals. *Honours:* Carl Sandburg Award for Poetry 1998. *Address:* Department of English, University of California, 417 Wheeler Hall, Berkeley, CA 94720, USA (office). *Telephone:* (510) 642-2736 (office). *Fax:* (510) 642-8738 (office). *E-mail:* csgiscombe@berkeley.edu (office). *Website:* english.berkeley.edu/profiles/30 (office).

GIVNER, Joan Mary, BA, MA, PhD; British fmr academic and writer; b. 5 Sept. 1936, Manchester, England; m. David Givner 1958; two d. *Education:* Univ. of London, Washington Univ., St Louis. *Career:* Prof. of English, Univ. of Regina 1965–95; Ed., Wascana Review 1984–92; Fellow, Bunting Inst., Radcliffe Coll., Harvard Univ. 1978–79; mem. Saskatchewan Writers' Guild. *Television:* Katherine Anne Porter: The Eye of Memory (USA 1986). *Plays:* Mazo and Caroline 1992. *Publications:* Katherine Anne Porter: A Life 1982, Tentacles of Unreason 1985, Katherine Anne Porter: Conversations (ed.) 1987, Unfortunate Incidents 1988, Mazo de la Roche: The Hidden Life 1989, Scenes from Provincial Life 1991, The Self-Portrait of a Literary Biographer 1993, In the Garden of Henry James 1996, Thirty Four Ways of Looking at Jane Eyre 1998, Half Known Lives 2001, Playing Sarah Bernhardt 2004, Ellen Fremedon: Journalist 2005, Ellen Fremedon 2007, Ellen's Book of Life 2010, A Girl Called Tennyson 2011. *E-mail:* dgivner@attglobal.net. *Website:* uregina.ca/givnerj/index.html.

GJESSING, Ketil, Cand.Philol; Norwegian poet and writer (retd); b. 18 Feb. 1934, Oslo. *Education:* Univ. of Oslo. *Career:* teacher, Atlantic Coll. (now United World Coll. of the Atlantic) 1965–66; dramaturg at the Radio Drama Dept, Norwegian Broadcasting Corp. 1966–99; adviser, Klassisk Musikkmagasion 2001; mem. Norwegian Authors' Asscn, Norwegian Authors' Centre, Norwegian Translators' Asscn. *Publications:* 10 collections of poetry, including Dans på roser og glass (Dance on Roses and Glass) 1996; contrib. to Aftenposten (newspaper), Vinduet, Samtiden (magazines) and others. *Honours:* Gyldendals Pris 1983, Språklig Samlings Litteraturpris 1996. *Address:* Dannevigsvn 12, 0463 Oslo, Norway (home). *Telephone:* (22) 382351 (home).

GLADWELL, Malcolm, BA; Canadian (b. British) writer; b. 1963, England. *Education:* Univ. of Toronto. *Career:* grew up in Canada; science writer, The Washington Post, later New York bureau chief 1987–96; staff writer, The New Yorker 1996–. *Publications:* The Tipping Point: How Little Things can Make a Big Difference 2000, Blink: The Power of Thinking Without Thinking 2005, Outliers: The Story of Success 2008, What the Dog Saw 2009. *Address:* The New Yorker, 4 Times Square, New York, NY 10036-6592, USA (office). *E-mail:* malcolm@gladwell.com (office). *Website:* www.gladwell.com.

GLAISTER, Lesley Gillian, BA, MA, FRSL; British writer and teacher; *Lecturer in Creative Writing, University of St Andrews*; b. 4 Oct. 1956, Wellingborough, Northamptonshire; three s. *Education:* Open Univ., Univ. of Sheffield. *Career:* teacher of Creative Writing, Sheffield Hallam Univ. 1993–2011; Writer-in-Residence, Univ. of Edinburgh 2008–11; lecturer in Creative Writing, Univ. of St Andrews 2011–. *Publications:* novels: Honour Thy Father, Trick or Treat, Digging to Australia, Limestone and Clay 1993,

Partial Eclipse 1994, The Private Parts of Women 1996, Easy Peasy 1997, Sheer Blue Bliss 1999, Now You See Me 2001, As Far As You Can Go 2004, Nina Todd Has Gone 2007, Chosen 2010; plays: Bird Calls (Crucible Theatre, Sheffield) 2003. *Honours:* Somerset Maugham Award, Betty Trask Award, Yorkshire Author of the Year Award 1993. *Address:* 8 Greenbank Loan, Edinburgh, EH10 5JH, Scotland (home).

GLANTZ, Margo, MA, PhD; Mexican writer, essayist, critic and academic; b. 28 Jan. 1930, Mexico City; d. of James Glantz and Elizabeth Shapiro; m. 1st Francisco Lopez Camara 1950 (divorced 1964); m. 2nd Luis Mario Schneider 1970; two d. *Education:* Universidad Nacional Autónoma de México, Univ. of Paris (Sorbonne), France. *Career:* fmr mem. Faculty of Philosophy and Letters, Universidad Nacional Autónoma de México, Prof. Emer. 1994–; Cultural Dir Mexican Cultural Inst. of Israel 1966–69; taught at Montclair State Coll., NJ 1971; Dir Directorate of Publs and Libraries, Ministry of Educ. 1982; Dir of Literature, Nat. Inst. of Fine Arts 1983; Cultural Attache, Embassy in London 1986; Fellow, Council of the Humanities, Princeton Univ. 1994; Dir Virtual Library Miguel de Cervantes, Univ. of Alicante 2005. *Publications:* narrative: Las mil y una calorías 1978, Las genealogías (relato autobiográfico) (Premio Magda Donato 1982) 1981, 1997 and 2006, Apariciones 1996, Zona de derrumbe 2001, El rastro (Premio Sor Juana Inés de la Cruz 2003) 2002, Historia de una mujer que caminó por la vida con zapatos de diseñador 2005, essays: Viajes en México. Crónicas extranjeras 1964, Tennessee Williams y el teatro norteamericano 1964, La aventura del Conde de Rousset Boulbon 1972, Doscientas ballenas azules, La Máquina de Escribir 1979, No pronunciarás 1980, Repeticiones. Ensayos sobre literatura mexicana 1980, Intervención y pretexto. Ensayos de literatura comparada e iberoamericana 1981, El día de tu boda 1982, La lengua en la mano 1983, De la amorosa inclinación de enredarse en cabellos 1984, Erosiones 1984, Síndrome de naufragios (Premio Xavier Villaurrutia) 1984, Borrones y borradores. Ensayos sobre literatura colonial 1992, Alvar Núñez Cabeza de Vaca 1993, Esguince de cintura (ensayos sobre narrativa mexicana del siglo XX) 1994, La Malinche 1994 and 2001, Obra selecta de Sor Juana Inés de la Cruz (selección y prólogo de Margo Glantz y cronología y bibliografía de María Dolores Bravo Arriaga) 1994, Sor Juana Inés de la Cruz, ¿hagiografía o autobiografía? 1995, Sor Juana Inés de la Cruz: saberes y place 1996, Sor Juana: La comparación y la hipérbole 2000; journals: La escritura como ceremonia 1997, La escritura como ceremonia 1997, Siempre es posible lo peor (políticas de la memoria) 1999, El segundo sexo 1999, Juan Gelman 2000, Salones de belleza 2000, Paul Celan, en el fondo... 2000, Feliz cumpleaños, Tito 2001, Brasil sigue 2002, Sigamos con Argentina 2002, Aniversarios aciagos 2002, Cómo aprovechar las vacaciones escolares 2002, ¿Qué hacer con el patrimonio cultural? 2002, Estaciones, fortificaciones y campos de concentración 2002, Libertades civiles y la tortura 2002, El espacio de lo público 2002, Irving Penn en el Metropolitan 2002, La austeridad de la abundancia 2002, Belice a vuelta de rueda 2002, A la memoria de Arreola por Margo Glantz 2002, Margo Glantz: la ética de la gratitud 2003, las palabras del cuerpo por Reina Roffé 2003, El fraude y su globalización 2003, Lilia Carillo en el Museo Cuevas 2003, Los perros héroes de Bellatin 2003, El nuevo orden mundial y la destrucción de la cultura 2003, La guerra de las palabras 2003, Historia natural de la destrucción 2003, Nacionalismo e impostura 2003, Santa: los pecados de la carne 2003, Una ballena llamada Ariel 2004, Y creímos que era inmortal 2004, La boda 2004, Mirando por el ojo de Bataille 2004, Pedro Páramo por Margo Glantz Babelia 2005, Catástrofes y desaguisados 2005, Un Apocalipsis de bolsillo 2005, Berlín, una extraña fascinación 2005, Gran investigadora: Dolores Bravo 2006, La celosa de sí misma 2006, Reivindicar ciencia y cultura 2006, Mi amigo Sergio Pitol 2006, ¿Cómo matar a una mujer 2006, Autobiografía de los otros, Esperanza López Parada, Una escritora de contrastes 2006. *Honours:* Dr hc (Universidad Nacional Autónoma de México) 2005; Premio Universidad Nacional 1991, Premio Nacional de Ciencias y Artes 2004. *Address:* c/o Academia de la Lengua Mexicana, AC Liverpool 76, 06600 México DF, Mexico (office).

GLANVILLE, Brian Lester; British writer and journalist; b. 24 Sept. 1931, London; s. of James A. Glanville and Florence Manches; m. Elizabeth De Boer 1959; two s. two d. *Education:* Charterhouse. *Career:* first sports columnist and football corresp., Sunday Times 1958–92; sports columnist, The People 1992–96, football writer, The Times 1996–98, Sunday Times 1998–; literary adviser, Bodley Head 1958–62. *Plays for radio:* The Rise of Gerry Logan, The Diary, I Could Have Been King, A Visit to the Villa. *Television:* original writer of That Was The Week That Was 1962; wrote BBC documentary European Centre Forward (winner Berlin Prize) 1963. *Publications:* novels: Along the Arno 1956, The Bankrupts 1958, Diamond 1962, The Rise of Gerry Logan 1963, A Second Home 1965, A Roman Marriage 1966, The Artist Type 1967, The Olympian 1969, A Cry of Crickets 1970, The Comic 1974, The Dying of the Light 1976, The Catacomb 1988, Dictators 2001; sport: Soccer Nemesis 1955, Champions of Europe 1991, Story of the World Cup 1993, The Arsenal Stadium History 2006, England Managers: The Toughest Job in Football 2007, For Club and Country (Obits) 2008, The Real Arsenal 2009; short stories: A Bad Streak 1961, The Director's Wife 1963, The King of Hackney Marshes 1965, The Thing He Loves 1985, Love Is Not Love; plays: A Visit to the Villa 1981, Underneath the Arches (musical, co-author) 1982, The Diary (radio play) 1986; other: Football Memories (autobiog.) 1999. *Honours:* Silver Bear Award, Berlin Film Festival, for European Centre Forward (BBC TV documentary) 1963. *Address:* 160 Holland Park Avenue, London, W11 4UH, England (home). *Telephone:* (20) 7603-6908 (home). *E-mail:* grandpam21@aol.com (home).

GLAVINIC, Thomas; Austrian writer; b. 2 April 1972, Graz; m.; one s. *Career:* fmr taxi driver and advertising copy writer. *Publications:* novels: Carl Haffners Liebe zum Unentschieden (trans. as Carl Haffner's Love of the Draw) 1998, Herr Susi 2000, Der Kameramörder (Friedrich-Glauser-Preis 2002) 2001, Wie man leben soll 2004, Die Arbeit der Nacht (trans. as Night Work) 2006, Das bin doch ich 2007, Das Leben der Wünsche 2009. *Honours:* Vienna Author's Scholarship 1995, Project Scholarship of the Austrian Fed. Chancellery 2001, Elias-Canetti Scholarship, Vienna 2002, Austrian Fed. Scholarship for Literature 2002, Great Austrian Fed. Prize for Literature 2006. *Address:* c/o Carl Hanser Verlag GmbH & Co. KG, Postfach 86 04 20, 81631 Munich, Germany (office). *Telephone:* (89) 998300 (office). *Fax:* (89) 99830-460 (office). *E-mail:* info@hanser.de (office). *Website:* www.hanser.de (office); www.thomas-glavinic.de.

GLEICK, James, BA; American author and journalist; b. 1 Aug. 1954, New York; s. of Donen Gleick and Beth Gleick; m. Cynthia Crossen. *Education:* Riverdale Country School, Harvard Univ. *Career:* Founder and fmr Man. Ed. Metropolis (weekly newspaper), Minneapolis; copy ed. and science and tech. reporter, New York Times 1986–88, later contrib.; McGraw Distinguished Lecturer, Princeton Univ. 1989–90; co-devised Pipeline Network (internet service) with Uday Ivatury 1993. *Publications include:* Chaos: Making a New Science 1987, Nature's Chaos (co-author) 1990, Genius: The Life and Science of Richard Feynman 1992, Faster: The Acceleration of Just About Everything 1999, What Just Happened: A Chronicle from the Electronic Frontier 2002, Isaac Newton 2003, The Information: A History, A Theory, A Flood (Hessell-Tiltman Prize for History 2012) 2011; contrib., Atlantic, Slate, Washington Post. *Literary Agent:* c/o Michael Carlisle, InkWell Management, 521 Fifth Avenue, 26th Floor, New York, NY 10175, USA. *Telephone:* (212) 922-3500. *Fax:* (212) 922-0535. *E-mail:* info@inkwellmanagement.com. *Website:* www.inkwellmanagement.com.

GLENDINNING, Hon. Victoria, CBE, MA, FRSL; British author and journalist; b. 23 April 1937, Sheffield, Yorks., England; d. of Baron Seebohm of Hertford and Lady Seebohm (née Hurst); m. 1st O. N. V. Glendinning 1959 (divorced 1981); four s.; m. 2nd Terence de Vere White 1981 (died 1994); m. 3rd Kevin O'Sullivan 1996. *Education:* St Mary's School, Wantage, Millfield School, Somerville Coll., Oxford and Univ. of Southampton. *Career:* part-time teaching 1960–69; part-time psychiatric social work 1970–73; Editorial Asst Times Literary Supplement 1974–78; Pres. English Centre of PEN 2001, Vice-Pres. 2001–; Vice-Pres. Royal Soc. of Literature 2000–. *Publications:* A Suppressed Cry 1969, Elizabeth Bowen: Portrait of a Writer 1977, Edith Sitwell: A Unicorn Among Lions 1981, Vita: A Biography of V. Sackville-West 1983, Rebecca West: A Life 1987, The Grown-Ups (novel) 1989, Hertfordshire 1989, Trollope 1992, Electricity (novel) 1995, Sons and Mothers (co-ed.) 1996, Jonathan Swift 1998, Flight (novel) 2001, Leonard Woolf (biog.) 2006, Love's Civil War: Elizabeth Bowen and Charles Ritchie, Letters and Diaries (ed.) 2008; articles in newspapers and journals. *Honours:* Hon. Fellow, Somerville Coll., Oxford; Hon. DLitt (Southampton) 1994; Dr hc (Ulster) 1995; Hon. LittD (Dublin) 1995; Hon. DUniv (York) 2000. *Literary Agent:* c/o David Higham Associates Ltd, 5–8 Lower John Street, Golden Square, London, W1F 9HA, England. *Telephone:* (20) 7434-5900. *Fax:* (20) 7437-1072. *E-mail:* dha@davidhigham.co.uk. *Website:* www.davidhigham.co.uk.

GLENDOWER, Rose (see Harris, Marion Rose)

GLICKMAN, James A., BA, MFA; American educator and writer; b. 29 Dec. 1948, Davenport, IA; m. Elissa Deborah Gelfand 1982; one s. *Education:* Univ. of Iowa Writers' Workshop. *Career:* Instructor, Univ. of Arizona Law School, Tucson 1972; English Teacher, Community Coll. of Rhode Island, Lincoln 1972–, now Prof. of English; Faculty mem., Radcliffe Seminars, Cambridge, Mass 1985–88. *Publications:* Sounding the Waters 1996; contrib. short stories to periodicals including Kansas Quarterly, Redbook, Ladies Home Journal, Worcester Review. *Literary Agent:* Kenneth Wright, Writers House, 21 West 26th Street, New York, NY 10010, USA. *Address:* 51 McGilpin Road, Sturbridge, MA 01566-1230, USA (home).

GLIORI, Debi, BA; British children's writer and illustrator; b. (Deborah Gliori), 21 Feb. 1959, Glasgow, Scotland; five c. *Education:* Edinburgh Coll. of Art. *Publications:* writer and illustrator: New Big Sister 1991, New Big House 1992, When I'm Big 1992, My Little Brother 1992, A Lion at Bedtime 1993, Mr Bear Babysits 1994, The Snowchild 1994, Mr Bear's Picnic 1995, Little Bear and the Wish Fish 1995, Mr Bear Says (series) 1995–, The Snow Lambs 1995, Princess and the Pirate King 1996, Mr Bear to the Rescue 1996, Hello, Baby Bear 1998, Mr Bear's New Baby 1998, Give him my Heart 1998, No Matter What 1999, Mr Bear's Holiday (Scottish Arts Council Children's Book Award) 2000, Flora's Blanket 2001, Pure Dead Magic 2001, Polar Bolero 2001, Where, Oh Where, is Baby Bear? 2001, Pure Dead Wicked 2002, Tickly Under There 2002, Can I Have a Hug? 2002, Flora's Flowers 2002, Debi Gliori's Bedtime Stories 2002, Penguin Post 2002, Flora's Surprise 2003, Little Owls Swim 2003, Little Fox's Picnic 2003, Hush, Little Chick 2003, Wake Up, Little Rabbit! 2003, Pure Dead Brilliant 2003, Deep Trouble 2004, Where Did That Baby Come From? 2004, Deep Water 2005, Pure Dead Trouble 2005, Deep Fear 2006, Pure Dead Batty 2006, Goodnight Baby Bat 2007, The Trouble With Dragons 2009, Stormy Weather 2010, The Scariest Thing of All 2011; illustrator of books by other authors, including: The Oxford A.B.C. Picture Dictionary 1990, Dulcie Dando (Sue Stops) 1990, Margery Mo (Margaret Donaldson) 1991, The Incredible Shrinking Hippo (Stephanie Baudet) 1991, Lizzie and Her Puppy (David Martin) 1993, Amazing Alphabets (Lisa Bruce)

1993, A Present for Big Pig (Kate Simpson) 1994, What Can I Give Him? (Christina Georgina Rossetti) 1998, Tell Me Something Happy Before I Go to Sleep (Joyce Dunbar) 1998, The Very Small (Joyce Dunbar) 2000, Tell Me What It's Like to be Big (Joyce Dunbar) 2001, Always and Forever (Alan Durant) 2003; poetry: Noisy Poems 1997, DK Book of Nursery Rhymes (ed.) 2000. *Address:* c/o Bloomsbury Publishing PLC, 50 Bedford Square, London, WC1B 3DP, England. *E-mail:* csm@bloomsbury.com (office).

GLOAG, Julian, BA, MA, FRSL, FRSA; British novelist; b. 2 July 1930, London; s. of John Gloag; one s. one d. *Education:* Rugby School, Magdalene Coll., Cambridge. *Television screenplays:* Only Yesterday 1986, The Dark Room 1988. *Publications:* Our Mother's House 1963, A Sentence of Life 1966, Maundy 1969, A Woman of Character 1973, Sleeping Dogs Lie 1980, Lost and Found 1981, Blood for Blood 1985, Only Yesterday 1986, Love as a Foreign Language 1991, Le passeur de la nuit 1996, Chambre d'ombre 1996. *Address:* 36 rue Gabrielle, 75018 Paris, France (home). *Telephone:* 1-42-55-86-55 (home).

GLOCER, Thomas (Tom) Henry, BA, JD; American lawyer and business executive; *CEO, Thomson-Reuters*; b. 8 Oct. 1959, NY; s. of Walter Glocer and Ursula Glocer (née Goodman); m. Maarit Leso 1988; one s. one d. *Education:* Columbia Univ., Yale Univ. Law School. *Career:* mergers and acquisitions lawyer, Davis Polk and Wardwell, New York, Paris and Tokyo 1985–93; joined Reuters 1993, mem. Legal Dept Gen. Counsel, Reuters America Inc., New York 1993–96, Exec. Vice-Pres., Reuters America Inc. and CEO Reuters Latin America 1996–98, CEO Reuters business in the Americas 1998–2001, Reuters Inc. 2000–01, CEO Reuters Group PLC (Thomson-Reuters following merger with Thomson 2007) 2001–; Dir New York City Investment Fund 1999–2003, Instinet Corpn 2000–; mem. Bd of Dirs Merck & Co. Inc. 2007–, Partnership for New York City, Int. Business Council, World Econ. Forum; mem. Advisory Bd Singapore Monetary Authority 2001–, Judge Inst. of Man., Univ. of Cambridge, European Business Leaders Council, Tate Gallery Corpn; mem. Int. Advisory Bd British American Business Inc., Madison Council, Library of Congress; mem. Corp. Council, Whitney Museum of American Art 2000–; mem. Council on Foreign Relations. *Publications include:* author of computer software, including Coney Island: A Game of Discovery (co-author) 1983. *Honours:* New York Hall of Science Award 2000, John Jay Alumni Award 2001. *Address:* Thomson-Reuters, Reuters Building, Canary Wharf, London, E14 5EP, England (office). *Telephone:* (20) 7250-1122 (office). *Fax:* (20) 7542-4064 (office). *Website:* www.reuters.com (office); www.thomsonreuters.com (office); www.tomglocer.com (home).

GLOVER, Douglas, BA, MLitt, MFA; Canadian writer and editor; *Faculty Member, Vermont College of Fine Arts*; b. 14 Nov. 1948, Simcoe, Ont.; s. of Murray Glover and Jean Ross; divorced; two s. *Education:* York Univ., Univ. of Edinburgh, UK, Univ. of Iowa, USA. *Career:* various writer-in-residencies; Lecturer, Skidmore Coll. 1992, 1993; Visiting Prof., Colgate Univ. 1995, State Univ. of NY, Albany 1996–98, 2000–01, Skidmore Coll. 1998–2000; Faculty mem., MFA in Writing Program, Vermont Coll. of Fine Arts 1994–; McGee Prof. of Writing, Davidson Coll. 2005; Ed. Coming Attractions 1991–95, Best Canadian Stories 1996–2006, Numéro Cinq Magazine 2010–; mem. Writers' Union of Canada, Authors' Guild. *Publications:* The Mad River 1981, Precious 1984, Dog Attempts to Drown Man in Saskatoon 1985, The South Will Rise at Noon 1988, A Guide to Animal Behaviour 1991, Coming Attractions (co-ed., five vols) 1991–95, The Life and Times of Captain N 1993, The Journey Prize Anthology (ed.) 1994, Best Canadian Stories (ed.) 1996–99, 2000–06, Notes from a Prodigal Son 1999, Sixteen Categories of Desire 2000, Elle 2003, Bad News of the Heart 2003, The Enamoured Knight 2004, Attack of the Copula Spiders 2012; contrib. to numerous journals and magazines. *Honours:* Canadian Fiction Magazine Contrib.'s Prize 1985, Literary Press Group Writers' Choice Award 1986, Nat. Magazine Award for Fiction 1990, Gov.-Gen.'s Award for Fiction 2003, Writers' Trust Timothy Findley Award 2006. *Literary Agent:* c/o Anne McDermid & Associates Ltd, 83 Willcocks Street, Toronto, ON M5S 1C9, Canada. *Telephone:* (416) 324-8845. *Fax:* (416) 324-8870. *E-mail:* info@mcdermidagency.com. *Website:* www.mcdermidagency.com. *E-mail:* dg@douglasglover.net (office). *Website:* www.douglasglover.net.

GLOVER, Jane Alison, CBE, MA, DPhil, FRCM; British conductor; *Director of Opera, Royal Academy of Music*; b. 13 May 1949, d. of the late Robert Finlay Glover and Jean Muir. *Education:* Monmouth School for Girls and St Hugh's Coll., Oxford. *Career:* Jr Research Fellow, St Hugh's Coll. 1973–75, Lecturer in Music 1976–84, Sr Research Fellow 1982–84; Lecturer, St Anne's Coll., Oxford 1976–80, Pembroke Coll. 1979–84; mem. Univ. of Oxford Faculty of Music 1979–; professional conducting debut at Wexford Festival 1975; operas and concerts for BBC, Glyndebourne 1982–, Royal Opera House 1988–, Covent Garden, ENO 1989–, London Symphony Orchestra, London Philharmonic Orchestra, Royal Philharmonic Orchestra, Philharmonia, Royal Scottish Orchestra, English Chamber Orchestra, Royal Danish Opera, Glimmerglass Opera, New York 1994–, Australian Opera 1996– and many orchestras in Europe and USA; Prin. Conductor London Choral Soc. 1983–2000; Artistic Dir London Mozart Players 1984–91; Prin. Conductor Huddersfield Choral Soc. 1989–96; Music Dir Music of the Baroque, Chicago, USA 2002–; Dir of Opera, RAM 2009–; mem. BBC Cen. Music Advisory Cttee 1981–85, Music Advisory Cttee, Arts Council 1986–88; Gov. RAM 1985–90, BBC 1990–95. *Television:* documentaries and series and presentation, especially Orchestra 1983, Mozart 1985. *Radio:* talks and series including Opera House 1995, Musical Dynasties 2000. *Publications:* Cavalli 1978, Mozart's Women: His Family, His Friends, His Music 2005; contribs to The New Monteverdi Companion 1986, Monteverdi 'Orfeo' Handbook 1986; articles in numerous journals. *Honours:* Hon. DMus (Exeter) 1986, (CNAA) 1991, (London) 1992, (City Univ.) 1995, (Glasgow) 1996; Hon. DLitt (Loughborough) 1988, (Bradford) 1992; Dr hc (Open Univ.) 1988, (Brunel) 1997. *Address:* Royal Academy of Music, Marylebone Road, London, NW1 5HT, England (office). *Telephone:* (20) 7873-7373 (office). *E-mail:* j.glover@ram.ac.uk (office). *Website:* www.ram.ac.uk (office); www.janeglover.co.uk; www.baroque.org.

GLOVER, Judith; British writer; b. 31 March 1943, Wolverhampton, West Midlands, England; two d. *Education:* Wolverhampton High School for Girls, Aston Polytechnic. *Career:* has worked for Wolverhampton Express & Star, Wolverhampton Chronicle, Sussex Express, Kent Messenger. *Publications:* Place Names of Sussex 1975, Place Names of Kent 1976, Sussex in Photographs 1976, Drink Your Own Garden 1979, The Sussex Quartet: The Stallion Man 1982, Sisters and Brothers 1984, To Everything a Season 1986; Birds in a Gilded Cage 1987, The Imagination of the Heart 1989, Tiger Lilies 1991, Mirabelle 1992, Minerva Lane 1994, Pride of Place 1995, Sussex Place-Names 1997; contrib.: Sussex Life, Surrey Life. *Address:* c/o Artellus Ltd, 30 Dorset House, Gloucester Place, London, NW1 5AD, England.

GŁOWACKI, Janusz; Polish writer, playwright and screenwriter; b. 13 Sept. 1938, Poznań; m.; one d. *Education:* Warsaw Univ. *Career:* columnist in Kultura weekly 1964–81; lecturer in many colls and univs in USA including Bennington, Yale, Cornell, Columbia; Playwright-in-Residence, New York Shakespeare Festival 1984 and Mark Taper Forum, Los Angeles 1989; Fellow in Writing, Univ. of Iowa 1977, 1982; Hon. mem. Univ. of Iowa 1977, 1982; mem. American and Polish PEN Club 1984–, Polish Film Union. *Publications:* short stories: Nowy taniec la-ba-da 1970, Paradis 1973, Polowanie na muchy 1974, My Sweet Raskolnikov 1977, Opowiadania wybrane 1978, Skrzek. Coraz trudniej kochać 1980, Rose Café 1997; novels: Moc truchleje 1981, Ostani cieć 2001; screenplays: Rejs 1970, Psychodrama (with Marek Piwowski) 1971, Polowanie na muchy 1971, Trzeba zabić tę miłość 1974, No Smoking Section (co-author) 1987, Hairdo (Tony Cox Screenwriting Award, Nantucket Film Festival, USA 1999) 1999; plays: Cudzołóstwo ukarane 1971, Mecz 1977, Obciach 1977, Kopciuch (Cinders) (Premio Molière, Argentina 1986) 1981, Fortinbras Gets Drunk 1986, Hunting Cockroaches (First Prize, American Theatre Critics Asscn 1986, Joseph Kesselring Award 1987, Hollywood Drama League Critics' Award 1987) 1986, Antigone in New York (Le Balladine Award for the Best Play of 1997) 1993, Ścieki, Skrzeki, karaluchy (selected works) 1996, Czwarta siostra (Grand Prize, Int. Theatre Festival, Dubrovnik 2001) 2000. *Honours:* Joseph Kesserling Award 1987, Drama League of New York Playwrighting Award 1987, Guggenheim Award 1988, Alfred Jurzykowski Foundation Award 1997. *Address:* ul. Bednarska 7 m. 4, 00-310 Warsaw, Poland; 845 West End Avenue, Apartment 4B, New York, NY 10025, USA. *Website:* www.januszglowacki.com.

GLÜCK, Louise Elisabeth; American poet, writer and academic; *Rosenkranz Writer-in-Residence, Yale University*; b. 22 April 1943, New York City; d. of Daniel Glück and Beatrice Glück (née Grosby); m. 1st Charles Hertz (divorced); one s.; m. 2nd John Dranow 1977 (divorced 1996). *Education:* Sarah Lawrence Coll., Bronxville, New York and Columbia Univ. *Career:* Artist-in-Residence, Goddard Coll., Plainfield, Vt 1971–72, faculty mem. 1973–74; Poet-in-Residence, Univ. of North Carolina at Greensboro 1973; Visiting Prof., Univ. of Iowa 1976–77; Elliston Prof. of Poetry, Univ. of Cincinnati 1978; Visiting Prof., Columbia Univ. 1979; Holloway Lecturer, Univ. of California, Berkeley 1982; Faculty mem. and Bd mem. MFA Writing Program at Warren Wilson Coll., Swannoa, NC 1980–84; Visiting Prof., Univ. of California, Davis 1983; Scott Prof. of Poetry, Williams Coll., Mass 1983, part-time Sr Lecturer in English 1984–97, Parish Sr Lecturer in English 1997–; Regents Prof. of Poetry, UCLA 1985–88; Baccalaureate Speaker, Williams Coll. 1993; Poet Laureate of Vt 1994; Visiting Mem. of Faculty, Harvard Univ. 1995; Hurst Prof., Brandeis Univ. 1996; Special Consultant in Poetry at Library of Congress, Washington, DC 1999–2000; Poet Laureate of the USA 2003–04; currently Rosenkranz Writer-in-Residence, Yale Univ.; Fellow, American Acad. of Arts and Sciences; mem. PEN, American Acad. and Inst. of Arts and Letters, Acad. of American Poets (mem. Bd of Chancellors 1999–2006). *Publications:* poetry: Firstborn 1968, The House on the Marshland 1975, The Garden 1976, Descending Figure 1980, The Triumph of Achilles 1985, Ararat 1990, The Wild Iris (Pulitzer Prize for Poetry 1993) 1992, Proofs and Theories: Essays on Poetry 1994, The First Four Books of Poems 1995, Meadowlands 1996, Vita Nova 1999, The Seven Ages 2001, October 2004, Averno 2007, A Village Life 2009; contrib. to many anthologies and periodicals. *Honours:* Hon. LLD (Williams Coll.) 1993, (Skidmore Coll.) 1995, (Middlebury Coll.) 1996; Acad. of American Poets Prize 1967, Rockefeller Foundation Grant 1968–69, Nat. Educ. Asscn grants 1969–70, 1979–80, 1988–89, Nat. Endowment for the Arts Fellowships 1969–70, 1979–80, 1988–89, Vt Council for the Arts Grant 1978–79, Lannan Foundation Grant, Eunice Tietjens Memorial Prize 1971, Guggenheim Foundation Grant 1975–76, 1987–88, American Acad. and Inst. of Arts and Letters Literary Award 1981, Nat. Book Critics' Circle Award for poetry 1985, Poetry Soc. of America Melville Cane Award 1986, Wellesley Coll. Sara Teasdale Memorial Prize 1986, Bobbitt Natil Prize, Library of Congress 1992, William Carlos Williams Award 1993, PEN/Martha Albrand Award 1995, New Yorker Magazine Award in Poetry 1999, English Speaking Union Amb. Award 1999, 2001, Bollingen Prize 2001, Wallace Stevens Award 2008. *Literary Agent:* Steven Barclay Agency, 12 Western Avenue, Petaluma, CA 94952, USA.

Telephone: (707) 773-0654. Fax: (707) 778-1868. Website: www.barclayagency.com. Address: 14 Ellsworth Park, Cambridge, MA 02139, USA (home).

GLUCKSMANN, André; French philosopher and essayist; b. 19 June 1937, Boulogne-Billancourt. Education: Lyon, Ecole Normale Supérieure de Saint Cloud. Career: researcher Centre National de la Recherche Scientifique (CNRS). Publications: non-fiction: Le Discours de la guerre 1967, La Cuisinière et le Mangeur d'hommes 1975, Maîtres penseurs 1977, Etat, le marxisme et les camps de concentration 1979, La Force du vertige 1983, La Fêlure du monde: éthique et sida 1994, Dostoïevski à Manhattan 2002, Ouest contre ouest 2003, Le Discours de la haine 2004, Une Rage d'Enfant 2006, Les deux chemins de la philosophie 2009; contrib. articles to numerous publications, including Wall Street Journal, Le Monde. Address: c/o Editions Plon, 76 rue Bonaparte, 75284 Paris Cedex 06, France.

GLYNN, Ian Michael, MD, PhD, FRS, FRCP; British scientist and academic; Professor Emeritus of Physiology, University of Cambridge; b. 3 June 1928, London; s. of Hyman Glynn and Charlotte Glynn; m. Jenifer Muriel Franklin 1958; one s. two d. Education: City of London School, Trinity Coll. Cambridge, Univ. Coll. Hosp. London. Career: House Physician, Cen. Middlesex Hosp. 1952–53; Nat. Service, RAF Medical Br. 1956–57; MRC Scholar, Physiological Lab., Cambridge 1956, Fellow, Trinity Coll. 1955–, Demonstrator in Physiology 1958–63, Lecturer 1963–70, Reader 1970–75, Prof. of Membrane Physiology 1975–86, Prof. of Physiology 1986–95, Prof. Emer. 1995–, Vice-Master Trinity Coll. 1980–86; Visiting Prof., Yale Univ. 1969; mem. British MRC 1976–80, Council of Royal Soc. 1979–81, 1991–92, Agric. Research Council 1981–86; Chair. Editorial Bd Journal of Physiology 1968–70. Publications: The Sodium Pump (with J. C. Ellory) 1985; An Anatomy of Thought: the Origin and Machinery of the Mind 1999; The Life and Death of Smallpox (with Jenifer Glynn) 2004; papers in scientific journals. Honours: Hon. Foreign mem. American Acad. of Arts and Sciences 1984, American Physiological Soc.; Hon. MD (Århus) 1988. Address: Trinity College, Cambridge, CB2 1TQ, England (office). Telephone: (1223) 353079 (office). E-mail: img10@cam.ac.uk (office). Website: www.trin.cam.ac.uk (office).

GODBER, John Harry, BEd, MA, PhD, FRSA; British playwright, film and theatre director and actor; Senior Lecturer, Dance, Drama and Performance Studies Department, Liverpool Hope University; b. 18 May 1956, Hemsworth, Yorks., England; s. of Harry Godber and Dorothy Godber; m. Jane Thornton; two d. Education: Minsthorpe High, Bretton Hall Coll., Wakefield, Univ. of Leeds. Career: fmr Head of Drama, Minsthorpe High; Artistic Dir Hull Truck Theatre Co. 1984–; apptd Prof. of Contemporary Theatre, Liverpool Hope Univ. 2004, currently Sr Lecturer, Dance, Drama and Performance Studies Dept; fmr Prof. of Drama, Univ. of Hull; est. John Godber Co. Plays: Happy Jack 1982, September in the Rain 1983, Up 'n' Under (Laurence Olivier Comedy of the Year Award 1984) 1984, Bouncers (seven Los Angeles Critics' Awards 1986) 1985, Blood, Sweat and Tears 1986, Shakers, Teechers 1987, Salt of the Earth 1988, On the Piste 1990, Happy Families 1991, April in Paris 1992, The Office Party, Passion Killers 1994, Lucky Sods 1995, Dracula 1995, Gym and Tonic 1996, Weekend Breaks 1997, It Started with a Kiss 1997, Unleashed 1998, Perfect Pitch, Thick as a Brick (music by John Pattison) 1999, Big Trouble in Little Bedroom 1999, Seasons in the Sun 2000, On a Night Like This 2000, This House 2001, Departures 2001, Moby Dick 2002, Men of the World 2002, Reunion 2002, Next Best Thing 2007, Sold 2007, Our House 2008, Funny Turns 2009, 20,000 Leagues Under the Sea 2010; also radio plays and TV programmes. Film: Up 'n' Under (writer and dir) 1998. Television: The Ritz (BBC 2 series) 1987, The Continental (BBC Christmas Special), My Kingdom for a Horse (BBC film) 1991, Chalkface (BBC series) 1991, Bloomin' Marvellous (BBC comedy series) 1997, Thunder Road (BBC 4 film) 2001, Portas, Os 2005; has also written numerous episodes of Brookside, Crown Court and Grange Hill. Honours: Hon. Lecturer, Bretton Hall Coll.; Hon. DLitt (Hull) 1988, (Lincoln) 1997, Hon. DUniv; Sunday Times Playwright Award 1981, Olivier Award 1984, Joseph Jefferson Award, Chicago 1988, Fringe First Winner (five times), BAFTA Awards for Best Schools Drama and for Best Original Drama 2005. Literary Agent: c/o Alan Brodie Representation Ltd, Paddock Suite, The Courtyard, 55 Charterhouse Street, London, EC1M 6HA, England. Telephone: (20) 7253-6226. Fax: (20) 7183-7999. E-mail: lisa@alanbrodie.com. Website: www.alanbrodie.com. Address: St Nicholas Swanland, North Ferriby, HU14 3QY, England (home). Telephone: (1482) 633854 (home). E-mail: johnhgodber@hotmail.com. Website: www.johngodber.co.uk.

GODBOUT, Jacques, OQ, BA, MA; Canadian author, poet and filmmaker; b. 27 Nov. 1933, Montréal; m. Ghislaine Reiher 1954; two c. Education: Univ. of Montréal. Career: apptd Lecturer, Univ. of Montréal 1969, Writer-in-Residence 1991–92; Visiting Lecturer, Univ. of California, Berkeley 1985; currently writes for L'Actualité (news magazine). Films: YUL 871 1966, Kid Sentiment 1967, IXE-13 1971, La gammick 1974. Publications: fiction: L'aquarium 1962, Le couteau sur la table 1965, Salut Galarneau! 1967, D'Amour, PQ 1972, L'isle au dragon 1976, Les tetes a Papineau 1981, Une histoire americaine 1986, Le temps des Galarneau 1993, Opération Rimbaud 1999, La Concierge du Panthéon (Prix Maurice-Genevoix 2007) 2006; poetry: Carton-pate 1956, Les pavés secs 1958, C'est la chaude loi des hommes 1960, La grande muraille de Chine (with J. R. Colombo) 1969, Souvenirs Shop 1984; non-fiction: Le réformiste 1975, Le murmure marchand 1984, Abécédaire Québécois 1988, L'écran du bonheur 1990, L'Ecrivain de province 1991, Le sort de l'Amérique 1997. Honours: Prix France-Canada 1962, Prix de l'Académie Française 1965, Gov.-Gen.'s Award for Fiction 1968, Prix Ludger-Duvernay 1973, Prix Belgique-Canada 1978, Prix du Québec Athanase-David 1985, various film prizes. Address: c/o L'Actualité, 1200 McGill College Avenue, Suite 800, Montreal H3B 4G7, Canada.

GODFREY, (William) Dave, BA, MFA, PhD; Canadian novelist; b. 9 Aug. 1938, Winnipeg; m. Ellen Swartz 1963; two s. one d. Education: Univ. of Iowa, Stanford Univ., Univ. of Chicago. Career: Ed. Canadian Writers Series, McClelland and Stewart 1968–72; Co-Founding Ed. News Press, Toronto 1969–73; Ed. Press Porcepic, Erin, Ontario 1972–; Co-founder House of Anansi Press; apptd Vice-Pres. Inter Provincial Asscn for Telematcis and Telidon 1982. Publications: The New Ancestors (Gov.-Gen.'s Award 1971) 1970; short stories: Death Goes Better with Coca Cola 1967, New Canadian Writing 1968, 1969, Dark Must Yield 1978, Gutenberg two (co-ed with Douglas Parkhill) 1979, The Telidon Book, Seaside Rock: The Resource Book 2002, Number Fun Song Resource Pack 2003, Rocky's Plaice 2009. Honours: Univ. of Western Ontario Pres.'s Medal 1965, Canada Council Award 1969.

GODFREY, Paul; British playwright and director; b. 16 Sept. 1960, Exeter, Devon, England. Publications: Inventing a New Colour 1988, A Bucket of Eels 1989, Once in a While the Odd Thing Happens 1990, The Panic 1991, The Blue Ball 1993, The Modern Husband 1994, The Candidate 1995, The Invisible Woman 1996, Catalogue of Misunderstanding 1997, Collected Plays (vol. 1) 1998, Tiananmen Square 1999, The Oldest Play 2000, Linda 2000, The Best Sex of my Life (screenplay) 2003.

GODINE, David R., MA, EdM; American publisher; Founder-President, David R. Godine, Inc.; b. 4 Sept. 1944, Cambridge, Mass; s. of Morton R. Godine and Bernice Beckwith; m. Sara Sangree Eisenman 1988; one s. one d. Education: Dartmouth Coll., Harvard Univ. Career: Founder-Pres. David R. Godine Inc. 1970–; mem. Bds Massachusetts Historical Soc., Massachusetts Horticultural Soc.; Fellow, Pierpoint Morgan Library. Publication: Renaissance Books of Science From the Collection of Albert E. Lownes (ed) 1970, The Red Pear Garden: Three Great Dramas of Revolutionary China 1973, 200 Years of American Sculpture 1976, The Field and Forest Handy Book: New Ideas for Out of Doors 2000, The Half-Life of An American Essayist (ed) 2008. Honours: Dwiggins Award 1984. Address: David R. Godine, Inc., Fifteen Court Square, Suite 320, Boston, MA 02108-4715 (office); 196 School Street, Milton, MA 02186, USA (home). Telephone: (617) 451-9600 (office). Fax: (617) 350-0250 (office). E-mail: info@godine.com (office). Website: www.godine.com (office).

GODLEE, Fiona N., MB, BChir, FRCP; British editor, writer and publisher; Editor, British Medical Journal; m.; two c. Career: apptd Asst Ed., British Medical Journal (BMJ) 1990, Editorial Dir, establishing open-access online publr BioMed Central, Current Science Group 2000–03, Head of Knowledge Div. BMJ Publishing Group 2003–04, Ed. British Medical Journal 2004–; fmr Pres. World Asscn of Medical Eds; Chair., Cttee on Publication Ethics 2004–05; Harkness Fellow, Harvard Univ. 1994. Address: BMJ Publishing Group Ltd, BMA House, Tavistock Square, London, WC1H 9JR, England (office). Website: www.bmjpg.com (office); www.publicationethics.org.uk (office).

GODWIN, Gail Kathleen, PhD; American writer; b. 18 June 1937, Birmingham, Ala; d. of Mose Godwin and Kathleen Krahenbuhl; m. 1st Douglas Kennedy Cole (divorced 1961); m. 2nd Ian Marshall 1965 (divorced 1966). Education: Peace Jr Coll. Raleigh, NC and Univs of North Carolina and Iowa. Career: news reporter, Miami Herald 1959–60; reporter and consultant, US Travel Service, London 1961–65; Editorial Asst Saturday Evening Post 1966; Fellow, Center for Advanced Study, Univ. of Illinois, Urbana 1971–72; Lecturer, Iowa Writers' Workshop 1972–73, Vassar Coll. 1977, Columbia Univ. Writing Program 1978, 1981; American specialist, USIS 1976; Guggenheim Fellow 1975–76; librettist for various productions; mem. PEN, Authors' Guild, Authors' League, Nat. Book Critics' Circle. Publications: novels including: The Perfectionists 1970, Glass People 1972, The Odd Woman 1974, Violet Clay 1978, A Mother and Two Daughters 1982, The Finishing School 1985, A Southern Family 1987, Father Melancholy's Daughter 1991, The Good Husband 1994, Evensong 1998, Evenings At Five 2003, Queen of the Underworld 2005, Unfinished Desires 2009; non-fiction: Heart 2001; The Making of A Writer: Journals (ed.) 1961–63 2006; also short stories, uncollected stories, novellas and librettos. Honours: American Acad. and Inst. of Arts and Letters Literature Award 1981. Address: PO Box 946, Woodstock, NY 12498-0946, USA (office). E-mail: gail@gailgodwin.com (office). Website: www.gailgodwin.com.

GODWIN, Parke; American novelist; b. 28 Jan. 1929, New York, NY. Education: American Univ., Washington, DC. Publications: The Masters of Solitude (co-author), 1978; Firelord, 1980; Wintermind (co-author), 1982; A Memory of Lions, 1983; A Cold Blue Light (co-author), 1983; Beloved Exile, 1984; The Fire When It Comes, 1984; The Last Rainbow, 1985; A Truce with Time (A Love Story with Occasional Ghosts), 1988; Invitation to Camelot: An Arthurian Anthology of Short Stories (ed.), 1988; Waiting for the Galactic Bus, 1988; The Snake Oil Wars: or, Scheherazade Ginsberg Strikes Again, 1989; Sherwood, 1991; Robin and the King, 1993; Limbo Search, 1995; The Tower of Beowulf, 1995; Lord of Sunset, 1998. As Kate Hawks: The Lovers, 1999; Watch by Moonlight, 2001, The Night You Could Hear Forever 2007. Honours: World Fantasy Award 1982. Address: 736 Auburn Ravine Terrace, No. 535, Auburn, CA 95603, USA. E-mail: petgod@foothill.net.

GODWIN, Rebecca Thompson, BA, MA; American writer; b. 9 July 1950, Charleston, South Carolina; m. 1st; two d.; m. 2nd Deane Bogardus 1988. *Education:* Coastal Carolina Coll., Middlebury Coll. *Career:* Ed. and Writer, Bennington magazine 1994–2002; teacher, Bennington Writing Workshops 1995, Wildacres Writing Workshops 1996; Faculty Ed. Plain China: The Bennington Literary Magazine 2009; Faculty Ed. Plain China: Best Undergraduate Writing 2009–; mem. of various Associated Writing Programs;. *Publications:* Private Parts 1992, Keeper of the House 1994; contribs to South Carolina Review, Paris Review, Iris, Crescent Review, First Magazine. *Literary Agent:* c/o Colleen Mohyde, The Doe Coover Agency, PO Box 668, Winchester, MA, USA. *Telephone:* (781) 721-6000. *Fax:* (781) 721-6727. *E-mail:* cmohyde@aol.com. *Website:* www.doecooveragency.com. *Address:* PO Box 211, Poestenkill, NY 12140, USA. *E-mail:* rgodwin@bennington.edu. *Website:* www.rebeccatgodwin.com.

GOERKE, Natasza; Polish short story writer and poet; b. 1960, Poznań. *Education:* Mickiewicz Univ., Poznań, Jagiellonian Univ., Kraków. *Publications:* Fractale 1994, Ksiega Pasztetów 1997, Pozegnania plazmy 1999, 47 na odlew 2002; contribs to The Eagle and the Crow (anthology) 1996, numerous magazines. *Honours:* Czas Kultury Prize 1993, Akademie Schloss Solitude six-month stipendium, Stuttgart 1995. *Address:* c/o Twisted Spoon Press, PO Box 21, Preslova 12, 150 21 Prague 5, Czech Republic.

GOFF, Martyn, OBE, CBE, FIAL, FRSA, FRSL; British author and bookseller; *Executive Director and Chairman, Henry Sotheran Ltd;* b. 7 June 1923, s. of Jacob Goff and Janey Goff. *Education:* Clifton Coll. *Career:* served in RAF 1941–46; worked in film industry 1946–48; bookseller 1948–70; established Booker Prize (later Man Booker Prize) 1969, Admin. 1970–2006, Chair. Advisory Cttee Man Booker Prize 2002–06, currently Pres. Booker Prize Foundation; CEO Book Trust 1970–88, Vice-Pres. 2000– (Deputy Chair. 1991–92, 1996–97, Chair. 1992–96); Fiction Reviewer, Daily Telegraph 1975–88, Non-fiction Reviewer 1988–; Dir and Exec. Chair. Henry Sotheran Ltd antiquarian bookseller 1988–; mem. Arts Council Literature Panel 1973–81, British Nat. Bibliography Research Fund 1976–88, British Library Advisory Council 1977–82, PEN Exec. Cttee 1978–, Exec. Cttee Greater London Arts Council 1982–88, Library and Information Services Council 1984–86; mem. Bd British Theatre Asscn 1983–85; Chair. Paternosters '73 Library Advisory Council 1972–74, New Fiction Soc. 1975–88, School Bookshop Asscn 1977–, Soc. of Bookmen 1982–84 (Pres. 1997–), 1890s Soc. 1990–99, Nat. Life Story Collections 1996–2004, Poetry Book Soc. 1996–99 (mem. Bd 1992–99), Wingate Scholarships 1988–2004, H. H. Wingate Foundation 1998–, Books for Keeps; Vice-Pres. Royal Overseas League 1996–; Dir Nat. Book League (mem. Prize Cttee 2008), Battersea Arts Centre 1992–97 (Trustee 1981–85), Trustee Cadmean Trust 1981–99, Nat. Literary Trust 1993–2004. *Publications:* fiction: The Plaster Fabric 1957, A Season With Mammon 1958, A Sort of Peace 1960, The Youngest Director 1961, Red on the Door 1962, The Flint Inheritance 1965, Indecent Assault 1967, The Liberation of Rupert Bannister 1978, Tar and Cement 1988; non-fiction: A Short Guide to Long Play 1957, A Further Guide to Long Play 1958, LP Collecting 1960, Why Conform? 1968, Victorian and Edwardian Surrey 1972, Record Choice 1974, Royal Pavilion 1976, Organising Book Exhibitions 1982, Publishing 1988, Prize Writing: An Original Collection of Writings by Past Winners to Celebrate 21 Years of the Booker Prize (ed.) 1989. *Honours:* Hon. DLitt (Oxford Brookes) 2003; The Bookseller Services to Bookselling Award 2001. *Address:* Henry Sotheran Ltd, 2 Sackville Street, London, W1S 3DP (office); 95 Sisters Avenue, London, SW11 5SW, England (home). *Telephone:* (20) 7734-1150 (office); (20) 7228-8164 (home). *Fax:* (20) 7434-2019 (office); (20) 7738-9893 (home).

GOKHALE, Namita; Indian writer and editor; b. 1956, Lucknow; m. Rajiv Gokhale (deceased); two d. *Career:* fmr co-ed. Super (film magazine); Founder Dir Jaipur Literature Festival, Yatra Books, Translating Bharat. *Publications include:* Paro: Dreams of Passion 1984, Gods, Graves and Grandmothers 1994, A Himalayan Love Story 1996, Mountain Echoes (essays) 1994, The Book of Shadows 1999, The Book of Shiva (essays) 2000, Shakuntala: The Play of Memory 2005, The Puffin Mahabharata 2009, In Search of Sita (co-ed) 2009. *Address:* c/o Marketing and Promotions Department, Penguin Books India Pvt. Ltd, 11 Community Centre, Panchsheel Park, New Delhi 110 017, India (office). *E-mail:* publicity@in.penguingroup.com (office). *Website:* www.penguinbooksindia.com (office); www.namitagokhale.com.

GOLD, Herbert, BA, MA, LèsL; American author; b. 9 March 1924, Cleveland; m. 1st Edith Zubrin 1948 (divorced 1956); two d.; m. 2nd Melissa Dilworth 1968 (divorced 1975); two s. one d. *Education:* Columbia Univ., Sorbonne, Univ. of Paris. *Career:* Lecturer, Western Reserve Univ. 1951–53; Faculty, Wayne State Univ. 1954–56; Visiting Prof., Cornell Univ. 1958, Univ. of California at Berkeley 1963, 1968, Harvard Univ. 1964, Stanford Univ. 1967; Mcguffey Lecturer in English, Ohio Univ. 1971; Regents Prof. 1973, Visiting Prof. 1974–79, Univ. of California at Davis. *Publications:* fiction: Birth of a Hero 1951, The Prospect Before Us 1954, The Man Who Was Not With It 1956, 15 x 3 (short stories with R. V. Cassill and James B. Hall) 1957, The Optimist 1959, Therefore Be Bold 1960, Love and Like (short stories) 1960, The Age of Happy Problems 1962, Salt 1963, Father: A Novel in the Form of a Memoir 1967, The Great American Jackpot 1969, Biafra Goodbye 1970, The Magic Will: Stories and Essays of a Decade 1971, My Last Two Thousand Years 1972, Swiftie the Magician 1974, Waiting for Cordelia 1977, Slave Trade 1979, He/She 1980, Family: A Novel in the Form of a Memoir 1981, A Walk on the West Side: California on the Brink 1981, True Love 1982, Mister White Eyes 1984, Stories of Misbegotten Love 1985, A Girl of Forty 1986, Lovers and Cohorts: Twenty Seven Stories 1986, Dreaming 1988, Travels in San Francisco 1990, Best Nightmare on Earth: A Life In Haiti 1991, Bohemia: Where Art, Angst, Love and Strong Coffee Meet 1993, She Took My Arm as if She Loved Me 1997, Daughter Mine 2000, Still Alive!: A Temporary Condition (memoir) 2008, Not Dead Yet: A Feisty Bohemian Explores the Art of Growing Old 2011; contribs to various periodicals. *Honours:* Ohioana Book Award 1957, Longview Foundation Award 1959, California Literature Medal 1968, Commonwealth Club Award for Best Novel, San Francisco 1982, Sherwood Anderson Prize for Fiction 1989; Hon. LHD (Baruch Coll., CUNY) 1988. *Address:* c/o Skyhorse Publishing, Inc. 307 West 36th Street, 11th Floor, New York, NY 10018, USA.

GOLDBARTH, Albert, BA, MFA; American poet, writer and academic; *Adele Davis Distinguished Professor of Humanities, Department of English,* Wichita State University; b. 31 Jan. 1948, Chicago, IL. *Education:* Univ. of Illinois, Univ. of Iowa, Univ. of Utah. *Career:* Instructor, Elgin Community Coll., IL 1971–72, Central YMCA Community Coll., Chicago 1971–73, Univ. of Utah 1973–74; Asst Prof., Cornell Univ. 1974–76; Visiting Prof., Syracuse Univ. 1976; Asst Prof. of Creative Writing, Univ. of Texas at Austin from 1977; currently Adele Davis Distinguished Prof. of Humanities in the Dept of English, Wichita State Univ. *Publications:* poetry: Under Cover 1973, Coprolites 1973, Opticks: A Poem in Seven Sections 1974, January 31 1974, Keeping 1975, A Year of Happy 1976, Comings Back: A Sequence of Poems 1976, Curve: Overlapping Narratives 1977, Different Flashes 1979, Eurekas 1980, Ink Blood Semen 1980, The Smuggler's Handbook 1980, Faith 1981, Who Gathered and Whispered Behind Me 1981, Goldbarth's Book of Occult Phenomena 1982, Original Light: New and Selected Poems 1973–1983 1983, Albert's Horoscope Almanac 1986, Arts and Sciences 1986, Popular Culture 1989, Delft: An Essay Poem 1990, Heaven and Earth: A Cosmology 1991, Across the Layers: Poems Old and New 1993, The Gods 1993, Marriage, and Other Science Fiction 1994, Adventures in Ancient Egypt 1996, Beyond 1998, Saving Lives 2001, Combinations of the Universe 2003, Budget Travel through Space and Time 2005, Kitchen Sink: New and Selected Poems 1972–2007 2007, To Be Read in 500 Years 2009; fiction: Pieces if Payne 2001; essays: A Sympathy of Souls 1990, Great Topics of the World: Essays 1994, Many Circles: New and Selected Essays 2001; editor: Every Pleasure: The 'Seneca Review' Long Poem Anthology 1979. *Honours:* Theodore Roethke Prize 1972, Ark River Review Prizes 1973, 1975, NEA grants 1974, 1979, Guggenheim Fellowship 1983, Nat. Book Critics Circle Award 2002. *Address:* c/o English Department, 620 Lindquist Hall, Box 14, Wichita State University, Wichita, KS 67260-0014, USA (office). *Telephone:* (316) 978-0014 (office). *Fax:* (316) 978-3548 (office). *Website:* www.wichita.edu (office).

GOLDBERG, Barbara June, MA, MEd, MFA; American poet, translator, teacher and speechwriter; *Senior Speechwriter, AARP;* b. 26 April 1943, Wilmington, Del.; d. of Eric Heymann and Emily Briess Heymann; m. 1st J. Peter Kiers 1963 (divorced 1970); m. 2nd Charles Goldberg 1971 (divorced 1990), two s. *Education:* Mt Holyoke Coll., Yeshiva Univ., Columbia Univ., American Univ. *Career:* Man. speechwriter, AARP (fmrly American Asscn of Retired Persons) 1998–2004, Sr Speechwriter 2004–; Dir Editorial Bd, The Word Works publrs 1987–99; Dir, Editorial Services American Speech-Language-Hearing Asscn 1988–98; Exec. Ed., Poet Lore 1990–98; mem. Poetry Soc. of America; individual mem. Associated Writing Programs. *Publications include:* Berta Broad Foot and Pepin the Short: A Merovingian Romance 1985, Cautionary Tales (Camden Award) 1990, Marvelous Pursuits (Violet Reed Hass Award) 1995, The Royal Baker's Daughter (Felix Pollak Poetry Prize) 2008; three books of poems in Hebrew translation including Night Watch; translations: The Stones Remember: Native Israeli Poetry 1996, After the First Rain: Israeli Poems on War and Peace 1998, The Fire Stays in Red: Poems of Ronny Someck (trans. with Moshe Dor) 2001; editor: The First Yes: Poems on Communication 1996; contribs to American Poetry Review, American Scholar, Gettysburg Review, Paris Review, Poetry, Virginia Quarterly. *Honours:* two Nat. Endowment for the Arts Fellowships, four Maryland State Art Council Fellowships for poetry, Armand G. Erpf Award of Columbia Univ.'s Trans. Center, Witter Bynner Foundation Award, Violet Reed Haas Poetry Award, Felix Pollak Poetry Prize. *Address:* 6703 Fairfax Road, Chevy Chase, MD 20815, USA (home). *Telephone:* (202) 434-2581 (office). *E-mail:* bjgoldberg@comcast.net (home).

GOLDBERG, Jacqueline; Venezuelan poet and novelist; b. 24 Nov. 1966, Maracaibo. *Publications:* Treinta soles desaparecidos 1985, De un mismo centro 1986, Luba 1988, Trastienda 1991, Una señora con sombrero (Premio los Mejores del Banco del Libro 1994) 1993, Mi bella novia voladora (Premio Nacional de Literatura Infantil Miguel Vicente Pata Caliente 1993) 1994, A fuerza de ciudad 1995, Insolaciones en Miami Beach 1995, Carnadas 1998, La casa sin sombrero 2001, La salud 2002, Una sal donde estoy de pie 2003, Historias sepultadas en un cementerio judío 2003, El Orden de las ramas 2003, Benjamin caballito de mar 2004, Exilio a la vida 2006, Verbos predadores 2007. *Address:* c/o Editorial Equinoccio, Universidad Simón Bolívar, valle de Sartenejas, Edificio Comunicaciones, ala sur, 1er piso, Caracas, Venezuela (office). *Telephone:* (212) 906-3162 (office). *E-mail:* equinoccio@usb.ve (office). *Website:* www.equinoccio.cultura.usb.ve (office).

GOLDEN, Arthur, MA; American writer; b. 6 Dec. 1956, Chattanooga, Tenn.; s. of Ruth Holmberg; m.; two c. *Education:* Harvard Coll., Columbia Univ., Boston Univ. *Career:* magazine journalist, Tokyo 1980–82; tutor in literature and creative writing, Boston Univ.; mem. Advisory Council, Grub Street, Inc. *Publications:* Memoirs of a Geisha 1997. *Literary Agent:* c/o Darhansoff &

Verrill Literary Agents, 236 West, 26th Street, Suite 802, New York, NY 10001, USA. *Telephone:* (917) 305-1300. *Fax:* (917) 305-1400. *E-mail:* info@dvagency.com.

GOLDEN, Mark, MA, PhD; Canadian academic and writer; *Professor of Classics, University of Winnipeg*; b. 6 Aug. 1948, Winnipeg, Man.; m. Monica Becker 1985; one s. *Education:* Univ. Coll., Toronto, Univ. of Toronto. *Career:* Lecturer, later Asst Prof., Univ. of British Columbia 1980–82; Asst Prof., later Prof. of Classics, Univ. of Winnipeg 1982–; Nat. Humanities Center Fellow, Research Triangle Park, NC 1987–88; Visiting Research Fellow, Univ. of New England, Armidale, NSW, Australia 1992; Visiting Fellow, Clare Hall, Cambridge, UK 1995; Center for Hellenic Studies Summer Scholar, Washington, DC 1996. *Publications:* Children and Childhood in Classical Athens 1990, Inventing Ancient Culture: Historicism, Periodization and the Ancient World (co-ed. with Peter Toohey) 1997, Sport and Society in Ancient Greece 1998, Sex and Difference in Ancient Greece and Rome (co-ed. with Peter Toohey) 2003, Sport in the Ancient World from A to Z 2004, Greek Sport and Social Status 2008; contrib. to scholarly books and journals. *Honours:* Rogers Award for Excellence in Research and Scholarship, Univ. of Winnipeg 1998, Ioannides Memorial Lecturer, Univ. of Western Ontario 1999, Fordyce Mitchel Memorial Lecturer, Univ. of Missouri, Columbia 2000, Stubbs Lecturer, Univ. Coll., Toronto 2004, Edson Memorial Lecturer, Univ. of Wisconsin, Madison 2005. *Address:* Department of Classics, University of Winnipeg, Winnipeg, Man. R3B 2E9, Canada (office). *E-mail:* m.golden@uwinnipeg.ca (office).

GOLDIN, Barbara Diamond, BA; American writer and teacher; b. 4 Oct. 1946, New York; m. Alan Goldin 1968 (divorced 1990); one s. one d. *Education:* Univ. of Chicago, Boston Univ., Western Washington Univ. *Publications:* Just Enough Is Plenty: A Hanukkah Tale 1988, The World's Birthday: A Story About Rosh Hashanah 1990, The Family Book of Midrash: Fifty-two Stories from the Sages 1990, Cakes and Miracles: A Purim Tale 1991, Fire!: The Beginnings of the Labor Movement 1992, The Magician's Visit: A Passover Tale 1993, The Passover Journey: A Seder Companion 1994, Red Means Good Fortune: A Story of San Francisco's China Town 1994, Night Lights: A Sukkot Story 1994, Bat Mitzvah: A Jewish Girl's Coming of Age 1995, Creating Angels: Stories of Tzedakah 1996, Coyote and the Fire Stick: A Pacific Northwest Indian Tale 1996, While the Candles Burn: Eight Stories for Hanukkah 1996, The Girl Who Lived with the Bears 1997, Journeys With Elijah 1999, A Mountain of Blintzes 2001, One Hundred and One Read-Aloud Jewish Stories 2001, The Best Hanukkah Ever 2007; contribs to various publications. *Honours:* Nat. Jewish Book Award 1989, Sydney Taylor Book Award 1991, Body-of-Work Award 1997, Asscn of Jewish Libraries Award 1992, American Library Asscn Notable Book Citation 1995. *E-mail:* barbaradiamond@rcn.com.

GOLDMAN, Paul Henry Joseph, BA, FRSA; British art historian; *Associate Fellow, Institute of English Studies, University of London*; b. 3 April 1950, London; m. Corinna Maroulis 1987. *Education:* Univ. of London, Postgraduate Diploma in Art Gallery and Museum Studies, Univ. of Manchester, Diploma, Museums Asscn in Art. *Career:* Asst Keeper, Dept of Prints and Drawings, British Museum, London 1974–97; Founder and Cttee mem. Imaginative Book Illustration Soc.; Fellow Museums Asscn; Assoc. Fellow, Inst. of English Studies, Univ. of London; mem. Soc. of Authors. *Publications:* Sporting Life: An Anthology of British Sporting Prints 1983, Looking at Prints, Drawings and Watercolours 1988, Victorian Illustrated Books 1850–1870: The Heyday of Wood-Engraving 1994, Victorian Illustration: The Pre-Raphaelites, the Idyllic School and the High Victorians 1996 (revised 2004), Retrospective Adventures, Forrest Reid, Author and Collector (ed. with Brian Taylor) 1998, John Everett Millais: Illustrator and Narrator 2004, Beyond Decoration – The Illustrations of John Everett Millais 2005, Lely to Turner: British Drawings and Watercolours 2007; contribs to Oxford Companion to the Book 2010 and Samuel Palmer Revisited 2010, and to journals, reviews, and quarterlies. *Honours:* Hon. Prof., School of English, Communication and Philosophy, Univ. of Cardiff. *Address:* Meadow View, East Orchard, Shaftesbury, Dorset, SP7 0LG, England (home).

GOLDMAN, William, MA; American author and screenwriter; b. 12 Aug. 1931, Chicago, Ill.; s. of M. Clarence Goldman and Marion Weil; m. Ilene Jones 1961; two d. *Education:* Oberlin Coll. and Columbia Univ. *Publications:* novels: The Temple of Gold 1957, Your Turn to Curtsy, My Turn to Bow 1958, Soldier in the Rain 1960, Boys and Girls Together 1964, The Thing of It Is 1967, No Way to Treat a Lady (under pseudonym Harry Longbaugh), Father's Day 1971, The Princess Bride 1973, Marathon Man 1974, Wigger 1974, Magic 1976, Tinsel 1979, Control 1982, The Silent Gondoliers 1983, The Color of Light 1984, Heat 1985, Brothers 1986; play: Blood, Sweat and Stanley Poole 1961 (with James Goldman); musical comedy: A Family Affair (with James Goldman and John Kander) 1962; non-fiction: Adventures in the Screen Trade 1983, Hype and Glory 1990, Four Screenplays 1995, Five Screenplays 1997, Which Lie Did I Tell? 2000; screenplays: Harper 1966, Butch Cassidy and the Sundance Kid 1969, Marathon Man 1976, All the President's Men 1976, A Bridge Too Far 1977, Magic 1978, Heat 1985, Brothers 1987, The Princess Bride 1987, Year of the Comet 1992, Memoirs of an Invisible Man 1992, Chaplin 1992, Indecent Proposal 1993, Maverick 1994, The Ghost and the Darkness 1996, Absolute Power 1997, Hearts in Atlantis 2001, Dreamcatcher 2003. *Honours:* Acad. Award for best original screenplay for Butch Cassidy and the Sundance Kid 1970, Acad. Award for best screenplay adaptation 1977, Laurel Award for Lifetime Achievement in Screenwriting 1983. *Literary*

Agent: Creative Artists Agency, 162 Fifth Avenue, 6th Floor, New York, NY 10010, USA. *Telephone:* (212) 277-9000. *Fax:* (212) 277-9099. *Website:* www.caa.com.

GOLDMARK, Peter Carl, Jr, BA; American newspaper executive and consultant; *Program Director, Climate and Air Program, Environmental Defense Fund*; b. 2 Dec. 1940, New York; s. of Peter Carl Goldmark and Frances Charlotte Trainer; m. Aliette Marie Misson 1964; three d. *Education:* Harvard Univ. *Career:* worked for US Office of Econ. Opportunity, Washington; fmr teacher of history Putney School, Vt; employed in Budget Office, City of New York for four years, later Asst Budget Dir Program Planning and Analysis then Exec. Asst to the Mayor 1971; Sec. Human Services, Commonwealth of Mass. 1972–75; Dir of Budget, NY State 1975–77; Exec. Dir Port Authority of NY and NJ 1977–85; joined Times Mirror Co., Los Angeles 1985, fmr Sr Vice-Pres. Eastern Newspapers Div.; Pres. Rockefeller Foundation 1988–97; Chair. and CEO Int. Herald Tribune 1998–2003; currently, Program Dir, Climate and Air Program, Environmental Defense Fund; mem. Bd of Dirs Financial Accounting Foundation, Lend Lease Corpn, Whitehead Inst. for Biomedical Research. *Address:* Environmental Defense Fund, 257 Park Avenue South, New York, NY 10010, USA (office). *Telephone:* (212) 505-2100 (office). *Fax:* (212) 505-2375 (office). *Website:* www.edf.org (office).

GOLDSMITH, Howard, (Ward Smith, Dayle Courtney), BA, MA; American author and editor; b. 24 Aug. 1945, New York, NY. *Education:* City Univ. of New York, Univ. of Michigan. *Career:* Editorial Consultant, Mountain View Center for Environmental Educ., Univ. of Colorado 1970–85; Sr Ed., Santillana Publishing Co. 1980–85; mem. Poets and Writers, SFWA, Soc. of Children's Book Writers and Illustrators. *Publications:* The Whispering Sea 1976, What Makes a Grumble Smile? 1977, The Shadow and Other Strange Tales 1977, Terror by Night 1977, Spine-Chillers 1978, Sooner Round the Corner 1979, Invasion: 2200 A.D. 1979, Toto the Timid Turtle 1980, The Ivy Plot 1981, Three-Ring Inferno 1982, Plaf Le Paresseux 1982, Ninon, Miss Vison 1982, Toufou Le Hibou 1982, Fourtou Le Kangourou 1982, The Tooth Chicken 1982, Mireille l'Abeille 1982, Little Dog Lost 1983, Stormy Day Together 1983, The Sinister Circle 1983, Shadow of Fear 1983, Treasure Hunt 1983, The Square 1983, The Circle 1983, The Contest 1983, Welcome, Makoto! 1983, Helpful Julio 1984, The Secret of Success 1984, Pedro's Puzzling Birthday 1984, Rosa's Prank 1984, A Day of Fun 1984, The Rectangle 1984, Kirby the Kangaroo 1985, Ollie the Owl 1985, The Twiddle Twins' Haunted House 1985, Young Ghosts 1985, Von Geistern Besessen 1987, The Further Adventures of Batman 1989, Visions of Fantasy 1989, The Pig and the Witch 1990, Mind-Stalkers 1990, Spooky Stories 1990, Little Quack and Baby Duckling 1991, The Proust Syndrome 1992, The President's Train 1991, The Future Light of the World 1993, Evil Tales of Evil Things 1991, The Twiddle Twins' Music Box Mystery 1996, The Gooey Chewy Contest 1996, The Twiddle Twins' Amusement Park Mystery 1997, McGraw-Hill Science Through Stories Series 1998, The Twiddle Twins' Single Footprint Mystery 1999, The Tooth Fairy Mystery 1999, Danger Zone 1999, Strike up the Band 2000, Thomas Edison to the Rescue 2003, Mark Twain at Work 2003, John F. Kennedy and the Stormy Sea 2005, Thomas Jefferson and the Ghost Riders 2008, Web of Fear 2008; contribs to periodicals, journals, magazines, reviews and newspapers. *Honours:* US Public Health Service Fellowship 1965, Rackham Predoctoral Fellowship, Univ. of Michigan 1966, Phi Sigma Science Award 1966. *Address:* 41-07 Bowne Street, Suite 6B, Flushing, NY 11355-5629, USA (office).

GOLDSTEIN, Laurence Alan, BA, PhD; American academic, writer, poet and editor; *Professor of English, University of Michigan*; b. 5 Jan. 1943, Los Angeles, Calif.; s. of Cecil Goldstein and Helen Goldstein; m. Nancy Jo Copeland 1968; two s. *Education:* Univ. of California, Los Angeles, Brown Univ. *Career:* instructor, Brown Univ. 1968–70; Asst Prof., Univ. of Michigan 1970–78, Assoc. Prof. 1978–85, Prof. of English 1985–; Ed. Michigan Quarterly Review 1977–2009. *Publications:* Ruins and Empire: The Evolution of a Theme in Augustan and Romantic Literature 1977, Altamira 1978, The Automobile and American Culture (co-ed. with David L. Lewis) 1983, The Flying Machine and Modern Literature 1986, The Three Gardens 1987, Writers and Their Craft: Short Stories and Essays on the Narrative (co-ed. with Nicholas Delbanco) 1991, Seasonal Performances: A Michigan Quarterly Review Reader (ed.) 1991, The Female Body: Figures, Styles, Speculations (ed.) 1992, The American Poet at the Movies: A Critical History 1994, The Male Body: Features, Destinies, Exposures (ed.) 1994, Cold Reading 1995, The Movies: Texts, Receptions, Exposures (co-ed. with Ira Konigsberg) 1996, Robert Hayden: Essays on the Poetry (co-ed. with Robert Chrisman) 2001, A Room in California 2005, Writing Ann Arbor: A Literary Anthology 2005; contribs to books, anthologies, reviews and journals. *Honours:* Distinguished Service Award, Univ. of Michigan 1977, Univ. of Michigan Press Book Award 1995. *Address:* Department of English, University of Michigan, Ann Arbor, MI 48109, USA (office). *E-mail:* lgoldste@umich.edu (office).

GOLDSTEIN, Rebecca Newberger, BA, PhD; American writer and academic; *Associate Professor, Harvard University*; b. 23 Feb. 1950, White Plains, NY; d. of Bezalel Newberger and Loretta Newberger; m. 1st Sheldon Goldstein 1969 (divorced); two d.; m. 2nd Steven Pinker 2007. *Education:* Princeton Univ. and Barnard Coll., Columbia Univ. *Career:* Asst Prof. of Philosophy, Barnard Coll. 1976–86; Visiting Prof. of Philosophy, Honours Programme, Rutgers Univ. 1988–90; Prof. of Creative Writing, MFA Program, Columbia Univ., New York 1993–96; Scholar-in-Residence, Brandeis Univ., Mass

1999–2000; Visiting Prof. of Philosophy, Trinity Coll., Hartford, Conn. 2001–06; currently Assoc. Prof., Harvard Univ.; Fellow, American Acad. of Arts and Sciences 2005; Radcliffe Fellow, Radcliffe Inst. for Advanced Study, Harvard Univ. 2006–07. *Publications:* fiction: The Mind-Body Problem (Feminista journal 100 Great 20th Century Works of Fiction by Women 2000) 1983, The Late-Summer Passion of a Woman of Mind 1989, The Dark Sister (Whiting Foundation Writer's Award 1994) 1993, Strange Attractors: Stories (Nat. Jewish Book Honor Award 1994) 1993, Mazel (Nat. Jewish Book Fiction Award 1995, Univ. of Hartford Edward Lewis Wallant Award 1996) 1995, Properties of Light: A Novel of Love, Betrayal and Quantum Physics (Massachusetts Book Award Honors in Fiction 2001) 2000, 36 Arguments for the Existence of God 2010; non-fiction: Incompleteness: The Proof and Paradox of Kurt Gödel 2005, Betraying Spinoza: The Renegade Jew Who Gave us Modernity 2006; contrib. short stories to journals, including Commentary, New Traditions, Prairie Schooner, Tikkun, and essays and reviews to newspapers, journals and magazines, including Black Clock, Commentary, Nature, NEST, New York Review of Books, New York Times, New York Times Book Review, Seed, Shma, Tikkun. *Honours:* Dr hc (Spertus Inst., Chicago) 2000, (Emerson Coll., Boston) 2008; NSF Fellowship Award for Philosophy of Science 1972–75, Whiting Foundation Fellowship Award in Philosophy 1975–76, American Council for Learned Socs Fellowship 1984, John D. and Catherine T. MacArthur Foundation Fellowship 1996–2001, Prairie Schooner Award for Best Short Story of 1997, Bogliasco Foundation Fellow 1998, Whiting Writers' Award, two Nat. Jewish Book Awards, Koret Int. Award for Jewish Thought, MacArthur Foundation 'Genius' Award, Acad. of Arts and Sciences, Guggenheim Fellowship 2006–07, Humanist Laureate, Humanist of the Year 2011, Free-thought Heroine. *E-mail:* rebegolds@gmail.com (home); rgold@wjh.harvard.edu (office). *Website:* www.rebeccagoldstein.com.

GOLDSTEIN, Robert Justin, BA, MA, PhD; American academic and writer; *Research Associate, University of Michigan*; b. 28 March 1947, Albany, NY. *Education:* Univ. of Illinois, Univ. of Chicago. *Career:* Research and Admin. Asst, Univ. of Illinois 1972–73; Lecturer, San Diego State Univ. 1974–76; Asst Prof., Assoc. Prof. then Full Prof., Oakland Univ., Rochester, Mich. 1976–2005, currently Prof. Emer.; Research Assoc., Univ. of Michigan 2003–. *Publications include:* Political Repression in Modern America 1978, Political Repression in Nineteenth Century Europe 1983, Censorship of Political Caricature in Nineteenth Century France 1989, Saving 'Old Glory': The History of the American Flag Desecration Controversy 1995, Burning the Flag: The Great 1989–90 American Flag Desecration Controversy 1996, Desecrating the American Flag: Key Documents from the Controversy from the Civil War to 1995 1996, Flag Burning and Free Speech: The Case of Texas v. Johnson 2000, The War for the Public Mind: Political Censorship in Nineteenth-Century Europe 2000, Political Censorship: The New York Times Twentieth Century in Review 2001, American Blacklist: The Attorney General's List of Subversive Organizations 2008, The Frightful Stage: Political Censorship of the Theater in Nineteenth-Century Europe (ed.) 2009. *Telephone:* (734) 996-8031 (office). *E-mail:* goldstei@oakland.edu (office).

GOLDSWORTHY, Peter, AM; Australian poet and writer; b. 12 Oct. 1951, Minlaton; m. Helen Louise Wharldall 1972; one s. two d. *Education:* Univ. of Adelaide. *Publications:* poetry: Number Three Friendly Street: Poetry Reader (co-ed.) 1979, Readings from Ecclesiastes (FAW Anne Elder Poetry Award, South Australian Premier's Award, Govt Biennial Literature Prize 1984) 1982, This Goes With That: Selected Poems 1970–1990 1991, After the Ball 1992, If, Then: Poems and Songs 1996, New Selected Poems 2001, Tattered Joys 2002; novel: Maestro (novel) 1989, Magpie 1992, Honk If You are Jesus 1992, Wish 1995, Keep it Simple, Stupid 1996, Three Dog Night (FAW Christina Stead Award 2004) 2003, Everything I Knew 2008; short stories: Archipelagoes 1982, Zooing 1986, Bleak Rooms 1988, Little Deaths 1993, The List of All Answers 2004, Gravel 2010. *Honours:* Commonwealth Poetry Prize 1982, Australian Bicentennial Literary Prize for Poetry 1988, ABC/ABA Bicentennial Literary Award 1998, Poetry Australia Literary Award 1998,. *Literary Agent:* c/o Fiona Inglis, Curtis Brown Pty Ltd, PO Box 19, Paddington, NSW 2021, Australia. *Telephone:* (2) 9331-5301. *Fax:* (2) 9360-3935. *Website:* www.curtisbrown.com.au; www.petergoldsworthy.com.

GOLDSWORTHY, Vesna, MA, PhD; Serbian/British broadcaster, writer and academic; *Professor of English Literature and Creative Writing, University of Kingston*; b. (Vesna Bjelogrlic), 1 July 1961, Belgrade, Serbia. *Education:* Univs of Belgrade and London. *Career:* emigrated to London 1980s; worked at BBC World Service; also teacher, Univ. of London and St Lawrence Univ., New York, USA; currently Prof. of English Literature and Creative Writing, Univ. of Kingston. *Publications:* Inventing Ruritania: The Imperialism of the Imagination 1998, Chernobyl Strawberries (memoir) 2005, Writing Worlds: Norwich Exchanges (ed.) 2006, The Angel of Salonika (poetry) (Crashaw Prize) 2011; contrib. of articles and chapters to Cambridge Guide to Women's Writing in English 1999, Representing Lives: Women and Autobiography 1999, Routledge International Encyclopedia of Women's Studies 2000, London Review of Books, The Guardian. *Address:* Department of English, University of Kingston, Penrhyn Road, Kingston-upon-Thames, Surrey, KT1 2EE, England (office). *Telephone:* (20) 8547-2000 (office). *Fax:* (20) 8547-7388 (office). *E-mail:* v.goldsworthy@kingston.ac.uk (office). *Website:* www.kingston.ac.uk (office).

GOLLANCZ, Livia Ruth, ARCM; British musician (French horn) and publishing executive; b. 25 May 1920, d. of Victor Gollancz and Ruth Lowy. *Education:* St Paul's Girls' School and Royal Coll. of Music, London. *Career:* French horn player, London Symphony Orchestra 1940–43, Hallé Orchestra 1943–45, Scottish Orchestra 1945–46, BBC Scottish Orchestra 1946–47, Royal Opera House, Covent Garden, London 1947, Sadler's Wells, London 1950–53; Editorial Asst, Typographer Victor Gollancz Ltd, Publrs, London 1953, Dir 1954–90, Governing Dir, Jt Man. Dir 1965–85, Chair. 1983–89, Consultant 1990–93. *Publication:* Victor Gollancz, Reminiscences of Affection (ed.) 1968. *Address:* 26 Cholmeley Crescent, London, N6 5HA, England (home).

GÖLLNER, Theodor, PhD, DrPhil, Habil.; German musicologist; *Professor Emeritus and Director, Commission of Music History, Bavarian Academy of Sciences*; b. 25 Nov. 1929, Bielefeld; s. of Friedrich Göllner and Paula Brinkmann; m. Marie Louise Martinez 1959; one s. one d. *Education:* Univs of Heidelberg and Munich. *Career:* Lecturer, Univ. of Munich 1958–62, Asst Prof. 1962–67, Assoc. Prof. 1967; Prof., Univ. of Calif., Santa Barbara 1967–73; Prof. and Chair. Inst. of Musicology, Univ. of Munich 1973–97; Prof. Emer. and Dir Comm. of Music History, Bavarian Acad. of Sciences 1982–; mem. European Acad. of Sciences and Arts 1991–. *Publications:* Formen früher Mehrstimmigkeit 1961, Die mehrstimmigen liturgischen Lesungen 1969, Die Sieben Worte am Kreuz 1986, Et incarnatus est in Bachs h-moll-Messe und Beethovens Missa solemnis 1996, Die Tactuslehre in den deutschen Orgelquellen des 15. Jahrhunderts 2003, Münchner Veröffentlichungen zur Musikgeschichte (ed.) 1977–2006, Münchner Editionen zur Musikgeschichte 1979–97, Die psalmodische Tradition bei Monteverdi und Schütz 2006. *Address:* Institute of Musicology, University of Munich, Geschwister-Scholl-Platz 1, 80539 Munich (office); Bahnweg 9, 82229 Seefeld, Germany (home). *Telephone:* (1089) 21802364 (office). *E-mail:* TheodorGoellner@aol.com (home).

GOMERY, Douglas, BS, MA, PhD; American academic and writer; *Resident Scholar, Library of American Broadcasting, University of Maryland*; b. 5 April 1945, New York; m. Marilyn Moon 1973. *Education:* Lehigh Univ., Univ. of Wisconsin at Madison. *Career:* Instructor to Assoc. Prof., Univ. of Wisconsin at Milwaukee 1974–81; Visiting Prof., Univ. of Wisconsin at Madison 1977, Northwestern Univ. 1981, Univ. of Iowa 1982, Univ. of Utrecht 1990, 1992; Assoc. Prof., Univ. of Maryland 1981–86, Prof., Dept of Radio-TV-Film 1987–92, Coll. of Journalism 1992–2005, currently Prof. Emer., also Resident Scholar, Library of American Broadcasting; Sr Researcher, Woodrow Wilson Center for Int. Scholars, Washington, DC 1988–92. *Publications:* High Sierra: Screenplay and Analysis 1979, Film History: Theory and Practice (with Robert C. Allen) 1985, The Hollywood Studio System 1986, The Will Hays Papers 1987, American Media (with Philip Cook and Lawrence W. Lichty) 1989, The Art of Moving Shadows (with Annette Michelson and Patrick Loughney) 1989, Movie History: A Survey 1991, Shared Pleasures 1992, The Future of News (with Philip Cook and Lawrence W. Lichty) 1992, A Media Studies Primer (with Michael Cornfield and Lawrence W. Lichty) 1997, Media in America (ed.) 1998, Who Owns the Media? (Robert Picard Award) 2000, The Coming of Sound 2004, Television Industries (with Luke Hockley) 2006, A History of Broadcasting in the United States 2008, Patsy Cline: The Making of an Icon 2011; contribs to books and scholarly journals. *Honours:* Jeffrey Weiss Literary Prize, Theatre Historical Soc. 1988, Prize, Theatre Library Asscn 1992. *Address:* Library of American Broadcasting, University of Maryland, MD 20742 (office); 4817 Drummond Avenue, Chevy Chase, MD 20815, USA (home). *Telephone:* (301) 405-9160 (office); (301) 951-4385 (home). *E-mail:* dgomery@umd.edu (office). *Website:* www.merrill.umd.edu/directory/douglas-gomery (office).

GOMES, Laurentino; Brazilian writer and journalist; b. 1956, Maringá, Paraná; m. Mara Ziravello. *Education:* Universidade de São Paulo. *Career:* fmr reporter and Ed., various publications including O Estado de São Paulo and Veja magazine. *Publications:* 1808 (Academia Brasileira de Letras prize, Prêmio Jabuti) 2007, 1822 2010. *E-mail:* lgomes@laurentinogomes.com.br (office). *Website:* www.laurentinogomes.com.br.

GOMEZ, Jewelle Lydia, BA, MS; American writer and poet; b. 11 Sept. 1948, Boston. *Education:* Northeastern Univ., Columbia Graduate School of Journalism. *Career:* Assoc. 1984–91, Dir of Literature 1991–93, New York State Council on the Arts; Adjunct Prof., New Coll. of California 1994, Menlo Coll. 1994; Writer-in-Residence, California Arts Council 1995–96; currently Dir Grants and Community Initiatives, Horizons Foundation; currently also Pres. San Francisco Library Comm.; Founding mem. Astraea Nat. Lesbian Foundation, James C. Hormel Endowment Cttee; mem. American Center of Poets and Writers; PEN. *Publications:* The Lipstick Papers 1980, Flamingos and Bears 1986, The Gilda Stories 1991, Forty-Three Septembers 1993, Oral Tradition: Selected Poems Old and New 1995, Swords of the Rainbow (co-ed with Eric Garber) 1996, Don't Explain 1997, Waiting for Giovanni 2011; contribs to various publications. *Address:* Horizons Foundation, 550 Montgomery Street, Suite 700, San Francisco, CA 94111, USA (office). *Telephone:* (415) 398-2333 (office). *Fax:* (415) 398-4733 (office). *E-mail:* jgomez@horizonsfoundation.org (office). *Website:* www.horizonsfoundation.org (office); www.jewellegomez.com.

GÖNCZ, Árpád, LLD; Hungarian writer and fmr head of state; b. 10 Feb. 1922, Budapest; s. of Lajos Göncz and Ilona Heimann; m. Mária Zsuzsanna Göntér 1946; two s. two d. *Education:* Pázmány Péter University of Arts and Sciences, Budapest. *Career:* early career as bank clerk with Nat. Land Credit Inst.; joined Ind. Smallholders, Landworkers and Bourgeois Party; leading positions in Ind. Youth Org.; Ed.-in-Chief Generation (weekly); sentenced in 1957 to life imprisonment as defendant in political Bibó trial; released under amnesty 1963; then freelance writer and literary translator, especially of English works; Pres. Hungarian Writers Fed. 1989–90, Hon. Pres. 1990–; Founding mem. Free Initiatives Network, Free Democratic Fed., Historic Justice Cttee; mem. Parl. 1990; Acting Pres. of Hungary May–Aug. 1990, Pres. of Hungary 1990–2000. *Publications include:* Men of God (novel) 1974, Encounters (short stories) 1980, Homecoming and Other Stories (short stories) 1991, Hungarian Medea (play), Balance (play), Iron Bars (play), A Pessimistic Comedy (play), Persephone (play), political essays; translated more than 100 works, mostly by British and American authors, including James Baldwin, Edgar Lawrence Doctorow, William Faulkner, William Golding, Ernest Hemingway, William Styron, Susan Sontag, John Updike, Edith Wharton and others. *Honours:* Hon. KCMG 1991; Dr hc (Butler) 1990, (Connecticut) 1991, (Oxford) 1995, (Sorbonne) 1996, (Bologna) 1997; Attila József Prize 1983, Wheatland Prize 1989, Premio Meditteraneo 1991, George Washington Prize 2000, Vision for Europe Award 2000, Pro Humanitate Award 2001, Polish Business Oscar Award 2002. *Address:* Office of the Former President, 1055 Budapest, Kossuth tér 4, Hungary (office). *Telephone:* (1) 441-3550 (office). *Fax:* (1) 441-3552 (office).

GONZÁLEZ, Justo Luis, MA, PhD, DDL; American theologian, writer and editor; b. 9 Aug. 1937, Havana, Cuba; m. 1st Erlantina Ramos 1959 (divorced 1972); one d.; m. 2nd Catherine Gunsalus 1973. *Education:* University of Havana, Seminario Evangélico de Teología, Matanzas, Yale University, University of Strasbourg, Seminario Evangélico de Puerto Rico. *Career:* Prof. of Historical Theology, Seminario Evangélico de Puerto Rico, 1961–69; Research Fellow, Yale University, 1968; Asst Prof. of World Christianity, 1969–71, Assoc. Prof., 1971–77, Emory University; Visiting Prof. of Theology, Interdenominational Theological Center, 1977–88; Ed., Apuntes, 1980–2000; Adjunct Prof. of Theology, Columbia Theological Seminary, 1988–91; mem. United Methodist Church; many ecumenical commissions and task forces. *Publications:* The Development of Christianity in the Latin Caribbean 1969, A History of Christian Thought, Vol. I, From the Beginnings to the Council of Chalcedon 1970, Vol. II, From Saint Augustine to the Eve of the Reformation 1971, Vol. III, From the Reformation to the Present 1979, Their Souls Did Magnify the Lord: Studies on Biblical Women (with Catherine Gunsalus González) 1977, Rejoice in Your Saviour: A Study for Lent-Easter (with Catherine Gunsalus González) 1979, Liberation Preaching: The Pulpit and the Oppressed (with Catherine Gonsalus González) 1980, In Accord: Let Us Worship (with Catherine Gonsalus González) 1981, The Story of Christianity, Vol. I, Early and Medieval Christianity 1984, Vol. II, From the Reformation to the Present 1985, Paul: His Impact on Christianity (with Catherine Gunsalus González) 1987, The Crusades: Piety Misguided 1988, Monasticism: Patterns of Piety 1988, The Theological Education of Hispanics 1988, Christian Thought Revisited: Three Types of Theology 1989, A Faith More Precious Than Gold: A Study of 1 Peter (with Catherine Gunsalus González) 1989, Faith and Wealth: A History of Early Christian Ideas on the Origin, Significance, and Use of Money 1990, Mañana: Christian Theology from a Hispanic Perspective 1990, Each in Our Own Tongue: A History of Hispanic Methodism (ed.) 1991, Voces: Voices from the Hispanic Church (ed.) 1992, Out of Every Tribe and Nation: Christian Theology at the Ethnic Roundtable 1992, The Liberating Pulpit (with Catherine Gunsalus González) 1994, Journey Through the Bible, Vol. 11, Luke 1994, Vol. 13, Acts of the Apostles 1995, When Christ Lives in Us 1995, Santa Biblia: The Bible Through Hispanic Eyes 1996, Church History: An Essential Guide 1996, Revelation (with Catherine Gunsalus González) 1997, For the Healing of the Nations: The Book of Revelation in an Age of Cultural Conflict 1999, Mark's Message for the New Millennium 2000, Acts: The Gospel of the Spirit 2001, The Changing Shape of Church History 2003, A Concise History of Christian Doctrine 2005, The Apostles' Creed for Today 2006, The Westminster Dictionary of Theologians 2006, Latin American Christianity: A History (with Ondina E González) 2008; other: many books in Spanish. Contributions: numerous books, reference works, journals, periodicals, etc. *Honours:* Hon. DDL (Seminario Evangélico de Puerto Rico) 1994; Hon. DD (Christian Theological Seminary) 2004, (Asbury Theological Seminary) 2005, (Wartburg Theological Seminary) 2006. *Address:* 336 S Columbia Drive, Decatur, GA 30030, USA (home). *E-mail:* justo325@aol.com (home).

GONZÁLEZ, Ray, MFA; American writer, editor and academic; *Professor of English, University of Minnesota, Minneapolis*; b. El Paso, Texas. *Education:* Univ. of Texas at El Paso, Southwest Texas State Univ. *Career:* Literary Dir Guadaloupe Cultural Arts Centre, San Antonio; currently Prof. of English, Creative Writing Program, Univ. of Minnesota, Minneapolis; Poetry Ed. Bloomsbury Review 1980–; Ed. Guadaloupe Review; Founder Luna poetry journal 1998. *Publications include:* poetry: The Heat of Arrivals (PEN Award, Josephine Miles Book Award 1997) 1996, Cabato Sentora 1999, Memory Fever 1999, Turtle Pictures (Minnesota Book Award 2001) 2000, The Hawk Temple at Tierra Grande (Minnesota Book Award 2003) 2002, Religion of Hands (Latino Heritage Award 2006) 2005, Consideration of the Guitar 2005, Faith Run 2009, Cool Auditor: Prose Poems 2009; non-fiction: Memory Fever 1999, The Underground Heart: Essays from Hidden Landscapes (Carr P. Collins Award, Texas Inst. of Letters 2003) 2002, Renaming the Earth: Personal Essays 2008; short story collections: The Ghost of John Wayne 2001, Circling the Tortilla Dragon 2002; Ed.: Touching the Fire: 15 Poets of the Latino Renaissance 1998; contrib. to Best American Poetry 1999–2000, The Pushcart Prize: Best of the Small Presses 2000, The Norton Anthology of Nature Writing. *Honours:* Amercian Book Award for Excellence in Editing 1993, Josephine Miles Book Award for Excellence in Literature 1997, Minnesota Book Award for Poetry 2001, Lifetime Achievement Award, Border Regional Library Asscn 2003. *Address:* Department of English, University of Minnesota, 310 E Lind Hall, 207 Church Street SE, Minneapolis, MN 55455, USA (office). *Telephone:* (612) 625-0332 (office). *E-mail:* gonza049@umn.edu (office). *Website:* english.cla.umn.edu/faculty/gonzalez (office).

GONZÁLEZ GALLEGO, Rubén David; Russian writer; b. 20 Sept. 1968, Moscow; s. of David Rafael González Oviedo and Aurora Gallego Rodríguez. *Career:* emigrated to Prague, Czech Repub. 2001; lived in Madrid, Spain 2002–05; now resident in Germany. *Publications:* Byeloye na chernom (trans. as White on Black) (Booker-Open Russia Prize) 2003, Ajedrez 2005. *Address:* c/o Alfaguara de Novela, Torrelaguna 60, 28043, Madrid, Spain. *Telephone:* (91) 7449060. *Fax:* (91) 7449224. *E-mail:* info@tea-at-5.com (office). *Website:* www.tea-at-5.com (office); www.alfaguara.santillana.es.

GOOCH, John, BA, PhD, FRHistS; British academic and writer; b. 25 Aug. 1945, Weston Favell, England; m. Catharine Ann Staley 1967; one s. one d. *Education:* King's Coll., London. *Career:* Asst Lecturer in History, King's Coll., Univ. of London 1966–67, apptd Asst Lecturer in War Studies 1969; Lecturer in History, Univ. of Lancaster 1969–81, Sr Lecturer 1981–84, Reader in History 1984–88, Prof. of History 1988–92; Ed. Journal of Strategic Studies 1978–; Sec. of the Navy Sr Research Fellow, US Naval War Coll. 1985–86; apptd Visiting Prof. of Military and Naval History, Yale Univ. 1988; apptd Prof. of International History, Univ. of Leeds 1992, Head, School of History 2006–09; mem. Army Records Soc.; Vice-Pres. 1990–94. *Publications:* The Plans of War: The General Staff and British Military Strategy c.1900–1916, Armies in Europe 1980, The Prospect of War: Studies in British Defence Policy 1847–1942 1981; Politicians and Defence: Studies in the Formulation of British Defence Policy 1847–1970 1981, Strategy and the Social Sciences 1981, Military Deception and Strategic Surprise 1982, Soldati e Borghesi nell' Europa Moderna 1982, Army, State and Society in Italy 1870–1915 1989, Decisive Campaigns of the Second World War 1989, Military Misfortunes: The Anatomy of Failure in War (with Eliot A Cohen) 1990, Airpower: Theory and Practice 1995, The Boer War: Direction, Experience, and Image (ed) 2000, The Unification of Italy 2002, Mussolini and his Generals: The Armed Forces and Fascist Foreign Policy 1922–1940 2007; contribs to scholarly journals. *Honours:* Premio Internazionale di Cultura, Città di Anghiari 1983, Kt, Royal Military Order of Vila Viçosa (Portugal) 1991, Kt, Order of the Star of Solidarity (Italy) 2011. *Address:* c/o School of History, University of Leeds, Leeds, LS2 9JT, England.

GOODALL, Dame Jane, DBE, PhD; British primatologist, ethologist and anthropologist; *Founder, Jane Goodall Institute*; b. (Valerie Jane Morris-Goodall), 3 April 1934, London; d. of Mortimer Herbert Morris-Goodall and Vanne Morris-Goodall (née Joseph); m. 1st Hugo Van Lawick 1964 (divorced 1974); one s.; m. 2nd M. Derek Bryceson 1975 (died 1980). *Education:* Uplands School, Univ. of Cambridge. *Career:* Sec. Univ. of Oxford; Asst Sec. to Louis Leakey, worked in Olduvai Gorge, then moved to Gombe Stream Game Reserve (now Gombe Nat. Park), Tanzania 1960, camp became Gombe Stream Research Centre 1964, Dir of Research, Gombe Nat. Park 1972–2003; Scientific Dir Gombe Stream Research Centre 1967–2003; studied social behaviour of the Spotted Hyena, Ngorongoro Conservation Area 1968–69; Founder, mem. Bd of Dirs and Trustee, Jane Goodall Inst. for Wildlife Research, Educ. and Conservation, USA 1976–; Scientific Gov. Chicago Acad. of Sciences 1981–; Int. Dir ChimpanZoo (research programme involving zoos and sanctuaries world-wide), USA 1984–; Vice-Pres. Animal Welfare Inst., British Veterinary Asscn, UK 1987–; Dir Humane Soc. of the US 1989–; mem. Int. Advisory Bd of Teachers Without Borders, USA 2001–; mem. Bd Orangutan Foundation, USA 1994–, Save the Chimps/Center for Captive Chimpanzee Care 2000–, North American Bear Center 2001–; mem. Hon. Cttee Farm Sanctuary, USA 2001–; mem. Bd of Dirs Cougar Fund 2002–, The Many One Foundation, USA 2002–; mem. Advisory Panel World Summit on Sustainable Devt 2002, and numerous other advisory bds and cttees; Visiting Prof., Dept of Psychiatry and Program of Human Biology, Stanford Univ. 1971–75; Adjunct Prof., Dept of Environmental Studies, School of Veterinary Medicine, Tufts Univ. 1987–88; Assoc., Cleveland Natural History Museum 1990; Distinguished Adjunct Prof., Depts of Anthropology and Occupational Therapy, Univ. of Southern California 1990; A.D. White Prof.-at-Large, Cornell Univ., NY 1996–2002; Scientific Fellow, Wildlife Conservation Soc., USA 2002–; Trustee, L. S. B. Leakey Foundation 1974–, Jane Goodall Inst., UK 1988–, Jane Goodall Inst., Canada 1993–; mem. Explorer's Club, New York 1981, American Philosophical Soc. 1988, Soc. of Women Geographers, USA 1988, Deutsche Akad. der Naturforscher Leopoldina 1990, Academia Scientiarium et Artium Europaea, Austria 1991; Foreign mem. Research Centre for Human Ethology, Max Planck Inst. for Behavioural Physiology 1984; speaker on conservation issues, appearing on numerous TV shows including: 20/20, Nightline, Good Morning America. *Films:* Miss Goodall and the Wild Chimpanzees 1963, Among the Wild Chimpanzees 1984, People of the Forest (with Hugo van Lawick) 1988, Chimpanzee Alert 1990, Chimps, So Like Us 1990, The Life and Legend of Jane Goodall 1990, The Gombe Chimpanzees 1990, Fifi's Boys 1995, My Life with the Wild Chimpanzees 1995, Chimpanzee Diary 1995, Animal Minds 1995, Jane Goodall: Reason For Hope 1999, Chimps R Us 2001, Jane Goodall's Wild Chimpanzees 2002, Jane Goodall's Return to Gombe 2004, Jane Goodall's State of the Great Ape 2004, Jane Goodall – When Animals Talk 2005, Jane Goodall's Heroes 2006.

Publications include: My Friends the Wild Chimpanzees 1967, Innocent Killers (with H. van Lawick) 1971, In the Shadow of Man 1971, The Chimpanzees of Gombe: Patterns of Behavior (R. R. Hawkins Award for the Outstanding Tech., Scientific or Medical Book of 1986, The Wildlife Soc. (USA) Award for Outstanding Publ. in Wildlife Ecology and Man. 1986) 1986, Through a Window: 30 Years Observing the Gombe Chimpanzees 1990, Visions of Caliban (with Dale Peterson) (New York Times Notable Book for 1993, Library Journal Best Sci-Tech Book for 1993) 1993, Brutal Kinship (with Michael Nichols) 1999, 40 Years at Gombe 2000, Africa in My Blood: An Autobiography in Letters (ed. by Dale Peterson) 2000, Beyond Innocence: An Autobiography in Letters, the Later Years (ed. by Dale Peterson) 2001, Performance and Evolution in the Age of Darwin: Out of the Natural Order 2002, Ten Trusts: What We Must Do to Care for the Animals We Love (with Marc Bekoff) 2002, Hope for Animals and Their World: How Endangered Species Are Being Rescued from the Brink (with Thane Maynard and Gail Hudson) 2009; for children: Grub: The Bush Baby 1972, My Life with the Chimpanzees (Reading-Magic Award for Outstanding Book for Children 1989) 1988, The Chimpanzee Family Book (UNICEF Award for the Best Children's Book of 1989, Austrian State Prize for Best Children's Book of 1990) 1989, Jane Goodall's Animal World: Chimps 1989, Animal Family Series, Jane Goodall: With Love 1994, Dr. White (illustrated by Julie Litty) 1999, The Eagle & the Wren (illustrated by Alexander Reichstein) 2000, Chimpanzees I Love: Saving Their World and Ours 2001, Rickie and Henri: A True Story (with Alan Marks) 2004; numerous book chapters and articles in scientific journals. *Honours:* Hon. Foreign mem. American Acad. of Arts and Sciences 1972; Hon. Fellow, Royal Anthropological Inst. of GB and Ireland 1991; Hon. mem. Ewha Acad. of Arts and Sciences 2006; Ordre nat. de la Légion d'honneur 2006; 22 hon. degrees; numerous awards including Franklin Burr Award, Nat. Geographic Soc. 1963–64, Conservation Award, New York Zoological Soc. 1974, Order of the Golden Ark, World Wildlife Award for Conservation 1980, J. Paul Getty Wildlife Conservation Prize 1984, Albert Schweitzer Award, Int. Women's Inst. 1987, Nat. Geographic Soc. Centennial Award 1988, Anthropologist of the Year Award 1989, AMES Award, American Anthropologist Asscn 1990, Gold Medal, Soc. of Women Geographers 1990, Inamori Foundation Award 1990, Washoe Award 1990, Kyoto Prize in Basic Science 1990, Rainforest Alliance Champion Award 1993, Hubbard Medal for Distinction in Exploration, Discovery, and Research, Nat. Geographic Soc. 1995, Lifetime Achievement Award, In Defense of Animals 1995, Silver Medal, Zoological Soc. of London 1996, Tanzanian Kilimanjaro Medal 1996, Conservation Award, Primate Soc. of GB 1996, William Proctor Prize for Scientific Achievement Kilimanjaro 1996, Commonwealth Award for Public Service 1997, Royal Geographical Soc./Discovery Channel Europe Award for A Lifetime of Discovery 1997, Roger Tory Peterson Memorial Medal, Harvard Museum of Natural History 2001, 2007, Benjamin Franklin Medal in Life Science 2003, Award of Harvard Medical School Center for Health and the Global Environment 2003, Prince of Asturias Award for Tech. and Scientific Achievement 2003, Life Time Achievement Award, Int. Fund for Animal Welfare 2004, UNESCO 60th Anniversary Gold Medal 2006, Lifetime Achievement Award, Jules Verne Adventures 2006, Hon. Medal of the City of Paris 2007, Lifetime Achievement Award, Heart of Green Awards 2011. *Address:* The Jane Goodall Institute for Wildlife Research, Education and Conservation, 4245 North Fairfax Drive, #600, Arlington, VA 22203, USA (office). *Telephone:* (703) 682-9220 (office). *Fax:* (703) 682-9312 (office). *E-mail:* info@janegoodall.org (office). *Website:* www.janegoodall.org.

GOODHEART, Eugene, MA, PhD; American professor of English and humanities and writer; *Edytha Macy Gross Professor Emeritus of Humanities, Brandeis University*; b. 26 June 1931, New York, NY; m. Joan Bamberger; one s. one d. *Education:* Columbia Coll., Univ. of Virginia, Sorbonne Univ., Paris, Columbia Univ. *Career:* Instructor, Bard Coll. 1958–60, Asst Prof. 1960–62; Asst Prof., Univ. of Chicago 1962–66; Assoc. Prof., Mount Holyoke Coll. 1966–67; Assoc. Prof., MIT 1967–70, Prof. 1970–74; Visiting Prof., Wellesley Coll. 1968; Prof., Boston Univ. 1974–83; Edytha Macy Gross Prof. Emer. of Humanities, Brandeis Univ. 1983–, also Dir Center for the Humanities 1986–; Adjunct Prof. of English, Columbia Univ. 1986; Corresp. Ed., Partisan Review 1978–; mem. PEN. *Publications include:* The Utopian Vision of D. H. Lawrence, 1963, The Cult of the Ego: The Self in Modern Literature, 1968, Culture and the Radical Conscience, 1978, The Failure of Criticism, 1978, The Skeptic Disposition in Contemporary Criticism, 1984, Pieces of Resistance, 1987, Desire and Its Discontents, 1991, The Reign of Ideology, 1996, Does Literary Studies Have a Future?, 1999, Confessions of a Secular Jew, 2001, Novel Practices: Classic Modern Fiction 2004, Darwinian Misadventures in the Humanities 2007; contribs to journals and periodicals. *Honours:* Fulbright Scholarship, Paris 1956–57, ACLS Fellowship 1965–66, Guggenheim Felowship 1970–71, Nat. Endowment for the Humanities Sr Fellowship 1981, Nat. Humanities Center Fellow 1987–88, Rockefeller Foundation Fellowship, Bellagio, Italy 1989. *Address:* Department of English, Brandeis University, Waltham, MA 02254, USA (office). *Telephone:* (781) 736-2160 (office). *Fax:* (781) 736-2179 (office). *E-mail:* goodhear@brandeis.edu (office).

GOODISON, Lorna Gaye; Jamaican poet, academic and writer; *Professor of English Language and Literature, University of Michigan*; b. 1 Aug. 1947, Kingston; one d. *Career:* teacher of Creative Writing, USA and Canada; fmr Assoc. Prof. of Creative Writing, Univ. of Michgan, currently Lemuel A Johnson Collegiate Prof. of English and Afroamerican and African Studies, Prof. of English Language and Literature, Prof. of Afroamerican and African Studies, Dept of English Language and Literature; has participated in literary festivals in New York, London and Erlangen. *Publications:* poetry: Poems 1974, Tamarind Season 1980, I Am Becoming My Mother 1986, Heartease 1988, Poems: Lorna Goodison 1989, Selected Poems 1992, To Us, All Flowers Are Roses 1995, Turn Thanks 1999, Guinea Women: New and Selected Poems 2000, Travelling Mercies 2001, Controlling the Silver 2005; short stories: Baby Mother and the King of Swords 1989, Fool-fool Rose is Leaving Labour-in-Vain Savannah 2005; other: From Harvey River (memoir) 2008. *Honours:* Inst. of Jamaica Centenary Prize 1981, Commonwealth Poetry Prize 1986, Musgrave Gold Medal 1999. *Address:* Department of English Language and Literature, 435 South State Street, 3187 Angell Hall, Ann Arbor, MI 48109-1003, USA (office). *Telephone:* (734) 764-5475. *E-mail:* goodison@umich.edu (office). *Website:* www.lsa.umich.edu/english/people/profile.asp?ID=251 (office).

GOODMAN, Elinor Mary; British political broadcaster and journalist; b. 11 Oct. 1946, d. of Edward Weston Goodman and Pamela Longbottom; m. Derek John Scott 1985. *Education:* pvt. schools and secretarial coll. *Career:* Consumer Affairs Corresp. Financial Times newspaper 1971–78, Political Corresp. 1978–82; Political Corresp. Channel Four News (TV) 1982–88, Political Ed. 1988–2005; freelance journalist 2006–; Chair., Affordable Rural Housing Commission 2005–06; mem. Bd, Commission for Rural Communities. *Address:* Commission for Rural Communities, John Dower House, Crescent Place, Cheltenham, Glos., GL50 3RA (office); Martinscote, Oare, Marlborough, Wilts. SN8 4JA, England (home). *Telephone:* (1242) 521381 (office). *E-mail:* info@ruralcommunities.gov.uk (office). *Website:* www.ruralcommunities.gov.uk (office).

GOODWEATHER, Hartley (see King, Thomas Hunt)

GOODWIN, Doris Helen Kearns, BA, PhD; American historian and writer; b. 4 Jan. 1943, Brooklyn, NY; m. Richard Goodwin 1973, three s. *Education:* Colby Coll., Harvard Univ. *Career:* Research Assoc., US Dept of Health, Educ. and Welfare, 1966; Special Asst, US Dept of Labor 1967, and to Pres. Lyndon B. Johnson, 1968; Asst Prof., Harvard Univ. 1969–71, Asst Dir, Inst. of Politics, 1971, Assoc. Prof. of Government 1972; Special Consultant to Pres. Lyndon B. Johnson 1969–73; mem. American Political Science Asscn, Council on Foreign Relations, Group for Applied Psychoanalysis, Signet Soc., Women Involved; Fulbright Fellow, 1966; White House Fellow, 1967. *Publications:* Lyndon Johnson and the American Dream, 1976, The Fitzgeralds and the Kennedys: An American Saga 1987, No Ordinary Time: Franklin and Eleanor Roosevelt: The Home Front in World War II (Pulitzer Prize for History 1995, Harold Washington Literary Award, New England Bookseller Asscn Award, Ambassador Book Award, The Washington Monthly Book Award) 1994, Wait Till Next Year: A Memoir, 1997, Every Four Years: Presidential Campaigns and the Media Since 1896 2003, Team of Rivals (Lincoln Prize, Book Prize for American History) 2005, The Political Genius of Abraham Lincoln 2009. *Honours:* Charles Frankel Prize, Nat. Endowment for the Humanities, Sara Josepha Hale Medal. *Literary Agent:* Beth Laski and Associates, 12930 Ventura Boulevard, Suite 513, Studio City, CA 91604, USA. *Telephone:* (818) 986-1105. *Fax:* (818) 986-1106. *E-mail:* beth@bethlaski.com. *Website:* www.doriskearnsgoodwin.com.

GOONERATNE, Malini Yasmine, AO, BA, PhD, DLitt; Australian academic, writer and poet; *Professor Emeritus, Macquarie University*; b. 22 Dec. 1935, Colombo, Sri Lanka; d. of S.J.F. Dias and Esther Mary (née Ramkeesoon) Bandaranaike; m. Brendon Gooneratne 1962; one s. one d. *Education:* Bishop's Coll. (Colombo), Univs of Ceylon and Cambridge (UK). *Career:* Lecturer in English Ceylon Univ. 1965–72; Sr Lecturer in English Macquarie Univ., NSW, Australia 1972, Assoc. Prof. 1979, Dir Postcolonial Literature and Language Research Centre 1988–93, Chair. of English Literature 1991–99, Prof. Emer. 1999–; Nat. Co-ordinator Commonwealth Visiting Fellowship 1989; Resident Fellow, Literary Criterion Centre, India 1990; Visiting Prof., Edith Cowan Univ., Western Australia 1991, Univ. of Michigan, USA 1991; Patron Jane Austen Soc. of Australia 1990–; Vice-Pres. Federation Internationale des Langues et Litteratures Modernes 1990–; mem. Australian Fed. of Univ. Women, Australian Soc. of Authors. *Publications include:* English Literature in Ceylon 1815–1878 1968, Jane Austen 1970, Word, Bird, Motif (poems) 1971, The Lizard's Cry and Other Poems 1972, Alexander Pope 1976, Diverse Inheritance: a Personal Perspective on Commonwealth Literature 1980, 6,000 Feet Death Dive: Poems 1981, Relative Merits: the Bandaranaike Family of Sri Lanka 1986, A Change of Skies (Marjorie Barnard Literary Award for Fiction 1992) 1991, Celebrations and Departures: Poems 1991, The Pleasures of Conquest 1995, This Inscrutable Englishman: Sir John D'Oyly, Baronet (1774–1824) (with B. Gooneratne) 1999, Masterpiece and Other Stories 2002, Celebrating Sri Lankan Women's English Writing 2002, The Sweet and Simple Kind 2006. *Honours:* Marjorie Barnard Literary Award for Fiction 1992, Raja Rao Award 2001. *Address:* Department of English, Faculty of Arts, Macquarie University, North Ryde, NSW 2109, Australia (office). *Telephone:* (2) 9850-8776 (office). *Fax:* (2) 9850-8240 (office). *E-mail:* yasmine.gooneratne@mq.edu.au (office). *Website:* www.engl.mq.edu.au/staff/people_gooneratne.htm (office).

GOOS, Maria; Dutch playwright, screenwriter and director; b. 1956, Breda; m. Peter Blok; two d. *Education:* Acad. of Dramatic Art, Maastricht. *Career:* Dir with theatre companies; Artistic Man., De Kompaan theatre group. *Screenplays include:* Familie 2001, Cloaca 2003. *Television screenplays:* De Keizerin van België 1990, Oog in oog (series) 1990, Klokhuis 1991, Hartslag 1991, Pleidooi (series) 1991–94, Oud geld (series) 1995–97, Familie 1999,

Icarus 1999, Ver van huis 2000, De Aanklacht 2000, Leef! (Golden Film Award 2006) 2002, Lieve Mensen (also dir) 2003. *Plays:* writer and dir: En toen Mamma 1982, Blessuretijd 1983, Tussen Zussen 1983, Een avond in Extase 1984, De Keizerin van België 1985, Helden 1986, De Kuba Walda's 1998, Nu Even Niet 2001, Smoeder (also actress) 2004, De Geschiedenis van de Familie Avenier, deel 3 en 4 2008; writer: Alles is liefde 1988, Eeuwig Jong 1988, Draaikonten 1997, Krambamboelie 1999, Familie 1999, Cloaca (Dutch Acad. Award) 2002, Nu Even Wel 2003, Smoeder 2004, Alte Freunde 2006, Baraka 2007; dir: In het uiterste geval by Paul Binnerts 1987. *Honours:* Acad. Award Nederland for Best Series 1998–99, for Best TV Drama 2004, Lira Script Award 2001, Golden Gate Award 2002, Publieksprijs en de speciale juryprijs 2003, De Gouden Ganzenveer in 2005, The Edmund Hustinxprijs 2008. *Literary Agent:* c/o Kik Productions, Postbus 13120, 3507 LC Utrecht, Netherlands. *Telephone:* (30) 2313416. *Fax:* (30) 2367416. *E-mail:* info@kikproductions.nl. *Website:* www.kikproductions.nl; www.mariagoos.nl.

GORALIK, Linor, BSc; Russian writer and journalist; b. 1975, Dnepropetrovsk, Ukraine. *Education:* Beer-Sheva Univ. *Career:* lived in Israel 1989–2000; worked as a computer programmer, IT man. and lecturer before becoming a full-time writer; Culture Ed. and columnist, Grani.ru online magazine; freelance contrib. to The Russian Journal, XXL, Elle, Paradox. *Publications:* Quote Pad 1999, Not local 2003, Book of Loneliness 2004, Talking 2004, Food for Adults Only 2004, Long Story Short 2008, No (with Sergey Kuznetsov) 2004, Half of the Sky (with Stanislav Lvovsky) 2004, The Hollow Woman: Barbie's World Inside and Outside 2005, Catch Them Piter! 2007, Food for Adults Only. No Dessert 2007, Agatha Returns Home 2008. *Honours:* Triumph Prize 2003. *E-mail:* linor@russ.ru.

GORDIMER, Nadine, FRSL; South African writer; b. 20 Nov. 1923, Springs, East Rand, Gauteng Prov.; d. of Isidore Gordimer and Nan Myers; m. 2nd Reinhold Cassirer 1954 (died); one s. one d. *Education:* convent school. *Career:* mem. African Nat. Congress 1990–; Vice-Pres. International PEN; Goodwill Amb. UNDP; mem. Congress of S African Writers; mem. jury Man Booker Int. Prize 2007. *Publications:* The Soft Voice of the Serpent (stories), The Lying Days (novel) 1953, Six Feet of the Country (stories) 1956, A World of Strangers (novel) 1958, Friday's Footprint (stories) 1960, Occasion for Loving (novel) 1963, Not For Publication (stories) 1965, The Late Bourgeois World (novel) 1966, South African Writing Today (co-ed.) 1967, A Guest of Honour (novel) 1970, Livingstone's Companions (stories) 1972, The Black Interpreters (literary criticism) 1973, The Conservationist (novel) 1974, Selected Stories 1975, Some Monday for Sure (stories) 1976, Burger's Daughter 1979, A Soldier's Embrace (stories) 1980, July's People (novel) 1981, Something Out There (novella) 1984, A Sport of Nature (novel) 1987, The Essential Gesture (essays) 1988, My Son's Story (novel) 1990, Jump (short stories) 1991, Crimes of Conscience (short stories) 1991, None to Accompany Me (novel) 1994, Writing and Being (lectures) 1995, The House Gun 1997, Living in Hope and History: Notes on our Century (essays) 1999, The Pickup 2001, Loot and Other Stories 2003, Telling Tales (ed. and contrib.) 2004, Get A Life 2005, Beethoven was One-Sixteenth Black (short stories) 2007, Telling Times: Writing and Living 1954–2008 2010, Life Times: Stories 1952–2007 (collection) 2010, No Time Like the Present (novel) 2012. *Honours:* Hon. Fellow, American Acad. of Arts and Letters, American Acad. of Arts and Sciences; Hon. mem. American Inst. of Arts and Letters; Commdr, Ordre des Arts et des Lettres 1987; Charles Eliot Norton Lecturer in Literature, Harvard Univ. 1994; Dr hc (Cambridge) 1992, (Oxford) 1994; WHSmith Literary Award 1961, Thomas Pringle Award, English Acad. of SA 1969, James Tait Black Memorial Prize 1971, Booker Prize (co-winner) 1974, Grand Aigle d'Or Prize (France) 1975, CNA Literary Award (S Africa) 1974, 1979, 1981, 1991, Scottish Arts Council Neil M. Gunn Fellowship 1981, Modern Language Asscn Award (USA) 1981, Premio Malaparte (Italy) 1985, Nelly Sachs Prize (Germany) 1985, Bennett Award (USA) 1987, Benson Medal, Royal Soc. of Literature 1990, Nobel Prize for Literature 1991, Primo Levi Award 2002, Mary McCarthy Award 2003, Bavarian State Premier's Hon. Award (part of the Corine Int. Book Prize), Grinzane Cavour Prize 2007. *Literary Agent:* c/o Linda Shaughnessy, AP Watt Ltd, 20 John Street, London, WC1N 2DR, England. *Telephone:* (20) 7405-6774. *Fax:* (20) 7831-2154. *E-mail:* apw@apwatt.co.uk. *Website:* www.apwatt.co.uk.

GORDON, Graeme, BA, DEJF; British writer; b. 21 June 1966, Epsom, England. *Education:* University of Sussex, University of Strasbourg, III. *Career:* mem. Writers' Guild of Great Britain. *Publications:* fiction: Bayswater Bodycount 1995, Barking Mad.

GORDON, Jaimy, BA, MA, DA; American academic and writer; *Professor of English, Western Michigan University*; b. 4 July 1944, Baltimore, MD; m. Peter Blickle 1988. *Education:* Antioch Coll., Brown Univ. *Career:* Writer-in-Residence, Rhode Island State Council on the Arts 1975–77; Dir, Creative Writing Program, Stephens Coll., Columbia, MO 1980–81; Asst Prof., Western Michigan Univ., Kalamazoo 1981–87, Assoc. Prof. 1987–92, Prof. of English 1992–; Prague Summer Program for Writers 2004–. *Publications:* Shamp of the City-Solo 1974, The Bend, the Lip, the Kid (narrative poem) 1978, Circumspections from an Equestrian Statue 1979, Maria Beig: Lost Weddings (trans. with Peter Blickle) 1990, She Drove Without Stopping 1990, Bogeywoman 1999, Lord of Misrule (Nat. Book Award for Fiction) 2010. *Honours:* Nat. Endowment for the Arts Fellowships 1979, 1991; Fellow, Fine Arts Work Center, Provincetown 1980–81, Bunting Inst., Harvard 1984–85; American Acad. and Inst. of Arts and Letters Award 1991. *Address:* Department of English, Western Michigan University, Kalamazoo, MI 49008-5432, USA (office). *Telephone:* (269) 387-2572 (office). *Fax:* (269) 387-2562 (office). *E-mail:* jaimy.gordon@wmich.edu (office). *Website:* www.wmich.edu/english/facultyandstaff/profiles/gordon.htm (office).

GORDON, John William; British writer; b. 19 Nov. 1925, Jarrow-on-Tyne, England; m. Sylvia Young 1954; one s. one d. *Career:* mem. Soc. of Authors. *Publications:* The Giant Under the Snow 1968, The House on the Brink 1970, The Ghost on the Hill 1976, The Waterfall Box 1978, The Spitfire Grave 1979, The Edge of the World 1983, Catch Your Death 1984, The Quelling Eye 1986, The Grasshopper 1987, Ride the Wind 1989, Secret Corridor 1990, Blood Brothers 1991, Ordinary Seaman (autobiog.) 1992, The Burning Baby 1992, Gilray's Ghost 1995, The Flesh Eater 1998, The Midwinter Watch 1998, Skinners 1999, The Ghosts of Blacklode 2002. *Address:* 99 George Borrow Road, Norwich, Norfolk, NR4 7HU, England (home).

GORDON, Lois, BA, MA, PhD; American academic and writer; *University Distinguished Professor of English, Fairleigh Dickinson University*; b. Englewood, NJ; m. Alan Lee Gordon 1961; one s. *Education:* Univs of Michigan and Wisconsin. *Career:* Lecturer in English, City Coll., CUNY, New York 1964–66; Asst Prof. of English, Univ. of Missouri, Kansas City 1966–68; Asst Prof., Fairleigh Dickinson Univ. 1968–71, Assoc. Prof. 1971–75, Prof. of English 1975–, Chair. Dept of English and Comparative Literature 1982–90, Distinguished Prof. 2002–07, Univ. Distinguished Prof. 2007–; Visiting Exchange Prof., Rutgers Univ., NJ 1994; mem. Acad. of American Poets, Authors' Guild, Harold Pinter Soc., Int. League for Human Rights, Modern Language Asscn, PEN, Samuel Beckett Soc. *Publications:* Stratagems to Uncover Nakedness: The Dramas of Harold Pinter 1969, Donald Barthelme 1981, Robert Coover: The Universal Fictionmaking Process 1983, American Chronicle: Six Decades in American Life 1920–1980 1987, American Chronicle: Seven Decades in American Life 1920–1990 1990, Harold Pinter Casebook 1990, The Columbia Chronicles of American Life 1910–1992 1995, The Columbia World of Quotations 1996, The World of Samuel Beckett 1906–1946 1996, American Chronicle: Year by Year Through the Twentieth Century 1999, Pinter at 70 2001, Reading Godot 2002, Nancy Cunard: Heiress, Muse, Political Idealist 2007; contrib. to journals, reviews and newspapers. *Honours:* Nat. Merit Scholar, Betsy Barbour Scholar, Dissertation Completion Fellowship, Univ. of Wisconsin. *Address:* Department of English, Fairleigh Dickinson University, Teaneck, NJ 07666 (office); 300 Central Park West, Apt 96, New York, NY 10024, USA (home). *Telephone:* (201) 692-2263 (office); (212) 362-4053 (home). *E-mail:* lgordon@fdu.edu (office); loisgord@aol.com (office). *Website:* www.fdu.edu (office).

GORDON, Lyndall Felicity, BA, PhD, FRSL; South African/British biographer and academic; *Senior Research Fellow, St Hilda's College, Oxford*; b. 4 Nov. 1941, Cape Town, South Africa; d. of Harry Getz and Rhoda Stella Press; m. Siamon Gordon 1963; two d. *Education:* Univ. of Cape Town, Columbia Univ., New York, USA. *Career:* Asst Prof. of English, Columbia Univ. 1975–76; Lecturer in English, Jesus Coll., Oxford 1977–84; Tutor in English 1984–95, Sr Research Fellow 1995–, St Hilda's Coll., Oxford. *Television:* Virginia Woolf: A Writer's Life (BBC 2) 1984, Charlotte Brontë Unmasked (BBC 2) 1995. *Publications:* Eliot's Early Years 1977, Virginia Woolf: A Writer's Life 1984, Eliot's New Life 1988, Shared Lives 1992, Charlotte Brontë: A Passionate Life 1994, A Private Life of Henry James: Two Women and His Art 1998, T.S. Eliot: An Imperfect Life 1998, Vindication: A Life of Mary Wollstonecraft 2005, Lives Like Loaded Guns: Emily Dickinson and Her Family's Feuds 2010. *Honours:* Rose Mary Crawshay Prize British Acad. 1978, James Tait Black Memorial Prize 1985, Southern Arts Prize 1989, Cheltenham Festival Prize 1994. *E-mail:* georges@gbagency.com (office); isobel@blakefriedmann.co.uk (office)*Website:* www.lyndallgordon.net.

GORDON, Mary Catherine, BA, MA; American writer; *Millicent C. McIntosh Professor of English, Barnard College*; b. 8 Dec. 1949, Far Rockaway, Long Island, NY; m. 1st James Brian 1974 (divorced); m. 2nd Arthur Cash 1979; one s. one d. *Education:* Barnard Coll., Syracuse Univ. *Career:* teacher of English, Dutchess Community Coll., Poughkeepsie, NY 1974–78, Amherst Coll., MA 1979; Millicent C. McIntosh Prof. of English, Barnard Coll. 1988–; State Author of New York 2008–; Guggenheim Fellowship 1993. *Publications:* Final Payments 1978, The Company of Women 1980, Men and Angels 1985, Temporary Shelter (short stories) 1987, The Other Side 1989, Good Boys and Dead Girls (essays) 1992, The Rest of Life: Three Novellas 1993, The Shadow Man: A Daughter's Search for her Father (memoir) 1996, Spending: A Utopian Divertimento 1998, Seeing Through Places: Reflections on Geography and Identity 2000, Joan of Arc 2000, Pearl 2005, The Stories of Mary Gordon (short stories) 2006, Circling My Mother (memoir) 2007, Reading Jesus: A Writer's Encounter with the Gospels 2009. *Honours:* Janet Heidinger Kafka Prize 1979, 1981, Lila Acheson Wallace-Readers' Digest Writers' Award 1992, O. Henry Award 1997, The Story Prize 2007, Edith Wharton Citation of Merit 2008. *Address:* 15 Claremont Avenue, New York, NY 10027, USA (home).

GORDON-REED, Annette, AB, JD; American academic and writer; *Professor of Law, New York Law School*; m.; one s. one d. *Education:* Dartmouth Coll., Harvard Law School. *Career:* fmr Assoc., Cahill Gordon & Reindel (law firm); fmrly Counsel to New York City Bd of Corrections; Prof. of Law, New York Law School 1992–. *Publications:* Thomas Jefferson and Sally Hemings: An American Controversy 1997, Vernon Can Read!: A Memoir (co-author) 2001, The Hemingses of Monticello: An American Family (Nat. Book Award, Pulitzer Prize for History 2009) 2008, Race on Trial: Law and Justice in American History (essays, ed.) 2009. *Honours:* MacArthur Fellowship 2010. *Address:* c/o Gemma Jacobs, New York Law School, 57 Worth Street, New

York, NY 10013, USA (office). *Telephone:* (212) 431-2120 (office). *E-mail:* gjacobs@nyls.edu (office). *Website:* www.nyls.edu (office).

GÓREC-ROSINSKI, Jan, MJ; Polish poet, writer, essayist and journalist; b. 6 Jan. 1920, Króglik; m. Maria Barbara Dobrzalska-Górec 1938; three s. *Education:* Nicolai Copernici Univ., Torun. *Career:* journalist, Polish radio 1957–58; Chief Ed. Fakty i Myśli 1958–74, Fakty 1974–88, Metafora (literary magazine) 1990; mem. Union of Polish Writers in Warsaw. *Publications:* Jamark arlekinów 1963, Ucieczka z Wiezy Babel 1964, Bluznierstwo garncarza 1965, Zaprzeszle horyzonty 1968, Molitwa za dobrinu 1968, Czas odnajdywania 1970, Zywa galaz 1971, W kamieniu 1973, Poezje wybrane 1976, Ulica Sokratesa 1978, Eroica 1980, Sen Syzyfa 1982, Wzejscie slonc 1985, Departures 1985, Czyje bedzie królestwo 1987, Kredowy Bóg 1987, Czlowiek Podzielony 1988, Czarnopis, poezje wybrane 1989, Siedem wieczerników 1990, Krzyczec beda kamienie 1991, Czarna perla 1992, Sloneczny splot 1993, Demony 1994, Przechodzien róz 1995, Rajska jablon 1995, Przychodzacy: sacrum et profanum 1997, Mesjasz zbuntowany: dramat mityczny 2001; contribs to many publications. *Honours:* Commander's Order and Star from Pres. of Poland 2002; Council Award, Bydgoszcz People's Province 1968, Workers' Publishing Co-operative Award 1979, Klemens Janicki Award 1986, Int. Poetic November Award 1987, Prof. T. Kotarbinski Prize 1989, Pres. of Bydgoszcz Artistic Award 2000.

GORES, Joseph Nicholas, MA; American writer, novelist and screenwriter; b. 25 Dec. 1931, Rochester, Minn.; m. Dori Corfitzen 1976, one s. one d. *Education:* Univ. of Notre Dame, Stanford Univ. *Career:* Story Ed., B. L. Stryker Mystery Movie Series, ABC-TV, 1988–89; mem. Mystery Writers of America (Pres. 1986), International Asscn of Crime Writers, Crime Writers' Asscn, Private Eye Writers of America. *Publications:* A Time of Predators 1969, Marine Salvage (non-fiction) 1971, Dead Skip 1972, Final Notice 1973, Interface 1974, Hammett 1975, Gone, No Forwarding 1978, Come Morning 1986, Wolf Time 1989, Mostly Murder (short stories) 1992, 32 Cadillacs 1992, Dead Man 1993, Menaced Assassin 1994, Contract Null and Void 1996, Cases 1998, Speak of the Devil (short stories) 1999, Stakeout on Page Street (short stories) 2000, Cons, Scams and Grifts 2001, Glass Tiger (novel) 2006, Spade and Archer: The Prequel to Dashiell Hammett's The Maltese Falcon 2009; contrib. to numerous magazines and anthologies; eight film scripts; television drama. *Honours:* Edgar Awards for Best First Novel 1969, for Best Short Story 1969, MWA for Best Episodic TV Drama 1975, Falcon, Maltese Falcon Soc. of Japan 1986. *Address:* PO Box 446, Fairfax, CA 94978, USA (office). *Telephone:* (415) 454-3462 (office). *Fax:* (415) 454-3143 (office).

GÖRGEY, Gábor; Hungarian poet, novelist and playwright. *Career:* fmr Minister of Cultural Heritage for Hungary. *Publications:* Lilla-Cápák Nyugalom 1976, Légifolyosó 1977, Találkozás egy fél kutyával 1980, Egy vacsora anatómiája 1981, A fél kutya másik fele 1983, Munkavilágitás 1984, A diva bosszúja 1988, Meteoropata nemzet 1989, Mindig újabb kuty ák jönnek 1991, Waterloo kellos közepén 1994. *Address:* c/o Széchenyi Academy of Letters and Arts, Hungarian Academy of Sciences, 1245 Budapest, Pf. 1000, Hungary (office).

GOSLING(-HARE), Paula Louise, (Ainslie Skinner, Holly Baxter), BA; American writer; b. 12 Oct. 1939, Michigan; d. of A. Paul Osius and Sylvie Van Slembrouck Osius; m. 1st Christopher Gosling 1968 (divorced 1978); two d.; m. 2nd John Hare 1982. *Education:* Wayne State Univ. *Career:* mem. CWA (chair. 1982), Soc. of Authors. *Publications:* A Running Duck (aka Fair Game, also film: Cobra) 1976, Zero Trap 1978, The Woman in Red 1979, Losers Blues 1980, Minds Eye (as Ainslie Skinner) 1980, Monkey Puzzle 1982, The Wychford Murders 1983, Hoodwink 1985, Backlash 1987, Death Penalties 1990, The Body in Blackwater Bay 1992, A Few Dying Words 1994, The Dead of Winter 1995, Death and Shadows 1999, Underneath Every Stone 2000, Richochet 2002, Tears of the Dragon 2004. *Honours:* CWA Gold Dagger, Arts Achievement Award, Wayne State Univ. *Literary Agent:* Greene & Heaton Ltd, 37 Goldhawk Road, London, W12 8QQ, England.

GOSPODINOV, Georgi, PhD; Bulgarian writer, poet and columnist; b. 1968, Jambol. *Education:* Bulgarian Acad. of Sciences Inst. for Literature. *Career:* weekly columnist in daily newspaper Dnevnik 2001–; guest writer Berlin arts programme DAAD 2008; Ed. in Chief Literaturen vestnik. *Play:* D.J.. *Publications:* seven books of poetry, fiction, literary and cultural research including Lapidarium (poems) 1992, Chereshata na edin narod (poems) (Book of the Year, Asscn of Bulgarian Writers) 1996, Estestven roman (trans. as Natural Novel) 1999, I drugi istorii (short stories) (trans. as And Other Stories) 2001, Inventarna kniga na sotsializma (co-author) 2006, Az zhiviakh sotsializma: 171 lichni istorii (Ed.) 2006. *Address:* c/o Dalkey Archive Press, Free Word Centre, 60 Farringdon Road, London, EC1R 3GA, England (office). *E-mail:* contact@dalkeyarchive.com (office).

GOSSETT, Philip, BA, MFA, PhD; American musicologist, academic and writer; *Robert W. Reneker Distinguished Service Professor Emeritus, University of Chicago*; b. 27 Sept. 1941, New York, NY; s. of Harold Gossett and Pear Gossett (née Lenkowsky); m. Suzanne S. Gossett 1963; two s. *Education:* Amherst Coll., Columbia Univ., Princeton Univ. *Career:* Asst Prof., Univ. of Chicago 1968–73, Assoc. Prof. 1973–77, Prof. 1977–84, Chair Dept of Music 1978–84, 1989, Robert W. Reneker Distinguished Service Prof. 1984–2010, Robert W. Reneker Distinguished Service Prof. Emer. 2010–, Dean Division of Humanities 1989–99; Visiting Assoc. Prof., Columbia Univ. 1975; Direttore dell'edizione, Edizione critica delle Opere di Gioachino Rossini 1978–2005; Meadows Visiting Prof., Southern Methodist Univ. 1980; Gen. Ed., Works of Giuseppe Verdi 1981–; Assoc. Prof., Universitá degli Studi, Parma 1983; Visiting Prof., Univ. of Paris 1988; Five-Coll. Visiting Prof. 1989; Gauss Seminars, Princeton Univ. 1991; Prof. di chiara fama, Univ. Roma, La Sapienza 2004–11; Gen. Ed. Works of Gioachino Rossini (Bärenreiter-Verlage) 2006–; 'Consulenza musicologica', Verdi Festival, Parma 2000–01; Hambro Visiting Prof. of Opera Studies, Univ. of Oxford 2001; Visiting Scholar, Phi Beta Kappa 2002–03; Fellow, American Acad. of Arts and Sciences 1989; Corresponding Fellow, British Acad. 2008–; Fellow, American Philosphical Soc. 2008–; Woodrow Wilson Fellowship 1963–64; Fulbright Scholar, Paris 1965–66; Martha Baird Rockefeller Fellowship 1967–68; Guggenheim Fellowship 1971–72; Nat. Endowment for the Humanities Sr Fellowship 1982–83; mem. Bd of Dirs American Inst. of Verdi Studies, American Musicological Soc. (Pres. 1994–96), Int. Musicological Soc. (Directorium 2006–), Società Italiana di Musicologia, Soc. for Textual Scholarship (Pres. 1993–95). *Publications:* The Operas of Rossini: Problems of Textual Criticism in Nineteenth-Century Opera (two vols) 1970, Treatise on Harmony, by Jean-Philippe Rameau (trans. and ed.) 1971, The Tragic Finale of Tancredi 1977, Early Romantic Opera (ed. with Charles Rosen) 1978–83, Le Sinfonie di Rossini 1981, Rossini Tancredi (critical edn) 1983, Italian Opera 1810–1840 (ed., 25 vols) 1984–92, 'Anna Bolena' and the Maturity of Gaetano Donizetti 1985, Il barbiere di Siviglia 1992, Rossini Ermione (with P. Brauner) 1995, Don Pasquale 1999, Semiramide (with A. Zedda) 2001, Divas and Scholars: Performing Italian Opera 2006, Petite Messe solennelle (with P. Brauner) 2009, Dive e maestri (2009); contribs to reference works, scholarly books and professional journals. *Honours:* Hon. DHL (Amherst Coll.) 1993; hon. mem. Accademia Filarmonica di Bologna 1992, Accademico Onorario Accademia di Santa Cecilia Rome 2003; Visiting Scholar, Phi Beta Kappa 2002–03; Foreign Mem. Ateneo Veneto 2001; American Musicological Soc. Alfred Einstein Award 1969, Medaglio d'Oro prima classe, Italy 1985, American Acad. of Composers, Authors and Publishers Deems Taylor Award 1986, Mellon Distinguished Achievement Award 2004, American Acad. of Composers, Authors and Publishers Deems Taylor Award 2007, Serena Prize, British Acad. 2008, Kinkeldey Award, American Musicological Soc. 2008, Palisca Award, American Musicological Soc. 2009; Grand Ufficiale dell'Ordine al Merito 1997, Cavaliere di Gran Croce 1998, Order of Rio Branca, Brazil 1998. *Address:* Department of Music, University of Chicago, 1010 East 59th Street, Chicago, IL 60637 (office); 5810 S. Harper Avenue, Chicago, IL 60637, USA (home). *Telephone:* (773) 834-4181 (office); (773) 955-3738 (home); (773) 710-7074 (mobile) (home). *Fax:* (773) 955-0247 (home). *E-mail:* phgs44@hotmail .com (office).

GÖTHE, (Lars) Staffan; Swedish playwright, actor, director and academic; *Actor, Royal Dramatic Theatre, Stockholm*; b. 20 Dec. 1944, Luleå; s. of the late Thorsten Göthe and of Margit Grape-Göthe; m. Kristin Byström 1969; one s. *Education:* Acad. of Performing Arts, Gothenburg. *Career:* actor and playwright, regional theatre of Växjö 1971, Folkteatern, Gothenburg 1974; Headmaster Acad. of Performing Arts, Malmö 1976; actor, Folkteatern, Gävleborg 1983; Dir The RTC Co. 1986–95; actor and playwright, Royal Dramatic Theatre, Stockholm 1995–2003, actor 2011–; Prof., Malmö Theatre Acad., Univ. of Lund 2003–11. *Plays:* En natt i februari 1972, Den gråtande polisen 1980, La strada dell'amore 1986, En uppstoppad hund 1986, Den perfekta Kyssen 1990, Arma Irma 1991, Boogie Woogie 1992, Blått Hus Med Röda Kinder 1995, Ruben Pottas Eländiga Salonger 1996, Ett Lysande Elände 1999, Temperance 2000, Byta Trottoar 2001, Stjärnan Över Lappland 2005, Kvart i fem-ekot 2010. *Publication:* Lysande Eländen (complete works) 2004. *Honours:* Royal Medal Litteris et Artibus, Award of Royal Swedish Acad. 2005. *Address:* Vindragarvägen 8, 117 50 Stockholm, Sweden (home). *Telephone:* (8) 668-38-18 (office). *Website:* staffangothe@gmail.com (office).

GOTO, Hiromi, BA; Canadian (b. Japanese) writer; b. 31 Dec. 1966, Chibaken; two c. *Education:* Univ. of Calgary. *Career:* Writer in Residence, Emily Carr Inst. of Art, Design and Media 2003–04, Simon Fraser Univ., BC 2008–09; mem. Writers' Union of Canada (co-chair., racial minority cttee 1995–97). *Publications:* Chorus of Mushrooms (Commonwealth Writers Prize Best First Book (Canada-Caribbean Region) 1995, co-winner, Canada-Japan Book Award 1995) 1994, The Water of Possibility 2001, The Kappa Child (James Tiptree Jr Memorial Award) 2001, Hopeful Monsters 2004, Half World 2009. *Literary Agent:* Transatlantic Literary Agency, 72 Glengowan Road, Toronto, ON M4N 1G4, Canada. *Telephone:* (416) 488-9214. *Fax:* (416) 488-4531. *E-mail:* info@tla1.com. *Website:* www.tla1.com.

GOTTLIEB, Robert Adams, BA; American editor and critic; b. 29 April 1931, New York; s. of Charles Gottlieb and Martha (née Kean) Gottlieb; m. 1st Muriel Higgins 1952; m. 2nd Maria Tucci 1969; two s. one d. *Education:* Columbia Coll. and Cambridge Univ. *Career:* employee Simon and Schuster 1955–65, Ed.-in-Chief 1965–68; Ed.-in-Chief Alfred A. Knopf 1968–87, Pres. 1973–87; Ed.-in-Chief The New Yorker 1987–92; now dance and book critic for New York Observer, New York Times, The New Yorker and New York Review of Books. *Publications:* Reading Jazz 1996, Reading Lyrics (co-author) 2000, George Balanchine – The Ballet Maker 2004, Reading Dance (ed.) 2008, Sarah: The Life of Sarah Bernhardt 2010. *Address:* 237 East 48th Street, New York, NY 10017-1538, USA (home).

GOULD, Alan David, BA, DipEd; British poet, novelist and essayist; b. 22 March 1949, London; s. of Ernest Clement Gould and Valgerdur Bjarnisdottir; m. Anne Langridge 1984; two s. *Education:* ANU, Canberra, Australia. *Career:* Creative Fellow, ANU 1978; Writer-in-Residence, Geelong Coll. 1978, 1980, 1982, 1985, Australian Defence Forces Acad. 1986, Lincoln Humberside

Arts Centre 1988; mem. Literature Bd of the Australia Council 2002–06. *Publications:* poetry: Icelandic Solitaries 1978, Astral Sea 1981, The Pausing of the Hours 1984, The Twofold Place 1986, Years Found in Likeness 1988, Former Light (selected poems) 1992, Momentum 1992, Mermaid 1996, Dalliance and Scorn 1999, A Fold in the Light 2001, The Past Completes Me, Selected Poems 1973–2003 (Grace Leven Prize for Poetry 2006) 2005; fiction: The Man Who Stayed Below 1984, The Enduring Disguises 1988, To The Burning City 1991, Close Ups 1994, The Tazyrik Year 1998, The Schoonermaster's Dance 2000; essays: The Totem Ship 1996; contrib. to various Australian publications. *Honours:* New South Wales Premier's Prize for Poetry 1981, Prizes for Fiction 1985, 1992, Philip Hodgins Memorial Medal 1999, Royal Blind Soc. Audio Book of the Year 1999, Co-winner, Courier-Mail Book of the Year 2001, Co-winner, ACT Book of the Year 2001. *Literary Agent:* c/o Sally Bird, Calidris Literary Agency, PO Boc 1014, Goulburn, NSW 2580, Australia. *E-mail:* sallybird@calidrislitagency.com. *Website:* www.calidrislitagency.com. *Address:* 198 Duffy Street, Ainslie, ACT 2602, Australia (home). *E-mail:* tazyrik@bigpond.com.au (home). *Website:* www.alangouldwriter.com.

GOULDEN, Joseph C., (Henry S. A. Becket); American writer; b. 23 May 1934, Marshall, TX; m. 1st; two s.; m. 2nd Leslie Cantrell Smith 1979. *Education:* Univ. of Texas, US Army Intelligence School, US Army Special Warfare School. *Career:* staff writer, Dallas Morning News, Philadelphia Inquirer 1958–68. *Publications:* The Curtis Caper 1965, Monopoly 1968, Truth is the First Casualty 1969, The Money Givers 1971, The Superlawyers 1972, Meany: The Unchallenged Strong Man of American Labor 1972, The Benchwarmers 1974, Mencken's Last Campaign (ed.) 1976, The Best Years 1976, The Million Dollar Lawyers 1978, Korea: The Untold Story of the War 1982, Myth-Informed (with Paul Dickson) 1983, The News Manipulators (with Reed Irvine and Cliff Kincaid) 1983, Jerry Wurf: Labor's Last Angry Man 1982, The Death Merchant 1984, There Are Alligators in Our Sewers (with Paul Dickson) 1984, Dictionary of Espionage (as Henry S. A. Becket) 1987, Fit to Print: A. M. Rosenthal and His Times 1988, The Money Lawyers 2006; contrib of over 200 articles to magazines. *Honours:* Nat. Magazine Award 1971. *Address:* 1534 29th Street, NW, Washington, DC 20007, USA (home). *E-mail:* josephg894@aol.com.

GOVIER, Katherine Mary, MA; Canadian writer; b. 4 July 1948, Edmonton, AB; d. of George Wheeler and Doris Eda Govier; m. John Allen Honderich 1981; one s. one d. *Education:* Univ. of Alberta and York Univ. (ON). *Career:* Writing first published 1972; fiction and non-fiction published by major British and Canadian magazines 1973–81; Lecturer in English Ryerson Polytech Inst., Toronto, ON 1973–74; Contrib., Ed. Toronto Life magazine 1975–77; Visiting Lecturer Creative Writing Programme, York Univ. 1982–86; Research Fellow Univ. of Leeds, UK 1986; Chair. Writers' Devt Trust 1990–91; mem. PEN Canada (Vice-Pres. 1996–97), Writers' Union of Canada; Nat. Magazine Award 1979; Foundation for the Advancement of Canadian Letters Authors' Award 1979. *Publications:* Going Through the Motions 1981, Random Descent (3rd edn) 1987; short stories: Fables of Brunswick Avenue 1985, Before and After (2nd edn) 1990; novels: Between Men 1987, Hearts of Flame 1991, The Immaculate Conception Photography Gallery 1994, Angel Walk 1996, Creation 2003, Three Views of Crystal Water 2005; short stories included in Oxford Book of Canadian Short Stories, Canadian Short Stories (ed R. Weaver) 1985, more Stories by Canadian Women (ed R. Sullivan) 1987, Oxford Book of Canadian Short Stories (ed M. Atwood and R. Weaver) 1995. *Literary Agent:* The Helen Heller Agency, 253 Eglinton Avenue W. Suite 202, Toronto, ON M4R 1B1, Canada. *Telephone:* (416) 489-0396. *E-mail:* info@helenhelleragency.com. *Website:* www.helenhelleragency.com. *Address:* 54 Farnham Ave, Toronto, ON M4V 1H4, Canada (home). *E-mail:* author@govier.com (office). *Website:* www.govier.com.

GOW, Michael; Australian playwright and writer; b. 14 Feb. 1955, Sydney. *Career:* Artistic Dir, Queensland Theatre Co. 1999–. *Publications:* The Kid 1983, The Astronaut's Wife 1984, Away (Australian Writer's Guild Awgie 1987) 1986, On Top of the World 1986, Europe 1987, 1841 1988, All Stops Out (juvenile) 1991, Furious (Sydney Theatre Critic's Circle Award) 1991, Sweet Phoebe 1994, Live Acts On Stage 1996, Up Here 2004, Toy Symphony 2007. *Honours:* Green Room Award 1986, NSW Premier's Literary Award 1986, Sydney Theatre Critic's Circle Award 1986. *Literary Agent:* c/o Shanahan Management, Level 3, Berman House, 91 Campbell Street, Surry Hills, NSW 2010, Australia. *Telephone:* (2) 8202-1800. *Fax:* (2) 8202-1801. *E-mail:* nellief@shanahan.com.au.

GOWDY, Barbara Louise, CM; Canadian novelist and short story writer; b. 25 June 1950, Windsor, Ont. *Education:* York Univ. *Career:* mem. PEN Canada, Writers' Union of Canada. *Publications:* Through the Green Valley (novel) 1988, Falling Angels (novel) 1989, We So Seldom Look on Love (short stories) 1992, Mister Sandman (novel) 1995, The White Bone (novel) 1998, The Romantic (novel) 2003, Helpless (novel) 2007; contrib. to Best American Short Stories, The New Oxford Book of Canadian Short Stories, The Penguin Anthology of Stories by Canadian Women. *Honours:* Marian Engel Award, Trillium Book Award. *Literary Agent:* c/o Westwood Creative Artists, 94 Harbord Street, Toronto, ON M5S 1G6, Canada.

GOWERS, Andrew, MA; British journalist, communications executive and consultant; b. 19 Oct. 1957, Reading, Berks.; s. of Michael Gowers and Anne Gowers; m. Finola Gowers (née Clarke); one s. one d. *Education:* Trinity School, Croydon and Univ. of Cambridge. *Career:* grad. trainee, Reuters 1980, Brussels Corresp. 1981, Zurich Corresp. 1982, joined Foreign Desk, Financial Times (FT), London 1983, Agric. Corresp. 1984, Commodities Ed. 1985, Middle East Ed. 1987, Foreign Ed. 1992, Deputy Ed. 1994, Acting Ed. 1997, Ed. FT Deutschland (German Language Business Paper) 1999, Ed. FT 2001–05; columnist, Evening Standard, Sunday Times 2005–06; Leader Gowers' Review of Intellectual Property for UK Government 2005–06; Head of Corp. Communications (Europe and Asia), Lehman Brothers 2006–07, Global Co-head of Corp. Communications, Marketing and Brand Man. 2007–08; Interim Head of External Relations, London Business School 2008–09, Head of Group Media, BP PLC 2009–10. *Publication:* Arafat, The Biography (co-author) 1991. *Address:* 4 Holmdene Avenue, London, SE24 9LF, England (home). *Telephone:* (20) 7733-4125 (home). *E-mail:* andrewgowers@btinternet.com (office).

GOYTISOLO, Juan; Spanish writer; b. 5 Jan. 1931, Barcelona; m. Monique Lange 1978 (died 1996). *Education:* Univs of Barcelona and Madrid. *Career:* emigrated to France 1957; reporter, Cuba 1965; assoc. with Gallimard Publishing Co.; Visiting Prof. at various univs in USA. *Writing for television:* Alquibla (series). *Publications:* fiction: Juegos de manos (trans. as The Young Assassins) 1954, Duelo en el Paraíso (trans. as Children of Chaos) 1955, El circo (El mañana efímero trilogy vol. one) 1957, Fiestas (El mañana efímero trilogy vol. two) 1958, La resaca (El mañana efímero trilogy vol. three) 1958, La isla 1961, La chanca 1962, Señas de identidad (trans. as Marks of Identity) 1966, Reivindicación del conde don Julián (trans. as Count Julian) 1970, Juan sin tierra (trans. as John the Landless) 1975, Colera de Aquines 1979, Makbara 1980, Paisajes después de la batalla (trans. as Landscapes After the Battle) 1982, Las virtudes del pájaro solitario (trans. as The Virtues of the Solitary Bird) 1988, La cuarentena (trans. as Quarantine) 1991, La saga de los Marx (trans. as The Marx Family Saga) 1993, Campos de Níjar 1993, Las semanas del jardín (trans. as The Garden of Secrets) 1997, Carajicomedia (trans. as A Cock-Eyed Comedy) 2000, Telón de boca 2003, El exiliado de aquí y allá (trans. as Exiled from Almost Everywhere) 2008; non-fiction: Crónicas Sarracinas (essays, trans. as Saracen Chronicles) 1982, Coto vedado (autobiography, trans. as Forbidden Territory) 1985, En los reinos de Taifa (autobiography, trans. as Realms of Strife) 1986, Cuaderno de Sarajevo (Premio francés Méditerranée) 1994, Reconocimiento (Gran Premio Proartes de Narrativa Iberoamericana) 1997, Pájaro que ensucia su propio nido (essays) 2001, Cinema Eden: Essays from the Muslim Mediterranean 2004, El Lucernario: La pasión crítica de Manuel Azaña 2004, La saga de los Marx 2005, Contra las sagradas formas 2007, Ensayos escogidos 2008; short stories, travel narratives, literary criticism, essays. *Honours:* Premio Europalia de la Comunidad Europea 1985, Premio Nelly-Sachs, Dortmund 1993, Premio Octavio Paz de Poesía y Ensayo, Mexico 2002, Premio Juan Rulfo 2004, Nat. Prize for Spanish Letters 2008, Prix Formento 2012. *Address:* c/o Eland Publishing Ltd, Third Floor, 61 Exmouth Market, London, EC1R 4QL, England. *E-mail:* jgoytiso@sauce.pntic.mec.es.

GRABER, Kathleen, BA, MFA; American poet and academic; *Assistant Professor of English, Virginia Commonwealth University.* *Education:* Hofstra Univ., New York Univ. *Career:* taught English in high school –1994 and at New York Univ.; currently Asst Prof. of English, Virginia Commonwealth Univ.; teacher, low residency MFA Program, Fairleigh Dickinson Univ. *Publications:* poetry collections: Correspondence (Saturnalia Books Poetry Prize) 2005, The Eternal City 2010; contrib. to The New Yorker, American Poetry Review and others. *Honours:* New Jersey State Council on the Arts Artists Fellowship, Rona Jaffe Foundation Writers Award, Hodder Fellowship in Creative Writing, Princeton Univ. 2007, Amy Lowell Travelling Scholarship 2008. *Address:* Hibbs Hall 324A, Virginia Commonwealth University, Richmond, VA 23284, USA (office). *Telephone:* (804) 827-8324 (office). *E-mail:* kjgraber@vcu.edu (office). *Website:* www.has.vcu.edu/eng (office).

GRACE, Dame Patricia Frances, DCNZM; New Zealand (Maori) writer; b. 17 Aug. 1937, Wellington; d. of Edward William Gunson and Joyce Frances Flan; m.; seven c. *Education:* St Mary's Coll., Wellington Teachers Coll. *Career:* Teacher, Primary and Secondary Schools, King Country, Northland and Porirua; Writing Fellow, Victoria Univ., Wellington, 1985. *Publications:* Mutuwhenua: The Moon Sleeps 1978, Potiki 1986, Cousins 1992, Baby No-Eyes 1998, Dogside Story 2001, Tu 2004, Ned & Katina 2009; short stories: Waiariki 1975, The Dream Sleepers and Other Stories 1980, Electric City and Other Stories 1980, Selected Stories 1991, The Sky People 1994, Collected Stories 1994, Small Holes in the Silence 2006; other: several books for children. *Honours:* Hon. HLD (Victoria Univ.) 1989; New Zealand Fiction Award 1987, Kiriyama Pacific Rim Prize for Literature 2001, Deutz Medal for Fiction 2005, Montana New Zealand Book Award 2005, Arts Foundation of New Zealand Icon Award 2005, Prime Minister's Award for Literature 2006, Neustadt Int. Prize for Fiction 2008. *Address:* c/o Pearson Education New Zealand Ltd, Private Bag 102908, NSMC, Auckland, New Zealand.

GRAEME, Roderic (see Jeffries, Roderic Graeme)

GRAFF, Henry Franklin, MA, PhD; American academic and writer; *Professor Emeritus of History, Columbia University;* b. 11 Aug. 1921, New York; m. Edith Krantz 1946; two d. *Education:* City Coll., City Univ. of New York, Columbia Univ. *Career:* Fellow in History, City Coll., CUNY 1941–42, Tutor in History 1946; Lecturer, Columbia Univ. 1946–47, Instructor to Assoc. Prof. 1946–61, Chair. Dept of History 1961–64, Prof. of History 1961–91, Prof. Emeritus 1991–; apptd Lecturer, Vassar Coll. 1953, Yale School of Medicine 1993; Presidential Appointee, Nat. Historical Publications Comm. 1965–71,

Pres. John F. Kennedy Assassination Records Review Bd 1993–98; Sr Fellow, Freedom Foundation Media Studies Center, New York City 1991–92; apptd Dean's Distinguished Lecturer in the Humanities, Columbia Univ. Coll. of Physicians and Surgeons 1992; mem. American Historical Asscn, Authors' Guild, Council on Foreign Relations, Org. of American Historians, PEN, Soc. of American Historians; Corresponding mem., Massachusetts Historical Soc. *Publications:* Bluejackets with Perry in Japan 1952, The Modern Researcher (with Jacques Barzun) 1962, American Themes (with Clifford Lord) 1963, Thomas Jefferson 1968, American Imperialism and the Philippine Insurrection 1969, The Tuesday Cabinet: Deliberation and Decision on Peace and War under Lyndon B. Johnson 1970, The Call of Freedom (with Paul J. Bohannan) 1978, The Promise of Democracy 1978, This Great Nation 1983, The Presidents: A Reference History 1984, America: The Glorious Republic 1985, Grover Cleveland 2002; contrib. to scholarly journals and to general periodicals. *Honours:* Townsend Harris Medal City Coll. CUNY 1966, Mark Van Doren Award 1981, Great Teacher Award 1982, Columbia Univ., Kidger Award New England History Teachers Asscn 1990, Presidential Medal George Washington Univ. 1997, James Madison Award American Library Asscn 1999, Lifetime Achievement Award Westchester Community Coll. Foundation 2000. *Address:* Department of History, Columbia University, 413 Fayerweather Hall, MC 2527, 1180 Amsterdam Avenue, New York, NY 10027 (office); 47 Andrea Lane, Scarsdale, NY 10583, USA (home). *Telephone:* (212) 854-4646 (office). *Fax:* (212) 851-5963 (office). *E-mail:* hfg1@columbia.edu (office); preshist@aol.com. *Website:* www.history.columbia.edu/faculty/Graff.html (office).

GRAFTON, Anthony Thomas, BA, MA, PhD; American historian, academic and writer; *Henry Putnam University Professor, Princeton University*; b. 21 May 1950, New Haven, CT; m. Louise Ehrlich 1972; one s. one d. *Education:* Univ. of Chicago. *Career:* Instructor in History, Cornell Univ. 1974–75; Asst Prof., Princeton Univ. 1975, Assoc. Prof. 1976–85, Prof. 1985–88, Andrew Mellon Prof. of History 1988–93, Dodge Prof. of History 1993–2000, Henry Putnam University Prof. 2000–; Exhibit Curator, New York Public Library, New York 1992; Meyer Schapiro Lecturer, Columbia Univ. 1996–96; mem. Renaissance Society of America. American Philosophical Society. *Publications:* Joseph Scaliger: A Bibliography, 1852–1982 (ed. with H. J. de Jonge) 1982, Joseph Scaliger: A Study in the History of Classical Scholarship, Vol. 1, Textual Criticism and Exegesis 1983, Vol. 2, Historical Chronology 1993, From Humanism to the Humanities: Education and the Liberal Arts in Fifteenth- and Sixteenth-Century Europe (with Lisa Jardine) 1986, Forgers and Critics: Creativity and Duplicity in Western Scholarship 1990, The Transmission of Culture in Early Modern Europe (with Ann Blair) 1990, Defenders of the Text: The Traditions of Scholarship in an Age of Science, 1450–1800 1991, New Worlds, Ancient Texts: The Power of Tradition and the Shock of Discovery (with April Shelford and Nancy Siraisi) 1992, The Foundations of Early Modern Europe, 1460–1559 (with Eugene F. Rice) 1994, The Footnote: A Curious History 1997, Cardano's Cosmos: The Worlds and Works of a Renaissance Astrologer 1999, Natural Particulars: Nature and the Disciplines in Renaissance Europe (ed. with Nancy Siraisi) 1999, Leon Battista Alberti: Master Builder of the Italian Renaissance 2000, Bring Out Your Dead: The Past as Revelation 2001, What Was History?: The Art of History in Early Modern Europe 2006, Worlds Made by Words: Scholarship and Community in the Modern West 2009, A Have Always Loved the Holy Tongue: Isaac Casaubon, the Jews, and a Forgotten Chapter in Renaissance Scholarship (with Joanna Weinberg) 2011; contributions: periodicals including: Proceedings of the American Philosophical Society, History and Theory, Journal of the Warburg and Courtauld Institutes, Journal of Roman Studies. *Honours:* Danforth Fellow 1971–75, Grant-in-Aid, ACLS 1977, Rollins Bicentennial Professorship, Princeton Univ. 1978, Guggenheim Fellow 1988–89, Fairchild Fellow, California Technical Institute 1988–89, Prize for History, Los Angeles Times 1993, Behrmann Fellow, Princeton Univ. 1994–95, Bainton Prize, Sixteenth-Century Studies Conference 1999, Marron Prize, American Historical Asscn 2000. *Address:* Department of History, 126 Dickinson Hall, Room 129, Princeton University, Princeton, NJ 08544, USA (office). *Telephone:* (609) 258-4182 (office). *Fax:* (609) 258-5326 (office). *E-mail:* grafton@princeton.edu (office). *Website:* www.princeton.edu/history (office).

GRAFTON, Sue, BA; American writer; b. 24 April 1940, Louisville, Ky; d. of C.W. Grafton and Vivian Harnsberger; m. 3rd Steven F. Humphrey; one s. two d. from previous marriages. *Education:* Univ. of Louisville, Ky. *Career:* worked as admissions clerk, cashier and clinic sec., St John's Hosp., Santa Monica, CA; receptionist, later medical educ. sec., Cottage Hosp., Santa Barbara, CA. *Television:* has written numerous films for TV, including Walking Through the Fire (Christopher Award) 1979, Sex and the Single Parent, Mark, I Love You, Nurse; also adaptations of Caribbean Mystery and Sparkling Cyanide by Agatha Christie. *Publications:* Keziah Dane 1967, The Lolly-Madonna War 1969, A is for Alibi 1982, B is for Burglar 1985, C is for Corpse 1986, D is for Deadbeat 1987, E is for Evidence 1988, F is for Fugitive 1989, G is for Gumshoe 1990, H is for Homicide 1991, I is for Innocent 1992, J is for Judgement 1993, K is for Killer 1994, L is for Lawless 1995, M is for Malice 1996, N is for Noose 1998, O is for Outlaw 1999, P is for Peril 2001, Q is for Quarry 2003, R is for Ricochet 2004, S is for Silence (RIO Award of Excellence 2007) 2006, T is for Trespass 2007, U is for Undertow 2009, V is for Vengeance 2011; Killer in the Family (jt author with S. Humphrey), Love on the Run (jt author with S. Humphrey). *Honours:* Cartier Diamond Dagger Award, Crime Writers' Asscn 2008, named Grand Master, Mystery Writers of America 2009. *Address:* PO Box 41447, Santa Barbara, CA 93140, USA (office). *Website:* www.suegrafton.com.

GRAHAM, Donald Edward, BA; American newspaper publisher; *Chairman and CEO, The Washington Post Company*; b. 22 April 1945, Baltimore, Md; s. of the late Philip L. Graham and of Katharine Meyer Graham; m. 1st Mary L. Wissler 1967 (divorced 2007); one s. three d.; m. 2nd Amanda Bennett 2012. *Education:* Harvard Univ. *Career:* joined the Washington Post 1971, Asst Man. Ed. (Sports) 1974–75, Asst Gen. Man. 1975–76, Exec. Vice-Pres. and Gen. Man. 1976–79, Publr 1979–2000, Chair. 2000–08; CEO The Washington Post Co. 1991–, Chair. 1993–; fmrly reporter and writer for Newsweek. *Address:* The Washington Post, 1150 15th Street, NW, Washington, DC 20071, USA (office). *Telephone:* (202) 334-6000 (office). *E-mail:* twpcoreply@washpost.com (office). *Website:* www.washpostco.com (office).

GRAHAM, Henry; British academic and poet; b. 1 Dec. 1930, Liverpool. *Education:* Liverpool Coll. of Art. *Career:* Lecturer in Art History, Liverpool Polytechnic 1968–90; Poetry Ed. Ambit, London 1969–. *Publications:* Good Luck to You Kafka/You'll Need It Boss 1969, Soup City Zoo 1969, Passport to Earth 1971, Poker in Paradise Lost 1977, Europe After Rain 1981, Bomb 1985, The Very Fragrant Death of Paul Gauguin 1987, Jardin Gobe Avions 1991, The Eye of the Beholder 1997, Bar Room Ballads 1999, Kafka in Liverpool 2002; contribs to Ambit, Transatlantic Review, Prism International Review, Evergreen Review; numerous anthologies world-wide. *Honours:* Arts Council Literature Awards 1969, 1971, 1975, Royal Literary Fund Awards 2003–07. *Address:* Flat 5, 23 Marmion Road, Liverpool, L17 8TT, England (home). *Telephone:* (151) 726-0741 (home).

GRAHAM, James (see Patterson, Harry)

GRAHAM, Jorie, BFA, MFA; American poet and academic; *Boylston Professor of Rhetoric and Oratory, Harvard University*; b. 9 May 1951, New York City; m. James Galvin. *Education:* New York Univ. and Univ. of Iowa. *Career:* Poetry Ed. Crazy Horse 1978–81, The Colorado Review 1990–; Contributing Ed., Boston Review, Conjunctions, Denver Quarterly; Asst Prof., Murray State Univ. 1978–79, Humboldt State Univ. 1979–81; Instructor, Columbia Univ. 1981–83; Bunting Fellow, Radcliffe Inst. 1982; staff mem. Writers' Workshop and Prof. of English, Univ. of Iowa 1983–1998; Chancellor, Acad. of American Poets 1997–2003; Boylston Prof. of Rhetoric and Oratory in the Dept of English and American Literature and Language, Harvard Univ. 1998–; mem. American Acad. of Arts and Letters 2009–. *Publications:* Hybrids of Plants and of Ghosts 1980, Erosion 1983, The End of Beauty 1987, The Best American Poetry (ed. with David Lehman) 1990, Region of Unlikeness 1991, Materialism 1993, The Dream of the Unified Field (Pulitzer Prize in Poetry 1996) 1995, Errancy 1997, Swarm 1999, Never 2002, Overlord 2004, Sea Change 2008. *Honours:* American Acad. of Poets Award 1977, Poetry Northwest Young Poets Prize 1980, Pushcart Prizes 1980, 1982, Ingram Merrill Foundation grant 1981, Great Lakes Colleges Asscn Award 1981, American Poetry Review Prize 1982, Guggenheim Fellowship 1983–84, John D. and Catherine T. MacArthur Foundation Fellowship 1990. *Address:* Department of English, Harvard University, 12 Quincy Street, Cambridge, MA 02138, USA (office). *Telephone:* (617) 495-2533 (office). *Fax:* (617) 496-8737 (office). *E-mail:* engdept@fas.harvard.edu (office). *Website:* www.fas.harvard.edu/~english (office).

GRAHAM, Robert (Bob) Donald; Australian writer and illustrator; b. 20 Oct. 1942, Sydney, NSW; m. Carolyn Smith 1968; one s. one d. *Education:* Julian Ashton School of Fine Art, Sydney. *Career:* mem. Australian Soc. of Authors, British Soc. of Authors. *Publications:* Pete and Roland 1981, Here Comes John 1983, Here Comes Theo 1983, Pearl's Place 1983, Libby, Oscar and Me 1984, Bath Time for John 1985, First There Was Frances 1985, Where is Sarah? 1985, The Wild 1986, The Adventures of Charlotte and Henry 1987, Crusher is Coming! (CBC Picture Book Award) 1987, The Red Woollen Blanket 1987, Has Anyone Here Seen William? 1988, Bringing Home the New Baby 1989, Grandad's Magic 1989, Greetings from Sandy Beach (CBC Picture Book Award) 1990, Rose Meets Mr Wintergarten (CBC Picture Book Award) 1992, Brand New Baby 1992, Spirit of Hope 1993, Zoltan the Magnificent 1994, Queenie the Bantam 1997, Buffy 1999, Max (Smarties Prize Gold Medal for Picture Book) 2000, Charlotte and Henry 2000, Let's Get a Pup (Early Childhood CBC Picture Book of the Year 2002, Boston Globe Horn Picture Book Award 2002) 2001, Jethro Byrde (Kate Greenaway Medal) 2002, Tales From the Waterhole 2004, Oscar's Half Birthday 2005, Dimity Dumpty 2006, How to Heal a Broken Wing (Charlotte Zolotow Picture Book Award 2009, CBC Early Childhood Award 2009) 2008, April Underhill 2010, A Bus Called Heaven 2011. *Honours:* Australian Picture Book of the Year 1988, 1991, 1993, 2002, 2009, Highly Commended, Kate Greenaway Medal 1997, Smarties Gold Medal 2000, Kate Greenaway Award 2002, Boston Globe Horn Award 2002, Charlotte Zolotow Award 2009. *Address:* c/o Walker Books Ltd, 87 Vauxhall Walk, London, SE11 5HJ, England. *Telephone:* (20) 7793-0909. *Website:* www.walkerbooks.co.uk.

GRAHAM, Sonia (see Sinclair, Sonia Elizabeth)

GRAINVILLE, Patrick; French novelist; b. 1 June 1947, Villers-sur-mer; s. of Jacques Grainville and Suzanne Grainville (née Laquerre); m. Françoise Lutgen 1971. *Education:* Lycée Deauville, Sorbonne. *Career:* Prof., Lycée de Sartrouville 1975–mem. CNRS literature section 1975; literary critic for Le Figaro. *Publications:* La toison 1972, La lisière 1973, L'abîme 1974, Les flamboyants (Prix Goncourt) 1976, La Diane rousse 1978, Le dernier viking

1980, Les fortresses noires 1982, La caverne céleste 1984, Le paradis des orages 1986, L'atelier du peintre 1988, L'orgie, La neige (Prix Guillaume le Conquérant) 1990, Colère 1992, Mathieu (jtly.) 1993, Les anges et les faucons 1994, Le lien 1996, Le tyran éternel 1998, Le tour de la fin du monde, Une femme me cache 2000, La joie d'Aurélie 2004, La main blessée 2005, Lumière du rat, 2008, Le Baiser de la pieuvre 2010. *Honours:* Officier, Ordre nat. du Mérite, Ordre des Arts et des lettres. *Address:* c/o Editions du Seuil, 27 rue Jacob, 75261 Paris cedex 06, France.

GRAN, Peter, BA, MA, PhD; American academic and writer; b. 14 Dec. 1941, Jersey City, New Jersey; m. Judith Abbott 1966. *Education:* Yale Univ., Univ. of Chicago. *Career:* Core Faculty, Friends World Coll. 1974–75; Visiting Asst Prof. of History, Univ. of California, Los Angeles 1975–77, Univ. of Texas, Austin 1977–79; Assoc. Prof. of History, Temple Univ. 1979–97, Full Prof. 1997–; Sr Fulbright Fellow, Cairo 1994. *Publications:* Islamic Roots of Capitalism: Egypt 1760–1840 1979, Beyond Eurocentrism: A New View of Modern World History 1996, The Rise of the Rich 2009; contribs to books and journals. *Honours:* Nat. Endowment for the Humanities Award, American Research Center Egypt 1992. *Address:* Department of History, Temple University, 844 Gladfelter Hall, 1115 West Berks Street, Philadelphia, PA 19122-6089, USA (office). *Telephone:* (215) 204-7461 (office). *Fax:* (215) 204-5891 (office). *E-mail:* pgran@temple.edu (office). *Website:* www.temple.edu/history/gran/index.html (office).

GRANDES HERNÁNDEZ, Almudena; Spanish writer; b. 7 May 1960, Madrid; m. Luis García Montero. *Education:* Universidad Complutense. *Publications:* Las edades de Lulú (novel) (Premio Sonrisa Vertical) 1989, Te llamaré Viernes (novel) 1991, Malena es un nombre de tango (novel) 1994, Modelos de mujer (short stories) 1996, Atlas de geografía humana (novel) 1998, Los aires difíciles (novel) 2002, Mercado de Barceló (stories and articles) 2003, Castillos de cartón (novel) 2004, Estaciones de paso (short stories) 2005, El corazón helado (novel) 2007, Ines y la alegria 2010, El Lector de Julio Verne 2012. *Honours:* Premio Rossone d'Oro, Italy 1997. *Address:* c/o Tusquets Editores SA, Cesare Cantù 8, 08023 Barcelona, Spain. *Website:* www.almudenagrandes.com.

GRANGÉ, Jean-Christophe; French writer; b. 15 July 1961, Paris. *Career:* fmr independent journalist, est. own news agency. *Publications:* Le Vol des cigognes (trans. as Flight of the Storks) 1994, Les Rivières pourpres (trans. as Blood-Red Rivers) 1997, Le Concile de pierre (trans. as The Stone Council) 2000, L'Empire des loups (trans. as Empire of the Wolves) 2003, La Ligne noire 2004, Le Serment des limbes 2007, Misérere 2008, La Fôret des Mânes 2009, Le Passager 2011, El Origen Del Mal 2011. *Address:* c/o Éditions Albin Michel, 22 rue Huyghens, 75014 Paris, France. *Website:* www.jc-grange.com.

GRANGE, Peter (see Nicole, Christopher Robin)

GRANN, Phyllis, BA; American publisher and editor; b. 2 Sept. 1937, London, England; d. of Solomon Grann and Louisa (Bois-Smith) Eitingon; m. Victor Grann 1962; two s. one d. *Education:* Barnard Coll. *Career:* Sec., Doubleday Publrs, New York 1958–60; Ed., William Morrow Inc., New York 1960–62, David McKay Co., New York 1962–70, Simon & Schuster Inc., New York 1970; Vice-Pres. Simon & Schuster Inc. 1976; Pres., Publr G. P. Putnam's & Sons, New York 1976–86; Pres. Putnam Publishing Group Inc. (now Penguin Putnam Inc.), New York 1986–96, CEO 1987–96, Chair. 1997–2001; Vice-Chair. Random House, Inc. 2001–02, Sr Ed. Doubleday 2003–11 (retd); currently Freelance Consultant and Ed.; apptd Dir, Warner Music Group Corpn 2006. *Address:* c/o Doubleday Books, Random House, Inc., 1745 Broadway, New York, NY 10019, USA.

GRANT, Anne Underwood, AB; American writer; b. 24 Feb. 1946, Savannah; m. Maxwell Berry Grant, Jr (divorced); one s. one d. *Education:* Univ. of North Carolina at Chapel Hill, Warren Wilson Coll. *Career:* Community Assoc., North Carolina Arts Council, Raleigh early 1970s; Communications Dir Good Will Publrs, Gastonia, North Carolina early 1980s; Pres. Underwood Grant Advertising, Charlotte, NC 1980s–mid-1990s; Pres. Tarra-diddle Players 1990s; mem. Bd of Dirs MWA 1997–99, Pres. Southeast Chapter 1997–99; Chair. Southern Mystery Gathering 1999. *Publications:* Multiple Listing 1998, Smoke Screen 1998, Cuttings 1999, Voices in the Sand 2000. *Address:* 587 George Chastain Road, Horse Shoe, NC 28742, USA. *E-mail:* annieug@sprynet.com.

GRANT, John, (Jonathan Gash, Graham Gaunt), BM, BS; British physician and writer; b. 30 Sept. 1933, Bolton, Lancashire, England; m. Pamela Richard 1955, three d. *Education:* University of London. *Career:* GP, London 1958–59; Pathologist, London and Essex 1959–62; Clinical Pathologist, Hannover and Berlin 1962–65; Lecturer in Clinical Pathology and Head of the Pathology Division, University of Hong Kong 1965–68; Microbiologist, Hong Kong and London 1968–71; Head of Bacteriology Unit, School of Hygiene and Tropical Medicine, University of London 1971–88; Fellow, International College of Surgeons, Royal Society of Tropical Medicine; mem. MRCS 1958; LRCP 1958. *Publications:* as Jonathan Gash: The Judas Pair 1977, Gold by Gemini 1978, The Grail Tree 1979, Spend Game 1981, The Vatican Rip 1981, The Sleepers of Erin 1983, Firefly Gadroom 1984, The Gondola Scam 1984, Pearlhanger 1985, The Tartan Ringers 1986, Moonspender 1987, Jade Woman 1989, The Very Last Gambado 1990, The Great California Game 1991, The Lies of Fair Ladies 1992, Paid and Loving Eyes 1993, The Sin Within Her Smile 1994, The Grace of Older Women 1995, The Possessions of a Lady 1996, The Rich and the Profane 1998, A Rag, a Bone, and a Hank of Hair 1999, Every Last Cent 2001, Ten Word Game 2003, The Year of the Woman 2004, Finding Davey 2005, Bad Girl Magdalene 2007, Faces in the Pool 2008; as Graham Gaunt: The Incomer 1982. *Honours:* CWA Award 1977. *Address:* Silver Willows, Chapel Lane, West Bergholt, Colchester, Essex CO6 3EF, England (home).

GRANT, John (see Barnett, Paul Le Page)

GRANT, Linda, MA; British novelist; b. 15 Feb. 1951, Liverpool, England. *Education:* Univ. of York, MacMaster Univ., Hamilton, Ont. and Simon Fraser Univ., Vancouver, Canada. *Publications:* fiction: The Cast Iron Shore (David Higham First Novel Award) 1996, When I Lived in Modern Times (Orange Prize for Fiction 2000) 2000, Still Here 2002, Suppose a City 2005, The Clothes on Their Backs 2008, We Had It So Good 2011; non-fiction: Sexing the Millennium: A Political History of the Sexual Revolution 1993, Remind Me Who I Am Again (MIND/Allen Lane Book of the Year, Age Concern Book of the Year) 1998, The People on the Street: A Writer's View of Israel 2006, The Thoughtful Dresser 2009; contrib. of essays in collections. *Honours:* Lettre Ulysses Prize for Literary Reportage. *Literary Agent:* c/o AP Watt Ltd, 20 John Street, London, WC1N 2DR, England. *Telephone:* (20) 7405-6774. *Fax:* (20) 7831-2154. *E-mail:* apw@apwatt.co.uk. *Website:* www.apwatt.co.uk. *Address:* c/o Virago Press, Little, Brown Book Group, 100 Victoria Embankment, London, EC4Y 0DY, England. *Telephone:* (20) 7911-8000. *Fax:* (20) 7911-8100. *E-mail:* virago.press@littlebrown.co.uk. *Website:* www.virago.co.uk; www.lindagrant.co.uk.

GRANT, Nicholas (see Nicole, Christopher Robin)

GRANT, Roderick; British author; b. 16 Jan. 1941, Forres, Morayshire, Scotland. *Publications:* Adventure in My Veins 1968, Seek Out the Guilty 1969, Where No Angels Dwell 1969, Gorbals Doctor 1970, The Dark Horizon (with Alexander Highlands) 1971, The Lone Voyage of Betty Mouat 1973, The Stalking of Adrian Lawford 1974, The Clutch of Caution 1975, The 51st Highland Division at War 1976, Strathalder: A Highland Estate 1978, A Savage Freedom 1978, The Great Canal 1978, A Private Vendetta 1978, But Not in Anger: The RAF in the Transport Role (with Christopher Cole) 1979, Clap Hands for the Singing Molecatcher: Scenes from a Scottish Childhood 1989, On the Rim of Time 2000, Wild Bird in My Open Hand 2001.

GRASS, Günter Wilhelm; German writer, poet and artist; b. 16 Oct. 1927, Danzig (now Gdańsk, Poland); m. 1st Anna Schwarz 1954 (divorced 1978); three s. one d.; m. 2nd Ute Grunert 1979. *Education:* Conradinum, Danzig, Kunstakademie, Düsseldorf, Hochschule für Bildende Künste, Berlin. *Career:* served in Luftwaffe 1944–45; adviser to Städtischen Bühnen Frankfurt am Main 1967–70; mem. Akad. der Künste, Berlin (pres. 1983–86), American Acad. of Arts and Sciences; mem. Social Democratic Party (resgnd Dec. 1992). *Plays:* Beritten, hin und zurück 1954, Hochwasser 1954, Die bösen Köche 1957, Noch Zehn Minuten bis Buffalo 1957, Onkel, Onkel 1958, Zweiunddreissig Zähne 1959, Die Plebejer proben den Aufstand 1965, Davor 1968, Die Vogelscheuchen (ballet) 1970. *Publications:* Die Vorzüge der Windhühner (poems, prose and drawings) 1955, Die Blechtrommel (novel, trans. as The Tin Drum) (Award for Best Foreign Novel, France 1962) 1959, Gleisdreieck (poems and drawings) 1960, Katz und Maus (novella, trans. as Cat and Mouse) 1961, Hundejahre (novel, trans. as Dog Years) 1963, Ausgefragt (poems and drawings) 1967, Über das Selbstverständliche 1968, Örtlich betäubt (novel) 1969, Aus dem Tagebuch einer Schnecke 1972, Dokumente zur politischen Wirkung 1972, Mariazuehren (poems and drawings) 1973, Die Bürger und seine Stimme 1974, Der Butt (novel, trans. as The Flounder) 1976, Denkzettel 1978, Das Treffen in Telgte (novel, trans. as The Meeting in Telgte) 1979, Kopfgeburten oder Die Deutschen sterben aus (novel, trans. as Headbirths, or the Germans are Dying Out) 1980, Aufsätze zur Literatur 1980, Zeichnen und Schreiben Band I 1982, Widerstand lernen-Politische Gegenreden 1980–83 1984 Band II 1984, On Writing and Politics 1967–83 1985, Die Rättin (novel) 1986, Züngezeigen 1987, Werkansgabe (10 vols) 1987, Die Gedichte 1955–1986 1988, Deutscher Lastenausgleich: Wider das dumpfe Einheitsgebot 1990, Two States—One Nation? 1990, Vier Jahrzehnte: Ein Werkstattbericht (drawings and notes) 1991, Unkenrufe (novel, trans. as The Call of the Toad) 1992, Rede vom Verlust: Über den Niedergang der politischen Kultur im geiinten Deutschland 1992, Der Ruf der Kröte (novel) 1992, Studienausgabe (12 vols) 1994, Ein weites Feld (trans. as Too Far Afield) 1995, Fundsachen für Nichtleser (poems) 1997, Auf ein anderes Blatt 1999, Vom Abenteuer der Aufklärung (jtly) 1999, Mein Jahrhundert (trans. as My Century) 1999, Nie wieder schweigen 2000, Fünf Jahrzehnte 2001, Im Krebsgang (novel, trans. as Crabwalk) 2002, Telling Tales (contrib. to charity anthology) 2004, Letzte Tänze (watercolours and drawings) 2003, Beim Häuten der Zwiebel (trans as Peeling the Onion, autobiog.) 2006, Dummer August (poems) 2007, Die Box (trans. as The Box: Tales from the Darkroom) 2008. *Honours:* Dr hc (Kenyon Coll.) 1965, (Harvard) 1976; Lyric Prize, Süddeutscher Rundfunk 1955, Group 47 Prize 1959, Literary Prize, Asscn of German Critics 1960, Georg-Büchner Prize 1965, Theodor-Heuss Prize 1969, Int. Feltrinelli Prize 1982, Karel Čapek Prize 1994, Sonning Arts Prize (Denmark) 1996, Thomas Mann Prize 1996, Hermann Kestan Medal 1995, Nobel Prize for Literature 1999, Premio Príncipe de Asturias 1999. *Address:* Glockengiesserstrasse 21, 23552 Lübeck, Germany.

GRAU, Shirley Ann, BA; American writer; b. 8 July 1929, New Orleans; d. of Adolph Eugene and Katherine Grau; m. James Feibleman 1955; two s. two d. *Education:* Tulane Univ. *Career:* Teacher of Creative Writing, Univ. of New Orleans 1966–67; Bd mem. St Martin's Episcopal School, New Orleans; mem. Authors Guild, Authors League of America. *Publications:* The Black Prince

1955, The Hard Blue Sky 1958, The House on Coliseum Street 1961, The Keepers of the House (Pulitzer Prize 1965) 1964, The Condor Passes 1971, The Wind Shifting West 1973, Evidence of Love 1977, Nine Women 1985, Roadwalkers 1994, The Condor Passes 2000; contribs to New Yorker, Saturday Evening Post. *Honours:* Dr hc (Rider Coll.), (Spring Hill Coll.); Louisiana Writer Award 2004. *Address:* 174 Sullivan Street, New York, NY, 10012, USA. *E-mail:* s.grau@worldnet.att.net.

GRAVER, Elizabeth, BA, MFA; American writer and academic; *Professor of English and Creative Writing, Boston College;* b. 2 July 1964, Los Angeles, Calif.; d. of Lawrence and Suzanne Graver; m. James Pingeor; two d. *Education:* Wesleyan Univ., Washington Univ. *Career:* Visiting Prof. of English and Creative Writing, Boston Coll. 1993–95, Asst Prof. of Creative Writing and English 1995–99, Assoc. Prof. 1999–2005, Full Prof. 2005–. *Publications:* Have You Seen Me? (story collection) 1991; novels: Unravelling 1997, The Honey Thief 1999, Awake 2004; contribs to Best American Short Stories, Story, Southern Review, Antaeus, Southwest Review, O. Henry Prize Stories, Ploughshares, Best American Essays, Pushcart Prize Anthology, Seneca Review, Boston Globe, other journals and anthologies. *Honours:* Fulbright Fellowship, Guggenheim Fellowship, Drue Heinz Literature Prize, Nat. Endowment for the Arts Fellowship, Best American Short Stories 1991 and 2001, Prize Stories, The O. Henry Awards 1994, 1996, 2001, Blue Mountain Center Residency 1995, 2007, 2008, MacDowell Fellow 1997, 2009, Best American Esssays 1998, Cohen Prize for the Short Story 2001, Pushcart Prize 2001. *Literary Agent:* c/o Richard Parks, The Richard Parks Agency, Box 693, Salem, NY 12865, USA. *Telephone:* (518) 853-9466. *E-mail:* rp@richardparksagency.com. *Website:* www.richardparksagency.com. *Address:* Carney Hall, English Department, Boston College, Chestnut Hill, MA 02167, USA (office). *Telephone:* (617) 552-4154 (office). *E-mail:* graver@bc.edu (office). *Website:* elizabethgraver.com.

GRAVES, Keller (see Rogers, Evelyn)

GRAVES, Richard Perceval, MA; British author; b. 21 Dec. 1945, Brighton, Sussex; two s. one d. *Education:* St John's Coll., Oxford. *Career:* Arnold Lodge School 1968; Harrow School 1969; Holme Grange School 1969–71; Ellesmere College 1971–73; mem. Housman Soc., Powys Soc. (Chair. 2001–05), Soc. of Authors. *Publications:* Lawrence of Arabia and His World 1976, A. E. Housman: The Scholar-Poet 1979, The Brothers Powys 1983, Robert Graves: The Assault Heroic 1986, Robert Graves: The Years with Laura Riding 1990, Richard Hughes 1994, Robert Graves and The White Goddess 1995, Changing Perceptions: The Poets of the Great War 2005. *Honours:* Hawthornden Fellowship 1999. *Literary Agent:* c/o The Sayle Literary Agency, 86 King's Parade, Cambridge, CB2 1SJ, England. *Address:* 7 Lilymead Avenue, Bristol, BS4 2BY, England (home). *Telephone:* (117) 972-4835 (home). *E-mail:* author@richardgraves.org (home). *Website:* www.richardgraves.org.

GRAVES, Roy Neil, (Giles Jimston, Margaret Medford), MA; American academic, poet and writer; *Professor of English, University of Tennessee at Martin;* b. 2 Feb. 1939, Medina, Tenn.; s. of Roy N. Graves Sr and Georgia Mae Reed Graves; m. Sue Lain Hunt 1965 (divorced 1982); one s. two d. *Education:* Princeton Univ., Duke Univ., Univ. of Mississippi. *Career:* Asst Prof. of English, Lynchburg Branch, Univ. of Virginia 1965–67; Asst Prof. 1967–68, Assoc. Prof. of English 1968–69, Central Virginia Community Coll., Lynchburg; Asst Prof., Univ. of Tennessee at Martin 1969–77, Assoc. Prof. 1977–82, Prof. of English 1982–. *Publications:* River Region Monographs: Reports on People and Popular Culture (ed.) 1975, Medina and Other Poems 1976, Hugh John Massey of the Royal Hall: The Lost Master Poet of Fourteenth-Century England and the Lost Runes 1977, Out of Tennessee: Poems, with an Introduction 1977, The Runic Beowulf and Other Lost Anglo-Saxon Poems, Reconstructed and Annotated 1979, Shakespeare's Lost Sonnets: The 154 Runic Poems Reconstructed and Introduced 1979, Somewhere on the Interstate (poems) 1987, Shakespeare's Sonnets Upside Down 1995, Always at Home Here: Poems and Insights from Six Tennessee Poets (ed by Ernest Lee) 1997, web publ. of Shakespeare's Lost Sonnets 2003; contribs to reference works and scholarly journals including Phylon, Spenser Studies, Upstart Crow and The Explicator; poems in anthologies and periodicals. *Honours:* Nat. Endowment for the Humanities Grant 1975, Cunningham Teacher/Scholar Award, Univ. of Tennessee at Martin 1997, First Place, Southern Poets over 50 Competition, Kennesaw State Univ. 2002. *Address:* Department of English, University of Tennessee at Martin, Martin, TN 38238, USA (office). *Telephone:* (731) 881-7301 (office). *Fax:* (731) 881-7276 (office). *E-mail:* ngraves@utm.edu (office). *Website:* www.utm.edu/staff/ngraves (office); www.utm.edu/staff/ngraves/shakespeare (office).

GRAY, Alasdair James; British writer and painter; b. 28 Dec. 1934, Glasgow; s. of Alexander Gray and Amy Fleming; m. 1st Inge Sørensen (divorced); one s.; m. 2nd Morag McAlpine 1991. *Education:* Glasgow School of Art. *Career:* art teacher, Glasgow and Lanarkshire 1958–62; scene painter, Pavilion and Citizens' theatres 1962–63; freelance writer and painter 1963–76; artist recorder, People's Palace Local History Museum, Glasgow 1976–77; Writer-in-Residence, Glasgow Univ. 1977–79; freelance writer and painter 1979–2001; Prof. of Creative Writing, Univ. of Glasgow 2001–2003; painter of mural decorations in Oran Mor Leisure Centre, Glasgow, 2003–; works in collections of People's Palace Local History Museum, Glasgow, Collin's Gallery, Strathclyde Univ., Hunterian Museum, Univ. of Glasgow; mural paintings in Palace Rigg Nature Reserve Exhibition Centre, New Cumbernauld, Abbot's House Local History Museum, Dunfermline, The Ubiquitous Chip Restaurant, Glasgow, Riverside Restaurant, Kirkfieldbank; mem. Soc. of Authors, Scottish Artists Union. *Exhibitions include:* Retrospective, Collins Gallery Glasgow 1974; Retrospective, Glasgow, Edinburgh and Aberdeen Art Galleries 1987–88. *Radio plays include:* Quiet People 1968, The Trial of Thomas Muir 1970, Dialogue 1971, Homeward Bound 1973, The Loss of the Golden Silence 1973, McGrothy and Ludmilla 1993, Working Legs 1998. *Television plays include:* The Fall of Kelvin Walker 1967, The Man Who Knew about Electricity 1973, The Story of a Recluse 1987. *Works include:* has designed and illustrated several books including Shoestring Gourmet 1986, Songs of Scotland 1997. *Publications include:* The Comedy of the White Dog (short story) 1979, Lanark: A Life in Four Books (novel) 1981, Unlikely Stories Mostly 1982, Janine (novel) 1984, The Fall of Kelvin Walker (novel) 1985, Lean Tales (co-writer) 1985, Five Scottish Artists (catalogue) 1986, Saltire Self-Portrait 4 (autobiographical sketch) 1988, Old Negatives (four verse sequences) 1989, Something Leather (novel) 1990, McGrotty and Ludmilla (novel) 1990, Poor Things (novel) 1992, Why Scots Should Rule Scotland (polemic) 1992, Ten Tales Tall and True (Short Stories) 1993, A History Maker (novel) 1994, Mavis Belfrage (novel) 1996, Working Legs (play) 1997, The Book of Prefaces 2000, Sixteen Occasional Poems 2000, A Study in Classic Scottish Writing 2001, The Ends of Our Tethers: 13 Sorry Stories 2003, How We Should Rule Ourselves (polemic, with Adam Tomkins) 2005, Old Men in Love 2007, A Gray Playbook (plays), Collected Verses 2010, A Life in Pictures (auto-biog.) 2010. *Honours:* Saltire Soc. Award 1981, Times Literary Supplement Award 1983, Whitbread and Guardian Awards 1992. *Literary Agent:* c/o Zoe Waldie, 20 Powis Mews, London, W11 1JN, England. *Address:* 2 Marchmont Terrace, Glasgow, G12 9LT, Scotland. *Telephone:* (141) 339-0093. *Website:* www.alasdairgray.co.uk.

GRAY, Angela (see Daniels, Dorothy)

GRAY, Caroline (see Nicole, Christopher Robin)

GRAY, Douglas, MA, FBA; British/New Zealand academic; *Professor Emeritus, Lady Margaret Hall, University of Oxford;* b. 17 Feb. 1930, Melbourne, Australia; s. of Emmerson Gray and Daisy Gray; m. Judith Claire Campbell 1959; one s. *Education:* Wellington Coll. NZ, Victoria Univ. of Wellington, Merton Coll., Oxford. *Career:* Asst Lecturer, Victoria Univ. of Wellington 1952–54, Lecturer in English, Pembroke and Lincoln Colls, Univ. of Oxford 1956–61, Fellow in English, Pembroke Coll. 1961–80, J. R. R. Tolkien Prof. of English Literature and Language and Fellow, Lady Margaret Hall, Oxford 1980–97, Prof. Emer. 1997–, Hon. Fellow, Lady Margaret Hall 1997–. *Publications:* Themes and Images in the Medieval English Lyric 1972, A Selection of Religious Lyrics 1974, Robert Henryson 1979, Oxford Book of Late Medieval Verse and Prose (ed.) 1985, J. A. W. Bennett, Middle English Literature (ed.) 1986, From Anglo-Saxon to Early Middle English (jt ed.) 1994, Selected Poems of Robert Henryson and William Dunbar (ed.) 1998, Oxford Companion to Chaucer (ed.) 2003, Later Medieval English Literature 2008, From the Norman Conquest to the Black Death 2011. *Honours:* Hon. LittD (Victoria Univ. of Wellington) 1995. *Address:* 31 Nethercote Road, Tackley, Oxford, OX5 3AW, England (home). *Telephone:* (1869) 331319 (home).

GRAY, Francine du Plessix, BA; American author; b. 25 Sept. 1930, Warsaw, Poland; d. of Bertrant du Plessix and Tatiana Yakovleva du Plessix; m. Cleve Gray 1957; two s. *Education:* Bryn Mawr Coll., Black Mountain Coll., Barnard Coll. *Career:* reporter, United Press International, New York City, 1952–54; Asst Ed., Realites Magazine, Paris, 1954–55; Book Ed., Art in America, New York City, 1962–64; Visiting Prof., CUNY 1975, Yale Univ. 1981, Columbia Univ. 1983, Princeton Univ., Brown Univ., Vassar Coll.; Ferris Prof., Princeton Univ. 1986; Annenberg Fellow, Brown Univ. 1997; Gladys Krieble Delmas Chair, Vassar Coll. 2001; mem. American Acad. of Arts and Letters, American Acad. of Arts and Sciences. *Publications:* Divine Disobedience: Profiles in Catholic Radicalism 1970, Hawaii: The Sugar-Coated Fortress 1972, Lovers and Tyrants 1976, World Without End 1981, October Blood 1985, Adam and Eve and the City 1987, Soviet Women: Walking the Tightrope 1991, Rage and Fire: A Life of Louise Colet 1994, At Home with the Marquis de Sade: A Life 1998, Simone Weil 2001, Them: A Memoir of Parents 2005, Madame de Staël: The First Modern Woman 2009. *Honours:* Officier, Ordre des Arts et des Lettres; Putnam Creative Writing Award, Barnard Coll. 1952, Nat. Book Critics' Circle Award 2006. *Literary Agent:* Janklow-Nesbitt Literary Agency, 445 Park Avenue, New York, 10022, USA. *Telephone:* (212) 355-1724. *Address:* c/o The Penguin Press, 375 Hudson Street, New York, NY 10024, USA.

GRAY, John; British philosopher, academic and writer. *Career:* staff, Inst. of Economic Affairs, London, Cato Inst., USA, Inst. for Humane Studies, USA, The Liberty Fund, USA, Social Philosophy and Policy Center, USA; Prof. of Politics, Univ. of Oxford; fmr Prof. of European Thought, LSE. *Publications include:* non-fiction: Hayek on LIberty 1984, Liberalism 1986, Voltaire 1998, False Dawn: The Delusions of Global Capitalism 1998, Two Faces of Liberalism 2000, Straw Dogs: Thoughts on Humans and Other Animals 2003, Al Qaeda and What it Means to be Modern 2003, Heresies: Against Progress and Other Illusions 2004, Black Mass: Apocalyptic Religion and the Death of Utopia 2007, Gray's Anatomy: Selected Writings 2009, The Immortalization Commission: Science and the Strange Quest to Cheat Death 2011; Ed.: On Liberty and other essays by John Stuart Mill 1998; contribs to The Guardian, TLS, Granta (Granta 77: What We Think of America), Journal of Ethics, Demos. *Honours:* Fellow, Jesus Coll., Oxford. *Address:* c/o London

School of Economics and Political Science, Houghton Street, London, WC2A 2AE, England.

GRAY, Stephen; South African novelist, poet and editor; *Professor Emeritus of English, University of Johannesburg*; b. 1941, Cape Town. *Education:* Univ. of Cape Town, Univ. of Cambridge, UK and Univ. of Iowa, USA. *Career:* Prof. of English, Rand Afrikaans Univ., Johannesburg –1992; Prof. Emer. of English, Univ. of Johannesburg 1993–. *Play:* Schreiner: A One-Woman Play 1983. *Publications:* fiction: Visible People 1977, Caltrop's Desire 1980, John Ross: The True Story 1987, Time of Our Darkness 1988, Born of Man 1989, War Child 1994, My Serial Killer and Other Stories 2005; poetry: It's About Time 1974, Hottentot Venus and Other Poems 1979, Love Poems: Hate Poems 1982, Apollo Café and Other Poems 1982–89 1989, Season of Violence 1992, Selected Poems 1960–92 1994, Gabriel's Exhibition 1998, Shelley Cinema and Other Poems 2006; non-fiction: Southern African Literature: An Introduction 1979, Human Interest and Other Pieces 1993, Accident of Birth: An Autobiography 1993, Freelancers and Literary Biography in South Africa 1999, Life Sentence: A Biography of Herman Charles Bosman 2005, Indaba: Interviews with African Writers 2005; editor: C. Louis Leipoldt's Stormwrack 1980, Modern South African Stories 1981, Modern South African Poetry 1984, The Penguin Book of Southern African Stories 1985, The Penguin Book of Southern African Verse 1988, South Africa Plays: New South African Drama 1994, The Natal Papers of 'John Ross' 1996, The Picador Book of African Stories 2000. *Honours:* Lifetime Achievement Award, S African Dept of Arts and Culture 2007. *Address:* PO Box 2633, Houghton 2041, South Africa (home). *Telephone:* (11) 6464917 (home). *E-mail:* humanhk@humanrousseau .com (office).

GRAYLING, (Anthony Clifford), BA, MA, DPhil, FRSL, FRSA; British philosopher, author and academic; *Founder and Master, New College of the Humanities*; b. 3 April 1949, s. of Henry Clifford Grayling and Ursula Adelaide Burns; m. Gabrielle Yvonne Smyth 1970 (divorced 1979); one s., one d.; pnr Katie Hickman; one d. *Education:* Univ. of Sussex, Univ. of London, Magdalen Coll. Univ. of Oxford. *Career:* Lecturer in Philosophy, St Anne's Coll., Univ. of Oxford 1983–91, Supernumerary Fellow 1991–; Lecturer, Inst. of Philosophy, Chinese Acad. of Social Sciences 1984; Lecturer in Philosophy, Birkbeck Coll., Univ. of London 1991–99, Reader, Professor of Philosophy 2005–11; Dir, Sino-British Summer School in Philosophy, Beijing 1988, 1993; Contributing Ed., Philosophical Annual of Chinese Acad. of Social Sciences; Visiting Prof., Univ. of Tokyo 1998; Lecturer, Univs of Chiba, Nagoya and Hokkaido, Japan and Lublin Univ., Poland 1993; Founder and First Master, New Coll. of the Humanities 2011–; Jan Hus Visiting Fellow, Inst. of Philosophy, Czech Acad. of Sciences 1994, 1996; mem. Aristotelian Soc. (Hon. Sec. 1993–2001), Fellow, World Econ. Forum 2001–04. *Play:* Grace/On Religion (with Mick Gordon), London 2006–07. *Radio:* current affairs and arts broadcasting. *Publications include:* An Introduction to Philosophical Logic 1982, The Refutation of Scepticism 1985, Berkeley: The Central Arguments 1986, Wittgenstein 1988, William Hazlitt 1989, The Long March to the Fourth of June 1990, China: A Literary Companion (with Susan Whitfield) 1994, Philosophy: A Guide Through the Subject (ed.) 1995, Russell 1996, Philosophy: Further Through the Subject 1998, Moral Values 1997, The Quarrel of the Age: The Life and Times of William Hazlitt 2000, Wittgenstein: A Very Short Introduction 2001, The Meaning of Things 2001, Russell: A Very Short Introduction 2002, The Reason of Things: Applying Philosophy to Life 2002, Meditations for the Humanist: Ethics for a Secular Age 2002, Life, Sex and Ideas: The Good Life Without God 2003, What is Good?: The Search for the Best Way to Live 2003, The Mystery of Things 2004, The Heart of Things: Applying Philosophy to the 21st Century 2005, Descartes 2005, Among the Dead Cities: Was the Allied Bombing of Civilians in WWII a Necessity or a Crime? 2006, The Form of Things 2006, On Religion/Grace 2007, Against All Gods 2007, The Choice of Hercules 2007, Towards the Light 2007, Ideas that Matter 2009, Liberty in the Age of Terror 2009, To Set Prometheus Free 2009, Thinking of Answers 2009, The Good Book: a Secular Bible 2011. *Literary Agent:* c/o Felicity Bryan, 2 North Parade, Banbury Road, Oxford, OX2 6LX, England. *Telephone:* (1865) 513816. *E-mail:* cc@felicitybryan.com. *Website:* www.felicitybryan.com. *Address:* New College of the Humanities, 27 Old Gloucester Street, London, WC1N 3AX, England (office). *Telephone:* (20) 7637-4550 (office). *E-mail:* info@nchum.org (office). *Website:* www.nchum.org (office); www.acgrayling.com.

GREAVES, Richard Lee, BA, MA, PhD, FRHistS; American academic and writer; b. 11 Sept. 1938, Glendale, CA; m. Judith Rae Dieker 1959; two d. *Education:* Bethel Coll., Berkeley Baptist Divinity School, Univ. of London, Univ. of Missouri. *Career:* Assoc. Prof. of History, Florida Memorial Coll. 1964–65; Asst Prof. of History, William Woods Coll. 1965–66, Eastern Washington State Coll. 1966–69; Assoc. Prof. of Humanities, Michigan State Univ. 1969–72; Prof. of History 1972–89, Robert O. Lawton Distinguished Prof. of History 1989–, Florida State Univ.; mem. American Historical Assen, American Philosophical Soc., American Soc. of Church History (pres. 1991), Baptist Historical Soc., Historians of Early Modern Europe, Int. John Bunyan Soc. (pres. 1992–95). *Publications:* The Puritan Revolution and Educational Thought: Background for Reform 1969, John Bunyan 1969, An Annotated Bibliography of John Bunyan Studies 1972, Elizabeth I: Queen of England (ed.) 1974, The Miscellaneous Works of John Bunyan (ed.), Vol. 2 1976, Vol. 8 1979, Vol. 9 1981, Vol. 11 1985, Theology and Revolution in the Scottish Reformation: Studies in the Thought of John Knox 1980, Society and Religion in Elizabethan England 1981, John Bunyan: A Reference Guide (ed. with James Forrest) 1982, Biographical Dictionary of British Radicals in the Seventeenth Century (ed. with Robert Zaller, three vols) 1982, 1983, 1984, Saints and Rebels: Seven Nonconformists in Stuart England 1985, Triumph Over Silence: Women in Protestant History (ed.) 1985, Deliver Us From Evil: The Radical Underground in Britain, 1660–1663 1986, Civilizations of the World: The Human Adventure (with Robert Zaller, Philip Cannistrano and Rhoads Murphey) 1990, Enemies Under His Feet: Radicals and Nonconformists in Britain, 1664–1677 1990, Civilization in the West (with Robert Zaller and Jennifer Roberts) 1992, Secrets of the Kingdom: British Radicals from the Popish Plot to the Revolution of 1688–89 1992, John Bunyan and English Nonconformity 1992, God's Other Children: Protestant Nonconformists and the Emergence of Denominational Churches in Ireland, 1660–1700 1997, Dublin's Merchant-Quaker: Anthony Sharp and the Community of Friends, 1643–1707 1998, Glimpses of Glory: John Bunyan and English Dissent 2002; contrib. to scholarly books and journals. *Honours:* Nat. Endowment for the Humanities grants 1967, 1980, Walter D. Love Memorial Prize, Conference on British Studies 1970, Andrew W. Mellon Fellow 1977, ACLS Fellow 1977, 1983, 1987, American Philosophical Soc. Fellow 1993, Albert C. Outler Prize, American Soc. of Church History 1996, Rockefeller Foundation Fellow, Bellagio Center, Italy 1998, Guggenheim Fellowship 2000. *Address:* Department of History, Florida State University, Tallahassee, FL 32306-2200, USA. *Website:* mailer.fsu.edu/~rgreaves.

GREELEY, Andrew Moran, AB, STB, STL, MA, PhD; American academic and writer; b. 5 Feb. 1928, Oak Park, IL. *Education:* St Mary of the Lake Seminary, Univ. of Chicago. *Career:* Ordained, Roman Catholic Priest 1954; Asst Pastor, Church of Christ the King, Chicago 1954–64; Sr Study Dir, Univ. of Chicago 1961–68, Program Dir for Higher Education 1968–70, Dir of Center for the Study of American Pluralism 1971–85, Research Assoc. 1985–, Prof. of Social Science 1991–; Prof. of Sociology, Univ. of Arizona at Tucson 1978–; mem. American Catholic Sociological Soc., American Sociological Assen, Religious Research Assen, Soc. for the Scientific Study of Religion. *Publications include:* non-fiction: The Catholic Experience: An Interpretation of the History of American Catholicism 1967, Uncertain Trumpet: The Priest in Modern America 1968, What Do We Believe?: The Stance of Religion in America (with Martin E. Marty and Stuart E. Rosenberg) 1968, Life for a Wanderer: A New Look at Christian Spirituality 1969, Come Blow Your Mind with Me (essays) 1971, The Jesus Myth 1971, What a Modern Catholic Believes about God 1971, The Denominational Society: A Sociological Approach to Religion in America ,1972, The Sinai Myth 1972, The Devil, You Say! Man and His Personal Devils and Angels 1974, The Sociology of the Paranormal: A Reconnaissance 1975, Death and Beyond 1976, The Great Mysteries: An Essential Catechism 1976, The Mary Myth: On the Femininity of God 1977, The Best of Times, The Worst of Times (with J. N. Kotre) 1978, Religion: A Secular Theory 1982, Confessions of a Parish Priest: An Autobiography 1986, God in Popular Culture 1989, Myths of Religion 1989, Complaints Against God 1989, Andrew Greeley (autobiog.) 1990, The Bible and Us: A Priest and a Rabbi Read Scripture Together (with Jacob Neusner) 1990, Faithful Attraction: Discovering Intimacy, Love and Fidelity in American Marriage 1991, Love Affair: A Prayer Journal 1992, The Sense of Love 1992, I Hope You're Listening God 1997, Furthermore (autobiog.) 1999, The Catholic Revolution 2004, Priests: A Calling in Crisis 2004, The Making of the Pope 2005, A Stupid, Unjust and Criminal War: Iraq 2001–2007 2008; fiction: Nora Maeve and Sebi 1976, The Magic Cup: An Irish Legend 1979, The Cardinal Sins 1981, Ascent into Hell 1984, God Game 1986, All About Women 1989, Fall from Grace 1993, Star Bright: A Christmas Story 1997, The Bishop at Sea 1997, A Midwinter's Tale 1998, The Bishop and the Three Kings 1998, Irish Mist 1999, Younger Than Springtime 1999, The Bishop and the Missing L Train 2000, A Christmas Wedding 2000, Irish Love 2001, The Bishop and the Beggar Girl of St Germain 2001, September Song 2001, Irish Stew 2002, The Bishop in the West Wing 2002, Second Spring 2003, The Bishop Goes to University 2003, Emerald Magic 2004, Priestly Sins 2004, The Golden Years 2004, Irish Cream 2005, Irish Crystal 2006, The Bishop in the Old Neighbourhood 2006, The Bishop at the Lake 2007, The Bishop in Andalusia 2008, Irish Tiger 2008, Irish Linen 2008, Irish Tweed 2009, Home for Christmas 2009. *Honours:* C. Albert Kobb Award, National Catholic Education Assen 1977, Mark Twain Award, Society for the Study of Midwestern Literature 1987; several hon. doctorates. *Address:* 1155 E 60th Street, Chicago, IL 60637, USA (office). *Telephone:* (773) 256-6281 (office). *Fax:* (773) 753-7866 (office). *E-mail:* agreel@aol.com (office). *Website:* www.agreeley .com.

GREEN, Brian (see Card, Orson Scott)

GREEN, Dan, BA; American book publishing executive; *Literary agent, Pom Inc.*; b. 28 Sept. 1935, Passaic, NJ; s. of Harold Green and Bessie Roslow; m. Jane Oliphant 1959; two s. *Education:* Syracuse Univ., NY. *Career:* Publicity Dir Dover Press 1957–58; Station WNAC-TV 1958–59; Bobbs-Merrill Co. 1959–62; Simon & Schuster Inc. 1962–85, Assoc. Publr 1976–80, Vice-Pres., Publr 1980–84; Pres. Trade Publishing Group 1984–85; Founder, Publr, Kenan Press 1979–80; CEO Grove Press and Weidenfeld & Nicolson, New York 1985–89; Pres. Kenan Books, New York 1989–, Pom Inc. (Literary Agency) 1989–. *Address:* Pom Inc., 21 Vista Drive, Great Neck, New York, NY 11021 (office); Kenan Books, 21 Vista Drive, Great Neck, New York, NY 11021, USA (home). *Telephone:* (516) 487-3441 (office). *E-mail:* dangreen@pomlit.com (office).

GREEN, Debbie Tucker; British playwright. *Career:* fmr stage man. *Plays:* Born Bad 2003, Dirty Butterfly 2003, Trade 2004, Generations 2005, Stoning Mary 2005, Generations 2007, random 2008. *Literary Agent:* c/o Leah Schmidt, The Agency, 24 Pottery Lane, London, W11 4LZ, England. *Telephone:* (20) 7727-1346. *Fax:* (20) 7727-9037. *E-mail:* info@theagency.co.uk. *Website:* www.theagency.com.

GREEN, Hannah (see Greenberg, Joanne)

GREEN, Jonathon, BA; British writer and broadcaster; b. 20 April 1948, Kidderminster, Worcs., England; two s. *Education:* Brasenose Coll., Oxford. *Publications:* Book of Rock Quotes I 1977, Famous Last Words 1979, The Book of Sports Quotes (with D. Atyeo) 1979, Directory of Infamy 1980, Don't Quote Me: The Other Famous Last Words (with D. Atyeo) 1981, The Book of Royal Quotes (with D. Atyeo) 1981, Book of Political Quotes 1982, Book of Rock Quotes II 1982, Contemporary Dictionary of Quotations 1982, What a Way to Go 1983, Newspeak: A Dictionary of Jargon 1983, revised edn as The Dictionary of Jargon 1987, The Dictionary of Contemporary Slang 1984, The Cynics' Lexicon 1984, Sweet Nothings: A Book of Love Quotes 1985, Consuming Passions: A Book of Food Quotes 1985, It Takes All Sports: Sporting Anecdotes (with D. Atyeo) 1986, The Slang Thesaurus 1986, The A to Z of Nuclear Jargon 1986, Says You: A Twentieth-Century Quotation Finder 1988, Day in the Life: Voices from the English Underground, 1961–71 1988, The Bloomsbury Good Word Guide 1988, The Encyclopedia of Censorship 1990, Them: Voices from the Immigrant Community in Contemporary Britain 1990, The Dictionary of Political Language 1991, Neologisms: A Dictionary of Contemporary Coinage 1991, It: The State of Sex Today 1992, All Dressed Up: The Sixties and the Counter-Culture 1998, Cassell Dictionary of Slang 1998, Big Book of Filth 1999, Big Book of Being Rude 2000, Cutting it Fine: Inside the Restaurant Business (with Andrew Parkinson) 2000, Big Book of Bodily Functions 2001, Cannabis: A History 2002, Talking Dirty: A Slang Phrasebook 2003, Getting Off at Gateshead: An A–Z of Filth 2008, Green's Dictionary of Slang (Dartmouth Medal 2012) 2010. *Literary Agent:* c/o Lucas Alexander Whitey, Elsinore House, 77 Fulham Palace Road, London, W6 8JA, England. *Address:* 117 Ashmore Road, London, W9 3DA, England (home).

GREEN, Martin Burgess, BA, DipEd, MA, PhD; British academic and writer; b. 21 Sept. 1927, London, England; m. Carol Elizabeth Hurd 1967; one s. two d. *Education:* St John's College, Cambridge, King's College, London, Sorbonne, Univ. of Paris, University of Michigan. *Career:* Instructor, Wellesley College, Massachussetts, USA 1957–61; Lecturer, Birmingham University 1965–68; Prof. of English, Tufts University, Medford, Massachusetts 1963-65, 1968–94. *Publications:* Mirror for Anglo-Saxons 1960, Reappraisals 1965, Science and the Shabby Curate of Poetry 1965, Yeats's Blessings on von Hugel 1968, Cities of Light and Sons of the Morning 1972, The von Richthofen Sisters 1974, Children of the Sun 1975, The Earth Again Redeemed (novel) 1976, Transatlantic Patterns 1977, The Challenge of the Mahatmas 1978, Dreams of Adventure, Deeds of Empire 1980, The Old English Elegies 1983, Tolstoy and Gandhi 1983, The Great American Adventure 1984, Mountains of Truth 1986, The Triumph of Pierrot (with J. Swan) 1986.

GREEN, Rose Basile, FRSA, MA, PhD; American poet and writer; b. 19 Dec. 1914, New Rochelle, NY; d. of Salvatore Basile and Caroline Basile; m. Raymond S. Green 1942; one s. one d. *Education:* Coll. of New Rochelle, Columbia Univ., New York, Univ. of Pennsylvania. *Career:* teacher, Torrington High School, Conn. 1936–42; writer, researcher, Cavalcade of America, NBC 1940–42; Assoc. Prof. of English and Registrar, Univ. of Tampa 1942–43; Special Lecturer in English, Temple Univ. 1953–57; Prof. of English, Cabrini Coll. 1957–70; Exec. Dir American Inst. of Italian Studies; Vice-Pres. and Dir Nat. Italian-American Foundation; Chair. Nat. Advisory Council for Ethnic Heritage Studies; mem. American Acad. of Political and Social Sciences, Acad. of American Poets, American Studies Asscn, Ethnic Studies Asscn, American Asscn of Univ. Women. *Publications include* Cabrinian Philosophy of Education 1967, Lauding the American Dream 1980, The Life of Mother Frances Xavier Cabrini 1984, The Pennsylvania People 1984, Challenger Countdown 1988, Five Hundred Years of America 1492–1992 1992, The Distaff Side: Great Women of American History 1995; poetry: To Reason Why 1972, Primo Vino 1974, 76 for Philadelphia 1975, Woman, The Second Coming 1977, Century Four 1981, Songs of Ourselves 1983; criticism: The Italian-American Novel: A Document of the Interaction of Two Cultures 1974. *Honours:* Cavalier of the Repub. of Italy; Hon. LHD (Gwynedd-Mercy Coll.) 1979, (Cabrini Coll.) 1982; Daughters of the American Revolution Nat. Bicentennial Award for Poetry 1976, Nat. Amita Award for Literature 1976. *Address:* 308 Manor Road, Lafayette Hill, PA 19444-1741, USA.

GREEN, Sharon, BA; American writer; b. 6 July 1942, New York; m. 1963 (divorced 1976); three s. *Education:* New York Univ. *Career:* started career as Shareowner Corresp. AT&T; then worked as Asst in construction co.; later sold bar steel for an import firm; full time writer 1984–; mem. SFWA. *Publications:* The Crystals of Mida 1982, The Warrior Within 1982, The Warrior Enchained 1983, An Oath to Mida 1983, Chosen of Mida 1984, The Warrior Rearmed 1984, Mind Guest 1984, Gateway to Xanadu 1985, The Will of the Gods 1985, To Battle the Gods 1986, The Warrior Challenged 1986, Rebel Prince 1986, The Far Side of Forever 1987, The Warrior Victorious 1987, Lady Blade, Lord Fighter 1987, Mists of the Ages 1988, Hellhound Magic 1989, Dawn Song 1990, Haunted House 1990, Silver Princess, Golden Knight 1993, The Hidden Realms 1993, Werewolfmoon 1993, Fantasy Man 1993, Flame of Fury 1993, Dark Mirror, Dark Dreams 1994, Silken Dreams 1994, Enchanting 1994, Wind Whispers, Shadow Shouts 1995, Game's End 1996, Convergence: Book One of The Blending 1996, Competitions: Book Two of The Blending 1997, Challenges: Book Three of The Blending 1998, Betrayals: Book Four of The Blending 1999, To Die For 2000, Haughty Spirit 2000, Intrigues: Book One of The Blending Enthroned 2000, Destiny: Book Three of The Blending Enthroned 2002; contribs to anthologies and magazines. *E-mail:* SharonGreen@integritytech.com. *Website:* www.integritytech.com/sharong.html.

GREEN, Simon Richard, BA, MA; British writer; b. 25 Aug. 1955, Bradford-on-Avon, Wiltshire. *Education:* Thames Polytechnic, Leicester Univ. *Publications:* Hawk and Fisher (aka No Haven for the Guilty) 1990, Winner Takes All (aka Devil Takes the Hindmost) 1991, The God Killer 1991, Blue Moon Rising 1991, Robin Hood: Prince of Thieves 1991, Guard Against Dishonour 1991, Wolf in the Fold (aka Vengeance from a Lonely Man) 1991, Mistworld 1992, Ghostworld 1993, Blood and Honour 1993, Down Among the Dead Men 1993, Shadows Fall 1994, Hellworld 1995, Deathstalker 1995, Deathstalker Rebellion 1996, Deathstalker War 1997, Deathstalker Honour 1998, Deathstalker Destiny 1999, Beyond the Blue Moon 2000, Drinking Midnight Wine 2001, Deathstalker Legacy 2003, Something from the Nightside 2003, Agents of Light and Darkness 2003, Deathstalker Return 2004, Nightingale's Lament 2004, Deathstalker Coda 2005, Hex and the City 2005, Paths not Taken 2005, Sharper than a Serpent's Tooth 2006, A Walk on the Nightside 2006, Hell to Pay 2006, The Man with The Golden Torc 2007, Daemons are Forever 2008, The Unnatural Inquirer 2008, The Dark Heart of the Nightside 2008, The Spy Who Haunted Me 2009, Just Another Judgement Day 2009, Ghost of a Chance 2010, The Good, the Bad and the Uncanny 2010, A Hard Day's Knight 2011. *Address:* 40 St Laurence Road, Bradford-on-Avon, Wiltshire BA15 1JQ, England (home). *E-mail:* info@simonrgreen.co.uk (office). *Website:* simonrgreen.co.uk.

GREEN, Terence Michael, BA, BEd, MA; Canadian writer and academic; *Lecturer in Creative Writing, University of Western Ontario;* b. 2 Feb. 1947, Toronto; m. 1st Penny Dakin 1968 (divorced 1990); two s.; m. 2nd Merle Casci 1994; one s. *Education:* Univ. of Toronto, Univ. Coll., Dublin. *Career:* fmr English teacher, East York Collegiate Inst., Toronto; juror for Philip K. Dick Award 1995; Writer-in-Residence, Mohawk Coll. 2003–04; Lecturer in Creative Writing, Univ. of Western Ontario 2005–; mem. SFWA, Writers' Union of Canada, Crime Writers of Canada. *Publications include:* The Woman Who is the Midnight Wind (short stories) 1987, Barking Dogs (novel) 1988, Children of the Rainbow (novel) 1992, Shadow of Ashland (novel) 1996, Blue Limbo (novel) 1997, A Witness to Life 1999, St. Patrick's Bed 2001, Sailing Time's Ocean 2006; contribs to anthologies including Northern Stars, Northern Frights, Ark of Ice, Dark Visions, Conversations with Robertson Davies, Tesseracts, The Writer's Voice 2, Aurora: The New Canadian Writing; contrib. of short stories, articles, interviews, reviews and poetry to periodicals including Globe and Mail, Books in Canada, Quarry, Magazine of Fantasy and Science Fiction, Isaac Asimov's SF Magazine, Twilight Zone, Unearth, Thrust, SF Review, SF Chronicle, Poetry Toronto, Leisure Ways. *Address:* Faculty of Arts and Humanities, University of Western Ontario, University College, Room 112, London, ON N6A 3K7, Canada (office). *Telephone:* (519) 850-2404 (office). *Fax:* (519) 661-3640 (office). *E-mail:* tmgreen@sympatico.ca. *Website:* www.uwo.ca/arts (office); www.tmgreen.com.

GREEN, Timothy Seton, BA; British writer; b. 29 May 1936, Beccles; m. Maureen Snowball 1959; one d. *Education:* Christ's Coll., Cambridge, Univ. of Western Ontario, Canada. *Career:* London Corresp., Horizon 1959–62, American Heritage 1959–62, Life, 1962–64; Ed. Illustrated London News 1964–66. *Publications:* The World of God 1968, The Smugglers 1969, Restless Spirit, UK edn as The Adventurers 1970, The Universal Eye 1972, World of Gold Today 1973, How to Buy Gold 1975, The Smuggling Business 1977, The World of Diamonds 1981, The New World of Gold 1982, The Prospect for Gold 1987, The World of Gold 1993, The Good Water Guide 1994, New Frontiers in Diamonds: The Mining Revolution 1996, The Gold Companion 1997, The Millennium in Gold 1999, The Millennium in Silver 1999, The Ages of Gold 2007. *Address:* 8 Ponsonby Place, London, SW1P 4PT, England (home).

GREENBERG, Alvin David, BA, MA, PhD; American academic, poet and writer; *Professor Emeritus of English, Macalester College;* b. 10 May 1932, Cincinnati, Ohio; m. 1st; two s. one d.; m. 2nd Janet Holmes 1993. *Education:* Univ. of Cincinnati, Univ. of Washington. *Career:* Faculty, Univ. of Kentucky 1963–65; Prof. of English, Macalester Coll. 1965–2002, Prof. Emer. 2002–, Chair, Dept of English 1988–93; Fulbright Lecturer, Univ. of Kerala, India 1966–67; Ed., Minnesota Review 1967–71. *Publications:* poetry: The Metaphysical Giraffe 1968, The House of the Would-Be Gardener 1972, Dark Lands 1973, Metaform 1975, In/Direction 1978, And Yet 1981, Heavy Wings 1988, Why We Live with Animals 1990, Hurry Back 2003; fiction: The Small Waves 1965, Going Nowhere 1971, The Invention of the West 1976, Time Lapse 2003; short stories: The Discovery of America and Other Tales of Terror 1980, Delta q 1982, The Man in the Cardboard Mask 1985, How the Dead Live 1998; plays: A Wall 1971, Opera Libretti: Horspfal 1969, The Jealous Cellist 1979, Apollonia's Circus 1994; memoir: The Dog Of Memory: A Family Album of Secrets and Silences 2002; contribs to many reviews, journals, and quarterlies. *Honours:* Associated Writing Programs Short Fiction Award 1982, Nimrod/Pablo Neruda Prize in Poetry 1988, Loft-McKnight Poetry Award 1991, Distinction in Poetry Award 1994, Chelsea Award for Poetry 1994. *Address:* c/o Department of English, Macalester College, 1600 Grand Avenue, St Paul, MN 55105-1899, USA.

GREENBERG, Joanne, (Hannah Green), BA; American writer and teacher; *Teacher of Cultural Anthropology and Fiction Writing, Colorado School of Mines*; b. 24 Sept. 1932, New York; m. Albert Greenberg 1955; two s. *Education:* Univ. of Colorado, Univ. of London, England. *Career:* currently Teacher of Cultural Anthropology and Fiction Writing, Colorado School of Mines; mem. Authors' Guild, PEN, Colorado Authors' League, Nat. Asscn of the Deaf. *Publications:* The King's Persons (Harry and Ethel Daroff Memorial Fiction Award, Jewish Book Council of America Award) 1963, I Never Promised You a Rose Garden 1964, The Monday Voices 1965, Summering: A Book of Short Stories 1966, In This Sign 1970, Rites of Passage 1972, Founder's Praise 1976, High Crimes and Misdemeanors 1979, A Season of Delight 1981, The Far Side of Victory 1983, Simple Gifts 1986, Age of Consent 1987, Of Such Small Differences 1988, With the Snow Queen (short stories) 1991, No Reck'ning Made 1993, Where the Road Goes 1998, Appearances 2006, Miri, Who Charms 2009; contribs to articles, reviews, short stories to numerous periodicals. *Honours:* William and Janice Epstein Fiction Award 1964, Marcus L. Kenner Award 1971, Christopher Book Award 1971, Freida Fromm Reichman Memorial Award 1971, Rocky Mountain Women's Inst. Award 1983, Denver Public Library Bookplate Award 1990, Hadassah's Women in the Arts Award 2008, Colorado School of Mines Medal. *Address:* Colorado School of Mines, 1500 Illinois Street, Golden, CO 80401, USA (office). *Telephone:* (303) 273-3000 (office). *Website:* www.mines.edu (office); www.mountaintopauthor.com.

GREENBERG, Martin, BA; American fmr academic, writer and translator; b. 3 Feb. 1918, Norfolk, Va; m. Paula Fox 1962; one s. *Education:* Univ. of Michigan. *Career:* Ed. Schocken Books 1946–49, Commentary magazine 1953–60; Lecturer, New School for Social Research, New York City 1961–67; Asst Prof. to Prof. of English, C. W. Post Coll. 1963–88; mem. Acad. of American Poets. *Publications:* The Terror of Art: Kafka and Modern Literature 1968, The Hamlet Vocation of Coleridge and Wordsworth 1986; translator: The Diaries of Franz Kafka 1914–23, The Marquise of O and Other Stories 1960, Five Plays 1988, Faust, Part One 1992, Faust, Part Two 1996, Four poems by Rainer Maria von Rilke 2001. *Honours:* Literature Award American Acad. and Inst. of Arts and Letters 1989, Harold Morton Landon Trans. Award 1989,. *Address:* 306 Clinton Street, New York, NY 11201, USA.

GREENBLATT, Stephen J., BA, PhD; American academic; *Cogan University Professor of the Humanities, Harvard University*; b. 7 Nov. 1943, Cambridge, Mass; s. of Harry Greenblatt and Mollie Brown; three s.; m. Ramie Targoff 1998. *Education:* Yale Univ., Pembroke Coll., Cambridge, UK. *Career:* Asst Prof. of English, Univ. of Calif., Berkeley 1969–74, Assoc. Prof. 1974–79, Prof. of English 1979–97; Prof. of English, Harvard Univ. 1997–, Cogan Univ. Prof. of the Humanities 2000–; numerous visiting professorships; Fellow, American Acad. of Arts and Sciences, American Acad. of Arts and Letters, American Philosophical Soc., Wissenschaftskolleg zu Berlin; mem. Int. Asscn of Univ. Profs of English, Modern Language Asscn, Renaissance Soc. of America. *Publications:* Three Modern Satirists: Waugh, Orwell and Huxley 1965, Sir Walter Raleigh: The Renaissance Man and his Roles 1970, Renaissance Self-Fashioning: From More to Shakespeare 1980, Allegory and Representation (ed.) 1981, Power of Forms 1982, Representing the English Renaissance 1988, Shakespearean Negotiations: The Circulation of Social Energy in Renaissance England 1988, Learning to Curse: Essays in Early Modern Culture 1990, Marvelous Possessions: The Wonder of the New World 1991, Redrawing the Boundaries of Literary Study in English 1992, New World Encounters 1992, The Norton Shakespeare (ed.) 1997, The Norton Anthology of English Literature (ed.) 2000, Practising New Historicism 2000, Hamlet in Purgatory 2001, Will in the World: How Shakespeare Became Shakespeare 2004, Cultural Mobility: A Manifesto 2009, Shakespeare's Freedom 2010; contribs to scholarly journals. *Honours:* Guggenheim Fellow 1975, 1983; Porter Prize 1969, British Council Prize 1982, James Russell Lowell Prize 1989, Distinguished Teaching Award, Erasmus Inst. Prize 2001, Mellon Distinguished Humanist Award 2002, Wilbur Cross Medal 2010. *Address:* Department of English, Harvard University, Cambridge, MA 02138, USA (office). *Telephone:* (617) 495-2101 (office). *Fax:* (617) 496-8737 (office). *E-mail:* greenbl@fas.harvard.edu (office). *Website:* www.fas.harvard.edu/~english (office).

GREENE, Brian R., PhD; American physicist and academic; *Professor of Mathematics and Physics, Columbia University*; b. 9 Feb. 1963, New York; s. of Alan Greene; m. Tracy Day. *Education:* Harvard Univ., Univ. of Oxford, UK. *Career:* Post-doctoral Fellow, Harvard Univ. 1987–90; Asst Prof., Cornell Univ. 1990, Assoc. Prof. 1995, later Prof.; currently Prof. of Math. and Physics, Columbia Univ., also Co-Dir Inst. for Strings, Cosmology, and Astroparticle Physics, Dir Theoretical Advanced Study Inst. 1996–; mem. Editorial Bd Physical Review D, Advance in Theoretical and Mathematical Physics. *Television:* The Theory of Everything 2003. *Publications:* journal papers: Duality in Calabi-Yau Moduli Space (with M. R. Plesser) 1990, Calabi-Yau Moduli Space, Mirror Manifolds and Spacetime Topology Change in String Theory (with P. S. Aspinwall and D. R. Morrison) 1994, Black Hole Condensation and the Unification of String Vacua (with D. R. Morrison and A. Strominger) 1995, Orbifold Resolution by D-Branes (with M. R. Douglas and D. R. Morrison) 1997, D-Brane Topology Changing Transitions 1998; books: The Elegant Universe (Aventis Prize for Science Books 2000) 1999, The Fabric of the Cosmos: Space, Time and the Texture of Reality 2004. *Address:* 910 Pupin, MC 5210, Box 10, 538 West 120 St, New York, NY 10027, USA (office). *Telephone:* (212) 854-3349 (office); (212) 854-4347 (office). *E-mail:* greene@phys.columbia.edu (office); greene@math.columbia.edu (office). *Website:* www.iscap.columbia.edu (office); www.phys.columbia.edu.

GREENE, Constance Clarke; American writer; b. 27 Oct. 1924, New York; m. Philip M. Greene 1946; two s. three d. *Education:* Skidmore Coll. *Publications:* A Girl Called Al 1969, Leo the Lioness 1970, The Good-Luck Bogie Hat 1971, Unmaking of Rabbit 1972, Isabelle the Itch 1973, The Ears of Louis 1974, Beat the Turtle Drum 1976, Getting Nowhere 1977, I and Sproggy 1978, Your Old Pal, Al 1979, Dotty's Suitcase 1980, Double-Dare O'Toole 1981, Al(exandra) the Great 1982, Ask Anybody 1983, Isabelle Shows Her Stuff 1984, Star Shine 1985, Other Plans 1985, The Love Letters of J. Timothy Owen 1986, Just Plain Al 1986, Isabelle and Little Orphan Frannie 1988, Monday I Love You 1988, Al's Blind Date 1989, Funny You Should Ask 1992, Odds on Oliver 1992; contribs to magazines and newspapers. *Honours:* American Library Asscn Notable Books 1970, 1977, 1987.

GREENE, Douglas G., BA, MA, PhD; American editor, historian and educator; *Publisher and Editor, Crippen and Landru Publishers*; b. 24 Sept. 1944, Middletown; m. Sandra Virginia Stangland 1966; one s. one d. *Education:* Univ. of Southern Florida, Univ. of Chicago. *Career:* Instructor in History, Univ. of Montana, Missoula 1970–71; Prof. of History, Old Dominion Univ., Norfolk, Virginia 1971–83, apptd Dir Inst. for Humanities 1983; currently Publisher and Ed. Crippen and Landru Publrs; mem. MWA. *Publications:* Bibliographia Oziana: A Concise Bibliographical Checklist of the Oz Books by L. Frank Baum and His Successors (co-author) 1976, W. W. Denslow (co-author) 1976, Diaries of the Popish Plot: Being the Diaries of Israel Tonge, Sir Robert Southwell, John Joyne, Edmund Warcup, and Thomas Dangerfield, and Including Titus Oates's 'A True Narrative of the Horrid Plot' (1679) (compiler) 1977, The Meditations of Lady Elizabeth Delaval: Written between 1661 and 1671 (ed.) 1978, John Dickson Carr, The Door to Doom, and Other Detections (ed.) 1980, John Dickson Carr, The Dead Sleep Lightly (ed.) 1983, Ruth Plumly Thompson, The Wizard of Way-Up and Other Wonders (co-ed.) 1985, Death Locked In: An Anthology of Locked Room Stories (co-ed.) 1987, The Collected Short Fiction of Ngaio March (ed.) 1989, John Dickson Carr, Fell and Foul Play (ed.) 1991, John Dickson Carr, Merrivale, March, and Murder (ed.) 1991, John Dickson Carr: The Man Who Explained Miracles 1995, Detection by Gaslight: Fourteen Victorian Detective Stories (ed.) 1997, Classic Mystery Stories (ed) 1999, Sissajig and other Surprises (ed) 2003. *Honours:* George N. Dove Award 2007. *Address:* Crippen & Landru Publishers, PO Box 9315, Norfolk, VA 23505-9315 (office); 627 New Hampshire Avenue, Norfolk, VA 23508-2132, USA (home). *Telephone:* (877) 622-6656 (office). *E-mail:* info@crippenlandru.com (office); Crippenl@pilot.infi.net. *Website:* www.crippenlandru.com (office).

GREENE, Graham Carleton, CBE, MA; British publisher; b. 10 June 1936, Berlin, Germany; s. of Sir Hugh Carleton Greene and Helga Mary Connolly; m. 1st Judith Margaret Gordon Walker 1957 (divorced); m. 2nd Sally Georgina Horton 1976 (divorced); one s.; also one step-s. one step-d. *Education:* Eton Coll. and Univ. Coll., Oxford. *Career:* Dir Jonathan Cape Ltd 1962–90, Man. Dir 1966–88; Dir Chatto, Virago, Bodley Head and Jonathan Cape Ltd 1969–88, Chair. 1970–88; Dir Book Reps (NZ) Ltd 1971–88, CVBC Services 1972–88, Australasian Publishing Co. Ltd 1969–88 (Chair. 1978–88), Guinness Peat Group PLC 1973–87, Triad Paperbacks 1975–88, Greene King PLC 1979–, Statesman and Nation Publishing Co. 1980–85 (Chair. 1981–85), Statesman Publishing Co. Ltd 1980–85 (Chair. 1981–85), Random House Inc. 1987–88, Jupiter Int. Investment Trust PLC 1989–2001, Henry Sotheran Ltd 1990–, Ed Victor Ltd 1991–, Rosemary Sandberg Ltd 1991–2002, Libra KFT (Budapest) 1991–, London Merchant Securities PLC 1996–2007 (Chair. 2000–07); Chair. Random House UK Ltd 1988–90, British Museum Devt Trust 1986–93 (Vice-Chair. 1993–2004), British Museum Publications (now British Museum Co.) Ltd 1998–2002, Museums and Galleries Comm. 1991–96, Vice-Pres. 1997–; Chair. Nation Pty Co. Ltd 1981–87, New Society 1984–86, Great Britain-China Centre 1986–1997; Dir Garsington Opera Ltd 1996–; mem. Bd of British Council 1977–88, Council of Publrs Asscn (Pres. 1977–79) 1969–88; Trustee, British Museum 1978–2002 (Chair. 1996–2002), Trustee Emer. 2002–), Open Coll. of the Arts 1990–97; mem. Int. Cttee of Int. Publrs Asscn 1977–88, Groupe des Editeurs de Livres de la CEE 1977–86 (Pres. 1984–86). *Honours:* Chevalier, Ordre des Arts et des Lettres; Hon. DLitt (Keele Univ.) 2002, Hon. DCL (Univ. E Anglia) 2002, Hon. DLitt (Buckingham) 2004. *Address:* D2 Albany, Piccadilly, London, W1J 0AP, England (home). *Telephone:* (20) 7734-0270 (home). *Fax:* (20) 7437-5251 (home). *E-mail:* grahamc.greene@virgin.net (home).

GREENE, Jonathan Edward, BA; American poet, writer, editor, publisher and book designer; *Publisher, Gnomon Press*; b. 19 April 1943, New York, NY; m. 1st Alice-Anne Kingston 1963 (divorced); one d.; m. 2nd Dobree Adams 1974. *Education:* Bard Coll. *Art exhibition:* Full Circle, with weavings and photographs by Dobree Adams. *Publications:* The Reckoning 1966, Instance 1968, The Lapidary 1969, A 17th Century Garner 1969, An Unspoken Complaint 1970, The Poor in Church, by Arthur Rimbaud (trans.) 1973, Scaling the Walls 1974, Glossary of the Everyday 1974, Peripatetics 1978, Jonathan Williams: A 50th Birthday Celebration (ed.) 1979, Once a Kingdom Again 1979, Quiet Goods 1980, Idylls 1983, Small Change for the Long Haul 1984, Trickster Tales 1985, Les Chambres des Poètes 1990, The Man Came to Haul Stone 1995, Of Moment 1998, Inventions of Necessity: Selected Poems 1998, Incidents of Travel in Japan 1999, A Little Ink in the Paper Sea 2001, Book of Correspondences 2002, Watching Dewdrops Fall 2003, Hummingbird's Water Trough 2003, Fault Lines 2004, On the Banks of Monks Pond: The Thomas Merton/Jonathan Greene Correspondence 2004, The Death of A Kentucky Coffee-Tree & Other Poems 2006, Gists, Orts, Shards: A Commonplace Book 2006, Hut Poems 2007, Heart Matters 2008, Feed the Lotus 2009, Distillations and Siphonings 2010; contribs to anthologies, reviews, quarterlies, and journals. *Honours:* Nat. Endowment for the Arts Fellowships 1969, 1978, Southern Fed. of State Arts Agencies Fellowship 1977, Kentucky Arts Council Fellowship 2003. *Address:* PO Box 475, Frankfort, KY 40602-0475, USA (home). *Telephone:* (502) 223-1858 (home). *Fax:* (502) 223-1858 (home). *E-mail:* jgnomon@bellsouth.net (home). *Website:* www.southernartistry.org; www.gnomonpress.com.

GREENE, Richard, BA, DPhil; Canadian poet, biographer, editor and academic; *Professor of English Literature, University of Toronto*; b. 17 July 1961, St John's, Newfoundland; s. of Richard Joseph Greene, QC and Anna Maureen Greene (née Healey); m. Marianne Marusic; one s. one d. and two step-d. *Education:* Memorial Univ., Christ Church, Oxford, UK (Rothermere Fellow). *Career:* taught for several years at Memorial Univ.; apptd mem. of staff, Univ. of Toronto 1995, currently Prof. of English Literature and Sr Fellow of Massey Coll.; Contributing Ed. Books in Canada. *Publications:* Mary Leapor: A Study in Eighteenth Century Women's Poetry (monograph) 1993, Republic of Solitude: Poems, 1984–1994 1994, Selected Letters of Edith Sitwell (ed) 1997, The Works of Mary Leapor (co-ed) 2003, Crossing the Straits (poems) 2004, Graham Greene: A Life in Letters (ed) 2007, Boxing the Compass (Gov.-Gen.'s Literary Award for Poetry 2010) 2009, Edith Sitwell: Avant Garde Poet, English Genius (biog.) 2011; contrib. reviews and poems to literary journals. *Literary Agent:* c/o Andrew Gordon, David Higham Associates Ltd, 5–8 Lower John Street, Golden Square, London, W1F 9HA, England. *Telephone:* (20) 7434-5900. *Fax:* (20) 7437-1072. *E-mail:* andrewgordon@davidhigham.co.uk. *Website:* www.davidhigham.co.uk. *Address:* Department of English, University of Toronto, Jackman Humanities Building, Room 712, 170 St George Street, 6th Floor, Toronto, ON M5R 2M8, Canada (office); c/o Virago Press, Little, Brown Book Group, 100 Victoria Embankment, London, EC4Y 0DY, England. *Telephone:* (905) 828-5439 (Toronto) (office); (20) 7911-8000 (London). *Fax:* (20) 7911-8100 (London). *E-mail:* richard.greene@utoronto.ca (office); virago.press@littlebrown.co.uk. *Website:* www.richardgreene.ca.

GREENFIELD OF OTMOOR, Baroness (Life Peer), cr. 2001, of Otmoor in the County of Oxfordshire; **Susan Adele Greenfield,** CBE, BA (Hons), MA, DPhil, FRSE; British pharmacologist; *Professor in Synaptic Pharmacology, University of Oxford*; b. 1 Oct. 1950, d. of Reginald Myer Greenfield and Doris Margaret Winifred Greenfield; m. Peter William Atkins 1991 (divorced 2005). *Education:* Godolphin and Latymer School for Girls, St Hilda's Coll., Oxford. *Career:* Dame Catherine Fulford Sr Scholarship, St Hugh's Coll. Oxford 1974; MRC Training Fellow, Univ. Lab. of Physiology, Oxford 1977–81; Collège de France, Paris; Royal Soc. Study Visit Award, 1978; MRC-INSERM French Exchange Fellow 1979–80; Jr Research Fellow, Green Coll. Oxford 1981–84, Lecturer in Synaptic Pharmacology 1985–96, currently Prof. in Synaptic Pharmacology; Dir Royal Inst. 1998–2010; Gresham Prof. of Physic, Gresham Coll. Oxford 1995–99; Visiting Fellow, Inst. of Neuroscience, La Jolla, Calif., USA 1995; Visiting Distinguished Scholar, Queen's Univ., Belfast 1996; Adelaide Thinker in Residence 2004–06; Chancellor Heriot-Watt Univ. 2006–; Co-founder Synaptica Ltd 1997, BrainBoost Ltd 2002; Dir (non-exec.) Britech Foundation Ltd 2002–06, Oxford Inspires Ltd 2002–05, Israel Britain Business Council 2002, Young Foresight Ltd 2003, Bank Leumi (UK) 2003–06, Cherwell Capital plc 2004–06, Enkephala Ltd 2005–; mem. Nat. Advisory Cttee on Cultural and Creative Educ. 1998–; Pres. Asscn for Science Educ. 2000; Vice-Pres. Asscn of Women in Science and Eng 2001; Fellow, Australian Davos Connection 2007, Science Museum 2010; Trustee, Science Museum, London 1998–2003. *Radio includes:* Start the Week, Any Questions and other discussion programmes; presenter of Turn On, Turn Off series on drugs and the brain, Today Programme. *Television includes:* Dimbleby Lecturer 1999, author and presenter of Brain Story 'Landmark' (BBC 2 series of programmes on the brain) 2000, Big Ideas in Science, Channel 5 (UK). *Publications include:* numerous articles in learned journals; Mindwaves (co-ed. with C. B. Blakemore) 1987, Journey to the Centres of the Brain (with G. Ferry) 1994, Journey to the Centres of the Mind 1995, The Human Mind Explained (ed.) 1996, The Human Brain: A Guided Tour 1997; Brainpower (ed.) 2000, Brain Story 2000, Private Life of the Brain 2000, Tomorrow's People: How 21st Century Technology is Changing the Way We Think and Feel 2003, ID: The Quest for Identity in the 21st Century 2008. *Honours:* Hon. Fellow, St Hilda's Coll. Oxford, Cardiff Univ. 2000; Hon. FRCP 2000; numerous hon. doctorates; Chevalier, Légion d'honneur 2003; Michael Faraday Medal, Royal Soc. 1998, Woman of Distinction, Jewish Care 1998, Hon. Australian of the Year 2006, Science and Tech. Award, British Inspiration Awards 2010, Australian Soc. for Medical Research Medal 2010. *Address:* Department of Pharmacology, Mansfield Road, Oxford, OX1 3QT (office). *Telephone:* (1865) 271852 (office). *Fax:* (1865) 271853 (office). *E-mail:* sagpa@pharm.ox.ac.uk (office).

GREENHALGH, Christopher David, BA, PGCE, PhD; British poet and writer; b. 17 March 1963, Bury, Lancashire. *Education:* Univ. of Hull, Univ. of East Anglia. *Career:* English teacher, International School, Athens 1987–90; currently Academic Deputy Head, Sevenoaks School, Kent; mem. Poetry Soc. *Publications:* poetry: Stealing the Mona Lisa 1994, Of Love, Death and the Sea-Squirt 2000, The Invention of Zero 2007; fiction: Coco and Igor 2002. *Honours:* First Prize, Thetford Open Poetry Competition 1987, Eric Gregory Award 1992. *Address:* Sevenoaks School, Sevenoaks, Kent TN13 1HU, England (office).

GREENLAND, Colin, MA, DPhil; British writer; b. 17 May 1954, Dover, Kent, England; s. of Harry Greenland and Kitty Greenland; m. Susanna Clarke. *Education:* Pembroke Coll., Oxford. *Career:* Writer-in-Residence, North East London Polytechnic 1980–82; mem. Science Fiction Foundation, Milford Science Fiction Writers' Conf.; Life mem. British Science Fiction Asscn. *Publications:* The Entropy Exhibition 1983, Daybreak on a Different Mountain 1984, Magnetic Storm (with Roger and Martyn Dean) 1984, Interzone: The First Anthology (co-ed.) 1985, The Freelance Writer's Handbook (with Paul Kerton) 1986, The Hour of the Thin Ox 1987, Storm Warnings (co-ed.) 1987, Other Voices 1988, Take Back Plenty 1990, Michael Moorcock: Death is No Obstacle 1992, Harm's Way 1993, Seasons of Plenty 1995, The Plenty Principle 1997, Mother of Plenty 1998, Spiritfeather 2000, Finding Helen 2002; contribs to numerous anthologies and periodicals. *Honours:* Eaton Award for Science Fiction Criticism 1985, Arthur C. Clarke Award 1992, BSFA Award 1992, Eastercon Award 1992, Guest of Honour, Evolution, Nat. Science Fiction Easter Convention 1996. *Literary Agent:* c/o MNLA, 7 Peacock Yard, Iliffe Street, London, SE17 3LH, England. *Telephone:* (20) 7708-3073. *E-mail:* colin.greenland@ntlworld.com. *Website:* www.goodreads.com/author/show/122629.Colin_Greenland.

GREENLAW, Lavinia, BA, MA, FRSL; British poet, novelist, critic and broadcaster; *Professor of Creative Writing, University of East Anglia*; b. 30 July 1962, London, England. *Education:* Kingston Polytechnic, London Coll. of Printing, Courtauld Inst. *Career:* British Council Fellow in Writing, Amherst Coll., Mass, USA 1995; Writer-in-Residence, Science Museum, London 1995, Wellington Coll. 1996, Mishcon de Reya solicitors 1997–98, Aldeburgh Poetry Festival 1998, Aldeburgh Festival 2003, Calouste Gulbenkian/Royal Soc. of Medicine 2005; Fellow in Writing, Sevenoaks School 1997; Reader-in-Residence, Royal Festival Hall 2000; Sr Lecturer in Creative Writing, Goldsmiths Coll., Univ. of London 2002–07; Prof. of Creative Writing, Univ. of E Anglia 2008–. *Music:* Hamelin (libretto for Ian Wilson/Schleswig-Holsteinisches Landestheater) 2003, Slow Passage, Low Prospect (song cycle for Richard Baker/Aldeburgh Festival) 2004, Minsk (libretto for Ian Wilson/Feldkirch Festival) 2005, Written on a Train (song cycle for Richard Baker/Borlotti-Buitoni Trust) 2006. *Radio:* drama: The Blood of Strangers (adaptation) 2002, Remembering Mum 2003, Night and Day: Virginia Woolf (adaptation) 2003, The Kamikaze Handbook 2004, The Innocence of Radium 2004, Troilus and Criseyde 2009; documentaries include Essex Rag, The Red in My Mind: Emily Dickinson, The Year's Four Corners, A Drink of Glass, The Land of Giving In, As Big As Life: Elizabeth Bishop's Childhood Landscape. *Publications:* poetry: The Cost of Getting Lost in Space (pamphlet) 1991, Love from a Foreign City (pamphlet) 1992, Night Photograph 1993, A World Where News Travelled Slowly (Forward Prize for Best Poem of the Year) 1997, Thoughts of a Night Sea (with photographs by Garry Fabian Miller) 2002, Minsk 2003, Signs and Humours: The Poetry of Medicine (ed.) 2007; prose: Mary George of Allnorthover (novel) (Prix du Premier Roman 2003) 2001, An Irresponsible Age (novel) 2006; other: The Importance of Music to Girls (memoir) 2007; contribs to TLS, London Review of Books, New Yorker, Paris Review, Poetry Review, Verse, New Statesman, The Observer, The Telegraph, The Guardian, The Financial Times, American Poet. *Honours:* Eric Gregory Award 1990, Arts Council of England Writers Award 1995, Wingate Scholarship 1998, NESTA Fellowship 2000, Spycher-Leuk Literaturpreis (Switzerland) 2002, Cholmondeley Award 2003, Prix du Premier Roman (France) 2003, Soc. of Authors Travelling Scholarship 2005. *Literary Agent:* c/o Derek Johns, AP Watt, 20 John Street, London, WC1N 2DR, England. *Telephone:* (20) 7405-6774. *Fax:* (20) 7831-2154. *E-mail:* djohns@apwatt.co.uk. *Website:* www.apwatt.co.uk; www.laviniagreenlaw.com.

GREENLEAF, Stephen Howell, BA, JD; American writer; b. 17 July 1942, Washington, DC; m. Ann Garrison 1968; one s. *Education:* Carleton Coll., Univ. of California at Berkeley, Univ. of Iowa. *Career:* admitted to the Bar, California 1968, Iowa 1977; Instructor in Writing, Univ. of Washington Extension 1993–96, Iowa Summer Writing Festival 1995–2000. *Publications:* Grave Error 1979, Death Bed 1980, Child Proof 1981, State's Evidence 1982, Fatal Obsession 1983, The Ditto List 1985, Beyond Blame 1986, Toll Call 1987, Impact 1989, Book Case (Maltese Falcon Award, Japan 1993) 1991, Blood Type 1992, Southern Cross 1993, False Conception 1994, Flesh Wounds 1996, Past Tense 1997, Strawberry Sunday 1999, Ellipsis 2000. *Address:* c/o Simon & Schuster Inc., 1200 Avenue of the Americas, New York, NY 10020, USA.

GREER, Bonnie, OBE; American/British writer and playwright; b. 1948, Chicago. *Education:* studied with David Mamet and Elia Kazan in New York. *Career:* theatre critic, Time Out, London; Gov., London Int. Film School; bd mem., Royal Opera House; judge for Orange Prize; regular contributor to radio, including Night Waves (BBC Radio 3), Front Row (BBC Radio 4) and television, including Booker Prize (Channel 4), Late Review and Newsnight Review/The Review Show (BBC2), Question Time (BBC 1); also contrib. to newspapers and women's magazines; Arts Council Playwright-in-Residence, Soho Theatre, Black Theatre Co-operative; Arts Council England Playwright-in-Residence, Pascal Theatre Co., London; Deputy Chair. Bd of Trustees, British Museum 2009–. *Plays:* Mundo Negra 1993, God Likes No Ugly, Marilyn and Ella 2007. *Publications:* Hanging by her Teeth (novel) 1994, Ways into Shakespeare 1996, Entropy (novel) 2009, Obama Music 2009.

Honours: Verity Bargate Award for Best New Play. *Literary Agent:* The Antell Agency, 5 Ruskin Road, London, N17 5ND, England. *Telephone:* (20) 7275-0234. *E-mail:* judith@theantellagency.co.uk. *Website:* www.theantellagency.co.uk.

GREER, Germaine, PhD; Australian feminist, author and broadcaster; b. 29 Jan. 1939, Melbourne; d. of Eric Reginald Greer and Margaret May Greer (née Lafrank). *Education:* Star of the Sea Convent, Vic., Melbourne, Sydney Univ., Univ. of Cambridge, UK. *Career:* Sr Tutor in English, Sydney Univ. 1963–64; Asst Lecturer then Lecturer in English, Univ. of Warwick 1967–72, Prof. of English and Comparative Studies 1998–2003; lecturer throughout N America with American Program Bureau 1973–78, to raise funds for Tulsa Bursary and Fellowship Scheme 1980–83; Visiting Prof., Grad. Faculty of Modern Letters, Univ. of Tulsa 1979, Prof. of Modern Letters 1980–83, Founder-Dir of Tulsa Centre for the Study of Women's Literature, Founder-Ed. Tulsa Studies in Women's Literature 1981; Dir Stump Cross Books 1988–; Special Lecturer and Unofficial Fellow, Newnham Coll., Cambridge 1989–98; broadcaster/journalist/columnist/reviewer 1972–; Jr Govt Scholarship 1952, Diocesan Scholarship 1956, Sr Govt Scholarship 1956, Teacher's Coll. Studentship 1956, Commonwealth Scholarship 1964; numerous television appearances and public talks including discussion with Norman Mailer in The Theatre of Ideas, New York. *Film appearance:* Rabbit Fever 2006. *Television:* The Late Review, Celebrity Big Brother. *Publications:* The Female Eunuch 1969, The Obstacle Race: The Fortunes of Women Painters and Their Work 1979, Sex and Destiny: The Politics of Human Fertility 1984, Shakespeare (co-ed.) 1986, The Madwoman's Underclothes (selected journalism 1964–85) 1986, Kissing the Rod: An Anthology of 17th Century Women's Verse (co-ed.) 1988, Daddy, We Hardly Knew You (J. R. Ackerly Prize and Premio Internazionale Mondello) 1989, The Uncollected Verse of Aphra Behn (ed.) 1989, The Change: Women, Ageing and the Menopause 1991, The Collected Works of Katherine Philips, the Matchless Orinda, Vol. III: The Translations (co-ed.) 1993, Slip-Shod Sybils: Recognition, Rejection and The Woman Poet 1995, The Surviving Works of Anne Wharton (co-ed.) 1997, The Whole Woman 1999, John Wilmot, Earl of Rochester 1999, 101 Poems by 101 Women (ed.) 2001, The Boy 2003, Poems for Gardeners (ed.) 2003, Whitefella Jump Up The Shortest Way to Nationhood 2004, Shakespeare's Wife 2007; articles for Listener, Spectator, Esquire, Harper's Magazine, Playboy, Private Eye and other journals. *Honours:* Dr hc (Univ. of Griffith, Australia) 1996, (Univ. of York, Toronto) 1999, (UMIST) 2000; hon. degrees (Melbourne) 2003, (Essex) 2003, (Anglia Polytechnic) 2003, (Sydney) 2005; Australian Living Treasure Nat. Trust Award Centenary Medal 2003. *Address:* The Mills, Walden Road, Stump Cross, nr. Saffron Walden, Essex, CB10 1PS, England.

GRÉGOIRE, Marie Menie, Licence d'Histoire; French journalist and writer; b. 15 Aug. 1919, Cholet; d. of Maurice Laurentin and Marie Laurentin (née Jactel); m. Roger Grégoire 1943 (deceased); three d. *Education:* Univ. de Paris (Sorbonne), Ecole des Hautes Etudes and Inst. d'Art et d'Archéologie, Paris. *Career:* psychoanalyst; speaker for the Alliance française in Finland, Italy, Sweden, USA 1950–; journalist with various newspapers and periodicals including Le Monde and Esprit; Editorial Writer Marie-Claire; presented two daily women's radio programmes on Radio-Télé Luxembourg (RTL) 1967–81, columnist 1981–86, Ed. 1980–86; presented Avec le temps (TV) 1984; columnist, France-Soir 1986–99; mem. Conseil supérieur de l'information sexuelle, de la régulation des naissances et de l'éducation familiale 1974–, various nat. comms. *Publications:* Le métier de femme 1964, Femmes (two vols) 1966, La belle Arsène, Passeport du couple 1967, Les cris de la vie 1971, Ménie Grégoire raconte... 1972, Telle que je suis 1976, Des passions et des rêves 1981, Tournelune 1983, Sagesse et folie des Français 1986, Nous aurons le temps de vivre 1987, La France et ses immigrés 1988, La Dame du Puy du Fou 1990, Le petit roi du Poitou 1992, La magicienne 1993, Le Bien aimé 1996, Les dames de la Loire 2001–03, Comme une lame de fond (100,000 lettres qui disent le mal-être des corps et des coeurs) 2007. *Honours:* Officier de la Légion d'honneur 1990. *Address:* 3 rue Chapon, 75003 Paris, France (home). *Telephone:* 1-42-77-53-81 (home).

GREGORY, Philippa, PhD; British writer; b. 9 Jan. 1954, Kenya; m.; two c. *Education:* Univ. of Sussex, Univ. of Edinburgh. *Career:* trained as a journalist and apprenticed at The News, Portsmouth; worked for BBC Radio for two years; has taught at Durham Univ., Open Univ., Teesside Polytechnic; f. The Gardens for Gambia (charity); Fellow, Kingston Univ. *Publications:* novels: Wideacre 1987, The Favoured Child 1989, Meridon 1990, The Wise Woman 1992, A Respectable Trade 1992, Fallen Skies 1993, Mrs Hartley and the Growth Centre 1995, Perfectly Correct 1996, The Little House 1997, Earthly Joys 1998, The Virgin Earth 1999, Midlife Mischief 1998, Zelda's Cut 2000, The Other Boleyn Girl (also adapted for TV) (Parker Romantic Novel of the Year) 2002, The Queen's Fool 2003, The Virgin's Lover 2004, The Constant Princess 2005, The Boleyn Inheritance 2006, The White Queen 2009, The Red Queen 2010, The Women of the Cousins' War 2011; contrib. short stories, features and reviews to newspapers and magazines. *Address:* c/o Simon and Schuster UK, 222 Gray's Inn Road, London, WC1X 8HE, England (office). *E-mail:* press@philippagregory.com (office). *Website:* www.philippagregory.com.

GREGSON, Julia; British writer and journalist; b. (Julia Sutton), 19 March 1947, London; d. of Group Captain Barry Sutton and Vicki Sutton; m. Richard Gregson; one d., one step s., two step d. *Career:* worked as a journalist in UK and foreign correspondent in Australia, Viet Nam, Bangladesh and USA; journalist, freelance writer, Rolling Stone, New York Times, Redbook, Good Housekeeping. *Publications:* The Water Horse 2005, East of the Sun (Romantic Novelists' Asscn Romantic Novel of the Year 2009, Le Prince Maurice Prize 2010) 2008; contrib. short stories to anthologies, magazines and radio. *Honours:* winner, Literary Review (Ryman's) Short Story Competition 2008, winner, Romantic Novelist of the Year 2008, Sydney Morning Herald Prize for English Literature 2008. *Literary Agent:* Aitken Alexander Associates, 18–21 Cavaye Place, London, SW10 9PT, England. *Telephone:* (20) 7373-8672. *Fax:* (20) 7373-6002. *E-mail:* reception@aitkenalexander.co.uk. *Website:* www.aitkenalexander.co.uk. *E-mail:* julia@juliagregson.net (office). *Website:* www.juliagregson.net.

GREIG, Andrew; British poet and writer; b. 1951, Bannockburn, Scotland; m. Lesley Glaister. *Education:* Univ. of Edinburgh. *Publications:* poetry: Men on Ice 1977, Surviving Passages 1982, A Flame in Your Heart (with Kathleen Jamie) 1986, The Order of the Day 1990, Western Swing 1994, Into You 2000, This Life, This Life: Selected Poems 1970–2006 2006; novels: Electric Brae 1992, The Return of John Macnab 1996, When They Lay Bare 1999, That Summer 2000, The Clouds Above 2002, In Another Light 2004, Romanno Bridge 2008; non-fiction: Summit Fever 1985, Kingdoms of Experience 1986, Preferred Lies: A Journey to the Heart of Scottish Golf 2006, At the Loch of the Green Corrie 2010. *Literary Agent:* c/o Capel and Land, 29 Wardour Street, London, W1V 3HB, England. *Website:* www.capelland.com.

GREIG, David; Scottish playwright. *Plays:* Maggie and the Cat, Savage Reminiscence, Stalinland (Citizens Stalls, Glasgow) 1993, Europe (Traverse Theatre, Edinburgh) 1994, One Way Street (Traverse Theatre, Edinburgh) 1995, Airport (Traverse Theatre, Edinburgh) 1996, The Architect (Traverse Theatre, Edinburgh) 1996, Caledonia Dreaming (Traverse Theatre, Edinburgh) 1997, Local (Tramway, Glasgow) 1998, Timeless (Donmar Warehouse, London) 1998, Mainstream (McRobert, Stirling) 1999, The Cosmonaut's Last Message to the Woman he Once Loved in the Former Soviet Union (Lyric Studio, London) 1999, Danny 306 + Me (4 Ever) (Traverse Theatre, Edinburgh) 1999, The Speculator (Traverse Theatre, Edinburgh) 1999, Candide 2000 (adaptation, Old Fruitmarket, Glasgow) 2000, The Greeks (translation, Tramway, Glasgow) 2000, Victoria (The Pit, London) 2000, Casanova (Tron, Glasgow) 2001, Dr Korczak's Example (Shawlands Academy) 2001, Outlying Islands (Traverse Theatre, Edinburgh) 2002, Caligula (translation, Donmar Warehouse, London) 2003, San Diego (Royal Lyceum, Edinburgh Festival) 2003, Suspect Culture (Tron Theatre, Glasgow) 2003, 8000m (Glasgow, Tramway) 2004, When The Bulbul Stopped Singing (adaptation, Traverse Theatre, Edinburgh) 2004, Pyrenees (Menier Chocolate Factory, London) 2005, The American Pilot (Other Place, Stratford-upon-Avon) 2005, Yellow Moon 2006, Dunsinane (RSC, Hampstead Theatre, London) 2010. *Literary Agent:* Casarotto Ramsay and Associates Ltd, National House, 60–66 Wardour Street, London, W1V 3HP, England. *Telephone:* (20) 7287-4450. *Fax:* (20) 7287-9128. *E-mail:* agents@casarotto.co.uk. *Website:* www.casarotto.co.uk.

GREIG, Geordie Carron, MA, FRSA; British journalist; *Editor, London Evening Standard*; b. 16 Dec. 1960, London; s. of Sir Carron Greig and Monica Greig (née Stourton); m. Kathryn Elizabeth Terry 1995; one s. two d. *Education:* Eton Coll. and St Peter's Coll., Oxford. *Career:* reporter, South East London and Kentish Mercury 1981–83, Daily Mail 1984–85, Today 1985–87; reporter, The Sunday Times 1987–89, Arts Corresp. 1989–91, New York Corresp. 1991–95, Literary Ed. 1995–99; Ed. of Tatler 1999–2009; Ed., London Evening Standard 2009–. *Publication:* Louis and the Prince 1999. *Address:* London Evening Standard, Northcliffe House, 2 Derry Street, London, W8 5TT, England (office). *Telephone:* (20) 7938-6000 (office). *Fax:* (20) 7937-2648 (office). *E-mail:* geordie.greig@standard.co.uk (office). *Website:* www.standard.co.uk (office).

GREILSAMER, Laurent, LèsL; French journalist; *Vice-President, Le Monde*; b. 2 Feb. 1953, Neuilly; s. of Marcel Greilsamer and Francine Alice Greilsamer; m. Claire Méheut 1979; three s. *Education:* Ecole Supérieure de Journalisme, Lille. *Career:* Le Figaro 1974–76, Quotidien de Paris 1976; ed., Le Monde 1977–84, Sr Reporter 1984–94, 1994–2005, Ed. 2005–07, now Vice Pres. *Publications:* Interpol, le siège du soupçon 1986, Un certain Monsieur Paul, L'affaire Touvier 1989, Hubert Beuve-Méry 1990, Enquête sur l'affaire du sang contaminé 1990, Les juges parlent 1992, Interpol, Policiers sans frontières 1997, Le Prince foudroyé, la vie de Nicholas de Staël 1998, Où vont les juges? 2002, L'Eclair au front, la vie de René Char 2004, Le dico de la présidentielle 2007. *Honours:* Prix des lectrices de Elle 1999, Grand Prix de la Critique 2004. *Address:* Le Monde, 80 Boulevard Blanqui, 75013 Paris, France (office). *Telephone:* 1-57-28-26-05 (office). *Fax:* 1-57-28-21-22 (office). *E-mail:* greilsamer@lemonde.fr (office). *Website:* www.lemonde.fr (office).

GRENNAN, Eamon, MA, PhD; Irish/American poet and professor of English; *Professor Emeritus of English, Vassar College*; b. 13 Nov. 1941, Dublin, Ireland; s. of Thomas Patrick Grennan and Evelyn Yourell Grennan; m. Joan Grennan (divorced); one s. two d.; pnr Rachel Kitzinger; one d. *Education:* Univ. Coll., Dublin, Harvard Univ. *Career:* Lecturer in English, Univ. Coll., Dublin 1966–67; Asst Prof., Lehman Coll., CUNY 1971–74; Asst Prof., Vassar Coll. 1974–83, Assoc. Prof. 1983–89, Prof. 1989, currently Prof. Emer.; Adjunct Prof. Columbia Univ., New York Univ. *Publications:* Wildly for Days 1983, What Light There Is 1987, Twelve Poems 1988, What Light There Is and Other Poems 1989, As If It Matters 1991, So It Goes 1995, Selected Poems of Giacomo Leopardi (trans.) 1995, 1997, Relations: New and Selected Poems 1998, Facing the Music: Irish Poetry in the 20th Century 1999, Still Life with

Waterfall 2001, The Quick of It 2004, Oedipus at Colonus (trans. with Rachel Kitzinger) 2004, Out of Breath 2007, Matter of Fact 2008, Out of Sight: New and Selected Poems 2010; contribs to anthologies and periodicals. *Honours:* Nat. Endowment for the Humanities Grant 1986, Nat. Endowment for the Arts Grant 1991, Guggenheim Fellowship 1995, PEN Translation Prize 1997, Lenore Marshall Poetry Prize 2003. *Address:* Department of English, Vassar College, Poughkeepsie, NY 12604, USA (office). *Telephone:* (845) 437-5655 (office). *Fax:* (845) 437-7578 (office). *E-mail:* grennan@vassar.edu (office).

GRENVILLE, Kate, BA (Hons), MA, DCA; Australian writer and teacher; b. 14 Oct. 1950, Sydney, NSW; d. of Kenneth Grenville Gee and Nance Russell; m. Bruce Petty 1986; one s. one d. *Education:* Univ. of Sydney, Univ. of Colorado, Boulder, USA, Univ. of Tech., Sydney. *Career:* ed. of documentary films, Film Australia 1971–76; freelance journalist, London and Paris 1977–80; Sub-Ed., Subtitling Unit, Multicultural TV, Sydney 1982–85; reviewer; journalist; writer-in-residence at univs and Nat. Film School, Sydney 1986–; Sr Fellowship, Australia Council Bicentennial Comm. *Publications:* Bearded Ladies 1984, Lilian's Story 1985, Dreamhouse 1986, Joan Makes History 1988, The Writing Book 1990, Making Stories 1992, Dark Places 1995, The Idea of Perfection (Orange Prize 2001) 1999, Writing From Start to Finish 2001, The Secret River (Commonwealth Writers' Prize 2006) 2005, Searching for The Secret River 2006, The Lieutenant 2008, Sarah Thornhill 2011. *Honours:* Hon. Assoc., Univ. of Sydney; Hon. DLitt (Univ. of New South Wales); Vogel/Australian Award 1985, Victorian Premier's Literary Award 1995, Soc. of Women Writers' Award 1998, the Orange Prize 2001, Christina Stead Prize 2005, NSW Premier's Prize 2005, Community Council Award 2005, Commonwealth Literature Prize (Overall) 2006. *Literary Agent:* c/o Barbara Mobbs Agency, PO Box 126, Edgecliff, NSW 2027, Australia. *Website:* www.kategrenville.com.

GRESHNEVIKOV, Anatoly Nikolaevich; Russian journalist and writer; b. 29 Aug. 1956, Borisoglebsky Dist, Yaroslavl region; m.; two c. *Education:* Leningrad State Univ. *Career:* head Correspondence Dept, Novoye Vremya newspaper, Borisoglebsk; elected to Yaroslavl Regional Soviet and Russian Soviet Federative Socialist Republic Congress of People's Deputies 1990; mem. RSFSR Supreme Soviet and Cttee on Ecological Issues and Rational Use of Natural Resources; apptd Deputy Chair. State Duma Cttee for Environment 1993; mem. Russian Way faction 1993–95, Narodovlastiye (Sovereignty of the People) parl. group 1995–99; stood as ind. 2003, then mem. Rodina (Motherland) faction (mem. Political Council); mem. Cttee for Environment 1993–95, Secr. 1995–99, apptd Deputy Chair. 1999; mem. Russian Writers' Union, Russian Creative Union of Cultural Workers. *Publications include:* Sound Ecosystem – Healthy Society, The President Doesn't Hear the Ecologists; 'The Era of Environmental Apocalypse' series: The Caspian in the Nets of Poachers, Sticks and Staves for Scenic Forests, The Call of Arctic, Sale: Beavers, Tigers, Falcons, Land Is Being Lost, Fighting Dolphins and Ring Dogs, Dangerous Climate, Save the Cranes 2001. *Honours:* Order of the Holy and Righteous Prince Daniil of Moscow (Rank III), Russian Orthodox Church; prizes from USSR Journalists' Union, Selskaya Zhizn newspaper 1989, Selskaya Nov and Novy Mir magazines, 850th Anniversary of Moscow Medal, 300th Anniversary of St Petersburg Medal. *Address:* c/o State Duma, Okhotny ryad 1, 103265 Moscow, Russia.

GREY, Amelia (see Skinner, Gloria Dale)

GREY, Anthony Keith, OBE; British writer, broadcaster and publisher; *Founder and Chairman, The Tagman Press, Tagman Worldwide Limited*; b. 5 July 1938, Norwich, Norfolk; m. Shirley McGuinn 1970; two d. *Education:* City of Norwich Grammar School, City Coll., Norwich. *Career:* journalist, Eastern Daily Press 1960–64; Foreign Correspondent, Reuters, East Berlin and Prague 1965–67, Beijing 1967–69; est. imprint, The Tagman Press, Norfolk, UK 1998; mem. PEN International, Royal Inst. of Int. Affairs, Soc. of Authors, Groucho Club, MCC, Royal Automobile Club; Life mem. Royal Soc. of St George. *Radio:* Himself (play) 1976, UFOs: Fact, Fiction or Fantasy (BBC World Service documentary series) 1997. *Television documentaries:* One Pair of Eyes – One Man's Freedom (BBC), The Lure of the Dolphin (ITV), Witness of the Long March (Channel 4), Return To Peking (BBC), Return To Saigon (BBC). *Publications:* autobiog./diaries: Hostage in Peking 1970, Hostage in Peking Plus 2004, The Hostage Handbook 2009–10; short stories: A Man Alone 1971, A Kindle For Sigmund 2011; novels: Some Put Their Trust in Chariots 1973, The Bulgarian Exclusive 1976, The Chinese Assassin 1978, Saigon 1982, The Prime Minister was a Spy 1983, Peking 1988, The Naked Angels 1990, The Bangkok Secret 1990, Tokyo Bay 1996; other: Crosswords from Peking (puzzles) 1975, What is the Universe In? 2004. *Honours:* UK Journalist of the Year 1970. *Address:* The Tagman Press, Lovemore House, PO Box 74, Norwich, Norfolk, NR1 4GY, England (office). *Telephone:* (845) 644-4186 (office). *Fax:* (845) 644-4187 (office). *E-mail:* editorial@tagmanpress.co.uk (office). *Website:* www.tagmanpress.co.uk (office).

GRIBBIN, John R., MSc, PhD; British astrophysicist and writer; b. 1946; m. Mary Gribbin; two s. *Education:* Sussex Univ., Univ. of Cambridge. *Career:* Ed., Nature magazine 1970–75; science journalist, The Times; Visiting Fellow in Astronomy, Univ. of Sussex. *Publications include:* fiction: Brother Esau 1982, Double Planet 1988, Father to the Man 1989, Ragnarok 1991, Reunion 1991, Innervisions 1993; non-fiction: The Jupiter Effect 1974, Forecasts, Famines and Freezes 1976, Timewarps 1979, Our Changing Universe 1977, The Death of the Sun 1980, The Monkey Puzzle 1983, Spacewarps 1984, In Search of Schrodinger's Cat 1984, Amateur Astronomer 1985, In Search of the Double Helix 1985, The Hole in the Sky 1988, The Omega Point 1988, Winds of Change 1989, Cosmic Coincidence 1989, Hothouse Earth 1990, Blinded by the Light 1991, The Matter Myth 1992, In Search of the Big Bang 1992, Being Human 1993, In the Beginning 1993, Einstein: a Life in Science (with Michael White) 1994, In Search of the Edge of Time 1995, Companion to the Cosmos 1996, Schrodinger's Kittens and the Search for Reality 1996, Fire on Earth (with Mary Gribbin) 1996, Mendel in 90 Minutes (with Mary Gribbin) 1997, Richard Feynman: A Life in Science (with Michael White) 1998, Almost Everyone's Guide to Science 1999, Q is for Quantum 1999, The Search for Superstrings, Symmetry and the Theory of Everything 2000, The Case of the Missing Neutrinos 2000, Darwin: A Life in Science (with Michael White) 2000, The Birth of Time 2000, Stardust (with Mary Gribbin) 2001, Space: Our Final Frontier 2001, Science: A History 1534–2001 2002, Ice Age: How a Change of Climate Made Us Human (with Mary Gribbin) 2003, Stephen Hawking: A Life in Science (with Michael White) 2003, Deep Simplicity: Chaos, Complexity and the Emergence of Life 2004, The Men who Measured the Universe 2004, Fitzroy: The Remarkable Story of Darwin's Captain and the Invention of the Weather Forecast (with Mary Gribbin) 2004, The Fellowship: the Story of a Revolution 2005, The Universe: A Biography 2007, The Flower Hunters (with Mary Gribbin) 2008, James Lovelock: In Search of Gaia (with Mary Gribbin) 2009; contrib. to New Destinies VII 1988, What's the Big Idea? Chaos and Uncertainty 1999, The Science of Philip Pullman's 'His Dark Materials' 2003, numerous journals, magazines and newspapers. *Honours:* Annual Award of the Gravity Research Foundation. *Literary Agent:* c/o Bruce Hunter, David Higham Associates, 5–8 Lower Street, Golden Square, London, W1F 9HA, England. *Telephone:* (20) 7434-5900. *Fax:* (20) 7437-1072. *Website:* www.biols.susx.ac.uk/home/John_Gribbin/.

GRICHKOVETS, Evguéni Valeryevich; Russian playwright; b. 17 Feb. 1967, Kémérovo; m.; one s. two d. *Films:* supporting actor: Progulka, Ne hlebom edinym, V kruge pervom. *Publications:* Gorod 2001, Comment j'ai mangé du chien 2002, Kak ya syel sobaku 2003, En même temps 2004, Rubashka 2004, Planète 2004, La Ville 2004, Zima 2005, Reki 2005, Planka 2006, La Chemise 2007, Le Taquet 2012. *Honours:* Moscow Festival Innovation Prize 2000.

GRIFFIN, Jasper, MA, FBA; British academic and writer; *Professor Emeritus of Classical Literature, Balliol College*; b. 29 May 1937, London; s. of Frederick William Griffin and Constance Irene Cordwell; m. Miriam Tamara Griffin (née Dressler) 1960; three d. *Education:* Balliol Coll., Oxford. *Career:* Jackson Fellow, Harvard Univ. 1960–61; Dyson Research Fellow, Balliol Coll., Oxford 1961–63, Fellow and Tutor in Classics 1963–2004, Sr Fellow 2000–04, Univ. Reader 1989–2004, Public Orator 1992–2004, Prof. of Classical Literature 1992–2004, Prof. Emer. 2004–. *Publications:* Homer on Life and Death 1980, Snobs 1982, Latin Poets and Roman Life 1985, The Mirror of Myth 1985, Virgil 1986, Homer: The Odyssey 1987, The Art of Snobbery 1998, Homer 2002, Latin Poets and Roman Life 2008; Ed. The Oxford History of the Classical World 1986, The Iliad: Book Nine 1995, Sophocles Revisited: Essays Presented to Sir Hugh Lloyd-Jones 1999,; contrib. to articles and reviews. *Address:* Balliol College, Oxford, OX1 3BJ, England (office). *Telephone:* (1865) 277777 (office). *Fax:* (1865) 277803 (office). *Website:* www.balliol.ox.ac.uk (office).

GRIFFIN, Keith Broadwell, BA, BPhil, DPhil, FAAS; British academic and writer; *Distinguished Professor Emeritus of Economics, University of California, Riverside*; b. 6 Nov. 1938, Colón, Panama; m. Dixie Beth Griffin 1956; two d. *Education:* Williams Coll., USA, Univ. of Oxford. *Career:* Fellow and Tutor in Econs, Magdalen Coll., Oxford 1965–76, Pres. 1979–88; apptd Cecil and Ida Green Visiting Prof., Univ. of British Columbia 1986; Prof. of Econs, Univ. of California, Riverside 1988–2004, Distinguished Prof. Emer. 2004–, Chair. Dept of Econs 1988–93. *Publications:* The Green Revolution: An Economic Analysis 1972, The Political Economy of Agrarian Change 1974, Land Concentration and Rural Poverty 1976, International Inequality and National Poverty 1978, The Transition to Egalitarian Development (with Jeffrey James) 1981, Growth and Equality in Rural China (with Ashwani Saith) 1981, World Hunger and the World Economy 1987, Alternative Strategies for Economic Development 1989, The Economy of Ethiopia 1992, The Distribution of Income in China (ed) 1993, Implementing a Human Development Strategy (with Terry McKinley) 1994, Studies in Globalization and Economic Transitions 1996, Economic Reform in Vietnam (ed.) 1998, Studies in Development Strategy and Systemic Transformation 2000, Poverty Reduction in Mongolia (ed.) 2003, Human Development in the Era of Globalization: Essays in Honor of Keith B. Griffin 2006; contribs to scholarly books and journals. *Honours:* Hon. Fellow, Magdalen Coll., Oxford 1988; Hon. DLitt (Williams Coll.) 1980. *Address:* Department of Economics, University of California, 4108 Sproul Hall, Riverside, CA 92521, USA (office). *Telephone:* (951) 827-4108 (office). *Fax:* (951) 827-5685 (office). *E-mail:* keith.griffin@mail.ucr.edu (office); keithdixiegriffin@sbcglobal.net. *Website:* www.economics.ucr.edu/people/griffin.html.

GRIFFITH, Patricia Browning, BA; American novelist and dramatist; *Associate Professor of English, The George Washington University*; b. 9 Nov. 1935, Fort Worth, Tex.; m. William Byron Griffith 1960; one d. *Education:* Baylor Univ. *Career:* currently Assoc. Prof. of English, The George Washington Univ.; fmr Pres. PEN/Faulkner Foundation Award for Fiction 1995–99, Co-Chair. PEN/Faulkner Foundation 2005–07. *Publications:* fiction: The Future is Not What it Used to Be 1970, Tennessee Blue 1981, The World Around Midnight (American Library Asscn Most Notable Book 1992) 1991,

Supporting the Sky 1996; plays: Outside Waco 1984, Safety 1987, Risky Games 1992; contribs to anthologies and periodicals. *Address:* Department of English, The George Washington University, Rome Hall, Room 667, Washington, DC 20052 (office); 1215 Geranium Street, NW, Washington, DC 20012, USA (home). *Telephone:* (202) 994-2135 (office); (202) 829-7780 (home). *E-mail:* pgrif@gwu.edu (office). *Website:* departments.columbian.gwu.edu/english/people/126 (office).

GRIFFITHS, Helen, (Helen Santos); British writer; b. 8 May 1939, London, England. *Publications:* Horse in the Clouds 1957, Wild and Free 1958, Moonlight 1959, Africano 1960, The Wild Heart 1962, The Greyhound 1963, Wild Horse of Santander 1965, Dark Swallows 1965, Leon 1966, Stallion of the Sands 1967, Moshie Cat 1968, Patch 1969, Federico 1970, Russian Blue 1973, Just a Dog 1974, Witch Fear 1975, Pablo 1976, Kershaw Dogs 1978, The Last Summer 1979, Blackface Stallion 1980, Dancing Horses 1981, Hari's Pigeon 1982, Rafa's Dog 1983, Jesus, As Told By Mark 1983, Dog at the Window 1984; as Helen Santos: Caleb's Lamb 1984, If Only 1987, Pepe's Dog 1996. *Honours:* Carnegie Medal Award 1966, Silver Pencil Award for Best Children's Book, Netherlands 1978. *Address:* 9 Ashley Terrace, Bath, BA1 3DP, England. *E-mail:* helensantos@lineone.net.

GRIFFITHS, Jay; British writer; b. Manchester. *Education:* Univ. of Oxford. *Publications:* non-fiction: Pip Pip: A Sideways Look at Time (Barnes and Noble Discover Award for Non-Fiction 2003) 1999, Wild: An Elemental Journey (Orion Book Award) 2007; fiction: Anarchipelago 2007. *Literary Agent:* Jessica Woollard, The Marsh Agency, 50 Albemarle Street, London, W1S 4BD, England. *Telephone:* (20) 7493-4361. *Fax:* (20) 7495-8961. *E-mail:* hannah@marsh-agency.co.uk. *Website:* www.marsh-agency.co.uk; www.jaygriffiths.com.

GRIFFITHS, Paul Anthony, BA, MSc; British music critic and writer; b. 24 Nov. 1947, Bridgend, Glam., Wales. *Education:* Lincoln Coll., Oxford. *Career:* music critic for various journals 1971–; Area Ed. 20th Century Music, New Grove Dictionary of Music and Musicians 1973–76; music critic, The Times 1982–92, New Yorker 1992–96, New York Times 1997–; compiled Mozart pasticcio The Jewel Box for Opera North 1991, Purcell pasticcio Aeneas in Hell 1995. *Publications:* A Concise History of Modern Music 1978, Boulez 1978, A Guide to Electronic Music 1979, Cage 1981, Peter Maxwell Davies 1982, The String Quartet 1983, György Ligeti 1983, Bartók 1984, Olivier Messiaen 1985, New Sounds, New Personalities: British Composers of the 1980s 1985, An Encyclopedia of 20th Century Music 1986, Myself and Marco Polo 1987, The Life of Sir Tristram (novel) 1991, The Jewel Box (opera libretto) 1991, Stravinsky 1992, Modern Music and After 1995, libretti for Tan Dun's opera, Marco Polo 1996, libretti for Elliott Carter's opera, What Next? 1999, Leda 2000, A Concise History of Western Music 2006, Horizons Touched: The Music of ECM (Ed., with Steve Lake) 2007, Let Me Tell You 2008. *E-mail:* paul@disgwylfa.com. *Website:* www.disgwylfa.com.

GRIFFITHS, Trevor, BA; British playwright; b. 4 April 1935, Manchester; s. of Ernest Griffiths and Anne Connor; m. 1st Janice Elaine Stansfield 1961 (died 1977); one s. two d.; m. 2nd Gillian Cliff 1992. *Education:* Univ. of Manchester. *Career:* taught English language and literature 1957–65; Educ. Officer, BBC 1965–72; Dir Saint Oscar 1990, The Gulf Between Us 1992, Who Shall be Happy...? 1995, Food for Ravens 1997. *Film scripts:* Reds (with Warren Beatty, Writers Guild of America Best Original Screenplay 1981) 1981, Fatherland 1986. *Plays include:* Occupations 1970, Apricots and Thermidor 1970, Sam Sam 1972, The Party 1974, Comedians 1976, The Cherry Orchard 1977, Oi for England 1981, Real Dreams 1984, Piano 1990, The Gulf Between Us 1992, Thatcher's Children 1993, Who Shall Be Happy 1994, Camel Station 2001, A New World: A Life of Thomas Paine 2009, Habaccuc Dreams 2011. *Television includes:* All Good Men 1974, Absolute Beginners 1974, Through the Night 1975, Bill Brand 1976, Country 1981, Sons and Lovers 1982, The Last Place on Earth 1985, Hope in the Year Two 1994, Food for Ravens 1997 (Royal Television Soc. Best Regional Programme 1998, Gwyn A. Williams Special Award, BAFTA Wales 1998). *Radio:* These Are The Times: A Life of Thomas Paine (BBC Radio) 2008. *Publications:* Occupations, Sam Sam 1972, The Party 1974, Comedians 1976, All Good Men, Absolute Beginners, Through the Night, Such Impossibilities, Thermidor and Apricots 1977, Deeds (co-author), The Cherry Orchard (trans.) 1978, Country 1981, Oi for England, Sons and Lovers (TV version) 1982, Judgement Over the Dead 1986, Fatherland, Real Dreams 1987, Collected Plays for TV 1988, Piano 1990, The Gulf Between Us 1992, Hope in the Year Two, Thatcher's Children 1994, Plays One (Collected Stage Plays) 1996, Food for Ravens 1998, These Are The Times 2005, Theatre Plays One 2007, Theatre Plays Two 2007, Bill Brand 2010. *Honours:* BAFTA Writer's Award 1981. *Literary Agent:* c/o United Agents, 12–26 Lexington Street, London, W1F 0LE, England. *Telephone:* (20) 3214-0800. *Fax:* (20) 3214-0801. *E-mail:* info@unitedagents.co.uk. *Website:* www.unitedagents.co.uk.

GRIMWOOD, Jonathan (Jon) David Giles Courtenay; British writer and journalist; b. Valetta, Malta; m. 1st (divorced); one s.; m. 2nd Sam Baker. *Career:* fmr ed. and publr; journalist, contrib. to newspapers and magazines, including Guardian, Times, Telegraph, Independent, Esquire, SFX, Focus. *Publications:* novels: neoAddix 1997, Lucifer's Dragon 1998, reMix 1999, redRobe 2000, Pashazade (Arabesk series Vol. I) 2001, Effendi (Arabesk series Vol. II) 2002, Felaheen (Arabesk series Vol. III) (British Science Fiction Asscn (BSFA) Award for Best Novel) 2003, Stamping Butterflies 2004, 9Tail Fox 2005, End of the World Blues (BSFA Award for Best Novel) 2006, Arabesk 2007, The Fallen Blade 2011, The Outcast Blade 2012; other: Mrs T's Bedside Book 1985, Royal Family Bedside Book 1986, Photohistory of the 20th Century 1986, Election Bedside Book 1987, assorted short fiction in Nature, New Scientist and others. *Literary Agent:* c/o Mic Cheetham Agency, 50 Albemarle Street, London, W1S 4BD, England. *E-mail:* jon@j-cg.co.uk (office). *Website:* www.j-cg.co.uk.

GRISEZ, Germain, MA, PhL, PhD; American academic; *Professor Emeritus of Christian Ethics, Mount Saint Mary's University;* b. 30 Sept. 1929, University Heights, Ohio; m. Jeannette Selby 1951 (deceased); four c.; m. Mariazinha Rozario 2006. *Education:* John Carroll Univ., Univ. Heights, Ohio, Dominican Coll. of St Thomas Aquinas, River Forest, Ill. and Univ. of Chicago. *Career:* Asst Prof. to Prof., Georgetown Univ. Washington, DC 1957–72; part-time Lecturer in Medieval Philosophy, Univ. of Virginia, Charlottesville 1961–62; Special Asst to HE Cardinal O'Boyle, Archbishop of Washington 1968–69; consultant (part-time) Archdiocese of Washington 1969–72; Prof. of Philosophy, Campion Coll. Univ. of Regina, Canada 1972–79; Most Rev. Harry J. Flynn Prof. of Christian Ethics, Mount St Mary's Univ., Emmitsburg, Md 1979–2009, Prof. Emer. 2009–; mem. American Catholic Philosophical Asscn. *Publications:* Contraception and the Natural Law 1964, Abortion: The Myths, the Realities and the Arguments 1970, Beyond the New Morality (with Russell Shaw) 1974, Free Choice (with others) 1976, Life and Death with Liberty Justice (with Joseph M. Boyle, Jr) 1979, The Way of the Lord Jesus, Vol. I, Christian Moral Principles (with others) 1983, Vol. II, Living a Christian Life (with others) 1993, Vol. III, Difficult Moral Questions (with others) 1997, Nuclear Deterrence, Morality and Realism (with J. Finnis and Joseph M. Boyle) 1987, Fulfilment in Christ (with Russell Shaw) 1991, Personal Vocation: God Calls Everyone by Name (with Russell Shaw) 2003, God: A Philosophical Preface to Faith 2005; numerous articles in learned journals. *Honours:* Hon. DD (Mount St Mary's, Emmitsburg) 2009; Pro ecclesia et pontifice Medal 1972; Cardinal Wright Award for service to the Church 1983 and other awards. *Address:* Mount Saint Mary's University, 16300 Old Emmitsburg Road, Emmitsburg, MD 21727-7799, USA (office). *Telephone:* (301) 447-5771 (office). *E-mail:* grisez@msmary.edu (office). *Website:* www.twotlj.org (office).

GRISHAM, John, BS, JD; American writer and lawyer; b. 8 Feb. 1955, Jonesboro, AR; m. Renée Jones; one s. one d. *Education:* Mississippi State Univ., Univ. of Mississippi, law school. *Career:* called to the Bar, Miss. 1981; attorney in Southaven, Miss. 1981–90; mem. Miss. House of Reps 1984–90. *Film screenplay:* The Gingerbread Man 1998. *Publications:* A Time to Kill 1989, The Firm 1991, The Pelican Brief 1992, The Client 1993, The Chamber 1994, The Rainmaker 1995, The Runaway Jury 1996, The Partner 1997, The Street Lawyer 1998, The Testament 1999, The Brethren 2000, A Painted House 2001, Skipping Christmas 2001, The Summons 2002, The King of Torts 2003, Bleachers 2003, The Last Juror 2004, The Broker 2005, The Innocent Man (non-fiction) 2006, Playing for Pizza 2007, The Appeal 2008, The Associate 2009, Ford County 2009, Theodore Boone: Kid Lawyer 2010, The Confession 2010, The Litigators 2011, Calico Joe 2012. *Honours:* Lifetime Achievement Award, British Book Awards 2007. *Address:* c/o Doubleday & Co. Inc., 1540 Broadway, New York, NY 10036, USA (office). *Website:* www.jgrisham.com.

GROENEWOLD, Sabine, DPhil; German publishing executive; b. 18 Oct. 1940, Hamburg; m. Kurt Groenewold. *Education:* Univs of Hamburg, Tübingen and Salamanca, Spain. *Career:* Asst Prof., later Assoc. Prof., Univs of New York, Hamburg, Kassel and Berlin 1969–88; Publr and Ed. Europäische Verlagsanstalt, Rotbuch Verlag, Hamburg 1989–; Founder Sabine Groenewold Verlage KG. *Publications:* numerous articles on Spanish and Latin-American literature 1972–. *Address:* Sabine Groenewold Verlage KG, Bei den Muhren 70, 20457 Hamburg, Germany (office). *Telephone:* (40) 4501940 (office). *Fax:* (40) 45019450 (office). *E-mail:* info@sabine-groenewold-verlage.de (office). *Website:* www.sabine-groenewold-verlage.de (office).

GROSS, Claudia; German novelist; b. 26 July 1956, Arolsen, Hesse. *Publications include:* Scholarium 2002. *Address:* c/o The Toby Press, PO Box 8531, New Milford, CT 06776-8531, USA.

GROSS, Philip John, BA; British writer, poet and creative writing teacher; b. 27 Feb. 1952, Delabole, England. *Education:* Univ. of Sussex, Polytechnic of North London. *Career:* numerous residencies and teaching posts. *Stage productions:* Rising Star (play) 1996, Snail Dreaming (opera, with composer Glyn Evans) 1997, Dancing the Knife (dance drama, with Medea Mahdavi) 2002. *Publications:* for children: Manifold Manor 1989, The Song of Gail and Fludd 1991, The All-Nite Café (Signal Award for Children's Poetry 1994) 1993, Plex 1994, The Wind Gate 1995, Scratch City (poems) 1996, Transformer 1996, Psylicon Beach 1998, Facetaker 1999, Going for Stone 2002, Marginaliens 2003, The Lastling 2003, The Storm Garden 2006; poetry: Familiars 1983, The Ice Factory 1984, Cat's Whisker 1987, The Air Mines of Mistila (with Sylvia Kantaris) 1988, The Son of the Duke of Nowhere 1991, I.D. 1994, A Cast of Stones 1996, The Wasting Game 1998, Changes of Address: Poems 1980–98 2001, Mappa Mundi 2003, The Egg of Zero 2006, I Spy Pinhole Eye (with Simon Denison) (Wales Book of the Year English language prize 2010) 2009, The Water Table (T.S. Eliot Prize for Poetry 2010) 2009. *Honours:* Eric Gregory Award 1981, Arts Council Bursary for Writing for Young People 1990. *E-mail:* contact@philipgross.co.uk (office). *Website:* www.philipgross.co.uk.

GROSSER, Alfred, Agrégé, Docteur d'Etat ès Lettres; French academic, writer and journalist; *Professor Emeritus, Institut d'Études Politiques;* b. 1 Feb. 1925,

Frankfurt, Germany; s. of the late Paul Grosser and Lily Grosser (née Rosenthal); m. Anne-Marie Jourcin 1959; four s. *Education:* Univs of Aix en Provence and Paris. *Career:* Asst Dir UNESCO Office in Germany 1950–51; Asst Prof., Univ. of Paris 1951–55; Lecturer, later Prof., Inst. d'études politiques 1954, Prof. Emer. 1992–; Dir Studies and Research, Fondation nat. des Sciences politiques 1956–92; with Ecole des hautes études commerciales 1961–66, 1986–88, with Ecole Polytechnique 1974–95; Visiting Prof., Bologna Center, Johns Hopkins Univ. 1955–69, Stanford Univ. 1964–67; political columnist, La Croix 1955–65, 1984–, Le Monde 1965–94, Ouest-France 1973–, L'Expansion 1979–89; Pres. Centre d'information et de recherche sur l'Allemagne contemporaine 1982–, Eurocréation 1986–92 (Hon. Pres. 1992–); Vice-Pres. Int. Political Science Asscn 1970–73; mem. Bd L'Express 1998–2003. *Publications include:* L'Allemagne de l'Occident 1953, La démocratie de Bonn 1958, Hitler, la presse et la naissance d'une dictature 1959, La Quatrième Republique et sa politique extérieure 1961, La politique extérieure de la Ve République 1965, Au nom de quoi? Fondements d'une morale politique 1969, L'Allemagne de notre temps 1970, les Occidentaux: Les pays d'Europe et les Etats Unis depuis la guerre 1978, Affaires extérieures: la politique de la France 1944–84, 1984 (updated 1989), L'Allemagne en Occident 1985, Mit Deutschen streiten 1987, Vernunft und Gewalt. Die französische Revolution und das deutsche Grundgesetz heute 1989, Le crime et la mémoire 1989 (revised 1991), Mein Deutschland 1993, Les identités difficiles 1996, Une Vie de Français (memoirs) 1997, Deutschland in Europa 1998, Les fruits de leur arbre: regard athée sur les Chrétiens 2001, L'Allemagne de Berlin 2002, La France, semblable et differente 2005, Die Früchte ihres Baumes 2005. *Honours:* Grosses Verdienstkreuz mit Stern 1995 und Schulterband 2003; Grand Officier, Légion d'honneur 2001; Dr hc (Aston, Birmingham, UK) 2001, (European Univ. of Humanities, Minsk, Belarus) 2001; Peace Prize, Union of German Publrs 1975, Grand Prix, Acad. des Sciences Morales et Politiques 1998. *Address:* 8 rue Dupleix, 75015 Paris, France (home). *Telephone:* 1-43-06-41-82 (home). *E-mail:* grosser.alfred@wanadoo.fr (home).

GROSSKURTH, Phyllis, OC, BA, MA, PhD; Canadian academic and writer; *Professor Emeritus of English, University of Toronto*; b. 16 March 1924, Toronto; m. 1st Robert A. Grosskurth; two s. one d.; m. 2nd Mavor Moore 1968 (divorced 1980); m. 3rd Robert McMullan 1986. *Education:* Univ. of Toronto, Univ. of Ottawa, Univ. of London. *Career:* Lecturer, Carleton Univ. 1964–65; Prof. of English, Univ. of Toronto 1965–87, Faculty, Humanities and Psychoanalysis Programme 1987–95, currently Prof. Emer.; mem. PEN. *Publications:* John Addington Symonds: A Biography (Gov.-Gen.'s Award for Non-Fiction 1965) 1964, Notes on Browning's Works 1967, Leslie Stephen 1968, Gabrielle Roy 1969, Havelock Ellis: A Biography 1980, The Memoirs of John Addington Symonds (ed.) 1984, Melanie Klein: Her World and Her Work 1986, Margaret Mead: A Life of Controversy 1988, The Secret Ring: Freud's Inner Circle and the Politics of Psychoanalysis 1991, Byron: The Flawed Angel 1997, Elusive Subject ...A Biographer's Life 1999; contribs to periodicals. *Honours:* Order of Ontario 2002; Dr hc (Trinity Coll., Univ. of Toronto) 1992, (St Mary's Univ., Halifax) 2002; Univ. of British Columbia Award for Biography 1965, Guggenheim Fellowships 1977–78, 1983, Rockefeller Foundation Fellowship 1982, Canada Council Arts Award 1989–90. *Address:* Department of English, University of Toronto, St. George Campus, 170 St. George Street, Toronto, ON M5R 2M8, Canada (office). *E-mail:* phyllis.grosskurth@utoronto.ca (office). *Website:* www.english.utoronto.ca (office).

GROSSMAN, David, BA; Israeli writer; b. 25 Jan. 1954, Jerusalem; m. Michal Grossman; two s. (one deceased) one d. *Education:* Hebrew Univ., Jerusalem. *Publications:* Hiyukh ha-gedi (trans. as The Smile of the Lamb) 1983, 'Ayen 'erekh–ahavah (trans. as See Under: Love) 1986, Ha-Zeman ha-tsahov (non-fiction, trans. as The Yellow Wind) 1987, Gan Riki: Mahazeh bi-shete ma'arakhot (play, trans. as Rikki's Kindergarten) 1988, Sefer hakikduk hapnimi (trans. as The Book of Intimate Grammar) 1991, Hanochachim hanifkadim (non-fiction, trans. as Sleeping on a Wire: Conversations with Palestinians in Israel) 1992, The Zigzag Kid (in trans.) (Premio Mondelo, Premio Grinzane), Duel (in trans.), Be My Knife (in trans.) 2002, Someone to Run With (in trans.) 2003, Death as a Way of Life: Dispatches from Jerusalem (non-fiction, in trans.) 2003, Her Body Knows (novel, in trans.), Lovers and Strangers (novel, in trans.) 2005, Dvash Arayiot (trans. as Lion's Honey: The Myth of Samson) 2005, Writing in the Dark (essays in trans.) 2009, To the End of the Land (novel, in trans.) 2010; also short stories, children's books, contribs to periodicals. *Honours:* Chevalier, Ordre des Artes et Lettres; Children's Literature Prize, Ministry of Educ. 1983, Prime Minister's Hebrew Literature Prize 1984, Israeli Publishers' Asscn Prize for Best Novel 1985, Vallombrosa Prize (Italy) 1989, Nelly Sachs Prize (Germany) 1992, Prix Eliette von Karajan (Austria), Premio Grinzane (Italy), Premio Mondelo (Italy), Vittorio de Sica Prize (Italy), Marsh Award for Children's Literature in Translation (UK), Juliet Club Prize (Italy), Buxtehuder Bulle (Germany), Sapir Prize (Israel), Italian Critics Prize (Italy), Nelly Sachs Prize (Germany), Mane Sperber Prize (Austria), Bernstein Prize (Israel), Bialik Prize (Israel), Emet Prize (Israel) 2007. *Literary Agent:* c/o Managing Editor, The Deborah Harris Agency, 9 Yael Street, Jerusalem 93502, Israel. *Telephone:* (2) 6722145; (2) 6722143. *Fax:* (2) 6725797. *E-mail:* iaustern@netvision.net.il.

GROULT, Benoîte Marie Rose, LèsL; French writer and journalist; b. 31 Jan. 1920, Paris; d. of André Groult and Nicole Groult (née Poiret); m. 1st Pierre Heuyer 1944 (died 1945); m. 2nd Georges de Caunes 1946; two d.; m. 3rd Paul Guimard 1951; one d. *Education:* Univ. of Paris-Sorbonne. *Career:* fmr teacher of Latin; journalist on Elle and Marie-Claire magazines; co-f. (with Claude Servan-Schreiber) F Magazine 1978; currently writer and freelance journalist; Pres. Comm. pour la Féminisation des noms de métiers 1985–; mem. Jury Prix Fémina 1979–. *Publications include:* La part des choses (Prix de l' Acad. de Bretagne) 1972, Ainsi soit-elle 1975, Le féminisme au masculin 1977, Les vaissaux du cœur (English title Salt on our Skin 1992, translated also to German) 1989, Olympe de Gouges (biog.), Pauline Roland (biog.), Histoire d'une evasion (autobiog.) 1998; With sister (Flora Groult): Journal à quatre mains (English title Double-Handed Diary) 1958, Le féminin pluriel (English title Feminine Plural) 1961, Il était deux fois, La touche étoile 2006, Mon Evasion (autobiog.) 2008. *Honours:* Officière de la Légion d'Honneur 1995, Commandeuse de l'Ordre Nat. du Mérite; Prix Bretagne 1975. *Address:* 54 rue de Bourgogne, 75007 Paris (office); 3 rue de la Croix, 83400 Hyères, France (home). *Telephone:* 1-47-05-33-30 (office); 4-94-65-19-53 (home). *Fax:* 4-94-65-81-95 (home).

GRUFFYDD, Peter, BA; British poet, writer, translator and actor; b. 12 April 1935, Liverpool, England; m. 1st; one s. one d.; m. 2nd Susan Soar 1974; two s. *Education:* Univ. of Wales, Bangor, Goethe Inst., Munich, Univ. of Bristol. *Career:* mem. Equity, PEN International (Founder-mem. Welsh Br. 1993), Yr Academi Gymraeg; fmr mem. Welsh Union of Writers. *Radio:* The Cuckoo (verse drama for four voices) (BBC Radio Wales) 1968, Wordsworth (poems) (BBC Radio 4) 2009. *Publications:* Triad 1963, Welsh Voices 1967, Poems 1969, The Lilting House 1970, Poems 1972, The Shivering Seed 1972, On Censorship 1985, Environmental Teletex 1989, Damned Braces 1993, Birds 2004, Corgi Series (Gwasg Carreg Gwalch) 2006–09, Poetry 1900-2000 (ed Meic Stephens) 2008; contribs to anthologies and periodicals. *Honours:* Eric Gregory Trust 1963, Second Prize, Young Poets Competition, Welsh Arts Council, 1969, First Prizes 1984, 1994, Third Prizes 1986, 1991, 1993, Aberystwyth Open Poetry Competitions, Duncan Lawrie Prize, Arvon-Observer Int. Poetry Competition 1994, Third Prize, Housman Soc. Open Poetry Competition 1998. *Address:* 10 Bower Ashton Terrace, Bristol, BS3 2LE, England (office).

GRUMBACH, Doris Isaac, AB, MA; American author, critic and fmr academic; b. 12 July 1918, New York; m. Leonard Grumbach 1941 (divorced 1972); four d. *Education:* Washington Square Coll., Cornell Univ. *Career:* Assoc. Ed., Architectural Forum 1942–43; Teacher of English, Albany Acad. for Girls, New York 1952–55; Instructor, Coll. of Saint Rose, Albany 1955–58, Asst Prof. 1958–60, Assoc. Prof. 1960–69, Prof. of English 1969–73; Visiting Univ. Fellow, Empire State Coll. 1972–73; Literary Ed., New Republic 1973–75; Adjunct Prof. of English, Univ. of Maryland 1974–75; Prof. of American Literature, American Univ., Washington, DC 1975–85; Columnist and reviewer for various publications, radio, and television; mem. PEN. *Publications:* The Spoil of the Flowers 1962, The Short Throat, the Tender Mouth 1964, The Company She Kept (biog. of Mary McCarthy) 1967, Chamber Music 1979, The Missing Person 1981, The Ladies 1984, The Magician's Girl 1987, Coming Into the End Zone 1992, Extra Innings: A Memoir 1993, Fifty Days of Solitude 1994, The Book of Knowledge: A Novel 1995, The Presence of Absence 1998, The Pleasure of Their Company 2000; contribs to books and periodicals.

GRÜNBAUM, Adolf, BA, MS, PhD; American academic and writer; *Chairman, Center for Philosophy of Science*; b. 15 May 1923, Cologne, Germany; m. Thelma Braverman 1949; one d. *Education:* Wesleyan and Yale Univs. *Career:* Faculty, Lehigh Univ. 1950–55, Prof. of Philosophy 1955–56, Selfridge Prof. of Philosophy 1956–60; Visiting Research Prof., Minnesota Center for the Philosophy of Science 1956, 1959; Andrew Mellon Prof. of Philosophy of Science, Univ. of Pittsburgh 1960–, Dir 1960–78, later Chair. Center for Philosophy of Science 1978–, Research Prof. of Psychiatry 1979–, Primary Research Prof., Dept of History and Philosophy of Science 2006–; Werner Heisenberg Lecturer, Bavarian Acad. of Sciences 1985; Gifford Lecturer, Univ. of St Andrews 1985; Visiting Mellon Prof., Calif. Inst. of Tech. 1990; Leibniz Lecturer, Univ. of Hannover 2003; Pres. Div. of Logic, Methodology and Philosophy of Science, Int. Union for History and Philosophy of Science 2004–05, Union Pres. 2006–07; mem. American Acad. of Arts and Sciences, American Philosophical Asscn (Pres. Eastern Div. 1982–83), Acad. Int. de Philosophie des Sciences, Philosophy of Science Asscn (Pres. 1965–67, 1968–70), AAAS (Vice-Pres. 1963). *Publications:* Philosophical Problems of Space and Time 1963 (also Russian edn), Modern Science and Zeno's Paradoxes, second edn 1968, Geometry and Chronometry in Philosophical Perspective 1968, The Foundations of Psychoanalysis: A Philosophical Critique 1984 (also several foreign language edns), Psicoanalisi: Obiezioni e Risposte 1988, Validation in the Clinical Theory of Psychoanalysis 1993, La Psychanalyse à l'Épreuve 1993; more than 400 contribs to books and scholarly journals. *Honours:* Dr hc (Konstanz, Germany) 1995; J. Walker Tomb Prize, Princeton Univ. 1958, Alumni Honour Citation, Wesleyan Univ. 1959, Festschriften published in his honour 1983, 1993, 2009, Sr US Scientist Prize, Alexander von Humboldt Foundation 1985, Fregene Prize for Science, Italian Parliament 1989, Master Scholar and Prof. Award, Univ. of Pittsburgh 1989, Wilbur Lucius Cross Medal, Yale Univ. 1990, Laureate, Int. Acad. of Humanism. *Address:* 7141 Roycrest Place, Pittsburgh, PA 15208-2737, USA (home). *Telephone:* (412) 241-7036 (home); (412) 624-5738 (office). *Fax:* (412) 371-6692 (home); (412) 648-1068 (office). *E-mail:* grunbaum@pitt.edu (office). *Website:* grunbaum.pitt.edu (office).

GRÜNBEIN, Durs; German poet and writer; b. 9 Oct. 1962, Dresden; m.; one d. *Publications:* Grauzone morgens (poems) 1988, Schädelbasislektion (poems) 1991, Den teuren Toten (poems) 1994, Falten und Fallen (poems)

(Peter-Huchel-Preis 1995) 1994, Galilei vermißt Dantes Hölle und bleibt an den Maßen hängen (essays) 1996, Nach den Satiren (poems) 1999, Das erste Jahr (essays) 2001, Erklärte Nacht (poems) 2002, Warum schriftlos leben (essays) 2003, Vom Schnee oder Descartes in Deutschland (poem) 2003, Der Misanthrop auf Capri (poems) 2005, Porzellan (poems) 2005, Antike Dispositionen (essays) 2005, Gedicht und Geheimnis - Aufsätze 1990–2006 (essays) 2007, Strophen für übermorgen (poems) 2007, Liebesgedichte (poems) 2008, Lob des Taifuns (poems) 2008, Der cartesische Taucher - Drei Meditationen (essays) 2008, Die Bars von Atlantis (essays) 2009. *Honours:* Nicolas-Born-Preis 1993, Georg-Büchner-Preis, Darmstadt 1995, Literaturpreis der Stadt Marburg 2000, Premio Nonino, Salzburg 2000, Friedrich-Nietzsche-Literaturpreis des Landes Sachsen-Anhalt 2004, Hölderlin-Preis der Stadt Bad Homburg 2005, Berliner Literaturpreis der Preußischen Seehandlung 2006, Samuel Bogumil Linde Preis 2008. *Address:* c/o Suhrkamp Verlag, Postfach 101945, 60019 Frankfurt am Main, Germany (office). *E-mail:* info@suhrkamp.de (office). *Website:* www.suhrkamp.de (office).

GRUNBERG, Arnon; Dutch writer; b. (Arnon Yasha Yves), 22 Feb. 1971, Amsterdam. *Education:* Vossius Gymnasium. *Television:* anchor, RAM 2004–05. *Films include:* de Kut van Maria 1989. *Publications:* Blauwe Maandagen (novel, trans. as Blue Mondays) (Anton Wachter-prijs) 1994, Figuranten 1997, De troost van de slapstick (essays) 1998, Het veertiende kippetje 1998, Liefde is business 1999, Fantoompijn (novel, trans. as Phantom Pain) (AKO-Literatuurprijs) 2000, The Asylum Seeker (Bordewijk Prestigious Prize) 2003, Grunberg The Bible 2005, Tirza 2006, Amuse-Bouche (short stories, in trans.) 2008, Chambermaids and Soldiers 2009. *Honours:* Constantijn Huygens Prize 2009. *Address:* c/o Nijgh & Van Ditmar, Singel 262, Amsterdam, Netherlands. *E-mail:* info@grunberg.nl. *Website:* www.grunberg.nl.

GRUNENBERG, Nina; German journalist; b. 7 Oct. 1936, Dresden; d. of Valentin and Dorothea Grunenberg; m. Reimar Lüst. *Career:* joined Die Zeit newspaper 1969, Head, Dept of Knowledge 1992–94, Deputy Ed. 1987–95; Chief Reporter 1995–2001; mem. Science Council 2000–09. *Publications:* Journalisten, Reportagen-Sammlung 1967, Schweden-Report (jtly) 1973, Japan-Report (jtly) 1981, Reise ins andere Deutschland (jtly) 1986, Die Chefs 1990, Wo die Macht Spielt 2000, Die Wundertäter 2006. *Honours:* Theodor-Wolff-Preis 1973, 2009, Quandt-Medienpreis 1990, Herbert Quandt Media Prize 1990. *Address:* c/o Random House Germany, Neumarkter Strasse 28, 81673 Munich, Germany.

GRUSHIN, Olga; American (b. Russian) novelist and essayist; b. (Olga Borisovna Grushina), 27 June 1971, Moscow; d. of Boris Grushin and Natalia Kartseva; m.; one s., one d. *Education:* Pushkin Museum of Fine Arts, Moscow State Univ., Emory Univ., Atlanta. *Career:* fmr personal interpreter for Pres. Jimmy Carter 1990; Trans. at the World Bank, law firm research analyst, Washington, DC; Ed., Dumbarton Oaks Research Library and Collection, Harvard Univ. 1996–2001; full-time writer 2001–. *Publications:* novels: The Dream Life of Sukhanov 2006, The Line (UK version as The Concert Ticket) 2010; short stories: Spiders Did It (in Happy) 1998, The Stamp Fever (in Green Mountains Review) 1998, At Thirteen Minutes to Three (in artisan: a journal of craft) 1999, The Night before Christmas (in Art Times) 2000, And the Third Glass (in Confrontation) 2001, The Last Offering (in Artful Dodge) 2002, Seven Variations of the Theme of Untied Shoelaces (in The Massachusetts Review) 2002, The Daughter of Kadmos (in Partisan Review) 2002, Exile (in Granta) 2007; also essays and reviews in The New York Times, The Moscow Times, Vogue (UK), Michigan Quarterly Review, Daily Mail, Farafina, Granta. *Honours:* Young Lions Fiction Award 2007, Best Young American Novelist, Granta Magazine. *Literary Agent:* c/o Warren Frazier, John Hawkins and Associates, 71 West 23rd Street, Suite 1600, New York, NY 10010, USA. *Telephone:* (212) 807-7040. *E-mail:* frazier@jhalit.com. *Website:* jhalit.com. *Address:* c/o Penguin Publicity, 375 Hudson Street, New York, NY 10014, USA (office). *E-mail:* olga@olgagrushin.com (office). *Website:* www.olgagrushin.com.

GRYZUNOV, Sergey Petrovich; Russian academic and fmr journalist; *Professor, Department of Journalism, Moscow State Institute for International Relations*; b. 23 July 1949, Kuybyshev; m.; one s. *Education:* Moscow State Univ., Acad. of Public Sciences, Cen. Communist Party Cttee. *Career:* worked for Ria-Novosti 1974–94, fmr ed. Novosti, then reviewer, then Deputy Head of Bureau, Yugoslavia; Deputy Chair. Cttee on Press April–Sept. 1994, Chair. 1994–95; mem. Pres. Yeltsin's Election Campaign March 1996; Vice-Pres. ICN Pharmaceutical Corpn 1996–2001; Vice-Pres. Moscow News Publrs 2001–03, Russian Asscn of Ind. Publishers 2004–05; fmr Deputy Gen. Dir Rumelco OOO; fmr Chair. Communications and Public Relations Cttee Novolipetsk Steel (NLMK); Ed.-in-Chief and Dir Gen. Novoe Russkoe Slovo Publishing House; Prof., Dept of Journalism, Moscow State Inst. for Int. Relations 2009–. *Address:* Department of Journalism, Moscow State Institute for International Relations, 119454 Moscow, Prospekt Vernadskogo, 76, Russia (office). *Telephone:* (495) 434-90-66 (office). *Website:* english.mgimo.ru (office).

GSTEIGER, Fredy, MBS; Swiss journalist and editor; *Diplomatic Correspondent, Schweizer Radio und Fernsehen (SRF)*; b. 1962, Berne. *Education:* Univ. of St Gallen, Switzerland, Univ. of Lyons, France and Univ. of Québec, Canada. *Career:* fmr Econ. Journalist, Der Bunde, Berne; Foreign Ed., St Galler Tagblatt 1988–89; Middle East Ed., Die Zeit, Hamburg, Germany 1989–93, Paris Corresp. 1997–2001; Ed.-in-Chief Die Weltwoche, Zürich 1997–2001; Diplomatic Corresp., Schweizer Radio und Fernsehen (SRF) (formed after merger of Schweizer Radio DRS and and Schweizer Fernsehen 2011) 2002–; Bd mem. International Press Inst. *Publication:* Blocher: Ein unschweizerisches Phänomen 2002. *Address:* Schweizer Radio und Fernsehen, Kundendienst Fernsehstrasse 1-4, 8052 Zürich, Switzerland (office). *Telephone:* 443661111 (office). *Fax:* 443055088 (office). *E-mail:* srf@srf.ch (office). *Website:* www.srf.ch (office).

GU, Hua; Chinese novelist; b. (Luo Hongyu), 20 June 1942, Jiahe Co., Hunan. *Education:* Chenzhou Agricultural School, Coll. for Young Writers. *Career:* research worker, Chenzhou Agricultural Research Inst. 1961–75; mem. writing staff, Chenzhou Song and Dance Ensemble 1975–79; mem. Writers' Asscn of Hunan Prov. 1981–87. *Publications include:* A Small Town Called Hibiscus 1983, Pagoda Ridge 1985, Virgin Widows 1996, A Log Cabin Overgrown with Creepers, The Prison for the Scholars, De kuise vrouw. *Honours:* Hon. Fellow, International Writing Program, Univ. of Iowa 1987.

GUARDIA DE ALFARO, Gloria, MA; Panamanian writer and journalist; b. 12 March 1940, San Cristóbal, Venezuela; d. of Carlos A. Guardia-Jaén and Olga Zeledón de Guardia; m. Ricardo A. Alfaro-Arosemena 1968; one d. *Education:* Colegio de las Esclavas del Sagrado Corazón (Panamá), Roycemore School for Girls (Evanston, IL), Vassar Coll. (NY), Columbia Univ. (NY, USA) and Univ. Complutense de Madrid (Spain). *Career:* began writing 1961; journalist Agencia Latinoamericana 1975–90; Columnist on La Prensa, Panamá 1980–83, El Panamá-América 1990; mem. Panamanian Acad. of Letters 1985, Librarian and mem. Bd of Dirs 1990; apptd mem. Editorial Bd Panorama Católico 1988, Editora Mariano Arosemena 1990; Hon. mem. Real Academia Española 1989; Hon. Scholarship Vassar Coll. 1958–1963; numerous awards including Honor al Mérito (Soc. of Spanish and Latin-American Writers) 1961, Premio Nacional Ricardo Miró 1966, Cen. American Book Award 1976. *Publications include:* novels: El último juego 1977, Libertad En Llamas 2001; Short stories: Otra vez Bach 1983, Cartas Apocrifas 1990, Hora Santa 1996; Essays: Estudios sobre el pensamiento poético de Pablo Antonio Cuadra 1971, La búsqueda del rostro 1983, El último juego y Lobos al anochecer 2006; editor: Palabras preliminares, Obras completas de María Olimpia de Obaldía 1976; numerous monographs. *Address:* CP 101830, Zona 10, Santa Fe de Bogotá; Calle 87, 11A –84, Santa Fe de Bogotá, Colombia (home). *Telephone:* (1) 256-1540 (home). *Fax:* (1) 218-4236.

GUARE, John, AB, MFA; American dramatist; b. 5 Feb. 1938, New York, NY; m. Adele Chatfield-Taylor 1981. *Education:* Georgetown Univ., Yale Univ. *Career:* Eugene O'Neill Theater Center, Waterford, Conn. 1965–68; resident playwright, New York Shakespeare Festival 1976; Seminar-in-Writing Fellow, Yale Univ. 1977–78, Adjunct Prof. 1978–81, 2004–10; Co-Ed. Lincoln Center New Theatre Review 1977–; Visiting Artist, Harvard Univ. 1990–91; Fellow, Juilliard School, New York 1993–94; Signature Theater 1998–99; Lecturer, Princeton Univ. 2010; judge, Yale Drama Series Prize 2011–12; mem. American Acad. of Arts and Letters, Dramatists Guild. *Publications:* plays: Theatre Girl 1959, The Toadstool Boy 1960, The Golden Cherub 1962, Did You Write My Name in the Snow? 1962, To Wally Pantoni, We Leave a Credenza 1964, The Loveliest Afternoon of the Year 1966, Something I'll Tell You Tuesday 1966, Muzeeka 1967, Cop-Out 1968, A Play by Brecht 1969, Home Fires 1969, Kissing Sweet 1969, The House of Blue Leaves 1971, as a musical 1986, Two Gentlemen of Verona 1971, A Day for Surprises 1971, Un Pape a New York 1972, Marco Polo Sings a Solo 1973, Optimism, or the Adventures of Candide 1973, Rich and Famous 1974, Landscape of the Body 1977, Take a Dream 1978, Bosoms and Neglect 1979, In Fireworks Lie Secret Codes 1981, Lydie Breeze 1982, Gardenia 1982, Stay a While 1984, Women and Water 1984, Gluttony 1985, The Talking Dog 1985, Moon Over Miami 1989, revised version as Moon Under Miami 1995, Six Degrees of Separation 1990, Four Baboons Adoring the Sun 1992, Chuck Close 1995, The War Against the Kitchen Sink (vol. of plays) 1996, Lake Hollywood 1999, Chaucer in Rome 2001, A Few Stout Individuals 2002, Blue Monologue 2007, A Free Man of Color (Pulitzer Prize 2011) 2010. *Honours:* Obie Awards 1968, 1971, 1990, New York Drama Critics Circle Awards 1969, 1971, 1972, 1990, Drama Desk Awards 1972, Tony Awards 1972, 1986, Joseph Jefferson Award 1977, Award of Merit, American Acad. of Arts and Letters 1981, Los Angeles Film Critics Award 1981, Nat. Soc. of Film Critics Circle Award 1981, New York Film Critics Award 1981, Venice Film Festival Grand Prize 1981, Olivier Best Play Award 1993, New York State Gov.'s Award 1996, PEN Master Dramatist Award 2003, American Acad. of Arts and Letters Gold Medal for Drama 2004, Greenfield Prize 2011. *Literary Agent:* c/o ICM, 730 Fifth Avenue, New York, NY 10019, USA. *Telephone:* (212) 556-5600. *Fax:* (212) 556-5677. *Website:* www.icmtalent.com.

GUARNIERI, Patrizia, MA, PhD; Italian historian and academic; *Associate Professor of Contemporary History, Department of Psychology, University of Florence*; b. 16 June 1954, Florence; one s. one d. *Education:* Univ. of Florence, Univ. of Urbino. *Career:* Lecturer, Univ. of Florence 1978–81, Stanford Univ. Programme in Italy 1982–93; Prof., History of Science, Univ. of Trieste 1988–91; Assoc. Prof. of Contemporary History, Dept of Psychology, Univ. of Florence 2004–; fmr Man. Ed. Medicina & Storia; mem. European Asscn of the History of Psychiatry; apptd CNR-NATO Fellow, Wellcome Centre of the History of Medicine 1983; apptd Jean Monnet Fellow, European Univ. Inst., Fiesole 1989. *Publications:* Introduzione a James 1985, Individualita' Difformi 1986, L'Ammazzabambini 1988, Between Soma and Psyche 1988, Theatre and Laboratory 1988, The Psyche in Trance 1990, Carta Penna e Psiche 1990, La Storia della Psichiatria 1991, Per Una Storia delle Scienze del Bambino 1996, Dangerous Girls, Family Secrets and Incest Law in Italy 1998, Children and

Health in Europe 1750–2000 (ed.) 2004, On Knowledge and Belief: Maternity Births and Abortions Between Experiences and Bioethics (ed.) 2009; contrib. to Kos, Physis, Nuncius, Belfagor, Medicina & Storia. *Address:* Department of Psychology, University of Florence, Via di San Salvi, 12 Complex of San Salvi, Hall 26, 50135 Florence, Italy (office). *Telephone:* 556237835 (office). *Fax:* 556236047 (office). *E-mail:* patrizia.guarnieri@unifi.it (office). *Website:* www.dpsico.unifi.it (office).

GUÐMUNDSSON, Einar Már, BA; Icelandic writer and poet; b. 18 Sept. 1954, Reykjavík; m.; five c. *Education:* Univ. of Iceland. *Career:* post-graduate work, Dept of Comparative Literature, Univ. of Copenhagen, Denmark. *Film scripts:* Börn náttúrunnar (Children of Nature), Bíódagar (Movie Days), Englar alheimsins (Angels of the Universe). *Publications:* novels: Riddara hringstigans (Almenna Bókafélagið prize 1985) 1982, Vængasláttur í þakrennum 1983, Eftirmáli Regndropanna (Epilogue of the Raindrops) 1986, Rauðir Dagar (Red Days) 1990, Englar alheimsins (Angels of the Universe) (DV Cultural Prize, Nordic Council Literary Award 1995) 1993, Fótspor á himnum 1997; poetry: Er nokkur í kórónafötum hér inni? 1980, Klettur í hafi (A Rock in the Ocean) 1991, Í auga óreiðunnar (The Eye of Chaos) 1995; other: Leitin að dýragarðinum (In Search of the Zoo) (short stories) 1988, Launsynir Orðanna (essays) 1998. *Honours:* Bröste's Optimism Award 1988, VISA Cultural Prize 1994, Giuseppe Acerbi Literary Prize, Italy 1999, The Karen Blixen Award 1999, Nat. Service Writer's Fund 2002, Nordic Prize, Swedish Acad. 2012.

GUELBENZU, José Maria; Spanish writer and academic; CEO Espasa Calpe SA; b. 14 April 1944, Madrid; m. Ana Rosa; two c. *Education:* Colegio Areneros de la Compañía de Jesús, Madrid, Universidad Complutense de Madrid, Univ. of Salamanca. *Career:* manufacturer and collaborator, Cuadernos for Dialogue 1964, head of production –1969; fmr mem. Bd of Dirs Cine-Club of Madrid; joined Taurus 1970, Ed. 1977–88; Literary Dir Alfaguara 1982–88; fmr Pres. and Prof. School of Arts, Madrid; currently CEO Editorial Espasa Calpe SA (publishing co.). *Publications:* EL Mercurio 1968, Antifaz 1970, El pasajero de ultramar 1976, La noche en casa 1977, El río de la luna (Premio de la Crítica) 1981, El esperado 1984, La mirada 1987, La Tierra Prometida (Premio Plaza & Janés) 1991, Ver Madrid 1991, El sentimiento 1995, Cuentos populares españoles 1996, Un peso en el mundo 1999, No acosen al asesino 2001, La cabeza del durmiente 2003, La muerte viene de lejos 2004, Esta pared de hielo 2005, 25 cuentos tradicionales españoles 2005, El cadáver arrepentido 2007, Un asesinato piadoso 2008, El amor verdadero 2010. *Honours:* Ruipérez Sánchez Foundation award for journalism 2007. *Address:* Espasa Calpe SA, Via De Las Dos Castillas 33, Complejo Atica, Edificio 4, 28224 Pozuelo de Alarcon, Madrid; Siruela Editions, 25 Almagro, 28010 Madrid, Spain. *Telephone:* (91) 3555720. *Fax:* (34) 9135522. *E-mail:* contacto@jmguelbenzu.com. *Website:* www.siruela.com.

GUÈNE, Faïza; French writer and filmmaker; b. 1985, Bobigny; m. 2007. *Education:* Lycée Marcelin Berthelot, Pantin, Université de Paris XIII, Université de Paris VIII, St Denis. *Career:* contributor, Le Monde Selon Wam, France Inter Radio 2004–; columnist, Respect magazine 2005–. *Short Films:* La Zonzonnière 1999, RTT 2002, Memories of October 17, 1961 2002, Rien que des mots 2004. *Publications:* novels: Kiffe Kiffe Demain (trans. as Just Like Tomorrow) 2004, Du rêve pour les oufs (trans. as Some Dream for Fools) 2006, Les Gens du Balto 2008. *Address:* c/o Hachette Littératures, 31, rue des Fleurus, 75006 Paris, France (office). *Website:* www.hachette-litteratures.com (office).

GUERIN, Orla, MA; Irish journalist; *Pakistan Correspondent, BBC Television;* b. May 1966, d. of the late Patrick James Guerin and Monica Guerin. *Education:* Coll. of Commerce, Dublin, Univ. Coll. Dublin. *Career:* newscaster, presenter and Foreign Corresp. with Irish State TV, RTE, Dublin 1987–94; joined BBC TV as news corresp. 1995, Southern Europe Corresp. covering the Balkans and conflict in the Basque country 1996–2000, Middle East Corresp. 2001–05, Africa Corresp. 2006–08, Pakistan Corresp. 2008–. *Honours:* Hon. MBE 2004; Hon. DUniv (Essex) 2002; Dr hc (Dublin Inst. of Tech.) 2005, (Open Univ.) 2007, (Queen's Univ. Belfast) 2009; Hon. DLitt (Ulster) 2009; The Jacobs Award for Broadcasters (Ireland) 1992, London Press Club Broadcaster of the Year Award 2002, News and Factual Award, Women in Film and Television (UK) 2003, David Bloom Award 2009. *Address:* c/o BBC Television Centre, Wood Lane, London, W12 7RJ, England (office).

GUERRA GARRIDO, Raúl, BPharm, PharmD; Spanish pharmacist and writer; b. 26 July 1935, Madrid. *Education:* Universidad Complutense de Madrid. *Career:* Founding mem. Foro Ermua (asscn of Basque academics and professionals). *Publications:* novels: Cacereño 1969, ¡Ay! 1972, Hipótesis 1975, Lectura insólita de El Capital (Premio Nadal) 1976, Pluma de pavo real, tambor de piel de perro 1977, Conpenhague no existe 1979, La costumbre de morir 1981, Escrito en un dólar 1982, El año del Wólfram 1984, La mar es mala mujer 1989, La carta 1990, El síndrome de Scot 1993, Tantos inocentes 1996, El otoño siempre hiere 2000, Cuaderno secreto 2003, La Gran Vía es New York 2004, La soledad del ángel de la guarda 2007, Quien sueña novela 2010; short stories: Micrófono oculto 1979, La sueca desnuda 1989, Dulce objeto de amor 1988, Viaje a una provincia interior 1990, Miento 2001; essays and travel books: Medicamentos españoles 1972, El telemirón 1982, Mis más bellas derrotas 1994, Esto no es un ensayo sobre Miró 1994, A los veinticinco años de Cacereño 1994, La muga en el horizonte 1996, Castilla en canal 1999. *Honours:* Pharmacist of the Year Award 2001, National Prize for Spanish Literature 2006, Medal of Merit Constitutional, Govt of Spain. *Address:* Alianza Editorial, 15 Juan Ignacio Luca de Tena, 28027 Madrid, Spain. *Telephone:* (91) 3938888. *Fax:* (91) 3207480. *E-mail:* alianzaeditorial@alianzaeditorial.es. *Website:* www.guerragarrido.es (office).

GUEST, Henry (Harry) Bayly, BA, D.E.S; British poet and writer; b. 6 Oct. 1932, Glamorganshire, Wales; m. Lynn Doremus Dunbar 1963; one s. one d. *Education:* Trinity Hall, Cambridge, Sorbonne, Univ. of Paris. *Career:* Lecturer, Yokohama Nat. Univ. 1966–72; Head of Modern Languages, Exeter School 1972–91; Teacher of Japanese, Exeter Univ. 1979–95; mem. Poetry Soc., General Council 1972–76; Hawthornden Fellow 1993, elected mem. Welsh Acad. 2001. *Publications:* Arrangements 1968, The Cutting-Room 1970, Post-War Japanese Poetry (ed. and trans.) 1972, A House Against the Night 1976, Days 1978, The Distance, the Shadows 1981, Lost and Found 1983, The Emperor of Outer Space (radio play) 1983, Lost Pictures 1991, Coming to Terms 1994, Traveller's Literary Companion to Japan 1994, So Far 1998, The Artist on the Artist 2000, A Puzzling Harvest 2002, Time After Time 2005, From a Condemned Cell 2008, Comparisons and Conversions 2009, Some Times 2010; contribs to reviews, quarterlies, and journals. *Honours:* Hon. Research Fellow, Univ. of Exeter 1994–; Hon. DLitt (Plymouth) 1998. *Address:* 1 Alexandra Terrace, Exeter, Devon, EX4 6SY, England (home). *Telephone:* (1392) 257142 (home).

GUHA, Ramachandra, MA, PhD; Indian writer and historian; b. 1958, Dehradun; s. of Subramaniam Rama Das Guha; m. Sujata Keshavan; two c. *Education:* St Stephen's Coll., Delhi, Delhi School of Econs, Indian Inst. of Man., Calcutta. *Career:* taught at Yale Univ. and Stanford Univ., USA; Fellow, Wissenschaftskolleg zu Berlin, Germany 1994–95; fmr Arné Naess Chair. Univ. of Oslo; fmr Indo-American Community Visiting Prof., Univ. of California, Berkeley, Sundaraja Visiting Prof. in the Humanities, Indian Inst. of Science, Bangalore 2003; fmr columnist, The Telegraph of Calcutta; currently full-time writer; Trustee, New India Foundation. *Publications:* The Unquiet Woods: Ecological Change and Peasant Resistance in the Himalaya 1989, This Fissured Land: An Ecological History of India (co-author) 1992, Wickets in the East 1992, Social Ecology (co-ed.) 1994, Spin and Other Turns 1994, An Indian Cricket Omnibus (co-ed.) 1994, Ecology and Equity (co-ed.) 1995, Nature, Culture, Imperialism: Essays on the Environmental History of South Asia (co-author) 1996, Varieties of Environmentalism: Essays North and South (co-author) 1997, Savaging the Civilized – Verrier Elwin, his tribals and India 1999, An Anthropologist Among the Marxists, and other essays 2000, Environmentalism: A Global History 2000, Institutions and Inequalities: Essays in Honour of André Béteille (co-author) 2000, A Corner of a Foreign Field (Daily Telegraph Cricket Soc. Book of the Year 2002) 2001, The Picador Book of Cricket (ed.) 2001, An Indian Cricket Century (ed.) 2002, The Last Liberal and Other Essays 2004, The States of Indian Cricket 2005, How Much Should a Person Consume?: Thinking Through the Environment 2006, Nature's Spokesman: M. Krishnan and Indian Wildlife (ed.) 2007, India after Gandhi: The History of the World's Largest Democracy 2007, The Miracle That Is India 2007; contrib. essays, articles and reviews to magazines. *Honours:* Padma Bhushan 2009; MacArthur Fellowship, Leopold-Hidy Prize, American Soc. of Environmental History 2001, Daily Telegraph Cricket Soc. Book of the Year 2002, Malcolm Adideshiah Award, R. K. Narayan Prize 2003. *Address:* 22A Brunton Road, Bangalore 560 025 (home); c/o Marketing and Promotions Department, Penguin Books India Pvt. Ltd, 11 Community Centre, Panchsheel Park, New Delhi 110017, India (office). *E-mail:* publicity@in.penguingroup.com (office). *Website:* www.penguinbooksindia.com (office).

GUIGNABODET, Lily (Liliane), LèsL; French writer; b. (Lily Lea Graciani), 26 March 1939, Paris; d. of Moïse Graciani and Olympia N. Graciani; m. Jean Guignabodet 1961; one s. two d. *Education:* primary school in Sofia, Bulgaria, Lycée Jules Ferry, Paris, Sorbonne and Univ. of London. *Career:* Prof. of French, San José, USA 1961–62; Prof. of Literature, Arts and Culture, Ecole Technique d'IBM France 1966–69; author 1977–; mem. PEN Club Français, Soc. des Gens de Lettres, Acad. Européenne des Sciences, des Arts et des Lettres, Acad. Valentin. *Publications:* L'écume du silence 1977, Le bracelet indien 1980, Natalia 1983, Le livre du vent 1984, Dessislava 1986, Car les hommes sont meilleurs que leur vie 1991, Un sentiment inconnu 1998. *Honours:* Prix George Sand 1977, Grand Prix du Roman, Acad. Française 1983, Grand prix du Roman, Ville de Cannes 1991. *Address:* 55 rue Caulaincourt, 75018 Paris, France. *Telephone:* 1-46-06-09-86. *Fax:* 1-46-06-09-86.

GUILLOU, Jan; Swedish writer and journalist; b. 17 Jan. 1944, Södertälje. *Television series:* Talismanen (with Henning Mankell) 2001. *Publications:* fiction: Om kriget kommer 1971, Det stora avslöjandet 1974, Ondskan (Prix France Culture 1990) 1981, Coq Rouge: berättelsen on en Svensk spion 1986, Den demokratiske terroristen 1987, I nationens intresse (Bästa svenska kriminalroman 1988) 1988, Fiendens fiende 1989, Den hedervärde mördaren 1990, Gudarnas Berg 1990, Vendetta 1991, Ingen mans land 1992, Den enda segern 1993, I hennes majestäts tjänst 1994, En medborgare höjd över varje misstanke 1995, Hamlon: en skiss till en möjlig fortsättning 1995, Vägen till Jerusalem 1998, Tempelriddaren 1999, Riket vid vägens slut 2000, Arvet efter Arn 2001, I Arns fotspår 2002, Tjuvarnas marknad 2004, Madame Terror 2006, Men inte om det gäller din dotter 2008; non-fiction: Handbok för rättslösa 1975, Journalistik 1976, Irak – det Nya Arabien 1977, Artister 1979, Reporter 1979, Berättelser från det Nya Riket 1982, Justitiemord 1983, Nya berättelser 1984, Åsikter 1990, Stora machoboken 1990, Grabbarnas stora presentbok 1991, On jakt och jägare: från fagerhult till sibirien 1996, Svenskarna, invandrarna och svartskallarna: mitt livs viktigaste reportage

1996, Antirasistiskt lexikon 1997, Häxornas försvarare 2002, Kolumnisten 2005. *Honours:* Stora Journalistpriset 1984, Aftonbladets TV Pris 1984, SKTF Pris-årets Författare 1998, Årets Bok-Månadens boks litterära pris 2000. *E-mail:* jan.guillou@aftonbladet.se.

GUISEWITE, Cathy Lee, BA; American cartoonist; b. 5 Sept. 1950, Dayton, OH; d. of William Lee and Anne Guisewite; m. Chris Wilkinson; one step-s. one d. *Education:* Univ. of Michigan, Ann Arbor. *Career:* worked as advertising writer for five years; cr. Cathy comic strip syndicated in around 500 newspapers 1976–; TV specials featuring cartoon characters (Emmy Award 1987). *Publications include:* The Cathy Chronicles 1978 (republished as What's a Nice Single Girl Doing with a Double Bed?! and, I Think I'm Having a Relationship with a Blueberry Pie! 1981), Motherly Advice from Cathy's Mom 1987, A Hand to Hold, an Opinion to Reject 1987, My Granddaughter Has Fleas 1989, $14 in the Bank and a $200 Face in My Purse 1990, Reflections (A Fifteenth Anniversary Collection) 1991, Only Love Can Break a Heart, but a Shoe Sale Can Come Close 1992, Revelations from a 45-Pound Purse 1993, Abs of Steel, Buns of Cinnamon 1997, I'd Scream Except I Look so Fabulous 1999, Shoes: Chocolate for the Feet 2000; collections of daily cartoon strips. *Honours:* several hon. degrees; numerous awards including Outstanding Communicator of the Year Award, Los Angeles Advertising Women 1982, named one of America's 25 Most Influential Women 1984, 1986, Reuben Award, Nat. Cartoonists Soc. 1993. *Address:* c/o Universal Press Syndicate, 1130 Walnut Street, Kansas City, MO 64106-2109, USA (office).

GULLAR, Ferreira; Brazilian writer and poet; b. (José Ribamar Ferreira), 10 Sept. 1930, São Luís, Maranhão; s. of Newton Ferreira and Alzira Ribeiro Goulart; m. Thereza Aragão (died 1993). *Career:* fmr newsreader Rádio Timbira, Maranhão; Ed. Manchete magazine 1954–55, Diário Carioca newapaper 1955–56; Founding mem. Neo-Concrete poetry movement 1959; Dir Cultural Foundation of Brasília 1961; Pres. Popular Centre for Culture (CPC) 1963; affiliated with Communist Party after military coup d'état of Brazil 1964; lived in exile in Moscow, Santiago, Lima and Buenos Aires 1971–77; Dir Brazilian Inst. of Art and Culture 1992–95. *Publications:* poetry: Um pouco acima do chão 1949, A luta corporal 1954, Poemas 1958, João Boa-Morte, cabra marcado pra morrer 1962, Quem matou Aparecida? 1962, História de um valente 1966, Por você por mim 1968, Dentro da noite veloz 1975, Poema Sujo 1976, Na vertigem do dia 1980, Toda poesía 1980, Crime na flora ou Ordem e progresso 1986, Barulhos 1987, O formigueiro 1991, Muitas vozes (Prêmio Jabuti, Prêmio Alphonsus de Guimarães) 1999, Um gato chamado Gatinho 2000, O rei que mora no mar 2001, Dr Urubu e outras fábulas 2005, Em alguma parte alguma (Prêmio Jabuti Book of the Year Award 2011) 2010; fiction: Gamação 1996, Cidades Inventadas 1997, Touro Encantada 2003; short stories: A estranha vida banal 1989, As melhores crônicas de Ferreira Gullar 2005, Resmungos (Prêmio Jabuti) 2007; non-fiction: Teoria do não-objeto 1959, Cultura posta em questão 1965, Vanguarda e subdesenvolvimento 1969, Augusto dos Anjos ou morte e vida noredestina 1976, Uma luz do chão 1978, Sobre Arte 1982, Etapas de arte contemporânea 1985, Indagações de hoje 1989, Argumentação contra a morte da arte 1993, O Grupo Frente e a reação neoconcreta 1998, Rabo de foguete - Os anos de exílio 1998, Cultura posta en questão 2002, Rembrandt 2002, Relâmpagos 2003. *Honours:* Literary Personality of the Year, Brazilian Book Council 1979, Prix Molière 1985, Prince Claus Fund, Netherlands 2002, Prêmio Fundação Conrado Wessel de Ciência e Cultura 2005, Prêmio Machado de Assis 2005, Camões Prize 2010. *Address:* c/o Livraria José Olympio Editora S.A., Rua da Gloria 344, 4° andar, Gloria, 20241-180 Rio de Janeiro, Brazil.

GULZAR; Indian filmmaker, poet and lyricist; b. (Sampooran Singh Kalra), 18 Aug. 1936, Deena, Jhelum Dist (now in Pakistan); s. of Makhan Singh Kalra and Sujan Kaur; m. Rakhee Gulzar; one d. *Career:* came to Delhi following partition; started as poet and was associated with Progressive Writers Asscn; joined Bimal Roy Productions in 1961; first break as lyricist came when he wrote Mora Gora Ang Lai Lae for Bimal Roy's Bandini 1963; began writing for films for dirs Hrishikesh Mukherjee and Asit Sen; turned filmmaker with first film Mere Apne 1971; began partnership with Sanjeev Kumar. *Films directed:* Shriman Satyawadi (Asst Dir) 1960, Kabuliwala (Chief Asst Dir) 1961, Bandini (Asst Dir) 1963, Mere Apne 1971, Parichay 1972, Koshish 1972, Achanak 1973, Mausam (Nat. Award for Best Dir, Filmfare The Best Dir Award) 1975, Khushboo 1975, Aandhi (Storm) 1975, Kitaab (also Producer) 1977, Kinara (also Producer) 1977, Meera 1979, Sahira 1980, Namkeen 1982, Angoor 1982, Suniye 1984, Aika 1984, Ek Akar 1985, Ijaazat (Guest) 1987, Ghalib (TV) 1988, Libaas 1988, Lekin... (But...) 1990, Ustad Amjad Ali Khan 1990, Pandit Bhimsen Joshi 1992, Maachis 1996, Hu Tu Tu 1999. *Film roles include:* Jallianwalla Bagh 1979, Grihapravesh (The Housewarming) (as himself) 1979, Wajood (guest appearance as himself) 1998, Chachi 420 (uncredited cameo appearance during end credits) 1998, Raincoat (voice) 2004, Yuvraaj (special appearance) 2008. *Film dialogue or scripts:* Sangharsh 1968, Aashirwad (The Blessing) 1968, Khamoshi 1969, Anand 1970, Guddi (Darling Child) 1971, Mere Apne 1971, Koshish (Nat. Award for Best Screenplay) 1972, Bawarchi 1972, Namak Haraam (The Ungrateful) 1973, Achanak 1973, Mausam 1975, Khushboo 1975, Chupke Chupke 1975, Aandhi (Storm) 1975, Palkon Ki Chhaon Mein 1977, Meera 1979, Grihapravesh (The Housewarming) 1979, Khubsoorat (Beautiful) 1980, Basera 1981, Namkeen 1982, Angoor 1982, Masoom (Innocent) 1983, New Delhi Times 1986, Ek Pal (A Moment) 1986, Ijaazat (Guest) 1987, Mirza Ghalib (TV) 1988, Lekin... (But...) 1990, Rudaal (The Mourner) 1993, Maachis 1996, Chachi 420 1998, Hu Tu Tu 1999, Saathiya 2002, Dus Kahaniya 2007. *Film song lyrics:* Swami Vivekananda 1955, Shriman Satyawadi 1960, Kabuliwala 1961, Prem Patra (Love Letter) 1962, Bandini 1963, Purnima 1965, Sannata 1966, Biwi Aur Makan 1966, Do Dooni Char 1968, Aashirwad (The Blessing) 1968, Rahgir 1969, Khamoshi 1969, Anand 1970, Guddi (Darling Child) 1971, Anubhav (Experience) 1971, Seema 1971, Mere Apne 1971, Parichay 1972, Koshish 1972, Doosri Seeta 1974, Chor Machaye Shor 1974, Mausam 1975, Khushboo 1975, Aandhi (Storm) 1975, Shaque 1976, Palkon Ki Chhaon Mein 1977, Kinara 1977, Gharaonda (The Nest) 1977, Ghar (Home) 1978, Meetha (Sweet and Sour) 1978, Devata 1978, Gol Maal (Hanky Panky) 1979, Ratnadeep (The Jewelled Lamp) 1979, Grihapravesh (The Housewarming) 1979, Sitara 1980, Thodisi Bewafaii 1980, Swayamvar 1980, Khubsoorat (Beautiful India) 1980, Garam 1981, Basera 1981, Namkeen 1982, Angoor 1982, Sadma 1983, Masoom (Innocent) 1983, Ghulami 1985, Jeeva 1986, Ek Pal (A Moment) 1986, Ijaazat (Guest) (Nat. Award for Best Lyricist) 1987, Libaas 1988, Lekin... (But...) 1990, Maya Memsaab (Maya: The Enchanting Illusion) 1992, Rudaali (The Mourner) 1993, Mammo 1994, Daayraa (The Square Circle, USA) 1996, Maachis 1996, Aastha (Aastha in the Prison of Spring) 1997, Satya 1998, Dil Se... (From the Heart, USA) 1998, Chachi 420 1998, Hu Tu Tu 1999, Khoobsurat 1999, Fiza 2000, Aks 2001, Asoka (Ashoka the Great, USA) 2001, Filhaal... 2002, Leela 2002, Lal Salaam (Red Salute) 2002, Dil Vil Pyar Vyar 2002, Makdee (The Web of the Witch) 2002, Saathiya 2002, Chupke Se 2003, Pinjar (The Cage) 2003, Jaan-E-Mann 2006, Guru 2007, Slumdog Millionaire (Jai Ho) (Academy Award for Best Original Song 2009, Grammy Award for Best Song Written for Motion Picture, Television or Other Visual Media 2010) 2008, Kaminey 2009, Veer 2010, Ishqiya 2010, Striker 2010. *Publications include:* poetry: Jaanam 1962, Kuch Aur Nazme 1980, Chand Pukhraj Ka 1995, Triveni 2001, Raat Pashmine Ki 2002 Raat Chand Aur Main 2004, Selected Poems 2008, Yaar Julaahe 2009, 100 Lyrics 2009; short stories: Raavi Paar 1999, Dhuaan (Sahitya Acad. Award 2003) 2001, Kharaashein 2003; 12 books for children, including Ekta (Nat. Council for Educ. Research and Training Award 1989). *Honours:* Lifetime Hon. Fellowship, Indian Inst. of Advanced Studies 2001; five Nat. Film Awards, more than 17 Filmfare Awards, including seven for Best Lyricist, Filmfare Lifetime Achievement Award 2002, Padma Bhushan 2004. *Address:* Boskiyana, Pali Hill, Bandra (W), Mumbai 400 050 (home); c/o Rupa and Co., 7/16 Ansari Road, Daryaganj, PO Box 7017, New Delhi 110 002, India (office). *Telephone:* (22) 6498351 (home). *E-mail:* info@rupapublications.com (office). *Website:* www.rupapublications.com (office).

GUNESEKERA, Romesh, FRSL; British (b. Sri Lankan) writer and poet; b. 1954, Colombo; m. Helen; two d. *Career:* Writer-in-Residence, Somerset House, London 2010; Writer-in-Residence, First Story, Highgate Wood School. *Publications include:* Monkfish Moon (short stories) 1992, Reef (novel) 1994, The Sandglass (novel) 1998, Heaven's Edge (novel) 2002, The Match (novel) 2006, The Spice Collector (short stories). *Honours:* New York Times Notable Book of the Year 1993, Yorkshire Post Best First Work Award 1994, Premio Mondello 1997, Ranjana, Sri Lanka 2005. *Literary Agent:* c/o Bill Hamilton, A. M. Heath & Company, 6 Warwick Court, Holborn, London, WC1R 5DJ, England. *Telephone:* (20) 7242-2811. *Fax:* (20) 7242-2711. *Website:* www.amheath.com. *E-mail:* rg@romeshgunesekera.com (home). *Website:* www.romeshgunesekera.com (home).

GUNNARS, Kristjana, MA; Icelandic/Canadian writer, poet, translator and academic; b. 19 March 1948, Reykjavík; d. of Gunnar Bodvarsson and Tove Christensen Bodvarsson; m. Charles Kang 1967 (divorced); one c. *Education:* Oregon State Univ., USA and Univ. of Regina, Sask., Canada. *Career:* family moved to Oregon 1964; Asst Ed. Iceland Review, Iceland 1980–81; freelance writer, translator and ed. 1981–; Writer-in-Residence, Regina Public Library, Canada 1988–89, Univ. of Alberta, Edmonton, Canada 1989–90, Assoc. Prof. of English 1991, Prof. of Creative Writing 1991–2004; Lecturer, Okanagan Coll., BC, Canada 1990–91; Visiting Prof., Univ. of Trier, Germany 1992, Oslo, Norway 1998; mem. PEN, Writers' Union of Canada, League of Canadian Poets, Composers', Authors' and Publishers' Asscn of Canada, Alliance of Canadian Cinema, TV and Radio Artists. *Publications:* Settlement Poems I and II 1980, 1981, One-Eyed Moon Maps 1981, Wake-Pick Poems 1982, Stephan G. Stephansson, In Retrospect (trans.) 1982, The Axe's Edge 1983, The Night Workers of Ragnarök 1985, The Papers of Dorothy Livesay (co-author) 1985, Crossing the River: Essays in Honor of Margaret Laurence (ed.) 1988, Stephan G. Stephansson, Selected Prose and Poetry (trans.) 1988, The Prowler 1989, Carnival of Longing 1989, Zero Hour 1991, Unexpected Fictions, New Icelandic Canadian Writing (ed.), The Guest House and Other Stories 1992, The Substance of Forgetting 1992, The Rose Garden: Reading Marcel Proust 1993, Exiles Among You 1996, Night Train to Nykøbing 1996, When Chestnut Trees Blossom 2002, Silence of the Country 2002, Stranger at the Door 2004. *Address:* 5593 Sans Souci Road, Halfmoon Bay, BC, V0N 1Y2, Canada (home).

GUNSTON, William (Bill) Tudor, OBE, FRAeS; British author and editor; b. 1 March 1927, London; m. Margaret Anne 1964; two d. *Education:* Univ. Coll., Durham, City Univ., London. *Career:* pilot, RAF 1946–48; editorial staff, Flight 1951–55, Tech. Ed. 1955–64; Tech. Ed., Science Journal 1964–70; team mem. Jane's All the World's Aircraft 1968–; freelance author 1970–; Dir So Few Ltd; Ed. Jane's Aero-Engines 1995–2008, now Asst Ed. *Publications:* more than 370 books, including The Development of Piston Aero Engines 1999, Modern Fighting Helicopters 1999, Aerospace Dictionary 1999, The Illustrated History of McDonnell Douglas Aircraft 2000 (companion works for Boeing and Lockheed), Hamlyn History of Military Aviation 2000, Soviet X-planes 2000, The Encyclopedia of Modern Warplanes 2001, Aviation Year by Year 2001, Rolls-Royce Aero Engines 2001, Aviation: The First 100 Years 2002, The Development of Jet and Turbine Aero Engines 2002, Flight Path (biog.) 2002, Night Fighters 2003, Cambridge Aerospace Dictionary 2004, Encyclopaedia of World Aircraft Constructors 2007, Faster than Sound 2008, Airbus 2009; contribs to 188 periodicals, 18 partworks, 75 video scripts. *Address:* High Beech, Kingsley Green, Haslemere, Surrey, GU27 3LL, England (home). *Telephone:* (1428) 644282 (home). *E-mail:* bill.gunston@tiscali.co.uk (home).

GUO, Xiaolu, MA; Chinese novelist, film director and screenwriter; b. 1973, Zhejiang Province; single. *Education:* Beijing Film Acad., Nat. Film and TV School, London. *Career:* moved to UK 2002. *Film and television:* Far and Near (documentary) (ICA/Becks Futures Prize) 2003, The Concrete Revolution (documentary) 2004, How Is Your Fish Today? (Grand Jury Prize, Creteil Int. Women's Film Festival, France 2007) 2006; as scriptwriter: Love in the Internet Age 1999, House 1999, A Boat in the Sea (TV series) 2000, Knowledge Can Change Your Fate (film series) 1998. *Publications:* novels: 20 Fragments of Fenfang's Youth (in Chinese) 2000, Village of Stone (in Chinese) 2004, A Concise Chinese-English Dictionary for Lovers (in English) 2007, 20 Fragments of a Ravenous Youth 2008; essay collections (in Chinese): Flying in my Dreams 2000, Movie Map 2001, Notes on Movie Theory 2002; single essays: Cinema and Adam's Rib 1999, A Chinese Writer's Journey to the West 2003, Blasting the Past in China 2003, Flashback of a Not-so-far-from home 2003, East Beast, West Beauty 2004; poems (in Chinese): Love and Middle Class Life 2001, Medicine 2002, Kew Garden 2002, Dear 2003, Scenery 2003, Notes 2004, Blindness 2004; other: Who is My Mother's Boyfriend (collected film scripts) 1999. *Literary Agent:* Toby Eady Associates Ltd, Third Floor, 9 Orme Court, London, W2 4RL, England. *Telephone:* (20) 7792-0092. *Fax:* (20) 7792-0879. *Website:* www.tobyeadyassociates.co.uk. *E-mail:* xiaolu@guoxiaolu.com. *Website:* www.guoxiaolu.com.

GUPPY, Stephen Anthony, BA, MA; Canadian writer, poet and academic; *Professor, Department of Creative Writing and Journalism, Vancouver Island University, Nanaimo*; b. 10 Feb. 1951, Nanaimo; m. Nelinda Kazenbroot 1986; one s. one d. *Education:* Univ. of Victoria. *Career:* teacher, School Dist No. 69, Qualicum 1982–85; currently Prof., Dept of Creative Writing and Journalism, Vancouver Island Univ., Nanaimo, also Prof., Dept of English. *Publications:* Ghostcatcher (poems) 1979, Rainshadow: Stories from Vancouver Island (anthology, co-ed.) 1982, Another Sad Day at the Edge of the Empire (short stories) 1985, Blind Date with the Angel (poems) 1998, Understanding Heaven 2002, The Fire Thief 2004, The Work of Mercy 2006; contrib. of short stories to anthologies including: Best Canadian Short Stories; The Journey Prize Anthology. *Honours:* Second Prize, Scottish International Open Poetry Competition 1997. *Address:* Department of Creative Writing and Journalism, Vancouver Island University, 900 Fifth Street, Building 340, Room No 127, Nanaimo, BC V9R 5S5, Canada (office). *Telephone:* (250) 753-3245 (office). *E-mail:* Steve.Guppy@viu.ca (office); steveguppy@shaw.ca. *Website:* www.viu.ca (office).

GUPTA, Tanika, MBE, BA; British playwright and screenwriter; b. 1 Dec. 1963, London; d. of the late Tapan Kumar Gupta and of Gairika Gupta; m.; three d. *Education:* Univ. of Oxford. *Career:* began her writing career in 1991 when she was a finalist in BBC Young Playwrights' Festival with 'Asha' (45-minute radio play); Writer-in-Residence, Soho Theatre 1996–98; Pearson Writer-in-Residence, Royal Nat. Theatre 2000–01; currently writing for BBC Asian Network's new soap, Silver Street and under comms with Birmingham Rep, Bolton Octagon and Nat. Youth Theatres. *Plays include:* Skeleton 1997, The Good Woman of Szechuan (trans.), Voices in the Wind, The Waiting Room (John Whiting Award 2000) 2000, Sanctuary 2002, Inside Out 2002, Fragile Land 2003, Hobson's Choice by Harold Brighouse (adaptation) 2003, The Country Wife 2004, Gladiator Games (Sheffield Crucible/Stratford East), Sugar Mummies (Royal Court, London) 2006, Catch (Group Play, Royal Court) 2006, White Boy (Nat. Youth Theatre) 2008, adaptation of Great Expectations (Soho Theatre, Watford Palace Theatre) 2011. *Radio:* Asha 1991, Badal and His Bike (Radio 5) 1993, Pankhiraj, The Bounty Hunter 1997, Ananda Sananda 1997, The Whispering Tree (Prix ex Aequeo Bratislava 1998), The Queen's Retreat 1999, Muse of Fusion 1999, The Book of Secrets (adaptation of novel by M. G. Vassanji) 1999, Betrayal – The Secret, The Trial of William Davidson, Stowaway 2001, ten-part adaptation of Arundhati Roy's The God of Small Things (Woman's Hour, Radio 4) 2004, The Parting (Radio 4) 2004; for BBC World Service and Radio 3: The Eternal Bubble, Voices On The Wind, Red Oleanders (adaptation of play by Rabindranath Tagore), A Second Chance 2003, Chitra (Amnesty International Media Award) 2005, Rudolpho's Zest (BBC Radio 3) 2009, Rescue Me 2010; regular contrib. to Westway. *Television:* Flight (BBC 2, Fipa D'argent Prize 1997, EMMA Award for Best TV Production 1998) 1995; pilot scripts for A Suitable Boy (Enigma/Channel 4/Cinema Verity), The Fiancee, The Rhythm of Raz and Bideshi 1995 (all award-winning short films); series: EastEnders (BBC 1), The Bill (Thames/ITV), Crossroads, Grange Hill and London Bridge; adaptation of J. M. Coetzee's The Lives of Animals (60-minute film for BBC 4) 2002; episodes of All About Me (sit-com for Celador), Banglatown Banquet (BBC 2) (Prix Europa Special Commendation) 2006. *Publications:* all her stage plays; Rebecca and the Neighbours (short story included in Asian Women Writers' Collective Anthology, Flaming Spirits). *Honours:* Hon. Fellow, Rose Bruford Coll. 2009; Asian Woman of Achievement (Arts and Culture) 2003. *Literary Agent:* c/o The Agency (London) Ltd, 24 Pottery Lane, Holland Park, London, W11 4LZ, England. *Telephone:* (20) 7727-1346. *Fax:* (20) 7727-9037. *E-mail:* info@theagency.co.uk. *Website:* www.theagency.co.uk.

GURGANUS, Allan, BA, MFA; American writer, artist and academic; b. 11 June 1947, Rocky Mount. *Education:* Monterey Language School, Radioman and Cryptography School, Univ. of Pennsylvania, Pennsylvania Acad. of Fine Arts, Harvard Univ., Sarah Lawrence Coll., Univ. of Iowa Writers' Workshop, Stanford Univ. *Career:* Prof. of Fiction Writing, Univ. of Iowa 1972–74, Writer's Workshop 1989–90; Prof. of Fiction Writing, Stanford Univ. 1974–76, Duke Univ. 1976–78, Sarah Lawrence Coll. 1978–86; Co-founder Writers Against Jesse Helms; mem. American Acad. of Arts and Sciences 2004, American Acad. of Arts and Letters 2007. *Publications:* Oldest Living Confederate Widow Tells All 1989, White People: Stories and Novellas 1991, Practical Heart 1993, Plays Well With Others 1997, The Practical Heart: Four Novellas (Lambda Literary Award) 2001; contribs to periodicals. *Honours:* Fellowship of Southern Writers 2004, John Simon Guggenheim Fellow 2006; Sue Kaufman Prize for First Fiction, American Acad. and Inst. of Arts and Letters 1990, Books Across the Sea Ambassador Book Award, English-Speaking Union of the US 1990, Los Angeles Times Book Prize 1991, Southern Book Prize. *E-mail:* agwebpost@gmail.com. *Website:* www.allangurganus.com.

GURLEY BROWN, Helen; American writer and editor; *Editor-in-Chief, Cosmopolitan International Editions*; b. 18 Feb. 1922, Green Forest, Ark.; d. of Ira M. Gurley and Cleo Gurley (née Sisco); m. David Brown 1959. *Education:* Texas State Coll. for Women, Woodbury Coll. *Career:* Exec. Sec. Music Corpn of America 1942–45, William Morris Agency 1945–47; Copywriter Foote, Cone & Belding advertising agency, Los Angeles 1948–58; advertisement writer and account exec. Kenyon & Eckhard advertising agency, Hollywood 1958–62; Ed.-in-Chief Cosmopolitan magazine 1965–97, Editorial Dir Cosmopolitan Int. Edns 1972–, Ed.-in-Chief 1997–; mem. Authors' League of America, American Soc. of Magazine Eds, AFTRA; est. Helen Gurley Brown Research Professorship at Northwestern Univ. 1986. *Publications:* Sex and the Single Girl 1962, Sex and the Office 1965, Outrageous Opinions 1967, Helen Gurley Brown's Single Girl's Cook Book 1969, Sex and the New Single Girl 1970, Having It All 1982, The Late Show: A Semiwild but Practical Survival Guide for Women over 50 1993, The Writer's Rules: The Power of Positive Prose 1998, I'm Wild Again: Snippets from My Life and a Few Brazen Thoughts 2000, Dear Pussycat: Personal Correspondence of Helen Gurley Brown 2004. *Honours:* Hon. LLD (Woodbury) 1987; Hon. DLitt (Long Island) 1993; Francis Holm Achievement Award 1956–59, Univ. of S. Calif. School of Journalism 1971, Special Award for Editorial Leadership of American Newspaper Woman's Club 1972, Distinguished Achievement Award in Journalism, Stanford Univ. 1977, New York Women in Communications Inc. Award 1985, Publrs' Hall of Fame 1988, Henry Johnson Fisher Award, Magazine Publrs of America 1995. *Address:* Cosmopolitan, 959 8th Avenue, New York, NY 10019 (office); 1 West 81st Street, New York, NY 10024, USA (home). *Telephone:* (212) 649-3555 (office). *Fax:* (212) 649-3529 (office). *Website:* www.cosmopolitan.com (office).

GURNAH, Abdulrazak, PhD, FRSL; Tanzanian novelist, literary critic and editor; *Lecturer in English Literature, School of English, University of Kent*; b. 1948, Zanzibar. *Career:* Lecturer, Bayero Univ. 1980–82; currently Lecturer in English Literature, School of English, Univ. of Kent; Contributing Ed. and mem. Advisory Bd Wasafiri (journal). *Publications:* Memory of Departure 1987, Pilgrim's Way 1988, Dottie 1990, Essays on African Writing: A Re-Evaluation (ed.) 1993, Paradise 1994, Essays on African Writing: Contemporary Literature (ed.) 1995, Admiring Silence 1996, By the Sea 2001, Desertion 2005, My Mother Lived on a Farm in Africa 2006, The Cambridge Companion to Salman Rushdie (ed) 2008; numerous works for radio; contrib. to Wole Soyinka: An Appraisal 1994, Modernism and Empire 1998, Essays and Criticism 2000, New Writing 9. *Address:* School of English, Rutherford College, University of Kent, Canterbury, Kent CT2 7NX, England (office). *Telephone:* (12) 2776-4000 (office). *E-mail:* A.S.Gurnah@ukc.ac.uk. *Website:* www.kent.ac.uk (office); www.wasafiri.org.

GURNEY, Albert Ramsdell, MFA; American playwright; b. 1 Nov. 1930, Buffalo, NY; s. of Albert R. Gurney and Marion Gurney (née Spaulding); m. Mary F. Goodyear 1957; two s. two d. *Education:* Williams Coll., Yale School of Drama. *Career:* joined MIT, Faculty of Humanities 1960–96, Prof. 1970–96; mem. American Acad. of Arts and Letters 2006. *Publications include:* plays: The Dining Room, The Cocktail Hour, Love Letters, Later Life, A Cheever Evening, Sylvia, Overtime; Let's Do It!, The Guest Lecturer, Labor Day, Far East, Ancestral Voices 1999, Human Events 2000, Buffalo Gal 2001, The Fourth Wall 2002, Big Bill 2004, Mrs Farnsworth 2004, Indian Blood 2006, Crazy Mary 2007, A Light Lunch 2009, The Grand Manner 2010, Office Hours 2010, Black Tie 2011; novels: The Gospel According to Joe, Entertaining Strangers, The Snow Ball; opera libretto: Stawberry Fields 1999. *Honours:* Hon. DDL (Buffalo State Univ., Williams Coll.); Drama Desk Award 1971, American Acad. of Arts and Letters Award 1987, Lucille Lortel Award 1992, William Inge Award 2000, Theatre Hall of Fame 2005, Drama Desk Award 2011. *Address:* 40 Wellers Bridge Road, PO Box 150, Roxbury, CT 06783-1616, USA (home). *Telephone:* (860) 354-3692 (home). *Fax:* (860) 354-3692 (home). *E-mail:* a.r.gurney@charter.net (home). *Website:* argurney.com.

GURR, Andrew John, BA, MA, PhD; British/New Zealand writer and academic; *Professor Emeritus, University of Reading*; b. 23 Dec. 1936, Leicester; m. Elizabeth Gordon 1961; three s. *Education:* Univ. of Auckland,

New Zealand, Univ. of Cambridge. *Career:* Lecturer, Victoria Univ. of Wellington 1959, Leeds Univ. 1962–69; Prof. of English, Univ. of Nairobi 1969–73, Univ. of Reading 1976–; mem. Int. Shakespeare Asscn, Asscn of Commonwealth Literature and Language Studies, Soc. for Theatre Research, Malone Soc. *Publications:* The Shakespeare Stage 1574–1642 1970, Writers in Exile 1982, Katherine Mansfield 1982, Playgoing in Shakespeare's London 1987, Studying Shakespeare 1988, Rebuilding Shakespeare's Globe 1989, The Shakespearian Playing Companies 1996, The Shakespeare Company 1594–1642 2004, Shakespeare's Opposites: The Admiral's Company 1594–1625 2009; Ed. Plays of Shakespeare, Beaumont and Fletcher; contrib. to scholarly journals and periodicals. *Honours:* Hon. DLitt (Auckland Univ.) 2004. *Address:* School of English and American Studies, University of Reading, PO Box 218, Reading, Berks., RG6 2AA, England (office).

GURR, David, (William Breton, D.G. Courtney), BSc; Canadian writer; b. 5 Feb. 1936, London, England; m. Judith Deverell 1958 (divorced 1991); two s. one d. *Education:* Canadian Naval Coll., Univ. of Victoria. *Career:* Career Officer, Royal Canadian Navy 1954–70; house designer and builder, Vancouver Island 1972–81; mem. Crime Writers of Canada, Writers' Guild of America, Writers' Union of Canada. *Plays:* Leonora 1982, The Ring Play 1992. *Films:* Cliffhanger (screen play). *Publications:* Troika 1979, A Woman Called Scylla 1981, An American Spy Story 1984, The Action of the Tiger 1984, On the Endangered List 1985, The Ring Master 1987, The Voice of the Crane 1989, Arcadia West: The Novel 1994, The Charlatan 2000, The Time of the Seventh Angel 2008; as William Breton: Ten Days to Zero Zero 1989, Countdown 1993; as D.G. Courtney: King's Cross 1993. *E-mail:* david@davidgurr.ca. *Website:* www.davidgurr.ca.

GUSEV, Pavel Nikolayevich; Russian journalist and publisher; *Editor-in-Chief, Moskovsky Komsomolets*; b. 4 April 1949, Moscow; s. of Nikolai Gusev and Alla Guseva; m. Yevgeniya Valeryevna Yefimova; two d. *Education:* Moscow Inst. of Geological Survey, Maxim Gorky Inst. of Literature. *Career:* First Sec. Komsomol Cttee of Krasnaya Presnya Region of Moscow 1975–80; Exec. Cen. Komsomol Cttee 1980–83; Ed.-in-Chief Moskovsky Komsomolets (newspaper) 1983–; Minister, Govt of Moscow, Head of Dept of Information and Mass Media Jan.–Oct. 1992; press adviser to Mayor of Moscow 1992–95; Chair. Comm. for the Politics of Information and Freedom of the Word of the Public Chamber, Public Council of Fed. Agency of Culture and Cinematography 2007–; currently Pres. Moscow Confed. of Journalists; also Prof. of Journalism, International Univ., Moscow. *Plays:* I Love You, Constance (Moscow Gogol Theatre) 1993, Cardinal's Coat (Maly Theatre) 2002. *Address:* Moskovsky Komsomolets, 1905 Goda 7, 123995 Moscow, Russia (office). *Telephone:* (495) 259-50-36 (office). *Fax:* (495) 259-46-39 (office). *E-mail:* letters@mk.ru (office). *Website:* www.mk.ru (office).

GUSMAN, Mikhail Solomonovich; Russian journalist; *First Deputy Director-General, ITAR-TASS News Agency*; b. 23 Jan. 1950, Baku, Azerbaijan; m.; one s. *Education:* Baku Higher CPSU School, Azerbaijan Inst. of Foreign Languages. *Career:* Deputy Chair. Cttee of Youth Orgs, Azerbaijan 1973–86; Head of Information Dept, then Head of Press Centre, USSR Cttee of Youth Orgs 1986–91; Head of Gen. Admin. of Information Co-operation INFOMOL 1991–95; Vice-Pres. International Analytic Press Agency ANKOM-TASS 1995–98; Head of Chief, Dept of International Co-operation, Public Contacts and Special Projects, ITAR-TASS News Agency 1998–99, Deputy Dir-Gen., First Deputy Dir-Gen. 1999–; Co-founder World Congress of Russian Press 1999; Exec. Dir World Asscn of Russian Press. *Honours:* Diploma of the USSR Supreme Soviet, numerous medals; Gold Medal for contrib. to devt of TV and radio, International Acad. of Radio and Television (Russia) 2007. *Address:* ITAR-TASS News Agency, Tverskoy Blvd 10-12, 103009 Moscow, Russia (office). *Telephone:* (495) 629-7925 (office). *Website:* www.itar-tass.com (office).

GUSTAFSSON, Lars Erik Einar, DPhil; Swedish writer, philosopher and academic; *Jamail Distinguished Professor Emeritus in the Plan II Program, University of Texas*; b. 17 May 1936, Västerås; s. of Einar Gustafsson and Margaretha Carlsson; m. 1st Madeleine Gustafsson 1962; m. 2nd Dena Alexandra Chasnoff 1982; two s. two d.; m. 3rd Agneta Blomqvist 2005. *Education:* Uppsala Univ. *Career:* Editor-in-Chief, Bonniers Litterära Magasin 1966–72; Research Fellow, Bielefeld Inst. of Advanced Studies 1980–81; Adjunct Prof., Univ. of Texas 1983–2006, Jamail Distinguished Prof. in the Plan II Program 1995, now Prof. Emer.; Aby Warburg Foundation Prof., Hamburg 1997; mem. Akad. der Wissenschaften und der Literatur, Mainz, Akad. der Künste, Berlin, Royal Swedish Acad. of Eng, Bayerische Akad. der schönen Künste, Munich; Fellow Berlin Inst. of Advanced Studies 2004–05. *Exhibitions include:* Galleri Händer, Stockholm 1989, 1991, Galerie am Savignyplatz, Berlin 2001, 2003. *Television:* 18th Century Pessimism (Swedish TV2), The Philosophers (syndicated). *Plays:* Celebration at Night, Zürich, Frankfurt, Berlin 1979. *Publications:* The Death of a Beekeeper 1978, Language and Lies 1978, Stories of Happy People 1981, Bernard Foy's Third Castle 1986, The Silence of the World before Bach (poems) 1988, Fyra Poeter 1988, Problemformuleringsprivilegiet 1989, Det sällsamma djuret från norr 1989, The Afternoon of a Tiler 1991, Historien med Hunden 1993, The Tail of the Dog 1997, Windy 1999, A Time in Xanadu 2003. *Honours:* Officier des Arts et des Lettres; Kommendör des Bundesverdienstzeichens, Literis et Artibus; Prix Charles Veillon, Heinrich Steffen Preis, Övralidspriset, Bellman Prize of Swedish Acad.; John Simon Guggenheim Memorial Fellow of Poetry 1993. *Address:* University of Texas, Waggener Hall, Room 413, Department of Philosophy, Austin, TX 78712 (office); PMB 317, 3112 Windsor Road, Austin, TX 78703, USA. *Telephone:* (512) 471-5632 (office). *E-mail:* lars.gustafsson@ownit.nu (office); lars.gustafsson@mail.utexas.edu (office). *Website:* www.utexas.edu/cola/depts/philosophy (office); www.utexas.edu/cola/depts/germanic (office).

GUTCHEON, Beth Richardson, BA; American writer; b. 18 March 1945, Sewickley; m. Jeffrey Gutcheon 1968; one s. *Education:* Radcliffe Coll. *Films:* scriptwriter: The Children of Theatre Street 1977, Without a Trace 1983, The Good Fight 1992. *Publications:* fiction: The New Girls 1979, Still Missing 1981, Domestic Pleasures 1991, Saying Grace 1995, Five Fortunes 1998, More Than You Know 2000, Leeway Cottage : A Novel 2005, Good-bye and Amen: A Novel 2009, Gossip: A Novel 2012; non-fiction: The Perfect Patchwork Primer 1973, Abortion: A Woman's Guide 1973, The Quilt Design Workbook (with Jeffrey Gutcheon) 1975; contribs to periodicals. *Address:* c/o HarperCollins, 10 E., 53rd Street, New York, NY 10022, USA.

GUTERSON, David, BA, MFA; American author; b. 4 May 1956, Seattle, Wash.; s. of Murray Guterson and Shirley Guterson (née Zak); m. Robin Ann Radwick 1979; three s. one d. *Education:* Univ. of Washington, Brown Univ. *Publications:* The Country Ahead of Us, The Country Behind (short stories) 1989, Family Matters: Why Home Schooling Makes Sense 1992, Snow Falling on Cedars (PEN/Faulkner Award for Fiction 1994, Barnes & Noble Discovery Award, Pacific NW Booksellers Award 1995) 1994, East of the Mountains 1998, Our Lady of the Forest 2003, The Other 2008. *Literary Agent:* c/o Georges Borchardt Inc., 136 East 57th Street, New York, NY 10020, USA. *E-mail:* georges@gbagency.com.

GUTIÉRREZ, Pedro Juan; Cuban novelist, poet, painter and journalist; b. 27 Jan. 1950, Matanzas. *Education:* Universidad de la Habana. *Career:* fmrly diverse range of employment, including ice-cream seller, soldier, sugar cane cutter, and many others; fmrly journalist, Bohemia journal, Havana; currently writer and painter. *Publications:* fiction: Dirty Havana Trilogy 2000, Dog Meat (Narrativa Sur del Mundo, Italy) 2003, Tropical Animal (Alfonso García-Ramos Prize, Spain) 2003, The King of Havana 2004, The Insatiable Spiderman 2005, Melancholy of Lions 2006, Corazon Mestizo: Apuntes de Viaje por Cuba 2007, Our GG in Havana 2010, Sabor a Mi 2011, The Snake's Nest (Prix des Amériques insulaires et de la Guyane 2008), Pobre Diablo and Other Stories; poetry: Espléndidos peces plateados, Fuego contra los herejes, Yo y una lujuriosa negra vieja, Lulu la perdida y otros poemas de John Snake, No tengas miedo, Lulú. *Address:* Apdo Postal 6239, 10600 Havana, Cuba (home). *Website:* www.pedrojuangutierrez.com.

GUTIÉRREZ ROMÁN, José; Spanish poet and novelist; b. 1977, Burgos. *Education:* Univ. of Burgos. *Publications:* poetry: Horarios de ausencia 2001, Alguien dijo tu nombre 2005, Los pies del Horizonte (Winner, Premio Adonais de Poesia 2010) 2010; novels: El equilibrio de los flamencos 2006, La vida en inglés 2008; appears in several anthologies. *Honours:* Premio Letras jóvenes de Castilla y León 2000, 2004, 2005. *Address:* c/o Ediciones RIALP SA, Alcalá 290, 28027 Madrid, Spain (office). *Telephone:* (91) 3260504 (office). *Fax:* (91) 3261321 (office). *E-mail:* ediciones@rialp.com (office). *Website:* www.rialp.com (office).

GUTIONTOV, Pavel Semenovich; Russian journalist; b. 23 Jan. 1953. *Education:* Moscow State Univ. *Career:* mem. of staff Moskovski Komsomolets 1970–75; fmr corresp. Komsomolskaya Pravda, then Head of Div. 1975–85; special corresp. Sovetskaya Rossiya 1985–87; political observer Izvestia; Co-Chair. Liberal Journalists Club –1997; Chair. Cttee for Defence of Freedom of Speech and Journalists' Rights; Sec. Russian Journalists' Union. *Publications:* Games in the Fresh Air of Stagnation 1990, Fate of Drummers 1997 and numerous articles. *Honours:* winner of numerous professional prizes. *Address:* Russian Journalists' Union, Zubovsky blvd 4, 119021 Moscow, Russia (office). *Telephone:* (495) 637-21-59 (office). *E-mail:* gutiontov@mail.ru (office).

GUTTERIDGE, Donald George, BA; Canadian poet, writer and academic; *Professor Emeritus, University of Western Ontario*; b. 30 Sept. 1937, Sarnia, Ont.; s. of William Gutteridge and Grace McWatters; m. Anne Barnett 1961; one s. one d. *Education:* Chatham Coll. Inst., Ont., Univ. of Western Ontario, London. *Career:* Asst Prof., Univ. of Western Ontario 1968–75, Assoc. Prof. 1975–77, Prof. of English Methods 1977–93, Prof. Emer. 1993–. *Publications:* poetry: Riel – A Poem for Voices 1968, The Village Within 1970, Death at Quebec and Other Poems 1972, Saying Grace: An Elegy 1972, Coppermine: The Quest for North 1973, Borderlands 1975, Tecumseh 1976, A True History of Lambton County 1977, God's Geography 1982, The Exiled Heart: Selected Narratives 1986, Love in the Wintertime 1982, Flute Music in the Cello's Belly 1997, Bloodlines 2001, Something More Miraculous 2004 Still Magical 2007; fiction: Bus-Ride 1974, All in Good Time 1980, St Vitus Dance 1986, Shaman's Ground 1988, How the World Began 1991, Summer's Idyll 1993, Winter's Descent 1996, Bewilderment 2001, Turncoat 2003, 2010, Solemn Vows 2003, 2011, Vital Secrets 2007. *Honours:* Pres.'s Medal, Univ. of Western Ontario 1971, Canada Council Travel Grant 1973. *Address:* 114 Victoria Street, London, ON N6A 2B5, Canada. *Telephone:* (519) 434-5843. *E-mail:* dongutteridge@rogers.com.

GUTTMAN, Robert, BA, MA; American journalist. *Education:* Indiana Univ., American Univ., Washington, DC. *Career:* fmr int. economist, Dept of Commerce; fmr Press Sec., White House; writer/researcher for presidential cands 1968, 1972 and 1976; Ed.-in-Chief, Pres. and Publr Political Profiles Inc. 1979–89; fmr Adjunct Prof. of Political Communications, George Washington Univ.; fmr Adjunct Prof. of American Politics and Communications, American

Univ.; Head of Pubs, EC Office, Washington, DC and Ed.-in-Chief, Europe magazine 1989–2003; Founder and Ed.-in-Chief Transatlantic magazine 2003–05, then Ed.; apptd Sr Fellow, Center for Transatlantic Relations, Johns Hopkins Univ. 2004, later Dir, Center on Politics and Foreign Relations, School of Advanced International Studies; fmr presenter, radio current affairs programme. *Publication:* Europe in the New Century: Visions of an Emerging Superpower 2001. *Address:* c/o Center on Politics and Foreign Relations, Paul H. Nitze School of Advanced International Studies, Johns Hopkins University, Nitze Building, 1740 Massachusetts Avenue, NW, Washington, DC 20036, USA.

GUY, John, PhD; British writer and historian; b. 1949, Australia; m. Julia Fox. *Education:* Univ. of Cambridge. *Career:* Research Fellow, Selwyn Coll., Cambridge 1970; writer and reviewer, The Sunday Times, The Guardian, The Economist, Times Literary Supplement, Financial Times, History Today; Fellow, Clare Coll., Cambridge. *Television:* presenter Timewatch: The King's Servant (BBC 2) 2001, Renaissance Secrets (four-part series, BBC 2); contrib. to Meet the Ancestors (BBC 2), Time Team (Channel 4), Royal Deaths and Diseases (Channel 4). *Publications:* non-fiction: The Cardinal's Court: The Impact of Thomas Wolsey in Star Chamber 1977, The Public Career of Sir Thomas More 1980, Law and Social Change in British History 1984, The Court of Star Chamber and its Records to the Reign of Elizabeth I 1985, Christopher St German on Chancery and Statute 1985, Reassessing the Henrician Age (with Alistair Fox) 1986, The Complete Works of St Thomas More, Vol. X: The Debellation of Salem and Bizance (co-ed.) 1987, Tudor England 1990, The Tudors and Stuarts (with John Morrill) 1992, The Reign of Elizabeth I: Court and Culture in the Last Decade 1995, The Tudor Monarchy 1997, Cardinal Wolsey 1998, Politics, Law and Counsel in Tudor and Early-Stuart England 2000, Thomas More 2000, The Tudors: A Very Short Introduction 2000, My Heart is My Own: The Life of Mary, Queen of Scots (Whitbread Biography Award) 2004, A Daughter's Love: Thomas and Margaret More 2008, Thomas Becket: Warrior, Priest, Rebel, Victim: A 900 Year Old Story Retold 2012; contrib. to The Oxford History of Britain 1988, The Oxford Illustrated History of Britain 1992, The Oxford Illustrated History of Tudor and Stuart Britain 2000, The Short Oxford History of the British Isles: The Sixteenth Century 1485–1603 2001. *Honours:* Hon. Prof., Univ. of St Andrews 2003; Yorke Prize 1976, Marsh Biography Award 2005. *Literary Agent:* c/o Rogers, Coleridge & White Literary Agency, 20 Powis Mews, London, W11 1JN, England. *Telephone:* (20) 7243-6326. *Fax:* (20) 7229-9084. *E-mail:* alex@rcwlitagency.com. *Website:* www.rcwlitagency.co.uk; www.johnguy.co.uk.

GWYN, Richard, OC; Canadian civil servant, journalist and writer; b. 1934, Bury St. Edmunds, England; s. of Brig. Philip Eustace Congreve Jermy-Gwyn and Elizabeth Edith Jermy-Gwyn (née Tilley); m. 1st Sandra Gwyn 1958 (died 2000); m. 2nd Carol Bishop Gwyn. *Education:* Stonyhurst Coll., Royal Military Acad., Sandhurst. *Career:* emigrated to Canada 1954; parl. corresp., United Press Int. 1957–59; worked for Thomson Newspapers 1959–60; Ottawa Ed., Maclean-Hunter Business Publications 1960–62; parl. corresp. and contributing ed. Time Canada 1962–68; exec. asst to Minister of Communications, Eric Kierans 1968–70; Dir-Gen., Socio-Economic Planning, Dept of Communications 1970–73; nat. affairs columnist, The Toronto Star 1973–85, int. affairs columnist 1985–92; Chancellor St Jerome's Univ. 2002; fmr mem. Bd of Dirs Canadian Journalists for Free Expression. *Publications:* The Shape of Scandal: A Study of a Government in Crisis 1965, Smallwood: The Unlikely Revolutionary 1965, The Northern Magus: Pierre Trudeau and Canadians 1980, The 49th Paradox: Canada in North America 1985, Nationalism Without Walls 1995, John A.: The Man Who Made Us (Charles Taylor Prize for Literary Non-Fiction 2008) 2007, Nation Maker (Shaughnessy Cohen Prize for Political Writing 2012) 2011. *Honours:* Hon. LLD (Univ. of King's Coll.) 1987. *Address:* c/o Random House of Canada Limited, One Toronto Street, Unit 300, Toronto ON M5C 2V6, Canada (office). *Telephone:* (416) 364-4449 (office). *Fax:* (416) 364-6863 (office). *Website:* www.randomhouse.ca (office).

GWYNN, Robert Samuel, BA, MA, MFA; American academic, writer, poet and editor; *Professor, Department of English and Modern Languages, Lamar University*; b. 13 May 1948, Eden, North Carolina; m. 1st Faye La Prade 1969 (divorced 1977); m. 2nd Donna Kay Skaggs Simon 1977; one s. *Education:* Davidson Coll., Univ. of Arkansas. *Career:* Instructor in English, Southwest Texas State Univ., San Marcos 1973–76; Prof., Dept of English and Modern Languages, Lamar Univ., Beaumont 1976–, named Univ. Prof. 1997, currently also Poet-in-Residence; many poetry readings throughout USA; mem. Associated Writing Programs, Poetry Soc. of America, Conf. of Coll. Teachers of English, Texas Asscn of Creative Writing Teachers, Texas Inst. of Letters; South Central MLA. *Publications:* Bearing and Distance (poems) 1977, The Narcissiad (poems) 1981, The Drive-In 1986, Dictionary of Literary Biography, Second Series (vol. 105), American Poets Since World War II (ed., contrib.) 1991, Drama: A HarperCollins Pocket Anthology (ed.) 1993, Fiction: A HarperCollins Pocket Anthology (ed.) 1993, Poetry: A HarperCollins Pocket Anthology (ed.) 1993, The Area Code of God (poems) 1994, The Advocates of Poetry: A Reader of American Poet-Critics of the Modern Era (ed.) 1996, No Word of Farewell (poems) 1996, Fiction: A Longman Pocket Anthology (ed., contrib.) 1997, Poetry: A Pocket Anthology (ed.) 2001, No Word of Farewell: Poems 1970–2000 2001, Contemporary American Poetry: A Pocket Anthology (ed.) 2005; anthologies including: Texas Poets in Concert: A Quartet, Rebel Angels: Twenty-Five Poets of the New Formation, The Store of Joys; more than 70 articles, poems and reviews to periodicals including: Sparrow, Tar River Poetry, Sewanee Review, Hudson Review, Poetry Northwest, Texas Monthly. *Honours:* Vereen Bell Award for Creative Writing, Davidson Coll., John Gould Fletcher Award for Poetry, Univ. of Arkansas, Michael Braude Award, American Acad. of Arts and Letters, Breakthrough Award, Univ. of Missouri Press. *Address:* Department of English and Modern Languages, Lamar University, PO Box 10023, Beaumont, TX 77710-0023, USA (office). *Telephone:* (409) 880-8575 (office). *E-mail:* RSGwynn@my.lamar.edu (office); rsgwynn@mail.com. *Website:* sites.google.com/site/rsgwynn (office).

GWYNNE, S. C. (Sam), MA; American journalist and author; m. Katie Gwynne; one d. *Education:* Princeton Univ., Johns Hopkins Univ. *Career:* fmr teacher of French and fmr int. banker; fmr Ed.-in-Chief California Business magazine; Bureau Chief, Nat. Corresp. and Sr Ed. Time magazine 1988–2000; Writer, Texas Monthly 2000–08; Sr Writer, Dallas Morning News 2010–; Lecturer, School of Journalism, Univ. of Texas; Pres. Bd of Dirs Caritas of Austin 2007–08. *Publications:* Selling Money 1986, The Outlaw Bank: A Wild Ride into the Secret Heart of BCCI (co-author) (one of Business Week's Top Ten Books of the Year) 2004, Empire of the Summer Moon: Quanah Parker and the Rise and Fall of the Comanches, the Most Powerful Indian Tribe in American History (Texas Book Award, Oklahoma Book Award) 2010; contrib. articles to New York Times, Harper's, California Magazine, San Francisco Chronicle, Los Angeles Times, The Boston Globe and others. *Honours:* Nat. Headliners Award, Gerald Loeb Award for Business Writing, Jack Anderson Award for Best Investigative Reporter, John Hancock Award for Distinguished Financial Writing, Nat. City and Regional Magazine Award for Writer of the Year 2008. *Literary Agent:* Amy Hughes, McCormick Williams, 37 West 20th Street, New York, NY 10011, USA. *Telephone:* (212) 691-9726. *E-mail:* ah@mccormickwilliams.com. *Website:* scgwynne.com.

H

HABERMAS, Jürgen, DPhil, Habilitation; German academic and writer; *Professor Emeritus of Philosophy, University of Frankfurt*; b. 18 June 1929, Düsseldorf; m. Ute Habermas-Wesselhoeft 1955; one s. two d. *Education:* Univs of Bonn and Göttingen. *Career:* Research Asst, Inst. für Soziale Forschung, Frankfurt 1956; Prof. of Philosophy, Univ. of Heidelberg 1961, of Philosophy and Sociology, Univ. of Frankfurt 1964; Dir Max Planck Inst., Starnberg, Munich 1971; Prof. of Philosophy, Univ. of Frankfurt 1983–94, Prof. Emer. 1994–; mem. Academia Europaea; Foreign mem. American Acad. of Arts and Sciences 1984, British Acad. of Science 1994. *Publications:* Strukturwandel der Öffentlichkeit 1962, Theorie und Praxis 1963, Erkenntnis und Interesse 1968, Legitimationsprobleme im Spätkapitalismus 1973, Theorie des kommunikativen Handelns 1981, Moralbewusstsein und Kommunikatives Handeln 1983, Der Philosophische Diskurs ober Moderne 1985, Eine Art Schadensabwicklüng 1987, Nachmetaphysisches Denken 1988, Nachholende Revolution 1990, Texte und Kontexte 1991, Erläuterungen zur Diskursetnik 1991, Faktizität und Geltung 1992, Vergangenheit als Zukunft 1993, Die Normalität einer Berliner Republik 1995, Die Einbeziehung des Anderen 1996, Vom sinnlichen Eindruck zum symbolischen Ausdruck 1997, Die postnationale Konstellation 1998, Wahrheit und Rechtfertigung 1999, Zeit und Übergänge 2001, Kommunikatives Handeln und Detranszendentalisierte Vernunft 2001, Die Zukunft der Menschlichen Natur 2001, Zeitdiagnosen 2003, Der gespaltene Westen 2004, Ach Europa 2008, Philosophische Texte (five vols) 2009, Zür Verfassung Europas 2011. *Honours:* Hon. DD (New School for Social Research) 1984; hon. degrees from Hebrew Univ. (Jerusalem), Univs of Hamburg, Buenos Aires, Evanston (Northwestern), Utrecht, Athens, Bologna, Paris, Tel-Aviv, Cambridge, Harvard; Hegel Prize 1972, Sigmund Freud Prize 1976, Adorno Prize 1980, Geschwister Scholl Prize 1985, Leibniz Prize 1986, Sonning Prize 1987, Jaspers Prize 1997, Culture Prize of the State of Hesse 1999, Friedenspreis des deutschen Buchhandels 2001, Prince of Asturias Award for Social Science 2003, Kyoto Prize for Philosophy 2004, Holberg Int. Memorial Prize 2005, Bruno Kreisky Prize 2006, Staatspreis des landes Nordheim-Westfalen 2006, Int. Brunet Prize, Pamplona 2008, Ulysses Medal, Dublin 2010. *Address:* Department of Philosophy, University of Frankfurt, Grüneburgplatz 1, 60629 Frankfurt am Main (office); Ringstrasse 8B, 82319 Starnberg, Germany (home). *Telephone:* (8151) 13537 (home). *Fax:* (8151) 13537 (home).

HABGOOD, Baron (Life Peer), cr. 1995, of Calverton in the County of Buckinghamshire; **Rt Rev. and Rt Hon. John Stapylton Habgood,** PC, MA, PhD, DD; British ecclesiastic (retd); b. 23 June 1927, Stony Stratford; s. of Arthur Henry Habgood and Vera Chetwynd-Stapylton; m. Rosalie Mary Anne Boston 1961; two s. two d. *Education:* Eton Coll., King's Coll. Cambridge Univ. and Cuddesdon Coll., Oxford. *Career:* Demonstrator in Pharmacology, Univ. of Cambridge 1950–53; Fellow, King's Coll. Cambridge 1952–55, Hon. Fellow 1984; Curate, St Mary Abbott's Church, Kensington 1954–56; Vice-Prin. Westcott House, Cambridge 1956–62; Rector, St John's Church, Jedburgh, Scotland 1962–67; Prin. Queen's Coll., Birmingham 1967–73; Bishop of Durham 1973–83; Archbishop of York 1983–95; Pres. (UK) Council on Christian Approaches to Defence and Disarmament 1976–95; Chair. WCCs' Int. Hearing on Nuclear Weapons 1981; mem. Council for Science and Society 1975–90, Council for Arms Control 1981–95; Moderator of Church and Soc. Sub-Unit, WCC 1983–90; Chair. UK Xenotransplantation Interim Regulatory Authority 1997–2003. *Publications:* Religion and Science 1964, A Working Faith 1980, Church and Nation in a Secular Age 1983, Confessions of a Conservative Liberal 1988, Making Sense 1993, Faith and Uncertainty 1997, Being a Person 1998, Varieties of Unbelief 2000, The Concept of Nature 2002. *Honours:* Hon. DD (Durham) 1975, (Cambridge) 1984, (Aberdeen) 1988, (Huron) 1990, (Hull) 1991, (Oxford) 1996, (Manchester) 1996, (London) 2005; Hon. DUniv (York) 1996; Hon. DHL (York, Pa) 1995; Bampton Lecturer, Univ. of Oxford 1999, Gifford Lecturer, Univ. of Aberdeen 2000. *Address:* 18 The Mount, Malton, N Yorks., YO17 7ND, England (home). *E-mail:* js.habgood@btinternet.com (home).

HABIB, Randa, MA; Lebanese/French journalist; *Director and Head, Agence France Presse, Jordan*; b. 16 Jan. 1952, Beirut, Lebanon; d. of Farid Habib; m. Adnan Gharaybeh 1973; one s. one d. *Education:* French Lycée, Rio de Janeiro and Univ. of Beirut. *Career:* corresp., Agence France Presse (AFP) 1980, Dir and Head of AFP Office, Amman 1987–; corresp., Radio Monte Carlo 1988–2006, columnist in local Jordanian papers, corresp. also for several int. publs and TV; Chair. Foreign Press Club, Jordan; mem. Bd of Dirs Jordan Media Inst.; Gov., Agence France Presse Foundation; mem. Bd Center to Protect Journalists. *Publications:* Hussein père et fils, 30 années qui ont changé le Moyen-Orient 2007, Hussein and Abdullah Inside the Jordanian Royal Family 2010. *Honours:* Chevalier, Ordre nat. du Mérite 2001, Légion d'honneur 2008; Médaille du Travail (France) 2000. *Address:* Agence France Presse, Jebel Amman, 2nd Circle, PO Box 3340, Amman 11181, Jordan (office). *Telephone:* (6) 4642976 (office). *Fax:* (6) 4654680 (office). *E-mail:* randa.habib@afp.com (office). *Website:* www.afp.com (office).

HABILA, Helon; Nigerian author and academic; *Faculty Member, Graduate Creative Writing Program, Department of English, George Mason University*; b. 17 Nov. 1967, Kaltungo, Gombe State; m. Susan Habila. *Education:* Univ. of Jos, Univ. of East Anglia, UK. *Career:* Lecturer in English and Literature, Fed. Polytechnic, Bauchi 1997–99; fmr contrib. to Hints magazine, Lagos; fmr Arts Ed. Vanguard newspaper, Lagos; African Writing Fellow, Univ. of East Anglia, UK 2002–04; Chinua Achebe Fellow of Africana Global Studies, Bard Coll., New York, USA 2005–06; Faculty mem. Dept of English, Grad. Creative Writing Program, George Mason Univ., USA 2007–; Contributing Ed. Virginia Quarterly Review. *Publications:* Mai Kaltungo (biog.) 1997, Prison Stories (short stories) 2000, Waiting for an Angel (Commonwealth Prize for Best First Book, African Region 2003) 2001, Measuring Time (Virginia Library Foundation Fiction Prize 2008) 2007, Oil on Water 2010; co-ed. New Writing 14 (British Council Anthology), Miracles, Dreams, and Jazz; short stories and poems in anthologies. *Honours:* First Prize, MUSON Festival Poetry Competition (for poem Another Age) 2000, Caine Prize for African Writing, UK (for short story Love Poems) 2001, Emily Balch Prize (for short story Hotel Malogo) 2008. *Address:* Graduate Creative Writing Program, Department of English, George Mason University, 4400 University Drive, MSN 3E4, Fairfax, VA 22030, USA (office). *Telephone:* (703) 993-9553 (office). *E-mail:* hngalaba@gmu.edu (office). *Website:* english.gmu.edu (office); www.helonhabila.com. *Literary Agent:* c/o David Godwin Associates, 55 Monmouth Street, London, WC2H 9DG, England. *Telephone:* (20) 7240-9992. *Fax:* (20) 7395-6110. *E-mail:* david@davidgodwinassociates.co.uk. *Website:* www.davidgodwinassociates.co.uk.

HACHETTE, Jean-Louis, LenD; French publisher; b. 30 June 1925, Paris; s. of Louis and Blanche (née Darbou) Hachette; m. Y. de Bouillé 1954; one s. two d. *Education:* Collège Stanislas, Paris and Faculté de Droit, Paris. *Career:* joined Librairie Hachette (f. by great-grandfather in 1826) 1946 (now Hachette Livre); entire career spent with Librairie Hachette, Admin. Dir 1971–; Pres. Librairie Générale Française 1954–. *Address:* Librairie Générale Française, 43 quai de Grenelle, 75905 Paris, Cédex 15, France (office). *Website:* www.hachette.com (office).

HACKER, Katharina; German writer; b. 1967, Frankfurt. *Education:* Freiburg Univ., Hebrew Univ., Jerusalem. *Career:* lived in Israel 1990–96; currently based in Berlin. *Publications include:* Tel Aviv 1997, Oder der Schnabelschuh (trans. as Morpheus) 1998, Der Bademeister (trans. as The Lifeguard) 2000, Eine Art Liebe 2003, Die Habenichtse (German Book Prize) (trans. as The Havenots) 2006, Überlandleitung 2007. *Address:* c/o Suhrkamp Insel, Lindenstasse 29–35, 60325 Frankfurt am Main, Germany (office). *Telephone:* (69) 756010 (office). *E-mail:* lektorat@suhrkamp.de (office). *Website:* www.suhrkamp.de (office).

HACKER, Marilyn, BA; American poet, writer, critic, editor and academic; *Chancellor, Academy of American Poets*; b. 27 Nov. 1942, New York, NY; one d. *Education:* New York Univ. *Career:* Ed. Quark: A Quarterly of Speculative Fiction 1969–71, The Kenyon Review 1990–94; Jenny McKean Moore Chair in Writing, George Washington Univ. 1976–77; mem. Editorial Collective, The Little Magazine 1977–80, Ed.-in-Chief 1979; teacher, School of General Studies, Columbia Univ., New York 1979–81; Visiting Artist, Fine Arts Work Center, Provincetown, Mass 1981; Visiting Prof., Univ. of Idaho 1982; Ed.-in-Chief, Thirteenth Moon: A Feminist Literary Magazine 1982–86; Writer-in-Residence, State Univ. of NY (SUNY), Albany 1988, Columbia Univ. 1988; George Elliston Poet-in-Residence, Univ. of Cincinnati 1988; Distinguished Writer-in-Residence, American Univ., Washington, DC 1989; Visiting Prof. of Creative Writing, SUNY, Binghamton 1990, Univ. of Utah 1995, Barnard Coll. 1995, Princeton Univ., NJ 1997; Fannie Hurst Poet-in-Residence, Brandeis Univ., Mass 1996; Prof. of English, City Coll. of New York 1999–2009; Prof. of French, CUNY Grad. Center 2003; Chancellor, Acad. of American Poets 2008–. *Publications:* Presentation Piece 1974, Separations 1976, Taking Notice 1980, Assumptions 1985, Love, Death and the Changing of the Seasons 1986, The Hang-Glider's Daughter: New and Selected Poems 1990, Going Back to the River 1990, Selected Poems: 1965–1990 1994, Winter Numbers 1994, Edge (trans. of poems by Claire Malroux) 1996, Squares and Courtyards 2000, A Long-Gone Sun (trans. of poems by Claire Malroux) 2000, Here There Was Once a Country (trans. of poems by Vénus Khoury-Ghata) 2001, She Says (trans. of poems by Vénus Khoury-Ghata) 2003, Desesperanto: Poems 1999–2002 2003, First Cities: Collected Early Poems 1960–1979 2003, Birds and Bison (trans. of poems by Claire Malroux) 2004, Poetry to Heal Your Blues (ed.) 2006, Essays on Departure: New and Selected Poems 1980–2005 2006, King of a Hundred Horsemen (trans. of poems by Marie Etienne) 2008, He and I (trans. of poems by Emmanuel Moses) 2009, Names 2009, Treason (trans. of poems by Hédi Kaddour) 2010; contrib. to numerous anthologies and other publications. *Honours:* Nat. Endowment for the Arts grants 1973–74, 1985–86, 1995, Nat. Book Award in Poetry 1975, Guggenheim Fellowship 1980–81, Ingram Merrill Foundation grant 1984–85, Robert F. Winner Award, Poetry Soc. of America 1987, 1989, John Masefield Memorial Award, Poetry Soc. of America 1994, Lambda Literary Award 1991, 1995, Lenore Marshall Award, Acad. of American Poets 1995, Poets' Prize, American Acad. of Arts and Letters 1995, Award in Literature, American Acad. of Arts and Letters 2004, PEN/Voelcker Award for Poetry 2010, Argana Int. Poetry Award 2011.

HACKER, Peter Michael Stephen, BA, MA, DPhil; British philosopher, librarian and writer; *Emeritus Research Fellow, St John's College, Oxford*; b. 15 July 1939, London, England; m. Sylvia Imhoff 1963; two s. one d.

Education: Queen's Coll., Oxford, St Antony's Coll., Oxford. *Career:* Jr Research Fellow, Balliol Coll., Oxford 1965–66; Fellow and Tutor in Philosophy, St John's Coll., Oxford 1966–2006, Librarian 1986–2006, Emer. Research Fellow 2006–; Visiting Prof., Swarthmore Coll., USA 1973, 1986, Univ. of Michigan, Ann Arbor, USA 1974, Queen's Univ., Kingston, Ont., Canada 1985, Visiting Sr Research Fellow, Inst. for Advanced Studies, Bologna Univ. 2009. *Publications:* Insight and Illusion: Wittgenstein and the Metaphysics of Experience 1972, second edn as Insight and Illusion: Themes in the Philosophy of Wittgenstein 1986, Law, Morality and Society: Essays in Honour of H. L. A. Hart (co-ed. and contrib.) 1977, Wittgenstein: Understanding and Meaning (with G. P. Baker) 1980, much revised 2nd edn 2004, Frege: Logical Excavations (with G. P. Baker) 1984, Language, Sense and Nonsense: A Critical Investigation into Modern Theories of Language (with G. P. Baker) 1984, Scepticism, Rules and Language (with G. P. Baker) 1984, Wittgenstein: Rules, Grammar and Necessity (with G. P. Baker) 1985, Appearance and Reality: A Philosophical Investigation into Perception and Perceptual Qualities 1987, The Renaissance of Gravure: The Art of S. W. Hayter (ed. and contributor) 1988, Wittgenstein: Meaning and Mind 1990, Gravure and Grace: The Engravings of Roger Vieillard (ed. and contributor) 1993, Wittgenstein: Mind and Will 1996, Wittgenstein's Place in Twentieth Century Analytic Philosophy 1996, Wittgenstein on Human Nature 1997, Wittgenstein: Connections and Controversies 2001, Philosophical Foundations of Neuroscience (with M. R. Bennett) 2003, Neuroscience and Philosophy: Language, Mind and Body (with M.R. Bennett, D. Dennet and J.R. Searle) 2007, Human Nature: the Categorial Framework 2007, History of Cognitive Neuroscience (with M. R. Bennett) 2008, Mind, Method and Morality: Essays in Honour of Anthony Kenny (co-ed.) 2009; contrib. to reference works, scholarly books and professional journals. *Honours:* Hon. Fellow, Queen's Coll., Oxford 2010 British Acad. Research Reader 1985–87, Leverhulme Sr Research Fellow 1991–94. *Address:* St John's College, Oxford, OX1 3JP, England (office). *Telephone:* (1865) 610876 (office).

HACKING, Ian MacDougall, CC, PhD, FRSC, FBA; Canadian academic; *Professor Emeritus, Collège de France*; b. 18 Feb. 1936, Vancouver; s. of Harold Eldridge Hacking and Margaret Elinore MacDougall; m. 1st Laura Anne Leach 1962; m. 2nd Judith Polsky Baker 1983; one s. two d. *Education:* Univ. of British Columbia, Univ. of Cambridge, UK. *Career:* Asst then Assoc. Prof., Univ. of British Columbia 1964–69; Univ. Lecturer in Philosophy, Univ. of Cambridge and Fellow of Peterhouse 1969–74; Prof., then Henry Waldgrave Stuart Prof. of Philosophy, Stanford Univ. 1975–82; Prof., Univ. of Toronto 1983–2003, Univ. Prof. 1991–2003, Prof. Emer. 2003–; Prof., Chair of Philosophy and History of Scientific Concepts Collège de France, Paris 2000–06, Prof. Emer. 2006–; Fellow American Acad. of Arts and Sciences 1991. *Publications:* Logic of Statistical Inference 1965, Why Does Language Matter to Philosophy? 1975, The Emergence of Probability 1975, Representing and Intervening 1983, The Taming of Chance 1991, Le plus pur nominalisme 1993, Rewriting the Soul: Multiple Personality and the Sciences of Memory 1995, Mad Travelers 1998, The Social Construction of What? 1999, Probability and Inductive Logic 2001, Historical Ontology 2002. *Honours:* Hon. Fellow, Trinity Coll., Cambridge 2000, Peterhouse, Cambridge 2002; Hon. LLD (Univ. of British Columbia) 2001, (McMaster Univ.) 2008, (Toronto) 2010; Hon. PhD (Univ. of Córdoba, Argentina) 2007; Molson Prize, Canada Council 2001, Killam Prize, Canada Council 2002, Holberg Int. Memorial Prize 2009. *Address:* 391 Markham Street, Toronto, Ont. M6G 2KB, Canada (office). *E-mail:* ian.hacking@college-de-france.fr (office). *Website:* www.college-de-france.fr (office).

HADAS, Rachel, BA, MA, PhD; American academic, poet and writer; *Board of Governors Professor of English, Rutgers University*; b. 8 Nov. 1948, New York, NY; m. 1st Stavros Kondilis 1970 (divorced) 1978; m. 2nd George Edwards 1978; one s. *Education:* Radcliffe Coll., Johns Hopkins Univ., Princeton Univ. *Career:* Asst Prof., Rutgers Univ. 1982–87, Assoc. Prof. 1987–92, Prof. of English 1992–2000, Bd of Govs Prof. of English 2000–; Adjunct Prof., Columbia Univ., New York 1992–93; Visiting Prof., Princeton Univ. 1995, 1996; Fellow, American Acad. of Arts and Sciences; mem. Modern Greek Studies Asscn, Modern Language Asscn, PEN, Poetry Soc. of America. *Publications:* Starting From Troy 1975, Slow Transparency 1983, A Son from Sleep 1987, Pass It On 1989, Living in Time 1990, Unending Dialogue 1991, Mirrors of Astonishment 1992, Other Worlds Than This 1994, The Empty Bed 1995, The Double Legacy 1995, Halfway Down the Hall (New and Selected Poems) 1998, Merrill Cavafy, Poems and Dreams 2000, Indelible 2001, Laws 2004, The River of Forgetfulness 2006; contribs to various periodicals. *Honours:* Ingram Merrill Foundation Fellowship 1976–77, Guggenheim Fellowship 1988–89, American Acad. and Inst. of Arts and Letters Award 1990, O. B. Hardison Award 2000, Scholars and Writers, New York Public Library 2000–01. *Address:* 838 West End Avenue, #3A, New York, NY 10025 (home); Department of English, Faculty of Arts and Sciences-Newark, 360 Dr Martin Luther King Jr Blvd, 520 Hill Hall, Newark, NJ 07102-1801, USA (office). *Telephone:* (212) 666-4482 (home); (973) 353-5279 ext. 520 (office). *Fax:* (212) 666-5533 (home); (973) 353-1450 (office). *E-mail:* rhadas@rutgers.edu (office). *Website:* www.rachelhadas.com.

HADDAD, Fawwaz, LLB; Syrian writer; b. 1947, Damascus. *Education:* Damascus Univ. *Publications:* nine novels including Mosaic, Damascus '39 1991, Teatro 1949 1994, Al-Risala al-Akhira (trans. as The Last Letter) 1994, Surat al-Rawee (trans. as The Image of the Narrator) 1998, Al-Walad al-Jahel (trans. as The Ignorant Child) 2000, Al-Daghina wa al-Hawa (trans. as Rancour and Affection) 2001, Mersal al-Gharam (trans. as The Love Messenger) 2004, Mashhad Aber (trans. as A Fleeting Scene) 2007, Al-Mutarjim Al-Khayn (trans. as The Unfaithful Translator) 2008, Azef Munfared 'ala al-Piano (trans. as A Solo Performance on the Piano) 2009. *Address:* c/o Riad El-Rayyes Books, Sanayeh, Union Building, Beirut, Lebanon (office). *E-mail:* info@elrayyesbooks.com (office). *Website:* www.elrayyesbooks.com (office).

HADDAD, Joumana; Lebanese journalist, poet and translator; b. 1970, Beirut. *Career:* arts journalist, an-Nahar newspaper 1997–, now Chief Ed. of the cultural pages. *Publications:* poetry collections: The Time of a Dream 1995, Invitation to a Secret Dinner 1998, Abyss 2000, I Haven't Sinned Enough (anthology) 2004, The Return of Lilith 2004; translations of poetry; contrib. to literary magazines, including Alhucema (Spain), Fornix (Peru), Hojas Sueltas (Colombia), Kalimat (Australia), Europe (France), Supérieur inconnu (France). *Honours:* Arab Press Prize, Dubai 2006. *E-mail:* contact@joumanahaddad.com (office). *Website:* www.joumanahaddad.com.

HADDON, Mark, MA; British writer and illustrator; b. 1962, Northampton; m. Sos Eltis; one s. *Education:* Merton Coll., Oxford, Edinburgh Univ. *Career:* positions at Mencap and other charity orgs; illustrator and cartoonist; painter; television work. *Screenwriting:* Microsoap (Royal Television Soc. Best Children's Drama), episodes of Starstreet, Fungus and the Bogeyman (adaptation). *Publications:* fiction: Gilbert's Gobstopper 1988, A Narrow Escape for Princess Sharon 1989, Toni and the Tomato Soup 1989, Agent Z Meets the Masked Crusader 1993, Gridzbi Spudvetch! 1993, In the Garden 1994, On Holiday (aka On Vacation) 1994, At Home 1994, At Playgroup 1994, Titch Johnson 1994, Agent Z Goes Wild 1994, Agent Z and the Penguin from Mars 1995, Real Porky Philips 1995, The Sea of Tranquillity 1996, Secret Agent Handbook 1999, Ocean Star Express 2001, Agent Z and the Killer Bananas 2001, The Ice Bear's Cave 2002, The Curious Incident of the Dog in the Night Time (Booktrust Teenage Prize 2003, Guardian Children's Fiction Prize 2003, South Bank Show Best Book Prize 2004, Whitbread Best Novel and Book of the Year 2004, Commonwealth Writers Prize for best first book 2004, Soc. of Authors McKitterick Prize 2004, WHSmith Children's Book of the Year 2004, Waterstone's Literary Fiction award 2004) 2003, A Spot of Bother 2006, The Red House 2012; poetry: The Talking Horse and the Sad Girl and the Village Under the Sea 2005. *Address:* 4 Farndon Road, Oxford, OX2 6RS, England. *Website:* www.markhaddon.com.

HADLOW, Janice; British broadcasting executive; *Controller, BBC Two.* *Career:* production trainee, BBC 1986, later producer on Radio 4, Ed. Late Show, Deputy Head music and arts dept, Jt Head of history dept –1999; Head of History, Arts and Religion, Channel 4 1999, later Head of Specialist Factual Group, Channel 4 –2004; Controller, BBC Four 2004–08, BBC Two 2008–. *Publication:* The Nunnery: The Six Daughters of George III (with Martin Davidson) 2004. *Address:* BBC Two, BBC Television Centre, Wood Lane, London, W12 7RJ, England (office). *Website:* www.bbc.co.uk (office).

HAEMAMOOL, Uthis; Thai author; b. 10 Jan. 1975, Kaeng Khoi. *Education:* Silpakorn Univ. *Career:* fmr short film maker; film reviewer, Movie Time magazine 2001–. *Films:* Pipop Buntoon, Dokmai Nai Tarng Puen (artistic dir). *Publications:* Luen: Joodjob Kong Name AunPenAuen 2001, Rabum Maytun 2005, Porimat Rampueng (short stories) 2005, Krajok Ngao/Ngao Krajok 2006, Mai Yorn Kuen (short stories) 2008, Lap Lae, Kaeng Khoi (Southeast Asian Writers Award 2009). *Address:* c/o Somsri Hansirisawasdi, SEA Write Award, Public Relations Department, The Oriental Bangkok, 48 Oriental Avenue, Bangkok 10500, Thailand.

HAGE, Rawi, BA; Lebanese/Canadian artist, photographer and writer; b. 1964, Beirut, Lebanon. *Education:* New York Inst. of Photography, USA, Dawson Coll., Montreal, Concordia Univ., Montreal. *Career:* emigrated to USA 1982, studied photography in New York City; moved to Canada 1991; has participated in solo and group exhbns in Canada, Lebanon, France, Colombia; works in perm. collections including Canadian Museum of Civilization, Musée de la civilisation de Québec; art works also include Care of Raymonde 1997. *Publications:* De Niro's Game (novel) (Paragraphe Hugh MacLennan Prize for Fiction, McAuslan First Book Prize, Int. IMPAC Dublin Literary Award 2008) 2006, Cockroach (Hugh MacLennan Prize for Fiction, Quebec Writers' Fed.) 2008; contrib. to Fuse Magazine, Mizna, Jouvert, The Toronto Review, Montreal Serai, Al-Jadid. *Address:* c/o House of Anansi Press, 110 Spadina Avenue, Suite 801, Toronto, ON M5V 2K4, Canada.

HAGÈGE, Claude, LèsL, TH; French linguist and author; *Professor, Collège de France*; b. 1 Jan. 1936, Carthage, Tunisia; s. of Edmond Hagège and Liliane Taïeb-Hagège. *Education:* Lycée Carnot, Tunis, Lycée Louis-le-Grand, Paris, Ecole Normale Supérieure, Paris, Harvard Univ. and Massachusetts Inst. of Tech., USA; diplômes de chinois, arabe, russe de l'Ecole Nationale des Langues Orientales, Paris. *Career:* teacher, Lycée Carnot, Tunis 1959–61, Lycées Victor Duruy et Saint-Louis, Paris 1963–66; Prof. of Linguistics, Univ. of Poitiers 1971–87; Chief of Confs, Univ. of Paris XII Val-de-Marne 1971–74, Univ. of Paris IV 1976–78, Univ. of Paris III 1977–78; Dir of Linguistic Studies, Ecole Pratique des Hautes Etudes 1977; Prof., Collège de France 1988–. *Publications:* La Structure des langues 1982, L'Homme de paroles 1985 (English trans.: The Dialogic Species 1990), Le Français et les siècles 1987, Le Souffle de la langue 1992, The Language Builder, An Essay on the Human Signature in Linguistic Morphogenesis 1993, L'Enfant aux deux langues 1996, Le Français, histoire d'un combat 1996, Halte à la mort des langues 2001 (English trans.: On the Death and Life of Languages 2009), Combat pour le français 2006, Adpositions, Function Marking in Human Languages 2010.

Honours: Hon. Dir of Studies, Ecole Pratique des Hautes Etudes, Paris; Officier, Ordre des Palmes académiques 1995, Chevalier, Ordre des Arts et des Lettres 1995, Officier, Légion d'honneur 2005; Prix Volney, Acad. des Inscriptions et Belles-Lettres 1981, Grand Prix de l'Essai, Soc. des Gens de Lettres 1986, CNRS Médaille d'or 1995, Prix du Mot d'or des langues 2003. *Address:* Collège de France, 11 place Marcelin Berthelot, 75231 Paris Cedex 05, France (office). *Telephone:* 1-44-27-17-03 (office). *Fax:* 1-44-27-13-29 (home). *E-mail:* claude.hagege@college-de-france.fr (office); claude-hagege@wanadoo.fr (home). *Website:* claude.hagege.wanadoo.fr.

HAGGER, Nicholas Osborne, MA; British poet, verse dramatist, short story writer and lecturer, author, philosopher and cultural historian; b. 22 May 1939, London, England; m. 1st Caroline Virginia Mary Nixon 1961; one d.; m. 2nd Madeline Ann Johnson 1974; two s. *Education:* Worcester Coll., Oxford. *Career:* Lecturer in English, Univ. of Baghdad 1961–62; Prof. of English Literature, Tokyo Univ. of Educ. and Keio Univ., Tokyo 1963–67, Tokyo Univ. 1964–65; Lecturer in English, Univ. of Libya, Tripoli 1968–70; freelance feature writer, The Times 1970–72; mem. Soc. of Authors. *Publications:* The Fire and the Stones: A Grand Unified Theory of World History and Religion 1991, Selected Poems: A Metaphysical's Way of Fire 1991, The Universe and the Light: A New View of the Universe and Reality 1993, A White Radiance: The Collected Poems 1958–93 1994, A Mystic Way: A Spiritual Autobiography 1994, Awakening to the Light: Diaries, Vol. 1 1958–67 1994, A Spade Fresh with Mud: Collected Stories, Vol. 1 1995, The Warlords: From D-Day to Berlin, A Verse Drama 1995, A Smell of Leaves and Summer: Collected Stories, Vol. 2 1995, Overlord, The Triumph of Light 1944–1945: An Epic Poem, Books 1–2 1995, Books 3–6 1996, Books 7–9, 10–12 1997, The One and the Many 1999, Wheeling Bats and a Harvest Moon: Collected Stories, Vol. 3 1999, Prince Tudor, A Verse Drama 1999, The Warm Glow of the Monastery Courtyard: Collected Stories, Vol. 4 1999, The Syndicate: The Story of the Coming World Government 2004, The Secret History of the West: The Influence of Secret Organisations on Western History from the Renaissance to the 20th Century 2005, Classical Odes: Poems on England, Europe and a Global Theme, and of Everyday Life in the One 2006, The Light of Civilization 2006, Overlord (one-vol. edn) 2006, Collected Poems 1958–2005 2006, Collected Verse Plays 2007, Collected Short Stories 2007, The Secret Founding of America: The Real Story of Freemasons, Puritans and the Battle for the New World 2007, The Rise and Fall of Civilizations: Why Civilizations Rise and Fall and What Happens When They End 2008, The Last Tourist in Iran 2008, The New Philosophy of Universalism, The Infinite and the Law of Order 2009, The Libyan Revolution, Its Origins and Legacy, A Memoir and Assessment 2009, Armageddon, The Triumph of Universal Order: An Epic Poem on the War on Terror and of Holy-War Crusaders 2010, The World Government: A Blueprint for a Universal World State 2010, The Secret American Dream: The Real Story of Liberty's Empire and the Rise of a World State 2011, A New Philosophy of Literature: The Fundamental Theme and Unity of World Literature 2012, A View of Epping Forest 2012. *E-mail:* info@nicholashagger.co.uk (office). *Website:* www.nicholashagger.com; www.nicholashagger.co.uk.

HAHN (GARCES), Oscar Arturo, MA, PhD; Chilean/American poet, writer and academic; b. 5 July 1938, Iquique, Chile; m. Nancy Jorquera 1971; one d. *Education:* University of Chile, University of Iowa, University of Maryland at College Park. *Career:* Prof. of Hispanic Literature, University of Chile 1965–73; Instructor, University of Maryland at College Park 1974–77; Asst Prof., University of Iowa 1977–79, Assoc. Prof. of Spanish-American Literature 1979, then Prof., now Prof. Emer.; mem. Instituto Internacional de Literatura Iberoamericana, Modern Language Asscn. *Publications:* Esta rosa negra (poems) 1961, Agua final (poems) 1967, Arte de morir (poems; trans. as The Art of Dying) 1977), El cuento fantástico hispanoamericano en el siglo XIX 1978, Mal de amor (trans. as Love Breaks) 1981, Imagenes nucleares 1983, Texto sobre texto 1984, Tratado de sortilegios 1992, Antología poética 1993, Antología virtual 1996, ¿Qué hacia yo el once de septiembre de 1973? (with Matias Rivas and Roberto Merino) 1997, Antología retroactiva 1998, Versos robados/Stolen Verses and Other Poems 2000, En un abrir y cerrar de ojos (Premio del Consejo Nacional del Libro) 2006, Ashes in Love 2009; contributions: literary journals. *Honours:* Hon. Fellow, International Writing Program 1972; Alerce Prize 1959, Premio Alerce 1961, Poetry Award, University of Chile 1966, Altazor Prize 2003, Pablo Neruda Prize 2011. *Address:* c/o Department of Spanish and Portuguese, University of Iowa, 111 Phillips Hall, Iowa City, IA 52242, USA (office). *E-mail:* oscar-hahn@uiowa.edu (office). *Website:* clas.uiowa.edu/dwllc/spanish-portuguese (office).

HAHN, Susan; American poet, playwright and editor; b. 11 Nov. 1947, Chicago; m. Frederic L. Hahn 1967; one s. *Career:* staff 1980–, Ed. 1997–, TriQuarterly literary magazine; Co-Founder/Co-Ed., TriQuarterly Books 1988–. *Publications:* Harriet Rubin's Mother's Wooden Hand 1991, Incontinence (Soc. of Midland Authors Award) 1993, Melancholia et cetera 1995, Confession 1997, Holiday 2001, Mother in Summer 2002, Golf (play) 2005, Self/Pity 2005, The Scarlet Ibis (also verse play, produced 2007, 2008) 2007, The Note She Left 2008; contrib. to many reviews, quarterlies and journals. *Honours:* Illinois Arts Council Literary Awards 1985, 1990, 1996, 1997, Soc. of Midland Authors Award for Poetry 1994, Pushcart Prizes for Poetry 2000, 2003, George Kent Prize, Poetry magazine 2000. *Address:* 1377 Scott Avenue, Winnetka, IL 60093, USA (home).

HAHN, Ulla, DPhil; German writer; b. 30 April 1946, Brachthausen, Sauerland. *Education:* Univs of Cologne and Hamburg. *Career:* Lecturer, Univs of Hamburg, Bremen, Oldenburg 1975–80; Radio Ed., Bremen 1979–91; freelance writer 1992–. *Publications include:* Herz über Kopf 1981, Spielende 1983, Freudenfeuer 1985, Unerhörte Nähe 1988, Ein Mann im Haus 1991, Galileo und zwei Frauen 1997, Das Verborgene Wort 2003. *Honours:* Leonce und Lena Award 1981, Hölderlin Award 1985, Roswitha von Sandersheim Medal 1986, Medal of FRG . *Address:* DVA, Neckarstrasse 121, Postfach 106012, 7000 Stuttgart 1 (Publr); Breitenfelderstrasse 86, 2000 Hamburg 20, Germany (home). *Telephone:* (40) 485495 (home).

HAIBLUM, Isidore, BA; American writer; b. 23 May 1935, New York. *Education:* City Coll., CUNY. *Publications:* The Tsaddik of the Seven Wonders 1971, The Return 1973, Transfer to Yesterday 1973, The Wilk Are Among Us 1975, Interworld 1977, Outerworld 1979, Nightmare Express 1979, Faster Than a Speeding Bullet: An Informal History of Radio's Golden Age (with Stuart Silver) 1980, The Mutants Are Coming 1984, The Identity Plunderers 1984, The Hand of Gantz 1985, Murder in Yiddish 1988, Bad Neighbors 1990, Out of Sync 1990, Specterworld 1991, Crystalword 1992, New York Confidential 2005, Murder In Gotham 2008; contribs to periodicals.

HAIDAR, Haidar; Syrian novelist and writer; b. 1936, Husain-al Bahr, nr Tartus. *Education:* Univ. of Damascus. *Career:* began publishing short stories in Syrian and Lebanese journals in 1960s; worked as a teacher in Algeria in early 1970s, then as a journalist, editor and book reviewer for publishing houses in Lebanon; moved to Cyprus 1980; now lives in Syria; his first novel was banned in several Arab countries; writes in Arabic. *Publications:* short stories including Al-Fahd (The Lynx) 1969, Al-Wamdh (The Flash) 1970, Hakaya an-Nawrass al-Muhajir (Tales of the Migrating Seagull), Az-Zaman al-Muhish (The Desolate Time) 1973, Ghasaq al-Aalihah (The Dusk of Gods) 1994, Al-Faiadhan (The Flood), At-Tamawujat (The Ripples), Pollen; novels: Walima Li Aashaab Al Bahr (Banquet for Seaweed) 1983, Maraya an-Nar (The Mirrors of Fire), Shumous al-Ghajar (The Suns of Gypsies) 1996, Haql Urjuwan (A Field of Purple) 2000, Marathi al-Ayyam (The Elegies of Days) 2001; non-fiction: Awraq al-Manfa (Exile Papers) 1993, Olumona (Our Sciences).

HAIGH, Christopher, BA, PhD, FRHistS; British academic and writer; *Lecturer in Modern History, Christ Church College, Oxford*; b. 28 Aug. 1944, Birkenhead, England; two d. *Education:* Univ. of Cambridge, Victoria Univ. of Manchester. *Career:* Lecturer in History, Victoria Univ. of Manchester 1969–79; Lecturer in Modern History, Christ Church Coll., Oxford 1979–; Univ. Lecturer, Oxford Univ. (retd). *Publications:* The Last Days of the Lancashire Monasteries 1969, Reformation and Resistance in Tudor Lancashire 1975, The Cambridge Historical Encyclopaedia of Great Britain and Ireland 1984, The Reign of Elizabeth l 1985, The English Reformation Revised 1987, Elizabeth l: A Profile in Power 1988, English Reformations: Religion, Politics and Society Under the Tudors 1993, The Plain Man's Pathway to Heaven: Kinds of Christianity in Post-Reformation England 1570–1640 2007. *Address:* Department of History, Christ Church College, St. Aldates, Oxford, OX1 1DP, England (office). *E-mail:* christopher.haigh@chch.ox.ac.uk (office). *Website:* www.chch.ox.ac.uk (office); www.history.ox.ac.uk/staff/postholder/haigh_ca.htm.

HAILEY, Elizabeth Forsythe, BA; American writer and dramatist; b. 31 Aug. 1938, Dallas, Tex.; m. Oliver Daffan Hailey 1960 (died 1993); two d. *Education:* Sorbonne, Univ. of Paris, Hollins Coll. *Career:* mem. Authors League of America, PEN USA. *Plays:* A Woman of Independent Means (Los Angeles Critics Award) 1984. *Publications:* fiction: A Woman of Independent Means 1978, Life Sentences 1982, Joanna's Husband and David's Wife 1986, Home Free 1991; contribs to books and periodicals. *Honours:* Silver Medal for Best First Novel, Commonwealth Club of California 1978, Los Angeles Drama Critics Award 1983. *Address:* 11747 Canton Place, Studio City, CA 91604, USA.

HAKIM, Seymour (Sy), AB, MA; American poet, writer, artist and educator; b. 23 Jan. 1933, New York; m. Odetta Roverso 1970. *Education:* Eastern New Mexico Univ., New York Univ. *Career:* Consultant Ed., Poet Gallery Press, New York 1970; Ed., Overseas Teacher 1977; mem. mem. Acad. of Poets and Writers; Nat. Photo Instructors' Asscn; Italo-Brittanica Asscn. *Publications:* The Sacred Family 1970, Manhattan Goodbye (poems) 1970, Under Moon 1971, In the Museum of the Mind 1971, Wine Theorem 1972, Substituting Memories 1976, Iris Elegy 1979, Balancing Act 1981, Birth of a Poet 1985, Eleanor, Goodbye 1988, Michaelangelo's Call 1999; other: Exhibits with accomanying writings: 1970, 1973, 1982–83; 1985; contribs Overseas Educator, California State Poetry Quarterly, American Writing, Dan River Anthology, Its On My Wall, Older Eyes, Art Exhibition and Reading, New York 1999, Life Shards 2006, Artwork/readings NYC 2000.

HAKOSHIMA, Shinichi; Japanese newspaper executive; *Adviser, The Asahi Shimbun Company*. *Career:* joined The Asahi Shimbun Co. (newspaper publr) 1962, posts included Chief of Econ. News section, Man. Ed. Tokyo Head Office, Exec. Man. Dir 1994, Pres. and CEO 1999–2005, Exec. Adviser –2005, Adviser 2005–; Dir NSK (Japanese Newspaper Publrs and Eds Asscn) 1999–2005, Chair. 2003–05. *Address:* The Asahi Shimbun Company, 5-3-2 Tsukiyi, Chuo-ku, Tokyo 104-8011, Japan (office). *Telephone:* (3) 5540-7724 (office). *Website:* www.asahi.com (office).

HALAM, Ann (see Jones, Gwyneth)

HALDEMAN, Joe William, BS, MFA; American novelist; b. 9 June 1943, Oklahoma City, Okla; m. Mary Gay Potter 1965. *Education:* Univs of Maryland and Iowa. *Career:* Assoc. Prof., Writing Programme, MIT 1983–;

mem. Science Fiction and Fantasy Writers of America, Authors' Guild, Poets and Writers, Nat. Space Inst., Writers' Guild. *Publications:* War Year 1972, Cosmic Laughter (ed.) 1974, The Forever War 1975, Mindbridge 1976, Planet of Judgement 1977, All My Sins Remembered 1977, Study War No More (ed.) 1977, Infinite Dreams 1978, World Without End 1979, Worlds 1981, There is No Darkness (co-author) 1983, Worlds Apart 1983, Nebula Awards 17 (ed.) 1983, Dealing in Futures 1985, Body Armour 2000 (co-ed.) 1986, Tool of the Trade 1987, Supertanks (co-ed.) 1987, Starfighters (co-ed.) 1988, The Long Habit of Living 1989, The Hemingway Hoax 1990, Worlds Enough and Time 1992, 1968, 1995, None So Blind 1996, Forever Peace 1997, Saul's Death and Other Poems 1997, Forever Free 1999, The Coming 2000, Guardian 2002, Camouflage 2004, Old Twentieth 2005, War Stories 2005, A Separate War 2006, The Accidental Time Machine 2007, Marsbound 2008, Starbound 2010. *Honours:* Purple Heart, US Army 1969; Nebula Awards 1975, 1990, 1993, 1998, 2005, Hugo Awards 1976, 1977, 1991, 1995, 1998, Rhysling Awards 1984, 1990, 2001, World Fantasy Award 1993, John Campbell Award 1998, Tiptree Award 2004, SESFA Awards 2003, 2004, Robert A. Heinlein Award 2009, Science Fiction Wrtiers of America Grandmaster Award 2010. *Address:* 5412 NW 14th Avenue, Gainesville, FL 32605, USA (home). *Website:* home.earthlink.net/~haldeman.

HALIM, Huri (see Offen, Yehuda)

HALL, Angus; British author and editor; b. 24 March 1932, Newcastle upon Tyne, England. *Career:* Ed., IPC Publishers, London 1971–; BPC Publishers, London 1972–. *Publications:* London in Smoky Region 1962, High-Bouncing Lover 1966, Live Like a Hero 1967, Comeuppance of Arthur Hearne 1967, Qualtrough 1968, Late Boy Wonder 1969, Devilday 1970, To Play the Devil 1971, Scars of Dracula 1971, Long Way to Fall 1971, On the Run 1974, Signs of Things to Come: A History of Divination 1975, Monsters and Mythic Beasts 1976, Strange Cults 1977, The Rigoletto Murder 1978, Self-Destruct 1985, The Crime Busters (ed) 1989.

HALL, Donald Andrew, BA, BLitt, LHD, DLitt; American poet, writer and academic; b. 20 Sept. 1928, New Haven, Conn.; s. of Donald A. Hall and Lucy Hall (née Wells); m. 1st Kirby Thompson 1952 (divorced 1969); one s. one d.; m. 2nd Jane Kenyon 1972 (died 1995). *Education:* Harvard Univ., Univ. of Oxford, Stanford Univ. *Career:* Jr Fellow, Harvard Univ. 1954–57; Asst Prof., Univ. of Michigan 1957–61, Assoc. Prof. 1961–66, Prof. of English 1966–75; Poetry Ed. Paris Review 1953–62; Consultant Harper & Row 1964–81; Poet Laureate of the USA 2006–07; Guggenheim Fellow 1963, 1972; mem. Authors' Guild, American Acad. of Arts and Letters. *Publications:* poetry: Poems 1952, Exile 1952, To the Loud Wind and Other Poems 1955, Exiles and Marriages 1955, The Dark Houses 1958, A Roof of Tiger Lilies 1964, The Alligator Bride: Poems New and Selected 1969, The Yellow Room: Love Poems 1971, A Blue Wing Tilts at the Edge of the Sea: Selected Poems 1964–1974 1975, The Town of Hill 1975, Kicking the Leaves 1978, The Toy Bone 1979, The Twelve Seasons 1983, Brief Lives 1983, Great Day at the Cows' House 1984, The Happy Man 1986, The One Day: A Poem in Three Parts (Nat. Book Circle Critic's Award 1989) 1988, Old and New Poems 1990, The One Day and Poems (1947–1990) 1991, The Museum of Clear Ideas 1993, The Old Life 1996, Without: Poems 1998, The Painted Bed 2000, White Apples and the Taste of Stone: Selected Poems 1946–2006 2006, The Back Chamber 2011; children's books: Ox-Cart Man (Caldecott Medal 1980) 1979, Lucy's Christmas 1994, I Am the Dog, I Am the Cat 1994, Lucy's Summer 1995; short stories: The Ideal Bakery 1987, Willow Temple 2002; prose: Henry Moore: The Life and Work of a Great Sculptor 1966, Marianne Moore: The Cage and the Animal 1970, The Gentleman's Alphabet Book 1972, Writing Well 1973, Goatfoot Milktongue Twinbird: Interviews, Essays and Notes on Poetry 1970–76 1978, The Weather for Poetry: Essays, Reviews and Notes on Poetry 1977–81 1982, Poetry and Ambition: Essays 1982–1988 1988, Here at Eagle Pond 1990, Their Ancient Glittering Eyes 1992, Life Work 1993, Death to Death of Poetry 1994, Principal Products of Portugal 1995, Breakfast Served Any Time All Day 2003, The Best Day The Worst Day (biog.) 2005, Unpacking the Boxes: A Memoir of a Life in Poetry 2008; editor: Harvard Advocate Anthology 1950, The New Poets of England and America (with L. Simpson and R. Pack) 1957, Second Selection (with R. Pack) 1962, A Poetry Sampler 1962, Contemporary American Poetry 1962, Poetry in English (with W. Taylor) 1963, A Concise Encyclopaedia of English and American Poets and Poetry (with S. Spender) 1963, Faber Book of Modern Verse 1966, The Modern Stylists 1968, A Choice of Whitman's Verse 1968, Man and Boy 1968, Anthology of American Poetry 1969, Pleasures of Poetry 1971, A Writer's Reader (with D. Emblen) 1976, Remembering Poets: Reminiscences and Opinions: Dylan Thomas, Robert Frost, T. S. Eliot, Ezra Pound 1978, To Read Literature 1981, To Read Poetry 1982, Oxford Book of American Literary Anecdotes 1981, Claims for Poetry 1982, Oxford Book of Children's Verse in America 1985, To Read Fiction 1987, Anecdotes of Modern Art (with Pat Corrigan Wykes) 1990. *Honours:* Univ. of Oxford Newdigate Prize for Poetry 1952, Acad. of American Poets Lamont Poetry Selection 1955, Edna St Vincent Millay Memorial Prize 1956, Longview Foundation Award 1960, Sarah Josepha Hale Award 1983, Leonore Marshal Award 1987, Los Angeles Times Book Award 1989, Poetry Soc. of America Robert Frost Silver Medal 1991, New Hampshire Writers and Publishers Project Lifetime Achievement Award 1992, New England Booksellers Asscn Award 1993, Ruth Lilly Prize 1994, Aiken Taylor Award for Modern American Poetry 2009, Nat. Medal of Art 2011.

HALL, Jane Anna; American writer, poet and artist; b. 4 April 1959, New London, Conn. *Education:* Barbizon School, Westbrook High School. *Career:* Founder-Ed. Poetry in Your Mailbox Newsletter 1989–; writer, presenter and producer, Book Time (TV show) 2009–; mem. Romance Writers of America, Conn. Poetry Soc. *Art works:* exhibited at 23 solo shows. *Compositions:* ten songs including lyrics (non-classical). *Publications include:* Cedar and Lace 1986, Satin and Pinstripe 1987, Fireworks and Diamonds 1988, Stars and Daffodils 1989, Sunrises and Stonewalls 1990, Mountains and Meadows 1991, Moonlight and Water Lilies 1992, Sunset and Beaches 1993, Under Par Recipes 1994, New and Selected Poems 1986–1994 1994, Poems for Children 1986–1995 1995, Butterflies and Roses 1996, Hummingbirds and Hibiscus 1997, Swans and Azaleas 1998, Damselflies and Peonies 1999, Egrets and Cattails 2000, Doves and Rhododendron 2001, Bluebirds and Mountain Laurel 2002, The Full Moon Looks Like (juvenile) 2002, Beach Poems Vol. I 2002, Spring Poems Vol. I 2003, Summer Poems Vol. I 2003, Autumn Poems Vol. I 2003, Winter Poems Vol. I 2003, Cardinals and Maples 2003, Wedding Poems Vol. I 2004, Sandpipers and Driftwood 2004, Emeralds and Gardenias 2005, Dragonflies and Pearls 2006, Rubies and Iris 2007, Robins and Oaks 2008, Selected Poems 1996–2006 2008, Amethyst and Lilacs 2009, Beeches and Beryls 2010; contrib. to several publs. *Honours:* second prizes, Conn. Poetry Soc. Contest 1983, 1986, various certificates. *Address:* PO Box 629, Westbrook, CT 06498, USA (office).

HALL, Sir Peter Geoffrey, Kt, MA, PhD, FBA; British geographer and academic; *Bartlett Professor of Planning and Regeneration, Bartlett School of Planning, University College London*; b. 19 March 1932, London; s. of Arthur Vickers and Bertha Hall (née Keefe); m. 1st Carla M. Wartenberg 1962 (divorced 1967); m. 2nd Magdalena Mróz 1967. *Education:* Blackpool Grammar School, St Catharine's Coll., Cambridge. *Career:* Asst Lecturer, Birkbeck Coll., Univ. of London 1956–60, Lecturer 1960–65; Reader in Geography with special reference to planning, LSE 1966–67; Prof. of Geography, Univ. of Reading 1968–89, Prof. Emer. 1989–; Prof. of City and Regional Planning, Univ. of California, Berkeley 1980–92, Prof. Emer. 1993–, Dir Inst. of Urban and Regional Devt 1989–92; Special Adviser to Sec. of State for the Environment 1991–94; Bartlett Prof. of Planning and Regeneration, Bartlett School of Planning, Univ. Coll., London 1992–; mem. South East Econ. Planning Council 1966–79, Social Science Research Council 1974–80, Urban Task Force 1998–99; mem. Academia Europaea; Fellow, British Acad. 1983. *Publications:* approx. 40 books on urban questions authored, co-authored or edited, including The Industries of London 1962, London 2000 1963, Labour's New Frontiers 1964, Land Values (ed.) 1965, The World Cities 1966, Von Thünen's Isolated State (ed.) 1966, Theory and Practice of Regional Planning 1970, The Containment of Urban England 1973, Planning and Urban Growth 1973, Urban and Regional Planning 1974, Europe 2000 1977, Growth Centres in the European System 1980, Great Planning Disasters 1980, The Inner City in Context (ed.) 1981, Silicon Landscapes (ed.) 1985, Can Rail Save the City? 1985, High-Tech America 1986, Western Sunrise 1987, Cities of Tomorrow 1988, The Carrier Wave 1988, London 2001 1989, The Rise of the Gunbelt 1992, Technopoles of the World 1993, Sociable Cities 1998, Cities in Civilization 1998, Urban Future 21 2000, Working Capital 2002, The Polycentric Metropolis 2006, London Voices London Lives 2007. *Honours:* Hon. Fellow, St Catherine's Coll. Cambridge 1988; 13 hon. degrees; Gill Memorial Prize, Royal Geographical Soc. 1968, Adolphe Bentinck Prize 1979, Founder's Medal, Royal Geographical Soc. 1988, Prix Vautrin Lud 2001, Gold Medal, Royal Town Planning Inst. 2003, Deputy Prime Minister's Lifetime Achievement Award 2005, Balzan Int. Prize 2005. *Address:* 12 Queens Road, London, W5 2SA (home); Bartlett School of Planning, University College London, Wates House, 22 Gordon Street, London, WC1H 0QB, England (office). *Telephone:* (20) 8997-3717 (home); (20) 8810-8723 (office). *Fax:* (20) 7679-7502 (office). *E-mail:* p.hall@ucl.ac.uk (office). *Website:* www.bartlett.ucl.ac.uk/planning (office).

HALL, Sir Peter Reginald Frederick, Kt, CBE, MA; British theatre director and film director; b. 22 Nov. 1930, Bury St Edmunds, Suffolk; s. of late Reginald Hall and Grace Hall; m. 1st Leslie Caron 1956 (divorced 1965); one s. one d.; m. 2nd Jacqueline Taylor 1965 (divorced 1981); one s. one d.; m. 3rd Maria Ewing 1982 (divorced 1989); one d.; m. 4th Nicola Frei 1990; one d. *Education:* Perse School and St Catharine's Coll., Cambridge. *Career:* produced and acted in over 20 plays at Cambridge; first professional production The Letter, Windsor 1953; produced in repertory at Windsor, Worthing and Oxford Playhouse; two Shakespearean productions for Arts Council; Artistic Dir Elizabethan Theatre Co. 1953; Asst Dir London Arts Theatre 1954, Dir 1955–57; formed own producing co., Int. Playwright's Theatre 1957; Man. Dir Royal Shakespeare Co., Stratford-upon-Avon and Aldwych Theatre, London 1960–68 (resgnd), Assoc. Dir –1973; mem. Arts Council 1969–73; Co-Dir, Nat. Theatre (now Royal Nat. Theatre) with Lord Olivier April-Nov. 1973, Dir 1973–88; f. Peter Hall Co. 1988; Artistic Dir Glyndebourne 1984–90; Artistic Dir The Old Vic 1997; Wortham Chair in Performing Arts, Houston Univ., Tex. 1999; Chancellor, Kingston Univ. 2000–; fmr Dir Kingston Theatre, now Dir Emer.; Assoc. Prof. of Drama, Warwick Univ. 1964–67; Patron, Canon's Mouth; mem. Bd Playhouse Theatre 1990–91; acted in The Pedestrian (film) 1973. *Productions include:* Blood Wedding, The Immoralist, The Lesson, South, Mourning Becomes Electra, Waiting for Godot, Waltz of the Toreadors, Camino Real, Gigi, Love's Labours Lost, Cymbeline, Twelfth Night, A Midsummer Night's Dream, Coriolanus, Two Gentlemen of Verona, Troilus and Cressida, Ondine, Romeo and Juliet, The Wars of the Roses (London Theatre Critics' Award for Best Dir 1963), Becket, Cat on a Hot Tin Roof, The Rope Dancers (on Broadway), The Moon and Sixpence (opera, Sadler's Wells), Henry VI (parts 1, 2 and 3), Richard III,

Richard II, Henry IV (parts 1 and 2), Henry V, Eh?, The Homecoming (London Theatre Critics' Award for Best Dir 1965, Antoinette Perry Award for Best Dir 1966), Moses and Aaron (opera, Covent Garden), Hamlet (London Theatre Critics' Award for Best Dir 1965), The Government Inspector, The Magic Flute (opera), Work is a Four Letter Word (film) 1968, Macbeth, Midsummer Night's Dream (film) 1969, Three into Two Won't Go (film) 1969, A Delicate Balance, Perfect Friday (film) 1971, La Calisto (opera, Glyndebourne Festival) 1970, The Knot Garden (opera, Covent Garden) 1970, Eugene Onegin (opera, Covent Garden) 1971, Old Times 1971, Tristan and Isolde (opera, Covent Garden) 1971, All Over 1972, Il Ritorno d'Ulisse (opera, Glyndebourne Festival) 1972, Alte Zeiten (Burgtheater, Vienna) 1972, Via Galactica (musical, Broadway) 1972, The Homecoming (film) 1973, Marriage of Figaro (opera, Glyndebourne) 1973, The Tempest 1973, Landscape (film) 1974, Akenfield (film) 1974, Happy Days 1974, No Man's Land 1975, Judgement 1975, Hamlet 1975, Tamburlaine the Great 1976, Don Giovanni (opera, Glyndebourne Festival) 1977, Volpone (Nat. Theatre) 1977, Bedroom Farce (Nat. Theatre) 1977, The Country Wife (Nat. Theatre) 1977, The Cherry Orchard (Nat. Theatre) 1978, Macbeth (Nat. Theatre) 1978, Betrayal (Nat. Theatre) 1978, Così Fan Tutte (opera, Glyndebourne) 1978, Fidelio (opera, Glyndebourne) 1979, Amadeus (Nat. Theatre) 1979, Betrayal (New York) 1980, Othello (Nat. Theatre) 1980, Amadeus (New York) (Tony Award for Best Dir 1981) 1980, Family Voices (Nat. Theatre) 1981, The Oresteia (Nat. Theatre) 1981, A Midsummer Night's Dream (opera, Glyndebourne) 1981, The Importance of Being Earnest (Nat. Theatre) 1982, Other Places (Nat. Theatre) 1982, The Ring (operas, Bayreuth Festival) 1983, Jean Seberg (musical, Nat. Theatre) 1983, L'Incoronazione di Poppea (opera, Glyndebourne) 1984, Animal Farm (Nat. Theatre) 1984, Coriolanus (Nat. Theatre) 1984, Yonadab (Nat. Theatre) 1985, Carmen (opera, Glyndebourne) 1985, (Metropolitan Opera) 1986, Albert Herring (opera, Glyndebourne) 1985, The Petition (New York and Nat. Theatre) 1986, Simon Boccanegra (opera, Glyndebourne) 1986, Salome (opera, Los Angeles) 1986, Coming in to Land (Nat. Theatre) 1986, Antony and Cleopatra (Nat. Theatre) 1987, Entertaining Strangers (Nat. Theatre) 1987, La Traviata (Glyndebourne) 1987, Falstaff (Glyndebourne) 1988, Salome (Covent Garden) 1988, Cymbeline (Nat. Theatre) 1988, The Winter's Tale (Nat. Theatre) 1988, The Tempest 1988, Orpheus Descending 1988, Salome (opera, Chicago) 1988, Albert Herring 1989, Merchant of Venice 1989, She's Been Away (TV) 1989, New Year (opera, Houston and Glyndebourne) 1989, Born Again (musical) 1990, The Homecoming 1990, Orpheus Descending (film) 1990, Twelfth Night 1991, The Rose Tattoo 1991, Tartuffe 1991, The Camomile Lawn (TV) 1991, Four Baboons Adoring the Sun (New York) 1992,All's Well That Ends Well (RSC) 1992, The Gift of the Gorgon (RSC) 1992, The Magic Flute (LA) 1993, Separate Tables 1993, Lysistrata 1993, She Stoops to Conquer 1993, Piaf (musical) 1993, An Absolute Turkey (Le Dindon) 1994, On Approval 1994, Hamlet 1994, Jacob (TV) 1994, Never Talk to Strangers (film) 1995, Julius Caesar (RSC) 1995, The Master Builder 1995, The Final Passage (TV) 1996, The Oedipus Plays (Nat. Theatre at Epidaurus and Nat. Theatre) 1996, A School for Wives 1995, A Streetcar Named Desire 1997, The Seagull 1997, Waiting for Godot 1997, 1998, King Lear 1997, The Misanthrope 1998, Major Barbara 1998, Simon Boccanegra (Glyndebourne) 1998, Amadeus 1998, Kafka's Dick 1998, Measure for Measure (LA) 1999, A Midsummer Night's Dream (LA) 1999, Lenny (Queens Theatre) 1999, Amadeus (LA, NY) 1999, Tantalus (Denver, Colo) 2000, Japes 2000, Romeo and Juliet (LA) 2001, Japes 2001, Troilus and Cressida (NY) 2001, A Midsummer Night's Dream (Glyndebourne) 2001, Otello (Glyndebourne) 2001, Japes (Theatre Royal) 2001, The Royal Family (Theatre Royal) 2001, Lady Windermere's Fan (Theatre Royal) 2002, The Bacchai (Olivier Theatre) 2002, Design for Living (Theatre Royal, Bath) 2003, Betrayal (Theatre Royal, Bath) 2003, The Fight for Barbara (Theatre Royal, Bath) 2003, As You Like It (Theatre Royal, Bath) 2003, Cuckoos (Theatre Royal, Bath) 2003, The Marriage of Figaro (Lyric Opera of Chicago) 2003, Happy Days (Arts Theatre, London) 2003, Man and Superman (Theatre Royal, Bath) 2004, Galileo's Daughter (Theatre Royal, Bath) 2004, The Vortex 2007, An Ideal Husband 2008, Pygmalion 2009. *Publications:* The Wars of the Roses 1970, Shakespeare's three Henry VI plays and Richard III (adapted with John Barton), John Gabriel Borkman (English version with Inga-Stina Ewbank) 1975, Peter Hall's Diaries: The Story of a Dramatic Battle 1983, Animal Farm: a stage adaptation 1986, The Wild Duck 1990, Making an Exhibition of Myself (autobiog.) 1993, An Absolute Turkey (new trans. of Feydeau's Le Dindon, with Nicki Frei) 1994, The Master Builder (with Inga-Stina Ewbank) 1995, Mind Millie for Me (new trans. of Feydeau's Occupe-toi d'Amélie, with Nicki Frei), The Necessary Theatre 1999, Exposed by the Mask 2000, Shakespeare's Advice to the Players 2003. *Honours:* Hon. Fellow, St Catharine's Coll. Cambridge 1964; Chevalier, Ordre des Arts et des Lettres 1965; Dr hc (York) 1966, (Reading) 1973, (Liverpool) 1974, (Leicester) 1977, (Essex) 1993, (Cambridge) 2003; Hon. DSocSc (Birmingham) 1989; Hamburg Univ. Shakespeare Prize 1967, Evening Standard Special Award 1979, Evening Standard Award for Outstanding Achievement in Opera 1981, Evening Standard Best Dir Award for The Oresteia 1981, Evening Standard Best Dir Award for Antony and Cleopatra 1987, South Bank Show Lifetime Achievement Award 1998, Olivier Special Award for Lifetime Achievement 1999, New York Shakespeare Soc. Medal 2003, Lifetime Achievement Award, Theater Hall of Fame 2006. *Address:* 48 Lamont Road, London, SW10 0HX, England. *E-mail:* phpetard@aol.com (office).

HALL, Philip David; British journalist and PR consultant; *Chairman, PHA Media;* b. 8 Jan. 1955, s. of Norman Philip Hall and Olive Jean Hall; m. Marina Thomson 1997; two c. *Education:* Beal Grammar School, Ilford. *Career:* reporter, Dagenham Post 1974–77, Ilford Recorder 1977–80; Sub-Ed. Newham Recorder 1980–84, Weekend Magazine 1984–85; reporter, The People 1985–86, Chief Reporter 1986–89, News Ed. 1989–92; News Ed. Sunday Express 1992–93; Asst Ed. (Features) News of the World 1993–94, Deputy Ed. 1994–95, Ed. 1995–2000; with Max Clifford Assocs 2000–01; Ed.-in-Chief Hello! 2001–02; Founder and Chair. Phil Hall Assocs. (public relations) (now PHA Media) 2004–; mem. Press Complaints Comm. 1998–2000, 2002–. *Address:* PHA Media, 117 Wardour Street, London, W1F 0UN, England (office). *Telephone:* (20) 7025-1350 (office). *Fax:* (20) 7025-1351 (office). *E-mail:* info@pha-media.com (office). *Website:* www.pha-media.com (office).

HALL, Rodney, AM; Australian writer, musician and actor; b. 18 Nov. 1935, s. of D. E. Hall; m. Maureen McPhail 1962; three d. *Education:* City of Bath School for Boys, UK, Brisbane Boys' Coll., Univ. of Queensland. *Career:* leader, Baroque Music Group; Creative Arts Fellow, ANU 1968, Literary Bd Fellow 1974–80, tutor, New England Univ. Summer School of Music 1967–71, 1977–80; Lecturer, Dept of Foreign Affairs; Recorder, Canberra School of Music 1979–83; Chair. Australia Council 1991–94. *Publications:* published over 500 poems in Australia, UK, USA, USSR, Philippines, France, India, several published books of poetry and novels; poetry: The Climber 1962, Penniless till Doomsday 1962, Forty Beads on a Hangman's Rope 1963, Eyewitness 1967, The Autobiography of a Gorgon 1968, The Law of Karma 1968, Australia 1970, Heaven, in a Way 1970, A Soapbox Omnibus 1973, Selected Poems 1975, Black Bagatelles 1978, The Most Beautiful World 1981; fiction: The Ship on the Coin 1972, A Place Among People 1975, Just Relations 1982, Kisses of the Enemy 1987, Captivity Captive 1988, The Second Bridegroom 1991, The Grisly Wife 1994, The Island in the Mind 1996, The Day We had Hitler Home 2000, The Last Love Story 2004, Love Without Hope 2007, The Lonely Traveller by Night 2009. *Honours:* Miles Franklin Award 1982, 1994. *Address:* c/o Publicity Department, Pan Macmillan Australia, Level 25, 1 Market Street, Sydney, NSW 2000, Australia (office). *Website:* www.panmacmillan.com.au (office).

HALL, Roger Leighton, QSO, BA, MA, DipEd; British dramatist; b. 17 Jan. 1939, Woodford, Wells, Essex, England; m. Dianne Sturm 1968; one s. one d. *Education:* Victoria Univ., Wellington, New Zealand. *Career:* emigrated to NZ 1958; public servant and teacher; Robert Burns Fellow, Otago Univ. 1977, 1978; Fullbright Visiting Lecturer, Georgetown Univ., Washington, DC, USA 2003; mem. PEN New Zealand, Scriptwriters' Guild. *Publications:* plays: Glide Time 1976, Middle Age Spread 1977, State of the Play 1978, Prisoners of Mother England 1979, The Rose 1981, Hot Water 1982, Fifty-Fifty 1982, Multiple Choice 1984, Dream of Sussex Downs 1986, The Hansard Show 1986, The Share Club 1987, After the Crash 1988, Conjugal Rites 1990, By Degrees 1993, Market Forces 1995, Social Climbers 1995, C'mon Black 1996, The Book Club 1999, You Gotta Be Joking 1999, Take a Chance on Me 2001, A Way of Life 2001, Spreading Out 2004, Taking Off 2004, Who Needs Sleep Anyway (with Pip Hall) 2007, Who wants to be a 100? 2007, Four Flat Whites in Italy 2009; other: musicals with Philip Norman and A. K. Grant, new pantomime versions of Cinderella, Aladdin, Jack and the Beanstalk, many plays for radio and TV and for children. *Honours:* Companion, NZ Order of Merit 2003; Hon. DLitt (Victoria) 1996; Fulbright Travel Award 1982, Turnovsky Award, Outstanding Contrib. to the Arts 1987. *Literary Agent:* c/o Casarotto Ramsay, Waverley House, 7–12 Noel Street, London, W1F 8GQ, England. *E-mail:* info@casarotto.co.uk. *Address:* c/o Playmarket, PO Box 9767, Wellington, New Zealand (office). *E-mail:* roger.h@xtra.co.nz (home).

HALL, Sarah, MLitt; British writer and poet; b. 1974, Cumbria; pnr Jacob Polley. *Education:* Univ. of Wales, Aberystwyth, St Andrews Univ. *Career:* tutor in creative writing, St Andrews Univ.; emigrated to North Carolina, USA; currently living in the Lake District, UK. *Publications:* Haweswater (Betty Trask Award, Commonwealth First Novel Prize 2003) 2002, The Electric Michelangelo 2004, The Carhullan Army 2007, How to Paint a Dead Man 2009, The Beautiful Indifference (short stories) 2011. *Honours:* John Llewellyn Rhys Prize 2007. *Address:* c/o Faber and Faber, Bloomsbury House, 74–77 Great Russell Street, London, WC1B 3DA, England (office). *Website:* www.faber.co.uk (office).

HALLIBURTON, David Garland, BA, MA, PhD; American academic and writer; *Professor Emeritus of English, Stanford University;* b. 24 Sept. 1933, San Bernardino, Calif.; m. 1960; three c. *Education:* Univ. of California-Riverside. *Career:* Asst Prof. of English, Univ. of California-Riverside, Riverside 1966–72, Assoc. Prof. of English, Comparative Literature, Modern Thought and Literature 1972–80; apptd Prof. of English, Stanford Univ., Stanford 2000, currently Prof. Emer.; mem. Modern Language Asscn; Fellow, American Council of Learned Socs 1971–72; Guest Ed. Studies in American Indian Literature. *Publications:* Edgar Allan Poe: A Phenomenological View 1973, Poetic Thinking: An Approach to Heidegger 1982, The Color of the Sky: A Study of Stephen Crane 1989, The Fateful Discourse of Worldly Things 1997; contribs to periodicals include: Modern Fiction Studies, Papers in Language and Literatures, Studies in Romanticism. *Address:* Department of English, Stanford University, 450 Serra Mall, Building 460, Room 201, Stanford, CA 94305-2087, USA (office). *Telephone:* (650) 723-2635 (office). *Fax:* (650) 725-0755 (office). *E-mail:* hallibur@stanford.edu (office). *Website:* english.stanford.edu/bio.php?name_id=60 (office).

HALLIDAY, Mark, BA, MA, PhD; American poet and academic; *Distinguished Professor of English, Ohio University*; b. 1949; m. J. Allyn Rosser. *Education:* Brown Univ., Brandeis Univ. *Career:* teacher, Wellesley Coll., Univ. of Pennsylvania, West Michigan Univ., Indiana Univ.; Prof. of English, Ohio Univ. 1996–, Distinguished Prof. 2012–; mem. of Council, Asscn of Literary Scholars, Critics and Writers. *Publications:* poetry: Little Star 1987, Tasket Street (Juniper Prize) 1992, Selfwolf 1999, Jab 2002, For Crying Out Loud 2004, Keep This Forever 2008; non-fiction: The Sighted Singer (with Allen Grossman) 1991, Stevens and the Interpersonal 1991. *Honours:* Lila Wallace-Reader's Digest Foundation Writer's Award, Rome Prize, American Acad. of Arts and Letters 2001. *Address:* Department of English, Ohio University, 357 Ellis Hall, Athens, OH 45701, USA (office). *Telephone:* (740) 593-2758 (office). *E-mail:* hallidam@ohio.edu (office). *Website:* www.english.ohiou.edu/directory/faculty_page/halliday (office).

HALLIGAN, Marion, AM, BA, DipEd; Australian writer; b. 16 April 1940, Newcastle, NSW; d. of Arthur James Crothall Mildred Alice Cogan; m. Graham James Halligan 1963 (died 1998); one s. one d. *Education:* Univ. of Newcastle. *Career:* several writer-in-residencies; Chair., Word Festival Canberra 1987–93, Literature Bd, Australia Council 1992–95; mem. Australian Soc. of Authors, Australian Symposium of Gastronomy. *Publications include:* Self Possession 1987, The Living Hothouse 1988, The Hanged Man in the Garden 1989, Spider Cup 1990, Eat My Words (essays) 1990, Lovers' Knots: A Hundred-Year Novel 1992, The Worry Box 1993, Wishbone 1994, Cockles of the Heart (essays) 1996, Out of the Picture 1996, Collected Stories 1997 Those Women Who Go to Hotels (co-author) 1997, The Midwife's Daughters (children's) 1997, The Golden Dress (novel) 1998, The Fog Garden (novel) 2001, The Point (novel) 2003, The Taste of Memory (autobiography) 2004, The Apricot Colonel 2006, Murder on the Apricot Coast 2008, Valley of Grace (novel) 2009, Shooting the Fox 2011; contribs to anthologies and periodicals. *Honours:* Australian Literature Bd Grants 1981, 1987, 1997–98, Braille Book of the Year Award 1989, Steele Rudd Award 1991, Age Book of the Year Award 1992, Australian Capital Territory Book of the Year Award, 1993, 2004, 2010, 3M Talking Book of the Year Award 1993, Nita B. Kibble Award 1993, Newcastle Univ. Newton John Award, Geraldine Pascall Award for Critical Writing. *Address:* 6 Caldwell Street, Hackett, ACT 2602, Australia (office). *Telephone:* (2) 6249-7120 (office). *E-mail:* marionhalligan@bigpond.com (office).

HALLINAN, Timothy, BA, MA; American author; b. 1942, Los Angeles. *Education:* Univ. of California, Los Angeles, California State Univ. *Career:* fmrly worked for public relations firms in American television industry; taught writing for many years; Founder, Hallinan Consulting LLC; cr. Simeon Grist series of mysteries, Junior Bender series of mysteries, Poke Rafferty series of thrillers. *Publications include:* The Four Last Things 1989, Everything But the Squeal 1990, Skin Deep 1991, Incinerator 1992, The Bone Polisher 1993, The Man with No Time 1994, A Nail Through the Heart: A Novel of Bangkok 2007, The Fourth Watcher: A Novel of Bangkok 2008, Breathing Water: A Bangkok Thriller 2009, The Queen of Patpong: A Poke Rafferty Thriller 2010, Crashed: A Junior Bender Novel 2010. *Address:* c/o Hallinan Consulting LLC, 15 26th Avenue, Venice, CA 90291, USA (office). *Telephone:* (310) 822-7229 (office). *Website:* www.timothyhallinan.com (home).

HALPERN, Daniel, MFA; American editor and writer; b. 11 Sept. 1945, Syracuse, NY; s. of Irving Halpern and Rosemary Halpern; m. Jeanne Carter 1982; one d. *Education:* California State Univ. and Columbia Univ., New York. *Career:* instructor in poetry and fiction workshops, New School of Social Research, New York 1971–76; Co-founder The Ecco Press (acquired by HarperCollins Publishers 1999) 1971, Ed.-in-Chief Antaeus magazine 1971–91, Editorial Dir 1991–94; Adjunct Prof., Columbia Univ. 1975–95; apptd Dir Nat. Poetry Series 1978; Visiting Prof., Princeton Univ. 1975–76, 1987–88; Nat. Endowment for the Arts Fellowship 1974, 1975, 1987; Robert Frost Fellowship, CAPS; Guggenheim Fellow 1988. *Publications:* poetry: Travelling on Credit 1972, Street Fire 1975, Life Among Others 1978, Seasonal Rights 1982, Tango 1987, Foreign Neon 1991, Selected Poems 1994, Antaeus 1970 1996, Something Shining 1998; ed. several anthologies including The Art of the Tale 1987, Reading the Fights 1990, Dante's Inferno: Translations by Twenty Contemporary Poets 1994, The Art of the Story 2000. *Honours:* numerous awards including Carey Thomas Award for Creative Publishing, Editor's Award 2009. *Address:* c/o HarperCollins Publishers, 10 East 53rd Street, New York, NY 10022, USA.

HALSEY, Alan, BA; British bookseller and poet; b. 22 Sept. 1949, Croydon, Surrey, England. *Career:* mem. David Jones Soc. *Publications:* Yearspace 1979, Another Loop in Our Days 1980, Present State 1981, Perspectives on the Reach 1981, The Book of Coming Forth in Official Secrecy 1981, Auto Dada Cafe 1987, A Book of Changes 1988, Five Years Out 1989, Reasonable Distance 1992, The Text of Shelley's Death 1995, A Robin Hood Book 1996, Fit to Print (with Karen McCormack) 1998, Days of '49 (with Gavin Selerie) 1999, Wittgenstein's Devil: Selected Writings, 1978–98 2000, Sonatas and Preliminary Sketches 2000, Dante's Barber Shop 2001, Lives of the Poets: A Preliminary Count (with Martin Corless-Smith) 2002, Death's Jest Book, by Thomas Lovell Beddoes (ed.) 2003, In Addition: Seventeen Lives of the Poets (trans.) 2004, The Epigrams & Fragments of Mercurialis the Younger 2004, Marginalien 2005, Not Everything Remotely 2006, Term as in Aftermath 2009, Lives of the Poets 2009, Collected Earlier Poems by Bill Griffiths (co-ed. with Ken Edwards) 2010, The Ivory Gate: Later Poems & Fragments by Thomas Lovell Beddoes (ed.) 2010, Even If Only Out Of 2011; contrib. to Critical Quarterly, Conjunctions, North Dakota Quarterly, Writing, Ninth Decade, Poetica, South West Review, Poetry Wales, Poesie Europe, O Ars, Figs, Interstate, Prospice, Reality Studios, Fragmente, Screens and Tasted Parallels, Avec, Purge, Grille, Acumen, Shearsman, Oasis, New American Writing, Agenda, Colorado Review, Talisman, PN Review, Resurgence, West Coast Line, The Gig, Boxkite, The Paper, Chicago Review, Envelope, Ecorché, Fence, Kiosk, New Arcadians Journal, Queen Street Quarterly, Fulcrum, Damn The Caesars, Golden Handcuffs Review. *Address:* 40 Crescent Road, Nether Edge, Sheffield, S Yorks., S7 1HN, England (home). *E-mail:* alan@nethedge.demon.co.uk (office). *Website:* www.westhousebooks.co.uk (office).

HALTER, Marek; French writer; b. 1936, Poland. *Career:* exiled in Russia with his Jewish family during Second World War, family emigrated to Paris, France 1950; studied mime with Marcel Marceau; as painter had works in numerous exhbns; f. Int. Cttee for a Negotiated Peace Agreement in the Near East 1967; f. (with Andrei Sakharov) the French Coll., Moscow 1991. *Publications:* novels: Le Fou et les rois (trans. as The Madman and the Kings) (Prix Aujourd'hui) 1976, Mais 1979, La Vie incertaine de Marco Mahler 1979, Argentina, Argenti' 1979, La Mémoire d'Abraham (trans. as The Book of Abraham (Prix du Livre Inter) 1983, Jérusalem 1986, Les Fils d'Abraham (trans. as The Children of Abraham) 1989, Jérusalem. La Poésie du Paradoxe 1990, Un homme, un cri 1991, La Force du Bien 1995, La Messie (trans. as The Messiah) 1996, Toulon 1998, Les Mystères de Jérusalem (trans. as The Mysteries of Jerusalem) 1999, Le Vent des Khazars (trans. as The Wind of the Khazars) 2001, Sarah 2004, Zipporah 2005, Lilah 2006, Marie 2006, Je me suis réveillé en colère 2007; non-fiction: Stories of Deliverance: Speaking with Men And Women Who Rescued Jews from the Holocaust 1998, Histoires du peuple juif (trans. as The Jewish Odyssey: An Illustrated History) 2010. *Address:* c/o Éditions Robert Laffont, 24 avenue Marceau, 75381 Paris, France (office). *Website:* www.laffont.fr (office).

HAMAD, Turki Al-, PhD; Saudi Arabian writer and academic; b. 1952, Jordan; m. Iman Al-Hamad; five c. *Education:* Univ. of Southern California, USA. *Career:* moved to Saudi Arabia as a child; taught political science, Riyadh –1995; full-time writer 1995–. *Publications include:* novels: Adama, Shumaisy, Karadeeb, East of the Valley, Wounds of a Memory, Winds of Paradise. *Address:* Saqi Books, 26 Westbourne Grove, London, W2 5RH, England; Saqi Books, PO Box 2388, Dammam 31451, Saudi Arabia. *Telephone:* (3) 584-3526 (Saudi Arabia). *E-mail:* hamad.turki@gmail.com (office); ibnalrawandy@hotmail.com. *Website:* www.saqibooks.com.

HAMBRICK-STOWE, Rev. Charles Edwin, BA, MDiv, MA, PhD; American writer and ecclesiastic; *Senior Minister, First Congregational Church of Ridgefield Connecticut;* b. 4 Feb. 1948, Worcester; m. Elizabeth Anne Hambrick-Stowe 1971; two s. one d. *Education:* Hamilton Coll., Pacific School of Religion, Boston Univ. Graduate School. *Career:* Religion Columnist, Evening Sun Newspaper, Carrol Co., Md 1982–85; Minister St Paul's United Church of Christ, Westminster, Md; Lead Pastor, Church of the Apostles, Lancaster, Pa; apptd Dir Doctor of Ministry Program, Pittsburgh Theological Seminary 2001; Dean, Northern Seminary, Lombard, Ill., also Vice-Pres. for Academic Affairs and Prof. of Christian History 2001–08; Sr Minister First Congregational Church of Ridgefield Connecticut 2008–; mem. American Historical Asscn, American Soc. of Church History; American Acad. of Religion. *Television:* The Scarlet Letter (Discovery Channel), Colonial House (PBS-TV), God in America (PBS-TV) 2010, Mary Siliman's War. *Publications:* Massachusetts Militia Companies and the Officers of the Lexington Alarm 1976, The Practice of Piety: Puritan Devotional Disciplines in 17th Century New England 1982, Early New England Meditative Poetry: Anne Bradstreet and Edward Taylor 1988, Theology and Identity: Traditions, Movements and Issues in the United Church of Christ 1990, Charles G. Finney and The Spirit of American Evangelicalism 1996, Living Theological Heritage: Colonial and Early National Beginnings (ed) 1998, Holding On to the Faith: Confessional Traditions in American Christianity (co-ed.) 2008; contribs to reference works, books and journals. *Honours:* Jamestown Prize for Early American History 1980. *Address:* First Congregational Church of Ridgefield Connecticut, 103 Main Street, Ridgefield, CT 06877, USA (office). *Telephone:* (203) 438-8077 (office). *Fax:* (203) 438-9678 (office). *E-mail:* charles@firstcongregational.com (office). *Website:* www.firstcongregational.com (office).

HAMBURGER, Anne Ellen, (Anne Beresford); British poet, writer, actress and teacher; b. (Anne Beresford), 10 Sept. 1928, Redhill, Surrey, England; m. Michael Hamburger 1951 (died 2007); one s. two d. *Education:* Central School of Dramatic Art, London. *Career:* actress, various repertory cos 1946–48, BBC Radio 1960–78; mem. Gen. Council Poetry Soc. 1976–78; mem. Cttee Aldeburgh Poetry Festival 1989, adviser on agenda, Editorial Bd 1993–. *Publications:* poetry: Walking Without Moving 1967, The Lair 1968, The Courtship 1972, Footsteps on Snow 1972, The Curving Shore 1975, Songs a Thracian Taught Me 1980, The Songs of Almut 1980, The Sele of the Morning 1988, Charm with Stones (Lyrik im Hölderlinturm) 1993, Landscape With Figures 1994, Selected and New Poems 1997, No Place for Cowards 1998, Hearing Things 2002, Collected Poems 2006, Whistling Through the Nightwood: Four Suffolk Poets 2008; other: Struck by Apollo (radio play, with Michael Hamburger) 1965, The Villa (radio short story) 1968, Alexandros Poems of Vera Lungu (trans.) 1974, Duet for Three Voices (dramatized poems for Anglia TV) 1982, Snapshots from an Album, 1884–1895 1992, Sonnenlicht im Obstgarten: Sunlight in the Orchard 2011; contribs to periodicals. *Address:* Riders Drift, 55 Judith Avenue, Knodishall, Suffolk, IP17 1UY, England (home). *Telephone:* (1728) 831895 (home).

HAMDARD, Peer Syed Sufaid Shah; Pakistani journalist; *Chief Editor, Daily Wabdat. Career:* started career as journalist with Anjam newspaper 1960, worked for Bang-i-Haram and Shahbaz; Founder-Ed. Alwahdat newspaper; currently Chief Ed. Daily Wabdat; Chair. Frontier Eds Council; Vice-Pres. CPNE. *Honours:* Tamgha-i-Imtiaz 1998; Pres.'s Award for Pride of Performance 2005, Lifetime Achievement Award, All Pakistan Newspapers Soc. 2012, Baba-e-Pashto Sahafat Award, World Pashto Conf. 2012. *Address:* Daily Wabdat, 20 Islamia Club Building, Khyber Bazar, Peshawar, Pakistan (office). *Website:* www.dailywahdat.com.pk (office).

HAMED, Abdul Samay; Afghan physician, writer and publisher; *Writer and Editor, Telaya magazine*; b. 1967, Badakhshan Prov. *Education:* trained as a physician. *Career:* helped start ten pubs in Afghanistan until forced into exile by the Taliban regime 1998; returned to Afghanistan 2002; f. Asscn for the Defence of Afghan Writers' Rights 2002; Founder, writer and ed. Telaya magazine 2002–; fmr Dir Mediothek media centre; Founder Kalak-e-Rhaastgoy newspaper. *Publications include:* Mountains of our Minds (with Bob McKerrow) 2004; poetry: Daaman-e Dosheeza-e Daryaacha, Hazaar-o Duomeen Shab, Dar Aakher-e Bayaanya-e Dood, Hendwaanah. *Honours:* Cttee to Protect Journalists Int. Press Freedom Award 2003. *E-mail:* samay_hamed1@hotmail.com.

HAMELIN, Claude, BSc, MSc, PhD; Canadian writer, academic and scientist; b. 25 Aug. 1943, Montréal; m. Renée Artinian 1970; one s. one d. *Career:* Demonstrator, Lab. of Genetics and Gen. Microbial Genetics, Univ. of Montreal 1970–74; apptd Lecturer in Human Genetics, Coll. of Gen. and Vocational Old Montreal 1972; apptd Lecturer in Cell Biology, Genetics and Molecular Biology, Univ. of Ottawa 1975; Prof., Centre for Research in Virology, Institut Armand-Frappier 1978–98, Assoc. Prof. 1985–86, Dir, Research and Devt Biotic, Div. of Biochemicals 1985–86, Prof., Centre for Research in Human Health 1998–2000; Pres. Biological Soc. of Montreal 1979–80; Pres. Canadian Soc. of Microbiologists 1986–87; Chair., Nominating Cttee, Genetics Soc. of Canada 1983–84. *Publications:* poetry: Fables des quatre-temps 1990, Lueurs froides 1991, Nef des fous 1992 Néant bleu/Nada azul/Blue Nothingness 1994, Silence du monde/Silencio del mundo/Silence of the World 1995, Coeur battant/Corazón palpitante/Beating Heart 1996, Hier comme demain: Poèmes (1962–71) 1996, Métamorphoses 1999; novel: Roman d'un quartier 1993; contribs to anthologies and journals. *Honours:* Leadership Award, Commemorative Medal of Honor, American Biographical Inst., USA, Bronze Plaque Award, International Biographical Centre. *Telephone:* (450) 622-1556. *E-mail:* cl_hamelin@yahoo.fr. *Website:* www.claudehamelin.com.

HAMID, Mohsin; Pakistani/British writer; b. 1971, Lahore; m. Zahra Hamid. *Education:* Princeton Univ., Harvard Law School. *Career:* worked as man. consultant, McKinsey & Co., New York, USA; fmr Man. Dir, Wolff Olins (branding consultancy), New York; worked as freelance journalist in Lahore; currently based in London, UK. *Publications:* novels: Moth Smoke (Betty Trask Award) 2000, The Reluctant Fundamentalist (Anisfield-Wolf Book Award, South Bank Show Award for Literature) 2007; contrib. to Time, New York Times, Guardian, Independent, Washington Post, La Repubblica, Paris Review, and others. *Literary Agent:* c/o Jay Mandel, William Morris Agency, 1325 Avenue of the Americas, New York, NY 10019, USA. *Telephone:* (212) 903-1119. *E-mail:* jman@wma.com. *Website:* www.wma.com; www.mohsinhamid.com.

HAMILL, (William) Pete; American journalist and writer; b. 24 June 1934, New York, NY; m. 1st Ramona Negron 1962 (divorced 1970); two d.; m. 2nd Fukiko Aoki 1987. *Education:* Pratt Inst., Mexico City Coll. *Career:* reporter, later columnist, 1960–74, 1988–93, New York Post; Contributing Ed. Saturday Evening Post 1963–64; Contributor, Village Voice and New York Magazine 1974–; Columnist, New York Daily News 1975–79, 1982–84, Esquire Magazine 1989–91; Ed. Mexico City News 1986–87; mem. Writers Guild of America. *Publications:* fiction: A Killing for Christ 1968, The Gift 1973, Flesh and Blood 1977, Dirty Laundry 1978, Deadly Piece 1979, The Guns of Heaven 1983, Loving Women 1990, Tokyo Sketches 1992, Snow in August 1997, Forever 2002, North River 2007; non-fiction: Irrational Ravings 1971, The Invisible City: A New York Sketchbook 1980, A Drinking Life: A Memoir 1994, Tools as Art: The Hechinger Collection 1995, Piecework 1996, News is a Verb 1998, Why Sinatra Matters 1998, Diego Rivera 1999, Subway Series Reader 2000, Downtown: My Manhattan 2004, They Are Us 2010; screenplays: Doc 1971, Badge 373 1973, Liberty 1986, Neon Empire 1987; Contribs to many periodicals. *Honours:* Meyer Berger Award, Columbia School of Journalism 1962, Newspaper Reporters Asscn Award 1962, 25 Year Achievement Award, Society of Silurians 1989; Peter Kihss Award 1992. *Address:* c/o Esther Newberg, International Creative Management, 40 West 57th Street, New York, NY 10019, USA (office). *Telephone:* (212) 556-5600 (office). *E-mail:* hamill@petehamill.com (home). *Website:* www.petehamill.com.

HAMILL, Sam Patrick; American poet, publisher, editor and translator; b. 9 May 1943, California; m. 1st Nancy Larsen 1964 (divorced); one d.; m. 2nd Tree Swenson 1973 (divorced); m. 3rd Gray Foster. *Education:* Los Angeles Valley Coll., Univ. of California, Santa Barbara. *Career:* co-f. Copper Canyon Press 1972, Ed. 1972–2004; Writer-in-Residence, Reed Coll., Univ. of Alaska, South Utah State Univ., South Oregon Coll., Austin Coll., Trinity Coll. 1974–; f. Poets Against the War 2003; mem. PEN American Center, Poetry Soc. of America, Acad. of American Poets. *Publications include:* poetry: Heroes of the Teton Mythos 1973, Petroglypics 1975, Uintah Blue 1975, The Calling Across Forever 1976, The Book of Elegaic Geography 1978, Triada 1978, Animae 1980, Fatal Pleasure 1984, The Nootka Rose 1987, Passport 1988, A Dragon in the Clouds 1989, Mandala 1991, Destination Zero: Poems 1970–1995, 1995, Gratitude 1998, Dumb Luck 2002, Almost Paradise: Selected Poems and Translations 2005, Measured by Stone 2007, Avocations: On Poets and Poetry; essays: At Home in the World 1980, Basho's Ghost 1989, A Poet's Work: The Other Side of Poetry 1990; ed. or co-ed. of anthologies, selected poems, collections, including: Endless River: Li Po and Tu Fu: A Friendship in Poetry 1993, Love Poems from the Japanese 1994, The Gift of Tongues: Twenty-Five Years of Poetry from Copper Canyon Press 1996, The Erotic Spirit 1999, Poets Against the War 2003, Selected Poems of Thomas McGrath, The Complete Poems of Kenneth Rexroth, Selected Poems of Hayden Carruth; trans. or co-trans. of Chinese, Estonian, Latin, Japanese and ancient Greek works; contrib. of poetry, essays and translations to numerous anthologies and literary magazines. *Honours:* Decoración de la Universidad de Carabobo, Venezuela; College Ed.'s Award, Best Coll. Journal, Co-ordinating Council of Literary Magazines 1972, Washington Gov.'s Arts Awards to Copper Canyon Press 1975, 1990, Pacific Northwest Booksellers' Award 1980, Guggenheim Fellowship 1983, Pushcart Prizes 1989, 1996, Lila Wallace-Reader's Digest Writing Fellowship 1992–93, Stanley Lindberg Lifetime Achievement Award for Editing, Lifetime Achievement Award for Poetry, Washington Poets Asscn, PEN American Freedom to Write Award.

HAMILTON, Carol Jean Barber, BS, MA; American writer, poet and educator (retd); b. (Carol Jean Barber), 23 Aug. 1935, Enid, Okla; d. of Clarence DeWitt Barber and Ruby Settles Barber; m. (divorced); two s. one d. *Education:* Phillips Univ., Univ. of Cen. Okla. *Career:* Prof. of English, Rose State Coll.; Prof. in Creative Studies, Univ. of Cen. Okla; Poet Laureate of Okla 1995–97; Trans., Variety Health Center; mem. Poetry Soc. of Okla, Individual Artists of Okla, Mid Okla Writers, American Acad. of Poetry, Soc. of Children's Book Writers and Illustrators, Authors' Guild, Sierra Club, First Christian Church. *Play:* The Quartet Performing Group. *Publications:* juvenile: The Dawn Seekers 1987, Legends of Poland 1993, The Mystery of Black Mesa 1995, I'm Not From Neptune 2003; poetry: Daring the Wind 1988, Once the Dust 1992, Breaking Bread, Breaking Silence, Legerdemain, Gold: Greatest Hits, I, People of the Llano, Vanishing Point, Shots On, Contrapuntal, Umberto Eco Lost His Gun, Master of Theater: Peter the Great; contrib. to Christian Science Monitor, Commonweal, New York Quarterly, Christian Century, Arizona Quarterly, Hawaii Review, Midwest Quarterly Review, Oklahoma Today, Kansas Quarterly, Arkansas Review, New Orleans Review, Poet Lore, South Carolina Review, Southern Poetry Review, Chariton Review, Windsor Review, Baltimore Review, Nimrod, Sojourners, Wisconsin Review, Southwester in American Literature, International Poetry Review, World Literature Today, Xavier Review, Quercus Review, Louisiana Literature, Tulane Review, Texas Poetry Calendar, Astronomy, Humpty Dumpty and others. *Honours:* Southwest Book Award 1987, Okla Book Award for Poetry 1992, Byline Literary Award for poetry 1994, for short story 1987, Cherubim Award 1995, Pegasus Award 1995, Chiron Review Chapbook Award 2000, David Ray Poetry Award 2000, Warren Keith Lewis Poetry Award 2002, Distinguished Alumni Award, Univ. of Central Oklahoma 2007. *Address:* 9608 Sonata Court, Midwest City, OK 73130, USA (home). *Telephone:* (405) 732-4336 (home); (405) 226-2106 (mobile). *E-mail:* hamiltoncj@earthlink.net (home). *Website:* www.carolhamilton.org.

HAMILTON, Hugo; Irish author; b. 1953, Dublin. *Publications include:* novels: Surrogate City 1990, The Last Shot 1991, The Love Test 1995, Headbanger 1996, Sad Bastard 1998, Sucking Diesel 2002, Disguise 2008, Hand in the Fire 2010; short stories: Dublin Where the Palm Trees Grow; memoirs: The Speckled People (Prix Femina Etranger, France 2004, Premio Giuseppe Berto 2004) 2003, The Sailor in the Wardrobe 2006. *Honours:* Rooney Prize for Irish Literature 1992. *Literary Agent:* c/o Peter Straus, Rogers, Coleridge & White Limited Literary Agency, 20 Powis Mews, London, W11 1JN, England. *Telephone:* (20) 7221-3717. *Fax:* (20) 7229-9084. *E-mail:* peters@rcwlitagency.com. *Website:* www.rcwlitagency.com. *E-mail:* info@hugohamilton.net (home). *Website:* www.hugohamilton.net (home).

HAMILTON, Jane, BA; American writer; b. 1957, Oak Park, IL; m. Robert Willard 1982; two c. *Education:* Carleton College, Northfield, MN. *Publications:* The Book of Ruth (PEN/Ernest Hemingway Foundation Award for Best First Novel) 1989, A Map of the World 1994, The Short History of a Prince 1999, Disobedience 2000, When Madeline Was Young 2007, Laura Rider's Masterpiece 2009. *Address:* c/o Random House Publicity Department, 1745 Broadway, New York, NY 10019, USA (office). *Website:* www.randomhouse.com/features/janehamilton/index.html (office).

HAMILTON, John Maxwell, BA, MS, PhD; American academic and writer; *Executive Vice-Chancellor and Provost, Louisiana State University*; b. 28 March 1947, Evanston, Ill.; s. of Maxwell M. Hamilton and Elizabeth C. Carlson; m. Regina Frances Nalewajek 1975; one s. *Education:* Marquette Univ., Univ. of New Hampshire, Boston Univ., George Washington Univ. *Career:* reporter, Milwaukee Journal 1967–69; journalist, Washington, DC 1973–75; foreign corresp., Latin America 1976–78; Special Asst and Asst Admin., Agency for Int. Devt, Washington, DC 1978–81; Staff Assoc., Foreign Affairs Sub-Cttee on Int. Econ. Policy and Trade, US House of Reps, Washington, DC 1981–82; Chief US Foreign Policy Corresp., Int. Reporting Information Systems, Washington, DC 1982–83; Dir, Main Street America and the Third World, Washington, DC 1985–87; Sr Counsellor, World Bank, Washington, DC 1983–85, 1987–92; commentator, Market Place Public Radio

1990–2003; Dean and Prof., Manship School of Mass Communication, Louisiana State Univ. 1992–2010, Hopkins Breazeale Foundation Prof. 1998, Exec. Vice-Chancellor and Provost Louisiana State Univ. 2010–; Dir, Treas., Int. Center for Journalists 1989–; mem. Bd Dirs, Lamar Advertising; Fellow, Shorenstein Center, Kennedy School, Harvard 2002; mem. Asscn of Schools of Journalism and Mass Communication, Soc. of Professional Journalists, Council on Foreign Relations 2004–. *Publications:* Main Street America and the Third World 1986, Edgar Snow: A Biography 1988, Entangling Alliances: How the Third World Shapes Our Lives 1990, Hold the Press: The Inside Story on Newspapers (with George Krimsky) 1996, Casanova Was a Book Lover: And Other Naked Facts and Provocative Curiosities About Reading, Writing and Publishing 2000, Journalism's Roving Eye: A History of American Foreign Reporting 2009; contrib. to books, scholarly journals and general periodicals and newspapers. *Honours:* numerous grants, Frank Luther Mott-Kappa Tau Alpha Research Award 1988, Marquette Univ. By-line Award 1993, Second Place, Green Eyeshade Awards 1999, 2000, Freedom Forum Journalism Admin. of the Year 2003, Goldsmith Prize 2010, Tankard Prize 2010. *Address:* Office of the Executive Vice-Chancellor and Provost, Louisiana State University, Baton Rouge, LA 70803-0001 (office); 3 Hidden Oak Lane, Baton Rouge, LA 70810, USA (home). *Telephone:* (225) 819-8510 (home). *Fax:* (225) 578-2125 (office). *E-mail:* jhamilt@lsu.edu (office).

HAMILTON, Peter F.; British writer; b. 2 March 1960, Rutland, England; m. Kate Hamilton; one s. one d. *Publications:* Mindstar Rising 1993, A Quantum Murder 1994, The Nano Flower 1995, The Reality Dysfunction (book one, Night's Dawn trilogy) 1996, The Neutronium Alchemist (book two, Night's Dawn trilogy) 1997, Escape Route (novella) 1997, The Web: Lightstorm (juvenile) 1998, A Second Chance at Eden 1998, The Naked God (book three, Night's Dawn trilogy) 1999, The Confederation Handbook 2000, Futures 2001, Fallen Dragon 2001, Watching Trees Grow 2002, Misspent Youth 2002, Pandora's Star 2004, Judas Unchained 2005, The Dreaming Void 2007, The Temporal Void 2008, The Evolutionary Void 2010, Manhattan in Reverse 2011; contrib. of short stories to magazines, including Fear, Interzone, and to anthologies, including In Dreams, New Worlds. *Address:* c/o Pan Macmillan, 20 New Wharf Road, London, N1 9RR, England. *Website:* www.peterfhamilton.co.uk.

HAMILTON, Priscilla (see Gellis, Roberta Leah)

HAMILTON, Steve; American author; b. 10 Jan. 1961, Detroit; m.; one s. one d. *Education:* Univ. of Michigan. *Career:* cr. Alex McKnight series of mystery novels 1998–; currently works full-time for IBM. *Publications include:* novels: Alex McKnight series: A Cold Day in Paradise (Private Eye Writers of America/St Martin's Press Award for Best First Mystery by an Unpublished Writer, Mystery Writers of America Edgar Award for Best First Novel 1998, Private Eye Writers of America Shamus Award for Best First Novel 1998) 1998, Winter of the Wolf Moon 2000, The Hunting Wind 2002, North of Nowhere 2003, Blood is the Sky (Gumshoe Award 2004) 2004, Ice Run 2005, A Stolen Season 2006, Misery Bay 2011, Beneath the Book Tower 2011, Die a Stranger 2012; other novels: Night Work 2007, The Lock Artist (Mystery Writers of America Edgar Award for Best Novel 2011) 2010. *Honours:* Mich. Author Award 2006. *Address:* c/o Minotaur Books, Macmillan, 175 Fifth Avenue, New York, NY 10010, USA (office). *E-mail:* steve@authorstevehamilton.com. *Website:* www.authorstevehamilton.com.

HAMILTON-PATERSON, James, BA; British writer and poet; b. 6 Nov. 1941, London, England. *Education:* Windlesham House, Sussex, Bickley Hall, Kent, King's School, Canterbury, Exeter Coll., Oxford, King's Coll., London. *Career:* teacher in Hertfordshire –1961, in Tripoli, Libya 1966; orderly, St Stephen's Hospital, London 1966–68; reporter, New Statesman 1969–74; features ed., Nova magazine 1974–75; science columnist, Das Magazin, Zürich 2000–02, Die Weltwocher 2002–. *Publications:* poetry: Option Three 1974, Dutch Alps 1984; novels: Playing with Water 1987, Gerontius (Whitbread First Novel Award) 1989, The Bell-Boy (aka That Time in Malomba) 1990, Griefwork 1993, Ghosts of Manila 1994, Loving Monsters 2001, Cooking with Fernet Branca 2004, Amazing Disgrace 2006, Rancid Pansies 2008; short story collections: The View from Mount Dog 1986, The Music 1995; juvenile: Flight Underground 1969, The House in the Waves 1970, Hostage! 1980; non-fiction: Very Personal War: The Story of Cornelius Hawkridge 1971, Mummies: Death and Life in Ancient Egypt (with Carol Andrews) 1978, Seven-Tenths 1992, The Great Deep: The Sea and Its Thresholds 1993, America's Boy: A Century of Colonialism in the Philippines 1998, Three Miles Down 1998, Empire of the Clouds: When Britain's Aircraft Ruled the World 2010. *Honours:* Oxford Newdigate Prize 1964. *Address:* Altwartenburg 16, Timelkam 4850, Austria.

HAMLYN, David Walter, BA, MA; British philosopher, academic and writer; *Professor Emeritus of Philosophy, Birkbeck College, London*; b. 1 Oct. 1924, Plymouth, England; m. Eileen Carlyle Litt 1949; one s. one d. *Education:* Exeter Coll., Oxford. *Career:* Research Fellow, Corpus Christi Coll., Oxford, 1950–53; Lecturer, Jesus Coll., Oxford 1953–54; Lecturer, Birkbeck Coll., Univ. of London 1954–63, Reader 1963–64, Prof. of Philosophy and Head of Dept of Philosophy 1964–88, Head of Dept of Classics 1981–86, Vice-Master 1983–88, Fellow 1988, Prof. Emer. of Philosophy 1988–; Ed., Mind 1972–84; Consulting Ed., Journal of Medical Ethics 1981–90; mem. Aristotelian Soc. (Pres. 1977–78), Univ. of London Senate 1981–87, Nat. Cttee for Philosophy 1986–92 (Hon. Vice-Pres. 1992–2003), Royal Inst. of Philosophy (mem. Council 1968–, mem. Exec. Cttee 1971–97, Vice-Chair. 1991–95). *Publications:* The Psychology of Perception 1957, Sensation and Perception 1961, Aristotle's De Anima, Books II–III 1968, The Theory of Knowledge 1970, Experience and the Growth of Understanding 1978, Schopenhauer 1980, Perception, Learning and the Self 1983, Metaphysics 1984, History of Western Philosophy 1987, In and Out of the Black Box 1990, Being a Philosopher 1992, Understanding Perception 1996; contribs to books and professional journals. *Address:* 38 Smithy Knoll Road, Hope Valley, Calver, Derbyshire, S32 3XW, England (home). *Telephone:* (1433) 631326 (home).

HAMMAD, Suheir; Palestinian/American poet and political activist; b. 25 Oct. 1973, Amman, Jordan. *Career:* emigrated with family to USA aged five; frequent readings and radio appearances. *Films:* Salt of this Sea 2008. *Television:* Russell Simmons Presents Def Poetry Jam on Broadway (original cast mem. and writer) (TONY Award for Special Theatrical Event) 2003. *Plays:* Blood Trinity (New York Hip Hop Theater Festival) 2002, ReOrientalism (libretto, commissioned by Center for Cultural Exchange) 2003, Half A Lifetime (producer, documentary). *Publications:* Born Palestinian, Born Black 1996, Drops of This Story 1996, ZaaraeDiva 2006, Breaking Poems 2008; contrib. to anthologies and periodicals, including The Amsterdam News, Black Renaissance/Renaissance Noire, Brilliant Corners, Clique, Drum Voices Revue, Essence, Long Shot, Atlanta Review, Bomb, Brooklyn Bridge, Fierce, Stress Hip-Hop Magazine, Quarterly Black Review of Books, Color Lines, Spheric, The Olive Tree Review, The Hunter Envoy, Meridians, Signs, 33 Things Every Girl Should Know About Women's History. *Honours:* Hunter Coll. Audre Lorde Writing Award 1995, 2000, Morris Center for Healing Poetry Award 1996, New York Mills Artist Residency 1998, Van Lier Fellowship 1999, Asian/Pacific/American Studies Inst. at NYU Emerging Artist Award 2001, American Book Award 2009. *E-mail:* suheir@suheirhammad.com. *Website:* www.suheirhammad.com.

HAMMARSTRÖM, Stina Margareta, MA; Swedish editor and fmr publishing executive; b. 21 Feb. 1945, Stockholm; d. of Sven Hammarström and Karin Hammarström; m. Gösta Åberg 1979; one d. *Career:* Ed., Bokförlaget Prisma AB (Publrs), Stockholm 1970–79; Publr, Hammarström & Åberg Bokförlag AB 1979–90; apptd Ed., AB Rabén & Sjögren Bokförlag, Stockholm 1990; now freelance ed. *Address:* Föreningsvägen 33, 12047 Enskede Gård, Sweden (home). *Telephone:* (8) 918894 (office). *E-mail:* stina.hammarstrom@telia.com (office).

HAMMER, David Lindley, BA, JD; American advocate and writer; b. 6 June 1929, Newton, Iowa; s. of Neal Paul Hammer and Agnes Marilyn Hammer (née Reece); m. Audrey Lowe 1953; one s. two d. *Education:* Grinnell Coll., Univ. of Iowa Law School. *Career:* served in US Army 1951–53; called to the Bar of Iowa 1956, Dist Court, Northern Dist, Iowa 1959, Dist Court, Southern Dist, Iowa 1969, Supreme Court 1977, Court of Appeals (8th Circuit) 1996; Partner, Hammer Simon & Jensen, Galena, Illinois and Iowa; mem. Grievance Comm., Iowa Supreme Court 1973–85, Advisory Rules Cttee 1986–92; mem. Bd of Dirs Linwood Cemetery Asscn 1973– (Pres. 1983–84), Dubuque Museum of Art 1998–2001 (Hon. Dir), Finley Hosp. (also fmr Pres. and Hon. Dir) Finley Foundation 1988–95; fmr Campaign Chair. and fmr Pres. United Way; fmr mem. Bd of Dirs Carnegie Stout Public Library; Fellow, American Coll. of Trial Lawyers; mem. ABA, Young Lawyers Iowa (fmr Pres.), Iowa Defense Counsel Asscn (Pres. 1991–92, Del. to Defense Research Inst. 1992–93), Asscn of Defense Trial Attorneys (mem. Exec. Council 1983–86, fmr Chair. Iowa Chapter), Iowa State Bar Asscn (fmr Chair. Continuing Legal Educ. Cttee), Iowa Acad. of Trial Lawyers, Dubuque Co. Bar Asscn (fmr Pres.), Baker Street Irregulars; Republican. *Publications:* Poems From the Ledge 1980, The Game is Afoot 1983, For the Sake of the Game 1986, The 22nd Man 1989, To Play the Game 1990, Skewed Sherlock 1992, The Worth of the Game 1992, The Quest 1993, My Dear Watson 1994, The Before Breakfast Pipe 1995, A Dangerous Game 1997, The Vital Essence 1999, A Talent for Murder 2000, Yonder in the Gaslight 2000, Straight Up With a Twist 2001, You Heard What Jesse Said 2002, Heaven Will Protect My Working Girl 2004, College Fairest of My Dreams 2004, Cases of Identity 2006; contrib. to American Journal of Philately, Baker Street Journal, Sherlock Holmes Journal. *Address:* Laurel Cottage, 720 Laurel Park Road, Dubuque, IA 52003, USA (home). *Telephone:* (563) 583-3730 (home).

HAMMES, Gordon G., PhD; American biochemist, academic and fmr university vice-chancellor; *Professor Emeritus and University Distinguished Service Professor Emeritus of Biochemistry, Medical Center, Duke University*; b. 10 Aug. 1934, Fond du Lac, Wis.; s. of Jacob Hammes and Betty (Sadoff) Hammes; m. Judith Ellen Frank 1959; one s. two d. *Education:* Princeton Univ. and Univ. of Wisconsin. *Career:* Postdoctoral Fellow, Max Planck Inst. für physikalische Chemie, Göttingen, FRG 1959–60; instructor, subsequently Assoc. Prof., MIT, Cambridge, Mass. 1960–65; Prof., Cornell Univ. 1965–88, Chair. Dept of Chem. 1970–75, Horace White Prof. of Chem. and Biochemistry 1975–88, Dir Biotechnology Program 1983–88; Prof., Univ. of Calif., Santa Barbara 1988–91, Vice-Chancellor for Academic Affairs 1988–91; Prof., Duke Univ., Durham, NC 1991–2008, Emer. 2008–, Vice-Chancellor Duke Univ. Medical Center 1991–98, Univ. Distinguished Service Prof. of Biochemistry 1996–2008, Emer. 2008–; mem. Physiological Chem. Study Section, Physical Biochemistry Study Section, Training Grant Cttee, NIH; mem. Bd of Counsellors, Nat. Cancer Inst. 1976–80, Advisory Council, Chem. Dept, Princeton 1970–75, Polytechnic Inst., New York 1977–78, Boston Univ. 1977–85; mem. Nat. Research Council, US Nat. Comm. for Biochemistry 1989–95; mem. ACS, American Soc. of Biochemistry and Molecular Biology

(Pres. 1994–95), NAS, American Acad. of Arts and Sciences; Ed. Biochemistry 1992–2003. *Achievements:* ACS est. the Gordon G. Hammes Lecture annual award 2008. *Publications:* Principles of Chemical Kinetics, Enzyme Catalysis and Regulation, Chemical Kinetics: Principles and Selected Topics (with I. Amdur), Thermodynamics and Kinetics for the Biological Sciences 2000, Spectroscopy for the Biological Sciences 2005, Physical Chemistry for the Biological Sciences 2007; numerous learned articles. *Honours:* ACS Award in Biological Chem. 1967, William C. Rose Award, American Soc. of Biochemistry and Molecular Biology 2002. *Address:* 11 Staley Place, Durham, NC 27705 (home); Department of Biochemistry, Duke University, Box 3711, Medical Center, Durham, NC 27710, USA (office). *Telephone:* (919) 684-8848 (office). *Fax:* (919) 684-9709 (office). *E-mail:* hamme001@mc.duke.edu (office). *Website:* medschool.duke.edu (office); www.biochem.duke.edu/modules/biochem_people/index.php?id=3 (office).

HAMMICK, Georgina; British writer and poet; b. 24 May 1939, Hants., England; m. 1961; one s. two d. *Education:* Académie Julian, Paris, Salisbury Art School. *Career:* mem. Writers' Guild. *Publications:* A Poetry Quintet (poems) 1976, People for Lunch 1987, Spoilt (short stories) 1992, The Virago Book of Love and Loss (ed.) 1992, The Arizona Game 1996, Green Man Running 2002, Fluchtwege 2005; contrib. to journals and periodicals. *Literary Agent:* c/o Sayle Literary Agency, Bickerton House, 25–27 Bickerton Road, London, N19 5JT, England. *Telephone:* (20) 7263-8681. *Fax:* (20) 7561-0529. *Address:* Bridgewalk House, Brixton, Deverill, Warminster, BA12 7EJ, England (home).

HAMMOND, Jane (see Poland, Dorothy Elizabeth Hayward)

HAMPSHIRE, Susan, OBE; British actress and writer; b. 12 May 1942, d. of the late George Kenneth Hampshire and June Hampshire; m. 1st Pierre Granier-Deferre 1967 (divorced 1974); one s. (one d. deceased); m. 2nd Sir Eddie Kulukundis 1981. *Education:* Hampshire School, Knightsbridge. *Stage roles include:* Expresso Bongo 1958, Follow that Girl 1960, Fairy Tales of New York 1961, Marion Dangerfield in Ginger Man 1963, Kate Hardcastle in She Stoops to Conquer 1966, On Approval 1966, Mary in The Sleeping Prince 1968, Nora in A Doll's House 1972, Katharina in The Taming of the Shrew 1974, Peter in Peter Pan 1974, Jeannette in Romeo and Jeannette 1975, Rosalind in As You Like It 1975, Miss Julie 1975, Elizabeth in The Circle 1976, Ann Whitefield in Man and Superman 1977, Siri Von Essen in Tribades 1978, Victorine in An Audience Called Edouard 1978, Irene in The Crucifer of Blood 1979, Ruth Carson in Night and Day 1979, Elizabeth in The Revolt 1980, Stella Drury in House Guest 1981, Elvira in Blithe Spirit 1986, Marie Stopes in Married Love, The Countess in A Little Night Music 1989, Mrs Anna in The King and I 1990, Gertie in Noel and Gertie 1991, The Countess of Marshwood in Relative Values 1993, Suzanna Andler in Suzanna Andler, Alicia Christie in Black Chiffon 1995–96, Sheila Carter in Relatively Speaking 2000–01, Felicity Marshwood in Relative Values 2002, Miss Shepherd in The Lady in the Van 2004–05, The Fairy Godmother in Cinderella, Wimbledon 2005–06, The Bargain 2007, Lady Kitty in The Circle 2008, Mrs Bennet in Pride and Prejudice 2009–10. *Television roles:* Andromeda in The Andromeda Breakthrough (series) 1962, Katy (series) 1962, Fleur Forsyte in The Forsyte Saga (mini-series) 1967, Becky Sharp in Vanity Fair (mini-series) 1967, Sarah Churchill, Duchess of Marlborough, in The First Churchills (mini-series) 1969, Baffled! 1973, Dr. Jekyll and Mr. Hyde 1973, Glencora Palliser in The Pallisers 1974, The Story of David 1976, Kill Two Birds 1976, Lady Melford in Dick Turpin 1981, Madeline Neroni in The Barchester Chronicles (mini-series) 1982, Martha in Leaving 1984, Martha in Leaving II 1985, Going to Pot 1985, Don't Tell Father (series) 1992, Esme Harkness in The Grand 1996–98, Miss Catto in Coming Home 1998–99, Miss Catto in Nancherrow 1999, Molly in Monarch of the Glen 1999–2005, Lucilla Drake in Sparkling Cyanide 2003, The Lady in the Van 2004, The Circle 2008, The Royal 2008–09, Bridge Celebrity Grand Slam 2009, Casualty 2011. *Films include:* The Woman in the Hall 1947, Idle on Parade (uncredited) 1959, Upstairs and Downstairs 1959, Expresso Bongo (uncredited) 1960, The Long Shadow 1961, During One Night 1961, The Three Lives of Thomasina 1964, Night Must Fall 1964, Wonderful Life 1964, Paris in August 1965, The Fighting Prince of Donegal 1966, Monte Carlo or Bust 1969, Malpertuis 1971, A Time for Loving 1971, Rogan, David Copperfield, Living Free 1972, Neither the Sea Nor the Sand 1972, Le fils 1973, Peccato mortale (aka Roses and Green Peppers) 1973, Bang! 1977. *Publications:* Susan's Story (autobiographical account of dyslexia) 1981, The Maternal Instinct, Lucy Jane at the Ballet 1985, Lucy Jane on Television 1989, Trouble Free Gardening 1989, Every Letter Counts 1990, Lucy Jane and the Dancing Competition 1991, Easy Gardening 1991, Lucy Jane and the Russian Ballet 1993, Rosie's First Ballet Lesson 1997. *Honours:* Hon. DLitt (City Univ., London) 1984, (St Andrews) 1986, (Exeter) 2001, Hon. DArts (Pine Manor Coll., Boston, USA) 1994, Dr hc (Kingston) 1994; Emmy Award, Best Actress for The Forsyte Saga 1970, for The First Churchills 1971, for Vanity Fair 1973, E. Poe Prize du Film Fantastique, Best Actress for Malpertius 1972. *Address:* c/o Rob Groves Personal Management, 33 Glasshouse Street, London, W1B 5DG, England.

HAMPTON, Angeline Agnes, (A. A. Kelly), BA, LèsL, DèsL; British writer; b. 28 Feb. 1924, London, England; m. George Hughan Hampton 1944; one s. three d. *Education:* Univ. of London, Univ. of Geneva, Switzerland. *Career:* mem. International Asscn for the Study of Anglo-Irish Literature, Society of Authors, PEN International. *Publications:* Liam O'Flaherty the Storyteller 1976, Mary Lavin: Quiet Rebel 1980, Joseph Campbell, 1879–1944, Poet and Nationalist 1988, The Pillars of the House (ed.) 1987, Wandering Women 1994, The Letters of Liam O'Flaherty (ed.) 1996; contributions: English Studies, Comparative Education, Eire, Ireland, Hibernia, Linen Hall Review, Geneva News and International Report, Christian. *Honours:* British Acad. grant 1987.

HAMPTON, Christopher James, CBE, MA, FRSL; British playwright; b. 26 Jan. 1946, Fayal, The Azores, Portugal; s. of Bernard Patrick and Dorothy Patience (née Herrington) Hampton; m. Laura Margaret de Holesch 1971; two d. *Education:* Lancing Coll., New Coll., Oxford. *Career:* wrote first play When Did You Last See My Mother? 1964; Resident Dramatist, Royal Court Theatre 1968–70; freelance writer 1970–. *Plays:* When Did You Last See My Mother? 1964, Total Eclipse 1969, The Philanthropist 1970, Savages 1973, Treats 1976, Able's Will (TV) 1978, Tales from Hollywood 1983, Les Liaisons Dangereuses 1985, The Ginger Tree (adaptation) 1989, The Philanthropist/Total Eclipse/Treats 1991, White Chameleon 1991, Sunset Boulevard 1993, Alice's Adventures Underground (adaptation) 1995, Carrington 1995, The Secret Agent/Nostromo (adaptation) 1996, The Talking Cure 2002. *Translations include:* Marya (Babel) 1967, Uncle Vanya, Hedda Gabler 1970, A Doll's House 1971 (film 1974), Don Juan 1972, Tales from the Vienna Woods 1977 (film 1979), Don Juan Comes Back from the War 1978, The Wild Duck 1980, Ghosts 1983, Tartuffe 1984, Faith, Hope and Charity 1989, Art 1996, An Enemy of the People 1997, The Unexpected Man 1998, Conversations After a Burial 2000, Life × Three 2001, Three Sisters 2005, Embers 2006. *Directed:* (films) Carrington 1995, The Secret Agent 1996, Imagining Argentina 2003. *Opera libretto:* Waiting for the Barbarians (music by Philip Glass) 2005. *Publications:* When Did You Last See My Mother? 1967, Total Eclipse 1969 (film 1995), The Philanthropist 1970, Savages 1973, Treats 1976, Able's Will (TV) 1978, The History Man (TV adaptation of novel by Malcolm Bradbury) 1981, The Portage to San Cristobal of A.H. (play adaptation of novel by George Steiner) 1983, Tales from Hollywood 1983, The Honorary Consul (film adaptation of a novel by Graham Greene) 1983, Les Liaisons Dangereuses (adaptation of a novel by Laclos) 1985, Hotel du Lac (TV adaptation of a novel by Anita Brookner q.v.) 1986, The Good Father (film adaptation of a novel by Peter Prince) 1986, Wolf at the Door (film) 1986, Dangerous Liaisons (film) 1988, The Ginger Tree (adaptation of novel by Oswald Wynd, TV) 1989, White Chameleon 1991, Sunset Boulevard (book and lyrics with Don Black) 1993, Alice's Adventures Underground (with Martha Clarke) 1994, Carrington (film) 1995, Mary Reilly (film) 1996, The Secret Agent (film) 1996, Nostromo (screenplay) 1997, The Quiet American (film) 2002, Collected Screenplays 2002, The Talking Cure 2002. Hampton on Hampton 2005. *Honours:* Officier, Ordre des Arts et des Lettres 1998; Evening Standard Award for Best Comedy 1970, 1983, for Best Play 1986, Plays and Players London Critics' Award for Best Play 1970, 1973, 1985; Los Angeles Drama Critics' Circle Award 1974, Laurence Olivier Award for Best Play 1986, New York Drama Critics' Circle Award for Best Foreign Play 1987, Prix Italia 1988, Writers' Guild of America Screenplay Award 1989, Academy Award for Best Adapted Screenplay 1989, BAFTA Award for Best Screenplay 1990, Special Jury Award, Cannes Film Festival 1995, Tony Awards for Best Original Score (lyrics) and Best Book of a Musical 1995, Scott Moncrieff Prize 1997. *Literary Agent:* Casarotto Ramsay and Associates Ltd., Waverley House, 7–12 Noel Street, London, W1F 8GQ, England. *Telephone:* (20) 7287-4450. *Fax:* (20) 7287-9128. *E-mail:* info@casarotto.co.uk. *Website:* www.casarotto.co.uk.

HAN, Ung-bin; North Korean writer. *Publications:* Hopes for Good Fortune, Second Thoughts 2002; contrib. of short fiction to Chosôn munhak magazine. *Address:* c/o Ministry of Culture, Pyongyang, Democratic People's Republic of Korea.

HAN SUYIN, MB, BS, LRCP, MRCS; British author and medical practitioner; b. 12 Sept. 1917, Xinyang, China; d. of Y. T. Chow (née Zhou) and M. Denis; m. 1st Gen. P. H. Tang 1938 (died 1947); m. 2nd L. F. Comber 1952 (divorced 1968); m. 3rd Col Vincent Ruthnaswamy 1971 (died 2003); two adopted d. *Education:* Yenching Univ., Peking, China, Univ. of Brussels, Belgium, Royal Free Hospital, Univ. of London. *Career:* in London 1945–49; employed Queen Mary Hospital, Hong Kong 1948–52, Johore Bahru Hospital, Malaya 1952–55; pvt. medical practice 1955–64; Lecturer in Contemporary Asian Literature, Nanyang Univ., Singapore 1958–60; Hon. Prof., Univ. of Alberta and six Chinese univs. *Publications:* Destination Chungking 1942, A Many-Splendoured Thing 1952, …And the Rain My Drink 1956, The Mountain is Young 1958, Cast but One Shadow 1962, Winter Love 1962, The Four Faces 1963, The Crippled Tree 1965, A Mortal Flower 1966, China in the Year 2001 1967, Birdless Summer 1968, Morning Deluge – Mao Tse-tung and the Chinese Revolution 1972, Wind in the Tower 1976, Lhasa, the Open City 1977, My House has Two Doors 1980, Phoenix Harvest 1980, Till Morning Comes 1982, The Enchantress (novel) 1985, A Share of Loving 1987, Tigers and Butterflies 1990, Fleur de Soleil, Les Yeux de Demain, La Peinture Chinoise, Chine Insolite, Wind in My Sleeve (autobiog.) 1992, Eldest Son: Zhou Enlai and the making of Modern China (1898–1976) 1994; three photography books. *Address:* Avenue de Montoie 37, 1007 Lausanne, Switzerland (home).

HANBURY-TENISON, (Airling) Robin, OBE, MA, FLS, FRGS, DL; British explorer, conservationist, writer, broadcaster and farmer; b. 7 May 1936, London, England; m. 1st Marika Hopkinson (died 1982); one d. one s.; m. 2nd Louella Edwards (née Williams) 1983; one s. two step s. *Education:* Eton Coll., Windsor, Magdalen Coll., Oxford. *Career:* has been on over 30 expeditions worldwide; Chief Exec. British Field Sports Soc., now Countryside Alliance 1995–98; mem. Royal Geographical Soc. (RGS) (Council mem. 1968–82, 1995–, Vice-Pres. 1982–86), Survival International (Pres. 1969–), Soc. of Authors;

Trustee, Ecological Foundation 1988–2005; Patron, Cornwall Heritage Trust. *Television films:* The Last Great Journey on Earth 1969, Trans-Africa Hovercraft Expedition 1970, A Time for Survival 1972, Mysteries of the Green Mountain 1978, Antiques at Home 1984, White Horse over France 1985, Great Wall of China 1987, Odyssey (series presenter) 1988, Collectors' Lot 1998, The Lost World of Mulu 1999, Reflections in the Sand 2000, Testament 2000, Land of Eagles 2009. *Publications:* The Rough and the Smooth 1969, A Question of Survival for the Indians of Brazil 1973, A Pattern of Peoples: A Journey Among the Tribes of the Outer Indonesian Islands 1975, Mulu: The Rain Forest 1980, The Aborigines of the Amazon Rain Forest: The Yanomami 1982, Worlds Apart (autobiog.) 1984, White Horses Over France 1985, A Ride Along the Great Wall 1987, Fragile Eden: A Ride Through New Zealand 1989, Spanish Pilgrimage: A Canter to St James 1990, The Oxford Book of Exploration 1993, Worlds Within 2005, The Seventy Great Journeys in History 2006, Land of Eagles: Riding Through Europe's Forgotten Country 2009, The Great Explorers 2010; children's books: Jake's Escape 1996, Jake's Treasure, Jake's Safari 1998; contrib. to The Times, Telegraph, Express, New Scientist, Field, Traveller, Spectator, Country Life, Literary Review and Frontiers Column, Geographical Magazine 1995–98. *Honours:* Dr hc (Univ. of Mons-Hainaut) 1991; RGS Gold Medal 1979, Krug Award for Excellence 1980, Thomas Cook Travel Book Award 1984, Mungo Park Medal RSGS 2001. *Address:* Cabilla Manor, Cardinham, Bodmin, Cornwall, PL30 4DW, England (office). *Telephone:* (1208) 821224 (office). *Fax:* (1208) 821267 (office). *E-mail:* robin@cabilla.co.uk (office). *Website:* www.cabilla.co.uk (office); www.robinsbooks.co.uk.

HANCOCK, Geoffrey White, BFA, MFA; Canadian writer and literary journalist; b. 14 April 1946, New Westminster; m. Gay Allison 1983; one d. *Education:* Univ. of British Columbia. *Career:* Ed.-in-Chief, Canadian Fiction Magazine 1975; Consulting Ed., Canadian Author and Bookman 1978; Fiction Ed., Cross-Canada Writers Quarterly 1980; Literary Consultant, CBC Radio 1980; mem. Periodical Writers of Canada. *Publications:* Magic Realism 1980, Illusion: Fables, Fantasies and Metafictions 1983, Metavisions 1983, Shoes and Shit: Stories for Pedestrians 1984, Moving Off the Map: From Story to Fiction 1986, Invisible Fictions: Contemporary Stories from Quebec 1987, Canadian Writers at Work: Interviews 1987, Singularities 1990, Fast Travelling 1995; contribs to Toronto Star, Writer's Quarterly, Canadian Author and Bookman, Books In Canada, Canadian Forum. *Honours:* Fiona Mee Award for Literary Journalism 1979.

HANDKE, Peter; Austrian writer, dramatist and poet; b. 6 Dec. 1942, Griffen-Altenmarkt; one d. *Education:* Univ. of Graz. *Publications:* Die Hornissen (novel) 1963, Begrüßung des Aufsichtsrats 1963, Sprechstücke 1964, Der Hausierer (novel) 1965, Kaspar (trans. as Kaspar and Other Plays) 1967, Das Mündel will Vormund sein 1968, Die Innenwelt der Außenwelt der Innenwelt (trans. as The Innerworld of the Outerworld of the Innerworld) 1968, Die Angst des Tormanns beim Elfmeter (trans. as The Goalie's Anxiety at the Penalty Kick) 1969, Wind und Meer 1970, Chronik der laufenden Ereignisse 1970, Der Ritt über den Bodensee 1970, Der kurze Brief zum langen Abschied (trans. as Short Letter, Long Farewell) 1971, Wunschloses Unglück (trans. as A Sorrow Beyond Dreams) 1972, Ich bin ein Bewohner des Elfenbeinturms 1972, Die Unvernünftigen sterben aus 1973, Als das Wünschen noch geholfen hat (trans. as Nonsense and Happiness) 1974, Die Stunde der wahren Empfindung (trans. as A Moment of True Feeling) 1974, Die linkshändige Frau (trans. as The Left-Handed Woman) 1976, Das Gewicht der Welt: Ein Journal 1977, Langsame Heimkehr 1979, Das Ende des Flanierens 1980, Die Lehre der Sainte-Victoire 1980, Kindergeschichte 1981, Über die Dörfer 1981, Die Geschicht des Bleistifts 1982, Phantasien der Wiederholung 1983, Der Chinese des Schmerzes 1983, Die Wiederholung 1986, Die Abwesenheit (trans. as Absence) 1987, Nachmittag eines Schriftstellers 1987, Das Spiel vom Fragen oder Die Reise zum sonoren Land 1989, Versuch über die Müdigkeit 1989, Versuch über die Jukebox 1990, Versuch über den geglückten Tag: Ein Wintertagtraum 1990, Die Stunde da wir nichts voneinander wußten 1991, Langsam im Schatten: Gesammelte Verzettelungen 1980–92 1992, Mein Jahre in der Niemandsbucht 1994, Noch einmal für Thukydides 1995, Zurüstungen für die Unsterblichkeit 1995, Eine winterliche Reise zu den Flüssen Donau, Save, Morawa und Drina oder Gerechtigkeit für Serbien (trans. as A Journey to the Rivers: Justice for Serbia) 1996, In einer dunklen Nacht ging ich aus meinem stillen Haus (novel) 1997, Lucie im Wald mit den Dingsda 1999, Die Fahrt im Einbaum oder Das Stück zum Film vom Krieg 1999, Unter Tränen fragend. Nachträgliche Aufzeichnungen von zwei Jugoslawien-Durchquerungen im Krieg, März und April 1999 2000, Der Bildverlust oder Durch die Sierra des Gredos (novel; trans. as Crossing the Sierra de Gredos) 2002, Mündliches und Schriftliches. Zu Büchern, Bildern und Filmen 1992–2002 2002, Untertagblues 2003, Don Juan (erzählt von ihm selbst) (Siegfried Unseld Preis) 2004, Spuren der Verirrten 2006, Kali 2007, Die morawische Nacht 2008. *Honours:* Gerhart Hauptmann Prize 1967, Peter Rosegger Literary Prize 1972, Schiller Prize, Mannheim 1972, Büchner Prize 1973, Prix Georges Sadoul 1978, Kafka Prize 1979, Salzburg Literary Prize 1986, Great Austrian (state) Prize 1987, Bremen Literary Prize, Hamburg 1991, Franz Grillparzer Prize, Hamburg 1991, Goethe Inst. Drama Prize, Munich 1993, Prize of Honour of the Schiller Memorial Prize 1995. *Address:* c/o Suhrkamp Verlag, Postfach 101945, 60019 Frankfurt am Main, Germany (office). *Website:* www.suhrkamp.de (office).

HANDLER, Daniel, (Lemony Snicket); American writer; b. 28 Feb. 1970, San Francisco, CA; m. Lisa Brown; one s. *Education:* Lowel High School, San Francisco and Wesleyan Univ. *Film screenplays:* Rick 2003, Lemony Snicket's A Series of Unfortunate Events 2004, Kill the Poor 2006. *Publications:* fiction: A Series of Unfortunate Events, Vol. 1: The Bad Beginning 1999, Vol. 2: The Reptile Room 1999, Vol. 3: The Wide Window 1999, Vol. 4: The Miserable Mill 2000, Vol. 5: The Austere Academy 2000, Vol. 6: The Ersatz Elevator 2001, Vol. 7: The Vile Village 2001, Vol. 8: The Hostile Hospital 2001, Vol. 9: The Carnivorous Carnival 2002, Vol. 10: The Slippery Slope 2003, Vol. 11: The Grim Grotto 2004, Vol. 12: The Penultimate Peril (Quill Book Award for Children's Chapter Book/Middle Grade 2006) 2004, Vol. 13: The End 2006; non-fiction: The Unauthorised Autobiography 2002, various other series tie-in books; adult novels: The Basic Eight 1999, Watch Your Mouth 2000, Adverbs 2006. *Address:* c/o Harper Collins Children's Books, 1350 Avenue of the Americas, New York, NY 10019, USA (office). *E-mail:* lsnicket@harpercollins.com. *Website:* www.lemonysnicket.com.

HANIKA, Iris, MA; German writer; b. 18 Oct. 1962, Wurzburg. *Education:* Free Univ. of Berlin. *Career:* staff writer (Berlin Pages), Frankfurter Allgemeine Zeitung 1999–2002; columnist, Merkur magazine 2000–08. *Publications include:* Katharina oder die Existenzverpflichtung (Katharina, or The Obligation to Exist) (story) 1992, Das Loch im Brot (The Hole in the Bread) (chronicle) 2003, Berlin im Licht. 24 Stunden Webcam (Berlin in the Light. 24 Hours of Webcam) (co-ed.) 2003, Musik für Flughäfen (Music for Airports) (short texts) (Hans Fallada Prize 2006) 2005, Die Wette auf das Unbewusste oder Was Sie schon immer über Psychoanalyse wissen wollten (The Bet on the Unconscious, or Everything You Always Wanted to Know about Psychoanalysis) (non-fiction, co-author) 2006, Treffen sich zwei, (When Two Meet) (novel) 2008, Das Eigentliche (The Bottom Line) (novel) (EU Prize for Literature 2010, LiteraTour North Prize 2011) 2010. *Address:* c/o Droschl Verlag, Stenggstrasse 33, 8043 Graz, Austria. *Telephone:* (316) 326404. *E-mail:* office@droschl.com; mail@iris-hanika.de (home). *Website:* www.droschl.com; www.iris-hanika.de.

HANKIN, Elizabeth Rosemary, (Elizabeth Gill); British writer and journalist; b. 16 Oct. 1950, Newcastle upon Tyne, England; m. Richard Hankin 1973 (divorced 1988); one d. *Education:* Emma Willard School. *Career:* Journalist in Durham 1970–75; Cttee mem. Romantic Novelists Asscn. *Publications:* fiction: The Singing Winds 1995, Far from My Father's House 1995, Under a Cloud-Soft Sky 1996, The Road to Berry Edge 1997, The Preacher's Son 2005, The Secret 2006, Swan Island 2007, Silver Street 2008, Sweet Wells 2008, Dream Breakers 2009, Paradise Lane 2010, Snow Hall 2010, Dragon's Field 2011. *Address:* c/o Severn House Publishers Limited, 9-15 High Street, Sutton, SM1 1DF, England.

HANNAH, Sophie, MA; British crime fiction writer and poet; *Fellow Commoner, Lucy Cavendish College, Cambridge*; b. 28 June 1971, Manchester, England; m. Dr Deiniol Jones; one s. one d. *Education:* Univ. of Manchester. *Career:* Fellow Commoner, Trinity Coll. Cambridge, Lucy Cavendish Coll. Cambridge; Fellow, Wolfson Coll. Oxford. *Television:* adaptation of The Point of Rescue (ITV 1) 2011. *Publications:* poetry: Early Bird Blues 1993, Second Helping of Your Heart 1994, Hero and the Girl Next Door 1995, Hotels Like House (Arts Council Writers' Award) 1996, Leaving and Leaving You 1999, First of the Last Chances 2003, Selected Poems 2006, Pessimism for Beginners 2007; fiction: Carrot the Goldfish 1992, Gripless 1999, Cordial and Corrosive 2000, The Superpower of Love 2001, Little Face 2006, Hurting Distance 2007, The Point of Rescue 2008, The Fantastic Book of Everyone's Secrets 2008, The Other Half Lives 2009, A Room Swept White 2010; trans.: The Book about Moomin, Mymble and Little My 2001, Who Will Comfort Toffle 2003; contrib. to The Box Poem 2001, Hyphen: An Anthology of Short Stories by Poets 2003, Leeds Stories 2 2004. *Honours:* Eric Gregory Award 1995. *Address:* c/o Carcanet Press, Fourth Floor, Alliance House, Cross Street, Manchester, M2 7AP; c/o Hodder & Stoughton, 338 Euston Road, London, NW1 3BH, England. *E-mail:* sophie@sophiehannah.com (office). *Website:* www.sophiehannah.com.

HANSEN, Erik Fosnes; Norwegian novelist; *Council Member and Head of Literary Department, Arts Council of Norway*; b. 6 June 1965, New York, USA; s. of the late Erik Fosnes Hansen Sr and Reidun Fosnes Hansen (née Ledang); m.; one s. *Career:* restaurant critic for Verdens Gang newspaper; mem. Norwegian Acad. *Music:* wrote lyrics and performed on album Neste stasjon Grorud (with Finn Kalvik) 2010. *Publications:* Falketårnet 1985, Salme ved reisens slutt (Psalm at Journey's End, novel) 1990, Beretninger om beskyttelse (Tales of Protection, novel) 1998, Underveis. Et portrett av Prinsesse Märtha Louise (non-fiction) 2001, Kokebok for Otto (cookery book) 2005, Løvekvinnen (The Lion Woman) 2006; contrib. of articles and columns in numerous magazines and newspapers. *Honours:* Riksmålsprisen 1998, Bokhandlerprisen 1998, NRK P2-lytternes Pris 1999, Bokhandlerprisen 2006. *Address:* c/o Secker & Warburg, Random House, 20 Vauxhall Bridge Road, London, SW1V 2SA, England.

HANSEN, Ron, BA, MFA, MA; American writer and academic; *Gerard Manley Hopkins, S.J. Professor in the Arts and Humanities, Department of English, Santa Clara University*; b. 8 Dec. 1947, Omaha, Nebraska; m. Bo Caldwell. *Education:* Creighton Univ., Univ. of Iowa, Stanford Univ., Santa Clara Univ. *Career:* taught at numerous univs including Stanford Univ., Univ. of Michigan, Univ. of Iowa, Univ. of Arizona, Cornell Univ.; currently Gerard Manley Hopkins, S.J. Prof. in the Arts and Humanities, Dept of English, Santa Clara Univ.; ordained perm. deacon of Catholic Church 2007; Fellow, Dominican School of Philosophy and Theology 2009. *Publications:* The

Desperadoes 1979, The Assassination of Jesse James by the Coward Robert Ford 1983, The Shadowmaker 1986, You Don't Know What Love Is 1987, Nebraska Stories 1989, Mariette in Ecstacy: A Novel 1992, Atticus 1996, Hitler's Niece 1999, Isn't it Romantic? An Entertainment 2003, Exiles 2008, A Wild Surge of Guilty Passion 2011. *Honours:* American Acad. and Inst. of Arts and Letters Award. *Address:* Department of English, Santa Clara University, Room No 303, Santa Clara, CA 95053, USA (office). *Telephone:* (408) 554-4130 (office). *Fax:* (408) 554-4837 (office). *E-mail:* RHansen@scu.edu (office). *Website:* www.scu.edu/cas/english/faculty/hansen.cfm?p=4268 (office).

HANSON, William Stewart, BA, PhD, FSA, FSA Scot; British archaeologist and writer; *Professor of Roman Archaeology, University of Glasgow*; b. 22 Jan. 1950, Doncaster, Yorks., England; m. Lesley Macinnes; one d. *Education:* Univ. of Manchester. *Career:* Sr Lecturer in Archaeology, Univ. of Glasgow 1990–2000, Prof. of Roman Archaeology 2000–. *Publications:* Rome's North-West Frontier: The Antonine Wall (co-author) 1983, Agricola and the Conquest of the North 1987, Scottish Archaeology: New Perceptions (co-ed.) 1991, Roman Dacia: The Making of a Provincial Society (co-ed.) 2004, Elginhaugh: A Flavian Fort and its Annexe 2007, A Roman Frontier Fort in Scotland: The First Century Fort at Elginhaugh 2007, The Army and Frontiers of Rome (ed.) 2009; contrib. to major academic archaeological and antiquarian journals and collected works. *Address:* Archaeology, School of Humanities, University of Glasgow, The Gregory Building, Lilybank Gardens, Glasgow, G12 8QQ, Scotland (office). *Telephone:* (141) 330-4915 (office). *Fax:* (141) 330-3544 (office). *E-mail:* william.hanson@glasgow.ac.uk (office). *Website:* www.gla.ac.uk/schools/humanities/staff/williamhanson (office).

HARADA, Masako, (Satoko Kizaki); Japanese writer; b. 14 Nov. 1939, Changchung, China; m. Hiroshi Harada 1962, two d. *Education:* Tokyo Women's Univ. Junior Coll. *Publications:* Rasoku 1982, Umi-to Rosoku 1985, Aogiri (trans. as The Phoenix Tree and Other Stories) 1985, Shizumeru tera (trans. as The Sunken Temple) 1987, Nami-Half-way 1988, Sanzoku-no-Haka 1989, Kagami-no-Tani 1990, Toki-no-Shizuku 1991, Atonaki-Niwa-ni 1991, Shiawase no chiisana tobira 1994. *Honours:* Akutagawa Prize 1985.

HARBACH, Chad, MFA; American author; b. 1975, Racine, Wis. *Education:* Harvard Univ., Univ. of Virginia. *Career:* Co-founder, ed. and writer, n + 1 literary journal 2004. *Publications:* The Art of Fielding 2011. *Address:* c/o Little, Brown and Co., Hachette Book Group, 237 Park Avenue, New York, NY 10017, USA (office). *Telephone:* (800) 759-0190 (office). *E-mail:* editors@nplusonemag.com (office). *Website:* www.hachettebookgroup.com (office); nplusonemag.com (office).

HARBISON, Peter, MA, DPhil, MRIA, FSA; Irish archaeologist, art historian and editor; *Honorary Academic Editor, Royal Irish Academy*; b. 14 Jan. 1939, Dublin; s. of Dr James Austin Harbison and Sheelagh Harbison (née McSherry); m. Edelgard Soergel 1969 (died 2008); three s. *Education:* St Gerard's School, Bray, Glenstal, Univ. Coll. Dublin and Univs of Marburg, Kiel and Freiburg, Germany. *Career:* awarded travelling scholarship by German Archaeological Inst. 1965; archaeological officer, Irish Tourist Bd 1966–84, editorial publicity officer 1984–86, Ed. Ireland of the Welcomes (magazine) 1986–95; Sec. Friends of the Nat. Collections of Ireland 1971–76; mem. Council, Royal Irish Acad. 1981–84, 1993–96, 1998–2001, 2004–, Vice-Pres. 1992–93, 2006–07, Hon. Academic Ed. 1997–; Prof. of Archaeology, Royal Hibernian Acad. of Arts; Chair. Nat. Monuments Advisory Council 1986–90, Dublin Cemeteries Cttee 1986–89, 1996–2002, Bunratty Castle Ownership and Furniture Trusts 2004–; Vice-Pres. for Leinster, Royal Soc. of Antiquities of Ireland 2005–07; Guest Prof., Univ. of Vienna summer 2004; Corresp. mem. German Archaeological Inst. *Publications:* Guide to National Monuments of Ireland 1970, The Archaeology of Ireland 1976, Irish Art and Architecture (co-author) 1978, Pre-Christian Ireland (Archaeological Book of the Year Award 1988) 1988, Pilgrimage in Ireland 1991, Beranger's Views of Ireland 1991, The High Crosses of Ireland 1992, Irish High Crosses 1994, Ancient Ireland (with Jacqueline O'Brien) 1996, Ancient Irish Monuments 1997, Beranger's Antique Buildings of Ireland, L'Art Médiéval en Irlande 1998, Spectacular Ireland 1999, The Golden Age of Irish Art 1999, The Crucifixion in Irish Art 2000, Cooper's Ireland 2000, Our Treasure of Antiquities 2002, Treasures of the Boyne Valley 2003, Ireland's Treasures 2004, Beranger's Rambles in Ireland 2004, A Thousand Years of Church Heritage in East Galway 2005; articles in books and journals. *Honours:* Hon. mem. Royal Hibernian Acad. of Arts 1998, Royal Inst. of Architects of Ireland; Hon. Fellow, Trinity Coll., Dublin 2000. *Address:* 5 St Damian's, Loughshinny, Skerries, Co. Dublin (home); Royal Irish Academy, 19 Dawson Street, Dublin 2, Republic of Ireland (office). *Telephone:* (1) 8490940 (home); (1) 6762570 (office). *Fax:* (1) 6762346 (office). *E-mail:* p.harbison@ria.ie (office). *Website:* www.ria.ie (office).

HARCOURT, Geoffrey Colin, AO, PhD, LittD, FASSA; Australian academic; *Emeritus Fellow, Jesus College and Reader Emeritus in the History of Economic Theory, University of Cambridge*; b. 27 June 1931, Melbourne; s. of Kenneth and Marjorie Harcourt (née Gans); m. Joan Bartrop 1955; two s. two d. *Education:* Univ. of Melbourne and Univ. of Cambridge, UK. *Career:* Lecturer in Econs, Univ. of Adelaide 1958–62, Sr Lecturer 1962–65, Reader 1965–67, Prof. (Personal Chair) 1967–85, Prof. Emer. 1988–; Lecturer in Econs and Politics, Univ. of Cambridge 1964–66, 1982–90, Reader in the History of Econ. Theory 1990–98, Reader Emer. 1998–, Dir of Studies in Econs and Fellow, Trinity Hall, Cambridge 1964–66, Fellow and Lecturer in Econs, Jesus Coll., Cambridge 1982–98, Fellow Emer. 1998–, Pres. 1988–92; Leverhulme Exchange Fellow, Keio Univ., Tokyo 1969–70; Visiting Fellow, Clare Hall, Cambridge 1972–73; Visiting Prof., Univ. of Toronto, Canada 1977, 1980, Univ. of Melbourne 2002; Visiting Fellow, ANU 1997; Pres. Econ. Soc. of Australia and New Zealand 1974–77; mem. Council Royal Econ. Soc. 1990–95, Life mem. 1998–; Distinguished Fellow, Econ. Soc. of Australia 1996, History of Econs Soc., USA 2004; Academician Acad. of Learned Socs for the Social Sciences (AcSS) 2003; Fellow, Acad. of the Social Sciences in Australia 1971 (exec. cttee mem. 1974–77). *Publications:* Economic Activity (with P. H. Karmel and R. H. Wallace) 1967, Readings in the Concept and Measurement of Income (ed., with R. H. Parker) 1969 (2nd edn with R. H. Parker and G. Whittington 1986), Capital and Growth, Selected Readings (ed., with N. F. Laing) 1971, Some Cambridge Controversies in the Theory of Capital 1972, The Microeconomic Foundations of Macroeconomics (ed.) 1977, The Social Science Imperialists, Selected Essays (edited by Prue Kerr) 1982, Keynes and his Contemporaries (ed.) 1985, Controversies in Political Economy, Selected Essays of G. C. Harcourt (edited by Omar Hamouda) 1986, International Monetary Problems and Supply-Side Economics: Essays in Honour of Lorie Tarshis (edited with Jon S. Cohen) 1986, On Political Economists and Modern Political Economy, Selected Essays of G. C. Harcourt (ed. by Claudio Sardoni) 1992, Post-Keynesian Essays in Biography: Portraits of Twentieth Century Political Economists 1993, The Dynamics of the Wealth of Nations. Growth, Distribution and Structural Change: Essays in Honour of Luigi Pasinetti (edited with Mauro Baranzini) 1993, Income and Employment in Theory and Practice. Essays in Memory of Athanasios Asimakopulos (ed. with Alessandro Roncaglia and Robin Rowley) 1994, Capitalism, Socialism and Post-Keynesianism. Selected Essays of G. C. Harcourt 1995, A 'Second Edition' of The General Theory (two vols, co-ed. with P. A. Riach) 1997, 50 Years a Keynesian and Other Essays 2001, Selected Essays on Economic Policy 2001, L'Economie rebelle de Joan Robinson (ed.) 2001, Joan Robinson: Critical Assessments of Leading Economists (five vols, ed. with Prue Kerr) 2002, Editing Economics: Essays in Honour of Mark Perlman (co-ed.) 2002, Capital Theory (3 Vols, ed. with Christopher Bliss and Avi Cohen) 2005, The Structure of Post-Keynesian Economics: The Core Contributions of the Pioneers 2006. *Honours:* Hon. Fellow, Queen's Coll., Melbourne 1998, Sugden Fellow 2002; Hon. Prof., Univ. of NSW 1997, 1999; Hon. mem. European Soc. for the History of Economic Thought 2004; Hon. LittD (De Montfort Univ.) 1997; Hon. DCom (Melbourne) 2003; Hon. Dr rer. pol (Fribourg) 2003; Wellington Burnham Lecturer, Tufts Univ., Medford, Mass 1975, Edward Shann Memorial Lecturer, Univ. of Western Australia 1975, Newcastle Lecturer in Political Economy, Univ. of Newcastle 1977, Acad. Lecturer, Acad. of the Social Sciences in Australia 1978, G.L. Wood Memorial Lecturer, Univ. of Melbourne 1982, John Curtin Memorial Lecturer, ANU 1982, Special Lecturer in Econs, Univ. of Manchester 1984, Lecturer, Nobel Conf. XXII, Gustavus Adolphus Coll., Minn. 1986, Laws Lecturer, Univ. of Tennessee at Knoxville 1991, Donald Horne Lecturer 1992, Sir Halford Cook Lecturer, Queen's Coll., Univ. of Melbourne, Kingsley Martin Memorial Lecturer, Cambridge 1996, Colin Clark Memorial Lecturer, Brisbane 1997, Bernard Hesketh Lecturer, Univ. of Minn., Kansas City 2006. *Address:* 43 New Square, Cambridge, CB1 1EZ (home); Jesus College, Cambridge, CB5 8BL, England (office). *Telephone:* (1223) 760353 (office). *E-mail:* fellows-secretary@jesus.cam.ac.uk (office); GCH3@cam.ac.uk (home).

HARDEN, Blaine Charles, BA, MA; American journalist and author; *Reporter, PBS Frontline*; b. 4 April 1952, Moses Lake, Wash.; m. Jessica Kowal; one s. one d. *Education:* Gonzaga Univ., Syracuse Univ. *Career:* Africa Corresp., Washington Post 1985–89, East European Corresp. 1989–93, reporter 1995–97, Nat. Corresp. covering American West, Seattle 2003–07, East Asia Bureau Chief covering Japan, Korea and SE Asia 2007–10; Nat. Corresp., New York Times 1997–2002; currently reporter, PBS Frontline. *Publications:* Africa: Dispatches From a Fragile Continent 1990, A River Lost: The Life and Death of Columbia 1996, Escape from Camp 14: A North Korean Odyssey 2011, Escape from Camp 14: One Man's Remarkable Odyssey from North Korea to Freedom in the West 2012; contribs to Washington Post, New York Times Magazine, Smithsonian Magazine, Discovery Magazine, National Geographic, The Economist. *Honours:* Livingston Award for Young Journalists 1986, American Asscn of Newspaper Editors Award for Non-deadline Writing 1987, Martha Albrand Citation for First Book of Non-Fiction, PEN 1991, Ernie Pyle Award for Human Interest Reporting 1993. *Telephone:* (206) 432-0961 (office). *E-mail:* hardenb@gmail.com (office).

HARDING, Paul, MFA; American writer and teacher; b. 1967, Wenham, Mass; m.; two s. *Education:* Univ. of Massachusetts at Amherst, Iowa Writers' Workshop. *Career:* fmr drummer with rock band, Cold Water Flat 1990–97; has taught writing at Iowa Writers' Workshop; teacher in expository writing program, Harvard Univ. 2001–08, teacher of fiction writing, Extension School 2002–. *Publications:* Tinkers (Pulitzer Prize for Fiction 2010, PEN/Robert Bingham Fellowship for Writers 2010) 2009. *Honours:* James E. Conway Excellence in Teaching Writing Award, Harvard Univ. 2009, Guggenheim Foundation Fellowship 2009. *Literary Agent:* Ms Arlynn Greenbaum, Authors Unlimited, 31 East 32nd Street #300, New York, NY 10016, USA. *E-mail:* arlynnj@cs.com. *Address:* c/o Bellevue Literary Press, Department of Medicine, New York University School of Medicine, 550 First Avenue, OBV 612, New York, NY 10016, USA (office). *E-mail:* erika.goldman@nyumc.org (office). *Website:* www.blpbooks.org (office).

HARDY, Barbara Gladys, BA, MA, FRSL, FBA; British academic and writer; b. 27 June 1924, England; m. Ernest Dawson Hardy (deceased); two d.

Education: Univ. Coll., London. *Career:* Prof. of English, Royal Holloway Coll., London 1965–70; Prof. of English Literature, Birkbeck Coll., London 1970–89, Prof. Emer. 1989–; mem. Welsh Acad.; Fellow, Royal Holloway Coll., London, Univ. of Wales, Swansea. *Publications:* The Novels of George Eliot: A Study in Form 1959, The Appropriate Form: An Essay on the Novel 1964, Middlemarch: Critical Appoaches to the Novel (ed.) 1967, Charles Dickens: The Later Novels 1968, Critical Essays on George Eliot (ed.) 1970, The Exposure of Luxury: Radical Themes in Thackeray 1970, Tellers and Listeners: The Narrative Imagination 1975, A Reading of Jane Austen 1975, The Advantage of Lyric: Essays on Feeling in Poetry 1977, Particularities: Readings in George Eliot 1982, Forms of Feeling in Victorian Fiction 1985, Narrators and Novelists: Collected Essays 1987, Swansea Girl 1993, London Lovers (novel) 1996, Henry James: The Later Writing 1996, Shakespeare's Storytellers 1997, Dylan Thomas: An Original Language 2000, Thomas Hardy: Imagining Imagination 2000, Severn Bridge: New and Collected Poems 2001, George Eliot: A Critic's Biography 2006, The Yellow Carpet: New and Collected Poems 2006, Dickens and Creativity 2008, London Rivers (with Kate Hardy) 2011, Dorothea's Daughter and Other Nineteenth-Century Postscripts 2011. *Honours:* Hon. mem. Modern Language Asscn 1973; Hon. DUniv (Open Univ.) 1982; Hon. Fellow, Birkbeck Coll., London 1991, Royal Holloway Coll. 1992, Swansea Metropolitan Univ. 2010; Hon. Prof. of English, Univ. of Wales, Swansea 1991; Rose Mary Crawshay Prize 1962, Sagittarius Prize 1997.

HARDY, Jules, MA, PhD; British novelist; b. Bristol. *Career:* publishing, teaching. *Publications:* novels: Altered Land 2001, Mister Candid 2003, Blue Earth 2005, Unforgiven 2007. *Honours:* WH Smith Fresh Talent Award 2003. *Address:* 33 Alexandra Park, Redland, Bristol, BS6 6QB, England.

HARDY, Justine; British journalist and writer. *Career:* documentary maker and presenter, Channel 4 1996, also projects with BBC and BBC World Service; fmr presenter, Travel TV; fmr co-presenter (with Jerry Hall), BBC series on Eastern philosophy; Dir Development Research and Action Group (NGO that sets up schools in slum areas of Delhi); f. Healing Kashmir (mental health project) 2008; worked with New Bridge (UK) for 22 years, foundation working on the rehabilitation of life sentence prisoners before release; teacher of yoga and philosophy, UK and India; conflict trauma therapist. *Radio:* Scoop-Wallah (BBC Radio 4) 1999, Goat: A Story of Kashmir and Notting Hill (BBC Radio 4) 2000, In the Valley of the Mist 2009. *Television:* Urban Jungle (Channel 4) 1996. *Publications:* The Ochre Border 1995, Scoop-Wallah 1999, Goat: A Story of Kashmir and Notting Hill 2000, Bollywood Boy 2002, In the Valley of Mist 2009; other: The Wonder House 2005 (novel); contrib. to Financial Times, India Express, The Times, Vanity Fair, Traveler, The Times of India, and others. *Literary Agent:* Elizabeth Sheinkman, Curtis Brown Group Ltd, Haymarket House, 28–29 Haymarket, London, SW1Y 4SP, England. *Telephone:* (20) 7393-4400. *Website:* www.curtisbrown.co.uk; www.justinehardy.com.

HARE, Sir David, Kt, MA, FRSL; British playwright and theatre director; b. 5 June 1947, Hastings, Sussex; s. of Clifford Theodore Rippon Hare and Agnes Cockburn Gilmour; m. 1st Margaret Matheson 1970 (divorced 1980); two s. one d.; m. 2nd Nicole Farhi 1992. *Education:* Lancing Coll., Jesus Coll., Cambridge. *Career:* Literary Man. and Resident Dramatist, Royal Court 1969–71; Resident Dramatist, Nottingham Playhouse 1973; f. Portable Theatre 1968, Joint Stock Theatre Group 1975, Greenpoint Films 1983; Assoc. Dir Nat. Theatre 1984–88, 1989–; UK/US Bicentennial Fellowship 1978. *Plays:* Slag, Hampstead 1970, Royal Court 1971, New York Shakespeare Festival (NYSF) 1971, The Great Exhibition, Hampstead 1972, Brassneck (with Howard Brenton q.v.), Nottingham Playhouse 1973 (also Dir), Knuckle, Comedy Theatre 1974, Fanshen, Inst. of Contemporary Arts 1975, Hampstead 1975, Nat. Theatre 1992, Teeth 'n' Smiles, Royal Court 1975 (also Dir), Wyndhams 1976 (also Dir), Plenty, Nat. Theatre 1978 (also Dir), NYSF and Broadway 1982 (also Dir), Albery 1999, A Map of the World, Nat. Theatre 1983 (also Dir) NYSF 1985 (also Dir), Pravda: A Fleet Street Comedy (with Howard Brenton), Nat. Theatre 1985 (also Dir), The Bay at Nice, Nat. Theatre 1986 (also Dir), The Secret Rapture, Nat. Theatre 1988, NYSF and Broadway 1989 (also Dir), Racing Demon, Nat. Theatre 1990, 1993, Broadway 1995, Murmuring Judges, Nat. Theatre 1992, 1993, The Absence of War, Nat. Theatre 1993, Skylight, Nat. Theatre 1995, Wyndhams and Broadway 1996, Vaudeville 1997, Amy's View, Nat. Theatre 1997, Aldwych 1998, Broadway 1999, The Judas Kiss, Almeida and Broadway 1998 (Dir on radio only), Via Dolorosa, Royal Court 1998 (also acted), Almeida and Broadway 1999 (also acted), My Zinc Bed, Royal Court 2000 (also Dir), The Breath of Life, Theatre Royal, Haymarket 2002, The Permanent Way, Nat. Theatre 2003, Stuff Happens, Nat. Theatre 2004, The Vertical Hour (Music Box Theatre, Broadway) 2006, Gethsemane, Nat. Theatre 2009. *Plays adapted:* The Rules of the Game, Nat. Theatre 1971, Almeida 1992, The Life of Galileo, Almeida 1994, Mother Courage and Her Children, Nat. Theatre 1995, Ivanov, Almeida and Broadway 1997 (Dir on radio only), The Blue Room, Donmar and Broadway 1998, Theatre Royal 2000, Platonov, Almeida 2001, The House of Bernarda Alba, Lorca 2005. *Plays directed:* Christie in Love, Portable Theatre 1969, Fruit, Portable Theatre 1970, Blowjob, Portable Theatre 1971, England's Ireland, Portable Theatre 1972 (Co-Dir), The Provoked Wife, Palace, Watford 1973, The Pleasure Principle, Theatre Upstairs 1973, The Party, Nat. Theatre 1974, Weapons of Happiness, Nat. Theatre 1976, Devil's Island, Joint Stock 1977, Total Eclipse, Lyric 1981, King Lear, Nat. Theatre 1986, The Designated Mourner, Nat. Theatre 1996, Heartbreak House, Almeida 1997. *Radio play:* Murder in Samarkand 2010. *TV screenplays:* Man Above Men (BBC) 1973, Licking Hitler (BBC) 1978 (also Dir), Dreams of Leaving (BBC) 1979 (also Dir), Saigon: Year of the Cat (Thames) 1983 (also Assoc. Producer), Heading Home (BBC) 1991 (also Dir), The Absence of War (BBC) 1995. *Film screenplays:* Wetherby 1985 (also Dir), Plenty 1985, Paris by Night 1989 (also Dir), Strapless 1990 (also Dir), Damage 1992, The Secret Rapture 1993 (also assoc. producer), Via Dolorosa 2000 (also actor), The Hours (adaptation of Michael Cunningham's novel) 2001, Lee Miller 2003, The Corrections (adaptation of Jonathan Franzen's novel) 2005. *Film directed:* The Designated Mourner 1996 (also Producer). *Opera libretto:* The Knife, New York Shakespeare Festival 1988 (also Dir). *Publications:* Writing Lefthanded 1991, Asking Around 1993, Acting Up: A Diary 1999, Obedience, Struggle and Revolt (collection of speeches) 2005. *Honours:* Hon. Fellow, Jesus Coll. Cambridge 2001; Officier, Ordre des Arts et des Lettres 1997; Evening Standard Drama Award 1970, John Llewellyn Rhys Prize 1974, BAFTA Best Play of the Year 1978, New York Critics' Circle Awards 1983, 1990, 1997, 1999, Golden Bear Award for Best Film 1985, Evening Standard Drama Award for Best Play 1985, Plays and Players Best Play Awards 1985, 1988, 1990, City Limits Best Play 1985, Drama Magazine Awards Best Play 1988, Laurence Olivier Best Play of the Year 1990, 1996, Time Out Award 1990, Dramalogue Award 1992, Time Out Award for Outstanding Theatrical Achievement 1998, Outer Critics' Circle Award 1999, Drama League Award 1999, Drama Desk Award 1999, Joan Cullman Award 1999, PEN Pinter Prize 2011. *Literary Agent:* c/o Casarotto Ramsay & Associates Ltd, Waverley House, 7–12 Noel Street, London, W1F 8GQ, England. *Telephone:* (20) 7287-4450. *Fax:* (20) 7287-9128. *E-mail:* info@casarotto.co.uk. *Website:* www.casarotto.co.uk.

HARGITAI, Peter, BA, MA, MFA; American/Hungarian writer and academic; *Senior Lecturer, Department of English, Florida International University;* b. 28 Jan. 1947, Budapest, Hungary; m. Dianne Kress 1967; one s. one d. *Education:* Univ. of Massachusetts. *Career:* Lecturer in English, Univ. of Miami 1980–85, Univ. of Massachusetts 1987–88; Asst Prof., Dept of English, Broward Community Coll. 1988–90; Instructor in Composition, Dept of English, Florida International Univ. 1990–97, apptd Lecturer of Writing and Rhetoric 1997, currently Sr Lecturer; mem. PEN International, Literary Network, New York. *Publications:* Forum: Ten Poets of the Western Reserve 1976, Perched on Nothings Branch 1986, Magyar Tales 1989, Budapest to Bellevue 1989, Budapesttöl New Yorkig és tovább… 1991, Fodois Budget Zion 1991, The Traveler 1994, Attila: A Barbarian's Bedtime Story 1994, Mother Tongue: A Broken Hungarian Love Song 2003, The Traveler 2003, Daughter of The Revolution 2006, Millie 2008, 2012 A Little Horn of Prophecy 2010, Approaching My Literature: Translations from the Hungarian Exilic Experience 2011; contribs to North Atlantic Review, Colorado Quarterly, Nimrod, College English, California Quarterly, Spirit, Prairie Schooner, Poetry East, Cornfield Review, Blue Unicorn. *Honours:* Acad. of American Poets Trans. Award 1988, Fust Milan Award, Hungarian Acad. of Sciences 1994, Pro Cultura Hungarica Medal 2000, Medal of Freedom, American Hungarian Fed., Washington, DC 2006, Silver Medal of Honor for teaching Literature of Exile, Hungarian House, Los Angeles 2009, Martin Luther King, Jr Poetry Award 2009. *Address:* Modesto Maidique Campus, DM 465A, 11200 SW, 8 Street, Miami, FL 33199, USA (office). *Telephone:* (305) 348-2874 (office). *E-mail:* hargitai@fiu.edu (office). *Website:* casgroup.fiu.edu/english/faculty.php?id=107 (office); www.freewebs.com/hargitai.

HARIHARAN, Githa, BA, MA; Indian writer, editor and academic; b. 1954, Coimbatore, Tamil Nadu; two s. *Education:* Bombay Univ., Fairfield Univ., USA. *Career:* fmr staff writer, WNET-Channel 13, New York; worked as ed. in publishing houses in Mumbai, Chennai and New Delhi 1979–84; freelance ed. 1985–; has taught, and been a fellow or writer-in-residence, at Dartmouth Coll., George Washington Univ., USA, Univ. of Kent, UK, Jamia Millia Islamia, India, Belagio, Italy; filed a writ petition in the Supreme Court of India against the Hindu Guardianship Act as discriminatory against women. *Publications:* novels: The Thousand Faces of Night (Commonwealth Writers Prize for Best First Book 1993) 1992, The Ghosts of Vasu Master 1994, When Dreams Travel 1999, In Times of Siege 2003, Fugitive Histories 2009; short stories: The Art of Dying 1993, The Winning Team 2004; numerous contribs to anthologies and columns in The Telegraph, Kolkata. *Literary Agent:* c/o Georges Borchardt, Georges Borchardt Inc., 136 East 47th Street, New York, NY 11022, USA. *Telephone:* (212) 753-5785. *Fax:* (212) 838-6518. *E-mail:* georges@gbagency.com. *Website:* www.gbagency.com. *E-mail:* contact@githahariharan.com (office). *Website:* www.githahariharan.com.

HARING, Firth (see Fabend, Firth Haring)

HARJO, Joy, BA, MFA; American poet, musician, lyricist, writer and screenwriter and playwright; b. 9 May 1951, Tulsa, Okla; d. of Allen W. Foster, Jr and Wynema Jewell Baker; one s. one d. *Education:* Inst. of American Indian Arts, Univ. of New Mexico, Univ. of Iowa. *Career:* Instructor, Inst. of American Indian Arts 1978–79, 1983–84, Santa Fe Community Coll. 1983–84; Lecturer, Arizona State Univ. 1980–81; Asst Prof., Univ. of Colorado at Boulder 1985–88; Assoc. Prof., Univ. of Arizona at Tucson 1988–90; Prof., Univ. of New Mexico 1991–97, Joseph M. Russo Prof. of Creative Writing 2005–09; Prof., UCLA 2001–; Nat. Endowment for the Arts Creative Writing Fellowships 1978, 1992; Arizona Comm. on the Arts Poetry Fellowship 1989; Woodrow Wilson Fellowship 1993; Witter Bynner Poetry Fellowship 1994; mem. PEN (Advisory Bd), Nat. Council of the Arts, Univ. of Arizona Sun Tracks Series Bd; mem. Native Arts and Cultures Foundation, Founding mem. Bd of Trustees 2007–. *Screenplay:* A Thousand Roads (signature film of the National Museum of the American Indian). *Compositions:* Letter From The End of The 20th Century, The Musician Who Became A Bear. *Recordings:* Letter From The End of The 20th Century, Eagle Song (video) 2002, Native Joy 2003, Native Joy for Real 2004, She Had Some Horses 2006, Winding Through the Milky Way 2008, Red Dreams 2010, A Trail Beyond Tears 2010. *Plays:* Wings of Night Sky, Wings of Night Morning 2007–09. *Publications:* The Last Song 1975, What Moon Drove Me To This? 1980, She Had Some Horses 1983, Secrets From the Center of the World (with Stephen Strom) 1989, In Mad Love and War 1990, Fishing 1992, The Woman Who Fell From the Sky 1994, Reinventing the Enemy's Language 1997, A Map to the Next World 2000, The Good Luck Cat 2000, How We Became Human 2002, For a Girl Becoming 2009, Soul Talk, Song Language, Conversations with Joy Harjo, with Tanaya Winder 2011; contrib. to many anthologies, magazines and recordings. *Honours:* Dr hc (Benedictine Coll.) 1992, (St Mary In the Woods); Pushcart Prize in Poetry 1987, in Poetry Anthology 1990, American-Indian Distinguished Achievement in the Arts Award 1990, Before Columbus Foundation American Book Award 1991, New York Univ. Delmore Schwartz Memorial Award 1991, Mountains and Plains Booksellers Award for Best Book of Poetry 1991, Poetry Soc. of America William Carlos Williams Award 1991, Native Writers Circle of the Americas Lifetime Achievement Award 1995, Oklahoma Book Arts Awards 1995, State of New Mexico Gov.'s Award for Excellence in the Arts 1997, Lila Wallace-Reader's Digest Writers Award 1998–2000, Eagle Spirit Award, American Indian Film Festival 2005, Rasmusson US Artist Fellowship 2008, Native American Contemporary Award, New Mexico Music Awards 2007, 2008, Native American Music Award for Best Female Artist of the Year 2009, Indian Summer Music Award for Best Instrumental 2011. *Literary Agent:* c/o Mekko Productions Inc., PO Box 348, Glenpool, OK 74033, USA. *E-mail:* joy.harjo@gmail.com (office). *Website:* www.joyharjo.com.

HARKNETT, Terry, (Frank Chandler, David Ford, George G. Gilman, William M. James, Charles R. Pike, James Russell, William Terry); British writer; b. 14 Dec. 1936, Rainham, Essex, England. *Career:* Ed., Newspaper Features Ltd 1958–61; Reporter and Features Ed., National Newsagent 1961–72. *Publications:* as George G. Gilman: Edge series: The Loner 1972, The Frightened Gun 1979, The Godforsaken 1982, Arapaho Revenge 1983, The Blind Side 1983, House of the Range 1983, Edge Meets Steele No. 3 Double Action 1984, The Moving Cage 1984, School for Slaughter 1985, Revenge Ride 1985, Shadow of the Gallows 1985, A Time for Killing 1986, Brutal Border 1986, Hitting Paydirt 1986, Backshort 1987, Uneasy Riders 1987, Eve of Evil 1991; Adam Steele series: Steele's War: The Preacher 1984, Canyon of Death 1985, High Stakes 1985, Rough Justice 1985, The Sunset Ride 1986, The Killing Strain 1986, The Big Gunfight 1987, The Hunted 1987, Code of the West 1987, The Outcasts 1987, The Long Shadow 1989; The Undertaker series: Three Graves to a Showdown 1982, Back from the Dead 1982, Death in the Desert 1982; as William Terry: Red Sun (novelization of screenplay) 1972; as Frank Chandler: A Fistful of Dollars (novelization of screenplay) 1972; as Charles R. Pike: Jubal Cade series: The Killing Trail 1974, Double Cross 1974, The Hungary Gun 1975, Vengeance Hunt 1976, Days of Blood 1977, Bounty Road 1978, Ashes and Blood 1979, The Death Pit 1980, Mourning Is Red 1981, Time of the Damned 1982, Gallows Bait 1983, Time of the Damned 1984; as William M. James: Apache series: The First Death 1974, Duel to the Death 1974, Fort Treachery 1975, Death Train 1978, Naked and the Savage 1977, Blood on the Tracks 1979, Texas Killing 1980, Fast Living 1981, Border Killing 1982, Death Ride 1983, Debt of Blood 1984; as Terry Harknett: The Caribbean 1972, Crown, The Sweet And Sour Kill 1974; as James Russell: The Balearic Islands 1972; as David Ford: Cyprus 1973. *Address:* Spring Acre, Springhead Road, Uplyme, Lyme Regis, Dorset, DT7 3RS, England (home).

HARLE, Elizabeth (see Roberts, Irene)

HARLEMAN, Ann, BA, MFA, PhD; American writer and educator; b. 28 Oct. 1945, Youngstown, OH; one d. *Education:* Rutgers Univ., Princeton Univ., Brown Univ. *Career:* Asst Prof. of English, Rutgers Univ. 1973–74; Asst Prof., Univ. of Washington 1974–79, Assoc. Prof. of English 1979–84; Visiting Prof. of Rhetoric, MIT 1984–86; Visiting Scholar, Program in American Civilization, Brown Univ. 1986–; Cole Distinguished Prof. of English, Wheaton Coll. 1992; Prof. of English, Rhode Island School of Design 1994–; mem. MLA (chair. of gen. linguistics exec. cttee), Poets and Writers, PEN American Center; Sr Fellow ACLS 1993. *Publications:* fiction: Happiness 1994, Bitter Lake 1996, Thoreau's Laundry 2007, The Year She Disappeared 2008; contrib. short stories to Alaska Quarterly Review, American Fiction, Boston Review, Chicago Tribune, Die Freundin, Glimmer Train, Good Housekeeping, Green Mountains Review, Greensboro Review, Hotel Amerika, Madison Review, MS, Nebraska Review, New England Review, The Ohio Review, Oxford Magazine, Ploughshares, Primavera, Southwest Review, Shenandoah, Story, Toyon Virginia Quarterly Review, Witness; contrib. poems to Apalachee Quarterly, Ascent, Greensboro Review, High Plains Literary Review, Kansas Quarterly, Southern Review, Yankee; non-fiction: Graphic Representation of Models in Linguistic Theory 1976; contrib. articles to journals and books. *Honours:* Guggenheim Fellowship 1976, Fulbright Fellowship 1980, MacDowell Colony Fellow 1988, Nat. Endowment for the Humanities Fellowship 1989, Rhode Island State Council on the Arts Fellowship 1990, 1997, 2007, PEN Syndicated Fiction Award 1991, Iowa Short Fiction Prize 1993, Bogliasco Foundation Fellowship 1998, 2004, Berlin Prize in Literature 2000, Civitella Ranieri Residency 2007. *Literary Agent:* Gail Hochman, Brandt & Hochman Literary Agency, 1501 Broadway, 23rd Floor, New York, NY 10036, USA. *Telephone:* (212) 840-5760. *Address:* 18 Imperial Place #5A, Providence, RI 02903, USA (home). *E-mail:* ann_harleman@brown.edu (office). *Website:* www.annharleman.com.

HARMAN, Gilbert Helms, BA, PhD; American academic and writer; *James S. McDonnell Distinguished University Professor of Philosophy, Princeton University*; b. 26 May 1938, East Orange, New Jersey; s. of William H. Harman, Jr and Marguerite Page; m. Lucy Newman 1970; two d. *Education:* Swarthmore Coll., Harvard Univ. *Career:* faculty mem. Dept of Philosophy, Princeton Univ. 1963–, apptd Stuart Prof. of Philosophy 1971, Co-Dir Cognitive Science Lab. 1986–2000, currently James S. McDonnell Distinguished Univ. Prof. of Philosophy; mem. American Philosophical Asscn, Philosophy of Science Asscn, Soc. for Philosophy and Psychology, American Psychological Soc., Linguistic Soc. of America, American Acad. of Arts and Sciences 2005; Fellow, Cognitive Science Soc. 2002, Asscn for Psychological Science 2011. *Publications:* Semantics of Natural Language (co-ed. with Donald Davidson) 1971, Thought 1973, On Noam Chomsky (ed.) 1974, The Logic of Grammar (ed. with Donald Davidson) 1975, The Nature of Morality: An Introduction to Ethics 1977, Change in View: Principles of Reasoning 1986, Skepticism and the Definition of Knowledge 1990, Conceptions of the Human Mind (ed.) 1993, Moral Relativism and Moral Objectivity (with Judith Jarvis Thomson) 1996, Reasoning, Meaning and Mind 1999, Explaining Values and other Essays in Moral Philosophy 2000, Reliable Reasoning: Induction and Statistical Learning Theory 2007, An Elementary Introduction to Statistical Learning Theory (with Sanjeev Kulkarni) 2011; contrib. to scholarly journals. *Honours:* Jean Nicod Prize 2005, Behrman Award 2009. *Address:* Department of Philosophy, Princeton University, 1879 Hall, Room 118, Princeton, NJ 08544-1006 (office); 106 Broadmead Street, Princeton, NJ 08540, USA (home). *Telephone:* (609) 258-4289 (office). *Fax:* (609) 258-1502 (office). *E-mail:* harman@princeton.edu (office). *Website:* www.princeton.edu/~harman (office).

HARMON, Maurice, BA, HDE, MA, AM PhD; Irish academic, poet, writer, editor and biographer; *Professor Emeritus, University College Dublin*; b. 21 June 1930, Dublin; m. Maura Lynch; one s. one d. *Education:* Univ. Coll., Dublin, Harvard Univ., USA. *Career:* Lecturer in English, Univ. Coll. Dublin 1964–76, Assoc. Prof. of Anglo-Irish Literature and Drama 1976–90, Prof. Emer. 1990–; Ed. University Review 1964–68, Irish University Review 1970–86, Poetry Ireland Review 2000–01; mem. Royal Irish Acad. 1976–. *Publications:* Seán O'Faoláin: A Critical Introduction 1966, Modern Irish Literature 1800–1967: A Reader's Guide 1967, Fenians and Fenianism: Centenary Papers (ed.) 1968, The Celtic Master: Contributions to the First James Joyce Symposium 1969, Romeo and Juliet, by Shakespeare (ed.) 1970, J.M. Synge Centenary Papers 1971 (ed.) 1971, King Richard II, by Shakespeare (ed.) 1971, Coriolanus, by Shakespeare (ed.) 1972, The Poetry of Thomas Kinsella 1974, The Irish Novel in Our Time (ed. with Patrick Rafroidi) 1976, Select Bibliography for the Study of Anglo-Irish Literature and Its Backgrounds 1976, Richard Murphy: Poet of Two Traditions (ed.) 1978, Irish Poetry After Yeats: Seven Poets (ed.) 1979, Image and Illusion: Anglo-Irish Literature and Its Contexts (ed.) 1979, A Short History of Anglo-Irish Literature From Its Origins to the Present (with Roger McHugh) 1982, The Irish Writer and the City (ed.) 1985, James Joyce: The Centennial Symposium (with Morris Beja et al) 1986, Austin Clarke: A Critical Introduction 1989, The Book of Precedence (poems) 1994, Seán O'Faoláin: A Life 1994, A Stillness at Kiawah (poems) 1996, No Author Better Served: The Correspondence of Samuel Beckett and Alan Schneider 1998, The Last Regatta (poems) 2000, Tales of Death (poems) 2001, The Colloquy of the Old Men (trans.) 2001, The Dolmen Press: A Celebration 2001, The Doll with Two Backs and Other Poems 2004, Selected Essays 2006, Thomas Kinsella: Designing for the Exact Needs 2008, The Mischievous Boy and Other Poems 2008, The Dialogue of the Ancients of Ireland (trans.) 2009, When Love is Not Enough: New and Selected Poems 2010. *Address:* 20 Sycamore Road, Mount Merrion, Blackrock, Co. Dublin, Ireland. *E-mail:* morris.harmon@ucd.ie.

HARPER, Michael Steven, BA, MA, MFA; American academic and poet; *University Professor, Brown University*; b. 18 March 1938, Brooklyn, NY; s. of Walter Warren Harper and Katherine Johnson Harper; m.; three c. *Education:* California State Univ. at Los Angeles, Univ. of Iowa Writers' Workshop, Brown Univ. *Career:* Visiting Prof., Lewis and Clark Coll. 1968–69, Reed Coll. 1968–69, Harvard Univ. 1974–77, Yale Univ. 1976; Prof. of English, later Univ. Prof., Brown Univ. 1970–; Benedict Distinguished Prof., Carleton Coll. 1979; Elliston Poet and Distinguished Prof., Univ. of Cincinnati 1979; Nat. Endowment for the Humanities Prof., Colgate Univ. 1985; Distinguished Minority Prof., Univ. of Delaware 1988, Macalester Coll. 1989; first Poet Laureate of the State of Rhode Island 1988–93; Phi Beta Kappa Visiting Scholar 1991; Berg Distinguished Visiting Prof., New York Univ. 1992; mem. American Acad. of Arts and Sciences. *Publications:* Dear John, Dear Coltrane 1970, History is Your Own Heartbeat 1971, History as Apple Tree 1972, Song: I Want a Witness 1972, Debridement 1973, Nightmare Begins Responsibility 1975, Images of Kin 1977, Healing Song for the Inner Ear 1985, Songlines: Mosaics 1991, Honorable Amendments 1995, Collected Poems 1996, Family Sequences 1998, Songlines in Michaeltree 1999, Selected Poems 2002, Sweet Homeland (with Rebecca Bella Wangh) 2002, I Do Believe in People: Remembrances of W. Warren Harper (1915–2004) 2004, The Fret Cycle 2006, Use Trouble 2008; editor: Chant of Saints (co-ed.) 1979, National Poetry Series: Collected Poems of Sterling A. Brown 1979, Eroding Witness 1985,

Every Shut Eye Ain't Asleep (co-ed.) 1994; audio: Double Take (with Paul Austerlitz, bass clarinet) 2004, Our Book of Trane (with Paul Austerlitz, bass clarinet) 2004, Selected Poems, Hear Where Coltrane Is (concert, with Ron De Vaugh, cello), The African Continuum (concert, Powell Hall, St Louis, Mo.), with nine musicians; contribs to Carleton Miscellany, Obsidian, The Vintage Anthology of African American Poetry 1750–2000. *Honours:* Hon. DLitt (Trinity Coll., CT, Coe Coll., IN, Notre Dame Coll., NH, Kenyon Coll., OH, Rhode Island Coll.); Black Acad. of Arts and Letters Award 1972, Nat. Inst. of Arts and Letters grants 1975, 1976, 1985, Guggenheim Fellowship 1976, Poetry Soc. of America Melville Cane Award 1978, Rhode Island Council of the Arts Governor's Poetry Award 1987, United Negro Coll. Fund Robert Hayden Memorial Poetry Award 1990, New York Public Library Literary Lion 1992, George Kent Poetry Award 1996, Claiborne Pell Award 1997, Robert Frost Medal for lifetime achievement, Poetry Soc. of America 2008. *Address:* Brown University, Box 1923, Providence, RI 02912-1923, USA (office). *Telephone:* (401) 863-2705 (office). *Fax:* (401) 863-2290 (office). *E-mail:* michael_harper@brown.edu (office).

HARRIES, Owen; British editor and fmr government official and academic; b. 1930, Wales. *Education:* Univs of Wales and Oxford. *Career:* taught for 20 years Univ. of Sydney, NSW; apptd Sr Adviser to Foreign Affairs Minister, Australia 1974, subsequently Dir of Policy Planning, Dept of Foreign Affairs; Sr Adviser to Prime Minister; Amb. to UNESCO 1982–83; Visiting Fellow, Heritage Foundation, USA 1983–85; Founder and Ed.-in-Chief The National Interest (journal) Washington, DC 1985–2001, later Consulting Ed. and Ed. Emer.; Sr Fellow, Centre for Ind. Studies, Australia; Visiting Fellow, Lowy Inst. for Ind. Studies; Sr Assoc. Center for Strategic and International Studies, USA. *Publications include:* Liberty and Politics (ed) 1976, Australia and the Third World (ed) 1979, America's Purpose (ed) 1991, China in the National Interest (ed) 2003, Benign or Imperial?: Reflections on American Hegemony 2004. *Address:* c/o Centre for Independent Studies, POB 92, St Leonards, NSW 1590, Australia.

HARRIES OF PENTREGARTH, Baron (Life Peer), cr. 2006, of Ceinewydd in the County of Dyfed; **Richard Douglas Harries,** DD, FRSL; British ecclesiastic; *Professor of Divinity, Gresham College;* b. 2 June 1936; Eltham, London, England; s. of Brig. W. D. J. Harries and G. M. B. Harries; m. Josephine Bottomley 1963; one s. one d. *Education:* Wellington Coll., Royal Mil. Acad., Sandhurst, Selwyn Coll., Cambridge, Cuddesdon Coll., Oxford. *Career:* Lt, Royal Corps of Signals 1955–58; Curate, Hampstead Parish Church 1963–69; Chaplain, Westfield Coll. 1966–69; Lecturer, Wells Theological Coll. 1969–72; Warden, Salisbury and Wells Theological Coll. 1971–72; Vicar, All Saints, Fulham, London 1972–81; Dean, King's Coll., London 1981–87, Fellow and Hon. Prof. of Theology; Bishop of Oxford 1987–2006; Prof. of Divinity, Gresham Coll., London 2008–; Vice-Chair. Council of Christian Action 1979–87, Council for Arms Control 1982–87; Chair. Southwark Ordination Course 1982–87, Shalom, End Loans to South Africa (ELSTA) 1982–87, Christian Evidence Soc.; Chair. Church of England Bd of Social Responsibility 1996–2001; Consultant to the Archbishops on Jewish-Christian Relations 1986–92; Chair. Council of Christians and Jews 1993–2001, House of Lords select Cttee on Stem Cell Research 2001–02; Visiting Prof., Liverpool Hope Coll. 2002; mem. Home Office Advisory Cttee for Reform of Law on Sexual Offences 1981–85, Bd Christian Aid 1994–2001, Royal Comm. on Lords Reform 1999–, Nuffield Council of Bioethics 2002–06, Human Fertilisation and Embryology Authority 2003–09. *Radio:* regular broadcaster, particularly on BBC Radio 4's Today Programme. *Publications include:* Prayers of Hope 1975, Turning to Prayer 1978, Prayers of Grief and Glory 1979, Being a Christian 1981, Should Christians Support Guerrillas? 1982, The Authority of Divine Love 1983, Praying Round the Clock 1983, Seasons of the Spirit (co-ed.) 1984, Prayer and the Pursuit of Happiness 1985, Reinhold Niebuhr and the Issues of Our Time (ed.) 1986, Christianity and War in a Nuclear Age 1986, C. S. Lewis: The Man and His God 1987, Is There a Gospel for the Rich? 1992, Art and the Beauty of God 1993, The Value of Business and its Values (co-author) 1993, Questioning Faith 1995, A Gallery of Reflections 1995, In the Gladness of Today 2000, Christianity: Two Thousand Years (co-ed.) 2000, God Outside the Box: Why Spiritual People Object to Christianity 2002, After the Evil: Christianity and Judaism in the Shadow of the Holocaust 2003, The Passion in Art 2005, The Re-Enchantment of Morality 2008, Faith in Politics? – Rediscovering the Christian Roots of Our Political Values 2010, Questions of Life and Death 2010, Reinhold Niebuhr and Contemporary Politics (co-ed. with Stephen Platten) 2010; contrib. to several books; numerous articles. *Honours:* Hon. Fellow, Selwyn Coll., Cambridge, St Anne's Coll. Oxford; Hon. FMedSci 2004; Hon. Fellow, Soc. of Biology 2009; Hon. DD (London) 1996; Hon. DUniv (Oxford Brookes) 2001, (Open Univ.), (Huddersfield) 2008; Sir Sigmund Steinberg Award 1989. *Address:* House of Lords, Westminster, London, SW1A 0PW, England (office). *Telephone:* (20) 7219-2910 (office). *E-mail:* harriesr@parliament.uk (office).

HARRIS, Charlaine; American writer; b. 25 Nov. 1951, Mississippi; three c. *Education:* Rhodes Coll. *Career:* mystery writer. *Publications:* Aurora Teagarden series: Real Murders 1990, A Bone to Pick 1992, Three Bedrooms, One Corpse 1994, The Julius House 1996, Dead over Heels 1997, A Fool and his Honey 1999, Last Scene Alive 2002, Poppy Done to Death 2003; Lily Bard Shakespeare series: Shakespeare's Landlord 1996, Shakespeare's Champion 1997, Shakespeare's Christmas 1998, Shakespeare's Trollop 2000, Shakespeare's Counselor 2001; Sookie Stackhouse series: Dead Until Dark 2001, Living Dead in Dallas 2002, Club Dead 2003, Dead to the World 2004, Dead as a Doornail 2005, Definitely Dead 2006, All Together Dead 2007, From Dead to Worse 2008, Dead and Gone 2009, Dead in the Family 2010, Death's Excellent Vacation 2011, Dead Reckoning 2011, Deadlocked 2012; Harper Connelly series: Grave Sight 2005, Grave Surprise 2006, An Ice Cold Grave 2007, Grave Secret 2009; other: Sweet and Deadly 1981, A Secret Rage 1984. *Literary Agent:* c/o Joshua Bilmes, JABberwocky Literary Agency, PO Box 4558, Sunnyside, NY 11104-0558, USA. *Telephone:* (718) 392-5985. *Fax:* (718) 392-5985. *E-mail:* jabagent@aol.com. *Website:* www.awfulagent.com; www.charlaineharris.com.

HARRIS, Jana, BS, MA; American writer, poet and teacher; *Editor, Switched-on Gutenberg;* b. 21 Sept. 1947, San Francisco; m. Mark Allen Bothwell. *Education:* Univ. of Oregon, San Francisco State Univ. *Career:* apptd Instructor in Creative Writing, New York Univ. 1980, Univ. of Washington 1986, Pacific Lutheran Univ. 1988; Founder-Ed. Switched-on Gutenberg (cyberspace poetry journal); Writer-in-Residence Univ. of Wyoming, St Catherine's Coll., Washington State Univ.; mem. PEN, Poetry Soc. of America, Nat. Book Critics Circle. *Publications:* This House That Rocks with Every Truck on the Road 1976, Pin Money 1977, The Clackamas 1980, Alaska 1980, Who's That Pushy Bitch? 1981, Running Scared 1981, Manhattan as a Second Language 1982, The Sourlands: Poems by Jana Harris 1989, Oh How Can I Keep on Singing: Voices of Pioneer Women (poems) (Washington State Governor's Writers Award) 1993, The Dust of Everyday Life: An Epic Poem of the Pacific Northwest (Andres Berger Award) 1998, The Pearl of Ruby City (novel) 1998, We Never Speak of It: Idaho-Wyoming Poems 1889 2003, Horses Never Lie about Love 2011; contribs to periodicals. *Honours:* Pushcart Prize for Poetry 2001, Prairie Schooner Reader's Choice Award 2004, Washington State Gov.'s Writers Award. *E-mail:* editor@switched-ongutenberg.org (office). *Website:* www.switched-ongutenberg.org (office); www.janaharris.org.

HARRIS, Jane, MA, PhD; British writer and scriptwriter; b. Belfast, Northern Ireland; m. Tom Shankland. *Education:* Univs of Glasgow and East Anglia. *Career:* fmr Writer-in-Residence, HM Prison, Durham and teacher of Creative Writing in univs and schools. *Film scripts include:* Bait 1999, Going Down 2000. *Publications:* The Observations (novel) 2006, Gillespie and I (novel) 2011; contrib. of short stories to anthologies and magazines. *Honours:* Arts Council England Writer's Award 2000, Waterstones Book of the Month April 2006, First Fiction Prize, USA Book of the Month Club 2007. *Address:* c/o Faber and Faber Ltd, Bloomsbury House, 74–77 Great Russell Street, London, WC1B 3DA, England. *Telephone:* (20) 7927-3800. *Fax:* (20) 7927-3801. *Website:* www.faber.co.uk.

HARRIS, Joanne; British writer; b. 1964, Yorks., England; m. Kevin; one d. *Education:* St Catharine's Coll., Cambridge. *Career:* fmr French teacher, Leeds Grammar School for 15 years. *Publications:* The Evil Seed 1989, Sleep, Pale Sister 1993, Chocolat 1999, Blackberry Wine 2000, Five Quarters of the Orange 2001, Coastliners 2002, The French Kitchen: A Cookbook, Holy Fools 2003, Jigs & Reels (short stories) 2004, The French Market: A Cookbook, Gentlemen & Players 2005, Runemarks (juvenile) 2006, The Lollipop Shoes 2007, Blueeyedboy 2010, Runelight (juvenile) 2011. *Honours:* Hon. DLitt (Huddersfield) 2003, (Sheffield) 2004. *Address:* c/o Transworld Publishers, 61–63 Uxbridge Road, London, W5 5SA, England. *Website:* www.joanne-harris.co.uk.

HARRIS, Jocelyn Margaret, MA, PhD; New Zealand academic and writer; *Professor Emeritus of English, University of Otago;* b. 10 Sept. 1939, Dunedin; one s. one d. *Education:* Univs of Otago, London. *Career:* fmr Personal Chair., Dept of English, Univ. of Otago, currently Prof. Emer.; mem. Australian and South Pacific 18th Century Soc. *Publications:* Samuel Richardson: Sir Charles Grandison (ed.) 1972, Samuel Richardson 1989, Jane Austen's Art of Memory 1989, Samuel Richardson's Published Commentary on Clarissa 1747–1765 (vol. I) (ed. with Tom Keymer), Approaches to Teaching the Novels of Samuel Richardson (co-ed.) 2006, Revolution Almost Beyond Expression: Jane Austen's Persuasion 2007, Rewriting the Long Eighteenth Century: Selected Papers from the Thirteenth David Nichol Smith Seminar (co-ed.) 2008; contribs to scholarly journals. *Honours:* Companion of the Order of Merit (New Zealand) 2009. *Address:* Department of English, University of Otago, PO Box 56, Dunedin 9054, New Zealand (office). *Telephone:* (3) 479-8952 (office). *Fax:* (3) 479-8558 (office). *E-mail:* jocelyn.harris@otago.ac.nz (office). *Website:* www.otago.ac.nz/english/staff/harris.html#top (office).

HARRIS, Marion Rose, (Rose Glendower, Rosie Harris, Marion Rose, Rose Young, Rosie Young); British writer; b. (Marion Rose Young), 12 July 1925, Cardiff, S Wales; m. Kenneth Mackenzie Harris 1943; two s. one d. *Career:* Ed./Owner Regional Feature Service 1964–74; Editorial Controller, W. Foulsham and Co. Ltd 1974–82; mem. Soc. of Authors, Romantic Novelists Asscn, Welsh Acad. *Publications:* as Marion Harris: Captain of Her Heart 1976, Just a Handsome Stranger 1983, The Queen's Windsor 1985, Soldiers' Wives 1986, Officers' Ladies 1987, Nesta 1988, Amelda 1989, Sighing for the Moon (also as Rose Glendower) 1991; as Rose Young: To Love and Love Again 1993, Secret of Abbey Place 1999, Love Can Conquer 1999; as Rosie Harris: Turn of the Tide 2002, Troubled Waters 2002, Patsy of Paradise Place 2003, One Step Forward 2003, Looking for Love 2003, Pins and Needles 2004, Winnie of the Waterfront 2004, At Sixes and Sevens 2005, The Cobbler's Kids 2005, Sunshine and Showers 2005, Megan of Merseyside 2006, The Power of Dreams 2006, A Mother's Love 2006, Sing For Your Supper 2007, Waiting for Love 2007, Love Against all Odds 2007, A Dream of Love 2008, A Love Like Ours 2008, Love Changes Everything 2009, The Quality of Love 2009,

Ambitious Love 2010, A Brighter Dawn 2011, The Price of Love 2011, The Web of Love 2011. *Address:* 11 Penn House, Jennery Lane, Burnham, Slough, Berks., SL1 8BN, England (office). *Telephone:* (1628) 605717 (office). *E-mail:* marionharris@btinternet.com (office); rosiebooks@btinternet.com (office). *Website:* www.rosiebooks.co.uk.

HARRIS, Randy Allen, BA, MA, MSc, MS, PhD; Canadian academic and writer; *Professor, University of Waterloo*; b. 6 Sept. 1956, Kitimat, BC; s. of Thomas Jefferson Harris and Dorthea Patricia Harris; m. Indira Naidoo-Harris 1984; one s. one d. *Education:* Queen's Univ., Dalhousie Univ., Univ. of Alberta, Rensselaer Polytechnic Inst. *Career:* Prof., Univ. of Waterloo, Ont. *Publications:* Acoustic Dimensions of Functor Comprehension in Broca's Aphasia 1988, Linguistics Wars 1993, Landmark Essays in Rhetoric of Science 1997, Voice Interaction Design 2005, Rhetoric and Incommensurability 2005; contrib. to College English, Perspectives on Science, Rhetoric Review, Historiographia Linguistica, Rhetoric Society Quarterly, Neuropsychologia. *Honours:* Killam Scholar 1980, 1991, 1992, Heritage Scholar (Sir James Lougheed Award of Distinction) 1985, Rensselaer Scholar 1986, Outstanding Performance Award, Univ. of Waterloo 2006. *Address:* Department of English, University of Waterloo, Waterloo, ON N2L 3G1, Canada (office). *E-mail:* raha@uwaterloo.ca (office). *Website:* www.arts.uwaterloo.ca/~raha (office).

HARRIS, Robert Dennis, FRSL; British journalist and writer; b. 7 March 1957, Nottingham; s. of the late Dennis Harris and Audrey Harris; m. Gill Hornby 1988; two s. two d. *Education:* Univ. of Cambridge. *Career:* Pres. Cambridge Union; Dir and reporter, BBC 1978–86; Political Ed. Observer 1987–89; columnist, Sunday Times 1989–92, 1996–97. *Publications:* non-fiction: A Higher Form of Killing (with Jeremy Paxman) 1982, Gotcha! 1983, The Making of Neil Kinnock 1984, Selling Hitler 1987, Good and Faithful Servant 1990; novels: Fatherland 1992, Enigma 1995 (film 2001), Archangel 1998, Pompeii 2003, Imperium 2006, The Ghost 2007, Lustrum 2009, Conspirata 2010, The Fear Index 2011. *Address:* Old Vicarage, Church Street, Kintbury, Berks., RG17 9TR, England (home).

HARRIS, Rosemary Jeanne; British writer; b. 20 Feb. 1923, London; d. of the late Sir Arthur Harris and Barbara Daisy Harris (née Kyrle Money). *Education:* privately and Chelsea School of Art, Courtauld Inst. *Career:* post-war reader for Metro-Goldwyn-Mayer; children's book reviewer, The Times, London 1970–73; mem. Soc. of Authors (fmr chair. children's writers group). *Television:* plays: Peronik 1976, The Unknown Enchantment 1982; adaptations: Jackanory: The Moon in the Cloud 1978. *Publications:* The Summer-House 1956, Voyage to Cythera 1958, Venus with Sparrows 1961, All My Enemies 1967, The Nice Girl's Story (aka Nor Evil Dreams) 1968, The Moon in the Cloud 1968, A Wicked Pack of Cards 1969, The Shadow on the Sun 1970, The Seal-Singing 1971, The Child in the Bamboo Grove 1972, The Bright and Morning Star 1972, The King's White Elephant 1973, The Double Snare 1974, The Lotus and the Grail: Legends from East to West (aka Sea Magic and Other Stories of Enchantment) 1974, The Flying Ship 1975, The Little Dog of Fo 1976, Three Candles for the Dark 1976, I Want to Be a Fish 1977, A Quest for Orion 1978, Beauty and the Beast (folklore) 1979, Green Finger House 1980, Tower of the Stars 1980, The Enchanted Horse 1981, Janni's Stork 1981, Zed 1982, Summers of the Wild Rose 1987, Love and the Merry-Go-Round 1988, Ticket to Freedom 1991, The Wildcat Strike 1995, The Haunting of Joey M'basa 1996. *Honours:* Library Asscn Carnegie Medal 1967.

HARRIS, Ruth Elwin; British writer; b. 22 June 1935, Bristol, England; m. Christopher J. L. Bowes 1964, two s. one d. *Education:* Bristol, England. *Career:* mem. Society of Authors. *Publications:* The Silent Shore 1986, The Beckoning Hills 1987, The Dividing Sea 1989, Billie: The Nevill Letters 1914–1916 1991, Beyond the Orchid House 1994, Frances' Story 2002, Gwen's Story 2002, Julia's Story 2002, Sarah's Story 2002.

HARRIS, Thomas; American writer; b. 11 April 1940, Jackson, Tenn.; s. of William Thomas Harris, Jr and Polly Harris; m. (divorced); one d. *Education:* Baylor Univ. *Career:* worked on news desk at Waco News-Tribune newspaper; mem. staff Associated Press, New York City 1968–74. *Publications:* Black Sunday 1975, Red Dragon 1981, The Silence of the Lambs (Bram Stoker Best Novel Award) 1988, Hannibal 1999, Hannibal Rising 2007. *Address:* c/o Arrow, Random House, 20 Vauxhall Bridge Road, London, SW1V 2SA, England. *Website:* www.thomasharris.com.

HARRIS, (Theodore) Wilson; Guyanese poet and novelist; b. 24 March 1921, New Amsterdam; m. 1st Cecily Carew 1945; m. 2nd Margaret Whitaker 1959. *Education:* Queen's Coll., Georgetown. *Career:* Visiting Lecturer, SUNY at Buffalo 1970; writer-in-residence, Univ. of the West Indies, Jamaica, Scarborough Coll., Univ. of Toronto 1970, Univ. of Newcastle, NSW 1979; Commonwealth Fellow in Caribbean Literature, Leeds Univ. 1971; Visiting Prof., Univ. of Texas, Austin 1972, 1981–82, Univ. of Mysore 1978, Yale Univ. 1979; Regents Lecturer, Univ. of California, Santa Cruz 1983. *Publications:* poetry: Fetish 1951, The Well and the Land 1952, Eternity to Season 1954; fiction: The Guyana Quartet 1960–63, Tumatumari 1968, Black Marsden 1972, Companions of the Day and Night 1975, Da Silva's Cultivated Wilderness 1977, Genesis of the Clowns 1977, The Tree of the Sun 1978, The Angel at the Gate 1982, The Carnival Trilogy 1985–90, Resurrection at Sorrow Hill 1993, The Dark Jester 2001, The Mask of the Beggar 2003, The Ghost of Memory 2006; short stories. *Address:* c/o Faber and Faber Ltd, Bloomsbury House, 74–77 Great Russell Street, London, WC1B 3DA, England (office). *Website:* www.faber.co.uk (office).

HARRIS, Zinnie, BA, MA; British playwright; b. (Zinnie Shaw), 23 Dec. 1972, Oxford; d. of Dr Mark Shaw and Francesca Shaw; m. John Harris 1995; two s., one d. *Education:* Univs of Oxford and Hull. *Plays:* By Many Wounds 1998, Further Than the Furthest Thing 2000, Nightingale and Chase 2001, Midwinter 2004, Solstice 2005, Julie 2006, Fall 2008, A Doll's House (new version of Ibsen's play) 2009. *Television scripts:* Born with Two Mothers (Windfall Films/Channel 4) 2005, Spooks (Kudos/BBC 1 Episode 5, Series 5) 2006, Richard is My Boyfriend (Windfall Films/Channel 4) 2007. *Publications:* By Many Wounds 1998, Further Than the Furthest Thing 2000, Nightingale and Chase 2001, Midwinter 2004, Solstice 2005, Fall 2008, A Doll's House (new version of Ibsen's play) 2009. *Honours:* Peggy Ramsay New Writing Award, John Whiting Award, Arts Foundation Fellowship Award, Pearson Bursary Scheme. *Literary Agent:* c/o Mel Kenyon, Casarotto Ramsay & Associates Ltd, Waverley House, 7–12 Noel Street, London, W1F 8GO, England. *Telephone:* (20) 7287-4450. *Fax:* (20) 7287-9128. *E-mail:* mel@casarotto.uk.com. *Website:* www.casarotto.uk.com.

HARRISON, Sir Brian Howard, Kt, MA, DPhil, FRHistS, FBA; British historian and academic; *Emeritus Fellow, Corpus Christi College and Professor Emeritus of Modern British History, University of Oxford*; b. 9 July 1937, Hampstead, London, England; s. of Howard Harrison and Mary Elizabeth Savill; m. Anne Victoria Greggain 1967. *Education:* Merchant Taylors' School, Northwood, St John's Coll., Oxford. *Career:* Nat. Service, 2nd Lt Malta Signal Squadron 1956–58; Sr Scholar, St Antony's Coll. Oxford 1961–64; Jr Research Fellow, Nuffield Coll. Oxford 1964–67; Fellow and Tutor in Modern History and Politics, Corpus Christi Coll. Oxford 1967–2000, Official Fellow 2000–04, Emer. Fellow 2004–, Sr Tutor 1984–86, 1988–90, Vice-Pres. 1992, 1993, 1996–98; Univ. Reader in Modern British History, Univ. of Oxford 1990–2000, Prof. of Modern British History 1996–2004, Prof. Emer. 2004–; Ed. Oxford Dictionary of National Biography 2000–04; Visiting Prof., Univ. of Michigan, Ann Arbor, USA 1970–71, Harvard Univ., USA 1973–74; Visiting Fellow, Univ. of Melbourne, Australia 1975, ANU, Australia 1995. *Publications include:* Drink and the Victorians 1971, Separate Spheres: The Opposition to Women's Suffrage in Britain 1978, Robert Lowery: Radical and Chartist (co-ed. with Patricia Hollis) 1979, Peaceable Kingdom: Stability and Change in Modern Britain 1982, A Hundred Years Ago: Britain in the 1880s in Words and Photographs (with Colin Ford) 1983, Prudent Revolutionaries: Portraits of British Feminists Between the Wars 1987, The History of the University of Oxford, Vol. 8: The Twentieth Century (ed. and contrib.) 1994, Corpuscles: A History of Corpus Christi College, Oxford in the Twentieth Century, Written by its Members (ed.) 1994, The Transformation of British Politics 1860–1995 1996, Civil Histories: Essays Presented to Sir Keith Thomas (co-ed. and contrib.) 2000, Oxford Dictionary of National Biography (co-ed.) 2004, contrib. of two vols to New Oxford History of England: Seeking a Role: The United Kingdom 1951–1970 2009, Finding a Role?: The United Kingdom 1970–1990 2010. *Honours:* Hon. Fellow, St John's Coll. Oxford 2010. *Address:* The Book House, Yarnells Hill, Oxford, OX2 9BG, England (home).

HARRISON, James (Jim) Thomas, BA, MA; American writer and poet; b. 11 Dec. 1937, Grayling, Mich.; s. of Winfield Sprague Harrison and Norma Olivia Harrison (née Wahlgren); m. Linda May King 1960; two d. *Education:* Michigan State Univ. *Career:* Asst Prof. of English, SUNY at Stony Brook 1965–66. *Film screenplays:* Cold Feet (with Tom McGuane) 1989, Revenge (with Jeffrey Fishkin) 1990, Wolf (with Wesley Strick) 1994. *Publications:* fiction: Wolf: A False Memoir 1971, A Good Day to Die 1973, Farmer 1976, Legends of the Fall 1979, Warlock 1981, Sundog 1984, Dalva 1988, The Woman Lit by Fireflies 1990, Sunset Limited 1990, Julip 1994, The Road Home 1998, The Beast God Forgot to Invent 2000, True North 2004, The Summer He Didn't Die 2005, Returning to Earth 2007, The English Major 2008, The Farmer's Daughter: Novellas 2010, The Great Leader 2011; poetry: Plain Song 1965, Locations 1968, Walking 1969, Outlyer and Ghazals 1971, Letters to Yesinin 1973, Returning to Earth 1977, New and Selected Poems, 1961–81 1982, The Theory and Practice of Rivers 1986, After Ikkyu and Other Poems 1996, The Shape of the Journey 1998, Braided Creek: A Conversation in Poetry 2003, Livingston Suite 2005, Saving Daylight 2006; non-fiction: Just Before Dark 1991, The Raw and the Cooked: Adventures of a Roving Gourmand 2001. *Honours:* NEA grant 1967–69, Guggenheim Fellowship 1968–69.

HARRISON, Sarah, BA; British author; b. 7 Aug. 1946, Exeter, Devon, England. *Education:* Univ. of London. *Career:* journalist, IPC Magazines, London 1967–71; freelance novelist/writer 1971–. *Publications:* fiction: Flowers of the Field 1980, A Flower That's Free 1984, Hot Breath 1985, An Imperfect Lady 1987, Cold Feet 1989, Foreign Parts 1991, The Forests of the Night 1992, Be An Angel 1993, Both Your Houses 1995, Life After Lunch 1996, Flowers Won't Fax 1997, That Was Then 1998, Heaven's On Hold 1999, The Grass Memorial 2002, The Dreaming Stones 2002, A Dangerous Thing 2003, The Divided Heart 2003, Swan Music 2004, The Nightingale's Nest 2006, A Spell of Swallows 2007, The Next Room 2005, The Red Dress 2006, Rose Petal Soup 2008, Matters Arising 2009, Returning the Favour 2010; children's fiction: In Granny's Garden 1980; Lark Rise series: Laura and Edmond 1986, Laura and Old Lumber 1986, Laura and the Lady 1986, Laura and the Squire 1986; non-fiction: How to Write a Blockbuster 1995. *Literary Agent:* c/o Sheila Crowley, Curtis Brown, Haymarket House, 28–29 Haymarket, London, England. *Telephone:* (20) 7393-4400. *E-mail:* sheila@curtisbrown.co.uk. *Tele-*

phone: (1462) 742056. *Fax:* (1462) 742549. *E-mail:* novel.sarah@virgin.net. *Website:* www.sarah-harrison.net.

HARRISON, Sue Ann, BA; American novelist; b. 29 Aug. 1950, Lansing, Mich.; d. of Charles Robert McHaney and Patricia Ann Sawyer McHaney; m. Neil Douglas Harrison 1969; one s. two d. (one deceased). *Education:* Lake Superior State Univ. *Career:* mem. Soc. of Midland Authors; mem. Bd of Regents, Lake Superior State Univ. 1994–2002. *Publications:* Mother Earth, Father Sky (chosen as one of the American Library Assen's Best Books for Young Adults 1991) 1990, My Sister the Moon 1992, Brother Wind 1994, Sisu 1997, Song of the River 1997, Cry of the Wind 1998, Call Down the Stars 2001. *Honours:* Lake Superior State Univ. Distinguished Alumni Award. *E-mail:* sue@sueharrison.com (office). *Website:* www.sueharrison.com.

HARRISON, Tony; British poet and dramatist; b. 30 April 1937, Leeds; s. of Harry Ashton Harrison and Florence Horner (née Wilkinson). *Education:* Leeds Grammar School and Univ. of Leeds. *Writing for television and film:* Yan Tan Tethera 1983, The Big H 1984, 'V' 1987, Loving Memory 1987, The Blasphemers' Banquet 1989, Black Daisies for the Bride 1993, A Maybe Day in Kazakhstan 1994, The Shadow of Hiroshima 1995, Prometheus 1998, Crossings 2002. *Plays:* Aikin Mata (with J. Simmons) 1965, The Misanthrope (version of Molière's play) 1973, Phaedra Britannica (version of Racine's Phèdre) 1975, The Passion 1977, Bow Down 1977, The Bartered Bride (libretto) 1978, The Oresteia (trans.) 1981, The Mysteries 1985, The Trackers of Oxyrhynchus 1990, The Common Chorus 1992, Square Rounds 1992, Poetry or Bust 1993, The Kaisers of Carnuntum 1995, The Labourers of Herakles 1995, The Prince's Play 1996, Fire and Poetry 1999, Fram 2008. *Publications include:* poetry: Earthworks 1964, Newcastle is Peru 1969, The Loiners 1970, Poems of Palladas of Alexandria (ed. and trans.) 1973, From the School of Eloquence and Other Poems 1978, Continuous 1981, A Kumquat for John Keats 1981, US Martial 1981, Selected Poems 1984, Fire-Gap 1985, 'V' 1985, Dramatic Verse, 1973–1985 1985, 'V' and Other Poems 1990, A Cold Coming: Gulf War Poems 1991, The Gaze of the Gorgon and other poems 1992, The Shadow of Hiroshima and other film/poems 1995, Permanently Bard 1995, Laureate's Block and other poems 2000, Under the Clock 2005, Collected Poems 2007, Collected Film Poetry 2007; collections of plays: Plays 1 1985, Theatre Works 1973–1985 1986, Plays 2 2002, Plays 3 1996, Plays 4 2002, Plays 5 2004, Hecuba 2005, Fram 2008. *Honours:* Cholmondeley Award for Poetry, Geoffrey Faber Memorial Award, European Poetry Translation Prize, Whitbread Poetry Prize 1993, Mental Health Award 1994, Prix Italia 1994, Northern Rock Foundation Writers' Award 2004, PEN/Pinter Award 2009, Wilfred Owen Award for Poetry 2008, European Prize for Literature (Strasbourg) 2011. *Address:* c/o Gordon Dickerson, 2 Crescent Grove, London, SW4 7AH, England (office). *Telephone:* (20) 7622-7666 (office). *E-mail:* gordondickerson@btinternet.com (office).

HARRISON, William Neal, BA, MA; American writer and academic; *University Professor Emeritus, University of Arkansas;* b. 29 Oct. 1933, Dallas, TX; m. Merlee Kimsey 1957; two s. one d. *Education:* Texas Christian Univ., Vanderbilt Univ., Univ. of Iowa. *Career:* Faculty, Dept of English, Univ. of Arkansas at Fayetteville 1964–99. *Publications:* The Theologian 1965, In a Wild Sanctuary 1969, Lessons in Paradise 1971, Roller Ball Murder and Other Stories 1974, Africana 1977, Savannah Blue 1981, Burton and Speke 1982, Three Hunters 1989, The Buddha in Malibu: New and Selected Stories 1998, The Blood Latitudes 1999, Texas Heat: Stories 2005, Black August 2012; other: screenplays, essays; contribs to anthologies and periodicals. *Honours:* Guggenheim Fellowship 1973–74, Nat. Endowment for the Arts Grant 1977, Christopher Award 1979. *Address:* 350 Sequoyah Drive, Fayetteville, AR 72701 (home); Department of English, University of Arkansas at Fayetteville, Fayetteville, AR 72701, USA (office). *E-mail:* billmerlee@earthlink.net (home).

HARRISS, Gerald Leslie, MA, DPhil, FBA; British historian and university teacher; b. 22 May 1925, London; s. of W. L. Harriss and M. J. O. Harriss; m. Margaret Anne Sidaway 1959; two s. three d. *Education:* Chigwell School, Essex, Magdalen Coll., Oxford. *Career:* war service in RNVR 1944–46; Univ. of Oxford 1946–53; Lecturer, Univ. of Durham 1953–65, Reader 1965–67; Fellow and Tutor in History, Magdalen Coll., Oxford 1967–92, Fellow Emer. 1992–, Reader in Modern History, Univ. of Oxford 1990–92. *Publications:* King, Parliament and Public Finance in Medieval England 1975, Henry V: the Practice of Kingship (ed.) 1985, Cardinal Beaufort 1988, K. B. McFarlane, Letters to Friends (ed.) 1997, Shaping the Nation: England 1360–1461 2005. *Address:* Fairings, 2 Queen Street, Yetminster, Sherborne, Dorset, DT9 6LL, England (home).

HARROWER, David; British playwright; b. 1967. *Plays:* Knives in Hens (Critics Award 1998) 1995, Kill the Old, Torture their Young (Meyer-Whitworth Award, Pearson Award) 1998, Begin Again 1999, Presence 2001, The Chysalids 2001, Ivanov (by Anton Chekhov) (adaptation) 2002, The Girl on the Sofa (by Jon Fosse) (adaptation) 2002, Dark Earth 2003, Tales from the Vienna Woods 2003, Purple, by Jon Fosse (adaptation) 2003, Blackbird (Best New Play, Laurence Olivier Awards 2007) 2005, Mary Stuart (by Friedrich Schiller) (adaptation) 2006, The Good Soul of Szechuan (by Bertolt Brecht) (adaptation) 2008, 365 2008, Sweet Nothings 2010, Good With People 2010, Government Inspector (adaptation) 2011, Slow Air 2011. *Publications:* Six Characters Looking for an Author (ed.) 2001. *Literary Agent:* c/o Mel Kenyon, Casarotto Ramsay & Associates Ltd, Waverley House, 7-12 Noel Street, London, W1F 8GQ, England. *Telephone:* (20) 7287-4450. *Fax:* (20) 7287-9128.

E-mail: mel@casarotto.co.uk; info@casarotto.co.uk. *Website:* www.casarotto.co.uk.

HARRS, (Margaret) Norma; Northern Irish writer; b. 15 Sept. 1935; m. Leonard Michael Harrs; two s. *Career:* mem. Playwrights Guild of Canada. *Publications:* A Certain State of Mind 1980, Love Minus One & Other Stories 1994, Where Dreams Have Gone 1997, Sonya (play), The 40th Birthday Party (play), Essential Conflict (play); contrib. to anthologies, including Ladies Start Your Engines 1997, Elements of English 1999; contrib. to journals, including Pittsburgh Review, Kairos, Antigonish Review, Room of One's Own. *Honours:* Ontario Literary Grant 1988, Canada Council Travel Grant 1997. *Address:* 171 Fifth Line, Fraserville, South Monaghan, ON K0L 1V0, Canada (home). *E-mail:* norharrs@nexicom.net (home). *Website:* www.normaharrs.com.

HARSENT, David, FRSL, FRSA; British poet; b. 9 Dec. 1942, Devonshire, England; m. 1st (divorced); two s. one d.; m. 2nd; one d. *Career:* fiction and poetry reviewer, Times Literary Supplement for 12 years; poetry reviewer, The Spectator for four years; poetry and TV reviewer, The New Review for three years; theatre critic, The New Statesman for two years; apptd Distinguished Writing Fellow, Hallam Univ., Sheffield 2005, now Visiting Prof. *Publications include:* novel: From an Inland Sea 1985; poetry: Tonight's Lover 1968, A Violent Country 1969, Ashridge 1970, After Dark 1973, Truce 1973, Dreams of the Dead 1977, Mister Punch 1984, Selected Poems 1989, Storybook Hero 1992, News From the Front 1993, The Sorrow of Sarajevo (trans. of poems by Goran Simic) 1996, The Potted Priest 1997, Sprinting from the Graveyard (trans. of poems by Goran Simic) 1997, Playback 1997, A Bird's Idea of Flight 1998, Marriage 2002, Legion (Forward Poetry Prize for Best Poetry Collection of the Year) 2005, New Selected Poems 2007, Night (Griffin Poetry Prize 2012) 2011; as ed.: New Poetry 7 1981, Poetry Book Society Supplement 1983, Savremena Britanska Poezija 1988, Another Round at the Pillars, a festschrift for Ian Hamilton 1999, Raising the Iron 2003; contrib. to Poetry Introduction 1 1968; words for music: Serenade the Silkie (music by Julian Grant) 1989, Gawain (opera, music by Harrison Birtwistle) 1991, The Woman and the Hare (music by Harrison Birtwistle) 1998, When She Died (opera for TV, music by Jonathan Dove) 2002, The Ring Dance of the Nazarene (music by Harrison Birtwistle) 2004, The Minotaur (opera, music by Harrison Birtwistle) 2008, Crime Fiction (opera, music by Huw Watkins) 2009, The Corridor (opera, music by Harrison Birtwistle) 2009. *Honours:* Eric Gregory Award 1967, Cheltenham Festival Prize 1968, Arts Council Bursaries 1969, 1984, Geoffrey Faber Memorial Prize 1978, Soc. of Authors Travel Fellowship 1989, Forward Prize 2005, Cholmondeley Award 2008. *Literary Agent:* c/o Charles Walker, United Agents, 12–26 Lexington Street, London, W1F 0LE, England. *Telephone:* (20) 3214-0800. *Fax:* (20) 3214-0801. *E-mail:* cwalker@unitedagents.co.uk. *Website:* unitedagents.co.uk.

HART, Anrea (see Freemantle, Brian Harry)

HART, Ellen, BA; American writer; b. 10 Aug. 1949, Minneapolis, MN; two d. *Education:* Ambassador Univ. *Career:* mem. Sisters in Crime. *Publications:* Hallowed Murder 1989, Vital Lies 1991, Stage Fright 1992, A Killing Cure 1993, The Little Piggy Went to Murder 1994, A Small Sacrifice 1994, Faint Praise 1995, For Every Evil 1995, Robber's Wine 1996, The Oldest Sin 1996, Murder in the Air 1997, Wicked Games 1998, Hunting the Witch 1999, Slice and Dice 2000, Dial M for Meatloaf 2001, The Merchant of Venus 2001, Immaculate Midnight 2002, Death on a Silver Platter 2003, An Intimate Ghost 2004, The Iron Girl 2005, No Reservations Required 2005, Night Vision 2006, The Mortal Groove 2007, Sweet Poison 2008, The Mirror and the Mask 2009, The Cruel Ever After 2010. *Honours:* Lambda Literary Award 1994, 1996, Minnesota Book Award 1995, 1996. *E-mail:* ellenhart@earthlink.net (office). *Website:* www.ellenhart.com.

HART, John; American author; b. 1965, Durham, NC; m.; two c. *Education:* Davidson Coll., Charlotte. *Career:* fmr banker, stockbroker, attorney. *Publications include:* novels: The King of Lies 2006, Down River (Edgar Allen Poe Award for Best Novel 2008) 2007, The Last Child (Ian Fleming Steel Dagger Award 2009, Edgar Allen Poe Award for Best Novel 2010, Barry Award for Best Novel 2010) 2009, Iron House 2011. *Literary Agent:* c/o Mickey Choate, The Choate Agency LLC, 1320 Bolton Road, Pelham Manor, NY 10803; c/o Esther Newberg, ICM Partners, 730 Fifth Avenue, New York, NY 10019, USA. *Telephone:* (914) 712-0801 (Choate Agency); (212) 556-5600 (ICM). *Fax:* (914) 712-0801 (Choate Agency). *E-mail:* mickey@thechoateagency.com. *Website:* www.thechoateagency.com; www.icmtalent.com. *Address:* c/o Stephen Lee, St Martin's Press, 175 Fifth Avenue, New York, NY 10010, USA (office). *Telephone:* (646) 307-5560 (office). *E-mail:* stephen.lee@stmartins.com (office); johnhartauthor@hotmail.com (home). *Website:* www.stmartins.com (office); www.johnhartfiction.com.

HART, Kevin John, BA, PhD, FAHA; Australian academic and poet; *Edwin B. Kyle Professor of Christian Studies, University of Virginia;* b. 5 July 1954, London, England, UK; s. of James Henry Hart and Rosina Mary Wootton; m. Rita Judith Hart; two d. *Education:* Australian Nat. Univ., Stanford Univ., USA, Univ. of Melbourne. *Career:* Lecturer in English, Univ. of Melbourne 1986–87; Lecturer to Sr Lecturer in Literary Studies, Deakin Univ., Vic. 1987–91; Assoc. Prof., Monash Univ. 1991–95, Prof. of English 1995–2002; Foundation Prof. of Australian and New Zealand Studies, Georgetown Univ., Washington, DC, USA 1996–97; Visiting Prof., Villanova Univ., USA 2001; Prof. of English, Univ. of Notre Dame, Ind., USA 2002–04, Notre Dame Prof. of Philosophy and Literature, Dept of Philosophy 2004–07; Edwin B. Kyle Prof. of Christian Studies, Univ. of Virginia, USA 2007–; Eric D'Arcy Prof. of

Philosophy, ANU 2011–; Fellow, Nanovic Inst.; mem. and Vice-Pres. Johnson Soc. of Australia. *Publications:* Nebuchadnezzar, 1976, The Departure 1978, The Lines of the Hand: Poems 1976–79, Your Shadow 1984, The Trespass of the Sign 1989, Peniel 1990, The Buried Harbour (trans.) 1990, A D. Hope 1992, The Oxford Book of Australian Religious Verse (ed.) 1994, New and Selected Poems 1995, Dark Angel 1996, Samuel Johnson and the Culture of Property 1999, Wicked Heat 1999, Flame Tree: Selected Poems 2002, The Impossible 2003, Postmodernism 2004, The Dark Gaze: Maurice Blanchot and the Sacred 2004, The Power of Contestation (with Geoffrey Hartman) 2004, Derrida and Religion (with Yvonne Sherwood) 2004, The Experience of God (with Barbara Wall) 2005, Counter-Experiences: Reading Jean-Luc Marion 2007, Young Rain 2008, The Exorbitant: Emmanuel Levinas between Jews and Christians 2009, Clandestine Encounters: Philosophy in the Narratives of Maurice Blanchot 2010, Morning Knowledge 2011, Jean-Luc Marion: The Essential Writings 2012; contribs to Arena Journal, The Critical Review, Boxkite, Heat, Verse, New Literary History, Faith and Philosophy, Virginia Quarterly Review. *Honours:* Australian Literature Bd Fellowship 1977, NSW Premier's Award 1985, Victorian Premier's Award for Poetry 1985, Grace Levin Awards for Poetry 1991, 1995, Christopher Brennan Award for Poetry 1999, Graybeal-Gowan Award for Poetry 2008. *Address:* Department of Religious Studies, University of Virginia, PO Box 400126, Charlottesville, VA 22904-4126, USA (office). *Telephone:* (434) 924-3741 (office). *Fax:* (434) 924-1467 (office). *E-mail:* kevinhart@virginia.edu (office). *Website:* www.virginia.edu/religiousstudies (office).

HART, Veronica (see Kelleher, Victor)

HART-DAVIS, Duff, BA; British writer; b. 3 June 1936, London, England. *Education:* Univ. of Oxford. *Career:* feature writer, Sunday Telegraph 1972–76, Literary Ed. 1976–77, Asst Ed. 1977–78; Country Columnist, The Independent 1986–2001. *Publications:* The Megacull 1968, The Gold of St Matthew (aka The Gold Trackers) 1968, Spider in the Morning 1972, Ascension: The Story of a South Atlantic Island 1972, Peter Fleming (biog.) 1974, Monarchs of the Glen 1978, The Heights of Rimring 1980, Fighter Pilot (with C. Strong) 1981, Level Five 1982, Fire Falcon 1984, The Man-Eater of Jassapur 1985, Hitler's Games 1986, End of an Era: Letters and Journals of Sir Alan Lascelles 1887–1920 (ed.) 1986, Armada 1988, In Royal Service: Letters and Journals of Sir Alan Lascelles Vol. 2 1920–1936 (ed.) 1989, The House the Berrys Built 1990, Horses of War 1991, Country Matters 1991, Wildings: The Secret Garden of Eileen Soper 1992, Further Country Matters 1993, When the Country Went to Town 1997, Raoul Millais 1998, Fauna Britannica 2002, Audubon's Elephant 2003, Honorary Tiger 2005, Pavilions of Splendour (ed.) 2005, King's Counsellor: Abdication and War: The Diaries of Sir Alan Lascelles (ed.) 2006, Philip de László: His Life and Art 2010, The War That Never Was 2011, Among the Deer 2011. *Address:* Owlpen Farm, Uley, Dursley, Glos., GL11 5BZ, England (home). *Telephone:* (1453) 860239 (home). *E-mail:* duff.hart@btinternet.com (office).

HARTILL, Rosemary Jane, BA; British writer and broadcaster; b. 11 Aug. 1949, Oswestry, Shropshire, England. *Education:* Univ. of Bristol. *Career:* BBC Religious Affairs Corresp. 1982–88, Presenter BBC World Service Meridian Books Programme 1990–92, 1994; ind. broadcaster 1989–; mem. Youth Justice Bd for England and Wales 2004–08; mem. Bd Shared Interest 1996–2005, Nat. Probation Service, Northumbria 2001–07, Strategic Health Authority, Northumberland, Tyne and Wear 2002–05, Northumbria Courts 2004–07. *Publications:* Emily Brontë: Poems (ed.) 1973, Wild Animals 1976, In Perspective 1988, Writers Revealed 1989, Were You There? 1995, Visionary Women: Florence Nightingale (ed.) 1996; contribs to various periodicals. *Honours:* Hon. DLitt (Hull) 1995, (Bristol) 2000; Sandford St Martin Trust Personal Award 1994. *Address:* Old Post Office, 24 Eglingham Village, Alnwick, Northumberland, NE66 2TX, England (home).

HARTLAND, Michael (see James, Michael Leonard)

HARTLEY, Aidan; writer; b. 1965. *Education:* Univ. of Oxford, Univ. of London. *Career:* grew up in Africa; foreign correspondent, Reuters, then freelance 1996–; currently columnist, The Spectator. *Publications:* The Zanzibar Chest: A Memoir of Love and War 2003, Wild Life 2008. *Address:* c/o Harper Perennial Publicity, Harper Collins Publishers, 77–85 Fulham Palace Road, London W6 8JB, England (office). *E-mail:* info@thezanzibarchest.com (office). *Website:* www.thezanzibarchest.com.

HÄRTLING, Peter; German writer and journalist; b. 13 Nov. 1933, Chemnitz; s. of Rudolf Härtling and Erika Härtling (née Häntzschel); m. Mechthild Maier 1959; two s. two d. *Education:* Gymnasium (Nürtingen/Neckar). *Career:* childhood spent in Saxony, Czechoslovakia and Württemberg; journalist 1953–; Literary Ed. Deutsche Zeitung und Wirtschaftszeitung, Stuttgart and Cologne; Ed. of magazine Der Monat 1962–70, also Co-publisher; Ed. and Man. Dir S. Fischer Verlag, Frankfurt 1968–74, Ed. Die Väter; mem. PEN, Akad. der Wissenschaften und der Literatur Mainz, Akad. der Künste Berlin, Deutsche Akad. für Sprache und Dichtung Darmstadt. *Publications:* Yamins Stationen (poetry) 1955, In Zeilen zuhaus (essays) 1957, Palmström grüsst Anna Blume (essays) 1961, Spielgeist-Spiegelgeist (poetry) 1962, Niembsch oder Der Stillstand (novel) 1964, Janek (novel) 1966, Das Familienfest (novel) 1969, Gilles (play) 1970, Ein Abend, Eine Nacht, Ein Morgen (novel) 1971, Neue Gedichte 1972, Zwettl – Nachprüfung einer Erinnerung (novel) 1973, Eine Frau (novel) 1974, Hölderlin (novel) 1976, Anreden (poetry) 1977, Hubert oder Die Rückkehr nach Casablanca (novel) 1978, Nachgetragene Liebe (novel) 1980, Die dreifache Maria 1982, Vorwarnung 1983, Sätze von Liebe 1983, Das Windrad (novel) 1983, Ich rufe die Wörter zusammen 1984, Der spanische Soldat oder Finden under Erfinden 1984, Felix Guttmann (novel) 1985, Waiblingers Augen (novel) 1987, Die Mösinger Pappel 1987, Der Wanderer (novel) 1988, Briefe von drinnen und draußen (poetry) 1989, Herzwand (novel) 1990, Brüder under Schwestern: Tagebuch eines Synodalen 1991, Schubert (novel) 1992, Božena (novel) 1994, Schumanns Schatten (novel) 1996, Grosse, Kleine Schwester (novel) 1998, Hoffmann oder Die vielfältige Liebe (novel) 2001, Leben lernen (autobiog.) 2004, Die Lebenslinie (autobiog.) 2005. *Honours:* Hon. Prof. 1996; Grosses Bundesverdienstkreuz 1996; Hon. DPhil 2001; Dr hc (Giessen) 2002; Literaturpreis des Deutschen Kritikerverbandes 1964, Literaturpreis des Kulturkreises der Deutschen Industrie 1965, Literarischer Förderungspreis des Landes Niedersachsen 1965, Prix du meilleur livre étranger, Paris 1966, Gerhart Hauptmann Preis 1971, Deutscher Jugendbuchpreis 1976, Stadtschreiber von Bergen-Enkheim 1978–79, Hölderlin-Preis 1987, Lion-Feuchtwanger-Preis 1992, Stadtschreiber von Mainz 1995, Leuschner-Medaille des Landes Hessen 1996, Eichendorff-Preis 1999, Deutsche Jugendbuchpreis 2001, Deutscher Bücherpreis 2002. *Address:* Finkenweg 1, 64546 Mörfelden-Walldorf, Germany. *Telephone:* (6105) 6109 (office). *Fax:* (6105) 74687 (office). *E-mail:* peter@haertling.de (office). *Website:* www.haertling.de.

HARTMAN, Geoffrey H., BA, PhD, FBA; American academic and writer; *Sterling Professor Emeritus of English and Comparative Literature, Yale University;* b. 11 Aug. 1929, Frankfurt am Main, Germany; m. Renee Gross 1956; one s. one d. *Education:* Queens Coll., City Univ. of New York, Yale Univ. *Career:* Fulbright Fellow, Univ. of Dijon 1951–52; Faculty mem., Yale Univ. 1955–62, Karl Young Prof. 1974–94, Sterling Prof. of English and Comparative Literature 1994–97, Sterling Prof. Emer. 1997–; Assoc. Prof., Univ. of Iowa 1962–64, Prof. of English 1964–65; Prof. of English and Comparative Literature, Cornell Univ. 1965–67; Gauss Seminarist, Princeton Univ., NJ 1968; Dir School of Theory and Criticism, Dartmouth Coll. 1982–87; Assoc. Fellow, Center for Research in Philosophy and Literature, Univ. of Warwick, UK 1993; Fellow, Woodrow Wilson Int. Center 1995; mem. American Acad. of Arts and Sciences, MLA. *Publications:* The Unmediated Vision 1954, André Malraux 1960, Wordsworth's Poetry 1964, Beyond Formalism 1970, The Fate of Reading 1975, Akiba's Children 1978, Criticism in the Wilderness 1980, Saving the Text 1981, Easy Pieces 1985, The Unremarkable Wordsworth 1987, Minor Prophecies 1991, A Critic's Journey 1999, Scars of the Spirit 2003; editor: Romanticism: Vistas, Instances, Continuities 1973, Psychoanalysis and the Question of the Text 1978, Shakespeare and the Question of Theory 1985, Bitburg in Moral and Political Perspective 1986, Midrash and Literature 1986, Holocaust Remembrance: The Shapes of Memory 1993. Monographs: The Longest Shadow: In the Aftermath of the Holocaust 1996, The Fateful Question of Culture 1997 (ACLA Renee Wellek Prize 1997), A Critic's Journey 1999, Scars of the Spirit: The Struggle Against Inauthenticity 2002, The Geoffrey Hartman Reader 2005, A Scholar's Tale: Intellectual Journey of a Displaced Child of Europe 2007, The Third Pillar: Essays in Jewish Studies 2011. *Honours:* Hon. DrPhil (Konstanz, Germany); Guggenheim Fellowships 1969, 1986; Hon. LHD (Queens College, CUNY) 1990, (Hebrew Union Coll., Cincinnatti) 2003; Keats-Shelley Asscn Distinguished Scholar Award 1997; Tanner Lectures, 1999; Haskins Lecturer, 2000. *Address:* 260 Everit Street, New Haven, CT 06511-1309, USA (home). *Telephone:* (203) 624-4410 (home).

HARTNETT, David William, BA, MA, DPhil; British writer, poet and editor; b. 4 Sept. 1952, London, England; m. Margaret R. N. Thomas 1976; one s. one d. *Education:* Univ. of Oxford. *Career:* Co-ed. Poetry Durham magazine; Dir, Contributing Ed., Leviathan Publishing Ltd, Leviathan Quarterly. *Publications:* poetry: A Signalled Love 1985, House of Moon 1988, Dark Ages 1992, At the Wood's Edge 1997; fiction: Black Milk 1994, Brother to Dragons 1998; contribs to TLS. *Honours:* TLS/Cheltenham Festival Poetry Competition 1989.

HARTNETT, Sonya, BA; Australian writer; b. 23 March 1968, Melbourne, Vic. *Education:* Royal Melbourne Inst. of Tech. *Career:* mem. St Martin's Theatre, Melbourne (bd mem.). *Publications:* Trouble All the Way 1984, Sparkle and Nightflower 1986, The Glass House 1990, Wilful Blue (Ena Noel Award 1996) 1994, Sleeping Dogs (Miles Franklin Kathleen Mitchell Award 1996, Victorian Premier's Literary Award, Sheaffer Pen Prize 1996, CBCA Children's Book of the Year Award 1996) 1995, The Devil Latch 1996, Black Foxes 1996, Princes 1997, Forest (CBCA Children's Book of the Year Award) 2001, Thursday's Child (Guardian Children's Fiction Prize, Aurealis Award) 2002, What the Birds See (The Age Book of the Year Award, Commonwealth Writers Prize) 2003, Stripes of the Sidestep Wolf 2004, The Silver Donkey (Courier Mail Award, CBCA Children's Book of the Year Award 2005) 2004, Surrender (Michael L. Printz Award, Victorian Premier's Literary Award) 2007) 2005, The Ghost's Child 2007, Sadie and Ratz 2008, Butterfly 2009, The Midnight Zoo 2010, The Boy and the Toy (Aurealis Award 2011) 2010, Come Down, Cat! 2011, The Children of the King 2012. *Honours:* Astrid Lindgren Memorial Award 2008. *Address:* c/o Penguin Books, PO Box 701, Hawthorn, Vic. 3122, Australia. *Website:* www.sonyahartnett.com.au.

HARTUNG, Harald; German poet, academic and critic; b. 29 Oct. 1932, Herne; s. of Richard Hartung and Wanda Hartung; m. Freia Schnackenburg 1979; two s. *Career:* secondary school teacher 1960–66; Prof., Pädagogische Hochschule Berlin 1971–80, Tech. Univ. Berlin 1971–98 (retd); mem. Akad. der Künste, Berlin, PEN. *Publications:* Experimentelle Literatur und

Konkrete Poesie 1975, Das Gewöhnliche Licht 1976, Augenzeit 1978, Deutsche Lyrik seit 1965 1985, Traum im Deutschen Museum 1986, Luftfracht 1991, Jahre mit Windrad 1996, Masken und Stimmen 1996, Jahrhundertgedächtnis.Deutsche Lyrik im 20.Jahrhundert 1998, Machen oder Entstehenlassen 2001, Langsamer träumen 2002, Aktennotiz meines Engels 2005, Ein Unterton von Glück – Über Dichter und Gedichte 2007, Wintermalerei. Gedichte 2010. *Honours:* Literature Promotion Prize of the Berlin Art Prize 1979, Annette von Droste-Hulshoff Prize 1987, Int. Poetry Prize Chianti Ruffino Antico Fattore 1999, Prize of the Frankfurt anthology 2002, Würth Prize for European Literature 2004, Johann Heinrich Merck Prize 2009. *Address:* Rüdesheimer Platz 4, 14197 Berlin, Germany.

HARUF, (Alan) Kent, BA, MFA; American writer; b. 24 Feb. 1943, Pueblo, CO; m. 1st Virginia Koon (divorced); m. 2nd Cathy Dempsey; three d. *Education:* Nebraska Wesleyan Univ., Univ. of Iowa. *Career:* Asst Prof., Nebraska Wesleyan Univ. 1986–91; Assoc. Prof., Southern Illinois Univ. 1991–2000. *Publications:* The Tie That Binds 1984, Where You Once Belonged 1991, Plainsong 1999, Eventide 2004, West of Last Chance (with Peter Brown) 2008; contrib. to anthologies and periodicals. *Honours:* Whiting Writer's Award 1986, Maria Thomas Award 1991, Mt Plains Booksellers Award 2000, Alex Award 2000, Dorothea Lange–Paul Taylor Prize, Duke Univ. 2005. *Address:* c/o Vintage Publicity, Random House Inc., 1745 Broadway, New York, NY 10019, USA (office). *Website:* www.randomhouse.com (office).

HARVEY, Anne Berenice; British actress, writer, poet, editor and broadcaster; b. 27 April 1933, London, England; m. Alan Harvey 1957; one s. one d. *Education:* Guildhall School of Music and Drama, London. *Career:* lectures, talks, readings at literary festivals, galleries; platform programmes, broadcasting; Dir, Guildhall Players, Perranporth, Cornwall 1954–59; Fellow Soc. of Teachers of Speech & Drama 2004; mem. Poetry Soc., Friends of the Dymock Poets, Eighteen Nineties Soc., Imaginative Book Illustration Soc., Walter de la Mare Soc. (founder mem.), Wilfred Owen Soc., John Masefield Soc., Children's Books History Soc.; Edward Thomas Fellowship, Charlotte Mary Yonge Fellowship; literary executor Eleanor Farjeon estate. *Radio:* as writer and presenter: A Life Kept Always Young: The Life of Eleanor Farjeon (BBC Radio 4), A Writer's Life: The Life of Noel Streatfeild (BBC Radio 4), Adlestrop Revisited (BBC Radio 4), Kings and Queens (BBC Radio 4); various Radio 2 Arts Programmes (BBC Radio 2). *Publications:* A Present for Nellie 1981, Poets in Hand 1985, Of Caterpillars, Cats and Cattle 1987, In Time of War: War Poetry 1987, Something I Remember (selected poetry of Eleanor Farjeon) 1987, A Picnic of Poetry 1988, The Language of Love 1989, Six of the Best 1989, Faces in the Crowd 1990, Headlines from the Jungle (with Virginia McKenna) 1990, Occasions 1990, Flora's Red Socks 1991, Shades of Green 1991, Elected Friends (poems for and about Edward Thomas) 1991, He Said, She Said, They Said (conversation poems, ed.) 1993; solo audition: Speeches for Young Actors, 1993, Criminal Records: Poetry of Crime (ed.) 1994, Methuen Book of Duologues 1995, Starlight, Starbright: Poems of Night 1995, Swings and Shadows: Poems of Times Past and Present 1996, Words Aloud, two vols (ed.) 1998, Eleanor Farjeon, The Last Four Years (ed.), Blackbird Has Spoken: Selected Poems of Eleanor Farjeon (ed.) 1999, Eleanor Farjeon, Come Christmas (ed.) 2000, Adlestrop Revisited (ed.) 2000, When Christmas Comes (anthology, ed.) 2002, Party Pieces (anthology; ed.) 2005; Series Editor: Poetry Originals 1992–95; contribs to radio, journals and magazines. *Honours:* Signal Poetry Award 1992. *Address:* 37 St Stephen's Road, Ealing, London, W13 8HJ, England (home). *Telephone:* (20) 8997-6443 (home). *E-mail:* harvey.anne@tiscali.co.uk.

HARVEY, Brett; American writer and critic; b. 28 April 1936, New York; one s. one d. *Education:* Northwestern Univ. *Career:* Drama and Literature Dir, WBAI-FM 1971–74; Publicity and Promotion Dir, The Feminist Press, Old Westbury 1974–80; fmr Exec. Dir American Soc. of Journalists and Authors. *Publications:* My Prairie Year 1986, Immigrant Girl 1987, Cassie's Journey: My Prairie Christmas 1990, The Fifties: A Women's Oral History 1993, Cassies Journey: Going West in the 1860s 1995, Farmers And Ranchers 1997; contribs to Village Voice, New York Times Book Review, Psychology Today, Voice Literary Supplement, Mirabella, Mother Jones, Mademoiselle. *Address:* c/o American Society of Journalists and Authors, Times Square, 1501 Broadway, Suite 403, New York, NY 10036, USA.

HARVEY, Caroline (see Trollope, Joanna)

HARVEY, Jack (see Rankin, Ian James)

HARVEY, John Barton, MA; British writer and poet; b. 21 Dec. 1938, London; three c. *Education:* Goldsmiths Coll., London, Hatfield Polytechnic, Univ. of Nottingham. *Career:* teacher of English in secondary schools 1965–75; part-time Lecturer in Film and Literature, Univ. of Nottingham 1980–86; fmrly tutor on residential writing courses, Arvon Foundation; teacher, Squaw Valley Community of Writers Fiction Workshop, Northern California 1995; Man. Slow Dancer Press 1977–99, Ed. Slow Dancer magazine –1993. *Radio:* Wasted Years 1995, Cutting Edge 1996, Slow Burn 1997, Cheryl 2001; adaptations of works by A.S. Byatt, Richard Ford, Bobbie Ann Mason, Jayne Anne Phillips, Paul Scott and Graham Greene (including The End of the Affair, winner of Silver Sony Radio Drama Award 1998. *Television:* Lonely Hearts (New York Festivals bronze medal for Screenplay for Best TV Drama Series 1992) 1991, Rough Treatment 1992, Hard Cases (series, Central TV); adaptations of Arnold Bennett works Anna of the Five Towns, Sophia and Constance. *Publications:* novels: Avenging Angel (as Thom Ryder) 1975, Angel Alone (as Thom Ryder) 1975, Kill Hitler! (as Jon Barton) 1976, Amphetamines and Pearls 1976, The Geranium Kiss 1976, River of Blood (as John J. McLaglen) 1976, Forest of Death (as Jon Barton) 1977, Lightning Strikes (as Jon Barton) 1977, The Raiders (as L. J. Coburn) 1977, Evil Breed (as J. B. Dancer) 1977, Black Blood (as Jon Hart) 1977, High Slaughter (as Jon Hart) 1977, Triangle of Death (as Jon Hart) 1977, Guerilla Attack (as Jon Hart) 1977, Shadow of Vultures (as John J. McLaglen) 1977, Death in Gold (as John J. McLaglen) 1977, Junkyard Angel 1977, Neon Madman 1977, Cross-Draw (as John J. McLaglen) 1978, Death Raid (as Jon Hart) 1978, Judgement Day (as J. B. Dancer) 1978, Bloody Shiloh (as L. J. Coburn) 1978, Blood Rising (as William M. James) 1979, Cannons in the Rain (as J. D. Sandon) 1979, Border Affair (as J. D. Sandon) 1979, The Hanged Man (as J. B. Dancer) 1979, Vigilante! (as John J. McLaglen) 1979, Frame 1979, Blood Money (as William S. Brady) 1979, Killing Time (as William S. Brady) 1980, Blood Kin (as William S. Brady) 1980, Cherokee Outlet (as John B. Harvey) 1980, Blood Trail (as John B. Harvey) 1980, Tago (as John B. Harvey) 1980, The Silver Lie (as John B. Harvey) 1980, Sun Dance (as John J. McLaglen) 1980, Billy the Kid (as John J. McLaglen) 1980, Till Death... (as John J. McLaglen) 1980, Blood Brother (as William M. James) 1980, Mazatlan (as J. D. Sandon) 1980, Death Dragon (as William M. James) 1981, Wheels of Thunder (as J. D. Sandon) 1981, Blind 1981, Blood on the Border (as John B. Harvey) 1981, Ride the Wide Country (as John B. Harvey) 1981, Desperadoes (as William S. Brady) 1981, Dead Man's Hand (as William S. Brady) 1981, Whiplash (as William S. Brady) 1981, Sierra Gold (as William S. Brady) 1982, Death and Jack Shade (as William S. Brady) 1982, Endgame (as James Mann) 1982, Arkansas Breakout (as John B. Harvey) 1982, John Wesley Hardin (as John B. Harvey) 1982, Dying Ways (as John J. McLaglen) 1982, Hearts of Gold (as John J. McLaglen) 1982, Durango (as J. D. Sandon) 1982, Death Ride (as William M. James) 1983, The Hanging (as William M. James) 1983, Border War (as William S. Brady) 1983, Killer! (as William S. Brady) 1983, War-Party (as William S. Brady) 1983, Wild Blood (as John J. McLaglen) 1983, California Bloodlines (as John B. Harvey) 1983, The Skinning Place (aka The Fatal Frontier) (as John B. Harvey) 1983, Dancer Draws a Wild Card (as Terry Lennox) 1985, Lonely Hearts 1989, Rough Treatment 1990, Cutting Edge 1991, Off Minor 1992, Wasted Years 1993, Cold Light (Grand Prix du Roman Noir Etranger du Cognac 2000) 1994, Living Proof 1995, Easy Meat 1996, Still Water 1997, Last Rites (Sherlock Award Winner for Best British Detective 1999) 1998, In a True Light 2001, Flesh and Blood (CWA Silver Dagger for Fiction) 2004, Ash and Bone 2005, Darkness and Light 2006, Gone to Ground 2007, Cold in Hand 2007, Far Cry 2009, A Darker Shade of Blue 2010; juvenile: What About It, Sharon? 1979, Reel Love 1982, Sundae Date 1983, What Game Are You Playing? 1983, Footwork 1984, Wild Love 1986, Last Summer 1986, Kidnap! 1987, Daylight Robbery! 1987, Hot Property! 1987, Terror Trap! 1988, Downeast to Danger 1988, Runner! Beaver 1988, Nick's Blues 2008; poetry: Provence (chapbook) 1978, The Old Postcard Trick (chapbook) 1985, Neil Sedaka Lied (chapbook) 1987, The Downeast Poems (chapbook) 1989, Sometime Other Than Now (with Sue Dymoke) (chapbook) 1989, Territory (chapbook) 1992, Ghosts of a Chance 1992, Bluer Than This 1998. *Honours:* CWA Silver Dagger 2004, CWA Cartier Diamond Dagger 2007. *Literary Agent:* Lutyens & Rubinstein, 231 Westbourne Park Road, London, W11 1EB, England. *Telephone:* (20) 7792-4855. *Address:* 37 Oakford Road, London, NW5 1AJ, England (office). *Website:* www.mellotone.co.uk.

HARVEY, John Robert, BA, MA, LittD; British academic and writer; *Life Fellow, Emmanuel College, Cambridge*; b. 25 June 1942, Bishops Stortford, Herts., England; m. Julietta Chloe Papadopoulou 1968; one d. *Education:* Univ. of Cambridge. *Career:* Vice-Master, Emmanuel Coll., Cambridge 2002–04, Univ. Reader in Literature and Visual Culture 2000–09, Life Fellow 2009–; Ed. Cambridge Quarterly 1978–86. *Publications:* non-fiction: Victorian Novelists and Their Illustrators 1970, Men in Black 1995, Clothes 2008; fiction: The Plate Shop 1979, Coup d'Etat 1985, The Legend of Captain Space 1990; contribs to London Review of Books, Sunday Times, Sunday Telegraph, Listener, Encounter, Cambridge Quarterly, Essays in Criticism, Royal Academy Magazine, Textual Practice, Fashion Theory, Cent. *Honours:* David Higham Prize 1979. *Address:* Emmanuel College, St Andrew's Street, Cambridge, CB2 3AP, England (office). *E-mail:* jrh49@cam.ac.uk (office).

HARVEY, Steven, BA, MA, PhD; American academic, writer and poet; *G. Milton Goolsby and Ophelia Roberts Goolsby Chair of English, Young Harris College*; b. 9 June 1949, Dodge City, KS; m. Barbara Hupfer 1971; two s. two d. *Education:* Wake Forest Univ., Johns Hopkins Univ., Middlebury Coll., Univ. of Virginia. *Career:* Prof. of English, Young Harris Coll. 1976–, currently also G. Milton Goolsby and Ophelia Roberts Goolsby Chair of English; Instructor in Writing, John C. Campbell Folk School 1995–; mem. Associated Writing Programs. *Publications:* Powerlines (poems) 1976, A Geometry of Lilies (non-fiction) 1993, Lost in Translation (non-fiction) 1997, In a Dark Wood: Personal Essays by Men on Middle Age (ed.) 1997, Bound for Shady Grove (non-fiction) 2000, It Started with a Steamboat 2005, Building America's Main Street Not Wall Street 2010; contribs to periodicals. *Honours:* MacDowell Colony Fellowship 1994. *Address:* Department of English, Young Harris College, 1 College Street, Young Harris, GA 30582, USA (office). *Telephone:* (800) 241-3754 (office). *E-mail:* sharvey@yhc.edu (office). *Website:* www.yhc.edu (office).

HARVOR, Erica Elisabeth Arendt, MA; Canadian writer; b. 26 June 1936, Saint John, NB; d. of Kjeld Deichmann and Erica Matthiesen; m. Stig Harvor 1957 (divorced 1977); two s. *Education:* Saint John High School and Concordia Univ. *Career:* Tutor Concordia Univ. 1986–87, currently Writer-in-Residence; Course Dir and Part-time Lecturer in Creative Writing, Div. of the Humanities, York Univ. (Toronto) 1987–93; mem. Canadian juries; reader and tutor in field; First Prize CBC's New Canadian Writing Series 1965, Ottawa Short Story Competition 1970, The League of Canadian Poets' Nat. Poetry Prize 1989, 1991; The Malahat Long Poem Prize 1990; Confed. Poets' Prize 1991, 1992. *Publications:* Women and Children 1973 (re-issued as Our Lady of All The Distances 1991), If Only We Could Drive Like This Forever 1988, Fortress of Chairs (poems) 1992, Let Me Be The One 1996, The Long Cold Green Evenings of Spring 1998, Excessive Joy Injures the Heart 2002, All Times have been Modern (novel) 2004; works featured in journals, magazines and anthologies. *E-mail:* eharvor@sympatico.ca (home). *Website:* www.elisabeth-harvor.com.

HARWOOD, Lee, BA; British poet, writer and translator; b. 6 June 1939, Leicester; m. (divorced); two s. one d. *Education:* Queen Mary Coll., London. *Career:* mem. Nat. Poetry Secr. (Chair. 1974–76), Poetry Soc., London (Chair. 1976–77). *Publications:* Title Illegible 1965, The Man with Blue Eyes 1966, The White Room 1968, The Beautiful Atlas 1969, Landscapes 1969, The Sinking Colony 1970, Penguin Modern Poets 19 (with John Ashbery and Tom Raworth) 1971, The First Poem 1971, New Year 1971, Captain Harwood's Log of Stern Statements and Stout Sayings 1973, Freighters 1975, HMS Little Fox 1975, Boston-Brighton 1977, Old Bosham Bird Watch and Other Stories 1977, Wish You Were Here (with A. Lopez) 1979, All the Wrong Notes 1981, Faded Ribbons 1982, Wine Tales (with Richard Caddel) 1984, Crossing the Frozen River: Selected Poems 1988, Monster Masks 1985, Dream Quilt (short stories) 1985, Rope Boy to the Rescue 1988, The Empty Hill: Memories and Praises of Paul Evans 1945–1991 (ed. with Peter Bailey) 1992, In the Mists: Mountain Poems 1993, Morning Light 1998, Evening Star 2004, Collected Poems 1964–2004 2004, Gifts Received 2007, Selected Poems 1965–2007 2008; trans of works by Tristan Tzara; contrib. to journals, reviews and magazines. *Honours:* Poetry Foundation Award, New York 1966, Alice Hunt Bartlett Prize, Poetry Soc., London 1976.

HARWOOD, Sir Ronald, Kt, CBE, FRSL; British author and playwright; b. (Ronald Horwitz), 9 Nov. 1934, Cape Town, South Africa; s. of the late Isaac Horwitz and Isobel Pepper; m. Natasha Riehle 1959; one s. two d. *Education:* Sea Point Boys' High School, Cape Town and Royal Acad. of Dramatic Art. *Career:* actor 1953–60; author 1960–; Artistic Dir Cheltenham Festival of Literature 1975; presenter, Kaleidoscope, BBC Radio 1973, Read All About It, BBC TV 1978–79, All The World's A Stage, BBC TV; Chair. Writers' Guild of GB 1969; Visitor in Theatre, Balliol Coll. Oxford 1986; Pres. PEN (England) 1989–93, Int. PEN 1993–97; Gov. Cen. School of Speech and Drama; author of numerous TV plays and screenplays; mem. Council Royal Soc. of Literature 1998–2001, chair. 2001–04; Trustee Booker Foundation 2002. *TV plays include:* The Barber of Stamford Hill 1960, Private Potter (with Casper Wrede) 1961, The Guests 1972, Breakthrough at Reykjavik 1987, Countdown to War 1989. *Screenplays include:* A High Wind in Jamaica 1965, One Day in the Life of Ivan Denisovich 1971, Evita Perón 1981, The Dresser 1983, Mandela 1987, The Browning Version 1994, Cry, Beloved Country 1995, Taking Sides 2002, The Pianist 2002 (Acad. Award for Best Adapted Screenplay 2003), The Statement 2003, Being Julia 2004, Oliver Twist 2005, Le Scaphandre et le Papillon (BAFTA Award for Best Adapted Screenplay 2008) 2007, Love in the Time of Cholera 2007. *Plays include:* Country Matters 1969, The Good Companions (musical libretto) 1974, The Ordeal of Gilbert Pinfold 1977, A Family 1978, The Dresser 1980, After the Lions 1982, Tramway Road 1984, The Deliberate Death of a Polish Priest 1985, Interpreters 1985, J. J. Farr 1987, Ivanov (from Chekhov) 1989, Another Time 1989, Reflected Glory 1992, Poison Pen 1994, Taking Sides 1995, The Handyman 1996, Equally Divided 1998, Quartet 1999, Mahler's Conversion 2002, An English Tragedy 2007. *Publications include:* fiction: All the Same Shadows 1961, The Guilt Merchants 1963, The Girl in Melanie Klein 1969, Articles of Faith 1973, The Genoa Ferry 1976, César and Augusta 1978, Home 1993; non-fiction: Sir Donald Wolfit, CBE: His Life and Work in the Unfashionable Theatre (biog.) 1971; editor: A Night at the Theatre 1983, The Ages of Gielfud 1984, Dear Alec: Guinness at Seventy-Five 1989, The Faber Book of the Theatre 1994; vols of essays and short stories. *Honours:* Chevalier des Arts et Lettres 1996; Hon. DLitt (Keele) 2002; New Standard Drama Award 1981, Drama Critics Award 1981, Molière Award for Best Play, Paris 1993. *Literary Agent:* Judy Daish Associates, 2 St Charles Place, London, W10 6EG, England. *Telephone:* (20) 8964-8811 (office).

HASAN, Anjum, MA; Indian writer and poet; *Communications Editor, India Foundation for the Arts;* b. 1972, Shillong, Meghalaya. *Education:* North-Eastern Hill Univ. *Career:* Communications Ed. and ed., ArtConnect magazine, India Foundation for the Arts, Bangalore; ed The Caravan. *Publications include:* Street on the Hill (poetry) (Sahitya Akademi) 2006, Lunatic in my Head (novel) 2007, Neti, Neti 2009; contrib. poems to anthologies, and criticism, essays and articles to journals and magazines including Hindu Literary Supplement, Outlook, Deccan Herald, Little Magazine. *Honours:* Indian Review of Books Award 1994, Outlook Picador Non-Fiction Contest Prize 2002. *Address:* India Foundation for the Arts, Apurva Ground Floor, 259 4th Cross, Raj Mahal Vilas, 2nd Stage 2nd Block, Bangalore 560 094, India (office). *Telephone:* (80) 23414681 (office). *Fax:* (80) 23412683 (office). *E-mail:* anjumhasan@indiaifa.org (office); jumhasan@yahoo.co.in (home). *Website:* www.indiaifa.org (office); www.anjumhasan.com.

HASHMI, (Aurangzeb) Alamgir, MA, DLit; Pakistani academic, poet, writer, editor and broadcaster; b. 15 Nov. 1951, Lahore. *Education:* Univ. of Louisville, Univ. of Punjab. *Career:* Instructor in English, Govt Coll., Lahore 1971–73; Lecturer, Forman Christian Coll., Lahore 1973–74; Davidson Int. Visiting Scholar, Univ. of North Carolina 1974–75; Lecturer in English, Univ. of Louisville 1975–78, Univ. of Zürich and Volkshochschule, Zürich 1980–85; Asst Prof. of English, Univ. of Bahawalpur, Pakistan 1979–80; Lecturer in English, Univ. of Basel, Univ. of Bern 1982; Prof. of English and Commonwealth Literature, Univ. of Geneva, Univ. of Fribourg 1985; Assoc. Prof. of English, Int. Islamic Univ., Islamabad 1985–86; Foundation Chair Prof. of English and Head, Dept of English, Univ. of Azad Jammu and Kashmir, Muzaffarabad 1986–87; Research Prof. of English, American, African and Comparative Literature, Quaid-i-Azam Univ., Islamabad 1986–2000; Prof. and Ed., PIDE, Islamabad 1988–2011; Course Dir, Foreign Service Acad., Islamabad 1988–; Prof. of English and Comparative Literature, Univ. of Iceland 2000; Founder and Chair. Standing Int. Cttee on English in S Asia; Founder and Chair. Townsend Poetry Prize Cttee 1986–; Judge, Commonwealth Writers Prize 1990, nat. literature prizes, Pakistan Acad. of Letters 1998–; jury mem., Neustadt Int. Prize for Literature; Ed., Advisory Ed., Editorial Adviser and referee for numerous int. scholarly and literary journals and book series; thesis supervisor and external examiner for many univs world-wide; broadcaster, scriptwriter, ed. Radio Pakistan and Pakistan TV 1968–; adviser, Nat. Book Council of Pakistan 1989–95, Nat. Book Foundation 1993–; Judge, Prime Minister's Award for Literature; Founding Pres. The Literature Podium; mem. Council Asscn for Commonwealth Studies, Bd of Govs Pakistan Acad. of Letters; mem. Poetry Soc., Associated Writing Programs, Asscn for Asian Studies, New York Acad. of Sciences, Council on Nat. Literatures, Asscn for Commonwealth Literature and Language Studies, Int. Asscn of Univ. Profs of English, Modern Language Asscn of America; Fellow, Int. Centre for Asian Studies, Int. PEN; Rockefeller Foundation Fellow; Life Fellow, Pakistan Acad. of Letters. *Publications:* poetry: The Oath and Amen: Love Poems 1976, America is a Punjabi Word 1979, An Old Chair 1979, My Second in Kentucky 1981, This Time in Lahore 1983, Neither This Time/Nor That Place 1984, Inland and Other Poems 1988, The Poems of Alamgir Hashmi 1992, Sun and Moon and Other Poems 1992, Others to Sport with Amaryllis in the Shade 1992, A Choice of Hashmi's Verse 1997, The Ramazan Libation: Selected Poems 2003; other: Pakistani Literature (two vols; ed., second edn as Pakistani Literature: The Contemporary English Writers) 1978, Ezra Pound 1983, Commonwealth Literature 1983, The Worlds of Muslim Imagination (ed.) 1986, The Commonwealth, Comparative Literature and the World 1988, Pakistani Short Stories in English (ed.) 1992, Postindependence Voices in South Asian Writings (co-ed.) 2001, Your Essence, Martyr (ed.) 2011; contrib. to many books, journals and periodicals. *Honours:* Hon. DLitt (Luxembourg, San Francisco); First Prize, All Pakistan Creative Writing Contest 1972, Patras Bokhari Award, Pakistan Acad. of Letters 1985, Roberto Celli Memorial Award 1994, inscribed in Academic Roll of Honour, Govt Coll., Lahore, Certificate of Merit, Univ. of the Punjab, Lahore, Pres. of Pakistan's Award for Pride of Performance (Medal for Literature); numerous other academic and literary distinctions, prizes and citations from different countries. *Address:* 1542 Service Road West, G-11/2, Islamabad, Pakistan (home). *E-mail:* alamgirhashmi@yahoo.co.uk (home).

HASLAM, Gerald William, MA, PhD; American writer and academic; *Professor Emeritus of English, Sonoma State University;* b. 18 March 1937, Bakersfield, Calif.; s. of Fredrick Martin Haslam and Lorraine Hope; m. Janice E. Pettichord 1961; three s. two d. *Education:* San Francisco State Coll., Washington State Univ., Union Grad. School. *Career:* Instructor in English, San Francisco State Coll. 1966–67; Prof. of English, Sonoma State Univ. 1967–97, Prof. Emer. 1997–; contributing writer, West (Los Angeles Times magazine) 2006–; Adjunct Prof., Fromm Inst., Univ. of San Francisco; Levan Distinguished Visiting Prof. in the Humanities, Bakersfield Coll. 2007; Pres. Western Literature Asscn 1984; mem. Bd of Dirs California Studies Asscn; Trustee, Yosemite Asscn. *Publications:* fiction: Okies: Selected Stories 1973, Masks: A Novel 1976, The Wages of Sin: Stories 1980, Hawk Flights: Visions of the West: Short Stories 1983, Snapshots: Glimpses of the Other California: Selected Stories 1985, The Man Who Cultivated Fire and Other Stories 1987, That Constant Coyote: California Stories 1990, Condor Dreams and Other Fictions 1994, The Great Tejon Club Jubilee: Stories 1995, Manuel and the Madman (with Janice E. Haslam) 2000, Straight White Male 2000; other: Forgotten Pages of American Literature (ed.) 1970, The Language of the Oilfields: Examination of an Industrial Argot 1972, Western Writings (ed.) 1974, Afro-American Oral Literature (ed.) 1974, California Heartland: Writing from the Great Central Valley (co-ed. with James D. Houston) 1978, Voices of a Place: The Great Central Valley 1986, A Literary History of the American West (co-ed. with J. Golden Taylor) 1987, Baiting the Hook 1990, Coming of Age in California: Personal Essays 1990, The Other California: The Great Central Valley in Life and Letters 1990, Many Californias: Literature from the Golden State (ed.) 1992, Out of the Slush Pile (with Stephen Glasser) 1993, The Horned Toad 1995, Where Coyotes Howl and Wind Blows Free: Growing Up in the West (co-ed. with Alexandra Russell) 1995, Workin' Man Blues: Country Music in California (with Alexandra Russell and Richard Chon) 1999, Straight White Male 2000, Haslam's Valley 2005, Grace Period 2006. *Honours:* Fulbright Sr Fellow, Spain 1986, California Arts Council Fellowship 1989, Josephine Miles Award, PEN 1990, 2006, Bay Area Book Reviewers' Award 1993, Benjamin Franklin Award, Publishers' Marketing Asscn 1993, Commonwealth Club Medal 1994, Award of Merit, Asscn for State and Local Historians 1994, Laureate, San Francisco Public Library 1998, Distinguished Achievement Award, Western Literature Asscn 1999, Ralph J. Gleason Award 2000, Western States Book Award for Fiction 2000, Carey

McWilliams Award 2001, Certificate for Citation, Asscn for State and Local History 2001, Sequoia: Giant of the Valley Award 2003, Delbert and Edith Wylder Award 2005, Certificate of Commendation Calif. Arts Council, Josephine Miles Award 2006. *Address:* PO Box 969, Penngrove, CA 94951, USA (home). *Telephone:* (707) 792-2944 (office). *Fax:* (707) 792-2944 (office). *E-mail:* ghaslam@sonic.net (office). *Website:* www.geraldhaslam.com.

HASLUCK, Nicholas Paul, AM; Australian writer and poet; b. 17 Oct. 1942, Canberra, ACT. *Education:* Univ. of Western Australia, Univ. of Oxford. *Career:* barrister, solicitor, Supreme Court of Western Australia 1968; Deputy Chair., Australia Council 1978–82; Chair., Literature Board 1998–2001; Chair., Commonwealth Writers Prize 2006–. *Publications:* fiction: Quarantine 1978, The Blue Guitar 1980, The Hand that Feeds You: A Satiric Nightmare 1982, The Bellarmine Jug 1984, The Country without Music 1990, The Blosseville File 1992, Offcuts From a Legal Literary Life 1993, A Grain of Truth 1994, Our Man K 1999, The Legal Labyrinth 2003, Somewhere in the Atlas 2005, Dismissal 2011; short stories: The Hat on the Letter O and Other Stories 1978; poetry: Anchor and Other Poems 1976, On the Edge 1980, Chinese Journey 1985, A Dream Divided 2005. *Honours:* Hon. DLitt (UWA) 2009; Age Book of the Year Award 1984, WA Premier's Prize 1990. *Address:* 14 Reserve Street, Claremont, WA 6010, Australia (home).

HASS, Robert Louis, BA, MA, PhD; American poet, writer, translator, editor and academic; *Professor of English, University of California, Berkeley*; b. 1 March 1941, San Francisco; m. Earlene Joan Leif 1962 (divorced 1986); two s. one d. *Education:* St Mary's Coll. of California, Stanford Univ. *Career:* Asst Prof., SUNY at Buffalo 1967–71; Prof. of English, St Mary's Coll. of California 1971–89, Univ. of California, Berkeley 1989–; Visiting Lecturer, Univ. of Virginia 1974, Goddard Coll. 1976, Columbia Univ. 1982, Univ. of California, Berkeley 1983; poet-in-residence, The Frost Place, Franconia, NH 1978; Poet Laureate of the USA 1995–97. *Publications:* poetry: Field Guide 1973, Winter Morning in Charlottesville 1977, Praise 1979, The Apple Tree at Olema 1989, Human Wishes 1989, Sun under Wood 1996, Time and Materials: Poems, 1997–2005 (Nat. Book Award for Fiction 2007, Pulitzer Prize for Poetry 2008) 2007, The Apple Trees at Olema: New and Selected Poems 2010; other: Twentieth Century Pleasures: Prose on Poetry 1984, Into the Garden – A Wedding Anthology: Poetry and Prose on Love and Marriage 1993; translations: Czesław Miłosz's The Separate Notebooks (with Robert Pinsky) 1983, Czesław Miłosz's Unattainable Earth (with Czesław Miłosz) 1986, Czesław Miłosz's Collected Poems 1931–1987 (with Louis Iribane and Peter Scott) 1988; editor: Rock and Hawk: A Selection of Shorter Poems by Robinson Jeffers 1987, The Pushcart Prize Xll (with Bill Henderson and Jorie Graham) 1987, Tomaz Salamun: Selected Poems (with Charles Simic) 1988, Selected Poems of Tomas Tranströmer, 1954–1986 (with others) 1989, The Essential Haiku: Versions of Basho, Buson and Issa 1994; contribs: anthologies and other publications. *Honours:* Woodrow Wilson Fellowship 1963–64, Danforth Fellowship 1963–67, Yale Series of Younger Poets Award, Yale University Press 1972, US-Great Britain Bicentennial Exchange Fellow in the Arts 1976–77, William Carlos Williams Award 1979, National Book Critics Circle Award 1984, Award of Merit, American Acad. of Arts and Letters 1984, John D. and Catherine T. MacArthur Foundation Grant 1984. *Literary Agent:* Steven Barclay Agency, 12 Western Avenue, Petaluma, CA 94952, USA. *Telephone:* (707) 773-0654. *Fax:* (707) 778-1868. *Website:* www.barclayagency .com. *Address:* PO Box 807, Inverness, CA 94937, USA (office). *E-mail:* bobhass@berkeley.edu (office).

HASSNER, Pierre; French writer and academic; b. 31 Jan. 1933, Bucharest, Romania. *Education:* École Normale Supérieure. *Career:* fmr Lecturer in International Relations and History of Political Thought, Institut d'Études Politiques, Paris; Emer. Research Dir Centre for International Studies and Research (CERI), Paris, Nat. Foundation of Political Science. *Publications:* La violence et la paix (trans. as Violence and Peace: From the Atomic Bomb to Ethnic Cleansing) 1995, La terreur et l'empire: La violence et la paix II 2003, Washington et le monde: Dilemmes d'une superpuissance (with Justin Vaisse) 2003, Guerre et Sociétés: Etats et violence aprés la guerre froide (ed with Roland Marchal) 2003, Justifier la guerre? De l'humanitaire au contre-terrorisme 2005; contrib. of articles to Revue de Synthèse, Critique Internationale, Commentaire, The Natinoal Interst, Cahiers de Chaillot, Esprit, Europe Unbound, Le Débat, Politique Internationale. *Honours:* Prix Tocqueville 2003. *Address:* c/o Center for International Studies and Research, 56 rue Jacob, 75006 Paris, France.

HASTINGS, Graham (see Jeffries, Roderic Graeme)

HASTINGS, March (see Levinson, Leonard)

HASTINGS, Sir Max Macdonald, Kt, FRSL, FRHistS; British writer and broadcaster; b. 28 Dec. 1945, London; s. of Macdonald Hastings and Anne Scott-James (Lady Lancaster); m. 1st Patricia Edmondson 1972 (divorced 1994); one s. (and one s. deceased) one d.; m. 2nd Penelope Grade 1999. *Education:* Charterhouse and Univ. Coll., Oxford. *Career:* reporter, London Evening Standard 1965–67, 1968–70; Fellow, US World Press Inst. 1967–68; reporter, current affairs, BBC Television 1970–73; freelance journalist, broadcaster and author 1973–; columnist, Evening Standard 1979–85, Daily Express 1981–83, Sunday Times 1985–86; Ed. Daily Telegraph 1986–95, Dir 1989–95, Ed.-in-Chief 1990–95; Ed. Evening Standard 1996–2002; Dir Evening Standard Ltd 1996–2002; columnist Daily Mail 2002–, Guardian 2004–; book reviewer Sunday Times 2006–; contributing Ed. Financial Times 2009–; mem. Press Complaints Comm. 1990–92; Trustee Liddell Hart Archive, King's Coll. London 1988–2004, Nat. Portrait Gallery 1995–2004; Pres. Council for the Protection of Rural England 2002–07. *Television:* documentaries: Ping-Pong in Peking 1971, The War About Peace 1983, Alarums and Excursions 1984, Cold Comfort Farm 1985, The War in Korea (series) 1988, We Are All Green Now 1990, Spies (in series Cold War) 1998, Churchill and His Generals (series) 2003, The Falklands Legacy 2012. *Publications:* America 1968: The Fire, The Time 1968, Ulster 1969, The Struggle for Civil Rights in Northern Ireland 1970, Montrose: The King's Champion 1977, Yoni: Hero of Entebbe 1979, Bomber Command 1979, The Battle of Britain (with Lee Deighton) 1980, Das Reich 1981, Battle for the Falklands (with Simon Jenkins) 1983, Overlord: D-Day and the Battle for Normandy 1984, Victory in Europe 1985, The Oxford Book of Military Anecdotes (ed.) 1985, The Korean War 1987, Outside Days 1989, Scattered Shots 1999, Going to the Wars 2000, Editor (memoir) 2002, Armageddon: The Battle for Germany 1944–45 2004, Warriors: Extraordinary Tales from the Battlefields 2005, Country Fair 2005, Nemesis: The Battle for Japan 1944–45 2007, Finest Years: Churchill as Warlord, 1940–45 2009, Did You Really Shoot the Television? A Family Fable 2010, All Hell Let Loose 2011. *Honours:* Hon. Fellow, King's Coll. London 2004; Hon. DLitt (Leicester) 1992, (Nottingham) 2005; Journalist of the Year 1982, Reporter of the Year 1982, Somerset Maugham Prize for Non-fiction 1979, Ed. of the Year 1988. *Literary Agent:* c/o PFD, Drury House, 34–43 Russell Street, London, WC2B 5HA, England. *Telephone:* (20) 7344-1000. *Fax:* (20) 7836-9539. *E-mail:* info@pfd.co.uk. *Website:* www.pfd.co.uk.

HASTINGS, Lady Selina, MA; British writer; b. 5 March 1945, Oxford, England; d. of 16th Earl of Huntingdon and Margaret Lane. *Education:* St Hugh's Coll., Oxford. *Career:* books page, Daily Telegraph 1968–82; Literary Ed., Harper's & Queen 1986–94. *Publications:* biographies: Nancy Mitford 1985, Evelyn Waugh 1994, Rosamond Lehmann: A Life 2002, The Secret Lives of Somerset Maugham 2009; children's books; contrib. to newspapers and periodicals. *Honours:* Marsh Biography Award 1993–96. *Literary Agent:* c/o Rogers, Coleridge & White Literary Agency, 20 Powis Mews, London, W11 1JN, England. *Telephone:* (20) 7221-3717. *Fax:* (20) 7229-9084. *E-mail:* info@ rcwlitagency.co.uk. *Website:* www.rcwlitagency.co.uk.

HASWELL, Chetwynd John Drake, (George Foster, Jock Haswell); British fmr soldier and writer; b. 18 July 1919, Penn, Bucks., England; m. Charlotte Annette Petter 1947; two s. one d. *Education:* Winchester Coll., Royal Mil. Coll., Sandhurst. *Career:* soldier 1939–60; author Service Intelligence, Intelligence Centre, Ashford 1966–84; Regimental Historian for the Queen's Regiment. *Publications:* as George Foster: Indian File 1960, Soldier on Loan 1961; as Jock Haswell: The Queen's Royal Regiment 1967, The First Respectable Spy 1969, James II, Soldier and Sailor 1972, British Military Intelligence 1973, Citizen Armies 1973, The British Army 1975, The Ardent Queen, Margaret of Anjou 1976, The Battle for Empire 1976, Spies and Spymasters 1977, The Intelligence and Deception of the D-Day Landings 1979, The Tangled Web 1985, The Queen's Regiment 1986, Spies and Spying 1986. *Address:* The Grey House, Lyminge, Folkestone, CT18 8ED, England (home). *Telephone:* (1303) 862232 (home).

HATCHER, Robin Lee; American novelist; b. 10 May 1951, Payette, Idaho; m. Jerrold W. Neu 1989; two d. *Career:* mem. Romance Writers of America, Pres. 1992–94; The Authors' Guild. *Publications:* Stormy Surrender 1984, Heart's Landing 1984, Thorn of Love 1985, Passion's Gamble 1986, Heart Storm 1986, Pirate's Lady 1987, Gemfire 1988, The Wager 1989, Dream Tide 1990, Promised Sunrise 1990, Promise Me Spring 1991, Rugged Splendor 1991, The Hawk and the Heather 1992, Devlin's Promise 1992, Midnight Rose 1992, A Frontier Christmas 1992, The Magic 1993, Where the Heart Is 1993, Forever, Rose 1994, Remember When 1994, Liberty Blue 1995, Chances Are 1996, Kiss me Katie 1996, Dear Lady 1997, Patterns of Love 1998, In His Arms 1998, The Forgiving Hour 1999, Hometown Girl, Taking Care of the Twins, Whispers from Yesterday, Daddy Claus 1999, The Shepherd's Voice (Excellence in Media Silver Angel Award, Inspirational Readers Choice Award, Booksellers' Best Award 2000) 2000, The Story Jar 2001, Ribbon of Years 2001, Firstborn 2002, Promised to Me (Golden Quill Award, Booksellers Best Award 2004) 2003, Speak to Me of Love (Inspirational Readers Choice Award 2004) 2003, Catching Katie (Carol Award, Write Touch Readers Award 2005) 2004, Beyond the Shadows 2004, Veterans Way 2005, The Victory Club (Award of Excellence 2006) 2005, Another Chance to Love You 2006, Diamond Place 2006, Sweet Dreams Drive 2007, Return to Me 2007, Trouble in Paradise 2007, Home to Hart's Crossing 2008, Wagered Heart (Holt Medallion Award 2009) 2008, The Perfect Life 2008, Bundle of Joy 2008, When Love Blooms (Inspirational Readers Choice Award 2010) 2009, A Vote of Confidence 2009, A Matter of Character (Inspirational Readers' Choice Award) 2010, Belonging 2011, A Home for Christmas 2011, Heart of Gold 2012; contribs to various publications. *Honours:* Idaho Writer of the Year Award 1984, Emma Merritt Award 1998, Heart of Romance Readers Choice Award 1996, RITA Award 1999, Christy Award for Excellence in Christian Fiction, 2000, Romance Writers of America Lifetime Achievement Award 2001, Writer of the Year, Idahope Christian Fiction Writers 2011. *Address:* RobinSong Inc., PO Box 1455, Meridian, ID 83680, USA. *E-mail:* rlhreadermail@gmail.com. *Website:* www.robinleehatcher.com.

HATOUM, Milton, MA; Brazilian academic, poet, writer and translator; b. 19 Aug. 1952, Manaus. *Education:* State Univ. of São Paulo, Sorbonne, Univ. of Paris, France. *Career:* Prof. of French Literature, Univ. of Amazonas Manaus 1983–99; apptd Visiting Prof. of Latin American Literature, Univ. of

California, Berkeley, USA 1996; Writer-in-Residence Yale Univ., New Haven, USA, Stanford Univ., USA, Univ. of California, Berkeley, USA. *Publications:* Um rio entre ruinas (poems) 1978, Relato de um Certo Oriente (novel) 1989, Dois Irmãos (novel) 2000, Cinzas do Norte 2005, Orfãos do Eldorado 2008; short stories: A cidade ilhada, Você tem medo do quê?, Varandas da Eva, Torn; contribs to periodicals. *Honours:* Multicultural Award 2001, Order of Cultural Merit 2008, APCA Award, Portugal Telecom Award, Impac-Dublin Prize, Tortoise Award, Portugal Telecom Award; Jabuti Prize 1990, 2001. *Address:* Ballantine Books, Rua Bandeira, Paulista 702, cj.32, 04532-002 São Paulo, Brazil. *Telephone:* (11) 3707-3500. *E-mail:* secretaria@companhiadasletras.com.br. *Website:* www.miltonhatoum.com.br.

HATTENDORF, John Brewster, AB, AM, DPhil, FRHistS; American academic and writer; *Ernest J. King Professor of Maritime History, U.S Naval War College;* b. 22 Dec. 1941, Hinsdale, Illinois; m. Berit Sundell 1978; three d. *Education:* Kenyon Coll., Brown Univ., Univ. of Oxford, London, England. *Career:* serving Officer, US Navy 1964–73; Prof. of Mil. History, Nat. Univ. of Singapore 1981–83; Ernest J. King Prof. of Maritime History, US Naval War Coll. 1984–, Chair. Maritime History Dept and Dir Naval War Coll. Museum 2003–; Sec. Navy Advisory Sub-Cttee for Naval History 2003–08, Vice-Chair. 2005, Chair. 2006–08; mem. Navy Records Soc., Hakluyt Soc., Academie du Var, Royal Swedish Acad. of Naval Science, Soc. for Nautical Research, Massachusetts Historical Soc. *Publications:* The Writings of Stephen B. Luce 1975, On His Majesty's Service 1983, Sailors and Scholars 1984, A Bibliography of the Works of A. T. Mahan 1986, England in the War of the Spanish Succession 1987, Maritime Strategy and the Balance of Power 1989, The Limitations of Military Power 1990, Mahan on Naval Strategy 1990, Mahan is Not Enough 1993, British Naval Documents (co-ed.) 1993, Ubi Sumnus: The State of Maritime and Naval History 1994, Doing Naval History 1995, Sea of Words (with Dean King) 1995, Maritime History: The Age of Discovery 1996, Maritime History: The Eighteenth Century 1996, Naval History and Maritime Strategy: Collected Essays 2000, The Evolution of the US Navy's Maritime Strategy 1977–1986 2004, Newport, the French Navy, and American Independence 2004, Oxford Encyclopedia of Maritime History (ed.-in-chief) (Dartmouth Medal, American Library Asscn 2008) 2007, Nineteen-Gun Salute: Case Studies of Operational, Strategic, and Diplomatic Naval Leadership during the 20th and Early 21st Centuries (co-ed with Bruce A. Elleman) 2010, Talking About Naval History: A Collection of Essays 2011; contribs to Naval War College Review, International History Review. *Honours:* Dr hc (Kenyon Coll.) 1997; Caird Medal, Nat. Maritime Museum 2000, K. Jack Bauer Award, North American Soc. for Oceanic History 2003, Navy Superior Civilian Service Award 2009, Samuel Eliot Morison Award, USS Constitution Museum, Alfred Thayer Mahan Award for Literary Achievement. *Address:* Maritime History Department, U.S Naval War College, 686 Cushing Road, Newport, RI 02841-1207, USA (office). *Telephone:* (401) 841-1310 (office). *E-mail:* john.hattendorf@usnwc.edu (office). *Website:* www.usnwc.edu (office).

HATTERSLEY, Baron (Life Peer), cr. 1997, of Sparkbrook in the County of West Midlands; **Roy Sydney George Hattersley,** PC, BSc (Econ.), FRSL; British politician, writer and broadcaster; b. 28 Dec. 1932, s. of the late Frederick Roy Hattersley and Enid Hattersley (née Brackenbury); m. Molly Loughran 1956. *Education:* Sheffield City Grammar School, Univ. of Hull. *Career:* journalist and health service exec. 1956–64; mem. Sheffield City Council 1957–65; MP for Sparkbrook Div. of Birmingham 1964–97; Parl. Pvt. Sec. to Minister of Pensions and Nat. Insurance 1964–67; Dir Campaign for European Political Community 1965; Jt Parl. Sec. Dept of Employment and Productivity 1967–69; Minister of Defence for Admin 1969–70; Opposition Spokesman for Defence 1970–72, for Educ. 1972–74, for the Environment 1979–80, for Home Affairs 1980–83, on Treasury and Econ. Affairs 1983–87, on Home Affairs 1987–92; Minister of State for Foreign and Commonwealth Affairs 1974–76; Sec. of State for Prices and Consumer Protection 1976–79; Deputy Leader of the Labour Party 1983–92; Pres. Local Govt Group for Europe 1998–; Public Affairs Consultant, IBM 1971, 1972; columnist, Punch, The Guardian, The Listener 1979–82; Visiting Fellow, Inst. of Politics, Harvard Univ. 1971, 1972, Nuffield Coll., Oxford 1984–; Labour. *Publications:* Nelson – A Biography 1974, Goodbye to Yorkshire – A Collection of Essays 1976, Politics Apart – A Collection of Essays 1982, Press Gang 1983, A Yorkshire Boyhood 1983, Choose Freedom: The Future for Democratic Socialism 1987, Economic Priorities for a Labour Government 1987, The Maker's Mark (novel) 1990, In That Quiet Earth (novel) 1991, Skylark's Song (novel) 1994, Between Ourselves (novel) 1994, Who Goes Home? 1995, Fifty Years On 1997, Buster's Diaries: As Told to Roy Hattersley 1998, Blood and Fire: The Story of William and Catherine Booth and their Salvation Army 1999, A Brand from the Burning: The Life of John Wesley 2002, The Edwardians 2004, Borrowed Time: The Story of Britain Between the Wars 2007, David Lloyd George: The Great Outsider 2010; contrib. to newspapers and journals. *Honours:* Hon. LLD (Hull) 1985; Dr hc (Aston) 1997. *Address:* House of Lords, Westminster, London, SW1A 0PW, England (office). *Telephone:* (20) 7219-3000 (office). *E-mail:* roy@royhattersley.com (office).

HATZFELD, Jean; French journalist and writer; b. 1949, Madagascar. *Career:* journalist, Libération newspaper 1977–2006; foreign corresp. specializing in war-affected countries; early postings included Czechoslovakia (covering the Velvet Revolution), Romania (fall of the Ceausescu regime); for 25 years worked in Middle East, especially Lebanon, Israel and Iraq; three years in countries of fmr Yugoslavia; also worked in Haiti, Congo, Algeria, Burundi, Iran; regular reports from Rwanda 1994–. *Publications:* non-fiction: L'Air de la guerre (Prix Novembre) 1994, Dans le nu de la vie (Prix Culture, Prix Pierre Mille, Prix France Culture) 2000, Une Saison de machetes (Prix Femina Essai 2003, Prix Jossef Kessel 2004) 2002, La stratégie des antilopes (Prix Medici) 2007; fiction: La guerre au bord du fleuve 1999, La ligne de flottaison 2005, La Stratégie des antilopes (Prix Médicis, Prix Ryszard Kapuściński 2010) 2007, Où en est la nuit (Grand Prix de littérature sportive) 2011. *Address:* c/o Editions du Seuil, 27 rue Jacob, 75006 Paris, France.

HAUG, Frigga, DPhil; German sociologist, publisher and teacher; b. (Frigga Langenberger), 28 Nov. 1937, Mülheim/Ruhr; d. of Heinz and Melanie Langenberger; m. 1st Mr Laudan 1959 (divorced 1965); one d.; m. 2nd Wolfgang Fritz Haug 1965. *Education:* Mädchengymnasium Mülheim/Ruhr and Free Univ. of Berlin. *Career:* nurse; social worker 1957–58; interviewer; interpreter; Ed. and Publr Das Argument (social sciences journal) 1968–; Lecturer Univs of Copenhagen, Berlin, Marburg (Germany) 1971–85; Distinguished Prof. Univs of Sydney, Australia 1985, Innsbruck, Austria 1988, Klagenfurt 1992, Ontario Inst. for Studies in Educ., Toronto 1992, Duke Univ., Durham, NC 1997; Prof. Hamburger Universität für Wirtschaft und Politik 1978–2001; Ed. Ariadne women's crime series 1988–1997; research into women's studies and labour; Pres., Berlin Inst. for Critical Theory; mem. women's editorial bd 1981–; co-Ed. Historical Critical Dictionary of Marxism; mem. Verdi (trade union), Linkspartei. *Publications include:* Kritik der Rollentheorie 1974, Gesellschaftliche Produktion und Erziehung 1977, Development of Work 1978, Education for Femininity 1980, Subjekt Frau 1985, Contradictions in Automated Labour 1987, Sexualisierung des Körpers 1988, (English 1987, 2000), Kitchen and State 1988, Erinnerungsarbeit 1990, Die andere Angst 1991, Beyond Female Masochism 1992, Hat die Leistung ein Geschlecht? 1993, Sündiger Genuß?, Filmerfahrungen von Frauen 1995, Frauen-Politiken 1996, Lustmolche und Köderfrauen 1997, Vorlesungen zur Einführung in die Erinnerungsarbeit 1999 (English 2002), Lernverhältnisse. Selbstbewegungen und Selbstblockierungen 2003, Rosa Luxemburg und die Kunst der Politik 2007, Die Vier-in-Einem-Perspektive, Eine Utopie von Frauen, die eine Utopie für alle ist 2008; approx. 150 articles in ten languages. *Address:* c/o Argument-Verlag, Eppendorfer Weg 95, 20259 Hamburg (office); Wittumhalde 5, 73732 Esslingen/N, Germany (home); Espigon del Mar 10, Las Indias, Fuencaliente, La Palma, Islas Canarias, Spain (home). *Telephone:* (711) 882-48-59 (home). *Fax:* (711) 88-48-63 (home). *E-mail:* FriggaHaug@aol.com (home). *Website:* www.friggahaug.inkrit.de (home).

HAUGEN, Paal-Helge; Norwegian poet, writer and dramatist; b. 26 April 1945, Valle. *Education:* Univ. of Oslo, studies in USA and France. *Career:* freelance writer; Chair. Norwegian State Film Production Board 1980–85, Bd of Literary Advisers, Asscn of Norwegian Authors 1984–88; Advisor, Norwegian Council of Culture 1992–2000. *Recording:* Pilegrimen 1995. *Television:* Som natt og dag (drama) 1972. *Publications include:* Anne (novel) 1968, Stone Fences 1986, Meditasjonar over Georges de la Tour (poems) 1990, Sone O (poems) 1992, Wintering with the Light 1995, Poesi: Collected Poems 1965–1995 1995, Kvartett (four separate vols of poetry) 2008; other: plays for stage, radio and TV, six opera libretti, including The Maid of Norway 2000, A. – a shadow opera 2001 (CD 2003), The Green Knight 2004; contribs to professional journals. *Honours:* Kt, First Class, Royal Norwegian Order of St Olav 2009; Dobloug Prize 1986, Richard Wilbur Prize, USA 1986, Norwegian Literary Critics Prize 1990, Norwegian National Brage Prize 1992, Grieg Prize for texts set to music 2001, Aschehoug Prize for Lifetime Achievement 2008, Gyldendal Prize 2009. *Literary Agent:* c/o CappelenDamm, PO Box 350, 0101 Oslo, Norway. *E-mail:* kirsten.lier@cappelendamm.no. *Website:* www.cappelendamm.no. *Address:* Skrefjellv 5, 4645 Nodeland, Norway. *E-mail:* phaugen@online.no.

HAUPTMAN, William Thornton, BFA, MFA; American dramatist and writer; b. 26 Nov. 1942, Wichita Falls, Texas; m. 1st Barbara Barbat 1968 (divorced 1977); one d.; m. 2nd Marjorie Endreich 1985; one s. *Education:* Univ. of Texas at Austin, Yale Univ. School of Drama. *Television:* A House Divided (series) 1981. *Publications:* Heat 1977, Domino Courts/Comanche Cafe 1977, Big River (with Roger Miller) 1986, Good Rockin' Tonight and Other Stories 1988, Gillette 1989, The Storm Season 1992, Charles Gleyre 1806–1874 1997, Ingres 2006, Hodler 2007, The Durango Flash. *Honours:* Boston Theatre Critics Circle Award 1984, Tony Award 1985, Drama-Lounge Award 1986, Jesse Jones Award, Texas Inst. of Letters 1989.

HAVIARAS, Stratis, MFA; Greek writer and fmr librarian; b. 28 June 1935, Nea Kios, Argos; s. of Christos Haviaras and Georgia Hadzikyriakos; m. 1st Gail Flynn 1967 (divorced 1973); m. 2nd Heather Cole 1990; one d. *Education:* Goddard Coll. *Career:* fmr construction worker; lived in USA 1959–61; went to USA following colonels' coup in Greece 1967, obtaining position at Harvard Univ. Library; Curator, Poetry Room, Harvard Univ. Library 1974–2000; Founder and Ed. Harvard Review 1992–2000, Founding Ed. Emer. 2000–; Faculty mem., Harvard Univ. Summer School; Admin. and Instructor, writing and translation workshops, Athens; Instructor, Aegean Arts Circle Workshop 2008–09; Teacher and Co-ordinator Nat. Book Centre; mem. PEN (New England), Signet, Soc. Imaginaire, Hellenic Authors' Soc., American Authors League, Modern Greek Studies Asscn, Greek Authors Soc. *Publications:* four vols of Greek poetry 1963, 1965, 1967, 1972, Crossing the River Twice (poems in English) 1976, Millennial Afterlives 2000; fiction: When the Tree Sings 1979, The Heroic Age 1984; other: The Canon by C. P. Cavafy (trans.) 2004, Seamus Heaney: a Celebration (ed.) 1996; contrib. to newspapers and magazines. *Honours:* Nat. Book Critics' Circle Awards. *Address:* 19 Clinton

Street, Cambridge, MA 02139, USA; 136 Em. Benaki Street, 11473 Athens, Greece. *Telephone:* (617) 354-4724.

HAWASS, Zahi, PhD; Egyptian archaeologist and Egyptologist; b. 28 May 1947, Damietta. *Education:* Alexandria Univ., Cairo Univ., Univ. of Pennsylvania, USA. *Career:* Inspector of Antiquities of Middle Egypt, Tuna El-Gebel and Mallawi 1969, Italian Expedition, Sikh Abada, Minia 1969, Edfu-Esna, Egypt 1969, Pennsylvania Yale Expedition at Abydos 1969, Western Delta at Alexandria 1970, Embaba, Giza 1972–74, Abu Simbel 1973–74, Pennsylvania Expedition, Malkata, Luxor 1974, Giza Pyramids (for Boston Museum of Fine Arts) 1974–75; First Inspector of Antiquities, Embaba and Bahariya Oasis 1974–79, Chief Inspector 1980, Gen. Dir 1987–98; Gen. Dir Saqqara and Bahariya Oasis 1987–98; apptd Archaeological Site Man. Memphis 1991; Under-Sec. of State for Giza Monuments 1998–2002; apptd Sec.-Gen. of the Supreme Council of Antiquities 2002; Goodwill Amb. to Japan 2008; Minister of State for Antiquities Affairs Jan.–July 2011; Dir of numerous excavations, conservation projects and discoveries including tombs of the pyramid builders at Giza and the Valley of the Golden Mummies in Bahariya; numerous consultancy roles; mem. Bd Egyptian Nat. Museum 1996–; Trustee, Egyptian Nat. Museum; Sound and Light Co. 1990; mem. German Archaeological Inst. 1991–, Russian Acad. of Natural Sciences 2001–, Austrian Archaeological Inst.; Explorer-in-Residence Nat. Geographic 2001; mem. of numerous cttees. *Television:* numerous appearances in documentaries and features on Egypt including BBC, CNN, Discovery Channel, History Channel, National Geographic, The Learning Channel. *Publications:* Valley of the Golden Mummies 2000, Silent Images: Women in Pharaonic Egypt 2000, Secrets from the Sand 2003, Hidden Treasures of Ancient Egypt 2004, The Curse of the Pharaohs (children's book), Tutankhamun and the Golden Age of the Pharaohs 2005, Mountains of the Pharaohs 2006, The Great Book of Ancient Egypt: In the Realm of the Pharaohs 2006, The Royal Tombs of Egypt 2006, The Archeaeology and Art of Ancient Egypt: Essays in Honor of David B. O'Connor 2007, Pyramids: Treasures, Mysteries, and New Discoveries in Egypt 2007, Treasures of Ancient Egypt 2007, King Tutankhamun: The Treasures of the Tomb 2007, Tutankhamun: The Golden King and the Great Pharaohs 2008, Royal Mummies: Immortality in Ancient Egypt 2008, Wonders of the Horus Temple: The Sound and Light of Edfu 2011; numerous papers on Egyptology and archaeology. *Honours:* Officier, Ordre des Arts et des Lettres 2007, Commdr, Order of Merit (Italy) 2008, Grand Decoration of Honour in Silver with Star (Austria), Order of the Sun (Peru); Hon. PhD (American Univ., Cairo) 2005, Dr hc (Catholic Univ. of Santo Domingo, Dominican Republic) 2009, (Bansomdejchaopraya Rajabhat Univ., Thailand) 2009, (Univ. of Veliko Tarnovo, Bulgaria) 2010, (New Univ. of Lisbon) 2011; Grantee Mellon Fellowship, Univ. of Pennsylvania, Presidential Medal 1988, Golden Plate Award, American Acad. of Achievement 2000, Distinguished Scholar of the Year Asscn of Egyptian-American Scholars 2000, Silver Medal Russian Acad. of Natural Sciences 2001, Achievement Award Mansoura Univ. 2002, named one of Five Distinguished Egyptians Egyptological Soc. of Spain 2002, Paestum Archaeology Award 2006, named amongst Top 100 Most Influential People of the Year by Time magazine 2005, Emmy Award Nat. Acad. of Television Arts and Sciences 2006, World Tourism Award 2008, Medal of the Spanish Order of Arts and Culture 2009, Personality of the Year Award 2010, Cape Breton Univ./Canadian International Coll. Special Award 2010. *Address:* 42 Aden Street, Mohandiseen, Cairo, Egypt (home). *E-mail:* pyramiza2004@yahoo.com. *Website:* www.drhawass.com.

HAWKING, Stephen William, CH, CBE, BA, PhD, FRS; British theoretical physicist, applied mathematician, academic and author; *Director of Research, Department of Applied Mathematics and Theoretical Physics, University of Cambridge*; b. 8 Jan. 1942, Oxford; s. of Dr F. Hawking and Mrs E. I. Hawking; m. 1st Jane Wilde 1965 (divorced); two s. one d.; m. 2nd Elaine Mason 1995 (divorced 2007). *Education:* St Albans School, Univ. Coll., Oxford, Trinity Hall, Cambridge. *Career:* Research Fellow, Gonville and Caius Coll., Cambridge 1965–69, Fellow for Distinction in Science 1969–; Research Asst, Inst. of Astronomy, Cambridge 1972–73; Research Asst, Dept of Applied Math. and Theoretical Physics, Univ. of Cambridge 1973–75, Reader in Gravitational Physics 1975–77, Prof. 1977–79, Lucasian Prof. of Applied Math. 1979–2009, Dir of Research 2009–; Distinguished Research Chair, Perimeter Inst. for Theoretical Physics, Waterloo, Ont., Canada 2009–; mem. Inst. of Theoretical Astronomy, Cambridge 1968–72; mem. Papal Acad. of Science 1986; Foreign mem. American Acad. Arts and Sciences 1984. *Publications:* The Large Scale Structure of Spacetime (with G. F. R. Ellis) 1973, General Relativity: An Einstein Centenary Survey (co-ed. with W. Israel) 1979, Is the End in Sight for Theoretical Physics?: An Inaugural Lecture 1980, Superspace and Supergravity: Proceedings of the Nuffield Workshop (co-ed. with M. Rocek) 1981, The Very Early Universe: Proceedings of the Nuffield Workshop (co-ed.) 1983, 300 Years of Gravitation (with W. Israel) 1987, A Brief History of Time: From the Big Bang to Black Holes 1988, Hawking on the Big Bang and Black Holes 1992, Black Holes and Baby Universes and Other Essays 1993, The Cambridge Lectures: Life Works 1995, The Nature of Space and Time (with Roger Penrose) 1996, The Universe in a Nutshell (Aventis Prize 2002) 2001, The Theory of Everything: The Origin and Fate of the Universe 2002, The Future of Spacetime (co-ed.) 2002, On the Shoulders of Giants 2002, A Briefer History of Time (with Leonard Mlodinow) 2005, George's Secret Key to the Universe (children's fiction; with Lucy Hawking) 2007, The Grand Design (with Leonard Mlodinow) 2010; also individual lectures, contrib. to scholarly books and journals. *Honours:* Hon. Fellow, Univ. Coll., Oxford 1977, Trinity Hall, Cambridge 1984; Hon. FRSA; several hon. degrees; Eddington Medal 1975, Pontifical Acad. of Sciences Pius XI Gold Medal 1975, Cambridge Philosophical Soc. William Hopkins Prize 1976, Wolf Foundation Prize for Physics 1988, Inst. of Physics Maxwell Medal 1976, Royal Soc. Hughes Medal 1976, Albert Einstein Award 1978, Royal Astronomical Soc. Gold Medal 1985, Inst. of Physics Paul Dirac Medal and Prize 1987, Sunday Times Special Award for Literature 1989, Britannica Award 1989, RSA Albert Medal 1999, Royal Soc. Copley Medal 2006, Fonseca Prize 2008, Presidential Medal of Freedom 2009. *Address:* Department of Applied Mathematics and Theoretical Physics, Centre for Mathematical Sciences, University of Cambridge, Wilberforce Road, Cambridge, CB3 0WA, England (office). *Telephone:* (1223) 337843 (office). *Website:* www.damtp.cam.ac.uk (office); www.hawking.org.uk.

HAWLICEK, Hilde; Austrian politician; b. 14 April 1942, Vienna. *Career:* mem. Nationalrat (Parl.) 1976–87, 1990–95, 1996; Minister of Educ., the Arts and Sport 1987–90; mem. European Parl. (Vice-Pres. PSE) 1995–99, Vice-Pres. Cttee on Culture, Youth, Educ. and the Media, mem. Del. for Relations with the Maghreb Countries and the Arab Maghreb Union; fmr Pres. International Inst. for Children's Literature and Reading Research. *Honours:* Grand Gold Medal of the Order of Merit (Austria), Grand Order of Merit of South Tyrol 2010. *Address:* c/o International Institute for Children's Literature and Reading Research, Mayerhofgasse 6, 1040 Vienna, Austria.

HAWTHORNE, Susan, DipEd, BA, MA, PhD; Australian academic, publisher, poet and writer; *Director, Spinifex Press*; b. 30 Nov. 1951, Wagga Wagga, New South Wales. *Education:* Melbourne Teachers Coll., La Trobe Univ., Univ. of Melbourne. *Career:* apptd Tutor, Koori Teacher Education Programme, Deakin Univ. 1986; Ed. and Commissioning Ed., Penguin Books, Australia 1987–91; Research Assoc., Victoria Univ. of Tech. 1990–2010; Founder-Dir Spinifex Press 1991–; Chair. Australian Women's Book Review 1993–99; apptd Asialink Literature Resident, Univ. of Madras, India 2009; currently Adjunct Prof., School of Arts and Social Sciences, James Cook Univ., Townsville; mem. International Advisory Bd, Women's Studies International Forum 1990–; mem. Editorial Bd, Strange Literary Magazine 2009–, Axon Literary Magazine 2011–; Bd mem. Australian Book Group 1998–2001, Asialink 2003–05; mem. Australian Soc. of Authors, Fellowship of Australian Authors, PEN International, Victoria Writers Centre. *Publications:* Difference (ed.) 1985, Moments of Desire 1989, The Exploring Frangipani 1990, Angels of Power 1991, The Falling Woman 1992, The Language in My Tongue: Four New Poets 1993, The Spinifex Quiz Book 1993, Australia for Women (co-ed.) 1994, Car Maintenance, Explosives and Love (co-ed.) 1997, CyberFeminism (co-ed.) 1999, Bird 1999, Wild Politics 2002, The Butterfly Effect 2005, Unsettling the Land (with Suzanne Bellamy) 2008, Earth's Breath 2009, Cow 2011; contribs to journals, reviews, and periodicals. *Address:* Spinifex Press, PO Box 212, 504 Queensberry St, North Melbourne, Melbourne, Vic. 3051, Australia (office). *Telephone:* (3) 9329-6088 (office). *Fax:* (3) 9329-9238 (office). *E-mail:* susan.hawthorne@bigpond.com.au. *Website:* www.spinifexpress.com.au (office).

HAYDEN, Dolores, BA, MArch; American architect, academic and writer; *Professor of Architecture, Urbanism and American Studies, Yale University*; b. 15 March 1945, New York, NY; m. Peter Marris 1975; one d. *Education:* Mount Holyoke Coll., Girton Coll., Cambridge, Harvard Grad. School of Design. *Career:* Lecturer, Univ. of California, Berkeley 1973; Assoc. Prof., MIT 1973–79; Prof., UCLA 1979–91; Prof. of Architecture, Urbanism and American Studies, Yale Univ. 1991–; Pres. Urban History Asscn; mem. American Studies Asscn; Djerassi Poetry Residency 2012. *Publications:* Seven American Utopias 1976, The Grand Domestic Revolution 1981, Redesigning the American Dream 1984, The Power of Place: Urban Landscapes as Public History 1995, Playing House 1998, Line Dance 2001, Building Suburbia 2003, A Field Guide to Sprawl 2004, Best American Poetry 2009, American Yard 2004, Nymph, Dun, and Spinner 2010; contribs to numerous journals. *Honours:* Nat. Endowment for the Humanities Fellowship 1976, Nat. Endowment for the Arts Fellowship 1980, Guggenheim Fellowship 1981, Rockefeller Foundation Fellowship 1981, ACLS-Ford Foundation Fellowship 1988, Asscn of American Publrs' Award 1995, Center for Advanced Study in the Behavioral Sciences Fellowship 2007, Virginia Center for the Creative Arts Fellowship 2010; awards from Poetry Soc. of America, New England Poetry Club. *Address:* School of Architecture, Yale University, PO Box 208242, 180 York Street, New Haven, CT 06520, USA (office). *Telephone:* (203) 432-4782 (office). *Fax:* (203) 432-7175 (office). *E-mail:* dolores.hayden@yale.edu (office). *Website:* www.architecture.yale.edu (office); www.doloreshayden.com.

HAYDEN TAYLOR, Drew; Canadian playwright and writer; b. 1962, Curve Lake, Ont. *Career:* Artistic Dir Native Earth Performing Arts 1994–97; fmr Writer-in-Residence, Univs of Michigan, Western Ontario, and Luneburg (Germany), and numerous theatre cos; stories and plays for theatre, TV and radio, also films. *Plays:* over 70 productions including (premiered by De-Ba-Jeh-Mu-Jig Theatre Group) Toronto at Dreamer's Rock 1989, Education is Our Right 1990, Talking Pictures 1990, The Bootlegger Blues 1990, Someday 1991, Three Tricksters 2009; other: A Contemporary Gothic Indian Vampire Story (Persephone Theatre) 1992, The Baby Blues (Arbour Theatre Festival) 1995, Girl Who Loved Her Horses (Theatre Direct) 1995, Only Drunks and Children Tell the Truth (Native Earth Performing Arts) 1996, alterNATIVES (Bluewater Theatre/Lighthouse Theatre) 1999, 400 Kilometres (Two Planks and a Passion Theatre) 1999, The Boy in the Treehouse (Manitoba Theatre for Young People) 2000, The Buzz'gem Blues (Lighthouse Theatre) 2001, Sucker Falls (Touchstone Theatre/Rubyslipper) 2001, Raven Stole the Sun (Red Sky

Performance) 2004, In a World Created by a Drunken God (Persephone Theatre) 2004, The Berlin Blues (Native Voices, Los Angeles) 2007, Spirit Horse (Roseneath Theatre) 2007, Dead White Writer on the Floor (Magnus Theatre, Thunder Bay) 2010, A Story Before Time (Winchester Street Theatre, Toronto) 2010. *Television includes:* several series including Mixed Blessings; In a World Created by a Drunken God (film, APTN) 2007. *Films include:* over 17 documentaries including Redskins, Tricksters and Puppy Stew. *Publications include:* plays: Toronto at Dreamer's Rock/Education is Our Right 1990, The Bootlegger Blues 1991, Someday 1993, Only Drunks and Children Tell the Truth 1998, The Baby Blues 1999, alterNATIVES 2000, Girl Who Loved Her Horses/The Boy in the Treehouse 2000, The Buzz'gem Blues 2002, 400 Kilometres 2005, In a World Created by a Drunken God 2006, The Berlin Blues 2007, Dead White Writer on the Floor 2011; novels: The Night Wanderer: A Native Gothic Novel (Jt First Prize for Young Adult Fiction, Independent Publisher Book Awards 2008, Book of the Year/Best Book for Kids & Teens, Canadian Children's Book Centre 2008) 2007, Motorcycles and Sweetgrass 2010; short stories: Fearless Warriors 1998; essay collections: Me Funny (Ed.), Me Sexy (Ed.) 2006, NEWS: Postcards From The Four Directions 2010, Funny, You Don't Look Like One (four vols) 1996–2004; ed/contrib. to numerous anthologies. *Literary Agent:* Aurora Artists, 19 Wroxeter Avenue, Toronto, ON M4K 1J5, Canada. *Telephone:* (416) 463-4634. *Fax:* (416) 463-4889. *E-mail:* aurora.artists@sympatico.ca. *Website:* www.drewhaydentaylor.com.

HAYDER, Mo, MA; British author; b. 1962, Essex; pnr Bob Randell; one d. *Education:* Loughton American Univ., Washington, DC, USA, Bath Spa Univ. *Career:* fmr barmaid, security guard, filmmaker, security guard, hostess in Tokyo club, educational administrator; fmrly taught English as a foreign language; devised DI Jack Caffery character and Walking Man series of novels 2008–; teacher of creative writing, Bath Spa Univ. *Publications include:* novels: Birdman 2000, The Treatment (WHSmith Thumping Good Read Award 2002) 2002, Tokyo (US title: The Devil of Nanking) (Elle magazine Crime Fiction Prize 2004, SNCF Prix Polar 2004) 2004, Pig Island 2006, Hanging Hill 2011; Walking Man series: Ritual 2008, Skin 2009, Gone (Edgar Award for Best Novel 2012) 2011, Quiet Day 2012. *Literary Agent:* c/o Gregory & Company Authors' Agents, 3 Barb Mews, Hammersmith, London, W6 7PA, England. *Telephone:* (20) 7610-4676. *Fax:* (20) 7610-4686. *E-mail:* info@gregoryandcompany.co.uk. *Website:* www.gregoryandcompany.co.uk; www.mohayder.net.

HAYES, Charles Langley (see Holmes, Bryan John)

HAYMAN, David, BA, PhD; American academic, writer and editor; *Professor Emeritus, University of Wisconsin-Madison*; b. 7 Jan. 1927, New York; m. Loni Goldschmidt 1951; two d. *Education:* New York Univ., Univ. of Paris. *Career:* Instructor 1955–57, Asst Prof. of English 1957–58, Assoc. Prof. 1958–65, Univ. of Texas; Prof. of English and Comparative Literature, Univ. of Iowa 1965–73; Prof. of Comparative Literature, Univ. of Wisconsin-Madison 1973–96, Eujire-Bascon Prof. in the Humanities 1990–96, Prof. Emer. 1997–. *Publications:* Joyce et Mallarmé 1956, A First-Draft Version of Finnegans Wake 1963, Configuration Critique de James Joyce (ed.) 1965, Ulysses: The Mechanics of Meaning 1970, Form in Fiction (with Eric Rabkin) 1974, Ulysses: Critical Essays (with Clive Hart) 1974, The James Joyce Archive (ed.) 1978, Philippe Sollers: Writing and the Experience of Limits (ed and co-translated) 1980, Reforming the Narrative 1987, The Wake in Transit 1990, Probes: Genetic Studies in Joyce (with Sam Slote) 1994, James Joyce: Epiphanias (ed.) 1996; contribs to many scholarly books and journals. *Honours:* Guggenheim Fellowship 1958–59, Nat. Endowment for the Humanities Fellowship 1979–80, Harry Levin Prize, American Comparative Literature Asscn 1989. *E-mail:* dhayman@facstaff.wisc.edu.

HAYMAN, Ronald, BA, MA; British writer; b. 4 May 1932, Bournemouth, Dorset; m. (divorced); two d. *Education:* Trinity Hall, Cambridge. *Career:* mem. Soc. of Authors. *Plays:* Playing the Wife, Chichester Festival Theatre 1995. *Publications:* Harold Pinter 1968, Samuel Beckett 1968, John Osborne 1968, John Arden 1968, Robert Bolt 1969, John Whiting 1969, Collected Plays of John Whiting (ed.), two vols 1969, Techniques of Acting 1969, The Art of the Dramatist and Other Pieces, by John Whiting (ed.) 1970, Arthur Miller 1970, Tolstoy 1970, Arnold Wesker 1970, John Gielgud 1971, Edward Albee 1971, Eugène Ionesco 1972, Playback 1973, The Set-Up 1974, Playback 2 1974, The First Thrust 1975, The German Theatre (ed.) 1975, How to Read a Play 1977, The Novel Today 1967–75 1976, My Cambridge (ed.) 1977, Tom Stoppard 1977, Artaud and After 1977, De Sade 1978, Theatre and Anti-Theatre 1979, British Theatre Since 1955: A Reassessment 1979, Nietzsche: A Critical Life 1980, K: A Biography of Kafka 1981, Brecht: A Biography 1983, Fassbinder: Film Maker 1984, Brecht: The Plays 1984, Günter Grass 1985, Secrets: Boyhood in a Jewish Hotel 1932–54 1985, Writing Against: A Biography of Sartre 1986, Proust: A Biography 1990, The Death and Life of Sylvia Plath 1991, Tennessee Williams: Everyone Else Is an Audience 1994, Thomas Mann 1995, Hitler and Geli 1997, Nietzsche's Voices 1997, A Life of Jung 1999. *Address:* The Penthouse, Highpoint, London, N6 4AZ, England (home).

HAYS, Robert Glenn, MS, PhD; American reporter, journalism educator and writer; *Emeritus Faculty in Journalism, University of Illinois*; b. 23 May 1935, Carmi, Ill.; m. Mary Elizabeth Corley 1957; two s. *Education:* Southern Illinois Univ. *Career:* reporter, Granite City Press-Record 1961–63; public relations writer, Southern Illinois Univ. 1963–66, Alumni Ed. 1966–71; Asst Scientist, Illinois Bd of Natural Resources and Conservation 1971–73; Journalism Faculty, Sam Houston State Univ. 1974–75, Univ. of Illinois 1975–86, 1987– (now Emer.), mem. Acad. of Teaching Excellence 1996; Chair. Dept of Mass Communications, Southeast Missouri Univ. 1986–87; Founding mem. Research Soc. of American Periodicals; mem. Asscn for Educ. in Journalism and Mass Communications, Illinois Press Asscn, Investigative Reporters and Eds, Missouri Press Asscn, Soc. of Professional Journalists, American Civil Liberties Union (Chapter Steering Cttee 1991–93), Nat. Org. for Women, South Carolina Writers Workshop. *Publications:* non-fiction: G-2: Intelligence for Patton 1971 (new edn 1999), Country Ed 1974, State Science in Illinois 1980, A Race at Bay: New York Times Editorials on the 'Indian Problem' 1860–1900 1997, Editorializing the 'Indian Problem' 2007; fiction: Early Stories From the Land 1995, Circles in the Water 2008, The Life and Death of Lizzie Morris 2009, The Baby River Angel 2009, Blood on the Roses 2011; contrib. to periodicals and journals. *Honours:* Int. ACE Award of Excellence 1993, 1994, Univ. of Illinois Karl E. Gardner Award 1996. *E-mail:* contactroberthays@gmail.com (office)*Address:* 2314 Glenoak Drive, Champaign, IL 61821, USA (home). *E-mail:* bobhays@illinois.edu (office). *Website:* home.comcast.net/~roberthayswriter/site.

HAYTHE, Justin, BA, MFA; British screenwriter and writer; b. 1973, London. *Education:* Middlebury Coll., Vermont, USA. *Career:* fmr Assoc. Ed. Fence magazine. *Films:* screenplays: The Clearing 2004, Revolutionary Road 2008. *Publications:* The Fabulous Wardrobe of Mrs Pat Campbell (short story) 2003, The Honeymoon (novel) 2004.

HAZEN, Robert Miller, PhD; American geophysicist, musician and writer; *Research Scientist, Geophysical Laboratory, Carnegie Institution for Science*; b. 1 Nov. 1948, Rockville Centre, New York; m. Margaret Hindle 1969; one s. one d. *Education:* Massachusetts Inst. of Tech., Harvard Univ. *Career:* NATO Fellow, Univ. of Cambridge, England 1975–76; Research Scientist, Geophysical Lab., Carnegie Inst. for Science, Washington, DC 1976–; Clarence Robinson Prof. of Earth Science, George Mason Univ.; trumpeter with many orchestras; mem. ACS, American Geophysical Union, History of Science Soc., International Guild of Trumpeters; Mineralogical Soc. of America. *Publications:* Comparative Crystal Chemistry 1982, Poetry of Geology 1982, Music Men 1987, The Breakthrough 1988, Science Matters 1990, Keepers of the Flame 1991, The New Alchemist 1993, The Sciences: An Integrated Approach 1995, Why Aren't Black Holes Black? 1997, The Diamond Makers 1999, Physics Matters: An Introduction to Conceptual Physics 2003, Genesis: The Scientific Quest for Life's Origin 2005, The Story of Earth: The First 4.5 Billion Years, From Stardust to Living Planet 2012; contrib. to many scientific journals and to periodicals. *Honours:* Mineralogical Soc. of America Award 1981, Ipatief Prize 1984, ASCAP-Deems Taylor Award 1988, Educ. Press Asscn Award 1992, Elizabeth Wood Science Writing Award 1998, Distinguished Public Service Medal, Mineralogical Soc. of America 2009. *Address:* Geophysical Laboratory, Carnegie Institution for Science, 5251 Broad Branch Road, NW, Washington, DC 20015-1305, USA (office). *Telephone:* (202) 478-8962 (office). *Fax:* (202) 478-8901 (office). *E-mail:* r.hazen@gl.ciw.edu (office). *Website:* hazen.gl.ciw.edu (office).

HAZLETON, Lesley, BA, MA; American/British writer; b. 20 Sept. 1945, Reading, England. *Education:* Manchester University, Hebrew University of Jerusalem. *Career:* mem. PEN American Center. *Publications:* Israeli Women 1978, Where Mountains Roar 1980, In Defence of Depression 1984, Jerusalem, Jerusalem 1986, England, Bloody England 1989, Confessions of a Fast Woman 1992, Everything Women Always Wanted to Know About Cars 1995, Driving to Detroit 1998, Mary 2004, Jezebel 2007, Karbala 2008, After the Prophet: The Epic Story of the Shia-Sunni Split in Islam 2009; contrib. to many periodicals and magazines. *Literary Agent:* Watkins Loomis Agency Inc., 133 E 35th Street, Suite 1, New York, NY 10016, USA. *Telephone:* (212) 532-0080. *Fax:* (212) 889-0506. *E-mail:* assistant@watkinsloomis.com. *Website:* www.watkinsloomis.com.

HAZO, Samuel John, BA, MA, PhD; American academic, writer and poet; *President and Director, International Poetry Forum*; b. 19 July 1928, Pittsburgh, Pa; m. Mary Anne Hazo; one s. *Education:* University of Notre Dame, Duquesne University, University of Pittsburgh. *Career:* Faculty mem., Duquesne University 1955–65, Dean College of Arts and Sciences 1961–66, Prof. of English 1965–; Pres. and Dir International Poetry Forum 1966–; State Poet, Commonwealth of Pennsylvania 1993–2003. *Publications include:* Discovery and Other Poems 1959, The Quiet Wars 1962, Hart Crane: An Introduction and Interpretation (revised edn as Smithereened Apart: A Critique of Hart Crane) 1963, The Christian Intellectual Studies in the Relation of Catholicism to the Human Sciences (ed.) 1963, A Selection of Contemporary Religious Poetry (ed.) 1963, Listen With the Eye 1964, My Sons in God: Selected and New Poems 1965, Blood Rights 1968, The Blood of Adonis (with Ali Ahmed Said) 1971, Twelve Poems (with George Nama) 1972, Seascript: A Mediterranean Logbook 1972, Once for the Last Bandit: New and Previous Poems 1972, Quartered 1974, Inscripts 1975, The Very Fall of the Sun 1978, To Paris 1981, The Wanton Summer Air 1982, Thank a Bored Angel 1983, The Feast of Icarus 1984, The Color of Reluctance 1986, The Pittsburgh That Starts Within You 1986, Silence Spoken Here 1988, Stills 1989, The Rest is Prose 1989, Lebanon 1990, Picks 1990, The Past Won't Stay Behind You 1993, The Pages of Day and Night 1995, The Holy Surprise of Right Now 1996, As They Sail 1999, Spying for God 1999, Mano a Mano: The Life of Manolete 2001, Just Once 2002, A Flight to Elsewhere 2005, The Power of Less 2005, The Song of the Horse: Selected Poems 1958–2008 2008, This Part of the World 2008. *Honours:* 10 hon. doctorates; Maurice English Poetry Award

2003, Griffin Award for Writing Univ. of Notre Dame 2005. *Address:* 785 Somerville Drive, Pittsburgh, PA 15243 (home); International Poetry Forum, 3333 Fifth Avenue, Pittsburgh, PA 15213, USA (office). *Telephone:* (412) 621-9893 (office). *Fax:* (412) 621-9898 (office). *E-mail:* ipf1@earthlink.net (office). *Website:* www.thepoetryforum.org (office).

HAZRA, Indrajit; Indian journalist and writer; b. Calcutta (now Kolkata). *Career:* fmr musician; currently Deputy Ed. The Hindustan Times. *Publications include:* The Burnt Forehead of Max Saul 2000, The Garden of Earthly Delights 2003, The Bioscope Man 2008. *Address:* Hindustan Times, 18–20 Kasturba Gandhi Marg, New Delhi 110 001, India (office). *Telephone:* (11) 23704666 (office). *Fax:* (11) 23704600 (office). *E-mail:* feedback@hindustantimes.com (office). *Website:* www.hindustantimes.com (office).

HAZZARD, Shirley, FRSL; Australian/American writer; b. 30 Jan. 1931, Sydney, Australia; d. of Reginald Hazzard and Catherine Hazzard; m. Francis Steegmuller 1963 (died 1994). *Education:* Queenwood School, Sydney. *Career:* Special Operations Intelligence, Hong Kong 1947–48; UK High Commr's Office, Wellington, NZ 1949–50; UN, New York (Gen. Service Category) 1952–61; novelist and writer of short stories and contrib. to The New Yorker 1960–; Guggenheim Fellow 1974; mem. American Acad. of Arts and Letters, American Acad. of Arts and Sciences. *Publications:* short stories: Cliffs of Fall 1963; novels: The Evening of the Holiday 1966, People in Glass Houses 1967, The Bay of Noon 1970, The Transit of Venus (Nat. Critics Circle Award for Fiction 1981) 1980, The Great Fire (Nat. Book Award for Fiction) 2003, Australia (Miles Franklin Prize 2004) 2004; non-fiction: Defeat of an Ideal: A Study of the Self-destruction of the United Nations 1973, Countenance of Truth: The United Nations and the Waldheim Case 1990, Greene on Capri (memoir) 2000, Ancient Shore: Dispatches from Naples (with Francis Steegmuller) 2009. *Honours:* Hon. Citizen of Capri 2000; American Acad. of Arts and Letters Award in Literature 1966, First Prize, O. Henry Short Story Awards 1976, Nat. Book Critics Award for Fiction, USA 1981, Boyer Lecturer, Australia 1984, 1988, Clifton Fadiman Medal for Literature 2001, Nat. Book Award for Fiction 2003, William Dean Howells Medal, American Acad. of Arts and Letters 2005.

HEADLEY, John Miles, MA, PhD; American historian and academic; b. 23 Oct. 1929, New York, NY. *Education:* Princeton and Yale Univs. *Career:* Instructor, Univ. of Massachusetts, Amherst 1959–61; Instructor then Asst Prof., Univ. of British Columbia, Vancouver 1962–64; Asst Prof., Univ. of North Carolina at Chapel Hill 1964–66, Assoc. Prof. 1966–69, Prof. 1969–2003, Prof. Emer. 2003–. *Publications include:* Luther's View of Church History 1963, Medieval and Renaissance Studies, Vol. III (ed.) 1968, Responsio ad Lutherum, Complete Works of St Thomas More, Vol. V (ed.) 1969, The Emperor and his Chancellor: A Study of the Imperial Chancellery under Gattinara 1983, San Carlo Borromeo: Catholic Reform and Ecclesiastical Politics in the Second Half of the Sixteenth Century (ed. and contributor) 1988, The Oxford Encyclopedia of the Reformation (assoc. ed.) 1996, Tommaso Campanella and the Transformation of the World 1997, Empire, Church and World: The Quest for Universal Order 1997, Confessionalization in Europe 1555–1700 (ed. and contrib.), The Europeanization of the World: On the Origins of Human Rights and Democracy 2007; contrib. to various scholarly books and journals. *Honours:* Guggenheim Fellowship 1974, Inst. for Arts and Humanities Fellowship 1989. *Address:* Department of History, University of North Carolina, Chapel Hill, NC 27599-3195 (office); 303 Oakland Lane, Chapel Hill, NC 27516, USA (home). *Telephone:* (919) 619-5514 (office); (919) 968-8365 (home). *Fax:* (919) 962-1403 (office). *E-mail:* headley@email.unc.edu (office).

HEALD, Timothy Villiers, (David Lancaster), MA, FRSL; British journalist and writer; b. 28 Jan. 1944, Dorset; m. 1st Alison Martina Leslie 1968 (divorced), two s. two d.; m. 2nd Penelope Byrne 1999. *Education:* Balliol Coll., Oxford. *Career:* reporter, Sunday Times 1965–67; Feature Ed. Town magazine 1967; feature writer, Daily Express 1967–72; Assoc. Ed. Weekend Magazine, Toronto 1977–78; columnist, Observer 1990; Visiting Fellow, Jane Franklin Hall 1997, 1999, Univ. Tutor in Creative Writing 1999, 2000, Univ. of Tasmania; Writer-in-Residence, Univ. of South Australia 2001; Visiting Fellow, St John's Coll., Sydney Univ. 2007; mem. CWA (Chair. 1987–88), PEN, Soc. of Authors. *Publications include:* It's a Dog's Life 1971, Unbecoming Habits 1973, Blue Book Will Out 1974, Let Sleeping Dogs Die 1976, The Making of Space 1976, John Steed: An Authorized Biography 1977, Just Desserts 1977, H.R.H.: The Man Who Will be King (with M. Mohs) 1977, Murder at Moose Jaw 1981, Caroline R 1981, Networks 1983, Class Distinctions 1984, Red Herrings 1985, The Character of Cricket 1986, The Newest London Spy (ed.) 1988, By Appointments: 150 Years of the Royal Warrant 1989, A Classic English Crime (ed.) 1990, My Lord's (ed.) 1990, The Duke: A Portrait of Prince Philip 1991, Honorable Estates 1992, Barbara Cartland: A Life of Love 1994, Denis: The Authorized Biography of the Incomparable Compton 1994, Brian Johnston: The Authorized Biography 1995, A Classic Christmas Crime (ed.) 1995, Beating Retreat: Hong Kong Under the Last Governor 1997, A Peerage for Trade 2001, Village Cricket 2004, Death and the Visiting Fellow 2004, Death and the D'Urbervilles 2005, Princess Margaret 2007, A Death on the Ocean Wave 2007, Death in the Opening Chapter 2011; contrib. to newspapers and periodicals. *Address:* 66 The Esplanade, Fowey, Cornwall, PL23 1JA, England (home). *Telephone:* (1726) 832781 (home). *Fax:* (1726) 833246 (home). *E-mail:* tim@timheald.com (office). *Website:* www.timheald.com (home).

HEALEY, Baron (Life Peer), cr. 1992, of Riddlesden in the County of West Yorkshire; **Denis Winston Healey,** PC, CH, MBE, FRSL, MA, DPhil; British politician; b. 30 Aug. 1917, Mottingham; s. of William Healey; m. Edna May Edmunds 1945 (died 2010); one s. two d. *Education:* Bradford Grammar School and Balliol Coll., Oxford. *Career:* Maj., Royal Engineers 1945; Sec. Labour Party Int. Dept 1945–52; MP 1952–92; Sec. of State for Defence 1964–70; Chancellor of the Exchequer 1974–79; Opposition Spokesman for Treasury and Econ. Affairs 1979–80, for Foreign and Commonwealth Affairs 1980–87; Chair. Interim Ministerial Cttee of IMF 1977–79; Deputy Leader of Labour Party 1980–83; Pres. Birkbeck Coll. London 1993–99. *Publications:* The Curtain Falls 1951, New Fabian Essays 1952, Neutralism 1955, Fabian International Essays 1956, A Neutral Belt in Europe 1958, NATO and American Security 1959, The Race Against the H Bomb 1960, Labour Britain and the World 1963, Healey's Eye (photographs) 1980, Labour and a World Society 1985, Beyond Nuclear Deterrence 1986, The Time of My Life (autobiog.) 1989, When Shrimps Learn to Whistle (collection of essays) 1990, My Secret Planet 1992, Denis Healey's Yorkshire Dales 1995, Healey's World (photographs) 2002. *Honours:* Hon. Fellow, Balliol Coll. Oxford 1980; Freeman of Leeds 1991; Grand Cross of Order of Merit (FRG) 1979; Hon. DLitt (Bradford) 1983; Hon. LLD, (Sussex) 1989, (Leeds) 1991. *Address:* House of Lords, Westminster, London, SW1A 0PW, England (office). *Telephone:* (20) 7219-3546 (office); (1323) 870028 (home).

HEALEY, Robin Michael, BA, MA; British historian and biographer; b. 16 Feb. 1952, London; s. of T.B.Healey and Vera Healey (née Paulson). *Education:* Univ. of Birmingham. *Career:* Documentation Officer, Tamworth Castle and Cambridge Museum of Archaeology and Anthropology 1977–79; Museum Asst, Saffron Walden Museum 1983–84; Research Asst, History of Parliament 1985–92; Ed. Herefords. Soc. Jubilee Yearbook 1986; Visiting Research Fellow, Univ. of Manchester 1997–2003; Ed. Lewisletter 2001–; apptd Co-Ed. ALS Journal 2006; mem. Charles Lamb Soc. (Exec. 1987–), Alliance of Literary Socs (press officer 1997–2005), Wyndham Lewis Soc. *Publications:* Hertfordshire: A Shell Guide 1982, Diary of George Mushet (1805–13) 1982, Grigson at Eighty 1985, A History of Barley School 1995, My Rebellious and Imperfect Eye: Observing Geoffrey Grigson 2002; contrib. to Biographical Dictionary of Modern British Radicals 1984, Domesday Book 1985, Secret Britain 1986, Dictionary of Literary Biography 1991, Encyclopaedia of Romanticism 1992, Consumer Magazines of the British Isles 1993, Postwar Literatures in English 1998–, I Remember When I Was Young 2003, Oxford Dictionary of National Biography 2004, Country Life, Hertfordshire Countryside, Guardian, Literary Review, Private Eye, Book and Magazine Collector, Independent, TLS, Art Newspaper, Mensa Magazine, Charles Lamb Bulletin, Cobbett's New Political Register, Rare Book Review, Lancet, Wyndham Lewis Annual, British Medical Association Journal. *Honours:* First Prize, Birmingham Post Poetry Contest 1974; various research awards. *Address:* 80 Hall Lane, Great Chishill, Royston, Herts., SG8 8SH, England. *Telephone:* (1763) 837058. *E-mail:* robinheal@aol.com (office).

HEALY, Jeremiah, (Terry Devane); American novelist. *Education:* Rutgers Coll., Harvard Law School. *Career:* Prof., New England School of Law; mem. Private Eye Writers of America (fmr Pres.) Shamus Awards (fmr chair.), International Asscn of Crime Writers (Pres. 2000–). *Publications:* as Jeremiah Healy: Blunt Darts 1984, The Staked Goat 1986, So Like Sleep 1987, Swan Dive 1988, Yesterday's News 1989, Right to Die 1991, Shallow Graves 1992, Foursome 1993, Act of God 1994, Rescue 1995, Invasion of Privacy 1996, The Only Good Lawyer 1998, The Stalking of Sheilah Quinn 1998, The Concise Cuddy (short stories) 1998, Spiral 1999, Turnabout 2001, Cuddy Plus One (short stories) 2003, Off-Season and Other Stories 2003; as Terry Devane: Uncommon Justice 2001, Juror Number Eleven 2002, A Stain Upon the Robe 2003; contrib. of shorts stories to collections, including Irreconcilable Differences, Blonde & Blue: Classic Private Eyes, Mom, Apple Pie, and Murder. *Honours:* Shamus Award 1986. *Literary Agent:* Sandy Balzo, Balzo Communications, 750 E Briar Ridge Drive, Brookfield, WI 53045, USA. *Telephone:* (262) 784-2591. *Fax:* (262) 784-3468. *E-mail:* balzocom@aol.com. *E-mail:* jeremiah_healy@yahoo.com. *Website:* www.jeremiahhealy.com.

HEANEY, Seamus, CLit; Irish poet and author; b. 13 April 1939, Northern Ireland; s. of Patrick Heaney and Margaret Heaney (née McCann); m. Marie Devlin 1965; two s. one d. *Education:* St Columb's Coll., Londonderry, Queen's Univ., Belfast. *Career:* Lecturer, St Joseph's Coll. of Educ., Belfast 1963–66; Queen's Univ., Belfast 1966–72; freelance writer 1972–75, Lecturer, Carysfort Coll. 1975–81, Sr Visiting Lecturer, Harvard Univ. 1982–84, Boylston Prof. of Rhetoric and Oratory 1985–97, Ralph Waldo Emerson Poet in Residence 1998–2006; Prof. of Poetry, Univ. of Oxford 1989–94. *Poems:* Eleven Poems 1965, Death of a Naturalist 1966, Door into the Dark 1969, Wintering Out 1972, North 1975, Field Work 1979, Selected Poems 1965–1975 1980, Station Island 1984, The Haw Lantern 1987, New Selected Poems 1966–1987 1990, Seeing Things 1991, The Spirit Level 1996 (Whitbread Book of the Year Award 1997), Opened Ground: Poems 1966–96 1998 (Irish Times Literary Award 1999), Beowulf: A New Verse Translation 1999, Electric Light 2001, The Testament of Cresseid (a retelling of Robert Henryson's poem) 2005, District and Circle (T.S. Eliot Prize for Poetry) 2006, Human Chain (Forward Prize for Best Collection) 2010. *Prose:* Preoccupations: Selected Prose 1968–1978 1980, The Government of the Tongue 1988, The Place of Writing 1990, The Redress of Poetry (lectures) 1995, Finders Keepers: Selected Prose 1971–2001 2002, The Midnight Verdict 2002. *Anthology:* The School Bag 1997 (co-ed. with Ted Hughes). *Plays:* The Cure at Troy 1991, The Burial at Thebes

(Abbey Theatre, Dublin) 2004. *Translations:* Sweeney Astray 1984, Sweeney's Flight 1992, Laments, by Jan Kochanowski (with Stanislaw Baranczak), Beowulf: a New Verse Translation (Whitbread Book of the Year 1999) 1999, The Testament of Cresseid and Seven Fables, by Robert Henryson 2009. *Honours:* Hon. DLitt (Oxford) 1997, (Birmingham) 2000; Commdr des Arts et Lettres; WH Smith Prize 1975, Bennet Award 1982, Sunday Times Award for Excellence in Writing 1988, Lannan Literary Award 1990, Nobel Prize for Literature 1996, Cunningham Medal, Royal Irish Acad. 2008, Lifetime Achievement Award, Queen's Univ., Belfast 2008, David Cohen Prize for Literature 2009. *Literary Agent:* Steven Barclay Agency, 12 Western Avenue, Petaluma, CA 94952, USA. *Telephone:* (707) 773-0654. *Fax:* (707) 778-1868. *Website:* www.barclayagency.com. *Address:* c/o Faber and Faber, Bloomsbury House, 74–77 Great Russell Street, London, WC1B 3DA, England (office). *Website:* www.faber.co.uk (office).

HEARON, Shelby, BA; American novelist; b. 18 Jan. 1931, Marion, Kentucky; m. 1st Robert Hearon, Jr 1953 (divorced 1976); one s. one d.; m. 2nd Billy Joe Lucas 1981 (divorced 1995); m. 3rd William Halpern 1995. *Education:* Univ. of Texas at Austin. *Career:* Visiting Lecturer, Univ. of Texas at Austin 1978–80; Visiting Assoc. Prof., Univ. of Houston 1981, Clark Univ. 1985, Univ. of California at Irvine 1987; Visiting Prof., Univ. of Illinois at Chicago 1993, Colgate Univ. 1993, Univ. of Massachusetts at Amherst 1994–96, Middlebury Coll. 1996–98; mem. Associated Writing Programs, Authors' Guild, Authors League, PEN American Centre, Poets and Writers, Texas Inst. of Letters. *Publications:* Armadillo in the Grass 1968, The Second Dune 1973, Hannah's House 1975 Now and Another Time 1976, A Prince of a Fellow 1978, Painted Dresses 1981, Afternoon of a Faun 1983, Group Therapy 1984, A Small Town 1985, Five Hundred Scorpions 1987, Owning Jolene (Literature Award, American Acad. of Arts and Letters) 1989, Hug Dancing 1991, Life Estates 1994, Footprints 1996, Ella in Bloom 2001, Year of the Dog 2007; other: Best Friends for Life (based on Life Estates), CBS-TV 1998; contribs to magazines. *Honours:* Guggenheim Fellowship in Fiction 1982, Nat. Endowment for the Arts Fellowship in Fiction 1983, Ingram Merrill Foundation Grant 1987, American Acad. of Arts and Letters Literature Award 1990. *Address:* 246 S Union Street, Burlington, VT 05401, USA (home). *Telephone:* (502) 660-4349 (home).

HEAT-MOON, William Least, (William Lewis Trogdon), BA, MA, PhD; American writer; b. 27 Aug. 1939, Kansas City, MO; m. 1st Lezlie (divorced 1978); m. 2nd Linda. *Education:* University of Missouri at Columbia. *Career:* Teacher of English, Stephens College, Columbia, MO 1965–68, 1972, 1978; Lecturer, School of Journalism, University of Missouri 1984–87. *Publications:* Blue Highways: A Journey into America 1982, PrairyErth (a deep map) 1991, River Horse 1999, Columbus in the Americas 2002, Roads to Quoz: An American Mosey 2008; contributions: newspapers and magazines. *Honours:* New York Times Notable Book Citations 1983, 1991, Books-Across-the-Sea Award 1984, Christopher Award 1984, American Library Asscn Best Non-Fiction Work 1991. *Address:* c/o Little, Brown and Co., 1271 Avenue of the Americas, New York, NY 10020, USA (office). *Website:* www.hachettebookgroup.com (office).

HEATER, Derek Benjamin, BA, PGCE; British writer; b. 28 Nov. 1931, Sydenham; one s. one d. *Education:* Univ. Coll. London, Inst. of Education, Univ. of London. *Career:* Ed. Teaching Politics 1973–79; Co-Ed. (with Bernard Crick) Political Realities Series 1974–93; Co-founder and mem. Politics Asscn 1969; mem. Council for Educ. in World Citizenship, Hon. Life mem.; Fellow, Politics Asscn 1994. *Publications:* Political Ideas in the Modern World 1960, Order and Rebellion 1964, World Affairs (with Gwyneth Owen) 1972, Contemporary Political Ideas 1974, Britain and the Outside World 1976, Essays in Political Education (with Bernard Crick) 1977, World Studies 1980, Our World This Century 1982, Peace Through Education 1984, Reform and Revolution 1987, Refugees 1988, Case Studies in Twentieth-Century World History 1988, Citizenship: The Civic Ideal in World History, Politics and Education 1990, The Idea of European Unity 1992 (Japanese trans. 2002, German trans. 2005), The Remarkable History of Rottingdean 1993, Introduction to International Politics (with G. R. Berridge) 1993, Foundations of Citizenship (with Dawn Oliver) 1994, National Self-Determination 1994, World Citizenship and Government 1996, The Theory of Nationhood: A Platonic Symposium 1998, Keeping Faith: History of Sutton Grammar School 1899–1999 1999, What is Citizenship? 1999 (Japanese trans. 2002, Chinese trans. 2009), World Citizenship: Cosmopolitan Thinking and Its Opponents 2002, A History of Education for Citizenship 2003 (Korean trans. 2007), A Brief History of Citizenship 2004 (Spanish trans. 2007, Arabic trans. 2008), Citizenship in Britain 2006, The Dying Man's Clues 2006, Murders in Brighton, Crisis in Britain 2008; contrib. to reference works, scholarly journals. *Honours:* Children's Book of the Year Award for Refugees 1988. *Address:* 3 The Rotyngs, Rottingdean, Brighton, BN2 7DX, England (home). *Telephone:* (1273) 307890 (home).

HEATH, Chris; British journalist and writer. *Career:* journalist, Jamming! 1984–85, Smash Hits 1984–89, The Guardian, The Face, The Daily Telegraph, The Sunday Telegraph, Empire, Rolling Stone, GQ; fmr Contributing Ed. Details magazine; official biographer, Pet Shop Boys, Robbie Williams. *Publications:* Pet Shop Boys, Literally 1990, Pet Shop Boys Vs America 1993, Feel: Robbie Williams 2004. *Address:* c/o Ebury Press, Random House, 20 Vauxhall Bridge Road, London, SW1V 2SA, England (office).

HEBALD, Carol, BA, MFA; American writer; b. 6 July 1934, New York, NY; d. of the late Henry Hebald and Ethel Miller. *Education:* Univ. of Iowa, City Coll., City Univ. of New York. *Career:* worked as actress 1952–64; Assoc. Prof. of English, Univ. of Kansas –1984; mem. PEN American Centre; Authors' Guild of America, Poets and Writers Inc. *Plays:* as actress: The Best House in Naples, Broadway 1956, Jane Eyre, Broadway 1958, Off Broadway: Playboy of the Western World, New York, Hanjo, Theatre des Lys, Maedchen in Uniform, Equity Library Theatre. *Publications:* Three Blind Mice (novella) 1989, Clara Kleinschmidt (novella) 1989, Martha (play) 1991, The Heart Too Long Suppressed (memoir) 2001, Little Monologs (poems) 2004, Spinster by the Sea (poems) 2005; contrib. to Commonweal, International Poetry Review, Antioch Review, Kansas Quarterly, Texas Quarterly, Massachusetts Review, The Humanist, New Letters, Confrontation, North American Review, New York Tribune, PEN International. *Honours:* William Bradley Otis Fellowship for Distinguished Contribs to American Literature. *Address:* 463 West Street, #660, New York, NY 10014, USA (home). *E-mail:* chebald@aol.com (office). *Website:* www.carolhebald.com.

HECKLER, Jonellen, BA; American writer and poet; b. 28 Oct. 1943, Pittsburgh; m. Lou Heckler 1968; one s. *Education:* Univ. of Pittsburgh. *Career:* mem. Authors' Guild. *Publications:* Safekeeping 1983, A Fragile Peace 1986, White Lies 1989, Circumstances Unknown 1993, Final Tour 1994; contrib. of numerous poems and short stories in Ladies Home Journal Magazine 1975–83.

HEDIN, Mary Ann, BS, MA; American writer and poet; b. 3 Aug. 1929, Minneapolis; m. Roger Willard Hedin; three s. one d. *Education:* Univ. of Minnesota, Univ. of California. *Career:* Fellow, Yaddo 1974; Writer-in-Residence Robinson Jeffers Town House Foundation 1984–85; mem. Authors' Guild; PEN; American Poetry Soc. *Publications:* Fly Away Home 1980, Direction, A Book of Poetry 1983; contribs to anthologies and journals. *Honours:* John H. McGinnis Memorial Award 1979, Iowa School of Letters Award for Short Fiction 1979.

HEDRICK, Joan Doran, AB, PhD; American academic and writer; b. 1 May 1944, Baltimore; m. Travis K. Hedrick 1967; two d. *Education:* Vassar Coll., Brown Univ. *Career:* Prof. of History, Trinity Coll., Hartford; mem. American Studies Asscn. *Publications:* Solitary Comrade: Jack London and His Work 1982, Harriet Beecher Stowe: A Life 1994, The Oxford Harriet Beecher Stowe Reader 1999. *Honours:* Pulitzer Prize in Biography 1995. *Address:* c/o Department of History, Trinity College, Hartford, CT 06106, USA.

HEESE, Marié, DLitt et Phil; South African writer, lecturer and educational consultant; b. 27 Sept. 1942, Cape Town; d. of Audrey Blignault; m. Chris Heese; three c. (one deceased). *Education:* Univ of Stellenbosch, Univ of South Africa. *Career:* taught Afrikaans and English at Empangeni and Richards Bay High Schools; lectured at Univs of Durban-Westville, Zululand and Pretoria; Lecturer, Dept of English, Univ. of South Africa (UNISA), later Dir of Academic Matters, Bureau for Univ. Teaching –1999; educational consultant, Wits, Int. Training in Communication, Readucate, Northern Cape Dept of Education, and in Ethiopia; examiner at doctoral level; fmr mem. Council Stellenbosch Univ. *Publications:* The Owl Critic: An Introduction to Literary Criticism (co-author) 1968, Tokkelspel (essays) 1972, Die Uurwerk Kantel (novel) 1976, Die Pikkewouters van Amper-Stamperland (juvenile) 1974, Avonture in Amper-Stamperland (juvenile) 1980, Tyd van Beslissing (novel) 1983, The Box Kite Summer (children's novel) 1984, Ons Geheim (juvenile) 1993, Practical Guide to Reading, Thinking and Writing Skills (co-author) 1995, Haiku for Africa 1997, Audrey Blignault: uit die dagboek van 'n vrou (auto-biog. essays, ed.) 2009, The Double Crown: Secret Writings of the Female Pharaoh (Commonwealth Writers Prize for Best Book, Africa region 2010), The Colour of Power (novel) 2011; also short stories and translations. *Address:* c/o NB Publishers, PO Box 5050, Cape Town 8000, South Africa (office). *Website:* www.nb.co.za (office).

HEFFER, Simon James, MA, PhD; British journalist and writer; *Editor, Mail Comment Online, and Columnist, Daily Mail*; b. 18 July 1960, Chelmsford, Essex; s. of the late James Heffer and of Joyce Mary Clements; m. Diana Caroline Clee 1987; two s. *Education:* King Edward VI School, Chelmsford and Corpus Christi Coll., Cambridge. *Career:* medical journalist 1983–85; freelance journalist 1985–86; Leader Writer, Daily Telegraph 1986–91, Deputy Political Corresp. 1987–88, political sketch writer 1988–91, political columnist 1990–91, Deputy Ed. 1994–96; Deputy Ed. The Spectator 1991–94; columnist, Evening Standard 1991–93, Daily Mail 1993–94, 1995–2005; Assoc. Ed. Daily Telegraph 2005–11; Ed. Mail Comment Online 2011–, columnist, Daily Mail 2011–. *Publications:* A Tory Seer (co-ed. with C. Moore) 1989, A Century of County Cricket (ed.) 1990, Moral Desperado: A Life of Thomas Carlyle 1995, Power and Place: The Political Consequences of King Edward VII 1998, Like the Roman: The Life of Enoch Powell 1998, Nor Shall My Sword; The Reinvention of England 1999, Vaughan Williams 2000, The Great British Speeches 2007, Strictly English: The Correct Way to Write and Why It Matters 2010, A Short History of Power 2011. *Honours:* Fellow Commoner, Corpus Christi Coll., Cambridge 2010; Charles Douglas-Home Prize 1993. *Address:* The Daily Mail, 2 Derry Street, London, W8 5TT, England (office). *Telephone:* (20) 7938-6000 (office). *E-mail:* simon.heffer@dailymail.co.uk (office). *Website:* www.dailymail.co.uk (office).

HEFFERNAN, Thomas Patrick Carroll, AB, MA, PhD; American/Irish academic, writer and poet; b. 19 Aug. 1939, Hyannis, Massachusetts; s. of Thomas Hugh Carroll Heffernan and Mary Elizabeth Sullivan Heffernan; m.

Nancy E. Iler 1972 (divorced 1977). *Education:* Boston Coll., Univ. of Manchester, England, Universita per Stranieri, Perugia, Italy, Sophia Univ., Tokyo. *Career:* Poet in Schools, North Carolina Dept of Public Instruction, Raleigh 1973–77; Visiting Artist, Poetry, North Carolina Dept of Community Colls 1977–81, South Carolina Arts Comm. 1981–82; Co-Ed., The Plover (Chidori), bilingual haiku journal, Japan 1989–92; fmr Prof. of English, Kagoshima Prefectural Univ., Japan; mem. Modern Language Assen, Japan English Literary Soc., Japan American Literary Soc., Renaissance Inst. (Tokyo), Japan Asscn of Language Teachers, Haiku Soc. of America. *Plays:* as actor: principal role in Solitaire, Double Solitaire, Harry Roat in Wait Until Dark; as mem. of Central Piedmont Repertory Co.: The Doctor in Something's Afoot, The Wizard in The Wizard of Oz. *Publications:* Mobiles 1973, A Poem is a Smile You Can Hear (ed.) 1976, A Narrative of Jeremy Bentham 1978, The Liam Poems 1981, City Renewing Itself 1983, Art and Emblem: Early Seventeenth Century English Poetry of Devotion 1991, Gathering in Ireland 1996, White Edge, Curling Wave 2002, Christmas Gifts in South Japan and Other Haiku Essays 2003; contribs to anthologies and other publications. *Honours:* Gordon Barber Memorial Award 1979, Portfolio Award 1983, Roanoke Chowan Prize 1982. *Telephone:* (99) 258-7502 (home). *E-mail:* thomasheffernan@yahoo.com.

HEFFRON, Dorris, BA, MA; Canadian novelist; b. 18 Oct. 1944, Noranda, QC; d. of William Heffron and Kathleen Heffron; m. 1st William Newton-Smith 1968 (divorced); two d.; m. 2nd D. L. Gauer 1980. *Education:* Queen's Univ., Kingston, Ont. *Career:* Tutor, Univ. of Oxford, UK 1968–80, The Open Univ. 1975–78, Univ. of Malaysia 1978; Writer-in-Residence, Wainfleet Public Library, 1989–90; mem. Authors Soc., Toronto Arts Council Literary Cttee, Nat. Writers' Union of Canada, fmr Chair. Foreign Affairs Cttee; mem. Bd of Dirs PEN, Writers' Trust of Canada, Na-Me-Res; book reviewer for Globe and Mail. *Publications:* A Nice Fire and Some Moonpennies 1971, Crusty Crossed 1976, Rain and I 1982, A Shark in the House 1996, City Wolves 2008; contrib. to various pubs. *Honours:* Canada Council Arts Grant 1974. *Address:* Little Creek Wolf Range, RR No. 1, Clarksburg, ON N0H 1J0, Canada (home). *E-mail:* dorrisheffron@sympatico.ca (office). *Website:* www.dorrisheffron.ca.

HEFNER, Hugh Marston, BS; American publisher; *Chairman Emeritus, Playboy Enterprises, Inc.*; b. 9 April 1926, Chicago, Ill.; s. of Glenn L. Hefner and Grace Hefner (née Swanson); m. 1st Mildred Williams 1949 (divorced 1959); one s. one d.; m. 2nd Kimberley Conrad 1989 (divorced); two s. *Education:* Univ. of Illinois. *Career:* Ed.-in-Chief Playboy Magazine 1953–, Oui Magazine 1972–81; Chair. Emer. Playboy Enterprises 1988–; Pres. Playboy Club Int. Inc. 1959–86. *Honours:* Int. Press Directory Int. Publisher Award 1997. *Address:* Playboy Enterprises Inc., 680 North Lake Shore Drive, Chicago, IL 60611, USA (office). *Telephone:* (312) 751-8000 (office). *Fax:* (312) 751-2818 (office). *Website:* www.playboyenterprises.com (home).

HEGARTY, Frances, (Frances Fyfield), BA, LLB; British writer and lawyer; b. 1949. *Education:* Univ. of Newcastle upon Tyne. *Career:* part-time lawyer 1987–2000; novelist 1987–; Helen West book series televised 1995–2001. *Publications include:* as Frances Fyfield: A Question of Guilt 1988, Deep Sleep (Silver Dagger Award) 1991, A Clear Conscience (Grand Prix de Littérature Policière 1998) 1994, Without Consent 1996, Blind Date 1998, Staring at the Light 1999, Undercurrents 2000, Helen West Omnibus 2001, The Nature of the Beast 2001, Seeking Sanctuary 2003, Looking Down 2004, Safer Than Houses 2005, The Art of Drowning 2006, Blood from Stone 2008, Cold to the Touch 2009; as Frances Hegarty: The Playroom 1991, Half Light 1992, Let's Dance 1995. *Literary Agent:* Rogers, Coleridge and White, 20 Powis Mews, London, W11 1JN, England.

HEGI, Ursula Johanna, BA, MA; German writer, poet and critic; b. 23 May 1946, Büderich; m. 1967 (divorced 1984); two s. *Education:* Univ. of New Hampshire. *Career:* Instructor, Univ. of New Hampshire 1980–84; book critic, Los Angeles Times, New York Times, Washington Post 1982–; Asst Prof., Eastern Washington Univ. 1984–89, Assoc. Prof. 1989–95, Prof. of English 1995–2001; visiting writer various univs; mem. Associated Writing Programs, Nat. Book Critics Circle (mem. bd of dirs 1992–94). *Publications:* fiction: Intrusions 1981, Unearned Pleasures and Other Stories 1988, Floating in My Mother's Palm (Pacific Northwest Booksellers Asscn Award) 1990, Stones from the River 1994, Salt Dancers 1995, The Vision of Emma Blau 1999, Hotel of the Saints (short stories) 2001, Trudi & Pia 2003, Sacred Time 2004, The Worst Thing I've Done 2007, Children and Fire 2011; non-fiction: Tearing the Silence: On Being German in America 1997; contribs to anthologies, newspapers, journals and magazines. *Honours:* Indiana Fiction Award 1988, Nat. Endowment for the Arts Fellowship 1990, New York Times Best Books Selections 1990, 1994, Pacific Northwest Booksellers Asscn Award 1991, Gov.'s Writers Awards 1991, 1994. *Address:* c/o Simon & Schuster Inc., 1230 Avenue of The Americas, 11th Floor, New York, NY 10020, USA.

HEIDSIECK, Bernard; French performance poet; b. 1928, Paris. *Education:* Istituto Politico. *Career:* co-creator sound poetry 1950s, action poems 1960s; fmr Vice-Pres. Banque Française du Commerce Extérieur, Paris; fmr Pres. Commission Poésie du Centre Nat. du Livre. *Recordings:* Poèmes Partition D2 and D3Z 1973, Partition V 1973, Trois Biopsies + Un Passe-Partout 1970, P Puissance B 1983, Canal Street 1986. *Publications:* poetry: Sitôt dit 1955, B2B3 1967, Portraits-Pétales 1973, D2 + D3Z 1973, Partition V 1973, Encoconnage 1975, Foules 1975, Dis-moi ton utopie 1975, Poésie action/ Poésie sonore 1955–75 1976, Participation à Tanger I 1978, Participation à Tanger II 1979, Poésie sonore et caves romaines suivi de Poème-Partition D4P 1984, Derviche/Le Robert 1988, Poème-Partition A 1992, Poème-Partition R 1994, Poème-Partition N 1995, Coléoptères and Co (with P.A.Gette) 1997, Poème-Partition T 1998, Vaduz 1999, Poème-Partition Q 1999, Respirations et brèves rencontres 2000, Nous étions bien peu en... 2001, Partition V 2001, Canal Street 2001, Poème-Partition F 2001, Le Carrefour de la chaussée d'Antin 2001, Notes convergentes 2001, La Poinçonneuse 2002, Ça ne sera pas long 2003, Lettre à Brion 2004, Démocratie II 2004. *Honours:* Grand Prix Nat. de Poésie 1991. *Address:* c/o Editions Al Dante, 2 La Charade, 23290 Saint-Etienne de Fursac, France. *E-mail:* aldante@club-internet.fr.

HEIGHTON, Steven, MA; Canadian author; b. 14 Aug. 1961, Toronto, Ont. *Education:* Silverthorn Coll. Inst., Queen's Univ. *Career:* Ed. Quarry magazine 1988–94; Writer-in-Residence, Concordia Univ. 2002–03; Jack McLelland Writer-in-Residence, Massey Coll., Univ. of Toronto 2004; participating author, American Movements II course, Univ. of New Orleans 2006; instructor Summer Literature Seminars, Herzen Univ., Russia 2007; Writer-in-Residence Univ. of Ottawa 2009, Royal Mil. Coll., Kingston 2010; Fellow, Cambridge Literary Seminars 1997; Ed. Quarry Magazine 1988–94. *Publications include:* Stalin's Carnival (poetry) 1989, Foreign Ghosts (travelogue/poetry) 1989, Flight Paths of the Emperor (stories) 1992, The Ecstasy of Skeptics (poetry) 1994, On earth as it is (stories) 1995, The Admen Move on Lhasa: Writing and Culture in a Virtual World (essays) 1997, The Shadow Boxer (novel) 2000, Musings: An Anthology of Greek-Canadian Literature (co-ed.) 2003, The Address Book (poetry) 2004, Afterlands (novel) 2006, Patient Frame (poetry) 2010, Every Lost Country (novel) 2010; poetry, fiction and critical articles in various periodicals and anthologies, including London Review of Books, Poetry, Tin House, New York Times Book Review, Best English Stories, Best Canadian Stories, Poetry London, Brick, etc. 1984–. *Honours:* Gerald Lampert Award for Best First Book of Poetry 1990, Air Canada Award 1990, Gold Medal for Fiction, Nat. Magazine Awards 1992, 2007, 2009, Petra Kenney Prize 2002, Gold Medal for Poetry, Nat. Magazine Awards 2003, K. M. Hunter Award (Literature Category) 2010. *Literary Agent:* c/o Anne McDermid Agency, 83 Willcocks Street, Toronto, ON M5S 1C9, Canada. *E-mail:* anne@mcdermidagency.com. *Website:* www.mcdermidagency.com. *E-mail:* sheighton@kos.net (office). *Website:* www.stevenheighton.com.

HEIKAL, Mohamed Hassanein; Egyptian journalist; b. 1923; m.; three s. *Career:* reporter, The Egyptian Gazette 1943, Akher Sa'a magazine 1945; Ed. Al-Akhbar daily newspaper 1956–57; Ed. Al-Ahram 1957–74, Chair. Bd of Dirs 1959–74; mem. Cen. Cttee, Arab Socialist Union 1968–74; Minister of Information and Foreign Affairs April–Oct. 1970; arrested Sept. 1981, released Nov. 1981. *Publications:* Nahnou wa America 1967, Nasser: The Cairo Documents 1972, The Road to Ramadan 1975, Sphinx and Commissar 1979, The Return of the Ayatollah 1981, Autumn of Fury 1983, Cutting the Lion's Tail 1986, Suez Through Egyptian Eyes 1986, Boiling Point 1988, (The) Explosion 1990, Illusions of Triumph 1992, Arms and Politics 1993, Secret Channels 1996.

HEIM, Scott, BA, MA, MFA; American writer and poet; b. 26 Sept. 1966, Hutchinson, Kansas. *Education:* Univ. of Kansas, Columbia Univ. *Publications:* Saved from Drowning: Poems 1993, Mysterious Skin (novel) 1995, In Awe (novel) 1997, We Disappear 2008. *Honours:* William Herbert Carruth Award for Poetry 1991, Edna Osborne Whitcomb Fiction Prize 1991. *Literary Agent:* c/o Dorian Karchmar, William Morris Agency, 1325 Avenue of the Americas, New York, NY 10019, USA. *Telephone:* (212) 586-5100. *Website:* heim.etherweave.com.

HEIN, Christoph; German novelist and playwright; b. 8 April 1944, Heinzendorf, Schlesien. *Education:* Gymnasium Berlin, Univ. of Leipzig, Humboldt Univ., Berlin. *Career:* dramatist and playwright, Volksbühne Berlin 1971–79; author 1979–. *Plays:* Schlötel oder Was solls 1974, Cromwell 1980, Lassalle fragt Herrn Herbert nach Sonja 1981, Die wahre Geschichte des Ah Q 1983, Passage 1987, Die Ritter der Tafelrunde 1989, Randow 1994, Bruch 1998, Himmel auf Erden 1998, In Acht und Bann 1998, Mutters Tag 2000, Noach (opera) 2001, Zur Geschichte des menschlichen Herzens 2002. *Publications:* fiction: Einladung zum Lever Bourgeois (stories) 1980, Nachfahrt und früher Morgen (juvenile) 1980, Der fremde Freund (novel) (trans. as The Distant Lover) 1982, Horns Ende (novel) 1985, Das Wildpferd unterm Kachelofen (juvenile) 1985, Der Tangospieler (novel) (trans. as The Tango Player) 1989, Die Vergewaltigung (stories) 1991, Matzeln 1991, Das Napoleonspiel (novel) 1993, Exekution eines Kalbes und andere Erzählungen 1994, Von allem Anfang an (novel) 1997, Willenbrock (novel) 2000, Mama ist gegangen (juvenile) 2003, Landnahme (trans. as Settlement) 2004, In seiner frühen Kindheit ein Garten (novel) 2005, Frau Paula Trosseau (novel) 2007; non-fiction: Die wahre Geschichte des Ah Q (plays/essays) 1984, Schlötel oder Was solls (essays) 1986, Öffentlich arbeiten. Essays und Gespräche 1987, Die fünfte Grundrechenart. Aufsätze und Reden 1986–1989 1990, Als Kind habe ich Stalin gesehen (essays/speeches) 1990, Die Mauern von Jerichow 1996. *Honours:* Chevalier, Ordre des Arts et des Lettres; Heinrich Mann-Preis der Akad. der Künste Berlin 1982, (westdeutscher) Kritikerpreis für Literatur Berlin 1983, Literaturpreis Hamburg 1985, Lessing Prize 1989, Stefan Andres Prize, Schweich 1989, Erich Fried Prize, Vienna 1990, Ludwig Mülheims Prize 1992, Berliner Literaturpreis der Stiftung Preussische Seehandlung 1992, Norddt. Literaturpreis 1998, Peter-Weiss-Preis 1998, Solothurner Literaturpreis 2000, Premio Grinzane Cavour Turin 2002, State Prize for European Literature Austria 2002, Schiller-Gedächtnispreis 2004, Verdi

Literaturpreis 2004. *Address:* c/o Suhrkamp-Verlag, Postfach 10 19 45, 60019 Frankfurt am Main, Germany.

HEINSEN, Geerd, PhD; German journalist; *Editor, Orpheus Oper International*; b. 29 Jan. 1945, s. of Prof. Hans Adolf Heinsen. *Education:* studies in Berlin, Freiburg, Harvard Univ. and Univ. of California, Los Angeles, USA, Berlin Free Univ. *Career:* Ed. Orpheus Oper International magazine. *Address:* Orpheus, Charlottenstrasse 53, 14059 Berlin, Germany (office). *E-mail:* heinsenorpheus@t-online.de (home); info@orpheusoper.de (office). *Website:* www.orpheusoper.de (office).

HEJDA, Zbyněk; Czech poet and translator; b. 2 Feb. 1930, Hradci Králové. *Education:* Charles Univ., Prague. *Career:* historian 1953–58; mem. Prague City Council 1958–68; ed. in a publishing house, lost his job after signing Charter 77 document calling for improved human rights 1977; various part-time positions –1989; full-time writer 1989–; taught medical ethics Charles Univ. 1990s; fmr Ed. Tvář literary journal; Co-Ed. Střední Evropa (Central Europe) 1985. *Publications include:* Všechna slast 1964, Blízkosti smrti 1978, Lady Felthamová 1979, Tři básně 1987, Pobyt v sanatoriu 1993, Nikoho tam nepotkám 1994, Valse mélancolique 995, Básně 1996, Překlady 1998, Cesta k Cerekvi 2004, Sny 2007; trans. of works by Emily Dickenson, Georg Trakl, Gottfried Benn. *Honours:* Jaroslav Seifert Prize 1996.

HEJINIAN, Lyn, BA; American poet and writer; *Professor, Department of English, University of California, Berkeley*; b. 17 May 1941, Alameda, California; m. 1st John P. Hejinian 1961 (divorced 1972); one s. one d.; m. 2nd Larry Ochs 1977. *Education:* Harvard Univ. *Career:* Founder-ed. Tuumba Press 1976–84; currently Co-founder and Co-ed. Atelos; currently Prof., Dept of English, Univ. of California at Berkeley; mem. Fellow, Acad. of American Poets. *Publications:* A Great Adventure 1972, A Thought is the Bride of What Thinking 1976, A Mask of Motion 1977, Gesualdo 1978, Writing is an Aid to Memory 1978, My Life 1980, The Guard 1984, Redo 1984, Individuals 1988, Leningrad: American Writers in the Soviet Union (with Michael Davidson, Ron Silliman, Barrett Watten) 1991, The Hunt 1991, The Cell 1992, The Cold of Poetry 1994, Two Stein Talks 1995, Guide, Grammar, Watch and the Thirty Nights 1996, The Little Book of a Thousand Eyes 1996, Wicker (with Jack Collom) 1996, The Traveler and the Hill (with Emilie Clark) 1998, Sight 1999, Sunflower (with Jack Collom) 2000, Chartings 2000, Happily 2000, The Beginner 2000, The Language of Enquiry 2000, A Border Comedy 2001, Slowly 2002, The Beginner 2002, The Fatalist 2003, My Life in the Nineties 2003, Saga/Circus 2008, The Book of a Thousand Eyes 2012; contribs to journals. *Address:* Department of English, University of California, 406 Wheeler Hall, Berkeley, CA 94720-1030, USA (office). *Telephone:* (510) 642-3467 (office). *Fax:* (510) 642-8738 (office). *Website:* english.berkeley.edu/profiles/38 (office).

HELD, Michael J., MA; American publisher; *Director, Division of Scholarly Journals and Professional Periodicals, American Academy of Pediatrics*. *Career:* fmr Pres. Council of Science Edn; fmr Exec. Dir Rockefeller Univ. Press; currently Dir Div. of Scholarly Journals and Professional Periodicals, American Acad. of Pediatrics. *Address:* American Academy of Pediatrics, 141 Northwest Point Blvd, Elk Grove Village, IL 60007-1098, USA (office). *Telephone:* (847) 434-4000 (office). *Fax:* (847) 434-8000 (office). *E-mail:* mheld@aap.org (office). *Website:* www.aap.org (office).

HELGADÓTTIR, Guðrun; Icelandic politician and writer; b. 7 Sept. 1935, Hafnarfjördur; d. of Helgi Guðlaugsson and Ingigerður Eyjólfsdóttir; two s. two d. *Education:* Reykjavík Grammar School and Univ. *Career:* worked as sec. at Reykjavík Grammar School 1957–70; Head of Dept, Nat. Social Security Inst. 1973–80; mem. Reykjavík City Council 1978–82; mem. Althingi (Parl., People's Alliance) 1979–95, Speaker (first woman) 1988–91; has written fiction for children and young adults since 1974; her children's play Óvitar (Infants) opened at Nat. Theatre of Iceland in 1979 (re-staged 1988) and has also been staged in the Faroe Islands. *Publications include:* 26 titles including, for children: Jón Oddur og Jón Bjarni (Jón Oddur and Jón Bjarni) 1974, Astarsaga ur fjöllunum (A Giant Love Story) 1981, Undan Illgresinu (From Beneath the Weeds) (The Nordic Prize for Children's Books) 1992, Ekkert að þakka (The Pleasure's Mine) 1995, Englajól (The Angels' Christmas Tree) 1997, Dagbladet; several illustrated books for young children with illustrations by known artists as well as a TV play and a novel for adults. *Honours:* Commdr's Cross, Order of the Falcon; numerous awards, including Thorbjörn Egner Fund Prize, IBBY Iceland Award. *Address:* Túngata 43, 101 Reykjavík, Iceland. *Telephone:* (1) 23124.

HELLENGA, Robert, BA, PhD; American writer and teacher; b. 5 Aug. 1941, Milwaukee; s. of Ted Hellenga and Marjorie Hellenga; m. Virginia Killion 1963; three d. *Education:* Univ. of Michigan, Queen's, Univ. of Belfast, Northern Ireland, Princeton Univ. *Career:* Knox Coll. 1968–; Dir Newberry Library Seminar in the Humanities, ACM programs, Florence; mem. Soc. of Midland Authors, Illinois Arts Alliance. *Publications:* fiction: The Sixteen Pleasures 1994, The Fall of a Sparrow 1998, Blues Lessons 2002, Philosophy Made Simple 2006, The Italian Lover 2007, Snakewoman of Little Egypt 2010; contribs to Iowa Review, Chicago Review, California Quarterly, Columbia, Ascent, Farmer's Market, Chicago Tribune Magazine, TriQuarterly, Crazyhorse, Mississippi Valley Review, Black Warrior Review, New York Times Magazine, The Gettysburg Review. *Honours:* several fellowships and grants from Illinois Arts Council, NEA Fellowship, PEN Syndicated Fiction Award 1988, Soc. of Midland Authors Award for Fiction 1995, Knox Coll. Faculty Achievement Award 1997–98. *Literary Agent:* c/o Henry Dunow, Dunow Carlson Lerner Literary Agency, 27 W 20th Street, Suite 1107, New York, NY 10011, USA. *Telephone:* (212) 645-7606. *E-mail:* henry@dclagency.com. *Website:* www.dclagency.com. *Address:* 85 S. Seminary Street #1, Galesburg, IL 61401, USA (home). *Telephone:* (309) 343-8957 (home); (309) 734-8758 (home). *E-mail:* rhelleng@knox.edu (home). *Website:* www.roberthellenga.com.

HELLER, Agnes, MA, PhD; Hungarian academic and writer; b. 12 May 1929, Budapest; m. 1st Istvan Hermann 1949, one d.; m. 2nd Ferenc Feher 1963, one s. *Education:* University of Budapest, Hungarian Acad. of Sciences. *Career:* Reader in Sociology, La Trobe University, Bundoora, Vic., Australia; Prof. of Philosophy, New School for Social Research, New York, 1985–2008, currently Emer. Prof.; mem. Société Européenne. *Publications:* Renaissance Man, 1978; A Theory of History, 1981; Hungary 1956 Revisited: The Message of a Revolution – A Quarter-Century After (co-author), 1983; Dictatorship Over Needs (co-author), 1983; Lukacs Reappraised, 1983, UK edn as Lukacs Revalued, 1983; The Power of Shame: A Rational Perspective, 1985; Reconstructing Aesthetics: Writings of the Budapest School (co-ed.), 1986; Doomsday or Deterrence?: On the Antinuclear Issue (co-author), 1986; Eastern Left, Western Left: Totalitarianism, Freedom and Democracy (co-author), 1987; Beyond Justice, 1987; The Postmodern Political Condition (co-author), 1988; General Ethics, 1988; A Philosophy of Morals, 1990; Can Modernity Survive?, 1990; From Yalta to Glasnost: The Dismantling of Stalin's Empire (co-author), 1991; The Grandeur and Twilight of Radical Universalism (co-author), 1991; A Philosophy of History in Fragments, 1993; The Limits to Natural Law and the Paradox of Evil, 1993; An Ethics of Personality, 1995, The Time is Out of Joint 2002, Immortal Comedy 2009, A Theory of Feeling 2010, A Short History of My Philosophy 2010; Contributions: Academic journals. *Honours:* Goethe Medal, Germany 2010; Hon. degrees (La Trobe, Melbourne, Australia) 1996, (Buenos Aires, Argentina) 1997, (Ben Gurion, Israel) 2008, (San Marcos, Peru); Lessing Prize, Hamburg 1991, Hannah Arendt Prize for Political Philosophy, Bremen 1995, Szechenyi National Prize, Hungary 1995, Sonning Prize 2006. *Address:* Gutenberg ter 4, u.4, Budapest 1088, Hungary. *Telephone:* 36205555788 (home). *E-mail:* aheller@emc.elte.hu (office); helleragnes@gmail.com (home).

HELLER, (Franz) André; Austrian poet, writer, singer and theatre producer; b. 22 March 1947, Vienna. *Career:* actor 1965–67; Co-founder, Ö3 radio station 1967; recording artist 1968–83; Dir TV documentaries 1978–. *Albums include:* No. 1 1970, Platte 1971, Das war André Heller 1972, Neue Lieder 1973, A Musi Musi A 1974, Bei lebendigem Leib 1975, Abendland 1976, Basta 1978, Bitter und Süß 1978, Ausgerechnet Helle 1979, Heurige und gestrige Lieder (with Helmut Qualtinger) 1979, Verwunschen 1980, Stimmenhören 1983, Narrenlieder 1985, Liebeslieder 1989, Kritische Gesamtausgabe 1967–1991 1991, Ruf und Echo 2003, Bestheller 1967–2007 2008. *Publications include:* Die Ernte der Schlaflosigkeit in Wien 1976, Auf und davon: Erzähites 1979, Schlamassel 1993, Sitzt ana und glaubt er is zwa (with Helmut Qualtinger) 1993, Bilderleben. Öffentliches & Privates 2000, Als ich ein Hund War. Liebesgeschichten und weitere rätselhafte Vorfälle 2001, Mein Garten. Flora-Führer durch den Giardino Botanico Gardone 2001, Augenweide. Der Garten der Gärten 2003, Afrika! Afrika! Das magische Zirkuserignis vom Kontinent des Stauens 2005, Vienna Warhol Vienna 2005, Wie ich lernte, bei mir selbst Kind zu sein 2008, Wienereien oder ein absichtlicher Schicksalsnarr 2012. *Honours:* Culture Award 1993, Amadeus Austrian Music Award 2004. *E-mail:* contact@andreheller.com. *Website:* www.andreheller.com.

HELLER, Michael, BS, MA; American poet, writer and teacher; b. 11 May 1937, New York, NY; m. 1st Doris Whytal 1962 (divorced 1978); m. 2nd Jane Augustine 1979; one s. *Education:* Rensselaer Polytechnic Inst., New York Univ. *Career:* Faculty mem., American Language Inst., New York Univ. 1967–99, Acting Dir 1986–87, Academic Co-ordinator 1987–91; Poet and Teacher, New York State Poets in the Schools 1970–; mem. American Acad. of Poets, Modern Language Asscn, New York State Poets in Public Service, PEN, Poetry Soc. of America, Poets and Writers, Poets House. *Publications:* Two Poems 1970, Accidental Center 1972, Figures of Speaking 1977, Knowledge 1979, Marble Snows, Origin 1979, Conviction's Net of Branches: Essays on the Objectivist Poets and Poetry 1985, Marginalia in a Desperate Hand 1986, In the Builded Place 1990, Carl Rakosi: Man and Poet (ed.) 1993, Wordflow: New and Selected Poems 1997, Living Root: A Memoir 2000, Exigent Futures: New and Selected Poems 2003, Uncertain Poetries: Essays on Poets, Poetry and Poetics, Speaking the Estranged: Essays on the Work of George Oppen, Two Novellas 2009, Eschaton 2009, Beckmann Variations, and Other Poems 2010; contribs to anthologies, reference books and journals. *Honours:* Coffey Poetry Prize, New School for Social Research 1964, Poetry in Public Places Award 1975, New York State Creative Artists Public Service Fellowship in Poetry 1975–76, Nat. Endowment for the Humanities Grant 1979, Di Castagnola Award, Poetry Soc. of America 1980, Outstanding Writer Citations, Pushcart Press 1983, 1984, 1992, New York Fellowship in the Arts 1989, Fund for Poetry Award 2003. *Address:* 346 East 18th Street, New York, NY 10003, USA (home). *Telephone:* (212) 533-1928 (office). *E-mail:* mh7@nyu.edu (office). *Website:* www.michaelhellerpoetry.com.

HELLER, Zoë Kate Hinde Mercedes, BA, MA; British novelist and journalist; b. 7 July 1965, London, England; d. of Lukas Heller and Caroline Carter; two d. *Education:* St Anne's Coll., Oxford, Columbia Univ., New York, USA. *Career:* worked as feature writer, critic and columnist for several newspapers, including Independent on Sunday, Sunday Times, Daily Telegraph 1993–; lives in New York. *Publications:* Everything You Know 1999, Notes on a Scandal (US edn as What Was She Thinking?) 2003, The Believers 2008; contrib. to Harper's Bazaar, The Independent, City Limits, Granta, Vogue, Vanity Fair, The New Yorker, The New Republic, London Review of Books. *Honours:* British Press Awards Columnist of the Year 2002. *Address:* c/o Fig Tree, 80 Strand, London, WC2R 0RL, England.

HELLIER, Trudy; Australian playwright, filmmaker and actress. *Education:* RMIT Univ., Melbourne. *Television appearances:* Welcher & Welcher, Marshall Law, Frontline, Round the Twist, Sea Change, The Games, Guinevere Jones, Blue Heelers, Halifax fp, Play School (presenter), Neighbours, The Secret Life of Us, State Coroner, Law of the Land, Driven Crazy. *Films:* screenplays: Break and Enter 1997, Trapped 2002, Dog Daze. *Publications:* Trapped 1996, Blind Faith 2001, The Family Trust (co-writer). *Honours:* Australian Film Inst. Award 1999. *Literary Agent:* c/o RGM Associates, PO Box 128, Surry Hills, NSW 2010, Australia. *Telephone:* (2) 9281-3911. *Fax:* (2) 9281-4705. *E-mail:* info@rgm.com.au. *Website:* www.rgm.com.au.

HELPRIN, Mark, AB, AM; American writer; b. 28 June 1947, New York, NY; m. Lisa Kennedy 1980; two d. *Education:* Harvard Univ., Magdalen Coll., Oxford. *Career:* fmrly served in the British Merchant Navy, Israeli infantry, Israeli Air Force; contributing ed., The Wall Street Journal; speechwriter for Senator Robert J. Dole 1996; mem. Council on Foreign Relations; Sr Fellow The Claremont Inst.; Fellow American Acad. in Rome; fmr Guggenheim Fellow. *Publications:* A Dove of the East and Other Stories 1975, Refiner's Fire: The Life and Adventures of Marshall Pearl, a Foundling 1977, Ellis Island and Other Stories 1981, Winter's Tale 1983, Best American Short Stories (ed. with Shannon Ravenel) 1988, Swan Lake 1989, A Soldier of the Great War 1991, Memoir from Antproof Case 1995, A City in Winter (novella) (World Fantasy Best Novella Award 1997) 1996, The Veil of Snows 1997, The Pacific and Other Stories 2005, Freddy and Fredericka 2005, Digital Barbarism: A Writer's Manifesto 2009; contrib. to The New Yorker, The Atlantic Monthly, The New Criterion, National Review, The American Heritage, The Wall Street Journal, The New York Times. *Honours:* American Acad. and Institute of Arts and Letters Prix de Rome 1982, Nat. Jewish Book Award 1982. *Address:* c/o The Claremont Institute, 937 W Foothill Boulevard, Suite E, Claremont, CA 91711, USA (office). *E-mail:* info@claremont.org (office). *Website:* www.claremont.org (office); www.markhelprin.com.

HELWIG, David Gordon, CM, MA; Canadian writer; b. 5 April 1938, Toronto, Ont.; s. of William Helwig and Ivy Helwig; m. Nancy Keeling 1959 (separated 1992); two d.; partner Judith Gaudet since 1996. *Education:* Univ. of Toronto, Univ. of Liverpool, UK. *Career:* Lecturer, then Asst Prof., Queen's Univ., Kingston, Ont. 1962–74, also Asst Prof. 1976–80; Literary Man., CBC 1974–76; Poet Laureate, Prince Edward Island 2008–09. *Radio plays:* many radio dramas for CBC. *Publications:* 41 books of poetry and novels, including Figures in a Landscape 1968, The Time of Her Life, This Human Day 2000, The Year One 2004, Coming Through 2007, The Sway of Otherwise 2008, Mystery Stories 2010. *Honours:* mem. Order of Canada; CBC Poetry Award 1983, Atlantic Poetry Award 2004, Matt Cohen Award. *Address:* Belfast, PEI C0A 1A0, Canada (home). *Telephone:* (902) 659-2942 (home). *E-mail:* dgh1938@gmail.com (home). *Website:* www.davidhelwig.com.

HELY-HUTCHINSON, Timothy Mark, MA; British publisher; *Group Chief Executive, Hodder Headline Ltd;* b. 26 Oct. 1953, London; s. of Earl of Donoughmore and Countess of Donoughmore (née Parsons). *Education:* Eton Coll. and Univ. of Oxford. *Career:* Man. Dir Macdonald & Co. (Publrs) Ltd 1982–86, Headline Book Publishing PLC 1986–93; Group Chief Exec. Hodder Headline Ltd 1993–; Dir W. H. Smith PLC 1999–, Chair. W. H. Smith News Ltd 2002–04; Group Chief Exec. Hachette Livre UK Ltd 2004–. *Honours:* Venturer of the Year (British Venture Capital Asscn) 1990, Publr of the Year (British Book Awards) 1992. *Address:* Hodder Headline Ltd, 338 Euston Road, London, NW1 3BH (office). *Telephone:* (20) 7873-6011 (office). *Fax:* (20) 7873-6012 (office). *Website:* www.hodderheadline.co.uk (office).

HELYAR, Jane Penelope Josephine, (Josephine Poole); British writer; b. 12 Feb. 1933, London; m. 1st T.R. Poole 1956; m. 2nd V.J.H. Helyar 1975; one s. five d. *Television scripts:* The Harbourer 1975, Touch and Go (for children) 1977, The Sabbatical 1981, The Breakdown 1981, Miss Constantine 1981, Ring a Ring a Rosie 1983, With Love, Belinda 1983, The Wit to Woo 1983, Fox 1984, Buzzard 1984, Dartmoor Pony 1984. *Publications:* A Dream in the House 1961, Moon Eyes 1965, The Lilywhite Boys 1967, Catch as Catch Can 1969, Yokeham 1970, Billy Buck 1972, Touch and Go 1976, When Fishes Flew 1978, Hannah Chance 1980, Diamond Jack 1983, The Country Diary Companion (to accompany Central TV series) 1983, Three for Luck 1985, Wildlife Tales 1986, The Loving Ghosts 1988, Angel 1989, This is Me Speaking 1990, Snow White (picture book) 1991, Paul Loves Amy Loves Christo 1992, Scared to Death 1994, Pinocchio (re-written) 1994, Deadly Inheritance 1995, The Water Babies (re-written) 1996, Hero 1997, Jack and the Beanstalk (picture book) 1997, Joan of Arc (picture book) 1998, Run Rabbit 1999, Fair Game 2000, Scorched 2003, Anne Frank (picture book) 2005. *Literary Agent:* c/o Celia Catchpole, 56 Gilpin Avenue, East Sheen, London, SW14 8QY, England. *E-mail:* celiacatchpole@yahoo.co.uk. *Address:* Poundisford Lodge, Poundisford, Taunton, TA3 7AE, England (home).

HEMLEY, Robin, BA, MFA; American academic and writer; *Director, Non-Fiction Writing Program, University of Iowa;* b. 28 May 1958, New York, NY; m. Beverly Bertling Hemley 1987, two d. *Education:* Indiana Univ., Univ. of Iowa. *Career:* Asst Prof. of English, Univ. of North Carolina at Charlotte 1986–92, Assoc. Prof. 1992–94; Asst Prof. of English, Western Washington Univ., Bellingham 1994–96, Assoc. Prof. 1996–99, Prof. 1999–2001; Viebranz Distinguished Visiting Chair., St Lawrence Univ. 2001; Faculty mem., Vermont Coll. 2000–05, Faculty Chair. 2002–05; Prof., Univ. of Utah 2001–04; Dir, Non-Fiction Writing Program, Univ. of Iowa 2004–. *Publications:* The Mouse Town 1987, All You Can Eat 1988, The Last Studebaker 1992, Turning Life Into Fiction 1994, The Big Ear 1995, Nola (Independent Press Book Award for Non-Fiction) 1998, Invented Eden 2003, Extreme Fiction: Fabulists and Formalists 2004, Do-Over! 2009. *Honours:* Pushcart Prizes 1990, 1994. *Address:* Non-Fiction Writing Program, Department of English, 425–B EPB, University of Iowa, Iowa City, IA 52242, USA (office). *Telephone:* (319) 335-0454 (office). *E-mail:* robin-hemley@uiowa.edu (office). *Website:* www.english.uiowa.edu/faculty/hemley (office).

HEMMING, John Henry, CMG, MA, DLitt, FSA; British/Canadian writer and publisher; *Joint Chairman, Hemming Group Ltd;* b. 5 Jan. 1935, Vancouver, BC; s. of H. Harold Hemming, OBE, MC and Alice L. Hemming, OBE; m. Sukie Babington-Smith 1979; one s. one d. *Education:* Eton Coll., UK, McGill Univ. and Univ. of Oxford, UK. *Career:* Dir and Sec. Royal Geographical Soc. 1975–96; Jt Chair. Hemming Group Ltd 1976–; Chair. Brintex Ltd, Newman Books Ltd; explorations in Peru and Brazil 1960, 1961, 1971, 1972, 1986–88, led Maracá Rainforest Project, Brazil (largest ever Amazon research programme by a European country) 1987–88. *Publications:* The Conquest of the Incas 1970, Tribes of the Amazon Basin in Brazil (with others) 1973, Red Gold: The Conquest of the Brazilian Indians 1978, The Search for El Dorado 1978, Machu Picchu 1982, Monuments of the Incas 1983, Change in the Amazon Basin (two vols) (ed.) 1985, Amazon Frontier: The Defeat of the Brazilian Indians 1987, Maracá 1988, Roraima, Brazil's Northernmost Frontier 1990, The Rainforest Edge (ed.) 1993, Royal Geographical Society Illustrated (ed.) 1997, The Golden Age of Discovery 1998, Die If You Must: Brazilian Indians in the Twentieth Century 2003, Tree of Rivers: The Story of the Amazon 2007. *Honours:* Hon. Fellow, Magdalen Coll. Oxford 2004; Commdr, Order of Southern Cross (Brazil) 1998, Grand Cross, Order of Merit (Peru) 2007; Hon. DLitt (Oxford) 1981, Dr hc (Warwick) 1989, (Stirling) 1991; Pitman Literary Prize 1970, Christopher Award (USA) 1971, Founder's Medal, Royal Geographical Soc. 1989, Bradford Washburn Medal, Boston Museum of Science 1989, Mungo Park Medal, Royal Scottish Geographical Soc. 1988, Special Award, Instituto Nacional de Cultura (Peru) 1996, Citation of Merit, Explorers' Club (New York) 1997. *Address:* 10 Edwardes Square, London, W8 6HE (home); Hemming Group Ltd, 32 Vauxhall Bridge Road, London, SW1V 2SS, England (office). *Telephone:* (20) 7602-6697 (home); (20) 7973-6634 (office). *Fax:* (20) 7233-5049 (office). *Website:* www.hgluk.com (office); www.johnhemming.net.

HEMON, Aleksandar; American writer and journalist; b. 1965, Sarajevo, Bosnia and Herzegovina; s. of Petar Hemon and Andja Hemon; m. Teri Boyd; one d. *Career:* fmr Cultural Ed. Dani magazine, Sarajevo; emigrated to Chicago, USA 1992; regular contrib., The New Yorker, Granta, The Paris Review, Best American Short Stories. *Publications:* fiction: The Question of Bruno (Los Angeles Times Book Review book of the year) 2000, Nowhere Man 2003, Pretext 7: Cut That Fence (ed.) 2003, The Lazarus Project 2008, Love and Obstacles (short stories) 2009, Best European Fiction (ed.) 2011 2010, Best European Fiction (ed.) 2012 2011. *Honours:* John C. Zacharis First Book Award 2001, Guggenheim Fellowship 2003, MacArthur 'Genius' Grant 2004, St Francis College Literary Prize 2009, PEN/W.G. Sebald Award 2011. *Literary Agent:* c/o Nicole Aragi, 143 West 27th Street, Suite 4F, New York, NY 10001, USA. *Address:* c/o Riverhead Books Publicity, Penguin Group USA, 375 Hudson Street, New York, NY 10014, USA (office). *E-mail:* sasha@aleksandarhemon.com (office). *Website:* www.aleksandarhemon.com.

HEN, Józef, (Korab); Polish writer and playwright; b. 8 Nov. 1923, Warsaw; s. of Rubin Cukier and Ewa Cukier; m. Irena Hen 1946; one s. one d. *Career:* self-educated; Lecturer, Sorbonne, France 1993 and Univ. of Warsaw 1995–96; mem. Acad. des Sciences, Belles Lettres et des Beaux Arts, Bordeaux, France; mem. Polish PEN Club. *Film screenplays include:* Krzyż walecznych (Cross of Valour) 1959, Kwiecień (April) 1961, Nikt nie woła (Nobody's Calling) 1961, Bokser i śmierć (The Boxer and Death), Prawo i pięść (Law and the Fist) and Don Gabriel. *Screenplays for TV serials:* Życie Kamila Kuranta (The Life of Kamil Kurant) 1983, Crimen and Królewskie Sny (Royal Dreams) 1987. *Theatre plays:* Ja, Michał z Montaigne (I, Michel de Montaigne) 1984, Justyn! Justyn!, Popołudnie kochanków (Lovers' Afternoon) 1994. *Publications include:* Skromny chłopiec w haremie (A Modest Boy in a Harem) 1957, Kwiecień (April) 1960 (Book of the Year 1961), Teatr Heroda (Herod's Theatre) 1966, Twarz pokerzysty (Pokerface) 1970, Oko Dajana (Dayan's Eye, as Korab) 1972, Yokohama 1973, Crimen 1975, Bokser i śmierć (The Boxer and Death) 1975, Ja, Michał z Montaigne (I, Michel de Montaigne) 1978, Milczące między nami (Silent between Us) 1985, Nie boję się bezsennych nocy (I'm Not Afraid of Sleepless Nights), 3 books 1987, 1992, 2001, Królenskie sny (Royal Dreams) 1989, Nikt nie woła (Nobody's Calling) 1990, Nowolipie 1991, Odejście Afrodyty (Aphrodite's Departure) 1995, Najpiękniejsze lata (The Most Beautiful Years) 1996, Niebo naszych ojcow (Sky of Our Fathers 1997, Błazen – wielki mąż (Jester – The Great Man) (ZAiKS Book of the Year Award 1999) 1998, Mójprzyjaciel Król (My Friend the King) (Booker's Club Book of the Year Award 2005) 2003, Bruliony profesora T. (The Bloch-notes of Professor T.) 2006, Ping-pomgista (The Ping-pongist) 2008, Dziennik na nowy wiek (A Diary for the New Age) 2009, Szóste, najmlodsze (The Sixth, The

Youngest) 2012. *Honours:* Great Literary Prize of Warsaw. *Address:* Al. Ujazdowskie 8 m. 2, 00-478 Warsaw, Poland (home). *Telephone:* (22) 629-19-03 (home). *E-mail:* jozef.hen@gmail.com (home).

HENDERSON, Neil Keir, MA; British writer and poet; b. 7 March 1956, Glasgow, Scotland. *Education:* Univ. of Glasgow. *Publications:* Maldehyde's Discomfiture, or A Lady Churned 1997, Fish-Worshipping – As We Know It 2001, An English Summer in Scotland and Other Unlikely Events 2005, Hormones A-Go-Go 2007; contrib. to anthologies, including Mystery of the City 1997, Loveable Warts: A Defence of Self-Indulgence, Chapman 87 1997, Red Candle Treasury 1998, Mightier Than the Sword: The Punch-Up of the Poses, Chapman 91 1998, Haggis: The Thinking Man's Buttock, Chapman 98 2001, Labyrinths 6 (showcased) 2002, Electric Sheep 2004, Spiders and Flies 2005. *Address:* 46 Revoch Drive, Knightswood, Glasgow, G13 4SB, Scotland (home).

HENDRY, Diana Lois, MLitt; British writer and poet; b. 2 Oct. 1941, Meols, Wirral, England; d. of Leslie McLonomy and Amelia McLonomy; m. George Hendry (divorced 1981); one s. one d.; partner Hamish Whyte 2000–. *Education:* West Kirby Grammar School for Girls, Wirral and Univ. of Bristol. *Career:* Reporter and Feature Writer for Western Mail, Cardiff 1960–65; freelance journalist 1965–80; teacher (part-time) Clifton Coll. 1987–90; Tutor in Literature (part-time), Open Univ. 1987–92, Bristol Polytechnic 1987–93; fmr Tutor in Creative Writing, Univ. of Bristol; Writer-in-Residence, Fairfield Grammar School and Dumfries & Galloway Royal Infirmary 1997–98; Tutor, Arvon Writing Course 2000–09; Royal Literary Fund Fellow, Univ. of Edinburgh 2007–10. *Radio:* various short stories and dramatization of Harvey Angell for BBC Radio 4. *Publications include:* children's fiction: Midnight Pirate 1984, Fiona Finds Her Tongue 1985, Double Vision 1989, The Not-Anywhere House 1989, The Rainbow Watchers 1989, The Carey Street Cat 1989, A Camel Called April 1990, Christmas in Exeter Street 1991, Harvey Angell (Whitbread Award for Junior Novel 1991) 1991, The Thing-in-a-Box 1992, Back Soon 1993, Why Father Christmas Was Late for Hartlepool 1993, Dog Dottington 1995, Happy Old Birthday, Owl 1995, The Thing-on-two-Legs 1995, Strange Goings-on 1995, The Awesome Bird 1995, Flower Street Friends 1995, Harvey Angell and the Ghost Child (Scottish Arts Council Award) 1997, Fiona Says 1998, Minders 1998, The Very Noisy Night 2000, The Very Busy Day 2001, The Very Snowy Christmas 2005, Catch a Gran 2006, Oodles of Noodles 2008, A Dragon in the House 2010; poetry: Making Blue 1995, Borderers 2001, Twelve Lilts 2003, Sparks! (with Tom Pow) 2003, No Homework Tomorrow 2003, Late Love and Other Whodunnits 2008. *Honours:* Third Prize, Peterloo Poetry Competition 1991, Second Prize 1993, First Prize, Housman Soc. Poetry Competition 1996, Robert Louis Stevenson Fellowship 2007. *Address:* 23 Dunrobin Place, Edinburgh, EH3 5HZ, Scotland (home). *Telephone:* (131) 332-3451 (office). *E-mail:* diana.hendry@btinternet.com (office). *Website:* www.dianahendry.co.uk.

HENLEY, Elizabeth (Beth) Becker, BFA, PhD; American playwright and actress; b. 8 May 1952, Jackson, Mississippi; d. of Charles and Lydy Henley; one s. *Education:* Southern Methodist Univ., Univ. of Illinois. *Film:* screenplays: Nobody's Fool 1986, Crimes of the Heart 1986, Miss Firecracker 1989, Signatures 1990, Revelers 1994, Impossible Marriage 1998. *Publications:* plays: Crimes of the Heart (Pulitzer Prize for Drama 1981) 1978, The Wake of Jamey Foster 1982, Am I Blue 1982, The Miss Firecracker Contest 1984, The Lucky Spot 1987, The Debutante Ball 1988, Abundance 1990, Signatures 1990, Beth Henley: Monologues for Women 1992, Control Freaks 1993, Revelers 1994, Collected Plays: Volume I, 1980–1989 2000, Collected Plays: Volume II, 1990–1999 2000, Family Week 2000, Ridiculous Fraud 2006. *Honours:* New York Drama Critics Circle Best Play Award 1981, George Oppenheimer/Newsday Playwriting Award 1980–81.

HENNESSY, Helen (see Vendler, Helen Hennessy)

HENNESSY, Peter John, BA, PhD, FBA, FRSA; British academic and writer; *Attlee Professor of Contemporary History, Queen Mary, University of London*; b. 28 March 1947, London, England; m. Enid Mary Candler 1969; two d. *Education:* St John's Coll., Cambridge, LSE, Harvard Univ., USA. *Career:* Sr Fellow 1984–85; Visiting Fellow 1986–91, Policy Studies Inst.; columnist, New Statesman 1986–87, The Independent 1987–91; Co-founder and Co-Dir 1986–89, Bd mem. 1989–98, Inst. of Contemporary British History; Visiting Fellow, Univ. of Reading 1988–94, Royal Inst. of Public Admin 1989–92, Univ. of Nottingham 1989–95; Visiting Prof. of Govt, Univ. of Strathclyde 1989–; Pnr, Intellectual R&D 1990–; Prof. of Contemporary History, Queen Mary, Univ. of London 1992–, currently Attlee Prof. of Contemporary History; Gresham Prof. of Rhetoric, Gresham Coll., London 1994–97; Chair., Kennedy Memorial Trust 1995–2000; Vice-Pres. Royal Histarial Soc. 1996–; mem. Johnian Soc. (Pres. 1995). *Publications:* States of Emergency (with Keith Jeffery) 1983, Sources Close to the Prime Minister (with Michael Cockerell and David Walker) 1984, What the Papers Never Said 1985, Cabinet 1986, Whitehall 1989, Never Again: Britain 1945–51 1992, The Hidden Wiring: Unearthing the British Constitution 1995, Muddling Through: Power, Politics and the Quality of Government in Postwar Britain 1996, The Prime Minister: The Office and its Holders Since 1945 2001, The Secret State: Whitehall and the Cold War 1945–70 2002, Having It So Good: Britain in the Fifties 2006, Cabinets and the Bomb 2007, The Secret State: Preparing For The Worst 1945–2010 2010; contribs to scholarly books and journals, to radio and television. *Honours:* Dr hc (Univ. of West of England) 1995, (Univ. of Westminster) 1996, (Kingston Univ.) 1998; Duff Cooper Prize 1993, NCR Book Award for Non-Fiction 1994. *Address:* School of History, Queen Mary, University of London, London, E1 4NS, England (office). *Telephone:* (20) 7882-8351 (office). *E-mail:* p.j.hennessy@qmul.ac.uk (office). *Website:* www.history.qmul.ac.uk/staff/hennessyp.html (office).

HENNING JOCELYN, Countess of Roden Ann Margareta Maria, BA; Swedish writer, dramatist, translator and broadcaster; b. 5 Aug. 1948, Göteborg; m. Earl of Roden Robert John Jocelyn 1986; one s. *Education:* Univ. of Lund. *Career:* Artistic Dir, Connemara Theatre Co.; fmr Chair. Translators' Asscn; mem. Irish Playwrights' and Scriptwriters' Guild, Irish Writers' Union. *Publications:* Modern Astrology 1983, The Connemara Whirlwind 1990, The Connemara Stallion 1991, The Connemara Champion 1994, Honeylove the Bearcub 1995, The Cosmos and You 1995, Keylines 2000, Keylines for Living 2007; plays: Smile 1972, Baptism of Fire 1997, The Alternative 1998; contribs to Swedish and Irish radio and television. *E-mail:* roden@ireland.com. *Website:* www.keylines2000.com.

HENRY, Stuart Dennis, BA, PhD; British academic, administrator, writer and editor; *Director, Interdisciplinary Studies Program and Professor, University of Texas, Arlington*; b. 18 Oct. 1949, London, England; s. of Lionel Victor Henry and Doris Knowles; m. Lee Doric 1988. *Education:* Univ. of Kent. *Career:* Research Sociologist, Univ. of London 1975–78; Research Fellow, Middlesex Univ. 1978–79; Sr Lecturer, Nottingham Trent Univ. 1979–83; Asst Prof., Old Dominion Univ., Norfolk, Va, USA 1984–87; Prof., Eastern Michigan Univ., USA 1987–98; Prof. of Sociology and Chair. of Dept of Sociology, Valparaiso Univ., Ind., USA 1998; Dir Interdisciplinary Studies Program and Assoc. Dean, Coll. of Lifelong Learning, then Chair. Dept of Interdisciplinary Studies, Coll. of Liberal Arts and Sciences, Wayne State Univ., USA 1999–2006; Dir School of Public Affairs, San Diego State Univ., USA 2006–10; Co-Dir Center for Ethics in Science and Tech. 2008–10; Dir Interdisciplinary Studies Program and Prof., Univ. of Texas, Arlington, USA 2010–; Co-Ed. Critical Criminologist 1997; mem. American Sociological Asscn, American Soc. of Criminology, Western Soc. of Criminology; mem. Bd, Asscn of Interdisciplinary Studies. *Publications:* Self-help and Health: Mutual Aid for Modern Problems (with D. Robinson) 1977, The Hidden Economy: The Context and Control of Borderline Crime 1978, Private Justice: Toward Integrated Theorizing in the Sociology of Law 1983, Making Markets: An Interdisciplinary Perspective on Economic Exchange (with R. Cantor and S. Rayner) 1992, The Deviance Process (with E. H. Pfuhl), third edn 1993, Criminological Theory (with W. Einstadter) 1995, Constitutive Criminology: Beyond Postmodernism (with D. Milovanovic) 1996, Essential Criminology (with M. Lanier) 1998 (revised edn 2010), Social Deviance 2009; editor: Informal Institutions: Alternative Networks in the Corporate State 1981, The Informal Economy (with L. Ferman and M. Hoyman) 1987, Degrees of Deviance: Student Accounts of their Deviant Behavior 1989, Work Beyond Employment in Advanced Capitalist Countries: Classic and Contemporary Perspectives on the Informal Economy (with L. Ferman and L. Berndt), 2 vols 1993, Social Control: Aspects of Non-State Justice 1994, Employee Dismissal: Justice at Work 1994, Inside Jobs: A Realistic Guide to Criminal Justice Careers for College Graduates 1994, The Criminology Theory Reader (with W. Einstadter) 1998, The Essential Criminology Reader (with M. Lanier) 2006, The Politics of Interdisciplinary Studies: Essays on Transformations in American Undergraduate Programs (with T. Augsburg) 2009, Recent Developments in Criminological Theory (with S. Lukas) 2009; contribs to scholarly books and journals. *Address:* Interdisciplinary Studies, College of Urban and Public Affairs, 501A University Hall, University of Texas, Arlington, TX 76019, USA (office). *Telephone:* (819) 272-5456 (office). *Fax:* (819) 272-7418 (office). *E-mail:* stuart.henry@uta.edu (office). *Website:* www.uta.edu/supa (office).

HENSCHEN, Helena; Swedish writer and illustrator; b. 21 March 1940, Stockholm. *Career:* worked as a graphic designer; writer and illustrator of children's books; co-f. design company Mah-Jong. *Publications:* I skuggan av ett brott (novel) (EU Prize for Literature 2009) 2004, Hon älskade 2008. *Address:* c/o Förlag Brombergs Bokförlag AB, Box 12886, 112 98 Stockholm, Sweden (office). *E-mail:* info@brombergs.se (office). *Website:* www.brombergs.se (office).

HENSHER, Philip Michael, BA, PhD, FRSL; British writer; b. 20 Feb. 1965, London. *Education:* Lady Margaret Hall, Oxford, Jesus Coll., Cambridge. *Career:* clerk, House of Commons 1990–96; Chief Book Reviewer, The Spectator 1994–; Art Critic, Mail on Sunday 1996–; columnist, The Independent; mem. RSL (mem. of Council 2000–). *Publications:* Other Lulus 1994, Kitchen Venom 1996, Pleasured 1998, The Bedroom of the Mister's Wife (short stories) 1999, The Mulberry Empire 2002, The Fit 2004, The Northern Clemency 2008, King of the Badgers 2011; other: libretto for opera Powder her Face, by Thomas Adès. *Honours:* Somerset Maugham Award 1996. *Literary Agent:* c/o AP Watt Ltd, 20 John Street, London, WC1N 2DR, England. *Address:* 83A Tennyson Street, London, SW8 3TH, England (home).

HERALD, Kathleen (see Peyton, Kathleen Wendy)

HERBERT, Brian Patrick, BA; American writer; b. 29 June 1947, Seattle, WA; s. of Frank Herbert. *Education:* Univ. of California at Berkeley. *Career:* mem. L-5 Soc., Nat. Writers' Club, SFWA, Horror Writers Asscn. *Publications:* Classic Comebacks 1981, Incredible Insurance Claims 1982, Sidney's Comet 1983, The Garbage Chronicles 1984, Sudanna, Sudanna 1985, Man of Two Worlds (with Frank Herbert) 1986, Prisoners of Arionn 1987, The Notebooks of Frank Herbert's Dune (ed.) 1988, Memorymakers (with Marie Landis) 1991, The Race for God 1990, Never as it Seems (ed.) 1992, Songs of Muad' Dib (ed.) 1992, Blood on the Sun (with Marie Landis) 1996, House Atreides (with Kevin J. Anderson) 1999, A Whisper of Caladan Seas (with Kevin J. Anderson) 1999, House Harkonnen (with Kevin J. Anderson) 2001, The Road to Dune (with Kevin J. Anderson) 2005, Hunters of Dune (with Kevin J. Anderson) 2006, Timeweb 2006, The Web and the Stars 2007, Sandworms of Dune (with Kevin J. Anderson) 2007, Paul of Dune (with Kevin J. Anderson) 2008, Webdancers 2008, The Winds of Dune (with Kevin J. Anderson) 2009; contrib. short stories in various anthologies and other publications. *Address:* PO Box 10164, Bainbridge Island, WA 98110, USA (office). *E-mail:* dunenews@dunenovels.com (office). *Website:* www.dunenovels.com.

HERBERT, James John, OBE; British writer; b. 8 April 1943, London, England; s. of Herbert Herbert and Catherine Herbert (née Riley). *Education:* St Aloysius Coll., Highgate, Hornsey Coll. of Art. *Career:* Art Dir Group Head Charles Barker Advertising. *Films:* The Rats 1982, The Survivor 1986, Fluke 1995, Haunted 1995. *Publications:* The Rats 1974, The Fog 1975, The Survivor 1976, Fluke 1977, The Spear 1978, Lair 1979, The Dark 1980, The Jonah 1981, Shrine 1983, Domain 1984, Moon 1985, The Magic Cottage 1986, Sepulchre 1987, Haunted 1988, Creed 1990, Portent 1992, James Herbert: By Horror Haunted 1992, James Herbert's Dark Places 1993, The City 1994, The Ghosts of Sleath 1994, '48 1996, Others 1999, Once... 2001, Devil in the Dark: Biography 2003, Nobody True 2003, The Secret of Crickley Hall 2006. *Literary Agent:* c/o David Higham Associates Ltd, 5–8 Lower John Street, Golden Square, London, W1F 9HA, England. *Telephone:* (20) 7434-5900. *Fax:* (20) 7437-1072. *E-mail:* dha@davidhigham.co.uk. *Website:* www.davidhigham.co.uk. *E-mail:* info@james-herbert.co.uk (office). *Website:* www.james-herbert.co.uk.

HERDMAN, John Macmillan, BA, MA, PhD; Scottish writer; b. 20 July 1941, Edinburgh, Scotland; m. 1st Dolina Maclennan 1983 (divorced); m. 2nd Mary Ellen Watson 2002. *Education:* Magdalene Coll., Cambridge. *Career:* Creative Writing Fellow, Univ. of Edinburgh 1977–79; William Soutar Fellow, Perth 1990–91. *Publications:* Descent 1968, A Truth Lover 1973, Memoirs of My Aunt Minnie/Clapperton 1974, Pagan's Pilgrimage 1978, Stories Short and Tall 1979, Voice Without Restraint: Bob Dylan's Lyrics 1982, Three Novellas 1987, The Double in Nineteenth-Century Fiction 1990, Imelda and Other Stories 1993, Ghostwriting 1996, Cruising (play) 1997, Poets, Pubs, Polls and Pillarboxes 1999, Four Tales 2000, The Sinister Cabaret 2001, Triptych 2004, My Wife's Lovers 2007. *Honours:* Scottish Arts Council Book Awards 1978, 1993. *Address:* 5A Barossa Place, Perth, PH1 5HG, Scotland (home). *Website:* www.johnherdman.co.uk.

HERMANN, Judith; German writer; b. 1970, Berlin. *Publications:* Sommerhaus Spaeter (short stories) 1999, Nicht als Gespenster (short stories) 2003, Alice 2009. *Honours:* Hugo Ball Förderpreis 1999, Förderpreis zum Bremer Literaturpreis 1999, Kleist Preis 2001, Friedricj Hölderlin Preis 2009. *Address:* c/o S. Fischer Verlag GmbH, Hedderichstrasse 114, 60596 Frankfurt, Germany (office). *Website:* www.fischerverlage.de (office).

HERMARY-VIEILLE, Catherine; French writer; b. 8 Oct. 1943, Paris; d. of Jacques and Jacqueline (née Dubois) Hermary; m. Jean Vieille 1962; one s. one d. *Education:* Coll. Ste Marie de Passy (Paris and Noisy), Ecole Nat des Langues Orientales (Paris), Univ. of Paris VIII–Vincennes à St-Denis, Manhattanville Coll. (NY, USA). *Career:* Asst Embassy of Cyprus, Paris 1968–69; began career as writer 1981; Reporter for various newspapers; mem. PEN-Club, Islam-Occident, Asscn des Ecrivains de Langue Française; Prix Georges Dufau de l' Acad. Française; Officier des Arts et des Lettres, Chevalier de la Légion d'honneur. *Publications:* Le grand vizir de la nuit (Prix Fémina) 1981, L'épiphanie des dieux (Prix Ulysse) 1982, La marquise des ombres 1984, L'infidèle (Prix Radio-Télé Luxembourg—RTL) 1986, Romy 1988, Le rivage des adieux 1989, Le jardin des Henderson 1990, Un amour fou (Prix des Maisons de la Presse) 1991, La piste des turquoises 1992, La pointe aux tortues 1994, Lola 1994, L'Initié 1996, L'Ange Noir 1998 (Prix Littéraire du Quartier Latin), Les Dames de Brières 1999, L'Etang du Diable 2000, La fille du Feu 2000, La Crépuscule des Rois (La Rose d'Anjou, Les Reines de Coeur, Les Lionnes d'Angleterre) 2004–06, Lord James 2006, Le Gardien du phare 2007, Le roman d'Alia 2008. *Address:* Shelton Mill, 371 Shelton Mill Road, Charlottesville, VA 22903-7367, USA (home). *E-mail:* catherinehv@yahoo.com (home).

HERNÁNDEZ PÉREZ, Francisco; Mexican poet; b. 1946, San Andres Tuxtla, Veracruz. *Publications include:* Gritar es cosa de mudos 1974, Textos criminales y Portarretratos 1976, Cuerpo disperse 1978, Textos criminales 1980, Mar de fondo (Premio Nacional de Poesía Aguascalientes) 1982, Oscura coincidencia 1986, De cómo Robert Schumann fue vencido por los demonios 1988, En las pupilas del que regresa 1991, Habla Scardanelli (Premio Carlos Pellicer) 1993, Moneda de tres caras (Premio Xavier Villaurrutia) 1994, Poesía reunida (1974–94) 1996, Mascarón de prosa 1997, Antojo de trampa (segunda antología personal) 1999, Las gastadas palabras de siempre 2000, Soledad al cubo 2001, Óptica la ilusión 2002, Diario invento 2003, Imán para fantasmas, El corazón en su avispero y Palabras más, palabras, menos 2004, Diario sin fechas de Charles B. Waite (Premio Jaime Sabines) 2005, Mi vida con la perra 2006, La isla de las breves ausencias 2009, Población de la máscara. 62 autorretratos 2010. *Honours:* Premio Ramón López Velarde 2008, Premio Mazatlán de Literatura 2010. *Address:* Almadia, Yucatan 56, Col. Roma Deleg. Cuauhtemoc, México DF, Mexico. *Telephone:* (55) 4429-0886. *E-mail:* informacion@almadia.com.mx. *Website:* www.almadia.com.mx.

HERNDON, Nancy Ruth, MA; American writer and lecturer; b. (Nancy Fairbanks), 29 May 1934, St Louis, MO; m. William C. Herndon 1956; two s. *Education:* Univ. of Missouri, Rice Univ. *Career:* Lecturer in English, Rice Univ. 1956–58, NY New York Univ. 1959–61, Univ. of Mississippi 1963–64, Florida Atlantic Univ. 1966, Univ. of Texas at El Paso 1976–81; mem. Sisters in Crime, Now, Planned Parenthood; Smithsonian Assoc. *Publications:* as Elizabeth Chadwick: Wanton Angel 1989, Widow's Fire 1990, Virgin Fire 1991, Bride Fire 1992, The Fourth Gift 1993, Reluctant Lovers 1993; as Nancy Herndon: Elusive Lovers 1994, Acid Bath 1995, Widows' Watch 1995, Lethal Statues 1996, Hunting Game 1996, Time Bombs 1997, C.O.P. Out 1998, Casanova Crimes 1999; as Nancy Fairbanks: Crime Brulee 2001, Truffled Feathers 2001, Death à l'orange 2002, Chocolate Quake 2003, The Perils of Paella 2004, Holy Guacamole 2004, Mozzarella Most Murderous 2005, Three-Course Murder 2006, Bon Bon Voyage 2006, French Fried 2006, Turkey Flambe 2007. *Honours:* Fellowship, Rice Univ. 1956–58, New York Univ. 1959–61, El Paso Writers Hall of Fame 1997. *Address:* 6504 Pino Drive, El Paso, TX 79912, USA (home). *Telephone:* (915) 581-6178 (office). *E-mail:* nherndon@elp.rr.com (home). *Website:* nancyfairbanks.com (home).

HERRALDE, Jorge; Spanish publisher; *Director, Editorial Anagrama*; b. Barcelona. *Career:* Founder-Dir Editorial Anagrama 1969–. *Publications:* Opiniones mohicanas (collection of articles) 2000, Flashes sobre escritores y otros textos editoriales 2003, El Observatorio editorial 2004, Para Roberto Bolaño 2005, Por orden alfabético. Escritores, editores, amigos 2006, Homenaje a Paul Auster (ed.) 2007, y Canutos con Copi. Aventuras de un editor 2008. *Honours:* Hon. Prof., Universidad Diego Portales in Santiago, Chile; Hon. OBE (UK) 2005, Commdr, Ordre des Arts et des Lettres 2006; Premio Nacional a la mejor labor editorial cultural de España 1994, Premio Tarda d'Argento al mejor editor europeo 1999, Premio Clarín 2000, Feria Int. del Libro de Guadalajara: Homenaje al mérito editorial 2002, Creu de Sant Jordi 2000, Premio Nazionale per la Traduzione Italia 2003, Premio Grinzane 2005, Silver Medal, Autonomous Univ. of Nuevo Leon, Mexico 2007, Legend Award 2008, London Book Fair Lifetime Achievement Award in Int. Publishing 2012. *Address:* Editorial Anagrama SA, Pedró de la Creu 58, 08034 Barcelona, Spain (office). *E-mail:* anagrama@anagrama-ed.es (office). *Website:* www.anagrama-ed.es (office).

HERRERA, Juan Felipe; American poet and writer; *Professor of Creative Writing, University of California, Riverside*; b. 27 Dec. 1948, Fowler, Calif. *Education:* Univ. of California, Los Angeles, Stanford Univ., Univ. of Iowa. *Career:* Instructor, Stanford Univ. 1979–80, De Anza Community Coll. 1986–88, New Coll. of California 1987–88; Teaching Fellow, Univ. of Iowa Writers' Workshop 1988–90; Assoc. Prof. of English, Univ. of Southern Illinois at Carbondale 1992–93; Prof. of Culture Studies and Creative Writing, California State Univ., Fresno 1990–2005; Prof. of Creative Writing, Univ. of California, Riverside 2005–. *Publications include:* Rebozos of Love 1974, Exiles of Desire 1985, Facegames 1987, Akrilika 1989, Memoria(s) from an Exile's Notebook of the Future 1993, The Roots of a Thousand Embraces 1994, Night Train to Tuxtla 1994, Calling the Doves 1995, Love After the Riots 1996, Mayan Drifter: Chicano Poet in the Lowlands of America 1997, Border Crosser with a Lamborghini Dream 1999, Loteria Cards and Fortune Poems 1999, Crashboomlove: A Novel in Verse 1999, The Upside Down Boy 2000, Thunderweavers 2000, Giraffe on Fire 2001, Grandma and Me at the Flea 2002, Notebooks of a Chile Verde Smuggler 2002, Cilantro Girl 2003, 187 Reasons Mexicanos Can't Cross the Border: Undocuments 1971–2007 2008, Half of the World in Light (Nat. Book Critics Circle Award in Poetry) 2008. *Address:* Department of Creative Writing, University of California, College of Humanities, Arts and Social Sciences, Riverside, CA 92521, USA (office). *Telephone:* (951) 827-4537 (office). *E-mail:* juan.herrera@ucr.edu (office). *Website:* www.creativewriting.ucr.edu/people/herrera (office).

HERSH, Burton David, BA; American author and biographer; b. 18 Sept. 1933, Chicago, IL; m. Ellen Eiseman 1957, one s. one d. *Education:* Harvard Univ. *Career:* mem. Authors' Guild; American Society of Journalists and Authors; PEN, Tampa Chapter of Cttee on Foreign Relations; Fellow, Florida Studies Program, Univ. of South Florida at St Petersburg. *Publications:* The Ski People 1968, The Education of Edward Kennedy 1972, The Mellon Family 1978, The Old Boys 1992, The Shadow President 1997, The Nature of the Beast (fiction; Writers Notes Award 2003) 2002, Bobby and J. Edgar 2007, Edward Kennedy: An Intimate Biography 2010. *Honours:* Fulbright Scholar 1955–56, Book Find Selection 1972, Book-of-the-Month Club 1978, First Bowdoin Prize. *Address:* 6673 30th Street S, Saint Petersburg, FL 33712-6517, USA (home). *E-mail:* bandehersh@aol.com (home).

HERSH, Seymour Myron, BA; American journalist and writer; b. 8 April 1937, Chicago, IL; m. Elizabeth Sarah Klein 1964; two s. one d. *Education:* Univ. of Chicago. *Career:* Chicago City News Bureau 1959; corresp. United Press International 1962–63, Associated Press 1963–67, The New Yorker 1992–; mem. of staff New York Times 1972–79; nat. corresp. Atlantic Monthly 1983–86. *Publications:* Chemical and Biological Warfare: America's Hidden Arsenal 1968, My Lai 4: A Report on the Massacre and Its Aftermath 1970, Cover-Up: The Army's Secret Investigation of the Massacre at My Lai 1972, The Price of Power: Kissinger in the Nixon White House 1983, The Target is Destroyed: What Really Happened to Flight 007 and What America Knew About It 1986, The Samson Option: Israel's Nuclear Arsenal and America's

Foreign Policy 1991, The Dark Side of Camelot 1997, Against All Enemies: Gulf War Syndrome: The War Between America's Ailing Veterans and Their Government 1999, Chain of Command: The Road from 9/11 to Abu Ghraib 2004; contribs to various magazines. *Honours:* Pulitzer Prize for Int. Reporting 1970, George Polk Memorial Awards 1970, 1973, 1974, 1981, Scripps-Howard Public Service Award 1973, Sidney Hillman Award 1974, John Peter Zenger Freedom of the Press Award 1975, Los Angeles Times Book Prize 1983, Nat. Book Critics Circle Award 1983, Investigative Reporters and Editors Prizes 1983, 1992, Nat. Magazine Award 2004. *Address:* 3214 Newark Street NW, Washington, DC 20008-3345, USA (home).

HERTMANS, Stefan, MA, PhD; Belgian novelist and poet; *Affiliated Researcher, University of Ghent;* b. 31 March 1951, Ghent. *Education:* Univ. of Ghent. *Career:* Prof., Acad. of Fine Arts, Ghent 1991–; Organiser, Studium Generale, Univ. Coll., Ghent 2002–10, Guest Prof. 2010–. *Plays:* Kopnaad, Mind the Gap, Dood van Empedokles (Death of Empedokles), Tyranny of Time. *Publications:* numerous titles, including: Ruimte (translated as Space) 1981, Melksteen 1986, Zoutsneeuw 1987, Gestolde wolken 1987, Bezoekingen Gedichten 1988, Oorverdovende Steen: Essays over literatuur 1988, Steden: Verhalen onderweg 1988, Sneeuwdoosjes 1989, De grenzen van woestijnen Verhalen 1989, Kopnaad: Eentekstvoor vier stemmen 1992, Muziek voor de overtocht: Gedichten 1994, Naar Merelbeke 1994, Francesco s paradox: Gedichten 1995, Fugas en pimpelmezen: Over actualiteit, kunst en Kritiek 1995, Annunciaties 1997, Het bedenkelijke 1999, Goya als hond 1999, Mind the Gap 2000, Intercities: Topographics London 2001, Als op de eerste dag (translated as Like the First Day) 2001, Harder Dan Sneeuw 2004, Kaneelvinfers 2005, Het zwijgen van de tragedie 2007, El Silencio de la Tragedia 2008, Het verborgen Weefsel (Hidden Fabric) (novel) 2008; contrib. to Modern Poetry in Translation 1997, short story in Review of Contemporary Fiction 1994, The Literary Review 1997, Chelsea 1999, Grand Street 70, Against Nature 2002. *Honours:* Multatuli Prize 1988, State Prize for Poetry 1995, Prize Maurice Gilliams 2002, Prize France Culture, Paris 2003, Five Years Prize Essay, Royal Acad. of Dutch Language and Literature 2008. *Address:* De Bezige Bij, PO Box 75184, 1070 AD Amsterdam, The Netherlands (office). *E-mail:* stefan.hertmans@telenet.be (office). *Website:* www.debezigebij.nl (office); www.stefanhertmans.be.

HERTZ, Noreena, BA, MBA, PhD; British economist, academic and writer; *Fellow, Judge Business School, University of Cambridge;* b. 24 Sept. 1967, London. *Education:* Univ. Coll., London, Univ. of Cambridge, Wharton School of the Univ. of Pennsylvania, USA. *Career:* attended business school in USA; helped establish first Leningrad (now St Petersburg) stock exchange 1991; Int. Finance Corpn adviser to Russian Govt on econ. reforms 1992; fmr head of research team working on prospects for regional econ. co-operation in the Middle East; fmr Distinguished Fellow and Assoc. Dir Centre for Int. Business and Man., Judge Inst. of Man. Studies, Univ. of Cambridge, currently Fellow, Judge Business School; also currently Duisenberg Prof. of Globalization, Sustainability and Finance, Duisenberg School of Finance, Erasmus Univ.; Belle van Zuylen Chair of Global Political Economy, Utrecht Univ. April–Sept. 2005; attended World Econ. Forum 2002; regular commentator on TV and radio. *Television includes:* documentary film of her book The Silent Takeover (Channel 4) 2001. *Publications include:* Russian Business in the Wake of Reform (doctoral thesis) 1996, The Silent Takeover: Global Capitalism and the Death of Democracy 2001, IOU: The Debt Threat and Why We Must Defuse It 2004; contribs to New Statesman, the Observer, the Guardian and the Washington Post. *Address:* Judge Business School, Trumpington Street, Cambridge, CB2 1AG (office). *Telephone:* (20) 7724-0829 (office). *Fax:* (20) 7724-1726 (office). *E-mail:* noreenah@yahoo.com (office). *Website:* www.jbs.cam.ac.uk (office).

HERVEY, Evelyn (see Keating, Henry Reymond Fitzwalter)

HERZBERG, Judith; Dutch poet, playwright and scriptwriter; b. 4 Nov. 1934, Amsterdam. *Education:* Montessori Lyceum. *Career:* teacher at film schools in Netherlands and Israel. *Film scripts:* scriptwriter: Charlotte, Leedvermaak, Qui Vive. *Publications:* Slow Boat 1964, Meadow Grass 1968, Flies 1970, Grazing Light 1971, 27 Love Songs 1973, Botshol 1980, Remains of the Day 1984, Twenty Poems 1984, But What: Selected Poems 1988, The Way 1992, What She Meant to Paint 1998, Small Catch 1999, Do You Know What Else I Never Know 2002, Sometimes Often 2004; plays: Near Archangel 1971, It Is Not a Dog 1973, That Day May Dawn 1974, Lea's Wedding 1982, The Fall of Icarus 1983, And/Or 1984, The Little Mermaid 1986, Scratch 1989, Lulu (adaptation of Wedekind) 1989, A Good Head 1991, Rijgdraad 1995, The Nothing-factory 1997, Wie Is Van Wie 1999, Simon 2002; children's book: Laika 2004; other: texts for the stage and film 1972–88, trans including The Trojan Women (Euripides), Ghosts (Ibsen), screenplays and TV plays. *Honours:* Jan Campert Prize 1980, Bayerische Filpreis 1980, Joost van der Vandel Prize 1984, Charlotte Koehler Prize 1988, Cestoda Prize 1988, Netherlands-Vlaamse Drama Prize 1989, Constantijn Huyens Prize 1995, P. C. Hooft Prize for Poetry 1997. *Address:* c/o De Harmonie, PO Box 3547, 1001 AH Amsterdam, The Netherlands.

HESSAYON, David Gerald, OBE, BSc, PhD; British writer; b. 13 Feb. 1928, Manchester, England; m. Joan Parker Gray 1951; two d. *Education:* Univs of Leeds and Manchester. *Career:* mem. Soc. of Authors. *Publications:* The House Plant Expert 1980, The Armchair Book of the Garden 1983, The Tree and Shrub Expert 1983, The Flower Expert 1984, The Indoor Plant Spotter 1985, The Garden Expert 1986, The Home Expert 1987, The Fruit Expert 1990, Be Your Own Greenhouse Expert 1990, The New House Plant Expert 1991, The Garden DIY Expert 1992, The Rock and Water Garden Expert 1993, The Flowering Shrub Expert 1994, The Greenhouse Expert 1994, The Flower Arranging Expert 1994, The Container Expert 1995, The Bulb Expert 1995, The Easy-Care Gardening Expert 1996, The New Bedding Plant Expert 1996, The New Rose Expert 1996, The New Vegetable and Herb Expert 1997, The New Lawn Expert 1997, The Evergreen Expert 1998, The New Flower Expert 1999, The Pocket Flower Expert 2001, The Pocket Garden Troubles Expert 2001, The Pocket Tree and Shrub Expert 2001, The Pocket House Plant Expert 2002, The Pocket Vegetable Expert 2002, The Garden Revival Expert 2004, The House Plant Expert Book 2 2005, The Pest and Weed Expert 2007, The Orchid Expert 2008, The Bedside Book of the Garden 2008, The Green Garden Expert 2009, The Expert Vegetable Notebook 2009. *Honours:* Nat. British Book Awards Lifetime Achievement Trophy 1992, Royal Horticultural Soc. Gold Veitch Memorial Medal 1992, Gardening Book of the Year Award 1993, Roy Hay Memorial Award 1998, Garden Writer's Guild Lifetime Achievement Award 2005. *Address:* c/o Expert, 61–63 Uxbridge Road, London, W5 5SA, England (office). *Website:* www.booksattransworld.co.uk/expertGarden/home.htm (office).

HETHERINGTON, Norriss Swigart, BA, MA, PhD; American academic and writer; b. 30 Jan. 1942, Berkeley, CA; m. Edith Wiley White 1966, one s. one d. *Education:* University of California, Berkeley, Indiana University. *Career:* Lecturer in Physics and Astronomy, Agnes Scott College, Decatur, GA, 1967–68; Asst Prof. of Mathematics and Science, York University, Toronto, Ontario, 1970–72; Administrative Specialist, National Aeronautics and Space Aministration, 1972; Asst Prof. of History, University of Kansas, 1972–76; Asst Prof. of Science, Technology and Society, Razi University, Sanandaj, Iran, 1976–77; Visiting Scholar, University of Cambridge, 1977–78; Research Assoc., Office for History of Science and Technology, University of Calfornia, Berkeley, 1978–; Assoc. Prof. of the History of Science, University of Oklahoma at Norman, 1981; Dir, Institute for the History of Astronomy, 1988–. *Publications:* Ancient Astronomy and Civilization, 1987; Science and Objectivity: Episodes in the History of Astronomy, 1988; The Edwin Hubble Papers, 1990; Encyclopedia of Cosmology, 1993; Cosmology: Historical, Literary, Philosophical, Religious and Scientific Perspectives, 1993; Hubble's Cosmology: A Guided Study of Selected Texts, 1996. *Honours:* Goddard Historical Essay Award 1974.

HETTICH, Michael, BA, MA, PhD; American academic, writer and poet; *Professor of English and Creative Writing, Miami Dade College;* b. 25 Sept. 1953, Brooklyn, NY; m. Colleen Ahern 1980; one s. one d. *Education:* Hobart Coll., Univ. of Denver, Univ. of Miami. *Career:* currently Prof. of English and Creative Writing, Miami Dade Coll.; mem. of Bd, Fla Literary Arts Coalition. *Publications:* Looking Out 1981, A Small Boat 1990, Immaculate Bright Rooms 1994, Many Simple Things 1997, Sleeping with the Lights on 2000, Singing with my Father 2001, Greatest Hits: 1987–2001 2002, The Point of Touching 2002, Behind our Memories 2003, Stationary Wind 2004, Summer Dreams 2005, Flock and Shadow: New and Selected Poems 2005, Many Loves 2007, Like Happiness 2010; contributions: Poetry East, Witness, Ploughshares, Orion, The Sun, Literary Review, Miami Herald, Salt Hills Journal. *Honours:* two State of Fla Artist Fellowships, The Tales Prize. *Address:* 561 NE 95th Street, Miami Shores, FL 33138, USA (home). *Telephone:* (305) 237-3187 (home). *E-mail:* mhettich@mdc.edu (home). *Website:* www.michaelhettich.com.

HEWETT, Dorothy Coade, AM, BA, MA; Australian poet, writer and dramatist; b. 21 May 1923, Perth, WA. *Education:* University of Western Australia. *Publications:* Bobbin Up (novel), 1959; What About the People? (poems with Merv Lilly), 1962; The Australians Have a Word for It (short stories), 1964; Windmill Country (poems), 1968; The Hidden Journey (poems), 1969; The Chapel Perilous, or The Perilous Adventures of Sally Bonner, 1971; Sandgropers: A Western Australian Anthology, 1973; Rapunzel in Suburbia (poems), 1975; Miss Hewett's Shenanigans, 1975; Greenhouse (poems), 1979; The Man from Mukinupin (play), 1979; Susannah's Dreaming (play), 1981; The Golden Oldies (play), 1981; Selected Poems, 1990; Wild Card (autobiog.), 1990.

HEYEN, William Helmuth, BS, MA, PhD; American academic, poet and writer; *Professor Emeritus of English, State University of New York, Brockport;* b. 1 Nov. 1940, Brooklyn, NY; s. of Henry Heyen and Wilhelmine Wormke Heyen; m. Hannelore Greiner 1962; one s. one d. *Education:* State Univ. of NY (SUNY), Brockport, Ohio Univ. *Career:* Asst Prof. to Prof. of English and Poet-in-Residence, SUNY, Brockport 1967–2000, currently Prof. Emer.; Sr Fulbright Lecturer in American Literature, Germany 1971–72; Visiting Creative Writer, Univ. of Wisconsin at Milwaukee 1980; Visiting Writer, Hofstra Univ. 1981, 1983, Southampton Coll. 1984, 1985; Visiting Prof. of English, Univ. of Hawaii 1985; Workshop Leader, Chautauqua Inst. 1993, 1996, 2000, 2004, 2007, 2010. *Publications:* Depth of Field 1970, Noise in the Trees: Poems and a Memoir 1974, American Poets in 1976 (ed.) 1976, The Swastika Poems 1977, Long Island Light: Poems and a Memoir 1979, The City Parables 1980, Lord Dragonfly: Five Sequences 1981, Erika: Poems of the Holocaust 1984, The Generation of 2000: Contemporary American Poets (ed.) 1984, Vic Holyfield and the Class of 1957: A Romance 1986, The Chestnut Rain: A Poem 1986, Brockport, New York: Beginning with 'And' 1988, Falling From Heaven (co-author) 1991, Pterodactyl Rose: Poems of Ecology 1991, Ribbons: The Gulf War 1991, The Host: Selected Poems 1965–1990 1994, With Me Far Away: A Memoir 1994, Crazy Horse in Stillness: Poems 1996, Pig

Notes and Dumb Music: Prose on Poetry 1998, Diana, Charles and the Queen: Poems 1998, September 11, 2001: American Writers Respond 2002, The Hummingbird Corporation: Stories 2002, The Rope: Poems 2004, Shoah Train: Poems 2004, Home: Autobiographies, Etc. 2005, Titanic & Iceberg: Early Essays & Reviews 2006, The Confessions of Doc Williams & Other Poems 2006, To William Merwin: A Poem 2007, A Poetics of Hiroshima 2008, The Cabin: Journal 1964–1985 2009; contribs to numerous anthologies, journals and magazines. *Honours:* Hon. DHumLitt (SUNY) 2011; Borestone Mountain Poetry Prize 1965, National Endowment for the Arts Fellowships 1973–74, 1984–85, American Library Asscn Notable American Book 1974, Ontario Review Poetry Prize 1977, Guggenheim Fellowship 1977–78, Eunice Tietjens Memorial Award 1978, Witter Bynner Prize for Poetry 1982, New York Foundation for the Arts Poetry Fellowship 1984–85, Lillian Fairchild Award 1996, Small Press Book Award for Poetry 1997, Andrew Eiseman Award 2004, Ohio Poet of the Year 2008, Arts and Cultural Council of Greater Rochester Award 2009. *Address:* 142 Frazier Street, Brockport, NY 14420, USA. *Telephone:* (585) 637-3867. *E-mail:* wheyen@rochester.rr.com.

HIAASEN, Carl Andrew; American novelist and journalist; *Columnist, Miami Herald*; b. 12 March 1953, Plantation, Fort Lauderdale, FL; s. of Odel Hiaasen and Patricia Hiaasen; m. 1st Connie Lyford 1970 (divorced 1996); one s.; m. 2nd Fenia Clizer 1999; one s. one step-s. *Education:* Emory Univ., Univ. of Florida. *Career:* reporter Cocoa Today, Florida 1974–76; reporter Miami Herald 1976–79, investigative reporter 1979–85, weekly columnist 1985–. *Publications:* fiction: Trap Line (with William Montalbano) 1981, Powder Burn (with William Montalbano) 1981, A Death in China (with William Montalbano) 1986, Tourist Season 1986, Double Whammy 1987, Skin Tight 1989, Native Tongue 1991, Strip Tease 1993, Stormy Weather 1993, Lucky You 1997, Sick Puppy 2000, Basket Case 2002, Hoot (Newbery Award 2003) (juvenile) 2002, Skinny Dip 2004, Flush (juvenile) 2005, Nature Girl 2007, The Downhill Lie: A Hacker's Return to a Ruinous Sport 2008, Scat (juvenile) 2009, Star Island 2010; non-fiction: Team Rodent: How Disney Devours the World 1998. *Honours:* Damon Runyon Award for services to journalism 2003. *Literary Agent:* The Lavin Agency, 77 Peter Street, Fourth Floor, Toronto, ON M5V 2G4, Canada. *E-mail:* tgagnon@thelavinagency.com. *Website:* www.thelavinagency.com; www.carlhiaasen.com.

HIATT, Fred, BA; American journalist; *Editorial Page Editor, The Washington Post*; b. 30 April 1955, Washington, DC; m. Margaret Shapiro; three c. *Education:* Harvard Univ. *Career:* City Hall reporter, Atlanta Journal-Constitution 1979–80; reporter, The Washington Star 1981; Va Reporter, The Washington Post 1981–83, Pentagon Reporter 1983–86, NE Asia Co-Bureau Chief 1987–90, Moscow Co-Bureau Chief 1991–95, Ed. editorial page 1996–. *Publications:* The Secret Sun 1992 (novel), If I Were Queen of the World 1997 (children's book), Baby Talk 1999. *Address:* The Washington Post, 1150 15th Street, NW, Washington, DC 20071, USA (office). *Telephone:* (202) 334-6000 (office). *E-mail:* twpcoreply@washpost.com (office). *Website:* www.washingtonpost.com (office).

HICK, John Harwood, MA, PhD, DPhil, DLitt; British academic; *Fellow, Institute for Advanced Research in Arts and Social Sciences, University of Birmingham*; b. 20 Jan. 1922, Scarborough, Yorks.; s. of Mark Day Hick and Mary Aileen Hirst; m. Joan Hazel Bowers 1953 (died 1996); three s. (one deceased) one d. *Education:* Bootham School, York, Univs of Edinburgh and Oxford, Westminster Theological Coll., Cambridge. *Career:* Minister, Belford Presbyterian Church, Northumberland 1953–56; Asst Prof. of Philosophy, Cornell Univ., USA 1956–59; Stuart Prof. of Christian Philosophy, Princeton Theological Seminary, USA 1959–64; Lecturer in Divinity, Univ. of Cambridge 1964–67; H.G. Wood Prof. of Theology, Univ. of Birmingham 1967–80, now Prof. Emer., Fellow, Inst. for Advanced Research in Arts and Social Sciences; Danforth Prof. of Philosophy of Religion, Claremont Grad. Univ., Calif., USA 1980–92, now Prof. Emer., Chair. Dept of Religion, Dir Blaisdell Programs in World Religions and Cultures 1983–92; Gifford Lecturer, Univ. of Edinburgh 1986–87; Guggenheim Fellow 1963–64, 1986–87; SA Cook Bye-Fellow, Gonville and Caius Coll., Cambridge 1963–64; Vice-Pres. World Congress of Faiths, British Soc. for the Philosophy of Religion. *Publications include:* Faith and Knowledge, Evil and the God of Love, God and the Universe of Faiths, Death and Eternal Life, Arguments for the Existence of God, Problems of Religious Pluralism, God Has Many Names, Philosophy of Religion, The Second Christianity, An Interpretation of Religion, Disputed Questions in Theology and the Philosophy of Religion, The Metaphor of God Incarnate, The Rainbow of Faiths, The Fifth Dimension, John Hick: An Autobiography, The New Frontier of Religion and Science, Who or What is God?, Between Faith and Doubt; Ed.: The Myth of God Incarnate, The Many-Faced Argument, The Myth of Christian Uniqueness, The Existence of God, Truth and Dialogue, Christianity and Other Religions, Faith and the Philosophers. *Honours:* Hon. DTheol (Uppsala) 1977; Hon. DD (Glasgow) 2002; Grawemeyer Award in Religion 1991. *Address:* 144 Oak Tree Lane, Selly Oak, Birmingham, B29 6HU, England (home). *Telephone:* (121) 689-4803 (home). *E-mail:* j.h.hick@bham.ac.uk (office). *Website:* www.johnhick.org.uk.

HICKEY, Christine Dwyer; Irish novelist and writer; b. Dublin. *Career:* Hon. Sec. Irish PEN. *Film screenplay:* No Better Man (adapted from short story). *Publications:* novels: The Dancer 1995, The Gambler 1996, The Gatemaker 2000, Tatty 2004. *Honours:* winner Listowel Writers' Week short-story competition (twice), winner Observer/Penguin short-story competition. *Address:* c/o New Island, 2 Brookside, Dundrum Road, Dublin 14, Ireland.

HICKOK, Gloria Vando (see Vando (Hickok), Gloria)

HICKSON, Jill Lesley Norton, MBA; Australian literary agent and business executive; b. 28 Sept. 1948, d. of Staveley Fredrick Norton Hickson and Jean Halse Rogers; m. Neville K. Wran 1976; one s. one d. *Education:* Univ. of Sydney and Australian Grad. School of Man. *Career:* programmer/announcer 2MBS FM 1975–76; Int. Relations Man. Quantas Airways 1976–81; Literary Agent and Man. Dir Hickson Assocs Pty Ltd 1983–99; consultant Curtis Brown Australia Pty Ltd 1999–; mem. Bd Dirs Ansett NZ, NSW Conservatorium of Music 1984–89, Sydney Opera House Trust 1985–89, Sydney Symphony Orchestra 1986; mem. Australian Inst. of Int. Affairs, Australian Soc. of Authors, Australian Writers' Guild, Grad. Man. Asscn; Patron Fellowship of Australian Writers, United Music Teachers' Asscn of NSW, 2MBS FM Music Foundation, Domestic Animal Birth Control Soc.; mem. Cttee State Library NSW Foundation, Art Gallery NSW Foundation. *Honours:* Cecil Hall Prize, Australian Inst. of Man. 1972, Schroder Darling Finance Prize, Inst. of Dirs Prize.

HIGASHINO, Keigo; Japanese author; b. 4 Feb. 1958, Osaka. *Education:* Osaka Prefectural Univ. *Career:* fmr engineer, Nippon Denso Co. (now DENSO); full-time writer in Tokyo; cr. Detective Galileo series of crime novels 2005–; Pres. Mystery Writers of Japan. *Publications include:* novels: Hōkago 1985, Naniwa shōnen tanteidan 1988, Nemuri no mori 1989, Henshin 1991, Parallel world love story 1994, Himitsu (The Secret) (Mystery Writers of Japan Award 1999) 1998, Byakuyakō 1999, Tegami 2003, Samayou Yaiba 2004, Gen'ya 2007, Ryūsei no Kizuna 2008, Kakkoh no Tamago ha Dare no Mono 2010, Platinum Data 2010; Detective Galileo novels: Yōgisha X no Kenshin (The Devotion of Suspect X) (Naoki Sanjugo Prize 2006, Honkaku Mystery Grand Prize 2006) 2005, Seijo no Kyūsai (Salvation of a Saint) 2008, Manatsu no Hōteishiki 2011; short story collections: Tantei Galileo 1998, Yochimu 2000, Galileo no Kunō 2008. *Honours:* Edogawa Rampo Award 1985. *Address:* c/o Minotaur Books, Macmillan, 175 Fifth Avenue, New York, NY 10010, USA (office). *Telephone:* (646) 307-5151 (office). *E-mail:* press.inquiries@macmillan.com (office). *Website:* us.macmillan.com/Minotaur.aspx (office).

HIGGINBOTHAM, (Prieur) Jay, BA; American archivist and writer; *Director Emeritus, Mobile Municipal Archives*; b. 16 July 1937, Pascagoula, Miss.; m. Alice Louisa Martin 1970; two s. one d. *Education:* Univ. of Mississippi, Hunter College, CUNY, American Univ., Washington, DC. *Career:* Head of Local History Dept, Mobile (Ala) Public Library 1973–83; Dir Mobile Municipal Archives 1983–2001, Dir Emer. 2001–; mem. and Chair. Mobile Assembly of Sages and Savants, 1983–2001. *Publications:* The Mobile Indians 1966, The World Around 1966, Family Biographies 1967, The Pascagoula Indians 1967, Pascagoula: Singing River City 1968, Mobile: City by the Bay 1968, The Journal of Sauvole 1969, Fort Maurepas: The Birth of Louisiana 1969, re-published 1998, Brother Holyfield 1972, A Voyage to Dauphin Island 1974, Old Mobile: Fort Louis de la Louisiane 1702–1711 1977, Fast Train Russia 1983, Autumn in Petrishchevo 1986, Discovering Russia 1989, Mauvila 1990, Kazula (play) 1991, Man, Nature and the Infinite 1998, Alma 2002, Narrow is the Way 2004, One Man in the Universe 2005, Selected Writings of Jay Higginbotham 2008; contrib. to Library Journal, The Humanist, Harvard International Review, Soviet Literature, Louisiana History, Encyclopaedia Britannica. *Honours:* General L. Kemper Williams Prize, Louisiana Historical Asscn 1977, Award of Merit, Mississippi Historical Soc. 1978, Alabama Library Asscn, Non-Fiction Award 1978, Gilbert Chinard Prize 1978, Elizabeth Gould Award 1981, Alabama Humanitarian Award 1999. *Address:* 60 N Monterey Street, Mobile, AL 36604, USA (home). *Telephone:* (251) 208-7735 (office); (251) 471-5276 (home). *Fax:* (251) 208-7428 (office).

HIGGINS, Aidan; Irish writer; b. 3 March 1927, Celbridge, County Kildare. *Education:* Clongowes Wood Coll., County Kildare. *Publications:* Stories Felo De Se 1960, Langrishe, Go Down (James Tait Black Memorial Prize 1967) 1966, Balcony of Europe 1972, Scenes from a Receding Past 1977, Bornholm Night Ferry 1983, Helsingor Station and Other Departures 1989, Ronda Gorge and Other Precipices: Travel Writings 1959–90, Lions of The Grunewald (novel) 1993, Donkey's Years (Memories of a Life as Story Told) 1995, Secker, Flotsam & Jetsam (collected stories) 1997, Dog Days 1998, A Bestiary 2004, Windy Arbours 2005. *Honours:* British Arts Council grant, Irish Acad. of Letters Award 1970, American Ireland Fund 1977. *Address:* c/o Dalkey Archive Press, Free Word Centre, 60 Farringdon Road, London, EC1R 3GA, England (office).

HIGGINS, Jack (see Patterson, Harry)

HIGGINS, Rita Ann; Irish poet and playwright; b. 1955, Galway. *Career:* Writer-in-Residence, Galway City Library 1987, National Univ. of Ireland, Galway 1994–95, Offaly County Council 1998–99; Green Honors Prof., Texas Christian Univ., USA 2000; mem. Aosdana 1996–. *Plays:* Face Licker Come Home 1991, God of the Hatch Man 1992, Colie Lally Doesn't Live in a Bucket 1993, Down All the Roundabouts 1999. *Publications include:* poetry: Goddess on the Mervue Bus 1986, Witch in the Bushes 1988, Goddess and Witch 1990, Philomena's Revenge 1992, Higher Purchase 1996, Sunny Side Plucked: New and Selected Poems 1996, An Awful Racket 2001; editor: Out the Clara Road: The Offaly Anthology 1999. *Honours:* Peadar O'Donnell Award 1989. *E-mail:* rahiggins@eircom.net (home). *Website:* www.ritaannhiggins.com.

HIGH, Peter Brown, BA, MA, PhD; American academic and writer; *Professor of Film and Literature, Nagoya University*; b. (Peter Brown), 6 Sept. 1944, New York, NY; m. 1972; one s. *Education:* American Univ., California State Univ., Nagoya Univ. *Career:* columnist, Asahi Shimbun, Japanese Language 1987–92; Prof. of Film and Literature, Nagoya Univ. 1987–. *Publications:* An Outline of American Literature 1985, Read All About It 1986, A Journalist Looks at Popular Culture 1991, Teikoku no Ginmaku: Jugo Nen Senso to Nihon Eiga 1995, A History of Cinema 1997, The Imperial Screen, Japanese Cinema in the Fifteen Years' War 2003; assorted language textbooks in the ESL field; contributions: journals. *Honours:* Soc. for Media and Cinema Studies Katherine Kovacs Best Book of 2004. *Address:* 12 Jalan Tukang Emas, 75100 Melaka, Malaysia (home). *Telephone:* (60) 129756841 (office). *E-mail:* peterbhigh2004@yahoo.com (home).

HIGHAM, Robin (David Stewart), AB, MA, PhD; American author, editor and academic (retd); b. 20 June 1925, London, England, UK; s. of (Frank) David Higham and Anne Stewart Higham; m. Barbara Davies 1950; one s. three d. (two deceased). *Education:* Harvard Univ., Claremont Grad. School, Calif. *Career:* Instructor, Univ. of Massachusetts 1954–57; Asst Prof., Univ. of North Carolina, Chapel Hill 1957–63; Assoc. Prof., Kansas State Univ. 1963–66, Prof. of History 1966–98; Ed. Military Affairs 1968–88, Ed. Emer. 1989; Ed. Aerospace Historian 1970–88, Ed. Emer. 1989; Founder-Pres. Sunflower University Press 1977–2004; Ed. and Co-Publr Journal of the West 1977–2004; mem. Int. Comm. of Mil. History 1975–. *Publications:* approx. 70 books, including Britain's Imperial Air Routes, 1918–39 1960, The British Rigid Airship, 1908–31 1961, Armed Forces in Peacetime: Britain, 1918–39 1963, The Military Intellectuals in Britain, 1918–39 1966, A Short History of Warfare (with David H. Zook) 1966, Air Power: A Concise History 1973, The Compleat Academic 1975, A Brief Guide to Scholarly Editing (with Mary Cisper and Guy Dresser) 1982, Diary of a Disaster: British Aid to Greece, 1940–41 1986, The Bases of Air Strategy 1915–1945 1998, 100 Years of Aviation and Air Power 1998; editor: various books, including: Civil Wars in the Twentieth Century 1972, A Guide to the Sources of British Military History 1971, A Guide to the Sources of US Military History 1975–1998, The Rise of the Wheat State: A History of Kansas Agriculture (with George E. Ham) 1986, Russian Aviation and Air Power (with John T. Greenwood and Von Handesty) 1998, A Military History of Tsarist Russia (with Frederick W. Kagan) 2001, A Military History of the Soviet Union (with Frederick W. Kagan) 2001, A Military History of China (with David Graff) 2001 (revised edn 2012), Why Air Forces Fail (with Stephen J. Harris) 2006; contrib. to reference works, scholarly books, and professional journals. *Honours:* First Prize, Calgary Stampede 1944, Social Science Research Council Nat. Security Policy Research Fellow 1960–61, Victor Gondos Award 1983, Samuel Eliot Morison Award 1986, Kansas Gov.'s Aviation Honor Award, American Mil. Inst. 2000. *Address:* 2961 Nevada Street, Manhattan, KS 66502, USA (home). *Telephone:* (785) 539-3668 (home). *E-mail:* rhigham@ksu.edu (office).

HIGHLAND, Monica (see See, Carolyn)

HIGSON, Philip Willoughby, BA, MA, PhD, PGCE, FRHistS, FRSA, FSA; British poet, translator, editor, historian and art historian and playwright; *President, The Baudelaire Society*; b. 21 Feb. 1933, Newcastle-under-Lyme, Staffs., England; s. of Roland Higson and E. Mary Higson. *Education:* Univs of Liverpool and Keele. *Career:* Lecturer, then Sr Lecturer in History, Univ. Coll., Chester (now Univ. of Chester) 1972–89, Visiting Lecturer 1989–90; Chair., Pres. and Anthology Ed. Chester Poets 1974–92; Pres. The Baudelaire Soc. 1992–; Chair. of Trustees, The Baudelaire Soc. and Limouse Foundation Ltd 2007–; mem. Soc. of Authors. *Publications:* The Bizarre Barons of Rivington 1965, The Riposte and Other Poems 1971, Sonnets to My Goddess 1983, Maurice Rollinat's Les Névroses: Selected English Versions (trans.) 1986, A Warning to Europe: The Testimony of Limouse (co-author) 1992, The Complete Poems of Baudelaire with Selected Illustrations by Limouse (ed. and principal trans.) 1992, Limouse Nudes 1994, Sonnets to My Goddess in This Life and the Next (two-part sequence) (David St John Thomas Poetry Publication Prize 1996) 1995, Poems on the Dee 1997, A Poet's Pilgrimage: The Shaping of a Creative Life 2000, Sonnets to My Goddess in This Life and the Next: The Prize-Winning Volume Expanded 2002, The Jewelled Nude: A Play About Baudelaire and Queen Pomaré 2002, Poems of Sauce and Satire: A Humorous Selection 2002, Maurice Rollinat: A Hundred Poems from Les Névroses 2003, Ut Pictura Poesis: Pictorial Poems 2004, Manichaean Contrasts (poems) 2004, Souvenir of a Triple Launch: Play, Translations, Sonnets 2004, D'Annunzio: Selected Poems Translated and Introduced 2005, Baudelaire and Limouse: Their Ennobling Mission for Art 2006, The Singular Lords Willoughby: A Lancashire Family Saga 2007, Evidence from the Beyond: a Historian's Testimony 2009, Rollinat: the Forgotten Country Poetry, Translated and Arranged for a Reading 2009, Rollinat: a Fuller Selection of Country Poetry, Translated and Introduced 2010, A Keele Idyll: Memories of Country Childhood 2010, A Spectrum of Poetry 2011, A Girl and a Garret 2011; contrib. of historical articles to Oxford Dictionary of National Biography and to journals, including Antiquaries Journal, Genealogists' Magazine, Coat of Arms, Northern History, Transactions of the Historic Society of Lancashire and Cheshire, and of the Lancashire and Cheshire Antiquarian Society; poems to The Picador Book of Erotic Verse 1978, Rhyme Revival 1982, Poet's England: Staffordshire 1987, Red Candle Treasury 1998, and to journals, including Critical Quarterly, Chester Poets Anthologies, Collegian, Candelabrum, The Eclectic Muse, Mandrake Poetry Review, Cadmium Blue Literary Journal, Lexikon, Rebirth, Solar Flame, Romantic Renaissance, Rubies in the Darkness, Quantum Leap, The Poet Tree, A Bard Hair Day, Metverse Muse, The LeaFlet, Bulletin de la Société 'Les Amis de Maurice Rollinat'. *Honours:* Charles Beard Research Studentship in Medieval History 1956, Research Fellowship in Modern History, Univ. of Liverpool 1963, First Prize for an Established Poet, The Eclectic Muse, Vancouver 1990, prizewinner, Lexikon Poetry Competition 1996, First Prize, Rubies in the Darkness Poetry Competition 2003, 2008. *Address:* 1 Westlands Avenue, Newcastle-under-Lyme, Staffs., ST5 2PU, England (home). *Telephone:* (1782) 612127 (home).

HIJUELOS, Oscar, BA, MFA; American writer and academic; *Professor of the Practice of Writing, Duke University*; b. 24 Aug. 1951, New York, NY; s. of Jose Pascual Hijuelos and Magalena Hijuelos Torrens; m. Lori Marie Carlson. *Education:* City Coll., City Univ. of New York. *Career:* currently Prof. of the Practice of Writing, Duke Univ. *Publications:* Our House in the Last World 1983, The Mambo Kings Play Songs of Love 1989, The Fourteen Sisters of Emilio Montez O'Brien 1993, Mr Ive's Christmas 1995, Empress of the Splendid Season 1999, A Simple Habana Melody (From When the World Was Good) 2002, Dark Dude 2008, Beautiful Maria of My Soul 2010, Thoughts Without Cigarettes 2011. *Honours:* Hon. DLitt (City Coll. of New York) 1996; Ingram Merrill Foundation Grant 1983, Nat. Endowment for the Arts Fellowship 1985, American Acad. in Rome Fellowship 1985, Pulitzer Prize in Fiction 1990, Guggenheim Fellowship 1990. *Literary Agent:* c/o Jennifer Lyons Literary Agency, 151 West 19th Street, 3rd Floor, New York, NY 10011, USA. *Telephone:* (212) 368-2812. *E-mail:* jenniferhlyons@earthlink.net. *Website:* www.jenniferlyonsliteraryagency.com.

HILDEBIDLE, John, BA, MA, PhD; American poet, writer and academic; b. 2 Feb. 1946, Hartford, Conn.; m. Nichola Gilsdorf 1978; one s. one d. *Education:* Harvard University. *Career:* Lecturer in English and American Literature, Harvard University 1980–83, mem. Extension Faculty 1981–; Asst Prof. of Literature, MIT 1983–; mem. MLA of America, National Council of Teachers of English, Thoreau Society. *Publications include:* Poetry: The Old Chore, 1981; One Sleep, One Waking, 1994; Defining Absence, 1999. Other: Modernism Reconsidered (ed. with Robert J. Kiely), 1983; Thoreau: A Naturalist's Liberty, 1983; Stubborness: A Field Guide, 1986; Five Irish Writers: The Errand of Keeping Alive, 1989; A Sense of Place; Poetry from Ireland (with Dorys Crow Grover and Michael D. Riley), 1995; contributions: anthologies and periodicals. *Honours:* Book Award, San Francisco Poetry Center 1982, Katherine Anne Porter Prize, Tulsa Arts and Humanities Council 1984; Anniversary Award for Poetry, Associated Writing Programs 1984, John Gardner Short Fiction Prize 1987.

HILL, Anthony Robert; Australian writer and journalist; b. 24 May 1942, Melbourne, Vic.; s. of Alan Hill and Elizabeth Hill (née Wardlaw); m. Gillian Mann 1965; one d. *Career:* mem. Australian Soc. of Authors. *Publications:* The Bunburyists 1985, Antique Furniture in Australia 1985, Birdsong 1988, The Burnt Stick 1994, Spindrift 1996, The Grandfather Clock 1996, Growing Up and Other Stories 1999, Soldier Boy 2001, Forbidden 2002, Young Digger 2002, The Shadow Dog 2003, Animal Heroes 2005, River Boy 2006, Harriet 2006, Lucy's Cat and the Rainbow Birds 2007, Captain Cook's Apprentice 2008, Billy 2011. *Honours:* Children's Book Council of Australia Honour Book 1995, 2002, NSW Premier's Award 2002, NSW Premier's Young People's History Prize 2009. *Address:* PO Box 7085, Yarralumla, ACT 2600, Australia (office). *Telephone:* (612) 6281-1358 (office). *E-mail:* anthony@anthonyhillbooks.com (office). *Website:* www.anthonyhillbooks.com.

HILL, Eric; British children's writer and illustrator; b. 7 Sept. 1927, London; m. Gillian Hill; one s. one d. *Career:* fmrly served with the RAF; drew cartoons for Illustrated and Lilliput magazines; worked in advertising and graphic design agencies before becoming a freelance art dir and illustrator; creator of Spot series of children's books 1980–. *Publications include:* Spot series: Where's Spot?, Spot's First Walk, Puppy Love, Spot's Birthday Party, Spot Tells the Time, Sweet Dreams, Spot!, Spot at the Fair, Spot Goes to the Farm, Spot's Baby Sister, Time for Bed, Spot, Spot's New Game, Spot and his Grandma, Spot's Tummy Ache, Spot's Garden, Spot's Camping Trip; other titles: The Park 1982, Help Your Child to Read series (including Poorly Pig, Bad Bear, Fast Frog, Double Ducks, Silly Sheep), Up There 1982, At Home 1982, My Pets 1982, Opposites 1983, Good Morning Baby Bear 1984, Eric Hill's Crazy Mix or Match 1984, My Day at Home 1998, My Animal Friends 2002. *Address:* c/o Ladybird Books, 80 Strand, London, WC2R 0RL, England (office). *E-mail:* ladybird@penguin.co.uk.

HILL, Sir Geoffrey William, Kt, MA, FRSL, FAAAS; British poet, critic and academic; *Professor of Poetry, University of Oxford*; b. 18 June 1932, s. of William George Hill and Hilda Beatrice Hill; m. 1st Nancy Whittaker 1956 (divorced 1983); three s. one d.; m. 2nd Alice Goodman 1987; one d. *Education:* County High School, Bromsgrove and Keble Coll., Oxford. *Career:* mem. academic staff, Univ. of Leeds 1954–80, Prof. of English Literature 1976–80; Univ. Lecturer in English and Fellow, Emmanuel Coll., Cambridge 1981–88; Univ. Prof. and Prof. of Literature and Religion, Boston Univ. 1988–2006, Emer. 2006–, Co-Dir Boston Univ. Editorial Inst. 1998–2004; Prof. of Poetry, Univ. of Oxford 2010–; Churchill Fellow, Univ. of Bristol 1980; Clark Lecturer, Trinity Coll., Cambridge 1986; Tanner Lecturer, Brasenose Coll., Oxford 2000; Assoc. Fellow, Centre for Research in Philosophy and Literature, Univ. of Warwick 2003; Empson Lecturer, Univ. of Cambridge 2005; Fellow, American Acad. of Arts and Sciences 1996. *Publications:* poetry: Poems 1952, For the Unfallen (Gregory Award 1961) 1959, Preghiere 1964, King Log

(Hawthornden Prize 1969, Geoffrey Faber Memorial Prize 1970) 1968, Mercian Hymns (Alice Hunt Bartlett Award) 1971, Somewhere is Such a Kingdom: Poems 1952–71 1975, Tenebrae (Duff Cooper Memorial Prize 1979) 1978, The Mystery of the Charity of Charles Péguy 1983, Collected Poems 1985, New and Collected Poems 1952–1992 1994, Canaan 1996, The Triumph of Love 1998, Speech! Speech! 2000, The Orchards of Syon 2002, Scenes from Comus 2005, Without Title 2006, Selected Poems 2006, A Treatise of Civil Power 2007, Oraclau/Oracles 2010, Clavic 2011, Odi Barbare 2012; poetic drama: Henrik Ibsen's Brand: a version for the English stage 1978 (produced at Nat. Theatre, London 1978); criticism: The Lords of Limit: essays on literature and ideas 1984, The Enemy's Country 1991, Style and Faith 2003, Collected Critical Writings 2008. *Honours:* Hon. Fellow, Keble Coll., Oxford 1981, Emmanuel Coll., Cambridge 1990; Hon. DLitt (Leeds) 1988, (Warwick) 2007, (Bristol) 2009, (Oxford) 2010, Hon. LittD (Cambridge) 2010; Whitbread Award 1971, RSL Award (W.H. Heinemann Bequest) 1971, Loines Award, American Acad. and Inst. of Arts and Letters 1983, Ingram Merrill Foundation Award in Literature 1985, Kahn Award 1998, T.S. Eliot Prize, Ingersoll Foundation 2000, Truman Capote Award for Literary Criticism 2009. *Address:* Faculty of English Language and Literature, University of Oxford, St Cross Building, Manor Road, Oxford, OX1 3UL, England (office). *Telephone:* (1865) 271055 (office). *Fax:* (1865) 271054 (office). *Website:* www.english.ox.ac.uk (office).

HILL, Jane Bowers, BA, MA, PhD; American academic, editor, writer and poet; *Professor and Chairman, University of West Georgia;* b. 17 Oct. 1950, Seneca, SC; m. Robert W. Hill 1980; one d. *Education:* Clemson Univ., Univ. of Illinois. *Career:* Assoc. Ed. Peachtree Publrs 1986–88; Sr Ed. Longstreet Press 1988–91; Dir Kennesaw Summer Writers' Workshop 1988–92; Asst Prof., Univ. of West Georgia 1992–; mem. Modern Language Asscn. *Publications:* An American Christmas: A Sampler of Contemporary Stories and Poems (ed.) 1986, Our Mutual Room: Modern Literary Portraits of the Opposite Sex (ed.) 1987, Songs: New Voices in Fiction (ed.) 1990, Cobb County: At the Heart of Change (ed.) 1991, Gail Godwin 1992; contrib. to numerous stories, poems, essays and reviews. *Honours:* Frank O'Connor Prize for Fiction 1989, Syvenna Foundation Fellow 1991, Monticello Fellowship for Female Writers 1992. *Address:* University of West Georgia, 1601 Maple Street, Carrollton, GA 30118 (office); 1419 Arden Drive, Marietta, GA 30008, USA (home). *Telephone:* (678) 839-6512 (office). *Fax:* (678) 839-4849 (office). *E-mail:* jhill@westga.edu (office); janehill@mindspring.com (home). *Website:* www.westga.edu/~jhill (office).

HILL, John (see Koontz, Dean Ray)

HILL, John Spencer, BA, MA, PhD; Canadian academic and writer; b. 22 Oct. 1943, Brantford, ON; m. 1966; two s. one d. *Education:* Queen's University, University of Toronto, Canada. *Career:* Asst Prof. of English, Royal Military College of Canada, 1967–69, 1972–73; Lecturer, University of Western Australia, 1973–79; Prof. of English Literature, University of Ottawa, 1979–. *Publications:* Imaginations in Coleridge, 1978; John Milton: Poet, Priest and Prophet, 1979; The Last Castrato (novel), 1995; Ghirlandaio's Daughter (novel), 1996; Infinity, Faith and Time, 1997. Contributions: scholarly journals. *Honours:* Critics' Choice Award, San Francisco Review of Books, 1995; Arthur Ellis Award, Crime Writers of Canada, 1996.

HILL, Justin, BA, MA; British novelist; *Assistant Professor, City University of Hong Kong;* b. 31 May 1971, Freeport, Grand Bahama; s. of Reginald Jerome Hill and Penelope Mary Hill; m. Elle Hill. *Education:* St Peter's School, York, Univs of Durham and Lancaster. *Career:* fmrly worked for an aid agency in Shanxi and Hunan, People's Repub. of China, as a teacher in Eritrea; currently Asst Prof., City Univ. of Hong Kong. *Theatre:* appearance in Macbeth, Galway Town Hall Theatre 2003. *Publications:* A Bend in the Yellow River 1997, The Drink and Dream Teahouse (Geoffrey Faber Memorial Prize 2002) 2001, Ciao Asmara 2002, Passing Under Heaven (Soc. of Authors Somerset Maugham Award 2005) 2004; contribs to The Independent, Asian Literary Review; reviews for The Guardian, TLS, South China Morning Post. *Honours:* Third XiaoXiang Friendship Award, Hunan Province (China), Betty Trask Award 2000, ranked by the Independent on Sunday amongst Top 20 Young British Writers 2001. *Literary Agent:* The Viney Agency, 23 Erlanger Road, Telegraph Hill, London, SE14 5TF, England. *E-mail:* charlie@thevineyagency.com. *Website:* www.thevineyagency.com. *Address:* c/o Little, Brown Book Group, 100 Victoria Embankment, London, EC2Y 0DY, England (office). *E-mail:* hi@justinhillauthor.com (office). *Website:* www.justinhillauthor.com.

HILL, Lawrence Arthur, BA, MA; Canadian writer; b. 24 Jan. 1957, Newmarket, Ont.; s. of Daniel Grafton Hill III and Donna Mae Bender Hill; m. Miranda Hill; one s., four d. *Education:* Laval Univ., Quebec, Johns Hopkins Univ. *Career:* worked as reporter, the Globe and Mail newspapers, parl. corresp., The Winnipeg Free Press; volunteer work in West Africa with Canadian Crossroads International. *Film:* Seeking Salvation: A History of the Black Church in Canada (American Wilbur Award 2005) 2004. *Publications:* Some Great Thing (novel) 1992, Any Known Blood (novel) 1997, Black Berry, Sweet Juice: On Being Black and White in Canada (memoir) 2001, The Deserter's Tale: The Story of an Ordinary Soldier Who Walked Away from the War in Iraq (with Joshua Key) (non-fiction) 2007, Someone Knows My Name/The Book of Negroes (novel) (Rogers Writers' Trust Fiction Prize 2008, Commonwealth Writers' Prize 2008, Canada Reads 2009) 2007; contrib. to The Beaver, The Walrus, MacLean's, Toronto Star, The Globe and Mail. *Honours:* National Magazine Award for best essay 2006, Ont. Library Asscn Evergreen Award 2008, Libris Award for Author of the Year, Canadian Booksellers Asscn 2008. *Literary Agent:* c/o Ellen Levine, Trident Media Group, 36th Floor, 41 Madison Avenue, New York, NY 10010, USA. *Telephone:* (212) 333-1517. *E-mail:* elevine@tridentmediagroup.com. *Website:* www.tridentmediagroup.com. *Address:* c/o The Writers' Union of Canada, 90 Richmond Street East, Suite 200, Toronto, ON M5C 1P1, Canada (office). *Telephone:* (416) 703-8982 (office). *E-mail:* mail@lawrencehill.com (office). *Website:* www.lawrencehill.com.

HILL, Pamela, (Sharon Fiske), BSc, DA; British writer; b. 26 Nov. 1920, Nairobi, Kenya. *Education:* Glasgow School of Art, Univ. of Glasgow. *Career:* mem. RSL, Society of Authors. *Publications:* Flaming Janet, 1954; The Devil of Aske, 1972; The Malvie Inheritance, 1973; Homage to a Rose, 1979; Fire Opal, 1980; This Rough Beginning, 1981; My Lady Glamis, 1981; Summer Cypress, 1981; The House of Cray, 1982; The Governess, 1985; Venables, 1988; The Sutburys, 1987; The Brocken, 1991; The Sword and the Flame, 1991; Mercer, 1992; The Silver Runaways, 1992; O Madcap Duchess, 1993; The Parson's Children, 1993; The Man from the North, 1994; Journey Beyond Innocence, 1994; The Charmed Descent, 1995; The Inadvisable Marriages, 1995; Saints' Names for Confirmation, 1995; Alice the Palace, 1996; Murder in Store, 1996; Widow's Veil, 1997. Contributions: periodicals.

HILL, Peter; British journalist and newspaper editor; *Editor, Daily Express.* *Career:* Ed. Daily Star 1998–2003, Daily Express 2003–11; mem. Press Complaints Comm. 2003–09. *Honours:* Ed. of the Year, What the Papers Say Awards 2002. *Address:* c/o Daily Express, 10 Lower Thames Street, London, EC3R 6EN, England.

HILL, Roberta, (Roberta Hill Whiteman), BA, MFA, PhD; American poet and academic; *Associate Professor of English and American Indian Studies, University of Wisconsin at Madison;* b. 1947; three c. *Education:* Univs of Wisconsin, Montana and Minnesota. *Career:* has taught at Oneida and Rosebud Native American reservations, Univ. of Wisconsin at Eau Claire, and Poet-in-the-Schools programmes in Minnesota, Arizona, Oklahoma; currently Assoc. Prof. of English and American Indian Studies, Univ. of Wisconsin at Madison; mem. Oneida Nation of Wisconsin; mem. Advisory Bd Wicazo Sa Review. *Publications:* poetry: Star Quilt 1984, Philadelphia Flowers 1996; contribs to The Southern Review, Northwest Review, American Poetry Review, The Nation. *Honours:* NEA grant, Lila Wallace Reader's Digest Fund Award, Univ. of Wisconsin Chancellor's Award. *Address:* Department of English, University of Wisconsin, 7187 Helen C. White Hall, 600 N Park Street, Madison, WI 53706, USA (office). *E-mail:* rhwhitm@wisc.edu. *Website:* www.wisc.edu/english.

HILL, Rosemary, MA, PhD, FSA, FRSL; British writer and historian; b. 10 April 1957, London, England; d. of Edward Hill and Barbara Hill (née Pegler); m. Christopher Logue (died 2011). *Education:* Newnham Coll., Cambridge, Queen Mary, Univ. of London. *Career:* editorial work, Quarto (literary magazine), Vole (ecological monthly) and freelance journalism 1979–81; writer/sub-ed., Country Life, also freelance writer/journalist, specializing in applied and decorative arts for The Times Literary Supplement, London Review of Books, Sunday Telegraph, Sunday Times 1982–87; fmr Contributing Ed., Crafts and occasional adviser to the Crafts Council Collection; ind. scholar 1987–2006; Visiting Fellow, All Souls Coll., Oxford 2004–05, Fellow 2009–11, Quondam Fellow 2011–; Co-Ed. Studies in Victorian Architecture and Design 2005–; mem. Editorial Bd London Review of Books 2000–, Journal of Modern Craft (Berg) 2008–; Trustee, London Library 1999–2002, Camberwell Residential and Academic Fellowship, Camberwell Coll. of Art 2000–, The Victorian Soc. 2003–; Brother, Artworkers Guild. *Publications:* God's Architect: Pugin and the Building of Romantic Britain (Wolfson History Prize 2007, Elizabeth Longford Prize for Historical Biography 2008, James Tait Black Memorial Prize 2008, Marsh Biography Prize 2009) 2007, Stonehenge 2008, The 1840s (co-author) 2008; contrib. essays and reviews to journals and newspapers. *Honours:* Soc. of Authors Award (British Literature Prize) 1993, Historians of British Art Prize for a subject before 1800 2010. *Literary Agent:* c/o David Godwin Associates Ltd, 55 Monmouth Street, London, WC2H 9DG, England. *Telephone:* (20) 7240-9992. *Fax:* (20) 7395-6110. *E-mail:* assistant@davidgodwinassociates.co.uk. *Website:* www.davidgodwinassociates.co.uk. *Address:* 41 Camberwell Grove, London, SE5 8JA, England. *Telephone:* 7747-800957 (mobile). *Website:* www.all-souls.ox.ac.uk/people.php?personid=270.

HILL, Tobias, BA; British writer, poet, editor and music critic; b. 30 March 1970, London, England. *Education:* Sussex Univ. *Career:* teacher, Apex School, Anjo, Aichi, Japan 1993–94; music critic, Telegraph on Sunday 1994–; Poetry Ed., Richmond Review 1995–96; Books Ed., Don't Tell It magazine 1995–96; Fellow, Royal Soc. Literature, Sussex Univ. *Publications:* Year of the Dog (poems) 1995, Midnight in the City (poems) 1996, Skin (short stories) (PEN-Macmillan Award for Fiction, Ian St James Award) 1997, Zoo (poems) 1998, Underground (novel) 1999, The Love of Stones (novel) 2002, The Cryptographer (novel) 2003, Nocturne in Chrome & Sunset Yellow 2006, The Lion who ate Everything (children's picture book) 2008, The Hidden (novel) 2009; contrib. to Observer, Times, Telegraph. *Honours:* Poetry Book Society Recommendation 1996, University of Cambridge Harper-Wood Studentship for Literature 1996, Eric Gregory Award, National Poetry Foundation 1996. *Literary Agent:* A.M. Heath and Co. Ltd, 6 Warwick Court, Holborn, London

WC1R 5DJ, England. *Telephone:* (20) 7242-2811. *Fax:* (20) 7242-2711. *Website:* www.amheath.com.

HILL WELLS, Susan Elizabeth, (Susan Hill), CBE, BA, MA, FRSL; British writer and playwright; b. 5 Feb. 1942, Scarborough, Yorks., England; d. of the late R. H. Hill and Doris Hill; m. Prof. Stanley W. Wells 1975; two d. (and one d. deceased). *Education:* grammar schools in Scarborough and Coventry and King's Coll. London. *Career:* literary critic, various journals 1963–; numerous plays for BBC 1970–; Fellow, King's Coll. London 1978; presenter, Bookshelf, BBC Radio 1986–87; Founder and Publr Long Barn Books 1996–. *Publications:* The Enclosure 1961, Do Me a Favour 1963, Gentleman and Ladies 1969, A Change for the Better 1969, I'm the King of the Castle 1970, The Albatross 1971, Strange Meeting 1971, The Bird of the Night 1972, A Bit of Singing and Dancing 1973, In the Springtime of the Year 1974, The Cold Country and Other Plays for Radio 1975, The Ramshackle Company (play) 1981, The Magic Apple Tree 1982, The Woman in Black 1983 (stage version 1989), One Night at a Time (for children) 1984, Through the Kitchen Window 1984, Through the Garden Gate 1986, Mother's Magic (for children) 1986, The Lighting of the Lamps 1987, Lanterns Across the Snow 1987, Shakespeare Country 1987, The Spirit of the Cotswolds 1988, Can it be True? (for children) 1988, Family (autobiog.) 1989, Susie's Shoes (for children) 1989, Stories from Codling Village (for children) 1990, I've Forgotten Edward (for children) 1990, I Won't Go There Again (for children) 1990, Pirate Poll (for children) 1991, The Glass Angels 1991, Beware! Beware! 1993, King of Kings 1993, Reflections from a Garden (with Rory Stuart) 1995, Contemporary Women's Short Stories (co-ed. with Rory Stuart) 1995, Listening to the Orchestra (short stories) 1996, The Second Penguin Book of Women's Short Stories 1997, The Service of Clouds 1998, The Boy Who Taught the Beekeeper to Read and Other Stories 2003, The Various Haunts of Men 2004, The Pure in Heart 2005, The Risk of Darkness 2006, The Man in the Picture 2007, Desperate Diary of a Country Housewife (non-fiction) 2007, The Battle for Gullywith (for children) 2008, The Beacon 2008, The Man in the Picture 2008, The Vows of Silence 2008, Howards End is On the Landing 2009, The Small Hand 2010, The Betrayal of Trust 2011, A Kind Man 2011. *Literary Agent:* c/o Sheil Land, 52 Doughty Street, London, WC1N 2LS, England. *E-mail:* vgreen@sheilland.co.uk. *E-mail:* mail@susan-hill.com. *Website:* www.susan-hill.com.

HILLES, Robert Edward, BA, MSc; Canadian poet, writer and academic; b. 13 Nov. 1951, Kenora, Ont.; m. Rebecca Susan Knight 1980; two c. *Education:* University of Calgary. *Career:* Prof. of Computer Programming, 1983–, Senior Prof., 1994–, DeVry Institute of Technology, Calgary; mem. League of Canadian Poets; Writers' Union of Canada; Writers' Guild of Alberta. *Publications:* Look the Lovely Animal Speaks, 1980; The Surprise Element, 1982; An Angel in the Works, 1983; Outlasting the Landscape, 1989; Finding the Lights On, 1991; A Breath at a Time, 1992; Cantos From a Small Room, 1993; Raising of Voices, 1993; Near Morning, 1995; Kissing the Smoke, 1996; Nothing Vanishes, 1996; Breathing Distance, 1997. Contributions: anthologies and periodicals. *Honours:* Gov.-Gen.'s Literary Award for Poetry, 1994; Best Novel Award, Writers' Guild of Alberta, 1994. *Address:* Booming Ground, UBC Creative Writing, Buch E-462, 1866 Main Mall, Vancouver, BC V6T 1Z1, Canada.

HILLIER, Bevis, FRSA; British writer and editor; b. 28 March 1940, s. of the late Jack Ronald Hillier and of Mary Louise Palmer. *Education:* Reigate Grammar School and Magdalen Coll., Oxford. *Career:* Editorial Staff, The Times 1963–68, Antiques Corresp. 1970–84, Deputy Literary Ed. 1981–84; Ed. British Museum Soc. Bulletin 1968–70; Guest Curator, Minn. Inst. of Arts 1971; Ed. The Connoisseur 1973–76; Assoc. Ed., Los Angeles Times 1984–88; Ed. Sotheby's Preview 1990–93. *Publications:* Master Potters of the Industrial Revolution: The Turners of Lane End 1965, Pottery and Porcelain 1700–1914 1968, Art Deco of the 1920s and the 1930s 1968, Posters 1969, Cartoons and Caricatures 1970, The World of Art Deco 1971, 100 Years of Posters 1972, Austerity-Binge 1975, The New Antiques 1977, Greetings from Christmas Past 1982, The Style of the Century 1900–1980 1983, John Betjeman: A Life in Pictures 1984, Young Betjeman 1988, Early English Porcelain 1992, Art Deco Style, A Tonic to the Nation: The Festival of Britain (co-ed.) 1951 1976, Betjeman: The Bonus of Laughter 2004. *Literary Agent:* The Maggie Noach Literary Agency, Unit 4, 246 Acklam Road, London, W10 5YG, England. *Telephone:* (20) 8748-2926. *E-mail:* info@mnla.co.uk. *Website:* www.mnla.co.uk.

HILLIS, Rick, BEd, MFA; Canadian writer, poet and teacher; b. 3 Feb. 1956, Nipawin, Sask.; m. Patricia Appelgren 1988; one s. one d. *Education:* University of Victoria, University of Saskatchewan, Concordia University, University of Iowa, Stanford University. *Career:* Stegner Fellow, Stanford University 1988–90, Jones Lecturer 1990–92; Lecturer, California State University at Hayward 1990, Chesterfield Film Writer's Fellowship 1991–92; Visiting Asst Prof. of English, Reed College 1992–96. *Publications include:* The Blue Machines of Night (poems) 1988, Coming Attractions (co-author) 1988, Canadian Brash (co-author) 1990, Limbo Stories 1990; contributions: anthologies and periodicals. *Honours:* Canada Council grant 1985, 1987, 1989, Drue Heinz Literature Prize 1990.

HILSUM, Lindsey, BA (Hons); British journalist; *International Editor, Channel 4 News (UK)*; b. 3 Aug. 1958, d. of Cyril Hilsum and Betty Hilsum. *Education:* Univ. of Exeter. *Career:* joined Oxfam working in Guatemala and Haiti 1979; began journalism career freelance reporting from Mexico and the Caribbean 1980; worked for three years as Information Officer for UNICEF, Nairobi; covered events in E Africa for BBC and The Guardian newspaper 1986–89; Sr Producer, BBC World Service 1990–93, reported from Rwanda, Middle East, Mexico, S Africa, S Pacific; Diplomatic Corresp., Channel 4 News 1996–2003, Int. Ed. 2003–, China Corresp. 2006–08; regular contrib. to Granta, Observer, Sunday Times. *Publication:* Sandstorm: Libya in the Time of Revolution 2012. *Honours:* Amnesty International Awards 1997, 2004, TV News Award 2004, Royal Television Soc. Specialist Journalist of the Year 2003, Emmy Award for coverage of fall of Saddam Hussein (co-recipient) 2004, Royal Television Soc. TV Journalist of the Year Award 2005, James Cameron Award 2005, Women in Film and Television Award 2005, Foreign Press Asscn Award 2010, Charles Wheeler Award 2011, One World Journalist of the Year 2011, Political Studies Asscn Award 2011. *Literary Agent:* c/o Knight Ayton Management, 35 Great James Street, London, WC1N 3HB, England. *Telephone:* (20) 7831-4400. *Fax:* (20) 7831-4455. *E-mail:* sueayton@knightayton.co.uk. *Website:* knightayton.co.uk. *Address:* Channel 4 News, ITN, 200 Grays Inn Road, London, WC1X 8XZ, England (office). *Telephone:* (20) 7430-4606 (office). *Fax:* (20) 7430-4607 (office). *E-mail:* c4foreign@itn.co.uk (office). *Website:* www.channel4.com/news (office).

HILTON, Suzanne McLean, BA; American writer; b. 3 Sept. 1922, Pittsburgh, Pa; m. Warren Mitchell Hilton 1946, one s. one d. *Education:* Beaver Coll. (now Arcadia Univ.). *Career:* Ed. Bulletin of Old York Road Historical Soc. 1976–92, Bulletin of Historical Soc. of Montgomery County 1987–89; Assoc. Ed. Montgomery County History 1983; now retd; mem. Soc. of Children's Book Writers and Illustrators, Philadelphia Children's Reading Round Table. *Publications:* How Do They Get Rid of It? 1970, How Do They Cope with It? 1970, Beat It, Burn It and Drown It 1974, Who Do You Think You Are? 1976, Yesterday's People 1976, Here Today and Gone Tomorrow 1978, Faster than a Horse: Moving West with Engine Power 1983, Montgomery County: The Second Hundred Years 1983, The World of Young Tom Jefferson 1986, The World of Young George Washington 1986, The World of Young Herbert Hoover 1987, The World of Young Andrew Jackson 1988, A Capital Capitol City 1991, Miners, Merchants and Maids 1995; contribs: hHistorical journals. *Honours:* Legion of Honour, Chapel of the Four Chaplains 1978; Award for Excellence in Non-Fiction, Drexel Univ. 1979, Golden Spur, Western Writers of America 1980, Gold Disc, Beaver Coll. (now Arcadia Univ.) 1981. *Address:* 3320 108th Street, NW, Gig Harbour, WA 98332, USA.

HILTON, Tessa; British newspaper editor; b. 18 Feb. 1951, d. of Michael Hilton and Phyllis Hilton; m. Graham Ball 1976; two s. one d. *Education:* St Mary's School, Gerrards Cross. *Career:* journalist, Sunday Mirror 1970–78, Ed. 1994; freelance writer 1978–85; Ed. Mother magazine 1985–87; Exec. Today 1987–91; Ed. Femail, Daily Mail 1991–94; Asst Ed. Sun 1994; Deputy Ed. Express then Ed. Express on Sunday magazine 1996–99; currently Features Ed.-at-Large Woman & Home; mem. judging panel, Penguin/Orange Reading Group Prize 2003, UKPG Award for Regional Newspaper of the Year and Free Newspaper of the Year 2004. *Publication:* The Great Ormond Street Book of Child Health 1990, The Great Ormond Street New Baby And Child Care Book: The Essential Guide for Parents of Children Aged 0–5 (co-author) 1997. *Address:* c/o Woman and Home, The Blue Fin Building, 110 Southwark Street, London, SE1 0SU, England (office). *Telephone:* (20) 3148-7836 (office). *E-mail:* wandhmail@ipcmedia.com (office). *Website:* www.womanandhome.com (office).

HIMMELFARB, Gertrude, PhD, FBA, FRHistS; American historian, academic and writer; *Professor Emerita, City University of New York*; b. 8 Aug. 1922, New York, NY; d. of Max Himmelfarb and Bertha Himmelfarb (née Lerner); m. Irving Kristol 1942; one s. one d. *Education:* Brooklyn Coll., CUNY, Univ. of Chicago, Girton Coll., Cambridge. *Career:* Distinguished Prof. of History, Graduate School, CUNY 1965–88, Prof. Emer. 1988–; Fellow, American Philosophical Soc., American Acad. of Arts and Sciences, Royal Historical Soc., etc.; many public and professional appts.; Guggenheim Fellow 1955–56, 1957–58; Nat. Endowment for the Humanities Fellowship 1968–69, American Council of Learned Socs. Fellowship 1972–73, Woodrow Wilson Int. Center Fellowship 1976–77, Rockefeller Foundation, Humanities Fellowship 1980–81, and other fellowships. *Publications:* Lord Acton: A Study in Conscience and Politics 1952, Darwin and the Darwinian Revolution 1959, Victorian Minds 1968, On Liberty and Liberalism: The Case of John Stuart Mill 1975, The Idea of Poverty 1984, Marriage and Morals Among the Victorians 1986, The New History and the Old 1987, Poverty and Compassion: The Moral Imagination of the Late Victorians 1991, On Looking Into the Abyss: Untimely Thoughts on Culture and Society 1994, The De-Moralization of Society from Victorian Virtues to Modern Values 1995, One Nation, Two Cultures 1999, The Road to Modernity: The British, French and American Enlightenments 2004, The Moral Imagination 2006. *Honours:* numerous hon. degrees including Hon. DHumLitt (Boston) 1987, (Yale) 1990; Hon. DLitt (Smith Coll.) 1977; Rockefeller Foundation Award 1962–63, Nat. Humanities Medal 2004. *Address:* 2510 Virginia Avenue, NW, Washington, DC 20037-1902, USA (home).

HINDE, Thomas (see Chitty, Sir Thomas Wiles)

HINE, (William) Daryl, MA, PhD; Canadian/American poet, writer and translator; b. 24 Feb. 1936, Burnaby, BC, Canada. *Education:* McGill Univ., Univ. of Chicago. *Career:* Asst Prof. of English, Univ. of Chicago 1967–69; Ed., Poetry magazine, Chicago 1968–78. *Publications:* poetry: Five Poems 1954, The Carnal and the Crane 1957, The Devil's Picture Book 1960, Heroics 1961,

The Wooden Horse 1965, Minutes 1968, Resident Alien 1975, In and Out: A Confessional Poem 1975, Daylight Saving 1978, Selected Poems 1980, Academic Festival Overtures 1985, Arrondissements 1988, Postscripts 1991, Recollected Poems: 1951–2004 2007, &: A Serial Poem 2010; novel: The Prince of Darkness and Co. 1961; other: Polish Subtitles: Impressions from a Journey 1962, The 'Poetry' Anthology 1912–1977 (ed. with Joseph Parisi) 1978; translator: The Homeric Hymns and the Battle of the Frogs and the Mice 1972, Theocritus: Idylls and Epigrams 1982, Ovid's Heroines: A Verse Translation of the Heroides 1991, Puerilities from the Greek Anthology 2001, Hesiod's Works 2005. *Honours:* Canada Foundation-Rockefeller Fellowship 1958, Canada Council Grants 1959, 1979, Ingram Merrill Foundation Grants 1962, 1963, 1983, Guggenheim Fellowship 1980, American Acad. of Arts and Letters Award 1982, John D. and Catherine T. MacArthur Foundation Fellowship 1986, Harold Morton Landon Translation Award 2005. *Address:* c/o Fitzhenry and Whiteside Ltd, 195 Allstate Parkway, Markham, ON L3R 4T8, Canada (office). *Website:* www.fitzhenry.ca (office).

HINES, Donald Merrill, BS, MAT, PhD; American writer and teacher; b. 23 Jan. 1931, St Paul, MN; m. Linda Marie Arnold 1961, three s. *Education:* Lewis and Clark Coll., Portland, OR, Reed Coll., Portland, OR, Indiana Univ. *Career:* faculty, Washington State University, 1968–77, King Saud University, Abha, Saudi Arabia, 1982–90, Blue Mountain Community College, Pendleton, Oregon, 1990–91; mem. American Folklore Society. *Publications:* Cultural History of the Inland Pacific Northwest Frontier, 1976; Tales of the Okanogans, 1976; Tales of the Nez Perce, 1984; The Forgotten Tribes: Oral Tales of the Tenino and Adjacent Mid-Columbia River Indian Nations, 1991; Ghost Voices: Yakima Indian Myths, Legends, Humor and Hunting Stories, 1992; Celilo Tales: Wasco Myths, Legends, Tales of Magic and the Marvelous, 1996. Contributions: journals. *Honours:* Ford Foundation Fellowship, 1965; Third Prize, Chicago Folklore Contest, University of Chicago, 1970.

HINOJOSA-SMITH, R. Rolando, BS, MA, PhD; American writer and academic; *Garwood Centennial Professor, University of Texas at Austin*; b. 21 Jan. 1929, Mercedes, Tex.; one s. two d. *Education:* Univ. of Texas at Austin, New Mexico Highlands Univ., Las Vegas, Univ. of Illinois. *Career:* worked as a civil servant for the Social Security Admin, as an office man. for a work clothing firm, as a data processor and as a labourer for a chemical co.; teaching asst, New Mexico Highlands Univ. 1962–63; Instructor, Univ. of Illinois 1966–68; Asst Prof., Trinity Univ., San Antonio 1968–70; Assoc. Prof. and Chair., Modern Languages, Texas A&I Univ., Kingsville 1970–74, Dean Coll. of Arts and Sciences 1974–76, Vice-Pres. for Academic Affairs 1976–77; Prof. and Chair. Dept of Chicano Studies, Univ. of Minnesota 1977–81; Prof., Dept of English, Univ. of Texas at Austin 1981–, Ellen Clayton Garwood Centennial Prof. 1985–; Mari Sabusawa Michener Chair 1990–94; Visiting Prof., Texas A&I Univ., Kingsville 1979, 1980, Univ. of Texas 1979, 1980, UCLA 1980; Distinguished Visiting Prof., Kansas Univ. 1994; Univ. of Illinois Kumbak/Homecoming Guest 1995; Will and Ariel Durant Professorship, St Peter's Coll. 1997–98; mem. American PEN, MLA, Academia Norte Americana de la Lengua Espanola, Hispanic Soc. of America, Texas Inst. of Letters, The Nat. Faculty 1988–, Texas Comm. for the Humanities 1990–95, Nat. Endowment for the Arts Panel 1990, 1991, 2001, Nat. Endowment for the Humanities Panel 1992; Fellow, Soc. of Spanish and Spanish American Studies; more than 300 presentations at confs etc. including formal papers, workshops, readings and consultant engagements. *Publications include:* Estampas del valle y otras obras 1973 (English trans. as Sketches of the Valley and Other Works 1980), The Valley 1983, Klail City y sus alrededores 1976 (English trans. as Klail City 1987), Korean Love Songs 1978, Generaciones, Notas, y Brechas (Generations, Notes, and Trails; translated by Fausto Avendafio) 1980, Claros varones de Belken 1981 (English trans. as Fair Gentlemen of Belken County 1987), Mi querido Rafa 1981 (English trans. as Dear Rafe 1985), Rites and Witnesses 1982, The Valley 1983, Partners in Crime 1985, This Migrant Earth (rendition of Tomas Rivera's . . .y no se lo tragó la tierra) 1987, Los amigos de Becky 1990 (English trans. as Becky and Her Friends 1990), The Useless Servants 1993, Ask a Policeman 1998, We Happy Few 2006; contribs to anthologies, reviews, journals and periodicals. *Honours:* Hon. DLitt (Texas A&M Univ.) 2007; Quinto Sol Literary Award for Best Novel 1972, Casa de las Americas Prize for Best Novel 1976, Univ. of Minnesota Grad. School Scholarship 1978, Univ. of Minnesota Reed-McMillan Scholarship 1979, Southern Fellowship 1979–80, Ford Foundation Scholarship 1979–80, Ford Fellow 1979–80, Southwest Conf. on Latin American Studies Award for Best Writing in the Humanities 1981, Univ. of Illinois/Coll. of Liberal Arts Distinguished Alumnus 1988–89, Lon Tinkle Lifetime Achievement Award, Texas Inst. of Letters 1998, Univ. of Illinois Alumni Award 1998, Celebrity Author, Scott Foresman Co. 1999–2000, Univ. of Illinois's Annual Lecture Series named after him 2005, Texas Literary Hall of Fame 2006, Bookend Award, Texas Literary Book Festival 2007. *Address:* Department of English, PAR 108, University of Texas, Austin, TX 78712 (office); 3111 Parker Lane #178, Austin, TX 78741, USA (home). *Telephone:* (512) 471-4991 (office); (512) 445-7379 (home). *Fax:* (512) 471-4909 (office). *E-mail:* rorro@mail.utexas.edu (office). *Website:* www.utexas.edu/research/eureka/faculty/view.php?pid=2533 (office).

HINSON, Edward Glenn, BA, BD, ThD, DPhil; American academic and writer; b. 27 July 1931, St Louis, Mo.; m. Martha Anne Burks 1956; one s. one d. *Education:* Washington Univ., St Louis, Southern Baptist Theological Seminary, Louisville, Univ. of Oxford, UK. *Career:* Prof., Southern Baptist Theological Seminary 1959–92, Wake Forest Univ. 1982–84; Visiting Prof., St John's Univ., Collegeville, Minn. 1983, Catholic Univ. of America 1987, Univ. of Notre Dame 1989; Prof. of Spirituality and John F. Loftis Prof. of Church History, Baptist Theological Seminary, Richmond, Va 1992–; mem. American Soc. of Church History, Asscn Internationale des Patristique, International Thomas Merton Soc., National Asscn of Baptist Profs of Religion (Pres. 1993–94), North American Patristics Soc., Societas Liturgica. *Publications include:* The Church: Design for Survival 1967, Seekers after Mature Faith 1968, A Serious Call to a Contemplative Life-Style 1974, Soul Liberty 1975, The Early Church Fathers 1978, The Reaffirmation of Prayer 1979, A History of Baptists in Arkansas 1980, The Evangelization of the Roman Empire 1981, Are Southern Baptists Evangelicals? 1983, Religious Liberty 1991, Spirituality in Ecumenical Perspective 1993, The Church Triumphant: A History of Christianity up to 1300 1995, The Early Church 1996, Love at the Heart of Things: A Biography of Douglas V. Steere 1998; contribs: Festschriften, reference works, and journals. *Honours:* American Asscn of Theological Schools Fellowship 1966–67, Prof. of the Year, Southern Baptist Theological Fellowship 1975–76, Johannes Quasten Medal, Catholic Univ. of America, Cuthbert Allen Award, Ecumenical Inst. of Belmont Abbey/Wake Forest Univ. 1992.

HINTON, Peter; Canadian playwright and director; *Artistic Director, National Arts Centre English Theatre. Career:* has held numerous posts in Canadian theatre, including Assoc. Artistic Dir Theatre Passe Muraille and Canadian Stage Co., Toronto, Artistic Dir Playwrights Theatre Centre, Vancouver, Dramaturg-in-Residence Playwrights' Workshop, Montréal, Artistic Assoc. Stratford Festival; Artistic Dir Nat. Arts Centre English Theatre 2005–; has taught at Ryerson Theatre School and Nat. Theatre School of Canada. *Plays:* Façade, Urban Voodoo (with Jim Millan), The Swanne trilogy: George III: The Death of Cupid 2002, Princess Charlotte: The Acts of Venus 2003, Queen Victoria: The Seduction of Nemesis 2004. *Libretti:* (with Peter Hannan): The Diana Cantata, 120 Songs for the Marquis de Sade (Alcan Performing Arts Award 2002). *Plays directed include:* Scary Stories by Gordon Armstrong (Jessie Richardson Award for Directing 1995), Hush and the Crimson Veil by Allen Cole, Serpent Kills by Blake Brooker, Possible Worlds by John Mighton, Geometry in Venice by Michael McKenzie, Burning Vision by Marie Clements, Frida K by Gloria Montero, Girls! Girls! Girls! by Greg MacArthur. *Publications:* essays in Theatrum, The Canadian Theatre Review, Between the Lines: a collection of interviews and articles on Dramaturgy in Canada. *E-mail:* phinton@nac-cna.ca (office). *Website:* www.nac-cna.ca/en/theatre/ (office).

HINTON, Susan Eloise (S. E.); American writer; b. 22 July 1948, Tulsa, OK; m. David Inhofe 1970; one s. *Career:* writer of teenage fiction and films. *Film appearances:* Tex. 1982, The Outsiders 1983. *Screenplay:* Rumble Fish (jtly). *Publications:* The Outsiders (Chicago Tribune Book, World Spring Festival Honour Book 1967, Media and Methods Maxi Award 1975, Massachusetts Children's Book Award 1979) 1967, That Was Then, This is Now (Chicago Tribune Book, World Spring Festival Honour Book 1971, Massachusetts Children's Book Award 1978) 1971, Rumble Fish (Land of Enchantment Award New Mexico Library Asscn 1982) 1975, Tex. (Sue Hefly Award 1983) 1979, Taming the Star Runner 1988, Big David, Little David 1994, The Puppy Sister 1997, Hawkes Harbor 2005, Some of Tim's Stories 2007. *Honours:* Golden Archer Award 1983, Author Award American Library Asscn Young Adult Services Div/School Library Journal 1988. *E-mail:* sehinton@sehinton.com (office). *Website:* www.sehinton.com.

HIPPOLYTE, Kendel; Saint Lucia poet; b. 9 Jan. 1952, Castries; s. of Kent Hippolyte and Geraldine Hippolyte; m. Jane King. *Career:* co-founder Lighthouse Theatre Co. 1984; fmr research and publs officer, Folk Research Centre; taught at St Mary's Coll. and Sir Arthur Lewis Community Coll. *Publications:* poetry: Island in the Sun, Side Two... 1980, Bearings 1986, The Labyrinth 1991, Night Vision 2006; contrib. poems to anthologies, including The Penguin Book of Caribbean Verse in English 1986, The Heinemann Book of Caribbean Poetry 1992, Wheel and Come Again 1998, Crossing Water 1999; editor: A Collection of Essays by St Lucian Writers (co-ed.) 1980, Nine St Lucian Poets (ed.) 1988. *Address:* c/o Peepal Tree Press, 17 King's Avenue, Leeds, LS6 1QS, England.

HIRANO, Keiichiro; Japanese writer; b. 22 June 1975, Kamagori, Aichi Pref. *Education:* studied law, Kyoto Univ. *Publications:* novels: Nisshoku (Eclipse) (Akutagawa Prize 1999) 1998, Ichigetsu Monogatari (A One Month Story) 1999, Soso (The Funeral) 2002; short stories: Takasegawa 2003, Shitatariochiru tokei-tachi no hamon (The Ripples of Dripping Clocks) 2005. *E-mail:* web@k-hirano.com. *Website:* www.k-hirano.com.

HIRSCH, Edward Mark, BA, PhD; American poet and writer; *President, Guggenheim Foundation*; b. (Edward Rubenstein), 20 Jan. 1950, Chicago, Ill.; m. Lauren Watel; one s. *Education:* Grinnell Coll., Univ. of Pennsylvania. *Career:* teacher, Poetry in the Schools Program, New York and Pennsylvania 1976–78; Asst Prof., Wayne State Univ. 1978–82, Assoc. Prof. of English 1982–85; Assoc. Prof., Univ. of Houston 1985–88, Prof. of English 1988–2002; Pres. Guggenheim Foundation 2002–; mem. Authors' Guild, Modern Language Asscn, PEN, Poetry Soc. of America, Texas Inst. of Letters. *Publications include:* For the Sleepwalkers 1981, Wild Gratitude 1986, The Night Parade 1989, Earthly Measures 1994, Transforming Vision (ed.) 1994, On Love 1998, How to Read a Poem and Fall in Love with Poetry 1999, Responsive Reading 1999, The Demon and the Angel: Searching for the Source of Artistic Expression 2002, Lay Back in Darkness 2003, Poet's Choice 2006, Special

Orders 2008, The Living Fire 2010; contrib. to numerous anthologies, books, journals and periodicals. *Honours:* Hon. DHumLitt (Grinnell Coll.) 1989, (Elon Coll.) 1994, (Lawrence Univ.) 2002, (Macalester Coll.) 2005, (Governors State Univ.) 2006, (Georgetown Univ.) 2007, (Grad. Center, CUNY) 2008; Peter I. B. Lavan Younger Poets Award, Acad. of American Poets 1983, Ingram Merrill Foundation Award 1978, American Council of Learned Socs Fellow 1981, Nat. Endowment for the Arts Fellowship 1982, Delmore Schwartz Memorial Poetry Award, New York Univ. 1985, Guggenheim Fellowship 1986–87, Award in Poetry, Texas Inst. of Letters 1987, Nat. Book Critics Circle Award 1987, Rome Prize, American Acad. and Inst. of Arts and Letters 1988, Robert and Hazel Ferguson Memorial Award for Poetry, Friends of Chicago Literature 1990, Lila Wallace-Reader's Digest Writing Fellow 1993, Woodrow Wilson Fellow 1994, 1995, Lyndhurst Prize 1994–96, MacArthur Fellowships 1998–2002. *Address:* 557 Carlton Avenue, #2, Brooklyn, NY 11238, USA (home). *Telephone:* (212) 687-4470 (office). *E-mail:* eh@gf.org (office). *Website:* www.gf.org (office).

HIRSCHMAN, Jack, BA, AM, PhD; American poet and translator; b. 13 Dec. 1933, New York, NY; m. 1st Ruth Epstein 1954 (divorced); one s. one d. *Education:* City Coll. CUNY, Indiana Univ. *Career:* editorial team of journal Left Curve 1983–, correspondent for The People's Tribune; Poet Laureate of San Francisco 2006–08. *Publications:* poetry: Fragments 1952, A Correspondence of Americans 1960, Two 1963, Interchange 1964, Kline Sky 1965, YOD 1966, London Seen Directly 1967, Wasn't Like This in the Woodcut 1967, William Blake 1967, A Word in Your Season (with Asa Benveniste) 1967, Ltd Interchangeable in Eternity: Poems of Jackruthdavidcelia Hirschman 1967, Jerusalem 1968, Aleph, Benoni and Zaddik 1968, Jerusalem Ltd 1968, Shekinah 1969, Broadside Golem 1969, Black Alephs: Poems 1960–68 1969, NHR 1970, Scintilla 1970, Soledeth 1971, DT 1971, The Burning of Los Angeles 1971, HNYC 1971, Les Vidanges 1972, The R of the Ari's Raziel 1972, Adamnan 1972, K'wai Sing: The Origin of the Dragon 1973, Cantillations 1973, Aur Sea 1974, Djackson 1974, Cockroach Street 1975, The Cool Boyetz Cycle 1975, Kashtaniyah Segodnyah 1976, Lyripol 1976, The Arcanes of Le Comte de St Germain 1977, The Proletarian Arcane 1978, The Jonestown Arcane 1979, The Caliostro Arcane 1981, The David Arcane 1982, Class Questions 1982, Kallatumba 1984, The Necessary Is 1984, The Bottom Line 1988, Sunsong 1988, The Tirana Arcane 1991, The Satin Arcane 1991, Endless Threshold 1992, The Back of a Spoon 1992, The Heartbeat Arcane 1993, The Xibalba Arcane 1994, The Arcane on a Stick 1995, The Graffiti Arcane 1995, Culture and Struggle 1995, The Green Chakra Arcane 1996, L'Arcano di Pasolini 1996, L'Arcano di Shupsl 1996, 36 1996, The Grit Arcane 1997, The Open Gate 1998, I Knew I Had a Brother 1999, The Archaic Now Arcane 2000, In the Crazy Hotel of My Last 2000, The Murder of Giordano Bruno 2001, The Lotus Bikini Arcane 2002, Front Lines 2002, Fists on Fire 2003, I Was Born Murdered 2004, Arcanes 2004, Wanted You to Know It 2004; editor: Hip Pocket Poems 1960–61, Artaud Anthology, 1965, Amerus Anthology 1978, Frammis 1979, Would You Wear My Eyes: A Tribute to Bob Kaufman, 1989, Partisans 1995, 500,000 Azaleas: The Selected Poems of Efrain Huerta 2001, Open Gate: An Anthology of Haitian Creole Poetry 2001, Art on the Line 2002; translator: over 50 vols 1970–2004. *Honours:* Antonio Vacaro Prize 2005. *Address:* 354 Columbus Avenue # 454, San Francisco, CA 94133, USA (home). *Telephone:* (415) 421-6776 (home). *E-mail:* aggiefalk@hotmail.com (home).

HIRSHFIELD, Jane, AB; American poet, writer, editor and lecturer; b. 24 Feb. 1953, New York, NY. *Education:* Princeton Univ. *Career:* California Poet in the Schools 1980–85; faculty, various writers' conferences 1984–; Artist-in-Residence, Djerassi Foundation 1987–90; Lecturer, Univ. of San Francisco 1991–; Visiting Poet-in-Residence, Univ. of Alaska, Fairbanks 1993; Adjunct Prof., Northern Michigan Univ. 1994; Assoc. Faculty, Bennington Coll. 1995; Visiting Assoc. Prof., Univ. of California at Berkeley 1995; Core Faculty, Bennington Coll., MFA Writing Seminars 1999–; Elliston Visiting Poet, Univ. of Cincinnati 2000; Poet-in-Residence, Duke Univ. 2009, Rea Visiting Poet-in-Residence, Univ. of Virginia 2012; Fellow Lindisfarne Asscn 1995–; mem. Associated Writing Programs, Authors' Guild, Djerassi Resident Artist Program (bd mem. 1996–), PEN American Center. *Publications:* Alaya (poems) 1982, Of Gravity and Angels (poems) 1988, The Ink Dark Moon: Poems by Ono no Komachi and Izumi Shikibu (trans. with Aratani) 1988, The October Palace (poems) 1994, Women in Praise of the Sacred: 43 Centuries of Spiritual Poetry by Women (ed.) 1994, The Lives of the Heart (poems) 1997, Nine Gates: Entering the Mind of Poetry (essays) 1997, Given Sugar, Given Salt (poems) 2001, Mirabai: Ecstatic Poems (trans. with Bly) 2004, After (poems) (Best Book of 2006, Washington Post, San Francisco Chronicle, Financial Times) 2006, Come, Thief (poems) 2011; contrib. to many anthologies, journals and reviews. *Honours:* Yaddo Fellowships 1983, 1985, 1987, 1989, 1992, 1996, 2002, Guggenheim Fellowship 1985, San Francisco Foundation Joseph Henry Jackson Award 1986, Columbia Univ. Trans. Center Award 1987, Poetry Soc. of America Awards 1987, 1988, Pushcart Prize 1988, Commonwealth Club of California Poetry Medals 1988, 1994, Dewar's Young Artists Recognition Award in Poetry 1990, MacDowell Colony Fellowship 1994, Bay Area Book Reviewers Awards 1994, 2001, Poetry Center Book Award 1995, Rockefeller Foundation Fellowship at Bellagio Study Center, Italy 1995, Acad. of American Poets Fellowship for Distinguished Achievement 2004, Nat. Endowment for the Arts Fellowship 2005. *Literary Agent:* Steven Barclay Agency, 12 Western Avenue, Petaluma, CA 94952, USA. *Telephone:* (707) 773-0654. *Fax:* (707) 778-1868. *Website:* www.barclayagency.com. *Address:* c/o Michael Katz, 367 Molino Avenue, Mill Valley, CA 94941, USA.

HIRSI ALI, Ayaan; Dutch/Somali politician; *Resident Fellow, American Enterprise Institute for Public Policy Research*; b. 13 Nov. 1967, Mogadishu. *Education:* Univ. of Leiden. *Career:* emigrated from Somalia to Netherlands 1992; trans. 1995–2001; staff mem. Wiardi Beckman Stichting 2001–02; mem. Partij van de Arbeid (PvdA) (Labour Party) 2001–02, Volkspartij voor Vrijheid en Democratie (VVD) (People's Party for Freedom and Democracy) 2002–; MP 2003–06; mem. Parl. Comms for Children and Welfare, Foreign Affairs and Devt, Integration, and Internal Affairs 2003–06; Resident Fellow, American Enterprise Inst. for Public Policy Research, Washington DC, USA 2006–. *Publications:* De Zoontjesfabriek (The Son Factory) 2002, The Caged Virgin (essays) 2006, Infidel (autobiog.) 2007, Adan and Eva (children's fiction) 2008, Nomad 2010. *Address:* The American Enterprise Institute, 1150 Seventeenth Street, N.W., Washington, DC 20036, USA (office). *Telephone:* (202) 862-5800 (office). *Fax:* (202) 862-7177 (office). *E-mail:* ayaan.hirsiali@aei.org (office). *Website:* www.aei.org (office).

HISLOP, Ian David, BA (Hons); British editor, writer and broadcaster; *Editor, Private Eye magazine*; b. 13 July 1960, s. of the late David Atholl Hislop and of Helen Hislop; m. Victoria Hamson 1988; one s. one d. *Education:* Ardingly Coll. and Magdalen Coll., Oxford. *Career:* joined Private Eye (satirical magazine) 1981, Deputy Ed. 1985–86, Ed. 1986–; columnist, The Listener magazine 1985–89, The Sunday Telegraph 1996–2003; TV critic, The Spectator 1994–96. *Radio:* The News Quiz (BBC Radio 4) 1985–90, Fourth Column 1992–96, Lent Talk 1994, Gush (scriptwriter, with Nick Newman) 1994, Words on Words 1999, The Hislop Vote (BBC Radio 2) 2000, A Revolution in 5 Acts (BBC Radio 4) 2001, The Real Patron Saints (BBC Radio 4) 2002, The Choir Invisible 2003, A Brief History of Tax (BBC Radio 4) 2003, Blue Birds over the White Cliffs of Dover (BBC Radio 4) 2004, Are We Being Offensive Enough? (BBC Radio 4) 2004, Looking for Middle England (BBC Radio 4) 2006. *TV scriptwriting:* Spitting Image (with Nick Newman; ITV) 1984–89, The Stone Age (with Nick Newman) 1989, Briefcase Encounter (with Nick Newman) 1990, Harry Enfield's Television Programme (with Nick Newman) 1990–92, Harry Enfield and Chums (with Nick Newman) 1994–98, Mangez Merveillac (with Nick Newman) 1994, Dead on Time (with Nick Newman) 1995, Gobble (with Nick Newman; BBC 1) 1996, Sermon from St Albions (ITV Granada) 1998, Songs and Praise from St Albions (with Nick Newman; ITV Granada) 1999, Confessions of a Murderer (with Nick Newman) 1999, My Dad's the Prime Minister (with Nick Newman; BBC) 2003, 2004. *TV performer:* Have I Got News for You (BBC 2) 1990–2000, (BBC 1) 2000–. *TV presenter:* Canterbury Tales (Channel 4) 1996, School Rules (Channel 4) 1997, Pennies from Bevan (Channel 4) 1998, Great Railway Journeys East to West (BBC) 1999, Who Do You Think You Are? (BBC 2) 2004, Not Forgotten (Channel 4) 2005, Not Forgotten: Shot at Dawn (Channel 4) 2007, Scouting for Boys (BBC 4) 2007. *Publications:* various Private Eye collections 1985–, contribs to newspapers and magazines on books, current affairs, arts and entertainment. *Honours:* Underhill Exhbn; Violet Vaughan Morgan Scholarship; BAFTA Award for Have I Got News for You 1991, Editors' Editor, British Soc. of Magazine Eds 1991, Magazine of the Year, What the Papers Say 1991, Editor of the Year, British Soc. of Magazine Eds 1998, Award for Political Satire, Channel 4 Political Awards 2004, Award for Political Comedy, Channel 4 Political Awards 2006. *Address:* Private Eye, 6 Carlisle Street, London, W1D 3BN, England (office). *Telephone:* (20) 7437-4017 (office). *Website:* www.private-eye.co.uk (office).

HITCHINGS, (Christian Nicholas) Henry, PhD; British writer and critic; b. 11 Dec. 1974. *Education:* Christ Church, Oxford, Univ. Coll., London. *Career:* Theatre Critic, London Evening Standard 2009–. *Publications:* Dr Johnson's Dictionary: The Extraordinary Story of the Book that Defined the World, aka Defining the World: The Extraordinary Story of Dr Johnson's Dictionary (Modern Language Asscn Prize) 2005, The Secret Life of Words: How English Became English (John Llewellyn Rhys Prize, Somerset Maugham Award) 2008, How to Really Talk About Books You Haven't Read 2008, The Language Wars: A History of Proper English 2011. *Literary Agent:* c/o Rogers, Coleridge & White, 20 Powis Mews, London, W11 1JN, England. *Telephone:* (20) 7221-3717. *Fax:* (20) 7229-9084. *E-mail:* info@rcwlitagency.com. *Website:* www.rcwlitagency.com. *Address:* c/o John Murray (Publishers) Ltd, 338 Euston Road, London, NW1 3BH, England. *E-mail:* enquiries@johnmurray.co.uk. *Website:* www.johnmurray.co.uk.

HJÖRNE, Lars Goran; Swedish newspaper editor and publisher; b. 20 Oct. 1929, Gothenburg; s. of the late Harry Hjörne; m. Lena Hjörne (née Smith); one s. one d. *Career:* Chief Ed. Göteborgs-Posten 1969–89, Chair. 1969–95, Hon. Chair. 1995–; Hon. British Consul-Gen. in Gothenburg 1991–98. *Honours:* Hon. OBE. *Address:* Göteborgs-Posten, Polhemsplatsen 5, 405 02 Gothenburg (office); Stora Vägen 43, 260 43 Arild, Sweden (home). *Telephone:* (31) 62-40-00 (office); (42) 34-68-03 (home). *Website:* www.gp.se (office).

HJÖRNE, Peter Lars; Swedish newspaper editor and publisher; *Editor-in-Chief, Göteborgs-Posten*; b. 7 Sept. 1952, Gothenburg; s. of Lars Hjörne and Anne Gyllenhammar; m. 2nd Karin Linnea Tufvesson Hjörne 1995; five d. *Education:* Göteborgs Högre Samskola and Univ. of Gothenburg. *Career:* Man. Trainee John Deere Co., USA 1978–79; Exec. Asst Göteborgs-Posten 1979–82, Deputy Man. Dir 1983–85, Man. Dir 1985–93, Owner, Publr and Ed.-in-Chief 1993–. *Address:* Göteborgs-Posten, Polhemsplatsen 5, 405 02 Gothenburg, Sweden (office). *Telephone:* 31-62-40-00 (office). *Fax:* 31-15-76-92 (office). *E-mail:* peter.hjorne@gp.se (office). *Website:* www.gp.se (office).

HO, Anh Thai, MA, PhD; Vietnamese novelist and diplomatist; b. 18 Oct. 1960, Hanoi. *Education:* Hanoi Inst. of Int. Studies. *Career:* served in India and the Middle East as a diplomat, currently working in Ministry of Foreign Affairs; Ed. World Affairs Weekly; Pres. Hanoi Writers' Union; lecturer and Indologist. *Publications include:* The Boy Who Waits at the Bus-stop (Chang trai o ben doi xe) (Short Story Prize, Van Nghe (Literature and Arts) newspaper) 1985, Men and Vehicle Run in the Moonlight (Nguoi va xe chay duoi anh trang) (Best Novel Award, Vietnam Writers' Asscn and the Vietnam Trade Union 1986–90) 1986, The Women on the Island (Nguoi dan ba tren dao) 1986, The Searches (Nhung cuoc kiem tim) 1988, Behind the Red Mist (Trong suong hong hien ra) 1989, Fragment of a Man (Manh vo cua dan ong) 1991, The Man Who Stood on One Leg (Nguoi dung mot chan) (Literature Award, Union of Literature and Art Asscns 1995) 1995, The Bastards (Lu con hoang) 1995, A Sigh through the Laburnums (Tieng tho dai qua rung kim tuoc) 1998, They Have Become My Characters (Ho tro thanh nhan vat cua toi) 2000, The Narration in 265 Days (Tu su 265 ngay) (Annual Prize, Vietnam Writers' Asscn 2002 (refused by author)) 2001, The Women on the Island 2001, The Apocalypse Bell Tolls in the Human World (Coi nguoi rung chuong tan the) 2002, Four Paths to the Fun House (Bon loi vao nha cuoi) 2004, The Hanoian Nights (Muoi le mot dem) 2006, The Buddha, Savitri and I (Duc Phat, nang Savitri va toi) 2007, Namaskar! Hail India (Namaskar! Xin chao An Do) 2008, Hanoi is Embraced by the Rivers (Huong nao Ha Noi cung song) 2009; co-ed.: Love After War: Contemporary Fiction from Viet Nam 2003. *Address:* c/o Curbstone Press, 321 Jackson Street, Willimantic, CT 06226-1738, USA. *E-mail:* info@curbstone.org.

HOAGLAND, Edward, AB; American author; b. 21 Dec. 1932, New York, NY; s. of Warren Eugene Hoagland and Helen Kelley Morley; m. 1st Amy J. Ferrara 1960 (divorced 1964); m. 2nd Marion Magid 1968 (died 1993); one d. *Education:* Harvard Univ. *Career:* Faculty mem. New School for Social Research, New York 1963–64, Rutgers Univ. 1966, Sarah Lawrence Coll., Bronxville, NY 1967, 1971, CUNY 1967, 1968, Univ. of Iowa 1978, 1982, Columbia Univ. 1980, 1981, Brown Univ. 1988, Bennington Coll., Bennington, Vt 1987–2005, Univ. of California, Davis 1990, 1992, Beloit Coll., Wis. 1995; Gen. Ed. Penguin Nature Library 1985–2004; Houghton Mifflin Literary Fellow 1954; American Acad. of Arts and Letters Travelling Fellow 1964; Guggenheim Fellow 1964, 1975; mem. American Acad. of Arts and Letters, American Acad. of Arts and Sciences. *Publications:* Cat Man 1956, The Circle Home 1960, The Peacock's Tail 1965, Notes from the Century Before: A Journal from British Columbia 1969, The Courage of Turtles 1971, Walking the Dead Diamond River 1973, The Moose on the Wall: Field Notes from the Vermont Wilderness 1974, Red Wolves and Black Bears 1976, African Calliope: A Journey to the Sudan 1979, The Edward Hoagland Reader 1979, The Tugman's Passage 1982, City Tales 1986, Seven Rivers West 1986, Heart's Desire 1988, The Final Fate of the Alligators 1992, Balancing Acts 1992, Tigers and Ice 1999, Compass Points 2001, Hoagland on Nature 2003, Early in the Season 2008, Sex and the River Styx 2011, Alaskan Travels: Far-Flung Tales of Love and Adventure 2012; numerous essays and short stories. *Honours:* Longview Foundation Award 1961, O. Henry Award 1971, Brandeis Univ. Citation in Literature 1972, New York State Council on Arts Award 1972, American Acad. of Arts and Letters Harold D. Vursell Memorial Award 1981, Nat. Endowment for the Arts Award 1982, NY Public Library Literary Lion Award 1988, Nat. Magazine Award 1989, Lannan Foundation Literary Award 1993, Boston Public Library Literary Lights Award 1995, John Burroughs Medal 2012. *Address:* POB 51, Barton, VT 05822 (office); POB 615, Edgartown, MA 02539, USA (home). *Telephone:* (508) 627-8803 (office).

HOAGLAND, Anthony Dey (Tony), BA, MFA; American poet, writer and academic; *Associate Professor of Creative Writing, University of Houston;* b. 19 Nov. 1953, Fort Bragg, NC. *Education:* Williams Coll., Univ. of Iowa, Univ. of Arizona. *Career:* currently Assoc. Prof. of Creative Writing, Univ. of Houston; also teaches on Warren Wilson Coll. MFA Program. *Publications:* chapbooks: A Change in Plans 1985, Talking to Stay Warm 1986, History of Desire 1990, Hard Rain 2005, Little Oceans 2009; poetry collections: Sweet Ruin (Brittingham Prize in Poetry 1992, John C. Zacharis First Book Award 1994) 1992, Donkey Gospel (Acad. of American Poets James Laughlin Award 1997) 1998, What Narcissism Means to Me 2003, Unincorporated Persons in the Late Honda Dynasty 2010; essays: Real Sofistikashun: Essays on Poetry and Craft 2006. *Honours:* Nat. Endowment of Arts Literature Fellowship in Poetry 1987, 1994, Guggenheim Fellowship in Poetry 2000, American Acad. of Arts and Letters Award in Literature 2002, Poetry Foundation Mark Twain Award 2005, Folger Shakespeare Library O.B. Hardison Jr Poetry Prize 2005, Poets & Writers Jackson Poetry Prize 2008. *Literary Agent:* c/o Alison Granucci, Blue Flower Arts, PO Box 1361, Millbrook, NY 12545, USA. *Address:* c/o Department of English, University of Houston, 223D Roy Cullen Building, 4800 Calhoun Road, Houston, TX 77004, USA (office). *Telephone:* (713) 743-3004 (office). *Fax:* (713) 743-3215 (office). *E-mail:* thglnd@aol.com. *Website:* www.uh.edu/class/english/faculty/hoagland/index.php (office).

HOARE, Philip, BA (Hons); British writer; b. (Patrick Kevin Moore), 22 May 1958, Southampton, Hants., England; s. of Leonard Joseph Moore and Theresa Marion Hoare. *Education:* St Mary's Coll., Bitterne Park, Southampton, St Mary's Coll. of Further Educ., Teddington, Middx. *Career:* ind. labels buyer, Virgin Records 1979–80; ind. labels buyer and sleeve design, Rough Trade Records 1980–81; formed ind. record label Operation Twilight (affiliated with Les Disques du Crepuscule) 1981–83, released 11 albums and singles, from artists including The Pale Fountains, 23 Skidoo, The Lost Jockey, Paul Haig, Tuxedomoon; co-managed Max rock group 1984–85; contrib. to Blitz, The Face, i-D and Harpers & Queen magazines, The Observer, The Guardian, and The Independent 1986–89; consultant and interviewee for BBC 2 Arena: The Noel Coward Trilogy 1997; co-curated Icons of Pop at Nat. Portrait Gallery (touring nationally through 2000) 1999; catalogue essay for the British Council touring exhbn, POSH and opened tour in Moscow 2003; catalogue essays for Linder, Cornerhouse, Alison Turnbull, Ruskin School and Oxford Botanic Gardens 2005; co-ed. Pet Shop Boys: Catalogue (UK, USA, Germany) 2006; catalogue essays for Gabriel Orozco, White Cube, Richard Wilson, Locus+, David Austen, Milton Keynes Gallery 2006; reviewed and wrote features for The Independent, The Independent on Sunday, The Observer, The Guardian, Sunday Telegraph, Times Literary Supplement, Frieze, Modern Painters 2007; catalogue essay for Peter Doig (Gavin Brown/Michael Werner Gallery) 2009; appeared at Edinburgh Science Festival 2010; Writer-in-Residence, Ruskin School, Oxford 2010; Creative Non-fiction tutor, HMP Albany, Isle of Wight 2010; appeared at Adelaide Literary Festival, Australia 2010, Wellington Literary Festival, NZ 2010; Leverhulme Artist-in-Residence, The Marine Inst., Plymouth Univ. 2011–12, co-curator (with Angela Cockayne) Dominion: A Whale Symposium, Peninsula Arts; Visiting Fellow, Univ. of Southampton 2011–12; appeared at Galle Literary Festival, Sri Lanka 2011. *Television:* writer/presenter, Travels with Pevsner: Hampshire and the Isle of Wight (BBC 2) 1998, writer/presenter, The Hunt for Moby-Dick (BBC 2) 2008, writer/dir, Philip Hoare's Guide to Whales (BBC 4) 2008. *Publications:* Serious Pleasures: The Life of Stephen Tennant 1990, Noel Coward: A Biography 1996, Wilde's Last Stand: Decadence, Conspiracy and the First World War 1997, Spike Island: The Memory of a Military Hospital 2001, England's Lost Eden: Adventures in a Victorian Utopia 2005, Leviathan or, The Whale (BBC Samuel Johnson Prize for Non-Fiction 2009) 2008 (published in USA 2010, Levithan O La Ballena published in Spain 2010), Dominion: A Whale Symposium (co-ed. with Angela Cockayne) 2012. *Honours:* Hon. Dr of Arts (Plymouth) 2012. *Literary Agent:* c/o Aitken Alexander Associates, 18–21 Cavaye Place, London, SW10 9PT, England. *Telephone:* (20) 7373-8672. *Fax:* (20) 7373-6002. *E-mail:* reception@aitkenalexander.co.uk. *Website:* www.aitkenalexander.co.uk; www.philiphoare.co.uk.

HOBB, Robin (see Ogden, Margaret Astrid Lindholm)

HOBSBAWM, Eric John Ernest, CH, MA, PhD, FBA; British academic (retd) and university administrator; *President, Birkbeck, University of London;* b. 9 June 1917, Alexandria, Egypt; s. of Leopold Percy Hobsbaum and Nelly Gruen; m. Marlene Schwarz 1962; one s. one d. *Education:* in Vienna, Berlin, London and Univ. of Cambridge. *Career:* Lecturer, Birkbeck Coll. 1947–59, Reader 1959–70, Prof. of Econ. and Social History 1970–82, Prof. Emer. 1982–, currently Pres.; Fellow, King's Coll. Cambridge 1949–55, Hon. Fellow 1973–; Andrew D. White Prof.-at-Large, Cornell Univ., USA 1976–82; Prof., New School for Social Research, New York, USA 1984–97. *Publications:* Primitive Rebels 1959, The Jazz Scene 1959 (revised edn 1992), The Age of Revolution 1962, Labouring Men 1964, Industry and Empire 1968, Captain Swing 1969, Bandits 1969 (revised edn 2000), Revolutionaries 1973, The Age of Capital 1975; Ed. Storia del Marxismo (five vols) 1978–82, Worlds of Labour 1984, The Age of Empire 1875–1914 1987, Politics for a Rational Left: Political Writing 1989, Nations and Nationalism since 1780 1990, Echoes of the Marseillaise 1990, The Age of Extremes 1914–1991 1994, On History 1997, Uncommon People: Resistance, Rebellion and Jazz 1998, On the Edge of the New Century 2000, Interesting Times 2002, Globalisation, Democracy and Terrorism 2007, How to Change the World: Tales of Marx and Marxism 1840–2011 2011. *Honours:* Hon. Foreign mem. American Acad. of Arts and Sciences, Hungarian Acad. of Sciences, Accad. delle Scienze, Turin, The Japan Acad.; Chevalier des Palmes académiques, Order of the Southern Cross (Brazil) 1996, Ehrenkreuz für Wissenschaft und Kunst (Austria) 2007; Dr hc (Stockholm) 1970, (Chicago) 1976, (East Anglia) 1982, (New School) 1982, (Bard Coll.) 1985, (York Univ., Canada) 1986, (Pisa) 1987, (London) 1993, (Essex) 1996, (Columbia Univ.) 1997, (Buenos Aires) 1997, (Univ. of ARCIS, Santiago, Chile) 1998, (Univ. de la República, Montevideo, Uruguay) 1999, (Turin) 2000, (Oxford) 2001, (Pennsylvania) 2002, (Thessaloniki) 2004, (Vienna) 2008, (Girona) 2009; Balzan Prize 2002. *Address:* Birkbeck, University of London, Malet Street, Bloomsbury, London, WC1E 7HX, England (office). *Telephone:* (20) 7631-6000 (office). *Fax:* (20) 7631-6270 (office). *Website:* www.bbk.ac.uk (office).

HOBSON, Charlotte; British writer; b. 23 Aug. 1970, Salisbury, Wilts.; d. of Anthony Hobson and Tanya Hobson (née Vinogradoff); m. Philip Marsden 1999; one s. one d. *Education:* Univ. of Edinburgh. *Publications:* Black Earth City: A Year in the Heart of Russia 2001; contrib. to Virgin Soil 2001, Granta 64: The Wild East, Poor People 2003, Petersburg Perspectives 2003. *Honours:* Somerset Maugham Award 2002. *Literary Agent:* c/o AP Watt Ltd, 20 John Street, London, WC1N 2DR, England. *Telephone:* (20) 7405-6774. *Fax:* (20) 7831-2154. *E-mail:* apw@apwatt.co.uk. *Website:* www.apwatt.co.uk. *Telephone:* (1326) 270273 (home).

HOBSON, Fred Colby, Jr, MA, PhD; American academic and writer; *Lineberger Professor in the Humanities, University of North Carolina;* b. 23 April 1943, Winston-Salem, NC; m. 1967 (divorced); one d. *Education:* Univ. of North Carolina, Duke Univ. *Career:* Prof. of English, Univ. of Alabama 1972–86; Prof. of English and Co-Ed., Southern Review, Louisiana State Univ. 1986–89; Prof. of English, Lineberger Prof. in the Humanities and Co-Ed., Southern Literary Journal, Univ. of North Carolina at Chapel Hill 1989–. *Publications:* Serpent in Eden: H. L. Mencken and the South 1974, Literature at the Barricades: The American Writer in the 1930s (co-ed.) 1983, Tell About the South: The Southern Rage to Explain 1984, South-Watching: Selected Essays of Gerald W. Johnson (ed.) 1984, The Southern Writer in the Post-Modern World 1990, Mencken: A Life 1994, Thirty-Five Years of Newspaper Work by H. L. Mencken (co-ed.) 1994, The Literature of the American South: A Norton Anthology (co-ed.) 1998, But Now I See: The Southern White Racial Conversion Narrative 1999, South to the Future: An American Region in the Twenty-First Century (ed.) 2002, Faulkner's Absalom, Absalom!: An Oxford Casebook (ed.) 2003, The Silencing of Emily Mullen and Other Essays 2005, Off the Rim: Basketball and Other Religions in a Carolina Childhood 2006; contributions: Virginia Quarterly Review, Sewanee Review, Atlantic Monthly, Kenyon Review, New York Times Book Review, American Literature, TLS. *Honours:* Lillian Smith Award, 1984; Jules F. Landry Awards, 1984, 1999. *Address:* 110 Hunters Ridge Road, Chapel Hill, NC 27517 (home); Department of English, University of North Carolina at Chapel Hill, NC 27599-3520, USA. *Telephone:* (919) 942-0417 (home); (919) 962-4005 (office). *E-mail:* fhobson@email.unc.edu.

HOCHGATTERER, Paulus, PhD; Austrian writer and psychiatrist; b. 16 July 1961, Amstetten, Niederösterreich. *Education:* Univ. of Wien. *Career:* Sr Consultant, Hospital for Neurology, Rosenhügel 1992–; Dir Institut für Erziehungshilfe, Wien. *Publications:* Rückblickpunkte (novel) 1983, Der Aufenthalt 1990, Über die Chirurgie (novel) 1993, Die Nystensche Rege (short stories) 1995, Wildwasser (short story) (Jugendbuchpreis der Jury der Jungen Leser 1998) 1997, Caretta Caretta (novel) (Österreichischer Jugendbuchpreis 2000) 1999, Über Raben (novel) 2002, Eine kurze Geschichte vom Fliegenfischen (short story) 2003, Die Süße des Lebens (novel) (trans. as The Sweetness of Life 2009) (EU Prize for Literature 2009) 2006, Das Matratzenhaus (novel) 2010. *Honours:* Harder Literaturpreis 1995, Österreichischen Förderpreis für Literatur 1998, Elias-Canetti-Stipendium 2001, Deutschen Krimi Preis 2007. *Address:* c/o Hanser Verlage Deuticke, Prinz-Eugen-Str. 30, 1040 Wien, Austria (office). *Website:* www.hanser-literaturverlage.de (office).

HOCHHUTH, Rolf; German playwright; b. 1 April 1931; m.; three s. *Career:* fmr publisher's reader; Resident Municipal Playwright, Basel 1963; mem. PEN of FRG. *Publications include:* plays: Der Stellvertreter: Ein christliches Trauerspiel (The Deputy, a Christian Tragedy) 1963, The Employer 1965, The Soldiers 1966, Anatomy of Revolution 1969, The Guerrillas 1970, The Midwife 1972, Lysistrata and NATO 1973, The Survivor 1981, Alan Turing 1987, Judith 1984, The Immaculate Conception 1989, Wessis in Weimar 1993, McKinsey is Coming 2004; novel: A Love in Germany 1980. *Literary Agent:* Agentur Hegmann, Essener Str. 32, 45529 Hattingen, Germany. *Telephone:* (23) 2443157. *E-mail:* ahegmann@web.de. *Website:* www.hegmann.de.tt; www.rolf-hochhuth.de.

HOCHSCHILD, Adam, AB; American author and journalist; b. 5 Oct. 1942, New York, NY; s. of Harold Hochschild and Mary Hochschild (née Marquand); m. Arlie Russell 1965; two s. *Education:* Harvard Univ. *Career:* reporter, San Francisco Chronicle 1965–66; ed. and writer, Ramparts Magazine 1966–68, 1973–74; Co-founder, ed., writer, Mother Jones Magazine 1974–81, 1986–87; commentator, Nat. Public Radio 1982–83, Public Interest Radio 1987–88; Regents Lecturer, Univ. of California at Santa Cruz 1987; Lecturer, Grad. School of Journalism, Univ. of California at Berkeley 1992–; Fulbright Lecturer, India 1997–98; mem. PEN. *Publications:* Half the Way Home: A Memoir of Father and Son 1986, The Mirror at Midnight: A South African Journey 1990, The Unquiet Ghost: Russians Remember Stalin 1994, Finding the Trapdoor: Essays, Portraits, Travels 1997, King Leopold's Ghost: A Story of Greed, Terror and Heroism in Colonial Africa 1998, Bury the Chains: Prophets and Rebels in the Fight to Free an Empire's Slaves 2005, To End All Wars: A Story of Loyalty and Rebellion, 1914–1918 2011; contrib. to New Yorker, Harper's, New York Times, Los Angeles Times, Washington Post, Progressive, Village Voice, Granta, New York Review of Books, Mother Jones. *Honours:* Dr hc (Curry Coll., Mass) 2004, (St Andrews) 2008; World Affairs Council Thomas Storke Award 1987, Overseas Press Club of America Madeleine Dane Ross Award 1995, Soc. of American Travel Writers Lowell Thomas Award 1995, PEN/Spielvogel-Diamonstein Award for the Art of the Essay 1998, California Book Awards Gold Medals 1999, 2006, J. Anthony Lukas Prize 1999, Lionel Gelber Prize, Canada 1999, 2006, Duff Cooper Prize, UK 2000, Soc. of Professional Journalists Award for best magazine article 2000, Lannan Literary Award 2005, Los Angeles Times Book Prize 2006, PEN USA Literary Award 2006, Theodor Roosevelt-Woodrow Wilson Award, American History Asscn 2009. *Literary Agent:* c/o Kate Johnson, Georges Borchardt Inc., Literary Agent, 136 E 57th Street, New York, NY 10022, USA. *Telephone:* (212) 753-5785. *Fax:* (212) 838-6518. *E-mail:* kate@gbagency.com. *Address:* 84 Seward Street, San Francisco, CA 94114, USA (home).

HOCKING, Mary Eunice, FRSL; British writer; b. 8 April 1921, London. *Career:* local govt officer 1946–70; mem. Soc. of Authors. *Publications:* The Winter City 1961, Visitors to the Crescent 1962, The Sparrow 1964, The Young Spaniard 1965, Ask No Question 1967, A Time of War 1968, Checkmate 1969, The Hopeful Traveller 1970, The Climbing Frame 1971, Family Circle 1972, Daniel Come to Judgement 1974, The Bright Day 1975, The Mind Has Mountains 1976, Look, Stranger! 1978, He Who Plays the King 1980, March House 1981, Good Daughters 1984, Indifferent Heroes 1985, Welcome Strangers 1986, An Irrelevant Woman 1987, A Particular Place 1989, Letters from Constance 1991, The Very Dead of Winter 1993, The Meeting Place 1996. *Address:* 3 Church Row, Lewes, Sussex, BN7 2PU, England (home).

HODAČOVÁ, Helena, PhD; Czech writer; b. 16 Sept. 1916, Jičín; d. of O. Homoláč; m. François Svoboda 1939; one s. one d. (deceased). *Education:* Charles Univ., Prague and Univ. of Paris (Sorbonne). *Career:* writer of poetry since age of 15; Publicist, Lidové Noviny; first books part of Czechoslovak Avant-Garde movt, later pubs deal with problems of everyday life. *Publications:* L'Harpe éolienne 1943, Ciel blanc – terre noire 1964, La Vie du peintre O. Homoláč, Demi-temps vertigineux, Les Oiseaux s'envolent: biographie d'une librettiste du compositeur Smetana, The Chinese 1996. *Address:* Pod lipkami 4, 150 00 Prague 5, Czech Republic. *Telephone:* (2) 523436.

HODGE, Roger D., MA; American editor; b. 12 Aug. 1967, Del Rio, TX; m. Deborah A. Hodge; two c. *Education:* Univ. of the South, Sewanee, TN and New School for Social Research, New York. *Career:* joined Harper's Magazine, New York as intern 1996, readings section 1997, Ed. readings section 1999–2003, Sr Ed. and author Harper's Weekly Review 2000–04, organized redesign of Harpers.org 2003, Deputy Ed. 2004–06, Ed. 2006–10. *Publication:* The Mendacity of Hope: Barack Obama and the Betrayal of American Liberalism 2010. *Address:* 266 Westminster Road, Brooklyn, NY 11218-4343, USA (home). *E-mail:* mendacity0fhope@gmail.com (office). *Website:* www.mendacityofhope.com.

HODGINS, Jack Stanley, BEd, FRSC; Canadian novelist and teacher; b. 3 Oct. 1938, Vancouver Island, BC; m. Dianne Child 1960, two s. one d. *Education:* Univ. of British Columbia. *Career:* mem. PEN, Writers' Union of Canada. *Publications:* Spit Delaney's Island, 1976; The Invention of the World, 1977; The Resurrection of Joseph Bourne, 1979; The Honorary Patron, 1987; Innocent Cities, 1990; Over Forty in Broken Hill, 1992; A Passion for Narrative, 1993; The Macken Charm, 1995; Broken Ground, 1998. *Honours:* Gibson First Novel Award 1978, Gov.-Gen.'s Award for Fiction 1980, Canada-Australia Literature Prize 1986, Commonwealth Literature Prize 1988, British Columbia Book Prizes Ethel Wilson Award 1999; Hon. DLitt (Univ. of British Columbia) 1995, (Malaspina Univ.) 1998.

HODROVÁ, Daniela, MA, PhDr, DrSc; Czech writer and literary theorist; b. 5 July 1946, Prague; d. of Zdeněk Hodr; m. 1st Karel Milota 1985 (died 2002); m. 2nd Jaroslav Skopek 2004 (died 2005). *Education:* Charles Univ., Prague. *Career:* mem. Literary Theory Dept, Inst. of Czech and World Literature, Prague 1974–. *Publications include:* Hledání románu 1989, Podobojí 1991, Visite Privée—Prague 1991, Kukly (Cocoons) 1991, Trýznivé město (The Suffering City, trilogy of novels) 1991–92, Roman zasvěcení (Novel of Initiation) 1994, Místa s tajemstulm (Mysterious Places) 1994, Perunův den (Perun's Day) 1994, Ztracené děti (Lost Children) 1997, ... na okraji chaosu... (On the Edge of Chaos) 2001, Komedie (Comedy) 2003. *Honours:* Franz Kafka Prize 2012. *Address:* Lucemburská 1, 130 00 Prague 3, Czech Republic (home).

HOE, Susanna Leonie, BA; British historian; b. 14 April 1945, Southampton, Hants., England; m. Derek Roebuck 1981. *Education:* London School of Econs, Univ. of Papua New Guinea. *Career:* campaign co-ordinator, British Section, Amnesty International 1977–80; Tutor, Dept of Anthropology and Sociology, Univ. of Papua New Guinea 1985–86; TEFL teacher, Women's Centre, Hong Kong 1991–97. *Publications:* Lady in the Chamber (novel) 1971, God Save the Tsar (novel) 1978, The Man Who Gave his Company Away (biog.) 1978, The Private Life of Old Hong Kong (history) 1991, Chinese Footprints (history) 1996, Stories for Eva (reader for learning English) 1997, The Taking of Hong Kong (history, with Derek Roebuck) 1999, Women at the Siege, Peking 1900 (history) 2000, At Home in Paradise (travel, autobiog.) 2003, Madeira: Women, History, Books and Places 2004, Crete: Women, History, Books and Places 2005, Watching the Flag Come Down (auto-biog.) 2007, Tasmania: Women, History, Books and Places 2010; contrib. to Times (Papua New Guinea), Liverpool Post, Women's Feature Service. *Honours:* Hon. Research Fellow, Centre of Asian Studies, Univ. of Hong Kong; Rangi Hiroa Pacific History Prize 1984. *Address:* 20A Plantation Road, Oxford, OX2 6JD, England (home). *Telephone:* (1865) 513681 (home). *Fax:* (1865) 554199 (home). *E-mail:* susanna@Lhoe.fsnet.co.uk (home). *Website:* www.holobooks.co.uk (home).

HØEG, Peter, MA; Danish writer; b. 1957, Copenhagen; m.; two d. *Education:* Univ. of Copenhagen. *Career:* worked as sailor, ballet dancer, athlete and actor before becoming full-time writer; f. Lolwe Foundation 1996. *Publications:* Forestilling om det Tyvende århundrede (trans. as The History of Danish Dreams) 1988, Fortællinger om natten (trans. as Tales of the Night; short stories) 1990, Frk. Smillas fornemmelse for sne (trans. as Miss Smilla's Feeling for Snow) 1992, De måske egnede (trans. as Borderliners) 1994, Kvinden og aben (trans. as The Woman and the Ape) 1996, Den stille pige (trans. as The Quiet Girl) 2006. *Address:* c/o Rosinante, Købmagergade 62, Postbox 2252, 1019 Copenhagen K, Denmark (office). *Telephone:* 33-41-18-00 (office). *E-mail:* rosinante@rosinante.dk (home). *Website:* www.rosinante.dk (office).

HOFFMAN, Adina; American writer; *Editor, Ibis Editions;* b. 1967, Miss.; m. Peter Cole. *Career:* Visiting Prof., Wesleyan Univ., Middlebury Coll.; Ed. Ibis Editions; fmr film critic for American Prospect, Jerusalem Post; essayist, various pubs; Franke Fellow, Whitney Humanities Center, Univ. of Yale. *Publications:* House of Windows: Portraits from a Jerusalem Neighbourhood 2000, My Happiness Bears No Relation to Happiness: A Poet's Life in the Palestinian Century 2009, Sacred Trash: The Lost and Found World of the Cairo Geniza (written with Peter Cole) 2011; contrib. to The Nation, Washington Post, TLS, Boston Globe, New York Newsday, Raritan, Tin House, The Forward, BBC World Service. *Honours:* Wingate Prize, Jewish

Quarterly 2010. *Address:* c/o Ibis Editions, PO Box 8074, German Colony, Jerusalem, Israel (office). *E-mail:* ibis@netvision.net.il (office). *Website:* www.ibiseditions.com/adinahoffman (office).

HOFFMAN, Alice, MA; American writer and screenwriter; b. 16 March 1952, New York, NY; m. Tom Martin; two s. *Education:* Adelphi Univ., Stanford Univ. *Screenplays:* Independence Day 1983, Practical Magic 1998, The River King 2005. *Publications:* novels: Property Of 1977, The Drowning Season 1979, Angel Landing 1980, White Horses 1982, Fortune's Daughter 1985, Illumination Night 1987, At Risk 1988, Seventh Heaven 1990, Turtle Moon 1992, Second Nature 1994, Practical Magic 1996, Here on Earth 1997, Local Girls 1999, Aquamarine 2001, The River King 2001, Blue Diary 2001, The Probable Future 2003, Blackbird House 2004, The Ice Queen 2005, Skylight Confessions 2007, The Third Angel 2009, The Story Sisters 2009, The Red Garden 2011, The Dovekeepers 2012; teenage and children's ficton: Horsefly, Fireflies, Aquamarine 2001, Indigo 2002, Water Tales 2003, Green Angel 2003, Moondog 2004, The Foretelling 2006, Incantation 2007, Green Witch 2010; contrib. to Redbook, American Review, Playgirl magazine. *Address:* c/o Penguin Putnam, 375 Hudson Street, New York, NY 10014, USA (office). *Website:* www.alicehoffman.com.

HOFFMAN, Daniel Gerard, MA, PhD; American poet and writer; b. 3 April 1923, New York; m. Elizabeth McFarland 1948; two c. *Education:* Columbia Univ. *Career:* Visiting Prof., Univ. of Dijon, France 1956–57; Asst Prof., Swarthmore Coll., Pa 1957–60, Assoc. Prof. 1960–65, Prof. of English 1965–66; Elliston Lecturer, Univ. of Cincinnati 1964; Lecturer, Int. School of Yeats Studies, Sligo, Ireland, 1965; Prof. of English, Univ. of Pennsylvania 1966–83, Poet-in-Residence 1978–, Felix E. Schelling Prof. of English 1983–93, Prof. Emer. 1993–; Consultant in Poetry, Library of Congress, Washington, DC 1973–74, Hon. Consultant in American Letters, 1974–77; Poet-in-Residence, Cathedral of St John the Divine, New York City, 1988–99; Visiting Prof. of English, King's Coll., London, 1991–92; mem. Acad. of American Poets (Chancellor 1973–97, Chancellor Emer. 1997–). *Oratorio:* libretto for Brotherly Love (music by Ezra Laderman) 2000. *Publications:* poetry: An Armada of Thirty Whales, 1954; A Little Geste and Other Poems, 1960; The City of Satisfactions, 1963; Striking the Stones, 1968; Broken Laws, 1970; Corgi Modern Poets in Focus 4 (with others), 1971; The Center of Attention, 1974; Able Was I Ere I Saw Elba: Selected Poems 1954–1974, 1977; Brotherly Love, 1981; Hang-Gliding from Helicon: New and Selected Poems 1948–1988, 1988; Middens of the Tribe 1995, Darkening Water 2002, Beyond Silence: Selected Shorter Poems 1948–2003 2003, Makes You Stop and Think: Sonnets 2005, The Whole Nine Yards: Longer Poems 2009; other: The Poetry of Stephen Crane 1957, Form and Fable in American Fiction 1961, Barbarous Knowledge: Myth in the Poetry of Yeats, Graves and Muir 1967, Poe Poe Poe Poe Poe Poe Poe 1972, Faulkner's Country Matters: Folklore and Fable in Yoknapatawpha 1989, Words to Create a World: Interviews, Essays and Reviews of Contemporary Poetry 1993, Zone of the Interior: A Memoir 1942–1947; editor: several books. *Honours:* American Acad. of Arts and Letters Grant, 1967; Ingram Merrill Foundation Grant, 1971; Nat. Endowment for the Humanities Fellowship, 1975–76; Guggenheim Fellowship, 1983; Hon. DHL (Swarthmore Coll.) 2005; Yale Series of Younger Poets Award, 1954; Ansley Prize, 1957; ACLS Fellowships, 1961–62, 1966–67; Columbia Univ. Medal for Excellence, 1964; Hungarian PEN Medal, 1980; Hazlett Memorial Award, 1984; Paterson Poetry Prize, 1989, Aiken Taylor Award for Modern American Poetry 2003, Rense Poetry Prize 2005. *Address:* 502 Cedar Lane, Swarthmore, PA 19081, USA (home). *Telephone:* (610) 544-4438 (home).

HOFFMAN, David E., BA; American writer; *Contributing Editor, The Washington Post;* b. Palo Alto, Calif.; m.; two c. *Education:* Univ. of Delaware, Oxford Univ., UK. *Career:* joined Capitol Hill News Service 1977; fmr mem. Washington bureau, San Jose Mercury News; joined The Washington Post as White House Corresp. 1982, Jerusalem Bureau Chief 1992–95, Moscow Bureau Chief 1995–2001, Foreign 2001–05, Asst Man. Ed. for foreign news 2005–09, currently Contrib. Ed.; Contrib. Ed., Foreign Policy magazine. *Publications:* The Oligarchs: Wealth and Power in the New Russia 2002, The Dead Hand: The Untold Story of the Cold War Arms Race and Its Dangerous Legacy (Pulitzer Prize for General Nonfiction 2010) 2009. *Honours:* three national journalism awards. *Address:* c/o The Washington Post, 1150 15th Street NW, Washington, DC 20071, USA (office). *Telephone:* (202) 334-6000 (office). *Website:* www.washingtonpost.com (office).

HOFFMAN, Eva Alfreda, PhD; Polish/American writer; b. 1 July 1945, Kraków, Poland. *Education:* Harvard Univ. *Career:* Ed. Week in Review, Arts and Leisure, New York Times 1981–87, The New York Times Book Review 1987–90; fmr Prof. of Literature and Creative Writing, Columbia Univ., Univ. of Minnesota, Tufts Univ.; Visiting Prof., Dept of the Humanities, MIT; broadcasts on BBC Radio 3; mem. PEN, New York Univ. Inst. for the Humanities. *Publications:* Lost in Translation: A Life in a New Language 1989, Exit Into History: A Journey Through the New Eastern Europe 1993, Shtetl: A History of a Small Town and an Extinguished World 1997, The Secret: A Fable for Our Time 2001, After Such Knowledge: Where Memory of the Holocaust Ends and History Begins 2004, Illuminations 2008, Time 2009; contrib. to newspapers and periodicals. *Honours:* American Acad. of Arts and Letters Award 1990, Whiting Award 1992, Guggenheim Fellowship 1993, Prix Italia. *Address:* 18 Goldhurst Terrace, London, NW6 3HU, England.

HOFFMAN, Mary Margaret Lassiter, BA, MA; British writer and journalist; b. 20 April 1945, Eastleigh, Hants., England; d. of Origen Herman Hoffman and Ivegh Cecilia May Lassiter; m. Stephen James Barber 1972; three d. *Education:* Newnham Coll., Cambridge, Univ. Coll., London. *Career:* Ed. Armadillo children's book review magazine online 1999–2009; judge, Guardian Children's Book Prize 2008; judge, Booktrust Teenage Book Prize 2010; mem. Soc. of Authors. *Publications:* approx. 100 books for teenagers and children, including: Amazing Grace 1991, Henry's Baby 1993, Grace and Family 1995, Song of the Earth 1995, An Angel Just Like Me 1997, Sun, Moon and Stars 1998, Three Wise Women 1999, Starring Grace 2000, Stravaganza: City of Masks 2002, Lines in the Sand (ed.) 2003, Stravaganza: City of Stars 2003, Encore, Grace! 2003, Bravo, Grace! 2005, Stravaganza: City of Flowers 2005, The Falconer's Knot 2007, Princess Grace 2007, Stravaganza: City of Secrets 2008, Troubadour 2009, Stravaganza: City of Ships 2010, David 2011; contrib. to Guardian, Daily Telegraph, Independent, Sunday Times, Specialist Children's Book Press. *Honours:* Hon. Fellow, Library Asscn 1998; Waldenbooks Best Children's Book Honor Award 1991, Primary English Award 1995, Prix Polar Jeunesse 2009, SLA Information Book Award (under sevens) 2011. *Literary Agent:* c/o Rogers, Coleridge & White Literary Agency, 20 Powis Mews, London, W11 1JN, England. *Telephone:* (20) 7221-3717. *Fax:* (20) 7229-9084. *E-mail:* info@rcwlitagency.co.uk. *Website:* www.rcwlitagency.co.uk; www.maryhoffman.co.uk; www.stravaganza.co.uk; bookmavenmary.blogspot.com.

HOFFMAN, William, BA; American writer; b. 12 April 1939, New York, NY. *Education:* City Coll., CUNY. *Career:* mem. American Society of Composers, Authors, and Publishers; Dramatists Guild; PEN; Writers Guild of America. *Publications:* As Is, 1985; The Ghosts of Versailles (libretto for opera by John Corigliano), 1991. Editor: New American Plays 2, 3, 4, 1968, 1970, 1971; Gay Plays, 1977. Contributions: journals and magazines. *Honours:* Drama Desk Award, 1985; Obie, 1985; International Classical Music Award, 1991; Emmy, 1992; WGA Award, 1992; Erwin Piscator Award, 1994.

HOFFMAN, Yoel; Israeli writer, translator and academic; *Professor of Eastern Philosophy and Literature, University of Haifa;* b. 1937, Hungary. *Career:* moved with family to pre-state Israel 1939; spent two years in a Buddhist monastery; currently Prof. of Eastern Philosophy and Literature, Univ. of Haifa. *Publications:* fiction: Sefer Yossef (trans. as The Book of Joseph) (stories) 1988, Be-Februar Kedai Liknot Pilim (children's fiction) 1988, Bernhard (novel) 1989, Kristus Shel Ha-Dagim (trans. as The Christ of Fish) (novel) 1991, Guttapercha 1993, Ma Shlomech Dolores? 1995, Ha-Lev Hu Katmandu (trans. as The Heart is Katmandu) (novel) 2000, Ephraim (novel) 2003, Curriculum Vitae (novel) 2007, The Shunra and the Schmetterling (in trans.) (novel); other: trans. of Japanese poetry. *Honours:* Koret Foundation Jewish Book Award, Bialik Prize 2002, Prime Minister's Prize 2007. *Address:* Department of Philosophy, University of Haifa, Eshkol Tower, 19th Floor, Room 1902 A, Mount Carmel, Haifa 31905, Israel (office). *Telephone:* (4) 8240989 (office). *Fax:* (4) 8249735 (office). *Website:* philo.haifa.ac.il (office).

HOFFMANN, Donald; American architectural critic and historian; b. 24 June 1933, Springfield, Ill.; m. Theresa McGrath 1958; four s. one d. *Education:* Univs of Chicago and Kansas City. *Career:* gen. assignment reporter, Kansas City Star 1956–65, Art Critic 1965–90; Asst Ed. Journal of the Society of Architectural Historians 1970–72; Life mem. Art Inst. of Chicago. *Publications:* The Meanings of Architecture: Buildings and Writings by John Wellborn Root (ed.) 1967, The Architecture of John Wellborn Root 1973, Frank Lloyd Wright's Fallingwater 1978, Frank Lloyd Wright's Robie House 1984, Frank Lloyd Wright: Architecture and Nature 1986, Frank Lloyd Wright's Hollyhock House 1992, Understanding Frank Lloyd Wright's Architecture 1995, Frank Lloyd Wright's Dana House 1996, Frank Lloyd Wright, Louis Sullivan and the Skyscraper 1998, Frank Lloyd Wright's House on Kentuck Knob, 2000, Mark Twain in Paradise: His Voyages to Bermuda 2006. *Honours:* Nat. Endowment for the Humanities Fellowship 1970–71, Nat. Endowment for the Arts Fellowship 1974, Graham Foundation Grant 1981. *Address:* 6441 Holmes Street, Kansas City, MO 64131-1110, USA. *Telephone:* (816) 333-0355. *E-mail:* donaldhffmnn@yahoo.com.

HOFFMANN, Roald, PhD; American chemist and academic; *Frank H.T. Rhodes Professor Emeritus of Humane Letters, Cornell University;* b. (Roald Safran), 18 July 1937, Złoczów, Poland; s. of Hillel Safran and Clara Rosen, step-s. of Paul Hoffmann; m. Eva Börjesson 1960; one s. one d. *Education:* Columbia and Harvard Univs. *Career:* Jr Fellow, Soc. of Fellows, Harvard Univ. 1962–65; Assoc. Prof. of Chem., Cornell Univ. 1965–68, Prof. 1968–74, John A. Newman Prof. of Physical Science 1974–96, Frank M. Rhodes Prof. of Humane Letters 1996–; mem. American Acad. of Arts and Sciences, NAS, American Philosophical Soc.; Foreign mem. Royal Soc., Indian Nat. Acad. of Sciences, Royal Swedish Acad. of Sciences; mem. USSR (now Russian) Acad. of Sciences, Societas Scientarum Fennica 1986. *Plays:* Oxygen (with Carl Djerassi), Should've. *Publications:* Conservation of Orbital Symmetry 1969, The Metamict State 1987, Solids and Surfaces 1988, Gaps and Verges 1990, Chemistry Imagined (co-author) 1993, The Same and Not the Same 1995, Old Wine, New Flasks (co-author) 1997, Memory Effects 1999, Soliton 2002, Catalísta (Spanish) 2002. *Honours:* Hon. DTech (Royal Inst. of Technology, Stockholm) 1977; Hon. DSc (Yale) 1980, (Columbia) 1982, (Hartford) 1982, (City Univ. of New York) 1983, (Puerto Rico) 1983, (Uruguay) 1984, (La Plata) 1984, (Colgate) 1985, (State Univ. of New York at Binghamton) 1985, (Ben Gurion Univ. of Negev) 1989, (Lehigh) 1989, (Carleton) 1989, (Md) 1990, (Ariz.) 1991, (Bar-Ilan Univ.) 1991, (Central Fla) 1991, (Athens) 1991, (Thessaloniki) 1991, (St Petersburg) 1991, (Barcelona) 1992, (Northwestern

Univ.) 1996, (The Technion) 1996, (Durham) 2000 and others; ACS Award 1969, Fresenius Award 1969, Harrison Howe Award 1969, Annual Award of Int. Acad. of Quantum Molecular Sciences 1970, Arthur C. Cope Award, ACS 1973, Linus Pauling Award 1974, Nichols Medal 1980, shared Nobel Prize for Chemistry 1981, Inorganic Chemistry Award, ACS 1982, Nat. Medal of Science 1984, Nat. Acad. of Sciences Award, in Chemical Sciences 1986, Priestley Medal 1990 and others. *Address:* Department of Chemistry and Chemical Biology, 222A Baker Laboratory, Cornell University, Ithaca, NY 14853-1301, USA (office). *Telephone:* (607) 255-3419 (office). *Fax:* (607) 255-5707 (office). *E-mail:* rh34@cornell.edu (office). *Website:* www.chem.cornell.edu (office); www.roaldhoffmann.com.

HOFMANN, Michael, BA, MA; German poet, reviewer, translator and academic; *Professor, Department of English, University of Florida*; b. 25 Aug. 1957, Freiburg, Germany; s. of Gert Hofmann. *Education:* Magdalene Coll., Trinity Coll., Cambridge. *Career:* Visiting Assoc. Prof., Creative Writing Dept, Univ. of Michigan 1994; Prof., Dept of English, Univ. of Florida 1994–; 2nd Craig-Kade Writer-in-Residence, Rutgers Univ. 2003; Visiting Assoc. Prof., Barnard Coll. and New School Univ. 2005. *Publications:* Nights in the Iron Hotel (Cholmondeley Award 1984) 1983, Acrimony (Geoffrey Faber Memorial Prize 1988) 1986, K.S. in Lakeland: New and Selected Poems 1990, Death in Rome (Schlegel-Tieck Prize, (Translators' Asscn) 1993, Corona, Corona 1993, After Ovid: New Metamorphoses (co-ed. with James Lasdun) 1994, The Film Explainer (Independent Foreign Fiction Prize) 1995, Approximately Nowhere (Arts Council Writers' Award) 1997, The Land of Green Plums (Int. IMPAC Dublin Literary Award for translation) 1998, Penguin Modern Poets 13 1998, The String of Pearls (PEN/Book of the Month Club Translation Prize) 1999, Behind the Lines 2002, Storm of Steel (Weidenfeld Translation Prize) 2004, Ashes for Breakfast (Weidenfeld Translation Prize) 2005, Faber Book of Twentieth Century German Poems (ed.) 2005, The Seventh Well (Jewish Quarterly Wingate Prize) 2008, Selected Poems 2008; plays: The Double Bass (adaptation of a play by Patrick Süskind, Schlegel-Tieck Prize, Translators' Asscn 1988) 1987, The Good Person of Sichuan (adaptation of a play by Brecht) 1989, Mother Courage (adaptation of a play by Brecht) 2006; others: The Voyage that Never Ends (ed.; collection of fiction, poems and letters of Malcolm Lowry) 2007; trans. from German: Child of All Nations 2008, Alone in Berlin 2009; contrib. to The London Review of Books, TLS, Guardian, Poetry (Chicago). *Address:* Department of English, Turlington Hall 4211D, University of Florida, Gainesville, FL 32611-7310, USA (office); c/o Faber and Faber Ltd, Bloomsbury House, 74–77 Great Russell Street, London, WC1B 3DA, England. *Telephone:* (352) 392-6650 (ext. 235) (office). *Fax:* (352) 392-0860 (office). *E-mail:* mhofmann@ufl.edu (office). *Website:* www.english.ufl.edu/faculty/mhofmann (office).

HOFSTADTER, Douglas Richard, BS, MS, PhD; American academic and writer; *Distinguished Professor, College of Arts and Sciences Professor of Cognitive Science and Computer Science, and Director, Center for Research on Concepts and Cognition, Indiana University, Bloomington*; b. 15 Feb. 1945, New York, NY; s. of Robert Hofstadter and Nancy Givan Hofstadter; m. Carol Ann Brush 1985 (died 1993); one s. one d. *Education:* Stanford Univ., Univ. of Oregon. *Career:* Visiting Scholar, Stanford Univ. 1975–77, 1980–81, Center for Computer-Assisted Research in the Humanities, Stanford Univ. 1997; Asst Prof. of Computer Science, Indiana Univ. 1977–80, Assoc. Prof. of Computer Science 1980–83; Distinguished Prof., Coll. of Arts and Sciences, Prof. of Cognitive Science and Computer Science, Adjunct Prof. of Comparative Literature, also Dir Center for Research on Concepts and Cognition, Indiana Univ., Bloomington 1988–; Visiting Scientist, Artificial Intelligence Laboratory, MIT 1983–84, Istituto per la Ricerca Scientifica e Technologica, Povo, Trento 1993–94; Walgreen Prof. for the Study of Human Understanding and Prof. of Psychology and Cognitive Science, Univ. of Michigan 1984–88; Visiting Prof., Dept of Slavic Languages and Literatures, Stanford Univ., and also Visiting Prof., Dept of Physics 1999–2000; Visiting Prof., Istituto di Studi Avanzati, Univ. degli Studi di Bologna, Italy 2001–02; mem. Cognitive Science Soc., Mathematical Asscn of America, American Asscn for Artificial Intelligence, Cttee for the Scientific Investigation of Claims of the Paranormal, Golden Key Nat. Honor Soc.; Fellow, American Acad. of Arts and Sciences 2009–, American Philosophical Soc. 2009–; Distinguished Fellow, The Cognitive Science Soc. 2010–; Foreign mem. Royal Soc. of Sciences, Uppsala, Sweden, in the Class for Physics and Math. 2010–. *Music:* compositions for piano. *Exhibitions:* The Nature of Whirly Art, Univ. of Calgary Art Museum 1991, For the Love of Line and Pattern: Studies Inspired by Alphabets and Music, Henry Radford Hope School of Fine Arts Gallery, Indiana Univ. 1998, and The Cooper Union's Great Hall Gallery, New York 1999, Wexner Gallery, Ohio State Univ., Columbus 1999, Ambigrammi e Creativita, Kaiser Arts Gallery, Genoa 2003. *Publications:* Gödel, Escher, Bach: an Eternal Golden Braid 1979, The Mind's I: Fantasies and Reflections on Self and Soul (co-ed. with Daniel C. Dennett) 1981, Metamagical Themas: Questing for the Essence of Mind and Pattern 1985, Ambigrammi: Un microcosmo ideale per lo studio della creativita 1987, Fluid Concepts and Creative Analogies: Computer Models of the Fundamental Mechanisms of Thought 1995, Rhapsody on a Theme by Clément Marot 1996, Le Ton beau de Marot: In Praise of the Music of Language 1997, Eugene Onegin: A Novel in Verse, by Alexander Sergeevich Pushkin, A Novel Versification by Douglas Hofstadter 1999, I Am a Strange Loop 2007, English trans. and foreword for La scoperta dell'alba (The Discovery of Dawn) by Walter Veltroni 2008, two books in one: That Mad Ache (English trans. from the French of La Chamade by Françoise Sagan) and Translator, Trader: An Essay on the Pleasantly Pervasive Paradoxes of Translation 2009; contribs to scholarly books and journals. *Honours:* Pulitzer Prize for General Non-Fiction 1980, American Book Award 1980, Guggenheim Fellowship 1980–81, Mathematical Asscn of America's Polya Prize for Best Article, Coll. Mathematics Journal 1981, Sr Fellow, Michigan Soc. of Fellows 1985, Arts and Sciences Alumni Fellows Award, Univ. of Oregon 1997, Tracy M. Sonneborn Award, Indiana Univ., Bloomington 1998, Los Angeles Times Book Award 2007. *Address:* Center for Research on Concepts and Cognition, Indiana University, 510 N Fess Street, Bloomington, IN 47408-3288, USA (office). *Telephone:* (812) 855-6965 (office). *Fax:* (812) 855-6966 (office). *E-mail:* dughof@indiana.edu (office). *Website:* www.cogsci.indiana.edu (office); prelectur.stanford.edu/lecturers/hofstadter (office).

HOGAN, Desmond, BA, MA; Irish writer and teacher; b. 10 Dec. 1950, Ballinasloe. *Education:* University College, Dublin. *Career:* Strode Fellow, University of Alabama 1989. *Publications:* novels: The Ikon Maker 1976, The Leaves on Grey 1980, A Curious Street 1984, A New Shirt 1984, Farewell to Prague 1995; other: A Short Walk to the Sea (play) 1976, A Link with the River (short stories) 1989, The Edge of the City (travel writing) 1993, Lark's Eggs: New and Selected Stories 2005, Old Swords and Other Stories 2009. *Honours:* John Llewellyn Memorial Prize 1980, Irish Post Award 1985, Deutscher Akademischer Austauschdienst Fellowship, Berlin 1991. *Address:* c/o The Lilliput Press, 62–63 Sitric Road, Arbour Hill, Dublin 7, Ireland (office). *E-mail:* info@lilliputpress.ie (office).

HOGAN, Kathleen (Kay) Margaret; Irish/American writer; b. 13 Feb. 1935, New York, NY; m. James P. Hogan, four s. one d. *Education:* high school. *Career:* started writing 1985. *Publications:* The El Train 1982, The Silent Men 1984, Widow Women 1985, Little Green Girl 1986, Of Saints and Other Things 1992, The Women Wore Black 1993, Roses 1994, Across the Clothesline 1997, The Letter 1995, Tulips in Ottawa 2004; contributions: Descant, Long Pond Review, Journal of Irish Literature, North Country Anthology, Catholic Girls Anthology, Glens Falls Review, Bless Me Father Anthology, Saratoga Anthology, Long Island Woman, Liguorian, Queen of Hearts, New York State Trooper, Back in the Bronx. *Honours:* Parnassus Award Coll. for Creative Writing 1997, Best Short Story of the Year Catholic Magazine Competition. *Address:* 154 East Avenue, Saratoga Springs, NY 12866, USA (home).

HOGAN, Linda, MA; American poet, novelist and academic; b. 16 July 1947, Denver, Colo; d. of Charles Henderson and Cleo Henderson; m. Pat Hogan (divorced); two d. *Education:* Univ. of Colorado at Boulder. *Career:* descended from Oklahoma Chickasaw tribe; Assoc., Rocky Mountain Women's Inst., Univ. of Denver 1979–80; Poet-in-the-Schools, Colorado and Oklahoma 1980–84; Asst Prof., Tribes Program, Colorado Coll. 1982–84; Assoc. Prof. of American and American Indian Studies, Univ. of Minnesota 1984–89; Assoc. Prof. of English, Univ. of Colorado at Boulder 1989–. *Publications:* poetry: Calling Myself Home 1979, Eclipse 1983, Seeing Through the Sun 1985, Savings 1988, The Book of Medicines 1993, Rounding the Human Corners: Poems 2008; fiction: A Piece of Moon (play) 1981, That Horse 1985, The Stories We Hold Secret: Tales of Women's Spiritual Development (ed. with Carol Bruchac and Judith McDaniel) 1986, Mean Spirit 1990, Solar Storms 1995, Power 1998, People of the Whale 2008; non-fiction: Dwellings: A Spiritual History of the Natural World 1995, Intimate Nature: The Bond Between Women and Animals 1998, Woman Who Watches Over the World: A Native Memoir 2001. *Honours:* Guggenheim Fellowship; Lannan Award for Poetry; Nat. Endowment for the Arts Grant; American Book Award 1986, Oklahoma Book Award for Fiction 1990, Colorado Book Awards 1994, 1997, Wordcraft Circle Writer of the Year 2002; mem. Authors' Guild, Nat. American Studies Program, Nat. Council of Teachers of English, PEN West, Writers Guild. *Address:* c/o Coffee House Press, 79 Thirteenth Avenue NE, Suite 110, Minneapolis, MN 55413, USA (home).

HOGGARD, James Martin, BA, MA; American academic, poet, writer and translator; *Perkins-Prothro Distinguished Professor of English, Midwestern State University*; b. 21 June 1941, Wichita Falls, Tex.; s. of Earl R. Hoggard and Helen C. Hoggard; m. Lynn Taylor Hoggard 1976; one s. one d. *Education:* Southern Methodist Univ., Univ. of Kansas. *Career:* teaching asst, Univ. of Kansas 1963–65; Instructor then Prof. of English, Midwestern State Univ. 1966–2000, Perkins-Prothro Distinguished Prof. of English 2000–; Guest Prof., Instituto Allende, San Miguel de Allende, Mexico, 1977, 1978, Univ. of Mosul, Iraq 1990; Exchange Prof., Instituto Tecnologico de Estudias Superiores de Monterrey, Chihuahua, Mexico 1993; mem. American Literary Trans. Asscn, American Studies Asscn of Texas, PEN, Conf. of Coll. Teachers of English, Texas Inst. of Letters (Pres. 1994–98), Texas Philosophical Soc.; Fellow, Texas Inst. of Letters 2011. *Publications:* poetry: Eyesigns: Poems on Letters and Numbers 1977, The Shaper Poems 1983, Two Gulls, One Hawk 1983, Breaking an Indelicate Statue 1986, Medea in Taos 2000, Rain in a Sunlit Sky 2000, Wearing the River: New Poems 2005, Triangles of Light: The Edward Hopper Poems 2011; fiction: Trotter Ross 1981, Riding the Wind and Other Tales 1997, Rev. 1999, Patterns of Illusion: Stories and a Novella 2002, The Mayor's Daughter: a novel 2011; non-fiction: Elevator Man 1983; trans.: The Art of Dying, Oscar Hahn 1988, Love Breaks, Oscar Hahn 1991, Chronicle of my Worst Years, Tino Villanueva 1994, Alone Against the Sea, Raul Mesa 1998, Splintered Silences, Greta de Leon 2000, Stolen Verses and Other Poems, Oscar Hahn, Ashes in Love, Oscar Hahn 2009; contribs to anthologies, reviews, quarterlies, journals and magazines. *Honours:* Soeurette Diehl Fraser Award, Stanley Walker Award, Brazos Bookstore (Houston) Short Story Award, NEA Creative Writing Fellowship, Stanley Walker Award for Newspaper Journalism, Lon Tinkle Award, PEN Texas Poetry Award 2007,

PEN Southwest Poetry Award 2007. *Address:* 3410 Taft, Department of English, Midwestern State University, Wichita Falls, TX 76308, USA (office). *Telephone:* (940) 397-4123 (office); (940) 761-5908 (home). *Fax:* (940) 397-4931 (office). *E-mail:* james.hoggard@mwsu.edu (office); jhoggard@sw.rr.com (home). *Website:* mwsu.edu.

HOGGART, Richard, MA, DLitt; British sociologist, writer and academic (retd); b. 24 Sept. 1918, Leeds; s. of Tom Longfellow Hoggart and Adeline Emma Hoggart (née Long); m. Mary Holt France 1942; two s. one d. *Education:* Cockburn Grammar School and Univ. of Leeds. *Career:* RA 1940–46; Staff Tutor and Sr Staff Tutor, Univ. Coll. of Hull and Univ. of Hull 1946–59; Sr Lecturer in English, Univ. of Leicester 1959–62; Visiting Prof., Univ. of Rochester, NY 1956–57; Prof. of English, Univ. of Birmingham 1962–73; Pres. British Assen of fmr UN Civil Servants 1978–86; Chair. European Museum of the Year Award Cttee 1977–, Broadcasting Research Unit 1980–90; mem. Albemarle Cttee on Youth Services 1958–60, Youth Service Devt Council 1960–62, Pilkington Cttee on Broadcasting 1960–62; Gov. Birmingham Repertory Theatre 1963–70; Dir Centre for Contemporary Cultural Studies 1964–73; mem. BBC Gen. Advisory Council 1959–60, 1964–70, Arts Council of GB 1976–81, Culture Advisory Cttee of UK Nat. Comm. to UNESCO 1966–70, Communications Advisory Cttee of UK Nat. Comm. to UNESCO 1977–79, Wilton Park Academic Council 1983–; Chair. Arts Council Drama Panel 1977–80, Vice-Chair. Arts Council 1980–81, Chair. Advisory Council for Adult and Continuing Educ. 1977–83, The Statesman and Nation Publishing Co. Ltd 1978–81; Gov. Royal Shakespeare Theatre 1966–88; Asst Dir-Gen. for Social Sciences, Humanities and Culture UNESCO 1970–75; Warden of Goldsmiths' Coll., London 1976–84; Chair. Book Trust 1995–97; Pres. Nat. Book Cttee 1997. *Publications:* Auden 1951, The Uses of Literacy 1957, W. H. Auden – A Selection 1961, Teaching Literature 1963, The Critical Moment 1964, How and Why Do We Learn 1965, Technology and Society 1966, Essays in Literature and Culture 1969, Speaking to Each Other 1970, Only Connect (Reith Lectures) 1972, An Idea and Its Servants 1978, An English Temper 1982, The Future of Broadcasting (ed. with Janet Morgan) 1978, An Idea of Europe (with Douglas Johnson) 1987, A Local Habitation (autobiog.) 1988, Liberty and Legislation (ed.) 1989, A Sort of Clowning 1990, An Imagined Life 1992, Townscape with Figures 1994, The Way We Live Now 1995, First and Last Things 1999, Hoggart en France 1999, Between Two Worlds 2001, Everyday Language and Everyday Life 2003, Mass Media in a Mass Society: Myth and Reality 2004, Promises to Keep: Thoughts in Old Age 2005. *Honours:* Hon. Visiting Prof., Univ. of E Anglia 1985–, Univ. of Surrey 1985–; Hon. Fellow, Sheffield City Polytechnic 1983, Goldsmiths' Coll. 1987, Ruskin Coll. Oxford 1994; Hon. DUniv (Open Univ.) 1972, (Surrey) 1981; Hon. DèsSc (Bordeaux) 1974, (Paris) 1987; Hon. LLD (CNAA) 1982, (York Univ., Toronto) 1988; Hon. LittD (E Anglia) 1986, (Metropolitan Univ. of London) 2003; Hon. DLitt (Leicester) (Hull) 1988, (Keele) 1995, (Metropolitan Univ. of Leeds) 1995, (Westminster) 1996, (Sheffield) 1999, (London) 2000; Hon. EdD (E London) 1998; BBC Reith Lecturer 1971. *Literary Agent:* Curtis Brown Ltd, Haymarket House, 28–29 Haymarket, London, SW1Y 4SP, England. *Telephone:* (20) 7393-4400. *Fax:* (20) 7393-4401. *E-mail:* info@curtisbrown.co.uk. *Website:* www.curtisbrown.co.uk.

HOGWOOD, Christopher Jarvis Haley, CBE, MA, FRSA; British musician, conductor, musicologist and keyboard player, writer, editor and broadcaster; b. 10 Sept. 1941, Nottingham, Notts.; s. of Haley Evelyn and Marion Constance Hogwood (née Higgott). *Education:* Univ. of Cambridge, Charles Univ., Prague, Czechoslovakia. *Career:* keyboard continuo, Acad. of St Martin-in-the-Fields 1965–76, keyboard soloist 1970–76, consultant Musicologist 1971–76; Founder-mem. Early Music Consort of London 1965–76; writer and presenter, The Young Idea (BBC Radio) 1972–82; Founder and Dir Acad. of Ancient Music 1973–2006, Dir Emer. 2006–; mem. Faculty of Music, Univ. of Cambridge 1975–; Artistic Dir King's Lynn Festival 1976–80; Dir Handel and Haydn Soc., Boston, USA 1986–2001, Conductor Laureate 2001–; Dir of Music, St Paul Chamber Orchestra, Minn., USA 1987–92, Prin. Guest Conductor 1992–98; Visiting Artist, Harvard Univ. 1988–89, Tutor, Mather House 1991–93; Artistic Adviser, Australian Chamber Orchestra 1989–93; Artistic Dir Summer Mozart Festival, Nat. Symphony Orchestra, USA 1993–2001; Assoc. Dir Beethoven Acad., Antwerp 1998–2002; Prin. Guest Conductor, Kammerorchester Basel, Switzerland 2000–07; Kayden Visiting Artist, Learning from Performers Programme, Harvard Univ. 2001; Prin. Guest Conductor, Orquesta Ciudad de Granada 2001–04, Orchestra Sinfonica di Milano Giuseppe Verdi 2003–06; Int. Prof. of Early Music Performance, RAM, London 1992–; Visiting Prof., Dept of Music, King's Coll., London 1992–96; Gresham Prof. of Music, Gresham Coll. 2010–; Series Ed. Music for London Entertainment 1983–97; Chair. Advisory Cttee and Gen. Ed. Francesco Geminiani Opera Omnia, Ut Orpheus Edizioni 2008–; mem. Editorial Cttee C.P.E. Bach Edn (Md) 1986–98, Chair. Advisory Bd C.P.E. Bach Complete Works 1999–; mem. Editorial Bd Early Music (Oxford Univ. Press) 1993–97, Early Music Performers, Peacock Press 2002, Bd Eds Bohuslav Martinu Foundation 2003–, Advisory Panel, Eighteenth-Century Music, Cambridge Univ. Press 2003; Pres. Early Music Wales 1996–, Nat. Early Music Assen (NEMA) 2000, The Handel Inst. 2000–. *Publications:* Music at Court 1977, The Trio Sonata 1979, Haydn's Visits to England 1980, Music in Eighteenth Century England (co-author) 1983, Handel 1984, Holmes' Life of Mozart (ed.) 1991, The Keyboard in Baroque Europe (ed.) 2003; many edns of musical scores; contribs to The New Grove Dictionary of Music and Musicians 1980 and 2001; numerous recordings. *Honours:* Hon. Prof. of Music, Univ. of Keele 1986–90, Univ. of Cambridge 2002–; Hon. Fellow, Jesus Coll., Cambridge 1989, Pembroke Coll., Cambridge 1992; Hon. mem. RAM 1995; Freeman, Worshipful Co. of Musicians 1989; Hon. DMus (Keele) 1991; Winner, Yorkshire Post Music Book Award 1984, Walter Willson Cobbett Medal, Worshipful Co. of Musicians 1986, UCLA Award for Artistic Excellence 1996, Scotland on Sunday Music Prize, Edin. Int. Festival 1996, Distinguished Musician Award, Inc. Soc. of Musicians 1997, Martinu Medal, Bohuslav Martinu Foundation, Prague 1999; Handel & Haydn Soc. Fellowship named 'The Christopher Hogwood Historically Informed Performance Fellowship' 2001, Regione Liguria per il suo contributo all'arte e alla filogia della musica 2003, Halle Hon. Handel Prize 2008. *Address:* 10 Brookside, Cambridge, Cambs., CB2 1JE, England (home). *Telephone:* (1223) 363975 (home). *Fax:* (1223) 327377 (home). *E-mail:* office@hogwood.org (office). *Website:* www.hogwood.org.

HOLDEN, Anne Jacqueline, QSO, JP, LLB, MA; New Zealand writer and lawyer; b. 11 May 1928, Whakatane; d. of Harold A. Dare and Mildred Dare; m. Henry Curran Holden 1954; two s. two d. *Education:* Auckland Girls' Grammar School, Hamilton High School, Univ. of Auckland, Victoria Univ. of Wellington, Auckland Coll. of Educ. *Career:* teacher of English and art history 1951–86; barrister and solicitor 1989–; case-worker, Wellington Community Law Centre 1990–; part-time Lecturer in Law, Wellington Polytechnic 1990; mem. Indecent Publications Tribunal 1991. *Film:* The Bedroom Window 1987. *Play:* Going Up, Mr Martin? 1965. *Publications:* novels: Rata 1965, The Empty Hills 1967, Death After School 1968, The Witnesses 1971, The Girl on the Beach 1973, No Trains at the Bay 1976. *Address:* 72 Amritsar Street, Khandallah, Wellington 4, New Zealand (home). *Telephone:* (4) 479-2621 (home).

HOLDEN, Anthony Ivan, MA; British journalist and writer; *President, International Federation of Poker;* b. 22 May 1947, Southport, Merseyside, England; m. 1st Amanda Warren 1971 (divorced 1988); m. 2nd Cynthia Blake 1990. *Education:* Merton Coll., Oxford. *Career:* corresp., Sunday Times 1973–77; columnist, Atticus 1977–79, Chief US Corresp. 1979–81, The Observer; Features Ed. and Asst Ed., The Times 1981–82; freelance journalist and author, broadcaster on radio and TV; Pres. Int. Fed. of Poker. *Publications:* Agememnon of Aeschylus 1969, The Greek Anthology 1973, The St Albans Poisoner 1974, Charles, Prince of Wales 1979, Their Royal Highnesses 1981, Of Presidents, Prime Ministers and Princes 1984, The Queen Mother 1985, Charles 1988, Olivier 1988, Big Deal 1990, The Last Paragraph (ed.) 1990, A Princely Marriage 1991, The Oscars 1993, The Tarnished Crown 1993, Tchaikovsky 1995, Diana: A Life, A Legacy 1997, Charles at Fifty 1998, William Shakespeare 2000, The Wit in the Dungeon 2005, The Man Who Wrote Mozart 2006, Bigger Deal: A Year on the New Poker Circuit 2007, Holden on Hold'em 2008. *Honours:* British Press Award for Columnist of the Year 1977, Fellow, Center for Scholars and Writers, New York Public Library 1999–2000. *Literary Agent:* c/o Rogers, Coleridge & White Literary Agency, 20 Powis Mews, London, W11 1JN, England. *Telephone:* (20) 7221-3717. *Fax:* (20) 7229-9084. *E-mail:* info@rcwlitagency.co.uk. *Website:* www.rcwlitagency.co.uk.

HOLDEN, Joan, BA, MA; American dramatist; b. 18 Jan. 1939, Berkeley, CA; m. 1st Arthur Holden 1958 (divorced); m. 2nd Daniel Chumley 1968, three d. *Education:* Reed College, Portland, OR, University of California at Berkeley. *Career:* Ed., Pacific News Service, 1973–75; Instructor in Playwriting, University of California at Davis, 1975, 1977, 1979, 1983, 1985, 1987. *Publications:* Americans, or, Last Tango in Huahuatenango (with Daniel Chumley), 1981; Factwindo Meets the Moral Majority (with others), 1981; Factwindo vs Armaggedonman, 1982; Steeltown, 1984; Spain/36, 1986; The Mozangola Caper (with others), 1986; Seeing Double, 1989; Back to Normal, 1990; Offshore, 1993. *Honours:* Obie Awards, 1973, 1990; Rockefeller Foundation Grant, 1985; Edward G. Robbins Playwriting Award, 1992.

HOLLAND, Cecelia Anastasia, BA; American writer; b. 31 Dec. 1943, Henderson, NV. *Education:* Pennsylvania State University, Connecticut College. *Publications:* The Firedrake 1966, Rakosy 1967, Kings in Winter 1968, Until the Sun Falls 1969, Ghost on the Steppe 1969, The King's Road 1970, Cold Iron 1970, Antichrist 1970, Wonder of the World 1970, The Earl 1971, The Death of Attila 1973, The Great Maria 1975, Floating Worlds 1976, Two Ravens 1977, Valley of the Kings 1977, The Earl 1979, City of God 1979, Home Ground 1981, The Sea Beggars 1982, The Belt of Gold 1984, Pillar of the Sky 1985, The Lords of Vaumartin 1988, The Bear Flag 1992, Pacific Street 1992, Jerusalem 1996, Railroad Schemes 1997, The Story of Anna and the King 1999, Lily Nevada 1999, An Ordinary Woman 1999, The Angel and the Sword 2000, The Soul Thief 2002, The Secret Eleanor 2010, Kings of the North 2010. *Honours:* Guggenheim Fellowship 1981–82. *E-mail:* ceceliaholland@sbcglobal.net (home). *Website:* www.thefiredrake.com.

HOLLAND, Norman Norwood, BS, LLB, JD, PhD; American scholar and writer; *Marston-Milbauer Eminent Scholar Emeritus, University of Florida;* b. 19 Sept. 1927, New York, NY; m. Jane Kelley 1954; one s. one d. *Education:* Massachusetts Inst. of Tech., Harvard Univ. *Career:* Instructor then Assoc. Prof., MIT 1955–66; McNulty Prof. of English, SUNY at Buffalo 1966–83; Assoc. Prof., Univ. of Paris 1971–72, 1985; Marston-Milbauer Eminent Scholar, Univ. of Florida, Gainesville 1983–, now Emer.; mem. American Acad. of Psychoanalysis, Boston Psychoanalytic Soc.; Fellow, American Council of Learned Socs 1974–75. *Publications:* The First Modern Comedies 1959, The Shakespearean Imagination 1964, Psychoanalysis and Shakespeare 1966, The Dynamics of Literary Response 1968, Poems in Persons: An

Introduction to the Psychoanalysis of Literature 1973, 5 Readers Reading 1975, Laughing: A Psychology of Humor 1982, The I 1985, The Brain of Robert Frost: A Cognitive Approach to Literature 1988, Holland's Guide to Psychoanalytic Psychology and Literature-and-Psychology 1990, The Critical I 1992, Death in a Delphi Seminar 1995, Meeting Movies 2006, Know Thyself: Delphi Seminars (with Murray Schwartz) 2008, Literature and the Brain 2009, The I and Being Human 2011. *Honours:* Guggenheim Fellowship 1979–80. *Address:* 5000 SW 25th Boulevard, Suite 3117, Gainesville, FL 32608-8931, USA (office). *Telephone:* (352) 371-9443 (office). *E-mail:* nholland@post.harvard .edu (office); normholland@gmail.com (office). *Website:* www.asharperfocus .com (office); www.normholland.com.

HOLLAND, Tom, BA, MA; British writer; b. 5 Jan. 1968, Oxford; s. of Martin Holland and Jans Holland; m. Sadie; two d. *Education:* Univ. of Cambridge. *Career:* previously worked in radio; Chair., Soc. of Authors 2009–10. *Publications:* Attis 1995, Lord of the Dead: The Secret History of Byron 1995, The Vampyre: Being the True Pilgrimage of George Gordon, Sixth Lord Byron 1995, Supping with Panthers 1996, Supping with Vampyres 1996, Deliver Us from Evil 1997, Importance of Being Frank 1997, Sleeper in the Sands 1998, The Bonehunter 2001, Rubicon: The Last Years of the Roman Republic (Hessel-Tiltman Prize 2004) 2003, Persian Fire: The First World Empire, Battle for the West (Runciman Prize) 2005, Millennium 2008. *Address:* c/o Little, Brown & Co., Time Warner Book Group, Brettenham House, Lancaster Place, London, WC2E 7EN, England (office).

HOLLANDER, John, PhD; American poet and academic; *Sterling Professor Emeritus of English, Yale University*; b. 28 Oct. 1929, New York, NY; s. of Franklin Hollander and Muriel Hollander (née Kornfeld); m. 1st Anne Loesser 1953 (divorced 1977); two d.; 2nd Natalie Charkow 1981. *Education:* Columbia, Harvard and Indiana Univs. *Career:* Lecturer in English, Connecticut Coll. 1957–59; Instructor in English, Yale Univ. 1959–61, Asst Prof. of English 1961–64, Assoc. Prof. 1964–66, Prof. 1977–85, A. Bartlett Giamatti Prof. 1986–95, Sterling Prof. of English 1995–2002, Sterling Prof. Emer. 2002–; Prof. of English, Hunter Coll., New York 1966–77; Christian Gauss Seminarian, Princeton Univ. 1962; Visiting Prof., School of Letters and Linguistic Inst., Indiana Univ. 1964; Visiting Prof., Seminar in American Studies, Salzburg, Austria 1965; Clark Lecturer, Trinity Coll., Cambridge 2000; editorial assoc. for Poetry Partisan Review 1959–65; mem. Poetry Bd Wesleyan Univ. Press 1959–62; Contributing Ed. Harper's magazine 1969–71; mem. Editorial Bd Raritan 1981–; Chancellor Acad. of American Poets 1981–, MacArthur Fellow 1990–95; Fellow, American Acad. of Arts and Sciences, Ezra Stiles Coll., Yale Univ. 1961–64, Nat. Endowment for Humanities 1973–, Silliman Coll. 1977–; Overseas Fellow, Churchill Coll., Univ. of Cambridge 1967–68; mem. American Acad. of Arts and Letters (Sec. 2000–03), Asscn of Literary Scholars and Critics (Pres. 2000). *Publications include:* A Crackling of Thorns 1958, The Untuning of the Sky 1961, Movie-Going and Other Poems 1962, Visions from the Ramble 1965, Types of Shape 1969 (enlarged edn 1991), The Night Mirror 1971, Town and Country Matters 1972, Selected Poems 1972, The Head of the Bed 1974, Tales Told of the Fathers 1975, Vision and Resonance 1975, Reflections on Espionage 1976, 1999, Spectral Emanations 1978, In Place 1978, Blue Wine 1979, The Figure of Echo 1981, Rhyme's Reason 1981 (enlarged edn 1989), Powers of Thirteen 1983, In Time and Place 1986, Harp Lake 1988, Some Fugitives Take Cover 1988, Melodious Guile 1988, William Bailey 1991, Tesserae 1993, Selected Poetry 1993, The Gazer's Spirit 1995, The Work of Poetry 1997, The Poetry of Everyday Life 1998, Figurehead and Other Poems 1999, Picture Window 2003, A Draft of Light 2008; contrib. of numerous poems and articles to journals; ed. and contributing ed. of numerous books including: Poems of Ben Jonson 1961, The Wind and the Rain 1961, Jiggery-Pokery 1966, Poems of Our Moment 1968, Modern Poetry: Essays in Criticism 1968, American Short Stories Since 1945 1968, The Oxford Anthology of English Literature (with Frank Kermode), 1973, For I. A. Richards: Essays in his Honor 1973, Literature as Experience (with Irving Howe and David Bromwich) 1979, The Essential Rossetti 1990, American Poetry: the Nineteenth Century 1993, Animal Poems (ed.) 1994, Garden Poems (ed.) 1996, Marriage Poems (ed.) 1997, Frost (ed.) 1997, Committed to Memory (ed.) 1999, Figurehead and Other Poems 1999, War Poems (ed.) 1999, Selected Poetry 1999, Sonnets (ed.) 2000, A Gallery of Poems 2001, American Wits (ed.) 2003, Selected Poems of Emma Lazarus 2005, Poems Haunted and Bewitched 2005. *Honours:* Hon. DLitt (Marietta Coll.) 1982; Hon. DHL (Indiana) 1990, (CUNY Grad. Center) 2001, (New School Univ.) 2003; Hon. DFA (Maine Coll. of Art) 1993; Nat. Inst. of Arts and Letters Award 1963, Levinson Prize 1964, Washington Monthly Prize 1976, Guggenheim Fellow 1979–80, Bollingen Prize 1983, Ambassador Book Award English Speaking Union 1994, Governor's Arts Award for Poetry, State of Connecticut 1997, Robert Penn Warren–Cleanth Brooks Award 1998, Poet Laureate State of Connecticut 2006–, Frost Medal, Poetry Soc. of America 2007. *Address:* Department of English, Yale University, PO Box 208302, New Haven, CT 06520, USA (office). *Telephone:* (203) 432-4566 (office). *Fax:* (203) 387-3497 (office). *E-mail:* john.hollander@yale.edu (office). *Website:* www.yale .edu/english (office).

HOLLANDER, Paul, BA, MA, PhD; American academic and writer; *Professor Emeritus, University of Massachusetts Amherst*; b. 3 Oct. 1932, Budapest, Hungary; s. of Jeno Hollander and Elsa Kaszab; m. Mina Harrison 1977; one d. *Education:* London School of Econs, UK, Univ. of Illinois, Princeton Univ. *Career:* Asst Prof., Harvard Univ. 1963–68, Research Fellow and Assoc., Russian Research Center 1963–68; Assoc. Prof., Univ. of Massachusetts at Amherst 1968–73, Prof. of Sociology 1973–2000, Prof. Emer. 2000–; Scholar-in-Residence, Rockefeller Study and Conf. Center, Bellagio, Italy 1984; Visiting Scholar, Hoover Inst. 1985, 1986, 1993; mem. Nat. Asscn of Scholars. *Publications:* American and Soviet Society: A Reader in Comparative Sociology and Perception (ed.) 1969, Soviet and American Society: A Comparison 1973, Political Pilgrims: Travels of Western Intellectuals to the Soviet Union, China and Cuba 1928–1978 1981, The Many Faces of Socialism 1983, The Survival of the Adversary Culture 1988, Decline and Discontent: Communism and the West Today 1992, Anti-Americans: Critiques at Home and Abroad 1965–1990 1992, Anti-Americanism: Irrational and Rational 1995, Political Will and Personal Belief: The Decline and Fall of Soviet Communism 1999, Discontents: Postmodern and Postcommunist 2002, Understanding Anti-Americanism: Its Origins and Impact at Home and Abroad (ed.) 2004, From the Gulag to the Killing Fields (ed.) 2006, The End of Commitment: Intellectuals, Revolutionaries and Political Morality 2006, Political Violence: Belief, Behavior and Legitimation 2008, The Only Super Power: Reflections on Strength, Weakness and Anti-Americanism 2009, Extravagant Expectations: New Ways to Find Romantic Love in America 2011; contrib. to scholarly and general publs. *Honours:* Guggenheim Fellowship 1974–75, Peter Shaw Award, Nat. Asscn of Scholars 2002. *Address:* 35 Vernon Street, Northampton, MA 01060, USA. *Telephone:* (413) 586-5546. *Fax:* (413) 584-4591. *E-mail:* hollanderaz@yahoo.com.

HOLLERAN, Andrew; American author; b. 1942. *Education:* Harvard Univ., Univ. of Iowa. *Publications:* Dancer from the Dance, 1978; Nights in Aruba, 1983; Ground Zero, 1988; The Beauty of Men, 1996; In September, the Light Changes, 1999. Contributions: anthologies and periodicals.

HOLLINGHURST, Alan James, BA, MLitt, FRSL; British writer; b. 26 May 1954, Stroud, Glos.; s. of the late James Kenneth Hollinghurst and of Elizabeth Lilian Hollinghurst (née Keevil). *Education:* Canford School, Dorset, Magdalen Coll., Oxford. *Career:* Asst Ed. Times Literary Supplement 1982–84, Deputy Ed. 1985–90, Poetry Ed. 1991–95; Visiting Prof., Univ. of Houston, Tex., USA 1998; Old Dominion Fellow, Princeton Univ., NJ, USA 2004. *Publications:* Confidential Chats with Boys (poems) 1982, The Swimming-Pool Library (novel) (Somerset Maugham Award 1989, American Acad. of Arts and Letters E.M. Forster Award 1989) 1988, Bajazet, by Racine (trans.) 1991, The Folding Star (novel) (James Tait Black Memorial Prize) 1994, New Writing 4 (co-ed. with A. S. Byatt) 1995, The Spell (novel) 1998, Three Novels, by Ronald Firbank (ed.) 2000, A. E. Housman: Poems Selected by Alan Hollinghurst (ed.) 2001, The Line of Beauty (novel) (Man Booker Prize for Fiction) 2004, The Stranger's Child (novel) (Galaxy Nat. Book Award for UK Author of the Year) 2011. *Literary Agent:* c/o Antony Harwood Ltd, 103 Walton Street, Oxford, OX2 6EB, England.

HOLLINGSHEAD, Gregory Albert Frank, BA, MA, PhD; Canadian academic and writer; b. 25 Feb. 1947, Toronto, ON; m. Rosa Spricer, one s. *Education:* University of Toronto, University of London. *Career:* Asst Prof., 1975–81, Assoc. Prof., 1981–93, Prof. of English University of Alberta 1993–2005; Dir of Writing Programs Banff Centre 1999–; mem. PEN Canada, Writers Guild of Alberta, Writers' Union of Canada. *Publications:* Famous Players, 1982; White Buick, 1992; Spin Dry, 1992; The Roaring Girl, 1995; The Healer, 1998, Bedlam 2004. *Honours:* Georges Bugnet Awards for Excellence in the Novel, 1993, 1999; Howard O'Hagan Award for Excellence in Short Fiction 1993, 1996; Gov.-Gen.'s Award for Fiction, 1995; Writers' Trust Rogers Fiction Prize, 1999. *Address:* c/o Department of English, University of Alberta, Edmonton, AB T6G 2E5, Canada. *Website:* www.greg.hollingshead.com (home).

HOLLINGWORTH, Clare, OBE; British journalist; b. 10 Oct. 1911, d. of John Albert Hollingworth and Daisy Gertrude Hollingworth; m. 1st Vyvyan Derring Vandeleur Robinson 1936 (divorced 1951); m. 2nd Geoffrey Spence Hoare 1952 (died 1966). *Education:* Girls' Collegiate School, Leicester, Grammar School, Ashby-de-la-Zouch, School of Slavonic Studies, Univ. of London. *Career:* mem. staff League of Nations Union 1935–38; worked in Poland for Lord Mayor's Fund for Refugees from Czechoslovakia 1939; Corresp. for Daily Telegraph Poland, Turkey, Cairo (covered Desert Campaigns, troubles in Persia and Iraq, Civil War in Greece and events in Palestine) 1941–50, for Manchester Guardian (covered Algerian War and trouble spots including Egypt, Aden and Viet Nam), based in Paris 1950–63; Guardian Defence Corresp. 1963–67; foreign trouble-shooter for Daily Telegraph (covering war in Viet Nam) 1967–73, Corresp. in China 1973–76, Defence Corresp. 1976–81; Far Eastern Corresp. in Hong Kong for Sunday Telegraph 1981–; Research Assoc. (fmrly Visiting Scholar), Centre for Asian Studies, Univ. of Hong Kong 1981–; currently Hon. Goodwill Amb. Foreign Corresps' Club of Hong Kong. *Publications include:* Poland's Three Weeks War 1940, There's A German Just Behind Me 1945, The Arabs and the West 1951, Mao and the Men Against Him 1984, Front Line 1990. *Honours:* Hon. DLitt (Leicester) 1993; Granada Journalist of the Year Award and Hannan Swaffer Award 1963; James Cameron Award for Journalism 1994. *Address:* 302 Ridley House, 2 Upper Albert Road, Hong Kong Special Administrative Region, People's Republic of China (home). *Telephone:* 28681838 (home).

HOLLIS, Matthew; British poet and editor; b. 1971, Norwich. *Career:* Asst Ed., Oxford Univ. Press 1998–2001; Ed., Faber and Faber Ltd 2002–. *Publications:* poetry: The Boy on the Edge of Happiness (pamphlet) 1996, Ground Water 2004; non-fiction: Edward Thomas – The Final Years 2010; co-editor: Strong Words 2000, 101 Poems Against War 2003. *Honours:* Eric

Gregory Award 1999, Jerwood Award 2009. *Address:* c/o Faber and Faber Ltd, Bloomsbury House, 74–77 Great Russell Street, London, WC1B 3DA, England (office). *Website:* www.faber.co.uk (office); www.matthewhollis.com.

HOLLO, Anselm; Finnish/American academic, poet, writer, translator and editor; *Professor of Poetry, Poetics and Translation, Naropa University, Boulder*; b. 12 April 1934, Helsinki, Finland; m. Jane Dalrymple-Hollo. *Education:* Univ. of Helsinki, Univ. of Tübingen, Germany. *Career:* Visiting Prof., State Univ. of NY, Buffalo 1967, Univ. of Iowa 1968–73, Bowling Green State Univ., OH 1971–73, Hobart and William Smith Colls, Geneva, NY 1973–75, Southwest Minnesota State Coll., Marshall 1977–78; Distinguished Visiting Poet, Michigan State Univ. 1974; Assoc. Prof. of Literature and Creative Writing, Univ. of Maryland 1975–77; Margaret Bannister Distinguished Writer-in-Residence, Sweet Briar Coll. 1978–81; Poet-in-Residence, Kerouac School of Poetics, Boulder, Colo 1981, Visiting Lecturer 1985–89; Visiting Lecturer in Poetics, New Coll. of California, San Francisco 1981–82; Book Reviewer, Baltimore Sun 1983–85; Distinguished Visiting Prof. of Poetry, Univ. of Colorado, Boulder 1985; Contributing Ed. The New Censorship 1989–; Assoc. Prof. of Poetry, Poetics and Trans., Naropa Univ., Boulder 1989–2000, Prof. of Poetry, Poetics and Trans. 2000–. *Publications:* poetry: Sojourner Microcosms: New and Selected Poems 1959–77, 1978, Finite Continued 1981, Pick Up the House: New and Selected Poems 1986, Outlying Districts: New Poems 1990, Near Miss Haiku 1990, Blue Ceiling 1992, High Beam: 12 Poems 1993, West is Left on the Map 1993, Survival Dancing 1995, Corvus: New Poems 1995, Hills Like Purple Pachyderms 1997, AHOE: And How on Earth 1997, Rue Wilson Monday 2000, Notes on the Possibilities and Attractions of Existence: New and Selected Poems 1965–2000 2001, Guests of Space 2007; prose: Caws and Causeries: Around Poetry and Poets 1999. *Honours:* Yaddo Residency Fellowship 1978, Nat. Endowment for the Arts Fellowship in Poetry 1979, PEN/American-Scandinavian Foundation Award for Poetry in Trans. 1980, American-Scandinavian Foundation Award for Poetry in Trans. 1989, Fund for Poetry Award for Contribs to Contemporary Poetry 1989, 1991, Stein Award in Innovative American Poetry 1996, Grez-sur-Loing Foundation Fellowship 1998, Baltic Centre for Writers and Trans Residency Fellowship 2002, San Francisco Poetry Center Award 2002, Acad. of American Poets Harold Norton Landon Poetry Trans. Prize 2004. *Address:* 3336 14th Street, Boulder, CO 80304, USA.

HOLLOWAY, Robin Greville, PhD, DMus; British composer, writer and academic; *Professor of Musical Composition, University of Cambridge*; b. 19 Oct. 1943, Leamington Spa; s. of Robert Charles Holloway and Pamela Mary Holloway (née Jacob). *Education:* St Paul's Cathedral Choir School, King's Coll. School, Wimbledon, King's Coll., Cambridge and New Coll., Oxford. *Career:* Lecturer in Music, Univ. of Cambridge 1975–, Reader in Musical Composition 1999–, Prof. 2001–; Fellow, Gonville and Caius Coll., Cambridge 1969–. *Compositions include:* Garden Music Op. 1 1962, First Concerto for Orchestra 1969, Scenes from Schumann Op. 13 1970, Evening with Angels Op. 17 1972, Domination of Black Op. 23 1973, Clarissa (opera) Op. 30 1976, Second Concerto for Orchestra Op. 40 1979, Brand (dramatic ballad) Op. 48 1981, Women in War Op. 51 1982, Seascape and Harvest Op. 55 1983, Viola Concerto Op. 56 1984, Peer Gynt 1985, Hymn to the Senses for chorus 1990, Serenade for strings 1990, Double Concerto Op. 68, The Spacious Firmament for chorus and orchestra Op. 69, Violin Concerto Op. 70 1990, Boys and Girls Come Out To Play (opera) 1991, Winter Music for sextet 1993, Frost at Midnight Op. 78, Third Concerto for Orchestra Op. 80 1994, Clarinet Concerto Op. 82 1996, Peer Gynt Op. 84 1984–97, Scenes from Antwerp Op. 85 1997, Gilded Goldberg for two pianos 1999, Symphony 1999, Missa Caiensis 2001, Cello Sonata 2001, Spring Music Op. 96 2002, String Quartet No. 1 2003, String Quartet No. 2 2004. *Recordings:* Sea Surface Full of Clouds chamber cantata, Romanza for violin and small orchestra Op. 31, 2nd Concerto for Orchestra Op. 40, Horn Concerto Op. 43, Violin Concerto Op. 70, Third Concerto for orchestra, Fantasy Pieces Op. 16, Serenade in DC Op. 41, Gilded Goldberg Op. 86, Missa Caiensis, Organ Fantasy, Woefully Arrayed. *Publications:* Wagner and Debussy 1978, On Music: Essays and Diversions 1963–2003 2004; numerous articles and reviews. *Address:* Gonville and Caius College, Cambridge, CB2 1TA (office); Finella, Queen's Road, Cambridge, CB3 9AH, England (home). *Telephone:* (1223) 335424. *E-mail:* rgh1000@cam.ac.uk (home). *Website:* www.rhessays.co.uk.

HOLMES, Bryan John, (Charles Langley Hayes, Ethan Wall, Jack Darby, Sean Kennedy), BA; British lecturer (retd) and writer; b. 18 May 1939, Birmingham; m. 1962; two s. *Education:* Univs of Keele and Birmingham. *Publications:* The Avenging Four 1978, Hazard 1979, Blood, Sweat and Gold 1980, Gunfall 1980, A Noose for Yanqui 1981, Shard 1982, Bad Times at Backwheel 1982, Guns of the Reaper 1983, On the Spin of a Dollar 1983, Another Day, Another Dollar 1984, Dark Rider 1987, I Rode with Wyatt 1989, Dollars for the Reaper 1990, A Legend Called Shatterhand 1990, Loco 1991, Shatterhand and the People 1992, The Last Days of Billy Patch 1992, Blood on the Reaper 1992, All Trails Lead to Dodge 1993, Montana Hit 1993, A Coffin for the Reaper 1994, Comes the Reaper 1995, Utah Hit 1995, Dakota Hit 1995, Viva Reaper 1996, The Shard Brand 1996, High Plains Death 1997, Smoking Star 1997, Crowfeeders 1999, North of the Bravo 2000, Bradford's Pocket Crossword Dictionary 2001, Bradford's Guide to Solving Crosswords 2002, Jake's Women 2002, Solving Cryptic Crosswords 2003, Bloomsbury's Pocket Crossword Dictionary 2003, Rio Grande Shoot-Out 2004, Trail of the Reaper 2004, The Expediter 2004, Three Graves to Fargo 2004, Trouble in Tucson 2005, Wyoming Hit 2005, Shotgun 2005, Black's Pocket Crossword Dictionary (second edn) 2005, Gunsmoke in Vegas 2006, Yuma Breakout 2008; contrib. to professional and academic journals. *Address:* c/o Robert Hale Ltd, Clerkenwell Green, London, EC1R 0HT, England (office).

HOLMES, Charlotte Amalie; American academic and writer; b. 26 April 1956, Georgia; m. James Brasfield 1983; one s. *Education:* BA, Louisiana State University, 1977; MFA, Columbia University, 1980. *Career:* Editorial Asst, Paris Review, 1979–80; Assoc. and Managing Ed., Ecco Press, 1980–82; Instructor, Western Carolina University, 1984–87; Asst Prof., 1987–93, Assoc. Prof., 1993–, Pennsylvania State University; mem. Associated Writing Programs. *Publications:* Gifts and Other Stories, 1994. Contributions: periodicals. *Honours:* Stegner Fellowship, Stanford University, 1982; North Carolina Arts Council Grant, 1986; Pennsylvania Council on the Arts Fellowships, 1988, 1993; Bread Loaf Writer's Conference National Arts Club Scholarship, 1990; Poets and Writers Award, 1993; DH Lawrence Fellowship, 2000. *Literary Agent:* Neil Olson, Donadio and Olson. *Address:* c/o Department of English, Pennsylvania State University, University Park, PA 16802, USA.

HOLMES, Diana, MA, DPhil; British academic, writer and editor; *Professor of French, University of Leeds*; b. 28 Jan. 1949, Preston, Lancs.; d. of the late Maurice F. Holmes and the late Marie W. Newsham; m. Nicolas W. Cheesewright 1983; one s. one d. *Education:* Univ. of Sussex, La Nouvelle Sorbonne Université de Paris III. *Career:* Lecturer in French, Wolverhampton Polytechnic 1975–80; Part-time Lecturer in French, N London Polytechnic 1981–84; Sr Lecturer in French, Wolverhampton Polytechnic 1984–90, Prin. Lecturer and Head of French 1990–92; Sr Lecturer, Keele Univ. 1992–95, Prof. of French and Head of French Studies 1995–99; Prof. of French, Univ. of Leeds 1999–; Visiting Scholar, Centre for Gender Studies, Univ. of British Columbia, Canada 2006; Ed. Modern and Contemporary France 1996–2003; Co-organiser Women in French. *Publications:* Colette 1991, French Women's Writing 1848–1994 1996, Truffaut (co-author) 1998, Rachilde – Gender, Decadence and the Woman Writer 2002, Romance and Readership in 20th Century France – Love Stories 2006; Ed.: 100 Years of European Cinema: Entertaining Ideologies 2000, A Belle Epoque? Women in French Society and Culture 1890–1914 2005, Stardom in Post-War France 2007, French Film Directors series (co-ed.). *Honours:* Chevalier des Palmes académiques 1998. *Address:* School of Modern Languages and Cultures, University of Leeds, Leeds LS2 9JT, England (office). *Telephone:* (113) 343-3496 (office). *E-mail:* d.holmes@leeds.ac.uk (office). *Website:* www.leeds.ac.uk/french/staff/diana_holmes.htm (office).

HOLMES, John (see Souster, (Holmes) Raymond)

HOLMES, Leslie Templeman, BA, MA, PhD; British academic and writer; b. 5 Oct. 1948, London, England; m. Susan Mary Bleasby 1971 (divorced 1989). *Education:* Hull University, Essex University. *Career:* Prof. of Political Science, University of Melbourne. *Publications:* The Policy Progress in Communist States, 1981; The Withering Away of the State? (ed.), 1981; Politics in the Communist World, 1986; The End of Communist Power, 1993; Post-Communism, 1997; Europe: Rethinking the Boundaries (co-ed.), 1998; Citizenship and Identity in Europe (co-ed.), 1999. *Honours:* Fellow, Acad. of the Social Sciences in Australia 1995. *E-mail:* leslieth@unimelb.edu.au.

HOLMES, Richard Gordon Heath, OBE, MA, FBA, FRSL; British writer and poet; *Professor of Biographical Studies, University of East Anglia*; b. 5 Nov. 1945, London; s. of Dennis Patrick Holmes and Pamela Mavis Gordon; partner Rose Tremain. *Education:* Downside School, Churchill Coll., Cambridge. *Career:* literacy features writer, The Times 1967–92; Visiting Fellow, Trinity Coll., Cambridge 2000; Prof. of Biographical Studies, Univ. of E Anglia 2001–. *Radio:* BBC Radio: Inside the Tower 1977, To the Tempest Given 1992, The Nightwalking (Sony Award) 1995, Clouded Hills 1999, Runaway Lives 2000, The Frankenstein Project 2002, A Cloud in a Paper Bag 2007. *Publications:* Thomas Chatterton: The Case Re-Opened 1970, One for Sorrows (poems) 1970, Shelley: The Pursuit 1974, Shelley on Love (ed.) 1980, Coleridge 1982, Nerval: The Chimeras (with Peter Jay) 1985, Footsteps: Adventures of a Romantic Biographer 1985, Mary Wollstonecraft and William Godwin (ed.) 1987, Kipling: Something Myself (ed. with Robert Hampson) 1987, Coleridge: Early Visions 1989, Dr Johnson and Mr Savage 1993, Coleridge: Selected Poems (ed.) 1996, The Romantic Poets and Their Circle 1997, Coleridge: Darker Reflections 1998, Sidetracks: Explorations of a Romantic Biographer 2000, Classic Biographies (series) 2004–, Insights: The Romantic Poets and Their Circle 2005, The Age of Wonder (Nat. Book Critics' Circle Award for General Nonfiction 2009, Royal Soc. Prize for Science Books 2009) 2008. *Honours:* Hon. DLitt (E Anglia) 2000, (Tavistock Inst.) 2001, (Kingston Univ.) 2008; Somerset Maugham Award 1977, James Tait Black Memorial Prize 1994, Whitbread Book of the Year Prize 1989, Duff Cooper Prize 1998. *Address:* c/o HarperCollins, 77–85 Fulham Palace Road, Hammersmith, London, W6 8JB, England.

HOLROYD, Sir Michael de Courcy Fraser, Kt, CBE, CLit; British writer; b. 27 Aug. 1935, London, England; s. of Basil Holroyd and Ulla Holroyd (née Hall); m. Margaret Drabble 1982. *Education:* Eton Coll. *Career:* Chair. Soc. of Authors 1973–74, Nat. Book League 1976–78; Pres. English Centre of PEN 1985–88; Chair. Strachey Trust 1990–95, Public Lending Right Advisory Cttee 1997–2000, Royal Soc. of Literature 1998–2001 (Pres. 2003–10); Vice-Pres. Royal Literary Fund 1997–; mem. Arts Council (Chair. Literature Panel) 1992–95; Gov. Shaw Festival Theatre, Niagara-on-the-Lake 1993–; Pres. Stephen Spender Trust 1998–; Trustee Laser Foundation 2001–03. *Publications:* Hugh Kingsmill: A Critical Biography 1964, Lytton Strachey: A Critical

Biography 1967–68 (new edn 1994), A Dog's Life (novel) 1969, The Best of Hugh Kingsmill (ed) 1970, Lytton Strachey by Himself: A Self-Portrait (ed) 1971, Unreceived Opinions (essays) 1973, Augustus John 1974–75 (new edn 1996), The Art of Augustus John (with Malcolm Easton) 1974, The Genius of Shaw (ed) 1979, The Shorter Strachey (ed with Paul Levy) 1980, William Gerhardie's God's Fifth Column (ed with Robert Skidelsky) 1981, Peterley Harveset: The Private Diary of David Peterley (ed) 1985, Bernard Shaw: Vol. 1: The Search for Love 1988, Vol. II: The Pursuit of Power 1989, Vol. III: The Lure of Fantasy 1991, Vol. IV: The Last Laugh 1992, Vol. V: The Shaw Companion 1992, Bernard Shaw 1997 (one-vol. biog.), Basil Street Blues 1999, The Art of Dora Carrington (with Jane Hill) 2001, (Works on Paper: The Craft of Biography and Autobiography 2002, Mosaic: Portraits in Fragments 2004, A Strange Eventful History: The Dramatic Lives of Two Remarkable Families (James Tait Black Memorial Prize for Biography) 2008, A Book of Secrets 2010. *Honours:* Hon. DLitt (Ulster) 1992, (Sheffield, Warwick) 1993, (East Anglia) 1994, (LSE) 1998, (Sussex) 2009; Saxton Memorial Fellowship 1964, Bollingen Fellowship 1966, Winston Churchill Fellowship 1971, Irish Life Arts Award 1988, Prix du Meilleur Livre Etranger 1996, Heywood Hill Prize 2001, David Cohen Prize for Literature 2005, The Sheridan Morley Prize 2009. *Literary Agent:* c/o A.P. Watt Ltd, 20 John Street, London, WC1N 2DL, England. *Telephone:* (20) 7405-6774. *Fax:* (20) 7831-2154. *E-mail:* apw@apwatt.co.uk. *Website:* www.apwatt.co.uk.

HOLT, Anne; Norwegian writer; b. 16 Nov. 1958, Larvik. *Career:* fmr lawyer, journalist, TV news ed. *Publications:* Blind Gudinne 1993, Salige er de som tørster 1994, Demonens død 1995, Mea culpa 1997, Løvens gap 1997, I hjertet av VM 1998, Død joker 1999, Bernhard Pinkertons store oppdrag 1999, Uten ekko 2000, Det som er mitt 2001, Sannheten bortenfor 2003, Det som aldri skjer 2004, Presidentens valg 2006, 1222 2010, Blind Goddess 2012. *E-mail:* webmaster@anne-holt.com. *Website:* www.anne-holt.com.

HOLT, Hazel, BA; British writer; b. 3 Sept. 1928, Birmingham, England; m. Geoffrey Louis Holt 1951; one s. *Education:* Newnham Coll., Cambridge. *Career:* ed., Int. African Inst., London 1950–74; reviewer, feature writer, Stage and Television Today, London 1975–80; writer 1989–. *Publications:* A Very Private Eye (ed.) 1984, Barbara Pym, Civil to Strangers and Other Writings (ed.) 1988, Gone Away 1989, A Lot to Ask: A Life of Barbara Pym 1991, The Cruellest Month 1991, The Shortest Journey 1992, Uncertain Death 1993, Murder on Campus 1994, Superfluous Death 1995, Death of a Dean 1996, The Only Good Lawyer 1997, Dead and Buried 1998, A Fatal Legacy 1999, Lilies that Fester 2000, Delay of Execution 2001, Leonora 2002, The Silent Killer 2003, Death in Practice 2004, No Cure for Death 2005, A Death in the Family 2006, A Time to Die 2008, Any Man's Death 2009, My Dear Charlotte 2009. *Address:* 7 Kinforde, Chard, Somerset, TA20 1DT, England (home). *Telephone:* (1640) 64414 (home). *E-mail:* holt369@btinternet.com (home).

HOMBERGER, Eric Ross, BA, MA, PhD; American academic and writer; *Professor Emeritus of American Studies, University of East Anglia;* b. 30 May 1942, Philadelphia, Pennsylvania; m. Judy Jones 1967, two s. one d. *Education:* Univ. of California at Berkeley, Univ. of Chicago, Univ. of Cambridge. *Career:* Temporary Lecturer in American Literature, Univ. of Exeter 1969–70, Lecturer 1970–88; Reader in American Literature, Univ. of East Anglia, later Prof. of American Studies, Prof. Emer. of American Studies 2007–; Visiting Faculty, Univ. of Minnesota 1977–78; Visiting Prof. of American Literature, Univ. of New Hampshire 1991–92. *Publications:* The Cambridge Mind: Ninety Years of the 'Cambridge Review' 1879–1969 (ed. with William Janeway and Simon Schama) 1970, Ezra Pound: The Critical Heritage (ed.) 1972, The Art of the Real: Poetry in England and America since 1939 1977, The Second World War in Fiction (ed. with Holger Klein and John Flower) 1984, John le Carre 1986, American Writers and Radical Politics, 1900–1939: Equivocal Commitments 1987, The Troubled Face of Biography (ed. with John Charmley) 1987, John Reed 1990, John Reed and the Russian Revolution: Uncollected Articles, Letters and Speeches in Russia, 1917–1920 (ed. with John Biggart) 1992, The Historical Atlas of New York City 1994, Scenes from the Life of a City: Corruption and Conscience in Old New York 1994, The Penguin Historical Atlas of North America 1995, New York City 2002, Mrs Astor's New York: Money and Social Power in a Gilded Age 2002, New York City: A Cultural History 2007; contribs: periodicals, The Guardian, The Independent. *Honours:* Leverhulme Fellowship 1978–79, Gilder Lehrman Institute Fellowship in American History 1999. *Address:* 74 Clarendon Road, Norwich, Norfolk, NR2 2PW, England (office). *Telephone:* (1603) 626603 (office). *E-mail:* eric.homberger@ntlworld.com (office).

HOME, Stewart Ramsay, (Harry Bates, Monty Cantsin, Karen Eliot); British writer; b. 24 March 1962, Merton, S London, England; s. of Julia Callan-Thompson. *Career:* mem. Soc. of Authors. *Exhibitions:* Humanity In Ruins, Central Space, London 1988, Vermeer II, workfortheeyetodo London 1996, Hallucination Generation: High Modernism in a Tripped Out World, Arnolfini, Bristol 2006, Again A Time Machine, White Columns, New York 2011; numerous group shows. *Films:* Eclipse & Re-Emergence of the Oedipus Complex 2004, Screams in Favour of De Sade 2002; numerous others, mainly shorts screened at specialist art cinemas and art events (not on commercial release). *Recordings:* Stewart Home Comes in Your Face 1998. *Publications:* Assault on Culture 1988, Pure Mania 1989, Defiant Pose 1991, No Pity 1993, Red London 1994, Neoism, Plagiarism & Praxis 1995, Cranked Up Really High 1995, Slow Death 1996, Come Before Christ & Murder Love 1997, Blow Job 1997, Cunt 1999, Confusion Incorporated: A Collection of Lies, Hoaxes and Hidden Truths 1999, Whips and Furs: My Life as a Bon Vivant Gambler and Love Rat 2000, 69 Things to Be Done with a Dead Princess 2002, Down and Out in Shoreditch and Hoxton 2004, Tainted Love 2005, Memphis Underground 2007, Blood Rites of the Bourgeoisie 2010; contrib. to Guardian, Big Issue, Independent, Art Monthly, Edinburgh Review, New Art Examiner, Konkret. *Honours:* Arts Council of England Writers' Award 2001, One to One Live Art Award 2005. *Literary Agent:* c/o Antony Harwood Ltd, 103 Walton Street, Oxford, OX2 6EB, England. *Telephone:* (1865) 559615. *Fax:* (1865) 310660. *E-mail:* mail@antonyharwood.com. *Website:* www.antonyharwood.com. *Address:* BM Senior, London, WC1N 3XX, England (office). *Website:* stewarthomesociety.org.

HOMEL, David; American/Canadian writer, journalist and translator; b. 1952, Chicago, Ill.; two s. *Education:* Univ. of Toronto, Indiana Univ. *Career:* Tutor in Translation, Concordia Univ., Toronto. *Screenplays:* Great North, Todo Incluido. *Publications:* fiction: Electrical Storms 1988, Rat Palms (Canadian Book and Periodical Marketers, Paperback of the Year 1993) 1992, Sonya and Jack (Prix Millepages for Best Foreign Literary Fiction, France) 1995, Get on Top 1999, The Speaking Cure (Hugh McLennan Prize for Fiction, Jewish Public Library Prize for Fiction 2004) 2003, Travels with my Family (with Marie-Louise Gay) 2006; non-fiction: Mapping Literature: The Art and Politics of Literary Translation 1988; contrib. to The Gazette, La Press. *Honours:* Gov.-Gen.'s Award for Translation 1995, 2001, QWF Prize for Translation 2003. *Telephone:* (514) 288-6690 (office). *E-mail:* dhomel@alcor.concordia.ca (office).

HOMES, A. M.; American writer; b. 1961, Washington, DC. *Films:* Wanted 1994, The Safety of Objects 2001, Freunde (aka The Whiz Kids) 2001, Jack (TV teleplay) 2004. *Publications:* Jack (Deutscher Jugendliteraturpreis) 1989, The Safety of Objects 1990, In a Country of Mothers 1993, The End of Alice 1995, Appendix A 1995, Music for Torching 1999, Things You Should Know (short stories) 2002, Los Angeles 2002, This Book Will Save Your Life (novel) 2006, The Mistress's Daughter 2007; contrib. to Vanity Fair, Art Forum, The New York Times, The New Yorker, Granta. *Honours:* fellowships from The Center for Scholars and Writers, New York Public Library, Guggenheim Foundation, NEA and New York Foundation for the Arts; Benjamin Franklin Award 2000. *Address:* Wylie Agency, 250 West 37th Street, New York, NY 10107, USA (office).

HONAN, Park, MA, PhD, FRSL; American biographer, writer and editor; *Professor Emeritus, University of Leeds;* b. 17 Sept. 1928, Utica, NY. *Education:* Univ. of Chicago, Univ. of London, UK. *Career:* Prof. of English and American Literature, Univ. of Leeds 1984–93, Prof. Emer. 1993–. *Publications:* Browning's Characters: A Study in Poetic Technique 1961, Shelley (ed.) 1963, Bulwer Lytton's Falkland (ed.) 1967, The Complete Works of Robert Browning (co-ed., nine vols) 1969–, The Book, The Ring and The Poet: A Biography of Robert Browning (co-author) 1975, Matthew Arnold: A Life 1981, Jane Austen: Her Life 1987, The Beats: An Anthology of 'Beat' Writing (ed.) 1987, Authors' Lives: On Literary Biography and the Arts of Language 1990, Shakespeare: A Life 1998, Christopher Marlowe: Poet & Spy 2005. *Honours:* British Acad. Awards, Leverhulme Award, Huntington Library Fellowship, Folger Shakespeare Library Fellowship 1991. *Address:* School of English, University of Leeds, Leeds, LS2 9JT, England (office).

HONAN, William Holmes, BA, MA; American journalist and writer; b. 11 May 1930, New York, NY; m. Nancy Burton 1975, two s. one d. *Education:* Oberlin College, University of Virginia. *Career:* Ed., The Villager, New York, 1957–60; Asst Ed., New Yorker Magazine, 1960–64, New York Times Magazine, 1969–70; Assoc. Ed., Newsweek, New York City, 1969; Travel Ed., 1970–72, 1973–74, Arts and Leisure Ed., 1974–82, Culture Ed., 1982–88, Chief Cultural Correspondent, 1988–93, National Higher Education Correspondent, 1993–2000, General Assignment, 2000–, New York Times; Managing Ed., Saturday Review, 1972–73. *Publications:* Greenwich Village Guide, 1959; Ted Kennedy: Profile of a Survivor, 1972; Bywater: The Man Who Invented the Pacific War, 1990; Visions of Infamy: The Untold Story of How Journalist Hector C. Bywater Devised the Plans that Led to Pearl Harbour, 1991; Fire When Ready, Gridley! – Great Naval Stories from Manila Bay to Vietnam (ed.), 1992; Treasure Hunt: A New York Times Reporter Tracks the Quedlinburg Treasures, 1997; Zingers (a play), 2002. Contributions: periodicals.

HONE, Joseph; British writer and broadcaster; b. 25 Feb. 1937, London; m. Jacqueline Mary Yeend 1963; one s. one d. *Education:* Kilkenny Coll., Sandford Park School, Dublin; St Columba's Coll., Dublin. *Career:* mem. Upton House Cricket Club. *Publications:* The Flowers of the Forest 1982, Children of the Country 1986, Duck Soup in the Black Sea 1988, Summer Hill 1990, Firesong 1997, Wicked Little Joe (memoir) 2009; contribs to periodicals. *Address:* Manor Cottage, Shutford, Oxfordshire, OX15 6PG, England (home).

HONEYMAN, Brenda (see Clarke, Brenda Margaret Lilian)

HONGO, Garrett, BA, MFA; American poet, writer and academic; *Distinguished Professor of Poetry, University of Oregon;* b. 1951, Volcano, HI; m.; two s. *Education:* Pomona Coll., Univ. of Michigan and Univ. of California, Irvine. *Career:* Founder and Dir Asian Exclusion Act theatre group, Seattle 1975–77; Dir of Creative Writing Program, Univ. of Oregon 1989–93, currently Distinguished Prof. of Poetry. *Publications:* poetry: Yellow Light 1982, The River of Heaven (Acad. of American Poets Lamont Prize) 1988, The Open Boat: Poems from Asian America (ed.) 1992; non-fiction: Volcano: A Memoir of

Hawaii (Oregon Book Award) 1995, Under Western Eyes: Personal Essays from Asian America (ed.); contribs to American Poetry Review, Antaeus, Field, Georgia Review, New England Review, Ploughshares, Parnassus, New York Times, Los Angeles Times, Hawaii Herald, The New Yorker. *Address:* Creative Writing Program, 5243 University of Oregon, Eugene, OR 97403-5243, USA (office). *E-mail:* crwrweb@darkwing.uoregon.edu (office).

HONORÉ, Christophe; French writer, critic and film director; b. 10 April 1970, Carhaix, Finistère. *Education:* Université de Rennes. *Plays:* Les Débutantes 1998, Le Pire du troupeau 2001. *Films:* Les Filles ne savent pas nager (writer) 2000, Nous deux (writer, dir) 2001, 17 fois Cécile Cassard (writer, dir) 2002, Tout contre Léo (writer, dir) 2002, Novo (writer) 2002, Ma mère (writer, dir) 2004, Le Clan (writer) 2004, Dans Paris (writer, dir) 2006, Les Chansons d'amour (writer, dir) 2007, Après lui (writer, dir) 2007, La Belle Personne 2008. *Publications:* novels: L'Infamille 1997, La Douceur 1999, Scarborough 2002, Le Livre pour enfants 2005; juvenile novels: Tout contre Léo 1995, C'est plus fort que moi 1996, Je joue très bien tout seul 1997, L'Affaire p'tit Marcel 1997, Zéro de lecture 1998, Une toute petite histoire d'amour 1998, Je ne suis pas une fille à papa 1998, Les Nuits où personne ne dort 1999, Mon cœur Bouleversé 1999, Bretonneries 1999, M'aimer 2003, Torse nu 2005, Noël, c'est couic! 2005, Viens 2006. *Literary Agent:* c/o Jean-François Gabard, ZELIG, 57 rue Réaumur, 75002 Paris, France. *Telephone:* 1-44-78-81-10. *Fax:* 1-44-78-07-65. *E-mail:* zelig@zelig-fr.com. *Website:* www.zelig-fr.com; christophehonore.free.fr.

HOOD, Daniel, BA; American writer and editor; b. 3 Nov. 1967, New Rochelle, NY. *Education:* Georgetown University. *Career:* Art Dir, IMP, publishers, New York City, 1989–94; Desktop Man., Wall Street Journal Europe, Brussels, Belgium, 1994–96; Managing Ed., Faulkner and Gray, publishers, New York City, 1996–2000; Business Ed., Daily News Express, New York, 2000–01; mem. SFWA. *Publications:* Fantasy Fiction: Fanuilh, 1994; Wizard's Heir, 1996; Beggar's Banquet, 1997; Scales of Justice, 1998; King's Cure, 2000. *Literary Agent:* Donald Maass Literary Agency, 157 W 57th Street, Suite 1003, New York, NY 10019, USA. *Address:* 315 E 92nd Street, No. 2E, New York, NY 10128, USA. *E-mail:* danhood@earthlink.net.com.

HOOJA, Rima, BA, MA, PhD; Indian historian, author, archaeologist and academic; *Director of Minnesota Studies in International Development, University of Minnesota*; b. 12 Nov. 1956. *Education:* MGD School, Kanoria Coll., Wolfson Coll., Univ. of 1st Div., Rajasthan, Univ. of Cambridge, UK. *Career:* Lecturer in History, Kanoria Coll., Japur 1979–81; Assoc. Ed. Indian Book Chronicle 1987–; Project Asst, Indian Nat. Trust for Art and Cultural Heritage 1987–89; Consultant, Dept of History, Kota Open Univ. 1988, Assoc. Prof. in Indian Tradition and Culture 1990–96; currently Dir Minn. Studies in Int. Devt, Univ. of Minnesota, USA; Visiting Fellow, Inst. of Devt Studies 1993–94, 1995–96; Fellow, Royal Asiatic Society 2001–; Founder mem. Int. Forum for Women in Archaeology; mem. Governing Bd Inst. of Rajasthan Studies, Japur 2001–. *Publications include:* The Ahar Culture and Beyond 1988, Prince, Patriot, Parliamentarian: Biography of Dr Karni Singh – Maharaja of Bikaner 1997, Crusader for Self-Rule: Tej Bahadur Sapru and the Indian National Movement 1999, A History of Rajasthan 2006; as co-ed.: Environment Degradation: Strategies for Control 1992; as translator: Mandan's Devata-Murti-Prakarnam 1999; numerous academic papers and newspaper articles. *Address:* Minnesota Studies in International Development, University of Minnesota, Learning Abroad Center, 230 Heller Hall, 271 19th Avenue South, Minneapolis, MN 55455, USA (office); c/o Rupa Publications, 161-B4 Gulmohar House, Yusuf Sarai Community Centre, New Delhi, 110049 (office); 11 Uniara Garden, Japur, 302004, India (home). *Telephone:* (612) 626-9000 (Minneapolis) (office); (14) 162005 (New Delhi) (office). *E-mail:* UMabroad@umn.edu (office); info@rupapublications.com (office); rimahooja@satyam.net.in (home). *Website:* www.umn.edu (office); www.rupapublications.com (office).

HOOKER, Jeremy Peter, BA, MA; British lecturer, poet and writer; *Reader in English Literature, Professor, University of Glamorgan*; b. 23 March 1941, Warsash, Hampshire, England. *Education:* University of Southampton. *Career:* Arts Council Creative Writing Fellow, Winchester School of Art, 1981–83; fmr Lecturer in English, Bath College of Higher Education, and Netherlands and USA; currently Reader in English Literature, Prof. Univ. of Glamorgan; mem. Fellow, Academi Gymreig, 2000; Richard Jefferies Society, pres., 1999. *Publications:* The Elements, 1972; Soliloquies of a Chalk Giant, 1974; Solent Shore: New Poems, 1978; Landscape of the Daylight Moon, 1978; Englishman's Road, 1980; Itchen Water, 1982; Poetry of Place, 1982; A View from the Source: Selected Poems, 1982; Master of the Leaping Figures, 1987; The Presence of the Past, 1987; In Praise of Windmills, 1990; Their Silence a Language (with Lee Grandjean), 1994; Writers in a Landscape, 1996; Our Lady of Europe, 1997; Groundwork (with Lee Grandjean), 1998. Contributions: Reviews and journals. *Honours:* Eric Gregory Award, 1969; Welsh Arts Council Literature Prize, 1975. *Address:* Old School House, 7 Sunnyside, Frome, Somerset BA11 1LD, England.

HOOKS, Bell, MA, PhD; American critic, writer, cultural theorist and activist; b. (Gloria Jean Watkins), 25 Sept. 1952, Hopkinsville, KY. *Education:* Crispus Attucks High School, Hopkinsville, Stanford Univ., Univ. of Wisconsin, Univ. of California at Santa Cruz. *Career:* English Prof. and Sr Lecturer in Ethnic Studies, Univ. of Southern California 1977–79; lead numerous courses at Univ. of California and San Fransisco State Univ. 1980s; tutor in African and Afro-American Studies, Yale Univ. 1985; Assoc. Prof. of Women's Studies and American Literature, Oberlin Coll., OH 1988; Distinguished Prof. of English, City Coll., New York 1994; Distinguished Prof. in Residence, Berea Coll., Kentucky; f. Hambone magazine. *Publications include:* poetry: And There We Wept (chapbook) 1978, The Woman's Mourning Song 1993; non-fiction: Ain't I a Woman: Black Women and Feminism 1981, Feminist Theory from Margin to Center 1984, Talking Back: Thinking Feminist, Thinking Black 1989, Yearning: Race, Gender and Cultural Politics 1990, Breaking Bread: Insurgent Black Intellectual Life (with Cornel West) 1991, Black Looks: Race and Representation 1992, Sisters of the Yam: Black Women and Self-recovery 1993, Teaching to Transgress: Education as the Practice of Freedom 1994, Outlaw Culture: Resisting Representations 1994, Art on my Mind: Visual Politics 1995, Killing Rage: Ending Racism 1995, Bone Black: Memories of Girlhood 1996, Reel to Real: Race, Sex and Class at the Movies 1996, Seduction and Surrender 1997, Wounds of Passion: A Writing Life 1997, Remembered Rapture: The Writer at Work 1999, Feminism is for Everybody: Passionate Politics 2000, Where We Stand: Class Matters 2000, Salvation: Black People and Love 2001, All About Love 2001, Communion: The Female Search for Love 2002, Rock my Soul: Black People and Self-Esteem 2002, Teaching Community: A Pedagogy of Hope 2003, We Real Cool: Black Men and Masculinity 2003, The Will to Change 2004; juvenile: Happy to be Nappy (with Christopher Raschka) 1999, Be Boy Buzz 2002, Homemade Love 2002; contrib. to numerous journals. *Honours:* Lila Wallace-Reader's Digest Fund Writer's Award 1994. *Address:* c/o Department of English, Berea College, Berea, KY 404041, USA.

HOOVER, Paul Andrew, BA, MA; American poet, writer, editor and educator; *Professor of Creative Writing, San Francisco State University*; b. 30 April 1946, Harrisonburg, Va; m. Maxine Chernoff 197; two s. one d. *Education:* Manchester Coll., Univ. of Illinois. *Career:* Ed. OINK! 1971–85; Founder-mem. 1974, mem. Bd Dirs 1974–87, Pres. 1975–78, The Poetry Center of Chicago at School of the Art Inst.; Poet-in-Residence, Columbia Coll. 1974–2003; Co-Founder and Ed. New American Writing 1986–; Fellow, Simon's Rock of Bard Coll. 1988–; Visiting Prof. in Creative Writing, San Francisco State Univ. 2003–06, Prof. of Creative Writing 2006–; mem. Associated Writing Programs, Co-ordinating Council of Literary Magazines, Modern Language Asscn of America. *Publications:* poetry: Hairpin Turns 1973, The Monocle Thugs 1977, Letter to Einstein Beginning Dear Albert 1979, Somebody Talks a Lot 1983, Nervous Songs 1986, Idea 1987, The Novel: A Poem 1990, Viridian 1997, Totem and Shadow: New and Selected Poems 1999, Rehearsal in Black 2001, Winter (Mirror) 2002; other: Saigon, Illinois (novel) 1988, Postmodern American Poetry: A Norton Anthology (ed.) 1993, Fables of Representation (essays) 2004, Poems in Spanish 2005, Edge and Fold 2006; contrib. to numerous anthologies, reviews, quarterlies and journals. *Honours:* Nat. Endowment for the Arts Poetry Fellowship 1980, Illinois Arts Council Artist's Fellowships 1983, 1984, 1986, General Electric Foundation Award for Younger Writers 1984, Carl Sandburg Award, Friends of the Chicago Public Library 1987, Gwendolyn Brooks Poet Laureate Award 1988, Shifting Foundation Grants 1990, 1991, Gertrude Stein Award in Innovative American Poetry 1994–95, Winner, Contemporary Poetry Series Competition, University of Georgia 1997, San Francisco Literary Laureate Award, Friends of the San Francisco Public Library 2000, Jerome J. Shestack Prize, American Poetry Review 2003. *Address:* 369 Molino Avenue, Mill Valley, CA 94941, USA (home). *Telephone:* (415) 338-3157 (office). *Fax:* (415) 384-0364. *E-mail:* viridian@hotmail.com (office). *Website:* www.newamericanwriting.com (office); www.paulhooverpoetry.blosspot.com (home).

HOPE, Christopher David Tully, MA, FRSL; South African writer; b. 26 Feb. 1944, Johannesburg; s. of Dudley Mitford Hope and Kathleen Mary Hope; m. Eleanor Marilyn Margaret Klein; two s. *Education:* Natal Univ., Univ. of the Witwatersrand. *Career:* Founder and Dir Franschhoek Literary Festival 2007–; mem. Soc. of Authors. *Publications:* A Separate Development 1981, Private Parts 1982, The King, the Cat and the Fiddle (with Yehudi Menuhin) 1983, Kruger's Alp (Whitbread Prize for Fiction 1985) 1984, The Dragon Wore Pink 1985, The Hottentot Room 1986, Black Swan 1987, White Boy Running 1988, My Chocolate Redeemer 1989, Moscow! Moscow! 1990, Serenity House 1992, The Love Songs of Nathan J. Swirsky 1993, Darkest England 1996; poetry: Cape Drives 1974, In the Country of the Black Pig 1981, Englishman 1985, Me, the Moon and Elvis Presley 1997, Signs of the Heart 1999, Heaven Forbid 2002, Brothers Under the Skin 2003, My Mother's Lovers 2006, The Garden of Bad Dreams 2008, Shooting Angels 2011; contrib. to TLS, London Magazine, Les Temps Modernes, BBC, Guardian. *Honours:* Cholmondeley Award 1972, David Higham Award 1981, Int. PEN Award 1983, Whitbread Award 1986, CNA Literary Award (S Africa) 1989, Travelex Travel Writer of the Year 1997. *Literary Agent:* Rogers, Coleridge & White Ltd, 20 Powis Mews, London, W11 1JN, England. *Telephone:* (20) 7221-3717. *Fax:* (20) 7229-9084. *E-mail:* christopher1hope@gmail.com (home).

HOPE, Ronald, CBE, BA, MA, DPhil, DEd; British writer; b. 4 April 1921, London; m. Marion Whittaker 1947; one s. one d. *Education:* New Coll., Oxford. *Career:* Fellow, Brasenose Coll., Oxford 1945–47, Dir Seafarers' Educ. Service, London 1947–76; Dir The Marine Soc. 1976–86. *Publications:* Spare Time at Sea 1954, Economic Geography 1956, Dick Small in the Half Deck, Ships 1958, The British Shipping Industry 1959, The Shoregoer's Guide to World Ports 1963, Seamen and the Sea 1965, Introduction to the Merchant Navy 1965, Retirement from the Sea 1967, In Cabined Ships at Sea 1969, Twenty Singing Seamen 1979, The Seamen's World 1982, A New History of

British Shipping 1990, Poor Jack: The Perilous History of the Merchant Seaman 2001. *Honours:* Hon. MA (Open Univ.) 1983, Hon. DEd (Council for Nat. Academic Awards) 1984. *Address:* 2 Park Place, Dollar, Clackmannanshire, FK14 7AA, Scotland (home). *Telephone:* (1259) 742045 (home).

HOPE-SIMPSON, Jacynth Ann, (Helen Dudley), MA, DipEd; British writer; b. 10 Nov. 1930, Birmingham, England. *Education:* Univ. of Lausanne, Univ. of Oxford. *Publications:* The Stranger in the Train 1960, The Bishop of Kenelminster 1961, The Man Who Came Back 1962, The Bishop's Picture 1962, The Unravished Bridge 1963, The Witch's Cave 1964, The Hamish Hamilton Book of Myths and Legends 1965, The Hamish Hamilton Book of Witches 1966, Escape to the Castle 1967, The Unknown Island 1968, They Sailed from Plymouth 1970, Elizabeth I 1971, Tales in School 1971, The Gunner's Boy 1973, Save Tarranmoor! 1974, Always on the Move 1975, The Hijacked Hovercraft 1975, Black Madonna 1976, Vote for Victoria 1976, The Making of the Machine Age 1978, The Hooded Falcon 1979, Island of Perfumes 1985, Cottage Dreams 1986.

HOPKINS, Antony, CBE, FRCM; British composer, writer and broadcaster (retd); b. 21 March 1921, London; s. of the late Hugh Reynolds and Marjorie Reynolds; m. 1st Alison Purves 1947 (died 1991); m. 2nd Beatrix Taylor 2012. *Education:* Berkhamsted School and Royal Coll. of Music (RCM) with Cyril Smith. *Career:* fmr Lecturer, RCM for 15 years; Dir Intimate Opera Co. 1952–64; composed incidental music for theatre (Old Vic, Stratford-upon-Avon), radio and cinema. *Radio:* presenter of series, Talking About Music (BBC) 1954–92. *Compositions include:* operas: Lady Rohesia, Three's Company, Hands Across the Sky, Dr Musikus, Ten o'clock Call, The Man from Tuscany; ballet music: Etude, Café des Sports; others: Psalm 42, Magnificat and Nunc Dimittis (for girls' choir), A Time for Growing, Early One Morning, Partita for solo violin, John and the Magic Music Man for narrator and orchestra (Grand Prix Besançon Film Festival) 1976, songs, recorder pieces, three piano sonatas; incidental music, including Oedipus, The Love of Four Colonels, Cast a Dark Shadow, Pickwick Papers, Billy Budd, Decameron Nights. *Publications:* Talking about Symphonies 1961, Talking about Concertos 1964, Music All Around Me 1967, Music Face to Face 1971, Talking about Sonatas 1971, Downbeat Guide 1977, Understanding Music 1979, The Nine Symphonies of Beethoven 1980, Songs for Swinging Golfers 1981, Sounds of Music 1982, Beating Time (autobiog.) 1982, Pathway to Music 1983, The Concertgoer's Companion Vol. I 1984, Vol. II 1986, The Seven Concertos of Beethoven 1996; contrib. to numerous books. *Honours:* Hon. FRAM; Hon. Fellow, Robinson Coll. Cambridge 1980; Hon. DUniv (Stirling) 1980; Hon. Dr of Arts (Bedford); Italia Prizes for composition 1952, 1957, City of Tokyo Medal for services to music 1973, Royal Coll. of Music Chappell Gold Medal 1943, Royal Coll. of Music Cobbett Prize. *Address:* Woodyard Cottage, Ashridge, Berkhamsted, Herts., HP4 1PS, England (home). *Telephone:* (1442) 842257 (home).

HOPKINSON, Simon; Australian playwright, director and writer. *Career:* Artistic Dir, Australian Theatre for Young People, New England Theatre Co., Darwin Theatre Group; fmr resident dramatist and Assoc. Dir, Melbourne Theatre Co.; founder, Theatre-in-Education Co., Australia; specialist consultant for children's television, Australian Broadcasting Authority. *Theatre includes:* Lipstick Dreams, Wedding Games, Happy Families. *Television includes:* Bananas in Pyjamas (co-creator, writer) 1991 (also subsequent stage shows), Driven Crazy, Chuck Finn, Fast Tracks, Gloria's House, Petals. *Films include:* The Magic Pudding. *Publications (on CD-ROM):* Oz – The Magical Adventure 2000, Bananas in Pyjamas: It's Fun Time, It's Party Time. *Literary Agent:* RGM Associates, PO Box 128, Surry Hills, NSW 2010, Australia. *Telephone:* (2) 9281 3911. *Fax:* (2) 9281 4705. *E-mail:* info@rgm.com.au. *Website:* www.rgm.com.au.

HOPKIRK, Joyce, FRSA; British journalist and editor (retd); b. Newcastle upon Tyne, England; d. of Walter Nicholson and Veronica Nicholson (née Keelan); m. 1st Peter Hopkirk 1962; one d.; m. 2nd William James Lear 1974; one s. *Education:* La Sagesse Convent and Middle St Secondary School, Newcastle upon Tyne. *Career:* reporter, Gateshead Post 1955; Founder-Ed. Majorcan News 1959; reporter, Daily Sketch 1960; Royal Reporter, Daily Express 1961; Ed. Fashion magazine 1967; Women's Ed. Sun newspaper 1967; Launch Ed. Cosmopolitan magazine 1971–72; Asst Ed. Daily Mirror 1973–78, Asst Ed. Sunday Mirror 1985; Women's Ed. Sunday Times 1982; Editorial Dir Elle magazine 1984; Ed.-in-Chief She magazine 1986–89; currently freelance journalist; Dir Editors Unlimited 1990–; Co-Chair. PPA Awards 1998–; mem. Competition Comm. 1999–2001, 2001–06. *Video cassette:* Successful Slimming 1978. *Publications:* Successful Slimming 1976, Successful Slimming Cookbook 1978, Splash (co-author) 1995, Best of Enemies 1996, Double Trouble 1997, Unfinished Business 1998, Relative Strangers 1999, The Affair 2000; six novels published as Val Hopkirk. *Honours:* Ed. of the Year 1972, Women's Magazines Ed. of the Year 1988. *Address:* Gadespring, 109 Piccotts End, Hemel Hempstead, Herts., HP1 3AT, England (home). *Telephone:* (1442) 245608 (home).

HOPPE, Felicitas; German author; b. 22 Dec. 1960, Hamelin. *Education:* Eberhard Karls Universität, Tübingen, Univ. of Oregon, USA, Freien Universität, Berlin. *Career:* fmr dramaturge and journalist; freelance writer 1996–; Visiting Scholar, Dartmouth Coll., USA 2006; taught at Georgetown Univ., Washington, DC 2010. *Publications include:* Unglückselige Begebenheiten 1991, Picknick der Friseure 1996, Das Richtfest 1997, Drei Kapitäne 1998, Pigafetta 1999, Vom Bäcker und seiner Frau 1999, Die Torte 2000, Fakire und Flötisten 2001, Paradiese, Übersee 2003, Die Reise nach Java 2003, Verbrecher und Versager 2004, Johanna 2006, Iwein Löwenritter 2008, Sieben Schätze. Augsburger Vorlesungen 2009, Der beste Platz der Welt 2009, Hoppe 2012. *Honours:* Alfred-Döblin-Stipendium Scholarship 1994, Aspekte-Literaturpreis 1996, Ernst-Willner-Preis 1996, Rauriser Literaturpreis 1997, Nicolas Born-Preis des Landes Niedersachsen 2004, Heimito von Doderer-Literaturpreis 2004, Spycher: Literaturpreis Leuk 2004, Brüder-Grimm-Preis der Stadt Hanau 2005, Literaturpreis der Stadt Bremen 2007, Roswitha-Preis 2007, Georg Büchner Prize 2012. *Address:* c/o S. Fischer Verlag GmbH, Hedderichstr. 114, 60596 Frankfurt am Main, Germany (office). *Telephone:* 696062-0 (office). *Fax:* 696062-214 (office). *Website:* www.fischerverlage.de/autor/14383 (office).

HORNBY, Nick; British journalist and novelist; b. 1957, London. *Recordings:* wrote lyrics for Ben Folds album, Lonely Avenue 2010. *Publications:* Contemporary American Fiction (essays) 1992, Fever Pitch (memoir) 1992, (screenplay) 1997, My Favourite Year: A Collection of New Football Writing (ed.) 1993, High Fidelity (novel) 1995, Speaking With the Angel (ed.) 2000, About a Boy (novel) 2000, How to be Good (novel) 2001, 31 Songs (non-fiction) 2003, A Long Way Down 2005, The Complete Polysyllabic Spree (collected columns) 2006, Slam (juvenile fiction) 2007, Juliet, Naked 2009; contrib. to Sunday Times, TLS, Literary Review, New York Times, New Yorker, the Believer. *Honours:* William Hill Sports Book of the Year Award 1992, Writers' Guild Best Fiction Book Award 1995, American Acad. of Arts and Letters E. M. Forster Award 1999, WHSmith Fiction Award 2002, London Award 2003. *Literary Agent:* United Agents, 12–26 Lexington Street, London, W1F 0LE, England. *Telephone:* (20) 3214-0800. *Fax:* (20) 3214-0801. *E-mail:* info@unitedagents.co.uk. *Website:* unitedagents.co.uk.

HORNE, Sir Alistair Allan, Kt, MA, DLitt (Cantab.); British writer, journalist and lecturer; b. 9 Nov. 1925, London; m. 1st Renira Margaret Hawkins; three d.; m. 2nd The Hon. Mrs Sheelin Eccles 1987. *Education:* Jesus Coll., Cambridge. *Career:* foreign correspondent, Daily Telegraph 1952–55; official biographer for Prime Minister Harold Macmillan 1979; mem. Soc. of Authors, RSL. *Publications:* Back into Power 1955, The Land is Bright 1958, Canada and the Canadians 1961, The Price of Glory - Verdun 1916, The Fall of Paris 1870–1871 1965, To Lose a Battle: France 1940 1969, Death of a Generation 1970, The Paris Commune 1971, Small Earthquake in Chile 1972, Napoleon, Master of Europe 1805–1807 1979, The French Army and Politics 1870–1970 1984, Macmillan, Vol. I 1894–1956 1985, Vol. II 1957–1986 1989, A Bundle from Britain 1993, The Lonely Leader: Monty 1944–45 1994, How Far from Austerlitz: Napoleon 1805–1815 1996, Telling Lives (ed.) 2000, Seven Ages of Paris: Portrait of a City 2002, The Age of Napoleon 2004, Friend or Foe: An Anglo-Saxon History of France 2004, The French Revolution 2008, Kissinger's Year: 1973 2009, But What Do You Actually Do? 2011; contrib. to various periodicals. *Honours:* Hawthornden Prize 1963, Yorkshire Post Book of Year Prize 1978, Wolfson Literary Award 1978, Enid Macleod Prize 1985; Chevalier, Légion d'honneur 1993. *Address:* The Old Vicarage, Turville, Nr Henley on Thames, Oxfordshire RG9 6QU, England (home).

HOROVITZ, Michael, OBE, BA, MA; British author, poet, editor and publisher, musician, singer, songwriter and visual artist and journalist; *Editor and Publisher, New Departures International Review of the Arts;* b. 4 April 1935, Frankfurt am Main, Germany; s. of Abraham Horovitz and Rosi Feist; m. Frances Horovitz (died 1983); one s. *Education:* Brasenose Coll., Oxford. *Career:* Ed. and Publr New Departures International Review 1959–; has performed duo on anglo-saxophone & voice with pianist-composer Stan Tracey since 1960; Founder, co-ordinator and torchbearer, Poetry Olympics Festivals 1980–; contrib. to Jazz Poetry SuperJams; mem. William Blake Klezmatrix Band 2002–. *Exhibitions:* various since 1960, including Royal Acad. Summer Shows, Retrospective in Art, @ 42, London 2010. *Film:* Peter Whitehead's Wholly Communion at First Int. Poetry Incarnation at Royal Albert Hall, London features performances of two poems 1965. *Radio:* A Good Read, Adventures in Poetry, The Bespoken Word, My Kind of Song, Poetry Now, Night Waves, Third Ear, The Poetry Olympian: Michael Horovitz at 75 (BBC Radio 4) 2010; numerous broadcasts in France, Germany, Canada and USA. *Television:* contribs to programmes on BBC 1, BBC 2, BBC 4, ITV, Channel 4 and to TV programmes in Europe and N America. *Publications:* Europa (trans.) 1961, Alan Davie 1963, Declaration 1963, Strangers: Poems 1965, Poetry for the People: An Essay in Bop Prosody 1966, Bank Holiday: A New Testament for the Love Generation 1967, Children of Albion (ed.) 1969, The Wolverhampton Wanderer: An Epic of Football, Fate and Fun 1970, Love Poems 1971, A Contemplation 1978, Growing Up: Selected Poems and Pictures 1951–1979 1979, The Egghead Republic (trans.) 1983, A Celebration of and for Frances Horovitz 1984, Midsummer Morning Jog Log 1986, Bop Paintings, Collages and Drawings 1989, Grandchildren of Albion (ed.) 1992, Wordsounds and Sightlines: New and Selected Poems 1994, Grandchildren of Albion Live (ed.) 1996, The POW! Anthology 1996, The POP! Anthology 2000, The POM! Anthology 2001, Jeff Nuttall's Wake 2004, A New Waste Land: Timeship Earth at Nillennium 2007. *Honours:* Arts Council Writers' Award 1976, Arts Council Translators' Award 1983, Poetry Book Soc. Recommendation 1986, Creative Britons Award 2000. *Address:* New Departures International Review, PO Box 9819, London, W11 2GQ, England (office). *E-mail:* info@poetryolympics.com (office). *Website:* www.poetryolympics.com (office).

HOROWITZ, Anthony; British writer and screenwriter; b. 5 April 1955, London; m. Jill Green; two s. *Education:* Orley Farm School London, Rugby School, Univ. of York. *Writing for television:* Dramarama, Boon, Robin of

Sherwood, Poirot, The Gift (adaptation), Murder Most Horrid, The Last Englishman, Chiller, Crime Traveller, Midsomer Murders, Murder in Mind (also creator), Menace, Foyle's War (also creator). *Film screenplay:* The Gathering 2002. *Play:* Mindgame 2000. *Publications:* The Sinister Secret of Frederick K. Bower 1979, Misha, the Magician and the Mysterious Amulet 1981, Devil's Door Bell 1983, Enter Frederick K. Bower 1985, Night of the Scorpion 1985, The Myths and Mythology 1985, Robin the Hooded Man (with Richard Carpenter) 1986, The Silver Citadel 1986, Public Enemy #2 1987, Adventurer 1987, Crossbow: The Adventures of William Tell 1987, The Falcon's Malteser 1987, Groosham Grange 1988, Just Ask for Diamond 1989, Day of the Dragon 1989, Groosham Grange II: The Unholy Grail 1991, South by South East 1991, The Puffin Book of Horror Stories (ed.) 1994, Granny 1994, The Switch 1996, Death Walks Tonight: Horrifying Stories 1996, The Devil and his Boy 1998, Horowitz Horror 1999, More Horowitz Horror 2000, Stormbreaker 2000, Point Blank 2001, Skeleton Key 2002, Eagle Strike 2003, Alex Rider 2003, I Know What You Did Last Wednesday 2003, Return to Groosham Grange 2003, The Blurred Man 2003, Scorpia 2004, Three of Diamonds 2004, The Killing Joke 2004, Ark Angel: Alex Rider Book 6 (British Book Awards Red House Children's Book of the Year 2006) 2005, The Power of Five: Raven's Gate 2005, The Power of Five: Evil Star 2006, The Power of Five: Nightrise 2007, Point Blanc (graphic novel) 2007, Snakehead 2007, The Power of Five: Necropolis 2008, Crocodile Tears 2009, House of Silk 2011. *Honours:* BA/Nielsen Book Data Author of the Year Award 2007. *Address:* c/o Walker Books Ltd, 87 Vauxhall Walk, London SE11 5HJ, England (office). *Website:* www.walker.co.uk (office); www.anthonyhorowitz.com.

HORROCKS, Paul John; British editor; b. 19 Dec. 1953, s. of Joe Horrocks and Eunice Horrocks; m. Linda Jean Walton 1976; two s. one d. one step-d. *Education:* Bolton School. *Career:* reporter, Daily Mail 1974–75; reporter, Manchester Evening News 1975–80, Crime Corresp. 1980–87, News Ed. 1987–91, Asst Ed. 1991–95, Deputy Ed. 1995–97, Ed. 1997–2009; Pres. UK Soc. of Editors; mem. Organizing Cttee, Commonwealth Games, Manchester 2002; Vice-Pres. Community Foundation for Greater Manchester; Patron Francis House Children's Hospice; mem. Bd New Children's Hosp.; Trustee Tatton Trust. *Address:* c/o Manchester Evening News, 1 Scott Place, Manchester, M3 3RN, England (office).

HORTON, Richard C., FRCP; British physician; *Editor, The Lancet. Career:* Visting Prof., London School of Hygiene and Tropical Medicine; Ed., publisher, The Lancet; bd mem. Council of Science Editors 1994–. *Publications:* non-fiction: Preventing Coronary Artery Disease (with Martin Kendall) 1997, How to Publish in Biomedicine 1997, Second Opinion: Doctors and Diseases 2003, Health Wars: On the Global Front Lines of Modern Medicine 2003, MMR: Science and Fiction 2004; contrib. to New York Review of Books, London Review of Books, The Lancet, journals. *Address:* The Lancet, 32 Jamestown Road, London, NW1 7BY, England (office). *Telephone:* (20) 7424-4910 (office). *Fax:* (20) 7424-4911 (office). *E-mail:* richard.horton@lancet.com (office). *Website:* www.lancet.com (office).

HORWITZ, Allan Kolski; South African writer, poet, singer, songwriter and political and cultural activist; *Co-ordinator, Botsotso Publishing*; b. 24 Feb. 1952, Vryburg. *Career:* f. and co-ordinator, Botsotso Publishing, mem. editorial board, Botsotso Magazine; f. Botsotso Jesters performance poetry group; f. All Clear music group. *Plays:* The Pump Room 2009. *Publications:* Call from the Free State (poems) 1979, Un/Common Ground (fiction) 2003, Saving Water (poems) 2005, Blue Wings (juvenile fiction) 2008, Out of the Wreckage (fiction) 2008; The Pump Room (play) 2009; contribs to Essential Things (poetry anthology), Throbbing Ink (poetry anthology), Unity in Flight (short story anthology) 2001, Botsotso (poetry anthology) 2009. *Address:* Botsotso, Box 30952, Braamfontein 2017, South Africa (office). *Telephone:* (11) 4872112 (office). *E-mail:* botsotso@artslink.co.za (office). *Website:* www.botsotso.org.za (office).

HORWOOD, William; British novelist; b. 1944, Oxford, England; m. 1st; m. 2nd; m. 3rd; six c. *Education:* Sir Roger Manwood's School, Sandwich, Univ. of Bristol. *Career:* frmly worked at trade magazine Campaign, feature ed. Daily Mail –1978. *Publications:* Duncton Wood 1980, The Stonor Eagles 1982, Callanish 1984, Skallagrigg 1987, Duncton Quest 1988, Duncton Found 1989, Duncton Tales 1991, The Book of Silence 1992, Duncton Rising 1993, Duncton Stone 1993, The Willows in Winter 1993, Toad Triumphant 1995, Journeys to the Heartland 1995, The Willows and Beyond 1996, Seekers at the Wulfrock 1997, Mole Gets Lost 1997, Flying into Danger 1997, Toad in Trouble 1997, Willows at Christmas 1998, The Boy With No Shoes (autobiog.) 2004, Dark Hearts of Chicago (with Helen Rappaport) 2007. *E-mail:* info@horwoodrappaport.com (office). *Website:* www.horwoodrappaport.com.

HOSKING, Geoffrey Alan, PhD, FBA, FRHistS; British historian and academic; *Professor Emeritus of Russian History, School of Slavonic and East European Studies, University College London*; b. 28 April 1942, Troon, Ayrshire, Scotland; s. of Stuart Hosking and Jean Smillie; m. Anne Lloyd Hirst 1970; two d. *Education:* Maidstone Grammar School, Moscow State Univ., Kings Coll., Cambridge, St Antony's Coll., Oxford. *Career:* Lecturer in Govt, Univ. of Essex 1966–71, Lecturer in History 1972–76, Sr Lecturer and Reader in History 1976–84; Prof. of Russian History, School of Slavonic and East European Studies, Univ. Coll. London 1984–99, 2004–07, Prof. Emer. of Russian History 2007–, Leverhulme Research Prof. 1999–2004, Deputy Dir School of Slavonic and East European Studies 1996–98; Visiting Prof. in Political Science, Univ. of Wisconsin-Madison, USA 1971–72, Slavisches Institut, Univ. of Cologne, Germany 1980–81; mem. Inst. for Advanced Studies, Princeton, USA 2006–07; mem. Booker Prize Jury for Russian Fiction 1993. *Publications include:* The Russian Constitutional Experiment 1973, Beyond Socialist Realism 1980, The First Socialist Society: A History of the Soviet Union from Within 1985, The Awakening of the Soviet Union 1990, The Road to Post-Communism: Independent Political Movements in the Soviet Union 1985–91 (with J. Aves and P. Duncan) 1992, Russia: People and Empire (1552–1917) 1997, Myths and Nationhood (co-ed. with George Schöpflin) 1997, Russian Nationalism Past and Present (co-ed. with Robert Service) 1998, Reinterpreting Russia (co-ed. with Robert Service) 1999, Russia and the Russians: A History 2001, Rulers and Victims: The Russians in the Soviet Union 2006, Trust: Money, Markets and Society 2010. *Honours:* Dr hc (Russian Acad. of Sciences) 2000; LA Times History Book Prize 1986, BBC Reith Lecturer 1988, US Ind. Publrs History Book Prize 2001, Alex Nove Book Prize 2008. *Address:* School of Slavonic and East European Studies, University College London, Gower Street, London, WC1E 6BT (office); 18 Camden Mews, London, NW1 9DA, England (home). *Telephone:* (20) 7267-5543 (home). *E-mail:* geoffreyhosking@mac.com (office).

HOSPITAL, Janette Turner, (Alex Juniper), MA; Australian/American writer and academic; *Carolina Distinguished Professor of English and Distinguished Writer-in-Residence, University of South Carolina*; b. 12 Nov. 1942, Melbourne, Vic.; d. of Adrian Charles Turner and Elsie Turner; m. Clifford Hospital 1965; one s. one d. *Education:* Univ. of Queensland and Queen's Univ., Canada. *Career:* high school teacher, Queensland 1963–66; librarian, Harvard Univ. 1967–71; Lecturer in English, St Lawrence Coll., Kingston, Ont., in maximum and medium-security fed. penitentiaries for men 1971–82; professional writer 1982–; Writer-in-Residence and Lecturer, Writing Program, MIT 1985–86, 1987, 1989, Writer-in-Residence, Univ. of Ottawa, Canada 1987, Univ. of Sydney, Australia 1989, Queen's Univ. at Herstmonceux Castle, UK 1994; Adjunct Prof. of English, La Trobe Univ., Melbourne 1990–93; Visiting Fellow and Writer-in-Residence, Univ. of E Anglia, UK 1996; O'Connor Chair. in Literature, Colgate Univ., Hamilton, NY 1999; Carolina Distinguished Prof. of English and Distinguished Writer-in-Residence, Univ. of S Carolina 1999–. *Publications:* The Ivory Swing (Seal First Novel Award 1982) 1982, The Tiger in the Tiger Pit 1983, Borderline 1985, Charades 1988, The Last Magician 1992, Oyster 1996, Due Preparations for the Plague (Qld Premier's Literature Award 2003) 2003; short story collections: Dislocations (Fellowship of Australian Writers Fiction Award 1988) 1986, Isobars 1990, Collected Stories 1995, North of Nowhere, South of Loss 2003; as Alex Juniper: A Very Proper Death 1991, Orpheus Lost 2007. *Honours:* Hon. DUniv (Griffith Univ., Qld) 1995; Hon. DLitt (Univ. of Queensland) 2003; Gold Medal, Nat. Magazine Awards (Canada) 1991 (for travel writing), First Prize, Magazine Fiction, Foundation for the Advancement of Canadian Letters 1982. *Address:* Department of English, University of South Carolina, Welsh Humanities Office Building, Room 504, Columbia, SC 29208, USA (office); c/o Barbara Mobbs, PO Box 126, Edgeclif, Sydney, NSW 2027, Australia. *Telephone:* (803) 777-2186 (office). *E-mail:* hospitjt@mailbox.sc.edu (office). *Website:* www.janetteturnerhospital.com. *Literary Agent:* c/o Elaine Markson, Literary Agent, 44 Greenwich Avenue, New York, NY 10011, USA.

HOSSEINI, Khaled; Afghan writer and physician; b. 1965, Kabul; m.; one s. one d. *Education:* Santa Clara Univ., UC San Diego School of Medicine. *Career:* moved to Paris, France aged 11, to San Jose, CA, USA in 1980; physician 1996–. *Publications:* The Kite Runner (novel) 2004, A Thousand Splendid Suns (British Book Award for Best Read 2008) 2007. *Literary Agent:* Judy Lubershane Agency, 2151 Massachusetts Avenue, Lexington, MA 02421, USA. *Telephone:* (781) 274-0717. *Fax:* (781) 274-0671. *E-mail:* jlubershane@rcn.com. *Address:* c/o Riverhead Books, 375 Hudson Street, New York, NY 10014, USA. *Website:* www.khaledhosseini.com.

HOTCHNER, Aaron Edward, LLB; American author and dramatist; b. 28 June 1920, St Louis, MO. *Education:* Washington University, St Louis. *Career:* mem. Authors League; Dramatists Guild; PEN, Century Asscn. *Films:* Adventures of a Young Man, King of the Hill. *Television:* Man Who Lived at the Ritz, For Whom Bell Tolls, The Killers, Looking for Miracles. *Publications:* The Dangerous American 1958, The White House (play) 1964, Papa Hemingway: A Personal Memoir 1966, The Hemingway Hero (play) 1967, Treasure 1970, Do You Take This Man? (play) 1970, King of the Hill 1972, Looking for Miracles 1974, Doris Day: Her Own Story 1976, Sophia: Living and Loving 1979, Sweet Prince (play) 1980, The Man Who Lived at the Ritz 1982, Choice People 1984, Hemingway and His World 1988, Welcome to the Club (musical) 1989, Blown Away 1990, Louisiana Purchase 1996, Exactly Like You (musical) 1998, After the Storm 2001, The Day I Fired Alan Ladd and Other World War Two Adventures 2002, Shameless Exploitation in Pursuit of the Common Good 2003, They All Come to Elaine's 2004, Dear Papa, Dear Hotch 2005, The World of Nick Adams (concert with music) 2002, 2003, Paul and Me: 53 Years of Adventure and Misadventures with My Pal Paul Newman 2010; contrib. to magazines. *Honours:* Hon. DHL, Washington University 1992; Distinguished Alumni Award, Washington University Law School 1992. *Address:* 14 Hillandale Road, Westport, CT 06880, USA (home). *Telephone:* (203) 227-9339 (home). *Fax:* (203) 226-5686 (home). *E-mail:* ahotchner@newmansown.com (home).

HOUELLEBECQ, Michel, DipAgr; French novelist, poet and film director; b. 26 Feb. 1958, Réunion; s. of René Thomas and Lucie Ceccaldi; m. 1st 1980 (divorced); one s.; m. 2nd Marie-Pierre Gauthier 1998. *Education:* Institut

Nat. Agronomique Paris-Grignon. *Career:* fmr Admin. Sec., French Nat. Ass.; first works (poetry) published in Nouvelle Revue de Paris 1985. *Films include:* Cristal de souffrance 1978, Déséquilibres 1982, La rivière 2001, La Possibilité d'une île 2008. *Publications include:* Contre le monde, contre la vie 1991, Rester vivant 1991, La poursuite de bonheur (Prix Tristan Tzara) 1992, Extension du domaine à la lutte 1994, Le sens du combat (Prix de Flore) 1996, Interventions, Les Particules élémentaires (Prix Novembre), Renaissance 1999, Lanzarote 2000, Plateforme (Int. Impac Dublin Literary Prize) 2002, La Possibilité d'une île (trans. as The Possibility of An Island) 2005, HP Lovecraft: Against the World, Against Life 2006, Ennemis Publics (with Bernard-Henri Lévy) 2008, La Carte et le Territoire (Prix Goncourt) 2010. *Honours:* Grand Prix Nat. des Lettres Jeune Talent 1998. *Address:* c/o Editions Fayard, 13 rue du Montparnasse, 75006 Paris, France.

HOUGHTON, Eric, Cert in Educ.; British teacher and author; b. 4 Jan. 1930, Shipley, West Yorks.; s. of Alfred William Houghton and Mary Elizabeth Houghton (née Meffen); m. Cecile Wolffe 1954; one s. one d. *Education:* Bradford Grammar School, Sheffield City Coll. of Educ., Univ. of Sheffield. *Career:* mem. Soc. of Authors, Children's Writers' Group. *Publications:* The White Wall 1961, Summer Silver 1963, They Marched with Spartacus 1963, Boy Beyond the Mist 1966, A Giant Can Do Anything 1975, The Mouse and the Magician 1976, The Remarkable Feat of King Caboodle 1978, Steps Out of Time 1979, Gates of Glass 1987, Walter's Wand 1989, The Magic Cheese 1991, The Backwards Watch 1991, Vincent the Invisible 1993, Rosie and the Robbers 1997, The Crooked Apple Tree 1999. *Honours:* American Jr Book Award 1964. *Address:* The Crest, 42 Collier Road, Hastings, East Sussex, TN34 3JR, England (home).

HOUSSI, Majid al-; Tunisian writer, poet and academic; *Professor and Chair of French, Università Ca' Foscari, Venice*; b. 1941. *Education:* Padua Univ. *Career:* moved to Italy 1962; fmr Lecturer in French Inst. des Langues et Littératures Romanes Padua Univ.; apptd Prof. and Chair of French Language, Faculté d'Economie, Ancona Polytechnic Univ. 1990, Dir Inst. des Langues 1990–99, Dir Centre Inter-Deptl des Services Linguistiques; currently Prof. and Chair of French Univ. Ca' Foscari, Venice. *Publications:* Je voudrais ésotériquement te conter 1972, Imagivresse (Prix Univ. di Padova) 1973, Iris-Ifriqiya 1981, Ahméta-O 1981, Pour une histoire du théâtre tunisien 1982, L'Espace scriptural de Tahar Ben Jelloun 1983, Maghreb: panorama letterario 1991, Albert Camus, un effet spatial algérien 1992, Le Verger des poursuites 1992, Albert Camus, le désir de Méditérranée 1993, L'Image du Maghreb dans les lettres françaises du XIXème siècle 1994, Préface et choix des textes à la Vie errante de Guy de Maupassant 1995, Regards sur la littérature tunisienne (co-author) 1997, La Cité méditérranéenne 1997, Pour une nouvelle pédagogie du français 1998, Des voix dans la traversée (Prix Comar 2000) 1999, Salammbô, le désir de perfection 1999, Regards sur la littérature marocaine de langue française (co-author) 2000, Les Arabismes dans la langue française: du moyen âge à nos jours 2001, Le Français pour les étudiants en sciences économiques 2001, Le Regard du coeur 2002; contrib. numerous articles to journals and chapters in books. *Honours:* Grand Officier au Mérite Educatif de la République Tunisienne. *Address:* c/o Università Ca' Foscari, Dorsoduro 3246, 30123 Venice, Italy.

HOUSTON, R. B. (see Rae, Hugh Crauford)

HOVANNISIAN, Richard G., BA, MA, PhD; American academic and writer; b. 9 Nov. 1932, Tulare, CA; m. Vartiter Kotcholosian 1957; four c. *Education:* University of California at Berkeley, Collège Armènien, Beirut, University of California at Los Angeles. *Career:* Lecturer, University of California at Los Angeles 1962–69, Prof. of Armenian and Near Eastern History 1969–, Assoc. Dir, G. E. von Grunebaum Center of Near Eastern Studies 1979–95; Assoc. Prof. of History, St Mary's College, Los Angeles 1965–69; Chair., Modern Armenian History, Armenian Educational Foundation 1987–; Guest Lecturer; Consultant; mem. American Asscn for the Advancement of Slavic Studies, American Historical Asscn, Armenian Acad. of Science, Middle East Studies Asscn, fellow; National Asscn of Armenian Studies, Oral History Asscn, Society for Armenian Studies, founder-pres. 1974–75, 1990–92. *Publications:* Armenia on the Road to Independence 1967, The Republic of Armenia Vol. I 1971, Vol. II 1982, Vols III–IV 1996, The Armenian Holocaust 1980, The Armenian Genocide in Perspective 1986, The Armenian Genocide: History, Politics, Ethics 1992, The Armenian People from Ancient to Modern Times, Vol. I, The Dynastic Periods: From Antiquity to the Fourteenth Century, Vol. II, Foreign Dominion to Statehood: The Fifteenth to Twentieth Century 1997; co-author: Transcaucasia: Nationalism and Social Change 1983, Le Crime de Silence: Le Gènocide des Armèniens 1984, Toward the Understanding and Prevention of Genocide 1984, A Crime of Silence 1985, Genocide: A Critical Bibliographic Review 1988, Embracing the Other: Philosophical, Psychological, and Historical Perspectives on Altruism 1992, Diasporas in World Politics 1993, Genocide and Human Rights 1993, Genocide: Conceptual and Historical Dimensions 1994, The Legacy of History in Russia and the New States of Eurasia 1994; contributions: many professional journals and to periodicals. *Honours:* Humanities Institute Fellow 1972, Guggenheim Fellowship 1974–75, National Endowment for the Humanities Grant 1981–82, California Council for the Humanities Grant 1985–86; numerous awards, citations, and recognitions. *Address:* 101 Groverton Place, Los Angeles, CA 90077, USA (home).

HOVE, Chenjerai, BA; Zimbabwean journalist and writer; b. 9 Feb. 1956, Zvishavane; s. of R. Muza Hove and Jessie Muza Hove; m. Thecla Hove 1978; three s. two d. *Education:* Gweru Teacher's Coll. *Career:* high school teacher 1978–81; Ed. Mambo Press, Gweru 1981; Sr Ed. Zimbabwe Publishing house, Harare 1985; Ed. Cultural Features, Interpress Service 1988; Writer-in-Residence, Univ. of Zimbabwe 1991–94; Visiting Prof. Lewis and Clark Coll., Oregon, USA 1995; full-time writer 1999–; in exile in France 2002–. *Publications:* Swimming in Floods of Tears (co-author) 1983, Red Hills of Home 1985, Bones (Zimbabwe Book Publishers Literary Award 1988, Noma Award for Publishing in Africa 1989) 1988, Shebeen Tales 1989, Shadows 1991, Guardians of the Soil 1996, Ancestors 1996, Shebeen Tales: Messages from Harare 1997, Rainbows in the Dust 1997, Palaver Finish (essays) 2003, Blind Moon 2004, The Keys of Ramb 2004. *Honours:* Democracy and Freedom of Speech in Africa Prize, Berlin 2001. *Address:* c/o Édition Actes Sud, BP 38, 13633 Arles Cedex, France (office).

HOWARD, Clark, (Rich Howard); American writer; b. 1934. *Career:* as Rich Howard: boxing columnist (On the Strip) The Ring magazine 1968–70; mem. MWA. *Publications:* The Arm 1967, A Movement Toward Eden 1969, The Doomsday Squad 1970, The Killings 1973, Last Contract 1973, Summit Kill 1975, Mark the Sparrow 1975, The Hunters 1976, The Last Great Death Stunt 1976, Six Against the Rock 1977, The Wardens 1979, Zebra: The True Account of the 179 Days of Terror in San Francisco 1979, UK edn as The Zebra Killings 1980, American Saturday 1981, Brothers in Blood 1983, Dirt Rich 1986, Hard City 1990, Love's Blood 1993, City Blood 1994, Crowded Lives and Other Stories of Desperation and Danger 2000, Challenge the Widow-Maker and Other Stories of People in Peril 2000. *Honours:* Edgar Allan Poe Award 1980, Ellery Queen Awards 1985, 1986, 1988, 1990, 1999, Derringer Award 2003. *Address:* Box 1527, Palm Springs, CA 92263, USA (home). *Fax:* (760) 327-1920 (office). *E-mail:* rchoward440@cs.com (home). *Website:* www.clarkhoward-author.com.

HOWARD, Deborah Janet, MA, PhD, FBA, FRSE, FSA; British academic and writer; *Professor of Architectural History, University of Cambridge*; b. 26 Feb. 1946, London, England; m. Malcolm S. Longair 1975; one s. one d. *Education:* Newnham Coll., Cambridge, Univ. of London. *Career:* Prof. of Architectural History, Univ. of Cambridge; Fellow, St John's Coll. Cambridge; Fellow, Soc. of Antiquaries of Scotland. *Publications:* Jacopo Sansovino: Architecture and Patronage in Renaissance Venice 1975, The Architectural History of Venice 1980 (revised and enlarged edn 2002), Scottish Architecture from the Reformation to the Restoration 1560–1660 1995, La Scuola Grande della Misericordia di Venezia (with G. Fabbri and S. Mason) 1999, Venice and the East: The Impact on the Islamic World on Venetian Architecture 1100–1500 2000; (with Laura Moretti): Sound and Space in Venetian Architecture: Architecture, Music, Acoustics; contribs to professional journals. *Honours:* Hon. Fellow, Royal Incorporation of Architects of Scotland. *Address:* St John's College, Cambridge, CB2 1TP, England (office). *Telephone:* (1223) 339360 (office). *Fax:* (1223) 332960 (office).

HOWARD, Elizabeth Jane, CBE, FRSL; British writer; b. 26 March 1923, London; d. of David Liddon and Katharine M. Howard; m. 1st Peter M. Scott 1942; one d.; m. 2nd James Douglas-Henry 1959; m. 3rd Kingsley Amis 1965 (divorced 1983, died 1995). *Education:* at home and at London Mask Theatre School. *Career:* BBC TV modelling 1939–46; Sec. Inland Waterways Asscn 1947; then professional writer, including plays for TV; Hon. Artistic Dir Cheltenham Literary Festival 1962; Artistic Co-Dir Salisbury Festival of Arts 1973; mem. Authors Lending and Copyright Soc. *Film scripts:* Getting It Right 1985, The Attachment 1986, The Very Edge. *Television:* Our Glorious Dead, Sight Unseen, Skittles, adaptations of After Julius (three plays for TV), Something in Disguise (six plays) 1982. *Publications:* The Beautiful Visit 1950, The Long View 1956, The Sea Change 1959, After Julius 1965, Something in Disguise 1969, Odd Girl Out 1972, Mr Wrong 1975, A Companion for Lovers (ed.) 1978, Getting It Right (Yorkshire Post Novel of the Year) 1982, Howard and Maschler on Food: Cooking for Occasions (co-author) 1987, The Light Years (The Cazalet Chronicle Vol. One) 1990, Green Shades (gardening anthology) 1991, Marking Time (The Cazalet Chronicle Vol. Two) 1991, Confusion (The Cazalet Chronicle Vol. Three) 1993, Casting Off (The Cazalet Chronicle Vol. Four) 1995, Falling 1999, Slipstream (autobiog.) 2002, Love All 2008; contrib. to The Times, Sunday Times, Telegraph, Encounter, Vogue, Harpers & Queen. *Honours:* John Llewellyn Rhys Memorial Prize 1950, Yorkshire Post Prize 1982. *Literary Agent:* c/o Jonathan Clowes Ltd, 10 Iron Bridge House, Bridge Approach, London, NW1 8BD, England. *Telephone:* (20) 7722-7674. *Fax:* (871) 528-3647. *E-mail:* admin@jonathanclowes.co.uk.

HOWARD, Ellen, BA; American writer; b. 8 May 1943, New Bern, NC; m. Charles Howard Jr 1975, four d. *Education:* University of Oregon, Portland State University. *Career:* mem. Authors' Guild; Society of Children's Book Writers and Illustrators. *Publications:* Circle of Giving, 1984; When Daylight Comes, 1985; Gillyflower, 1986; Edith Herself, 1987; Her Own Song, 1988; Sister, 1990; The Chickenhouse House, 1991; The Cellar, 1992; The Tower Room, 1993; The Big Seed, 1993; Murphy and Kate, 1995; The Log Cabin Quilt, 1996; A Different Kind of Courage, 1996. *Honours:* Golden Kite Honor Book, 1984; Christopher Award, 1997.

HOWARD, Lynette Desley (see Stevens, Lynsey)

HOWARD, Maureen, BA; American lecturer and writer; *Professor of Writing, Columbia University*; b. 28 June 1930, Bridgeport, CT; m. 1st Daniel F. Howard 1954 (divorced 1967); one d.; m. 2nd David J. Gordon 1968 (divorced); m. 3rd Mark Probst 1981. *Education:* Smith Coll. *Career:* Lecturer, New

School for Social Research, New York 1967–68, 1970–71, 1974–, Univ. of California at Santa Barbara 1968–69, Amherst Coll., Brooklyn Coll., CUNY; Assoc. Prof. then Prof. of Writing, Columbia Univ. 1993–. *Publications:* fiction: Not a Word About Nightingales 1961, Bridgeport Bus 1966, Before My Time 1975, Grace Abounding 1982, Expensive Habits 1986, Natural History 1992, A Lover's Almanac 1998, Big as Life: Three Tales for Spring 2001, The Silver Screen 2004, The Rags of Time 2009; non-fiction: Facts of Life (autobiog.) 1978; editor: Seven American Women Writers of the Twentieth Century 1977, Contemporary American Essays 1984. *Honours:* Guggenheim Fellowship 1967–68, Radcliffe Inst. Fellow 1967–68, Nat. Book Critics Circle Award 1980, Ingram Merrill Foundation Fellow 1988, New York Public Library Literary Lion 1993. *Address:* Writing Department, School of the Arts, Columbia University, 415 Dodge Hall, 2690 Broadway, New York, NY 10027, USA (office). *Telephone:* (212) 854-4391 (office). *E-mail:* writing@columbia.edu (office). *Website:* www.columbia.edu (office).

HOWARD, Sir Michael Eliot, Kt, CH, CBE, MC, MA, DLitt, FBA, FRHistS; British historian; *Regius Professor Emeritus of Modern History, University of Oxford*; b. 29 Nov. 1922, London; s. of the late Geoffrey Eliot Howard and of Edith Howard (née Edinger). *Education:* Wellington Coll., Christ Church, Oxford. *Career:* served in army 1942–45; Asst Lecturer, Lecturer in History, King's Coll., London 1947–53; Lecturer, Reader in War Studies, Univ. of London 1953–63; Prof. of War Studies, Univ. of London 1963–68; Fellow in Higher Defence Studies, All Souls Coll., Oxford 1968–77; Chichele Prof. of the History of War, Univ. of Oxford 1977–80; Regius Prof. of Modern History, Univ. of Oxford 1980–89, Prof. Emer. 1989–; Robert A. Lovett Prof. of Mil. and Naval History, Yale Univ. 1989–93; Leverhulme Lecturer 1996; Lee Kuan Yew Distinguished Visitor, Nat. Univ. of Singapore 1996; Founder and Pres. Emer. Int. Inst. for Strategic Studies; mem. The Literary Soc. (Pres. –2004); Foreign mem. American Acad. of Arts and Sciences. *Publications:* The Coldstream Guards 1920–1946 (with John Sparrow) 1951, Disengagement in Europe 1958, Wellingtonian Studies 1959, The Franco-German War 1961, The Theory and Practice of War 1965, The Mediterranean Strategy in the Second World War 1967, Studies in War and Peace 1970, Grand Strategy, Vol. IV (in UK History of Second World War) 1972, The Continental Commitment 1973, War in European History 1976, Clausewitz on War (trans. with Peter Paret) 1976, War and the Liberal Conscience 1978, Restraints on War (ed.) 1979, The Causes of Wars 1983, Clausewitz 1983, Strategic Deception: British Intelligence in the Second World War 1990, The Lessons of History (essays) 1991, The Oxford History of the Twentieth Century (co-ed. with W. R. Louis) 1998, The Invention of Peace 2000, The First World War 2001, Captain Professor: A Life in War and Peace 2006, Liberation or Catastrophe?: Reflections on the History of the Twentieth Century 2007. *Honours:* Hon. Fellow, Oriel Coll., Oxford 1990; Hon. Student Christ Church 1990; Order of Merit; Hon. LittD (Leeds) 1979; Hon. DLitt (London) 1988; Duff Cooper Memorial Prize 1961, Wolfson Foundation History Award 1972, NATO Atlantic Award 1989, Chesney Memorial Gold Medal, Royal United Services Inst., Samule Eliot Morrison Prize, Soc. for Mil. History 1992, Paul Nitze Award, Center for Naval Analysis 1994, Political Book Prize, Friedrich Ebert Stiftung 2002. *Address:* The Old Farm, Eastbury, Hungerford, Berks., RG17 7JN, England (home). *Telephone:* (1488) 71387 (home). *Fax:* (1488) 71387 (home).

HOWARD, Philip Nicholas Charles, MA, FRSL; British editor, journalist and writer; *Leader Writer and Columnist, The Times*; b. 2 Nov. 1933, London, England; m. Myrtle Janet Mary Houldsworth 1959; two s. one d. *Education:* Trinity College, Oxford. *Career:* Staff, Glasgow Herald, 1959–64; Staff, 1964–, Literary Ed., 1978–92, Leader Writer and Columnist, 1992–, The Times; London Ed., Verbatim, 1977–; mem. Classical Asscn, pres., 2002; Friends of Classics, founder-patron; Horatian Society; Literary Society; Society of Bookmen, Garrick Club. *Publications:* The Black Watch, 1968; The Royal Palaces, 1970; London's River, 1975; New Words for Old, 1977; The British Monarchy, 1977; Weasel Words, 1978; Words Fail Me, 1980; A Word in Your Ear, 1983; The State of the Language: English Observed, 1984; The Times Bicentenary Stamp Book (co-author), 1985; We Thundered Out: 200 Years of the Times, 1785–1985, 1985; Winged Words, 1988; Word-Watching, 1988; London: The Evolution of a Great City (co-author), 1989; A Word in Time, 1990; The Times Bedside Book (ed.), 1991; Reading a Poem, 1992, The British Library, a Treasure House of Knowledge 2008. *Address:* The Times, 3 Thomas More Square, London E98 1XY (office); Flat 1, 47 Ladbroke Grove, London W11 3AR, England (home). *Telephone:* (20) 7782-7175 (office); (20) 7727-1077 (home). *Fax:* (20) 7782-5229 (home). *E-mail:* philip.howard@thetimes.co.uk.

HOWARD, Richard Joseph, BA, MA; American poet, critic, editor and translator; *Professor of Writing, Columbia University*; b. 13 Oct. 1929, Cleveland, OH. *Education:* Columbia Univ., Sorbonne, Univ. of Paris. *Career:* lexicographer, World Publishing Co. 1954–58; Poetry Ed., New American Review, New Republic, Paris Review, Shenandoah, Western Humanities Review; Luce Visiting Scholar, Whitney Humanities Center, Yale Univ. 1983; Ropes Prof. of Comparative Literature, Univ. of Cincinnati; Univ. Prof. of English, Univ. of Houston 1987–97; Poet Laureate for New York State 1994–97; Prof. of Writing, School of the Arts, Columbia Univ. 1997–; Pres., PEN American Center 1979–80; mem. American Acad. of Arts and Letters 1983–. *Publications:* poetry: Quantities 1962, The Damages 1967, Untitled Subjects (Pulitzer Prize in Poetry 1970) 1969, Findings 1971, Two-Part Inventions 1974, Fellow Feelings 1976, Misgivings 1979, Lining Up 1984, Quantities/Damages 1984, No Traveller 1989, Like Most Revelations: New Poems 1994, Trappings 1999, Talking Cures 2002, Inner Voices: Selected Poems, 1963–2003 2004, Without Saying 2008; criticism: Alone with America: Essays on the Art of Poetry in the United States Since 1950 1969, Passengers Must Not Ride on Fenders 1974, Paper Trail: Selected Prose, 1965–2003 2004; editor: Preferences: Fifty-One American Poets Choose Poems from Their Own Work and from the Past 1974, The War in Algeria 1975, The Silent Treatment 2006; translator: over 150 works, from French; contributions: magazines and journals. *Honours:* Chevalier, Ordre Nationale du Mérite, France 1982; Guggenheim Fellowship 1966–67, Harriet Monroe Memorial Prize 1969, Levinson Prize 1973, Cleveland Arts Prize 1974, American Acad. and Institute of Arts and Letters Medal for Poetry 1980, American Book Award for Trans. 1983, PEN American Center Medal for Trans. 1986, France-American Foundation Award for Trans. 1987, National Endowment for the Arts Fellowship 1987, MacArthur Fellowship 1996. *Address:* Writing Division, School of the Arts, Columbia University, 415 Dodge Hall, 2690 Broadway, New York, NY 10027, USA (office). *Telephone:* (212) 854-4391 (office). *E-mail:* writing@columbia.edu (office). *Website:* www.app.cc.columbia.edu (office).

HOWARD, Roger, MA; British dramatist, poet, author and lecturer; b. 19 June 1938, Warwick, England; m. Anne Mary Zemaitis 1960; one s. *Education:* RADA, London, Univs of Bristol and Essex. *Career:* teacher, Nankai Univ., Tientsin, People's Repub. of China 1965–67; Lecturer, Univ. of Beijing 1972–74; Fellow in Creative Writing, Univ. of York 1976–78; Writing Fellow, Univ. of East Anglia 1979; Founder-Dir Theatre Underground, Univ. of Essex 1979–2003, Lecturer in Literature 1979–93, Ed. New Plays series 1980–90, Sr Lecturer in Literature 1993–2003. *Publications:* A Phantastic Satire (novel) 1960, From the Life of a Patient (novel) 1961, To the People (poems) 1966, Praise Songs (poems) 1966, The Technique of the Struggle Meeting 1968, The Use of Wall Newspapers 1968, New Short Plays I 1968, Fin's Doubts 1968, Episodes from the Fighting in the East 1971, The Hooligan's Handbook 1971, Slaughter Night and Other Plays 1971, Method for Revolutionary Writing 1972, Culture and Agitation: Theatre Documents (ed.) 1972, Contemporary Chinese Theatre 1977, Mao Tse-tung and the Chinese People 1978, The Society of Poets 1979, A Break in Berlin 1980, The Siege 1981, Partisans 1983, Ancient Rivers 1984, The Speechifier 1984, Contradictory Theatres 1985, Senile Poems 1988, The Tragedy of Mao and Other Plays 1989, Britannia and Other Plays 1990, Selected Poems 1966–96 1997, Three War Plays 2004; contrib. to anthologies, newspapers and journals. *Address:* c/o Theatre Underground, Department of Literature, University of Essex, Wivenhoe Park, Colchester, Essex, CO4 3SQ, England (office).

HOWATCH, Susan, LLB; British writer; b. 14 July 1940, Leatherhead, Surrey; d. of G. S. Sturt and Ann Sturt; m. Joseph Howatch 1964 (separated 1975); one d. *Education:* Sutton High School, King's Coll., London. *Career:* emigrated to USA 1964, lived in Ireland 1976–80, returned to UK 1980; first book published 1965; Fellow, King's Coll. London 1999–; f. Starbridge Lectureship in Theology and Natural Science Univ. of Cambridge 1992. *Publications:* novels: The Dark Shore 1965, The Waiting Sands 1966, Call in the Night 1967, The Shrouded Walls 1968, April's Grave 1969, The Devil on Lammas Night 1970, Penmarric 1971, Cashelmara 1974, The Rich are Different 1977, Sins of the Fathers 1980, The Wheel of Fortune 1984, Glittering Images 1987, Glamorous Powers 1988, Ultimate Prizes 1989, Scandalous Risks 1991, Mystical Paths 1992, Absolute Truths 1994, A Question of Integrity (US title: The Wonder Worker) 1997, The High Flyer 1999, The Heartbreaker 2003. *Honours:* Winifred Mary Stanford Memorial Prize 1991. *Literary Agent:* Aitken Alexander Associates Ltd, 18–21 Cavaye Place, London, SW10 9PT, England. *Telephone:* (20) 7373-8672. *Fax:* (20) 7373-6002. *E-mail:* reception@aitkenalexander.co.uk. *Website:* www.aitkenalexander.co.uk.

HOWE, Daniel W., AB, MA, PhD, FRHistS; American historian, academic and writer; *Professor Emeritus of History, University of California, Los Angeles*; b. 10 Jan. 1937, Ogden, Utah; m. Sandra Shumway; two s. one d. *Education:* Harvard Univ., Univ. of California, Berkeley, Univ. of Oxford, UK. *Career:* taught at Yale Univ. 1966–73; Assoc. Prof. of History, UCLA 1973–77, Prof. 1977–92, Chair. Dept of History 1983–87, currently Prof. Emer.; Rhodes Prof. of History, Univ. of Oxford 1992–2002; Emer. Fellow, St Catherine's Coll. Oxford; fmr Dir Oxford Inst. for American Studies; Pres. Soc. for Historians of the Early American Repub. 2000–01; mem. Editorial Bd, Religion and American Culture, Journal of the Early Republic, American Nineteenth Century History, Modern Intellectual History; mem. American Acad. of Arts and Sciences. *Publications:* The Unitarian Conscience: Harvard Moral Philosophy, 1805–1861 (American Soc. of Church History's Brewer Prize) 1970, Sourcebooks in American Social Thought (six vols) (co-ed.), The American Whigs: An Anthology 1973, Victorian America 1976, The Political Culture of the American Whigs 1980, American History in an Atlantic Context 1993, Making the American Self: Jonathan Edwards to Abraham Lincoln 1997, What Hath God Wrought: The United States, 1815–1848 (The Oxford History of the United States) (Pulitzer Prize for History 2008) 2007; numerous chapters and articles in books and journals. *Address:* Department of History, University of California, Los Angeles, 6265 Bunche Hall, Box 951473, Los Angeles, CA 90095-1473, USA (office). *Telephone:* (818) 907-0135 (office). *Fax:* (310) 907-0135 (office). *E-mail:* howe@history.ucla.edu (office). *Website:* www.history.ucla.edu (office).

HOWE, Fanny; American academic, author, poet and dramatist; *Professor Emerita of Writing and American Literature, University of California, San Diego*; b. 15 Oct. 1940, Buffalo, NY; one s. two d. *Education:* Stanford

University. *Career:* Lecturer, Tufts University 1968–71, Emerson College 1974, Columbia University Extension and School of the Arts 1975–78, Yale University 1976, Harvard University Extension 1977, MIT 1978–87; Prof. of Writing and American Literature, University of California at San Diego 1987–, now Emer.; Assoc. Dir, Study Center, University College London 1993–95; Distinguished Visiting Writer-in-Residence, Mills College 1996–97. *Publications:* fiction: Forty Whacks 1969, First Marriage 1975, Bronte Wilde 1976, Holy Smoke 1979, The White Slave 1980, In the Middle of Nowhere 1984, Taking Care 1985, The Lives of a Spirit 1986, The Deep North 1988, Famous Questions 1989, Saving History 1992, Nod 1998, The Lives of a Spirit/Glasstown: Where Something Got Broken 2005; young adult fiction: The Blue Hills 1981, Yeah, But 1982, Radio City 1983, The Race of the Radical 1985; poetry: Eggs 1980, The Amerindian Coastline Poem 1976, Poem from a Single Pallet 1980, Alsace Lorraine 1982, For Erato 1984, Introduction to the World 1985, Robeson Street 1985, The Vineyard 1988, The Quietist 1992, The End 1992, O'Clock 1995, One Crossed Out 1997, Q 1998, Forged 1999, Selected Poems 2000, On the Ground 2004, The Lyrics 2007; essays: The Wedding Dress: Meditations on Word and Life 2003, The Winter Sun: Notes from a Vacation 2009; contributions: many anthologies, reviews, quarterlies, journals, and magazines. *Honours:* MacDowell Colony Fellowships 1965, 1990, National Endowment for the Arts Fellowships in Fiction 1969, and in Poetry 1991, Bunting Institute Fellowship 1974, St Botolph Award for Fiction 1976, Writer's Choice Award for Fiction 1984, Village Voice Award for Fiction 1988, California Council on the Arts Award for Poetry 1993, Lenore Marshall Poetry Prize, Acad. of American Poets 2001, Ruth Lilly Poetry Prize, Poetry Foundation 2009. *Address:* c/o Department of Literature, University of California, 9500 Gilman Drive, Room 0410, La Jolla, CA 92093-0410, USA (office). *E-mail:* litug@ucsd.edu (office). *Website:* literature.ucsd.edu (office).

HOWE, Susan, BFA; American poet and academic; b. 10 June 1937. *Education:* Museum of Fine Arts, Boston. *Career:* Butler Fellow in English, 1988, Prof. of English, 1991–, SUNY at Buffalo; Visiting Scholar and Prof. of English, Temple University, Philadelphia, 1990, 1991; Visiting Poet and Leo Block Prof., University of Denver, 1993–94; Visiting Brittingham Scholar, University of Wisconsin at Madison, 1994; Visiting Poet, University of Arizona, 1994; Visiting Prof., Stanford University, 1998; mem. Acad. of American Poets, board of chancellors, 2000–; American Acad. of Arts and Sciences. *Publications:* Poetry: Hinge Picture, 1974; The Western Borders, 1976; Secret History of the Dividing Line, 1978; Cabbage Gardens, 1979; The Liberties, 1980; Pythagorean Silence, 1982; Defenestration of Prague, 1983; Articulation of Sound Forms in Time, 1987; A Bibliography of the King's Book, or Eikon Basilike, 1989; The Europe of Trusts: Selected Poems, 1990; Singularities, 1990; The Nonconformist's Memorial, 1993; Frame Structures: Early Poems 1974–1979, 1996; Pierce-Arrow, 1999; Bad-Hangings, 2000. Other: My Emily Dickinson, 1985; Incloser, 1990; The Birthmark: Unsettling the Wilderness in American Literary History, 1993. *Honours:* Before Columbus Foundation American Book Awards, 1980, 1986; New York State Council of the Arts Residency, 1986; Pushcart Prize, 1987; New York City Fund for Poetry Grant, 1988; Roy Harvey Pearce Award, 1996; Guggenheim Fellowship, 1996–97; Distinguished Fellow, Stanford Humanities Centre, 1998; Hon. degrees, National Univ. of Ireland, 2000, St Joseph Coll., Hartford, CT, 2003; State of New York Distinguished Prof., 2002.

HOWE, Tina, BA; American playwright; b. 1937, New York; d. of Quincy and Mary (née Post) Howe; m. Norman Levy 1961; one s. one d. *Education:* Sarah Lawrence Coll. (Bronxville, NY) and Columbia and Chicago Teacher Training Colls. *Career:* Adjunct Prof., Goldberg Dept of Dramatic Writing, New York Univ. 1983–; Visiting Prof., Hunter Coll. Dept of Theatre 1990–; mem. Council Dramatists' Guild; Guggenheim Fellow 1990. Plays include: Closing Time 1959, The Nest 1969, Birth and After Birth 1973, Museum 1976, The Art of Dining 1979, Appearances (unpublished) 1982, Painting Churches 1983, Coastal Disturbances 1986, Approaching Zanzibar 1989, One Shoe Off 1989, Swimming 1991, Teeth 1991, Birth and After Birth 1995, Pride's Crossing (New York Drama Critics Circle Award for Best Play 1998) 1997, Divine Fallacy 1999, Rembrandt's Gift 2002, Such Small Hands 2003. *Honours:* Dr hc (Bowdoin Coll) 1988; Obie for Distinguished Playwriting 1983; Outer Critics Circle Award 1983; Tony nomination for Best Play 1987; American Acad. of Arts and Letters Award in Literature 1993. *Address:* Hunter College Department of Theatre, North Building 522, New York, NY 10021; Goldberg Department of Dramatic Writing, New York University, 721 Broadway, 7th Floor, New York, NY 10003; c/o ICM, 825 8th Avenue, New York, NY 10019, USA. *Telephone:* (212) 998-1940 (NYU); (212) 556-5600 (ICM). *E-mail:* theater@icmtalent.com. *Website:* www.hunter.cuny.edu/theatre; www.hunter.cuny.edu/theatre/grad.shtml.

HOWELL, Anthony; British poet, writer and editor; b. 20 April 1945, London, England. *Education:* Leighton Park School, Royal Ballet School, London. *Career:* Lecturer, Grenoble Univ., Cardiff School of Art; Ed., Softly, Loudly Books, London, Grey Suit. *Publications:* poetry: Inside the Castle 1969, Femina Deserta 1971, Oslo: A Tantric Ode 1975, The Mekon 1976, Notions of a Mirror: Poems Previously Uncollected 1964–82 1983, Winter's Not Gone 1984, Why I May Never See the Walls of China 1986, Howell's Law 1990, Near Cavalry: Selected Poems of Nick Lafitte (ed.) 1992, Dancers in Daylight 2003; fiction: In the Company of Others 1986, First Time in Japan 1995. *Honours:* Welsh Arts Council Bursary 1989. *E-mail:* anthony@ther00m.wanadoo.co.uk. *Website:* www.anthonyhowell.org.

HOWELLS, Coral Ann, MA, PhD; British/Australian academic and writer; *Professor of English and Canadian Literature, University of Reading;* b. 22 Oct. 1939, Maryborough, Qld, Australia; m. Robin Jonathan Howells 1963; two d. *Education:* Univ. of Queensland and Univ. of London. *Career:* Prof. of English and Canadian Literature, Univ. of Reading 1996–; mem. British Asscn for Canadian Studies, Pres. 1992–94; Assoc. Ed. Int. Journal for Canadian Studies, 1998–; mem. Council, Foundation for Canadian Studies in the UK 1998–, Canadian Memorial Scholarship Academic Selection Cttee 1999–. *Publications:* Love, Mystery and Misery: Feeling in Gothic Fiction 1978, Private and Fictional Words: Canadian Women Novelists of the 1970s and 80s 1987, Jean Rhys 1991, Margaret Atwood 1996, Alice Munro 1998, Contemporary Canadian Women's Fiction: Refiguring Identities 2003, Cambridge Companion to Margaret Atwood (ed.) 2006; contribs to many academic journals. *Honours:* Margaret Atwood Soc. Best Book Award 1997. *Address:* School of English and American Literature, University of Reading, Whiteknights, Reading, RG6 6AA, Berks., England (office). *Telephone:* (118) 378-7001 (office). *Fax:* (118) 378-6561 (office). *E-mail:* c.a.howells@reading.ac.uk (office). *Website:* www.rdg.ac.uk/english (office).

HOYLAND, Michael David; British academic (retd), author and poet; b. 1 April 1925, Nagpur, India; m. Marette Nicol Fraser 1948; two s. two d. *Career:* school teacher 1951–63; Lecturer, Kesteven College of Education 1963–65, Sr Lecturer in Art 1963–80; mem. Stamford Writers Group; PEN; Welland Valley Art Society; East Anglian Potters Asscn. *Publications:* Introduction Three, 1967; Art for Children, 1970; Variations: An Integrated Approach to Art, 1975; A Love Affair with War, 1981; The Bright Way In, 1984; Dominus-Domina (play); Poems in journals and a collection; 6 Short Stories. Contributions: Reviewing for Ore; Jade.

HOYLE, Peter, BA; British writer and fmr librarian; b. 25 Oct. 1939, Accrington, Lancs.; m. Barbara Croop; one s. one d. *Education:* Univ. of Liverpool. *Radio:* stories broadcast on BBC Radio 3 and Radio 4's Morning Story. *Publications:* The Man in the Iron Mask 1984, Brantwood 1986, Missing Man 2002; contrib. to Stand, PN Review, New Stories 1, New Statesman. *Honours:* North West Arts Bursary 1984. *Address:* 19 Hexham Avenue, Bolton, Lancs., BL1 5PP, England (home). *Telephone:* (1204) 847147 (home).

HOYLE, Trevor; British writer; b. Rochdale, England; m. 1962; one s. one d. *Career:* mem. Soc. of Authors. *Radio:* drama: GIGO 1990, Conflagration 1991, Randle's Scandals 1992, Haunted Hospital 2006. *Television:* Whatever Happened to the Heroes (Granada). *Publications:* The Relatively Constant Copywriters 1972, The Adulterer 1972, Rule of Night 1975, Rock Fix 1977, Seeking the Mythical Future 1977, Through the Eye of Time 1977, The Gods Look Down 1978, The Man Who Travelled on Motorways 1979, Earth Cult 1979, The Stigma 1980, Bullet Train 1980, The Last Gasp 1983, Vail 1984, K.I.D.S. 1988, Blind Needle 1994, Mirrorman 1999, Rule of Night (reissue) 2003, (Italian edition) 2006. Other: several film and television adaptations and radio dramas; contribs to periodicals, Oxford Good Fiction Guide 2001. *Honours:* Radio Times Drama Award 1991, British Winner, Transatlantic Review Story Competition. *Literary Agent:* Tanja Howarth Literary Agency, 19 New Row, London, WC2N 4LA, England.

HUANG, Yongyu; Chinese artist and poet; b. 1924, Fenghuang Co., Hunan Prov. *Career:* best known for his satirical picture Maotouying (Owl) of an owl with its left eye closed, produced during the 'Gang of Four' era; Vice-Chair. Chinese Artists' Asscn 1985–; mem. Nationalities Cttee 7th CPPCC. *Works include:* Maotouying (Owl), Ahshima, Spring Tide, Collected Woodcarvings, World Peace (donated to UN), China = MC2 2008. *Publications:* A Can of Worms, An Old Man who is Older than Me 2003. *Honours:* Olympic Art Prize 2008; Commendatore (Italy) 1986. *Address:* c/o Central Academy of Fine Arts, Beijing, People's Republic of China (office).

HUCKER, Hazel Zoë, JP, BSc (Econ); British economics teacher and novelist; b. 7 Aug. 1937, London; m. Michael Hucker 1961, two s. (one deceased) one d. *Education:* LSE. *Career:* mem. Soc. of Authors. *Publications:* The Aftermath of Oliver 1993, La Herencia del Recuerdo 1994, A Dangerous Happiness 1994, Cousin Susannah 1995, Trials of Friendship 1996, The Real Claudia Charles 1998, Changing Status 2000. *Literary Agent:* MBA Literary Agents Ltd, 62 Grafton Way, London, W1T 5DW, England. *Address:* 11 Waterhouse Close, Twyford, Winchester, Hampshire SO21 1PN (home). *Telephone:* (1962) 712796 (home).

HUDDLE, David, BA, MA, MFA; academic, writer and poet; *Visiting Distinguished Professor of Creative Writing, Hollins University;* b. 11 July 1942, Ivanhoe, Va; m. Lindsey M. Huddle; two d. *Education:* Univ. of Virginia, Hollins Coll., Columbia Univ. *Career:* Faculty, Warren Wilson Coll. 1981–85; Prof. of English, Univ. of Vermont 1982–2009, Prof. Emer. 2009–; currently Visiting Distinguished Prof. of Creative Writing, Hollins Univ.; Ed. New England Review 1993–94. *Publications:* A Dream With No Stump Roots In It 1975, Paper Boy 1979, Only the Little Bone 1986, Stopping by Home 1988, The High Spirits 1992, The Writing Habit: Essays on Writing 1992, The Nature of Yearning 1992, Intimates 1993, Tenorman 1995, Summer Lake: New and Selected Poems 1999, The Story of a Million Years 1999, Not: A Trio – A Novella and Two Stories 2000, La Tour Dreams of the Wolf Girl 2002, Grayscale (poems) 2004, Glory River 2008, Nothing Can Make Me Do This (novel) 2011; contribs to Esquire, Harper's, The New Yorker, New York Times Book Review, Kentucky Poetry Review, Texas Quarterly, Poetry, Shenandoah, American Poetry Review. *Honours:* Hon. DH (Shenandoah Coll.) 1989;

Bread Loaf School of English Commencement Speaker 1989. *Literary Agent:* c/o 34 North Williams Street, Burlington, VT 05401, USA. *Telephone:* (802) 864-6111 (office). *E-mail:* david.huddle@uvm.edu (office); dhuddle@hollins.edu (office).

HUDES, Quiara Alegría, BA, MFA; American playwright and teacher; m. Ray Beauchamp; one d. *Education:* Yale Univ., Brown Univ. *Career:* raised in W Philadelphia; resident writer, New Dramatists; Visiting Writer, Theater Dept, Wesleyan Univ., Middletown, Conn., teacher of advanced intensive course in playwriting 2011–12; mem. Bd Philadelphia Young Playwrights. *Plays include:* Yemaya's Belly (Clauder Prize 2003, Paula Vogel Award in Playwriting 2003, Kennedy Center/ACTF Latina Playwriting Award 2003), Elliot, a Soldier's Fugue 2007, In the Heights (book for musical) (Tony Award for Best Musical 2008, Lucille Lortel Award 2008, Outer Critics Circle Award for Best Musical 2008) 2008, 26 Miles 2009, Barrio Grrrl! 2009, Water by the Spoonful (Pulitzer Prize for Drama 2012) 2011. *Publications include:* Yemaya's Belly 2008, Welcome to My Neighborhood! A Barrio ABC (co-author) 2010, 26 Miles 2011, Water by the Spoonful 2012, Elliot, A Soldier's Fugue 2012. *Honours:* United States Artists Fellow 2010, Roe Green Award 2012. *Literary Agent:* c/o John Buzzetti, William Morris Endeavor Entertainment, 1325 Avenue of the Americas, New York, NY 10019, USA. *Telephone:* (212) 903-1166. *E-mail:* jbuzzetti@wmeentertainment.com. *Website:* www.wmeentertainment.com.

HUDGINS, Andrew Leon, Jr, BA, MA, MFA; American academic, poet and writer; *Humanities Distinguished Professor of English, Ohio State University;* b. 22 April 1951, Killeen, TX; m. Erin McGraw. *Education:* Huntingdon College, Univ. of Alabama, Syracuse Univ., Univ. of Iowa. *Career:* Adjunct Instructor, Auburn Univ. 1978–81; Teaching-Writing Fellow, Univ. of Iowa 1981–83; Lecturer, Baylor Univ. 1984–85; Prof. of English, Univ. of Cincinnati 1985–92; Prof. of English, Ohio State Univ. 1992–, currently Humanities Distinguished Prof. of English; mem. Texas Institute of Letters. *Publications:* poetry: Saints and Strangers 1985, After the Lost War: A Narrative 1988, The Never-Ending: New Poems 1991, The Glass Hammer: A Southern Childhood 1994, Babylon in a Jar 1998, Ecstatic in the Poison 2003, Shut Up, You're Fine: Poems for Very, Very Bad Children 2009, American Rendering: New and Selected Poems 2010; non-fiction: The Glass Anvil (essays) 1997; contributions: numerous journals. *Honours:* Wallace Stegner Fellow in Poetry, Stanford Univ. 1983–84, Yaddo Fellowships 1983, 1985, 1987, 1988, 1991, Acad. of American Poets Award 1984, MacDowell Colony Fellowship 1986, National Endowment for the Arts Fellowships 1986, 1992, Ingram Merrill Foundation Grant 1987, Poets' Prize 1988, Witter Bynner Award, American Acad. and Institute of Arts and Letters 1988, Alfred Hodder Fellow, Princeton Univ. 1989–90, Poetry Award, Texas Institute of Letters 1991, Ohioana Poetry Award 1997. *Address:* Department of English, Ohio State University, 164 Denney Hall, 164 West 17th Avenue, Columbus, OH 43210, USA (office). *Telephone:* (614) 247-6103 (office). *E-mail:* hudgins.6@osu.edu (office). *Website:* english.osu.edu (office).

HUDSON, Christopher; British writer; b. 29 Sept. 1946, England; m. Kirsty McLeod 1978; one s. *Education:* Jesus Coll., Cambridge. *Career:* ed., Faber and Faber 1968; Literary Ed. The Spectator 1971, The Standard 1981; Editorial Page Ed. The Daily Telegraph 1992, 1994. *Publications:* Overlord 1975, The Final Act 1980, Insider Out 1982, The Killing Fields 1984, Colombo Heat 1986, Playing in the Sand 1989, Spring Street Summer 1993. *Address:* Domons, Higham Lane, Northiam, Rye, East Sussex, TN31 6JT, England (home).

HUDSON, Helen (see Lane, Helen)

HUELLE, Paweł; Polish writer and journalist; b. 10 Sept. 1957, Gdańsk. *Education:* Gdańsk Univ. *Career:* Dir Polish Television Centre, Gdańsk 1994–99; columnist for Gazety Wyborczej; teacher of literature, philosophy and history. *Publications:* Weiser Dawidek (trans. as Who was David Weiser?) 1987, Opowiadania na czas przeprowadzki (trans. as Stories for a Time of Relocation) 1991, Wiersze (poems) 1994, Pierwsza miłość i inne opowiadania (trans. as First Love and Other Stories) 1996, Inne Historie (Different Stories) 1999, Mercedes-Benz. Z listów do Hrabala (trans. as Mercedes Benz) 2001, Byłem samotny i szczęśliwy 2002, Hans Castorp w Sopocie. Zaginiony rozdział z 'Czarodziejskiej Góry' (trans. as Castorp) 2004, Ostatnia Wieczerza (trans. as The Last Supper) 2007. *Address:* c/o Gazety Wyborczej, ul. Czerska 8/10, 00-732 Warsaw, Poland.

HUFANA, Alejandrino, AB, MA, MS; Philippine editor, writer, poet and dramatist; b. 22 Oct. 1926, San Fernando. *Education:* University of the Philippines, University of California at Berkeley, Columbia University. *Career:* Co-Founding Ed., Signatures Magazine, 1955, Comment Magazine, 1956–67; Co-Founding Ed., 1967–68, Literary Ed., 1987–, Heritage Magazine; Dir, Cultural Center of the Philippines Library, 1970–85; Prof., 1975, Dir, Creative Writing Center, 1981–85, University of the Philippines. *Publications:* 13 Kalisud, 1955; Man in the Moon, 1956; Sickle Season, 1948–58, 1959; Poro Point, 1955–60, 1961; Curtain Raisers: First Five Plays, 1964; A Philippine Cultural Miscellany, 1970; The Wife of Lot and Other New Poems, 1971; Notes on Poetry, 1973; Sieg Heil, 1975; Philippine Writing, 1977; Shining On, 1985; Dumanon, 1994; No Facetious Claim: Notes on Writers and Writing, 1995; Enuegs, 1999; Survivor, 1999; Kaputt, 1999. *Address:* c/o Heritage Magazine, 20218 Tajauta Avenue, Carson, CA 90746, USA.

HUGGAN, (Jean) Isabel, BA; Canadian writer; b. 21 Sept. 1943, Kitchener, Ont.; d. of Cecil Ronald Howey and Catherine Innes Howey; m. Bob Huggan 1970; one d. *Education:* Univ. of Western Ontario. *Career:* Editorial Asst, Macmillan Publishing Co. 1965–66; teacher 1968–72; reporter, photographer and columnist, The Belleville Intelligencer 1973–76; teacher of creative writing, Univ. of Ottawa 1985–87. *Publications include:* First Impressions 1980, Best Canadian Stories (contrib) 1983, The Elizabeth Stories 1984, 1987, Stories by Canadian Women (Vol. II) 1987, New American Short Stories 1988, Soho Square 1990, The Time of Your Life (contrib) 1992, You Never Know 1993, Unbecoming Daughters of the Empire 1993, Gates of Paradise II (contrib) 1994, Serpent à Plumes 1994, The Seasons of Women 1996, When We Were Young 1997, Altre Terre 1997, Penguin Anthology of Stories by Canadian Women 1999, Dropped Threads 2000, Belonging (Charles Taylor Prize for Political Non-Fiction) 2004. *Honours:* First Prize for film script Nat. Film Bd contest for women writers 1977, Joe Savago Award—New Voice of 1987 (Quality Paperback Book Club) 1987, Alan Swallow Literary Award 1987. *Address:* c/o Vintage Canada, Random House of Canada Ltd, One Toronto Street, Unit 300, Toronto, ON M5C 2V6, Canada (office). *Website:* www.randomhouse.ca (office).

HUGHES, Frieda, BA (Hons); British/American poet, artist and children's author; b. 1 April 1960, England; d. of Ted Hughes and Sylvia Plath. *Education:* St Martin's School of Art, London. *Career:* worked for HM Collector of Taxes, Ministry of Defence, Galleon Publications; self-employed writer and artist 1988–; Poetry Columnist, The Times 2006–08. *Solo exhibitions:* Anna Mei Chadwick Gallery, Fulham, London 1993, 1995, Provenance Gallery, Sydney, Australia 1995, exhbn sponsored by Lloyds Bank plc 1996, The Gallery, 27 Cork Street, London 1997, 2010, exhbn sponsored by The Royal Commonwealth Soc., London 1998, Studio Exhbn, London 1999, 2001, 2002, Soan Gallery, Fulham, London 2003, Studio Exhbn, Powys, Wales 2008. *Group exhibitions:* Chris Beetles Gallery, St James's, London 1989, Milne and Moller Gallery at Art Expo 1991, London 1991, Milne and Moller Gallery at Art Expo 1992, London 1992, jt exhbn, The Delaney Gallery, Perth, WA 1993, Perth Galleries, Perth 1993, Gomboc Gallery, Middle Swan, WA 1994, Gallery Savah, Sydney 1994. *Artistic achievement:* project of 45 paintings and 45 poems depicting her life story – one painting and poem per year, resulting in a painting 4ft high and 225ft long in 45 panels (award from Nat. Endowment for Science, Tech. and the Arts). *Publications:* poetry: Wooroloo 1999, Stonepicker 2001, Waxworks 2002, Forty-Five 2006, The Book of Mirrors 2008; juvenile fiction: Getting Rid of Aunt Edna (short stories) 1986, The Meal A Mile Long 1989, Waldorf and the Sleeping Granny (picture book) 1990, The Thing in the Sink 1992, Rent-a-Friend 1994, The Tall Story 1997, Three Scary Stories 2001; adult fiction: Keeper of the Keys (short story, published in Exile) 1986; numerous newspaper and magazine articles on poetry, gardening and motorbikes for various publs, including The Times, Guardian, Daily Mail, among others. *Literary Agent:* c/o Rebecca Lukacs, PO Box 128, Welshpool, Powys, SY21 1AA, Wales. *E-mail:* rebeccalukacs@btinternet.com. *Address:* c/o Bloodaxe Books Ltd, Highgreen, Tarset, Northumberland NE48 1RP, England. *Website:* www.friedahughes.com.

HUGHES, Ian (see Paterson, Alistair Ian)

HUGHES, John Lawrence, BA; American publisher; b. 13 March 1925, New York; s. of John C. Hughes and Margaret Kelly; m. Rose M. Pitman 1947; three s. one d. *Education:* Yale Univ. *Career:* reporter, Nassau Review Star, Rockville Centre, Long Island, NY 1949; Asst Sr Ed., Pocket Books, Inc. New York 1949–59; Vice-Pres. Washington Square Press 1958; Sr Ed., Vice-Pres. and Dir William Morrow & Co. 1960–65, Pres. and CEO 1965–85; Pres. The Hearst Trade Book Group 1985–87, Chair. and CEO 1988–90, Ed.-at-Large, Group Adviser 1990; Consultant and Ed.-at-Large HarperCollins Publrs, NY 1999–2001; Trustee, Yale Univ. Press, Pierpont Morgan Library, Library of America, Acad. of American Poets; mem. Bd Asscn of American Publishers 1986–90 (Chair. 1988–90); mem. Bd Nat. Book Awards 1982–94 (Chair. 1988–89). *Honours:* mem. Publrs Hall of Fame 1989. *Address:* PO Box 430, Southport, CT 06490, USA (home). *Telephone:* (203) 259-8957 (home). *Fax:* (203) 259-8142 (home).

HUGHES, Linda Jean, BA; Canadian newspaper publisher; b. 27 Sept. 1950, d. of Edward Rees and Madge Preston; m. George Ward 1978; one s. one d. *Education:* Univs of Victoria and Toronto. *Career:* Reporter on Victoria Times 1972–73, Head Legislature Bureau 1974–76; City Hall Reporter, Copy Ed. on The Edmonton Journal 1976–77, Editorial Writer 1978–80, Head Legislature Bureau, Asst City Ed. 1980, City Ed. 1981–84, Asst Man. Ed. 1984–87, Ed. 1987–91, Publr and Pres. 1992–2006 (retd); Southam News Services, Ottawa 1979; Southam Fellow Univ. of Toronto 1977–78; mem. Bd of Dirs, Royal Alexandra Hospital Foundation 2007–. *Honours:* Hon. DLitt (Athabasca) 1997, Hon. DIur (Univ. of Alberta) 2003, Grant MacEwan Community Coll. Hon. Diploma in Journalism and Distinguished Citizen Award (Grant MacEwan Community Coll.) 1999, Distinguished Alumni Award, Univ. of Vic. 2000 Jr Achievement Alberta Business Hall of Fame 2004. *Address:* c/o Royal Alexandra Hospital Foundation, 10240 Kingsway, Edmonton, Alberta, T5H 3V9, Canada (office).

HUGHES, Richard Edward, BA, MEd; American writer, poet and teacher; b. 31 Oct. 1950, Los Angeles, CA; m. Dalcy Beatriz Camacho 1989; one c. *Education:* California State University, University of Hawaii. *Career:* Prof. of English as a Second Language, American Samoa Community College, Pago Pago, 1984–86; Instructor in English, Cambria English Institute, Los Angeles,

1986–88; Freelance Writer, 1988–; mem. PEN; Poets and Writers. *Publications:* Isla Grande (novel), 1994; Legends of the Heart (novel), 1997. Contributions: poems to magazines and anthologies. *Honours:* Henri Coulette Award for Poetry, Acad. of American Poets, 1981.

HUGHES, Robert Studley Forrest, AO; Australian art critic and writer; b. 28 July 1938, Sydney, NSW; m. Victoria Whistler 1981; one s. *Education:* Saint Ignatius Coll., Sydney and Univ. of Sydney. *Career:* staff, Time magazine, New York 1970–; writer and narrator of art documentaries, BBC-TV, London 1974–. *Publications:* The Art of Australia 1966, Heaven and Hell in Western Art 1970, The Fatal Shore 1987, Nothing if Not Critical 1990, Frank Auerbach 1990, Barcelona 1992, Culture of Complaint 1993, American Visions: The Epic History of Art in America 1997, Goya (biog.) 2003, Things I Didn't Know (memoir) 2006; contrib. to various publications. *Honours:* College Art Asscn of America Frank Jewett Mather Awards 1982, 1985, Duff Cooper Prize 1987, WHSmith Literary Award 1987, first prize Olimpiada Cultural, Spain 1992. *Address:* c/o Time Magazine, Time-Life Building, Rockefeller Center, New York, NY 10020, USA.

HUGHES, Shirley, OBE, FRSL; British writer and illustrator; b. 16 July 1927, Hoylake, Wirral; d. of Thomas James Hughes and Kathleen Hughes (née Dowling); m John Sebastian Papendrek Vulliamy 1952; two s. one d. *Education:* West Kirby High School for Girls, Liverpool Art School and Ruskin School of Drawing and Fine Art, Oxford. *Career:* freelance writer and illustrator; lecturer in field; Advisory Cttee Public Lending Rights Registrar 1984–88; Library and Information Services Council 1989–92; mem. Soc. of Authors (man. cttee 1983–86). *Art exhibitions:* Ashmolean Museum, Oxford 2002, Walker Art Gallery, Liverpool 2003. *Publications:* Lucy & Tom Series: Lucy & Tom's Day, Lucy & Tom's Christmas, Lucy & Tom at the Seaside, Lucy & Tom Go To School, Lucy & Tom's abc, Lucy & Tom's 123 1960–87; Dogger, The Trouble with Jack 1970, Sally's Secret 1973, Helpers, It's Too Frightening for Me 1977, Moving Molly 1978, Up and Up 1979, Here Comes Charlie Moon, Charlie Moon and the Big Bonanza Bust Up 1982, Alfie Gets in First, Alfie's Feet, Alfie Gives a Hand 1983, An Evening at Alfie's 1984, The Nursery Collection (six vols) 1985–86, Chips and Jessie 1985, Another Helping of Chips 1986, The Big Alfie and Annie Rose Story Book 1988, Out and About 1988, Angel Mae 1989, The Big Concrete Lorry 1989, The Snow Lady 1990, Wheels 1991, The Big Alfie Out of Doors Story Book 1992, Stories by Firelight 1993, Giving, Bouncing, Chatting, Hiding 1994, Rhymes for Annie Rose 1995, Enchantment in the Garden 1996, Alfie and the Birthday Surprise 1997, The Lion and the Unicorn 1998, Mother and Child Treasury (ed.) 1998, Abel's Moon 1999, Alfie's Numbers 1999, The Shirley Hughes Collection 2000, Alfie Weather 2001, Annie Rose is My Little Sister 2002, A Life Drawing: Recollections of an Illustrator (autobiog.) 2002, Ella's Big Chance: A Fairy Tale Retold 2003, Olly and Me 2004, Alfie Wins a Prize 2004, A Brush With the Past 1900–1950: The Years That Changed Our Lives 2005, Alfie's World – A Celebration 2006, Alfie Wins a Prize 2006, Alfie and the Big Boys 2007, Jonadab and Rita 2008, Bye Bye Birdie 2009, Don't Want to Go! 2010, The Christmas Eve Ghost 2010. *Honours:* Hon. Fellow Library Asscn 1997, Hon. Fellow Liverpool John Moores Univ. 2003; Hon. DLitt (East Anglia) 2004, (Liverpool) 2004; Children's Rights Award 1976, Kate Greenaway Medal 1978, 2004, Silver Pencil Award, Netherlands 1980, Eleanor Farjeon Award 1984, Greenaway of Greenaways Medal 2007. *Address:* c/o Random House Children's Books, 61–63 Uxbridge Road, London, W5 5SA, England (office).

HULME, Keri; New Zealand novelist; b. 9 March 1947, Christchurch, NZ. *Education:* Canterbury Univ., Christchurch. *Career:* worked as tobacco picker, fish and chip cook, TV dir and woollen mill worker and studied law, before becoming full-time writer 1972; Writer-in-Residence Otago Univ. 1978, Univ. of Canterbury, Christchurch 1985. *Publications:* The Bone People 1984, Te Kaihau 1987, Homeplaces 1989, Strands (poems) 1992, Bait 1996, Te Whenua Te Iwi 1987, Homeplaces 1989, Stonefish 2004. *Honours:* awarded New Zealand Book of the Year Award 1984, Mobil Pegasus Prize 1984, Booker McConnell Prize for Fiction, UK 1985. *Address:* PO Box 1, Whataroa, South Westland, Aotearoa, New Zealand.

HULSE, Michael William, MA; British poet, writer, translator, editor and publisher; b. 12 June 1955, Stoke-on-Trent, Staffordshire, England. *Education:* University of St Andrews. *Career:* Lecturer, University of Erlangen-Nuremberg 1977–79, Catholic University of Eichstätt 1981–83; Part-time Lecturer, University of Cologne 1985–95; Trans., Deutsche Welle TV, Cologne 1986–2000; Assoc. Ed., Littlewood Arc, Todmorden 1992–98; Visiting Lecturer, University of Zürich 1994; Founder-Editorial Dir, Leviathon publishing house, Amsterdam 2000–; currently teacher of poetry, Warwick Univ.; mem. Poetry Society; Society of Authors. *Publications:* poetry: Monochrome Blood 1980, Dole Queue 1981, Knowing and Forgetting 1981, Propaganda 1985, Eating Strawberries in the Necropolis 1991, Monteverdi's Photographs 1995; other: The New Poetry (with David Kennedy and David Morley) 1993; numerous trans.; contrib. to anthologies. *Honours:* First Prize, National Poetry Competition 1978, Second Prize, TLS/Cheltenham Literature Festival Poetry Competition 1987, First Prizes, Bridport Poetry Competition 1988, 1994, Hawthornden Castle Fellowship 1991. *Address:* Department of English and Comparative Literary Studies, Warwick University, Room H544, Coventry CV4 7AL, England (office). *Telephone:* (2476) 524928 (office). *E-mail:* m.w.hulse@warwick.ac.uk (office). *Website:* www.warwick.ac.uk (office).

HUMAYDANE-YOUNES, Iman, MA; Lebanese writer, novelist, researcher and anthropologist; b. (Iman Humaydan), 18 Dec. 1956, Ain Enoub; three c. *Education:* American Univ. of Beirut. *Career:* Founder ARRAWI Centre for Cultural Devt and Publishing; participated in creative writing workshops in the Netherlands, France and Int. Writing Program, Univ. of Iowa, USA; literary and academic work related especially to the theme of war memories. *Films:* co-writer of scenario of Lebanese film Here Comes the Rain (won nine awards) 2010, researcher and scenario writer for documentary film on the life of the Arab Diva Asmahan, killed in a car accident in Egypt in 1944. *E-mail:* ihumaydan@yahoo.com (office)*Address:* PO Box 16-5805, Ashrafieh, Beirut, Lebanon (office); 138 rue Nationale, 75013 Paris, France (home). *Telephone:* (1) 323234 (Beirut) (office); 6-16-30-49-85 (France, mobile) (home); 3-717534 (Beirut, mobile). *E-mail:* imanhumaydan@yahoo.com; info@arrawi.com (office). *Website:* www.arrawi.com (office).

HUMPHREYS, Emyr Owen, FRSL; British author and poet; b. 15 April 1919, Clwyd, Wales; m. Elinor Myfanwy 1946; three s. one d. *Education:* Univ. Coll., Aberystwyth and Univ. Coll., Bangor. *Publications:* The Little Kingdom 1946, The Voice of a Stranger 1949, A Change of Heart 1951, Hear and Forgive 1952, A Man's Estate 1955, The Italian Wife 1957, A Toy Epic 1958, The Gift 1963, Outside the House of Baal 1965, Natives 1968, Ancestor Worship 1970, National Winner 1971, Flesh and Blood 1974, Landscapes 1976, The Best of Friends 1978, The Kingdom of Bran 1979, The Anchor Tree 1980, Pwyll a Riannon 1980, Miscellany Two 1981, The Taliesin Tradition 1983, Salt of the Earth 1985, An Absolute Hero 1986, Open Secrets 1988, The Triple Net 1988, Bonds of Attachment 1990, Outside Time 1991, Unconditional Surrender 1996, The Gift of a Daughter 1998, Collected Poems 1999, Dal Pen Rheswm 1999, Ghosts and Strangers 2001, Conversations and Reflections 2002, Old People Are a Problem 2003, The Shop 2005, Welsh Time 2009, The Woman in the Window 2009. *Honours:* Hon. Prof. of English, Univ. Coll. of N Wales, Bangor; Hon. DLitt (Univ. of Wales) 1990, (Univ. of Glamorgan) 2005, Somerset Maugham Award 1953, Hawthornden Prize 1959, Soc. of Authors Travel Award 1978, Welsh Arts Council Prize 1983, Welsh Book of the Year 1992, 1999, Cymmrodorion Medal 2003. *Address:* Llinon, Penyberth, Llanfairpwll, Ynys Môn, Gwynedd, LL61 5YT, Wales (home). *Telephone:* (1248) 714540 (home).

HUMPHREYS, Josephine, AB, MA; American novelist; b. 2 Feb. 1945, Charleston, SC; m. Thomas A. Hutcheson 1968, two s. *Education:* Duke University, Yale University. *Publications:* Dreams of Sleep, 1984; Rich in Love, 1987; The Fireman's Fair, 1991; Nowhere Else on Earth, 2000. Contributions: newspapers and periodicals. *Honours:* PEN, Ernest Hemingway Foundation, 1985; Guggenheim Fellowship, 1985; Lyndhurst Prize, 1986.

HUMPHRIES, (John) Barry, AO, CBE; Australian entertainer and author; b. 17 Feb. 1934, s. of J. A. E. Humphries and L. A. Brown; m. 1st Rosalind Tong 1959; two d.; m. 2nd Diane Millstead; two s.; m. 3rd Lizzie Spender 1990. *Education:* Melbourne Grammar and Univ. of Melbourne. *Career:* repertory seasons at Union Theatre, Melbourne 1953–54, Phillip Street Revue Theatre, Sydney 1956, Demon Barber Lyric, Hammersmith 1959, Oliver, New Theatre 1960; one-man shows (author and performer): A Nice Night's Entertainment 1962, Excuse I 1965, Just a Show 1968, A Load of Olde Stuffe 1971, At Least You Can Say That You've Seen It 1974, Housewife Superstar 1976, Isn't It Pathetic at His Age 1979, A Night with Dame Edna 1979, An Evening's Intercourse with Barry Humphries 1981–82, Tears Before Bedtime 1986, Back with a Vengeance, London 1987–88, Look at Me When I'm Talking to You 1993–94, Edna: The Spectacle 1998, Dame Edna: The Royal Tour, San Francisco 1998, Remember You're Out 1999; numerous plays, films and broadcasts; best-known for his comic characterizations of Dame Edna Everage, Sir Les Patterson and Sandy Stone; Pres. Frans de Boewer Soc. (Belgium); Vice-Pres. Betjeman Soc. 2001–. *Publications:* Bizarre 1964, Innocent Austral Verse 1968, The Wonderful World of Barry McKenzie (with Nicholas Garland) 1970, Bazza Holds his Own (with Nicholas Garland) 1972, Dame Edna's Coffee Table Book 1976, Les Patterson's Australia 1979, Treasury of Australian Kitsch 1980, A Nice Night's Entertainment 1981, Dame Edna's Bedside Companion 1982, The Traveller's Tool 1985, The Complete Barry McKenzie 1988, My Gorgeous Life: The Autobiography of Dame Edna Everage 1989, The Life and Death of Sandy Stone 1991, More Please: An Autobiography 1992, Women in the Background (novel) 1996, My Life As Me (autobiography). *Honours:* Dr hc (Melbourne Univ., Griffith Univ.), Hon. LLD (Melbourne) 2003; J.R. Ackerley Prize, Golden Rose of Montreux, Outer Critics Circle Award. *Literary Agent:* c/o Claire Ningale, PBJ Management, 5 Soho Street, London, W1D 3QA, England. *Telephone:* (20) 7287-1112. *Fax:* (20) 7287-1191. *E-mail:* general@pbjmgt.co.uk. *Website:* www.pbjmgt.co.uk.

HUMPHRY, Derek John; American/British journalist, author, broadcaster and publisher; *President, Euthanasia Research and Guidance Organization*; b. 29 April 1930, Bath, England. *Education:* municipal schools, UK. *Career:* Messenger Boy, Yorkshire Post, London 1945–46; Cub Reporter, Evening World, Bristol 1946–51; Jr Reporter, Evening News, Manchester 1951–55; Reporter, Daily Mail 1955–61; Deputy Ed. The Luton News 1961–63; Ed. Havering Recorder 1963–67, World Federation of Right-To-Die Societies Newsletter 1980; Hemlock Quarterly 1983–92, Euthanasia Review 1986–88, World Right to Die Newsletter 1992–94; Home Affairs Corresp., The Sunday Times 1966–78; Special Writer, Los Angeles Times 1978–79; Pres. Norris Lane Press, Oregon USA; Founder Hemlock Soc., USA 1980, Exec. Dir 1980–92; Founder Euthanasia Research and Guidance Org. 1993, Pres. 1993–; Dir World Fed. of Right-To-Die Socs 1980–, The Final Exit Network

2003–; contrib. to Is This The Day? (theatre), Good Bye, My Love (drama). *Publications:* Because They're Black 1971, Police Power and Black People 1972, Passports and Politics 1974, The Cricket Conspiracy 1976, False Messiah 1977, Jean's Way 1978, Let Me Die Before I Wake 1982, The Right to Die!: Understanding Euthanasia 1986, Final Exit 1991 (also English, Italian and Spanish edns), Dying with Dignity 1992, Lawful Exit 1993, Freedom to Die 1998, The Good Euthanasia Guide 2003, Good Life, Good Death (memoir) 2008. *Honours:* Martin Luther King Memorial Prize 1972, Socrates Award 1997, Saba Medal for contrib. to the World Right-to-Die Movement 2000. *Address:* 24829 Norris Lane, Junction City, OR 97448-9559, USA (home). *Telephone:* (541) 999-1873 (home). *Fax:* (541) 998-1873 (home). *E-mail:* ergo@finalexit.org (office); derekhumphry@starband.net (home). *Website:* www.finalexit.org/dhumphry (office); www.assistedsuicide.org (office).

HUNEBELLE, Danielle; French journalist, writer and television producer; b. 10 May 1922, Paris; d. of André Weill and Germaine Weill (née Cordon); two d. *Education:* Lycées Racine and Molière, Paris and Univ. of Paris-Sorbonne. *Career:* actress 1945–48; journalist 1948–; war corresp. in Greece 1948; worked in army information office in Indochina 1951; Special Envoy for Le Monde newspaper 1951; Sr Reporter for Réalités magazine 1952–72; TV Producer, made documentaries about Ho Chi Minh and Henry Kissinger and produced Jeux de Société series and docu-dramas; Founder Société des Publications Danielle Hunebelle 1973, Publr in French and English of La Lettre Int. de Danielle Hunebelle; now retd. *Publications include:* Philippine, Les plumes du paon, Rien que les hommes, Dear Henry. *Honours:* Chevalier de la Légion d'honneur, des Arts et Lettres. *Address:* Elia, 06190 Cap Martin, France (home). *Telephone:* (4) 93-57-77-47 (home). *E-mail:* a.hunebelle@laposte.net (home).

HUNT, Gill (see Tubb, Edwin Charles)

HURD OF WESTWELL, Baron (Life Peer), cr. 1997, of Westwell in the County of Oxfordshire; **Douglas Richard Hurd,** CH, CBE, PC, BA (Hons); British politician, diplomatist, banker and author; b. 8 March 1930, Marlborough, Wilts.; s. of the late Anthony Hurd, Baron Hurd and Stephanie Corner; m. 1st Tatiana Elizabeth Michelle Eyre 1960 (divorced 1982); three s.; m. 2nd Judy Smart 1982 (died 2008); one s. one d. *Education:* Eton Coll., Trinity Coll., Cambridge. *Career:* fmr Pres. Cambridge Union Soc.; joined diplomatic service 1952; served in Beijing 1954–56, UK Mission to UN 1956–60, Pvt. Sec. to Perm. Under-Sec. of State, Foreign Office 1960–63, in British Embassy, Rome 1963–66; joined Conservative Research Dept 1966, Head of Foreign Affairs Section 1968; Pvt. Sec. to Leader of the Opposition 1968–70, Political Sec. to the Prime Minister 1970–74; MP for Mid-Oxon 1974–83, for Witney 1983–97; Opposition Spokesman on European Affairs 1976–79, Minister of State, FCO 1979–83, Home Office 1983–84; Sec. of State for NI 1984–85; Home Sec. 1985–89; Sec. of State for Foreign and Commonwealth Affairs 1989–95; mem. Constitutional Comm. 1998–99, Royal Comm. on the Reform of the House of Lords 1999–2001, House of Lords Appointments Comm. 2000–10; Deputy Chair. NatWest Markets 1995–98; Dir NatWest Group 1995–99; Chair. British Invisibles 1997–2000; Deputy Chair. Coutts and Co. 1998–2010; cand. for Conservative Leadership 1990; Chair. Prison Reform Trust 1997–2001 (Pres.), Booker Prize Cttee 1998, Archbishop of Canterbury's Review 2000–01, Council for Effective Dispute Resolution 2001–04; Sr Adviser to Hawkpoint Partners Ltd 1999–; Pres. Montrose Strategic Consultancy, London; Chair. Advisory Council, FIRST Magazine (Forum For Decision Makers) (int. affairs org.), London; High Steward Westminster Abbey 2000–10; Pres. German-British Forum; Co-Pres. Royal Inst. Int. Affairs 2002–10; Vice-Pres. Falkland Islands Asscn 1996–2000 (Pres. 2000–), Commonwealth Parl. Asscn (UK Br.); mem. Global Leadership Foundation, Top Level Group of UK Parliamentarians for Multilateral Nuclear Disarmament and Non-proliferation 2009–; f. charity, Crime Concern 1988 (merged with young people's charity Rainer to become Catch22 2008); Fellow, Nuffield Coll. Oxford. *Publications:* non-fiction: The Arrow War 1967, An End to Promises 1979, The Search for Peace 1997, Memoirs 2003, Robert Peel, a Biography 2007, Choose Your Weapons: The British Foreign Secretary (with Edward Young) 2010; fiction: Send Him Victorious (with Andrew Osmond) 1968, The Smile on the Face of the Tiger 1969, Scotch on the Rocks (with Andrew Osmond) 1971, Truth Game 1972, Vote to Kill 1975, War Without Frontiers (with Andrew Osmond) 1982, Palace of Enchantments (with Stephen Lamport) 1985, The Last Day of Summer 1992, The Shape of Ice 1998, Ten Minutes to Turn the Devil (short stories) 1999, Image in the Water 2001. *Honours:* Hon. DLitt (Aston) 2009, (Brunel) 2009; Spectator Award for Parliamentarian of the Year 1990. *Address:* House of Lords, Westminster, London, SW1A 0PW, England (office).

HURST, Frances (see Mayhar, Ardath)

HUSSAIN, Fahmida, PhD; Pakistani writer, literary critic and academic; *Director, Shah Abdul Latif Bhitai Chair, University of Karachi. Education:* Univ. of Sindh and Univ. of Karachi. *Career:* teacher in Sindhi Dept, Univ. of Karachi for over 20 years, currently Dir Shah Abdul Latif Bhitai Chair; mem. Co-ordination Council for Promotion of Shah Abdul Latif Bhitai Studies; mem. of jury, Kamal-i-Fun literary award 2003. *Publications:* Shah Abdul Latif Bhitai Jee Shairee Ma Aurt Jo Roop (Pakistan Acad. of Letters Book of the Year), Adabi Tanqeed Fun Aeen Tareekh 1996, numerous articles in journals and magazines. *Honours:* President's Award for Pride of Performance 2005. *Address:* Department of Sindhi, University of Karachi, Karachi, Pakistan (office). *E-mail:* saleem@sindhi.ku.edu.pk. *Website:* www.uok.edu.pk.

HUSSEIN, Aamer, BA, FRSL; British writer, academic and literary critic; *Professorial Writing Fellow, University of Southampton;* b. 8 April 1955, Karachi, Pakistan; s. of The Nawab Ahmed Husain and Begum Sabiha (née Malik). *Education:* School of Oriental and African Studies, Univ. of London. *Career:* moved to London, England aged 15; researcher on films for MIP and TV documentaries 1981–87; first fiction and reviews published in arts journals Artrage and Bazaar 1986–; Visiting Lecturer at various univs, including Postcolonial Writing Fellow, Univ. of Southampton 2000; Royal Literary Fund Writing Fellow, Imperial Coll., London 2003–06; Lecturer, Inst. of English Studies, Univ. of London 2004–06, Dir Nat. and Int. Literatures in English, Inst. of English Studies 2006–09; Sr Lecturer in English/Creative Writing, Univ. of Southampton 2006–09, Professorial Writing Fellow 2010; Contrib. Ed., Wasafiri literary journal. *Publications:* short story collections: Mirror to the Sun 1993, This Other Salt 1999, Hoops of Fire: Fifty Years of Fiction by Pakistani Women (co-ed.) 2000, Cactus Town and Other Stories 2002, Turquoise 2002, Insomnia 2007; novels: Another Gulmohar Tree 2009, The Cloud Messenger 2011; contrib. to The Independent, TLS, New Statesman. *Address:* c/o Saqi Books, 26 Westbourne Grove, London, W2 5RH, England (office). *E-mail:* aamerhussein@btinternet.com (home).

HUSTON, Charlie; American crime novelist; b. Oakland, Calif.; m. Virginia Louise Smith. *Career:* writer of crime fiction (devised Henry Thompson trilogy and Joe Pitt Casebooks) and comic book titles; contrib. for Marvel Comics, Ultimates, Wolverine. *Publications include:* novels: Henry Thompson trilogy: Caught Stealing 2004, Six Bad Things 2005, A Dangerous Man 2006; Joe Pitt Casebooks: Already Dead 2005, No Dominion 2006, Half the Blood of Brooklyn 2007, Every Last Drop 2008, My Dead Body 2009; other novels: The Shotgun Rule 2007, The Mystic Arts of Erasing All Signs of Death 2009, Sleepless 2010. *Literary Agent:* c/o Simon Lipskar, Writers House, 21 West 26th Street, New York, NY 10010, USA. *Telephone:* (212) 685-2400. *Fax:* (212) 685-1781. *E-mail:* queries@circleofconfusion.com. *Website:* www.circleofconfusion.com; www.writershouse.com.

HUSTON, Nancy Louise, OC, BA, MA; Canadian/French writer; b. 16 Sept. 1953, Calgary, AB; m. Tzvetan Todorov 1981; one s. one d. *Education:* Sarah Lawrence Coll., École des Hautes Études. *Career:* Writer-in-Residence, American Univ., Paris 1989; facilitator, South African Writers Workshop 1994; Visiting Prof., Harvard Univ. 1994. *Publications:* Désirs et réalités: textes choisis (essay) 1978–94, Jouer au papa et à l'amant (essay) 1979, Dire et interdire: éléments de jurologie (essay) 1980, Les Variations Goldberg (novel, trans. as The Goldberg Variations) 1981, Mosaïque de la pornographie (essay) 1982, À l'amour comme à la guerre (non-fiction) 1984, Histoire d'Omaya (novel, trans. as The Story of Omaya) 1985, Lettres parisiennes (non-fiction) 1986, Trois fois septembre (novel) 1989, Journal de la création (essay) 1990, Véra veut la vérité (juvenile) 1992, Dora demande des détails (juvenile) 1993, Cantique des plaines (novel, trans. as Plainsong) (Prix Canada-Suisse 1995) 1993, La Virevolte (novel) 1994, Tombeau de Romain Gary (essay) 1995, Pour un patriotisme de l'ambiguïté (essay) 1995, Instrument des ténèbres (novel, trans. as Instrument of Darkness) (Prix Goncourt des Lycéens 1996, Prix du Livre Inter 1997) 1996, L'Empreinte de l'ange (novel, trans. as The Mark of the Angel) (Grand prix des lectrices de Elle 1999) 1998, Les Souliers d'or (juvenile) 1998, Prodige: polyphonie (novel) 1999, Nord Perdu (essay) 1999, Limbes (essay) 2000, Dolce agonia (novel) 2001, Une adoration (novel) 2003, Professeurs de désespoir (essay) 2004, Lignes de faille (Fault Lines; novel) (Prix Femina, Prix France Télévisions) 2006, Passions d'Annie Leclerc 2007, L'Espèce fabulatrice (trans. as The Tale-Tellers 2009) 2008, Infrarouge (trans. as Infrared 2011) 2010, Ultraviolet 2011. *Honours:* Officier, Ordre des Arts et des Lettres; Dr hc (Montréal, Guelph, McGill, Ottawa, Liège, Belgium); Prix Binet Sangle de l' Acad. Française 1980, Prix Contrepoint 1981, Prix du Gouverneur-Général 1993, Prix Louis Hémon 1995. *Address:* c/o Actes Sud, 18 rue Séguier, 75006 Paris, France.

HUSTVEDT, Siri, PhD; American poet, novelist and essayist; b. 19 Feb. 1955, Northfield, Minn.; d. of the late Lloyd Hustvedt and of Ester Vegan Hustvedt; m. Paul Auster 1981; one d. *Education:* Columbia Univ. *Career:* worked as ed. and trans. *Publications:* Reading to You (poems) 1982, The Blindfold (novel) 1990, The Enchantment of Lily Dahl (novel) 1996, Yonder: Essays 1998, What I Loved (novel, Prix des Libraires de Québec) 2003, Mysteries of the Rectangle (essays) 2005, A Plea for Eros (essays) 2006, The Sorrows of an American (novel) 2008, The Shaking Woman or a History of My Nerves (non-fiction) 2010, The Summer Without Men (novel) 2011; contrib. to Paris Review, Modern Painters, The Guardian, The Yale Review, Conjunctions and many other publs; fiction translated into 25 languages. *Literary Agent:* c/o ICM International Creative Management, 40 West 57th Street, New York, NY 10019; c/o ICM International Creative Management, 825 Eighth Avenue, New York, NY 10019, USA; c/o Curtis Brown, Haymarket House, 28–29 Haymarket, London, SW1Y 4SP, England. *Telephone:* (212) 556-5764 (New York); (212) 556-5600 (New York); (20) 7393-4400 (London). *Fax:* (212) 556-5624 (New York); (20) 7393-4401 (London). *Website:* www.icmtalent.com; www.curtisbrown.co.uk.

HUTCHEON, Linda Ann Marie, OC, MA, PhD, FRSC; Canadian writer and academic; *University Professor Emeritus, University of Toronto;* b. (Linda Bortolotti), 24 Aug. 1947, Toronto, Ont.; d. of Roy Bortolotti and Elisa Rossi; m. Michael Alexander Hutcheon 1970. *Education:* Univ. of Toronto, Cornell Univ., USA. *Career:* Asst, Assoc. and Full Prof. of English, McMaster Univ. 1976–88; Prof. of English and Comparative Literature, Univ. of Toronto 1988–96, Distinguished Univ. Prof. 1996–2010, Univ. Prof. Emer. 2010–;

mem. Modern Language Asscn of America, American Acad. of Arts and Sciences. *Publications:* Narcissistic Narrative 1980, Formalism and the Freudian Aesthetic 1984, A Theory of Parody 1985, A Poetics of Postmodernism 1988, The Canadian Postmodern 1988, The Politics of Postmodernism 1989, Splitting Images 1991, Irony's Edge 1995, A Theory of Adaptation 2006, Opera: Desire, Disease, Death (with Michael Hutcheon) 1996, Bodily Charm: Living Opera (with Michael Hutcheon), 2000, Opera: The Art of Dying (with Michael Hutcheon), 2004. Ed.: Other Solitudes 1990, Double-Talking 1992, Likely Stories 1992, A Postmodern Reader 1993, Rethinking Literary History: A Forum on Theory 2002; contribs to Diacritics, Textual Practice, Cultural Critique and other journals. *Honours:* Hon. LLD 1995, Hon. DLitt 1999, 2000, 2005, 2007, 2008, 2011; Killam Prize 2005, Molson Prize 2010. *Address:* Department of English, University of Toronto, Toronto, ON M5R 2M8, Canada (office). *Telephone:* (416) 978-6616 (office). *Fax:* (416) 978-2836 (office). *E-mail:* l.hutcheon@utoronto.ca (office). *Website:* individual.utoronto.ca/lindahutcheon (office).

HUTCHINSON, Gregory Owen, BA, MA, DPhil; British writer; *Professor of Greek and Latin Languages and Literature, Oxford University*; b. 5 Dec. 1957, London, England; m. Yvonne Downing 1979, one d. *Education:* Balliol and Christ Church Colleges, Oxford. *Career:* Tutor and Fellow, Exeter Coll., Oxford 1984–98, Prof. of Greek and Latin Languages and Literature, Oxford Univ. 1998–. *Publications:* Aeschylus, Septem Contra Thebas (ed.) 1985, Hellenistic Poetry 1988, Latin Literature from Seneca to Juvenal: A Critical Study 1993, Cicero's Correspondence: A Literary Study 1998, Greek Lyric Poetry: A Commentary on Selected Larger Pieces 2001, Propertius, Elegies Book IV 2006, Talking Books: Readings in Hellenistic and Roman Books of Poetry 2008. *Address:* Exeter College, Oxford, OX1 3DP, England (office).

HUTTERLI, Kurt; Canadian/Swiss writer, poet and artist; b. 18 Aug. 1944, Bern, Switzerland; m. Marianne Büchler 1966; one s. one d. *Education:* Secondary School Teacher Diploma Univ. of Bern 1966. *Career:* mem. PEN Switzerland, Autorinnen und Autoren der Schweiz, Berner Schriftsteller-Verein. *Publications:* Aber 1972, Herzgrün 1974, Felsengleich 1976, Die Faltsche 1977, Das Matterköpfen 1978, Ein Hausmann 1980, Finnlandisiert 1982, Überlebenslust 1984, Elchspur 1986, Baccalà 1989, Gaunerblut 1990, Mir kommt kein Tier ins Haus 1991, Stachelflieder 1991, Katzensprung 1993, Die sanfte Piratin 1994, Im Fischbauch 1998, Hotel Goldtown 2000, Der Clown im Mond 2000, Arche Titanic 2000, Der Rocky Mountain King 2003, Das Centovalli Brautgeschenk 2004, Omleto 2004, Wie es euch nicht gefällt 2006, Der Salon der Witwe Rusca 2008; contrib. to Der Bund, Stuttgarter Zeitung, Drehpunkt, Einspruch. *Honours:* Poetry Prize City of Bern 1971, Book Prizes City of Bern 1972, 1978, Theatre Awards 1976, 1982, 1987. *Address:* RR5, S53/C9, Oliver, BC V0H 1T0, Canada (home).

HUTTON, Ronald Edmund, FRHistS, FSA, MA, DPhil; British historian; *Professor of History, Bristol University*; b. 19 Dec. 1953, Ootacamund, India; s. of Geoffrey Edmund Hutton and Elsa Edwina Hansen; m. Lisa Radulovic 1988 (divorced 2003). *Education:* Univ. of Cambridge, Univ. of Oxford. *Career:* Prize Fellow, Magdalen Coll., Oxford 1979–81; Lecturer, Bristol Univ. 1981–89, Reader 1989–96, Prof. of History 1996–; Commr, English Heritage; Chair., Nat. Advisory Cttee on Designation of Historic Buildings. *Publications:* The Royalist War Effort 1981, The Restoration 1985, Charles II 1989, The British Republic 1990, The Pagan Religions of the Ancient British Isles 1991, The Rise and Fall of Merry England 1994, The Stations of the Sun 1996, The Triumph of the Moon: A History of Modern Pagan Witchcraft 1999, Shamans 2001, Witches, Druids and King Arthur: Studies in Paganism, Myth and Magic 2003, Debates in Stuart History 2004, The Druids: A History 2007, Blood and Mistletoe: The History of Druids in Britain 2009; contrib. to journals. *Honours:* Benjamin Franklin Prize 1993. *Address:* 13 Woodland Road, Bristol BS8 1TB, England (office). *Telephone:* (117) 928-7595 (office). *E-mail:* r.hutton@bristol.ac.uk (office).

HUTTON, Will Nicholas, MBA; British writer and broadcaster; *Chief Executive, Work Foundation*; b. 21 May 1950, London; s. of the late William Hutton and Dorothy Haynes; m. Jane Atkinson 1978; one s. two d. *Education:* Chislehurst and Sidcup Grammar School, Univ. of Bristol and Institut Européen d' Admin des Affaires (INSEAD), Fontainebleau, France. *Career:* with Phillips & Drew (stockbrokers) 1971–77; Sr Producer Current Affairs, BBC Radio 4 1978–81; Dir and Producer The Money Programme, BBC 2 1981–83; Econs Corresp. Newsnight, BBC 2 1983–88; Ed. European Business Channel 1988–90; Econs Ed. The Guardian 1990–95, Asst Ed. 1995–96; Ed. The Observer 1996–98, Ed.-in-Chief 1998–2000; Chief Exec. The Work Foundation (fmrly The Industrial Soc. –2002) 2000–; Gov. LSE 2000–. *Publications:* The Revolution That Never Was: An Assessment of Keynesian Economics 1986, The State We're In 1994, The State to Come 1997, The Stakeholding Society 1998, The World We're In 2002, The Writing on the Wall: China and the West in the 21st Century 2007, Them and Us: Politics, Greed and Inequality—Why We Need a Fair Society 2010. *Honours:* Hon. DLitt (Kingston) 1995, (De Montfort) 1996; Political Journalist of the Year, What the Papers Say 1993. *Address:* The Work Foundation, 21 Palmer Street, London, SW1H 0AD (office); 34 Elms Avenue, London, N10 2JP, England (home). *Telephone:* (20) 7004-7103 (office). *Fax:* (20) 7004-7111 (office). *E-mail:* aharris@theworkfoundation.com (office). *Website:* www.theworkfoundation.com (office).

HWANG, David Henry, BA; American dramatist and screenwriter; b. 11 Aug. 1957, Los Angeles, CA; m. 1st Ophelia Chong 1985; m. 2nd Kathryn Layng 1993; one s. *Education:* Stanford Univ., Yale Drama School. *Career:* dramaturg, Asian American Theatre Centre, San Francisco 1987–; mem. Dramatists' Guild (bd of dirs 1988–). *Plays:* FOB 1980, The Dance and the Railroad 1981, Family Devotions 1981, Sound and Beauty 1983, The Sound of a Voice 1984, As the Crow Flies 1986, Rich Relations 1986, M Butterfly 1988, Bondage 1992, Face Value 1993, Trying to Find Chinatown 1996, Golden Child (Obie Award 1997) 1996, Yellow Face 2007. *Screenplays:* M Butterfly 1993, Golden Gate 1993, Possession. *Other works:* 1000 Airplanes on the Roof (musical) 1988, Forbidden Nights (TV play) 1990, The Voyage (libretto) 1992, Elton John and Tim Rice's Aida (co-librettist, Broadway) 2000, Flower Drum Song (revised libretto, Broadway) 2002, The Fly (opera libretto). *Honours:* Drama-Logue Awards 1980, 1986, Obie Award 1981, Rockefeller Foundation Fellowship 1983, Guggenheim Fellowship 1984, Nat. Endowment for the Arts Fellowship 1987, Tony Award for Best Play 1988, Outer Critics Circle Award for Best Broadway Play 1988, John Gassner Award 1988. *Literary Agent:* c/o William Craver, Paradigm, 360 Park Avenue South, 16th Floor, New York, NY 10010, USA. *Telephone:* (212) 897-6400. *Fax:* (212) 764-8941. *Website:* www.paradigmagency.com.

HWANG, Sok-yong; South Korean novelist; b. 1943, Zhanchung, Manchuria, China. *Career:* drafted into Korean army, fought in Viet Nam war 1966–69; fmr labourer and political activist in S Korea; took part in cultural exchange with N Korea 1989; went into voluntary exile in Germany and USA, imprisoned on his return to Seoul 1993, pardoned 1998. *Publications:* The Pagoda (short story) (Chosun Ilbo New Year Prize) 1970, The Chronicle of a Man Named Han (novel) 1970, The Road to Sampo (short stories) 1974, Chang Kil-san (serialised novel) 1974–84, The Shadow of Arms (novel) 1985, The Old Garden (novel) (Danjae Award, Yi San Literary Award) 2000, The Guest (novel) 2001. *Honours:* Manhae Grand Prize for Literature 2004. *Address:* c/o Seven Stories Press, 140 Watts Street, New York, NY 10013, USA (office). *E-mail:* info@sevenstories.com (office). *Website:* www.sevenstories.com (office).

HYDE, Lewis, BA, MA; American academic, author, poet, editor and translator; *Richard L. Thomas Professor of Creative Writing, Kenyon College*; b. 16 Oct. 1945, Boston, Mass; m. Patricia Auster Vigderman 1981; one step-s. *Education:* University of Minnesota, University of Iowa. *Career:* Instructor in Literature, University of Iowa 1969–71; Lecturer in Expository Writing, Harvard University 1983–85, Briggs-Copeland Asst Prof. of English 1985–89, Dir, Creative Writing Programme 1988–89; Henry R. Luce Prof. of Art and Politics, Kenyon College 1989–2001, Richard L. Thomas Prof. of Creative Writing 2001–; Fellow, Berkman Center for Internet and Soc., Harvard Univ. *Publications include:* Twenty Poems of Vicente Aleixandre (ed. and trans. with Robert Bly) 1977, A Longing for the Light: Selected Poems of Vicente Aleixandre (ed. and trans. with others) 1979, World Alone, by Vicente Aleixandre (trans. with David Unger) 1982, The Gift: Imagination and the Erotic Life of Property 1983, On the Work of Allen Ginsberg (ed.) 1984, Alcohol and Poetry: John Berryman and the Booze Talking 1986, This Error is the Sign of Love (poems) 1988, Trickster Makes This World: Mischief, Myth, and Art 1998, Selected Essays of Henry D. Thoreau (ed. and annotator) 2002, Common as Air: Revolution, Art and Ownership 2010; contribs to numerous journals, quarterlies, reviews. *Honours:* Hon. DFA, San Francisco Art Institute 1997; Acad. of American Poets Prize 1966, National Endowment for the Arts Creative Writing Fellowships 1977, 1982, 1987, Columbia University Trans. Center Award 1979, National Endowment for the Humanities Fellowship for Independent Study and Research 1979, Massachusetts Council on the Arts and Humanities Fellowship In Poetry 1980, MacDowell Colony Fellowships 1989, 1991, 1996, 1999, 2000, Scholar-in-Residence, Rockefeller Study and Conference Center, Bellagio, Italy 1991, John D. and Catherine T. MacArthur Foundation Fellowship 1991–96, Getty Scholar 1993–94, Osher Fellow 1998. *Address:* Bailey House, 11, Kenyon College, Gambier, OH 43022-9623, USA (office). *Telephone:* (740) 427-5343 (office). *Fax:* (740) 427-5673 (office). *E-mail:* hyde@kenyon.edu (office). *Website:* www.kenyon.edu (office); www.lewishyde.com.

HYLAND, M. J. (Maria Joan), BA, LLB, MA; Irish/British writer and academic; *Lecturer, Centre for New Writing, University of Manchester*; b. 6 June 1968, London; pnr Trevor Byrne. *Education:* Univ. of Melbourne. *Career:* brought up in Ireland and Australia; worked as a lawyer for six years; fmr Ed. Nocturnal Submissions (literary magazine); based in London 2005–; worked in Rome on an Australia Council scholarship 2006; currently Lecturer, Manchester Centre for New Writing, Univ. of Manchester. *Publications:* novels: How The Light Gets In (Best Young Novelist Award, Sydney Morning Herald) 2003, Carry Me Down (Encore Award, Hawthornden Prize 2007) 2006, This is How 2009; contrib. to New York Stories, Australian Short Stories, Zoetrope: All-Story, The London Review of Books, The Scottish Herald, The Financial Times. *Honours:* Hawthornden Prize, Encore Award, Australia Council grants 2002, 2004, 2006. *Literary Agent:* Rogers, Coleridge and White Ltd, 20 Powis Mews, London, W11 1JN, England. *Telephone:* (20) 7221-3717. *Fax:* (20) 7229-9084. *E-mail:* info@rcwlitagency.com. *Website:* www.rcwlitagency.co.uk. *Address:* Centre for New Writing, School of Arts, Histories and Cultures, The University of Manchester, Oxford Road, Manchester, M13 9PL, England (office). *Telephone:* (161) 860-4819 (office). *E-mail:* hylandbyrne@yahoo.com (office). *Website:* www.arts.manchester.ac.uk/newwriting (office); www.editingfirm.com (office); www.mjhyland.com.

HYLAND, Paul, BSc; British poet and travel writer; b. 15 Sept. 1947, Poole, Dorset. *Education:* Univ. of Bristol. *Career:* mem. Soc. of Authors, Poetry Soc.,

PEN, The Magic Circle, Int. Brotherhood of Magicians. *Publications:* Purbeck: The Ingrained Island 1978, Wight: Biography of an Island 1984, The Black Heart 1988, Indian Balm 1994, Backwards Out of the Big World 1996, Discover Dorset: Isle of Purbeck 1998, Ralegh's Last Journey 2003; poetry: Poems of Z 1982, The Stubborn Forest 1984, Getting into Poetry 1992, Kicking Sawdust 1995, Art of the Impossible 2004. *Honours:* Eric Gregory Award 1976, Alice Hunt Bartlett Award 1985, Authors' Foundation 1995. *Literary Agent:* c/o David Higham Associates Ltd, 5–8 Lower John Street, Golden Square, London, W1F 9HA, England. *Telephone:* (20) 7434-5900. *Fax:* (20) 7437-1072. *E-mail:* dha@davidhigham.co.uk. *Website:* www.davidhigham.co.uk. *E-mail:* write@paul-hyland.co.uk (office).

HYMAN, Harold Melvin, BA, MA, PhD; American academic and author; b. 24 July 1924, New York, NY; m. Ferne Beverly Handelsman 1946, two s. one d. *Education:* Univ. of California at Los Angeles, Columbia Univ. *Career:* Asst Prof., Earlham Coll. 1952–55; Visiting Asst Prof., Univ. of California at Los Angeles 1955–56, Prof. 1963–68; Assoc. Prof., Arizona State Univ., Tempe 1956–57; Prof. of History, Univ. of Illinois 1963–68; William P. Hobby Prof. of History, Rice Univ. 1968–96, Prof. Emeritus 1997–; Graduate Faculty in Political Science, Univ. of Tokyo 1973; Faculty of Law, Keio Univ. 1973; Adjunct Prof. of Legal History, Bates Coll. of Law, Univ. of Houston 1977, and of American Legal History, School of Law, Univ. of Texas 1986; Meyer Visiting Distinguished Prof. of Legal History, School of Law, New York Univ. 1982–83; mem. American Historical Asscn, American Society of Legal History (pres. 1994–95), Organization of American Historians, Southern Historical Asscn. *Publications:* Era of the Oath: Northern Loyalty Tests During the Civil War and Reconstruction 1954, To Try Men's Souls: Loyalty Tests in American History 1959, Stanton: The Life and Times of Lincoln's Secretary of War (with Benjamin P. Thomas) 1962, Soldiers and Spruce: The Loyal Legion of Loggers and Lumbermen, the Army's Labor Union of World War I 1963, A More Perfect Union: The Impact of the Civil War and Reconstruction on the Constitution 1973, Union and Confidence: The 1860s 1976, Equal Justice Under Law: Constitutional History, 1835–1875 (with William Wiecek) 1982, Quiet Past and Stormy Present?: War Powers in American History 1986, American Singularity: The 1787 Northwest Ordinance, the 1862 Homestead-Morrill Acts, and the 1944 G.I. Bill 1986, Oleander Odyssey: The Kempners of Galveston, 1870–1980 1990, The Reconstruction Justice of Salmon P. Chase: In Re Turner and Texas v White 1997, Craftsmanship and Character: A History of the Vinson & Elkins Law Firm of Houston, 1917–1990s 1998; editor: several books; contributions: scholarly journals. *Honours:* Albert J. Beveridge Award, American Historical Asscn 1952, Coral H. Tullis Memorial Prize, Texas A & M Univ. Press 1990, T. R. Fehrenbach Book Award, Texas Historical Commission 1990, Ottis Lock Endowment Award, East Texas Historical Asscn 1991.

HYMAN, Timothy, RA; British painter and writer; b. 17 April 1946, Hove; s. of Alan Hyman and Noreen Gypson; m. Judith Ravenscroft 1982. *Education:* Charterhouse and Slade School of Fine Art, London. *Career:* Curator Narrative Paintings at Arnolfini and ICA Galleries, etc. 1979–80; public collections include Arts Council, Bristol City Art Gallery, British Council Collection, Museum of London, Contemporary Art Soc., British Museum, Govt Art Collection, Los Angeles Co. Museum; Visiting Prof. at Baroda, India, two British Council lecture tours 1981–83; Artist-in-Residence, Lincoln Cathedral 1983–84, Sandown Racecourse 1992, Maggie's Cancer Caring Centres 2011–12; Purchaser for Arts Council Collection 1985; selector, John Moores Prize 1995; Lead Curator Stanley Spencer retrospective exhbn, Tate Gallery, London 2001–; Co-curator British Vision, Museum of Fine Arts, Ghent 2007. *Exhibitions:* started to exhibit at Blond 1980, solo exhbns 1981, 1983 and 1985; Austin/Desmond (solo exhbn 1990, 2000, 2003, 2006, 2009), Castlefield Gallery, Manchester 1993, Gallery Chemould, Bombay 1994, Gallery M, Flowers East 1994; group exhbns at Royal Acad., Hayward Gallery, Whitechapel Art Gallery, Nat. Portrait Gallery, Museum of London. *Publications:* Hodgkin 1975, Kitaj 1977, Beckmann 1978, Balthus 1980, Narrative Paintings 1979, English Romanesque 1984, Kiff 1986, Domenico Tiepolo 1987, Bhupen Khakhar (monograph) 1998, Bonnard (monograph) 1998, Carnivalesque (catalogue) 2000, Stanley Spencer (catalogue) 2001, Sienese Painting (monograph) 2003; numerous articles on contemporary figurative painting in London Magazine, Artscribe, Times Literary Supplement 1975–. *Honours:* Leverhulme Award 1992, Rootstein Hopkins Foundation Award 1995, Wingate Award 1998, Medaglio Beato Angelico, Florence 2005, Nat. Portrait Gallery/BP Travel Award 2007. *Address:* 62 Myddelton Square, London, EC1R 1XX, England (home). *Telephone:* (20) 7837-1933 (home).

HYNES, Samuel, DFC, PhD, FRSL; American academic and writer; *Professor Emeritus, Department of English, Princeton University;* b. 29 Aug. 1924, Chicago; s. of Samuel Lynn and Margaret Hynes (née Turner); m. Elizabeth Igleheart 1944 (died 2008); two d. *Education:* Univ. of Minnesota, Columbia Univ. *Career:* served in USMCR 1943–46, 1952–53; mem. faculty, Swarthmore Coll. 1949–68, Prof. of English Literature 1965–68; Prof. of English, Northwestern Univ., Evanston, Ill. 1968–76; Prof. of English, Princeton Univ. 1976–90, Woodrow Wilson Prof. of Literature 1978–90, Prof. Emer. 1990–. *Publications:* The Pattern of Hardy's Poetry (Explicator Award 1962) 1961, William Golding 1964, The Edwardian Turn of Mind 1968, Edwardian Occasions 1972, The Auden Generation 1976, Flights of Passage: Reflections of a World War Two Aviator 1988, A War Imagined: The First World War and English Culture 1990, The Soldiers' Tale (Robert F. Kennedy Book Award 1998) 1997, The Growing Seasons: An American Boyhood Before the War 2003; Ed.: Further Speculations by T. E. Hulme 1955, The Author's Craft and Other Critical Writings of Arnold Bennett 1968, Romance and Realism 1979, Complete Poetical Works of Thomas Hardy, Vol. I 1982, Vol. II 1984, Vol. III 1985, Vols IV, V 1995, Thomas Hardy 1984, Complete Short Fiction of Joseph Conrad (Vol. I–III) 1992, (Vol. IV) 1993. *Honours:* Fulbright Fellow 1953–54; Guggenheim Fellow 1959–60, 1981–82; Bollingen Fellow 1964–65; American Council of Learned Socs Fellow 1969, 1985–86; Nat. Endowment for Humanities Sr Fellow 1973–74, 1977–78; American Acad. of Arts and Letters Award in Literature 2004. *Address:* 130 Moore Street, Princeton, NJ 08540 (home); Department of English, 22 McCosh Hall, Princeton University, Princeton, NJ 08544-1006, USA (office). *Website:* web.princeton.edu/sites/english/new_web/index.htm (office).

I

IACUB, Marcela; French (b. Argentine) lawyer, researcher and writer; b. 1964; m. Patrice Maniglier. *Career:* moved to France 1989; researcher at CNRS, mem. Centre de Recherches Historiques (CRH—Centre for Historical Research), Ecole des Hautes Etudes en Sciences Sociales. *Publications include:* Au-delà du Pacs: l'expertise familiale à l'épreuve de l'homosexualité (co-ed.) 1999, Juger la vie: Le choix médicaux en matière de procréation (co-author) 2001, Le crime était presque sexuel 2002, Penser les droits de la naissance 2002, Qu'avez-vous fait de la révolution sexuelle? 2002, L'empire du ventre 2004, Aimer tue (novel) 2005, Bêtes et victimes et autres chroniques de Libération 2005, Antimanuel d'éducation sexuelle (co-author with Patrice Maniglier) 2005, Une journée dans la vie de Lionel Jospin 2006, Par le trou de la serrure: Une histoire de la pudeur publique, XIXème-XXIème siècle 2008. *Address:* Centre de Recherches Historiques (CRH), 54 blvd Raspail, 75270 Paris Cedex 06 (office); 117 boulevard Bessières, 75017 Paris, France. *Telephone:* 1-49-54-24-42 (office); 1-53-11-00-83. *Fax:* 1-49-54-23-99 (office). *E-mail:* marcela.iacub@wanadoo.fr.

IANNUCCI, Armando, OBE, MA; British screenwriter, author and producer; b. 28 Nov. 1963, Glasgow, Scotland; s. of Armando Iannucci; m. Rachael Jones 1990; two s. one d. *Education:* Univ. of Glasgow, University Coll., Oxford. *Career:* has produced, presented, written and appeared in numerous programmes for radio (BBC) and TV (BBC, Channel 4); Visiting Prof. of Broadcast Media, Univ. of Oxford 2006; columnist, The Observer. *Radio includes:* for BBC Radio 4, as producer: Quote... Unquote 1989–90, Week Ending 1991, The News Quiz 1989–90, On The Hour (also creator, co-writer) 1991–92, Knowing Me Knowing You (also writer) 1992–93; as actor: Lionel Nimrod's Inexplicable World (various characters) 1992, 1993; for others: No' The Archie McPherson Show (BBC Radio Scotland, also presenter, writer) 1988, The Mary Whitehouse Experience (BBC Radio 1) 1990, Loose Talk 1991–92, Armando Iannucci Show (BBC Radio 1, also writer, presenter) 1993–97; as presenter: Bite the Wax 1988–89, In Excess 1993–94, Scraps with Iannucci 1998, The News Quiz (regular guest), The 99p Challenge, The Unbelievable Truth, Armando Iannucci's Charm Offensive 2005–07. *Television includes:* for BBC 2: The Day Today (co-writer/producer) 1993, Knowing Me Knowing You with Alan Partridge (co-writer/producer) 1994, The Saturday Night Armistice (writer/co-presenter) 1995, The Friday Night Armistice (two series) 1996–98, I'm Alan Partridge (co-writer/producer) (two series) 1997, 2002, Clinton: His Struggle With Dirt (writer/dir) 1998, Britain's Best Sitcom (guest presenter) 2004, The Thick of It (writer/dir) (three series) 2005–09, Time Trumpet (co-writer/dir/performer) 2006, Comics Britannia (narrator) 2007, Lab Rats (exec. producer) 2008, Stewart Lee's Comedy Vehicle (exec. producer, and appears in 'Comedy Extra' segments on red button) 2009; regular contrib. to Daily Politics; for Channel 4: Loose Talk, The Armando Iannucci Shows 2001, Channel 4's 2010 Alternative Election (guest); other: Paradise Lost (presenter and writer), Veep (HBO) (writer, dir, producer) 2012, Armando Iannucci on Dickens (writer, presenter) 2012. *Music:* wrote libretto for Skin Deep 2009. *Films:* Tube Tales (writer and dir of 'Mouth') 1999, In the Loop (dir) 2009. *Publications:* Facts and Fancies 1997, Alan Partridge: Every Ruddy Word (with others) 2003, The Audacity of Hype: Bewilderment, Sleaze and Other Tales of the 21st Century 2009. I, Partridge: We Need to Talk About Alan 2011. *Honours:* two Sony Radio Awards, three British Comedy Awards. *Literary Agent:* c/o Lucy Fairney, PBJ Management, 5 Soho Square, London, W1D 3QA, England. *Telephone:* (20) 7287-1112. *Fax:* (20) 7287-1191. *E-mail:* lucy@pbjmgt.co.uk. *Website:* www.pbjmgt.co.uk.

IBRAGIMBEKOV, Maksud Mamed Ibragim ogli; Azerbaijani/Russian writer, scriptwriter and playwright; *Chairman, National Peace Committee of Azerbaijan;* b. 1935, Baku; s. of Mamed Ibragim Ibragimbekov and Fatima Alekper-kyzy Meshadibekova; brother of Rustam Ibragimbekov; m. Anna Yuryebna Ibragimbekova (née Gerulaitis); one s. *Education:* Baku Polytechnic Inst., High Scenario and Directoral Courses, Moscow. *Career:* Supt Aztyazhpromstroi 1960–62; freelance scriptwriter, theatre dir 1964–; mem. USSR (now Russian) Union of Writers 1965–; mem. Azerbaijan Parl. 1985–2010; Pres. PEN Club, Azerbaijan 1991–2009; Chair. Nat. Peace Cttee of Azerbaijan 1984–, Nobility Ass. of Azerbaijan 1995–. *Plays:* Mesozoic Story (Moscow Maly Theatre) 1975, Death of All the Good (Leningrad Theatre of Young Spectator) 1978, Men for Young Woman (Dramatic Theatre) 1992, The Oil Boom is Smiling on Everyone 2002, Restoran Final (Restaurant Final) (Baku Dramatic Theatre) 2006, Rolls Royce of Her Majesty (Baku Dramatic Theatre) 2009. *Films:* 23 films, including Latest Night of Childhood, Djabishmuallim, Who is Going to Travel to Truskavets?, Latest Interview, Etc. 23 films. *Television:* Gold Voyage 1993, The History with Happy End 1998. *Publications:* Who is Going to Travel to Truskavets?, There Was Never a Better Brother, Let Him Stay With Us; novels and prose in magazines and separate editions. *Honours:* Amb. for Peace; Order of Labour Red Banner 1981, Order of Glory of Azerbaijan Repub. 1995, Pope of Rome Praise 2002, Order of Independence (Azerbaijan) 2005, Order of Friendship (Russia) 2005, Order of Glory and Honor (Russia) 2010; State Prize of Azerbaijan Repub. 1975, People's Writer of Azerbaijan 1998. *Address:* 28 Boyuk Qala Str., 370004 Baku (office); 38 Kutkashenli Str., 370006 Baku, Azerbaijan (home). *Telephone:* (12) 4929843 (office); (12) 4975300 (home). *Fax:* (12) 4928459 (office). *E-mail:* maksud@planet-az.com (office); maksud@azeurotel.com (home).

IBRAHIM, Sonallah; Egyptian writer; b. 1937, Cairo; m. 1975; one step-d. *Education:* Cairo Univ. *Career:* fmr journalist; full-time writer since 1975; Visiting Assoc. Prof. Dept of Near Eastern Studies, Univ. of California at Berkeley 1999. *Publications:* Tilka al-Raiha (The Smell of It) 1966, Star of August 1974, The Committee 1981, Beirut Beirut 1984, Zaat (also in trans. 2004) 1992, Sharaf (Best Egyptian Novel 1998) 1997, Cairo From Edge to Edge 1998, Warda 2000, Amrikanli 2004, Al-talassos (trans. as Stealth) 2007. *Honours:* Eweiss Prize 1994, Galeb Halasa Prize 1995, Ibn Rush Prize 2004. *Address:* Ali Fahmi Kamel St 2, 11351 Heliopolis, Cairo, Egypt (home); c/o Syracuse University Press, 621 Skytop Road, Suite 110, Syracuse, NY 13244-5290, USA (office). *Telephone:* (202) 633-2301 (home). *E-mail:* selorfaly@hotmail.com (home).

IDLE, Eric, BA; British writer, lyricist and actor; b. 29 March 1943, South Shields, Tyne and Wear, England; m. 1st Lynn Ashley (divorced); one s.; m. 2nd Tania Kosevich; one d. *Education:* Royal School, Wolverhampton and Pembroke Coll., Cambridge. *Films:* Albert Carter, Q.O.S.O. (writer) 1968, And Now for Something Completely Different (actor, writer) 1971, Monty Python and the Holy Grail (actor, writer, exec. prod.) 1975, Life of Brian (actor, writer) 1979, The Meaning of Life (actor, writer) 1983, Yellowbeard (actor) 1983, European Vacation (actor) 1985, The Transformers: The Movie (voice) 1986, The Adventures of Baron Munchausen (actor) 1988, Nuns on the Run (actor) 1990, Missing Pieces (actor) 1991, Too Much Sun (actor) 1991, Mom and Dad Save the World (actor) 1992, Splitting Heirs (actor, writer, exec. prod.) 1993, Casper (actor) 1995, The Wind in the Willows (actor) 1996, Quest for Camelot (voice) 1998, Rudolph the Red-Nosed Reindeer: The Movie (voice) 1998, The Secret of NIMH 2: Timmy to the Rescue (voice) 1998, Pirates: 3D Show (actor, writer) 1999, Journey into Your Imagination (actor) 1999, Hercules: Zero to Hero (voice) 1999, South Park: Bigger Longer & Uncut (voice) 1999, Dudley Do-Right (actor) 1999, Brightness (actor) 2000, 102 Dalmatians (voice) 2000, Pinocchio (voice) 2002, Hollywood Homicide (actor) 2003, Ella Enchanted (actor) 2004, The Nutcracker and the Mouseking (voice) 2004, Delgo (voice) 2007, Shrek the Third (voice) 2007, Delgo (voice) 2008. *Television:* Alice in Wonderland (actor) 1966, The Frost Report (series, writer) 1966, No, That's Me Over Here! (series, writer) 1967, At Last the 1948 Show (series, actor) 1967, Do Not Adjust Your Set (series, actor and writer) 1967–69, Simply Sheila (writer) 1968, According to Dora (series, writer) 1968, We Have Ways of Making You Laugh (series, actor and writer) 1968, Broaden Your Mind (series, writer) 1968, Hark at Barker (series, writer) 1969, Monty Python's Flying Circus (four series, actor and writer) 1969–74, Euroshow 71 (actor) 1971, The Two Ronnies (series, writer) 1971, The Ronnie Barker Yearbook (writer) 1971, Ronnie Corbett in Bed (writer) 1971, Monty Python's Fliegender Zirkus (actor, writer) 1972, Christmas Box (writer) 1974, Commander Badman (writer) 1974, Rutland Weekend Television (series, actor and writer) 1975, The Rutles (actor, writer, dir) 1978, The Mikado (film, actor) 1987, Nearly Departed (series, actor) 1989, Around the World in 80 Days (series, actor) 1989, Mickey Mouse Works (series, voice) 1999, Suddenly Susan (series, actor) 1999–2000, House of Mouse (series, voice) 2001, The Scream Team (film, actor) 2002, Rutles 2: Can't Buy Me Lunch (writer, dir) 2002, Christmas Vacation 2: Cousin Eddie's Island Adventure (film, actor) 2003, The Simpsons (voice) 2003–07, Super Robot Monkey Team Hyperforce Gol (voice) 2004–05. *Stage productions:* I'm Just Wild About Harry (actor, Edinburgh Festival) 1963, Monty Python Live at the Hollywood Bowl (actor, writer) 1982, The Mikado (actor, ENO) 1987, (actor, Houston Opera House) 1989, Monty Python's Spamalot (writer, The Shubert Theatre, Broadway) 2005. *Compositions:* songs for Monty Python's Flying Circus series 1969, Always Look on the Bright Side of Life.. (for Life of Brian film) 1979, Bruces' Philosophers Song (for Monty Python Live at the Hollywood Bowl) 1982, Sit On My Face (for Monty Python Live at the Hollywood Bowl) 1982, songs for The Meaning of Life film 1983, The Adventures of Baron Munchausen (song, for film) 1988, One Foot in the Grave (TV series theme song) 1990, That's Death (song for video game, Discworld II: Missing Presumed...!?) 1996, songs for Monty Python's Spamalot stage production 2005. *Publications include:* Hello Sailor 1975, The Rutland Dirty Weekend Book 1976, Pass the Butler 1982, Monty Python's Flying Circus: Just the Words (co-author, two vols) 1989, The Fairly Incomplete and Rather Badly Illustrated Monty Python Song Book (co-author) 1994, The Quite Remarkable Adventures of the Owl and the Pussycat (co-author) 1996, The Road to Mars 1998, The "Pythons" Autobiography by the "Pythons" (co-author) 2003, The Greedy Bastard Diary: A Comic Tour of America 2005. *Website:* pythonline.com.

IERONIM, Ioana; Romanian poet, translator and diplomatist; *Programme Director, Fulbright Exchange, Bucharest;* b. 1947, Transylvania. *Education:* Univ. of Bucharest. *Career:* fmr ed. and trans. for various scientific and encyclopedic publs; apptd Cultural Counsellor, Romanian Embassy in the USA; currently Programme Dir Fulbright Exchange, Bucharest. *Publications:* poetry: The Curtain 1983, Monday Mornings 1987, Poems 1986, The Fool's Triumph 1992, The Triumph of the Water Witch (co-trans.) 2000, Munci, zile, alunecari de teren: Poeme/proze 1970–2000 2001. *Address:* c/o Fulbright Commission, Ing. Costinescu Street, Nr.2 Sector 1, Bucharest, Romania.

IGGERS, Georg Gerson, BA, AM, PhD; German/American historian and academic; *Distinguished Professor Emeritus, State University of New York at*

Buffalo; b. 7 Dec. 1926, Hamburg, Germany; m. Wilma Abeles 1948, three s. *Education:* Univ. of Richmond, Va, Univ. of Chicago, New School for Social Research, New York. *Career:* Instructor, Univ. of Akron 1948–50; Assoc. Prof., Philander Smith Coll. 1950–56; Visiting Prof., Univ. of Arkansas 1956–57, 1964, Univ. of Rochester, NY 1970–71, Univ. of Leipzig 1992; Assoc. Prof., Dillard Univ., New Orleans, La 1957–63; Visiting Assoc. Prof., Tulane Univ. 1957–60, 1962–63; Assoc. Prof., Roosevelt Univ., Chicago 1963–65; Prof., State Univ. of NY, Buffalo 1965–78, Distinguished Prof. 1978–97, Distinguished Prof. Emer. 1997–; Visiting Scholar, Technische Hochschule, Darmstadt 1991, Forschungsschwerpunkt Zeithistorische Studien, Potsdam 1993, 1998, Univ. of Århus, Denmark 1998, Univ. of New England, Australia 1999, Univ. of Vienna, Austria 2002; Fellow, Int. Inst. of Cultural Studies, Vienna 2000; mem. Int. Comm. for the History and Theory of Historiography (Pres. 1995–2000). *Publications:* Cult of Authority: Political Philosophy of the Saint Simonians 1958, German Conception of History 1968, Leopold von Ranke: The Theory and Practice of History (co-ed.) 1973, New Directions in European Historiography 1975, International Handbook of Historical Studies (co-ed.) 1979, Social History of Politics (ed.) 1985, Aufklärung und Geschichte (co-ed.) 1986, Leopold von Ranke and the Shaping of the Historical Discipline (co-ed.) 1990, Marxist Historiography in Transition: Historical Writings in East Germany in the 1980s (ed.) 1991, Geschichtswissenschaft 20. Jahrhundert 1993, Historiography in the Twentieth Century: From Scientific Objectivity to the Postmodern Challenge 1997, Zwei Seiten der Geschichte (autobiog. with Wilma Iggers) 2002, Turning Points in Historiography (co-ed.) 2002, A Global History of Modern Historiography (co-author) 2008; contrib. to scholarly journals. *Honours:* Foreign mem. Acad. of Sciences of GDR 1990–92; Medal of Merit, First Class, Order of the Merit (FRG) 2007; Alexander von Humboldt Foundation Research Prize 1995–96; Hon. PhD (Univ. of Richmond) 2001, (Darmstadt Tech. Univ.) 2006. *Address:* 100 Ivyhurst Road, Amherst, NY 14226, USA (home). *Telephone:* (716) 836-1216 (home). *E-mail:* iggers@buffalo.edu (office).

IGGULDEN, John (Jack) Manners; Australian writer and industrialist; b. 12 Feb. 1917, Brighton, Vic.; m. Helen Carroll Schapper; one s. (deceased) two d. *Career:* man. family-owned manufacturing cos 1940–59; writer 1959–70; businessman 1970–; part-time writer 1980–; currently Chair. Planet Lighting, Lucinda Glassworks, Bellingen, NSW. *Publications:* Breakthrough 1960, The Storms of Summer 1960, The Clouded Sky 1964, Dark Stranger 1965, Summer's Tales 3 1966, Manual of Standard Procedures, Gliding Federation of Australia 1964, Gliding Instructor's Handbook 1968, The Promised Land Papers Vol. 1: The Revolution of the Good 1986, Vol. 2: How Things Are Wrong and How to Fix Them 1988, Vol. 3: The Modification of Freedom 1993, Silent Lies 1997, Good World 1998, The Good World Reader 2004; memoir series: Second Son 2005, Equal Partners 2005, The Blue Skies 2006, The Dark Clouds 2006, Late Starter 2007, Catching Up 2008, Open Ticket 2008. *Address:* 'Evandale', Promised Land, Bellingen, NSW 2454, Australia (home). *Telephone:* (2) 6655-1184 (home). *E-mail:* cjmhc@bordernet.com.au (home).

IGLORIA, Luisa A., PhD; Philippine/American poet and academic; *Director of MFA Creative Writing Program, Department of English, Old Dominion University*; b. (Maria Luisa B. Aguilar), 1961, Makati, Rizal, Philippines; d. of Gabriel Zafra Aguilar and Zosima Rillera Buccat. *Education:* Baguio Coll.-Univ. of the Philippines, Ateneo de Manila Univ., Univ. of Ill. at Chicago. *Career:* currently Dir of MFA Creative Writing Program, Dept of English, Old Dominion Univ. *Publications include:* poetry: Cordillera Tales (Nat. Book Award for Poetry 1991) 1990, Cartography: A Collection of Poetry on Baguio (Nat. Book Award 1993) 1992, Encanto 1994, In the Garden of the Three Islands 1995, Blood Sacrifice (Nat. Book Award for Poetry 1998) 1997, Songs for the Beginning of the Millennium 1999, Not Home, But Here: Writing from the Filipino Diaspora (ed) 2003, Juan Luna's Revolver (Ernest Sandeen Prize in Poetry, Univ. of Notre Dame) 2009; prose: Wedding Night (special mention The Pushcart Prize Anthology: Best of the Small Presses) 2003, The Birdcage Maker (poem) (first prize Fugue Award Competition in Poetry) 2004, Trill & Mordent (Second Prize, Editions Prize for Poetry, WordTech Editions 2004) 2005; contrib. to numerous anthologies, journals and periodicals, including Poetry East, Crab Orchard Review, The Missouri Review, Smartish Pace, New Letters, Our Own Voice electronic literary journal for Philippine people in the diaspora www.oovrag.com. *Honours:* 11 Palanca Awards for Literature in three genres (poetry, essay, fiction), Palanca Hall of Fame Distinction. *Address:* MFA Creative Writing Program and Department of English, 5000 Batten Arts and Letters, Old Dominion University, Hampton Boulevard, Norfolk, VA 23529, USA (office). *Telephone:* (757) 683-3991 (office). *Fax:* (757) 683-3241 (office). *E-mail:* ligloria@odu.edu (office). *Website:* al.odu.edu/english/mfacw (office); www.luisaigloria.com.

IGNATENKO, Vitaly Nikitich; Russian journalist; *Director-General, ITAR-TASS News Agency*; b. 19 April 1941, Sochi; m. Svetlana Ignatenko; one s. *Education:* Moscow Univ. *Career:* corresp., Deputy Ed.-in-Chief Komsomolskaya Pravda 1963–75; Deputy Dir-Gen. TASS (USSR Telegraph Agency) 1975–78; Deputy Head of Int. Information Section, CPSU Cen. Cttee 1978–86; Ed.-in-Chief Novoe Vremya 1986–90; Asst to fmr Pres. Gorbachev, Head of Press Service 1990–91; Dir-Gen. ITAR-TASS News Agency 1991–; Deputy Chair. Council of Ministers 1995–97; Pres., Chair. of Bd Russian Public TV (ORT) 1998–; Pres. World Asscn of Russian Press; mem. Int. Acad. of Information Science, Russian Fed. Comm. on UNESCO Affairs, Union of Russian Journalists, Union of Russian Cinematographers. *Publications:* several books and more than 30 film scripts. *Honours:* Order of the Friendship of Peoples (twice) 1996, Order of Merit to the Fatherland 1999; Lenin Prize 1978, Prize of USSR Journalists' Union 1975. *Address:* ITAR-TASS, 125993 Moscow, Tverskoy blvd 10-12, Russia (office). *Telephone:* (495) 202-29-81 (office). *Fax:* (495) 202-54-74 (office). *E-mail:* worldmarket@itar-tass.com (office). *Website:* www.itar-tass.com (office).

IGNATIEFF, Michael, BA, MA, PhD; Canadian writer, historian, academic and fmr politician; b. 12 May 1947, Toronto, Ont.; m. 1st Susan Barrowclough 1977; one s. one d.; m. 2nd Zsuzsanna Zsohar. *Education:* Univ. of Toronto, Harvard Univ., USA, Univ. of Cambridge, UK. *Career:* reporter, Globe and Mail newspaper, Toronto 1966–67; Teaching Fellow, Harvard Univ. 1971–74; Asst Prof., Univ. of British Columbia, Vancouver 1976–78; Sr Research Fellow, King's Coll., Cambridge, UK 1978–84; Visiting Prof., École des Hautes Études, Paris 1985; editorial columnist, The Observer, London 1990–93; corresp. for BBC, The Observer, New Yorker 1984–2000; mem. Int. Comm. on Sovereignty and Intervention; Carr Prof. of Human Rights Practice, Harvard Univ. 2000–05; Dir Carr Center for Human Rights Policy, John F. Kennedy School of Govt 2001–05; Chancellor Jackman Visiting Prof. in Human Rights Policy, Univ. of Toronto 2005; MP (Liberal) for Etobicoke-Lakeshore 2006–11, assoc. critic for Human Resources and Skills Devt in Official Opposition Shadow Cabinet 2006; unsuccessful campaign for leadership of Liberal Party of Canada 2006, Deputy Leader 2006–08, interim Leader of Liberal Party of Canada 2008–09, Leader 2009–11 (resgnd); residence at Massey Coll., Univ. of Toronto 2011–. *Television:* host of Thinking Aloud (BBC) 1986, Voices (Channel Four) 1986, The Late Show (BBC 2) 1989. *Publications:* A Just Measure of Pain: The Penitentiary in the Industrial Revolution 1978, Wealth and Virtue: The Shaping of Classical Political Economy in the Scottish Enlightenment (co-ed. with Istvan Hont) 1983, The Needs of Strangers: An Essay on the Philosophy of Human Needs 1984, The Russian Album: A Family Memoir (RSL W. H. Heinemann Award, UK, Governor-General Award, Canada 1988) 1987, Asya 1991, Scar Tissue (novel) 1993, Blood and Belonging: Journeys into the New Nationalism 1993, Isaiah Berlin: A Life 1998, The Warrior's Honor: Ethnic War and the Modern Conscience 1998, Virtual War: Kosovo and Beyond 2000, The Rights Revolution (Massey Lectures 2000) 2001, Human Rights as Politics and Idolatry (Tanner Lectures) 2001, Charlie Johnson in the Flames 2003, The Lesser Evil: Political Ethics in an Age of Terror 2004, After Paradise 2005; contribs to New York Times, New Yorker, New York Review of Books. *Honours:* Dr hc (Bishop's Univ.) 1995; Lionel Gelber Award 1994. *Address:* Massey College, 4 Devonshire Place, Toronto, ON M5S 2E1, Canada.

IGNATIUS, David, AB, Dipl.Econ.; American journalist and novelist; *Associate Editor, The Washington Post*; b. 1950, Cambridge, Mass; m. Dr Eve Ignatius; three d. *Education:* Harvard Univ., King's Coll., Cambridge, UK. *Career:* Ed. The Washington Monthly magazine 1975; reporter, The Wall Street Journal 1976–86, assignments included Steelworkers Corresp., Pittsburgh, Senate Corresp., Washington, DC, Middle East Corresp., Chief Diplomatic Corresp.; Ed. Sunday Outlook, The Washington Post 1986–90, Foreign Ed. 1990–93, apptd Asst Man. Business Ed. 1993, Assoc. Ed. 2004–; Exec. Ed. International Herald Tribune 2000–03; columnist, The Washington Post and Washington Post Writers Group 2003–. *Film:* Body of Lies. *Publications include:* Agents of Innocence 1987, SIRO 1991, The Bank of Fear 1994, A Firing Offense 1997, The Sun King 1999, Body of Lies 2007, The Increment 2009, Bloodmoney 2011; contribs to The New York Times Magazine, The Atlantic Monthly, Foreign Affairs and The New Republic. *Honours:* Chevalier, Légion d'honneur 2010; Frank Knox Fellow, Harvard-Cambridge Univs 1973–75, Edward Weintal Prize for Diplomatic Reporting 1985, Gerald Loeb Award for Commentary 2000, Edward Weintal Certificate 2006, Urbino Press Award 2010, Founder's Award, Int. Cttee for Foreign Journalism 2010. *Address:* Washington Post Writers Group, 1150 15th Sreet NW, Washington, DC 20071, USA (office). *Telephone:* (202) 334-6548 (office). *Fax:* (202) 334-5269 (office). *E-mail:* davidignatius@washpost.com (office). *Website:* www.postwritersgroup.com (office).

IHIMAERA-SMILER, Witi, BA; New Zealand (Maori) author; b. 7 Feb. 1944, Gisborne, New Zealand. *Education:* Univ. of Auckland, Victoria Univ. *Career:* fmr diplomat, New Zealand Ministry of Foreign Affairs 1973–89; faculty mem., Univ. of Auckland 1990–, now Prof. and Distinguished Creative Fellow in Maori Literature. *Publications:* Pounamu, Pounamy 1972, Tangi 1973, Whanau 1974, Maori 1975, The New Net Goes Fishing 1977, Into the World of Light 1980, The Matriarch 1986, The Whale Rider 1987, Dear Miss Mansfield 1989. *Honours:* Distinguished Companion of the New Zealand Order of Merit 2005. *Address:* Arts 1 Building, 5 Room 517, University of Auckland, 14a Symonds Street, Auckland 1142, New Zealand (office). *E-mail:* w.ihimaera@auckland.ac.nz (office).

IJUIN, Shizuka; Japanese novelist; b. 9 Feb. 1950, Yamaguchi Pref.; m. 1st Natsume Masako; m. 2nd Shino Hiroko. *Education:* Rikkyo Univ. *Career:* fmr freelance dir of TV commercials. *Films:* scriptwriter on adaptions of his own novels, Chibusa 1993, Kikansha sensei 2004. *Publications:* novels: Chibusa (Breasts) (Yoshikawa Eiji Prize for New Writers) 1991, Kaikyo (The Strait) 1991, Ukezuki (The Crescent Moon) (Naoki Prize) 1992, Toge no koe 1992, Hakushu 1992, Ukezuki 1992, Kikansha sensei 1994, Kinou Sukecchi (Yesterday Sketch) 1999, Goro-goro (Rolling Away) (Yoshikawa Prize for Literature) 2002. *E-mail:* info@ijuin-shizuka.com. *Website:* www.ijuin-shizuka.com.

IKEDA, Daisaku; Japanese Buddhist philosopher, peace activist and author; *President, Soka Gakkai International*; b. 2 Jan. 1928, Tokyo; s. of Nenokichi Ikeda and Ichi Ikeda; m. Kaneko Shiraki 1952; two s. *Education:* Fuji Coll. *Career:* Pres. Soka Gakkai 1960–79, Hon. Pres. 1979–, Pres. Soka Gakkai Int. 1975–; Founder Soka Univ., Soka Univ. of America, Soka Women's Coll., Tokyo and Kansai Soka Schools, Soka Kindergartens (Japan, Hong Kong, Singapore, Malaysia, Brazil and S Korea), Makiguchi Foundation for Educ., Inst. of Oriental Philosophy, Ikeda Center for Peace, Learning and Dialogue, Toda Inst. for Global Peace and Policy Research, Tokyo Fuji Art Museum, Min-On Concert Asscn, Victor Hugo House of Literature and Komeito Party; mem. Advisory Bd World Centres of Compassion for Children International, Ireland 2004–; Poet Laureate, World Acad. of Arts and Culture 1981–; World People's Poet, World Poetry Soc. Intercontinental, India 2007–; Foreign mem. Künstlerhaus, Austria 1991–, Brazilian Acad. of Letters 1993–. *Exhibition:* Dialogue with Nature (photographic exhbn shown in more than 40 countries 1988–). *Publications include:* The Human Revolution Vols I–VI 1972–99, The Living Buddha 1976, Choose Life (with A. Toynbee) 1976 (revised edn 2007), Buddhism: The First Millennium 1977 (revised edn 2009), Glass Children and Other Essays 1979, A Lasting Peace Vols I–II 1981, 1987, Before It Is Too Late (with A. Peccei) 1984 (revised edn 2009), Buddhism and the Cosmos 1985, The Flower of Chinese Buddhism 1986, Human Values in a Changing World (with B. Wilson) 1987 (revised edn 2008), Unlocking the Mysteries of Birth and Death 1988 (revised edn 2003), A Lifelong Quest for Peace (with L. Pauling) 1992 (revised edn 2009), Choose Peace (with J. Galtung) 1995, A New Humanism: The University Addresses of Daisaku Ikeda 1996 (revised edn 2010), The New Human Revolution, Vols I–XXIII (in Japanese) 1998–2011, The Wisdom of the Lotus Sutra, Vols I–VI 2000–03, Diálogo sobre José Martí (with C. Vitier) 2001, Choose Hope (with D. Krieger) 2002, Alborada del Pacífico (with P. Aylwin) 2002, On Being Human (with R. Simard and G. Bourgeault) 2002, Global Civilization: A Buddhist–Islamic Dialogue (with M. Tehranian) 2003, Planetary Citizenship (with H. Henderson) 2004, Moral Lessons of the Twentieth Century (with M. Gorbachev) 2005, A Quest for Global Peace (with J. Rotblat) 2006, A Dialogue between East and West (with R. Díez-Hochleitner) 2008, Embracing the Future 2008, Search for A New Humanity (with J. Derbolav) 2008, Ode to the Grand Spirit (with C. Aitmatov) 2009, Human Rights in the Twenty-first Century (with A. de Athayde) 2009, The Persistence of Religion (with H. G. Cox) 2009, Ikeda-Abdurrahman Wahid Dialogue (in Japanese) 2010, New Horizons in Eastern Humanism (with Tu Weiming) 2011 and other writings on Buddhism, civilization, life and peace. *Honours:* Hon. Prof., Nat. Univ. of San Marcos 1981, Peking Univ. 1984, Tsinghua Univ. 2010 and others; Hon. Senator, European Acad. of Sciences and Arts 1997–; Hon. Adviser, World Fed. of UN Asscns 1999–; Hon. mem. The Club of Rome 1996–, Inst. of Oriental Studies of Russian Acad. of Sciences 1996–, Photographic Soc. of Singapore 1999–, Russian Acad. of Arts 2007–; Hon. Dir, Jao Tsung-I Petite Ecole, Univ. of Hong Kong 2011– and others; Grand Cross, Order of the Sun of Peru 1984, Grand Cross, Order of May for Merit (Argentina) 1990, Commdr, Nat. Order of Southern Cross (Brazil) 1990, Kt Grand Cross of the Most Noble Order of the Crown (Thailand) 1991, Austrian Cross of Honour for Science and Art, First Class 1992, Grande Officiale, Ordine al Merito (Italy) 2006, Order of Friendship (Russia) 2008, Hwa-Gwan Order of Cultural Merit (Repub. of Korea) 2009 and others; more than 25 hon. degrees; UN Peace Award 1983, Kenya Oral Literature Award 1986, UNHCR Humanitarian Award 1989, Rosa Parks Humanitarian Award (USA) 1993, Simon Wiesenthal Center Int. Tolerance Award (USA) 1993, Tagore Peace Award, The Asiatic Soc. (India) 1997, Peace Gold Medal, Sydney Peace Foundation 2009, Goethe Medal, Goethe Soc., Weimar 2009 and others. *Address:* 32 Shinano-machi, Shinjuku-ku, Tokyo 160-8583, Japan (office). *Telephone:* (3) 5360-9831 (office). *Fax:* (3) 5360-9885 (office). *E-mail:* contact@sgi.org (office). *Website:* www.sgi.org (office); www.daisakuikeda.org.

IKHLASSI, Walid; Syrian novelist, short story writer, playwright and politician; b. 1935, Alexandretta (then part of Syria, ceded to Turkey 1939). *Education:* Univ. of Alexandria, Egypt. *Career:* moved to Aleppo when Alexandretta ceded to Turkey; fmr Lecturer, Coll. of Agric., Univ. of Aleppo; mem. Parl. *Publications:* short stories: The Cock 1954, The Dead Afternoon; short story collections: Stories 1963, The Time of Short Migrations 1970, Whatever Happened to Antara: And Other Syrian Stories (in trans.) 2004; 11 novels including A Winter of the Dry Sea 1965, The Lap of the Beautiful Lady 1969, Dar el Mit3a, The Minor Epic of Death 1993; The Path (play) (in trans.). *Address:* c/o University of Texas Press, PO Box 7819, Austin, TX 78713-7819, USA (office). *E-mail:* utpress@uts.cc.utexas.edu (office). *Website:* www.utexas.edu/utpress.

IKSTENA, Nora, BA; Latvian writer; b. 1969, Rīga. *Education:* Univ. of Latvia. *Career:* Guest Ed. Review of Contemporary Fiction (special issue on new Latvian fiction), USA 1995–97; columnist Diena newspaper; Pres. Latvian Centre for Literature. *Publications:* novels: Dzīves svinēšana (trans. as A Celebration of Life) 1998, Jaunavas mācība (trans. as The Education of the Virgin) 2001; short stories: Nieki un izpriecas (trans. as Trifles and Amusements) 1995, Maldīgas romances (trans. as Misleading Romances) 1997; non-fiction: Pānākšana: Grāmata par Annu Rūmani Keninu (biog., trans. as The Homecoming) 1993, Brīnumainā kārtā (trans. as But Then, Miraculously...) 1999, Vija Vētra: Deja un dvēsele (trans. as Vija Vētra: The Dance and the Soul) 2001; contrib. to reviews, journals and anthologies. *Honours:* Hans Christian Andersen Amb. for 2005 bicentenary (Denmark); Ministry of Culture Award for achievements in literature 1998, Baltic Assembly Prize 2006. *Address:* c/o Atena Publishers Ltd, Blaumana iela 16/18-2a, 1011 Rīga, Latvia (office). *Telephone:* 6728-3973 (office). *Fax:* 6728-2375 (office). *E-mail:* atena@atena.lv (office).

ILDEFONSO HUANCA, Miguel Dante, BA, MA; Peruvian poet, novelist and literary critic; b. 5 Jan. 1970, Lima. *Education:* Pontificia Universidad Católica del Perú, Univ. of Texas-El Paso, USA. *Career:* with online magazine El Malhechor Exhausto. *Publications:* poems: Vestigios 1999, Canciones de un Bar en la Frontera 2001, Las ciudades fantasmas 2002, M.D.I.H. 2004, Heautontimoroumenos 2005, Los Desmoronamientos Sinfónicos 2008, Himnos 2008, Libro de Exilio (Premio Nacional PUCP en la categoría poesía 2009) 2009, Todos los Trágicos Desiertos 2010, Dantes 2010; novels: El Paso 2005, Hotel Lima 2006, El último viaje de Camilo 2009; features in anthologies. *Honours:* Primer Puesto en los Juegos Florales de la Universidad Católica del Perú 1995, Primer Puesto del I Premio de Poesía "Luces de Bohemia" del Departamento de Literatura de la Universidad de Texas El Paso 1999, Primer Puesto del III Premio de Poesía "Luces de Bohemia" del Departamento de Literatura de la Universidad de Texas El Paso 2001, Ganador del X Premio COPE de Oro de Poesía (Petroperú) 2001, Ganador del II Concurso de Cuentos ACJ – Alfredo Bryce 2003, Ganador del Concurso de Cuentos de la Asociación Peruano-Japonés 2004. *Website:* miguelildefonso.blogspot.co.uk.

ILICHEVSKY, Alexander; Russian writer, poet and fmr physicist; b. 1970, Sumgait, Azerbaijan. *Education:* Moscow Univ. *Career:* worked in scientific research in Israel and USA 1991–98; currently Ed. Radio Svoboda. *Publications include:* Matisse (novel) (Russian Booker Prize) 2007; contrib. to Novyi mir, Oktiabr. *Address:* c/o Novyi Mir, 103806 Moscow, M. Putinkovskii per. 1/2, Russia (office). *Telephone:* (495) 200-08-29 (office). *E-mail:* nmir@aha.ru (office). *Website:* magazines.russ.ru/novyi_mi (office).

IMPEY, Rosemary (Rose) June; British writer; b. 7 June 1947, Northwich, Cheshire, England; two d. *Education:* teacher's certificate. *Publications:* Who's a Clever Girl, Then 1985, The Baked Bean Queen 1986, The Girls Gang 1986, Desperate for a Dog 1988, The Flat Man 1988, Letter to Father Christmas 1988, Instant Sisters 1989, Joe's Cafe 1990, Revenge of the Rabbit 1990, First Class 1992, Trouble with the Tucker Twins 1992, Orchard Book of Fairytales 1992, Animal Crackers 1993, Sir Billy Bear and Other Friends 1996, Potbelly and the Haunted House 1996, Fireballs from Hell 1996, Sleepover Club 1997, Feather Pillows 1997. *Address:* c/o Egmont, 239 Kensington High Street, London, W8 6SA, England. *E-mail:* info@egmont.co.uk.

INDRIÐASON, Arnaldur, BA; Icelandic journalist, film critic, historian and writer; b. 8 Jan. 1961, Reykjavík; m.; three c. *Education:* Univ. of Iceland. *Career:* journalist Morgunbladid newspaper 1981–82, film critic 1986–2001; freelance scriptwriter 1982–86. *Publications:* novels: Synir duftsins (trans. as Sons of Earth) 1997, Dauðarósir (Silent Kill) 1998, Napóleonsskjölin (Operation Napoleon) 1999, Mýrin (trans. as Jar City) (Skandinaviska Kriminalselskapet Glass Key 2002) 2000, Leyndardómar Reykjavíkur2000 (The Reykjavik 2000 Mystery) 2000, Grafarþögn (trans. as Silence of the Grave) (Skandinaviska Kriminalselskapet Glass Key 2003, CWA Gold Dagger 2005) 2001, Röddin (The Voice) (The Martin Beck Award for Translation, Sweden 2005) 2002, Bettý (Betty) 2003, Kleifarvatn (The Draining Lake) 2004, Vetrarborgin (Arctic Chill) 2005, Harðskafi (Hypothermia) 2007, Myrká 2008, Svörtuloft 2009. *Address:* c/o Harvill Press, Random House, 20 Vauxhall Bridge Road, London, SW1V 2SA, England (office).

INGALLS, Rachel Holmes, BA; American author; b. 13 May 1940, Boston, MA. *Education:* Radcliffe College. *Career:* mem. American Acad. and Institute of Arts and Letters, fellow. *Publications:* Theft, 1970; The Man Who Was Left Behind, 1974; Mediterranean Cruise, 1973; Mrs Caliban, 1982; Binstead's Safari, 1983; I See a Long Journey, 1985; The Pearlkillers, 1986; The End of the Tragedy, 1987; Something to Write Home About, 1990; Black Diamond, 1992; Be My Guest, 1992; Days Like Today, 2001. *Honours:* First Novel Award, Author's Club, England, 1971; British Book Marketing Council Best Book Award, 1986.

INGHAM, Kenneth, OBE, MC, MA, DPhil, FRHistS; British writer; *Professor Emeritus, University of Bristol*; b. 9 Aug. 1921, Harden, England; m. Elizabeth Mary Southall 1949; one s. one d. *Education:* Keble Coll., Oxford. *Career:* Lecturer, Makerere Coll., Uganda 1950–56, Prof. 1956–62; Dir of Studies, Royal Mil. Acad., Sandhurst 1962–67; Prof. of History, Univ. of Bristol 1967–84, Head Dept of History 1970–84, part-time Prof. of History 1984–86, Prof. Emer. 1986–; mem. Royal African Soc., Royal Historical Soc. *Publications:* Reformers in India 1956, The Making of Modern Uganda 1958, A History of East Africa 1962, The Kingdom of Toro in Uganda 1975, Jan Christian Smuts: The Conscience of a South African 1986, Politics in Modern Africa 1990, Obote: A Political Biography 1994; contrib. to reference books and professional journals. *Address:* The Woodlands, 94 West Town Lane, Bristol, BS4 5DZ, England (home). *Telephone:* (117) 977-6588 (home). *E-mail:* ingham65@btinternet.com (home).

INGLE, Stephen James, BA, DipEd, MA (Econ), PhD; British writer and academic; *Professor Emeritus of Politics, University of Stirling*; b. 6 Nov. 1940, Ripon, Yorks., England; s. of James Ingle and Violet Grace Ingle (née Stephenson); m. Margaret Anne Farmer 1964; two s. one d. *Education:* Univ. of Sheffield, Victoria Univ., NZ. *Career:* Lecturer, then Sr Lecturer, Dept of Politics, Univ. of Hull –1991; Prof. of Politics, Univ. of Stirling 1991–2006, Head, Dept of Politics 1991–2002, Vice-Dean, Faculty of Arts 1995–2001, Prof. Emer. 2006–; Visiting Lecturer, Univ. of Osnabruck 1979–83; Visiting

Research Fellow, Victoria Univ., NZ 1993; Overseas Scholar, State Univ. of Tbilisi 2005–08; Panel mem. Arts & Humanities Research Council (History) 2008–; mem. Political Studies Asscn, British Politics Group (American Political Science Asscn), Soc. of Authors. *Publications:* Socialist Thought in Imaginative Literature 1979, Parliament and Health Policy 1981, British Party System 1987, 1989, 2000, 2008, George Orwell: A Political Life 1993, Narratives of British Socialism 2002, The Social and Political Thought of George Orwell 2006; contrib. to many publs in the fields of politics and literature. *Honours:* Commonwealth Scholar 1964–67, Erasmus Scholar 1989, Visiting Overseas Fellow, Open Soc. 2005–08. *Address:* Department of Politics, University of Stirling, Stirling, FK9 4LA, Scotland (office). *Telephone:* (1786) 467593 (office). *Fax:* (1786) 466266 (office). *E-mail:* s.j.ingle@stir.ac.uk (office). *Website:* www.politics.stir.ac.uk (office).

INGRAMS, Richard Reid; British journalist; *Editor, The Oldie*; b. 19 Aug. 1937, London; s. of Leonard St Clair and Victoria Ingrams (née Reid); m. Mary Morgan 1962 (divorced 1993); two s. (one deceased) one d. *Education:* Shrewsbury School, Univ. Coll., Oxford. *Career:* co-founder Private Eye 1962, Ed. 1963–86, Chair. 1974–; founder and Ed. The Oldie 1992–; TV critic The Spectator 1976–84; columnist The Observer 1988–90, 1992–2005, The Independent 2005–. *Publications:* Private Eye on London (with Christopher Booker and William Rushton) 1962, Private Eye's Romantic England 1963, Mrs Wilson's Diary (with John Wells) 1965, Mrs Wilson's Second Diary 1966, The Tale of Driver Grope 1968, The Bible for Motorists (with Barry Fantoni) 1970, The Life and Times of Private Eye (ed.) 1971, Harris in Wonderland (as Philip Reid with Andrew Osmond) 1973, Cobbett's Country Book (ed.) 1974, Beachcomber: the works of J. B. Morton (ed.) 1974, The Best of Private Eye 1974, God's Apology 1977, Goldenballs 1979, Romney Marsh (with Fay Godwin) 1980, Dear Bill: The Collected Letters of Denis Thatcher (with John Wells) 1980, The Other Half 1981, Piper's Places (with John Piper) 1983, Dr Johnson by Mrs Thrale (ed.) 1984, Down the Hatch (with John Wells) 1985, Just the One (with John Wells) 1986, John Stewart Collis: A Memoir 1986, The Best of Dear Bill (with John Wells) 1986, Mud in Your Eye (with John Wells) 1987, The Eye Spy Look-alike Book (ed.) 1988, The Ridgeway 1988, You Might As Well Be Dead 1988, England: An Anthology 1989, No. 10 1989, On and On... Further Letters of Denis Thatcher (with John Wells) 1990, The Oldie Annual (ed.) 1993, The Oldie Annual II (ed.) 1994, Malcolm Muggeridge (ed.) 1995, I Once Met (ed.) 1996, The Oldie Annual III (ed.) 1997, Jesus: Authors Take Sides (anthology) 1999, The Oldie Annual IV (ed.) 1999, The Life and Adventures of William Cobbett (biog.) 2005. *Address:* The Oldie, 65 Newman Street, London, W1T 3EG, England. *Telephone:* (20) 7436-8801. *Fax:* (20) 7436-8804. *E-mail:* editorial@theoldie.co.uk. *Website:* www.theoldie.co.uk.

INKSTER, Tim; Canadian poet, printer, designer and publisher; b. 26 Sept. 1949, Toronto, Ont.; m. Elke Inkster. *Education:* University of Toronto. *Career:* designer and printer, Press Porcepic, Erin, Ont 1971–74; Co-owner, The Porcupine's Quill, Erin 1974–; mem. League of Canadian Poets, American Institute of Graphic Arts, Society of Graphic Designers of Canada. *Publications:* poetry: For Elke, 1971; The Topolobampo Poems and Other Memories, 1972; Mrs Grundy, 1983; The Coach House Press, 1974; The Crown Prince Waits for a Train, 1976; Blue Angel, 1981; Other: Letters, Riddles and Miscellany, 1976; The Porcupine's Quill Reader (co-ed.), 1997; Autobiographic films: Print Shop, 1976; Tim Inkster: Colours of a Poet, 1976. *Address:* 68 Main Street, Erin, ON N0B 1T0, Canada.

INNAURATO, Albert Francis, BA, BFA, MFA; American playwright, writer and stage director; b. 2 June 1947, Philadelphia, PA. *Education:* Temple University, California Institute of the Arts, Yale University. *Career:* Playwright-in-Residence, Public Theatre, New York City, 1977, Circle Repertory Theatre, New York City, 1979, Playwright's Horizons, New York City, 1983; Adjunct Prof., Columbia University, Princeton University, 1987–89; Instructor, Yale School of Drama, 1993; mem. Dramatists Guild; Writers Guild of America. *Publications:* Plays: Earthworms, 1974; Gemini, 1977; The Transfiguration of Bennon Blimpie, 1977; Verna the USO Girl, 1980; Gus and Al, 1988; Magda and Callas, 1988. Other: Coming of Age in Soho, 1985. Contributions: newspapers and journals. *Honours:* Guggenheim Fellowship, 1976; Rockefeller Foundation Grant, 1977; Obie Awards, 1977, 1978; Emmy Award, 1981; National Endowment for the Arts Grants, 1986, 1989; Drama League Award, 1987.

INNES, Brian, BSc, MRSC; British writer and publisher (retd); b. 4 May 1928, Croydon, Surrey, England; m. 1st Felicity McNair Wilson 1956; m. 2nd Eunice Lynch 1971; three s. *Education:* King's Coll. London. *Career:* Asst Ed. Chemical Age 1953–55; Assoc. Ed. The British Printer 1955–60; Art Dir Hamlyn Group 1960–62; Dir Temperance Seven Ltd 1961–; Proprietor Brian Innes Agency 1964–66, Immediate Books 1966–70, FOT Library 1970–; Creative Dir and Deputy Chair. Orbis Publishing Ltd 1970–86; Editorial Dir Mirror Publishing 1986–88; numerous recordings, films, radio and television broadcasts; many photographs published; mem. Arts Club, Chartered Soc. of Designers, RSA, Inst. of Paper, Printing and Publishing, CWA, British Actors' Equity, RSL, Royal Soc. of Chemistry. *Publications:* Book of Pirates 1966, Book of Spies 1967, Book of Revolutions 1967, Book of Outlaws 1968, Flight 1970, Saga of the Railways 1972, Horoscopes 1976, The Tarot 1977, Book of Change 1979, The Red Baron Lives 1981, Red Red Baron 1983, The Havana Cigar 1983, Crooks and Conmen 1993, Catalogue of Ghost Sightings 1996, The History of Torture 1998, Death and The Afterlife 1999, Dreams 1999, Bodies of Evidence 2000, A Long Way from Pasadena 2001, Snapshots of the Sixties 2002, United Kingdom 2002, Myths of Ancient Rome 2002, Profile of a Criminal Mind 2003, The Body in Question 2005; contrib. to Man, Myth & Magic, Take Off, Real Life Crimes, Fire Power, The Story of Scotland, Discover Scotland, Marshall Cavendish Encyclopaedia of Science. *Honours:* Royal Variety Command Performance 1961. *Address:* 21 Southwick Mews, London, W2 1JG, England (office); Les Forges de Montgaillard, 11330 Montgaillard, France (home). *Telephone:* (4) 68-45-09-43 (home). *Fax:* (4) 68-45-09-43 (home). *E-mail:* binnes1@compuserve.com.

INUKAI, Tomoko, BA; Japanese journalist and writer; b. 18 April 1931, Tokyo; d. of Mototake and Katsuko Hatano; m. Yasuhiko Inukai 1953 (divorced 1978); one s. one d. *Education:* Univs of Gakushin and Illinois (USA). *Career:* Journalist Far E. Bureau, Chicago Daily News 1957–60; published first book 1968; mem. Cttee Social Policy Council, Econ. Planning Agency 1988, Cttee Tokyo Metropolitan Marine Park 1990; solo art exhibition Tokyo 1992; Del. to Jt Japan Inst. for Social and Econ. Affairs and Swiss Inst. of Int. Studies Japan Symposium, Zurich, Switzerland 1979. *Publications include:* How to Avoid Housekeeping: to be free from the house 1968, Men and Women: new relationships 1982, Suspicious Circuit 1986, Japan Rediscovering Kabuki 1989. *Address:* 25-19 Kamiyama-cho, Shibuya-ku, Tokyo 150, Japan. *Telephone:* (3) 469-4691. *Fax:* (3) 460-3040.

IOANNIDOU-ADAMIDOU, Irena; Cypriot writer and translator; b. 5 Feb. 1939, Famagusta; d. of the late Cleanthis Ioannides and of Anastasia Ioannides (née Galanou); m. Panos Adamides 1961; two d. *Education:* Brillantmont International Coll., Acad. of Music, Lausanne, Switzerland and Univ. of Vienna, Austria. *Career:* writer since the age of 16; collaboration with Cyprus Broadcasting Corpn and numerous other TV and radio stations and theatres 1962–; mem. Public Relations Cttee, Cyprus PEN 1980–86; mem. Cyprus Center of the Inst. of Translating and Interpreting, PEN Club Cyprus Center, Nat. Asscn of Greek Authors, Cyprus, Asscn of Playwrights, Cyprus, Asscn of Greek Playwrights and Literary Translators. *Publications include:* novels: Hommes, chemins et destin (People, Ways and Destiny) 1959, Maria Cristina 1960, Symphonie Héroïque (Heroic Symphony) 1961, Dans les bras de la mer (In the Arms of the Sea) 1962, Mme Rime (Mrs. Rima) 1963, Mattinata 1964, Nous vivrons/Un ciel comme le nôtre (We Shall Live/A Sun Like Ours) 1981, The Hair/The Last Card 2001, Duel with the Wind 2003, The Nightingale of Smyrna 2006, Roads of the East 2009; Plays: The World of the Mythology 1967, Le parfum 1968, Le suicide 1970, La vengeance 1975, Visite 1977, Conflit 1978, Le cerf-volant 1980, Le champ 1982, Délit prémédité 1983, Post mortem 1986, Lutte secrète 1987, Syméos 1989, Le conseil conjugal (First Prize, Cyprus Radio) 1990, The Suspects (winner VII Third World International Playwright Competition 1994), The Robbery; short stories: Short Stories 1968, Ups and Downs 1973, Syméos (Pan-Hellenic Prize, Athens) 1985, La Fille de Théodore (Theodor's Daughter) 1992, Uncle Alexander (Third Prize, Le culture del Mediterraneo, Genova) 2005, The Nightingale of Smyrna 2006, Roads of the East 2009, Student Short Story International (12); has translated works from French, English, Spanish, etc by writers including Alfred de Musset, Molière, Boris Vian, Romain Rolland, Diego Fabbri, Strindberg, Natalia Ginzburg, Arthur Miller. *Honours:* Cavaliere dell'Ordine della Stella della Solidarieta Italiana 2004; numerous awards and prizes. *Address:* Vontyza Street 8, Flat 402, 1076 Nicosia, Cyprus (home). *Telephone:* (2) 2422181 (home). *E-mail:* pkadam@cytanet.com.cy.

IOANNOU, Susan, BA, MA; Canadian writer, editor and poet; *Director, Wordwrights Canada*; b. 4 Oct. 1944, Toronto, Ont.; m. Lazaros Ioannou 1967; one s. one d. *Education:* Univ. of Toronto. *Career:* Managing Ed. Coiffure du Canada 1979–80; Assoc. Ed. Cross-Canada Writers' Magazine 1980–89; Poetry Ed. Arts Scarborough Newsletter 1980–85; Poetry Instructor, Toronto Bd of Educ. 1982–94, Univ. of Toronto 1989–90; Dir Wordwrights Canada 1985–; mem. League of Canadian Poets, Writers' Union of Canada, Arts and Letters Club of Toronto. *Publications include:* Spare Words 1984, Motherpoems 1985, The Crafted Poem 1985, Familiar Faces, Private Griefs 1986, Ten Ways to Tighten Your Prose 1988, Writing Reader-Friendly Poems 1989, Clarity Between Clouds 1991, Read-Aloud Poems: For Students from Elementary through Senior High School 1993, Polly's Punctuation Primer 1994, Where the Light Waits 1996, A Real Farm Girl 1998, A Magical Clockwork: The Art of Writing the Poem 2000, Coming Home 2004, An Old Love Story 2004, Who Would be God? (with Lenny Everson) 2004, Balkan Poems 2005, O Canada: Three Poems 2005, The Merla Poems 2006, Catalysts & Catastrophes: Feline Poems 2007, Looking Through Stone: Poems about the Earth 2007, Holding True: Essays on Being a Writer 2008, Nine to Ninety: stories across the generations 2009. *Honours:* Arts Scarborough Poetry Award 1987, Media Club of Canada Memorial Award 1990, Okanagan Short Story Award 1997. *E-mail:* susanio@sympatico.ca (office). *Website:* www3.sympatico.ca/susanio/WWC.html (office).

IPARRAGUIRRE, Sylvia; Argentine novelist; b. 4 July 1947, Junín, Buenos Aires; m. Abelardo Castillo 1976. *Career:* Prof. of Modern Literature, Instituto de Literatura Hispanoamericana de la Facultad de Filosofía y Letras, Universidad de Buenos Aires 1986–; co-founder of literary journal El Ornitorrinco. *Publications:* En el invierno de las ciudades (short stories) (Premio Municipal de Literatura) 1988, Probables lluvias por la noche (short stories) 1993, El Parque (novel) 1996, Tierra del Fuego: una biografía del fin del mundo (novel) (Sor Juana Inés de la Cruz Prize) 2000, Narrativa Breve 2006, El muchacho de los Senos de Goma 2007; contrib. short stories and essays to newspapers and literary journals, including El Escarabajo de Oro, Clarín, Página\12, ETC, Contexto, Puro Cuento, Tramas, Cuadernos Hispanoamericanos, and short stories to numerous anthologies. *Address:* c/o

Alfaguara, Grupo Santillana Argentina, Avenida L.N. Alem 720, 1001 Buenos Aires, Argentina (office). *E-mail:* info@alfaguara.com.ar (office). *Website:* www.alfaguara.com.ar (office).

IRBY, Kenneth Lee, BA, MA, MLS, PhD; American writer, poet and teacher; b. 18 Nov. 1936, Bowie, Tex. *Education:* University of Kansas, Harvard University, University of California. *Career:* Assoc. Prof. of English, University of Kansas, Lawrence. *Publications include:* The Roadrunner Poem 1964, Kansas-New Mexico 1965, Movements/Sequences 1965, The Flower of Having Passed Through Paradise in a Dream 1968, Relation 1970, To Max Douglas 1971, Archipelago 1976, Catalpa 1977, Orexis 1981, Riding the Dog 1982, A Set 1983, Call Steps 1992, Antiphonal and Fall to Fall 1994; contributions: anthologies and magazines.

IRELAND, David Neil, AM; Australian novelist; b. 24 Aug. 1927, Lakemba, NSW. *Education:* state schools in NSW. *Publications:* Image in the Clay (play) 1962, The Chantic Bird 1968, The Unknown Industrial Prisoner 1971, The Flesheaters 1972, Burn 1974, The Glass Canoe 1976, The Wild Colonial Boy (short story) 1979, A Woman of the Future 1979, City of Women 1981, Archimedes and the Eagle 1984, Bloodfather 1987, The Chosen 1997. *Honours:* Adelaide Advertiser Award 1966, Age Book of the Year Award 1980. *Address:* c/o Penguin Group (Australia), 250 Camberwell Road, Camberwell, Vic. 3124, Australia.

IRELAND, Kevin Mark, OBE; New Zealand poet and writer; b. 18 July 1933, Auckland; m. Phoebe Caroline Dalwood (deceased); two s. *Career:* Writer-in-Residence, Canterbury Univ. 1986; Sargeson Fellow, Auckland Univ. 1987; Literary Fellow 1989; Russell Henderson Arts Fellow 2010; mem. NZSA (PEN) (Nat. Pres. PEN 1990–92); Vice-Chair. Sargeson Trust 2005; Vice-Pres. North Shore Cricket Club 2000; Patron Torpedo Bay Indoor Bowling Club 2000. *Publications:* poetry: Face to Face 1964, Educating the Body 1967, A Letter From Amsterdam 1972, Orchids, Hummingbirds and Other Poems 1974, Poems 1974, A Grammar of Dreams 1975, Literary Cartoons 1978, The Dangers of Art: Poems 1975–80 1980, Practice Night in the Drill Hall 1984, The Year of the Comet 1986, Selected Poems 1987, Tiberius at the Beehive 1990, Skinning a Fish 1994, Anzac Day: Selected Poems 1997, Fourteen Reasons for Writing 2001, Walking the Land 2003, Airports and Other Wasted Days 2007, How to Survive the Morning 2008, Table Talk 2009; other: Sleeping with the Angels (short stories) 1995, Blowing My Top (novel) 1996, The Man Who Never Lived (novel) 1997, Under the Bridge and Over the Moon (memoir) 1998, The Craymore Affair (novel) 2000, Backwards to Forwards (memoir) 2002, Getting Away With It (novel) 2004, On Getting Old (essays) 2005, How to Catch a Fish (essays) 2005, The Jigsaw Chronicles (novel) 2008, Daisy Chains (novel) 2010. *Honours:* Hon. DLitt 2000; NZ Nat. Book Award for Poetry 1979, Commemorative Medal 1990, Montana Award for History and Biography 1999, NZ Prime Minister's Award for Literary Achievement (Poetry) 2004, A. W. Reed Award 2006. *Address:* 3A Everest Street, Devonport, Auckland 0624, New Zealand (home). *E-mail:* kireland@xtra.co.nz (home).

IRVING, Clifford Michael, (John Luckless), BA; American writer and screenwriter; b. 5 Nov. 1930, New York, NY; m. 3rd Julie Irving; three s. *Education:* Cornell University. *Publications:* On a Darkling Plain 1956, The Losers 1957, The Valley 1962, The 38th Floor 1965, Spy 1969, The Battle of Jerusalem 1970, Fake 1970, Global Village Idiot 1973, Project Octavio 1978, The Death Freak 1979, The Hoax 1981, Tom Mix and Pancho Villa 1982, The Sleeping Spy 1983, The Angel of Zin 1984, Daddy's Girl 1988, Trial 1990, Final Argument 1993, The Spring 1995, I Remember Amnesia. *Address:* c/o Hyperion Editorial Department, 77 West 66th Street, 11th Floor, New York, NY 10023, USA (office). *Website:* www.hyperionbooks.com (office); www.cliffordirving.com.

IRVING, Janet Turnbull, MA; Canadian literary agent; b. 16 April 1954, Toronto; d. of Donald Gibson and Joan Heloise Turnbull; m. John Irving 1987; one s. *Education:* Univ. of Toronto. *Career:* Ed. Authors' Marketing Services Ltd 1979; Ed. Doubleday Canada Ltd 1980, Man. Ed. 1981; Vice-Pres., Publr and Dir Seal Books 1984–87; Pres. The Turnbull Agency 1987–, Curtis Brown Canada Ltd 1989–99; Ed. Bantam Canada Inc.; Founding-Pres. The Canadian Business Task Force on Literacy; Co-founder (with her husband) and Chair. Bd of Trustees Maple Street School (ind. primary school), Vt. *Address:* Turnbull Agency, PO Box 757, Dorset, VT 052551-0757, USA (office).

IRVING, John Winslow, BA, MFA; American writer; b. 2 March 1942, Exeter, NH; s. of Colin F. N. Irving and Frances Winslow; m. 1st Shyla Leary 1964 (divorced 1981); two s.; m. 2nd Janet Turnbull 1987; one s. *Education:* Univs of Pittsburgh, Vienna, New Hampshire and Iowa. *Career:* Asst Prof. of English, Mount Holyoke Coll. 1967–72, 1975–78; Writer-in-Residence, Univ. of Iowa 1972–75; with Bread Loaf Writers' Conf. 1976, Brandeis Univ.; Rockefeller Foundation grantee 1971–72; Nat. Endowment for Arts Fellow 1974–75, Guggenheim Fellow 1976–77; mem. American Acad. of Arts and Letters 2001. *Publications:* novels: Setting Free the Bears 1969, The Water-Method Man 1972, The 158-Pound Marriage 1974, The World According to Garp (Nat. Book Award 1980 for paperback fiction 1980) 1978, The Hotel New Hampshire 1981, The Cider House Rules 1985, screenplay (Acad. Award for the best adapted screenplay 2000) 1999, A Prayer for Owen Meany 1989, A Son of the Circus 1994, A Widow for One Year 1998, The Cider House Rules 1999, The Fourth Hand 2001, Until I Find You 2005, Last Night in Twisted River 2009, In One Person 2012; non-fiction: An Introduction to Great Expectations 1986, Trying to Save Piggy Sneed (memoirs, short stories and essays) 1996, An Introduction to A Christmas Carol 1996, My Movie Business (memoir) 1999; contrib. to New York Times Book Review, New Yorker, Rolling Stone, Esquire, Playboy. *Honours:* , O. Henry Award 1981. *Literary Agent:* Turnbull Agency, PO Box 757, Dorset, VT 05251, USA. *Website:* www.john-irving.com.

ISAACS, Anne, BA, MS; American writer; b. 2 March 1949, Buffalo, NY; one s. two d. *Education:* University of Michigan, SUNY at Buffalo. *Career:* numerous positions in environmental education 1975–90. *Publications:* Swamp Angel, 1994, (broadcast adaptation, 1995); Treehouse Tales, 1997; Cat up a Tree, 1998; Torn Thread, 2000. *Honours:* Ralph Caldecott Honor Book, American Library Asscn Notable Books Selection, New York Times Best Illustrated Books Citation, School Library Journal Best Books, Publishers Weekly Best Books, Honor Book, Boston Globe-Horn Book, Children's Book of the Year List, Child Study Children's Book Committee, National Council of Teachers of English Notable Trade Book in Language Arts.

ISAACS, Susan; American novelist and screenwriter; b. 7 Dec. 1943, New York, NY; m. Elkan Abramowitz 1968, one s. one d. *Education:* Queens Coll., CUNY. *Career:* mem. Authors' Guild, International Asscn of Crime Writers, MWA, National Book Critics Circle, PEN, Poets and Writers, Creative Coalition, American Society of Journalists and Authors. *Publications:* Compromising Positions 1978, Close Relations 1980, Almost Paradise 1984, Shining Through 1988, Magic Hour 1991, After All These Years 1993, Lily White 1996, Lily White 1996, Red, White and Blue 1998, Brave Dames and Wimpettes: What Women are really doing on Page and Screen 1999, Long Time No See 2001, Any Place I Hang My Hat 2004, Past Perfect 2007, As Husbands Go 2010; contributions: newspapers and magazines. *Honours:* Hon. DLitt (Dowling Coll.) 1988; Hon. DHumLitt (Queens Coll., CUNY) 1996; Barnes & Noble Writers for Writers Award 1996, John Steinbeck Award 1999. *Address:* c/o Scribner Publicity Department, Simon & Schuster, Inc., 1230 Avenue of the Americas, New York, NY 10020, USA (office). *E-mail:* katherine.monaghan@simonandschuster.com (office). *Website:* www.susanisaacs.com.

ISEGAWA, Moses; Dutch writer; b. 1963, Kampala, Uganda. *Career:* fmr secondary school teacher; resettled in Netherlands 1990; returned to Uganda 2006. *Publications:* Abyssinian Chronicles (in trans.) 1999, Slangenkuil (trans. as Snakepit) 1999, Twee chimpansees (trans. as Two Chimpanzees, non-fiction) 2001.

ISHIGURO, Kazuo, OBE, MA, DLitt, FRSL; British writer; b. 8 Nov. 1954, Nagasaki, Japan; s. of Shizuo Ishiguro and Shizuko Ishiguro; m. Lorna Anne Macdougall 1986; one d. *Education:* Woking Grammar School, Univs of Kent and East Anglia. *Career:* fmr community worker, Renfrew; writer 1980–. *Publications include:* A Pale View of Hills (RSL Winifred Holtby Prize 1983) 1982, A Profile of Arthur J. Mason (TV play) 1985, An Artist of the Floating World (Whitbread Book of the Year, Fiction Prize 1986) 1986, The Gourmet (TV play) 1987, The Remains of the Day (Booker Prize 1989) 1989, The Unconsoled (Cheltenham Prize 1995) 1995, When We Were Orphans (novel) 2000, The Saddest Music in the World (screenplay, co-author) 2003, Never Let Me Go (novel) (Premio Serono 2006, Corine Int. Book Prize 2006, Casino de Santiago European Novel Prize 2007) 2005, White Countess (screenplay) 2005, Nocturnes: Five Stories of Music and Nightfall 2009. *Honours:* Hon. DLit (Kent) 1990, (East Anglia) 1995, (St Andrews) 2003; Chevalier, Ordre des Arts et des Lettres 1998; Premio Scanno 1995, Premio Mantova 1998. *Literary Agent:* c/o Rogers, Coleridge & White Literary Agency, 20 Powis Mews, London, W11 1JN, England. *Telephone:* (20) 7221-3717. *Fax:* (20) 7229-9084. *E-mail:* info@rcwlitagency.co.uk. *Website:* www.rcwlitagency.co.uk.

ISKANDER, Fazil Abdulovich; Russian/Abkhaz writer; b. 6 March 1929, Sukhumi, Georgian SSR; m.; one s. one d. *Education:* Maxim Gorky Inst. of Literature, Moscow. *Career:* first works Publ 1952; USSR People's Deputy 1989–91; Pres. Asscn of Authors and Publrs against Piracy; Head, World of Culture Asscn; Vice-Pres. Russian Acad. of Arts; Academician of RAN, Natural Sciences Dept, Bayerische Akad. der Schönen Künste. *Films include:* Time of Lucky Finds, Crime Kings 1986, A Little Giant of Big Sex, A Night with Stalin. *Plays:* Djamchuch: A Son of a Deer 1986, A Greeting from Zürüpa (The One Who Thinks About Russia) 1999. *Publications include:* Green Rain 1960, Youth of the Sea 1964, Goatibex Constellation 1966, Forbidden Fruit 1966 (English trans. 1972), Summer Forest 1969, Time of Lucky Finds 1970, Tree of Childhood and Other Stories 1970, Sandro from Chegem 1978, Metropol (co-ed.) 1979, Small Giant of the Big Sex 1979, The Path (poems) 1987, Rabbits and Boa Constrictors 1989, School Waltz or the Energy of Shame 1990, Poets and Tsars 1991, Man and His Surroundings 1992, Pshada 1993, Sofichka 1996, The One Who Thinks About Russia and the American 1997, Poet 1998, The Swallow's Nest 2000 and other stories. *Honours:* Dr hc (Norwich Univ., USA); Malaparti Prize (Italy) 1985, USSR State Prize 1989, State Prize of Russia 1993, A. Sakharov Prize, A. Pushkin Prize (Germany) 1994, Moscow-Penne Prize (Italy) 1996, Triumph Prize (Russia) 1998. *Address:* Leningradski prosp. 26, korp. 2, Apt. 67, 125040 Moscow, Russia. *Telephone:* (495) 973-94-53 (office); (495) 212-73-60. *Fax:* (495) 973-94-53 (office).

ISLAM, Mazhar ul; Pakistani writer and folklorist; *Director, Lok Virsa*. *Education:* Punjab Univ., Lahore. *Career:* writer of short stories, novels and works on folklore studies; Dir, Lok Virsa (Nat. Inst. of Folk and Traditional Heritage). *Publications:* short stories: Baton ki Barish mein Bheegti Larki, Gurya ki Aankh say Shehrko Daykho, Ghoron kay Shehr mein Akela Aadmi, Bolian, Khat mein post ki Huye Dophr, Aye Khuda; novel: Mohabbat Murda Phoolon ki symphony; non-fiction: Folklore ki Pahli Kitab, Lok Punjab.

Honours: President's Award for Pride of Performance 2005. *Address:* Lok Virsa, POB 1184, Shakarparian, Islamabad 81, Pakistan (office).

ISLER, Alan David, BA, MA, PhD; American academic; b. (writer), 12 Sept. 1934, London, England. *Education:* Hunter Coll., CUNY, Columbia Univ. *Career:* Asst Prof. of English, Huron Coll., Univ. of Western Ontario, Canada 1965–67; Assoc. Prof. of English, Queens Coll. CUNY 1967–95; Visiting Lecturer, Univ. of Tel-Aviv 1971–72; mem. Renaissance Soc. of America. *Publications:* novels: The Prince of West End Ave 1994, Kraven Images 1996, Clerical Errors 2001, The Living Proof 2005; short story collections: The Bacon Fancier: four tales 1997, Op.Non.Cit 1997; contrib. to periodicals, including Univ. of Toronto Quarterly. *Honours:* Nat. Jewish Book Award 1994.

ISMAT, Riad, PhD; Syrian diplomatist, politician, playwright, short-story writer and critic and stage director; b. 11 July 1947, Damascus; m. Azzah Konbaz; two s. one d. *Education:* Damascus Univ., studied briefly at Drama Centre, London, UK, Univ. Coll., Cardiff, UK, World Univ. *Career:* studied mime with Adam Darius and TV production and direction at the BBC, UK; also apprentice in actor training with Joseph Chaikin, Camille Howard, Jean Shelton and Mark Epstein in USA; Rector, Acad. for Dramatic Arts, Damascus 2000–02; apptd Dir Gen. Syrian State Radio and Television 2003; Vice-Minister of Culture 2004–05; Amb. to Pakistan 2005–10, to Qatar 2010; Minister of Culture 2010–12; has directed 15 theatrical productions, including interpretations of Shakespeare, Tennessee Williams, Bertolt Brecht, Frank Wedekind and Ariel Dorfman, as well as own version of The Arabian Nights; f. first mime troupe in Damascus; also directed trilogy for Syrian TV. *Plays include:* The Game of Love and Revolution, Was Dinner Good My Sister, Mourning Becomes Antigone, Sinbad, Shahryar's Nights, Abla & Antar, Banana Republic, In Search of Zenobia, Mata Hari. *Television:* scripts for seven serials. *Publications:* 35 books, including short stories, nine books critiquing Arab and World drama, a book on Nobel Prize laureate Naguib Mahfouz and a book on cinema. *Honours:* Dr hc (Greenwich Univ., UK) 2007; honouree of Cairo and Damascus int. theatre festivals. *Address:* PO Box 60049, Damascus; c/o Ministry of Culture, rue George Haddad, Rawda, Damascus, Syria.

ISRAEL, Jonathan Irvine, DPhil, FBA; British historian, academic and writer; *Professor of Modern European History, School of Historical Studies, Institute for Advanced Study*; b. 22 Jan. 1946, London, England; one s. one d. by previous m.; m. 2nd Anette Munt. *Education:* Queens' Coll., Cambridge, St Antony's Coll., Oxford. *Career:* Asst Lecturer, Univ. of Hull 1972–73, Lecturer 1973–74; Lecturer, Univ. Coll., London 1974–81, Reader 1981–85, Prof. of Dutch History and Insts 1985–2000; Prof. of Modern European History, School of Historical Studies, Inst. for Advanced Study, Princeton, NJ, USA 2001–; Corresp. Fellow, Royal Netherlands Acad. of Arts and Sciences. *Publications:* Race, Class and Politics in Colonial Mexico 1975, The Dutch Republic and the Hispanic World 1982, European Jewry in the Age of Mercantilism 1550–1750 1985, Dutch Primacy in World Trade 1585–1740 1989, Empires and Entrepots: The Dutch, the Spanish Monarchy and the Jews 1585–1713 1990, The Anglo-Dutch Movement: Essays on the Glorious Revolution and its World Impact (ed.) 1991, The Dutch Republic 1995, Conflict of Empires: Spain, the Low Countries and the Struggle for World Supremacy 1585–1713 1997, Radical Enlightenment, 2001, Enlightenment Contested: Philosophy, Modernity, and the Emancipation of Man 1670–1752 2006, A Revolution of the Mind: Radical Enlightenment and the Intellectual Origins of Modern Democracy 2009; numerous contributions to scholarly books and journals. *Honours:* Hon. Prof., Univ. of Amsterdam; Kt, Order of the Dutch Lion 2004; Dr hc (Antwerp), (Univ. Jean Monnet), (Rotterdam); Wolfson Literary Award for History 1986, Leo Gershoy Award, American Historical Assen 2001, Dr A.H. Heineken Prize in History, Royal Netherlands Acad. of Arts and Sciences 2008, Benjamin Franklin Medal 2010. *Address:* School of Historical Studies, Institute for Advanced Study, Einstein Drive, Princeton, NJ 08540, USA (office). *Telephone:* (609) 734-8000 (office). *E-mail:* jisrael@ias.edu (office). *Website:* www.hs.ias.edu (office).

ISTARÚ, Ana, BA; Costa Rican poet, playwright and actress; b. 1960, San José. *Education:* Univ. of Costa Rica. *Plays:* El vuelo de la grulla 1984, Madre nuestra que estás en la tierra 1988, Baby Boom en el Paraíso 1996, Hombres en escabeche 2000. *Film:* screenplay: Caribe 2004. *Publications:* poetry: La estación de fiebre 1983, Le muerte y otros efímeros agravios 1989, Verbo Madre 1995, Raíces del aire 1996, Poesía Escogida 2002. *Honours:* Guggenheim Fellowship 1990, Nat. Prize for a debut actress 1990, Premio María Teresa León 1995, Premio Machado de Teatro 1999. *Address:* c/o Editorial Costa Rica, Costado oeste del cementerio, Guadalupe de Goicoechea, Apdo 10010, San José, Costa Rica (office). *E-mail:* difusion@editorialcostarica.com (office). *Website:* www.editorialcostarica.com (office).

ITANI, Frances, RN, BA, MA; Canadian novelist, short story writer, poet and teacher; b. Belleville, Ont. *Education:* Univs of Alberta and New Brunswick, McGill Univ., Montréal Gen. Hosp. School of Nursing. *Career:* nursing, then teaching and writer-in-residence positions at Univ. of Ottawa, Trent Univ., The Banff Centre, Nepean Public Library; full-time writer. *Radio:* The Keeper of the Cranes (drama). *Publications:* poetry: No Other Lodgings 1978, Rentee Bay 1983, A Season of Mourning 1988; juvenile: Linger by the Sea 1979; short story collections: Pack Ice 1989, Truth or Lies 1989, Man Without Face 1994, Leaning, Leaning Over Water 1998, Poached Egg on Toast 2004; novels: Deafening 2003, Remembering the Bones 2007, Missing 2011, Requiem 2011. *Honours:* Mem. Order of Canada; Canadian Fiction Magazine Best Short Story 1987, Ottawa Book Award for Fiction 1995, 2005, First Prize, CBC/Tilden Literary Award for Fiction 1995, 1996, Drummer-Gen.'s Award for Fiction 2004, Commonwealth Writers' Prize (Caribbean & Canada Region) for Best Book 2004, Grant MacEwan Coll./Book of the Year 2004–05, CAA Jubilee Award for Best Book (Short Stories) 2005, Kingston Reads Award 2007. *Literary Agent:* c/o Agent, WCA, 94 Harbord Street, Toronto, ON M5S 1G6, Canada. *Telephone:* (416) 964-3302. *Fax:* (416) 975-9209.

IVĂNESCU, Mircea; Romanian poet and translator; b. 26 March 1931, Bucharest. *Education:* Univ. of Bucharest. *Career:* fmr Ed. World Literature Press; has translated works by F. Scott Fitzgerald and William Faulkner, and James Joyce's Ulysses. *Publications:* poetry: Versuri 1968, Poesii 1970, Alte versuri 1972, Alte poeme 1973, Poeme 1973, Amintiri 1973, Alte poesii 1976, Poesii nouă 1982, Poeme nouă 1983, Alte poeme nouă 1986, Versuri vechi 1988, Poeme vechi, nouă 1989, Versuri 1996, Poezii 1997, Poesii vechi şi nouă 1999; contrib. poems to anthologies and journals, including Square Lake, Harvard Review. *Address:* c/o Minerva Editura, 46–56 Bd. Metalurgiei, sector 4, OP 82, CP 92, Bucharest 041833, Romania.

IVANJI, Ivan; Serbian writer and translator; b. 24 Jan. 1929, Zrenjanin, Yugoslavia (now in Serbia). *Career:* deported to Auschwitz and Buchenwald 1944; worked as building technician, teacher, and in journalism, publishing, theatre and diplomatic service; embassy-counsellor Yugoslav Embassy, Bonn 1974–78; interpreter for Josip Broz Tito, including at KSZE founding conf., Helsinki 1975, summit of Communist and Workers Parties, East Berlin 1976, summit of bloc-free states, Havana 1979; writes in German and Serbian; Sec.-Gen. Yugoslav Writers' Asscn 1982–88. *Publications include:* Das Kinderfräulein (novel) 1998, Der Aschenmensch von Buchenwald (novel) 1999, Die Tänzerin und der Krieg (novel) 2002; short stories, essays, plays, poems and trans. *Address:* c/o Picus Verlag, Friedrich-Schmidt-Platz 4, 1080 Vienna, Austria.

IVANOVA, Natal'ya Borisovna, PhD; Russian editor and literary critic; *Deputy Editor-in-Chief, Znamya*; b. 17 May 1945; m. 3rd Alexandr Rybakov (deceased); one d. *Education:* Moscow State Univ. *Career:* journalist, Znamya (monthly) 1972–86, Deputy Ed.-in-Chief 1991–; journalist, Druzhba Narodov; mem. Exec. Cttee European Forum, Moscow; mem. Aprel'lit movt, Moscow Asscn, Russian Fed. Writers' Union, PEN Centre, Commonwealth of Writers' Unions 1992–, European Cultural Centre, Geneva, Switzerland. *Television:* Boris Pasternak 2007, Pasternak and Others 2009. *Publications include:* The Prose of Jurij Grifonov 1984, Laugh Against Terror, or Fazil 1990, Nowstalgia 2002, Pasternak and Others 2003; Co-ordinator Caucasus in Search of the Future project 2000. *Honours:* literary awards from Literaturnaja Gazeta, DruzbaNarodov and Znamya, Tsarskosel'skaya Award 2004. *Address:* Znamya, ul Bolshaja Sadovaja, 2/46, 123001 Moscow (office); Prospect Mira 49–86, 129110 Moscow, Russia (home). *Telephone:* (495) 699-39-60 (office); (495) 593-03-54 (home). *Fax:* (495) 699-52-83 (office). *E-mail:* ivanova@znamlit.ru (office). *Website:* magazines.russ.ru/znamia (office).

IVASHKIN, Alexander Vasilevich, BMus, MMus, DMus, PhD; British/New Zealand cellist, conductor, writer and critic; *Professor of Music and Director of the Centre for Russian Music, University of London*; b. 17 Sept. 1948, Blagoveshchensk, Russia; m. Natalia Mikhailovna Pavlutskaya 1969. *Education:* Gnessin Special Music School, Russian Acad. of Music, Moscow, Russian Art History Inst. *Career:* solo cellist, Bolshoi Theatre Orchestra, Moscow 1971–91; mem. Bd Dirs Bolshoi Opera Co. 1987–91; solo recitals and appearances with orchestras, chamber music concerts, recording in over 40 countries in Europe, Russia, USA, Australia, Japan and NZ 1975–; Artistic Dir Bolshoi Soloists 1978–91; Prof. of Cello, Univ. of Canterbury, NZ 1990–99; Artistic Dir Adam Int. Festival/Competition 1995–; Prof. of Music and Dir Centre for Russian Music, Univ. of London 1999–; Chair. VTB Capital Int. Competition 2008–. *Recordings include:* Shostakovich, Cello Concertos Nos 1 and 2 1998/2006, Schnittke, Complete Cello Music 1998–2002, Schumann, Gretchaninov, Cello Concertos 1999–2000, Prokofiev, Complete Cello Music 1996–2003, Tcherepnin, Complete Cello Music 2000, Roslavets, Complete Cello Music 2001, Rachmaninov, Complete Cello Music 2003, Kancheli, Cello Concertos 2002–05, Ivashkin plays Schnittke (Complete Cello Concertos and Sonatas) 2007, Due Celli (Music by Pergolesi, Boccherini, Mozart, Boismortier, Vivaldi with Natalia Pavlutskaya) 2008, Ivashkin plays Prokofiev (Complete Cello Concertos and Sonatas) 2008, Pacific Voyage (Improvisations with Polynesian musicians Ora Barlow and Kim Halliday) 2009, Schnittke Discoveries 2010, Russian Cello Concertos 1960–2000 2010, Nikolai Korndorf (Complete Cello Music) 2012. *Publications:* Krzysztof Penderecki 1983, Charles Ives and 20th Century Music 1991, Conversation with Alfred Schnittke 1994, Alfred Schnittke 1996, Rostrospective (on M. Rostropovich) 1997, A. Schnittke Reader 2002, Rostropovich 2007, Contemplating Shostakovich: Life, Music and Film (with Andrew Kirkman) 2012. *Literary Agent:* c/o Salpeter Artists Management, 4 Denman Drive, London, NW11 6RG, England; c/o Ivy Artists, Groot Hertoginnenlaan 217, 2517 The Hague, The Netherlands. *Telephone:* (70) 392-5271 (The Hague). *Fax:* (70) 365-9021 (The Hague). *E-mail:* judithsalpeter@gmail.com; marjon@ivyartists.com. *Website:* www.ivyartists.com. *Address:* Music Department, Goldsmiths College, University of London, London, SE14 6NW, England (office). *Telephone:* (20) 7919-7646 (office). *Fax:* (20) 7919-7247 (office). *E-mail:* a.ivashkin@gold.ac.uk (office). *Website:* www.alexanderivashkin.com.

IVIMY, May (see Badman, May Edith)

IWAI, Katsuhito, BA, PhD; Japanese economist and writer; *Visiting Professor, International Christian University*; b. 2 March 1947, Tokyo. *Education:* Univ. of Tokyo, Massachusetts Inst. of Tech., USA. *Career:* Asst Prof. of Econs, Yale Univ. 1973–79, Sr Research Assoc., Cowles Foundation for Research in Econs 1979–81; Assoc. Prof. of Econs, Univ. of Tokyo 1981–89, Prof. of Econs 1989–2010, Prof. Emer. 2010–, Dean Grad. School of Econs 2001–03; Visiting Assoc. Prof. of Int. Affairs, Princeton Univ., USA 1988–89; Visiting Prof., Univ. of Pennsylvania 1988–89; Visiting Fellow, Dipartimento di Economia Politica, Università di Siena, Italy 1997; Sr Research Assoc., Tokyo Foundation 2007–; Visiting Prof., Int. Christian Univ. 2010–; Specially Appointed Prof., Musashiro Univ. 2010–; mem. Science Council of Japan 2005–12. *Publications include:* in English: Disequilibrium Dynamics: A Theoretical Analysis of Inflation and Unemployment (Grand Prix, Nikkei Econ. Books Cultural Award 1982) 1981; in Japanese: Venice no Shonin no Shihon Ron (Capitalism According to the Merchant of Venice) 1985, Kahei Ron (Ontology of Money) (Suntory Academic Award 1993) 1993, Gendai no Keizai Riron (Modern Economic Theory, co-ed.) 1994, Shihonshugi wo Kataru (Talks on Capitalism) 1994, 21 Seiki no Shihonshugi Ron (On 21st Century Capitalism) 2000, Kaisha ha Korekara Dounaru no ka (What Will Become of the Corporation?) (Kobayashi Hideo Award 2003, Shûkan Daiyamondo Best Economics Book of the Year) 2003, Kaisha ha Dareno Mono ka (To Whom Does the Corporation Belong) 2005, Shihonshugi kara Shiminshugi he (From Capitalism to Civil Society) 2006, M&A Kokufuron (MA Forum Prize) 2008; contrib. of numerous articles to professional journals and to newspapers and magazines. *Honours:* Medal with Purple Ribbon, Japan 2007; Dr hc (Univ. of Belgrade) 2009. *Address:* International Christian University, 3-10-2 Osawa, Mitaka-shi, Tokyo 181-8585, Japan (office). *E-mail:* iwai@icu.ac.jp (office). *Website:* www.iwai-k.com.

IYAYI, Festus, PhD; Nigerian novelist; b. 29 Sept. 1947, Ibadan. *Education:* Annunciation Catholic College, Kiev Institute of Economics, University of Bradford, Yorkshire. *Career:* Lecturer, University of Benin. *Publications:* Violence, 1979; The Contract, 1982; Heroes, 1986; Awaiting Court Martial, 1996. *Honours:* Asscn of Nigerian Authors Prize, 1987; Commonwealth Writers Prize, 1988; Pius Okigbo Africa Prize for Literature, 1996; Nigerian Author of the Year, 1996.

IZRAELEWICZ, Erik, DEcon; French journalist; *Editor-in-Chief, La Tribune*; b. 6 Feb. 1954, Strasbourg. *Education:* Haute Ecole de Commerce, Centre de Formation des Journalistes and Univ. de Paris I. *Career:* journalist, L'Expansion 1981–85; Banking Finance Ed. Le Monde 1986–88, Head of Econ. Service 1989–92, Deputy Ed.-in-Chief 1992–94, New York Corresp. 1993–94, Econs Reporter, Europe 1994–95, leader writer 1994, Ed.-in-Chief 1996–2000; Ed.-in-Chief Les Echos 2000–08, La Tribune 2008–. *Address:* La Tribune, 51 rue Vivienne, 75095 Paris, Cedex 02, France. *Telephone:* 1-44-82-16-16 (office). *E-mail:* directiondelaredaction@latribune.fr (office). *Website:* www.latribune.fr (office).

J

JACCOTTET, Philippe; Swiss poet and writer; b. 30 June 1925, Moudon. *Education:* University of Lausanne. *Publications:* Poetry: Requiem, 1947; L'Effraie et autres poésies, 1953; L'ignorant: Poèmes 1952–56. Airs: Poèmes 1961–64; Poésie 1946–67; Leçons, 1969; Chants d'en bas, 1974; Breathings, 1974; Pensées sous les nuages, 1983; Selected Poems, 1987; Cahier de verdure, 1990; Libretto, 1990. Other: Through the Orchard, 1975; Des Histoires de passage: Prose 1948–78; Autres Journées, 1987; Trans. of works by Robert Musil, Thomas Mann, Leopardi, Homer and Hölderlin. *Honours:* Larbaud Prize 1978. *Address:* c/o Editions Gallimard, 5 rue Sebastien-Bottin, 75007 Paris, France.

JACK, Ian; British writer and journalist; b. 7 Feb. 1945, Farnworth, Lancs.; s. of Harry Jack and Isabella Jack (née Gillespie); m. 1st 1979; m. 2nd Rosalind Sharpe 1998; one s. one d. *Career:* newspaper journalist in Scotland 1960s; variously reporter, feature writer, Foreign Corresp., Sunday Times 1970–86; co-f. Independent on Sunday 1989, Ed. 1991–95; Ed. Granta magazine 1995–2007; currently writes for The Guardian newspaper. *Publications include:* Before the Oil Ran Out 1987, The Crash that Stopped Britain 2001, The Country Formerly Known as Great Britain 2009; various Granta anthologies. *Honours:* Journalist of the Year 1986, Reporter of the Year 1989, Editor of the Year 1992. *Address:* The Guardian, Kings Place, 90 York Way, London, N1 9GU, England (office). *Telephone:* (20) 3353-2000 (office). *Fax:* (20) 3353-3193 (office). *E-mail:* ian.jack@guardian.co.uk (office); iangjack@blueyonder.co.uk (home). *Website:* www.guardian.co.uk (office).

JACK, Ronald Dyce Sadler, MA, DLitt, PhD, FRSE; British academic and writer; *Professor Emeritus, University of Edinburgh*; b. 3 April 1941, Ayr, Scotland; s. of the late Muirice Jack; m. Kirsty Nicolson 1967; two d. *Education:* Univ. of Glasgow, Univ. of Edinburgh. *Career:* Lecturer, Univ. of Edinburgh 1965–78, Reader 1978–87, Prof. 1987–2004, Prof. Emer. 2004–; Visiting Prof., Univ. of Virginia 1973–74, Univ. of Strathclyde 1993; Distinguished Visiting Prof., Univ. of Connecticut 1998; W. Ormiston Roy Fellow, Univ. of S Carolina 2003; Fellow, English Asscn 2000, Asscn for Scottish Literary Studies; mem. Medieval Acad. of America, Scottish Text Soc. *Publications:* Scottish Prose 1550–1700 1972, The Italian Influence on Scottish Literature 1972, A Choice of Scottish Verse 1560–1660 1978, The Art of Robert Burns (co-author) 1982, Sir Thomas Urquhart (co-author) 1984, Alexander Montgomerie 1985, Scottish Literature's Debt to Italy 1986 (revised edn 2010), The History of Scottish Literature, Vol. I 1988, Patterns of Divine Comedy 1989, The Road to the Never Land 1991, Of Lion and Unicorn 1993, The Poems of William Dunbar 1997, Mercat Anthology of Early Scottish Literature 1997 (revised edn 2010), Oxford Dictionary of National Biography (asst ed.) 2004, Scotland in Europe (ed.) 2005, Myths and the Myth Maker 2010; contrib. to Review of English Studies, Modern Language Review, Comparative Literature, Studies in Scottish Literature, and others. *Honours:* Robert Bruce Award 1986. *Address:* University of Edinburgh, David Hume Tower, George Square, Edinburgh, EH8 9JX (office); 54 Buckstone Road, Edinburgh, EH10 6HN, Scotland (home). *Telephone:* (131) 445-3498 (home). *E-mail:* r.d.s.jack@ed.ac.uk (office); RDSJack@aol.com (home).

JACKMAN, Brian; British journalist and writer; b. 25 April 1935, Epsom, Surrey, England; m. 1st 1964 (divorced 1992); one d.; m. 2nd 1993. *Education:* grammar school. *Career:* staff, Sunday Times 1970–90; Contributing Ed., Condé Nast Traveller; mem. RGS, Fauna and Flora Preservation Soc.; patron Tusk Trust. *Publications:* We Learned to Ski 1974, Dorset Coast Path 1977, The Marsh Lions 1982, The Countryside in Winter 1986, My Serengeti Years 1987, Roaring at the Dawn 1996, The Big Cat Diary 1996, Touching the Wild 2003; contrib. to Sunday Times, The Times, Daily Telegraph, Daily Mail, Country Living, Country Life, BBC Wildlife, Travel Africa. *Honours:* TTG Travel Writer of the Year 1982, Wildscreen Award 1982, AITO Travel Writer of the Year 2005. *Address:* Spick Hatch, West Milton, Nr Bridport, Dorset, DT6 3SH, England (home). *E-mail:* brian@spickhatch.freeserve.co.uk.

JACKMAN, Stuart Brooke; British clergyman, editor and writer; b. 22 June 1922, Manchester, England. *Career:* Congregational Minister, Barnstaple, Devon, 1948–52, Pretoria, 1952–55, Caterham, Surrey, 1955–61, Auckland, 1961–65, Upminster, Essex, 1965–67, Oxford, Surrey, 1969–; Ed., Council for World Mission, 1967–71, Oxted, Surrey, 1969–81, Melbourne, Cambridgeshire, 1981–87. *Publications:* Portrait in Two Colours, 1948; But They Won't Lie Down, 1954; The Numbered Days, 1954; Angels Unawares, 1956; One Finger for God, 1957; The Waters of Dinyanti, 1959; The Daybreak Boys, 1961; The Desirable Property, 1966; The Davidson Affair, 1966; The Golden Orphans, 1968; Guns Covered with Flowers, 1973; Slingshot, 1975; The Burning Men, 1976; Operation Catcher, 1980; A Game of Soldiers, 1981; The Davidson File, 1981; Death Wish, 1998. *Address:* 114 Balland Field, Willingham, Cambs., CB4 5JU, England.

JACKOWSKA, Nicki, ANEADip, BA, MA; British poet, novelist, writer and teacher; b. 6 Aug. 1942, Brighton, Sussex, England; m. Andrzej Jackowski 1970 (divorced); one d. *Education:* Univ. of Sussex. *Career:* founder and tutor, Brighton Writing School; Writer-in-Residence at various venues; mem. Poetry Society. *Publications:* The House That Manda Built 1981, Doctor Marbles and Marianne 1982, Earthwalks 1982, Letters to Superman 1984, Gates to the City 1985, The Road to Orc 1985, The Islanders 1987, News from the Brighton Front 1993, Write for Life 1997, Lighting a Slow Fuse, New and Selected Poems 1998, Write for Life 2002, Behold 2009; contributions to various publications. *Honours:* winner Stroud Festival Poetry Competition 1972, Continental Bursary, South East Arts 1978, C. Day-Lewis Fellowship 1982, Arts Council Writer's Fellowship 1984–85, Arts Council of England Writer's Bursary 1994. *Address:* c/o Enitharmon Press, 26B Caversham Road, London, NW5 2DU, England (office). *Website:* www.enitharmon.co.uk (office).

JACKSON, Belle (see Carr, Margaret)

JACKSON, Everatt (see Muggeson, Margaret Elizabeth)

JACKSON, Jane (see Pollard, Jane)

JACKSON, Kenneth Terry, BA, MA, PhD; American academic and writer; *Barzun Professor of History and Social Sciences, Columbia University*; b. 27 July 1939, Memphis, TN; m. Barbara Ann Bruce 1962; two s. (one deceased). *Education:* Univ. of Memphis, Univ. of Chicago. *Career:* Asst Prof. 1968–71, Assoc. Prof. 1971–76, Prof. 1976–87, Mellon Prof. 1987–90, Barzun Prof. of History and Social Sciences 1990–, Chair., Dept of History 1994–97, Columbia Univ.; Visiting Prof., Princeton Univ. 1973–74, George Washington Univ. 1982–83, Univ. of California at Los Angeles 1986–87; Chair., Bradley Commission on History in the Schools 1987–90, Nat. Council for History Education 1990–92; Woodrow Wilson Foundation Fellow 1961–62, Nat. Endowment for the Humanities Sr Fellow 1979–80; Guggenheim Fellowship 1983–84; mem. American Historical Asscn, Urban History Asscn (pres. 1994–), Soc. of American Historians (pres. 1998–2000), Organization of American Historians (pres. 2000–01), New York Historical Soc. (pres. and CEO 2001–04). *Publications:* The Ku Klux Klan in the City 1915–1930 1967, American Vistas (ed. with L. Dinnerstein, two vols) 1971, Cities in American History (ed. with S. K. Schultz) 1972, Atlas of American History 1978, Columbia History of Urban Life (general ed.) 1980–, Crabgrass Frontier: The Suburbanization of the United States 1985, Silent Cities: The Evolution of the American Cemetery (with Camilo Verqara) 1989, Dictionary of American Biography (ed.-in-chief) 1991–95, Scribner's Encyclopedia of American Lives (ed.-in-chief) 1995–2005; Encyclopaedia of New York City 1995, Empire City: New York Through the Centuries 2001; contribs to scholarly books and professional journals. *Honours:* four hon. doctorates; Bancroft Prize 1986, Francis Parkman Prize 1986, Columbia Univ. Mark Van Doren Great Teaching Award 1989, Univ. of Memphis Outstanding Alumni Award 1989, New York State Scholar of the Year 2001, Columbia Univ. Nicholas Murray Butler Medal. *Address:* c/o Department of History, 603 Fayerweather Hall, Columbia University, New York, NY 10027, USA (office). *Telephone:* (212) 854-2555 (office); (914) 666-5721 (home). *Fax:* (212) 932-0602 (office); (914) 666-4310 (home). *E-mail:* ktj1@columbia.edu (office).

JACKSON, Kevin, BA, MA, FRSA; British journalist, author, broadcaster, critic and academic; *Visiting Professor of English, University College London*; b. 1955, London. *Education:* Emanuel School, Pembroke Coll., Univ. of Cambridge. *Career:* producer, writer and presenter for TV and radio; Assoc. Arts Ed. and film critic, The Independent newspaper 1987–; fmr Contributing Ed. Arena magazine; currently freelance writer, broadcaster, lecturer; currently Visiting Prof., Univ. Coll. London; contrib. to many newspapers and periodicals including Sunday Telegraph, Vogue, Modern Review, Harpers and Queen, Literary Review. *Radio includes:* People Be Good (BBC Radio 3) 2000. *Television includes:* Burgess at Seventy (BBC 2), 1987, The Burgess Variations (BBC 2) 2000. *Publications include:* Schrader on Schrader 1990, The Language of Cinema 1998, Invisible Forms – a Guide to Literary Curiosities 1999, A Russian Alphabet 2000, Letters of Introduction 2004, Humphrey Jennings 2004, Withnail and I: BFI Film Classics 2004, Fast 2006, The Book of Hours 2007, The Pataphysical Flook 2007, Lawrence of Arabia 2007, Moose 2008, Bite: A Vampire Handbook: A Vampire Miscellany 2009, The Worlds of John Ruskin 2009, Moose 2009, Chronicles of Old London: Exploring England's Historic Capital 2012; as ed.: The Humphrey Jennings Film Reader 1993, The Oxford Book of Money 1995. *Honours:* Hon. Prof., Univ. Coll. London. *Literary Agent:* c/o Peter Straus, Rogers, Coleridge & White Ltd, 20 Powis Mews, London, W11 1JN, England. *Telephone:* (20) 7221-3717. *Fax:* (20) 7229-9084. *E-mail:* info@rcwlitagency.com. *Website:* www.rcwlitagency.com. *Address:* c/o University College London, Department of English, Gower Street, London, WC1E 6BT, England (office). *Telephone:* (20) 7679-3134 (office). *Website:* www.ucl.ac.uk/english/about/staff/index.htm (office).

JACKSON, Richard Paul, BA, MA, PhD; American writer, poet, academic and editor; *UC Foundation Professor of English, University of Tennessee, Chattanooga*; b. 17 Nov. 1946, Lawrence, Mass; s. of Richard Jackson and Mary Jackson; m. Theresa Harvey 1999; one d. *Education:* Merrimack Coll., Middlebury Coll., Yale Univ. *Career:* UC Foundation Prof. of English, Univ. of Tennessee, Chattanooga; Faculty, Vermont Coll., MFA 1988–; Dir Meacham Writing Workshops; Univ. of Tennessee, Chattanooga; Faculty, Vermont Coll., MFA 1988–; Journal Ed. Poetry Miscellany; readings in Israel, Czech Repub., Hungary, UK, Romania, Serbia, Slovenia, Bosnia, Switzerland, and throughout USA; mem. PEN, Associated Writing Programs. *Publications:* Part of the Story 1983, Acts of Mind 1983, Worlds Apart 1987, Dismantling Time in Contemporary Poetry 1989, Alive All Day 1993, Heart's Bridge 1999,

Heartwall 2000, Half Lives 2001, Unauthorized Autobiography: New and Selected Poems 2004; contrib. to Georgia Review, Antioch Review, North American Review, New England Review. *Honours:* Order of Freedom (Slovenia); Nat. Endowment for the Humanities Fellowship 1980, Nat. Endowment for the Arts Fellowship 1985, Fulbright Exchange Fellowships 1986, 1987, Agee Prize 1989, CSU Poetry Award 1992, Juniper Prize 2000, five Pushcart Prizes, Guggenheim Fellowship, Witter-Bynner Fellowship, Teaching Awards from Univ. of Tennessee, Chattanooga and Vermont Coll., AWP George Garrett Award. *Address:* 3413 Alta Vista Drive, Chattanooga, TN 37411, USA (home). *Telephone:* (423) 624-7279 (office). *E-mail:* svobodni@aol.com (office). *Website:* members.authorsguild.net/svobodni.

JACKSON, Robert Louis, BA, MA, PhD; American academic, writer and editor; b. 10 Nov. 1923, New York, NY; s. of Eugene Jackson and Ella Fred; m. Elizabeth Mann Gillette 1951; two d. *Education:* Cornell Univ., Russian Institute, Columbia Univ., Univ. of California at Berkeley. *Career:* Instructor, Yale Univ. 1954–58, Asst Prof. 1958–67, Prof. of Russian Literature 1967–91, B. E. Bensinger Prof. of Slavic Languages and Literatures 1991–2000, retd 2002; mem. N. American Dostoevsky Soc. (Pres. 1971–77); Pres. Int. Dostoevsky Soc. 1977–83; f. and Pres.N. American Chekhov Soc. 1988, Vyacheslav Ivanov Convivium 1981–. *Publications:* Dostoevsky's Underground Man in Russian Literature 1958, Dostoevsky's Quest for Form: A Study of His Philosophy of Art 1966, The Art of Dostoevsky 1981, Dialogues with Dostoevsky: The Overwhelming Questions 1993; Editor: Chekhov: Collected Critical Essays 1967, Crime and Punishment: Collected Critical Essays 1974, Dostoevsky: Collected Critical Essays 1984, Russian Formalism: A Retrospective Glance (co-ed.) 1985, A New Word on the Brothers Karamazov 2004, Vyacheslav Ivanov: Poet, Critic and Philosopher 1986, Reading Chekhov's Text 1993, A New Word on the Brother's Karamazov 2004; contributions: over 100 essays in books and journals including Russian Literature, Yale Review, Sewanee Review, Yale French Studies, Slavic and East European Journal, Comparative Literature, Slavic Review, Dostoevsky Studies etc. *Honours:* Hon. MA (Yale) 1967, Hon. Doctorate (Moscow State Univ.) 1994, (Petrozavodsk Univ.) 2000; Ford Foundation Grant 1958, Guggenheim Fellowship 1967, Nat. Endowment for the Humanities Fellowship 1974, Distinguished Scholarly Career Award 1993, Prize for Outstanding Work in the field of Slavic Languages and Literature, American Asscn of Teachers of Slavic and East European Languages 1994, Alexander von Humboldt Award 1999. *Address:* c/o Dept of Slavic Languages and Literatures, Yale University, PO Box 208236, New Haven, CT 06520, USA.

JACOBS, Barbara, BA, PGCE; British journalist and writer; b. 6 Feb. 1945, St Helens, England; m. Mark Jacobs 1968, divorced, one s. *Education:* Leicester University. *Career:* freelance journalist 1978–. *Publications:* Ridby Graham, 1982; Two Times Two, 1984; The Fire Proof Hero, 1986; Desperadoes, 1987; Listen to My Heartbeat, 1988; Stick, 1988; Goodbye My Love, 1989; Just How Far, 1989; Loves a Pain, 1990; Not Really Working, 1990. Contributions: periodicals.

JACOBS, Leah (see Gellis, Roberta Leah)

JACOBS, Steve, BA, LLB; South African/Australian writer, journalist and barrister; *Chief Sub-Editor and Environment Editor, The Sydney Morning Herald*; b. Port Elizabeth, S Africa. *Education:* Univ. of Cape Town. *Career:* Chief Sub-Ed. and web producer, The Sydney Morning Herald, Herald online; also works for The Sun-Herald, Sydney, Australia. *Publications:* Light in a Stark Age (short stories) 1984, Diary of an Exile (two novellas) 1986, Under the Lion (novel) 1993, The Enemy Within (novel) 1995. *Address:* c/o African Writers Series, Heinemann Educational Publishers, Halley Court, Jordan Hill, Oxford, OX2 8EJ, England (office).

JACOBSON, Dan, BA, FRSL; British (b. South African) author; *Professor Emeritus of English, University College London*; b. 7 March 1929, Johannesburg, S Africa; s. of Hyman Michael Jacobson and Liebe Jacobson (née Melamed); m. Margaret Pye 1954; two s. one d. *Education:* Boys' High School, Kimberly, Univ. of Witwatersrand, S Africa. *Career:* worked in business and journalism in SA, settled in England 1955; Fellow in Creative Writing, Stanford Univ., Calif. 1956–57; Prof. of English, Syracuse Univ., New York 1965–66; Visiting Fellow, State Univ. of NY 1971, Humanities Research Centre, ANU, Canberra 1981; Lecturer, Univ. Coll. London 1975–79, Reader in English, Univ. of London 1979–87, Prof. of English, Univ. Coll. London 1988–94, Prof. Emer. 1995–, Fellow 2005–. *Publications:* fiction: The Trap 1955, A Dance in the Sun 1956, The Price of Diamonds 1957, The Evidence of Love 1960, The Beginners 1965, The Rape of Tamar 1970, The Wonder-Worker 1973, Inklings (short stories) 1973, The Confessions of Josef Baisz 1977, Her Story 1987, Hidden in the Heart 1991, The God-Fearer 1992, All For Love 2005; non-fiction: The Story of the Stories (criticism) 1982, Time and Time Again (autobiog.) 1985, Adult Pleasures (criticism) 1988, The Electronic Elephant (travel) 1994, Heshel's Kingdom (travel) 1998, A Mouthful of Glass (trans.) 2000, Ian Hamilton in Conversation with Dan Jacobson (interview) 2002, A Month in the Country (poems) 2009, Invictus (Beginning Again), British Studies (University of Texas). *Honours:* Hon. DLitt (Witwatersrand) 1997; John Llewellyn Rhys Award 1958, W. Somerset Maugham Award 1961, Jewish Chronicle Award 1971, H.H. Wingate Award 1978, J.R. Ackerley Award for Autobiography 1986, Mary Eleanor Smith Poetry Prize 1992. *Address:* c/o A.M. Heath & Co., 79 St Martin's Lane, London, WC2N 4RE, England. *Telephone:* (20) 7836-4271.

JACOBSON, Howard, BA, MA; British novelist and critic; b. 25 Aug. 1942, Manchester, England; s. of Max Jacobson and Anita Black; m. 1st Barbara Starr 1964 (divorced 1972); one s.; m. 2nd Rosalin Sadler 1978 (divorced 2004); m. 3rd Jenny De Yong 2005. *Education:* Downing Coll., Cambridge. *Career:* Lecturer, Univ. of Sydney 1965–68; Supervisor, Selwyn Coll., Cambridge 1969–72; Sr Lecturer, Wolverhampton Polytechnic 1974–80; TV critic, The Sunday Correspondent 1989–90; columnist, The Independent 1998–. *Television:* writer, presenter: Into the Land of Oz (Channel 4) 1990, Yo, Mrs Askew! (BBC 2) 1991, Roots Schmoots (Channel 4) 1993, Sorry, Judas (Channel 4) 1993, Seriously Funny: An Argument for Comedy (Channel 4) 1997, Howard Jacobson Takes on the Turner (Channel 4) 2000, Why the Novel Matters (South Bank Show special, LWT) 2002, Jesus the Jew (Channel 4) 2009, Creation (Channel 4) 2010, The Genius of British Art: Flesh (Channel 4) 2010. *Publications:* Shakespeare's Magnanimity: Four Tragic Heroes, Their Friends and Families 1978, Coming From Behind 1983, Peeping Tom 1984, Redback 1986, In the Land of Oz 1987, The Very Model of a Man 1992, Roots Schmoots 1993, Seeing With the Eye: The Peter Fuller Memorial Lecture 1993, Seriously Funny 1997, No More Mister Nice Guy 1998, The Mighty Walzer 1999, Who's Sorry Now 2002, The Making of Henry 2004, Kalooki Nights 2006, The Act of Love 2008, The Finkler Question (Man Booker Prize 2010) 2010, Whatever It Is, I Don't Like It 2011, Zoo Time 2012. *Honours:* Jewish Quarterly and Wingate Prize 2000, 2007, Bollinger Everyman Wodehouse Prize 2000. *Literary Agent:* c/o Curtis Brown Ltd, 28–29 Haymarket, London, SW1Y 4SP, England. *Telephone:* (20) 7393-4400. *Fax:* (20) 7393-4401. *E-mail:* info@curtisbrown.co.uk. *Website:* www.curtisbrown.co.uk.

JACOBUS, Lee A., BA, MA, PhD; American academic and writer; b. 20 Aug. 1935, Orange, NJ; m. Joanna Jacobus 1958, two c. *Education:* Brown University, Claremont Graduate University. *Career:* Faculty, Western Connecticut State University, 1960–68; Asst Prof., 1968–71, Assoc. Prof., 1971–76, Prof. of English, 1976–, University of Connecticut; Visiting Prof., Brown University, 1981; Visiting Fellow, Yale University, 1983, 1996. *Publications:* Improving College Reading, 1967; Issues and Responses, 1968; Developing College Reading, 1970; Humanities Through the Arts (with F. David Martin), 1974; John Cleveland: A Critical Study, 1975; Sudden Apprehension: Aspects of Knowledge in Paradise Lost, 1976; The Paragraph and Essay Book, 1977; The Sentence Book, 1980; Humanities: The Evolution of Values, 1986; Writing as Thinking, 1989; Shakespeare and the Dialectic of Certainty, 1993; Substance, Style and Strategy, 1998. Editor: Aesthetics and the Arts, 1968; 17 From Everywhere: Short Stories from Around the World, 1971; Poems in Context (William T. Moynihan), 1974; Longman Anthology of American Drama, 1982; The Bedford Introduction to Drama, third edn, 1997; A World of Ideas, fourth edn, 1994; Teaching Literature: An Introduction to Critical Reading, 1996. Contributions: scholarly books, journals, and other publications.

JACOBUS, Mary Longstaff, CBE, BA, MA, DPhil, FBA; British academic and writer; *Grace 2 Professor of English, University of Cambridge*; b. 4 May 1944, Cheltenham, Glos., England. *Education:* Univ. of Oxford. *Career:* Lecturer, Dept of English, Univ. of Manchester 1970–71; Fellow and Tutor in English, Lady Margaret Hall, Oxford 1971–80, Lecturer in English, Univ. of Oxford 1971–80; Assoc. Prof., Cornell Univ., Ithaca, NY 1980–82, Prof. 1982–, John Wendell Anderson Prof. of English 1989–2000; Grace 2 Prof. of English, Univ. of Cambridge 2000–, Professorial Fellow, Churchill Coll., Dir Centre for Research in the Arts, Social Sciences and Humanities (CRASSH) 2005–11; mem. Modern Language Asscn. *Publications:* Tradition and Experiment in Wordsworth's Lyrical Ballads (1798) 1976, Women Writing and Women about Women (ed.) 1979, Reading Women 1986, Romanticism, Writing, and Sexual Difference: Essays on The Prelude 1989, Body/Politics: Women and the Discourses of Science (co-ed.) 1989, First Things: The Maternal Imaginary 1995, Psychoanalysis and the Scene of Reading 1999, The Poetics of Psychoanalysis: In the Wake of Klein 2005; contrib. to numerous magazines and journals. *Honours:* Hon. Fellow, Lady Margaret Hall, Oxford 2000–; Guggenheim Fellowship 1988–89, Nat. Endowment for the Humanities Award 2000–01. *Address:* Faculty of English, Univ. of Cambridge, 9 West Road, Cambridge, CB3 9DP, England (office). *Telephone:* (1223) 335070 (office). *Fax:* (1223) 335075 (office). *E-mail:* mlj25@cam.ac.uk (office). *Website:* www.english.cam.ac.uk (office).

JACOBY, Hildegard (Hilla); German writer and photographer; b. 20 April 1922, Berlin; d. of Heinrich Gerberding and Else Gerberding (née Klein); m. Max-Moshe Jacoby. *Education:* Oberlyzeum Weissensee, Berlin. *Career:* actress, dir children's theatre and artistic producer 1945–; lecturer, writer, photographer for illustrated books (with Max-Moshe Jacoby) 1973–; exhbns of photographs in Berlin and London 1990. *Publications include:* Shalom 1978, The Land of Israel 1978, Sweden 1978, Hallelujah Jerusalem 1980, New York 1981, The Last Hours with Jesus 1982, The Jews, God's People 1983, Who Saves Tina? (for children) 1985, Do Not Fear 1985, I Am With You 1985, The Ten Commandments – That We May Live 1987, Israel, the Miracle 1988, Walking With Jesus in the Holy Land 1989, Mit Jesus unterwegs 1990, Nächstes Jahr in Jerusalem 1995, The Land of the Bible 1997, A Camera Trip through the Holy Land 1999; also children's books. *Honours:* two Kodak Photo Book Prizes (with Max-Moshe Jacoby) 1978, 1981. *Address:* Spessartstrasse 15, 14197 Berlin, Germany (home). *Telephone:* (30) 8211815 (home). *Fax:* (30) 8211815 (home).

JACOBY, Russell, BA, MA, PhD; American historian and writer; b. 23 April 1945, New York, NY; m. Naomi Glauberman, one s. one d. *Education:*

University of Chicago, University of Wisconsin at Madison, University of Rochester, École Pratique des Hautes Études, Paris. *Career:* Lecturer in Social Science, Boston University, 1974–75; Scholar-in-Residence, Brandeis University, 1975–76; Lecturer in History, 1976–79, Visiting Assoc. Prof. of History, 1992–, University of California at Los Angeles; Visiting Asst Prof. of History, University of California at Irvine, 1979–80; Visiting Assoc. Prof. of Humanities, Simon Fraser University, 1983–84; Visiting Scholar-Assoc. Prof., Longergan University College-Liberal Arts College, Concordia University, 1985–86; Visiting Senior Lecturer, University of California at San Diego, 1986–87; Visiting Assoc. Prof. of History, University of California at Riverside, 1988–90. *Publications:* Social Amnesia: A Critique of Conformist Psychology from Adler to Laing, 1975; Dialectic of Defeat: Contours of Western Marxism, 1981; The Repression of Psychoanalysis: Otto Fenichel and the Political Freudians, 1983; The Last Intellectuals: American Culture in the Age of Academe, 1987; Dogmatic Wisdom: How the Culture Wars Divert Education and Distract America, 1994; The Bell Curve Debate: History, Documents, Opinions (ed. with Naomi Glauberman), 1995; The End of Utopia: Politics and Culture in an Age of Apathy, 1999. Contributions: anthologies, reviews, quarterlies and journals. *Honours:* National Endowment for the Humanities Fellowship, 1976; Mellon Postdoctoral Fellowship, 1976–77; Guggenheim Fellowship, 1980–81.

JACQUEMARD, Simonne; French novelist, poet and essayist; b. 6 May 1924, Paris; d. of André Jacquemard and Andrée Jacquemard (née Raimondi); m. 2nd Jacques Brosse 1955. *Education:* Inst. Saint-Pierre, Univ. of Paris. *Career:* teacher of music; collaborator, Laffont-Bompiani Dictionaries; contrib. to Figaro Littéraire, La Table Ronde; travelled in USSR, Egypt, Greece, Italy, N Africa and Spain. *Dance:* Sacred dances of India; flamenco dance shows 1982–2000. *Publications:* Les fascinés 1951, Sable 1952, La leçon des ténèbres 1954, Planant sur les airs 1960, Compagnons insolites 1961, Le veilleur de nuit 1962 (Prix Renaudot 1962), L'orangerie 1963, Les derniers rapaces 1965, Dérive au zénith 1965, Exploration d'un corps 1965, Navigation vers les îles 1967, A l'état sauvage 1967, L'éruption du Krakatoa 1969, La thessalienne 1973, Des roses pour mes chevreuils 1974, Le mariage berbère 1975, Danse de l'orée 1979, Le funambule 1981, Lalla Zahra 1983, La fête en éclats 1985, Les belles échappées 1987, L'huître dans la perle 1993, Le Jardin d'Hérodote 1995, L'Éphèbe couronné de lierre 1995, La Gloire d'Ishwara 1996, Vers l'estuaire ébloui 1996, Trois mystiques grecs 1997, Orphée ou l'initiation mystique (jtly) 1998, L'Oiseau 1963, 1998 (Prix Jacques Lacroix, l'Académie française 1999), Héraclite d'Ephèse 2003, Rituels 2004, Pythagore et l'Harmonie des Sphères 2004. *Honours:* Officier Ordre des Arts et des Lettres 1993, Chevalier Légion d'honneur 1999; Prix Renaudot 1962, Grand prix Thyde-Monnier 1984. *Address:* Le Verdier, 24620 Sireuil, France.

JACQUES, Paula; French author and broadcaster; b. 8 May 1949, Cairo, Egypt; d. of Jacques Abadi and Esther Sasson; m. (divorced 1970). *Career:* worked as comedienne in Africa; joined Radio France Internationale as reporter, worked on Après-midi de France-Culture, L'Oreille en coin 1975–90; presenter, Nuits-noires France-Inter radio 1997–, Cosmopolitaine 2000–; sometime writer, F Magazine; mem. jury Prix Femina 1996–, Prix des Cinq Continents. *Play:* Zanouba. *Publications:* Lumière de l'oeil 1980, Un baiser froid comme la lune 1983, L'Heritage de Tante Carlotta 1987, Deborah et les anges dissipés (Prix Femina 1991), La Déscente au Paradis (Prix Nice Baie des Anges) 1995, Les femmes avec leur amour 1997, Gilda Stambouli souffre et se plaint... (Prix Europe 1) 2001, Rachel-Rose et l'officier arabe (Prix des Sables d'Olonne) 2006, Kairo Jacobi, juste avant l'oubli 2011. *Address:* France-Inter, 116 avenue du Président Kennedy, 75220 Paris cedex 16, France.

JAFFE, Harold; American writer and academic. *Career:* Prof. of Creative Writing and Literature, San Diego State Univ.; Ed.-in-Chief, Fiction Int. *Publications:* fiction: Mole's Pity 1979, Mourning Crazy Horse 1982, Dos Indios 1983, Beasts 1986, Madonna and Other Spectacles 1988, Eros Anti-Eros 1990, Straight Razor 1995, Othello Blues 1996, Sex for the Millennium 1999, False Positive 2002, 15 Serial Killers 2003, Terror-Dot-Gov 2005, Jesus Coyote 2008; non-fiction: Beyond the Techno-Cave 2007. *Honours:* two Nat. Endowment of the Arts grants, California Arts Council grant, Rockefeller Fellowship, NY CAPS grant, two Fulbright grants. *Address:* Department of English and Comparative Literature, San Diego State University, Arts and Letters Building, Office AL-269, 5500 Campanile Drive, San Diego, CA 92182-6020, USA (office). *E-mail:* hjaffe@mail.sdsu.edu (office). *Website:* www.jaffeantijaffe.com (office).

JAFFREY, Madhur, CBE; Indian actress and cookery writer; b. 13 Aug. 1937, Delhi; m. 1st Saeed Jaffrey (divorced 1965); three c.; m. 2nd Sanford Allen 1969. *Education:* Univ. of Delhi, Royal Acad. of Dramatic Art, London. *Career:* has appeared in numerous radio and TV plays and acted on Broadway and in several films; writes on Indian cookery for the New York Times and other publications; currently living in the UK. *Films include:* Shakespeare Wallah (Best Actress Award, Berlin International Film Festival, Germany) 1965, Guru 1969, Autobiography of a Princess 1975, Heat and Dust 1983, The Assam Garden 1985, The Perfect Murder 1988, Six Degrees of Separation 1993, Vanya on 42nd Street 1994, Cotton Mary 1999, Chutney Popcorn 1999, Cosmopolitan 2003, Prime 2005. *Play:* Medea, A Tenth of an Inch Makes the Difference 1962, The Guide 1969, Conduct Unbecoming 1970, Two Rooms 1993, Last Dance at Dum Dum 1999, Bombay Dreams on Broadway 2004, India Awakening 2005. *TV appearances include:* Madhur Jaffrey's Indian Cookery (series), Madhur Jaffrey's Far Eastern Cookery 1989, Firm Friends 1992, Madhur Jaffrey's Flavours of India 1995. *Publications include:* cookery books: Invitation to Indian Cooking 1973, Madhur Jaffrey's Indian Cooking 1973, Madhur Jaffrey's World of the East: Vegetarian Cooking 1981, Eastern Vegetarian Cooking 1983, A Taste of India 1988, Madhur Jaffrey's Cook Book: Food for Family and Friends 1989, Indian Cooking 1989, A Taste of the Far East 1993, Madhur Jaffrey's Spice Kitchen 1993, Madhur Jaffrey's Indian Recipes 1994, Entertaining with Madhur Jaffrey 1994, Madhur Jaffrey's Flavours of India 1995, Food for Family and Friends 1995, Quick and Easy Indian Cookery 1996, Madhur Jaffrey Cooks Curries 1996, The Essential Madhur Jaffrey 1999, Madhur Jaffrey's Step-by-Step Cooking 2001, Foolproof Indian Cooking 2002, Madhur Jaffrey Indian Cooking 2003, From Curries to Kebabs 2003 (James Beard Award, Cookery Book of the Year), Ultimate Curry Bible 2003, Curry Easy 2010; others: Seasons of Splendour 1995, Market Days 1995, Robi Dobi 1997, Climbing the Mango Trees: A Memoir of a Childhood in India 2006. *Honours:* Hon. CBE 2004; Taraknath Das Foundation Award 1993, Muse Award 2000.

JAGIELSKI, Wojciech; Polish journalist and author; b. 12 Sept. 1960. *Education:* Wladyslaw IV High School, Warsaw Univ. *Career:* fmrly worked in television; journalist, Polish Press Agency 1986–91; journalist and foreign correspondent, Gazeta Wyborcza (ind. daily newspaper) 1991–2012, reported from conflict zones in Transcaucasus, Cen. Asia and Africa; contrib., BBC, Le Monde. *Publications include:* Modlitwa o deszcz (Pray for the Rain) (Amber Butterfly Award in Arkady Fiedler Competition 2003, Józef Tischner Award 2003) 2002, Dobre miejsce do umierania (A Good Place to Die) 2004, Towers of Stone: The Battle of Wills in Chechnya (Italian Literatura Frontera Award 2009) 2009, The Night Wanderers 2012. *Honours:* Bene Merito distinction, Ministry of Foreign Affairs 2009; Polish Journalists Asscn (SDP) Award 1996, Ksawery Pruszynski Award of Polish PEN Club 1996, Warsaw Literary Premiere Award 2002, Dariusz Fikus Award 2002, Polish Grand Press Special Achievement Award 2011. *Address:* c/o Seven Stories Press, 140 Watts Street, New York, NY 10013, USA (office). *Telephone:* (212) 226-8760 (office). *Fax:* (212) 226-1411 (office). *E-mail:* publicity@sevenstories.com (office). *Website:* www.sevenstories.com (office).

JAHR-STILCKEN, Angelika; German publishing executive; *Publisher, Editor-in-Chief and Journalist Member, Executive Board, Gruner + Jahr AG;* b. 26 Oct. 1941; m. Rudolf Stilcken 1977; one s. one d. *Education:* Univs of Hamburg and Munich. *Career:* began as trainee journalist at Die Welt; spent time in USA at McCall's, Glamour, Vogue and Time Magazine; began career in Germany as Deputy Ed.-in-Chief at es, Petra, Schöner Wohnen 1969, later Ed.-in-Chief; launched Essen und Trinker 1972, Schöner Essen 1985; Ed.-in-Chief Häuser; helped develop concept of Schöner Wohnen Decoration 1989; Gen. Man. Living publishing group 1994–, publishing Flora Garten 1996–, Living at Home 2000–, Essen und Trinken für Jeden Tag 2003–; mem. Supervisory Bd Nestlé Deutschland AG 1996–; Publr, Ed.-in-Chief and Journalist mem. Exec. Bd Gruner + Jahr AG 2000–. *Address:* Gruner + Jahr AG & Co. KG, Druck- und Verlagshaus, Am Baumwall 11, Postfach 110011, 20459 Hamburg, Germany (office). *Telephone:* (40) 37032700 (office). *Fax:* (40) 37035851 (office). *E-mail:* Jahr.Angelika@guj.de (office). *Website:* www.guj.de (office).

JAKES, John William, AB, MA; American writer; b. 31 March 1932, Chicago, IL; m. Rachel Ann Payne 1951; one s. three d. *Education:* DePauw Univ., Ohio State Univ. *Career:* Research Fellow, Univ. of South Carolina 1989; mem. Authors' Guild, Authors' League of America, Dramatists' Guild, PEN, Western Writers of America, Century Asscn. *Publications:* Brak the Barbarian 1968, Brak the Barbarian Versus the Sorceress 1969, Brak Versus the Mark of the Demons 1969, Six Gun Planet 1970, On Wheels 1973, The Bastard 1974, The Rebels 1975, The Seekers 1975, The Titans 1976, The Furies 1976, The Best of John Jakes 1977, The Warriors 1977, Brak: When the Idols Walked 1978, The Lawless 1978, The Americans 1980, Fortunes of Brak 1980, North and South 1982, Love and War 1984, Heaven and Hell 1988, California Gold 1989, The Best Western Stories of John Jakes 1991, Homeland 1993, New Trails (co-ed.) 1994, American Dreams 1998, On Secret Service 2000, Charleston 2002, Savannah (or A Gift for Mr Lincoln) 2004; contrib. to magazines. *Honours:* Hon. LLD (Wright State Univ.) 1976, Hon. LittD (DePauw Univ.) 1977, Hon. LDH (Winthrop Coll.) 1985, (Univ. of South Carolina) 1993, Hon. DH (Ohio State Univ.) 1996; Porgie Award 1977, Ohioana Book Award 1978, Ohio State Univ. Distinguished Alumni Award 1995, Cowboy Hall of Fame Western Heritage Literature Award 1995, Ohio State Univ. Alumni Asscn Professional Achievement Award 1997, South Carolina Humanities Asscn Career Achievement Award 1998, Univ. of South Carolina Thomas Cooper Library Soc. Medal 2002. *Address:* c/o Rembar and Curtis, 19 W 44th Street, New York, NY 10036, USA (office). *E-mail:* jjfiction@aol.com (office). *Website:* www.johnjakes.com.

JAMES, Canute W., BA, PhD; Jamaican journalist and lecturer; *Director, Caribbean Institute of Media and Communication (CARIMAC), University of the West Indies;* b. St Ann. *Education:* Manchester School, Mandeville, Univ. of the West Indies. *Career:* sub-ed., The Gleaner; reporter, producer and news reader, BBC Radio, London, UK 1971–73; Head of Current Affairs Programming, Jamaica Broadcasting Corpn 1973; Sr Reporter, Jamaica Daily News 1973–76, Ed. 1976–80; Caribbean Corresp., Financial Times 1980–2003; Dir Caribbean Inst. of Media and Communication (CARIMAC), Univ. of the West Indies. *Publications:* contribs to The Journal of Commerce, Time, The Miami Herald and others. *Honours:* Maria Moors Cabot Prize, Grad. School of Journalism, Columbia Univ., New York 1995. *Address:* CARIMAC, University of the West Indies, Mona Campus, 3 Sherlock Drive, Kingston 7, Jamaica (office). *Telephone:* 977-0898 (office). *Fax:* 977-1597 (office). *E-mail:* canute.james@uwimona.edu.jm (office). *Website:* mona.uwi.carimac.com (office).

JAMES, Clive Vivian Leopold, CBE, AM, FRSL; Australian writer, broadcaster, journalist and poet; b. (Vivian James), 7 Oct. 1939, Kogarah, Sydney, NSW; s. of Albert A. James and Minora M. Darke; m. Prue Shaw; two d. *Education:* Sydney Technical High School, Sydney Univ. and Pembroke Coll. Cambridge. *Career:* Asst Ed. Morning Herald, Sydney 1961; Pres. of Footlights at Cambridge, UK; TV critic, The Observer 1972–82, feature writer 1972–; Dir Watchmaker Productions 1994–; as lyricist for Pete Atkin, record albums include Beware of the Beautiful Stranger, Driving Through Mythical America, A King at Nightfall, The Road of Silk, Secret Drinker, Live Libel, The Master of the Revels; also songbook, A First Folio (with Pete Atkin); Patron Burma Campaign UK. *Television series include:* Cinema, Up Sunday, So It Goes, A Question of Sex, Saturday Night People, Clive James on Television, The Late Clive James, The Late Show with Clive James, Saturday Night Clive, Fame in the 20th Century, Sunday Night Clive, The Clive James Show, Clive James on Safari; numerous TV documentaries including Clive James meets Katharine Hepburn 1986, Clive James meets Jane Fonda, Clive James meets Mel Gibson 1998, Clive James meets the Supermodels 1998, Postcard series 1989–. *Publications:* non-fiction: The Metropolitan Critic 1974, The Fate of Felicity Fark in the Land of the Media 1975, Peregrine Prykke's Pilgrimage through the London Literary World 1976, Britannia Bright's Bewilderment in the Wilderness of Westminster 1976, Visions Before Midnight 1977, At the Pillars of Hercules 1979, First Reactions 1980, The Crystal Bucket 1981, Charles Charming's Challenges on the Pathway to the Throne 1981, From the Land of Shadows 1982, Glued to the Box 1982, Flying Visits 1984, Snakecharmers in Texas 1988, The Dreaming Swimmer 1992, Clive James on Television 1993, Fame 1993, The Speaker in Ground Zero 1999, Even as We Speak (essays) 2000, Reliable Essays 2001, The Meaning of Recognition: New Essays 2001–2005 2005, North Face of Soho 2006, Alone in the Café 2007, Cultural Amnesia 2007, The Revolt of the Pendulum 2009, The Blaze of Obscurity: The TV Years 2009, The Revolt of the Pendulum: Essays 2005–2008 2010, A Point of View 2011; novels: Brilliant Creatures 1983, The Remake 1987, The Silver Castle 1996; autobiography: Unreliable Memoirs 1980, Falling Towards England: Unreliable Memoirs Vol. II 1985, Unreliable Memoirs Vol. III 1990, May Week was in June 1990, Brrm! Brrm! or The Man from Japan or Perfume at Anchorage 1991, Fame in the 20th Century 1993, The Metropolitan Critic 1993; poetry: Fanmail 1977, Poem of the Year 1983, Other Passports: Poems 1958–85 1986, The Book of My Enemy: Collected Verse 1958–2003 2004, Opal Sunset: Selected Poems 1958–2008 2008, Angels Over Elsinore 2008; contribs to numerous pubs including Commentary, Encounter, Listener, London Review of Books, Nation, New Review, New Statesman, New York Review of Books, New Yorker, TLS. *Honours:* Dr hc (Sydney), (East Anglia); Philip Hodgins Memorial Medal for Literature 2003, Orwell Prize for Lifetime Achievement in Journalism 2008. *Literary Agent:* c/o United Agents, 12–26 Lexington Street, London, W1F 0LE, England. *Telephone:* (20) 3214-0800. *Fax:* (20) 3214-0801. *E-mail:* info@unitedagents.co.uk. *Website:* unitedagents.co.uk; www.clivejames.com.

JAMES, Dana (see Pollard, Jane)

JAMES, E(rika). L.; British writer; b. 1963, London; m. Niall Leonard; two s. *Education:* Univ. of Kent. *Career:* fmr Asst, National Film and Television School, London; fmr TV exec. *Publications include:* Fifty Shades of Grey 2011, Fifty Shades Darker 2012, Fifty Shades Freed 2012. *Address:* c/o Valerie Hoskins, Valerie Hoskins Associates Limited, 20 Charlotte Street, London, W1T 2NA, England. *E-mail:* author.eljames@gmail.com. *Website:* www.eljamesauthor.com.

JAMES, Erica; British novelist; b. 1960, Hampshire; two s. *Publications:* novels: A Breath of Fresh Air 1996, Time for a Change 1997, Airs and Graces 1997, A Sense of Belonging 1998, Act of Faith 1999, The Holiday 2000, Precious Time 2001, Hidden Talents 2002, Paradise House 2003, Love and Devotion 2004, Gardens of Delight (Romantic Novelists' Asscn Romantic Novel of the Year 2006) 2005, The Real Katie Lavender 2011. *Address:* c/o Orion Publishing Group, Orion House, 5 Upper St Martin's Lane, London, WC2H 9EA, England. *E-mail:* publicity.enquiries@orionbooks.co.uk.

JAMES, Marlon, BA; Jamaican novelist and essayist; b. 26 Nov. 1970, Kingston. *Education:* Univ. of the West Indies. *Career:* Prof. of Literature and Creative Writing, Macelester Coll., St Paul, Minn., USA. *Publications:* John Crow's Devil 2005, The Book of Night Women (Dayton Literary Peace Prize 2010) 2009. *Literary Agent:* Ellen Levine, Trident Media Group, 41 Madison Avenue Floor 36, New York, NY 10010, USA. *Telephone:* (212) 333-1517. *E-mail:* levine.assistant@tridentmediagroup.com. *Website:* www.tridentmediagroup.com. *Address:* c/o Lizzie Curtin, Publicity Manager, Oneworld Publications, 10 Fitzroy Square, London, W1T 5HP, England (office). *Telephone:* (1865) 310597 (office). *Fax:* (1865) 310598 (office). *E-mail:* lcurtin@oneworld-publications.com (office). *Website:* www.marlonjames.com; marlon-james.blogspot.com.

JAMES, Michael Leonard, (Michael Hartland, Ruth Carrington), MA, FRSA; British government official, writer and broadcaster; b. 7 Feb. 1941; m. Jill Tarján 1975; two d. *Education:* Christ's Coll., Cambridge. *Career:* entered govt service (GCHQ) 1963; Pvt. Sec. to Rt Hon. Jennie Lee, Minister for the Arts 1966–68; DES 1968–71; Planning Unit of Rt Hon Margaret Thatcher, Sec. of State for Educ. and Science 1971–73, Asst Sec. 1973; Deputy Chief Scientific Officer 1974; served in London, Milan, Paris, Tokyo 1973–78; Dir, IAEA Vienna 1978–83; Adviser, Int. Relations to Comm. of the European Union, Brussels 1983–85; Chair. Civil Service Selection Bds 1983–93; Gov. East Devon Coll. of Further Educ., Tiverton 1985–91, Colyton Grammar School 1985–90, Sidmouth Community Coll. 1988–2004, Chair. Bd of Govs 1998–2001; Chair. Gen. Medical Council Fitness to Practise Cttee 2000–06; Chair. Kennaway House Trust 2001–11, Pres. 2011–; mem. Immigration Appeal Tribunal 1987–2005, Devon and Cornwall Rent Assessment Panel 1990–, Asylum and Immigration Tribunal 2005–; feature writer and book reviewer, The Times (thriller critic 1989–90, travel corresp. 1993–), Daily Telegraph (thriller critic 1993–2000), Sunday Times, Guardian. *TV and radio include:* Seven Steps to Treason (BBC Radio 4) 1990, Sonja's Report (ITV documentary) 1990, Masterspy: interviews with KGB defector Oleg Gordievsky (BBC Radio 4) 1991. *Publications:* Internationalization to Prevent the Spread of Nuclear Weapons (co-author) 1980; novels as Michael Hartland: Down Among the Dead Men 1983, Seven Steps to Treason (South West Arts Literary Award) 1985, The Third Betrayal 1986, Frontier of Fear 1989, The Year of the Scorpion 1991, The Verdict of Us All (short stories) (co-author) 2006; other: Masters of Crime – Lionel Davidson and Dick Francis 2006; novel as Ruth Carrington: Dead Fish 1998. *Honours:* Hon. Fellow, Univ. of Exeter 1985–. *Address:* Cotte Barton, Branscombe, Devon, EX12 3BH, England (home). *E-mail:* michael@hartlandpress.freeserve.co.uk (office).

JAMES, Peter; British crime novelist and film producer; b. 1948, Brighton, Sussex; s. of Cornelia James. *Education:* Charterhouse, Ravensbourne Film School. *Career:* Co-founder Quadrant Films (production co.) 1971–78; full-time writer 1979–; co-f. Pavilion Internet plc 1993–98; co-f. Ministry of Vision 1997–; Chair. Crime Writers Asscn. *Films include:* as co-producer: Dead of Night, Sunday in the Country, The Neptune Factor, Malachi's Cove, The Blockhouse, Find The Lady, Spanish Fly, Biggles 1985. *Publications include:* Possession 1988, Sweet Heart 1990, Dreamer 1989, Twilight 1991, Prophecy 1992, Host 1993, Alchemist 1996, The Truth 1997, Denial 1998, Faith 2000, Dead Simple (trans. as Comme Une Tombe, Le Prix Polar Int. 2006, Le Prix Coeur Noir 2007) 2005, Looking Good Dead, Not Dead Enough 2007, Dead Man's Footsteps 2008, Dead Tomorrow 2009, The Perfect Murder (Quick Reads Readers' Favourite Award) 2010, Dead Like You 2010, Dead Man's Grip 2011. *Honours:* Hon. DLit (Brighton) 2009; FHS Emer. Award, Hypnotherapy Soc. 1999. *Literary Agent:* c/o Carole Blake, Blake Friedmann Agency, 122 Arlington Road, London, NW1 7HP, England. *Telephone:* (20) 7284-0408. *Fax:* (20) 7284-0442. *E-mail:* carole@blakefriedmann.co.uk. *Website:* www.blakefriedmann.co.uk. *E-mail:* scary@pavilion.co.uk (office). *Website:* www.peterjames.com.

JAMES, Russell; British writer; b. 5 Oct. 1942, Gillingham, Kent, England; m. Jill Redfern 1978; one s. two d. *Publications:* Undergound 1989, Daylight 1990, Payback 1991, Slaughter Music 1995, Count Me Out 1996, Oh, No, Not My Baby 1999, Painting in the Dark 2000, Pick Any Title 2002, The Annex 2002, No One Gets Hurt 2003, Underground and Collected Stories 2006, The Maud Allan Affair 2008, Great British Fictional Detectives 2008, Great British Fictional Villains 2009, The Pocket Guide to Victorian Writers and Poets 2010, The Pocket Guide to Victorian Artists and Their Models 2011, Requiem for a Daughter 2012, The Exhibitionists 2012; contrib. to periodicals. *Literary Agent:* c/o Jane Conway-Gordon, 38 Cromwell Grove, London, W6 7RG, England. *Telephone:* (20) 7602-4690. *E-mail:* jane@conway-gordon.co.uk. *E-mail:* findrj@lineone.net (office). *Website:* www.russelljames.co.uk; russelljamesbooks.wordpress.com.

JAMES, William M. (see Harknett, Terry)

JAMES OF HOLLAND PARK, Baroness (Life Peer), cr. 1991, of Southwold in the County of Suffolk; **Phyllis Dorothy (P. D.) James,** OBE, JP, FRSL, FRSA; British author; b. 3 Aug. 1920, Oxford; d. of Sidney Victor James and Dorothy Amelia Hone; m. Ernest Connor Bantry White 1941 (deceased 1964); two d. *Education:* Cambridge Girls' High School. *Career:* Admin., Nat. Health Service 1949–68; Prin., Home Office 1968; Police Dept 1968–72; Criminal Policy Dept 1972–79; JP, Willesden 1979–82, Inner London 1984; Chair. Soc. of Authors 1984–86, Pres. 1997–; mem. BBC Gen. Advisory Council 1987–88, Gov. BBC 1988–93; Assoc. Fellow, Downing Coll., Cambridge 1986; mem. Bd of British Council 1988–93, Arts Council; Chair. Arts Council Literary Advisory Panel 1988–92; mem. Detection Club; mem. Church of England Liturgical Comm. 1991–2000; Hon. Fellow, St Hilda's Coll., Oxford 1996, Downing Coll., Cambridge 2000, Girton Coll., Cambridge 2000, Kellogg Coll., Oxford 2006. *Publications:* Cover Her Face 1962, A Mind to Murder 1963, Unnatural Causes 1967, Shroud for a Nightingale 1971, The Maul and the Pear Tree (with T. A. Critchley) 1971, An Unsuitable Job for a Woman 1972, The Black Tower 1975, Death of an Expert Witness 1977, Innocent Blood 1980, The Skull Beneath the Skin 1982, A Taste for Death 1986, Devices and Desires 1989, The Children of Men 1992, Original Sin 1994, A Certain Justice 1997, Time To Be in Earnest 1999, Death in Holy Orders 2001, The Murder Room 2003, The Lighthouse 2005, The Private Patient 2008, Talking About Detective Fiction 2009, Death Comes to Pemberley 2011. *Honours:* Hon. Bencher Inner Temple 2009; Hon. DLitt (Buckingham) 1992, (Herts.) 1994, (Glasgow) 1995, (Durham) 1998, (Portsmouth) 1999; Hon. LitD (London) 1993; Dr hc (Essex) 1996; Grand Master Award, Mystery Writers of America 1999. *Literary Agent:* c/o Greene & Heaton Ltd, 37A Goldhawk Road, London, W12 8QQ, England.

JAMIE, Kathleen, MA; Scottish poet and writer; b. 13 May 1962, Johnston, Renfrewshire; m. Phil Butler; two c. *Education:* Currie High School, Univ. of

Edinburgh. *Career:* part-time Lecturer in Creative Writing, Univ. of St Andrews 1999–. *Publications:* poetry: Black Spiders 1982, The Way We Live 1987, The Queen of Sheba 1994, Mr & Mrs Scotland are Dead: Selected Poems 1980–94 1994, Jizzen 1999, The Tree House (Forward Prize 2004, Scottish Arts Council Book of the Year 2005) 2004, Findings 2005; non-fiction: The Golden Peak: Travels in Northern Pakistan 1992, The Autonomous Region: Poems and Photographs from Tibet (with Sean Mayne Smith) 1993, Among Muslims: Meetings at the Frontiers of Pakistan 2002, Findings (essays) 2005. *Honours:* Eric Gregory Award 1981, Scottish Arts Council Book Award 1982, 1988, Somerset Maugham Award 1995, Forward Poetry Prize 1996, Geoffrey Faber Memorial Prize 1996, 2000, Scottish Arts Council Creative Scotland Award 2001. *Literary Agent:* Peter Straus, Rogers, Coleridge and White, 20 Powis Mews, London, W11 1JN, England. *E-mail:* peters@rcwlitagency.co.uk. *Address:* The School of English, Castle House, The Poetry House, University of St Andrews, St Andrews, Fife KY16 9AL, Scotland.

JAMIESON, Kathleen Hall, BA, MA, PhD; American academic and writer; b. 24 Nov. 1946, Minneapolis, MN; m. Robert Jamieson, 1968, two s. *Education:* Marquette University, University of Wisconsin. *Career:* Prof. of Communications, University of Maryland, 1971–86, University of Texas at Austin, 1986–89; Prof. of Communications, 1989–, Dir, Annenberg School of Communications, 1993–, University of Pennsylvania, Philadelphia; Assoc. Ed., several journals; Television news appearances as Political Analyst. *Publications:* Debating Crime Control (co-author), 1967; A Critical Anthology of Public Speeches (compiler), 1978; Form and Genre: Shaping Rhetorical Action (co-ed.), 1978; Age Stereotyping and Television (ed.), 1978; Televised Advertising and the Elderly, 1978; The Interplay of Influence: Mass Media and Their Publics in News, Advertising, and Politics (co-author), 1982; Packaging the Presidency: A History and Criticism of Presidential Campaign Advertising, 1984; Eloquence in an Electronic Age: The Transformation of Political Speechmaking, 1988; Presidential Debates: The Challenge of Creating an Informed Electorate (co-author), 1988; Deeds Done in Words: Presidential Rhetoric and the Genres of Governance (co-author), 1990; Dirty Politics: Deception, Distraction, and Democracy, 1992; 1-800-President: The Report of the Twentieth Century Fund Task Force on Television and the Campaign of 1992 (co-author), 1993; Beyond the Double Bind: Women and Leadership, 1995; Spiral of Cynicism: The Press and the Public Good, 1996. Contributions: periodicals and professional journals. *Honours:* numerous fellowships, grants and teaching, research and academic awards; Golden Anniversary Book Award, 1984, Winans-Wichelns Book Award, 1989, Speech Communication Asscn.

JANČAR, Drago; Slovenian playwright and writer; *Chief Editor, Slovenská Matica;* b. 13 April 1948, Maribor. *Education:* studied law. *Career:* ed student journal Katedra, worked on Večer newspaper; arrested for possessing a booklet critical of Tito's regime, sentenced to one year's imprisonment, released after three months; moved to Ljubljana to pursue full-time writing career; Pres. Slovene PEN 1987–91; currently Chief Ed. Slovenská Matica publishing house; mem. Slovenian Acad. of Sciences and Arts. *Plays:* Disident Arno in njegovi (Dissident Arno and his Band) 1982, Veliki briljantni valček (The Great Brilliant Waltz) 1985, Vsi tirani mameluki so hud konec vzeli ... (All Mameluk Tyrants had a Bad End ...) 1986, Daedalus 1988, Klementov padec (Klement's Fall) 1988, Zalezujoč Godota (After Godot) 1988, Halštat (Hallstadt) 1994. *Publications:* novels: Petintrideset stopinj (Thirty-five Degrees) 1974, Galjot (The Galley Slave) 1978, Severni sij (Northern Lights) 1984, Pogled angela (Angel's Gaze) 1992, Posmehljivo pozelenje (trans. as Mocking Desire) 1993, Zvenenje v glavi (Ringing in the Head) 1998, Katarina, pav in jezuit 2000, Graditelj (The Builder) 2006; short stories: The Day Tito Died (in trans.) 1996, Joyce's Pupil (in trans.) 2006; essays: Razbiti vrč (The Broken Jug) 1992, Egiptovski lonci mesa (Egyptian Pots of Meat) 1994, Kratko porocilo iz dolgo obleganega mesta (Short Report on a City Long Besieged) 1996, Brioni 2002, Duša Evrope (Europe's Soul) 2006. *Honours:* Cross of Honour for Science and Art (Austria) 2005; Prešeren Award, European Short Story Award Augsburg 1994, Herder Prize for literature 2003, Fulbright Fellowship 2005, Jean Améry Prize 2007. *Address:* Slovenská Matica, 1000 Ljubljana, Kongresni trg 8, Slovenia (office). *Telephone:* (1) 4224340 (office). *E-mail:* drago.jancar@siol.net (office). *Website:* www.slovenska-matica.si (office).

JANÉS, Clara, LicenFil, MA; Spanish poet, writer and translator; b. 6 Nov. 1940, Barcelona; d. of the late Josep Janés. *Education:* Pamplona Univ. and Sorbonne, Univ. of Paris. *Publications:* Isla del suicidio (poems), Las estrellas vencidas (poems) 1964, La noche de Abel Micheli (novel) 1965, Desintegración (novel) 1969, La vida callada de Federico Monpou (biog.) (Premio Ciudad de Barcelona de Ensayo 1972) 1972, Tentativa de encuentro y tentativa de olvido (short story) (Premio Café Gijón 1972) 1972, Límite humano (poems) 1973, Aprender a envejecer (essay) 1973, En busca de Cordelia y Poemas rumanos (poems) 1975, Cartas a Adriana (novel) 1976, Antología personal 1959–1979 (poems) 1979, Libro de alienaciones (poems) 1980, Sendas de Rumanía (novel) 1981, Eros (poems) 1981, Pureza canelo (biog.) 1981, Vivir (poems) (Premio Ciudad de Barcelona de Poesía 1983) 1983, Kampa: poesía, música y voz (poems) 1986, Las primeras poetisas en lengua castellana (poems) 1986, Fósiles (poems) 1987, Federico Mompou: vida, textos y documentos (essay) 1987, Lapidario (poems) 1988, Creciente fértil (poems) 1989, Los caballos del sueño (novel) 1989, Jardín y laberinto (biog.) 1990, Esbozos (poems) 1990, El hombre de Adén (novel) 1991, Emblemas (poems) 1991, Espejismos (novel) 1991, Las palabras de la tribu: escritura y habla (essay) 1993, Rosas de fuego (poems) 1996, Cirlot, el no mundo y la poesía imaginal (essay) 1996, Diván del ópalo de fuego (poems) 1996, Espejos de agua (short stories) 1997, La indetenible quietud (poems) 1998, El libro de los pájaros (poems) 1999, Arcángel de sombra (poems) (Premio Ciudad de Melilla 1998) 2000, Los secretos del bosque (Premio de Poesía Gil de Biedma 2002) 2001, Paralajes (poems) 2002; contrib. numerous short stories to anthologies; translations, particularly of Czech poetry, also French, English, and Persian and Turkish verse. *Honours:* Premio Nacional de Traducción 1997. *Address:* c/o Ediciones Bassarai, Apdo No. 1630-01080, Vitoria-Gasteiz, Spain.

JANES, J(oseph) Robert, BASc, MEng; Canadian writer; b. 23 May 1935, Toronto, Ont.; m. Gracia Joyce Lind 1958; two s. two d. *Education:* Univ. of Toronto. *Career:* qualified as mining engineer and geologist; worked in industry and research, then as teacher and univ. lecturer –1970; full-time writer 1970–; mem. Crime Writers of the United Kingdom, Historical Novel Soc. (UK), Int. Asscn of Crime Writers (N American Br.). *Publications:* juvenile fiction: The Tree-Fort War 1976, Theft of Gold 1980, Danger on the River 1982, Spies for Dinner 1984, Murder in the Market 1985; adult fiction: The Toy Shop 1981, The Watcher 1982, The Third Story 1983, The Hiding Place 1984, The Alice Factor 1991, Mayhem (St Cyr/Kohler series) 1992, Carousel (St Cyr/Kohler series) 1992, Kaleidoscope (St Cyr/Kohler series) 1993, Salamander (St Cyr/Kohler series) 1994, Mannequin (St Cyr/Kohler series) 1994, Dollmaker (St Cyr/Kohler series) 1995, Stonekiller (St Cyr/Kohler series) 1995, Sandman (St Cyr/Kohler series) 1996, Gypsy (St Cyr/Kohler series) 1997, Madrigal (St Cyr/Kohler series) 1999, Beekeeper (St Cyr/Kohler series) 2001, Flykiller (St Cyr/Kohler series) 2002; non-fiction: Holt Geophoto Resource Kits 1972, Rocks, Minerals and Fossils 1973, Earth Science 1974, Geology and New Global Tectonics 1976, Searching for Structure (co-author) 1977, Teachers' Guide: Searching for Structure (co-author) 1977, The Great Canadian Outback 1978, Airphoto Interpretation and the Canadian Landscape (with J. D. Mollard) 1984; contrib. to Toronto Star, Toronto Globe and Mail, The Canadian, Winnipeg Free Press, Canadian Children's Annual. *Honours:* Canadian Inst. of Mining and Metallurgy Thesis Award 1958, grants from J. P. Bicknell Foundation 1975, Canada Council 1977, Ontario Arts Council 1981, Canada Council travel grant 2002. *Literary Agent:* c/o Acacia House, 62 Chestnut Avenue, Brantford, ON N3T 4C2, Canada. *Website:* www.jrobertjanes.com.

JÁNOSHÁZY, György, LLB; Romanian writer and editor; b. 20 June 1922, Cluj; m. Annamária Biluska 1980; one s. *Education:* Bolyai Univ., Cluj, Acad. of Dramatic Arts, Tg Mures, Bolyai Univ. *Career:* journalist 1945–48; art sec. and stage man. Hungarian Opera, Cluj 1949–59; Ed. Korunk (monthly) 1958–63, Igaz Szó monthly 1963–90, Deputy Gen. Ed. 1969–; mem. Writers' Union of Romania, Tg Mures Asscn (Sec. 1981–90), Hungarian Writers' Union. *Publications include:* Lepkék szekrényben (trans. as Butterflies in a Glass Case) 1994, Innen semerre (trans. as From Here in No Direction) 1995, Böllérek miséje (trans. as Butchers' Mass) 1999, Úszó sziget (trans. as Floating Island) 2002, Bagolytükör (trans. as Owe Mirror) 2003, Vízöntö (trans. as Water-carrier) 2005; numerous translations, essays on literature and the arts; contrib. to anthologies, reviews and journals. *Honours:* Order of Labour 1968, Gold Merit Cross (Hungary) 1997, Kt's Cross (Hungary) 2007, Pro Libro Senator 2009; Tg Mures Writers' Asscn Prize 1974, Cultural Merit Medal 1981, Látó Prize 1992, 1999, Szentgyörgyi Albert Soc. Prize 1995, Writers' Union of Romania Prize 2000, Hungarian Journalists' Asscn Golden Feather, Romania 2002, Hungarian Writers' Union Arany János Prize 2003. *Address:* Str Parangului 24/9, 540369 Tg Mures, Romania (home). *Telephone:* (365) 407697 (home). *E-mail:* janoshazy@rdslink.ro; janoshazy@gmail.com.

JANOWITZ, Tama, MA; American writer; b. 12 April 1957, San Francisco, Calif.; d. of Frederick Janowitz and Phyllis Janowitz (née Winer). *Education:* Lexington High School, Barnard Coll., Hollins Coll., Roanoke and Yale School of Drama. *Career:* fmr model; Asst Art Dir Kenyon and Eckhardt advertising agency 1977; Alfred Hodder Fellow, Princeton Univ. 1988–89. *Publications:* short stories: Slaves of New York (also screenplay) 1986, Sunpoisoning; novels: American Dad 1981, A Cannibal in Manhattan 1987, The Male Crossdresser Support Group, By the Shores of Gitchee Gumee 1996, A Certain Age 2000, Peyton Amberg 2003, They Is Us 2009; non-fiction: Area Code 212 – New York Days, New York Nights 2002; for children: Hear That? (illustrated by Tracy Dockery) 2001; contribs to Vogue, Elle, New York Times Sunday Magazine. *Honours:* Hon. MFA (Columbia) 1985. *Address:* 92 Horatio Street, Suite 5E, New York, NY 10014, USA (home).

JAPIN, Arthur; Dutch writer and actor; b. 26 July 1956, Haarlem; s. of Bert Japin and Annie Japin-van Arnhem. *Education:* Univ. of Amsterdam, Webber-Douglas Acad. of Dramatic Arts, London, Amsterdam Theatre School. *Career:* for a short period was opera singer at De Nederlandse Opera, Amsterdam; has acted extensively on stage, screen and tv; writer-in-residence, univs of Hull, Sheffield, Cambridge, Cen. London, New York. *Films:* as writer: Hoerenpreek 1996, De Wolkenfabriek 1996, Magonia 2000. *Publications:* novels: De zwarte met het witte hart (trans. as The Two Hearts of Kwasi Boachi) (Lucy B. en C.W. van der Hoogtprijs, ECI-prijs voor Schrijvers van Nu) 1997, De droom van de leeuw (trans. as The Lion Dreaming) 2002, Een schitterend gebrek (trans. as In Lucia's Eyes) (Libris Prize, De Inktaap) 2003, De klank van sneeuw 2006, De grote wereld (novella) 2006, De overgave (trans. as Someone Found) 2007; other: De vierde wand (travel) 1998, Dooi & Zeep (two stories, illustrated) 2004, Alle verhalen (short stories) 2005, De klank van sneeuw (two stories) 2006, De Grote Wereld 2006, The Two Hearts of Kwasi Boachi (opera libretto, music by Jonathan Dove)

2007, Alle verhalen 2008, Zoals dat gaat met wonderen (essays) 2008. *Honours:* Gorcumse Literatuurprijs 1990, LIRA-prijs 1995, Literaire prijs van de provincie Gelderland 1995, Halewijn-literatuurprijs van de stad Roermond 1998. *Address:* Stichting Schrijver School en Samenleving (SSS), Huddestraat 7, 1018 HB Amsterdam (office); c/o Uitgeverij De Arbeiderspers, Herengracht 370-72, 1016 CH Amsterdam, Netherlands (office). *Telephone:* (20) 6234923 (office); (20) 5247500 (office). *Fax:* (20) 4206319 (office). *E-mail:* info@sss.nl (office); info@arbeiderspers.nl (office). *Website:* www.sss.nl (office); www.arthurjapin.nl.

JARAMILLO AGUDELO, Darío; Colombian poet and author; b. 28 July 1947, Santa Rosa de Osos, Antioquia. *Education:* Universidad Javeriana, Bogotá. *Career:* mem. of several editorial bds including Golpe de Dados magazine, Simón y Lola Guberek Foundation. *Publications:* poetry: Historias 1974, Tratado de retórica (Premio Nacional de Poesia 1978) 1978, Poemas de amor 1986, Del ojo a la lengua 1995, Cantar por cantar 2001, Gatos 2005, Cuadernos de Música 2008; prose: La muerte de Alex 1983, Guía para viajeros, 1991, Cartas cruzadas 1993, El juego del alfiler 2002, Novela con fantasma 2004, Historia de una pasión 2006, La voz interior 2006, Memorias de un hombre feliz 2010, Historia de Simona (Premio de Novela Corta José Maria de Pereda 2010) 2010; essays: Poesia en la canción popular latinoamericana 2009. *Address:* c/o Editoria Pre-Textos, Luis Santángel 10, 1-C, 46005 Valencia, Spain (office). *Telephone:* (96) 3333226 (office). *Fax:* (96) 3955477 (office). *E-mail:* info@pre-textos.com (office). *Website:* www.pre-textos.com (office).

JARDINE, Lisa Anne, CBE, BA, MA, PhD, FRHistS, FRSA; British historian; *Centenary Professor of Renaissance Studies, Queen Mary, University of London;* b. 12 April 1944; m. 1st Nicholas Jardine 1969 (divorced 1979); one s. one d.; m. 2nd John Robert Hare 1982; one s. *Education:* Cheltenham Ladies' Coll., Newnham Coll., Cambridge, Univ. of Essex. *Career:* Resident Fellow, Warburg Inst., Univ. of London 1971-74; Lecturer in Renaissance Literature, Univ. of Essex 1974; Resident Fellow, Cornell Univ. 1974-75; Resident Fellow, Girton Coll., Cambridge 1974-75, Fellow, King's Coll. 1975-76, Jesus Coll. 1976-89, Lecturer in English Univ. of Cambridge 1976-89, Reader in Renaissance English 1989; Davis Center Fellow, Princeton Univ. 1987-88; Centenary Prof. of Renaissance Studies, Queen Mary, Univ. of London 1989-, Dir Centre for Editing Lives and Letters 2002-; mem. Arts and Humanities Research Council (AHRC—fmrly Arts and Humanities Research Bd) 2002- (Chair. working party on public understanding of the arts and humanities 2002, Chair. Museums and Collections Cttee 2004-); Trustee Victoria & Albert Museum 2003- (chair. collections cttee 2004-, mem. Bethnal Green Museum Cttee 2004-), United Westminster Schools Foundation; Chair. Bd of of Govs Westminster City School 1999-, Human Fertilisation and Embryology Authority 2008-. *Television and radio:* presenter Night Waves (BBC Radio 3) 1992-96, regular appearances on TV and radio programmes. *Publications:* Francis Bacon: Discovery and the Art of Discourse 1974, Still Harping on Daughters: Women and Drama in the Age of Shakespeare 1983, From Humanism to the Humanities (with Anthony Grafton) 1986, What's Left?: Women in Culture and the Labour Movement (with Julia Swindells) 1989, Erasmus: Man of Letters 1993, Reading Shakespeare Historically 1996, Wordly Goods: A New History of the Renaissance 1996, Erasmus: The Education of a Christian Prince (ed.) 1997, Hostage To Fortune: The Troubled Life of Francis Bacon (with Alan Stewart) 1998, Ingenious Pursuits: Building the Scientific Revolution 1999, Francis Bacon: The New Organon and Other Writings (ed. with M. Silverthorne) 1999, Global Interests: Renaissance Art Between East and West (with Jerry Brotton) 2000, On a Grander Scale: The Outstanding Career of Sir Christopher Wren 2002, Living History (series ed. with Amanda Foreman) 2002-, The Curious Life of Robert Hooke: The Man Who Measured London (biog.) 2003, London's Leonardo (ed. with J. Bennett, M. Cooper and M. Hunter) 2003, The Awful End of Prince William the Silent: The First Assassination of a Head of State with a Hand-Gun 2005, A Point of View 2008, Going Dutch: How England Plundered Holland's Glory 2008. *Honours:* Hon. Fellow, King's Coll., Cambridge 1995; Dr hc (Sheffield Hallam Univ.). *Address:* AHRC Centre for Editing Lives and Letters, Arts Research Centre, Queen Mary, Mile End Road, London, E1 4NS, England (office). *E-mail:* l.a.jardine@qmul.ac.uk (office). *Website:* www.livesandletters.ac.uk/people/lisajardine (office).

JARMAN, Douglas, BA, PhD; British lecturer and writer; b. 21 Nov. 1942, Dewsbury, Yorkshire, England; m. Angela Elizabeth Brown 1970; two d. *Education:* Hull Univ., Durham Univ., Liverpool Univ. *Career:* Lecturer in Music, Univ. of Leeds 1970-71; Lecturer, Royal Northern Coll. of Music, Manchester 1974-86, Principal Lecturer in Academic Studies 1986-2008, Prof. Emer. 2008-; Visiting Distinguished Scholar, Univ. of Manchester 2010; Artistic Dir, Young Musicians' Chamber Music Festival; Chair., Psappha; mem. advisory bd, Music Analysis. *Recording:* Talk, Lulu, The Historical Background (recording of The Complete Lulu). *Publications:* The Music of Alban Berg 1979, Kurt Weill 1982, Wozzeck 1989, The Berg Companion 1989, Alban Berg, Lulu 1991, Expressionism Reassessed 1993, Alban Berg: Violin Concerto (critical edn) 1998, Hans Werner Henze at the RNCM (vols 1-3) 1999, The Twentieth Century String Quartet 2002, Alban Berg: Chamber Concerto (critical edn) 2004; contrib. to Perspectives of New Music, Musical Quarterly, Musical Times, Music Review, Journal of Royal Musical Association, Newsletter of International Alban Berg Society, Alban Berg Studien vols 2 and 6. *Honours:* Hon. Fellow, Royal Northern Coll. of Music 1986; Hon. Prof. of Music, Univ. of Manchester 2002. *Address:* 1 Birch Villas, Birchcliffe Road, Hebden Bridge, HX7 8DA, England (home).

JARMAN, Mark Foster, BA, MFA; American academic and poet; *Professor of English, Vanderbilt University;* b. 5 June 1952, Mt Sterling, Ky; m. Amy Kane Jarman 1974; two d. *Education:* University of California, Santa Cruz, University of Iowa. *Career:* Teacher and Writing Fellow, University of Iowa 1974-76; Instructor, Indiana State University, Evansville 1976-78; Visiting Lecturer, University of California, Irvine 1979-80; Asst Prof., Murray State University 1980-83; Asst Prof., Vanderbilt University 1983-86, Assoc. Prof. 1986-92, Prof. of English 1992; mem. Associated Writing Programs, MLA, Poetry Society of America, Poets Prize Committee. *Publications:* Poetry: North Sea, 1978; The Rote Walker, 1981; Far and Away, 1985; The Black Riviera, 1990; Iris, 1992; Questions for Ecclesiastes, 1997; Unholy Sonnets, 2000; To the Green Man, 2004. Other: The Reaper Essays (with Robert McDowell), 1996; Rebel Angels: 25 Poets of the New Formalism (ed. with David Mason), 1996; The Secret of Poetry, 2001; Body and Soul: Essays on Poetry, 2002; contributions: journals, periodicals, and magazines. *Honours:* Joseph Henry Jackson Award, 1974; Acad. of American Poets Prize, 1975; National Endowment for the Arts Grants, 1977, 1983, 1992; Robert Frost Fellowship, Bread Loaf Writers' Conference, 1985; Guggenheim Fellowship, 1991-92; Lenore Marshall Poetry Prize, 1998. *E-mail:* mark.jarman@vanderbilt.edu (office).

JARMUSCH, Jim; American film director and screenwriter; b. 22 Jan. 1953, Akron, OH. *Education:* Medill School of Journalism, Northwestern Univ., Evanston, Ill., Colombia Coll., SC. *Career:* teaching asst to Nicholas Ray at New York Univ. Graduate Film School 1976-79; has worked on several films as sound recordist, cameraman and actor. *Films:* Permanent Vacation (writer, dir) 1980, You Are Not I (writer) 1981, The New World (dir) 1982, Stranger Than Paradise (writer, dir) (Camera d'Or Award, Cannes Film Festival 1984) 1983, Down By Law (writer, dir) 1986, Coffee and Cigarettes (short film, writer and dir) 1986, Mystery Train (writer, dir) 1989, Coffee and Cigarettes II (short film, writer and dir) 1989, Night on Earth (writer, dir) 1992, Coffee and Cigarettes III (short film, writer and dir) 1993, Dead Man (writer, dir) 1995, Year of the Horse (dir) 1997, Ghost Dog: The Way of the Samurai (writer, dir) 1999, Ten Minutes Older: The Trumpet (writer, dir) 2002, Coffee and Cigarettes (writer, dir) 2003, Broken Flowers 2005, The Limits of Control 2009. *Music videos directed include:* The Lady Don't Mind (Talking Heads) 1985, Sightsee MC! (Big Audio Dynamite) 1987, It's Alright With Me (Tom Waits) 1991, I Don't Wanna Grow Up (Tom Waits) 1992, Dead Man Theme (Neil Young) 1995, Big Time (Neil Young and Crazy Horse) 1996. *Literary Agent:* c/o Bart Walker, Creative Artists Agency LLC, 162 5th Avenue, 6th Floor, New York, NY 10010, USA. *Telephone:* (212) 277-9000.

JARRAR, Nada Awar; Lebanese/Australian novelist; b. Australia; m. Bassem; one d. *Career:* has lived in the USA, Australia, France and UK; returned to Lebanon 2001. *Publications:* novels: Somewhere, Home (Commonwealth Best First Book Award) 2004, Dreams of Water 2007, A Good Land 2009; contrib. to newspapers and anthologies. *Address:* c/o Harper Collins Publicity, 77-85 Fulham Palace Road, Hammersmith, London, W6 8JB, England (office). *Website:* www.harpercollins.co.uk (office).

JARVIS, Sharon, BFA; American literary agent, publisher, editor and writer; b. 1 Oct. 1943, New York, NY. *Education:* Hunter College, CUNY. *Career:* Copy Ed., Ace Books, 1969; Asst Managing Ed., Popular Library, 1971; Ed., Ballantine Books, 1972, Doubleday and Co, 1975; Senior Ed., Playboy Books, 1978; mem. International Fortean Organization; The Holistic Consortium; American Booksellers Asscn; Artists for Art. *Publications:* The Alien Trace (with K. Buckley), 1984; Time Twister, 1984; Inside Outer Space, 1985; True Tales of the Unknown, 1985; True Tales of the Unknown: The Uninvited, 1989; True Tales of the Unknown: Beyond Reality, 1991; Dead Zones, 1992; Dark Zones, 1992; Pitching Your Project, 1999; The Cosmic Countdown, 2003.

JASINSKA-JEDROSZ, Elzbieta Maria; Polish musicologist; b. 11 Jan. 1949, Katowice; d. of Edward Jasinka and Wanda Jasinka; m. Janusz Jedrosz 1970; one s. *Education:* Warsaw Univ. *Career:* engaged in bibliographic documentation of Polish musical works and in other tasks at Archive of Polish Composers, Polish Composers Archive, Warsaw Univ. Library Music Collection 1973-, currently Head of Polish Composers Archives; mem. Polish Composers' Union, Karol Szymanowski Music Asscn, Zakopane, Polish Librarians' Asscn, Asscn of Polish Musicians. *Publications:* Music and Polish Musicians in French 1925-1950 1977, Karol Szymanowski 1882-1937 1983, The Manuscripts of Karol Szymanowski's Musical Works (catalogue) 1983, Karol Szymanowski in the Polish Collections (guide-book, co-author) 1989, Karol Szymanowski: Writer-Poet-Thinker 1997, The Manuscripts of the Young Poland's Composers (catalogue) 1997, Collection of the 20th Century Polish Composers' Archives 1999, Four Seasons: Selected Poetry 2004; contrib. to Muzyka 1981, Ruch Muzyczny 1980, 1981, 1983, 1988-89, 1998-99, 2002-07, Pagine 1989, Przeglad Biblioteczny 1989, 2002, Polski Rocznik Muzykologiczny 2004. *Honours:* hons for popularization of Karol Szymanowski's compositions 1998. *Address:* Biblioteka Uniwersyteka w Warszawie, ul. Dobra 56/66, 00312 Warsaw (office). *Telephone:* (22) 5525746 (office). *Fax:* (22) 5525659 (office). *E-mail:* e.m.jasinska@uw.edu.pl (office). *Website:* www.buw.uw.edu.pl (office).

JASPER, David, MA, DD, PhD; British academic, ecclesiastic and writer; *Professor of Literature and Theology, University of Glasgow;* b. 1 Aug. 1951, Stockton on Tees, England; m. Alison Elizabeth Collins 1976; three d.

Education: Jesus Coll., Cambridge, St Stephen's House, Oxford, Keble Coll., Oxford, Hatfield Coll., Durham. *Career:* Dir Centre for the Study of Literature and Theology, Univ. of Durham 1986–91; Dir Centre for the Study of Literature and Theology, Univ. of Glasgow 1991–, Prof. of Literature and Theology 1998–; Ed. Literature and Theology; Gen. Ed. Macmillan series Studies in Religion and Culture; Ida Cornelia Beam Distinguished Visiting Prof., Univ. of Iowa 2002–03; Dana Fellow, Emory Univ., Atlanta, Ga 1991; Fellow and Dir Soc. for Arts, Religion and Culture 2000; mem. European Soc. for Literature and Religion (Sec.), American Acad. of Religion, MLA. *Publications:* Coleridge as Poet and Religious Thinker 1985, The New Testament and the Literary Imagination 1987, The Study of Literature and Religion 1989, Rhetoric Power and Community 1992, Reading in the Canon of Scripture 1995, The Sacred and Secular Canon in Romanticism 1999, The Sacred Desert 2004, A Short Introduction to Hermeneutics 2004. *Honours:* Hon. Fellow, Research Foundation, Univ. of Durham 1991. *Address:* Netherwood, 124 Old Manse Road, Wishaw, Lanarkshire, ML2 0EP, Scotland. *Telephone:* (141) 330-4405 (office); (1698) 373286 (home). *Fax:* (141) 330-4943 (office). *E-mail:* D.Joseph@arts.gla.ac.uk (office). *Website:* www.religions.divinity.gla.ac.uk (office).

JASSO, David; Spanish writer; *President, Asociación Española de Escritores de Terror*; b. 1961, Zaragoza; m.; one d. *Career:* teaches numerous workshops for children and others; Pres. Asociación Española de Escritores de Terror. *Publications:* La silla 2006, Cazador de Mentiras 2007, Día de perros (Premio IGNOTUS 2009) 2008, Feral—preferirias estar muerto 2010. *Address:* Sirius Team, 2 Antequera, 28041 Madrid, Spain. *Telephone:* (91) 7107349. *Fax:* (91) 4751305. *E-mail:* davidjassog@gmail.com; autores@equiposirius.com. *Website:* www.davidjasso.es; www.equiposirius.com.

JAY, Sir Antony Rupert, CVO, BA, MA, DBA, FRSA; British writer and producer; b. 20 April 1930, London, England; m. Rosemary Jill Watkins 1957, two s. two d. *Education:* St. Paul's School, Magdalene Coll., Cambridge. *Career:* staff mem., BBC 1955–64, Ed., Tonight 1962–63; Chair., Video Arts Ltd 1972–89; writer (with Jonathan Lynn), Yes, Minister and Yes, Prime Minister (BBC TV series) 1980–88. *Plays:* as co-author (with Jonathan Lynn): Yes, Prime Minister, Gielgud Theatre, London (What's On Stage Award for Best Comedy 2011) 2010–11. *Publications:* Management and Machiavelli 1967, To England With Love (with David Frost) 1967, Effective Presentation 1970, Corporation Man 1972, The Householder's Guide to Community Defence Against Bureaucratic Aggression 1972, Yes, Minister (with Jonathan Lynn, three vols) 1981–83, The Complete Yes, Minister (with Jonathan Lynn) 1984, Yes, Prime Minister (with Jonathan Lynn, two vols) 1986–87, The Complete Yes, Prime Minister (with Jonathan Lynn) 1989, Elizabeth R 1992, Oxford Dictionary of Political Quotations (ed.) 1996– (published as Lend Me Your Ears: The Oxford Dictionary of Political Quotations 2010), How to Beat Sir Humphrey 1997. *Honours:* Hon. MA (Sheffield Univ.) 1987, Hon. Dr of Business Admin. (Int. Management Centre, Buckingham) 1988; Companion, Inst. of Management 1992. *Address:* c/o Oxford University Press, Great Clarendon Street, Oxford, OX2 6DP, England (office).

JAY, Martin Evan, BA, PhD; American writer and academic; *Sidney Hellman Ehrman Professor, University of California, Berkeley*; b. 4 May 1944, New York, NY; s. of Edward Jay and Sari Jay; m. Catherine Gallagher 1974; two d. *Education:* Union Coll., Harvard Univ. *Career:* Asst Prof., Univ. of California, Berkeley 1971–76, Assoc. Prof. 1976–82, Prof. of History 1982–, Sidney Hellman Ehrman Prof. 1997–; mem. American Historical Assn, American Acad. of Arts and Sciences 1986. *Publications:* The Dialectical Imagination: A History of the Frankfurt School and the Institute of Social Research, 1923–1950 1973, Adorno 1984, Marxism and Totality 1984, Permanent Exiles 1985, Fin de Siècle Socialism 1989, Downcast Eyes 1993, Force Fields 1993, Cultural Semantics 1997–98, Refractions of Violence 2003, Songs of Experience 2004, The Virtues of Mendacity 2010, Essays from the Edge 2011; contrib. to Salmagundi. *Honours:* Herbert Baxter Adams Award, American Historical Assn 1973, Aby Warburg Stiftung Wissenschaftspreis, Hamburg 2003, Berlin Prize, American Acad., Berlin 2010. *Address:* 718 Contra Costa Avenue, Berkeley, CA 94707, USA (home). *Telephone:* (510) 642-7218 (office). *Fax:* (510) 643-5323 (office). *E-mail:* martjay@berkeley.edu (office).

JEAL, Tim, MA; British writer; b. 27 Jan. 1945, London, England; m. Joyce Timewell 1969; three d. *Education:* Christ Church, Oxford. *Career:* mem. Soc. of Authors. *Publications:* For Love of Money 1967, Somewhere Beyond Reproach 1969, Livingstone 1973, Cushing's Crusade (Llewelyn Rhys Memorial Prize (jtly) 1974) 1974, Until the Colours Fade 1976, A Marriage of Convenience 1979, Baden-Powell 1989, The Missionary's Wife 1997, Deep Water 2000, Swimming with my Father 2004, Stanley: The Impossible Life of Africa's Greatest Explorer (Nat. Book Critics' Circle Award for Best Biography, USA 2007) 2007. *Honours:* Writers' Guild Laurel Award. *Address:* c/o Faber and Faber Ltd, Bloomsbury House, 74–77 Great Russell Street London, WC1B 3DA, England (office). *Website:* www.faber.co.uk (office).

JEAMBAR, Denis; French journalist and publisher; *Chairman, Institut pratique de journalisme*. *Career:* mem. staff, Paris-Match 1970–73, Le Point 1973–95 (Ed. 1993–95); Ed. Radio station Europe 1 1995–96; Ed.-in-Chief weekly L'Express 1996–2006; CEO Editions du Seuil 2006–10; Chair. Institut pratique de journalisme 2007–. *Publications:* Sur la route de Flagstaff 1980, George Gershwin 1982, Le PC dans la maison 1984, Dieu s'amuse 1985, Eloge de la trahison (with Yves Roucaute) 1988, Le Poisson pourrit par la tête (with José Frèches) 1992, Le Self-service électoral (with Jean-Marc Lech) 1993, Le Jour ou la girafe s'est assise 1994, La Grande Lessive: anarchie et corruption (with Jean-Marc Lech) 1995, L'Inconnu de Goa 1996, Questions de France 1996, Un Secret d'état 1997, Les Dictateurs à penser et autres donneurs de leçons 2004, Accusé Chirac, levez vous! 2005, Le Défi du monde avec Claude Allègre 2006, Nos enfants nous haïront (with Jacqueline Rémy) 2006. *Address:* Institut pratique de journalisme, 24, rue Saint-Georges, 75009 Paris, France (office). *Website:* www.ipj.eu (office).

JEBREAL, Rula; Palestinian/Italian journalist, broadcaster and author; b. 24 April 1973, Haifa; one d. *Education:* Univ. of Bologna. *Career:* fmr newspaper journalist in Italy, Il Resto del Carlino, Il Giorno e La Nazione, Il Messaggero; TV journalist in Italy for 12 years, became first foreign anchorwoman to broadcast evening news bulletin 2000. *Television includes:* as presenter: Omnibus (talk show) 2004, as co-presenter: Anno Zero 2006; as writer/producer: Pernesso di Soggiorno (documentary on the death penalty) 2008; created own show for Al-Qahira Wai-Nas station, Cairo, Egypt 2009. *Film:* screenplay: Miral 2011. *Publications include:* fiction: Miral 2003, La Sposa di Assuan (The Bride of Aswan) (Winner, Int. Fenice Europa Prize 2007) 2007; non-fiction: Rejected (aka Divieto di Soggiorno) 2007. *Honours:* Media Watch Award (for TV coverage of Iraq War) 2004, Int. Ischia Award for Journalist of the Year 2005. *Literary Agent:* c/o Thomas Colchie, The Colchie Agency, 324 85th Street, Brooklyn, New York, NY 11209; c/o Office of Ari Emanuel, William Morris Endeavor LLC, Beverly Hills, CA 90210, USA. *Telephone:* (718) 921-7468 (New York); (310) 248-3064 (Beverly Hills). *E-mail:* colchieagency@gmail.com; AEmanuel_Sched@wmeentertainment.com. *Website:* www.wma.com; rulajebreal.net.

JEFFREYS, Diarmuid; British writer, journalist and television producer; m. *Career:* producer of current affairs and documentary programs for the BBC, Channel 4 and other television channels. *Publications:* The Bureau: Inside the Modern FBI 1995, Aspirin: The Remarkable Story of a Wonder Drug 2004, Hell's Cartel: I.G. Farben and the Making of Hitler's War Machine 2008. *Address:* c/o Bloomsbury Publishing Plc, 38 Soho Square, London, W1D 3HB, England (office). *Website:* www.bloomsbury.com (office).

JEFFRIES, Roderic Graeme, (Peter Alding, Jeffrey Ashford, Hastings Draper, Roderic Graeme, Graham Hastings); British writer and barrister; b. 21 Oct. 1926, London, England; s. of Bruce Graeme Jeffries and Lorna Hélène Jeffries; m. Rosemary Powys Woodhouse 1958; one s. one d. *Education:* Univ. of Southampton. *Career:* served at sea 1943–49; barrister-at-law, Gray's Inn 1953. *Publications:* Evidence of the Accused 1961, Exhibit No. Thirteen 1962, Police and Detection 1962, The Benefits of Death 1963, An Embarrassing Death 1964, Dead Against the Lawyers 1965, Police Dog 1965, Death in the Coverts 1966, A Deadly Marriage 1967, Police Car 1967, A Traitor's Crime 1968, River Patrol 1969, Dead Man's Bluff 1970, Police Patrol Boat 1971, Trapped 1972, Mistakenly in Mallorca 1974, Two Faced Death 1976, The Riddle in the Parchment 1976, The Boy Who Knew Too Much 1977, Troubled Deaths 1977, Murder Begets Murder 1978, Eighteen Desperate Hours 1979, The Missing Man 1980, Just Desserts 1980, Unseemly End 1981, Voyager into Danger 1981, Peril at Sea 1983, Deadly Petard 1983, Three and One Make Five 1984, Layers of Deceit 1985, Sunken Danger 1985, Meeting Trouble 1986, Almost Murder 1986, Relatively Dangerous 1987, The Man Who Couldn't Be 1987, Death Trick 1988, Dead Clever 1989, Too Clever by Half 1990, A Fatal Fleece 1991, Murder's Long Memory 1992, Murder Confounded 1993, Death Takes Time 1994, An Arcadian Death 1995, An Artistic Way to Go 1996, A Maze of Murders 1997, The Ambiguity of Murder 1999, An Enigmatic Disappearance 2000, Definitely Deceased 2001, Seeing is Deceiving 2002, An Intriguing Murder 2002, An Air of Murder 2003, A Sunny Disappearance 2005, Murder Delayed 2006, Murder Needs Imagination 2007, Sun, Sea and Murder 2008, A Question of Murder 2010, Murder, Majorcan Style 2011, Murdered by Nature 2012; as Peter Alding: The C.I.D. Room 1967, Circle of Danger 1968, Murder Among Thieves 1969, Guilt Without Proof 1971, Despite the Evidence 1971, Call Back to Crime 1972, Field of Fire 1973, The Murder Line 1974, Six Days to Death 1975, Murder Is Suspected 1978, Ransom Town 1979, A Man Condemned 1981, Betrayed by Death 1982, One Man's Justice 1983; as Jeffrey Ashford: Counsel for the Defence 1960, Investigations Are Proceeding 1961, The Burden of Proof 1962, Will Anyone Who Saw the Accident. . . 1963, Enquiries Are Continuing 1964, The Hands of Innocence 1965, Consider the Evidence 1966, Hit and Run 1966, Forget What You Saw 1967, Grand Prix Monaco 1968, Prisoner at the Bar 1969, Grand Prix Germany 1970, To Protect the Guilty 1970, Bent Copper 1971, Grand Prix United States 1971, A Man Will Be Kidnapped Tomorrow 1972, Grand Prix Britain 1973, The Double Run 1973, Dick Knox at Le Mans 1974, The Color of Violence 1974, Three Layers of Guilt 1975, Slow Down the World 1976, Hostage to Death 1977, The Anger of Fear 1978, A Recipe for Murder 1979, The Loss of the Culion 1981, Guilt with Honour 1982, A Sense of Loyalty 1983, Presumption of Guilt 1984, An Ideal Crime 1985, A Question of Principle 1986, A Crime Remembered 1987, The Honourable Detective 1988, A Conflict of Interests 1989, An Illegal Solution 1990, Deadly Reunion 1991, Twisted Justice 1992, Judgement Deferred 1993, The Bitter Bite 1994, The Price of Failure 1995, Loyal Disloyalty 1996, A Web of Circumstances 1997, The Cost of Innocence 1998, An Honest Betrayal 1999, Murder Will Out 2000, Looking-glass Justice 2001, A Truthful Injustice 2002, Fair Exchange is Robbery 2003, Evidentially Guilty 2004, Deadly Corruption 2005, Jigsaw Guilt 2009, Criminal Innocence 2010, Justice Deferred 2011; as Hastings Draper: Wiggery Pokery 1956, Wigged and Gowned 1958, Brief Help 1961; as Roderic Graeme: Brandy Ahoy! 1951, Concerning Blackshirt 1952, Where's Brandy?

1953, Blackshirt Wins the Trick 1953, Blackshirt Passes By 1953, Salute to Blackshirt 1954, Brandy Goes a Cruising 1954, The Amazing Mr Blackshirt 1955, Blackshirt Meets the Lady 1956, Paging Blackshirt 1957, Blackshirt Helps Himself 1958, Double for Blackshirt 1958, Blackshirt Sets the Pace 1959, Blackshirt Sees it Through 1960, Blackshirt Finds Trouble 1961, Blackshirt Takes the Trail 1962, Blackshirt on the Spot 1963, Call for Blackshirt 1963, Blackshirt Saves the Day 1964, Danger for Blackshirt 1965, Blackshirt at Large 1966, Blackshirt in Peril 1967, Blackshirt Stirs Things Up 1969, as Graham Hastings: Twice Checked 1959, Deadly Game 1961. *Address:* Apartado 5, Ca Na Paiaia, 07460 Pollensa, Spain (home). *Telephone:* (944) 530782. *E-mail:* paiaia@arrakis.es.

JELINEK, Elfriede; Austrian writer, dramatist and poet; b. 20 Oct. 1946, Mürzzuschlag, Styria; m. Gottfried Hüngsberg. *Education:* Vienna Conservatory, Albertsgymnasium, Vienna and Univ. of Vienna. *Career:* mem. Graz Writers' Asscn. *Screenplays:* Die Ausgesperrten (TV) 1982, Malina (from novel by Ingeborg Bachmann) 1991. *Plays include:* Raststätte, Wolken. Heim, Das Werk, Totenauberg: ein Stück, Ein Sportstück, Das Lebewohl, In den Alpen. *Radio:* numerous pieces for radio, including wenn die sonne sinkt ist für manche schon büroschluss (radio play) 1974. *Publications:* Lisas Schatten (poems) 1967, wir sind lockvögel baby! (novel) 1970, Michael: ein Jugendbuch für die Infantilgesellschaft (novel) 1972, Die Liebhaberinnen (novel, trans. as Women as Lovers) 1975, bukolit (novel) 1979, Die Ausgesperrten (novel, trans. as Wonderful, Wonderful Times) 1980, ende: gedichte von 1966–1968 1980, Die endlose Unschuldigkeit (essays) 1980, Was geschah, nachdem Nora ihren Mann verlassen hatte oder Stützen der Gesellschaft 1980, Die Klavierspielerin (novel, trans. as The Piano Teacher) 1983, Burgtheater 1984, Clara S 1984, Oh Wildnis, oh Schutz vor ihr (non-fiction) 1985, Krankeit oder moderne Frauen 1987, Lust (novel) 1989, Wolken. Heim 1990, Die Kinder der Toten (novel) 1995, Macht nichts: eine kleine Trilogie des Todes 1999, Gier: ein Unterhaltungsroman 2000, Der Tod und das Mädchen I–V: Prinzessinnendramen 2003, Greed (novel) 2006; translations of other writers' works, including Thomas Pynchon, Georges Feydeau, Eugène Labiche, Christopher Marlowe; film scripts and an opera libretto. *Honours:* The Young Austrian Culture Week Poetry and Prose Prize 1969, Austrian Univ. Students' Poetry Prize 1969, Austrian State Literature Stipendium 1972, City of Stadt Bad Gandersheim Roswitha Memorial Medal 1978, West German Interior Ministry Prize for Film Writing 1979, West German Ministry of Education and Art Appreciation Prize 1983, City of Cologne Heinrich Böll Prize 1986, Province of Styria Literature Prize 1987, City of Vienna Literature Appreciation Prize 1989, City of Aachen Walter Hasenclever Prize 1994, City of Bochum Peter Weiss Prize 1994, Rudolf Alexander Schroder Foundation Bremen Prize for Literature 1996, Georg Büchner Prize 1998, Berlin Theatre Prize 2002, City of Düsseldorf Heinrich Heine Prize 2002, Mülheim and der Ruhr Festival of Theatre Dramatist of the Year 2002, 2004, Else Lasker Schüler Prize, Mainz 2003, Lessing Critics' Prize, Wolfenbüttel 2004, Stig Dagerman Prize, Älvkarleby 2004, The Blind War Veterans' Radio Theatre Prize, Berlin 2004, Franz Kafka Prize 2004, Nobel Prize for Literature 2004. *Address:* Jupiterweg 40, 1140 Vienna, Austria. *Website:* www.elfriedejelinek.com.

JELLICOE, (Patricia) Ann, OBE; British playwright and director; b. 15 July 1927, Middlesborough, Yorkshire, England; m. 1st C. Knight-Clarke 1950 (divorced 1961); m. 2nd Roger Mayne 1962; one s. one d. *Education:* Polam Hall, Darlington, Queen Margaret's, York and Cen. School of Speech and Drama, London. *Career:* actress, stage man., and dir 1947–51; founder and Dir Cockpit Theatre Club 1952–54; teacher, Cen. School of Speech and Drama 1954–56; Literary Man. Royal Court Theatre 1973–75; founder and Dir Colway Theatre Trust 1979–85, Pres. 1986; Pres. Dorchester Community Plays Asscn 1997. *Plays:* The Sport of My Mad Mother 1958, The Knack 1961, Shelley, or The Idealist 1965, The Rising Generation 1967, The Giveaway 1969, You'll Never Guess! 1973, Clever Elsie, Smiling John, Silent Peter 1974, A Good Thing or a Bad Thing 1974, Flora and the Bandits 1976, The Reckoning 1978, The Bargain 1979, The Tide 1980, The Western Women 1984, Mark og Mønt 1988, Under the God 1989, Changing Places; translations: Rosmersholm 1960, The Lady From the Sea 1961, The Seagull (jtly) 1963, Der Freischütz 1964. *Publications:* non-fiction: Some Unconscious Influences in the Theatre 1967, Shell Guide to Devon (with Roger Mayne) 1975, Community Plays: How to Put Them On 1987. *Address:* Colway Manor, Lyme Regis, Dorset DT7 3HD, England (home).

JEN, Gish, MFA; American writer; b. (Lillian Constance Jen), 12 Aug. 1955, Long Island, NY; d. of Norman Jen and Agnes Jen; m. David O'Connor; two c. *Education:* Harvard Univ., Iowa Writers' Workshop. *Career:* Prof. of English, Brandeis Univ. 2008; Fellow, American Acad. of Arts and Sciences 2009–. *Publications:* novels: Typical American 1991, Mona in the Promised Land 1996, The Love Wife 2004, World and Town 2010; short stories: Who's Irish? 1999; contrib. to Best American Short Stories 1988, 1996, Best American Short Stories of the Century, Ploughshares, The New Yorker, Atlantic Monthly, The New Republic, Los Angeles Times, New York Times, The Paris Review, Granta, Daedalus. *Honours:* Dr hc (Emerson Coll.); Radcliffe Bunting Fellowship 1986, Nat. Endowment for the Arts Fellowship 1988, Guggenheim Fellowship 1992, Lannan Award for Fiction 1999, Radcliffe Inst. for Advanced Study Fellowship 2001, Fulbright Fellowship 2003, Strauss Living Award, American Acad. of Arts and Letters 2003, Massachusetts Book Award 2011. *Literary Agent:* c/o Melanie Jackson, Melanie Jackson Literary Agency, 41 West 72nd Street #3F, New York, NY 10023, USA. *E-mail:* gishjen@me.com (office). *Website:* www.gishjen.com.

JENCKS, Charles Alexander, BA, MA, PhD, FRSE; American architectural historian and designer; b. 1939, Baltimore, Md; m. Maggie Keswick (deceased); three s. one d. *Education:* Harvard Univ., Univ. of London, UK. *Career:* studied under Siegfried Giedon and Reyner Banham; with Architectural Asscn 1968–88; Lecturer, UCLA 1974–; has lectured at over forty univs including Univs of Peking, Shanghai, Paris, Tokyo, Milan, Venice, Frankfurt, Montréal, Oslo, Warsaw, Barcelona, Lisbon, Zurich, Vienna, Edinburgh, Columbia, Princeton, Yale and Harvard; producer of furniture designs for Sawaya & Moroni, Milan 1986–; currently Ed. Consultant Architectural Design and Ed. Academy Editions, London; contrib. to Sunday Times Magazine, Times Literary Supplement, The Observer, The Independent (all UK); mem. Selection Cttee Venice Biennale 1980; Juror for Phoenix City Hall 1985; Curator Wight Art Centre, LA and Berlin 1987; mem. RSA, London, Acad. Forum of Royal Acad., London. *Furniture designs include:* 'Architecture in Silver': Tea and Coffee Service, Alessi, Italy 1983, Symbolic Furniture exhbn, Aram Designs, London 1985; other furniture and drawings collected by museums in Japan and Victoria & Albert Museum, London. *Architectural works include:* Garagia Rotunda, Truro, MA 1976–77, The Elemental House (with Buzz Yudell), LA, The Thematic House (with Terry Farrell), London 1979–84, The Garden of Six Senses 1998, The Garden of Cosmic Speculation, Scotland 2001, Landform Veda, Scottish Gallery of Modern Art, Edinburgh 2002, Portello Park, Milan 2003. *Television includes:* two feature films written for BBC on Le Corbusier and Frank Lloyd Wright. *Publications include:* Meaning in Architecture (co-ed.) 1969, Architecture 2000: Predictions and Methods 1971, Adhocism (co-author) 1972, Modern Movements in Architecture 1973, Le Corbusier and the Tragic View of Architecture 1974, The Language of Post-Modern Architecture 1977, The Daydream Houses of Los Angeles 1978, Bizarre Architecture 1979, Late-Modern Architecture 1980, Signs, Symbols and Architecture (co-author) 1980, Skyscrapers-Skycities 1980, Architecture Today 1982, Kings of Infinite Space 1983, Towards a Symbolic Architecture 1985, What is Post-Modernism? 1987, Post-Modernism – The New Classicism in Art and Architecture 1987, The Prince, The Architects and New Wave Monarchy 1988, The New Moderns 1990, The Post-Modern Reader (ed.) 1992, The Architecture of the Jumping Universe 1995, Theories and Manifestos of Contemporary Architecture 1997, New Science – New Architecture? 1997, The Chinese Garden (with Maggie Keswick), Le Corbusier and the Architecture of Continual Revolution 2000, The New Paradigm in Architecture 2002, The Garden of Cosmic Speculation 2003. *Honours:* Fulbright Scholarship (Univ. of London) 1965–67, NARA Gold Medal for Architecture 1992. *Address:* c/o Royal Academy Forum, Royal Academy of Arts, Burlington House, Piccadilly, London, W1J 0BD, England (office). *Website:* www.charlesjencks.com.

JENKINS, Alan, FRSL, BA, MA; British poet, critic and editor; *Deputy Editor, The Times Literary Supplement*; b. 1955, Kingston, Surrey, England; s. of Donald F. Jenkins and Deirdre Yvonne Jenkins (née Herrick). *Education:* Univ. of Sussex. *Career:* Poetry and Fiction Ed., later Deputy Ed., TLS 1981–; poetry critic Observer, then Independent on Sunday 1985–90; taught creative writing, Bread Loaf, Princeton, Arvon Foundation, Poetry Soc., American Univ., Paris. *Publications:* In the Hot-House 1988, Greenheart 1990, Harm 1994, The Drift 2000, The Little Black Book 2003, A Shorter Life 2005, Drunken Boats 2007, The Lost World 2010, Blue Days 2010; ed.: Collected Poems of Ian Hamilton 2009; contrib. to Times Literary Supplement, London Review of Books, numerous newspapers and journals. *Honours:* Eric Gregory Award for Poetry 1981, Forward Prize for Best Collection 1994, Cholmondeley Award 2006. *Address:* The Times Literary Supplement, Times House, 3 Thomas More Square, London, E98 1BS, England (office). *Telephone:* (20) 7782-5000 (office). *Fax:* (20) 7782-4966 (office). *E-mail:* deputy@the-tls.co.uk (office).

JENKINS, Catherine Anne May, BA, MA; Canadian writer and poet; b. 18 Feb. 1962, Hamilton, Ont. *Education:* Trent Univ., Peterborough, Ont., Ryerson Univ., York Univ. *Career:* mem. The Writers' Union of Canada. *Publications:* Submerge (chapbook) 1997, Written in the Skin (anthology, contrib.) 1998, Blood, Love and Boomerangs (poems) 1999, Swimming in the Ocean (novel) 2002, In Our Own Words: A Generation Defining Itself (anthology, contrib.) 2005; contrib. to Descant, Pottersfield Portfolio, Lichen, Rampike, Queen Street Quarterly, Room of One's Own, Blood and Aphorisms, Carleton Arts Review, Quill and Quire, The Toronto Star, The Globe and Mail, Dream Catcher, Magma Poetry Magazine, Poetry Croydon, Books in Canada, Canadian Bookseller. *E-mail:* solidus@sympatico.ca (home). *Website:* www.catherinejenkins.com.

JENKINS, Sir Simon David, Kt, BA; British journalist and organization official; *Chairman, The National Trust*; b. 10 June 1943, Birmingham; s. of Daniel Jenkins; m. Gayle Hunnicutt 1978; one s. one step-s. *Education:* Mill Hill School, St John's Coll., Oxford. *Publications:* A City at Risk 1971, Landlords to London 1975, Newspapers: The Power and the Money 1979, The Companion Guide to Outer London 1981, Images of Hampstead 1982, The Battle for the Falklands 1983, With Respect, Ambassador 1985, The Market for Glory 1986, The Selling of Mary Davies and other writings 1993, Against the Grain 1994, Accountable to None: The Tory Nationalization of Britain 1995, England's Thousand Best Churches 1999, England's Thousand Best Houses 2003, Big Bang Localism 2004, Thatcher and Sons 2006, Wales: Churches, Houses, Castles 2008. *Honours:* Hon. DLitt (Univ. of London, City Univ.); Edgar Wallace Prize 1997, Rio Tinto David Watt Memorial Prize 1998; Journalist of the Year, Granada Awards 1988, Columnist of the Year 1993.

Address: The National Trust, 32 Queen Anne's Gate, London, SW1H 9AB, England (office). Telephone: (20) 7799-4521 (office). E-mail: simon.jenkins@nationaltrust.org.uk (office). Website: www.nationaltrust.org.uk (office).

JENKINS, Terence Andrew, BA, PhD, FRHistS; British historian, writer and editor; b. 30 May 1958, England. Education: Univ. of East Anglia, Norwich and Univ. of Cambridge. Career: British Acad. Postdoctoral Fellow, Univ. of Cambridge 1987–90; Lecturer, Univ. of East Anglia 1990–91, 1992–93, 1995–96, Univ. of Exeter 1991–92, Univ. of Bristol 1996–97; Sr Research Officer, History of Parliament, London 1998–. Publications: Gladstone, Whiggery and the Liberal Party, 1874–1886 (Univ. of Cambridge Prince Consort Prize for History) 1988, The Parliamentary Diaries of Sir John Trelawny (ed.), Vol. 1 1858–1865 1990, Vol. 2 1868–1873 1994, The Liberal Ascendency, 1830–1886 1994, Disraeli and Victorian Conservatism 1996, Parliament, Party and Politics in Victorian Britain 1996, Sir Robert Peel 1999, Britain: A Short History 2001; contrib. to periodicals, including Historical Journal, English Historical Review, History Today, Parliamentary History, BBC History magazine. Address: History of Parliament, 18 Bloomsbury Square, London, WC1A 2NS, England (office). E-mail: tjenkins@histparl.ac.uk (office). Website: www.histparl.ac.uk (office).

JENNI, Alexis; French author and biology teacher; Professor in Life Sciences, Lycée Saint-Marc, Lyon; b. 1963, Lyon. Career: currently Prof. in Life Sciences, Lycée Saint-Marc, Lyon. Publication: L'Art français de la guerre (The French Art of War) (Prix Goncourt 2011) 2011. Address: c/o Lycée Saint-Marc, 10 rue Sainte Hélène, 69287 Lyon, cedex 02 (office); c/o Éditions Gallimard, 5 rue Gaston-Gallimard, 75328 Paris cedex 07, France (office). Telephone: (4) 78-38-06-06 (office); (1) 49-54-42-00 (office). Fax: (4) 78-38-72-59 (office); (1) 45-44-94-03 (office). E-mail: webmaster@galliard.fr (office). Website: www.lyceesaintmarc.org (office); www.gallimard.fr (office); jalexis2.blogspot.co.uk (home).

JENS, Walter, (Walter Freiburger, Momos), DPhil; German critic, philologist and novelist; Honorary President, Akademie der Künste Berlin-Brandenburg; b. 8 March 1923, Hamburg; s. of Walter Jens and Anna Jens (née Martens); m. Inge Puttfarcken 1951; two s. Education: Hamburg and Freiburg im Breisgau Univs. Career: Asst, Univs of Hamburg and Tübingen 1945–49; Dozent, Univ. of Tübingen 1949–56, Prof. of Classical Philology and Rhetoric 1956–88, Prof. Emer. 1988–; Visiting Prof., Univ. of Stockholm 1964, Univ. of Vienna 1984; Dir Seminar für Allgemeine Rhetorik (Tübingen) 1967–; mem. Gruppe 47 1950, German PEN 1961– (Pres. 1976–82, Hon. Pres. 1982–), Berliner Akad. der Künste 1961–, Deutsche Akad. für Sprache und Dichtung 1962–, Deutsche Akad. der Darstellenden Künste (Frankfurt) 1964–, Freie Akad. der Künste (Hamburg) 1964; Pres. Akad. der Künste Berlin-Brandenburg 1989–97, Hon. Pres. 1997–. Publications include: Nein–Die Welt der Angeklagten (novel) 1950, Der Blinde (novel) 1951, Vergessene Gesichter (novel) 1952, Der Mann, der nicht alt werden wollte (novel) 1955, Die Stichomythie in der frühen griechischen Tragödie (diss.) 1955, Hofmannsthal und die Griechen 1955, Das Testament des Odysseus (novel) 1957, Statt einer Literaturgeschichte (Essays on Modern Literature) 1957, Die Götter sind sterblich (Diary of a Journey to Greece) 1959, Deutsche Literatur der Gegenwart 1961, Zueignungen 1962, Herr Meister (Dialogue on a Novel) 1963, Euripides-Büchner 1964, Von deutscher Rede 1969, Die Verschwörung (TV play) 1970, Am Anfang der Stall, am Ende der Galgen 1973, Der tödliche Schlag (TV play) 1974, Der Prozess Judas (novel) 1975, Der Ausbruch (libretto) 1975, Republikanische Reden 1976, Eine deutsche Universität, 500 Jahre Tübinger Gelehrtenrepublik 1977, Zur Antike 1979, Die Orestie des Aischylos 1979, Warum ich Christ bin (ed.) 1979, Ort der Handlung ist Deutschland (essays) 1979, Die kleine grosse Stadt Tübingen 1981, In letzter Stunde (ed.) 1982, Aufruf zum Frieden 1983, In Sachen Lessing 1983, Momos am Bildschirm 1984, Dichtung und Religion (with H. Küng) 1985, Roccos Erzählung 1985, Die Friedensfrau 1986, Theologie und Literatur 1986, Das A und das O–die Offenbarung der Johannes 1987, Feldzüge eines Republikaners 1988, Juden und Christen in Deutschland 1988, Reden 1989, Schreibschule 1991, Die sieben letzten Worte am Kreuz 1992, Die Friedensfrau 1992, Mythen der Dichter 1993, Am Anfang das Wort 1993, Menschenwürdig sterben 1995, Macht der Erinnerung 1997, Aus gegebenem Anlass 1998, Wer am besten red't ist der reinste Mensch 2000, Der Römerbrief 2000, 'Der Teufel lebt nicht mehr, mein Herr': Erdachte Monologe – imaginäre Gespräche 2001, Pathos und Präzision, Texte zur Theologie 2002, Frau Thomas Mann: Das Leben der Katharina Pringsheim (with I. Jens) 2003, Katias Mutter: Das ausserordentliche Leben der Hedwig Pringsheim (with I. Jens) 2005, Auf der Suche nach dem verlorenen Sohn. Die Südamerika-Reise der Hedwig Pringsheim (with I. Jens) 2006, Psalm 104 (to G. Klebe, Composition 104 Psalm) 2007. Honours: Hon. DPhil; Prix Amis de la Liberté 1951, Schleussner Schüller Prize 1956, Kulturpreis der deutschen Industrie 1959, Lessing Prize 1968, DAG Prize 1976, Tübinger Universitätsmedaille 1979, Heinrich-Heine Prize 1981, Adolf-Grimme 1984, Theodor-Heuss Prize (with I. Jens) 1988, Alternativer Büchnerpreis 1989, Hermann-Sinsheimer Prize 1989, Österreichischer Staatspreis für Kulturpublizistik 1990, Frankfurter Poetik-Vorlesungen 1992, Österreichisches Verdienstzeichen 1993, Bruno-Snell-Plakette, Univ. of Hamburg 1997, Ernst-Reuter-Plakette 1998, Deutscher Predigtpreis 2002, Corine Int. Buchpreis (with I. Jens) 2003. Address: Sonnenstrasse 5, 72076 Tübingen, Germany (home). Fax: (7071) 600693 (home). E-mail: danielseger@web.de.

JENSEN, Liz, BA, FRSL; British writer, critic and creative writing teacher; b. (Elisabeth Jensen), 26 Nov. 1959, Oxon., England; d. of Niels Rosenvinge Jensen and Valerie Corcos; Carsten Jensen; two s. Education: Univ. of Oxford. Career: fmr journalist in the Far East and France, BBC producer, sculptor. Publications: novels: Egg Dancing 1995, Ark Baby 1998, The Paper Eater 2000, War Crimes for the Home 2002, The Ninth Life of Louis Drax 2004, My Dirty Little Book of Stolen Time 2006, The Rapture 2009, The Uninvited 2012. Literary Agent: c/o Aitken Alexander Associates, 18–21 Cavaye Place, London, SW10 9PT, England. Telephone: (20) 7373-8672. E-mail: clare@aitkenalexander.co.uk. Website: www.aitkenalexander.co.uk. Address: c/o Bloomsbury Publishing, 38 Soho Square, London, W1D 3HB, England. Website: www.lizjensen.com.

JENSEN, Ruby Jean; American author; b. 1 March 1930; m. Vaughn Jensen, one d. Publications: The House That Samuel Built, 1974; The Seventh All Hallows Eve, 1974; Dark Angel, 1978; Hear the Children Cry, 1981; Such a Good Baby, 1982; Mama, 1983; Home Sweet Home, 1985; Annabelle, 1987; Chain Letter, 1987; House of Illusions, 1988; Jump Rope, 1988; Death Stone, 1989; Baby Dolly, 1991; Celia, 1991; The Reckoning, 1992; The Living Exile, 1993; The Haunting, 1994.

JERSILD, Per Christian; Swedish writer; b. 1935, Katrineholm; m. Ulla Flyxe 1960; two s. Education: Karolinska Institute. Career: Staff, Institute of Social Medicine, Stockholm, 1963–66; Stockholm Civil Service Welfare Dept; social psychiatrist, Huddinge hospital, 1974–78; Asst Prof. of Social and Preventive Medicine and medical adviser, National Govt Administration Board; writer, 1977–. Publications: Räknelära (short stories), 1960; Till Varmare Länder, 1961; Ledig Lördag, 1963; Calvinols Resa Genom Världen, 1965; Pyton (with Lars Ardelius), 1966; Prins Valiant Ock Konsum, 1966; Till Varmare Länder, 1967; Obs! Sammanträde Pågår, 1967; Sammanträde Pågor (TV play), 1967; Grisjakten, 1968; Fänrik Duva, 1969; Vi Ses I Song My, 1970; Drömpojken: En Paranoid Historia (Recovery in Schizophrenia), 1970; Uppror Bland Marsinen, 1972; Stumpen, 1973; Djurdoktorn (The Animal Doctor), 1973; Den Elektriska Kaninen, 1974; Barnens Ö (Children's Island), 1976; Moskvafeber, 1977; Babels Hus (House of Babel), 1978; Gycklarnas Hamlet. Och Monologerna Balans Och En Rolig Halvtimme, 1980; En Levande Själ (A Living Soul), 1980; Professionella Bekännelser, 1981; Efter Floden (After the Flood), 1982; Lit De Parade, 1983; Den Femtionde Frälsaren, 1984; Geniernas Återkomst, 1987; Svarta Villan, 1987; Ryktet Smittar: En Monolog An Aids, 1988; Ett Ensamt Öra, 1989; Fem Hjärtan In En Tändsticsask, 1989; Humpty-Dumpty's Fall, En Livsåskådsningsbok, 1990; Alice Och Nisse I Lustiga Huset, 1991; Holgerssons, 1991; Röda Hund, 1991; Hymir, 1993; En Gammal Kärlek, 1995; En Gammal Kylskåp Och Enförkyld Hund, 1995; Sena Sagor, 1998; Darwins Ofullbordade: Om Människans Biologiska Natur, 1999; Ljusets Drottning, 2000; Hundra Friståände Kolumner I Dagens Nyheter, 2002. Contributions: Dagens Nyheter; FIB/Kulturfront. Honours: Swedish Society for Promotion of Literature grand prize, 1981; De Nio prize, 1998. Address: c/o University of Nebraska Press, 233 N Eighth Street, Lincoln, NE 68588-0255, USA.

JESIH, Boris, PhD; Slovenian artist and poet; b. 8 Aug. 1943, Škofja Loka; s. of Svetoslav Jesih and Kristina Jesih; m. Bojana Žokalj 1970 (divorced 1981); one s. one d. Education: Acad. of Fine Arts, Ljubljana, Berlin. Career: works appear in numerous collections; has published several books of poetry; Ed.-in-Chief Razprave in Gradivo. Exhibitions include: 37th Biennale, Venice 1978, Premio le Arti 1971, 11–15th Biennale of Graphic Arts, Ljubljana 1975–83, 6–10th Biennale of Graphic Art, Cracow 1976–84, Premio Biella 1976, British Print Biennale, Bradford 1980, 1982, 1984, Die Kunst vom Stein, Vienna 1985. Publications include: The Apple Tree and the Grafts 1979. Honours: 10 nat. and 10 int. awards. Address: Department of Fine Arts Education, University of Ljubljana, Kardeljeva Ploscad 16, 1000 Ljubljana (office). Telephone: (1) 589-22-00 (office). Fax: (1) 589-22-33 (office). Website: www.pef.uni-lj.si (office).

JESSUP, Frances, BA (Hons); British novelist, poet, playwright and critic; b. 29 July 1936, d. of John Gray Jessup and Elsie Overy; m. Clive Turner 1960 (divorced 1996); one s. three d. Education: King's Coll., London. Career: organizer, Theatre Writing, Haslemere, UNA 1992, Healthy Planet Poems, Electric Theatre 2001, 2006; Programme Sec., Wey Poets 2000 (UNA SCR Wey Poets Cttee 2007–10), Signing the Charter, Haslemere UNA Br. Theatre; mem. UNA SC Exec., PEN, MEND 2004–. Television: Unusual Afternoon (BBC 2 30 Minute Theatre) 1972. Publications include: The Fifth Child's Conception 1970, Deutsch Penguin 1972, The Car: A Fable for Voices 1999, Three Short Plays, Fry/Eliot Era of British Verse Drama: A Dramatic Reassessment 2009; contribs to anthologies and magazines, including Hard Lines 3, Acumen, The Lantern, Weyfarers, Manifold, New Poems 6, Earth Love, Savoir Faire, Contemporary Review, Vol. 289. Honours: Moor Park Coll. First Prize for Fiction and Poetry 1972, UNA Trust Award for Peace Play Festival 1988, Univ. of Surrey Arts Cttee Literary Festival Award 1991, Nuffield Theatre Writing Bursary 1993, Arvon Foundation Award 1999, Skyros Poetry Award 2005. Address: 20 Heath Road, Haslemere, GU27 3QN, England (home). Telephone: (1428) 654319 (office). E-mail: francesjess@clara.co.uk (home).

JETER, K. W., BA, MA; American novelist; b. 1950, Los Angeles, CA; m. Geri Jeter. Education: San Francisco State University. Publications: Seeklight, 1975; The Dreamfields, 1976; Morlock Night, 1979; Soul Eater, 1983; Dr Adder, 1984; The Glass Hammer, 1985; Night Vision, 1985; Death Arms, 1987; Infernal Devices: A Mad Victorian Fantasy, 1987; Mantis, 1987; Dark Seeker, 1987; Farewell Horizontal, 1989; In the Land of the Dead, 1989; The Night

Man, 1990; Madlands, 1991; Wolf Flow, 1992; Dark Horizon: Alien Nation, 1993; Warped: Star Trek, Deep Space Nine, 1995; Blade Runner 2: The Edge of Human, 1995; Blade Runner: Replicant Night, 1996. *Literary Agent:* c/o Russ Galen, Scovil, Chichak, Galen Literary Agency, 381 Park Avenue South, Suite 1020, New York, NY 10016, USA. *Telephone:* (212) 679-8686. *Fax:* (212) 679-6710. *E-mail:* russellgalen@scglit.com. *Website:* www.kwjeter.com.

JHA, Radhika, MA; Indian writer; b. 1970, Delhi; m.; two c. *Education:* Amherst Coll. and Univ. of Chicago, USA. *Career:* worked for Hindustan Times and BusinessWorld, writing on culture, the environment and the economy; worked for Rajiv Gandhi Foundation, on Interact project for the educ. of children of victims of terrorism in India; currently lives in Tokyo. *Publications:* Smell (novel) (Prix Guerlain) 1999, The Elephant and the Maruti (short stories) 2003, Lanterns on Their Horns (novel) 2009. *Literary Agent:* The Susijn Agency Ltd, 3rd Floor, 64 Great Titchfield Street, London, W1W 7QH, England. *Telephone:* (20) 7580-6341. *Fax:* (20) 7580-8626. *E-mail:* info@thesusijnagency.com. *Website:* www.thesusijnagency.com.

JHA, Raj Kamal, BE MA; Indian writer and journalist; *Executive Editor, Indian Express, New Delhi*; b. 1 Jan. 1966, Kolkata; m. *Education:* St Joseph's Coll., Kolkata, Indian Inst. of Tech., Kharagpur, Univ. of Southern California, USA. *Career:* journalist, The Statesman, India Today; Deputy Ed., currently Exec. Ed., Indian Express, New Delhi; mem. Yaddo Residency, New York, 2005; Visiting Prof. of Journalism, Univ. of Calif., Berkeley. *Publications:* novels: The Blue Bedspread (Commonwealth Writers Prize for Best First Book, Eurasia region 2000) 1999, If You are Afraid of Heights 2003, Zwischen den Welten 2006, Die durchs Feuer gehen 2006, Wenn du dich fürchtest vor dem Fall 2006, Fireproof 2007. *Address:* c/o The Indian Express Group, 9–10 Bahadurshah Zafar Marg, Express Building, ITO, New Delhi 110 002, India (office). *E-mail:* editor@expressindia.com (office). *Website:* www.expressindia.com (office).

JHABVALA, Ruth Prawer, CBE, MA; British/American author and screenwriter; b. 7 May 1927, Cologne, Germany; d. of Marcus Prawer and Eleonora Cohn; sister of Siegbert Salomon Prawer (q.v.); m. C. S. H. Jhabvala 1951; three d. *Education:* Hendon Co. School and London Univ. *Career:* born in Germany of Polish parentage; refugee to England 1939; lived in India 1951–75, in USA 1975–; Neill Gunn Int. Fellowship 1979. *Film screenplays:* Shakespeare-Wallah 1965, The Guru 1969, Bombay Talkie 1970, Autobiography of a Princess 1975, Roseland 1977, Hullabaloo over Georgie and Bonnie's Pictures (TV) 1978, The Europeans 1979, Jane Austen in Manhattan 1980, Quartet 1981, The Courtesans of Bombay (TV) 1983, The Bostonians 1984, A Room with a View 1986, Madame Sousatzka 1988, Mr & Mrs Bridge 1989, Howards End 1992, The Remains of the Day 1993, Jefferson in Paris 1995, Surviving Picasso 1996, A Soldier's Daughter Never Cries 1998, The Golden Bowl 2000, Le Divorce 2003, The City of Your Final Destination 2010. *Publications:* novels: To Whom She Will 1955, Nature of Passion 1956, Esmond in India 1958, The Householder (also screenplay) 1960, Get Ready for Battle 1962, A Backward Place 1962, A New Dominion 1971, Heat and Dust (also screenplay) 1975, In Search of Love and Beauty 1983, Three Continents 1987, Poet and Dancer 1993, Shards of Memory 1995, My Nine Lives 2004; short story collections: A Stronger Climate 1968, An Experience of India 1970, How I Became a Holy Mother 1976, Out of India: Selected Stories 1986, East into Upper East 1998, My Nine Lives 2004, A Lovesong for India 2011. *Honours:* Booker Award for best novel 1975, MacArthur Foundation Award 1984, Acad. Award for Best Screenplay 1986, 1992. *Address:* 400 East 52nd Street, New York, NY 10022, USA (home).

JIANG, Rong; Chinese novelist; b. (Lu Jiamin), 1946, Beijing; m. Zhang Kangkang. *Career:* lived with nomadic communities on the Inner Mongolian steppe 1967–78; returned to Beijing; founding mem., Beijing Spring reform movement 1978; Prof. of Political Economy, Beijing Univ. *Publication:* Lang Tuteng (novel, trans. as The Wolf Totem; Man Asian Literary Prize 2007) 2004. *Address:* Penguin Chinese Division, c/o Penguin Group Australia, PO Box 701, Hawthorn, Australia.

JIANG, Zilong; Chinese writer; *Vice-Chairman, Chinese Writers' Association*; b. 2 June 1941, Cang Xian, Hebei; s. of Jiang Junsan and Wei Huanzhang; m. Zhang Qinglian 1968; one s. one d. *Career:* worker Tianjin Heavy Machinery Plant 1958; navy conscript 1960–65; Vice-Chair. Chinese Writers' Asscn 1996–. *Publications:* A New Station Master 1965, One Day for the Chief of the Bureau of Electromechanics 1976, Manager Qiao Assumes Office 1979, Developer 1980, Diary of a Plant Secretary 1980, All the Colours of the Rainbow 1983, Yan-Zhao Dirge 1985, Serpent Deity 1986, Jiang Zilong Works Collection (eight vols) 1996, Human Vigour 2000, Ren Qi 2000, Empty Hole 2001. *Honours:* Nat. Short Story Prize 1979. *Address:* No. 7 Dali Road, Heping District, Tianjin (home); Tianjin Writers' Association, Tianjin, People's Republic of China. *Telephone:* (22) 23304153 (office); (22) 23306250 (home). *Fax:* (22) 23304159 (office); (22) 23306250 (home). *E-mail:* jzltj@hotmail.com (home).

JIANG AN DAO (see Parkin, Andrew Terence Leonard)

JILES, Paulette, BA; Canadian/American poet and writer; b. 1943, Salem, Mo. *Education:* University of Missouri. *Career:* teacher, David Thompson University, Nelson, BC 1984–85; Writer-in-Residence, Phillips Acad., Andover, Massachusetts 1987–; mem. Writers' Union of Canada. *Publications:* poetry: Waterloo Express 1973, Celestial Navigation 1983, The Jesse James Poems 1987, Flying Lessons: Selected Poems 1995; prose: Sitting in the Club Car Drinking Rum & Karma-Kola 1986, The Late Great Human Roadshow 1986, Blackwater 1988, Song to the Rising Sun 1989, Cousins 1991, North Spirit 1995, Enemy Women (Rogers Writers' Trust Award) 2001, Stormy Weather (Canadian Authors' Asscn Award for Fiction 2008) 2007, The Color of Lightning 2009. *Honours:* Governor-General's Award 1984, Gerald Lampert Award 1984, Pat Lowther Award 1984, ACTRA Award for Best Original Drama 1989. *Address:* c/o Author Mail, 7th Floor, HarperCollins Publishers, 10 East 53rd Street, New York, NY 10022, USA (office).

JIMÉNEZ LOZANO, José; Spanish writer, poet and journalist; b. 13 May 1930, Langa, Ávila. *Education:* Universidad de Valencia, Universidad de Valladolid. *Career:* Ed., El Norte de Castilla (newspaper) 1962–78, Deputy Ed. 1978–92, Ed.-in-Chief 1992–95. *Publications:* Historia de un otoño 1971, El sambenito 1972, La salamandra 1973, El santo de Mayo 1976, Duelo en la Casa Grande 1982, El grano d maíz rojo 1988, Sara de Ur 1989, Estampas y memorias 1990, El Medujarillo 1992, Los Grandes relatos 1992, La boda de Ángela 1993, Cogedor de acianos 1993, Relación topográfica 1993, Objetos Perdidos 1993, Teorema de Pitágoras 1995, La luz de una candela 1996, Las sandalias de plata 1996, Un dedo en los labios 1996, Los compañeros 1997, El faro 1997, El balneario 1998, Ronda de noche 1998, Las señoras 1999, Maestro Huidobro 1999, Un Hombre en la Raya 2000, Le lobeznos 2001, El viaje de Jonás 2002, Yo vi una vez a Ícaro 2002, Los cuadernos de letra pequeña 2003, Cartas e Tesa 2004, Antología de cuentos 2004, Las gallinas del licenciado 2005, El ajuar de mamá 2006, La piel de los tomates 2007, Libro de visitantes 2007; poetry: Oficio Parvo 1979, Tantas devastaciones 1992, Un fulgor tan breve 1995, El tiempo de Eurídice 1996, Pájaros 2000, Elegías menores 2002, Elogios y celebraciones 2005, Libro de visitantes 2007, El azul sobrante 2009. *Honours:* Medalla del Oro al Mérito en las Bellas Artes 1998; Premio Nacional de las Letras Españolas 1992, Premio Miguel de Cervantes 2002. *Address:* c/o Ediciones Encuentro, Ramírez de Arellano 17, 10°, 28043 Madrid, Spain (office). *E-mail:* encuentro@ediciones-encuentro.es (office). *Website:* www.ediciones-encuentro.es (office).

JIN, Ha, BA, MA, PhD; American/Chinese writer, poet and academic; *Professor, Department of English, Boston University*; b. (Jin Xuefei), 21 Feb. 1956, Jinzhou, China; m. Lisah Bian 1982; one c. *Education:* Heilongjian Univ., Harbin, Shangdong Univ., Jinan, Brandeis Univ. *Career:* faculty mem. Dept of English, Emory Univ. 1993–2002, Boston Univ. 2002–; wrote libretto for opera (with Tan Dun), The First Emperor (Metropolitan Opera, New York) 2006; Fellow, American Acad. of Arts and Sciences 2006. *Publications:* fiction: Ocean of Words: Army Stories 1996, Under the Red Flag 1997, In the Pond 1998, Waiting 1999, The Bridegroom (short stories) 2000, The Crazed 2002, War Trash (novel) 2004, A Free Life 2007, A Good Fall (short stories) 2009; poetry: Between Silences 1990, Facing Shadows 1996, Wreckage 2001; essays: The Writer as Migrant 2008. *Honours:* PEN/Hemingway Award 1997, Flannery O'Connor Award 1997, Nat. Book Award 1999, PEN/Faulkner Award 2000, 2005, Asian American Literary Award 2001, Townsend Prize for Fiction 2002. *Address:* c/o Department of English, College of Arts and Sciences, Boston University, 236 Bay State Road, Boston, MA 02215, USA (office). *Telephone:* (617) 353-2506 (office). *Fax:* (617) 353-3653 (office). *E-mail:* xjin@bu.edu (office). *Website:* www.bu.edu/english (office).

JIN, Yong; Chinese writer, journalist and newspaper publisher; b. (Louis Cha Liang Yong), 6 Feb. 1924, Haining, Zhejiang Prov.; m. three times. *Education:* Dongwu Law School. *Career:* writer, Ta Kung Pao newspaper, Shanghai, later Hong Kong; later became film reviewer and screenwriter; first martial arts novel serialised in Xin Wan Bao newspaper, Hong Kong 1955; f. newspaper Ming Bao Daily, Hong Kong; ceased writing novels in 1972. *Publications:* (titles translated) Legend of the Book and the Sword 1955, The Sword Stained With Royal Blood (Vol. I Crimson Sabre Saga) 1956, Flying Fox of the Snowy Mountain 1959, The Young Flying Fox, Legend of the Condor Heroes (Vol. I Condor trilogy) 1957, Return of the Condor Heroes (Vol. II Condor trilogy) 1959, Heavenly Sword Dragon Sabre (Vol. III Condor trilogy) 1961, Demi Gods Semi Devils 1963, Way of the Heroes, Requiem of Ling Sing, The Proud Smiling Wanderer 1967, The Duke of Mount Deer (Vol. II Crimson Sabre Saga), The Deer and the Cauldron 1969, Sword of the Yue Maiden 1970. *Honours:* several hon. degrees; Chevalier de la Légion d'Honneur 1992, Commdr de l'Ordre des Arts et des Lettres 2004. *Address:* c/o The Chinese University Press, The Chinese University of Hong Kong, Sha Tin, N.T., Hong Kong Special Administrative Region, People's Republic of China (office). *Website:* www.chineseupress.com (office).

JIRGL, Reinhard; German author; b. 16 Jan. 1953, Berlin. *Education:* Humboldt Univ., Adlershofer Acad. *Career:* lighting technician, Volksbühne, E Berlin 1978–89, Berlin 1989–95; banned from publishing manuscripts in GDR –1989; began publishing works 1990–. *Publications include:* Mutter Vater Roman 1990, Uberich 1990, Im offenen Meer 1991, Zeichenwende (co-author) 1993, Das obszöne Gebet 1993, Abschied von den Feinden 1995, Hundsnächte 1997, Die atlantische Mauer 2000, Genealogie des Tötens 2002, Die Unvollendeten 2003, Gewitterlicht 2003, Abtrünnig (Literaturpreis der Stadt Bremen 2006) 2005, Land und Beute 2008, Die Stille (Grimmelshausen-Preis 2009) 2009. *Honours:* Alfred-Döblin-Preis 1993, Literaturpreis der Stadt Marburg 1994, Joseph-Breitbach-Preis 1999, Kranichsteiner Literaturpreis 2003, Rheingau Literaturpreis 2003, Dedalus Preis 2004, Literaturpreis der Stadt Bremen 2006, Lion-Feuchtwanger-Preis 2009, Georg Büchner Prize 2010, Sudetendeutscher Kulturpreis 2011. *Address:* c/o Carl Hanser Verlag GmbH & Co., KG, Kolbergerstrasse 22, 81679 Munich, Germany (office).

Telephone: (89) 99830-0 (office). *Fax:* (89) 984809 (office). *E-mail:* info@hanser.de (office). *Website:* www.hanser-literaturverlage.de (office).

JOFFE, Josef, PhD; German journalist, editor and international relations scholar; *Publisher-Editor, Die Zeit;* b. 15 March 1944, Łódź, Poland; m. Dr Christine Joffe; two d. *Education:* Swarthmore Coll., Johns Hopkins Univ., Harvard Univ., USA. *Career:* Foreign and Editorial Page Dir Suddeutsche Zeitung 1985–2000; Publr-Ed. Die Zeit newspaper 2000–; Professorial Lecturer, Johns Hopkins Univ. 1982–84; Adjunct Prof. of Political Science, Stanford Univ. 2004–, Fellow, Inst. for Int. Studies, Stanford 2004, now Sr Fellow; Fellow, Hoover Inst.; Visiting Prof. of Govt, Harvard Univ. 1999–2000, Assoc., Olin Inst. for Strategic Studies; Visiting Lecturer, Princeton Univ., Dartmouth Univ.; Founding Bd mem. The National Interest 1995–2005, The American Interest; mem. Editorial Bd International Security, Prospect. *Publications include:* The Limited Partnership: Europe, the United States and the Burdens of Alliance 1987, The Great Powers 1998, Überpower: The Imperial Temptation of America 2006; numerous articles in scholarly journals and chapters in books. *Honours:* Order of Merit 1998; hon. degree (Swarthmore Coll.) 2002, (Lewis and Clark Coll.) 2005; Theodor-Wolff-Prize in Journalism (Germany), Ludwig Börne Prize in Essays/Literature (Germany). *Address:* Die Zeit, Speersort 1, 20095 Hamburg, Germany (office). *Telephone:* (40) 328-00 (office). *Fax:* (40) 3280-596 (office). *E-mail:* dagmar.gentsch@zeit.de (office). *Website:* www.zeit.de (office).

JOHANSEN, Hanna; Swiss (b. German) writer; b. (Hanna Margarete Meyer), 17 June 1939, Bremen, Germany; m. Adolf Muschg 1967–90; two s. *Education:* Univs of Marburg and Göttingen and Ithaca Univ., NY, USA. *Career:* writer of novels and children's stories 1978–. *Publications include:* novels: Die Stehende Uhr 1978, Trocadero 1980, Die Analphabetin 1982, Zurück nach Orambi 1986, Ein Mann vor der Tür 1988, Kurnovelle 1994, Ein Maulwurf kommt immer allein 1994, Universalgeschichte der Monogamie 1997, Halbe Tage, ganze Jahre 1998, Sei doch mal still! 2001, Lena 2002, Icn bin hier bloss die Katze 2007, Der schwarze Chirm 2007; short stories: Über den Wunsch, sich Wohlzufühlen 1985, Die Schöne am Unteren Bildrand 1990, Dinosaurier gibt es nicht 1992, Über den Himmel 1993, Die Hühneroper (jtly) 2004; five children's books 1983–89, Henrietta and the Golden Eggs 2002, Omps! – ein Dinosaurier zu viel 2003; other: Der Füsch, München (with Rotraut Susanne Berner) 1995, Die Hexe zieht den Schlafsack enger (with Käthi Bhend) 1995, Bist du schon wach? (with Rotraut Susanne Berner) 1998, Vom Hühnchen, das goldene Eier legen wollte (with Käthi Bhend) 1998, Maus, die Maus, liest ein langes Buch (with Klaus Zumbühl) 2000, Maus, die Maus, liest und liest (with Klaus Zumbühl) 2000. *Honours:* Ehrengabe des Kantons Zürich 1980, Marie-Louise Kaschnitz Prize 1986, Conrad Ferdinand Meyer Prize 1987, Swiss Youth Book Prize 1990, Schiller Prize 1991, 2002, Children's Book Prize Nordrhein-Westphalia 1991, Austrian Children's and Youth's Book Prize 1993, Literature Prize, Kärnten beim Ingeborg-Bachmann-Wettbewerb, Klagenfurt 1993, Phantastik Prize, Wetzlar 1993, Solothurner Literature Prize 2003. *Address:* Vorbühlstrasse 7, 8802 Kilchberg, Switzerland (home). *Telephone:* 447153029 (home).

JOHANSSON-BACKE, Karl Erik, BEd; Swedish teacher (retd), writer, dramatist and poet; b. 24 Nov. 1914, Stockholm; m. Kerstin Gunhild Bergquist 1943, one s. three d. *Career:* mem. Swedish Authors' Federation. *Publications:* fiction: A Pole in the River 1950, Daybreak 1954, The Mountain of Temptation 1983, The Tree and the Bread 1987, King of the Mountains 1993; poetry: Lust and Flame 1981. *Honours:* many literary awards 1961–93; hon. mem. Swedish Playwrights' Federation.

JOHN, Katherine (see Watkins, Karen Christna)

JOHNSON, (Alexander) Boris (de Pfeffel); British politician and journalist; *Mayor of London;* b. 19 June 1964, New York City, NY, USA; s. of Stanley Patrick Johnson and Charlotte Fawcett; m. 1st Allegra Mostyn-Owen; m. 2nd Marina Wheeler 1993; two s. two d. *Education:* Eton Coll. and Balliol Coll., Oxford. *Career:* journalist with The Times 1987–88; EC Corresp., The Daily Telegraph 1989–94, Asst Ed. and Chief Political Columnist 1994–99, currently columnist; Ed. The Spectator 1999–2005; MP (Conservative) for Henley 2001–08; Vice-Chair. Conservative Party 2003–04; Shadow Minister for the Arts 2004; Shadow Minister for Higher Educ. 2005–07; Mayor of London 2008–. *Television includes:* Have I Got News for You 1998, 2004, 2006, The Dream of Rome 2006, Who Do You Think You Are? 2008, After Rome 2008. *Publications:* Friends, Voters, Countrymen 2001, Seventy-Two Virgins (novel) 2004, The Dream of Rome 2006, The British 2007, Life in the Fast Lane: The Johnson Guide to Cars 2007, Johnson's Life of London 2011. *Honours:* What the Papers Say Award for Columnist of the Year 2006. *Address:* The Mayor's Office, Greater London Authority, City Hall, The Queen's Walk, London, SE1 2AA, England (office). *Telephone:* (20) 7983-4100 (office). *Fax:* (20) 7983-4057 (office). *E-mail:* mayor@london.gov.uk (office). *Website:* www.london.gov.uk (office); www.boris-johnson.com (office).

JOHNSON, Alison Findlay, BPhil, MA; British author; b. 19 Nov. 1947, Stafford, England; m. Andrew J. D. Johnson 1973, one d. *Education:* Aberdeen University, University of Oxford. *Publications:* A House by the Shore, 1986; Scarista Style, 1987; Children of Disobedience, 1989; Islands in the Sound, 1989; The Wicked Generation, 1992. Contributions: West Highland Press; The Times.

JOHNSON, Charles Richard, BS, MA, PhD; American author and academic; *Professor Emeritus, Department of English, University of Washington, Seattle;* b. 23 April 1948, Evanston, Ill.; m. Joan New 1970; one s. one d. *Education:* Southern Illinois Univ., State Univ. of NY, Stoneybrook. *Career:* fmr cartoonist and filmmaker; Lecturer, Univ. of Washington, Seattle 1975–79, Assoc. Prof. of English 1979–82, Prof. 1982, then Pollock Endowed Prof. of English, now Prof. Emer.; Co.-Dir Twin Tigers (martial arts studio). *Publications include:* novels: Faith and the Good Thing 1974, Oxherding Tale 1982, Middle Passage (Nat. Book Award 1990) 1990; The Sorcerer's Apprentice (short stories); Being and Race: Black Writing Since 1970 1988, The Middle Passage 1990, All This and Moonlight 1990, In Search of a Voice (with Ron Chernow) 1991; Black Humor, Half-Past Nation Time (drawings); Booker, Charlie Smith and the Fritter Tree (broadcast plays); numerous reviews, essays and short stories. *Address:* University of Washington, Department of English, PDL A-406, Seattle, WA 98105, USA (office). *E-mail:* chasjohn@u.washington.edu. *Website:* depts.washington.edu/engl (office).

JOHNSON, Colin; Australian novelist; b. 23 July 1939, Beverley, WA. *Career:* Lecturer, University of Queensland, St Lucia. *Publications:* Wild Cat Falling, 1965; Long Live Sandawara, 1979; Before the Invasion: Aboriginal Life to 1788, 1980; Doctor Wooreddy's Prescription for Enduring the End of the World, 1983; Doin' Wildcat, 1988; Dalwurra: The Black Bittern, 1988; Writing from the Fringe, 1990. *Honours:* Wieckhard Prize, 1979; Western Australia Literary Award, 1989.

JOHNSON, Denis; American writer and poet; b. 1949, Munich, Germany. *Publications:* poetry: The Man Among the Seals 1969, Inner Weather 1976, The Incognito Lounge and Other Poems 1982, The Veil 1987, The Throne of the Third Heaven of the Nations Millennium General Assembly: Poems Collected and New 1995; other: Angels 1983, Fiskadoro 1985, The Stars at Noon 1986, Resuscitation of a Hanged Man 1991, Jesus' Son 1993, Already Dead: A Californian Gothic 1997, The Name of the World 2000, Seek: Reports from the Edges of America & Beyond 2001, Train Dreams (novella, Aga Khan Prize for Fiction) 2002, Tree of Smoke (Nat. Book Award for Fiction) 2007, Nobody Move 2009. *Honours:* Whiting Writers' Award 1986, American Acad. of Arts and Letters Literature Award 1993, several grants. *Address:* Farrar, Straus & Giroux, 19 Union Square West, New York, NY 10003, USA (office). *Telephone:* (212) 741-6900 (office). *Website:* www.fsgbooks.com (office).

JOHNSON, Diane Lain, AA, BA, MA, PhD; American novelist and essayist; b. (Diane Lain), 28 April 1934, Moline, Ill.; m. 1st B. Lamar Johnson Jr 1953; four c.; m. 2nd John Frederick Murray 1969. *Education:* Stephens Coll., Univ. of Utah, Univ. of California at Los Angeles. *Career:* Asst Prof. to Prof. of English, Univ. of California, Davis 1968–87; mem. International PEN, Writers' Guild of America, American Acad. of Arts and Sciences, American Acad. of Arts and Letters. *Plays:* An Apple, An Orange. *Film screenplay:* The Shining (co-author) 1979. *Publications:* Fair Game 1965, Loving Hands at Home 1968, Burning 1971, Lesser Lives: The True History of the First Mrs Meredith 1972, The Shadow Knows 1975, Lying Low 1978, Terrorists and Novelists 1982, Dashiell Hammett: A Life 1983, Persian Nights 1987, Health and Happiness 1990, Natural Opium: Some Travelers' Tales 1993, Le Divorce (California Book Awards Gold Medal for Fiction) 1997, Le Mariage 2000, L'Affaire 2003, Lulu in Marrakesh 2008; contrib. to newspapers, periodicals and magazines, including New York Times, New York Review of Books, Vogue, Food and Wine. *Honours:* Guggenheim Fellowship 1977–78, Rosenthal Award 1979, Harold and Mildred Strauss Living Stipend 1988–92, American Acad. of Arts and Letters, Los Angeles Times Medal 1994. *Literary Agent:* c/o Lynn Nesbit, Janklow and Nesbit Associates, 445 Park Avenue, No. 13, New York, NY 10022, USA. *Telephone:* (212) 421-1700. *Website:* www.janklowandnesbit.co.uk (home). *Address:* 1000 Green Street, San Francisco, CA 94133, USA (home); 8 rue Bonaparte, 75006 Paris, France (home). *E-mail:* DJohn54134@aol.com (home).

JOHNSON, Elizabeth Ann, BA, MA, PhD; American theologian and writer; *Distinguished Professor of Theology, Fordham University;* b. 6 Dec. 1941, New York, NY. *Education:* Brentwood Coll., Manhattan Coll., Catholic Univ. of America. *Career:* Prof. of Theology, Catholic Univ. of America 1981–91; Distinguished Prof. of Theology, Fordham Univ. 1991–; mem. Catholic Theological Soc. of America (Pres. 1996–97), American Acad. of Religion, Coll. Theology Soc., American Theological Soc. (Pes. 2006–07). *Publications:* Consider Jesus: Waves of Renewal in Christology 1990, She Who Is: The Mystery of God in Feminist Theological Discourse 1992, Women, Earth, and Creator Spirit 1993, Friends of God and Prophets: A Feminist Theological Reading of the Communion of Saints 1998, The Church Women Want 2002, Truly Our Sister: A Theology of Mary in the Communion of Saints 2003, Dangerous Memories: A Mosaic of Mary in Scripture 2004, Quest for the Living God 2007; contrib. to scholarly books and journals. *Honours:* Dr hc (St Mary's Coll.) 1994, (Maryknoll School of Theology) 1995, (Chicago Theological Union) 1996, (Siena Coll.) 1998, (LeMoyne Coll.) 1999, (St Joseph Coll., NY) 2001, (Manhattan Coll.) 2002, (Jesuit School of Theology, Berkeley) 2003, (Coll. of New Rochelle) 2004, (Villanova Univ.) 2005, (St Joseph's Coll., Conn.) 2006, (St Paul Univ.) 2008, (Univ. of St Michael's Coll. at Univ. of Toronto) 2010; Grawemeyer Award in Religion, Univ. of Louisville, Crossroad Women's Studies Award 1992, Award for Excellence in the Study of Religion, American Acad. of Religion 1999, Outstanding Book Award, Coll. Theology Soc. 2004, Loyola Mellon Award, Loyola Univ., Chicago, John Courtney Murray Award, CTSA, Jerome Award, CLA, Monika Hellwig Award, ACCU, Yves Congar Award, Barry Univ., Sophia Award, Washington Theological Union, Marianist Award, Univ. of Dayton. *Address:* Department of Theology, Fordham University, 441 East Fordham Road, Bronx, New York, NY 10458, USA (office). *Telephone:* (718) 817-3247 (office). *Fax:* (718) 817-5787 (office). *E-mail:* ejohnson@fordham.edu (office).

JOHNSON, George Laclede, BA, MA; American writer; b. 20 Jan. 1952, Fayetteville, AR. *Education:* Univ. of New Mexico, Albuquerque and American Univ., Washington, DC. *Career:* reporter, The Albuquerque Journal 1975–77; special assignment reporter, The Minneapolis Star 1979–82; staff ed., The Week in Review, The New York Times 1986–94; writer, The New York Times 1995–. *Publications:* Architects of Fear: Conspiracy Theories and Paranoia in American Politics (PEN Los Angeles Center Special Achievement in Nonfiction) 1984, Machinery of the Mind: Inside the New Science of Artificial Intelligence 1986, In the Palaces of Memory: How We Build the Worlds Inside Our Heads 1991, Fire in the Mind: Science, Faith and the Search for Order 1995, Strange Beauty: Murray Gell-Mann and the Revolution in 20th-Century Physics 1999, A Shortcut Through Time: The Path to the Quantum Computer 2003, Miss Leavitt's Stars: The Untold Story of the Woman Who Discovered How to Measure the Universe 2005, The Ten Most Beautiful Experiments 2008; contrib. to journals and newspapers, including Atlantic Monthly, New York Times, Scientific American, Slate, Time, Wired. *Honours:* Alicia Patterson Journalism Fellow 1984, New York Times Publr's Award 1991, AAAS Science Journalism Award 1999, Templeton-Cambridge Journalism Fellowships in Science and Religion, Cambridge, UK 2005. *Literary Agent:* c/o Ms Esther Newberg, International Creative Management, 40 West 57th Street, New York, NY 10019, USA. *Telephone:* (212) 556-5622. *Fax:* (212) 556-5624. *E-mail:* johnson@santafe.edu (office). *Website:* sciwrite.org/glj; santafereview.com.

JOHNSON, Haynes Bonner, BJ, MS; American journalist, academic and writer; b. 9 July 1931, New York, NY; m. 1st Julia Ann Erwin 1954 (divorced); two s. three d.; m. 2nd Kathryn Anne Oberly. *Education:* Univs of Missouri and Wisconsin. *Career:* 1st Lt Artillery, US Army, Korean War 1952–55; reporter, Wilmington News-Journal, Del. 1956–57; Reporter to Special Assignments Corresp., Washington Star 1957–69; Commentator, Washington Week in Review 1967–94, The News Hour with Jim Lehrer 1994–, PBS TV; Nat. Corresp., Washington Post 1969–73, Asst Man. Ed. 1973–77, Columnist 1977–94; Ferris Prof. of Journalism and Public Affairs, Princeton Univ. 1975–78; Guest Scholar, Brookings Inst., Washington, DC 1987–91; Regents Lecturer, Univ. of California, Berkeley 1992; Prof. of Political Commentary and Journalism, George Washington Univ. 1994–96; Knight Chair, Prof. of Journalism, Univ. of Maryland, College Park 1998–; mem. Nat. Acad. of Public Admin. *Publications:* Dusk at the Mountain 1963, The Bay of Pigs 1964, Fulbright: The Dissenter (with Bernard M. Gwertzman) 1968, Army in Anguish (with George C. Wilson) 1972, Lyndon (with Richard Harwood) 1973, The Fall of a President (ed.) 1974, The Working White House 1975, In the Absence of Power 1980, The Landing (with Howard Simons) 1986, Sleepwalking Through History 1991, Divided We Fall 1994, The System (with David S. Broder) 1996, The Best of Times: America in the Clinton Years 2001, The Age of Anxiety: McCarthyism to Terrorism 2005, The Battle for America 2008: The Story of an Extraordinary Election (with Dan Balz) 2009, Herblock: The Life and Works of the Great Political Cartoonist (with Harry Katz) 2009. *Honours:* Hon. DH (Wheeling Jesuit Univ.) 1997; Hon. DHumLitt (Univ. of Missouri) 1999, (St Norbert Coll.) 2009; Pulitzer Prize for Nat. Reporting 1966. *Address:* Philip Merrill College of Journalism, University of Maryland, 2207 Knight Hall, College Park, MD 20742-7111, USA (office). *Telephone:* (301) 405-2408 (office). *Fax:* (202) 387-3902 (office). *E-mail:* hjohnson@jmail.umd.edu (office).

JOHNSON, Hugh Eric Allan, OBE, MA; British writer, editor and broadcaster; b. 10 March 1939, London; s. of the late Guy F. Johnson CBE and Grace Kittel; m. Judith Eve Grinling 1965; one s. two d. *Education:* Rugby School, King's Coll., Cambridge. *Career:* feature writer, Condé Nast Magazines 1960–63; Wine Corresp., Sunday Times 1962–67, Travel Ed. 1967; Ed. Wine and Food Magazine 1963–65; Ed. Queen Magazine 1968–70; Wine Ed., Gourmet Magazine 1971–72, Cuisine Magazine, New York 1983–84; Chair. Winestar Productions Ltd 1984–2009, The Hugh Johnson Collection Ltd, The Movie Business; Pres. Sunday Times Wine Club 1973–, Circle of Wine Writers 1997–2007; Founder-mem. Tree Council 1974; Founder The Plantsman (quarterly) 1979; Dir Château Latour 1986–2001; Editorial Consultant, The Garden (Royal Horticultural Soc. Journal) 1975–2005; columnist, Tradescant's Diary 1975–; Sec. Wine and Food Soc. 1962–63; Gardening Corresp., New York Times 1986–87; Pres. Metropolitan Public Gardens Asscn 2011; Vice-Pres. Int. Dendrology Soc. 2010–. *Television includes:* Wine – A User's Guide (series) 1986, Vintage – A History of Wine (series) 1989, Return Voyage 1992. *Publications:* Wine 1966, Frank Schoonmaker's Encyclopaedia of Wine (ed. of English edn) 1967, The World Atlas of Wine 1971 (sixth edn with Jancis Robinson 2007), The International Book of Trees 1973, The California Wine Book (with Bob Thompson) 1976, Understanding Wine (Sainsbury Guide) 1976, Hugh Johnson's Pocket Wine Book (annually since 1977), The Principles of Gardening 1979 (revised edn with new title, Hugh Johnson's Gardening Companion 1996), Hugh Johnson's Wine Companion 1983 (sixth edn with Stephen Brook 2009), How to Handle a Wine (video) 1984, Hugh Johnson's Cellar Book 1986, The Atlas of German Wines 1986, How to Enjoy Your Wine 1985, The Wine Atlas of France (with Hubrecht Duijker) 1987, The Story of Wine 1989, The Art and Science of Wine (with James Halliday) 1992, Hugh Johnson on Gardening: The Best of Tradescant's Diary 1993, Tuscany and Its Wines 2000, Wine: A Life Uncorked 2005, Hugh Johnson in the Garden 2009, Trees: A Lifetime's Journey through Forests, Woods and Gardens (Garden Media Guild Reference Book of the Year 2011) 2010, Wine Journal 2011. *Honours:* Hon. Chair. Wine Japan 1989–93; Hon. Pres. Int. Wine and Food Soc. 2004–08, Wine & Spirit Educ. Trust 2009–11; Fellow Commoner, King's Coll. Cambridge 2001; Hon. Freeman of the Vintner's Co. 2003; Chevalier, Ordre nat. du Mérite 2003; Dr hc (Acad. du Vin de Bordeaux) 1987, (Essex) 1998; André Simon Prize 1967, 1989, 2005, Glenfiddich Award 1972, 1986, 1990, Marqués de Cáceres Award 1984, Wines and Vines Trophy 1982, Grand Prix de la Communication de la Vigne et du Vin 1992, 1993, Decanter Magazine Man of the Year 1995, Von Rumor Award, Gastronomische Akad., Germany 1998, Gold Veitch Memorial Medal, Royal Horticultural Soc. 2000. *Address:* 73 St James's Street, London, SW1A 1PH; Saling Hall, Great Saling, Essex, CM7 5DT, England. *Telephone:* (1371) 850243. *Website:* www.salinghall.com; www.tradsdiary.com.

JOHNSON, Linton Kwesi, BA; British poet and writer; b. 24 Aug. 1952, Chapeltown, Jamaica. *Education:* Goldsmiths Coll., London. *Career:* family emigrated to London 1963; involved in Black Panther movement, London; wrote for NME and Melody Maker in 1970s and 1980s; regular TV/radio apppearances as an authority on reggae; C. Day-Lewis Fellowship 1977, Assoc. Fellow, Warwick Univ. 1985; Founder LKJ Records and LKJ Music Publishers; Trustee, George Padmore Inst. *Recordings include:* Dread Beat An' Blood, Forces of Victory, More Time, LKJ Live in Paris. *Publications:* Voices of the Living and the Dead 1974, Dread Beat an' Blood 1975, Inglan is a Bitch 1980, Tings an' Times: Selected Poems 1991, Mi Revalueshanary Fren: Selected Poems 2002; contrib. to recordings, television. *Honours:* Hon. Fellow, Wolverhampton Polytechnic 1987, Goldsmiths Coll., London 2002; Hon. Visiting Prof., Middlesex Univ. 2004; Italian literary awards 1990, 1998, Silver Musgrave Medal Inst. of Jamaica 2005. *Address:* PO Box 623, Herne Hill, London, SE24 OLS, England (office). *Telephone:* (20) 7738-7647 (office). *Fax:* (20) 7738-7647 (office). *E-mail:* info@lkjrecords.com (office). *Website:* www.lkjrecords.com (office).

JOHNSON, Nora, BA; American author; b. 31 Jan. 1933, Los Angeles, CA; m. 1st Leonard Siwek 1955; m. 2nd John A. Milici 1965, two s. two d. *Education:* Smith College. *Career:* mem. Authors' Guild; PEN. *Publications:* The World of Henry Orient, 1958; A Step Beyond Innocence, 1961; Love Letter in the Dead Letter Office, 1966; Flashback, 1979; You Can Go Home Again, 1982; The Two of Us, 1984; Tender Offer, 1985; Uncharted Places, 1988; Perfect Together, 1991. Contributions: newspapers and magazines. *Honours:* McCall's Short Story Prize, 1962; O. Henry Award Story, 1982; New York Times Best Book Citations, 1982, 1984.

JOHNSON, Paul Bede, BA, MA; British historian and broadcaster; b. 2 Nov. 1928, Barton; s. of William Aloysius and Anne Johnson; m. Marigold Hunt 1957; three s. one d. *Education:* Stonyhurst and Magdalen Coll., Oxford. *Career:* Asst Exec. Ed. Réalités, Paris 1952–55; Asst Ed. New Statesman 1955–60, Deputy Ed. 1960–64, Ed. 1965–70, Dir 1965; DeWitt Wallace Prof. of Communications, American Enterprise Inst., Washington, DC 1980; mem. Royal Comm. on the Press 1974–77, Cable Authority 1984–90; freelance writer. *Publications:* The Offshore Islanders 1972, Elizabeth I: a Study in Power and Intellect 1974, Pope John XXIII 1975, A History of Christianity 1976, Enemies of Society 1977, The National Trust Book of British Castles 1978, The Civilization of Ancient Egypt 1978, Civilizations of the Holy Land 1979, British Cathedrals 1980, Ireland: Land of Troubles 1980, The Recovery of Freedom 1980, Pope John Paul II and the Catholic Restoration 1982, Modern Times 1983 (revised 1991), History of the Modern World: From 1917 to the 1980s 1984, The Pick of Paul Johnson 1985, The Oxford Book of Political Anecdotes (ed.) 1986, The History of the Jews 1987, Intellectuals 1988, The Birth of the Modern: World Society 1815–1830 1991, Wake Up Britain! 1994, The Quest for God 1996, To Hell with Picasso and other essays 1996, A History of the American People 1997, The Renaissance 2000, Napoleon 2002, Art: A New History 2003, The Vanished Landscape: A 1930s Childhood in the Potteries 2004, Creators: From Chaucer to Walt Disney 2006, Heroes: From Alexander the Great to Mae West 2009, Churchill 2009, Humorists: From Hogarth to Noel Coward 2010. *Honours:* Book of the Year Prize, Yorkshire Post 1975, Francis Boyer Award for Services to Public Policy 1979, King Award for Excellence (Literature) 1980, Pilkington Literary Award 2003, Presidential Medal of Freedom, USA 2006. *Address:* 29 Newton Road, London, W2 5JR; The Coach House, Over Stowey, nr Bridgwater, Somerset TA5 1HA, England. *Telephone:* (20) 7229-3859 (London); (1278) 732393 (Somerset). *Fax:* (20) 7792-1676 (London).

JOHNSON, (John) Stephen, MA, DPhil; British writer; b. 3 June 1947, Mansfield, England. *Education:* Univ. of Oxford. *Publications:* The Roman Fort of the Saxon Shore 1976, Later Roman Britain 1980, Late Roman Fortifications 1983, Hadrian's Wall 1989, Rome and its Empire 1989. *Address:* 49 Branksome Road, Norwich, NR4 6SW, England.

JOHNSON, Susan Ruth, BA; Australian writer; b. 30 Dec. 1956, Brisbane; d. of John Joseph Johnson and Barbara Ruth Johnson (née Bell); m. 1st John Patrick Burdett 1989 (divorced 1991); m. 2nd Leslie William Webb 1994; one s. *Education:* Clayfield Coll., Brisbane and Univ. of Queensland. *Career:* journalist, The Courier-Mail 1975, The Australian Women's Weekly 1977–78, The Sun-Herald 1980–81, The Sydney Morning Herald 1981–82, The National Times 1982–84; full-time writer 1984–; resident Keesing Studio, Cité Int. des Arts, Paris (awarded by Literature Bd, Australia Council) –1992; Ed. Saturday Extra, in The Age 1999–2001; mem. Australian Soc. of Authors; several fellowships awarded by Australia Council 1986–92. *Publications:*

fiction: Latitudes: New Writing from the North (ed. with Mary Roberts) 1986, Message from Chaos 1987, Flying Lessons 1990, A Big Life 1993, WomenLoveSex (ed., short stories) 1996, Hungry Ghosts 1996, Life in Seven Mistakes 2007; non-fiction: A Better Woman (memoir) 1999, The Broken Book (biog.) 2005. *Address:* Margaret Connolly and Associates, POB 945, Wahroonga, NSW 2076, Australia. *E-mail:* sjreaders@hotmail.com. *Website:* margaretconnolly.com; www.abetterwoman.net.

JOHNSON, Terry, BA; British dramatist and screenwriter; b. 20 Dec. 1955, England. *Education:* Univ. of Birmingham. *Plays:* Insignificance 1982, Cries from the Mammal House 1984, Unsuitable for Adults 1985, Tuesday's Child (with Kate Lock) 1987, Imagine Drowning 1991, Hysteria 1993, Dead Funny 1994, Cleo, Camping, Emmanuelle and Dick 1998, The London Cuckolds 1998, Hitchcock Blonde 2003, Piano/Forte 2006. *Film screenplays:* Insignificance 1985, Absolute Beginners (with others) 1986, Killing Time 1985, Way Upstream 1987. *Television screenplays:* Time Trouble 1985, Tuesday's Child (with Kate Lock) 1985, Way Upstream 1987, 99-1 (with others) 1994, Blood and Water 1995, The Bite 1996, Cor Blimey! 2000, Not Only But Always 2004. *Honours:* Evening Standard Drama Award 1983. *Literary Agent:* Curtis Brown Ltd, Haymarket House, 28–29 Haymarket, London, SW1Y 4SP, England. *Telephone:* (20) 7393-4400. *Fax:* (20) 7393-4401. *E-mail:* info@curtisbrown.co.uk. *Website:* www.curtisbrown.co.uk.

JOHNSON, William Stacy, AB, JD, MDiv, PhD; American theologian and lawyer; b. 13 July 1956, Pinehurst, NJ. *Education:* Davidson College, Wake Forest University, Union Theological Seminary, Harvard University. *Career:* Assoc. Prof. of Theology, Austin Presbyterian Theological Seminary, Austin, Texas, 1992–; Attorney-at-Law; mem. Karl Barth Society of North America; American Acad. of Religion; American Asscn for the Advancement of Science. *Publications:* Theology, History, and Culture (ed.), 1996; The Mystery of God: Karl Barth and the Postmodern Foundations of Theology, 1997. *Address:* Austin Presbyterian Theological Seminary, 100 E 27th St, Austin, TX 78705, USA. *E-mail:* wsjnson@ix.netcom.com.

JOHNSON-DAVIES, Denys; Canadian translator and writer; b. 1922, Vancouver. *Education:* Univ. of Cambridge. *Career:* fmrly worked for the BBC Arabic Service, teacher at Fouad al-Awwal Univ., Cairo; Arabic–English translator. *Publications include:* Memories in Translation (memoir) 2006; editor: Arabic Short Stories, The Mountain of Green Tea (with Yahya al-Tahir 'Abd Allah), The Island of Animals (with Khemir Sabiha), The Anchor Book of Modern Arabic Fiction 2006; translations: Short Stories, by Mahmoud Teymour 1947, The Tree Climber, by Tawfiq al-Hakim, Bandarshah, by al-Tayyib Salih, Houses Behind the Trees, by Mohamed el-Bisatie, The Slave's Dream and Other Stories, by Nabil Naoum Gorgy, Blood Feud and Other Stories, by Yusuf Sharouni and Yusuf Sharuni, Season of Migration to the North, by Tayeb Salih, The Time and the Place, and Other Stories, by Naguib Mahfouz, Arabian Nights and Days, by Naguib Mahfouz and Najib Mahfuz, The Wiles of Men and Other Stories, by Salwa Bakr, The Journey of Ibn Fattouma, by Naguib Mahfouz and Najib Mahfuz, Echoes of an Autobiography, by Naguib Mahfouz and Nadine Gordimer. *Address:* c/o Anchor Publicity, 1745 Broadway, 20th Floor, New York, NY 10019, USA (office).

JOHNSTON, George Benson, BA, MA; Canadian poet and translator; b. 7 Oct. 1913, Hamilton, ON; m. Jeanne McRae 1944; three s. three d. *Education:* University of Toronto. *Career:* Faculty, Dept of English, Mount Allison University, Sackville, New Brunswick, 1947–49, Carleton College, later University, Ottawa, 1949–79. *Publications:* poetry: The Cruising Auk, 1959; Home Free, 1966; Happy Enough: Poems 1935–1972, 1972; Between, 1976; Taking a Grip, 1979; Auk Redivivus: Selected Poems, 1981; Ask Again, 1984; Endeared by Dark: The Collected Poems, 1990; What is to Come: Selected and New Poems, 1996. Prose: Carl: Portrait of a Painter, 1986. Translator: Over 10 vols, 1963–94. *Honours:* hon. doctorates.

JOHNSTON, Jennifer; Irish writer; b. 12 Jan. 1930, Dublin; d. of Denis Johnston and Shelah Richards; m. 1st Ian Smyth; two s. two d.; m. 2nd David Gilliland. *Education:* Park House School, Dublin, Trinity Coll., Dublin. *Plays:* The Desert Lullaby, Moonlight and Music; several radio and TV programmes. *Publications:* How Many Miles to Babylon?, The Old Jest, The Christmas Tree, The Invisible Worm 1991, The Illusionist 1995, Two Moons, The Railway Station Man 1986, Shadows on Our Skin, The Gingerbread Woman, The Porch 1986, The Invisible Man 1986, The Desert Lullaby 1996, This is Not a Novel 2003, Grace and Truth 2005, Foolish Mortals 2008, Truth or Fiction 2009, Shadowstory 2011. *Honours:* Hon. Fellow Trinity Coll., Dublin; Hon. DLitt (New Univ. of Ulster, Queen's Univ., Belfast, Trinity Coll., Dublin, Nat. Univ. of Ireland); Whitbread Prize 1980, Giles Cooper Award 1989, Premio Giuseppe Acerbi 2003. *Address:* Brook Hall, Culmore Road, Derry, BT48 8JE, Northern Ireland (home). *Telephone:* (28) 7135-1297 (home).

JOHNSTON, Julia Ann; Canadian writer; b. 21 Jan. 1941, Smith Falls, ON; m. Basil W. Johnston 1963, four d. *Education:* University of Toronto, Trent University. *Career:* mem. Canadian Society of Children's Authors; Writers' Union of Canada. *Publications:* There's Going to be a Frost 1979, Don't Give Up the Ghosts 1981, Tasting the Alternative 1982, After 30 Years of Law, Ken Starvis Sculpts New Career 1990, Hero of Lesser Causes 1992, The Interiors of Pots 1992, Adam and Eve and Pinch Me 1994, The Only Outcast 1998, Love Ya Like A Sister (Ed.) by Katie Ouniour, In Spite of Killer Bees 2001. *Honours:* Hon. DLitt (Trent) 1996; Governor-General's Literary Award 1992, School Library Best Book 1993, Joan Fassler Memorial Award 1994, Ruth Schwartz Young Adult Book Award 1995, Canadian Library Asscn Young Adult Book Award 1995, Vicky Metcalf Award for body of work inspirationial to youth 2003. *Address:* 463 Hunter Street W, Peterborough, ON K9H 2M7, Canada.

JOHNSTON, Kenneth Richard, BA, MA, PhD; American academic and writer; *Ruth N. Halls Chair of English, Indiana University*; b. 20 April 1938, Marquette, MI; m. 1st Elizabeth Louise Adolphson (divorced); two s. one d.; m. 2nd Ilinca Marina Zarifopol (deceased); one s. *Education:* Augustana College, Univ. of Chicago, Yale Univ. *Career:* Instructor in English, Augustana College 1962–63; Asst Prof., Indiana Univ. 1966–70, Assoc. Prof. 1970–75, Prof. of English 1975–2002, Ruth N. Halls Chair of English 2002–; Sr Fulbright Lecturer, Univ. of Bucharest 1974–75; Cox Family Distinguished Scholar, Univ. of Colorado 2003; mem. British Asscn for Romantic Studies, MLA, North American Soc. for the Study of Romanticism, Wordsworth-Coleridge Asscn. *Publications:* The Rhetoric of Conflict (ed.) 1969, Wordsworth and 'The Recluse' 1984, Wordsworth and Romanticism (with Gene W. Ruoff) 1987, The Age of William Wordsworth: Critical Essays on the Romantic Tradition (ed. with Gene W. Ruoff) 1988, Romantic Revolutions: Criticism and Theory (ed. with Karen Hanson) 1990, The Hidden Wordsworth: Poet, Lover, Rebel, Spy 1998; contrib. to scholarly books and journals. *Honours:* Hon. Fellow Inst. for Advanced Study in the Humanities, Univ. of Edinburgh 1998; Guggenheim Fellowship, Nat. Endowment for the Humanities Fellowships, Fulbright Fellow, UK 2005–06, Mellon Emer. Fellow 2006–07. *Address:* c/o Department of English, Indiana University, Bloomington, IN 47405, USA (office). *E-mail:* johnstonk@indiana.edu (office).

JOHNSTON, Ronald John, OBE, MA, PhD, FBA; British geographer and academic; *Professor of Geography, University of Bristol*; b. 30 March 1941, Swindon, Wilts.; s. of Henry Louis Johnston and Phyllis Joyce Johnston (née Liddiard); m. Rita Brennan 1963; one s. one d. *Education:* The Commonweal Co. Secondary Grammar School, Swindon, Univ. of Manchester, Monash Univ., Australia. *Career:* Teaching Fellow, then Lecturer, Dept of Geography, Monash Univ. 1964–66; Lecturer then Reader, Dept of Geography, Univ. of Canterbury, NZ 1967–74; Prof. of Geography, Univ. of Sheffield 1974–92, Pro-Vice-Chancellor for Academic Affairs 1989–92; Vice-Chancellor Univ. of Essex 1992–95; Prof. of Geography, Univ. of Bristol 1995–; Ed. New Zealand Geographer 1969–74, Proceedings of the British Academy 2007–; Co-Ed. Environment and Planning 1979–2005, Progress in Human Geography 1979–2007. *Publications:* author or co-author of more than 50 books, including Geography and Geographers, Philosophy and Human Geography, City and Society, The Geography of English Politics, A Nation Dividing?, Bell-ringing: The English Art of Change-Ringing, An Atlas of Bells; ed. or co-ed. of more than 40 books, including Geography and the Urban Environment (six vols), The Dictionary of Human Geography; author or co-author of more than 850 articles in academic journals. *Honours:* Hon. DUniv (Essex) 1996; Hon. LLD (Monash) 1999; Hon. DLitt (Sheffield) 2002; Hon. DLH (Bath) 2005; Murchison Award, Royal Geographical Soc. (RGS) 1984, RGS Victoria Medal 1990, Hons Award for Distinguished Contribs, Asscn of American Geographers 1991, Prix Vautrin Lud 1999, Lifetime Achievement Award, Asscn of American Geographers 2010. *Address:* School of Geographical Sciences, University of Bristol, Bristol, BS8 1SS, England (office). *Telephone:* (117) 928-9116 (office). *Fax:* (117) 928-7878 (office). *E-mail:* r.johnston@bris.ac.uk (office). *Website:* www.bris.ac.uk/geography (office).

JÓKAI, Anna, BA; Hungarian writer; b. 24 Nov. 1932, Budapest; d. of Gyula Jókai and Anna Jókai (née Lukács); m. 3rd Sándor Kapocsi 1983; one s. one d. *Education:* Univ. Eötvös Loránd, Budapest. *Career:* accountant 1951–61; teacher 1961–76; freelance writer 1976–; Pres. Hungarian Writers' Asscn 1990–93. *Publications include:* 4447 (novel) 1968, Tartozik és követel (Debit and Credit, novel) 1970, Napok (Days, novel) 1972, A reimsi angyal (The Angel from Reims, short-stories) 1975, Jákob lajtorjája (Jacob's Ladder, novel) 1982, A feladat (The Task, novel) 1985, Az együttlét (The Being Together, novel) 1987, Szegény Sudár Anna (Poor Anna Sudár, novel) 1989, Ne féljetek (Fear Not, novel) (Book of the Year Prize 1998), Virágvasárnap alkonyán (Sunset of Flower-Sunday, poems) 2004, Majd (The Future, short stories) 2005, Breviarium 2005, Godot megjött (Godot Has Come, novel) 2007, Elbezréltem (I Have Told, short stories) 2007. *Honours:* Jòzsef Attila Prize 1971, Int. Pietrczak Pax Literary Prize, Poland 1980, Kossuth Prize 1994, Hungarian Heredity Prize 1998, The Book of the Year Prize 1998, Centre for European Times Prize 1999, Hungarian Art Prize 2000, Arany János Grand-Prize 2004, Prima Primissima Prize 2004, Stephanus Prize 2006, Árpad Prize 2007, Prize for the Arts 2009. *Address:* Vas Gereben u. 211, 1194 Budapest, Hungary (home). *Telephone:* (1) 357-2411 (home).

JOLLY, James; British writer. *Education:* Univ. of Bristol, Univ. of Reading. *Career:* producer, Record Review (BBC Radio 3); Asst Ed. Gramophone –1989, Ed. 1990–2005, Ed.-in-Chief 2006–; co-presenter The Classical Collection (BBC Radio 3) 2007. *Publications as editor:* The Greatest Classical Recordings of All Time 1995, The Gramophone Opera 75: The 75 Best Opera Recordings of All Time 1997, The Gramophone Opera Good CD Guide 1998, The Gramophone Classical 2001 Good CD Guide (co-ed.) 2002. *Address:* Gramophone, Haymarket Magazines Ltd, PO Box 568, Haywards Heath, Sussex RH16 3XQ, England (office). *Website:* www.gramophone.co.uk.

JONAS, Manfred, BS, AM, PhD; American historian and academic; *John Bigelow Professor Emeritus of History, Union College*; b. 9 April 1927, Mannheim, Germany; s. of Walter Jonas and Antonie Jonas; m. Nancy Jane Greene 1952; two s. two d. *Education:* City Coll. of New York, Harvard Univ. *Career:* Visiting Prof. for North American History, Free Univ. of Berlin,

1959–62; Asst Prof. to Prof. of History, Union Coll., Schenectady, NY 1963–81, Washington Irving Prof. in Modern Literary and Historical Studies 1981–86, John Bigelow Prof. of History 1986–96, Emer. 1996–; Dr Otto Salgo Visiting Prof. of American Studies, Eötvös Lorand Univ., Budapest, Hungary 1983–84. *Publications:* Die Unabhängigkeitserklärung der Vereingten Staaten 1964, Isolationism in America 1935–1941 1966, American Foreign Relations in the 20th Century 1967, Roosevelt and Churchill: Their Secret Wartime Correspondence 1975, New Opportunities in the New Nation 1982, The United States and Germany: A Diplomatic History 1984; contribs to Diplomatic History, The Historian, Mid-America, American Studies, Maryland Historical Magazine, Essex County Historical Collections, Jahrbuch für Amerikastudien, The Origins of the Second World War: An International Perspective 2011. *Address:* Department of History, Union College, Schenectady, NY 12308, USA (office). *E-mail:* jonasm@union.edu (office).

JONES, Arthur (Alun) Gwynne (see CHALFONT)

JONES, Alys, BA; Welsh writer; b. 15 Sept. 1944, Newborough, Anglesey, North Wales; m. Robin Jones 1973; one s. one d. *Education:* Univ. Coll., Bangor, North Wales. *Career:* teacher in Welsh, Maesteg Comprehensive School 1966–67, Machynlleth Secondary School, Powys 1967–70, Ysgol Dyffryn Conwy, Llanrwst 1970–74, Ysgol Glan Clwyd, Llanelwy 1974–75. *Publications:* Ysbrydion y Môr 1982, Storiau Non 1982, Storiau Huw a'i Ffrindiau 1987, Dirgelwch Neuadd Henffordd 1987, Mac Pync 1987, Storiau Cornel y Cae 1988, Yr Ysbryd Arian 1989, Y Gadwyn 1989, Jetsam 1991, Straeon Cornel y Stryd 1994, Cuthbert Caradog 1998, Pwtyn Escapes 1998, Pwtyn ar Goll 2001, Clymau Ddoe 2001, Pwtyn and Pwtan go to School 2001, Pwtyn and Pwtan Meet 2002, Achub Myrffi 2005, Storïau Cornel yr Ardd 2009; contributions: CIP, Heno Heno (short story anthology) 1990, group reading booklet, Isle of Anglesey County Council 2000. *Address:* Llys Alaw, 18 Ystad Eryri, Bethel, Caernarfon, Gwynedd, North Wales (home).

JONES, Charlotte; British playwright and writer; m. Paul Bazely. *Education:* Balliol Coll., Oxford. *Career:* fmr actress. *Plays:* Airswimming (Battersea Arts Centre, London) 1997, In Flame (Bush Theatre, London) 1999, Martha, Josie and the Chinese Elvis (Octagon, Bolton) 1999, Humble Boy (Royal Nat. Theatre, London) 2001, The Dark (Donmar Warehouse, London) 2004, The Woman in White (The Book) 2004, The Lightening Play (Almeida Theatre) 2006. *Radio:* for BBC Radio 4: The Sound of Solitary Waves, Mary Something Takes the Veil, Future Perfect, A Seer of Sorts, Sea Symphony for Piano and Child 2001, Blue Air Love and Flowers. *Television:* Bessie and the Bell (Carlton) 2000, Mother's Ruin (Carlton) 2001. *Film:* Dogstar 2000. *Publications:* In Flame 2001, Martha, Josie and the Chinese Elvis 1999, Humble Boy 2001, The Woman in White (book to musical, based on Wilkie Collins' novel) 2004. *Honours:* Manchester Evening News Best Play Award 1999, Pearson TV Best Play Award 1999, Critics' Circle Award for Most Promising Playwright 2000, Susan Smith Blackburn Award 2001, Critics' Circle Best New Play Award 2002, People's Choice Best New Play Award 2002. *Literary Agent:* United Agents, 12–26 Lexington Street, London, W1F 0LE, England. *Telephone:* (20) 3214-0800. *Fax:* (20) 3214-0801. *E-mail:* info@unitedagents.co.uk. *Website:* unitedagents.co.uk.

JONES, Christopher Dennis, BA; American playwright; b. 13 Dec. 1949, New York; m. Gwendoline Shirley Rose 1979. *Education:* University of Pittsburgh. *Career:* Resident Playwright, Carnaby Street Theatre, London, 1975–76, New Hope Theatre, London, 1977– 78; mem. Writer's Guild of Great Britain. *Publications:* Plays: Passing Strangers, 1975; Nasty Corners, 1977; New Signals, 1978; In Flight Reunion, 1979; Sterile Landscape, 1982; Ralph Bird's River Race, 1985; Dying Hairless With a Rash, 1985; Bitter Chalice, 1987; Begging the Ring, 1989; Burning Youth, 1989. Contributions: Country Life; Arts Review.

JONES, Douglas Gordon, OC, BA, MA; Canadian poet and academic (retd); b. 1 Jan. 1929, Bancroft; m. Monique Grandmangin; one step-s.; four c. from previous m. *Education:* McGill Univ., Queen's Univ., Kingston. *Career:* Prof., Univ. of Sherbrooke, Québec 1963–94. *Publications include:* poetry: Frost on the Sun 1957, The Sun is Axeman 1961, Phrases from Orpheus 1967, Under the Thunder the Flowers Light Up the Earth 1977, A Throw of Particles: Selected and New Poems 1983, Balthazar and Other Poems 1988, The Floating Garden 1995, Wild Asterisks in Cloud 1997, Grounding Sight 1999; other: Butterfly on Rock: A Study of Themes and Images in Canadian Literature 1970. *Honours:* Hon. DLitt (Guelph Univ.) 1982; Univ. of Western Ontario Pres.'s Medal 1976, Gov.-Gen.'s Award for Poetry 1977, and for Translation 1993. *Address:* 120 Houghton Street, North Hatley, QC J0B 2C0, Canada (home). *Telephone:* (819) 842-2404 (home). *Fax:* (819) 842-1106 (home). *E-mail:* dgjones@abacom.com (home).

JONES, Dylan; British journalist; *Editor-in-Chief, GQ magazine*; m. *Career:* Ed., Arena 1989–92; fmrly Ed. i-D magazine, Group Ed. Wagadon (publisher of Arena, The Face, etc.), Sr Ed. The Sunday Times, The Observer, Ed.-at-Large The Sunday Times Magazine; has also worked for The Independent and The Guardian; currently Editor-in-Chief, GQ; Chair. British Soc. of Magazine Editors. *Publications include:* Jim Morrison: Dark Star 1991, Sex, Power and Travel: 10 Years of Arena (ed. and contrib.) 1996, Meaty, Beaty, Big and Bouncy: Classic Rock and Pop Writing from Elvis to Oasis 1996, Ultra Lounge: The Lexicon of Easy Listening 1997, iPod, Therefore I Am 2005, Mr Jones' Rules for the Modern Man 2006, Cameron on Cameron 2008. *Honours:* seven Magazine Editor of the Year awards 1993–2007. *Address:* GQ, The Condé Nast Publications Ltd, Vogue House, Hanover Square, London, W1S 1JU, England (office). *Telephone:* (20) 7499-9080 (office). *Fax:* (20) 7495-1679 (office). *Website:* www.gq-magazine.co.uk (office).

JONES, Edward Paul, BA, MFA; American writer; b. 5 Oct. 1950, Arlington, Va. *Education:* Holy Cross Coll., Univ. of Virginia. *Career:* teaches periodically at George Washington University, Washington, DC; Morgan Writer-in-Residence, Univ. of North Carolina 2010. *Publications:* Lost in the City (short stories) (PEN/Hemingway Award) 1992, The Known World (novel) (Pulitzer Prize for Fiction 2004, Lannan Literary Award , Int. IMPAC Dublin Literary Award 2005) 2003, All Aunt Hagar's Children 2006. *Address:* c/o Department of English, George Washington University, 801 22nd Street, NW, Suite 760, Washington, DC 20052, USA (office).

JONES, Evan Lloyd, BA, MA; Australian poet, writer and photographer; b. 20 Nov. 1931, Preston, Vic.; m. 1st Judith Anne Dale 1954; one s.; m. 2nd Margot Sanguinetti 1966; three d. *Education:* Univ. of Melbourne, Stanford Univ., USA. *Publications include:* poetry: Inside the Whale 1960, Understandings 1967, Recognitions 1978, Left at the Post 1984, Alone at Last! (CD); prose: Kenneth Mackenzie 1969, The Poems of Kenneth Mackenzie (ed. with Geoffrey Little) 1972, Alone at Last! 2010; contrib. of innumerable essays and reviews in publs ranging from learned journals to newspapers, on topics ranging from literature to physics. *Address:* PO Box 122, Carlton North, Vic. 3054 (office); 104 Garton Street, Carlton North, Vic. 3054, Australia (home). *Telephone:* (3) 9380-6664 (home). *Fax:* (3) 9388-1283 (home). *E-mail:* jonesel@ihug.com.au (home).

JONES, (Everett) Le Roi, (Amiri Baraka); American poet and dramatist; *Editor, Unity & Struggle Newspaper*; b. 7 Oct. 1934, Newark, NJ; s. of Coyette L. Jones and Anna Lois (Russ) Jones; m. 1st Hettie R. Cohen 1958 (divorced 1965); two d.; m. 2nd Sylvia Robinson (Bibi Amina Baraka) 1966; five c.; two step-c. *Education:* Howard Univ., New School and Columbia Univ. *Career:* served with USAF; taught poetry at New School Social Research, drama at Columbia Univ., literature at Univ. of Buffalo; Visiting Prof., San Francisco State Univ.; began publishing 1958; f. Black Arts Repertory Theater School, Harlem 1964, Spirit House, Newark 1966; Whitney Fellowship 1963, Guggenheim Fellowship 1965; Fellow, Yoruba Acad. 1965; Visiting Lecturer, Afro-American Studies, Yale Univ. 1977–78; Asst Prof. of African Studies, State Univ. of New York 1980–83, Assoc. Prof. 1983–85, Prof. 1985–; Ed. Unity & Struggle Newspaper; mem. Int. Co-ordinating Cttee of Congress of African Peoples; mem. Black Acad. of Arts and Letters; Fellow, American Acad. of Arts and Letters; Poet Laureate of NJ 2002–04. *Publications include:* Preface to a Twenty Volume Suicide Note 1961, Dante 1962, Blues People 1963, The Dead Lecturer 1963, Dutchman 1964, The Moderns 1964, The System of Dante's Hell 1965, Home 1965, Jello 1965, Experimental Death Unit 1965, The Baptism–The Toilet 1966, Black Mass 1966, Mad Heart 1967, Slave Ship 1967, Black Music 1967, Tales 1968, Great Goodness of Life 1968, Black Magic, Four Black Revolutionary Plays 1969, Black Art 1969, In Our Terribleness 1970, Junkies are Full of Shhh …, Bloodrites 1970, Raise 1971, It's Nation Time 1971, Dutchman + the Slave 1971, Kawaida Studies 1972, Spirit Reach 1972, Afrikan Revolution 1973, Hard Facts: Excerpts 1975, Spring Song 1979, AM/TRAK 1979, In the Tradition: For Black Arthur Blythe 1980, Reggae or Not! Poems 1982, The Autobiography of Le Roi Jones/Amiri Baraka 1984, Thornton Dial: Images of the Tiger 1993, Shy's, Wise, Y's: The Griot's Tale 1994, Transbluesency 1996, Funk Lore 1996, Home 1998, Black Music 1998, The Essence of Reparations 2003, Somebody Blew up America 2004, Tales of the Out and Gone (PEN Faulkner Award 2008) 2006, Digging: Afro American Soul of American Classical Music 2009, Razor: Revolutionary Art for Cultural Revolution 2009; several film scripts; ed. Hard Facts 1976. *Honours:* James Weldon Johnson Medal for outstanding contribution to the Arts. *Literary Agent:* Celeste Bateman and Associates, PO Box 4071, Newark, NJ 07114-4071, USA. *Telephone:* (973) 705-8253. *E-mail:* celestebateman@aol.com. *Website:* www.celestebateman.com. *Address:* 808 South 10th Street, Newark, NJ 07108, USA (office). *Telephone:* (973) 242-1572 (office). *Fax:* (973) 242-1509 (office). *E-mail:* amirib@aol.com (office). *Website:* www.amiribaraka.com.

JONES, Frederick Malcolm Anthony, MA, PhD; British academic, writer and poet; *Senior Lecturer, School of Archaeology, Classics and Egyptology, University of Liverpool*; b. 14 Feb. 1955, Middx, England; two s. *Education:* Univs of Newcastle upon Tyne, Leeds and St Andrews. *Career:* Asst Lecturer, Univ. of Cape Town, SA 1982–86; Teacher of Classics, Cobham Hall, Kent 1987–89; Lecturer in Classics and Ancient History, Univ. of Liverpool 1989–96; Sr Lecturer in Classics, School of Archaeology, Classics and Egyptology 1996–; mem. Cambridge Philological Soc., Soc. for the Promotion of Roman Studies. *Publications:* Congreve's Balsamic Elixir 1995, Nominum Ratio 1996; contribs to journals, reviews and periodicals. *Honours:* one of ten jt winners, Northern Poetry Competition 1991, Felicia Hemans Prize for Lyrical Poetry 1991. *Address:* School of Archaeology, Classics and Egyptology, University of Liverpool, Room 2.08, 12 Abercromby Square, Liverpool, L69 3BX, England (office). *Telephone:* (151) 794-2347 (office). *Fax:* (151) 794-2442 (office). *E-mail:* fjones@liv.ac.uk (office). *Website:* www.liv.ac.uk/sace/organisation/people/jones.htm (office); www.jonesprints.co.uk (home).

JONES, Gail; Australian academic and writer; *Professor in Writing and Society, University of Western Sydney*; b. 17 June 1955. *Education:* Univ. of Western Australia. *Career:* fmr Lecturer in the Dept of English, Univ. of Western Australia; currently Prof. in Writing, Univ. of Western Sydney. *Publications:* novels: Black Mirror (Nita B. Kibble Award, Western Australian

Premier's Book Awards Fiction Prize) 2003, Sixty Lights (Fiction and Premier's Prize, Western Australian Premier's Book Awards 2004, Age Book of the Year Award for Fiction 2005, South Australian Festival Award for Literature 2006) 2004, Dreams of Speaking 2006, Sorry 2007, Family Secrets 2008, Family Fear 2010, Five Bells 2011; short stories: The House of Breathing 1992, Fetish Lives 1997; non-fiction: The Piano (film criticism). *Address:* Writing and Society Research Group, Bankstown 1.1.136, University of Western Sydney, Locked Bag 1797, Penrith, NSW 2751, Australia (office). *Telephone:* (2) 9772-6709 (office). *Fax:* (2) 9772-6733 (office). *E-mail:* gail.jones@uws.edu.au (office). *Website:* www.uws.edu.au/writing_society/writing_and_society (office).

JONES, Gwyneth Ann, (Ann Halam), BA; British writer and critic; b. 14 Feb. 1952, Manchester, England; d. of the late Desmond Jones and Rita Jones (née Dugdale); m.; one s. *Education:* Univ. of Sussex. *Publications:* novels: Divine Endurance 1984, Escape Plans 1986, The Hidden Ones 1988, Kairos 1988, White Queen 1991, Flowerdust 1993, North Wind 1994, Seven Tales and a Fable 1995, Phoenix Cafe 1997, Bold as Love 2001, Castles Made of Sand 2002, Midnight Lamp 2003, Band of Gypsys 2004, Life 2004, Rainbow Bridge 2006, Spirit 2008; criticism: Deconstructing The Starships – Science Fiction and Reality 1999, Imagination/Space 2009; juvenile: The Haunting of Jessica Raven 1997, Don't Open Your Eyes (illustrator) 2000; other: Identifying the Object – A Collection of Short Stories 1993, Grazing the Long Acre (short stories) 2009, The Universe of Things (short stories) 2011; as Ann Halam: novels: Ally Ally Aster 1981, The Alder Tree 1982, King Death's Garden 1986, The Daymaker 1987, Transformations 1988, The Skybreaker 1990, Dinosaur Junction 1991, The Haunting of Jessica Raven 1993, The Fear Man 1995, The Powerhouse – A Horror Story 1997, Crying in the Dark 1998, The N.I.M.R.O.D. Conspiracy 1999, Don't Open Your Eyes 2000, The Shadow on the Stairs 2000, Dr Franklin's Island 2001, Taylor Five 2002, Finders Keepers 2004, Siberia 2005, The Visitor 2006, Snakehead 2007; contrib. to Wild Hearts in Uniform, in Fictions (ed Darko Suvin) 2005. *Honours:* two World Fantasy Awards, BFSA Short Story Award, Tiptree Award 1992, Arthur C. Clarke Award 2001; as Ann Halam: Children of the Night Award 1995, W Sussex Book Award 2001, Philip K. Dick Award 2004, Pilgrim Award 2008. *Literary Agent:* c/o David Higham Associates, 5–8 Lower John Street, Golden Square, London, W1F 9HA, England. *Telephone:* (20) 7434-5900. *Fax:* (20) 7437-1072. *E-mail:* dha@davidhigham.co.uk. *Website:* www.davidhigham.co.uk. *E-mail:* gwyneth.jones@ntlworld.com (home). *Website:* www.boldaslove.co.uk; homepage.ntlworld.com/gwynethann.

JONES, Ivor Wynne; British journalist, author and lecturer; b. 28 March 1927, Liverpool, England; m. Marion-Jeannette Wrighton 1958, one s. one d. *Education:* Caernarfon Grammar School and BBC Engineering Training School. *Career:* co-founder of broadcasting in Cyprus; Ed. Caernarvon and Denbigh Herald 1953; Columnist 1955–, Welsh Political Correspondent 1969–92, Chief Welsh Correspondent 1980–92, Liverpool Daily Post; Research Ed. Llechwedd Slate Caverns, Blaenau Ffestiniog 1972–; mem. Yr Academi Gymreig (Welsh Acad.), Royal Historical Soc., Lewis Carroll Soc., UK, Lewis Carroll Soc. of North America, Lewis Carroll Soc. of Japan. *Publications:* Money for All 1969, Arian I Bawb 1969, Betws-y-coed, The Mountain Resort 1972, Shipwrecks of North Wales 1973, Betws-y-coed and the Conway Valley 1974, Llandudno, Queen of the Welsh Resorts 1975, America's Secret War in Welsh Waters 1976, Luftwaffe Over Clwyd 1977, U-Boat Rendezvous at Llandudno 1978, Minstrels and Miners 1986, Wales and Israel 1988, Baden-Powell, The Welsh Dimension 1992, The Order of St John in Wales 1993, Colwyn Bay: A Brief History 1995, Gold, Frankenstein and Manure 1997, BFBS Cyprus 1948–98 1998, Alice's Welsh Wonderland 1999, Wilder Wales 2001, Llandudno Queen of Welsh Resorts 2002, Victorian Slate Mining 2003, The Cairo Eisteddfod 2003, Money Galore 2003; contrib. to various historical journals. *Honours:* European Architectural Year Book Design Award 1975. *Address:* Pegasus, Llandudno Road, Penrhyn Bay, Llandudno, LL30 3HN, Wales (home).

JONES, J. Farragut (see Levinson, Leonard)

JONES, J. Steve, PhD; British geneticist and writer; *Professor of Genetics, University College London;* b. 24 March 1944, Aberystwyth, Wales. *Education:* Wirral Grammar School, studied in Edinburgh and Chicago. *Career:* currently Prof. of Genetics, Univ. Coll. London; UCL representative to London Regional Science Centre; Pres. Galton Inst.; several visiting professorships, including Harvard Univ., Univ. of Chicago, Univ. of California at Davis, Univ. of Botswana, Fourah Bay Coll., Sierra Leone and Flinders Univ., Adelaide. *Radio and television includes:* gave Reith Lectures on 'The Language of the Genes' 1991, Blue Skies (BBC Radio 3), In the Blood (six-part TV series on human genetics) 1996. *Publications:* Genetics for Beginners (with B. van Loon) 1991, The Cambridge Encyclopedia of Human Evolution (ed. with R. D. Martin, D. Pilbeam) 1992, The Language of the Genes (Rhone-Poulenc Book Prize, Yorkshire Post First Book Prize 1994) 1993, In The Blood 1995, Almost like a Whale: The Origin of Species Updated (aka Darwin's Ghost) 1999, Y: The Descent of Men 2002, The Single Helix: A Turn Around the World of Science 2005; also around 100 scientific papers in a variety of journals and contrib. column, View from the Lab, to The Daily Telegraph. *Honours:* Royal Soc. Faraday Medal for public understanding of science 1997, BP Natural World Book Prize 1999, 2000, Inst. of Biology Charter Medal 2002. *Address:* Department of Biology, University College London, Gower Street, London, WC1E 6BT, England (office). *E-mail:* j.s.jones@ucl.ac.uk (office). *Website:* www.ucl.ac.uk/biology/academic-staff/jones/jones.htm (office).

JONES, Joanna (see Burke, John Frederick)

JONES, J(on) Sydney, BA; American writer and teacher; b. 6 April 1948, Britton, SD. *Education:* Williamette University, University of Oregon, University of Vienna, Austria. *Career:* Journalist, 1971–76; Instructor, English as a Second Language and Writing, 1977–; mem. American Society of Journalists and Authors; Authors' Guild. *Publications:* Bike and Hike: Sixty Tours around Great Britain and Ireland, 1977; Vienna Inside-Out: Sixteen Walking Tours, 1979; Hitler in Vienna, 1983; Tramping in Europe: A Walking Guide, 1984; Viennawalks, 1985; Time of the Wolf, 1990; The Hero Game, 1992; Frankie, 1997. Contributions: articles to over 100 newspapers in the USA and Europe. *Literary Agent:* Evan Marshall, 6 Tristam Place, Pine Brook, NJ 07058, USA. *E-mail:* sjones@cats.ucsc.edu.

JONES, Julia; British writer and dramatist; b. 27 March 1923, Liverpool, England; m. Edmund Bennett 1950, one s. one d. *Education:* RADA, London. *Career:* mem. Dramatist Club, Writers' Guild of Great Britain. *Publications:* The Navigators 1986; over 50 plays for stage, film, radio and television. *Honours:* Prague Television Festival First Prize for Drama 1970.

JONES, Lloyd; New Zealand writer and publisher; b. 23 March 1955, Lower Hutt. *Education:* Victoria Univ. of Wellington. *Career:* f. The Four Winds Press 2002. *Publications:* fiction: Gilmore's Dairy 1985, Splinter 1988, Swimming to Australia and Other Stories 1991, Biografi: An Albanian Quest 1993, This House Has Three Walls (three novellas) 1997, Choo Woo 1998, Book of Fame (Deutz Medal for Fiction 2001) 2000, Here at the End of the World We Learn to Dance 2002, Napoleon and the Chicken Farmer (Honour Award, NZ Post Book Awards for Children and Young Adults 2004) 2003, Paint Your Wife 2004, Everything You Need to Know About the World by Simon Eliot (juvenile) 2004, Mister Pip (Commonwealth Writers' Prize, South East Asia and South Pacific Region and Overall Winner 2007, Montana Medal for Fiction 2007, Kiriyama Prize for Fiction 2008) 2006, Hand Me Down World 2010; other: Into the Field of Play: New Zealand Writers on the Theme of Sport (ed.) 1992, Last Saturday (essay) 1994; contrib. to Landfall, Listener, Sport, New Zealand Herald, Booknotes. *Honours:* Hon. DLitt 2008; Katherine Mansfield Memorial Fellowship 1988, Creative New Zealand Berlin Writers' Residency 2007, Arts Foundation of New Zealand Laureate 2008. *Literary Agent:* c/o Lutyens and Rubinstein, 231 Westbourne Park Road, London, W11 1EB, England. *Telephone:* (20) 7792-4855. *Fax:* (20) 7792-4833. *E-mail:* info@lutyensrubinstein.co.uk. *Website:* www.lutyensrubinstein.co.uk.

JONES, Madison Percy, BA, MA; American writer and academic (retd); b. 21 March 1925, Nashville, TN; m. Shailah McEvilley 1951, three s. two d. *Education:* Vanderbilt Univ., Univ. of Florida. *Career:* Instructor, Miami Univ. of Ohio 1953–54, Univ. of Tennessee 1955–56; Prof. of English and Writer-in-Residence, Auburn Univ. 1956–87; mem. Alabama Acad. of Distinguished Authors, Fellowship of Southern Writers. *Publications:* The Innocent 1957, Forest of the Night 1960, A Buried Land 1963, An Exile 1967, A Cry of Absence 1971, Passage Through Gehenna 1978, Season of the Stranger 1983, Last Things 1989, To the Winds 1996, Nashville 1864: The Dying of the Light 1997, Herod's Wife 2003, The Adventures of Douglas Bragg 2008; contrib. to journals and magazines. *Honours:* Sewanee Review Writing Fellowship 1954–55, Rockefeller Foundation Fellowship 1968, Alabama Library Asscn Book Award 1968, Guggenheim Fellowship 1973–74, Sewanee Review Lytle Annual Short Story Prize 1994, Ingersol Foundation T. S. Eliot Award 1998, US Civil War Center Michael Shaara Award 1998, Alabama Arts Foundation Harper Lee Award 1999. *Address:* 800 Kuderna Acres, Auburn, AL 36832, USA (home). *Telephone:* (334) 887-6380 (home). *E-mail:* madisonjones@bellsouth.net (home).

JONES, Malcolm Vince, BA, PhD; British professor of Slavonic studies and writer; *Professor Emeritus of Slavonic Studies, University of Nottingham;* b. 7 Jan. 1940, Stoke-sub-Hamdon, Somerset, England; s. of Reginald Cross Jones and Winifred Ethel Jones; m. Jennifer Rosemary Durrant 1963; one s. one d. *Education:* Univ. of Nottingham. *Career:* Prof. Emer. of Slavonic Studies, Univ. of Nottingham; Hon. mem. British Asscn for Slavonic and East European Studies (Vice-Pres. 1988–91), British Univs' Asscn of Slavists (Pres. 1986–88), Int. Dostoyevsky Soc. (Pres. 1995–98, Hon. Pres. 2010–). *Publications:* Dostoyevsky: The Novel of Discord 1976, New Essays on Tolstoy (ed.) 1978, New Essays on Dostoyevsky (co-ed. with Garth M. Terry) 1983, Dostoyevsky After Bakhin 1990, The Cambridge Companion to the Classic Russian Novel (co-ed. with Robin Feuer Miller) 1998, Dostoevsky and the Dynamics of Religious Experience 2005, Slavianskii mir, the story of Slavonic Studies at the University of Nottingham 2009; contribs to scholarly journals in many countries. *Address:* Department of Russian and Slavonic Studies, University of Nottingham, University Park, Nottingham, NG7 2RD, England (office). *Telephone:* (115) 928-3392 (home). *E-mail:* malcolmvjones@btinternet.com (home).

JONES, Marie, OBE; Northern Irish playwright and actress; b. 1951, Belfast; three c. *Career:* co-founder, writer-in-residence, Charabanc Theatre Co. 1983–90; co-founder, Double Joint Theatre Co. 1991. *Film appearances include:* In the Name of the Father, Best, Rebel Heart. *Plays:* Lay Up Your Ends 1983, Oul' Delf and False Teeth 1984, Now You're Talking 1985, Gold on the Streets 1986, Girls in the Big Picture 1987, Somewhere over the Balcony 1988, Under Napoleon's Nose 1988, The Hamster Wheel 1990, Weddings Wee'ins and Wakes 1990, The Government Inspector (adaptation of Gogol) 1994, A Night in November 1994, Ethel Workman is Innocent 1995, Women on the Verge of HRT 1996, A Night to Remember 1998, Stones in his Pockets

1999, The Blind Fiddler 2000, A Very Weird Manner 2003, The Blood of the Lamb 2007. *Writing for television:* Tribes 1990, The Hamster Wheel 1991, Fighting the Shadows 1992, Wingnut and the Sprog 1994. *Honours:* Hon. DLitt (Queen's Belfast, Ulster); Evening Standard Award for Best West End Comedy, John Hewitt Award, Olivier Award, Irish Times Theatre Award, Glasgow Mayfest Award. *Telephone:* (20) 7393-4400. *E-mail:* ben@curtisbrown.co.uk.

JONES, Michael Frederick; British journalist; b. 3 July 1937, Gloucester, Glos.; s. of Glyn F. Jones and Elizabeth Jones (née Coopey); m. Sheila Dawes 1959; three s. *Education:* Crypt Grammar School, Gloucester. *Career:* reporter on prov. newspapers 1956–64; Financial Times 1964–65; Daily Telegraph 1965–67; Business News Asst Ed. The Times 1967–70; Man. Ed. The Asian, Hong Kong 1971; News Ed. Sunday Times 1972, Political Corresp. 1975, Political Ed. 1984, Assoc. Ed. 1990–95, Assoc. Ed. (Politics) 1995–2002; Chair. Parl. Press Gallery, House of Commons 1989–91; Media Adviser, Memorial to the Women of World War II Cttee, London 2004–05; Visiting Fellow, Goldsmith's Coll., Univ. of London 2000–02; currently Research Asst to Baroness Boothroyd, House of Lords. *Publication:* Betty Boothroyd: The Autobiography (collaborated) 2001. *Address:* 43 Hillview Road, Orpington, Kent, BR6 0SE, England (home). *Telephone:* (1689) 820796 (home). *E-mail:* micjon1937@hotmail.com (home).

JONES, Richard Andrew, III, BA, MA, MFA; American academic, poet, writer and editor; *Professor of English, DePaul University*; b. 8 Aug. 1953, London, England; s. of Richard Jones and Flora Jones; m. Dr Laura Stahl Jones; two s. one d. *Education:* Univ. of Virginia, Vermont Coll. *Career:* Prof. of English, DePaul Univ. 1987–. *Publications:* Windows and Walls 1982, Poetry and Politics (ed.) 1984, Innocent Things 1985, The Inward Eye: The Photographs of Ed Roseberry (ed., with S. Margulies) 1986, Walk On 1986, Country of Air 1986, Sonnets 1990, At Last We Enter Paradise 1991, A Perfect Time 1994, The Abandoned Garden 1997, 48 Questions 1998, The Last Believer in Words (ed.) 1998, The Stone It Lives On 1999, They Say This (ed.), The Blessing: New and Selected Poems 2000, Who are the Rich and Where do they Live? (ed.), Apropos of Nothing 2006, The Correct Spelling and Exact Meaning 2010; contrib. to numerous publications. *Honours:* Swedish Writers' Union Excellence Prize 1982, Co-ordinating Council of Literary Magazines Eds' Award 1985, and Citation of Special Commendation 1988, Council for Wisconsin Writers Posner Award for Best Book of Poetry 1986, Illinois Arts Council Awards 1991, 1995, 1996, 1997, 2000, 2002, Soc. of Midland Authors Award for Best Book of Poetry 2000, Via Sapentia Lifetime Achievement Award 2000. *Literary Agent:* Copper Canyon Press, PO Box 271, Port Townsend, WA 98368, USA. *Telephone:* (360) 385-4925. *E-mail:* michael@coppercanyonpress.org. *Website:* www.coppercanyonpress.org. *Address:* c/o Department of English, DePaul University, 802 W Belden Avenue, Chicago, IL 60614, USA (office). *Website:* www.poetryeast.org (office).

JONES, Robert (Bobi) Maynard, BA, MA, PhD, DLitt, FBA; Welsh academic and writer; *Professor Emeritus, University of Wales, Aberystwyth*; b. 20 May 1929, Cardiff; m. Anne Elizabeth James 1952; one s. one d. *Education:* Univ. of Wales, Cardiff. *Career:* Lecturer, Trinity Coll., Carmarthen 1956–58; Lecturer, Univ. of Wales, Aberystwyth 1959–67, Sr Lecturer to Reader 1967–79, Prof. of Welsh and Head of Dept 1980–89, Prof. Emer. 1989–; Chair. Yr Academi Gymreig 1975–79. *Publications:* Y Gân Gyntaf 1956, Nid yw Dŵr Yn Plygu 1958, Rhwng Taf A Thaf 1960, Allor Wydn 1971, Tafod Y Llenor 1974, Llên Cymru A Chrefydd 1977, Seiliau Beirniadaeth 1984–85, Hunllef Arthur 1986, Llenyddiaeth Gymraeg 1902–1936 1987, Selected Poems 1987, Casgliad o Gerddi 1989, Crio Chwerthin 1990, Cyfriniaeth Gymraeg 1994, Canu Arnaf 1994, 1995, Ysbryd Y Cwlwm 1998, Ynghylch Tawelwch 1998, Tair Rhamant Arthuraidd 1998, O'r Bedd i'r Crud 2000, Mawl a'i Gyfeillion 2000, Mawl a Gelynion ei Elynion 2002, Ôl Troed 2003, Beirniadaeth Gyfansawdd 2003, Rhy Iach 2004, Y Fadarchen Hudol 2005, Meddwl y Gynghanedd 2005, Yr Amhortreadwy 2009. *Honours:* Hon. Pres., Yr Academi Gymreig 2010; Welsh Arts Council Prizes 1956, 1959, 1971, 1987, 1990, 1998. *Address:* Tandderwen, Ffordd Llanbadarn, Aberystwyth, SY23 1HB, Wales (home). *Telephone:* (1970) 623603 (home). *Fax:* (1970) 623603 (home). *E-mail:* rjones34@btinternet.com (home).

JONES, Rodney, BA, MFA; American poet and writer; *Professor of English and Distinguished Scholar, Southern Illinois University at Carbondale*; b. 11 Feb. 1950, Hartselle, Ala; m. 1st Virginia Kremza 1972 (divorced 1979); m. 2nd Gloria Nixon de Zepeda 1981, two c. *Education:* University of Alabama, University of North Carolina at Greensboro. *Career:* currently Prof. of English and Distinguished Scholar, Southern Illinois Univ. at Carbondale; mem. Associated Writing Programs, MLA. *Publications include:* Going Ahead, Looking Back 1977, The Story They Told Us of Light 1980, The Unborn 1985, Transparent Gestures 1989, Apocalyptic Narrative and Other Poems 1993, Things that Happen Once 1996, Elegy for the Southern Drawl (Southeast Booksellers Asscn Award) 1999, Kingdom of the Instant Poems 2004, Salvation Blues: 100 Poems, 1985–2005 (Kingsley Tuft Award 2007) 2006, Imaginary Logic 2011; numerous contribs to journal and periodicals. *Honours:* Lavan Younger Poets Award, Acad. of American Poets 1986, Younger Writers Award, General Electric Foundation 1986, Jean Stein Prize, American Acad. and Institute of Arts and Letters 1989, National Book Critics Circle Award 1989, Harper Lee Award 2003. *Address:* Department of English, Faner Hall 2225, Mail Code 4503, Southern Illinois University, 1000 Faner Drive, Carbondale, IL 62901, USA (office). *Telephone:* (618) 453-6841 (office). *E-mail:* rodjones@siu.edu (office). *Website:* www.siuc.edu (office).

JONES, Russell Celyn, MA; British novelist and critic; *Professor of Creative Writing, Birkbeck College, London*; b. 1955, Swansea, Wales; one s. two d. *Education:* Univ. of London and Iowa Univ., USA. *Career:* Lecturer in Creative Writing, Univ. of East Anglia, Univ. of Warwick, Western Cape Univ., South Africa; Prof. in Creative Writing, Birkbeck Coll., London 2003–, Chair. in Creative Writing 2006–; book reviewer, The Times; mem. Judging Panel, John Llewellyn Rhys Prize 1998, Booker Prize 2002, Royal Soc. of Litaerature Ondaatji Prize; Dir Soc. of Authors 2004–07. *Publications:* novels: Soldiers and Innocents 1990, Small Times 1992, An Interference of Light 1995, The Eros Hunter 1998, Surface Tension 2001, Ten Seconds from the Sun 2005; short fiction in anthologies: Time Out Book of New York Stories 1997, The Ex-Files 1998, Time Out Book of London Short Stories 2000, Summer Magic 2003, Journey to the Sea 2005; non-fiction: Dylan Thomas's Wales, The Atlas of Literature (ed. Malcolm Bradbury) 1996, Standards in Creative Writing Teaching, The Creative Writing Coursebook 2001. *Honours:* Fellowships at Iowa Univ., USA, Univ. of E Anglia; David Higham Prize for Best First Novel 1990, Welsh Arts Council Fiction Award 1991, Soc. of Authors Award 1996. *Literary Agent:* c/o AP Watt Ltd, 20 John Street, London, WC1N 2DR, England. *Telephone:* (20) 7405-6774. *Fax:* (20) 7831-2154. *E-mail:* apw@apwatt.co.uk. *Website:* www.apwatt.co.uk. *Address:* School of English and Humanities, Birkbeck, University of London, Malet Street, London, WC1E 7HX, England (office). *Telephone:* (20) 7679-1063 (office). *E-mail:* r.jones@bbk.ac.uk (office).

JONES, Sadie; British writer and screenwriter; b. London, England; d. of Evan Jones and Joanna Jones; m. Tim Boyd; two c. *Education:* Godolphin and Latymer School, London, Bath Tech. Coll. *Publications:* novels: The Outcast (Costa Book Award for First Novel) 2008, Small Wars 2009, The Uninvited Guests 2012. *Literary Agent:* c/o Felicity Bryan Literary Agency, 2A North Parade Avenue, Oxford, OX2 6LX, England. *Telephone:* (1865) 513816. *Fax:* (1865) 310055. *E-mail:* agency@felicitybryan.com. *Website:* www.felicitybryan.com.

JONES, Sally Roberts, BA; British author and publisher; *Publisher, Alun Books*; b. 30 Nov. 1935, London, England. *Education:* Univ. Coll. of North Wales, North-Western Polytechnic, Swansea Univ. *Career:* Sr Asst Reference Library, London Borough of Havering 1964–67; Reference Librarian, Borough of Port Talbot, Wales 1967–70; Publr Alun Books 1977–; Royal Literary Fund Fellow, Univ. of Wales, Swansea 1999–2009; Chair. Port Talbot Historical Soc.; Pres. Allen Raine Celebration Soc.; Sec. Cymdeithas Owain Glyn Dwr. *Publications include:* Turning Away 1969, Elen and the Goblin 1977, The Forgotten Country 1977, Books of Welsh Interest 1977, Allen Raine 1979, Relative Values 1985, The History of Port Talbot 1991, Pendarvis 1992, Kiki is Not Well 2005, Notes for a Life 2010. *Honours:* Welsh Arts Council Literature Prize 1970. *Address:* 3 Crown Street, Port Talbot, SA13 1BG, Wales (office). *E-mail:* srjones@alunbooks.co.uk (office).

JONG, Erica Mann, BA, MA; American writer and poet; b. 26 March 1942, New York, NY; d. of Seymour Mann and Eda Mann (née Mirsky); m. 1st Michael Werthman 1963 (divorced 1965); m. 2nd Allan Jong 1966 (divorced 1975); m. 3rd Jonathan Fast 1977 (divorced 1983); one d.; m. 4th Kenneth David Burrows 1989. *Education:* Barnard Coll. and Columbia Univ., New York; studied poetry with Mark Strand and Stanley Kunitz. *Career:* Lecturer in English, City Coll. of New York 1965–66, 1969–70; Poetry Instructor, Poetry Center of the 92nd Street Y 1966–69; Lecturer in English, Overseas Div., Univ. of Md, Heidelberg, Germany 1970–72; Bread Loaf Writers Conf., Middlebury, Vt 1970–73; mem. Literature Panel, NY State Council on Arts 1972–74; mem. of Faculty, Salzburg Seminar, Austria 1993; Visiting Writer, Ben Gurion Univ., Beersheva, Israel 1998, Bennington Coll. 1998, Marymount Coll. Writers Workshop Poetry Seminar 2007. *Publications:* poetry: Fruits and Vegetables 1971, Half-Lives 1973, Loveroot 1975, At the Edge of the Body 1979, Ordinary Miracles 1983, Becoming Light: Poems New and Selected 1991, Love Comes First 2009; novels: Fear of Flying 1973, How to Save Your Own Life 1977, Fanny: Being the True History of Fanny Hackabout-Jones 1980, Parachutes and Kisses 1984, Serenissima: A Novel of Venice (aka Shylock's Daughter: A Novel of Love in Venice) 1987, Any Woman's Blues 1990, Inventing Memory: A Novel of Mothers and Daughters 1997, Sappho's Leap 2004; non-fiction: Witches 1981, Megan's Book of Divorce (for children) 1984, The Devil at Large: Erica Jong on Henry Miller 1993, Fear of Fifty: A Midlife Memoir 1994, Composer Zipless: Songs of Abandon from the Erotic Poetry of Erica Jong 1995, What Do Women Want? Bread. Roses. Sex. Power. 1998, Seducing the Demon: Writing for my Life 2006. *Honours:* Hon. Fellow (Welsh Coll. of Music and Drama) 1994; New York State Council on the Arts Grants 1971, Nat. Endowment of the Arts grant 1973; Hon. PhD (CUNY) 2006; Acad. of American Poets Prize 1971, Poetry magazine Bess Hokin Prize 1971, Poetry Soc. of America Alice Faye di Castagnola Award 1972, Freud Award for Literature, Italy 1975, UN Award for Excellence in Literature 1995, Prix Littéraire de Deauville Film Festival (France) 1998, Fernanda Pivano Award for Literature (Italy) 2009. *Address:* 205 East 68th Street, Suite T3G, New York, NY 10021, USA. *Telephone:* (212) 517-2907. *Fax:* (212) 517-6478. *Website:* www.ericajong.com.

JOOLZ (see Denby, Joolz)

JORDAN, Leonard (see Levinson, Leonard)

JORDAN, Neil Patrick, BA; Irish writer and film director; b. 25 Feb. 1950, Sligo; three s. two d. *Education:* St Paul's Coll. Raheny, Dublin and Univ. Coll., Dublin. *Career:* co-f. Irish Writers' Co-operative, Dublin 1974. *Films* *directed:* Angel 1982, Company of Wolves 1984, Mona Lisa 1986, High Spirits 1988, We're No Angels 1989, The Miracle 1990, The Crying Game 1992, Interview with the Vampire 1994, Michael Collins (Golden Lion, Venice 1996) 1995, The Butcher Boy 1997, In Dreams 1999, The End of the Affair 1999, Not I 2000, The Good Thief 2002, Breakfast on Pluto (Best Dir, Best Writer, IFTA 2007) 2005, The Brave One 2007, Ondine 2009. *Television includes:* The Borgias (series) 2011. *Publications:* Night in Tunisia and Other Stories (Guardian Fiction Award 1979) 1976, The Past 1979, The Dream of a Beast 1983, Sunrise with Sea Monster 1994, Nightlines 1995, Shade (novel) 2004, Mistaken 2011. *Honours:* Dr hc (Univ. Coll. Dublin) 2005; London Film Critics' Circle Award 1984, London Evening Standard Most Promising Newcomer Award 1982, Los Angeles Film Critics' Circle Award 1992, NY Film Critics' Circle Award 1992, Writers Guild of America Award 1992, BAFTA Awards 1992, 2000, Golden Lion, Venice Film Festival 1996, Silver Bear, Berlin Film Festival 1997, Irish Film and Television Awards (IFTA) 2003, Gemini Awards 2011. *E-mail:* pa@neiljordan.com (office). *Address:* 6 Sorrento Terrace, Dalkey, Co. Dublin, Ireland.

JOSE, Francisco Sionil; Philippine writer, social activist and publisher; b. 3 Dec. 1924, Rosales; m. Teresita 1949. *Education:* Univ. of Santo Tomas. *Career:* fmr journalist and ed. The Commonwealth, United States Information Service, The Manila Times Sunday Magazine, Progress, Comment, Manila; Man. Ed. The Asia Magazine, Hong Kong 1961–62; Information Officer The Colombo Plan, Sri Lanka 1962–64; correspondent The Economist 1968–69; f. of publishing house, Solidaridad 1965–, journal Solidarity 1966–, Chair. Solidarity Foundation 1987–; fmr Lecturer Univ. of The Philippines, Manila, De La Salle Univ., Manila, Far Eastern Univ., Manila, Univ. of Santo Tomas, Univ. of Calif. at Berkeley, USA; writer-in-residence Nat. Univ. of Singapore 1987, Stanford Univ., USA 2005; founder and nat. sec. PEN (Philippines branch). *Publications:* novels: Rosales Saga: The Pretenders 1962, Tree 1978, My Brother, My Executioner 1979, Two Filipino Women 1981, Mass 1982, Po-on (Dusk) 1984, Ermita 1988, Gagamba 1991, Three Filipino Women 1992, Viajero 1993, Sin 1994, Sins 1996, Ben Sinngkol 2002; short story collections: The God Stealer and Other Stories 1968, Waywaya, Eleven Filipino Short Stories 1980, Platinum, Ten Filipino Stories 1983, Olvidon and Other Short Stories 1988, Puppy Love 1999, The Molave and the Orchid 2004; poetry: Questions 1988; non-fiction: In Search of the Word: Selected Essays of F. Sionil Jose, We Filipinos: Our Moral Malaise, Our Moral Heritage 1999; editor: Equinox I 1965, Asian PEN Anthology 1966, A Filipino Agenda for the 21st Century 1987. *Honours:* Order of Sacred Treasure, Japan 2001; Hon. PhD (Univ. of the Philippines, Manila) 1992, (De La Salle Univ., Manila) 1995, (Far Eastern Univ., Manila) 2000; three Nat. Press Club Annual Journalism Awards, three first prizes Palanca Annual Award for the English Short Story, City of Manila Award for Literature 1979, Cultural Centre of the Philippines Novel Award 1979, Literature Award (Gawad para sa Sining) 1989, Ramon Magsaysay Award for Journalism, Literature and Creative Communication Arts 1980, Tawid Award for Literature 1980, Palanca Annual Award for the English Novel 1981, National Artist for Literature, The Philippines 2001, Pablo Neruda Award, Chile 2004. *Address:* Solidariad Publishing House, 531 Padre Faura, Ermita, Manila, The Philippines (office). *Telephone:* (2) 523-0870 (office). *Fax:* (2) 525-5038 (office). *E-mail:* soli@skyinet.net (office).

JOSEPH, Ammu, BA, BSc; Indian journalist; *Co-ordinator, Network of Women in Media*; d. of Dr K. C. Joseph and Anna Joseph. *Education:* Women's Christian Coll., Chennai, Syracuse Univ., New York, USA. *Career:* fmr Asst Ed. Eve's Weekly 1977; fmr Magazine Ed. The India Post; Visiting Lecturer in Journalism, Sophia Coll. Polytechnic 1981–85–; Visiting Prof., Asian Coll. of Journalism, Chennai 2000–03; currently teaching at Convergence Inst. of Media Man. and Information Tech. Studies, Bangalore; Press Fellow, Wolfson Coll., Univ. of Cambridge, UK 1988; Media Fellow, Nat. Foundation for India 1995; columnist for The Hindu's Young World 1996–, India Together; Editorial Consultant for Voices for Change (quarterly); freelance writer for various publs; Co-founder Network of Women in Media, currently Co-ordinator; Regional Co-ordinator for South Asia, Int. Women's Media Foundation Global Report on Women in the News Media. *Publications include:* Whose News? The Media and Women's Issues (co-author and co-editor) 1994, Women in Journalism: Making News 2000, Terror, Counter-Terror: Women Speak Out (co-editor) 2003, Storylines: Conversations with Women Writers 2003, Just Between Us: Women Speak about their Writing 2003. *Honours:* Donna Allen Award, Comm. of the Status of Women of the Asoc. for Educ. in Journalism and Mass Communication 2003. *Address:* c/o Convergence Institute of Media, Management and Information Technology Studies, #7, IV Main, Tavarekere Main Road, Bangalore 560 029, Karnataka, India. *E-mail:* ammujo2003@yahoo.co.in. *Website:* www.nwmindia.org.

JOSEPH, Jenny, BA, FRSL; British writer, poet and lecturer; b. 7 May 1932, Birmingham, England; m. C. A. Coles 1961 (died 1985); one s. two d. *Education:* St Hilda's Coll., Oxford. *Career:* mem. council Nat. Poetry Soc. of Great Britain 1975–78. *Publications:* The Unlooked-for Season 1960, 'Warning' 1961, Boots 1966, Rose in the Afternoon 1974, The Thinking Heart 1978, Beyond Descartes 1983, Persephone 1986, The Inland Sea 1989, Beached Boats 1991, Selected Poems 1992, Ghosts and Other Company 1995, Extended Similes 1997, Warning 1997, All the Things I See (poems for children) 2000, Led by the Nose: a garden of smells 2002, Extreme of Things 2006, Nothing Like Love 2009; contrib. to anthologies and magazines. *Honours:* Eric Gregory Award 1962, Cholmondeley Award 1974, Arts Council of Great Britain Award 1975, James Tait Black Memorial Prize for Fiction 1986, Soc. of Authors Travelling Scholarship 1995, Forward Prize 1995. *Literary Agent:* c/o Johnson & Alcock Ltd, Clerkenwell House, 45–47 Clerkenwell Green, London, EC1R 0HT, England. *Address:* 17 Windmill Road, Minchinhampton, Gloucestershire, GL6 9DX, England (home). *Telephone:* (1453) 886311 (office). *Fax:* (1453) 886311 (office).

JOSEPH, Lawrence, BA, JD, MA; American poet, essayist, critic and academic; b. 10 March 1948, Detroit, Mich.; m. 1976. *Education:* University of Michigan, University of Cambridge, UK. *Career:* Law Clerk, Michigan Supreme Court, Justice G. Mennen Williams; Litigator, Shearman Sterling, New York City; Creative Writing Prof., Princeton University; Prof. of Law, St John's University School of Law, Jamaica, New York 1987–; mem. PEN American Centre, Poetry Society of America, Poets House, National Writers Voice. *Publications include:* Shouting at No One, 1983; Curriculum Vitae, 1988; Before Our Eyes, 1993; Lawyerland: What Lawyers Talk about When They Talk about Law, 1997; contributions: Paris Review; Nation; Village Voice; Partisan Review; Poetry; Boulevard; Kenyon Review. *Honours:* Hopwood Award for Poetry, 1970; Agnes Lynch Starrett Poetry Prize, 1982; National Endowment for the Arts Poetry Award, 1984; Fellowship, University of Cambridge.

JOSIPOVICI, Gabriel David, BA, FRSL, FBA; British novelist, dramatist, critic and academic; b. 8 Oct. 1940, Nice, France; s. of Jean Josipovici and Sacha Rabinovitch. *Education:* St Edmund Hall, Oxford. *Career:* Lord Northcliffe Lecturer, Univ. of London 1981; Weidenfeld Visiting Prof. of Comparative Literature, Univ. of Oxford 1996–97. *Plays:* Dreams of Mrs Fraser, Royal Court 1972, Evdence of Intimacy, Soho Poly 1972, Flow, Edinburgh Lyceum 1973, 1975, Twenty Years, Lyttleton Platform 1978. *Radio:* BBC Radio 3: Playback 1972, AG 1977, A Little Portable Pocket Requiem 1987, Mr Vee 1988. *Publications:* fiction: The Inventory 1968, Words 1971, Mobius the Stripper 1974, The Present 1975, Migrations 1977, The Air We Breathe 1981, Contre-Jour 1986, In the Fertile Land 1987, The Big Glass 1990, In a Hotel Garden 1993, Moo Pak 1994, Now 1997, Goldberg: Variations 2002, Only Joking 2004, Everything Passes 2006, After 2009, Making Mistakes 2009, Heart's Wings 2010, Infinity 2012; essays: The World and the Book 1971, The Lessons of Modernism 1977, The Book of God: A Response to the Bible 1988, Text and Voice 1992, Touch 1996, On Trust 1998, A Life 2000, The Singer on the Shore 2005, Whatever Happened to Modernism? 2010; plays: Dreams of Mrs Frazer 1973, AG 1976, Vergil Dying 1977, Mr Vee 1991; contrib. to Encounter, New York Review of Books, London Review of Books, TLS. *Honours:* South-East Arts Book Award 1978. *Literary Agent:* c/o Johnson & Alcock Ltd, Clerkenwell House, 45–47 Clerkenwell Green, London, EC1R 0HT, England. *Address:* 60 Prince Edwards Road, Lewes, Sussex, BN7 1BH, England (home). *E-mail:* gabriel@josipovici.plus.com.

JOUANNEAU, Joël; French writer and director; b. 7 Nov. 1946, Celle, Loir-et-Cher. *Career:* f. amateur theatre collective, Grand Luxe 1970–; journalist, Révolution early 1980s; Assoc. Artist, Théâtre de Sartrouville 1989–, Co-Dir 1999–2003; teacher, École du Théâtre Nat. de Strasbourg 1992–2000, Conservatoire d'art dramatique, Paris 2000–05. *Plays directed include:* La Dédicace (Théâtre Gérard Phillipe) 1984, L'Hypothèse (Festival d'Avignon) (also film) 1987, Minetti (also film) 1988, Les Enfants Tanner (also film) 1990, En attendant Godot 1991, Au coeur des ténèbres 1992, Le Rayon vert 1994, Compagnie 1995, Fin de partie 1995, L'Idiot 1995, Les Reines 1997, Coriolanus (Théâtre de l'Athénée, Paris) 1998, Juste la fin du monde (Théâtre Vidy Lausanne) 1999, Oh! les beaux jours 2001, Les Trois jours de la queue du dragon (opera for children) 2001, Madame on meurt ici! (Théâtre Vidy Lausanne) 2002, J'étais dans ma maison et j'attendais que la pluie vienne (Théâtre du peuple, Bussang) 2004, Kaddish pour l'enfant qui ne naîtra pas (with Jean-Quentin Châtelain) (Théâtre ouvert de Lucien et Micheline Attoun, Paris) 2004, Embrasser les ombres (Théâtre du Vieux-Colombier – Comédie Française) 2004, Atteintes à sa Vie (Festival d'Automne, Paris) 2008, Sous l'oeil d'Oedipe (Festival d'Avignon) 2010. *Plays written include:* Nuit d'orage sur Gaza 1985, Le Bourrichon (Prix du Syndicat de la critique dramatique et musicale 1989) 1987, Kiki l'Indien 1987, Mamie Ouate en Papouasie (co-writer) 1990, Gauche Uppercut (Prix de la Critique de la SACD) 1991, Le Marin perdue en mer 1992, Le Condor 1994, Opus Allegria 147 (Prix du Syndicat de la Critique 1996) 1993, Dernier Rayon 1998, La Main bleue, Les Dingues de Knoxville 1999, L'Inconsolé 2001, Yeul le jeune 2001, L'Adoptée 2003, L'Ebloui 2004, Sous l'oeil d'Oedipe 2010. *Radio:* Palais de glace (adaptation de Vessas-France Culture 2010) L'enfant cachée dans l'encrier (France-culture 2009). *Films:* as director: L'Hypothèse (Prix spécial du jury du Festival de Riccione, Italy) 1987, Simon Tanner 1993, Endspiel 1996, Les Amants 2005, Mamie Ouate en Papoâsie 2010. *Literary Agent:* c/o L'Eldorado, 28 rue des Dames, 56290 Port-Louis, France. *Address:* 26 rue des Dames, 56290 Port-Louis, France (home). *E-mail:* joeljouanneau@wanadoo.fr (home).

JOYCE, Graham, (William Heaney), BEd, MA, ML, PhD; British writer; b. (Graham William Joyce), 22 Oct. 1954, Keresley, Coventry, England; s. of William Joyce and Josephine Joyce; m. Suzanne Lucy Johnsen 1988; one s. one d. *Education:* Bishop Lonsdale Coll., Univ. of Leicester, Nottingham Trent Univ. *Career:* mem. Soc. of Authors. *Publications:* Dreamside 1991, Dark Sister 1992, House of Lost Dreams 1993, Requiem 1995, The Tooth Fairy 1996, Spiderbite (juvenile) 1997, The Stormwatcher 1998, Indigo 1999, Leningrad Nights (short stories) 2000, Smoking Poppy 2001, The Facts of Life 2003, The Limits of Enchantment 2005, TWOC 2005, Do the Creepy Thing 2006, Three Ways to Snog an Alien (juvenile) 2008, Memoirs of a Master Forger (as

William Heaney) 2008, The Devil's Ladder (juvenile) 2008, Simple Goalkeeping Made Spectacular (non-fiction) 2009, The Silent Land 2010. *Honours:* Hon. MLitt (Derby) 2008; Derleth Awards 1993, 1996, 1997, 1999, 2009, World Fantasy Award 2004, Grand Prix de l'Imaginaire 2004, Angus Award 2006, O. Henry Award 2009. *Literary Agent:* c/o Luigi Bonomi, Luigi Bonomi Associates, 91 Great Russell Street, London, WC1B 3BS, England. *E-mail:* graham@grahamjoyce.net (office). *Website:* www.grahamjoyce.net.

JUDD, Alan, (Holly Budd), FRSL; British writer; b. 1946, Kent, England; m.; one d. *Education:* Univ. of Oxford. *Career:* army, Foreign Office; motoring correspondent, The Spectator. *Publications:* as Alan Judd: A Breed of Heroes 1981, Short of Glory 1984, The Noonday Devil 1987, Tango 1989, Ford Madox Ford 1990, The Devil's Own Work 1991, First World War Poets (with David Crane) 1997, The Quest for 'C': Sir Mansfield Cumming and the Founding of the British Secret Service 1999, Legacy 2001, The Kaiser's Last Kiss 2003, Dancing with Eva 2007, Seabed Fluid Flow: The Impact on Geology, Biology and the Marine Environment (with Martin Hovland) 2009, Uncommon Enemy 2012; as Holly Budd: The Office Life Little Instruction Book 1996. *Honours:* RSL Award 1982, W. H. Heinemann Literature Award 1990, Guardian Fiction Award 1991. *Literary Agent:* David Higham Associates, 5–8 Lower John Street, Golden Square, London, W1F 9HA, England. *Telephone:* (20) 7434-5900. *Fax:* (20) 7437-1072. *E-mail:* dha@davidhigham.co.uk. *Website:* www.davidhigham.co.uk.

JUDD, Denis Onan, BA, PGCE, PhD, FRHistS; British historian and writer; b. 28 Oct. 1938, Byfield, Northants.; m. Dorothy Woolf 1964; three s. one d. *Education:* Univs of Oxford and London. *Career:* awarded professorship 1990; Prof. Emer. of History, London Metropolitan Univ.; Fellow, Royal Historical Soc. *Publications:* Balfour and the British Empire 1968, The Boer War 1977, 2002, Radical Joe: Joseph Chamberlain 1977, Prince Philip 1981, Lord Reading 1982, Alison Uttley 1986, Jawaharlal Nehru 1993, Empire: The British Imperial Experience 1996, The Boer War 2002, The Lion and the Tiger: The Rise and Fall of the British Raj 2004; other: two books for children; other history books and biographies; ed.: The Private Diaries of Alison Uttley 2009; contrib. to History Today, History, Journal of Imperial and Commonwealth History, Literary Review, Daily Telegraph, New Statesman, International Herald Tribune, Independent, BBC History Magazine, Mail on Sunday. *Address:* 20 Mount Pleasant Road, London, NW10 3EL, England (home). *E-mail:* denisjudd@ntlworld.com (home).

JUDSON, John, BA, MFA; American educator, editor, writer and poet; b. 9 Sept. 1930, Stratford, Conn. *Education:* Colby College, University of Maine, University of Iowa. *Career:* Ed., Juniper Press, Northeast/Juniper Books, literary magazine and chapbook series, 1961–; Prof. of English, University of Wisconsin, La Crosse 1965–93. *Publications:* Two From Where It Snows (co-author), 1963; Surreal Songs, 1968; Within Seasons, 1970; Voyages to the Inland Sea, six vols, 1971–76; Finding Worlds in Winter; West of Burnam South of Troy, 1973; Ash Is the Candle's Wick, 1974; Roots from the Onion's Dark, 1978; A Purple Tale, 1978; North of Athens, 1980; Letters to Jirac II, 1980; Reasons Why I Am Not Perfect, 1982; The Carrabassett Sweet William Was My River, 1982; Suite for Drury Pond, 1989; Muse(sic), 1992; The Inardo Poems, 1996.

JUERGENSMEYER, Mark Karl, BA, MDiv, MA, PhD; American academic and writer; *Director, Orfalea Center of Global and International Studies*; b. 13 Nov. 1940, Carlinville, IL; m. Sucheng Chan 1969. *Education:* University of Illinois at Urbana-Champaign, Columbia University, Union Theological Seminary, New York, University of California at Berkeley. *Career:* Lecturer, 1971–72, Dir, Religious Studies Program, 1977–89, University of California at Berkeley; Lecturer, 1973–74, Assoc. Prof., 1974–84, Prof., 1984–89, Dir, Comparative Religion Program, 1984–89, Graduate Theological Union, Berkeley; Distinguished Visiting Prof., University of California at Santa Cruz, 1988; Dean, Asian and Pacific Studies, and Prof. of Religion and Political Science, University of Hawaii, 1989–93; Prof. of Sociology, 1993–, Dir, Orfalea Center of Global and International Studies, 1995–, University of California at Santa Barbara; Chair, Pacific Rim Research Program, University of California System, 1994–97; Halle Distinguished Visiting Prof. of Global Learning, Emory University, 2002. *Publications:* Sikh Studies: Comparative Perspectives on a Changing Tradition (co-ed.), 1979; Religion as Social Vision: The Movement Against Untouchability in 20th-Century Punjab, 1982; Fighting with Gandhi, 1984, revised edn as Gandhi's Way: A Handbook of Conflict Resolution, 2002; Songs of the Saints of India (co-trans.), 1988; Imagining India: Essays on Indian History by Ainslie Embres (ed.), 1989; Teaching the Introductory Course in Religious Studies (ed.), 1991; A Bibliographic Guide to the Comparative Study of Ethics (co-ed.), 1991; Radhasoami Reality: The Logic of a Modern Faith, 1991; Violence and the Sacred in the Modern World (ed.), 1992; The New Cold War?: Religious Nationalism Confronts the Secular State, 1993; Terror in the Mind of God: The Global Rise of Religious Violence, 2000. *Contributions:* Reference works, scholarly books and professional journals. *Honours:* International Fellow, Columbia University, 1963–65; Indo-American Fellowship, India, 1978; American Institute of Indian Studies Senior Research Grants, 1979, 1983, 1985, 1986; Fellow, Woodrow Wilson International Center for Scholars, Washington, DC, 1986; Guggenheim Fellowship, 1988–90; Fellow, United States Institute of Peace, 1989–91; Fellow, ACLS, 1996. *Address:* c/o Global and International Studies, 3042 Humanities and Social Sciences Bldg, University of California at Santa Barbara, Santa Barbara, CA 93106, USA.

JULY, Miranda; American performance artist, filmmaker and writer; b. (Miranda Jennifer Grossinger), 15 Feb. 1974, Barre, Vt; d. of Lindy Hough and Richard Grossinger. *Career:* set up Joanie4Jackie women's film making project 1996; performance art pieces include Love Diamond (with composer Zac Love and artist Jamie Isenstein) 1998, The Swan Tool (with Zac Love and Mitsu Hadeishi) 2000, Things We Don't Understand and Definitely are Not Going To Talk About 2006; f. art website Learning to Love You More with Harrell Fletcher and Yuri Ono 2002. *Art Exhibitions:* has performed at galleries and festivals including New York Video Festival, The Kitchen, Museum of Modern Art, Guggenheim Museum, New York, Whitney Biennial 2002, 2004, Portland Inst. for Contemporary Art, Walker Art Center, Minneapolis, Rotterdam Int. Film Festival, ICA, London. *Films:* short films: Atlanta 1996, Amateurist 1998, Nest of Tens 2000, Getting Stronger Every Day 2001, Haysha Royko 2004; feature film: Me and You and Everyone We Know 2005. *Recordings:* Margie Ruskie Stops Time EP 1996, 10 Million Hours A Mile 1997, Binet-Simon Test 1998. *Publications:* The Boy from Lam Kien (short story) 2005, No One Belongs Here More Than You (short stories) (Frank O'Connor Int. Short Story Award) 2007; contrib. to The Paris Review, Harper's, The New Yorker. *Address:* POB 26596, Los Angeles, CA 90026, USA (office). *E-mail:* secretary@mirandajuly.com (office). *Website:* mirandajuly.com.

JULY, Serge; French journalist; b. 27 Dec. 1942, Paris; one s. *Career:* journalist Clarté 1961–63; Vice-Pres. Nat. Union of Students 1965–66; French teacher Coll. Sainte-Barbe, Paris 1966–68; Asst Leader Gauche prolétarienne 1969–72 (disbanded by the Govt); co-f. newspaper, Libération 1973, Chief Ed. 1973–2006, Publishing Dir 1974–75, Jt Dir 1981, Man. Dir 1987–2006; Reporter Europe 1983; mem. Club de la presse Europe 1976–. *Publications:* Vers la guerre civile (with Alain Geismar and Erlyne Morane) 1969, Dis maman, c'est quoi l'avant-guerre? 1980, Les Années Mitterrand 1986, La Drôle d'Année 1987, Le Salon des artistes 1989, La Diagonale du Golfe 1991, Entre quatre z'yeux (with Alain Juppé).

JUNGER, Sebastian, BA; American author and journalist; b. 1962, Belmont, MA. *Education:* Wesleyan Univ., CT. *Career:* climber and arborist 1989–96; foreign reporter 1996–; author 1997–. *Films:* Restrepo (dir and producer, with Tim Hetherington) (Grand Jury Prize, Sundance Film Festival) 2010. *Publications:* novels: The Perfect Storm 1997, Fire 2001, A Death in Belmont 2006, War 2010; contrib. to Outside, City Paper, American Heritage, Men's Journal, Vanity Fair. *Honours:* Nat. Magazine Award, SAIS-Novartis Award, New England PEN Award 2007. *Address:* c/o Twelve, Grand Central Publishing, 237 Park Avenue, New York, NY 10017, USA (office). *E-mail:* twelve.books@hbgsua.com (office). *Website:* www.twelvebooks.com.

JUNGK, Peter Stephan; American/Austrian writer, translator and filmmaker; b. 19 Dec. 1952, Santa Monica, Calif; s. of Robert Jungk; m Lillian Birnbaum; one d. *Education:* Univ. of California, Los Angeles, American Film Inst. *Career:* Prof. for Germanic Language and Literatures, Washington Univ., St Louis, Mo. *Films:* documentary films for German TV. *Publications:* Stechpalmenwald 1978, Rundgang 1981, Franz Werfel: A Life in Prague, Vienna, and Hollywood 1990, Shabbat: A Rite of Passage in Jerusalem, A Life Torn by History: Franz Werfel 1890–1945 1990, Tigor 1991, Die Unruhe der Stella Federspiel 1996, Die Erbschaft (trans. as The Inheritance) 1999, Der König von Amerika 2001, The Snowflake Constant 2002, The Perfect American 2004, Die Reise über den Hudson (trans. as Crossing the Hudson) 2005, Das elektrische Herz 2011, Le Coeur électrique 2012. *Honours:* Stefan Andres Prize 2001, Literature Prize, Salzburger Wirtschaft 2011. *Literary Agent:* c/o Anna Webber, United Agents, 12–26 Lexington Street, London, W1F 0LE, England. *Telephone:* (20) 3214-0876. *Website:* unitedagents.co.uk. *Address:* 9B rue Michel Chasles, 75012 Paris, France. *Fax:* 1-43-42-26-93 (office); 1-43-45-48-99 (office). *E-mail:* peterjungk@gmail.com (home). *Website:* www.peterstephanjungk.com.

JUNKINS, Donald Arthur, BA, STB, STM, AM, PhD; American poet, writer and academic; b. 19 Dec. 1931, Saugus, Mass; m. 1st; two s. one d.; m. 2nd Kaimei Zheng 1993; one step-s. *Education:* University of Massachusetts, Boston University. *Career:* Instructor, Emerson College, Boston 1961–62, Asst Prof. 1962–63; Asst Prof., Chico State College 1963–66; Asst Prof., University of Massachusetts, Amherst 1966–69, Assoc. Prof. 1969–74, Dir, Master of Fine Arts Program in English 1970–78, 1989–90, Prof. of English 1974–95, Prof. Emeritus, 1995–; mem. PEN, Hemingway Society, Fitzgerald Society. *Publications include:* The Sunfish and the Partridge, 1965; The Graves of Scotland Parish, 1969; Walden, One Hundred Years After Thoreau, 1969; And Sandpipers She Said, 1970; The Contemporary World Poets (ed.), 1976; The Uncle Harry Poems and Other Maine Reminiscences, 1977; Crossing By Ferry: Poems New and Selected, 1978; The Agamenticus Poems, 1984; Playing for Keeps: Poems, 1978–1988, 1989; Andromache, by Euripides (trans.), 1998; Journey to the Corrida, 1998; Lines from Bimini Waters, 1998; contributions: Longman Anthology of American Poetry: Colonial to Contemporary; reviews, journals and magazines. *Honours:* Bread Loaf Writers Conference Poetry Scholarship, 1959; Jennie Tane Award for Poetry, 1968; John Masefield Memorial Award, 1973; National Endowment for the Arts Fellowships, 1974, 1979.

JUNQUEIRA, Ivan; Brazilian poet, journalist and literary critic; b. 3 Nov. 1934, Rio de Janeiro. *Career:* became journalist 1963, worked for several newspapers and periodicals including Tribuna da Imprensa, Correio da Manhã, Jornal do Brasil, O Globo; Advisor Fundacen 1987–90, Funarte 1991–;

Dir UN Information Center, Rio de Janeiro 1970–77; fmr Deputy Ed. and Exec. Ed. Poetry Forever; mem. PEN Club of Brazil, Academia Brasileira de Letras. *Publications include:* poetry: Os Mortos 1964, Três Meditações na Corda Lírica 1977, A Rainha Arcaica 1980, Cinco Movimentos 1982, O Grifo 1987, A Sagração dos Ossos 1994, Poemas Reunidos 1999, Os Melhores Poemas de Ivan Junqueira 2003, Poesia Reunida 2005, O Tempo além do Tempo 2007, O Outro Lado 2007; work appears in numerous anthologies. *Honours:* Cruz e Sousa Medal 1998, Paul Claudel Medal 1999; INL Prêmio Nacional de Poesia 1981, ABL Prêmio Assis Chateaubriand 1985, INL Prêmio Nacional de Ensaísmo Literário 1985, Prêmio da Associação Paulista de Críticos de Arte 1991, Prêmio da Biblioteca Nacional 1992, Prêmio José Sarney de poesia inédita 1994, Prêmio Jabuti, da Câmara Brasileira do Livro 1995, PEN Club of Brazil Prêmio Luísa Cláudio de Sousa 1995, UBE Prêmio Oliveira Lima 1999, UBE Prêmio Jorge de Lima 2000. *Address:* c/o Academia Brasileira de Letras, Av. Presidente Wilson 203, Castelo, Rio de Janeiro, RJ 20030-021, Brazil (office). *Telephone:* (21) 3974-2500 (office). *E-mail:* academia@academia.org.br (office). *Website:* www.academia.org.br (office).

JUST, Ward Swift; American writer; b. 5 Sept. 1935, Michigan City, IN. *Education:* Lake Forest Acad., IL, Cranbrook School, Michigan, Trinity Coll., Hartford, CT. *Career:* reporter, Waukegan News-Sun, IL 1957–59; reporter 1962–63, correspondent 1963–65, Newsweek magazine; correspondent, Washington Post 1965–70; Berlin Prize Fellowship 1998. *Publications:* To What End: Report from Vietnam 1968, A Soldier of the Revolution 1970, Military Men 1970, The Congressmen Who Loved Flaubert and Other Washington Stories 1973, Stringer 1974, Nicholson at Large 1975, A Family Trust 1978, Honor, Power, Riches, Fame and the Love of Women 1979, In the City of Fear 1982, The American Blues 1984, The American Ambassador 1987, Jack Gance 1989, Twenty-One Selected Stories 1990, The Translator 1991, Ambition and Love 1994, Echo House 1997, A Dangerous Friend 1999, Lowell Limpett 2001, The Weather in Berlin 2002, An Unfinished Season 2004, Forgetfulness 2006, Exiles in the Garden 2009; contrib. to anthologies and periodicals. *Honours:* O. Henry Awards 1985, 1986. *Address:* Vineyard Haven, MA 02568, USA (home).

JUTEAU, Monique, MA; Canadian poet and writer; b. 8 Jan. 1949, Montréal; d. of Aldéo Juteau and Jeanne Tranquil. *Education:* Université du Québec à Trois-Rivières. *Career:* Author's Residency, Ottawa Univ., Canada Council for the Arts; mem. Soc. des Écrivains de la Mauricie, Union des écrivaines et des écrivains québécois, PEN. *Exhibition:* The Great Silence, with artist Mylène Gervais, Trois-Rivières, Québec 2010. *Play:* The Red Light, with sculptors Annie Pelletier and Henri Morissette. *Publications:* poetry: La Lune Aussi 1975, Regards Calligraphes 1986, Trop Plein d'Angles 1990, Des jours de chemins perdus et retrouvés 1997, Des lieux des villes un chou-fleur 2008; fiction: En Moins de Deux 1990, L'Emporte-Clé 1994, La Fin des Terres 2001, Une histoire pour chaque jour de la semaine 2003, Le voyage a dit 2005, Un pied dans le vide 2010; contrib. to various publs. *Honours:* Prix Gerald-Godin 1998, Prix Félix-Antoine-Savard 2001, Télé-Québec Prix Daring 2002, Second Prize, Radio-Canada Grands Prix Littéraires 2002, Télé-Québec Amb. 2003, Prix du Conseil des Arts et des Lettres à la Création artistique, Région Centre-du-Québec. *Address:* 19200 Forest, Bécancour, PQ G9H 1P9, Canada (home). *Telephone:* (819) 233-2983 (home). *E-mail:* monique.juteau@uqtr.ca (office). *Website:* www.litterature.org/recherche/ecrivains/juteau-monique-265.

K

KAAVERI (see Kannan, Lakshmi)

KABAKOV, Alexander Abramovich; Russian writer and journalist; *Departmental Editor, Commersant Publishing*; b. 22 Oct. 1943, Novosibirsk; m.; one d. *Education:* Dniepropetrovsk Univ. *Career:* engineer, space rocket production co. 1965–70; journalist, Gudok 1972–88; columnist, then Deputy Ed.-in-Chief Moscow News 1988–97; special corresp., Commersant Publishing 1997–2000, Departmental Ed. 2000–; columnist, New Media Publishing Group 2002–; Chief Ed. journal Sak Voyazh; Chair. jury for Russian Booker Prize 2006; first literary publ. 1975. *Publications:* Cheap Novel 1982, Cafe Yunost 1984, Oil, Comma, Canvas 1986, Approach of Kristapovich (trilogy) 1985, Obviously False Fabrications (collection of short stories) 1989, No Return 1989, Story-Teller 1991, Imposter 1992, The Last Hero (novel) 1995, Selected Prose 1997, One Day from the Life of a Fool 1998, The Arrival Hall 1999, Youth Café 2000, The Journey of an Extrapolator 2000, The Tardy Visitor 2001, Qualified as Escape 2001, Survivor 2003, Everything Corrected (novel) (Apollon Grigoryev Prize 2005, Big Book Prize 2006) 2004, Moscow Stories (Prose of the Year Prize 2005, Ivan Bunin Prize 2006) 2005. *Honours:* Moscow Journalists' Union Prize 1989, Best Pens of Russia Award 1999, Short Story of the Year Award 1999. *Address:* New Media Publishing Group, Pyatnitzkaya str. 55, Moscow, Russia (office). *Telephone:* (495) 411-63-90 (office); (495) 994-83-45 (home); (495) 101-77-24.

KACEM, Abdelaziz; Tunisian essayist; b. 1933. *Career:* taught at Sorbonne, Univ. of Paris. *Publications:* Le Frontal 1983, Culture Arabe/Culture Française: La Parenté Reniée 2002, Le voile est-il islamique? 2004; contrib. to Bulletin du Centre Culturel Arabe, La Gazette de la Presse Francophone. *Honours:* Hon. Curator, Bibliothèque de Tunis' Grand Prix de l'Académie Française 1998. *Address:* c/o Editions Harmattan, 5–7 rue de l'Ecole Polytechnique, Paris 75005, France.

KACHACHI, Inaam, PhD; Iraqi writer and journalist; *Paris Correspondent, Asharq Al-Awsat and Kol Al-Usra newspapers*; b. 1952, Baghdad. *Education:* Univ. of Sorbonne, Paris. *Career:* worked in Iraqi press and radio; moved to Paris to work as journalist 1979–; Paris correspondent of Asharq Al-Awsat and Kol Al-Usra newspapers. *Film:* documentary about Naziha Al Dulaimi. *Publications:* novels: Sawaqi al-Quloob 2005, Al-Hafeeda al-Amreekiya 2008; other: Lorna, her years with Jawad Selim, Paroles d'Irakiennes (ed.) 2003. *Address:* c/o Bloomsbury Qatar Foundation Publishing, Qatar Foundation, Education City, Villa No. 3, PO Box 5825, Doha, Qatar (office). *E-mail:* bqfp@qf.org.qa (office). *Website:* www.bqfp.com.qa (office).

KADARÉ, Ismail; Albanian writer; b. 28 Jan. 1936, Gjirokastër; s. of Halit Kadaré; m. Elena Gushi 1963; two d. *Education:* Univ. of Tirana and Gorky Inst., Moscow. *Career:* full-time writer since 1963; works translated into more than 30 languages; sought political asylum in Paris 1990; mem. Albanian Acad.; Corresponding, then Assoc. Prof. mem. Acad. des sciences morales et politiques; mem. Acad. of Arts, Berlin, Acad. Mallarmé. *Plays:* Mauvaise saison pour Olymp. *Publications:* fiction: Gjenerali i ushtërisë së vdekur (trans. as The General of the Dead Army) 1963, Këshjtella (trans. as The Castle, later as The Siege) 1970, Kronikë në gur (trans. as Chronicle in Stone) 1971, The Great Winter (novel, in trans.) 1973, Ura më tri harque (trans. as The Three-Arched Bridge) 1978, The Twilight (in trans.) 1978, The Niche of Shame (in trans.) 1978, Kush e solli doruntinen (trans. as Who Brought Back Doruntine?) 1980, Prilli i thyer (trans. as Broken April) 1980, Nëpunësi I pallatit të ëndrrave (trans. as The Palace of Dreams) 1980, Nje dosje per Homerin (trans. as The H Dossier) 1980, Koncert në fund të dimrit (trans. as The Concert) 1985, Eschyle or The Eternal Loser (in trans.) 1988, Albanian Spring (in trans.) 1991, Le Monstre (in trans.) 1991, Piramida (trans. as The Pyramid) 1992, La Grande muraille 1993, Le Firman aveugle 1993, Clair de Lune 1993, L'Ombre 1994, L'Aigle 1996, Spiritus 1996, Oeuvres 1993–97 (12 vols) 1997, Temps barbares, de l'Albanie au Kosovo 1999, Il a fallu ce deuil pour se retrouver 2000, Froides fleurs d'avril (trans. as Spring Flowers, Spring Frost) 2000, L'envol du migrateur 2001, Vie, jeu et mort de Lul Mazrek 2002, La fille d'Agamemnon 2003, Le successeur 2003, L'Accident 2010; six vols of poetry 1954–80, criticism, essays. *Honours:* Dr hc (Grenoble III) 1992, (St Etienne) 1997, (South East European Univ.) 2005; Prix Mondial Cino del Duca 1992, Int. Booker Prize 2005, Premio Príncipe de Asturias, Spain 2009. *Address:* 63 blvd Saint-Michel, 75005 Paris (home); c/o Librairie Arthème Fayard, 75 rue des Saints Pères, 75006 Paris, France (office). *Telephone:* 1-43-29-16-20 (home).

KADMON, Jean Ball Kosloff, BA; American/Israeli poet, novelist and painter; b. 1 Aug. 1922, Denver, Colo; m. 1945, two s. *Education:* University of Alberta, University of Chicago. *Career:* anthropologist, International Centre for Community Development, Haifa, Israel 1964–65; Sociologist, Jewish Agency, Israel 1966–68; mem. Israel Asscn of Writers in English, Voices Israel Poetry Asscn. *Publications include:* Moshav Segev, 1972; Clais and Clock, 1988; Peering Out, 1996; MacKenzie Breakup, 1997; High Grandeur (poem) 2005, Commentary (poem) 2005, Lyric (poem) 2005, Solar Heater (poem) 2005, Guru (poem) 2005, Bus Voyage Station (novel) 2005, Summer Madness (novel) 2005, Shadows of the Oleander (novel) 2006. *Honours:* Second Prize, New Zealand International Writers Workshop 1981, First Prize, Ruben Rose International Poetry Contest 2001. *Address:* 12 Zerubavel Street, Jerusalem 93504, Israel. *Telephone:* (2) 6733048. *E-mail:* kadmonj@yahoo.com.

KADOHATA, Cynthia Lynn, BA; American writer; b. 7 Feb. 1956, Chicago, IL; m. 1992. *Education:* Univ. of Southern California. *Publications:* fiction: The Floating World 1989, In the Heart of the Valley of Love 1992; juvenile fiction: Kira-Kira (Newbery Medal 2005) 2004, Weedflower (Jane Addams Children's Book Award 2007) 2006, Cracker! 2007; contributions: newspapers and magazines. *Honours:* National Endowment for the Arts grant 1991, Whiting Writers Award 1991. *E-mail:* cynthia@kira-kira.us (office). *Website:* www.kira-kira.us.

KAGAN, Andrew Aaron, BA, MA, PhD; American art historian, art adviser and writer; b. 22 Sept. 1947, St Louis, MO; m. Jayne Wilner 1987. *Education:* Washington Univ., Harvard Univ. *Career:* Advisory Ed., Arts Magazine, 1975–89; Critic of Art, Music, Architecture, St Louis Globe Democrat, 1978–81; mem. Wednesday Night Society, founder, dir. *Publications:* Paul Klee/Art and Music, 1983; Rothko, 1987; Trova, 1988; Marc Chagall, 1989; Paul Klee at the Guggenheim, 1993; Absolute Art, 1995. Contributions: McMillan Dictionary of Art; Arts Magazine; Burlington Magazine; Others. *Honours:* Harvard Prize Fellowship, 1970–77; Kingsbury Fellowship, 1977–78; Goldman Prize, 1985.

KAGAN, Donald, AB, MA, PhD; American academic and writer; *Sterling Professor of Classics and History, Yale University*; b. 1 May 1932, Kurshan, Lithuania; m. Myrna Dabrusky 1955; two s. *Education:* Brooklyn Coll., Brown Univ., Ohio State Univ. *Career:* part-time Instructor in History, Capital Univ., Columbus, OH 1957–58; Instructor in History, Pennsylvania State Univ. 1959–60; Asst Prof. of History, Cornell Univ. 1960–63, Assoc. Prof. of History 1964–66, Prof. of History 1967–69; Prof. of History and Classics, Yale Univ. 1969–, Chair. 1972–75, Acting Chair. Dept of Classics 1986–87, Master, Timothy Dwight Coll. 1976–78, Richard M. Colgate Prof. of History and Classics 1979–90, Dean, Yale Coll. 1989–92, Bass Prof. of History and Western Civilization 1991–95, Hillhouse Prof. of History and Classics 1995–2002, Sterling Prof. of Classics and History 2002–; Fellow, Center for Advanced Study in the Behavioural Sciences, Stanford, Calif. 1992–93; Guest Scholar, Woodrow Wilson Int. Center for Scholars 1996. *Publications:* The Decline and Fall of the Roman Empire in the West (ed.) 1962 (third edn as The End of the Roman Empire, Decline or Transformation? 1992), The Great Dialogue: A History of Greek Political Thought From Homer to Polybius 1965, Readings in Greek Political Thought (ed.) 1965, Problems in Ancient History (ed.), two vols 1966, Great Issues in Western Civilization (co-ed. with L. P. Williams and Brian Tierney), two vols 1967, The Outbreak of the Peloponnesian War 1969, Hellenic History, by Botsford and Robinson, revised edn 1969, The Archidamian War 1974, The Western Heritage (with Steven Ozment and Frank M. Turner) 1979, The Peace of Nicias and the Sicilian Expedition 1981, The Heritage of World Civilizations (with Albert Craig, William Graham, Steven Ozment and Frank M. Turner) 1986, The Fall of the Athenian Empire 1987, Pericles of Athens and the Birth of Democracy 1990, On the Origins of War and Preservation of Peace 1995, While America Sleeps (with Frederick W. Kagan) 2000, The Peloponnesian War 2003, Thucydides: The Reinvention of History 2009; contribs to scholarly books and professional journals, and to general periodicals. *Honours:* Dr hc (New Haven) 1988, (Adelphi) 1990, (Dallas) 2001; Fulbright Fellowship 1958–59, Center for Hellenic Studies Fellowship, Washington, DC 1966–67, Nat. Endowment for the Humanities Sr Fellowship 1971–72, Sidney Hook Memorial Award, National Asscn of Scholars 1994, Harwood Byrnes '08/Richard B. Sewall Teaching Prize, Yale Coll. 1998, Nat. Humanities Medal 2002, Jefferson Lecturer, Nat. Endowment for the Humanities 2005. *Address:* 37 Woodstock Road, Hamden, CT 06517, USA (home). *Website:* donald.kagan@yale.edu (office).

KAGAN, Robert, BA, MA; American writer and journalist; b. 28 Sept. 1958, Athens, Greece; m. Victoria Nuland; one s. one d. *Education:* Yale Coll., Harvard Univ. *Career:* foreign policy adviser to Congressman Jack Kemp 1983; policy planning staff at US State Dept and principal speechwriter to Sec. of State George P. Schultz 1984–88; Sr Assoc. at the Carnegie Endowment for International Peace 1997–, Dir, US Leadership Project; mem., Council on Foreign Relations. *Publications:* non-fiction: A Twilight Struggle – American Power and Nicaragua (1977–1990) 1996, Present Dangers – Crisis and Opportunity in American Foreign and Defense Policy (ed. with William Kristol) 2000, Of Paradise and Power - America and Europe in the New World Order 2003, Dangerous Nation: America and the World 1600–1900 2006, The Return of History and the End of Dreams 2008; contrib. journalism to Foreign Affairs, Foreign Policy Commentary, New York Times, New Republic, Wall Street Journal, National Interest, Policy Review, Weekly Standard (contrib. ed.); columnist, The Washington Post. *Address:* c/o Carnegie Endowment for International Peace, 1779 Massachusetts Avenue NW, Washington, DC 20036, USA. *Telephone:* (202) 483-7600. *Fax:* (202) 483-1840. *E-mail:* info@ceip.org. *Website:* www.ceip.org.

KAHN, James, BA, MD; American physician and writer; b. 30 Dec. 1947, Chicago, IL. *Education:* University of Chicago. *Career:* resident, Los Angeles County Hospital, 1976–77; University of California at Los Angeles, 1978–79; Physician, Emergency Room, Rancho Encino Hospital, Los Angeles, 1978–.

Publications: Diagnosis Murder 1978, Nerves in Patterns (with Jerome McGann) 1978, World Enough and Time 1982, Time's Dark Laughter 1982, Poltergeist 1982, Return of the Jedi 1983, Indiana Jones and the Temple of Doom 1984, Goonies 1985, Timefall 1986, Poltergeist II 1986, Melrose Place (writer-producer) 1995–1999, Star Trek: Voyager (writer-producer) 2001–02. *Address:* c/o Danielle Egan-Miller, 410 S Michigan Avenue, Suite 460, Chicago, IL 60605, USA (office).

KAHORA, Billy, BA, MSc; Kenyan poet, author and editor. *Education:* Rhodes Univ., Univ. of Edinburgh, UK. *Career:* fmr Editorial Asst, AllAfrica.com, Washington, DC; currently Man. Ed. Kwani? (literary journal); work has appeared in Granta, Vanity Fair, Chimurenga; Regional Judge, Commonwealth Writers' Prize 2009. *Publications include:* The True Story of David Munyakei 2009; as ed.: Kenya Burning 2009; anthologies: African Violet: The 2012 Caine Prize Anthology 2012. *Address:* c/o Kwani Trust, PO Box 2895, 00100 Nairobi, Kenya (office). *Telephone:* 204441801 (office); 704832379 (mobile). *E-mail:* info@kwani.org (office). *Website:* kwani.org (office).

KAKAR, Sudhir, BE, Dipl.Kfm, PhD; Indian psychoanalyst, author and academic; *Adjunct Professor, INSEAD*; b. 1938, Nainital, Uttarakhand; m. Katharina Kakar; two c. *Education:* Gujarat Univ., Univ. of Mannheim, Germany, Sigmund Freud Inst., Frankfurt. *Career:* Lecturer in Gen. Educ., Faculty of Arts and Sciences, Harvard Univ. 1966–67; Asst Prof., Indian Inst. of Man., Ahmedabad 1968–71; Visiting Lecturer, Sigmund Freud Inst., Frankfurt 1972; Visiting Prof. of Behavioural Sciences, Univ. of Econs, Vienna 1974–75; Prof. and Chair. Dept of Humanities and Social Sciences, Indian Inst. of Tech., New Delhi 1976–77; Visiting Prof., Dept of Psychology, Coll. and School of Divinity, Univ. of Chicago 1989–93; Adjunct Prof., INSEAD, Fontainbleau, France 1994–; Research Fellow, Program for Applied Psychoanalysis, Grad. School of Business Admin, Harvard Univ. 1967–78; Sr Fellow, Center for Study of Developing Socs, New Delhi 1980–90; Sr Fellow, Center for Study of World Religions, Harvard Univ. 2001–02; Fellow, Insts of Advanced Study, Princeton and Berlin; mem. Int. Psychoanalytical Asscn, New York Acad. of Sciences, Indian Psychological Soc. *Publications include:* non-fiction: Fredrick Taylor: A Study in Personality and Innovation 1970, Conflict and Choice: Indian Youth in a Changing Society (co-author) 1971, The Inner World: A Psychoanalytic Study of Childhood and Society in India 1978, Shamans, Mystics and Doctors 1982, Tales of Love, Sex and Danger (co-author) 1986, Intimate Relations: Exploring Indian Sexuality 1989, The Analyst and the Mystic 1991, The Colours of Violence 1995, The Indian Psyche 1996, Culture and Psyche: Selected Essays 1996, The Indians: Portrait of a People (co-author) 2007, Mad and Divine: Spirit and Psyche in the Modern World 2008; fiction: novels: The Ascetic of Desire 1998, Ecstasy 2001, Mira and the Mahatma 2004, The Crimson Throne 2010; as ed.: Indian Love Stories 1999; as trans.: Kamasutra: A New Translation (co-author) 2002. *Honours:* Karolyi Foundation Award for Young Writers 1963, Boyer Prize for Psychological Anthropology, American Anthropological Asscn Award 1987, Goethe Medal of Goethe Institut Germany 1998, Abraham Kardiner Award, Columbia Univ. 2002, Distinguished Service Award of Indo-American Psychiatric Asscn 2007. *Address:* INSEAD, Boulevard de Constance, 77305 Fontainebleau, France (office); Pulwaddo Pequeno, Benaulim, Salcete, Goa, 403716, India (home). *Telephone:* (1) 60-72-43-68 (office). *Fax:* (1) 60-74-55-00/01 (office). *E-mail:* sudhir.kakar@insead.edu (home); sudhir_kakar@rediffmail.com. *Website:* www.insead.edu/facultyresearch/faculty/profiles/skakar (office); www.sudhirkakar.com (home).

KAKU, Michio, BS, PhD; American theoretical physicist, academic, writer, broadcaster and television presenter; *Henry Semat Professor of Theoretical Physics, City College, City University of New York*; b. 24 Jan. 1947, San Jose, Calif. *Education:* Harvard Univ., Univ. of California, Berkeley Radiation Lab. *Career:* Lecturer, Princeton Univ. 1973; fmr Visiting Prof., Inst. for Advanced Study, Princeton Univ. and New York Univ.; co-founder of string field theory; currently Henry Semat Prof. of Theoretical Physics, City Coll., CUNY, New York. *Radio:* host of Explorations in Science (weekly programme on WBAI), Science Fantastic (broadcasting to 130 radio stations across USA and the Internet). *Television:* Making Time (BBC four-part series) 2006, numerous appearances and contribs to documentaries. *Publications:* Nuclear Power: Both Sides (with Jennifer Trainer) 1982, To Win a Nuclear War: The Pentagon's Secret War Plans (with Daniel Axelrod) 1986, Beyond Einstein: The Cosmic Quest for the Theory of the Universe 1987, Introduction to Superstrings and M-Theory 1988, Strings, Conformal Fields and M-Theory 1991, Quantum Field Theory: A Modern Introduction 1993, Hyperspace: A Scientific Odyssey Through Parallel Universes, Time Warps and the Tenth Dimension 1994, Visions: How Science Will Revolutionize the 21st Century 1997, Einstein's Cosmos: How Albert Einstein's Vision Transformed Our Understading of Space and Time 2004, Parallel Worlds: A Journey Through Creation, Higher Dimensions and the Future of the Cosmos 2004, Physics of the Impossible 2008, Physics of the Future 2011; contrib. of numerous articles to journals and magazines, including Astronomy, Discover, BBC Focus Magazine (UK), Cosmos (Australia), New Scientist (UK), TIME magazine, Wall Street Journal, Popular Mechanics, New York Times, Daily Telegraph (UK), The Times (UK), Boston Globe. *Honours:* hon. degrees from Hofstra Univ., State Univ. of NY, Old Westbury; Award for Outstanding Educator, American Asscn of Physics Teachers. *Address:* Department of Physics, City College of New York, 160 Convent Avenue, New York, NY 10031, USA (office). *E-mail:* kaku@sci.ccny.cuny.edu (office); mkaku@aol.com (home). *Website:* www1.ccny.cuny.edu/prospective/science/physics (office); www.mkaku.org.

KALB, Jonathan, BA, MFA, DFA; American theatre critic and academic; b. 30 Oct. 1959, Englewood, NJ; m. Julie Heffernan 1988; two s. *Education:* Wesleyan Univ., Yale School of Drama. *Career:* Theatre Critic, The Village Voice, 1987–97; Asst Prof. of Performance Studies, 1990–92, Asst Prof. of Theatre, 1992–95, Assoc. Prof. of Theatre, 1996–2002, Prof. of Theatre, 2003–, Hunter College, CUNY; Chief Theatre Critic, New York Press, 1997–2001; mem. MLA; PEN American Centre. *Publications:* Beckett in Performance, 1989; Free Admissions: Collected Theater Writings, 1993; The Theater of Heiner Müller, 1998; Play by Play: Theater Essays and Reviews 1993–2002, 2003. Contributions: newspapers and journals. *Honours:* Fulbright Hays Grant, 1988–89; T. C. G. Jerome Fellowship, 1989–90; George Jean Nathan Award for Dramatic Criticism, 1990–91.

KALECHOFSKY, Roberta, BA, MA, PhD; American writer and publisher; b. 11 May 1931, New York, NY; m. Robert Kalechofsky 1953, two s. *Education:* Brooklyn College, CUNY, New York University. *Career:* Literary Ed., Branching Out, Canada, 1973–74; Contributing Ed., Margins, 1974–77, On the Issues, 1987–94; charter mem. National Writers Union; mem. Authors' Guild. *Publications:* Stephen's Passion, 1975; La Hoya, 1976; Orestes in Progress, 1976; Solomon's Wisdom, 1978; Rejected Essays and Other Matters, 1980; The 6th Day of Creation, 1986; Bodmin 1349, 1988; Haggadah for the Liberated Lamb, 1988; Autobiography of a Revolutionary: Essays on Animals and Human Rights, 1991; Justice, My Brother, 1993; Haggadah for the Vegetarian Family, 1993; K'tia: A Savior of the Jewish People, 1995; A Boy, a Chicken and the Lion of Judah: How Ari Became a Vegetarian (children's book), 1995; Vegetarian Judaism: A Guide for Everyone, 1998. Contributions: Confrontation; Works; Ball State University Forum; Western Humanities Review; Rocky Mountain Review; Between the Species; So'western; Response; Reconstructionist. *Honours:* National Endowment for the Arts Fellowship, 1962; Hon. Mem., Israel Bibliophile Society, 1982; Literary Fellowship in Fiction, Massachusetts Council on the Arts, 1987.

KALETSKY, Anatole, MA; British journalist; *Editor-at-Large and Principal Economic Commentator, The Times (UK)*; b. 1 June 1952, Moscow, Russia; s. of Jacob Kaletsky and Esther Kaletsky; m. Fiona Murphy 1985; two s. one d. *Education:* Melbourne High School, Australia, Westminster City School and King's Coll., Cambridge, UK and Harvard Univ., USA. *Career:* Hon. Sr Scholar, King's Coll., Cambridge 1973–74; Kennedy Scholar, Harvard Univ., USA 1974–76; financial writer, The Economist 1976–79; leader writer, Financial Times 1979–81, Washington Corresp. 1981–83, Int. Econs Corresp. 1984–86, Chief, New York Bureau 1986–90, Moscow Assignment 1990; Econs Ed. The Times 1990–96, Assoc. Ed. and econ. commentator 1992–, now Ed.-at-Large and principal econ. commentator; Dir Kaletsky Econ. Consulting 1997–; mem. Advisory Bd UK Know-How Fund for E Europe and fmr Soviet Union 1991–, Royal Econs Soc. 1999–. *Publications:* The Costs of Default 1985, In the Shadow of Debt 1992, Capitalism 4.0 2010. *Honours:* Specialist Writer of the Year, British Press Awards 1980, 1992, Press Awards Commentator of the Year 1995, What the Papers Say 1996, Financial Journalist of the Year, Wincott Foundation Award 1997. *Address:* The Times, 1 Pennington Street, London, E1 9XY, England (office). *Telephone:* (20) 7782-5000 (office). *Fax:* (20) 7782-5046 (office). *Website:* www.timesonline.co.uk (office).

KAMANDA, Kama Sywor, DipHumLit, BJ, BA, LèsL, HD; Democratic Republic of the Congo writer, poet, novelist, playwright and essayist and lecturer; b. 11 Nov. 1952, Luebo; s. of the late Malaba Kamenga and Kony Ngalula. *Education:* Journalism School, Kinshasa, Univ. of Kinshasa, Univ. of Liège, Belgium. *Career:* political leader; freelance journalist; lecturer at various univs, schools, etc.; literary critic for several newspapers; mem. French Soc. of Men of Letters, Conseil Int. d'Etudes Francophones, Belgian Soc. of Authors, Composers and Editors (SABAM), Maison de la poésie (MAPI – Dakar, Senegal), SCAM. *Publications:* Les Contes des veillées africaines 1967, Chants de brumes 1986, Les Résignations 1986, Éclipse d'étoiles 1987, Les Contes du griot Vol. 1 1988, Vol. 2: La Nuit des griots 1991, Vol. 3: Les Contes des veillées africaines 1998, La Somme du néant 1989, L'Exil des songes 1992, Les Myriades des temps vécus 1992, Les Vents de l'épreuve 1993, Quand dans l'âme les mers s'agitent 1994, Lointaines sont les rives du destin 1994, L'Étreinte des mots 1995, Œuvre poétique 1999, Les Contes du crépuscule 2000, Le Sang des solitudes 2002, Contes (édition illustrée) 2003, Contes (œuvres complètes) 2004, La Traversée des mirages 2006, La Joueuse de Kora 2006, Contes africains (Grund) 2006, Au-delà de Dieu, au-delà des chimères 2007, Oeuvre poétique (édition intégrale) 2008. *Honours:* Acad. française Paul Verlaine Award 1987, Acad. française Théophile Gautier Award 1993, Louise Labé Award 1990, Black African Asscn of French-Speaking Writers Award 1991, Acad. Inst. of Paris Special Poetry Award 1992, Silver Jasmine for Poetic Originality 1992, Gen. Council Agen Special Prize for French-Speaking Countries 1992, Greek Poets and Writers Asscn Melina Mercouri Award 1999, Int. Poets Acad. India Poet of the Millennium Award 2000, Joal Fadiouth hon. citation, Senegal 2000, Int. Soc. of Greek Writers Poetry Award 2002, Int. Council for French Studies Maurice-Cagnon Exceptional Contribution Honour Certificate 2005, World Acad. of Letters Master Diploma for Specialty Honors in Writing, USA 2006, United Cultural Convention Int. Peace Prize, USA 2006, Golden Medal Youth Book (Czech Repub.) 2008, Heredia Award, French Acad. 2009. *Address:* 18 Am Moul, 7418 Buschdorf, Luxembourg (office). *Telephone:* 26610948 (office); (621) 301611 (mobile) (office). *E-mail:* kamanda@pt.lu (office). *Website:* www.kamanda.jp (office); webplaza.pt.lu/public/kamanda (office); www.kamanda.net.

KAMATH, Madhav Vittal, BSc; Indian journalist and broadcasting executive; *Honorary Director, Manipal Institute of Communications, Manipal University*; b. 7 Sept. 1921, Udupi. *Education:* St Xavier's Coll., Mumbai. *Career:* worked for five years as chemist; changed careers and became reporter, then special adviser, then Ed. Free Press Journal, Mumbai 1946–54; Foreign Corresp. Times of India reporting from Germany and France, Ed. Sunday Times 1967–69, US Corresp., Times of India, Washington, DC 1969–78; Ed. Illustrated Weekly 1978–81; columnist in numerous newspapers and magazines 1981–; mem. Bd of Dirs Prasar Bharati (Broadcasting Corpn of India) 2002, Chair. 2003–09; fmr Dir Manipal Inst. of Communications, Manipal Univ., now Hon. Dir; fmr Chair. Vigyan Prasar. *Publications include:* over 45 books including The United States and India 1776–1976 1976, Philosophy of Death and Dying 1978, The Other Face of India 1988, A Banking Odyssey: The Canara Bank Story 1991, Ganesh Vasudeo Mavalankar 1992, Management Kurien-Style: The Story of the White Revolution, Points and Lines, Charat RAM: A Biography 1994, Journalist's Handbook 1995, Gandhi's Coolie: Life and Times of Ramkrishna Bajaj 1995, Professional Journalism 1996, Some of Us are Lucky 1996, Milkman from Anand: The Story of Verghese Kurien 1996, Sai Baba of Shirdi: A Unique Saint (co-author) 2005, A Reporter at Large (autobiog.), Collection of Articles on Politics, Media and Literature 2009. *Honours:* Hon. DLit (Mangalore Univ.) 2007; Padma Bhushan 2004. *Address:* c/o Manipal Institute of Communications, Manipal University, Manipal 576 104 (office); Kalyanpur House, 3rd Road, Near Railway Station, Kar, Mumbai, India (home). *Telephone:* (820) 2922080 (office); (22) 26483418 (home). *E-mail:* mv.kamath@manipal.edu (office). *Website:* www.manipal.edu (office).

KAMINER, Wladimir; German writer, journalist and DJ; b. 1967, Moscow, USSR; m.; two c. *Career:* moved to Germany 1990; DJ, Russian Disco, Berlin. *Publications:* Russendisko (short stories) 2000, Frische Goldjungs (ed.) 2001, Schönhauser Allee 2001, Militärmusik 2001, Die Reise nach Trulala 2002, Helden des Alltags (with Helmut Höge) 2002, Dschungelbuch 2003, Ich mache mit Sorgen, Mama 2004, Karaoke 2005, Küche totalitas 2006; contrib. to FAZ, taz and the Frankfurter Rundschau. *Address:* c/o Random House UK Ltd, Random House, 20 Vauxhall Bridge Road, London, SW1V 2SA, England. *Website:* www.russendisko.de.

KAMPFNER, John, BA (Hons); British writer and journalist; *Adviser, Freedom of Expression and Culture, Google Inc.*; b. 27 Dec. 1962, Singapore; s. of Fred Kampfner and Elizabeth Kampfner (née Andrews); m. Lucy Ash; two d. *Education:* Westminster School, London, The Queen's Coll., Oxford. *Career:* fmr foreign corresp. with Reuters and Daily Telegraph; Chief Political Corresp., Financial Times mid-1990s; fmr political commentator, Today programme (BBC Radio 4); Political Ed. New Statesman 2002–05, Ed. 2005–08; CEO Index on Censorship 2008–12, Trustee 2012–; Chair. Turner Contemporary Trustees 2008–; Adviser, Freedom of Expression and Culture, Google Inc. 2012–; regular appearances on radio and TV. *Television documentary films:* (all for BBC) Israel Undercover 2002, The Ugly War: Children of Vengeance (Foreign Press Asscn Award for Film of the Year and Journalist of the Year) 2002, War Spin 2003, Robin Cook: The Lost Leader (profile) 2003, Clare Short: The Conscientious Objector (profile) 2003, Who Runs Britain (series) 2004. *Publications:* Inside Yeltsin's Russia: Corruption, Conflict, Capitalism 1995, Robin Cook 1999, Blair's Wars 2003, Freedom for Sale 2009; contrib. to The Times, Sunday Times, Observer, Independent, Guardian, Financial Times, Daily Telegraph, Daily Mail, Mail on Sunday, Evening Standard, Washington Post, Los Angeles Times, Time, Newsweek, Prospect, New Statesman, Spectator. *Honours:* British Soc. of Magazine Eds. Ed. of the Year Award for Current Affairs Magazines 2006. *Address:* Index on Censorship, Free Word Centre, 60 Farringdon Road, London, EC1R 3GA, England (office). *Telephone:* (20) 7324-2522 (office). *E-mail:* john@jkampfner.net (office). *Website:* www.indexoncensorship.org (office); www.jkampfner.net.

KAN, Sergei, BA, MA, PhD; American academic and writer; *Professor of Anthropology and Native American Studies, Dartmouth College*; b. 31 March 1953, Moscow, Russia; m. Alla Glazman 1976; one d. *Education:* Moscow State University, Boston University, University of Chicago. *Career:* Lecturer, Sheldon Jackson College, Sitka, AK 1979–80, University of Massachusetts, Boston 1982–83; Part-time Asst Prof., Northeastern University 1981–83; Asst Prof., University of Michigan 1983–89; Asst Prof., Dartmouth College 1989–92, Assoc. Prof. of Anthropology and of Native American Studies 1992–98, Prof. of Anthropology and Native American Studies 1998–; mem. Alaska Anthropological Asscn, American Asscn for the Advancement of Slavic Studies, American Ethnological Society, American Society for Ethnohistory, International Arctic Social Science Asscn. *Publications:* Symbolic Immortality: The Tlingit Potlatch of the Nineteenth Century 1989, Memory Eternal: Tlingit Culture and Russian Orthodox Christianity Through Two Centuries 1999, Coming to Shore: Northwest Coast Ethnology, Traditions and Visions 2004, Perspectives on Native North America: Cultures, Histories and Representations (co-ed) 2006; contributions: books and scholarly journals. *Honours:* Robert F. Heizer Prize, American Society for Ethnohistory 1987, American Book Award, Before Columbus Foundation 1990, ACLS Fellowship 1993–94, National Endowment for the Humanities Fellowships 1993–94, 1999–2000. *Address:* Department of Anthropology, Dartmouth College, 6047 Silsby Hall, Hanover, NH 03755, USA (office). *Telephone:* (603) 646-2550 (office). *Fax:* (603) 646-1140 (office). *E-mail:* sergei.kan@dartmouth.edu (office). *Website:* www.dartmouth.edu/~anthro (office).

KANAKK, Atul, MA; Indian author and fmr editor; b. 16 Feb. 1967, Ramganj Mandi, Kota district. *Career:* Sub-ed. Desh ki Dharti (Hindi daily newspaper) 1983–90, fmr Sr Ed.; trans. and writer, drama, satire, poetry; writes in Hindi and Rajasthani. *Publications include:* Tubhyam Namostu (play) 1988, Pooruya (poetry) 1998, Joon-Jatra (novel) (Sahitya Akademi Award 2011) 2011. *Website:* www.atulkanak.blog.co.in; www.vyangyavagairah.blog.co.in.

KANDEL, Michael, PhD; American editor and writer; b. 24 Dec. 1941, Baltimore, MD. *Education:* Indiana Univ. *Career:* Asst Ed., MLA; Consultant Science Fiction Ed., Harcourt; Trans. of Stanislaw Lem; mem. PEN Club; SFWA. *Publications:* Strange Invasion, 1989; In Between Dragons, 1991; Captain Jack Zodiac, 1993; Panda Ray, 1996. *Address:* Modern Language Association, 26 Broadway, Third Floor, New York, NY 10004-1789, USA. *E-mail:* mkandel@mla.org.

KANE, Cheikh Hamidou; Senegalese novelist; b. 1928, Mataru, Senegal. *Education:* Univ. of Paris, Ecole Nationale de la France d'Outre-Mer. *Career:* frmly Dir, Dept of Economic Planning and Development, Governor, Thies Region, Commissioner of Planning; worked for UNICEF. *Publications:* L'Aventure Ambiguë (Ambiguous Adventure) 1961, Les Gardiens du Temple 1995. *Honours:* Grand Prix Litteraire de l'Afrique Noir, 1962.

KANE, Paul, BA, MA, MPhil, PhD; American poet, critic and academic; b. 23 March 1950, Cobleskill, NY; m. Christine Reynolds 1980. *Education:* Yale University, University of Melbourne. *Career:* Instructor, Briarcliff College, 1975–77; Assoc., Institute for World Order, 1982; Dir of Admissions and Instructor, Wooster School, 1982–84; Part-time Instructor, Yale University, 1988–90; Prof. of English, Vassar College, 1990–; mem. Acad. of American Poets; PEN; Poetry Society of America. *Publications:* The Farther Shore, 1989; A Hudson Landscape (with William Cliff), 1993; Ralph Waldo Emerson: Collected Poems and Translations, 1994; Poetry of the American Renaissance, 1995; Australian Poetry: Romanticism and Negativity, 1996; Emerson: Essays and Poems, 1996; Drowned Lands, 2000. Contributions: articles, poems, and reviews in New Republic; Paris Review; Poetry; Sewanee Review; Partisan Review; Raritan; Antipodes; The New Criterion. *Honours:* Fulbright Scholar, 1984–85; National Endowment for the Humanities Grant, 1998; Guggenheim Fellowship, 1999.

KANEHARA, Hitomi; Japanese novelist; b. 1983, Tokyo. *Publications:* Hebi ni Piasu (trans. as Snakes and Earrings) (Akutagawa Prize (jtly) 2004) 2003, Ash Baby 2004, Amebic 2005, Autofiction 2007; contrib. to Subaru magazine. *Address:* Azusa Takagi, c/o Shueisha Inc, 3-13-1 Jinbocho, Chiyoda-ku, Tokyo 101-8050 (office); 3-28-12 Bubaicho, Fuchushi, Tokyo 183-0033, Japan (home). *Telephone:* (3) 3230-6092 (office). *Fax:* (3) 3221-1387 (office). *E-mail:* takagi-bungei@shueisha.co.up (office).

KANENGONI, Alexander; Zimbabwean author; b. 1951, Chivhu. *Education:* Saint Paul's Teacher Training College, Univ. of Zimbabwe. *Career:* Project Officer, Ministry of Education and Culture 1983; Head of Research Services, Zimbabwe Broadcasting Corpn 1988–. *Publications:* Vicious Circle (novel) 1983, When the Rainbird Cries (novel) 1988, Effortless Tears (short stories) 1993, Echoing Silences (novel) 1998. *Honours:* Zimbabwe Book Publishers' Literary Awards 1994.

KANIGEL, Robert, BS; American writer and fmr academic; b. 28 May 1946, New York, NY; s. of Charles Kanigel and Beatrice Kanigel; m. 1st Judith Schiff Pearl 1981 (divorced); one s.; m. 2nd Sarah Merrow. *Education:* Rensselaer Polytechnic Inst., Troy, NY. *Career:* freelance writer 1970–; Instructor, Johns Hopkins Univ. School of Continuing Studies 1985–91; Visiting Prof. of English, Univ. of Baltimore, Sr Fellow, Inst. of Publications Design 1991–99; Prof. of Science Writing, MIT 1999–2012, Dir Grad. Program in Science Writing 2001–08; now ind. writer of general non-fiction; mem. Authors' Guild, American Conf. for Irish Studies, Soc. for the History of Technology. *Publications:* Apprentice to Genius: The Making of a Scientific Dynasty 1986, The Man Who Knew Infinity: A Life of the Genius Ramanujan 1991, The One Best Way: Frederick Winslow Taylor and the Enigma of Efficiency 1997, Vintage Reading: From Plato to Bradbury, a Personal Tour of Some of the World's Best Books 1998, High Season: How One French Riviera Town Has Seduced Travelers for Two Thousand Years 2002, Faux Real: Genuine Leather and 200 Years of Inspired Fakes 2007, On an Irish Island 2012; contrib. to New York Times Magazine, The Sciences, Health, Psychology Today, Science 85, Johns Hopkins Magazine, Washington Post, Civilization. *Honours:* Grady-Stack Award 1989, Alfred P. Sloan Foundation grant 1991, 2005, Elizabeth Eisenstein Prize 1994, Author of the Year, American Soc. of Journalists and Authors 1998, John Simon Guggenheim Memorial Foundation Fellowship 2008. *Address:* 2634 North Calvert Street, Baltimore, MD 21218, USA (office). *Telephone:* (410) 243-0776 (office). *E-mail:* kanigel@mit.edu (office). *Website:* robertkanigel.com.

KANN, Mark E., BA, MA, PhD; American academic and writer; b. 24 Feb. 1947, Chicago, Ill.; m. Kathy Michael 1969; one s. *Education:* Univ. of Wisconsin, Madison. *Career:* Asst Prof., 1975–81, Assoc. Prof., 1981–88, Prof. of Political Science 1988–, Univ. of Southern California, Los Angeles. *Publications:* Thinking About Politics: Two Political Sciences 1980, The American Left: Failures and Fortunes 1983, Middle Class Radicals in Santa Monica 1986, On the Man in Question: Gender and Civic Virtue in America 1991, A Republic of Men: The American Founders, Gendered Language, and Political Patriachy 1998, The Gendering of American Politics 1999, Punishment, Prisons, and Patriarchy: Liberty and Power in the Early National American Republic 2005;

contrib. to numerous newspapers, journals and magazines. *Honours:* various research and teaching awards. *Address:* Department of Political Science, University of Southern California, Los Angeles, CA 90089, USA (office).

KANN, Peter Robert; American journalist, publisher and business executive; b. 13 Dec. 1942, New York; s. of Robert Kann and Marie Kann (née Breuer); m. 1st Francesca Mayer 1969 (died 1983); m. 2nd Karen House 1984; one s. three d. *Education:* Harvard Univ. *Career:* joined Wall Street Journal 1964, worked as journalist in New York 1964–67, in Viet Nam 1967–68, in Hong Kong 1968–75, Publr and Ed. Wall Street Journal Asian Edn 1976–79, Assoc. Publr 1979–88, Exec. Vice-Pres. Dow Jones & Co. 1986, Pres. int. and magazine groups 1986–89, mem. Bd of Dirs 1987, Pres. Dow Jones & Co., New York 1989–91, Publr and Editorial Dir The Wall Street Journal 1989–2002, CEO Dow Jones & Co. 1991–2006, Chair. 1991–2007 (retd); Chair. Bd Far Eastern Econ. Review 1987–89; Trustee Asia Soc. 1989–94, Inst. for Advanced Study, Princeton 1990–, Aspen Inst. 1994–98; mem. Pulitzer Prize Bd 1987–96. *Honours:* Pulitzer Prize for int. reporting 1972 for his coverage of the 1971 India-Pakistan War. *Address:* 58 Cleveland Lane, Princeton, NJ 08540, USA.

KANNAN, Lakshmi, (Kaaveri (for writings in Tamil), MA, PhD; Indian poet, novelist, short story writer and translator; b. 13 Aug. 1947, Mysore; m. L. V. Kannan (deceased); two s. *Career:* taught English at several colls and univs; participant Int. Writing Program, Iowa Univ., USA; Writer-in-Residence on Charles Wallace Trust Fellowship, Univ. of Kent at Canterbury, UK 1993; Fellow, Indian Inst. of Advanced Study, Shimla; Sahitya Akademi Writer-in-Residence, Jamia Millia Islamia Univ., Delhi; mem. Governing Bd, Poetry Soc. of India, New Delhi; mem. India Int. Centre, Delhi. *Publications include:* written more than 21 books including poems: Impressions 1974, The Glow and the Grey 1976, Exiled Gods 1985, Unquiet Waters 2005; fiction: Rhythms (short stories) 1986, Parijata (short stories) 1992, India Gate (short stories) 1993, Going Home (novel) 1998, Nandanvan & Other Stories 2011, six collections of short stories; one novel in Tamil and three collections of short fiction in Hindi trans. *Honours:* Hon. Fellow in Writing, Univ. of Iowa, USA; Ilakkiya Chintani Award for Best Short Story in Tamil, Chennai, Katha Award for Best Translation, New Delhi. *Address:* B-XI/8193, Vasant Kunj, New Delhi 110 070, India (home). *Telephone:* (11) 26897793 (home). *E-mail:* lakshmi_kaaveri@yahoo.com.

KANO, Kenia; Mexican poet and visual artist; b. 21 June 1972, Mexico City. *Exhibitions include:* solo: Danzan Los Cuerpos Su Quietud Ociosa, France 1997, Oración De Pájaros, Zarco Gallery, Morelos 2004, Artkéo 1, Galerie Positions Aix, France 2007, Cuaderno De Los Gansos, LITM Gallery, New York 2008; group: Colectiva, Casa de la Cultura de Tlalpan, México 1997, Perú-México, Centro Cultural Latinoamericano Expresso, Aix-en-Provence 1998, C'est Bon Le Café Fort, Colectiva Francia-México, Universidad Marseille III, Aix-en-Provence 1998, Salón Estatal De La Acuarela, Jardín Borda, Cuernavaca 2002 and 2004, Abstractamente Tuyo, Galería Punto Rojo, Morelos 2005, Colectiva De Otoño, La Tallera 2005, Kakemonos, Museo Nacional de la Acuarela, México 2005, Sintonías, danza y poesía visual, Museo Na Bolom, San Cristóbal de las Casas 2005, Qué Rollo Con Estos Rollos, Galería CCC, Morelos 2006, No Se Puede Vivir Sin Amar, Museo La Casona Spencer 2007. *Publications:* Hojas De Una Sibarita Indiscreta 1994, Tiempo De Hojas 1995, Acantilado 2000, Ganador del Fondo para la Publicación de Obra Inédita 2003, Oración De Pájaros 2005, Del Amor Ileso 2008. *Address:* Instituto De Cultura De Morelos, Callejon Borda 1, Col. Centro Cuernavaca, 62000 Morelos, Mexico (office). *E-mail:* info@institutodeculturademorelos.gob.mx (office), keniacano72@hotmail.com; keniacano@pintoresmexicanos.com. *Website:* www.institutodeculturademorelos.gob.mx (office).

KANON, Joseph; American author and fmr publishing executive; b. 1946, Pa; m. Robin Straus; two s. *Education:* Harvard Univ., Trinity Coll., Univ. of Cambridge, UK. *Career:* stories published in Atlantic Monthly; fmr Ed. in Chief, CEO and Pres. Houghton Mifflin and E.P. Dutton publishing houses, New York; began writing novels 1995. *Publications include:* novels: Los Alamos (Edgar Award for Best First Novel) 1997, The Prodigal Spy 1998, The Good German 2001, Alibi (Int. Hammett Prize for Literary Excellence in Crime Writing 2005) 2005, Stardust 2009, Istanbul Passage 2012. *Honours:* Anne Frank Human Writers Award 2007. *Literary Agent:* c/o Amanda Urban, International Creative Management (ICM), 730 Fifth Avenue, New York, NY 10019, USA. *Telephone:* (212) 556-5600. *E-mail:* msouthard@icmtalent.com. *Website:* www.icmtalent.com; josephkanon.com.

KANT, Hermann Paul Karl, BA; German writer; b. 14 June 1926, Hamburg; m. Marion Meyer 1962; two s. two d. *Education:* Univ. of Berlin. *Career:* mem. PEN Centre, Germany, Writers' Asscn (pres. 1979–89). *Publications:* Ein bisschen Südsee 1962, Die Aula 1965, In Stockholm 1971, Eine Übertretung 1971, Das Impressum 1972, Der Aufenthalt 1977, Der dritte Nagel 1980, Zu den Unterlagen 1981, Bronzezeit 1986, Die Summe 1988, Abspann (memoir) 1991, Kormoran 1992, Escape 1994, Okarina 2002, Kino 2005. *Honours:* Hon. DrPhil (Greifswald) 1980; Heinrich Heine Prize 1962, Heinrich Mann Prize 1967, Nat. Prizes 1973, 1977, Goethe Prize 1985. *Address:* Prälank-Dorf 4, 17235 Neustrelitz, Germany (home). *Telephone:* (3981) 202975 (home). *E-mail:* HMYRONK@aol.com (home).

KANTARIS, Sylvia, CertEd, MA, PhD; British poet, writer, teacher, reviewer and essayist and university lecturer (retd); b. (Sylvia Mosley), 9 Jan. 1936, Grindleford, Derbyshire, England; m. Emmanuel Kantaris 1958; one s. one d. *Education:* Sorbonne, Univ. of Paris, Univ. of Bristol, Univ. of Queensland, Australia. *Career:* school teacher, Bristol 1957–58, London 1958–62; Tutor, Univ. of Queensland 1963–66, Open Univ., UK 1974–84; Extra-Mural Lecturer, Univ. of Exeter 1974–; Writer in the Community, Cornwall 1986–87; mem. Poetry Soc. of GB, South West Arts (literature panel 1983–87, literary consultant 1990–). *Publications:* Time and Motion 1975, Stocking Up 1981, The Tenth Muse 1983, News From the Front (with D. M. Thomas) 1983, The Sea at the Door 1985, The Air Mines of Mistila (with Philip Gross) 1988, Dirty Washing: New and Selected Poems 1989, Lad's Love 1993; contribs to many anthologies, newspapers and magazines and numerous academic and literary essays and reviews published in UK, USA, France and Australia, translated into many languages. *Honours:* Hon. DLitt (Exeter) 1989; Nat. Poetry Competition Award 1982, Major Arts Council Literature Award 1991, Soc. of Authors Award 1992. *Address:* 14 Osborne Parc, Helston, Cornwall, TR13 8PB, England (home). *Telephone:* (1326) 574578 (home). *E-mail:* sylvia@kantaris.com (home). *Website:* www.kantaris.com/sylvia.

KÁNTOR, Péter, MA; Hungarian poet, editor and translator; b. 5 Nov. 1949, Budapest; s. of László Kántor and Zsuzsa Kántor; m. Valéria Huszti. *Education:* Budapest ELTE Univ. *Career:* Literary Ed. Kortars magazine 1984–86; Poetry Ed. Élet és Irodalom magazine 1997–2000; mem. Writers' Asscn, International PEN. *Publications:* Kavics 1976, Halmadar 1981, Sebbel Lobbal 1982, Gradicsok 1985, Hogy no az eg 1988, Naplo, 1987–89 1991, Font lomb, lent avar 1994, Mentafü (selected poems) 1994, Bucsu és Megérkezés 1997, Lóstaféta 2002, Kétszáz lépcső föl és le 2005, Trója-variacók 2008, Megtanulni élni (selected and new poems) 2009; contribs to various publications. *Honours:* George Soros Fellowship 1988–89, Wessely Laszlo Award 1990, Dery Tibor Award 1991, Fulbright Fellowship 1991–92, Fust Milan Award 1992, József Attila Award 1994, George Soros Award 1999, Vas István Award 2004, Babérkoszorú Award 2007, Palládium Award 2009. *Address:* Stollar Bela u 3/a, Budapest 1055, Hungary (home). *Telephone:* (1) 332-0828 (home); (30) 561-2711 (home). *E-mail:* peterkantor@freemail.hu; peterkantor1@gmail.com.

KANTŮRKOVÁ, Eva; Czech writer; b. 11 May 1930, Prague; d. of Jiří Síla and Dobromila Sílová; m. 1st Mr Štern 1949; m. 2nd Mr Kantůrek; two s. *Education:* Charles Univ., Prague. *Career:* writer 1964–, unable to publish works in Czechoslovakia 1970–89; imprisoned by Czechoslovak authorities because of book which was printed abroad 1981–82; mem. Czech Parl. 1990–92; mem. Czech Centrum PEN Club, Asscn of Czech Writers; numerous novels, short stories, essays, plays and screenplays. *Screenplays include:* Funeral Ceremony (Second Prize, Film Festival, Montréal, Canada) 1990, My Friends in the Black House (TV) (First and Second Prizes, Cannes Film Festival). *Honours:* Tom Stoppard Prize 1985, Jan Palach Prize 1989, Egon Hostovsky Prize 1998, Ladislav Fuks Prize 2008. *Address:* Xaveriova 13, 150 00 Prague 5, Czech Republic (home).

KAPLAN, Harold, BA, MA; American academic and writer; b. 3 Jan. 1916, Chicago, IL; m. Isabelle M. Ollier 1962; one s. two d. *Education:* Univ. of Chicago. *Career:* Instructor of English, Rutgers Univ. 1946–49; Prof. of English, Bennington Coll. 1950–72; Prof. of English, Northwestern Univ. 1972–86, Prof. Emeritus 1986–; Visiting Prof. in American Literature in France, Italy, Israel; Chair. Studies in American Culture 1972–74. *Publications:* The Passive Voice 1966, Democratic Humanism and American Literature 1972, Power and Order 1981, Conscience and Memory: Meditations in a Museum of the Holocaust 1994, Poetry, Politics and Culture 2006. *Honours:* Fulbright Lecturer 1967, 1981, Rockefeller Foundation Humanities Fellowship 1982. *Address:* 219 Meadowbrook Drive, Bennington, VT 05201, USA (home). *Telephone:* (802) 442-7148 (home). *Fax:* (802) 442-7148 (home). *E-mail:* harkap@sover.net (home).

KAPLAN, Justin, BS; American biographer and editor; b. 5 Sept. 1925, New York, NY; m. Anne F. Bernays 1954, three d. *Education:* Harvard University. *Career:* Senior Ed., Simon & Schuster Inc, New York City, 1954–59; Lecturer in English, Harvard University, 1969, 1973, 1976, 1978; Writer-in-Residence, Emerson College, Boston, 1977–78; Visiting Lecturer, Griffith University, Brisbane, Australia, 1983; Jenks Prof. of Contemporary Letters, College of the Holy Cross, Worcester, Massachusetts, 1992–95; mem. American Acad. of Arts and Letters; American Acad. of Arts and Sciences, fellow; Society of American Historians, fellow. *Publications:* Mr Clemens and Mark Twain, 1966; Lincoln Steffens: A Biography, 1974; Mark Twain and His World, 1974; Walt Whitman: A Life, 1980; The Language of Names (with Anne Bernays), 1997; Back Then (with Anne Bernays), 2002. Editor: Dialogues of Plato, 1948; With Malice Toward Women, 1949; The Pocket Aristotle, 1956; The Gilded Age, 1964; Great Short Works of Mark Twain, 1967; Mark Twain: A Profile, 1967; Walt Whitman: Complete Poetry and Collected Prose, 1982; The Harper American Literature, 1987; Best American Essays, 1990. General Editor: Bartlett's Familiar Quotations, 17th edn, 2002. Contributions: newspapers, journals and magazines. *Honours:* Pulitzer Prize for Biography, 1967; National Book Award, 1967; Guggenheim Fellowship, 1975–76; American Book Award, 1981; Hon. DHL, Marlboro College, 1984; Bellagio Study and Conference Center Residency, 1990.

KAPLAN, Morton A., BS, PhD; American political scientist, academic, writer, editor and publisher; *Professor Emeritus, University of Chicago;* b. 9 May 1921, Philadelphia, Pa; m. Azie Mortimer 1967. *Education:* Temple Univ., Columbia Univ. *Career:* Fellow 1952–53, Research Assoc. 1958–62, Center of Int. Studies, Princeton, NJ; Asst Prof., Haverford Coll. 1953–54; Fellow, Center for Advanced Study in the Behavioral Sciences, Stanford, Calif.

1955–56; Asst Prof., Univ. of Chicago 1956–61, Assoc. Prof. 1961–65, Prof. of Political Science 1965–89, Distinguished Service Prof. 1989–91, Prof. Emer. 1991–; Visiting Assoc. Prof., Yale Univ. 1961–62; mem. staff, Hudson Inst. 1961–78, Consultant 1978–80; Dir Center for Strategic and Foreign Policy Studies 1976–85; Ed. and Publr The World and I 1985–2004; mem. American Political Science Asscn. *Publications:* System and Process in International Politics 1957, Some Problems in the Strategic Analysis of International Politics 1959, The Communist Coup in Czechoslovakia (co-author) 1960, The Political Foundations of International Law (with N. de B. Katzenbach) 1961, Macropolitics: Essays on the Philosophy and Science of Politics 1969, On Historical and Political Knowing: An Enquiry into Some Problems of Universal Law and Human Freedom 1971, On Freedom and Human Dignity: The Importance of the Sacred in Politics 1973, The Rationale for NATO: Past and Present 1973, Alienation and Identification 1976, Justice, Human Nature and Political Obligation 1976, Towards Professionalism in International Theory: Macrosystem Analysis 1979, Science, Language and the Human Condition 1984, The Soviet Union and the Challenge of the Future (co-ed.), four vols 1988–89, Morality and Religion (co-ed.) 1992, Law in a Democratic Society 1993, The World of 2044: Technological Development and the Future of Society (co-ed.) 1994, Character and Identity: Philosophical Foundations of Political and Sociological Perspectives (ed. and co-author) 1998, Character and Identity: Sociological Foundations of Literary and Historical Perspectives 2000; contrib. to many books and professional journals. *Address:* 5446 S Ridgewood Court, Chicago, IL 60615, USA (home).

KAPLAN, Nelly; French (b. Argentine) film director and writer; b. 11 April 1936, Buenos Aires, Argentina; d. of Julio Kaplan and Sima Kaplan (née Efron). *Education:* Univ. of Buenos Aires. *Career:* began as a film archivist, went to Paris as a writer for Argentine film journals, met and collaborated with film dir Abel Gance 1950s; journalist for various Argentine newspapers; Asst Dir, Cythère Films, Paris 1957–64, Dir 1967—; has written and directed numerous short films on art 1961–, and several feature films and documentaries 1967–; also writer under pseudonym Belen. *Films include:* Magirama (asst dir), La Tour de Nesle (asst dir) 1954, Austerlitz (asst dir) 1960, Gustave Moreau 1961, Cyrano et D'Artagnan (asst dir) 1963, Rodolphe Bresdin 1961, Abel Gance, hier et demain 1963, Dessins et merveilles 1964, A la source, la femme aimée 1965, le Regard Picasso (Golden Lion, Venice Film Festival 1967) 1967, La fiancée du pirate (Médaille d'Or, Venice Film Festival 1969) 1969, Papa, les petits bateaux 1971, Il faut vivre dangereusement 1975, Néa 1976, Charles et Lucie 1979, Abel Gance et son Napoléon 1983, Le regard dans le miroir 1985, Pattes de velours 1986, Plaisir d'amour 1991. *Television includes:* Docteur Teyran 1980, Livingstone 1981, Ce fut un bel été 1982, Un fait d'hiver 1982, Le regard dans le miroir (mini-series) 1985, Crépuscule des loups 1987, Les mouettes 1991, Honorin et la Loreleï 1992, Polly West est de retour 1993, Honorin et l'enfant prodigue 1994, La petite fille en costume marin (mini-series) 1999. *Publications:* Le Manifeste d'un art nouveau: la Polyvision 1956, Le sunlight d'Austerlitz 1960, Le réservoir des sens 1965, Le collier de Ptyx 1971, Mémoires d'une liseuse de draps 1974, Napoléon d'Abel Gance, Aux orchidées sauvages 1998, Un manteau de fou rire 1998, Ils furent une étrange comète 2002, Cuisses de grenouille 2005, Et Pandore en avait deux! 2008, Ecris-moi tes hauts faits et tes crimes 2009. *Honours:* Officier, Ordre nat. du Mérite, Chevalier de la Légion d'honneur, Commdr des Arts et des Lettres. *Address:* Cythère Films, 34 avenue des Champs Elysées, 75008 Paris, France.

KAPLAN, Robert D., BA; American author; *Senior Fellow, Center for a New American Security*; b. 23 June 1952, New York, NY; m. Maria Cabral; one s. *Education:* Univ. of Connecticut. *Career:* Nat. Corresp., The Atlantic Monthly magazine; Sr Fellow, Center for a New American Security 2008–. *Publications include:* Surrender or Starve: The Wars Behind the Famine 1988, Soldiers of God: With the Mujahidin in Afghanistan 1990, Balkan Ghosts: A Journey Through History 1993, The Arabists: The Romance of an American Elite 1993, The Ends of the Earth: A Journey at the Dawn of the Twenty-First Century 1996, An Empire Wilderness: Travels Into America's Future 1998, The Coming Anarchy: Shattering the Dreams of the Post Cold War 2000, Eastward to Tartary: Travels in the Balkans, the Middle East, and the Caucasus 2000, Imperial Grunts 2005, Hog Pilots: Blue Water Grunts: The American Military in the Air, at Sea, and on the Ground 2007, Monsoon: The Indian Ocean and the Future of American Power 2010; contrib. to periodicals. *Honours:* Greenway-Winship Award for Excellence in Int. Reporting 2001, United States State Dept Distinguished Public Service Award 2002. *E-mail:* dlockyer@nycap.rr.com*Address:* Center for a New American Security (CNAS), 1301 Pennsylvania Avenue NW, Suite 403, Washington, DC 20004, USA (office). *Telephone:* (202) 457-9400 (office). *Fax:* (202) 457-9401 (office). *E-mail:* info@cnas.org (office). *Website:* www.cnas.org (office); www.robertdkaplan.com.

KAPLINSKI, Jaan; Estonian poet, writer, linguist and translator (retd); b. 22 Jan. 1941, Tartu (Dorpat); s. of Jerzy Kaplinski and Nora Raudsepp; one s.; m. Tiia Toomet 1969; three s. one d. *Education:* Univ. of Tartu. *Career:* mem. Riigikogu (State Ass.) 1992–95; Lecturer in History of Western Civilization, Univ. of Tartu; columnist at various Estonian and Scandinavian newspapers; has written around 900 poems, 20 stories and some plays; mem. Universal Acad. of Cultures, Estonian Writers' Union, European Acad. of Poetry, Finnish Literature Soc. *Publications include:* poetry: Ma vaatasin päikese aknasse 1976, Uute kivide kasvamine 1977, The New Heaven & Earth of Jaan Kaplinski 1981, Raske on kergeks saada 1982, Tule tagasi helmemänd 1984, Õhtu toob tagasi kõik 1985, Käoraamat: Luulet 1956–80 1986, The Wandering Border 1987, The Same Sea in Us All 1990, Sjunger näktergalen än i Dorpat?: En brevväxling 1990, I Am The Spring in Tartu and other poems in English 1991, Non-Existent Frontier 1995, Võimaluste võimalikkus 1997, Öölinnud, öömõtted yölintuja, yöajatuksia: Luuletusi 1995–97 1998, Evening Brings Everything Back 2004; novel: Seesama jõgi 2007 (English trans. The Same Sea 2009). *Honours:* IV Class Order of Nat. Coat of Arms 1997, Chevalier, Légion d'honneur 2000, Order of the Lion of Finland 2003; Dr hc; several Estonian awards, Baltic Ass. Prize for Literature 1997, Prix Max Jacob Etranger 2003. *Literary Agent:* c/o Bloodaxe Books Ltd, Highgreen, Tarset, Northumberland, NE48 1RP, England. *E-mail:* editor@bloodaxebooks.com. *Address:* Nisu 33-9, 50407 Tartu, Estonia (home). *Telephone:* (7) 425755 (Estonia) (home). *E-mail:* jaan.kaplinski@gmail.com (home). *Website:* jaan.kaplinski.com; jaankaplinski.blogspot.com.

KAPPACHER, Walter; Austrian writer; b. 1938, Salzburg. *Career:* apprenticed as a car mechanic and trained as a travel agent before starting to write full-time 1978–; contrib. regular stories to Stuttgarter Zeitung; Deutsche Akademie für Sprache und Dichtung. *Publications:* novels: Morgen 1975, Rosina 1978, Der lange Brief 1982, Touristomania 1990, Ein Amateur 1993, Wer zuerst lacht 1997, Silberpfeile 2000, Selina oder das andere Leben 2005, Der Fliegenpalast 2009. *Honours:* Dr hc (Salzburg); Hermann Lenz Prize 2004, Großer Kunstpreis des Landes Salzburg 2006, Georg Buchner Prize 2009. *Address:* c/o Renate Anderle, Residenz Verlag, Gutenbergstrasse 12, 3100 St Pölten, Austria (office). *Telephone:* (274) 28021411 (office). *E-mail:* r.anderle@residenzverlag.at (office). *Website:* www.residenzverlag.at (office); www.walter-kappacher.at.

KAPUR, Manju, MA, MPhil; Indian writer; b. Amritsar, Punjab; m.; three d. *Education:* Dalhousie Univ., Canada, Univ. of Delhi. *Career:* fmr Prof. of English Literature, Miranda House Coll., Delhi Univ. *Publications:* Difficult Daughters (Commonwealth Writers Prize, Eurasia region) 1998, A Married Woman 2002, Home 2006, The Immigrant 2009. *Address:* c/o Department of English, Miranda House College, University of Delhi, Delhi 110 007, India.

KARAHASAN, Dževad; Bosnia and Herzegovina writer and dramatist; *Professor, University of Sarajevo*; b. 25 Jan. 1953, Duvno, Yugoslavia; m. Dragana. *Education:* Univ. of Sarajevo, Univ. of Zagreb. *Career:* worked at Zenica theatre 1976–78; Ed., Odjek magazine, Sarajevo 1979–86; Prof. of Drama, Univ. of Sarajevo 1986–93, currently Prof., Dept of Philology; Visiting Prof., Univ. of Salzburg, Austria 1994–95, Univ. of Innsbruck, Austria 1995–97, Univ. of Göttingen, Germany 1995–97; Stadtschreiber Graz, Austria 1997–2003. *Plays:* Al-Mukaffa, Klagenfurt/Salzburg 1994, Der entrückte Engel – Povuceni Andjeo, Salzburg 1995, Das Konsert der Vögel – Koncert ptica, Vienna 1997, Snow and Death 2002. *Publications:* novels: Istočni Diwan (The Eastern Diwan) 1989, Sahrijarov prsten (Shahrijar's Ring) 1994, Sara i Serafina (Sarah and Seraphine) 1999, Nocno vijece (The Nights Council) 2006, Izvjestaji iz tamnog vilajeta (Tales from the Dark World) 2007; non-fiction: Sarajevo: Exodus of a City 1994, Knjiga vrtova (trans. as The Book of Gardens) 2002, Die Schatten der Städte (The Shadows of the Citys) 2010. *Honours:* Leipzig European Understanding Literary Award, Charles Veillon Prize for Essay, France 1995, Bruno Kreisky Prize for Politics Book of the Year, Austria 1995, Int. Prize for Dialogue 1997, Herder Prize 1999, Vilenica Prize 2010. *Address:* Insel Verlag, Lindenstrasse 29–35, 60325 Frankfurt am Main, Germany (office); Augusta Brauna 1, 71000 Sarajevo, Bosnia Herzegovina (home). *Telephone:* (30) 740744-294 (Germany) (office); (33) 445899 (BH) (home). *Fax:* (30) 740744-299 (Germany) (office). *E-mail:* jann@suhrkamp.de (office); dragana.tomasevic@gmx.at (home). *Website:* www.suhrkamp.de (office).

KARBO, Karen Lee, BA, MA; American writer; b. 1956, Detroit, Mich.; m. 1st (divorced); m. 2nd Kelley Baker 1988. *Education:* University of Southern California, Los Angeles. *Publications include:* Trespassers Welcome Here 1989, The Diamond Lane 1991, Motherhood Made a Man Out of Me 2000, Generation Ex: Tales from the Second Wives Club 2001; contributions: periodicals.

KARIM, Fawzi, BA; Iraqi/British poet, writer and painter; b. 1 July 1945, Baghdad; m. 1980; two s. *Education:* Coll. of Arts, Baghdad. *Career:* Ed.-in-Chief and Publr Al-laza Al-Shiria quarterly, London; freelance writer; mem. Poetry Soc., England, Union of Iraqi Writers. *Exhibition:* The Room, London 2008. *Publications:* poetry: Where Things Begin 1969, I Raise My Hand in Protest 1973, Madness of Stone 1977, Stumbling of a Bird 1985, We Do Not Inherit the Earth 1988, Schemes of Adam 1991, Pestilential Continents 1995 (French trans. Continent de douleurs 2003, Swedish trans. Epidemiemas Kontinent 2005), Selected Poems, 1968–1995 1995, Cairo 1995, Collected Poems (two vols) 2000, The Foundling Years 2003, Selected Poems 2004, The Last Gypsies 2005, The Night of Abil Alaa 2007; prose: From Exile to Awareness 1972, City of Copper 1995, The Emperor's Clothes, on Poetry 2000, The Musical Virtues 2002, Return to Gardenia 2004, Diary of the End of a Nightmare 2005, Breakdown of the Generation of the Sixties, Dangers of Intellectual Passions 2006, The Gods Companion 2009; reviews of classical music, Art and English poetry in Arabic newspapers. *E-mail:* fawzi46@hotmail.com (home). *Website:* fawzi-karim.com.

KARKARIA, Bachi J.; Indian editor; *Consulting Editor, The Times of India*; m.; two s. *Education:* Loreto Coll., Calcutta, Calcutta Univ. *Career:* began career at Illustrated Weekly of India 1969; Asst Ed. The Statesman, Calcutta (first woman) 1980; Group Editorial Dir, Mid Day Multimedia Ltd 2000–02;

Ed. Sunday Times of India 1998–2000, Resident Ed. The Times of India 2003, in charge of Delhi section, then Nat. Metro Ed., now Consulting Ed. and columnist; mem. Int. Women's Media Foundation; mem. Bd World Editors' Forum 2002–, India AIDS Initiative of Bill and Melinda Gates Foundation; Jefferson Fellow, East West Center, Honolulu; mem. Professional Women's Advisory Bd, American Biographical Inst. *Publications include:* Dare to Dream: The Life of M.S. Oberoi 2007, To a Grand Design. *Honours:* Media India Award (for human interest stories) 1992, Mary Morgan-Hewitt Award for Lifetime Achievement 1994. *Address:* The Times of India, 7 Bahadur Shah Zafar Marg, New Delhi 110 002, India (office). *Telephone:* (11) 23492049 (office). *Fax:* (11) 23351606 (office). *E-mail:* bachi.karkaria@timesgroup.com (office). *Website:* www.timesofindia.com (office).

KARLIN, Wayne Stephen, BA, MA; American writer, teacher and editor; *Professor of Languages and Literature, College of Southern Maryland*; b. 13 June 1945, Los Angeles, Calif.; s. of Louis Karlin and Rhoda Karlin; m. Ohnmar Thein 1977; one s. *Education:* American Coll., Jerusalem, Goddard Coll., Vt. *Career:* Pres., Co-Ed. First Casualty Press 1972–73; Prof. of Languages and Literature, Coll. of Southern Maryland 1984–; Visiting Writer, William Joiner Center for the Study of War and Social Consequences, Univ. of Massachusetts, Boston 1989–93; Dir of Fiction, Literary Festival, St Mary's Coll. 1994–2002; Ed. Curbstone Press Vietnamese Writers series 1996–; mem. Associated Writing Programs. *Film:* scriptwriter and actor, Song of the Stork 2002. *Radio:* producer, writer, Shared Weight series (Center for Emerging Media, NPR) 2006; producer, writer, Wandering Souls broadcast (Center for Emerging Media, NPR) 2009. *Publications:* Crossover 1984, Lost Armies 1988, The Extras 1989, US 1993, Rumors and Stones: A Journey 1996, Prisoners (Paterson Prize for Fiction 1999) 1998, The Wished-for Country 2002, War Movies 2005, Marble Mountain 2008, Wandering Souls 2009; contrib. to anthologies, newspapers and periodicals. *Honours:* Air Medal, Combat Aircrew Badge; Maryland State Arts Council Fellowship in Fiction and Individual Artist Award 1988, 1991, 1993, 2001, Nat. Endowment for the Arts Fellowship 1993, 2003, Critics' Choice Award 1995–96, Paterson Prize in Fiction 1999, Vietnam Veterans of America, Excellence in the Arts Award 2005. *Literary Agent:* c/o Phyllis Westberg, Harold Ober Associates, 425 Madison Avenue, New York, NY 10017, USA. *Telephone:* (212) 759-5600. *Address:* PO Box 239, St Mary's City, MD 20686, USA (home). *Telephone:* (240) 725-5451 (office). *E-mail:* waynek@csmd.edu (office).

KARNAD, Girish, MA; Indian playwright, filmmaker and actor; b. 19 May 1938, Matheran; s. of Raghunath Karnad and Krishnabai Karnad; m. Saraswarthy Ganapathy 1980; one s. one d. *Education:* Karnatak Coll., Dharwad, Magdalene Coll., Univ. of Oxford. *Career:* Rhodes Scholar, Oxford 1960–63; Pres. Oxford Union Soc. 1963; Asst Man. Oxford Univ. Press, Madras 1963–69, Man. 1969–70; Homi Bhabha Fellow 1970–72; Dir Film & TV Inst. of India, Pune 1974–75; Pres. Karnataka Nataka Acad. 1976–78; Visiting Prof. and Fulbright Scholar-in-Residence, Univ. of Chicago 1987–88; Indian Co-Chair., Media Cttee, Indo-US Subcomm. 1984–93; Chair. Sangeet Natak Akademi (Nat. Acad. of Performing Arts) 1988–93; Dir The Nehru Centre, London 2000; World Theatre Amb., Int. Theatre Inst. of UNESCO 2008; Fellow, Sangeet Natak Acad. 1994. *Plays include:* Yayati (Mysore State Award 1962) 1961, Tughlaq 1964, Hayavadana (Kamaladevi Award Bharatiya Natya Sangh 1972) 1971, Anjumallige 1976, Nagamandala 1988, Taledanda (Writer of the Year Award 1990, B.H. Sridhar Award 1992, Karnataka Sahitya Acad. Award 1992, Sahitya Acad. Award 1994) 1990, Agni Mattu Male 1995, Tipu Sultan Kanda Kanasu 2000, Bali 2002, Broken Images 2005, Flowers 2008, Wedding Album 2009. *Films include:* Samskara (President's Gold Medal 1970) 1970, Vamsha Vriksha (Nat. Award 1972, Mysore State Award 1972) 1971, Kaadu (President's Silver Medal 1974) 1973, Tabbaliyu Neenade Magane 1977, Swami (Best Bengal Film Journalists' Asscn Award 1978) 1977, Ondanondu Kaaladalli (Nat. Award 1978) 1978, Utsav 1984, Cheluvi 1992, Kanooru Heggadithi 1999, Iqbal (as actor) 2005, Dor (as actor) 2006, 8 x 10 Tasveer (as actor) 2009, Life Goes On (as actor) 2009. *Radio:* Ma Nishada 1986, The Dreams of Tipu Sultan 1997. *Television:* Antaraal 1996, Swarajnama 1997, Kanooru Ki Thakurani 1999, wrote and presented The Bhagavad Gita for BBC Two 2002. *Honours:* Hon. DLitt (Univ. of Karnataka) 1994, (Univ. of Vidyasagar, Midnapur) 2010, (Univ. of Ravenshaw, Bhubaneshwar) 2011; Dr hc (Univ. of Southern Calif.) 2011; several awards for film work; Govt of Mysore Rajyotsava Award 1970, Sangeet Natak Acad. (Nat. Acad. of Performing Arts) Award 1972, Padma Shri 1974, Karnataka Nataka Acad. Award 1984, Nandikar, Calcutta Award 1989, Padma Bhushan 1992, Booksellers and Publishers Asscn of South India Award 1992, Bharatiya Jnanpith Award 1999, Sahitya Acad. Award 1994, Gubbi Veeranna Award 1996–97. *Address:* 697, 15th Cross, JP Nagar Phase II, Bangalore 560 078, India (home). *Telephone:* (80) 26590463 (home). *Fax:* (80) 26590019 (home). *E-mail:* karnad.girish@gmail.com (home).

KARNOW, Stanley, BA; American journalist and writer; b. 4 Feb. 1925, New York, NY; m. 1st Claude Sarraute 1948 (divorced 1955); m. 2nd Annette Kline 1959; two s. one d. *Education:* Harvard Univ., Univ. of Paris. *Career:* correspondent, Time magazine, Paris 1950–57; Bureau Chief, North Africa 1958–59, Hong Kong 1959–62, Time-Life; special correspondent, Observer, London 1961–65, Time Inc 1962–63, NBC News 1973–75; Far East correspondent, Saturday Evening Post 1963–65; Far East correspondent 1965–71, diplomatic correspondent 1971–72, Washington Post; Assoc. Ed., New Republic 1973–75; columnist, King Features 1975–88, Le Point, Paris 1976–83, Newsweek International 1977–81; Ed., International Writers Service 1976–86; Chief Correspondent, Viet Nam: A Television History (series, PBS) 1983; Chief Correspondent and narrator, The US and the Philippines: In Our Image (series, PBS) 1989; mem. Asia Soc., Council on Foreign Relations, PEN American Centre, Soc. of American Historians. *Publications:* Southeast Asia 1963, Mao and China: From Revolution to Revolution 1972, Vietnam: A History 1983, In Our Image: America's Empire in the Philippines 1989, Asian Americans in Transition (co-author) 1992, Paris in the Fifties 1997; contrib. to books, newspapers, journals and magazines. *Honours:* Neiman Fellow 1957–58, East Asian Research Center Fellow 1970–71, Peabody Award 1984, Pulitzer Prize in History 1990, Shorenstein Lifetime Achievement Award 2001. *Address:* 10850 Spring Knowlls Drive, Rockville, MD 20854, USA (home). *Telephone:* (301) 299-3116 (home). *Fax:* (301) 299-4834 (home). *E-mail:* karnow@erols.com (home).

KARUNATILAKA, Shehan, BA; Sri Lankan author and advertising executive; b. 1975, Galle. *Education:* St Thomas' Preparatory School, Kollupitiya, Massey Univ., New Zealand. *Career:* copywriter, Grant McCann-Erickson, Colombo 1997–2002, Creative Dir 2006–08; freelance writer, ARC Leo Burnett, TMP Worldwide, London 2003; copywriter, Springer & Jacoby and BoyMeetsGirl, London 2004–05; Creative Group Head, Iris, Singapore 2010–11; first novel The Painter unpublished but shortlisted for Gratiaen Prize 2000; fmr bass guitarist for rock groups in Sri Lanka including Independent Square and Powercut Circus; feature writer for Guardian, Newsweek, National Geographic, Economic Times, Rolling Stone, Wisden, The Cricketer. *Publication:* Chinaman: The Legend of Pradeep Mathew (Gratiaen Prize 2008, Commonwealth Book Prize 2012, DSC Prize for S Asian Literature 2012) 2008. *Address:* c/o Vintage Publishing, The Random House Group, 20 Vauxhall Bridge Road, London, SW1V 2SA, England (office). *Telephone:* (20) 7840-8400 (office). *Fax:* (20) 7840-8778 (office). *Website:* www.vintage-books.co.uk (office); www.randomhouse.co.uk (office); www.shehanwriter.com.

KASHU'A, Said; Israeli writer and journalist; b. 1975, Tira. *Education:* Israel Arts and Sciences Acad. High School, Jerusalem, Hebrew Univ., Jerusalem. *Career:* columnist, Ha'aretz newspaper; Fellow, John Simon Guggenheim Memorial Foundation. *Publications include:* Dancing Arabs (Grinzane Cavour Award for First Novel 2004) 2002, Let it be Morning 2004, Zweite Person Singular (Bernstein Prize) 2011. *Honours:* President's Prize for Literature 2004. *Address:* c/o Grove Press, 841 Broadway, 4th Floor, New York, NY 10003, USA (office). *Website:* www.groveatlantic.com (office).

KASISCHKE, Laura, BA, MFA; American poet, writer and teacher; *Associate Professor of English, University of Michigan*; b. 5 Dec. 1961, Lake Charles, La; m. William Abernethy 1994; one s. *Education:* Univ. of Michigan, Columbia Univ. *Career:* Instructor in Writing, South Plains Coll., Levelland, Texas 1987–88; Visiting Lecturer in Creative Writing and Literature, Eastern Michigan Univ. 1989–90; Instructor in Creative Writing and Literature, Washtenaw Community Coll., Ann Arbor 1990; Assoc. Prof., Univ. of Nevada, Las Vegas 1994–95; currently Assoc. Prof. of English, Univ. of Michigan. *Publications:* poetry: Brides, Wives, and Widows 1990, Wild Brides 1992, Housekeeping in a Dream 1995, What it Wasn't 2002, Dance and Disappear 2002, Gardening in the Dark 2004, Lilies Without 2007; fiction: Suspicious River 1996, White Bird in a Blizzard 1999, The Life Before Her Eyes 2002, Boy Heaven 2006, Be Mine 2007, Feathered 2008, In a Perfect World 2009, Eden Springs 2010, Space, in Chains 2011; contributions: numerous periodicals. *Honours:* Michael Gutterman Poetry Award 1983, Marjorie Rapaport Poetry Award 1986, Michigan Council for the Arts Individual Artist Grant 1990, Ragdale Foundation Fellowships 1990–92, Elmer Holmes Bobst Award for Emerging Writers 1991, Bread Loaf Fellow in Poetry 1992, MacDowell Colony Fellow 1992, Creative Artists Award, Arts Foundation of Michigan 1993, Alice Fay DiCastagnola Award 1993, Pushcart Prize 1993, Barbara Deming Memorial Award 1994, National Endowment for the Arts Fellowship 1994, Poets & Writers Exchange Fellowship 1994. *Address:* Department of English, University of Michigan, 435 South State Street, 3187 Angell Hall, Ann Arbor, MI 48109-1003, USA (office). *Telephone:* (734) 764-6370 (office). *E-mail:* laurakk@umich.edu (office). *Website:* www.lsa.umich.edu/english (office).

KASSABOVA, Kapka, BA, MA; Bulgarian poet, novelist and journalist; b. 1973, Sofia. *Education:* Univ. of Otago, Dunedin, Victoria Univ. of Wellington, New Zealand. *Career:* teacher of English, Marseilles, France 1998; currently lives in Edinburgh. *Publications:* poetry: All Roads Lead to the Sea 1997, Dismemberment 1998, Someone Else's Life 2003, Geography for the Lost 2007; novels: Reconnaissance 1999, Love in the Land of Midas 2000; travel writing: Globetrotter's Guide to Dheli, Jaipur and Agra 2002, Globetrotter's Guide to Bulgaria 2007, Street Without a Name 2008; contrib. to Critic, NZ Listener. *Honours:* Buddie Finlay Sargeson Fellowship 1999; New Zealand Soc. of Authors Jessie McKay Award for the Best First Book of Poetry, Commonwealth Writers' Prize for Best First Book in the SE Asia-Pacific Region 2000, Cathay Pacific NZ Travel Writer of the Year Award 2002, 2004, winner, Landfall New Zealand Essay Competition 2002. *Literary Agent:* c/o Isobel Dixon, Blake Friedmann Literary Agency, 122 Arlington Road, London NW1 7HP, England. *Telephone:* (20) 7284-0408. *Fax:* (20) 7284-0442. *E-mail:* isobel@blakefriedmann.co.uk. *Website:* www.blakefriedmann.co.uk. *E-mail:* kapka.kassabova@googlemail.com (office). *Website:* www.kapka-kassabova.com.

KASSEM, Louise (Lou) Sutton Morrell; American writer; b. 10 Nov. 1931, Elizabethton, TN; m. Shakeep Kassem 1951; four d. *Education:* East

Tennessee State Univ., Univ. of Virginia, Vassar Coll. *Career:* mem. Soc. of Children's Book Writers, Writers in Virginia, Appalachian Writers, Nat. League of American Pen Women, Authors' Guild. *Publications:* Dance of Death 1984, Middle School Blues 1986, Listen for Rachel 1986, Secret Wishes 1989, A Summer for Secrets 1989, A Haunting in Williamsburg 1990, The Treasures of Witch Hat Mountain 1992, Odd One Out 1994, The Druid Curse 1994, The Innkeeper's Daughter 1996, Sneeze on Monday 1997; contrib. to Alan Review, Signal, Chicken Soup for Kids' Souls, Chicken Soup for Pre-Teen Souls, The Writer, North Carolina Educ. Asscn. *Honours:* American Library Asscn Notable Book in Social Studies 1986, Virginia State Reading Asscn Best Book for Young Readers. *Address:* 715 Burruss Drive NW, Blacksburg, VA 24060-3205, USA (home). *Telephone:* (540) 552-2241 (home). *E-mail:* lmk1931@aol.com (home).

KATRAGADDA, Siddharth; Indian/American poet, author, painter and filmmaker; b. 1972, Bangalore, India; m. *Education:* Univ. of Texas, Arlington. *Career:* software engineer with telecommunications co.; contrib. to Grey Sparrow Press, A Generation Defining Itself, Carter Street Review, Eastown Fiction, WriteFromWrong Journal. *Film:* as screenwriter and dir: The Girl Upstairs 2012. *Publications include:* Dark Rooms: A Novel in Verse 2002, The Other Wife: A Novel in Verse 2003. *Website:* www.siddharthkatragadda.blogspot.com; www.siddharthfilms.com.

KATTAN, Naïm, OC, FRSC; Canadian writer; b. 26 Aug. 1928, Baghdad, Iraq; s. of the late Nessim and Hela Kattan; m. Gaetane Laniel 1961; one s. *Education:* Univ. of Baghdad and Sorbonne, Paris. *Career:* newspaper corresp. in Near East and Europe, broadcaster throughout Europe; emigrated to Canada 1954; Int. Politics Ed. for Nouveau Journal 1961–62; fmr teacher at Laval Univ.; fmr Sec. Cercle Juif de langue française de Montreal; freelance journalist and broadcaster; Prof., Univ. of Québec, Montreal; Assoc. Dir Canada Council; mem. Académie Canadienne-Française; Pres. Royal Soc. of Canada. *Plays:* Avant le ceremonie 2009. *Publications:* (novels) Adieu Babylone 1975, Les Fruits arrachés 1981, La Fiancée promise 1983, La Fortune du passager 1989, La Célébration 1997, L'Anniversaire 2000; (essays) Le Réel et le théâtral 1970, Ecrivains des Amériques, Tomes I-III, Le Repos et l'Oubli 1987, Le Père 1990, Farida 1991, La Reconciliation 1992, A. M. Klein 1994, La Distraction 1994, Culture: Alibi ou liberté 1996, Idoles et images 1996, Figures bibliques 1997, L'Amour reconnu 1999, Le Silence des adieux 1999, Le gardien de mon frère 2003, La Parole et le lieu 2004, Les Villes de naissance, L'Ecrivain migrant, Farewell Babylon: Coming of Age in Jewish Baghdad 2007; also numerous short stories and criticisms. *Honours:* Chevalier Légion d'honneur; Officier des Arts et Lettres de France; Chevalier Ordre nat. du Québec; Dr. hc (Middlebury Coll.), (Concordia). *Address:* 2463 rue Sainte Famille No. 2114, Montreal, PQ, H2X 2K7, Canada. *Telephone:* (514) 499-2836. *Fax:* (514) 499-9954. *E-mail:* kattan.naim@uqam.ca. *Website:* www.uqam.ca.

KATZ, Steve, (Stephanie Gatos), BA, MA; American writer, poet, screenwriter and academic; *Professor Emeritus of English, University of Colorado, Boulder;* b. (Steven Robert Katz), 14 May 1935, New York, NY; s. of Alexander Katz and Sally Goldstein; m. Patricia Bell 1956 (divorced); three s. *Education:* Cornell Univ., Univ. of Oregon. *Career:* English Language Inst., Lecce, Italy 1960; overseas faculty, Univ. of Maryland, Lecce, Italy 1961–62; Asst Prof. of English, Cornell Univ. 1962–67; Lecturer in Fiction, Univ. of Iowa 1969–70; Writer-in-Residence, Brooklyn Coll., CUNY 1970–71, Co-Dir Projects in Innovative Fiction 1971–73, Adjunct Asst Prof., Queens Coll., CUNY 1973–75; Assoc. Prof. of English, Univ. of Notre Dame 1976–78; Assoc. Prof. of English, Univ. of Colorado at Boulder 1978–82, Prof. of English 1982–2010, Prof. Emer. 2010–; mem. Authors' League of America, PEN International, Writers' Guild. *Publications:* fiction: The Lestriad 1962, The Exaggerations of Peter Prince 1968, Posh 1971, Saw 1972, Moving Parts 1977, Wier and Pouce 1984, Florry of Washington Heights 1987, Swanny's Ways 1995, Antonello's Lion 2005, Kissssss: A Miscellany 2007; autobiography: Memoir: Time's Wallet 2010; short story collections: Creamy and Delicious: Eat my Words (in Other Words) 1970, Stolen Stories 1985, 43 Fictions 1991; poetry: The Weight of Antony 1964, Cheyenne River Wild Track 1973, Journalism 1990; screenplay: Grassland 1974. *Honours:* PEN grant 1972, Creative Artists Public Service grant 1976, Nat. Educational Asscn grants 1976, 1982, GCAH Book of the Year 1991, America Award in Fiction 1995. *Address:* 669 Washington Street, No. 602, Denver, CO 80203, USA. *Telephone:* (303) 832-2534. *E-mail:* elbonoz@earthlink.net. *Website:* stevekatzwrites.com.

KAUFMAN, Alan, BA; American/Israeli/French writer, poet, editor and journalist; b. 12 Jan. 1952, New York, NY; s. of George Kaufman and Marie Jucht; one d. *Education:* City College, CUNY, Columbia University. *Career:* founder Jewish Arts Quarterly 1974–75; founder and Ed. Davka: Jewish Cultural Revolution 1996–97; founder TATTOOJEW.COM 1998–2001; Ed.-in-Chief Jewish Frontier 1987–88; American Ed. Tel Aviv Review 1989; freelance feature writer for Los Angeles Times, San Francisco Chronicle, Partisan Review, San Francisco Examiner, Salon.com, Huffington Post, Evergreen Review etc; mem. PEN American Center. *Exhibition:* Acrylic Paintings (exhibited with David Newman and Tim Wicks), San Francisco 2003, 2004, Himmelberger Gallery, San Francisco 2007. *Publications:* The New Generation: Fiction for Our Time from America's Writing Programs (ed.) 1987, Who Are We? (poems) 1997, The Outlaw Bible of American Poetry (ed.) 1999, 2004, Jew Boy: A Memoir 2000, The Outlaw Bible of American Literature (ed.) 2004, Matches (novel) 2005, The Outlaw Bible of American Essays (ed.) 2006; contrib. to anthologies and periodicals. *Honours:* Firecracker Alternative Book Award 2000. *E-mail:* akpoem2@aol.com (office). *Website:* www.pen.org/MemberProfile.php/prmProfileID/19319 (office); www.redroom.com/author/alan-kaufman (office).

KAUFMAN, Charles (Charlie) Stewart; American screenwriter; b. Nov. 1958, W Hartford, Conn.; m. Denise Kaufman; one d. *Education:* Boston Univ., New York Univ. *Career:* worked in newspaper circulation dept, The Star Tribune, Minneapolis, Minn. 1986–90; contrib. to National Lampoon 1991; began scriptwriting 1991; cr. short films shown on Late Night with David Letterman TV show 1990s; writer 30 episodes for TV shows 1991–96; Producer, Misery Loves Company (TV series) 1995. *Screenplays include:* films: Being John Malkovich 1999, Human Nature 2001, Adaptation (Best Screenplay, Broadcast Film Critics Asscn, Chicago Film Critics Asscn, Nat. Bd of Review, Toronto Film Critics Asscn) 2002, Confessions of a Dangerous Mind 2002, Eternal Sunshine of the Spotless Mind (Nat. Bd of Review Best Original Screenplay Award 2004, BAFTA Award 2005, Writers' Guild of America Award for Best Original Screenplay 2005, Acad. Award for Best Original Screenplay 2005) 2004, Synecdoche, New York 2008; TV: Get A Life 1991–92, The Edge 1992–93, The Trouble with Larry 1993, Ned and Stacey 1996–97, The Dana Carvey Show 1996. *Literary Agent:* United Talent Agency, 9560 Wilshire Boulevard, Fifth Floor, Beverly Hills, CA 90212, USA.

KAUFMAN, Sir Gerald Bernard, Kt, PC, MA, MP; British politician; b. 21 June 1930, s. of Louis Kaufman and Jane Kaufman. *Education:* Leeds Grammar School and Queen's Coll., Oxford. *Career:* Asst Gen. Sec. Fabian Soc. 1954–55; political staff, Daily Mirror 1955–64; Political Corresp., New Statesman 1964–65; Parl. Press Liaison, Labour Party 1965–70; MP for Manchester, Ardwick 1970–83, for Manchester, Gorton 1983–; Under-Sec. of State for the Environment 1974–75, for Industry 1975; Minister of State, Dept of Industry 1975–79; mem. Parl. Cttee of Labour Party 1980–92; Opposition Spokesman for Environment 1980–83, Home Affairs 1983–87; Shadow Foreign Sec. 1987–92; Chair. House of Commons Nat. Heritage Select Cttee 1992–97, Culture, Media and Sport Select Cttee 1997–2005; mem. Labour Party Nat. Exec. Cttee 1991–92; mem. Royal Comm. on House of Lords Reform 1999; Chair. Booker Prize Judges 1999. *Publications:* How to Live under Labour (co-author) 1964, To Build the Promised Land 1973, How to Be a Minister 1980 (revised edn 1997), Renewal: Labour's Britain in the 1980s 1983, My Life in the Silver Screen 1985, Inside the Promised Land 1986, Meet Me in St Louis 1994. *Honours:* Hillal-e-Pakistan 1999. *Address:* House of Commons, Westminster, London, SW1A 0AA (office); 87 Charlbert Court, Eamont Street, London, NW8 7BX, England (home). *Telephone:* (20) 7219-5145 (office). *Fax:* (20) 7219-6825 (office).

KAUFMANN, Thomas DaCosta, BA, MA, MPhil, PhD; American academic and writer; b. 7 May 1948, New York, NY; m. Virginia Burns Roehrig 1974 (divorced 1998); one d. *Education:* Yale University, Warburg Institute, London and Harvard University. *Career:* Asst Prof., 1977–83, Assoc. Prof., 1983–89, Prof. of Art History, 1989–, Princeton University; Visiting professorships and curatorships; mem. College Art Asscn of America; Renaissance Society of America; Verband Deutscher Kunsthistorien. *Publications:* Variations on the Imperial Theme, 1978; Drawings From the Holy Roman Empire 1540–1650, 1982; L'Ecole de Prague, 1985; Art and Architecture in Central Europe 1550–1620, 1985; The School of Prague: Painting at the Court of Rudolf II, 1988; Central European Drawings 1680–1800, 1989; The Mastery of Nature, 1993; Court, Cloister and City, 1995. Contributions: books and professional journals. *Honours:* Marshall-Allison Fellow, 1970; David E. Finley Fellow, National Gallery of Art, Washington, DC, 1974–77; ACLS Award, 1977–78, and Fellowship, 1982; Senior Fellow, Alexander von Humboldt Stiftung, Berlin and Munich, 1985–86, 1989–90; Guggenheim Fellowship, 1993–94; Herzog August Bibliothek Fellow, Wolfenbüttel, 1994.

KAUR, Prabhjot (see Prabhjot Kaur)

KAVALER, Lucy Estrin, BA; American writer; b. 29 Aug. 1930, New York, NY; m. 1948; one s. one d. *Education:* Oberlin College, OH; Fellowship, Advanced Science Writing, Columbia University Graduate School. *Publications:* Private World of High Society, 1960; Mushrooms, Molds and Miracles, 1965; The Astors, 1966; Freezing Point, 1970; Noise the New Menace, 1975; A Matter of Degree, 1981; The Secret Lives of the Edmonts, 1989; Heroes and Lovers, 1995. Contributions: Smithsonian; Natural History; McCall's; Reader's Digest; Redbook; Primary Cardiology; Woman's Day (encyclopaedia); Skin Cancer Foundation Journal; Memories; Female Patient. *E-mail:* lucykavaler@lucykavaler.com. *Website:* www.lucykavaler.com.

KAVALER, Rebecca, AB; American writer; b. 26 July 1930, Atlanta, GA; m. Frederic Kavaler 1955; two s. *Education:* University of Georgia. *Career:* mem. PEN. *Publications:* Further Adventures of Brunhild 1978, Doubting Castle 1984, Tigers in the Woods 1986, A Little More Than Kin 2002; contrib. short stories to anthologies and magazines including Best of Nimrod 1957–69 and Best American Short Stories 1972. *Honours:* Award for Short Fiction, Associated Writing Programs, 1978; National Endowment for the Arts Fellowships, 1979, 1985. *Address:* 425 Riverside Drive, New York, NY 10025, USA (home). *E-mail:* rkavaler@msn.com (home).

KAVANAGH, Dan (see Barnes, Julian Patrick)

KAVANAGH, Patrick Joseph, MA, FRSL; British poet, writer and editor; b. 6 Jan. 1931, Worthing, Sussex, England; m. 1st Sally Philipps 1956 (died 1958); m. 2nd Catherine Ward 1965; two s. *Education:* Merton Coll., Oxford. *Career:* columnist, The Spectator 1983–96, Times Literary Supplement 1996–2002.

Publications: poetry: One and One 1960, On the Way to the Depot 1967, About Time 1970, Edward Thomas in Heaven 1974, Life Before Death 1979, Selected Poems 1982, Presences: New and Selected Poems 1987, An Enchantment 1991, Collected Poems 1992, Something About 2004; fiction: A Song and Dance 1968, A Happy Man 1972, People and Weather 1978, Scarf Jack: The Irish Captain 1978, Rebel for Good 1980, Only By Mistake 1980; non-fiction: The Perfect Stranger 1966, People and Places 1988, Finding Connections 1990, Voices in Ireland: A Traveller's Literary Companion 1994, A Kind of Journal 2003, Selected Prose 2003; editor: The Collected Poems of Ivor Gurney 1982, The Oxford Book of Short Poems (with James Michie) 1985, The Bodley Head G. K. Chesterton 1985, Selected Poems of Ivor Gurney 1990, A Book of Consolations 1992. *Honours:* Richard Hillary Prize 1966, Guardian Fiction Prize 1968, Cholmondeley Poetry Prize 1993. *Literary Agent:* c/o PFD, Drury House, 34–43 Russell Street, London, WC2B 5HA, England. *Telephone:* (20) 7344-1000. *Fax:* (20) 7836-9539. *E-mail:* info@pfd.co.uk. *Website:* www.pfd.co.uk.

KAVANAUGH, Cynthia (see Daniels, Dorothy)

KAWADA, Junzo; Japanese anthropologist and writer; *Professor of Cultural Anthropology, Hiroshima City University*; b. 1934, Tokyo. *Education:* Tokyo Univ. *Career:* Prof. of Cultural Anthropology, Hiroshima City Univ.; mem. Universal Acad. of Cultures, Inst. for the Study of the Languages and Cultures of Asia and Africa, Tokyo; Assoc. Ed. Anthropological Science. *Publications:* non-fiction: Kotoba kotoba kotoba: Moji to Nihongo o kangaeru (Words, Native and Imported: Orthography and the Japanese Language), Koe (Voices) 1988, Nishi no kaze, minami no kaze (West Wind, South Wind) 1992, Oto-Kotoba-Ningen (Sound-Word-Man) (with Toru Takemitsu) 1992, Genese et Dynamique de la Royaute: Les Mosi Merdionaux 2002; translations: Claude Lévi-Strauss: L'anthropologie face aux problèmes du monde moderne (jtly); contrib. numerous articles to scholarly journals, including Dialogue Among Civilisations Vol. II, Annales: Histoire, Sciences Sociales, Revue Gabonaise des Sciences de l'Homme. *Honours:* Koizumi Fumio Prize 2001. *Address:* Faculty of International Studies, Hiroshima City University, 3-4-1 Ozuka-Higashi, Asa-Minami-Ku, Hiroshima 731-3194, Japan (office). *E-mail:* j-kawada@intl.hiroshima-cu.ac.jp (office).

KAWAMOTO, Koji; Japanese author and critic. *Career:* Pres., International Comparative Literary Asscn (ICLA); Vice-Pres., Oternae Univ.; teaches literature at the Univ. of Tokyo. *Publications:* non-fiction: The Poetics of Japanese Verse - Imagery, Structure and Meter 1999. *Address:* c/o Paola Mildonian, Letterature Comparate, Dipartim. di Studi Anglo-Americani e Ibero-Americani, Universitè Ca' Foscari-Venezia, Ca' Garzoni, S. Marco 3417, 30124, Venice, Italy.

KAY, Guy Gavriel, BA, LLB; Canadian writer; b. 7 Nov. 1954, Weyburn, SK; m. Laura Beth Cohen 1984; two s. *Education:* Univ. of Manitoba, Univ. of Toronto. *Career:* prin. writer and Assoc. Prod., The Scales of Justice (CBC Radio drama) 1981–90; mem. Asscn of Canadian Radio and TV Artists, Law Soc. of Upper Canada. *Publications:* The Summer Tree 1984, The Darkest Road 1986, The Wandering Fire 1986, Tigana 1990, A Song for Arbonne 1992, The Lions of Al-Rassan 1995, The Last Light of the Sun 2004, Ysabel 2007, Under Heaven 2010; contrib. to journals. *Honours:* Aurora Prizes 1986, 1990. *Address:* c/o Viking Canada, Penguin Group, 90 Eglington Avenue East, Suite 700, Toronto, ON M4P 2Y3, Canada (office). *Website:* www.guygavrielkay.ca.

KAY, Jackie, MBE, BA, PhD; British writer and poet; *Professor of Creative Writing, Newcastle University*; b. 9 Nov. 1961, Edinburgh; d. of John and Helen Kay; pnr Denise Else. *Education:* Stirling Univ., Scotland. *Career:* Literature Touring Co-ordinator Arts Council 1991–93; currently Prof. of Creative Writing, Newcastle Univ.; mem. Poetry Soc., Writers' Guild. *Publications:* poetry: The Adoption Papers (Eric Gregory Award, Saltire and Forward Prizes) 1991, Other Lovers (Somerset Maugham Award) 1993, Off Colour 1998, New and Selected Poems 2003, Life Mask 2005, Darling: New and Selected Poems 2007; juvenile: Two's Company 1992, Three Has Gone 1994, The Frog Who Dreamed She Was an Opera Singer 1998, Strawgirl 2002, Red Cherry 2007; other: Outlines: Bessie Smith (biog.) 1997, Trumpet (Guardian Fiction Prize, Scottish Arts Council Book Award) 1998, Why Don't You Stop Talking (short stories) 2003, Wish I Was Here (short stories) 2006, The Lamplighter 2008, Red Dust Road (memoirs) 2010, Fiere 2011; also several TV documentaries; contribs to Poetry Review, Spare Rib, Conditions, Poetry Wales, Chapman, Rialto, Poetry Matters, London Poetry Newsletter, City Limits. *Honours:* Dr hc (St Andrews), (Warwick), (Stirling), (Open Univ.); British Book Award for Writer of the Year 2007. *Literary Agent:* The Wylie Agency, 17 Bedford Square, London WC1B 3JA, England. *Telephone:* (20) 7908-5900. *Fax:* (20) 7908-5901. *E-mail:* schalfant@wylieagency.co.uk. *Website:* www.wylieagency.com. *Address:* c/o Bloodaxe Books, Highgreen, Tarset, Northumberland, NE48 1RP, England (office). *Telephone:* (1434) 240500 (office). *Fax:* (1434) 240505 (office). *Website:* www.bloodaxebooks.com (office).

KAY, John, PhD, FBA, FRSE; British economist, academic and writer; b. 3 Aug. 1948, Edinburgh, Scotland. *Education:* Royal High School, Edinburgh, Edinburgh Univ., Nuffield Coll., Oxford. *Career:* Fellow, St John's Coll., Oxford 1970–, Lecturer in Econs 1971–78, Peter Moores Dir, Said Business School 1997–99; Research Dir Inst. for Fiscal Studies 1979–81, Dir 1981–86; Prof. of Econs, London Business School 1986–96, Dir Centre for Business Strategy 1986–91; Visiting Prof., LSE 2000–; f. London Economics 1986, Exec. Chair. 1986–96, Dir 1986–2000; Chair. SVM UK Active Fund PLC 1994–2005, Clear Capital Ltd 2004–08; Dir Foreign & Colonial Special Utilities Investment Trust PLC 1993–2003, Value and Income Trust PLC 1994–, Halifax PLC 1996–2000; Dir Law Debenture Corpn PLC 2004–; mem. Council and Exec. Cttee Nat. Inst. for Econ. and Social Research 1989–97; mem. Council of Econ. Advisers to Scottish Govt 2007–; now full-time writer; lecturer and broadcaster; columnist, Financial Times. *Publications:* Concentration in Modern Industry (co-author) 1977, The British Tax System (co-author) 1978, The Reform of Social Security (co-author) 1984, The Economic Analysis of Accounting Profitability (co-author) 1987, Foundations of Corporate Success 1993, Why Firms Succeed 1995, The Business of Economics 1996, The Truth about Markets 2003, Everlasting Light Bulbs (collected articles) 2004, The Hare and the Tortoise (collected articles) 2006, The Long And The Short Of It 2009, Obliquity 2010; contrib. articles to journals. *Honours:* Hon. DLitt (Heriot-Watt). *E-mail:* info@johnkay.com (office). *Website:* www.johnkay.com.

KAYE, Geraldine Hughesdon, BSc; British writer; b. 14 Jan. 1925, Watford, Herts, England; m. 1948 (divorced 1975); one s. two d. *Education:* LSE. *Career:* mem. PEN, West Country Writers, Society of Authors. *Publications:* Comfort Herself, 1985; A Breath of Fresh Air, 1986; Summer in Small Street, 1989; Someone Else's Baby, 1990; A Piece of Cake, 1991; Snowgirl, 1991; Stone Boy, 1991; Hands Off My Sister, 1993; Night at the Zoo, 1995; Forests of the Night, 1995; Late in the Day, 1997; The Dragon Upstairs, 1997; My Second Best Friend, 1998; Between Us (adult novel), 1998. *Honours:* The Other Award 1986.

KAYE, Marvin Nathan, BA, MA; American writer; b. 10 March 1938, Philadelphia, PA; m. Saralee Bransdorf 1963, one d. *Education:* Pennsylvania State University, University of Denver. *Career:* Senior Ed., Harcourt Brace Jovanovich; Artistic Dir, Open Book Theatre Company 1975–; Adjunct Prof. of Creative Writing, New York University, 1975–; Seminar Dir, Smithsonian Institution, Washington, DC, 1998–; mem. several professional organizations. *Publications:* The Histrionic Holmes, 1971; A Lively Game of Death, 1972; A Toy is Born, 1973; The Stein and Day Handbook of Magic, 1973; The Grand Ole Opry Murders, 1974; The Handbook of Mental Magic, 1974; Bullets for Macbeth, 1976; The Incredible Umbrella, 1977; Catalog of Magic, 1977; My Son the Druggist, 1977; The Laurel and Hardy Murders, 1977; My Brother the Druggist, 1979; The Amorous Umbrella, 1981; The Possession of Immanuel Wolf, 1981; The Soap Opera Slaughters, 1982; Ghosts of Night and Morning, 1985; Fantastique, 1993. With Parke Godwin: The Masters of Solitude, 1978; Wintermind, 1982; A Cold Blue Light, 1983. Editor: Fiends and Creatures, 1975; Brother Theodore's Chamber of Horrors, 1975; Ghosts, 1981; Masterpieces of Terror and the Supernatural, 1985; Ghosts of Night and Morning, 1987; Devils and Demons, 1987; Weird Tales, the Magazine That Never Dies, 1988; Witches and Warlocks, 1989; 13 Plays of Ghosts and the Supernatural, 1990; Haunted America, 1991; Lovers and Other Monsters, 1991; Sweet Revenge, 1992; Masterpieces of Terror and the Unknown, 1993; Frantic Comedy, 1993; The Game is Afoot, 1994; Angels of Darkness, 1995; Readers Theatre: How to Stage It, 1995; The Resurrected Holmes, 1996; Page to Stage, 1996; The Best of Weird Tales, 1923, 1997; The Confidential Casebook of Sherlock Holmes, 1998; Don't Open This Book, 1998. Contributions: Amazing; Fantastic; Galileo; Family Digest; Columnist, Science Fiction Chronicle.

KAYO, Patrice, BA, MA, PhD; Cameroonian writer and poet; b. 1942, Bandjoun, W Prov.; m. Celine; six c. *Education:* Univ. of Yaounde, Univ. of Paris, Sorbonne. *Career:* fmr journalist; arrested and condemned to death for writing a poem in honour of a rebel leader, verdict was later annulled; Chair. Nat. Asscn of Poets and Writers of Cameroon 1969–81; co-founder Int. Fed. of French-speaking Writers, Quebec, Canada 1982. *Publications:* La sagesse bamiléké 1964, Fables et devinettes de mon enfance 1979, Dechirements 1983, Les sauterelles (novel) 1986, En attendant l'Aurore (poems) 1988, Chansons populaires bamileke 1996, Fables des Montagnes (children's fiction) 1998, Tout le long des saisons (novel) 2001, Les fetes tragiques (novel) 2007; contrib. to Penguin Book of Modern African Poetry. *Address:* c/o Presses Universitaires d'Afrique, BP 8106, Yaoundé, Cameroon (office). *E-mail:* aes@iccnet.cm (office).

KAYSEN, Susanna; American writer; b. 11 Nov. 1948, Cambridge, MA. *Publications:* Asa, as I Knew Him 1987, Far Afield 1990, Girl, Interrupted 1993, The Camera My Mother Gave Me 2001. *Address:* c/o Knopf Publishing/Author Mail, 1745 Broadway, New York, NY 10019, USA (office). *Website:* www.randomhouse.com/knopf (office).

KAZANTZIS, Judith; British poet and novelist; b. 14 Aug. 1940, Oxford, England; m. 2nd Irving Weinman; one d. one s. (from previous marriage). *Education:* Univ. of Oxford. *Career:* Royal Literary Fund Fellow, Univ. of Sussex 2005–06; judge of several poetry prize competitions; mem. Soc. of Authors, English PEN, Palestine Solidarity Campaign, Nicaragua Solidarity Campaign, Campaign for Nuclear Disarmament. *Publications:* poetry: Minefield 1977, The Wicked Queen 1980, Touch Papers (co-author) 1982, Let's Pretend 1984, Flame Tree 1988, A Poem for Guatemala (pamphlet) 1988, The Rabbit Magician Plate 1992, Selected Poems 1977–92 1995, Swimming Through the Grand Hotel 1997, The Odysseus Poems: Fictions on the Odyssey of Homer 1999, In Cyclop's Cave (trans. of book IX of The Odyssey) 2002, Just After Midnight 2004, Some Poetical Thoughts by Mad King George (contrib.) 2009; prose: Of Love and Terror (novel) 2002; non-fiction: introduction to Eminent Victorian Women, Elizabeth Longford 2008; contribs to anthologies and periodicals. *Honours:* Cholmondeley Award 2007. *E-mail:* judith@judithkazantzis.com. *Website:* www.judithkazantzis.com.

KEANE, Fergal Patrick, OBE; Irish journalist and broadcaster; b. 6 Jan. 1961, s. of the late Eamon Brendan Keane and of Mary Hasset; m. Anne Frances Flaherty 1986; one s. *Education:* Terenure Coll., Dublin and Presentation Coll., Cork. *Career:* trainee reporter with Limerick Leader 1979–82; reporter Irish Press Group, Dublin 1982–84, Radio Telefis Eireann, Belfast 1986–89 (Dublin 1984–86); NI Corresp. BBC Radio 1989–91, South Africa Corresp. 1991–94, Asia Corresp. 1994–97, Special Corresp. Radio 4 1997–; presenter, Fergal Keane's Forgotten Britain (BBC) 2000; columnist The Independent newspaper. *Publications:* Irish Politics Now 1987, The Bondage of Fear 1994, Season of Blood: A Rwandan Journey 1995, Letter to Daniel 1996, Letters Home 1999, A Stranger's Eye 2000, There will be Sunlight Later: A Memoir of War 2004, All of These People (memoir) 2005, Road of Bones 2010. *Honours:* Hon. DLitt (Strathclyde) 2001, (Staffs.) 2002; James Cameron Prize 1996, Bayeux Prize for war reporting 1999; Reporter of the Year Sony Silver Award 1992 and Sony Gold Award 1993, Int. Reporter of the Year 1993, Amnesty Int. Press Awards, RTS Journalist of the Year 1994, BAFTA Award 1997. *Address:* BBC Radio, Broadcasting House, Portland Place, London, W1A 1AA, England. *Website:* www.bbc.co.uk/radio4/presenters/fergal_keane.shtml.

KEARNEY, Martha Catherine; British journalist; *Presenter, The World at One, BBC Radio 4*; b. 8 Oct. 1957, d. of Hugh Kearney and Catherine Kearney; m. Christopher Thomas Shaw 2001. *Education:* Brighton and Hove High School, George Watson's Ladies' Coll., Edinburgh and St Anne's Coll., Oxford. *Career:* worked for LBC/IRN Radio 1980–87, as reporter AM breakfast show, presenter AM and Nightline phone-in, lobby correspondent for IRN; worked on A Week in Politics (Channel 4) 1987–88; worked for BBC from 1988, reporter On the Record (BBC 1) 1988–94, Panorama 1993, presenter Woman's Hour (BBC Radio 4) 1999–, reporter Newsnight 1994–2000, Political Ed. Newsnight 2000–07, presenter The World at One (BBC Radio 4) 2007–. *Honours:* TRIC Radio Presenter of the Year 2003, House Magazine Political Commentator of the Year 2005. *Address:* BBC TV Centre, Wood Lane, London, W12 7RJ, England (office). *E-mail:* martha.kearney@bbc.co.uk (office). *Website:* www.bbc.co.uk (office).

KEARNS, Marguerite, (Marguerite Culp), BA; American writer; b. 17 Feb. 1943, Norristown, PA. *Education:* Beaver Coll., Glenside, Temple Univ., Philadelphia. *Career:* mem. National Writers' Union, PEN. *Publications:* Freedom Deferred (online) 2002, Big Brother 2002, For Love's Sake Only 2002; contrib. to newspapers and journals. *Honours:* New York State Bar Asscn Award in Journalism 1974.

KEAY, John Stanley Melville, BA; British writer and broadcaster; b. 18 Sept. 1941, Devon; m. Julia Keay; four c. *Education:* Ampleforth Coll., York, Magdalen Coll., Oxford. *Career:* Corresp. The Economist 1966–71; fmr writer and presenter BBC Radio. *Publications include:* Into India 1973, When Men and Mountains Meet 1977, The Gilgit Game 1979, India Discovered 1981, Eccentric Travellers 1982, Highland Drove 1984, Explorers Extraordinary 1985, The Royal Geographical Society's History of World Exploration 1991, The Honourable Company 1991, Collins Encyclopaedia of Scotland (with Julia Keay) 1994, Indonesia: From Sabang to Merauke 1995, The Explorers of the Western Himalayas 1996, Last Post: Empire's End 1997, India: A History 2000, The Great Arc 2000, Sowing the Wind: The Seeds of Conflict in the Middle East 2003, Mad About the Mekong: Exploration and Empire in South East Asia 2005, The Spice Route 2005, China: A History 2008, The London Encyclopaedia (co-author) 2008, Mammoth Book of Travel in Dangerous Places 2010. *Honours:* Sir Percy Sykes Memorial Medal, Royal Soc. for Asian Affairs 2009. *Address:* Succoth, Dalmally, Argyll, Scotland.

KEE, Robert, CBE, MA; British journalist, writer and broadcaster; b. 5 Oct. 1919, Calcutta, India; s. of late Robert Kee and Dorothy F. Kee; m. 1st Janetta Woolley 1948 (divorced 1950); one d.; m. 2nd Cynthia Judah 1960 (divorced 1989); one s. (and one s. deceased) one d.; m. 3rd Catherine M. Trevelyan 1990. *Education:* Rottingdean School, Stowe School and Magdalen Coll., Oxford. *Career:* journalist, Picture Post 1948–51; picture ed. Who 1952; foreign corresp. Observer 1956–57, Sunday Times 1957–58; literary ed. Spectator 1957; TV reporter, Panorama, BBC 1958–62; TV Reporters Int., This Week, Faces of Communism (four parts, also for Channel 13, USA) ITV 1962–78; Ireland: a TV history (13 parts, also for Channel 13, USA), Panorama, BBC 1979–82; TVam 1982–83, Presenter, 7 Days (Channel 4), ITV 1984–88; mem. BECTU, Equity. *Publications:* A Crowd Is Not Company 1947, The Impossible Shore 1949, A Sign of the Times 1955, Broadstrop in Season 1959, Refugee World 1960, The Green Flag 1972, Ireland: A History 1980, The World We Left Behind 1984, The World We Fought For 1985, Trial and Error 1986, Munich: The Eleventh Hour 1988, The Picture Post Album 1989, The Laurel and the Ivy: Parnell and Irish Nationalism 1993. *Honours:* BAFTA Richard Dimbleby Award 1976, Jacobs Award (Dublin) for BBC Ireland 1981. *Address:* c/o Rogers, Coleridge and White, 20 Powis Mews, London, W11 1JN, England.

KEEBLE, Neil Howard, BA, DPhil, DLitt, FRSE, FEA, FRHistS, FRSA; British academic, writer and editor; *Professor Emeritus of English Studies, University of Stirling*; b. 7 Aug. 1944, London, England; m. Jenny Bowers 1968; two s. one d. *Education:* Univs of Lampeter, Oxford and Stirling. *Career:* Lecturer in English, Univ. of Århus, Denmark 1969–74; Lecturer, Univ. of Stirling 1974–88, Reader in English 1988–95, Prof. of English 1995–2010, Prof. Emer. of English Studies 2010–, Deputy Prin. 2001–03, Sr Deputy Prin. 2003–10; Fellow, English Asscn 2000. *Publications:* Richard Baxter: Puritan Man of Letters 1982, The Literary Culture of Nonconformity 1987, Calendar of the Correspondence of Richard Baxter (co-author) 1991, The Restoration: England in the 1660s 2002; editor: The Autobiography of Richard Baxter 1974, The Pilgrim's Progress 1984, John Bunyan: Conventicle and Parnassus 1988, The Cultural Identity of Seventeenth-Century Woman 1994, Lucy Hutchinson, Memoirs of the Life of Colonel Hutchinson 1995, The Cambridge Companion to Writing of the English Revolution 2001, Daniel Defoe, Memoirs of the Church of Scotland 2002, John Bunyan: Reading Dissenting Writing 2002, Andrew Marvell, Remarks Upon a Late Disingenuous Discourse 2003, Memoirs of a Cavalier 2008; numerous articles on cultural history 1500–1700 in academic journals and symposia. *Honours:* Hon. Fellow, Univ. of Wales, Lampeter 2000. *Address:* 12 Pine Crescent, Menstrie, Clackmannanshire, FK11 7DT, Scotland (home). *E-mail:* n.h.keeble@stir.ac.uk (office); nhk@logres.co.uk (office).

KEEFFE, Barrie Colin; British dramatist, novelist, director and university tutor; *Tutor, City University, London*; b. 31 Oct. 1945, London; s. of the late Edward Thomas Keeffe and Constance Beatrice Keeffe (née Marsh); m. 1st Sarah Dee (Truman) 1969 (divorced 1975); m. 2nd Verity Eileen Bargate 1981 (died 1981); two step-s.; m. 3rd Julia Lindsay 1983 (divorced 1991). *Education:* East Ham Grammar School. *Career:* fmr actor with Nat. Youth Theatre, journalist; has written plays for theatre, TV and radio; fmr Resident Writer, Shaw Theatre, London, RSC; Assoc. Writer, Theatre Royal, Stratford East, also mem. Bd; Assoc. Soho Theatre Co.; Writers' Mentor, Nat. Theatre 1999–2002; Tutor, City Univ., London 2001–; Bye-Fellow, Christ's Coll., Cambridge 2003–04; UN Amb., 50th Anniversary Year 1995; mem. Soc. des auteurs et compositeurs dramatiques. *Theatre plays include:* Only a Game 1973, A Sight of Glory 1975, Scribes 1975, Here Comes the Sun 1976, Gimme Shelter 1977, A Mad World My Masters 1977, Barbarians 1977, Frozen Assets 1978, Sus 1979, Heaven Scent 1979, Bastard Angel 1980, She's So Modern 1980, Black Lear 1980, Chorus Girls 1981, Better Times 1985, King of England 1988, My Girl 1989, Not Fade Away 1990, Wild Justice 1990, I Only Want to Be With You 1995, Shadows on The Sun 2001. *Plays directed include:* A Certain Vincent, A Gentle Spirit, Talking of Chekov (Amsterdam and London), My Girl (London and Bombay), The Gary Oldman Fan Club (London). *Film:* The Long Good Friday (screenplay) 1980, Sus (screenplay) 2010. *Television plays include:* Substitute 1972, Not Quite Cricket 1977, Gotcha 1977, Nipper 1977, Champions 1978, Hanging Around 1978, Waterloo Sunset 1979, No Excuses (series) 1983, King 1984. *Radio plays include:* Good Old Uncle Jack 1975, Pigeon Skyline 1975, Self- Portrait 1977, Paradise 1990, On the Eve of the Millennium 1999, Tales 2000, Feng Shui and Me 2000, The Five of Us 2002. *Publications:* novels: Gadabout 1969, No Excuses 1983; screenplay: The Long Good Friday 1998; Barrie Keeffe Plays I 2001. *Honours:* Dr hc (Univ. of Warwick) 2010; French Critics' Prix Révélation 1978, Thames TV Playwright Award 1979, Giles Cooper Award Best Radio Plays, Mystery Writers of America Edgar Allan Poe Award 1982. *Address:* 110 Annandale Road, London, SE10 0JZ, England. *E-mail:* barriekeeffe@aol.com (office).

KEEGAN, Sir John, Kt, OBE; British military historian and journalist; b. 15 May 1934, London; s. of Francis Joseph Keegan and Eileen Mary Bridgman; m. Susanne Keegan; two s. two d. *Education:* privately and Balliol Coll. Oxford. *Career:* awarded travel grant to study American Civil War in USA; writer of political reports for US Embassy, London 1957–59; Lecturer, then Sr Lecturer, War Studies Dept, Royal Mil. Acad., Sandhurst 1959–86; war corresp. for Atlantic Monthly Telegraph, Beirut 1984; Defence Ed. Daily Telegraph 1986–2009; Delmas Prof. of History, Vassar Coll. 1997–98; Contributing Ed. US News and World Report 1986–; Dir E Somerset NHS Trust 1991–97; Commr Commonwealth War Graves Comm. 2000–; Trustee, Heritage Lottery Fund 1994–2000; Fellow, Princeton Univ. 1984. *Publications include:* The Face of Battle 1976, The Nature of War 1981, Six Armies in Normandy: From D-Day to the Liberation of Paris 1982, Zones of Conflict: An Atlas of Future Wars 1986, Soldiers: A History of Men in Battle 1986, The Mask of Command 1987, Who's Who in Military History (with A. Wheatcroft) 1987, The Price of Admiralty: The Evolution of Naval Warfare 1989, The Second World War 1990, Churchill's Generals (ed.) 1991, A History of Warfare 1993, Warpaths: Travels of a Military Historian in North America 1995, Who's Who in World War 2 1995, The Battle for History: Re-fighting World War II 1995, Warpaths 1996, The First World War 1998, The Penguin Book of War 1999, Winston Churchill 2002, Intelligence in War 2003, The Iraq War 2004, The American Civil War: A Military History 2009; ed. and co-ed. of several mil. reference works. *Honours:* Hon. Fellow, Balliol Coll. Oxford 1995; Hon. LLD (New Brunswick) 1997; Hon. LittD (Queen's Univ. Belfast) 2000; Hon. DLitt (Bath) 2001; Samuel Eliot Morrison Prize, US Soc. for Mil. History 1996, BBC Reith Lecturer 1998. *Address:* The Manor House, Kilmington, nr Warminster, Wilts., BA12 6RD, England. *Telephone:* (1985) 844856.

KEEGAN, William James, CBE, MA; British journalist and writer; *Senior Economics Commentator, The Observer*; b. 3 July 1938, London; m. 1st Tessa Ashton 1967 (divorced 1982); two s. two d.; m. 2nd Hilary Stonefrost 1992; one s. two d. *Education:* Wimbledon Coll., Trinity Coll., Cambridge. *Career:* Economics Ed. 1977, Assoc. Ed. 1983–2003, Sr Econs Commentator 2003–; The Observer; Visiting Prof. of Journalism, Sheffield Univ. 1989–; mem. Dept of Applied Economics, Univ. of Cambridge, mem. Advisory Bd 1988–93. *Publications include:* Consulting Father Wintergreen (novel) 1974, A Real Killing (novel) 1976, Who Runs the Economy? 1979, Mrs Thatcher's Economic Experiment 1984, Britain Without Oil 1985, Mr Lawson's Gamble 1989, The Spectre of Capitalism 1992, 2066 and All That 2000, The Prudence of Mr Gordon Brown 2003; contrib. to The Tablet; Frequent Broadcaster. *Honours:*

Hon. DLit (Sheffield), (London) 1995, (City) 1998. *Address:* 76 Lofting Road, London, N1 1JB, England (home). *Telephone:* (20) 7607-3590 (home). *E-mail:* william.keegan@observer.co.uk (office).

KEELEY, Edmund Leroy, BA, DPhil; American academic, writer and translator; *Charles Barnwell Straut Professor of English Emeritus, Princeton University*; b. 5 Feb. 1928, Damascus, Syria; m. Mary Stathatos-Kyris 1951. *Education:* Princeton Univ., Univ. of Oxford. *Career:* instructor, Brown Univ. 1952–53; Fulbright Lecturer, Univ. of Thessaloniki 1953–54, 1986; instructor, Princeton Univ. 1954–57, Asst Prof. 1957–63, Assoc. Prof. 1963–70, Prof. of English and Creative Writing 1970–92, Charles Branwell Straut Class of 1923 Prof. of English 1992–94, Prof. Emeritus 1994–; Visiting Lecturer, Univ. of Iowa 1962–63, Univ. of the Aegean 1988; writer-in-residence, Knox Coll. 1963; Visiting Prof., New School for Social Research, New York 1980, Columbia Univ. 1981, King's Coll. London 1996; Fulbright Lecturer 1985, and Research Fellow 1987, Univ. of Athens; Sr Assoc. mem., St Antony's Coll., Oxford 1996; mem. American Acad. of Arts and Sciences, Acad. of Athens, American Literary Trans Asscn, Authors' Guild, Modern Greek Studies Asscn (pres. 1969–73, 1982–84), PEN American Center (pres. 1991–93), Poetry Soc. of America. *Publications:* fiction: The Libation 1958, The Gold-Hatted Lover 1961, The Impostor 1970, Voyage to a Dark Island 1972, A Wilderness Called Peace 1985, School for Pagan Lovers 1993, Some Wine for Remembrance 2001; non-fiction: Cavafy's Alexandria 1976, Modern Greek Poetry: Voice and Myth 1982, The Salonika Bay Murder: Cold War Politics and the Polk Affair 1989, Albanian Journal: The Road to Elbasan 1996, George Seferis and Edmund Keeley: Correspondence, 1951–1971 1997, Inventing Paradise: The Greek Journey, 1937–1947 1999, On Translation: Reflections and Conversations 2000, Borderlines: A Memoir 2005; translator: Six Poets of Modern Greece (with Philip Sherrard) 1960, Vassilis Vassilikos: The Plant, the Well, the Angel (with Mary Keeley) 1964, George Seferis: Collected Poems (with Philip Sherrard) 1967, Odysseus Elytis: The Axion Esti (with George Savidis) 1974, C. P. Cavafy: Collected Poems (with Philip Sherrard and George Savidis) 1975, 1992, 2009, Angelos Sikelianos: Selected Poems (with Philip Sherrard) 1979, Odysseus Elytis: Selected Poems (with Philip Sherrard) 1981, Yannis Ritsos: Repetitions, Testimonies, Parentheses 1991, A Greek Quintet (with Philip Sherrard) 1992, A Century of Greek Poetry (ed. with Peter Bien, Peter Constantine, Karen Van Dyck) 2004, The Greek Poets: Homer to the Present (ed. with Peter Constantine, Rachel Hadas, Karen Van Dyck) 2010; contrib. to books and journals. *Honours:* Dr hc (Univ. of Athens) 1994, (Univ. of Cyprus) 2010, Hon. DHumLitt (Richard Stockton Coll. of New Jersey) 2006; Commander, Order of the Phoenix (Greece) 2001; American Acad. of Arts and Letters Rome Prize Fellow 1959–60, American Acad. of Arts and Letters Award in Literature 1999, Guggenheim Fellowships 1959–60, 1973, Columbia Univ. Trans. Center –PEN Award 1975, Harold Morton Landon Trans. Award 1980, Nat. Endowment for the Arts Fellowships 1981, 1988–89, Bellagio Study Center Rockefeller Foundation Scholar, Italy 1982, 1989, Research Fellow Virginia Center for the Creative Arts 1983, 1984, 1986, 1990, Pushcart Prize Anthology 1984, First European Prize for Trans. of Poetry 1987, PEN-Ralph Manheim Medal for Trans. 2000, London Hellenic Soc. Criticos Prize 2000, The Yale Review Prize 2003, Gennadius Library Trustees' Annual Award 2003, Hellenic Public Radio Phidippides Award 2004, Dido Sotiriou Cultural Prize, Hellenic Authors' Soc. 2008, Lord Byron Award, Hellenic Coll. 2008, Amb. of Hellenism Award, Normarchy of Athens 2010. *Address:* 140 Littlebrook Road, Princeton, NJ, USA (home).

KEEN, Geraldine (see Norman, Geraldine Lucia)

KEEN, Suzanne Parker, AB, AM, MA, PhD; American academic and poet; *Thomas H. Broadus Professor of English, Washington and Lee University, Lexington*; b. 10 April 1963, Bethlehem, Pa; d. of William Parker Keen and Sarah Lowell Whitcomb Keen; m. Francis MacDonnell 1992; one s. *Education:* Brown and Harvard Univs. *Career:* Asst Prof. of English, Yale Univ. 1990–95; Assoc. Prof., Washington and Lee Univ., Lexington, Va 1995–2001, Prof. 2001–05, Thomas H. Broadus Prof. 2005–; Past Pres. Int. Soc. for Study of Narrative; Vice-Pres. Thomas Hardy Asscn; mem. MLA, N American Victorian Socs Asscn, Asscn of the Study of the Arts of the Present, Rotary International. *Publications:* Victorian Renovations of the Novel: Narrative Annexes and the Boundaries of Representation 1998, Romances of the Archive in Contemporary British Fiction 2001, Narrative Form 2003, Empathy and the Novel 2007, Milk Glass Mermaid 2007; Ed.: double-special issue of Poetics Today, 'Narrative and the Emotions'; contrib. to anthologies, reviews and journals. *Honours:* Brown Univ. Kim Ann Arstark Poetry Prize 1985, Acad. of American Poets Prize 1987, Virginia Comm. for the Arts Individual Artist Fellowship 1998, Nat. Endowment for the Humanities Fellowship 1999, Outstanding Faculty Award, State Council of Higher Educ. for Virginia 2008. *Address:* Department of English, Payne Hall, Washington and Lee University, Lexington, VA 24450, USA (office). *Telephone:* (540) 458-8759 (office). *Fax:* (540) 458-8708 (office). *E-mail:* skeen@wlu.edu (office). *Website:* www.wlu.edu/x23945.xml?InsertFile=x23417 (office).

KEENAN, Brian, BA, MA, PhD; Northern Irish writer; b. 28 Sept. 1950, Belfast, Northern Ireland; m. Audrey Doyle 1993; two s. *Education:* Ulster Univ., Queen's Univ., Belfast. *Career:* Instructor in English, American Univ., Beirut, Lebanon 1985–86; Writer-in-Residence, Trinity Coll., Dublin 1993–94. *Publications:* An Evil Cradling: The Five-Year Ordeal of a Hostage 1992, Blind Fight (screenplay) 1995, Between Extremes 1999, Turlough 2000, Four Quarters of Light 2004. *Honours:* Time/Life International PEN Award 1992, Ewart Biggs Award 1992, Irish Times Award 1992, Christopher Award, New York 1993. *Address:* c/o Elaine Steel, 110 Gloucester Avenue, London, NW1 8JA, England (office). *Telephone:* (20) 8348-0918 (office). *Fax:* (20) 8341-9807 (office). *E-mail:* ecmsteel@aol.com (office).

KEENE, Donald, BA, MA, PhD, DLitt; American academic, writer and translator; *Shincho Professor Emeritus of Japanese, Columbia University*; b. 18 June 1922, New York, NY. *Education:* Columbia Univ., New York, Univ. of Cambridge, UK. *Career:* Lecturer, Univ. of Cambridge 1948–53; Guest Ed., Asahi Shimbun, Tokyo, Japan; Prof., Columbia Univ. 1953–1992, Shincho Prof. Emer. of Japanese 1992–; mem. Japan Soc., New York (Dir 1979–82), American Acad. of Arts and Letters, Japan Acad. (Foreign mem.). *Publications:* The Battles of Coxinga 1951, The Japanese Discovery of Europe 1952, Japanese Literature: An Introduction for Western Readers 1953, Living Japan 1957, Bunraku, the Puppet Theater of Japan 1965, No: The Classical Theatre of Japan 1966, Landscapes and Portraits 1971, Some Japanese Portraits 1978, World Within Walls 1978, Meeting with Japan 1978, Travels in Japan 1981, Dawn to the West 1984, Travellers of a Hundred Ages 1990, Seeds in the Heart 1993, On Familiar Terms 1994, Modern Japanese Diaries 1995, Emperor of Japan 2002, Yoshimasa and the Silver Pavilion 2003, A Frog in the Well 2006; editor: Anthology of Japanese Literature 1955, Modern Japanese Literature 1956, Sources of Japanese Tradition 1958, Twenty Plays of the No Theater 1970; translator: The Setting Sun 1956, Five Modern No Plays 1957, No Longer Human 1958, Major Plays of Chikamatsu 1961, The Old Woman, the Wife and the Archer 1961, After the Banquet 1965, Essays in Idleness 1967, Madame de Sade 1967, Friends 1969, The Man Who Turned into a Stick 1972, Three Plays of Kobo Abe 1993, The Narrow Road to Oku 1997, The Tale of the Bamboo Cutter 1998, The Breaking Jewel 2003, Chronicles of My Life 2008, So Lovely a Country will not Perish 2010. *Honours:* Bunka Kunsko, Japan; Hon. DLitt (Tohoku) 1997, (Waseda) 1998, (Tokyo Univ. of Foreign Languages) 1999, (Keiwa) 2000, (Kyoto Sangyō) 2002. *Address:* 407 Kent Hall, Columbia University, New York, NY 10027 (office); 445 Riverside Drive, New York, NY 10027, USA (home). *Telephone:* (212) 222-1449 (home). *Fax:* (212) 222-1449 (home). *E-mail:* dk8@columbia.edu (office).

KEHLMANN, Daniel, PhD; German/Austrian novelist; b. 13 Jan. 1975, Munich, Germany; s. of Michael Kehlmann. *Career:* moved to Vienna 1981; Guest Lecturer in Poetics, Johannes Gutenberg Univ., Mainz 2001, FH Wiesbaden 2005–06; writer-in-residence, New York Univ. 'Deutsches Haus' 2006, Univ. of Göttingen 2006–07; mem. Mainzer Akademie der Wissenschaften und der Literatur. *Publications:* Beerholms Vorstellung (novel) (Förderpreis des Kulturkreises der deutschen Wirtschaft) 1997, Unter der Sonne (short stories) 1998, Mahlers Zeit (novel) 1999, Der fernste Ort (novel) 2001, Ich und Kaminski (novel; trans. as Me and Kaminski) 2003, Die Vermessung der Welt (novel; trans. as Measuring the World) (Heimito von Doderer Prize) 2005, Wo ist Carlos Montúfar? (essays) 2005, Ruhm (novel, trans. as Fame) 2009; contrib. to Süddeutsche Zeitung, Frankfurter Rundschau, Frankfurter Allgemeine Zeitung, Literaturen. *Honours:* Candide Award 2005. *Address:* c/o Rowohlt Verlag, Hamburgerstrasse 17, 21465 Reinbek, Germany (office). *E-mail:* info@rowohlt.de (office). *Website:* www.rowohlt.de (office).

KEILLOR, Garrison Edward, BA; American author and broadcaster; b. (Gary Edward Keillor), 7 Aug. 1942, Anoka, Minn.; s. of John P. Keillor and Grace R. Keillor (née Denham); m. 1st Mary Guntzel (divorced 1976, died 1998); one s.; m. 2nd Ulla Skaerved (divorced); m. 3rd Jenny Lind Nilsson; one d. *Education:* Anoka High School and Univ. of Minnesota. *Career:* journalist 1962–63; radio announcer and presenter 1969–73; creator and host A Prairie Home Companion radio show 1974–87, 1993–; host American Radio Co. 1989–93; staff writer, The New Yorker 1987–92. *Film:* A Prairie Home Companion 2006. *Publications:* Happy to Be Here 1982, Lake Wobegon Days (Grammy Award for best non-musical recording 1987) 1985, Leaving Home 1987, We Are Still Married: Stories and Letters 1989, WLT: A Radio Romance 1991, Wobegon Boy The Book of Guys 1993, Cat, You Better Come Home (children's book) 1995, The Old Man Who Loved Cheese 1996, The Sandy Bottom Orchestra 1996, Wobegon Boy 1997, ME by Jimmy (Big Boy) Valente as told to Garrison Keillor 1999, Lake Wobegon Summer 1956 2001, Love Me 2004, Pontoon 2007, Liberty: A Lake Wobegon Novel 2008, Pilgrims: A Lake Wobegon Romance 2010; contrib. to newspapers and magazines. *Honours:* George Foster Peabody Award 1980, Ace Award for best musical host (A Prairie Home Companion) 1988, Best Music and Entertainment Host Awards 1988, 1989, American Acad. and Institute of Arts and Letters Medal 1990, Music Broadcast Communications Radio Hall of Fame 1994, Nat. Humanities Medal 1999, John Steinbeck Award 2007. *Address:* A Prairie Home Companion, Minnesota Public Radio, 480 Cedar Street, St Paul, MN 55101, USA (office). *Website:* prairiehome.publicradio.org (office).

KEIN, Sybil, BS, MA, PhD; American academic, poet, dramatist and musician; b. 29 Sept. 1939, New Orleans, La; m. Felix Provost 1960 (divorced 1969); one s. two d. *Education:* Xavier University, Aspen School of Arts, Louisiana State University, University of Michigan. *Career:* Instructor, University of Michigan at Flint 1972–75, Asst Prof. 1975–78, Assoc. Prof. 1979–88, Prof. of English 1988–. *Publications:* Bessie, Bojangles and Me, 1975; Visions from the Rainbow, 1979; Gombo People: Poésies Créoles de la Nouvelle Orleans, 1981; Delta Dancer, 1984; An American South, 1997; contributions: anthologies and journals. *Honours:* several teaching awards; Creative Artist Awards for Poetry, Michigan Council for the Arts, 1981, 1984, 1989; Chercheur Associé, Centre d'Etudes Afro-Americaines, Université de la Sorbonne Nouvelle, 1990. *E-mail:* sybkein@aol.com.

KEITH, William John, BA, MA, PhD, FRSC; Canadian fmr academic, literary critic and poet; b. 9 May 1934, London, England; m. Hiroko Teresa Sato 1965. *Education:* Jesus Coll., Cambridge, Univ. of Toronto. *Career:* Lecturer, McMaster University 1961–62, Asst Prof. 1962–66; Assoc. Prof., University of Toronto 1966–71, Prof. of English 1971–95, Prof. Emeritus 1995–; Ed., University of Toronto Quarterly 1976–85; mem. Richard Jefferies Society, hon. pres. 1974–91. *Publications:* Richard Jefferies: A Critical Study 1965, Charles G. D. Roberts 1969, The Rural Tradition 1974, Charles G. D. Roberts: Selected Poetry and Critical Prose (ed.) 1974, The Poetry of Nature 1980, The Arts in Canada: The Last Fifty Years (co-ed.) 1980, Epic Fiction: The Art of Rudy Wiebe 1981, A Voice in the Land: Essays by and About Rudy Wiebe (ed.) 1981, Canadian Literature in English 1985 (revised and expanded edn, 2 vols 2007), Regions of the Imagination 1988, Introducing The Edible Woman 1989, A Sense of Style: Studies in the Art of Fiction in English-Speaking Canada 1989, An Independent Stance: Essays on English-Canadian Criticism and Fiction 1991, Echoes in Silence (poems) 1992, Literary Images of Ontario 1992, The Jefferies Canon 1995, In the Beginning and Other Poems 1999, Canadian Odyssey: A Reading of Hugh Hood's The New Age/Le nouveau siècle 2002; contributions: journals. *Address:* University College, University of Toronto, Toronto, ON M5S 3H7, Canada (office).

KELEK, Necla; German (b. Turkish) sociologist and writer; b. 1957, Istanbul, Turkey. *Publications:* Islam im Alltag 2002, Die verlorenen Söhne (Lost Sons), Die fremde Braut (The Foreign Bride) (Geschwister-Scholl-Preis) 2005. *Address:* c/o Verlag Kiepenheuer & Witsch GmbH & Co. KG, Rondorfer Str. 5, Cologne 50968, Germany. *E-mail:* verlag@kiwi-koeln.de.

KELLEHER, Victor, (Veronica Hart), BA, DipEd, MA, DLitt; Australian writer; b. 19 July 1939, London, England; m. Alison Lyle 1962, one s. one d. *Education:* Univ. of Natal, Univ. of St Andrews, Univ. of the Witwatersrand, Univ. of South Africa. *Career:* Jr Lecturer in English, Univ. of the Witwatersrand 1969; Lecturer, Univ. of South Africa, Pretoria 1970–71, Senior Lecturer in English 1972–73; Lecturer in English, Massey Univ., Palmerston North, New Zealand 1973–76; Lecturer, Univ. of New England, Armidale, Australia 1976–79, Senior Lecturer 1980–83, Assoc. Prof. of English 1984–87; mem. Australian Society of Authors. *Publications:* Voices from the River 1979, Forbidden Paths of Thual 1979, The Hunting of Shadroth 1981, Master of the Grove 1982, Africa and After 1983, The Beast of Heaven 1983, Papio 1983, The Green Piper 1984, Taronga 1986, The Makers 1987, Em's Story 1988, Baily's Bones 1988, The Red King 1989, Wintering 1990, Brother Night 1990, Del-Del 1991, To the Dark Tower 1992, Micky Darlin 1992, Where the Whales Sing 1994, Parkland 1994, Double God (as Veronica Hart) 1994, The House that Jack Built (as Veronica Hart) 1994, Earthsong 1995, Storyman 1996, Fire Dancer 1996, Slow Burn 1997, Into the Dark 1999, Riding the Whales 1999, The Ivory Trail 1999, Billy the Baked Bean Kid 2002, Born of the Sea 2003, The Grimes Family 2004, Dogboy 2006, The Gorilla Suit 2007; contributions: anthologies and magazines. *Address:* c/o Penguin Group (Australia), PO Box 701, Hawthorn, Vic. 3122, Australia (office). *Website:* www.penguin.com.au (office).

KELLENBERGER, James, PhD; American academic and writer; *Professor of Philosophy Emeritus, California State University at Northridge;* b. 4 May 1938, San Francisco, Calif.; m. Anne Dunn 1981; one s. one d. *Education:* San Jose State Univ., Univ. of California, Berkeley, Univ. of Oregon. *Career:* Lecturer in Logic, Cameroon Coll. of Arts and Science 1962–64; Asst Prof., California State Univ. at Northridge 1967–71, Assoc. Prof. 1971–75, Prof. of Philosophy 1975–2008, Emer. 2008–; Visiting Prof., Albion Coll., Michigan 1971–72; Adjunct Prof. of Religion, Claremont Grad. School 1991; mem. American Philosophical Asscn, Soc. of Christian Philosophers. *Publications include:* Religious Discovery, Faith and Knowledge 1972, The Cognitivity of Religion: Three Perspectives 1985, God-Relationships With and Without God 1989, Inter-Religious Models and Criteria (ed.) 1993, Relationship Morality 1995, Kierkegaard and Nietzsche: Faith and Eternal Acceptance 1997, Moral Relativism, Moral Diversity, and Human Relationships 2001, Introduction to Philosophy of Religion 2007, Introduction to Philosophy of Religion: Readings 2007, Moral Relativism: A Dialogue 2008; contrib. to scholarly books, reviews, quarterlies and journals. *Address:* Department of Philosophy, California State University at Northridge, 18111 Nordhoff Street, Northridge, CA 91330, USA (office). *E-mail:* james.kellenberger@csun.edu (office).

KELLER, Bill, BA; American newspaper editor; *Executive Editor, The New York Times;* b. 18 Jan. 1949, s. of George M. Keller, fmr Chair. and Chief Exec. Chevron Corpn; m. Emma Gilbey 1999; one s. two d. *Education:* Junípero Serra High School, San Mateo, Calif., Pomona Coll., Wharton School, Univ. of Pennsylvania. *Career:* reporter, The Portland Oregonian 1970–79, Congressional Quarterly Weekly Report, Washington, DC 1980–82, The Dallas Times Herald 1982–84; domestic corresp., The New York Times 1984–86, Russian Corresp., Moscow 1986–88, Bureau Chief 1988–91, Bureau Chief, Johannesburg, SA 1992–95, Foreign Ed., New York 1995–97, Man. Ed. 1997–2001, Op-Ed. Columnist and Sr Writer 2001–03, Exec. Ed. 2003–; Trustee, Pomona Coll. *Publication:* Tree Shaker: the Story of Nelson Mandela 2008. *Honours:* Pulitzer Prize for coverage of the USSR 1989, ranked by Forbes magazine amongst The World's Most Powerful People (51st) 2009, (50th) 2010. *Address:* The New York Times, 620 Eighth Avenue, New York, NY 10018, USA (office). *Telephone:* (212) 556-1234 (office). *E-mail:* executive-editor@nytimes.com (office). *Website:* www.nytimes.com (office).

KELLER, Evelyn Fox, PhD; American historian, philosopher of science and academic; *Professor of History and Philosophy of Science Emerita, Massachusetts Institute of Technology;* b. 20 March 1936, New York, NY; d. of Albert Fox and Ray Fox; m. Joseph B. Keller 1964 (divorced); one s. one d. *Education:* Radcliffe Coll., Brandeis and Harvard Univs. *Career:* Asst Research Scientist, New York Univ. 1963–66, Assoc. Prof. 1970–72; Assoc. Prof., State Univ. of New York, Purchase 1972–82; Prof. of Math. and Humanities, Northwestern Univ. 1982–88; Prof., Univ. of California, Berkeley 1988–92; Prof. of History and Philosophy of Science, MIT 1992–2009, Emer. 2009–; mem. Inst. of Advanced Studies, Princeton 1987–88; Visiting Fellow, later Scholar, MIT 1979–84, Visiting Prof. 1985–86; Pres. West Coast History of Science Soc. 1990–91. *Publications include:* A Feeling for the Organism 1983, Reflections on Gender and Science 1985, Secrets of Life, Secrets of Death 1992, Keywords in Evolutionary Biology (ed.) 1994, Refiguring Life 1995, Feminism and Science (co-author) 1996, The Century of the Gene 2000, Making Sense of Life 2002, The Mirage of a Space between Nature and Nurture 2010. *Honours:* Dr hc (Mount Holyoke Coll.) 1991, (Univ. of Amsterdam) 1993, (Simmons Coll.) 1995, (Rensslaer Polytechnic Inst.) 1995, (Tech. Univ. of Luleå, Sweden) 1996, (New School Univ.) 2000, (Allegheny Coll.) 2000, (Wesleyan Univ.) 2001, (Dartmouth Coll.) 2007; MacArthur Fellow 1992–97, Guggenheim Fellowship 2000–01, Moore Scholar, California Inst. Tech. 2002, Winton Chair, Univ. of Minnesota 2002–05, Dibner Fellow 2003, Radcliffe Inst. Fellow 2005, Rothschild Lecturer, Harvard Univ. 2005, Plenary Speaker, Int. History of Science Congress, Beijing 2005; numerous awards, including Mina Shaughnessey Award 1981–82, Radcliffe Grad. Soc. Medal 1985, Medal of the Italian Senate 2001, Chaire Blaise Pascal 2005–07. *Address:* Massachusetts Institute of Technology, E51-171, 77 Massachusetts Avenue, Cambridge, MA 02139, USA (office). *Telephone:* (617) 324-2095 (office). *Fax:* (617) 253-8118 (office). *E-mail:* efkeller@mit.edu (office). *Website:* web.mit.edu.sts (office).

KELLERMAN, Jonathan Seth, AB, AM, PhD; American writer, clinical child psychologist and academic; *Clinical Professor of Pediatrics, Keck School of Medicine, University of Southern California;* b. 9 Aug. 1949, New York, NY; m. Faye Kellerman; one s. three d. *Education:* Univ. of California at Los Angeles, Univ. of Southern California at Los Angeles. *Career:* freelance illustrator 1966–72, Dir Psychsocial Program 1976–81, staff psychologist 1975–81, Children's Hospital of Los Angeles; Clinical Assoc. Prof., Univ. of Southern California School of Medicine, Los Angeles 1979–, now Clinical Prof. of Pediatrics; Head Jonathan Kellerman PhD and Assocs, Los Angeles 1981–88. *Publications:* fiction: When the Bough Breaks 1985, Blood Test 1986, Over the Edge 1987, The Butcher's Theatre 1988, Silent Partner 1989, Time Bomb 1990, Private Eyes 1992, Devil's Waltz 1993, Bad Love 1994, Daddy, Daddy Can You Touch the Sky? 1994, Self-Defense 1995, The Web 1996, Survival of the Fittest 1997, Billy Straight 1999, Monster 2000, On Death 2000, Flesh and Blood 2001, The Murder Book 2002, The Conspiracy Club 2003, Therapy 2004, Twisted 2004, Rage 2005, Gone 2006, Capital Crimes (with Faye Kellerman) 2006, Obsession 2007, Compulsion 2008, Bones 2008, True Detectives 2009, Evidence 2009, Deception 2010; non-fiction: Psychological Aspects of Childhood Cancer 1980, Helping the Fearful Child: A Parents' Guide to Everyday Problem Anxieties 1981. *Honours:* MWA Edgar Allen Poe Award 1985, Anthony Boucher Award 1986. *Address:* Department of Pediatrics, Keck School of Medicine, MS 71, 4650 Sunset Boulevard, Los Angeles, CA 90027, USA (office). *Telephone:* (323) 669-2303 (office). *Fax:* (323) 953-8566 (office). *Website:* www.usc.edu/schools/medicine/departments/pediatrics (office); www.jonathankellerman.com.

KELLEY, Kitty, BA; American writer; b. 4 April 1942, Spokane, Wash.; m. Michael Edgley (divorced). *Education:* Univ. of Washington. *Career:* worked for four years as press asst to US Senator Eugene McCarthy; editorial asst, Washington Post 1969–71; freelance journalist and writer of biogs 1971–; currently developing TV show The Kitty Kelley Show. *Publications:* The Glamour Spas 1973, Jackie Oh! 1978, Elizabeth Taylor: The Last Star 1981, His Way: The Unauthorized Biography of Frank Sinatra 1986, Nancy Reagan: The Unauthorized Biography 1991, The Royals 2001, The Family: The Real Story of the Bush Dynasty 2004, Oprah: A Biography 2010; contribs to magazines and newspapers, including New York Times, The Washington Post, Wall Street Journal, Newsweek, People, Ladies Home Journal, McCall's, Los Angeles Times, Chicago Tribune. *Honours:* Outstanding Author Award, American Soc. of Journalists and Authors 1987, Philip M. Stern Award. *Address:* c/o Crown Publishing Group, Random House, 1745 Broadway, New York, NY 10019, USA (office).

KELLEY, Leo Patrick, BA; American author; b. 10 Sept. 1928, Wilkes Barre, PA. *Education:* New School for Social Research, New York. *Publications:* The Counterfeits, 1967; Odyssey to Earthdeath, 1968; Time Rogue, 1970; The Coins of Murph, 1971; Brother John, 1971; Mindmix, 1972; Time: 110100, 1972, UK edn as The Man From Maybe, 1974; Themes in Science Fiction: A Journey Into Wonder (ed.), 1972; The Supernatural in Fiction (ed.), 1973; Deadlocked (novel), 1973; The Earth Tripper, 1973; Fantasy: The Literature of the Marvellous (ed.), 1974. Science fiction novels for children: The Time Trap, 1977; Backward in Time, 1979; Death Sentence, 1979; Earth Two, 1979; Prison Satellite, 1979; Sunworld, 1979; Worlds Apart, 1979; Dead Moon, 1979; King of the Stars, 1979; On the Red World, 1979; Night of Fire and Blood, 1979; Where No Star Shines, 1979; Vacation in Space, 1979; Star Gold, 1979; Goodbye to Earth, 1979. Western novels: Luke Sutton series, 9 vols, 1981–90; Cimarron series, 20 vols, 1983–86; Morgan, 1986; A Man Named Dundee, 1988; Thunder Gods Gold, 1988.

KELLMAN, Steven G., BA, MA, PhD; American literary critic and academic; *Professor of Comparative Literature, University of Texas, San Antonio*; b. 15 Nov. 1947, Brooklyn, NY. *Education:* State Univ. of NY at Binghamton, Univ. of California, Berkeley. *Career:* Ed.-in-Chief Occident 1969–70; Asst Prof., Bemidji State Univ., Minnesota 1972–73; Lecturer, Univ. of Tel-Aviv, Israel 1973–75; Visiting Lecturer, Univ. of California, Irvine 1975–76; Asst Prof., Univ. of Texas, San Antonio 1976–80, Assoc. Prof. 1980–85, Prof. 1985–, Ashbel Smith Prof. of Comparative Literature 1995–2000; Fulbright Sr Lecturer, USSR 1980; Visiting Assoc. Prof., Univ. of California, Berkeley 1982; Literary Scene Ed. USA Today; Partners of the Americas Lecturer, Peru 1988, 1995; Nat. Endowment for the Humanities Summer Seminar, Natal, SA 1996; John E. Sawyer Fellow, Longfellow Inst., Harvard Univ. 1997; Fulbright Distinguished Chair, Bulgaria 2000; mem. Nat. Book Critics' Circle (mem. Bd Dirs 1996–2002). *Publications:* The Self-Begetting Novel 1980, Approaches to Teaching Camus's The Plague (ed.) 1985, Loving Reading: Erotics of the Text 1985, The Modern American Novel 1991, The Plague: Fiction and Resistance 1993, Perspectives on Raging Bull 1994, Into The Tunnel (co-ed.) 1998, Leslie Fiedler and American Culture (co-ed.) 1999, The Translingual Imagination 2000, UnderWords: Perspectives on Don DeLillo's Underworld (co-ed.) 2002, Switching Languages: Translingual Writers Reflect on Their Craft (ed.) 2003, Redemption: The Life of Henry Roth 2005; contrib. to Chicago Tribune, San Antonio Light, Nation, Georgia Review, Newsweek, Modern Fiction Studies, Midstream, New York Times Book Review, Washington Post Book World, Gettysburg Review, The American Scholar, Atlantic Monthly, Forward, Atlanta Journal and Constitution, San Francisco Chronicle, Texas Observer, Film Critic, San Antonio Current. *Honours:* H.L. Mencken Award 1986, Fulbright travel grant, People's Repub. of China 1995, inducted into Texas Inst. of Letters 2005, Arts and Letters Award San Antonio Public Library Foundation 2005, New York Soc. Library Award for Biog. 2006, First Place, Art Criticism, Asscn of Alternative Newsweeklies 2006. *Address:* 302 Fawn Drive, San Antonio, TX 78231, USA (office). *Telephone:* (210) 458-5216 (office). *Fax:* (210) 458-5366 (office). *E-mail:* kellman@lonestar.utsa.edu (office).

KELLOGG, Marjorie Bradley, BA,; American academic and writer; b. 30 Aug. 1946, Cambridge, MA. *Education:* Vassar College 1967, University of California at Los Angeles 1967–68. *Career:* Scenic Designer, on and off Broadway, regional theatres and films 1970–; Visiting Prof., Princeton University 1983–84, 1985–86; Resident Designer, Alliance Theater 1992–94; Adjunct Prof., Columbia University 1993–95; Assoc. Prof. of Design, Colgate University 1995–; mem. Science Fiction Writers of America, United Scenic Artists. *Publications:* A Rumor of Angels 1983, Lear's Daughters, two vols 1986, The Book of Earth 1995, The Book of Water 1997. *Honours:* several awards for design. *Address:* RD 1, PO Box 62-A, Sidney Center, NY 13839, USA (office). *E-mail:* mkellogg@wpe.com (office).

KELLS, Susannah (see Cornwell, Bernard)

KELLY, A. A. (see Hampton, Angeline Agnes)

KELLY, Cathy; Irish writer; b. Belfast. *Career:* fmr journalist in Dublin, first as news and feature reporter, then film critic and agony aunt; apptd UNICEF Ireland Amb. 2005. *Publications include:* Woman to Woman 1997, She's the One 1998, Never Too Late 1999, Someone Like You (Parker Romantic Novel of the Year) 2000, What She Wants 2001, Just Between Us 2002, Best of Friends 2003, Always and Forever 2005, Past Secrets 2006, Lessons in Heartbreak 2008, Once in a Lifetime 2009. *Address:* c/o HarperCollins Publishers (author mail), 77–85 Fulham Palace Road, London, W6 8JB, England (office). *Website:* www.cathykelly.com.

KELLY, Christopher Paul, MA; British novelist and producer; b. 24 April 1940, Cuddington, Cheshire, England; m. Vivien Ann Day 1962; one s. one d. *Education:* Clare Coll., Cambridge. *Career:* mem. Writer's Guild. *Radio:* as writer/presenter: The Uncommon Garden, Twinkle Twinkle Little Star, The Life of Rylands, Kelly's Heroes. *Television as producer:* Soldier, Soldier (two series, ITV), Kavanagh QC (five series, ITV), Monsignor Renard (series, ITV), Without Motive (series), Clapperboard. *Publications:* The War of Covent Garden 1989, The Forest of the Night 1991, Taking Leave 1995, A Suit of Lights 2000. *Literary Agent:* c/o Broo Doherty, Wade and Doherty Literary Agency, 33 Cormorant Lodge, Thomas More Street, London, E1W 1AU, England. *Telephone:* (20) 7488-4177 (office). *E-mail:* xtopherkelly@hotmail.co.uk (home).

KELLY, Jim; American journalist; b. 15 Dec. 1953, Brooklyn, New York; m. Lisa Henricksson; one s. *Education:* Princeton Univ. *Career:* joined Time magazine 1977, as writer in Nation section, Foreign Ed. early 1990s, Deputy Man. Ed. 1996–2000, Man. Ed. 2001–06, Man. Ed. Time Inc. 2006–09, consultant to Time Inc. 2009–; Ed. Corporate Welfare series 1998, Visions 21 series 1999–2000; mem. Bd of Visitors Columbia Univ. Grad. School of Journalism. *Address:* Time Inc., Time-Life Building, Rockefeller Center, 1271 Avenue of the Americas, New York, NY 10020-1393, USA (office). *Telephone:* (212) 522-1212 (office). *Fax:* (212) 522-0323 (office). *Website:* www.time.com (office).

KELLY, Milton Terrence, BA, BEd; Canadian writer, poet and dramatist; b. 30 Nov. 1946, Toronto, Ont. *Education:* York University, University of Toronto. *Career:* reporter, Moose Jaw Times Harald 1974–75; columnist, Globe and Mail newspaper 1979–80; Teacher of Creative Writing, York University, 1987–92, 1995; Writer-in-Residence, North York Public Library 1992, Metropolitan Toronto Reference Library 1993; mem. International PEN, Writers' Union of Canada. *Publications include:* Fiction: I Do Remember the Fall, 1978; The More Loving One, 1980; The Ruined Season, 1982; A Dream Like Mine, 1987; Breath Dances Between Them, 1990; Out of the Whirlwind, 1995; Save Me, Joe Louis, 1998. Poetry: Country You Can't Walk In, 1979; Country You Can't Walk In and Other Poems, 1984. Other: The Green Dolphin (play), 1982; Wildfire: The Legend of Tom Longboat (screenplay), 1983. Contributions: many anthologies, reviews, quarterlies, and journals. *Honours:* Canada Council Grants, Ontario Arts Council Grants, Toronto Arts Council Award for Poetry 1986, Governor-General's Award for Fiction 1987, Award for Journalism 1995. *Address:* 60 Kendal, Toronto, ON M5R 1L9, Canada.

KELLY, Robert, AB, LittD; American poet, writer and teacher; *Asher B. Edelman Professor of Literature and Co-Director, The Wrutten Arts Program, Bard College*; b. 24 Sept. 1935, Brooklyn, NY; s. of Samuel Jason Kelly and Margaret Rose Kane; m. Charlotte Mandell. *Education:* City Coll., City Univ. of New York, Columbia Univ. *Career:* Ed. Chelsea Review 1957–60, Matter magazine and Matter publishing 1964–, Los 1 1977; Advisory Ed., Alcheringa: Ethnopoetics, Conjunctions, Poetry International; Lecturer, Wagner Coll. 1960–61; Founding Ed. (with George Economou), Trobar magazine 1960–64, Trobar Books, 1962–65; Instructor, Bard Coll. 1961–64, Asst Prof. 1964–69, Assoc. Prof. 1969–74, Prof. of English 1974–86, Founding Dir Writing Program, Milton Avery Grad. School of the Arts 1980–93, Asher B. Edelman Prof. of Literature 1986–; Asst Prof., State Univ. of NY at Buffalo 1964; Visiting Lecturer, Tufts Univ. 1966–67; Poet-in-Residence, Yale Univ./Calhoun Coll. 1967, California Inst. of Tech., Pasadena 1971–72, Univ. of Kansas 1975, Dickinson Coll. 1976. *Plays:* Oedipus after Colonus, produced 2010, Monologues for Orpheus, in production. *Publications:* poetry: Armed Descent 1961, Her Body Against Time 1963, Round Dances 1964, Tabula 1964, Entasy 1964, Matter/Fact/Sheet/1 1964, Matter/Fact/Sheet/2 1964, Lunes 1964, Lectiones 1965, Words in Service 1966, Weeks 1966, Songs XXIV 1967, Twenty Poems 1967, Devotions 1967, Axon Dendron Tree 1967, Crooked Bridge Love Society 1967, A Joining: A Sequence for H D 1967, Alpha 1968, Finding the Measure 1968, From the Common Shore, Book 5 1968, Songs I–XXX 1969, Sonnets 1969, We Are the Arbiters of Beast Desire 1969, A California Journal 1969, The Common Shore, Books I–V: A Long Poem About America in Time 1969, Kali Yuga 1971, Flesh: Dream: Book 1971, Ralegh 1972, The Pastorals 1972, Reading Her Notes 1972, The Tears of Edmund Burke 1973, Whaler Frigate Clippership 1973, The Bill of Particulars 1973, The Belt 1974, The Loom 1975, Sixteen Odes 1976, The Lady of 1977, The Convections 1978, The Book of Persephone 1978, The Cruise of the Pnyx 1979, Kill the Messenger Who Brings the Bad News 1980, Sentence 1980, The Alchemist to Mercury 1981, Spiritual Exercises 1981, Mulberry Women 1982, Under Words 1983, Thor's Thrush 1984, Not This Island Music 1987, The Flowers of Unceasing Coincidence 1988, Oahu 1988, A Strange Market 1992, Mont Blanc 1994, Red Actions: Selected Poems 1960–1993 1995, Lapis 2005, May Day 2007, Sainte Terre 2008, Fire Exit 2009, Uncertainties 2011, Runaway Horses 2011; fiction: The Scorpions 1967, Cities 1971, Wheres 1978, A Transparent Tree: Ten Fictions 1985, Doctor of Silence 1988, Cat Scratch Fever: Fictions 1990, Queen of Terrors: Fictions 1994, The Logic of the World and other Fictions 2011; other: A Controversy of Poets: An Anthology of Contemporary American Poetry (co-ed. with Paris Leary) 1965, Statement 1968, In Time 1971, Sulphur 1972, A Line of Sight 1974, Atlantis Manifesto (with Peter Lamborn Wilson) 2009. *Honours:* Los Angeles Times Book Prize 1980, American Acad. of Arts and Letters Award 1986. *Address:* Department of Literature, Bard College, Hopson 101, PO Box 5000, Annandale-on-Hudson, NY 12504-5000, USA (office). *Telephone:* (845) 758-7205 (office). *E-mail:* kelly@bard.edu (office). *Website:* rk-ology.com.

KELMAN, James; British writer; b. 9 June 1946, Glasgow; m. Marie Connors; two d. *Education:* Greenfield Public School, Govan. *Plays:* Hardie and Baird, The Last Days 1991, One, Two – Hey (R and B musical, toured 1994). *Radio:* The Art of the Big Bass Drum (play, BBC Radio 3) 1998. *Publications include:* novels: The Bus Conductor Hines 1984, A Chancer 1985, A Disaffection (James Tait Black Memorial Prize) 1989, How Late It Was, How Late (Booker Prize) 1994, Translated Accounts 2001, You Have to be Careful in the Land of the Free 2004, Kieron Smith, Boy (Saltire Soc's Book of the Year 2008, Scottish Mortgage Investment Trust Book of the Year 2009) 2008; short stories: An Old Pub Near the Angel 1973, Short Tales from the Nightshift 1978, Not Not While the Giro 1983, Lean Tales 1985, Greyhound for Breakfast (Cheltenham Prize) 1987, The Burn (Scottish Arts Council Book Award) 1991, Busted Scotch 1997, The Good Times (Scottish Writer of the Year Award) 1998, If It is Your Life 2010; plays: The Busker 1985, In the Night 1988; other: And the Judges Said (essays) 2002. *Honours:* Spirit of Scotland Award. *Literary Agent:* Rogers, Coleridge and White Ltd, 20 Powis Mews, London, W11 1JN, England. *Telephone:* (20) 7221-3717. *E-mail:* info@rcwlitagency.com. *Website:* www.rcwlitagency.com.

KELMAN, Judith Ann, BS, MA, MS; American writer; b. (Judith Edelstein), 21 Oct. 1945, New York, NY. *Education:* Cornell Univ., , New York Univ., Southern Connecticut CT State Univ. *Career:* mem. American Society of Journalists and Authors; MWA; Authors' Guild. *Publications:* Prime Evil, 1986; Where Shadows Fall, 1988; While Angels Sleep, 1990; Hush Little Darlings, 1991; Someone's Watching, 1992; The House on the Hill, 1994; If I Should Die, 1995; One Last Kiss, 1996; More Than You Know, 1998; Fly Away Home, 1999, After the Fall 2000, Summer of Storms 2002, Every Step You Take 2003, Dr. Peter Scardino's Prostate Book 2004, Backward in High Heels

2005, The First Stone 2007; contrib.: anthologies and periodicals. *Honours:* Mary Higgins Clark Award, Presidential Medal, Southern Conn. State Univ. *Literary Agent:* Peter Lampack Agency, 551 Fifth Avenue, New York, NY 10176, USA. *Telephone:* (212) 687-9106 (office). *E-mail:* lampackag@verizon.net (office). *Address:* 345 East 68th Street, New York, NY 10065, USA. *Telephone:* (212) 535-3985 (office). *E-mail:* jkelman@jkelman.com.

KELNER, Simon; British newspaper editor; *Editor-in-Chief, The Independent and The Independent on Sunday;* b. 9 Dec. 1957, Manchester. *Education:* Bury Grammar School, Preston Polytechnic. *Career:* Trainee Reporter, Neath Guardian 1976–79; Sports Reporter, Extel 1979–80; Sports Ed., Kent Evening Post 1980–83; Asst Sports Ed., The Observer 1983–86; Deputy Sports Ed., The Independent 1986–89; Sports Ed., Sunday Corresp. 1989–90; Sports Ed., The Observer 1990–93; Sports Ed., The Independent on Sunday 1993–95, Night Ed., The Independent 1995, Features Ed. 1995–96; Ed. Night and Day Magazine, Mail on Sunday 1996–98; Ed., The Independent 1998–2008, 2010–, The Independent on Sunday 1998–2008, Ed.-in-Chief 2008–, Man. Dir 2008–10, Ed.-in-Chief The Independent May 2010– and i Oct. 2010–. *Publications:* To Jerusalem and Back 1996. *Honours:* Hon. Fellowship, Univ. of Cen. Lancashire; Ed. of the Year, What the Papers Say Awards 1999, 2003, Newspaper Ed. of the Year, What the Papers Say Awards 2004, Edgar Wallace Award 2000, 2004, Newspaper of the Year, British Press Awards 2004, GQ Editor of the Year 2004, 2010, Media Achiever of the Year, Campaign Media Awards 2004, Marketeer of the Year, Marketing Week Effectiveness Awards 2004, Editorial Intelligence Comment Award 2010. *Address:* The Independent, 2 Derry Street, London, W8 5HF, England (office). *Telephone:* (20) 7005-2300 (office). *Fax:* (20) 7005-3859 (office). *E-mail:* s.kelner@independent.co.uk (office). *Website:* www.independent.co.uk (office).

KELSALL, Malcolm Miles, BA, BLitt, MA; British academic, writer and editor; *Professor Emeritus of English, University of Cardiff;* b. 27 Feb. 1938, London, England; m. Mary Emily Ives 1961. *Education:* Univ. of Oxford. *Career:* Asst Lecturer, Univ. of Exeter 1963–64; Lecturer, Univ. of Reading 1964–75; Prof. of English, Univ. of Cardiff 1975–2003, Prof. Emer. 2003–. *Publications:* Christopher Marlowe 1981, Studying Drama 1985, Byron's Politics 1987, Encyclopedia of Literature and Criticism (ed.) 1990, The Great Good Place: The Country House and English Literature 1992, Jefferson and the Iconography of Romanticism 1999, Literary Representations of the Irish Country House 2003; ed. of several plays; contrib. to Cambridge Companion to Pope, Cambridge Companion to Byron, scholarly journals. *Honours:* Elma Dangerfield Prize 1991; British Acad. Warton Lecturer 1992, Marchand Lecturer 2005.

KEMAL, Yaşar; Turkish writer and journalist; b. (Kemal Sadık Gökçel), 1926, Adana; m. 1st Thilda Serrero 1952 (deceased); one s.; m. 2nd Ayse Semiha Baban 2002. *Career:* self-educated; mem. Académie Universelle des Cultures, Paris. *Publications:* (in English) Memed, My Hawk 1961, The Wind from the Plain 1963, Anatolian Tales 1968, They Burn the Thistles 1973, Iron Earth, Copper Sky 1974, The Legend of Ararat 1975, The Legend of the Thousand Bulls 1976, The Undying Grass 1977, The Lords of Akchasaz (Part I), Murder in the Ironsmiths' Market 1979, The Saga of a Seagull 1981, The Sea-Crossed Fisherman 1985, The Birds Have Also Gone 1987, To Crush the Serpent 1991, Salman the Solitary 1997, The Story of an Island Vols I–IV 1998; novels, short stories, plays and essays in Turkish. *Honours:* Commdr, Légion d'honneur 1984; Dr hc (Strasbourg) 1991, (Akdeniz Univ., Antalya) 1991, (Mediterranean Univ.) 1992, (Free Univ., Berlin) 1998, (Bilkent Univ.) 2002; Prix Mondial Cino del Duca 1982, VIII Premi Internacional Catalunya, Barcelona 1996, Hellman-Hammett Award, New York 1996, Peace Prize of German Book Trade 1997, Prix Nonino, Percoto, Italy 1997, Stig Dagerman Prize, Sweden 1997, Norwegian Authors Union Prize 1997, Prix Ecureuil de littérature étrangère, Bordeaux 1998, Z. Homer Poetry Award 2003, Soranos Prize (Thessalonika, Greece) 2003, Turkish Publisher's Asscn Lifetime Achievement Award 2003. *Address:* P.K. 14, Basinköy, Istanbul, Turkey. *Website:* www.yasarkemal.net.

KEMP, Rev. Anthony Eric, LTCL, FTCL, LMusTCL, DipEd, MA, DPhil; British priest, music educator, chartered psychologist and counsellor; *Assistant Priest, St Paul's Parish Church, Wokingham;* b. 2 Jan. 1934, Tanga, Tanzania; m. Valerie Francis 1964; one s. one d. *Education:* Coll. of St Mark and St John, Plymouth, Trinity Coll. of Music, London, Univ. of Sussex. *Career:* Head of Music, Forest Hill School 1959; Lecturer in Music, Brighton Coll. of Educ. 1964, Sr Lecturer 1967; Prin. Lecturer and Head of Music, Coll. of St Mark and St 1972; Lecturer, Univ. of Reading 1973, Sr Lecturer 1987, Prof. 1996, Prof. Emer. 1999–; Sr Research Fellow, Univ. of Surrey, Roehampton 1999; Visiting Prof., Sibelius Acad., Helsinki 1995–2003; Curate, All Saints Church, Wokingham 1998–2005; Asst Priest, St Paul's Parish Church, Wokingham 2005–; mem. Inc. Soc. of Musicians, Int. Soc. for Music Educ. (Chair. Research Comm. 1988–90), Music Educ. Council (Chair. 1989–92), Soc. of Catholic Priests. *Publications include:* Fun to Make Music 1975, Considering the Mind's Ear 1984, Some Approaches to Research in Music Education 1992, The Musical Temperament: Psychology and Personality of Musicians 1996; contrib. to Psychology of Music 1981, 1982, 1999, International Journal of Music Education 1984, 1986, 1988, Council for Research in Music Education Bulletin 1985, 1987, British Journal of Music Education 1987, 1990, Quarterly Journal of Music Teaching and Learning 1995, Musical Performance: An International Journal 2000, New Grove Dictionary of Music and Musicians 2001, Advances in Social Psychology and Music Education Research 2011. *Honours:* Hon. MusDoc (Sibelius Acad., Helsinki) 2003; Hon. Fellow, London Coll. of Music 1983, British Psychological Soc. 1997; Univ. of Hong Kong Raysen Huang Fellowship 1989, Univ. of British Columbia Distinguished Scholars Fellowship 1990. *Address:* 18 Blagrove Lane, Wokingham, Berks., RG41 4BA, England (home); St Paul's Parish Church, Reading Road, Wokingham, Berks., RG41 1HE, England (office). *Telephone:* (118) 978-2756 (home); (118) 979-2122 (office). *E-mail:* a.e.kemp@btinternet.com (home).

KEMP, Martin John, MA, DLitt, FBA, FRSA, FRSE; British art historian, academic, author and exhibition curator; *Professor Emeritus, University of Oxford;* b. 5 March 1942, Windsor, Berks.; s. of Frederick Maurice Kemp and Violet Anne Kemp (née Tull); m. Jill Lightfoot 1966 (divorced 2003); one s. one d. *Education:* Windsor Grammar School, Downing Coll., Cambridge and Courtauld Inst. of Art, London. *Career:* Lecturer in History of Western Art, Dalhousie Univ., NS, Canada 1965–66; Lecturer in History of Fine Art, Univ. of Glasgow 1966–81; Prof. of Fine Arts, Univ. of St Andrews 1981–90; Prof. of History, Royal Scottish Acad. 1985–; Prof. of History and Theory of Art, Univ. of St Andrews 1990–95; Prof. of History of Art, Univ. of Oxford 1995, now Emer. Prof. and Head of Dept; Fellow Trinity Coll. Oxford 1995–; Provost St Leonard's Coll., Univ. of St Andrews 1991–95; mem. Inst. for Advanced Study, Princeton, NJ, USA 1984–85; Slade Prof., Univ. of Cambridge 1987–88; Benjamin Sonenberg Visiting Prof., Inst. of Fine Arts, New York Univ. 1988; Wiley Visiting Prof., Univ. of N Carolina, Chapel Hill 1993; British Acad. Wolfson Research Prof. 1993–98; Trustee, Nat. Galleries of Scotland 1982–87, Victoria and Albert Museum, London 1986–89, British Museum 1995–, Ashmolean Museum 1995–; Pres. Leonardo da Vinci Soc. 1988–97; Chair. Asscn of Art Historians 1989–92; mem. Exec. Scottish Museums Council 1990–95; Dir and Chair. Graeme Murray Gallery 1990–92; Dir Wallace Kemp/Artakt 2001; mem. Bd Interalia 1992–, Bd Museum Training Inst. 1993–98, Council British Soc. for the History of Science 1994–97; mem. Visual Arts Advisory Panel, Arts Council of England 1996–; Visiting mem. Getty Center, Los Angeles 2002; Mellon Sr Fellow, Canadian Centre for Architecture, Montreal 2004; Trustee, Wilhelmina Barns-Graham Trust 2000–; Fellow, Royal Soc. of Sciences, Uppsala 1995. *Publications:* Leonardo da Vinci: The Marvellous Works of Nature and Man 1981, Leonardo da Vinci (co-author) 1989, Leonardo on Painting (co-author) 1989, The Science of Art: Optical Themes in Western Art from Brunelleschi to Seurat 1990, Behind the Picture: Art and Evidence in the Italian Renaissance 1997, Immagine e Verità 1999, The Oxford History of Western Art (ed.) 2000, Spectacular Bodies (with Marina Wallace) 2000, Visualizations: The Nature Book of Science and Art 2001, Leonardo 2004, Leonardo da Vinci: Experience, Experiment and Design 2006, Seen/Unseen 2006, The Human Animal 2007, Leonardo da Vinci: La Bella Principessa 2010; regular column on Science in Culture in Nature 1997–. *Honours:* Hon. mem. American Acad. of Arts and Sciences 1996–, Hon. Fellow, Downing Coll. 1999, Trinity Coll. Oxford 2008; Hon. DLitt (Heriot Watt) 1995, (Uppsala) 2009; Mitchell Prize 1981, Armand Hammer Prize for Leonardo Studies 1992, Pres.'s Prize, Italian Asscn of America 1992. *Address:* Trinity College, Oxford, OX1 3BH, England (home). *Telephone:* (1993) 811364 (office). *E-mail:* martin.kemp@trinity.ox.ac.uk (office). *Website:* www.martinjkemp.co.uk.

KEMP, Patricia (Penn), (Penny Chalmers, Penny Kemp), BA, MEd; Canadian writer, poet, performer, playwright and editor; *Series Editor, Pendas Productions;* b. 4 Aug. 1944, Strathroy, Ont.; d. of Jim Kemp and Anne Kemp; m. Gavin Stairs; one s. one d. *Education:* Univ. of Western Ontario, Univ. of Toronto. *Career:* has taught creative writing and sounding in Canadian schools, from kindergarten to univ. since 1966; as sound poet and playwright, performs in arts festivals around the world, giving readings and workshops; various writer-in-residencies; Publr Pendas Productions; Series Ed. Pendas Poets Series; Asscn of Canadian Studies speaker in Brazil, India; Writer-in-Residence, Univ. of Western Ontario 2009–10; inaugural Poet Laureate, City of London, Ont. 2010–12; mem. League of Canadian Poets, Playwrights' Guild of Canada, Writers' Union. *Plays:* Angel Makers, The Epic of Toad and Heron, What the Ear Hears Last. *Music:* several of her series of Sound Operas produced for Artword Theatre in Toronto and London, Ont., Aeolian Hall's Summer Music Festival 2005–11, Brescia Univ. Coll. 2009, 2010; mytown.ca/poemforpeace includes video of her Poem for Peace in Many Voices (and many of the 129 trans. of the poem; video shows one of the Poem for Peace performances in London). *Radio:* programmes on CBC, CIUT stations, campus radio; presenter and host, Gathering Voices (CHRW Radio). *Publications:* 25 books of poetry and plays as well as 10 CDs of Sound Opera and Sound Poetry, including Bearing Down 1972, Binding Twine 1984, Some Talk Magic 1986, Eidolons 1990, Throo 1990, The Universe is One Poem 1990, What the Ear Hears Last 1994, Four Women 1999, Vocal Braidings 2001, Sarasvati Scapes 2002, Poem for Peace in Two Voices 2003, C'Loud 2004, Gathering Voice 2004, SoundSpoke 2005, Trance Dance Form 2006, Darkness Visible 2007, Helwa! 2008, Luminous Entrance 2010. *Honours:* Canada Council Arts grants 1979–80, 1981–82, 1991–92, 1994, 1999, 2001, Ontario's Grad. Scholarship 1987–88, videopoem won Vancouver Videopoem Festival's Voice Award, proclaimed a foremother of Canadian poetry by The League of Poets, OAC Media Arts grant 2010. *Telephone:* (519) 434-8555 (office). *E-mail:* pendas@pennkemp.ca (office). *Address:* Pendas Productions, 525 Canterbury Road, London, ON N6G 2N5, Canada (office). *E-mail:* penn@pennkemp.ca (office). *Website:* www.mytown.ca/pennkemp (office); www.mytown.ca/pennletters (office); www.chrwradio.com/talk/gatheringvoices (office); pennkemp.ca.

KEMSKE, Floyd, BA, MA; American writer; b. 11 March 1947, Wilmington, DE; m. Alice Geraldine Morse 1968. *Education:* University of Delaware, Michigan State University. *Career:* mem. National Writers' Union. *Publications:* Lifetime Employment, 1992; The Virtual Boss, 1993; Human Resources, 1995; The Third Lion, 1997; Jigsaw Puzzles: Hole in One, 1997; Unbridled Fear, 1997; Cooking Commando, 1997; Purrfect Medicine, 1998; Murder on the Hindenburg, 1999; Labor Day, 2000.

KENANI, Stanley Onjezani; Malawian author, poet and accountant; b. 1976. *Education:* Univ. of Malawi. *Career:* fmr accountant, Malawi Govt; fmr Internal Auditor, Tambala Food Products, Lilongwe Water Bd; fmr Asst Accountant, Sunbird Malawi; fmr Group Finance Man., Khupe Group of Cos; fmr Finance and Admin Officer, African Union Comm., Addis Ababa; currently Auditor, UN; currently Malawi and S African editor, AuthorMe.com; numerous stories published in newspapers and magazines in Malawi; fmr Pres. Malawi Writers Union. *Publications include:* For Honour and Other Stories 2011; featured in: African Violet: The 2012 Caine Prize Anthology (features story Love on Trial) 2012. *Address:* c/o United Nations, Palais de Nations, 1211 Geneva 10, Switzerland (office); c/o eKhaya, Random House Struik (Pty) Limited, PO Box 1144, Cape Town 8000, South Africa (office). *Telephone:* (22) 917-1234 (Geneva) (office). *Fax:* (22) 917-0123 (Geneva) (office). *E-mail:* webmaster@unog.ch (office); ekhaya@randomstruik.co.za (office); stanleyk@lemeridienmalawi.com (home). *Website:* www.unog.ch (office); www.randomstruik.co.za (office).

KENEALLY, Thomas Michael, AO, FRSL; Australian writer; b. 7 Oct. 1935, Sydney; s. of Edmund Thomas and Elsie Margaret Keneally; m. Judith Mary Martin 1965; two d. *Education:* St Patrick's Coll., Strathfield, NSW. *Career:* Lecturer in Drama, Univ. of New England, Armidale, NSW 1968–70; Visiting Prof. Univ. of Calif., Irvine 1985, Prof. Dept of English and Comparative Literature 1991–95; Berg Prof. Dept of English, New York Univ. 1988; Pres. Nat. Book Council of Australia –1987; Chair. Australian Soc. of Authors 1987–90, Pres. 1990–; mem. Literary Arts Bd 1985–; mem. Australia-China Council; mem. American Acad. of Arts and Sciences; Founding Chair. Australian Republican Movt 1991–93. *Publications:* The Place at Whitton 1964, The Fear 1965, Bring Larks and Heroes 1967, Three Cheers for the Paraclete 1968, The Survivor 1969, A Dutiful Daughter 1970, The Chant of Jimmie Blacksmith 1972, Blood Red, Sister Rose 1974, Gossip from the Forest 1975, Moses and the Lawgiver 1975, Season in Purgatory 1976, A Victim of the Aurora 1977, Ned Kelly and the City of Bees 1978, Passenger 1978, Confederates 1979, Schindler's Ark (Booker Prize 1982) 1982, Outback 1983, The Cut-Rate Kingdom 1984, A Family Madness 1985, Australia: Beyond the Dreamtime (contrib.) 1987, The Playmaker 1987, Towards Asmara 1989, Flying Hero Class 1991, Now and in Time to Be: Ireland and the Irish 1992, Woman of the Inner Sea 1992, The Place Where Souls Are Born: A Journey into the American Southwest 1992, Jacko: The Great Intruder 1993, The Utility Player – The Story of Des Hassler (non-fiction) 1993, Our Republic (non-fiction) 1993, A River Town 1995, Homebush Boy: A Memoir 1995, The Great Shame: And the Triumph of the Irish in the English-Speaking World 1998, Bettany's Book 2000, An American Scoundrel: The Life of the Notorious Civil War General Dan Sickles (non-fiction) 2002, An Angel in Australia 2002, Abraham Lincoln (biog.) 2003, The Office of Innocence 2003, The Tyrant's Novel 2004, The Commonwealth of Thieves: The Story of the Founding of Australia (non-fiction) 2006, The Widow and Her Hero 2007, Searching for Schindler: A Memoir 2008, The People's Train 2009. *Honours:* Hon. DLit (Univ. of Queensland), (Nat. Univ. of Ireland) 1994; Hon. DLitt (Fairleigh Dickenson Univ., USA) 1996, (Rollins Coll., USA) 1996; Royal Soc. of Literature Prize, Los Angeles Times Fiction Prize 1983. *Literary Agent:* Curtis Brown (Australia) Pty Ltd, PO Box 19, Paddington, NSW 2021, Australia.

KENNEDY, Adrienne Lita, BS; American dramatist; b. 13 Sept. 1931, Pittsburgh, PA; m. Joseph C. Kennedy 1953 (divorced 1966); two s. *Education:* Ohio State University, Columbia University, New School for Social Research, American Theatre Wing, Circle in the Square Theatre School, New York. *Career:* Playwright, Actors Studio, New York City, 1962–65; Lecturer, Yale University, 1972–74; Princeton University, 1977; CBS Fellow, School of Drama, New York City, 1973; Visiting Assoc. Prof., Brown University, 1979–80; Distinguished Lecturer, University of California, Berkeley, 1980, 1986; Visiting Lecturer, 1990, 1991, Visiting Prof., 1997–2000, Harvard University; mem. PEN. *Publications:* Plays: Funnyhouse of a Negro, 1964; Cities in Bezique, 1965; A Rat's Mass, 1966; A Lesson in Dead Language, 1966; The Lennon Plays, 1968; Sun, 1969; An Evening With Dead Essex, 1972; A Movie Star Has to Star in Black and White, 1976; In One Act, 1988; Deadly Triplets, 1990; She Talks to Beethoven, 1990; Ohio State Murders, 1992; The Alexander Plays, 1992; Sleep Deprivation Chamber: A Theatre Piece (with Adam Kennedy), 1996; Adrienne Kennedy Reader, 2001. Other: People Who Led to My Plays, 1987; Letter to My Students, 1992. Contributions: anthologies. *Honours:* Obie Awards, 1964, 1996; Guggenheim Fellowship, 1968; Rockefeller Foundation Fellowships, 1968, 1974; National Endowment for the Arts Fellowships, 1973, 1993; Manhattan Borough Pres.'s Award, 1988; American Acad. of Arts and Letters Award, 1994; Lila Wallace-Reader's Digest Award, 1994; Pierre Lecomte du Novy Award, Lincoln Center for the Performing Arts, New York, 1994.

KENNEDY, A(lison) L(ouise), BA (Hons); British writer and academic; *Associate Professor, Creative Writing Programme, University of Warwick*; b. 22 Oct. 1965, Dundee, Scotland; d. of Robert Alan Kennedy and Edwardene Mildred Price. *Education:* Univ. of Warwick. *Career:* community arts worker for Clydebank & Dist 1988–89; writer 1988–; Writer-in-Residence, Hamilton & East Kilbride Social Work Dept 1989–91, for Project Ability, Arts & Special Needs 1989–95, Copenhagen Univ. 1995; book reviewer for The Scotsman, Glasgow Herald, BBC, STV, The Telegraph 1990–; Ed. New Writing Scotland 1993–95; part-time Lecturer, St Andrews Univ. 2002–07; Assoc. Prof., Creative Writing Programme, Univ. of Warwick 2007–; columnist, The Guardian; stand-up comedian, reviewer 2005–. *Plays:* The Audition (Fringe First Award) 1993, Delicate (performance piece for Motionhouse dance co.) 1995, True (performance project for Fierce Productions and Tramway Theatre) 1998. *Film:* Stella Does Tricks (writer) 1997. *Radio:* Born a Fox (BBC Radio 4 drama) 2002, Like an Angel (BBC Radio 4 drama) 2004, Confessions of a Medium (BBC Radio drama) 2010, Blood Empire (SWR, Germany, drama) 2010, That I Should Rise 2012, Love Love Love Like The Beatles (BBC Radio 4) 2012. *Television:* Ghostdancing (BBC drama/documentary, writer and presenter) 1995, Dice (series I and II, with John Burnside, CBC TV). *Publications:* Night Geometry and the Garscadden Trains 1991, Looking for the Possible Dance 1993, Now That You're Back 1994, So I Am Glad 1995, Tea and Biscuits 1996, Original Bliss 1997, The Life and Death of Colonel Blimp 1997, Everything You Need 1999, On Bullfighting 1999, Indelible Acts 2002, Paradise 2004, Day (Saltire Scottish Book of the Year Award 2007, Costa Book of the Year Award 2007) 2007, What Becomes 2009, The Blue Book 2011. *Honours:* Hon. DLit (Glasgow); Somerset Maugham Award, Encore Award, SAC Book Award (four times), Saltire Scottish Book of the Year Award, Best of Young British Novelists (twice), Lannan Literary Award for Fiction 2007, Austrian State Prize for European Literature, Eifel Literature Prize. *Literary Agent:* c/o Antony Harwood Ltd, 103 Walton Street, Oxford, OX2 6EB, England. *Telephone:* (1865) 559615. *Fax:* (1865) 554173; (1865) 310660. *E-mail:* mail@antonyharwood.com. *Website:* www.antonyharwood.com. *E-mail:* info@a-l-kennedy.co.uk (office). *Website:* www.a-l-kennedy.co.uk.

KENNEDY, David Michael, BA, MA, PhD; American academic and writer; *Donald J. McLachlan Professor of History, Stanford University*; b. 22 July 1941, Seattle, WA; m. Judith Ann Osborne 1970; two s. one d. *Education:* Stanford Univ., Yale Univ. *Career:* Asst Prof. 1967–72, Assoc. Prof. 1972–80, Prof. 1980–, William Robertson Coe Prof. of History and American Studies 1988–93, Chair, Dept of History 1990–94, Donald J. McLachlan Prof. of History 1993–, Stanford Univ.; Harmsworth Prof. of American History, Univ. of Oxford 1995–96; Ed., The Oxford History of the United States 1999–; Fellow, American Acad. of Arts and Sciences, American Philosophical Soc. *Publications:* Birth Control in America: The Career of Margaret Sanger 1970, Social Thought in America and Europe (ed. with Paul A. Robinson) 1970, Progressivism: The Critical Issues (ed.) 1971, The American People in the Depression 1973, The American People in the Age of Kennedy 1973, The American Pageant: A History of the Republic (with Thomas A. Bailey and Lizabeth Cohen, sixth to 13th edns) 1979–2005, Over Here: The First World War and American Society 1980 (revd 2004), The American Spirit: United States History as Seen by Contemporaries (ed. with Thomas A. Bailey, fifth to 11th edns) 1983–2005, Power and Responsibility: Case Studies in American Leadership (ed. with Michael Parrish) 1986, Freedom from Fear: The American People in Depression and War, 1929–1945 1999; contrib. to reference works, scholarly books, learned journals, periodicals, etc. *Honours:* Guggenheim Fellowship 1975–76, Center for Advanced Study in the Behavioural Sciences Fellowship 1986–87, Stanford Humanities Center Fellowship 1989–90, Hon. DLitt (LaTrobe Univ.) 2001; John Gilmary Shea Prize 1970, Bancroft Prize 1971, Ambassador's Book Award, English-Speaking Union 2000, Francis Parkman Prize, Soc. of American Historians 2000, Pulitzer Prize in History 2000. *Address:* c/o Department of History, Stanford University, Stanford, CA 94305, USA. *Telephone:* (650) 723-0351. *Fax:* (650) 725-0597. *E-mail:* dmk@stanford.edu. *Website:* history.stanford.edu/faculty/dkennedy.

KENNEDY, Donald, MA, PhD; American biologist, academic, editor and fmr university administrator; *President Emeritus, Stanford University*; b. 18 Aug. 1931, New York; s. of William D. Kennedy and Barbara (Bean) Kennedy; m. 1st Barbara J. Dewey 1953; two d.; m. 2nd Robin Beth Wiseman 1987; two step-s. *Education:* Harvard Univ. *Career:* Asst Prof., Syracuse Univ. 1956–59, Assoc. Prof. 1959–60; Asst Prof., Stanford Univ. 1960–62, Assoc. Prof. 1962–65, Prof. 1965–77, Chair. Dept of Biological Sciences 1965–72, Benjamin Crocker Prof. of Human Biology 1974–77, Vice-Pres. and Provost 1979–80, Pres. 1980–92, Pres. Emer. and Bing Prof. of Environmental Science Emer. 1992–; Sr Consultant, Office of Science and Tech. Policy, Exec. Office of the Pres. 1976–77; Commr of Food and Drug Admin. 1977–79; Ed.-in-Chief Science Magazine 2000–; Fellow, American Acad. of Arts and Sciences; mem. NAS. *Publications:* The Biology of Organisms (with W. M. Telfer) 1965, Academic Duty 1997; over 60 articles in scientific journals. *Honours:* Hon. DSc (Columbia Univ., Williams Coll., Michigan, Rochester, Ariz., Whitman Coll., Coll. of William and Mary); Dinkelspiel Award 1976. *Address:* Stanford University, Encina Hall E401, Stanford, CA 94305 (office); 532 Channing Avenue, #302, Palo Alto, CA 94301, USA (home). *E-mail:* kennedyd@stanford .edu (office). *Website:* fsi.stanford.edu/people/donaldkennedy (home).

KENNEDY, (George) Michael (Sinclair), CBE, MA, CRNCM, FIJ; British journalist and music critic; b. 19 Feb. 1926, Chorlton-cum-Hardy, Manchester; s. of Hew G. Kennedy and Marian F. Kennedy; m. 1st Eslyn Durdle 1947 (died 1999); m. 2nd Joyce Bourne 1999. *Education:* Berkhamsted School. *Career:*

staff music critic, The Daily Telegraph 1941–50, Northern Music Critic 1950–60, Northern Ed. 1960–86, Jt Chief Music Critic 1986–89; Chief Music Critic, The Sunday Telegraph 1989–2005; Gov. Royal Northern Coll. of Music. *Publications:* The Hallé Tradition: A Century of Music 1960, The Works of Ralph Vaughan Williams 1964, Portrait of Elgar 1968, Elgar: Orchestral Music 1969, Portrait of Manchester 1970, History of the Royal Manchester College of Music 1971, Barbirolli: Conductor Laureate 1971, Mahler 1974, The Autobiography of Charles Hallé, with Correspondence and Diaries (ed.) 1976, Richard Strauss 1976, Britten 1980, Concise Oxford Dictionary of Music (ed.) 1980, The Hallé 1858–1983 1983, Strauss: Tone Poems 1984, Oxford Dictionary of Music (ed.) 1985, Adrian Boult 1987, Portrait of Walton 1989, Music Enriches All: The First 21 Years of the Royal Northern College of Music, Manchester 1994, Richard Strauss: Man, Musician, Enigma (French critics prize for musical biog. 2003) 1999, The Life of Elgar 2004, Buxton: an English Festival 2004; contrib. to newspapers and magazines, including Gramophone, Listener, Musical Times, Music and Letters, The Sunday Telegraph, BBC Music Magazine. *Honours:* Hon. mem. Royal Manchester Coll. of Music 1971, Hon. mem. Royal Philharmonic Soc. 2006; Hon. MA (Manchester) 1975; Hon. MusD (Manchester) 2003. *Address:* The Bungalow, 62 Edilom Road, Manchester, M8 4HZ, England (home). *Telephone:* (161) 740-4528 (home). *E-mail:* majkennedy@bungalow62.fsnet.co.uk.

KENNEDY, Geraldine; Irish journalist; *Editor, The Irish Times;* b. 7 Sept. 1951, Tramore, Co. Waterford; d. of James Kennedy and Nora McGrath; m. David J. Hegarty; two d. *Education:* Convent S.H.M., Ferrybank, Waterford. *Career:* Political Corresp. The Sunday Tribune 1980–82, The Sunday Press 1982–87; mem. Dáil Éireann (Irish Parl.) 1987–89; Public Affairs Corresp. The Irish Times 1990–93, Political Corresp. 1993–99, Political Ed. 1999–2002, Duty Ed. 2000–02, Ed. 2002–, Dir Irish Times Ltd 2002–. *Honours:* Hon. mem., Royal Irish Acad.; Hon. DUniv (Queen's Univ., Belfast) 2005, Hon. DPhil (Dublin Inst. of Tech.) 2007, Hon. DrIur (Univ. Coll., Dublin) 2008; Journalist of the Year 1994. *Address:* The Irish Times, PO Box 74, 24–28 Tara Street, Dublin 2, Ireland (office). *Telephone:* (1) 6758000 (office). *Fax:* (1) 6758035 (office). *E-mail:* editor@irish-times.ie (office). *Website:* www.irishtimes.com (office); www.ireland.com.

KENNEDY, James C., BBA; American publishing and media executive; *Chairman and CEO, Cox Enterprises Inc.;* b. 1947, Honolulu; m. *Education:* Univ. of Denver. *Career:* with Atlanta Newspapers 1976–79; Pres. Grand Junction Newspapers 1979–80, Publr Grand Junction Daily Sentinel 1980–85; Vice-Pres. Newspaper Div. Cox Enterprises Inc. 1985–86, Exec. Vice-Pres. then Pres. 1986–87, COO then Chair. 1987–; Chair. and CEO Cox Enterprises Inc. 1988–, also Chair. Cox Communications and Cox Radio. *Cycling achievements:* past Masters Nat., Pan American and World Champion in 3000 meter pursuit; served as capt. of four-man team that won Race Across AMerica (RAAM) 1992, setting world record. *Address:* Cox Enterprises Inc., 6205 Peachtree Dunwoody Road, Atlanta, GA 30328 (office); 1601 W Peachtree Street NE, Atlanta, GA 30309, USA (home). *Telephone:* (678) 645-0000 (office). *Fax:* (678) 645-1079 (office). *Website:* www.coxenterprises.com (office).

KENNEDY, Moorhead, AB, JD; American foundation administrator and writer; b. 5 Nov. 1930, New York, NY; m. Louisa Livingston 1955, four s. *Education:* Princeton University, Harvard University, National War College. *Career:* Foreign Service Officer, 1961–69, 1975–78, Dir, Office of Investment Affairs, 1971–74, US Dept of State; Exec. Dir, Cathedral Peace Institute, New York City, 1981–83, Council for International Understanding, New York City, 1983–90; Pres., Moorhead Kennedy Institute, New York City, 1990–97; mem. American Foreign Service Asscn; Americans for Middle East Understanding; International Advisory Committee, International Centre, New York. *Publications:* The Ayatollah in the Cathedral, 1986; Terrorism: The New Warfare, 1988; Hostage Crisis, 1989; Death of a Dissident, 1990; Fire in the Forest, 1990; Metalfabriken, 1993; Grocery Store, 1993; Nat-Tel, 1995; The Moral Authority of Government, 2000. Contributions: books and professional journals. *Honours:* Medal for Valor, US Dept of State, 1981; Gold Medal, National Institute of Social Sciences, 1991; many hon. doctorates.

KENNEDY, Pagan, MA; American writer and teacher; b. 7 Sept. 1962, Washington, DC. *Education:* Wesleyan, Conn. and Johns Hopkins Univs, Md. *Career:* Publr Pagan's Head magazine 1988–93; columnist, Village Voice 1990–93; Adjunct Instructor, Boston Coll. 1995–; contribs to The Nation, Spin, Seventeen, Interview, etc. *Publications:* Elvis's Bathroom (short stories) 1989, Stripping and Other Stories 1994, 'Zine 1995, Spinsters (novel) 1996, The Exes (novel) 1998, Confessions of a Memory Eater 2006; non-fiction: Platforms: A Microwaved Cultural Chronicle of the 1970s 1994, Pagan Kennedy's Living: A Handbook for Maturing Hipsters 1997, Black Livingstone: A True Tale of Adventure in the Nineteenth-Century Congo 2002, The First Man-Made Man 2007. *Honours:* Nat. Endowment for the Arts Award 1993. *E-mail:* paganken@gmail.com (office). *Website:* www.pagankennedy.net.

KENNEDY, Paul Michael, CBE, MA, DPhil, FRHistS, FBA; British historian and academic; *J. Richardson Dilworth Professor of History and Director, International Security Studies, Yale University;* b. 17 June 1945, Wallsend; s. of John Patrick Kennedy and Margaret (née Hennessy) Kennedy; m. 1st Catherine Urwin 1967 (died 1998); three s., m. 2nd Cynthia Farrar 2001. *Education:* St Cuthbert's Grammar School, Newcastle-upon-Tyne, Univ. of Newcastle and Oxford Univ. *Career:* Research Asst to Sir Basil Liddell Hart 1966–70; Lecturer, Reader and Prof., Univ. of E Anglia 1970–83; J. Richardson Dilworth Prof. of History, Yale Univ. 1983–, Dir Int. Security Studies 1988–; Visiting Fellow, Inst. for Advanced Study, Princeton 1978–79; Fellow, Alexander von Humboldt Foundation, American Philosophical Soc., American Acad. of Arts and Sciences. *Publications:* The Samoan Tangle 1974, The Rise and Fall of British Naval Mastery 1976, The Rise of the Anglo-German Antagonism 1980, The Realities Behind Diplomacy 1981, Strategy and Diplomacy 1983, The Rise and Fall of the Great Powers 1988, Grand Strategy in War and Peace 1991, Preparing for the Twenty-First Century 1993, Pivotal States: A New Framework for US Policy in the Developing World (ed.) 1998, The Parliament of Man: The United Nations and the Quest for World Government 2006. *Honours:* Hon. DHL (New Haven, Alfred, Long Island, Connecticut); Hon. DLitt (Newcastle, East Anglia); Hon. LLD (Ohio); Hon. MA (Yale, Union, Quinnipiac); Dr hc (Leuven). *Address:* Department of History, Yale Univ., PO Box 208353, New Haven, CT 06520-8353, USA (office). *Telephone:* (203) 432-6242 (office). *Fax:* (203) 432-6250 (office). *E-mail:* paul.kennedy@yale.edu (office). *Website:* www.yale.edu/iss (office).

KENNEDY, Thomas Eugene, MFA, PhD; American writer, editor, translator and teacher; *Core Faculty in Fiction and Creative Nonfiction, MFA Program, Fairleigh Dickinson University;* b. 9 March 1944, New York, NY; s. of the late George Ryan Kennedy and Ethel May Paris; m. Monique M. Brun 1974 (divorced 1997); one s. one d. *Education:* Fordham Univ., New York, Vermont Coll., Norwich Univ., Copenhagen Univ., Denmark. *Career:* Guest Ed. Nordic Section Frank magazine 1987; International Ed. Cimarron Review 1989–99; Contributing Ed. Pushcart Prize 1990–; Advisory Ed. Short Story 1990–95, Literary Review 1996–; mem. Editorial Bd International Quarterly 1994, Absinthe: New European Writing 2002–; Int. Ed. Story Quarterly 2000–07; Co-Ed. Best New Writing/Eric Hoffer Awards 2007–08; mem. panel, Thomas E. Kennedy: A Lifetime in Literature, US Asscn of Writers & Writing Programs, Atlanta, Ga 2007; Co-founder and Co-Ed. Serving House Books 2009–; Contributing Ed. Serving House Journal 2009–; mem. Core Faculty in Fiction and Creative Nonfiction, MFA Program, Fairleigh Dickinson Univ. *Music:* song lyrics recorded on record album Hammer, San Francisco/Atlantic label 1970. *Films:* Thomas E. Kennedy: Copenhagen Quartet (documentary) 2004, In the Company of Angels (documentary) 2010. *Publications:* Andre Dubus: A Study 1988, Crossing Borders (novel) 1990, The American Short Story Today 1991, Robert Coover: A Study 1992, Index American Award Stories 1993, A Weather of the Eye (novel) 1996, Unreal City (short stories) 1996, New Danish Fiction (ed.) 1995, The Book of Angels (novel) 1997, Drive, Dive, Dance and Fight (short stories) 1997, New Irish Writing (ed.) 1997, Stories and Sources (ed.) 1998, Poems and Sources (ed.) 2000, Realism and Other Illusions (essays) 2002, Kerrigan's Copenhagen, A Love Story (novel) 2002, The Secret Life of the Writer (co-ed.) 2002, Bluett's Blue Hours (novel) 2003, Greene's Summer (novel) 2004, Danish Fall (novel) 2005, The Literary Traveler (essays) 2005, A Passion in the Desert (novel) 2007, Cast Upon the Day (stories) 2007, Writers on the Job: Tales of Nonwriting Life (essays, co-ed) 2008, New Danish Writing (ed) 2008, Riding the Dog: A Look Back at America (essays) 2008, In the Company of Angels (novel) 2010, Last Night My Bed a Boat of Whiskey Going Down (novel in essays) 2010, Last Walk Through the City (poetry trans.) 2010, The Girl with Red Hair (co-ed) 2010, Falling Sideways (novel) 2011, Winter Tales: Men Write about Ageing 2011; other: The Literary Traveler (online column) 2001–, Writers on the Job (online column) 2004–, A Shout from Copenhagen (blog in Absinthe: New European Writing and on Facebook) 2007–; hundreds of short stories, essays, translations etc. in American and European magazines since 1984. *Honours:* Angoff Award 1988, Emerging Writer Award, Passages North 1988, Pushcart Prize 1990, O. Henry Prize 1994, European Competition Winner 1995, Gulf Coast Short Story Prize 2002, Frank Expatriate Writing Award 2002, Copenhagen Poetry Day Grass Prize 2006, Eric Hoffer Book Award 2007, First Runner Up (General Fiction) and Winner Micro Press Award 2007, US National Magazine Award (essay) 2008. *Literary Agent:* c/o Nat Sobel, Sobel Weber Associates, Inc., 146 East 19th Street, New York, NY 10003-2404, USA. *Telephone:* (212) 410-8585. *E-mail:* NSobel@sobelweber.com. *E-mail:* KennedyCopenhagen@gmail.com (office); info@thomasekennedy.com (office). *Website:* www.thomasekennedy.com; www.copenhagenquartet.com.

KENNEDY, William Joseph, BA; American author and academic; *Professor of Creative Writing and Director, New York State Writers' Institute, University at Albany, State University of New York;* b. 16 Jan. 1928, Albany, New York; s. of William J. Kennedy and Mary E. McDonald; m. Ana Segarra 1957; one s. two d. *Education:* Siena Coll., New York. *Career:* Asst Sports Ed. and columnist, Glens Falls Post Star, New York 1949–50; reporter, Albany Times-Union, New York 1952–56, special writer 1963–70; Asst Man. Ed. and columnist, P.R. World Journal, San Juan 1956; reporter, Miami Herald 1957; corresp., Time-Life Publs, Puerto Rico 1957–59; reporter, Knight Newspapers 1957–59; Founding Man. Ed. San Juan Star 1959–61; Lecturer, State Univ. of New York, Albany 1974–82, Prof. of English 1983–; Visiting Prof., Cornell Univ. 1982–83; Exec. Dir and Founder, NY State Writers' Inst. 1983–; Nat. Endowment for Arts Fellow 1981, MacArthur Foundation Fellow 1983. *Publications include:* The Ink Truck 1969, Legs 1975, Billy Phelan's Greatest Game 1978, Ironweed (Pulitzer Prize and Nat. Book Critics Circle Award 1984) 1983, O Albany! (non-fiction) 1983, Charlie Malarkey and the Belly Button Machine (children's book) 1986, Quinn's Book 1988, Very Old Bones 1992, Riding the Yellow Trolley Car 1993, Charlie Malarkey and the Singing Moose (children's book) 1994, The Flaming Corsage 1996, Grand View (play) 1996, Roscoe 2002, Chango's Beads and Two-Tone Shoes 2011; film scripts, The Cotton Club 1984, Ironweed 1987; also short stories, articles in professional journals. *Honours:* several hon. degrees; Gov. of New York Arts Award 1984, Creative Arts Award, Brandeis Univ. 1986. *Address:* Department of English, University at Albany, State University of New York, Humanities 333, 1400 Washington Avenue, Albany, NY 12222; New York State Writers Institute, New Library, LE 320, University at Albany, State University of New York, Albany, NY 12222, USA (office). *Telephone:* (518) 442-4055 (office). *Fax:* (518) 442-4599 (office). *E-mail:* writers@uamail.albany.edu (office). *Website:* www.albany.edu/writers-inst (office); www.albany.edu/english (office).

KENNEDY, X. J. (Joseph Charles), BSc, MA; American poet and writer; b. 21 Aug. 1929, Dover, NJ; s. of Joseph Francis Kennedy and Agnes Rauter; m. Dorothy Mintzlaff 1962; four s. one d. *Education:* Seton Hall Univ., Columbia Univ. and Sorbonne Univ. of Paris. *Career:* Teaching Fellow, Univ. of Michigan 1956–60, Instructor 1960–62; Lecturer in English, Women's Coll. of the Univ. of North Carolina 1962–63; Asst Prof. of English, Tufts Univ. 1963–67, Assoc. Prof. 1967–73, Prof. 1973–79; freelance writer 1979–; Poetry Ed., The Paris Review 1961–64. *Publications:* Nude Descending a Staircase (Acad. of American Poets Lamont Award) 1961, An Introduction to Poetry (with Dana Gioia) 1968, The Bedford Reader 1982, Cross-Ties: Selected Poems (Los Angeles Times Book Award) 1985, Dark Horses: New Poems 1992, The Lords of Misrule: Poems 1992–2002 (Poets' Prize 2004) 2003, In a Prominent Bar in Secaucus: New and Selected Poems 2007, Peeping Tom's Cabin: Comic Verse 2007, City Kids 2009; contrib. to newspapers and journals. *Honours:* Dr hc (Lawrence Univ., Adelphi Univ., Westfield State Coll.); Univ. of the South and The Sewanee Review Aiken-Taylor Award for Modern American Poetry, Guggenheim Fellowship, Nat. Arts Council Fellowship, American Acad. and Inst. of Arts and Letters Michael Braude Award, Shelley Memorial Award, New England Poetry Club Golden Rose, Nat. Council of Teachers of English Award for Excellence in Children's Poetry 2000, Robert Frost Medal, Poetry Soc. of America 2009. *Address:* 22 Revere Street, Lexington, MA 02420, USA (home). *Website:* www.xjanddorothymkennedy.com.

KENNEDY OF THE SHAWS, Baroness (Life Peer) cr. 1997, of Cathcart in the City of Glasgow; **Helena Ann Kennedy,** QC, FRSA; British lawyer; b. 12 May 1950, Glasgow, Scotland; d. of Joshua Kennedy and Mary Jones; pnr (Roger) Iain Mitchell 1978–84; one s.; m. Dr Iain L. Hutchison 1986; one s. one d. *Education:* Holyrood Secondary School, Glasgow and Council of Legal Educ. *Career:* called to the Bar, Gray's Inn 1972; mem. Bar Council 1990–93; mem. CIBA Comm. into Child Sexual Abuse 1981–83; mem. Bd City Limits Magazine 1982–84, New Statesman 1990–96, Counsel Magazine 1990–93; mem. Council, Howard League for Penal Reform 1989–, Chair. Comm. of Inquiry into Violence in Penal Insts for Young People (report 1995); Commr BAFTA inquiry into future of BBC 1990, Hamlyn Nat. Comm. on Educ. 1991–; Visiting lecturer, British Postgrad. Medical Fed. 1991–; Adviser, Mannheim Inst. on Criminology, LSE 1992–; Leader of inquiry into health, environmental and safety aspects of Atomic Weapons Establishment, Aldermaston (report 1994); Chancellor, Oxford Brookes Univ. 1994–2001; Chair. British Council 1998–2004, Human Genetics Comm. 2000–; author of official report (Learning Works) for Further Educ. Funding Council on widening participation in further educ. 1997; Pres. School of Oriental and African Studies, London Univ. 2002–; mem. Advisory Bd, Int. Centre for Prison Studies 1998; Chair. London Int. Festival of Theatre, Standing Cttee for Youth Justice 1992–97; Chair. Charter 88 1992–97; Pres. London Marriage Guidance Council, Birth Control Campaign, Nat. Children's Bureau, Hillcroft Coll.; Vice-Pres. Haldane Soc., Nat. Ass. of Women; mem. British Council's Law Advisory Cttee Advisory Bd for Study of Women and Gender, Warwick Univ., Int. Bar Asscn's Task Force on Terrorism; presenter of various programmes on radio and TV and creator of BBC drama series Blind Justice 1988; Patron, Liberty; mem. Acad. de Cultures Internationales. *Publications:* The Bar on Trial (jtly) 1978, Child Abuse within the Family (jtly) 1984, Balancing Acts (jtly) 1989, Eve was Framed 1992, Just Law: the Changing Face of Justice and Why it Matters to Us All 2004; articles on legal matters, civil liberties and women. *Honours:* Hon. Fellow, Inst. of Advanced Legal Studies, Univ. of London 1997; Hon. mem. Council, Nat. Soc. for Prevention of Cruelty to Children; 18 hon. LLD from British and Irish univs; Women's Network Award 1992, UK Woman of Europe Award 1995; Campaigning and Influencing Award, Nat. Fed. of Women's Insts 1996, Times Newspaper Lifetime Achievement Award in the Law (jtly) 1997; Spectator Magazine's Parl. Campaigner of the Year 2000. *Address:* House of Lords, London, SW1A 0PW, England (office). *Telephone:* (20) 7219-5353 (office); (1708) 379482 (home). *Fax:* (20) 7219-5979 (office); (1708) 379482 (home). *E-mail:* info@helenakennedy.co.uk (home). *Website:* www.parliament.uk (office); www.helenakennedy.co.uk (home).

KENNELL, Nigel M., BA, MA, PhD; Canadian classicist; b. 29 Nov. 1955, London, England; m. Stefanie Adelaide Hillert Suszko 1985. *Education:* University of British Columbia, University of Toronto, American School of Classical Studies, Athens, Greece. *Career:* Lecturer in Classics, Brock University, St Catherine's, Ontario, Canada 1985–86; Asst Prof., Memorial University, St John's University, NF 1986–92, Assoc. Prof. of Classics 1992–; Research Asst, Institute for Advanced Study, Princeton, NJ 1992–93; Research Assoc., Collège de France, Paris 1993; mem. Archeological Institute of America, Classical Asscn of Canada, Society for the Promotion of Hellenic Studies, Canadian Academic Centre in Athens, Asscn of Ancient Historians, American School of Classical Studies Alumni Asscn. *Publications:* The Gymnasium of Virtue 1996, Ancient Greece at the Turn of the Millennium (jt ed.) 2005, Ephebeia 2006; contributions: American Journal of Archaeology, American Journal of Philology, Classical Philology, Epigraphica Anatolica, Hesperia, Journal of Jewish Studies, Phoenix, Tyche, Zeitschrift für Papyrologie und Epigraphik. *Honours:* Choice Outstanding Academic Book 1996. *Address:* c/o College Year in Athens, PO Box 390890, Cambridge, MA 02139, USA (office). *E-mail:* nkennell@teledomenet.gr (office); nigelk@myway.com (home).

KENNELLY, (Timothy) Brendan, MA, PhD, DLitt; Irish academic, poet, writer and dramatist; *Professor Emeritus of Modern Literature and Fellow Emeritus, Trinity College, Dublin*; b. 17 April 1936, Ballylongford, Co. Kerry. *Education:* Trinity Coll., Dublin, Leeds Univ., England. *Career:* Fellow, Trinity Coll., Dublin 1967–73, Prof. of Modern Literature and Sr Fellow 1973–2005, Prof. Emer. and Fellow Emer. 2005–. *Publications:* poetry: Cast a Cold Eye (with Rudi Holzapfel) 1959, The Rain, The Moon (with Rudi Holzapfel) 1961, The Dark About Our Loves (with Rudi Holzapfel) 1962, Green Townlands: Poems (with Rudi Holzapfel) 1963, Let Fall No Burning Leaf 1963, My Dark Fathers 1964, Up and At It 1965, Collection One: Getting Up Early 1966, Good Souls to Survive 1967, Dream of a Black Fox 1968, Selected Poems 1969, A Drinking Cup: Poems from the Irish 1970, Bread 1971, Love Cry 1972, Salvation, the Stranger 1972, The Voices 1973, Shelley in Dublin 1974, A Kind of Trust 1975, New and Selected Poems 1976, Islandman 1977, The Visitor 1978, A Girl: 22 Songs 1978, A Small Light 1979, In Spite of the Wise 1979, The Boats Are Home 1980, The House That Jack Didn't Build 1982, Cromwell: A Poem 1983, Moloney Up and At It 1984, Selected Poems 1985, Mary: From the Irish 1987, Love of Ireland: Poems From the Irish 1989, A Time for Voices: Selected Poems 1960–1990 1990, The Book of Judas: A Poem 1991, Breathing Spaces: Early Poems 1992, Poetry My Arse 1995, The Man Made of Rain 1998, The Singing Tree 1998, Begin 1999, Glimpses 2001, The Little Book of Judas 2002, Martial Art 2003, Familiar Strangers: New and Selected Poems 1960–2004, Now 2006, Reservoir Voices 2009; fiction: The Crooked Cross 1963, The Florentines 1967; plays: Medea 1991, The Trojan Women 1993, Antigone 1996, Blood Wedding 1996, When Then Is Now: Three Greek Plays 2006; criticism: Journey into Joy: Selected Prose 1994; other prose: Real Ireland 1984, Ireland Past and Present (ed.) 1985; contrib. poems to anthologies, including The Penguin Book of Irish Verse 1970, Landmarks of Irish Drama 1988, Joycechoyce: The Poems in Verse and Prose of James Joyce (with A. Norman Jeffares) 1992, Irish Prose Writings: Swift to the Literary Renaissance (with Terence Brown) 1992, Between Innocence and Peace: Favourite Poems of Ireland 1993, Dublines (with Katie Donovan) 1994, Ireland's Women: Writings Past and Present (with Katie Donovan and A. Norman Jeffares) 1994. *Honours:* AE Monorial Prize for Poetry 1967, Critics' Special Harveys Award 1988, American Ireland Funds Literary Award 1999. *Address:* School of English, Trinity College, Dublin 2, Ireland (office); 38 Trinity College, Dublin 2 (home). *Telephone:* (1) 8961111.

KENNELLY, Laura B., BA, MA, PhD; American writer, poet and editor; *Associate Editor, BACH: Journal of the Riemenschneider Bach Institute, Baldwin Wallace University*; b. Denton, Tex. *Education:* Univ. of North Texas. *Career:* Adjunct Prof., Univ. of North Texas 1976–94, Texas Woman's Univ. 1995; Ed. Grasslands Review 1989–2006; Assoc. Ed., BACH: Journal of the Riemenschneider Bach Institute, Baldwin-Wallace Univ.; music reviewer, WCLV radio; arts columnist, Morning Journal 2000–11; mem. Texas Asscn of Creative Writing Teachers (Pres. 1993–95), Music Critics' Asscn of North America. *Publications:* The Passage of Mrs Jung (chapbook) 1990, A Certain Attitude 1995; contrib. to San Jose Studies, Studies in Contemporary Satire, Exquisite Corpse, New Mexico Humanities Review, Australian Journal of Communication. *Honours:* First Place, North Central Texas Coll. Poetry Contest 1988, First Place, Univ. of North Texas Centennial Poem Award 1990, Nat. Endowment for the Arts Classical Music and Opera Fellowship, Columbia Univ. 2005. *Address:* PO Box 626, Berea, OH 44017-1102, USA (home). *Telephone:* (440) 826-8071 (office). *E-mail:* LKennell@bw.edu (home).

KENNEY, Catherine, MA, PhD; American writer, academic and arts administrator; *President, Proudfoot Press*; b. 3 Oct. 1948, Memphis, Tennessee, USA; d. of J. D. and Norma Kirby McGehee; one s. *Education:* Siena Coll., Loyola Univ., Chicago. *Career:* fmr Chair. and Prof. of English, Mundelein Coll., Loyola Univ.; fmr Exec. Dir, Irish American Heritage Center, Chicago; Dir of Devt, Apple Tree Theatre, Highland Park, IL 2005–; Pres., Proudfoot Press 2006–; mem., Faculty of the American Man. Asscn. *Publications:* Thurber's Anatomy of Confusion 1984, The Remarkable Case of Dorothy L. Sayers 1990, Dorothy L. (play) 1993; contributions: books, scholarly journals and newspapers. *Honours:* American Asscn of University Women Grant 1983, Kilby Award, Wheaton Coll. 1984. *Address:* 228 Stanley Avenue, Park Ridge, IL 60068, USA (office). *Telephone:* (847) 207-4004 (office). *E-mail:* proudfootproduct@sbcglobal.net (office).

KENNY, Adele, BA, MA; American poet, writer, editor, academic and consultant; *Poetry Editor, Tiferet Journal of Spiritual Literature*; b. 28 Nov. 1948, Perth Amboy, NJ; s. of William Kenny and Adele Kenny. *Education:* Kean Univ., Coll. of New Rochelle. *Career:* Artist-in-Residence, Middlesex Co. Arts Council 1979–80; Prof. of Creative Writing, Coll. of New Rochelle Grad. School 1981–85; Poetry Ed., New Jersey ArtForm magazine 1981–83, Tiferet Journal of Spiritual Literature 2006–; Founder and Dir Carriage House Poetry Reading Series 1998–; Arts Council Dir Kuran Arts Center 1999–; Instructor, Stamler Police Acad. 1998–2008; Contributing Ed. The Antiques News 2000–02; Assoc. Ed. The Antiquer: Fine Arts and Antiques 2002–05. *Exhibitions:* Jailhouse Revival, NJ Inst. of Tech. 2006, Double Exposures,

Silconas Poetry Center and Art Gallery 2009. *Publications:* An Archeology of Ruins 1982, Illegal Entries 1984, The Roses Open 1984, Between Hail Marys 1986, Migrating Geese 1987, The Crystal Keepers Handbook 1988, Counseling Gifted, Creative and Talented Youth Through the Arts 1989, Castles and Dragons 1990, Questi Momenti 1990, Starship Earth 1990, We Become By Being 1994, Staffordshire Spaniels 1997, At the Edge of the Woods 1997, Staffordshire Animals 1998, Photographic Cases: Victorian Design Sources 2001, Chosen Ghosts 2001, Staffordshire Figures: History in Earthenware 1740–1900 2004, What Matters 2011; poems in books and anthologies from Crown, McGraw-Hill, Tuttle and Shambhala; contrib. to periodicals. *Honours:* Writer's Digest Award 1981, New Jersey State Council on the Arts Fellowships 1982, 1987, Merit Book Awards 1983, 1986, 1987, 1991, Henderson Award 1984, Roselip Award 1988, Haiku Quarterly Award 1989, Allen Ginsberg Poetry Award 1993, 2006, Merton Poetry of the Sacred Prize 2007, Women of Excellence Award in the Arts and Humanities 2011. *Telephone:* (908) 889-7223 (office). *E-mail:* adelekenny@verizon.net (office). *Website:* www.adelekenny.com; adelekenny.blogspot.com.

KENNY, Sir Anthony John Patrick, Kt, DPhil, FBA; British philosopher and academic; b. 16 March 1931, Liverpool; s. of John Kenny and Margaret Kenny (née Jones); m. Nancy Caroline Gayley 1966; two s. *Education:* Gregorian Univ., Rome, Italy, St Benet's Hall, Oxford. *Career:* ordained Catholic priest, Rome 1955; curate, Liverpool 1959–63; returned to lay state 1963; Asst Lecturer, Univ. of Liverpool 1961–63; Lecturer in Philosophy, Exeter and Trinity Colls, Oxford 1963–64; Tutor in Philosophy, Balliol Coll., Oxford 1964, Fellow 1964–78, Sr Tutor 1971–72, 1976–77, Master 1978–89; Warden Rhodes House 1989–99; Professorial Fellow, St John's Coll., Oxford 1989–99; Pro-Vice-Chancellor, Univ. of Oxford 1984–99, Pro-Vice Chancellor for Devt 1999–2001; Wilde Lecturer in Natural and Comparative Religion, Oxford 1969–72; Jt Gifford Lecturer, Univ. of Edinburgh 1972–73; Stanton Lecturer, Univ. of Cambridge 1980–83; Speaker's Lecturer in Biblical Studies, Univ. of Oxford 1980–83; Visiting Prof., Stanford, Cornell and Rockefeller Univs and Univs of Chicago, Washington and Michigan; Vice-Pres. British Acad. 1986–88, Pres. 1989–93; Chair. Bd British Library 1993–96 (mem. Bd 1991–96); Pres. Royal Inst. of Philosophy 2005–09; Del. and mem. of Finance Cttee, Oxford Univ. Press 1986–93; Ed. The Oxford Magazine 1972–73; mem. Royal Norwegian Acad. 1993–, American Philosophical Soc. 1994–, American Acad. of Arts and Sciences 2003–. *Publications:* Action, Emotion and Will 1963, Responsa Alumnorum of English College, Rome (two vols) 1963, Descartes 1968, The Five Ways 1969, Wittgenstein 1973, The Anatomy of the Soul 1974, Will, Freedom and Power 1975, Aristotelian Ethics 1978, Freewill and Responsibility 1978, The God of the Philosophers 1979, Aristotle's Theory of the Will 1979, Aquinas 1980, The Computation of Style 1982, Faith and Reason 1983, Thomas More 1983, The Legacy of Wittgenstein 1984, A Path from Rome 1985, The Logic of Deterrence 1985, The Ivory Tower 1985, Wyclif – Past Master 1985, Wyclif's De Universalibus 1985, Rationalism, Empiricism and Idealism 1986, Wyclif in His Times 1986, The Road to Hillsborough 1986, Reason and Religion (essays) 1987, The Heritage of Wisdom 1987, God and Two Poets 1988, The Metaphysics of Mind 1989, Mountains 1991, What is Faith? 1992, Aristotle on the Perfect Life 1992, Aquinas on Mind 1992, The Oxford Illustrated History of Western Philosophy (ed.) 1994, Frege 1995, A Life in Oxford 1997, A Brief History of Western Philosophy 1998, Essays on the Aristotelian Tradition 2001, Aquinas on Being 2002, The Unknown God 2003, A New History of Western Philosophy (one vol.) 2003, A New History of Western Philosophy Vol. 1: Ancient Philosophy 2004, Vol. 2: Medieval Philosophy 2005, Arthur Hugh Clough: A Poet's Life 2005, What I Believe 2006, Life, Liberty and the Pursuit of Utility (with C. Kenny) 2006, The Rise of Modern Philosophy 2006, Philosophy in the Modern World 2007, Can Oxford Be Improved? (with R. Kenny) 2007, From Empedocles to Wittgenstein: Historical Essays in Philosophy 2008. *Honours:* Hon. Bencher, Lincoln's Inn 1999; Hon. DLitt (Bristol) 1982, (Denison Univ.) 1986, (Liverpool) 1988, (Glasgow) 1990, (Lafayette) 1990, (Trinity Coll., Dublin) 1992, (Hull) 1993, (Belfast) 1994; Hon. DCL (Oxford) 1987; Hon. DLit (London) 2002; Hon. DD (Liverpool Hope) 2010; Aquinas Medal 1996. *Address:* 1a Larkins Lane, Headington, Oxford, OX3 9DW, England (home). *Telephone:* (1865) 764174 (home). *E-mail:* ajpk@f2s.com (home).

KENNY, Maurice, PhD; American (Mohawk) poet, writer and teacher; *Associate Visiting Professor and Writer in Residence, State University of New York, Potsdam;* b. 1929, Watertown, NY. *Education:* Butler Univ., St Lawrence Univ. and New York Univ. *Career:* founder and fmr Ed. Contact II literary magazine; fmr Ed. and Publisher Strawberry Press; fmr Poetry Ed. Adirondac Magazine; Visiting Prof. Univ. of Oklahoma at Norman, En'owkin Center at Univ. of Victoria, Paul Smith's Coll.; currently Assoc. Visiting Prof. and writer-in-residence State Univ. of New York (SUNY) at Potsdam; numerous appointments as writer-in-residence, including American Indian Community House, New York, Oneida Indian Nation, Wisconsin, Univ. of California at Berkeley, Columbia Univ., St Lawrence Univ., Gettysburg Coll., North Country Community Coll., Syracuse Community Writers, SUNY at Fredonia, Silver Bay Asscn; served on panels, including New York Foundation for the Arts, North Carolina Arts Council, New York State Council on the Arts, Educational Testing Service Arts Recognition and Talent Search; fmr mem. bd of dirs Co-ordinating Council of Literary Magazines, New York Foundation for the Arts, WSLU-FM radio station; currently Art Dir Blue Moon Cafe, Saranac Lake. *Radio:* Dug-Out (New American Radio) 1990, Black Robe: Saint Isaac Jogues. *Television:* Reno Hill... Little Big Horn (NBC), Poems, Poets and the Song (CBS). *Publications:* poetry: Dead Letters Sent 1958, I Am the Sun 1976, North: Poems of Home 1977, Dancing Back Strong the Nations 1979, Rivers 1979, Only as Far as Brooklyn 1979, Kneading the Blood 1981, Boston Tea Party 1982, The Smell of Slaughter 1982, Black Robe 1983, The Mama Poems (American Book Award) 1984, Between Two Rivers: Selected Poems 1956–84 1985, Prayer for Philip Deer in the Sierras 1987, Wounds Beneath the Flesh: Fifteen Native American Poets (ed.) 1987, Humans and/or Not So Humans 1988, Greyhounding This America 1989, The Short and Long of It 1990, Last Mourning in Brooklyn 1991, Tekonwatonti: Molly Brant 1992, On Second Thought: A Compilation (poems and essays) 1995, In the Time of the Present 2000, Carving Hawk: New and Selected Poems 1953–2000 2002, Connotations 2008; contrib. poems to numerous anthologies; short stories: Rain and Other Fictions 1985, Stories for a Winter's Night 1999, Tortured Skins and Other Fictions 2000; non-fiction: Backward to Forward (essays) 1997; contrib. to Trends, Calaloo, World Literature Today, American Indian Quarterly, Blue Cloud Quarterly, Wicazo Sa Review, Saturday Review, New York Times. *Honours:* Dr hc (St Lawrence Univ.); Wordcraft Circle of Native Writers Elder Recognition Award 2000, Nat. Public Radio Award for Broadcasting. *Address:* SUNY Potsdam, 44 Pierrepont Avenue, Potsdam, NY 13676-2294 (office); Apt 4, 49 Pierrepont Avenue, Potsdam, NY 13676-2120, USA (home). *Telephone:* (315) 267-2950 (office); (315) 268-1607 (home). *E-mail:* kennymf@potsdam.edu (office).

KENRICK, Tony; Australian author; b. 23 Aug. 1935, Sydney, NSW. *Career:* Advertising Copywriter, Sydney, Toronto, San Francisco, New York, London, 1953–72. *Publications:* The Only Good Body's a Dead One, 1970; A Tough One to Lose, 1972; Two for the Price of One, 1974; Stealing Lillian, 1975; The Seven Day Soldiers, 1976; The Chicago Girl, 1976; Two Lucky People, 1978; The Nighttime Guy, 1979; The 81st Site, 1980; Blast, 1983; Faraday's Flowers, 1985; China White, 1986; Neon Tough, 1988; Glitterbug, 1991; Round Trip, 1996.

KENT, Alexander (see Reeman, Douglas Edward)

KENT, Helen (see Polley, Judith Anne)

KENT, Jeffrey (Jeff) John William, BSc (Econ) (Hons), PGCE; English writer, musician (keyboards, percussion), singer, lecturer and campaigner; *Director, Witan Creations;* b. 28 July 1951, Stoke-on-Trent, Staffs., England; s. of Cyril Kent and Helen Kent; m. Rosalind Ann Downs 1987. *Education:* Univ. of London, Crewe Coll. of Educ. *Career:* freelance writer and ed. 1972–; Lecturer in Humanities, various Staffordshire colls 1974–2010; performing musician and songwriter 1975–; guest speaker 1986–; Lecturer in Writing and Publishing, Stoke on Trent Coll. 1994–2010; performances include Dragon Fair 1984, Open Air Concert, Chamberlain Square, Birmingham 1984, Green Party Conf. Concert 1987, Artists for the Planet Concert 1989; appearance on BBC Midlands TV, launching album 1992; Only One World tour 2000; Co-ordinator, The Mercia Movement 1993–; Convener The Mercian Constitutional Convention 2001–03, The Acting Witan of Mercia 2003–; Br. Sec., Stoke on Trent Coll., Univ. and Coll. Union 2006–10. *Films:* Up the Vale! The Story of Port Vale FC (historical adviser) 1998, Millennium Documentary: Port Vale Football Club (historical adviser) 2000. *Recordings include:* albums: Tales from the Land of the Afterglow Part 1, Part 2 1984, Port Vale Forever 1992, Only One World 2000; single: Butcher's Tale/Annie with the Dancing Eyes 1981. *Publications:* The Rise and Fall of Rock 1983, Principles of Open Learning 1987, Routes to Change: A Collection of Essays for Green Education (co-author) 1988, The Last Poet: The Story of Eric Burdon 1989, Back to Where We Once Belonged! 1989, The Valiants' Years: The Story of Port Vale 1990, Port Vale Tales 1991, Port Vale Forever 1992, 100 Walks in Staffordshire (co-author) 1992, The Port Vale Record 1879–1993 1993, Port Vale Personalities 1996, The Mercia Manifesto: A Blueprint for the Future Inspired by the Past (prin. author and ed.) 1997, Port Vale Grass Roots (ed.) 1997, The Potteries Derbies 1998, A Draft Constitution for Mercia (prin. author and ed.) 2001, The Mysterious Double Sunset 2001, The Constitution of Mercia (prin. author and ed.) 2003, A Potteries Past (ed.) 2010, What If There Had Been No Port in the Vale?: Startling Port Vale Stories! 2011; contribs to Alsager Chronicle, Education Now, Eric Burdon Connection Newsletter, First Hearing, Hard Graft, NATFHE Journal, The Sentinel, TAG-mag etc. *Address:* Cherry Tree House, 8 Nelson Crescent, Cotes Heath, via Stafford, Staffs., ST21 6ST, England (office). *Telephone:* (1782) 791673 (office). *E-mail:* witan@mail.com (office). *Website:* www.witancreations.com (office).

KENYON, Bruce Guy, (Meredith Leigh); American writer; b. 16 Aug. 1929, Cadillac, Michigan, USA; m. Marian Long 1950 (divorced 1954). *Career:* mem. Authors' Guild, Authors League. *Publications:* Rose White, Rose Red 1983, The Forrester Inheritance 1985, Fair Game 1986, A Marriage of Inconvenience 1986, Wild Rose 1986, The Counterfeit Lady 1987, An Elegant Education 1987, A Lady of Qualities 1987, Return to Cheyne Spa 1988, A Certain Reputation 1990; contributions: periodicals.

KEOGH, Dermot Francis, BA, MA, PhD; Irish academic and historian; b. 12 May 1945, Dublin; m. Ann 1973; two s. two d. *Education:* Univ. Coll., Dublin, European Univ. Inst., Florence. *Career:* Lecturer in History, Univ. Coll., Cork 1970–, Jean Monnet Prof. of Modern Integration 1990–, Acting Head, School of Modern History 1999–2000, Head 2003–09; Sr Research Fellow, Queens Univ., Belfast 1995–96; Visiting Prof. Dept of History, Colby Coll., USA 1998; Jean Monnet Fellow Dept of History and Civilisation, European Univ. Inst., Florence, Italy 2001–02; Fulbright Prof. Boston Coll. Social Welfare Research Inst. Boston, USA summer 2002; Visiting Prof., Univ. of NSW 2007; mem. Royal Irish Acad. 2002–, Archives Advisory Group Dept of Justice 2006.

Publications: The Rise of the Irish Working Class 1890–1914 1982, The Vatican, the Bishops and Irish Politics 1919–1939 1986, Ireland and Europe 1919–1948 1989, Church and Politics in Latin America 1990, Ireland, 1922–1993 1993, Jews in Twentieth Century Ireland 1998, Documents on Irish Foreign Policy, Vols I-IV, The Making of the Irish Constitution 1937 2007, Jack Lynch: A Biography 2008; contrib. to academic journals and national press. *Honours:* Fellow, Woodrow Wilson Centre for Scholars, Washington, DC 1988; James S. Donnelly Sr Prize, American Conf. for Irish Studies, Oleinin Medal, Nat. Library of Russia 2008. *Address:* School of Modern History, University College Cork, Tyrconnell, Perrott Avenue, Cork, Ireland (office). *Telephone:* (21) 4902687 (office). *Fax:* (21) 4273369 (office). *E-mail:* d.keogh@ucc.ie (office). *Website:* www.ucc.ie/academic/history (office).

KEOHANE, Robert Owen, BA, MA, PhD; American political scientist and academic; *Professor of International Affairs, Woodrow Wilson School, Princeton University*; b. 3 Oct. 1941, Chicago, Ill.; s. of Robert Emmet Keohane and Marie Irene Keohane (née Pieters); m. Nannerl Overholser 1970; three s. one d. *Education:* Shimer Coll., Illinois, Harvard Univ. *Career:* Fellow, Harvard Univ., Woodrow Wilson School of Public and Int. Affairs, Princeton Univ. 1961–62; mem. Woodrow Wilson Award Cttee 1982, Chair. Nominating Cttee 1990–91, Chair. Minority Identification Project 1990–92; Instructor, then Assoc. Prof., Swathmore Coll. 1965–73; Assoc. Prof., then Prof., Stanford Univ. 1973–81; Ed. Int. Org. 1974–80, mem. Bd Eds 1968–77, 1982–88, 1992–97, 1998–, Chair. 1986–87; Prof., Brandeis Univ. 1981–85; Pres. Int. Studies Asscn 1988–89, Chair. Nominations Cttee 1985; Prof., then Stanfield Prof. of Int. Peace, Harvard Univ. 1985–96, Chair. Dept of Govt 1988–92; James B. Duke Prof. of Political Science, Duke Univ. –2004; Prof. of Int. Affairs, Woodrow Wilson School, Princeton Univ. 2004–; Sherill Lecturer, Yale Univ. Law School 1996; Pres. American Political Science Asscn 1999–2000; mem. NAS 2005; Fellow, American Acad. of Arts and Sciences 1983–, Center for Advanced Study in Behavioral Sciences 1977–78, 1987–88, 2004–05; Frank Kenan Fellow, Nat. Endowment for the Humanities 1995–96. *Publications include:* After Hegemony: Cooperation and Discord in the World Political Economy 1984, Neorealism and Its Critics 1986, International Institutions and State Power: Essays in International Relations Theory 1989; (as co-author): Power and Interdependence: World Politics in Transition 1977, Institutions for the Earth: Sources of Effective International Environmental Protection 1993, After the Cold War: State Strategies and International Institutions in Europe, 1989–91 1993, Designing Social Inquiry: Scientific Inference in Qualitative Research 1994; (as co-ed.): Transnational Relations and World Politics 1972, The New European Community: Decision-Making and Institutional Change 1991, Ideas and Foreign Policy 1993, From Local Commons to Global Interdependence 1994, Institutions for Environmental Aid: Pitfalls and Promises 1996, Internationalization and Domestic Politics 1996, Imperfect Unions: Security Institutions Across Time and Space 1999, Exploration and Contestation in the Study of World Politics 1998, Legalization and World Politics 2000. *Honours:* Bell Research Fellow, German Marshall Fund 1977–78; Fellow, Council on Foreign Relations 1967–69, Guggenheim Foundation 1992–93, Sr Foreign Policy Fellow, Social Science Research Council 1986–88; Bellagio Resident Fellow 1993; Hon. PhD (Univ. of Århus, Denmark) 1988; Grawemeyer Award for Ideas Improving World Order 1989, First Mentorship Award, Soc. for Women in Int. Political Economy 1997, Skytte Prize, Johan Skytte Foundation, Uppsala, Sweden 2005. *Address:* Woodrow Wilson School, 408 Robertson Hall, Princeton University, Princeton, NJ 08544-1013, USA (office). *Telephone:* (609) 258-1856 (office). *Fax:* (609) 258-0019 (office). *E-mail:* rkeohane@princeton.edu (office). *Website:* www.wws.princeton.edu/rkeohane (office).

KEPEL, Gilles; French sociologist and writer; *Professor of the Middle East, Institut d'Études Politiques*. *Career:* Visiting Prof., New York Univ. 1994, Columbia Univ. 1995–96; currently Prof. of the Middle East, Institut d'Études Politiques, Paris. *Publications:* non-fiction: Muslim Extremism in Egypt: The Prophet and Pharaoh 1985, The Revenge of God: Resurgence of Islam, Christianity and Judaism in the Modern World 1993, Allah in the West: Islamic Movements in America and Europe 1997, Jihad: The Trail of Political Islam 2002, Bad Moon Rising: A Chronicle of the Middle East Today 2003, The War for Muslim Minds: Islam and the West 2004, The Roots of Radical Islam 2004, Du jihad à la fitna 2005. *Honours:* Tel-Aviv Prize for Literature 1990, Newman Prize 2003. *Address:* Institut d'Études Politiques de Paris, 2002 - 27 rue Saint-Guillaume, 75337 Paris Cédex 07, France (office). *E-mail:* gilles.kepel@sciences-po.fr (office). *Website:* www.ceri-sciences-po.org/cherlist/kepel.htm (office).

KERBER, Linda Kaufman, AB, MA, PhD; American academic and writer; *May Brodbeck Professor of Liberal Arts and Professor of History, University of Iowa*; b. 23 Jan. 1940, New York, NY; m. Richard Kerber 1960; two s. *Education:* Barnard Coll., New York Univ., Columbia Univ. *Career:* Lecturer, Stern Coll. for Women, Yeshiva Univ. 1963–67, Asst Prof. 1968; Asst Prof., San Jose State Coll. 1969–70; Visiting Asst Prof., Stanford Univ. 1970–71; Assoc. Prof., Univ. of Iowa 1971–75, Prof. of History 1975–, May Brodbeck Prof. of Liberal Arts 1985–; Visiting Prof., Univ. of Chicago 1991–92; Harmsworth Prof. of American History, Oxford Univ. 2006–07; mem. American Antiquarian Soc., American Studies Asscn (pres. 1988), Org. of American Historians (pres. 1997), Soc. of American Historians, PEN American Center, American Historical Asscn (pres. 2006). *Publications:* Federalists in Dissent: Imagery and Ideology in Jeffersonian America, 1970; Women of the Republic: Intellect and Ideology in Revolutionary America, 1980; Women's America: Refocusing the Past (co-ed.), 1982; The Impact of Women on American Education, 1983; History Will Do It No Justice: Women's Lives in Revolutionary America, 1987; US History as Women's History: New Feminist Essays (co-ed.), 1995; Toward an Intellectual History of Women: Essays, 1997; No Constitutional Right to Be Ladies: Women and the Obligations of Citizenship, 1998. Contributions: Professional journals. *Honours:* elected mem. American Philosophical Soc., American Acad. of Arts and Sciences; Nat. Endowment for the Humanities Fellowships 1976, 1983–84, 1994, Nat. Humanities Center Fellowship 1990–91, Guggenheim Fellowship 1990–91. *Address:* c/o Department of History, University of Iowa, Iowa City, IA 52242, USA (office). *Telephone:* (319) 335-2299 (office). *E-mail:* linda-kerber@comcast.net (home).

KERET, Etgar; Israeli writer, screenwriter and actor; *Lecturer Department of Film and Television, Tel-Aviv University*; b. 1967, Tel-Aviv. *Career:* currently Lecturer, Dept of Film and Television, Tel-Aviv Univ.; also columnist for a Jerusalem weekly newspaper and draws a comic strip for a Tel-Aviv newspaper. *Film screenplays:* Devek Metoraf 1994, Ha-Chavera Shel Korbi 1994, Breaking the Pig (voice) 1998, Mashehu Totali 2000, A Buck's Worth 2005, Wristcutters: A Love Story 2006, Three Towers 2006. *Films as actor:* Malka Lev Adom (Skin Deep, also dir) 1996, Clara Hakedosha 1996, Mashehu Totali 2000, Meduzot (also dir, Caméra d'Or, Cannes Film Festival 2007) 2007. *Television screenplays:* Ha-Hamishia Hakamerit 1994, Aball'e 2001, Eretz Nehederet (series) 2003. *Publications include:* short stories: Pipelines 1992, Gaza Blues (with Samir el-Youssef) 2004, The Nimrod Flip-Out 2005, The Bus Driver Who Wanted to be God 2005, Missing Kissinger 2007, The Girl on the Fridge 2008, Suddenly, a Knock on the Door 2012; also four graphic novels. *Address:* c/o Department of Film and Television, Tel-Aviv University, POB 39040, Tel-Aviv 69978, Israel. *Website:* www.etgarkeret.com.

KERMAN, Joseph Wilfred, BA, PhD; American musicologist, writer, critic and editor; *Professor Emeritus of Music, University of California at Berkeley*; b. (Joseph Wilfred Zukerman), 3 April 1924, London, England; m. Vivian Shaviro 1945; two s. one d. *Education:* New York Univ., Princeton Univ. *Career:* Dir of Graduate Studies, Westminster Choir Coll., Princeton 1949–51; Asst Prof. 1951–56 Univ. of California at Berkeley, Assoc. Prof. 1956–60, Prof. of Music 1960–71, 1974–94, Emer. 1994–, Chair., Dept of Music 1960–63, 1991–93; Heather Prof. of Music, Univ. of Oxford 1971–74; Fellow, Wadham Coll., Oxford 1972–74; founder/Co-Ed., 19th Century Music 1977–89; Ed. California Studies in 19th Century Music 1980–; Charles Eliot Norton Prof. of Poetry, Harvard Univ. 1997–98; Fellow, American Acad. of Arts and Sciences 1973, American Philosophical Soc. 2001. *Publications:* Opera as Drama 1956, The Elizabethan Madrigal: A Comparative Study 1962, Beethoven Quartets 1967, A History of Art and Music (with Horst W. Janson and Dora Jane Janson) 1968, Listen (with Vivian Kerman and Gary Tomlinson) 1972, Beethoven Studies (ed. with Alan Tyson) 1973, The Masses and Motets of William Byrd 1981, The New Grove Beethoven (with Alan Tyson) 1983, Contemplating Music: Challenges to Musicology 1985, Music at the Turn of the Century (ed.) 1990, Write All These Down: Essays on Music 1994, Concerto Conversations 1999, The Art of Fugue: Bach Fugues for Keyboard 1715–1750 2005, Opera and the Morbidity of Music 2008; contrib. to scholarly journals, including Hudson Review, New York Review of Books. *Honours:* Guggenheim Fellowship 1960, Fulbright Fellowship 1966; National Inst. and American Acad. of Arts and Letters Award 1956, Hon. Fellow, Royal Acad. of Music, London 1972, hon. mem. American Musicological Soc. 1995. *Address:* Music Department, University of California, Berkeley, CA 94720-1200 (office); 107 Southampton Avenue, Berkeley, CA 94707, USA (home). *Telephone:* (510) 526-7977 (office). *E-mail:* josephkerman@comcast.net (home). *Website:* music.berkeley.edu/Kerman (office).

KERN, E. R. (see Kerner, Fred)

KERNAGHAN, Eileen Shirley; Canadian writer; b. 6 Jan. 1939, Enderby, BC; m. Patrick Walter Kernaghan 1959, two s. one d. *Education:* University of British Columbia. *Career:* mem. Burnaby Writers Society; Federation of British Columbian Writers; Writers Union of Canada. *Publications:* The Upper Left-Hand Corner: A Writer's Guide for the Northwest (co-author), 1975; Journey to Aprilioth, 1980; Songs for the Drowned Lands, 1983; Sarsen Witch, 1988; Walking After Midnight, 1991. Contributions: journals and periodicals. *Honours:* Silver Porgy Award, West Coast Review of Books, 1981; Canadian Science Fiction and Fantasy Award, 1985.

KERR, (Anne) Judith, OBE; British children's writer and illustrator; b. 14 June 1923, Berlin, Germany; m. Nigel Kneale; one s. one d. *Education:* Central School of Art, London. *Career:* Sec., Red Cross, London, UK 1941–45; teacher and textile designer 1948–53; script ed., scriptwriter, BBC TV, London 1953–58. *Publications:* The Tiger Who Came to Tea 1968, Mog the Forgetful Cat 1970, When Hitler Stole Pink Rabbit 1971, When Willy Went to the Wedding 1972, The Other Way Round (aka Bombs on Aunt Dainty) 1975, Mog's Christmas 1976, A Small Person Far Away 1978, Mog and the Baby 1980, Mog in the Dark 1983, Mog and Me 1984, Mog's Family of Cats 1985, Mog's Amazing Birthday Caper 1986, Mog and Bunny 1988, Mog and Barnaby 1990, How Mrs Monkey Missed the Ark 1992, The Adventures of Mog 1993, Mog on Fox Night 1993, Mog in the Garden 1994, Mog's Kittens 1994, Mog and the Vee Ee Tee 1996, The Big Mog Book 1997, Birdie Halleluyah 1998, Mog's Bad Thing 2000, The Other Goose 2001, Goodbye Mog 2002, Goose in a Hole 2005, Twinkles, Arthur and Puss 2007, One Night in the Zoo 2009, My Henry 2011. *Honours:* Officer's Cross, Order of Merit (Germany) 2007; German

Youth Book Prize (Jugendbuchpreis) 1974, Peter Pan Prize 2006. *Address:* c/o Harper Collins Publishers, 77–85 Fulham Palace Road, London, W6 8JB, England (office).

KERR, Carole (see Carr, Margaret)

KERR, David; British writer and academic; *Associate Professor of English, University of Botswana*; b. 1942, Carlisle, Cumbria. *Career:* Founder and dir of theatre cos in UK, Malawi, Zambia and Botswana; Assoc. Prof. of English, Univ. of Botswana. *Publications:* non-fiction: African Popular Theatre 1996; poetry: Tangled Tongues 2003. *Address:* c/o Flambard Press, Stable Cottage, East Fourstones, Hexham, Northumberland, NE47 5DX, England. *Telephone:* (1434) 674360. *Fax:* (1434) 674178. *E-mail:* flambardpress@btinternet.com. *Website:* www.flambardpress.co.uk.

KERR, Katharine; American novelist; b. (Katharine Nansi Brahtin), 3 Oct. 1944, Cleveland; m. Howard Kerr 1973. *Education:* Stanford Univ., Univ. of California at Santa Barbara. *Publications:* Daggerspell 1986, Darkspell 1987, The Bristling Wood (aka Dawnspell: The Bristling Wood) 1989, The Dragon Revenant (aka Dragonspell: The Southern Sea) 1990, Polar City Blues 1991, A Time of Exile: A Novel of the Westlands 1991, A Time of Omens: A Novel of the Westlands 1992, Resurrection 1992, Days of Blood and Fire: A Novel of the Westlands (aka A Time of War: Days of Blood and Fire) 1993, Days of Air and Darkness: A Novel of the Westlands (aka A Time of Justice: Days of Air and Darkness) 1994, Freeze Frames 1995, Snare 2003, Gold Falcon 2006, Spirit Stone 2007, Shadow Isle 2008, The Silver Mage 2009; ed. of anthologies: Weird Tales from Shakespeare, Enchanted Forests, Sorceries, Palace (co-author) 2002, Polar City Nightmare (co-author) 2004. *Literary Agent:* Larsen-Pomada Literary Agency, 1029 Jones Street (between California and Pine Streets), San Francisco, CA 94109, USA. *Telephone:* (415) 673-0939 (office). *E-mail:* larsenpoma@aol.com. *E-mail:* caddacerrmor@aol.com (office). *Website:* www.deverry.com; www.deepgenre.com.

KERR, Philip Ballantyne, LLM; British writer; b. 22 Feb. 1956, Edinburgh, Scotland; s. of William Kerr and Ann Brodie; m. Jane Thynne 1991; two s. one d. *Education:* Northampton Grammar School and Birmingham Univ. *Career:* film critic, New Statesman. *Play:* Bluesbreakers 2002. *Publications:* adult fiction: March Violets 1989, The Pale Criminal 1990, The Penguin Book of Lies (ed.) 1990, A German Requiem 1991, A Philosophical Investigation 1992, The Penguin Book of Fights, Feuds, and Heartfelt Hatreds: An Anthology of Antipathy (ed.) 1992, Dead Meat 1993, Gridiron (aka The Grid) 1993, Esau 1996, A Five-Year Plan 1997, The Second Angel 1998, The Shot 1999, Dark Matter 2002, The One from the Other 2007, A Quiet Flame 2008, If the Dead Rise Not (CWA Ellis Peters Historical Award) 2009, Field Grey 2010; juvenile fiction (as P.B. Kerr): Children of the Lamp series: The Akhenaten Adventure 2004, The Blue Djinn of Babylon 2005, The Cobra King of Kathmandu 2006, The Day of the Djinn Warriors 2007, The Eye of the Forest 2009. *Honours:* Prix de Romans L'Aventures, Deutsches Krimi Prize. *Literary Agent:* A. P. Watt Literary Agents, 20 John Street, London, WC1N 2DR, England. *Telephone:* (20) 7405-6774. *Fax:* (20) 7430-1952. *Website:* www.apwatt.co.uk. *E-mail:* pbk@pbkerr.com (office). *Website:* www.pbkerr.com.

KERSHAW, Sir Ian, BA, DPhil, FBA, FRHistS; British academic and writer; b. 29 April 1943, Oldham, England; m. Dame Janet Elizabeth Murray Gammie 1966; two s. *Education:* Univ. of Liverpool, Merton Coll., Oxford. *Career:* Asst Lecturer in Medieval History, Univ. of Manchester 1968–70, Lecturer 1970–74, Lecturer in Modern History 1974–79, Sr Lecturer 1979–87, Reader Elect 1987; Visiting Prof. of Contemporary History, Ruhr-Univ., Bochum, Germany 1983–84; Prof. of Modern History, Univ. of Nottingham 1987–89, Univ. of Sheffield 1989–2008; Fellow, Alexander von Humboldt-Stiftung 1976, Wissenschaftskolleg zu Berlin 1989–90. *Television:* consultant to historical series on BBC 2, ZDF, Spiegel TV 1994–. *Publications:* Rentals and Ministers' Accounts of Bolton Priory, 1473–1539 (ed.) 1969, Bolton Priory: The Economy of a Northern Monastery 1973, Der Hitler-Mythos: Volksmeinung und Propaganda im Dritten Reich 1980, Popular Opinion and Political Dissent in the Third Reich: Bavaria, 1933–1945 1983, The Nazi Dictatorship: Problems and Perspectives of Interpretation 1985, Weimar: Why Did German Democracy Fail? (ed.) 1990, Hitler: A Profile in Power 1991, Stalinism and Nazism (co-ed. with M. Lewin) 1997, Hitler 1889–1936: Hubris 1998, Hitler 1936–1945: Nemesis 2000, The Bolton Priory Compotus 1286–1325 (co-ed. with D. Smith) 2001, Making Friends with Hitler: Lord Londonderry and Britain's Road to War (Soc. of Authors Elizabeth Longford Prize for Historical Biog. 2005) 2004, Fateful Choices 2007, Hitler, the Germans and the Final Solution 2008, Luck of the Devil 2009; contrib. to scholarly journals. *Honours:* Bundesverdienstkreuz (Germany) 1994; Hon. Fellow, Merton Coll. Oxford 2006; Dr hc (Manchester) 2004, (Stirling) 2004, (Belfast) 2007; Wolfson Literary Award 2000, Bruno Kreisky Prize (Austria) 2000, British Acad. Book Prize 2001. *E-mail:* b.eaton@sheffield.ac.uk (office).

KERTÉSZ, Imre; Hungarian writer and translator; b. 9 Nov. 1929, Budapest; m. 2nd Magda Kertész. *Career:* deported to Auschwitz, then Buchenwald during World War II 1944; worked for newspaper Világosság, Budapest 1948–51 (dismissed when it adopted CP line); mil. service 1951–53; ind. writer and trans. of German authors such as Nietzsche, Schnitzler, Freud, Roth, Wittgenstein and Canetti 1953–; has also written theatre musicals; works have been translated into German, Spanish, French, English, Czech, Russian, Swedish and Hebrew. *Publications include:* Sorstalanság (trans. as Fatelessness) (Jewish Quarterly Wingate Literary Prize 2006) (made into film 2005) 1975, A nyomkeresö (The Pathfinder) 1977, Detektívtörténet (Detective Story) 1977, A kudarc (Fiasco) 1988, Kaddis a meg nem születetett gyermekért (Kaddish for a Child not Born 1997) 1990, Az angol labogó (The English Flag) 1991, Gályanapló (Galley Diary) 1992, A Holocaust mint kultúra (The Holocaust as Culture) 1993, Jegyzökönyv 1993, Valaki más: a változás kró'nikája (I, Another: Chronicle of a Metamorphosis) 1997, A gondolatnyi csend, amig kivégzöoztag újratölt (Moment of Silence while the Execution Squad Reloads) 1998, A számüzött nyelv (The Exiled Language) 2001, Felszámolás: regény (Liquidation) 2003. *Honours:* Brandenburg Literary Prize 1995, Leipzig Book Prize for European Understanding 1997, WELT-Literaturpreis 2000, Ehrenpreis der Robert-Bosch-Stiftung 2001, Hans-Sahl-Preis 2002, Nobel Prize in Literature 2002. *Address:* c/o Magvetõ Press, Balassi B.U. 7, 1055 Budapest, Hungary (office); c/o Northwestern University Press, 625 Colfax Street, Evanston, IL 60208-4210, USA (office).

KERTZER, David I., PhD; American historian, anthropologist, writer and academic; *Provost, Brown University*; b. 20 Feb. 1948, New York City; s. of Morris Kertzer and Julia Hoffman Kertzer; m. Susan; one d. one s. *Education:* Brown Univ., Brandeis Univ. *Career:* Asst Prof. of Anthropology, Bowdoin Coll. 1973–79, Assoc. Prof. 1979–84, Prof. 1984–89, William R. Kenan, Jr Prof. 1989–92, Chair. Dept of Sociology and Anthropology 1979–81, 1984–86, 1987–88, 1992; Paul Dupee, Jr Univ. Prof. of Social Science, Brown Univ. 1992–, also Prof. of Anthropology 1992–, of History 1992–2001, of Italian Studies 2001–, Provost Brown Univ. 2006–; Fulbright Sr Lecturer, Univ. of Catania 1978; Professore a contratto, Univ. of Bologna 1987; Visiting Fellow Trinity Coll., Cambridge, UK 1991; Visiting Scholar, Posthumous Inst. and Univ. of Amsterdam 1994; Visiting Dir of Studies, Ecole des Hautes Etudes en Sciences Sociales, Paris 1994; Prof. of Educ., American Acad. of Rome 1999; Fulbright Chair, Univ. of Bologna 2000; Visiting Prof., Ecole Normale Superieure, Paris 2002; guest lecturer at over 40 univs world-wide; Co-Founder and Co-Ed. Journal of Modern Italian Studies 1994–; Ed. Book Series: New Perspectives in Anthropological and Social Demography 1996–2007; Pres. Soc. for the Anthropology of Europe 1994–96; mem. Editorial Bd Social Science History 1987–96, 2001–04, Journal of Family History 1990–, Continuity and Change 1996–2000, Int. Studies Review 1998–2002; mem. Jury Lynton History Prize 2000–01; mem. Exec. Bd American Anthropological Asscn 1995–96, NIH Population Review Cttee 1996–99, Nat. Research Council Cttee on Population 1999–2005, German Marshall Fund Advisory Bd 2000–02; Vice-Pres. Social Science History Asscn 2005–06, Pres. 2006–07; Fellow, American Acad. of Arts and Sciences 2005–. *Publications include:* Comrades and Christians: Religion and Political Struggle in Communist Italy 1980, Famiglia Contadina e Urbanizzazione 1981, Family Life in Central Italy 1880–1910: Sharecropping, Wage Labour and Coresidence (Marraro Prize, Soc. for Italian Historical Studies 1985) 1984, Ritual, Politics and Power 1988, Family, Political Economy and Demographic Change (Marraro 1990) 1989, Sacrificed for Honor: Italian Infant Abandonment and the Politics of Reproductive Control 1993, Politics and Symbols: The Italian Communist Party and the Fall of Communism, 1996, The Kidnapping of Edgardo Mortara (Nat. Jewish Book Award 1997, Best Books of the Year, Publishers Weekly, Toronto Globe and Mail 1997; stage version 'Edgard Mine' by Alfred Uhry premiered 2002) 1997, The Popes Against the Jews (UK edn The Unholy War 2002) 2001, Prisoner of the Vatican 2004, Amelia's Take 2008; contrib. to numerous nat. and state newspapers, contrib., ed. or co-ed. of numerous books, author of over 60 journal articles and 50 academic papers. *Honours:* Fellowship Center for Advanced Studies, Stanford 1982–83, Guggenheim Fellowship 1986, Nat. Endowment for the Humanities Fellowship 1995, Rockefeller Foundation Fellowship, Bellagio, Italy 2000. *Address:* Office of the Provost, University Hall, Room 114, One Prospect Street, Box 1862, Brown University, Providence, RI 02912, USA (office). *Telephone:* (401) 863-2706 (office). *Fax:* (401) 863-1928 (office). *E-mail:* provost@brown.edu (office). *Website:* www.davidkertzer.com (office).

KESSLER, Jascha Frederick, BA, MA, PhD, LittD; American academic, poet, writer, dramatist and critic; *Professor Emeritus of Modern English and American Literature, University of California, Los Angeles*; b. 27 Nov. 1929, New York, NY; m. 1950; two s. one d. *Education:* Univ. of Heights Coll. of New York Univ., Univ. of Michigan. *Career:* Faculty, Univ. of Michigan 1951–54, New York Univ. 1954–55, Hunter Coll., CUNY 1955–56, Hamilton Coll. 1957–61; Ed. Education Texts, Harcourt Brace & Co. 1956–57; Prof. of Modern English and American Literature, UCLA 1961–1992, Prof. Emer. 1992–; Fulbright Research Scholar, Italy 1963–64; Univ. of California Pres.'s Scholar 1963–64; Fulbright Lecturer in American Literature, Italy 1970; Vice-Pres. Los Angeles PEN Club 1980s; Arts Commr City of Santa Monica, Calif. 1990–96; mem. The American Soc. of Composers, Authors and Publrs (ASCAP). *Publications:* poetry: Whatever Love Declares 1969, After the Armies Have Passed 1970, In Memory of the Future 1976, revised edn as Collected Poems 2000; fiction: An Egyptian Bondage (short stories) 1967, Death Comes for the Behaviorist (novellas) 1983, Classical Illusions (short stories) 1985, Transmigrations: 18 Mythologems 1985, Siren Songs and Classical Illusions (short stories) 1992, Rapid Transit 1948: An Unsentimental Education (novel) 2000; plays: Selected Plays 1998, Christmas Carols and Other Plays 2000; other: The Anniversary (opera libretto), numerous translations of poetry collections and fairy tales, including The Magician's Garden: 24 Stories by Geza Csáth (Translation Prize, Colombia Univ.) 1980, Rose of Mother-of-Pearl (translated with author Grozdana Olujic) 1983, Bride of Acacias: The Poetry of Forugh Farrokhzad (with Amin Banani) 1983, Under Gemini: The Selected Poetry of Miklós Radnóti 1985, Medusa: The Selected Poetry of Nicolai Kantchev 1986, The Face of Creation: 23 Contemporary

Hungarian Poets 1988, Catullun Games (poetry of Sándor Rákos, Translation Center George Soros Foundation Prize) 1989, Sophocles' Oedipus Rex 1999, Tataga's Children: 23 Fairy Tales (Grozdana Olujic) 2000, Traveling Light: Selected Poems of Kirsti Simonsuuri (Finnish Literary Trans. Centre Award 2001), Our Bearings at Sea: A Novel in Poems (Otto Orban) 2001, Tahirih: A Portrait in Poetry 2004. *Honours:* Major Hopwood Award for Poetry, Univ. of Michigan 1952, Nat. Endowment for the Arts Fellowship 1974, Rockefeller Foundation Fellowship 1979, Hungarian PEN Club Memorial Medal 1979, California Arts Council Fellowship 1993–94, many trans. prizes. *Address:* Department of English, UCLA, Los Angeles, CA 90095-1530 (office); 218 16th Street, Santa Monica, CA 90402-2216, USA (home). *Fax:* (310) 393-4648 (home). *E-mail:* jkessler@ucla.edu (office); urim.urim@gmail.com (home). *Website:* www.jfkessler.com.

KESSLER, Lauren Jeanne, BS, MS, PhD; American writer and academic; b. 4 April 1951, New York, NY; m. Thomas Hager 1984; two s. one d. *Education:* Northwestern Univ., Univ. of Oregon, Univ. of Washington. *Career:* Dir, Grad. Program in Literary Nonfiction, School of Journalism and Communications, Univ. of Oregon; Ed. Etude magazine. *Publications:* The Dissident Press: Alternative Journalism in American History 1984, When Worlds Collide 1984, Aging Well 1987, Mastering the Message 1989, After All These Years: Sixties Ideals in a Different World 1990, The Search 1991, Stubborn Twig: A Japanese Family in America 1993, Full Court Press 1997, Happy Bottom Riding Club: The Life and Times of Pancho Barnes 2000, Clever Girl: Elizabeth Bentley, the Spy Who Ushered in the McCarthy Era 2003, Dancing with Rose: Finding Life in the Land of Alzheimer's (Pacific Northwest Book Award) 2007; contribs: NY Times magazine, Los Angeles Times magazine, O magazine, Utne Reader, Salon, The Nation, Writer's Digest. *Honours:* Excellence in Periodical Writing Award, Council for the Advancement of Secondary Educ. 1987, Frances Fuller Victor Award for Literary Non-Fiction 1994. *Address:* School of Journalism and Communication, University of Oregon, Eugene, OR 97403, USA. *Website:* www.laurenkessler.com.

KEYES, Daniel, BA, MA; American author; b. 9 Aug. 1927, New York, NY; m. Aurea Georgina Vazquez 1952; two d. *Education:* Brooklyn Coll. *Career:* Lecturer, Wayne State Univ. 1962–66; Prof. of English, Ohio Univ. 1966–2000, Prof. Emer. 2000–. *Publications:* Flowers for Algernon 1966, The Touch 1968, The Fifth Sally 1980, The Minds of Billy Milligan (non-fiction) 1986, Unveiling Claudia (non-fiction) 1986, Daniel Keyes Short Stories 1993, Daniel Keyes Reader 1994, The Milligan Wars (non-fiction) 1995, Until Death 1998, Algernon, Charlie and I 2000, The Asylum Prophecies 2009. *Honours:* Distinguished Alumnus of Honor, Brooklyn Coll. 1988. *Address:* c/o Editorial Department, Dorchester Publishing Co., Inc., 200 Madison Avenue, Suite 2000, New York, NY 10016, USA (office). *Website:* www.danielkeyesauthor.com.

KEYES, Marian; Irish writer; b. 10 Nov. 1963, Limerick; m. Tony. *Education:* Univ. Coll. Dublin. *Publications:* novels: Watermelon 1995, Lucy Sullivan is Getting Married 1996, Rachel's Holiday 1998, Last Chance Saloon 1999, No Dress Rehearsal (novella) 2000, Sushi for Beginners 2000, Angels 2002, The Other Side of the Story 2004, Anybody Out There? 2006, This Charming Man 2008, The Brightest Star in the Sky 2009; other: Under the Duvet (non fiction) 2001, Further Under the Duvet (non fiction) 2005; contrib. to Yeats is Dead!, Irish Girls About Town, Big Night Out. *Address:* c/o Penguin Publicity, 80 Strand, London WC2R 0RL, England (office). *Website:* www.penguin.co.uk (office); www.mariankeyes.com.

KHADER, Hassan; Palestinian writer, translator and editor; Managing Editor, al-Karmel; b. 1953, Gaza. *Education:* univ. in Cairo. *Career:* fmr Ed. literary journal of the Palestinian Liberation Org.; currently Man. Ed. al-Karmel literary magazine; Asst Prof. an-Najah Nat. Univ.; Dir of Creative Writing, Ministry of Culture. *Publications:* non-fiction: Time and Hostages: Theories of Literary Criticism, Memoirs of Exile, Splinters of Reality and Glass (essays) 2002; contrib. to al-Ahram weekly. *E-mail:* editor@alkarmel.org (office). *Website:* www.alkarmel.org.

KHADRA, Yasmina; Algerian writer; b. (Mohammed Moulessehoul), 10 Jan. 1955, Kenadsa; m.; three c. *Education:* Ecole Nationale des Cadets de la Révolution, Acad. Inter-armes de Cherchell. *Career:* spent 36 years serving in Algerian army. *Films:* L'attentat (Zied Doueri), Ce que le jour doit à la nuit (Alexandre Aracady), Morituri (Okasha Touita). *Publications include:* fiction: Houria 1984, La Fille du poet 1985, El Kahira 1986, De l'autre côté de la ville 1988, Le Privilège du phénix 1989, Le Dingue au bistouri 1990, La Foire des Enfoirés 1993, Les Agneaux du seigneur (trans. as In the Name of God) 1998, Morituri 1997, Double blanc (trans. as Double Blank) 1998, L'Automne aux chimères (trans. as Autumn of the Phantoms) 1998, A quoi rêvent les loups (trans. as Wolf Dreams) 1999, L'Imposture des mots 2002, Les Hirondelles de Kaboul (trans. as The Swallows of Kabul) 2002, Cousine K 2003, La Part du mort (trans. as Dead Man's Share) 2004, L'Attentat (trans. as The Attack; Prix des Libraires) 2005, Les Sirènes de Bagdad (trans. as The Sirens of Baghdad) 2006, Ce que le jour doit à la nuite (trans. as What the Day Owes the Night) 2008, L'Olympe des Infortunes 2010, L'Equation Africaine 2011, Les Chants cannibales (short stories) 2012; non-fiction: L'Écrivain (autobiog.) 2001. *Honours:* Chevalier, Légion d'honneur 2008, Officier des Arts et des Lettres; Prix des Libraires Algériens 2003, Prix des Libraires, France 2005, Prix Meilleur Livre de l'année 2008, Prix France Television 2008, Trophée Createur sans Frontières, Time for Peace Literature Award 2012. *Address:* c/o Éditions Julliard, 24 avenue Marceau, 75381 Paris, France. *Telephone:* 1-53-67-14-00. *Fax:* 1-53-67-15-40. *E-mail:* yasminakhadra@yahoo.fr. *Website:* www.laffont.fr/julliard; yasmina-khadra.com.

KHAKETLA, Masechele; Lesotho teacher and writer; m. Makalo Bernard Khaketla (died 2000). *Education:* Morija Training Coll. and Univ. of Fort Hare. *Career:* Co-Founder and Propr Iketsetseng Primary School; teacher, Basutholand High School; High Court Assessor. *Publications include:* Mosali eo o'nehileng Eena, Mahlopha a senya, Ka u Lotha, Khotosoaneng, Selibelo sa Nkhono, Pelo ea monna, Ho isa Lefung, Mosiuoa Masilo, Mantsopa, Molamu oa kotjana. *Honours:* Hon. DLitt (Nat. Univ. of Lesotho) 1983, (Univ. of Fort Hare) 2002. *Address:* Patlong Thotaneng, Qacha's Nek, Lesotho (home).

KHAL, Abdo; Saudi Arabian writer; b. 1962, Al-Majanah. *Education:* King Abdulaziz Univ., Jeddah. *Career:* teaches Arabic at a government school, Jeddah; arts and culture Ed. and daily columnist, Okaz (daily newspaper); co-Publr Ar Rawi (magazine); mem. Bd of Dirs Jeddah Literary Club. *Publications:* novels in trans.: Cities Eating Grass, Immorality, The Mud, Death Passes from Here, Days Don't Hide Anyone, Barking, Spewing Sparks As Big As Castles (Int. Prize for Arab Fiction 2010); several collections of short stories. *Address:* c/o Okaz, POB 1508, Seaport Rd, Jeddah 21441, Saudi Arabia (office).

KHALIFA, Khaled, BA; Syrian writer and film and tv scriptwriter; b. 1964, Aleppo. *Education:* Aleppo Univ. *Career:* Int. Writing Program Fellow, Univ. of Iowa, USA 2007. *Television:* scriptwriter: Serat Al-Jalali 1999, Kaws Kozah 2001, City People 2005, The Age of Fear 2007, Shadow of a Woman 2007. *Films:* scriptwriter: Bab al-Maqam (Best Script, Valencia Film Festival) 2005, Black Stone (documentary) (also co-producer) 2006. *Publications:* novels: Haress al-Khadeiaa (trans. as Guard of Deceit) 1993, Dafater Al-Qarbatt (trans. as The Al-Qarbatt Notebooks) 2000, Madeeh al-Karahiya (trans. as In Praise of Hatred) 2006. *Honours:* Ismaiiliyah Int. Documentary Festival Award. *Address:* c/o Dar Al Asmaa, PO Box 36267, Damascus, Syria (office). *Telephone:* (11) 2224279 (office). *Fax:* (11) 2457554 (office).

KHALIFA, Sahar, BA, MA, PhD; Palestinian writer and feminist; b. 1941, Nablus; m. 1959 (divorced); two d. *Education:* Rosary Coll. and Bir Zeit Univ., Univ. of North Carolina and Univ. of Iowa, USA. *Career:* began writing 1967–; moved to USA to study; returned to Nablus 1988; f. Women's Affairs Center, Nablus, Gaza City 1991, Amman 1994; Fulbright Scholar 1980. *Publications include:* novels (in trans.): We Are Not Your Slave Girls Anymore 1974, Wild Thorns 1975, The Sunflower 1980, Memoirs of an Unrealistic Woman 1986, The Door of the Courtyard 1990, The Inheritance 1997. *Honours:* Naguib Mahfouz Prize. *Address:* c/o Pontas Literary and Film Agency, Sèneca, 31, 08006 Barcelona, Spain.

KHAN, Haseena Moin, BEd, MA; Pakistani screenwriter, author and playwright; b. 20 Nov. 1938, Kanpur, India; d. of the late Moinuddin Khan and Aziz Fatima. *Education:* Univ. of Karachi. *Career:* began writing stories and plays in coll.; playwright, Pakistan TV Corpn 1971–; headmistress of a girls' high school; has written numerous plays, TV serials, two radio serials for village women on agric. and health. *Television serials:* Shahzori 1972, Kiran Kahani 1973, Zer Zabar Pesh 1974, Uncle Urfi 1975, Roomi 1976, Parchaiyan 1977, Dhund 1978, Ankahi 1979, Tanhaiyan 1981, Dhoop Kinarey 1983, Aahat 1987, Tansen 1991, Pal Do Pal, Aik Umeed 2001, Des Pardes, Aansoo Dua, Shayed Ke Bahar Aye, Kash in Kash 2007, Tanha 2007, Mere Dard Ko Jo Zuban Miley 2007, Watan Kahani (President's Award 2008) 2007, Dhoop Kinaray 2011, Saray Mausam Apre 2012. *TV plays include:* Sangsar, Gurya Ralta, Paani Pe Likha tha, Chup Darya, Despardis, Aanso Dua, Aik Naye Mod Por, Shayed Ke Bahor Aye, Kuchto Kaha Hata. *Films:* Henna for Rajkapoor. *Publications:* Pulsarat ka Safar (novel); short stories and articles in English and Urdu newspapers; plays published in BookShape, Unkalri Tanhaiyan and Dhoop Kinarey. *Honours:* awards include PTV Best Writer Award 1975, 1982, 1985, 1987, TV Writer Award, Awami Award, Civil Award, Governor Award, Pride of Performance Nat. Award 1988, Nigar Award, Johns Hopkins Univ. Award 1992, Lifetime Achievement Award 1998. *Address:* A 190, Block I, North Nazimabad, Karachi, Pakistan (home). *Telephone:* (21) 6630168 (home); 300-9272117 (mobile). *E-mail:* haseenamoin@hotmail.com (home).

KHANFAR, Wadah; Palestinian journalist and broadcasting executive; b. Jinin. *Education:* Univ. of Jordan. *Career:* joined Al-Jazeera 1999, fmr corresp., Africa Bureau, New Delhi, war corresp., Afghanistan 2001–02, Baghdad Bureau Chief 2003, Man. Dir Al-Jazeera 2003–06, Dir-Gen. Al-Jazeera Satellite Network 2006–11 (resgnd). *Honours:* ranked 13th by arabianbusiness.com in Power 100 list of The World's Most Powerful Arabs 2010, ranked 54th by Forbes magazine amongst The World's Most Powerful People 2009. *Address:* c/o Al-Jazeera Satellite Network, PO Box 23123, Doha, Qatar.

KHARRAT, Edwar al-, LLB; Egyptian author and translator; b. 16 March 1926, Alexandria; s. of Kolta Faltas Youssef al-Kharrat; m. 1958; two s. *Education:* Alexandria Univ. *Career:* storehouse asst, Royal Navy Victualling Dept, Alexandria 1944–46; clerk, Nat. Bank of Egypt 1946–48; clerk, Nat. Insurance Co. 1950–55; published first collection of stories 1958; Dir of Tech. Affairs Afro-Asian People's Solidarity Org. 1959–67, Asst Sec.-Gen. 1967–73, Pres. 1967–; mem. Afro-Asian Writers' Assen (Asst Sec.-Gen. 1967–72), Egyptian Writers' Union, Egyptian PEN; trans. and broadcaster for Egyptian Broadcasting Service; Assoc. Sr mem. St Antony's Coll., Oxford 1979; Ed. The Lotus, Afro-Asian Writings. *Publications include:* short stories: High Walls 1959, Hours of Pride 1972 (State Prize), Suffocations of Love and Mornings

1983; novels: Rama and the Dragon 1979, The Railway Station 1985, The Other Time 1985, Saffron Dust 1986, The Ribs of Desert 1987, Girls of Alexandria 1990, Creations of Flying Desires 1990, Waves of the Nights 1991, Stones of Bobello 1992, Penetrations of Love and Perdition 1993, My Alexandria 1994, Ripples of Salt Dreams 1994, Fire of Phantasies 1995, Soaring Edifices 1997, Certitude of Thirst 1997, Throes of Facts and Folly 1998, Boulders of Heaven 2000, Path of Eagle, Stones of Bobello 2005; poetry: Cry of the Unicorn 1998, Seven Clouds 2000; literary criticism: Transgeneric Writing 1994, The New Sensibility 1994, From Silence to Rebellion 1994, Hymn to Density 1995, Beyond Reality 1998, Voices of Modernity in Fiction 1999, Modernist Poetry in Egypt 2000, Fiction and Modernity 2003, The Fiction Scene 2003. *Honours:* State Story Award 1973, Franco-Arab Friendship Prize 1991, Ali Al Owais Award (for fiction) 1994/95, Cavifis Prize 1998, Naguib Mahfouz Award for Fiction, American Univ. of Cairo in 1999, State Merit Award for Literature 2000, Cairo Arab Novel Award 2008. *Address:* 45 Ahmad Hishmat Street, Zamalek, Cairo, Egypt. *Telephone:* (2) 7366367. *Fax:* (2)7366367.

KHATCHADOURIAN, Haig, BA, MA, PhD; American philosopher, academic, writer and poet; *Professor Emeritus of Philosophy, University of Wisconsin at Milwaukee*; b. 22 July 1925, Old City, Jerusalem, Palestine; s. of Apraham Khatchadourian and Elizabeth Khatchadourian; m. Arpiné Yaghlian 1950; two s. one d. *Education:* American Univ. of Beirut, Lebanon, Duke Univ., USA. *Career:* American Univ. of Beirut, Lebanon 1948–49, 1951–67; Andrew Mellon Postdoctoral Fellow, Dept of Philosophy, Univ. of Pittsburgh 1963–64; Prof. of Philosophy, Univ. of Southern California at Los Angeles 1968–69; Prof. of Philosophy, Univ. of Wisconsin at Milwaukee 1969–94, Emeritus Prof. 1994–; Visiting Prof., Univ. of Hawaii, Manua 1968; Distinguished Visiting Prof., Univ. of New Mexico 1978–79; Liberal Arts Fellow in Philosophy and Law, Harvard Law School 1982–83; mem. Fellow, Royal Soc. for the Encouragement of Arts, Manufacture and Commerce, Nat. Acad. of Sciences, Armenia; Foreign mem. Armenian Acad. of Philosophy; Founding mem. Int. Acad. of Philosophy, Yerevan. *Publications:* The Coherence Theory of Truth: A Critical Evaluation 1961 (revised edn 2010), Traffic with Time (co-author, poems) 1963, A Critical Study in Method 1967, The Concept of Art 1971, Shadows of Time (poems) 1983, 2010, Music, Film and Art 1985 (revised edn 2010), Philosophy of Language and Logical Theory: Collected Papers 1996, The Morality of Terrorism 1998, Community and Communitarianism 1999, The Quest for Peace Between Israel and the Palestinians 2000, War, Terrorism, Genocide and the Quest for Peace: Contemporary Problems in Political Ethics 2003, Meaning and Criteria: With Applications to Various Philosophical Problems 2007, The Raven and the Cardinal (poems) 2010, Truth: Its Nature, Criteria and Conditions 2011; contribs to numerous professional and literary journals, including Mind, Philosophy, Journal of Philosophy, Phil of Science, American Philosophy Quarterly, Armenian Mind, Quest, Ararat, Raft. *Honours:* J. Walker Tomb Prize, Princeton Univ. 1958, Outstanding Educators of America Award 1973, Univ. of Wisconsin Alumni Asscn Award for Teaching Excellence 1987, Ernest Spaighs Plaza Award, Univ. of Wisconsin 2005, 'David the Invincible Medal', Armenian Acad. and Int. Acad. of Philosophy 2005. *Address:* Department of Philosophy, University of Wisconsin, Milwaukee, WI 53201, USA (office). *Telephone:* (414) 964-8865 (office). *E-mail:* haigkhat@uwm.edu (home).

KHELLADI, Aissa; Algerian novelist, journalist, playwright and poet; *Director, Algérie Littérature/Action*; b. 1953. *Education:* Université d'Alger. *Career:* co-founder Nouvel Hebdo 1990, Hebdo Libéré 1991; fmr journalist, Ruptures weekly publ.; exiled in France 1994; co-founder and Dir Algérie Littérature/Action literary journal 1996–. *Play:* Le Paradis des fausses espérances 1999. *Publications:* novels: Peurs et mensonges 1996, Rose d'abîme 1998, Spoliation 1998; non-fiction: Algérie: les islamistes face au pouvoir 1992; contrib. to Les Temps modernes. *Address:* Algérie Littérature/Action, c/o Marsa Editions, 103 Boulevard MacDonald, Paris 75019, France (office). *E-mail:* algerie.litterature@free.fr (office). *Website:* www.algerie-litterature.com.

KHERDIAN, David, BS; American author and poet; b. 17 Dec. 1931, Racine, Wis.; m. 1st Kato Rozeboom 1968 (divorced 1970); m. 2nd Nonny Hogrogian 1971. *Education:* University of Wisconsin. *Career:* Founder-Ed. Giligia Press 1966–72, Press at Butterworth Creek 1987–88, Fork Roads: Journal of Ethnic American Literature 1995–96; Rare Book Consultant, Fresno State College 1968–69, Lecturer, 1969–70; Poet-in-the-Schools, State of New Hampshire 1971; Dir, Two Rivers Press 1978–86; Founder Ed. Stopinder: A Gurdjieff Journal for Our Time 2000; mem. PEN. *Publications:* On the Death of My Father and Other Poems, 1970; Homage to Adana, 1970; Looking Over Hills, 1972; The Nonny Poems, 1974; Any Day of Your Life, 1975; Country Cat, City Cat, 1978; I Remember Root River, 1978; The Road from Home: The Story of an Armenian Girl, 1979; The Farm, 1979; It Started With Old Man Bean, 1980; Finding Home, 1981; Taking the Soundings on Third Avenue, 1981; The Farm Book Two, 1981; Beyond Two Rivers, 1981; The Song of the Walnut Grove, 1982; Place of Birth, 1983; Right Now, 1983; The Mystery of the Diamond in the Wood, 1983; Root River Run, 1984; The Animal, 1984; Threads of Light: The Farm Poems Books III and IV, 1985; Bridger: The Story of a Mountain Man, 1987; Poems to an Essence Friend, 1987; A Song for Uncle Harry, 1989; The Cat's Midsummer Jamboree, 1990; The Dividing River/The Meeting Shore, 1990; On a Spaceship with Beelzebub: By a Grandson of Gurdjieff, 1990; The Great Fishing Contest, 1991; Junas's Journey, 1993; Asking the River, 1993; By Myself, 1993; Friends: A Memoir, 1993; My Racine, 1994; Lullaby for Emily, 1995; ed. of several books. *Honours:* Jane Addams Peace Award, 1980; Banta Award, 1980; Boston Globe/Horn Book Award, 1980; Lewis Carroll Shelf Award, 1980; Newbery Honor Book Award, 1980; Friends of American Writers Award, 1982.

KHOURI, Callie; American screenwriter and film director; b. 27 Nov. 1957, San Antonio, Tex. *Films:* Thelma & Louise (screenwriter, prod.) (Acad. Award 1992) 1991, Something to Talk About (screenwriter) 1995, Divine Secrets of the Ya-Ya Sisterhood (screenwriter, dir) 2002, Hollis & Rae (screenwriter, prod., dir) 2006, Mad Money (dir) 2008. *Literary Agent:* c/o International Creative Management, 10250 Constellation Boulevard, Los Angeles, CA 90067, USA.

KHOURY, Elias; Lebanese novelist and literary critic; b. 1948, Ashrafiyyeh, nr Beirut. *Education:* Lebanese Univ., Beirut, Univ. of Paris, France. *Career:* with PLO Research Centre, Beirut 1973–79; Publr Su'un filastiniya (Palestinian Affairs) journal 1976–79; Editorial Dir Al-Karmel 1981–82; Ed. culture section of As-Safir journal 1983–90, Al-Mulhaq cultural supplement of an-Nahar daily newspaper 1992–2009; Dir Masrah Beyrut theatre 1993–98; Global Distinguished Prof. of Middle Eastern and Islamic Studies, New York Univ. 2004–05; fmr Prof., Columbia Univ., Lebanese Univ., American Univ. of Beirut, Lebanese American Univ. *Publications:* An 'ilaqat al-da'irah (novel) 1975, Al-Jabal al-Saghir (novel) 1977, Dirasat fi naqd al-shi'r (criticism) 1979, Abwab al-Madinah (novel) 1981, Al-wujuh al-baida' (novel, trans. as White Masks 2010) 1981, Al-dhakira al-mafquda (criticism) 1982, Al-mubtada' wa'l-khabar (short stories) 1984, Tajribat al-ba'th 'an ufq (criticism) 1984, Zaman al-ihtilal (criticism) 1985, Rahlat Gandhi al-Saghir (novel) 1989, Mamlakat al-Ghuraba (novel) 1993, Majma' al-Asrar (novel) 1994, Bab al-Shams (novel, trans. as Gate of the Sun 2006) (Palestine Prize 1998) 1998, Ra'ihat al-Sabun (novel) 2000, Yalo (novel) 2002, Ka'anaha Nae'ma (novel) 2007. *Honours:* Lettre Ulysses Award 2005. *Address:* c/o An-Nahar (The Day), Immeuble An-Nahar, place des Martyrs, Marfa', Beirut 2014 5401, Lebanon. *Telephone:* (1) 994888. *Fax:* (1) 996777. *E-mail:* webmaster@annahar.com.lb. *Website:* www.annaharonline.com.

KHOURY-GHATA, Vénus; Lebanese/French novelist and poet; b. 1937, Bsherre; m. 1st (divorced); three c.; m. 2nd Jean Ghata (died 1981); one d. *Education:* in Lebanon. *Career:* fmr journalist; moved to France 1973; fmr contrib. and trans., Europe magazine; Pres. Prix des Cinq Continents, Prix Yvon Goll, Prix France Liban; mem. selection cttee, Prix Mallarmé, Prix Max-Pol-Fouchet, Prix Max-Jacob; frequent radio broadcaster. *Publications:* poetry: (first collection) 1966, Les Ombres et leurs cris (Prix Guillaume-Apollinaire) 1980, Monologue du mort (Prix Mallarmé) 1987, Fable pour un peuple d'argile (Grand Prix de la Société des gens de lettres) 1992, Anthologie person-elle 1997, Elle dit 1999, Here There Was Once a Country (anthology in trans.) 2001, La Compassion des pierres 2001, She Says (trans.) 2003, Quelle est la nuit parmi les nuits 2007, Les obscurcis (Grand Prix de Poésie, Acad. Française 2009) 2008, À quoi sert la neige – Poèmes pour enfants 2008; novels: Vacarme pour une lune morte 1983, Bayarmine 1990, Mortemaison 1992, La maitresse du notable (Liberatturpreis) 1992, La Maestra 1994, Les Fiancées du Cap Ténès 1995, Une maison au bord des larmes (trans. as A House on the Edge of Tears 2006) 1998, Privilège des morts 2001, Le Moine, l'ottoman et la femme du grand argentier 2003, La Maison aux orties 2006, Sept pierres pour la femme adultère 2007, La Fille qui marchait dans le désert 2010; contrib. in trans. to Ambit, Banipal: A Journal of Modern Arab Literature, Columbia, Field, Contemporary Poetry and Poetics, Gobshite Quarterly, Jacket, Luna, The Manhattan Review, Metre, The New Yorker, Poetry, Shenandoah, Verse, Poetry London. *Honours:* Officier, Ordre nat. du Mérite 2003, Officier, Légion d'honneur 2010; Prix Guillaume Apollinaire, Prix Mallarmé, Grand Prix Guillevic de Poésie de Saint-Malo 2010, Grand Prix Doha, Qatar 2010. *Address:* 16 avenue Raphael, 75016 Paris, France (home). *Telephone:* 1-45-04-06-37 (home). *Fax:* 1-45-04-06-37 (home).

KHRISTOV, Boris Kirilov; Bulgarian poet and writer; b. 1945, Krapets, Pernik. *Education:* Univ. of Tŭrnovo. *Career:* worked as a teacher, journalist and editor; work was frequently banned by govt –1989. *Publications:* poetry: Vecheren trompet (Evening Trumpet) 1977, Chesten krŭst (Cross My Heart) 1982, Dumi i grafiti (Words and Graffiti) 1991, Dumi vŭrkhu drugi dumi (Words on Words) 1991, Cherni bukvi vŭrkhu cheren list (Black Letters on a Black Page) 1997; prose: Izpitanieto: Spomeni za protsesa i sudbata na Traicho Kostov i negovata grupa 1995.

KHWAJA, Waqas Ahmad, BA, LLB, MA, PhD; American (b. Pakistani) academic, lawyer, writer, poet and translator and editor; *Professor of English, Agnes Scott College*; b. 14 Oct. 1952, Lahore, Pakistan; s. of Khwaja Sultan Ahmad and Irshad Sultan Ahmad; m. Maryam Khurshid 1978; four c. *Education:* Govt Coll., Lahore, Punjab Univ. Law Coll., Emory Univ., Atlanta, USA. *Career:* lawyer, Advocate High Court 1982–93; Visiting Prof., Quaid-e-Azam Law Coll. 1988–91, Punjab Law Coll. 1988–92; Visiting Faculty, Lahore Coll. for Arts and Sciences 1989–90, Punjab Univ. 1990–91; Visiting Asst Prof. of English, Agnes Scott Coll. 1995–2000, Asst Prof. 2001–04, Assoc. Prof. 2004–09, Prof. 2010–, mem. Pres.'s Cttee on Community Diversity 2000, Chair. English Dept 2004–07; Founding mem. Writers Group, Lahore 1984, Convener and Gen. Ed. 1984–92; Foreign Faculty and Approved PhD Supervisor, Higher Educ. Comm., Pakistan (assigned to Fatima Jinnah Women's Univ.) 2007–08 (declined); mem. Modern Language Asscn, South Asian Literary Asscn. *Publications:* Cactus: An Anthology of Recent Pakistani Literature (ed.) 1984, Six Geese from a Tomb at Medum (poems) 1987,

Mornings in the Wilderness (ed. and trans.) 1988, Writers and Landscapes (prose travelogue and poems) 1991, Mariam's Lament and Other Poems 1992, Short Stories from Pakistan (ed. and trans.) 1992, No One Waits for the Train (poems) 2007, Modern Poetry of Pakistani (ed. with translations) 2010; contribs to journals, newspapers and magazines, web publs since 1979. *Honours:* Hon. Fellow, Univ. of Iowa 1988; Rotary Foundation Scholar, Emory Univ. 1979–80, Int. Writing Fellowship, US Information Agency and Univ. of Iowa 1988, Jessie Ball duPont Grant for developing first-year seminar course on Strangers in the Metropolis: Diaspora Cultures in Post-imperial London, Agnes Scott Coll. 2001, Rotary Int. Visiting Prof. Fellowship for teaching in Bangladesh 2002, Professional Devt Grant for ongoing research in Post-colonial Studies in the UK, Agnes Scott Coll. 2003, for research on Pakistani vernacular writers 2005, for research on Oriental influences on British writers of the Romantic period 2006, for research on William Jones and participation in the Oxford Roundtable, Oxford, UK, Agnes Scott Coll. 2008, Catherine Sims Faculty Enrichment Fund Award for research and travel 2006, 2008. *Address:* English Department, Agnes Scott College, 141 East College Avenue, Decatur, GA 30030, USA (office). *Telephone:* (404) 471-5056 (office). *Fax:* (404) 471-6369 (office). *E-mail:* wkhwaja@agnesscott.edu (office). *Website:* ecademy .agnesscott.edu/~wkhwaja (office).

KIAROSTAMI, Abbas, BA; Iranian film director, producer, writer and photographer; b. 22 June 1940, Tehran; m. (divorced); two s. *Education:* Tehran Coll. of Fine Arts. *Career:* worked as designer and illustrator (commercials, film credit titles and children's books); involved in establishment of film making Dept at Inst. for Intellectual Devt of Children and Young Adults (Kanoon); ind. film maker from early 1990s; has made over 20 films, including shorts, educational films, documentaries. *Exhibitions include:* Forest Without Leaves (installation, V&A, London) 2005, Trees in Snow (photographs, V&A, London) 2005. *Films directed:* Nan va koucheh (Bread and Alley, short) (debut production of Kanoon film Dept) 1970, Zangu-e tafrih (Breaktime) 1972, Tajrobeh (The Experience) 1973, Mossafer (The Traveller) 1974, Man ham mitoumam (So Can I, short) 1975, Do rah-e hal baraye yek massaleh (Two Solutions for One Problem, short) 1975, Lebasi bara-ye arusi (A Wedding Suit) 1976, Rang-ha (Colours, short) 1976, Bozorgdasht-e mo'allem (Tribute to the Teachers, documentary) 1977, Az oghat-e faraghat-e khod chegouneh estefadeh konim: Rang-zanie (How to Make Use of Leisure Time: Painting, short) 1977, Gozarech (The Report) 1977, Rah-e hal (Solution, short) 1978, Ghazieh-e shekl-e aval, ghazieh-e shekl-e douuom (First Case, Second Case) 1979, Dandan-dard (Toothache, short) 1979, Beh tartib ya bedoun-e tartib (Orderly or Disorderly, short) 1981, Hamsorayan (The Chorus, short) 1982, Hamshahri (Fellow Citizen) 1983, Avali-ha (First-Graders, documentary) 1984, Khaneh-je doost kojast? (Where Is the Friend's House?, first film of the 'Koker trilogy') 1987, Mashq-e shab (Homework, documentary) 1989, Namay-eh nazdik (Close-Up, documentary) 1990, Zendegi va digar hich (And Life Goes On…, second film of the 'Koker trilogy') (aka Va zendegi edemah darad—Life and Nothing More) (Cannes Film Festival Rossellini Prize) 1991, Zir-e darakhtan-e zeyton (Through the Olive Trees, final film of the 'Koker trilogy') 1994, Tavalod-e noor (Plus Dinner for One, short) 1996, Ta'am-e gilas (The Taste of Cherry) (Cannes Film Festival Palme d'Or) 1997, Bad mara khahad bourd (The Wind Will Carry Us) (Venice Film Festival Grand Jury Prize) 1999, ABC Africa (documentary) 2001, Ta'ziyeh 2002, 10 (also writer) 2002, Five (also writer) 2003, Ten Minutes Older (short) 2003, 10 on Ten (also writer) 2004, Tickets (with others, also writer) 2004, Kargaran mashghoole karand (also writer) 2006, Roads of Kiarostami (also writer) 2006, Kojast jaye residan (also writer) 2007. *Film screenplays:* The Key 1987, The Journey 1995, Badkonak-e sefid (The White Balloon) (Cannes Film Festival Caméra d'Or) 1995, Istgah-e matrouk (The Deserted Station) 2002, Talaye sorgh (Crimson Gold) 2003. *Publications:* Walking with the Wind: Poems 2001. *Honours:* more than 50 int. prizes including special prize of the Pasolini Foundation 1995, UNESCO Fellini Medal 1997, Lifetime Achievment Award, Yerevan Int. Film Festival 2005. *Address:* c/o Zeitgeist Films Ltd, 247 Center Street, Second Floor, New York, NY 10013, USA.

KIBEDI VARGA, Aron, PhD; Dutch/Hungarian academic and poet; *Professor of French Literature, Vrije Universiteit*; b. 4 Feb. 1930, Szeged, Hungary; m. 1st T. Spreij 1954; m. 2nd K. Agh 1964; m. 3rd S. Bertho 1991; four s. one d. *Education:* Univs of Amsterdam, Leiden, Sorbonne. *Career:* Lecturer in French Literature, Vrije Universiteit, Amsterdam 1954–66, currently Prof.; Prof. of French Literature, Univ. of Amsterdam 1966–95; Visiting Prof., Univ. of Iowa, USA 1971, Yale Univ., USA 1975, Princeton Univ., USA 1980, Rabat Univ., Morocco 1985, Coll. de France 1992, Isparta Univ., Turkey 2006; mem. Cttee Int. Soc. for the History of Rhetoric 1979–83; Pres. Int. Assn Word and Image Studies 1987–93; mem. Royal Netherlands Acad. of Sciences 1981–; mem. Hungarian Acad. of Sciences 1990–. *Publications:* criticism: Les Constantes du Poème 1963, Rhétorique et Littérature 1970, Théorie de la Littérature (ed.) 1981, Discours récit, image 1989, Les Poétiques du classicisme (ed.) 1990, Le Classicisme 1998, Szavak, világok 1998, Noé könyvei 1999, Amszterdami krónika 2000, És felébred aminek neve van 2002, A jelen 2003; poetry (in Hungarian): Kint és Bent 1963, Téged 1975, Szépen 1991, Hántani, fosztani 2000, Oldás 2004, Történések 2008. *Honours:* Officer, Nederlandse Leeuw 1993, Officer, Merit of Hungarian Repub. 2006; Dr hc (Pécs) 1994. *Address:* Burgunder Strasse 19, 79104 Freiburg im Breisgau, Germany. *Telephone:* (67) 11371862.

KIBERD, Declan, MRIA, MA, DPhil; Irish literary critic and educator; *Professor of Anglo-Irish Literature and Drama, School of English, Drama and Film, University College Dublin*; b. 24 May 1951, Dublin. *Education:* Trinity Coll., Dublin, Univ. of Oxford, UK. *Career:* Lecturer in English and Prof. of Anglo-Irish Literature and Drama, Univ. Coll. Dublin. *Publications:* Synge and the Irish Language 1979, Men and Feminism in Modern Literature 1985, Omnium Gatherum – Essays for Richard Ellmann (co-ed.) 1989, An Crann Faoi Bhlath-The Flowering Tree – Contemporary Irish Poems with Verse Translations (co-ed.) 1991, The Student's Annotated Ulysses (ed.) 1992, Idir Dhá Chúltur 1993, Inventing Ireland – The Literature of the Modern Nation 1996, Irish Classics 2000, The Irish Writer and the World 2005, Ulysses and Us: The Art of Everyday Life in Joyce's Masterpiece 2009. *Honours:* Irish Times Literature Prize 1997, American Cttee of Irish Studies Award 1997, 2001, Truman Capote Award for Literary Criticism 2002. *Address:* J203, School of English, Drama and Film, University College, Belfield, Dublin 4, Ireland (office). *Telephone:* (1) 7168348 (office). *Website:* www.ucd.ie/englishanddrama (office).

KIBIROV, Timur Yuryevich; Russian poet; b. (Zapoyev), 15 Feb. 1955, Shepetovka, Ukraine; m. Yelena Ivanovna Borisova; one d. *Education:* Krupskaya Moscow Regional Pedagogical Inst. *Career:* Jr Researcher, All-Union Research Inst. of Arts 1981–93; Ed. Tsikady (publr) 1993–; first poems published in Yunost and Continent 1989. *Publications:* collections of poetry: Calendar 1990, Verses about Love 1993; Sentiments 1994; verses in leading literary journals. *Honours:* Pushkin Prize (Germany) 1993, Prize of Druzhba Narodov (magazine) 1993. *Address:* Ostrovityanova str. 34, korp. 1, Apt. 289, Moscow, Russia (home). *Telephone:* (495) 420-6175 (home).

KIDDER, Tracy, AB, MFA; American writer; b. 12 Nov. 1945, New York, NY; m. Frances Toland 1971; one s. one d. *Education:* Harvard Univ., Univ. of Iowa. *Career:* fmr army officer; Contributing Ed., Atlantic Monthly 1982–2009. *Publications:* The Road to Yuba City: A Journey into the Juan Corona Murders 1974, The Soul of a New Machine 1981, House 1985, Among Schoolchildren 1989, Old Friends 1993, Home Town 1999, Mountains Beyond Mountains 2003, My Detachment (memoir) 2005, Strength in What Remains: A Journey of Remembrance and Forgiveness 2009. *Honours:* Atlantic Monthly Atlantic First Award 1978, Sidney Hillman Foundation Prize 1978, Pulitzer Prize in General Non-Fiction 1982, American Book Award 1982, Ambassador Book Award 1990, Robert F. Kennedy Award 1990, New England Book Award 1994. *Literary Agent:* c/o Georges Borchardt Inc., 136 East 57th Street, New York, NY 10022, USA. *Telephone:* (212) 753-5785. *Fax:* (212) 838-6518. *Website:* www.gbagency.com.

KIDMAN, Dame Fiona Judith, DNZM, OBE; New Zealand writer; b. 26 March 1940, Hawera; d. of Hugh Eric Eakin and Flora Cameron Eakin (née Small); m. Ian Kidman 1960; one s. one d. *Education:* small rural schools in the north of NZ. *Career:* Founding Sec./Organizer NZ Book Council 1972–75, Pres. 1992–95, Pres. of Honour 1997–; Sec. NZ Centre, PEN 1972–76, Pres. 1981–83; f. Writers in Schools, Words on Wheels (touring writing co.), Writers Visiting Prisons, Randell Cottage Writers Trust; mem. Bd of Dirs Randell Cottage Writers Trust; Deputy Chair. French Cultural Trust. *Publications:* A Breed of Women 1979, Mandarin Summer 1981, Mrs. Dixon and Friend (short stories) 1982, Paddy's Puzzle 1983, The Book of Secrets 1986, Unsuitable Friends (short stories) 1988, True Stars 1990, Wakeful Nights (poems selected and new) 1991, The Foreign Woman (short stories) 1994, Palm Prints (autobiog. essays) 1995, Ricochet Baby 1996, The House Within 1997, The Best of Fiona Kidman's Short Stories 1998, New Zealand Love Stories; An Oxford Anthology (ed.) 1999, A Needle in the Heart (short stories) 2002, Songs from the Violet Café (novel) 2003, Captive Wife 2004; The Best New Zealand Fiction Vols 1, 2 and 3 (ed.) 2004, 2005, 2006, At the End of Darwin Road: A Memoir 2008, The Trouble with Fire (short stories) 2011. *Honours:* Chevalier, Ordre des Arts et des Lettres 2009, Légion d'Honneur (France) 2009; numerous literary prizes including NZ Book Awards (fiction category), Queen Elizabeth II Arts Council Award for Achievement, Victoria Univ. Writers' Fellow; NZ Scholarship in Letters; A. W. Reed Award for Lifetime Achievement 2001, Meridian Energy Katherine Mansfield Fellow 2006, Creative NZ Michael King Fellowship 2008. *Literary Agent:* Random House NZ Ltd, Private Bag 102950, North Shore Mail Centre, Auckland, New Zealand. *Telephone:* (9) 444-7197. *Fax:* (9) 444-7524. *E-mail:* admin@randomhouse.co .nz. *Fax:* (4) 386-1895 (home). *E-mail:* fionakidman@yahoo.com (home); fiona@ fionakidman.co.nz (office). *Website:* www.fionakidman.co.nz.

KIERAN, Sheila Harriet; Canadian writer and consultant; b. 4 May 1930, Toronto, Ont.; d. of Seymour Ginzler and Ida Ginzler (née Schulman); m. 1951 (divorced 1968); four s. two d. (and one d. deceased). *Education:* Columbia Univ., USA and Univ. of Toronto. *Career:* Dir Public Participation, Royal Comm. on Violence in the Communications Industry 1975–77; Sr Policy Adviser Ministry of the Environment 1985–87; Speech-writer to several govt ministers 1987–90; writer of govt reports; Sr Editorial Adviser to Gov.-Gen. of Canada; Ed. Royal Comm. on the Future of the Toronto Waterfront and other govt reports and documents; numerous articles for TV, radio and journals. *Publications include:* The Non-Deductible Woman: A Handbook for Working Wives and Mothers 1970, The Chatelaine Guide to Marriage (contrib.) 1974, The Family Matters: Two Centuries of Family Law and Life in Ontario 1986. *Address:* 1 Concorde Place, Toronto, Ontario, M3C 3K6, Canada (home).

KILALEA, Rory, (Murungu); Zimbabwean writer, playwright and film producer. *Career:* Prod., own co. Rory Kilalea Films, producer of films and numerous advertisements; fmrly taught broadcasting and writing, Univ. of Zimbabwe; currently lives in Middle East. *Films produced:* A Dry White Season (also man.) 1989, A Far Off Place 1993. *Plays:* Zimbabwe Boy, Ashes, Diary of David and Ruth, Colours, Friends. *Publications:* novel: The Disappointed Diplomat; short stories: The Arabian Princess and Other Stories 2002; contribs of short stories Whine of a Dog in The New Writer 1998, Zimbabwe Boy in Asylum 98 and Other Stories 2001, Unfinished Business in Writing Now 2005.

KILGUS, Martin A., MA, PhD; German journalist; *Editor, SWR Public Radio, Television & Internet*; b. 15 March 1963, Stuttgart; s. of Alfred Kilgus and Charlotte-Pauline Hofmann. *Education:* Wirtemberg-Gymnasium, Stuttgart, Univ. of Stuttgart and The American Univ., Washington, DC, USA. *Career:* traineeship, NBC Radio; joined Dept for Ethnic Broadcasting, SDR Radio & TV, Stuttgart 1989; worked as ed. for migrants' audio broadcasts 1991; now Ed. with SWR (fmrly SDR) Radio, TV & Internet; Chair. Int. Educ. Information Exchange, Stuttgart 1996–2004; Vice-Chair. German Asscn for the UN BW; mem. Bd Stiftung Geissstrasse Stuttgart, Konrad-Adenauer-Foundation; special field of research and activity include Digital Audio Broadcasting (DAB) and multi-lingual broadcasts, European integration and int. migration. *Honours:* Caritas Prize for Journalism. *Address:* SWR Public Radio, TV & Internet, Neckarstrasse 230, 70190 Stuttgart, Germany (office). *Telephone:* (711) 9292648 (office). *Fax:* (711) 929182648 (office). *E-mail:* martin.kilgus@swr.de (office). *Website:* www.swr.de/international (office).

KILLDEER, John (see Mayhar, Ardath)

KILLOUGH, (Karen) Lee; American writer; b. 5 May 1942, Syracuse, KS. *Career:* mem. SFWA, MWA, Sisters In Crime. *Publications:* A Voice Out of Ramah, 1979; The Doppelganger Gambit, 1979; The Monitor, the Miners, and the Shree, 1980; Aventine, 1981; Deadly Silents, 1982; Liberty's World, 1985; Spider Play, 1986; Blood Hunt, 1987; The Leopard's Daughter, 1987; Bloodlinks, 1988; Dragon's Teeth, 1990; Bloodwalk, 1997; Bridling Chaos, 1998; Blood Games, 2001; Wilding Nights, 2002. *Address:* PO Box 1167, Manhattan, KS 66505, USA. *E-mail:* klkillo@flinthills.com.

KILROY, Thomas, BA, MA, FRSL; Irish writer, dramatist and academic; b. 23 Sept. 1934, Callan; m. 1st; three s.; m. 2nd Julia Lowell Carlson 1981; one d. *Education:* University College, Dublin. *Career:* Emeritus Prof. of Modern English, NUI Galway, 2002; mem. Irish Acad. of Letters 1973. *Publications:* Death and Resurrection of Mr Roche (play), 1968; The Oneill (play), 1969; The Big Chapel (novel), 1971; Talbots' Box (play), 1977; The Seagull (play adaptation), 1981; Double Cross (play), 1986; Ghosts, 1989; The Madame McAdam Travelling Theatre (play), 1990; Gold in the Streets (television), 1993; Six Characters in Search of An Author (adaptation), 1996; The Secret Fall of Constance Wilde (play), 1997; My Scandalous Life, 2001; The Shape of Metal (play), 2003, Henry (play) 2005; Contributions: Radio, television, journals, and magazines. *Honours:* Guardian Fiction Prize, 1971; Heinemann Award for Literature, 1971; Irish Acad. of Letters Prize, 1972; American-Irish Foundation Award for Literature, 1974. *Address:* c/o Aosdána, The Arts Council, 70 Merrion Square, Dublin 2, Ireland. *E-mail:* aosdana@artscouncil.ie.

KILWORTH, Garry Douglas, (Garry Douglas), BA; British writer; b. 5 July 1941, York; m. Annette Jill Bailey 1962; one s. one d. *Career:* mem. PEN, Crimean War Soc. *Publications:* In Solitary 1977, The Night of Kadar 1979, Split Second 1979, Theatre of Timesmiths 1984, Songbirds of Pain 1984, Witchwater Country 1986, Spiral Winds 1987, The Wizard of Woodworld 1987, Abandonati 1988, Hunter's Moon 1989, In the Hollow of the Deep-Sea Wave 1989, The Foxes of First Dark 1990, Standing on Samshan 1992, Angel 1993, In The Country of Tattooed Men 1993, Hogfoot Right And Bird-Hands 1993, Archangel 1994, A Midsummer's Nightmare 1996, The Roof of Voyaging 1996, The Princely Flower 1997, Land-of-Mists 1998, Thunder Oak 1998, Windjammer Run 1998, Castle Storm 1998, Shadow-Hawk 1999, The Devil's Own 2001, The Winter Soldiers 2002, The Silver Claw 2005, Attica 2006, Moby Jack and Other Tall Stories 2006, Jigsaw 2007, Rogue Officer (Charles Whiting Award for Literature 2008) 2007, The Hundred Towered City 2008, Kiwi Wars 2008, Scarlet Sash 2010, Tales from a Fragrant Harbour 2010, Vampire Voles 2011, Dragoons 2011, The Sculptor 2011; as Garry Douglas: Highlander 1986, The Street 1988, Soldiers in the Mist 2000; contrib. to magazines and newspapers. *Honours:* Gollancz Short Story Award, Sunday Times 1974, Carnegie Medal Commendation, Librarian Asscn 1991, Lancashire Children's Book of the Year Award 1995. *Address:* c/o Caroline Sheldon Literary Agency, 71 Hillgate Place, London W8 7SS, England. *Website:* www.garry-kilworth.co.uk.

KIM, Hong-ik; North Korean writer. *Career:* lives in Seoul, Republic of Korea. *Publications:* He's Alive (in trans.). *Address:* c/o Korean PEN Centre, Room 1105, Oseong B/D, 13-5 Youido-dong, Yongdungpo-ku, Seoul, 150-010, Republic of Korea.

KIM, Ji-woon; South Korean filmmaker and screenwriter; b. 6 July 1964, Seoul. *Films:* Choyonghan kajok (The Quiet Family, writer, dir) 1998, Banchikwang (The Foul King, writer, dir) 2000, Coming Out (writer, dir) 2001, Saam gaang (Three, segment 'Memories', dir, writer) 2002, Janghwa, Hongryeon (A Tale of Two Sisters, writer, dir) 2003, Dalkomhan insaeng (A Bittersweet Life, writer, dir) 2005, The Good, the Bad, the Weird 2008, I Saw the Devil 2010,.

KIM, Suji Kwock, BA, MFA; Korean/American writer, translator, editor and academic; *Assistant Professor of English, University of Massachusetts*. *Education:* Yale Univ., Univ. of Iowa, Seoul Nat. Univ., Yonsei Univ., Stanford Univ. *Career:* fmr Visiting Prof., Sarah Lawrence Coll., Asst Prof. of English, Drew Univ.; currently Asst Prof. of English, Univ. of Massachusetts; Kingsley Tufts Award preliminary judge, Claremont-McKenna Grad. Coll.; fmr Mrs Giles Whiting Foundation Fellow, Nat. Endowment for the Arts (NEA) Fellow, Fulbright Scholar, Wallace Stegner Fellow, NEA-Japan Creative Artists, Fellow, Blakemore Foundation for Asian Studies Fellow, Korea Foundation Fellow, Asscn for Asian-American Studies Fellow, Mid-Atlantic Arts Foundation Fellow, New York Foundation for the Arts Fellow, California Arts Council Fellow, San Francisco Arts Comm. Fellow, Fine Arts Work Center in Provincetown Fellow; fmr Visiting Writer, American Acad. in Rome, Bogliasco Foundation, Genova. *Compositions:* libretti for three compositions by Mayako Kubo, performed by the Tokyo Philharmonic Chorus at Pablo Casals Hall, Tokyo 2007; libretti for five compositions for voice and piano by Jerome Blais, performed at Dalhousie Univ., Nova Scotia 2007; text for composition for violin, chorus and orchestra by Mark Grey, performed by the Los Angeles Philharmonic and Los Angeles Master Chorale (forthcoming). *Play:* Private Property (co-author) 1993. *Publications:* Notes from the Divided Country 2003; contrib. to more than 25 anthologies, including American Religious Poems (ed. Harold Bloom), American War Poetry (ed. Lorrie Goldensohn), The Future Dictionary of America (ed. Dave Eggers), Contemporary American Poetry (ed. R.S. Gwynn), The Griffin Poetry Prize Anthology (ed. Billy Collins), An Introduction to Poetry (ed. Dana Gioia); contrib. to New York Times, Washington Post, Los Angeles Times, The New Statesman, SLATE, The Nation, The New Republic, Paris Review, Poetry, Yale Review, Harvard Review, Salmagundi, Kenyon Review, Threepenny Review, Ploughshares, Southwest Review and other periodicals. *Honours:* Addison Metcalf Award, American Acad. of Arts and Letters, Whiting Writer's Award, Walt Whitman Award, Acad. of American Poets, The Nation/Discovery Award, Bay Area Book Reviewers' Award. *Address:* c/o National Endowment for the Arts, Literature Division, 1100 Pennsylvania Avenue, NW, #722, Washington, DC 20004-2501, USA (office). *Telephone:* (202) 682-5551 (office).

KINCAID, Jamaica; Antigua and Barbuda writer and academic; *Visiting Lecturer on African and African American Studies and on English and American Literature and Language, Harvard University*; b. (Elaine Potter Richardson), 25 May 1949, St John's; d. of Annie Richardson; m. Allen Shawn; one s. one d. *Career:* staff writer, The New Yorker 1976; currently Visiting Lecturer on African and African American Studies and on English and American Literature and Language, Harvard Univ.; mem. American Acad. of Arts and Letters; Fellow, American Acad. of Arts and Sciences 2009–. *Publications include:* At the Bottom of the River (short stories; American Acad. and Inst. of Arts and Letters Morton Dauwen Zabel Award) 1983, Annie John (novel) 1985, A Small Place (non-fiction) 1988, Lucy (novel) 1990, The Autobiography of My Mother 1995, My Brother 1997, My Favorite Plant 1998, Poetics of Place (with Lynn Geesaman) 1998, My Garden (non-fiction) 1999, Talk Stories 2001, Mr Potter 2002, Among Flowers: A Walk in the Himalaya 2005. *Honours:* numerous hon. degrees; Lila Wallace-Reader's Digest Fund Annual Writer's Award 1992. *Address:* Barker Center, Harvard University, 12 Quincy Street, 2nd Floor, Cambridge, MA 02138 (office); c/o Farrar Straus & Giroux, 19 Union Square West, New York, NY 10003, USA. *Telephone:* (617) 496-8543 (office). *Fax:* (617) 496-2872 (office). *E-mail:* jkincaid@fas.harvard.edu (office). *Website:* aaas.fas.harvard.edu (office).

KING, Cynthia; American writer and editor; b. (Cynthia Bregman), 27 Aug. 1925, New York, NY; m. Jonathan King 1944 (died 1997); three s. *Education:* Bryn Mawr Coll., Univ. of Chicago, New York Univ. Writers' Workshop. *Career:* Assoc. Ed., Hillman Periodicals 1945–50; Managing Ed., Fawcett Publications 1950–55; Co-curator Exhbn Children's Book Art, Contemporary Arts Museum, Houston, Tex. 1975; mem. Authors' Guild, Poets and Writers, Detroit Working Writers (Pres. 1979–81). *Publications:* In the Morning of Time 1970, 2010, The Year of Mr Nobody 1978, Beggars and Choosers 1980, Sailing Home 1982; contrib. of book reviews to New York Times Book Review, Detroit News, Houston Chronicle, LA Daily News, short fiction to Good Housekeeping, Texas Stories & Poems, Quartet; numerous mass market publs. *Honours:* Michigan Council for the Arts grant 1986, Detroit Working Writers Spring Readings Award 2002. *Address:* 365 North Main Street, Cottage M-2, West Lebanon, NH 03784, USA (home). *Telephone:* (603) 277-9555 (home); (713) 503-9123 (mobile). *E-mail:* t.king.vt@gmail.com (home). *Website:* www.cynthiakingbooks.com.

KING, Daren, BA; British screenwriter, novelist, journalist and illustrator; b. 8 March 1972, Herts. *Education:* Bath Univ. *Publications:* fiction: Boxy an Star 1999, Jim Giraffe 2004, Tom Boler 2005, Manual 2008; cartoon humour: Smally's Party (illustrated) 2005; juvenile fiction: Mouse Noses on Toast (Nestlé Children's Book Prize) 2006, Sensible Hare and the Case of Carrots 2007, Peter the Penguin Pioneer 2008, Frightfully Friendly Ghosties 2009; contrib. of short stories to Arena magazine, and to books, All Hail the New Puritans, Piece of Flesh, New Writing 13. *Literary Agent:* c/o Tibor Jones and Associates, Unit 12b, Piano House, 9 Brighton Terrace, London, SW9 8DJ, England. *E-mail:* hello@darenking.co.uk (office). *Website:* www.darenking.co.uk.

KING, Sir David Anthony, Kt, BSc, MA, PhD, ScD, FRS, FRSC, FInstP; British academic and research scientist; *Director, Smith School of Enterprise and the Environment, University of Oxford*; b. 12 Aug. 1939, Durban, South Africa; s.

of Arnold King and Patricia Vardy; m. Jane Lichtenstein 1983; three s. one d. *Education:* St John's Coll., Johannesburg, Univ. of Witwatersrand, Johannesburg, Imperial Coll. London. *Career:* Lecturer in Chemical Physics, Univ. of E Anglia, Norwich 1966–74; Brunner Prof. of Physical Chem., Univ. of Liverpool 1974–88, Head, Dept of Inorganic, Physical and Industrial Chem. 1983–88; 1920 Prof. of Physical Chem., Dept of Chem., Univ. of Cambridge 1988–, Head, Dept of Chem. 1993–2000; Fellow, St John's Coll. 1988–95, Queen's Coll. 2001–; Master of Downing Coll. 1995–2000; Chief Scientific Adviser to UK Govt and Head, Office of Science and Tech. 2000–07; Dir Smith School of Enterprise and the Environment, Univ. of Oxford 2008–; Ed. Chemical Physics Letters 1990–2001; Pres. Asscn of Univ. Teachers 1976–77; Chair. British Vacuum Council 1982–85; mem. Comité de Direction, Centre Cinétique et Physique, Nancy 1974–81, Research Awards Advisory Cttee Leverhulme Trust 1980–91 (Chair. 1995–2001), Direction Cttee (Beirat) Fritz Haber Inst., Berlin 1981–93; Chair. European Science Foundation Programme 'Gas–Surface Interactions' 1991–96, Kettle's Yard Gallery, Cambridge 1989–2001; Sr Scientific Adviser to UBS; Pres. BAAS; Assoc. Fellow, Third World Acad. of Sciences 2000; Foreign mem. American Acad. of Arts and Sciences 2002. *Publications:* The Chemical Physics of Solid Surfaces and Heterogeneous Catalysis (seven vols) (co-ed. with D. P. Woodruff) 1980–94, The Hot Topic: How to Tackle Global Warming and Still Keep the Lights On (with Gabrielle Walker) 2008; over 450 original pubs in the scientific literature. *Honours:* Hon. Fellow, Indian Acad. of Sciences, Downing Coll., Univ. of Cardiff 2001; Hon. Prof., Qingdao Univ., People's Repub. of China; Hon. Life Fellow, Royal Soc. of Arts 2006; Hon. DSc (Liverpool) 2001, (East Anglia) 2001, (Stockholm) 2003, (Genoa) 2002, (Leicester) 2002, Cardiff (2002), (Witwatersrand) 2003, (St Andrews) 2003, (York) 2004, (Oxford Brookes) 2007; Shell Scholar 1963–66, RSC Awards, Surface Chem. 1978, RSC Tilden Lecturer 1988, Medal for Research, British Vacuum Council 1991, Liversidge Lectureship and Medal 1997–98, Royal Soc. Rumford Medal 2003. *Address:* Smith School of Enterprise and the Environment, Hayes House, 75 George Street, Oxford, OX1 2BQ (office); Department of Chemistry, University of Cambridge, Lensfield Road, Cambridge, CB2 1EN (office); 20 Glisson Road, Cambridge, CB1 2EW, England (home). *Telephone:* (1865) 614964 (Oxford) (office); (1223) 336338 (Cambridge) (office); (1223) 315629 (Cambridge) (home). *Fax:* (1865) 614960 (Oxford) (office); (1223) 762829 (Cambridge) (office). *E-mail:* director.smithschool@admin.ox.ac.uk (office); director@smithschool.ox.ac.uk (office); dak10@cam.ac.uk (office). *Website:* www.smithschool.ox.ac.uk (office); www.ch.cam.ac.uk (office).

KING, (David) Clive; British novelist; b. 28 April 1924, Richmond, Surrey, England; m. 1st Jane Tuke 1948; one s. one d.; m. 2nd Penny Timmins 1974; one d. *Education:* Downing Coll. *Career:* mem. Soc. of Authors. *Publications:* The Town That Went South 1959, Stig of the Dump 1963, The Twenty-Two Letters 1966, The Night the Water Came 1973, Snakes and Snakes 1975, Me and My Million 1976, Ninny's Boat 1980, The Sound of Propellers 1986, The Seashore People 1987; seven other books. *Honours:* Boston Globe-Horn Book Award, Honour Book 1980. *Address:* Pond Cottage, Low Road, Thurlton, Norwich, NR14 6PZ, England.

KING, Janey, (Rosie Thomas), BA; British novelist; b. 22 Oct. 1947, Denbigh, Wales; m. Caradoc King 1975 (divorced); one s. one d. *Education:* St Hilda's College, Oxford. *Publications:* Love's Choice 1982, Celebration 1982, Follies 1983, Sunrise 1984, The White Dove 1985, Strangers 1986, Bad Girls, Good Women 1988, A Woman of Our Times 1990, All My Sins Remembered 1991, Other People's Marriages 1993, A Simple Life 1996, The Potter's House 2002, Sun at Midnight 2004, Iris and Ruby 2006, Constance 2007. *Honours:* Romantic Novel of the Year Award, Romantic Novelists Asscn, 1985, 2007. *Address:* 74 Canal Building, 135 Shepherdess Walk, London, N1 7RR, England.

KING, Janey (see Thomas, Rosie)

KING, Larry L.; American playwright, author and actor; b. 1 Jan. 1929, Putnam, TX; m. Barbara S. Blaine, two s. three d. *Education:* Texas Technical University, Harvard University, Duke University. *Career:* Visiting Ferris Prof. of Journalism and Political Science, Princeton University, 1973–74; Poet Laureate (life), Monahans (Texas) Sandhills Literary Society, 1977–. *Publications:* Plays: The Kingfish, 1979; The Best Little Whorehouse in Texas, 1978; Christmas: 1933, 1986; The Night Hank Williams Died, 1988; The Golden Shadows Old West Museum, 1989; The Best Little Whorehouse Goes Public, 1994; The Dead Presidents' Club, 1996. Other: The One-Eyed Man (novel), 1966; . . .And Other Dirty Stories, 1968; Confessions of a White Racist, 1971; The Old Man and Lesser Mortals, 1974; Of Outlaws, Whores, Conmen, Politicians and Other Artists, 1980; Warning: Writer at Work, 1985; None But a Blockhead, 1986; Because of Lozo Brown, 1988. Contributions: Harper's; Atlantic Monthly; Life; New Republic; Texas Monthly; Texas Observer; New York; Playboy; Parade; Esquire; Saturday Evening Post; National Geographic.

KING, Laurie R., (Leigh Richards), BA, MA; American writer; b. (Laurie Lee Richardson), 19 Sept. 1952, Oakland, Calif.; d. of Roger Romeyne Richardson and Mary Richardson (née Dickson); m. Noel Q. King 1977; one s. one d. *Education:* Univ. of California, Santa Cruz, Grad. Theological Union, Berkeley. *Career:* mem. MWA, Sisters in Crime, Int. Asscn of Crime Writers, Crime Writers Asscn. *Publications:* A Grave Talent 1993, The Beekeeper's Apprentice 1994, To Play the Fool 1995, A Monstrous Regiment of Women 1995, With Child 1996, A Letter of Mary 1997, The Moor 1998, A Darker Place 1999, O Jerusalem 1999, Night Work 2000, Folly 2001, Justice Hall 2002, Keeping Watch 2003, The Game 2004, Califia's Daughters (as Leigh Richards) 2004, Locked Rooms 2005, The Art of Detection 2006, Touchstone 2008, The Language of Bees 2009, The God of the Hive 2010, Beekeeping for Beginners (novella) 2011, Pirate King 2011, Garment of Shadows 2012. *Honours:* Dr hc (Church Divinity School of the Pacific) 1997; Edgar Award for Best First Novel 1993, Creasey Award for Best First Novel 1995, Nero Wolfe Award for Best Novel 1996, Macavity Award 2002, Jack Reacher Award 2008, inducted into Baker Street Irregulars 2010. *Address:* PO Box 1152, Freedom, CA 95019, USA (office). *E-mail:* info@laurieking.com (office). *Website:* www.laurieking.com.

KING, Paul (see Drackett, Philip Arthur)

KING, Philip (see Levinson, Leonard)

KING, Stephen Edwin, (Richard Bachman), BS; American writer and screenwriter; b. 21 Sept. 1947, Portland, ME; s. of Donald King and Nellie R. King (née Pillsbury); m. Tabitha J. Spruce 1971; two s. one d. *Education:* Univ. of Maine. *Career:* teacher of English, Hampden Acad., ME 1971–73; writer-in-residence, Univ. of Maine at Orono 1978–79; mem. Authors' Guild of America, Screen Artists' Guild, Screen Writers of America, Writers' Guild. *Television:* Kingdom Hospital. *Publications:* novels: Carrie 1974, Salem's Lot 1975, The Shining 1976, The Stand 1978, The Dead Zone 1979, Firestarter 1980, Cujo 1981, Different Seasons 1982, The Dark Tower I: The Gunslinger 1982, Christine 1983, Pet Cemetery 1983, The Talisman (with Peter Straub) 1984, It 1986, The Eyes of the Dragon 1987, Misery 1987, The Dark Tower II: The Drawing of the Three 1987, Tommyknockers 1987, The Dark Half 1989, The Dark Tower III: The Waste Lands 1991, Needful Things 1991, Gerald's Game 1992, Dolores Claiborne 1992, Insomnia 1994, Rose Madder 1995, Desperation 1996, The Green Mile (serial novel) 1996, The Dark Tower IV: Wizard and Glass 1997, Bag of Bones 1997, The Girl Who Loved Tom Gordon 1999, Hearts in Atlantis 1999, Riding the Bullet 2000, The Plant (serial novel) 2000, Dreamcatcher 2001, Black House (with Peter Straub) 2001, From a Buick 8 2002, The Dark Tower V: Wolves of the Calla 2003, The Dark Tower VI: Song of Susannah 2004, The Dark Tower VII: The Dark Tower 2004, The Colorado Kid 2005, Cell 2006, Lisey's Story 2006, Duma Key 2008, Under the Dome 2009, Full Dark, No Stars 2010, The Wind Through the Keyhole 2012; other: Night Shift (short stories) 1978, Danse Macabre (non-fiction) 1980, Different Seasons (short stories) 1982, Creepshow (comic book) 1982, Cycle of the Werewolf (illustrated novel) 1984, Skeleton Crew (short stories) 1985, Four Past Midnight (short stories) 1990, Nightmares and Dreamscapes (short stories) 1993, Head Down (story) 1993, Six Stories (short stories) 1997, Storm of the Century (screenplay) 1999, On Writing: A Memoir of the Craft (revised edn as Secret Windows) 2000, Everything's Eventual: 14 Dark Tales (short stories) 2002, Faithful (non-fiction, with Stewart O'Nan) 2005, Just After Sunset (short stories) 2008, Blockade Billy (novella) 2010, Full Dark, No Stars (short stories) 2010, 11/22/63 2011, numerous short stories, screenplays and television plays; as Richard Bachman: Rage 1977, The Long Walk 1979, Roadwork 1981, The Running Man 1982, Thinner 1984, The Regulators 1996, Blaze 2007. *Honours:* Medal for Distinguished Contribution to American Letters, Nat. Book Foundation 2003. *Address:* 49 Florida Avenue, Bangor, ME 04401, USA (office). *Website:* www.stephenking.com (office).

KING, Thomas Hunt, (Hartley Goodweather), CM, MA, PhD; American/Canadian academic, writer and photographer; *Professor Emeritus of English, University of Guelph*; b. 24 April 1943, Sacramento, Calif.; m. Kristine Adams 1970 (divorced 1980); one s.; partner, Helen Hoy 1984; one s. one d. *Education:* Chico State Univ., Univ. of Utah. *Career:* Dir Native Studies, Univ. of Utah 1971–73, Co-ordinator History of the Indians of the Americas Program 1977–79; Assoc. Dean Student Services, Humboldt State Univ. 1973–77; Asst Prof. of Native Studies, Univ. of Lethbridge 1978–89, Chair Native Studies 1985–87; Assoc. Prof. of American Studies/Native Studies, Univ. of Minnesota 1989–95, Chair Native Studies 1991–93; Assoc. Prof. of English, Univ. of Guelph 1995–2003, Prof. of English 2003–11, Prof. Emer. 2011–. *Exhibitions:* Native American Humour, Weisman Museum, Minneapolis 1997–98, New Voices/New Visions, Ansel Adams Center for Photography, San Francisco 1998–99. *Films:* Medicine River 1993, I'm Not the Indian You Had in Mind 2007, Totem 2009. *Radio:* Dead Dog Cafe Comedy Hour (CBC Radio) 1996–2003, Dead Dog in the City (CBC Radio) 2006. *Publications:* The Native in Literature: Canadian and Comparative Perspectives (ed. with Helen Hoy and Cheryl Calver) 1987, An Anthology of Short Fiction by Native Writers in Canada (ed.) 1988, All My Relations: An Anthology of Contemporary Canadian Native Fiction (ed.) 1990, Medicine River 1990, A Coyote Columbus Story 1992, Green Grass, Running Water 1993, One Good Story, That One 1993, Coyote Sings to the Moon 1998, Truth and Bright Water 1999, Dreadful Water Shows Up (as Hartley Goodweather) 2002, The Truth about Stories 2003, Coyote's New Suit 2004, A Short History of Indians in Canada 2005, The Red Power Murders (as Hartley Goodweather) 2006, A Coyote Solstice Tale 2009; other: films and radio and television drama; contribs to reference works, books, anthologies, reviews, quarterlies and journals. *Honours:* Univ. of Guelph Presidential Distinguished Prof. Award 2004–06; Writers' Guild of Alberta Best Novel Award 1991, Oakland PEN Josephine Miles Award 1991, Canadian Authors Award for Fiction 1994, Aboriginal Radio Award 2000, American Library Asscn Notable Book Citation 2001, Nat. Aboriginal Achievement Award 2003, Ontario Trillium Book Award 2004, Western Literature Asscn Distinguished Achievement Award 2004. *Literary Agent:* c/o Jackie Kaiser, Westwood Creative Artists, 94 Harbord Street, Toronto, ON

M5S 1G6, Canada. *Telephone:* (416) 964-3302. *Fax:* (416) 975-9209. *Address:* 82 Water Street, Guelph, ON N1G 1A5, Canada (home). *Telephone:* (519) 824-2634 (office). *E-mail:* thking@uoguelph.ca (office).

KING-ARIBISALA, Karen; Nigerian writer; b. Guyana; m.; one s. *Career:* Prof. of English, Univ. of Lagos. *Publications:* Our Wife and Other Stories (short stories) (Commonwealth Writers' Prize Best First Book, Africa Region) 1990, Kicking Tongues 1998, The Hangman's Game (Commonwealth Writers' Prize for Best Book, Africa Region 2008) 2007. *Address:* Peepal Tree Press, 17 King's Avenue, Leeds, LS6 1QS, England (office). *Telephone:* (113) 245-1703 (home). *E-mail:* contact@peepaltreepress.com (office). *Website:* www.peepaltreepress.com (office).

KING-HELE, Desmond George, MA, FRS; British writer and scientist; b. 3 Nov. 1927, Seaford, Sussex; s. of late S. G. King-Hele and Mrs B. King-Hele; m. Marie Newman 1954 (separated 1992); two d. *Education:* Epsom Coll. and Trinity Coll., Cambridge. *Career:* Royal Aircraft Establishment, Farnborough 1948–88 (research on earth's gravity field and upper atmosphere by analysis of satellite orbits), Deputy Chief Scientific Officer, Space Dept 1968–88; mem. Int. Acad. of Astronautics 1961–; Chair. British Nat. Cttee for the History of Science, Medicine and Tech. 1985–89, History of Science Grants Cttee 1990–93; Ed. Notes and Records of the Royal Soc. 1989–96; Bakerian Lecturer, Royal Soc. 1974, Wilkins Lecturer, Royal Soc. 1997. *Radio:* dramas: A Mind of Universal Sympathy 1973, The Lunaticks 1978. *Publications:* Shelley: His Thought and Work 1960, Satellites and Scientific Research 1960, Erasmus Darwin 1963, Theory of Satellite Orbits in an Atmosphere 1964, Observing Earth Satellites 1966, Essential Writings of Erasmus Darwin 1968, The End of the Twentieth Century? 1970, Poems and Trixies 1972, Doctor of Revolution 1977, Letters of Erasmus Darwin 1981, Animal Spirits 1983, Erasmus Darwin and the Romantic Poets 1986, Satellite Orbits in an Atmosphere 1987, The R.A.E. Table of Earth Satellites 1957–1989, 1990, A Tapestry of Orbits 1992, John Herschel 1992, Erasmus Darwin: A Life of Unequalled Achievement 1999, Antic and Romantic 2000, Charles Darwin's The Life of Erasmus Darwin 2002, The Collected Letters of Erasmus Darwin 2006; more than 300 scientific or literary papers in various learned journals. *Honours:* Hon. DSc (Univ. of Aston) 1979, Hon. DUniv (Univ. of Surrey) 1986; Soc. of Authors' Medical History Prize 1999; Eddington Medal, Royal Astronomical Soc. 1971, Chree Medal, Inst. of Physics 1971, Nordberg Medal, Int. Cttee on Space Research 1990. *Address:* 7 Hilltops Court, 65 North Lane, Buriton, Hants., GU31 5RS, England (home). *Telephone:* (1730) 261646 (home).

KINGDON, Robert McCune, AB, MA, PhD; American historian, academic and writer; b. 29 Dec. 1927, Chicago, Ill. *Education:* Oberlin Coll., OH, Columbia Univ., New York, Univ. of Geneva, Switzerland. *Career:* Instructor to Asst Prof., Univ. of Massachusetts 1952–57; Visiting Instructor, Amherst Coll. 1953–54; Asst Prof. to Prof. of History, Univ. of Iowa 1957–65; Visiting Prof., Stanford Univ. 1964, 1980; Prof. of History, Univ. of Wisconsin, Madison 1965–, Hilldale Prof. of History 1988–98; Ed. Sixteenth Century Journal 1973–97; mem. Inst. for Research in the Humanities 1974–, Dir 1975–87; mem. American Soc. of Reformation Research (Pres. 1971), Int. Fed. of Socs and Insts for the Study of the Renaissance, Renaissance Soc. of America (mem. Exec. Bd 1972–92), American Soc. of Church History (Pres. 1980). *Publications:* Geneva and the Coming of the Wars of Religion in France 1555–1563 1956, Registres de la Compagnie des Pasteurs de Genève au Temps de Calvin (co-ed. with J.-F. Bergier) (two vols) 1962, 1964, William Cecil: Execution of Justice in England (ed.) 1965, William Allen: A True, Sincere and Modest Defence of English Catholics (ed.) 1965, Geneva and the Consolidation of the French Protestant Movement 1564–1572 1967, Calvin and Calvinism: Sources of Democracy (co-ed. with R. D. Linder) 1970, Theodore de Béze: Du Droit des magistrats (ed.) 1971, Transition and Revolution: Problems and Issues of European Renaissance and Reformation History (ed.) 1974, The Political Thought of Peter Martyr Vermigli 1980, Church and Society in Reformation Europe 1985, Myths About the St Bartholomew's Day Massacres 1572–1576 1988, A Bibliography of the Works of Peter Martyr Vermigli (co-ed. with J. P. Donnelly) 1990, Adultery and Divorce in Calvin's Geneva 1995, Registres du Consistoire de Genève au temps de Calvin (co-ed.), Vol. I 1996, Vol. II 2001, Vol. III 2004, Vol. IV 2007; contrib. to scholarly journals. *Address:* 4 Rosewood Circle, Madison, WI 53711, USA (home). *E-mail:* rkingdon@wiscmail.wisc.edu (office).

KINGSOLVER, Barbara, MS; American writer; b. 8 April 1955, Annapolis, Md; m. Steven Hopp; two d. *Education:* DePauw Univ., Indiana, Univ. of Arizona. *Career:* scientific writer, Office of Arid Land Studies, Univ. of Ariz. 1981–85; freelance journalist 1985–87, novelist 1987–; book reviewer, New York Times 1988–, Los Angeles Times 1989–, San Francisco Chronicle, The Nation, The Progressive, The Washington Post, Women's Review of Books and others; Woodrow Wilson Foundation/Lila Wallace Fellowship 1992; est. The Bellwether Prize for Fiction: In Support of a Literature of Social Change 1997. *Publications:* The Bean Trees (Enoch Pratt Library Youth-to-Youth Books Award) 1988, Holding the Line 1989, Homeland and Other Stories 1989, Animal Dreams (Edward Abbey Award for Ecofiction, PEN/USA West Fiction Award) 1990, Another America 1992, Pigs in Heaven (Mountains and Plains Booksellers Award for Fiction, Los Angeles Times Fiction Prize) 1993, High Tide in Tucson 1995, The Poisonwood Bible (Village Voice Best Books 1998, New York Times Top Ten Books 1998, Los Angeles Times Best Books for 1998, Independence Publisher Brilliance Audio 1999, Booksense Prize 1999, Nat. Book Award (SA) 2000) 1998, Prodigal Summer 2000, Small Wonder 2002, Last Stand 2002, Animal, Vegetable, Miracle: Our Year of Seasonal Eating (American Booksellers Book of the Year Award, James Beard Foundation Award) 2007, The Lacuna (Orange Prize for Fiction 2010) 2009. *Honours:* Hon. LittD (DePauw) 1994; Nat. Writers Union Andrea Egan Award 1998, Arizona Civil Liberties Union Award 1998, Nat. Humanities Medal 2000, Best American Science and Nature Writing 2001, Gov.'s Nat. Award in the Arts, Kentucky 2002, John P. McGovern Award for the Family 2002, Physicians for Social Responsibility Nat. Award 2002. *Address:* PO Box 160, Meadowview, VA 24361 (office); c/o Harper Collins, 10 East 53rd Street, New York, NY 10022, USA.

KINGSTON, Maxine Hong, BA; American author and academic; *Professor Emerita, Department of English, University of California, Berkeley*; b. 27 Oct. 1940, Stockton, Calif.; d. of Tom and Ying Lan Hong (née Chew); m. Earl Kingston 1962; one s. *Education:* Univ. of California, Berkeley. *Career:* taught English, Sunset High School, Hayward, Calif. 1965–66, Kahuku High School, Hawaii 1967, Kahaluu Drop-In School 1968, Kailua High School 1969, Honolulu Business Coll. 1969, Mid-Pacific Inst., Honolulu 1970–77; Prof. of English, Visiting Writer, Univ. of Hawaii, Honolulu 1977; Thelma McCandless Distinguished Prof., Eastern Mich. Univ., Ypsilanti 1986; Chancellor's Distinguished Prof., Univ. of California, Berkeley 1990–, now Prof. Emer. *Art Exhibitions:* Cowra Gallery, Australia 2007, The Writers Brush, New York and Boston 2008. *Publications:* The Woman Warrior: Memoirs of a Girlhood Among Ghosts (Nat. Book Critics Circle Award for non-fiction) 1976, China Men (Nat. Book Award) 1981, Hawaii One Summer (Ka Palapola Po'okela Award 1999) 1987, Through The Black Curtain 1988, Tripmaster Monkey – His Fake Books (PEN USA West Award in Fiction) 1989, The Literature of California (ed.) 2001, To Be The Poet 2002; The Fifth Book of Peace 2004, Veterans of War, Veterans of Peace (ed., Northern California Book Award 2007, Pacific Justice and Reconciliation Center Peace Book Award) 2006, I Love a Broad Margin to My Life 2011; short stories, articles and poems. *Honours:* Mademoiselle Magazine Award 1977, Anisfield-Wolf Book Award 1978, Stockton (Calif.) Arts Comm. Award 1981, Hawaii Award for Literature 1982, NEA Writing Fellow 1980, Guggenheim Fellow 1981, named Living Treasure of Hawaii 1980, American Acad. and Inst. Award in Literature 1990, Nat. Humanities Medal 1997, Fred Cody Lifetime Achievement Award 1998, John Dos Passos Prize 1998, Ka Palapola Po'okela Award 1999, Commonwealth Club Silver Medal 2001, California State Library Gold Medal 2002, Spirituality and Health Book Award, KPFA Peace Award 2005, Red Hen Press Lifetime Achievement Award 2006, Los Angeles Times Book Festival Lifetime Achievement Award 2007, Nat. Book Foundation Medal for Distinguished ContribS to American Letters 2008. *Address:* Department of English, University of California, 413 Wheeler Hall, Berkeley, CA 94720, USA (office). *Telephone:* (510) 643-5127 (office). *E-mail:* yinglan@berkeley.edu (office). *Website:* english.berkeley.edu (office).

KINLOCH, David, MA, DPhil; British academic, poet and editor; *Reader in English, University of Strathclyde*; b. 21 Nov. 1959, Glasgow, Scotland. *Education:* Univ. of Glasgow, Balliol Coll., Oxford. *Career:* Jr Research Fellow, St Anne's Coll. Oxford 1985–87; Research Fellow, Univ. of Wales 1987–89; Lecturer, Univ. of Salford 1989–90; Lecturer, Univ. of Strathclyde 1990–94, Sr Lecturer 1994–2006, Reader in English 2006–; Ed. Southfields Magazine; Founder/Co-Ed. Verse Poetry Magazine. *Publications:* Other Tongues (co-author) 1990, Dustie-Fute 1992, Paris-Forfar 1994, Un Tour d'Ecosse 2001, In My Father's House 2005; contrib. to reviews, journals and magazines. *Honours:* Robert Louis Stevenson Memorial Fellowship 2004, Scottish Arts Council Writer's Bursary 2006. *Address:* Department of English Studies, University of Strathclyde, Livingstone Tower, 26 Richmond Street, Glasgow, G1 1XH, Scotland (office). *Telephone:* (141) 548-3572 (office). *Fax:* (141) 548-3602 (office). *E-mail:* d.p.kinloch@strath.ac.uk (office). *Website:* www.strath.ac.uk/english/membersofthedepartment/kinlochdaviddr (office).

KINNELL, Galway, MA; American writer and academic; b. 1 Feb. 1927, Providence, RI; s. of James S. Kinnell and Elizabeth Mills; m. 1st Inés Delgado de Torres 1965; (divorced) one s. two d.; m. 2nd Barbara K. Bristol 1997. *Education:* Princeton Univ. and Univ. of Rochester. *Career:* Guggenheim Fellow 1963–64, 1974–75, MacArthur Fellow 1984; Dir Writing Programme, New York Univ. 1981–84, Samuel F. B. Morse Prof. of Arts and Sciences 1985–92, Erich Maria Remarque Prof. of Creative Writing 1992–2005; fmr Chancellor, Acad. of American Poets; named Vt State Poet 1989–93; mem. Nat. Inst., Acad. of Arts and Letters. *Publications:* poetry: What a Kingdom it Was 1960, Flower Herding on Mount Monadnock 1963, Body Rags 1966, The Book of Nightmares 1971, The Avenue Bearing the Initial of Christ into the New World 1974, Mortal Acts, Mortal Words 1980, Selected Poems 1982, The Past 1985, Imperfect Thirst 1994; novel: Black Light 1966; children's story: How the Alligator Missed Breakfast 1982; trans.: The Poems of François Villon 1965, On the Motion and Immobility of Douve by Yves Bonnefoy 1968, The Lackawanna Elegy by Yvan Goll 1970, The Essential Rilke; interviews: Walking Down the Stairs 1977. *Honours:* Award of Nat. Inst. of Arts and Letters 1962, Cecil Hemley Poetry Prize 1969, Medal of Merit 1975, Pulitzer Prize 1983, Nat. Book Award 1983, Frost Medal 2001, Wallace Stevens Award 2010. *Address:* 1218 Town Road 16, Sheffield, VT 05866, USA (home).

KINNEY, Arthur Frederick, MA, PhD; American academic, writer and editor; *Thomas W. Copeland Professor of Literary History, University of Massachusetts at Amherst*; b. 5 Sept. 1933, Cortland, NY; s. of Arthur Kinney and Gladys Kinney. *Education:* Syracuse Univ., Columbia Univ., Univ. of Michigan. *Career:* Instructor, Yale Univ. 1963–66; Asst Prof., Univ. of

Massachusetts at Amherst 1966–69, Assoc. Prof. 1969–73, Prof. 1973–85, Thomas W. Copeland Prof. of Literary History 1985–; Founder-Ed. English Literary Renaissance journal 1971–; Adjunct Prof. Clark University 1973–, New York University 1992–; Dir Massachusetts Center for Renaissance Studies 1996–; mem. MLA; Renaissance English Text Society, pres. 1985–; Renaissance Society of America; Shakespeare Asscn of America, trustee 1995–98; Sixteenth-Century Studies Conference Asscn. *Radio recordings:* Renaissance Reflections (CD of broadcasts on NPR Morning Edition, WFCR). *Publications:* On Seven Shakespearean Tragedies 1968, On Seven Shakespearean Comedies 1968, Rogues, Vagabonds, and Sturdy Beggars 1973, Elizabethan Backgrounds 1974, Faulkner's Narrative Poetics: Style As Vision 1978, William Faulkner: The Compson Family (ed.) 1982, Flannery O'Connor's Library: Resources of Being 1985, William Faulkner's The Sartoris Family (ed.) 1985, Poetics & Praxis, Understanding and Imagination: The Collected Essays of O.B. Hardison (ed.) 1986, Essential Articles for the Study of Sir Philip Sidney 1986, Humanist Poetics 1986, John Skelton: Priest as Poet 1987, Renaissance Historicism 1987, Continental Humanist Poetics 1989, William Faulkner: The McCaslin Family (ed.) 1990, Dorothy Parker's The Coast of Illyria (ed.) 1990, Classical, Renaissance, and Postmodern Acts of the Imagination: Essays in Honor of O. B. Hardison Jr (ed.) 1994, William Faulkner: The Sutpen Family (ed.) 1996, Go Down, Moses: The Miscegenation of Time 1997, Dorothy Parker Revisited 1998, Shakespeare, Text and Theatre (ed.) 1999, Renaissance Drama: An Anthology of Plays and Performances Edited from Manuscript and Early Quartos (ed.) 1999, The Cambridge Companion to English Literature 1500–1600 2000, Tudor England: An Encyclopaedia 2000, Blackwell Companion to Renaissance Drama (ed.) 2001, Lies Like Truth: Shakespeare, Macbeth and the Cultural Moment 2001, New Essays on Hamlet 2001, Shakespeare by Stages 2003, Shakespeare's Webs: Networks of Meaning in Renaissance Drama 2004, Shakespeare and Cognition 2006, Challenging Humanism: Essays in Honor of Dominic Baker-Smith 2006; contributions to scholarly books and professional journals. *Honours:* Senior Huntington Library Fellow 1973–74, 1978, 1983, Senior National Endowment for the Humanities Fellow 1973–74, 1987–88, Senior Folger Shakespeare Library Fellow 1974, 1990, 1992, Fulbright Fellow, Christ Church, Oxford 1977–78, Chancellor's Medal, University of Massachusetts at Amherst 1985, Outstanding Teacher Award 1990, Paul Oskar Kristeller Lifetime Achievement Award 2006. *Address:* Center for Renaissance Studies, POB 2300, Amherst, MA 01004, USA (office). *Telephone:* (413) 577-3600 (office). *Fax:* (413) 577-3605 (office).

KINNEY, Harrison Burton, BA, MA; American writer; b. 16 Aug. 1921, Mars Hill, ME; s. of Charles Kinney; m. Doris Getsinger 1952; one s. three d. *Education:* Washington and Lee Univ., Columbia Univ. *Career:* mem. Authors' Guild. *Publications:* The Lonesome Bear 1949, The Last Supper of Leonardo da Vinci by Lumen Martin Winter 1953, Has Anybody Seen My Father? 1960, The Kangaroo in the Attic 1960, James Thurber: His Life and Times 1993, The Thurber Letters: The Wit, Wisdom and Surprising Life of James Thurber 2003; contrib. to periodicals. *E-mail:* hk@harrisonkinney.com (office). *Website:* www.harrisonkinney.com.

KINSELLA, John; Australian poet, writer, editor and publisher; b. 1963, Perth, WA. *Education:* Univ. of Western Australia. *Career:* Writer-in-Residence, Churchill Coll., Cambridge 1997; Ed. Salt literary journal; Publr and Ed. Folio (Salt) Publishing; Richard L. Thomas Prof. of Creative Writing, Kenyon Coll., USA 2001, then Prof. of English; Adjunct Prof., Edith Cowan University, Western Australia, and Prin. of the Landscape and Language Centre; Consultant Ed. Westerly (journal); Int. Ed. The Kenyon Review; Fellow, Churchill Coll., Cambridge. *Publications:* poetry: The Frozen Sea 1983, Night Parrots 1989, The Book of Two Faces 1989, Poems 1991, Ultramarine (with Anthony Lawrence) 1992, Eschatologies 1991, Full Fathom Five 1993, Syzygy 1993, Erratum/Frame(d) 1995, Intensities of Blue (with Tracy Ryan) 1995, The Silo: A Pastoral Symphony 1995, The Radnoti Poems 1996, The Undertow: New and Selected Poems 1996, Lightning Tree 1996, Graphology (ed.) 1997, Poems: 1980–1994 1997, voice-overs (with Susan Schultz) 1997, The Hunt 1998, Kangaroo Virus (with Ron Sims) 1998, Sheep Dip 1998, Pine (with Keston Sutherland) 1998, alterity: poems without tom raworth 1998, The Benefaction (ed.) 1999, Fenland Pastorals 1999, Visitants 1999, Counter-Pastorals 1999, Wheatlands 2000, Zone 2000, Zoo (with Coral Hull) 2000, The Hierarchy of Sheep 2001, Auto 2001, Speed Factory (with Bernard Cohen, McKenzie Wark and Terri-ann White) 2002, Rivers (with Peter Porter and Sean O'Brien) 2002, Outside the Panopticon 2002, Lightning Tree 2003, Peripheral Light: New and Selected Poems (Western Australian Premier's Book Award for Poetry 2004) 2003, Four Australian Poets (with others) 2003, Doppler Effect 2004, The New Arcadia 2005, Shades of the Sublime and Beautiful 2008, Armour 2011; prose: Genre (novel) 1997, Grappling Eros (short stories) 1998, Crop Circles (play in verse) 1998, Paydirt (play), The Wasps (play), From Poetry to Politics and Back Again 2000, Divinations: Four Plays 2003, Peter Porter in Conversation with John Kinsella (with Peter Porter) 2003. *Honours:* Western Australia Premier's Award for Poetry 1993, Harri Jones Memorial Prize for Poetry, Adelaide Festival John Bray Poetry Award 1996, Sr Fellowships Literature Bd of the Australia Council, Young Australian Creative Fellowship, Grace Leven Poetry Prize, The Age Poetry Book of the Year. *Address:* Salt Publishing Ltd, PO Box 937, Great Wilbraham, Cambridge, CB21 5JX, England (office). *Telephone:* (1223) 882220 (office). *Fax:* (1223) 882260 (office). *Website:* www.saltpublishing.com (office); www.johnkinsella.org.

KINSELLA, Thomas; Irish poet; b. 4 May 1928, Dublin; s. of John Paul Kinsella and Agnes Casserly Kinsella; m. Eleanor Walsh 1955; one s. two d. *Career:* with Irish Civil Service 1946–65, resgnd as Asst Prin. Officer, Dept of Finance 1965; Artist-in-Residence, Southern Ill. Univ. 1965–67, Prof. of English 1967–70; Prof. of English, Temple Univ., Philadelphia 1970–90; Dir Dolmen Press Ltd, Cuala Press Ltd, Dublin; f. Peppercanister (pvt. publishing co.) Dublin 1972; mem. Irish Acad. of Letters 1965–, American Acad. of Arts and Sciences 2000–; Guggenheim Fellowship 1968–69, 1971–72. *Publications include:* Poems 1956, Another September (poems) 1958, Downstream (poems) 1962, Nightwalker and Other Poems 1966, Notes from the Land of the Dead (poems) 1972, Butcher's Dozen (poem) 1972, Selected Poems 1956–1968 1973, Song of the Night and Other Poems 1978, The Messenger (poem) 1978, Fifteen Dead (poems) 1979, One and Other Poems 1979, Poems 1956–1973, Peppercanister Poems 1972–1978 1979; Songs of the Psyche (poems) 1985, Her Vertical Smile (poem) 1985, St Catherine's Clock (poem) 1987, Out of Ireland (poems) 1987, Blood and Family (collected poems from 1978) 1988, Poems from Centre City 1990, Personal Places (poems) 1990, One Fond Embrace (poem) 1990, Madonna and other Poems 1991, Butcher's Dozen (anniversary reissue) 1992, From Centre City (collected poems from 1990) 1994, The Dual Tradition: an Essay on Poetry and Politics in Ireland 1995, Collected Poems 1956–94, The Pen Shop (poem) 1997, The Familiar (poems) 1999, Godhead (poems) 1999, Citizen of the World (poems) 2001, Marginal Economy (poems) 2006, Readings in Poetry (essays) 2006, A Dublin Documentary 2006, Man of War (poems) 2007, Belief and Unbelief (poems) 2007, Prose Occasions 1951–2006 2009, Fat Master 2012, Love Joy Peace 2012; The Táin (trans.) 1969; Selected Poems of Austin Clarke 1976; co-ed. Poems of the Dispossessed 1600–1900 (with 100 translations from the Irish) 1981; Ed.: Ireland's Musical Heritage: Sean O'Riada's Radio Talks on Irish Traditional Music 1981, The New Oxford Book of Irish Verse (including all new trans from the Irish) 1986. *Honours:* Hon. Sr Fellow, School of English, Univ. Coll. Dublin 2003; Hon. DLitt (Nat. Univ. of Ireland) 1985, (Turin) 2005; Guinness Poetry Award 1958, Irish Arts Council Triennial Book Award 1960, Denis Devlin Memorial Award 1966, 1969, 1992, First European Poetry Award 2001, Freedom of City of Dublin 2007, Ulysses Medal, Univ. Coll. Dublin 2008.

KINSELLA, William Patrick, OC, BA, MFA; Canadian writer and poet; b. 25 May 1935, Edmonton, Alberta; s. of John M. Kinsella and Olive M. Elliot; m. 1st Myrna Salls 1957; m. 2nd Mildred Heming 1965; m. 3rd Ann Knight 1978; m. 4th Barbara L. Turner 1999, three d. *Education:* Eastwood High School, Edmonton, Univ. of Victoria, Univ. of Iowa, USA. *Career:* Houghton Mifflin Literary Fellowship 1982. *Publications:* stories: Dance Me Outside 1977, Scars 1978, Shoeless Joe Jackson Comes to Iowa 1980, Born Indian 1981, The Moccasin Telegraph 1983, The Thrill of the Grass 1984, The Alligator Report 1985, The Fencepost Chronicles 1986, Five Stories 1987, Red Wolf, Red Wolf 1987, The Further Adventures of Slugger McBatt (reissued as Go the Distance 1995) 1988, The Miss Hobbema Pageant 1988, Dixon Cornbelt League 1993, Brother Frank's Gospel Hour 1994, The Secret of the Northern Lights 1998, The Silas Stories 1998, Japanese Baseball 2000; novels: Shoeless Joe 1982, The Iowa Baseball Confederacy 1986, Box Socials 1991, The Winter Helen Dropped By 1995, If Wishes Were Horses 1996, Magic Time 1998; other works: The Ballad of the Public Trustee 1982, The Rainbow Warehouse (poetry, with Ann Knight) 1989, Two Spirits Soar: The Art of Allen Sapp 1990, Even at This Distance (poetry, with Ann Knight) 1993. *Honours:* Order of BC 2005; Hon. DLitt. (Univ. of Victoria) 1991; Books in Canada First Novel Award 1982; Canadian Authors' Asscn Award for Fiction 1982; Writers Guild Alberta Award for Fiction 1982, 1983; Vancouver Award for Writing 1987; Stephen Leacock Award for Humour 1987; Canadian Booksellers Asscn Author of the Year 1987. *Address:* #201, 14881 Marine Drive, White Rock, BC V4B 1C2, Canada (office); PO Box 3067, Sumas, WA 98295, USA.

KINSLEY, Michael, BA, JD; American journalist; b. 9 March 1951, Detroit, Mich.; m. Patty Stonesifer. *Education:* Cranbrook Kingswood School, Mich., Harvard Univ., Magdalen Coll., Oxford, UK and George Washington Univ. *Career:* journalist, The New Republic (magazine), Ed. 1978–95, writing 'TRB from Washington' column; editorial posts at Washington Monthly, Harper's, The Economist; Co-host Crossfire TV program (CNN) 1989–95; Founding Ed. Slate online magazine 1995–2002, columnist 2002–04; Editorial and Opinion Ed. Los Angeles Times 2004–05; columnist Time magazine 2006–09, Politico 2009–; fmr columnist Wall Street Journal, The Times (London), Washington Post; contrib. to New Yorker, Reader's Digest, Condé Nast Traveler, Vanity Fair; American Ed. Guardian Unlimited (London) 2006. *Publication:* Please Don't Remain Calm: Provocations and Commentaries 2008, Creative Capitalism (ed) 2009. *Honours:* Columbia Journalism Review Editor of the Year 1999. *Address:* c/o Politico, 1100 Wilson Boulevard, Suite 601, Arlington, VA 22209, USA. *Telephone:* (703) 647-7999. *Website:* www.politico.com.

KINZIE, Mary, BA, MA, PhD; American poet, editor, critic and academic; *Professor of English*, Northwestern University. *Education:* Northwestern Univ., Free Univ. of Berlin, Johns Hopkins Univ. *Career:* Exec. Ed., TriQuarterly magazine 1975–78; instructor 1975–78, Lecturer 1978–85, Assoc. Prof. 1985–90, Martin J. and Patricia Koldyke Outstanding Teaching Prof. 1990–92, Prof. of English 1990–, Dir of Creative Writing Program 1979–, Northwestern Univ.; Sr Fellowship, Nat. Humanities Center 2005–06; mem. PEN, Poetry Soc. of America, Soc. of Midland Authors. *Publications:* poetry: The Threshold of the Year 1982, Summers of Vietnam 1990, Masked Women 1990, Autumn Eros and Other Poems 1991, Ghost Ship 1996, Drift 2003, California Sorrow 2007; criticism: The Cure of Poetry in an Age of Prose:

Moral Essays on the Poet's Calling 1993, The Judge is Fury: Dislocation and Form in Poetry 1994, A Poet's Guide to Poetry 2000, A Poet's Prose: Selected Writings of Louise Bogan 2005, California Sorrow 2007; contrib. to various books, anthologies, reviews, quarterlies, journals and magazines. *Honours:* Fulbright Fellowship, Woodrow Wilson Fellowship, Illinois Arts Council Awards 1977, 1978, 1980, 1982, 1984, 1988, 1990, 1993, and Artist grant 1983, DeWitt Wallace Fellow MacDowell Colony 1979, Devins Award for a First Vol. of Verse 1982, Guggenheim Fellowship 1986, Southwest Review Elizabeth Matchett Stover Memorial Award in Poetry 1987, Poetry Soc. of America Celia B. Wagner Award 1988, Pres.'s Fund for the Humanities Research grant 1990–91, Levinson Award 2007, Hardison Poetry Award, Folger Shakespeare Library 2008. *Address:* Department of English, Northwestern University, University Hall, Room 224, Evanston, IL 60208-2240, USA (office). *Telephone:* (847) 491-5618 (office). *Fax:* (847) 467-1545 (office). *E-mail:* mkinzie@northwestern.edu (office). *Website:* www.english.northwestern.edu/people/kinzie.html (office).

KIRALY, Sherwood; American writer and editor; b. 23 Oct. 1949, Chicago, IL; m. 1st; one s. one d.; m. 2nd Patti J. Reynolds 1987. *Education:* Knox College. *Publications:* California Rush, 1990; Diminished Capacity, 1995; Big Babies, 1996. Contributions: newspapers and television.

KIRANOVA, Evgenia, LLB; Bulgarian journalist and magazine editor; *President, Women's Union for Dignity and Equality*; b. 23 Jan. 1929, Sofia; m. 1st Dencho Denchev 1948 (divorced 1967); one s. one d.; m. 2nd Ivan Delchev 1973. *Education:* Univ. of Sofia. *Career:* Sec. World Democratic Fed. of Women 1954–57; Deputy Ed. Bulgarian-Soviet Friendship 1957–66; Head Foreign Dept Bulgarian Writers' Union 1966–67; Ed. Pogled (Review) 1968–72; Foreign Commentator Bulgarian Radio and TV 1972–73; World Peace Council Sec., Helsinki 1973–82; Sec-Gen., Vice-Pres. Int. Cttee of Solidarity with Cyprus 1975; Political Observer and Deputy Gen. Dir Sofia Press Agency 1985–90; Ed-in-Chief Nie Zhenite women's magazine 1990–; Founder, Pres. Women's Union for Dignity and Equality; Vice-Pres. Bulgarian section Int. Women's Fed. of Business and Professional Women. *Publications:* Well Known and Beloved 1960, Legal Defence of Motherhood 1965, Cyprus Drama, Women in the Contemporary World, Fight for Peace, Suomi, The River Run Back (ed.), Our Tzvetana (ed.). *Address:* 1712 Sofia, J. K. Mladost 3, bl 316, vh A, Bulgaria (home). *Telephone:* (2) 8814022 (home). *E-mail:* jenyk@cablebg.net (home).

KIRINO, Natsuo; Japanese novelist; b. 1951, Kanazawa; m.; one c. *Publications include:* novels: Kao ni Furikakaru Ame (Edogawa Ranpo Prize 1993) 1993, Tenshi ni Misuterareta Yoru 1994, Fire Ball Blues 1995, Mizu no Nemuri Hai no Yume 1995, Out (Mystery Writers of Japan Award) 1997, Yawarakana hohu (Soft Cheeks) (Naoki Prize) 1999, Kogen 2000, Fire Ball Blues 2 2001, Gyokuran 2001, Dark 2002, Real World 2003, Grotesque (Izumi Kyoka Literary Award) 2003, Zangyakuki (What Remains) 2004, I'm Sorry, Mama 2004, Tamamoe! 2005, Boken no Kuni 2005, Grotesque 2007; short story collections: Sabiru Kokor 1997, Diorama 1998, Rose Gaden 2000, Ambos Mundos 2005. *Address:* c/o International Creative Management Inc., 40 West 57th Street, New York, NY 10019, USA (office). *Telephone:* (212) 556-5665 (office). *Fax:* (212) 556-5665 (office). *Website:* www.icmtalent.com/flash.html (office).

KIRK, Pauline Marguerite, MA; British writer and poet; b. 14 April 1942, Birmingham, England; m. Peter Kirk 1964; one s. one d. *Education:* Nottingham University, Sheffield University, Monash University, Bretton Hall College, Leeds University. *Career:* Teacher, Methodist Ladies College, 1965–66; Teaching Fellow, Monash University, 1965–69; Tutor-Counsellor, Asst Senior Counsellor, Open University, 1971–88; Senior Officer, Leeds Dept of Social Service, 1988–95; Partner, Fighting Cock Press, 1996–; mem. Aireings, Partner, Fighting Cock Press, 1997–; Pennine Poets; Society of Authors. *Publications:* Fiction: Waters of Time, 1988; The Keepers, 1996. Poetry: Scorpion Days, 1982; Red Marl and Brick, 1985; Rights of Way, 1990; Travelling Solo, 1995; Return to Dreamtime, 1996; No Cure in Tears, 1997; Owlstone, 2002. Criticism: Brian Merrikin Hill: Poet and Mentor, 1999. Editor: A Survivor Myself: Experiences of Child Abuse, 1994; Local history booklets for Leeds City Council; Poetry Collections: Dunegrass, Brakken City, 1997; Chernobyl's Cloud, Natural Light, Kingfisher Days, 1998; The Imaginator, 2000; Imaginary Gates, 2001; Patterns in the Dark (second edn), 2001; Webbed Skylights of Tall Oaks (with Clare Chapman), 2002. Contributions: anthologies and other publications. *Honours:* Yorkshire and Humberside Arts New Beginnings Award, 1994. *Address:* 45 Middlethorpe Drive, York YO24 1NA, England.

KIRK-GREENE, Anthony Hamilton Millard, (Nicholas Caverhill), CMG, MBE, BA, MA, FRHistS; British academic, writer and editor; *Emeritus Fellow, St Antony's College, Oxford*; b. 16 May 1925, Tunbridge Wells, England; m. Helen Sellar 1967. *Education:* Clare Coll., Cambridge, Univ. of Edinburgh. *Career:* District Officer (Colonial Service) N Nigeria 1950–66; Sr Lecturer in Government, Inst. of Administration, Zaria, Nigeria 1957–62; Prof. of Government, Ahmadu Bello Univ., Nigeria 1962–65; Univ. Lecturer and Fellow, St Antony's Coll., Oxford 1967–92, Emer. Fellow 1992–; Dir Oxford Colonial Records Project 1980–85; Dir Foreign Service Programme, Univ. of Oxford 1986–90; Assoc. Ed., New Dictionary of Nat. Biography 1996–2002); mem. Council of Britain – Nigeria Asscn 1985–2008; mem. African Studies Asscn UK (pres. 1988–90) Int. African Inst., Royal African Soc. (vice-pres. 1992–2013). *Publications:* Barth's Travels in Nigeria 1962, The Emirates of Nigeria 1966, Conflict and Crisis in Nigeria 1971, A Biographical Dictionary of the British Colonial Service 1939–66 1991, Diplomatic Initiative: A History of the Foreign Service Programme 1994, On Crown Service 1999, Britain's Imperial Administrators 2000, The British Intellectual Engagement with Africa in the 20th Century (co-ed.) 2000, Symbol of Authority 2006; contrib. to various reference books and scholarly journals. *Honours:* Harkness Fellow 1958–59, Hans Wolff Memorial Lecturer 1973, Festschrift 1993, Leverhulme Emeritus Fellowship 1993; African Studies Asscn (USA) Best Text Prize 1997, African Studies Asscn (UK) Distinguished Africanist Award 2005. *Address:* c/o St Antony's College, Oxford, OX2 6JF, England (office).

KIRKPATRICK, Sidney Dale, BA, MFA; American writer and filmmaker; b. 4 Oct. 1955, New York, NY; m. 2005; two s. two d. *Education:* Hampshire Coll., Amherst, New York Univ. *Career:* Reader, Huntington Library 1992; mem. PEN Center West, Bd of Dirs 1991–92. *Film:* My Father the President (Dir; Winner, American Film Festival 1982). *Television:* The Indomitable Teddy Roosevelt (NBC, Assoc. Producer) 1985. *Publications:* A Cast of Killers 1986, Turning the Tide 1991, Lords of Sipan 1992, Edgar Cayce, an American Prophet 2000, The Revenge of Thomas Eakins 2006, Hitler's Holy Relics 2010; contribs to Los Angeles Times, American Film. *Literary Agent:* c/o Richard Morris, Janklow and Nesbit, 445 Park Avenue, New York, NY 10022, USA. *Telephone:* (212) 421-1700. *E-mail:* sidneykirkpatrick@verizon.net (office). *Website:* SidneyKirkpatrick.com.

KIRSCH, Jonathan, BA, JD; American novelist, writer, reviewer and attorney; b. 19 Dec. 1949, Los Angeles, CA; m. Ann Benjamin 1970, one s. one d. *Education:* University of California, Santa Cruz, Loyola University School of Law. *Career:* book reviewer, Los Angeles Times Book Review 1968–; Ed., California magazine, formerly New West 1977–83; correspondent, Newsweek 1979–80; Attorney, Kirsch and Mitchell, Los Angeles 1988–. *Publications:* Bad Moon Rising (novel), 1977; Lovers in a Winter Circle (novel), 1978; Kirsch's Handbook of Publishing Law: For Authors, Publishers, Editors, and Agents, 1995; The Harlot by the Side of the Road: Forbidden Tales of the Bible, 1997; Moses: A Life, 1998. Contributions: More than 1,000 articles and book reviews to newspapers and magazines. *Literary Agent:* Laurie Fox, Linda Chester Literary Agency, Rockefeller Center, 630 Fifth Ave, New York, NY 10111, USA. *Address:* Kirsch and Mitchell, 2029 Century Park E, Suite 2750, Los Angeles, CA 90067, USA. *E-mail:* ursus@aol.com.

KIRSCH, Sarah, DipA; German author and poet; b. 16 April 1935, Limlingerode; m. Rainer Kirsch 1958 (divorced 1968); one s. *Education:* University of Halle, Johannes R. Becher Institute, Leipzig. *Publications:* Landaufenthalt, 1967; Die Vögel signen im Regen am Schönsten, 1968; Zaubersprüche, 1973; Es war der merkwürdigste Sommer, 1974; Musik auf dem Wasser, 1977; Rückenwind, 1977; Drachensteigen, 1979; Sieben Häute: Ausgewählte Gedichte 1962–79, 1979; La Pagerie, 1980; Erdreich, 1982; Katzenleben, 1984; Hundert Gedichte, 1985; Landwege: Eine Auswahl 1980–85, 1985; Irrstern, 1986; Allerlei-Rauh, 1988; Schneewärme, 1989; Die Flut, 1990; Spreu, 1991; Schwingrasen, 1991; Sic! natur!, 1992; Erlkönigs Tochter, 1992; Das simple Leben, 1994; Winternachtigall, 1995; Ich Crusoe, 1995; Nachtsonnen, 1995; Bodenlos, 1996. *Honours:* Petrarca Prize, 1976; Austrian State Prize for Literature, 1981; Austrian Critics Prize, 1981; Gandersheim Literary Prize, 1983; Hölderlin Prize, Bad Homburg, 1984; Art Prize, Schleswig-Holstein, 1987; Author-in-Residence, City of Mainz, 1988; Heinrich-Heine-Gesellschaft Award, Düsseldorf, 1992; Peter Huchel Prize, 1993; Konrad Adenauer Foundation Literature Prize, 1993; Büchner Prize, 1996.

KISSINGER, Henry Alfred, MA, PhD; American academic, international consultant and fmr government official; *Chairman, Kissinger McLarty Associates*; b. 27 May 1923, Fuerth, Germany; s. of Louis Kissinger and Paula Stern; m. 1st Anne Fleisher 1949 (divorced 1964); one s. one d.; m. 2nd Nancy Maginnes 1974. *Education:* George Washington High School, Harvard Coll., Harvard Univ. *Career:* went to USA 1938; naturalized US Citizen 1943; US Army 1943–46; Dir Study Group on Nuclear Weapons and Foreign Policy, Council of Foreign Relations 1955–56; Dir Special Studies Project, Rockefeller Brothers Fund 1956–58; Consultant, Weapons System Evaluation Group, Joint Chiefs of Staff 1956–60, Nat. Security Council 1961–63, US Arms Control and Disarmament Agency 1961–69, Dept of State 1965–68 and to various other bodies; Faculty mem. Harvard Univ. 1954–69; Dept of Govt and Center for Int. Affairs; faculty Harvard Univ. Center for Int. Affairs 1960–69; Dir Harvard Int. Seminar 1951–69, Harvard Defense Studies Program 1958–69, Asst to Pres. of USA for Nat. Security Affairs 1969–75; Sec. of State 1973–77; prominent in American negotiations for the Viet Nam settlement of Jan. 1973 and in the negotiations for a Middle East ceasefire 1973, 1974; Trustee, Center for Strategic and Int. Studies 1977–; Chair. Kissinger Assocs Inc. (since 1999 Kissinger McLarty Assocs Inc.) 1982–; mem. Pres.'s Foreign Intelligence Advisory Bd 1984–90; Chair. Nat. Bipartisan Comm. on Cen. America 1983–84; fmr Chair. US Comm. investigating Sept. 11 attacks; Counsellor to J. P. Morgan Chase Bank and mem. of its Int. Advisory Council; Hon. Gov. Foreign Policy Asscn; Sr Fellow, Aspen Inst., syndicated columnist LA Times 1984–; Adviser to Bd of Dirs American Express, Forstmann Little & Co., Dir Emer. Freeport McMoran Copper and Gold Inc., Conti Group Cos Ltd, The TCW Group, US Olympic Cttee, Int. Rescue Cttee; Chair. American Int. Group, Int. Advisory Bd; mem. Exec. Cttee Trilateral Comm.; Chair. Eisenhower Exchange Fellowships; Chancellor The Coll. of William and Mary; Hon. Chair. World Cup USA 1994. *Publications:* Nuclear Weapons and Foreign Policy 1956, A World Restored: Castlereagh, Metternich and the

Restoration of Peace 1812–22 1957, The Necessity for Choice: Prospects of American Foreign Policy 1961, The Troubled Partnership: A Reappraisal of the Atlantic Alliance 1965, American Foreign Policy (3 essays) 1969, White House Years 1979, For the Record 1981, Years of Upheaval 1982, Observations: Selected Speeches and Essays 1982–84 1985, Diplomacy 1994, Years of Renewal 1999, Does America Need a Foreign Policy? 2001, Ending the Vietnam War 2003, Crisis 2003; and numerous articles on US foreign policy, international affairs and diplomatic history. *Honours:* Woodrow Wilson Book Prize 1958, American Inst. for Public Service Award 1973, Nobel Peace Prize 1973, American Legion Distinguished Service Medal 1974, Wateler Peace Prize 1974, Presidential Medal of Freedom 1977, Medal of Liberty 1986, Hon. KCMG 1995, and many other awards and prizes. *Address:* 350 Park Avenue, New York, NY 10022; Suite 400, 1800 K Street, NW, Washington, DC 20006, USA. *Telephone:* (212) 759-7919 (NY); (202) 822-8182 (DC). *Website:* www.kmaglobal.com.

KITAMURA, Kaoru; Japanese writer; b. 1950, Saitama. *Publications:* Yoru No Semi (Night Locust) 1990, Autumn Flower 2007, Sagi to Yuki (Herons and Snow) (Naoki Prize) 2009. *Address:* c/o Bungei Shunju Ltd, Bungei Shunju Building, 3-23 Kioi-cho, Chiyoda-ku, Tokyo 102-8008, Japan (office). *E-mail:* i-homu@bunshun.co.jp (office). *Website:* www.bunshun.co.jp (office).

KITAMURA, So; Japanese playwright; b. 5 July 1952, Ohtsu-shi; m. Konomi Kitamura; one d. *Career:* Leader, Project Navi 1986–2003; Dir Shiga Prefecture Center for Creation of Art for Citizens, Kusatsu 2006–07. *Films:* Tokiwa-so no seishun 1996, The Angel's Egg 2006. *Publications:* plays include: Hogiuta, So-Ko Gingatetsudo no yoru; novels include: Kaijin nijumenso den (Shincho sha), Seido no majin (Shincho sha), Kenji (Kadokawa). *Honours:* Kishida Gikyoku-sho 1984, Kinoleuni-ya engeki-sho 1989.

KITANO, Takeshi; Japanese film director, actor, comedian and screenwriter; b. 18 Jan. 1947, Tokyo. *Education:* Meiji Univ. *Films:* Makoto-chan (actor) 1980, Danpu wataridori (actor) 1981, Manon (actor) 1981, Sukkari... sono ki de! (actor) 1981, Merry Christmas, Mr. Lawrence (actor) 1983, Jukkai no mosquito (actor) 1983, Kanashii kibun de joke (actor) 1985, Yasha (actor) 1985, Komikku zasshi nanka iranai! (actor) 1986, Anego (actor) 1988, Sono otoko, kyobo ni tsuki (writer, director, actor) 1989, Hoshi tsugu mono (actor) 1990, 3-4x jugatsu (writer, director, actor) 1990, Ano natsu, ichiban shizukana umi (writer, director) 1991, Sakana kara daiokishin! (actor) 1992, Erotikkuna kankei (actor) 1992, Sonatine (writer, director, actor) 1993, Kyôso tanjô (writer, actor) 1993, Minnâ-yatteruka! (writer, director, actor) 1995, Johnny Mnemonic (actor) 1995, Gonin (actor) 1995, Kidzu ritan (writer, director) 1996, Hana-bi (writer, director, actor) (Venice Film Festival Golden Lion) 1997, Tokyo Eyes (actor) 1998, Kikujiro no natsu (writer, director, actor) 1999, Gohatto (actor) 1999, Brother (writer, director, actor) 2000, Batoru rowaiaru (Battle Royale) (actor) 2000, Dolls (writer, director) 2002, Asakusa Kid (writer) 2002, Battle Royale II (actor) 2003, Zatôichi (writer, director, actor) (Venice Film Festival Silver Lion) 2003, Izô: Kaosu mataha fujôri no kijin (actor) 2004, Chi to hone 2004, Takeshis' 2005, Gegege no Kitano 2007, Achilles and the Tortoise 2008, Outrage 2010. *Address:* Office Kitano Inc., Tokyo, Japan. *E-mail:* office@office-kitano.co.jp. *Website:* www.office-kitano.co.jp.

KITCHEN, Martin, BA, PhD, FRHistS, FRSC; British/Canadian academic and writer; *Professor Emeritus, Simon Fraser University*; b. 21 Dec. 1936, Nottingham, Notts., England; m. Bettina Franke. *Education:* Magdalen Coll., Oxford, Univ. of London. *Career:* Faculty mem. Simon Fraser Univ., Burnaby, BC 1966–76, Prof. of History 1976–. *Publications:* The German Officer Corps 1890–1914 1968, A Military History of Germany 1975, The Silent Dictatorship: The Politics of the German High Command Under Hindenburg and Ludendorff 1976, Fascism 1976, The Political Economy of Germany 1815–1914 1978, The Coming of Austrian Fascism 1980, Germany in the Age of Total War 1981, British Policy Towards the Soviet Union During the Second World War 1986, Europe Between the Wars 1988, The Origins of the Cold War in Comparative Perspective: American, British and Canadian Relations with the Soviet Union, 1941–48 1988, Nazi Germany at War 1994, The British Empire and Commonwealth: A Short History 1996, The Cambridge Illustrated History of Germany 1996, Kasper Hauser 2001, The German Offensives of 1918 2001, Nazi Germany: A Critical Introduction 2004, A History of Modern Germany 1800–2000 2006, The Third Reich: Charisma and Community 2007, Rommel's Desert War: Waging World War II in North Africa, 1941–1943 2009; contribs to professional journals. *Honours:* Moncado Prize, American Mil. Acad. 1978. *Address:* Department of History, Simon Fraser University, Burnaby, BC V5A 1S6 (office); 24B – 6128 Patterson Avenue, Burnaby, BC V5H 4P3, Canada (home). *Telephone:* (604) 291-3521 (office); (604) 433-0119 (home). *Fax:* (604) 291-5837 (office); (604) 433-0119 (home). *E-mail:* kitchen@sfu.ca (office).

KITSIKIS, Dimitri, MA, PhD, FRSC; Canadian/French/Greek poet, historian and academic; *Professor Emeritus, Department of History, University of Ottawa*; b. 2 June 1935, Athens, Greece; s. of the late Nikolas Kitsikis and Beata Petychakis; m. 1st Anne Hubbard 1955 (divorced 1973); one s. one d.; m. 2nd Ada Nikolaros 1975; one s. one d. *Education:* American Coll. Athens, Ecole des Roches, Normandy, Lycée Lakanal and Lycée Carnot, Paris and Sorbonne, Paris. *Career:* Research Assoc. Grad. Inst. of Int. Studies, Geneva 1960–62, Centre for Int. Relations, Nat. Foundation of Political Science, Paris 1962–65, Nat. Centre for Scientific Research, Paris 1965–70; Assoc. Prof. of History of Int. Relations, Univ. of Ottawa 1970–83, Prof. 1983–96, Prof. Emer. 1996–; Sr Research Scholar, Nat. Centre of Social Research, Athens 1972–74; Founder, Ed. Intermediate Region (journal) 1996–; adviser to Govts of Greece and Turkey; numerous visiting professorships, including at Univ. of Bogazici, Istanbul, Univ. of Bilkent, Ankara, Univ. of Gediz, Izmir, Sun Yat-Sen Univ., Guangzhou, and other appointments; Founder and Pres. Dimitri Kitsikis Public Foundation and Library, Athens 2008. *Publications include:* 37 books, including Propaganda and Pressure in International Politics 1963, The Role of the Experts at the Paris Peace Conference of 1919 1972, A Comparative History of Greece and Turkey in the 20th Century 1978, History of the Greek-Turkish Area 1981, The Ottoman Empire 1985, The Third Ideology and Orthodoxy 1990, The Old Calendarists 1995, Turkish-Greek Empire 1996, The Byzantine Model of Government 2001, J.-J. Rousseau and the French Origins of Fascism 2006, Bektashism and Alevism 2006, A Comparative History of Greece and China 2007, The Rise of National-Bolshevism in the Balkans 2008, National Bolshevism 2010; co-author of 40 other books; six vols of poetry, including Omphalos 1977, L'Orocc dans l'age de Kali 1985, Le Paradis Perdu sur les Barricades 1993, two vols of poetry and painting; hundreds of scholarly articles. *Honours:* First Prize in Poetry, Abdi Ipekçi Peace and Friendship Prize 1992. *Address:* Department of History, University of Ottawa, Ottawa, ON K1N 6N5 (office); 2104 Benjamin Avenue, Ottawa, ON K2A 1P4, Canada (home); Dimitri Kitsikis Foundation, Hagiou Ioannou Theologou 22, Zographou, Athens 15772 (office); 29 Travlantoni, Zographou, Athens 15772, Greece (home). *Telephone:* (613) 562-5735 (Ottawa) (office); (210) 778-0225 (Athens) (office); (613) 842-9175 (Ottawa) (home); (613) 729-9814 (Ottawa) (home); (210) 777-6937 (Athens) (home); (27310) 83096 (Pikoulianika, Greece) (home); 1-40-31-32-34 (Paris) (home). *Fax:* (613) 562-5995 (Ottawa) (office). *E-mail:* dimitri.kitsikis@uottawa.ca (office). *Website:* www.idkf.gr (office).

KITTREDGE, William Alfred, (Owen Rountree), BS, MFA; American academic and writer; *Professor Emeritus of English, University of Montana*; b. 14 Aug. 1932, Portland, OR; one s. one d. *Education:* Oregon State Univ., Univ. of Iowa. *Career:* Prof. Emeritus of English, Univ. of Montana. *Publications:* The Van Gogh Field 1977, We Are Not In This Together 1982, Owning It All 1984, Hole in the Sky 1992, Who Owns the West? 1996, Portable Western Reader (ed.) 1998, Balancing Water 2000, The Nature of Generosity 2000, Southwestern Homelands 2002, The Best Short Stories of William Kittredge 2002, The Willow Field 2006; contrib. to Time, Newsweek, New York Times, Wall Street Journal, Esquire, Outside, Paris Review. *Honours:* NEH Charles Frankel Award 1994, Los Angeles Times Lifetime Achievement Kirsch Award 2007, Lifetime Achievement Award, Western Literature Asscn 2008. *Literary Agent:* Amanda Urban, ICM, 40 West 57th Street, New York, NY 10019, USA. *Address:* Brookside Way, Missoula, MT 59802, USA. *Telephone:* (406) 549-6605 (home). *E-mail:* Kittredgeb@aol.com (home).

KIZAKI, Satoko (see Harada, Masako)

KIZER, Carolyn Ashley, BA; American writer; b. 10 Dec. 1925, Spokane, Wash.; d. of Benjamin Kizer and M. Kizer (née Ashley); m. 1st Stimson Bullitt 1948 (divorced); one s. two d.; m. 2nd John Woodbridge 1975. *Education:* Sarah Lawrence Coll., Columbia Univ., New York and Univ. of Washington. *Career:* Writer-in-Residence, Ohio Univ. 1974, Center Coll., Ky 1979, Eastern Washington Univ. 1980, Bucknell Univ. 1982, State Univ. of New York 1982; Prof. of Poetry, Univ. of Maryland 1976–77, Univ. of Cincinnati 1981, Univ. of Louisville 1982, Columbia Univ. 1982, Stanford Univ. 1986; Sr Fellow, Princeton Univ. 1986; Visiting Prof., Univ. of Arizona 1989, 1990, Univ. of California, Davis 1991; Cole Royalty Chair., Univ. of Alabama 1995; mem. PEN, Poetry Soc. of America, Acad. of American Poets, Amnesty International. *Publications include:* The Ungrateful Garden 1961, Knock Upon Silence 1965, Midnight Was My Cry 1971, Mermaids in the Basement: Poems for Women 1984, Yin: New Poems (Pulitzer Prize for Poetry 1985) 1984, The Nearness of You (Theodore Roethke Prize 1988) 1987, The Essential Clare (ed) 1993, On Poems and Poets 1994, Picking and Choosing: Prose on Prose 1995, 100 Great Poems by Women (ed) 1995, Cool, Calm and Collected 2003. *Honours:* Hon. DLitt (Whitman Coll.) 1986, (St Andrew's) 1989, (Mills) 1990; American Acad. and Inst. of Arts and Letters Award 1985, Gov.'s Award, State of Washington 1965, 1985, 1995, 1998, Theodore Roethke Memorial Poetry Award 1988, Frost Medal, John Masefield Memorial Award. *Address:* 19772 Eighth Street East, Sonoma, CA 95476-3849, USA (home). *Telephone:* (707) 996-7436 (home).

KJAERSTAD, Jan; Norwegian writer and essayist; b. 6 March 1953, Oslo; s. of Leif Asbjørn Kjærstad and Ragnhild Jensen; m. Astrid Nøstvik 1988 (divorced), two d.; pnr Terese Moe Leiner, two d. *Education:* MF Norwegian School of Theology, Univ. of Oslo. *Career:* Ed. literary journal Vinduet 1985–89; co-creator literary journal BØK. *Publications:* novels: Speil: leseserie fra det 20. århundre 1982, Homo Falsus, eller, det perfekte mord 1984, Det store eventyret 1987, Rand 1990, Forføreren (Aschehoug Prize) (trans. as The Seducer) 1993, Erobreren (Henrik Steffens Prize, Germany 1998) (trans. as The Conqueror) 1996, Oppdageren (Dobloug Prize 2000, Nordic Council Literature Prize 2001) (trans. as The Discoverer) 1999, Tegn til kjærlighet 2002, Kongen av Europa 2005, Jeg er brødrene Walker 2008; other: Kloden dreier stille rundt (short stories) 1980, Jakten på de skjulte vaffelhjertene (juvenile) 1989, Menneskets matrise: litteratur i 80-årene (essays) 1989, Hos Sheherasad, fantasiens dronning (juvenile) 1995, Menneskets felt (essays) 1997; contrib. to Aftenposten. *Address:* c/o W.Nygaard, H. Aschehoug & Co., PO Box 363 Sentrum, N-0102, Oslo, Norway (office). *E-mail:* epost@aschehoug.no (office). *Website:* www.aschehoug.no (office).

KLAM, Matthew; American writer; b. 1964. *Education:* Univ. of New Hampshire, Hollins Coll., Va. *Career:* teacher of creative writing, St Albans School, American Univ., Stockholm Univ., Sweden. *Publications:* Sam the Cat and other stories 2000; contrib. to The New Yorker, Harpers, Allure, USA Weekend, Nerve, The Washington Post Magazine, New York Times Magazine. *Honours:* Robert Bingham/PEN Award, Nat. Endowment for the Arts grant, Whiting Writer's Award, O'Henry Award. *Address:* c/o Random House Inc., 1745 Broadway, New York, NY 10019, USA (office). *E-mail:* MattKlam@gmail.com (home). *Website:* www.matthewklam.com.

KLAPPERT, Peter, BA, MA, MFA; American academic, poet and writer; *Professor Emeritus, George Mason University*; b. 14 Nov. 1942, Rockville Center, Nassau Co., NY; s. of Herman E. Klappert, Jr and Grace Barbara Klappert. *Education:* Cornell Univ., Univ. of Iowa. *Career:* Instructor, Rollins Coll. 1968–71; Briggs-Copeland Lecturer, Harvard Univ. 1971–74; Visiting Lecturer, New Coll. 1972; Writer-in-Residence, Coll. of William and Mary 1976–77, Asst Prof. 1977–78; Asst Prof., George Mason Univ. 1978–81, Dir Grad. Writing Program 1979–81, 1985–88, Assoc. Prof. 1981–91, Prof. 1991–2007, Prof. Emer. 2007–, Dir MFA Degree Program in Poetry 1995–98; mem. Acad. of American Poets, Associated Writing Programs, Asscn of Literary Scholars and Critics, PEN, Poetry Soc. of America, Writers' Center, Bethesda, Md. *Publications:* On a Beach in Southern Connecticut 1966, Lugging Vegetables to Nantucket 1971, Circular Stairs, Distress in the Mirrors 1975, 2008, Non Sequitur O'Connor 1977, The Idiot Princess of the Last Dynasty 1984, 2010, '52 Pick-Up: Scenes From the Conspiracy, A Documentary 1984, Chokecherries: New and Selected Poems 1966–1999 2000; contribs: many anthologies, books, journals, and magazines. *Honours:* Yale Series of Younger Poets Prize 1970, Yaddo Resident Fellowships 1972, 1973, 1975, 1981, MacDowell Colony Resident Fellowships 1973, 1975, Nat. Endowment for the Arts Fellowships 1973, 1979, Lucille Medwick Award, Poetry Soc. of America 1977, Virginia Center for the Creative Arts Resident Fellowships 1978, 1979, 1981, 1983, 1984, 1987, 1993, 1995, Millay Colony for the Arts Resident Fellowship 1981, Ingram Merrill Foundation Grant 1983, Klappert-Ai Poetry Award established in his honour by Gwendolyn Brooks, George Mason Univ. 1987, Poet-Scholar, American Library Asscn-Nat. Endowment for the Humanities Voices and Visions Project 1988. *Address:* 911 Silver Palm Way, Apollo Beach, FL 33572, USA. *Telephone:* (202) 483-3822; (813) 645-5601.

KLASS, Perri Elizabeth, AB, MD; American writer, paediatrician and academic; *Professor of Journalism and Pediatrics, New York University*; b. 1958, Trinidad; d. of Morton Klass and Sheila Klass; two s. one d. *Education:* Radcliffe Coll., Harvard Univ., Harvard Medical School. *Career:* mem. American Acad. of Pediatrics, Academic Pediatrics Asscn, PEN American Centre, Barbara Pym Soc.; currently Prof. of Journalism and Pediatrics, New York Univ.; Nat. Medical Dir, Reach Out and Read. *Publications:* Recombinations (novel) 1985, I Am Having An Adventure (short stories) 1986, A Not Entirely Benign Procedure (essays) 1987, Other Women's Children (novel) 1990, Baby Doctor (essays) 1992, Love and Modern Medicine (short stories) 2001, Quirky Kids: Understanding and Helping Your Child Who Doesn't Fit In (non-fiction with Eileen Costello) 2003, Two Sweaters for My Father (essays) 2004, The Mystery of Breathing (novel) 2004, Every Mother is a Daughter (non-fiction with Sheila Solomon Klass) 2006, Treatment Kind and Fair: Letters to a Young Doctor (essays) 2007, The Mercy Rule (novel) 2008; contribs to New York Times, New England Journal of Medicine, Washington Post, Massachusetts Medicine, Discover, Vogue, Glamour, Esquire, Boston Globe Magazine, Mademoiselle, TriQuarterly, North American Review, Gourmet, Diversion, Knitters Magazine. *Honours:* Hon. MD (Univ. of South Florida) 2010; O. Henry Award 1983, 1984, 1991, 1992, 1995, Honors Award, New England chapter, American Medical Writers Asscn 1995, James Beard Journalism Award 2000, Women's Nat. Book Asscn Award 2006, American Acad. of Pediatrics Educ. Award 2007. *Literary Agent:* c/o Elaine Markson Agency, 44 Greenwich Avenue, New York, NY 10011, USA. *Address:* Reach Out and Read National Center, 56 Roland Street, Suite 100, Boston, MA 02129-1243, USA (office). *Telephone:* (617) 455-0600 (office). *E-mail:* info@reachoutandread.org (office). *Website:* www.reachoutandread.org (office); journalism.nyu.edu (office); www.perriklass.com.

KLEIN, Étienne, DèsSc, PhD; French physicist and writer; *Physicist, Commissariat à l'énergie atomique*; b. 1 April 1958, Paris; two c. *Education:* Ecole centrale, Univ. de Paris VII. *Career:* physicist CEA 1983–, Dir Sciences de la Matière, teacher Ecole Centrale; worked in Proton Accelerator Study Group CERN 1992–93. *Publications:* Conversations avec le Sphinx: Les paradoxes en physique 1991, Regards sur la matière: des quanta et des choses 1993, Le Temps et sa flèche (with Michel Spiro) 1994, Prédiction et probabilité 1998, La Quête de l'unité (with Marc Lachièze-Rey) 2000, L'Atome au pied du mur et autres nouvelles 2000, L'Unité de la physique 2000, Le Temps existe-t-il? 2002, Les Tactiques de Chronos 2003, La Science nous menace-t-elle? 2003, Quand la science a dit c'est bizarre! 2003, Petit voyage dans le monde des quantas (Prix Jean Rostand) 2004, Il était sept fois la Révolution: Albert Einstein et les autres... 2005, Les Atomes de l'univers 2005, Le Facteur temps ne sonne jamais deux fois 2007, Les secrets de la matière 2008, Galilée et les Indiens 2008, Pourquoi je suis devenu chercheur scientifique 2009. *Honours:* Officer, Ordre des Palmes Académiques; Prix Jean Perrin 1997, Prix Grammaticakis-Neumann 2000. *Address:* c/o CEA/Saclay (Essonne), 91191 Gif-sur-Yvette Cédex, France (office). *Telephone:* 1-69-08-74-12 (office); 1-45-65-09-24 (home). *E-mail:* etienne.klein@cea.fr (office). *Website:* www.cea.fr.

KLEIN, Joseph (Joe), AB; American journalist and writer; b. 7 Sept. 1946, New York; m. Janet Eklund 1967 (divorced 1975); two s. *Education:* Univ. of Pennsylvania. *Career:* reporter, Beverly/Peabody Times, Mass 1969–72, WGBH-TV, Boston 1972; News Ed., The Real Paper, Boston 1972–74; Contributing Ed., Rolling Stone Magazine 1975–80, Washington Bureau Chief 1975–77; Political Columnist, New York Magazine 1987–92; Senior Ed. Newsweek Magazine 1992–96, Contributing Ed. 1996–2003; columnist, New Yorker Magazine 1996–, Time Magazine 2003–. *Publications:* Woody Guthrie: A Life 1980, Payback: Five Marines After Vietnam 1984, Primary Colors: A Novel of Politics (published anonymously) 1996, The Running Mate 2000, The Natural (non-fiction) 2001, Politics Lost 2006. *Honours:* Robert Kennedy Journalism Award 1973, Washington Monthly Journalism Award 1989, National Headliner Award 1994; Hon. DLitt (Franklin and Marshall Coll., Lancaster, PA) 1990. *Address:* Time Magazine, Time and Life Building, Rockefeller Center, 1271 Avenue of the America, New York, NY 10020-1393, USA (office). *Telephone:* (212) 522-1212 (office). *Fax:* (212) 522-0023 (office). *E-mail:* letters@time.com (office). *Website:* www.time.com (office).

KLEIN, Naomi; Canadian writer, journalist and social critic; b. 1970, Montréal. *Career:* syndicated columnist for The Globe and Mail, Canada and The Guardian, UK; contrib. to numerous publs including The Nation, The Guardian, New Statesman, Newsweek International, New York Times, Village Voice and Ms. Magazine; campaigner on issues of devt econs, corp. accountability and consumer affairs; has travelled throughout N America, Asia, Latin America and Europe giving lectures and workshops on corp. branding and econ. globalization 1996–; frequent media commentator; guest lecturer at Harvard Univ., Yale Univ., McGill Univ. and New York Univ. *Publication:* No Logo: Taking Aim at the Brand Bullies (translated into 22 languages) 2000, The Shock Doctrine: The Rise of Disaster Capitalism (Warwick Prize for Writing 2009) 2007. *Honours:* Canadian Nat. Business Book Award 2001, Le Prix Médiations, France 2001, Ms. Magazine's Women of the Year Award 2001. *Address:* c/o Random House of Canada Ltd., 1 Toronto Street, Unit 300, Toronto, ON M5C 2V6, Canada (office). *E-mail:* admin@nologo.org (office). *Website:* www.nologo.org (office).

KLEIN, Richard; American writer; b. 1941, USA. *Publications:* Cigarettes are Sublime, 1993; Eat Fat, 1996; Pop Surrealism (non-fiction, with Dominique Nahas), 1998; Jewelry Talks, 2001.

KLEIN, Robin; Australian writer; b. 28 Feb. 1936, Kempsey, NSW; d. of Lesley Macquarie and Mary (née Cleaver) McMaugh; m. Karl Klein 1956 (divorced 1980); two s. two d. *Education:* Newcastle Girls' High School, NSW. *Career:* has written numerous children's books. *Publications* include: The Giraffe in Pepperell Street 1978, Honoured Guest 1979, Thing (Jr Book of the Year, Children's Book Council of Australia 1983) 1982, Sprung! 1982, Junk Castle 1983, Penny Pollard's Diary 1983, Oodoolay 1983, Hating Alison Ashley (Special Award, W Australian Young Readers' Book Award, Winner Sr Category, KOALA Awards 1987) 1984, Thalia the Failure 1984, Thingnapped 1984, Brock and the Dragon 1984, Penny Pollard's Letters 1984, Ratbags and Rascals 1984, People Might Hear You 1984, Seeing Things 1984, Hating Alison Ashley 1985, Battlers 1985, Halfway Across the Country and Turn Left 1985, The Enemies 1985, Annabel's Ghost 1985, Snakes and Ladders 1985, Boss of the Pool 1986, The Princess Who Hated It 1986, Games 1986, Penny Pollard in Print 1986, Halfway Across the Galaxy and Turn Left 1986, The Lonely Hearts Club 1987, Robin Klein's Crookbook 1987, Get Lost 1987, The Last Pirate 1987, Christmas 1987, I Shot an Arrow 1987, Birk the Berserker 1987, Stanley's Smile 1988, Annabel's Party 1988, Irritating Irma 1988, The Kidnapping of Clarissa Montgomery 1988, Jane's Mansion 1988, Laurie Loved Me Best 1988, Penny Pollard's Passport 1988, Dear Robin 1988, Against the Odds 1989, The Ghost in Abigail Terrace 1989, Came Back to Show You I Could Fly (Human Rights Award for Literature 1989, Australian Children's Book of the Year Award, Older Readers 1990, named a White Raven Book at Bologna Children's Book Fair 1990) (filmed as Say A Little Prayer 1993) 1989, Penny Pollard's Guide to Modern Manners 1989, Tearaways 1990, Boris And Borsch (Honour Book, Australian Children's Book Council Awards 1991) 1990, The Listmaker 1990 (South Australian Festival Award for Literature 1990), All in the Blue Unclouded Weather 1991, Dresses of Red and Gold 1992, Seeing Things 1993, Turn Right for Zyrgow 1994, The Sky in Silver Lace 1995. *Honours:* Dr hc (Univ. of Newcastle) 2004; Dromkeen Medal 1991. *Address:* c/o Penguin Group (Australia), PO Box 701, Hawthorn, Vic. 3124, Australia (office). *Website:* www.penguin.com.au (office).

KLEIN, Theodore Eibon Donald, AB, MFA; American writer and editor; b. 15 July 1947, New York, NY. *Education:* Brown University, Columbia University. *Career:* Ed.-in-Chief, Brown Daily Herald, 1968; Twilight Zone magazine, 1981–85, Crime Beat magazine, 1991–93; mem. Arthur Machen Society. *Publications:* The Ceremonies (novel), 1984; Dark Gods (story collection), 1985. Contributions: New York Times; New York Daily News; Washington Post Book World; Film column, Night Cry Magazine; Writer's Digest. *Honours:* British Fantasy Society Award for Best Novel 1985, World Fantasy Award for Best Novella 1986.

KLEIN, Zachary; American writer; b. 6 July 1948, New Brunswick, NJ; two s. *Education:* Hillel Acad., Jewish Educational Centre, Mirrer Yeshia and University of Wisconsin. *Publications:* Still Among the Living, 1990; Two Way Toll, 1991; No Saving Grace, 1994. *Honours:* Notable Book of 1990, New York Times; Ed.'s Choice, Drood Review.

KLEINZAHLER, August Benjamin, BA; American poet and writer; b. 10 Dec. 1949, Jersey City, NJ; s. of Marvin Kleinzahler and Isabel Reznitzky Kleinzahler. *Education:* Univ. of Wisconsin, Madison, Univ. of Victoria. *Career:* Visiting Holloway Lecturer, Univ. of California, Berkeley 1987; Visiting Writer on Grad. Programs, Brown Univ. 1996, Univ. of Iowa 1997, Univ. of Texas 1999, 2006, Stanford Univ. 2000. *Publications:* A Calendar of Airs 1978, News and Weather: Seven Canadian Poets (ed.) 1982, Storm Over Hackensack 1985, On Johnny's Time 1988, Earthquake Weather 1989, Red Sauce, Whiskey and Snow 1995, Live from the Hong Kong Nile Club: Poems, 1975–1990 2000, The Strange Hours Travelers Keep (Griffin Int. Poetry Prize) 2004, Cutty, One Rock (prose) 2004, Sleeping It Off in Rapid City: Poems New and Selected (Nat. Book Critics Circle Award in Poetry) 2008, Music: I-LXXVII 2009; contrib. to newspapers and magazines. *Honours:* Gen. Electric Award for Younger Writers 1983, Bay Area Book Reviewers Award 1985, Guggenheim Fellowship 1989, Lila Wallace-Reader's Digest Writers' Awards 1991–94, Award in Literature American Acad. of Arts and Letters 1997, Commonwealth Club of Calif. Gold Medal for Poetry 2004, 2008, Griffin Int. Poetry Prize 2004, Lannan Literary Award for Poetry 2008, Nat. Book Critics' Poetry Award 2008.

KLIKOVAC, Igor; Bosnia and Herzegovina poet and editor; b. 16 May 1970. *Education:* University of Sarajevo. *Career:* Ed., Literary Review, Sarajevo, 1991–92; Ed., Stone Soup Magazine, London, 1995–. *Publications:* Last Days of Peking (poems), 1996. *Contributions:* Literary Review; Echo; Bridge; Transitions; Stone Soup; New Iowa Review. *Address:* 37 Chesterfield Road, London W4 3HQ, England.

KLÍMA, Ivan, MA; Czech author and dramatist; b. 14 Sept. 1931, Prague; s. of Vilém Klíma and Marta Klíma; m. Helena Malá-Klímová 1958; one s. one d. *Education:* Charles Univ., Prague. *Career:* Ed. Československy spisovatel (publishing house) 1958–63; Ed. Literární noviny 1963–67, Literární Listy 1968, Listy 1968–69; Visiting Prof., Univ. of Michigan, Ann Arbor, USA 1969–70, Univ. of California, Berkeley, USA 1998; freelance author publishing abroad 1970–89; columnist, Lidove Noviny newspaper; mem. Council, Czech Writers 1989–, Ed.'s Council, Lidové noviny 1996–97; Exec. Pres. Czech PEN Centre 1990–93, Deputy Pres. 1993–. *Publications:* Ship Named Hope 1968, A Summer Affair 1972, My Merry Mornings (short stories) 1979, My First Loves (short stories) 1985, Love and Garbage 1987, Judge on Trial 1987, My Golden Trades (short stories) 1992, The Island of Dead Kings 1992, The Spirit of Prague (essays) 1994, Waiting for the Dark, Waiting for the Light 1996, The Ultimate Intimacy (novel) 1997, No Saints or Angels 1999, Between Security and Insecurity: Prospects for Tomorrow 2000, Lovers for a Day: New and Collected Stories on Love 2000, Karel Capek: Life and Work 2002, The Premier and the Angel (in Czech) 2004; plays: The Castle 1964, The Master 1967, The Sweetshop Myriam 1968, President and the Angel, Klara and Two Men 1968, Bridegroom for Marcela 1968, The Games 1975, Kafka and Felice 1986, My Crazy Century 2009; contribs to magazines. *Honours:* Hostovský Award, New York 1985, George Theiner Prize (UK) 1993, Franz Kafka Prize 2002, Medal for Outstanding Service to the Czech Repub. 2002, Karel Capek Prize 2010. *Address:* Na Dubině 5, 14700 Prague 4, Czech Republic. *Telephone:* 73-7788981 (mobile).

KLINKOWITZ, Jerome, BA, MA, PhD; American writer and academic; *Professor of English, University of Northern Iowa;* b. 24 Dec. 1943, Milwaukee, Wis.; m. 1st Elaine Ptaszynski 1966; m. 2nd Julie Huffman 1978; one s. one d. *Education:* Marquette Univ., Univ. of Wisconsin. *Career:* Asst Prof., Northern Illinois Univ. 1969–72; Assoc. Prof., Univ. of Northern Iowa 1972–75, Prof. of English 1975–, Univ. Distinguished Scholar 1985–; Fellow, Univ. of Wisconsin 1968–69; mem. PEN American Center, MLA, Authors' Guild, Eighth Air Force Historical Soc., Frank Lloyd Wright Asscn, Walter Burley Griffin Soc. *Publications:* Literary Disruptions 1975, The Life of Fiction 1977, The American 1960s 1980, The Practice of Fiction in America 1980, Kurt Vonnegut 1982, Peter Handke and the Postmodern Transformation 1983, The Self Apparent Word 1984, Literary Subversions 1985, The New American Novel of Manners 1986, Rosenberg/Barthes/Hassan: The Postmodern Habit of Thought 1988, Short Season and Other Stories 1988, Their Finest Hours: Narratives of the RAF and Luftwaffe in World War II 1989, Slaughterhouse-Five: Reinventing the Novel and the World 1990, Listen: Gerry Mulligan/An Aural Narrative in Jazz 1991, Donald Barthelme: An Exhibition 1991, Writing Baseball 1991, Structuring the Void 1992, Basepaths 1995, Yanks Over Europe 1996, Here at Ogallala State U. 1997, Keeping Literary Company 1998, Vonnegut in Fact 1998, Owning a Piece of the Minors 1999, With the Tigers Over China 1999, You've Got To Be Carefully Taught: Relearning and Relearning Literature 2001, The Vonnegut Effect 2004, Pacific Skies 2004, The Enchanted Quest of Dana and Ginger Lamb 2006, Kurt Vonnegut's America 2009; contrib. of more than 250 essays to Partisan Review, New Republic, Nation, American Literature; short stories to North American Review, Chicago Tribune, San Francisco Chronicle. *Honours:* PEN Syndicated Fiction Prizes 1984, 1985. *Address:* Department of English, University of Northern Iowa, Cedar Falls, IA 50614-0502, USA (office). *Telephone:* (319) 273-2571 (office). *Fax:* (319) 273-5807 (office). *Website:* www.uni.edu/english (office).

KLUBACK, William, AB, AM, PhD; American writer and academic; b. 6 Nov. 1927, New York, NY. *Education:* George Washington University, Columbia University, Hebrew University, Jerusalem. *Publications:* Paul Valéry, 6 vols, 1987–97; Juan Ramon Jiménez, 1995; Benjamin Fondane, 1996; Emil Cioran, 1997; Léopold Sédar Senghor, 1997. *Contributions:* Midstream; Shofar; Archives de Philosophie.

KLUGE, Paul Frederick, BA, MA, PhD; American writer; *Writer-in-Residence, Kenyon College;* b. 24 Jan. 1942, Berkeley Heights, NJ; s. of Walter Kluge and Maria Kluge; m. Pamela Hollie 1977. *Education:* Kenyon Coll., Univ. of Chicago. *Career:* Visiting Prof., Kenyon Coll. 1987–97, Writer-in-Residence 1997–; Contributing Ed., National Geographic Traveler 2000–. *Films:* Eddie and The Cruisers (based on author's second novel), Dog Day Afternoon (based on article in LIFE magazine). *Publications:* The Day That I Die 1976, Eddie and the Cruisers 1980, Season for War 1984, MacArthur's Ghost 1987, The Edge of Paradise: America in Micronesia 1991, Alma Mater: A College Homecoming 1993, Biggest Elvis 1996, Final Exam 2005, Gone Tomorrow 2008, A Call from Jersey 2010; contrib. to periodicals. *Honours:* Fulbright Fellowship, Univ. of Bucharest, Romania 2006. *Address:* Department of English, Kenyon College, Finn House 104, Gambler, OH 43022, USA (office). *Telephone:* (740) 427-5407 (office). *E-mail:* klugef@kenyon.edu (office). *Website:* www.pfkluge.com.

KLUGER, Steve; American writer and dramatist; b. 24 June 1952, Baltimore, MD. *Education:* University of Southern California. *Publications:* Changing Pitches, 1984; Lawyers Say the Darndest Things, 1990; Last Days of Summer, 1998. Stage Plays: Cafe 50s, 1988–89; James Dean Slept Here, 1989; Pilots of the Purple Twilight, 1989; Jukebox Saturday Night, 1990; Yank: World War II From The Guys Who Brought You Victory, 1990; Bullpen, 1990; Bye Bye Brooklyn, 1997. Films: Once Upon a Crime, 1992; Yankee Doodle Boys, 1996; Bye Bye Brooklyn, 1997; Almost Like Being in Love, 1997. *Contributions:* Chicago Tribune; Los Angeles Times; Sports Illustrated; Inside Sports; Diversion; Playboy; Science Digest.

KNAAK, Richard Allen, BA; American author; b. 28 May 1961, Chicago, IL. *Education:* University of Illinois. *Career:* mem. SFWA. *Publications:* The Legend of Huma, 1988; Firedrake, 1989; Ice Dragon, 1989; Kaz the Minotaur, 1990; Wolfhelm, 1990; Shadow Steed, 1990; The Shrouded Realm, 1991; Children of the Drake, 1991; Dragon Tome, 1992; The Crystal Dragon, 1993; King of the Grey, 1993; The Dragon Crown, 1994; Frostwing, 1995.

KNAUSGÅRD, Karl Ove; Norwegian author; b. 6 Dec. 1968, Oslo; m.; three c. *Education:* Univ. of Bergen. *Career:* consultant, new Norwegian trans. of The Bible; wrote six autobiographical novels under series title Min kamp (My Struggle) 2009–11. *Publications include:* novels Ute av verden (Out of the World) (Norwegian Critics Prize for Literature 2004) 1998, En tid for alt (A Time to Every Purpose Under Heaven) 2004, Min kamp 1 (My Struggle Vol. 1) (Brage Prize 2009) 2009, Min kamp 2 (My Struggle Vol. 2) 2009, Min kamp 3 (My Struggle Vol. 3) 2009, Min kamp 4 (My Struggle Vol. 4) 2010, Min kamp 5 (My Struggle Vol. 5) 2010, Min kamp 6 (My Struggle Vol. 6) 2011. *Honours:* Southern Norway Literature Prize 2005, 2010, NRK P2 Listeners' Prize 2009, Morgenbladet Book of the Year Prize 2010, Gyldendal Prize 2011. *Address:* c/o Aschehoug Agency, Sehesteds gate 3, PO Box 363, Sentrum, 0102 Oslo, Norway. *E-mail:* epost@aschehougagency.no. *Website:* www.aschehougagency.no. *Address:* c/o Forlaget Oktober AS, PO Box 6848, St. Olavs plass, 0130 Oslo, Norway (office). *Telephone:* (23) 35-46-20 (office). *Fax:* (23) 35-46-21 (office). *E-mail:* oktober@oktober.no (office). *Website:* oktober.no/nor/In-English (office).

KNEALE, Matthew Nicholas Kerr, BA; British writer; b. 24 Nov. 1960, London, England; m. Shannon Russell 2000. *Education:* Magdalen Coll., Oxford. *Publications:* Whore Banquets 1987, Inside Rose's Kingdom 1989, Sweet Thames 1992, English Passengers 2000, Small Crimes in an Age of Abundance 2005, When We Were Romans 2007. *Honours:* Somerset Maugham Award 1988, John Llewellyn Rhys Prize 1993, Whitbread Book of the Year 2000, Prix Relay du roman d'évasion 2002. *Literary Agent:* Rogers, Coleridge & White Ltd, 20 Powis Mews, London, W11 1JN, England.

KNECHT, Robert Jean, MA, DLitt, FRHistS; British academic and writer; *Professor of French History Emeritus, University of Birmingham;* b. 20 Sept. 1926, London, England; m. 1st Sonia Hodge 1956 (died 1984); m. 2nd Maureen White 1986. *Education:* Univ. of London. *Career:* Asst Lecturer 1956–59, Lecturer 1959–68, Sr Lecturer in Modern History 1969–78, Reader 1978–85, Prof. of French History 1985–92, Prof. Emeritus and Hon. Sr Research Fellow 1992–, Univ. of Birmingham; Dir d'études associe, École des Hautes Études en Sciences Sociales, Paris 1994; mem. Société de l'Histoire de France, Soc. for Renaissance Studies (chair. 1989–92), Soc. for the Study of French History (co-founder 1987, chair. 1995–98). *Publications:* The Voyage of Sir Nicholas Carewe to the Emperor Charles V in the Year 1529 (ed.) 1959, Francis I and Absolute Monarchy 1969, Renaissance and Reformation 1969, The Fronde 1975, Francis I 1982, revised edn as Renaissance Warrior and Patron: The Reign of Francis I 1994, French Renaissance Monarchy: Francis I and Henry II 1984, The French Wars of Religion 1559–1598 1989, Richelieu 1991, The Rise and Fall of Renaissance France 1996, Catherine de'Medici 1998, Un Prince de la Renaissance: François 1er et son royaume 1998, The French Civil Wars 2000, The French Religious Wars 2002, Catherine de Médicis: pouvoir royal, amour maternel 2003, The Valois Kings of France 1328–1589 2004; contrib. to reference works, scholarly books and professional journals. *Honours:* Chevalier, Ordre des Palmes Académiques. *Address:* 79 Reddings Road, Moseley, Birmingham, B13 8LP, England. *Telephone:* (121) 449-1916 (home).

KNIGHT, Andrew Stephen Bower, MA; British editor and business executive; *Chairman, J. Rothschild Capital Management;* b. 1 Nov. 1939, s. of M. W. B. Knight and S. E. F. Knight; m. 1st Victoria Catherine Brittain 1966 (divorced); one s.; m. 2nd Begum Sabiha Rumani Malik 1975 (divorced 1991); two d.; m. 3rd Marita Georgina Phillips Crawley 2006. *Education:* Ampleforth Coll., York, Balliol Coll., Oxford. *Career:* Ed. The Economist 1974–86; Chief Exec. Daily Telegraph 1986–89, Ed.-in-Chief 1987–89; Chair. News Int. PLC 1990–94; Chair. Ballet Rambert 1984–87; Chair. Times Newspaper Holdings 1990–94; Dir News Corpn 1991–; Dir Rothschild Investment Trust CP 1996–2008, Chair. J. Rothschild Capital Management 2008–; Chair. Shipston Home Nursing 1996–2006; Chair. Jerwood Charity 2003–06; mem. Advisory Bd Center for Econ. Policy Research, Stanford Univ., USA 1981–; Gov. mem. Council of Man. Ditchley Foundation 1982–; Founder-Trustee Spinal Muscular Atrophy Trust; now farms in Warwicks. and Dannevirke, NZ. *Address:* J. Rothschild Capital Management Ltd, 27 St James's Place, London, SW1A 1NR (office); Compton Scorpion Manor, Shipston-on-Stour, Warwicks., CV36 4PJ, England (home).

KNIGHT, Arthur Winfield, AA, BA, MA; American academic (retd), writer, poet and film critic; b. 29 Dec. 1937, San Francisco; m. Kit Duell 1976; one d. *Education:* Santa Rosa Junior Coll., San Francisco State Univ. *Career:* Prof. of English, California Univ. of Pennsylvania 1966–93; film critic, Russian River News, Guerneville, Calif. 1991–92, Anderson Valley Advertiser, Boonville, Calif. 1992–2006, Potpourri, Prairie Village, Kan. 1993–95; part-time Prof., Univ. of San Francisco 1995–2000, Univ. of California, Davis 2004–05; ran writing workshop Western Nevada Community Coll., Yerington Sept. 2006; mem. Western Writers of America. *Publications include:* A Marriage of Poets (with Kit Knight) 1984, King of the Beatniks 1986, The Beat Vision (co-ed.) 1987, Wanted! 1988, Basically Tender 1991, Cowboy Poems (aka Outlaws, Lawmen and Bad Women) 1993, Tell Me An Erotic Story 1993, The Darkness Starts Up Where You Stand 1996, The Secret Life of Jesse James 1996, The Cruelest Month 1997, Johnnie D. (novel) 2000, Blue Skies Falling (novel) 2001, James Dean's Diaries (novel) 2005; contrib. to reviews, quarterlies and journals. *Honours:* First Place Joycean Lively Arts Guild Poetry Competition 1982. *Literary Agent:* c/o Nat Sobel, Sobel Weber Associates Inc, 146 East 19th Street, New York, NY 10003-2404, USA. *Address:* 303 Sherry Way, Yerington, NV 89447, USA (home). *Telephone:* (775) 463-4773 (home).

KNIGHT, Bernard, CBE, MB, BCh, MD, MRCP, FRCPath; British academic and writer; *Professor Emeritus of Forensic Pathology, Cardiff University;* b. 3 May 1931, Cardiff, Wales; s. of Harold Knight and Doris Lawes; m. Jean Gwenllian Knight. *Education:* Univ. of Wales, Gray's Inn, London, Diploma in Medical Jurisprudence (Pathology). *Career:* Lecturer in Forensic Medicine, Univ. of London 1959–62; Medical Ed. Medicine, Science and the Law 1960–63; Lecturer, Coll. of Medicine, Univ. of Wales 1962–65, Sr Lecturer 1965–76, Reader to Prof. and Consultant in Forensic Pathology 1976–96, Prof. Emer. 1996–; Sr Lecturer in Forensic Pathology, Univ. of Newcastle 1965–68; Home Office Pathologist 1965–98; Man. Ed. 1992–96, Pathology Ed. 1980–92, Forensic Science International; writer of fiction, non-fiction, biography, radio and TV scripts 1963–; mem. Crime Writers Asscn (CWA), The Medieval Murderers' Promotion Group. *Radio:* numerous plays for BBC Radio. *Television:* scripts and technical advice for several dramas and documentaries. *Publications:* fiction: The Lately Deceased 1963, Thread of Evidence 1965, Mistress Murder 1968, Policeman's Progress 1969, Tiger at Bay 1970, Murder, Suicide or Accident 1971, Deg Y Dragwyddoldeb 1972, The Sanctuary Seeker 1998, The Poisoned Chalice 1998, Crowner's Quest 1998, The Awful Secret 1999, The Tinner's Corpse 2000, The Grim Reaper 2001, Fear in the Forest 2003, Brennan 2003, The Witch Hunter 2004, Figure of Hate 2005, The Tainted Relic (co-author) 2005, The Elixir of Death 2006, The Sword of Shame (co-author) 2006, The Noble Outlaw 2007, The Manor of Death 2008, Crowner Royal 2009, A Plague of Heretics 2010, Where Death Delights 2010, According to the Evidence 2011, Grounds for Appeal 2011, Crowner's Crusade 2012, Dead in the Dog 2012; non-fiction: Legal Aspects of Medical Practice 1972, Discovering the Human Body 1980, Forensic Radiology 1981, Lawyer's Guide to Forensic Medicine 1982, Sudden Death in Infancy 1983, Post-Modern Technicians Handbook 1984, Pocket Guide to Forensic Medicine 1985, Simpson's Forensic Medicine (10th edn) 1991, (11th edn) 1996, Forensic Pathology 1991, The Estimation of the Time Since Death (ed.) 1995; contrib. to Red Herrings (CWA monthly bulletin). *Honours:* Hon. DSc 1996, Hon. LLD 1998, Hon. DM 2000, 2009, Hon. PhD 2001; CWA Leo Harris Award 2005. *E-mail:* knight.j4@sky.com (home). *Website:* bernardknight.homestead.com.

KNIGHT, David Marcus, MA, DPhil; British academic and writer; *Professor Emeritus of History and Philosophy of Science, Durham University;* b. 30 Nov. 1936, Exeter, Devon, England; s. of Rev. Marcus Knight, subsequently Dean of Exeter, and Claire Hewett; m. Sarah Prideaux 1962; two s. four d. *Education:* Univ. of Oxford. *Career:* Lecturer, Durham Univ. 1964–75, Sr Lecturer 1975–88, Reader 1988–91, Prof. of History and Philosophy of Science 1991–, now Prof. Emer.; Gen. Ed. Cambridge Science Biographies 1996–; mem. British Asscn, British Soc. for the History of Science (Pres. 1995–96), Royal Inst. *Publications:* Atoms and Elements: A Study of Theories of Matter in England in the 19th Century 1967, Natural Science Books in English 1600–1900 1972, Sources for the History of Science 1660–1914 1975, The Nature of Science: The History of Science in Western Culture since 1600 1977, Zoological Illustration: An Essay Towards a History of Printed Zoological Pictures 1977, The Transcendental Part of Chemistry 1978, Ordering the World: A History of Classifying Man 1981, The Age of Science: The Scientific World View in the 19th Century 1986, A Companion to the Physical Sciences 1989, Ideas in Chemistry: A History of the Science 1992, Humphry Davy: Science and Power 1992, Science in the Romantic Era 1998, The Making of the Chemist 1789–1914 1998, Science and Spirituality: The Volatile Connection 2003, Public Understanding of Science: A History of Communicating Scientific Ideas 2006; contrib. to scholarly books and journals. *Honours:* Templeton Foundation Award for teaching science and religion courses 1998, ACS Edelstein Award for history of chem. 2003. *Address:* Department of Philosophy, University of Durham, 50 Old Elvet, Durham, DH1 3HN, England (office). *Telephone:* (191) 334-6550 (office). *Fax:* (191) 334-6551 (office). *E-mail:* d.m.knight@durham.ac.uk (office). *Website:* www.durham.ac.uk/philosophy (office).

KNIGHT, Gareth (see Wilby, Basil Leslie)

KNIGHT, Kathleen (Kit), BA; American writer, poet and film critic; b. 21 Sept. 1952, North Kingston, RI; m. Arthur Winfield Knight 1976; one d. *Education:* California Univ. of Pennsylvania. *Career:* Co-Ed. Unspeakable Visions of the Individual 1976–88; poet and columnist, Russian River News, Guerneville, Calif. 1988–92; poet/columnist, film critic, Russian River Times, Monte Rio, Calif. 1997–99; reviewer, Citizen's Echo, Calif. 2000–09; film critic, City Times, Gold River News, Citrus Heights, Calif. 2002–05, Douglas Times 2007–08, Carson Times, Dayton Courier (all three out of Carson City, Nev.) 2007–09; guest columnist, Sr Spectrum, Sacramento, Calif. 2006–; now lives with her husband in Yerington, Nev. *Publications:* A Marriage of Poets (with Arthur Winfield Knight) 1984, Women of Wanted Men 1994, The Greatest Kisser in the Northern Hemisphere (poems) 2004; contrib. to periodicals. *Honours:* Perry Award for Best Achievement in Poetry 1994. *Address:* 303 Sherry Way, Yerington, NV 89447, USA (home). *Telephone:* (775) 463-4773 (home).

KNIGHT, Steven, BA; British screenwriter and playwright; b. 5 Aug. 1959. *Education:* Univ. Coll., London. *Career:* writer and producer, Capital Radio 1983–87; writer for TV 1990–; now screenwriter. *Play:* The President of An Empty Room (Nat. Theatre, London) 2005. *Film screenplays:* Gypsy Woman 2001, Dirty Pretty Things (Variety Ten Screenwriters to Watch Award 2002, British Ind. Film Awards Best British Screenplay 2003, Edgar Award for Best Motion Picture Screenplay, Best Cinema South Bank Show Awards 2003, London Film Critics' Circle Best British Screenwriter Award 2003, Evening Standard British Film Award for Best Film, Humanitas Award 2004) 2002, Amazing Grace 2006, Eastern Promises 2006. *Television writing includes:* Carrott's Commercial Breakdown (series) 1989, Canned Carrott (series) 1990, The Detectives (series, also dir) 1993, Who Wants To Be A Millionaire (series co-creator) 1998, All About Me (series, also creator) 2002. *Publications:* The Movie House (WHSmith Fresh Talent Award) 1993, Alphabet City 1995, Out of the Blue 1997. *Literary Agent:* c/o Natasha Galloway, United Agents, 12–26 Lexington Street, London, W1F 0LE, England. *Telephone:* (20) 3214-0800. *Fax:* (20) 3214-0801. *E-mail:* info@unitedagents.co.uk. *Website:* unitedagents .co.uk.

KNIGHT, William Edwards, BA, MA; American writer and publisher; b. 1 Feb. 1922, Tarrytown, NY; m. Ruth L. Lee 1946, two s. *Education:* Yale College, US Army Air Force, Yale University, Industrial College of the Armed Forces, State Dept Senior Seminar in Foreign Policy. *Career:* B-24 Co-Pilot, 1944–45; Foreign Service Officer, US Dept of State, 1946–75; Pres. and CEO, Araluen Press, 1982–; mem. Yale Club; Washington Independent Writers; Diplomatic and Consular Officers Retired; American Foreign Service Asscn; Army/Navy Country Club; Randolph Mountain Club. *Publications:* The Tiger Game, 1986; The Bamboo Game, 1993; Footprints in the Sand (light verse), 1995; Letter to the Twenty-Second Century: An American Family's Odyssey, 1998; The Devil's End Game, 2002. Contributions: journals.

KNIGHTLEY, Phillip George, AO; Australian journalist and writer; b. 23 Jan. 1929, Sydney, NSW; s. of Phillip James Knightley and Alice May Iggleden; m. Yvonne Fernandes 1964; one s. two d. *Education:* Canterbury Boys' High School, Sydney. *Career:* reporter, Northern Star, Lismore 1948–49, Herald, Melbourne 1952–54; reporter, Daily Mirror, Sydney 1954–56, Foreign Corresp. 1956–60; Ed. Imprint, Mumbai 1960–62; Special Corresp., Sunday Times 1965–85; Visiting Prof. of Journalism, Univ. of Lincoln; mem. Soc. of Authors, Royal Overseas League, The Queen's Club. *Publications:* Philby: The Spy Who Betrayed a Generation (with Bruce Page and David Leitch) 1968, The Games (with Hugh Atkinson) 1968, The Secret Lives of Lawrence of Arabia (with Colin Simpson) 1969, The First Casualty: The War Correspondent as Hero Propagandist and Myth-Maker, Crimea to Vietnam 1975, Lawrence of Arabia 1976, The Death of Venice (with Stephen Fay) 1976, Suffer the Children (ed.) 1979, The Vestey Affair 1981, The Second Oldest Profession: The Spy as Bureaucrat, Patriot, Fantasist, and Whore 1986, An Affair of State: The Profumo Case and the Framing of Stephen Ward (with Caroline Kennedy) 1987, Philby: KGB Masterspy 1988, A Hack's Progress 1997, Australia: A Biography of a Nation 2000. *Honours:* Hon. Doctor of Arts (City Univ., Sydney Univ.); Overseas Press Club of America Award for Best Book on Foreign Affairs 1975, British Journalist of the Year Awards 1980, 1988. *Literary Agent:* c/o The Sayle Literary Agency, 8B Kings Parade, Cambridge, CB2 1SJ, England. *Telephone:* (1223) 303035. *Fax:* (1223) 301638. *Address:* 4 Northumberland Place, London W2 5BS, England (home). *Telephone:* (20) 7229-2179 (office). *E-mail:* phillipgk@aol.com (home). *Website:* phillipknightley.com.

KNOPP, Lisa, BA, MA, PhD; American academic, writer and poet; b. 4 Sept. 1956, Burlington, Ia; m. Colin Ramsay 1990 (divorced 1996); one s. one d. *Education:* Iowa Wesleyan College, Western Illinois University, University of Nebraska, Lincoln. *Career:* Teaching Asst, University of Nebraska, Lincoln 1988–93, Lecturer, 1994–95; Asst Prof., Southern Illinois University 1995; mem. Associated Writing Programs, Asscn for the Study of Literature and the Environment, Western Literature Asscn. *Publications include:* Field of Vision (essays) 1996; contributions: anthologies, newspapers and periodicals. *Honours:* Frank Vogel Scholar in Non-Fiction, Bread Loaf Writers Conference 1992, Second Place, Society of Midland Authors 1996.

KNOX, Elizabeth, BA; New Zealand novelist; b. 15 Feb. 1959, Wellington; m. Fergus Barrowman 1989; one s. *Education:* Victoria University, Wellington. *Career:* Writer-in-Residence Victoria Univ. of Wellington 1997. *Publications:* After Z Hour 1987, Paremata 1989, Treasure 1992, Pomare 1994, Glamour and the Sea 1996, Tawa 1998, The Vintner's Luck 1998, Black Oxen 2000, The High Jump: A New Zealand Childhood 2000, Billie's Kiss 2001, Daylight 2003; essays: Origins, Authority and Imaginary Games 1988, Afraid 1991, Take As Prescribed 1991, The Receding Lion: A Vulgar Manifesto 1992, Going to the Gym 1992, Privacy: the Art of Julia Morison 1993, Heat 1993, Where We Stopped 1995, Reuben Avenue 1996, On Being Picked Up 2000, Getting Over It 1998, On the Am Track 2000, Assemble in Bunny Street 1999, A Stilled Cascade 1999, Beverages 2000, Provenance 2000, Starling 2002, The Love School 2003, Patience 2003, Hands and Hooves 2004; other: The Dig (short film script), 1994. *Honours:* Officer of the New Zealand Order of Merit; ICI Bursary 1988, PEN Award 1988, PEN Fellowship 1991, QEII Arts Council Scholarship in Letters 1993, New Zealand Book Council Lecture Award 1998, Katherine Mansfield Memorial Fellowship 1999, Deutz Medal for Fiction 1999, Arts Foundation of NZ Laureate Award 2000, Tasmania Pacific Region Prize 2001. *Literary Agent:* AP Watt Ltd, 20 John Street, London, WC1N 2DR, England. *Address:* PO Box 11-806, Wellington, New Zealand.

KNOX-JOHNSTON, Sir Robin, CBE, MA, RD, FRIN; British master mariner and author; b. 17 March 1939, Putney, London, England; s. of David Robert Knox-Johnston and Elizabeth Mary Knox-Johnston; m. 1962 (died 2003); one d. *Education:* Berkhamsted School. *Career:* currently Chair. Clipper Ventures PLC; mem. Younger Brother, Trinity House; Honourable Co. of Master Mariners, Royal Inst. of Navigation, Nat. Maritime Museum, Cornwall. *Publications:* A World of My Own 1969, Sailing 1974, Twilight of Sail 1978, Last But Not Least 1978, Seamanship 1986, The BOC Challenge 1986–87 1987, The Cape of Good Hope 1989, The History of Yachting 1990, The Columbus Venture 1991, Sea Ice Rock (with Chris Bonington) 1992, Cape Horn 1994, Beyond Jules Verne 1995, Force of Nature 2007; contrib. to Yachting World, Cruising World, Guardian. *Honours:* Hon. DTech (Nottingham Trent Univ.) 1993, Hon. DSc (Maine Maritime Acad.) 1993. *Literary Agent:* c/o Curtis Brown Ltd, Haymarket House, 28–29 Haymarket, London, SW1Y 4SP, England. *Telephone:* (20) 7393-4400. *Fax:* (20) 7393-4401. *E-mail:* info@curtisbrown.co.uk. *Website:* www.curtisbrown.co.uk. *Address:* St Francis Cottage, Torbryan, Newton Abbot, Devon, TQ12 5UR, England (home). *Website:* www.robinknox-johnston.co.uk.

KNUDSEN, Lisbeth; Danish newspaper editor and executive manager; *Editor-in-Chief, Berlingske Tidende;* b. 7 June 1953, Copenhagen. *Career:* Political Ed. Berlingske Tidende 1975–84, Business Ed. 1984–88, Sunday Ed. 1988–89, Ed. 1989–90, Ed.-in-Chief 2007–; Ed.-in-Chief and Exec. Man. Apressen/Det Friaktuelt 1990–98; Man. Dir Danish Broadcasting Corpn 1998–2007; CEO Mecom Denmark 2007–; Chair. Bd, Danish School of Journalism. *Address:* Berlingske Tidende, Pilestræde 34, 1147 Copenhagen K, Denmark (office). *Telephone:* 33-75-75-75 (office). *Fax:* 33-75-20-20 (office). *E-mail:* knudsen.lisbeth@gmail.com (home); redaktionen@berlingske.dk (office). *Website:* www.berlingske.dk (office); lisbethknudsen.blogspot.com.

KO, Un; South Korean writer, poet and academic; b. 1933, Kunsan; m. Lee Sang-wha 1983. *Career:* teacher of Korean language and art, Kunsan Middle School 1950; served as Buddhist monk 1952–62; Sec.-Gen. Asscn of Writers for Practical Freedom 1974; arrested many times for political activities and served several prison terms; Resident Prof., Grad. School, Kyonggi Univ., Seoul 1994–98, Resident Poetry Prof., Dangook Univ. 2008; Pres. Asscn of Korean Artists 1989–90, Asscn of Writers for Nat. Literature 1992–94, Co-Pres. Nat. Trust of Korea 2000; Chair. South and North Korea Writers' Conf. 2004; Visiting Research Scholar, Yenching Inst., Harvard Univ., USA 1999. *Publications include:* Maninbo (Ten Thousand Lives) (poetry) 30 vols., has written numerous books of poetry, novels, non-fiction, literary criticism, travel books, biographies, translation; I, Ko Un (autobiography, three vols.) 1993, My Bronze Period (autobiography) 1995. *Honours:* Silver Order of Merit in Culture 2002, Bjornson Order for Literature (Norway) 2005; Dr hc (Dankook Univ.) 2010; Korean Literature Prize 1974, 1987, Manhae Prize in Literature 1989, Joong-Ang Prize for Literature 1991, Daesan Prize for Literature 1994, Manhae Grand Prize 1998, Buddhist Literature Prize 1999, Danjae Prize 2004, Unification Award 2005, Cikada Prize (Sweden) 2006, Young-Rang Poetry Award 2007, Yusim Literature Prize 2008, Lifetime Achievement Award, Griffin Fund for Excellence in Poetry (Canada) 2008, Korea Acad. of Arts Award 2008. *Address:* 173 Changmikol, Daerimdongsan Ansong, Kyonggi-do, 456–820, South Korea. *Telephone:* (31) 618-1783. *Fax:* (31) 618-1781. *E-mail:* koun_poet@yahoo.co.kr. *Website:* www.koun.co.kr.

KOCH, Christopher John, BA, DLitt; Australian author; b. 16 July 1932, Hobart, Tasmania; m. Irene Vilnonis 1960, one s. *Education:* University of Tasmania. *Publications:* The Boys in the Island, 1958; Across the Sea Wall, 1965; The Doubleman, 1965; The Year of Living Dangerously, 1978; Crossing the Gap (essays), 1987; Highways to War, 1995; Out of Ireland, 1999. *Honours:* National Book Council Award for Australian Literature, 1979; Miles Franklin Prize, 1985, 1996; AO, 1995. *Address:* c/o 16 Winton Street, Warrawee, Sydney, NSW 2074, Australia.

KOCH, Joanne Barbara, (Joanna Z. Adams), BA, MA, PhD; American writer, dramatist and academic; *Professor of English and Director, Graduate Writing Program, National-Louis University;* b. 28 March 1941, Chicago; d. of Ceil Schapiro and Isadore Schapiro; m. Lewis Z. Koch 1964; one s. two d. *Education:* Cornell Univ., Columbia Univ., Southern Illinois Univ. *Career:* syndicated columnist, with Lewis Z. Koch, for Newspaper Enterprise Asscn 1971–75; Prof. of English, Nat.-Louis Univ., Chicago 1998–, Dir of Grad. Writing Program 2002–; Guest Lecturer on Women's Studies and Screenwriting, Northwestern Univ., Columbia Coll., Chicago; mem. Dramatists' Guild, Soc. of Midland Authors, Women in Film, Women in Theatre. *Plays:* Haymarket: Footnote to a Bombing (Piscator Foundation-SIU Int. Playwriting Award) 1985, Teeth (Illinois Arts Council Grant) 1988, Hearts in the Wood (musical, with James Lucas) (Illinois Arts Council Playwriting Fellowship) 1992, Saul Bellow's Stories on Stage: A Silver Dish and The Old System (adaptations, with Sarah Cohen) (Streisand Festival Award) 1995, Nesting Dolls (PBS Broadcast, SIU Best New Play Award) 1994, Sophie, Totie & Belle (with Sarah Cohen) 1995; off-Broadway and other productions: Soul Sisters (with Sarah Cohen) 1997, Safe Harbor 1999, A Leading Woman (Driehaus Foundation grant) 2002, Henrietta Szold: Woman of Valor (with Sarah Cohen) (Brandeis Univ. Hadassah Inst. Research grant) 2002, Courage Like a Wild Horse 2004, American Klezmer (musical, with Sarah Cohen, Owen Kalt, Ilya Levinson) 2004, Belle Barth: If I Embarrass You, Tell Your Friends 2007, Stardust (Nantucket Short Play Contest winner) 2007. *Television:* Flying Feathers, The Thirty-Six and Abigail & Brewster (part of Magic Door Series broadcast on CBS-WBBM-TV) 1985–86, High Top Tower (Fox TV) (Midwest Emmy Award 1991, First Place American Film and Video Award 1991) 1990, Today I Am A Person (Nat. Angel Award) 1986, The Price of Daffodils 1985, Baby, You're Okay (Excalibur Award). *Publications:* The Marriage Savers (with Lewis Z. Koch) 1976, Readings in Psychology Today (contributor) 1978, Children: development through adolescence (with Allison Clarke-Stewart) 1983, Marriage and Family (with Diane Levande, Lewis Z. Koch) 1983, Child Psychology (with Allison Clarke-Stewart) 1985, Good Parents for Hard Times (with Linda Freeman) 1991, Shared Stages: Ten American Dramas of Blacks and Jews (co-ed. with Sarah Blacher Cohen) 2008, Stardust 2009, A Silver Dish 2010; novels, as Joanna Z. Adams: Makeovers 1987, Rushes 1988, Intimate Connections 1989, A Silver Dish (adaptation) 2010. *Honours:* Family Service Asscn Award for writing 1974, American Psychoanalytic Asscn/Harris Media Award for Psychology Today article 1978, Piscator Playwriting Award 1980, Best New Play Award, Southern Illinois Univ. 1994, Illinois Arts Council Award 1995, Evanston Arts Council Award 2000, American Film and Video Award. *Address:* 343 Dodge Avenue, Evanston, IL 60202, USA (home). *Telephone:* (847) 864-5357 (home). *Fax:* (847) 864-2312 (home). *E-mail:* jkoch@nl.edu (home). *Website:* www.lzkoch.com/kochandcohen (office).

KOEGLER, Hans-Herbert, MA, DrPhil; German philosopher, writer and academic; *Professor of Philosophy and Chairperson, Department of Philosophy, University of North Florida;* b. 13 Jan. 1960, Darmstadt; one d. *Education:* Johann Wolfgang von Goethe Univ., Frankfurt am Main. *Career:* Dissertation Fellow, German Fellowship Foundation 1987–91; Research Fellow, Visiting Scholar, Northwestern Univ., New School for Social Research, Univ. of California, Berkeley 1989–90; Asst Prof., Univ. of Illinois at Urbana-Champaign 1991–97; Asst Prof., Univ. of North Florida 1997–99, Assoc. Prof. of Philosophy 1999–2008, Chair. Dept of Philosophy 2007–, Prof. of Philosophy 2008–; Visiting Prof., Univ. of Boston, USA 1997, Charles Univ., Prague, Czech Repub. 2003, Alpe Adria Univ., Klagenfurt 2004, 2006, 2010. *Publications:* Die Macht des Dialogs: Kritische Hermeneutik nach Gadamer 1992, Michel Foucault: Ein antihumanistischer Aufklarer 1994, 2004, The Power of Dialogue: Critical Hermeneutics After Gadamer and Foucault 1996, 1999, Empathy and Agency: The Problem of Understanding in the Human Sciences 2000, Kultura, Kritika, Dialog 2006; contrib. to journals, reviews, periodicals, magazines and handbooks. *Address:* Building 10, Room 2325, Department of Philosophy and Religious Studies, University of North Florida, 4567 St Johns Bluff Road S, Jacksonville, FL 32224-2645, USA (office). *Telephone:* (904) 620-1330 (office). *Fax:* (904) 620-1187 (office). *E-mail:* hkoegler@unf.edu (office). *Website:* www.unf.edu/~hkoegler (office).

KOELB, Clayton, BA, MA, PhD; American academic and writer; *Guy B. Johnson Distinguished Professor of German and Chairman, Department of Germanic and Slavic Languages and Literatures, University of North Carolina, Chapel Hill;* b. 12 Nov. 1942, New York, NY; m. 1st Barbara Dublin 1965; one d.; m. 2nd Susan J. Noakes 1979; one s.; m. 3rd Janice Koelb (née Hewlett) 1999. *Education:* Harvard Univ. *Career:* Asst Prof., Assoc. Prof., Prof. of German and Comparative Literature, Univ. of Chicago 1969–91, Chair. Dept of Germanic Languages 1978–82; Visiting Prof., Purdue Univ. 1984–85, Princeton Univ. 1985–86; Visiting Eugene Falk Prof., Univ. of N Carolina, Chapel Hill 1990, Guy B. Johnson Distinguished Prof. of German 1991–, Chair. Dept of Germanic Languages 1997–2011, Dept of Germanic and Slavic Languages and Literatures 2011–; mem. Modern Language Asscn of America, Int. Asscn for Philosophy and Literature, Semiotics Soc. of America, Kafka Soc. of America, Asscn of Literary Scholars and Critics, German

Studies Asscn, American Asscn of Teachers of German. *Publications:* The Incredulous Reader 1984, Thomas Mann's Goethe and Tolstoy 1984, The Current in Criticism 1987, Inventions of Reading 1988, The Comparative Perspective on Literature 1988, Kafka's Rhetoric 1989, Nietzsche as Post-modernist 1990, Thomas Mann's Death in Venice: A Critical Edition 1994, Legendary Figures 1998, Camden House History of German Literature: The 19th Century 2005, A Franz Kafka Encyclopedia 2005, The Revivifying Word 2008, Kafka Guide for the Perplexed 2010; contribs to professional journals. *Honours:* Germanistic Soc. of America Fellow 1964–65, Woodrow Wilson Foundation Fellow 1965, Danforth Foundation Fellow 1965–69, Susan Anthony Potter Prize, Harvard Univ. 1970, Guggenheim Fellowship 1993–94. *Address:* University of North Carolina, 443 Dey Hall, Chapel Hill, NC 27599, USA (office). *Telephone:* (919) 962-0470 (office). *E-mail:* ckoelb@email.unc.edu (office). *Website:* gsll.unc.edu/people/current-faculty/clayton-koelb (office).

KOESTENBAUM, Wayne, BA, MA, PhD; American academic, poet, writer and critic; *Distinguished Professor of English, City University of New York*; b. 20 Sept. 1958, San Jose, Calif. *Education:* Harvard Coll., Johns Hopkins Univ., Princeton Univ. *Career:* Assoc. Prof. of English, Yale Univ. 1988–97, Morse Fellowship 1990–91, Co-Ed. The Yale Journal of Criticism 1991–96; Prof. of English, CUNY 1997–, now Distinguished Prof.; Whiting Fellowship in the Humanities 1987–88. *Publications include:* Double Talk: The Erotics of Male Literary Collaboration 1989, Ode to Anna Moffo and Other Poems 1990, The Queen's Throat: Opera, Homosexuality, and the Mystery of Desire 1993, Rhapsodies of a Repeat Offender 1994, Jackie Under My Skin: Interpreting an Icon 1995, The Milk of Inquiry 1999, Cleavage: Essays on Sex, Stars and Aesthetics 2000, Andy Warhol 2001, Model Homes 2004, Moira Orfei in Aigues-Mortes 2004, Best-Selling Jewish Porn Films 2006, Hotel Theory 2007, Humiliation 2011; other: Jackie O (libretto for the opera by Michael Daugherty) 1997; contribs to anthologies, books, newspapers, reviews, quarterlies and journals. *Honours:* Twentieth Century Literature Prize in Literary Criticism 1988, Discovery/The Nation Poetry Contest (jtly) 1989, New York Times Book Review Notable Book 1993, Whiting Writer's Award 1994. *E-mail:* wkoestenbaum@aol.com. *Address:* c/o English Program, Graduate School and University Center, City University of New York, 365 Fifth Avenue, New York, NY 10016, USA.

KOGAN, Norman, BA, PhD; American academic (retd) and writer; b. 15 June 1919, Chicago, Ill.; m. Meryl Reich 1946; two s. *Education:* Univ. of Chicago. *Career:* Faculty, Univ. of Connecticut 1949–88, Dir Center for Italian Studies 1967–76; Visiting Prof., Univ. of Rome 1973, 1979, 1987; Pres. Conf. Group on Italian Politics 1975–77; Chair. Southern Europe Comm., Council for the Int. Exchange of Scholars 1976–80; mem. Soc. for Italian Historical Studies (Exec. Sec., Treas. 1966–76), Connecticut State Chapter of the Fulbright Asscn (Pres. 1990–95). *Publications:* Italy and the Allies 1956, The Government of Italy 1962, The Politics of Italian Foreign Policy 1963, A Political History of Postwar Italy 1966, Storia Politica dell' Italia Repubblicana 1982, A Political History of Italy: The Postwar Years 1983; contrib. to Yale Law Journal, Il Ponte, Western Political Quarterly, Journal of Politics, Comparative Politics, Indiana Law Journal. *Honours:* Kt, Order of Merit (Italy) 1971; Career Achievement Award, Italian Studies 2003.

KOGAWA, Joy Nozomi, CM; Canadian writer; b. (Nozomi Joy Nakayama), 6 June 1935, Vancouver, BC; d. of the late Gordon Goichi and Lois Masui Nakayama (née Yao); one s. one d. *Education:* R. I. Baker School, Alberta and Univ. of Alberta. *Career:* writer, Prime Minister's Office 1974–76; Writer-in-Residence, Univ. of Ottawa 1978; Dir Canadian Civil Liberties Asscn; mem. Writers' Union of Canada, PEN Int.; Fellow, Ryerson Polytechnical Univ. 1991; fmr Pres. Toronto Dollar Community Projects, Inc. *Publications include:* poetry: The Splintered Moon 1967, A Choice of Dreams 1974, Jericho Road 1977, Woman in the Woods 1985, A Song of Lilith 2000, A Garden of Anchors 2003; novels: Obasan (Books in Canada First Novel Award 1981, Canadian Authors' Asscn Book of the Year Award 1982, Notable Book, American Library Asscn 1982, American Book Award, Before Columbus Foundation 1983, Periodical Distributors of Canada and Foundation for the Advancement of Canadian Letters Award for Paperback Fiction 1983) 1981, Itsuka 1992, The Rain Ascends 1995, Emily Kato 2005; children's fiction: Naomi's Road 1986, Naomi's Tree 2008. *Honours:* Hon. LLD (Lethbridge) 1991, (Simon Fraser) 1993, (Queen's) 2003, (Windsor) 2003; Hon. DLitt (Guelph) 1992, (British Columbia) 2001; Hon. DD (Knox Coll., Toronto) 1999; Urban Alliance Race Relations Award 1994, Grace MacInnis Visiting Scholar Award 1995, Asscn of Asian-American Studies Lifetime Achievement Award 2001, Nat. Asscn of Japanese Canadians Nat. Award 2001. *Address:* #1418, 25 The Esplanade, Toronto, ON M5E 1W5 (home); #308, 1050 Jervis Street, Vancouver, BC V6E 2C1, Canada (home). *Telephone:* (416) 363-9130 (Toronto) (home); (604) 687-3554 (Vancouver) (home). *E-mail:* joy.kogawa@rogers.ca (home).

KOHAN, Martín, (Miguel Cané), BA, MA, PhD; Argentine academic and writer; b. 1967, Buenos Aires. *Career:* Prof. of Literary Theory, Univ. of Buenos Aires. *Publications:* fiction: La Pérdida de Laura 1993, El informe 1997, Los cautivos 2000, Dos veces junio 2002, Segundos afuera 2005, Museo de la Revolución 2006, Ciencias Morales (Premio de Herralde de Novela) 2007; non-fiction: Eva Perón, cuerpo y política 1998, Zona urbana: Ensayo de lectura sobre Walter Benjamin 2004, Narra a San Martín 2005; short stories: Muero contento 1994, Una pena extraordinaria 1998. *Address:* Departamento de Letras, Facultad de Filosofía y Letras, Universidad de Buenos Aires, Puán 470, 3°, 1406 Buenos Aires, Argentina (office). *E-mail:* deletras@filo.uba.ar (office). *Website:* www.filo.uba.ar (office).

KOHLER, Sheila May, MA, MFA; South African author and academic; *Lecturer in Creative Writing, Lewis Center for the Arts, Princeton University*; b. 13 Nov. 1941, Johannesburg; d. of Max Kohler and Sheila Kohler; m. 1st Boris Troyan 1961 (divorced); m. 2nd William Tucker 1986; three c. *Education:* Sorbonne, Paris, Institut Catholique, Columbia Univ., USA. *Career:* left South Africa for Europe aged 17; moved to USA 1981; first story published 1987; teacher at Writer's Voice 1991–99; instructor, New School, NY 1995–2000; Writer-in-Residence, State Univ. of New York, Purchase 1996, International Inkwell, Montolieu 1997, Sarah Lawrence Coll. 1999–2001, City Coll., CUNY 2000–02; mem. of core faculty, Bennington Coll., Bennington Vt 2000–06; Adjunct Faculty Mem., Columbia Univ. 2006; currently Lecturer in Creative Writing, Lewis Center for the Arts, Princeton Univ.; work published in numerous journals including The Quarterly, Ontario Review, Antioch Review, Story Magazine, Yale Review; essays published in Boston Globe, Salmagundi, Bellevue Literary Magazine, O Magazine. *Publications:* novels: The Perfect Place 1989, The House on R Street 1994, Cracks 1999, The Children of Pithiviers 2001, Crossways 2004, Bluebird or the Invention of Happiness 2007, Becoming Jane Eyre 2009, Bay of Foxes 2012; short story collections: Miracles in America 1990, One Girl (Willa Cather Prize 1998) 1998, Stories from Another World 2003. *Honours:* O'Henry Prize 1988, 2008, Open Voice Award 1991, Smart Family Foundation Prize 2000, Dorothy and Lewis B. Cullman Institute Fellowship 2003, Antioch Review Prize 2004. *Literary Agent:* c/o Robin Straus Agency Inc., 229 East 79 Street, Suite 5A, New York, NY 10075, USA. *Telephone:* (212) 472-3282. *E-mail:* info@robinstrausagency.com. *Website:* www.robinstrausagency.com. *Address:* c/o Lewis Center for the Arts, Princeton University, New South Building, Floor 6, Princeton, NJ 08544, USA (office). *Telephone:* (609) 258-8561 (office). *Fax:* (609) 258-0377 (office). *E-mail:* skohler@princeton.edu (office); sheila@sheilakohler.com (home). *Website:* www.princeton.edu/arts/arts_at_princeton/creative_writing/professor_bios/kohler/ (office); www.sheilakohler.com.

KOHOUT, Pavel; Czech novelist, playwright and poet; b. 20 July 1928, Prague; m. 1st Alena Vránová; m. 2nd Anna Kohoutová; m. 3rd Jelena Mašínová 1970; one s. one d. *Career:* fmr mem. Communist Party of Czechoslovakia, subsequently reformist, then dissident; co-author Charter 77 human rights manifesto; expelled to Austria; playwright Divadlo na Vinohradech theatre 1963–66; ed. of periodicals; worked at Assoc. Centre for Economics and Politics (CEP), Prague; mem. Deutsche Akademie für Sprache und Schöpfung. *Plays:* Poor Murderer (Ethel Barrymore Theater, New York, USA) 1976, Fool's Mate (New End Theatre, Hampstead, London, UK) 1990, Fire in the Basement (Traverse Theatre, Edinburgh, UK) 1998. *Publications:* Taková láska (Such a Love) 1958, Dvanáct: Dvanáct obrazu ze zivota dvanácti mladých hercu (Divadlo) 1963, Z deníku kontrarevolucionáře (From the Diary of a Counterrevolutionary) 1968, Pat aneb Hra králů (Stalemate or the Game of Kings 1978, Atest (Testimonial) 1979, Katyne 1980, The Hangwoman 1981, Kde je zakopán pes (Where the Dog is Buried, memoirs) 1987, Ecce Constantia 1990, I Am Snowing: The Confessions of a Woman of Prague 1994, The Widow Killer 1998; contrib. to numerous anthologies and literary and political periodicals. *Honours:* Grosser Staatspreis für Europäische Literatur, Austria.

KOHUT, Thomas August, BA, MA, PhD; American historian, academic, writer and college administrator; *Sue and Edgar Wachenheim III Professor of History, Williams College*; b. (Thomas Alan Kohut), 11 March 1950, Chicago, Ill.; s. of Heinz Kohut and Elizabeth Meyer Kohut; m. Susan Neeld Kohut 1975; one s. one d. *Education:* Oberlin Coll., Univ. of Minnesota, Cincinnati Psychoanalytic Inst. *Career:* Asst Clinical Prof. of Psychiatry, Univ. of Cincinnati 1982–84; Asst Prof., Williams Coll. 1984–90, Assoc. Prof. 1990–95, Sue and Edgar Wachenheim III Prof. of History 1995–, Dean of the Faculty 2000–06, Acting Provost 2003; Guest Prof., Univ. of Munich 1988, Univ. of Siegen 1991–92, 1995–96; mem. American Historical Asscn, German Studies Asscn; mem. Bd of Trustees, Austen Riggs Center, Stockbridge, Mass. *Publications:* Wilhelm II and the Germans: A Study in Leadership 1991, A German Generation: An Experiential History of the Twentieth Century 2012; contribs to scholarly books, journals and anthologies. *Honours:* Deutscher Akademischer Austauschdienst Grant 1978–79, Int. Research and Exchanges Board Grant 1979, Fulbright Scholarship 1987–88, Köhler Foundation Grant 1996. *Address:* Department of History, Williams College, Williamstown, MA 01267, USA (office). *Telephone:* (413) 597-2108 (office). *E-mail:* thomas.a.kohut@williams.edu (office). *Website:* history.williams.edu/profile/tkohut (office).

KOKH, Alfred Reingoldovich, CandEconSci; Russian economist, media executive, writer and fmr government official; b. 28 Feb. 1961, Zyryanovsk, Kazakhstan; m.; two d. *Education:* Leningrad Inst. of Finance and Econs. *Career:* fmr Sr Researcher, Prometey Inst.; Asst, Leningrad Polytech. Inst. 1987–90; Chair. Sestroretsk Dist Exec. Cttee, Leningrad 1990–91; Deputy Dir Cttee on Man. of State Property of St Petersburg 1991–93; First Deputy Chair. State Cttee on Property in Russian Fed. 1993–96, Chair. 1996–97; Vice-Chair. Russian Fed. Govt responsible for Privatization and Budget 1997 (resgnd); Chair. Bd of Dirs Montes Auri Investment Co. 1997–; Dir-Gen. Gasprom-Media 1998–2001 (resgnd), with NTV Broadcasting 2001–03; mem. Exec. Cttee Union of Rightist Forces (SPS) party, led SPS parl. election campaign 2003; Contributing Ed. Medved magazine. *Publications:* History of Privatization in Russia (with A. Chubais and M. Boyko) 1997, Sale of Soviet Empire 1998, A Crate of Vodka (co-author) 2006. *Address:* Medved, c/o Forward Media

Group, 123022 Moscow, ul. Rochdelskaya, 15, p. 10, Russia. *Telephone:* (495) 620-08-00. *Fax:* (495) 620-08-01. *Website:* medved-magazine.ru.

KOLBE, Uwe; German poet and writer; b. 17 Oct. 1957, Berlin; three s. *Education:* Johannes R. Becher Inst., Leipzig. *Career:* early work published in Sinn und Form and Mitteldeutsche Verlag journals; Co-Ed. Mikado literary journal 1982–87; Visiting Lecturer, Univ. of Austin, Texas, USA and Univ. of Vienna, Austria; Dir Studio of Literature and Theatre, Tübingen Univ. 1997–2004; Poet-in-Residence, Oberlin Coll., Ohio, USA 2007, Allegheny Coll., Pa, USA 2010. *Publications:* poetry: Hineingeboren (Born Into) 1980, Abschiede und andere Liebesgedichte (Farewells and Other Love Poems) 1983, Bornholm II 1986, Vaterlandkanal: Ein Fahrtenbuch (Fatherland-Channel: A Logbook) 1990, Nicht wirklich platonisch (Not Really Platonic) 1994, Vineta 1998, Die Farben des Wassers (The Colours of Water) 2001, Sailor's Home (co-author) 2005, Diese Frau, Lovepoems 2007, Heimliche Feste 2008; essays: Die Situation 1994, Renegatentermine: 30 Versuche, die eigene Erfahrung zu behaupten (Renegade's Appointments: 30 Attempts at Asserting One's Own Experience) 1998, Vinetas Archive (Vineta's Archives) 2011; novel: Thrakische Spiele 2005; prose: Storiella. Das Maerchen von der Unruhe (Storiella. A Fairytale of Unrest) 2008. *Honours:* City of Berlin (West) Arts Award 1987, Förderpreis zum Friedrich Hoelderlin Preis 1987, Henschel Translation Award 1988, Nicolas-Born Prize, Munich 1988, Berlin Literature Award 1992, Friedrich Hölderlin Award, Tübingen 1993, Literaturhaeuser Award 2006. *Literary Agent:* c/o S. Fischer Verlag, Hedderichstr. 114, 60596 Frankfurt am Main, Germany. *Telephone:* (69) 6062-0. *E-mail:* kolbeuwe@web.de (office).

KOLLER, James, BA; American writer, poet and artist; b. 30 May 1936, Oak Park, Ill.; m. (divorced); two s. four d. *Education:* North Central Coll., Naperville, Ill. *Publications include:* poetry: Two Hands 1965, Brainard and Washington Street Poems 1965, The Dogs and Other Dark Woods 1966, Some Cows 1966, I Went To See My True Love 1967, California Poems 1971, Bureau Creek 1975, Poems for the Blue Sky 1976, Messages-Botschaften 1977, Andiamo 1978, O Didn't He Ramble-O ware er nicht unhergezogen 1981, Back River 1981, One Day at a Time 1981, Great Things Are Happening-Grossartoge Dinge passieren 1984, Give the Dog a Bone 1986, Graffiti Lyriques (with Franco Beltrametti), graphics and texts 1987, Openings 1987, Fortune 1987, Roses Love Sunshine 1989, This Is What He Said (graphics and texts) 1991, In the Wolf's Mouth, Poems 1972–88 1995, The Bone Show 1996, Travaux de Voirie 1997, Iron Bells 1999, After Days of Rain 1999, Close to the Ground 2000, Looking for his Horses 2003, Crows Talk to Him 2003, Hungry Wolf 2004, Ashes & Embers 2004, Snows Gone By 2004, How Close Can You Get 2006, La canzone delle volpe 2006; other: Messages 1972, Working Notes 1960–82 1985, Gebt dem alten Hund'nen Knochen (Essays, Gedichte und Prosa 1959–85) 1986, The Natural Order (essay and graphics) 1990, Like It Was (selected poems, prose and fiction) 2000, Un Reading di Poesie 2002; fiction: If You Don't Like Me You Can Leave Me Alone 1974, Shannon Who Was Lost Before 1975, The Possible Movie (with Franco Beltrametti) 1997. *Address:* PO Box 629, Brunswick, ME 04011, USA.

KOLM, Ronald Akerson, (Rank Cologne), BA; American writer, editor and publisher; *Manager, Posmanbooks, Grand Central Station, New York City*; b. 21 May 1947, Pittsburgh, Pa; s. of Roger Edward Kolm and Martyne C. Kolm; m. Donna Sterling 1984; two s. *Education:* Albright Coll. *Career:* Ed. Appearances magazine; Man. Posmanbooks, Grand Central Station, New York City; Contributing Ed. Sensitive Skin magazine; papers in the Fales Collection, New York Univ. Library, also archived in Ohio State Univ., State Univ. of NY Poetry and Rare Books Collection, Museum of Modern Art Library, New York. *Publications:* Plastic Factory 1989, Welcome to the Barbecue 1990, Suburban Ambush 1991, Rank Cologne 1991, The Unbearables (ed.) 1995, Crimes of the Beats (ed.) 1998, Help Yourself! (ed.) 2002, Neo Phobe (co-author) 2006, Up is Up, But So is Down (co-ed.) 2006, The Worst Book I Ever Read (ed.) 2009, The Unbearables Big Book of Sex (ed.) 2011. *Address:* 30–73 47th Street, Long Island City, NY 11103, USA (home). *E-mail:* kolmrank@verizon.net (office).

KOLYADA, Nikolai Vladimirovich; Russian actor, writer and playwright; b. 4 Dec. 1957, Presnogorkovka, Kustanai region, Kazakhstan. *Education:* Sverdlovsk Higher School of Theatre Arts. *Career:* actor Sverdlovsk Drama theatre 1972–77; mem. USSR Writers' Union 1989–; teacher Yekaterinburg Inst. of Theatre Arts 1998–; Ed.-in-Chief Ural Journal 1999–. *Plays:* Forfeits, Our Unsociable Sea or A Fool's Vessels, Barakb Lashkaldak, Parents' Day, Slingshot, Chicken, Polonaise, Mannequin, A Tale About the Dead Tsarina, Persian Lilac; *Theatre:* Chicken Blindness. *Publications:* Plays for Beloved Theatre 1994. *Honours:* Sverdlovsk Komsomol Cttee Prize 1978, Teatralnaya Zhizn (magazine) Prize 1988, Schloss Solitude Academy Award, Stuttgart, Germany 1992. *Address:* Ural Journal, Malysheva str. 24, 620219 GSP 352, Yekaterinburg, Russia. *Telephone:* (3432) 759754. *Fax:* (3432) 769741. *E-mail:* editor@mail.ru. *Website:* www.koljada.uralinfo.ru/.

KOMUNYAKAA, Yusef, BA, MA, MFA; American academic and poet; *Global Distinguished Professor of English, New York University*; b. 29 April 1947, Bogalusa, La. *Education:* Univ. of Colorado, Colorado State Univ., Univ. of California, Irvine. *Career:* Correspondent, then Ed. The Southern Cross (military newspaper); fmrly taught poetry, New Orleans schools, and creative writing, Univ. of New Orleans; Visiting Prof., Indiana Univ. at Bloomington 1985, Assoc. Prof. of Afro-American Studies 1987–96; Prof. of Creative Writing, Princeton Univ. 1997–2006, also Prof. of the Council of the Humanities and Creative Writing Program; Global Distinguished Prof. of English, New York Univ. 2006–; mem. Bd of Chancellors, Acad. of American Poets 1999–; mem. American Acad. of Arts and Letters 2009–. *Publications:* poetry: Dedications and Other Darkhorses 1977, Lost in the Bonewheel Factory 1979, Copacetic 1984, I Apologize for the Eyes in My Head (San Francisco Poetry Center Award) 1986, Toys in a Field 1987, Dien Cai Dau (Dark Room Poetry Prize) 1988, February in Sydney 1989, Magic City 1992, Neon Vernacular: New and Selected Poems 1977–1989 (Université de Rennes William Faulkner Prize 1994, Pulitzer Prize in Poetry 1994, Kingsley Tufts Poetry Award 1994) 1993, Thieves of Paradise (Southern Literary Asscn Hanes Poetry Prize 1997, Poetry Magazine Levinson Prize 1998, Poetry Soc. of America Shelley Memorial Award) 1998, Talking Dirty to the Gods 2000, Pleasure Dome: New and Collected Poems 1975–1999 2001, Scandalize My Name 2002, Taboo: Wishbone Trilogy Part One 2004, Warhorses 2009, The Chameleon Couch 2011; prose: The Jazz Poetry Anthology (ed. with J. A. Sascha Feinstein) 1991, The Second Set: The Jazz Poetry Anthology Vol. 2 (ed. with J. A. Sascha Feinstein) 1996, Blue Notes: Essays, Interviews and Commentaries 2000, Gilgamesh: A Verse Play 2009, The Chameleon Couch 2011. *Honours:* two NEA Creative Writing Fellowships 1981, 1987, Thomas Forcade Award, Union League Civic Arts and Poetry Prize, Chicago 1998, Ruth Lilly Poetry Prize 2001, Wallace Stevens Award 2011. *Address:* Department of English, New York University, 19 University Place, 5th Floor, New York, NY 10003, USA (office). *Telephone:* (212) 998-8800 (office). *Fax:* (212) 995-4019 (office). *E-mail:* yk24@nyu.edu (office). *Website:* english.fas.nyu.edu.

KONI, Ibrahim al-; Libyan writer; b. 1948, Ghadamis Oasis. *Education:* Maxim Gorky Literature Inst., Moscow. *Career:* brought up in the desert, later lived in Russia and Poland; living in Switzerland 1993–; worked at Libyan Cultural Inst., Moscow; and as journalist in Warsaw. *Publications:* over 80 publs including A Myth of Love for Switzerland, The Divan of the Mainland and the Ocean, The Seven Veils of Seth (in trans.), The Bleeding of the Stone (in trans.) 2003, Anubis: A Desert Novel (in trans.) 2005, Gold Dust (in trans.) 2008, The Seven Veils of Seth (novel, in trans.) 2008, The Puppet (in trans.) 2010, The Animists (in trans.) 2012. *Honours:* Chevalier Ordre des Arts et des Lettres (France) 2006; State Award 1996, Mohamed Zafzaf Award for the Arabic Novel 2005, Shaikh Zayed Creativity Award 2008, Cairo Arab Novel Award 2010. *Address:* c/o American University in Cairo Press, 113 Kasr el Aini Street, POB 2511, Cairo, Egypt (office). *E-mail:* aucpress@aucegypt.edu (office). *Website:* www.aucpress.com (office).

KÖNIG, Hans; German writer; b. 30 Sept. 1925, Erlangen; m. 1949; one s. *Career:* mem. Verband Fränkischer Schriftsteller; Pegnesischer Blumenorden. *Publications:* Der Pelzermärtl kummt, 1977; Woss wissd denn ihr, 1981; Anekdoten Erzählungen Originale aus Erlangen, 1981–84; Burschen, Knoten und Philister – Erlanger Studentenleben von 1843–1983, 1984; Erlangen vorwiegend heiter – ein unterhaltsamer Streifzug dürch die Stadt und ihre Geschichte, 1988; Wie es Lem so is, 1994. Contributions: anthologies, journals and periodicals. *Honours:* Verdienstmedaille und Verdienstkreuz der Bundesrepublik Deutschland, 1985–91; Kultureller Ehrenbrief der Stadt Erlangen, 1989; Ehrenkrenz des Pegnesischen Blumenordens, 1995; Frankenwurtel, 1999.

KONRÁD, György; Hungarian novelist and essayist; b. 2 April 1933, Berettyóújfalu, nr Debrecen; s. of József Konrád and Róza Klein; m. Judit Lakner; three s. two d. *Education:* Debrecen Reform Coll., Madách Gymnasium, Budapest, Eötvös Loránd Univ., Budapest. *Career:* teacher at general gymnasium in Csepel; Ed. Életképek 1956; social worker, Budapest 7th Dist Council 1959–65; Ed. Magyar Helikon 1960–66; urban sociologist on staff of City Planning Research Inst. 1965–73; full-time writer 1973–; Pres. Akad. der Künste Berlin-Brandenburg 1997; Visiting Prof. of Comparative Literature, Colorado Springs Coll. 1988; Corresp. mem. Bayerische Akad., Munich; fmr Pres. Int. PEN. *Publications include:* novels: A látogató (The Case Worker) 1969, A városlapító (The City Builder) 1977, A cinkos (The Loser) 1982, Kerti mulatság (Feast in the Garden) (Vol. 1 of trilogy Agenda) 1989, Kóóra (Stone Dial) (Vol. 2 of Agenda) 1995; essays: Új lakótelepek szociológiai problémái 1969, Az értelmiség utja az osztályhatalomhoz (The Intellectuals on the Road to Class Power) 1978, Az autonómia kisértése (The Temptation of Autonomy) 1980, Antipolitics 1986, Esszék 91–93 (Essays 1991–93) 1993, The Melancholy of Rebirth 1995, Várakozás (Expectation) 1995, Áramló leltár 1996, Láthatatlan hang (The Invisible Voice: Meditations on Jewish Themes) 2000. *Honours:* Herder Prize, Vienna-Hamburg 1984, Charles Veillon European Essay, Zürich 1985, Fredfonden Peace Foundation, Copenhagen 1986, Fed. Critics' Prize for Novel of the Year (FRG) 1986, Maecenas Prize 1989, Manès-Sperber Prize 1990, Kossuth Prize, Friedens-Preis des Deutschen Buchhandels 1991, Karlspreis zu Aachen 2001; numerous scholarships. *Address:* Torockó utca 3, 1026 Budapest, Hungary. *Telephone:* (1) 560-425.

KONWICKI, Tadeusz; Polish writer, film director and screenwriter; b. 22 June 1926, Nowa Wilejka, USSR (now in Lithuania); m. Danuta Lenica (deceased). *Education:* Jagiellonian Univ., Kraków, Warsaw Univ. *Career:* partisan with Home Army detachment 1944–45; mem. Polish Writers' Asscn 1949–, Polish Language Council; mem. editorial staff Nowa Kultura (weekly) 1950–57. *Films directed:* Ostatni dzień lata (Last Day of Summer) 1958, Zaduszki 1962, Salto 1965, Jak daleko stąd jak blisko 1972, Dolina Issy 1982, Lawa 1989. *Publications:* novels: Władza 1954, Godzina smutku 1954, Z oblężonego miasta 1955, Rojsty 1956, Dziura w niebie 1959, Sennik współczesny (A Dreambook of Our Time) 1963, Ostatni dzień lata (filmscript)

1966, Wniebowstąpienie 1967, Zwierzoczłekoupiór 1969, Nic albo nic 1971, Kronika wypadków miłosnych 1974, Kalendarz i klepsydra (The Calendar and the Sand-Glass) 1976, Kompleks polski 1977, Mała apokalipsa 1979, Wschody i zachody Księżyca 1982, Rzeka podziemma, podziemne ptaki 1984; Nowy Świat i okolice 1986, Bohiń 1987, Zorze wieczorne 1991, Czytadło 1994, Pamflet na samego siebie (Slander Against Myself) 1995, Pamietam, ze bylo goraco (I Remember It Was Hot) 2001; filmscripts: Zimowy zmierzch (Winter Twilight), Matka Joanna od aniołów 1961, Faraon 1965, Jowita 1968, Austeria 1982, Chronicle of Amorous Incidents 1985. *Honours:* Officer's Cross, Order of Polonia Restituta 1964; State Prize, 3rd Class 1950, 1954, 1st Class 1966; Mondello Prize for Literature 1981 and many other awards and prizes at int. film festivals, including Venice 1958. *Address:* ul. Górskiego 1 m. 68, 00-033 Warsaw, Poland.

KOOMSON, Dorothy, MA; British novelist and journalist; b. 1971, London, England. *Education:* Univ. of Leeds, Goldsmiths Coll. *Publications:* The Cupid Effect 2003, The Chocolate Run 2004, My Best Friend's Girl 2006, Marshmallows for Breakfast 2007, Goodnight, Beautiful 2008, The Ice Cream Girls 2010, The Woman He Loved Before 2011; contrib. to numerous magazines and newspapers, including the Guardian, The Independent on Sunday, New Woman, Red, J17 and Cosmopolitan. *Literary Agent:* c/o Antony Harwood Ltd, 103 Walton Street, Oxford, OX2 6EB, England. *Telephone:* (1865) 559615. *Fax:* (1865) 310660. *E-mail:* mail@antonyharwood.com. *Website:* www.antonyharwood.com; www.dorothykoomson.co.uk (office).

KOONTZ, Dean Ray, (David Axton, Brian Coffey, Deanna Dwyer, K. R. Dwyer, John Hill, Leigh Nichols, Anthony North, Richard Paige, Owen West), BS; American writer; b. 9 July 1945, Everett, PA; s. of Raymond Koontz and Florence Logue; m. Gerda Ann Cerra 1966. *Education:* Shippensburg Univ. *Career:* fmr teacher of English; freelance author 1969–; work includes novels, short stories, science fiction/fantasy, social commentary/phenomena and journalism. *Publications include:* Star Quest 1968, The Fall of the Dream Machine 1969, Fear That Man 1969, Anti-Man 1970, Beastchild 1970, Dark of the Woods 1970, The Dark Symphony 1970, Hell's Gate 1970, The Crimson Witch 1971, A Darkness in My Soul 1972, The Flesh in the Furnace 1972, Starblood 1972, Time Thieves 1972, Warlock 1972, A Werewolf Among Us 1973, Hanging On 1973, The Haunted Earth 1973, Demon Seed 1973, Strike Deep 1974, After the Last Race 1974, Nightmare Journey 1975, The Long Sleep 1975, Night Chills 1976, The Voice of the Night 1980, Whispers 1980, The Funhouse 1980, The Eyes of Darkness 1981, The Mask 1981, House of Thunder 1982, Phantoms 1983, Darkness Comes 1984, Twilight 1984, The Door to December 1985, Strangers 1986, Shadow Fires 1987, Watchers 1987, Twilight Eyes 1987, Oddkins 1988, Servants of Twilight 1988, Lightning 1988, Midnight 1989, The Bad Place 1990, Cold Fire 1991, Hideaway 1992, Dragon Tears 1992, Winter Moon 1993, The House of Thunder 1993, Dark Rivers of the Heart 1994, Mr Murder 1994, Fun House 1994, Strange Highways 1994, Icebound 1995, Intensity 1995, The Key to Midnight 1995, Ticktock 1996, Santa's Twin 1996, Sole Survivor 1996, Fear Nothing 1997, Seize the Night 1998, False Memory 1999, From the Corner of his Eye 2001, One Door Away From Heaven 2001, By the Light of the Moon 2002, The Face 2003, Odd Thomas 2003, Life Expectancy 2004, Frankenstein Book 1: Prodigal Son (with Kevin J. Anderson) 2004, Frankenstein Book 2: City of Night (with Ed Gorman) 2005, Forever Odd 2005, The Husband 2006, Brother Odd 2006, The Good Guy 2007, The Darkest Evening of the Year 2007, Odd Hours 2008, Bliss to You 2008, In Odd We Trust 2008, Shadowfires 2008, The Bad Place 2008, Your Heart Belongs to Me 2008, Relentless 2009, Frankenstein Book 3: Dead and Alive 2009, Breathless 2009, A Big Little Life 2009, Frankenstein Book 4: Lost Souls 2010, Odd is On Our Side 2010, Darkness Under the Sun 2010, What the Night Knows 2011, Frankenstein Book 5: The Dead Town 2011, The Moonlit Mind 2011, 77 Shadow Street 2011, House of Odd 2012, Odd Apocalypse 2012. *Honours:* Hon. DLitt (Shippensburg) 1989. *Address:* POB 9529, Newport Beach, CA 92658, USA (office). *E-mail:* dean@deankoontz.com (office). *Website:* www.deankoontz.com.

KOOSER, Theodore (Ted), BS, MA; American poet and writer; b. 25 April 1939, Ames, Ia; m. 1st Diana Tresslar 1962 (divorced 1969); one s.; m. 2nd Kathleen Rutledge 1977. *Education:* Iowa State Univ., Univ. of Nebraska. *Career:* Underwriter, Bankers Life Nebraska 1965–73; part-time instructor in creative writing 1970–, Sr Underwriter, Lincoln Benefit Life 1973–84, Vice-Pres. 1984–98; currently Prof., Univ. of Neb., Lincoln; Ed. and Publr, Windflower Press; Poet Laureate of the USA 2004–06. *Publications include:* Official Entry Blank 1969, Grass County 1971, A Local Habitation and a Name 1974, Shooting a Farmhouse: So This is Nebraska 1975, Not Coming to be Barked At 1976, Voyages to the Inland Sea (with Harley Elliott) 1976, Hatcher 1978, Old Marriage and New 1978, Cottonwood County (with William Kloefkorn) 1979, Windflower Home Almanac of Poetry (ed.) 1980, Sure Signs: New and Selected Poems (Soc. of Midland Authors Poetry Prize) 1980, One World at a Time 1985, As Far as I Can See: Contemporary Writers of the Middle Plains (ed.) 1989, Etudes 1992, Weather Central 1994, A Book of Things 1995, A Decade of Ted Kooser Valentines 1996, Riding with Colonel Carter 1999, Winter Morning Walks: 100 Postcards to Jim Harrison (Nebraska Book Award for poetry 2001) 2000, Braided Creek: A Conversation in Poetry (with Jim Harrison) 2003, Local Wonders: Seasons in the Bohemian Alps (Friends of American Writers Chicago Award, ForeWord Magazine Gold Award for Autobiography, Nebraska Book Award for Nonfiction 2003) 2002, Delights and Shadows (Pulitzer Prize for Poetry 2005) 2004, The Poetry Home Repair Manual 2004, Flying at Night: Poems 1965–1985 2005, Valentines 2008; contrib. to The American Poetry Review, Antioch Review, Cream City Review, The Hudson Review, Kansas Quarterly, The Kenyon Review, Midwest Quarterly, The New Yorker, Poetry Northwest, Poetry, Prairie Schooner, Shenandoah, Tailwind. *Honours:* John H. Vreeland Award for Creative Writing 1964, Prairier Schooner Prizes in Poetry 1976, 1978, NEA Literary Fellowships 1976, 1984, Columbia Magazine Stanley Kunitz Poetry Prize 1984, Governor's Arts Award 1988, Mayor's Arts Award 1989, Poetry Northwest Richard Hugo Prize 1994, Nebraska Arts Council Merit Award 2000, Pushcart Prize, James Boatwright Prize. *Website:* www.blueflowerarts.com*Address:* 1820 Branched Oak Road, Garland, NE 68360-9303, USA (home). *E-mail:* kr84428@windstream.net (home). *Website:* www.tedkooser.net (home).

KOPIT, Arthur, AB; American dramatist and screenwriter; b. 10 May 1937, New York, NY; m. Leslie Ann Garis; two s. one d. *Education:* Harvard University. *Career:* Fellow, 1974–75, Playwright-in-Residence, 1975–76, Wesleyan University; CBS Fellow, 1976–77, Adjunct Prof. of Playwriting, 1977–80, Yale University; Adjunct Prof. of Playwriting, City College, CUNY, 1981–; mem. Dramatists Guild; Hasty Pudding Society; PEN; Signet Society; Writers Guild of America. *Publications:* Plays: Questioning of Nick, 1957; Gemini, 1957; Don Juan in Texas, 1957; On the Runway of Life You Never Know What's Coming Off Next, 1957; Across the River and Into the Jungle, 1958; Sing to Me Through Open Windows, 1959; To Dwell in a Place of Strangers, 1959; Aubade, 1959; Oh Dad, Poor Dad, Mamma's Hung You in the Closet and I'm Fellin' So Sad, 1960; Asylum, or What the Gentlemen Are Up To, and As For the Ladies, 1963; Mhil'daim, 1963; Chamber Music, 1965; Sing to Me Through Open Windows, 1965; The Day the Whores Came Out to Play Tennis, 1965; Indians, 1968; What's Happened to the Thorne's House, 1972; The Conquest of Everest, 1973; The Hero, 1973; Louisiana Territory, or Lewis and Clark Lost and Found, 1975; Secrets of the Rice, 1976; Wings, 1978; End of the World, 1984; Road to Nirvana, 1991. Contributions: Films and television. *Honours:* Vernon Rice Award, 1960; Outer Critics Circle Award, 1960; Guggenheim Fellowship, 1967; Rockefeller Foundation Grant, 1968; American Institute of Arts and Letters Award, 1971; National Endowment for the Humanities Grant, 1974; Prix Italia, 1978; Tony Award, 1982.

KOPS, Bernard; British poet, writer and dramatist; b. 28 Nov. 1926, London; m. Erica Gordon 1956; four c. *Career:* Lecturer, Spiro Inst. 1985–86, Surrey Educ. Authority, Ealing Educ. Authority, Inner London Educ. Authority, Arts Educational School/Acting Co. 1989–90, City Literary Inst. 1990–93. *Publications:* poetry: Poems 1955, Poems and Songs 1958, Anemone for Antigone 1959, Erica, I Want to Read You Something 1967, For the Record 1971, Barricades in West Hampstead 1988, Grandchildren and Other Poems 2000; other: Awake for Mourning 1958, Motorbike 1962, Autobiography, The World is a Wedding 1963, Yes From No Man's Land 1965, By the Waters of Whitechapel 1970, The Passionate Past of Gloria Gaye 1971, Settle Down Simon Katz 1973, Partners 1975, On Margate Sands 1978; 32 plays, including The Hamlet of Stepney Green 1958, Goodbye World 1959, Change for the Angel 1960, Stray Cats and Empty Bottles 1961, Enter Solly Gold 1962, The Boy Who Wouldn't Play Jesus 1965, More Out Than In 1980, Ezra 1981, Simon at Midnight 1982, Some of These Days 1990, Sophie: Last of the Red Hot Mamas 1990, Playing Sinatra 1991, Androcles and the Lion 1992, Dreams of Anne Frank 1992, Who Shall I Be Tomorrow? 1992, Call in the Night 1995, Green Rabbi 1997, Cafe Zeitgeist 1998, Collected Plays (three vols) 1998, 2000, 2002, Shalom Bomb 2000, Returning We Hear the Larks 2004, I Am Isaac Babel 2005, The Opening 2005, Knocking on Heaven's Door 2005–06. *Honours:* Arts Council Bursaries 1957, 1979, 1985, and Awards 1991, 2003, 2006, C. Day-Lewis Fellowship 1981–83, London Fringe Award 1993, Writer's Guild of GB Best Radio Play Awards 1995, 1996. *Literary Agent:* c/o Emily Hayward, Sheil Land Associates, 52 Doughty Street, London, WC1N 2LS, England. *Telephone:* (20) 7405-9351. *Fax:* (20) 7831-2127. *E-mail:* ehayward@sheilland.co.uk. *Address:* 41B Canfield Gardens, London, NW6 3JL, England (home). *Telephone:* (20) 7624-2940 (home); (20) 7624-2840 (home). *E-mail:* bernardkops@tiscali.co.uk (home).

KORDA, Michael Vincent, BA; American publishing executive (retd); *Editor-in-Chief Emeritus, Simon & Schuster Inc.*; b. 8 Oct. 1933, London, England; s. of Vincent Korda and Gertrude Korda (née Musgrove); m. Carolyn Keese 1958; one s. *Education:* Magdalen Coll., Oxford, UK. *Career:* served in RAF 1952–54; joined Simon and Schuster, New York 1958–, first as Ed., then Sr Ed., Man. Ed., Exec. Ed., Sr Vice-Pres. and Ed.-in-Chief, Ed.-in-Chief Emer. 2005–; mem. Nat. Soc. of Film Critics, American Horse Shows Assn. *Publications:* Male Chauvinism: How It Works 1973, Power: How to Get It, How to Use It 1975, Success! 1977, Charmed Lives 1979, Worldly Goods 1982, The Fortune 1989, Man to Man: Surviving Prostate Cancer 1997, Another Life, 2000, Making the List 2001, Country Matters 2002, Horse People 2004, Ulysses S. Grant: The Unlikely Hero 2004, Marking Time: Collecting Watches and Thinking about Time 2004, Journey to a Revolution: A Personal Memoir and History of the Hungarian Revolution of 1956 2006, Cat People (with Margaret Korda) 2006, Ike: An American Hero 2007, With Wings Like Eagles 2009, Hero: The Life and Legend of Lawrence of Arabia 2010. *Address:* c/o Simon and Schuster, 1230 Avenue of the Americas, New York, NY 10020, USA.

KORG, Jacob, MA, PhD; American academic and writer; *Professor Emeritus of English, University of Washington, Seattle*; b. 21 Nov. 1922, New York, NY. *Education:* City Coll., CUNY, Columbia Univ., New York. *Career:* Bard Coll. 1948–50; City Coll., CUNY 1950–55; Asst and later Assoc. Prof., Univ. of

Washington, Seattle 1955–65, Prof. of English 1965–91, Prof. Emer. 1991–; mem. Int. Asscn of Univ. Profs of English, Modern Language Asscn, Asscn of Literary Scholars and Critics. *Publications:* Westward to Oregon (co-ed. with S. F. Anderson) 1958, Thought in Prose (co-ed. with R. S. Beal) 1958, An Introduction to Poetry 1959, London in Dickens's Day (ed.) 1960, The Complete Reader (co-ed. with R. S. Beal) 1961, George Gissing's Commonplace Book (ed.) 1962, George Gissing: A Critical Biography 1963, Dylan Thomas 1965, The Force of Few Words 1966, Twentieth Century Interpretations of Bleak House (ed.) 1968, The Poetry of Robert Browning (ed.) 1971, George Gissing: Thyrza (ed.) 1974, George Gissing: The Unclassed (ed.) 1978, Language in Modern Literature 1979, Browning and Italy 1983, Ritual and Experiment in Modern Poetry 1995, Winter Love: Ezra Pound and H. D. 2003; contribs to professional journals. *Address:* Department of English, University of Washington, 900 University Street, Apt 14–0, Seattle, WA 98101, USA (office). *Telephone:* (206) 525-2276 (office). *E-mail:* korg@u.washington.edu (office).

KORHONEN, Riku; Finnish writer; b. 1972, Turku; m. Anna-Leena Härkönen 2009. *Career:* fmr high school teacher of Finnish language, then teacher of creative writing, Univ. of Turku 2004–08; freelance writer and columnist, Helsingin Sanomat (newspaper). *Play:* Two Stories in One Night (Turku City Theatre 2008). *Publications include:* Kahden ja yhden yön tarinoita (And Two Stories in One Night) (Helsingin Sanomat First Novel Prize) 2003, Savumerkkejä lähtöä harkitseville (Smoke Signals for Those Considering Leaving) (poems) 2005, Lääkäriromaani (The Doctor Novel) (Kalevi Jäntti Prize for Young Authors, Turku Cultural Bd Aboa Award, EU Prize for Literature 2010) 2008, Hyvästi tytöt (Goodbye Girls) (short stories) 2009. *Address:* c/o Kustannusosakeyhtiö Sammakko, Puutarhakatu 25, 20100 Turku, Finland (office). *Telephone:* 22306031 (office). *Website:* kauppa .sammakko.com.

KORMONDY, Edward John, BA, MS, PhD; American academic and writer; b. 10 June 1926, Beacon, NY. *Education:* Tusculum Coll., Univ. of Michigan. *Career:* Instructor in Zoology and Curator of Insects, Museum of Zoology, Univ. of Michigan 1955–57; Asst Prof. to Prof. of Biology, Oberlin Coll. 1957–68; Dir Comm. on Undergraduate Educ. in the Biological Sciences and the Office of Biological Educ., American Inst. of Biological Sciences 1968–71; mem. Faculty, Evergreen State Coll., Olympia, Wash. 1971–79, Interim Acting Dean 1972–73, Vice-Pres. and Provost 1973–78; Sr Professional Assoc., NSF 1979; Provost and Prof. of Biology, Univ. of Southern Maine, Portland 1979–82; Vice-Pres. for Academic Affairs and Prof. of Biology, California State Univ., Los Angeles 1982–86; Sr Vice-Pres. Univ. of Hawaii 1991–93, Chancellor and Prof. of Biology, Univ. of Hawaii at Hilo and at West Oahu 1986–93; Pres. Univ. of West Los Angeles 1995–97; Special Asst to the Pres., Pacific Oaks Coll. 2000–05. *Publications:* Introduction to Genetics 1964, Readings in Ecology (ed.) 1965, Readings in General Biology (ed., two vols) 1966, Concepts of Ecology 1969, Population and Food (ed. with R. Leisner) 1971, Pollution (co-ed. with R. Leisner) 1971, Ecology (co-ed. with R. Leisner) 1971, Environmental Education: Academia's Response (with J. Aldrich) 1972, General Biology: The Natural History and Integrity of Organisms (with others) 1977, Handbook of Contemporary Developments in World Ecology (with F. McCormick) 1981, Environmental Sciences: The Way the World Works (with B. Nebel) 1981, Biology (with B. Essenfield) 1984, International Handbook of Pollution Control 1989, Environmental Education: Academia's Response (with P. Corcoran) 1997, Fundamentals of Human Ecology (with D. Brown) 1998, University of Hawaii-Hilo: A College in the Making (with F. Inouye) 2001; contrib. to professional journals. *Honours:* Hon. DSc (Tusculum Coll.) 1997. *Address:* 1388 Lucile Avenue, Los Angeles, CA 90026-1520, USA (home). *Telephone:* (323) 666-6372 (home). *Fax:* (323) 666-1258 (home). *E-mail:* ekor@aol.com (home).

KORNFELD, Robert Jonathan, BA; American dramatist, writer and poet; b. 3 March 1919, Newtonville, Mass; m. Celia Seiferth 1945; one s. *Education:* Harvard Univ., Columbia Univ., Tulane Univ., New York Univ., New School for Social Research, Circle-in-the-Square School of Theatre, Playwrights' Horizons Theatre School and Laboratory. *Career:* Visiting Artist, American Acad., Rome 1996; Playwright-in-Residence, Univ. of Wisconsin 1998; mem. Authors' League, Dramatists' Guild, Nat. Arts Club, New York Drama League, PEN, Theater for the New City (bd mem. 2002), Bronx County Democratic Cttee, Times Square Playwrights. *Plays written:* A Dream Within a Dream (opera libretto) 1987, Ligeia (opera libretto) 1987, Music For Saint Nicholas 1992, Hot Wind From the South 1995, The Hanged Man 1996. *Plays produced:* Hot Wind From the South 1995, The Hanged Man 1996, Father New Orleans 1997, The Queen of Carnival 1997, The Art of Love 1998, The Celestials 1998, Passage in Purgatory, Shanghai, China 2000, The Gates of Hell 2002. *Publications include:* non-fiction: Great Southern Mansions 1977, Landmarks of the Bronx (jtly) 1990; fiction and poetry; contrib. to various publications. *Honours:* numerous awards and prizes. *Address:* The Withers Cottage, 5286 Sycamore Avenue, Riverdale, NY 10471, USA (home). *Telephone:* (718) 549-6643 (home). *E-mail:* rojokosr@aol.com (home).

KOROTYCH, Vitaliy Alekseyevich; Russian/Ukrainian writer and poet; *Editor, Boulevard magazine*; b. 26 May 1936, Kiev; s. of Aleksey Korotych and Zoa Korotych; m. Zinaida Korotych 1958; two s. *Education:* Kiev Medical Inst. *Career:* physician 1959–66; Ed. Ukrainian literary journal Ranok 1966–77; Ed.-in-Chief Vsesvit magazine 1978–86; Ed.-in-Chief Ogonyok weekly magazine 1986–91; Sec. of Ukrainian Writers' Union 1966–69; mem. USSR Writers' Union 1981–90; USSR People's Deputy 1989–91; Prof. Boston Univ., USA 1991–98, returned to Moscow; ed. Boulevard magazine and others 1998–. *Publications include:* Golden Hands 1961, The Smell of Heaven 1962, Cornflower Street 1963, O Canada! 1966, Poetry 1967, Metronome (novel) 1982, The Face of Enmity (novel) 1984, Memory, Bread and Love 1986, Le Visage de la haine (travel essays) 1988, Glasnost und Perestroika 1990, The Waiting Room (memoirs, Vol. I) 1991, On My Behalf (memoirs, Vol. II) 2000, Selected Poems 2005, Selected Essays 2005; many translations from English into Ukrainian and other Slavonic languages. *Honours:* several Russian, Ukrainian, Polish and Bulgarian decorations and medals including two USSR State Prizes, A. Tolstoy Prize 1982, Int. Julius Fuchik Prize 1984, Wiental Prize, Georgetown Univ. (USA) 1987, Int. Ed. of the year, W P Revue (USA) 1989, Johann Wolfgang von Goethe Medallion, European Acad. of Natural Sciences 2006, Moscow Writers' Union Prize 2007. *Address:* Trifonovskaya str. 11, Apt. 256, 127018 Moscow, Russia (home). *Telephone:* (495) 689-03-84 (home); (496) 462-67-44 (home). *Fax:* (495) 689-03-84 (home). *E-mail:* vkorotich@yandex.ru (home); vak1137@mail.ru (home).

KORZENIK, Diana, BA, EdD; American academic, writer and artist; *Professor Emerita, Massachusetts College of Art, Boston*; b. 15 March 1941, New York, NY. *Education:* Oberlin Coll., Vassar Coll., Columbia Univ., Harvard Univ. Grad. School of Educ. *Career:* Prof. Emer., Massachusetts Coll. of Art, Boston; Founder, first Pres. and Bd mem. Friends of The Longfellow House; mem. Advisory Bd Teen Voices magazine; mem. American Antiquarian Soc., Massachusetts Historical Soc.; participating artist in The Art Connection, Boston, Mass. *Art exhibitions include:* Writers' Room of Boston 2003. *Publications:* Art and Cognition (co-ed. with Leondar & Perkins) 1977, Drawn to Art 1986, Art Making and Education (with Maurice Brown) 1993, The Cultivation of American Artists (co-ed. with Sloat and Barnhill) 1997, Objects of American Art Education (Leab Award, American Library Asscn) 2004; contrib. to professional journals and to magazines. *Honours:* Woodrow Wilson Fellow 1962, Boston Globe L.L. Winship Literary Award 1986, Nat. Art Educ. Asscn Lowenfeld Award 1998. *Address:* 7 Norman Road, Newton Highlands, MA 02461, USA (home). *Telephone:* (617) 965-9338 (home). *E-mail:* dkorzenik@comcast.net (home).

KORZHAVIN, Naum; Russian author and poet; b. (Mandel Emmanuel Moiseyevich Korzhavin), 14 Oct. 1925, Kiev. *Education:* Karaganda Mining Inst. and Gorky Inst. of Literature, Moscow 1959. *Career:* first publication 1941; exiled to USA 1974; revisited Moscow 1989; citizenship and membership of Writers' Union restored 1990. *Publications include:* The Years 1963, Where Are You? 1964, Bread, Children in Auschwitz, Autumn in Karaganda, Verse 1981, Selected Verse 1983, Interlacements 1987, Letter to Moscow 1991, The Time is Given 1992, To Myself 1998; contributor to émigré dissident journal Kontinent. *Honours:* Big Book Nat. Literary Award 2006. *Address:* 28c Colborne Road, Apt 2, Brighton, MA 02135, USA.

KOSICE, Gyula; Argentine artist and poet; b. 26 April 1924, Košice, Czechoslovakia (now Slovakia); s. of Joseph F. Falk and Eta Falk (née Berger); m. Haydée Itzkovitz 1947; two d. *Education:* Acad. of Arts, Buenos Aires. *Career:* co-f. Arturo magazine 1944, Concrete Art Invention 1945; f. Madí Art Movt 1946, Founder and Ed. Universal Madí Art magazine 1947; first use of neon gas in art 1946; introduction of water as essential component of his work 1948; creator Hydrospatial City (concept) 1948–; works include sculptures, hydrospatial courses, hydromurals; works in museums and pvt. collections in Argentina, Latin America, USA, Europe and Asia. *Exhibitions:* more than 35 solo and 600 group exhbns, including Madí Art Exhbn Salon des Réalités Nouvelles, Paris 1948, 50-year retrospective Museum of Fine Arts, Buenos Aires 1991, Homenaje a Kosice, Museo Arte Moderno Buenos Aires 1994, anthology exhbn (120 works) Centro Recoleta, Buenos Aires 1999–, Digital Works Centro Recoleta, Buenos Aires 2003. *Publications:* Invención 1945, Madí Manifesto 1946, Golse-Se (poems) 1952, Peso y Medida de Alberto Hidalgo 1953, Antología Madí 1955, Geocultura de la Europa de Hoy 1959, Poème hydraulique 1960, Arte Hidrocinético 1968, La Ciudad Hidroespacial 1972, Arte y Arquitectura del Agua 1974, Arte Madí 1982, Obra Poética 1984, Entrevisiones 1984, Teoría sobre el Arte 1987, Arte y Filosofía Porvenirista 1996, Madí grafías 2001, Autobiography 2010, 500 Places to Live (Hydrospatial City) 2010. *Honours:* Hon. Citizen of Buenos Aires, Hon. Citizen of Košice; Chevalier des Arts et des Lettres; Best Art Book, Asscn of Art Critics for Arte Madi 1982, Ordre des Arts et des Lettres 1989, Premio Trayectoria en el Arte, Nat. Arts Foundation 1994, Ciudadano Ilustre de la Ciudad de Buenos Aires 1997, Homenaje por Trayectoria de 62 Años, Centro Recoleta 2003. *Address:* Humahuaca 4662, Buenos Aires (office); República de la India 3135 6° A, 1425 Buenos Aires, Argentina (home). *Telephone:* (11) 4867-1240 (office); (11) 4801-8615 (home). *Fax:* (11) 4801-8615 (home). *E-mail:* gyula@kosice.com .ar (home). *Website:* www.kosice.com.ar (office).

KOSTASH, Myrna Ann, BA, MA; Canadian writer; b. 2 Sept. 1944, Edmonton, Alberta; d. of William Kostash and Mary Maksymiuk. *Education:* Univs of Alberta and Toronto. *Career:* Writer-in-Residence, The Loft, Minneapolis, Minn. 1993, Regina Public Library 1996–97, Saskatoon Public Library 2002–03, Univ. of Alberta 2003–04; documentary writer/researcher, CBC; mem. Writers' Union of Canada (Chair. 1993–94), Writers' Guild of Alberta (Pres. 1989–90), Canadian Conf. of the Arts (mem. Bd of Govs 1996–), PEN Canada, Parkland Inst. (mem. Bd of Dirs 2001–); Founder and Pres. Creative Nonfiction Collective, Program Cttee, Edmonton Int. Nonfiction Literary Festival 2006–. *Plays:* several stage plays. *Radio:* several documentaries. *Publications:* All of Baba's Children 1977, Long Way From Home 1980, No Kidding 1988, Bloodlines 1993, The Doomed Bridgeroom: A Memoir 1998,

The Next Canada: In Search of the Future Nation 2000, Reading the River: A Traveller's Companion to the North Saskatchewan River 2005, The Frog Lake Reader 2009, Prodigal Daughter: A Journey to Byzantium 2010; contrib. to Saturday Night, Canadian Forum, Brick, Border Crossings, Canadian Geographic, Prairie Fire, Journal of Canadian Studies, Signs, mostovi, Literature na swiece. *Honours:* Hon. Lifetime mem. Canadian Conf. of the Arts; Queen's Silver Jubilee Medal 1977; Canada Council Sr Artist Grants, Nat. Magazine Silver Prize, Alberta Achievement Award, Writers Trust Matt Cohen Award for Life of Writing. *Address:* 110, 11716-100 Avenue, Edmonton, AB T5K 2G3, Canada (home). *E-mail:* kostashm@yahoo.ca (office). *Website:* www.myrnakostash.com (office).

KOSTELANETZ, Richard Cory, AB, MA; American writer, poet, critic, artist and composer; b. 14 May 1940, New York, NY. *Education:* Brown Univ., King's Coll., London, Columbia Univ., Morley Coll., London, New School for Social Research, New York. *Career:* Literary Dir, Future Press, New York 1976–; sole proprietor, Archae Editions, New York 1978–; contributing ed. to various journals; guest lecturer and reader at many colls and univs; numerous exhibitions as an artist; Pollock-Kraser Master Artist Foundation 2001, Atlantic Center for the Arts, New Smyrna Beach, Fla 2002; Woodrow Wilson Fellowship 1962–63; Fulbright Fellowship 1964–65; Pulitzer Fellowship 1965–66; Guggenheim Fellowship 1967; Fellow New Asscn of Sephardic/Mizrahi Artists and Writers Int. 2000–02; mem., American Soc. of Composers, Authors and Publishers (ASCAP), Int. Asscn of Art Critics. *Audio art (radio):* Praying to the Lord 1981, Invocations 1981, Die Evangelien 1982, The Gospels 1982, The Eight Nights of Hanukah 1983, New York City 1984, The Gospels Abridged 1986, Le Bateau Ivre 1986, Ululation 1992, Epiphanies 1992. *Film and video:* Alternative Views 2005, More Wordworks 2005, Furtherest Fictions 2007. *Publications include:* poetry: Visual Language 1970, I Articulations/Short Fictions 1974, Portraits From Memory 1975, Numbers: Poems and Stories 1976, Rain Rains Rain 1976, Illuminations 1977, Numbers Two 1977, Richard Kostelanetz 1980, Turfs/Arenas/Fields/Pitches 1980, Arenas/Fields/Pitches/Turfs 1982, Fields/Pitches/Turfs/Arenas 1990, Solos, Duets, Trios, and Choruses 1991, Wordworks: Poems Selected and New 1993, Paritions 1993, Repartitions 1994, More Wordworks 2004; fiction: In the Beginning (novel) 1971, Constructs (five vols) 1975–91, One Night Stood (novel) 1977, Tabula Rasa: A Constructivist Novel 1978, Exhaustive Parallel Intervals (novel) 1979, Fifty Untitled Constructivist Fictions 1991, 3-Element Stories 1998, Kaddish and Other Short Pieces 2004; non-fiction: Recyclings: A Literary Autobiography (two vols) 1974, 1984, The End of Intelligent Writing: Literary Politics in America 1974, Metamorphosis in the Arts 1980, The Old Poetries and the New 1981, The Grants-Fix: Publicly Funded Literary Granting in America 1987, The Old Fictions and the New 1987, On Innovative Music(ian)s 1989, Unfinished Business: An Intellectual Nonhistory 1990, The New Poetries and Some Old 1991, Published Encomia 1967–91 1991, On Innovative Art(ist)s 1992, A Dictionary of the Avant-Gardes 1993, On Innovative Performance(s) 1994, Fillmore East: 25 Years After: Recollections of Rock Theatre 1995, An ABC of Contemporary Reading 1995, Crimes of Culture 1995, Radio Writings 1995, John Cage (Ex)plain(ed) 1996, Thirty Years of Critical Engagement with John Cage 1996, One Million Words of Booknotes 1958–1993 1996, Political Essays 1999, Three Canadian Geniuses 2001, SoHo: The Rise and Fall of an Artists' Colony 2003, Dis/sections 2003, Thirty-Five Years of Visible Writing, 2004, Autobiographies at 60 2004, Autobiographies at 50 2006; plays: Collected Performance Texts 1998; e-books: The Maturity of American Thought 2006, Home and Away 2006, Book-Art, Anthologies and Alternative Publishing 2006, A Book of Kostis 2006, Jewish Writings So Far 2006, On Sports and Sportsmen 2006, A Special Time 2006; editor of many books; films, videotapes, radio scripts, recordings; contribs to many anthologies, numerous poems, articles, essays, reviews in journals and other publications. *Honours:* Nat. Endowment for the Arts grants 1976, 1978–79, 1981–82, 1985 (twice), 1986, 1990–91, American Inst. of Graphic Arts One of Best Books award 1976, Pushcart Prize 1977, Deutscher Akademischer Austauschdienst Stipend, Berlin 1981–83, ASCAP Awards 1983–91, 1992–2004, 2005–. *Address:* PO Box 444, Prince Street Station, New York, NY 10012-0008, USA. *E-mail:* richkostelanetz@aol.com. *Website:* www.richardkostelanetz.com.

KOSTENKO, Lina Vasilievna; Ukrainian poet; b. 19 March 1930, Rzhischevo, Kiev Region. *Education:* Kiev Pedagogical Inst. and Maxim Gorky Inst. of Literature, Moscow. *Publications:* Rays of the Earth 1957, Sails 1958, Wanderings of the Heart 1961, On the Shores of the Eternal River 1977, Inimitability 1980, Marusya Churay (novel in verse) 1979–82, The Integral of the Cosmos, The Scythian Odyssey 1981, Snow in Florence, A Duma About the Non-Azov Brothers, The Garden of Unmelting Sculptures 1987, Selected Works 1989, Berestechko (historical poem) 2000, Landscapes of Memory: The Selected Later Poetry of Lina Kostenko 2002; children's verse: The Lilac King; numerous publs in literary magazines. *Honours:* Hon. Prof., Nat. Univ. of Kyiv-Mohyla Acad. Taras Shevchenko Prize 1987. *Address:* Chkalova str. 52, Apt 8, 252054 Kiev, Ukraine (home). *Telephone:* (44) 224-70-38 (home).

KOSTOVA, Elizabeth, MFA; American writer; b. 26 Dec. 1964, New London, Conn.; m. Georgi Kostov. *Education:* Yale Univ., Univ. of Michigan. *Career:* taught English as a second language, creative writing and composition at univs in Phila, Pa. *Publications:* novels: The Historian (Quill Award for Debut Author of the Year, Book Sense Award for Best Adult Fiction 2006) 2005, The Swan Thieves 2010. *Honours:* Hopwood Award for Novel-in-Progress. *Literary Agent:* c/o Amy Williams, McCormick Williams, 37 West 20th Street, New York, NY 10011, USA. *Telephone:* (212) 691-9726. *Website:* www.mccormickwilliams.com. *Address:* c/o Author Mail, Little, Brown and Company, 237 Park Avenue, New York, NY 10017, USA (office). *Website:* www.theswanthieves.com.

KOTHARI, Rita, BA, MA, MPhil, PhD; Indian author, translator and academic; *Associate Professor, Humanities and Social Studies Department, Indian Institute of Technology, Gandhinagar*. *Education:* Gujarat Univ., Univ. of Poona. *Career:* Lecturer, Sadguna Girls Coll., Ahmedabad 1991–92; Lecturer, St Xavier's Coll., Ahmedabad 1992–2007; Assoc. Prof., Mudra Inst. of Communications, Ahmedabad 2007–09, Prof. 2009–11; Assoc. Prof., Humanities and Social Sciences Dept, Indian Inst. of Tech., Gandhinagar 2011–; Research Fellow, Indian Inst. of Advanced Studies, Shimla 2010. *Publications include:* as author: Translating India: The Cultural Politics of English 2005, The Burden of Refuge: The Sindhi Hindus of Gujarat 2007, Partition, Memories and Movements: Borders and Communities in Banni, Kutch, Gujarat (forthcoming); as co-ed.: Decentring Translation Studies: India and Beyond 2009, Chutnefying English: The Phenomenon of Hinglish 2011; as trans.: numerous novels and poetry anthologies. *Honours:* numerous including: Fellowship, S Asia Regional Council (Ford Foundation) Project on Stigmatised Identities 2005, Int. Centre for Writing and Trans. Grant, Univ. of Calif., Irvine 2006. *Address:* Indian Institute of Technology Gandhinagar, Vishwakarma Government Engineering College Complex, Chandkheda, Visat-Gandhinagar Highway, Ahmedabad, Gujarat 382424, India (office). *Telephone:* (79) 23972324 (office). *Fax:* (79) 23972622 (office). *E-mail:* rita@iitgn.ac.in (office). *Website:* www.iitgn.ac.in/faculty/humanities/rita.htm (office).

KOTKER, (Mary) Zane, (Maggie Strong); American writer; b. 2 Jan. 1934, Waterbury, CT; m. Norman Kotker 1965; one s. one d. *Education:* MA, Columbia University 1959–60. *Publications:* novels: Bodies in Motion 1972, A Certain Man 1976, White Rising 1981, Mainstay (as Maggie Strong) 1988, Try to Remember 1997. *Honours:* National Endowment for the Arts Grant 1972.

KOTZWINKLE, William; American writer; b. 22 Nov. 1938, Scranton, Pennsylvania; m. Elizabeth Gundy 1970. *Education:* Rider College, Pennsylvania State University. *Publications include:* Elephant Bangs Train, 1971; Hermes 3000, 1971; The Fat Man, 1974; Night-Book, 1974; Swimmer in the Secret Sea, 1975; Doctor Rat, 1976; Fata Morgana, 1977; Herr Nightingale and the Satin Woman, 1978; Jack in the Box, 1980; Christmas at Fontaine's, 1982; E.T., the Extra-Terrestrial: A Novel, 1982; Superman III, 1983; Queen of Swords, 1983; E.T., the Book of the Green Planet: A New Novel, 1985; Seduction in Berlin, 1985; Jewell of the Moon, 1985; The Exile, 1987; The Midnight Examiner, 1989; Hot Jazz Trio, 1989; The Game of Thirty, 1994; other: many children's books. *Honours:* National Magazine Award for Fiction 1972, 1975, O. Henry Prize 1975, World Fantasy Award for Best Novel 1977, North Dakota Children's Choice Award 1983, Buckeye Award 1984.

KOUDIL, Hafsa Zinai; Algerian writer, film-maker and actress; b. 1951. *Career:* living in Tunisia; campaigns for the rights of women and against the Islamicization of Algeria. *Films:* Le démon au féminin (writer and dir) 1994, Viva Laldjérie (actress) 2004, Morituri (actress) 2007, Délice Paloma (actress) 2007. *Publications include:* La Fin d'un rêve (autobiog.) 1984, Le Passé décomposé 1993, Le Mariage de jouissance (screenplay).

KOUMI, Margaret (Maggie); British journalist; b. 15 July 1942, d. of the late Yiasoumis Koumi and Melexidia Paraskeva; m. Ramon Sola 1980. *Education:* Buckingham Gate, London. *Career:* sec. Thomas Cook 1957–60; sub-ed., feature and fiction writer Visual Features Ltd 1960–66; sub-ed. TV World 1966–67; Production Ed. 19 Magazine 1967–69, Ed. 1969–86, concurrently Ed. Hair Magazine; Man. Ed. Practical Parenting, Practical Health, Practical Hair and Beauty 1986–87; Jt Ed. Hello! 1988–93, Ed. 1993–2001, Consultant Ed. 2001–. *Publications:* Beauty Care 1981, Claridges – Within The Image 2004. *Honours:* Jt Ed. of the Year Award 1991.

KOURVETARIS, George A., BS, MA, PhD; American/Greek academic, writer and editor; *Professor of Sociology, Northern Illinois University, DeKalb and Editor of the Journal of Political and Military Sociology*; b. 21 Nov. 1933, Eleochorion, Arcadia, Greece; m. 1st Toula Savas 1966 (divorced 1987); two s. one d.; m. 2nd Vassia Dumas Siapkaris 1998. *Education:* Teacher's Coll., Tripolis, Greece, Loyola Univ., Chicago, USA, Roosevelt Univ., Chicago, Northwestern Univ., Evanston, IL. *Career:* Asst Prof., Chicago City Coll. 1967; Fellow and Lecturer, Northwestern Univ. 1967–68; Asst Prof. 1969–73, Assoc. Prof. 1973–78, Prof. of Sociology 1978–, Northern Illinois Univ., DeKalb; Founder-Ed., The Journal of Political and Military Sociology 1973–; founder video/DVD production co. The Paideia Projects-NFP 2003–; mem. American Sociological Asscn, European Community Studies Asscn, Modern Greek Studies Asscn, Southeast European Asscn. *Recordings:* series on the Golden Age of Pericles (Paideia Projects, production of video/DVD). *Publications:* First and Second Generation Greeks in Chicago: An Inquiry Into Their Stratification and Mobility Patterns 1971, Social Origins and Political Orientations of Officer Corps in a World Perspective (co-author) 1973, World Perspectives in the Sociology of the Military (co-ed.) 1977, Political Sociology: Readings in Research and Theory (co-ed.) 1980, Society and Politics: An Overview and Reappraisal of Political Sociology (co-author) 1980, A Profile of Modern Greece: In Search of Identity (co-author) 1987, Social Thought 1994, The Impact of European Integration: Political, Sociological, and Economic Changes (co-ed.) 1996, Political Sociology: Structure and Process 1997, Studies on Greek Americans 1997, Studies in Modern Greek Society and

Politics 1999, The New Balkans: Disintegration and Reconstruction (co-ed.) 2002; poetry: Nostalgias Kai Xenitias 1992, Stohasmoi (Conjectures) 2004; contrib. to various scholarly books, journals and encyclopaedias, over 70 articles and over 35 book reviews; several poems in Greek and English in journals and newspapers. *Honours:* various academic grants and awards, Greek American Community Services Heritage Award, Chicago 1987, Hellenic Council on Education Recognition Award, Chicago 1991, Recognition Award for the Silver Anniversary of the Founding of the Journal of Political and Military Sociology 1998, American Sociological Asscn Award for 30 Years of Distinguished Publication (for The Journal of Political and Military Sociology) 2002, Pan Arcadian Fed. of America Award 2004. *Address:* 109 Andresen Court, DeKalb, IL 60115, USA (home). *Telephone:* (815) 753-6433 (office); (815) 756-2152 (home). *Fax:* (815) 753-6302 (office). *E-mail:* ykourvet@niu.edu (office).

KOZER, José, BA, MA, PhD; Cuban/American academic, poet and writer; b. 28 March 1940, Havana, Cuba; s. of David Kozer and Ana Kozer; m. Guadalupe Kozer 1974; two d. *Education:* Univ. of Havana, New York Univ., Queens Coll., CUNY. *Career:* Prof. of Spanish Literature and Language, Queens Coll., CUNY 1960–97; fmr Co-Ed. Enlace magazine, New York. *Publications:* poetry: Padres y otras profesiones 1972, Por la libre 1973, Este judío de números y letras 1975, Y así tomaron posesión en las ciudades 1978, La rueca de los semblantes 1980, Jarrón de las abreviaturas 1980, Antología breve 1981, The Ark Upon the Number 1982, Bajo este cien 1983, La garza sin sombras 1985, Díptico de la restitucion 1986, El carillón de los muertos 1987, Carece de causa 1988, Prójimos/Intimates 1990, De donde oscilan los seres en sus proporciones 1990, Una índole 1993, Trazas del lirondo 1993, A Caná 1995, Et mutabile 1995, Los paréntesis 1995, La maquinaria ilimitada 1996, AAA1144 1997, Réplicas 1997, Dípticos 1998, Farándula 1999, Al traste 1999, No buscan reflejarse: Antología poética (1972–1980) 2001, Rupestres 2001, Rosa cúbica 2002, Anima 2002, Madame Chu & Outros Poemas 2002, Un caso llamado FK 2002, Ogi No Mato 2005, Y Del Esparto la Invariabilidad 2005, Stet 2005, Trasvasando 2006, Mueca la Muerte 2007, Práctica 2007, Ibis amarelo sobre fundo negro 2007, Trazas/Spuren 2007, Semovientes 2007, 22 poems 2007; prose: Mezcla para dos tiempos, Una huella destartalada; anthology: Medusario Muestra de Poesia Latinoamericana (co-ed. with Roberto Echavarren, Jacobo Sefamí) 1996; contrib. to numerous poetry magazines, literary journals and newspapers in N and S America, Spain. *Honours:* Gulbenkian Prize, Portugal 1967, CINTAS Foundation Award 1973, Julio Tovar Poetry Prize 1974, CUNY/PSC Foundation Award 1991. *Address:* 500 Three Islands Blvd, Apt 1209, Hallandale, FL 33009, USA (home). *Telephone:* (954) 456-3961 (office). *E-mail:* josekozer@comcast.net (home).

KOZIOŁ-PRZYBYLAK, Urszula, BA; Polish writer and poet; b. 20 June 1931, Rakówka; d. of Hipolit Kozioł and Czestawa Kozioł (née Kargol); m. Feliks Przybylak 1960. *Education:* Univ. of Wrocław. *Career:* high school teacher 1954–71; Literary Ed. Poglądy (Opinions) 1956; Literary Ed. Odra 1971–. *Publications include:* poetry: Gumowe klocki (Rubber Blocks) 1957, W rytmie korzeni (In the Rhythm of the Roots) 1963, Smuga i promień (A Trace and a Ray) 1965, Lista obecności (Attendance Record) 1967, W rytmie słońca (In the Rhythm of the Sun) 1974, Wybór wierszy (Select Poetry) 1976, Poezje wybrane (second edn) 1986, Żalnik (Laments) 1989, Postoje słowa (Stations of Words) 1995, Wielka Pauza (A Great Pause) 1996, W płynnym stanie 1998, Stany nieoczywistośći 1999, Supliki 2005; prose: Osobnego sny i przypowieści 1997; novels: Postoje pamięci (Stations of Memory, third edn) 1964–2004, Ptaki dla myśli (Birds for Thought, second edn) 1971; short stories: Z poczekalni (From the Waiting Room) 1978, Osobnego sny i przypowieści (The Dreams and Parables of the Separate One) 1978, Król malowany (The Painted King) 1978, Trzy Światy (Three Worlds) 1981, Podwórkowcy (Yard Kids) 1982, Spartolino 1982, Psujony (Spoilers) 1982, Zbieg z Bobony (Escapee from Bobona) 1983, Noli me tangere 1984, Dziwna podróż Bączka do Gryslandii (Strange Voyage of Bug to Grysland) 1984, Magiczne imię (A Magic Name) 1985, O stołku (About a Chair) 1987, Zgaga 1990. *Honours:* Kommandeur-Kreuz zum Orden der Wiedergelurf Polens 1997; Dr hc (Wrocław) 2003; Autumnal Encounters Festival of Gdańsk Literary Prize 1963, Polish Students' Asscn Władysław Broniewski Prize 1964, Literary Prize of Wrocław 1965, Kościelski Foundation of Geneva Prize 1969, Polish Ministry of Culture Literary Prize 1971, Kultur Preis Schlesien, Hanover 1998, PEN-Club Award 1998, Joseph von Eichendorff Prize, Wangen, Germany 2002. *Address:* Komandorska 37/6, 53-342 Wrocław, Poland (home). *Telephone:* (71) 3435516 (office); (71) 3673853 (home). *Fax:* (71) 3435516 (office). *E-mail:* odra@odra.net.pl (office). *Website:* www.odra.net.pl.

KOZOL, Jonathan, BA; American writer; b. 5 Sept. 1936, Boston; s. of Dr Harry L. Kozol and Ruth Massell Kozol. *Education:* Harvard Coll. and Magdalen Coll., Oxford, UK. *Career:* Rhodes Scholar 1958; teacher in Boston area 1964–72; lecturer at numerous univs 1973–2006; Guggenheim Fellow 1972, 1984; Field Foundation Fellow 1973, 1974; Rockefeller Fellow 1978, Sr Fellow 1983; f. Education Action! (non-profit org.); mem. Editorial Bd Greater Good Magazine. *Publications:* Death At An Early Age (Nat. Book Award 1968) 1967, Free Schools 1972, The Night Is Dark 1975, Children of the Revolution 1978, On Being a Teacher 1979, Prisoners of Silence 1980, Illiterate America 1985, Rachel and Her Children: Homeless Families in America (Robert F. Kennedy Book Award 1989, Conscience in Media Award of the American Soc. of Journalists and Authors 1989) 1988, Savage Inequalities: Children in America's Schools (New England Book Award 1992) 1991, Amazing Grace (Anisfield-Wolf Book Award 1996) 1995, Ordinary Resurrections 2000, The Shame of the Nation: The Restoration of Apartheid Schooling in America (Nation Magazine Book Award) 2005, Letters to a Young Teacher 2007. *Address:* PO Box 145, Byfield, MA 01922; Education Action!, A Project of The Cambridge Institute for Public Education, 16 Lowell Street, Cambridge, MA 02138, USA (office). *Telephone:* (617) 945-5568 (office). *Fax:* (617) 945-5562 (office); (978) 462-8557 (home). *E-mail:* jonathankozol@gmail.com; educationactioninfo@gmail.com. *Website:* ed-action.org.

KRALL, Hanna; Polish journalist and writer; b. 20 May 1935, Warsaw; m. Jerzy Szperkowicz; one d. *Education:* Univ. of Warsaw. *Career:* reporter, Życie Warszawy 1955–66, Polityka 1966–, corresp. in Moscow 1966–69; corresp., Tygodnik Powszechny, Gazeta Wyborcza; freelance writer early 1980s–. *Publications include:* Na wschód od Arbatu (East of the Arbat) 1972, Zdążyć przed Panem Bogiem (Shielding the Flame) 1977, Sześć odcieni bieli (Six Shades of White) 1978, Sublokatorka (The Sub-tenant) 1985, Hipnoza (Hypnosis) 1989, Trudności ze wstawaniem (Difficulties Getting Up) 1990, Taniec na cudzym weselu (Dance at a Stranger's Wedding) 1993, Co się stało z naszą bajką (What's Happened to Our Fairy Tale) 1994, Dowody na istnienie (Proofs of Existence) 1996, Tam już nie ma żadnej rzeki (There is No River There Anymore) 1998, To ty jesteś Daniel (So You Are Daniel) 2001, Wyjątkowo długa linia (Incredible Long Line) 2004, Król kier znów na wylocie (King of Hearts) 2006, Różowe Strusie Pióra (Rosy Ostrich Feathers) 2009 (books translated into over 18 languages). *Honours:* Solidarity Cultural Prize 1985, Prize of Minister of Culture and Art 1989, J. Shocken Literary Prize (Germany), Kulture Foundation Award 1999, Leipzig Book Fair Award 2000, Herder Prize 2005, Ricarda Huch Award (Germany) 2008. *Address:* Stowarzyszenie Pisarzy Polskich, ul. Krakowskie Przedmieście 87/89, 00-079 Warsaw, Poland (office). *Telephone:* (22) 6433164 (home). *Fax:* (22) 6433164 (home).

KRAMBERGER, Nataša; Slovenian writer and journalist; b. 1983, Maribor. *Career:* reporter, Večer Daily (newspaper) and 7dn (magazine); columnist, Kažin magazine; writes literary diary for Mentor magazine; f. Green Central (eco-art collective). *Publications include:* Nebesa v Robidah: roman v zgodbah (Heaven in a Blackberry Bush: Novel in Stories) (EU Prize for Literature 2010) 2007, Dva tedna s smetarji (Two Weeks' Tour of Waste) (essay) (Young Euro Connect Prize) 2009, Polne vreče zgodb (Bags of Stories) 2009; contrib. articles, essays and columns to newspapers in Slovenia and Italy, literary texts to magazines and radio, also documentary screenplays. *Honours:* Slovenian Young Authors Prize 2006, Anna Lindh Foundation A Sea of Words Int. Short Story Competition 2008. *Address:* c/o Dragica Breskvar, Mentor, Štefanova 5, 1000 Ljubljana, Slovenia (office). *Telephone:* (1) 2410516 (office). *E-mail:* dragica.breskvar@jskd.si (office). *Website:* www.jskd.si (office).

KRAMER, Aaron, BA, MA, PhD; American academic, author, poet and translator; b. 13 Dec. 1921, New York, NY; m. Katherine Kolodny 1942; two d. *Education:* Brooklyn College, CUNY, New York University. *Career:* Instructor, 1961–63, Asst Prof., 1963–66, Adelphi University; Lecturer, Queens College, CUNY, 1966–68; Assoc. Prof., 1966–70, Prof. of English, 1970–91, Prof. Emeritus, 1991–, Dowling College, Oakdale, New York; mem. American Society of Composers, Authors and Publishers; Asscn for Poetry Therapy; Edna St Vincent Millay Society; e. e. cummings Society; International Acad. of Poets; PEN; Walt Whitman Birthplace Asscn, exec. board, 1969–85. *Publications:* The Glass Mountain, 1946; Poetry and Prose of Heine, 1948; Denmark Vesey, 1952; The Tinderbox, 1954; Serenade, 1957; Tune of the Calliope, 1958; Moses, 1962; Rumshinsky's Hat, 1964; Rilke: Visions of Christ, 1967; The Prophetic Tradition in American Poetry, 1968; Poetry Therapy (co-author), 1969; Melville's Poetry, 1972; On the Way to Palermo, 1973; Poetry the Healer (co-author), 1973; The Emperor of Atlantis, 1975; O Golden Land, 1976; Death Takes a Holiday, 1979; Carousel Parkway, 1980; The Burning Bush, 1983; In the Suburbs, 1986; A Century of Yiddish Poetry, 1989; Indigo, 1991; Life Guidance Through Literature (co-author), 1991; Dora Teitelboim: Selected Poems (ed. and trans.), 1995. Contributions: professional journals. *Honours:* Hart Crane Memorial Award, 1969; Eugene O'Neill Theatre Center Prize, 1983; National Endowment for the Humanities Grant, 1993; Festschrift published in his honour, 1995.

KRAMER, Dale Vernon, BS, MA, PhD; American academic and writer; b. 13 July 1936, Mitchell, SD; m. Cheris Gamble Kramarae 1960; two c. *Education:* South Dakota State Univ., Case Western Reserve Univ. *Career:* Instructor, Ohio Univ. 1962–63, Asst Prof. 1963–65; Asst Prof., Univ. of Illinois 1965–67, Assoc. Prof. 1967–71, Prof. of English 1971–96, Acting Head, Dept of English 1982, 1986–87, Assoc. Dean, College of Arts and Sciences 1992–95; Assoc. Mem., Center for Advanced Study, Urbana, IL 1971; Assoc. Vice-Provost, Univ. of Oregon 1990; mem. Bd of Eds Cambridge Edn of Joseph Conrad 1995–; Vice-Pres. The Thomas Hardy Asscn; mem. Asscn of American Univ. Profs, Asscn for Documentary Editing, Soc. for Textual Scholarship. *Publications:* Charles Robert Maturin 1973, Thomas Hardy: The Forms of Tragedy 1975, Critical Approaches to the Fiction of Thomas Hardy (ed.) 1979, Thomas Hardy: The Woodlanders (ed.) 1981, Thomas Hardy: The Mayor of Casterbridge (ed.) 1987, Critical Essays on Thomas Hardy: The Novels (ed.) 1990, Thomas Hardy: Tess of the d'Urbervilles 1991, The Cambridge Companion to Thomas Hardy 1999; contributions: professional journals. *Honours:* American Philosophical Society Grants 1969, 1986, National Endowment for the Humanities Grant 1986, Boydston Prize, Asscn for Documentary Editing 1997. *Address:* c/o Dept of English, University of Illinois at Urbana-Champaign, Urbana, IL 61801, USA (home).

KRAMER, Larry D., BA; American writer; b. 25 June 1935, Bridgeport, Conn. *Education:* Yale Univ. *Career:* Production Exec. Columbia Pictures Corpn, London 1961–65; Asst to Pres. United Artists, New York; producer-screenwriter, Women in Love 1970; Co-founder Gay Men's Health Crisis Inc., New York 1981; Founder ACT UP-AIDS Coalition to Unleash Power, New York 1988. *Publications:* Faggots 1978, The Normal Heart (play) 1985, Just Say No 1988, The Furniture of Home 1989, The Destiny of Me 1993, The People Themselves: Popular Constitutionalism and Judicial Review 2005.

KRAMER, Lawrence Eliot, BA, MPhil, PhD; American academic, author, composer and editor; *Professor of English and Music, Fordham University*; b. 21 Aug. 1946, Philadelphia, Pa; m. Nancy S. Leonard 1973. *Education:* Univ. of Pennsylvania, Yale Univ. *Career:* Asst Prof. of English, Univ. of Pennsylvania 1972–78; Asst Prof., Fordham Univ. 1978–81, Assoc. Prof. 1981–87, Prof. of English and Comparative Literature 1987–95, Prof. of English and Music 1995–2011; Ed. 19th Century Music; Visiting Prof., Yale Univ. 1994, Columbia Univ. 2001, 2004, Univ. of Newcastle-upon-Tyne, UK 2003, 2004, Franz Liszt Acad., Budapest, Hungary 2010; mem. American Musicological Soc., Int. Asscn for Word and Music Studies, American Music Center. *Performances:* six song cycles in Oxford, Edinburgh, Vienna and New York 2007–11; short opera in Hartford, Conn. 2010; instrumental performances in New York 2007 and Keele, UK. *Publications:* Music and Poetry: The Nineteenth Century and After 1985, Music as Cultural Practice, 1800–1900 1990, Classical Music and Postmodern Knowledge 1995, After the Lovedeath: Sexual Violence and the Making of Culture 1997, Franz Schubert: Sexuality, Subjectivity, Song 1998, Walt Whitman and Modern Music: War, Desire, and the Trials of Nationhood (ed.) 2000, Musical Meaning: Toward a Critical History 2001, Opera and Modern Culture: Wagner and Strauss 2004, Why Classical Music Still Matters 2007, Beyond the Soundtrack: Representing Music in Cinema (ed.) 2007, Musical Meaning and Human Values (co-ed. with Keith Chapin) 2009, Interpreting Music 2010, Hart Crane's The Bridge: An Annotated Edition 2011; contribs to scholarly books and journals. *Honours:* Special Guest of Honor, Tenth Annual Mannes Inst. of Musical Aesthetics, Chicago 2010. *Address:* 791 Slate Quarry Road, Rhinebeck, NY 12572, USA (home). *E-mail:* lkramer@fordham.edu (office). *Website:* www.amc.net/Lawrence_Kramer (office).

KRAMER, Dame Leonie Judith, AC, DBE, DPhil, FAHA, FACE; Australian academic; *Professor Emerita of Australian Literature, University of Sydney*; b. 1 Oct. 1924, d. of the late A. L. Gibson and G. Gibson; m. Harold Kramer 1952 (deceased); two d. *Education:* Presbyterian Ladies Coll., Melbourne and Univs of Melbourne and Oxford. *Career:* Tutor, St Hugh's Coll., Oxford 1949–52; Assoc. Prof. Univ. of NSW 1963–68; Prof. of Australian Literature, Univ. of Sydney, 1968–89, Prof. Emer. 1989–; Deputy Chancellor, Univ. of Sydney 1988–91, Chancellor 1991–2001; Vice-Pres. Australian Asscn for Teaching of English 1967–70; Vice-Pres. Australian Soc. of Authors 1969–71; mem. Nat. Literature Bd of Review 1970–73; mem. Council, Nat. Library of Australia 1975–81; Pres., then Vice-Pres. Australian Council for Educ. Standards 1973–; mem. Univs Comm. 1974–86; Commr Australian Broadcasting Comm. (ABC) 1977–81, Chair. 1982–83, Dir Australia and NZ Banking Group 1983–94, Western Mining Corpn 1984–96, Quadrant Magazine Co. Ltd 1986–99 (Chair. 1988–99); mem. Council Nat. Roads and Motorists' Asscn 1984–95, Council Foundation for Young Australians 1989–2000, Asia Soc. 1991–2000; Nat. Pres. Australia-Britain Soc. 1984–93, Order of Australia Asscn 2001–04; mem. Council ANU 1984–87; mem. Bd of Studies, NSW Dept. of Educ. 1990–2001; Chair. Bd of Dirs Nat. Inst. of Dramatic Art 1987–91, Deputy Chair. 1991–95; Sr Fellow, Inst. of Public Affairs 1988–96; Commr Electricity Comm. (NSW) 1988–95; mem. World Book Encyclopaedia Advisory Bd 1989–99, Int. Advisory Cttee Encyclopaedia Britannica 1991–99, NSW Council of Australian Inst. of Co. Dirs 1992–2001; Chair. Operation Rainbow Australia Ltd 1996–2003; mem. Governing Council Old Testament House, Canberra 1998–2001; Gov. Medical Benefits Fund 2005–; Patron, United World Colleges Australia. *Publications include:* (as L. J. Gibson): Henry Handel Richardson and Some of Her Sources 1954; (as Leonie Kramer): Australian Poetry 1961 (ed.) 1962, Companion to Australia Felix 1962, Myself When Laura 1966, A Guide to Language and Literature (with Robert D. Eagleson) 1977, A. D. Hope 1979, The Oxford History of Australian Literature (ed.) 1981, The Oxford Anthology of Australian Literature (ed. with Adrian Mitchell) 1985, My Country: Australian Poetry and Short Stories – Two Hundred Years (two vols) 1985, James McAuley: Poetry, Essays etc. (ed.) 1988, David Campbell: Collected Poems (ed.) 1989, Collected Poems of James McAuley 1995. *Honours:* Hon. Fellow, St Hugh's Coll. Oxford 1994, St Andrew's Coll., Univ. of Sydney, Hon. Prof. Dept of English (Sydney) 2002, Janet Clarke Hall, Univ. of Melbourne 2005; Hon. DLitt (Tasmania), 1977 (Queensland) 1991, (NSW) 1992, (Sydney) 2009; Hon. LLD (Melbourne) 1983, (ANU) 1984; Hon. MA (Sydney) 1989; Britannica Award 1986. *Address:* A20–John Woolley, Room S365, University of Sydney, Sydney NSW 2006 (office); 12 Vaucluse Road, Vaucluse, NSW 2030 Australia (home). *Telephone:* (2) 93514164 (office). *Fax:* (2) 93514773 (office). *E-mail:* L.Kramer@staff.unisyd.edu.au (office).

KRAMER, Lotte Karoline; British poet and painter; b. 22 Oct. 1923, Mainz, Germany; m. Frederic Kramer 1943; one s. *Education:* studied art and history of art. *Career:* mem. Decorative and Fine Arts Soc., PEN, Peterborough Museum Soc., Poetry Soc., Ver Poets, Writers in Schools. *Publications:* Scrolls 1979, Ice Break 1980, Family Arrivals 1981, A Lifelong House 1983, The Shoemaker's Wife 1987, The Desecration of Trees 1994, Earthquake and Other Poems 1994, Selected and New Poems 1980–1997, Heimweh/Homesick 1999, The Phantom Lane 2000, Poem on London Underground Trains 2003, Black Over Red 2005, Kindertransport, Before and After 2007, Selected Poems in Japan in Translation 2007, Turning the Key 2009; contrib. to anthologies, newspapers, reviews, quarterlies and journals. *Honours:* Second Prize, York Poetry Competition 1972, Eastern Arts Board Bursary 1999, Second Prize, Manchester Cathedral Poetry Competition 2002. *Address:* 4 Apsley Way, Longthorpe, Peterborough, PE3 9NE, England (home). *Telephone:* (1733) 264378 (home).

KRANTZ, Judith, BA; American author; b. 9 Jan. 1928, New York City; d. of Jack David Tarcher and Mary Brager; m. Stephen Krantz 1954 (died 2007); two s. *Education:* Wellesley Coll. *Career:* contrib. to Good Housekeeping 1948–54, McCalls 1954–59, Ladies Home Journal 1959–71; Contributing Ed. Cosmopolitan 1971–79. *Publications:* Scruples 1978, Princess Daisy 1980, Mistral's Daughter 1982, I'll Take Manhattan 1986, Till We Meet Again 1988, Dazzle 1990, Scruples Two 1992, Lovers 1994, Spring Collection 1996, The Jewels of Teresa Kant 1998, Sex & Shopping: Confessions of a Nice Jewish Girl 2000. *Literary Agent:* c/o Esther Newberg, International Creative Management Inc. (ICM), 825 Eighth Avenue, New York, NY 10019, USA. *Telephone:* (212) 556-5600. *Website:* www.icmtalent.com.

KRAPF, Norbert, MA, PhD; American academic and writer; *Emeritus Professor of English, Long Island University;* b. 14 Nov. 1943, Jasper, IN; m. 1970; one s. one d. *Education:* St Joseph's Coll., Ind., Univ. of Notre Dame. *Career:* Faculty 1970–84, Prof. of English 1984–95, Prof. Emer. 1995–, Long Island Univ.; Fulbright Prof. of American Poetry, Univ. of Freiburg 1980–81, Univ. of Erlangen, Nuremburg 1989–90. *Recordings:* Imagine – Indiana in Music and Words (with Monika Herzig) 2007. *Publications:* poetry: Arriving on Paumanok 1979, Lines Drawn from Durer 1981, Circus Songs 1983, A Dream of Plum Blossoms 1985, Under Open Sky: Poets on William Cullen Bryant (ed.) 1986, Beneath the Cherry Sapling: Legends from Franconia (ed. and trans.) 1988, Shadows on the Sundial: Selected Early Poems of Rainer Maria Rilke (ed. and trans.) 1990, Somewhere in Southern Indiana: Poems of Midwestern Origins 1993, Finding the Grain: Pioneer Journals and Letters from Dubois County, IN 1996, Blue-eyed Grass: Poems of Germany 1997: Bittersweet Along the Expressway: Poems of Long Island 2000, The Country I Come From: Poems 2002, Looking for God's Country: Poems 2005, Bloodroot: Indiana Poems 2008; non-fiction: The Ripest Moments: A Southern Indiana Childhood (memoir) 2008; contribs to professional journals. *Honours:* Poetry Soc. of America Lucille Medwick Memorial Award 1999. *Address:* c/o Department of English, Long Island University, Brookville, NY 11548 (office); 356 Miami Street, Indianapolis, IN 46204, USA (home). *Telephone:* (317) 636-0943 (home). *E-mail:* nkrapf@indy.rr.net (home). *Website:* www.krapfpoetry.com.

KRATT, Mary, BA, MA; American writer and poet; b. (Mary Randolph Norton), 7 June 1936, Beckley, W Va; d. of William Randolph Norton and Martha Norton (née Hood); m. Emil F. Kratt 1959; one s. two d. *Education:* Agnes Scott Coll., Univ. of North Carolina at Charlotte. *Career:* mem. N Carolina Writers' Conf. (Chair. 1991–92), N Carolina Writers' Network (Bd mem.), Poets and Writers. *Publications include:* Southern Is 1985, Legacy: The Myers Park Story 1986 (revised edn 2009), The Imaginative Spirit: Literary Heritage of Charlotte and Mecklenburg County 1988, A Little Charlotte Scrapbook 1990, A Bird in the House 1991, The Only Thing I Fear is a Cow and a Drunken Man (poems and prose) 1991, Charlotte: Spirit of the New South 1992, On the Steep Side (poems) 1993, Small Potatoes (poems) 1999, Valley (poems) 2000, Remembering Charlotte: Postcards from a New South City 1905–50 2000, New South Women 2001, Edward M. O'Herron, Jr.: An Extraordinary Life 2006, Charlotte, North Carolina: A Brief History 2009; contrib. to newspapers, reviews and magazines. *Honours:* Lyricist Prize 1982, Oscar Arnold Young Award for Best Original Poetry Book by a North Carolinian 1983, N Carolina Poetry Soc. Sidney Lanier Award 1985, St Andrews Writer and Community Award 1994, Agnes Scott Coll. Distinguished Alumnae Writer Award 1994, MacDowell Colony residency 1996, Brockman Poetry Book Award 2000. *Address:* 3328 Providence Plantation Lane, Charlotte, NC 28270, USA. *Website:* www.marykratt.net.

KRAUSS, Nicole; American poet and writer; b. 1974, New York, NY; m. Jonathan Safran Foer; two c. *Education:* Stanford Univ., Univ. of Oxford, Courtauld Inst., London. *Publications:* Future Emergencies (short story, in Esquire), Man Walks into a Room (novel) 2003, The Future Dictionary of America (with Dave Eggers and Jonathan Safran Foer) 2004, The History of Love (novel) 2005, Great House 2010; contrib. poems to pubs, including Ploughshares, Doubletake, PN Review, and fiction to The New Yorker, Esquire, Best American Short Stories. *Address:* c/o W.W. Norton & Company, Inc., 500 Fifth Avenue, New York, NY 10110, USA (office). *Website:* www.wwnorton.com (office).

KRAUSSER, Helmut; German novelist; b. 11 July 1964, Esslinger. *Education:* Univ. of Munich. *Career:* fmrly nightwatchman, pop singer, radio announcer, journalist; Prof. of Poetry, Ludwig-Maximillians-Universität München 2007–08. *Publications:* novels: Thanatos: Das schwarze Buch 1986, Könige über dem Ozean 1989, Fette Welt (Fat World) 1992, Der grosse Bagarozy (trans. as The Great Bagarozy) 1997, Schweine und Elefanten 1999, UC (Ultrachronos) 2003, Eros 2006, Die kleinen Gärten des Maestro Puccini 2008, Einsamket und Sex und Mitleid 2009. *Address:* c/o DuMont Buchverlag GmbH and Co., Amsterdamer Strasse 192, D–50735 Köln, Germany (office). *E-mail:* info@dumont-buchverlag.de (office). *Website:* www.dumontliteraturundkunst.de (office).

KRAUTHAMMER, Charles, MD; American psychiatrist and journalist; b. 13 March 1950, New York; s. of Shulim Krauthammer and Thea Krauthammer; m. Robyn Trethewey; one s. *Education:* McGill Univ., Balliol Coll. Oxford and Harvard Univs, Medical School. *Career:* Resident in Psychiatry, Mass. Gen. Hosp., Boston 1975–78; Scientific Adviser, Dept of Health and Human Services, Washington, DC 1978–80; speech writer to Vice-Pres. Walter Mondale, Washington, DC 1980–81; Sr Ed. The New Republic, Washington, DC 1981–88, now Contributing Ed.; Contributing Ed. Weekly Standard; fmr essayist, Time Magazine; syndicated columnist, The Washington Post 1984–; commentator, Fox News; mem. Bd of Advisers, The Nat. Interest, Public Interest; mem. President's Council on Bioethics 2002–. *Publications:* Cutting Edges 1985; contribs to psychiatric journals. *Honours:* Nat. Magazine Award (for essays), American Soc. of Magazine Eds 1984, First Amendment Award, People for the American Way 1985, Pulitzer Prize (for commentary) 1987. *Address:* c/o The Washington Post Writers Group, 1150 15th Street, NW, Washington, DC 20071, USA. *Website:* www.washingtonpost.com.

KRAUZER, Steven Mark, (Terry Nelson Bonner), BA, MA; American writer; b. 9 June 1948, Jersey City, NJ; m. Dorri T. Karasek 1992; two d. *Education:* Yale University, University of New Hampshire. *Career:* mem. Writers Guild of America West; Authors' Guild; Authors League; MWA. *Publications:* The Cord Series, 1982–86; The Executioner Series, 1982–83; Blaze, 1983; The Diggers, 1983; The Dennison's War Series, 1984–86; Framework, 1989; Brainstorm, 1991; Rojak's Rule, 1992. Anthologies: Great Action Stories, 1977; The Great American Detective, 1978; Stories into Film, 1979; Triquarterly 48: Western Stories, 1980. Contributions: Magazines.

KRAWIEC, Richard, BS, MA; American writer; b. 9 May 1952, Brockton, MA; m. Mary Sturrock 1983, two s. *Education:* Suffolk University, University of New Hampshire. *Career:* mem. Associated Writing Programs; Authors' Guild; Poets and Writers. *Publications:* Time Sharing, 1986; Cardinal: A Contemporary Anthology from North Carolina (ed.), 1986; Faith in What?, 1996; And Fools of God, 2000. Contributions: newspapers and magazines. *Honours:* National Endowment for the Arts Fellowship, 1992; North Carolina Arts Council Fellowship, 1999.

KREMP, Herbert, DPhil; German journalist; b. 12 Aug. 1928, Munich; s. of Johann Kremp and Elisabeth Kremp; m. Brigitte Steffal 1956; two d. (one deceased). *Education:* Munich Univ. *Career:* reporter, Frankfurter Neue Presse 1956–57; Political Ed. Rheinische Post 1957–59; Dir Political Dept, Der Tag, Berlin 1959–61; Bonn Corresp. Rheinische Post 1961–63; Ed.-in-Chief Rheinische Post 1963–68; Ed.-in-Chief Die Welt 1969–77, Co-Ed. 1981, Co-Publr 1984–87, Chief Corresp. in Beijing 1977–81, Ed.-in-Chief 1981–85, apptd Chief Corresp. in Brussels 1987, Co-Ed., Springer Group newspapers 1984–87, commentator, Die Welt, Berliner Morgenpost, Welt am Sonntag, Bild, B.Z. Berlin, Hamburger Abendblatt; currently associated with Axel Springer publishing house. *Publications:* Am Ufer der Rubikon: Eine politische Anthropologie, Die Bambusbrücke: Ein asiatisches Tagebuch 1979, Wir brauchen unsere Geschichte 1988. *Honours:* Bundesverdienstkreuz 1988; Konrad Adenauer Prize 1984, Theodor-Wolff Prize 1978, 2003. *Address:* c/o Axel Springer Verlag AG, Axel-Springer-Str. 65, 10888 Berlin, Germany.

KRESS, Nancy, BS, MS, MA; American teacher and writer; b. 20 Jan. 1948, Buffalo, NY; m. 1st Michael Kress (divorced); two s.; m. 2nd Mark P. Donnelly 1988. *Education:* SUNY at Plattsburgh, SUNY at Brockport. *Career:* elementary school teacher, Penn Yan 1970–73; Adjunct Instructor, SUNY at Brockport 1980–; sr copywriter, Stanton and Hucko, Rochester 1984–; mem. SFWA. *Publications:* The Prince of Morning Bells, 1981; The Golden Grove, 1984; The White Pipes, 1985; Trinity and Other Stories, 1985; An Alien Light, 1988; Brain Rose, 1990; Maximum Light, 1998. Contributions: anthologies and periodicals. *Honours:* SFWA Nebula Award 1985.

KRIPKE, Saul Aaron, BA, LHD; American philosopher, logician and academic; *Distinguished Professor, Graduate Program in Philosophy, City University of New York*; b. 13 Nov. 1940, Bay Shore, NY; s. of Myer Samuel Kripke and Dorothy Kripke; m. Margaret P. Gilbert 1976 (divorced 1998). *Education:* Harvard Univ. *Career:* Soc. of Fellows, Harvard Univ. 1963–66, concurrently Lecturer with rank of Asst Prof., Princeton Univ. 1964–66; Lecturer, Harvard Univ. 1966–68; Assoc. Prof., Rockefeller Univ. 1968–72, Prof. 1972–76; McCosh Prof. of Philosophy, Princeton Univ. 1977–98, now Emer.; currently Distinguished Prof., Grad. Program in Philosophy, CUNY; Fulbright Fellow 1962–63; Guggenheim Fellow 1968–69, 1977–78; Visiting Fellow, All Souls Coll., Oxford, UK 1977–78, 1989–90; Visiting Prof., The Hebrew Univ. 1998–; mem. American Philosophical Soc. 2004–; Fellow, American Acad. of Arts and Sciences; Corresp. Fellow, British Acad. *Publications:* Naming and Necessity 1980, Wittgenstein on Rules and Private Language 1982; numerous papers in professional journals and anthologies. *Honours:* Hon. DHumLitt (Univ. of Neb. at Omaha) 1977, (Johns Hopkins Univ.) 1997, (Univ. of Haifa) 1998, (Univ. of Penn) 2005; Detur Prize 1960, Charles J. Wister Prize 1962, Howard Behrman Award 1988, Schock Prize in Logic and Philosophy 2001. *Address:* Graduate Program in Philosophy, CUNY Graduate Center, 365 Fifth Avenue, New York, NY 10016, USA (office). *Telephone:* (212) 817-8615 (home). *E-mail:* skripke@gc.cuny.edu (office). *Website:* web.gc.cuny.edu/philosophy/people/kripke.html (office).

KRIST, Gary Michael, AB; American writer; b. 23 May 1957, New Jersey; m. Elizabeth Cheng 1983; one d. *Education:* Princeton Univ., Fulbright Scholar at Universität Konstanz. *Career:* mem. PEN, Nat. Book Critics' Circle. *Publications:* The Garden State (short stories) 1988, Bone by Bone (short stories) 1994, Bad Chemistry (novel) 1998, Chaos Theory (novel) 1999, Extravagance (novel) 2002, The White Cascade (non-fiction); contribs to New York Times Book Review, Wall Street Journal, Salon Internet, Washington Post, Hudson Review, New Republic. *Honours:* Sue Kaufman Prize, American Acad. of Arts and Letters 1989, Stephen Crane Award 2000. *E-mail:* gary@garykrist.com (home). *Website:* www.garykrist.com.

KRISTEVA, Julia, DèsL; French psychoanalyst and writer; b. 24 June 1941, Silven, Bulgaria; m. Philippe Sollers 1967; one s. *Education:* Univ. of Sofia and Ecole des Hautes Etudes en Sciences Sociales, Paris, Univ. of Paris VII. *Career:* researcher in linguistics and French literature, Lab. of Social Anthropology, Ecole des Hautes Etudes en Sciences Sociales 1967–73; Prof., Univ. of Paris VII 1973–99, Prof. classe exceptionelle 1999–, Dir Ecole Doctorale Langue, Littérature, Image, civilisations et sciences humaines; Chargé de mission auprès du Pres. for the handicapped; Visiting Prof., Columbia Univ., New York 1974, Univ. of Toronto 1992; mem. Editorial Bd Telquel 1970–82; mem. Soc. psychanalytique de Paris, American Acad. of Arts and Sciences, Inst. Universitaire de France, British Acad., Acad. universelle des cultures. *Publications include:* Séméiotike: Recherches pour une sémanalyse 1969, Le Texte du roman, approche sémiologique d'une structure discursive transformationnelle 1970, La Révolution du langage poétique: l'avant-garde à la fin du XIXème siècle, Lautréamont et Mallarmé 1974, Des chinoises 1974, Polylogue 1977, Folle Vérité (with Jean Michel Ribettes) 1979, Pouvoirs de l'horreur: Essai sur l'abjection 1980, Le Langage, cet inconnu 1981, Histoires d'amour 1985, Au commencement était l'amour 1985, Soleil noir, dépression et mélancolie 1987, Etrangers à nous-mêmes (Prix Henri Hertz 1989) 1988, Les Samouraïs 1990, Lettre ouverte à Harlem Désir 1990, Le Vieil homme et les loups 1991, Les Nouvelles maladies de l'âme 1993, Le Temps sensible: Proust et l'expérience littéraire (essay) 1994, Possessions 1996, Sens et non-sens de la révolte 1996, La Révolte intime 1997, L'Avenir d'une révolte 1998, Le Génie féminin, Vol. 1: Hannah Arendt 1999, Vol. 2: Melanie Klein 2000, Colette 2002, Meurtre à Byzance 2004, La Haine et le Pardon: Pouvoirs et limites de la psychanalyse III 2005, Thérèse mon amour 2008. *Honours:* Chevalier, Ordre des Arts et des Lettres 1987, Chevalier, Légion d'honneur 1997, Officier, Ordre nat. du Mérite 2004, Officier de la Légion d'honneur 2008; Dr hc (Western Ont., Canada) 1995, (Victoria, Toronto) 1997, (Harvard) 1999, (Univ. Libre de Belgique) 2000, (Bayreuth) 2000, (Toronto) 2000, (Sofia) 2002, (New School, New York) 2003; Prix Henri Hertz Chancellerie des Universités de Paris 1989, Holberg Int. Memorial Prize, Norway 2004, Grande Médaille de Vermeil de la Mairie de Paris 2005, Award of Merit, Bucknell Univ. 2006. *Address:* Université de Paris VII, Grands Moulins, 7th Floor, bureau 777C, 16, rue Marguerite Duras, 75205 Paris cedex 13, France (office). *Telephone:* 1-57-27-64-42 (office). *Fax:* 1-57-27-64-44 (office). *E-mail:* julia.kristeva@univ-paris-diderot.fr (office). *Website:* www.kristeva.fr.

KRISTOF, Agota; Swiss (b. Hungarian) writer; b. 30 Oct. 1935, Csikvánd; d. of Kristof Kálmán and Antonia Turchányi; m. 1st Jean Béri 1954; m. 2nd Jean-Pierre Baillod 1963; two d. one s. *Education:* Szombathely (Hungary). *Career:* writer since age of 14; left Hungary 1956; began writing plays in French 1970; factory worker 1983–88; first book published 1986; full-time writer 1988–. *Publications:* Un rat qui passe, La fille de l'arpenteur, L'expiation, Le grand cahier 1986, La preuve 1988, Le troisième mensonge 1991, Hier 1995, L'analphabète 2004: C'est égal 2005. *Honours:* Prix Européen ADELF 1986, Prix France-Inter 1992. *Address:* c/o 13 rue de Vieux-Châtel, 2000 Neuchâtel, Switzerland.

KRISTOF, Nicholas D., BA, MA; American journalist; *Columnist, The New York Times*; b. 27 April 1959, Chicago; s. of Ladis Kristof and Jane Kristof; m. Sheryl WuDunn; two s. one d. *Education:* Harvard Coll., Magdalen Coll., Oxford, UK. *Career:* joined The New York Times 1984, corresp. in Los Angeles, Hong Kong, Beijing, Tokyo, later Assoc. Man. Ed., columnist 2001–. *Films:* Reporter (documentary) 2009. *Publications:* with Sheryl WuDunn: China Wakes: The Struggle for the Soul of a Rising Power 1994, Thunder from the East: Portrait of a Rising Asia 2000, Half the Sky: Turning Oppression into Opportunity for Women Worldwide 2009. *Honours:* Pulitzer Prize for International Reporting (jtly) 1990, for Commentary 2006, George Polk Award, Overseas Press Club Award, Dayton Literary Peace Prize (jtly) 2009. *Address:* The New York Times, 620 Eighth Avenue, New York, NY 10018, USA (office). *Website:* www.nytimes.com/kristof (office).

KRIVAK, Andrew, MFA; American author, poet and academic; m.; three c. *Education:* St John's Coll., Annapolis, Columbia Univ. *Career:* fmr teacher, Harvard Univ., Coll. of Holy Cross; mem. Soc. of Jesus, Syracuse 1990–98; currently teaches on Honors Program, Boston Coll. *Publications include:* Islands (poetry) 1999, A Long Retreat: In Search of a Religious Life 2008, The Sojourn (Chautauqua Prize 2012) 2010; as ed.: The Letters of William Carlos Williams to Edgar Irving Williams 1902–1912 (Louis Martz Prize 2009) 2009. *Literary Agent:* c/o Betsy Lerner, Dunow Carlson & Lerner, 27 West 20th Street, Suite 1107, New York, NY 10011, USA. *Telephone:* (212) 645-7606. *E-mail:* mail@dclagency.com. *Website:* www.dclagency.com. *Address:* Carney 113, College of Arts and Sciences, Boston College, 140 Commonwealth Avenue, Chestnut Hill, MA 02467, USA (office). *Website:* andrewkrivak.com (home).

KROG, Antjie, BA, MA; South African writer, poet and translator; *Extraordinary Professor, Faculty of the Arts, University of the Western Cape*; b. (Anna Elizabeth Krog), 23 Oct. 1952, Kroonstad; d. of Willem Krog and Susanna Jacoba (Dot) Serfontein; m. John Samuel; three s., one d. *Education:* Univ. of the Orange Free State, Univ. of Pretoria, Univ. of South Africa. *Career:* fmr

Ed. Die Suid-Afrikaan journal; reporter on SA's Truth and Reconciliation Comm. (as Antjie Samuel), AM Live radio show, SA Broadcasting Corpn (SABC), subsequently Parl. Ed. SABC; Extraordinary Prof., Faculty of the Arts, Univ. of the Western Cape 2004–. *Plays:* Waarom is dié wat voor toyi-toyi altyd vet? 1999. *Publications:* prose: Relaas van 'n Moord 1995, Account of a Murder 1997, Country of my Skull 1998, A Change of Tongue ('N Ander Tongval) 2003, Begging to Be Black 2009; poetry: Dogter van Jefta 1970, Januarie-suite 1972, Beminde Antarktika 1974, Mannin 1974, Otters in Bronslaai 1981, Jerusalemgangers 1985, Lady Anne 1989, Mankepank en ander Monsters 1989, Voëls van anderster vere 1992, Gedigte 1989–1995 1995, Kleur kom nooit alleen nie 2000, Down to my last skin 2000, Body Bereft 2006, Met woorde soos met kerse 2002, Die Sterre Se 'Tsau' (trans. as The Stars Say 'Tsau'), Verweerskrif 2006; children's poetry: Mankepank en ander Monsters 1989, Voëls van anderster vere (trans. as Birds of a Different Feather) 1992, Fynbos feetjies 2007; trans.: Long Walk to Freedom by Nelson Mandela, Een Mond vol Glas by Henk van Woerden, Mamma Medea by Tom Lanoye, Met woorde soos met kerse 2002. *Honours:* Dr hc (Univ. of East London), (Stellenbosch), (Freestate), (Nelson Mandela Univ.), (Metropolitan Univ.); Eugene Marais Prize 1973, Reina Prinsen-Geerligs Prijs 1976, Rapport Prize 1987, Hertzog Prize 1990, Foreign Corresp. Award 1996, Pringle Award 1996, Alan Paton Award 1996, Booksellers Award 1999, Hiroshima Peace Culture Foundation Award 2000, RAU-Prys vir Skeppende Skryfwerk 2001, South African Translators' Inst. Award for Outstanding Translation 2003, Nielsen Book Data Booksellers Award 2004, Protea Prize for Best Poetry Volume 2006, Open Soc. Award, Central European Univ., Budapest 2006, Wissenschaftskolleg zu Berlin Fellowship 2007–08. *Address:* Faculty of the Arts, The University of the Western Cape, Private Bag X17, Bellville, Cape Town 7535, South Africa (office). *Telephone:* (21) 9592911 (office). *E-mail:* akrog@uwc.ac.za (office). *Website:* www.uwc.ac.za (office).

KROKER, Arthur W., BA, MS, PhD; Canadian academic, writer and editor; b. 27 Aug. 1945, Winnipeg, MB; m. Marilouise DiRusso, 9 Aug. 1975, one c. *Education:* University of Windsor, Purdue University, McMaster University. *Career:* Asst Prof., 1975–80, Dir, Canadian Studies, 1979–80, Assoc. Prof. of Political Science, 1980–81, University of Winnipeg; Founding Ed., Canadian Journal of Political and Social Theory, 1975–93, renamed CTHEORY: Theory, Technology, and Culture, 1993–; Assoc. Prof., 1981–87, Prof. of Political Science, 1987–, Concordia University, Montréal; Guest Lecturer, colleges, universities, art museums; mem. Canadian Political Science Asscn; Canadian Communication Asscn; Asscn for Canadian Studies; Conference for the Study of Political Thought. *Publications:* Technology and the Canadian Mind: Innis, McLuhan and Grant, 1984; Panic Encyclopedia: The Definitive Guide to the Postmodern Scene, 1989; The Possessed Individual: Technology and the French Postmodern, 1992; Spasm: Virtual Reality, Android Music, and Electric Flesh, 1993; Data Trash: The Theory of the Virtual Class (co-author), 1994; Hacking the Future: Stories for the Flesh-Eating 90s (co-author), 1996; Digital Delirium (co-ed.), 1997. Contributions: anthologies; Articles and reviews to periodicals. *Honours:* Grants, Social Sciences and Humanities Research Council of Canada; Invited Distinguished Fellow, Society of the Humanities, Cornell University, 1999. *Address:* University of Victoria, Department of Political Science, PO Box 1700 STN CSC, Victoria, BC V8W 2Y2, Canada.

KRONENFELD, Judy Zahler, BA, MA, PhD; American poet and writer; *Lecturer Emerita, Creative Writing Department, University of California, Riverside*; b. 17 July 1943, New York, NY; d. of Samuel Zahler and Stella Jupiter Zahler; m. David Brian Kronenfeld 1964; one s. one d. *Education:* Smith Coll., Oxford UK, Stanford Univ. *Career:* Visiting Scholar, Univ. of California, Riverside 1977–78, 1981–83, Instructor 1978, Visiting Asst Prof., English Dept 1980–81, 1988–89, Lecturer, Creative Writing Dept 1984–2009, Lecturer Emerita 2009–; Lecturer, Univ. of California, Irvine 1972–73, 1978–79, 1984, 1985–86, Visiting Assoc. Prof., English and Comparative Literature 1987; Asst Prof., Purdue Univ. 1976–77. *Publications:* Shadow of Wings (poems) 1991, King Lear and the Naked Truth: Rethinking the Language of Religion and Resistance 1998, Disappeared Down Dark Wells and Still Falling (poems) 2000, Ghost Nurseries 2005, Light Lowering in Diminished Sevenths (Litchfield Review Book Award for Poetry) 2007; contrib. of articles in scholarly books and journals, poems in anthologies, reviews, quarterlies and magazines. *Honours:* Award for the Best Undergraduate Thesis in English, Smith Coll. 1964, Leverhulme Trust Fund Fellowship 1968–69, Squaw Valley Community of Writers Scholarship 1983, Non-Senate Academic Distinguished Researcher Award, Univ. of California at Riverside 1996–97, Co-Winner first Annual Poetry Contest, The dA Center for the Arts, Pomona, Calif. 2002. *Address:* 3314 Celeste Drive, Riverside, CA 92507, USA (home). *E-mail:* judy.kronenfeld@ucr.edu (office). *Website:* judykronenfeld.com.

KRÜGER, Manfred Paul, DPhil; German writer, academic and editor; *Lecturer, Institute for Spiritual Science and Arts, Nuremberg*; b. 23 Feb. 1938, Köslin; s. of Paul Krüger and Hildegard Krüger; m. Christine Petersen 1962; three s. four d. *Education:* Oberrealschule Ansbach, Heidelberg Univ., Tübingen Univ. *Career:* Asst Prof., Erlangen Univ. 1966–73; Lecturer, Inst. for Spiritual Science and Arts, Nuremberg 1972–; Lecturer, Fachhochschule Ottersberg 1980–2010; Co-Ed. Goetheanum weekly 1984–96. *Publications:* Gérard de Nerval 1966, Wandlungen des Tragischen 1973, Nora Ruhtenberg 1976, Bilder und Gegenbilder 1978, Wortspuren 1980, Denkbilder 1981, Literatur und Geschichte 1982, Mondland 1982, Nah ist er 1983, Meditation 1983, Rosenroman 1985, Meditation und Karma 1988, Anthroposophie und Kunst 1988, Ästhetik der Freiheit 1992, Ichgeburt 1996, Das Ich und seine Masken 1997, Die Verklärung auf dem Berge 2003. *Address:* Rieterstrasse 20, 90419 Nuremberg, Germany (home). *Telephone:* (911) 338678 (home).

KRUGMAN, Paul Robin, PhD; American economist and academic; *Professor of Economics and International Affairs, Princeton University*; b. 28 Feb. 1953, Albany, NY; s. of David Krugman and Anita Krugman; m. Robin Leslie Bergman 1983. *Education:* Yale Univ., Massachusetts Inst. of Tech. *Career:* taught at Stanford Univ.; Asst Prof., Yale Univ. 1977–79; Asst Prof., MIT 1979–80, Assoc. Prof. 1980–82, Ford Int. Prof. of Econs 1983–2000; Sr Int. Economist for Pres.'s Council of Econ. Advisers, under Ronald Reagan 1982–83; Op-Ed Columnist, New York Times 1999–; Prof. of Econs and Int. Affairs, Princeton Univ. 2000–; Centenary Prof., LSE, UK; Research Assoc., Nat. Bureau of Econ. Research; mem. Group of Thirty Consultative Group on Int. Econ. and Monetary Affairs, Inc. (G-30), Washington, DC; has served as a consultant to Fed. Reserve Bank of New York, World Bank, IMF, UN, as well as to several countries, including Portugal and the Philippines; Fellow, Econometric Soc. *Publications:* author, co-author or ed. or more than 23 books, including Market Structure and Foreign Trade (with E. Helpman) 1985, International Economics, Theory and Policy (with M. Obsfeld) 1988, The Age of Diminished Expectations 1990, Rethinking International Trade 1990, Geography and Trade 1991, Currencies and Crises 1992, Peddling Prosperity 1994, The Great Unravelling: From Boom to Bust in Three Short Years (New York Times best-seller) 2003, Microeconomics (with Robin Wells) 2004, Macroeconomics (with Robin Wells) 2005, The Conscience of a Liberal 2007, The Return of Depression Economics and the Crisis of 2008 2009; more than 200 professional journal articles, many of them on int. trade and finance; monthly column, The Dismal Science, for online magazine Slate, columnist for Fortune and has published articles in The New Republic, Foreign Policy, Newsweek and The New York Times Magazine. *Honours:* John Bates Clark Medal, American Econ. Asscn 1991, Nobel Prize for Econs 2008, named by The Washington Monthly as "the most important political columnist in America", named by The Asia Times as "the Mick Jagger of political/economic punditry", named by The Economist as "the most celebrated economist of his generation", Asturias Award from the King of Spain. *Address:* Department of Economics, 414 Robertson Hall, Princeton University, Princeton, NJ 08544, USA (office). *E-mail:* pkrugman@princeton.edu (office). *Website:* www.princeton.edu/~pkrugman (office); www.econ.princeton.edu (office); www.krugmanonline.com.

KRUKOWSKI, Lucian Wladyslaw, BA, BFA, MS, PhD; American academic, artist and writer; *Professor Emeritus of Philosophy, Washington University, St Louis*; b. 22 Nov. 1929, New York, NY; m. Marilyn Denmark 1955; one d. *Education:* Brooklyn Coll., CUNY, Yale Univ., Pratt Inst., Washington Univ., St Louis. *Career:* Faculty, Pratt Inst. 1955–69; Dean School of Fine Arts 1969–77, Prof. of Philosophy 1977–96, Chair Dept of Philosophy 1986–89, Prof. Emeritus of Philosophy 1996–, Washington Univ., St Louis; mem. American Philosophical Asscn, Soc. for Aesthetics. *Art Exhibitions:* one-person shows in New York and St Louis, paintings in museums and pvt. collections. *Publications:* Art and Concept 1987, Aesthetic Legacies 1992; anthologies, including The Arts, Society, and Literature 1984, The Reasons of Art 1985, Cultural Literacy and Arts Education 1990, Ethics and Architecture 1990, The Future of Art 1990, Schopenhauer, Philosophy and the Arts 1996; contrib. to professional journals. *Address:* 6003 Kingsbury, St Louis, MO 63112, USA (home). *Telephone:* (314) 863-5094 (home).

KRUPAT, Arnold, BA, MA, PhD; American academic, writer and editor; *Professor of Literature, Sarah Lawrence College*; b. 22 Oct. 1941, New York, NY; one s. one d. *Education:* New York Univ., Columbia Univ. *Career:* Prof. of Literature, Sarah Lawrence Coll. 1968–. *Publications:* For Those Who Come After 1985, I Tell You Now (co-ed. with Brian Swann) 1987, Recovering the Word (co-ed. with Brian Swann) 1987, The Voice in the Margin 1989, Ethnocriticism: Ethnography, History, Literature 1992, New Voices: Essays on Native American Literature (ed.) 1993, Native American Autobiography (ed.) 1993, Woodsmen, or Thoreau and the Indians (novel) 1994, The Turn to the Native: Studies in Culture and Criticism 1996, Here First: Autobiographical Essays by Native American Writers (co-ed. with Brian Swann) 1997, Red Matters: Native American Studies 2002, All that Remains: Varieties of Indigenous Expression 2009; contribs to numerous critical journals. *Honours:* Fulbright Fellowship, Woodrow Wilson Fellowship, Nat. Endowment for the Humanities Fellowship, Guggenheim Fellowship 2005, Sarah Lawrence Excellence in Teaching Award 2007, Nat. Endowment for the Humanities Fellowship 2009. *Address:* Sarah Lawrence College, Gilbert Building 03, 1 Mead Way, Bronxville, NY 10708, USA (office). *Telephone:* (914) 395-2309 (office). *E-mail:* akrupat@slc.edu (office); akrupat@verizon.net (home). *Website:* pages.slc.edu/~akrupat (office).

KRUZHKOV, Grigory; Russian poet, children's writer and translator; b. 1945. *Education:* Tomsk Univ., Siberia and post-graduate studies in physics at Serpukhov nr Moscow. *Career:* translator of English language poetry, including collections by W. B. Yeats, John Donne, John Keats, Robert Frost, Lewis Carroll; Visiting Lecturer Columbia Univ., USA 2001; jury mem. British Council Russia Poetry Translation Competition 2006; mem. PEN Russia. *Publications include:* The Book of Nonsense, Nostalgia for Obelisks: Literary Dreams; juvenile: Guillaum the Gnome and the Moon Kitten, The Rainy Island, Where Things Came From 1995, Big Ben Tales (compiler and trans.) (Int. Bd on Books for the Young Diploma 1996); contrib. to Amerika: Contemporary Russian Writers on the US 2004, Glas: New Russian Writing.

Honours: State Prize for Literature (translation) 2006. *E-mail:* ftm@litagent.ru. *Website:* www.litagent.ru.

KUBAISI, Tarrad al-; Iraqi journalist; b. 1937, Hit; m. Widdad Al-Jourani 1962; one s. two d. *Education:* Coll. of Literature, Univ. of Baghdad. *Career:* Ed.-in-Chief, Al-Mawsu'a Al-Sagira (small encyclopaedia) 1976–77; Ed.-in-Chief, Al-Aqlam (magazine) 1978–81, Al-Maurid (magazine) 1984–87, 1989–90; Man. and Ed.-in-Chief, Afaq Arabia (magazine) 1991; Press Office and Iraq Cultural Centre, London 1982–84; Press Attaché, Morocco 1988–89; later Chair. Cultural Affairs Office. *Publications:* Introductions in Sumerian Sufi-African Poetry 1971, The New Iraqi Poetry 1972, The Stony Forest Trees 1975, The Forest and Seasons 1979, Al-Munzalat Book (Vol. I) 1992, (Vol. II) 1995, The Artistic Construction in Epic Literature 1994. *Address:* c/o PO Box 4032, Adhamiya, Baghdad, Iraq. *Telephone:* 4436044 (office); 5544746 (home).

KUCBELOVÁ, Katarína, MA; Slovak poet and screenwriter; b. 1979, Banská Bystrica. *Education:* Acad. of Dramatic Art, Bratislava. *Career:* works as a script ed.; has written scripts for two short films, also writes poetry, prose and film reviews. *Publications:* poetry: Duály (Duals); contrib. to anthologies, including A Fine Line: New Poetry from Eastern and Central Europe 2004. *Address:* c/o Literarne Informacne Centrum, Nam. SNP 12, Bratislava 812 24, Slovakia. *E-mail:* lic@litcentrum.sk.

KULSHRESHTHA, Manisha, MPhil; Indian author and translator; b. Rajasthan. *Education:* Univ. of Udaipur. *Career:* Kathak dancer; popular story Kathputaliyan (based on life in Thar Desert, Rajasthan) translated into 12 languages. *Publications include:* novels: Shigaf (The Slit) 2010, Shalbhanjika; five collections of stories; as trans. into Hindi: numerous works including titles by Maya Angelou, N. Scott Momaday. *Address:* c/o Rajkamal Prakashan Pvt. Limited, 1-B Netaji Subhash Marg, Daryaganj, New Delhi, 110002, India. *Telephone:* (11) 23274463. *Fax:* (11) 23278144. *E-mail:* info@rajkamalprakashan.com. *Website:* www.rajkamprakashan.com.

KULTERMANN, Udo, PhD; American academic and writer; *Professor Emeritus of Architecture, Washington University, St Louis*; b. 14 Oct. 1927, Stettin, Germany; s. of Georg Kultermann and Charlotte Kultermann (née Schultz). *Education:* Univ. of Greifswald, Univ. of Münster. *Career:* Dir City Art Museum, Leverkusen 1959–64; study tour, Nigeria, Ghana, Senegal, Morocco 1962; lecture, First Int. Congress for African Culture, Harare, Zimbabwe (fmrly Salisbury, Rhodesia) 1962; Prof. of Architecture 1967–94, Prof. Emer. 1994–, Washington Univ., St Louis; Int. Corresp., MIMAR, Singapore/London 1981–92; mem. Nat. Faculty of Humanities, Arts, and Sciences, Atlanta 1986–; Corresp. mem. Croatian Acad. of Sciences and Arts, Zagreb 1997–. *Publications:* Architecture of Today 1958, Hans und Wassili Luckhardt: Bauten und Projekte 1958, Dynamische Architektur 1959, New Japanese Architecture 1960, Junge deutsche Bildhauer 1963, Der Schlüssel zur Architektur von heute 1963, New Architecture in Africa 1963, New Architecture in the World 1965, Geschichte der Kunstgeschichte: Der Weg einer Wissenschaft 1966, Architektur der Gegenwart 1967, The New Sculpture 1967, Gabriel Grupello 1968, The New Painting 1969, New Directions in African Architecture 1969, Kenzo Tange: Architecture and Urban Design 1970, Modern Architecture in Color (with Werner Hofmann) 1970, Art and Life: The Function of Intermedia 1970, New Realism 1972, Ernest Trova 1977, Die Architektur im 20. Jahrhundert 1977, I Contemporanei: Storia della scultura nel mondo 1979, Architecture in the Seventies 1980, Architekten der Dritten Welt 1980, Contemporary Architecture in Eastern Europe 1985, Kleine Geschichte der Kunsttheorie 1987, Visible Cities-Invisible Cities: Urban Symbolism and Historical Continuity 1988, Art and Reality: From Fiedler to Derrida: Ten Approaches 1991, Architecture in the 20th Century 1993, Die Maxentius Basilika: Ein Schlüsselwerk Spätantiker Architektur 1996, Architektur der Welt (ed.) 1996–, St James Modern Masterpieces: The Best of Art, Architecture, Photography and Design Since 1945 (ed.) 1998, Contemporary Architecture in the Arab States: Renaissance of a Region 1999, Architecture in South and Central Africa in World Architecture: A Critical Mosaic 1900–2000 (ed.) 2000, Thirty Years After: The Future of the Past 2002, Architecture and Revolution – The Visions of Boullée and Ledoux 2003, Tradition, Globalization, Intercultural Exchange and Regional Identity 2007; contrib. to books, encyclopedias and periodicals. *Honours:* Dr hc (Acad. of Art, Tallinn) 2004; Distinguished Faculty Award Washington Univ., St Louis 1985. *Address:* 300 Mercer Street, Apt 17B, New York, NY 10003, USA (home). *E-mail:* ukulter@rcn.com (home).

KUMIN, Maxine Winokur, MA; American writer and poet; b. 6 June 1925, Germantown, Philadelphia; d. of Peter Winokur and Doll Simon; m. Victor M. Kumin 1946; one s. two d. *Education:* Radcliffe Coll. *Career:* consultant in poetry, Library of Congress 1981–82; Fellow, Acad. of American Poets, Chancellor 1995–; Visiting Prof., MIT 1984, Univ. of Miami 1995, Pitzer Coll. 1996; McGee Prof. of Writing, Davidson Coll. 1997; Writer-in-Residence, Fla Int. Univ. 1998; Poet Laureate, State of New Hampshire 1989; Nat. Endowment for the Arts Grant 1966, Nat. Council on the Arts Fellowship 1967, Acad. of American Poets Fellowship 1985; mem. Poetry Soc. of America, PEN America, Authors' Guild, Writers' Union. *Publications:* poetry: Halfway 1961, The Privilege 1965, The Nightmare Factory 1970, Up Country: Poems of New England, New and Selected 1972, House, Bridge, Fountain, Gate 1975, The Retrieval System 1978, Our Ground Time Here Will Be Brief 1982, Closing the Ring 1984, The Long Approach 1985, Nurture 1989, Looking for Luck 1992, Connecting the Dots 1996, Selected Poems 1960–1990 1997, The Long Marriage 2001, Bringing Together: Uncollected Early Poems 2003, Jack and Other New Poems 2005, Still to Mow 2007, Where I Live: New and Selected Poems 1990–2010 2010; fiction: Through Dooms of Love 1965, The Passions of Uxport 1968, The Abduction 1971, The Designated Heir 1974, Why Can't We Live Together Like Civilised Human Beings? 1982; other: In Deep: Country Essays 1987, To Make a Prairie: Essays on Poets, Poetry, and Country Living 1989, Women, Animals, and Vegetables: Essays and Stories 1994, Quit Monks or Die! 1999, Inside the Halo and Beyond (memoir) 2000, Always Beginning (essays) 2000, The Roots of Things: Essays 2010; also short stories, children's books and poetry contribs to nat. magazines. *Honours:* various hon. doctorates; Lowell Mason Palmer Award 1960, William Marion Reedy Award 1968, Eunice Tietjens Memorial Prize 1972, Pulitzer Prize for Poetry 1973, American Acad. of Arts and Letters Award 1980, Poetry magazine Levinson Award 1987, American Acad. and Inst. of Arts Award 1989, Sarah Josepha Hale Award 1992, The Poet's Prize 1994, Aiken Taylor Poetry Prize 1995, Harvard Grad. School of Arts and Sciences Centennial Award 1996, Ruth Lilly Poetry Prize 1999, Arts Medal, Harvard Univ. 2005. *Literary Agent:* Giles Anderson, The Giles Anderson Agency, 435 Convent Avenue, Suite 5, New York, NY 10031, USA. *Telephone:* (212) 234-0692. *Fax:* (212) 234-0693. *E-mail:* gilesacanderson@gmail.com. *Website:* www.maxinekumin.com.

KUMMINGS, Donald D., BA, MA, PhD; American poet, writer and academic; *Professor Emeritus of English, University of Wisconsin, Parkside*; b. 28 July 1940, Lafayette, Ind.; m. 1st (divorced) 1978; m. 2nd 1987; two s. *Education:* Purdue Univ., Indiana Univ. *Career:* Teaching Asst, Purdue Univ. 1963–64; Instructor, Adrian Coll., Mich. 1964–66; Assoc. Instructor, Indiana Univ. 1966–70; Asst Prof., Univ. of Wisconsin, Parkside 1970–75, Chair. Dept of English 1974–76, 1991–94, Assoc. Prof. 1975–85, Prof. of English 1985–2006, Prof. Emer. 2006–; Book Review Ed. The Mickle Street Review 1983–90. *Publications:* Walt Whitman, 1940–1975: A Reference Guide 1982, The Open Road Trip: Poems 1989, Approaches to Teaching Whitman's Leaves of Grass 1990, The Walt Whitman Encyclopedia (ed. with J. R. LeMaster) 1998, A Companion to Walt Whitman 2006; contrib. to anthologies, reviews, quarterlies and journals. *Honours:* Acad. of American Poets Prize 1969, Council for Wisconsin Writers Posner Poetry Prize 1990, Carnegie Foundation for the Advancement of Teaching Wisconsin Prof. of the Year 1997. *Address:* Department of English, University of Wisconsin, Parkside, Kenosha, WI 53141, USA (office). *E-mail:* kumming@uwp.edu (office).

KUNDERA, Milan; Czech/French novelist; b. 1 April 1929, Brno; s. of Dr Ludvik Kundera and Milada Kunderová-Janosikova; m. Věra Hrabánková 1967. *Education:* Film Faculty, Acad. of Music and Dramatic Arts, Prague. *Career:* Asst, later Asst Prof., Film Faculty, Acad. of Music and Dramatic Arts, Prague 1958–69; Prof., Univ. of Rennes 1975–80; Prof., Ecole des hautes études en sciences sociales, Paris 1980–94; mem. Union of Czechoslovak Writers 1963–69; mem. Editorial Bd Literární noviny 1963–67, 1968. *Publications:* drama: Jacques and his master, an homage to Diderot 1971–81; short stories: Laughable Loves (Czechoslovak Writers' Publishing House Prize) 1970; novels: The Joke (Union of Czechoslovak Writers' Prize 1968) 1967, Life is Elsewhere (Prix Médicis) 1973, La Valse aux adieux (The Farewell Waltz) (Premio letterario Mondello 1978) 1976, Livre du rire et de l'oubli (The Book of Laughter and Forgetting) 1979, The Unbearable Lightness of Being (Los Angeles Times Prize) 1984, Immortality (The Independent Prize, UK 1991) 1989, Slowness 1995, L'Identità (Identity) 1997, La Ignorancia (Ignorance) 2000; essays: The Art of the Novel 1987, Les Testaments trahis (Aujourd'hui Prize, France) 1993, Le Rideau (The Curtain) 2005, Une rencontre (The Encounter) 2009. *Honours:* Dr hc (Michigan) 1983; Commonwealth Award 1981, Prix Europa-Littérature 1982, Jerusalem Prize 1985, Prix de la critique de l' Acad. française 1987, Nelly Sachs Preis 1987, Österreichische Staatspreis für Europäische Literatur 1988, Jaroslav-Seifert Prize (Czech Repub.) 1994, Medal of Merit (Czech Repub.) 1995, J. G. Herder Prize (Austria) 2000, Grand Prize Acad. française (for novels Slowness, Identity and Ignorance) 2001. *Website:* www.faber.co.uk (office).

KUNERT, Günter; German writer and painter; *President, PEN Centre of German-speaking Writers Abroad*; b. 6 March 1929, Berlin; s. of Adolf Kunert and Edith Warschauer; m. 1st Marianne Todten 1951; m. 2nd Erika Hinckel. *Education:* Basic-School, Berlin. *Career:* Visiting Assoc. Prof., Univ. of Texas at Austin, USA 1972; Writer-in-Residence, Univ. of Warwick, UK 1975; mem. Akad. der Künste (Hamburg and Mannheim), Akad. für Sprache und Dichtung, Darmstadt; Pres. PEN Centre of German-speaking Writers Abroad 2005–. *Film:* Abschied and others. *Play:* The Time Machine (based on the novel by H. G. Wells). *TV screenplays include:* King Arthur 1990, An Obituary of the Wall 1991, Endstation: Harembar 1991 and 13 others. *Radio:* 10 radio plays. *Publications:* 60 volumes of poetry, prose, satire, essays, novels, short stories and lectures. *Honours:* Bundesverdienstkreuz (First Class); Dr hc (Allegheny Coll., Pa) 1988, (Juniata Coll.) 2005, (Univ. of Turin) 2005, (Dickinson Coll., Pa) 2010; Heinrich Mann Prize, Akad. der Künste (East Berlin) 1962, Becher Prize for Poetry 1973, Heinrich Heine Prize (City of Düsseldorf) 1985, Hölderlin Prize 1991, E.R. Curtius Prize 1991, Hans-Sahl-Preis 1996, Georg-Trakl-Preis (Austria) 1997, EU Prix Aristeion 1999, Preis der Frankfurter Anthologie 2012, America Award. *Address:* Schulstrasse 7, 25560 Kaisborstel, Germany (home). *Telephone:* (4892) 1414 (home). *Fax:* (4892) 8403 (home).

KÜNG, Dinah Lee, BA, MA; American journalist and author; b. Detroit, MI; m.; three c. *Education:* Univ. of California at Santa Cruz, Univ. of California at Berkeley. *Career:* reporter, Washington Post, National Public Radio, International Herald Tribune, The Economist; Hong Kong bureau chief, Business Week; mem. Council on Foreign Relations, PEN Int., Overseas Press Club, Foreign Correspondents Club of Hong Kong. *Publications:* novels: Left in the Care of 1998, A Visit from Voltaire 2003, Under Their Skin 2006. *Honours:* Overseas Press Club Award for Best Human Rights Coverage 1992. *Address:* c/o Peter Halban Publishers Ltd, 22 Golden Square, London, W1F 9JW, England (office). *Telephone:* (20) 7437-9300 (office). *Fax:* (20) 7437-9512 (office). *E-mail:* books@halbanpublishers.com (office). *Website:* www.halbanpublishers.com (office); www.dinahleekung.com (home).

KÜNG, Hans, DTheol; Swiss theologian and academic; *President, Global Ethic Foundation*; b. 19 March 1928, Sursee, Lucerne. *Education:* Gregorian Univ., Rome, Italy, Inst. Catholique and Univ. of the Sorbonne, Paris, France. *Career:* ordained priest 1954; mem. practical ministry, Lucerne Cathedral 1957–59; Scientific Asst for Dogmatic Catholic Theology, Univ. of Münster Westfalen 1959–60; Prof. of Fundamental Theology, Univ. of Tübingen 1960–63; Prof. of Dogmatic and Ecumenical Theology and Dir, Inst. Ecumenical Research 1963–80, Prof. of Ecumenical Theology, Dir Inst. of Ecumenical Research (under direct responsibility of Pres. and Senate Univ. of Tübingen) 1980–96, Prof. Emer. 1996–; Guest Prof., Univ. of Chicago 1981, of Mich. 1983, of Toronto 1985, of Rice Univ., Houston 1987; numerous guest lectures at univs worldwide; mem. PEN; Pres. Global Ethic Foundation, Germany 1995–, Switzerland 1997–; Co-Pres. World Conf. on Religion and Peace, New York; Founding mem. Int. Review of Theology, Concilium. *Publications:* The Council: Reform and Reunion 1961, That the World May Believe 1963, The Council in Action 1963, Justification: The Doctrine of Karl Barth and a Catholic Reflection 1964, (with new introductory chapter and response of Karl Barth 1981), Structures of the Church 1964, (with new preface) 1982, Freedom Today 1966, The Church 1967, Truthfulness 1968, Menschwerdung Gottes 1970, Infallible? – An Inquiry 1971, Why Priests? 1972, Fehlbar? – Eine Bilanz 1973, On being a Christian 1976, Signposts for the Future 1978, The Christian Challenge 1979, Freud and the Problem of God 1979, Does God Exist? 1980, The Church – Maintained in Truth 1980, Eternal Life? 1984, Christianity and the World Religions: Paths to Dialogue with Islam, Hinduism and Buddhism (with others) 1986, The Incarnation of God 1986, Church and Change: The Irish Experience 1986, Why I am still a Christian 1987, Theology for the Third Millennium: An Ecumenical View 1988, Christianity and Chinese Religions (with Julia Ching) 1989, Paradigm Change in Theology: A Symposium for the future 1989, Reforming the Church Today 1990, Global Responsibility: In Search of a New World Ethic 1991, Judaism 1992, Credo: The Apostles' Creed Explained for Today 1993, Great Christian Thinkers 1994, Christianity 1995, A Dignified Dying: a plea for personal responsibility (with Walter Jens) 1995, Yes to a Global Ethic (ed.) 1996, A Global Ethic for Global Politics and Economics 1997, Breaking Through (with others) 1998, The Catholic Church: A Short History 2001, Women in Christianity 2001, Tracing the Way: Spiritual Dimensions of the World Religions 2002, My Struggle for Freedom (memoirs) 2003, Islam: Past, Present and Future 2006, The Beginning of all Things: Science and Religion 2006, Disputed Truth (memoirs) 2008, How to Do Good and Avoid Evil. A Global Ethic from the Sources of Judaism (with Walter Homolka) 2009, What I Believe 2010. *Honours:* Hon. Citizen City of Syracuse, Italy 2002, Tübingen, Germany 2002, Mozart Hon. Chair, European Acad. of Yuste, Spain 2004; Grosses Bundesverdienstkreuz mit Stern 2003; numerous hon. doctorates, including Hon. DD (Univ. of Wales) 1998, (Florida Int. Univ.) 2002, (Ecumenical Theological Seminary, Detroit) 2003, Hon. LHD (Ramapo Coll., NY) 1999, (Hebrew Union Coll., Cincinnati) 2000, Hon. DPhil (Genoa) 2004, (Universidad Nacional de Educación a Distancia, Madrid) 2011; Ludwig-Thoma Medal 1975, Oskar Pfister Award, American Psychiatric Asscn 1986, Karl Barth Prize, Evangelische Kirche der Union, Berlin 1992, Hirt Prize, Zürich 1993, Prize for Zivilcourage Zürich 1995, Univ. of Tübingen 1996, Theodor Heuss Prize, Stuttgart 1998, Interfaith Gold Medallion of the Int. Council of Christians and Jews 1998, Martin Luther Towns Prize 1999, Ernst-Robert-Curtius Literary Award Bonn 2001, Göttingen Peace Award 2002, Juliet Hollister Award of the Temple of Understanding 2004, Niwano Peace Prize 2005, Lev Kopelev Prize 2006, Cultural Award, German Freemasons 2007, Croatian Academic Soc. Award 2007, Steiger Award 2008, Lifetime Achievement Award, Prince Alwaleed Bin Talal Center for Muslim-Christian Understanding, Georgetown Univ., Washington 2008, Award for Civil Courage, Freundeskreis Heinrich Heine 2008, Otto Hahn Peace Medal 2008, Abraham Geiger Award 2009, Nonino Prize 2012. *Address:* Waldhäuserstrasse 23, 72076 Tübingen, Germany (office). *Telephone:* (7071) 62646 (office). *Fax:* (7071) 610140 (office). *E-mail:* office@global-ethic.org (office). *Website:* www.global-ethic.org (office).

KUNHI, Bolwar Mohammed; Indian writer and scriptwriter; b. 1951, Bangalore. *Education:* Mysore Univ. *Career:* Kannada writer; currently Chief Publicity Manager, Syndicate Bank, Bangalore office. *Plays:* Pandita Fakeera – Ondu Gazal, Swatantryada Oota. *Publications include:* short story collections: Atta Ittagala Mutta, Devarugala Rajyadalli, Anka, Akashakke Neeli Parade, Ondu Tundu Gode; novel: Jehad; non-fiction: Punnapra Vayalar Samara; six children's books. *Honours:* Bharathiya Sahitya Samsthana Award 1981, three Karnataka Sahitya Akademi Awards including Lifetime Achievement Award 1997, Parashurama 2001, Nat. Award for Kannada films 2002, 2003. *Address:* Syndicate Bank, Corporate Office, II Cross, Gandhinagar, Bangalore 560 009, India (office). *Telephone:* (80) 22267545 (office); (80) 22267548. *E-mail:* inrc@syndicatebank.co.in (office). *Website:* www.syndicatebank.in.

KUNKEL, Thor; German novelist and theatre director; b. 1963, Frankfurt. *Education:* studied in Frankfurt, San Francisco. *Career:* moved to London, worked in the media; apptd Creative Head of an int. advertising agency, Netherlands 1992; freelance writer, playwright and dir 1996–. *Publications:* The Black Light Terranium 2000, Ein Brief an Hanny Porter 2001, Final Stage 2004, bin Shoppen 2006. *Honours:* Ernst-Willner Award, Literaturstipendium der Preuβische Seehandlung. *Literary Agent:* Bakker, Friedbergstr. 12, 14057 Berlin-Charlottenburg, Germany. *Telephone:* (49) 69 2560 0358 (office). *E-mail:* thor@thorkunkel.de (office). *Website:* www.thorkunkel.de.

KUNSTLER, James Howard, BS; American writer; b. 19 Oct. 1948, New York, NY; m. 1996. *Education:* Brockport State Coll. *Publications:* The Wampanaki Tales 1979, A Clown in the Moonlight 1981, The Life of Byron Jaynes 1983, An Embarrassment of Riches 1985, Blood Solstice 1986, The Halloween Ball 1987, The Geography of Nowhere 1993, Home From Nowhere 1996, The City in Mind: Notes on the Urban Condition 2002, The Long Emergency 2005, World Made by Hand 2008, The Witch of Hebron 2010; contrib. to Atlantic Monthly, New York Times Sunday Magazine. *Honours:* Humanities Prize 1995. *Address:* c/o Atlantic Books, Ormond House, 26–27 Boswell Street, London, WC1N 3JZ, England (office). *Website:* www.kunstler.com.

KUNZE, Reiner; German writer; b. 16 Aug. 1933, Oelsnitz/Erzgebirge; s. of Ernst Kunze and Martha Kunze (née Friedrich); m. Dr Elisabeth Mifka 1961; one s. one d. *Education:* Univ. of Leipzig. *Career:* mem. Bavarian Acad. of Fine Arts, Acad. of Arts, West Berlin 1975–92, German Acad. for Languages and Literature, Darmstadt, Free Acad. of Arts Mannheim, Sächsische Akad. der Künste, Dresden. *Photography:* solo exhibitions in Berlin, Düsseldorf, Frankfurt, Offenbach, Würzburg and other cities in Germany and Austria. *Publications:* Sensible Wege 1969, Der Löwe Leopold 1970, Zimmerlautstärke 1972, Brief mit blauem Siegel 1973, Die wunderbaren Jahre 1976, Auf eigene Hoffnung 1981, Eines jeden einziges Leben 1986, Das weisse Gedicht 1989, Deckname 'Lyrik' 1990, Wohin der Schlaf sich schlafen legt 1991, Mensch ohne Macht 1991, Am Sonnenhang 1993, Wo Freiheit ist… 1994, Steine und Lieder 1996, Der Dichter Jan Skácel 1996, Bindewort 'deutsch' 1997, Ein Tag auf dieser Erde 1998, Die Aura der Wörter 2002, Der Kuss der Koi 2002, Wo wir zu Hause das Salz haben 2003, Die Chausseen der Dichter (with Mireille Gansel) 2004, Bleibt nur die eigene Stirn 2005, Lindennacht 2007, Mensch im Wort 2008, Die Sprache, die die Sprache spricht 2009, Was macht die Biene auf dem Meer? 2011, Wenn wieder eine Wende kommt 2011. *Honours:* Hon. mem. Collegium Europaeum Jenense of Friedrich-Schiller-Universität Jena; Dr hc; numerous awards and prizes including Literary Prize of Bavarian Acad. of Fine Arts 1973, Georg Trakl Prize (Austria) 1977, Andreas Gryphius Prize 1977, Georg Büchner Prize 1977, Bavarian Film Prize 1979, Eichendorff Literature Prize 1984, Bayerischer Verdienstorden 1988, Grosses Verdienstkreuz der BRD 1993, Weilheimer Literaturpreis 1997, Europapreis für Poesie, Serbia 1998, Friedrich Hölderlin-Preis 1999, Hans Sahl Prize 2001, Bayerischer Maximiliansorden für Wissenschaft und Kunst 2001, Kunstpreis zur Deutsch-tschechischen Verständigung 2002, Ján Smrek Preis 2003, STAB Preis 2004, Übersetzer Preis 'Premia Bohemica' 2004, Thüringer Verdienstrorden 2008, Memminger Freiheitspreis 2009, Thüringer Literaturpreis 2009. *Address:* Am Sonnenhang 19, 94130 Obernzell, Germany. *Telephone:* 8591-2989 (home). *Website:* www.reiner-kunze.com (home).

KUNZIG, Robert; American science journalist. *Career:* Contributing Ed., Discover magazine. *Publications:* The Restless Sea 1999, Mapping the Deep (Aventis Prize 2001) 2000, Fixing Climate (with Wallace S. Broecker) 2008. *Honours:* American Asscn for the Advancement of Science Westinghouse Science Journalism Award, American Geophysical Union Walter Sullivan Award for Excellence in Science Journalism. *Address:* Discover Magazine, 90 Fifth Avenue, New York, NY 10011, USA (office). *E-mail:* editorial@discover.com (office). *Website:* www.discover.com (office).

KUNZRU, Hari Mohan Nath, BA, MA; British writer and journalist; b. 1969, Woodford Green, Essex, England; s. of Krishna Mohan Nath Kunzru and Hilary Ann David. *Education:* Wadham Coll., Oxford and Univ. of Warwick. *Career:* fmr journalist, Music Ed. Wallpaper magazine, Assoc. Ed. Wired magazine, Contrib. Ed. Mute magazine. *Publications:* novels: The Impressionist (Observer Young Travel Writer of the Year 1999, Betty Trask Prize 2002) 2002, Transmission 2004, My Revolutions 2007; other: short stories, journalism; contrib. to Wired, London Review of Books, Guardian, Observer, New York Times, Daily Telegraph, BBC Midnight Review. *Honours:* Somerset Maugham Award 2003, John Llewellyn Rhys Prize 2003, Granta Best of Young British Novelists 2003, Lire 50 Écrivains Pour Demain 2005, British Book Award for Decibel Writer of the Year 2005. *Address:* 435 West 23rd Street, Apt 7D, New York, NY 10011, USA. *Website:* www.harikunzru.com.

KUPPNER, Frank; British writer and poet; b. 1951, Glasgow, Scotland. *Education:* Univ. of Glasgow. *Career:* Writer-in-Residence, Edinburgh Univ. 1998–2001; Writing Fellow, Strathclyde Univ. 2002–03. *Publications:* fiction: Ridiculous! Disgusting! 1989, A Very Quiet Street 1989, A Concussed History of Scotland 1990, Something Very Like Murder 1994; poetry: A Bad Day for the Sung Dynasty 1984, The Intelligent Observation of Naked Women 1987, Everything is Strange 1994, A God's Breakfast 2004. *Honours:* McVitie's Prize for Scottish Writer of the Year 1996. *Address:* c/o Carcanet Press, Fourth Floor, Alliance House, Cross Street, Manchester, M2 7AP, England (office). *Website:* www.carcanet.co.uk (office).

KÜR, Pinar, DèsL; Turkish writer, screenwriter and academic; b. 15 April 1943, Bursa; d. of Behram Kür and Halide Ismet Kür (née Zerluhan); m. Can Kolukisaoğlu 1964 (divorced 1979); one s. *Education:* Forest Hills High School and Queens Coll., New York and Univs of the Bosphorus, Istanbul and Paris (Sorbonne). *Career:* writer, State Theatre of Ankara 1971–73; apptd Lecturer in English, Istanbul Univ. 1979; Lecturer in Literature, Istanbul Bilgi Universifesi 1996. *Films:* Bir kadin, bir hayat 1985, Asılacak Kadan (A Woman to Hang) 1986, Yarin, Yarin (Tomorrow, Tomorrow) 1987. *Publications include:* novels: Yarin, Yarin (Tomorrow, Tomorrow) 1976, Küçük Oyuncu (Petty Player) 1977, Asılacak Kadan (A Woman to Hang) 1979, Bitmeyen Aşk (Unending Love) 1986, Bir Cinayet Romanı (A Crime Novel) 1989, Sonuncu Sonbahar (The Last Fall); short stories: Bir Deli Ağaç (A Tormented Tree) 1981, Akışi Olmayan Sular (Still Waters, Sait Faik Award 1984) 1983; numerous magazine and newspaper articles and translations into Turkish. *Honours:* Sait Faik Award 1984. *Address:* Turna Sokak 7/3, Elmadağ, 80230 Istanbul, Turkey (home). *Telephone:* (1) 2415148 (home). *E-mail:* kurpinar@hotmail.com (home).

KURAHASHI, Yumiko; Japanese writer; b. 1935, Shikoku. *Education:* Meiji Univ., Univ. of Iowa, USA. *Career:* writer of experimental Japanese fiction 1960–; pioneered post-War Japanese fantasy literature; technique ranges from parodies of classical literature to gothic erotica, ghost stories, futuristic science and avant-garde works; first short story Parutai (The Party) won Meiji Univ. Intramural Fiction Competition 1960; Fulbright Scholar, Univ. of Iowa 1966. *Publications:* Parutai (The Party) 1961, Kai no naka (Inside the Shell), Hebi (Snake), Kon'yaku (The Engagement), Baajinia (Vriginia) 1968, Sumiyakisuto Q no bōken (The Adventure of Sumiyakist Q) 1989, Yume no ukihashi (Bridge of Dreams) 1971, Han higeki (Anti-tragedies) 1972, Shiro no naka no shiro (A Castle within a Castle), Shunposhion (Symposium), Kōkan (Fraternity), Amanonkoku ōkanki (The Record of the Journey to the Amanon Empire), Otona no tame no zankoku dōwa (Cruel Fairy Tales for Adults) 1984, Creepy Little Stories 1985, The Woman with the Flying Head and Other Stories 1997. *Honours:* Women's Literary Prize, Tamura Toshiko Prize, Izumi Kyoka Prize and others.

KUREISHI, Hanif, CBE, BA; British writer and dramatist; b. 5 Dec. 1954, Bromley; m. Tracey Scoffield; three c. *Education:* King's Coll., London. *Career:* worked as typist at Riverside Studios; Writer-in-Residence, Royal Court Theatre, London 1981, 1985–86. *Stage plays:* Soaking the Heat 1976, The Mother Country (Thames TV Playwright Award) 1980, The King and Me 1980, Outskirts (RSC) 1981, Cinders (after the play by Janusz Glowacki) 1981, Borderline (Royal Court) 1981, Artists and Admirers (after a play by Ostrovsky, with David Leveaux) 1981, Birds of Passage (Hampstead Theatre) 1983, Mother Courage (adaptation of a play by Brecht, RSC) 1984, Sleep With Me (Nat. Theatre) 1999, When the Night Begins (Hampstead Theatre) 2004. *Screenplays:* My Beautiful Laundrette (Evening Standard Best Film Award 1986, New York Critics' Best Screenplay Award 1987) 1986, Sammy and Rosie Get Laid 1988, London Kills Me (also directed) 1991, My Son The Fanatic 1997, The Mother 2002. *Television:* The Buddha of Suburbia (BBC) 1993. *Publications:* fiction: The Buddha of Suburbia (Whitbread Award for Best First Novel) 1990, The Black Album 1995, Love in a Blue Time (short stories) 1997, Intimacy 1998, Midnight All Day (short stories) 1999, Gabriel's Gift 2000, The Body 2002, Telling Tales (contrib. to charity anthology) 2004, Something to Tell You 2008, Collected Stories 2010; non-fiction: The Rainbow Sign (autobiog.) 1986, Eight Arms to Hold You (essay) 1991, Dreaming and Scheming: Reflections on Writing and Politics (essays) 2002, My Ear at his Heart (autobiog.) (Prix France Culture littérature étrangère, France 2005) 2004, The Word and The Bomb (essays) 2005; ed.: The Faber Book of Pop (co-ed.) 1995; stories in Granta, Harpers (USA), London Review of Books and The Atlantic; regular contrib. to New Statesman and Society. *Honours:* Chevalier, Ordre des Arts et Lettres 2002; George Devine Award 1981, PEN/Pinter Prize 2010. *Literary Agent:* c/o Rogers, Coleridge & White Ltd, 20 Powis Mews, London, W11 1JN, England.

KURKOV, Andrey; Ukrainian author and screenwriter; b. 1961, St Petersburg, USSR. *Education:* Foreign Language Inst., Kiev. *Career:* fmr journalist, film cameraman. *Publications:* novels in trans.: A Matter of Death and Life 1996, Death and the Penguin 1996, The Case of the General's Thumb 2003, Penguin Lost 2003, The President's Last Love 2007, The Good Angel of Death 2009; other: four children's books, various screenplays. *Address:* c/o Harvill Secker, Random House, 20 Vauxhall Bridge Road, London, SW1V 2SA, England (office). *Website:* www.randomhouse.co.uk/harvillsecker (office).

KURTZ, Katherine Irene, BS, MA; American writer; b. 18 Oct. 1944, Coral Gables, FL; m. Scott Roderick MacMillan 1983; one s. *Education:* Univ. of Miami, Univ. of California, Los Angeles. *Career:* mem. Authors' Guild, Science Fiction and Fantasy Writers of America, Inc. *Publications:* Deryni Rising 1970, Deryni Checkmate 1972, High Deryni 1973, Camber of Culdi 1976, Saint Camber 1978, Camber the Heretic 1981, Lammas Night 1983, The Bishop's Heir 1984, The King's Justice 1985, The Quest for Saint Camber 1986, The Legacy of Lehr 1986, The Deryni Archives 1986, The Harrowing of Gwynedd 1989, Deryni Magic: A Grimoire 1990, King Javan's Year 1992, The Bastard Prince 1994, Two Crowns for America 1996, King Kelson's Bride 2000, St Patrick's Gargoyle 2001, In the King's Service 2003, Childe Morgan 2006; with Deborah Turner Harris: The Adept 1991, Lodge of the Lynx 1992, The Templar Treasure 1993, Dagger Magic 1994, Death of an Adept 1996, The Temple and the Stone 1998, The Temple and the Crown 2001; with Robert Reginald: Codex Derynianus 1998; editor: Tales of the Knights Templar 1995, On Crusade 1998, Deryni Tales 2002, Crusade of Fire 2002; various short stories. *Honours:* Edmund Hamilton Memorial Award 1977, Balrog Award 1982. *Address:* 1417 North Augusta Street, Staunton, VA 24401, USA (home). *E-mail:* kkurtz@iol.ie (home). *Website:* www.deryni.net.

KURUMATANI, Chokitsu; Japanese novelist; b. 1 July 1945, Himeji City, Hyogo Pref. *Education:* Keio Univ. *Career:* fmrly worked in advertising and publishing cos and as a cook's helper. *Publications:* novels: Shiotsubo no saji (The Salt Bowl Spoon) (Mishima Yukio Prize) 1992, Hyoryubutsu (Drifting Object) (Hirabayashi Taiko Award) 1995, Akame Shijuuyataki Shinju Misui (Naoki Sanjugo Award), Musashimaru, Han jidaiteki dokumushi 2004, Hibari no su o sagashita hi 2005. *Address:* c/o Kodansha International, Otowa YK Building, 1-17-14 Otowa, Bunkyo-ku, Tokyo 112-8652, Japan. *E-mail:* sales@kodansha-intl.co.jp.

KURZWEIL, Raymond (Ray) C., BS; American computer scientist and business executive; *Chairman and CEO, Kurzweil Technologies*; b. 12 Feb. 1948, Queens, NY; m. Sonya R. Kurzweil. *Education:* Massachusetts Inst. of Tech. *Career:* aspired to become an inventor from age of five; built and programmed his own computer to compose original melodies aged 15; founder and fmr CEO Kurzweil Computer Products, Inc. 1974–80, Kurzweil Music Systems, Inc. 1982–90, Kurzweil Applied Intelligence, Inc. 1982–97, Kurzweil Educational Systems, Inc. 1996; Chair. Strategy and Tech. Cttee Bd Dirs, Wang Laboratories, Inc. 1993–98; Founder, Chair. and CEO Kurzweil Technologies, Inc. 1995–, FAT KAT, Inc. 1999–, Kurzweil Cyber Art Technologies, Inc. 2000–; Founder, Pres. and CEO Medical Learning Co., Inc. and FamilyPractice.com 1997; Founder, CEO and Ed.-in-Chief www.KurzweilAI.net 2001–; Co-Founder, Chair. and Co-CEO Ray & Terry's Longevity Products, Inc. 2003; mem. Bd Dirs Medical Manager Corpn 1997–2000, Inforte 1999–, United Therapeutics 2002–; Chair. and Founder The Kurzweil Foundation; Dir Massachusetts Computer Software Council; fmr Dir Boston Computer Soc.; mem. MIT Corpn Visiting Cttee, MIT School of Humanities, MIT School of Music, Bd of Overseers, New England Conservatory of Music; developed first computerized Four-Way Analysis of Variance (statistical program) 1964, first computer-based Expert System for College Selection 1967, first Text-to-Speech speech synthesis 1975, first CCD Flatbed Scanner 1975, first Print-to-Speech Reading Machine for the Blind (Kurzweil Reading Machine) 1976, first Omni-Font (any-type font) Optical Character Recognition (now Xerox TextBridge) 1976, first Computer Music Keyboard capable of accurately reproducing sounds of the grand piano and other orchestral instruments (Kurzweil 250) 1984, first Knowledge Base System for Creating Medical Reports (Kurzweil VoiceMED) 1985, first commercially marketed Large Vocabulary Speech Recognition (Kurzweil Voice Report) 1987, first Speech Recognition Dictation System for Windows (Kurzweil Voice for Windows) 1994, first Continuous Speech Natural Language Command and Control Software (Kurzweil VoiceCommands) 1997, first Print-to-Speech Reading System for Persons with Reading Disabilities (Kurzweil 3000), first Virtual Performing and Recording Artist (Ramona) to perform in front of a live audience with a live band 2001, first 'host/hostess' Avatar on the Web to combine lifelike photo-realistic, moving and speaking facial image with a conversational engine 2001; Fellow, American Acad. of Arts and Sciences 2009–. *Film:* The Age of Intelligent Machines (The Chris Plaque, Columbus Int. Film Festival 1987, Creative Excellence Award, US Industrial Film and Video Festival 1987, Gold Medal – Science Educ., Int. Film and TV Festival of New York 1987, CINE Golden Eagle Award 1987, Tech. Culture Award, Int. Festival of Scientific Films, Belgrade 1988, Prize of the President of the Festival, Int. Film Festival of Czechoslovakia 1988) 1987. *Publications:* The Age of Intelligent Machines (MIT Press Best Seller 1991, Silicon Valley Best Seller 1991, Most Outstanding Computer Science Book of 1990 Award, Asscn of American Publishers 1991) 1990, The 10% Solution for a Healthy Life (Regional Best Seller 1993) 1993, The Age of Spiritual Machines, When Computers Exceed Human Intelligence (Nat. and Regional Best Sellers 1999, 2000, Literary Lights Prize, Boston Public Library 1999) 1999, Are We Spiritual Machines, Ray Kurzweil versus the Critics of Strong AI 2002, Fantastic Voyage: Live Long Enough to Live Forever (co-author) 2004, The Singularity is Near, When Humans Transcend Biology 2005. *Honours:* Hon. Chair. for Innovation, White House Conf. on Small Business 1986; Hon. DHumLitt (Hofstra Univ.) 1982, (Misericordia Coll.) 1989, (Landmark Coll.) 2002, Worcester Polytechnic Inst. 2005; Hon. DMus (Berklee Coll. of Music) 1987; Hon. DSc (Northeastern Univ.) 1988, (Rensselaer Polytechnic Inst.) 1988, (New Jersey Inst. of Tech.) 1990, (City Univ. of New York) 1991, (Dominican Coll.) 1993; Hon. DEng (Merrimack Coll.) 1989; Dr hc in Science and Humanities (Michigan State Univ.) 2000; numerous awards including Mass's Gov.'s Award 1977, Grace Murray Hopper Award, Asscn for Computing Machinery (ACM) 1978, Nat. Award, Johns Hopkins Univ. 1981, admitted to Computer Industry Hall of Fame 1982, Pres.'s Computer Science Award 1982, The White House Award for Entrepreneurial Excellence 1986, Inventor of the Year Award, awarded by MIT, Boston Museum of Science and Boston Patent Law Asscn 1988, MIT Founders Award 1989, Engineer of the Year Award, Design News magazine 1990, Louis Braille Award, Associated Services for the Blind 1991, Massachusetts Quincentennial Award for Innovation and Discovery 1992, ACM Fellow Award 1993, Gordon Winston Award, Canadian Nat. Inst. for the Blind 1994, Dickson Prize, Carnegie Mellon Univ. 1994, Software Industry Achievement Award, Massachusetts Software Council 1996, Pres.'s Award, Asscn on Higher Educ. and Disability 1997, Stevie Wonder/SAP Vision Award for Product of the Year (for the Kurzweil 1000) 1998, Nat. Medal of Tech. 1999, Lemelson-MIT Prize 2000, inducted into Nat. Inventors' Hall of Fame, US Patent Office 2002. *Address:* Kurzweil Technologies, Inc., PMB 193 733, Turnpike Street, North Andover, MA 01845 (office); Kurzweil Technologies, Inc., 15 Walnut Street, Wellesley Hills, MA 02481, USA (office). *Telephone:* (718) 263-0000 (office). *Fax:* (718) 263-9999 (office). *E-mail:* raymond@kurzweiltech.com (office). *Website:* www.KurzweilTech.com (office); www.KurzweilAI.net (office).

KUSHNER, Aleksandr Semyonovich; Russian poet; b. 14 Sept. 1936, Leningrad; s. of Semyon Semyonovich Kushner and Asya Aleksandrovna Kushner; m. Elena Vsevolodovna Nevzglyadova 1981; one s. *Education:* Leningrad Pedagogical Inst. *Career:* lecturer in literature 1959–69. *Publications include:* First Impression 1962, Night Watch 1966, Omens 1969, Letter 1974, Direct Speech 1975, Voice 1978, Canvas 1981, The Tavrichesky Garden 1984, Daydreams 1986, Poems 1986 (Selected Poems), The Hedgerow 1988, A Night Melody 1991, Apollo in the Snow (selected essays on Russian literature of the nineteenth and twentieth centuries and personal memoirs) 1991, Apollo in the Snow (selected poems trans. into English) 1991, On the Gloomy Star (State Prize) 1995, Selected Poetry 1997, The Fifth Element 1999, The Bush 2002, Cold Month of May 2005, Selected Poems 2005, Apollo in the Grass (essays on poetry) 2005, In the New Century 2006, The Time is Not to Be Chosen 2007, Clouds Opt for Anapest 2008; essays in literary journals. *Honours:* Northern Palmira Award 1995, Russian Fed. State Award 1995, German Pushkin Award, Alfred Toepfer Foundation 1999, Russian Fed. Alexander Pushkin Award 2001, Nat. 'The Poet' Award 2005. *Address:* Kaluzhsky pereulok No. 9, Apt 48, 193015 St Petersburg, Russia (home). *Telephone:* (812) 577-32-56 (home). *E-mail:* kushner@mail.lanck.net (home).

KUSHNER, Tony, BA, MFA; American playwright; b. 16 July 1956, New York, NY. *Education:* Columbia Univ., New York Univ. *Career:* Playwright-in-Residence, Juilliard School, New York 1990–92. *Publications:* Yes, Yes, No, No 1985, Actors on Acting 1986, Stella 1987, A Bright Room Called Day 1987, Hydriotaphia 1987, The Illusion 1988, The Persistence of Prejudice 1989, Widows (with Ariel Dorfman) 1991, Angels in America: A Gay Fantasia on National Themes, Part One: Millennium Approaches (Pulitzer Prize 1993) 1991, Part Two: Perestroika 1992, Slavs! 1994, Holocaust and the Liberal Imagination 1994, Thinking About the Longstanding Problems of Virtue and Happiness 1995, Homebody/Kabul 2001, Caroline, or Change (Best New Musical, Olivier Awards 2007) 2006, The Intelligent Homosexual's Guide to Capitalism and Socialism with a Key to the Scriptures 2009. *Honours:* Tony Award 1993, 1994, Critics' Circle Award, London Evening Standard Award, Steinberg Distinguished Playwright Award 2008. *Literary Agent:* Steven Barclay Agency, 12 Western Avenue, Petaluma, CA 94952, USA. *Telephone:* (707) 773-0654. *Fax:* (707) 778-1868. *E-mail:* steven@barclayagency.com. *Website:* www.barclayagency.com.

KÜTHEN, Hans-Werner, MA, PhD; German musicologist and editor; b. 26 Aug. 1938, Cologne; m. Annette Magdalena Leinen; one s. *Education:* Bonn Univ., studied in Bologna. *Career:* Ed., Beethoven Archives; mem. Gesellschaft für Musikforschung, VG Musikedition; Patron of the Verein Beethoven-Haus Bonn. *Films:* Beethoven's Hair 2005. *Publications:* On Beethoven: Article Beethoven Herder, Das Grosse Lexikon der Musik 1978, Complete edition, Henle, München: Ouverturen und Wellingtons Sieg 1974, Critical Report, separately 1991, Klavierkonzerte I (nos 1–3) 1984, Klavierkonzerte II (nos 4–5) 1996, Klavierkonzerte III (WoO 4, WoO 6, op. 61a) 2004, each with Critical Report; contrib. to int. professional publications, including Beethoven yearbooks, congress reports, scholarly periodicals; journal contribs include: Gradus ad partituram; Erscheinungsbild und Funktionen der Solostimme in Beethovens Klavierkonzerten, Gradus ad Partituram: Appearance and Essence in the Solo Part of Beethoven's Piano Concertos, Beethoven Forum Vol. 9 No. 2, Urbana-Champaign, Ill. 2002; Ein unbekanntes Notierungsblatt Beethovens aus der Entstehungszeit der Mondscheinsonate, Prague, 1996; Rediscovery and reconstruction of an authentic version of Beethoven's Fourth Piano Concerto for pianoforte and 5 strings, see Beethoven Journal Vol. 13 No. 1, San José, 1998 and Bonner Beethoven-Studien Vol. 1, Bonn 1999; Hudebuí věda 1, Prague 1999; On Viadana: Article V in Herder-Lex, 1982, id in Lexikon für Theologie und Kirche, Herder, 2000; Co-Editor, Beethoven im Herzen Europas. Leben und Nachleben in den Böhmischen Ländern, Prague 2000; Ed., Beethoven und die Rezeption der Alten Musik, Die hohe Schule der Überlieferung, Report of the Int. Symposium, Bonn 2000; A Lost Sonority: Beethoven's imitation of the Aeolian Harp, Arietta Vol. 4, London 2004; Ein verlorener Registerklang Beethoven's Imitation der Aeolsharfe, Musik & Ästhetik 34 2005; Wer schrieb den Endtext des Violinkonzerts op. 61 von Beethoven? Franz Alexander Pössinger als letzte Instanz für den Komponisten, Bonner Beethoven-Studien Vol. 4, Bonn 2005; Coriolanus Overture, conducting score with Preface, Wiesbaden 2005. *Address:* Am Hofgarten 7, 53113 Bonn, Germany. *E-mail:* hans-werner@kuethen.de (home).

KUTTNER, Paul; American publicity director (retd) and writer; b. 20 Sept. 1922, Berlin, Germany; s. of Paul Kuttner and Margarete Fraenkel-Kuttner; m. Ursula Timmermann 1963 (divorced 1970); one s. *Education:* Bryanston Coll., Dorset, UK. *Career:* child actor in films of Fritz Lang, G. W. Pabst, and Gerhard Lamprecht, Germany 1930–31; US Publicity Dir, Guinness Book of World Records 1964–89; Publicity Dir, Sterling Publishing Co. Inc. 1989–98. *Films include:* M 1931, Kameradschaft, Emil und die Detektive; appeared in documentaries, including The Kindertransport: My Knees Were Jumping 1991, Into the Arms of Strangers 2000, Die Rote Kapelle (The Red Orchestra) 2003. *Publications:* The Man Who Lost Everything 1976, Condemned 1983, Absolute Proof 1984, The Iron Virgin 1985, History's Trickiest Questions 1990, Arts & Entertainment's Trickiest Questions 1993, Science's Trickiest Questions 1994, The Holocaust: Hoax or History? – The Book of Answers to Those Who Would Deny the Holocaust 1997, An Endless Struggle: Reminiscences and Reflections (auto-biog.) 2010; several trans of books; contrib. to Der Weg, London Week, London News Chronicle. *Address:* 3726 87th Street, Apt 5C, Jackson Heights, NY 11372, USA (home). *Telephone:* (718) 446-2179 (home).

KWEI-ARMAH, Kwame, OBE; British actor, playwright, singer and broadcaster; *Artistic Director, Centerstage, Baltimore, Md;* b. (Ian Roberts), 24 March 1967, Hillingdon, London, England; m.; four c. *Education:* Barbara Speake Stage School. *Career:* Writer-in-Residence, Bristol Old Vic 1999–2001; fmrly writer on attachment as Assoc. Artist to Nat. Theatre Studio; took part in Celebrity Fame Academy (BBC TV) 2003; named an Assoc. Artist at Centerstage, Baltimore, Md, directing debut with Naomi Wallace's Things of Dry Hours, has since Esa Davis's ten-minute play Dave Chappelle was Right for the 24 Hour Plays on Broadway, Artistic Dir Centerstage 2011–; took part in the Bush Theatre's project Sixty Six (wrote a piece based upon a chapter of the King James Bible) 2011; judge, BBC World Service's Int. Radio Playwriting Competition 2009; mem. Bd Royal Nat. Theatre, Tricycle Theatre; named Goodwill Amb. for Trade for Christian Aid; Chancellor Univ. of the Arts London. *Plays as writer:* Big Nose (adaptation of Rostand's Cyrano De Bergerac, Belgrade Theatre, Coventry) 1999, Blues Brother Soul Sister (musical, Bristol Old Vic) 2000, A Bitter Herb (Peggy Ramsey Bursary, Bristol Old Vic) 2001, Hold On (Durham Theatre Royal) 2002, Elmina's Kitchen (Royal Nat. Theatre, Charles Wintour Award for Most Promising Playwright, Evening Standard Theatre Awards 2004) 2003, Fix Up (Royal Nat. Theatre) 2004, Statement of Regret (Royal Nat. Theatre) 2007, Let There Be Love (Tricycle Theatre) 2008, Seize the Day. *Plays as actor:* Mozart and Salieri (Crucible, Sheffield). *Films:* Once Upon a Time (short) (dir and producer) 1991; as actor: Cutthroat Island 1995, Il mio West 1998, The 3 Kings 2000, Fade to Black 2006. *Television:* as actor Ian Roberts: The Latchkey Children (series) 1980, Birth of a Nation (film) 1983, The Bill (series) 1989; as actor Kwame Kwei-Armah: Between The Lines (series) 1994, Casualty (series) 1994–2004, Expert Witness (series documentary) 1996, An Unsuitable Job for a Woman (series) 1998, Der Clown (series) 1999, Holby City (series) 2000–01, The Afternoon Play (series) – Sons, Daughters and Lovers 2004, Pride (film) (voice) 2004, Robin Hood (series) 2006, Cold Blood 2 (film) 2007, Lewis (series) – The Great and the Good 2008, Hotel Babylon (series) 2008, Walter's War (film) (BBC Four) (also writer) 2008, Horne & Corden (series) 2009, Skins (series) 2010; as writer: Elmina's Kitchen (film) 2005, Christianity: A History (series documentary) 2009. *Recordings:* album: Kwame 2003. *Honours:* Dr hc (Open Univ.) 2008; Evening Standard Charles Wintour Award for Most Promising Playwright 2003. *Address:* Centerstage, 700 North Calvert Street, Baltimore, MD 21202, USA (office). *Telephone:* (410) 986-4000 (office). *E-mail:* info@centerstage.org (office). *Website:* www.centerstage.org (office).

KYLE, Susan Eloise Spaeth, (Diana Blayne, Diana Palmer), BA; American author; b. 12 Dec. 1946, Cuthbert, GA; d. of William Kyle and Eloise Spaeth; m. James Edward Kyle 1972; one s. *Education:* Piedmont Coll. *Career:* mem. Authors' Guild. *Publications include:* as Diana Palmer: Now and Forever 1979, Storm Over the Lake 1979, To Have and To Hold 1979, Sweet Enemy 1980, September Morning 1982, Snow Kisses 1983, Diamond Girl 1983, Heart of Ice 1984, The Rawhide Man 1984, Love By Proxy 1985, The Australian 1985, Eye of the Tiger 1986, Loveplay 1986, Betrayed by Love 1987, The Humbug Man 1987, Woman Hater 1988, Miss Greenhorn 1990, Nelson's Brand 1991, Trilby 1992, Calamity Moon 1993, Nora 1994, That Burke Man 1995, Anabelle's Legacy 1996, The Patient Nurse 1997, The Bride Who Was Stolen 1998, Beloved 1999, Circle of Gold 2000, The Eye of the Tiger 2001, Garden Cop 2002, The Marrying Kind 2003, Before Sunrise 2005, Fearless 2008, Diamond in the Rough 2009, Miss Greenhorn 2009, Tough to Tame 2010, Dangerous 2010, Merciless 2011, True Blue 2011; as Diana Blayne: A Waiting Game 1982, A Loving Arrangement 1983, White Sand, Wild Sea 1983, Dark Surrender 1984, Denim and Lace 1986, Tangled Destinies 1986; as Katy Currie: Blind Promises 1984; as Susan Kyle: Diamond Spur 1988, Night Fever 1990, True Colors 1991, Escapade 1992, After Midnight 1993, All that Glitters 1995; contrib. to journals and magazines. *Honours:* seven Waldenbooks nat. sales awards, four B. Dalton nat. sales awards, two Bookrak nat. sales awards, several Affaire de Coeur awards, two Romance Writers of America awards, Lifetime Achievement Award, Romantic Times, Distinguished Alumni Award, Piedmont Coll. 2012. *Website:* www.dianapalmer.com.

KYNASTON, David, PhD; British historian and writer; *Visiting Professor, Kingston University;* b. 30 July 1951, Aldershot. *Education:* Wellington Coll., New Coll., Oxford, LSE. *Career:* Visiting Prof. Kingston Univ. 2001–. *Publications:* King Labour: British Working Class 1850–1914 1976, The Financial Times: a centenary history 1988, Cazenove & Co.: a history 1991, The Bank of England: money, power, and influence 1694–1994 1995, The City of London: A World of Its Own 1815–90 1995, Golden Years 1890–1914 1995, Illusions of Gold 1914–45 2000, Club No More 1945–2000 (co-author) 2002, W.G's Birthday Party 1990, Tales of a New Jerusalem: Austerity Britain 1945–1951 2007, Family Britain 1951–1957 2009; contrib. articles to newspapers. *Address:* c/o Bloomsbury Publishing Plc, 36 Soho Square, London, W1D 3QY, England (office). *Website:* www.bloomsbury.com (office).

L

LA PLANTE, Lynda, CBE; British television dramatist and novelist; *Chairman, La Plante Productions Ltd*; b. 15 March 1946, Formby; m. Richard La Plante (divorced). *Education:* Royal Coll. of Dramatic Art. *Career:* fmr actress; appeared in The Gentle Touch, Out, Minder; founder and Chair. La Plante Productions 1994–. *Television includes:* Prime Suspect 1991, 1993, 1995, Civvies, Framed, Seekers, Widows (series), Comics (two-part drama) 1993, Cold Shoulder 2 1996, Cold Blood, Bella Mafia 1997, Trial and Retribution 1997–, Killer Net 1998, Mind Games 2000, The Warden 2001, Framed 2002, Widows (mini-series) 2002, The Commander 2003. *Publications include:* The Widows 1983, The Widows II 1985, The Talisman 1987, Bella Mafia 1991, Framed 1992, Civvies 1992, Prime Suspect 1992, Seekers 1993, Entwined 1993, Prime Suspect 2 1993, Lifeboat 1994, Cold Shoulder 1994, Prime Suspect 3 1994, She's Out 1995, The Governor 1996, Cold Blood 1996, Trial and Retribution 1997, Cold Heart 1998, Trial and Retribution 2 1998, Trial and Retribution 3 1999, Trial and Retribution 4 2000, Sleeping Cruelty 2000, Trial and Retribution 5 2002, Trial and Retribution 6 2002, Royal Flush 2002, Like a Charm (short stories) 2004, Above Suspicion (novel) 2004, The Red Dahlia 2006, Clean Cut 2007, Deadly Intent 2008, Silent Scream 2009, Blind Fury 2011. *Address:* La Plante Productions Ltd, Paramount House, 162–170 Wardour Street, London, W1F 8ZX, England (office). *Telephone:* (20) 7734-6767 (office). *Fax:* (20) 7734-7878 (office). *E-mail:* admin@laplanteproductions.com (office). *Website:* www.laplanteproductions.com (office); www.lyndalaplante.com.

LAABI, Abdellatif; Moroccan poet, novelist, essayist and translator; b. 1942, Fès; m. Jocelyne Lécuelle 1964; three c. *Education:* Rabat Univ., Bordeaux III Univ. *Career:* French teacher at coll. in Rabat; Founder Souffles literary journal 1966–72 (publ. banned); Founder Atlantes Publishing Co. and Asscn de Recherche Culturelle; imprisoned for "crimes of opinion", Kénitra 1972–80; exiled in France 1985–. *Plays:* Le Baptême chacaliste, Exercices de tolérance, Le Juge de l'ombre. *Publications:* poetry: Le Règne de barbarie 1980, Histoire des sept crucifiés de l'espoir 1980, Sous le bâillon le poème 1981, Discours sur la colline arabe 1985, L'Ecorché vif 1986, Tous les déchirements 1990, L'Etreinte du monde 1993, Le Spleen de Casablanca 1996, Fragments d'une genèse oubliée 1998, Poèmes périssables 2000, Petit musée portatif 2002, L'Automne promet 2003, Les Fruits du corps 2003, Ruses de vivant 2004, Ecris la vie 2005, Oeuvre poétique I 2006, Mon cher double 2007, Tribulations d'in rêveur attitré 2008, Jardinier de l'âme 2008, Oeuvre poétique II 2010, Zone de turbulences 2012; novels: L'Oeil et la nuit 1969, Le Chemin des ordalies 1982, Les Rides du lion 1989, Le Fond de la jarre 2002, Le Livre imprévu 2010; non-fiction: La Parole confisquée 1982, La Brûlure des interrogations 1985, Un continent humain 1997, L'Ecriture au tournant 2000, Rimbaud et Shéhérazade 2000, Les Rêves sont têtus 2001, Chroniques de la citadelle d'exil 2005, Pourquoi cours-tu après la goutte d'eau? 2006, Combat pour la culture 2011, Maroc, quel projet démocratique? 2012; juvenile: Saida et les voleurs de soleil 1987, L'Orange bleue 1995, Comment Nassim a mangé sa première tomate 2001, Devine 2007; translator: La Poésie palestinienne contemporaine (anthology, co-ed. and trans.) 1990, La Poésie marocaine: de l'indépendance à nos jours (anthology, ed. and trans.) 2005, poetry by Aïcha Arnaout, Qassim Haddad, Mohammed Bennis, Saadi Youssef, Faraj Bayrakdar, Mohamed al-Maghout, Hassan Hamdane, Mahmoud Darwich, Samih al-Qassim, Abdelwahab al-Bayati, Abdallah Zrika, Aïcha Bassry, novels by Ghassan Kanafani, Hanna Mina, Issa Makhlouf. *Honours:* Commdr, Ordre des Arts et des Lettres 1985; Dr hc (Univ. de Rennes II); Prix de l'amitié franco-arabe 1979, Prix international de poésie de la Fondation nationale des arts, Rotterdam 1979, Prix de la liberté PEN Club français 1980, Prix Albert Droin de la Société des gens de lettres, France 1981, African Literature Asscn Fonlon Nichols Prize 1999, Wallonie-Bruxelles poetry prize 1999, Prix de l'Afrique méditerranéenne de l'ADELF 2002, Prix de poésie Alain Bosquet 2006, Prix de poésie Robert Ganzo 2008, Prix de poésie Naim Frasheri 2008, Prix Goncourt de Poésie 2009, Prix de la francophonie Benjamin Fondane 2010, Grand Prix de la francophonie de l' Acad. française 2011. *Address:* 8 rue de Mesly, 94000 Créteil, France (home). *Telephone:* 1-48-99-26-40 (home). *E-mail:* jalaabi@free.fr. *Website:* www.laabi.net.

LABERGE, Andrée, PhD; Canadian novelist; b. 1953, Québec City. *Career:* doctor of epidemiology, also trained and worked as a social worker; combines writing with career as public health researcher; full-time writer 2008–. *Publications include:* Les Oiseaux de verre 2000, L'Aguayo 2001, La Rivière du loup (Gov.-Gen.'s Literary Award) 2006, Le Fin Fond de L'Histoire 2008. *Address:* 8645 Avenue de Montcourt, Quebec, PQ G1G 5A5 (home); c/o XYZ Publishing, 1781 Saint Hubert Street, Montréal, PQ H2L 3Z1, Canada (office). *Telephone:* (418) 624-9294 (home). *E-mail:* alaberge1@sympatico.ca (home); info@editionsxyz.com (office).

LABERGE, Marie; Canadian dramatist, author, poet and editor; b. 29 Nov. 1950, Québec. *Education:* Université Laval, Conservatoire d'art dramatique de Québec. *Career:* Pres., Centre d'essai des auteurs dramatiques, 1987–89; Theatre Ed., Editions du Boréal, 1991–. *Publications:* Avec l'hiver qui s'en vient, 1981; Ils étaient venus pour. . ., 1981; C'était avant la guerre à l'Anse à Gilles, 1981, English trans. as Before the War, Down at l'Anse à Gilles, 1986; Jocelyne Trudelle trouvée morte dans ses larmes, 1983; Deux tangos pour toute une vie, 1985; L'homme gris, 1986, English trans. as Night, 1988; Le Night Cap Bar, 1987; Oublier, 1987, English trans. as Forgetting, 1988; Aurélie, ma soeur, 1988, English trans. as Aurélie, My Sister, 1989; Le Blanc, 1989; Juillet, 1989; Quelques adieux, 1992; Pierre, ou, La consolation, 1992; Annabelle, 1996; Le gout du bonheur, 2000. Contributions: Film, radio, television and various publications. *Honours:* Gov.-Gen.'s Award for Drama, 1982; Chevalier, Ordre des Arts et des Lettres, 1989; Prix des Lectrices de Elle-Québec, 1992.

LaBUTE, Neil; American playwright, film writer and director; b. 19 March 1963, Detroit, Mich.; m.; two c. *Education:* Brigham Young Univ., Univ. of Kan., New York Univ. *Films include:* In the Company of Men (writer, dir) (Sundance Film Festival Filmmakers' Trophy, Soc. of Tex. Film Critics Best Original Screenplay Award, New York Film Critics' Circle Best First Film) 1997, Your Friends and Neighbors (writer, dir) 1998, Tumble (writer) 2000, Nurse Betty (dir) 2000, Possession (screenplay writer, dir) 2002, The Shape of Things (writer, dir) 2003, The Wicker Man 2006, Lakeview Terrace 2008. *Theatre productions include:* Woyzeck, Dracula, Sangguinarians & Sycophants, Ravages, Rounder, Lepers, Filthy Talk For Troubled Times, In the Company of Men (Asscn for Mormon Letters Award for Drama 1993) 1992, Bash: Latterday Plays 2000, The Shape of Things 2001, The Distance From Here (Almeida, London) 2002, The Mercy Seat 2002, Merge 2003, Wrecks (Everyman Palace, Cork) 2005, This is How it Goes (New York, and Donmar Warehouse London) 2005, Some Girl(s) 2005, Land of the Dead/Helter Skelter 2007, Reasons to be Pretty 2008. *Television includes:* Bash: Latter-Day Plays 2001. *Publications include:* In the Company of Men 1998, Your Friends and Neighbors 1999, Bash: Latterday Plays 2000, The Shape of Things 2001, The Distance from Here 2003, The Mercy Seat 2003, Seconds of Pleasure (short stories) 2004. *Literary Agent:* William Morris Agency, One William Morris Place, Beverly Hills, CA 90212, USA. *Telephone:* (310) 859-4000. *Fax:* (310) 859-4462. *Website:* www.wma.com.

LACEY, Robert, BA, DipEd, MA; British writer; b. 3 Jan. 1944, Guildford, Surrey, England. *Education:* Selwyn Coll., Cambridge. *Career:* Asst Ed., Sunday Times Magazine 1969–73; Ed., Look! pages, Sunday Times 1973–74; Co-Ed., Co-Publisher Cover magazine 1999–2000. *Publications:* The French Revolution (two vols) 1968, The Rise of Napoleon 1969, The Peninsular War 1969, 1812: The Retreat From Moscow 1969, Robert, Earl of Essex: An Elizabethan Icarus 1971, The Life and Times of Henry VIII 1972, The Queens of the North Atlantic 1973, Sir Walter Raleigh 1973, Sir Francis Drake and the Golden Hinde 1975, Heritage of Britain (ed., contrib.) 1975, Majesty: Elizabeth II and the House of Windsor 1977, The Kingdom: Arabia and the House of Saud 1981, Princess 1982, Aristocrats 1983, Ford: The Men and the Machine 1986, God Bless Her: Her Majesty Queen Elizabeth the Queen Mother 1987, Little Man: Meyer Lansky and the Gangster Life 1991, Grace 1994, Sotheby's: Bidding for Class 1998, The Year 1000 (with Danny Danziger) 1999, Royal: Her Majesty Queen Elizabeth II 2002, Great Tales from English History: Cheddar Man to the Peasants' Revolt 2003, From Chaucer to the Glorious Revolution 2004, Battle of the Boyne to DNA 2006, Inside the Kingdom: Kings, Clerics, Modernists, Terrorists, and the Struggle for Saudi Arabia 2009. *E-mail:* robert@robertlacey.com (office). *Website:* www.robertlacey.com.

LÄCKBERG, Camilla; Swedish writer; b. 30 Aug. 1974, Fjällbacka; m. Martin Melin; one s.; one s. one d. (from previous marriage). *Education:* Gothenburg Univ. of Economics. *Career:* worked as an economist before becoming full-time crime writer. *Television:* presenter, Läckberg & Rudberg. *Publications include:* Isprinsessan (trans. as The Ice Princess) (Silver Pocket Winner, Guldpocketgalan 2008, Int. Grand Prix de Littérature Policière 2008) 2002, Predikanten (trans. as The Preacher) 2004, Stenhuggaren (trans. as The Stonecutter) (Swedish Novelist of the Year) 2005, Olycksfågeln (trans. as The Jinx) 2006, Tyskungen 2007, Sjöjungfrun 2008, Fyrvaktaren 2009, The Scent of Almonds 2009, The Angel Maker's Wife 2011; children's book: Super-Charlie 2012; non-fiction: The Taste of Fjällbacka (co-author) 2008, Feast, Food and Love 2011. *Honours:* SKTF Prize for Author of the Year 2005, People's Literature Award 2006. *Literary Agent:* Nordin Agency, Götgatan 58, POB 4022, 102 61 Stockholm, Sweden. *Telephone:* (8) 57168525. *E-mail:* joakim@nordinagency.se. *Website:* www.nordinagency.se; www.camillalackberg.com.

LACKEY, Mercedes, BS; American writer; b. 24 June 1950, Chicago, IL; m. 1st Anthony Lackey 1972 (divorced); m. 2nd Larry Dixon 1990. *Education:* Purdue Univ. *Career:* mem. SFWA. *Publications include:* Arrow's Flight 1987, Arrows of the Queen 1987, Arrow's Fall 1988, Oathbound 1988, Magic's Pawn 1989, Oathbreakers 1989, Reap the Whirlwind 1989, Children of the Night 1990, Knight of Ghosts and Shadows 1990, Magic's Price 1990, Magic's Promise 1990, By the Sword 1991, The Elvenbane 1991, Jinx High 1991, Winds of Fate 1991, Born to Run 1992, Castle of Deception 1992, The Lark and the Wren 1992, The Last Herald Mage 1992, Summoned to Tourney 1992, The Ship Who Searched 1992, Wheels of Fire 1992, Winds of Change 1992, Wing Commander: Freedom Flight 1992, Burning Water 1993, Fortress of Frost and Fire 1993, If I Pay Thee Not in Gold 1993, Prison of Souls 1993, Rediscovery: A Novel of Darkover 1993, The Robin and the Kestrel 1993, When the Bough Breaks 1993, Winds of Fury 1993, The Black Gryphon 1994, A Cast of Corbies 1994, Chrome Circle 1994, Sacred Ground 1994, Storm Warning 1994, The

Eagle and the Nightingales 1995, Elvenblood 1995, The Fire Rose 1995, Storm Rising 1995, Tiger Burning Bright 1995, The White Gryphon 1995, Firebird 1996, Lammas Night 1996, The Silver Gryphon 1996, Storm Breaking 1996, Four and Twenty Blackbirds 1997, Owlflight 1997, Owlsight 1998, The Black Swan 1999, The Chrome Bone 1999, Owlknight 1999, The River's Gift 1999, Werehunter 1999, Brightly Burning 2000, Beyond the World's End 2001, The Serpent's Shadow 2001, Spirits White as Lightning 2001, Take a Thief 2001, Elvenborn 2002, Exile's Honor 2002, The Gates of Sleep 2002, The Shadow of the Lion 2002, Charmed Destinies 2003, Exile's Valor 2003, Jouse 2003, Mad Maudlin 2003, The Outstretched Shadow 2003, This Rough Magic 2003, Alta 2004, The Fairy Godmother 2004, To Light a Candle 2004, Phoenix and Ashes 2004, Sword of Knowledge 2004, This Scepter'd Isle 2004, Wizard of Karres 2004, Bedlam's Edge 2005, Crossroads 2005, Ill Met by Moonlight 2005, Music to my Sorrow 2005, Sanctuary 2005, Stoned Souls 2005, Wizard of London 2005, Aerie 2006, One Good Knight 2006, When Darkness Falls 2006, Fortune's Fall 2007, By Slanderous Tongue 2007, Reserved for the Cat 2007, The Phoenix Unchained 2007, And Less Than Kind 2008, Foundation 2008, Moving Targets 2008, The Phoenic Endangered 2008, The Snow Queen 2008, The Phoenix Transformed 2009, Gwenhwyfar 2009; contributions: many anthologies and periodicals. *Website:* www.mercedeslackey.com.

LACOUTURE, Jean Marie-Gérard, DenSoc; French writer; b. 9 June 1921, Bordeaux; s. of Antoine-Joseph Lacouture and Anne-Marie Servantie; m. Simonne Grésillon; one d. *Career:* journalist 1946–72; Press Attaché, Résidence-Générale of France, Morocco 1947–49; Diplomatic Ed. Combat 1950–51; reporter, Le Monde 1951–72; corresp., France-Soir, Egypt 1954–56; Research Fellow, Harvard Univ. 1966; Dir of Collections, Editions du Seuil 1962–80. *Publications include:* Cinq Hommes et la France 1961, De Gaulle 1965, Le Vietnam entre deux paix 1965, Hô Chi Minh 1967, Nasser 1971, André Malraux, une vie dans le siècle 1973, Un sang d'encre 1974, Léon Blum 1977, Survive le peuple cambodgien! 1978, Signes du Taureau 1979, François Mauriac (two vols) 1980, Pierre Mendès France 1981, Le Piéton de Bordeaux 1981, Profils perdus 1983, De Gaulle (three vols) 1984–86, Algérie: la guerre est finie 1985, Champollion: Une vie de lumières 1989, Enquête sur l'auteur 1989, Jésuites (two vols) 1991–92, Voyous et gentlemen: une histoire du rugby 1993, le Désempire (jtly) 1993, Une adolescence du siècle 1994, Mes héros et nos monstres 1995, Montaigne à cheval 1996, Histoire de France en cent tableaux 1997, Mitterrand (two vols) 1998, Greta Garbo: la dame aux caméras 1999, Stendhal – Le bonheur vagabond 2004; several works in collaboration with Simonne Lacouture and others. *Honours:* Officer, Légion d'honneur, Commdr des Arts et Lettres; Prix Sola Cabiati de la Ville de Paris 1996. *Address:* 37 quai des Grands Augustins, 75006 Paris, France.

LADJALI, Cécile, DLit; French writer and teacher; b. 1971, Lausanne. *Education:* Sorbonne, Univ. of Paris. *Career:* student teacher, Institut universitaire de formation des maîtres, Créteil; now French teacher, Lycée Évariste-Gallois, Noisy-le-Grand. *Publications:* Murmures (poems) 2001, Tohu-Bohu (tragic play) 2002, Les Souffleurs (novel) 2002, Éloge de la transmission: le maître et l'élève (non-fiction, with George Steiner) 2003, La Chapelle Ajax (novel) 2005. *Address:* c/o Actes Sud, 18 rue Séguier, 75006 Paris, France. *E-mail:* accueil.paris@actes-sud.fr.

LAFERRIÈRE, Dany; Canadian (b. Haitian) writer; b. 17 April 1953, Port-au-Prince, Haiti. *Career:* journalist for Petit Samedi Soir and Radio Haïti; went into exile 1976, moving to Montréal, Canada, where worked as journalist, TV presenter for Télévision Quatre Saisons network; now lives in Miami, USA; writes in French. *Films:* Voodoo Taxi (writer) 1991, Vite, je n'ai pas que cela à faire (writer), Le Violon rouge (actor) 1998, Le Goût des jeunes filles (adaptation of novel) 2004, Comment conquérir l'Amérique en une nuit (writer, dir) 2004, Vers le sud (writer) 2005. *Publications include:* Comment faire l'amour avec un nègre sans se fatiguer (novel, trans. as How to Make Love to a Negro Without Getting Tired) 1985, Éroshima (novel, trans. as Eroshima) 1987, L'Odeur du café (trans. as An Aroma of Coffee) (Prix Carbet de la Caraïbe) 1991, Le Goût des jeunes filles (novel, trans. as Dining with the Dictator) (Prix Edgar-l'Espérance) 1992, Cette grenade dans la main du jeune nègre est-elle une arme ou un fruit? (novel, trans. as Why Must a Black Writer Write About Sex?) (Prix RFO du Livre 2002) 1993, Chronique de la dérive douce (poems, trans. as A Drifting Year) 1994, Pays sans chapeau (novel, trans. as Down Among the Dead Men) 1996, La Chair du maître 1997, Le Charme des après-midi sans fin (novel) 1997, Dans l'oeil du cyclone 1999, Le Cri des oiseaux foux (novel) (Marguerite Yourcenar Prize 2001) 2000, Je suis fatigué 2000, Les Annees 80 dans ma vieille Ford 2005, Vers le sud 2006, J'écris comme je vis 2006, Je suis fou de Vava (juvenile) (Governor-General's Literary Award) 2006, Je suis en écrivain japonais 2008, L'enigme du Retour (Prix Médicis) 2009, Tout bouge autour de moi 2010. *Address:* c/o Éditions Grasset, 61 rue des Saints-Pères, 75006 Paris, France (office). *Website:* www.grasset.fr (office).

LAFFIN, John Alfred Charles, MA, DLitt; Australian author, journalist and lecturer; b. 21 Sept. 1922, Sydney, NSW; m. Hazelle Stonham 1943 (died 1997); one s. two d. *Career:* Battlefield Archaeologist; Adviser/Consultant, War, Military History and Islam; Founder, John Laffin Australian Battlefield Museum, 1988; mem. Society of Authors, UK; Australian Society of Authors; Pres., Families and Friends of the First A I F. *Publications:* Return to Glory, 1953; Digger: Story of the Australian Soldier, 1959; Codes and Ciphers, 1964; Anzacs at War, 1965; Jackboot: Story of the German Soldier, 1965; The Hunger to Come, 1966; Women in Battle, 1967; Devil's Goad, 1970; Americans in Battle, 1972; The Arab Mind, 1974; Dagger of Islam, 1979; Damn the Dardanelles!, 1980; Fight for the Falklands, 1982; The PLO Connections, 1982; Australian Army at War 1899–1975, 1982; The Man the Nazis Couldn't Catch, 1984; On the Western Front, 1985; Know the Middle East, 1985; Brassey's Battles, 1986; War Annual 1, 1986; War Annual 2, 1987; Battlefield Archaeology, 1987; War Annual 3, 1987; Western Front, 1916–17: The Price of Honour, 1988; Western Front, 1917–18: The Cost of Victory, 1988; Holy War – Islam Fights, 1988; War Annual 4, 1988; British Butchers and Bunglers of World War I, 1989; War Annual 5, 1991; The Western Front Illustrated, 1991; Dictionary of Africa Since 1960, 1991; Guidebook to Australian Battlefields of France and Flanders 1916–18, 1992; Digging up the Diggers, War, 1993; Panorama of the Western Front, 1993; A Western Front Companion, 1994; Forever Forward, 1994; War Annual 6, 1994; Aussie Guide to Britain, 1995; Hitler Warned Us, 1995; War Annual 7, 1995; Brassey's Book of Espionage 1996; War Annual 8, 1997; British VCs of World War II, 1997; The Spirit and the Source (poems), 1997; Gallipoli, 1999; The Somme, 1999; Raiders: Great Exploits of the Second World War, 1999; The Battle of Hamel: Australians' Finest Victory, 1999; Combat Surgeons, 1999; A Kind of Immortality (autobiog.), Vol. 1, 2000. Contributions: newspapers, magazines and journals.

LAGNADO, Lucette Matalon, (Loulou), BA; American journalist and writer; *Investigative Reporter, The Wall Street Journal*; b. Cairo, Egypt; d. of the late Leon Lagnado and Edith Lagnado; m. Douglas Feiden 1995. *Education:* Vassar Coll., Poughkeepsie, NY. *Career:* worked as investigative reporter for columnist Jack Anderson 1980–87; reporter, The New York Post 1987–90; columnist, the Village Voice 1990–93; Sr Ed., Forward weekly Jewish newspaper 1993–96; joined The Wall Street Journal as health care reporter 1996, sr special writer New York bureau, covering hospital and health systems 2000–. *Publications:* non-fiction: Children of the Flames: Dr. Mengele and the Untold Story of the Twins of Auschwitz (co-author) 1991, The Man in the White Sharkskin Suit: A Jewish Family's Exodus from Cairo to the New World (Sami Rohr Prize for Jewish Literature 2008) 2007, The Arrogant Years: One Girl's Search for Her Lost Youth, from Cairo to Brooklyn 2011. *Honours:* Big Apple Journalism Award for reporting 2001, New York Press Club Heart of New York Award 2001, three Newswomen's Club of New York Front Page awards 2001–03, Mike Berger Award, Columbia Univ. Graduate School of Journalism 2002, Columbia Journalism Review 'Laurel' 2003, New York Press Club Feature Award 2003, Exceptional Merit Media Award for Exceptional Feature Story 2003. *Address:* The Wall Street Journal, 200 Liberty Street, New York, NY 10281, USA (office). *Telephone:* (212) 416-3727 (office). *E-mail:* lucette.lagnado@wsj.com (office). *Website:* www.wsj.com (office).

LAGO, Eduardo, MA, PhD; Spanish writer and academic; *Professor of Spanish and Latin American Literature, Sarah Lawrence College*; b. 1954, Madrid. *Education:* Universidad Autónoma de Madrid, Grad. Center, City Univ. of NY. *Career:* Prof. of Spanish and Latin American Literature, Sarah Lawrence Coll. 1993–; Exec. Dir Instituto Cervantes, New York 2006–; Co-founder Order of Finnegans. *Publications:* Cuaderno de México 2000, Cuentos Dispersos 2000, Llámame Brooklyn (Premio Nadal Prize 2006, City of Barcelona Literary Prize for Literature 2007, National Critics Award 2007, Lara Foundation Award for Best Critical Reception 2007) 2006, Ladrón de mapas 2008. *Honours:* Bartolomé March Award for Excellence in Literary Criticism 2001. *Address:* Office of the Director, Instituto Cervantes, 211 East 49th Street, New York, NY 10017, USA (office). *Telephone:* (212) 308-7720 (office). *E-mail:* dirny@cervantes.org (office). *Website:* www.nuevayork.cervantes.es (office).

LAGZDINS, Viktors, DipEd; Latvian writer; b. 28 Aug. 1926, Rīga; s. of Oto Lagzdins and Adele Freiberga; m. Dzidra Reita 1952; one d. *Education:* Pedagogic School, Liepaja, Riga Pedagogic Inst. *Career:* teacher 1947–58; journalist, Liepaja newspaper 1958–63, Riga magazine 1963–82; mem. Writers' Union of Latvia (chair. of the prose section 1979–80). *Publications include:* Parbaude (trans. as The Test) 1959, Indianu Virsaitis Drossirdigais Kikakis 1963, Kedes Loks 1972, Nakts Mezazos (trans. as A Night at Elk Farm) 1976, Zili Zala (trans. as The Blue and the Green) 1986, Nulles gada odiseja (trans. as Year Zero Odyssey, WWII) 2006. *Honours:* IBA Award of Excellence (UK) 2006. *Address:* Agenskalna iela 22-48, Rīga 1046, Latvia (home). *Telephone:* 6762-4242 (home).

LAHIRI, Jhumpa, BA, MA, PhD; British/American novelist and teacher; b. 1967, London, England; m.; one s. *Education:* Barnard Coll. and Boston Univ. *Career:* fmr tutor in Creative Writing, Boston Univ., Rhode Island School of Design. *Publications:* novels: Interpreter of Maladies (Pulitzer Prize for Fiction 2000) 1999, The Namesake 2003, Unaccustomed Earth (Commonwealth Writers' Prize, Europe Region 2009) 2008; short story contrib. to The New Yorker 1998. *Honours:* PEN/Hemingway Award, the New Yorker Debut of the Year award, American Academy of Arts and Letters Addison Metcalf Award, Guggenheim Fellowship 2002. *Address:* c/o Knopf Publishing/Author Mail, 1745 Broadway, New York, NY 10019, USA (office). *Website:* www.randomhouse.com/kvpa/jhumpalahiri (office).

LAI, Jimmy; Hong Kong business executive, journalist and publisher; *Proprietor, Next Media*. *Career:* Propr Giordano (retail clothing chain) 1980–, Chair. 1980–94; Propr Next Magazine 1990–, Apple Daily 1995–, Sharp Daily 2006–. *Address:* Apple Daily, 6/F Garment Centre, 576–586 Castle Peak Road, Cheung Sha Wan (office). *Telephone:* 29908388 (office). *Fax:* 27410830 (office). *E-mail:* adnews@appledaily.com (office). *Website:* appledaily.atnext.com (office).

LAI, Larissa, BA; Canadian writer and poet; b. 13 Sept. 1967, La Jolla, Calif., USA. *Education:* University of British Columbia. *Career:* Asst Curator, Yellow Peril: Reconsidered 1990; Co-ordinator, Saw Video Co-op 1991; Television and Video Assoc., Banff Centre for the Arts 1994; Ed. Front Magazine 1994–95; Gallery Animateur, Vancouver Art Gallery 1996–97; Writer-in-Residence, University of Calgary 1997–98; mem. Writers Union of Canada, Asian Canadian Writers Workshop. *Publications include:* fiction: New Reeboks, 1994; The Home Body, 1994; Water, and Other Measures of Distance, 1996; The Voice of the Blind Concubine, 1996; The Peacock Hen, 1996. Poetry: The Birdwoman, 1990; Lullabye for the Insect Catcher, 1990; Eighty Years Bathing, 1991; Where, 1991; Trap I, 1991; Trap II, 1991; Bone China, 1991; Nora, 1991; Glory, 1991; Arrangements, 1991; Shade, 1991; Nostalgia, 1992; Calling Home, 1992; The Escape, 1992; Tell: Longing and Belonging, 1994. *Honours:* Astraea Foundation Emerging Writers Award, 1995.

LAIRD, Elizabeth, BA, MLitt; British writer; b. 21 Oct. 1943, Wellington, New Zealand; m. David Buchanan McDowall 1975; two s. *Education:* Bristol Univ., Edinburgh Univ. *Publications:* Red Sky in the Morning 1988, Arcadia 1990, Kiss the Dust 1991, Hiding Out 1993, Secret Friends 1996, Jay 1997, The Wild Things Series 1999–2000, Jake's Tower 2001, The Garbage King 2003, A Little Piece of Ground 2003, Paradise End 2004, Oranges in No Man's Land 2006, Crusade 2007, A Fistful of Pearls and other tales from Iraq 2008, The Ogress and the Snake and other tales from Somalia 2009, The Witching Hour 2009, Pea Boy 2009. *Honours:* Children's Book Award 1992, Glass Globe Award Dutch Royal Geographical Soc. 1992, Smarties Young Judges Award 1994, Lancashire Book Award 1997, Scottish Arts Council Children's Book of the Year 2004. *Literary Agent:* c/o Hilary Delamere, The Agency, 24 Pottery Lane, London, W11 4LZ, England. *Telephone:* (20) 7727-1346. *E-mail:* hd-office@theagency.co.uk. *Website:* www.theagency.co.uk; www.elizabethlaird.co.uk.

LAIRD, Nick; Northern Irish writer, lawyer, poet and critic; b. 1975, Cookstown, Co. Tyrone; m. Zadie Smith 2004. *Education:* Univ. of Cambridge. *Career:* writer Times Literary Supplement; fmr Visiting Fellow Harvard Univ. *Publications:* Firmhand the Queried 2004, The Last Saturday in Ulster 2004, To A Fault (poems) 2004, Utterly Monkey (novel) (Soc. of Authors Betty Trask Prize 2006) 2005, On Purpose (poems) (Somerset Maugham Award 2008, Geoffrey Faber Memorial Prize 2008) 2007, Glover's Mistake 2009; contrib. poems to various journals in UK and USA, including London Review of Books, TLS, New Writing 11. *Honours:* Quiller-Couch Award for Creative Writing, Eric Gregory Award 2004, Rooney Prize for Irish Literature 2005, Irish Chair of Poetry Prize 2005, Aldeburgh First Collection Award 2005. *Address:* c/o Faber and Faber Ltd, Bloomsbury House, 74–77 Great Russell Street, London, WC1B 3DA, England (office). *Website:* www.faber.co.uk (office).

LAKE, David John, BA, MA, DipEd, PhD; Australian writer and academic; b. 26 March 1929, Bangalore, India; m. Marguerite Ivy Ferris 1964; one d. three step-c. *Education:* Trinity Coll., Cambridge, Univ. of Wales, Bangor, Univ. of Queensland, Australia. *Publications include:* Hornpipes and Funerals (poems) 1973, The Canon of Thomas Middleton's Plays 1975, Walkers on the Sky 1976, The Right Hand of Dextra 1977, The Wildings of Westron 1977, The Gods of Xuma 1978, The Man who Loved Morlocks 1981, The Changelings of Chaan 1985; editor: H.G.Wells, The Invisible Man, The First Men in the Moon; contrib. to Extrapolation, Science Fiction Studies, Foundation, Notes and Queries, Explicator, Ring Bearer, Wellsian. *Honours:* Ditmar Award for Best Australian Science Fiction Novel 1977, 1982, and for Short Fiction 1999. *Address:* 7 Eighth Avenue, St Lucia, Qld 4067, Australia (home). *E-mail:* djlake@optusnet.com.au (home).

LAKO, Natasha; Albanian politician and writer; b. 13 May 1948, Korça; m. Sjevlan Shanaj 1970; one s. one d. *Education:* Univ. of Tirana. *Career:* teacher 1966–68; journalist 1968–71; scriptwriter 1976–88; freelance writer 1989–91; worked for New Albania Film Studios, Tirana; fmr Dir Nat. Archive of Albanian Film; mem. Parl. (Kuvendi Popullor—Democratic Party) 1991. *Films include:* Nusja dhe shtetërrethimi (script supervisor) 1978, Ballë për ballë (script supervisor and line producer) 1979, Mësonjëtorja 1979, Partizani i vogël Velo 1980, Rruga e lirisë 1982, Një emër midis njerzëve 1983, Fjalë pa fund 1986, Një vitë i gjatë 1987, Muri i gjallë 1989, Lule të kuqe, lule të zeza (aka Black Flowers) 2003. *Television includes:* Koha nuk pret 1984, Fletë të bardha 1990. *Publications include:* poetry: Marsi brenda nesh (March within us) 1972, E para fjalë e botë (The World's First Word) 1979, Këmisha e pranverës (The Spring Shirt) 1984, Yllësia e fjalëve (Constellation of Words) (Migjeni Prize 1986) 1986, Natyrë e qetë (Quiet Nature) 1990, Thesi me pëllumba (The Bag of Doves) 1995; novel: Stinët e jetës (The Seasons of Life) 1977; poems translated into German and Dutch. *Honours:* Film Festival Prize for Screenplays 1980. *Telephone:* (42) 23502. *Fax:* (42) 22540.

LAKSHMI, C. S. (see Ambai)

LAL, Deepak Kumar, MA, BPhil; British academic; *James S. Coleman Professor Emeritus of International Development Studies, Department of Economics, University of California, Los Angeles;* b. 3 Jan. 1940, Lahore, India; s. of the late Nand Lal and of Shanti Devi; m. Barbara Ballis 1971; one s. one d. *Education:* Doon School, Dehra Dun, St Stephen's Coll., Delhi, India, Jesus Coll., Oxford. *Career:* Indian Foreign Service 1963–65; Lecturer, Christ Church, Oxford 1966–68; Research Fellow, Nuffield Coll., Oxford 1968–70; Lecturer, Univ. Coll. London 1970–79, Reader 1979–84, Prof. of Political Economy, Univ. of London 1984–93, Prof. Emer. 1993–; James S. Coleman Prof. of Int. Devt Studies, UCLA 1991–2010, Prof. Emer. 2010–; Consultant, Indian Planning Comm. 1973–74; Research Admin., World Bank, Washington, DC 1983–87; Dir Trade Policy Unit, Centre for Policy Studies 1993–96, Trade and Devt Unit, Inst. of Econ. Affairs 1997–2002; Pres. Mont Pelerin Soc. 2008–10; consultancy assignments ILO, UNCTAD, OECD, IBRD Ministry of Planning, Sri Lanka, Repub. of Korea 1970–2002. *Publications:* Wells and Welfare 1972, Methods of Project Analysis 1974, Appraising Foreign Investment in Developing Countries 1975, Unemployment and Wage Inflation in Industrial Economies 1977, Men or Machines 1978, Prices for Planning 1980, The Poverty of "Development Economics" 1983, Labour and Poverty in Kenya (with P. Collier) 1986, Stagflation, Savings and the State (co-ed. with M. Wolf) 1986, The Hindu Equilibrium (two vols) 1988, 1989, Public Policy and Economic Development (co-ed. with M. Scott) 1990, Development Economics (four vols) (ed.) 1991, The Repressed Economy 1993, Against Dirigisme 1994, The Political Economy of Poverty, Equity and Growth (with H. Myint) 1996, Unintended Consequences 1998, Unfinished Business 1999, Trade, Development and Political Economy (co-ed. with R. Snape) 2001, In Praise of Empires 2004, The Hindu Equilibrium 2005, Reviving the Invisible Hand: The Case for Classical Liberalism in the 21st Century 2006, Poverty and Progress: Reality and Myths about Third World Poverty 2012, Lost Causes: The Retreat from Classical Liberalism 2012. *Honours:* Dr hc (Univ. Paul Cezanne, Aix-Marreille III) 2009; Int. Freedom Award for Econs, Società Liberia (Italy) 2007. *Address:* Department of Economics, 8369 Bunche Hall, UCLA, Box 951477, Los Angeles, CA 90095-1477, USA (office); A30 Nizamuddin West, New Delhi 110013, India (home); 2 Erskine Hill, London, NW11 6HB, England (home). *Telephone:* (310) 825-1011 (office); (11) 41827013 (New Delhi) (home); (20) 8458-3713 (London) (home). *Fax:* (310) 825-9528 (office). *Website:* www.econ.ucla.edu/faculty/regular/Lal.html (office); www.econ.ucla.edu/lal (office).

LALWANI, Nikita, MA; British/Indian writer; b. 1973, Kota, Rajasthan; m.; one c. *Education:* Bristol Univ., Bath Spa Univ. *Publications include:* Gifted (Desmond Elliott Prize for New Fiction 2008) 2007; contrib. the Guardian, Observer, New Statesman and AIDS Sutra anthology. *Literary Agent:* The Wylie Agency, 17 Bedford Square, London WC1B 3JA, England. *Telephone:* (20) 7908-5900. *Fax:* (20) 7908-5901. *E-mail:* tbohan@wylieagency.co.uk. *Website:* www.wylieagency.co.uk. *E-mail:* email@nikitalalwani.com (home). *Website:* www.nikitalalwani.com.

LAM, Vincent; Canadian writer and physician; b. 5 Sept. 1974, London, ON; m. Margarita Lam; one s. *Education:* Univ. of Toronto. *Career:* emergency room physician Toronto East General Hospital. *Publications:* Bloodletting and Miraculous Cures (short stories) (Scotiabank Giller Prize for Excellence in English-language Canadian Fiction, Royal Conservatory of Music Cecilia Zhang Award) 2006, The Flu Pandemic and You (non-fiction, with Colin Lee) 2006, A Quiet Snow (short story) 2007, Cholon, Near Forgotten (novel) 2007, Bloodletting and Miraculous Cures 2007; contrib. fiction to Carve and non-fiction to the Globe and Mail, National Post, Toronto Star, Toronto Life Magazine, University of Toronto Medical Journal. *Honours:* Young Writer's Development Trust short story competition award. *Literary Agent:* Anne McDermid & Associates, 83 Willcocks Street, Toronto, ON M5S 1C9, Canada. *Telephone:* (416) 324-8845. *Fax:* (416) 324-8870. *E-mail:* info@mcdermidagency.com. *E-mail:* contact2007@vincentlam.ca. *Website:* www.vincentlam.ca.

LAMB, Andrew Martin, MA, DLitt, FIA; British writer, musicologist and broadcaster; b. 23 Sept. 1942, Oldham, Lancs., England; s. of Harry Lamb and Winifred Lamb (née Emmott); m. Wendy Ann Davies 1970; one s. two d. *Education:* Corpus Christi Coll., Oxford. *Career:* noted authority on lighter forms of music theatre; extensive writings on wide range of musical topics, including musical comedy, zarzuela, operetta, American musical theatre, Arthur Sullivan, the Strauss family, Jacques Offenbach, Jerome Kern and the Waldteufels; Life mem. Lancashire Co. Cricket Club. *Publications:* Jerome Kern in Edwardian London 1985, Gänzl's Book of the Musical Theatre (with Kurt Gänzl) 1988, Skaters' Waltz: The Story of the Waldteufels 1995, An Offenbach Family Album 1997, Shirley House to Trinity School 1999, 150 Years of Popular Musical Theatre 2000, Leslie Stuart: Composer of Florodora 2002, Fragson: The Triumphs and the Tragedy (with Julian Myerscough) 2004, The Merry Widow at 100 2005, A Life on the Ocean Wave: The Story of Henry Russell 2007; ed.: The Moulin Rouge 1990, Light Music from Austria 1992, Leslie Stuart: My Bohemian Life 2003; contrib. to The New Grove Dictionary of Music and Musicians, The New Grove Dictionary of American Music, The New Grove Dictionary of Opera, Gramophone, Musical Times, Classic CD, American Music, Music and Letters, Wisden Cricket Monthly, Cricketer, Listener, Notes. *Address:* 1 Squirrel Wood, West Byfleet, Surrey, KT14 6PE, England. *Telephone:* (1932) 342566. *E-mail:* andrewmlamb@gmail.com.

LAMB, Christina, MA; British journalist; *Foreign Affairs Correspondent, Sunday Times;* b. 15 May 1965, London; d. of Kenneth Ernest Edward and Anne Doreen Lamb; m. one s. *Education:* Univ. Coll., Oxford. *Career:* News Reporter Cen. TV 1987–88; Financial Times Corresp. in Afghanistan and Pakistan 1988–89, in Brazil 1990; currently Foreign Affairs Corresp., Sunday Times; Fellow, Royal Geographical Soc. *Publications:* Waiting for Allah 1991, The Africa House 2000, The Sewing Circles of Herat 2003, House of Stone 2006, Small Wars Permitting 2008. *Honours:* Young Journalist of the Year, British Press Awards 1988, Foreign Corresp. of the Year, British Press Awards 2002, 2007. *Literary Agent:* c/o David Godwin, David Godwin Associates, 55 Monmouth Street, London WC2H 9DG, England. *Telephone:* (20) 7240-9992. *Fax:* (20) 7395-6110. *E-mail:* david@davidgodwinassociates.co

.uk. *Website:* www.davidgodwinassociates.co.uk. *E-mail:* info@christinalamb.net (office). *Website:* www.christinalamb.net.

LAMBDIN, Dewey Whitley, II, BS; American writer; b. 21 Jan. 1945, San Diego, CA; m. 1st Melinda Alice Phillips 1971; m. 2nd Julie Dawn Pascoe 1984. *Education:* Montana State Univ. *Career:* mem. Sisters in Crime, US Naval Inst., US Navy Memorial Foundation, Nat. Maritime Historical Soc.; Friend of the Nat. Maritime Museum (UK). *Publications:* The King's Coat 1989, The French Admiral 1990, King's Commission 1991, King's Privateer 1992, The Gun Ketch 1993, For King and Country 1994, HMS Cockerel 1995, King's Commander 1997, Jester's Fortune 1999, The King's Captain 2000, Sea of Grey 2002, Havoc's Sword 2003, The Captain's Vengeance 2004, A King's Trade 2006, Troubled Waters 2008, The Baltic Gambit 2009, King, Ship and Sword 2010, The Invasion Year 2011, Reefs & Shoals 2012; contributions: newspapers and periodicals. *Honours:* Theme Vault, Univ. of Tennessee 1963. *Address:* 141 Neese Drive, Apartment G20, Nashville, TN 37211-2755, USA (home). *Telephone:* (615) 781-8219 (home).

LAMBERT, Sir Richard Peter, Kt, BA; British journalist, organization official and university chancellor; *Chancellor, University of Warwick;* b. 23 Sept. 1944, Bucks., England; s. of Peter Lambert and Mary Lambert; m. Harriet Murray-Browne 1973; one s. one d. *Education:* Fettes Coll., Edinburgh, Balliol Coll. Oxford. *Career:* mem. staff, Financial Times 1966–2001, Lex Column 1972, Financial Ed. 1978, New York Corresp. 1982, Deputy Ed. 1983, Ed. Financial Times 1991–2001; lecturer and contrib. to The Times 2001–; external mem. Bank of England Monetary Policy Cttee 2003–06; Dir-Gen. CBI, London 2006–11; Chancellor Univ. of Warwick 2008–; Dir (non-exec.) London Int. Financial Futures Exchange (LIFFE), AXA Investment Mans, Int. Rescue Cttee UK; Chair. Visiting Arts; Gov. Royal Shakespeare Co.; UK Chair. Franco-British Colloque; mem. UK-India Round Table; mem. Int. Advisory Bd British-American Business Inc., Bd of British Museum. *Honours:* Hon. DLitt (City Univ. London) 2000; Dr hc (Warwick, Brighton, Exeter), (York) 2007; Princess of Wales Amb. Award 2001, World Leadership Forum Business Journalist Decade of Excellence Award 2001. *Address:* Office of the Chancellor, University of Warwick, Coventry, CV4 7AL, England (office). *Telephone:* (24) 7652-3523 (office). *Fax:* (24) 7646-1606 (office). *Website:* www2.warwick.ac.uk (office).

LAMBRON, Marc; French journalist and writer; b. 4 Feb. 1957, Lyon; s. of Paul Lambron and Jacqueline Lambron (née Denis); m. Sophie Missoffe 1983; one s. two d. *Education:* Ecole normale supérieure, Institut d'etudes politiques, Ecole nationale d' admin. *Career:* columnist, Point 1986–, Madame Figaro; mem. Conseil d'Etat 1985–. *Publications:* L'Impromptu de Madrid 1988, La nuit des masques 1990, Carnet de bal 1992, L'oeil du silence 1993, 1941 1997, Etrangers dans la nuit 2001, Carnet de bal II 2003, Les Menteurs 2004, Une saison sur la terre 2006, Mignonne, allons voir 2006, Eh bien, dansez maintenant 2008, Théorie du chiffon 2010. *Honours:* Officier, Ordre des Arts et des Lettres, Chevalier, Légion d'honneur 2004; Prix des Deux Magots 1989, Prix Colette 1991, Prix Fémina 1993. *Address:* 17 rue Lagrange, 75005 Paris, France. *Telephone:* 1-40-51-02-12. *Fax:* 1-46-33-43-18.

LAMM, Donald Stephen, BA; American publisher; *Literary Agent, Carlisle & Company;* b. 31 May 1931, New York; s. of Lawrence W. Lamm and Aleen A. Lassner; m. Jean S. Nicol 1958; two s. one d. *Education:* Fieldston School, Yale Univ. and Univs of Oxford, UK. *Career:* Counter-intelligence Corps, US Army 1953–55; joined W.W. Norton & Co. Inc. 1956, college rep. 1956–59, Ed. 1959–2000, Dir 1964–2000, Vice-Pres. 1968–76, Chair. 1984–2000; Pres. Yale Univ. Press 1984–2000; currently Literary Agent, Fletcher & Parry; mem. Editorial Bd The American Scholar; Regents Lecturer, Univ. of Calif., Berkeley 1997–99; mem. Advisory Council Inst. of Early American History and Culture 1979–82; mem. Council on Foreign Relations 1978–; mem. Council, Woodrow Wilson Center, Int. Advisory Bd, Logos; Guest Fellow, Yale Univ. 1980, 1985; Trustee, The Roper Center 1984–; Fellow, Branford Coll. Yale Univ. 1985–2000, Center for Advanced Study in Behavioral Sciences 1998–99; Guest Fellow Woodrow Wilson Center 1996; Pres. Bd of Govs Yale Univ. 1986–; Ida H. Beam Distinguished Visiting Prof. Univ. of Iowa 1987–88; mem. American Acad. of Arts and Sciences (first book publisher elected in AAAS history); Vice-Pres. Phi Beta Kappa Soc. 2003–; Trustee Univ. of Calif. Press. *Publications:* Economics and the Common Reader 1989, Beyond Literacy 1990, Book Publishing in the United States Today 1997, Perception, Cognition and Language 2000. *Address:* Fletcher & Parry, 78 Fifth Avenue, Co., 24 East 64th Street, New York, NY 10011, USA (office).

LAMMING, George Eric; Barbadian novelist; b. 8 June 1927, Carrington Village. *Career:* Writer-in-Residence, University of the West Indies, Jamaica 1967–68. *Publications:* In the Castle of My Skin, 1953; The Emigrants, 1955; Of Age and Innocence, 1958; Water with Berries, 1971; Natives of My Person, 1972. Short Stories: David's Walk, 1948; A Wedding in Spring, 1960; Birthday Weather, 1966; Birds of a Feather, 1970. *Honours:* Guggenheim Fellowship, 1954; Maugham Award, 1957; Canada Council Fellowship, 1962; DLitt, University of the West Indies, 1980.

LAMMON, Martin, BA, MA, PhD; American academic and poet; b. 19 June 1958, Wilmington, OH; m. Frances Elizabeth Davis 1996. *Education:* Wittenberg University, Ohio University. *Career:* Visiting Instructor in English, Juniata College, Huntingdon, Pennsylvania, 1988–91; Asst Prof., then Assoc. Prof. of English, Fairmont State College, West Virginia, 1991–97; Co-Founder and Co-Ed., Kestrel: A Journal of Literature and Art, 1992–97; Prof. of English and Fuller E. Callaway Endowed Flannery O'Connor Chair in Creative Writing, Georgia College and State University, Milledgeville, 1997–; mem. Associated Writing Programs. *Publications:* Written in Water, Written in Stone: Twenty Years of Poets on Poetry (ed.), 1996; News From Where I Live: Poems, 1998. Contributions: periodicals. *Honours:* Fellow, West Virginia Commission on the Arts, 1994; Arkansas Poetry Award, University of Arkansas Press, 1997; Neruda Prize for Poetry, Nimrod International Journal, 1997. *Address:* 103 Cambridge Drive S, Milledgeville, GA 31061-9047, USA. *E-mail:* mlammon@mail.gac.peachnet.edu.

LAMONT-BROWN, Raymond, MA, JP, FSA Scot; British writer and broadcaster; b. 20 Sept. 1939, Horsforth; m. 2nd Dr Elizabeth Moira McGregor 1985. *Career:* Managing Ed., Writers Monthly 1984–86; mem., Soc. of Authors, Scotland, Rotary Int. (Pres. St Andrews Branch 1984–85); Fellow, Soc. of Antiquaries of Scotland; Justice of the Peace 1999–; City of Dundee Bench and Sheriffdom of Tayside, Central and Fife. *Publications include:* Discovering Fife 1988, The Life and Times of Berwick-upon-Tweed 1988, The Life and Times of St Andrews 1989, Royal Murder Mysteries 1990, Scottish Epitaphs 1990, Scottish Superstitions 1990, Scottish Witchcraft 1994, Scottish Folklore 1996, St Andrews 1996, Kamikaze: Japan's Suicide Samurai 1997, Scotland of One Hundred Years Ago 1998, Kempeitai: Japan's Dreaded Military Police 1998, Edward VII's Last Loves 1998, Tutor to the Dragon Emperor 1999, John Brown: Queen Victoria's Highland Servant 2000, Royal Poxes and Potions 2001, Ships from Hell 2002, Fife in History and Legend 2003, Villages of Fife 2003, Humphry Davy 2004, Andrew Carnegie 2005, St Andrews: City by the Northern Sea 2006, How Fat Was Henry VIII 2009; contrib. to magazines and newspapers, TV and radio scripts. *Address:* 76T Strathern Road, Broughty Ferry, Dundee, DD5 1PH, Scotland (home).

LAMPITT, Dinah, (Deryn Lake); British author; b. 6 March 1937, Essex, England; m. L. F. Lampitt 1959 (deceased); one s. one d. *Education:* Putney High School, Regent Street Polytechnic, London. *Career:* mem. Crime Writers Asscn. *Publications:* Sutton Place 1983, The Silver Swan 1984, Fortune's Soldier 1985, To Sleep No More 1987, Pour the Dark Wine 1989, The King's Women 1992, As Shadows Haunting 1993, Banishment 1994, Death in the Dark Walk 1995, Death at the Beggar's Opera 1996, Death at the Devil's Tavern 1997, Death on the Romney Marsh 1998, Death in the Peerless Pool 1999, Death at Apothecaries Hall 2000, Death in the West Wind 2001, Death at St James's Palace 2002, Death in the Valley of Shadows 2003, Death in the Setting Sun 2005, Death and the Cornish Fiddler 2006, The Governor's Ladies 2006, Death in Hellfire 2007, Death and the Black Pyramid 2009, The Mills of God 2010; serials: The Moonlit Door; The Gemini Syndrome; The Staircase; The Anklets; The Wardrobe; contrib. of numerous short stories to women's magazines. *Literary Agent:* c/o Vanessa Holt Ltd, 59 Crescent Road, Leigh-on-Sea, Essex, SS9 2PF, England. *Telephone:* (1702) 473787. *E-mail:* info@vanessaholt.eclipse.co.uk. *Website:* www.derynlake.com (home).

LAMPLUGH, Lois Violet, BA; British writer; b. 9 June 1921, Barnstaple, Devon, England; m. Lawrence Carlile Davis 1955; one s. one d. *Education:* Open University. *Career:* Editorial Staff, Jonathan Cape Publishers 1946–56; mem. West Country Writers' Asscn. *Publications:* The Pigeongram Puzzle 1955, Nine Bright Shiners 1955, Vagabond's Castle 1957, Rockets in the Dunes 1958, Sixpenny Runner 1960, Midsummer Mountains 1961, Rifle House Friends 1965, Linhay on Hunter's Hill 1966, Fur Princess and Fir Prince 1969, Mandog 1972, Sean's Leap 1979, Winter Donkey 1980, Falcon's Tor 1984, Barnstaple: Town on the Taw 1983, History of Ilfracombe 1984, Minehead and Dunster 1987, A Shadowed Man: Henry Williamson 1990, Take Off From Chivenor 1990, Sandrabbit 1991, Lundy: Island Without Equal 1993, A Book of Georgeham and the North West Corner of Devon 1995, Ilfracombe in Old Photographs 1996, Two Rivers Meeting 1998, Four Centuries of Devon Dialect 1999; contributions: Western Morning News.

LAN, David Mark, BA, BSc, PhD; British writer, dramatist, artistic director and social anthropologist; *Artistic Director, Young Vic Theatre, London;* b. 1 June 1952, Cape Town, South Africa. *Education:* Univ. of Cape Town and LSE, England. *Career:* academic researcher 1979–84; Writer-in-Residence, Royal Court Theatre 1995–97; Artistic Dir Young Vic Theatre 2000–. *Plays:* Painting a Wall 1974, Bird Child 1974, Homage to Been Soup 1975, Paradise 1975, The Winter Dancers 1977, Not in Norwich 1977, Red Earth 1978, Sergeant Ola and his Followers 1979, Flight 1986, A Mouthful of Birds (with Caryl Churchill) 1986, Desire 1990, The Ends of the Earth 1996; adaptations: Ghetto 1989, Hippolytos 1991, Ion 1993, The She Wolf 1996, Uncle Vanya 1998, The Cherry Orchard 2000. *Plays directed include:* for Young Vic: Julius Caesar 2000, A Raisin in the Sun 2001 (Lyric Hammersmith and UK tour 2005), Doctor Faustus 2002, The Daughter-in-Law 2002, The Skin of Our Teeth 2004, The Soliders' Fortune 2007; other: Pericles (Nat. Theatre Studio), The Glass Menagerie (Watford) 1998, As You Like It (Wyndhams) 2005. *Radio play:* Charley Tango 1995. *Television:* The Sunday Judge (film) 1985, The Crossing (film) 1988, Welcome Home Comrades (film) 1990, Dark City (film) 1990, Artist Unknown (writer, dir) 1996, Royal Court Diaries (writer, dir) 1997. *Publications:* Guns and Rain, Guerrillas and Spirit Mediums in Zimbabwe 1985. *Honours:* John Whiting Award 1977, George Orwell Memorial Award 1983, Zürich Int. Television Prize 1990, Olivier Award 2004. *Literary Agent:* c/o Judy Daish Associates, 2 St Charles Mews, London, W10 6EG, England.

LANCASTER, David (see Heald, Timothy Villiers)

LANCASTER-BROWN, Peter; Australian author; b. 13 April 1927, Cue, WA; m. Johanne Nyrerod 1953, one s. *Education:* studied astronomy, surveying, mining engineering and civil engineering. *Career:* mem. Society of Authors. *Publications:* Twelve Came Back, 1957; Call of the Outback, 1970; What Star is That?, 1971; Astronomy in Colour, 1972; Australia's Coast of Coral and Pearl, 1972; Comets, Meteorites, and Men, 1973; Megaliths, Myths, and Men, 1976; Planet Earth in Colour, 1976; Megaliths and Masterminds, 1979; Fjord of Silent Men, 1983; Astronomy, 1984; Halley and His Comet, 1985; Halley's Comet and the Principia, 1986; Skywatch, 1993. Contributions: Blackwood's Nature; New Scientist; Sky and Telescope.

LANCHESTER, John; British novelist and journalist; b. 1962, Hamburg, Germany; m. Miranda Carter; two s. *Education:* football writer, obituary writer, book ed., restaurant critic; editorial bd, London Review of Books. *Publications:* The Debt to Pleasure 1996, Mr Phillips 2000, Fragrant Harbour 2002, Family Romance: A Memoir 2007, Whoops! Why Everyone Owes Everyone and No One Can Pay 2010, Capital 2012; contrib. to Granta, New York Times Book Review, New York Times Magazine, The New Yorker. *Honours:* Whitbread First Novel Award, Hawthornden Prize. *Address:* c/o London Review of Books, 28 Little Russell Street, London, WC1A 2HN, England (office).

LANDES, David S., PhD; American economist and academic; *Professor Emeritus, Department of Economics, Harvard University;* b. 29 April 1924, New York; s. of Harry Landes and Sylvia Landes; m. Sonia Tarnopol 1943; one s. two d. *Education:* City Coll., New York, Harvard Univ. *Career:* Jr Fellow, Soc. of Fellows, Harvard Univ. 1950–53; Asst Prof. of Econs, Columbia Univ., New York 1952–55, Assoc. Prof. 1955–58; Fellow, Center for Advanced Study in Behavioral Sciences, Stanford, Calif. 1957–58; Prof. of History and Econs, Univ. of Calif., Berkeley 1958–64; Prof. of History, Harvard Univ. 1964–72, LeRoy B. Williams Prof. of History and Political Science 1972–75, Robert Walton Goelet Prof. of French History 1975–81, Prof. of Econs 1977–98, Coolidge Prof. of History 1981, now Prof. Emer.; Chair. Faculty Cttee on Social Studies 1981; Pres. Council on Research in Econ. History 1963–66; Dir Center for Middle Eastern Studies, Harvard Univ. 1966–68; Acting Dir Center for West European Studies, Harvard Univ. 1969–70; Pres. Econ. History Assen 1976–77; Ellen McArthur Lecturer, Univ. of Cambridge 1964; Visiting Prof., Univ. of Paris IV 1972–73, Univ. of Zürich and Eidgenössische Technisch Hochschule, Zürich 1978; Richards Lectures, Univ. of Virginia 1978, Janeway Lectures, Princeton Univ. 1983; mem. Bd of Eds, various journals of history; Fellow, NAS, American Acad. of Arts and Sciences, American Philosophical Soc., British Acad., Royal Historical Soc.; Overseas Fellow, Churchill Coll., Cambridge 1968–69; Visiting Fellow, All Souls, Oxford 1985; mem. American Historical Assen, Econ. History Assen (also Trustee), Econ. History Soc., Soc. for French Historical Studies, Soc. d'Histoire Moderne and others; Assoc. mem. Fondation Royaumont pour le Progrès des Sciences de l'Homme. *Publications:* Bankers and Pashas 1958, The Unbound Prometheus 1968, Revolution in Time: Clocks and the Making of the Modern World 1983, The Wealth and Poverty of Nations: Why Some Are So Rich and Some So Poor 1998, Dynasties: Fortune & Misfortune in the World's Greatest Family Businesses 2007, and other books and articles on econ. and social history. *Honours:* Dr hc (Lille) 1973. *Address:* 24 Highland Street, Cambridge, MA 02138, USA (home). *Telephone:* (617) 354-6308 (office); (617) 354-6308 (home). *Fax:* (617) 354-5335 (home). *E-mail:* soniatl@aol.com (home). *Website:* www.economics.harvard.edu (office).

LANDIS, J(ames) D(avid), BA; American publisher and writer; b. 30 June 1942, Springfield, MA; m. 1st Patricia Lawrence Straus 1964 (divorced); one d.; m. 2nd Denise Evelyn Tillar 1982; two s. *Education:* Yale Coll. *Career:* Asst Ed., Abelard Schuman 1966–67; Ed. to Sr Ed. 1967–80, Sr Vice-Pres. 1985–91, Publisher and Ed.-in-Chief 1988–91, William Morrow & Co.; Editorial Dir, Sr Vice-Pres. and Publisher, Quill Trade paperbacks 1980–85; mem. PEN. *Publications:* The Sisters Impossible 1979, Love's Detective 1984, Daddy's Girl 1984, Joey and the Girls 1987, The Band Never Dances 1989, Looks Aren't Everything 1990, Lying in Bed (American Acad. of Arts and Letters Morton Dauwen Zabel Award for Fiction 1996) 1995, Longing 2001, Artist of the Beautiful 2005, The Valley 2006, The Last Day 2009. *Honours:* Roger Klein Award for Editing 1973, Advocate Humanitarian Award 1977. *Address:* c/o Snowbooks, 120 Pentonville Road, London N1 9JN, England (office). *Website:* www.snowbooks.com (office).

LANDIS, Jill Marie, BA; American writer and teacher; b. 8 Nov. 1948, Clinton, IN; m. Stephen Landis 1971. *Education:* California State Univ. at Long Beach. *Career:* teacher, various writing workshops and seminars; mem. Romance Writers of America, Novelists Inc, Authors' Guild. *Publications:* Sunflower 1988, Wildflower 1989, Rose 1990, Jade 1991, Come Spring 1992, Past Promises 1993, Until Tomorrow 1994, After All 1995, Last Chance 1995, Day Dreamer 1996, Just Once 1997, Glass Beach 1998, Blue Moon 1999, The Orchid Hunter 2000, Summer Moon 2001, Magnolia Creek 2002, Lover's Lane 2003, Heat Wave 2004, Heartbreak Hotel 2005, Destination: Marriage 2008, Homecoming 2008, The Accidental Lawman 2009, Heart of Stone 2010; contributions: anthologies, including Loving Hearts, Sweet Hearts, Three Mothers and a Cradle, Heartbreak Ranch, Summer Love. *Address:* c/o Zondervan, 5300 Patterson Avenue, Grand Rapids, MI 49530, USA (office). *Website:* www.jillmarielandis.com.

LANDSMAN, Anne Leora, BA, MFA; South African writer and screenwriter; b. 1959, Worcester, Western Cape; m. James Wagman; one s. one d. *Education:* Univ. of Cape Town, Columbia Univ., New York, USA. *Career:* Adjunct Prof. of English, Borough of Manhattan Community Coll. 1990–93; Prof. of Screenwriting, New School for Social Research, New York 1993–2001; Adjunct Prof. of Writing, MFA Program, Columbia Univ. 2008–. *Films:* screenplays: Honest Arrogance 1985–86, The Devil's Chimney 1999–2001. *Publications:* novels: The Devil's Chimney 1997, The Rowing Lesson (Sunday Times Literary Award for Fiction 2009) 2007; short story and essay contribs to An Uncertain Inheritance, The Honeymoon's Over, Touch anthologies; contribs to Oprah magazine, Jewish Book World, Poets and Writers Magazine, The Believer, Psychologies, The Sunday Times, Red, The Sunday Telegraph, The Guardian, PEN America Journal. *Honours:* M-Net Literary Award (English Category) 2009. *Address:* c/o Soho Press Inc., 853 Broadway, New York, NY 10003, USA. *Website:* www.sohopress.com; www.annelandsman.com.

LANE, Helen, (Helen Hudson), BA, MA, PhD; American writer; b. 31 Jan. 1920, New York, NY; m. Robert Lane 1944; two s. *Education:* Bryn Mawr Coll., Columbia Univ. *Career:* mem. Authors' Guild, Authors' League, American PEN. *Publications:* Tell the Time to None 1966, Meyer Meyer 1967, The Listener 1968, Farnsbee South 1971, Criminal Trespass 1986, A Temporary Residence 1987, Dinner at Six: Voices from the Soup Kitchen 2002, Night Voices 2009; contrib. to Antioch Review, Sewanee Review, Virginia Quarterly, Northwest Review, Mademoiselle, Quarterly Review of Literature, Red Book, Ellery Queen, Mid-Stream, Best American Short Stories, O. Henry Prize Stories, Ploughshares, Mediterranean Review. *Honours:* Virginia Quarterly Prize Story 1963. *Address:* 200 Leeder Hill Drive, No. 600B, Hamden, CT 06517-2749, USA (home). *Telephone:* (203) 230-2443 (home). *E-mail:* helen.lane@snet.net (home).

LANE, Millicent Elizabeth Travis, (M. Travis Lane), BA, MA, PhD; Canadian poet and writer; b. (Millicent Elizabeth Travis), 23 Sept. 1934, San Antonio, Tex., USA; m. Lauriat Lane 1957; one s. one d. *Education:* Vassar Coll., Cornell Univ. *Career:* assistantships, Cornell Univ., Univ. of New Brunswick; poetry reviewer, Fiddlehead Magazine; mem. League of Canadian Poets (Life mem. 2003–), Writers' Federation of New Brunswick (Hon. Pres.). *Publications include:* Five Poets: Cornell 1960, An Inch or So of Garden 1969, Poems 1969–72 1973, Homecomings 1977, Divinations and Shorter Poems, 1973–78 1980, Walking Under the Nebulae 1981, Reckonings: Poems 1979–83 1988, Solid Things: Poems New and Selected 1993, Temporary Shelter 1993, Night Physics 1994, Keeping Afloat 2001, Touch Earth 2004, The Crisp Day Closing on My Hand 2007, The Book of Widows 2010, The All-Nighter's Radio 2010, Ash Steps 2012; contrib. to reviews, quarterlies and journals. *Honours:* Hon. Research Assoc., Univ. of New Brunswick; Pat Lowther Prize, League of Canadian Poets 1980, Atlantic Poetry Prize 2002, Alden Nowlan Prize for Literary Excellence 2003, Bliss Carman Poetry Award 2006. *Address:* 807 Windsor Street, Fredericton, NB E3B 4G7, Canada (office). *E-mail:* travlane@nb.sympatico.ca (home).

LANE, Nick, BSc, PhD; British writer and academic; m. Ana Hidalgo; two s. *Education:* Imperial Coll., London and Royal Free Hospital Medical School, London. *Career:* Scientific Officer, MRC Clinical Research Centre, Northwick Park Hospital 1988–91; medical writer, Oxford Clinical Communications 1995–96; sr writer and prod., Medi Cine Int. 1996–99, Strategic Dir, Adelphi Medi Cine 1999–2002; science writer and freelance communications consultant 2002–. *Publications include:* Monitoring of mitochondrial NADH levels by surface fluorometry as an indication of ischaemia during hepatic and renal transplantation (chapter in Oxygen Transport to Tissue Vol. XVII, with others) 1996, Oxygen: The Molecule that Made the World 2002, Life in the Frozen State (chapter: The Future of Cryobiology; also co-ed.) 2004, Power, Sex, Suicide: Mitochondria and the Meaning of Life 2005, Mitochondria: Key to Complexity (chapter in Origins of Mitochondria and Hydrogenosomes) 2006, Life Ascending: The Ten Great Inventions of Evolution (Royal Soc. Prize for Science Books 2010) 2009; contrib. to journals, including Biochemical Pharmacology, Biochemical Society Transactions, Biologist, British Medical Journal, Journal of the Royal Society of Medicine, Journal of Theoretical Biology, Kidney International, The Lancet, New Scientist, The Sciences, Scientific American, Transplantation. *Honours:* Hon. Sr Research Fellow, Univ. Coll. London 1997–; Daily Telegraph Young Science Writer of the Year Award 1993, New Scientist Millennial Science Essay Competition prize winner 1994. *Website:* www.nick-lane.net.

LANE, Patrick; Canadian writer; b. 26 March 1939, Nelson, BC; s. of Albert Stanley Lane and Eileen Mary Titsworth; m. Lorna Crozier; four s., one d. *Education:* Vernon Sr High School. *Career:* Ed., Very Stone House, Publrs, Vancouver 1966–72; Writer-in-Residence, Univ. of Manitoba, Winnipeg 1978–79, Univ. of Ottawa 1980, Univ. of Alberta Edmonton 1981–82, Saskatoon Public Library 1982–83, Concordia Univ. 1985, Globe Theatre Co., Regina, Sask. 1986–90; Adjunct Prof., Writing Dept, Victoria Univ. 1991–2004; mem. League of Canadian Poets, Writer's Union of Canada, PEN Canada. *Publications:* Letters From the Savage Mind 1966, For Rita: In Asylum 1969, Calgary City Jail 1969, Separations 1969, Sunflower Seeds 1969, On the Street 1970, Mountain Oysters 1971, Hiway 401 Rhapsody 1972, The Sun Has Begun to Eat the Mountain 1972, Passing into Storm 1973, Beware the Months of Fire 1974, Certs 1974, Unborn Things: South American Poems 1975, For Riel in That Gawdam Prison 1975, Albino Pheasants 1977, If 1977, Poems, New and Selected 1978, No Longer Two People (with Lorna Uher) 1979, The Measure 1980, Old Mother 1982, Woman in the Dust 1983, A Linen Crow, a Caftan Magpie 1985, Selected Poems 1987, Milford and Me 1989, Winter 1990, Mortal Remains 1991, How do you Spell Beautiful? 1992, Too Spare, Too Fierce 1995, Selected Poems, 1978–1997 1997, The Bare Plum of Winter Rain 1997, There is a Season (British Columbia Award for Canadian Non-Fiction 2005) 2004, Go Leaving Strange 2004, Last Water Song 2006, Red Dog, Red Dog 2008; contribs to most major Canadian magazines, American and English journals. *Honours:* Gov.-Gen.'s Award for Poetry 1979, Canadian Authors' Asscn Award 1985, British Columbia Book Award 1997, 2005, Drummer Gen.'s Award 2005, Lt Gov.'s Award for Literary Excellence 2007, Butler Prize for Fiction 2009. *Literary Agent:* c/o Dean Cooke, The Cooke Agency, 278 Bloor Street East, Suite 305, Toronto, ON M4W 3M4, Canada. *Telephone:* (416) 406-3390. *Fax:* (416) 406-3389. *E-mail:* agents@cookeagency.ca. *Website:* www.cookeagency.ca. *Address:* 9185 Inverness Road, North Saanich, BC V8L 5G1, Canada (office). *Telephone:* (250) 652-3956 (office). *E-mail:* plane@shaw.ca (office). *Website:* www.patricklane.ca.

LANE, Roumelia; British writer; b. 31 Dec. 1927, Bradford, West Yorkshire, England; m. Gavin Green 1949, one s. one d. *Career:* mem. Society of Authors of Great Britain, Writers Guild of Great Britain, Writers Guild of America (East and West). *Publications:* Sea of Zanj; Rose of the Desert; Cafe Mimosa; Harbour of Deceit; Desert Haven; Bamboo Wedding; Night of the Beguine; The Chasm; The Nawindi Flier. Television and film scripts: Stardust; The Chasm; Tender Saboteur; Chantico; Turn of the Tide; Gilligan's Last Gamble; Where Are the Clowns?; Death From the Past. Contributions: various journals and magazines. *Address:* Casa Mimosa, Santa Eugenia, Majorca, Beleares, Spain.

LANG-DILLENBURGER, Elmy, (Elmy Lang); German writer and painter; b. 13 Aug. 1921, Pirmasens; d. of Hermann Lang and Else Lang (née Haber); one s. *Education:* Munich, Göttingen, Paris and Salzburg, Austria. *Career:* fmr foreign corresp.; currently freelance writer and journalist; stories have appeared in newspapers, magazines and anthologies; mem. Die Kogge (writers' assen), European Authors Asscn, Asscn Européenne François Mauriac, Regensburg Int. *Plays:* The Ground Looking Children. *Publications include:* novels: Frühstück auf französisch 1971, Der Rabenwald 1985, Ich – Vincent van Gogh 1990, Bis der Adler stürzt 1997, Nele und der Arnikadoktor 2003, Ohne Liebe läuft nichts 2005, Ansichten eines Hundes 2005; poetry: Mitternachtsspritzer 1970, Ping-pong Pinguin (also English), Blick ins Paradies 1978, 1980, Das Wort 1980, Limericks 1984, Stufen zum Selbst 1986, Lebenszeichen 1988, Der Schäfer von Madrid 1992, Verdammt geliebtes Leben, Vie maudite bien aimée 1993, Hieroglyphen des Lebens 1999, Lebensboot 2006; short stories: Paradies mit Streifen 1994; plays: Die Bodenguckkinder (The Ground Looking Children), Er Sprach Immer von Tauben, Die Puppe Darf Nicht Mehr Tanzen 2002; essays and stories: Alles aus Vergesslichkeit 2010; also children's books. *Honours:* Diploma di Merito dell' Univ. delle Arti, Salsomaggiore (Italy) 1982; Landgrafenmedaille der Stadt Pirmasens 1986; Gran Premio d'Europa La Musa dell'Arte 1990; ELK-Feder 1991. *Address:* Lemberger str. 20, 66955 Pirmasens, Germany (home). *Telephone:* (6331) 41425 (home). *Fax:* (6331) 41425 (home).

LANGA, Mandla; South African writer, poet and fmr politician; *Chairman, MultiChoice Africa;* b. 1950, Stanger, Northern KwaZulu-Natal. *Education:* Fort Hare Univ. *Career:* fmr teacher, Nhlakanipho School; arrested, escaped to exile 1976; joined Umkhonto we Sizwe; lived in several countries in Africa and held posts in African Nat. Congress abroad; fmrly weekly columnist, Sunday Independent, Programme Dir, later mem. bd, South Africa Broadcasting Corpn; Chair., Independent Communications Authority of SA (Icasa) 1999–2005; currently Chair., MultiChoice Africa; Dir, Contemporary African Music and Arts; mem. bd, Inst. for the Advancement of Journalism, Foundation for Global Dialogue and Business, Arts South Africa; Trustee, Nation's Trust, Read Educational Trust, South African Screenwriters' Laboratory. *Musical opera:* Milestones (Standard Bank Festival, Grahamstown 2000). *Publications:* novels: Tenderness of Blood 1987, A Rainbow on a Paper Sky 1989, The Naked Song and Other Stories 1997, The Memory of Stones 2000, The Lost Colours of the Chameleon (Commonwealth Writers' Prize for Best Book, Africa region 2009) 2008; other: The Dead Men Who Lost Their Bones (winner, Drum magazine Story Contest) 1980, The Tenderness of Blood (poems) 1987, A Rainbow on a Paper Sky (poems) 1989. *Honours:* Order of Ikhamanga in Silver 2009; Arts Council of GB Bursary 1991. *Address:* MultiChoice, PO Box 1502, Randburg 2125, South Africa (office). *Telephone:* (11) 2893000 (office). *Fax:* (11) 7897804 (office). *E-mail:* corporateaffairs@multichoice.co.za (office). *Website:* www.multichoice.co.za (office).

LANGE, Hartmut; German author and dramatist; b. 31 March 1937, Berlin; s. of Karl Lange and Johanna Lange; m. Ulrike Ritter 1971. *Education:* Babelsberg Film School. *Career:* playwright at Deutsches Theater, Berlin 1961–65; freelance writer, W Berlin 1965–. *Publications:* Die Revolution als Geisterschiff 1974, Die Selbstverbrennung 1982, Deutsche Empfindungen 1983, Die Waldsteinsonate 1984, Das Konzert 1986, Die Ermüdung 1988, Vom Werden der Vernunft 1988, Gesammelte Theaterstücke (Collected Plays) 1988, Die Wattwanderung 1990, Die Reise nach Triest 1991, Die Stechpalme 1993, Schnitzlers Würgeengel 1995, Der Herr im Café 1996, Italienische Novellen 1998, Eine andere Form des Glücks 1999, Die Bildungsreise 2000, Das Streichquartett 2001, Irrtum als Erkenntnis 2002, Leptis Magna 2003, Der Wanderer 2005, Der Therapeut 2007, Der Abgrund des Endlichen 2009, Im Museum 2010. *Honours:* Gerhart-Hauptmann-Preis 1968, Literatur Preis der Adenauer Stiftung 1998, Ehrengabe der Schiller-Stiftung von 1859 2000, Italo Svevo Preis 2003, Preis der LiteraTour Nord 2004. *Address:* Hohenzollerndamm 197, 10717 Berlin, Germany (home); 06010 Niccone, Perugia, Italy (home).

LANGE, Mechthild, MA; German journalist; b. Hamburg. *Education:* in Hamburg, Berlin, Munich and Geneva, Switzerland. *Career:* freelance journalist; Dramatic Adviser, Deutsches Schauspielhaus, Hamburg 1986–89; mem. editorial staff and producer NDR-Fernsehen TV 1972–; has written numerous theatre reviews for Frankfurter Rundschau nat newspaper; Adolf-Grimme Preis 1972. *Publication:* Regie im Theater (jtly) 1989. *Address:* NDR-Fernsehen, Norddeutscher Rundfunk, Rothenbaumchaussee 132, 20149 Hamburg (office); Isestr 134, 20149 Hamburg, Germany (home). *Telephone:* (40) 4603738 (home). *E-mail:* ndr@ndr.de (office). *Website:* www.ndr.de (office).

LANGER, Lawrence Lee, BA, MA, PhD; American academic and writer; b. 20 June 1929, New York, NY; m. Sondra Weinstein 1951; one s. one d. *Education:* City College, CUNY, Harvard University. *Career:* Instructor, Simmons College 1956–61, Asst Prof. 1961–66, Assoc. Prof. 1966–72, Prof. 1972–76, Alumnae Chair Prof. 1976–92, Prof. Emeritus 1992–; mem. PEN, MLA. *Publications:* The Holocaust and the Literary Imagination 1975, The Age of Atrocity: Death in Modern Literature 1978, Versions of Survival: The Holocaust and the Human Spirit 1982, Holocaust Testimonies: The Ruins of Memory 1991, Admitting the Holocaust: Collected Essays 1994, Art from the Ashes: A Holocaust Anthology 1994, Pre-empting the Holocaust 1998, Using and Abusing the Holocaust 2006; contributions: journals. *Honours:* National Book Critics Circle Award 1991. *Address:* 249 Adams Avenue, West Newton, MA 02165, USA (home). *E-mail:* lllanger@verizon.net (home).

LANGFORD, Gary Raymond, BA, MA, DipEd; New Zealand writer, dramatist, poet and academic; b. 21 Aug. 1947, Christchuch; one d. *Education:* University of Canterbury, Christchurch Secondary Teachers College. *Career:* Senior Lecturer in Creative Writing, University of Western Sydney, 1986; Writer-in-Residence, University of Canterbury, 1989. *Publications:* over 20 books, including novels and poetry. *Other:* Plays and scripts for stage, radio, and television. Contributions: anthologies and other publications. *Honours:* Australia Council Young Writers Fellowship, 1976; Alan Marshall Award, 1983.

LANGFORD GINIBI, Ruby, (Ginibi, Black Swan); Australian (aboriginal) writer and poet; b. 26 Jan. 1934, Box Ridge Mission, Coraki, NSW; m. (divorced); four s. five d. (three deceased). *Education:* Casino High School, NSW. *Career:* mem. Australian Soc. of Authors. *Publications:* Don't Take Your Love to Town 1988, Real Deadly 1992, My Bundjalung People 1994, Haunted by the Past 1998, All my Mob, Only Gammoa, Koori Voices, Language and Legends of the Bundjalung Tribes and Nation; contrib. to Women's Weekly, HQ, Sun Herald, Meanjin, Best of Independent (monthly) 1990, A to Z Authorship by Ken Methold, Aboriginal English 1996, Australian Literary Studies, Canonozities by Southerlys 1997. *Honours:* Human Rights Literature 1988, Hon. Fellowship 1995. *Literary Agent:* Level 7, 61 Marlborough Street, Surry Hills, NSW 2010, Australia. *Telephone:* (2) 9319-7199. *E-mail:* info@cameronsmanagement.com.au. *Website:* members.dodo.com.au/~ginibi (home).

LANGLAND, Joseph Thomas, BA, MA; American academic and writer; b. 16 Feb. 1917, Spring Grove, Minn.; m. Judith Gail Wood 1943; two s. one d. *Education:* Santa Ana College, University of Iowa, Harvard University, Columbia University. *Career:* Instructor, Dana College 1941–42, University of Iowa 1946–48; Asst, then Assoc. Prof., University of Wyoming 1948–49; Assoc. Prof. to Prof., University of Massachusetts 1959–80, Prof. Emer. 1980–. *Publications:* A Dream of Love 1986, Twelve Poems 1991, Selected Poems 1992; contributions: reviews, quarterlies, journals, and magazines. *Honours:* Ford Foundation Faculty Fellowship, Amy Lowell Poetry Fellowship, New England Living Legend, Chancellor's Prize. *Address:* 18 Morgan Circle, Amherst, MA 01002, USA.

LANGSLET, Lars Roar, MA; Norwegian writer and politician; *Chairman, National Ibsen Committee;* b. 5 March 1936, Nesbyen; s. of Knut Langslet and Alma Langslet. *Education:* Univ. of Oslo. *Career:* Assoc. Prof. 1969–89; MP 1969–89; Minister of Culture and Science 1981–86; writer Aftenposten newspaper 1990–97; Ed. Ordet 1997–; State Scholarship 1997–99; Pres. of Norwegian Acad. for Language and Literature 1995–; Chair., Nat. Ibsen Cttee. *Publications:* Karl Marx 1963, Conservatism 1965, (biogs of) John Lyng 1989, King Olav V 1995, St Olav 1995, King Christian IV 1997, King Christian VIII 1998–99, Ludvig Holberg 2001. *Honours:* Commdr Order of St Olav, Dannebrog, Order of Gregory the Great, etc. *Address:* Ibsen.net, c/o The National Library of Norway, PO Box 2674, Solli, 0203 Oslo, Norway (office). *Telephone:* 23-27-60-15 (office). *Fax:* 23-27-60-10 (office). *Website:* www.ibsen.net (office).

LANGTON, Jane Gillson, BA, MA; American writer; b. 30 Dec. 1922, Boston, Mass; m. William Langton 1943 (died 1997); three s. *Education:* Wellesley Coll., Univ. of Michigan, Radcliffe Coll. *Publications:* The Transcendental Murder 1964, Dark Nantucket Noon 1975, The Memorial Hall Murder 1978, Natural Enemy 1982, Emily Dickinson is Dead 1984, Good and Dead 1986, Murder at the Gardner 1988, The Dante Game 1991, God in Concord 1992, Divine Inspiration 1993, The Shortest Day 1995, Dead as a Dodo 1996, The Face on the Wall 1998, The Thief of Venice 1999, Murder at Monticello 2001, The Escher Twist 2002, The Deserter, Murder at Gettysburg 2003, Steeple Chase 2005; juvenile: Her Majesty, Grace Jones 1961, Diamond in the Window 1962, The Swing in the Summerhouse 1967, The Astonishing Stereoscope 1971, The Boyhood of Grace Jones 1972, Paper Chains 1977, The Fledgling 1980, The Fragile Flag 1984, The Time Bike 2000, The Mysterious Circus

2005, The Abominable Encyclopedia. *Honours:* Newbery Honor Book 1981, Nero Wolfe Award 1984, Boucheron Lifetime Achievement Award 2000. *Address:* 9 Baker Farm Road, Lincoln, MA 01773, USA (home). *Telephone:* (781) 259-9148 (home). *E-mail:* janelangton@verizon.net (home). *Website:* www.janelangton.com.

LANSDALE, Joe Richard; American writer; b. 28 Oct. 1951, Gladwater, TX; m. 1st Cassie Ellis 1970 (divorced 1972); m. 2nd Karen Ann Morton 1973; one s. one d. *Education:* Tyler Junior Coll., Univ. of Texas at Austin, Stephen F. Austin State Univ. *Career:* mem. Horror Writers of America (vice-pres. 1987–88), Western Writers of America (treas. 1987). *Television writing:* four episodes Batman: The Animated Series (Critters (with Steve Gerber), Read My Lips, Showdown, Perchance to Dream), one episode Superman: The Animated Series (Identity Crisis). *Publications:* Act of Love (novel) 1980, The Nightrunners (novel) 1983, Texas Night Riders (novel, as Ray Slater) 1983, Dead in the West (novel) 1986, Magic Wagon (novel) 1986, The Drive-In (novel) 1988, The Best of the West (anthology ed.) 1989, By Bizarre Hands (short stories) 1989, Cold in July (novel) 1989, The Drive-In 2 (novel) 1989, New Frontier (anthology ed.) 1989, Razored Saddles (anthology, ed. with Pat Lo Brutto) 1989, Savage Season (novel) 1990, Batman: Captured by the Engines (novel) 1991, On the Far Side of the Cadillac Desert with Dead Folks 1991, Stories by Mama Lansdale's Youngest Boy (short stories, aka Best Sellers Guaranteed) 1991, The Steel Valentine 1991, Batman in Terror on the High Skies (juvenile novel) 1992, Dark at Heart (anthology, ed. with Karen Lansdale) 1992, Steppin' Out, Summer '68 1992, Tight Little Stitches on a Dead Man's Back 1992, Drive-By (with Andrew H. Vachss) 1993, Jonah Hex: Two-Gun Mojo (five-issue comic series) 1993, Lone Ranger and Tonto (four-issue comic series) 1993, Dead in the West (two-issue comic series, with Neil Barrett Jr) 1993, Electric Gumbo (short stories) 1994, Mucho Mojo (novel) 1994, Weird Business (anthology, ed. with Richard Klaw) 1994, The West That Was (non-fiction, ed. with Thomas W. Knowles) 1994, Wild West Show (non-fiction, ed. with Thomas W. Knowles) 1994, Writer of the Purple Rage (short stories) 1994, My Dead Dog Bobby (short story) 1995, Tarzan: The Lost Adventure (novel, with Edgar Rice Burroughs) 1995, Two-Bear Mambo (novel) 1995, Blood and Shadows (four-issue comic series) 1996, Fist Full of Stories (and Articles) 1996, Supergirl Annual #2 (comic book, with Neil Barrett) 1996, Weird War Tales #2 (short story) 1996, Atomic Chili (novel) 1997, Bad Chili (novel) 1997, The Good, the Bad & the Indifferent (short stories) 1997, The Boar (novel) 1998, Gangland #4 (comic book, with Rick Klaw) 1998, Private Eye Action As You Like It (short stories, with Lewis Shiner) 1998, Rumble Tumble (novel) 1998, Freezer Burn (novel) 1999, Something Lumber This Way Comes (juvenile novel) 1999, Waltz of Shadows (novel) 1999, The Bottoms (novel) 2000, Zeppelins West (novel) 2000, Captains Outrageous (novel) 2001, Sunset and Sawdust (novel) 2004, The Drive In: The Bus Tour (novel) 2005, Flaming London (novel) 2006, A Fine Dark Line (novel) 2006, Lost Echoes (novel) 2007, Leather Maiden (novel) 2008, Vanilla Ride (novel) 2009, Unchained and Unhinged (novel) 2009, The Best of Joe R. Lansdale (short stories) 2010. *Address:* 199 Country Road 508, Nacogdoches, TX 75961-0170, USA (home). *Website:* www.joerlansdale.com.

LAPHAM, Lewis H., BA; American writer and editor; *Editor, Lapham's Quarterly;* b. 8 Jan. 1935, San Francisco; m.; three c. *Education:* Yale Univ., Univ. of Cambridge, UK. *Career:* reporter San Francisco Examiner newspaper 1957–59, New York Herald Tribune 1960–62; Ed. Harper's Magazine 1976–81, 1983–2006, Ed. Emer. and columnist 2006–; syndicated newspaper columnist 1981–87; univ. lecturer; founder and Ed., Lapham's Quarterly magazine 2008–; appearances on American and British TV, broadcasts on nat. public radio. *Publications:* Fortune's Child (essays) 1980, Money and Class in America 1988, Imperial Masquerade 1990, Hotel America: Scenes in the Lobby of the Fin-de-Siècle 1995, Waiting for the Barbarians 1997, The Agony of Mammon 1999, Lapham's Rules of Influence 1999, Theater of War 2002, 30 Satires 2003, Gag Rule 2004, Pretensions to Empire: Notes on the Criminal Folly of the Bush Administration 2007; contrib. 'Notebook' monthly essay Harper's Magazine; also contrib. to Commentary, Nat. Review, Yale Literary Magazine, Elle, Fortune, Forbes, American Spectator, Vanity Fair, Parade, Channels, Maclean's, London Observer, New York Times, Wall Street Journal. *Honours:* Nat. Magazine Award for Essays 1995, Thomas Paine Journalism Award 2002. *Address:* Lapham's Quarterly, 33 Irving Place, Eighth Floor, New York, NY 10003, USA (office). *E-mail:* editorial@laphamsquarterly.org (office). *Website:* laphamsquarterly.org (office).

LAPID, Haim; Israeli writer and critic; b. 1967, nr Tel-Aviv. *Education:* Tel-Aviv Univ. *Career:* served in the Israeli army as paratrooper; fmrly taught Social and Behavioural Psychology; Lecturer on Negotiation Theory, organizational consultant for hi-tech industries. *Publications include:* novels: Reshimotav Ha-Nistarot (trans. as The Secret Notes of my Deputy) 1983, Breznitz 1992, Pesha Ha-Ketivah (trans. as The Crime of Writing) 1998, Ha-Mehila (trans. as The Burrow) 2002, Ha-Tzvi Ha-Boer (trans. as The Burning Deer) 2007; short story collections: Meshicha Negdit (trans. as Opposite Attraction) 1995; non-fiction: Ahavot Rishonot (trans. as First Loves) 1993. *Honours:* Prime Minister's Prize 2002. *Address:* c/o Am Oved Publishers Ltd, 22 Mazeh Street, Tel Aviv 65213, Israel (office). *Website:* www.am-oved.co.il (office).

LAPIERRE, Dominique; French journalist, writer and philanthropist; b. 30 July 1931, Châtelaillon, Charente-Maritime; s. of Jean Lapierre and Luce Lapierre (née Andreotti); m. 2nd Dominique Conchon 1980; one d. (by first m.). *Education:* Lycée Condorcet, Paris and LaFayette Univ., Easton, USA. *Career:* Ed. Paris Match Magazine 1954–67; founder and Pres. Action Aid for Lepers' Children of Calcutta. *Publications:* Un dollar les mille kilomètres 1949, Honeymoon around the World 1953, En liberté sur les routes d'U.R.S.S. 1957, Russie portes ouvertes 1957, Les Caïds de New York 1958, Chessman m'a dit 1960, The City of Joy 1985, Beyond Love 1991, A Thousand Suns 1998, Five Past Midnight in Bhopal 2002, It Was Once the USSR 2006, Un Arc-en-Ciel dans la Nuit 2008; with Larry Collins: Is Paris Burning? 1964, ...Or I'll Dress You In Mourning 1967, O Jerusalem 1971, Freedom at Midnight 1975, The Fifth Horseman 1980, Is New York Burning? 2004. *Honours:* Citizen of Honour of the City of Calcutta; Chevalier, Légion d'honneur 2000; Commdr, Confrérie du Tastevin 1990; Grand Cross of the Order of Social Solidarity (Spain) 2002; Dr hc (Lafayette Univ.) 1982; Christopher Book Award 1986, 2002, Gold Medal of Calcutta, Int. Rainbow Prize, UN 2000, Vatican Prize for Peace 2000, Gold Medal of the City of Milan 2006. *Address:* 37 Rue Charles-Laffitte, 92200 Neuilly; Les Bignoles, Val de Rian, 83350 Ramatuelle, France. *Telephone:* 1-46-37-34-34 (Neuilly); (4) 94-97-17-31 (Ramatuelle). *Fax:* (4) 94-97-38-05. *E-mail:* D.Lapierre@wanadoo.fr (home). *Website:* cityofjoyaid.org (office).

LAPINE, James Elliot, BA, MFA; American dramatist and film and stage director; b. 10 Jan. 1949, Mansfield, OH; m. Sarah Marshall Kernochan 1985, one d. *Education:* Franklin and Marshall College, California Institute of the Arts. *Career:* Dir of several plays and films; Lecturer on drama; mem. Dramatists Guild. *Publications:* Photographs, 1977; Table Settings, 1980; Twelve Dreams, 1983; Sunday in the Park with George, 1984; Into the Woods, 1987; Falsettoland, 1990; Luck, Pluck and Virtue, 1993; Passion, 1994. *Honours:* Obie Award, 1977; George Oppenheimer/Newsday Award, 1983; Pulitzer Prize for Drama, 1984; New York Critic's Circle Awards, 1984, 1988; Tony Awards, 1988, 1992, 1994.

LAPPÉ, Frances Moore, BA; American lecturer, writer, environmentalist and institute director; *Co-Director, Small Planet Institute;* b. 10 Feb. 1944, Pendleton, Ore.; d. of John Moore and Ina Moore; m. 1st Marc Lappé 1967 (divorced 1977, died 2005); one s. one d.; m. 2nd J. Baird Callicott 1985 (divorced 1991); m. 3rd Paul Martin DuBois 1991 (divorced 1999, died 2005). *Education:* Earlham Coll., Ind. *Career:* Co-founder and mem. staff, Inst. for Food and Devt Policy, San Francisco, Calif. 1975–90; Co-founder and Co-Dir Centre for Living Democracy, Brattleboro, VT 1990, Small Planet Inst., Cambridge, Mass; adviser to Simple Living, Project Censored, Fairness and Accuracy in Reporting, Earthsave, Union of Concerned Scientists. *Publications include:* Diet for a Small Planet 1971, Now We Can Speak 1982, What To Do After You Turn Off the TV: Fresh Ideas for Enjoying Family Time 1985, What Can We Do? 1980, Aid as Obstacle 1980, Nicaragua: What Difference Could a Revolution Make?, Mozambique and Tanzania: Asking the Big Questions (co-author) 1980, Food and Farming in the New Nicaragua 1982, World Hunger: Ten Myths 1982, World Hunger: Twelve Myths (co-author) 1986, Casting New Molds: First Steps Toward Worker Control in a Mozambique Factory (co-author) 1980, Food First: Beyond the Myth of Scarcity (co-author) 1977, Betraying the National Interest (co-author) 1987, Rediscovering America's Values 1989, Taking Population Seriously (co-author) 1990, The Quickening of America: Rebuilding Our Nation, Remaking Our Lives 1994, Hope's Edge – The Next Diet for a Small Planet (co-author) (Nautilus Award 2003) 2002, You Have the Power – Choosing Courage in a Culture of Fear 2004, Democracy's Edge 2005; co-author of chapter in Feeding The Future – From Fat to Famine: How to Solve the World's Food Crises 2004, Getting a Grip – Clarity, Creativity, and Courage in a World Gone Mad 2007, Getting a Grip 2 – Clarity, Creativity and Courage for the World We Really Want 2010; contribs to The New York Times, Los Angeles Times, Readers' Digest, Christian Century, Chemistry, Le Monde Diplomatique, National Civic Review, Tikkun, Harper's, Huffington Post, Alternet. *Honours:* 18 hon. doctorates, including Hon. PhD (St Mary's Coll.) 1983, (Lewis and Clark Coll.) 1983, (Macalester Coll.) 1986, (Hamline Univ.) 1987, (Earlham Coll.) 1989, (Kenyon Coll.) 1989, (Univ. of Michigan) 1990, (Nazareth Coll.) 1990, (Niagara Coll.) 1993, (Allegheny Coll.); named to Nutrition Hall of Fame, Center for Scientific and Public Interest 1981, Mademoiselle Magazine Award 1977, World Hunger Media Award 1982, Henry George Award, Right Livelihood Award (Sweden) 1987, inducted into Natural Health Magazine's Hall of Fame 2000, Rachel Carson Award, Nat. Nutritional Foods Asscn 2003, Nonino Rist D'Aur Prize 2011. *Address:* The Small Planet Institute, 25 Mt Auburn Street, Suite 203, Cambridge, MA 02138, USA (office). *Telephone:* (617) 871-6609 (office). *Fax:* (617) 441-6307 (office). *E-mail:* info@smallplanet.org (office). *Website:* www.smallplanet.org (office).

LAPPING, Brian Michael, CBE, BA; British television producer and journalist; *Chairman, Brook Lapping Productions, Teachers' TV;* b. 13 Sept. 1937, London, England; s. of Max Lapping and Doris Lapping; m. Anne Shirley Lucas Lapping CBE; three d. *Education:* Pembroke Coll., Cambridge. *Career:* reporter, Daily Mirror, London 1959–61; reporter and Deputy Commonwealth Corresp., The Guardian, London 1961–67; Ed. Venture, Fabian Soc. monthly journal 1965–69; feature writer, Financial Times, London 1967–68; Deputy Ed. New Society, London 1968–70; TV producer, Granada Television Ltd 1970–88; Chief Exec. Brian Lapping Assocs 1988–; Chair. Brook Lapping Productions 2003–, Teachers' TV 2003–. *Television productions:* Exec. Producer: World in Action 1976–78, The State of the Nation 1978–80, End of Empire 1980–85, Countdown to War 1989, Hypotheticals (three programmes annually for BBC 2), The Second Russian Revolution (eight programmes for BBC 2) 1991, Question Time (weekly for BBC 1)

1991–94, The Washington Version (for BBC 2) 1992, Watergate (for BBC 2) 1994, Fall of the Wall (for BBC 2) 1994, The Death of Yugoslavia 1995, The 50 Years War: Israel and the Arabs 1998, Hostage 1999, Endgame in Ireland 2002, Tackling Terror 2002, The Fall of Milosevic 2003, Elusive Peace, Israel and the Arabs 2005, Iran and the West 2009. *Publications:* More Power to the People (co-ed.) 1968, The Labour Government 1964–70 1970, The State of the Nation: Parliament (ed.) 1973, The State of the Nation: The Bounds of Freedom 1980, End of Empire 1985, Apartheid: A History 1986. *Honours:* three Broadcasting Press Guild Awards, four Royal Television Soc. Awards, three Emmy, Peabody, DuPont batons, three Golden Gate Awards, four New York TV Festival Awards, British Documentary Award, 12 int. awards 1995. *Address:* Brook Lapping Productions, 6 Angler's Lane, London, NW5 3DG (office); 61 Eton Avenue, London, NW3 3ET, England (home). *Telephone:* (20) 7428-3117 (office); (20) 7586-1047 (home). *E-mail:* bmlapping@aol.com (home). *Website:* www.teachers.tv (office).

LAPTEV, Ivan Dmitrievich, DPhilSc; Russian editor and journalist; b. 15 Oct. 1934, Sladkoye, Omsk Dist; m. Tatyana Kareva 1966; one d. *Education:* Siberian Road Transport Inst., Acad. of Social Sciences. *Career:* worked for CPSU Cen. Cttee; mem. CPSU 1960–91; worked at Omsk River Port 1952–60; teacher 1960–61; instructor, Soviet Army Sports Club 1961–64, literary collaborator and special corresp. Sovietskaya Rossiya 1964–67; Consultant for Kommunist (later named Free Thought) 1967–73; work with CPSU Cen. Cttee 1973–78; Section Ed. Pravda 1978–82, Deputy Ed. 1982–84; Chief Ed. Izvestiya 1984–90; mem. USSR Supreme Soviet 1989–91; People's Deputy of the USSR 1989–91; Chair. Council of Union 1990–91; Gen. Man. Izvestiya Publrs 1991–94; Deputy Chair. Fed. Press Cttee 1994–95, Chair. 1995–99; Head of Sector Professional Acad. of State Service to Russian Presidency 1995–; mem. Int. Acad. of Information 1993; Pres. Asscn of Chief Eds and Publrs 1993–. *Publications:* Ecological Problems 1978, The World of People in the World of Nature 1986; over 100 scientific articles on ecological problems. *Address:* Academy of State Service, Vernadskogo prosp. 84, 117606 Moscow, Russia. *Telephone:* (495) 436-99-07.

LAQUEUR, Walter; American historian, academic, editor and political commentator; *Academic Director, Center for Strategic and International Studies*; b. 26 May 1921, Breslau, Germany (now Wrocław, Poland); s. of Fritz Laqueur and Else Berliner; m. 1st Barbara Koch 1941 (deceased); m. 2nd C. S. Wichmann; two d. *Career:* Ed. Survey 1955–65; Dir Inst. of Contemporary History and Wiener Library, London 1964–91; Founding Ed. Journal of Contemporary History 1965–; Prof. of History Brandeis Univ. 1967–72; Prof. of History, Tel-Aviv Univ. 1970–87; Prof. of Govt Georgetown Univ. 1977–90; Chair. Int. Research Council, Center for Strategic and Int. Studies, Washington DC 1973–2001, currently Academic Dir; Ed. Washington Papers 1973–2001, Washington Quarterly 1978–2001; Visiting Prof. of History, Harvard Univ. 1977; Rockefeller Fellow, Guggenheim Fellow. *Publications:* Young Germany 1962, The Road to War 1967 1968, Europe Since Hitler 1970, A History of Zionism 1972, Confrontation 1974, Weimar 1974, Guerrilla 1976, Terrorism 1977, A Continent Astray: Europe 1970–78 1979, The Missing Years (novel) 1980, The Terrible Secret 1981, Farewell to Europe (novel) 1981, Germany Today 1985, A World of Secrets 1985, Breaking the Silence 1986, The Age of Terrorism 1987, The Long Road to Freedom 1989, Stalin 1990, Thursday's Child has Far to Go (autobiog.) 1993, Black Hundred 1993, The Dream That Failed 1994, Fascism 1997, Generation Exodus 2001, Yale Encyclopedia of the Holocaust (Ed.) 2001, No End to War 2003, The Changing Face of Antisemitism 2006, The Last Days of Europe 2007, Best of Times, Worst of Times 2009. *Honours:* several hon. degrees. *E-mail:* walter@laqueur .net (home).

LARA BOSCH, José Manuel; Spanish economist and media executive; *President, Grupo Planeta*; b. Barcelona; s. of the late José Manuel Lara Hernández and María Teresa Bosch Carbonell; m.; four c. *Career:* CEO Grupo Planeta (owns TV and radio stations, publishing imprints, chain of bookshops, newspapers and real estate firms) 1998–2003, Pres. 2003–; Pres. Antena 3; fmr Pres. Quiero TV, UTECA; Chair. Inst. of Family Businesses 2000–03, Fundación José Manuel Lara; Pres. Círculo de Economía 2005–08. *Address:* Grupo Planeta SA, Edificio Planeta, Diagonal 662–664, 08034 Barcelona, Spain (office). *Telephone:* (93) 4928999 (office). *Fax:* (93) 4928562 (office). *E-mail:* direccion@planeta.es (office).

LARSEN, Eric, BA, MA, PhD; American writer and academic; *Publisher, The Oliver Arts and Open Press*; b. 29 Nov. 1941, Northfield, Minn.; m. Anne Schnare 1965; two d. *Education:* Carleton Coll. . and Univ. of Iowa. *Career:* Prof. of English, John Jay Coll. of Criminal Justice, CUNY 1971–2006, Prof. Emer. 2006–; Founder and Publr The Oliver Arts & Open Press. *Publications:* fiction: An American Memory 1988, I Am Zoe Handke 1992; non-fiction: A Nation Gone Blind: America in an Age of Simplification and Deceit 2006, Homer for Real: A Reading of the Iliad 2009, The Skull of Yorick: The Emptiness of American Thinking at a Time of Grave Peril – Studies in the Cover-up of 9/11; contrib. to Harper's, New Republic, Nation, Los Angeles Times Book Review; North American Review, New England Review. *Honours:* Heartland Prize, Chicago Tribune 1988. *Address:* The Oliver Arts and Open Press, 2578 Broadway, Suite 102, New York, NY 10025, USA (office). *Telephone:* (212) 866-7425 (office). *Fax:* (212) 222-3269 (office). *E-mail:* oliveropenpress@nyc.rr.com (office). *Website:* www.oliveropenpress.com (office).

LARSEN, Jeanne Louise, BA, MA, PhD; American academic, writer, poet and translator; *Professor of English, Hollins University*; b. 9 Aug. 1950, Washington, DC; m. Thomas Hugh Mesner 1977; one step-s. one step-d. *Education:* Oberlin College, Hollins College, Nagasaki University, University of Iowa. *Career:* Lecturer, Tunghai University, 1972–74; Asst Prof., 1975, 1980–86, Assoc. Prof., 1986–92, Prof. of English, 1992–98, Hollins College; Prof. of English, Hollins University, 1998–; mem. Asscn for Asian Studies; Authors' Guild; International Asscn for the Fantastic in the Arts; PEN; Poets and Writers. *Publications:* Fiction: Silk Road, 1989; Bronze Mirror, 1991; Manchu Palaces, 1996. Poetry: James Cook in Search of Terra Incognita: A Book of Poems, 1979. Other: Brocade River Poems: Selected Works of the Tang Dynasty Courtesan Xue Tao (trans. and ed.), 1987; Engendering the Word: Feminist Essays in Psychosexual Poetics (ed. with others), 1989. Contributions: scholarly books, anthologies, learned journals and periodicals. *Honours:* First Selection, Associated Writing Programs' Annual Poetry Book Competition, 1979; Resident Fellowships, Virginia Center for the Creative Arts, 1982, 1986, 1987, 1989, 1990, 1995; John Gardner Fellowship in Fiction, Bread Loaf Writers' Conference, 1990; William L. Crawford Award for Year's Best New Novelist, International Asscn for the Fantastic in the Arts, 1990; National Endowment for the Arts Fellowship in Trans., 1995. *E-mail:* jlarsen@hollins .edu (office).

LARSSON, Åsa; Swedish crime writer; b. 1966, Kiruna; m.; two c. *Education:* studied in Uppsala. *Career:* fmr tax lawyer; full-time writer. *Publications:* (titles in translation) The Savage Altar (aka Sun Storm) (Award for Best First Crime Novel, Sweden) 2006, The Blood Spilt 2007. *Address:* c/o Penguin Books, 80 Strand, London, WC2R 0RL, England (office).

LARUE, Monique, BPh, MA, DèsL; Canadian writer and teacher; b. 1948, Montréal, QC. *Education:* Univ. of Montréal, Sorbonne, Univ. of Paris. *Career:* teacher Dept of French, Collège Edouard Montpetit, Montréal 1974–; mem. Académie des Lettres du Québec. *Publications:* La cohorte fictive 1979, Les faux fuyants 1982, Copies conformes (trans. as True Copies) 1989, Promenades littéraires dans Montréal (with Jean-Francois Chassay) 1989, La démarche du crabe 1995, La Gloire de cassiodore 2002. *Honours:* Grand Prix du livre de Montréal 1990, Prix du Journal de Montréal 1996, Prix du roman du Gouverneur Général du Canada 2002. *Address:* c/o Union des écrivaines et des écrivains québécois, La Maison des écrivains, 3492 avenue Laval, Montréal, QC H2X 3C8, Canada.

LASICA, Milan, AM; Slovak actor, dramatist and scriptwriter; b. 3 Feb. 1940, Zvolen; s. of Vojtech Lasica and Edita Šmáliková; m. Magdalena Vašáryová; two d. *Education:* Univ. of Musical Arts, Bratislava. *Career:* dramatist Slovak TV 1964–67; actor with theatres Divadlo na Korze 1967–71, Divaldo Večerní Brno 1971–72, Nová scéna 1972–89; f. Štúdio S-Bratislava 1989, Dir 1989–; co-operation as actor, dramatist and scriptwriter with Slovak and Czech TV, radio and theatres Semafor, Divadlo bez zábradlí and Labyrint. *Films include:* Sladké hry minulého léta (TV) 1969, Srdečný pozdrav ze zeměkoule (also screenwriter) 1982, Tři veteráni (Three Veterans) 1983, Vážení přátelé 1989, Tajomstvo alchymistu Storitza 1991, Vystrel na Bonaparta (TV) 1992, O psíckovi a macicke 1993, Mimozemšťané, Saturnin 1994, Výchova dívek v Čechách (Bringing Up Girls in Bohemia) 1997, Pasti, pasti, pasticky (Traps) 1998, Hanele 1999, Talár a ptačí zob 2003, Konečná stanica 2005, Obsluhoval jsem anglického krále 2006. *Films directed include:* Úlet (TV) 2002. *Plays include:* Cyrano, Don Juan, Mrtvé duše. *Honours:* TV Prize Monte Carlo Festival. *Address:* Stúdio Lasica-Satinský, Nám 1 Mája 5, Bratislava, Slovakia (office). *Telephone:* (2) 5292-1584 (office). *Fax:* (2) 5292-5082 (office).

LASKOWSKI, Jacek Andrzej, MagPhil; British dramatist and translator; *Literature Officer, Arts Council England, East Midlands*; b. 4 June 1946, Edinburgh, Scotland; m. Anne Grant Howieson 1978; two d. *Education:* Jagiellonian Univ., Kraków, Poland. *Career:* Literary Man., Haymarket Theatre, Leicester 1984–87; mem. Soc. of Authors, (Vice-Chair., Broadcasting Cttee 1983–83), Writers' Guild of Great Britain; Literature Officer, Arts Council England, East Midlands. *Publications:* plays produced: Dreams to Damnation (BBC Radio 3) 1977, Pawn Takes Pawn (BBC Radio 4) 1978, The Secret Agent (BBC Radio 4) 1980, Nostromo (BBC Radio 4) 1985, Phoney Physician (after Molière) 1986, Orestes/Electra (with Nancy Meckler) 1987, Wiseguy Scapino (after Molière) 1993. *Address:* 52 Holme Road, West Bridgford, Nottingham NG2 5AD, England (home). *E-mail:* jalaskowski@ tiscali.co.uk (home); jacek.laskowski@artscouncil.org.uk (office).

LATHAM, Alison Mary, BMus; British editor and writer; b. (Alison Mary Goodall), 13 July 1948, Southsea, Hants., England; m. Richard Latham; three s. *Education:* The Maynard School, Exeter, Univ. of Birmingham. *Career:* Sr Copy Ed., The New Grove Dictionary of Music and Musicians 1971–77, Asst Ed., The Grove Concise Dictionary of Music 1986–88; Co-Ed., The Musical Times 1977–88; Publs Ed., Royal Opera House, Covent Garden 1989–2000; Ed. Edinburgh Int. Festival programmes 2003–; mem. Royal Soc. of Arts, Royal Musical Asscn, Soc. of Authors, Critics' Circle. *Publications:* The Cambridge Music Guide (with Stanley Sadie) 1985, Verdi in Performance (co-ed. with Roger Parker) 2001, The Oxford Companion to Music (ed.) 2002, Sing Ariel: Essays and Thoughts for Alexander Goehr's Seventieth Birthday (ed.) 2003, The Oxford Dictionary of Musical Terms 2004, The Oxford Dictionary of Musical Works 2004. *Address:* c/o Joanna Harris, Oxford University Press, Walton Street, Oxford, OX2 6DP, England. *Telephone:* (1865) 556767. *Fax:* (1865) 354635. *E-mail:* joanna.harris@oup.com.

LATYNINA, Yuliya Leonidovna; Russian journalist and writer; b. 16 June 1966, Moscow; d. of Leonid Latynin and Alla Latynina. *Career:* presenter, Yest Mneniye, TVS (current affairs programme); worked for Izvestia 1995–97, Expert 1997–98, Top Secret (Editor-in-Chief Artyom Borovik), Novaya Gazeta newspaper 2001–03, Kommersant 2006–, currently writes for The Moscow Times; writer of crime novels; also worked for TV Channels V drugoe vremya 2001–02, Est' Mneniye 2002–033), Nedelya 2003–04; host, Access Code, Echo of Moscow radio station 2003–; mem. Committee 2008 2004–. *Publications include:* Tale of the Holy Grail 1990, Case of the Missing God 1991, Clearchus and Heraclea 1994, Preacher 1994, Bomb for the Banker 1995, A Hundred Fields 1996, Tale of the Golden Emperor 1996, Hunting Elk 1999, Tale of the Empress Cassius 1999, Case of the Azure Letter 1999, Locust 2000, Steel King 2000, Draw 2001, Industrial Area 2003, Only the Pigeons Fly Free 2004, Jahannam, or See You in Hell 2005, The Land of War 2007, Alien 2007, No Time For Glory 2009. *Honours:* Freedom Defenders Award, US Dept of State 2008, awards for best business journalism. *Address:* Novaya Gazeta, 10100 Moscow, Petapovskii per. 3, Russia (office). *Telephone:* (495) 921-5739 (office). *Fax:* (495) 923-6888 (office).

LAU, Evelyn Yee-Fun; Canadian writer; b. 2 July 1971, Vancouver. *Career:* Published poems and short stories in magazines from the age of 12; Air Canada Award for Most Promising Writer Under 30; Vantage Women of Originality Award 1999. *Publications include:* Runaway: Diary of a Street Kid (autobiog., adapted for TV as The Diary of Evelyn Lau) 1989, You Are Not Who You Claim (Milton Acorn People's Poetry Award) 1990, Oedipal Dreams 1992, Fresh Girls & Other Stories 1993, Choose Me (short stories) 1999, Inside Out 2001, Treble 2005. *Address:* c/o Raincoast Books, 9050 Shaughnessy Street, Vancouver, BC V6P 6ES, Canada (office). *E-mail:* info@raincoast.com (office). *Website:* www.raincoast.com (office).

LAURENS, André Antoine; French journalist; *Vice-President and Director-General, L'Indépendant;* b. 7 Dec. 1934, Montpellier (Hérault); s. of André Laurens and Mme Laurens (née Raymonde Balle). *Education:* Lycée de Montpellier. *Career:* journalist, L'Eclaireur Meridional (fortnightly), Montpellier 1953–54, Agence centrale de Presse, Paris 1958–62; mem. political staff, Le Monde 1963–69, Asst to head of political Dept 1969–82; Dir Le Monde 1982–84, Chief writer 1986–, Ombudsman 1994–; Vice-Pres. Soc. des Rédacteurs; Vice-Pres. and Dir-Gen. L'Indépendant 2000–. *Publications:* Les nouveaux communistes 1972, D'une France à l'autre 1974, Le Métier politique ou la conquête du pouvoir 1980. *Address:* L'Independant, Mas de la Garrigue, 2 avenue Alfred Sauvy, BP 105, 66605 Rivesaltes (office); 58 rue de la Roquette, Paris 75011 (home); 1 Espace Mediterraneé, Perpignan 66605, France (home). *Telephone:* 4-68-64-88-88 (office). *Fax:* 4-68-64-88-49 (office). *Website:* www.lindependant.com (office).

LAURENS, Joanna, BA; British playwright; b. 1978. *Education:* Queen's Univ., Belfast. *Career:* writer on attachment at the Nat. Theatre, London; currently writer-in-residence, RSC. *Plays:* The Three Birds (Critics' Circle Most Promising Playwright Award, Time Out Award for Most Outstanding New Talent) 2000, Five Gold Rings (Almeida, London) 2003, Poor Beck (RSC) 2004. *Literary Agent:* United Agents, 12–26 Lexington Street, London, W1F 0LE, England. *Telephone:* (20) 3214-0800. *Fax:* (20) 3214-0801. *E-mail:* info@unitedagents.co.uk. *Website:* unitedagents.co.uk.

LAURIE, (James) Hugh Callum, OBE; British actor, writer and musician; b. 11 June 1959, Oxford, England; s. of the late (William George) Ranald (Mundell) Laurie and Patricia Laurie (née Laidlaw); m. Jo Green 1989; two s. one d. *Education:* Eton Coll., Windsor, Univ. of Cambridge. *Career:* fmr Pres. Footlights, Univ. of Cambridge. *Films:* Peter's Friends 1992, A Pin for the Butterfly 1994, Sense and Sensibility 1995, 101 Dalmatians 1996, The Snow Queen's Revenge 1996, The Borrowers 1997, Spice World 1997, The Ugly Duckling 1997, The Man in the Iron Mask 1998, Cousin Bette 1998, Stuart Little 1999, Carnivale 2000, Maybe Baby 2000, Lounge Act 2000, The Piano Tuner 2001, Chica de Río 2001, Stuart Little 2 2002, Flight of the Phoenix 2004, Valiant (voice) 2005, Street Kings 2008, Monsters vs Aliens (voice) 2009, The Oranges 2011. *Television appearances include:* Alfresco (series, also writer) 1983, The Crystal Cube (also writer) 1983, Mrs Capper's Birthday (film) 1985, Saturday Live (writer) 1986, A Bit of Fry and Laurie (series, also writer) 1986–95, The Laughing Prisoner (also writer) 1987, Blackadder the Third (series) 1987, Up Line 1987, Blackadder: The Cavalier Years 1988, Les Girls (series) 1988, Blackadder's Christmas Carol 1988, Blackadder Goes Forth (series) 1989, Hysteria 2! 1989, Jeeves and Wooster (series) 1990–92, Treasure Island (series) 1993, All or Nothing at All 1993, Look at the State We're In! (series, also dir) 1995, The Adventures of Mole 1995, The Best of Tracey Takes On… 1996, The Place of Lions 1997, Blackadder Back & Forth 1999, Santa's Last Christmas (series) 1999, Little Grey Rabbit (series) 2000, Preston Pig (series) 2000, Life with Judy Garland: My and My Shadows 2001, Second Star to the Left 2001, Family Guy (series) 2001–09, Spooks (series) 2002, Stuart Little (series) 2003, Fortysomething (series, also dir) 2003, The Young Visiters [sic] 2003, House (Satellite Award for Outstanding Actor in a Series, Drama 2005, 2006, Television Critics Association Award for Individual Achievement in Drama 2005, 2006, Golden Globe Award for Best Performance in a Drama TV Series 2006, Golden Globe Award for Best Actor in a Drama TV Series 2007, Screen Actors' Guild Award for Outstanding Performance by a Male Actor in a Drama Series 2007, 2009, Teen Choice Award for TV Actor: Drama 2007, People's Choice Award for Favourite Male TV Star 2008, 2009, for Favourite TV Drama Actor 2010, 2011, for Favourite TV Doctor 2011) 2004–, Monsters vs Aliens: Mutant Pumpkins from Outer Space (film) 2009, The Simpsons (voice) 2010, Fry and Laurie Reunited 2010. *Publications:* Fry and Laurie 4 (with Stephen Fry) 1994, The Gun Seller 1996, The Paper Soldier 2009. *Literary Agent:* c/o Lorraine Hodell, Hamilton Hodell Ltd, 5th Floor, 66–68 Margaret Street, London, W1W 8SR, England. *Telephone:* (20) 7636-1221. *Fax:* (20) 7636-1226. *E-mail:* info@hamiltonhodell.co.uk. *Website:* www.hamiltonhodell.co.uk.

LAURO, Shirley, BS, MS; American actress, playwright and teacher; b. (Shirley Shapiro), 18 Nov. 1933, Des Moines, IA; m. 1st Norton Mezvinsky (divorced); m. 2nd Louis Paul Lauro 1973. *Education:* Northwestern Univ., Univ. of Wisconsin at Madison. *Career:* actress on stage and in films and television; Instructor, City College, CUNY, 1967–71, Yeshiva University, 1971–76, Manhattan Community College, 1978, Marymount Manhattan College, 1978–79; Literary Consultant, 1975–80, Resident Playwright, 1976–, Ensemble Studio Theatre, New York City; Resident Playwright, Alley Theatre, Houston, 1987; Adjunct Prof. of Playwrighting, Tisch School of the Arts, New York University, 1989–; mem. Authors' Guild; Authors League; Dramatists Guild; League of Professional Theatre Women; PEN; Writers' Guild of America. *Publications:* The Edge, 1965; The Contest, 1975; Margaret and Kit, 1979; In the Garden of Eden, 1982; Sunday Go to Meetin', 1986; Pearls on the Moon, 1987; A Piece of My Heart, 1992; A Moment in Time, 1994; The Last Trial of Clarence Darrow, 1997; Railing it Uptown, 1997. *Contributions:* periodicals.

LaVALLE, Victor, MFA; American writer; b. 1972, New York City. *Education:* Cornell Univ., Columbia Univ. *Publications:* Slapboxing with Jesus (short stories) (PEN Open Book Award) 1999, The Ecstatic (novel) 2002, Big Machine (novel) (Los Angeles Times' Best Science Fiction, Washington Post's Best Science Fiction & Fantasy, The Nation's Most Valuable Fiction Book, Chicago Tribune Favorite Fiction, Shirley Jackson Award for Best Novel, American Book Award 2010, Ernest J. Gaines Award for Literary Excellence 2010) 2009; contrib. to journals including Granta. *Honours:* Whiting Award for Emerging Writers 2004, US Artists Ford Fellowship 2006, Guggenheim Fellowship. *Address:* c/o Jynne Martin, Associate Publicity Director, Random House Publishing Group, 1745 Broadway, 17th Floor, New York, NY 10019, USA. *E-mail:* JyMartin@randomhouse.com (office). *Website:* www.victorlavalle.com.

LAVEN, Mary; British academic and writer. *Education:* Univs of Cambridge, London and Leicester. *Career:* Sr Lecturer in History, Univ. of Cambridge, Fellow, Jesus Coll., Cambridge. *Publications:* Virgins of Venice: Enclosed Lives and Broken Vows in the Renaissance Convent 2002, Mission to China: Matteo Ricci and the Jesuit Encounter with the East 2011. *Honours:* John Llewellyn Rhys Prize, Mail on Sunday. *Address:* c/o Jesus College, Cambridge, CB5 8BL, England (office). *Telephone:* (1223) 339781 (office). *Fax:* (1223) 324910 (office). *E-mail:* mr125@cam.ac.uk (office). *Website:* www.hist.cam.ac.uk (office).

LAVENTHOL, David, MA; American publisher; b. 15 July 1933, Philadelphia; s. of Jesse Laventhol and Clare Horwald; m. Esther Coons 1958; one s. one d. *Education:* Yale Univ. and Univ. of Minnesota. *Career:* reporter, later News Ed., St Petersburg Times 1957–63; City Ed. New York Herald Tribune 1963–66; Asst Man. Ed. The Washington Post 1966–69; Assoc. Ed. Newsday 1969, Exec. Ed. 1969–70, Ed. 1970–78, Publr and CEO 1978–86, Chair. 1986–87; Group Vice-Pres. Times Mirror 1981–86, Sr Vice-Pres. 1986, Pres. 1987–93; CEO and Publr LA Times 1989–93; Ed.-at-Large Times Mirror Co., LA 1994–98, Consultant Ed. 1998–99; Ed. and Publr Columbia Journalism Review 1999–2003; Chair. Pulitzer Prize Bd 1988–89; Vice-Chair. Int. Press Inst. 1985–92, Chair. 1992–95; Chair. Museum of Contemporary Art, LA 1993–97, Cttee to Protect Journalists –2005; Dir Newspaper Advertising Bureau, American Press Inst. 1988–, LA Times Washington Post/News Service, Times Mirror Foundation, United Negro Coll. Fund; mem. Bd Dirs Assoc. Press 1993–96, Columbia Journalism School 1995–, Nat. Parkinson Foundation 1995–, Saratoga Performing Arts Center 1993–96; mem. American Soc. of Newspaper Eds Writing Awards Bd, American Newspaper Publr Asscn, Century Asscn, Council on Foreign Relations. *Address:* c/o Columbia Journalism Review, Columbia University, 2950 Broadway, New York, NY 10027, USA (office).

LAVERS, Norman, BA, MA, PhD; American teacher and writer; b. 21 April 1935, Berkeley, CA; m. Cheryl Dicks 1967, one s. *Education:* San Francisco State Univ., Univ. of Iowa. *Publications:* Mark Harris (criticism) 1978; Selected Short Stories, 1979; Jerzy Kosinski (criticism) 1982; The Northwest Passage (novel), 1984; Pop Culture Into Art: The Novels of Manuel Puig (criticism), 1988; Growing up in Berkeley with the Bomb (autobiog.), 1998. *Contributions:* Ed., Arkansas Review; Contributing Ed., Bird Watcher's Digest. *Honours:* National Endowment for the Arts Fellowships, 1982, 1991; Ed.'s Choice Award, 1986; Hohenberg Award, 1986; O. Henry Award, 1987; Pushcart Award, 1992; William Peden Prize, 1992; Porter Fund Award, 1995.

LAVERY, Bryony; British playwright; b. 1947, Dewsbury. *Career:* Tutor-Lecturer on MA playwriting course, Birmingham Univ. 1989–92; Artistic Dir, various theatre seasons and festivals. *Plays:* Of All Living (London) 1967, Days at Court (London) 1968, Warbeck (London) 1969, Germany Calling (with Peter Leabourne, London) 1976, I was too Young at the Time to Understand Why my Mother was Crying (London) 1976, Sharing (London) 1976, The Catering Service (Edinburgh Festival) 1976, Snakes (London) 1977, Bag (Young Vic Theatre) 1977, Grandmother's Footsteps (King's Head Theatre, London) 1977, Floorshow (cabaret with Caryl Churchill, Monstrous Regiment,

London) 1977, Helen and her Friends (London) 1978, Missing (Sheffield Crucible) 1979, Sugar and Spice (Ipswich, Suffolk) 1979, The Wild Bunch (Women's Theatre Group, London) 1979, Time Gentlemen Please (London) 1979, Unemployment: An Occupational Hazard (London) 1979, Gentlemen Prefer Blondes (adaptation, London) 1980, Hot Time (Common Stock Theatre Tour) (Pink Paper Play of the Year 1991) 1980, The Family Album (London) 1980, The Joker (London) 1980, Zulu (with Patrick Barlow, ICA, London) 1981, Female Trouble (cabaret, Theatrespace, London) 1981, More Female Trouble (Drill Hall, London) 1982, For Maggie, Betty and Ida (Drill Hall, London) 1982, Götterdämmerung (adaptation, Nat. Theatre of Brent) 1982, The Black Hole of Calcutta (Drill Hall, London) 1982, Calamity (Tricycle Theatre, London) 1983, The Zulu Hut Club (London) 1984, Origin of the Species (Birmingham Repertory Theatre) 1984, Over and Out (on tour) 1985, Witchcraze (BAC, London) 1985, Getting Through (musical, on tour) 1985, Sore Points (London) 1986, Mummy (with Sally Owen and L. Ortolja, Drill Hall, London) 1987, Madagascar (London) 1987, The Headless Body (London) 1987, The Dragon Wakes (London) 1988, Frozen (Birmingham Repertory Theatre) (TMA Best New Play, Eileen Anderson Central TV Award for Best Play) 1998, The Two Marias (Theatre Centre, London) 1988, Puppet States (Riverside Studios, London) 1988, The Drury Lane Ghost (with Nona Sheppard, London) 1989, Wicked (Oval House Theatre, London) 1990, Her Aching Heart (Oval House Theatre, London) 1990, Kitchen Matters (Royal Court, London) 1990, Flight (Perspectives Theatre, Denmark) 1991, The Way to Cook a Wolf (BAC Studio, London) 1993, Nothing Compares to You (Birmingham Repertory Theatre) 1995, Down Among the Mini-Beasts (Polka, London) 1996, Ophelia 1996, Goliath (Newcastle Playhouse) 1997, More Light (Royal Nat. Theatre) 1997, Shot Through the Heart (Ludlow Castle) 2000, Illyria (ACT, San Francisco) 2000, A Wedding Story (Birmingham Repertory Theatre) 2000, Behind the Scenes at the Museum (adaptation, Theatre Royal, York) 2000, The Magic Toyshop (Wolsey, Ipswich) 2001, Cherished Disappointments in Love (trans., Soho Theatre, London) 2001, Precious Bane (Pentabus) 2003, Thyestes (Furies) (RSC) 2003, Discontented Winter (Old Rep, Birmingham) 2004, A Dolls House (adaptation, Birmingham Repertory Theatre) 2004, Last Easter (Lucille Lortel Theatre, New York) 2004, Dracula (adaptation, Birmingham Rep.) 2005, Discontented Winter: House Remix (Royal Nat. Theatre, London) 2005, Smoke (New Vic Theatre) 2006, Last Easter (Birmingham Rep.) 2007, Stockholm 2007. *Radio plays:* Laying Ghosts 1992, Wuthering Heights (adaptation) 1994, My Cousin Rachel (adaptation) 1994, Twelve Days of Christmas 1994, Velma and Therese 1996, No Joan of Arc 1997, The Smell of Him 1998, A High Wind in Jamaica (adaptation) 2000, Requiem 2000, Lady Audley's Secret (adaptation) 2000, Wise Children (adaptation) 2003. *Television and film:* Revolting Women (for BBC2), Buy (for Channel 4) 2000, Restless Farewell 2003, Goodbye? 2003. *Honours:* Hon. DArts (De Montfort Univ.). *Literary Agent:* United Agents, 12–26 Lexington Street, London, W1F 0LE, England. *Telephone:* (20) 3214-0800. *Fax:* (20) 3214-0801. *E-mail:* info@unitedagents.co.uk. *Website:* unitedagents.co.uk.

LAVIN, S. R., BA, MA; American poet and writer; b. 2 April 1945, Springfield, Mass; two s. four d. *Education:* AIC, Trinity Coll. *Career:* Poet-in-Residence, Clark Univ., Worcester, Mass 1972; Prof. of English, Castleton State Coll., Vermont 1987–99; Priest of the Order of Melchizedek. *Songs:* published with Peer Corpn 1972–78. *Publications include:* poetry: The Stonecutters at War with the Cliff Dwellers 1972, Cambodian Spring 1973, Let Myself Shine 1979; fiction: Metacomet; translation: I and You, by Martin Buber; contrib. to Cold Drill, Hiram, I.P.R., Mandrake, Stand, Vermont Literary Magazine, Chinese Poetry International. *Honours:* Leonardo da Vinci Award for Poetry, Firenze, Italy 1976. *Address:* c/o Parchment Press, 52 South River Street, Coxsackie, NY 12051, USA (office). *Telephone:* (202) 577-3641 (office). *E-mail:* srlavin@hotmail.com (office).

LAW, Michael, (Michael Kreuzenau), BA; British dramatist, writer and translator; b. 17 April 1925, Kerman, Iran; s. of Henry D.G. Law and Jean Law; m. Dorothea V. Schön 1954; four s.; m. Elizabeth Yarnold 2005. *Education:* Peterhouse, Cambridge. *Career:* Lecturer in Educ., Univ. of Leeds 1969–83; mem. Soc. of Authors, Writers' Guild. *Plays:* Two or Three Ghosts 1997, A Companion for Claire (premiered Questors Theatre, Ealing 1993) 1997, Helen of Rhodes 1997, Aquarium (premiered Mercury Theatre, Colchester 1980) 1997, The Magic Man 1997, A Guest for the Sabbath 1997, Have-You-Any-Idea-What-Time-It-Is! 1998, Just Us (premiered Questors Theatre, Ealing 1993) 1998, The Nurses' Tale 1998, The Wench is Dead 1998, Come and Get Me! 1998, Looking After Molly (premiered Questors Theatre, Ealing 1999) 1999, As Time Goes By 2004, The Sci Fi Man 2004, The Dissonance Quartet 2006, The Serving-Maid's Story 2006. *Publications:* The Vienna Opera House (trans.) 1955, Caricature from Leonardo to Picasso (trans.) 1957, Seven German Readers for Schools 1960–75, How to Read German (textbook) 1963; 13 published plays 1997–2004; contrib. to numerous educational journals. *Honours:* numerous drama prizes, including First and Second Prizes, London Writers' Competition, AJ Gooding Award, Understanding Play Competition, First and Third Prizes, Drama Asscn of Wales. *Address:* 4 Summers Way, Waterside, London Colney, St Albans, Herts., AL2 1QY, England (home). *Telephone:* (1727) 826894 (home). *E-mail:* michael.law9@btinternet.com (office).

LAWRENCE, Clifford Hugh, MA, DPhil, FRHistS; British academic and writer; *Professor of Medieval History Emeritus, University of London*; b. 28 Dec. 1921, London; m. Helen Maud Curran 1953; one s. five d. *Education:* Univ. of Oxford. *Career:* Asst Lecturer, Bedford Coll., London 1951, Lecturer 1953–63, Reader in Medieval History 1963–70; External Examiner, Univ. of Newcastle upon Tyne 1972–74, Univ. of Bristol 1975–77, Univ. of Reading 1977–79; Prof. of Medieval History, Univ. of London 1970–87, Prof. Emeritus 1987–; mem. Soc. of Antiquaries. *Publications:* St Edmund of Abingdon: A Study in Hagiography and History 1960, The English Church and the Papacy in the Middle Ages 1965, The University in State and Church (Vol. 1 of The History of the University of Oxford) 1984, Medieval Monasticism: Forms of Religious Life in Western Europe in the Middle Ages 1984, The Friars: The Impact of the Early Mendicant Movement on Western Society 1994, The Life of St Edmund, by Matthew Paris (trans.) 1996, The Letters of Adam Marsh (ed. and trans.) (two vols) 2006–10; contrib. to reference works, scholarly books and journals. *Address:* 11 Durham Road, London, SW20 0QH, England (home). *Telephone:* (20) 8964-3820 (home).

LAWRENCE, Karen Ann, BA, MA; Canadian/American writer and editor; b. 5 Feb. 1951, Windsor, Ont.; d. of Kenneth Lawrence and Wanda Klapowich; m. Robert Gabhart 1982; one s. *Education:* Univs of Windsor and Alberta. *Career:* Editorial Consultant, iUniverse; currently freelance writer/ed.; mem. Writers' Union of Canada, Asscn of Canadian Radio and TV Artists. *Publications:* Nekuia; The Inanna Poems 1980, The Life of Helen Alone (also screenplay) 1986, Springs of Living Water 1990. *Honours:* WHSmith/Books in Canada First Novel Award 1987, PEN Los Angeles Center Best First Novel Award 1987, Canada Council recipient. *Address:* 2153 Pine Street, San Diego, CA 92103, USA (home). *Telephone:* (619) 291-8753 (office). *E-mail:* klawrence25@gmail.com (home).

LAWRENCE, Louise; British novelist; b. 5 June 1943, Surrey, England; m. Graham Mace 1987, one s. two d. *Publications:* Andra, 1971; Power of Stars, 1972; Wyndcliffe, 1974; Sing and Scatter Daisies, 1977; Star Lord, 1978; Cat Call, 1980; Earth Witch, 1981; Calling B for Butterfly, 1982; Dram Road, 1983; Children of the Dust, 1985; Moonwind, 1986; Warriors of Taan, 1986; Extinction is Forever, 1990; Ben-Harran's Castle, 1992; The Disinherited, 1994.

LAWS, Stephen; British writer and local council administrator; b. 13 July 1952, Newcastle upon Tyne, England; m. Lyn Hunter 1980 (divorced 1989); one d. *Education:* College of Arts and Technology. *Career:* County and Borough Council administrative positions; Senior Committee Administrator for Central Administration, Newcastle City Council, Newcastle upon Tyne, 1982–; mem. British Fantasy Society; National Asscn of Local Government Officers. *Publications:* Ghost Train, 1985; Spectre, 1985; The Wyrm, 1987; The Frighteners, 1990; Darkfall, 1992; Voyages into Darkness (co-author), 1993; Macabre, 1994; Annabel Says, 1997. Contributions: articles and short stories to periodicals. *Honours:* Three Sunday Sun Awards, for short stories; Radio Newcastle Award, for short story. *Address:* c/o Publicity Director, Souvenir Press Ltd, 43 Great Russell Street, London, WC1B 3PA, England.

LAWSON, Hon. Dominic Ralph Campden, BA, FRSA; British journalist and editor; b. 17 Dec. 1956, London; s. of Nigel Lawson, now Lord Lawson of Blaby and the late Lady (Vanessa) Ayer; m. 1st Jane Fiona Wastell Whytehead 1982 (divorced 1991); m. 2nd Hon. Rosamond Monckton 1991; two d. *Education:* Westminster School, Christ Church, Oxford. *Career:* mem. staff World Tonight and The Financial World Tonight, BBC 1979–81; mem. staff Financial Times (Energy Corresp. and Lex column) 1981–87; Deputy Ed. The Spectator 1987–90, Ed. 1990–95; Ed. The Sunday Telegraph 1995–2005; columnist, Sunday Corresp. 1990, The Financial Times 1991–94, Daily Telegraph 1994–95, The Independent 2006–, The Sunday Times 2008–. *Publications:* Korchnoi, Kasparov 1983, Britain in the Eighties (jtly) 1989; ed. The Spectator Annual 1992, 1993, 1994, The Inner Game 1993. *Honours:* Harold Wincott Prize for Financial Journalism, Ed. of the Year, Soc. of Magazine Eds. 1990. *Address:* The Sunday Times, 1 Pennington Street, London, E98 1ST, England (home). *Telephone:* (20) 7782-5000 (office). *Fax:* (20) 7782-5658 (office). *Website:* www.sunday-times.co.uk (home).

LAWSON, Nigella Lucy, BA; British journalist, food writer and broadcaster; b. 6 Jan. 1960, d. of Lord Lawson of Blaby and the late Lady (Vanessa) Ayer; m. 1st John Diamond 1992 (died 2001); two c.; m. 2nd Charles Saatchi 2003. *Education:* Univ. of Oxford. *Career:* began writing restaurant column, The Spectator 1985; fmr Deputy Literary Ed. The Sunday Times; journalist or columnist for numerous publs, including Evening Standard, The Guardian, The Daily Telegraph, The Observer, The Times Magazine, Vogue, Gourmet magazine (USA), Bon Appetit (USA). *Television includes:* Nigel Slater's Real Food (UK Channel 4) 1998, Nigella Bites (Channel 4) 2000–01, Forever Summer (Channel 4) 2002, Nigella (ITV 1) 2005, Nigella Express 2007, Nigella Christmas 2008. *Publications:* How to Eat: The Pleasures and Principles of Good Food 1998, How To Be A Domestic Goddess: Baking and the Art of Comfort Cooking 2000, Nigella Bites 2001, Forever Summer 2002, Feast: Food that Celebrates Life 2004, Nigella Express 2007, Nigella Christmas 2008, Kitchen: Recipes from the Heart of the Home 2010. *Honours:* Illustrated Book of the Year, British Book Awards 1998, Author of the Year, British Book Awards 2000, Cookery Book of the Year, Guild Food Writers 2001, Gold Ladle for Best TV Food Show, World Food Media Awards 2001, Lifestyle Book of the Year, WH Smith Book Awards 2002. *Address:* Pabulum Productions Ltd, 5 Elstree Gate, Elstree Way, Borehamwood, Herts., WD6 1JD, England (office). *Website:* www.nigella.com (office).

LAWSON, Philip (see Bishop, Michael Lawson)

LAWSON, Sarah Anne, MA, PhD; American/British writer, poet and translator; b. 4 Nov. 1943, Indianapolis, Ind., USA; d. of Lindol Lawson and Fern Reed Lawson; m. Alastair Pettigrew 1969 (deceased 1992). *Education:* Indiana Univ., Univ. of Pennsylvania, Univ. of Glasgow. *Career:* mem. English PEN, Poetry Soc., RSL, Soc. of Authors, Translators' Asscn. *Play:* Gertrude, Queen of Denmark 2007. *Publications:* poetry: Dutch Interiors 1985, Down Where the Willow is Washing her Hair 1995, Below the Surface 1996, Twelve Scenes of Malta 2000, Friends in the Country 2004, All the Tea in China 2006, The Wisteria's Children 2009; translations: The Treasure of the City of Ladies, by Christine de Pisan 1985, A Foothold in Florida, by René de Laudonnière 1992, The Girls' Consent, by Leandro Fernández de Moratín 1997, Jacques Prévert, Selected Poems 2002, All My Friends are Crazy, by Sera Anstadt 2006; other: A Fado for My Mother 1996, The Ripple Effect 2009; contrib. to anthologies, including New Writers and Writing 16 1979, Poetry Introduction 6 1986, reviews, quarterlies and journals. *Honours:* C. Day-Lewis Fellowship 1979–80, Hawthornden Fellowship 2005. *Address:* 186 Albyn Road, London, SE8 4JQ, England (home). *Website:* www.sarah-lawson.net.

LAYARD, Baron (Life Peer), cr. 2000, of Highgate in the London Borough of Haringey; **Peter Richard Grenville Layard,** BA, MSc, FBA; British economist and academic; *Director, Wellbeing Programme, Centre for Economic Performance, London School of Economics*; b. 15 March 1934, Welwyn Garden City, Herts., England; s. of John Willoughby Layard and Doris Layard; m. Molly Meacher 1991. *Education:* Univ. of Cambridge, London School of Econs. *Career:* school teacher, London Co. Council 1959–61; Sr Research Officer, Robbins Cttee on Higher Educ. 1961–64; Deputy Dir Higher Educ. Research Unit, LSE 1964–74, Lecturer, LSE 1968–75, Reader 1975–80, Prof. of Econs 1980–99, Prof. Emer. 1999–, Hon. Fellow 2000–, Head, Centre for Labour Econs 1974–90, Co-Dir Centre for Econ. Performance 1990–2003, currently Dir Wellbeing Programme; Consultant, Centre for European Policy Studies, Brussels 1982–86; mem. Univ. Grants Cttee 1985–89; Chair. Employment Inst. 1987–92; Co-Chair., World Economy Group of the World Inst. for Devt Econs Research 1989–93; Econ. Adviser to Russian Govt 1991–97; Fellow, Econometric Soc. 1986, European Econ. Asscn 2004. *Publications:* Cost Benefit Analysis 1973, Causes of Poverty (with D. Piachaud and M. Stewart) 1978, Microeconomic Theory (with A. A. Walters) 1978, More Jobs, Less Inflation 1982, The Causes of Unemployment (co-ed. with C. Greenhalgh and A. Oswald) 1984, The Rise in Unemployment (co-ed. with C. Bean and S. Nickell) 1986, How to Beat Unemployment 1986, Handbook of Labor Economics (co-ed. with Orley C. Ashenfelter) 1987, The Performance of the British Economy (co-author) 1988, Unemployment: Macroeconomic Performance and the Labour Market (co-author) 1991 (second edn 2005), East-West Migration: the alternatives (co-author) 1992, Post-Communist Reform: Pain and Progress 1993 (co-author), Macroeconomics: A Text for Russia 1994, The Coming Russian Boom 1996 (co-author), What Labour Can Do 1997, Tackling Unemployment 1999, Tackling Inequality 1999, What the Future Holds (co-ed. with R. Cooper), Happiness: Lessons from a New Science 2005, A Good Childhood (with J. Dunn) 2009. *Honours:* W.W. Leontief Medal, Russian Acad. of Natural Sciences for "achievements in economics" 2005, IZA Prize in Labor Econs (co-recipient with S. Nickell), Inst. for the Study of Labor 2008. *Address:* Centre for Economic Performance, London School of Economics, Houghton Street, London, WC2A 2AE (office); 45 Cholmeley Park, London, N6 5EL, England (home). *Telephone:* (20) 7955-7281 (office). *Fax:* (20) 7955-7595 (office). *E-mail:* r.layard@lse.ac.uk (office). *Website:* cep.lse.ac.uk/layard (office).

LAZARUS, Arnold Leslie, BA, BS, MA, PhD; American writer and poet; b. 20 Feb. 1914, Revere, Mass; m. Keo Felker 1938; two s. two d. *Education:* University of Michigan, Middlesex Medical School, University of California, Los Angeles. *Career:* mem. Acad. of American Poets, American Society for Theatre Research, Comparative Literature Asscn, MLA, Poetry Society of America. *Publications include:* Entertainments and Valedictions 1970, Harbrace Adventures in Literature (ed. with R. Lowell and E. Hardwick) 1970, Modern English (co-ed.) 1970, A Suit of Four 1973, The Indiana Experience 1977, Beyond Graustark (with Victor H. Jones) 1981, Glossary of Literature and Composition (ed. with H. Wendell Smith) 1983, Best of George Ade (ed.) 1985, Some Light: New and Selected Verse 1988, A George Jean Nathan Reader (ed.) 1990; contributions: numerous periodicals. *Honours:* Ford Foundation Fellow, 1954; Kemper McComb Award, 1976.

LAZARUS, Henry (see Slavitt, David Rytman)

LAZENBY, John Francis, MA; British academic and writer; *Professor Emeritus of Ancient History, University of Newcastle upon Tyne*; b. 14 April 1934, Tiruchirapalli, Tamil Nadu, India; m. Elizabeth Mary Leithead 1967; one s. one d. *Education:* Keble Coll., Oxford, Magdalen Coll., Oxford. *Career:* Lecturer in Ancient History, King's Coll., Newcastle upon Tyne, Univ. of Durham 1959–62; Lecturer 1962–71, Sr Lecturer 1971–79, Reader 1979–94, Prof. 1994–99, of Ancient History, Prof. Emeritus 1999–, Univ. of Newcastle upon Tyne. *Publications:* The Catalogue of the Ships in Homer's Iliad 1970, Hannibal's War 1978, The Spartan Army 1985, The Defence of Greece 490–479 BC 1993, The First Punic War 1996, The Peloponnesian War 2004; contrib. to scholarly journals. *Address:* 15 Rectory Terrace, Gosforth, Newcastle upon Tyne, NE3 1YB, England (home). *Telephone:* (191) 285-8000 (home). *Fax:* (191) 285-8000 (home).

LE, Minh Khue; Vietnamese writer and editor. *Career:* war corresp., Tien Phong (Vanguard), Giaia Phong (Liberation); Chief Fiction Ed., Vietnam Writers' Asscn. *Publications:* The Stars, The Earth, The River 1997; as co-ed.: The Other Side of Heaven: Post-War Fiction by Vietnamese and American Writers 1995. *Address:* c/o Vietnam Writers' Association, Nguyen Dinh Chieu Street, Hanoi, Viet Nam. *E-mail:* nhavan.bdn@fpt.vn.

LE, Nam, BA/LLB; Vietnamese writer; b. 1978, Rach Gia. *Education:* Melbourne Univ., Australia. *Career:* grew up in Australia; admitted to Supreme Court of Vic. 2003, practised law in Melbourne; currently divides his time between Australia and USA; Fiction Ed., Harvard Review; readings and festivals world-wide. *Publications:* The Boat (short stories) (Michener-Copernicus Soc. of America Award 2007, Dylan Thomas Prize 2008, US Nat. Book Foundation's '5 under 35' Award 2008, Australian Literary Review's Fiction Book of the Year 2008, Sydney Morning Herald Best Young Novelist Award (co-recipient) 2009, Anisfield-Wolf Book Award for Fiction (co-recipient) 2009, NSW Premier's Literary Award for Book of the Year 2009, Arts Queensland Steele Rudd Award for Australian Short Story Collection, Queensland Premier's Literary Awards 2009, Australian Prime Minister's Literary Award for Fiction 2009, Melbourne Prize for Literature (Best Writing Award) 2009) 2008; contrib. to anthologies and journals including Zoetrope: All-Story, A Public Space, Conjunctions, One Story, NPR's Selected Shorts, Prospect Magazine. *Honours:* fellowships include Iowa Writers' Workshop, Fine Arts Work Center in Provincetown, Phillips Exeter Acad., Univ. of East Anglia (UK); Pushcart Prize (for short story, Cartagena) 2007, Australian Book Industry Award for Newcomer of the Year 2009, PEN/Malamud Award for Excellence in the Short Story (co-recipient) 2010, Kathleen Mitchell Award 2010. *Literary Agent:* c/o Eric Smirnoff, William Morris Agency, 1325 Avenue of the Americas, New York, NY 10019, USA. *Telephone:* (212) 903-1160; (212) 586-5100. *Fax:* (212) 246-3583. *E-mail:* esimonoff@wmeentertainment.com. *Website:* www.wma.com. *E-mail:* namletheboat@gmail.com (office). *Website:* www.namleonline.com.

Le CARRÉ, John (see Cornwell, David John Moore)

LE CLÉZIO, Jean Marie Gustave; British/French writer; b. 13 April 1940, Nice; s. of Raoul Le Clézio and Simone Le Clézio; m. 1st Rosalie Piquemal 1961; one d.; m. 2nd Jemia Jean 1975. *Education:* Bristol Univ., Univ. de Nice, Univ. de Provence, Univ. de Perpginan. *Career:* lived in Nigeria as a child 1948–50; has taught at univs in Bangkok, Mexico City, Boston, Austin, Albuquerque. *Publications:* Le procès-verbal (The Interrogation) 1963, Le jour où Beaumont fit connaissance avec sa douleur 1964, La fièvre (Fever) 1965, Le procès 1965, Le déluge 1966, L'extase matérielle 1967, Terra amata 1967, Le livre des fuites 1969, La guerre 1970, Haï 1971, Conversations 1971, Les géants 1973, Mydriase 1973, Voyages de l'autre côté 1975, Mondo et autres histoires 1978, L'inconnu sur la terre 1978, Vers les Icebergs 1978, Voyages au pays des arbres 1978, Désert 1980, Trois villes saintes 1980, Lullaby 1980, Celui qui n'avait vu la mer suivi de la Montagne du dieu vivant 1982, La ronde et autres faits divers 1982, Journal du chercheur d'or 1985, Balaabilou 1985, Villa Aurore 1985, Voyage à Rodrigues 1986, Le rêve mexicain ou la pensée interrompue 1988, Printemps et autres saisons 1989, La Grande Vie 1990, Sirandanes, Suivi de Petit lexique de la langue créole et des oiseaux (jtly) 1990, Onitsha 1991, Étoile errante 1992, Pawana 1992, Diego et Frida 1993, La Quarantaine 1995, Le Poisson d'or 1997, La Fête chantée 1997, Hasard et Angoli Mala 1999, Coeur brûlé et autres romances 2000, Révolutions 2003, L'Africain 2004, Ourania 2005, Raga: approche du continent invisible 2006, Ballaciner 2007, Ritornelle de la faim 2008. *Honours:* Chevalier des Arts et Lettres, Légion d'honneur; Prix Renaudot 1963, Prix Larbaud 1972, Grand Prix Paul Morand (Acad. française) 1980, Grand Prix Jean Giono 1997, Prix Prince de Monaco 1998, Stig Dagermanpriset 2008, Nobel Prize for Literature 2008. *Address:* c/o Editions Gallimard, 5 rue Sébastien-Bottin, 75328 Paris, France (office). *Website:* www.gallimard.fr (office).

LE COZ, Martine; French novelist; b. Sept. 1955. *Publications include:* Gilles de Raiz ou La confession imaginaire 1989, Le pharaon qui n'avait pas d'ombre 1992, Hypnose et graphologie 1993, La palette du jeune Turner 1993, Le journal de l'autre 1995, Gilles de Rais ignoble et chrétien 1995, Les confins du jour 1996, Léo la nuit 1997, Le Briquet 1997, Le chagrin du zèbre 1998, Le nègre et la Méduse 1999, Catherine d'Alexandrie ou La philosophie défaite par la foi 1999, La beauté 2000, Le rire de l'arbre au milieu du jardin 2000, Céleste (Prix Renaudot) 2001, Gilles de Rais ou la confession imaginaire 2002, Hosana! 2003, Nos lointains et nos proches 2004, La reine écarlate 2007, Le Jardian d'Orient 2008, L'Homme Électrique 2009. *Address:* c/o Les Éditions Michalon, 34 rue de Lancry, 75010 Paris, France (office). *Website:* www.michalon.fr (office).

LE GENDRE, Bertrand; French journalist; b. 25 Feb. 1948, Neuilly-sur-Seine; s. of Bernard Le Gendre and Catherine Chassaing de Borredon; m. 1st Jacqueline de Linares 1987 (divorced 1995); one s.; m. 2nd Nadia du Luc-Baccouche 1995; one s. *Education:* Collège Sainte-Croix-de-Neuilly, Univ. of Paris X, Institut d'études politiques, Paris, Institut des hautes études de défense nationale. *Career:* joined Le Monde as journalist 1974, in charge of judicial desk 1983, Reporter 1987, Ed.-in-Chief 1993–2000; Visiting Assoc. Prof., Univ. de Paris II 2000–; Sub-Ed. Gallimard 1986–89. *Honours:* Prix de la Fondation Mumm pour la presse écrite 1986. *Address:* Le Monde, 80 Boulevard Auguste-Blanqui, 75707 Paris Cedex 13 (office); 16 rue de la Glacière, 75013 Paris, France (home). *Telephone:* 1-57-28-26-14 (office). *E-mail:* legendre@lemonde.fr (office).

LE GOFF, Jacques Louis; French fmr historian and fmr academic; b. 1 Jan. 1924, Toulon; s. of Jean Le Goff and Germaine Ansaldi; m. Anna Dunin-

Wasowicz 1962 (died 2004); one s. one d. *Education:* Ecole française de Rome, Italy, lycées in Toulon, Marseilles and Louis-le-Grand, Paris, Ecole normale supérieure, Paris. *Career:* history teacher 1950; Fellow of Lincoln Coll., Oxford 1951–52; mem. Ecole française de Rome 1953–54; Asst at Univ. of Lille 1954–59; Prof., then Dir of Studies, 6th Section, Ecole des hautes études (EHE) 1960–72, Pres. Ecole des hautes études en sciences sociales (fmr 6th Section of EHE) 1972–77; mem. Comité nat. de la recherche scientifique 1962–70, Comité des travaux historiques 1972, Conseil supérieur de la Recherche 1985–87; Co-Dir reviews Annales-Economies, sociétés, civilisations and Ethnologie Française 1972; Pres. commission scientifique Ecole Nationale du Patrimoine; mem. Acad. Culturelles des Cultures 1990. *Publications:* Marchands et banquiers du Moyen Age 1956, Les Intellectuels au Moyen Age 1957, Le Moyen Age 1962, La Civilisation de l'occident médiéval 1964, Pour un autre Moyen Age (trans. as Time, Work and Culture in the Middle Ages) 1978, La Naissance du purgatoire 1981, L'Apogée de la chrétienté 1982, L'Imaginaire médiéval (trans. as The Medieval Imagination) 1985, La Bourse et la vie 1986, Histoire de la France religeuse (co-author) 1988, L'Homme médiéval (trans. as Medieval Callings) 1989, L'Etat et les pouvoirs 1989, St Louis 1996, Une Vie pour l'histoire 1996, L'Europe racontée aux jeunes 1996, Un Autre Moyen Age 1999, Saint François d'Assise 1999, Dictionnaire raisonné de l'Occident médiéval 1999, La Vieille Europe et la nôtre 2000, Le Moyen Age en images 2001, A la recherche du Moyen Age 2002, Dieu au Moyen Age 2003, Héros du Moyen Age: le Saint et le Roi 2004, Vu long Moyen Age 2004, Héros et Merveilles du Moyen Age 2004, Le Moyen Age expliqué aux enfants 2006, Avec Anka 2008, Le Moyen Age et l'argent 2010. *Honours:* Grand Prix Nat. 1987, Gold Medal, CNRS 1991, Grand Prix Gobert 1996, Grand Prix d'Histoire 1997, Prix d'Histoire Heineken 2004, Dan David Prize 2007. *Address:* c/o Ecole des Hautes Etudes en Sciences Sociales, 54 Boulevard Raspail, 75006 Paris (office); 5 rue de Thionville, 75019 Paris, France (home). *Telephone:* 1-49-54-23-00 (office). *Fax:* 1-49-54-26-86 (office). *E-mail:* gahom@ehess.fr (office). *Website:* gahom.ehess.fr (office).

LE GUIN, Ursula Kroeber, BA, MA; American writer and poet; b. 21 Oct. 1929, Berkeley, Calif.; d. of Alfred L. Kroeber and Theodora K. Kroeber; m. Charles A. Le Guin 1953; one s. two d. *Education:* Radcliffe Coll., Columbia Univ. *Career:* taught French, Mercer Univ., Univ. of Idaho 1954–56; teacher, resident writer or visiting lecturer at numerous univs, including Bennington Coll., Portland State Univ., Pacific Univ., Reading Univ., Univ. of California, San Diego, Indiana Writers' Conf., Kenyon Coll., Clarion West Writers' Workshop, First Australian Workshop in Speculative Fiction, Beloit, Haystack, Flight of the Mind, Stanford, etc. 1971–; Mellon Prof., Tulane Univ. 1986; mem. Science Fiction Research Asscn, Authors' League, Writers' Guild West, PEN; Fellow, Columbia Univ. 1952, Fulbright Fellow 1953; Arbuthnot Lecturer, American Library Asscn 2004. *Films:* King Dog (screenplay) 1985. *Television:* The Lathe of Heaven. *Publications:* fiction: Rocannon's World 1966, Planet of Exile 1966, City of Illusion 1967, A Wizard of Earthsea (Earthsea series) (Boston Globe-Horn Award) 1968, The Left Hand of Darkness (Nebula Award, Hugo Award) 1969, The Tombs of Atuan (Earthsea series) (Newbery Silver Medal 1972) 1970, The Lathe of Heaven (Locus Award 1973) 1971, The Farthest Shore (Earthsea series) (Nat. Book Award) 1972, The Dispossessed: An Ambiguous Utopia (Hugo Award, Nebula Award) 1974, The Wind's Twelve Quarters (short stories) 1975, The Word for World is Forest 1976, Very Far Away from Anywhere Else 1976, Orsinian Tales (short stories) 1976, Malafrena 1979, The Beginning Place 1980, The Compass Rose (short stories) (Locus Award 1984) 1982, The Eye of the Heron 1983, Always Coming Home (Kafka Award 1986) 1985, Buffalo Gals (short stories) (Hugo Award 1988, Int. Fantasy Award 1988) 1987, Tehanu (Earthsea series) (Nebula Award) 1990, Searoad (short stories) (H. L. Davis Award 1992) 1991, A Fisherman of the Inland Sea (short stories) 1994, Four Ways to Forgiveness (short stories) (Locus Award) 1995, Unlocking the Air (short stories) 1996, The Telling (Locus Award, Endeavor Award) 2000, Tales from Earthsea (Earthsea series) (Locus Award, Endeavor Award) 2001, The Other Wind (Earthsea series) 2001, The Birthday of the World (short stories) (Locus Readers' Award) 2002, Changing Planes (short stories) 2003, Kalpa Imperial (translation) 2003, Gifts 2004, Voices 2006, Powers 2007, Lavinia 2008; juvenile fiction: Leese Webster 1979, Cobbler's Rune 1983, Solomon Leviathan 1988, Catwings 1988, A Visit from Dr Katz 1988, Fire and Stone 1989, Catwings Return 1989, Fish Soup 1992, A Ride on the Red Mare's Back 1992, Wonderful Alexander and the Catwings 1994, Jane on her Own 1999, Tom Mouse 2002; poetry: Wild Angels 1974, Walking in Cornwall (chapbook) 1976, Tillai and Tylissos (chapbook, with Theodora Kroeber) 1979, Hard Words 1981, In the Red Zone (chapbook, with Henk Pander) 1983, Wild Oats and Fireweed 1988, No Boats (chapbook) 1992, Blue Moon over Thurman Street (with Roger Dorband) 1993, Going out with Peacocks 1994, Sixty Odd 1999, Selected Poems of Gabriela Mistral (translation) 2003, Incredible Good Fortune 2006; non-fiction: Dancing at the Edge of the World (criticism) 1989, The Language of the Night (criticism) 1992, A Winter Solstice Ritual for the Pacific Northwest (chapbook, with Vonda N. McIntyre) 1991, Findings (chapbook) 1992, The Art of Bunditsu (chapbook) 1993, Lao Tzu: Tao Te Ching: A Book About the Way and the Power of the Way (trans.) 1997, The Twins, The Dream/Las Gemelas, El Sueño (trans. with Diana Bellessi) 1997, Steering the Craft (criticism) 1998, The Wave in the Mind (criticism) 2004, Cheek by Jowl: Talks and Essays on How and Why Fantasy Matters 2009; contrib. to periodicals, including New Yorker, Omni, Redbook, Fantasy and Science Fiction, Fantastic, Amazing, Playboy, Playgirl, Tri-Quarterly, Kenyon Review, Calyx, Milkweed, Mr Cogito, Seattle Review, NW Review, Open Places, Backbone, Orion, Parabola, Paradoxa, Yale Review, Antaeus Foundation, SF Studies, Critical Inquiry. *Honours:* Hon. DLitt (Bucknell Univ., Lawrence Univ.); Hon. DHumLitt (Lewis and Clark Coll., Occidental Coll., Emory Univ., Univ. of Ore., Western Ore. State, Kenyon, Portland State); Hugo Awards 1969, 1974, 1975, Jupiter Awards 1975, 1976, Nebula Awards 1969, 1975, 1990, 1996, 2008, Gandalf Award 1979, Lewis Carroll Shelf Award 1979, Prix Lectures-Jeunesse 1987, American Acad. and Inst. of Arts and Letters Harold Vursell Award 1991, Pushcart Prize 1991, Hubbub annual poetry award 1995, Asimov's Reader's award 1995, Theodore Sturgeon Award 1995, James Tiptree Jr Retrospective Award 1996, Locus Award 1973, 1984, 1995, 1996, 2001, 2002, 2003, Bumbershoot Arts Award, Seattle, WA 1998, LA Times Robert Kirsch Lifetime Achievement Award 2000, Pacific NW Booksellers' Asscn Lifetime Achievement Award 2001, Willamette Writers' Lifetime Achievement Award 2002, PEN/Malamud Award for Short Fiction 2002, World Fantasy Award 2002, SFWA Grand Master 2003, YALSA Margaret A. Edwards Award for Lifetime Achievement 2004, PEN Center USA Award for Children's Literature 2005, Maxine Cushing Gray Award for Literary Achievement 2006, ICON Gallun Award 2007. *Address:* Virginia Kidd Agency, PO Box 278, Milford, PA 18337, USA (office). *E-mail:* vkagency@ptd.net (office). *Website:* www.ursulakleguin.com.

LE MAR, Angie; British writer and performer. *Education:* Univ. of Cambridge. *Television:* The Real McCoy (BBC2), Get Up Stand Up (Channel 4). *Radio:* The Ladies' Room, The Saturday Morning Show (Choice FM London). *Plays:* Funny Black Women on the Edge (writer, dir and performer) 2003, Live at the Palladium (performer) 2003, Sisters Under the Skin (writer) 2004, The Brothers (writer) 2005, Do You Know Where Your Daughter Is? (writer) 2006. *Honours:* BECA Best Stand-Up Female 2000, BECA Most Original Material 2001, Men & Women of Merit 2002, European Federation of Black Women (EFBWO) in Business 2002. *E-mail:* office@angielemarschoolofexpression.com (office). *Website:* www.angielemarschoolofexpression.com (office); www.angielemar.com.

LE PLASTRIER, Robert (see Warner, Francis)

LEACH, Penelope, PhD; British psychologist and writer; *Honorary Senior Research Fellow, Birkbeck, University of London*; b. (Penelope Balchin), 19 Nov. 1937, London, England; d. of the late Nigel Marlin Balchin and Elisabeth Balchin; m. Gerald Leach (deceased 2004) 1963; one s. one d. *Education:* The Perse School, Cambridge, Newnham Coll., Cambridge and London School of Econs. *Career:* mem. staff, Home Office 1960–61; Lecturer in Psychology, LSE 1965–67; Research Officer and Research Fellow, MRC 1967–76; Medical Ed. Penguin Books 1970–78; Research Consultant, Int. Centre for Child Studies 1984–90; Founder and Dir Lifetime Productions (childcare videos) 1985–87; Founder and Parent Educ. Co-ordinator End Physical Punishment for Children 1989–; Commr Comm. on Social Justice 1993–95; Vice-Pres. Pre-School Playgroups Asscn 1977, Health Visitors Asscn 1982–98; Pres. Child Devt Soc. 1992–93 (Chair. 1993–95), Nat. Childminding Asscn 1999–2009; mem. Voluntary Licensing Authority on In-vitro Fertilisation 1985–89, Advisory Council American Inst. for Child, Adolescent and Family Studies 1993–; Prin. Investigator and Dir Families Children and Childcare Study 2000–07; Fellow, British Psychological Soc. 1988. *Television:* Your Baby and Child with Penelope Leach (winner 14th Annual Nat. Cable ACE Award for Informational or Documentary Host). *Publications include:* Babyhood 1974, Baby and Child 1977, 1989, Who Cares? 1979, The Parents' A–Z 1984, The First Six Months 1987, The Babypack 1990, Children First 1994, Your Baby and Child: New Version For a New Generation 1997, Child Care Today 2009, Your Baby and Child (new edn) 2010, The Essential First Year 2010. *Honours:* Hon. Sr Research Fellow, Leopold Muller Univ. Dept of Child and Family Mental Health, Royal Free and Univ. Coll. Medical School 1998–2002, Tavistock Centre 2000–, Univ. of Oxford 2002, Birkbeck, Univ. of London 2004–; Hon. DEd. *Address:* Birkbeck College, 7 Bedford Square, London, WC1 3RA (office); 2 Bull Lane, Lewes, East Sussex, BN7 1UA, England (home). *E-mail:* pen.leach@btinternet.com (home).

LEAKEY, Richard Erskine Frere, FRAI; Kenyan politician, palaeontologist and conservationist; b. 19 Dec. 1944, Nairobi; s. of the late Louis Leakey and Mary Leakey; m. 1st Margaret Cropper 1965; m. 2nd Meave Gillian Epps 1970; three d. *Education:* Duke of York School (later known as Lenana School), Nairobi. *Career:* trapper of primates for research 1961–65; co-leader of research expeditions to Lake Natron 1963–64, Omo River 1967; Dir Root & Leakey Safaris (tour co.) 1965–68; archaeological excavation, Lake Baringo 1966; Admin. Dir Nat. Museums of Kenya 1968–74, Dir and Chief Exec. 1974–89; research in Nakali/Suguta Valley 1978; leader of research projects, Koobi Fora 1979–81, W Turkana 1981–82, 1984–89, Buluk 1983; Dir Wildlife Conservation and Man. Dept 1989–90; Dir Kenya Wildlife Service 1990–94, 1998–99; Man. Dir Richard Leakey & Assocs Ltd 1994–98; Co-Founder and Gen.-Sec. Safina Party 1995–98; nominated MP Nat. Ass. –1999; Perm. Sec., Sec. to the Cabinet, Head of the Public Service, Office of the Pres., Rep. of Kenya 1999–2001; interim Chair. Transparency International (Kenya br.) 2007; numerous hon. positions including Chair. Wildlife Clubs of Kenya 1969–80 (Trustee 1980–), Foundation for Research into the Origins of Man (USA) 1971–85, Kenya Nat. Cttee of the United World Colls 1982–, E African Wildlife Soc. 1984–89, SAIDIA 1989–; Chair. Bd of Trustees, Nat. Museums of Kenya 1989–94; Co-founder and mem. Bd Dirs Wildlife Direct 2004–; Life Trustee, L.S.B. Leakey Foundation; Trustee, Nat. Fund for Disabled in Kenya 1980–95, Agricultural Research Foundation, Kenya 1986–; has given more than 750 public and scholarly Lectures. *TV documentaries:* Bones of Contention, Survival Anglia 1975, The Making of Mankind, BBC 1981, Earth Journal (presenter), NBC 1992. *Publications:* numerous articles on finds in the field of palaeontology in scientific journals, including Nature, Journal of World History, Science, American Journal of Physical Anthropology, etc.; contrib. to General History of Africa (Vol. I), Perspective on Human Evolution and Fossil Vertebrates of Africa; Origins (book, with R. Lewin) 1977, People of the Lake: Man, His Origins, Nature and Future (book, with R. Lewin) 1978, The Making of Mankind 1981, Human Origins 1982, One Life 1983, Origins Reconsidered (with R. Lewin) 1992, Origins of Humankind (with R. Lewin) 1995, The Sixth Extinction (with R. Lewin) 1995, Wildlife Wars: My Fight to Save Africa's Natural Treasures (with V. Morrell) 2001, Wildlife Wars: My Battle to Save Kenya's Elephants 2011. *Honours:* Foreign Hon. mem. American Acad. of Arts and Sciences 1998; Order of the Burning Spear, Kenya 1993; nine hon. degrees; numerous awards and honours, including James Smithsonian Medal, USA 1990, Gold Medal, Royal Geographical Soc., UK 1990, World Ecology Medal, Int. Centre for Tropical Ecology, USA 1997. *Address:* Africa Conservation Fund, PO Box 24926, Karen 00502, Nairobi, Kenya (office). *Telephone:* (3) 865120 (office). *E-mail:* info@wildlifedirect.org (office); leakey@wananchi .com (home). *Website:* www.leakey.com; www.leakeyfoundation.org; richardleakey.wildlifedirect.org.

LEALE, B(arry) C(avendish); British poet; b. 1 Sept. 1930, Ashford, Middlesex, England; s. of Charles Frederick Leale and Winifred May Leale (née Burrows). *Education:* Municipal Coll., Southend-on-Sea. *Publications:* Under a Glass Sky 1975, Preludes 1977, Leviathan and Other Poems 1984, The Colours of Ancient Dreams 1984; contrib. to anthologies and periodicals. *Address:* Flat 38, Davey's Court, 33 Bedfordbury, London, WC2N 4BW, England (home).

LEAPMAN, Michael Henry; British writer and journalist; b. 24 April 1938, London, England; m. Olga Mason 1965; one s. *Career:* journalist, The Times 1969–81; mem. RSA, Soc. of Authors, Nat. Union of Journalists. *Publications:* One Man and His Plot 1976, Yankee Doodles 1982, Companion Guide to New York 1983, Barefaced Cheek 1983, Treachery 1984, The Last Days of the Beeb 1986, Kinnock 1987, The Book of London (ed.) 1989, London's River 1991, Treacherous Estate 1992, Eyewitness Guide to London 1993, Master Race (with Catrine Clay) 1995, Witnesses to War 1998, The Ingenious Mr Fairchild 2000, The World for a Shilling 2001, Inigo: The Troubled Life of Inigo Jones, Architect of the English Renaissance 2003, The Biggest Beetroot in the World 2008; contribs to numerous magazines and journals. *Honours:* Campaigning Journalist of the Year, British Press Award 1968, Thomas Cook Travel Book Award, Best Guide Book of 1983, Garden Writers Guild Award 1995, Times Education Supplement Sr Book Award 1999. *Literary Agent:* c/o Felicity Bryan, 2A North Parade, Oxford, OX2 6PE, England. *Address:* 13 Aldebert Terrace, London, SW8 1BH, England (home). *E-mail:* mhleapman@msn.com (home).

LEAR, Peter (see Lovesey, Peter)

LEAVITT, David, BA; American writer; *Professor of English, University of Florida*; b. 23 June 1961, Pittsburgh, PA; s. of Harold Leavitt and Gloria Rosenthal Leavitt; pnr Mark Mitchell. *Education:* Yale Univ. *Career:* Prof. of English, Univ. of Florida 2000–; currently Ed. Subtropics (journal); mem. PEN, Authors' Guild. *Publications:* Family Dancing 1984, The Lost Language of Cranes 1986, Equal Affections 1989, A Place I've Never Been 1990, While England Sleeps 1993, The Penguin Book of Gay Short Stories (ed. with Mark Mitchell) 1994, Arkansas 1997, The Page Turner 1998, Martin Bauman 2000, Florence: A Delicate Case 2002, The Body of Jonah Boyd 2004, The Stories of David Leavitt 2005, The Man Who Knew Too Much: Alan Turing and the Invention of the Computer 2006, The Indian Clerk 2007; contrib. to periodicals. *Honours:* O. Henry Award 1984, Nat. Endowment for the Arts grant 1985, Guggenheim Fellowship 1990, New York Public Library Literary Lion 1995. *Literary Agent:* The Wylie Agency, 250 W 57th Street, Suite 2114, New York, NY 10107, USA. *Address:* Department of English, 4101 Turlington Hall, PO Box 117310, Gainesville, FL 32611-7310, USA (office). *Telephone:* (352) 392-6650 (office). *Fax:* (352) 392-0860 (office). *E-mail:* dleavitt@ufl.edu (office). *Website:* www.english.ufl.edu/faculty/dleavitt (office).

LEBOW, Jeanne, AB, MA, PhD; American writer, poet, teacher and photographer; b. 29 Jan. 1951, Richmond, Va; m. 1st Howard Lebow 1975 (divorced 1981); m. 2nd Steve Shepard 1985. *Education:* Coll. of William and Mary, Hollins Coll., Univ. of Southern Mississippi. *Career:* Instructor, Memphis State Univ. 1982–84; Teaching Asst, Univ. of Southern Mississippi 1984–87, Adjunct Prof. 1992–93, 1994–95, Visiting Prof. 1993–94; Fulbright Lecturer in American Studies, Univ. of Ouagadougou, Burkina Faso 1987–88; Asst Prof., Northeast Missouri State Univ. 1988–92; freelance nature columnist 1991–; Instructor, Miss. School of the Arts. *Exhibitions:* numerous photography exhibitions. *Publications include:* The Outlaw James Copeland and the Champion-Belted Empress (poems) 1991; contributions: anthologies, books, reviews, and journals including Bird Watcher's Digest. *Honours:* Nat. Award, Georgia State Poetry Soc. 1983, Miss. Humanities Council Grants 1994, 1995. *Address:* PO Box 1295, Gautier, MS 39553, USA (home). *E-mail:* shepart@ datasync.com (home).

LEBRECHT, Norman; British writer; b. 11 July 1948, London; m. Elbie Spivack 1977; three d. *Education:* Bar Ilan Univ., Israel. *Career:* radio and television producer 1969–78; writer 1978–; Asst Ed., Evening Standard, London 2002–09; presenter, Lebrecht.live, The Lebrecht Interview, BBC Radio 3 1999–; mem. Soc. of Authors. *Publications:* Discord 1982, Hush! Handel's in a Passion 1985, The Book of Musical Anecdotes 1985, Mahler Remembered 1987, The Book of Musical Days 1987, The Maestro Myth 1991, Music in London 1991, The Companion to Twentieth-Century Music 1992, When the Music Stops 1996, Who Killed Classical Music? 1997, Covent Garden: Dispatches from the English Culture War, 1945–2000 2000, The Song of Names (Whitbread First Novel Award) 2002, Maestros, Masterpieces and Madness: The Secret Life and Shameful Death of the Classical Record Industry 2007, The Game of Opposites 2009, Why Mahler? 2010. *Literary Agent:* c/o Curtis Brown Ltd, Haymarket House, 28–29 Haymarket, London, SW1Y 4SP, England. *Telephone:* (20) 7393-4400. *Fax:* (20) 7393-4401. *E-mail:* info@curtisbrown.co.uk. *Website:* www.curtisbrown.co.uk. *Address:* 3 Bolton Road, London, NW8 0RJ, England (home). *E-mail:* norman@normanlebrecht .com (office). *Website:* www.normanlebrecht.com.

LEBRUN HOLMES, Sandra; Australian writer, film-maker and researcher; b. 24 April 1924, Bulcoomatta Station, NSW; m. Cecil William Holmes 1956; two s. one d. *Education:* Sydney Univ. *Career:* mem. Australian Soc. of Authors, Film Directors' Guild. *Recordings:* Sound of Melanesia 1954, Land of the Morning Star: Songs and Music of Arnhem Land 1962, Hunter of the Black 1989. *Publications:* Yirawala: Artist and Man 1972, Yirawala: Painter of the Dreaming 1992, Faces in the Sun (autobiog.) 1999; contrib. to various publications. *Address:* Box 439 PO, Potts Pt, NSW 2011, Australia. *Telephone:* 93604194 (office).

LEDERMAN, Leon M., PhD; American physicist and academic; *Pritzker Professor of Science, Department of Biology, Chemistry and Physical Sciences, Illinois Institute of Technology*; b. 15 July 1922, New York City; s. of the late Morris Lederman; m. 1st Florence Gordon; two d. one s.; m. 2nd Ellen Lederman. *Education:* City Coll. of New York, Columbia Univ., New York. *Career:* entered US Army 1943, rank of 2nd Lt Signal Corps 1946; grad. research involved building a Wilson Cloud Chamber for Cyclotron Project, Columbia Univ. 1948–51, Asst Prof. of Physics 1951–58, Prof. of Physics 1958–79; organised g-2 experiment, CERN 1958; Dir Nevis Labs 1961–78; Dir Fermi Nat. Accelerator Laboratory 1979–89, Dir Emer. 1989–; Prof. of Physics, Univ. of Chicago 1989–; currently Pritzker Prof. of Science, Illinois Inst. of Tech.; apptd Science Adviser to Gov. of Illinois 1989; Pres. American Asscn for the Advancement of Science 1991–; Resident Scholar IMSA Great Minds Program 1998; Founding mem. High Energy Physics Advisory Panel, Int. Cttee on Future Accelerators; Co-Founder and mem. Bd Trustees Illinois Math. and Science Acad.; mem. American, Finnish and Argentine Nat. Acads of Science; serves on 13 bds of dirs of museums, schools, science orgs and govt agencies; recipient of fellowships from Ford, Guggenheim, Ernest Kepton Adams and Nat. Science Foundations. *Publications include:* Nuclear and Particle Physics (with J. Weneser) 1969, From Quarks to the Cosmos: Tools of Discovery (with David N. Schramm) 1989, Portraits of Great American Scientists 2001, Symmetry and the Beautiful Universe (with Christopher T. Hill) 2004; numerous scientific articles. *Honours:* Hon. DSc (City Coll. of New York, Univ. of Chicago, Illinois Inst. of Tech., Northern Illinois Univ., Lake Forest Coll., Carnegie Mellon Univ., Univ. of Pisa, Univ. of Guanajuarto); Nat. Medal of Science 1965, Elliot Cresson Medal, Franklin Inst. 1976, Wolf Prize for Physics 1982, Nobel Prize for Physics 1988, Enrico Fermi Prize. *Address:* Illinois Institute of Technology, LS 106, 3300 South Federal Street, Chicago, IL 60616-3793 (office); Fermilab, PO Box 500, Batavia, IL 60510-0500, USA (office). *Telephone:* (312) 567-8920 (office); (630) 840-3000 (Fermilab) (office). *Fax:* (630) 840-4343 (Fermilab) (office). *E-mail:* lederman@iit.edu (office); lederman@fnal.gov (office). *Website:* www.iit.edu (office); www.fnal.gov (office).

LEE, Chang-rae, BA, MFA; American novelist; *Director, Program in Creative Writing, Lewis Center for the Arts, Princeton University*; b. 29 July 1965, Seoul, Republic of Korea; m. Michelle Branca 1993. *Education:* Phillips Exeter, Yale Univ., Univ. of Oregon. *Career:* moved to USA 1968; fmr Asst Prof., Univ. of Oregon; fmr Prof. and Dir, MFA program, Hunter Coll., CUNY; currently Dir Program in Creative Writing and Prof. of Creative Writing, Lewis Center for the Arts, Princeton Univ. *Publications:* Native Speaker 1995 (PEN/Hemingway Award for First Fiction), A Gesture Life 1999 (screenplay 2000), Aloft 2004, The Surrendered 2010; contribs to The New York Times Magazine. *Honours:* American Book Award, Before Columbus Foundation 1995, American Library Asscn Notable Book of the Year Award 1995, Barnes & Noble Discover Great New Writers Award 1995, one of New Yorker magazine's best fiction writers under 40. *Address:* c/o Program in Creative Writing, Lewis Center for the Arts, Princeton University, 185 Nassau Street, Princeton, NJ 08544, USA (office). *Telephone:* (609) 258-8561 (office). *E-mail:* changlee@princeton.edu (office). *Website:* www.princeton.edu/arts/ arts_at_princeton (office).

LEE, (William) David, BA, PhD; American poet and academic; b. 13 Aug. 1944, Matador, Tex.; m. Jan M. Lee 1971; one s. one d. *Education:* Colorado State University, Idaho State University, University of Utah. *Career:* Prof. of English, Southern Utah University 1971–, Chair. 1973–82, Acting Chair. 1984–85, Dept of English, Head, 1987; Poetry Ed., Weber Studies, 1986–; John Neihardt Distinguished Lectureships, State of Nebraska 1990, 1996; First Poet Laureate, State of Utah 1997; mem. National Foundation for Advancement of the Arts (mem. Bd of Dirs) 1996–, Western States Foundation, Writers at Work (mem. Bd of Advisors) 1993–. *Publications include:* The Porcine Legacy 1978, Driving and Drinking 1979, Shadow Weaver 1984, The Porcine Canticles 1984, Paragonah Canyon Autumn 1990, Day's Work 1990, My Town 1995, Covenants 1996, The Fish 1997, The Wayburne Pig 1998, A Legacy of Shadows: Poems 1979–1999 1999; contributions: numerous anthologies, reviews, quarterlies, journals, and magazines. *Honours:* National Endowment for the Arts Fellowship 1985, First Place, Poetry, Creative Writing Competition, Utah Arts Council 1988, Publication Prize, Utah Arts Council 1989, Outstanding Utah Writer, Utah Endowment for the Humanities and National Council of Teachers of English 1990, Governor's Award for Lifetime Achievement, Utah 1994, Western States Book Award 1995; Mountain and Plain Booksellers Award 1995, Governor's Award in the Humanities 2001, Bronze Minuteman Award for Lifetime Service to State and Nation 2000, Ward Roylance Award 2005.

LEE, Dennis Beynon, CM, BA, MA; Canadian poet and writer; b. 31 Aug. 1939, Toronto, Ont.; m. 1st; one s. one d.; m. 2nd Susan Perly 1985. *Education:* University of Toronto. *Career:* Lecturer, University of Toronto 1963–67; Ed., House of Anansi Press 1967–72; Consulting Ed., Macmillan of Canada 1972–78; Poetry Ed., McClelland and Stewart 1981–84; mem. PEN, Canada; Writers' Union of Canada. *Publications:* Poetry: Kingdom of Absence 1967, Civil Elegies (Governor General's Award for Poetry in 1972) 1972, The Gods 1979, The Difficulty of Living on Other Planets 1998, Riffs 1993, Nightwatch: New and Selected Poems, 1968–1996 1996; children's poetry: Wiggle to the Laundromat 1970, Alligator Pie 1974, Nicholas Knock 1974, Garbage Delight 1977, Jelly Belly 1983, Lizzy's Lion 1984, The Ice Cream Store 1991, Un 2003, Yesno 2003, Testament: Poems 2000–2011 2012; non-fiction: Savage Fields 1977, Body Music (essays) 1998; contributions: journals and magazines. *Address:* c/o House of Anansi Press, 110 Spadina Avenue, Suite 801, Toronto, ON M5V 2K4, Canada.

LEE, Hamilton, BS, MA, DEd; Chinese/American academic, poet and writer; b. 10 Oct. 1921, Zhouxian, Shandong, China; m. Jean C. Chang 1945; one s. three d. *Education:* Beijing Normal University, University of Minnesota, Wayne State University, Detroit. *Career:* teacher of English, High Schools, Taiwan, 1948–56; Research Assoc., Wayne State University, Detroit, 1958–64; Visiting Prof. of Chinese Literature, Seton Hall University, summer, 1964; Asst Prof., Moorhead State University, 1964–65; Visiting Scholar, Harvard University, 1965 and Summer 1966; Assoc. Prof., University of Wisconsin at La Crosse, 1965–66; Prof., 1966–84, Prof. Emeritus, 1984–, East Stroudsburg University, Pennsylvania; Visiting Fellow, Princeton University, 1976–78; mem. Acad. of American Poets; distinguished mem., mem. of advisory panel, International Society of Poets; Poetry Society of America; Pennsylvania Poetry Society; World Literary Acad., fellow; World Future Society. *Publications:* Readings in Instructional Technology, 1970; Reflection (poems), 1989; Revelation (poems), 1991. Contributions: numerous anthologies, journals, and literary magazines. *Honours:* many poetry contest awards; Ed.'s Choice, National Library of Poetry, 1994.

LEE, (Nelle) Harper; American writer; b. 28 April 1926, Monroeville, Ala; d. of Amasa Coleman Lee and Frances Finch Cunningham Lee. *Education:* Huntingdon Coll., Univ. of Ala and Univ. of Oxford, UK. *Career:* worked as airline reservation clerk for Eastern Airlines and BOAC (NY) 1950s; accompanied the late Truman Capote to Holcombe, Kan., as research asst for his novel In Cold Blood; mem. Nat. Council of Arts 1966–71. *Publications include:* fiction: To Kill A Mockingbird (Pulitzer Prize for Fiction 1961, Best Sellers' Paperback of the Year Award 1962) 1960; essays: Love: In Other Words (essay in Vogue) 1961, Christmas to Me (essay in McCalls) 1961, When Children Discover America (essay in McCalls) 1965, High Romance and Adventure (essay, part of Ala History and Heritage Festival) 1983; contribs to numerous magazines. *Honours:* Hon. DHumLitt (Spring Coll., Ala) 1997, (Notre Dame) 2006; Alabama Library Assen Award 1961, Nat. Conf. of Christians and Jews Brotherhood Award 1961, Los Angeles Public Library Literary Award 2005, Presidential Medal of Freedom 2007, National Medal of Arts 2011. *Address:* PO Box 278, Monroeville, AL 36461, USA.

LEE, Hermione, CBE, MA, FRSL, FBA; British writer, broadcaster and academic; *President, Wolfson College, University of Oxford;* b. 29 Feb. 1948, Winchester; d. of Dr Benjamin Lee and Josephine Lee; m. John Barnard 1991. *Education:* Univ. of Oxford. *Career:* Instructor, Coll. of William and Mary, Williamsburg, Va 1970–71; Lecturer, Dept of English, Univ. of Liverpool 1971–77; Lecturer, Dept of English, Univ. of York 1977–87, Sr Lecturer 1987–90, Reader 1990–93, Prof. 1993–98; Goldsmiths' Chair of English Literature and Fellow of New Coll., Oxford 1998–2008, Pres. Wolfson Coll., Univ. of Oxford 2008–; presenter of Book Four on Channel Four TV (UK) 1982–86; Chair. judges Man Booker Prize for Fiction 2006; Mel and Lois Tukman Fellow, Dorothy and Lewis B. Cullman Center for Scholars and Writers, New York Public Library 2004–05. *Publications include:* The Novels of Virginia Woolf 1977, Elizabeth Bowen 1981 (2nd. ed. 1999), Philip Roth 1982, The Secret Self I 1985 and II 1987, The Mulberry Tree: Writings of Elizabeth Bowen 1986, Willa Cather: A Life Saved Up 1989, Virginia Woolf 1996, Virginia Woolf: Moments of Being (ed.) 2002, Body Parts: Essays on Life-Writing 2005, Virginia Woolf's Nose 2005, Edith Wharton (biog.) 2007, Biography: A Very Short Introduction 2009. *Honours:* Foreign Hon. mem. American Acad. of Arts and Sciences; Hon. Fellow, St Hilda's Coll. Oxford 1998, St Cross Coll. Oxford 1998; Hon. DLitt (Liverpool) 2002, (York) 2007. *Literary Agent:* United Agents, 12-26 Lexington Street, London, W1F 0LE, England. *Address:* Wolfson College, Linton Road, Oxford, OX2 6UD, England (office). *Telephone:* (18) 6527-4100 (office). *Fax:* (18) 6527-4125 (office). *E-mail:* hermione.lee@wolfson.ox.ac.uk (office). *Website:* www.wolfson.ox.ac.uk (office); www.hermionelee.com.

LEE, John Darrell, BA, MSJ; American writer and fmr academic; b. 12 March 1931, Indiahoma, Oklahoma. *Education:* Texas Technological College, West Virginia University. *Career:* Former Prof. of Journalism. *Publications:* Caught in the Act 1968, Diplomatic Persuaders 1968, Assignation in Algeria 1971, The Ninth Man 1976, The Thirteenth Hour 1978, Lago 1980, Stalag Texas 1990. *Literary Agent:* Don Congdon Associates Inc, 156 Fifth Avenue, Suite 625, New York, NY 10010, USA.

LEE, Kuei-shien; Taiwanese poet, essayist, translator, chemical engineer and patent agent; b. 19 June 1937, Taipei; m. Wang Huei-uei 1965; one s. one d. *Education:* Taipei Inst. of Technology, European Language Center, Ministry of Education. *Career:* Chair. Nat. Culture and Arts Foundation 2005–07; Dir Int. Writers and Artists Asscn; mem. Int. Acad. of Poets (founder-fellow), Li Poetry Soc., Rilke Gesellschaft, Taiwan PEN (pres. 1995). *Publications:* (in Chinese): poetry: 16 works 1963–2001; essays: 23 works 1971–2002; translator: 35 works 1969–2001; contrib. to anthologies and other publications. *Honours:* Hon. PhD in chemical engineering (Marquis Giuseppe Scicluna Int. Univ. Foundation) 1985; Albert Einstein Int. Acad. Foundation Alfred Nobel Medal for Peace 1991, Li Poetry Soc. Poetic Creation Award 1994, Sec.-Gen. Asian Poets Conference 1995, Best World Poet of the Year 1997, 1998, Poet of the Millennium Award 2000, New Millennium Michael Madhusudan Award 2002, Taiwan Premier Culture Award 2002, Mongolian Cultural Foundation Poet Medal 2005, Chinggis Khaan Gold Medal for 800th Anniversary of the Mongolian State 2006. *Address:* Room 705, Asia Enterprise Center, No. 142 Minchuan East Road, Sec 3, Taipei 10542, Taiwan (office).

LEE, Lance Wilds, BA, MFA; American poet, dramatist, writer and editor; b. 25 Aug. 1942, New York, NY; s. of the late David Levy and of Lucile Levy (née Wilds); m. Jeanne Barbara Hutchings 1962; two d. *Education:* Boston Univ., Brandeis Univ., Yale School of Drama. *Career:* Lecturer, Univ. of Bridgeport 1967–68; Asst Prof., UCLA 1971–73, California State Univ. at Northridge 1981–2005; Instructor, Southern Connecticut State Coll. 1968; Sr Lecturer, then Asst Prof., Univ. of Southern California, Los Angeles 1968–71; freelance writer since 1971. *Plays:* Rasputin, Gambits, Fox Hound and Huntress, Time's Up. *Publications:* Fox, Hound and Huntress (play) 1973, Time's Up (play) 1979, The Understructure of Screenwriting (with Ben Brady) 1988, Wrestling with The Angel (poems) 1990, A Poetics for Screenwriters 2001, Second Chances (novel) 2001, Time's Up and Other Plays 2001, Becoming Human (poems) 2001, On the Waterfront 2003; with others: The Death and Life of Drama 2005, Human/Nature 2006, Seasons of Defiance (poems) 2010; contribs to reviews, quarterlies, journals, and periodicals, in England and USA. *Honours:* Arts of the Theatre Foundation Fellowship 1967, Univ. of Southern California Research and Publication Grants 1970, 1971, Rockefeller Foundation Grant, Office for Advanced Drama Research 1971, Theatre Devt Fund Grant 1976, Nat. Endowment for the Arts Fellowship 1976, Squaw Valley Scholarships in Poetry 1982, 1983, Port Townsend Writers Conf. Scholarship in Poetry 1985. *Literary Agent:* c/o Reece Halsey Agency, 8733 Sunset Boulevard, Los Angeles, CA 90069, USA. *Telephone:* (310) 652-7595 (office). *Website:* lanceleeauthor.com.

LEE, Li-Young; American poet; b. 19 Aug. 1957, Jakarta, Indonesia; m. Donna Lee 1978; two c. *Education:* Univ. of Pittsburgh, Univ. of Arizona, SUNY at Brockport. *Publications:* Rose 1986, The City in Which I Love You 1990, The Winged Seed: A Remembrance 1995, Book of My Nights 2001. *Honours:* New York Univ. Delmore Schwartz Memorial Poetry Award 1986, Ludwig Vogelstein Foundation Fellowship 1987, Mrs Giles Whiting Foundation Writer's Award 1988, Acad. of American Poets Lamont Poetry Selection 1990. *Address:* c/o BOA Editions Ltd, 260 East Avenue, Rochester, NY 14604, USA. *E-mail:* info@boaeditions.org.

LEE, Stewart Graham, BA; British writer, comedian and director; b. 5 April 1968, Solihull, West Midlands, England. *Education:* Univ. of Oxford. *Career:* writer-performer, The Oxford Revue 1987–89; solo stand-up work 1989–; writer-performer with Richard Herring in double act Lee & Herring 1991–99; rock music critic, The Sunday Times 1995–. *Theatre:* Jerry Springer – The Opera (co-writer and dir) 2002, Standup Comedian 2004, Stewart Lee: '90s Comedian (Soho Theatre) 2005, 41st Best Standup Ever 2007, If You Prefer a Milder Comedian, Please Ask for One 2009, Carpet Remnant World 2011, writer-performer for Edinburgh Festival shows, including Club Zarathustra, Pea Green Boat, King Dong vs Moby Dick. *Radio:* On The Hour (writer, BBC Radio 4) 1991–92, Lionel Nimrod's Inexplicable World (BBC Radio 4) 1992–93, Lee & Herring's Fist Of Fun (BBC Radio 1) 1993, Lee & Herring (BBC Radio 1) 1994–95, patron and regular presenter for Resonance FM London 2002–. *Television:* Fist of Fun (BBC 2) 1995–96, Harry Hill (script ed., Avalon TV/Channel 4) 1997–2000, This Morning with Richard Not Judy (BBC 2) 1998–99, Attention Scum (writer and dir, BBC 2) 2000, Time Gentlemen Please (script ed.) 2001, Stewart Lee's Comedy Vehicle (BBC 2) 2009, (BAFTA Award for Best Comedy Programme 2012) 2011. *Publications:* Lee & Herring's Fist Of Fun (with Richard Herring) 1995, The Perfect Fool 2001, How I Escaped My Certain Fate: The Life and Deaths of a Stand-Up Comedian 2010, If You Prefer a Milder Comedian, Please Ask for One 2012; contrib. to Vox, Q, The Guardian. *Honours:* Writers' Guild Award 1992, Sony Gold Award 1992, Evening Standard Theatre Awards 2003, Critics Circle Theatre Awards 2003, British Comedy Award for Best Male TV Comic 2011, British Comedy Award for Best Comedy Entertainment Programme 2011. *Literary Agent:* c/o Debi Allen Associates, 22 Torrington Place, London, WC1E 7HP, England. *Telephone:* (20) 7255-6123. *E-mail:* debi@debiallenassociates.com. *Website:* www.debiallenassociates.com; www.stewartlee.co.uk.

LEE, Tanith, (Esther Garber); British writer and playwright; b. 19 Sept. 1947, London; d. of Bernard Lee and Hylda Lee; m. John Kaiine 1992. *Education:* Prendergast Grammar School. *Television and radio writing:* two episodes of Blake's Seven (BBC TV), several radio plays. *Publications:* The Betrothed (short stories) 1968, The Dragon Hoard (juvenile) 1971, Princess Hynchatti and Some Other Surprises (juvenile) 1972, Animal Castle (juvenile) 1972, Companions on the Road (juvenile) 1975, The Birthgrave 1975, Don't Bite the Sun 1976, The Storm Lord 1976, The Winter Players (juvenile) 1976, East of Midnight (juvenile) 1977, Drinking Sapphire Wine 1977, Volkhavaar 1977, Vazkor, Son of Vazkor 1978, Quest for the White Witch 1978, Night's Master 1978, The Castle of Dark (juvenile) 1978, Shon the Taken (juvenile) 1979, Death's Master 1979, Electric Forest 1979, Sabella (aka The Blood Stone) 1980, Kill the Dead 1980, Day by Night 1980, Delusion's Master 1981, The Silver Metal Lover 1982, Cyrion (short stories) 1982, Prince on a White Horse (juvenile) 1982, Sung in Shadow 1983, Anackire 1983, Red as Blood, or Tales from the Sisters Grimmer 1983, The Dragon Hoard 1984, The Beautiful Biting Machine (short stories) 1984, Tamastara, or the Indian Nights (short stories) 1984, Days of Grass 1985, The Gorgon and Other Beastly Tales 1985, Dreams of Dark and Light 1986, Women as Demons: The Male Perception of Women Through Space and Time 1989, Blood of Roses 1990, Black Unicorn 1995, The Book of the Mad 1998, The Book of the Dead 1998, White as Snow 2000, East of Midnight 2001, Queen of the Wolves 2001, Faces Under Water 2002, Wolf Wing 2002, Piratica (juvenile) 2004, Fatal Woman (short stories) 2004, Thirty-Four (novel) 2004, Death of the Day 2004, Lionwolf Trilogy: Cast a Bright Shadow 2004, Here in Cold Hell 2005, No Flame But Mine 2007, Piratica 2 (juvenile) 2005, L'Amber 2006, Piratica 3 (juvenile) 2007, Indigara 2007. *Honours:* August Derleth Award 1985, World Fantasy Award. *Address:* c/o Pan Macmillan, 20 New Wharf Road, London, N1 9RR, England. *Website:* www.tanithlee.com.

LEE, Warner (see Battin, B. W.)

LEE, Wayne C., (Lee Sheldon); American writer; b. 2 July 1917, Lamar, NE. *Career:* mem. Western Writers of America (pres. 1970–71), Nebraska Writers' Guild (pres. 1974–76). *Publications:* Prairie Vengeance 1954, Broken Wheel Ranch 1956, Slugging Backstop 1957, His Brother's Guns 1958, Killer's Range 1958, Bat Masterson 1960, Gun Brand 1961, Blood on the Prairie 1962, Thunder in the Backfield 1962, Stranger in Stirrup 1962, The Gun Tamer 1963, Devil Wire 1963, The Hostile Land 1964, Gun in His Hand 1964, Warpath West 1965, Fast Gun 1965, Brand of a Man 1966, Mystery of Scorpion Creek 1966, Trail of the Skulls 1966, Showdown at Julesburg Station 1967, Return to Gunpoint 1967, Only the Brave 1967, Doomed Planet (as Lee Sheldon) 1967, Sudden Guns 1968, Trouble at Flying H 1969, Stage to Lonesome Butte 1969, Showdown at Sunrise 1971, The Buffalo Hunters 1972, Suicide Trail 1972, Wind Over Rimfire 1973, Son of a Gunman 1973, Scotty Philip: The Man Who Saved the Buffalo (non-fiction) 1975, Law of the Prairie 1975, Die Hard 1975, Law of the Lawless 1977, Skirmish at Fort Phil Kearney 1977, Gun Country 1978, Petticoat Wagon Train 1978, The Violent Man 1978, Ghost of a Gunfighter 1980, McQuaid's Gun 1980, Trails of the Smoky Hill (non-fiction) 1980, Shadow of the Gun 1981, Guns at Genesis 1981, Putnam's Ranch War 1982, Barbed Wire War 1983, The Violent Trail 1984, White Butte Guns 1984, War at Nugget Creek 1985, Massacre Creek 1985, The Waiting Gun 1986, Hawks of Autumn 1986, Wild Towns of Nebraska (non-fiction) 1988, Arikaree War Cry 1992, Bad Men and Bad Towns (non-fiction) 1993, Deadly Days in Kansas (non-fiction) 1997. *Address:* PO Box 906, Imperial, NE 69033, USA (home).

LEECH, Geoffrey Neil, BA, MA, DLitt, PhD, FBA; British academic and writer; *Professor Emeritus of Linguistics and English Language, University of Lancaster*; b. 16 Jan. 1936, Gloucester, Glos., England; s. of Charles Richard Leech and Dorothy Eileen Leech; m. Frances Anne Berman 1961; one s. one d. *Education:* Univ. Coll., London, Univ. of Lancaster. *Career:* Asst Lecturer, Univ. Coll. London 1962–64, Lecturer 1965–69; Reader, Univ. of Lancaster 1969–74, Prof. of Linguistics and English Language 1974–1996, Research Prof. in English Linguistics 1996–2002, Prof. Emer. of Linguistics and English Language 2002–; Visiting Prof., Brown Univ., USA 1972, Kobe Univ., Japan 1984, Kyoto Univ., Japan 1991, Meikai Univ., Japan 1999; mem. Academia Europaea, Det Norske Videnskaps-Akademi. *Publications:* English in Advertising 1966, A Linguistic Guide to English Poetry 1969, Towards a Semantic Description of English 1969, Meaning and the English Verb 1971, A Grammar of Contemporary English (with R. Quirk, S. Greenbaum and J. Svartvik) 1972, Semantics 1974, A Communicative Grammar of English (with J. Svartvik) 1975, Explorations in Semantics and Pragmatics 1980, Studies in English Linguistics (co-ed. with S. Greenbaum and J. Svartvik) 1980, Style in Fiction (with Michael H. Short) 1981, English Grammar for Today (with R. Hoogenraad and M. Deuchar) 1982, Principles of Pragmatics 1983, A Comprehensive Grammar of the English Language (with R. Quirk, S. Greenbaum and J. Svartvik) 1985, Computers in English Language Teaching and Research (co-ed. with C. N. Candlin) 1986, The Computational Analysis of English (co-ed. with R. Garside and G. Sampson) 1987, An A–Z of English Grammar and Usage 1989, Introducing English Grammar 1992, Statistically-driven Computer Grammars in English (co-ed. with E. Black and R. Garside) 1993, Spoken English on Computer (co-ed. with G. Myers and J. Thomas) 1995, Corpus Annotation (co-ed. with R. Garside and T. McEnery) 1997, Longman Grammar of Spoken and Written English (with D. Biber, S. Johansson, S. Conrad and E. Finegan) 1999, Word Frequency in Written and Spoken English (with P. Rayson and A. Wilson) 2001, Longman Student Grammar of Spoken and Written English (with D. Biber and S. Conrad) 2002, A Glossary of English Grammar 2006, English: One Tongue, Many Voices (with Jan Svartvik) 2006, Language in Literature: Style and Foregrounding 2008, Change in Contemporary English: a Grammatical Study (with M. Hundt, C. Mair and N. Smith) 2009; contrib. to A Review of English Literature, International Journal of Corpus Linguistics, Language Learning, Lingua, New Society, Linguistics, Dutch Quarterly Review of Anglo-American Letters, TLS, Prose Studies, The Rising Generation, Transactions of the Philological Society, English Language and Linguistics, International Journal of Pragmatics, Journal of Foreign Language Teaching, ICAME Journal, Journal of Politeness Research. *Honours:* Hon. Fellowship, Lancaster Univ. 2009–; Hon. FilDr (Univ. of Lund) 1987; Hon. DLitt (Univ. of Wolverhampton) 2002; Harkness Fellowship 1964–65. *Address:* Department of Linguistics and English Language, University of Lancaster, Lancaster, LA1 4YL, England (office). *Telephone:* (1524) 593036 (office). *Fax:* (1524) 843085 (office). *Website:* www.ling.lancs.ac.uk/profiles/296 (office).

LEEDOM-ACKERMAN, Joanne, MA; American writer; b. 7 Feb. 1947, Dallas, TX; d. of John Nesbit Leedom and Joanne Shriver Leedom; m. Peter Ackerman 1972; two s. *Education:* Principia Coll., Johns Hopkins Univ., Brown Univ. *Career:* mem. Int. PEN (Vice-Pres., Writers in Prison Cttee 1993–97, Int. Sec. 2004–07). *Publications:* No Marble Angels 1985, The Dark Path to the River 1988, Women for All Seasons (ed.) 1989; contrib. to anthologies, newspapers and magazines. *Fax:* (202) 965-9869 (home). *E-mail:* jlajoanne@aol.com (home). *Website:* www.joanneleedom-ackerman.com.

LEESON, Robert Arthur, BA; British journalist and writer; b. 31 March 1928, Barnton, Cheshire; m. Gunvor Hagen 1954; one s. one d. *Education:* Univ. of London. *Career:* Literary Ed., Morning Star, London 1960–80; mem. Int. Bd of Books for Young People, British Section (Treas. 1972–91), Writers' Guild of Great Britain (Chair. 1985–86). *Publications:* Third Class Genie 1975, Silver's Revenge 1978, Travelling Brothers 1979, It's My Life 1980, Candy for King 1983, Reading and Righting 1985, Slambash Wangs of a Compo Gormer 1987, Coming Home 1991, Zarnia Experiment 1–6 1993, Robin Hood 1994, Red, White and Blue 1996, Liar 1999, The Song of Arthur 2000, My Sister Shahrazad 2001, Onda Wind Rider 2003, Partners in Crime 2003; contrib. to newspapers and journals. *Honours:* Eleanor Farjeon Award for Services to Children and Literature 1985. *Address:* 18 McKenzie Road, Broxbourne, Hertfordshire, EN10 7JH, England (home).

LEFFLAND, Ella Julia, BA; American writer; b. 25 Nov. 1931, Martinez, CA. *Education:* San Jose State College. *Publications:* Mrs Munck, 1970; Love out of Season, 1974; Last Courtesies, 1979; Rumors of Peace, 1980; The Knight, Death and the Devil, 1990. Contributions: New Yorker; Harper's; Atlantic Monthly; Mademoiselle; New York Magazine; New York Times. *Honours:* Gold Medals for Fiction, 1974, 1979, Silver Medal, 1991, Commonwealth Club of California; O. Henry First Prize, 1977; Bay Area Book Reviewers Award for Fiction, 1990.

LEGGATT, Alexander Maxwell, BA, MA, PhD, FRSC; Canadian academic and writer; *Professor Emeritus of English, University College, University of Toronto*; b. 18 Aug. 1940, Oakville, Ont.; m. Anna Thomas 1964; four d. *Education:* Univ. of Toronto, Shakespeare Inst., Stratford-on-Avon (affiliated with Univ. of Birmingham), UK. *Career:* Lecturer, University Coll., Univ. of Toronto 1965–67, Asst Prof. 1967–71, Assoc. Prof. 1971–75, Prof. of English 1975–2006, Prof. Emer. 2006–; Assoc. Ed., Modern Drama 1972–75; mem. Editorial Bd English Studies in Canada 1984–91, Univesity of Toronto Quarterly 1996–2006, Studies in Theatre and Performance 1999–2006, Renaissance and Reformation 2000–06; mem. Amnesty International, Anglican Church of Canada (lay reader 1979–), Int. Asscn of Univ. Profs of English, Int. Shakespeare Asscn (Exec. Cttee 1987–96), PEN Canada, Arts and Letters Club of Toronto. *Publications:* Citizen Comedy in the Age of Shakespeare 1973, Shakespeare's Comedy of Love 1974, Ben Jonson: His Vision and his Art 1981, English Drama: Shakespeare to the Restoration 1988, Shakespeare's Political Drama 1988, Harvester-Twayne New Critical Introductions to Shakespeare: King Lear 1988, Coriolanus: An Annotated Bibliography (co-author) 1989, Craft and Tradition: Essays in Honour of William Blissett (co-ed.) 1990, Shakespeare in Performance: King Lear 1991, Jacobean Public Theatre 1992, English Stage Comedy 1490–1990 1998, Introduction to English Renaissance Comedy 1999, Cambridge Companion to Shakespearean Comedy (ed.) 2002, Approaches to Teaching English Renaissance Drama (co-ed.) 2002, Shakespeare's Tragedies 2005, William Shakespeare's Macbeth: A Sourcebook (ed.) 2005; contrib. to many scholarly journals. *Honours:* Guggenheim Fellowship 1985–86, Killam Research Fellowship 1995, Univ. of Toronto Outstanding Teaching Award 1995, Univ. of Toronto Alumni Awards of Excellence Faculty Award 1998, Chancellor Jackman Research Fellowship in the Humanities 2004. *Address:* 2593 St Clair Avenue East, Toronto, ON M4B 1M2, Canada. *Telephone:* (416) 755-2325.

LEGRAS, Anny, (Anny Duperey); French actress and writer; b. 28 June 1947, Rouen; d. of Lucien Legras and Ginette Legras; fmr pnr Bernard Giraudeau; one s. one d. *Education:* Conservatoire d'Art Dramatique, Rouen and Paris. *Career:* numerous appearances on stage, in films and on TV. *Plays include:* La guerre de Troie n'aura pas lieu (Prix Gérard Philipe, Best Foreign Theatre Actress, Canada) 1975–78, Attention fragile (co-adaptor) 1978–80, Duo pour une soliste 1984, Le secret 1987, Le plaisir de rompre, Le pain de ménage 1990, Quand elle dansait 1994, Un mari idéal 1995; Sarah 2003–04. *Films include:* Stavisky 1973, Un éléphant ça trompe énormément 1976, Psy

1981, Le grand pardon 1982, Mille milliards de dollars 1982, Meurtres à domicile 1982, Les compères 1983, La triche 1984, Danse avec lui 2007. *Television includes:* Un château au soleil (Sept d'or for Best Actress) 1988, La face de l'ogre (also dir) 1988, Une famille formidable (Sept d'or for Best Actress) 1992, Charlemagne 1994, La vocation d'Adrienne 1997, Chère Marianne 1999; Le voyage de la grande Duchesse 2002, Familles formidables 2002, Une vie en retour 2005, Forailles formidables 2005, Le otre: Oscar et la dorae rose 2005–06. *Publications:* L'Admiroir (Acad. française Prix Alice Barthou) 1976, Le Nez de Mazarin 1986, Le Voile noir 1992, Je vous écris… 1993, Les chats de hasard 1999, Allons voir plus loin, veux-tu 2002, Une Soirée 2005. *Honours:* Chevalier, Légion d'honneur; Prix Dussane 1984. *Address:* c/o Danielle Gain, Cinéart, 36 rue de Ponthieu, 75008 Paris, France (office). *Telephone:* 1-56-69-33-00 (office). *E-mail:* d.gain@cineart.fr (office). *Website:* anny-duperey.chez-alice.fr.

LEHANE, Dennis; American novelist; b. 1966, Dorchester, Boston, MA. *Publications:* A Drink Before the War 1994, Darkness Take My Hand 1996, Sacred 1997, Gone Baby Gone 1998, Prayers for Rain 1999, Mystic River 2001, Shutter Island 2003, Coronado 2006, The Given Day 2008, Midnight Mile 2010. *Honours:* Anthony Award, Barry Award for Best Novel, Massachusetts Book Award in Fiction. *Address:* c/o Author Mail, 7th Floor, Harper Collins Publishers, 10 East 53rd Street, New York, NY 10022, USA (office). *Website:* www.dennislehanebooks.com.

LEHMAN, David Cary, BA, MA, PhD; American writer, poet and editor; *Professor and Poetry Coordinator, New School Graduate Writing Program*; b. 11 June 1948, New York, NY; s. of Joseph Lehman and Anne Lehman (née Lusthaus); m. 1st Stefanie Green 1978 (divorced 1993); one s.; m. 2nd Stacey Harwood 2005. *Education:* Columbia Univ., Univ. of Cambridge, UK. *Career:* Instructor, Brooklyn Coll., CUNY 1975–76; Asst Prof., Hamilton Coll., Clinton, New York 1976–80; Fellow, Soc. for the Humanities, Cornell Univ. 1980–81; Lecturer, Wells Coll., Aurora, New York, 1981–82; Book Critic and Writer, Newsweek 1982–89; Series Ed., The Best American Poetry 1988–, Poets on Poetry, Univ. of Michigan Press 1994–2006; Core Faculty, Bennington Coll. MFA Program 1994–2006; Adjunct Prof. of English, Columbia Univ. 1995–98, New York Univ. 1997–2007; Prof. and Poetry Coordinator, New School Graduate Writing Program, New York 1996–. *Publications:* Some Nerve 1973, Day One 1979, Beyond Amazement: New Essays on John Ashbery (ed.) 1980, James Merrill: Essays in Criticism (ed.) 1983, An Alternative to Speech 1986, Ecstatic Occasions, Expedient Forms: 65 Leading Contemporary Poets Select and Comment on Their Poems (ed.) 1987, Twenty Questions 1988, The Best American Poetry (co-ed.) annually 1988–2011, The Perfect Murder: A Study in Detection 1989, Operation Memory 1990, The Line Forms Here 1992, Signs of the Times: Deconstruction and the Fall of Paul de Man 1992, The Big Question 1995, Valentine Place 1996, The Daily Mirror 2000, The Evening Sun 2003, Great American Prose Poems: From Poe to the Present (ed.) 2003, When a Woman Loves a Man 2005, The Oxford Book of American Poetry (ed.) 2006, The Best American Erotic Poems: From 1800 to the Present (ed.) 2008, A Fine Romance: Jewish Songwriters, American Songs 2009, Yeshiva Boys 2009; contrib. to anthologies, newspapers, reviews and journals, including the New York Times, Washington Post, The New Yorker, The Atlantic, the Times Literary Supplement, Harper's, The Paris Review, Poetry, American Poetry Review, Art in America, American Heritage, Smithsonian, The Wall Street Journal, The Los Angeles Times. *Honours:* Van Rensselaer Poetry Prize 1967, 1970, Bennett A. Cerf Prize 1973, Acad. of American Poets Prize 1974, Ingram Merrill Foundation Grants 1976, 1982, 1984, 1993, Nat. Endowment for the Humanities Grant 1979, Nat. Endowment for the Arts Fellowship 1987, American Acad. of Arts and Letters Award 1990, Lila Wallace-Reader's Digest Fund Writers Award 1991–94, Deems Taylor Award (ASCAP) 2010. *Address:* c/o Glen Hartley, Writers' Representatives, 116 West 14 Street, 11th Floor, New York, NY 10011, USA. *Telephone:* (212) 229-5611 (office). *E-mail:* lehmand@newschool.edu (office). *Website:* bestamericanpoetry.com (office).

LEHRER, Keith Edward, BA, AM, PhD; American philosopher, academic, writer and artist; *Research Professor, University of Miami*; b. 10 Jan. 1936, Minneapolis, Minn.; s. of Abraham Lehrer and Estelle Lehrer; m. Adrienne Lehrer; two s. *Education:* Univ. of Minnesota, Brown Univ. *Career:* Instructor and Asst Prof., Wayne State Univ. 1960–63; Asst Prof. to Prof., Univ. of Rochester 1963–73; Visiting Assoc. Prof., Univ. of Calgary, Canada 1966; Prof., Univ. of Arizona 1974–90, Regents Prof. of Philosophy 1990–2007, Emer. 2007–; Research Prof., Univ. of Miami 2007–; Assoc., CREA, École Polytechnique, Paris 1993–94; Visiting Fellow, Univ. of London 1996, ANU 1997; mem. American Philosophical Asscn (Pres. 1989, Chair. Nat. Bd of Officers) 1992–95), Council for Philosophical Studies, Institut Int. de Philosophie, Paris and Lund, American Acad. of Arts and Sciences 2005–; Fellow, AAAS 2005–, Center for Advanced Behavioural Studies 2007–08. *Exhibitions:* Univ. of Graz Library 2005, Univ. of Santa Clara Library 2005. *Publications:* Philosophical Problems and Arguments: An Introduction (with James Cornman) 1968, Knowledge 1978, Rational Consensus in Science and Society: A Philosophical and Mathematical Study (with Carl Wagner) 1981, Thomas Reid 1989, Metamind 1990, Theory of Knowledge 1990, 2000, Self-Trust: A Study of Reason, Knowledge and Autonomy 1997; ed. several books; contrib. to numerous books and journals. *Honours:* Hon. Prof., Karl-Franzens Univ., Graz 1985–; Dr hc (Graz) 1997; Hon. Mem. Vereinigung für Wissenschaftliche Grundlagen-forschung, Austria; ACLS Fellowship 1973–74, Nat. Endowment for the Humanities Fellowship 1980, Guggenheim Fellowship 1983–84, Brown Univ. Citation for Distinguished Achievement 1988,. *Address:* 65 Sierra Vista Drive, Tucson, AZ 85719, USA (home). *E-mail:* lehrer@email.arizona.edu (office). *Website:* web.arizona.edu/~phil/faculty/klehrer.htm (office).

LEIGH, Danny; British writer and critic; b. 1972; m. *Career:* fmr musician; journalist, writing about music and film (contrib. to Sight and Sound, The Guardian). *Publications:* novels: The Greatest Gift 2004, The Monsters of Gramercy Park 2005. *Address:* c/o The Guardian, Kings Place, 90 York Way, London, N1 9GU, England (office). *Telephone:* (20) 3353-2000 (office). *Website:* www.guardian.co.uk (office).

LEIGH, Julia; Australian novelist, film director and screenwriter; b. 1970, Sydney, NSW. *Education:* Univ. of Sydney. *Career:* initially studied law but changed to writing; worked at Australian Soc. of Authors; mentors have included Frank Moorhouse, Toni Morrison and Jane Campion; directorial debut with screenplay for Sleeping Beauty 2011; film selected for main competition at Cannes Film Festival 2011. *Film screenplays include:* Sleeping Beauty 2011, The Hunter 2011. *Television:* appeared as herself in episode of Cinema 3 (series) May 2011. *Publications:* novels: The Hunter (Betty Trask Award, Prix de l'Astrolabe 2001, New York Times Notable Book of the Year) (adapted into feature film 2011) 2001, Disquiet 2009. *Honours:* chosen by the Observer newspaper as one of 21 writers to watch in the millennium. *Address:* c/o Faber and Faber Ltd (Editorial Dept), Bloomsbury House, 74–77 Great Russell Street, London, WC1B 3DA, England. *Telephone:* (20) 7927-3800. *Fax:* (20) 7927-3801. *Website:* www.faber.co.uk.

LEIGH, Meredith (see Kenyon, Bruce Guy)

LEIGH, Mike, OBE; British dramatist and film and theatre director; b. 20 Feb. 1943, Salford, Lancs.; s. of the late A. A. Leigh and the late P. P. Leigh (née Cousin); m. Alison Steadman 1973 (divorced 2001); two s. *Education:* Royal Acad. of Dramatic Art, Camberwell School of Arts and Crafts, Cen. School of Art and Design, London Film School. *Career:* Chair. Govs London Film School 2001–. *Plays:* The Box Play 1965, My Parents Have Gone to Carlisle, The Last Crusade of the Five Little Nuns 1966, Nenaa 1967, Individual Fruit Pies, Down Here and Up There, Big Basil 1968, Epilogue, Glum Victoria and the Lad with Specs 1969, Bleak Moments 1970, A Rancid Pong 1971, Wholesome Glory, The Jaws of Death, Dick Whittington and His Cat 1973, Babies Grow Old, The Silent Majority 1974, Abigail's Party 1977 (also TV play), Ecstasy 1979, Goose-Pimples (London Evening Standard and London Drama Critics' Choice Best Comedy Awards 1981) 1981, Smelling A Rat 1988, Greek Tragedy 1989 (in Australia), 1990 (in UK), It's a Great Big Shame! 1993, Two Thousand Years (Cottlesloe Theatre, London) 2005. *Television films:* A Mug's Game 1972, Hard Labour 1973, The Permissive Society, The Birth of the 2001 F.A. Cup Final Goalie, Old Chums, Probation, A Light Snack, Afternoon 1975, Nuts in May 1976, Knock for Knock 1976, The Kiss of Death 1977, Abigail's Party 1977, Who's Who 1978, Grown-Ups 1980, Home Sweet Home 1981, Meantime 1983, Four Days in July 1984, The Short and Curlies 1987. *Feature films:* Bleak Moments (Golden Leopard, Locarno Film Festival, Golden Hugo, Chicago Film Festival 1972) 1971, High Hopes (Int. Critics' Prize, Venice Film Festival 1989, London Evening Standard Peter Sellers Best Comedy Film Award 1990) 1989, Life is Sweet 1991, Naked (Best Dir Cannes Film Festival 1993) 1993, Secrets and Lies (winner Palme d'Or) 1996, (Alexander Korda Award, BAFTA 1997), Career Girls 1997, Topsy-Turvy 1999 (London Evening Standard Best Film 1999, Los Angeles Film Critics' Circle Best Film 1999, New York Film Critics' Circle Best Film 1999), All or Nothing 2002, Vera Drake (Best British Ind. Film, Best Dir, British Ind. Film Awards, Best Film, Evening Standard British Film Awards 2005, David Lean Award for Achievement in Direction, BAFTA Awards 2005) 2004, Happy-Go-Lucky 2008, Another Year 2010. *Radio play:* Too Much of a Good Thing 1979. *Publications:* Abigail's Party and Goose-Pimples 1982, Ecstasy and Smelling a Rat 1989, Naked and other Screenplays 1995, Secrets and Lies 1997, Career Girls 1997, Topsy-Turvy 1999, All or Nothing 2002, Two Thousand Years 2006, Vera Drake 2008, Mike Leigh on Mike Leigh 2008. *Honours:* Officier des Arts et des Lettres; Hon. MA (Salford) 1991, (Northampton) 2000; Hon. DLitt (Staffs.) 2000, (Essex) 2002. *Literary Agent:* United Agents, 12–26 Lexington Street, London W1F 0LE, England. *Telephone:* (20) 3214-0800. *Fax:* (20) 3214-0801. *E-mail:* info@unitedagents.co.uk. *Website:* unitedagents.co.uk.

LEITH, Linda, BA, PhD; Canadian writer; *President, Linda Leith Publishing*; b. 13 Dec. 1949, Belfast, Northern Ireland; d. of John Desmond Fitzhugh Leith and Annie May McClure; three s. *Education:* McGill Univ., Univ. of Paris-Sorbonne, Queen Mary Coll., London. *Career:* Founder Blue Metropolis Foundation, fmr Artistic Dir Blue Metropolis Montreal Int. Literary Festival; Pres. Linda Leith Publishing. *Publications:* Telling Differences: New English Fiction From Quebec (anthology) 1989, Introducing Hugh MacLennan's 'Two Solitudes' (essay) 1990, Birds of Passage (novel) 1993, The Tragedy Queen (novel) 1995, Travels with an Umbrella: An Irish Journey (translation) 2000, Epouser la Hongrie (memoir) 2004, The Desert Lake (novel) 2007, Marrying Hungary (memoir) 2008, Writing in the Time of Nationalism (literary history/memoir) 2010. *Honours:* First Award of Excellence, Linguistic Duality Commr of Official Languages. *E-mail:* leith.lindaleith@gmail.com. *Website:* www.lindaleith.com.

LEITHAUSER, Brad, BA, JD; American poet, writer and academic; *Professor, Writing Seminars, Johns Hopkins University*; b. 27 Feb. 1953, Detroit, Mich.; m. Mary Jo Salter 1980; two d. *Education:* Harvard Univ. *Career:* Research

Fellow, Kyoto Comparative Law Center 1980–83; Visiting Writer, Amherst Coll. 1984–85; Lecturer, Mount Holyoke Coll. 1987–2007; Prof., Writing Seminars, Johns Hopkins Univ. 2008–. *Publications include:* poetry: Hundreds of Fireflies 1982, A Seaside Mountain: Eight Poems from Japan 1985, Cats of the Temple 1986, Between Leaps: Poems 1972–1985 1987, The Mail from Anywhere: Poems 1990, The Odd Last Thing She Did 1998, Lettered Creatures 2005, Curves and Angels 2006, Toad to a Nightingale 2007; fiction: The Line of Ladies 1975, Equal Distance 1985, Hence 1989, Seaward 1993, A Few Corrections 2001, Darlington's Fall 2002, The Art Student's War 2009; non-fiction: Penchants & Places: Essays and Criticism 1995; editor: The Norton Book of Ghost Stories 1994, No Other Book 1999. *Honours:* Order of the Falcon (Iceland) 2005; Harvard Univ.-Acad. of American Poets Prize 1973, 1975, Harvard Univ. McKim Garrison Prize 1974, 1975, Amy Lowell Traveling Scholarship 1981–82, Guggenheim Fellowship 1982–83, Lavan Younger Poets Award 1983, John D. and Catherine T. MacArthur Foundation Fellowship 1983–87, 2004, Meribeth E. Cameron Faculty Award for Scholarship, Mount Holyoke Coll. 2004. *Address:* 100 University Parkway, 9–B, Baltimore, MD 21210, USA (home). *Telephone:* (443) 449-6920 (home). *E-mail:* bleithau@jhu.edu (office). *Website:* writingseminars.jhu.edu/faculty_directory/leithauser.html (office).

LELAND, Christopher Towne, BA, MA, PhD; American writer and academic; b. 17 Oct. 1951, Tulsa, Oklahoma. *Education:* Pomona College, University of California at San Diego. *Career:* Prof. of English, Wayne State University, 1990–; mem. Poets and Writers; MLA. *Publications:* Mean Time, 1982; The Last Happy Men: The Generation of 1922, Fiction and the Argentine Reality, 1986; Mrs Randall, 1987; The Book of Marvels, 1990; The Prof. of Aesthetics, 1994; Letting Loose, 1996; The Art of Compelling Fiction, 1998. Contributions: Principal Translator, Open Door by Luise Valenzvela 1988. *Honours:* Fellow, Massachusetts Artists Foundation, 1985. *Address:* c/o Dept of English, Wayne State University, Detroit, MI 48202, USA.

LELCHUK, Alan, BA, MA, PhD; American writer and teacher; b. 15 Sept. 1938, New York, NY; m. Barbara 1981; two s. *Education:* Brooklyn Coll., CUNY, Stanford Univ. *Career:* has taught at Brandeis Univ. 1966–81; Amherst Coll. 1982–84; Dartmouth Coll. 1985–; Visiting Writer, Prof., Haifa Univ. 1986–87, CUNY 1993; Visiting Writer, Univ. of Rome II 1996; Salgo Prof. in American Literature, ELTE University, Budapest 1999–2000; Fulbright Prof., Int. Univ. of Moscow 2003; Fulbright Sr Specialist Prof. in Creative Writing and American Literature, Moscow State Univ., Univ. of Naples, Free Univ. of Berlin 2005–; co-founder and Ed., Steerforth Press 1993–. *Publications:* fiction: American Mischief 1973, Shrinking 1978, Miriam in Her Forties 1985, Brooklyn Roy 1990, Playing the Game 1995, Ziff: A Life? 2003; for young adults: On Home Ground 1987, Eight Great Hebrew Short Novels (co-ed.) 1982; contributions: New York Times Book Review, New Republic, Dissent, Atlantic Monthly, New York Review of Books. *Honours:* Guggenheim Fellowship 1976–77, Fulbright Award 1986–87. *Literary Agent:* c/o Georges Borchardt, 136 E 57th Street, New York, NY 10022, USA. *Address:* Steerforth Press, 45 Lyme Road, Suite 208, Hanover, NH 03755, USA (office). *Telephone:* (603) 643-4787 (office). *Fax:* (603) 643-4788 (office). *E-mail:* info@steerforth.com (office); alan.leichuk@dartmouth.edu (office). *Website:* www.steerforth.com (office).

LELCHUK, Alan, BA, MA, PhD; American writer; *Professor of Literature and Writing, Dartmouth College*; b. 15 Sept. 1938, New York, NY; m. Barbara Kreiger 1979; two s. *Education:* Brooklyn Coll., Stanford Univ. *Career:* Brandeis Univ. 1966–81; Assoc. Ed. Modern Occasions 1980–82; Amherst Coll. 1982–84; Prof. of Literature and Writing, Dartmouth Coll. 1985–; Fulbright Writer-in-Residence, Haifa Univ., Israel 1986–87; Visiting Writer, City Coll., CUNY 1991; Ed., Publr Steerforth Press, South Royalton, Vt 1993–; Salgo Prof. of American Literature and Writing, ELTE Univ., Budapest, Hungary 1999–2000; Fulbright Prof., Int. Univ. of Moscow 2003–04; Fulbright Sr Specialist Prof., Moscow State Univ. 2005; mem. PEN, Authors' Guild. *Publications:* American Mischief 1973, Miriam at Thirty-Four 1974, Shrinking: The Beginning of My Own Ending 1978, 8 Great Hebrew Short Novels (co-ed.) 1983, Miriam in her Forties 1985, On Home Ground 1987, Brooklyn Boy 1989, Playing the Game 1995, Ziff: A Life? 2003; contrib. to New York Times Book Review, Sewanee Review, Atlantic, New Republic, Dissent, New York Review of Books. *Honours:* Guggenheim Fellowship 1976–77, Mishkenot Sha'Ananim Resident Fellow 1976–77, Fulbright Awards 1986–87, (Russia) 2003–04, Manuscript Collection Mugar Memorial Library, Boston Univ. *Address:* RFD 2, Canaan, NH 03741 (office); 176 Fethwood Farms Road, Canaan, NH 03741, USA (home). *Telephone:* (603) 523-4241 (home). *E-mail:* alan.lelchuk@dartmouth.edu (office).

LELYVELD, Joseph Salem; American journalist; b. 5 April 1937, Cincinnati; s. of Arthur Joseph Lelyveld and Toby Bookholz; m. Carolyn Fox 1958; two d. *Education:* Columbia Univ., New York. *Career:* reporter, Ed. New York Times 1963–, Foreign Corresp. Johannesburg, New Delhi, Hong Kong, London 1965–86, columnist, staff writer 1977, 1984–85, Foreign Ed. 1987–89, Deputy Man. Ed. 1989–90, Man. Ed. 1990–94, Exec. Ed. 1994–2001, Interim Exec. Ed. 2003. *Publication:* Move Your Shadow (Pulitzer Prize) 1985, Omaha Blues: A Memory Loop 2005. *Honours:* George Polk Memorial Award 1972, 1984. *Address:* c/o New York Times, 229 W 43rd Street, New York, NY 10036, USA.

LEMASTER, Jimmie Ray, BS, MA, PhD; American academic, poet, writer and editor; *Professor Emeritus of English, Baylor University*; b. 29 March 1934, Pike Co., Ohio; m. Wanda May Ohnesorge 1966; one s. two d. *Education:* Defiance Coll., Bowling Green State Univ., OH. *Career:* Faculty, Defiance Coll. 1962–77; Prof. of English and Dir of American Studies, Baylor Univ. 1977–2006, Prof. Emer. 2006–; Assoc. Ed., JASAT (Journal of the American Studies Association of Texas) 1988–90, Ed. 1992–96; mem. American Studies Asscn, Conf. of Coll. Teachers of English, Jesse Stuart Foundation (Bd of Dirs 1989–99), Mark Twain Circle of America, Modern Language Asscn. *Publications:* poetry: The Heart is a Gypsy 1967, Children of Adam 1971, Weeds and Wildflowers 1975, First Person, Second 1983, Purple Bamboo 1986, Journey to Beijing 1992, Journeys Around China 2004; other: Jesse Stuart: A Reference Guide 1979, Jesse Stuart: Kentucky's Chronicler-Poet 1980, The New Mark Twain Handbook (with E. Hudson Long) 1985; editor: Poets of the Midwest 1966, The World of Jesse Stuart: Selected Poems 1975, Jesse Stuart: Essays on His Work (with Mary Washington Clarke) 1977, Jesse Stuart: Selected Criticism 1978, Jesse Stuart on Education 1992, The Mark Twain Encyclopedia (with James D. Wilson) 1993, Walt Whitman: An Encyclopedia (with Donald D. Kummings) 1998, China Teacher: An Intimate Journal 2005, Walt Whitman and the Persian Poets (with Sabahat Jahan) 2009. *Honours:* Hon. DLitt (Defiance Coll.) 1988; South and West Inc. Publishers Award 1970, Ohio Poet of the Year 1976, American Library Asscn Outstanding Reference Source Citation 1993. *Telephone:* (254) 772-9829 (home). *E-mail:* j_r_lemaster@baylor.edu.

LENKIEWICZ, Rebecca; British playwright and actress; b. 1969, Plymouth. *Education:* Central School of Speech and Drama, London, Kent Univ. *Plays as actress:* Tales from Ovid, Bollocks, A Midsummer Night's Dream, Flight, Half Moon, King Lear, Twelfth Night, Two Gentlemen of Verona, Soho. *Television as actress:* State of Play, Casualty, Doctors, Down to Earth, The Inspector Lynley Mysteries. *Film as actress:* Wonderland 1999. *Plays as writer:* Soho 2000, The Night Season (Critics Circle Theatre Award for Most Promising Playwright 2005) 2004, Shoreditch Madonna (Soho Theatre, London) 2005. *Radio as writer:* Fighting for Words (BBC Radio 4) 2004. *Honours:* Fringe First, Edinburgh Festival 2000, Critics' Circle award for most promising playwright 2004. *Literary Agent:* c/o Georgina Ruffhead, David Higham Associates, 5–8 Lower John Street, Golden Square, London, W1F 9HA, England. *Telephone:* (20) 7434-5900. *Fax:* (20) 7437-1072. *E-mail:* dha@davidhigham.co.uk. *Website:* www.davidhigham.co.uk.

LENTRICCHIA, Frank, BA, MA, PhD; American academic and writer; *Gilbert Professor of Literature, Duke University*; b. 23 May 1940, Utica, NY; m. 1st Karen Young 1967 (divorced 1973); two c.; m. 2nd Melissa Christensen 1973 (divorced 1992); m. 3rd Johanna McAuliffe 1994; one c. *Education:* Utica Coll. of Syracuse Univ., Duke Univ. *Career:* Asst Prof., UCLA 1966–68; Asst Prof., Univ. of California, Irvine 1968–70, Assoc. Prof. 1970–76, Prof. 1976–82; Autrey Prof. of Humanities, Rice Univ. 1982–84; Gilbert Prof. of Literature, Duke Univ. 1984–; mem. MLA, PEN. *Publications:* The Gaiety of Language: An Essay on the Radical Poetics of W. B. Yeats and Wallace Stevens 1968, Robert Frost: Modern Poetics and the Landscapes of Self 1975, Robert Frost: A Bibliography, 1913–1974 (co-ed. with Melissa Christensen Lentricchia) 1976, After the New Criticism 1980, Criticism and Social Change 1983, Ariel and the Police 1988, Critical Terms for Literary Study 1990, New Essays on White Noise 1991, Introducing Don DeLillo 1991, The Edge of Night: A Confession 1994, Modernist Quartet 1994, Johnny Critelli and The Knifemen: Two Novels 1996, The Music of the Inferno: A Novel 1999, Lucchesi and The Whale 2001, Dissent from the Homeland (with Stanley Hauerwas) 2002, Close Reading: The Reader (with Andrew DuBois) 2003, Modernist Lyric in the Culture of Capital (with Andrew DuBois) 2003, Crimes of Art and Terror (with Jody McAuliffe) 2003, The Book of Ruth 2005, The Italian Actress 2008; contribs to professional journals. *Address:* Literature Program, Duke University, Box 90670, Room 101, Friedl Building, Durham, NC 27708-0001, USA (office). *Telephone:* (919) 684-6172 (office). *E-mail:* frll@duke.edu (office). *Website:* literature.aas.duke.edu (office).

LENZ, Siegfried; German writer; b. 17 March 1926, Lyck, East Prussia; m. Liselotte Lenz. *Education:* High School, Samter and Univ. of Hamburg. *Career:* Cultural Ed. Die Welt 1949–51; freelance writer 1952–. *Publications include:* Es waren Habichte in der Luft 1951, Duell mit dem Schatten 1953, So zärtlich was Suleyken 1955, Das schönste Fest der Welt 1956, Das Kabinett der Konterbande 1956, Der Mann im Strom 1957, 1958, Jäger des Spotts 1958, Lukas, sanftmütiger Knecht 1958, Brot und Spiele 1959, Das Feuerschiff 1960, Zait der Schuldlosen 1961, Stimmungen der See 1962, Stadtgespräche 1963, Das Gesicht 1964, Lehmanns Erzählungen 1964, Der Spielverderber 1965, Haussuchung 1967, Deutschstunde 1968, Leute von Hamburg 1968, Die Augenbinde 1970, Das Vorbild 1973, Wie bei Gogol 1973, Einstein überquert die Elbe bei Hamburg 1975, Heimatmuseum 1978, Drei Stücke 1980, Der Verlust 1981, Ein Kriegsende 1984, Das serbische Mädchen 1987, Die Auflehnung 1994, Ludmilla 1996, Arnes Nachlass 1999, Fundbüro 2003, Zaungast 2004, Die Erzählungen 2006, Ein Freund der Regierung 2006, Schweigeminute 2008, Kummer mit jütländischen Kaffeetafeln 2008, Der Anfang von etwas 2009; stories: So zärtlich war Suleyken 1955, Jäger des Spotts 1958, Das Feuerschiff 1960, Der Spielverderber 1965, Einstein überquert die Elbe bei Hamburg 1975; plays: Zeit der Schuldlosen 1961, Das Gesicht 1963, Haussuchung (radio plays) 1967. *Honours:* Hon. Citizen of Hamburg 2001–; Gerhart Hauptmann Prize 1961, Bremer Literaturpreis 1962, German Freemasons' Literary Prize 1970, Kulturpreis, Goslar 1978, Bayern Literary Prize 1995, Goethe Prize 1999, Lev Kopelev Prize for Peace and Human Rights 2009. *Address:* c/o Hoffman und Campe Verlag, Harvestehuder Weg 42, 20149 Hamburg, Germany (office). *E-mail:* email@hoca.de (office). *Website:* www.hoca.de (office).

LEON, Donna; American writer; b. 29 Sept. 1942, New Jersey. *Career:* has worked as a teacher in Switzerland, Saudi Arabia, Iran and China; fmrly lecturer in English Literature, Univ. of Maryland Univ. Coll. – Europe; currently lives in Venice, Italy. *Publications:* Death at La Fenice 1992, Death in a Strange Country 1993, The Anonymous Venetian (aka Dressed for Death) 1994, A Venetian Reckoning (aka Death and Judgment) 1995, Acqua Alta (aka Death in High Water) 1996, The Death of Faith (aka Quietly in Their Sleep) 1997, A Noble Radiance 1997, Fatal Remedies 1999, Friends in High Places (CWA Macallan Silver Dagger for Fiction) 2000, A Sea of Troubles 2001, Wilful Behaviour 2002, Uniform Justice 2003, Doctored Evidence 2004, Blood From A Stone 2005, Through A Glass, Darkly 2006, Suffer the Little Children 2007, The Girl of His Dreams 2008, A Question of Belief 2010. *Literary Agent:* c/o Diogenes Verlag AG, Sprecherstrasse 8, 8032 Zürich, Switzerland. *Telephone:* (44) 2548511. *Fax:* (44) 2528407. *E-mail:* info@diogenes.ch. *Website:* www.diogenes.ch; www.donnaleon.co.uk.

LEONARD, Elmore, PhB; American novelist and screenwriter; b. 11 Oct. 1925, New Orleans; s. of Elmore John and Flora Amelia Leonard (née Rivé); m. 1st Beverly Claire Cline 1949 (divorced 1977); three s. two d.; m. 2nd Joan Leanne Lancaster 1979 (died 1993); m. 3rd Christine Kent 1993. *Education:* Univ. of Detroit. *Career:* mem. Writers' Guild of America, Authors' Guild, MWA, Western Writers of America, PEN. *Television includes:* Justified (series) (exec. producer) 2010–. *Publications:* novels: The Bounty Hunters 1953, The Law at Randado 1954, Escape from Five Shadows 1956, Last Stand at Saber River 1959, Hombre 1961, The Big Bounce 1969, The Moonshine War 1969, Valdez is Coming 1970, Forty Lashes Less One 1972, Mr Majestyk 1974, Fifty-Two Pickup 1974, Swag 1976, Unknown Man #89 1977, The Hunted 1977, The Switch 1978, Gold Coast 1980, Gun Sights 1979, City Primeval 1980, Split Images 1981, Cat Chaser 1982, Stick 1983, La Brava 1983, Glitz 1985, Bandits 1986, Touch 1987, Freaky Deaky 1988, Killshot 1989, Get Shorty 1990, Maximum Bob 1991, Rum Punch 1992, Pronto 1993, Riding the Rap 1995, Out of Sight 1996, Jackie Brown 1997, Cuba Libre (also film screenplay) 1998, Be Cool (also film screenplay) 1999, Pagan Babies 2000, Tishomingo Blues 2002, When the Women Come Out to Dance 2002, A Coyote's in the House (juvenile) 2004, Mr Paradise 2004, The Hot Kid 2005, Comfort to the Enemy 2005, Up In Honey's Room 2007, Road Dogs 2009, Djibouti 2010, Raylan: A Novel 2012; short story collections: Dutch Treat 1985, Double Dutch Treat 1986, The Tonto Woman and Other Stories 1998, The Complete Western Stories 2006. *Honours:* Hon. DLitt (Florida Atlantic Univ.) 1995, (Univ. of Detroit Mercy) 1997; MWA Edgar Allan Poe Award 1984, MWA Grand Master Award 1992, Mich. Foundation for the Arts Award for Literature 1985, Cartier Diamond Dagger Award 2006, PEN Lifetime Achievement Award 2009. *Address:* c/o Michael Siegel, 9150 Wilshire Blvd, Suite 350, Beverly Hills, CA 90212, USA. *Website:* www.elmoreleonard.com.

LEONARD, Mark; British research institute director; *Senior Research Associate, Foreign Policy Centre. Career:* worked on policy and strategy devt for several nat. govts, int. governmental assocs and cos; Dir of European Programme, Demos –1998; Founding Dir. Foreign Policy Centre 1998, now Sr Research Assoc.; currently Dir of Foreign Policy Centre for European Reform. *Publications include:* research reports: Rebranding Britain, Network Europe 1998, The Future Shape of Europe 2000, Public Diplomacy (co-author) 2000, Public Diplomacy in the Middle East, Re-Ordering the World: The Long-Term Implications of September 11 (collection of essays), What Does China Think? 2007; 24 articles, including Rebranding Europe; Why Europe Will Run the 21st Century 2004. *Address:* Foreign Policy Centre, Suite 14, 2nd Floor, 23-28 Penn Street, Hoxton, London, N1 5DL, England (office). *Telephone:* (20) 7729-7566 (office). *Fax:* (20) 7729-7668 (office). *E-mail:* info@fpc.org.uk (office). *Website:* www.fpc.org.uk (office).

LEONARD, Richard (Dick) Lawrence, MA; British journalist, editor, broadcaster and writer; *Senior Research Associate, Foreign Policy Centre;* b. 12 Dec. 1930, Ealing, Middlesex; m. Irene Heidelberger 1963; one s. one d. *Education:* Inst. of Education, London and Essex Univ. *Career:* Sr Research Fellow, Essex Univ. 1968–70; MP Labour Party, Romford 1970–74; Asst Ed., The Economist 1974–85; Visiting Prof., Free Univ. of Brussels 1988–96; Brussels and European Union Correspondent, The Observer 1989–96; Sr Adviser, Center for European Policy Studies 1994–2000; Sr Research Assoc., Foreign Policy Centre 2004–; mem. Fabian Soc. (chair. 1977–78), Reform Club. *Publications:* Elections in Britain 1968, The Backbencher and Parliament (co-ed.) 1972, Paying for Party Politics 1975, The Socialist Agenda (co-ed.) 1981, World Atlas of Elections (co-author) 1986, Pocket Guide to the EEC 1988, Elections in Britain Today 1991, The Economist Guide to the European Community (10th edn as The Economist Guide to the European Union) 2010, Replacing the Lords 1995, Eminent Europeans (co-author) 1996, Crosland and New Labour (ed.) 1998, The Pro-European Reader (co-ed.) 2001, A Century of Premiers: Salisbury to Blair 2004, 19th Century Premiers: Pitt to Rosebery 2008, 18th Century Premiers: Walpole to the Younger Pitt 2010; contrib. to newspapers and periodicals worldwide. *Address:* 16 Albert Street, London NW1 7NZ, England (home).

LEONARD, Tom, MA; Scottish writer and poet; b. 22 Aug. 1944, Glasgow; m. Sonya Maria O'Brien 1971; two s. *Education:* Univ. of Glasgow. *Career:* Writer-in-Residence, Renfrew Dist Libraries 1986–89, Univ. of Glasgow/Univ. of Strathclyde 1991–92, Bell Coll. of Tech. 1993–94; Prof. of Creative Writing, Univ. of Glasgow 2001–09. *Publications:* Intimate Voices (Writing 1965–83) 1984, Situations Theoretical and Contemporary 1986, Radical Renfrew (ed.) 1990, Nora's Place 1990, Places of the Mind: The Life and Work of James Thomson 'BV' 1993, Reports From the Present 1995, access to the silence 2004, Being a Human Being 2006, Outside the Narrative: Poems 1965–2009. *Honours:* Jt Winner, Saltire Scottish Book of the Year Award 1984, Scottish Book of the Year Award 2010. *Address:* 56 Eldon Street, Glasgow, G3 6NJ, Scotland (home). *E-mail:* mail@tomleonard.co.uk (office). *Website:* www.tomleonard.co.uk.

LEONG, Russell Charles, (Wallace Lin), BA, MFA; American writer, poet and editor; *Adjunct Full Professor of English, University of California, Los Angeles;* b. 7 Sept. 1950, San Francisco. *Education:* San Francisco State Coll., Nat. Taiwan Univ., Univ. of California, Los Angeles. *Career:* Adjunct Full Prof. of English, Dept of English, UCLA, also Ed. Amerasia Journal, Asian American Studies Center. *Publications:* fiction: Phoenix Eyes and Other Stories (American Book Award 2001) 2000; poetry: The Country of Dreams and Dust (PEN Josephine Miles Literature Award) 1993; non-fiction: A History Reclaimed: An Annotated Bibliography of Chinese Language Materials on the Chinese of America (ed. with Jean Pang Yip) 1986, Frontiers of Asian American Studies: Writing, Research, and Criticism (ed. with G. Nomura, R. Endo and S. Sumida) 1989, Moving the Image: Independent Asian Pacific American Media Arts 1970–1990 (ed.) 1991, Los Angeles—Struggle toward Multiethnic Community: Asian America, African America, and Latino Perspectives (ed. with Edward T. Chang) 1995, Asian American Sexuality: Dimensions of the Gay and Lesbian Experience 1996; contrib. to anthologies and periodicals. *Address:* Asian American Studies Center, 3227 Campbell Hall, University of California, Los Angeles, CA 90095-1546, USA (office). *Telephone:* (310) 206-2892 (office). *Fax:* (310) 206-9844 (office). *E-mail:* rleong@ucla.edu (office). *Website:* www.aasc.ucla.edu/people/rleong.htm.

LEONTYEV, Mikhail Vladimirovich; Russian journalist; b. 12 Oct. 1958, Moscow; m.; two c. *Education:* Moscow Plekhanov Inst. of Nat. Econs. *Career:* political reviewer Kommersant (newspaper) 1987–90; on staff newspaper Atmoda (Riga) and Experimental Creative Cen. in Moscow 1989–91; Ed. Div. of Politics Nezavisimaya Gazeta (newspaper) 1990–92; First Deputy Ed.-in-Chief Business MN (daily) 1992–93; First Deputy Ed.-in-Chief Segodnya (newspaper) 1993–97; political reviewer TV-Cen. Channel 1997–98, ORT Channel 1999–; Ed.-in-Chief journal Fas 2000–. *Address:* Obshchestvennoye Rossiyskoe Televideniye (ORT), Akademika Koroleva str. 12, 127000 Moscow, Russia (office). *Telephone:* (495) 217-94-72 (office); (495) 217-94-73 (office).

LEOTTA, Guido; Italian writer, poet, publisher and musician; b. 2 May 1957, Faenza; one s. *Career:* Pres., Tratti/Mobydick Cultural Co-operative and Publishing House, 1987; Author and Co-ordinator, Tratti Folk Festival, 1989–2007; plays saxophone and flute with blues-jazz quintet Faxtet. *Recordings:* CDs and audio books: Villes Visions (with French poet Sylviane Dupuis), Blue Notebook (with Flemish poet Willem M. Roggeman) 2007. *Publications:* Sacsaphone (collected novels), 1981; Anatre (short stories), 1989; Il Bambino Ulisse (children's stories), 1995; Passo Narrabile (novel), 1997; Leviatamo (poems), 1999; Doppio Diesis (novel), 2000, Inverni Dispari (poems) 2001, Il Silenzio del Trombone (short stories) 2003, Il Tempo è un Cerchio infinito epaziente (novel) 2007; contrib. to anthologies and magazines. *Honours:* Premio Leonforte for Children's Stories, 1991; Oun Laoghaire Poetry Prize, Ireland, 1994; Premio Selezione Bancarellino, 1996. *Address:* Via San Michele 3, 48018 Faenza, Italy. *Telephone:* (546) 681819. *E-mail:* tratti@fastwebnet.it.

LEPSCHY, Anna Laura, MA, BLitt; Italian writer and academic; *Adjunct Professor, University of Toronto;* b. (Anna Laura Momigliano), 30 Nov. 1933, Turin; d. of Arnaldo Momigliano and Gemma Segre; m. 1962. *Education:* Somerville Coll., Oxford. *Career:* Prof. of Italian, Univ. Coll., London, now Prof. Emer.; Visiting Prof., Univ. of Cambridge; currently Adjunct Prof., Univ. of Toronto; mem. Pirandello Soc. (Pres. 1988–92), Soc. for Italian Studies (Chair. 1988–95), Asscn for the Study of Modern Italy, Associazione Internazionale di Lingua e Letteratura Italiana (Vice-Pres. 1998–). *Publications include:* Viaggio in Terrasanta 1480 1966, The Italian Language Today (co-author) 1977, Tintoretto Observed 1983, Narrativa e Teatro fra due Secoli 1984, Varietà linguistiche e pluralità di codici nel Rinascimento 1996, Davanti a Tintoretto 1998, L'amanuense analfabeta e altri saggi (co-author) 1999, Nell'officina del dizionario (co-ed.) 2008, Freud and Italian Culture (co-ed.) 2009, Into and Out of Italy: Lingua e cultura della migrazione italiana (co-ed.) 2010; contrib. to Italian Studies, Romance Studies, Studi Francesi, Studi sul Boccaccio, Studi Novecenteschi, Yearbook of the Pirandello Society, Modern Languages Notes, Lettere Italiane. *Honours:* Hon. Research Fellow, Univ. of Cambridge; Hon. Fellow, Somerville Coll., Oxford; Hon. Prof., Univ. of Bangor; Ufficiale al Merito della Repubblica Italiana 1994, Commendatore della Repubblica Italiana 2003; Serena Medal, British Acad. 2010. *Address:* Department of Italian, University College, Gower Street, London, WC1E 6BT, England (office). *Telephone:* (20) 7679-7784 (office). *E-mail:* a.lepschy@ucl.ac.uk (office).

LERMAN, Rhoda, BA; American writer; b. 18 Jan. 1936, Far Rockaway, NY; m. Robert Lerman 1957, one s. two d. *Education:* University of Miami. *Career:* National Endowment for the Arts Distinguished Prof. of Creative Writing, Hartwick College, Oneonta, New York, 1985; Visiting Prof. of Creative Writing, 1988, 1990, Chair in English Literature, 1990, SUNY at Buffalo.

Publications: Call Me Ishtar, 1973; Girl That He Marries, 1976; Eleanor, a Novel, 1979; Book of the Night, 1984; God's Ear, 1989; Animal Acts, 1994.

LERNER, Laurence David, MA, FRSL; British retd academic, writer and poet; b. 12 Dec. 1925, Cape Town, South Africa; m. Natalie Winch 1948; four s. *Education:* Univ. of Cape Town, Pembroke Coll., Cambridge. *Career:* Lecturer, Univ. Coll. of the Gold Coast 1949–53, Queen's Univ. 1953–62; Lecturer to Prof., Univ. of Sussex 1962–84; Kenan Prof., Vanderbilt Univ., Nashville, Tennessee 1985–95; several visiting professorships. *Publications:* Poems 1955, Domestic Interior and Other Poems 1959, The Directions of Memory: Poems 1958–63 1964, Selves 1969, A.R.T.H.U.R.: The Life and Opinions of a Digital Computer 1974, The Man I Killed 1980, A.R.T.H.U.R. and M.A.R.T.H.A., or, The Loves of the Computer 1980, Chapter and Verse: Bible Poems 1984, Selected Poems 1984, Rembrandt's Mirror 1987; fiction: The Englishmen 1959, A Free Man 1968, My Grandfather's Grandfather 1985; play: The Experiment 1980; non-fiction: The Truest Poetry 1960, The Truthtellers: Jane Austen, George Eliot, Lawrence 1967, The Uses of Nostalgia 1973, An Introduction to English Poetry 1975, Love and Marriage: Literature in its Social Context 1979, The Frontiers of Literature 1988, Angels and Absences 1997, Philip Larkin 1997, Wandering Prof. 1999; contributions: newspapers, reviews, journals, and magazines. *Honours:* South-East Arts Literature Prize 1979. *Address:* Abinger, 1-B Gundreda Road, Lewes, East Sussex BN7 1PT, England (home).

LERNER, Rabbi Michael Phillip, AB, MA, PhD; American writer; b. 7 Feb. 1943, Newark, NJ. *Education:* Columbia Univ., Univ. of California at Berkeley. *Career:* Rabbi of Beyt Tikkun synagogue; founder Ed., TIKKUN magazine 1986–. *Publications:* Surplus Powerlessness 1986, Jewish Renewal 1994, Blacks and Jews 1995, The Politics of Meaning 1995, Spirit Matters: Global Healing and the Wisdom of the Soul 2000, Best Contemporary Jewish Writing (ed.) 2001, Healing Israel/Palestine 2003, The Geneva Accord and Other Strategies for Middle East Peace 2004, The Left Hand of God: Taking Our Country Back from the Relligious Right 2006; contrib. to newspapers and magazines. *Honours:* PEN Award 2001. *Address:* c/o Tikkun Magazine, 2342 Shattuck Avenue, #1200, Berkeley, CA 94704, USA. *E-mail:* RabbiLerner@tikkun.org. *Website:* www.tikkun.org.

LERNER, Robert Earl, BA, MA, PhD; American academic and writer; *Peter B. Ritzma Professor in the Humanities Emeritus, Northwestern University*; b. 8 Feb. 1940, New York, NY; m. Erdmut Krumnack 1963; two d. *Education:* Univ. of Chicago, Princeton Univ. and Univ. of Münster. *Career:* Instructor, Princeton Univ. 1963–64; Asst Prof., Western Reserve Univ. 1964–67; Asst Prof., Northwestern Univ. 1967–71, Assoc. Prof. 1971–76, Prof. 1976–, Peter B. Ritzma Prof. in the Humanities 1993–, now Emer.; Fellow, Woodrow Wilson Center for Scholars 1996–97. *Publications:* The Age of Adversity: The Fourteenth Century 1968, The Heresy of the Free Spirit in the Later Middle Ages 1972, Western Civilizations (co-author, ninth–12th edns) 1980–98, World Civilizations (co-author, sixth–ninth edns) 1982–97, The Powers of Prophecy: The Cedar of Lebanon Vision from the Mongol Onslaught to the Dawn of the Enlightenment 1983, Weissagungen über die Päpste (with Robert Moynihan) 1985, Johannes de Rupescissa, Liber secretorum eventuum: Edition critique, traduction et introduction historique (with C. Morerod-Fattebert) 1994, Propaganda Miniata: Le origini delle profezie papali 'Ascende Calve' (with Orit Schwartz) 1994, Neue Richtungen in der hoch – und spätmittelalterlichen Bibelexegese (ed.) 1995, The Feast of Saint Abraham 2000; contrib. to professional journals, Times Literary Supplement. *Honours:* Fulbright Sr Fellowship 1967–68, Nat. Endowment for the Humanities research grant 1972–73, American Acad. in Rome Fellowship 1983–84, Guggenheim Fellowship 1984–85, Rockefeller Foundation Study Center Residency, Bellagio, Italy 1989, Historisches Kolleg, Munich, Forschungspreis 1992, Stipendiat 1992–93, Max-Planck-Gesellschaft Prize for Int. Co-operation 1998. *Address:* Department of History, Northwestern University, Evanston, IL 60208, USA (office). *E-mail:* rlerner@northwestern.edu (office).

LEROI, Armand Marie, BSc, PhD; Dutch evolutionary biologist; *Reader in Evolutionary Developmental Biology, Imperial College London*; b. 16 July 1964, Wellington, New Zealand. *Education:* Dalhousie Univ., Halifax, Canada, Univ. of California at Irvine, USA. *Career:* postdoctoral work at the Albert Einstein Coll. of Medicine, New York; Lecturer Imperial Coll. London 1996–2001, Reader in Evolutionary Developmental Biology 2001–. *Television:* Mutants (three-part series, Channel 4) 2004. *Publications:* Mutants: On the Form, Varieties and Errors of the Human Body (Guardian First Book Award 2004) 2003; contrib. to London Review of Books; numerous research papers. *Address:* Department of Biological Sciences, Silwood Park Campus, Imperial College London, Ascot, Berkshire SL5 7PY, England (office). *Telephone:* (20) 7594-2396 (office). *Fax:* (20) 7594-2339 (office). *E-mail:* a.leroi@imperial.ac.uk (office). *Website:* www.armandleroi.com.

LEROY, Gilles; French writer; b. 28 Dec. 1958, Bagneux. *Publications:* Habibi (novel) 1987, Maman est morte 1990, Les Derniers seront les premiers (short stories) 1991, Madame X (novel) 1992, Les Jardins publics (novel) 1994, Les Maîtres du monde (novel) 1996, Machines à sous (novel) 1998, Soleil noir (novel) 2000, L'amant russe (novel) 2002, Grandir (novel) 2004, Le Jour des fleurs (play) 2004, Champsecret (novel) 2005, Alabama Song (Prix Goncourt 2007) 2007, Zola Jackson (novel) 2010. *Honours:* Chevalier des Arts et des Lettres, Ordre nat. du Mérite; Prix Valery-Larbaud 1999, Prix Millepages 2004, Prix du roman de Cabourg 2004, Prix Eté du Livre 2010. *Address:* c/o Mercure de France SA, Editions Gallimard, 26 rue de Conde, 75006 Paris (office); 53 rue Pernety, 75014 Paris, France (home). *Telephone:* 6-88-32-81-59 (mobile). *E-mail:* contact@gillesleroy.net (office). *Website:* gillesleroy.net.

LESCHAK, Peter, BA; American writer and fireman; b. 11 May 1951, Chisholm, MN; m. Pamela Cope May 1974. *Education:* Ambassador Coll., TX. *Career:* Contributing Ed., Twin Cities magazine 1984–86, Minnesota Monthly 1984–89; mem. Authors' Guild. *Publications:* Letters from Side Lake 1987, The Bear Guardian 1990, Bumming with the Furies 1993, Seeing the Raven 1994, Hellroaring 1994, The Snow Lotus 1996, Rogues and Toads 1999, Trials by Wildfire 2000, Ghosts of the Fireground 2002. *Honours:* Minnesota Book Award 1991. *Address:* PO Box 51, Side Lake, MN 55781, USA. *E-mail:* pleschak@cpinternet.com.

LESOURNE, Jacques François; French newspaper editor, economist and academic; *President, Futuribles International*; b. 26 Dec. 1928, La Rochelle; s. of André Lesourne and Simone Lesourne (née Guille); m. Odile Melin, 1961; one s. two d. *Education:* Lycée Montaigne, Bordeaux, École Polytechnique, École Nationale Supérieure des Mines de Paris. *Career:* Head Econ. Service of French Collieries 1954–57; Dir Gen., later Pres. METRA Int. and SEMA 1958–75; Prof. of Econs École des Mines de Saint-Étienne 1958–61; Prof. of Industrial Econs École Nationale Supérieure de la Statistique 1960–63; Pres. Asscn Française d'Informatique et de Recherche Operationnelle 1966–67; mem. Council Int. Inst. of Applied Systems Analysis, Vienna 1973–79, Inst. of Man. Science 1976–79; Prof. Conservatoire Nat. des Arts et Métiers 1974–; Dir Projet Interfuturs OECD 1976–79; Dir of Studies, Inst. Auguste Comte 1979–81; Pres. Comm. on Employment and Social Relations of 8th Plan 1979–81; mem. Comm. du Bilan 1981, Council European Econ. Asscn 1984–89; Pres. Asscn Française de Science Économique 1981–83, Int. Federation of Operational Research Socs 1986–89; Dir and Man. Ed. Le Monde 1991–94; Pres. Futuribles Int. 1993–, Centre for Study and Research on Qualifications 1996–; Bd mem. Acad. des Technologies. *Publications:* Economic Technique and Industrial Management 1958, Du bon usage de l'étude économique dans l'entreprise 1966, Les systèmes du destin 1976, L'entreprise et ses futurs 1985, Éducation et société, L'après-Communisme, de l'Atlantique à l'Oural 1990, The Economics of Order and Disorder 1991, Vérités et mensonges sur le chômage 1995, Le Modèle français: Grandeur et Décadence 1998, Un Homme de notre Siècle 2000, Ces Avenirs qui n'ont pas eu lieu 2001, Leçons de Microéconomie évolutionniste (with André Orléan and Bernard Walliser) 2002, Democratie: Marché et Gouvernance, Quels Avenirs? 2004, Evolutionary Microeconomics (with André Orléan and Bernard Walliser) 2006, La recherche et l'innovation en France (with Denis Radet) 2007, 2008, 2009, Les crises et le XXIème siècle 2009, L'humanité face au changement climatique (with R. Dautray) 2009. *Honours:* Officier, Légion d'honneur 1993, Commdr 2009, Commdr, Ordre nat. du Mérite, Officier des Palmes académiques. *Address:* 52 rue de Vaugirard, 75006 Paris, France. *Telephone:* 1-43-25-66-05. *Fax:* 1-56-24-47-98. *E-mail:* jolesourne@wanadoo.fr. *Website:* www.futuribles.com.

LESSARD, Suzannah, BA; American writer; b. 12 Jan. 1944, Islip, NY; one s. *Education:* Columbia School of General Studies. *Career:* Ed., Contributor, Washington Monthly, 1969–73; Staff Writer, New Yorker, 1975–95; mem. PEN. *Publications:* The Architect of Desire: Beauty and Danger in the Stanford White Family. *Honours:* Whiting Award, 1995; Woodrow Wilson International Center for Scholars Fellow, 2001–02; Jenny Moore Writer's Fellowship, George Washington University, 2002–03. *Address:* c/o The Dial Press, 1540 Broadway, New York, NY 10036, USA.

LESSER, Rika Ellen, BA, MFA; American poet, translator and educator; b. 21 July 1953, Brooklyn, NY; d. of Milton Lesser and Celia Lesser. *Education:* Yale Univ., Univ. of Göteborg, Sweden, Columbia Univ. *Career:* Visiting Lecturer, Yale Univ. 1976, 1978, 1987–88, Baruch Coll., CUNY 1979; poetry workshop instructor, 92nd Street Y, New York 1982–85, 2003–07, trans. workshop instructor 2002; Jenny McKean Moore Visiting Lecturer in English, George Washington Univ. 1985–86; Master Artist-in-Residence, Atlantic Center for the Arts, New Smyrna Beach, Fla 1998; Adjunct Assoc. Prof. of Trans., Columbia Univ. 1998, 2005; featured poet, Geraldine R. Dodge Poetry Festival 2000; Guest Lecturer, Literary Trans., Grad. Writing Program, The New School 2003–06; mem. Acad. of American Poets, PEN American Center, ASCAP, Associated Writing Programs, Asscn. of Literary Scholars, Critics and Writers, Authors' Guild, Poets and Writers, Poetry Soc. of America. *Publications:* poetry: Etruscan Things 1983, All We Need of Hell 1995, Growing Back: Poems 1972–1992, 1997, Questions of Love: New and Selected Poems 2008; as trans.: Holding Out: Poems by Rainer Maria Rilke 1975, Hours in the Garden and Other Poems by Hermann Hesse 1979, Guide to the Underworld by Gunnar Ekelöf 1980, Rilke: Between Roots 1986, A Child Is Not a Knife: Selected Poems of Göran Sonnevi 1993, What Became Words by Claes Andersson 1996, Siddhartha: An Indic Poem by Hermann Hesse 2007, Mozart's Third Brain by Göran Sonnevi 2009; as ed.: Pictor's Metamorphoses and Other Fantasies by Hermann Hesse 1982, Hansel and Gretel (Retelling of the Grimms' tale) 1984 (ALA Notable Book and Caldecott Honor 1985), The Hideout by Sigrid Heuck 1988, A Living Soul by P. C. Jersild 1988, A Hand Full of Stars by Rafik Schami 1990, Agnes Cecilia by Maria Gripe 1990, Prose Translations and Retellings: My Sister Lotta and Me (retelling of Swedish picture book Min syster Lotta och jag) 1993, The New European Poets (Wayne Miller & Kevin Prufer, Eds) 2008; editor & sometimes translator for the Swedish-language poets of Sweden and Finland; co-editor for Sami poetry. *Honours:* Amy Lowell Poetry Traveling Scholarship 1974, John Courtney Murray Fellowship, Yale Univ. 1974, David Oliker Award, American Review

1974, Ingram Merrill Foundation Award (Poetry) 1978–79, Harold Morton Landon Trans. Prize for Poetry, Acad. of American Poets 1982, grants 1981–91 from Swedish Inst., Swedish Information Services, Finnish Literature Information Center to work on translations of various Swedish and Finland-Swedish writers; Batchelder Award 1990, American-Scandinavian Foundation Trans. Prize 1992, 2002, George Bogin Memorial Award, Poetry Soc. of America 1992, Stover Award (Southwest Review) for poetry 1993, Swedish Writers' Foundation Award 1995, Swedish Acad. Poetry Trans. Prize 1996, Fulbright-Hays Sr Scholar Award, English Dept, Stockholm Univ. 1999, Nat. Endowment for the Arts Literature Fellowship 2001, Yaddo residency 2001, grants from Barbro Osher Pro Suecia Foundation and American-Scandinavian Foundation 2006, grant from Swedish Arts Council to attend WALTIC 2008. *Address:* 133 Henry Street, Apt 5, New York, NY 11201, USA (home). *Telephone:* (718) 852-1163 (office). *E-mail:* rika.lesser.mc.74@aya.yale.edu (office). *Website:* rikalesser.com.

LESSING, Doris May, CH, CLit; British author; b. 22 Oct. 1919, Kermanshah, Persia; d. of Alfred Cook Tayler and Emily Maude Tayler (née McVeagh); m. 1st F. A. C. Wisdom 1939–43; m. 2nd Gottfried Anton Nicolai Lessing 1944 (divorced 1949; two s. (one deceased) one d. *Education:* Roman Catholic Convent and Girls' High School, Salisbury, Southern Rhodesia. *Career:* Assoc. mem. American Acad. of Arts and Letters 1974, Nat. Inst. of Arts and Letters (USA) 1974; mem. Inst. for Cultural Research 1974; Pres. Book Trust 1996–. *Publications:* novels: The Grass is Singing 1950, Children of Violence (Martha Quest 1952, A Proper Marriage 1954, A Ripple from the Storm 1965, The Four-Gated City 1969), Retreat to Innocence 1956, The Golden Notebook (Prix Médicis for French trans., Carnet d'Or 1976) 1962, Landlocked 1965, Briefing for a Descent into Hell 1971, The Summer Before the Dark 1973, The Memoirs of a Survivor 1974, Canopus in Argos series (Re: Colonised Planet 5, Shikasta 1979, The Marriages between Zones Three, Four and Five 1980, The Sirian Experiments 1981, The Making of the Representative for Planet 8 1982, The Sentimental Agents in the Volyen Empire 1983), The Diary of a Good Neighbour (as Jane Somers) 1983, If the Old Could (as Jane Somers) 1984, The Diaries of Jane Somers 1984, The Good Terrorist (WHSmith Literary Award 1986, Palermo Prize and Premio Internazionale Mondello 1987) 1985, The Fifth Child 1988, Love, Again 1996, Playing the Game 1996, Mara and Dann: an Adventure 1999, Ben, in the World 2000, The Old Age of El Magnifico 2000, The Sweetest Dream 2001, The Story of General Dann and Mara's Daughter, Griot and the Snow Dog 2005, The Cleft 2007; short stories: Collected African Stories: Vol. 1, This Was the Old Chief's Country 1951, Vol. 2, The Sun Between Their Feet 1973, Five 1953, The Habit of Loving 1957, A Man and Two Women 1963, African Stories 1964, Winter in July 1966, The Black Madonna 1966, The Story of a Non-Marrying Man and Other Stories 1972, A Sunrise on the Veld 1975, A Mild Attack of the Locusts 1977, Collected Stories: Vol. 1, To Room Nineteen 1978, Vol. 2, The Temptation of Jack Orkney 1978, London Observed: Stories and Sketches 1992, The Grandmothers 2003; non-fiction includes: Going Home 1957 (revised edn 1968), In Pursuit of the English 1960, Particularly Cats 1967, Particularly Cats and More Cats 1989, African Laughter: Four Visits to Zimbabwe 1992, Under My Skin: Volume One of My Autobiography to 1949 (Los Angeles Times Book Prize 1995, James Tait Memorial Prize 1995) 1994, Walking in the Shade: Volume Two of My Autobiography 1949–62 1997, Time Bites 2004, Alfred and Emily 2008; plays: Each His Own Wilderness 1958, Play with a Tiger 1962, The Singing Door 1973; other: Fourteen Poems 1959, A Small Personal Voice 1974, Doris Lessing Reader 1990. *Honours:* Hon. Fellow, MLA 1974; Distinguished Fellow in Literature, Univ. of East Anglia 1991; Hon. DLitt (Princeton) 1989, Durham (1990), (Warwick) 1994, (Bard Coll. New York State) 1994, (Harvard) 1995, (Oxford) 1996; Somerset Maugham Award 1954, Soc. of Authors 1954–, Austrian State Prize for European Literature 1981, Shakespeare Prize, Hamburg 1982, Grinzane Cavour Award, Italy 1989, Woman of the Year, Norway 1995, Premio Internacional Cataluña, Spain 1999, David Cohen Literary Prize 2001, Príncipe de Asturias Prize, Spain 2001, PEN Award 2002, Nobel Prize in Literature 2007. *Literary Agent:* c/o Jonathan Clowes Ltd, Literary Agents, 10 Iron Bridge House, Bridge Approach, London, NW1 8BD, England. *Telephone:* (20) 7722-7674. *Fax:* (871) 5283647. *E-mail:* admin@jonathanclowes.co.uk. *Website:* www.jonathanclowes.co.uk; www.dorislessing.org.

LESTARI, Dewi, (Dee); Indonesian novelist and singer; b. 20 Jan. 1976, Bandung; m.; one s. *Education:* grad. of political and social sciences. *Career:* f. singing trio RSD (Rida, Sita, Dewi); f. Truedee Books to publish her first novel 2001–. *Recordings:* albums: with RSD: Antara Kita 1995, Bertiga 1997, Satu 1999; solo: Out of Shell 2006. *Publication:* Supernova (novel) 2001, Supernova 2.1: Akar 2003, Supernova: petir 2005, Rectus Verso. *Website:* dewilestari.com.

LETHEM, Jonathan Allen; American writer and editor; b. 19 Feb. 1964, New York, NY. *Education:* High School for Music and Art, New York; Bennington Coll., Vermont. *Publications:* Gun, with Occasional Music (novel) 1994, Amnesia Moon (novel) 1995, The Wall of the Sky, The Wall of the Eye (short stories) 1996, As She Climbed Across the Table (novel) 1997, Girl in Landscape (novel) 1998, Motherless Brooklyn (novel) 1999, This Shape We're In (novel) 2000, The Vintage Book of America (ed.) 2000, Da Capo Best Music Writing (ed. with Paul Bresnick) 2002, The Fortress of Solitude (novel) 2003, Men and Cartoons (short stories) 2004, The Disappointment Artist 2005, You Don't Love Me Yet (novel) 2007, Chronic City 2009, They Live (novel) 2010, The Ecstasy of Influence 2011. *Honours:* CWA Silver Dagger Award, The Salon Book Award, Nat. Book Critics' Circle Award.

LETTE, Kathy; Australian author and playwright; b. 11 Nov. 1958, Sydney; d. of Mervyn Lette and Val Lette; m. Geoffrey Robertson (q.v.) 1990; one s. one d. *Career:* fmr columnist, Sydney and NY; fmr satirical news writer and presenter Willasee Show, Channel 9; fmr TV sitcom writer Columbia Pictures, LA; fmr guest presenter This Morning with Richard and Judy, ITV; writer-in-residence, The Savoy, London 2003. *Plays include:* Wet Dreams 1985, Perfect Mismatch 1985, Grommits 1986, I'm So Happy For You, I Really Am 1991. *Films:* Puberty Blues 1982, Mad Cows 2001. *Publications:* Puberty Blues (with G. Carey) 1979, Hit and Ms 1984, Girls' Night Out 1987, The Llama Parlour 1991, Foetal Attraction 1993, Mad Cows 1996, She Done Him Wrong (essays), The Constant Sinner by Mae West (introduction) 1995, Altar Ego 1998, Nip 'n Tuck 2001, Dead Sexy 2003, How to Kill Your Husband 2005, A Stitch in Time 2005, To Love, Honour, and Betray 2009; contribs to Sydney Morning Herald, The Bulletin, Cleo Magazine. *Honours:* Australian Literature Board Grant 1982. *Address:* c/o Ed Victor, 6 Bayley Street, London, WC1B 3HB, England. *Telephone:* (20) 7304-4100 (office). *Fax:* (20) 7304-4111 (office). *E-mail:* kathy.lette@virgin.net (office). *Website:* www.kathylette.com.

LETTS, Tracy; American actor and playwright; b. 4 July 1965, Tulsa, Okla; s. of Dennis and Billie Letts. *Career:* debut play Killer Joe premiered at Next Lab Theater, Chicago 1993; ensemble mem. Steppenwolf Theatre Co. 2002–. *Plays as writer:* Bug, Killer Joe, Man from Nebraska, August: Osage County (Pulitzer Prize for Drama 2008), Superior Donuts. *Plays as actor:* O Dammit, The Glass Menagerie 1988, Picasso At The Lapin Agile 1994, Three Days Of Rain 1999, Glengarry Glen Ross 2001, The Dazzle 2002, Homebody/Kabul 2003, Man From Nebraska 2003, The Dresser 2004, The Pain and the Itch 2005, Last of the Boys 2005, The Well-Appointed Room 2006, The Pillowman 2006, Betrayal 2007. *Television:* actor: 1998, Judging Amy 1999, Profiler 2000, Strong Medicine 2001, The District 2001. *Films as writer:* Bug 2007, Cop Show 2007. *Films as actor:* Paramedics 1988, Straight Talk 1992, U.S. Marshals 1998, Chicago Cab 1998, Guinevere 1999. *Address:* Steppenwolf Theatre Company, 758 W. North Avenue, 4th floor, Chicago, IL 60610, USA (office). *Telephone:* (312) 335-1888 (office). *Fax:* (312) 335-1888 (office). *Website:* www.steppenwolf.org (office).

LEUTENEGGER, Gertrud; Swiss writer; b. 7 Dec. 1948, Schwyz; m. M. von Wartburg 1989; one d. *Education:* Schauspielakademie (Zurich). *Publications include:* Vorabend 1975, Ninive 1977, Lebewohl, Gute Reise 1980, Gouverneur 1981, Komm ins Schiff 1983, Kontinent 1985, Das verlorene Monument 1985, Meduse 1988, Acheron 1994, Sphärenklang 1999, Pomona 2004, Gleich nach dem Gotthard kommt der Mailänder Dom 2006, Matutin 2008. *Honours:* Ingeborg Bachmann Critics' Prize 1978, Drostepreis 1979.

LEVEL, Brigitte Marie Adélaïde, (Anne Acoluthe), DèsL; French writer; b. 31 Oct. 1918, Paris; d. of Maurice Level and Jacqueline Level (née Ancey de Curnieu); m. Christian Léon-Dufour 1941 (died 1983); four s. (two deceased) four d. (one deceased). *Education:* Cours du Colisée, Paris and Univ. of Paris (Sorbonne). *Career:* Prof., Univ. of Paris 1959–85; participant in numerous confs since retirement 1985; Producer Radio-Courtoisie 1988–; Pres. Acad. of Still Life Art 1994; Pres. French Poets Soc. 1985; Vice-Pres. Défense de la langue française, Hon. Vice-Pres. 2005– (Pres. Cercle Paul-Valéry). *Publications include:* as Anne Acoluthe, Geneviève Minne, Zoé Zou: poetry: La girafe dépeignée, L'oiseau bonheur, L'arche de Zoé, Le temps des guitares 1990, Le Zoo de Zoulou 1994; prose: Le caveau 1729–1939, Guillaume Apollinaire, André Level: lettres 1976, Masques 1990, Le poète et l'oiseau 1991, Le poète à la pêche, La bestiaire de Lais, Fables et fabulettes. *Honours:* Officier des Palmes Académiques 1971, Officier du Mérite Agricole 1981, Officier Ordre des Arts et des Lettres 1986, Chevalier Ordre nat. du mérite 1989; numerous other awards including Prix Acad. française, Prix Acad. des Jeux floraux (églantine), Grand Prix Pascal Bonetti 1988, Grand Prix des Poètes français 1996, Prix Daudet 1998 and Médaille de Vermeil de la Ville de Paris. *Address:* 22 rue Legendre, 75017 Paris, France. *Telephone:* (1) 46-22-71-25.

LEVENSON, Christopher, BA, MA; Canadian poet, editor, translator and educator; b. 13 Feb. 1934, London, England. *Education:* University of Cambridge, University of Bristol, University of Iowa. *Career:* teacher, University of Münster 1958–61, Carleton University, Ottawa 1968–99; Ed.-in-Chief, ARC magazine 1978–88; Founder-Dir, ARC Reading Series, Ottawa 1981–91; Series Ed., Harbinger Poetry Series 1995–99; Poetry Ed., Literary Review of Canada 1997; mem. League of Canadian Poets. *Publications:* poetry: In Transit 1959, Cairns 1969, Stills 1972, Into the Open 1977, The Journey Back 1978, Arriving at Night 1986, The Return 1986, Half Truths 1990, Duplicities: New and Selected Poems 1993, The Bridge 2000, Belvédère (trans.) 2002; other: Seeking Heart's Solace (trans.) 1981, Light of the World (trans.) 1982, Reconcilable Differences: The Changing Face of Poetry by Canadian Men Since 1970 (ed.) 1994, Requiem 53 (contributed texts to requiem for 50th anniversary of Dutch floods of 1953) 2003; contributions: various anthologies, reviews, quarterlies, and journals. *Honours:* Eric Gregory Award 1960, Archibald Lampman Award 1987. *Address:* 333 St Andrew Street, Ottawa, ON K1N 5G9, Canada (home). *E-mail:* clevenson@rogers.com (home).

LEVER, Sir (Tresham) Christopher Arthur Lindsay, Bt , MA, FRGS, FLS; British naturalist and writer; b. 9 Jan. 1932, London; s. of Sir Tresham Lever, Bt and Frances Yowart Goodwin; m. 1st 1970; m. 2nd Linda Weightman McDowell Goulden 1975. *Education:* Eton, Trinity Coll., Cambridge. *Career:*

fmrly stockbroker, accountant, co. dir 1954–64; Fellow WWF UK 2005–; consultant, trustee and council mem. various conservation and animal welfare organizations. *Publications:* Goldsmiths and Silversmiths of England 1975, The Naturalised Animals of the British Isles 1977, Naturalised Mammals of the World 1985, Naturalised Birds of the World 1987, The Mandarin Duck 1990, They Dined on Eland: The Story of the Acclimatisation Societies 1992, Naturalised Animals: The Ecology of Successfully Introduced Species 1994, Naturalised Fishes of the World 1996, The Cane Toad: The History and Ecology of a Successful Colonist 2001, Naturalised Reptiles and Amphibians of the World 2003, Naturalised Birds of the World 2005, The Naturalized Animals of Britain and Ireland 2009; contrib. to many books, professional journals and general publications. *Honours:* Hon. life mem., Brontë Soc. 1988, Hon. life Pres. Tusk Trust 2004–. *Address:* Newell House, Winkfield, Berkshire, SL4 4SE, England (home). *Telephone:* (1344) 882604 (home). *Fax:* (1344) 891744 (home).

LÉVESQUE, Anne-Michèle, BSc; Canadian writer; b. 29 May 1939, Val d'Or, QC; m. (deceased); two d. *Education:* Univ. of Montréal, Outremont Business Coll. *Career:* mem. Union des écrivaines et des écrivains québécois, Conseil de la Culture de l'Abitibi-Térniscamingue, Cercle des Écrivains de l'Abitibi-Térniscamingue. *Publications:* Persil Frisé 1992, A La Recherche d'un Salaud 1995, Fleurs de Corail 1995, La Maison du Puits Sacré 1997, Quartiers divers 1997, Meurtres à la sauce tomate 1999, Rapt 2000, Abitibissimo 2000, Fleur Invitait au Troisième 2001, La Revanche des Dieux 2002, Rumeurs et Marées 2002, AZ-3 (poems) Vol. I 2003, Vol. II 2004, Le Sang sur la Chantepleure 2004, Gabrielle en vancances au Mexique 2008, Crapules et Cie 2008, Météo surprise 2008, Dragons.com 2009, Les Enfants de Roches-Noires 2009, Escapade Météo 2010, Gabrielle et la visiteuse de l'au-dela 2010; contrib. to Lumière d'Encre, Arcade magazines. *Honours:* First Prize, Concours Littéraire 1991, Arthur Ellis Award for Best Mystery Novel in French (Canada) 2002. *Address:* 184 Williston Street, Val d'Or, QC J9P 4S7, Canada (office). *Telephone:* (819) 825-4190 (office). *E-mail:* mauve@amlevesque.ca (office). *Website:* www.amlevesque.ca.

LEVI, Arrigo, PhD; Italian journalist and political writer; b. 17 July 1926, Modena; s. of Enzo Levi and Ida Levi (née Donati); m. Carmela Lenci 1952; one d. *Education:* Univs of Buenos Aires and Bologna. *Career:* refugee in Argentina 1942–46; Negev Brigade, Israeli Army 1948–49; BBC European Services 1951–53; London Corresp. Gazzetta del Popolo and Corriere d'Informazione 1952–59; Moscow Corresp. Corriere della Sera 1960–62; news anchorman on Italian State Television 1966–68; special corresp. La Stampa 1969–73, Ed. in Chief 1973–78, Special Corresp. 1978–; columnist on int. affairs, The Times 1979–83; Leader Writer, Corriere della Sera 1988–. *Publications:* L'economia degli Stati Uniti oggi 1966, Il potere in Russia 1965, La televisione all'italiana 1969, Viaggio fra gli economisti 1970, PCI, la lunga marcia verso il potere 1971, Un'idea dell'Italia 1983, La Democrazia nell'Italia che cambia 1984, Intervista sulla Dc 1986, Noi: gli italiani 1988, Tra Est e Ovest 1990, Yitzhak Rabin 1996, Le due fedi 1996, La vecchiaia può attendere 1997, Rapporto sul Medio Oriente 1998, Russia del '900 1999, Dialoghi di fine Millennio 1999, Dialoghi sulla fede 1999, America Latina 2004, Cinque discorsi tra due secoli 2004. *Honours:* Premio Trento 1987, Premio Luigi Barzini 1995, Premio Ischia Internazionale di Giornalismo 2001.

LEVIN, Gabriel; French/Israeli/American poet, translator and editor; b. 13 Dec. 1948, France. *Career:* mem. Editorial Bd Ibis Editions, Jerusalem; Joseph B. Glossberg Visiting Israeli Scholar, Knox Coll., Galesburg, Ill. 2008. *Publications include:* poetry: Sleepers of Beulah 1992, Ostraca 1999, The Maltese Dreambook 2008; prose: Hezekiah's Tunnel 1997, Pleasant if Somewhat Rude Views 2005, The Maltese Dreambook 2008; translations: Poems from the Diwan, by Yehuda Halevi 2002, The Little Bookseller Oustaz Ali, by Ahmed Rassim 1997, Never Mind, by Taha Muhammad Ali 2000; editor: Found in Translation: A Hundred Years of Modern Hebrew Poetry 1999; contrib. to Times Literary Supplement, American Poetry Review, American Book Review, Boston Review, Parnassus, PN Review, Raritan. *Address:* c/o Ibis Editions, PO Box 8074, German Colony, Jerusalem, Israel (office). *E-mail:* ibis@netvision.net.il (office). *Website:* www.ibiseditions.com (office).

LEVIN, Gerald Manuel, BA, LLB; American fmr media executive; *Presiding Director, Moonview Sanctuary*; b. 6 May 1939, Philadelphia, Pa; s. of David Levin and Pauline Schantzer; m. 1st Carol S. Needlemam 1959 (divorced 1970), two s. (one s. deceased), one d.; m. 2nd Barbara Riley 1970, one s. one d.; m. 3rd Laurie Perlman 2005. *Education:* Haverford Coll. and Univ. of Pa. *Career:* Assoc. Simpson, Thatcher & Bartlett, New York 1963–67; Gen. Man., COO Devt and Resources Corpn New York 1967–71; Rep. Int. Basic Economy Corpn Tehran 1971–72; Vice-Pres. Programming, Home Box Office, New York 1972–73, Pres., CEO 1973–76, Chair., CEO 1976–79; Group Vice-Pres. (Video), Time Inc. New York 1979–84, Exec. Vice-Pres. 1984–88, Vice-Chair., Dir 1988–90; Vice-Chair., Dir Time-Warner Inc. 1990–92, Jt CEO 1992–93, CEO and Chair. 1992–2001, CEO AOL Time Warner (created after merger of Time Warner and American Online 2000) 2001–02 (retd); currently Presiding Dir Moonview Sanctuary (spiritual healing firm). *Honours:* Hon. LLD (Texas Coll.) 1985, (Middlebury Coll.) 1994, Hon. LHD (Univ. of Denver) 1995; Media Person of the Year Award, Cannes Lions Int. Advertising Festival 2001. *Address:* Moonview Sanctuary, PO Box 1518, Santa Monica, CA 90406, USA (office). *Telephone:* (866) 601-0601 (office). *E-mail:* glevin@moonviewsanctuary.com (office). *Website:* www.moonviewsanctuary.com (office).

LEVINE, Ellen; American magazine editor; *Editorial Director, Hearst Magazines;* b. 19 Feb. 1943, d. of Eugene Jack and Jean Jacobson; m. Richard U. Levine 1964; two s. *Education:* Wellesley Coll. *Career:* reporter The Record, Hackensack, NJ 1964–70; Ed. Cosmopolitan, New York 1976–82; Ed-in-Chief Cosmopolitan Living 1980–81, Woman's Day 1982–91, Redbook 1991–94, Good Housekeeping 1994–2006, Editorial Dir Hearst Magazines 2006–; mem. Bd of Dirs New York Restoration Project, Gaylord Entertainment and Finlay Enterprises, Inc., Lifetime Television; mem Bd of Advisors New York Women in Communications; fmr Dir NJ Bell, Newark; Commr Attorney-Gen's Comm. on Pornography 1985–86; mem. Exec. Cttee Sen. Bill Bradley 1984. *Publications:* Planning Your Wedding, Waiting for Baby, Rooms That Grow With Your Child. *Honours:* New York Women in Communications Inc. Matrix Award 1989, Birmingham Southern Coll. Honor Award 1991, Leadership in Media Award, American Legacy Foundation 2003, WISER Award, Heinz Family Philanthropies 2003, Wind Beneath My Wings Leadership Award, New York Restoration Project 2003, Wellesley Coll. Alumnae Achievement Award 2005. *Address:* The Hearst Corporation, Hearst Tower, 12th Floor, 300 West 57th Street, New York, NY 10019, USA (office). *Telephone:* (212) 649-4190 (office). *Fax:* (212) 649-2108 (office). *Website:* www.hearst.com/magazines (office).

LEVINE, Paul, BA, JD; American writer and lawyer; b. 9 Jan. 1948, Williamsport, PA; m. Alice Holmstrom 1975 (divorced 1992); one s. one d. *Education:* Pennsylvania State Univ., Univ. of Miami. *Career:* admitted to the Bar, State of Florida, 1973, US Supreme Court, 1977, District of Columbia, 1978, Commonwealth of Pennsylvania, 1989; Attorney and/or Partner, various law firms, 1973–91; mem. American Bar Asscn; American Trial Lawyers Asscn; Authors' Guild. *Publications:* What's Your Verdict?, 1980; To Speak for the Dead, 1990; Night Vision, 1992; False Dawn, 1994; Mortal Sin, 1994; Slashback, 1995; Fool Me Twice, 1996.

LEVINE, Philip, BA, AM, MFA; American poet, writer and academic (retd); b. 10 Jan. 1928, Detroit, Mich.; m. Frances Artley 1954; three s. *Education:* Wayne State Univ., Detroit, Univ. of Iowa, studied with John Berryman. *Career:* worked in several automobile mfg plants, Detroit; Instructor, California State Univ. at Fresno 1958–69, Prof. of English 1969–92; Elliston Prof. of Poetry, Univ. of Cincinnati 1976; Poet-in-Residence, ANU, Canberra 1978; Visiting Prof. of Poetry, Columbia Univ. 1978, 1981, 1984, New York Univ. 1984, 1991, Brown Univ. 1985; Poet Laureate of the US 2011–12; Chair. Literature Panel, Nat. Endowment for the Arts 1985; NEA grants 1969, 1976, 1981, 1987; Guggenheim Fellowships 1974, 1981; mem. American Acad. of Arts and Letters, Acad. of American Poets (Chancellor 2000–). *Publications:* poetry: On the Edge 1961, Silent in America: Vivas for Those Who Failed 1965, Not This Pig 1968, 5 Detroits 1970, Thistles: A Poem of Sequence 1970, Pili's Wall 1971, Red Dust 1971, They Feed, They Lion 1972, 1933 1974, New Season 1975, On the Edge and Over: Poems Old, Lost, and New 1976, The Names of the Lost 1976, 7 Years from Somewhere 1979, Ashes: Poems New and Old 1979, One for the Rose 1981, Selected Poems 1984, Sweet Will 1985, A Walk with Tom Jefferson 1988, New Selected Poems 1991, What Work Is (Nat. Book Award for Poetry 1991) 1991, The Simple Truth: Poems (Pulitzer Prize in Poetry 1995) 1994, The Mercy 1995, Breath 2004, News of the World 2009; non-fiction: Don't Ask (interviews) 1979, Earth, Stars, and Writers (with others, lectures) 1992, The Bread of Time: Toward an Autobiography 1994; contrib. to many anthologies and reviews. *Honours:* San Francisco Foundation Joseph Henry Jackson Award 1961, Frank O'Hara Prizes 1973, 1974, American Acad. of Arts and Letters Award of Merit 1974, Levinson Prize 1974, Univ. of Chicago Harriet Monroe Memorial Prize for Poetry 1976, Leonore Marshall Award for Best American Book of Poems 1976, American Book Award for Poetry 1979, Nat. Book Critics Circle Prize 1979, American Library Asscn Notable Book Award 1979, New England Poetry Soc. Golden Rose Award 1985, Ruth Lilly Award 1987, New York Univ. Elmer Holmes Bobst Award 1990, Commonwealth Club of California Silver Medal in Poetry 1992, 2000. *Address:* 4549 North Van Ness Blvd, Fresno, CA 93704, USA (home). *Telephone:* (209) 226-3361 (home). *E-mail:* pl24@nyu.edu (home). *Website:* www.loc.gov.poetry.

LEVINE, Stuart George, (Esteban O'Brien Córdoba), PhD; American academic, writer and musician; *Professor Emeritus, University of Kansas;* b. 25 May 1932, New York, NY; s. of Mex Levine and Jean Levine; m. Susan Fleming Matthews 1963; two s. one d. *Education:* Harvard and Brown Univs. *Career:* Instructor, Univ. of Kansas 1958–61, Asst Prof. 1961–65, Assoc. Prof. 1965–69, Chair. Dept of American Studies 1965–70, Prof. 1969–92, Prof. Emer. 1992–; Visiting Prof., Kansas State Univ. 1964, Univ. of Missouri at Kansas City 1966, 1974, California State Univ. at Los Angeles 1969, 1971; Fulbright Distinguished Lecturer, Naples, Italy 1995; Fulbright Professorships, Argentina, Mexico, Costa Rica, Chile; Guest Professorship, Univ. of the West Indies, Mona; Founder-Ed. American Studies 1959–90; many engagements as a professional French horn player. *Achievements:* several one-man shows of his paintings. *Radio:* Portfolio (writer and host, weekly music programme). *Publications:* Materials for Technical Writing 1963, The American Indian Today (with Nancy O. Lurie) 1968, Edgar Poe, Seer and Craftsman 1972, The Short Fiction of Edgar Allan Poe: An Annotated Edition (with Susan F. Levine) 1976, The Monday-Wednesday-Friday Girl and Other Stories 1994, Eureka: Edgar Allan Poe (with Susan F. Levine) 2004, Poe's Critical Theory: The Major Documents (ed. with Susan F. Levine) 2009; contribs to various scholarly reviews, quarterlies and journals. *Honours:* Anisfield-Wolf Award in Race Relations 1968, Theodore Blegen Award 1975, Citation for 30-year editorship of American Studies 1989, Gross Award for Short Fiction 1994. *Address:* Department of English, University of Kansas, Lawrence, KS 66045 (office); 1644 University Drive, Lawrence, KS 66044, USA (home). *Telephone:* (785) 864-4520 (office); (785) 842-0356 (home). *E-mail:* slevine@ku.edu (office); stuartglevine@gmail.com (home).

LEVINSON, Jerrold, BS, PhD; American academic and writer; *Professor, University of Maryland at College Park*; b. 11 July 1948, New York, NY; m. Karla Hoff 1985 (divorced 2004); one d. *Education:* Massachusetts Inst. of Tech., Univ. of Michigan. *Career:* Asst Prof., State Univ. of NY, Albany 1974–75; Asst Prof. 1976–81, Assoc. Prof. 1981–91, Prof. 1991–, Univ. of Maryland, College Park; Visiting Prof., Univ. of London, UK 1991, Johns Hopkins Univ. 1993, Univ. of Rennes, France 1998, Columbia Univ., New York 2000, Université Libre de Bruxelles, Belgium 2006, Univ. of Kent, UK 2008–09, Univ. of Leuven, Belgium 2010–11; mem. American Soc. for Aesthetics (Pres. 2001–03). *Publications:* Music, Art, and Metaphysics 1990 (second edn 2011), The Pleasures of Aesthetics 1996, Music in the Moment 1998, Aesthetics and Ethics (ed.) 1998, Oxford Handbook of Aesthetics (ed.) 2003, Contemplating Art 2006. *Honours:* Nat. Endowment for the Humanities Fellowship 1980, Chaire Francqui 2010–11, Premio della Società Italiana d'Estetica 2010. *Address:* 4209 Underwood Street, University Park, MD 20782, USA (office). *Telephone:* (301) 405-5693 (office). *E-mail:* august@umd.edu (office).

LEVINSON, Leonard, (Nicholas Brady, Clay Dawson, Josh Edwards, J. Farragut Jones, Leonard Jordan, Philip King, John Mackie, Bruno Rossi, Cynthia Wilkerson), BA; American writer; b. 1935, New Bedford, MA. *Education:* Michigan State Univ. *Career:* other pseudonyms include Michael Bodren, Frank Burleson, Lee Chang, Glen Chase, Richard Hale Curtis, Gordon Davis, Richard Gallagher, March Hastings, Robert Novak, Philip Rawls, Jonathon Scofield, Jonathon Trask. *Publications:* Worst Way To Die 1974, Headcrusher 1974, Shark Fighter 1975, Operation Perfida 1975, Without Mercy 1981, Sweeter Than Candy 1978, The Fast Life 1979, Hydra Conspiracy 1979, The Battle of the Bulge 1981, Hit the Beach 1983, Nightmare Alley 1985, Gold Town 1989, 40 Fathoms Down 1990, Searcher 1990, Warpath 1991, Fort Hays Bustout 1992, Bloody Sunday 1993. *Literary Agent:* Lowenstein-Yost Associates Inc, 121 West, 27th Street, Suite 501, New York, NY 10001, USA. *Telephone:* (212) 206-1630. *Fax:* (212) 727-0280. *Website:* www.lowensteinassociates.com.

LEVITT, Steven D., BA, PhD; American economist, academic and writer; *Alvin H. Baum Professor of Economics, University of Chicago*; b. 29 May 1967; m. Jeannette Levitt; four c. *Education:* Harvard Univ., MIT. *Career:* Man. Consultant, Corporate Decisions, Inc. 1989–91; Junior Fellow, Harvard Soc. of Fellows 1994–97; Research Fellow, American Bar Foundation 1997–; Asst Prof., Dept of Econs, Univ. of Chicago 1997–98, Assoc. Prof. 1998–99, Prof. 1999–2002, Alvin H. Baum Prof. 2002–, Dir, Becker Center on Chicago Price Theory 2004–; Ed., Journal of Political Economy 1999–; Faculty Research Fellow, Nat. Bureau of Econ. Research 1994–; Nat. Fellow, Hoover Univ. Program in Inequality and Social Policy 1998–; Alfred P. Sloan Research Fellow 1999; Fellow, American Acad. of Arts and Sciences 2002. *Publications:* Freakonomics: A Rogue Economist Explores the Hidden Side of Everything (with Stephen J. Dubner) (Booksense Ind. Booksellers Nonfiction Book of the Year, Quill Award for Best Business Book of the Year) 2005, Superfreakonomics: Global Cooling, Patriotic Prostitutes and Why Suicide Bombers Should Buy Life Insurance 2009; contrib. to Slate magazine, New York Times; numerous chapters/articles in academic books/journals. *Honours:* Quantrell Award for undergraduate teaching, Univ. of Chicago 1998, Nat. Science Foundation CAREER Award 1999, Duncan Black Prize (jtly) 2000, Nat. Science Foundation Presidential Early Career Award for Scientists and Engineers 2000, Garvin Prize, Univ. of Calif., Berkeley Law and Econs Workshop 2003, John Bates Clark Medal 2003. *Address:* Department of Economics, University of Chicago, 1126 East 59th Street, Chicago, IL 60637, USA (office). *Telephone:* (773) 834-1862 (office). *Fax:* (773) 834-8490 (office). *E-mail:* slevitt@uchicago.edu (office). *Website:* pricetheory.uchicago.edu/levitt/home.html (office); www.freakonomics.com (office).

LEVY, Andrea, BA (Hons); British writer; b. 7 March 1956, London; d. of Winston Levy and Amy Levy; m. Bill Mayblin; two step-d. *Education:* Highbury Hill High School, London and Middlesex Polytechnic. *Career:* fmr graphic designer. *Publications:* Every Light in the House Burnin' 1994, Never Far from Nowhere 1996, Fruit of the Lemon 1999, Small Island (Orange Prize 2004, Whitbread Novel of the Year and Whitbread Prize 2005, Commonwealth Writers Prize 2005, Orange Prize for Fiction tenth anniversary award 2005) 2004, The Long Song 2010. *Honours:* Dr hc (Middlesex); Arts Council Award 1998. *Literary Agent:* David Grossman Literary Agency, 118B Holland Park Avenue, London, W11 4VA, England. *Telephone:* (20) 7221-2770. *Fax:* (20) 7221-1445. *Address:* c/o Review Press, Hodder Headline, 338 Euston Road, London, NW1 3BH, England.

LÉVY, Bernard-Henri; French writer and philosopher; b. 5 Nov. 1948, Beni-Saf, Algeria; s. of André Lévy and Ginette Lévy; m. 1st Sylvie Bouscasse 1980; one s. one d.; m. 2nd Arielle Sonnery 1993. *Education:* Ecole Normale Supérieure (rue d'Ulm), Paris. *Career:* War Corresp. for Combat 1971–72; Lecturer in Epistemology, Univ. of Strasbourg, in Philosophy, Ecole Normale Supérieure 1973; mem. François Mitterrand's Group of Experts 1973–76; joined Editions Grasset as Ed. 'nouvelle philosophie' series 1973; Ed. Idées section, Quotidien de Paris; Contrib. to Nouvel Observateur and Temps Modernes 1974; co-founder Action Int. contre la Faim 1980, Radio Free Kabul 1981, SOS Racisme; f. and Dir Règle du jeu 1990–; Pres. Supervisory Council Sept-Arte 1993–; seconded by French Govt to Kabul, Afghanistan 2002. *Film directed:* Le Jour la Nuit 1997. *Publications:* Bangladesh: Nationalisme dans la révolution 1973, Les Indes rouges 1973, La barbarie à visage humain 1977 (Prix d'honneur 1977), Le testament de Dieu 1979, L'idéologie française 1981, Questions de principe 1983, Le diable en tête (Prix Médicis) 1984, Impressions d'Asie 1985, Questions de principe II 1986, Eloge des intellectuels 1987, Les derniers jours de Charles Baudelaire (Prix Interallié) 1988, Questions de principe III 1990, Frank Stella: Les années 80 1990, Les bronzes de César 1991, Les aventures de la liberté 1991, Piet Mondrian 1992, Piero Della Francesca 1992, Le jugement dernier (play) 1992, Questions de principe IV 1992, Les hommes et les femmes (jtly) 1993, Un jour dans la mort de Sarajevo (screenplay, jtly) 1993, Bosna! (screenplay, jtly) 1994, La pureté dangereuse 1995, Questions de principe V 1995, Le lys et la cendre 1996, Comédie 1997, The Rules of the Game 1998 (revised edn What Good Are Intellectuals?: 44 Writers Share Their Thoughts 2000), Le siècle de Sartre 2000, Réflexion sur la guerre, Le mal et la fin de l'histoire 2001, Mémoire vive 2001, Qui a tué Daniel Pearl? 2003, American Vertigo 2006, Ce grand cadavre à la renverse 2007, Ennemis publics (with Michel Houellebecq) 2008. *Address:* c/o Editions Grasset et Fasquelle, 61 rue des Saint-Pères, 75006 Paris, France (office). *Telephone:* 1-44-39-22-00 (office). *Fax:* 1-42-22-64-18 (office). *Website:* www.grasset.fr (office).

LEVY, Marc; French writer; b. 16 Oct. 1961, Boulogne Billancourt. *Education:* Université Paris-Dauphine. *Career:* worked for the Red Cross 1980–83; f. Logitec 1983; moved to USA and launched computer graphics co. 1984; currently based in UK. *Publications:* Et si c'était vrai... 2000, Où es-tu? 2001, Sept jours pour une éternité... 2003, La Prochaine fois 2004, Vous revoir 2005, Mes amis Mes amours 2006, Les enfants de la liberté 2007, Toutes ces choses qu'on ne s'est pas dites 2008. *Literary Agent:* Susanna Lea Associates, 28 rue Bonaparte, 75006 Paris, France. *Telephone:* 1-53-10-28-40. *Fax:* 1-53-10-28-49. *E-mail:* postmaster@susannalea.com. *Website:* www.susannalea.com; www.marclevy.info.

LEVY, Peter B., BA, MA, PhD; American historian; b. 11 May 1956, Burlingame, CA; m. Diane Krejsa 1984, one s. one d. *Education:* University of California, Berkeley, Columbia University. *Career:* Visiting Assistant Prof. of History, Rutgers University, Newark Campus, NJ, 1986–88; Assoc. Prof. of History, York College, Pennsylvania, 1989–; mem. American Historical Assen; Organization of American Historians. *Publications:* Let Freedom Ring: A Documentary History of the Modern Civil Rights Movement (co-ed.), 1992; The New Left and Labor in the 1960s, 1994; Encyclopedia of the Reagan-Bush Years, 1996; The Civil Rights Movement, 1998; America in the Sixties: Right, Left, and Center, 1999. *Address:* 1214 Temfield Road, Towson, MD 21286, USA. *E-mail:* plevy@ycp.edu.

LEWIN, Hugh; South African writer; b. 1939, Eastern Transvaal. *Career:* joined African Resistance Movement 1964; imprisoned 1965–72; on release, moved to London, later Zimbabwe; returned to South Africa 1990; fmr Dir, Inst. for the Advancement of Journalism; mem. Truth Commission Human Rights Violations Cttee; currently a media trainer. *Publications include:* Bandiet: Seven Years in a South African Jail 1974, Jafta 1989, The Picture That Came Alive 1993, Bandiet Out of Jail 2001. *Honours:* Olive Schreiner Prize 2001–02. *Address:* c/o Umizi-Random House Inc, PO Box 6810, Roggebai 8012, South Africa (office). *E-mail:* umuzi@randomhouse.co.za (office). *Website:* www.umuzi-randomhouse.co.za (office).

LEWIN, Michael Zinn, AB; American/British writer and dramatist; b. 21 July 1942, Cambridge, Mass; one s. one d. *Education:* Harvard Univ., Churchill Coll., Cambridge. *Career:* Co-Ed. CWA Annual Anthology 1992–94; mem. Detection Club, Authors' Guild. *Radio plays:* The Loss Factor, The Way We Die Now, The Enemies Within, Arrest is as Good as a Change, Rainey Shines, Ask the Right Question, Missing Woman, Cross Rems Of, Rough Cider (adapted from Peter Lovesey novel), Keystone (adapted from Peter Lovesey novel), The Silent Salesman, Who Killed Gnutley Almond?, Place of Safety, The Interests of the Child, Jingle. *Plays:* Deadlock (for Dr Fosters Travelling Theatre) 1990, Who Killed Frankie Almond? 1995, Whooodunnit? 1998. *Publications:* novels: Ask the Right Question 1971, The Way we Die Now 1973, The Enemies Within 1974, Night Cover 1976, The Next Man (novelization of a film) 1976, The Silent Salesman 1978, Outside In 1980, Missing Woman 1981, Hard Line (Maltese Falcon Award for Best Foreign Novel of the Year, Japan 1987) 1982, Out of Season (aka Out of Time) 1984, Late Payments 1986, And Baby Will Fall (aka Child Proof) 1988, Called by a Panther (Raymond Chandler Soc. of Germany Marlowe Award for Best PI Novel 1992) 1991, Underdog 1993, Family Business 1995, Cutting Loose 1999, Family Planning 1999, Eye-Opener 2004, Oh Joe 2008; short story collections: Telling Tales 1994, Rover's Tales 1998, The Reluctant Detective and Other Stories 2001; non-fiction: How to Beat College Tests: A Guide to Ease the Burden of Useless Courses 1970; contrib. of numerous short stories to magazines and anthologies. *Honours:* Falcon Award 1987, Marlowe Award 1992, Mid-America Mystery Conf. Mystery Masters Award 1994. *Address:* Garden Flat, 15 Bladud Buildings, Bath, BA1 5LS, England. *Website:* www.michaelzlewin.com.

LEWIN, Roger A., BA, MD; American psychiatrist, teacher, writer and poet; b. 22 Jan. 1946, Cleveland, OH; m. 1st Julia Vandivort 1977 (died 1988); one d.; m. 2nd Joan Lilienthal 1990. *Education:* Harvard Coll., Wright State Univ.

Career: resident, Sheppard and Enoch Pratt Hosp., Towson, Md 1981–85, psychiatrist 1985–91, teacher and supervisor 1991–; pvt. practice of psychiatry 1981–. *Publications:* Losing and Fusing (co-author) 1992, Compassion 1996, New Wrinkles (poems) 1996, Creative Collaboration in Psychotherapy 1997, Spring Fed Pond 2003. *Honours:* Ford Foundation Grant 1965, Ginsburg Fellow Group for the Advancement of Psychiatry 1981–85. *Address:* 504 Club Lane, Towson, MD 21286, USA (home). *Telephone:* (410) 828-7045 (office). *Fax:* (410) 938-4444 (office). *E-mail:* oaktree@comcast.net (home). *Website:* rogerlewin.com.

LEWING, Anthony Charles, (Mark Bannerman); British writer; b. 12 July 1933, Colchester, Essex, England; s. of Maj. H. C. Lewing Mrs G. M. Lewing; m. Françoise Faury 1966; one s. one d. *Education:* King's Coll. School, Wimbledon. *Career:* Royal Army Ordnance Corps 1951–53, Royal Army Pay Corps 1958–89; civil service 1989–95. *Publications:* Grand Valley Feud 1995, The Beckoning Noose 1996, Escape to Purgatory 1996, The Early Lynching 1997, Renegade Rose 1997, Ride into Destiny 1997, Goose Pimples 1997, Man Without a Yesterday 1998, Trail to Redemption 1998, Bridges to Cross (as Rowena Carter) 1998, Short Story World 1999, Comanchero Rendezvous 1999, The Cornish Woman 1999, Frank Riddle – Frontiersman 1999, Pinkerton Man 2000, Galvanized Yankee 2001, Railroaded 2001, Lust to Kill 2003, Blind Trail 2004, Bender's Boot 2004, The Frontiersman 2004, Hog-Tied Hero 2005, Fury at Troon's Ferry 2005, Legacy of Lead 2005, Gunsmoke at Adobe Walls 2006, The Mavericks 2007, The Modoc Kid 2006, Shadow of Guilt 2012, The Headhunters 2012; contrib. of more than 300 short stories to magazines, newspapers and anthologies. *Address:* Greenmantle, Horseshoe Lane, Ash Vale, Surrey, GU12 5LJ, England. *Telephone:* (1252) 679779. *E-mail:* anthony.lewing@ntlworld.com.

LEWIS, Anthony, AB; American journalist and academic; *James Madison Visiting Professor, Columbia University*; b. 27 March 1927, New York, NY; m. 1st Linda Rannells 1951 (divorced); one s. two d.; m. 2nd Margaret H. Marshall 1984. *Education:* Harvard Univ. *Career:* deskman, Sunday Dept 1948–52, reporter, Washington Bureau 1955–64, Chief London Bureau 1965–72, editorial columnist 1969–2001, New York Times; reporter, Washington Daily News 1952–55; Lecturer on Law, Harvard Univ. 1974–89; James Madison Visiting Prof., Columbia Univ. 1983–; mem. American Acad. of Arts and Sciences. *Publications:* Gideon's Trumpet 1964, Portrait of a Decade: The Second American Revolution 1964, Make No Law: The Sullivan Case and the First Amendment 1991, Written into History: Pulitzer Prize Reporting of the Twentieth Century from the New York Times (ed.) 2001, Freedom for the Thought that We Hate: A Biography of the First Amendment 2008; contrib. to professional journals. *Honours:* Hon. DLitt (Adelphi Univ.) 1964, (Rutgers Univ.) 1973, (Williams Coll.) 1978, (Clark Univ.) 1982, Hon. LLD (Syracuse Univ.) 1979, (Colby Coll.) 1983, (Northeastern Univ.) 1987; Heywood Broun Award 1955, Pulitzer Prizes for Nat. Reporting 1955, 1963, Nieman Fellow 1956–57, MWA Best Fact-Crime Book Award 1964, Presidential Citizen's Medal 2001. *Address:* 1010 Memorial Drive, Cambridge, MA 02138, USA (home). *Telephone:* (617) 354-2229 (office). *Fax:* (617) 354-2458 (office); (617) 876-3641 (home).

LEWIS, Anthony Robert (Tony), CBE, DL, MA; British sports commentator, writer and fmr cricketer and opera administrator; *Director, Welsh National Opera*; b. 6 July 1938, Swansea, Wales; s. of Wilfrid Lewis and Florence Lewis (née Flower); m. Joan Pritchard 1962; two d. *Education:* Neath Grammar School, Christ's Coll. Cambridge. *Career:* right-hand batsman; teams: Glamorgan, Cambridge Univ.; double blue and debut at int. level; led Glamorgan to their second Co. Championship title 1969; played in nine Tests (eight as Capt. 1972–73) scoring 457 runs (average 32.64, highest score 125) including one hundred; scored 20,495 First-class runs (average 32.42, highest score 223) including 30 hundreds; retd 1974; became cricket commentator and journalist; Pres. Marylebone Cricket Club (MCC) 1998–2000, secured admission of women into MCC Club, Trustee 2002–; fmr Chair. Glamorgan Co. Cricket Club, Pres. 1987–93, 2003–; Chair. Welsh Tourist Bd 1992–2000; led successful Welsh campaign to host 2010 Ryder Cup; Chair. (non-exec.) World Snooker Ltd 2003–; Dir Welsh Nat. Opera 2003–. *Publications:* A Summer of Cricket 1976, Playing Days 1985, Double Century 1987, Cricket in Many Lands 1991, MCC Masterclass 1994, Taking Fresh Guard 2003. *Honours:* Hon. Fellow, St David's Univ. Coll., Lampeter 1993, Univ. of Glamorgan 1995, Univ. of Wales, Swansea 1996, Univ. of Cardiff 1999. *Address:* Castellau, Near Llantrisant, Mid Glamorgan, CF72 8LP, Wales (home); c/o Angie Bainbridge Management, 3 New Cottages, The Holt, Washington, West Sussex, RH20 4AW, England (office). *Telephone:* (1903) 8933748 (office). *Fax:* (1903) 891320 (office). *E-mail:* angie.bainbridge@btopenworld.com (office).

LEWIS, Arnold, MA, PhD; American architectural historian, art historian and academic; b. 13 Jan. 1930, New Castle, Pa; m. Beth Irwin 1958; two s. one d. *Education:* Allegheny Coll., Univ. of Wisconsin, Univ. of Bonn and Univ. of Munich, Germany. *Career:* Wells Coll., Aurora, New York 1962–64; Coll. of Wooster, OH 1964–96; mem. Coll. Art Asscn, Soc. of Architectural Historians (Dir 1979–82). *Publications:* American Victorian Architecture 1975, Wooster in 1876 1976, American Country Houses of the Gilded Age 1983, American Interiors of the Gilded Age (with James Turner and Steven McQuillin) 1987, An Early Encounter with Tomorrow: Europeans, Chicago's Loop, and the World's Columbian Exposition 1997; contrib. to Journal of the Society of Architectural Historians. *Honours:* Founder's Award, Journal of the Society of Architectural Historians 1974, Western Reserve Book Award, Soc. of Architectural Historians 1977, Barzun Prize in Cultural History, American Philosophical Soc. 1998. *Address:* 614 Kieffer Street, Wooster, OH 44691, USA (home). *Telephone:* (330) 264-3515 (home). *E-mail:* lewisda@sssnet.com (home); alewis@wooster.edu (office).

LEWIS, Bernard, PhD, FBA, FRHistS; American writer and academic; b. 31 May 1916, London, England; m. Ruth Hélène Oppenhejm 1947 (divorced 1974); one s. one d. *Education:* Univs of London and Paris. *Career:* Lecturer in Islamic History, School of Oriental Studies, Univ. of London 1938; served in RAC and Intelligence Corps 1940–41; attached to Foreign Office 1941–45; Prof. of History of the Near and Middle East, Univ. of London 1949–74; Cleveland E. Dodge Prof. of Near Eastern Studies, Princeton Univ. 1974–86, later Prof. Emer.; Dir Annenberg Research Inst., Philadelphia 1986–90; Visiting Prof. of History, UCLA 1955–56, Columbia Univ. 1960, Ind. Univ. 1963, Princeton Univ. 1964, Univ. of Calif. at Berkeley 1965, Coll. de France 1980, École des Hautes Études en Sciences Sociales, Paris 1983, 1988, Univ. of Chicago 1985; Visiting mem. Inst. for Advanced Study, Princeton Univ. 1969, mem. 1974–86; A.D. White Prof.-at-Large, Cornell Univ. 1984–90; mem. Bd of Dirs, Institut für die Wissenschaften von Menschen, Vienna 1988; Jefferson Lecturer in the Humanities, US Nat. Endowment for the Humanities 1990; Tanner Lecturer, Brasenose Coll., Oxford 1990; Henry M. Jackson Memorial Lecturer (Seattle) 1992; mem. British Acad., American Philosophical Soc. 1973, American Acad. of Arts and Sciences 1983; American Oriental Soc., Corresp. mem. Inst. d'Egypte, Cairo 1969, Inst. de France 1994; Fellow, Univ. Coll., London 1976. *Publications:* The Origins of Ismā'ilism: A Study of the Historical Background of the Fatimid Caliphate 1940, Turkey Today 1940, British Contributions to Arabic Studies 1941, Handbook of Diplomatic and Political Arabic 1947, Land of Enchanters (ed.) 1948, The Arabs in History 1950, Notes and Documents from the Turkish Archives: A Contribution to the History of the Jews in the Ottoman Empire 1952, Encyclopedia of Islam (co-ed.) 1956–86, The Emergence of Modern Turkey 1961, The Kingly Crown 1961, Historians of the Middle East (co-ed. with P.M. Holt) 1962, Istanbul and the Civilization of the Ottoman Empire 1963, The Middle East and the West 1964, The Assassins: A Radical Sect in Islam 1967, The Cambridge History of Islam (ed. with P. M. Holt and Ann K. S. Lambton, two vols) 1970, Race and Colour in Islam 1971, Islam in History: Ideas, Men and Events in the Middle East 1973, Islamic Civilization (ed.) 1974, Islam from the Prophet Muhammad to the Capture of Constantinople (ed. and trans., two vols) 1974, History: Remembered, Recovered, Invented 1975, Studies in Classical and Ottoman Islam: Seventh to Sixteenth Centuries 1976, The World of Islam: Faith, People, Culture (ed.) 1976, Population and Revenue in the Towns of Palestine in the Sixteenth Century (with Amnon Cohen) 1978, The Muslim Discovery of Europe 1982, Christians and Jews in the Ottoman Empire (two vols) 1982, The Jews of Islam 1984, Semites and Anti-Semites: An Inquiry into Conflict and Prejudice 1986, As Others See Us (co-ed.) 1986, The Political Language of Islam 1988, Race and Slavery in the Middle East: A Historical Enquiry 1990, Islam and the West 1993, The Shaping of the Modern Middle East 1994, Cultures in Conflict: Christians, Muslims and Jews in the Age of Discovery 1995, The Middle East: Two Thousand Years of History from the Rise of Christianity to the Present Day 1995, The Future of the Middle East 1997, The Multiple Identities of the Middle East 1998, A Middle East Mosaic: Fragments of Life, Letters and History 2000, Music of a Distant Drum, Classical Arabic, Persian, Turkish and Hebrew Poems 2001, What Went Wrong? Western Impact and Middle Eastern Response 2002, The Crisis of Islam: Holy War and Unholy Terror 2003, From Babel to Dragomans: Interpreting the Middle East 2004, Political Words and Ideas in Islam 2008, Islam: The Religion and The People (co-author) 2008, Faith and Power: Religion and Politics in the Middle East 2010, The End of Modern History in the Middle East 2011, Notes on a Century: Recollections of a Middle East Historian (co-author) 2012; numerous contribs to professional journals. *Honours:* Hon. mem. Turkish Historical Soc., Société Asiatique, Paris, Atatürk Acad. of History, Language and Culture, Ankara, Turkish Acad. of Sciences, Hon. Fellow, SOAS, London 1986; 15 hon. doctorates including (Hebrew Univ., Jerusalem) 1974, (Tel-Aviv) 1979, (State Univ. of New York, Binghamton, Univ. of Penn., Hebrew Union Coll., Cincinnati) 1987, (Univ. of Haifa, Yeshiva Univ., New York) 1991 (Bar-Ilan Univ.) 1992, (Brandeis) 1993, (Ben-Gurion, Ankara) 1996, (Princeton Univ.) 2002; Citation of Honour, Turkish Ministry of Culture 1973, Harvey Prize, Technion-Israel Inst. of Tech. 1978, Educ. Award for Outstanding Achievement in Promotion of American-Turkish Studies 1985, Atatürk Peace Prize 1998, Golden Plate Award, Acad. of Achievement, Washington, DC 2004, Nat. Endowment for the Humanities 2007, Irving Kristol Award 2007. *Telephone:* (609) 258-4280.

LEWIS, Beverly Marie; American writer; b. Lancaster, Pa; m. David Lewis. *Education:* Evangel Univ. *Career:* Amish writer; fmr teacher. *Publications:* fiction: for adults: The Shunning 1997, The Confession 1997, The Reckoning 1998, The Postcard 1999, The Crossroad 1999, Sanctuary 2001, The Covenant 2002, The Betrayal 2003, The Sacrifice 2004, The Prodigal 2004, The Revelation 2005, The Preacher's Daughter 2005, The Englisher 2006, The Brethren 2006, The Parting 2007, The Forbidden 2008, The Longing 2008, The Secret 2009, The Missing 2009, The Telling 2010, The Thorn 2010; for children: The Double Dabble Surprise 1995, The Chicken Pox Panic 1995, The Crazy Christmas Angel Story 1995, No Grown-Ups Allowed 1995, Frog Power 1995, The Mystery of Case D. Luc 1995, The Stinky Sneakers Mystery 1996, Pickle Pizza 1996, Mailbox Mania 1996, The Mudhole Mystery 1997, Fiddlesticks 1997, The Crabby Cat Caper 1997, Tarantula Toes 1997, Green Gravy 1997, Backyard Bandit Mystery 1997, Tree House Trouble 1997, The Creepy Sleep-Over 1997, The Great TV Turn-Off 1997, Piggy Party 1998, The

Granny Game 1999, Mystery Mutt 2000, Big Bad Beans 2000, The Upside-Down Day 2000, The Midnight Mystery 2000, also Girls Only series, Holly's Heart series, Summerhill Secrets series. *Honours:* eight Evangelical Christian Publishers Asscn awards. *Address:* c/o Bethany House, Baker Publishing Group, 6030 East Fulton Road, Ada, MI 49301, USA (office). *Website:* www.bethanyhouse.com (office); www.beverlylewis.com.

LEWIS, Charles (see Dixon, Roger)

LEWIS, David Levering, BA, MA, PhD; American academic and writer; *Julius Silver University Professor and Professor of History, New York University*; b. 25 May 1936, Little Rock, AR; s. of John Henry Lewis and Urnestine Alice Lewis; m. 1st Sharon Siskind 1966 (divorced 1988); two s. one d.; m. 2nd Ruth Ann Stewart 1994; one d. *Education:* Fisk Univ., Columbia Univ., LSE. *Career:* Lecturer, Univ. of Ghana 1963–64, Howard Univ., Washington, DC 1964–65; Asst Prof., Univ. of Notre Dame 1965–66; Assoc. Prof., Morgan State Coll., Baltimore 1966–70, Federal City Coll., Washington, DC 1970–74; Prof. of History, Univ. of the District of Columbia 1974–80, Univ. of California at San Diego, La Jolla 1981–85; Martin Luther King Jr Prof. of History, Rutgers Univ. 1985–2003; Julius Silver Univ. Prof. and Prof. of History, New York Univ. 2003–; mem. African Studies Asscn, American Asscn of Univ. Profs, American Historical Asscn, Authors' Guild, Organization of American Historians, Soc. for French Historical Studies, Southern Historical Asscn, American Acad. of Arts and Sciences, American Philosophical Soc. *Publications:* Martin Luther King: A Critical Biography 1971, Prisoners of Honor: The Dreyfus Affair 1973, District of Columbia: A Bicentennial History 1977, When Harlem Was in Vogue: The Politics of the Arts in the Twenties and the Thirties 1981, Harlem Renaissance: Art of Black America (with others) 1987, The Race to Fashoda: European Colonialism and African Resistance in the Scramble for Africa 1988, W. E. B. Du Bois: Biography of a Race, 1868–1919 1994, The Portable Harlem Renaissance Reader (ed.) 1994, W. E. B. Du Bois: A Reader (ed.) 1995, W. E. B. Du Bois: The Fight for Equality and the American Century 2001, God's Crucible: Islam and the Making of Europe, 570 to 1215 2008. *Honours:* Hon. DLitt (Lafayette Coll.) 1995, Hon. DH (Pittsburgh Univ.) 1999, Hon. DHumLitt (Lehman Coll.) 1995, (Bard Coll.) 2002, (Wheaton Coll.) 2003, (Emory Univ.) 2003, (Bates Coll.) 2004, (Marymount Manhattan Coll.) 2004, (New School Univ.) 2005; American Philosophical Soc. grant 1967, Social Science Research Council grant 1971, Nat. Endowment for the Humanities grant 1975, Woodrow Wilson Int. Center for Scholars Fellow 1977–78, Guggenheim Fellowship 1986, Bancroft Prize 1994, Ralph Waldo Emerson Prize 1994, Pulitzer Prizes for Biography 1994, 2001, Francis Parkman Prize 1994, Fellow John D. and Catherine T. MacArthur Foundation 1999, John Hope Franklin Award 2004. *Address:* Department of History, King Juan Carlos I Center, New York University, 53 Washington Square South, New York, NY 10012-1098 (office); Hill House, 195 South Road, Stanfordville, NY 12581, USA (home). *Telephone:* (212) 998-8619 (office). *Fax:* (845) 758-0208 (home). *E-mail:* david.levering.lewis@nyu.edu (office); dleveringlewis@msn.com (office). *Website:* history.fas.nyu.edu/object/davidleveringlewis (office).

LEWIS, Desmond Francis, BA; British poet and writer; b. 18 Jan. 1948, Colchester, Essex, England; m. Denise Jean Woolgar 1970; one s. one d. *Education:* Lancaster University. *Publications:* contrib. hundreds of prose poems and stories to various UK and US publications.

LEWIS, Gwyneth, MA, DPhil, FRSL; British poet and writer; b. 1959, Cardiff, Wales; d. of Gwilym Lewis and Ann Eryl James; m. Leighton Denver Davies. *Education:* Girton Coll., Cambridge, Harvard and Columbia Univs, USA, Balliol Coll., Oxford. *Career:* fmr freelance journalist in New York, USA and documentary prod. and dir, BBC Wales; composed the bilingual inscription on the front of Cardiff's Wales Millennium Centre, opened in 2004; Nat. Poet of Wales 2005–06; Fellow, Radcliffe Inst. for Advanced Studies, Harvard Univ. 2008–09, Stanford Humanities Center 2009–10; Mary Amelia Cummins Harvey Visiting Fellow Commonership, Girton Coll. Cambridge 2011; Writing Fellow, Centre for New Writing, Univ. of Manchester 2012. *Play:* Clytemnestra (Sherman Cymru). *Radio:* Sunbathing in the Rain (BBC Radio 4), Stardust: A Love Story (BBC Radio 4). *Television:* Zero Gravity (BBC 2). *Publications:* Llwybrau bywyd (poetry) 1977, Ar y groesfford (poetry) 1978, Sonedau Redsa a Cherddi Eraill 1990, Parables and Faxes (poetry) (Aldeburgh Poetry Festival Prize) 1995, Cyfrif Un ac Un yn Dri (poetry) 1996, Zero Gravity (poetry) 1998, Y Llofrudd Iaith (poetry) (Welsh Arts Council Book of the Year) 2000, Sunbathing in the Rain: A Cheerful Book About Depression (non-fiction) 2002, Keeping Mum (poetry) 2003, Redflight/Barcud (libretto) 2005, The Most Beautiful Man from the Sea (oratorio) 2005, Two in a Boat: A Marital Voyage 2005, Tair mewn Un (poetry) 2005, Chaotic Angels (poetry) 2005, Dolffin (libretto) 2006, The Hospital Odyssey (poetry) 2010, The Meat Tree (stories) 2010, Sparrow Tree 2011. *Honours:* Hon. Fellow, Univ. of Cardiff 2005, Univ. of Liverpool 2011, Bangor Univ. 2012; Harkness Fellow 1982–84, Eric Gregory Award 1987, Nat. Endowment for Science, Technology and the Arts Fellowship 2002–07, Wellcome Trust Sciart Award, Creative Wales Award, Cholmondeley Award 2010. *Literary Agent:* c/o David Miller, Rogers, Coleridge & White Literary Agency, 20 Powis Mews, London, W11 1JN, England. *Telephone:* (20) 7243-9504. *E-mail:* davidmiller@rcwlitagency.com. *Website:* www.rcwlitagency.com. *E-mail:* gl@gwynethlewis.com. *Website:* www.gwynethlewis.info.

LEWIS, Jeremy Morley, MA, FRSL; British writer and editor; b. 15 March 1942, Salisbury, Wiltshire; m. Petra Lewis 1968, two d. *Education:* Trinity Coll., Dublin and Sussex Univ. *Career:* Ed., Andre Deutsch Ltd 1969–70, OUP 1977–79; Literary Agent, AP Watt Ltd 1970–76; Dir, Chatto and Windus 1979–89; Deputy Ed., London Magazine 1991–94; Editorial Consultant, Peters, Fraser & Dunlop Group Ltd 1994–2002; Commissioning Ed. The Oldie 1997–; Ed.-at-Large, Literary Review 2004–; mem. R. S. Surtees Soc. (Sec.). *Publications:* Playing for Time 1987, Chatto Book of Office Life 1992, Kindred Spirits 1995, Cyril Connolly: A Life 1997, Tobias Smollett 2003, Penguin Special: The Life and Times of Allen Lane 2005, Grub Street Irregular 2008, Shades of Greene 2010. *Address:* 3 Percival Road, London, SW14 7QE, England (home). *Telephone:* (20) 8876-2807 (office). *E-mail:* jeremy.lewis5@btinternet.com (office).

LEWIS, Mervyn (see Frewer, Glyn Mervyn Louis)

LEWIS, Russell T., BA, JD; American newspaper executive; b. 1948. *Education:* State Univ. of New York at Stony Brook, Brooklyn Law School. *Career:* joined New York Times as a copy boy, while attending coll. 1966; litigation assoc. Cahill, Gordon and Reindel 1973; staff attorney New York Times legal dept 1977; Pres., Gen. Man. The New York Times, New York 1993–97, Pres., CEO 1997–2004 (retd). *Honours:* Acad. of Man. Distinguished Exec. of the Year 2002, American Lung Asscn of NY Life & Breath Award 2002, Nat. Human Relations Award, American Jewish Cttee 2003. *Address:* c/o The New York Times, 229 West 43rd Street, New York, NY 10036, USA (office).

LEWIS, Warn B., Jr, BA, MA, PhD; American academic and writer; b. 8 May 1938, Minneapolis, Minnesota; m. Erika Cornehl 1961, three d. *Education:* Amherst College, University of Minnesota at Twin Cities, University of Pennsylvania. *Career:* Asst Prof. of German, University of Iowa, Iowa City, 1968–71; Asst Prof., 1971–73, Assoc. Prof. of German, 1973–99, Prof. of German, 1999–, University of Georgia, Athens; mem. International Brecht Society; Modern Language Asscn of America; German Studies Asscn; Society for Exile Studies; Eugene O'Neill Society; Northeast MLA, Chair., German-American Literary Relations, 1985–86, 1989–90; South Atlantic MLA. *Publications:* Poetry and Exile: An Annotated Bibliography of the Works and Criticism of Paul Zech, 1975; Eugene O'Neill: The German Reception of America's First Dramatist, 1984; German and International Perspectives on the Spanish Civil War: The Aesthetics of Partisanship (contributor), 1992; Paul Zech's The Bird in Langfoot's Belfry (ed.), 1993; The Ironic Dissident: Frank Wedekind in the View of His Critics, 1997. Contributions: Comparative Literature Studies; Modern Language Studies; German Quarterly; German Life and Letters; Modern Drama. *Honours:* Fellow, Alexander von Humboldt Foundation, 1979–80. *Address:* 490 S Milledge Avenue, Athens, GA 30605, USA. *E-mail:* wlewis@arches.uga.edu.

LEWIS, William (Bill) Edward; British poet, writer, editor, artist and storyteller and mythographer; b. 1 Aug. 1953, Maidstone, Kent; s. of Edward Francis Lewis and Helen Lewis; m. Ann Frances Morris 1981. *Career:* Writer-in-Residence, Brighton Festival 1985; Creative Writing Tutor, HM Prison, Maidstone 1984–86; teacher (mythology courses), Kent Children's Univ. and Adult Educ. 1994–2003; Guest Lecturer on Myth, Univ. of Eastern Connecticut, Univ. of Rhode Island, USA; Founder-mem. Medway Poets, Stuckist Group, Urban Fox, Collective Re-modernist Group, Inst. for Remodernism. *Exhibitions include:* photography: Fire in the Dust, The Brook Chatham 1990, Faces from Turtle Island, Medway Festival 1993; paintings: Stuck! Stuck! Stuck!, Gallery 108, London 1999, The First Art Show of the New Millennium, Salon des Arts, London 2000, The Resignation of Sir Nicholas Serota, Gallery 108, London, The Real Turner Prize Show, The Pure Gallery, London 2000, Vote Stuckist, Artbank and The Fridge Gallery, London 2001, Stuck up North, Newcastle Arts Centre, The Stuckists, Musée d'Adzac, Paris 2001 and 2005, Punk Victorian, Walker Gallery, Liverpool 2004, Triumph of Stuckism Symposium, John Moores Univ. 2006, Collective Remodernist and the Shadow Group (Joint Exhibition), Lauderdale House, London 2010. *Recordings:* Blackberry Ghosts 1994, The Medway Poets Album 1998, Collected Poems Vol. 1 2005, Collected Prose Vol. 1 2005. *Illustrations:* The Winter Solstice by John Matthews, The Green Man by John Matthews. *Publications:* Poems 1975–83 1983, Night Clinic 1984, Communion 1986, Rage Without Anger 1987, Skyclad Christ 1992, Paradigm Shift (ed.) 1992, Coyote Cosmos (short stories) 1994, Translation Women 1996, Industry of Letters, The Book of North Kent Writers (co-ed.) 1996, The Wine of Connecting (poems) 1996, Intellect of the Heart (poems) 1997, Shattered English: Complete North Kent Poems 1998, Leaving the Autoroute (short stories) 1999, Beauty is the Beast (poems) 2000, Blackberry Ghosts: Collected Poems 1975–2003 2003, The Book of Misplaced but Imperishable Names (prose) 2003, The Medway Scene (co-ed. and contrib.), The Arts in Medway Vols I and II (co-ed. and contrib.) 2004, The Stuckist Anthology 2010; contrib. to Best Horror and Fantasy 1997, 1998, The Green Man 2003, Jungewelt, numerous anthologies, reviews and journals. *Address:* The Medway Delta Press, PO Box 479, Chatham, Kent, ME4 5WX, England (office). *Telephone:* (1634) 827308 (home). *E-mail:* medwaydeltapress@yahoo.co.uk (office). *Website:* medwaydeltapress.co.uk (office).

LEWIS-SMITH, Anne Elizabeth, (Emily Devereaux, A. McCormick, Quilla Slade); British poet, writer, editor and publisher; b. 14 April 1925, London; m. Peter Lewis-Smith 1944; one s. two d. *Career:* Asst Ed. 1967–83, Ed. 1983–91, Envoi; Ed., Aerostat 1973–78, British Asscn of Friends of Museums Yearbook 1985–91; Publisher, Envoi Poets Publications 1986–; mem. PEN. *Publications:* Seventh Bridge 1963, The Beginning 1964, Flesh and Flowers 1967,

Dandelion Flavour 1971, Dinas Head 1980, Places and Passions 1986, In the Dawn 1987, Circling Sound 1996, Feathers, Fancies and Feelings 2000, Off Duty! 2006, Every Seventh Wave 2006, Red Shoes 2008; contrib. to newspapers and magazines. *Honours:* Tissadier Diploma for Services to Int. Aviation, Debbie Warley Award for Services to Int. Aviation, Dorothy Tutin Award for Services to Poetry. *Address:* Pen Ffordd, Newport, Pembrokeshire SA42 0QT, Wales (home).

LEWYCKA, Marina, BPhil, MA; British writer and fmr university lecturer; b. 12 Oct. 1946, Kiel, Germany; m.; one d. *Education:* Univs of Keele, York and Leeds, Sheffield Hallam Univ. *Career:* b. of Ukrainian parents in refugee camp in Germany at the end of World War II; moved to England 1948; Lecturer in English and Journalism, Sheffield Hallam Univ. –2011 (retd). *Publications:* A Short History of Tractors in Ukrainian (novel) (Bollinger Everyman Wodehouse Prize for Comic Fiction 2005, Saga Award for Wit 2005, British Book Awards Waterstones Newcomer of the Year 2006) 2005, Two Caravans 2007, We Are All Made of Glue 2009, Various Pets Alive and Dead 2012. *Honours:* Hon. DLitt (Leeds Metropolitan Univ.). *Literary Agent:* c/o Bill Hamilton, A.M. Heath & Co. Ltd, 6 Warwick Court, Holborn, London, WC1R 5DJ, England. *Telephone:* (20) 7242-2811. *Fax:* (20) 7242-2711. *E-mail:* bill.hamilton@amheath.co.uk. *Website:* www.amheath.com; marinalewycka.com.

LEY, Alice Chetwynd, DipSoc; British novelist and teacher; b. 12 Oct. 1913, Halifax, Yorkshire, England; m. Kenneth James Ley 1945, two s. *Education:* Univ. of London. *Career:* Tutor in Creative Writing, Harrow Coll. of Further Education 1962–84, Lecturer in Sociology and Social History 1968–71; mem. Jane Austen Soc., Romantic Novelists' Asscn (chair. 1971–73, hon. life mem. 1987–), Soc. of Women Writers and Journalists. *Publications:* The Jewelled Snuff Box 1959, The Guinea Stamp (aka The Courting of Joanna) 1961, Master of Liversedge (aka The Master and the Maiden) 1966, The Clandestine Betrothal 1967, The Toast of the Town 1969, A Season at Brighton 1971, Tenant of Chesdene Manor (aka Beloved Diana) 1974, An Advantageous Marriage 1977, The Sentimental Spy 1977, A Regency Scandal 1979, A Conformable Wife 1981, A Reputation Dies 1982, The Intrepid Miss Haydon 1983, A Fatal Assignation 1987, Masquerade of Vengeance 1989. *Honours:* Gilchrist Award 1962.

LEYS, Simon (see Ryckmans, Pierre)

LEYSHON, Nell; British playwright and writer; b. Glastonbury, Somerset; two s. *Education:* Univ. of Southampton. *Career:* Visiting Fellow in English, Univ. of Southampton; first female playwright to have work commissioned and performed at Globe Theatre, London. *Radio:* plays: Milk (co-writer) (Richard Imison Award for Best First Radio Play) 2002, The Home Field 2003, Michael 2004, The House in the Trees 2004, Soldier Boy 2005, War Bride 2008, Sons 2009. *Plays:* The Farm 2002, Comfort Me with Apples (London Evening Standard Most Promising Playwright Award) 2005, Glass Eels 2007, Don't Look Now (adaptation) 2007, Winter 2007, Paradise 2009, Bedlam 2010. *Publications:* fiction: Black Dirt 2004, Devotion 2008, The Voice (short stories) 2008. *Literary Agent:* United Agents, 12–26 Lexington Street, London, W1F 0LE, England. *Telephone:* (20) 3214-0800. *Fax:* (20) 3214-0801. *E-mail:* info@unitedagents.co.uk. *Website:* unitedagents.co.uk. *E-mail:* nell@nellleyshon.co.uk (office). *Website:* www.nellleyshon.co.uk.

LEYTON, Sophie (see Walsh, Sheila)

L'HEUREUX, John Clarke, AB, LPhil, LTheol, MA; American academic and writer; b. 26 Oct. 1934, South Hadley, MA; m. Joan Ann Polston 1971. *Education:* Weston College, Boston College, Woodstock College, Harvard University. *Career:* Writer-in-Residence, Georgetown University, 1964–65, Regis College, 1968–69; Ordained Roman Catholic Priest, 1966, laicized, 1971; Staff Ed., 1968–69, Contributing Ed., 1969–83, The Atlantic; Visiting Prof., Hamline University, 1971, Tufts College, 1971–72; Visiting Asst Prof., Harvard University, 1973; Asst Prof., 1973–79, Dir, Creative Writing Programme, 1976–89, Assoc. Prof., 1979–81, Prof., 1981–, Lane Prof. of the Humanities, 1985–90, Stanford University. *Publications:* Quick as Dandelions, 1964; Rubrics for a Revolution, 1967; Picnic in Babylon, 1967; One Eye and a Measuring Rod, 1968; No Place for Hiding, 1971; Tight White Collar, 1972; The Clang Birds, 1972; Family Affairs, 1974; Jessica Fayer, 1976; Desires, 1981; A Woman Run Mad, 1988; Comedians, 1990; An Honorable Profession, 1991; The Shrine at Altamira, 1992; The Handmaid of Desire, 1996; Having Everything, 1999; The Miracle, 2002.

LHOMEAU, Franck; French editor and publisher; *Founder Director, Editions Joseph K;* b. 1955, Nantes. *Education:* Univ. de Paris VIII. *Career:* co-f. Le Temps Singulier publishing house –1982; f. Editions Joseph K 1994–; created Temps noir review 1998–. *Publications:* Marcel Proust à la recherche d'un éditeur (with Alain Coelho) 1988, Dictionnaire des littératures policières 2003. *Address:* Editions Joseph K, 21/25 rue Geoffrey Drouet, 44000 Nantes, France (office). *Telephone:* 2-40-74-42-84 (office). *E-mail:* editions.josephk@free.fr (office). *Website:* www.editions-josephk.com (office).

LI, Bihua, (Lilian Lee); Taiwanese novelist and screenwriter. *Films:* screenplays: Yin ji kau 1987, Chuan dao fang zi 1990, Ba wang bie ji 1993, You Seng 1993, Ching Se 1993, Gaau ji 2004. *Publications:* over 30 books including Her Pao chu yen hua 1983, Yanzhi Kou (Rouge) 1985, Qingshe (Black Snake) 1985, Bawang bieji (Farewell my Concubine) 1986, The Last Princess of Manchuria 1992, Farewell my Concubine (also co-writer of screenplay) 1993, Yanhua Sanyue (The Red String), Hong er zhui 2006.

LI, Renchen; Chinese journalist; b. Oct. 1941, Changyi County, Shandong Prov. *Education:* Fudan Univ. *Career:* mem. CCP 1975–; Features and Photos Service, Comm. for Cultural Relations with Foreign Countries 1964–66; Ed. Huizhou Bao, Anhui Prov., Ed. People's Daily and Deputy Dir Commentary Dept People's Daily 1983–86; Deputy Ed.-in-Chief, then Ed.-in-Chief, Renmin Ribao (People's Daily) 1986; writes under pen name Chen Ping; Sr Visiting Prof. Tsinghua Univ.; Standing mem. CPPCC Nat. Cttee; Vice-Chair. CPPCC Learning and Historical & Cultural Data Cttee. *Address:* c/o Renmin Ribao, 2 Jin Tai Xi Lu, Choo Yong Men Nai, Beijing 100733, People's Republic of China. *Telephone:* (1) 65092121. *Fax:* (1) 65091982.

LI, Xiao; Chinese writer; b. 1950, Shanghai; s. of Ba Jin. *Education:* Fudan Univ. *Publications:* novels: Tianqiao (The Overpass) 1989, Zuihou de wancan (The Last Supper) 1993, Yao a yao yao dao waipo qiao 1995, Sishi er li (A Man is Established at Forty) 1996; over 20 short stories published. *Address:* c/o Ministry of Culture, 10 Chaoyangmen Bei Jie, Dongcheng Qu, Beijing 100020, People's Republic of China.

LI, Yiyun; Chinese/American writer; b. Beijing; m.; two s. *Career:* emigrated to USA 1996; Contrib. Ed., A Public Space (literary magazine); currently teaches at Univ. of California, Davis. *Publications:* A Thousand Years of Good Prayers (short stories) (Frank O'Connor Int. Short Story Award, PEN/Hemingway Award, Guardian First Book Award, California Book Award for First Fiction) 2006, The Vagrants (novel) 2009, Gold Boy, Emerald Girl (short stories) 2010; contrib. short stories and essays to The New Yorker, Best American Short Stories, O. Henry Prize Stories and others. *Honours:* Lannan Foundation Fellowship, Whiting Foundation Writers' Award, one of Granta's 21 Best Young American Novelists under 35, MacArthur Fellowship 2010. *Address:* c/o Publicity Dept, Random House Inc., 1745 Broadway, New York, NY 10019, USA (office). *E-mail:* bfillon@randomhouse.com (office); yiyun.write@gmail.com (home). *Website:* www.randomhouse.com (office); www.yiyunli.com.

LIBBY, Ronald Theodore, BA, MA, PhD; American academic, writer and consultant; *Professor of Political Science, University of North Florida;* b. 20 Nov. 1941, Los Angeles, Calif.; s. of Theodore Harold Libby and Patricia M. Griswold; two d. *Education:* Washington State Univ., Pullman, Univ. of Washington, Seattle. *Career:* Lecturer, Univ. of Botswana, Lesotho, and Swaziland 1973–75, Malawi 1975–76, Zambia 1976–79; Visiting Asst Prof., Univ. of Notre Dame 1981–83; Sr Lecturer, Univ. of the West Indies, Jamaica 1983–85, Victoria Univ. of Wellington, NZ 1987–89; Visiting Assoc. Prof., Northwestern Univ. 1985–86; Sr Research Fellow, ANU 1986–87; Prof. and Chair. Dept of Political Science, Southwest State Univ., Marshall, Minn. 1989–96, Saint Joseph's Univ., Phila 1996–2000; Prof. of Political Science, Univ. of N Florida, Jacksonville 2000–; Research Fellow, Blue Cross/Blue Shield Center of Medical Ethics. *Publications:* Towards an Africanized US Policy for Southern Africa 1980, The Politics of Economic Power in Southern Africa 1987, Hawke's Law: The Politics of Mining and Aboriginal Land Rights in Australia 1989, Protecting Markets: US Policy and the World Grain Trade 1992, Eco-Wars: Political Campaigns and Social Movements 1999, Treating Doctors as Drug Dealers 2005, The Criminalization of Medicine: America's War on Doctors 2008; contrib. to scholarly books and journals. *Honours:* grants include Carnegie Endowment for Int. Peace, Visiting Research Scholar, Univ. of California at Irvine 1972, Choice magazine Outstanding Academic Book 1990. *Address:* Department of Political Science and Public Administration, University of North Florida, 4567 St Johns Bluff Road, South Jacksonville, FL 32224-2645 (office); 117 Turtle Bay Lane, Ponte Verde Beach, FL 32082, USA (home). *Telephone:* (904) 620-1927 (office); (904) 808-4612 (home). *Fax:* (904) 620-2979 (office); (904) 824-5913 (home). *E-mail:* rlibby@unf.edu (office); rtl2129@aol.com (home). *Website:* www.unf.edu/~rlibby (office).

LICHTENSTEIN, Nelson, PhD; American historian; *Professor of History, University of California at Santa Barbara;* b. 15 Nov. 1944, Frederick, MD; m. Eileen Boris 1979, one s. *Education:* Univ. of California at Berkeley. *Career:* Asst Prof., Assoc. Prof., Catholic Univ. of America 1981–89; Prof., Univ. of Virginia 1989–2001; Prof. of History, Univ. of California at Santa Barbara 2001–; mem. American Historical Asscn, Organization of American Historians. *Publications:* Political Profiles: The Kennedy Years (ed.) 1976, Political Profiles: The Johnson Years (ed.) 1976, Labor's War at Home: The CIO in World War II 1982, On the Line: Essays in the History of Auto Work (co-ed.) 1989, Major Problems in the History of American Workers: Documents and Essays (ed.) 1991, Industrial Democracy in America: The Ambiguous Promise (co-ed.) 1993, Walter Reuther: the Most Dangerous Man in Detroit 1995, The United States, 1940–2000 2000, State of the Union: A Century of American Labor 2002, Wal-Mart: The Face of the Twenty-First Century Capitalism (ed.) 2006, American Capitalism: Social Thought and Political Economy in the Twentieth Century (ed.) 2006, The Retail Revolution: How Wal-Mart Created a Brave New World of Business 2009. *Address:* Department of History, University of California, Santa Barbara 93106-9410, USA (office). *Telephone:* (805) 893-4822 (office). *Fax:* (805) 893-8795 (office). *E-mail:* nelson@history.ucsb.edu (office). *Website:* www.history.ucsb.edu (office).

LICKONA, Thomas Edward, BA, MA, PhD; American developmental psychologist, academic and writer; b. 4 April 1943, Poughkeepsie, NY; m. Judith Barker 1966, two s. *Education:* Siena College, Ohio University, SUNY at Albany. *Career:* Instructor, SUNY at Albany, 1968–70; Asst Prof., 1970–75, Assoc. Prof., 1975–82, Prof. of Education, 1982–, SUNY at Cortland; Visiting

Prof., Harvard University, 1978–79, Boston University, 1979–80; numerous radio and television talk show appearances; mem. Asscn for Moral Education; Character Counts Coalition, advisory board; Character Education Partnership, board of dirs; Medical Institute for Sexual Health, advisory board. *Publications:* Open Education: Increasing Alternatives for Teachers and Children (ed. with Jessie Adams, Ruth Nickse, and David Young), 1973; Moral Development and Behavior: Theory, Research, and Social Issues (ed.), 1976; Raising Good Children: Helping Your Child Through the Stages of Moral Development, 1983; Educating for Character: How Our Schools Can Teach Respect and Responsibility, 1991; Sex, Love and You (with Judith Lickona and William Boudreau), 1994. Contributions: journals and magazines. *Honours:* Distinguished Alumni Award, SUNY at Albany; Christopher Award, 1992.

LIDDLE, Peter Hammond, BA, PGCE, MLitt, PhD, FRHistS; British historian, writer and archivist; *Director, The Second World War Experience Centre, Leeds*; b. 26 Dec. 1934, Sunderland, England. *Education:* Univ. of Sheffield, Univ. of Nottingham, Loughborough Coll. of Physical Education, Univ. of Newcastle, Univ. of Leeds. *Career:* History Teacher, Havelock School, Sunderland 1957; Head, History Dept, Gateacre Comprehensive School, Liverpool 1958–67; Lecturer, Notre Dame Coll. of Educ. 1967; Lecturer in History, Sunderland Polytechnic 1967–70, Sr Lecturer 1970–88; Keeper of the Liddle Collection, Univ. of Leeds 1988–99; Dir, The Second World War Experience Centre, Leeds 1999–; mem. British Audio Visual Trust, British Military History Comm. *Publications:* Men of Gallipoli 1976, World War One: Personal Experience Material for Use in Schools 1977, Testimony of War 1914–18 1979, The Sailor's War 1914–18 1985, Gallipoli: Pens, Pencils and Cameras at War 1985, 1916: Aspects of Conflict 1985, Home Fires and Foreign Fields 1985, The Airman's War 1914–18 1987, The Soldier's War 1914–18 1988, Voices of War 1988, The Battle of the Somme 1992, The Worst Ordeal: Britons at Home and Abroad 1914–18 1994, Facing Armageddon: The First World War Experienced (co-ed. and contributor) 1996, Passchendaele in Perspective: The Third Battle of Ypres (ed. and contributor) 1997, At the Eleventh Hour (co-ed. and contributor) 1998, For Five Shillings a Day (co-ed. and contributor) 2000, The Great World War, 1914–45 (co-ed. and contributor), two vols 2000–01, D Day: By Those Who Were There 2004; contrib. to journals and books; Founder and Ed. of following journals: The Poppy and the Owl 1988–99, Everyone's War 1999–. *Honours:* MLitt Univ. of Newcastle 1975, PhD Univ. of Leeds 1997; Distinguished Lecturer Sam Houston State Univ., Huntsville, TX 2003. *Address:* The Second World War Experience Centre, 5 Feast Field, Horsforth, Leeds LS18 4TJ (office); Prospect House, 39 Leeds Rd, Rawdon, Leeds LS19 6NW, England (home). *Telephone:* (113) 2584993 (office); (113) 2505829 (home). *Fax:* (113) 2582557 (office). *E-mail:* enquiries@war-experience.org (office); peterhliddle@yahoo.co.uk (home). *Website:* www.war-experience.org (office).

LIDSTONE, John Barrie Joseph, FCIM; British writer and business executive; b. 21 July 1929; m. Primrose Vivien 1957; one d. *Education:* Univ. of Manchester, RAF Education Officers' Course. *Career:* nat. service, RAF 1947–48; English Master, Repton 1949–52; Shell-Mex and BP and Assoc. cos 1952–62; Deputy Man. Dir Vicon Agricultural Machinery Ltd 1962–63; Dir and Gen. Man. Marketing Selections Ltd 1969–72; Dir Marketing Improvements Group plc 1968–93, Dir and Gen. Man. 1972–74, Deputy Man. Dir 1974–88, Deputy Chair. 1988–89, Dir (non-exec.) 1989–93; mem. Chemical and Allied Products Industrial Training Bd 1975–79, Nat. Inter-Active Video Centre 1988–90; Dartnell lecture tours, USA 1978–82; mem. UK Management Consultancies Asscn 1978–88 (Chair. 1986–87); Ed. Lidstorian 1985–88; mem. Nat. Exec. Cttee Chartered Inst. of Marketing 1985–90; Dir (non-exec.) Kalamazoo plc 1986–91, North Hampshire Trust Co. Ltd 1986–93, St Nicholas' School Fleet Educational Trust Ltd 1982–90, 1995–96; Sr Visiting Lecturer, Univ. of Surrey 1990–98; gave expert evidence to House of Commons Public Admin Select Cttee on reform of honours system 2004 (included in report, A Matter of Honour: Reforming the Honours System); mem. Court of Assts, Guild of Man. Consultants 1993; Marketing Ed. Pharm Times 1994–; mem. BAFTA; Fellow, Inst. of Man. Consultants, Inst. of Man. *Films:* film and video technical adviser and scriptwriter for The Persuaders 1975, Negotiating Profitable Sales 1979, Training Salesmen on the Job 1981, Marketing for Managers 1985, Marketing Today 1985, Reaching Agreement and Interviewing 1987. *Publications:* Training Salesmen on the Job 1975, Recruiting and Selecting Successful Salesmen 1976, Negotiating Profitable Sales 1977, Motivating Your Sales Force 1978, Making Effective Presentations 1985, The Sales Presentation (co-author) 1985, Profitable Selling 1986, Marketing Planning for the Pharmaceutical Industry 1987, Manual of Sales Negotiation 1991, Manual of Marketing for University of Surrey 1991, Beyond the Pay Packet 1992, Face the Press 1992, Presentation and Media Planning for the Pharmaceutical Industry 2003; contrib. chapters to The Best of Dilemma and Decision 1985, Marketing in the Service Industries 1985, Marketing Handbook (third edn) 1989, Gower Book of Management Skills (second edn) 1992, The Director's Manual 1992, The Marketing Book (third edn) 1994, Ivanhoe Guide to Management Consultants 1994, International Encyclopedia of Business and Management 1988, The Reform of the Honours System (Churchill Lecture) 1998; contrib. articles to The Times, Sunday Times, Daily Telegraph, Sunday Telegraph, Financial Times, Observer, Long Range Planning, International Management, Management Today, Marketing, Marketing Week. *Honours:* Freeman of City of London, Liveryman Worshipful Co. of Marketers; US Industrial Film Festival Award for Creative Excellence 1982.

LIEBENBERG, Lauren, MBA; South African writer; b. 3 Aug. 1972, Zimbabwe. *Education:* Univ. of Witwatersrand. *Career:* grew up in Rhodesia (now Zimbabwe); moved with family to Johannesburg, SA; worked for Rand Merchant Bank. *Publications include:* The Electronic Financial Markets of the Future: Survival Strategies of the Broker-Dealers 2002, The Voluptuous Delights of Peanut Butter and Jam (novel) 2008, The West Rand Jive Cats Boxing Club (novel) 2011. *Address:* c/o Penguin Group (South Africa), 24 Sturdee Avenue, Rosebank, Johannesburg 2196, South Africa. *E-mail:* info@za.penguingroup.com. *Website:* www.penguinbooks.co.za.

LIEBER, Robert James, BA, PhD; American academic and writer; *Professor of Government and International Affairs, Georgetown University*; b. Chicago, Ill.; m. Nancy Lieber; two s. *Education:* Univ. of Wisconsin, Univ. of Chicago, Harvard Univ. *Career:* Asst Prof., Univ. of California, Davis 1968–72, Assoc. Prof. 1972–77, Chair. Dept of Political Science 1975–76, 1977–80, Prof. 1977–81; Visiting Prof., Fudan Univ., Shanghai, People's Repub. of China 1988; Postdoctoral Fellow, St Antony's Coll., Oxford, UK 1969–70; Research Assoc., Center for Int. Affairs, Harvard Univ. 1974–75; Fellow, Woodrow Wilson Int. Center for Scholars, Washington, DC 1980–81, 1999–2000; Prof. of Govt and Int. Affairs, Georgetown Univ., Washington, DC 1982–, Chair. Dept of Govt 1990–96, Acting Chair. Dept of Psychology 1997–99; foreign policy adviser in various presidential campaigns; mem. American Political Science Asscn, Int. Political Science Asscn, Council on Foreign Relations. *Television appearances:* The News Hour with Jim Lehrer on PBS TV, ABC TV's Good Morning America and Nightline, NBC and CBS network news, The O'Reilly Factor on Fox TV, Voice of America, BBC World Service, Al Jazeera, and radio and TV programmes in Europe, the Arab world and Israel. *Publications:* British Politics and European Unity: Parties, Elites, and Pressure Groups 1970, Theory and World Politics 1972, Contemporary Politics: Europe (co-author) 1976, Oil and the Middle East War 1976, Eagle Entangled: US Foreign Policy in a Complex World (co-ed. and contrib.) 1979, Will Europe Fight for Oil? (ed.) 1983, Eagle Defiant: US Foreign Policy in the 1980s (co-ed. and contrib.) 1983, The Oil Decade: Conflict and Cooperation in the West 1986, Eagle Resurgent?: The Reagan Era in American Foreign Policy (co-ed. and contrib.) 1987, Eagle in a New World: American Grand Strategy in the Post-Cold War Era (co-ed. and contrib.) 1992, Eagle Adrift: American Foreign Policy at the End of the Century (ed. and contrib.) 1997, No Common Power: Understanding International Relations (fourth edn) 2001, Eagle Rules? Foreign Policy and American Primacy in the 21st Century (ed. and contrib.) 2002, The American Era: Power and Strategy for the 21st Century (Book of the Year Award (Bronze) in Political Science, ForeWord magazine 2005) 2005 (revised edn 2007), Power and Willpower in the American Future: Why the U.S. is Not Destined to Decline 2012; contrib. to scholarly books, professional journals and gen. periodicals. *Honours:* William Jennings Bryan Prize for Best Undergraduate Essay on a Political Subject, Univ. of Wisconsin, Graduate Fellowship Prize, Harvard Univ. 1964–68, Council on Foreign Relations Int. Affairs Fellowship 1973–74, Guggenheim Fellowship 1973–74, Rockefeller Int. Relations Fellowship 1978–79, Ford Foundation grant 1981, Public Policy Scholar, Woodrow Wilson Int. Center for Scholars 1999–2000, 21st Annual Jerome Nemer Lecturer, The Casden Inst., Univ. of Southern California 2001, 14th Annual Laura Blanche Jackson Lecturer in World Affairs, Baylor Univ. 2007. *Address:* Department of Government, Georgetown University, ICC 681, Washington, DC 20057-1034, USA (office). *Telephone:* (202) 687-5920 (office). *E-mail:* lieberr@georgetown.edu (office). *Website:* government.georgetown.edu/lieberr (office).

LIEBERMAN, Herbert Henry, AM; American novelist and playwright; b. 22 Sept. 1933, New Rochelle, NY; m. Judith Barsky 1963; one d. *Education:* City College, CUNY, Columbia Univ. *Career:* mem. Mystery Writers of America, Int. Asscn of Crime Writers. *Plays:* Matty and the Moron and Madonna, Tigers in Red Weather. *Publications:* The Adventures of Dolphin Green 1967, Crawlspace 1971, The Eighth Square 1973, Brilliant Kids 1975, City of the Dead 1976, The Climate of Hell 1978, Nightcall from a Distant Time Zone 1982, Night Bloom 1984, The Green Train 1986, Shadow Dancers 1989, Sandman Sleep 1993, The Girl with the Botticelli Eyes 1996, The Concierge 1998, The Vagabond of Holmby Park 2003. *Honours:* First Prize for Playwriting, Univ. of Chicago 1963, Guggenheim Fellowship 1964, Grand Prix de Littérature Policière, Paris 1978. *Literary Agent:* c/o Georges Borchardt, 136 East 57th Street, New York, NY 10022, USA. *Telephone:* (212) 753-5785.

LIEBERMAN, Laurence, BA, MA; American academic, poet, writer and editor; *Professor Emeritus of English, University of Illinois at Urbana-Champaign*; b. 16 Feb. 1935, Detroit, Mich.; m. Bernice Braun 1956; one s. two d. *Education:* Univ. of Michigan, Univ. of California. *Career:* Assoc. Prof. of English, Coll. of the Virgin Islands 1964–68; Assoc. Prof. of English, Univ. of Illinois at Urbana-Champaign 1968–70; Prof. of English and Creative Writing 1970–2005, Prof. Emer. 2005–; Poetry Ed., Univ. of Illinois Press 1971–2009; mem. Acad. of American Poets, Associated Writing Programs, Poetry Soc. of America. *Publications:* The Unblinding (poems) 1968, The Achievement of James Dickey 1968, The Osprey Suicides (poems) 1973, Unassigned Frequencies: American Poetry in Review 1964–77 1977, God's Measurements 1980, Eros at the World Kite Pageant: Poems 1979–83 1983, The Mural of Wakeful Sleep (poems) 1985, The Creole Mephistopheles (poems) 1990, New and Selected Poems: 1962–92 1993, The St Kitts Monkey Feuds (poem) 1995, Beyond the Muse of Memory: Essays on Contemporary American Poets 1995, Dark Songs: Slave House and Synagogue 1996, Compass of the Dying (poems)

1998, The Regatta in the Skies: Selected Long Poems 1999, Flight from the Mother Stone 2000, Hour of the Mango Black Moon 2004, Carib's Leap: Selected and New Poems 2006; contribs to anthologies, reviews, journals and magazines. *Honours:* Yaddo Foundation Fellowship 1964, Illinois Arts Council Fellowship 1981, Nat. Endowment for the Arts Fellowship 1986–87, Jerome J. Shestack Poetry Prize, American Poetry Review 1986–87. *Address:* 1304 Eliot Drive, Urbana, IL 61801, USA (home). *Telephone:* (217) 367-7186 (home); (217) 333-2390 (office). *Fax:* (217) 333-4321 (office). *E-mail:* llieberm@illinois.edu (home).

LIEBERMANN, Berta R.; Austrian poet; b. 16 March 1921, Glashütten; m. Albert Liebermann 1967. *Publications include:* Heimweh, Planet der Glücklichkeit, Traumnetz der silberner Spinne, Spätlicht, Verwehte Spuren, Rückruf der Vergangenheit, Roter Oleander, Urlaute der Schöpfung, Urwind der Frühe, Verstreute Blüten III, Gespräche mit einem Engel; contribs to newspapers on the arts. *Honours:* Hon. DLitt (Albert Einstein Acad., Mo., USA); Salsomaggiore Award 1982, Albert Einstein Medal (USA) 1990. *Address:* Kieferbachstraße 6, 83088 Kiefersfelden, Germany (home). *Telephone:* (8033) 8104 (home).

LIEBERTHAL, Kenneth Guy, BA, MA, PhD; American political scientist, academic and writer; *Senior Fellow and Director, John L. Thornton China Center, Brookings Institution*; b. 9 Sept. 1943, Asheville, NC; s. of Milton Lieberthal and Naomi Lieberthal; m. Jane Lindsay 1968; two s. *Education:* Dartmouth Coll., Columbia Univ. *Career:* Instructor, Political Science Dept, Swarthmore Coll. 1972, Asst Prof. 1972–75, Assoc. Prof. 1976–82, Prof. 1982–83; Visiting Prof., Univ. of Michigan, Ann Arbor 1983, Prof. 1983–2009, Political Science Dept, William Davidson Prof. of Business Admin, Univ. of Michigan Business School 1995–2009, Arthur F. Thurnau Prof. of Political Science 1995–2009; Special Asst to the Pres. and Sr Dir for Asia, Nat. Security Council, The White House, Washington, DC 1998–2000; Visiting Fellow, Brookings Inst. 2008–09, Sr Fellow in Foreign Policy and Global Economy and Devt 2009–, Dir John L. Thornton China Center 2009–; Sr Advisor, The Cowen Group; Sr Dir, Albright-Stonebridge Group; mem. Dept of Defense Jt Strategy Review Sr Review Panel 2004–07; mem. or fmr mem. Bd of Dirs/Advisors, Nat. Cttee on US-China Relations, East-West Center, US-China Policy Foundation, Nat. Bureau of Asian Research, US Advisory Bd of the Council on East Asian Affairs (Seoul), Tsinghua Univ.'s Center for China in the World Economy, Research Center for Contemporary China at Peking Univ., CSIS-IIE China Futures Initiative, Asian Studies Visiting Cttee at Harvard Univ., East Asian Inst. of the Nat. Univ. of Singapore, William Davidson Inst., The Pyle Center, Forum on Northeast Asia Security of the Nat. Cttee on American Foreign Policy, China Vitae web site; Fellow, Beijing Univ. Political Devt and Govt Man. Research Inst.; mem. Editorial Bd, Asia Policy, China: An International Journal, The China Quarterly, The China Economic Review, Foreign Policy Bulletin, Journal of Contemporary China, Journal of International Business Education. *Publications:* Revolution and Tradition in Tinentsin 1980, Policy Making in China: Leaders, Structures and Processes (with Michel Oksenberg), 1988; Research Guide to Central Party and Government Meetings in China 1949–86 (with Bruce Dixon) 1989, Perspectives on Modern China: Four Anniversaries (co-ed.) 1991, Bureaucracy, Politics and Policy Making in Post-Mao China (co-ed.) 1991, Governing China 2004, China's Search for Energy Security: Implications for US Policy 2006, Overcoming Obstacles to US-China Cooperation on Climate Change (with David Sandalow) 2009; contribs: Foreign Affairs, China Quarterly, Harvard Business Review; book reviews in American Political Science Review, China Economic Review, China Quarterly. *Publications include* Bureaucratic Politics and Chinese Energy Development (with Michel Oksenberg) 1986, Policy Making in China: Leaders, Structures, and Processes (with Michel Oksenberg) 1988, Paths to Sino-American Cooperation in the Automotive Sector (with Michael Flynn, et al.) 1989, Research Guide to Central Party and Government Meetings in China, 1949–1986 (with Bruce Dixon) 1989, Perspectives on Modern China: Four Anniversaries (co-ed. and contrib.) 1991, Bureaucracy, Politics and Policy Making in Post-Mao China (co-ed. with David M. Lampton and contrib.) 1991, Governing China: From Revolution through Reform 1995 (second revised edn 2004, translated as Zhili Zhongguo 2010), Constructing China: The Interaction of Culture and Economics (co-ed. with Shuen-fu Lin and Ernest Young), Univ. of Michigan Center for Chinese Studies Monograph Series, Vol. No. 78 1997, China's Search for Energy Security and Implications for US Policy (with Mikkal Herberg) 2006, Overcoming Obstacles to US-China Cooperation on Climate Change (with David Sandalow) 2009, The U.S. Intelligence Community and Foreign Policy: Getting Analysis Right 2009, Chinese Politics: New Sources, Methods, and Field Strategies (contributing co-ed.) 2010, Managing the China Challenge: How to Achieve Corporate Success in the People's Republic 2011; contribs to Foreign Affairs, China Quarterly, Harvard Business Review; book reviews in American Political Science Review, China Economic Review, China Quarterly. *Honours:* Hon. Sr Fellow, Inst. of American Studies, Chinese Acad. of Social Sciences 2008; Guest Prof., Chinese Acad. of Governance 2011; Bailey Morris-Eck Lecturer, Salzburg, Austria 2006, Rosenfield Lecturer, Grinnell Coll. 2007; McKenzie Prize Harvard Business Review 1998, Distinguished Faculty Achievement Award Univ. of Michigan 2004. *Address:* Brookings Institution, 1775 Massachusetts Avenue NW, Washington, DC 20036, USA (office). *Telephone:* (202) 797-2494 (office). *E-mail:* klieberthal@brookings.edu (office). *Website:* www.brookings.edu (office).

LIEBESCHUETZ, John Hugo Wolfgang Gideon, BA, PhD; British academic (retd) and writer; b. 22 June 1927, Hamburg, Germany; m. Margaret Rosa Taylor 1955; one s. three d. *Education:* Univ. of London. *Career:* Prof. and Head of Dept of Classical and Archaeological Studies, Univ. of Nottingham 1979–92; Fellow, British Acad. 1992–; Corresponding Fellow, German Archaeological Inst. 1994–; Fellow, Univ. Coll. London 1997; Fellow, Soc. of Antiquaries; mem. Princeton Inst. of Advanced Studies 1993. *Publications:* Antioch 1972, Continuity and Change in Roman Religion 1979, Barbarians and Bishops 1992, From Diocletian to the Arab Conquest 1992, Decline and Fall of the Roman City 2001, Ambrose of Milan: Political Letters and Speeches 2005. *Address:* 1 Clare Valley, The Park, Nottingham, NG7 1BU, England (home). *E-mail:* wolf.lieb@btinternet.com (home).

LIEBLER, Michael Lynn, BA, MA; American lecturer and poet; b. 24 Aug. 1953, Detroit, Mich.; m. Pamela Mary Liebler 1976; one s. one d. *Education:* Oakland University, Rochester, Mich. *Career:* part-time Instructor, Henry Ford Community College 1980–86; Lecturer, Wayne State University, Detroit 1981–92, Senior Lecturer 1992–; Dir National Writers' Voice Project 1995–; Arts and Humanities Dir YMCA of Metro Detroit; mem. American Asscn of University Profs, Associated Writing Programs, MLA, National Council of Teachers of English, National Writers Voice Project, National Writers Corp Program, Poetry Resource Center of Michigan (Pres. 1987–93), Popular Culture Asscn. *Publications include:* Measuring Darkness 1980, Breaking the Voodoo: Selected Poems 1990, Deliver Me 1991, Stripping the Adult Century Bare 1995, Brooding the Heartlands 1998; contributions: Rattle, Exquisite Corpse, Cottonwood Review, Relix Magazine, Christian Science Monitor, Detroit Sunday Journal, Review of Contemporary Fiction, American Book Review. *Address:* PO Box 120, Roseville, MI 48066, USA.

LIEHU, Rakel Maria; Finnish poet and writer; b. 3 Sept. 1939, Nivala. *Career:* newspaper columnist and translator. *Publications include:* Kubisseja (poems, trans. as Cubisms) 1992, Murehtimatta! Smaragdinen (poems, trans. as Grieve Not! Emerald) 1993, Readymade (poems) 1995, Skorpionin sydän (poems, trans. as Scorpion's Heart) 1997, Helene (novel) 2003; also trans. of German and Swedish poetry; contrib. to Zeitschrift für Literatur, Kunst und Zeitkritik. *Honours:* Asscn of Authors Prize 1992. *Address:* c/o Penumbra Press, POB 940, Manotick, ON K4M 1A8, Canada (office).

LIFSHIN, Lyn Diane, BA, MA; American poet and teacher; b. 12 July 1944, Burlington, Vt. *Education:* Syracuse Univ., Univ. of Vermont. *Career:* Instructor, SUNY at Cobleskill 1968, 1970; Writing Consultant, New York State Mental Health Dept, Albany 1969, Empire State Coll. of SUNY at Saratoga Springs 1973; Poet-in-Residence, Mansfield State Coll., Pennsylvania 1974, Univ. of Rochester, New York 1986, Antioch's Writers' Conference, Ohio 1987. *Publications include:* poetry: over 120 collections, including: Upstate Madonna: Poems 1970–74 1975, Shaker House Poems 1976, Some Madonna Poems 1976, Leaning South 1977, Madonna Who Shifts for Herself 1983, Kiss the Skin Off 1985, Many Madonnas 1988, The Doctor Poems 1990, Apple Blossoms 1993, Blue Tattoo 1995, The Mad Girl Drives in a Daze 1995, Barbie Poems, Marilyn Monroe, Lost in the Fog 2008, Desire 2008, Drifting 2008, Nutley Pond 2008, Ballet Madonnas 2009, Barbaro: Beyond Brokenness 2009, Lost Horses 2009, Light at the End 2009, Katrina 2010; ed.: Tangled Vines: A Collection of Mother and Daughter Poems 1978, Ariadne's Thread: A Collection of Contemporary Women's Journals 1982, Unsealed Lips 1988; other: In Mirrors, Upstate: An Unfinished Story, The Daughter I Don't Have, Cold Comfort (Paterson Review Award) 1997, Before It's Light (Paterson Review Award) 2000, The Licorice Daughter: My Year With Ruffian (Texas Review Award) 2006, Another Woman Looks Like Me 2007, 92 Rapple Drive 2007, When a Cat Dies 2007, In the Darkness of Night 2007, What Matters Most 2007; contributions: many books and numerous other publications, including journals. *Honours:* Hart Crane Award, Bread Loaf Scholarship, Yaddo Fellowship 1970, 1971, 1975, 1979, 1980, MacDowell Fellowship 1973, Millay Colony Fellowships 1975, 1979, Jack Kerouac Award 1984, Centennial Review Poetry Prize 1985, Madeline Sadin Award, New York Quarterly 1986, Footwork Award 1987, Estersceffler Award 1987. *Address:* 2719 Baronhurst Drive, Vienna, VA 22181, USA (home). *Telephone:* (703) 242-3829 (home). *Fax:* (703) 242-0127 (home). *Website:* www.lynlifshin.com.

LIFTON, Robert Jay, MD; American psychiatrist, academic and writer; *Lecturer in Psychiatry, Cambridge Health Alliance/Harvard Medical School*; b. 16 May 1926, New York, NY; s. of Harold A. Lifton and Ciel Roth Lifton; m. Betty Jean Kirschner 1952; one s. one d. *Education:* Cornell Univ., New York Medical Coll. *Career:* intern, Jewish Hosp. of Brooklyn, New York 1948–49; Resident, State Univ. Medical Center, VA Program, Northport and Brooklyn, NY 1949–51; Resident Fellow, Washington School of Psychiatry, Hong Kong and Washington, DC 1954–55; Research Assoc. in Psychiatry, Harvard Medical School 1955–61; Foundation's Fund for Research Assoc. Prof. of Psychiatry 1961–67; Prof. of Psychiatry, Yale Univ. School of Medicine, New Haven, Conn. 1967–85; Distinguished Prof. of Psychiatry and Psychology and Dir Center on Violence and Human Survival, John Jay Coll. of Criminal Justice, Grad. School and Univ. Center, and Mount Sinai School of Medicine, CUNY 1985–2003; Lecturer in Psychiatry, Cambridge Health Alliance/Harvard Medical School 2003–; several guest lectureships; mem. American Psychiatric Asscn, Asscn of Asian Studies, Fed. of American Scientists, Soc. for Psychological Study of Social Issues; Fellow, American Acad. of Arts and Sciences 1970. *Publications:* Thought Reform and the Psychology of Totalism: A Study of Brainwashing in China 1961, The Woman in America (ed.) 1965, America and the Asian Revolutions (ed.) 1966, Revolutionary Immorality:

Mao Tse-Tung and the Chinese Cultural Revolution 1968, Death in Life: Survivors of Hiroshima 1969, History and Human Survival 1970, Boundaries: Psychological Man in Revolution 1970, Crimes of War (co-ed. with R. A. Falk and G. Kolko) 1971, Home from the War: Vietnam Veterans–Neither Victims Nor Executioners 1973, Living and Dying (with Eric Olson) 1974, Explorations in Psychohistory: The Wellfleet Papers (co-ed. with E. Olson) 1975, The Life of the Self 1976, Six Lives, Six Deaths: Portraits from Modern Japan (with Shuichi Kato and Michael Reich) 1979, The Broken Connection: On Death and the Continuity of Life 1979, Indefensible Weapons: The Political and Psychological Case Against Nuclearism (with Richard A. Falk) 1982, Last Aid: Medical Dimensions of Nuclear War (co-ed. with E. Chivian, S. Chivian and J. E. Mack) 1982, In a Dark Time: Images for Survival (co-ed. with N. Humphrey) 1984, The Nazi Doctors: Medical Killing and Psychology of Genocide 1986, The Future of Immortality and Other Essays for a Nuclear Age 1987, The Genocidal Mentality: Nazi Holocaust and Nuclear Threat (with Eric Markusen) 1990, The Protean Self: Human Resilience in an Age of Fragmentation 1993, Hiroshima in America: Fifty Years of Denial 1995, Destroying the World to Save It: Aum Shinrikyo, Apocalyptic Violence and the New Global Terrorism 1999, Who Owns Death?: Capital Punishment, the American Conscience and the End of Executions (with Greg Mitchell) 2000, Beyond Invisible Walls: The Psychological Legacy of Soviet Trauma (co-ed. with J. D. Lindy) 2001, Superpower Syndrome: America's Apocalyptic Confrontation with the World 2003, Crimes of War: Iraq (co-ed. with R. Falk and I. Gendzier) 2006; contrib. to professional journals. *Honours:* various hon. degrees, Hon. DHumLitt or Hon. DSc, including those from Lawrence Univ., Appleton, Wis. 1971, New York Medical Coll. 1977, Univ. of Vermont 1984, Universität-Munchen, Munich, Germany 1989, State Univ. of NY Coll. at New Paltz 1991, Saybrook Inst. Grad. School and Research Center, San Francisco, Calif. 1995, Colgate Univ., Hamilton, NY 1999, Lifetime Achievement Award, Int. Soc. for Traumatic Stress Studies 2004; Nat. Book Award in the Sciences 1969, Van Wyck Brooks Award 1969, Hiroshima Gold Medal 1975, Gandhi Peace Award 1984, Bertrand Russell Soc. Award 1985, Holocaust Memorial Award 1986, Nat. Jewish Book Award 1987, Los Angeles Times Book Prize for History 1987, Lisl and Leo Eitinger Award, Oslo 1988, American Orthopsychiatrists Asscn Max A. Hayman Award 1992, Psychiatric Inst. Nat. Living Treasure Award 1994, Outstanding Achievement Award, Armenian-American Soc. for Studies on Stress and Genocide 1996, Pioneer Award, Int. Soc. for Traumatic Stress Studies 1985, Boston Public Library Literary Lights Award 2006. *Address:* Department of Psychiatry, Cambridge Health Alliance, 1493 Cambridge Street, Cambridge, MA 02139, USA (office).

LIGHTMAN, Alan Paige, AB, PhD; American physicist, writer and academic; *Professor of the Practice of the Humanities, Massachusetts Institute of Technology;* b. 28 Nov. 1948, Memphis, Tenn.; s. of Richard Lightman and Jeanne Lightman (née Garretson); m. Jean Greenblatt 1976; two d. *Education:* Princeton Univ., California Inst. of Technology. *Career:* Postdoctoral Fellow, Cornell Univ. 1974–76; Asst Prof., Harvard Univ. 1976–79; staff scientist Smithsonian Astrophysical Observatory, Cambridge 1979–88; Prof. of Science and Writing, MIT 1988–2002, John E. Burchard Chair 1995–2001, f. Grad. Program in Science Writing 2001, Adjunct Prof. of Humanities, Creative Writing, Physics 2002–12, Prof. of the Practice of the Humanities 2012–; Founding Dir Harpswell Foundation to empower women leaders in Cambodia 2003; Fellow, American Acad. of Arts and Sciences, American Physical Soc.; mem. American Astronomical Soc. *Publications:* fiction: Einstein's Dreams 1993, Good Benito 1994, The Diagnosis 2000, Reunion 2003, Ghost 2007, Song of Two Worlds 2009, Mr g 2012; non-fiction: Problem Book in Relativity and Gravitation 1974, Radiative Process in Astrophysics (with George B. Rybicki) 1976, Time Travel and Papa Joe's Pipe 1984, A Modern Day Yankee in a Connecticut Court and Other Essays on Science 1986, Origins: The Lives and Worlds of Modern Cosmologists (with Roberta Brawer) 1990, Ancient Light: Our Changing View of the Universe (adapted from Origins) 1991, Great Ideas in Physics 1992, Time for the Stars: Astronomy in the 1990s 1992, The World is Too Much with Me: Finding Private Space in the Wired World 1992, Dance for Two: Selected Essays 1996, A Sense of the Mysterious: Science and the Human Spirit 2005, The Discoveries 2005; editor: Revealing the Universe: Prediction and Proof in Astronomy (with James Cornell) 1982, The Best American Essays 2000; contrib. to professional journals and literary magazines. *Honours:* Hon. DLitt (Bowdoin Coll.) 2005, Hon. DFA (Memphis Coll. of Arts) 2006; Hon. Dr of Humanities (Univ. of Maryland) 2006, Hon. DHumLitt (Univ. of Massachusetts) 2010; Asscn of American Publishers Most Outstanding Science Book in the Physical Sciences Award 1990, Boston Globe Winship Book Prize 1993, American Inst. of Physics Andrew Gemant Award 1996, Nat. Public Radio Book of the Month 1998, Distinguished Alumnus Award, California Inst. of Tech. 2003, Sigma Xi John P. McGovern Award, 2006, Gold Medal for Humanitarian Service, Govt of Cambodia 2008, Sydney Award for Best Essays 2011. *Address:* Massachusetts Institute of Technology, Room 14E-303, 77 Massachusetts Avenue, Cambridge, MA 02139, USA (office). *Telephone:* (617) 253-2308 (office). *Website:* www.harpswellfoundation.org (office); www.alanlightman.com.

LIKHANOV, Albert Anatolyevich; Russian writer, journalist and human rights activist; *President, International Association of Children's Funds;* b. 13 Sept. 1935, Kirov; m. Liliya Alexandrovna; one c. *Education:* Urals Gorky State Univ., Yekaterinburg. *Career:* Contrib. Kirovskaya Pravda newspaper 1958–61; Ed. Komsomolskoye Plemya 1961–64; Corresp. for Western Siberia Komsomolskaya Pravda, Novosibirsk 1964–66; various posts central cttee of Komsomol (Young Communists' League) 1966; Exec. Sec. Smena magazine 1967–75, Ed.-in-Chief 1975–88; Chair. All-Union Creative Youth Council 1979; Pres. Asscn of Literary and Artistic Figures for Children and Youth, Union of Soviet Socs for Friendship and Cultural Relations with Foreign Countries 1982–87; Chair. Lenin Soviet Children's Fund 1987; Dir Research Inst. of Childhood 1989–; People's Deputy of the USSR 1989–92, mem. USSR Supreme Soviet; founder Dom Children's Fund; founder Bozhiy Mir, Ditna Chelovecheskoye and Putevodnaya Zvezda journals; Chair. Russian Children's Fund 1991–; Pres. Int. Asscn of Children's Funds 1992–. *Publications include:* Semeinye Obstoyatelstva (trilogy, trans. as Family Circumstances) 1974, selected works (two vols) 1976, essays (four vols) 1986–87, Russkiye Malchiki (trans. as Russian Boys) 1995, Mushskaya Shkola (trans. as Boys' School) 1995, essays (six vols) 2000, Nikto (trans. as Nobody) 2000, Slomannaya Kukla (trans. as A Broken Doll) 2002. *Honours:* Order of the Red Banner of Labour, Order of the Badge of Honour, Russian Orthodox Church Order of the Holy and Righteous Prince Daniil of Moscow, Russian Orthodox Church Order of Sergiy of Radonezh, Order for Service to the Fatherland (Rank IV), Russian Orthodox Church Order of St Innokentiy 2002; Russian State Prize, Lenin Komsomol Prize, Ostrovsky Prize, Polevoy Prize, Int. Korchak Prize, Int. Gorky Prize, Victor Hugo Prize (France), Tolstoy Int. Gold Medal 1995. *Address:* c/o International Association of Children's Funds, Russian Children's Fund, Armyansky per. 11/2a, 101963 Moscow, Russia. *Telephone:* (495) 9258200. *Fax:* (495) 2002276.

LIKING, Werewere; Cameroonian playwright, poet, writer and painter; *Artistic Director, Village et Fondation Ki-Yi Mbock;* b. (Nicole Eddy-Njock), 1 May 1950, Bondé; d. of Daniel Njock and Berthe Ngwe; m. Gnepo Gnepa Ganthier; two c. *Career:* f. Ki-Yi Group, Abidjan, Côte d'Ivoire 1985; several art exhbns in Africa and Europe; singer with Reines Mères group. *Plays:* La puissance de Um (trans. as The Power of Um) 1979, Une nouvelle terre (A New Earth) 1980, Singue Mura 1990, Un Touareg s'est Marie a une Pygmee 1992, Heros d'Eau 1993, The Amputated Memory 2004. *Films:* Dieu Chose 1988, L'enfant Lion. *Recordings:* Carnet & B with Ki-Yi Group 1995, Les Reines Mères Oh la la! & Profession Femme 2010. *Publications:* novels: A la rencontre de ... 1980, Orphée Dafric 1981, Elle sera de jaspe et de corail (trans. as It shall be of jasper and coral) 1983, L'Amour-cent-vies (trans. as Love hundred lives) 2000, La mémoire amputée (Noma Award 2005) 2004; poetry: On ne raisonne pas avec le venin 1977. *Honours:* Chevalier, Ordre des Arts et des Lettres 1992, Officer, Ordre de la Culture (Cameroon), Chevalier, Ordre Nat. (Cameroon); Prince Claus Award 2000. *Address:* Village et Fondation Ki-Yi Mbock, 08 BP 21 Cidex 02, Abidjan 08, Côte d'Ivoire (office). *Telephone:* 22-43-09-93 (office); 22-43-59-47 (office); 1-10-82-13 (mobile). *E-mail:* kiyivillage@yahoo.fr (office); contact@lesreinesmeres.com (office). *Website:* www.kiyi-village.org (office); lesreinesmeres.com (office).

LIKSOM, Rosa; Finnish author, playwright, artist and filmmaker; b. (Anni Ylävaara), 7 Jan. 1958, Ylitornio. *Education:* Univ. of Moscow. *Exhibitions:* numerous solo and group exhbns. *Films include:* Ordinary Life in Cosmic Kitchen 1990, Six Feet High in Puppet Love 1990, Freaky Crew 1990, Dyve In 1991, Cut Up Doble 1991, La Tour Eiffel 1991, Lollipop 1992, Hair-Tonic for Pony 1992, Hindumama and the Plastic Academy 1992, How to Clean Up in American Style 1992, Vampirella 1996, Shopping 1996, Cosmetic Boat 1996, Risto (documentary) 1999, Finlandia – National Landscape 2008, Finlandia – Suburban Landscape 2009, Finlandia – Historical Monuments 2010; screenplays: Kadonneet kakarat 1989, Mari 17 1990, Missä on suuri pohjoinen (Where is the Big North) 1991, Hysteria 1993, Aino 1996. *Plays:* Family Affairs 1993, Reitari 2005, Jepata Nasta Pohjoisnavalla 2011, Rikos 2012; several stage monologues. *Publications include:* short story collections: Yhden yön pysäkki (Erkko Literature Prize 1985) 1985, Unohdettu vartti 1986, Väliasema Gagarin 1987, Go Moskova go 1988, Tyhjän tien paratiisit 1989, Bamalama 1993, Perhe 2000, Maa 2006; novels: Kreisland 1996, Reitari 2002; play: Family Affairs 2008; children's books: Jepata Nastan lentomatka 2002, Tivoli Tähtisade 2004, Jepata Nasta Pohjoisnavalla 2008, Neko 2009. *Honours:* Awards: Weilin + Göös Literature Prize 1986, Kalevi Jäntti Literature Prize 1986, Art Prize of Province of Lapland 1987, EBU Screenplay Prize 1987, State Prize for Literature 1987, Scandinavian Literature Prizes 1989, 1990, Uudet kirjat Book Club Prize 1990, Vuoden kiila 1991, EU Literature Prizes 1995, 1998, Dublin Literature Prize 1995, WSOY Literature Prize 2006, Finlandia Literary Prize 2011. *Address:* c/o WSOY, PO Box 222, 00121 Helsinki, Finland. *Fax:* (9) 6168-3560. *E-mail:* foreign.rights@wsoy.fi; rosa@rosaliksom.com. *Website:* www.wsoy.fi; www.rosaliksom.com.

LILIENTHAL, Alfred Morton, BA, LLD; American author, historian, attorney and academic; b. 25 Dec. 1913, New York, NY. *Education:* Cornell University, Columbia University School of Law. *Career:* Ed., Middle East Perspective, 1968–85; mem. University Club; Cornell Club; National Press Club; Capital Hill Club. *Publications:* What Price Israel?, 1953; There Goes the Middle East, 1958; The Other Side of the Coin, 1965; The Zionist Connection I, 1978; The Zionist Connection II, 1982. Contributions: numerous journals. *Honours:* National Press Club Book Honours 1982.

LILLINGTON, Kenneth James; British author, dramatist and academic (retd); b. 7 Sept. 1916, London, England. *Education:* St Dunstan's Coll., Wandsworth Training Coll. *Career:* fmr Lecturer in English Literature, Brooklands Technical Coll., Weybridge, Surrey. *Publications:* The Devil's Grandson 1954, Soapy and the Pharoah's Curse 1957, Conjuror's Alibi 1960, The Secret Arrow 1960, Blue Murder 1960, A Man Called Hughes 1962, My Proud Beauty 1963, First (and Second) Book of Classroom Plays 1967–68,

Fourth (and Seventh) Windmill Book of One-Act Plays 1967–72, Cantaloup Crescent 1970, Olaf and the Ogre 1972, Nine Lives (ed.) 1977, For Better for Worse 1979, Young Map of Morning 1979, What Beckoning Ghost 1983, Selkie 1985, Full Moon 1986, A Trick of the Dark 1995. *Address:* c/o Faber and Faber Ltd, Bloomsbury House, 74–77 Great Russell Street, London, WC1B 3DA, England (office). *Website:* www.faber.co.uk (office).

LIM, Catherine, PhD; Singaporean writer and political commentator; b. 23 March 1942, Malaya; one s. one d. *Education:* Univ. of Malaya, Univ. of Singapore. *Career:* writer, first book published 1978; columnist, The Straits Times 1994–. *Publications include:* Little Ironies: Stories of Singapore 1978, Or Else: The Lightning God and Other Stories 1980, The Serpent's Tooth 1982, They do Return 1983, The Shadow of a Shadow of a Dream: Love Stories of Singapore 1987, O Singapore! Stories in Celebration 1989, Love's Lonely Impulses 1992, Deadline for Love & Other Stories 1992, The Best of Catherine Lim 1993, The Woman's Book of Superlatives 1993, Meet Me on the Queen Elizabeth II 1993, The Bondmaid 1995, The Teardrop Story Woman 1997, The Howling Silence 1999, Following the Wrong God Home 2001, The Song of Silver Frond 2003, Unhurried Thoughts at my Funeral 2005, Humoresque 2006. *Honours:* Dr hc (Murdoch Univ.); South-East Asia Write Award. *Address:* c/o Horizon Books Pte Ltd, Block 5, Ang Mo Kio Industrial Park 2A, #05-12/14, AMK Tech II, Singapore 567760, Singapore (office). *E-mail:* contact@catherinelim.sg (office); horizon@horizonbooks.com.sg (office). *Website:* www.horizonbooks.com.sg (office); catherinelim.sg (home).

LIM, Shirley Geok-Lin, MA, PhD; Malaysian/American academic, author and poet; *Professor of English, University of California, Santa Barbara;* b. 27 Dec. 1944, Malacca, Malaysia; m. Dr Charles Bazerman 1972; one s. *Education:* Univ. of Malaya, Brandeis Univ. *Career:* Lecturer and Teaching Asst, Univ. of Malaya 1967–69; Teaching Fellow, Queens College, CUNY 1972–73; Asst Prof., Hostos Community Coll., CUNY 1973–76; Lecturer, Universiti Sains, Penang, Malaysia 1974; Assoc. Prof., SUNY at Westchester 1976–90; Writer-in-Residence, Univ. of Singapore 1985, East West Center, Honolulu 1988; Prof. of Asian American Studies, Univ. of California, Santa Barbara 1990–93, Prof. of English and Women's Studies 1993–2002, Prof. of English 1993–; Fulbright Distinguished Lecturer, Nanyang Technological Univ. 1996; Chair and Prof. of English, Univ. of Hong Kong 1999–2001; Visiting Prof., MIT 2003; mem. American Studies, Asscn for Asian American Studies, Asscn for Commonwealth Languages and Literatures, MLA, Multi-Ethnic Literatures of the United States, Nat. Women's Studies Asscn; numerous grants and fellowships, Fulbright Scholarship, Wien Int. Fellowship 1969–72, ISEAS Fellowship 1985-86, Distinguished Lecturer, Univ. of Western Australia 1999, Salzburg American Studies Lecturer 2003; ISEAS Writer-in-Residence NUS 1982, East-West Center 1984, Hedgebrook 1999. *Publications:* Crossing the Peninsula and Other Poems 1980, Another Country and Other Stories 1982, No Man's Grove and Other Poems 1985, Modern Secrets: New and Selected Poems 1989, Nationalism and Literature: Literature in English from the Philippines and Singapore 1993, Monsoon History: Selected Poems 1994, Writing Southeast/Asia in English: Against the Grain 1994, Life's Mysteries: The Best of Shirley Lim 1995, Among the White Moon Faces: An Asian-American Memoir of Homelands 1996, Two Dreams: Short Stories 1997, What the Fortune Teller Didn't Say 1998, Joss and Gold 2001, Sister Swing 2006, Listening to the Singer 2007; editor: The Forbidden Stitch: An Asian American Women's Anthology 1989, Approaches to Teaching Kingston's The Woman Warrior 1991, Reading the Literatures of Asian America 1992, One World of Literature 1993, Transnational Asia Pacific 1999, Asian American Literature: An Anthology 2000, Tilting the Continent 2000, Power, Race and Gender in Academe 2000, Moving Poetry 2001, Transnational Asian American Literature 2006; ed journals: ARIEL 2001, Tulsa Studies in Women's Writing 2004, Studies in the Literary Imagination 2004, Life Writing 2006, Concentric 2007; contribs to anthologies, books, reviews, quarterlies and journals. *Honours:* Research Lecturer Award, Univ. of California, Santa Barbara 2002, Professorial Award 2007, Commonwealth Poetry Prize 1980, Asiaweek Short Story Competition 1982, American Book Awards 1990, 1997, J. T. Stewart Award 1999. *Address:* English Department, University of California, Santa Barbara, Santa Barbara, CA 93106, USA. *Telephone:* (805) 893-8584 (office). *Fax:* (805) 893-4622. *E-mail:* slim@english.ucsb.edu (office).

LIM, Suchen Christine; Malaysian teacher, writer and dramatist; b. 15 July 1948; two s. *Education:* National University of Singapore. *Publications:* Ricebowl, 1984; The Amah: A Portrait in Black and White (play), 1986; Gift From the Gods, 1990; Fistful of Colours, 1993; A Bit of Earth, 2000. Contributions: anthologies and journals. *Honours:* Shell Short Play Award, National University of Singapore, 1986; Singapore Literature Prize, 1992; Fulbright Award, 1996. *E-mail:* suchenchristinelim@hotmail.com.

LIMA, Robert, BA, MA, PhD; American academic, writer, poet and dramatist, translator, editor and bibliographer; *Fellow Emeritus, Institute for the Arts and Humanistic Studies, Pennsylvania State University;* b. (Roberto Alfredo Lima Millares), 7 Nov. 1935, Havana, Cuba; s. of Robert F. Lima and Juanita Millares; m. Sally Murphy 1964; two s. two d. *Education:* Villanova Univ., New York Univ. *Career:* Lecturer, Hunter Coll., CUNY 1962–65; Asst Prof., Pennsylvania State Univ. 1965–69, Assoc. Prof. 1969–73, Prof. of Spanish and Comparative Literature 1973–2002, Prof. Emer., Fellow Emer. 2002–; Sr Fulbright Scholar and Visiting Prof., Pontifica Universidad Católica del Peru 1976–77; Poet-in-Residence, Universidad de San Marcos, Peru 1976–77; Visiting Scholar and Lecturer, Univ. of Yaoundé, Cameroon 1986; USIA Lecturer in Peru, Cameroon, Equatorial Guinea; mem. Poetry Soc. of America, International PEN, American Center; Academician, Academia Norteamericana de la Lengua Española; Corresp. mem. Real Academia Española; Fellow Emer., Inst. for the Arts and Humanistic Studies. *Art exhibitions:* Eye of the Beholder: The Poetry of Robert Lima & the Photography of Margaret Duda, Penn State Univ. 1993, The Poetic World of Robert Lima: A Retrospective, Penn State Univ. 2004, Framed Poetry, State Theatre Gallery, State Coll., Pa 2010, Betsy Rogers Gallery, Schlow Library, State Coll. 2012. *Plays:* Episode in Sicily (premiered at UNESCO Int. Drama Festival, PA) 1959, The Lesson 1960, The Inmates of St Mary Egyptian (premiered at Pennsylvania State Univ., also performed at Edinburgh Fringe Festival) 1980, numerous translations of Spanish plays from the Siglo de Oro through modern times. *Films:* Eye of the Beholder (DVD) 1993, Shared Stories of World War II – Robert Lima (DVS) (WPSU-TV) 2008. *Radio:* SU-FM radio broadcasts on Hispanic Heritage Month, Columbus Day, museum exhibits, etc., Tracking the Minotaur – Poems read by Robert Lima and recorded at WPSU Studios on CD 2011. *Recording:* Santa Rosalía – Cantata for Voices and Chamber Orchestra, Spanish libretto by Robert Lima 2007 (premiered in Bogotá, Colombia). *Publications:* Reader's Encyclopedia of American Literature (co-ed., revised edn) 1962, The Theatre of García Lorca 1963, Borges the Labyrinth Maker (ed. and trans.) 1965, Ramón del Valle-Inclán 1972, An Annotated Bibliography of Ramón del Valle-Inclán 1972, Dos ensayos sobre teatro español de los veinte (co-author) 1984, Valle-Inclán: The Theatre of his Life 1988, Savage Acts: Four Plays (ed. and trans.) 1993, Borges and the Esoteric (ed. and contrib.) 1993, Valle-Inclán: El teatro de su vida 1995, Dark Prisms: Occultism in Hispanic Drama 1995, Homenaje a/Tribute to Martha T. Halsey (co-ed. and contrib.) 1995, Ramón del Valle-Inclán, An Annotated Bibliography, Vol. I: The Works 1999, The Alchemical Art of Leonora Carrington, Special Issue of Cauda Pavonis, Studies in Hermeticism (ed. and contrib.) 2001, The Dramatic World of Valle-Inclán 2003, Stages of Evil: Occultism in Western Theater and Drama 2005, The International Bibliography of Studies on the Life and Works of Ramón del Valle-Inclán 2008, Dark Prisms: Occultism in Hispanic Drama 2009, Prismas oscuros. El ocultismo en el teatro hispánico 2010; poetry: Fathoms 1981, The Olde Ground 1985, Mayaland 1992, Sardinia/Sardegna 2001, Tracking the Minotaur 2003, The Pointing Bone 2008, The Rites of Stone 2010; contrib. to many books, reference works, anthologies, newspapers, reviews, quarterlies and journals. *Honours:* Kt Commdr, Orden de Isabel la Católica 2003, Enxebre Orden da Vieira 2002, initiated Fon, Menda-Nkwe Nation, Bamenda (Camoroun); Cintas Fellowship in Poetry, Sr Fulbright Fellowship 1976–77, Fellowships, Villanova Univ. Coll. of Arts and Sciences Distinguished Alumnus Medal 1999. *Address:* 485 Orlando Avenue, State College, PA 16803, USA (home). *Telephone:* (814) 238-8359 (office). *E-mail:* rxl2@psu.edu (office). *Website:* www.personal.psu.edu/rxl2.

LIMONOV, Eduard; Russian/French writer, poet and politician; *Chairman, National Bolshevik Party;* b. (Eduard Venyaminovich Savenko), 22 Feb. 1943, Dzerzhinsk, Gorkii (now Nizhnii Novgorod) Oblast; m. 1st Yelena Limonova Shchapova 1971 (divorced); m. 2nd Natalya Medvedeva (divorced); m. 6th Yekaterina Volkova 2006; one s. one d. *Career:* first wrote poetry at age of 15; in Kharkov 1965–67, moved to Moscow in 1967, worked as a tailor; left USSR 1974; settled in New York, USA 1975; moved to Paris, France 1982; participant in Russian nationalist movt 1990–; returned to Russia 1991; Chair. Nat. Radical Party 1992–93; Chair. Nat. Bolshevik Party (banned political party) 1994–; arrested on terrorism and conspiracy charges 2001, sentenced by Saratov Oblast Court to four years' imprisonment for illegal acquisition and possession of arms April 2003, released June 2003; f. Russia without Putin movt Jan. 2004. *Publications include:* verse and prose in Kontinent, Ekho, Kovcheg, Apollon –1977 (in trans. in England, USA, Austria and Switzerland); over 40 books including It's Me – Eddie (novel) 1979, Russian (Russkoye) (verse) 1979, Diary of a Failure 1982, Teenager Savenko: Memoir of a Russian Punk 1983, The Young Scoundrel (memoir) 1986, The Death of Contemporary Heroes 1993, The Murder of the Sentry 1993, Selected Works (three vols) 1999, The eXile: Sex, Drugs and Libel in the New Russia (with Mark Ames and Matt Taibbi) 2000, My Political Biography; articles in Russian Communist and nationalist newspapers 1989–. *E-mail:* nbpinfo@gmail.com (office). *Website:* www.nazbol.ru (office); limonov2012.ru.

LIN, Lin; Chinese writer; b. 27 Sept. 1910, Zhao'an Co., Fujian Prov.; s. of Lin Hede and Zhen Yilian; m. 1st Wu Lanjiao 1930 (deceased); m. 2nd Chen Ling 1950; two s. two d. *Education:* Zhao'an middle school, Chinese Univ., Beijing, Waseda Univ. Tokyo, Japan. *Career:* joined Left-Wing Movt in Literature, 1934–36; returned to Shanghai 1936; Ed., Jiuwang Daily, Shanghai 1937, Guangzhou 1938, Guilin 1939–41; Chief Ed. of Huaqiao Guide, Manila, Philippines 1941–47; Prof., Dept of Chinese Literature, Dade Coll., Hong Kong 1947–49; Cultural Counsellor, Embassy, New Delhi, India 1955–58; Vice-Pres. of the China-Japan Friendship Asscn 1965–; Vice-Pres. Chinese People's Asscn for Friendship with Foreign Countries 1973–86; Pres. China Soc. for Study of Japanese Literature 1980–94, Hon. Pres. 1994–; mem. 5th, 6th and 7th Nat. Cttees CPPCC 1978–93. *Publications:* Poems of India 1958, Essays about Japan 1982, A Selection of Japanese Classical Haiku 1983, The Sea and the Ship (essays) 1987, A Selection of Japanese Modern Haiku 1990, Amaranthus (poems) 1991, Cutting Clouds (Chinese haiku) 1994, Continued Essays About Japan 1994, Memoirs of My First 88 Years 2002. *Honours:* Hon. mem. Nat. Cttee, Chinese Writers' Asscn 2002–; Yakushi Inoue Cultural Exchange Award 1996. *Address:* Room 402, Building 22, Congwenmen Dongdajie Street, Beijing 100062, People's Republic of China (home).

LIN, Wallace (see Leong, Russell Charles)

LIN, Yanni; Hong Kong writer. *Publications include:* Ming yue 1985, Song jun he chu 1989, Qing chun zhi zang 1990, Wei wo er sheng 1990, Xue si gu ren ren si xue 1991.

LINACRE, Sir (John) Gordon Seymour, Kt, CBE, AFC, DFM, CCMI; British newspaper executive; b. 23 Sept. 1920, Sheffield; s. of John J. Linacre and Beatrice B. Linacre; m. Irene A. Gordon 1943; two d. *Education:* Firth Park Grammar School, Sheffield. *Career:* served RAF, rank of Squadron Leader 1939–46; journalistic appointments Sheffield Telegraph/Star 1937–47; Kemsley News Service 1947–50; Deputy Ed. Newcastle Journal 1950–56, Newcastle Evening Chronicle 1956–57; Ed. Sheffield Star 1958–61; Asst Gen. Man. Sheffield Newspapers Ltd 1961–63; Exec. Dir Thomson Regional Newspapers Ltd, London 1963–65; Man. Dir Yorkshire Post Newspapers Ltd 1965–83, Deputy Chair. 1981–83, Chair. 1983–90, Pres. 1990–2009; Dir United Newspapers PLC 1969–91, Deputy Chair. 1981–91, Chief Exec. 1983–88; Deputy Chair. Express Newspapers PLC 1985–88; also fmr Chair. United Provincial Newspapers Ltd, Sheffield Newspapers Ltd, Lancashire Evening Post Ltd, Northampton Mercury Co. Ltd, East Yorkshire Printers Ltd etc.; Dir Yorkshire TV 1969–90; Chair. Leeds Univ. Foundation 1989–2000; Chair. Chameleon TV Ltd 1994–2008; Chair. Opera North Ltd 1978–98, Pres. 1998–; many other professional and public appointments. *Honours:* Commendatore, Ordine al Merito della Repubblica Italiana 1973, Grand Ufficiale 1987; Kt Order of the White Rose, Finland 1987; Hon. LLD (Leeds) 1991.

LINCOLN, Bruce Kenneth, BA, PhD; American academic and writer; *Caroline E. Haskell Professor of the History of Religions, University of Chicago;* b. 5 March 1948, Philadelphia; s. of William D. Lincoln and Geraldine Kovsky Lincoln; m. Louise Gibson Hassett 1971; two d. *Education:* Haverford Coll., Univ. of Chicago. *Career:* Asst Prof. of Humanities, Religious Studies and South Asian Studies, Univ. of Minnesota 1976–79, Assoc. Prof. 1979–84, Prof. and Chair, Religious Studies Programme 1979–86, Prof. of Comparative Studies in Discourse and Society 1986–93; Visiting Prof., Università degli Studi di Siena, Italy, 1984–85, Univ. of Uppsala, Sweden 1985, Novosibirsk State Pedagogical Inst., Russia 1991, Univ. of Copenhagen, Denmark 1998, Collège de France, 2003; Prof. of the History of Religions, Anthropology, Classics and Middle Eastern Studies, Univ. of Chicago 1993–2000, Caroline E. Haskell Prof. of the History of Religions 2000–. *Publications:* Priests, Warriors, and Cattle: A Study in the Ecology of Religions 1981, Emerging from the Chrysalis: Studies in Rituals of Women's Initiation 1981, Religion, Rebellion, Revolution: An Interdisciplinary and Crosscultural Collection of Essays (ed.) 1985, Myth, Cosmos, and Society: Indo-European Themes of Creation and Destruction 1986, Discourse and the Construction of Society: Comparative Studies of Myth, Ritual, and Classification 1989, Death, War, and Sacrifice: Studies in Ideology and Practice 1991, Authority: Construction and Corrosion 1994, Theorizing Myth: Narrative, Ideology and Scholarship 1999, Holy Terrors: Thinking about Religion after September 11 2002, Religion, Empire and Torture: The Case of Achaemenian Persia 2007; contribs: professional journals. *Honours:* Dr hc (Univ. of Copenhagen); ACLS Grant 1979, Rockefeller Foundation Grant 1981, Best New Book in History of Religion Citation, ACLS 1981, Guggenheim Fellowship 1982–83, Nat. Endowment for the Humanities Grant 1986, Outstanding Academic Book Citation, Choice 1989, Scholar of the Coll., Univ. of Minnesota 1990–93, Excellence in the Study of Religion (Analytical-Descriptive Studies), American Acad. of Religion 2000, Gordon J. Laing Prize, Univ. of Chicago Press 2003, Frank Moore Cross Award, American Soc. for Oriental Research 2008. *Address:* Swift Hall, 1025 East 58th Street, University of Chicago, Chicago IL 60637, USA (office). *Telephone:* (773) 703-5083 (office). *E-mail:* blincoln@uchicago.edu (office).

LINDBERG, Tod, BA; American writer and journalist; *Editor, Policy Review;* b. 1960, Syracuse, NY; m. Tina Linberg: two d. *Education:* Univ. of Chicago. *Career:* fmr Exec. Ed. National Interest, Man. Ed. Public Interest; Deputy Man. Ed. Insight Magazine –1991; Ed. Editorial Page, The Washington Times 1991–98, weekly columnist 1996–; Ed. Policy Review, Washington, DC 1999–; fmr Media Fellow and Lecturer on Politics, Hoover Inst., Stanford Univ., currently Research Fellow; contribs to Commentary, Nat. Review, Wall St Journal, USA Today, Los Angeles Times; mem. Bd of Educ., Chicago 1978–81; mem. Bd of Visitors, Inst. on Political Journalism, Georgetown Univ.; mem. Council on Foreign Relations; media appearances on public affairs TV programmes including Evening Exchange, Nightline, Dateline, Hardball and Crossfire. *Honours:* Associated Press Best Editorial Award 1997. *Address:* Policy Review, 21 Dupont Circle, NW, Suite 310, Washington, DC 20036, USA (office). *Telephone:* (202) 466-6730 (office). *Fax:* (202) 466-6733 (office). *E-mail:* polrev@hoover.stanford.edu (office). *Website:* www.policyreview.org (office).

LINDBLOM, Charles Edward, BA, PhD; American academic and writer; b. 21 March 1917, Turlock, Calif.; m. Rose K. Winther 1942 (died 2002); two s. one d. *Education:* Stanford Univ., Calif., Univ. of Chicago. *Career:* instructor, Univ. of Minnesota 1939–46; Asst Prof. to Prof., Yale Univ. 1946–; Pres. American Political Science Asscn. *Publications:* Unions and Capitalism 1949, Politics, Economics and Welfare 1953, The Intelligence of Democracy 1965, The Policy Making Process 1968, Politics and Markets 1977, Usable Knowledge 1979, Democracy and the Market System 1988, Inquiry and Change 1990, The Market System 2001; contrib. to professional journals. *Address:* 3940 Old Santa Fe Trail, Santa Fe, NM 87505, USA (home). *Telephone:* (505) 820-2353 (home).

LINDE, Nancy, BA, MA; American academic, writer and poet; b. 21 Dec. 1949, New York, NY; m. Stephan A. Khinoy 1980 (divorced 1990). *Education:* CUNY. *Career:* Lecturer, College of Staten Island, CUNY, 1978–85, 1988–; Mem., Board of Dirs, Woodstock Writers Worskhop, 1980–; mem. American Aikido Federation. *Publications:* Arabesque (screenplay) 1969, The Orange Cat Bistro (novel) 1996; contrib. poems to periodicals. *Honours:* CUNY Poetry Prize 1970.

LINDEMAN, Jack, BS; American academic, poet and writer; b. 31 Dec. 1924, Philadelphia, Pa. *Education:* West Chester State Coll., Univ. of Pennsylvania, Univ. of Mississippi, Villanova Univ. *Career:* Ed. Whetstone 1955–61; Faculty, Lincoln Univ., Pa 1963–64, Temple Univ. 1964–65; Faculty, Kutztown Univ., Pa 1969–85, Prof. Emer. 1985–; Poetry Ed. Time Capsule 1981–83; mem. Poets and Writers. *Publications:* Twenty-One Poems, The Conflict of Convictions, Appleseed Hollow 2001, As If 2005, Lincoln: The Black Man's Advocate 2012; contrib. to anthologies, quarterlies, reviews, journals and magazines, including Apocalypse, Bellowing Ark, Beloit Poetry Journal, Blueline, Blue Unicorn, Bryant Literary Review, California Poetry Quarterly, California Quarterly, Christian Science Monitor, Colorado Quarterly, Commonweal, Contemporary Literary Criticism, Dickinson Review, Eureka Literary Magazine, Harper's Bazaar, High Plains Review, Hollins Critic, International Poetry Review, Kansas Quarterly, Massachusetts Review, Nation, New World Writing, Oregon East, Poetry, Prairie Schooner, Red Hawk Review, Rocky Mountain Review, Slant, South Carolina Review, Southern Poetry Review, Southwest Review, Calapooya, Chiron Review, Poetry Motel, The Poet's Page, San Fernando Poetry Journal, Southwest Review, White Pelican Review, CommonSense2, Concho River Review, Kerf, Phantasmagora, Rambunctious Review, RiverSedge. *Honours:* Achievement Award For Outstanding Achievement, A Peace of Mind Poetry: Expedition 2003–04. *Address:* 133 South Franklin Street, Fleetwood, PA 19522-1810, USA (home). *Telephone:* (610) 944-9554 (home). *Fax:* (610) 944-9554 (home). *E-mail:* jacklindeman@verizon.net.

LINDEY, Christine, BA; art historian; b. 26 Aug. 1947, France. *Education:* Courtauld Institute, London. *Career:* currently Tutor in Art History, Birkbeck, Univ. of London. *Publications:* Superrealist Painting and Sculpture 1980, 20th Century Painting: Bonnard to Rothko 1981, Art in the Cold War 1990. *Address:* c/o HAFVM, Birkbeck College, 43 Gordon Square, London WC1H 0PD, England (office). *Website:* www.bbk.ac.uk/hafvm (office).

LINDHOLM, Megan (see Ogden, Margaret Astrid Lindholm)

LINDNER, Carl Martin, BS, MA, PhD; American academic and poet; *Professor of English, University of Wisconsin at Parkside;* b. 31 Aug. 1940, New York, NY; one s. one d. *Education:* City College, CUNY, Univ. of Wisconsin at Madison. *Career:* Asst Prof. 1969–74, Assoc. Prof. 1974–87, Prof. of English 1987–, Univ. of Wisconsin at Parkside. *Publications:* Vampire 1977, The Only Game 1981, Shooting Baskets in a Dark Gymnasium 1984, Angling into Light 2001, Eat and Remember 2001; contrib. reviews to journals and periodicals. *Honours:* Wisconsin Arts Board Creative Writing Fellowship for Poetry, 1981; Stella C. Gray Teaching Excellence Awards, 1990–91, 2000–01; University of Wisconsin at Parkside Award for Excellence in Research and Creative Activity, 1996. *Address:* c/o Department of English, University of Wisconsin at Parkside, PO Box 2000, Wood Road, Kenosha, WI 53141, USA.

LINDOP, Grevel Charles Garrett, MA, BLitt, PhD; British academic, poet, writer and editor; b. 6 Oct. 1948, Liverpool, England; m. Amanda Therese Marian Cox 1981; one s. two d. *Education:* Liverpool Coll., Wadham and Wolfson Colls, Oxford, Univ. of Manchester. *Career:* Lecturer, Univ. of Manchester 1971–84, Sr Lecturer 1984–93, Reader in English Literature 1993–96, Prof. of Romantic and Early Victorian Studies 1996–2001; Dir Temenos Acad. and Ed. Temenos Acad. Review 2000–03; Fellow, Temenos Acad., Wordsworth Trust; mem. Soc. of Authors. *Publications:* poetry: Against the Sea 1970, Fools' Paradise 1977, Moon's Palette 1984, Tourists 1987, A Prismatic Toy 1995, Selected Poems 2000, Touching the Earth: Books I–IV 2001, Playing With Fire 2006; prose: British Poetry Since 1960 (with Michael Schmidt) 1971, The Opium-Eater: A Life of Thomas De Quincey 1981, A Literary Guide to the Lake District 1993, The Path and the Palace: Reflections on the Nature of Poetry 1996, Travels on the Dance Floor 2008; editor: British Poetry Since 1960 (with Michael Schmidt) 1970, Selected Poems, by Thomas Chatterton 1971, Confessions of an English Opium-Eater and Other Writings, by Thomas De Quincey 1985, The White Goddess, by Robert Graves 1997, The Works of Thomas De Quincey, 21 vols 2000–03, Graves and the Goddess (with Ian Firla) 2003; contrib. to Poetry Nation Review, TLS, Stand, Poetry London, The Economist, Guardian, Independent, Warwick Review. *Honours:* Lakeland Book of the Year Award 1993, Poetry London Prize 2005, Stafford Poetry Prize 2009. *Address:* 216 Oswald Road, Chorlton-cum-Hardy, Manchester, M21 9GW, England (home). *E-mail:* gcglindop@aol.com (home). *Website:* www.grevel.co.uk.

LINDQVIST, Sven, PhD; Swedish writer; b. 1932, Stockholm; m. Agneta Stark 1986; one s. one d. *Education:* Stockholm Univ. *Publications include:* China in Crisis 1965, The Myth of Wu Tao-tzu 1967, The Shadow: Latin America Faces the Seventies 1972, Dig Where You Stand: How to Research a Job 1978, Land and Power in South America 1979, Exterminate All the Brutes 1996, The Skull Measurer's Mistake 1997, Desert Divers 2000, A History of Bombing 2001, Bench Press 2003, Terra Nullius 2007. *Honours:* awarded Hon. Professorship from Swedish Govt; Dr hc (Uppsala Univ.). *Address:* c/o Granta

Books, 12 Addison Avenue, London, W11 4QR, England (office). *E-mail:* mail@svenlindqvist.net (home). *Website:* www.svenlindqvist.net.

LINDSEY, David L., BA; American writer and editor; b. 6 Nov. 1944, Kingsville, Texas; m. Joyce Lindsey. *Education:* University of North Texas. *Career:* freelance ed. 1972–80; founder, Heidelberg Publishers; Acquisitions Ed. for the Humanities, University of Texas Press. *Publications:* Mysteries: Black Gold, Red Death, 1983; A Cold Mind, 1983; Heat from Another Sun, 1984; Spiral, 1986; In the Lake of the Moon, 1988; Mercy, 1990; Body of Truth, 1992; An Absence of Light, 1994; Requiem for a Glass Heart, 1996; The Color of Night, 1999; Animosity, 2001. *Honours:* Bochumer Krimi Archiv Award, Best Suspense Novel of the Year, Germany, 1992. *Literary Agent:* Aaron Priest Literary Agency, 708 Third Avenue, 23rd Floor, New York, NY 10017, USA. *E-mail:* dlindsey1@austin.rr.com.

LINDSTRØM, Merethe; Norwegian author; b. 26 May 1963, Bergen. *Publications include:* short story collections: Sexorcisten og andre fortellinger 1983, Borte, men savnet (Gone, But Missed) 1988, Kannibal-leken (The Cannibal Game) 1990, Svømme under vann (Swimming Under Water) 1994, Jeg kjenner dette huset (I Know This House) 1999, Gjestene' (The Guests) 2007; novels: Regnbarnas rike (The Kingdom of the Children of Rain) 1992, Steinsamlere (The Stone Collectors) 1996, Stedfortrederen (The Substitute) 1997, Natthjem (A Shelter for the Night) 2002, Ingenting om mørket (Nothing About the Dark) 2003, Barnejegeren (The Child Searcher) 2005, Dager i stillhetens historie (Days in the History of Silence) (Nordic Council Literature Prize and Critics' Prize 2012) 2011; juvenile: Mille og den magiske kringlen (co-author) (Mille and the Magic Pretzel) 1997. *Honours:* Mads Wiel Nygaards Endowment 1994, NotaBenes litteraturpris 1996, Tanums kvinnestipend 1997, Dobloug Prize 2008. *Literary Agent:* c/o Aschehoug Agency, Sehesteds gate 3, PO Box 363, Sentrum, 0102 Oslo, Norway. *E-mail:* epost@aschehougagency.no. *Website:* www.aschehougagency.no.

LINETT, Deena, DEd; American academic and writer; b. 30 Aug. 1938, Boston, MA; two s. one d. *Education:* Rutgers Univ. *Career:* Prof. of English, Montclair State University; Fellowship, Centre for Writers and Translators, Gotland, Sweden 2004–; mem. PEN American Center, Poets and Writers, Acad. of American Poets, Poetry Society of America. *Publications:* On Common Ground, 1983; The Translator's Wife, 1986; Rare Earths: Poems, 2001. Contributions: journals. *Honours:* Yaddo Fellowships, 1981, 1985; PEN-Syndicated Fiction Project, 1990; Residency, Hawthornden Castle International Retreats for Writers, 1996, 2001. *Address:* c/o Department of English, Montclair State University, Upper Montclair, NJ 07043, USA. *Telephone:* (973) 655-7320 (office). *Fax:* (973) 746-2236 (home).

LINGARD, Joan Amelia, DipEd, MBE; British author; b. 8 April 1932, Edinburgh, Scotland; three d. *Education:* Moray House Training College, Edinburgh. *Career:* mem. Society of Authors in Scotland (chair. 1982–86); Hon. Vice-Pres., Scottish PEN; Dir, Edinburgh Book Festival. *Publications:* children's books: The Twelfth Day of July, 1970; Frying as Usual, 1971; Across the Barricades, 1972; Into Exile, 1973; The Clearance, 1974; A Proper Place, 1975; The Resettling, 1975; Hostages to Fortune, 1976; The Pilgrimage, 1976; The Reunion, 1977; The Gooseberry, 1978; The File on Fraulein Berg, 1980; Strangers in the House, 1981; The Winter Visitor, 1983; The Freedom Machine, 1986; The Guilty Party, 1987; Rags and Riches, 1988; Tug of War, 1989; Glad Rags, 1990; Between Two Worlds, 1991; Hands Off Our School!, 1992; Night Fires, 1993; Lizzie's Leaving, 1995; Dark Shadows, 1998; A Secret Place, 1998; Tom and the Tree House, 1998; The Egg Thieves, 1999; River Eyes, 2000; Natasha's Will, 2000; Me and My Shadow, 2001; Tortoise Trouble, 2002; Tell the Moon to Come Out, 2003, Tilly and the Wild Goats 2005, The Sign of the Black Dagger 2005, Tilly and the Badgers 2006, The Eleventh Orphan 2008, What to Do About Holly 2009, The Chancery Lane Conspiracy 2010, The Stolen Sister 2011; fiction: Liam's Daughter, 1963; The Prevailing Wind, 1964; The Tide Comes In, 1966; The Headmaster, 1967; A Sort of Freedom, 1968; The Lord on Our Side, 1970; The Second Flowering of Emily Mountjoy, 1979; Greenyards, 1981; Sisters by Rite, 1984; Reasonable Doubts, 1986; The Women's House, 1989; After Colette, 1993; Lizzie's Leaving, 1995; Dreams of Love and Modest Glory, 1995; The Kiss 2002, Encarnita's Journey 2005, After You've Gone 2007. *Honours:* Scottish Arts Council Bursary, 1967–68; Preis der Leseratten ZDF, Germany, 1986; Buxtehuder Bulle, Germany, 1987; Scottish Arts Council Award, 1994. *Literary Agent:* David Higham Associates, 5–8 Lower John Street, Golden Square, London, W1F 9HA, England.

LINGEMAN, Richard Roberts, BA; American editor and writer; b. 2 Jan. 1931, Crawfordsville, IN; m. Anthea Judy Nicholson 1965; one d. *Education:* Haverford Coll., Yale Law School, Columbia Univ. Graduate School. *Career:* Exec. Ed., Monocle magazine 1960–69; Sr Ed., The Nation 1978–; Assoc. Ed. and columnist, The New York Times Book Review 1969–78; mem. Authors' Guild, Nat. Book Critics Circle, New York Historical Soc., PEN, Soc. of American Historians. *Publications:* Drugs from A to Z 1969, Don't You Know There's a War On? The American Home Front 1941–1945 1971, Small Town America: A Narrative History 1620–Present 1980, Theodore Dreiser: At the Gates of the City, 1871–1907 1986, Theodore Dreiser: An American Journey, 1908–1945 1990, Sinclair Lewis: Rebel from Main Street 2002, Double Lives: American Writers' Friendships 2006. *Honours:* Chicago Sun-Times Book of the Year Award 1990. *Address:* c/o The Nation, 33 Irving Place, New York, NY 10003, USA (office).

LINK, Daniel, BA, MA, PhD; Argentine academic, writer and editor; *Professor of Twentieth Century Literature, University of Buenos Aires.* *Career:* Ed. Magazín Literaria 1997, Radar Libros 1998–2004; currently Prof. of Twentieth Century Literature, Univ. of Buenos Aires; mem. Brazilian Asscn of Comparative Literature, Latin American Studies Asscn. *Publications:* non-fiction: El juego de los cautos 1992, La chancha con cadenas 1994, Escalera al cielo 1994, Carta la padre y otras escritos intimos 2002, Cómo se lee 2003, Clases 2005, Leyenda. Literatura argentina: cuatro cortes 2006; fiction: Los años noventa 2001, La ansiedad 2004, Montserrat 2006. *Honours:* Guggenheim Fellowship 2004. *Address:* Departamento de Letras, Facultad de Filosofía y Letras, Universidad de Buenos Aires, Puán 470, 3°, 1406 Buenos Aires, Argentina (office). *E-mail:* deletras@filo.uba.ar (office). *Website:* www.filo.uba.ar (office).

LINKLATER, Magnus Duncan, BA, FRSE; British journalist, broadcaster and writer; *Scotland Editor, The Times*; b. 21 Feb. 1942, Orkney, Scotland; m. Veronica Lyle 1967; two s. one d. *Education:* Univ. of Freiburg; Sorbonne, Univ. of Paris; Trinity Hall, Cambridge. *Career:* reporter, Daily Express, Manchester 1965–66, London Evening Standard, 1966–67; Diary Ed., Evening Standard 1967–69, Spectrum Ed., Sunday Times 1969–72, Ed., Sunday Times Colour Magazine 1972–75, News Ed., Sunday Times 1975–79, Exec. Ed., Features, Sunday Times 1979–83; Managing Ed., News, The Observer 1983–86; Ed., London Daily News 1987, The Scotsman 1988–94; columnist, The Times 1994–, Scotland Ed. 2007–; broadcaster, Radio Scotland 1994–96; Chair. Scottish Arts Council 1996–2001, Little Sparta Trust 2001–. *Publications:* Hoax: The Inside Story of the Howard Hughes/Clifford Irving Affair (with Stephen Fay and Lewis Chester) 1972, Jeremy Thorpe: A Secret Life (with Lewis Chester and David May) 1979, Massacre: The Story of Glencoe 1982, The Falklands War (with others) 1982, The Fourth Reich: Klaus Barbie and the Neo-Fascist Connection (with Isabel Hilton and Neal Ascherson) 1984, Not With Honour: Inside Story of the Westland Scandal (with David Leigh) 1986, For King and Conscience: The Life of John Graham of Claverhouse, Viscount Dundee (with Christian Hesketh) 1989, Anatomy of Scotland (co-ed.) 1992, Highland Wilderness (with Colin Prior) 1993, People in a Landscape 1997, Great Cities of the World (contrib.) 2010, Edinburgh (introduction) 2010. *Honours:* Hon. DArts (Napier) 1994; Hon. LLD (Aberdeen) 1997; Hon. DLitt (Glasgow) 2001, (Queen Margaret). *Address:* 5 Drummond Place, Edinburgh, EH3 6PH, Scotland. *Telephone:* (131) 5575705 (office). *E-mail:* magnus.linklater@blueyonder.co.uk.

LINS, Paulo; Brazilian writer and screenwriter; b. 1958, Rio de Janneiro. *Education:* Federal Univ. of Rio de Janeiro. *Career:* mem. Cooperativa de Poetas 1980s; researcher for anthropologist, Alba Zaluar, studying the favelas of Rio de Janeiro 1986–93; currently screenwriter. *Films:* screenplays: Orfeu 1999, Cidade de Deus 2002, Quase Dois Irmãos 2004, Maré, Nossa História do Amor 2007. *Television:* screenplay: Cidade dos Homens 2002. *Publications:* poetry: Sobre o Sol 1986; fiction: Cidade de Deus 1997, Desde que o samba é samba é assim 2008. *Honours:* Vitae de Artes Grant 1995. *Address:* c/o Editora Companhia das Letras, Departamento de Divulgação, Rua Bandeira Paulista, 702, cj. 32, São Paulo, SP 04532-002, Brazil (office). *E-mail:* divulgacao@companhiadasletras.com.br (office). *Website:* www.companhiadasletras.com.br (office).

LINSCOTT, Gillian; British journalist and writer; b. 27 Sept. 1944, Windsor; m. Tony Geraghty 1988. *Education:* Somerville Coll., Oxford. *Career:* mem. Soc. of Authors, Crime Writers Asscn (CWA). *Publications:* A Healthy Body 1984, Murder Makes Tracks 1985, Knightfall 1986, A Whiff of Sulphur 1987, Unknown Hand 1988, Murder, I Presume 1990, Sister Beneath the Sheet 1991, Hanging on the Wire 1992, Stage Fright 1993, Widow's Peak 1994, Crown Witness 1995, Dead Man's Music 1996, Dance on Blood 1998, Absent Friends 1999, The Perfect Daughter 2000, Dead Man Riding 2002, The Garden 2002, Blood on the Wood 2003. *Honours:* CWA Ellis Peters Historical Dagger 2000, Herodotus Award, Historical Mystery Appreciation Soc.

LIPMAN, Elinor, AB; American writer; b. 16 Oct. 1950, Lowell, Mass; d. of Louis Saul Lipman and Julia Mazur Lipman; m. Robert M. Austin 1975 (died 2009); one s. *Education:* Simmons Coll., Boston. *Career:* has taught at Simmons Coll., Smith Coll., Hampshire Coll., Mass; Elizabeth Drew Chair. in Creative Writing, Smith Coll. 2011–12; mem. Authors' Guild. *Publications:* Into Love and Out Again (short stories) 1987, Then She Found Me 1990, The Way Men Act 1992, Isabel's Bed 1995, The Inn at Lake Devine 1998, The Ladies' Man 1999, The Dearly Departed 2001, The Pursuit of Alice Thrift 2003, My Latest Grievance (Paterson Fiction Prize 2007) 2006, The Family Man 2009; contribs to Yankee, Playgirl, Ascent, Ladies Home Journal, Cosmopolitan, Self, Good Housekeeping, Gourmet, Washington Post, Boston Globe, New York Times. *Honours:* Hon. DLitt (Simmons Coll.); Distinguished Story Citations, Best American Short Stories 1984, 1985, New England Book Award 2001. *Address:* 67 Winterberry Lane, Florence, MA 01062-9702, USA (home). *E-mail:* author@elinorlipman.com (office). *Website:* www.elinorlipman.com.

LIPPMAN, Laura; American novelist; b. 31 Jan. 1959, Atlanta, Ga; d. of Theo Lippman Jr and Madeline Lippman; m. David Simon. *Education:* Wilde Lake High School. *Career:* fmr reporter, San Antonio Light and Baltimore Sun newspapers; cr. series of detective novels featuring the Tess Monaghan character; currently teacher, Goucher Coll., Md. *Publications include:* novels: Tess Monaghan series: Baltimore Blues 1997, Charm City 1997, Butchers Hill 1998, In Big Trouble 1999, The Sugar House 2000, In a Strange City 2001, The

Last Place 2002, By a Spider's Thread 2004, No Good Deeds 2006, Another Thing to Fall 2008, The Girl in the Green Raincoat 2011; other novels: Every Secret Thing 2003, To the Power of Three 2005, What the Dead Know (aka Little Sister) 2007, Life Sentences 2009, I'd Know You Anywhere (aka Don't Look Back) 2010, The Most Dangerous Thing 2011; short story collections: Hardly Knew Her: Stories 2008; appearances in several anthologies. *Address:* c/o Sharyn Rosenblum, William Morrow, HarperCollins Publishers, 10 East 53rd Street, New York, NY 10022 (office); Goucher College, 1021 Dulaney Valley Road, Baltimore, MD 21204, USA (office). *Telephone:* (212) 207-7000 (New York) (office); (410) 337-6000 (Baltimore) (office). *E-mail:* sharyn.rosenblum@harpercollins.com (office); laura@lauralippman.com. *Website:* www.harpercollins.com (office); www.goucher.edu (office); www.lauralippman.com.

LIPPY, Charles Howard, MA, MDiv, PhD; American academic (retd), writer and editor; b. 2 Dec. 1943, Binghamton, NY; s. of Charles Augustus Lippy and Natalie Grace Setzer Lippy. *Education:* Dickinson Coll., Union Theological Seminary, Princeton Univ. *Career:* Asst Prof., Oberlin Coll. 1972–74, West Virginia Wesleyan Coll. 1975–76; Visiting Assoc. Prof., Miami Univ. 1974–75; Asst Prof., Clemson Univ. 1976–80, Assoc. Prof. 1980–85, Prof. of History and Religion 1985–88, Prof. of Religion 1988–94; Visiting Scholar, Univ. of North Carolina at Chapel Hill 1984; Visiting Prof. of Religion, Emory Univ. 1990–91, Visiting Research Scholar 2000–01; LeRoy A. Martin Distinguished Prof. of Religion Studies, Univ. of Tennessee at Chattanooga 1994–2008 (retd); mem. American Acad. of Religion, American Catholic Historical Asscn, American Soc. of Church History (Pres. 2009), American Studies Asscn, Organization of American Historians, Soc. for the Scientific Study of Religion, South Carolina Acad. of Religion (Pres. 1981–82), United Methodist Historical Soc. *Publications:* Seasonable Revolutionary: The Mind of Charles Chauncy 1981, A Bibliography of Religion in the South 1985, Religious Periodicals of the United States: Academic and Scholarly Journals (ed.) 1986, Encyclopedia of the American Religious Experience (co-ed. with Peter W. Williams, three vols) 1988, Twentieth-Century Shapers of American Popular Religion (ed.) 1989, The Christadelphians in North America 1989, Christianity Comes to the Americas, 1492–1776 (with Robert Choquette and Stafford Poole) 1992, Religion in South Carolina (ed.) 1993, Being Religious, American Style: A History of Popular Religiosity in the United States 1994, Popular Religious Magazines of the United States (co-ed. with P. Mark Fackler) 1995, Modern American Popular Religion: A Critical Assessment and Annotated Bibliography 1996, The Evangelicals: A Historical, Thematic and Biographical Guide (with Robert H. Krapohl) 1999, Pluralism Comes of Age: American Religion in the Twentieth Century 2000, Where Rivers Run and Mountains Rise (co-ed. with John L. Topolewski and Nancy Topolewski) 2002, Do Real Men Pray? 2005, Encyclopedia of Religion in the South (co-ed. with Samuel S. Hill) 2005, Faith in America (ed., three vols) 2006, Introducing American Religion 2009, Encyclopedia of Religion in America (co-ed. with Peter W. Williams, four vols) 2010; contrib. to reference works, scholarly books and journals. *Honours:* several grants, Outstanding Academic Book Citations, Choice 1987, 1989, 2001, 2011, American Library Asscn Outstanding Reference Work Citation 1988, 2010, Excellence in Research Award, Coll. of Arts and Sciences, Univ. of Tennessee at Chattanooga 2001. *Address:* 1589 Teague Street, Charleston, SC 29407, USA (home). *Telephone:* (843) 766-5954 (home). *E-mail:* charles-lippy@utc.edu (office).

LIPSEY, Baron (Life Peer), cr. 1999; **David Lawrence;** British journalist and writer; b. 21 April 1948, Cheltenham, Gloucestershire, England; m. Margaret Robson 1982, one d. *Education:* Magdalen Coll., Oxford. *Career:* Research Asst, General and Municipal Workers' Union 1970–72; Special Adviser to Anthony Crosland, MP 1972–77; staff, Prime Minister, 1977–79; journalist, New Society 1979–80, Ed. 1986–88; political staff, The Sunday Times 1980–82, Economics Ed. 1982–86; Co-Founder and Deputy Ed., The Sunday Correspondent 1988–90; Assoc. Ed., The Times 1990–92; journalist, The Economist 1992–, Political Ed. 1994–; mem. Fabian Society, chair. 1981–82. *Publications:* Labour and Land 1972, The Socialist Agenda: Crosland's Legacy (ed. with Dick Leonard) 1981, Making Government Work 1982, The Name of the Rose 1992. *Address:* House of Lords, London, SW1A 0PW, England (office).

LIPSKA, Ewa; Polish poet; b. 8 Oct. 1945, Kraków. *Education:* Acad. of Fine Arts, Kraków. *Career:* Co-Ed. Pismo 1981–83; mem. editorial Bd Dekada Literacka 1990–92; First Sec. Polish Embassy, Vienna 1991–95, Adviser 1995–97; Deputy Dir Polish Inst., Vienna 1991–95, Dir 1995–97; mem. Asscn of Polish Writers, Polish and Austrian PEN Club. *Publications include:* Wiersze (Poems) 1967, Drugi zbiór wierszy (Second Vol. of Poems) 1970, Trzeci zbiór wierszy (Third Vol. of Poems) 1972, Czwarty zbiór wierszy (Fourth Vol. of Poems) 1974, Piaty zbiór wierszy (Fifth Vol. of Poems) 1978, Zywa smierc (Living Death) 1979, Dom Spokojnej Mlodosci (House of the Quiet Youth) 1979, Nie o smierc tutaj chodzi, lecz o bialy kordonek 1982, Utwory wybrane (Selected Poems) 1986, Przechowalnia ciemnosci 1985, Strefa ograniczonego postoju 1990, Wakacje Mizantropa (Misantrope's Holidays) 1993, Stypendysci czasu 1994, Wspólnicy zielonego wiatraczka 1996, Ludzie dla poczatkujacych (People for Beginners) 1997, Zycie zastepcze (Substitute Life) (Polish-German edition 1998), Godziny poza godzinami (After-hours Hours) 1999, Biale truskawki (White Strawberries) 2000, Sklepy zoologiczne (Pet Shops) 2001, Uwaga stopien 2002; selections of poems translated include Versei (Hungary) 1979, Vernisaz (Czechoslovakia) 1979, Such Times (Canada) 1981, Huis voor een vredige jeugd 1982, Auf den Dächern der Mausoleen (Germany) 1983, En misantrops ferie (Denmark) 1990, Meine Zeit. Mein Leib. Mein Leben (Austria) 1990, Poet? Criminal? Madman? (UK) 1991, Wakancitie na mizantropa (Bulgaria) 1994, Zon (Sweden) 1997, Stipiendisti Wremiena (Yugoslavia) 1998, Mennesker for Begyndere (Denmark) 1999, Mesohu me vdekjen (Albania) 2000, Menseen voor beginners (Netherlands) 2000, Sedemnast cervenych vevericiek (Slovakia) 2001, Selection of Poems (Israel) 2001, Fresas Blancas (Spain) 2001, Pet Shops (UK) 2002, Uwaga 2002, Ja 2003, Wiersze do Piosenek. Serca na rowerach 2004, Gdzie indziej 2005, Drzazga 2006. *Honours:* Koscielscy Foundation Award (Switzerland) 1973, Robert Graves PEN Club Award 1979, Ind. Foundation of Supporting of Polish Culture—Polcul Foundation Award 1990, PEN Club Award 1992, Alfred Jurzykowski Foundation Award (USA) 1993, City of Kraków Award 1995, Andrzej Bursa Award 1997, Literary Laurel 2002. *Address:* c/o Wydawnictwo Literackie (Literary Publishing House), 31-147 Kraków, ul. Długa 1, Poland (office). *E-mail:* redakcja@wl.net.pl (office). *Website:* www.wl.net.pl (office); lipska.wydawnictwoliterackie.pl.

LIPSKEROV, Dmitry; Russian writer and playwright. *Career:* co-f., Debut Prize 2001. *Publications:* Gotlib's Space; The Forty Years of Chanchzhoe (novel), 2001; Relatives (novel), 2001. *Address:* c/o EKSMO Publishing House, Klari Tsetkin ul., d.18/5, Moscow 127299, Russia. *E-mail:* info@eksmo.ru.

LISLE, Holly; American writer; b. Oct. 1960, Salem, OH. *Education:* Richmond Community College. *Career:* mem. SFWA. *Publications:* Fire in the Mist 1992, Bones of the Past 1993, Mind of the Magic 1995, Minerva Wakes 1993, When the Bough Breaks (co-author) 1993, The Rose Sea (co-author) 1994, Mall, Mayhem and Magic 1995, Glenraven (co-author) 1996, Sympathy for the Devil 1996, The Devil and Dan Cooley (co-author) 1996, Hell on High (co-author) 1997, Hunting the Corrigan's Blood 1997, Thunder of the Captains (co-author) 1996, Wrath of the Princes (co-author) 1997, Curse of the Black Heron 1998, Diplomacy of Wolves 1998, Vengeance of Dragons 1999, Courage of Falcons 2000, Vincalis the Agitatot 2002, Memory of Fire 2002, The Wreck of Heaven 2003, Gods Old and Dark 2004, Talyn 2005, Hawkspar 2008, The Ruby Key 2008, The Silver Door 2009; contributions include short stories to anthologies including Women of War, The Enchanter Reborn, Chicks in Chainmail. *Honours:* Compton Crook Award for Best First Novel 1993. *Literary Agent:* c/o Robin Rue, Writer's House, 21 West 26th Street, New York, NY 10010, USA. *Telephone:* (212) 685-2400. *Fax:* (212) 685-1781. *Website:* writershouse.com; hollylisle.com.

LISNYANSKAYA, Inna Lvovna; Russian writer and poet; b. 24 June 1928, Baku, Azerbaijan SSR, USSR; d. of Lev Lisnyansky, Raisa Adamova; m. Semen I. Lipkin (died 2003); one d. *Education:* Baku Univ., literary courses, Moscow. *Career:* began writing poetry aged 10; first works published 1948; poems published in Moscow literary journal Novyi mir (New World) and Yunost (Youth) 1957–; in internal exile 1979–89, following contribs to literary almanac Metropole; resgnd from Union of Writers 1980 (membership restored 1989); Chair. Bd, 'Poet' Award of Russia 2010; mem. Russian PEN Centre. *Publications include:* This Happened to Me 1957, Faithfulness 1958, Not Simply Love 1963, At First Hand 1966, Grape Light 1978, Rains and Mirrors 1983, Verse 1970–83, 1984, On the Edge of Sleep 1984, The Circle 1985, Airy Layer 1990, Poetry 1991, The Music of Akhmatova's 'Poem without a Hero' 1991, After Everything 1994, The Lonely Gift 1995, 2003, The Box with a Triple Bottom (Study on Akhmatova's Poem without the Hero) 1995, The First-hand Word 1996, Wind of Calmness 1998, Selected Poetry 2000, Far from Sodom 2002 (English trans. 2005), Without You 2003, The Echo 2005 (Bulgarian trans. 2010), Dreams of Old Eve 2005, She-Boaster 2006, Inna Lisnyanskaya 2009, Replaced Windows 2011, Verses (Chinese) 2010, Color Visions 2011; contribs to literary journals including Novyi mir, Oktiabr, Znamia, etc. *Honours:* Arion Prize 1994, Streletz Prize 1995, Druzhba Narodov magazine Prize 1996, State Literary Prize of Russia 1998, Alexander Solzhenitsyn Prize 1999, Znamya magazine Prize 2000, 'Poet' Award of Russia 2009. *Address:* c/o Russian PEN Centre, 107031 Moscow, Neglinnaya str. 18/1, p. 2; 125315 Moscow, Usievicha Street 8, Apt 16, Russia (home); Hess Street 33, Apt 5, 33397 Haifa, Israel (home). *Telephone:* 77-5633023 (Voip, Internet phone) (home); 547-994732 (Israel, mobile) (office). *Fax:* (495) 625-35-73 (office). *E-mail:* penrussian@mail.ru; inlist@rambler.ru.

LISTER, Gwen, BA; Namibian journalist; *Editor, The Namibian*; b. 5 Dec. 1953, East London, S Africa; one s. one d. *Education:* Univ. of Cape Town. *Career:* began career as journalist with Windhoek Advertiser 1975; Co-founder (with Hannes Smith) Windhoek Observer 1978, Political Ed. 1978–84 (S African authorities banned newspaper during coverage of independence talks 1984, ban defeated, resgnd because of accusations by newspaper sr staff 1984); Founder The Namibian newspaper 1985, Ed. 1985– (copies confiscated by authorities, advertising boycott by business community, office bldg burned down 1988, prohibition of govt advertising in newspaper 2001); Co-founder Media Inst. of Southern Africa, fmr Chair. Governing Council and mem. Trust Funds Bd; mem. UNESCO Press Freedom Council, African Advisory Bd Int. Women's Media Foundation, Advisory Bd Int. Consortium of Investigative Journalists. *Honours:* Inter Press Service Int. Journalism Award 1988, S African Soc. of Journalists Pringle Prize for Journalism 1988, Cttee to Protect Journalists Int. Journalism Award 1991, Nieman Fellowship, Harvard Univ. 1995–96, Media Inst. of S Africa Press Freedom Award 1997, named Int. Press Inst. Press Freedom Hero 2000, Int. Women's Media Foundation Courage in Journalism Award 2004. *Address:* The Namibian, POB 20783, 42 John Meinert Street, Windhoek, Namibia (office). *Telephone:* (61) 279600 (office).

Fax: (61) 279602 (office). *E-mail:* gwen@namibian.com.na (office). *Website:* www.namibian.com.na (office).

LISTER, Richard Percival, BSc, FRSL; British author, poet and painter; b. 23 Nov. 1914, Nottingham; m. Ione Mary Wynniatt-Husey 1985. *Education:* Manchester Univ. *Career:* author, painter, poet since 1949. *Publications:* fiction: The Way Backwards 1950, The Oyster and the Torpedo 1951, Rebecca Redfern 1953, The Rhyme and the Reason 1963, The Questing Beast 1965, One Short Summer 1974; poetry: The Idle Demon 1958, The Albatross 1986; travel: A Journey in Lapland 1965, Turkey Observed 1967, Glimpses of a Planet 1997; biography: The Secret History of Genghis Khan 1969, Marco Polo's Travels 1976, The Travels of Herodotus 1979; short story collections: Nine Legends 1991, Two Northern Stories 1996; contrib. to Punch, New Yorker, Atlantic Monthly. *Address:* Flat 11, 42 St James Gardens, London, W11 4RQ, England (home). *Telephone:* (20) 7371-3856 (home).

LITT, Toby; British writer; b. 1968, Ampthill, Beds., England. *Education:* Worcester Coll., Oxford, Univ. of East Anglia. *Career:* lived in Prague 1990–93; currently Lecturer in Creative Writing, Birkbeck Coll.; mem. English PEN. *Publications:* Adventures in Capitalism (short stories) 1996, Beatniks (novel) 1997, Corpsing (novel) 2000, deadkidsongs (novel) 2001, Exhibitionism (short stories) 2002, Finding Myself (novel) 2003, Ghost Story (novel) 2004, Hospital (novel) 2007, I Play The Drums in a Band Called Okay 2008, Journey into Space (novel) 2009, King Death 2010; contribs to numerous anthologies; contribs to The Idler, The Erotic Review, Interzone, Ambit, Concrete, The Guardian, Big Issue, Modern Painters, Art Quarterly. *Honours:* Curtis Brown Fellowship 1995, Granta Best of Young British Novelists 2003, Manchester Fiction Prize 2009. *Literary Agent:* Mic Cheetham, 50 Albemarle Street, London, W1S 4BD, England. *Telephone:* (20) 7495-2002. *E-mail:* mic@miccheetham.com. *Website:* www.miccheetham.com; www.tobylitt.com.

LITTELL, Jonathan; American/French novelist; b. 10 Oct. 1967, New York; s. of Robert Littell; m.; two c. *Education:* Yale Univ. *Career:* spent most of childhood in France; worked for int. humanitarian organization, Action Against Hunger 1994–2001, head of mission in Chechnya. *Publications:* fiction: Bad Voltage 1989, Les Bienveillantes (Prix Goncourt, Grand Prix du Roman de l'Académie française) 2006, Die Wohlgesinnten 2008, Georgisches Reisetagebuch 2008, Récit sur Rien 2009, The Invisible Enemy 2011, Triptych: How to Look at Francis Bacon 2011; non-fiction: The Security Organs of the Russian Federation – A Brief History 1991–2005 2006. *Address:* c/o Editions Gallimard, 5 rue Sébastien-Bottin, 75328 Paris, France.

LITTELL, Robert; American writer; b. 1935, New York, NY. *Career:* journalist Newsweek 1964; writer of Cold War espionage fiction. *Publications include:* Read America First 1968, If Israel Lost the War (with Richard Z. Cheznoff and Edward Klein) 1969, The Czech Black Book 1969, The Defection of A. J. Lewinter 1973, Sweet Reason 1974, The October Circle 1976, Mother Russia 1978, The Debriefing 1979, The Amateur 1981, The Sisters 1985, The Revolutionist 1988, The Once and Future Spy 1990, An Agent in Place 1991, The Visiting Professor 1994, Walking Back the Cat 1996, For the Future of Israel (with Shimon Peres) 1998, The Company 2002, Legends: A Novel of Dissimulation 2005, Vicious Circles 2007, The Stalin Epigram 2009. *Address:* c/o Author Mail, Simon and Schuster, 1230 Avenue of the Americas, 11th Floor, New York, NY 10020, USA (office). *Website:* www.simonandschuster.com (office).

LITTLE, Charles Eugene, BA; American writer; *Director, American Land Publishing Project*; b. 1 March 1931, Los Angeles, CA; m. Ila Dawson. *Education:* Wesleyan Univ. *Career:* began career as Advertising Exec., Foote, Cone & Belding, New York; Editorial Dir, Open Space Action Magazine 1968–69; Ed.-in-Chief, American Land Forum 1980–86; full-time writer 1986–; Books Ed., Wilderness Magazine 1987–97; Consulting Ed., Johns Hopkins Univ. Press 1989–97; Dir, American Land Publishing Project 2000–; Adjunct Faculty mem., Geography Dept, Univ. of New Mexico 2001–. *Publications:* Challenge of the Land 1969, Space for Survival (with J. G. Mitchell) 1971, A Town is Saved... (with photos by M. Mort) 1973, The American Cropland Crisis (with W. Fletcher) 1980, Green Fields Forever 1987, Louis Bromfield at Malabar (ed.) 1988, Greenways for America 1990, Hope for the Land 1992, Discover America: The Smithsonian Book of the National Parks 1995, The Dying of the Trees 1995, An Appalachian Tragedy 1998, Encyclopedia of Environmental Studies 2001, Sacred Lands of Indian America 2001; contributions: magazines and journals. *Address:* 33 Calle del Norte, Placitas, NM 87043, USA (home).

LIU, Shahe; Chinese poet; b. (Wu Xuntan), 11 Nov. 1931, Chengdu, Sichuan Prov.; m. 1st 1966; one s. one d.; m. 2nd 1992. *Education:* Sichuan Univ. *Career:* mem. editorial staff The Stars (poetry magazine) –1957 and 1979–; satirical poem Verses of Plants (1957) led to condemnation as 'bourgeois rightist'; in labour camp during Cultural Revolution 1966–77, rehabilitated 1979. *Publications include:* Night on the Farm 1956, Farewell to Mars 1957, Liu Shahe Poetic Works 1982, Travelling Trace 1983, Farewell to my Home 1983, Sing Alone 1989, Selected Poems of Seven Chinese Poets 1993, Random Notes by Liu Shahe 1995, River of Quicksand (poetry) 1995, River of Quicksand (short texts) 2001. *Address:* 30 Dacisi Road, Chengdu City, Sichuan Province, People's Republic of China. *Telephone:* (28) 6781738 (home).

LIU, Timothy, BA, MA; American poet, writer and academic; *Associate Professor of English, William Paterson University*; b. 2 Oct. 1965, San Jose, Calif.; s. of Ching C. Liu and Lida Liu; partner, Christopher Arabadjis. *Education:* Brigham Young Univ., Univ. of Houston. *Career:* Asst Prof., Cornell Coll. 1994–98; Asst Prof., William Paterson Univ. 1998–2003, Assoc. Prof. 2003–; Holloway Lecturer, Univ. of California 1997; Distinguished Visiting Writer, Univ. of N Carolina, Wilmington 2001; Core Faculty mem. Bennington Coll. 2005–; Distinguished Visiting Writer, Tulane Univ. 2008; mem. Associated Writing Programs, PEN American Center. *Publications:* A Zipper of Haze 1988, Vox Angelica 1992, Burnt Offerings 1995, Say Goodnight 1998, Word of Mouth: An Anthology of Gay American Poets 2000, Hard Evidence 2001, Of Thee I Sing 2004, For Dust Thou Art 2005, Bending the Mind Around the Dream's Blown Fuse 2009, Polytheogamy 2009; contribs to reviews, quarterlies and journals. *Honours:* Norma Farber First Book Award, Poetry Soc. of America 1992, John Ciardi Fellowship, Bread Loaf Writers' Conf. 1993, Holloway Lecturer, Univ. of California, Berkeley 1997, Judge's Choice Award, Bumbershoot Festival 1998, Open Book Beyond Margins Award, PEN America Center 2000, Book of the Year Award, Publishers' Weekly 2004. *Address:* Department of English, William Paterson University, 300 Pompton Road, Wayne, NJ 07470, USA (office). *Telephone:* (973) 720-3567 (office). *Fax:* (973) 720-2189 (office). *E-mail:* liut@wpunj.edu (office). *Website:* timothyliu.comuf.com (office).

LIU, Xinwu; Chinese writer; b. 4 June 1942, Chengdu, Sichuan Prov.; s. of Liu Tianyan and Wang Yuntao; m. Lu Xiaoge 1970; one s. *Education:* Beijing Teachers' Coll. *Career:* school teacher 1961–76; with Beijing Publishing House 1976–80; lived in Beijing 1950–; Ed.-in-Chief People's Literature 1987–89; professional writer 1980–; mem. Standing Cttee, China All Nation Youth Fed. –1992; mem. Council, Chinese Writers' Asscn. *Publications:* short stories: Class Counsellor (Nationwide Short Story Prize) 1977, The Position of Love 1978, I Love Every Piece of Green Leaves (Nationwide Short Story Prize) 1979, Black Walls 1982, A Scanning over the May 19th Accident 1985; novels: Ruyi (As You Wish) 1980, Overpass 1981, Drum Tower (Mao Dun Literature Prize) 1984; Liu Xinwu Collected Works (eight vols) 1993, A Small Block of Wood, Four Decorated Archways, Wind Passing through the Ear; non-fiction: Construction and Environment in My Eyes 1998, The Beauty of Material 2004. *Address:* 8 Building No. 1404, Anding Menwai Dongheyan, Beijing 100011, People's Republic of China. *Telephone:* 4213965 (home).

LIVELY, Dame Penelope Margaret, DBE, CBE, OBE, FRSL; British writer; b. (Penelope Margaret Low), 17 March 1933, Cairo, Egypt; d. of Roger Low and Vera Greer; m. Jack Lively 1957; one s. one d. *Education:* St Anne's Coll. Oxford. *Career:* mem. Bd British Library 1993–99, Bd British Council 1998–; Vice-Pres. Friends of the British Library; mem. Soc. of Authors, PEN. *Publications:* juvenile fiction: Astercote 1970, The Whispering Knights 1971, The Wild Hunt of Hagworthy 1971, The Driftway 1972, Going Back 1973, The Ghost of Thomas Kempe (Carnegie Medal) 1973, The House in Norham Gardens 1974, Boy Without a Name 1975, Fanny's Sister 1976, The Stained Glass Window 1976, A Stitch in Time (Whitbread Award) 1976, Fanny and the Monsters 1978, The Voyage of QV66 1978, Fanny and the Battle of Potter's Piece 1980, The Revenge of Samuel Stokes 1981, Uninvited Ghosts and Other Stories 1984, Dragon Trouble, Debbie and the Little Devil 1984, A House Inside Out 1987, The Cat, the Crow and the Banyan Tree 1994, Good Night, Sleep Tight 1995, Two Bears and Joe 1995, Staying with Grandpa 1995, A Martian Comes to Stay 1995, Heatwave 1996, Lost Dog 1996, One, Two, Three... Jump! 1998, Beyond the Blue Mountains: Stories 1997, Spiderweb 1998, In Search of a Homeland: The Story of the Aeneid 2001; adult fiction: The Road to Lichfield 1977, Nothing Missing but the Samovar and Other Stories (Southern Arts Literature Prize) 1978, Treasures of Time (Nat. Book Award) 1979, Judgement Day 1980, Next to Nature, Art 1982, Perfect Happiness 1983, Corruption and Other Stories 1984, According to Mark 1984, Moon Tiger (Booker-McConnell Prize 1987) 1986, Pack of Cards: Stories 1978–86 1986, Passing On 1989, City of the Mind 1991, Cleopatra's Sister 1993, The Photograph 2003, Making It Up 2005, Family Album 2009, How It All Began 2011; non-fiction: The Presence of the Past: An Introduction to Landscape History 1976, Oleander, Jacaranda: A Childhood Perceived (autobiog.) 1994, A House Unlocked (memoir) 2001, Consequences 2007; TV and radio scripts; contrib. to numerous journals and magazines. *Honours:* Hon. Fellow, Swansea Univ. 2002, St Anne's Coll., Oxford 2007; Hon. DLitt (Tufts Univ.) 1993, (Warwick) 1998. *Literary Agent:* c/o David Higham Associates, 5–8 Lower John Street, Golden Square, London, W1F 9HA, England. *Telephone:* (20) 7434-5900. *Fax:* (20) 7437-1072. *E-mail:* dha@davidhigham.co.uk. *Website:* www.davidhigham.co.uk; www.penelopelively.net.

LIVINGS, Henry; British writer and playwright; b. 20 Sept. 1929, Prestwich, Lancashire, England. *Education:* Liverpool University. *Publications:* Stop it Whoever You Are, 1961; Nil Caborundum, 1963; Kelly's Eye and Other Plays, 1965; Eh?, 1965; The Little Mrs Foster Show, 1967; Good Grief!, 1968; Honour and Offer, 1969; The Ffinest Ffamily in the Land, 1970; Pongo Plays 1–6, 1971; The Jockey Drives Late Nights, 1972; Six More Pongo Plays, 1974; Jonah, 1975; That the Medals and the Baton Be Put in View: The Story of a Village Band 1875–1975, 1975; Cinderella, 1976; Pennine Tales, 1983; Flying Eggs and Things: More Pennine Tales, 1986; The Rough Side of the Boards, 1994.

LJUNGGREN, Olof, LLB; Swedish publisher and business executive; b. 5 Jan. 1933, Eskilstuna; s. of Lars Ljunggren and Elisabeth Ljunggren; m. 1st Lena Carlsöö; m. 2nd Margreth Bäcklund; three s. *Education:* Univ. of Stockholm. *Career:* Sec. Tidningarnas Arbetsgivareförening (Swedish Newspaper Employers' Asscn) 1959–62, Pres. and CEO 1962–66; Deputy Pres. and

CEO Allers Förlag AB 1967–72, Pres. and CEO 1972–74; Pres. and CEO Svenska Dagbladet 1974–78; Pres. and CEO Svenska Arbetsgivareföreningen (Swedish Employers' Confed.) 1978–89; Chair. of Bd Askild & Kärnekull Förlag AB 1971–74, Nord Artel AB 1971–78, Centralförbundet Folk och Försvar (Vice-Chair. 1978–83) 1983–86, Richard Hägglöf Fondkommission AB 1984–87, Svenska Dagbladet 1989–91, Liber AB 1990–98 (Vice-Chair. 1998–), Intentia AB 1994–, AMF 1995–, AFA 1995–2001, Addum AB 1996–99, Consolis AB Oy 1997–; mem. Bd, SPP 1978–93, Investor 1989–92, Providentia 1989–92, Alfa Laval 1989–92, Trygg Hansa 1990–95, and numerous other bds. *Honours:* Kt Commdr Order of the White Rose of Finland 1982, The King's Medal of the 12th Dimension with the Ribbon of the Order of the Seraphim 1987, Kommendörskorset av Den Kgl. Norske Fortjenstorden; Hon. MD. *Address:* Skeppargatan 7, 114 52 Stockholm, Sweden. *Telephone:* (707) 472346 (office); (8) 6678785 (home). *Fax:* (8) 6678785 (home). *E-mail:* olof.ljunggren@gmail.com (home).

LLEWELLYN, Sam, BA, MA; British novelist, columnist and editor; b. 2 Aug. 1948, Isles of Scilly, England; m. Karen Wallace 1975; two s. *Education:* St Catherine's Coll., Oxford. *Career:* Ed., Picador 1973–76; Sr Ed., McClelland & Stewart 1976–79; Pres. and Publr Arch Books 1982–, New Hat Books 2006–; Ed. The Marine Quarterly 2011–; Capt., SY Lucille 1993–, SY Daisy 2005–; mem. Soc. of Authors, Campaign to Protect Rural England, The Corryvreckan Cruising Club. *Publications:* Hell Bay 1980, The Worst Journey in the Midlands 1983, Dead Reckoning 1987, Blood Orange 1988, Death Roll 1989, Pig in the Middle 1989, Deadeye 1990, Blood Knot 1991, Riptide 1992, Clawhammer 1993, Maelstrom 1994, The Rope School 1994, The Magic Boathouse 1994, The Iron Hotel 1996, Storm Force from Navarone 1996, The Polecat Cafe 1998, The Shadow in the Sands 1998, Thunderbolt from Navarone 1998, The Sea Garden 2000, Wonderdog 2000, The Malpas Legacy 2001, Little Darlings 2004, Nelson 2004, Bad, Bad Darlings 2005, Emperor Smith, The Man Who Built Scilly 2005, The Return of Death Eric 2005, The Haunting of Death Eric 2005, Abbot Dagger's Academy and the Quest for the Holy Grail 2007, The Well Between the Worlds 2009, The Minimum Boat 2010, Darksolstice 2010, Black Fish 2010; contribs to The Times, The Telegraph, Classic Boat, Practical Boat Owner, Yachting Monthly. *Honours:* Premio di Letteratura per l'Infanzia 1992. *Literary Agent:* c/o Araminta Whitley, LAW, 14 Vernon Street, London, W14 0RJ, England. *Telephone:* (20) 7471-7900. *Fax:* (20) 7471-7900. *E-mail:* sam@samllewellyn.com. *Website:* www.samllewellyn.com.

LLOYD, Sir Geoffrey Ernest Richard, Kt, PhD, FBA; British academic; *Professor Emeritus of Ancient Philosophy and Science, University of Cambridge*; b. 25 Jan. 1933, London, England; s. of William Ernest Lloyd and Olive Irene Neville Lloyd; m. Janet Elizabeth Lloyd 1956; three s. *Education:* Charterhouse and King's Coll. Cambridge. *Career:* Asst Lecturer in Classics, Univ. of Cambridge 1965–67, Lecturer 1967–74, Reader in Ancient Philosophy and Science 1974–83, Prof. 1983–2000, Prof. Emer. 2000–; Master, Darwin Coll., Cambridge 1989–2000, Hon. Fellow 2000–; Fellow, King's Coll. 1957–89, Hon. Fellow 1990–; A. D. White Prof.-at-Large, Cornell Univ., Ithaca, NY, USA 1990–96; Chair. East Asian History of Science Trust 1992–2002; mem. Japan Soc. for the Promotion of Science, Int. Acad. of the History of Science; Zhu Kezhen Visiting Prof., Inst. for the History of Natural Science, Beijing 2002. *Publications:* Polarity and Analogy 1966, Aristotle, the Growth and Structure of his Thought 1968, Early Greek Science: Thales to Aristotle 1970, Greek Science after Aristotle 1973, Hippocratic Writings (ed.) 1978, Aristotle on Mind and the Senses (co-ed. with G. E. L. Owen) 1978, Magic, Reason and Experience 1979, Science, Folklore and Ideology 1983, Science and Morality in Greco-Roman Antiquity 1985, The Revolutions of Wisdom 1987, Demystifying Mentalities 1990, Methods and Problems in Greek Science 1991, Adversaries and Authorities 1996, Aristotelian Explorations 1996, Greek Thought (ed.) 2000, The Ambitions of Curiosity 2002, The Way and the Word (with N. Sivin) 2002, In the Grip of Disease, Studies in the Greek Imagination 2003, Ancient Worlds, Modern Reflections 2004, The Delusions of Invulnerability 2005, Principles and Practices in Ancient Greek and Chinese Science 2006, Cognitive Variations, Reflections on the Unity and Diversity of the Human Mind 2007, Disciplines in the Making, Cross-Cultural Perspectives on Elites, Learning and Innovation 2009. *Honours:* Foreign Hon. mem. American Acad. of Arts and Sciences 1995; Hon. LittD (Athens) 2003; Sarton Medal 1987, Kenyon Medal 2007. *Address:* Needham Research Institute, 8 Sylvester Road, Cambridge, CB3 9AF (office); 2 Prospect Row, Cambridge, CB1 1DU, England (home). *Telephone:* (1223) 311545 (office); (1223) 355970 (home). *E-mail:* eahost1@hotmail.com (office); gel20@cam.ac.uk (office).

LLOYD, John Nicol Fortune, MA; British journalist; *Contributing Editor, Financial Times*; b. 15 April 1946, s. of Christopher Lloyd and Joan A. Fortune; m. 1st Judith Ferguson 1974 (divorced 1979); m. 2nd Marcia Levy 1983 (divorced 1997); one s. *Education:* Waid Comprehensive School and Univ. of Edinburgh. *Career:* Ed. Time Out 1972–73; reporter, London Programme 1974–76; Producer, Weekend World 1976–77; industrial reporter, labour corresp., industrial and labour ed., Financial Times 1977–86; Ed. New Statesman 1986–87, Assoc. Ed. 1996–2003; with Financial Times 1987–, posts include East Europe Ed., Financial Times Magazine Ed., Moscow Corresp. 1991–95, currently Contributing Ed.; freelance journalist 1996–; Dir East-West Trust, New York 1997–, Foreign Policy Centre 1999–. *Publications:* The Politics of Industrial Change (with Ian Benson) 1982, The Miners' Strike: Loss without Limit (with Martin Adeney) 1986, In Search of Work (with Charles Leadbeater) 1987, Counterblasts (contrib.) 1989, Rebirth of a Nation: an Anatomy of Russia 1998, Re-engaging Russia 2000, The Protest Ethic 2001, What the Media are Doing to Our Politics 2004, The Republic of Entertainment 2005. *Honours:* Journalist of the Year, Granada Awards 1984, Specialist Writer of the Year, IPC Awards 1985; Rio Tinto David Watt Memorial Prize 1997. *Address:* Financial Times, One Southwark Bridge, London, SE1 9HL, England (office). *Telephone:* (20) 7873-3000 (office). *E-mail:* john.lloyd@ft.com (office). *Website:* www.ft.com (office).

LLOYD, Kathleen Annie, (Kathleen Conlon, Kate North), BA; British writer; b. 4 Jan. 1943, Southport, Merseyside, England; m. Frank Lloyd 1962 (divorced); one s. *Education:* King's Coll., Durham. *Career:* mem. Soc. of Authors. *Publications:* Apollo's Summer Look 1968, Tomorrow's Fortune 1971, My Father's House 1972, A Twisted Skein 1975, A Move in the Game 1979, A Forgotten Season 1980, Consequences 1981, The Best of Friends 1984, Face Values 1985, Distant Relations 1989, Unfinished Business 1990; as Kate North: Land of My Dreams 1997, Gollancz 1997, Eva Shell 2008; contribs to Atlantic Review, Cosmopolitan, Woman's Journal, Woman, Woman's Own. *Address:* 26A Brighton Road, Birkdale, Southport, PR8 4DD, England.

LLOYD, Trevor Owen, MA, DPhil; Canadian/British professor of history and writer; *Professor Emeritus of History, University of Toronto*; b. 30 July 1934, London. *Education:* Merton Coll., Oxford, Nuffield Coll., Oxford. *Career:* Lecturer Dept of History, Univ. of Toronto 1959–63, Asst Prof. 1963–67, Assoc. Prof. 1967–73, Prof. 1973–97, Prof. Emeritus 1997–; mem. William Morris Soc., Victorian Studies Asscn of Ontario, Royal Historical Soc. *Publications:* Canada in World Affairs 1957–59 1968, The General Election of 1880 1968, Suffragettes International 1971, The Growth of Parliamentary Democracy in Britain 1973, Empire, Welfare State, Europe: English History 1906–1992 (revised edn as Empire, Welfare State, Europe: The United Kingdom 1906–2001) 2002, The British Empire 1558–1995 1996, Empire: The History of the British Empire 2001; contrib. to various journals. *Honours:* Guggenheim Fellowship 1978–79. *Address:* Department of History, University of Toronto, Toronto, M5S 3G3 (office); 15 McMurrich Street, Apt 502, Toronto, M5R 3M6, Canada (home). *Telephone:* (416) 978-8482 (office); (416) 960-5556 (home). *Fax:* (416) 978-4810 (office).

LLYWELYN, Robin, BA; Welsh writer; b. 24 Nov. 1958, Bangor. *Education:* Univ. Coll. Wales, Aberystwyth. *Publications:* Seren Wen ar Gefndir Gwyn (trans. as White Star) (Nat. Eisteddfod Prose Medal) 1992, O'r harbwr gwag i'r cefnfor gwyn (trans. as From Empty Harbour to White Ocean) 1994, Y Dwr Mawr Llwyd (short stories, trans. as The Big Grey Water), Y Filltir Sgwar 1996, Gwartheg ar y Drafford 1999, Gwr y Plas 2000, Y Syrcas 2004, Un Diwrnod yn yr Eisteddfod 2004. *Honours:* Welsh Arts Council Book of the Year 1993, BBC Wales Writer of the Year Award 1994, Daniel Owen Memorial Prize. *Address:* c/o Parthian Books, The Old Surgery, Napier Street, Cardigan, SA43 1ED, Wales. *E-mail:* robin@swyddfa.co.uk. *Website:* www.llywelyn.com.

LO LIYONG, Taban, BA, MFA; Ugandan novelist, poet and essayist; b. 1939, Kajokaji, Sudan. *Education:* Nat. Teachers' Coll., Kampala, Uganda, Howard Univ., Washington, DC and Univ. of Iowa, USA. *Career:* taught at univs in Kenya, Tanzania, Papua New Guinea, Sudan, Japan and Australia; currently Prof. of Literature, Univ. of Venda, South Africa. *Publications:* poetry: Frantz Fanon's Uneven Ribs: With Poems More and More 1971, Another Nigger Dead 1972, Ballads of Underdevelopment: Poems and Thoughts 1974, To Still a Passion 1977, The Cows of Shambat 1992, Carrying Knowledge up a Palm Tree 1997, Homage to Onyame 1998; prose: Fixions 1969, Eating Chiefs: Lwo Culture from Lolwe to Malkal 1970, Uniformed Man: Essays 1977, Thirteen Offensives Against our Enemies: Essays 1977, Meditations 1978, Images of Women in Folktales and Short Stories of Africa, Another Last Word 1990. *Address:* University of Venda, Private bag X5050, Thohoyandou 0950, Northern Province, South Africa.

LOADES, David Michael, MA, PhD, DLitt, FRHistS; British academic (retd) and writer; b. 19 Jan. 1934, Cambridge; m. Judith Anne Atkins 1987. *Education:* Emmanuel Coll., Cambridge. *Career:* Lecturer in Political Science, Univ. of St Andrews 1961–63; Lecturer in History, Univ. of Durham 1963–70; Sr Lecturer 1970–77, Reader 1977–80, Prof. of History 1980–96, Univ. College of North Wales, Bangor; Dir, British Acad. John Foxe Project 1993; fellow Soc. of Antiquaries of London. *Publications:* Two Tudor Conspiracies 1965, The Oxford Martyrs 1970, The Reign of Mary Tudor 1979, The Tudor Court 1986, Mary Tudor: A Life 1989, The Tudor Navy 1992, John Dudley: Duke of Northumberland 1996, Tudor Government 1997, England's Maritime Empire 2000, Elizabeth: The Golden Reign of Gloriana 2003, Elizabeth I 2003, Intrigue and Reason: The Tudor Court 1547–1558 2004; Ed.: The Papers of George Wyatt 1968, The End of Strife 1984, Faith and Identity 1990, John Foxe and the English Reformation 1997, John Foxe: An Historical Perspective 1999, The Anthony Roll of Henry VIII (with C. S. Knighton) 2000, Letters from the Mary Rose (with C. S. Knighton) 2002, The Chronicles of the Tudor Queens 2002, John Foxe: at Home and Abroad 2004, Henry VIII: Court, Church and Conflict 2007; contrib. to journals. *Address:* The Cottage, Priory Lane, Burford, Oxon. OX18 4SG, England.

LOBO, Tatiana; Chilean/Costa Rican writer; b. 1939, Puerto Montt, Chile. *Education:* studied in Germany and Spain. *Career:* lived in Costa Rica 1967–. *Play:* El Caballero del V Centenario 1989. *Publications:* novels: Asalto al paraiso (trans. as Assault on Paradise) 1993, Calypso 1996, El año del laberinto 2000, El corazón del silencio (Premio Aquileo J. Echeverría) 2004; short stories: Tiempo de Claveles 1989, Entre Dios y el Diablo 1993; non-fiction: Entre Dios y el Diablo: Mujeres de la colonia: crónicas 1993, Negros y

Blancos: Todo Mezclado (with Mauricio Meléndez) 1997. *Address:* c/o Grupo Editorial Norma, Zona Franca Metropolitana Local 7B, Barreal de Heredia, Heredia, Costra Rica (office). *E-mail:* gerencia@farben.co.cr (office). *Website:* www.norma.com (office).

LOBO ANTUNES, António, MD; Portuguese novelist; b. 1 Sept. 1942, Lisbon; s. of João Alfredo Lobo Antunes and Maria Margarida Almeida Lima; three d. *Education:* higher educ. in Portugal. *Career:* fmr doctor and psychiatrist; now full-time writer (his experience of the Portuguese colonial war in Angola being a major influence). *Publications include:* novels: Memória de Elefante 1979, Os Cus de Judas 1979, Conhecimento do Inferno 1980, Explicação dos Pássaros 1981, Fado Alexandrino 1983, Auto dos Danados 1985, As Naus 1988, Tratado das Paixões da Alma 1990, A Ordem Natural das Coisas 1992, A Morta de Carlos Gardek 1994, O Manual dos Inquisidores 1996, O Esplendor de Portugal 1997, Livro de Crónicas 1998, Exortação aos Crocodilos 1999, Não Entres Tão Depressa Ness Noite Excura 2000, Que Farei Quando Tudo Arde? 2001, Segundo Livro de Crónicas 2002, Boa Tarde ás Coisas Aqui em Baixo 2003, Eu Hei-de Amar Uma Pedra 2004, Terceiro Livro de Crónicas 2006, Ontem Não Te Vi em Babilónia 2006, O Meu Nome é Legião 2007, O Arquipélago da Insónia 2008; short stories: A História do Hidroavião 1994–2005 2005, The Fat Man and Infinity and Other Writings (in trans.) 2009; other: Letrinhas de Cantigas 2002, Apontar com o dedo o centro da terra 2002, D'este Viver Aqui Neste Papel Descripto 2005, Quem me assassinou para que eu seja tão doce? 2008. *Honours:* French Culture Prize 1996, 1997, Prix du Meilleur Livre Etranger, Rosália de Castro Prize 1999, European Literature Prize of Austria 2000, Latin Union Int. Prize 2003, Jerusalem Prize 2005, Premio Camões 2007. *Address:* c/o Publicações Dom Quixote, Rua Cidade de Códova 2, 2610-038 Alfragide, Portugal (office). *Website:* www.dquixote.pt (office).

LOCHHEAD, Douglas Grant, MA, BLS, FRSC; Canadian poet, writer and academic; *Professor Emeritus of Canadian Studies, Mount Allison University*; b. 25 March 1922, Guelph, Ont.; m. Jean St Clair 1949 (deceased); two d. *Education:* McGill Univ., Univ. of Toronto. *Career:* Librarian, Victoria Coll., BC 1951–52, Cornell Univ., Ithaca, New York 1952–53, Dalhousie Univ., Halifax, NS 1953–60, York Univ., Toronto 1960–63; Librarian and Fellow, Massey Coll. 1963–75; Prof. of English, Univ. Coll., Univ. of Toronto 1963–75; Davidson Prof. of Canadian Studies and Dir of the Centre for Canadian Studies Mount Allison Univ., Sackville, NB 1975–87, Prof. Emer. 1987–; Visiting Prof., Univ. of Edinburgh 1983–84; mem. League of Canadian Poets; Life mem. Bibliographical Soc. of Canada. *Publications include:* The Heart is Fire 1959, It is all Around 1960, Millwood Road Poems 1970, The Full Furnace: Collected Poems 1975, A & E 1980, Battle Sequence 1980, High Marsh Road 1980, The Panic Field 1984, Tiger in the Skull: New and Selected Poems 1959–85 1986, Dykelands 1989, Upper Cape Poems 1989, Black Festival: A Long Poem 1991, Homage to Henry Alline & Other Poems 1992, Breakfast at Mel's and Other Poems of Love and Places 1997, All Things Do Continue (poems) 1997, Cape Enragé: Poems on a Raised Beach 2000, Weathers: New and Selected Poems 2002, Orkney: October Diary 2002: Midgic: A Place, A Poem 2003, La Strada di Tantramar, versi per un diario 2004, That Place By Tantramar, Sackville New Brunswick 2006, Love on the Marsh 2008; contrib. to various publications. *Honours:* Hon. DLitt (St Mary's) 1987, (New Brunswick) 2006, Hon. LLD (Dalhousie) 1987; Golden Dog Award 1974, NB Govt Award in English Literature 2001, Poet Laureate of Sackville, NB 2003, Carlo Betochi Int. Poetry Prize, Florence, Italy 2005. *Address:* 9 Quarry Lane, Sackville, NB E4L 4G3, Canada (office). *Telephone:* (506) 536-1189 (home).

LOCHHEAD, Liz; British poet, playwright, screenwriter and teacher; *Scots Makar*; b. 26 Dec. 1947, Motherwell. *Career:* fmr art school teacher, Glasgow and Bristol; Lecturer, Univ. of Glasgow; Scots Makar (Nat. Poet of Scotland) 2011–. *Television includes:* Damages (BBC). *Publications include:* poetry: Memo for Spring 1972, The Grimm Sisters 1981, Dreaming of Frankenstein and Collected Poems 1984, True Confessions and True Clichés 1985, Bagpipe Muzak 1991, Cuba/Dog House (with Gina Moxley) 2000, The Colour of Black and White: Poems 1984–2003 2003; plays: Blood and Ice 1982, Silver Service 1984, Dracula (adaptation) 1989, Mary Queen of Scots Got Her Head Chopped Off 1989, Molière's Tartuffe (Scots trans. in rhyming couplets), Perfect Days 1998, Medea (adaptation) 2000, Misery Guts (adaptation) 2002, Thebans 2003, Good Things 2006; screenplay: Now and Then 1972; anthology contribs: Penguin Modern Poets Vols 3 and 4, Shouting It Out 1995. *Honours:* Dr hc (Edinburgh) 2000; BBC Scotland Prize 1971, Scottish Arts Council Award 1972. *Literary Agent:* 57 Productions, 57 Effingham Green, Lee Green, London, SE12 8NT, England. *Telephone:* (20) 8463-0866. *E-mail:* paul@57productions.com. *Website:* www.57productions.com.

LOCKE, Hubert Gaylord, BA, BD, MA; American academic and writer; *Professor Emeritus of Public Service, University of Washington, Seattle*; b. 30 April 1934, Detroit, Mich.; two d. *Education:* Wayne State Univ., Univ. of Chicago, Univ. of Michigan. *Career:* Asst Dir, Office of Religious Affairs, Wayne State Univ. 1957–62, Dir 1967–70, Adjunct Asst Prof. of Urban Education 1970–72; Assoc. Prof. of Urban Studies and Dean Coll. of Public Affairs and Community Service, Univ. of Nebraska 1972–75; Prof., Univ. of Washington, Seattle 1976–, Assoc. Dean Coll. of Arts and Sciences 1976–77, Vice-Provost for Academic Affairs 1977–82, Dean Grad. School of Public Affairs 1982–87, John and Marguerite Corbally Prof. of Public Service 1996–, now Prof. Emer.; mem. Bd of Dirs Nat. Council on Crime and Delinquency, Seattle Symphony; mem. Comm. on Judicial Conduct, State of Wash., The Russell Family Foundation. *Publications:* The Detroit Riot of 1967 1969, The Care and Feeding of White Liberals 1970, The German Church Struggle and the Holocaust (ed. with Franklin H. Littell) 1974, The Church Confronts the Nazis (ed.) 1984, Exile in the Fatherland: The Prison Letters of Martin Niemöller (ed.) 1986, The Barmen Confession: Papers from the Seattle Assembly (ed.) 1986, The Black Antisemitism Controversy: Views of Black Protestants (ed.) 1992, Learning from History 2000, Searching for God in God-Forsaken Times and Places 2003; contrib. to books and professional journals. *Honours:* Hon. Dr of Divinity (Payne Theological Seminary) 1968, (Chicago Theological Seminary) 1971; Hon. DHumLitt (Univ. of Akron) 1971, (Univ. of Nebraska) 1992, (Univ. of Bridgeport) 1997; Hon. Dr of Public Service (Christian Theological Seminary) 2011; Michigan Bar Asscn Liberty Bell Award 1967, Wayne State Univ. Distinguished Alumni Award 1979. *Address:* 2801 First Avenue 609, Seattle, WA 98121, USA. *Telephone:* (206) 374-0863.

LOCKE, Ralph Paul, MA, PhD; American musicologist, teacher and writer; *Professor of Musicology, Eastman School of Music, University of Rochester*; b. 9 March 1949, Boston, Mass; m. Lona M. Farhi 1979; two d. *Education:* Harvard Univ., Univ. of Chicago. *Career:* Faculty, Eastman School of Music, Univ. of Rochester, NY 1975–, Sr Ed. Eastman Studies in Music; mem. Editorial Bd University of Rochester Press, Journal of Musicological Research, Ad Parnassum, Journal of the American Musicological Society, Journal of Music History Pedagogy, Revista Brasileira de Música; mem. American Musicological Soc., Int. Musicological Soc., Soc. for American Music. *Publications:* Music, Musicians, and the Saint-Simonians 1986 (French trans. 1992), Cultivating Music in America: Women Patrons and Activists Since 1860 1997, Musical Exoticism: Images and Reflections 2009, chapter in a book that won the Ruth Solie Award, American Musicological Society 2010; contribs to reference books and professional journals. *Honours:* Best Article Citation, Music Library Asscn 1980, Galler Dissertation Prize 1981, ASCAP-Deems Taylor Awards 1992, 1996, 1999, 2003, 2007, H. Colin Slim Award for article on Aida, American Musicological Soc. 2006. *Address:* Department of Musicology, Eastman School of Music, 26 Gibbs Street, Rochester, NY 14604-2599, USA (office). *Telephone:* (585) 274-1455 (office). *Website:* www.esm.rochester.edu/faculty/locke_ralph (office).

LOCKE, Robert Howard, (Clayton Bess), BA, MA, MS; American librarian, playwright and author; b. 30 Dec. 1944, Vallejo, CA. *Education:* California State Univ., San Francisco State Univ., Simmons Coll., Boston. *Career:* Peace Corps Volunteer, Liberia 1967–70; Bibliographic Asst, French and Italian Acquisitions, Harvard Coll. Library 1970–72; Reference Librarian, Thesis Ed., California State Univ., Chico 1974–76; Ed. and Man. Hollywood Reporter 1980–83; Reference Librarian California State Univ. Libary, Sacramento 1987–89, Sacramento County Public Library 1987–89; Playwriting Instructor, Univ. of California, Davis 1994–95; Actor Singer-Baritone 1967–; Stage Dir 1986–; Playwright and Novelist 1971–; Reference Librarian and Research Technician, California State Univ. Library, Sacramento 1989–2002. *Plays:* In the First Place ..., The Dolly, Play, Rose Jewel and Harmony, Murder and Edna Redrum, On Daddy's Birthday, Premiere, Howling Twain, Love, Bob. *Publications:* as Robert Locke: X Xx Zero (co-author with William Roy Harp, III), The Blood Gospels; as Clayton Bess: Story for a Black Night 1982, The Truth About the Moon 1984, Big Man and the Burn-Out 1985, Tracks 1986, The Mayday Rampage 1993, A Ghost in Silence, Lonely Island. *Honours:* Best First Novel, Commonwealth Club of California 1982, Best Book for Young Adults, American Library Asscn 1987. *E-mail:* boblocke@csus.edu. *Website:* webpages.csus.edu/~boblocke/.

LOCKERBIE, D(onald) Bruce, AB, MA; American scholar and writer; *Chairman, Paideia Inc.*; b. 25 Aug. 1935, Capreol, ON, Canada. *Education:* New York University. *Career:* Scholar-in-Residence, Stony Brook School, New York, 1957–91; Visiting Consultant at American Schools in Asia and Africa, 1974; Visiting Lecturer/Consultant to American universities; Chair. Paideia, Inc. 1984–. *Publications:* Billy Sunday 1965, Patriarchs and Prophets 1969, Hawthorne 1970, Melville 1970, Twain 1970, Major American Authors 1970, Success in Writing (with L. Westdahl) 1970, Purposeful Writing 1972, The Way They Should Go 1972, The Liberating Word 1974, The Cosmic Center: The Apostles' Creed 1977, A Man under Orders: Lt Gen William K. Harrison 1979, Who Educates Your Child? 1980, The Timeless Moment 1980, Asking Questions 1980, Fatherlove 1981, In Peril on the Sea 1984, The Christian, the Arts and Truth 1985, Thinking and Acting Like a Christian 1989, Take Heart (with L. Lockerbie) 1990, College: Getting In and Staying In (with D. Fonseca) 1990, A Passion for Learning 1994, From Candy Sales to Committed Donors 1996, Dismissing God 1998, A Christian Paideia 2005. *Honours:* Hon. DHL (Eastern Coll.) 1985, (Taylor Univ.) 1993. *Address:* PO Box 26, Stony Brook, NY 11790, USA.

LOCKLEY, John, MA, MB BChir; British doctor and writer; b. 10 Feb. 1948, Sale, Cheshire; m. Mavis June Watt 1972; two s. one d. *Education:* Gonville and Caius Coll., Cambridge. *Career:* House Surgeon, Royal London Hospital 1972; Vocational Training Course for General Practice, Colchester 1973; General Practitioner, Ampthill, Bedfordshire, England 1976–; Ed., Torus 2000; Fellow Soc. of Medical Writers; mem. Soc. of Authors. *Publications:* The Complete BBC Computer User Handbook 1988, Acorn to PC: Changing from DFS and ADFS to DOS 1990, A Practical Workbook for the Depressed Christian 1991, Headaches – A Comprehensive Guide to Relieving Headaches and Migraine 1993, After the Fire 1994, After the Fire II – A Still Small Voice 1996, After the Fire III – Chronicles 1998; contrib. many articles to General Practitioner, Daily Telegraph, Daily Mail and Guardian, Doctor Magazine.

Honours: Medeconomics GP Writer of the Year 1989. *Address:* 107 Flitwick Road, Ampthill, Bedfordshire MK45 2NT, England. *Telephone:* (1525) 631395 (office). *E-mail:* john.lockley@gmail.com.

LOCKLIN, Gerald, BA, MA, PhD; American author, poet, dramatist, literary critic and academic; *Professor Emeritus of English, California State University of Long Beach*; b. 17 Feb. 1941, Rochester, NY. *Education:* St John Fisher College, University of Arizona. *Career:* Instructor in English, California State College at Los Angeles, 1964–65; Asst Prof. to Prof. of English, California State University at Long Beach, 1965–; mem. Associated Writing Programs; e. e. cummings Society; Hemingway Society; PEN; Western Literature Asscn. *Publications:* Sunset Beach, 1967; The Toad Poems, 1970; Poop and Other Poems, 1973; Toad's Europe, 1973; Locked In, 1973; Son of Poop, 1974; Tarzan and Shane Meet the Toad (with others), 1975; The Chase: A Novel, 1976; The Criminal Mentality, 1976; The Four-Day Week and Other Stories, 1977; Pronouncing Borges, 1977; A Weekend on Canada, 1979; The Cure: A Novel for Speed Readers, 1979; Two Summer Sequences, 1979; Two Weeks on Mr Stanford's Farm, 1980; The Last of Toad, 1980; Two for the Seesaw and One for the Road, 1980; Scenes from a Second Adolescence, 1981; A Clear and Present Danger to Society, 1981; By Land, Sea, and Air, 1982; Why Turn a Perfectly Good Toad into a Prince?, 1983; Fear and Paternity in the Pauma Valley, 1984; The Ensenada Poems (with Ray Zepada), 1984; The Case of the Missing Blue Volkswagen, 1984; The Phantom of the Johnny Carson Show, 1984; We Lose L.A. (with Ray Zepeda), 1985; The English Mini-Tour, 1987; Gringo and Other Poems, 1987; Gerald Haslam, 1987; A Constituency of Dunces, 1988; Children of a Lesser Demagogue, 1988; On the Rack, 1988; Lost and found, 1989; The Treasure of the Sierra Faulkner, 1989; The Gold Rush and Other Stories, 1989; The Rochester Trip, 1990; The Conference, 1990; The Illegitimate Son of Mr Madman, 1991; The Firebird Poems, 1992; A New Geography of Poets (ed. with Edward Field and Charles Stetler), 1992; The Old Mongoose and Other Poems, 1994; Big Man on Canvas, 1994; The Cabo Conference, 1995; Charles Bukowski: A Sure Bet, 1996; The Pittsburgh Poems, 1996; The Macao/Hong Kong Trip, 1996; The Hospital Poems, 1998; Two Novellas (with Donna Hilbert), 1998; Down and Out: A Novel for Adults, 1999; Hemingway Colloquium: The Poet Goes to Cuba, 1999; Candy Bars, 2000; A Simpler Time, a Simpler Place: Three Mid-Century Stories, 2000; The Iceberg Theory, 2000; Four Jazz Women, 2000; Art and Life, 2000; The Sixth Jazz Chapbook, 2001; Familiarities, 2001; The Life Force Poems, 2002; The Mystical Exercycle, 2002; The Pocket Book, 2003; Henry's Gift, 2003; Takes on Bill Evans, 2003; More Takes on Bill Evans, 2003; The Dorset Poems, 2003, The Modigliani/Montparnasse Poems 2003, Retirement Blues 2003, The Ultimate Pessimist 2003, Two Jazz Poems 2004, Jimmy Abbey Stays for the Drum Circle 2004, The Spirit of the Struggle 2005, New Orleans, Chicago, and Points Elsewhere 2006, Open Thy Effing Ears (Please) 2006; contrib. to periodicals. *Address:* c/o Department of English, California State University at Long Beach, Long Beach, CA 90840, USA. *Telephone:* (542) 985-5285 (office). *E-mail:* glocklin@csulb.edu (office). *Website:* www.geraldlocklin.com (home).

LOCKRIDGE, Ernest Hugh, BA, MA, PhD; American academic, novelist and artist; b. 28 Nov. 1938, Bloomington, IN; m. Laurel Richardson 1981; two s. three d. *Education:* Indiana Univ., Yale Univ. *Career:* Prof., Yale Univ. 1963–71, Ohio State Univ. 1971–. *Publications:* fiction: Hartspring Blows his Mind 1968, Prince Elmo's Fire 1974, Flying Elbows 1975; non-fiction: 20th Century Studies of the Great Gatsby 1968, Travels with Ernest 2004; contrib. to professional journals. *Honours:* Book-of-the-Month Club Selection 1974, Ohio State Univ. Distinguished Teaching Award 1985. *Address:* 143 W South Street, Worthington, OH 43085, USA (home). *E-mail:* lockridge.1@osu.edu (office).

LOCKWOOD, Lewis Henry, BA, MFA, PhD; American musicologist, writer, editor and academic; b. 16 Dec. 1930, New York, NY; s. of Gerald Lockwood and Madeline Lockwood; m. 1st Doris Hoffmann Lockwood (deceased); m. 2nd Ava Bry Penman; one s. one d. *Education:* Queens Coll., City Univ. of New York, Princeton Univ. *Career:* Faculty, Princeton Univ. 1958–65, Assoc. Prof. 1965–68, Prof. 1968–80, Chair. Dept of Music 1970–73; Ed. Journal of the American Musicological Society 1963–66, Beethoven Forum 1991–2007; Prof. of Music, Harvard Univ. 1980–2002, Chair. Dept of Music 1988–90; Gen. Ed. Studies in Musical Genesis and Structure 1984–98; mem. American Acad. of Arts and Sciences, American Musicological Soc. (Pres. 1987–88, Hon. mem. 1993–). *Publications:* Music in Renaissance Ferrara, 1400–1505 1984, Beethoven Essays: Studies in Honor of Elliot Forbes (co-ed.) 1984, Essays in Musicology: A Tribute to Alvin Johnson (co-ed.) 1990, Beethoven: Studies in the Creative Process 1992, Beethoven: The Music and the Life 2003, Inside Beethoven's Quartets (co-authored with the Juilliard Quartet); contrib. to scholarly books and journals on studies in Renaissance musicology and on Beethoven. *Honours:* Dr hc (Università degli Studi, Ferrara) 1991, (New England Conservatory of Music) 1998, (Wake Forest Univ.) 2004; Nat. Endowment for the Humanities Sr Fellowships 1973–74, 1984–85, Guggenheim Fellowship 1977–78; Deems Taylor Award, The American Soc. of Composers, Authors and Publrs (ASCAP) 1993, Festschrift published in his honour 1997, Award in his name est. by American Musicological Soc. 2005, Lifetime Achievement Award, Renaissance Soc. of America 2008. *Address:* Department of Music, Harvard University, Cambridge, MA 02138, USA (office). *E-mail:* llockw@fas.harvard.edu (office).

LODGE, David John, CBE, PhD, FRSL; British writer and academic; *Professor Emeritus of English Literature, University of Birmingham*; b. 28 Jan. 1935, London; s. of William F. Lodge and Rosalie M. Lodge (née Murphy); m. Mary Frances Jacob 1959; two s. one d. *Education:* St Joseph's Acad., Blackheath and Univ. Coll., London. *Career:* asst, British Council, London 1959–60; Asst Lecturer in English, Univ. of Birmingham 1960–62, Lecturer 1963–71, Sr Lecturer 1971–73, Reader 1973–76, Prof. of English Literature 1976–87, Hon. Prof. 1987–2000, Prof. Emer. 2001–; Chair. Booker Prize Cttee 1989; Harkness Commonwealth Fellow, 1964–65; Visiting Assoc. Prof. Univ. of Calif. at Berkeley 1969; Henfield Writing Fellow, Univ. of E Anglia 1977; Fellow, Univ. Coll. London 1982, Goldsmith's Coll. 1992. *Publications:* fiction: The Picturegoers 1960, Ginger, You're Barmy 1962, The British Museum is Falling Down 1965, Out of the Shelter 1970, Changing Places: A Tale of Two Campuses 1975, How Far Can You Go? (aka Souls and Bodies) (Whitbread Book of Year Award) 1980, Small World: An Academic Romance 1984, Nice Work (Sunday Express Book of the Year Award) 1988, The Writing Game (play) 1991, Paradise News 1991, Therapy 1995, Home Truths (novella) 1999, Thinks… (novel) 2001, Author, Author 2004, Deaf Sentence (novel) 2008, A Man of Parts (H. G. Wells) 201; non-fiction: Language of Fiction 1966, Graham Greene 1966, The Novelist at the Crossroads and Other Essays on Fiction and Criticism 1971, Evelyn Waugh 1971, Twentieth-Century Literary Criticism: A Reader (ed.) 1972, The Modes of Modern Writing: Metaphor, Metonymy and the Typology of Modern Literature 1977, Working with Structuralism: Essays and Reviews on Nineteenth- and Twentieth Century Literature 1981, Write On: Occasional Essays 1986, Modern Criticism and Theory: A Reader (ed.) 1988, After Bakhtin: Essays on Fiction and Criticism 1990, The Art of Fiction: Illustrated from Classic and Modern Texts 1992, The Practice of Writing: Essays, Lectures, Reviews, and a Diary 1996, Consciousness and the Novel 2002, The Year of Henry James 2006. *Honours:* Chevalier, Ordre des Arts et des Lettres 1997; Yorkshire Post Fiction Prize 1975, Hawthornden Prize 1976, RTS Award for Best Drama Serial 1990. *Address:* c/o Department of English, University of Birmingham, Birmingham, B15 2TT, England (office). *Telephone:* (121) 414-5670 (office). *Fax:* (121) 414-5668 (office). *E-mail:* english@bham.ac.uk (office). *Website:* www.english.bham.ac.uk (office).

LOEWE, Michael Arthur Nathan, MA, PhD; British academic (retd) and writer; b. 2 Nov. 1922, Oxford. *Education:* Magdalen Coll., Oxford, Univ. of London, Univ. of Cambridge. *Career:* Lecturer in History of the Far East, Univ. of London 1956–63; Lecturer in Chinese Studies, Univ. of Cambridge 1963–90. *Publications:* Imperial China: The Historical Background to the Modern Age 1966, Records of Han Administration (two vols) 1967, Everyday Life in Early Imperial China During the Han Period, 202 BC–AD 220 1968, Crisis and Conflict in Han China, 104 BC–AD 9 1974, Ancient Cosmologies (ed. with Carmen Blacker) 1975, Ways to Paradise: The Chinese Quest for Immortality 1979, Divination and Oracles (ed. with Carmen Blacker) 1981, Chinese Ideas of Life and Death: Faith, Myth, and Reason in the Han Period (202 BC–AD 220) 1982, The Ch'in and Han Empires, 221 BC–AD 220, Vol. 1 of The Cambridge History of China (ed. with Denis Twichett) 1986, The Pride That Was China 1990, Early Chinese Texts: A Bibliographical Guide 1993, Divination, Mythology and Monarchy in Han China 1994, The Cambridge History of Ancient China (ed. with E. Shaughnessy) 1999, A Biographical Dictionary of the Qin, Former Han and Xin Periods 2000, The Men Who Governed Han China 2004, The Government of the Qin and Han Empires 221 BCE–220 CE 2006, China's Early Empires (ed. with Michael Nylan) 2010; contrib. to scholarly publications. *Honours:* Fellow, Soc. of Antiquaries, 1972; Fellow, Clare Hall, 1968–90; Foreign Hon. Mem., American Acad. of Arts and Sciences, 2002. *Address:* Willow House, Grantchester, Cambridge CB3 9NF, England (home).

LÖFFELHOLZ, Thomas, DrJur; German journalist and editor. *Career:* Chair. German Press Asscn, Bonn 1982–83; Chief Ed. Stuttgarter Zeitung 1983–95; Ed., then Chief Ed. Die Welt 1995–98, re-apptd. Ed.-in-Chief 2001–08. *Honours:* Chevalier Ordre de la Couronne (Belgium); Karl Bräuer Prize 1981, Ludwig Erhard Prize 1984, Franz Karl Maier Prize 1992, Theodor Wolff Prize 1972, 1998, Bundesverdienstkreuz (First Class) 1999. *Address:* c/o Die Welt, Axel-Springer-Strasse 65, 10888 Berlin, Germany.

LÖFGREN, Lars, PhD; Swedish theatre, film and television director, playwright and poet; *Lord Chamberlain;* b. 6 Sept. 1935, The Arctic Circle; m. Anna-Karin Gillberg 1963; one s. two d. *Education:* Gustavus Adolphus Coll., USA, Stanford Univ., USA, Sorbonne, France, Uppsala Univ., Sweden. *Career:* Dir Royal Dramatic Theatre of Sweden 1985–97, Nordic Museum 1997–2001; Lord Chamberlain 1999–. *Publications:* various plays, filmscripts, TV scripts, poetry, novels, Svensk Teater — Artistry of the Swedish Theater 2003. *Honours:* Lord-in-Waiting to His Majesty the King; Commdr, Légion d'honneur 2001; Royal Prize of Swedish Acad. 1996. *Address:* The Office of the Marshal of the Court of the Royal Palace, 11130 Stockholm (office); Sjötullsbacken 27, 11525 Stockholm, Sweden (home). *Telephone:* (8) 402-6000 (office); (8) 855822 (home). *E-mail:* lars.lofgren@pof.se (home).

LOGAN, Mark (see Nicole, Christopher Robin)

LOMAX, Marion (see Bolam, Robyn)

LOMPERIS, Timothy John, MA, PhD; American academic and writer; *Professor of Political Science, St Louis University*; b. 6 March 1947, Guntur, India; s. of Rev. Clarence Lomperis and Marjorie Lomperis; m. Ana Maria Turner 1976; one s. one d. *Education:* Augustana Coll., School of Advanced Int. Studies, Johns Hopkins Univ., Duke Univ. *Career:* Instructor and Asst Prof., Louisiana State Univ. 1980–84; Visiting Asst Prof., Duke Univ., 1983–84, Asst Prof. of Political Science 1984–94; John M. Olin Postdoctoral

Fellow, Harvard Univ., 1985–86; Fellow, Woodrow Wilson Int. Center for Scholars, Washington, DC 1988–89; Assoc. Prof. of Political Science, United States Military Acad., West Point, New York, 1994–96; Prof. of Political Science, St Louis Univ. 1996–, also Chair. Dept of Political Science 1996–2004. *Publications:* The War Everyone Lost – and Won: America's Intervention in Viet Nam's Twin Struggles 1984, Hindu Influence on Greek Philosophy: The Odyssey of the Soul from the Upanishads to Plato 1984, 'Reading the Wind': The Literature of the Vietnam War 1987, From People's War to People's Rule: Insurgency, Intervention, and the Lessons of Vietnam 1996, The Vietnam War From the Rear Echelon: An Intelligence Officer's Memoir 2011; contribs to scholarly journals, book chapters. *Honours:* United States Army Bronze Star 1973, Vietnamese Army Staff Medal First Class 1973, Presidential Outstanding Community Achievement Award for Vietnam Era Veterans, Chapel Hill, NC 1979, Helen Dwight Reid Award, American Political Science Asscn 1982, Civilian Superior Service Award, United States Military Acad., West Point, New York 1996, Faculty Excellence Award, St Louis Univ. 2004. *Address:* Department of Political Science, St Louis University, St Louis, MO 63103, USA (office). *Telephone:* (314) 977-3044 (office). *E-mail:* lomperis@slu.edu (office). *Website:* www.slu.edu/x21655.xml (office).

LONDON, Joan; Australian writer; b. 1948, Perth, WA. *Publications:* Sister Ships (short stories) (Age Book of the Year, Western Australia Week Literary Award) 1986, Letter to Constantine (short stories) (Steele Rudd Award, West Australian Premier's Award for Fiction) 1994, Gilgamesh (novel) (Age Book of the Year for Fiction 2002) 2001, The New Dark Age (short stories) 2004, The Good Parents (novel) 2008. *Address:* c/o Vintage Publicity Department, Random House Australia, Level 3 100 Pacific Highway, North Sydney, NSW 2060, Australia (office). *E-mail:* media@randomhouse.com.au (office). *Website:* www.randomhouse.com.au (office).

LONG, Elizabeth (Lisa) Valk, BA, MBA; American publishing executive; b. 29 April 1950, Winston-Salem, NC. *Education:* Hollins Univ., Harvard Business School. *Career:* mem. circulation staff Time Inc., New York 1979–80, Circulation Dir Fortune Magazine 1982–84, Sports Illustrated 1984–85, Time magazine 1985–86, Publr Life magazine (first woman publr at Time Inc.) 1986–88, Publr People magazine 1988–91, Publr Time magazine 1991–93, Pres. Time magazine 1993–95, Exec. Vice Pres. Time Inc. 1995–2001 (retd); mem. Bd of Dirs Steelcase Inc., J.M. Smucker Co., Belk Inc., Jefferson Pilot Corpn; Chair. Bd of Trustees Hollins Univ. *Honours:* Matrix Women in Communications Award 1992, Hollins Medal, Hollins Univ. 2007. *Address:* c/o Steelcase Inc., PO Box 1967, Grand Rapids, MI 49501, USA (office).

LONG, Robert Emmet, BA, MA, PhD; American literary critic and writer; b. 7 June 1934, Oswego, NY, USA. *Education:* Columbia Univ., Syracuse Univ. *Career:* Instructor, SUNY 1962–64; Asst Prof., Queens Coll., CUNY 1968–71. *Publications:* The Achieving of the Great Gatsby: F. Scott Fitzgerald 1920–25, 1979; The Great Succession: Henry James and the Legacy of Hawthorne, 1979; Henry James: The Early Novels, 1983; John O'Hara, 1983; Nathanael West, 1985; Barbara Pym, 1986; James Thurber, 1988; James Fenimore Cooper, 1990; Ingmar Bergman: Film and Stage, 1994; The Films of Merchant Ivory, 1999; Broadway, the Golden Years: Jerome Robbins and the Great Choreographers and Dirs, 1940 to the Present, 2001; John Huston: Interviews, 2001; George Cukor; Interviews, 2001. Editor: American Education, 1985; Drugs and American Society, 1985; Vietnam, Ten Years After, 1986; Mexico, 1986; The Farm Crisis, 1987; The Problem of Waste Disposal, 1988; AIDS, 1989; The Welfare Debate, 1989; Energy and Conservation, 1989; Japan and the USA, 1990; Censorship, 1990; The Crisis in Health Care, 1991; The State of US Education, 1991; The Reunification of Germany, 1992; Immigration to the United States, 1992; Drugs in America, 1993; Banking Scandals: The S&L and BCCI, 1993; Religious Cults in America, 1994; Criminal Sentencing, 1995; Suicide, 1995; Immigration, 1996; Affirmative Action, 1996; Multiculturalism, 1997; Right to Privacy, 1997; First Impressions: Observations on Theater and Books 2003; An Enlarging Vision: Early Essays and Stories 2003; James Ivory in Conversation 2005; Gallagher Horse 2005; Liv Ullmann: Interviews (Ed.) 2005, Working in the Theatre (ed., four vols) 2006; contrib. several hundred articles to magazines, journals and newspapers. *Address:* 254 South Third Street, Fulton, NY 13069, USA.

LONG, Robert Hill, BA, MFA; American poet, writer and university administrator; *Assistant Director of Faculty Research, University of Oregon*; b. 23 Nov. 1952, Raleigh, NC; m. Sandra Morgen 1980; one s. one d. *Education:* Davidson Coll., Warren Wilson Coll. *Career:* Visiting Lecturer, Clark Univ., Univ. of Hartford, Smith College, Univ. of Connecticut at Torrington 1987–91; Sr Lecturer in Creative Writing, Univ. of Oregon 1991–2006, currently Asst Dir of Faculty Research; Sr Instructor, Penn State Univ. 2006–08. *Publications:* The Power to Die (poems) 1987, The Work of the Bow (poems) 1997, The Effigies (fiction) 1998, The Kilim Dreaming (poems) 2010; contributions: various anthologies and journals. *Honours:* Aspen Writers' Conference Poetry Fellowship 1981, First Prize, North Carolina Poetry Award 1986, Grand Prize, A Living Culture in Durham Anthology 1986, North Carolina Arts Council Literary Fellowship 1986, Nat. Endowment for the Arts Fellowship 1988, 2005, Cleveland State Univ. Poetry Center Prize 1995, Oregon Arts Commission Literary Fellowship 1997, Balch Prize, Virginia Quarterly Review 1999, War Poetry Prize 2004, 2009, Dorothy Brunsman Prize 2010. *Address:* 208 Agate Hall, University of Oregon, Eugene, OR 97403, USA (office). *Telephone:* (541) 346-2293 (office). *E-mail:* rohilong@gmail.com (office). *Website:* roberthilllong.wordpress.com.

LONGLEY, Edna, MRIA, FBA; Irish poet, academic and critic; *Emerita Professor, Queen's University*; m. Michael Longley; one s. two d. *Education:* Trinity Coll., Dublin. *Career:* Lecturer 1964–76, Sr Lecturer 1976–87, Reader 1987–91, Prof. 1991–2002, Emerita Prof. 2002–, School of English, Queen's Univ., Belfast; editorial bd mem., Fortnight and Yeats Annual. *Publications:* poetry: Poetry in the Wars 1986, Alice in Wormland: Selected Poems 1990, From Kathleen to Anorexia 1990, The Living Stream: Literature and Revisionism in Ireland 1994; editor: Language Not to Be Betrayed 1985, The Biggest Egg in the World 1987, Yeats Annual: That Accusing Eye, Yeats and his Irish Readers (with others) 1996, The Bloodaxe Book of 20th Century Poetry from Britain and Ireland 2000, Poetry and Posterity 2000, Edward Thomas: The Annotated Collected Poems 2008; contrib. reviews to TLS, The Irish Times, Poetry Review, Thumbscrew, Metre, BBC Radio. *Address:* c/o Bloodaxe Books Ltd, Highgreen, Tarset, Northumberland NE48 1RP, England. *Website:* www.bloodaxebooks.com.

LONGLEY, Michael George, CBE, BA; Northern Irish poet; b. 27 July 1939, Belfast; m. Edna Broderick 1964; one s. two d. *Education:* Royal Belfast Academical Institution, Trinity Coll. Dublin. *Career:* teacher, Avoca School, Blackrock 1962–63, Belfast High School and Erith Secondary School 1963–64, Royal Belfast Academical Institution 1964–69; Asst Dir, Arts Council of Northern Ireland, Belfast 1970–91; Ireland Chair of Poetry 2007–10. *Publications:* poetry: Ten Poems 1965, Room To Rhyme (with Seamus Heaney and David Hammond) 1968, Secret Marriages: Nine Short Poems 1968, Three Regional Voices (with Barry Tebb and Ian Crichton-Smith) 1968, No Continuing City: Poems 1963–1968 1969, Lares 1972, An Exploded View: Poems 1968–72 1973, Fishing in the Sky 1975, Man Lying on a Wall 1976, The Echo Gate: Poems 1975–1978 1979, Selected Poems 1963–1980 1980, Patchwork 1981, Poems 1963–1983 1985, Gorse Fires 1991, The Ghost Orchid 1995, Selected Poems 1998, The Weather in Japan (T. S. Eliot Prize) 2000, Snow Water 2004, Collected Poems 2006, A Jovial Hullabaloo 2008; editor: Causeway: The Arts in Ulster 1971, Under the Moon, Over the Stars: Young People's Writing from Ulster 1971, Selected Poems by Louis MacNeice 1988; contrib. to periodicals. *Honours:* Foreign Hon. Fellow, American Acad. of Arts and Sciences 2009; Hon. DLitt (Queen's Univ., Belfast) 1995; Eric Gregory Award 1965, Commonwealth Poetry Prize 1985, Whitbread Poetry Award 1991, Hawthornden Prize 2000, Irish Times Poetry Prize 2000, Queen's Gold Medal for Poetry 2001. *Address:* c/o Jonathan Cape, Random House UK, 20 Vauxhall Bridge Road, London SW1V 2SA, England (office). *Website:* www.randomhouse.co.uk (office).

LONGMATE, Norman Richard, BA, MA, FRHistS; British writer; b. 15 Dec. 1925, Newbury, Berkshire, England. *Education:* Worcester Coll., Oxford. *Career:* Leader Writer, Evening Standard, 1952; Feature Writer, Daily Mirror, 1953–56; Schools Radio Producer, 1963–65, Senior, subsequently Chief Asst, BBC Secretariat, 1965–83; mem. Oxford Society; Society of Authors; Fortress Study Group; United Kingdom Fortification Club; Historical Asscn; Ramblers Asscn; Society of Sussex Downsmen; Prayer Book Society. *Publications:* A Socialist Anthology (ed.), 1953; Oxford Triumphant, 1955; King Cholera, 1966; The Waterdrinkers, 1968; Alive and Well, 1970; How We Lived Then, 1971; If Britain had Fallen, 1972; The Workhouse, 1974; The Real Dad's Army, 1974; The GI's, 1975; Milestones in Working Class History, 1975; Air Raid, 1976; When We Won the War, 1977; The Hungry Mills, 1978; The Doodlebugs, 1981; The Bombers, 1982; The Breadstealers, 1984; Hitler's Rockets, 1985; Defending the Island from Caesar to the Armada, 1989.

LONGWORTH, Philip, MA; British/Canadian historian; b. 17 Feb. 1933, London. *Education:* Balliol Coll., Oxford. *Career:* Prof. of History, McGill Univ., Montréal 1984–2003. *Publications:* A Hero of Our Time, by Lermontov (trans.) 1962, The Art of Victory 1965, The Unending Vigil 1967, The Cossacks 1969, The Three Empresses 1971, The Rise and Fall of Venice 1974, Alexis, Tsar of All the Russias 1984, The Making of Eastern Europe 1992 (2nd Edn 1997), The Rise and Fall of Russia's Empires: From Prehistory to Putin 2005; contributions to periodicals. *Address:* A. M. Heath & Co, 6 Warwick Court, London, WC1R 5DV, England (office). *E-mail:* prlongworth@virgin.net (office). *Website:* www.philiplongworth.com.

LONGYEAR, Barry B.; American writer; b. 12 May 1942, Harrisburg, PA. *Publications:* City of Baraboo, 1980; Manifest Destiny (short stories), 1980; Circus World (short stories), 1980; Elephant Song, 1981; The Tomorrow Testament, 1983; It Came from Schenectady, 1984; Sea of Glass, 1986; Enemy Mine, 1988; Saint MaryBlue, 1988; Naked Came the Robot, 1988; The God Box, 1989; Infinity Hold, 1989; The Homecoming, 1989; Slag Like Me, 1994; The Change, 1994; Yesterday's Tomorrow, 1997; The Enemy Papers, 1998.

LOPATE, Phillip, BA, PhD; American writer and poet; *Professor of English, Hofstra University*; b. 16 Nov. 1943, New York, NY; m. Cheryl Cipriani 1990; one c. *Education:* Columbia Coll., Union Inst. *Career:* Assoc. Prof. of English, Univ. of Houston 1980–88; Assoc. Prof. of Creative Writing, Columbia Univ. 1988–90; Prof. of English, Bennington Coll. 1990, Hofstra Univ. 1991–. *Publications:* fiction: Confessions of Summer 1979, The Rug Merchant 1987, Two Marriages (novellas) 2008; poetry: The Eyes Don't Always Want to Stay Open 1972, The Daily Round 1976; non-fiction: Being with Children (memoir) 1975, Journal of a Living Experiment (ed.) 1979, Bachelorhood (essays) 1981, The Art of the Personal Essay (ed.) 1994, Against Joie de Vivre (essays) 1989, Portrait of My Body (essays) 1996, The Anchor Essay Annual (ed.) 1997–99, Totally, Tenderly, Tragically (film criticism) 1998, Writing New York (ed.)

1998, Getting Personal 2003, Waterfront 2003, Rudy Burckhardt (biog.) 2004, American Movie Critics (ed.) 2006; contrib. to anthologies, newspapers, reviews, quarterlies, journals and magazines. *Honours:* Guggenheim Fellowship, Nat. Endowment for the Arts grants, New York Foundation for the Arts grants, New York Public Library Center for Scholars and Writers Fellowship; Christopher Medallion, Texas Inst. of Letters Award. *Address:* 402 Sackett Street, New York, NY 11231, USA (home). *E-mail:* plopate@aol.com (home). *Website:* www.philliplopate.com.

LOPÈS, Henri Marie Joseph; Republic of the Congo author, politician and diplomatist; *Ambassador to France;* b. 12 Sept. 1937, Léopoldville, Belgian Congo (now Kinshasa, Democratic Repub. of the Congo); s. of Jean-Marie Lopès and Micheline Vulturi; m. Nirva Pasbeau 1961; one s. three d. *Education:* France. *Career:* Minister of Nat. Educ. 1968–71, of Foreign Affairs 1971–73; mem. Political Bureau, Congolese Labour Party 1973; Prime Minister and Minister of Planning 1973–75, of Finance 1977–80; UNESCO Asst Dir-Gen. for Programme Support 1982–86, UNESCO Asst Dir-Gen. for Culture and Communication 1986–90, for Culture 1990–94, for Foreign Affairs 1994–95, Deputy Dir-Gen. 1996–98; Amb. to France (also accred to Portugal, Spain, UK and The Holy See (Vatican City) 1998–; mem. Haut Conseil de la Francophonie. *Publications:* Tribaliques (short stories), La Nouvelle Romance (novel), Learning to be (with others), Sans tam-tam (novel) 1977, Le Pleurer Rire (novel) 1982, Le Chercheur d'Afriques (novel) 1990, Sur l'autre Rive (novel) 1992, Le Lys et le flamboyant (novel) 1997. *Honours:* Chevalier, Légion d'honneur, Commdr du Mérite Congolais, etc.; Prix littéraire de l'Afrique noire 1972, Prix SIMBA de littérature 1978, Prix de littérature du Président (Congo), Prix de l' Acad. de Bretagne et des Pays de la Loire 1990, Grand Prix de la Francophonie de l' Acad. française 1993. *Address:* Embassy of the Republic of the Congo, 37 bis rue Paul Valéry, 75116 Paris, France (office). *Telephone:* 1-45-00-60-57 (home). *Fax:* 1-40-67-17-33 (office). *E-mail:* ambacongo_france@yahoo.fr (office). *Website:* www.ambacongo.org (office).

LOPEZ, Barry Holstun, BA, MA; American writer; b. 6 Jan. 1945, Port Chester, NY; s. of Adrian Bernard and Mary Frances (Holstun) Lopez; m. Debra Gwartney. *Education:* Univ. of Notre Dame. *Career:* Visiting Distinguished Scholar, Texas Tech. Univ. 2003–. *Publications include:* Desert Notes 1976, Giving Birth to Thunder 1978, Of Wolves and Men (John Burroughs Medal 1979, Christopher Medal 1979, Pacific NW Booksellers Award 1979) 1978, River Notes 1979, Winter Count 1981, Arctic Dreams (Nat. Book Award 1987, Christopher Medal 1987, Pacific NW Booksellers Award 1987, Frances Fuller Victor Award 1987) 1986, Crossing Open Ground 1988, Crow and Weasel 1990, The Rediscovering of North America 1991, Field Notes (Pacific NW Booksellers Award 1995, Critics' Choice Award 1996) 1994, Lessons from the Wolverine 1997, Apologia 1997, About this Life 1998, Light Action in the Caribbean 2000, Resistance (H. L. Davis Award 2005) 2004; ed.: Home Ground (with Debra Gwartney); contrib. to many periodicals. *Honours:* Fellow, The Explorers Club 2002; Hon. LDH (Whittier Coll.) 1988, (Univ. of Portland) 1994, (Texas Tech. Univ.) 2000, (Utah State Univ.) 2002; numerous awards including American Acad. of Arts and Letters Award 1986, Guggenheim Fellowship 1987, Lannan Foundation Award 1990. *Literary Agent:* c/o Peter Mason, Sterling Lord Literistic, 65 Bleecker Street, New York, NY 10012; Steven Barclay Agency, 12 Western Avenue, Petaluma, CA 94952, USA. *Telephone:* (212) 780-6050 (Sterling Lord); (707) 773-0654 (Steven Barclay). *Fax:* (707) 778-1868. *E-mail:* peter@sll.com. *Website:* www.barclayagency.com; www.barrylopez.com.

LÓPEZ, Lorraine M., BA, MA, PhD; American writer and academic; *Associate Professor of English, Vanderbilt University;* b. Los Angeles, Calif. *Education:* California State Univ., Northridge, Univ. of Georgia. *Career:* currently Assoc. Prof. of English, Vanderbilt Univ.; Assoc. Ed. Afro-Hispanic Review. *Publications:* Soy la Avon Lady and Other Stories (Miguel Marmól Prize for Fiction) 2002, Call Me Henri (novel) (Paterson Prize for Young Adult Literature) 2006, The Gifted Gabaldón Sisters (novel) 2008, An Angle of Vision: Women Writers on Their Poor and Working-Class Roots (essays, Ed.) 2009, Homicide Survivors Picnic and Other Stories 2009, The Realm of Hungry Spirits (novel) 2011; contrib. stories to Prairie Schooner, Voices of Mexico, CrazyHorse, Image, Cimarron Review, Alaska Quarterly Review, StoryQuarterly/Narrative Magazine, Latino Boom. *Honours:* Ind. Publisher Book Award for Multicultural Fiction, Int. Latino Book Award for Short Stories. *Address:* Benson Hall 425, 2301 Vanderbilt Place, Vanderbilt University, Nashville, TN 37235-1654, USA (office). *Telephone:* (615) 322-2328. *E-mail:* lorraine.lopez@vanderbilt.edu. *Website:* www.lorrainelopez.net (home).

LOPEZ, Tony, BA, PhD; British academic, poet and writer; b. 5 Nov. 1950, London, England; m. Sara Louise Banham 1985; one s. one d. *Education:* Univ. of Essex, Gonville & Caius Coll., Cambridge. *Career:* Lecturer in English, Univ. of Leicester, 1986–87, Univ. of Edinburgh, 1987–89; Lecturer to Reader in Poetry, Univ. of Plymouth 1989–99, first Prof. of Poetry 2000–09; self-employed writer 2009–. *Publications:* more than 20 books of poetry, fiction and criticism, including Snapshots 1976, Change 1978; The English Disease 1979, A Handbook of British Birds 1982, Abstract and Delicious 1983, The Poetry of W. S. Graham 1989, A Theory of Surplus Labour 1990, Stress Management 1994, Negative Equity 1995, False Memory 1996, Devolution 2000, False Memory 2003, Meaning Performance: Essays on Poetry 2006, Covers, 2007, Poetry and Public Language (co-ed.) 2007, Darwin 2009; contribs to anthologies and periodicals. *Honours:* Blundel Award 1990, Wingate Scholarship 1996, British Academy Research Travel Grant 2001, Arts and Humanities Research Council Award 2005, Arts Council England Writers Award 2010. *Website:* www.tonylopez.org.uk.

LÓPEZ MILLS, Tedi, BPhil, MA; Mexican poet, translator and essayist; b. Aug. 1959, Mexico City. *Education:* Universidad Nacional Autónoma de México, Univ. of Paris (Sorbonne), France. *Career:* Man. Ed. La Gaceta (magazine) 1994–99; Fellow, FONCA 1994; mem. Sistema Nacional de Creadores de Arte 2000–. *Publications:* Cinco estaciones 1989, Un lugar ajeno 1993, Segunda persona (Premio Nacional de Literatura Efraín Huerta) 1994, Glosas 1997, Horas (Poetry Fellowship Foundation Octavio Paz 1999) 2000, Luz por aire y agua 2002, La noche en blanco de Mallarmé 2006, Contracorriente (Premio Nacional de Literatura José Fuentes Mares) 2006, Muerte en la rúa Augusta (Premio Xavier Villaurrutia) 2009. *Address:* c/o Ediciones Era SA de CV, Calle Labour 31, Col. Fame, 14269 México DF, Mexico.

LORD, Graham John, BA (Hons); British writer; b. 16 Feb. 1943, Umtali, Southern Rhodesia (now Zimbabwe); s. of the late Harold Reginald Lord and Ida Frances McDowall; m. Jane Carruthers 1962 (died 2000); two d.; partner Juliet Lewis. *Education:* Falcon Coll., Essexvale, Bulawayo, Southern Rhodesia, Univ. of Cambridge. *Career:* Reporter, Sunday Express 1965–69; Literary Ed. Sunday Express, London 1969–92; Originator, Sunday Express Book of the Year Award 1987, Judge 1987–92; columnist and arts corresp., The Daily Telegraph 1992–94; Ed. Raconteur short story magazine 1994–95; regular contrib. to The Times, Daily Mail 1994–96; full-time novelist and biographer 1996–. *Publications:* Marshmallow Pie 1970, A Roof Under Your Feet 1973, The Spider and the Fly 1974, God and All His Angels 1976, The Nostradamus Horoscope 1981, Time Out of Mind 1986, Ghosts of King Solomon's Mines 1991, Just the One: The Wives and Times of Jeffrey Bernard 1992, A Party to Die For 1997, James Herriot: The Life of a Country Vet 1997, Sorry, We're Going to have to Let You Go 1999, Dick Francis: A Racing Life 1999, Arthur Lowe 2002, Niv: The Authorised Biography of David Niven 2003, John Mortimer: The Devil's Advocate 2005, Joan Collins: The Biography of an Icon 2007, Under a Hammock Moon 2012, Gossiping With Legends 2012. *E-mail:* pelicans@sisterisles.kn (office). *Website:* www.graham-lord.com; www.graham-lord.com/Serendipity/PAGES/Home.htm.

LORIGA, Ray; Spanish writer, screenwriter and film director; b. 1967, Madrid. *Films include:* Live Flesh (writer, with Pedro Almodóvar) 1997, La pistola de mi hermano (Dir) 1997, Todos los aviones del mundo (writer) 2001, El Séptimo día (writer) 2004, Ausentes (writer) 2005, Teresa, el cuerpo de Cristo (Dir) 2007. *Publications include:* Lo Peor de todo 1993, Heroes 1994, My Brother's Gun: A Novel of Disposable Lives, Immediate Fame and a Big Black Automatic 1997, Tokyo Doesn't Love Us Anymore 2004; contrib. to Crime Hamper. *Address:* c/o Canongate Books, 14 High Street, Edinburgh, EH1 1TE, Scotland.

LORRIMER, Claire (see Clark, Patricia Denise)

LOSHAK, Victor Grigoryevich; Russian journalist; *Editor-in-Chief, Ogoniok;* b. 20 April 1952, Zaporozhye, Ukraine; s. of Grigory Abramovich Loshak and Anna Davydovna Loshak; m. Marina Devovna Loshak; one d. *Education:* Odessa State Univ. *Career:* corresp. for various Odessa newspapers 1973–83; special corresp. Izvestia 1983–86; political observer Moskovskye Novosti 1986–91, First Deputy Ed. 1991–92, Ed.-in-Chief 1992–2003; Ed.-in-Chief Ogoniok (periodical) 2003–; broadcaster for Kultura (TV channel); mem. Int. Inst. of Press (Vice-Pres. Russian br.). *Honours:* Prize of Journalists' Union of Moscow, Order of Honour. *Address:* Ogoniok, Krasnokazarmennaya str. pb. 14, 111250 Moscow, Russia (office). *Telephone:* (495) 540-47-10 (office). *Fax:* (495) 775-41-06 (office). *E-mail:* pochta@ovarpress.ru (office). *Website:* www.ogoniok.com (office).

LOTT, Bret, BA, MFA; American academic and writer; *Professor of English, College of Charleston;* b. 8 Oct. 1958, Los Angeles, CA; m. Melanie Kai Swank 1980, two s. *Education:* California State Univ. at Long Beach, Univ. of Massachusetts at Amherst. *Career:* reporter, Daily Commercial News, Los Angeles 1980–81; Instructor in Remedial English, Ohio State Univ., Columbus 1984–86; Prof. of English, also Writer-in-Residence, Coll. of Charleston 1986–2004, 2007–; Ed. and Dir, The Southern Review, Louisiana State Univ. 2004–07; Fulbright Sr American Scholar, Bar Ilan Univ. 2006–07; apptd to Nat. Council on the Arts (Presidential appointment); mem. Associated Writing Programs, Poets and Writers. *Publications:* The Man Who Owned Vermont 1987, A Stranger's House 1988, A Dream of Old Leaves 1989, Jewel 1991, Reed's Beach 1994, How to Get Home 1996, Fathers, Sons and Brothers 1997, The Hunt Club 1999, A Song I Knew by Heart 2004, The Difference Between Women and Men 2005, Before We Get Started: A Practical Memoir of the Writer's Life 2005, Ancient Highway 2008, Dead Low Tide 2012; contribs to anthologies and periodicals. *Honours:* Chancellor's Medal, Univ. of Massachusetts at Amherst 2000, Denise Levertov Medal 2006. *Address:* Department of English, College of Charleston, 96 Wentworth Street, Room 309, Charleston, SC 29424, USA (office). *Telephone:* (843) 953-6494 (office). *E-mail:* lottb@cofc.edu (office). *Website:* english.cofc.edu/about/faculty-staff-listing/lott-bret.php (office).

LOTT, Tim; British writer and broadcaster; b. 1956, London. *Education:* Harlow Coll. and LSE. *Career:* journalist, Sounds magazine, City Limits magazine; television producer; panellist, Newsnight Review (BBC2) 2001–. *Publications:* The Scent of Dried Roses (memoir) 1996, White City Blue (Whitbread First Novel Award) 1999, Rumours of a Hurricane (novel) 2002,

The Love Secrets of Don Juan (novel) 2003, The Seymour Tapes 2005, Fearless (juvenile) 2007, Under the Same Stars (novel) 2012; contrib. 'What Young Men Do', Granta 62 1998. *Honours:* J.R. Ackerley Prize for Autobiography. *Address:* c/o Viking, Penguin Books Ltd, 80 Strand, London, WC2R 0RL, England. *Website:* www.penguin.co.uk.

LOUW, Raymond; South African publishing executive and editorial consultant; b. 13 Oct. 1926, Cape Town; s. of George K. E. Louw and Helen K. Louw (née Finlay); m. Jean Ramsay Byres 1950; two s. one d. *Education:* Parktown Boys' High School, Johannesburg, University of Cape Town Programme for Management Development. *Career:* reporter on Rand Daily Mail 1946–50, Worthing Herald 1951–52, North-Western Evening Mail 1953–54, Westminster Press Provincial Newspapers (London) 1955–56; Night News Ed. Rand Daily Mail 1958–59, News Ed. 1960–65, Ed. 1966–77; News Ed. Sunday Times 1959–60; Chair. SA Morning Newspaper Group 1975–77; Gen. Man. SA Associated Newspapers 1977–82, City Press, Johannesburg 1982–84; mem. Man. Cttee, South African Press Asscn 1977–82; Chair. South African Newspaper Press Conciliation Bd 1979–82; Ed. and Publr Southern Africa Report 1982–2011; Rapporteur, Five Freedoms Forum mission to Lusaka to meet banned African National Congress leaders 1989; Chair. Media Defence Fund 1989–94, Campaign for Open Media 1985–94 (now merged as Freedom of Expression Inst., Chair. 1994–96); New Era Schools Trust; Director Media Business Training Foundation 1992-4; Trustee of Institute for Advancement of Journalism 1992–; Africa Consultant, World Press Freedom Cttee 2003–09; mem. Task Group on Govt Communications 1996; mem. Exec. Bd, Int. Press Inst., London, 1979–87, Fellow 1994; mem. Independent Media Comm. 1994; chosen by Int. Press Inst. to travel to Cameroon to make plea for release from jail of Pius Njawe (Ed. of Le Messager) 1998, Njawe freed six months later; mem. IPI delegations to the Pres. of Indonesia 2000, Zimbabwean Govt 2001, Israeli Govt 2003, Ethiopian Govt 2004 on media freedom issues; addressed UN Human Rights Comm. on need for press freedom to be declared a human right 1987; as mem. South African Nat. Editors' Forum, made numerous representations to parl. cttees against proposed legislation that would restrict media freedom 2002–; Vice-Pres. South African PEN 2005–, South African PEN rep. at confs in Dakar, Senegal 2007, Berlin 2008; as mem. of FXI, described role of South African press between 1960 and 1994 to Truth and Reconciliation Comm. 1997; made representations on media issues to govt comms of inquiry; persuaded World Asscn of Newspapers to issue Declaration of Table Mountain at WAN annual conf., Cape Town 2007; as rep. of WAN, addressed Pan African Parl.'s Human Rights Cttee, Midrand on need to repeal "insult laws" in Africa 2011. *Publications:* Four Days in Lusaka – Whites from 'Home' in talks with the ANC 1989, Report on the media situation in South Africa (for UNESCO) 1994; narrative for Nelson Mandela, Man of Destiny – A Pictorial Biography (by Peter Magubane) 1996; Undue Restriction: Laws Impacting on Media Freedom in the SADC (ed.); numerous papers and articles on the media and press freedom. *Honours:* Pringle Medal for services to journalism 1976, 1992, Media Freedom Award, Media Inst. of Southern Africa 2005, Wrottesley Award, South African Nat. Editors' Forum 2006, 2008, 2010; Mondi-Shanduka Newspaper Lifetime Achiever Award 2007, Vodacom Journalist of the Year Lifetime Achiever Award 2010, Award for Press Freedom Campaigning, Int. Press Inst. 2010, World Press Freedom Hero Award, Int. Press Inst. 2011. *Address:* 23 Duncombe Road, Forest Town, PO Box 261579, Johannesburg 2193, South Africa (office). *Telephone:* (11) 646-8790 (office). *Fax:* (11) 646-6085 (office). *E-mail:* rlouw@sn.apc.org (office).

LOVE, William F., BA, MBA; American writer; b. 20 Dec. 1932, Oklahoma City, OK; m. Joyce Mary Athman 1970; two d. *Education:* St John's Univ., Collegeville, Minnesota, Univ. of Chicago. *Career:* mem. Authors' Guild, Int. Asscn of Crime Writers, MWA, PEN Midwest, Private Eye Writers of America, Soc. of Midland Authors. *Publications:* The Chartreuse Clue 1990, The Fundamentals of Murder 1991, Bloody Ten 1992.

LØVEID, Cecilie Meyer; Norwegian playwright and poet; b. 21 Aug. 1951, Mysen; d. of Erik Løveid and Ingrid Meyer; m. Bjørn H. Ianke 1978; one s. two d. *Education:* arts and crafts school in Bergen and studies in graphic design, theatre history and drama. *Career:* mem. editorial staff, Profil (magazine) 1969; Sec. Norsk Forfattersentrum, Vestlandsardelingen 1974; Teacher, Writing Arts Centre, Bergen 1986; mem. Literary Council, Den norske Fordatterforening 1987. *Publications:* Most (novel) 1972, Sug (novel) 1979, Måkespisere (radio play) 1982, Balansedame (play) 1986, Maria Q. (play) 1991, Rhindøtrene (play) 1996, Osterrike (play) 1998. *Honours:* Prix Italia 1982; Aschehons Prize; Donblans Prize.

LOVELACE, Col Merline A., BA, MS; American fmr air force officer and writer; b. 9 Sept. 1946, Northampton, Mass; d. of Merlin S. and Alyce S. Thoma; m. Cary A. Lovelace 1970. *Education:* Ripon Coll., Troy State Univ., Middlebury Coll., Princeton Univ., Kennedy School of Govt, Harvard Univ., Squadron Officers' School, Armed Forces Staff Coll., Air War Coll. *Career:* served to Col, USAF 1968–91; novelist, mainly romances 1991–; mem. Romance Writers of America (Pres. Oklahoma Chapter). *Publications:* Bits and Pieces 1993, Maggie and Her Colonel 1994, Alena 1994, Sweet Song of Love 1994, Dreams and Schemes 1994, Siren's Call 1994, Somewhere in Time 1994, His Lady's Ransom 1995, Night of the Jaguar 1995, Cowboy and the Cossack 1995, Undercover Man 1996, Perfect Double 1996, Lady of the Upper Kingdom 1996, Line of Duty 1996, Beauty and the Bodyguard 1996, Halloween Honeymoon 1996, Wrong Bride, Right Groom 1996, The 14th and Forever 1997, Duty and Dishonor 1997, Countess in Buckskin 1998, Return to Sender 1998, Call of Duty 1998, The Tiger's Bride 1998, If A Man Answers 1998, A Drop of Frankincense 1998, The Mercenary and the New Mom 1999, His First Father's Day 1999, River Rising 1999, Undercover Groom 1999, A Man of His Word 1999, Mistaken Identity 2000, Some Like It Hot 2000, The Harder They Fall 2000, Mismatched Hearts 2000, Final Approach to Forever 2000, Dark Side of Dawn 2001, The Horse Soldier 2001, The Spy Who Loved Him 2001, The Major's Wife 2001: Twice in a Lifetime 2001, The Colonel's Daughter 2002, Hot As Ice 2002, Texas Hero 2002, Undercover Ops 2002, The Captain's Woman 2003, After Midnight 2003, Texas Now and Forever 2003, To Love A Thief 2003, A Military Affair 2003, A Savage Beauty 2003, A Question of Intent 2003, Full Throttle 2004, The Right Stuff 2004, Sailor's Moon 2004, Untamed 2004, A Bridge for Christmas 2004, The First Mistake 2005, The Middle Sin 2005, The Last Bullet 2005, Eye of the Beholder 2005, Diamonds Can Be Deadly 2006, Devlin and the Deep Blue Sea 2006, Closer Encounters 2006, Ex Marks the Spot 2007, Stranded with a Spy 2007, Risky Business 2008, Match Play 2008, Mind Game 2008, Undercover Wife 2008, The CEO's Christmas Proposition 2008, The Duke's New Year Resolution 2008, A Christmas Kiss 2008, The Executive's Valentine Seduction 2009, The Hello Girl 2009, The Protector 2009, All the Wrong Moves 2009. *Honours:* Bronze Star, Legion of Merit with one Oak Leaf Cluster, Defense Meritorious Service Medal; Distinguished Grad., Squadron Officers' School, Air War Coll., Southwest Writers Workshop Prize for Best Historical Novel 1992, Best Romance, Romantic Times 1993, 2002, Romance Writers of America RITA Award 2001, Oklahoma Writer of the Year 1998, Oklahoma Woman Veteran of the Year 2000. *E-mail:* lovelace@swbell.net (home). *Website:* www.merlinelovelace.com.

LOVELL, Sir (Alfred Charles) Bernard, Kt, OBE, PhD, MSc, FRS; British radio astronomer; b. 31 Aug. 1913, Oldland Common, Glos.; s. of Gilbert Lovell and Emily Laura Lovell (née Adams); m. Mary Joyce Chesterman 1937 (died 1993); two s. three d. *Education:* Bristol Univ. *Career:* Asst Lecturer in Physics, Univ. of Manchester 1936–39, Lecturer 1945–47, Sr Lecturer 1947–49, Reader 1949–51, Prof. of Radio Astronomy 1951–81, Emer. Prof. 1981–; with Telecommunications Research Est. 1939–45; Founder and Dir Nuffield Radio Astronomy Labs, Jodrell Bank 1945–81; Fellow, Royal Soc. 1955; Pres. Royal Astronomical Soc. 1969–71, British Asscn 1974–75; Vice-Pres. Int. Astronomical Union 1970–76; mem. Aeronautical Research Council 1955–58, Science Research Council 1965–70; Pres. Guild of Church Musicians 1976–89; Master Worshipful Co. of Musicians 1986–87. *Publications:* Science and Civilisation 1939, World Power Resources and Social Development 1945, Radio Astronomy 1952, Meteor Astronomy 1954, The Exploration of Space by Radio 1957, The Individual and the Universe (The Reith Lectures 1958), The Exploration of Outer Space 1962, Discovering the Universe 1963, Our Present Knowledge of the Universe 1967; Ed. (with Tom Margerison) The Explosion of Science: The Physical Universe 1967, The Story of Jodrell Bank 1968, The Origins and International Economics of Space Exploration 1973, Out of the Zenith: Jodrell Bank 1957–1970 1973, Man's Relation to the Universe 1975, P. M. S. Blackett – A Biographical Memoir 1976, In the Centre of Immensities 1978, Emerging Cosmology 1981, The Jodrell Bank Telescopes 1985, Voice of the Universe 1987, Pathways to the Universe (with Sir Francis Graham-Smith) 1988, Astronomer by Chance 1990, Echoes of War 1991. *Honours:* Hon. Foreign mem. American Acad. of Arts and Sciences 1955; Hon. mem. New York Acad. of Sciences 1960, Royal Northern Coll. of Music; Hon. Fellow Royal Swedish Acad. 1962, Inst. of Electrical Engineers 1967, Inst. of Physics 1975; Hon. Freeman City of Manchester 1977; Ordre du Mérite pour la Recherche et l'Invention 1962; Polish Order of Merit 1975; Hon. LLD (Edin.) 1961, (Calgary) 1966, (Liverpool) 1999; Hon. DSc (Leicester) 1961, (Leeds) 1966, (Bath, London) 1967, (Bristol) 1970; Hon. DUniv (Stirling) 1974, (Surrey) 1975; Royal Medal of Royal Soc. 1960, Daniel and Florence Guggenheim Int. Astronautics Award 1961. Maitland Silver Medal, Inst. of Structural Engineers 1964, Churchill Gold Medal, Soc. of Engineers 1964, Benjamin Franklin Medal, Royal Soc. of Arts 1980, Gold Medal, Royal Astronomical Soc. 1981. *Address:* The Quinta, Swettenham, nr Congleton, Cheshire, CW12 2LD, England (home). *Telephone:* (1477) 571254 (home). *Fax:* (1477) 571954 (home).

LOVELL, Mary Sybilla, FRGS; British writer; b. Prestatyn, North Wales; m. 2nd Geoffrey A. H. Watts 1991; one s. two step-s. two step-d. *Career:* fmr accountant and co. dir; mem. Soc. of Authors, R. S. Surtees Soc. (Vice-Pres. 1980–). *Publications:* Hunting Pageant 1980, Cats as Pets 1982, Boys Book of Boats 1983, Straight on Till Morning 1987, The Splendid Outcast 1988, The Sound of Wings 1989, Cast No Shadow 1991, A Scandalous Life 1995, The Rebel Heart 1996, A Rage to Live 1998, The Mitford Girls 2001, Bound to a Star 2004, Bess of Hardwick 2005. *Address:* c/o Little, Brown Book Group, 100 Victoria Embankment, London, EC4Y 0DY, England. *Telephone:* (20) 7911-8000. *Fax:* (20) 7911-8100. *E-mail:* mlovell2002@yahoo.com (home). *Website:* www.marylovell.com.

LOVELOCK, James Ephraim, CH, CBE, PhD, DSc, FRS; British scientist, inventor, writer and academic; *Honorary Visiting Fellow, Green College, Oxford;* b. 26 July 1919, Letchworth Garden City, Herts.; s. of Tom Arthur Lovelock and Nellie Ann Elizabeth Lovelock (née March); m. 1st Helen Mary Hyslop 1942 (died 1989); two s. two d.; m. 2nd Sandra Jean Orchard 1991. *Education:* Strand School, Univ. of Manchester, London School of Hygiene and Tropical Medicine. *Career:* staff scientist, Nat. Inst. for Medical Research, London 1941–61; Prof. of Chem., Baylor Univ. Coll. of Medicine, Tex., USA 1961–64; ind. scientist 1964–; Hon. Visiting Fellow, Green Coll., Oxford 2004–; Rockefeller Travelling Fellowship in Medicine, Harvard Univ., USA

1954; Visiting Scientist, Yale Univ. Medical School 1958–59; Visiting Prof., Univ. of Reading 1967–90; Pres. Marine Biology Asscn 1986–90; mem. Environmentalists for Nuclear Energy. *Achievements include:* inventor of the electron capture detector (which made possible the detection of CFCs and other atmospheric nano-pollutants) and of the microwave oven; originator of the 'Gaia hypothesis' during 1960s as a result of work for NASA concerned with detecting life on Mars; hypothesis proposes that living and non-living parts of the Earth form a complex interacting system that can be thought of as a single organism; named after Greek goddess Gaia, hypothesis postulates that biosphere has a regulatory effect on the Earth's environment that acts to sustain life. *Publications:* Gaia: A New Look at Life on Earth 1979, The Great Extinction (co-author) 1983, The Greening of Mars (co-author) 1984, The Ages of Gaia 1988, Gaia: The Practical Science of Planetary Medicine 1991, Homage to Gaia: The Life of an Independent Scientist 2000, Gaia: Medicine for an Ailing Planet 2005, The Revenge of Gaia: Why the Earth is Fighting Back – and How We Can Still Save Humanity 2006, The Vanishing Face of Gaia 2009. *Honours:* Hon. DSc (Univ. of East Anglia) 1982, (Plymouth Polytechnic) 1988, (Univ. of Exeter) 1988, (Stockholm Univ.) 1991, (Univ. of Edinburgh) 1993, (Univ. of Kent) 1996, (Univ. of East London) 1996, (Univ. of Colorado) 1997; CIBA Foundation Award for Research in Ageing 1955, three NASA Certificates of Recognition for: Gas Chromatograph Interface System and Method, Vapor Phase Detectors, Combined Carrier Gas Separator and Generator for Gas Chromatographic Systems 1972, Tswett Medal for Chromatography 1975, ACS Chromatography Award 1980, Stephen Dal Nogare Award 1985, Norbert Gerbier Prize, Silver Medal and Prize, Plymouth Marine Lab. 1986, World Meteorological Asscn 1988, Dr A. H. Heineken Prize for the Environment, Royal Netherlands Acad. of Arts and Sciences 1990, Rosenstiel Award in Oceanographic Science 1990, Nonino Prize 1996, Volvo Environment Prize 1996, The Blue Planet Prize 1997, Goi Peace Prize 2000, Discovery Lifetime Award, Royal Geographical Soc. 2001, Wollaston Medal, Geological Soc. 2006. *Address:* Coombe Mill, St Giles on the Heath, Launceston, Cornwall, PL15 9RY, England. *Website:* www.jameslovelock.org.

LOVESEY, Peter, (Peter Lear), BA; British writer; b. 10 Sept. 1936, Whitton, Middx, England; m. Jacqueline Ruth Lewis 1959; one s. one d. *Education:* Univ. of Reading. *Career:* mem. Crime Writers Asscn of GB (chair. 1991–92), Detection Club, Soc. of Authors. *Publications:* The Kings of Distance 1968, Wobble to Death 1970, The Detective Wore Silk Drawers 1971, Abracadaver 1972, Mad Hatters Holiday 1973, Invitation to a Dynamite Party 1974, A Case of Spirits 1975, Swing, Swing Together 1976, Goldengirl 1977, Waxwork 1978, Official Centenary History of the Amateur Athletic Association 1979, Spider Girl 1980, The False Inspector Dew 1982, Keystone 1983, Butchers (short stories) 1985, The Secret of Spandau 1986, Rough Cider 1986, Bertie and the Tinman 1987, On the Edge 1989, Bertie and the Seven Bodies 1990, The Last Detective 1991, Diamond Solitaire 1992, Bertie and the Crime of Passion 1993, The Crime of Miss Oyster Brown (short stories) 1994, The Summons 1995, Bloodhounds 1996, Upon a Dark Night 1997, Do Not Exceed the Stated Dose (short stories) 1998, The Vault 1999, The Reaper 2000, Diamond Dust 2002, The Sedgemoor Strangler and Other Stories of Crime 2002, The House Sitter 2003, The Circle 2005, The Secret Hangman 2007, The Headhunters 2008, Murder on the Shortlist (short stories) 2008, Skeleton Hill 2009, Stagestruck 2011, Cop to Corpse 2012. *Honours:* Macmillan/Panther First Crime Novel Award 1970, CWA Silver Dagger 1978, 1995, 1996 and Gold Dagger 1982 and Cartier Diamond Dagger 2000, Grand Prix de Littérature Policière 1985, Prix du Roman D'Aventures 1987, Anthony Award 1992, Macavity Award 1997, 2004, CWA Short Story Award 2007. *Literary Agent:* Vanessa Holt Ltd, 59 Crescent Road, Leigh-on-Sea, Essex, SS9 2PF, England. *E-mail:* p.lovesey@virgin.net (office). *Website:* peterlovesey.com.

LOW(-WESO), Denise, MA, MFA, PhD; American poet, writer, academic and administrator; *Interim Dean of Humanities and Arts, Haskell Indian Nations University;* b. (Denise Lea Dotson), 9 May 1949, Emporia, Kan.; d. of William Francis Dotson and Dorothy Dotson; m. Thomas F. Weso; two s. one step-d. *Education:* Univ. of Kansas ,Wichita State Univ. *Career:* Asst Instructor, Univ. of Kansas 1970–72, Lecturer 1977–84, Visiting Lecturer 1988; Temp. Instructor, Kansas State Univ. 1975–77; part-time Instructor, Washburn Univ., Topeka, Kan. 1982–84; Instructor of Humanities, Haskell Indian Nations Univ., Lawrence, Kan. 1984–, Chair. English Dept 2002–04, currently Interim Dean of Humanities and Arts; Visiting Prof., Univ. of Richmond 2005; Poet Laureate of State of Kansas 2007–09; mem. Associated Writing Programs, Modern Language Asscn, Poets and Writers, Imagination & Place Cttee, Lawrence Arts Center. *Publications:* Dragon Kite 1981, Quilting 1984, Spring Geese and Other Poems 1984, Learning the Language of Rivers 1987, Starwater 1988, Selective Amnesia: Stiletto I 1988, Vanishing Point 1991, Tulip Elegies: An Alchemy of Writing 1993, Touching the Sky: Essays 1994, New and Selected Poems: 1980–99 1999, Thailand Journal 2003, Teaching Leslie Maron Silko's Ceremony (co-ed.), Words of a Prairie Alchemist: Essays 2006; contrib. to anthologies, books, reviews, quarterlies, journals, and magazines. *Honours:* several grants and fellowships. *Address:* Haskell Indian Nations University, Lawrence, KS 66046, USA (office). *Telephone:* (785) 749-8431 (office). *E-mail:* dlow@haskell.edu (office). *Website:* www.haskell.edu (office); deniselow.blogspot.com.

LOW, Rachael, BSc, PhD; British film historian; b. 6 July 1923, London, England. *Education:* LSE. *Career:* researcher, British Film Inst., London 1945–48; Gulbenkian Research Fellow 1968–71, Fellow Commoner 1983, Lucy Cavendish Coll., Cambridge. *Publications:* History of the British Film 1896–1906 1948, Films of Comment and Persuasion of the 1930s 1979, Documentary and Educational Films of the 1930s 1979, History of the British Film (with Roger Manvell) 1906–1914 1949, 1914–1918 1950, 1918–1929 1971, 1929–1939 Vols I and II 1979, Vol. III 1985.

LOW, Robert Nicholas, BA; British journalist and writer; b. 15 Aug. 1948, Addlestone, Surrey, England; m. Angela Levin 1983, one s. *Education:* Fitzwilliam College, Cambridge. *Career:* teacher, University of Chile, La Serena, 1970–72; Journalist, Birmingham Post & Mail, 1973–77, The Observer, 1977–93; Senior Ed.-Deputy Ed., British Edition, 1994–98, European Bureau Chief, 1998–, Reader's Digest. *Publications:* The Kidnap Business (with Mark Bles), 1987; The Observer Book of Profiles (ed.), 1991; La Pasionaria, The Spanish Firebrand, 1992; W. G.: A Life of W. G. Grace, 1997. *Literary Agent:* Curtis Brown Ltd, Haymarket House, 28–29 Haymarket, London, SW1Y 4SP, England. *Telephone:* (20) 7393-4400. *Fax:* (20) 7393-4401. *E-mail:* info@curtisbrown.co.uk. *Website:* www.curtisbrown.co.uk. *Address:* 33 Canfield Gardens, London, NW6 3JP, England (home). *E-mail:* bob.low@readersdigest.co.uk.

LOWDEN, Desmond Scott; British writer; b. 27 Sept. 1937, Winchester, Hampshire, England; m. 1962, one s. one d. *Career:* mem. CWA. *Publications:* Bandersnatch, 1969; The Boondocks, 1972; Bellman and True, 1975; Boudapesti 3, 1979; Sunspot, 1981; Cry Havoc, 1984; The Shadow Run, 1989; Chain, 1990. *Honours:* CWA Silver Dagger Award 1989.

LOWE, Barry; Australian playwright, writer and scriptwriter; b. 16 May 1947, Sydney, NSW; pnr Walter Figallo 1972. *Career:* mem. Australian Writers' Guild, Australian Soc. of Authors. *Publications:* plays: Writers Camp, first performed, 1982; Tokyo Rose, 1989; The Death of Peter Pan, 1989; Seeing Things, 1994; Relative Merits, 1994; The Extraordinary Annual General Meeting of the Size-Queen Club, 1996. Contributions: various publications.

LOWE, Stephen, BA; British playwright; *Artistic Director, Meeting Ground Theatre, Nottingham;* b. (Stephen James Wright), 1 Dec. 1947, Nottingham, England; s. of Harry Wright and Minnie Wright; m. 1st Tina Barclay; one s.; m. 2nd Tanya Myers; two d. *Education:* Univ. of Birmingham. *Career:* Sr Tutor in Writing for Performance, Dartington Coll. of Arts Performance 1978–82; Resident Playwright, Riverside Studios, London 1982–84; Sr Tutor, Univ. of Birmingham 1987–88; mem. Nottingham Trent Univ. Advisory Bd to Theatre Design Degree 1987–; Chair. East Midlands Arts 2001–02; Trustee and Gov. Arts Council England, Chair. Arts Council England, East Midlands 2002–; mem. Theatre Writers Union, Writers Guild, PEN. *Plays:* more than 40 plays for the theatre. *Radio:* Empty Bed Blues (BBC Radio 4) 2006. *Television:* numerous films, including adaptations. *Publications:* Cards 1983, Moving Pictures and Other Plays 1985, Body and Soul in Peace Plays (two vols) 1985, 1990, Divine Gossip/Tibetan Inroads 1988, Ragged Trousered Philanthropists 1991, Revelations 2004. Spirit of the Man 2005, Touched 2006; contribs books and journals. *Honours:* George Devine Award for Playwriting 1977. *Literary Agent:* c/o Howard Gooding, Judy Daish Associates, 2 St Charles Place, London, W10 6EG, England. *Telephone:* (20) 8964-8811. *E-mail:* steplowe.1@ntlworld.com (office). *Website:* www.meetinggroundtheatre.org.uk (office); www.stephenlowe.co.uk.

LOWELL, Susan Deborah, BA, MA, PhD; American writer; b. 27 Oct. 1950, Chihuahua, Mexico; m. William Ross Humphreys 1975, two d. *Education:* Stanford University, Princeton University. *Career:* mem. Southern Arizona Society of Authors. *Publications:* Ganado Red: A Novella and Stories, 1988; I am Lavinia Cumming, 1993. *Honours:* Milkweed Editions National Fiction Prize, 1988; Mountain and Plains Booksellers Asscn Regional Book Award, Children's Writing, 1994. *Address:* c/o Rio Nuevo Publishers, Treasure Chest Books, PO Box 5250, Tucson, AZ 85703, USA.

LOWERY, Joanne, AB, MA; American educator, writer and editor; b. 30 July 1945, Cleveland, OH; m. Stephen Paul Lowery 1968 (divorced 1988); one s. one d. *Education:* University of Michigan, University of Wisconsin. *Career:* part-time Instructor of English, Elgin College, 1986–91, College of DuPage, Glen Ellyn, 1991–96, St Mary's College, Notre Dame, 1997–98; Poetry Ed., Black Dirt, literary magazine, 1994–99. *Publications:* Coming to This, 1990; Corinth, 1990; Heroics, 1996; Double Feature, 2000. Contributions: Magazines. *Honours:* New Letters Literary Award, 1993. Address 412 Evelyn Ave, Kalamazoo, MI 49001, USA.

LOWNIE, Andrew James Hamilton, MA, MSc; British literary agent, writer and editor; b. 11 Nov. 1961, Kenya; s. of His Honour Ralph Hamilton Lownie and Claudine Lecrocq; m. Angela Doyle 1998; one s. one d. *Education:* Magdalene Coll., Cambridge, Univ. of Edinburgh, Coll. of Law, London. *Career:* mem. John Farquharson Literary Agents 1985–86, Dir 1986–88; Dir Andrew Lownie Literary Agency Ltd 1988–; Partner, Denniston and Lownie 1991–93; Dir Thistle Publishing 1996–; mem. Asscn of Authors' Agents, Soc. of Authors; Sec. The Biographer's Club 1998–2008, Pres. 2008–; mem. Exec. Cttee PEN 2000–04. *Publications:* North American Spies 1992, Edinburgh Literary Guide 1992, John Buchan: The Presbyterian Cavalier 1995, John Buchan's Collected Poems (ed.) 1996, The Complete Short Stories of John Buchan, Vols 1–3 (ed.) 1997–98, The Literary Companion to Edinburgh 2000, The Edinburgh Literary Companion 2005; contribs books and periodicals. *Honours:* English Speaking Union Scholarship 1979–80. *Address:* 36 Great Smith Street, London, SW1P 3BU, England (home). *Telephone:* (20) 7222-7574 (office). *Fax:* (20) 7222-7576 (office). *E-mail:* lownie@globalnet.co.uk (office). *Website:* www.andrewlownie.co.uk.

LOWRY, Beverly Fey, BA; American writer; b. 10 Aug. 1938, Memphis, TN; m. Glenn Lowry 1960, two s. *Education:* Univ. of Mississippi, Memphis State Univ. *Career:* fmr Lecturer, Univs of Houston, Montana, and Alabama; currently Dir, Creative Nonfiction Studies, George Mason Univ., Va. *Publications:* Come Back, Lolly Ray 1977, Emma Blue 1978, Daddy's Girl 1981, The Perfect Sonya 1987, Breaking Gentle 1988, Crossed Over: The True Story of the Houston Pickax Murders 1992, The Track of Real Desire 1994, Harriet Tubman: Imagining a Life 2007; contrib. to newspapers and magazines. *Honours:* Richard Wright Literary Excellence Award 2007. *Address:* Graduate Creative Writing Program, George Mason University, 4400 University Drive, Fairfax, VA 22030 USA (office). *Telephone:* (703) 993-1180 (office). *E-mail:* writing@gmu.edu (office). *Website:* creativewriting.gmu.edu (office).

LOWRY, Lois, BA; American writer; b. 20 March 1937, Honolulu, HI; m. Donald Grey Lowry 1956 (divorced 1977); two s. two d. *Education:* Brown Univ., Univ. of Southern Maine. *Publications:* children's books: A Summer to Die 1977, Find a Stranger, Say Goodbye 1978, Anastasia Krupnik 1979, Autumn Street 1979, Anastasia Again! 1981, Anastasia at Your Service 1982, Taking Care of Terrific 1983, Anastasia Ask Your Analyst 1984, Us and Uncle Fraud 1984, One Hundredth Thing About Caroline 1985, Anastasia on her Own 1985, Switcharound 1985, Anastasia Has the Answers 1986, Rabble Starkey 1987, Anastasia's Chosen Career 1987, All About Sam 1988, Number the Stars 1989, Your Move J.P.! 1990, Anastasia at This Address 1991, Attaboy Sam! 1992, The Giver 1993, Anastasia Absolutely 1995, See You Around, Sam 1996, Stay! Keeper's Story 1997, Looking Back 1998, Zooman Sam 1999, Gathering Blue 2000, Gooney Bird Greene 2002, The Silent Boy 2003, Messenger 2004, Gooney Bird and the Room Mother 2006, Gossamer 2006, Gooney the Fabulous 2007, The Willoughbys 2008, Gooney Bird is So Absurd 2009, Crow Call 2009, The Birthday Ball 2010. *Honours:* Int. Reading Asscn Children's Literature Award 1978, American Library Asscn Notable Book Citation 1980, Boston Globe-Horn Book Award 1987, Nat. Jewish Book Award 1990, Newbery Medals 1990, 1994, American Library Asscn Margaret A. Edwards Award for Lifetime Achievement 2007. *Address:* 205 Brattle Street, Cambridge, MA 02138, USA (home). *E-mail:* info@loislowry.com (office). *Website:* www.loislowry.com.

LUANDINO VIEIRA, José; Angolan writer, poet and translator; b. (José Mateus Vieira da Graça), 4 May 1935, Lagoa de Furadoura, Portugal. *Education:* studied in Luanda. *Career:* moved to Angola aged three; fmr marketing man.; imprisoned on charges of anti-colonial activity and links to the Popular Movement for the Liberation of Angola (MPLA) 1959–61, 1961–75 (transferred to Cape Verde 1964–72, to Lisbon 1972–75); returned to Angola 1975; Dir Angolan Television 1975–78; Dir Angolan Institute of Cinema 1979–84; Gen. Sec., Writers' Union of Angola 1975–80, 1985–92, Afro-Asiatic Writers Asscn 1979–84. *Publications:* A cidade e a infância (Prêmio Literário da Sociedade Cultural de Angola 1961, Prêmio da Casa dos Estudantes do Império de Lisboa 1961) 1957, Duas histórias de pequenos burgueses 1961, A vida verdadeira de Domingos Xavier 1961, Luuanda (Grande Prêmio de Novelística, Sociedade Portuguesa de Escritores 1965) 1963, Vidas Novas 1968, Velhas estórias 1974, Nós, os du Makulusu 1974, Duas estórias 1974, Macamdumba 1978, João Vêncio. Os seus amores 1979, Lourentinho, Dona Antónia de Sousa Neto e Eu 1981, Estória da baciazinha de Quitaba 1986, Kapapa: pássaros e peixes 1998, À espera do luar 1998, Nosso Musseque 2003, A guerra dos fazedores de chuva com os caçadores de nuvens 2006, O livro dos rios 2006. *Address:* c/o Editorial Caminho S.A, Estrada de Paço de Arcos, 66-A, 2735-336 Cacém, Portugal (office). *E-mail:* info@editorial-caminho.pt (office). *Website:* www.editorial-caminho.pt (office).

LUCARELLI, Carlo; Italian novelist; b. 26 Oct. 1960, Parma. *Career:* Co-Ed., Stile libero Noir; singer of group, Progetto K; Ed., Incubatoio 16 (online); Lecturer in Creative Writing, Scuola Holden di Alessandro Baricco, Turin; mem. Italian chapter of AIEP (Int. Asscn Police Writers), Associazione Scrittori-Bologna. *Radio:* Radio Bellablù (scriptwriter, for RadioTre). *Plays:* Radiogiallo (Teatro Comunale, Mordano) 1989, Il Delitto di Via Marconi (Teatro Comunale, Mordano) 1991, Finestra sul Cortile (Teatro Comunale, Mordano) 1993, Viva l'Itaglia 1994, Asasini!!! 1997, Via delle Oche (Teatro delle Moline, Bologna) 1999, La Profezia (Teatro Comunale, Mordano) 2001, Belfagor (Teatro Comunale, Mordano) 2001, Delitto a Teatro (Teatro Duse, Bologna) 2002. *Publications:* Compagni di sangue (with Michele Giuttari), Almost Blue, Carta bianca 1990, L'estate torbida 1991, Falange Armata 1993, Indagine non autorizzata (Premio Alberto Tedeschi) 1993, Vorrei essere il pilota di uno zero 1994, Nikita 1994, Il Giorno del lupo 1994, Lupo Mannaro 1995, Via delle Oche (Premio Mistery) 1996, Guernica 1996, Febbre Gialla 1997, Autosole 1998, Il Trillo del diavolo 1998, L'Isola dell'Angelo Caduto (Premio Franco Fedeli 2000) 1999, Mistero in Blu 1999, Un Giorno dopo l'altro 2000, Laura di Rimini 2001, Medical Thriller (with Eraldo Baldini and Giampiero Rigosi) 2002, Misteri d'Italia - i casi di Blu Notte 2002, Serial Killer - Storie di ossessione omicida (with Massimo Picozzi) 2003, Il Lato sinistro del cuore 2003, La Scena del crimine 2005, Tracce criminali (with Massimo Picozzi) 2006. *Address:* c/o Giulio Einaudi Editore, Via Biancamano 2, 10121 Turin, Italy. *E-mail:* eirights@einaudi.it. *Website:* www.carlolucarelli.net.

LUCAS, Celia, BA; British writer; b. 23 Oct. 1938, Bristol, England; m. Ian Skidmore 1971. *Education:* St Hilda's College, Oxford. *Career:* mem. Welsh Acad. 1989–. *Publications:* Prisoners of Santo Tomas 1975, Steel Town Cats 1987, Glyndwr Country (with Ian Skidmore) 1988, Anglesey Rambles (with Ian Skidmore) 1989, The Adventures of Marmaduke Purr Cat 1990, The Terrible Tale of Tiggy Two 1995, Madoc's Prickly Problem 2000, Steel Town Kittens 2004; contributions: numerous journals and magazines. *Honours:* Tir Na nOg Award for Junior Fiction 1988, Irma Chilton Award for Junior Fiction 1995. *Address:* 1 Elwyn Court, March, Cambs. PE15 9BZ, England (home). *Telephone:* (1354) 652586 (home). *E-mail:* celia.skidmore1@btinternet.com (home).

LUCAS, Craig, BFA; American playwright and screenwriter; b. 30 April 1951, Atlanta, Ga; s. of Charles Samuel Lucas and Eleanore Alltmont Lucas. *Education:* Boston Univ. *Career:* Rockefeller and Guggenheim Fellowships; mem. Dramatists' Guild, PEN, Writers' Guild of America. *Plays:* Missing Persons 1980, Reckless 1983, Blue Window 1984, Prelude to a Kiss 1987 and The Scare 1989, God's Heart 1994, The Dying Gaul 1996, Savage Light (with David Schulner) 1996. *Musicals:* Marry Me a Little (anthology of songs by Stephen Sondheim) 1981, Three Postcards (music and lyrics by Craig Carnelia) 1987, The Light in the Piazza 2004. *Films:* Blue Window 1987, Longtime Companion 1990, Prelude to a Kiss 1991, Reckless 1995, Secret Lives of Dentists 2002, The Dying Gaul 2005. *Honours:* Sundance Audience Award, Obie and Outer Critics' Award, Los Angeles Drama Critics' Award, two Tony nominations. *Address:* c/o Peter Franklin, William Morris Agency, 1325 Aveue of the Americas, New York, NY 10019, USA. *E-mail:* craig.lucas@mac.com (home).

LUCAS, Georges, LenD; French publisher; b. 29 Aug. 1915, Rennes; s. of René and Madeleine (Bazin) Lucas; m. Evelyne Torres 1941; one s. *Career:* Man. Dir and Pres. Livraria Bertrand-Amadora, Lisbon 1948–75; Pres. Franco-Portuguese Chamber of Commerce, Lisbon 1963–72; mem. Bd Editions Robert Laffont 1967–75, Man. Dir 1976–79; Vice-Pres. and Man. Dir Banque Franco-Portuguaise d'Outre-Mer 1966–73; Chair. and Man.-Dir Librairie Larousse 1979–83, Adviser 1984–86; Conseiller Nat. du Commerce Extérieur 1973–86. *Honours:* Chevalier, Légion d'honneur, Croix de Guerre. *Address:* 5 avenue Emile Deschanel, 75007 Paris, France (home).

LUCAS, John, BA, PhD, FRSA; British academic, poet, writer and publisher; *Professor Emeritus, Loughborough University and Nottingham Trent University*; b. 26 June 1937, Exeter, Devon; m. 1961; one s. one d. *Education:* Univ. of Reading. *Career:* Asst Lecturer, Univ. of Reading 1961–64; Lecturer, Sr Lecturer, Reader, Univ. of Nottingham 1964–77; Visiting Prof., Univ. of Maryland and Indiana Univ. 1967–68; Prof. of English, Loughborough Univ. 1977–96, Prof. Emer. 1996–; Research Prof., Nottingham Trent Univ. 1996–2003, Prof. Emer. 2003–; Lord Byron Visiting Prof., Univ. of Athens 1984–85; Visiting Prof. of English, Univ. of Birmingham 2009–; Publr, Shoestring Press 1994–; mem. John Clare Soc., Poetry Book Soc. (Chair. 1988–92), Robert Bloomfield Soc. *Publications:* over 40 books of a critical and scholarly nature, including studies of Dickens, Arnold Bennett, the 1920s, and romantic and modern poetry; About Nottingham 1971, A Brief Bestiary 1972, Egils Saga: Versions of the Poems 1975, The Days of the Week 1983, Studying Grosz on the Bus 1989, Flying to Romania 1992, One for the Piano 1997, The Radical Twenties 1997, On the Track: Poems 2000, A World Perhaps: New and Selected Poems 2002, Starting to Explain: Essays on 20th-Century British and Irish Poetry 2003, The Long and the Short of It 2004, Flute Music 2006, Shakespeare's Second Tetralogy 2007, 92 Acharnon Street 2007, I, the Poet Egil 2008, All My Eye and Betty Martin 2009, Things to Say: Poems 2010, Next Year Will Be Better: A Memoir of England in the 1950s 2010; contrib. to anthologies, newspapers, reviews; BBC Radio 3 and 4. *Honours:* Poetry Prize for Best First Full Vol. of Poetry, Aldeburgh Festival 1990, Authors' Club Dolman Award for Best Travel Book 2008. *Address:* 19 Devonshire Avenue, Beeston, Nottingham NG9 1BS, England (home). *Telephone:* (115) 925-1827 (home). *Fax:* (115) 925-1827 (home).

LUCAS, John Randolph, MA, FBA; British academic (retd), writer and inventor; b. 18 June 1929, England; s. of the late Rev. E. de G. Lucas and J. M. Lucas; m. Morar Portal 1961, two s. two d. *Education:* St Mary's Coll., Winchester, Balliol Coll., Oxford. *Career:* Jr Research Fellow, Merton Coll. Oxford 1953–56, Fellow and Tutor 1960–96; Fellow and Asst Tutor, Corpus Christi Coll. Cambridge 1956–59; Jane Eliza Procter Visiting Fellow, Princeton Univ., USA 1957–58; Leverhulme Research Fellow, Univ. of Leeds 1959–60; Giffford Lecturer, Univ. of Edinburgh 1971–73; Margaret Harris Lecturer, Univ. of Dundee 1981; Harry Jelema Lecturer, Calvin Coll., Grand Rapids, Mich., USA 1987; Reader in Philosophy, Univ. of Oxford 1990–96; mem. British Acad. (Fellow), British Soc. for the Philosophy of Science (Pres. 1991–93). *Publications:* Principles of Politics 1966, The Concept of Probability 1970, The Freedom of the Will 1970, The Nature of Mind 1972, The Development of Mind 1973, A Treatise on Time and Space 1973, Essays on Freedom and Grace 1976, Democracy and Participation 1976, On Justice 1980, Space, Time and Causality 1985, The Future 1989, Spacetime and Electromagnetism 1990, Responsibility 1993, Ethical Economics 1996, The Conceptual Roots of Mathematics 1999, An Engagement with Plato's Republic 2003, Reason and Reality 2006, Economics as a Moral Science 2011; contrib. to scholarly journals. *Address:* Lambrook House, East Lambrook, Somerset, TA13 5HW, England (home). *E-mail:* john.lucas@merton.ox.ac.uk (office). *Website:* users.ox.ac.uk/~jrlucas (office).

LUCAS, Stephen E., MA, PhD; American academic and writer; *Evjue-Bascom Professor in the Humanities, University of Wisconsin at Madison*; b. 5 Oct. 1946, White Plains, NY; m. Patricia Vore 1969; two s. *Education:* Univ. of California at Santa Barbara, Pennsylvania State Univ. *Career:* Asst Prof., Univ. of Wisconsin at Madison 1972–76, Assoc. Prof. 1976–82, Prof. 1982–, Evjue-Bascom Prof. in the Humanities 2001–; Visiting Assoc. Prof., Univ. of

Virginia 1979; Advisory Prof., East China Normal Univ. 2009; mem. Int. Soc. for the History of Rhetoric, Org. of American Historians, Nat. Communication Asscn. *Publications:* Portents of Rebellion: Rhetoric and Revolution in Philadelphia 1765–1776 1976, The Art of Public Speaking 1983, George Washington: The Wisdom of an American Patriot 1998, Words of a Century: The Top 100 American Speeches 1900–1999 2009, The Art of Public Speaking for Chinese Readers 2010; contribs to scholarly books and journals. *Honours:* Hon. Prof., Univ. of Int. Business and Econs, Beijing 2001, East China Univ. of Science and Tech. 2009, J. Jeffrey Auer Lecturer, Indiana Univ. 1988; Nat. Communication Asscn Golden Anniversary Book Award 1977, Nat. Communication Asscn Golden Anniversary Monograph Award 1999, Donald H. Ecroyd Award for Outstanding Teaching in Higher Education, Nat. Communication Asscn 2001, Text and Academic Authors Asscn Textbook Excellence Award 2004, William Holmes McGuffey Award 2004, Distinguished Scholar, Nat. Communication Asscn 2009. *Address:* Department of Communication Arts, University of Wisconsin at Madison, Madison, WI 53706, USA (office). *Telephone:* (608) 262-2543 (office). *E-mail:* selucas@wisc.edu (office).

LUCIE-SMITH, (John) Edward (McKenzie), MA, FRSL; British art critic and poet; b. 27 Feb. 1933, Kingston, Jamaica; s. of John Dudley Lucie-Smith and Mary Lushington. *Education:* King's School, Canterbury, Merton Coll., Oxford. *Career:* officer in RAF 1954–56; fmrly worked in advertising and as freelance journalist and broadcaster; contributes to The Times, Sunday Times, Independent, Mail on Sunday, Spectator, New Statesman, Evening Standard, Encounter, London Magazine, Illustrated London News, La Vanguardia (Barcelona); now works as a freelance art historian and exhbn curator. *Solo photographic exhibitions:* Zlato Oko, Novi Sad, Vojvoidina, Serbia 1998, Adonis Art, London 1998, Art Kiosk, Brussels 1999, Rivington Gallery, London 1999, Toni Berini Gallery, Barcelona 2000, Rosenfeld Gallery, Tel-Aviv 2001, Plus 1, Plus 2 Gallery, London 2001, Il Polittico, Rome 2002, D-137 Gallery, St Petersburg 2002, Butler Inst. of Art, Youngstown, Ohio 2003, Valentine Willie Fine Art, Kuala Lumpur 2003, Albemarle Gallery, London 2003, Art Gallery, Univ. of Buckingham 2003, Labiola Gallery, Ljubljana 2003, O'Connor, A Gallery, Toronto 2004, Museu de Arte Moderna, Rio de Janeiro 2004, Wunderkammer, Valencia 2005, Museum of Contemporary Art, Skopje, Macedonia 2005, Galerija Svetega Donalda, Piran, Slovenia 2006, O'Connor, A Gallery, Toronto 2007, City Art Museum, Helsinki 2007, Gallery Kontrast, Stockholm 2007, Piramid Sanat, Istanbul 2007, Galleria Forni, Bologna 2007, Grafiki Kolektiv, Belgrade 2008, Nat. Gallery, Kingston, Jamaica 2010. *Publications as sole author include:* A Tropical Childhood and Other Poems 1961, Confessions and Histories 1964, What is a Painting? 1966, Thinking About Art 1968, Towards Silence 1968, Movements in Art Since 1945 1969, Art in Britain 69–70 1970, A Concise History of French Painting 1971, Symbolist Art 1972, Eroticism in Western Art 1972, The First London Catalogue 1974, The Well Wishers 1974, The Burnt Child (autobiog.) 1975, The Invented Eye (early photography) 1975, World of the Makers 1975, Joan of Arc 1976, Fantin-Latour 1977, The Dark Pageant (novel) 1977, Art Today 1977, A Concise History of Furniture 1979, Super Realism 1979, Cultural Calendar of the Twentieth Century 1979, Art in the Seventies 1980, The Story of Craft 1981, The Body 1981, A History of Industrial Design 1983, Art Terms: An Illustrated Dictionary 1984, Art in the Thirties 1985, American Art Now 1985, Lives of the Great Twentieth Century Artists 1986, Sculpture Since 1945 1987, Art in the Eighties 1990, Art Deco Painting 1990, Fletcher Benton 1990, Jean Rustin 1991, Harry Holland 1992, Art and Civilisation 1992, Andres Nagel 1992, Wendy Taylor 1992, Alexander 1992, British Art Now 1993, Race, Sex and Gender: Issues in Contemporary Art 1994, American Realism 1994, Art Today 1995, Visual Arts in the Twentieth Century 1996, Arts Erotica: an Arousing History of Erotic Art 1997, Adam 1998, Stone 1998, Zoo 1998, Judy Chicago: an American Vision 2000, Flesh and Stone 2000, Changing Shape (poems) 2002, Censoring the Body 2008; has edited numerous anthologies. *Honours:* John Llewellyn Rhys Memorial Prize. *Literary Agent:* c/o Pat White, Rogers, Coleridge and White, 20 Powis Mews, London, W11 1JN, England. *Telephone:* (20) 7221-3717. *Fax:* (20) 7229-9084. *E-mail:* info@rcwlitagency.com. *Website:* www.rcwlitagency.com. *E-mail:* edward@edwardlucie-smith.co.uk (office). *Website:* www.edwardlucie-smith.co.uk.

LUCKLESS, John (see Irving, Clifford Michael)

LUDWIKOWSKI, Rett Ryszard, LLM, PhD, Habil.; American (b. Polish) academic and writer; *Professor of Law and Director, Comparative and International Law Institute, Catholic University of America*; b. 6 Nov. 1943, Skawina-Kraków, Poland; m. Anna Ludwikowski 1995; one s. one d. *Education:* Jagiellonian Univ., Kraków. *Career:* Sr Lecturer, Jagiellonian Univ., Kraków 1967–71, Adjunct Prof. 1971–76, Asst Prof. 1976–81, Assoc. Prof. of Law 1981; Visiting Prof., Elizabethtown Coll., Pennsylvania 1982–83, Alfred Univ. 1983; Visiting Scholar, Hoover Inst., Stanford Univ. 1983, Max Planck Inst., Hamburg, 1990; Visiting Prof. of Politics, Catholic Univ. of America, Washington, DC 1984, Visiting Prof. of Law 1985, Ordinary Prof. of Law 1986–, Dir Comparative and Int. Law Inst. 1987–; Sr Fulbright Scholar 1997, 2004. *Publications:* The Crisis of Communism: Its Meaning, Origins and Phases 1986, Continuity and Change in Poland 1991, Constitutionalism and Human Rights (co-ed. with Kenneth Thompson) 1991, The Beginning of the Constitutional Era: A Comparative Study of the First American and European Constitution (with William Fox Jr) 1993, Constitution Making in the Countries of Former Soviet Dominance 1996, Regulations of International Trade and Business, two vols 1996, 1998, Comparative Constitutional Law 2000, Comparative Rights and Fundamental Freedoms Vol. I (with Gisbert Flanz, Man. Ed.) 2002, International Trade 2006, The Courts in the United States: Structure and Jurisdiction (with Anna M. Ludwikowska) 2008; contribs to scholarly books and journals. *Honours:* Officer, Medal of Merits (Poland) 2005, Medals of Merit, Copernicus Univ., Torun 2006, Univ. of Wroclaw 2007; various grants and awards. *Address:* Columbus School of Law, Catholic University of America, Washington, DC 20064, USA (office). *Telephone:* (202) 319-5140 (office). *Fax:* (202) 319-4459 (office). *E-mail:* ludwikowski@law.edu (office).

LUEBKE, Frederick Carl, BS, MA, PhD; American academic and writer; b. 26 Jan. 1927, Reedsburg, WI. *Education:* Concordia University, River Forest, IL, Claremont Graduate University, University of Nebraska. *Career:* Assoc. Prof., 1968–72, Prof., 1972–87, Charles Mach Distinguished Prof. of History, 1987–94, Prof. Emeritus, 1994–, University of Nebraska; Ed., Great Plains Quarterly, 1980–84; Dir, Center for Great Plains Studies, 1983–88. *Publications:* Immigrants and Politics, 1969; Ethnic Voters and the Election of Lincoln (ed.), 1971; Bonds of Loyalty: German-Americans and World War I, 1974; The Great Plains: Environment and Culture (ed.), 1979; Ethnicity on the Great Plains (ed.), 1980; Vision and Refuge: Essays on the Literature of the Great Plains (co-ed.), 1981; Mapping the North American Plains (co-ed.), 1987; Germans in Brazil: A Comparative History of Cultural Conflict During World War I, 1987; Germans in the New World: Essays in the History of Immigration, 1990; A Harmony of the Arts: The Nebraska State Capital (ed.), 1990; Nebraska: An Illustrated History, 1995; European Immigration in the American West: Community Histories (ed.), 1998. Contributions: Professional journals.

LUELLEN, Valentina (see Polley, Judith Anne)

LUHRMANN, Bazmark (Baz) Anthony; Australian film and theatre director; b. 17 Sept. 1962, NSW; s. of Leonard and Barbara Luhrmann; m. Catherine Martin 1997; one d. *Education:* Narrabeen High School, Sydney. *Career:* theatre work with Peter Brook; owns Bazmark Inq. production co., Sydney; acting roles in films The Winter of Our Dreams 1982, The Dark Room 1984; directed advertisement for Chanel No. 5 2004. *Recording:* Something for Everybody (concept album, including track Everybody's Free To Wear Sunscreen) (Platinum Album, Australia, Gold Album, USA). *Films:* Strictly Ballroom 1992 (Cannes Film Festival Prix de la Jeunesse, Toronto Film Festival People's Choice Award, Chicago Film Festival Award for Best Feature Film), La Bohème (TV) 1993, Romeo + Juliet 1996, Moulin Rouge 2001 (numerous awards including Golden Globe, Producers' Guild of America Film of the Year, Hollywood Film Festival Best Movie). *Plays:* Strictly Ballroom, Haircut. *Operas directed:* La Bohème, Sydney 1990, New York 2002–03, San Francisco 2002, A Midsummer Night's Dream, Sydney 1993. *Television includes:* A Country Practice (actor) 1981–82. *Screenplays written:* Strictly Ballroom 1992, Romeo + Juliet 1996, Moulin Rouge (also story) 2001. *Literary Agent:* Bazmark Inq, PO Box 430, Kings Cross, NSW 1340, Australia; c/o Robert Newman, The Endeavor Agency, 9601 Wilshire Blvd., 10th Floor, Beverly Hills, CA 90212, USA. *Telephone:* (2) 9361-6668. *Fax:* (2) 9361-6667. *Website:* www.bazmark.com.

LUHRMANN, Tanya Marie, BA, MPhil, PhD; American academic and writer; *Professor of Anthropology, Stanford University*; b. 24 Feb. 1959, Dayton, OH. *Education:* Harvard Univ., Univ. of Cambridge. *Career:* Research Fellow, Christ's Coll., Cambridge 1985–89; Assoc. Prof. of Anthropology, Univ. of California at San Diego 1989–98, Prof. of Anthropology 1998–2007; Prof. Cttee on Human Development, Univ. of Chicago 2000–07; Prof. of Anthropology, Stanford Univ. 2007–; mem. American Anthropology Asscn, Soc. for Psychological Anthropology, Royal Anthropological Inst. *Publications:* Persuasions of the Witch's Craft 1989, The Good Parsi 1996, Of Two Minds: The Growing Disorder in American Society 2000; contribs to professional journals. *Honours:* Bowdoin Prize 1981, Nat. Science Foundation Graduate Fellow 1982–85, Emanuel Miller Prize 1983, Partingdon Prize 1985, Stirling Prize 1986, Fulbright Award 1990, Turner Prize 2000, John Simon Guggenheim Fellowship 2007–08. *Address:* Building 10, Main Quad, Stanford University, Stanford, CA 60637, USA (office).

LUKACS, John Adalbert, PhD; American academic (retd) and historian; b. 31 Jan. 1924, Budapest, Hungary; m. 1st Helen Schofield 1953 (died 1970); one s. one d.; m. 2nd Stephanie Harvey 1974 (died 2003); m. 3rd Pamela Hall 2005. *Education:* Palatine Joseph Univ., Budapest. *Career:* Prof. of History, Chestnut Hill Coll., Philadelphia 1947–94, Chair. Dept of History 1947–93; Visiting Prof., La Salle Coll. 1949–82, Columbia Univ. 1954–55, Univ. of Toulouse 1964–65, Univ. of Pennsylvania 1964, 1967, 1968, 1995–97, Johns Hopkins Univ. 1970–71, Fletcher School of Law and Diplomacy 1971–72, Princeton Univ. 1988, Univ. of Budapest 1991, Univ. of Pennsylvania 1994–96; Fellow Soc. of American Historians; mem. American Catholic History Asscn (pres. 1977), American Philosophical Soc. *Publications:* The Great Powers and Eastern Europe 1953, A History of the Cold War 1961, The Decline and Rise of Europe 1965, Historical Consciousness 1968, The Passing of the Modern Age 1970, The Last European War, 1939–41 1976, 1945: Year Zero 1978, Philadelphia: Patricians and Philistines, 1900–1950 1981, Outgrowing Democracy: A Historical Interpretation of the US in the 20th Century 1984, Budapest 1900 1988, Confessions of an Original Sinner 1990, The Duel: Hitler vs. Churchill, 10 May–31 August 1940 1991, The End of the 20th Century and the End of the Modern Age 1993, Destinations Past 1994, George P. Kennan and the Origins of Containment: The Kennan/Lukacs Correspondence 1997, The Hitler of History 1997, A Thread of Years 1998, Five Days in London 1999, At the End of an Age 2002, Churchill: Visionary, Statesman, Historian 2002, A New Republic 2004, Democracy and Populism 2005, The Remembered Past 2005, June 1941: Hitler and Stalin 2006, George Kennan: A Study of Character 2007, Last Rites 2009, The Legacy of the Second World War 2010, Through the History of the Cold War: The Correspondence of George F. Kennan and John Lukacs (ed.) 2010; contrib. many scholarly journals. *Honours:* three hon. doctorates; Ingersoll Prize 1991; Order of Merit, Republic of Hungary 1994, Ordre of the Corvinus Chain 2001. *Address:* 129 Valley Park Road, Phoenixville, PA 19460, USA (home). *Telephone:* (610) 933-7495 (home). *Fax:* (610) 917-0871 (home).

LUKAS, Richard Conrad, MA, PhD; American historian and academic; b. 29 Aug. 1937, Lynn, Massachusetts; s. of Frank Lukas and Elizabeth Lukas; m. Marita Lukas (née Rokicki). *Education:* Florida State Univ. *Career:* Research Consultant, US Air Force Historical Archives, 1957–58; Asst Prof., Tennessee Tech. Univ., Cookeville 1963–66, Assoc. Prof. 1966–69, Prof. 1969–83, Univ. Prof. of History 1983–89; Prof. Wright State Univ., Lake Campus 1989–92; Adjunct Prof. Univ. of South Florida, Fort Myers 1993–96; Consultant (documentary films) Zegota: A Time to Remember 1997, Burning Questions 1998. *Publications:* Eagles East: The Army Air Forces and the Soviet Union 1941–45 1970, From Metternich to the Beatles (ed.) 1973, The Strange Allies: The United States and Poland 1941–45 1978, Bitter Legacy: Polish-American Relations in the Wake of World War II 1982, Forgotten Holocaust: The Poles under German Occupation 1986, Out of the Inferno: Poles Remember the Holocaust 1989, Did the Children Cry?: Hitler's War Against Jewish and Polish Children 1994, Zapomnany Holocaust: Polacy pod okupacja Niemiecka 1939–1944 1995, Forgotten Survivors: Polish Christians Remember the Nazi Occupation 2004. *Honours:* Polonia Restituta 1988; Hon. DHumLitt 1987; American Inst. of Aeronautics and Astronautics History Book Award 1971, American Council for Polish Culture Cultural Achievement Award 1994, Janusz Korczak Literary Award 1996, Waclaw Jedrzejewicz History Award 2000, Kosciuszko Foundation's Joseph Slotkowski Achievement Award 2001, Catholic Press Asscn Award 2009. *Address:* 5894 NW 26th Lane, Ocala, FL 34482, USA (home). *E-mail:* marich@embarqmail.com (home).

LUKER, Nicholas John Lydgate, MA, PhD; British academic, writer, editor and translator; *Senior Lecturer in Russian, University of Nottingham*; b. 26 Jan. 1945, Leeds; one s. *Education:* Hertford Coll., Oxford, Univ. of Grenoble, Univ. of Nottingham. *Career:* Lecturer, Univ. of Nottingham 1970–88, Sr Lecturer in Russian 1988–; various visiting lectureships and fellowships in Australia, New Zealand and USA; mem. British Asscn of Slavists. *Publications:* Alexander Grin 1973, The Seeker of Adventure, by Alexander Grin (trans. with B. Scherr) 1978, A I Kuprin 1978, The Forgotten Visionary 1982, An Anthology of Russian Neo-Realism: The 'Znanie' School of Maxim Gorky (ed. and trans.) 1982, Fifty Years On: Gorky and His Time (ed.) 1987, Alexander Grin: Selected Short Stories (ed. and trans.) 1987, From Furmanov to Sholokhov: An Anthology of the Classics of Socialist Realism (ed. and trans.) 1988, In Defence of a Reputation: Essays on the Early Prose of Mikhail Artsybashev 1990, The Russian Short Story 1900–1917 (ed.) 1991, Urban Romances, by Yuri Miloslavsky (ed. and co-trans.) 1994, After the Watershed: Russian Prose 1917–1927 (ed.) 1996, Out of the Shadows: Neglected Works in Soviet Prose (ed.) 2003; contrib. to numerous scholarly journals. *Address:* c/o Department of Russian and Slavonic Studies, University of Nottingham, Nottingham NG7 2RD, England. *Telephone:* (115) 951-5151 (office). *E-mail:* nicholas.luker@nottingham.ac.uk (office).

LUKYANOV, Anatoliy Ivanovich, DJurSc; Russian politician and poet; b. 7 May 1930; m.; one d. *Education:* Moscow Univ. *Career:* mem. CPSU 1955–91; mem. CP of Russian Fed. 1992–; Chief Consultant on Legal Comm. of USSR Council of Ministers 1956–61; Deputy Head of Dept of Presidium of USSR Supreme Soviet 1969–76, Head of Secr. 1977–83; mem. of editorial staff of Sovietskoe Gosudarstvo i Pravo 1978; mem. Cen. Auditing Comm. CPSU 1981–86, 1986–89; Deputy of RSFSR Supreme Soviet 1984–91; Head of Gen. Dept of Cen. Cttee CPSU 1985–87, Sec. of Cen. Cttee 1987–88; Cand. mem. Political Bureau 1988–90; First Vice-Chair. of Presidium, USSR Supreme Soviet 1988–90, Chair. 1990–91; Chief Adviser on Legal Reform in USSR 1986–89; mem. Cen. Cttee CPSU 1986–91; People's Deputy of USSR 1989–91; arrested 1991 following failed coup d'état; charged with conspiracy Jan. 1992; released on bail Dec. 1992, on trial 1993–94; mem. State Duma (Parl.) 1993–2003, mem. Cttee for Legis. and Judicial Reform 1994, Chair. 1996–99; Chair. Cttee for State Org. 2000–2002; mem. Presidium, Cen. Exec. Cttee CP of Russian Fed. *Publications include:* many articles and books on Soviet legal system and Soviet constitution, three vols of poetry (under pseudonym A. Osenev). *Address:* c/o Communist Party of the Russian Federation, per. M. Sukharevskii 3/1, 103051 Moscow, Russia. *Telephone:* (495) 928-71-29. *Fax:* (495) 292-90-50.

LUMSDEN, Lynne Ann; American publishing executive; b. 30 July 1947, Battle Creek, Mich.; d. of Arthur Lumsden and Ruth Pandy; m. Jon Harden 1986; one d. *Education:* Univ. of Paris, Sarah Lawrence Coll., City Grad. Center and New York Univ. *Career:* copy ed., Harcourt, Brace, Jovanovich, New York 1970–71; ed., Appleton-Century Crofts, New York 1971–73; Coll. Div. Prentice Hall 1974–78, Sr Ed. Coll. Div. 1978–81; Asst Vice-Pres. and Ed.-in-Chief, Spectrum Books 1981–82, Vice-Pres. and Editorial Dir, Gen. Publishing Div. 1982–85; Exec. Vice-Pres., Publr and co-owner, Dodd, Mead & Co., Inc. New York 1985–89; owner, Chair. JBH Communications Inc. Hartford, Conn. 1989–; Publr Hartford News and Southside Media 1989–. *Address:* JBH Communications Inc., 99 Hanmer Street, Suite A, Hartford, CT 06114, USA (office).

LUND, Gerald Niels, BA, MS; American educator (retd) and writer; b. 12 Sept. 1939, Fountain Green, UT; m. Lynn Stanard 1963; three s. four d. *Education:* Brigham Young Univ., Pepperdine Coll., Univ. of Judaism. *Career:* educator 1965–99; mem. Asscn of Mormon Letters, Hon. Lifetime mem. 1997. *Publications:* The Coming of the Lord 1971, This is Your World 1973, One in Thine Hand 1981, The Alliance 1983, Leverage Point 1986, The Freedom Factor 1987, The Work and the Glory (nine vols) 1990–2000 (also made into a film), The Kingdom and the Crown (three vols) 2000, 2002, 2003, Fire of the Covenant 2001, The Scholarly Writings of Gerald N. Lund 2002; contribs to monographs and periodicals. *Honours:* Best Novel Awards, Asscn of Mormon Letters 1991, 1993, Frankie and John K. Orton 1994, LDS Ind. Booksellers Asscn Awards 1994, 1997, 2000, 2001. *Address:* 47 E. South Temple Street, Salt Lake City, UT 89150-1700 (home); PO Box 30178, Salt Lake City, UT 84130, USA (home).

LUNN, Janet Louise Swoboda, CM; Canadian writer and editor; b. (Janet Louise Swoboda), 28 Dec. 1928, Dallas, TX, USA; d. of Herman A. Swoboda and Margaret Swoboda; m. Richard Lunn 1950; four s. one d. *Education:* Queen's Univ., Ont. *Career:* literary consultant, Ginn and Co. 1968–78; Children's Ed. Clarke, Irwin and Co. 1972–75; conducted writers' workshops with Ontario Arts Council; Writer-in-Residence, Regina Public Library 1982–83, Kitchener Public Library 1988; mem. Bd Dirs The Canadian Children's Book Centre 1990–93, (Vice-Pres. 1990), IBBY Canada 1989; Second Vice-Chair. Writers' Union of Canada 1979–80, Vice-Chair. 1983–84, Chair. 1984–85; mem. Canadian Soc. of Children's Authors, Illustrators and Performers, PEN Int. *Publications include:* The County (jtly) 1967, Double Spell (first published as Twin Spell 1968), Larger Than Life 1979, The Twelve Dancing Princesses (IODE Toronto Br. Children's Book Award) 1979, The Root Cellar (Book of the Year, Canadian Library Asscn 1982, Booklist's Reviewers' Choice, Teachers' Choice, American Nat. Council of Teachers of English 1983, Honour List Int. Bd of Books for Young People 1984, chosen in Jr High Category, California Young Reader Medal programme 1988), Shadow in Hawthorn Bay (Children's Book Award, Canadian Library Asscn, Young Adult Book of the Year Award, Saskatchewan Library Asscn, Children's Book of the Year, IODE Nat. Chapter, Honour List, Int. Bd of Books for Young People 1984, one of 40 books of the year, Int. Children's Library, Munich, Germany 1986), Amos's Sweater (Ruth Schwartz Award, Canadian Booksellers' Asscn 1989, Amelia Frances Howard Gibbon Award, Gov-Gen's Award) 1988, Duck Cakes for Sale 1989, One Hundred Shining Candles 1990, The Story of Canada for Children 1992, The Hollow Tree, Umbrella Birthday, Come to the Fair 1997, Charlotte 1998, Laura Secord 2001, Maud's House of Dreams 2003, A Rebel's Daughter (City of Ottawa Book of the Year) 2006. *Honours:* Order of Ontario 1996; Hon. LLD (Queen's) 1992; Hon. Diploma (Loyalist Coll., Belville, Ont.) 1993. *Address:* 115–3260 Southgate Road, Ottawa, Ontario, K1V 8W9, Canada (home). *E-mail:* janetlunn@sympatico.ca (home). *Website:* www.johnlunn.com/janetlunn.

LUPOFF, Richard Allen, BA; American writer; b. 21 Feb. 1935, New York, NY; m. Patricia Enid Loring 1958; two s. one d. *Education:* Univ. of Miami at Coral Gables. *Career:* Ed., Canaveral Press 1963–70; Contributing Ed., Crawdaddy Magazine 1968–71, Science Fiction Eye 1988–90; Ed., Canyon Press 1986–. *Publications:* Edgar Rice Burroughs: Master of Adventure 1965, All in Color for a Dime 1971, Sword of the Demon 1977, Space War Blues 1978, Sun's End 1984, Circumpolar! 1984, Lovecrafts Book 1985, The Forever City 1987, The Comic Book Killer 1988, The Classic Car Killer 1992, The Bessie Blue Killer 1994, The Sepia Siren Killer 1994, The Cover Girl Killer 1995, The Silver Chariot Killer 1996, The Radio Red Killer 1997, The Tinpan Tiger Killer 1998, One Murder at a Time 2001, Claremont Tales 2001, Claremont Tales II 2002, Terrors 2005, Master of Adventure: The Worlds of Edgar Rice Burroughs 2005, Marblehead 2007, Quintet 2008, Deep Space 2009, Visions 2009, The Compleat Ova Hamlet 2009, Killer's Dozen 2010, The Emerald Cat Killer 2010; contrib. Ramparts, Los Angeles Times, Washington Post, San Francisco Chronicle, New York Times, Magazine of Fantasy and Science Fiction. *Honours:* Hugo Award 1963. *Address:* c/o Minotaur Books, Publicity Department, 175 Fifth Avenue, New York, NY 10010, USA (office). *Website:* us.macmillan.com/minotaur.aspx (office).

LURAGHI, Raimondo, MD, PhD; Italian historian, academic and writer; *Professor Emeritus of American History, University of Genoa*; b. 16 Aug. 1921, Milan; m. 1950; one s. one d. *Education:* Univ. of Turin, Univ. of Rome. *Career:* Prof. of History, Junior Coll. 1954–64; Prof. of American History, Univ. of Genoa 1964–96, Prof. Emer. 1996–; mem. Italian Asscn for Mil. History (Pres.). *Publications:* Storia della Guerra Civile Americana 1966, Gli Stati Uniti 1972, The Rise and Fall of the Plantation South 1975, Marinai del Sud 1993, A History of the Confederate Navy 1861–1865 1995; contrib. to Italian, French, American and Chinese historical magazines. *Honours:* Gold Medal, Pres. of the Italian Repub., Arts and Sciences 1999. *Address:* Corso Regina Margherita 155, 10122 Turin, Italy (home). *Telephone:* (1) 4374678. *E-mail:* luraghiraimondo@libero.it (home).

LURIE, Alison, AB; American novelist and academic; *Frederic J. Whiton Professor of American Literature Emerita, Cornell University*; b. 3 Sept. 1926, Chicago; d. of Harry Lawrence Lurie and Bernice Stewart Lurie; m. 1st Jonathon Peale Bishop 1948 (divorced 1985); three s.; m. 2nd Edward Hower 1996. *Education:* Radcliffe Coll., Mass. *Career:* Editorial Asst, Oxford

University Press 1946; worked as receptionist and sec.; Lecturer in English, Cornell Univ. 1969–73, Adjunct Assoc. Prof. 1973–76, Assoc. Prof. 1976–79, Frederic J. Whiton Prof. of American Literature 1979, now Prof. Emer.; Yaddo Foundation Fellow 1963, 1964, 1966, 1984, Guggenheim Fellow 1965, Rockefeller Foundation Fellow 1967. *Publications:* V. R. Lang: a Memoir 1959, Love and Friendship 1962, The Nowhere City 1965, Imaginary Friends 1967, Real People 1969, The War Between the Tates 1974, Only Children 1979, Clever Gretchen and Other Forgotten Folktales (juvenile) 1980, The Heavenly Zoo (juvenile) 1980, Fabulous Beasts (juvenile) 1981, Foreign Affairs 1984 (Pulitzer Prize in Fiction 1985), The Man with a Shattered World 1987, The Truth about Lorin Jones 1988, Women and Ghosts 1994, The Last Resort 1998, Familiar Spirits 2001, Truth and Consequences 2005; non-fiction: The Language of Clothes 1981, Don't Tell the Grown Ups, Subversive Children's Literature (essays) 1990, Boys and Girls Forever: Reflections on Children's Classics (essays) 2003. *Honours:* New York State Cultural Council Foundation Grant 1972; American Acad. of Arts and Letters Literature Award 1978, Prix Femina Étranger 1989, Parents' Choice Foundation Award 1996. *Address:* Department of English, 263 Goldwin Smith Hall, Cornell University, Ithaca, New York, NY 14853-3201, USA (office). *Telephone:* (607) 255-4235 (office). *E-mail:* al28@cornell.edu (office). *Website:* www.writers.cornell.edu/entirelist/#lurie (office).

LURIE, Morris; Australian writer; b. 30 Oct. 1938, Melbourne, Vic. *Career:* Writer-in-Residence, Latrobe Univ. 1984, Holmesglen Tafe 1992. *Screenplays:* Cactus (additional dialogue) 1986, Two Brothers Running 1988. *Publications:* novels: Rappaport 1966, The London Jungle Adventures of Charlie Hope 1968, Rappaport's Revenge 1973, Flying Home 1978, Seven Books for Grossman 1983, Madness 1991, To Light Attained 2008; short stories: Happy Times 1969, Inside the Wardrobe 1975, Running Nicely 1979, Dirty Friends 1981, Outrageous Behaviour 1984, The Night We Ate the Sparrow 1985, Two Brothers Running 1990, The String 1995, Welcome to Tangier 1997, The Secret Strength of Children 2001; children's books: The Twenty-Seventh Annual African Hippopotamus Race 1969, Arlo the Dandy Lion 1971, The Story of Imelda Who Was Small 1984, Night-Night! 1986, What's That Noise? What's That Sound? 1991, Racing the Moon 1993, Zeeks Alive! 1997, Boy in a Storm at Sea 1997; autobiog.: Whole Life 1987; contribs to Virginia Quarterly Review, The New Yorker, The New York Times, Antaeus, The Times, Punch, Telegraph Magazine, The Age (Australia); stories broadcast and plays telecast. *Honours:* State of Victoria Short Story Award 1973, Nat. Book Council Selection 1980, Children's Book Council Honour Book 1983, Bicentennial Banjo Award 1988, Patrick White Award 2006. *Address:* 141 Woodhouse Grove, Box Hill North, Vic. 3129, Australia (home). *Telephone:* (3) 9890-7435 (home). *E-mail:* morrislurie@y7mail.com (office).

LUSTBADER, Eric Van, BA; American writer; b. 24 Dec. 1946, New York, NY; s. of Melvin Harry Lustbader and Ruth Lustbader (née Aaronson); m. Victoria Lustbader. *Education:* Stuyvesant High School and Columbia Coll., New York. *Career:* writer of thriller and fantasy novels; has continued writing Jason Bourne novels, with permission from estate of Robert Ludlum, from where Ludlum left off in The Bourne Ultimatum 2004; second-level Reiki master. *Film:* The Bourne Legacy 2012. *Publications:* The Sunset Warrior Cycle: The Sunset Warrior 1977, Shallows of Night 1978, Dai-San 1978, Beneath an Opal Moon 1980, Dragons on the Sea of Night 1997; The Nicholas Linnear/Ninja Cycle: The Ninja 1980, The Miko 1984, White Ninja 1990, The Kaisho 1993, Floating City 1994, Second Skin 1995; The China Maroc Series: Jian 1986, Shan 1988; The Pearl Saga: The Ring of Five Dragons 2001, The Veil of a Thousand Tears 2002, The Cage of Nine Banestones (US title: Mistress of the Pearl) 2004; continuation of The Bourne Series by Robert Ludlum: The Bourne Legacy 2004, The Bourne Betrayal 2007, The Bourne Sanction 2008, The Bourne Deception 2009, The Bourne Objective 2010, The Bourne Dominion 2011, The Bourne Imperative 2012; others: Sirens 1981, Black Heart 1983, Zero 1987, French Kiss 1989, Angel Eyes 1991, Batman: The Last Angel (DC Comics graphic novel) 1992, Black Blade 1993, Dark Homecoming 1997, Pale Saint 1999, Art Kills 2002, The Testament 2006, First Daughter 2008, Last Snow 2010, Blood Trust 2011; anthologies containing stories by Eric Van Lustbader: David Copperfield's Beyond Imagination 1982, Peter S. Beagle's Immortal Unicorn 1984, David Copperfield's Tales of the Impossible 1995, Excalibur 1995, Murder by Revenge 1996, Vampires 1997, 999 1999, Thriller 2006, Women of the Night 2007; short stories: In Darkness, Angels 1983, The Devil on Myrtle Ave 1995, Lassorio 1995, The Singing Tree 1995, 16 Mins. 1996, An Exaltation of Termagants 1999. *Literary Agent:* c/o Henry Morrison Inc., 105 South Bedford Road, Mount Kisco, NY 10549, USA. *Telephone:* (914) 666-3500. *Fax:* (914) 241-7845. *E-mail:* HMorrison1@aol.com. *E-mail:* EVL@EricVanLustbader.com (office). *Website:* www.ericvanlustbader.com.

LUTTWAK, Edward Nicolae, PhD; American academic, international consultant and writer; *Senior Fellow, Center for Strategic and International Studies;* b. 4 Nov. 1942, Arad, Romania; s. of Joseph Luttwak and Clara Baruch; m. Dalya Iaari 1970; one s. one d. *Education:* elementary schools in Palermo and Milan, Carmel Coll., Wallingford, UK, London School of Econs and Johns Hopkins Univ. *Career:* Lecturer, Univ. of Bath, UK 1965–67; Consultant, Walter J. Levy SA (London) 1967–68; Visiting Prof., Johns Hopkins Univ. 1974–76; Sr Fellow, Center for Strategic and Int. Studies, Washington, DC 1977–87, Burke Chair. of Strategy 1987–92, Sr Fellow 1992–; Consultant to Office of US Sec. of Defense 1975, to Policy Planning Council, US Dept of State 1981, Nat. Security Council, The White House 1987, US Dept of Defense 1987, to Govts of Italy, Korea, Spain; Prin., Edward N. Luttwak Inc. Int. Consultants 1981–; Pres. Servicios Agricolas Tupinamba, Bolivia; Int. Assoc. Inst. of Fiscal and Monetary Policy, Japan Ministry of Finance (Okurasho); mem. editorial Bd The American Scholar, Journal of Strategic Studies, The National Interest, Géopolitique, The Washington Quarterly, Orbis. *Publications:* Coup d'Etat 1968, Dictionary of Modern War 1972, The Israeli Army 1975, The Political Uses of Sea Power 1976, The Grand Strategy of the Roman Empire 1978, Strategy and Politics: Collected Essays 1979, The Grand Strategy of the Soviet Union 1983, The Pentagon and the Art of War 1985, Strategy and History: collected essays 1985, International Security Yearbook 1984/85 (with Barry M. Brechman) 1985, On the Meaning of Victory 1986, Strategy: The Logic of War and Peace 1987, The Dictionary of Modern War (with Stuart Koehl) 1991, The Endangered American Dream 1993, Il Fantasma della Povertà (co-author) 1996, Cose è davvero la Democrazia 1996, La Renaissance de la puissance aérienne stratégique 1998, Turbo-Capitalism 1999, Il Libro della Libertà 2000, Strategy: The Logic of War and Peace (ed.) 2002, The Grand Strategy of the Byzantine Empire 2010; books have been translated into 16 languages. *Honours:* Hon. LLD (Bath) 2007; Nimitz Lectureship, Univ. of Calif. 1987, Tanner Lecturer, Yale Univ. 1989, Rosenstiel Lecturer, Grinner Coll. 1992. *Address:* Center for Strategic and International Studies, 1800 K Street, NW, Washington, DC 20006, USA (office). *Telephone:* (301) 656-1972 (office); (202) 775-3145 (office). *Fax:* (202) 775-3199 (office). *Website:* www.csis.org (office).

LUTZ, John Thomas; American writer; b. 11 Sept. 1939, Dallas, Tex.; m. Barbara Jean Bradley 1958; one s. two d. *Education:* Meramac Community Coll. *Career:* mem. MWA (fmr. Pres.); Private Eye Writers of America (mem. bd of dirs, fmr Pres.), American Crime Writers League, Int. Asscn of Crime Writers. *Film:* Single White Female (adapted from novel), The Ex (adapted from novel). *Publications:* The Truth of the Matter 1971, Buyer Beware 1976, Bonegrinder 1977, Lazarus Man 1979, Jericho Man 1980, The Shadow Man 1981, Exiled (with Steven Greene) 1982, Nightlines 1985, The Right to Sing the Blues 1986, Tropical Heat 1986, Ride the Lightning (short story) 1987, Scorcher 1987, Kiss (Private Eye Writers of America Shamus Award) 1988, Shadowtown 1988, Time Exposure 1989, Flame 1990, Diamond Eyes 1990, SWF Seeks Same 1990, Bloodfire 1991, Hot 1992, Dancing with the Dead 1992, Spark 1993, Shadows Everywhere (short stories) 1994, Thicker Than Blood 1994, Death by Jury 1995, Torch 1995, Burn 1996, Lightning 1996, Final Seconds (with David August) 1998, Oops! 1998, Until You are Dead (short stories) 1998, The Nudger Dilemmas (short stories) 2001, The Night Caller 2001, The Night Watcher 2002, The Night Spider 2003, Endless Road 2003, Darker Than Night 2004, Fear the Night 2005, Chill of Night 2006, In for the Kill 2007, Night Kills 2008, Urge to Kill 2009, Mister X 2010; contrib. to anthologies and magazines. *Honours:* Hon. DLitt (Univ. of Missouri-St Louis) 2007; MWA Scroll 1981, 2003, Private Eye Writers of America Shamus Award 1982, MWA Edgar Award 1983, Private Eye Writers of America Life Achievement Award 1995, Short Mystery Fiction Soc. Golden Derringer Lifetime Achievement Award 2000. *E-mail:* dominick@dalinc.com *Telephone:* (314) 394-1616 (office). *Fax:* (314) 394-1616 (office). *E-mail:* jlutz65151@aol.com (office); john@johnlutzonline.com (office). *Website:* johnlutzonline.com.

LUX, Thomas, BA; American poet and teacher; *Margaret T. and Henry C. Bourne Chair in Poetry, Georgia Institute of Technology;* b. 10 Dec. 1946, Northampton, Mass; m. Jean Kilbourne 1983; one d. *Education:* Emerson Coll., Boston and Univ. of Iowa. *Career:* Managing Ed., Iowa Review 1971–72, Ploughshares 1973; Poet-in-Residence, Emerson Coll. 1972–75; Faculty mem. Sarah Lawrence Coll. 1975, Warren Wilson Coll. 1980, Columbia Univ. 1980; currently Margaret T. and Henry C. Bourne Chair in Poetry, Georgia Inst. of Tech. *Publications include:* The Land Sighted 1970, Memory's Handgrenade 1972, The Glassblower's Breath 1976, Sunday 1979, Like a Wide Anvil from the Moon the Light 1980, Massachusetts 1981, Tarantulas on the Lifebuoy 1983, Half Promised Land 1986, Sunday: Poems 1989, The Drowned River 1990, A Boat in the Forest 1992, Pecked to Death by Swans 1993, Split Horizon 1994, The Sanity of Earth and Grass (ed. with Jane Cooper and Sylvia Winner) 1994, The Cradle Place 2004, God Particles 2008. *Honours:* Bread Loaf Scholarship 1970, MacDowell Colony Fellowship 1973, 1974, 1976, 1978, 1980, 1982, Nat. Endowment for the Arts grant 1976, 1981, 1988, Guggenheim Fellowship 1988, Kingsley Tufts Poetry Award 1995. *Address:* Ivan Allen College of Liberal Arts, Georgia Institute of Technology, 781 Marietta Street, Atlanta, GA 30332-0525, USA (office). *Telephone:* (404) 385-2418 (office). *E-mail:* thomas.lux@lcc.gatech.edu (office). *Website:* www.iac.gatech.edu/faculty (office).

LUXON, Thomas H., BA, AM, PhD; American educator and writer; b. 26 April 1954, Darby, PA; m. 1st Nancy Ellen Gray 1980 (divorced 1985); m. 2nd Ivy Schweitzer 1988; one s. one d. *Education:* Brown University, University of Chicago. *Career:* William Rainey Harper Instructor, University of Chicago, 1984–85; Visiting Asst Prof. of English, St Lawrence University, Canton, New York, 1985–86; Asst Prof. of English, Franklin and Marshall College, Lancaster, Pennsylvania, 1987–88; Assoc. Prof. of English, 1988–, Dept Vice-Chair, 1994–96, Dartmouth College, Hanover, NH; mem. John Bunyan Society of North America; MLA of America; Milton Society of America. *Publications:* Literal Figures: Puritan Allegory and the Reformation, 1995; Milton and Manliness: Friends and Lovers, 1999. Contributions: Prose Studies: Literature, History, Theory. *Honours:* Fellow, National Endowment for the Humanities 1985–86.

LYKIARD, Alexis Constantine, (Celeste Piano), BA, MA; British poet, writer and translator; b. 2 Jan. 1940, Athens, Greece. *Education:* King's Coll., Cambridge. *Career:* Creative Writing Tutor, Arvon Foundation 1974–; Writer-in-Residence, Sutton Cen. Library 1976–77, Loughborough Art Coll. 1982–83, Tavistock, Devon Libraries 1983–85, HM's Prison (HMP) Channings Wood 1988–89, HMP Haslar 1993–94; mem. Soc. of Authors. *Publications:* Lobsters 1961, Journey of the Alchemist 1963, The Summer Ghosts 1964, Wholly Communion (ed.) 1965, Zones 1966, Paros Poems 1967, A Sleeping Partner 1967, Robe of Skin 1969, Strange Alphabet 1970, Best Horror Stories of J. Sheridan Le Fanu (ed.) 1970, Eight Lovesongs 1972, The Stump 1973, Greek Images 1973, Lifelines 1973, Instrument of Pleasure 1974, Last Throes 1976, Milesian Fables 1976, A Morden Tower Reading 1976, The Drive North 1977, New Stories 2 (ed.) 1977, Scrubbers 1983, Cat Kin 1985, Out of Exile 1986, Safe Levels 1990, Living Jazz 1991, Beautiful is Enough 1992, Omnibus Occasions 1995, Selected Poems 1956–96 1997, Jean Rhys Revisited 2000, Skeleton Keys 2003, Jean Rhys Afterwords 2006, Judging By Disappearances 2007, Unholy Empires 2008, Haiku Of Five Decades 2009, Haiku At Seventy 2011, Getting On 2012; many French translations including Apollinaire, Aragon, Artaud, Lautréamont, Jarry, Mac Orlan etc. *Honours:* C. Day Lewis Fellowship 1976; Arts Council Awards 1973, 1978. *Address:* 77 Latimer Road, Exeter, EX4 7JP, England (home). *E-mail:* alexis.lykiard@gmail.com. *Website:* www.alexis.lykiard.co.uk.

LYNCH, Frances (see Compton, David Guy)

LYNCH, John, MA, PhD, FRHistS; British historian and academic; *Professor Emeritus of Latin American History, University of London*; b. 11 Jan. 1927, Boldon. *Education:* Univ. of Edinburgh, Univ. of London. *Career:* Lecturer in History, Univ. of Liverpool 1954–61; Lecturer, Reader and Prof. of Latin American History, Univ. Coll. London 1961–74, Prof. of Latin American History and Dir Inst. of Latin American Studies, Univ. of London 1974–87, Prof. Emer. 1987–. *Publications:* Spanish Colonial Administration 1782–1810: The Intendant System in the Viceroyalty of the Río de la Plata 1958, Spain Under the Habsburgs (two vols) 1964, 1967, The Origins of the Latin American Revolutions 1808–1826 (with R. A. Humphreys) 1965, The Spanish American Revolutions 1808–1826 1973, Argentine Dictator: Juan Manuel de Rosas 1829–1852 1981, The Cambridge History of Latin America (with others), Vol. 3 1985, Vol. 4 1986, Bourbon Spain 1700–1808 1989, Caudillos in Spanish America 1800–1850 1992, Latin American Revolutions 1808–1826: Old and New World Origins 1994, Massacre in the Pampas 1872: Britain and Argentina in the Age of Migration 1998, Latin America Between Colony and Nation 2001, UNESCO Historia General de América Latina, Vol. V (with others) 2003, Simón Bolívar: A Life 2007. *Honours:* Encomienda Isabel La Católica, Spain 1988, Order of Andrés Bello, First Class, (Venezuela) 1995; Dr hc (Seville) 1990. *Address:* 8 Templars Crescent, London, N3 3QS, England (home). *E-mail:* johnlynch53@msn.com (home).

LYNCH, Thomas; American writer, poet and funeral director; b. 16 Oct. 1948, Detroit, Mich.; s. of Edward J. Lynch and Rosemary Lynch; m. Mary Lynch; three s. one d. *Education:* Oakland Univ., Wayne State Univ. *Career:* Pres. Lynch & Sons Funeral Dirs. *Play:* Lacrimae Rerum 2010. *Publications include:* Skating with Heather Grace (poems) 1986, Grimalkin and Other Poems 1994, The Undertaking: Life Studies from the Dismal Trade (non-fiction) 1997, Still Life in Milford (poems) 1998, Bodies in Motion and at Rest (poems) 2000, Booking Passage (memoir) 2005, Apparition and Late Fictions: A Novella and Stories 2010, Walking Papers (poems) 2010. *Honours:* Hon. DH (Oakland Univ.); American Book Award, Heartland Prize for Non-Fiction, Great Lakes Book Award. *Address:* 404 East Liberty, Milford, MI 48381, USA (home). *Telephone:* (248) 684-6645 (office). *E-mail:* thoslynch@aol.com (home). *Website:* www.thomaslynch.com.

LYNN, Jonathan, MA; British theatre and film director, actor and writer; b. 3 April 1943, Bath, England. *Education:* Pembroke College, Cambridge. *Career:* Artistic Dir, Cambridge Theatre Co, 1976–81; Company Dir, National Theatre, 1987. *Publications:* A Proper Man, 1976; The Complete Yes Minister, 1984; Yes Prime Minister, Vol. I, 1986; Yes Prime Minister, Vol. II, 1987; Mayday, 1993. *Other:* various screenplays and television series.

LYNTON, Ann (see Rayner, Claire Berenice)

LYNTON, H. Ronken, AB; American writer and consultant; b. 22 May 1920, Rochester, Minn.; m. Rolf P. Lynton 1955; one s. two d. *Education:* Radcliffe Coll. *Career:* mem. Faculty, Harvard Business School 1945–54; consultant in Indonesia, India, Botswana, Sri Lanka 1955–90; mem. North Carolina Writers Network. *Publications:* Administering Changes 1952, Training for Human Relations 1954, The Days of the Beloved 1974, My Dear Nawab Sahib 1991, Born to Dance 1995, The Sawdust House 2005, Mission to Kabul 2006, Veiled Destinies 2009; contribs to The Homesteaders, Potpourri, The Literary Arts. *Address:* 458 Fearrington Post, Pittsboro, NC 27312, USA (home). *Telephone:* (919) 542-0020 (home). *Fax:* (919) 542-0020 (home). *E-mail:* ronlynton@gmail.com (home).

LYONS, Elena (see Fairburn, Eleanor M.)

LYONS, Garry Fairfax, BA, MA; British dramatist and academic; *Lecturer in Writing for Performance and Performance Production, School of Performance and Cultural Industries, University of Leeds*; b. 5 July 1956, Kingston-upon-Thames; m. Ruth Caroline Willis 1985; one s. one d. *Education:* Univ. of York, Univ. of Leeds. *Career:* Playwright-in-Residence, Major Road Theatre Co. 1983; Fellow in Theatre, Univ. of Bradford 1984–88; Theatre Adviser, National Theatre Education Dept 1988–93; Drama Advisor, Yorkshire Arts 1990–96; Drama Producer, Chameleon Television 1995–98; Visiting Lecturer in Screenwriting, Northern Film School, Leeds Metropolitan University 1992–2002; currently Lecturer in Writing for Performance and Performance Production, University of Leeds; mem. Screenwriting Research Network, Theatre Writers' Union. *Productions include:* Echoes from the Valley 1983, Mohicans 1984, St Vitus' Boogie 1985, Urban Jungle 1985, The Green Violinist 1986, Irish Night 1987, Divided Kingdoms 1989, The People Museum 1989, Dream Kitchen 1992, Frankie and Tommy 1992, Wicked Year 1994. *Address:* Room 1.08, School of Performance and Cultural Industries, University of Leeds, Leeds, LS2 9JT (office); c/o Lisa Foster Alan Brodie Representation, Paddock Suite, The Courtyard, 55 Charterhouse Street, London, EC1M 6HA, England. *Telephone:* (113) 343-8735 (office). *E-mail:* g.f.lyons@leeds.ac.uk (office). *Website:* www.leeds.ac.uk/pci (office).

M

MA, Jian; Chinese writer; b. 1953, Qingdao; one d. (from previous m.); pnr Flora Drew; one s. one d. *Career:* left Beijing for Hong Kong 1987, shortly before his books were banned in China; moved to Europe 1997, now lives in London. *Publications (in translation):* Red Dust (memoir) (Thomas Cook Travel Book Award 2002) 2001, The Noodle Maker (novel) 2004, Stick Out Your Tongue (short stories) 2006, Beijing Coma (novel) 2008. *Address:* c/o Vintage, Random House, 20 Vauxhall Bridge Road, London, SW1V 2SA, England (office).

MA, Van Khang; Vietnamese writer; b. (Dinh Trong Doan), 1 Dec. 1936, Kim Lien, nr Hanoi. *Education:* Hanoi Pedagogical Univ. *Career:* fmr headmaster in Lao Cai Prov.; Deputy Ed.-in-Chief, Lao Cai newspaper; Ed.-in-Chief, Labor Publishing House 1976; Ed.-in-Chief, Foreign Literary Review section, Viet Nam Writers' Asscn, mem. Exec. Cttee 1995–2000. *Publications in translation:* novels: The French Silver Coin 1979, Summer Rain 1982, The Athlete in his Arena 1982, Border Area 1983, Young Moon 1984, The Garden in the Season of Falling Leaves 1986, The Lonely Orphan 1989, A Marriage Without Certificate 1989, Bi, The Wandering Dog 1992, Against the Flood 1999; short story collections: A Beautiful Day 1986, Ripe Fruits in Autumn 1988, The Strong Breeze 1992, Moonlight on the Small Yard 1995, Suburb 1996, The Classical Circle 1997, Lotus Marsh 1997, A Windy Afternoon 1998. *Honours:* Viet Nam Writers' Asscn Best Novel 1986, Best Short Story Collection 1995, ASEAN Literary Prize 1998. *Address:* c/o Curbstone Press, 321 Jackson Street, Willimantic, CT 06226-1738, USA. *E-mail:* info@curbstone.org. *Website:* www.curbstone.org.

MAALOUF, Amin, Maîtrise en Sociologie; Lebanese/French writer; b. 25 Feb. 1949, Beirut, Lebanon; s. of the late Ruchdi Maalouf and of Odette Ghossein; m. Andrée Abouchdid 1971; three c. *Education:* Univ. Saint-Joseph, Beirut, Univ. de Lyon. *Career:* journalist, an-Nahar 1971–76, Economia 1976–77; Ed. Jeune Afrique 1978–79, 1982–84; mem. Acad. française 2011. *Publications:* Les Croisades vues par les Arabes 1983, Léon l'Africain 1986, Samarcande 1988, Les Jardins de lumière 1991, Le premier siècle après Béatrice 1992, Le Rocher de Tanios 1993, Les Echelles du Levant 1996, Les Identités meurtrières 1998, Le Périple de Baldassare 2000, L'Amour de Loin (opera libretto) 2001, Origines 2004, Adriana Mater (opera libretto) 2006, Le Dérèglement du monde 2009, Émilie (opera libretto) 2010. *Honours:* Commdr, Ordre du Cèdre (Lebanon); Officier, Ordre nat. du Mérite; Chevalier, Légion d'honneur, Commdr des Arts et des Lettres; Kt, Order of the Lion of Finland; hon. degrees from Univ. Catholique de Louvain, Belgium, American Univ. of Beirut, Lebanon, Tarragona Univ., Spain, Evora Univ., Portugal; Prix France-Liban 1986, Grand Prix de l' UNICEF 1991, Prix Goncourt 1993, Premio Nonino 1997, Premio Elio Vittorini 1997, Prix européen de l'essai 1998, Premio Grinzane Cavour 2001, Premio Antonio de Sancha 2003, Prix Méditerranée 2004, Premio Grupo de Compostela 2009, Prix du livre des Droits de l'Homme 2009, Premio Príncipe de Asturias 2010. *Address:* c/o Académie française, 23 quai de Conti, 75006 Paris, France.

MABANCKOU, Alain, DEA; French writer and academic; *Professor of French and Francophone Studies, University of California, Los Angeles*; b. 24 Feb. 1966, Mouyondzi, Repub. of Congo; s. of Kimangou Roger and Pauline Kengué. *Education:* Univ. of Paris – Dauphine (Paris IX). *Career:* adviser, Lyonnaise des Eaux (now SUEZ) 1992–2002; Writer-in-Residence, Univ. of Michigan 2001; Asst Prof. of French and Francophone Literature, UCLA 2002–06, Visiting Prof. Dept of French and Francophone Studies 2006, Prof. of French and Francophone Studies 2007–. *Publications include:* poetry: Au jour le jour 1993, L'Usure des lendemains (Prix Jean-Christophe de la Société des Poètes françaises) 1995, La Légende de l'errance 1995, Les Arbres aussi versent des larmes 1997, Quand le coq annoncera l'aube d'un autre jour... 1999, Tant que les arbres s'enracineront dans la terre 2004; novels: Bleu Blanc Rouge (Grand prix littéraire de l'Afrique noire) 1998, Et Dieu seul sait comment je dors 2001, Les Petits-fils nègres de Vercingétorix 2002, African Psycho 2003, Verre Cassé (also adapted for theatre) (trans. as Broken Glass) (Prix des Cinq continents de la Francophonie, Prix Ouest-France/Etonnants Voyageurs, Prix RFO du livre) 2006, Mémoires de porc-épic (Prix Renaudot, Prix Aliénor d'Aquitaine, Prix de la rentrée littéraire française) 2006, Black Bazar 2009; prose: L'Enterrement de ma mère (essay); contrib. short stories and articles to anthologies, newspapers and magazines, including Transfuge. *Honours:* Fellow in Humanities Council and French and Italian Dept, Princeton Univ., Tam-Tam D'Or, Ministry of Culture, Repub. of Congo 2007, Prix des Créateurs Sans Frontières, Ministry of Foreign Affairs, France 2007. *Address:* 833 16th Street, Apt B, Santa Monica, CA 90403, USA (home). *E-mail:* mabanckou@humnet.ucla.edu (office). *Website:* www.alainmabanckou.net.

MABBETT, Ian William, MA, DPhil; British historian and academic; *Adjunct Research Fellow, Monash University*; b. 27 April 1939, London, England; s. of F. W. Mabbett and Phyllis M. Mabbett; m. Jacqueline Diana June Towns 1971; two d. *Education:* Univ. of Oxford. *Career:* Faculty mem. Monash Univ., Melbourne, Australia 1965–, currently Adjunct Research Fellow; Prof., Aichi Bunkyo Univ., Aichi, Japan 2000–02, Prof. Emer. 2002–; Pres. IXth World Sanskrit Conf. 1994; mem. Inst. for Advanced Study, Princeton, NJ, USA 2005–06. *Publications:* A Short History of India 1968, Modern China, The Mirage of Modernity 1985, Kings and Emperors of Asia 1985, Patterns of Kingship and Authority in Traditional Asia (ed.) 1985, The Khmers (co-author) 1995, Sociology of Early Buddhism (co-author) 2003, Writing History Essays: A Student's Guide 2007, The Iconic Female (co-ed.) 2008, History of State and Religion in India (co-author) 2012; contrib. to Hemisphere (Canberra), Asian Pacific Quarterly (Seoul), History Today (London) The Cambridge History of Southeast Asia. *Honours:* Asiatic Soc. Gold Medal 1999. *Address:* Monash Asia Institute, Monash University, PO Box 197, Caulfield East, Vic. 3145, Australia (office). *Fax:* (3) 9905-5370 (office). *E-mail:* ian.mabbett@monash.edu (office). *Website:* www.arts.monash.edu.au/mai (office).

MABEY, Richard Thomas, BA, MA; British writer and broadcaster; b. 20 Feb. 1941, Berkhamsted, Hertfordshire, England. *Education:* St Catherine's Coll., Oxford. *Career:* Sr Ed., Penguin Books 1966–73; mem. Botanical Soc. of British Isles (council 1981–83), Nature Conservancy (council 1982–86), London Wildlife Trust (pres. 1982–92), Plantlife (advisory council 1990–), Open Spaces Soc. (vice-pres. 2003–), Richard Jefferies Soc. (pres. 1996–98), Norfolk and Norwich Naturalists' Soc. (pres. 2005–06). *Publications:* The Pop Process 1969, Food for Free 1972, Unofficial Countryside 1973, Street Flowers 1976, Plants with a Purpose 1977, The Common Ground 1980, The Flowering of Britain 1980, In a Green Shade 1983, Oak and Company 1983, Frampton Flora 1985, Gilbert White 1986, The Flowering of Kew 1988, Home Country 1990, Whistling in the Dark 1993, Oxford Book of Nature Writing (ed.) 1995, Flora Britannica 1996, Nature Cure 2005, Birds Britannica (with Mark Cocker) 2005, Beechcombings: The Narratives of Trees 2007, The Full English Cassoulet 2008, Weeds 2010; contrib. to Times, Telegraph, Sunday Times, Observer, Guardian, Nature, Modern Painters, Independent. *Honours:* Hon. DSc (St Andrews) 1997; TES Information Book Award 1977, New York Acad. of Sciences Children's Book Award 1984, Whitbread Biography Award 1986, Nat. Book Award 1997. *Address:* Sheil Land Associates, 43 Doughty Street, London, WC1N 2LF, England.

McADAM, Douglas John, BA, MA, PhD; American academic and writer; *Professor of Sociology and Director of Urban Studies, Stanford University*; b. 31 Aug. 1951, Pasadena, CA; m. Tracy Lynn Stevens 1988. *Education:* Occidental Coll., Los Angeles, SUNY at Stony Brook. *Career:* instructor, Occidental Coll., Los Angeles 1975, SUNY at Stony Brook 1977–79; Asst Prof., George Mason Univ., Fairfax, Virginia 1979–82; Asst Prof., Univ. of Arizona 1983–86, Assoc. Prof. 1986–90, Prof. of Sociology 1990–98; Fellow, Center for Advanced Study in the Behavioral Sciences, Yale Univ 1991–92, 1997–98, Udall Center for Studies in Public Policy 1994–95, Hollingshead Lecturer 1997; Prof. of Sociology, Stanford Univ. 1998–, Dir Center for Advanced Study in the Behavioral Sciences 2001–05, Dir of Urban Studies 2005–; mem. American Sociological Asscn, Sociological Research Asscn; mem. American Acad. of Arts and Sciences 2003–. *Publications:* The Politics of Privacy (with James Rule, Linda Stearns and David Uglow) 1980, Political Process and the Development of Black Insurgency 1930–1970 1982, Freedom Summer 1988, Collective Behavior and Social Movements (with Gary Marx) 1994, Comparative Perspectives on Social Movements: Political Opportunities, Mobilizing Structures, and Cultural Framings (ed. with John McCarthy and Mayer Zald) 1996, Social Movements: Readings on Their Emergence, Mobilization and Dynamics (with David Snow) 1996, How Movements Matter: Theoretical and Comparative Studies on the Consequences of Social Movements (ed. with Marco Giugni and Charles Tilly) 1998, From Contention to Democracy (ed. with Marco Guigni and Charles Tilly) 1999, Dynamics of Contention (with Sydney Tarrow and Charles Tilly) 2001, Silence and Voice in the Study of Contentious Politics (with others) 2001, Social Movements and Networks (ed with Mario Diani) 2003, Social Movements and Organizations (ed with Gerald Davis, W. Richard Scott and Mayer N. Zald) 2005; contrib. to scholarly books and professional journals. *Honours:* Guggenheim Fellowship 1984–85, Gustavus Myers Center Outstanding Book 1988, C. Wright Mills Award 1990. *Address:* Stanford University, Sociology Department MC 2047, Main Quad – 450 Serra Mall, Building 120, Room 160, Stanford, CA 94305-2047, USA (home). *Telephone:* (650) 723-9401 (office). *Fax:* (650) 725-6471 (office). *E-mail:* mcadam@stanford.edu (office). *Website:* www.stanford.edu/dept/soc (office).

MacALAN, Peter (see Ellis, Peter Berresford)

McALLISTER, Casey (see Battin, B. W.)

MacAULAY, David Alexander, BArch; British/American writer and illustrator; b. 2 Dec. 1946, Burton-on-Trent, England; m. 1st Janice Elizabeth Michel 1970 (divorced); one d.; m. 2nd Ruth Marris 1978 (divorced); m. 3rd Charlotte Valerie. *Education:* Rhode Island School of Design. *Publications:* Cathedral: The Story of Its Construction, 1973; City: A Story of Roman Planning and Construction, 1974; Pyramid, 1975; Underground, 1976; Castle, 1977; Great Movements in Architecture, 1978; Motel of the Mysteries, 1979; Unbuilding, 1980; Electricity, 1983; Mill, 1983; BAAA, 1985; Why the Chicken Crossed the Road, 1987; The Way Things Work, 1988; Black and White, 1990; Ship, 1993; Shortcut, 1995. *Honours:* Caldecott Honor Books, 1973, 1977; Christopher Medal, 1991. *Address:* c/o Houghton Mifflin Co, 222 Berkeley Street, Boston, MA 02116, USA.

McAULEY, James John; Irish academic and poet; b. 8 Jan. 1936, Dublin; m. Deirdre O'Sullivan 1982. *Education:* Univ. Coll. Dublin, Univ. of Arkansas, Fayetteville. *Career:* Ed., Dolmen Press, Dublin 1960–66; Prof., Eastern

Washington Univ., Cheney 1978–; Dir, Eastern Washington Univ. Press 1993. *Publications:* poetry: Observations 1960, A New Address 1965, Draft Balance Sheet 1970, Home and Away 1974, After the Blizzard 1975, The Exile's Recurring Nightmare 1975, Recital, Poems, 1975–80 1982, The Exile's Book of Hours 1982, Coming and Going: New and Selected Poems, 1968–88 1989, Meditations, with Distractions: Poems 1988–98 2001, New and Selected Poems 2005; play: The Revolution 1966; libretto: Praise 1981. *Honours:* NEA grant 1972, Washington Governor's Award 1976. *Address:* c/o The Dedalus Press, 13 Moyclare Road, Baldoyle, Dublin 13, Republic of Ireland (office). *Telephone:* (1) 8392034 (office). *E-mail:* editor@dedaluspress.com (office). *Website:* www.dedaluspress.com (office).

McAULEY, Paul J., BSc, PhD; British biologist and writer; b. 23 April 1955, Stroud, Gloucestershire, England. *Education:* Univ. of Bristol. *Publications:* Four Hundred Billion Stars 1988, Secret Harmonies 1989, Eternal Light 1991, The King of the Hill and Other Stories 1991, In Dreams (ed. with Kim Newman) 1992, Red Dust 1993, Pasquale's Angel 1994, Fairyland 1995, The Invisible Country 1996, Child of the River 1997, Ancients of Days 1998, Shrine of Stars 1999, The Secret of Life 2001, Whole Wide World 2001, White Devils 2004, Mind's Eye 2005, Players 2007, The Quiet War 2008, Gardens of the Sun 2010; contrib. to magazines. *Honours:* Philip K. Dick Memorial Award for Best New Novel 1989, Arthur C. Clarke Award for Best British Novel 1995, Sidewise Award 1995, British Fantasy Soc. Short Story Award 1995, John W. Campbell Award 1996. *Literary Agent:* Antony Harwood Ltd, Office 109, Riverbank House, 1 Putney Bridge Approach, London, SW6 3JD, England.

MAC AVOY, Roberta Ann, BA; American writer; b. 13 Dec. 1949, Cleveland, Ohio. *Education:* Case Western Reserve University. *Publications:* Tea with the Black Dragon, Damiano, 1983; Damiano's Lute, Raphael, 1984; The Book of Kells (co-author), 1985; Twisting the Rope, 1986; The Grey Horse, 1987; The Third Eagle, 1989; Lens of the World, 1990.

McBRIDE, James; American writer, journalist and musician; b. New York, NY; m.; two c. *Education:* Oberlin Conservatory of Music, OH, Columbia Univ., NY. *Career:* fmr staff writer, Washington Post, People magazine, Boston Globe; songwriter for artists, including Anita Baker, Grover Washington Jr, Gary Burton; mem. Nat. Council on the Arts. *Publications:* The Color of Water: A Black Man's Tribute to his White Mother 1996, Autobiography of Quincy Jones (with Quincy Jones) 2001, Miracle at St Anna 2002, Song Yet Sung 2008; contrib. to Essence, Rolling Stone, New York Times. *Honours:* Dr hc (Whitman Coll., Coll. of New Jersey); Ansfield-Wolf Book Award for Literary Excellence 1997. *Address:* PO Box 829, New York, NY 10108, USA (home). *E-mail:* jamesmcbride@jamesmcbride.com (office). *Website:* www.jamesmcbride.com.

McBRIDE, Jule, BA, MFA; American writer; b. 27 Oct. 1959, Charleston, West Virginia. *Education:* West Virginia State College, University of Pittsburgh. *Publications:* Wild Card Wedding, 1993; Baby Trap, 1993; The Wrong Wife, 1994; The Baby and the Bodyguard, 1994; Bride of the Badlands, 1995; The Baby Maker, 1995; The Bounty Hunter's Baby, 1996; Baby Romeo, 1996; Cole in My Stocking, 1996; Mission: Motherhood, 1997; Verdict: Parenthood, 1997; Wed to a Stranger, 1997; Who's Been Sleeping in My Bed?, 1997; Diagnosis: Daddy, 1998; How the West Was Wed, 1998; AKA: Marriage, 1998; Smoochin' Santas, 1998; Santa Slept Over, 1999; The Strong Silent Type, 1999. Contributions: anthologies. *Honours:* Reviewer's Choice Award for Best Series Romance, Romantic Times, 1993. *Literary Agent:* Karen Solem, Writers House Inc, 21 W 26th Street, New York, NY 10010, USA.

McBRIEN, Rev. Richard Peter, MA, STD; American theologian and academic; *Crowley-O'Brien Professor of Theology, University of Notre Dame*; b. 19 Aug. 1936, Hartford, Conn.; s. of the late Thomas H. McBrien and Catherine Botticelli. *Education:* St Thomas Seminary, Bloomfield, Conn., St John Seminary, Brighton, Mass, Pontifical Gregorian Univ., Rome, Italy. *Career:* Prof. of Theology and Dean of Studies Pope John XXIII Nat. Seminary, Weston, Mass 1965–70; Prof., Boston Coll., Newton, Mass 1970–80; Chair. Dept of Theology, Univ. of Notre Dame, Ind. 1980–91, Crowley-O'Brien Prof. of Theology 1980–. *Publications:* Do We Need the Church? 1969, Church: The Continuing Quest 1970, The Remaking of the Church 1973, Catholicism (two vols) (Christopher Award 1981) 1980, Caesar's Coin: Religion and Politics in America 1987, Report on the Church: Catholicism after Vatican II 1992, Catholicism (new edn) 1994, The HarperCollins Encyclopedia of Catholicism (Gen. Ed.) 1995, 101 Questions and Answers on the Church 1996, Lives of the Saints: From Mary and St Francis of Assisi to John XXIII and Mother Teresa 2001, Lives of the Popes: The Pontiffs from St Peter to Benedict XVI 2006, The Church: The Evolution of Catholicism 2008. *Honours:* Hon. DLitt (Quincy Coll., Ill.) 1989, Hon. DD (Muhlenberg Coll., Pa) 1997, Hon. DHumLitt (Coll. of Liberal Arts & Sciences, DePaul Univ., Chicago) 2008; John Courtney Murray Award, Catholic Theology Soc. of America 1976. *Address:* Department of Theology, University of Notre Dame, 130 Malloy Hall, Notre Dame, IN 46556, USA (office). *Telephone:* (574) 631-5151 (office). *Fax:* (574) 631-4169 (office). *E-mail:* rmcbrien@nd.edu (office). *Website:* theology.nd.edu/people/all/mcbrien-richard-p (office).

McCABE, Patrick; Irish writer; b. 27 March 1955, Clones, Co. Monaghan; m. Margot Quinn 1981; two d. *Education:* St Patrick's Teacher Training Coll., Dublin. *Career:* fmr teacher of disabled children. *Play:* has written plays for BBC radio, Frank Pig Says Hello (stage play, based on novel The Butcher Boy). *Film screenplay:* The Butcher Boy (co-writer). *Publications:* The Adventures of Shay Mouse 1985, Music on Clinton Street 1986, Carn 1989, The Butcher Boy (Irish Times/Aer Lingus Fiction Prize) 1992, Frank Pig Says Hello (play based on The Butcher Boy) 1992, The Dead School 1995, Breakfast on Pluto 1997, Mondo Desperado 1998, Emerald Gems of Ireland 2000, Call Me the Breeze 2003, Winterwood (Hughes and Hughes/Irish Independent Irish Novel of the Year 2007) 2006, The Holy City 2009, The Stray Sod Country 2010; contrib. to anthologies, periodicals. *Honours:* Irish Press Hennessy Award 1979, Sunday Independent Arts Award. *Address:* c/o Bloomsbury Publishing, 36 Soho Square, London, W1D 3QY, England (office). *Telephone:* (20) 7494-2111 (office). *Fax:* (20) 7434-0151 (office). *Website:* www.bloomsbury.com (office).

McCALL, Carolyn, OBE, BA, MA; British media executive; *CEO, easyJet plc*; b. 13 Sept. 1961; m.; three c. *Education:* Univ. of Kent, Univ. of London. *Career:* teacher Holland Park School 1982–84; Risk Analyst, Costain Group PLC 1984–86; Planner, Guardian Newspapers Ltd (GNL) 1986–88, Advertisement Exec. 1988–89, Advertisement Man. 1989–91, Product Devt Man. 1991–92, Display Advertisement Man. 1992, Advertisement Dir Wired UK 1992–94, Deputy Advertisement Dir 1994–95, Advertisement Dir 1995–97, Commercial Dir 1997–98 (with responsibility for internet strategy – launched Guardian Unlimited 1999), Deputy Man. Dir 1998–2000, CEO of GNL 2000–06, and mem. Bd of Dirs Guardian Media Group PLC (GMG) 2000–10, Chief Exec. GMG 2006–10; CEO easyJet plc 2010–; mem. Bd of Dirs New Look Group PLC 1999–2004, Tesco PLC 2005–; Chair. Opportunity Now (gender equality and diversity org.) 2005–; Trustee Tools for Schools (educ. charity) 2000–05. *Address:* easyJet plc, Hanger 89, Luton Airport, Luton, Bedfordshire LU2 9PF, England (office). *Website:* www.easyjet.com (office).

McCALL SMITH, Alexander, CBE; British writer and academic; *Professor Emeritus of Medical Law, University of Edinburgh*; b. 1948, Southern Rhodesia (now Zimbabwe); m. Elizabeth; two d. *Career:* currently Emer. Prof. of Medical Law, Univ. of Edinburgh; fmr mem. Human Genetics Comm. (fmr Vice-Chair.), UNESCO Int. Bioethics Comm., British Medical Journal Ethics Cttee (fmr Chair.), Roslin Inst. Ethics Cttee (fmr Chair.). *Publications:* fiction: The No. 1 Ladies' Detective Agency 1998, Tears of the Giraffe 2000, Morality for Beautiful Girls 2001, The Kalahari Typing School for Men 2002, The Full Cupboard of Life (Saga Award for Wit) 2003, At the Villa of Reduced Circumstances 2003, Portuguese Irregular Verbs 2003, In the Company of Cheerful Ladies 2004, 44 Scotland Street (serialized in The Scotsman) 2004, The Sunday Philosophy Club 2004, The $2\frac{1}{2}$ Pillars of Wisdom 2004, Friends, Lovers, Chocolate 2005, Blue Shoes and Happiness 2006, Dream Angus: The Celtic God of Dreams 2006, Love Over Scotland 2007, The World According to Bertie 2007, The Right Attitude to Rain 2007, The Careful Use of Compliments 2007, The Miracle at Speedy Motors 2008, Corduroy Mansions 2008, Tea Time for the Traditionally Built 2009, The Unbearable Lightness of Scones 2009, La's Orchestra Saves the World 2009, The Comfort of Saturdays 2009, The Lost Art of Gratitude 2010, The Double Comfort Safari Club 2010, The Charming Quirks of Others 2010, The Forgotten Affairs of Youth 2011, The Dog Who Came in From the Cold 2012; non-fiction: Law and Medical Ethics (with J. K. Mason) 1983, The Duty to Rescue: The Jurisprudence of Aid (with Michael A. Menlowe) 1993, Forensic Aspects of Sleep (with C. Shapiro) 1997, Justice and the Prosecution of Old Crimes: Balancing Legal, Psychological, and Moral Concerns (with Daniel W. Shuman) 2000, The Criminal Law of Botswana; children's fiction includes: White Hippo 1980, The Perfect Hamburger 1982, Jeffrey's Joke Machine 1990, The Five Lost Aunts of Harriet Bean 1990, Marzipan Max 1991, Uncle Gangster 1991, The Spaghetti Tangle 1992, Harriet Bean and the League of Cheats 1991, The Ice-Cream Bicycle 1992, Akimbo and the Lions 1992, The Doughnut Ring 1992, Springy Jane 1992, The Princess Trick 1992, The Cowgirl Aunt of Harriet Bean 1993, My Chameleon Uncle 1993, The Muscle Machine 1993, Paddy and the Ratcatcher 1994, The Banana Machine 1994, Akimbo and the Crocodile Man 1995, Billy Rubbish 1995, The Watermelon Boys 1996, Calculator Annie 1996, The Bubblegum Tree 1996, Bursting Balloons Mystery 1997, The Popcorn Pirates 1999, Chocolate Money Mystery 1999, Precious and the Puggles 2010; short story collections: Children of Wax: African Folk Tales 1991, Heavenly Date and Other Stories (revised edn as Heavenly Date: And Other Flirtations) 1995, The Girl Who Married a Lion (short stories) 2004, One City (contrib.) 2006. *Honours:* Hon. DIur (Edinburgh) 2007; British Books Awards Author of the Year 2004, Booksellers' Asscn Author of the Year 2004, Waterstone's Author of the Year 2004. *Literary Agent:* c/o David Higham Associates, 5–8 Lower John Street, Golden Square, London, W1F 9HA, England. *Website:* www.alexandermccallsmith.co.uk.

McCANN, Colum; Irish writer; b. 1965; m. Allison Hawke; two s. one d. *Education:* Clonkeen Coll., Dublin Inst. of Technology and Univ. of Texas at Austin, USA. *Career:* began career as journalist; currently mem. Creative Writing Faculty, Hunter Coll., New York; mem. Aosdana 2009–. *Film:* Everything in this Country Must 2004. *Publications:* Fishing the Sloe-Black River 1993, Songdogs 1995, This Side of Brightness 1998, Everything in This Country Must 2000, Dancer 2003, Zoli 2006, Let the Great World Spin (Nat. Book Award for Fiction) 2009; contrib. to books and newspapers. *Honours:* Chevalier, Ordre des Arts et des Lettres 2009; Hennessy/Sunday Tribune Award for Best First Fiction, Best New Writer 1991, Rooney Prize for Irish Literature 1994, Irish Book of the Year 2000, Princess Grace Memorial Literary Award 2002, Esquire Magazine Writer of the Year 2003, Sunday Independent Hughes & Hughes Irish Novel of the Year 2003, Deauville Festival of Cinema Literary Prize 2009. *Literary Agent:* c/o Sarah Chalfant, The Wylie Agency, 250 West 57th Street, Suite 2114, New York, NY 10107,

USA. *Telephone:* (212) 246-0069. *E-mail:* mail@wylieagency.com. *Website:* www.wylieagency.com; www.colummccann.com.

McCARRY, Charles; American journalist, government official, editor and writer; b. 14 June 1930, Pittsfield, Mass; m. Nancy Neill 1953; four s. *Career:* reporter and Ed. Lisbon Evening Journal, OH 1952–55; reporter and columnist, Youngstown Vindicator, OH 1955–56; Asst to US Sec. of Labor, Washington, DC 1956–57; Operations Officer, CIA 1958–67; Ed.-at-Large, National Geographic magazine 1983–90. *Publications:* fiction: The Miernik Dossier 1973, The Tears of Autumn 1975, The Secret Lovers 1977, The Better Angels 1979, The Last Supper 1983, The Bride of the Wilderness 1988, Second Sight 1991, Shelley's Heart 1995, Lucky Bastard 1998, Old Boys 2004, Christopher's Ghosts 2007; non-fiction: Citizen Nader 1972, Double Eagle 1979, Isles of the Caribbean (co-author) 1979, The Great Southwest 1980, Caveat (with Alexander M. Haig, Jr) 1983, For the Record (with Donald T. Regan) 1988, Inner Circles: How America Changed the World (with Alexander M. Haig, Jr) 1992; contrib. to periodicals. *Literary Agent:* c/o WME Entertainment, 1325 Avenue of the Americas, New York, NY 10019, USA. *Telephone:* (212) 586-5100. *Fax:* (212) 246-3583. *Website:* www.wma.com.

McCARTHY, Cormac; American writer; b. 1933, Rhode Island; s. of Charles Joseph McCarthy and Gladys McGrail; m. 1st Lee Holleman 1961 (divorced); one s.; m. 2nd Annie DeLisle (divorced); m. 3rd Jennifer Winkley 1998. *Education:* Univ. of Tennessee. *Career:* USAF 1953–57; MacArthur Fellowship 1981; Guggenheim Fellowship; Rockefeller Fellowship. *Play:* The Stonemason 1994. *Publications:* novels: The Orchard Keeper 1965, Outer Dark 1968, Child of God 1973, Suttree 1979, Blood Meridian 1985, All the Pretty Horses (Vol. 1 of The Bouden Trilogy) 1992, The Crossing (Vol. 2 of The Bouden Trilogy) 1994, Cities of the Plain (Vol. 3 of The Bouden Trilogy) 1998, No Country for Old Men 2005, The Road (James Tait Black Memorial Prize for Fiction 2007, Pulitzer Prize for Fiction 2007, Quill Award for General Fiction 2007) 2006. *Honours:* PEN/Saul Bellow Award for Lifetime Achievement 2009. *Address:* c/o Santa Fe Institute, 1399 Hyde Park Road, Santa Fe, NM 87501, USA.

MacCARTHY, Fiona, OBE, MA, FRSL; British biographer and cultural historian; b. 23 Jan. 1940, London, England; m. 1st Ian White-Thomson 1961 (divorced 1966); m. 2nd David Mellor 1966 (died 2009); one s. one d. *Education:* Wycombe Abbey School, Univ. of Oxford. *Career:* Design Correspondent The Guardian 1963–70; Women's Ed. Evening Standard 1970–71; reviewer The Times 1981–91, The Observer 1991–2000; mem. PEN Club, RSL. *Publications:* The Simple Life: C. R. Ashbee in the Cotswolds 1981, The Omega Workshops: Decorative Arts of Bloomsbury 1984, Eric Gill 1989, William Morris: A Life for our Time 1994, Stanley Spencer 1997, Byron: Life and Legend 2002, Last Curtsey: The End of the Debutantes 2006, The Last Pre-Raphaelite: Edward Burne-Jones and the Victorian Imagination; contrib. to Guardian, TLS, New York Review of Books. *Honours:* Hon. DLitt (Sheffield) 1996, Dr hc (Sheffield Hallam) 2001; RSA Bicentenary Medal 1987, Hon. Fellowship Royal Coll. of Art 1989, Wolfson History Prize 1995, Sr Fellowship Royal Coll. of Art 1997. *Address:* The Round Building, Hathersage, Sheffield, S32 1BA, England (office). *Telephone:* (1433) 650220 (office). *Fax:* (1433) 650944 (office). *E-mail:* fionamacarthy@davidmellordesign.co.uk (office).

McCARTHY, Gary, BS, MS; American writer; b. 23 Jan. 1943, South Gate, CA; m. Virginia Kurzwell 1969; one s. three d. *Education:* California State University, University of Nevada. *Career:* Labour Economist, State of Nevada, Carson City, 1970–77; Economist, Copley International Corp, La Jolla, CA, 1977–79. *Publications:* The Derby Man, 1976; Showdown at Snakegrass Junction, 1978; The First Sheriff, 1979; Mustang Fever, 1980; The Pony Express War, 1980; Winds of Gold, 1980; Silver Shot, 1981; Explosion at Donner Pass, 1981; The Legend of the Lone Ranger, 1981; North Chase, 1982; Rebel of Bodie, 1982; The Rail Warriors, 1983; Silver Winds, 1983; Wind River, 1984; Powder River, 1985; The Last Buffalo Hunt, 1985; Mando, 1986; The Mustangers, 1987; Transcontinental, 1987; Sodbuster, 1988; Blood Brothers, 1989; Gringo Amigo, 1990; Whiskey Creek, 1992; The American River, 1992; Comstock Camels, 1993; The Gila River, 1993; Yosemite, 1995; Grand Canyon, 1996; Mesa Verde, 1997.

McCARTHY, Patrick A., BA, MA, PhD; American academic and writer; *Chairman, English Department, University of Miami at Coral Gables*; b. 12 July 1945, Charlottesville, VA; m. 1st; three c.; m. 2nd Yolanda A. Armstrong 1997. *Education:* Univ. of Virginia, Univ. of Wisconsin at Milwaukee. *Career:* Instructor in English, Murray State Univ., Ky 1968–69, William Paterson Coll. of New Jersey 1973–74, Broome Community Coll., Binghamton, NY 1975–76; Visiting Prof. of English, State Univ. of NY at Binghamton 1974–75; Asst Prof., Univ. of Miami at Coral Gables 1976–81, Assoc. Prof. 1981–84, Prof. of English 1984–, Acting Chair. History Dept 2002–03, Chair. English Dept 2005–. *Publications:* The Riddles of 'Finnegans Wake' 1980, Olaf Stapledon 1982, Critical Essays on Samuel Beckett (ed.) 1986, The Legacy of Olaf Stapledon: Critical Essays and an Unpublished Manuscript (ed. with Charles Elkins and Martin H. Greenberg) 1989, 'Ulysses': Portals of Discovery 1990, Critical Essays on James Joyce's 'Finnegans Wake' (ed.) 1992, Forests of Symbols: World, Text and Self in Malcolm Lowry's Fiction 1994, Malcolm Lowry's La Mordida: A Scholarly Edition (ed.) 1996, Joyce/Lowry: Critical Perspectives (ed. with Paul Tiessen) 1997, Star Maker (ed.) 2004, Joyce, Family, 'Finnegans Wake' 2005. *Address:* Department of English, University of Miami, Coral Gables, FL 33124-4632, USA (office). *Telephone:* (305) 284-3818 (office). *E-mail:* p.mccarthy@miami.edu (office).

McCARTHY, Tom, BA; British author and artist; b. 1969. *Education:* Dulwich Coll., New Coll., Oxford. *Career:* lived in Prague in the early 1990s, and worked in Amsterdam as literary ed., Time Out, also as script ed. in British television; Co-ed Mute magazine; f. The International Necronautical Society (art group); installations and exhibitions in galleries and museums world-wide, including Tate Britain and ICA, London, Moderna Museet, Stockholm, Drawing Center, New York; has tutored and lectured at the Architectural Asscn, Central St Martin's School of Art and RCA. *Film script:* Double Take 2010. *Publications:* novels: Remainder (Believer Book Award 2008) 2005, Men in Space 2007, C 2010; literary criticism: Tintin and the Secret of Literature 2006; contrib. stories to anthologies and essays and articles to newspapers including The Observer, Times Literary Supplement, London Review of Books, Artforum and The New York Times. *Literary Agent:* c/o Jonathan Pegg Literary Agency, 32 Batoum Gardens, London, W6 7QD, England. *Telephone:* (20) 7603-6830. *Fax:* (20) 7348-0629. *E-mail:* info@jonathanpegg.com. *Address:* c/o Jonathan Cape, Random House, 20 Vauxhall Bridge Road, London, SW1V 2SA, England (office). *Telephone:* (20) 7840-8400 (office). *Fax:* (20) 7840-8778 (office). *Website:* www.surplusmatter.com; www.vintage-books.co.uk/authors/2468607/tom-mccarthy.

McCARTHY, Wil, BS; American engineer and writer; b. 16 Sept. 1966, Princeton, NJ; m. 1st Kumiko McCarthy (divorced 1990); m. 2nd Cathy Polk; one s. *Education:* University of Colorado, Boulder. *Career:* Space Launch Systems Engineer, 1988–97, Flight Systems Engineer, 1997–, Lockheed-Martin Corporation, Denver, CO; Creative Writing Instructor, Colorado Free University and Jefferson Adult and Continuing Education Programme; mem. SFWA; North Colorado Writers Workshop, former Pres. *Publications:* Aggressor Six, 1994; A Midnight Clear (co-author), 1994; Flies from the Amber, 1995; Murder in the Solid State, 1996; The Fall of Sirius, 1996; Bloom, 1998. Contributions: anthologies; Periodicals including: Colorado Engineer; Aboriginal SF; Interzone; Analog; Isaac Asimov's Science Fiction Magazine; ComputerEdge; SF Age; SFWA Bulletin. *Address:* c/o Lockheed-Martin Astronautics, PO Box 179, Denver, CO 80201, USA.

McCARTHY, William Edward John, BA, PhD; British writer; b. 30 July 1925, London, England. *Education:* Ruskin College, Merton College, Oxford, Nuffield College, Oxford. *Career:* Research Fellow, Nuffield College, 1959–63; Staff Lecturer, Tutor, Industrial Relations, 1964–65, Fellow, Nuffield College and Centre for Management Studies, 1968–, University of Oxford; Dir of Research, Royal Commission on Trade and Unions and Employers Asscn, London, 1965–68; Senior Economic Adviser, Dept of Employment, 1968–70; Special Adviser, European Economic Commission, 1974–75. *Publications:* The Future of the Unions, 1962; The Closed Shop in Britain, 1964; The Role of Shop Stewards in British Industrial Relations: A Survey of Existing Information and Research, 1966; Disputes Procedures in Britain (with Arthur Ivor Marsh), 1966; Employers' Associations: The Results of Two Studies (with V. G. Munns), 1967; The Role of Government in Industrial Relations, Shop Stewards and Workshop Relations: The Results of a Study, 1968; Industrial Relations in Britain: A Guide for Management and Unions (ed.), 1969; The Reform of Collective Bargaining: A Series of Case Studies, 1971; Trade Unions, 1972; Coming to Terms with Trade Unions (with A. J. Collier), 1972; Management by Agreement (with N. D. Ellis), 1973; Wage Inflation and Wage Leadership (with J. F. O'Brien and V. C. Dowd), 1975; Making Whitley Work, 1977; Change in Trade Unions (co-author), 1981; Strikes in Post War Britain (with J. W. Durcun), 1985; Freedom at Work, 1985; The Future of Industrial Democracy, 1988; Employee Relations Audits (co-author), 1992; Legal Intervention in Industrial Relations (ed.), 1992; New Labour at Work, 1997; Fairness at Work and Trade Union Recognition, 1998. *Address:* 4 William Orchard Close, Old Headington, Oxford, England.

McCAUGHREAN, Geraldine, BEd, FRSL, FEA; British writer; b. (Geraldine Margaret Jones), 6 June 1951, Enfield, North London, England; m. John McCaughrean; one d. *Education:* Christ Church Coll. of Educ., Canterbury. *Career:* writer for Thames Television Ltd 1970–77, Marshall Cavendish Partworks Ltd 1977–89; freelance writer 1989–; Fellow, English Asscn. *Plays:* Dazzling Medusa, Polka Children's Theatre 2006, Gilgamesh, Bristol Old Vic 2006, Thingummyjig, Theatre Royal, Portsmouth 2006, Not The End of the World, Bristol Old Vic 2006. *Publications:* juvenile: A Little Lower than the Angels (Whitbread Children's Book Award 1987), A Pack of Lies (Carnegie Medal, Guardian Children's Fiction Award 1988), Gold Dust (Whitbread Children's Book Award 1994), Plundering Paradise (Smarties Book Prize Bronze Award 1996), Forever X (UK Reading Asscn Children's Book Award 1998) The Stones Are Hatching, The Kite Rider (Smarties Book Prize Bronze Award 2001), Stop the Train (Smarties Book Prize Bronze Award) 2002, Show Stopper! 2003, Jalopy 2003, Not the End of the World (Whitbread Children's Book Award 2005) 2004, The White Darkness 2005, Peter Pan in Scarlet (the official sequel to J. M. Barrie's 'Peter Pan', commissioned by Great Ormond Street Hospital, London) 2006, Tamburlaine's Elephants 2007, The Death Defying Pepper Roux 2009, Pull Out All The Stops 2010; illustrated books: Saint George and the Dragon, Little Angel, Unicorns, Unicorns, Never Let Go, Beauty and the Beast, The Nutcracker, Grandma Chicken Legs, How the Reindeer Got Their Antlers, My Grandmother's Clock, Bright Penny, Jesse Tree, One Thousand and One Arabian Nights, The Canterbury Tales, El CID, The Odyssey, Moby Dick, A Pilgrim's Progress, Myths and Legends of the World (The Golden Hoard, The Silver Treasure, The Bronze Cauldron, The Crystal Pool, Golden Myths and Legends of the World, Silver Myths and Legends of the World, Greek Myths, Greek Gods and Goddesses, Roman

Myths, The Greeks on Stage), Starry Tales, Love and Friendship, King Arthur, On the Day the World Began, Tales of Robin Hood, Britannia, Brave Magic, The Quest of Isis, Gilgamesh the Hero, Dog Days 2003, Hercules 2003, Perseus 2003, The Orchard Book of Roman Myths 2004, Theseus 2004, Odysseus 2004, Peter Pan in Scarlet 2006, Monocello 2011; other: plays and radio plays, poems, books for younger children; adult fiction: The Maypole 1989, Fires' Astonishment 1990, Vainglory 1991, Lovesong 1996, The Ideal Wife 1997; contrib. short stories to anthologies. *Honours:* Hon. Fellow, Canterbury Christ Church Univ. 2006. *Literary Agent:* c/o David Higham Associates Ltd, 5–8 Lower John Street, Golden Square, London, W1F 9HA, England. *Telephone:* (20) 7434-5900. *Fax:* (20) 7437-1072. *E-mail:* dha@davidhigham.co.uk. *Website:* www.davidhigham.co.uk; www.geraldinemccaughrean.co.uk.

McCAULEY, Martin, BA, PhD, MRICS; British academic and writer; b. 18 Oct. 1934, Omagh, Northern Ireland; s. of Isaac Edmund McCauley and Levena McCauley (née Anderson); m Marta (née Kring); one s. *Education:* Univ. of London. *Career:* Sr Lecturer in Soviet and East European Studies, School of Slavonic and East European Studies, Univ. Coll. London 1968–91, Sr Lecturer in Politics 1991–98, Chair. Dept of Social Sciences 1993–96; mem. Economic and Social Research Council, Politics and Society Group; mem. Royal Inst. of Chartered Surveyors. *Publications:* The Russian Revolution and the Soviet State 1917–1921 (ed.) 1975, Khrushchev and the Development of Soviet Agriculture: The Virgin Land Programme 1953–64 1976, Communist Power in Europe 1944–1949 (ed. and contrib.) 1977, Marxism-Leninism in the German Democratic Republic: The Socialist Unity Party (SED) 1978, The Stalin File 1979, The Soviet Union Since 1917 1981, Stalin and Stalinism 1983, Origins of the Cold War 1983, The Soviet Union Since Brezhnev (ed. and contrib.) 1983, The German Democratic Republic Since 1945 1984, Octobrists to Bolsheviks: Imperial Russia 1905–1917 1984, Leadership and Succession in the Soviet Union, East Europe and China (ed. and contrib.) 1985, The Origins of the Modern Russian State 1855–1881 (with Peter Waldron) 1986, The Soviet Union under Gorbachev (ed.) 1987, Gorbachev and Perestroika (ed.) 1990, Khrushchev 1991, The Soviet Union 1917–1991 1991, Directory of Russian MPs (ed.) 1993, Longman Biographical Directory of Decision Makers in Russia and the Successor States (ed.) 1994, Who's Who in Russia and the Soviet Union 1997, Russia 1917–1941 1997, Longman Companion to Russia since 1914 1997, Gorbachev 1998, America, Russia and the Cold War 1949–1991 1998, Afghanistan and Central Asia 2001, Bandits, Gangsters and the Mafia: Russia, the CIS and the Baltic States 2002, The Origins of the Cold War 1941–1949 2003, Stalin and Stalinism 2003, Russia, America and the Cold War 1949–1991 2004, The Rise and Fall of the Soviet Union 2008; contrib. to professional journals. *Address:* UCL School of Slavonic and East European Studies, 16 Taviton Street, London, WC1H 0BW, England (office). *Telephone:* (845) 349-7668 (home). *E-mail:* andermccauley@hotmail.com (home). *Website:* stirringtroubleinternationally.com.

McCLANE, Kenneth Anderson, Jr, AB, MA, MFA; American academic, poet and writer; b. 19 Feb. 1951, New York, NY; m. Rochelle Evette Woods 1983. *Education:* Cornell University. *Career:* Instructor, Colby College, 1974–75; Luce Visiting Prof., Williams College, 1983; Assoc. Prof., 1983–89, Prof., 1989–93, W. E. B. DuBois Prof., 1993–, Cornell University; Visiting Prof., Wayne State University, 1987, University of Michigan, 1989, Washington University, 1991; mem. Associated Writing Programs; Poets and Writers. *Publications:* Take Five: Collected Poems, 1988; Walls: Essays 1985–90, 1991. Contributions: journals. *Honours:* George Harmon Coxe Award, 1973; Corson Morrison Poetry Prize, 1973. *Address:* c/o Department of English, Cornell University, Rockefeller Hall, Ithaca, NY 14853, USA.

McCLARY, Susan Kaye, BMus, MA, PhD; American academic and writer; *Professor of Musicology, University of California at Los Angeles*; b. 2 Oct. 1946, St Louis, MO. *Education:* Southern Illinois Univ., Harvard Univ. *Career:* Lecturer, Trinity Coll., Hartford, CT 1977; Asst Prof. 1977–83, Assoc. Prof. 1983–90, Prof. of Musicology 1990–92, Univ. of Minnesota; Prof. of Musicology, McGill Univ. 1992–94, Univ. of California at Los Angeles 1994–; Ernest Bloch Visiting Prof., Univ. of California at Berkeley 1993; mem. American Musicological Soc. *Publications:* The Transition from Modal to Tonal Organization in the Works of Monteverdi 1976, Music and Society: The Politics of Composition, Performance and Reception (ed. with R. Leppert) 1987, Feminine Endings: Music, Gender, and Sexuality 1991, Georges Bizet: Carmen 1992, Conventional Wisdom: The Content of Musical Form 2000; contrib. to scholarly books and journals. *Honours:* John D. and Catherine T. MacArthur Foundation Fellowship 1995. *Address:* c/o Department of Musicology, University of California at Los Angeles, Los Angeles, CA 90095, USA.

McCLATCHY, Joseph Donald, Jr, AB, PhD; American poet, writer and editor; *Adjunct Professor of English, Yale University*; b. 12 Aug. 1945, Bryn Mawr, Pennsylvania. *Education:* Georgetown Univ., Yale Univ. *Career:* Instructor, LaSalle Coll., Philadelphia 1968–71; Assoc. Ed., Four Quarters 1968–72; Asst Prof., Yale Univ. 1974–81; Poetry Ed., The Yale Review 1980–91, Ed. 1991–; Lecturer in Creative Writing, Princeton University 1981–93; Adjunct Prof. of English, Yale Univ. 2002–; mem. American Acad. of Arts and Letters (Pres. 2009–), American Acad. of Arts and Sciences, International PEN, Acad. of American Poets (chancellor 1996–2003). *Libretti:* 13 works, including A Question of Taste, Our Town, Miss Lonelyhearts, Grendel, 1984, Little Nemo in Slumberland, The Secret Agent, Vincent, An Inconvenient Truth. *Publications:* Anne Sexton: The Artist and Her Critics 1978, Scenes from Another Life (poetry) 1981, Stars Principal (poetry) 1986, James Merrill: Recitative: Prose (ed.) 1986, Kilim (poetry) 1987, Poets on Painters: Essays on the Art of Painting by Twentieth-Century Poets (ed.) 1988, White Paper: On Contemporary American Poetry 1989, The Rest of the Way (poetry) 1990, The Vintage Book of Contemporary American Poetry (ed.) 1990, Woman in White: Selected Poems of Emily Dickinson (ed.) 1991, The Vintage Book of Contemporary World Poetry (ed.) 1996, Ten Commandments (poetry) 1998, Twenty Questions (essays) 1998, Hazmat (poetry) 2002, Selected Poems of Edna St Vincent Millay 2003, Division of Spoils (poetry) 2003, American Writers at Home (essays) 2004, Mercury Dressing (poetry) 2009, The Whole Difference: Selected Writings of Hugo von Hofmannsthal (ed.) 2009; contributions: anthologies and magazines. *Honours:* Woodrow Wilson Fellowship 1967–68, O. Henry Award 1972, Ingram Merrill Foundation Grant 1979, Michener Award 1982, Gordon Barber Memorial Award 1984, Melville Cane Award, Poetry Society of America 1991, Eunice Tietjens Memorial Prize, Poetry Magazine 1985, Witter Bynner Poetry Prize, American Acad. of Arts and Letters 1985, Nat. Endowment for the Arts Fellowship 1986, Guggenheim Fellowship 1988, Oscar Blumenthal Prize 1988, Levinson Prize 1990, Award in Literature 1991, Acad. of American Poets Fellowship 1991. *Address:* Department of English, Yale University, 63 High Street, Room 109, PO Box 208302, New Haven, CT 06520-8302, USA (office). *Telephone:* (203) 432-0499 (office). *E-mail:* j.d.mcclatchy@yale.edu (office). *Website:* www.yale.edu/english/profiles/mcclatchy.html (office).

McCLURE, Gillian Mary, BA; British children's writer and illustrator; b. (Gillian Mary Coltman), 29 Oct. 1948, Bradford, England; three s. *Education:* Horsham High School for Girls, Bristol Univ., Moray House. *Career:* mem. CWIG Soc. of Authors (cttee mem. 1989–95), PLR Advisory Cttee 1992; Royal Literary Fund Writing Fellow, Kent Univ. 2005–08; Escalator Judge and Mentor, New Writing Partnership 2006–; f. Plaister Press 2010; Royal Literary Fund Writing Fellow, Essex Univ. 2011–12. *Publications:* The Emperor's Singing Bird 1974, Prickly Pig 1976, Fly Home McDoo 1979, What's The Time Rory Wolf? 1982, Tog The Ribber (illustrator, by Paul Coltman) 1985, What Happened To The Picnic? 1986, Witch Watch (illustrator, by Paul Coltman) 1989, Cat Flap 1990, Tinker Jim (illustrator, by Paul Coltman) 1992, The Christmas Donkey 1993, Norse Myths (illustrator, by Kevin Crossley-Holland) 1993, Poems That Go Bump In The Night 1994, The Little White Hen (illustrator, by Philippa Pearce) 1995, Selkie (Parent's Guide to Children's Media Award, USA 2000) 1999, Tom Finger 2001, Bruna (illustrator, by Anne Cottringer) 2003, Mario's Angels (illustrator, by Mary Arrigan) 2006, The Land of the Dragon King and other Korean Stories (illustrator) 2008, Selkie 2010, The Little White Sprite 2011, Zoe's Boat 2012. *Honours:* US Parents' Guide to Children's Media Award 2000. *Address:* 9 Trafalgar Street, Cambridge, CB4 1ET (home); Curtis Brown Ltd, Haymarket House, 28–29 Haymarket, London, SW1Y 4SP, England (office). *Telephone:* (20) 7393-4400 (office); (1223) 575406 (home). *Fax:* (20) 7393-4401 (office). *E-mail:* gillianmcclure@ntlworld.com (home); info@curtisbrown.co.uk (office). *Website:* www.gillianmcclure.com.

McCLURE, Michael Thomas, BA; American academic, poet, dramatist and writer; b. 20 Oct. 1932, Marysville, Kan.; m. Joanna Kinnison 1954; one d. *Education:* University of Wichita, University of Arizona, San Francisco State College. *Career:* Asst Prof., California College of Arts and Crafts, Oakland 1962–77, Assoc. Prof. 1977–78, Prof. 1978–; Playwright-in-Residence, American Conservatory Theatre, San Francisco 1975; Assoc. Fellow, Pierson College, Yale University 1982. *Publications include:* poetry: Passage, 1956; For Artaud, 1959; Hymns to St Geryon and Other Poems, 1959; The New Book: A Book of Torture, 1961; Dark Brown, 1961; Ghost Tantras, 1964; 13 Mad Sonnets, 1964; Hail Thee Who Play, 1968; The Sermons of Jean Harlow and the Curses of Billy the Kid, 1969; Star, 1971; The Book of Joanna, 1973; Rare Angel (writ with raven's blood), 1974; September Blackberries, 1974; Jaguar Skies, 1975; Antechamber and Other Poems, 1978; The Book of Benjamin, 1982; Fragments of Perseus, 1983; Selected Poems, 1986; Rebel Lions, 1991; Simple Eyes and Other Poems, 1994. Plays: The Growl, in Four in Hand, 1964; The Blossom, or Billy the Kid, 1967; The Beard, 1967; The Shell, 1968; The Cherub, 1970; Gargoyle Cartoons (11 plays), 1971; The Mammals, 1972; The Grabbing of the Fairy, 1973; Gorf, 1976; General Gorgeous, 1975; Goethe: Ein Fragment, 1978; The Velvet Edge, 1982; The Beard and VKTMs: Two Plays, 1985; fiction: The Mad Club, 1970; The Adept, 1971; other: Meat Science Essays, 1963; Freewheelin' Frank, Secretary of the Angels, as Told to Michael McClure by Frank Reynolds, 1967; Scratching the Beat Surface, 1982; Specks, 1985; Lighting the Corners: On Art, Nature, and the Visionary: Essays and Interviews, 1993. *Honours:* National Endowment for the Arts Grant 1967, 1974, Guggenheim Fellowship 1971, Magic Theatre Alfred Jarry Award 1974, Rockefeller Foundation Fellowship 1975, Obie Award 1978. *Website:* www.thing.net/~grist/l&d/mcclure/mcclure.htm.

MACCOBY, Michael Moses Isaac, BA, PhD; American consultant, writer, psychoanalyst and academic; *President, The Maccoby Group*; b. 5 March 1933, Mt Vernon, NY; s. of Max Maccoby and Dora Maccoby; m. Sandylee Weille 1959; one s. three d. *Education:* Harvard Univ., New Coll., Oxford, UK, Univ. of Chicago, Mexican Inst. of Psychoanalysis. *Career:* Pres. The Maccoby Group; Assoc. Fellow, Said Business School, Univ. of Oxford, UK; mem. PEN, Signet Soc., Cosmos, American Psychological Asscn, American Anthropological Asscn, Nat. Acad. of Public Admin; Fellow, Center for Advanced Study in the Behavioral Sciences 1968. *Publications:* Social Change and Character in Mexico and the United States 1970, Social Character in a Mexican Village (with E. Fromm) 1970, The Gamesman 1977, The Leader 1981, Why Work 1988, Sweden at the Edge 1991, A Prophetic Analyst (with M. Cortina) 1996, Agents of Change (with C. Heckscher, R. Ramirez, P. E. Tixier) 2003, The Productive Narcissist 2003, Narcissistic Leaders 2007, The Leaders We Need 2007. *Honours:* Commdr, Royal Order of the Polar Star (Sweden) 2007; Woodrow Wilson Fellowship 1954, McKinsey Award 2000, General von Steuben Medal for American History. *Address:* 4825 Linnean Avenue NW, Washington, DC 20008, USA (office). *Telephone:* (202) 895-8922 (office). *Fax:* (202) 895-8923 (office). *E-mail:* michael.maccoby@gmail.com (office). *Website:* www.maccoby.com (office).

McCOLLEY, Diane Kelsey, AB, PhD; American academic and writer; *Distinguished Professor Emerita, Rutgers University*; b. (Diane Laurene Kelsey), 9 Feb. 1934, Riverside, CA; m. Robert M. McColley 1958; one s. five d. *Education:* Univ. of California at Berkeley, Univ. of Illinois at Urbana-Champaign. *Career:* Teaching Asst, Univ. of Illinois at Urbana-Champaign 1966–74, Visiting Lecturer 1975–78; Asst Prof., Camden College of Arts and Sciences, Rutgers Univ. 1979–84, Assoc. Prof. 1984–93, Prof. of English 1993–2002, Distinguished Prof. Emer. 2002–; Visiting Fellow, Lucy Cavendish College, Univ. of Cambridge 1990; mem. Asscn for the Study of Literature and the Environment, Asscn of Univ. Profs of English, Milton Soc. of America, (Pres. 1990, Honoured Scholar 1999). *Publications:* Milton's Eve 1983, A Gust for Paradise: Milton's Eden and the Visual Arts 1993, Poetry and Music in Seventeenth-Century England 1997; contributions: scholarly books and journals. *Honours:* Nat. Endowment for the Humanities Fellowship 1989–90, American Philosophical Soc. Research Grant 1990, James Holly Hanford Award, Milton Soc. of America 1993, 2008, Mellon Fellowship, Huntington Library 1999–2000; Clark Library Fellowship 2000. *Address:* 1050 14th Street, Santa Rosa, CA 95404, USA (home). *Telephone:* (707) 528-7678 (home). *E-mail:* mccolley@camden.rutgers.edu (home).

McCONCHIE, Lyn, (Jan Bishop, Elizabeth Underwood); New Zealand writer; b. 3 April 1946, Auckland. *Career:* served in Justice Dept, Agriculture and Fisheries Dept, Probation Dept; writer 1991–. *Publications:* Farming Daze 1993, The Key of the Kelian 1995, The Lonely Troll (also as The Troll's New Jersey) 1997, Tales From the Marrigan Trade House (collection) 1998, Ciara's Song 1998, The Troll and the Taniwha 1998, Beastmaster's Ark (Sir Julius Vogel Award 2002), Daze on the Land 2003, Beast Master's Circus (Sir Julius Vogel Award) 2004, The Duke's Ballad (Sir Julius Vogel Award 2005), Silver May Tarnish 2005, Beast Master's Quest 2006, Tiger Daze 2007, Daze in the Country 2008, South of Rio Chama 2009, Rural Daze and Knights 2009, Summer of Dreaming (Best Young Adult Novel 2011) 2010, The Questing Road (Sir Julius Vogel Award 2011) 2010, Field Daze 2011, Vestiges of Flames, Queen of Iron Years 2011; short stories: Swan Song 1996, Lullaby 1999, Other Agendas 1999, One Righteous One in the City, Deathsong, Tiger Dreaming, A Tale of Two Kitties, Chasing China Cats, Death Song (Jonny Cat Award, Exel Mineral Co. in America 1997), Opener of Doors (Certificate of Excellence, Muse Medallion 2011), and numerous others; contribs to New Zealand Cat Fancy Yearbook; Disinformation. *Honours:* Australasion Medal 1992, New York Public Library Best Books for Teenagers Listing 1995, Music Medallion, Int. Cat Writers Award 1996, 1997, 1998, 1999, 2002. *Literary Agent:* c/o Sternig and Bryne Literary Agency, 2370 South 107th Street, Apartment 4, Milwaukee, WI 53227-2036, USA. *Telephone:* (414) 328-8034. *Fax:* (414) 328-8034. *Address:* Farside Farm, Norsewood 5491, New Zealand (home). *Website:* www.lynmcconchie.com.

McCONICA, James Kelsey, OC, MA, DPhil, FRHistS, FRSC, FBA; Canadian historian and academic; *Professor Emeritus, Pontifical Institute of Mediaeval Studies*; b. 24 April 1930, Luseland, Sask.; s. of Thomas Henry McConica and Edith Wilma Crates. *Education:* Univ. of Saskatchewan, Univ. of Oxford, Univ. of Toronto. *Career:* instructor, Univ. of Saskatchewan 1956–57, Asst Prof. 1957–62; Assoc. Prof., Pontifical Inst. of Mediaeval Studies, Toronto 1967–70, Prof. of History 1971–90, Prof. Emer. 1990–, Pres. 1996–2008; ordained Roman Catholic Priest 1968; Visiting Fellow, All Souls Coll., Oxford 1969–71, 1977, Special Ford Lecturer 1977, Research Fellow 1978–84, 1990–97, Academic Dean 1990–92; Fellow, Davis Center for Historical Studies, Princeton Univ. 1971; Prof., Univ. of Toronto 1972–90; Pres. Univ. of St Michael's Coll., Toronto 1984–90; Vice-Pres. Int. Council of Critical Edn of Opera Omnia 1998–; mem. American Soc. for Reformation Research, Canadian Soc. for Renaissance Studies, Oxford Historical Soc., Renaissance Soc. of America; Foreign mem. Royal Belgian Acad. *Publications:* English Humanists and Reformation Politics under Henry VIII and Edward VI 1965, The Correspondence of Erasmus (ed.), Vol. III 1976, Vol. IV 1977, Thomas More: A Short Biography 1977, The History of the University of Oxford (ed.), Vol. III 1986, Erasmus 1991; contribs to books and professional journals. *Honours:* Hon. Fellow, Exeter Coll. Oxford 2002; Hon. LLD (Saskatchewan) 1986, (St Francis Xavier) 1999, (Regina) 1999, Hon. DLitt (Windsor) 1989, Hon. DUniv (St Paul) 2002, Hon. Dr of Sacred Letters (Univ. of Trinity Coll.) 2010; Rhodes Scholar 1951, Guggenheim Fellowship 1969–70, Killam Sr Research Scholar 1976–77. *Address:* Pontifical Institute of Mediaeval Studies, 59 Queen's Park Crescent East, Toronto, ON M5S 2C4, Canada (office). *Telephone:* (416) 926-7288 (office). *Fax:* (416) 926-7292 (office). *E-mail:* james.mcconica@utoronto.ca (office). *Website:* www.pims.ca (office).

McCONKEY, James Rodney, MA, PhD; American professor of English and writer; *Professor Emeritus, Cornell University*; b. 2 Sept. 1921, Lakewood, Ohio; s. of Clayton Delano McConkey and Grace Baird McConkey; m. Gladys Jean Voorhees 1944; three s. *Education:* Cleveland Coll., Western Reserve Univ., Univ. of Iowa. *Career:* Asst Prof. to Assoc. Prof., Morehead State Coll., Ky 1950–56; Dir Morehead Writer's Workshop 1951–56, Antioch Seminar in Writing and Publishing, Yellow Springs, OH 1957–60; Asst Prof. to Assoc. Prof., Cornell Univ. 1956–62, Prof. of English 1962–87, Goldwin Smith Prof. of English Literature 1987–92, Prof. Emer. 1992–; mem. PEN. *Publications:* The Novels of E. M. Forster 1957, The Structure of Prose (ed.) 1963, Night Stand 1965, Crossroads: An Autobiographical Novel 1968, A Journal to Sahalin (novel) 1971, The Tree House Confessions (novel) 1979, Court of Memory 1983, To a Distant Island (novel) 1984, Chekhov and Our Age: Responses to Chekhov by American Writers and Scholars (ed.) 1984, Kayo: The Authentic and Annotated Autobiographical Novel from Outer Space 1987, Rowan's Progress 1992, Stories from My Life with the Other Animals 1993, The Anatomy of Memory (ed.) 1996, The Telescope in the Parlor (essays) 2004; contribs to magazines. *Honours:* Eugene Saxton Literary Fellow 1962–63, Nat. Endowment for the Arts Essay Award 1967, Ohioana Book Award 1969, Guggenheim Fellowship 1969–70, American Acad. of Arts and Letters Award 1979. *Address:* 402 Aiken Road, Trumansburg, NY 14886, USA (home). *E-mail:* jrm9@cornell.edu (office).

McCORMICK, A. (see Lewis-Smith, Anne Elizabeth)

McCOURT, James, BA; American writer; b. 4 July 1941, New York, NY. *Education:* Manhattan College, New York University, Yale University. *Publications:* Mawrdew Czgowchuz, 1975; Kaye Wayfaring, 1984; Time Remaining, 1993; Delancey's Way, 2000. Contributions: anthologies and magazines. *Literary Agent:* Elaine Markson, 44 Greenwich Avenue, New York, NY 10011, USA.

McCRACKEN, Elizabeth, BA, MA, MFA, MS; American writer and teacher; b. 1966. *Education:* Boston University, University of Iowa. *Career:* Adjunct Asst Lecturer, Drexel University and Evening College, Philadelphia 1991–92; mem., Writing Committee, Fine Arts Work Center, Provincetown 1993–, Instructor, Summer Program 1996–98; Community Writing Instructor, Sommerville Arts Council 1995, 1996; Writing Instructor, Iowa Summer Writing Festival 1997, 1998; Writer-in-Residence, Western Michigan University 1998. *Publications:* Here's Your Hat What's Your Hurry? 1993, The Giant's House 1996, Niagara Falls All Over Again 2001, The Giant's House 2007, An Exact Replica of a Figment of my Imagination: A Memoir 2008; contributions: anthologies and periodicals. *Honours:* James Michener Grant 1990, Fine Arts Work Centre Fellowships, Provincetown 1990–91, 1992–93, National Endowment for the Arts Fellowship 1992, MacDowell Colony Fellowship 1993, Notable Book of the Year, American Library Asscn 1996, Discovery Award, Barnes and Noble 1997, Harold D. Vursell Memorial Award, American Acad. of Arts and Letters 1997, Guggenheim Fellowship 1998. *Literary Agent:* Dunow, Carlson and Lerner Literary Agency, 27 West 20th Street, Suite 1107, New York, NY 10011, USA. *Telephone:* (212) 645-7606. *E-mail:* mail@dclagency.com. *Website:* www.dclagency.com. *Address:* c/o Author Mail, Little, Brown and Company, 237 Park Avenue, New York, NY 10017, USA (office). *Website:* www.hachettebookgroupusa.com (office).

McCRACKEN, Kathleen Luanne, PhD; Canadian poet and literary critic; *Lecturer in English and Creative Writing, University of Ulster at Coleraine*; b. 26 Oct. 1960, Dundalk, Ont.; d. of Robert Ivan McCracken and Shirley Marguerite Hardy. *Education:* York Univ. and Univ. of Toronto, Ont. *Career:* Teaching Asst, Course Dir and Lecturer Univ. of Toronto and Ryerson Polytechnic Inst. 1985–89; Course Dir Dept of English, York Univ. 1988–89; Postdoctoral Fellowship, Social Sciences and Humanities Research Council, Univ. Coll. Dublin, Ireland 1989–91; Lecturer in American Studies Univ. of Ulster at Jordanstown, Belfast, NI 1992–2005; Lecturer in English and Creative Writing, Univ. of Ulster at Coleraine, NI 2005–; has presented papers at confs in Canada, Ireland and USA; Ontario Arts Council Writers' Grantee (four times); Univ. of Toronto Open Fellowship; Ontario Grad. Scholarships; mem. League of Canadian Poets, Modern Language Asscn, Anglo-Irish Literature. *Publications include:* Reflections 1978, Into Celebration 1980, The Constancy of Objects 1980, Reflections: A Creative History of the One-Room Schoolhouse in Proton Township (jtly) 1978, A Geography of Souls 2002, Mooncalves 2007, Tattoo Land 2009; poetry and literary criticism published in various Canadian, American, Irish and British journals. *Address:* School of Languages and Literature, University of Ulster at Coleraine, Cromore Road, Coleraine, Co. Londonderry, Northern Ireland (office). *Telephone:* (28) 7032-3031 (office). *E-mail:* kl.mccracken@ulster.ac.uk (office).

McCRANEY, Tarell Alvin, BFA; American playwright and actor; b. 17 Oct. 1980, Miami. *Education:* New World School of the Arts High School, Miami, DePaul Univ. Theater School, Yale School of Drama. *Career:* commissions from Southern Rep Theater, New Orleans, Foundry Theater, New York, Young Vic, London; mem. New Dramatists and Teo Castellanos/D Projects Theater Co., Miami; Int. Playwright in Residence, Royal Shakespeare Co. 2008; mem. Steppenwolf Theatre Ensemble, Chicago 2010–. *Plays:* Choir Boy, Again and Again, A Meditation on Antigone, The Breach 2006, The Brothers Size 2006, In The Red and Brown Water 2006, Marcus; or The Secret of the Sweet, Without/Sin, Run Mourner, Run, Wig Out! 2008. *Honours:* Paula Vogel Playwriting Award, Steinberg Distinguished Playwright Award 2009. *Address:* c/o Steppenwolf Theater Ensemble, 758W North Avenue, 4th floor, Chicago, IL 60610, USA (office). *Telephone:* (312) 335-1888 (office). *Fax:* (312) 335-0808 (office).

McCRAW, Thomas Kincaid, BA, MA, PhD; American academic, writer and editor; b. 11 Sept. 1940, Corinth, Mississippi; m. Susan Morehead 1962; one s.

one d. *Education:* University of Mississippi, University of Wisconsin. *Career:* Asst Prof., 1970–74, Assoc. Prof., 1974–78, University of Texas at Austin; Newcomen Fellow, 1973–74, Visiting Assoc. Prof., 1976–78, Prof., 1978–89, Isidor Straus Prof. of Business History, 1989–, Harvard University; Ed., Business History Review, 1994–; mem. American Economic Asscn; Business History Conference, trustee, 1986–95, pres., 1989; Economic History Asscn; Massachusetts Historical Society; Organization of American Historians. *Publications:* Morgan Versus Lilienthal: The Feud Within the TVA, 1970; TVA and the Power Fight, 1933–39, 1971; Regulation in Perspective: Historical Essays (ed.), 1981; Prophets of Regulation, 1984; America Versus Japan (ed.), 1986; The Essential Alfred Chandler (ed.), 1988; Management Past and Present (co-author), 1996; Creating Modern Capitalism (ed.), 1997; The Intellectual Venture Capitalist: John H. McArthur and the Work of the Harvard Business School, 1980–1995 (co-ed.), 1999; American Business, 1920–2000: How It Worked, 2000. Contributions: scholarly books and journals. *Honours:* Woodrow Wilson Fellow, 1966–67; William P. Lyons Master's Essays Award, Loyola University, Chicago, 1969; Younger Humanist Award, National Endowment for the Humanities, 1975; Pulitzer Prize in History, 1985; Thomas Newcomen Book Award, 1986; Inducted, Alumni Hall of Fame, University of Mississippi, 1986. *Address:* c/o Harvard University Business School, Soldiers Field, Boston, MA 02163, USA.

McCRORIE, Edward Pollitt, PhD; American academic, poet and translator; b. 19 Nov. 1936, Central Falls, RI; m. 1995. *Education:* Brown Univ. *Career:* Prof. of English, Providence College, RI. *Publications:* After a Cremation (poems), 1974; The Aeneid of Virgil (trans.), 1995. Contributions: journals. *Address:* c/o Department of English, Providence College, Providence, RI 02918, USA.

McCRUM, (John) Robert, MA; British writer and newspaper editor; b. 7 July 1953, s. of Michael William McCrum and Christine Mary Kathleen fforde; m. 1st Olivia Timbs (divorced 1984); m. 2nd Sarah Lyall 1995; two d. *Education:* Sherborne School, Corpus Christi Coll., Cambridge and Univ. of Pennsylvania. *Career:* house editor Chatto & Windus 1977–79; Editorial Dir Faber and Faber Ltd 1979–89, Ed.-in-Chief 1990–96; Literary Ed. Observer newspaper 1996–2008; scriptwriter and co-producer The Story of English TV series 1980–86. *Publications:* In the Secret State 1980, A Loss of Heart 1982, The Fabulous Englishman 1984, The Story of English 1986, The World is a Banana 1988, Mainland 1991, The Psychological Moment 1993, Suspicion 1996, My Year Off 1998, Wodehouse: A Life (biog.) 2004, Globish: How the English Language Became the World's Language 2010. *Honours:* Tony Godwin Prize 1979, Peabody Award 1986, Emmy Award 1987. *Address:* c/o Viking, Penguin Publicity, 80 Strand, London, WC2R 0RL, England (office). *Website:* www.penguin.co.uk (office).

McCRYSTAL, Cahal (Cal); Northern Irish journalist, writer, critic and broadcaster; b. 20 Dec. 1935, Belfast; m. Stella Doyle 1958; three s. *Education:* St Mary's Coll., Dundalk, St Malachy's Coll., Belfast. *Career:* fmr reporter with Northern Herald; fmr corresp. with Belfast Telegraph; crime reporter, chief reporter, foreign corresp., New York Bureau Chief, News Ed., Foreign Features Ed. and columnist, Sunday Times, London; sr writer and columnist, Independent on Sunday; sr writer, The Observer; literary critic, Financial Times, Independent on Sunday; mem. Editorial Bd, British Journalism Review. *Publications:* Watergate: The Full Inside Story (co-author) 1973, Reflections on a Quiet Rebel 1997; contrib. to Canadian and Australian publs, British magazines, London Evening Standard, The Guardian, Poetry Ireland, Vanity Fair, Poetry Ireland Review and British Journalism Review. *Honours:* various journalism awards, Belfast Arts Council Literary Award 1998. *Literary Agent:* c/o Greene & Heaton Ltd, 37 Goldhawk Road, London, W12 8QQ, England.

McCULLAGH, Sheila Kathleen, MBE, MA; British writer; b. 3 Dec. 1920, Surrey, England. *Education:* Bedford Froebel College, Univ. of Leeds. *Career:* Lecturer, Univ. of Leeds Institute of Education, 1949–57; mem. Society of Authors. *Publications:* Pirate Books, 1957–64; Tales and Adventures, 1961; Dragon Books, 1963–70; One, Two, Three and Away, 1964–92; Tim Books, 1974–83; Into New Worlds, 1974; Hummingbirds, 1976–92; Whizzbang Adventurers, 1980; Buccaneers, 1980; New Buccaneers, 1984; Where Wild Geese Fly, 1981; Puddle Lane, 1985–88; The Sea Shore (and other information books), 1992. *Literary Agent:* AP Watt Ltd, 20 John Street, London WC1N 2DR, England. *Address:* 27 Royal Crescent, Bath, NE Somerset BA1 2LT, England.

MacCULLOCH, Sir Diarmaid, Kt, MA, DD, PhD, FRHistS, FSA, FBA; British writer, editor, academic and broadcaster; *Professor of the History of the Church, St Cross College, Oxford;* b. 31 Oct. 1951, Folkestone, Kent, England; s. of Rev. Nigel MacCulloch and Jennie MacCulloch. *Education:* Univs of Cambridge, Liverpool and Oxford. *Career:* Jr Research Fellow, Churchill Coll., Cambridge 1976–78; Tutor in History, Wesley Coll., Bristol 1978–90; Lecturer in Theology, Univ. of Bristol 1978–95; Lecturer in Theology, St Cross Coll. Oxford 1995–97; Sr Tutor 1996–2000, Prof. of the History of the Church 1997–; Co-Ed. Journal of Ecclesiastical History 1995–. *Television:* A History of Christianity (BBC 4/BBC 2) 2009, The English: How God Made Them (BBC 2) 2011. *Publications:* The Chorography of Suffolk (ed.) 1976, Suffolk and the Tudors: Politics and Religion in an English County, 1500–1600 1986, Groundwork of Christian History 1987, How to Read Church History, Vol. II (with J. Comby) 1988, The Later Reformation in England, 1547–1603 1990, The Reign of Henry VIII: Politics, Policy, and Piety (ed.) 1995, Thomas Cranmer: A Life 1996, Tudor Rebellions (with Anthony Fletcher, fifth edn) 2004, Tudor Church Militant: Edward VI and the Protestant Reformation 2000, Reformation: Europe's House Divided 1490–1700 (US title: The Reformation: A History 2004) 2003, A History of Christianity: the First Three Thousand Years 2009; contrib. to learned books and journals. *Honours:* Hon. DLitt (East Anglia) 2003, Hon. DD (Virginia Theological Seminary) 2011; Royal Historical Soc. Whitfield Prize 1986, Duff Cooper Prize 1996, Whitbread Biography Prize 1996, James Tait Black Memorial Prize 1996, Wolfson History Prize 2004, British Acad. Prize 2004, Non-Fiction Award, Nat. Book Critics Circle of America 2004, Longman/History Today Trustees Award 2009, Hessell-Tiltman Prize 2010, Radio Times Readers Award 2010, Cundill Prize for History 2010. *Address:* Faculty of Theology, University of Oxford, 41 St Giles, Oxford, OX1 3LW, England (office). *Telephone:* (1865) 270795 (office). *E-mail:* diarmaid.macculloch@stx.ox.ac.uk (office). *Website:* www.stx.ox.ac .uk/general/fellows/macculloch_diarmaid (office); www.theology.ox.ac.uk/ people/staff-list/prof-diarmaid-macculloch.html (office).

McCULLOUGH, Colleen; Australian author; b. 1 June 1937, Wellington, NSW; m. Ric Robinson 1984. *Education:* Holy Cross Coll., Woollahra, Sydney Univ., Inst. of Child Health, London Univ. *Career:* trained as neuroscientist and worked in Sydney and English hospitals; researcher lecturer Dept of Neurology, Yale Univ. Medical School, USA 1967–77; moved to Norfolk Island, S Pacific 1979; mem. New York Acad. of Sciences, Bd of Visitors Int. Programs Center Dept of Political Science, Univ. of Oklahoma; Fellow, AAAS; fmr Patron Gerontology Foundation of Australia; currently Patron Macular Degeneration Foundation of Australia. *Publications:* novels: Tim 1974, The Thorn Birds 1977, An Indecent Obsession 1981, A Creed for the Third Millennium 1985, The Ladies of Missalonghi 1987, The First Man in Rome 1990, The Grass Crown 1991, Fortune's Favourites 1993, Caesar's Women 1996, Caesar 1997, The Song of Troy 1998, Morgan's Run 2000, The October Horse 2002, The Touch 2003, Angel 2005, On, Off 2006, Antony and Cleopatra 2007, The Independence of Miss Mary Bennett 2008, Too Many Murders 2009; non-fiction: Cooking with Colleen McCullough and Jean Easthope 1982, Roden Cutler, VC – The Biography 1998 (aka The Courage and the Will 1999). *Honours:* Hon. Founding Gov. Prince of Wales Medical Research Inst.; Hon. DLitt (Macquarie) 1993; designated one of Australia's Living National Treasures. *Address:* 'Out Yenna', Norfolk Island, Oceania (via Australia). *Fax:* (6723) 23313. *Website:* www.colleenmccullough.com.

McCULLOUGH, David Gaub, BA; American historian and writer; b. 7 July 1933, Pittsburgh; m. Rosalee Ingram Barnes 1954; three s. two d. *Education:* Yale Univ. *Career:* Ed., Time Inc., New York 1956–61, United States Information Agency, Washington, DC 1961–64, American Heritage Publishing Co., New York 1964–70; Scholar-in-Residence, Univ. of New Mexico 1979, Wesleyan Univ. 1982, 1983; Visiting Prof., Cornell Univ. 1989; Marian McFadden Memorial Lecturer, Indianapolis-Marion County Public Library 2002; mem. Jefferson Legacy Foundation, Nat. Trust for Historic Preservation, Soc. of American Historians, Harry S. Truman Library Inst. *Television:* host, Smithsonian World 1984–88, The American Experience 1988– (both PBS). *Publications:* The Johnstown Flood 1968, The Great Bridge 1972, The Path Between the Seas (Nat. Book Award for History 1978, Samuel Eliot Morison Award 1978, Cornelius Ryan Award 1978, Francis Parkman Prize 1978) 1977, Mornings on Horseback (Nat. Book Award) 1981, Brave Companions 1991, Truman (Pulitzer Prize in Biography 1993, Harry S. Truman Public Service Award 1993) 1992, John Adams 2001 (Pulitzer Prize 2002), 1776 2005, The Course of Human Events 2005. *Honours:* various hon. doctorates. *Literary Agent:* Janklow & Nesbit Associates, 445 Park Avenue, New York, NY 10022, USA. *Website:* www.davidmccullough.com.

McCULLOUGH, Kenneth (Ken), BA, MFA; American poet, writer and teacher; b. 18 July 1943, Staten Island, NY. *Education:* University of Delaware, University of Iowa. *Career:* Teacher, Montana State University, 1970–75, University of Iowa, 1983–95, Kirkwood Community College, Cedar Rapids, 1987, St Mary's University, Winona, Minnesota, 1996; Writer-in-Residence, South Carolina ETV Network, 1975–78; Participant, Artist-in-the-Schools Program, Iowa Arts Council, 1981–96; mem. Associated Writing Programs; Asscn of American University Profs; National Asscn of College Academic Advisers; Renaissance Artists and Writers Asscn and Renaissance International; Rocky Mountain MLA; SFWA. *Publications:* Poetry: The Easy Wreckage, 1971; Migrations, 1972; Creosote, 1976; Elegy for Old Anna, 1985; Travelling Light, 1987; Sycamore Oriole, 1991; Walking Backwards, 1997. Contributions: numerous publications. *Honours:* Acad. of American Poets Award, 1966; Second Place, Ark River Awards, 1972; Helene Wurlitzer Foundation of New Mexico Residencies, 1973, 1994; National Endowment for the Arts Fellowship, 1974; Second Prize, Sri Chinmoy Poetry Awards, 1980; Writers' Voice Capricorn Book Award, 1985; Second Place, Pablo Neruda Award, Nimrod magazine 1990; Third Prize, Kudzu Poetry Contest, 1990; Ucross Foundation Residency, WY, 1991; Witter Bynner Foundation for Poetry Grant, 1993; Iowa Arts Council Grants, 1994, 1996.

McCULLY, Emily Arnold, (Emily Arnold), BA, MA; American writer and illustrator; b. 7 Jan. 1939, Galesburg, IL; two s. *Education:* Brown University, Columbia University. *Career:* mem. PEN Society; Authors' Guild. *Publications:* A Craving, 1982; Picnic, 1985; Life Drawing, 1986; Mirette on the High Wire, 1992; The Amazing Felix, 1993; Little Kit, or, the Industrious Flea Circus Girl, 1995; The Pirate Queen, 1995. *Honours:* O. Henry Award Collection, 1977; Caldecott Award, 1993. *Literary Agent:* Harriet Wasserman, 137 E 36th Street, New York, NY 10026, USA.

McCUNN, Ruthanne Lum, BA, DipEd; American writer; b. 21 Feb. 1946, San Francisco, Calif.; m. Donald H. McCunn 1965. *Education:* Univ. of Texas at Austin, San Francisco State Coll. *Career:* Guest Lecturer, Univ. of California, Santa Cruz 1988, Cornell Univ. 1989, Univ. of San Francisco 1993, 1996; mem. American Civil Liberties Union, Amnesty International, Chinese for Affirmative Action, Chinese Historical Soc., Int. Inst. of San Francisco. *Play:* Wooden Fish Songs: A Concert Reading 1998. *Publications include:* An Illustrated History of the Chinese in America 1979, Thousand Pieces of Gold 1981, Pie-Biter 1983, Sole Survivor 1985, Chinese American Portraits: Personal Histories, 1828–1888 1988, Chinese Proverbs 1991, Wooden Fish Songs 1995, The Moon Pearl 2000, God of Luck 2007, Him Mark Lai: Autobiography of a Chinese American Historian (co-ed.) 2011; contrib. to journals. *Honours:* Before Columbus Foundation American Book Award 1984, Southwestern Booksellers Asscn Best Non-Fiction Adventure Book 1985, Choice Best Non-Fiction Book Citation 1989, Nat. Women's Political Caucus Distinguished Achievement Award 1991, Women's Heritage Museums Jeanne Fair McDonnell Best Fiction Award 1997, Kiriyama Notable Book 2008, Chinese American Librarians Asscn Best Fiction Award 2008. *Address:* 1007 Castro, San Francisco, CA 94114, USA (home). *Website:* www.mccunn.com.

McCURRY, Stephanie, MA, PhD; British historian, educator, author and academic; *Professor of History, University of Pennsylvania*; b. Belfast. *Education:* Univ. of Western Ontario, Canada, Univ. of Rochester, State Univ. of New York at Binghamton, USA. *Career:* mem. faculty, Univ. of California, San Diego 1993–2002; mem. faculty and Dir Alice Berline Kaplan Center for the Humanities, Northwestern Univ. 2002–03; joined Univ. of Pennsylvania 2003, currently Prof. of History; Visiting Prof., Princeton Univ. 2006–07; Dir California History Project 1996–98; Program Cttee Co-Chair Org. of American Historians 2003, Distinguished Lecturer 2005–. *Publications:* Masters of Small Worlds: Yeoman Households and the Political Culture of the Antebellum South Carolina Low Country (American Studies Asscn John Hope Franklin Prize, Southern Historical Asscn Charles Sydnor Award) 1995, Confederate Reckoning: Power and Politics in the Civil War South 2010; contrib. articles, reviews and essays to anthologies and journals including Journal of American History, Signs: Journal of Women in Culture and Society and The Women's Review of Books. *Honours:* fellowships from Smithsonian Inst., American Asscn of Univ. Women, American Council of Learned Socs, Guggenheim Foundation. *Address:* Department of History, School of Arts & Sciences, University of Pennsylvania, College Hall 208A, Philadelphia, PA 19104-6379, USA (office). *Telephone:* (215) 898-3427 (office). *Fax:* (215) 573-2089 (office). *E-mail:* smccurry@sas.upenn.edu (office). *Website:* www.history.upenn.edu/faculty/mccurry (office).

McDERMID, Val, MA; British writer; b. 4 June 1955, Fife, Scotland; only d. of James McDermid and Davina McDermid (née McCall); one s.; civil partnership with Kelly Smith 2006. *Education:* St Hilda's Coll., Oxford. *Career:* began career as journalist, Plymouth and South Devon Times 1975–77; worked at Daily Record, Glasgow 1977–79, then at Sunday People, Manchester, becoming Northern Bureau Chief –1991; crime fiction reviewer, Manchester Evening News, also for other national newspapers; regular broadcasts on BBC Radio 4 and BBC Radio Scotland. *Plays:* Like A Happy Ending (Plymouth Theatre Co.) 1977, Clean Break 1998, The Right Chemistry 1999, Village SOS 2011, Stranded 2012. *Television:* Wire in the Blood (six series), A Place of Execution. *Publications:* fiction: Report for Murder 1987, Common Murder 1989, Final Edition 1991, Dead Beat 1992, Union Jack 1993, Kick Back 1993, Crack Down 1994, Clean Break 1995, The Mermaids Singing (Crime Writers' Asscn Macallan Gold Dagger for Fiction) 1995, Blue Genes 1996, Booked for Murder 1996, The Wire in the Blood 1997, Star Struck (Grand Prix des Romans d'Adventure 1998) 1997, A Place of Execution (Barry Award for Best British Mystery 2000, Los Angeles Times Book Prize for Mystery/Thriller, Mystery Readers of America Macavity Award, Dilys Award, Anthony Award for Best Novel 2001) 1998, Killing the Shadows 2001, The Last Temptation 2002, The Distant Echo (Barry Award for Best British Crime Novel, Sherlock Award for Best Crime Novel 2004) 2003, Hostage to Murder 2003, The Torment of Others (Theakston's Old Peculier Crime Novel of the Year 2006) 2004, The Grave Tattoo (Portico Prize for Fiction) 2006, Beneath the Bleeding (Stonewall Writer of the Year) 2007, A Darker Domain 2008, Fever of the Bone (Lambda Literary Foundation Award for Best Lesbian Mystery 2010) 2009, Trick of the Dark 2010; short stories: Writing on the Wall and Other Stories 1997, Stranded 2005; non-fiction: A Suitable Job for a Woman: Inside the World of Women Private Eyes 1994. *Honours:* Hon. Fellow, St Hilda's Coll., Oxford 2010; Hon. DLitt (Sunderland) 2011; Trainee Journalist of the Year 1977, Scotland Magazine Icon of Scotland 2004, inducted into Saints and Sinners LGBT Hall of Fame 2004, Alice B Award 2008, Crime Writers' Asscn Cartier Diamond Dagger Award 2010, inducted into ITV 3 Crime Writers' Hall of Fame 2010, Lambda Literary Foundation Pioneer Award 2011. *Literary Agent:* c/o Gregory & Co., 3 Barb Mews, London, W6 7PA, England. *Telephone:* (20) 7610-4676. *E-mail:* jane@gregoryandcompany.co.uk. *Address:* c/o Little, Brown Book Group, 100 Victoria Embankment, London, EC4Y 0DY, England. *E-mail:* info@valmcdermid.com (office). *Website:* www.littlebrown.co.uk; www.valmcdermid.com.

McDERMOTT, Alice, BA, MA; American writer; *Richard A. Macksey Professor, Johns Hopkins University*; b. 27 June 1953, Long Island, NY; m. David Armstrong; two c. *Education:* SUNY, Univ. of New Hampshire. *Career:* mem. staff Houghton Mifflin publrs; writer, short stories published in Ms, Redbook, Seventeen and Mademoiselle magazines; teacher writing workshops American Univ. (DC); currently Richard A. Macksey Prof., Johns Hopkins Univ.; mem. Associated Writing Programs, PEN, Poets and Writers, Writers' Guild. *Publications:* A Bigamist's Daughter 1982, That Night 1987, At Weddings and Wakes 1991, Charming Billy (Nat. Book Award) 1998, Child of My Heart 2002, After This 2006. *Honours:* Whiting Writers Award 1987. *Address:* The Writing Seminars, Johns Hopkins University, Dell House, Suite 702, 3400 North Charles Street, Baltimore, MD 21218, USA (office). *Telephone:* (410) 516-5273 (office). *Fax:* (410) 516-6828 (office). *Website:* writingseminars.jhu.edu (office).

McDEVITT, Jack, BA, MA; American writer; b. (John McDevitt), 14 April 1935, Philadelphia, Pa; s. of John McDevitt and Elizabeth McDevitt; m. Maureen McAdams 1967; two s. one d. *Education:* La Salle Coll., Wesleyan Univ. *Career:* mem. Science Fiction and Fantasy Writers of America, US Chess Fed., Mil. Officers Asscn of America. *Publications:* Time Travelers Never Die (Best Novella Award), The Hercules Text 1986, A Talent for War 1989, The Engines of God 1994, Ancient Shores 1996, Standard Candles 1996, Eternity Road 1997, Moonfall 1998, Infinity Beach 2000, Deepsix (Southeastern Science Fiction Achievement Award for Best Science Fiction Novel 2004) 2001, Chindi 2002, Omega (John W. Campbell Memorial Award for Best Novel 2004) 2003, Polaris 2004, Seeker (Southeastern Science Fiction Achievement Award for Best Novel 2005, Nebula Award for Best Science Fiction Novel 2006) 2005, Odyssey 2006, Cauldron 2007, The Devil's Eye 2008, Cryptic: The Best Short Fiction of Jack McDevitt 2008, Time Travelers Never Die 2009, Echo 2010, Firebird 2011; contrib. to various publs. *Honours:* Philip K. Dick Special Award 1986, UPC Grand Prize 1992, Phoenix Award for Lifetime Achievement 2000, Southeastern Science Fiction Achievement Lifetime Achievement Award 2006. *Address:* 57 Sunset Blvd, Brunswick, GA 31525, USA (office). *Telephone:* (912) 265-5610 (office). *E-mail:* cryptic@gate.net (office). *Website:* www.jackmcdevitt.com.

McDONAGH, Martin; Irish playwright and film director; b. 1970, London, England. *Career:* fmr resident playwright, Royal Nat. Theatre, London; mem. Acad. of Motion Picture Arts and Sciences. *Plays:* The Beauty Queen of Leenane (Evening Standard Award for Most Promising Playwright 1996, George Devine Award for Most Promising Playwright 1996, Drama Desk Award for Outstanding Play 1998) 1996, The Cripple of Inishmaan 1997, The Lonesome West 1997, A Skull In Connemara 1997, The Lieutenant of Inishmore (Olivier Award for Best New Comedy 2003, Obie Award for Best Play 2006) 2001, The Pillowman (Olivier Award for Best New Play 2004) 2003. *Films include:* Six Shooter (writer and dir) 2004, In Bruges (writer and dir) (BAFTA Award for Original Screenplay 2009) 2008. *Publications:* Plays One 1999, Plays Two 2004. *Literary Agent:* c/o The Rod Hall Agency Ltd, 3 Charlotte Mews, London, W1T 4DZ, England. *Telephone:* (20) 7637-0706. *Fax:* (20) 7637-0807. *E-mail:* office@rodhallagency.com. *Website:* www.rodhallagency.com.

MacDONALD, Cynthia, BA, MA; American poet and lecturer; b. 2 Feb. 1928, New York, NY; m. E. C. Macdonald 1954 (divorced 1975); one s. one d. *Education:* Bennington College, Vermont, Mannes College of Music, New York, Sarah Lawrence College. *Career:* Asst Prof., Sarah Lawrence College 1970–74, Assoc. Prof. and Acting Dean of Studies 1974–75; Prof., Johns Hopkins University 1975–79; Consultant, University of Houston 1977–78, Co-Dir, Writing Program 1979–; Guest Lecturer at various universities, colleges, seminars, etc; mem. American Society of Composers, Authors, and Publishers; Associated Writing Programs. *Publications:* Amputations 1972, Transplants 1976, Pruning the Annuals 1976, (W)holes 1980, Alternate Means of Transport 1985, Living Wills: New and Selected Poems 1991, I Can't Remember 1997; contributions: anthologies and other publications. *Honours:* MacDowell Colony Grant 1970, National Endowment for the Arts Grants 1973, 1979, Yaddo Foundation Grants 1974, 1976, 1979, CAPS Grant 1976, American Acad. and Institute of Arts and Letters Award 1977, Rockefeller Foundation Fellow 1978. *Address:* c/o Alfred A. Knopf Inc, 1745 Broadway, Suite 81, New York, NY 10019-4305, USA (office).

McDONALD, Forrest, PhD; American academic; *Distinguished Research Professor, University of Alabama*; b. 7 Jan. 1927, Orange, Tex.; s. of John Forrest and Myra M. McGill; m. Ellen Shapiro 1963; five c. *Education:* Orange High School and Univ. of Tex. (Austin). *Career:* State Historical Soc. of Wis. 1953–58; Assoc. Prof., Brown Univ. 1959–64, Prof. 1964–67; Prof., Wayne State Univ. 1967–76; Prof., Univ. of Ala 1976–87, Distinguished Research Prof. 1976, 1987–; J. P. Harrison Visiting Prof., Coll. of William and Mary 1986–87; Jefferson Lecturer Nat. Endowment for the Humanities 1987; Guggenheim Fellow 1962–63; mem. American Antiquarian Soc., Philadelphia Soc., The Historical Soc. *Publications:* We The People: The Economic Origins of the Constitution 1958, Insull 1962, E Pluribus Unum: The Formation of the American Republic 1965, Presidency of George Washington 1974, The Phaeton Ride 1974, Presidency of Thomas Jefferson 1976, Alexander Hamilton: A Biography 1980, A Constitutional History of the United States 1982, Novus Ordo Seclorum: The Intellectual Origins of the Constitution 1985, Requiem: Variations on Eighteenth-Century Themes 1988, The American Presidency: An Intellectual History 1994, States' Rights and the Union 2000, Recovering the Past: A Historian's Memoir 2004. *Honours:* George Washington Medal (Freedom's Foundation) 1980, Frances Tavern Book Award 1980, American Revolution Round Table Book Award 1986, 16th Jefferson Lecturer in the Humanities (Nat. Endowment for the Humanities) 1987, Ingersoll Prize, Richard M. Weaver Award 1990, Salvatori Award for

Academic Excellence 1992. *Address:* P.O. Box 155, Coker, AL 35452, USA. *Telephone:* (205) 339-0317.

MACDONALD, Hugh John, MA, PhD, FRCM; British musicologist and academic; *Avis Blewett Professor of Music, Washington University, St Louis*; b. 31 Jan. 1940, Newbury, Berks., England; m. 1st Naomi Butterworth 1963; one s. three d.; m. 2nd Elizabeth Babb 1979; one s. *Education:* Pembroke Coll., Cambridge. *Career:* Lecturer in Music, Univ. of Cambridge 1966–71, Univ. of Oxford 1971–80; Visiting Prof., Indiana Univ., USA 1979; Gardiner Prof. of Music, Univ. of Glasgow 1980–87; Avis Blewett Prof. of Music, Washington Univ., St Louis, Mo., USA 1987–. *Publications:* New Berlioz Edition (Gen. Ed., complete works) 1965–2006, Berlioz Orchestral Music 1969, Skryabin 1978, Berlioz 1982, Berlioz: Correspondance générale (ed.) Vol. 4 1984, Vol. 5 1989, Vol. 6 1995, Vol. 7 2001, Vol. 8 2002, Selected Letters of Berlioz 1995, Berlioz's Orchestration Treatise 2002, Beethoven's Century: Essays on Composers and Themes 2008; contrib. to The New Grove Dictionary of Music and Musicians, The New Grove Dictionary of Opera, many journals. *Honours:* Szymanowski Medal 1982, Grand Prix de Littérature Musicale Charles Cros 1985, 1996, Médaille de Rayonnement Culturel 2010. *Address:* Department of Music, Washington University, St Louis, MO 63130, USA (office).

McDONALD, Ian A., BA, MA, FRSL; Trinidad and Tobago poet, writer, dramatist and editor; b. 18 April 1933, St Augustine, Trinidad; s. of John Archie McDonald and Thelma McDonald (neé Seheult); m. Mary Angela Callender 1984; three s. *Education:* Queen's Royal Coll., Trinidad, Univ. of Cambridge, UK. *Career:* Dir, Theatre Co. of Guyana, Georgetown 1981–; Ed., Kyk-Over-Al West Indian literary journal 1984–; Chair. Demerara Publrs 1988–; CEO Sugar Asscn of the Caribbean 2000–07. *Films:* The Humming Bird Tree (BBC film) 1992. *Publications:* The Tramping Man (play) 1969, The Humming Bird Tree (novel) 1969, Selected Poems 1983, Mercy Ward 1988, Essequibo 1992, Jaffo the Calypsonian (poems) 1994, Between Silence and Silence (poems), The Heinemann Book of Caribbean Poetry (co-ed.) 1994, The Collected Poems of A. J. Seymour (co-ed.) 2000, Poems by Martin Carter (co-ed.) 2006. *Honours:* Hon. DLitt (Univ. of the West Indies) 1997; Golden Arrow of Achievement (Guyana Nat. Award) 1987. *Address:* c/o Demerara Sugar Terminal, River View, Ruimveldt, Georgetown, Guyana (office). *Telephone:* 2272051 (office). *Fax:* 2266104 (office). *E-mail:* dstgsc@guyana.net.gy (office).

MacDONALD, Malcolm (see Ross-MacDonald, Malcolm John)

MACDONALD, Marianne, BA, BLitt, PhD; Canadian writer; b. 9 July 1934, Kenora, Ont.; m. Erik Korn 1958 (divorced 1998); two s. *Education:* McGill Univ., Univs of Oxford and Keele, UK. *Career:* Lecturer in English, Univ. of Toronto 1960–62; Lecturer in American Studies, Univ. of Keele 1964–69; Prin. Lecturer in English, Middlesex Polytechnic 1972–86; mem. Crime Writers Asscn, Crime Writers of Canada, Sisters in Crime. *Publications:* fiction: Death's Autograph 1996, Ghost Walk 1997, Smoke Screen 1999, Road Kill 2000, Blood Lies 2001, Die Once 2002, Three Monkeys 2005, Faking It 2006; juvenile fiction: Black Bass Rock 1952, Smugglers Cove 1955, The Treasure of Ur 1958, The Pirate Queen 1991, The Eighty-Nine Pennies of Emma Jones 1992, The Witch Repair 1995; non-fiction: The State of Literary Theory Today (ed.) 1982, Ezra Pound: purpose/form/meaning 1983, Ezra Pound and History (ed.) 1985. *Honours:* Woodrow Wilson Fellowship 1954–55. *Literary Agent:* c/o David Higham Associates, 5–8 Lower John Street, Golden Square, London, W1F 9HA, England. *Website:* www.marianne-macdonald.com.

MacDONALD, Sharman, MA; British writer, playwright and screenwriter; b. 8 Feb. 1951, Glasgow; d. of Joseph Henry Hosgood MacDonald and Janet Rewat Macdonald (née Williams); m. Will Knightly 1976; one s. one d. *Education:* Hutchesons' Girls' Grammar School, Glasgow, George Watson's Ladies' Coll., Edinburgh and Univ. of Edinburgh. *Career:* actress with 7:84 at Royal Court Theatre 1972–84; Thames TV Writer-in-Residence 1985. *Plays:* When I Was A Girl I Used To Scream And Shout 1984, The Brave 1987, When We Were Women 1987, All Things Nice 1990, Shades 1992, The Winter Guest 1995, Borders of Paradise 1995, Sea Urchins 1998, After Juliet 1999, The Girl with Red Hair (Lyceum Theatre, Edinburgh) 2005, Broken Hallelujah 2006. *Film screenplays:* Wild Flowers 1988, The Edge of Love 2008. *Radio:* Sea Urchins (adapted for stage 1998), Gladly My Cross-Eyed Bear 2000. *Opera libretto:* Hey Persephone! 1998. *Publications:* novels: The Beast 1984, Night, Night 1987. *Honours:* London Evening Standard Award for Most Promising Playwright 1984. *Literary Agent:* United Agents, 12–26 Lexington Street, London W1F 0LE, England. *Telephone:* (20) 3214-0800. *Fax:* (20) 3214-0801. *E-mail:* info@unitedagents.co.uk. *Website:* www.unitedagents.co.uk.

McDONALD, Sir Trevor, Kt, OBE; British broadcast journalist; b. 16 Aug. 1939, Trinidad; m.; two s. one d. *Career:* worked on newspapers, radio and TV, Trinidad 1960–69; Producer BBC Caribbean Service and World Service, London 1969–73; reporter Ind. TV News 1973–78, sports corresp. 1978–80, diplomatic corresp. 1980–87, newscaster 1982–87, Diplomatic Ed. Channel Four News 1987–89, newscaster News at 5.40 1989–90, News at Ten 1990–99, ITV Evening News 1999–2000, ITV News at Ten 2001–04, 2008, News at 10.30 2004–05; Chair. Better English Campaign 1995–97, Nuffield Language Inquiry 1998–2000; Gov. English-Speaking Union of the Commonwealth 2000–; Pres. European Year of Languages 2000; Chancellor South Bank Univ. 1999–. *Publications:* Clive Lloyd: A Biography 1985, Vivian Richards: A Biography 1987, Queen and Commonwealth 1989, Fortunate Circumstances (autobiog.) 1993, Favourite Poems 1997, World of Poetry 1999. *Honours:* Hon. Fellow, Liverpool John Moores Univ. 1998; Hon. DLitt (South Bank) 1994, (Plymouth) 1995, (Southampton Inst.) 1997, (Nottingham) 1997; Dr hc (Surrey) 1997, (Open Univ.) 1997; Hon. LLD (Univ. of West Indies) 1996; Newscaster of the Year TV and Radio Industries Club 1993, 1997, 1999; Gold Medal, Royal TV Soc. 1998, Richard Dimbleby Award for outstanding contrib. to TV, BAFTA 1999, Royal Television Soc. lifetime achievement award 2005. *Address:* c/o ITN, 200 Gray's Inn Road, London, WC1X 8XZ, England. *Telephone:* (20) 7833-3000 (office). *Website:* www.itv.com/news (office).

McDONALD, Walter Robert, BA, MA, PhD; American academic, poet and writer; b. 18 July 1934, Lubbock, Tex.; m. Carol Ham 1959; two s. one d. *Education:* Texas Technological College, University of Iowa. *Career:* Faculty mem. US Air Force Acad., University of Colorado; Paul W. Horn Prof. of English and Poet-in-Residence, Texas Tech University, Lubbock; mem. Texas Asscn of Creative Writing Teachers, PEN, Poetry Society of America, Assoc. Writing Programs, Texas Institute of Letters, Conference of College Teachers of English of Texas. *Publications include:* poetry: Caliban in Blue, 1976; One Thing Leads to Another, 1978; Anything, Anything, 1980; Working Against Time, 1981; Burning the Fence, 1981; Witching on Hardscrabble, 1985; Flying Dutchman, 1987; After the Noise of Saigon, 1988; Rafting the Brazos, 1988. Fiction: A Band of Brothers: Stories of Vietnam, 1989; Night Landings, 1989; The Digs in Escondido Canyon, 1991; All That Matters: The Texas Plains in Photographs and Poems, 1992; Where Skies Are Not Cloudy, 1993; Counting Survivors, 1995; contributions: numerous journals and magazines. *Honours:* Poetry Award, Texas Institute of Letters 1976, 1985, 1987, George Elliston Poetry Prize 1987, Juniper Prize 1988, Western Heritage Award for Poetry, National Cowboy Hall of Fame 1990, 1992; 1993. *Address:* Department of English, Texas Tech University, Lubbock, TX 79409, USA.

MacDONOGH, Giles Malachy Maximilian, BA, MA; British writer and journalist; b. 6 April 1955, London, England; m. Candida Brazil; one s. one d. *Education:* Balliol Coll., Oxford, École des Hautes Études Pratiques, France. *Career:* freelance journalist 1983–; Ed., Made in France 1984; columnist, Financial Times 1989–; mem. International PEN, Octagon of Wine Writers. *Publications:* A Palate in Revolution: Grimod de La Reynière and the Almanach des Gourmands 1987, A Good German: Adam von Trott zu Solz 1990, The Wine and Food of Austria 1992, Brillat Savarin: The Judge and his Stomach 1992, Syrah Grenache, Mourvèdre 1992, Prussia, the Perversion of an Idea 1994, Austria: New Wines from the Old World 1997, Berlin: A Portrait of its History, Architecture and Society 1997, Frederick the Great 1999, The Last Kaiser: The Life of Wilhelm II 2000, Portuguese Table Wines 2001, After the Reich: from the Liberation of Vienna to the Berlin Airlift 2007, 1938: Hitler's Gamble 2009; contributions: reference works, books, and periodicals. *Honours:* Glenfiddich Special Award 1988. *Website:* www.macdonogh.co.uk.

MacDOUGALL, Ruth Doan, BEd; American writer; b. 19 March 1939, Laconia, NH; m. Donald K. MacDougall 1957. *Education:* Bennington Coll., Keene State Coll. *Career:* mem. NH Writers' Project. *Publications:* The Lilting House 1965, The Cost of Living 1971, One Minus One 1971, The Cheerleader 1973, Wife and Mother 1976, Aunt Pleasantine 1978, The Flowers of the Forest 1981, A Lovely Time Was Had By All 1982, Snowy 1993, The Cheerleader: 25th Anniversary Edition 1998, A Woman Who Loved Lindbergh 2001, Henrietta Snow 2004, Fifty Hikes in the White Mountains 2004, Fifty More Hikes in New Hampshire 2006, the Husband Bench or Bev's Book 2007, Mutual Aid 2009; contrib. book reviews to New York Times Book Review, Newsday and others. *Honours:* winner PEN Syndicated Fiction Project 1983, 1984, 1985, NH Writers' Project Lifetime Achievement Award 2005, Keene State Coll. Alumni Achievement Award 2006. *Address:* 285 Range Road, Center Sandwich, NH 03227, USA (home). *Website:* www.ruthdoanmacdougall.com.

McDOUGALL, Walter Allan, BA, MA, PhD; American academic and writer; *Professor of History and Alloy-Ansin Professor of International Relations, University of Pennsylvania*; b. 3 Dec. 1946, Washington, DC; m. 2nd Jonna van Zanten 1988; two c. *Education:* Amherst Coll., Univ. of Chicago. *Career:* US Army, Viet Nam 1968–70; Asst Prof., Univ. of California, Berkeley 1975–83, Assoc. Prof. 1983–87, Prof. of History 1987–; Prof. of History and Alloy-Ansin Prof. of Int. Relations, Univ. of Pennsylvania 1988–; Sr Fellow and Dir Center for America and the West, Foreign Policy Research Inst., Phila 1991–; Ed. Orbis, 1999–2001; mem. American Church Union, Pumpkin Papers Irregulars. *Publications:* France's Rhineland Diplomacy 1914–1924: The Last Bid for a Balance of Power in Europe 1978, The Grenada Papers (co-ed. with Paul Seabury) 1984, Social Sciences and Space Exploration: New Directions for University Instruction (contrib.) 1984, …The Heavens and the Earth: A Political History of the Space Age 1985, Let the Sea Make a Noise 1993, Promised Land, Crusader State: The American Encounter with the World Since 1776 1997, Throes of Democracy: The American Civil War Era, 1829–1877 2008; contribs to numerous articles and reviews to periodicals. *Honours:* Pulitzer Prize for History 1986, Visiting Scholar, Hoover Inst. 1986, One of America's Ten Best College Profs, Insight 1987, Dexter Prize for Best Book, Soc. for the History of Tech. 1987. *Address:* 208 College Hall, University of Pennsylvania, Philadelphia, PA 19104-6379, USA (office). *Telephone:* (215) 898-2185 (office); (215) 898-0452 (office). *Fax:* (215) 573-2089 (office). *E-mail:* wamcd@sas.upenn.edu (office). *Website:* www.history.upenn.edu/faculty/mcdougall.htm (office).

MacDOWELL, John (see Parks, Timothy Harold)

McDOWELL, John Henry, MA, FBA, FAAS; British academic; *University Professor, University of Pittsburgh*; b. 7 March 1942, Boksburg, South Africa; s. of Sir Henry McDowell and Norah McDowell (née Douthwaite); m. Andrea

Lehrke 1977. *Education:* St John's Coll. Johannesburg, Univ. Coll. of Rhodesia and Nyasaland, New Coll., Oxford. *Career:* Fellow, Praelector in Philosophy, Univ. Coll., Oxford 1966–86; Prof. of Philosophy, Univ. of Pittsburgh 1986–88, Univ. Prof. 1988–. *Publications:* Ed. (with Gareth Evans) Truth and Meaning, Ed. (with Philip Pettit) Subject, Thought and Context, Mind and World, Mind, Value and Reality, Meaning, Knowledge and Reality, Having the World in View, The Engaged Intellect; trans of Plato, Theaetetus. *Honours:* Hon. DHumLitt (Chicago) 2008. *Address:* Department of Philosophy, University of Pittsburgh, Pittsburgh, PA 15260, USA. *Telephone:* (412) 624-5792.

McELDOWNEY, Eugene, (Kate McCabe, Carol Magill), BA; Irish writer and journalist; b. 27 June 1950, Belfast, Northern Ireland; m. Maura Magill 1970; one s. one d. *Education:* St Mary's Grammar School, Belfast, Queen's Univ., Belfast. *Career:* journalist, Night Ed., Irish Times, Dublin 1972–2002; mem. Nat. Union of Journalists, Howth Singing Circle and Goilin Club, Dublin. *Publications:* A Kind of Homecoming 1994, A Stone of the Heart 1995, The Sad Case of Harpo Higgins 1996, Murder at Piper's Gut 1997, The Faloorie Man 1999, Stella's Story 2002, Hotel Las Flores 2005, The Beach Bar 2006, The Book Club (writing as Kate McCabe) 2007, Forever Friends (as Kate McCabe) 2008, Sleep Softly, Baby (as Carol Magill) 2008. *Address:* c/o Poolbeg Press, Baldoyle, Dublin 13, Ireland.

McELROY, Colleen Johnson, BS, MS, PhD; American academic, poet and writer; b. 30 Oct. 1935, St Louis, Mo.; m. (divorced); one s. one d. *Education:* Kansas State University, University of Washington, Seattle. *Career:* Ed., Dark Waters, 1973–79; Prof., University of Washington, Seattle, 1973–. *Publications:* Music From Home, 1976; The Halls of Montezuma, 1979; The New Voice, 1979; Winters Without Snow, 1979; Lie and Say You Love Me, 1981; Queen of the Ebony Isles, 1984; Jesus and Fat Tuesday, 1987; What Madness Brought Me Here, 1990; contributions: various journals. *Address:* c/o Creative Writing Program, Department of English, University of Washington, Seattle, WA 98195, USA.

McELROY, Joseph Prince, BA, MA, PhD; American writer; b. 21 Aug. 1930, New York, NY. *Education:* Williams College, Columbia University. *Publications:* A Smuggler's Bible, 1966; Hind's Kidnap, 1969; Ancient History, 1971; Lookout Cartridge, 1974; Plus, 1977; Ship Rock, 1980; Women and Men, 1987; Actress in the House, 2003. *Address:* c/o Georges Borchardt, 136 E 57th Street, New York, NY 10022, USA.

McELROY, Lee (see Kelton, Elmer Stephen)

MACER-STORY, Eugenia, (Zephyr Fidelis), BS, MFA; American writer, dramatist and poet; b. 20 Jan. 1945, Minneapolis, Minn.; m. Leon A. Story 1970 (divorced 1975); one s. *Education:* Northwestern Univ., Columbia Univ. *Career:* mem. Dramatists' Guild, US Psychotronics Asscn, Poet's House, New York, American Soc. for Psychical Research. *Plays:* Meister Hemmelin 1994, Double or Nothing 1994, Radish 1995, Conquest of the Asteroids 1996, Mister Shooting Star 1997, Wild Dog Casino 1998, Holy Dragonet 1998–99, Old Gaffer from Boise 2000, Redecoration According to Currier 2000, Ars Chronicon Sylvestre 2002, Just 45 Minutes from Paradise 2004, Honky Tonk Tornado Warnings 2005, The Liberation of Little Lulu or Martin Luther King Detained in Limbo 2006, The Poison Man 2007. *Publications:* Congratulations: The UFO Reality 1978, Angels of Time: Astrological Magic 1981, Du Fu Man Chu Meets the Lonesome Cowboy: Sorcery and the UFO Experience 1991, Legacy of Daedalus 1995, Cattle Bones and Coke Machines (anthology) 1995, The Dark Frontier 1997, Crossing Jungle River (poems) 1998, Troll: Other Interdimensional Invasions (short stories) 2000, Vanishing Questions (poems) 2000, Carrying Thunder 2002, Doing Business in the Adrondocks (metaphysical travelogue) 2002, The Merry Piper's Hollow Hills (chapbook) 2004, Struck by Green Lightning, aka Project Midas (novel) 2004, The Sin of Love (novel) 2005, Theatre Cosmos (poetry) 2006, Lucky Hurricane (novel) 2006, On Nada (novel) 2006, Fast Luck Botanica (poetry) 2007; contrib. to numerous publications. *Honours:* Shubert Fellowship 1968. *Address:* Magick Mirror Communications, PO Box 741, JAF Bldg, New York, NY 10116, USA. *Telephone:* (212) 355-2111 (office); (845) 679-7968 (home). *E-mail:* magickmirror@aol.com (office); e.macer-story@att.net (home).

McEWAN, Ian Russell, CBE, MA, FRSL; British writer; b. 21 June 1948, Aldershot, Hants.; s. of the late David McEwan and Rose Moore; m. 1st Penny Allen 1982 (divorced 1995); two s. and two step-d.; m. 2nd Annalena McAfee 1997. *Education:* Woolverstone Hall, Univs of Sussex and E Anglia. *Screenplays:* The Imitation Game & Other Plays 1981, The Ploughman's Lunch 1985, Sour Sweet 1989. *Publications:* novels: The Cement Garden 1978, The Comfort of Strangers 1981, Rose Blanche (juvenile) 1985, The Child in Time (Whitbread Novel of the Year 1987, Prix Fémina Etranger 1993) 1987, The Innocent 1989, Black Dogs 1992, The Daydreamer (juvenile) 1994, Enduring Love 1997, Amsterdam (Booker Prize for Fiction 1998) 1998, Atonement (WHSmith Literary Award 2002, Nat. Book Critics Circle Fiction Award 2002, Los Angeles Times Prize for Fiction 2003, Santiago Prize for the European Novel 2004) 2001, Saturday (James Tait Black Memorial Prize 2006) 2005, On Chesil Beach (British Book Award for Book of the Year 2008) 2007, Solar (Bollinger Everyman Wodehouse Prize for Comic Fiction) 2010, Sweet Tooth 2012; short stories: First Love, Last Rites (Somerset Maugham Award 1976) 1975, In Between the Sheets 1978; librettos: Or Shall We Die? (oratorio) 1983, For You (opera) 2008. *Leisure interest:* hiking. *Honours:* Hon. Fellow American Acad. of Arts and Sciences 1997; Hon. DPhil (Sussex) 1989, (E Anglia) 1993, (London) 1998; Primo Letterario, Prato 1982, Shakespeare Prize, Germany 1999, British Book Award for Author of the Year 2008, Jerusalem Prize 2011. *Address:* c/o Jonathan Cape, Random Century House, 20 Vauxhall Bridge Road, London, SW1V 2SA, England. *Website:* www.ianmcewan.com.

McFADDEN, David William; Canadian poet and writer; b. 11 Oct. 1940, Hamilton, Ont. *Career:* began his career as proofreader, Hamilton Spectator newspaper, later became a reporter; full-time writer 1976–; founder Mountain literary magazine; writer-in-residence Simon Fraser Univ. 1979; instructor, writing program, David Thompson Univ. Centre, Nelson, BC 1979–82. *Publications:* poetry: The Poem Poem 1967, Letters from the Earth to the Earth 1968, Poems Worth Knowing 1971, Intense Pleasure 1972, The Ova Yogas 1972, The Poet's Progress 1977, The Saladmaker 1977, I Don't Know 1978, A Knight in Dried Plums 1978, On the Road Again 1978, A New Romance 1979, My Body Was Eaten By Dogs 1981, Country of the Open Heart 1982, Three Stories and Ten Poems 1982, A Pair of Baby Lambs 1983, The Art of Darkness 1984, Gypsy Guitar 1987, Anonymity Suite 1992, There'll Be Another 1995, The Death of Greg Curnoe 1995, Five Star Planet 2002, Why Are You So Sad? 2007; fiction: The Great Canadian Sonnet 1974, Animal Spirits 1983, Canadian Sunset 1986; travel writing: A Trip Around Lake Huron 1980, A Trip Around Lake Erie 1980, A Trip Around Lake Ontario 1988, An Innocent in Ireland 1995, Great Lakes Suite 1997, An Innocent in Scotland 1999. *Literary Agent:* c/o The Helen Heller Agency Inc., 4-216 Heath Street West, Toronto, ON M5P 1N7, Canada. *Telephone:* (416) 489-0396. *Website:* www.helenhelleragency.com.

McFARLAND, Ronald (Ron) Earl, AA, BA, MA, PhD; American academic, poet and writer; *Professor of English, University of Idaho*; b. 22 Sept. 1942, Bellaire, OH; s. of Earl A. McFarland and Mary Maxine Stullenburger McFarland; m. 1st Elsie Roseland Watson 1966 (divorced 2002); one s. two d.; m. 2nd Georgia Tiffany 2003. *Education:* Brevard Junior Coll., Florida State Univ., Univ. of Illinois. *Career:* Teaching Asst, Florida State Univ. 1964–65, Univ. of Illinois 1967–70; Instructor, Sam Houston State Coll. 1965–67; Asst Prof., Assoc. Prof., Univ. of Idaho 1970–79, Prof. of English 1979–; Idaho State Writer-in-Residence 1984–85; Exchange Prof., Ohio Univ. 1985–86; mem. Acad. of American Poets, Hemingway Society, Pacific Northwest American Studies Asscn. *Publications:* poetry: Certain Women 1977, Composting at Forty 1984, The Haunting Familiarity of Things 1993, Stranger in Town 2000, The Hemingway Poems 2000, The Mad Waitress Poems 2000, Ballygloves 2000, Ron McFarland: Greatest Hits, 1946–2002 2003, At the Ballpark 2006; fiction: Catching First Light (short stories) 2001; non-fiction: The Villanelle: Evolution of a Poetic Form 1988, David Wagoner 1989, Norman Maclean 1993, Tess Gallagher 1995, The World of David Wagoner 1997, Understanding James Welch 2000, William Kittredge 2002, Confessions of a Night Librarian and Other Embarrassments 2005, The Rockies in First Person 2008, The Long Life of Evangeline 2009; editor: Eight Idaho Poets 1979, James Welch 1987, Norman Maclean (with Hugh Nichols) 1988, Idaho's Poetry: A Centennial Anthology (with William Studebaker) 1988, Deep Down Things: Poems of the Inland Pacific Northwest (with Franz Schneider and Kornel Skovajsa) 1990; contributions: scholarly books and journals, poetry anthologies, reviews, quarterlies and periodicals. *Honours:* National Endowment for the Arts Grant 1978, Asscn for the Humanities in Idaho Grant 1983, Burlington-Northern Faculty Achievement Award 1990, Alumni Award for Faculty Excellence 1991, Distinguished Alumnus, Brevard Community Coll. 1996, Univ. of Idaho Faculty Award for Creative Excellence 2002. *Address:* Department of English, University of Idaho, Moscow, ID 83844-1102 (office); 932 East 7th Street, Moscow, ID 83843, USA (home). *Telephone:* (208) 885-6937 (office); (208) 882-2220 (home). *Fax:* (208) 885-5944 (office). *E-mail:* ronmcf@uidaho.edu (office).

MacFARLANE, Robert; British writer and academic; b. 1976, Nottingham. *Education:* Nottingham High School, Emmanuel Coll., Cambridge. *Career:* Fellow, Emmanuel Coll., Cambridge. *Publications:* Mountains of the Mind: A History of a Fascination (Guardian First Book Award, Somerset Maugham Award 2004) 2003, Wild Eyed 2005, The Wild Places 2007; contrib. to The Sunday Times, The Observer, TLS, The Spectator, Evening Standard. *Literary Agent:* Toby Eady Associates Ltd, Third Floor, 9 Orme Court, London, W2 4RL, England. *Telephone:* (20) 7792-0092. *Fax:* (20) 7792-0879. *E-mail:* toby@tobyeady.demon.co.uk. *Website:* www.tobyeadyassociates.co.uk. *Address:* c/o Emmanuel College, University of Cambridge, St Andrew's Street, Cambridge, CB2 3AP, England.

McFEELY, William Shield, BA, MA, PhD; American academic and writer; b. 25 Sept. 1930, New York, NY; m. Mary Drake 1952; one s. two d. *Education:* Amherst College, Yale University. *Career:* Asst Prof., 1966–69, Assoc. Prof., 1969–70, Yale University; Prof. of History, 1970–80, Rodman Prof. of History, 1980–82, Andrew W. Mellon Prof. in the Humanities, 1982–86, Mount Holyoke College; Visiting Prof., University College London, 1978–79, Amherst College, 1980–81; Visiting Prof., 1984–85, John J. McCloy Prof., 1988–89, University of Massachusetts; Richard B. Russell Prof. of American History, 1986–94, Abraham Baldwin Prof. of the Humanities, 1994–, University of Georgia; mem. American Historical Asscn; Authors' Guild; Century Asscn; Organization of American Historians; PEN; Southern Historical Asscn. *Publications:* Yankee Stepfather: General O. O. Howard and the Freedmen, 1968; The Black Man in the Land of Equality (with Thomas J. Ladenburg), 1969; Grant: A Biography, 1981; Ulysses S. Grant: Memoirs and Selected Letters 1839–1865 (ed. with Mary Drake McFeely), 1990; Frederick Douglass, 1991; Sapelo's People: A Long Walk into Freedom, 1994, Portrait: A Life of Thomas Eakins (biog.) 2006. *Honours:* Morse Fellow, 1968–69; Fellow, ACLS,

1974–75; Pulitzer Prize in Biography, 1982; Francis Parkman Prize, 1982; Guggenheim Fellowship, 1982–83; National Endowment for the Humanities Grant, 1986–87; Avery O. Craven Award, 1992; Lincoln Prize, 1992.

McGARRY, Jean, BA, MA; American writer and academic; *Professor of Fiction, Johns Hopkins University*; b. 18 June 1952, Providence, RI; m. Wayne Biddle. *Education:* Harvard Univ., Johns Hopkins Univ. *Career:* Prof. of Fiction, Johns Hopkins Univ.; academic cand., Baltimore-Washington Psychoanalytic Inst. *Publications:* Airs of Providence 1985, The Very Rich Hours 1987, The Courage of Girls 1992, Gallagher's Travels 1995, Home at Last 1998, Dream Date 2001, A Bad and Stupid Girl 2006, Ocean State 2010; contribs to Yale Review, Boulevard, Southern Review, Southwest Review, Sulfur, New Orleans Review. *Honours:* Short Fiction Prize, Southern Review-Louisiana State Univ. 1985, Nat. Endowment for the Arts grant 1987, Univ. of Michigan Fiction Prize 2005. *Address:* The Writing Seminars, Johns Hopkins University, Baltimore, MD 21218, USA (office). *E-mail:* mcgarry@jhu.edu (office).

McGINN, Bernard John, BA, STL, PhD; American academic, writer, translator and editor; *Naomi Shenstone Donnelley Professor Emeritus, Divinity School, University of Chicago*; b. 19 Aug. 1937, Yonkers, NY; m. Patricia Ferris 1971; two s. *Education:* St Joseph's Seminary and Coll., Yonkers, NY, Pontifical Gregorian Univ., Rome, Columbia Univ., Univ. of Munich, Brandeis Univ. *Career:* Lecturer, Regis Coll., Weston, Mass 1966–67; Instructor, Catholic Univ. of America, Washington, DC 1968–69; Instructor, Divinity School, Univ. of Chicago1969–70, Asst Prof. 1970–75, Assoc. Prof. 1975–78, Prof. of Historical Theology and the History of Christianity 1978–, Naomi Shenstone Donnelley Prof. 1992–2003, Emer. 2003–; mem. American Soc. of Church History (Pres. 1995–), Eckhart Soc., Int. Soc. for the Promotion of Eriugenean Studies (Pres.); Fellow, Medieval Acad. of America 1994–, Nat. Humanities Centre 1999–2000, American Acad. of Arts and Sciences 2002–; Research Fellow, Inst. for Advanced Studies, Hebrew Univ., Jerusalem 1988–89, Inst. for Ecumenical and Cultural Research, St John's Univ. 1992. *Publications:* The Golden Chain: A Study in the Theological Anthropology of Isaac of Stella 1972, The Crusades 1973, Visions of the End: Apocalyptic Traditions in the Middle Ages 1979, The Calabrian Abbot: Joachim of Fiore in the History of Western Thought 1985, The Presence of God: A History of Christian Mysticism, 4 vols 1991, 1994, 1998, 2007, Apocalypticism in the Western Tradition 1994, Antichrist: Two Thousand Years of the Human Fascination with Evil 1994; translator: Apocalyptic Spirituality 1979, Meister Eckhart: The Essential Sermons, Commentaries, Treatises and Defense (with Edmund Colledge) 1981, Meister Eckhart: Teacher and Preacher (with Frank Tobin and Elvira Borgstadt) 1986; editor: Three Treatises on Man: A Cistercian Anthropology 1977, Christian Spirituality: Origins to the Twelfth Century (with John Meyendorff and Jean Leclercq) 1985, Christian Spirituality: High Middle Ages and Reformation (with Jill Raitt and John Meyendorff) 1987, Mystical Union and Monotheistic Faith: An Ecumenical Doctrine (with Moshe Idel) 1989, God and Creation: An Ecumenical Symposium (with David B. Burrell) 1990, The Apocalypse in the Middle Ages (with Richard K. Emmerson) 1992, Meister Eckhart and the Beguine Mystics: Hadewijch of Brabant, Mechthild of Magdeburg, and Marguerite Porete 1994, Eriugena: East and West: Papers of the Eighth International Colloquium of the Society for the Promotion of Eriugenean Studies: Chicago and Notre Dame, 18–20 October 1991 (with Willemiem Otten) 1994, The Encyclopedia of Apocalypticism, Vol. 2: Apocalypticism in Western History and Cultures 1998; contrib. articles in many books and journals. *Honours:* Fulbright-Hays Research Fellowship 1967–68, Phi Beta Kappa Lecturer 2005–06. *Address:* 5701 South Kenwood, Chicago, IL 60637, USA (home). *Fax:* (773) 288-7911 (home).

McGINN, Colin, MA, BPhil; British academic; *Professor, Department of Philosophy, University of Miami*; b. 10 March 1950, s. of Joseph McGinn and June McGinn; one s. *Education:* Manchester and Oxford Univs. *Career:* lecturer, Univ. Coll. London 1974–85; Wilde Reader in Mental Philosophy, Oxford Univ. 1985–90; Prof., Rutgers Univ., USA 1990–2005, Univ. of Miami 2005–. *Publications:* The Character of Mind 1981, The Subjective View 1982, Wittgenstein on Meaning 1984, Mental Content 1989, The Problem of Consciousness 1991, The Space Trap 1992, Moral Literacy 1992, The Space Trap 1992, Problems in Philosophy 1993, Minds and Bodies: Philosophers and their Ideas 1997, Ethics, Evil and Fiction 1997, Knowledge and Reality 1998, The Mysterious Flame 1999, Logical Properties 2000, The Making of a Philosopher 2002, Consciousness and its Objects 2004, Mindsight: Image, Dream, Meaning 2004, The Power of Movies 2005, Shakespeare's Philosophy 2006, Mindfucking 2008. *Honours:* John Locke Prize 1973. *Address:* Department of Philosophy, University of Miami, PO Box 248054, Coral Gables, FL 33124-4670 (office); 270 West End Avenue, Apt 9E, New York, NY 10023, USA. *Telephone:* (305) 284-4757 (office). *E-mail:* cmcginn@mail.as.miami.edu (office). *Website:* www.as.miami.edu/phi (office); www.colinmcginnblog.com (home).

McGINNISS, Joe, BS; American writer; b. 9 Dec. 1942, New York, NY. *Education:* Holy Cross College. *Career:* newspaper reporter 1964–68. *Publications:* The Selling of the President 1968, The Dream Team 1972, Heroes 1976, Going to Extremes 1980, Fatal Vision 1983, Blind Faith 1989, Cruel Doubt 1991, The Last Brother 1993, The Miracle of Castel di Sangro 1999, The Big Horse 2004, Never Enough 2007. *Address:* c/o Simon and Schuster Publicity Department, Simon and Schuster, Inc., 1230 Avenue of the Americas, NY 10020, USA (office). *Website:* www.simonsays.com (office).

McGONIGAL, James, MA, MPhil, PhD, DPSE; British educator and poet; *Professor Emeritus, University of Glasgow*; b. 20 May 1947, Dumfries, Scotland; m. Mary Alexander 1970; one s. three d. *Education:* Univ. of Glasgow, Diploma in Professional Studies in Educ. *Career:* high school English teacher 1971–84; coll. lecturer 1985–91; Head, Dept of Language and Literature, St Andrew's Coll. of Educ., Glasgow 1992–2003; Prof. of English in Educ., Univ. of Glasgow 2004–09, Prof. Emer. 2009–; Ed. SCROLL (Scottish Cultural Review of Language and Literature) Rodopi, Amsterdam and New York; Fellow, Asscn for Scottish Literary Studies 2010. *Publications:* A Sort of Hot Scotland: New Writing Scotland 12 (with A. L. Kennedy) 1994, Last Things First: New Writing Scotland 13 (with A. L. Kennedy) 1995, Sons of Ezra: British Poets and Ezra Pound (with M. Alexander) 1995, Full Strength Angels: New Writing Scotland 14 (with K. Jamie) 1996, Driven Home: Selected Poems 1998, Across the Water: 'Irishness' in Contemporary Scottish Literature (co-ed.) 2000, Scottish Religious Poems: From Columba to the Present (co-ed.) 2000, The Star You Steer By: Basil Bunting and British Modernism (co-ed.) 2000, Passage/An Pasaíste: Poems in Scots and Irish 2004, Ethically Speaking: voice and values in modern Scottish writing (co-ed.) 2006, Learning to Read a New Culture (with E. Arizpe) 2008, Beyond the Last Dragon: A Life of Edwin Morgan 2010, Cloud Pibroch (Michael Marks Poetry Award 2010) 2010. *Address:* School of Education, St Andrew's Building, University of Glasgow, 11 Eldon Street, Glasgow, G3 6NH, Scotland (office). *E-mail:* james.mcgonigal@glasgow.ac.uk (office).

McGOUGH, Roger Joseph, CBE, MA, DLitt, FRSL; British poet and children's writer; b. 9 Nov. 1937, Liverpool; s. of Roger McGough and Mary McGarry; m. 1st Thelma Monaghan 1970 (divorced 1980); m. 2nd Hilary Clough 1986; three s. one d. *Education:* St Mary's Coll., Liverpool, Hull Univ. *Career:* Poetry Fellow Univ. of Loughborough 1973–75; writer-in-residence Western Australia Coll. of Educ., Perth 1986, Univ. of Hamburg 1994; Vice-Pres. The Poetry Society 1996–2011 (mem. Exec. Council 1989–93), Pres. 2012–; Fellow John Moores Univ. 1999; Trustee Chelsea Arts Club 1987–, fmr Chair.; Freeman City of Liverpool 2001. *Music:* wrote and performed Top Twenty hits Lily the Pink and Thank U Very Much 1968–69. *Plays include:* The Sound Collector and My Dad's a Fire-eater (for children); wrote lyrics for Broadway production of The Wind in the Willows 1984; adaptations of Molière's Tartuffe and The Hypochondriac. *Plays for radio include:* Summer with Monika, FX, Walking the Dog. *Television:* Kurt, Mungo, B. P. and Me (Thames Television) 1985, The Elements (Channel 4) (Royal Television Soc. Award) 1993. *Art installation:* Liverpool Doors, Museum of Liverpool 2012. *Publications:* The Mersey Sound (with Brian Patten and Adrian Henri) 1967, Watchwords 1969, After the Merrymaking 1971, Out of Sequence 1972, Gig 1972, Sporting Relations 1974, In the Glassroom 1976, Summer with Monika 1978, Holiday on Death Row 1979, Unlucky for Some 1981, Waving at Trains 1982, Melting into the Foreground 1986, Blazing Fruit: Selected Poems 1967–1987 1989, You at the Back 1991, Defying Gravity 1992, The Spotted Unicorn 1998, The Way Things Are 1999, Everyday Eclipses 2002, Collected Poems of Roger McGough 2003, Said and Done (memoir) 2005, Selected Poems 2006, That Awkward Age 2009, As Far As I Know 2012; for children: Mr Noselighter 1977, The Great Smile Robbery 1982, Sky in the Pie 1983, The Stowaways 1986, Noah's Ark 1986, Nailing the Shadow 1987, An Imaginary Menagerie 1988, Helen Highwater 1989, Counting by Numbers 1989, Pillow Talk 1990, The Lighthouse That Ran Away 1991, My Dad's a Fire-eater 1992, Another Custard Pie 1993, Lucky 1993, Stinkers Ahoy! 1995, The Magic Fountain 1995, The Kite and Caitlin 1996, Bad Bad Cats 1997, Until I Met Dudley 1998, Good Enough to Eat 2002, Moonthief 2002, The Bees' Knees 2002, Dotty Inventions 2002, What On Earth Can It Be? 2003; editor: Strictly Private 1981, The Kingfisher Book of Comic Verse 1986, The Kingfisher Books of Poems About Love 1997, The Ring of Words (anthology) 1998, Wicked Poems 2002, All the Best 2002, Sensational (anthology) 2004. *Honours:* Hon. Prof. Thames Valley Univ. 1993; Hon. MA (Nene Coll.) 1998, Hon. DLitt (Hull Univ.) 2004, (Univ. of Surrey) 2006; Signal Award 1984, 1998, BAFTA Awards 1984, 1992, Cholmondeley Award 1998, Centre for Literacy in Primary Educ. Award for Best Book of Poetry for Children 2004, 2005. *Literary Agent:* United Agents, 12–26 Lexington Street, London, W1F 0LE, England. *Telephone:* (20) 3214-0800. *Fax:* (20) 3214-0801. *E-mail:* info@unitedagents.co.uk. *Website:* unitedagents.co.uk. *E-mail:* personal@rogermcgough.org.uk (office). *Website:* www.rogermcgough.org.uk.

McGOVERN, Ann, BA; American writer, poet, collage artist and lecturer; b. 25 May 1930, New York, NY; m. Martin L. Scheiner 1970 (died 1992); three s. one d. *Education:* Univ. of New Mexico. *Career:* Publr The Privileged Traveler 1986–90; mem. Explorers Club, PEN, Authors' Guild, Soc. of Children's Book Writers, Women's Forum. *Publications include:* If You Lived in Colonial Times 1964, Too Much Noise 1967, Stone Soup 1968, The Secret Soldier 1975, Sharks 1976, Shark Lady, The Adventures of Eugenie Clark 1978, Playing with Penguins and Other Adventures in Antarctica 1994, Lady in the Box 1997, Adventures of the Shark Lady Eugenie Clark Around the World 1998; contrib. to Signature, Saturday Review, poetry in various literary magazines. *Honours:* Nat. Science Teachers Asscn Outstanding Science Books 1976, 1979, 1984, 1993, Scholastic Publishing Inc. Author of the Year 1978, Cuffie Award 1998, First Prize, Artella's Poetry Contest.

MacGOWAN, Christopher John, BA, MA, PhD; British writer, editor and academic; *Professor of English, College of William and Mary*; b. 6 Aug. 1948, London, England; m. Catherine Levesque 1988. *Education:* King's Coll., Cambridge, Princeton Univ., USA. *Career:* Teaching Asst, Pennsylvania State

Univ. 1976–77; Research Asst, The Writings of Henry D. Thoreau 1981–83; Asst Prof., Coll. of William and Mary, Williamsburg, Va 1984–90, Assoc. Prof. 1990–96, Prof. 1996–, also currently Assoc. Chair of English Dept; mem. Modern Language Asscn, William Carlos Williams Soc. (Pres. 1989–91). *Publications:* William Carlos Williams' Early Poetry: The Visual Arts Background 1984, The Collected Poems of William Carlos Williams, Vol. I 1909–1939 (co-ed.) 1986, Vol. II 1939–1962 (ed.) 1988, William Carlos Williams' Paterson (ed.) 1992, The Letters of Denise Levertov and William Carlos Williams (ed.) 1998, Poetry for Young People: William Carlos Williams (ed.), Twentieth-Century American Poetry 2003, Twentieth Century American Fiction 2011; contrib. to reference works and journals. *Honours:* King's Coll., Cambridge James Prize 1976, 1977, Princeton Univ. Graduate Fellowship 1977–81, Coll. of William and Mary Summer Grants 1985, 1987, 1989, Nat. Endowment for the Humanities Summer Stipend 1986, Fellowship 1990–91. *Address:* Tyler Hall 318C, Department of English, College of William and Mary, Williamsburg, VA 23187, USA (office). *E-mail:* cjmacg@wm.edu (office). *Website:* www.wm.edu/as/english (office).

McGOWAN, Margaret Mary, CBE, PhD, FBA; British professor of French; *Research Professor of French, University of Sussex*; b. 21 Dec. 1931, d. of George McGowan and Elizabeth McGowan; m. Sydney Anglo 1964. *Education:* Stamford High School for Girls, Univs of Reading and Strasbourg, France. *Career:* Lecturer, Univ. of Glasgow 1957–64, Univ. of Sussex 1964–74, Research Prof. of French 1974–, Dean 1979–82, Pro-Vice-Chancellor (Arts and Social Studies) 1982–87, Sr Pro-Vice-Chancellor 1989–96; fmr Vice-Pres. British Acad., fmr Chair. Pictures, Portraits and Decoration Cttee. *Publications:* L'Art du ballet de cour 1963, Montaigne's Deceits 1974, Louis XIII's Ballets 1986, Ideal Forms in the Age of Ronsard 1985, Moy qui me voy 1989, The Vision of Rome in Late Renaissance France 2000, Dance in the Renaissance, European Fashion, French Obsession (Wolfson History Prize) 2008. *Honours:* Freedom of the City of Tours, France 1982; Hon. DLitt (Sussex) 1998. *Address:* Arts A007 (School Office), University of Sussex, Falmer, Brighton, BN1 9SH, England (office).

McGRATH, Alister Edgar, BA, BD, MA, DD, DPhil, FRSA; British theologian, academic and writer; *Professor of Theology, Ministry and Education, King's College London*; b. 23 Jan. 1953, Belfast, Northern Ireland; m. Joanna Ruth Collicutt 1980; one s. one d. *Education:* Univ. of Oxford. *Career:* Curate, St Leonard's Parish Church, Wollaton, Nottingham 1980–83; Lecturer in Historical and Systematic Theology, Wycliffe Hall, Oxford 1983–95, Prin. 1995–2004; mem. Faculty of Theology, Univ. of Oxford 1983–2008, Univ. Research Lecturer in Theology 1993–99, Prof. of Historical Theology 1999–2008; Research Prof. of Systematic Theology, Regent Coll., Vancouver, BC, Canada 1993–97; Prof. of Theology, Ministry and Educ., King's Coll., London 2008–. *Publications:* Luther's Theology of the Cross 1985, Iustitia Dei: A History of the Christian Doctrine of Justification 1986, The Intellectual Origins of the European Reformation 1987, Reformation Thought: An Introduction 1988, Explaining Your Faith Without Losing Your Friends 1989, revised edn as Explaining Your Faith 1996, A Life of John Calvin 1990, The Genesis of Doctrine 1990, Making Sense of the Cross 1992, What Was God Doing on the Cross? 1992, The Dilemna of Self-Esteem: The Cross and Christian Confidence 1992, Suffering 1992, Understanding Doctrine: Its Relevance and Purpose for Today 1992, The Blackwell Encyclopedia of Modern Christian Thought (ed.) 1993, The Renewal of Anglicanism 1993, Intellectuals Don't Need God and Other Modern Myths: Building Bridges to Faith Through Apologetics 1993, The Making of Modern German Christology, 1750–1990 1994, Spirituality in an Age of Change: Rediscovering the Spirit of the Reformers 1994, Christian Theology: An Introduction 1994, How Shall We Reach Them? (with Michael Green) 1995, Evangelicalism and the Future of Christianity 1995, Beyond the Quiet Time: Practical Evangelical Spirituality 1995, Suffering and God 1995, The Christian Theology Reader (ed.) 1995, A Passion for Truth: The Intellectual Coherence of Evangelicalism 1996, An Introduction to Christianity 1997, The NIV Bible Companion: A Basic Commentary on the Old and New Testaments 1997, J. I. Packer: A Biography (UK edn as To Know and Serve God) 1997, The Foundations of Dialogue in Science and Religion 1998, Historical Theology: An Introduction to the History of Christian Thought 1998, 'I Believe': Exploring the Apostles' Creed 1998, Christian Spirituality: An Introduction 1999, The Unknown God: Searching for Spiritual Fulfilment 1999, Science and Religion: An Introduction 1999, The Hodder Dictionary of Bible Themes (gen. ed.) 1999, The NIV Thematic Reference Bible (gen. ed.) 1999, Christian Literature: An Anthology (ed.) 2000, The J. I. Packer Collection (ed.) 2000, The Journey: A Pilgrim in the Lands of the Spirit 2000, In the Beginning: The Story of the King James Bible 2001, The Re-enchantment of Nature: Science, Religion and the Human Sense of Wonder 2003, The Twilight of Atheism 2004, Dawkins' God 2004, The Dawkins Delusion? (with Joanna Collicutt McGrath) 2007, Theology: The Basics 2011. *Address:* Harris Manchester College, Oxford OX1 3TD, England (office).

McGRATH, Patrick, BA; British writer; b. 7 Feb. 1950, London, England; m. Maria Aitken. *Education:* Univ. of London and Simon Fraser Univ., Burnaby, BC. *Career:* Managing Ed., Speech Technology magazine 1982–87. *Publications:* The Lewis and Clark Expedition 1985, Blood and Water and Other Tales (short story collection) 1988, The Grotesque (novel) 1989, New York Life or, Friends and Others 1990, Spider (novel and screenplay) 1990, Dr Haggard's Disease (novel) 1993, Asylum (novel) 1996, Martha Peake: A Novel of the Revolution (novel) 2000, Port Mungo (novel) 2004, Ghost Town: Tales of Manhattan Then and Now (non-fiction) 2005, Trauma (novel) 2008; contrib. to periodicals. *Literary Agent:* c/o Deborah Rogers, Rogers, Coleridge & White, 20 Powis Mews, London, W11 1JN, England. *Telephone:* (20) 7221-3717. *Fax:* (20) 7229-9084.

MacGREGOR, David Roy, BA, MA, ARIBA, FRHistS; British writer; b. 26 Aug. 1925, London, England; m. Patricia Margaret Aline Purcell-Gilpin 1962. *Education:* Trinity College, Cambridge, Hammersmith School of Building. *Career:* mem. Soc. of Nautical Research (council mem. 1959–63, 1965–69, 1974–77, 1980–85, hon. vice-pres. 1985), Maritime Trust. *Publications:* The Tea Clippers, 1952; The China Bird, 1961; Fast Sailing Ships 1775–1875, 1973; Clipper Ships, 1977; Merchant Sailing Ships 1775–1815, 1980; Merchant Sailing Ships 1815–1850, 1984; Merchant Sailing Ships 1858–1875, 1984. Contributions: Mariner's Mirror; Journal of Nautical Archaeology. *Honours:* Gold Medal, Daily Express 1973. *Address:* 99 Lonsdale Road, London SW13 9DA, England.

McGREGOR, Iona, BA; British writer; b. 7 Feb. 1929, Aldershot, England. *Education:* University of Bristol. *Career:* mem. Scottish PEN. *Publications:* Fiction: Death Wore a Diadem, 1989; Alice in Shadowtime, 1992. Children's Fiction: An Edinburgh Reel, 1968; The Popinjay, 1969; The Burning Hill, 1970; The Tree of Liberty, 1972; The Snake and the Olive, 1974. Non-Fiction: Edinburgh and Eastern Lowlands, 1979; Wallace and Bruce, 1986; Importance of Being Earnest, 1987; Huckleberry Finn, 1988. *Honours:* Writer's Bursary, Scottish Arts Council, 1989.

McGREGOR, Jon, BSc; British novelist and short story writer; b. Feb. 1976, Bermuda; m. *Education:* Univ. of Bradford. *Publications:* novels: If Nobody Speaks of Remarkable Things (Betty Trask Award, Somerset Maugham Award) 2002, So Many Ways To Begin 2006, Even the Dogs 2010; short story collections: Cinema 100 1998, Everyone Is Fine, And Lying To Everyone Else 1999; short stories: Jonas, What the Sky Sees 2002, The First Punch 2004, The First Thing That Happened 2004, Which Reminded Her, Later 2007, If It Keeps On Raining (BBC Nat. Short Story Award) 2010, Even the Dogs 2010 (International Impac Dublin Literary Award 2012); contrib. stories/articles to Granta, Guardian Weekend and Sunday Times magazines, Conjunctions, Observer. *Honours:* British Antarctic Survey/Arts Council England Artists and Writers Fellowship 2004. *Literary Agent:* c/o Tracy Bohan, Wylie Agency, 17 Bedford Square, London, WC1B 3JA, England. *E-mail:* tbohan@wylieagency.co.uk. *Website:* www.wylieagency.co.uk. *Address:* c/o Bloomsbury Publishing, 36 Soho Square, London, W1D 3QY, England (office). *Website:* www.jonmcgregor.com.

McGUANE, Thomas Francis, III, BA, MFA; American writer; b. 11 Dec. 1939, Wyandotte, MI; m. 1st Portia Rebecca Crockett 1962 (divorced 1975); one s.; m. 2nd Margot Kidder 1976 (divorced 1977); one d.; m. 3rd Laurie Buffett 1977; one step-d. one d. *Education:* Univ. of Michigan, Olivet Coll., Michigan State Univ., Yale Univ., Stanford Univ. *Career:* mem. American Acad. of Arts and Letters. *Publications include:* The Sporting Club 1969, The Bushwacked Piano 1971, Ninety-Two in the Shade 1973, Panama 1977, An Outside Chance: Essays on Sports (revised edn as An Outside Chance: Classic and New Essays on Sports) 1980, Nobody's Angel 1982, In the Crazies: Book and Portfolio 1984, Something to Be Desired 1984, To Skin a Cat 1986, Silent Seasons: Twenty-One Fishing Stories 1988, Keep the Change 1989, Nothing but Blue Skies 1992, Some Horses 1999, Upstream: Fly Fishing in the American Northwest 1999, The Longest Silence 2000, The Cadence of Grass 2002, Horses 2005, Gallatin Canyon 2006, Driving on the Rim 2010. *Honours:* Wallace Stegner Fellowship Stanford Univ. 1966–67, Dr hc (Montana State Univ.) 1993, (Rocky Mountain Coll.) 1995; American Acad. of Arts and Letters Richard and Hinda Rosenthal Foundation Award 1971. *Address:* PO Box 25, McLeod, MT 59052-0025, USA (home). *Website:* tommcguane.com.

McGUCKIAN, Medbh, BA, MA; Northern Irish poet and teacher; b. 12 Aug. 1950, Belfast; m. John McGuckian 1977; three s. one d. *Education:* Queen's Univ., Belfast. *Career:* teacher, Dominican Convent, Fortwilliam Park, Belfast 1974; instructor, St Patrick's Coll., Knock, Belfast 1975–; writer-in-residence, Queen's Univ., Belfast 1986–88. *Publications:* poetry: Single Ladies: Sixteen Poems 1980, Portrait of Joanna 1980, Trio Poetry (with Damian Gorman and Douglas Marshall) 1981, The Flower Master 1982, The Greenhouse 1983, Venus and the Rain 1984, The Big Striped Golfing Umbrella: Poems by Young People from Northern Ireland (ed.) 1985, On Ballycastle Beach 1988, Two Women, Two Shores 1989, Marconi's Cottage 1991, The Flower Master and Other Poems 1993, Captain Lavender 1994, Drawing Ballerinas 2001, The Face of the Earth 2004. *Honours:* Nat. Poetry Competition Prize 1979, Eric Gregory Award 1980, Rooney Prize 1982, Ireland Arts Council Award 1982, Alice Hunt Bartlett Award 1983, Cheltenham Literature Festival Poetry Competition Prize 1989. *Address:* c/o Gallery Press, Oldcastle, County Meath, Ireland.

McGUINNESS, Frank, MPhil; Irish playwright and academic; *Lecturer in English Literature, University College Dublin*; b. 29 July 1953, Buncrana, Donegal; s. of Patrick McGuinness and Celine McGuinness. *Education:* University Coll. Dublin. *Career:* Lecturer in English, Univ. of Ulster, Coleraine 1977–79, Univ. Coll. Dublin 1979–80, St Patrick's Coll., Maynooth 1984–97; Writer-in-Residence, School of English and Drama, Univ. Coll. Dublin 1997–; Dir Abbey Theatre, Dublin 1992–96. *Publications:* The Factory Girls 1982, Observe the Sons of Ulster Marching towards the Somme 1985, Baglady 1985, Innocence 1986, Rosmersholm, A Version 1987, Scout 1987, Yerma: A Version 1987, Carthaginians 1988, The Hen House 1989, Peer Gynt, A Version 1989, Mary and Lizzie 1989, Three Sisters, A Version 1990, The

Bread Man 1990, The Threepenny Opera, A Version 1991, Someone Who'll Watch Over Me 1992, The Bird Sanctuary 1994, Hedda Gabler, A Version 1994, Uncle Vanya, A Version 1995, Booterstown: Poems 1995, Selected Plays: Vol. I 1996, The Dazzling Dark: Introduction 1996, A Doll's House: A Version 1996, The Caucasian Chalk Circle: A Version 1997, Electra: A Version 1997, Mutabilitie 1997, Dancing at Lughnasa: A Screenplay 1998, The Storm: A Version 1998, Dolly West's Kitchen 1999, The Sea With No Ships: Poems 1999, Miss Julie: A Version 2000, The Barbaric Comedies 2000, Gates of Gold 2002, The Stone Jug (poems) 2003, Hecuba 2004, Speaking Like Magpies 2005, Phaedra 2006, There Came a Gypsy Riding 2007, Ghosts (A Version) 2007, Supper With Judas 2007. *Honours:* Officier des Arts et Lettres; Hon. DLitt (Ulster) 2000; Harvey's Award, Evening Standard Drama Award, Ewart-Biggs Peace Prize, Cheltenham Literary Prize, Fringe First, Irish American Literary Prize 1992, Independent on Sunday Best Play 1992, New York Drama Critics' Award 1993, Writers' Guild Award 1993, Tony Award for Best Revival 1997. *Address:* School of English and Drama, Department of Anglo-Irish Literature, University College Dublin, Belfield, Dublin 4, Ireland (office). *Telephone:* (1) 7168420 (office). *E-mail:* englishdramafilm@ucd.ie (office). *Website:* www.ucd.ie/englishanddrama (office).

McGURN, Barrett, AB; American writer; b. 6 Aug. 1914, New York, NY; s. of William Barrett McGurn Sr and Alice Schnieder; m. Janice Ann McLaughlin 1962; five s. one d. *Education:* Fordham Univ., New York. *Career:* reporter New York and Paris Herald Tribune 1935–66; Bureau Chief Herald Tribune, Rome, Paris, Moscow 1946–62; mem. Overseas Press Club of America (pres. 1963–65), Foreign Press Asscn in Italy (pres. 1961, 1962), Nat. Press Club, Cosmos Club (Washington, DC). *Publications:* Decade in Europe 1958, A Reporter Looks at the Vatican 1960, A Reporter Looks at American Catholicism 1966, America's Court, The Supreme Court and the People 1997, Pilgrim's Guide to Rome 1999, Yank, The Army Weekly, Covering the Greatest Generation 2004; contrib. to Reader's Digest, Catholic Digest, Commonweal, Colliers, Yank. *Honours:* Hon. DLitt (Fordham Univ.) 1958; Long Island Univ. Polk Award 1956, Overseas Press Club Award 1957; Cavaliere Ufficiale, Italian Nat. Order of Merit 1961, Meritorious Honor Award, US State Dept 1971. *Address:* 5229 Duvall Drive, Bethesda, MD 20816-1875, USA (home). *Telephone:* (301) 229-7439 (home). *E-mail:* jmcgurn@erols.com (home).

MccGWIRE, Michael Kane, OBE, BSc; British writer, fmr Royal Navy Commander, fmr academic and foreign policy analyst; b. 9 Dec. 1924, Madras (now Chennai), India; m. Helen Jean Scott 1952; two s. three d. *Education:* Royal Naval Coll., Dartmouth and Univ. of Wales. *Career:* officer, Royal Navy 1942–67; Prof., Dalhousie Univ. 1971–79; Sr Fellow, Brookings Institution, Washington, DC 1979–90; Visiting Prof., Univ. of Cambridge 1990–93; Hon. Prof. of Int. Politics, Univ. of Wales 1997–. *Publications:* Military Objectives and Soviet Foreign Policy 1987, Perestroika and Soviet National Security 1991, NATO Expansion and European Security 1997; Ed: Soviet Naval Developments 1973, Soviet Naval Policy 1975, Soviet Naval Influence 1977; contrib. to over 40 books and numerous journals, most recently Int. Affairs. *Address:* Hayes, Durlston, Swanage, Dorset BH19 2JF, England (home).

McHUGH, Heather, BA, MA; American academic, poet, writer and translator; *Professor of English, University of Washington*; b. 20 Aug. 1948, San Diego, Calif. *Education:* Radcliffe Coll. at Harvard Univ., Univ. of Denver. *Career:* Assoc. Prof., SUNY at Binghamton 1974–83; Core Faculty, MFA Program for Writers, Warren Wilson Coll. 1976–; Milliman Distinguished Writer-in-Residence, later Pollock Prof. of Creative Writing, Univ. of Washington 1984–; Holloway Lecturer in Poetry, Univ. of California, Berkeley 1987; Coal-Royalty Chair in Poetry, Univ. of Alabama, Tuscaloosa 1992; Elliston Prof. of Poetry, Univ. of Cincinnati 1993; Visiting Prof., Univ. of Iowa 1991–92, 1995, UCLA 1994, Univ. of California, Irvine 1994, Stanford Univ.; Visiting Lecturer, Univ. of Bergen, Norway 1994; mem. Acad. of American Poets (mem. Bd of Chancellors 1999–), American Acad. of Arts and Sciences. *Publications include:* poetry: Dangers 1977, A World of Difference 1981, To the Quick 1987, Shades 1988, Hinge & Sign: Poems 1968–1993 1994, The Father of the Predicaments (Poems 1993–1998) 1999, Eyeshot 2003, Upgraded to Serious 2009; essays: Broken English: Poetry and Partiality 1993; translator: D'Après Tout: Poems by Jean Follain 1981, Because the Sea is Black: Poems by Blaga Dimitrova (with Niko Boris) 1989, Glottal Stop: 101 Poems by Paul Celan (with Nikolai B. Popov); other: Where Are They Now? (with Tom Phillips) 1990, Best American Poems (co-ed. with David Lehman) 2007; contrib. to many anthologies and journals. *Honours:* Nat. Endowment for the Arts Grants 1974, 1979, 1981, Pushcart Prizes 1978 et seq, Guggenheim Fellowship 1989, Woodrow Wilson Nat. Poetry Fellow 1992–93, Daniel A. Pollack Prize, Harvard Univ. and Harvard Coll. Library 1995, Bingham Prize, Boston Book Review 1995, TLS Int. Book of the Year List 1995, Lila Wallace/Reader's Digest Writing Award 1996–99, O.D. Hardison Award 1998, PEN Voelker Prize 2000, MacArthur Fellowship 2009, Griffin Int. Poetry Prize 2000. *Address:* Department of English, Box 354330, University of Washington, Seattle, WA 98195, USA (office). *E-mail:* postcocious@gmail.com (home). *Website:* depts.washington.edu/engl/people/profile.php?id=71 (office); spondee.com (home).

McILVANNEY, William, MA; Scottish writer and poet; b. 25 Nov. 1936, Kilmarnock, Ayrshire. *Education:* Univ. of Glasgow. *Career:* English teacher 1960–75. *Publications:* novels: Remedy is None (Geoffrey Faber Memorial Prize 1967) 1966, A Gift from Nessus (Scottish Arts Council Book Award) 1968, Docherty (Whitbread Novel Award, Scottish Arts Council Book Award) 1975, Laidlaw (CWA Macallan Silver Dagger for Fiction) 1977, The Papers of Tony Veitch (CWA Macallan Silver Dagger for Fiction) 1983, The Big Man 1985, In Through the Head 1988, Strange Loyalties 1991, The Kiln (Saltire Soc. Scottish Book of the Year Award) 1996, Weekend 2006; poetry: The Longships in Harbour: Poems 1970, Landscapes and Figures (poems to accompany eight etchings by Norman Ackroyd) 1973, These Words: Weddings and After (essay and poems) 1984, Walking Wounded (Glasgow Herald People's Prize 1990) 1989, Surviving the Shipwreck (poems and essays) 1991; non-fiction: Shades of Grey: Glasgow 1956–1987 1990. *Address:* c/o Sceptre, 338 Euston Road, London, NW1 3BH, England (office).

McINERNEY, Jay; American writer; b. 1955; m. 1st Linda Rossiter; m. 2nd Merry Raymond; m. 3rd Helen Bransford 1991; one s. one d. *Education:* Williams Univ. *Publications include:* Bright Lights, Big City 1984, Ransom 1986, Story of My Life 1988, Brightness Falls 1992, The Last of the Savages 1996, Model Behavior 1998, How It Ended 2000, The Good Life (novel) 2006, A Hedonist in the Cellar: Adventures in Wine 2006, The Last Bachelor 2009, How it Ended: New and Collected Stories 2009. *Address:* c/o Bloomsbury Publishing Plc, 36 Soho Square, London, W1D 3QY, England (office). *Website:* www.bloonsbury.com (office).

McINNIS, (Harry) Donald, AB; American writer and dramatist; b. 18 April 1916, Worcester, MA; m. Marjorie E. Graber 1948; two s. two d. *Education:* Clark University, American University, Johns Hopkins University. *Career:* mem. Australian Writers Guild; US Dramatists Guild. *Publications:* The Running Years, 1986; Cobwebs and Twigs, 1990; Will – Man from Stratford (play), 1992; New Work No Lines (play), 1994. *Honours:* special awards, US Government, Government of Guatemala, Republic of Korea. *Address:* 22 Chauvel Circle, Chapman, ACT 2611, Australia.

McINTOSH, Fiona; British (b. Australian) magazine editor; m.; two d. *Career:* worked on Melbourne Herald; moved to UK, where London correspondent for Australian newspapers; feature writer, Daily Mirror newspaper, later Ed. women's page and Deputy Features Ed.; Ed. Company magazine 1995–98; Ed. Elle magazine 1998–2001, including launch Ed. Elle Girl magazine 2001; fmr Ed. ES magazine; launch Ed.-in-Chief Grazia magazine 2005–07; columnist, Sunday Mirror 2007–, Grazia 2007–; Consultant Creative Dir, my-wardrobe.com 2010–. *Address:* Sunday Mirror, 1 Canada Square, Canary Wharf, London, E14 5AP, England (office). *Telephone:* (20) 7293-3000 (office). *Fax:* (20) 7822-3587 (office). *Website:* www.sundaymirror.co.uk (office).

MacINTYRE, Alasdair, BA, MA; British philosopher, academic and writer; *Professor Emeritus of Philosophy, University of Notre Dame*; b. 12 Jan. 1929, Glasgow, Scotland. *Education:* Queen Mary Coll., London, Univs of Manchester and Oxford. *Career:* Lecturer, Univ. of Manchester 1951–57, Univ. of Leeds 1957–61; Research Fellow, Nuffield Coll., Oxford 1961–62; Sr Fellow, Princeton Univ., NJ, USA 1962–63; Fellow, University Coll., Oxford 1963–66; Riddell Lecturer, Newcastle Univ. 1964; Bampton Lecturer, Columbia Univ., New York 1966; Prof. of the History of Ideas, Brandeis Univ., USA 1969–72; Dean Coll. of Liberal Arts, Boston Univ. 1972–73, Prof. of Philosophy and Political Science 1972–80; Henry Luce Prof., Wellesley Coll., USA 1980–82; W. Alton Jones Prof., Vanderbilt Univ. 1982–88; Henry Luce Scholar, Yale Univ. 1988–89; McMahon/Hank Prof., Univ. of Notre Dame, Ind. 1988–94, Research Prof. of Philosophy 2000–10, Prof. Emer. 2010–; Prof. of Arts and Sciences, Duke Univ. 1995–2000; Research Fellow, London Metropolitan Univ. 2010–; Corresp. mem. British Acad.; mem. American Acad. of Arts and Sciences. *Publications:* Marxism and Christianity 1953, The Unconscious 1957, Short History of Ethics 1966, Against the Self-Images of the Age 1971, After Virtue: A Study in Moral Theory 1981, Whose Justice? Which Rationality? 1988, Three Rival Versions of Moral Enquiry 1990, First Principles, Final Ends and Contemporary Philosophy 1990, Dependent-Rational Animals 1999, Edith Stein: A Philosophical Prologue 1913–22 2006, God, Philosophy, Universities 2009. *Honours:* Hon. MRIA; Gifford Lecturer, Univ. of Edinburgh 1988. *Address:* Philosophy Department, University of Notre Dame, Notre Dame, IN 46556, USA.

McINTYRE, Ian James, BA, MA; British writer and broadcaster; b. 9 Dec. 1931, Banchory, Kincardineshire, Scotland; s. of Hector Harold McIntyre and Annie Mary Michie; m. Leik Sommerfelt Vogt 1954; two s. two d. *Education:* St John's Coll., Cambridge, College of Europe, Bruges, Belgium. *Career:* Ed. At Home and Abroad 1959; Programme Services Officer, ITA 1961; Dir of Information Research, Scottish Conservative Cen. Office 1964–70, contested Roxburgh, Selkirk and Peebles 1966; writer, broadcaster 1970–76; Main Presenter Analysis programme, BBC Radio 4 1970–76, Controller BBC Radio 4 1976–78, BBC Radio 3 1978–87; Assoc. Ed. The Times, London 1989–90. *Radio includes:* writer and presenter of several BBC Radio 3 and Radio 4 programmes including Aspects of India, Yanks & Limeys, Speaking for Myself, Analysis. *Publications:* The Proud Doers: Israel After Twenty Years 1968, Words: Reflections on the Uses of Language (ed. and contrib.) 1975, Dogfight: The Transatlantic Battle over Airbus 1992, The Expense of Glory: A Life of John Reith 1993, Dirt and Deity: A Life of Robert Burns 1996, Garrick 1999, Joshua Reynolds: The Life and Times of the First President of the Royal Academy 2003, Hester: The Remarkable Life of Dr Johnson's Dear Mistress 2008, Robert Burns: A Life 2009; contribs to The Listener, The Times, The Independent, The Spectator, The New Statesman, Oxford Dictionary of National Biography. *Honours:* Theatre Book Prize 1999. *Address:* Spylaw House, Newlands Avenue, Radlett, Herts., WD7 8EL, England (home). *Telephone:* (1923) 853532 (home). *E-mail:* ian.mcintyre@waitrose.com (home).

MACINTYRE, Linden, BA; Canadian journalist, broadcaster and novelist; *Co-host, The Fifth Estate (CBC TV)*; b. 29 May 1943, St Lawrence; s. of Dan Rory MacIntyre and Alice Donohue; m. Carol Off; five c. *Education:* St Francis Xavier Univ., St Mary's Univ., Univ. of King's Coll., Halifax. *Career:* Parl. reporter, Halifax Herald, Ottawa 1964–67; Parl. reporter, Financial Times of Canada 1967–70; correspondent, Chronicle Herald, Cape Breton 1970–76; various roles at CBC, including host, The MacIntyre File 1976–79, news producer and journalist, The Journal 1982–90, co-host, The Fifth Estate 1990–, frequent guest host, The Current (CBC Radio One). *Television:* documentaries include: To Sell A War (Int. Emmy Award), A Toxic Company (Peabody Award, George Polk Award). *Publications:* novels: The Long Stretch 1999, The Bishop's Man (Scotiabank Giller Prize 2009, Dartmouth Book Award for Fiction, Atlantic Ind. Booksellers' Choice Award 2010) 2009, Why Men Lie 2012; non-fiction: Who Killed Ty Conn (co-author) 2000, Causeway: A Passage from Innocent (memoir) (Edna Staebler Award for Creative Non-Fiction, Evelyn Richardson Prize for Non-Fiction) 2006. *Honours:* nine Gemini Awards for broadcast journalism, Gordon Sinclair Award. *Address:* c/o The Canadian Broadcasting Corporation, 250 Front Street West, Toronto, ON M5W 1E6 (office); c/o Random House of Canada Limited, One Toronto Street, Unit 300, Toronto, ON M5C 2V6, Canada (office). *Telephone:* (416) 364-4449 (Random House) (office). *Fax:* (416) 364-6863 (Random House) (office). *Website:* www.randomhouse.ca (office).

MACINTYRE, Stuart Forbes, MA, PhD; Australian academic and writer; *Ernest Scott Professor of History, University of Melbourne*; b. 21 April 1947, Melbourne, Vic.; m. 1st Margaret Joan Geddes 1970; m. 2nd Martha Adele Bruton 1976; two d. *Education:* Univ. of Melbourne, Monash Univ., Univ. of Cambridge. *Career:* Tutor in History, Murdoch Univ., Perth 1976, Lecturer in History 1979; Research Fellow, St John's Coll., Cambridge 1977–78; Lecturer, Univ. of Melbourne 1980–84, Sr Lecturer 1984–86, Reader in History 1987–90, Ernest Scott Prof. 1990–, Dean Faculty of Arts 1999–2006; Visiting Prof., Harvard Univ. 2007–08; mem. Acad. of the Social Sciences in Australia (Pres. 2006–09), Australian Acad. of the Humanities. *Publications:* A Proletarian Science: Marxism in Britain 1917–1933 1980, Little Moscows 1980, Militant: The Life and Times of Paddy Troy 1983, Ormond College Centenary Essays (ed.) 1983, Making History (ed.) 1984, Winners and Losers: The Pursuit of Social Justice in Australian History 1985, The Oxford History of Australia, Vol. IV 1986, Foundations of Arbitration (ed.) 1989, The Labour Experiment 1989, Through White Eyes (ed.) 1990, A Colonial Liberalism: The Lost World of Three Victorian Visionaries 1990, A History for a Nation 1995, The Discovery of Australian History (ed.) 1995, The Reds: The Communist Party of Australia, from Origins to Illegality 1998, The Oxford Companion to Australian History (ed.) 1998, A Concise History of Australia 1999, True Believers (ed.) 2001, A Short History of the University of Melbourne 2003, The History Wars 2003, The Historian's Conscience (ed.) 2004, The New Province for Law and Order (ed.) 2004, What If? (ed.) 2006, The Life of the Past (ed.) 2006, The Poor Relation 2010; contrib. to professional journals. *Address:* c/o Department of History, University of Melbourne, Parkville, Vic. 3052 (office); 10 Ferriman Street, W Brunswick, Vic. 3055, Australia (home). *Telephone:* (3) 8344-5242 (office); (3) 9380-2650 (home). *E-mail:* s.macintyre@unimelb.edu.au (office).

McIVER, Susan Bertha, BA, MSc, PhD; Canadian (b. American) writer, biologist and coroner; b. 6 Nov. 1940, Hutchinson, Kan.; d. of Ernest D. McIver and Thelma Faye McIver (née McCrory); m. Robin Wyndham. *Education:* Univ. of California, Riverside and Washington State Univ. *Career:* Research Scientist and Asst Prof. of Parasitology, Univ. of Toronto 1967–72, Assoc. Prof. of Microbiology and Parasitology 1972–80, Prof. of Zoology and of Microbiology 1980–84; Prof. and Chair. of Environmental Biology, Univ. of Guelph 1984–90; Consultant in Entomology, US Army 1975–79, 1986–89; mem. Consultant Study Group on Tropical Medicine and Parasitology, NIH 1983–85; Coroner, BC Coroners Service 1993–2003; freelance journalist 2003–; publicist Agur Lake Camp Soc. 2007–; Dir Women-in-Crisis 1980–87, Chair. 1988–89; mem. Entomological Soc., Biological Council of Canada, Entomological Soc. of America, Canadian Soc. of Zoology, American Soc. of Parasitology, Canadian Microscopic Soc., Mosquito Control Asscn; Int. Fellowship in Tropical Medicine 1973; Medical Research Council Fellowship 1978. *Publications include:* Medical Nightmares: The Human Face of Error 2001; more than 100 scientific research papers and articles 1964–90 and numerous short stories 1990–; approx. 600 articles on agriculture and civic affairs for gen. public in newspapers and magazines. *Honours:* C. Gordon Hewitt Award, Entomological Soc. of Canada 1978, 125th Confed. Anniversary Silver Medal for Contribs to Community, Compatriots and Canada. *Address:* PO Box 968, Penticton, BC V2A 7N7 (office); 10214 Haddrell Avenue, Summerland, BC V0H 1Z8, Canada (home). *Telephone:* (250) 494-9081 (office). *Fax:* (250) 494-9081 (office). *E-mail:* smciver@shaw.ca (office).

MACK, William P., BS; American naval officer (retd) and writer; b. 6 Aug. 1915, Hillsboro, IL; m. Ruth McMillian 1939, one s. one d. *Education:* US Naval Acad., National War College, George Washington University. *Career:* US Naval Officer, 1935–75; Deputy Asst Secretary of Defense, 1968–71. *Publications:* Non-Fiction: Naval Officers Guide, 1958; Naval Customs, Traditions and Usage, 1978; Command at Sea, 1980. Fiction: South to Java, 1988; Pursuit of the Sea Wolf, 1991; Checkfire, 1992; New Guinea, 1993; Straits of Messina, 1994; Lieutenant Christopher Captain Kulburnie. Contributions: various publications. *Honours:* Alfred Thayer Mahan Award for Literary Excellence, Navy League, 1982.

McKAY, Donald Fleming, CM, BA, MA, PhD; Canadian poet, writer, editor and academic; b. 25 June 1942, Owen Sound, Ont.; m. (divorced); one s. one d. *Education:* Bishop's Univ., Univ. of Western Ontario, Univ. Coll., Swansea, Wales. *Career:* mem. staff, Univ. of Western Ontario 1970–90; Teacher, Univ. of New Brunswick 1990–96; Assoc. Dir of Poetry, The Banff Centre for the Arts 1996–; Jack McClelland Writer-in-Residence, Univ. of Toronto 2007; Ed., The Fiddlehead; mem. League of Canadian Poets, PEN, Writers' Union of Canada. *Publications include:* Air Occupies Space 1973, Long Sault 1975, Lependu 1978, Lightning Ball Bait 1980, Birding, or Desire 1983, Sanding Down This Rocking Chair on a Windy Night 1987, Night Field 1991, Apparatus 1997, Another Gravity 2000, Vis à Vis 2001, Camber 2004, Strike/Slip (Dorothy Livesay Poetry Prize) 2007, Deactivated West 100 2007; contributions: periodicals. *Honours:* Canadian Authors' Asscn Award for Poetry 1983, Governor-General's Award for Poetry 1991, 2000, National Magazine Award for Poetry 1991, Griffin Award for Poetry 2007. *Address:* 28 Barnes Road, St Johns, NL, A1C 3X2, Canada (home).

MACKAY, Shena, FRSL; British writer; b. 6 June 1944, Edinburgh, Scotland; d. of Benjamin Mackey and Morag Mackey (née Carmichael); m. Robin Brown 1964 (divorced 1982); three d. *Education:* Tonbridge Girls' Grammar School, Kent and Kidbrooke Comprehensive, London. *Career:* began career working in antique shop, Chancery Lane, London. *Publications:* Dust Falls on Eugene Schlumberger 1964, Toddler on the Run 1964, Music Upstairs 1965, Old Crow 1967, An Advent Calendar 1971, Babies in Rhinestones 1983, A Bowl of Cherries 1984, Redhill Rococo 1986, Dreams of Dead Women's Handbags 1987, Dunedin 1992, The Laughing Academy 1993, Such Devoted Sisters (ed) 1993, Collected Stories 1994, The Orchard on Fire 1996, Friendship (ed) 1997, The Artist's Widow 1998, The World's Smallest Unicorn 1999, Heligoland 2003, The Atmospheric Railway 2008. *Honours:* Hon. Visiting Prof. to MA in Writing, Univ. of Middlesex 2000–03; Fawcett Prize 1987, Scottish Arts Council Awards, Soc. of Authors Award. *Literary Agent:* c/o Rogers, Coleridge & White Literary Agency, 20 Powis Mews, London, W11 1JN, England. *Telephone:* (20) 7221-3717. *Fax:* (20) 7229-9084. *Website:* www.rcwlitagency.co.uk.

MACKAY, Simon (see Nicole, Christopher Robin)

McKEAN, John Maule Laurie, (Laurie Melville), BArch, MA, ARIBA, ARIAS, MCSD; British academic and writer; b. 7 Nov. 1943, Glasgow, Scotland; m. Mary Tetlow; two s. one d. *Education:* Univs of Strathclyde and Essex. *Career:* architect in practice 1966–67, 1969–71; Teacher of Architectural Design, Univ. of Ceylon 1968–69, Univ. of East London, 1976–80, Univ. of North London 1980–90; Teacher of Design and Architectural History, Univ. of North London 1983–88, Univ. of Middlesex 1984–88; Dir of Interior Architecture, Univ. of Brighton 1990–95, Prof. of Architecture 1996–2008; mem. Critics' Circle of Int. Asscn of Architects, 1990. *Publications:* Architecture of the Western World (co-author) 1980, Learning from Segal 1989, Royal Festival Hall 1991, Crystal Palace 1994, Leicester Engineering Building 1994, Alexander Thomson (co-author) 1995, The Parthenon 1996, C. R. Mackintosh (co-author) 1996, Mackintosh Pocket Guide (8th edition) 1998, C.R. Mackintosh: Architect, Artist, Icon 2000, Giancarlo De Carlo, Layered Places 2004, La Modernite Critique autour du CIAM9 (co-author) 2006, The Man-Made Future (co-author) 2007; contribs to Architects' Journal, Building Design, Spazio e Società, Milan, Architectural History, Journal of Architecture. *Honours:* two AIA Int. Book Awards 1994, 1995, Architects' Journal Books of the Year 2001, 2004. *E-mail:* john.mckean@clara.co.uk (home); NBF@clara.co.uk (office).

McKEE, David, (Roc Almirall, Violet Easton); British children's writer and illustrator; b. Devon. *Education:* Plymouth Art Coll. *Career:* started career drawing cartoons for Punch, Reader's Digest, Times Educational Supplement; created popular children's characters for books and TV, including Mr Benn, King Rollo, Elmer the Patchwork Elephant; co-founder King Rollo Films; illustrated numerous Paddington Bear books. *Television:* Mr Benn (series), King Rollo (series), also co-writer Towser, Spot the Dog children's series. *Publications include:* Two Can Toucan 1964, Tusk Tusk 1978, Not Now, Bernard 1980, I Hate My Teddybear 1982, King Rollo and the Letter 1984, Two Monsters 1985, The Hill and the Rock 1985, The Sad Story of Veronica 1987, Snow Woman 1987, Who's a Clever Baby Then? 1988, The Monster and the Teddy Bear 1989, Zebra's Hiccups 1991, Elmer 1989, Elmer Again 1991, Elmer on Stilts 1993, The School Bus Comes at 8 o'clock 1993, Isabel's Noisy Tummy 1994, Elmer and Wilbur 1994, Elmer in the Snow 1995, Charlotte's Piggy Bank 1996, Elmer and the Wind 1997, Prince Peter and the Teddy Bear 1997, Elmer Plays Hide and Seek 1998, Elmer and the Lost Teddy 1999, Mary's Secret 1999, Elmer and the Stranger 2000, Elmer and Grandpa Eldo 2001, King Rollo and the New Stockings 2001, Mr Benn – Gladiator 2001, Elmer's Concert 2001, Elmer and Butterfly 2002, Elmer's New Friend 2002, Elmer and the Hippos 2003, The Adventures of Charmin the Bear 2003, Who is Mrs Green? 2003, The Conquerors 2004, Charlotte's Piggy Bank 2004, Three Monsters 2005, Four Red Apples 2006. *Address:* c/o Andersen Press Publicity Department, 20 Vauxhall Bridge Road, London, SW1V 2SA, England (office). *E-mail:* andersenpress@randomhouse.co.uk (office).

McKEE, Louis, BA; Irish-American poet, writer, editor and teacher; b. (Louis Charles McKee, Jr), 31 July 1951, Philadelphia; s. of Louis Charles McKee and Mary Jane McKee; m. Christine Caruso 1978 (divorced 1982). *Education:* LaSalle Coll., Temple Univ. *Career:* Ed. Painted Bride Quarterly 1984–88, One Trick Pony 1997–2006; Founding Co-Ed. Axe Factory Review 1984–;

mem. Acad. of American Poets, PEN, Poetry Soc. of America, Poets and Writers. *Publications:* Schuylkill County 1982, The True Speed of Things 1984, Safe Water 1986, No Matter 1987, Oranges 1989, Angelus 1990, Three Poems 1993, River Architecture: Poems from Here and There: Selected Poems, 1973–1993 1999, Right as Rain 2000, Greatest Hits 1973–2003 2003, Near Occasions of Sin 2006, Still Life 2008, Marginalia (trans. of Old Irish monastic poems) 2008, Jamming 2009; contrib. to anthologies, reviews, quarterlies and journals. *Address:* 8460 Frankford Avenue, Philadelphia, PA 19136, USA (home). *Telephone:* (215) 331-7389 (office). *E-mail:* lmckee4148@aol.com (home). *Website:* www.louismckee.com.

MacKENNEY, Richard, BA, PhD, FRHistS; British historian and educator; b. 2 April 1953, Aylesbury, Buckinghamshire, England. *Education:* Queens' College, Cambridge, University of Edinburgh. *Career:* Sr Lecturer in History, University of Edinburgh. *Publications:* Tradesmen and Traders: The World of the Guilds in Venice and Europe, c. 1250–c. 1650, 1987; The City-State, 1500–1700: Republican Liberty in an Age of Princely Power, 1989; Sixteenth-Century Europe: Expansion and Conflict, 1993; Renaissance Italians, 1300–1600, 1997. Contributions: various specialised articles to journals and periodicals. *Honours:* Graduate Fellow, Rotary Foundation, Rotary International, 1975–76. *Literary Agent:* David Higham Associates, 5–8 Lower John Street, Golden Square, London W1F 9HA, England. *Address:* Department of History, University of Edinburgh, William Robertson Building, George Square, Edinburgh, EH8 9JY, Scotland.

MacKENZIE, David, AB, MA, PhD; American academic; *Professor of History Emeritus, University of North Carolina at Greensboro*; b. 10 June 1927, Rochester, NY; m. Patricia Williams 1953; three s. *Education:* Univ. of Rochester, Columbia Univ. *Career:* Prof. of History, US Merchant Marine Acad. 1953–58, Princeton Univ. 1959–61, Wells Coll. 1961–68; Prof. of History, Univ. of North Carolina, Greensboro 1969–2000, Prof. Emer. 2000–. *Publications:* The Serbs and Russian Pan-Slavism 1875–1878 1967, The Lion of Tashkent: The Career of General M. G. Cherniaev 1974, Ilija Garasanin: The Balkan Bismarck 1985, IIija Garasanin Drzavnik i Diplomata 1987, Apis: The Congenial Conspirator 1989, Imperial Dreams/Harsh Realities: Tsarist Russian Foreign Policy, 1815–1917 1993, From Messianism to Collapse: Soviet Foreign Policy 1917–1991 1994, The Black Hand on Trial: Salonika 1917 1995, Violent Solutions: Revolutions, Nationalism, and Secret Societies in Europe to 1918 1996, Serbs and Russians 1996, Solunski proces 1997, Exonerating the Black Hand 1917–1953 1999, Obnova Solunshog procesa 2001, Count N. P. Ignat'ev: Father of Lies? 2002, A History of Russia, the Soviet Union and Beyond (sixth edn) 2002, Russia and the USSR in the Twentieth Century (fourth edn) 2002, One Foot in Russia, the Other in Yugoslavia: a Memoir 2003, Jovan Ristic, Evropski Drzavnik 2004, Jovan Ristic, European Diplomat 2006, Jovan Marinovic 2006, Milovan Milovanovic: Talented and Peace Loving Serbian Diplomat, Stojan Protic: The Brain of the Serbian Radical Party 1857–1923 2007; contrib. to books and professional journals. *Address:* 870 Library Tower, University of North Carolina, Greensboro, NC (office); 1000 Fairmont Street, Greensboro, NC 27401, USA (home). *Telephone:* (336) 275-1229 (home). *Fax:* (336) 334-5910 (office).

McKEOWN, Tom S., MA, MFA; American poet, writing consultant and college instructor; b. 29 Sept. 1937, Evanston, Ill.; m. Patricia Haebig 1989; one s. one d. *Education:* Univ. of Michigan, Vermont Coll. *Career:* teacher, Alpena Community Coll. 1962–64, Univ. of Wisconsin, Oshkosh 1964–68; Writer-in-Residence, Stephens Coll. 1968–74; Poet-in-Residence, Savannah Coll. of Art and Design 1982–83, Univ. of Wisconsin, Oshkosh 1983–87, Univ. of Wisconsin at Madison 1989–94; ind. consultant in writing 1999–. *Performances:* Circle of the Eye (Carnegie Hall 1979, Library of Congress 1979); Poetry Readings (Journalism Club, Moscow 1979, Leningrad 1979, Tallinn 1979). *Art:* August Garden (acrylic on canvas) 1992. *Publications:* The Luminous Revolver 1973, The House of Water 1974, Driving to New Mexico 1974, Certain Minutes 1978, Circle of the Eye 1982, Three Hundred Tigers 1994, The Oceans in the Sleepwalker's Hands 2008; contrib. to newspapers, reviews and magazines. *Honours:* Avery Hopwood Award 1968, Wisconsin Arts Fellowship 1980, Montserrat/Dragonfly Press Award for Lifetime Achievement in Poetry 2003.

McKERNAN, Llewellyn McKinnie, MA; American poet and children's writer; b. 12 July 1941, Hampton, Ark.; m. John Joseph McKernan 1967; one d. *Education:* Hendrix College, University of Arkansas, Brown University. *Career:* Instructor of English, Georgia Southern College, 1966–67; Adjunct Prof. of English, Marshall University, 1980–86, 1991; Prof. of English, St Mary's College, 1989; mem. West Virginia Writers; Poetry Society of West Virginia; Society of Children's Book Writers and Illustrators. *Publications:* Short and Simple Annals 1979, More Songs of Gladness 1987, Bird Alphabet 1988, Many Waters 1993, This is the Day and This is the Night 1994, Llewellyn McKernan's Greatest Hit 2005; contributions: Reviews and journals. *Honours:* Third Prize, Chester H. Jones National Poetry Competition 1982, West Virginia Humanities Artist Grant 1983, Second Prize, National Founders Award Contest, NFSPS 1994. *Address:* Route 10, PO Box 4639B, Barboursville, WV 25504, USA.

MACKERRAS, Colin Patrick, AO, FAHA, BA (Hons), MLitt, PhD; Australian author, editor and academic; *Professor Emeritus, Department of International Business and Asian Studies, Griffith University*; b. 26 Aug. 1939, Sydney, NSW; s. of Alan Patrick Mackerras and Catherine Brearcliffe MacLaurin Mackerras; m. Alyce Barbara Brazier 1963; two s. three d. *Education:* Univ. of Melbourne, Australian Nat. Univ., Univ. of Cambridge, UK. *Career:* Foreign Expert, Beijing Inst. of Foreign Languages 1964–66, Beijing Foreign Studies Univ. 1986, 2005, 2006–07, 2008–09, 2010, 2011–12; Prof., Renmin Univ. of China 2011, Chair Prof. 2012–13; Research Scholar, ANU 1966–69, Research Fellow 1969–73, Sr Research Fellow 1973; Prof., School of Modern Asian Studies, Griffith Univ. 1974–2004, Chair. School of Modern Asian Studies 1979–85, Head School of Modern Asian Studies 1988–89, 1996–2000, Prof. Emer., Dept of Int. Business and Asian Studies 2004–; mem. Asian Studies Asscn of Australia (Pres. 1992–95), Chinese Studies Asscn (Pres. 1991–93), Queensland History Teachers Asscn, Queensland-China Council 2007–11; Founding Ed.-in-Chief Asian Ethnicity (journal) 2000–07. *Television:* Dragon's Tongue 1990–91. *Publications include:* The Rise of the Peking Opera 1972, The Chinese Theatre in Modern Times 1975, The Performing Arts in Contemporary China 1981, Modern China – A Chronology from 1842 to the Present 1982, From Fear to Friendship: Australia's Policies Towards the People's Republic of China 1966–1982 (with Edmund S. K. Fung) 1985, Western Images of China 1989, Portraits of China 1989, Dragon's Tongue: Communicating in Chinese (with Peter Chang, Yu Hsiu-ching and Alyce Mackerras, two vols) 1990–91, Chinese Drama: A Historical Survey 1990, The Cambridge Handbook of Contemporary China (with Amanda Yorke) 1991, Unlocking Australia's Language Potential: Profiles of Nine Key Languages in Australia, Vol. 2: Chinese (with Doug Smith, Ng Bee Chin, and Kam Louie) 1993, China Since 1978: Reform, Modernisation, and 'Socialism with Chinese Characteristics' (with Pradeep Taneja and Graham Young) 1994, China's Minorities: Integration and Modernization in the Twentieth Century 1994, China's Minority Cultures: Identities and Integration Since 1912 1995, Peking Opera 1997, China in Transformation 1900–1949 1998, revised 2008, The New Cambridge Handbook of Contemporary China 2001, China's Ethnic Minorities and Globalisation 2003; editor: Essays on the Sources for Chinese History (with Donald Leslie and Wang Gungwu) 1973, China: The Impact of Revolution: A Survey of Twentieth Century China 1976, Chinese Theater from its Origins to the Present Day 1983, Marxism in Asia (with Nick Knight) 1985, Drama in the People's Republic of China (with Constantine Tung) 1987, Chinese Language Teaching and its Application (with Hugh Dunn) 1987, Contemporary Vietnam: Perspectives from Australia (with Robert Cribb and Allan Healy) 1988, Eastern Asia: An Introductory History 1992, Asia Since 1945: History Through Documents 1992, China in Revolution: History Through Documents 1993, Imperialism, Colonialism and Nationalism in East Asia: History Through Documents 1994, Australia and China: Partners in Asia 1996, Dictionary of the Politics of the People's Republic of China (with Donald H. McMillen and Andrew Watson) 1998, Culture and Society in the Asia-Pacific (with Richard Maidment) 1998, Sinophiles and Sinophones, Western Views of China: An Anthology 2000, Ethnicity in Asia 2003, China, Xinjiang and Central Asia (with Michael Clarke) 2009, Ethnic Minorities in Modern China, Critical Concepts in Asian Studies (four vols) 2011; contrib. to numerous scholarly books, journals and encyclopaedias. *Honours:* Dr hc (Kyrgyz-Turkish Manas Univ.) 2004, Hon. DUniv (Griffith Univ.) 2006; co-recipient, UN Asscn of Australia Gold Citation for the Media Peace Prize 1981, Albert Einstein Int. Acad. Foundation Cross of Merit Award 1993, Medal for Outstanding Contribs to Australia-China Cultural Relations 1999, Centenary Medal Australia 2003. *Address:* Department of International Business and Asian Studies, Griffith University, Nathan, Qld 4111, Australia (office). *Telephone:* (7) 3735-7446 (office); (7) 3735-1647 (home). *Fax:* (7) 3735-5111 (office); (7) 3390-1641 (home). *E-mail:* c.mackerras@griffith.edu.au (office); colinmackerras@hotmail.com.

MACKESY, Piers Gerald, MA, DPhil, DLitt, FBA; British historian and writer; *Emeritus Fellow, Pembroke College, University of Oxford*; b. 15 Sept. 1924, Cults, Aberdeenshire, Scotland; s. of Maj.-Gen. P. J. Mackesy, CB, DSO, MC and Dorothy Cook; m. 1st Sarah Davies; one s. two d.; m. 2nd Patricia Timlin. *Education:* Christ Church, Oxford, Oriel Coll., Oxford. *Career:* Lt, Royal Scots Greys 1944–47; Harkness Fellow, Harvard Univ. 1953–54; Fellow 1954–87, Emeritus 1988–, Pembroke Coll., Oxford; Visiting Fellow, Inst. for Advanced Study, Princeton, NJ 1961–62; Visiting Prof., California Inst. of Technology 1966; mem. Nat. Army Museum (council mem. 1983–92), Soc. for Army Historical Research (Vice-Pres. 1994–), Royal Scots Dragoon Guards Asscn (Chair. N. of Scotland Br. 1992–2007). *Publications:* The War in the Mediterranean 1803–1810 1957, The War for America 1775–1783 1964, Statesmen at War: The Strategy of Overthrow 1798–1799 1974, The Coward of Minden: The Affair of Lord George Sackville 1979, War without Victory: The Downfall of Pitt 1799–1802 1984, British Victory in Egypt, 1801: The End of Napoleon's Conquest 1995. *Honours:* Templer Medal 1995. *Address:* Westerton Farmhouse, Dess, by Aboyne, Aberdeenshire AB34 5AY, Scotland (home). *Telephone:* (13398) 84415 (home).

MACKEY, James Patrick, BA, LPh, BD, STL, DD, PhD; Irish philosopher, theologian and academic; *Visiting Professor, Trinity College Dublin*; b. 9 Feb. 1934, Waterford; s. of Peter Mackey and Esther Morrissey; m. Noelle Quinlan 1973; one s. one d. *Education:* Mount St Joseph Coll., Nat. Univ. of Ireland, Pontifical Univ., Maynooth and Queen's Univ., Belfast, doctoral Research at Univ. of Oxford, UK and Univ. of Strasbourg, France. *Career:* ordained priest 1958; Lecturer in Philosophy, Queen's Univ., Belfast 1960–66; Lecturer in Philosophy and Theology, St John's Coll., Waterford 1966–69; Assoc. Prof. of Philosophical and Systematic Theology, Univ. of San Francisco, USA 1969–73, Prof. 1973–79; Visiting Prof., Univ. of California, Berkeley, USA 1974–75; Thomas Chalmers Prof. of Theology, Univ. of Edin., UK 1979–99, Dean of Faculty of Divinity 1984–88, Dir Grad. School and Assoc. Dean 1995–98, Prof.

Emer. 1999–, Fellow, Faculty of Divinity 1999–2002; Visiting Prof., Univ. of Dublin Trinity Coll. 2000–; curricular consultant, Univ. Coll., Cork 2000–04; Visiting Prof., Dartmouth Coll., NH, USA 1989, Univ. of San Francisco 1990; mem. Ind. Assessment Panel and jt author of Report on NI Policing Bd 2005; Dir Derry City Int. Conf. on the Cultures of Europe 1992; mem. Consultative Group on the Past of N Ireland 2007–09; Assoc. Ed. Herder Correspondence 1966–69, Concilium 1965–73, Horizons 1973–79, Monograph Series: Biblical Foundations of Theology 1985–91; Founding Ed. Studies in World Christianity: the Edinburgh Review of Theology and Religion 1995–2001. *Television:* scripted and presented two eight-part series on world religions for Channel 4, The Hall of Mirrors 1984, The Gods of War 1986, two six-part series for the BBC, Perspectives (on Northern Ireland) 1986, Perspectives II 1987, numerous other contribs to TV and radio. *Publications:* The Modern Theology of Tradition 1962, Life and Grace 1966 (American edn, The Grace of God, the Response of Man 1967, Spanish trans., Vida y Gracia 1969), Tradition and Change in the Church 1968 (French trans., Tradition et Evolution de la Foi 1969, Polish trans., Tradycja i Zmiana w Kosciele 1974), Morals, Law and Authority (ed.) 1969 (Italian trans., Il Magistero Morale; Compiti e Limite 1973), The Church: Its Credibility Today 1970, The Problems of Religious Faith 1972, Jesus, The Man and the Myth 1979 (German trans., Jesus der Mensch und der Mythos 1981, 1991), The Christian Experience of God as Trinity 1983, Religious Imagination (ed.) 1986, New Testament Theology in Dialogue (with J. D. G Dunn) 1987, Modern Theology 1987, An Introduction to Celtic Christianity (ed.) 1989, Power and Christian Ethics 1994, The Cultures of Europe (ed.) 1994, The Critique of Theological Reason 2000, Religion and Politics in Ireland at the Turn of the Millennium (ed.) 2003, Christianity and Creation 2006, The Scientist and the Theologian 2007, Jesus of Nazareth 2008. *Honours:* British Acad. Research Scholarship, Univs of Oxford and Strasbourg 1964–65. *Address:* School of Religions and Theology, Trinity College, Dublin 2 (office); 15 Glenville Park, Dunmore Road, Waterford, Ireland (home). *Telephone:* (1) 6081297 (office); (51) 844624 (home). *E-mail:* jpmackey_ie@yahoo.co.uk (home).

MACKEY, Mary, (Kate Clemens), BA, MA, PhD; American novelist, poet and academic; *Professor Emeritus of English, California State University at Sacramento*; b. 21 Jan. 1945, Indianapolis, Ind.; d. of John Mackey and Jean Mackey; m. Angus Wright. *Education:* Harvard Coll., Univ. of Michigan. *Career:* Asst Prof., California State Univ., Sacramento 1972–76, Assoc. Prof. 1976–80, apptd Prof. of English 1980, currently Prof. Emer., also Writer-in-Residence; Visiting Prof., California Inst. for Integral Studies 2009, 2011; mem. Feminist Writers' Guild, Nat. Book Critics' Circle, PEN American Center West (Pres. 1989–92, mem. Bd PEN Oakland 2000–06), Writers' Guild of America, Northern Calif. Book Reviewers Asscn, Authors' Guild, Women's Nat. Book Asscn; Fellow, Virginia Center for the Creative Arts. *Publications:* novels: Immersion 1972, McCarthy's List 1979, The Last Warrior Queen 1983, A Grand Passion 1986, The Kindness of Strangers 1988, Season of Shadows 1991, The Year the Horses Came 1993, The Horses at the Gate 1996, The Fires of Spring 1998, The Stand In (as Kate Clemens) 2003, Sweet Revenge (as Kate Clemens) 2004, The Notorious Mrs Winston 2007, The Widow's War 2009; poetry: Split Ends 1974, One Night Stand 1977, Skin Deep 1978, The Dear Dance of Eros 1987, Breaking the Fever 2006, Sugar Zone 2011; other: Chance Music (co-ed. with Mary MacArthur) 1977; contrib. to periodicals. *Honours:* Woodrow Wilson Fellowship 1966–67, Virginia Center for the Creative Arts Fellowship 1999, 2002. *Literary Agent:* c/o Barbara Lowenstein, Lowenstein Associates Literary Agency, 121 West 27th Street, Suite 601, New York, NY 10001, USA. *Telephone:* (212) 236-8196. *Website:* www.lowensteinassociates.com. *Address:* 1563 Solano Avenue, PMB 545, Berkeley, CA 94707, USA (office). *Telephone:* (916) 278-6586 (office). *E-mail:* mackeym@mindspring.com. *Website:* www.marymackey.com.

MACKEY, Nathaniel, AB, PhD; American academic, poet, writer and editor; *Professor, University of California, Santa Cruz*; b. 25 Oct. 1947, Miami, Fla; m. Pascale Gaitet 1991; one d. one step-s. *Education:* Princeton Univ., Stanford Univ. *Career:* Asst Prof., Univ. of Wisconsin at Madison 1974–76; Ed., Hambone literary magazine 1974–; Asst Prof. and Dir of Black Studies, Univ. of Southern California 1976–79; Visiting Prof., Occidental Coll. 1979; Asst Prof., Bd of Studies in Literature and American Studies Program, Univ. of California, Santa Cruz 1979–81, Assoc. Prof. 1981–87, Prof. 1987–; Writer-in-residence, Washington, DC Project for the Arts 1986, Inst. of American Indian Arts, Santa Fe, NM 1987, 1988, Brown Univ. 1990, Intersection for the Arts, San Francisco 1991; Faculty mem. Naropa Inst., Boulder Summers 1991, 1993; Visiting Foreign Artist, Kootenay School of Writing, Vancouver, BC 1994; mem. Acad. of American Poets (mem. Bd of Chancellors 2001–). *Publications:* poetry: Four for Trane 1978, Septet for the End of Time 1983, Eroding Witness 1985, Outlandish 1992, School of Udhra 1993, Song of the Andoumboulou: 18–20 1994, Whatsaid Serif 1998, Splay Anthem (Nat. Book Award for Poetry) 2006; fiction: From a Broken Bottle Traces of Perfume Still Emanate Vol. I: Bedouin Hornbook 1986, Vol. II: Djbot Baghostus's Run 1993, Vol. III: Atet A.D. 2001, Vol. IV: Bass Cathedral 2008; non-fiction: Discrepant Engagement: Dissonance, Cross-Culturality and Experimental Writing 1993; other: Moment's Notice: Jazz in Poetry and Prose (ed. with Art Lange) 1993, Strick: Song of the Andoumboulou 16–25 (poems with musical accompaniment) 1995; contrib. to anthologies, scholarly journals and magazines. *Honours:* Co-ordinating Council of Literary Magazines Editor's Grant 1985, Whiting Writer's Award 1993. *Address:* c/o New Directions Publishing, 80 Eighth Avenue, New York, NY 10011, USA (office).

McKIBBEN, William (Bill); American environmental activist and author; *Scholar-in-Residence in Environmental Studies, Middlebury College*; b. 1960, Lexington, Mass; m. Sue Halpern; one d. *Career:* fmr Pres. Harvard Crimson newspaper; joined New Yorker magazine as staff writer, wrote much of 'Talk of the Town' column 1982–87 (resgnd); moved to Adirondack Mountains, upstate NY; led five-day walk across Vt to demand action on global warming Summer 2006; f. stepitup07.org to demand that Congress enact curbs on carbon emissions to cut global warming pollution 80 per cent by 2050; co-organized 1,400 global warming demonstrations across all 50 states of USA 14 April 2007; second day of action held 3 Nov. 2007; f. new campaign called 350.org to highlight need to reduce atmospheric CO_2 concentration from 385 ppm to at most 350 ppm March 2008; mem. Bd Grist Magazine; Scholar-in-Residence, Middlebury Coll., directs Middlebury Fellowships in Environmental Journalism. *Publications:* The End of Nature 1989, The Age of Missing Information 1992, Hope, Human and Wild: True Stories of Living Lightly on the Earth 1995, American Earth, Maybe One: A Personal and Environmental Argument for Single Child Families 1998, Hundred Dollar Holiday 1998, Long Distance: Testing the Limits of Body and Spirit in a Year of Living Strenuously 2001, Hope, Human and Wild, Enough: Staying Human in an Engineered Age 2003, Wandering Home 2005, The Comforting Whirlwind: God, Job, and the Scale of Creation 2005, Fight Global Warming Now: The Handbook for Taking Action in Your Community 2007, Deep Economy: The Wealth of Communities and the Durable Future 2007, The Bill McKibben Reader (essays) 2008, American Earth: Environmental Writing Since Thoreau (ed.) 2008, Eaarth: Making a Life on a Tough New Planet 2010; numerous articles on global warming, alternative energy and the need for more localized economies; frequent contrib. to The New York Times, The Atlantic Monthly, Harper's, Orion Magazine, Mother Jones, The New York Review of Books, Granta, Rolling Stone, Outside, Grist Magazine. *Honours:* hon. degrees from Sterling Coll., Green Mountain Coll., Unity Coll., State Univ. of NY, Colgate Univ., Lebanon Valley Coll.; Guggenheim Fellowship 1993, Lyndhurst Fellowship, Lannan Literary Award for nonfiction writing 2000. *Address:* Franklin Environmental Center at Hillcrest 205, Middlebury College, Middlebury, VT 05753, USA (office). *Telephone:* (802) 443-3489 (office). *E-mail:* mckibben.bill@gmail.com; wmckibbe@middlebury.edu (office). *Website:* www.billmckibben.com; www.middlebury.edu/academics/ump/majors/es (office).

MACKIE, John (see Levinson, Leonard)

MacKINNON, Catharine Alice, BA, JD, PhD; American academic, writer, lawyer and activist; *Elizabeth A. Long Professor of Law, University of Michigan Law School*; b. 7 Oct. 1946, Minneapolis, Minn.; d. of George E. MacKinnon and Elizabeth Davis MacKinnon. *Education:* Smith Coll., Yale Univ., Yale Law School. *Career:* Asst Prof. of Law, Univ. of Minnesota 1982–84; Prof. of Law, York Univ., Toronto 1988–90; Prof. of Law, Univ. of Michigan at Ann Arbor 1990–; Elizabeth A. Long Prof. of Law, Univ. of Michigan Law School; Visiting Prof., Univ. of Chicago 1997–2004; Roscoe Pound Visiting Prof. of Law, Harvard Univ. 2007; Wisenschaftskolleg zu Berlin 1992–93; Fellow, Center for Advanced Study, Stanford 2005–06; Fellow, AAAS 2005. *Achievement:* one of the most widely cited legal scholars writing in the English language. *Publications:* Sexual Harrassment of Working Women: A Case of Sex Discrimination 1979, Feminism Unmodified: Discourses on Life and Law 1987, Pornography and Civil Rights: A New Day for Women's Equality (with Andrea Dworkin) 1988, Toward a Feminist Theory of the State 1989, Only Words 1993, In Harm's Way: The Pornography Civil Rights Hearings (with Andrea Dworkin) 1998, Sex Equality 2001, rev. 2007, Directions in Sexual Harassment Law (with Reva Siegel) 2002, Women's Lives, Men's Laws 2005, Are Women Human? 2006; contribs to journals. *Honours:* several hon. degrees; Smith Medal, Wilber Lucius Cross Medal, Yale, American Bar Foundation Distinguished Research Award 2007. *Address:* University of Michigan Law School, 625 S State Street, Ann Arbor, MI 48109-1215, USA (office). *Telephone:* (734) 647-3595 (office). *E-mail:* camtwo@umich.edu (office).

MACKINNON, Lachlan; British poet, critic and literary journalist; b. 1956, Aberdeen, Scotland; pnr Wendy Cope. *Education:* Charterhouse School, Univ. of Oxford. *Career:* teacher of English, Winchester Coll. –2011; reviewer, Times Literary Supplement. *Plays:* Sixty Six (for Bush Theatre, London) 2011. *Publications:* Eliot: Auden, Lowell: Aspects of the Baudelairean Inheritance 1983, Monterey Cypress 1988, Shakespeare the Aesthete: An Exploration of Literary Theory 1988, The Coast of Bohemia 1991, The Lives of Elsa Triolet 1992, The Jupiter Collisions 2003, Small Hours 2010. *Honours:* Eric Gregory Award 1986, Cholmondeley Award 2011. *Address:* c/o Faber & Faber, Bloomsbury House, 74–77 Great Russell Street, London, WC1B 3DA, England (office). *Telephone:* (20) 7927-3800 (office). *Fax:* (20) 7927-3801 (office). *E-mail:* webmaster@faber.co.uk (office). *Website:* www.faber.co.uk (office).

McKINSTRY, Nancy, BA, MBA; American publishing executive; *Chairman of the Executive Board and CEO, Wolters Kluwer NV*; b. 4 Jan. 1959, Conn. *Education:* Univ. of Rhode Island, Kingston and Columbia Univ., New York. *Career:* held man. positions with Booz Allen Hamilton (int. man. consulting firm) 1980s; held a succession of man. positions with Wolters Kluwer cos in North America 1991–99, Vice-Pres. Product Man. and Sr Officer for CCH Inc. and Asst Vice-Pres. Electronic Products Div. for CCH –1996, Pres. and CEO CCH Legal Information Services 1996, CEO Wolters Kluwer's operations in North America –2001, mem. Exec. Bd Wolters Kluwer NV 2001–, Chair. Exec. Bd Wolters Kluwer NV, responsible for Wolters Kluwer's Divs, Business Devt,

Strategy and Tech. 2001–03, Chair. Exec. Bd and CEO 2003–; CEO SCP Communications (medical information co.) 1999; mem. Bd of Dirs Ericsson 2004–, MortgageIT, American Chamber of Commerce in the Netherlands 2004–, TiasNimbas Business School; mem. Advisory Council of Amsterdam Inst. of Finance, Dutch Advisory Council of Institut Européen d' Admin des Affaires (INSEAD), Advisory Bd Univ. of Rhode Island, Bd of Overseers of Columbia Business School, University Club of New York City. *Honours:* Hon. LLD (Univ. of Rhode Island) 2005; ranked by Fortune magazine as one of the 50 Most Powerful Women in Business outside the US (10th) 2007, (13th) 2008–11, ranked by Forbes magazine amongst The World's 100 Most Powerful Women (53rd) 2007, (82nd) 2008, (43rd) 2009, (77th) 2010, ranked by the Financial Times amongst Top 25 Businesswomen in Europe (eighth) 2006, (14th) 2007, and 16th in Top 50 Women in World Business 2009; included in Wall Street Journal's 50 Women to Watch 2007. *Address:* Zuidpoolsingel 2, PO Box 1030, 2400 BA Alphen aan den Rijn, The Netherlands (office). *Telephone:* (172) 641400 (office). *Fax:* (172) 474889 (office). *E-mail:* info@wolterskluwer.com (office). *Website:* www.wolterskluwer.com (office).

McKISSACK, Frederick Lemuel, BS; American writer; b. 12 Aug. 1939, Nashville, TN; m. Patricia McKissack 1964; three s. *Education:* Tennessee Agricultural and Industrial State Univ. *Career:* fmrly civil engineer. *Publications:* with Patricia McKissack: Abram, Abram, Where Are We Going? 1984, A Long Hard Journey: The Story of the Pullman Porter (Coretta Scott King Award) 1990, Martin Luther King, Jr: Man of Peace 1991, Carter G. Woodson: The Father of Black History 1991, Sojourner Truth: Ain't I a Woman (Boston Globe Horn Book Award for Non-Fiction 1993, Coretta Scott King Award 1993) 1992, Jesse Owens: Olympic Star 1992, Paul Robeson: A Voice to Remember 1992, Langston Hughes: Great American Poet 1992, African-American Inventors 1994, Black Diamond (Coretta Scott King Award) 1994, Christmas in the Big House, Christmas in the Quarters (Coretta Scott King Award 1995, ABC Children's Booksellers Choices Award 1995) 1994, George Washington Carver: The Peanut Scientist 1994, Red-Tail Angels: The Story of the Tuskegee Airmen of World War II (Carter G. Woodson Outstanding Merit Book 1996) 1995, Rebels Against Slavery: American Slave Revolts (Coretta Scott King Award 1997) 1996, Let My People Go (with illustrations by James E. Ransome) 1998, Young, Black and Determined: a biography of Lorraine Hansberry 1998, Black Hands, White Sails: The Story of African-American Whalers (Carter G. Woodson Book Award 2000, Coretta Scott King Award 2000, Soc. of Midland Authors Book Award for Juvenile Non-fiction 2000) 1999, Bugs! 2000, Nzingha: Warrior Queen of Matamba 2000, Ida B. Wells-Barnett: A Voice Against Violence (Soc. of School Librarians Int. Book Award) 2001, Messy Bessey's Garden (with illustrations by Dana Regan) 2002, Ralph J. Bunche: Peacemaker 2002, Satchel Paige: The Best Arm in Baseball 2002, Zora Neale Hurston, Writer and Storyteller 2002, Hard Labor: The First African Americans 1619 2004. *Honours:* Jane Addams Children's Book Award, 1990; Boston Globe/Horn Book Award, 1993. *Address:* c/o Scholastic, 557 Broadway, New York, NY 10012, USA.

McKISSACK, Patricia L'Ann Carwell, BA, MA; American writer; b. 9 Aug. 1944, Smyrna, TN; m. Frederick Lemuel McKissack 1964; three s. *Education:* Tennessee Agricultural and Industrial State Univ., Webster Univ. *Career:* fmrly teacher and children's book ed. *Publications:* The Inca 1985, Flossie & the Fox 1986, A Picture of Freedom: The Diary of Clotee, a Slave Girl, Belmont Plantation, Virginia, 1859, The Dark Thirty: Southern Tales of the Supernatural (Coretta Scott King Award 1993, John Newbery Medal 1993) 1992, Run Away Home 1997, Ma Dear's Aprons (with illustrations by Floyd Cooper) 1997, Can You Imagine (with photographs by Myles Pinkney) 1997, Color Me Dark 2000, The Honest-to-Goodness Truth (with illustrations by Giselle Potter) (Soc. of School Librarians Int. Book Award 2000, Storytelling World Award 2001) 2000, Nzingha: Warrior Queen of Matamba 2000, Goin' Someplace Special (with illustrations by Jerry Pinkney) (Coretta Scott King Award 2002, ABC Children's Booksellers Choices Award 2002) 2001; with Frederick McKissack: Abram, Abram, Where Are We Going? 1984, A Long Hard Journey: The Story of the Pullman Porter (Coretta Scott King Award) 1990, Martin Luther King, Jr: Man of Peace 1991, Carter G. Woodson: The Father of Black History 1991, Sojourner Truth: Ain't I a Woman (Boston Globe Horn Book Award for Non-Fiction 1993, Coretta Scott King Award 1993) 1992, Jesse Owens: Olympic Star 1992, Paul Robeson: A Voice to Remember 1992, Langston Hughes: Great American Poet 1992, African-American Inventors 1994, Black Diamond (Coretta Scott King Award) 1994, Christmas in the Big House, Christmas in the Quarters (Coretta Scott King Award 1995, ABC Children's Booksellers Choices Award 1995) 1994, George Washington Carver: The Peanut Scientist 1994, Red-Tail Angels: The Story of the Tuskegee Airmen of World War II (Carter G. Woodson Outstanding Merit Book 1996) 1995, Rebels Against Slavery: American Slave Revolts (Coretta Scott King Award 1997) 1996, Let My People Go (with illustrations by James E. Ransome) 1998, Young, Black and Determined: a biography of Lorraine Hansberry 1998, Black Hands, White Sails: The Story of African-American Whalers (Carter G. Woodson Book Award 2000, Coretta Scott King Award 2000, Soc. of Midland Authors Book Award for Juvenile Non-fiction 2000) 1999, Bugs! 2000, Nzingha: Warrior Queen of Matamba 2000, Ida B. Wells-Barnett: A Voice Against Violence (Soc. of School Librarians Int. Book Award) 2001, Messy Bessey's Garden (with illustrations by Dana Regan) 2002, Ralph J. Bunche: Peacemaker 2002, Satchel Paige: The Best Arm in Baseball 2002, Zora Neale Hurston, Writer and Storyteller 2002, Hard Labor: The First African Americans 1619 2004. *Honours:* Jane Addams Children's Book Award, 1990; Boston Globe/Horn Book Award 1993. *Address:* c/o Scholastic, 557 Broadway, New York, NY 10012, USA.

MACKRELL, Judith, BA, DPhil; British journalist and writer; b. 26 Oct. 1954, London, England; m. Simon Henson 1977; two s. *Education:* Univs of York and Oxford. *Career:* fmr Lecturer in English Literature; Dance Critic The Independent 1986–95, The Guardian 1995–; regular broadcasts for TV and radio and author of several books. *Publications:* Out of Line: The History of British New Dance 1992, Reading Dance 1995, Life in Dance (with Darcey Bussell) 1998, Oxford Dictionary of Dance (jtly) 2000, Bloomsbury Ballerina: The Life of Lydia Lopokova 2008. *Honours:* Hon. Fellow, Laban Centre. *Address:* The Guardian, Kings Place, 90 York Way, London, N1 9GU, England (office). *Telephone:* (20) 3353-2000 (office). *E-mail:* judith.mackrell@guardian.co.uk (office).

McKUEN, Rod; American writer and composer; b. 29 April 1933, Oakland, Calif. *Career:* has appeared in numerous films, concerts and on TV; composer of film scores and background music for TV shows; composer-lyricist of many songs; Pres. of numerous record and book cos; mem. Bd of Dirs American Nat. Theater of Ballet, Animal Concern; mem. Bd of Govs Nat. Acad. of Recording Arts and Sciences; mem. American Soc. of Composers, Authors and Publishers (ASCAP), Writers Guild, AFTRA, MPA, NARAS; Pres. of American Guild of Variety Artists (AGVA); mem. Bd of Dirs Calif. Music Theater. *Works include:* Symphony Number One, Concerto for Guitar and Orchestra, Concerto for Four Harpsichords, Seascapes for Piano and Orchestra, Adagio for Harp and Strings, Piano Variations, Concerto Number Three for Piano and Orchestra 1972, The Plains of My Country (ballet) 1972, The City (orchestral suite) 1973, Ballad of Distances (orchestral suite) 1973, Bicentennial Ballet 1975, Symphony Number Three 1975, over 200 record albums. *Film scores:* Joanna 1968, The Prime of Miss Jean Brodie 1969, Me, Natalie 1969, A Boy Named Charlie Brown 1970, Come to Your Senses 1971, Scandalous John 1971, Wildflowers 1971, The Borrowers 1973, Lisa Bright and Dark 1973, Awareness of Emily 1976, The Unknown War 1979, Man to Himself 1980, Portrait of Rod McKuen 1982, Death Rides this Trail 1983, The Living End 1983, The Beach 1984. *Publications:* And Autumn Came 1954, Stanyan Street and Other Sorrows 1966, Listen to the Warm 1967, Twelve Years of Christmas 1968, In Someone's Shadow 1969, With Love 1970, Caught in the Quiet 1970, Fields of Wonder 1971, The Carols of Christmas 1971, And to Each Season 1972, Beyond the Boardwalk 1972, Come to Me in Silence 1973, America–An Affirmation 1974, Seasons in the Sun 1974, Alone, Moment to Moment 1974, The McKuen Omnibus 1975, Celebrations of the Heart 1975, My Country 200 1975, I'm Strong but I Like Roses, Sleep Warm, Beyond the Boardwalk 1976, The Sea Around Me... The Hills Above 1976, Finding My Father (biographical) 1977, Coming Close to Earth 1977, Hand in Hand... 1977, Love's Been Good to Me 1979, We Touch the Sky 1979, Looking for a Friend 1980, An Outstretched Hand 1980, The Power Bright and Shining 1980, Too Many Midnights 1981, Rod McKuen's Book of Days 1981, The Beautiful Strangers 1981, The Works of Rod McKuen, Vol. 1, Poetry 1982, Watch for the Wind... 1982, Rod McKuen – 1984 Book of Days 1983, The Sound of Solitude 1983, Suspension Bridge 1984, Another Beautiful Day 1985, Valentines 1985, Intervals 1986. *Honours:* Grand Prix du Disque 1966, 1974, 1975, 1982, Golden Globe 1969, Motion Picture Daily Award 1969; LA Shrine Club Award 1975, Freedoms Foundation 1975, Horatio Alger Award 1976; Brandeis Univ. Literary Trust Award 1981, Freedoms Foundation Patriot Medal 1981, Salvation Army Man of the Year 1983, Rose d'Or, Cannes 1986, Myasthenia Gravis Community Service Award 1986. *Address:* PO Box 2783, Los Angeles, CA 90028, USA.

McLAREN, Colin Andrew, BA, MPhil, DipArch; British writer; b. 14 Dec. 1940, Middlesex, England; one s. one d. *Education:* University of London. *Career:* Librarian, Univ. of Aberdeen –1999; mem. Society of Authors. *Publications:* Rattus Rex, 1978; Crows in a Winter Landscape, 1979; Mother of the Free, 1980; A Twister over the Thames, 1981; The Warriors under the Stone, 1983; Crown and Gown: An Illustrated History of the University of Aberdeen (with J. J. Carter), 1994; Rare and Fair: A Visitor's History of Aberdeen University Library, 1995. Contributions: BBC Radio 3 and 4. *Honours:* Society of Authors Award for Best Adaptation, 1986.

McLAREN, John David, BEd, MA, PhD; Australian academic, writer and editor; *Professor Emeritus, Victoria University;* b. 7 Nov. 1932, Melbourne, Vic.; s. of David Lawrence McLaren and Katherine Euphemia McLaren; m. Shirley Marion McLaren (deceased); two s. *Education:* Univ. of Melbourne, Monash Univ. *Career:* Assoc. Ed. Overland 1966–93, Ed. 1993–97, Consulting Ed. 1997–; Head, Dept of Gen. Studies, Darling Downs Inst. of Advanced Educ. 1972–75, Dept of Humanities 1975–76, Foundation Chair., School of the Arts 1973–76; Head, Dept of Humanities, Footscray Inst. of Tech. 1976–89; Ed. Australian Book Review 1978–86; Prin. Lecturer, Footscray Inst. of Tech./Victoria Univ. of Tech. 1989–91; Prof. of Humanities, Victoria Univ. 1991–97, Hon. Prof. 1997–2001, Prof. Emer. 2001–; mem. Asscn for the Study of Australian Literature, Australian Studies Asscn for South Asia (Vice-Pres. 1997), South Pacific Asscn for Commonwealth Language and Literature Studies. *Publications:* Our Troubled Schools 1968, Dictionary of Australian Education 1974, Australian Literature: An Historical Introduction 1989, The New Pacific Literatures: Culture and Environment in the European Pacific 1993, Prophet from the Desert: Critical Essays on Patrick White (ed.) 1995, Writing in Hope and in Fear: Postwar Australian Literature as Politics, 1945–72 1996, States of Imagination 2001, Free Radicals 2003, Not in Tranquillity 2005, Journey Without Arrival: the Life and Work of Vincent Buckley 2009; contribs to scholarly books and journals. *Honours:* Hon. Life mem. Int. Australian Studies Asscn; Fulbright Sr Scholar 1990, Australian Research Council Research Grants 1991, 1993, 1996, 2006, Humanities Research Centre Scholar, ANU 1994, Walter McRae Russell Award for the best work of literary scholarship on an Australian subject published in the previous two years 2011. *Address:* FAEHD, Footscray Park Campus, Victoria University, PO Box 14428, MCMC, Melbourne, Vic. 8001, Australia (office). *E-mail:* john.mclaren@vu.edu.au (office). *Website:* (office).

MacLAVERTY, Bernard, BA, DipEd; Irish writer and dramatist; b. 14 Sept. 1942, Belfast, Northern Ireland; s. of John MacLaverty and Mary MacLaverty; m. Madeline McGuckin 1967; one s. three d. *Education:* Queen's Univ., Belfast. *Career:* fmrly medical lab. technician, English teacher; fmr Writer-in-Residence, Univ. of Aberdeen; mem. Aosdána. *Stage:* opera libretti: The King's Conjecture 2008, The Letter 2010. *Television:* plays: My Dear Palestrina 1980, Phonefun Limited 1982, The Daily Woman 1986, Sometime in August 1989; documentary: Hostages 1992; adaptation: The Real Charlotte, by Somerville and Ross 1989. *Screenplays:* Cal (London Evening Standard Award for Screenplay 1984) 1984, Lamb 1985, Bye-Child (short film, also Dir) (Best First Dir, BAFTA Scotland 2004) 2003. *Radio plays:* My Dear Palestrina 1980, Secrets 1981, No Joke 1983, The Break 1988, Some Surrender 1988, Lamb 1992, Grace Notes 2003, The Woman from the North 2007, Winter Storm 2009. *Publications:* novels: Lamb 1980, Cal 1983, Grace Notes (Saltire Scottish Book of the Year Award 1997) 1997, The Anatomy School 2001; short story collections: Secrets and Other Stories 1977, A Time to Dance and Other Stories 1982, The Great Profundo and Other Stories 1987, Walking the Dog and Other Stories 1994, Matters of Life & Death and Other Stories 2006; juvenile fiction: A Man in Search of a Pet 1978, Andrew McAndrew 1988. *Honours:* NI and Scottish Arts Councils Awards, Irish Sunday Independent Award 1983, Scottish Writer of the Year (co-recipient) 1988, Soc. of Authors Travelling Scholarship 1994, Stakis Scottish Writer of the Year, Creative Scotland Award 2003. *Literary Agent:* c/o Gill Coleridge, Rogers, Coleridge & White, 20 Powis Mews, London, W11 1JN, England. *Telephone:* (20) 7221-3717. *Fax:* (20) 7229-9084. *E-mail:* info@rcwlitagency.co.uk. *Website:* www.rcwlitagency.co.uk; www.bernardmaclaverty.com.

MacLEAN, Rory, BA (Hons), FRSL; Canadian/British author and broadcaster; b. 5 Nov. 1954, Vancouver, BC; m. Katrin Latta 1992; one s. *Education:* Upper Canada Coll., Toronto, Ryerson Univ., Toronto. *Radio:* Itchy Feet, Out-takes, Following Durrell, Building Icarus, Magic Bus (all for BBC). *Publications:* Stalin's Nose 1992, The Oatmeal Ark 1996, Under the Dragon 1998, Next Exit Magic Kingdom 2000, Falling for Icarus 2004, Magic Bus 2006, Missing Lives 2010, Gift of Time 2011. *Honours:* Canada Council Independent Travel Writing Award, Yorkshire Post Best First Book Award, Arts Council of England Writers' Award 1998; awards for short films at Cannes Int. Festival du Film Amateur, Los Angeles Filmex, Mannheim and Canadian Television Commercials Festival. *Literary Agent:* c/o Peter Straus, Rogers, Coleridge & White Literary Agency, 20 Powis Mews, London, W11 1JN, England. *Telephone:* (20) 7221-3717. *Fax:* (20) 7229-9084. *Website:* www.rcwlitagency.co.uk; www.rorymaclean.com.

McLELLAN, David Thorburn, LLB, MA, DPhil; British political philosopher, writer and academic; *Professor of Political Theory, Goldsmiths College, London*; b. 10 Feb. 1940, Hertford, Herts.; m. Annie Brassart 1967; two d. *Education:* St John's Coll., Oxford. *Career:* fmr Prof. of Political Theory, Univ. of Kent; Fellow and Prof. of Political Theory, Goldsmiths Coll., London. *Publications:* The Young Hegelians and Karl Marx 1969, Karl Marx: His Life and Thought 1974, Engels 1977, Marxism After Marx 1980, Ideology 1986, Marxism and Religion 1987, Simone Weil: Utopian Pessimist 1989, Unto Caesar: The Political Importance of Christianity 1993, Political Christianity 1997, Karl Marx: A Biography 2006, Marxism after Marx 2007; contrib. to professional journals. *Address:* 13 Ivy Lane, Canterbury, Kent, CT1 1TU, England (home).

MacLENNAN, Murdoch; British newspaper executive; *CEO, Telegraph Group Ltd*. *Career:* started career as graduate trainee The Scotsman newspaper; Production Dir Scottish Daily Record and Sunday Mail 1982–84; Dir of Production Mirror Group 1984–85; Production and Tech. Dir Express Newspapers 1985–89, Man. Dir 1989–92; Group Operations Dir Mirror Group Newspapers and Man. Dir Scottish Daily Record and Sunday Mail 1992–94; Group Man. Dir Associated Newspapers 1994–2004; CEO Telegraph Group Ltd 2004–; fmr Pres. IFRA (newspaper publishers' asscn); Chair. Press Asscn Remuneration Cttee; Vice-Pres. and Appeals Chair. Newspaper Press Fund; Chair. (non-exec.) PA Group 2010–; Companion Inst. of Man.; Freeman of the City of London. *Honours:* Dr hc (Paisley). *Address:* Telegraph Group Ltd, 1 Canada Square, Canary Wharf, London, E14 5DT, England (office). *Telephone:* (20) 7538-5000 (office). *Fax:* (20) 7513-2512 (office). *Website:* www.pressoffice.telegraph.co.uk.

MACLEOD, Alison; British writer; b. 12 April 1920, Hendon, Middlesex. *Publications:* The Heretics (aka The Heretic) 1965, The Hireling (aka The Trusted Servant) 1968, City of Light (aka No Need of the Sun) 1969, The Muscovite 1971, The Jesuit (aka Prisoner of the Queen) 1972, The Portingale 1976, The Death of Uncle Joe 1997. *Address:* Room 27, Mary Feilding Guild, 1 View Road, London, N6 4DJ, England (home). *Telephone:* (20) 3213-0129 (home).

MacLEOD, Alistair, BA, BEd, MA, PhD; Canadian writer and academic; *Professor Emeritus of English, University of Windsor*; b. 20 July 1936, North Battleford, SK; m. Anita MacLellan 1971; six s. *Education:* Nova Scotia Teachers Coll., St Francis Xavier Univ., Univ. of New Brunswick, Univ. of Notre Dame. *Career:* Prof. of English, Nova Scotia Teachers Coll. 1961–63; Faculty, Indiana Univ., Fort Wayne 1966–69; Prof. of English, Univ. of Windsor 1969–2000, Prof. Emer. 2000–. *Publications:* The Lost Salt Gift of Blood 1976, As Birds Bring Forth the Sun and Other Stories 1986, No Great Mischief 2000, Island 2000, To Every Thing There Is a Season 2004; Contribs: anthologies and periodicals. *Honours:* Hon. doctorates, St Francis Xavier Univ. 1987, Univ. Coll., Cape Breton 1991; Best Book of the Year, Publisher's Weekly 1988, International IMPAC Dublin Literary Award 2001. *Address:* c/o Department of English, University of Windsor, Windsor, ON N9B 3P4, Canada.

MacLEOD, Joan, BA, MA; Canadian playwright and academic; *Assistant Professor of Writing, University of Victoria*; b. 1954, Vancouver, BC; m. Bill Loach; one d. *Education:* Univ. of Victoria, Univ. of British Columbia. *Career:* fmr Playwright-in-Residence, Tarragon Theatre, Toronto; Asst Prof. of Writing, Univ. of Victoria 2004–; Senior Playwright-in-Residence, Banff Centre Playwrights' Colony 2009. *Television:* scripted episodes for Edgemont (CBC TV) 2001–05. *Plays:* Jewel 1987, Toronto, Mississippi 1987, Amigo's Blue Guitar (Governor General's Award in Drama 1991) 1990, The Hope Slide (Chalmers' Award for Best Canadian Play 1993) 1992, Little Sister (Chalmers' Award for Best Canadian Play 1995) 1992, 2000 1996, The Shape of a Girl (Betty Mitchell Award for Best New Play 2001, Jessie Richardson Award for Best New Play 2002) 2001, Homechild 2006, Another Home Invasion 2009. *Publications:* Jewel/Toronto, Mississippi 1989, Amigo's Blue Guitar 1991, The Hope Slide/Little Sister 1995, The Shape of a Girl/Jewel 1995, 2000 1997, Homechild 2008, Another Home Invasion 2009; The Secret Garden (Dora Mavor Moore Award) 1986. *Honours:* Univ. of Victoria R.H. Petch Memorial Prize for Creative Writing 1978, Univ. of BC Douglas Bankson Prize for Long Fiction 1980, Siminovitch Prize 2011. *Literary Agent:* Pam Winter, Gary Goddard Agency, 10 St Mary Street, Suite 305, Toronto, ON M4Y 1P9, Canada. *Telephone:* (416) 928-0299. *Fax:* (416) 924-9593. *E-mail:* goddard@canadafilm.com. *Website:* www.garygoddardagency.com. *Address:* c/o University of Victoria, Office FIA 251, PO Box 1700, STN CSC, Victoria, BC V8W 2Y2, Canada (office). *Telephone:* (250) 721-7306 (office). *Fax:* (250) 721-7212 (office). *E-mail:* macleodj@uvic.ca (office). *Website:* finearts.uvic.ca/writing/faculty/macleod (office); www.joanmacleod.com.

McLEOD, Wallace Edmond, BA, AM, PhD; Canadian academic and writer; *Professor Emeritus of Classics, Victoria College, Toronto*; b. 30 May 1931, East York, Ont.; s. of Angus Edmond McLeod and Mary Ann Elta Shier; m. Elizabeth Marion Staples 1957; three s. one d. *Education:* Univ. of Toronto, Harvard Univ. *Career:* instructor, Trinity Coll., Hartford, Conn. 1955–56, Univ. of British Columbia 1959–61; Lecturer, Univ. of Western Ontario 1961–62; Special Lecturer, Victoria Coll., Univ. of Toronto 1962–63, Asst Prof. 1963–66, Assoc. Prof. 1966–74, Anson Jones Lecturer 1984, Prof. of Classics 1974–96, Prof. Emer. 1996–, ANZMRC Lecturer 1997, Inaugural Sam Houston Lecturer 1998, Walter Calloway Lecturer 2002, John Ross Robertson Lecturer 2005; mem. Freemasons, Philalethes Soc. (Pres. 1992), Soc. of Blue Friars, Grand Abbot, Classical Asscn of Canada, American Philological Asscn, Archaeological Inst. of America. *Publications:* Composite Bows from the Tomb of Tut'ankhamun 1970, Beyond the Pillars: More Light on Freemasonry (ed. and contrib.) 1973, Meeting the Challenge: The Lodge Officer at Work (ed. and contrib.) 1976, The Sufferings of John Coustos (ed.) 1979, Whence Come We?: Freemasonry in Ontario 1764–1980 (ed. and contrib.) 1980, Self Bows and Other Archery Tackle from the Tomb of Tut'ankhamun 1982, The Old Gothic Constitutions (ed.) 1985, The Old Charges 1986, A Candid Disquisition (ed.) 1989, For the Cause of Good 1990, The Grand Design: Selected Masonic Addresses and Papers 1991, The Quest for Light: Selected Masonic Addresses 1997, Freemasonry on Both Sides of the Atlantic: Essays Concerning the Craft in the British Isles, Europe, the United States, and Mexico (Assoc. Ed.) 2002, A Daily Advancement in Masonic Knowledge: The Collected Blue Friar Lectures (ed. and contrib.) 2003; contrib. to numerous books and journals. *Honours:* Philalethes Certificate of Literature 1984. *Address:* Victoria College, University of Toronto, 73 Queen's Park, Toronto, ON M5S 1K7 (office); 399 St Clements Avenue, Toronto, ON M5N 1M2, Canada (home). *Telephone:* (416) 585-4488 (office). *Fax:* (416) 585-4584 (office). *E-mail:* w.mcleod@utoronto.ca (office).

McLERRAN, Alice, BA, MS, MPH, PhD; American writer; b. 24 June 1933, West Point, NY; m. Larry Dean McLerran 1976; two s. one d. *Education:* Stanford Univ., Univ. of California at Berkeley, Harvard School of Public Health (Certification in Psychiatric Epidemiology). *Career:* mem. Authors' Guild, Soc. of Children's Book Writers and Illustrators. *Publications:* The Mountain that Loved a Bird 1985, Secrets 1990, Roxaboxen 1991, I Want to go Home 1992, Dreamsong 1992, Hugs 1993, Kisses 1993, The Ghost Dance 1995, The Year of the Ranch 1996, The Legacy of Roxaboxen: A Collection of Voices 1998, Dragonfly 2000. *Honours:* Southwest Book Award 1991, Notable Children's Trade Book in Field of Social Studies 1996, 1997, Southwest Book Award 2005, Judy Goddard Children's Author Award, Ariz. Library Asscn 2005, Kroeber Prize. *Address:* 70 S Country Road, Bellport, NY 11713, USA (home). *E-mail:* alicemclerran@mac.com (home). *Website:* alicemclerran.us.

McLOUGHLIN, Merrill, BA; American journalist; b. 6 Jan. 1945, Skowhegan, Maine; d. of Comerford W. McLoughlin and Elizabeth M. McLoughlin; m. Michael A. Ruby 1986. *Education:* Smith Coll. *Career:* Educ. Ed. Newsweek Magazine 1973–78, Tech. Writer 1978–1982, Nat. Affairs Ed.

1982–1986; Asst Man. Ed. US News & World Report 1986–89, Co-Ed (with Michael A. Ruby) 1989–96; now freelance journalist in Milwaukee, Wis.; judge, Award for Excellence in Economic Reporting, Fund for American Studies 2005. *Publication:* The Impeachment and Trial of President Clinton 1999, A Good Fight (with Sarah Brady) 2002.

McMANUS, (I.) Chris; British author and academic; *Professor of Psychology and Medical Education, University College London. Career:* fmrly at Univ. Coll. London, Imperial Coll. School of Medicine; Prof. of Psychology and Medical Education, Dept of Psychology, Univ. of London 1997; Assoc. Ed. of Laterality 1995–2000; Assoc. Ed., British Journal of Psychology; editorial bd mem., Journal of Health Psychology, Psychology – Health and Medicine, Developmental Neuropsychology, Perception, Medical Education. *Publications:* Psychology in Medicine 1992, Right Hand Left Hand (Aventis Prize 2003) 2002; contrib. to British Journal of Psychology, British Medical Journal, Journal of Hygiene, The Lancet, Nature, New Scientist, Perception, Times Higher Education Supplement, TLS. *Honours:* Wellcome Trust Prize 2002. *Address:* Department of Psychology, University College London, 26 Bedford Way, London, WC1H 0AP, England (office). *Telephone:* (20) 7679-5390 (office). *Fax:* (20) 7436-4276 (office). *E-mail:* i.mcmanus@ucl.ac.uk (office). *Website:* www.psychol.ucl.ac.uk (office); www.righthandleftland.com.

McMANUS, James, BA, MA; American poet, writer and teacher; b. 22 March 1951, New York, NY; m. Jennifer Arra 1992; one s. three d. *Education:* Univ. of Illinois at Chicago. *Career:* faculty mem., School of the Art Inst., Chicago 1981–; Rockefeller Foundation Bellagio Residency 1997; Lois Mackey Distinguished Prof. of Writing, Beloit Coll. 2010; mem. Associated Writing Programs, PEN. *Publications:* Going to the Sun (novel) 1996, Positively Fifth Street (non-fiction) 2003, Physical: An American Checkup 2006, Cowboys Full: The Story of Poker (non-fiction) 2009. *Honours:* Guggenheim Fellowship 1994–95; Carl Sandburg Prize 1996, Soc. of Midland Authors Nonfiction Awards 2004, 2009. *Address:* 544 Sterling Road, Kenilworth, IL 60043 (home); School of the Art Institute, 37 South Wabash, Chicago, IL 60603, USA (office). *Telephone:* (847) 256-4109 (home). *E-mail:* jmcmanus@saic.edu (office); arramc@msn.com.

McMANUS, Jason Donald, BA, MPA; American journalist; b. 3 March 1934, Mission, Kan.; s. of John A. McManus and Stella F. Gosney; m. 1st Patricia A. Paulson 1958 (divorced 1966); one s.; m. 2nd Deborah H. Murphy 1973; two d. *Education:* Davidson Coll., Princeton Univ. and Univ. of Oxford (Rhodes Scholar). *Career:* Common Market Bureau Chief, Time Magazine, Paris 1962–64; Assoc. Ed. Time Magazine, New York 1964–68, Sr Ed. 1968–75, Asst Man. Ed. 1975–78, Exec. Ed. 1978–83; Corporate Ed. Time Inc. 1983–85; Man. Ed. Time Magazine 1985–87; Ed.-in-Chief, Time Inc. 1987–95. *Honours:* Hon. LittD (Davidson Coll.) 1979.

McMASTER, Juliet Sylvia, BA, MA, PhD; Canadian academic and writer; *University Professor Emerita, University of Alberta*; b. 2 Aug. 1937, Kisumu, Kenya; m. Rowland McMaster 1968; one s. one d. *Education:* St Anne's Coll., Oxford, Univ. of Alberta. *Career:* Asst Prof., Univ. of Alberta 1965–70, Assoc. Prof. 1970–76, Prof. 1976–86, Univ. Prof. 1986–, Univ. Prof. Emer. 2000–; Gen. Ed. Juvenilia Press 1994–; mem. Jane Austen Soc. of N America, Asscn of Canadian Univ. Teachers of English. *Publications:* Thackeray: The Major Novels 1971, Jane Austen's Achievement 1976, Trollope's Palliser Novels 1978, Jane Austen on Love 1978, The Novel from Sterne to James 1981, Dickens the Designer 1987, The Beautifull Cassandra 1993, Jane Austen the Novelist 1995, Cambridge Companion to Jane Austen (co-ed.) 1997, Reading the Body in the Eighteenth-Century Novel 2004; contrib. to 19th-Century Fiction, Victorian Studies, Modern Language Quarterly, English Studies in Canada. *Honours:* Canada Council Post-Doctoral Fellowship 1969–70, Guggenheim Fellowship 1976–77, McCalla Professorship 1982–83, Univ. of Alberta Research Prize 1986, Killam Research Fellowship 1987–88, Molson Prize 1994. *Address:* Department of English, University of Alberta, Edmonton, AB T6G 2E5, Canada (office). *Telephone:* (780) 436-5284 (home). *Fax:* (780) 492-8142 (office). *E-mail:* juliet.mcmaster@ualberta.ca (office). *Website:* www.arts.ualberta.ca/~jchook (office).

McMASTER, Susan, (S. M. Page), BA; Canadian poet and editor; *Senior Book Editor, National Gallery of Canada*; b. 11 Aug. 1950, Toronto, Ont.; m. Ian McMaster 1969; two d. *Education:* Carleton Univ., Ottawa Teachers' Coll. *Career:* Founding Ed. magazine for women, Branching Out 1973–75; Sr Book Ed., Nat. Gallery of Canada 1989–98, 2002–; Ed.-in-Chief Vernissage 1999–2002; mem. League of Canadian Poets, PEN, Writers' Union of Canada, Writers' Fed. of Nova Scotia, Writers' Trust (Canada). *Recordings:* Wordmusic 1986, Dangerous Graces 1997, Sugar Beat music and poetry (CD) 1999, Geode music and poetry (CD) 2000, Until the Light Bends (CD) 2004. *Publications:* Pass This Way Again (co-author) 1983, Dark Galaxies 1986, North/South (co-author) 1987, Dangerous Graces (ed.) 1987, Women and Language (ed.) 1990, Two Women Talking, Erin Mouré and Bronwen Wallace 1991, Illegitimate Positions (ed.) 1991, The Hummingbird Murders 1992, Learning to Ride 1994, Dangerous Times (ed.) 1996, Uncommon Prayer 1997, Siolence: Poets on Violence and Silence (ed.) 1998, Waging Peace: Poetry and Political Action (ed.) 2002, La Deriva del Pianeta/World Shift (in English with Italian trans.) 2003, Until the Light Bends 2004, The Gargoyle's Left Ear: Writing in Ottawa 2007, Crossing Arcs: Alzheimer's, My Mother, and Me 2009, Paper Affair: Poems Selected and New 2010, Pith and Wry: Canadian Poetry (ed.) 2010; contrib. to magazines, journals, broadcasts, scripts and anthologies. *Honours:* various awards from Canada Council for the Arts, Ontario Arts Council, Regional Municipality of Ottawa Carleton, Canadian Authors' Asscn, League of Canadian Poets. *Address:* 43 Belmont Avenue, Ottawa, ON K1S 0T9 (home); National Gallery of Canada, 380 Sussex Drive, POB 427, Stn A, Ottawa, ON K1N 9N4, Canada (office). *E-mail:* smcmaster@ncf.ca (home); smcmaster@gallery.ca (office). *Website:* web.ncf.ca/smcmaster.

McMILLAN, James Reid, (Coriolanus), MA; British journalist (retd); b. 30 Oct. 1925, England; m. Doreen Smith 1953; three s. one d. *Education:* Univ. of Glasgow. *Career:* fmr leader writer, Daily Express. *Publications:* The Glass Lie 1964, American Take-Over 1967, Anatomy of Scotland 1969, The Honours Game 1970, Roots of Corruption 1971, British Genius (with Peter Grosvenor) 1972, The Way We Were 1900–1950 (trilogy) 1977–80, Five Men at Nuremberg 1984, The Dunlop Story 1989, From Finchley to the World – Margaret Thatcher 1990. *Address:* Thurlestone, Fairmile Park Road, Cobham, Surrey, KT11 2PL, England. *Telephone:* (1932) 862180.

MacMILLAN, Margaret Olwen, OC, BA, BPhil, DPhil, FRSL; Canadian university administrator, historian and writer; *Warden, St Antony's College Oxford*; b. Dec. 1943, Toronto, Ont. *Education:* Univ. of Toronto, St Antony's Coll., Oxford, UK. *Career:* Prof. of History, Ryerson Univ., Toronto 1975–2002; Provost and Vice Chancellor, Trinity Coll., Univ. of Toronto 2002–07; Warden St Antony's Coll., Oxford 2007–; Ed. International Journal 1995–2003; Sr Fellow, Massey Coll., Univ. of Toronto. *Publications:* Women of the Raj 1988, Canada and NATO: Uneasy Past, Uncertain Future 1990, Peacemakers: Six Months that Changed the World 2001, Paris 1919 2002, Parties Long Estranged: Canada and Australia in the 20th Century (co-ed.) 2003, Canada's House: Rideau Hall and the Invention of a Canadian Home (with Marjorie Harris and Anne L. Desjardins) 2004, Seize the Hour: When Nixon Met Mao 2006, Nixon and Mao 2007, Dangerous Games: The Uses and Abuses of History 2009. *Honours:* Hon. Fellow, St Antony's Coll. Oxford; Gov.-Gen.'s Literary Award 2003, BBC 4 Samuel Johnson Prize for Non-Fiction, Duff Cooper Award, Hessell-Tiltman Prize. *Address:* Office of the Warden, St Antony's College, 62 Woodstock Road, Oxford, OX2 6JF, England (office). *Telephone:* (1865) 284717 (office). *Fax:* (1865) 274526 (office). *E-mail:* margaret.macmillan@sant.ox.ac.uk (office). *Website:* www.sant.ox.ac.uk (office).

McMILLAN, Terry, BA; American writer; b. 18 Oct. 1951, Port Huron, Mich.; d. of Edward McMillan and Madeline Tillman; one s. *Education:* Univ. of Calif., Berkeley and Columbia Univ. Film School. *Career:* fmr sec.; Guest Columnist 'Hers' column, New York Times; book reviewer for New York Times Book Review, Atlanta Constitution, Philadelphia Inquirer; fmr Assoc. Prof. of English, Univ. of Arizona, Prof. 1988–91; fmr Visiting Prof. in Creative Writing, Univ. of Wyoming, Stanford Univ.; Fiction Judge Nat. Book Awards 1990; Nat. Endowment for the Arts Fellow 1988; mem. PEN USA; Doubleday/Columbia Univ. Literary Fellow; Fellow, Yaddo Artist Colony, Macdowell Colony. *Publications:* Mama (Nat. Book Award, Before Columbus Foundation) 1987, Disappearing Acts 1989, Breaking Ice (ed) 1990, Waiting To Exhale 1995 (co-writer screenplay), How Stella Got Her Groove Back 1996, A Day Late and a Dollar Short 2002, The Interruption of Everything 2005, It's Okay if You're Clueless 2006, Getting to Happy 2010. *Honours:* NY Woman of the Year in Books 1993, Glamour Magazine Woman of the Year 1996. *Address:* c/o Publicity, Author Mail, Viking Penguin, 375 Hudson Street, New York, NY 10014-3657, USA (office). *E-mail:* fanmail@terrymcmillan.com (office). *Website:* www.terrymcmillan.com.

McMILLEN, Neil Raymond, BA, MA, PhD; American academic and writer; *Professor Emeritus, University of Southern Mississippi, Hattiesburg*; b. 2 Jan. 1939, Lake Odessa, MI; m. Beverly J. Smith 1960; one s., one d. *Education:* Univ. of Southern Mississippi, Vanderbilt Univ. *Career:* Asst Prof. of History, Ball State Univ., Muncie 1967–69; Asst Prof., Univ. of Southern Mississippi, Hattiesburg 1969–70, Assoc. Prof. 1970–78, Prof. of History 1978–2001, Prof. Emer. 2001–. *Publications:* The Citizens' Council: Organized Resistance to the Second Reconstruction 1971, Thomas Jefferson: Philosopher of Freedom 1973, Dark Journey: Black Mississippians in the Age of Jim Crow 1989, A Synopsis of American History (with Charles Bolton, eighth edn) 1997, Remaking Dixie: The Impact of World War II on the American South (ed.) 1997. *Honours:* Bancroft Prize 1990. *Address:* 509 Bay Street, Hattiesburg, MS 39401-3934, USA (home). *Telephone:* (601) 544-8047 (home). *E-mail:* nmcmillen@aol.com (home).

MacMULLEN, Ramsay, AB, AM, PhD; American writer and academic (retd); *Professor Emeritus, Yale University*; b. 3 March 1928, New York, NY; s. of Charles William MacMullen and Margaret Richmond MacMullen; m. 1st Edith Merriman Nye 1954 (divorced 1991); two s. two d.; m. 2nd Margaret McNeill 1992. *Education:* Harvard Univ. *Career:* Instructor then Asst Prof., Univ. of Oregon 1956–61; Assoc. Prof. then Prof., Brandeis Univ. 1961–67, Chair. Dept of Classics 1965–66, Pres. Faculty Senate; Fellow, Inst. for Advanced Study, Princeton, NJ 1964–65; Prof., Yale Univ. 1967–93, Prof. Emer. 1993–, Chair., Dept of History 1970–72, Dunham Prof. of History and Classics 1979–93, Master, Calhoun Coll. 1984–90; Fulbright Fellowship 1960–61; Guggenheim Fellowship 1964; Sr Fellow, Nat. Endowment for the Humanities 1974–75; mem. Asscn of Ancient Historians (Pres. 1978–81), Friends of Ancient History, Soc. for the Promotion of Roman Studies. *Publications:* Soldier and Civilian in the Later Roman Empire 1963, Enemies of the Roman Order 1966, Constantine 1969, Roman Social Relations 1974, Roman Government's Response to Crisis 1976, Paganism in the Roman Empire 1981, Christianizing the Roman Empire 1984, Corruption and the

Decline of Rome 1988, Changes in the Roman Empire 1990, Paganism and Christianity (with E. N. Lane) 1992, Christianity and Paganism 1997, Sisters of the Brush 1997, Romanisation in the Time of Augustus 2001, Sarah's Choice, 1828–32 2001, Feeling in History, Ancient and Modern 2003, Voting About God in Early Church Councils 2006, The Second Church: Popular Christianity A.D. 200–400 2009, The Earliest Romans 2011; contribs to professional journals. *Honours:* Porter Prize, Coll. Art Asscn 1964, Lifetime Award for Scholarly Distinction, American Historical Asscn 2000. *Address:* 25 Temple Court, New Haven, CT 06511, USA (home). *E-mail:* ramsay.macmullen@yale.edu (office).

McMULLEN, Sean Christopher, BA, MA, PhD; Australian writer; b. (John Christopher McMullen), 21 Dec. 1948, Sale, Vic.; one d. *Education:* Univ. of Melbourne, Canberra Coll. of Adult Educ., Latrobe Univ., Deakin Univ. *Career:* computer systems analyst, Bureau of Meteorology 1981–; speaker to various groups; mem. SFWA, Boobooks. *Publications:* Call to the Edge 1992, Voices in the Light 1994, Mirror Sun Rising 1995, The Centurion's Empire 1998, Souls in the Great Machine 1999, The Miocene Arrow 2000, Eyes of the Calculor 2001, Voyage of the Shadowmoon 2002, Glass Dragons 2004, Voidfarer 2005, Before the Storm 2007, The Time Engine 2008; Non-Fiction: Strange Constellations: A History of Australian Science Fiction (with Russell Blackford and Van Ikin) 1999; contributions: anthologies, including Year's Best Science Fiction 2005, Dreaming Again 2008; Periodicals, including: Eidolon; Sirius; Aurealis; Analog Science Fiction and Fact; Magazine of Fantasy and Science Fiction; Interzone. *Honours:* Writing Prize, World Science Fiction Convention, 1985, Ditmar Awards 1991, 1992, 1996, William Atheling Awards 1992, 1993, 1996, 1998, 2000, Aurealis Awards 1998, 2000, 2003, Analog Readers Award 2002, Nova Fantasy KA Award 2003. *Literary Agent:* Chris Lotts, Ralph M. Vicinaga Ltd, 303 W 18th Street, New York, NY 10010, USA. *Address:* GPO Box 2653, Melbourne, Vic. 3001, Australia (home). *Telephone:* (4) 11439847 (home). *E-mail:* scm@unite.com.au (home). *Website:* www.seanmcmullen.net.au.

McMURTRY, Larry Jeff; American writer; b. 3 June 1936, Wichita Falls, Tex.; s. of William Jefferson McMurtry and Hazel McIver; m. Josephine Ballard 1959 (divorced 1966); one s. *Television includes:* co-writer and co-producer with Diana Ossana of CBS mini-series Streets of Laredo and ABC mini-series Dead Man's Walk 1996. *Publications:* Horseman Pass By (aka Hud) 1961, Leaving Cheyenne 1963, The Last Picture Show 1966, In a Narrow Grave (essays) 1968, Moving On 1970, All My Friends Are Going to be Strangers 1972, It's Always We Rambled (essay) 1974, Terms of Endearment 1975, Somebody's Darling 1978, Cadillac Jack 1982, The Desert Rose 1983, Lonesome Dove 1985, Texasville 1987, Film Flam: Essay on Hollywood 1987, Anything for Billy 1988, Some Can Whistle 1989, Buffalo Girls 1990, The Evening Star 1992, Streets of Laredo 1993, Pretty Boy Floyd (with Diana Ossana) 1993, The Late Child 1995, Dead Man's Walk 1995, Zeke and Ned (novel, with Diana Ossana) 1996, Comanche Moon 1997, Duane's Depressed 1998, Walter Benjamin at the Dairy Queen 1999, Boone's Lick 2000, Sin Killer: The Berrybender Narratives, Book One 2002, The Wandering Hill: The Berrybender Narratives, Book Two 2003, Folly and Glory: The Berrybender Narratives, Book Three 2004, Loop Group 2004, When the Light Goes 2007, Books: A Memoir 2008, Rhino Ranch 2009, Literary Life: A Second Memoir 2010, Hollywood: A Third Memoir 2010. *Address:* Saria Co. Inc., 2509 North Campbell Avenue, Suite 95, Tucson, AZ 85719, USA (office).

McNAB, Andy; British writer; b. 1959. *Career:* joined the army 1976, mem. 22 SAS Regiment, B Squadron 1984–93; writer 1993–; currently Dir, security co. running a specialist training course for individuals working in hostile environments. *Publications:* adult fiction: Remote Control 1997, Crisis Four 1999, Firewall 2000, Last Light 2001, Liberation Day 2002, Dark Winter 2003, Deep Black 2004, Aggressor 2005, Recoil 2006, Crossfire 2007; juvenile fiction: Boy Soldier (with Robert Rigby) 2005, Payback (with Robert Rigby) 2005, Avenger (with Robert Rigby) 2006; non-fiction: Bravo Two Zero (autobiog.) 1993, Immediate Action (autobiog.) 1995. *Honours:* DCM, MM. *Address:* c/o Transworld, 61–63 Uxbridge Road, London, W5 5SA, England. *Website:* www.booksattransworld.co.uk/andymcnab/home.htm.

McNAIR, Wesley, BA, MA, MLitt; American academic and poet; *Professor Emeritus and Writer-in-Residence, University of Maine at Farmington*; b. 19 June 1941, Newport, NH; s. of Wilbur Frank McNair and Eileen Ruth McNair; m. Diane Reed McNair 1962; three s. one d. *Education:* Keene State Coll., Middleton Coll. *Career:* Assoc. Prof., Colby Sawyer Coll. 1968–87; Sr Fulbright Prof., Catholic Univ. of Chile 1977–78; Visiting Prof., Dartmouth Coll. 1984, Colby Coll. 2000–04; Assoc. Prof. to Prof., Univ. of Maine at Farmington 1987–98, Prof. Emer. and Writer-in-Residence 2005–. *Publications:* poetry: The Town of No 1989, Twelve Journeys in Maine 1992, My Brother Running 1993, Talking in the Dark 1998, Mapping the Heart: Reflections on Place and Poetry 2002, Fire: Poems (Jane Kenyon Award 2004) 2002, A Place on Water (essays, co-author) 2004, The Ghosts of You and Me 2006, Lovers of the Lost: New and Selected Poems 2010, The Words I Chose: A Memoir of Family and Poetry 2010; anthologies: The Quotable Moose (ed.) 1994, The Maine Poets (ed.) 2003, Contemporary Maine Fiction (ed.) 2005, Maine in Four Seasons (ed.) 2010; contribs to anthologies, reviews, quarterlies and journals. *Honours:* Hon. DHumLitt (Colby Sawyer Coll.) 2003, (Keene State Coll.) 2003, (Univ. of Southern New Hampshire) 2009; Nat. Endowment for the Humanities Fellowship in Literature 1970–71, Nat. Endowment for the Arts Fellowships 1980, 1990, Devins Award 1984, Eunice Tietjens Prize 1984, Guggenheim Fellowship 1986, Pushcart Prize 1986, Robert Frost Prize 1987, New England Emmy Award 1991, Rockefeller Residency, Bellagio, Italy 1993, 2005, Theodore Roethke Prize 1993, Distinguished Faculty Award, Univ. of Maine at Farmington 1994, 1996, Yankee Magazine Poetry Prize 1995, Sarah Josepha Hale Medal 1997, Jane Kenyon Award 2002, Ind. Book Publrs' Award 2006, US Artists' Fellowship 2006. *Address:* Creative Writing Program, University of Maine at Farmington, Farmington, ME 04938 (office); 43 Main Street, Mercer, ME 04957, USA (home). *Fax:* (207) 587-4241 (home). *E-mail:* wesleymcnair@yahoo.com (home). *Website:* www.wesleymcnair.com.

McNALLY, Terrence; American playwright; b. 3 Nov. 1939, St Petersburg, FL; pnr Tom Kirdahy. *Career:* Stage Man., Actors Studio, New York 1961; tutor 1961–62; film critic, The Seventh Art 1963–65; Asst Ed., Columbia Coll. Today 1965–66. *Publications:* Apple Pie, Sweet Eros Next and Other Plays 1969, Three Plays: Cuba Si!, Bringing It All Back Home, Last Gasps 1970, Where Has Tommy Flowers Gone? 1972, Bad Habits: Ravenswood and Dunelawn 1974, The Ritz and Other Plays 1976, The Rink 1985, And Things That Go Bump in the Night 1990, Frankie and Jonny in the Clair de Lune 1990, Kiss of the Spider Woman (with John Kander and Fred Ebb) 1992, Lips Together, Teeth Apart 1992, Until Your Heart Stops 1993, Love! Valour! Compassion! 1994, Masterclass 1995, Ragtime (with Stephen Flaherty and Lynn Ahrens) 1997, Corpus Christi 1998, Dead Man Walking (libretto) 2000, The Stendhal Syndrome 2003, Some Men 2006, Deuce 2007, Unusual Acts of Devotion 2008. *Honours:* Stanley Award 1962, Obie Award 1974, American Acad. of Arts and Letters Citation, Nat. Inst. of Arts and Letters Citation, Four Tony Awards, Pulitzer Award, two Guggenheim Awards. *Address:* 218 W 10th Street, New York, NY 10014, USA.

McNAMARA, Eugene Joseph, BA, MA, PhD; American academic, editor, poet and writer; b. 18 March 1930, Oak Park, Ill.; m. Margaret Lindstrom 1952; four s. one d. *Education:* DePaul University, Northwestern University. *Career:* Ed., University of Windsor Review, 1965–, Mainline, 1967–72, Sesame Press, 1973–80; Prof. of English, University of Windsor. *Publications:* poetry: For the Mean Time, 1965; Outerings, 1970; Dillinger Poems, 1970; Love Scenes, 1971; Passages, 1972; Screens, 1977; Forcing the Field, 1980; Call it a Day, 1984. Short Stories: Salt, 1977; Search for Sarah Grace, 1978; Spectral Evidence, 1985; The Moving Light, 1986; contributions: Queens Quarterly; Saturday Night; Chicago; Quarry; Denver Quarterly. *Address:* 166 Randolph Place, Windsor, ON N9B 2T3, Canada.

McNAMARA, Robert James, MA, PhD; American academic and poet; *Senior Lecturer in English, University of Washington, Seattle*; b. 28 March 1950, New York, NY; s. of James McNamara and Doris Maier; m. Judith Lightfoot 1993; one d. *Education:* Amherst Coll., Colorado State Univ., Univ. of Washington, Seattle. *Career:* Founder-Ed. L'Epervier Press 1977; Sr Lecturer in English, Univ. of Washington, Seattle 1985–; Univ. Dir, Puget Sound Writing Project; mem. Acad. of American Poets, PEN West. *Publications:* Second Messengers (poems) 1990, The Body and the Day (poems) 2007, The Cat under the Stairs (translations) 2010, Incomplete Strangers (poems) 2012; contribs to anthologies, reviews, quarterlies and journals. *Honours:* Nat. Endowment for the Arts Fellowship 1987–88, Fulbright Grant, Jadavpur Univ., Kolkata, India 1993. *Address:* Department of English, Box 354330, University of Washington, Seattle, WA 98195-4330, USA (office). *Telephone:* (206) 543-7131 (office). *E-mail:* rmcnamar@uw.edu (office). *Website:* sites.google.com/site/bobmcnamarapoet.

MacNEACAIL, Aonghas; Scottish writer and poet; b. 7 June 1942, Uig, Isle of Skye; m. Gerda Stevenson 1980; one s. *Education:* University of Glasgow. *Career:* Writing Fellowships, The Gaelic College, Isle of Skye, 1977–79, An Comunn Gaidhealachm Oban, 1979–81, Ross-Cromarty District Council, 1988–90; mem. Scottish Poetry Library Asscn, council mem., 1984–. *Publications:* Poetry Quintet, 1976; Imaginary Wounds, 1980; Sireadh Bradain Sicir/Seeking Wise Salmon, 1983; An Cathadh Mor/The Great Snowbattle, 1984; An Seachnadh/The Avoiding, 1986; Rocker and Water, 1990. Contributions: many publications. *Honours:* Grampian TV Gaelic Poetry Award; Diamond Jubilee Award, Scottish Asscn for the Speaking of Verse, 1985; An Comunn Gaidhealach Literary Award, 1985. *E-mail:* aonghasd@smo.uhi.ac.uk.

McNEILL, Daniel Richard, AB, JD; American writer; b. 1 June 1947, San Francisco, CA; m. Rosalind Gold 1984. *Education:* University of California at Berkeley, Harvard Law School. *Career:* mem. Authors' Guild. *Publications:* Fuzzy Logic, 1993; The Face, 1998. *Honours:* Los Angeles Times Book Prize in Science and Technology 1993. *Address:* c/o Author Mail, Grand Central Publishing, 237 Park Avenue, New York, NY 10017, USA.

McNEISH, Sir James Henry Peter, BA, KNZM; New Zealand writer; b. 23 Oct. 1931, Auckland; s. of Arthur McNeish and Ina McNeish (née Bosworth); m. 1st Felicity Wily; one d.; m. 2nd Helen Schnitzer; one step-s. *Education:* Univ. of Auckland. *Career:* Journalist, NZ Herald, Auckland, 1953–57; Theatre Workshop, Stratford East and teaching, London, 1958–59; writer and documentary maker, BBC Home Service & Third Programme 1963–67; Katherine Mansfield Fellow, Menton, France 1973; Co-founder and Dir (with Helen McNeish) Bridge in NZ (educational trust) 1974–82; author, penal report for Justice Dept 1976; Visiting Writer, Berlin DAAD Kunstler-program 1983; Research Fellow, Nat. Library of New Zealand 1999; Berlin residency, Creative NZ 2009; Pres. of Honour, NZ Soc. of Authors 2012–. *Plays:* The Rocking Cave 1973, The Mouse Man 1975, Eighteen-Ninety-Five 1975, Thursday Bloody Thursday 1998. *Publications include:* Tavern in the Town 1957, Fire Under the Ashes: A Life of Danilo Dolci 1965, Mackenzie 1970, The Mackenzie Affair 1972, The Rocking Cave 1973, Larks in a Paradise (co-author) 1974, The Glass Zoo 1976, As for the Godwits 1977, Art of the Pacific (with Brian Brake) 1980, Belonging: Conversations in Israel 1980, Joy 1982, Walking on My Feet: Portrait of A.R.D. Fairburn 1983, Ahnungslos in Berlin: A Berlin Diary 1985, Lovelock 1986 (enlarged edn 2009), Penelope's Island 1990, The Man from Nowhere and Other Prose 1991, My Name is Paradiso 1995, Mr Halliday and the Circus Master 1996, The Mask of Sanity: The Bain Murders 1997, An Albatross Too Many 1998, Dance of the Peacocks: New Zealanders in Exile in the Time of Hitler and Mao Tse-tung 2003, The Sixth Man: The Extraordinary Life of Paddy Costello 2007, The Crime of Huey Dunstan 2010. *Honours:* Prime Minister's Award for Literary Achievement in Non-Fiction 2010, Pres.-of-Honour, New Zealand Soc. of Authors 2012. *Literary Agent:* Andrew Hewson, Johnson & Alcock Ltd, Clerkenwell House, 45 Clerkenwell Green, London, EC1R 0HT, England. *E-mail:* andrew@johnsonandalcock.co.uk. *Address:* Michael Gifkins, PO Box 6496, Auckland, 1, New Zealand (office). *Telephone:* (9) 523-5032 (office). *Fax:* (9) 523-5033 (office). *E-mail:* michael.gifkins@xtra.co.nz (office).

McNICHOLAS, Conor, BA; British journalist; b. 1973, Bradford, West Yorkshire, England; m. Susan McNicholas; one s. *Education:* Manchester Victoria Univ. *Career:* staff mem. CD Rom Magazine 1994–95, Escape magazine 1995–96; Features Ed., Ministry magazine 1996–97; account exec., Powerhouse PR 1997–98; News Ed., Mixmag 1998–2001; Ed., Muzik 2001–02, NME (New Musical Express) 2002–09; Ed., Top Gear magazine 2009–10; Cttee mem. BSME (Chair. 2009–). *Honours:* PPA Award for Consumer Magazine Editor of the Year, BSME Award for Entertainment Magazine Ed. of the Year 2005. *Address:* c/o Top Gear Magazine, Second Floor A, Energy Centre, Media Centre, 201 Wood Lane, London, W12 7TQ, England (office).

MACOMBER, Debbie; American writer; b. 1948, Yakima, Wash.; m. Wayne; four c. *Career:* romance writer 1983–. *Publications:* fiction: Let it Snow 1986, A Season of Angels 1993, Morning Comes Softly 1993, The Trouble with Angels 1995, Someday Soon 1995, Sooner or Later 1996, Mrs Miracle 1996, This Matter of Marriage 1997, Lonesome Cowboy 1998, Texas Two-Step 1998, Caroline's Child 1998, Nell's Cowboy 1998, Dr Texas 1998, Lone Star Baby 1998, Montana 1998, Can This be Christmas? 1998, Moon Over Water 1999, Promise Texas 1999, Shirley, Goodness and Mary 1999, Dakota Born 2000, Dakota Home 2000, Return to Promise 2000, Always Dakota 2001, 16 Lighthouse Road 2001, Thursdays at Eight 2001, Buffalo Valley 2001, 204 Rosewood Lane 2002, Between Friends 2002, The Christmas Basket (Romance Writers of America RITA Award 2005) 2002, 311 Pelican Court 2003, Changing Habits 2003, The Snow Bride 2003, 44 Cranberry Point (Quill Award for Romance 2005) 2004, The Shop on Blossom Street 2004, When Christmas Comes 2004, 50 Harbor Street 2005, A Good Yarn 2005, There's Something About Christmas 2005, 6 Rainier Drive 2006, Susannah's Garden 2006, Christmas Letters 2006, 74 Seaside Avenue 2007, Back on Blossom Street 2007, Where Angels Go 2007, 8 Sandpiper Way 2008, Twenty Wishes 2008, A Cedar Cove Christmas 2008, Summer on Blossom Street 2009, The Perfect Christmas 2009, 92 Pacific Boulevard 2009, Angels at Christmas 2009, Hannah's List 2010, Call me Mrs Miracle 2010; non-fiction: One Simple Act: Discovering the Power of Generosity 2009, God's Guest List 2010. *Honours:* Romantic Times Career Achievement Award 1992–93. *Literary Agent:* Nancy Berland Public Relations, 2816 NW 57th Street, Suite 101, Oklahoma City, OK 73118, USA. *Telephone:* (800) 308-3160. *E-mail:* nancy@nancyberland.com. *Website:* www.nancyberland.com; www.debbiemacomber.com.

McPHEE, John Angus, AB; American academic and writer; *Ferris Professor of Journalism, Princeton University;* b. 8 March 1931, Princeton, NJ; m. 1st Pryde Brown 1957; four d.; m. 2nd Yolanda Whitman 1972; two step-s. two step-d. *Education:* Princeton Univ., Univ. of Cambridge. *Career:* dramatist, Robert Montgomery Presents television programme 1955–57; Assoc. Ed., Time magazine, New York 1957–64; staff writer, The New Yorker magazine 1965–; Ferris Prof. of Journalism, Princeton Univ. 1975–; Fellow, Geological Soc. of America; mem. American Acad. of Arts and Letters. *Publications:* A Sense of Where You Are 1965, The Headmaster 1966, Oranges 1967, The Pine Barrens 1968, A Roomful of Hovings 1969, The Crofter and the Laird 1969, Levels of the Game 1970, Encounters with the Archdruid 1972, Wimbledon: A Celebration 1972, The Deltoid Pumpkin Seed 1973, The Curve of Binding Energy 1974, Pieces of the Frame 1975, The Survival of the Bark Canoe 1975, The John McPhee Reader 1977, Coming into the Country 1977, Giving Good Weight 1979, Alaska: Images of the Country (with Galen Rowell) 1981, Basin and Range 1981, In Suspect Terrain 1983, La Place de la Concorde Suisse 1984, Table of Contents 1985, Rising from the Plains 1986, Outcroppings 1988, The Control of Nature 1989, Looking for a Ship 1990, Assembling California 1993, The Ransom of Russian Art 1994, The Second John McPhee Reader 1996, Irons in the Fire 1997, Annals of the Former World 1998, The Founding Fish 2002, Uncommon Carriers 2006, Silk Parachute 2010. *Honours:* various hon. doctorates; American Acad. and Inst. of Arts and Letters Award 1977, Princeton Univ. Woodrow Wilson Award 1982, American Asscn of Petroleum Geologists Journalism Award 1982, 1986, United States Geological Survey John Wesley Powell Award 1988, American Geophysical Union Walter Sullivan Award 1993, Pulitzer Prize for Non-Fiction 1999, Geological Soc. of America Public Service Award 2002, Acad. of Natural Sciences Gold Medal for Distinction in Natural History Art 2005, George Polk Career Award 2008. *Address:* Joseph Henry House, Princeton University, Princeton, NJ 08544 (office); 475 Drake's Corner Road, Princeton, NJ 08540, USA (home).

McPHERSON, Conor; Irish dramatist; b. 6 Aug. 1971, Dublin. *Education:* Univ. Coll., Dublin. *Career:* writer-in-residence, Bush Theatre, London 1996; co-f., Fly by Night Theatre Co. Dublin. *Plays:* Taking Stock 1989, Michelle Pfeiffer 1990, Scenes Federal 1991, Radio Play 1992, A Light in the Window of Industry 1993, Rum & Vodka 1994, The Good Thief 1994, The Stars Lose Their Glory 1994, Inventing Fortune's Wheel 1994, This Lime Tree Bower 1995, The Weir (Laurence Olivier Award) 1997, St Nicholas 1997, Dublin Carol 2000, Port Authority 2001, Come on Over 2001, Shining City 2004, The Seafarer 2006. *Films:* I Went Down (writer) (San Sebastian Film Festival Best Screenplay Award) 1997, Endgame (TV, dir) 2000, Saltwater (writer, dir) 2000, The Actors (writer, dir) 2003. *Honours:* Evening Standard Most Promising Playwright Award 1997, Stewart Parker Trust Award 1995, Guiness/National Theatre Ingenuity Award, Outer Critics Circle Award for Best Play, George Devine Award for Best New Play in London. *Address:* 10 Adelaide Street, Dun Laoghaire, Dublin, Republic of Ireland.

McPHERSON, James A., BA, LLB, MFA; American academic and writer; *Professor of English, University of Iowa;* b. 16 Sept. 1943, Savannah, GA; m. (divorced); one d. *Education:* Morris Brown Coll., Harvard Law School, Univ. of Iowa. *Career:* Rhetoric Program and Law School, Univ. of Iowa 1968–69; Lecturer, Univ. of California at Santa Cruz 1969–72; Asst Prof., Morgan State Univ. 1975–76; Assoc. Prof., Univ. of Virginia, Charlottesville 1976–81; Visiting Scholar, Yale Law School, New Haven 1978; Prof. of English, Writers' Workshop, Univ. of Iowa 1981–; Lecturer, Meiji Univ., Tsuda Coll., Chiba Univ. 1989–90, Japan; Fellow Center for Advanced Studies, Stanford Univ. 1997–98, 2002–03; mem. American Civil Liberties Union, PEN, Writers' Guild, Nat. Asscn for the Advancement of Colored People, American Acad. of Arts and Sciences. *Publications:* fiction and essays: Hue and Cry 1969, Railroad 1976, Elbow Room 1977, Crabcakes 1998, A Region Not Home 1999; contrib. to Atlantic, Harvard Advocate, Ploughshares, Nimrod, New York Times, Esquire, Reader's Digest, Washington Post, World Literature Today, Doubletake, Harper's. *Honours:* Guggenheim Fellowship 1973, Pulitzer Prize for Fiction 1978, MacArthur Prize Fellows Award 1981, Univ. of Iowa Award for Excellence in Teaching 1990, Soc. of Southern Journalists Green Eyeshades Award for Excellence in Print Commentary 1994. *Address:* 102 Dey House, 507 S. Clinton Street, Iowa City, IA 52242-1000 (office); 711 Rundell Street, Iowa City, IA 52240, USA (home). *Telephone:* (319) 335-0416 (office); (319) 354-2737 (home). *Fax:* (319) 335-0420 (office). *E-mail:* james.mcpherson@uiowa.edu (office). *Website:* www.uiowa.edu/~iww (office).

McPHERSON, James Munro, PhD; American historian, academic and writer; *George Henry Davis '86 Professor Emeritus of History, Princeton University;* b. 11 Oct. 1936, Valley City, ND; s. of James M. McPherson and Miriam O. McPherson; m. Patricia Rasche 1957; one d. *Education:* Gustavus Adolphus Coll. and Johns Hopkins Univ. *Career:* Instructor Princeton Univ. 1962–65, Asst Prof. 1965–66, Assoc. Prof. 1966–72, Prof. of History 1972–82, Edwards Prof. of American History 1982–91, George Henry Davis '86 Prof. of American History 1991, now Prof. Emer.; Pres. Soc. of American Historians 2000–01; Woodrow Wilson Fellow and Danforth Fellow 1958–62; Guggenheim Fellow 1967–68; Huntingdon Library-Nat. Endowment for the Humanities Fellowship 1977–78; Center for Advanced Study in the Behavioural Sciences Fellowship 1982–83; Huntington Seaver Fellow 1987–88; Pres. American Historical Asscn 2003; mem. American Philosophical Soc. 1991; Fellow, American Acad. of Arts and Sciences 2009. *Publications:* The Struggle for Equality: Abolitionists and the Negro in the Civil War and Reconstruction 1964, The Negro's Civil War 1965, Marching Toward Freedom 1968, The Anti-Slavery Crusade in America (co-ed, 59 vols) 1969, Blacks in America (essays) 1971, The Abolitionist Legacy 1975, Ordeal by Fire: The Civil War and Reconstruction 1982, Religion, Race and Reconstruction (essays, co-ed) 1982, Battle Cry of Freedom: The Civil War Era 1988, Battle Chronicles of the Civil War (ed, six vols) 1989, Abraham Lincoln and the Second American Revolution 1991, Images of the Civil War 1992, Gettysburg 1993, What They Fought For 1861–1865 1994, The Atlas of the Civil War 1994, Drawn With the Sword: Reflections on the American Civil War 1996, The American Heritage New History of the Civil War (ed) 1996, For Cause and Comrades: Why Men Fought in the Civil War 1997, Lamson of the Gettysburg: The Civil War Letters of Lt Roswell H. Lamson, US Navy 1997, Is Blood Thicker Than Water? Crises of Nationalism in the Modern World 1998, The Encyclopedia of Civil War Biographies (ed, three vols) 1999, To the Best of My Ability: The American Presidents (ed) 2000, Crossroads of Freedom: Antietam, The Battle That Changed the Course of the Civil War 2002, Hallowed Ground: A Walk at Gettysburg 2003, The Illustrated Battle Cry of Freedom 2003, Into the West (juvenile) 2006, Tried by War: Abraham Lincoln as Commander in Chief (Lincoln Prize, Gettysburg Coll. 2009) 2008, This Mighty Scourge: Perspectives on the Civil War 2009, Abraham Lincoln 2009; contrib. to reference works, scholarly books and professional journals. *Honours:* 10 hon. degrees from American colls and univs; Anisfield-Wolf Prize in Race Relations 1965, Pulitzer Prize in History 1989, Christopher Award 1989, Best Book Award, American Military Inst. 1989, Lincoln Prize 1998, Theodore and Franklin D. Roosevelt Prize in Naval History 1998, Jefferson Lecturer 2000, Pritzker Mil. Library Literature Award for lifetime achievement in mil. writing 2007, Lincoln Prize 2009. *Literary Agent:* c/o 41 William Street, Princeton, NJ 08540, USA. *Address:* Department of History, 130 Dickinson Hall, Princeton University, Princeton, NJ 08544 (office); 15 Randall Road, Princeton, NJ 08540, USA (home). *Telephone:* (609) 258-4173 (office); (609) 924-9226 (home). *Fax:* (609) 258-5326 (office). *E-mail:* jmcphers@princeton.edu (office). *Website:* his.princeton.edu (office).

McPHERSON, Sandra Jean, BA; American academic (retd), poet, writer and publisher; b. (Helen Todd), 2 Aug. 1943, San Jose, Calif.; adoptive parents, Walter McPherson and Frances McPherson; m. 1st Henry D. Carlile 1966 (divorced 1985); one d.; m. 2nd Walter D. Pavlich 1995 (died 2002). *Education:* San Jose State Univ., Univ. of Washington. *Career:* Visiting Lecturer, Univ. of Iowa 1974–76, 1978–80; Holloway Lecturer, Univ. of California, Berkeley 1981; teacher, Oregon Writers' Workshop, Portland 1981–85; Prof. of English, Univ. of California, Davis 1985–2008 (retd); Ed. and Publr Swan Scythe Press 1999–2009. *Publications:* Elegies for the Hot Season 1970, Radiation 1973, The Year of Our Birth 1978, Patron Happiness 1983, Streamers 1988, The God of Indeterminacy 1993, Edge Effect 1996, The Spaces Between Birds 1996, A Visit to Civilisation 2002, Expectation Days 2007; contrib. to periodicals. *Honours:* Ingram Merrill Foundation grants 1972, 1984, Nat. Endowment for the Arts grants 1974, 1980, 1985, Guggenheim Fellowship 1976, Oregon Arts Comm. Fellowship 1984, American Acad. and Inst. of Art and Letters Award 1987. *Telephone:* (530) 752-9672 (home). *E-mail:* sandyjmc@mindspring.com (home).

McQUAIN, Jeffrey Hunter, AA, BA, MA, PhD; American writer, researcher and word historian; b. 23 Nov. 1955, Frederick, MD. *Education:* Montgomery College, University of Maryland, American University. *Career:* researcher to William Safire, New York Times; mem. MLA. *Publications:* The Elements of English 1986, Guide to Good Word Usage 1989, Power Language 1996, Coined by Shakespeare 1998, Never Enough Words 1999, Homegrown English 2002, Coined by God 2003, The Bard on the Brain 2003; contributions: New York Times Magazine. *Honours:* Words From Home Award 1996. *Address:* 8410 Victory Lane, Potomac, MD 20854-3559, USA (home).

McQUEEN, Priscilla (Cilla) Muriel, MA; New Zealand (b. British) poet and artist; b. 22 Jan. 1949, Birmingham, England; m. Ralph Hotere 1974 (divorced 1986); one d. *Education:* Columba Coll., Dunedin, Otago Univ., Dunedin. *Career:* moved with family to NZ aged four; NZ Poet Laureate 2009–11; mem. Australasian Performing Rights Asscn, PEN. *Publications:* Homing In 1982, Anti Gravity 1984, Wild Sweets 1986, Benzina 1988, Berlin Diary 1990, Crikey 1994, Markings 2000, Axis 2001, Soundings 2002, Fire-Penny 2005, A Wind Harp (CD) 2006, The Radio Room 2010; contribs to various publs. *Honours:* Hon. DLitt (Otago) 2008; New Zealand Book Awards for Poetry 1983, 1989, 1991, Fulbright Visiting Writers Fellowship 1985, Robert Burns Fellowships 1985, 1986, Australia-New Zealand Exchange Writers' Fellowship 1987, Goethe Institute Scholarship, Berlin 1988, Queen Elizabeth II Arts Council Scholarship in Letters 1992, Southland Art Foundation Artist in Residence 1999, Prime Minister's Awards for Literary Achievement (Poetry) 2010. *Address:* c/o Otago University Press, PO Box 56, Dunedin 9054, New Zealand (office). *E-mail:* university.press@otago.ac.nz (office). *Website:* www.otago.ac.nz/press (office).

McRAE, Hamish Malcolm Donald, MA; British journalist and writer; b. 20 Oct. 1943, Barnstaple, Devon, England; m. Frances Anne Cairncross 1971; two d. *Education:* Fettes Coll., Edinburgh, Trinity Coll., Dublin. *Career:* Ed. Euromoney 1972; Financial Ed. The Guardian 1975; Business and City, The Independent 1989; Assoc. Ed. The Independent 1991–. *Publications:* Capital City – London as a Financial Centre (with Frances Cairncross) 1973, The Second Great Crash (with Frances Cairncross) 1975, Japan's Role in the Emerging Global Securities Market 1985, The World in 2020 1994, What Works 2010; contrib. to numerous magazines and journals. *Honours:* Wincott Foundation Financial Journalist of the Year 1979, Amex Bank Review Essays Special Merit Award 1987, Periodical Publishers Asscn Award for Columnist of the Year 1996, David Watt Prize 2005, Business and Financial Journalist of the Year, British Press Awards 2006. *Address:* The Independent, 2 Derry Street, London, W8 5HF (office); 6 Canonbury Lane, London, N1 2AP, England (home). *Telephone:* (20) 7005-2635 (office). *E-mail:* h.mcrae@independent.co.uk (office).

McSHARRY, Deirdre Mary; Irish journalist, editor and curator; b. 4 April 1932, London, England; d. of the late Dr John McSharry and Mary O'Brien; m. Ian Coulter Smyth. *Education:* Dominican Convent, Wicklow, Trinity Coll., Dublin Univ. *Career:* actress at Gate Theatre, Dublin 1953–55; freelance with The Irish Times 1953; mem. staff Evening Herald, Dublin 1955–56; with bookshop Metropolitan Museum of Art, New York 1956; Reporter Women's Wear Daily, New York 1956–58; mem. staff Woman's Own 1959–62; Fashion Ed. Evening News 1962; Woman's Ed. Daily Express 1963–66; Fashion Ed. The Sun 1967–71; Fashion Ed. Cosmopolitan 1972, Ed. 1973–85; Ed.-in-Chief Country Living 1986–89; Consultant Nat. Magazine Co. and Magazine Div. The Hearst Corpn 1990–92; Ed. Countryside magazine, New York 1991–92; Chair. Bath Friends of The American Museum in Britain, Bath; mem. Council of the American Museum, Council of the Bath Festivals Trust 2002; Trustee The American Museum (in Britain) 2002–04. *Art Exhibitions (as curator):* Inspirations – The Textile Tradition (The American Museum) 2001, Quilt Bonanza (The American Museum) 2003. *Publication:* Inspirations: The Textile Tradition Then and Now (American Museum Catalogue) 2001. *Honours:* Ed. of the Year (Periodical Publrs Asscn) 1981, 1987, Mark Boxer Award: Editor's Ed. 1991. *Address:* Southfield House, 16 High Street, Rode, BA11 6NZ, England. *Telephone:* (1373) 831263 (home). *Fax:* (1373) 831263 (home). *E-mail:* deirdre.mcsharry@btopenworld.com.

MACSOVSZKY, Peter, DipEd, MA; Slovak teacher and writer; b. 4 Nov. 1966. *Education:* Teacher Training Coll., Mitra, Univ. of Constantine the Philosopher. *Career:* mem. Obec Slovensky Spisovatelov. *Publications:* Strach z Utopie (trans. as Fear of Utopia) 1994, Ambit 1995, Somrak Cudnosti (trans. as The Dusk of Chastity) 1996, Cvicna Pitva (trans. as Training Autopsy) 1997, A'lbonctan (trans. as False Pathology) 1998.

MacTHÒMAIS, Ruaraidh (see Thomson, Derick Smith)

McTRUSTRY, Christifor John; Australian screenwriter and novelist; b. 29 Oct. 1960, Wellington, NSW; m. Patricia Rose Dravine 1986; one s. one d. *Education:* Bachelor of Creative Arts, 1989, Master of Creative Arts, 1990, University of Wollongong. *Career:* mem. Australian Writers Guild; Australian National Playwrights Centre; Australian Society of Authors; MWA; Crime Writers Asscn of Australia. *Publications:* The Cat Burglar, 1995; The Card Shark, 1996; Axeman!, 1997; Frankenkid, 1997; George and the Dragon, 1997; Susie Smelly-Feet, 1997. Other: Television and radio series. *Address:* 22 Stanleigh Crescent, West Wollongong, NSW 2500, Australia.

MacVEY, John Wishart, BA; Scottish writer; b. 19 Jan. 1923, Kelso. *Education:* diploma in applied chemistry, University of Strathclyde, Open University, Milton Keynes. *Career:* fmr technical information officer. *Publications:* Speaking of Space (with C. P. Snow, B. Lovell and P. Moore), 1962; Alone in the Universe?, 1963; Journey to Alpha Centauri, 1965; How We Will Reach the Stars, 1969; Whispers from Space, 1973; Interstellar Travel: Past, Present and Future, 1977; Space Weapons/Space War, 1979; Where We Will Go When the Sun Dies?, 1980; Colonizing Other Worlds, 1984; Time Travel, 1987. *Address:* Mellendean, 15 Adair Avenue, Saltcoats, Ayrshire KA21 5QS, Scotland.

McWHIRTER, George, BA, DipEd, MA; Canadian (b. Northern Irish) writer, poet and translator; *Professor Emeritus, University of British Columbia;* b. 26 Sept. 1939, Belfast, Northern Ireland; s. of James McWhirter DCM and Margaret McWhirter; m. Angela Mairead Coid 1963; one s. one d. *Education:* Queen's Univ., Belfast, Univ. of British Columbia. *Career:* asst teacher, Kilkeel Secondary 1962–64, Bangor Grammar School 1964–65; instructor, Escuela de Idiomas, Univ. of Barcelona 1965–66; teacher, Alberni Dist Secondary School 1966–68; Visiting Lecturer, Univ. of British Columbia 1970–71, Asst Prof. 1971–76, Assoc. Prof. 1976–82, Prof. 1982–2004, Head of Creative Writing 1983–93, Prof. Emer. 2004–; Co-Ed.-in-Chief, Prism International Magazine 1977, Advisory Ed. 1978–; Inaugural Poet Laureate of Vancouver 2007–09; Life mem. League of Canadian Poets; mem. Writers' Union of Canada, PEN. *Play:* translator: Euripides' Hecuba, Blackbird Theatre, Vancouver 2009. *Radio:* The Listeners (CBC), Don't Go Walking on the Water (CBC). *Publications:* Catalan Poems 1971, Bodyworks 1974, Queen of the Sea 1976, God's Eye 1981, Coming to Grips with Lucy 1982, Fire Before Dark 1983, Paula Lake 1984, Cage 1987, The Selected Poems of José Emilio Pacheco (ed. and trans.) 1987, The Listeners 1991, A Bad Day to be Winning 1992, A Staircase for All Souls 1993, Incubus: The Dark Side of the Light 1995, Musical Dogs 1996, Fab 1997, Where Words Like Monarchs Fly (ed. and trans.) 1998, Ovid in Saskatchewan 1998, Eyes to See Otherwise: The Selected Poems of Homero Aridjis, 1960–2000 (co-ed. and trans.) 2001, The Book of Contradictions (poems) 2002, The Incorrection (poems) 2007, The Anachronicles (poems) 2008, A Verse Map of Vancouver with photos by Derek von Essen (ed. and contrib.) 2009, Poemas solares/Solar Poems by Homero Aridjis (trans.) 2010; contrib. to numerous magazines and journals. *Honours:* McMillan Prize 1969, Commonwealth Poetry Prize 1972, F. R. Scott Prize for Trans. 1988, Ethel Wilson Fiction Prize 1988, Killan Prize for Teaching, Univ. of British Columbia 1998, Winner League of Canadian Poets Canadian Poetry Chapbook Competition 1998, Killan Prize for Mentoring 2004, Sam Black Prize for contrib. to Fine Arts 2005. *E-mail:* mcwhirte@interchange.ubc.ca (office). *Website:* www3.telus.net/GeorgeMcWhirter.

McWILLIAM, Candia Frances Juliet, BA; British writer; b. 1 July 1955, Edin.; d. of Colin McWilliam and Margaret McWilliam; m. 1st Quentin Gerard Carew Wallop (now Earl of Portsmouth) 1981; one s. one d.; m. 2nd Fram Dinshaw; one s. *Education:* Sherborne School, Dorset and Girton Coll., Cambridge. *Publications:* A Cast of Knives 1988, A Little Stranger 1989, Debatable Land 1994, Change of Use 1996, Wait till I Tell You 1997, Lady Rose and Mrs Memmary (with Ruby Ferguson) 2004, What to Look For in Winter 2010. *Address:* 62/5 Great King Street, Edinburgh, EH3 6QY, Scotland.

MADDEN, David, BS, MA; American writer, critic, editor, poet and dramatist and academic; *Robert Penn Warren Professor Emeritus of Creative Writing, Louisiana State University;* b. 25 July 1933, Knoxville, Tenn.; m. Roberta Margaret Young 1956; one s. *Education:* Univ. of Tennessee, San Francisco State Coll., Yale Drama School. *Career:* mem. Faculty, Appalachian State Teachers Coll. ., Boone, North Carolina 1957–58, Centre Coll. 1964–66, Ohio Univ. 1966–68; Asst Ed. Kenyon Review 1964–66; Writer-in-Residence, Louisiana State Univ. 1968–92, Dir Creative Writing Program 1992–94, and US Civil War Center 1992–99, Alumni Prof. 1994, Donald and Veliva Crunbley Prof. of Creative Writing 2000–07, Robert Penn Warren Prof. of Creative Writing 2007, now Prof. Prof. Emer.; Chair. Louisiana Abraham Lincoln Comm. 2009–; mem. Associated Writing Programs, Authors' League. *Publications:* fiction: The Beautiful Greed 1961, Cassandra Singing 1969, The Shadow Knows 1970, Brothers in Confidence 1972, Bijou 1974, The Suicide's Wife 1978, Pleasure-Dome 1979, On the Big Wind 1980, The New Orleans of Possibilities 1982, Sharpshooter 1995; non-fiction: Wright Morris 1964, The Poetic Image in 6 Genres 1969, James M. Cain 1970, Creative Choices: A Spectrum of Quality and Technique in Fiction 1975, Harlequin's Stick: Charlie's Cane: A Comparative Study of Commedia dell' arte and Silent

Slapstick Comedy 1975, A Primer of the Novel: For Readers & Writers 1980, Writer's Revisions (with Richard Powers) 1981, Cain's Craft 1986, Revising Fiction 1988, The Fiction Tutor 1990; editor: Proletarian Writers of the Thirties 1968, Tough Guy Writers of the Thirties 1968, American Dreams, American Nightmares 1970, Rediscoveries 1971, The Popular Culture Explosion (with Ray B. Browne) 1972, The Contemporary Literary Scene (assoc. ed.) 1973, Nathanael West: The Cheaters and the Cheated 1973, Remembering James Agee 1974, Studies in the Short Story (fourth–sixth editions) 1975–84, Rediscoveries II (with Peggy Bach) 1988, The World of Fiction 1990, Eight Classic American Novels 1990, Classics of Civil War Fiction 1991, Beyond the Battlefield (ed.), A Pocketful of Prose: Vintage 1992, A Pocketful of Prose: Contemporary 1992, A Pocketful of Plays 1995, A Pocketful of Poems 1995, The Legacy of Robert Penn Warner 2000, Thomas Wolfe's Civil War 2004, Losses of the Sultana 2004, Touching the Web of Southern Novelists 2006; contrib. poems, plays, essays and short stories to various publications. *Honours:* John Golden Fellow in Playwriting 1959, Rockefeller Foundation grant in fiction 1969, Nat. Council on the Arts Award 1970, Robert Penn Warren Fiction Award 2005. *Address:* 118 Church Street, Black Mountain, NC 28711, USA. *Telephone:* (828) 669-2757. *E-mail:* dmadden33@yahoo.com. *Website:* www.davidmadden.net (home).

MADELEY, John, BA; writer and broadcaster; b. 14 July 1934, Salford, Greater Manchester, England; m. Alison Madeley 1962; one s. one d. *Education:* Univ. of Manchester. *Career:* broadcaster, BBC and Deutsche Welle. *Publications:* Human Rights Begin with Breakfast 1981, Diego Garcia: Contrast to the Falklands 1982, When Aid is No Help 1991, Trade and the Poor 1992, Big Business, Poor People: The Impact of Transnational Corporations on the World Poor 1999, Hungry for Trade: How the Poor Pay for Free Trade 2000, Food for All: The Need for a New Agriculture 2001, A People's World: Alternatives to Economic Globalization 2003, 100 Ways to Make Poverty History 2005, 50 Reasons to Buy Fair Trade (with Miles Litvinoff) 2007, Big Business, Poor Peoples 2008, Beyond Reach? 2009, Let Live: A Bike Ride, Climate Change and the CIA 2011; contrib. to newspapers and magazines. *Address:* 19 Woodford Close, Caversham, Reading, Berks., RG4 7HN, England (office). *Telephone:* (118) 947-6063 (office). *E-mail:* john.madeley@gmail.com (office). *Website:* www.johnmadeley.co.uk.

MADGETT, Naomi Long, BA, MEd, PhD; American poet, publisher and academic; b. 5 July 1923, Norfolk, Va; m. Leonard P. Andrews Sr. *Education:* Virginia State Coll., Wayne State Univ., Int. Inst. for Advanced Studies. *Career:* Research Assoc., Oakland Univ.; Lecturer in English, Univ. of Michigan; Assoc. Prof., Eastern Michigan Univ., now Prof. Emer.; Ed., Lotus Press. *Publications:* Songs to a Phantom Nightingale, 1941; One and the Many, 1956; Star by Star, 1965; Pink Ladies in the Afternoon, 1972; Exits and Entrances, 1978; Phantom Nightingale, 1981; A Student's Guide to Creative Writing, 1990; contributions: numerous anthologies and journals.

MADHAVAN, N. S., BSc, MSc; Indian writer and civil servant; b. 1948, Ernakulam, Kerala; m.; one d. *Education:* Sree Rama Varma High School, Maharaja Coll., Ernakulam, Univ. of Kerala. *Career:* Malayalam writer; joined Indian Admin. Service 1975. *Publications include:* short stories: Sisu 1970, Choolaimedile Savangal 1983, Higuita (Kerala Sahitya Akademi Award 1995) 1990, Vanmarangal, Thiruthu, Paryaya Kathakal, Nilavili; novel: Lanthanbatheriyile Luthiniyakal (Kerala Sahitya Akademi Award 2004, Book of the Year, Malayalam Manorama 2004) 2003; play: Randu Natangangal 2006. *Honours:* Muttathu Varkey Award 2009. *Literary Agent:* David Godwin Associates, 55 Monmouth Street, London, WC2H 9DG, England. *Telephone:* (20) 7240-9992. *Fax:* (20) 7395-6110. *E-mail:* assistant@davidgodwinassociates.co.uk. *Website:* www.davidgodwinassociates.co.uk.

MADSEN, Richard Paul, BD, MTh, MA, PhD; American writer and academic; *Distinguished Professor of Sociology, University of California, San Diego*; b. 2 April 1941, Alameda, Calif.; m. Judith Rosselli 1974. *Education:* Maryknoll Coll., Glen Ellyn, Ill., Maryknoll Seminary, Ossining, NY, Harvard Univ. *Career:* ordained RC priest 1968; Maryknoll missioner, Taiwan 1968–71; left priesthood 1974; Lecturer in Sociology, Harvard Univ. 1977–78; Asst Prof., Univ. of California, San Diego 1978–83, Assoc. Prof. 1983–85, Prof. of Sociology 1985, now Distinguished Prof.; mem. American Sociological Asscn, Asscn of Asian Studies, Governing Council for China and Inner Asia 1989–91. *Publications:* Chen Village: The Recent History of a Peasant Community in Mao's China (with Anita Chan and Jonathan Unger) 1984, revised edn as Chen Village Under Mao and Deng 1992, Morality and Power in a Chinese Village 1984, Habits of the Heart: Individualism in American Life (with Robert N. Bellah, William M. Sullivan, Ann Swidler and Steven M. Tipton) 1985, Individualism and Commitment in American Life: A Habits of the Heart Reader (with Robert N. Bellah, William M. Sullivan, Ann Swidler and Steven M. Tipton) 1987, Unofficial China (ed. with Perry Link and Paul Pickowicz) 1989, The Good Society (with Robert N. Bellah, William M. Sullivan, Ann Swidler and Steven M. Tipton) 1991, China and the American Dream: A Moral Inquiry 1995, China's Catholics: Tragedy and Hope in a Emerging Civil Society 1998, Meaning and Modernity: Religion, Polity and Self (with William M. Sullivan, Ann Swidler and Steven M. Tipton) 2002, Popular China: Unofficial Culture in a Globalising Society (with Perry Link and Paul Pickowicz) 2002, The Many and the One: Religious and Secular Perspectives in Ethical Pluralism in the Modern World (with Tracy B. Strong) 2003, Democracy's Dharma: Religious Renaissance and Political Development in Taiwan 2007; contribs to journals. *Honours:* C. Wright Mills Award, Soc. for the Study of Social Problems 1985, Current Interest Book Award, Los Angeles Times 1985, Book Award, Asscn of Logos Bookstores 1986. *Address:* Department of Sociology, University of California, San Diego, La Jolla, CA 92093, USA (office). *E-mail:* rmadsen@ucsd.edu (office). *Website:* sociology.ucsd.edu (office).

MAFFIA, Dante; Italian poet and author; b. 17 Jan. 1946, Roseto Capo Spulico (Cosenza). *Education:* graduated in Rome. *Career:* Founder and Ed. Il Policordo and Poetica magazines; contrib. to books of RAI and many periodicals, including Nuova Antologia, Misure critiche, Belfagor, Otto/Novecento, Cartolaria, Il Bel Paese, Hortus, Lunarionuovo, Idea, Poiesis; Ed. Rivista di Italianistica (S Africa), Il Belli; Corresp., La Naciòn; currently working at Univ. of Salerno. *Publications:* poetry: Il leone non mangia l'erba (Premio Viareggio, Pino d'Oro) 1974, Le favole impudiche 1977, Passeggiate romane (Premio Trastevere) 1979, L'eredità infranta (Premio Brutium) 1981, Caro Baudelaire (Prizes: Tarquinia-Cardarelli, Martina Franca, Rhegium Julii) 1983, Il ritorno di Omero (Premio Alfonso Gatto) 1984, A vite i tutte i jùrne (Premio Acireale e Premio Lentini) 1987, U ddÌje poverìlle (Premio Brutium del Presidente e Premio Lanciano) 1990, L'educazione permanente (with an intoructory essay by Giacinto Spagnoletti) (Premio Città di Cariati, Premio Calliope, Premio Circe-Sabaudia) 1992, La castità del male (Premio Montale, Premio Città di Venezia) 1993, Confessione (with an aquatint by Antonio Bobò) 1993, Racconto (with a recording by Giacomo Soffiantino; edited by Fabrizio Mugnaini) 1994, I rùspe cannarùte 1995; prose: Corradino, «La clessidra» 1990, La danza del adiós (in Spanish) 1991, La barriera semantica (written in dialect poetry of the 20th century) 1996, Le donne di Courbet racconti (with a note by Alberto Moravia and a preface by Alberto Bevilacqua) 1996, Il romanzo di Tommaso Campanella (preface by Norberto Bobbio) (Premio Cirò Marina, Premio Stresa, Premio Palmi) 1996; other: exhbn catalogues and monographs of important painters and sculptors; works have been translated into many languages; ed.: Poesie alla Calabria, La narrativa calabrese dell'Otto/Novecento, Una simpatia di Giulio Carcano, Torquato Tasso di Carlo Goldoni, Torquato Tasso di Francesco De Sanctis (anthology). *Honours:* Calliope Award for literary fiction 1995. *Address:* P. le Caduti della Montagnola 50, 00142 Rome, Italy. *Telephone:* (339) 6567133 (mobile). *E-mail:* dantemaffia@libero.it (office). *Website:* www.dantemaffia.com (office).

MAGANI, Mohamed, BA, MA; Algerian writer. *Education:* Univ. of Algiers, Univ. of London, UK. *Career:* exiled 1995–2002; Lecturer, Univ. of Algiers 2002–; founder and Dir Algerian PEN Club, elected to bd Int. PEN 2005–. *Publications:* novels: La Faille du ciel (Grand Prix Littéraire International de la Ville d'Alger) 1983, Esthétique de boucher (The Aesthetic of the Butcher) 1998, Un Temps berlinois 2001, Le Refuge des ruines 2002, Une Guerre se meurt 2004, Scène de pêche en Algérie 2006; short stories: An Icelandic Dream 1993, Please Pardon our Appearance Whilst we Redress the Window Display 1995; contrib. to Freedom to Publish, Responsibility for a Human Right 1998, Metronome, Lettre International, Nouvelle/Nouvelle, Neuwer Rundshau, Si Scrive. *Address:* B2/59 cité Rabia Tahar, Bab Ezzouar, Algiers, Algeria (office). *Telephone:* (73) 27-55-55 (office). *E-mail:* mohmagani@yahoo.fr (home).

MAGARY, Drew; American writer and journalist; b. New York; m.; three c. *Career:* fmr advertising copywriter; sports writer, journalist and blogger for many publs and websites including Deadspin, Maxim, Kissing Suzy Kolber (Co-founder), GQ, New York Magazine, ESPN, Yahoo!, Playboy. *Publications include:* Men With Balls 2008, The End Specialist (US title: The Postmortal) 2011. *Address:* c/o Harper Voyager, HarperCollins Publishers LLC, 10 East 53rd Street, New York, NY 10022, USA (office). *Website:* www.harpercollins.com (office); harpervoyagerbooks.com/category/voyager-us (office).

MAGDALEN, I. I. (see Botsford, Keith)

MAĞDEN, Perihan; Turkish writer; b. 1960, Istanbul; one d. *Education:* Boğaziçi Univ. *Career:* columnist for various Turkish newspapers including Radikal 1997–2000. *Publications:* Haberci Çocuk Cinayetleri (trans. as The Messenger Boy Murders) (novella) 1991, Refakatçi (The Companion) (novel) 1994, Mutfak Kazaları (Kitchen Accidents) (poetry) 1995, Hiç Bunları Kendine Dert Etmeye Değer mi? (Is it Worth Bothering With These?) 1997, Kapı Açık Arkanı Dön ve Çık (Turn Around and Walk Out the Door) 1998, Fakat Ne Yazık ki Sokak Boştu (Unfortunately, However, The Street was Empty) 1999, İki Genç Kızın Romanı (trans. as Two Girls) (novel) 2002, Politik Yazılar (essays) 2006, Biz Kimden Kaçıyorduk Anne? (Escape) (novel) 2007. *Literary Agent:* Istanbul Copyright Agency (Istanbul Telif Ofisi), Akyol Caddesi No 29/13, Cihangir, 34427 Istanbul, Turkey. *Telephone:* (212) 2926754. *Fax:* (212) 2920401. *Website:* www.istanbultelifofisi.com.

MAGEE, Bryan, MA, DLitt; British author; b. 12 April 1930, London; s. of Frederick Magee and Sheila Lynch; m. Ingrid Söderlund 1954 (died 1986); one d. *Education:* Christ's Hosp., UK, Lycée Hôche, Versailles, France, Keble Coll. Oxford, UK, Yale Univ., USA. *Career:* served with Army Intelligence Corps 1948–49; fmr TV reporter, This Week; music and theatre critic, Musical Times and The Listener; Lecturer in Philosophy, Balliol Coll., Oxford 1970–71; Visiting Fellow, All Souls Coll. Oxford 1973–74; MP for Leyton 1974–83; Pres. Critics Circle of GB 1983–84, Hon. mem. 2012–; Hon. Sr Research Fellow, King's Coll. London 1984–94, Visiting Prof. 1994–2000; Fellow, Queen Mary and Westfield Coll. London 1989–; Visiting Fellow, Wolfson Coll., Oxford 1991–94, New Coll. Oxford 1995, Merton Coll., Oxford 1998, St Catherine's Coll., Oxford 2000, Peterhouse, Cambridge 2001, Clare Hall, Cambridge (Life Mem.) 2004; Visiting Prof., Univ. of Otago, Dunedin, New Zealand 2006, 2009, 2012, also fmr Visiting Fellow at Yale Univ., Harvard Univ., Univ. of Sydney, LSE; newspaper columnist; mem. Arts Council of GB and Chair. Music Panel

1993–94; mem. Soc. of Authors. *Television:* Men of Ideas 1978, The Great Philosophers 1987. *Publications:* Crucifixion and Other Poems 1951, Go West Young Man 1958, The New Radicalism 1962, The Democratic Revolution 1964, Towards 2000 1965, One in Twenty 1966, The Television Interviewer 1966, Aspects of Wagner 1968 (revised edn 1988), Modern British Philosophy 1971 (re-issued as Talking Philosophy 2001), Popper 1973, Facing Death 1977, Men of Ideas 1978, The Philosophy of Schopenhauer 1983, 1997, The Great Philosophers 1987, On Blindness 1995 (re-issued as Sight Unseen 1998), Confessions of a Philosopher 1997, The Story of Philosophy 1998, Wagner and Philosophy 2000, Clouds of Glory: A Hoxton Childhood (J. R. Ackerley Prize for autobiog. 2004) 2003, Growing Up In a War 2007. *Honours:* Hon. Fellow, Queen Mary Coll. London 1988–, Keble Coll. Oxford 1994–; Hon. DLitt (Univ. of Leicester) 2005; Silver Medal, Royal TV Soc. 1978, J. R. Ackerley Prize for Autobiography 2004. *Address:* Wolfson College, Oxford, OX2 6UD, England (office).

MAGEE, Wesley (Wes) Leonard Johnston; British poet and writer; b. 20 July 1939, Greenock, Scotland; m. Janet Elizabeth Parkhouse 1967; one s. one d. *Education:* Goldsmiths Coll., Univ. of London, Univ. of Bristol. *Career:* mem. Poetry Soc. of Great Britain, Philip Larkin Soc.; Cole Scholar, FL 1985. *Publications:* over 80 books for children 1972–; contribs: reviews and journals. *Honours:* New Poets Award 1972, Poetry Book Soc. Recommendation 1978, Children's Poetry Bookshelf Choice 2001, Poetry Archive (recording) 2004. *Address:* Crag View Cottage, Thorgill, Rosedale, North Yorkshire, YO18 8SG, England (home). *Telephone:* (1751) 417633 (home). *E-mail:* wes@wesmagee.fsnet.co.uk (home).

MAGER, Donald Northrop, BA, MA, PhD; American academic, poet and writer; *Dean, College of Arts and Letters, Johnson C. Smith University*; b. 24 Aug. 1942, Santa Rita, NM; m. Barbara Feldman (divorced); two s.; pnr William McDowell. *Education:* Drake Univ., Syracuse Univ., Wayne State Univ. *Career:* Instructor, Syracuse Univ.; Assoc. Prof., Johnson C. Smith Univ., Prof. of English 1994–, Dean, Coll. of Arts and Letters 2003–; mem. MLA. *Publications:* poetry: To Track the Wounded One: A Journal 1988, Glosses: Twenty-four Preludes and Etudes 1995, That Which is Owed to Death 1998, Borderings 1998, Good Turns 2001, Akhmatova (opera libretto) 2002, Elegance of the Ungraspable 2003, Drive Time 2008, Birth Day 2008, Us Four Plus Four: Eight Russian Poets Conversing 2009; contributions: anthologies, books, reviews, quarterlies, journals, and magazines. *Honours:* first prize, Hallmark Competition 1965, Approach Magazines Award 1978, Tompkings Award First Prize for Poetry, Wayne State Univ. 1986, first prize, The Lyricist Statewide Poetry Competition, Campbell Univ. 1992, Assoc. Artist Residency, Atlantic Center for the Arts, New Smyrna Beach, FL 1994, winner, Union County Writers Club Chapbook Contest 1998. *Address:* c/o Johnson C. Smith University, UPO 2441, Charlotte, NC 28216, USA (office). *Telephone:* (704) 378-1238 (office).

MAGNUSSON, Sigurdur A., BA; Icelandic writer and poet; b. 31 March 1928, Reykjavík; m. 1st (divorced); m. 2nd (divorced); two s. three d. *Education:* Univ. of Iceland, Univ. of Copenhagen, Univ. of Athens, Univ. of Stockholm , New School for Social Research, New York. *Career:* Literary and Drama Critic, Morgunbladid 1956–67; Ed.-in-Chief, Samvinnan 1967–74; mem. Int. Writing Programme, Univ. of Iowa, 1976, 1977; mem. Int. Artists' Programme, West Berlin 1979–80; mem. Jury, Nordic Council Prize for Literature 1990–98; mem. Amnesty Int. (Chair. 1988–89, 1993–95), mem. Greek-Icelandic Soc. (Chair. 1985–88), Soc. of Icelandic Drama Critics (Chair. 1963–71), Writers' Union of Iceland (Chair. 1971–78, Hon. mem. 1999–); Hon. mem. Union of Translators and Interpreters 2006–. *Plays:* Visiting (Nat. Theatre 1962). *Publications include:* in Icelandic: Grískir reisudagar 1953, Krotad í sand 1958, Nýju fötin keisarans 1959, Thanatos tou Balder kai alla poiemata 1960, Hafid og kletturinn 1961, Næturgestir 1961, Gestagangur 1962, Vid elda Indlands 1962, Sjónvarpid 1964, Smárædi – Tólf thættir 1965, Sád í vindinn 1967, Thetta er thitt líf 1974, Í ljósi næsta dags 1978, Fákar – Íslenski hesturinn í blídu og strídu 1978, Undir kalstjörnu – Uppvaxtarsaga 1979, Möskvar morgundagsins 1981, Bilder aus einer Kindheit 1981, Í svidsljósinu – Leikdómar 1962–1973 1982, Jakobsglíman – Uppvaxtarsaga 1983, Skilningstréd – Uppvaxtarsaga 1985, Úr snöru fuglarans – Uppvaxtarsaga 1986, Hvarfbaugar – Úrval ljóða 1952–1982 1988, Sigurbjörn biskup – Ævi og starf 1988, Ísland er nafn thitt 1990, Grikklandsgaldur 1992, Írlandsdagar 1995, Með hálfum huga – Throskasaga 1997, Í tíma og ótíma – Rædur og ritgerdir 1998, Lousia Matthíasdóttir 1999, Undir dagstjörnu – Athafnasaga 2000, Á hnífsins egg – Átakasaga 2001, Ljósatími – Einskonar uppgjör 2003, Gardur gudsmódur. Munkríkid Athos. Elsta lýdveldi í heimi 2006, Fótatak í fjarska – Bókmenntapistlar 1962–2008 2008, Örlagavaldar 20. aldar 2008; in English: Handy Facts on Iceland 1972, Northern Sphinx: Iceland and the Icelanders from the Settlement to the Present 1977, Iceland: Country and People 1978, The Iceland Horse 1978, Iceland Crucible: A Modern Artistic Renaissance 1985, The Icelanders 1990, Iceland: Isle of Light 1995, The Natural Colours of the Iceland Horse 1996; more than 33 translations into Icelandic from English, Danish, German and Greek; contribs to professional journals. *Honours:* Golden Cross, Royal Order of the Phoenix, Greece 1955, Golden Cross of the Greek Republic 2006; Cultural Council Prize for Best Play 1961, and Best Novel 1980, European Jean Monnet Prize for Literature 1995. *Address:* Grettisgata 24, 101 Reykjavik, Iceland (home). *Telephone:* 552-5922 (home). *E-mail:* sambar@isl.is (home).

MAGORIAN, James, BS, MS; American poet and writer; b. 24 April 1942, Palisade, Neb. *Education:* Univ. of Nebraska, Illinois State Univ., Univ. of Oxford, UK, Harvard Univ. *Publications:* poetry: Hitchhiker in Hall County 1968, The Garden of Epicurus 1971, Safe Passage 1977, Phases of the Moon 1978, Tap Dancing on a Tightrope 1981, Taxidermy Lessons 1982, The Walden Pond Caper 1983, The Emily Dickinson Jogging Book 1984, Weighing the Sun's Light 1985, The Hideout of the Sigmund Freud Gang 1987, Borderlands 1992, The Yellowstone Meditations 1996, Haymarket Square 1998, Littorals 2004, Voices 2006; fiction: America First 1992, The Man Who Wore Layers of Clothing in the Winter 1994, Hearts of Gold 1996, Souvenir Pillows From Mars 1996; also children's books; contrib. to reviews, quarterlies and journals. *Address:* 2626 North 49th Street, #402, Lincoln, NE 68504, USA.

MAGORIAN, Michelle Jane, Dip; British writer and actress; b. 6 Nov. 1947, Southsea, Portsmouth, Hants., England; d. of William Magorian and Freda Magorian; m. Peter Keith Venner 1987 (divorced 1998); two s. *Education:* Rose Bruford Coll. of Speech and Drama, Kent, École Internationale de Mime Marcel Marceau, Paris. *Career:* mem. PEN, British Actors' Equity, Soc. of Authors. *Television:* Just Henry (ITV). *Publications:* fiction: Goodnight Mister Tom (also libretto for musical 2001) 1981, Back Home 1984, A Little Love Song 1991, Cuckoo in the Nest 1994, A Spoonful of Jam 1998, Just Henry (Costa Award for Best Children's Book) 2008; poetry: Waiting for My Shorts to Dry 1989, Orange Paw Marks 1991; short stories: In Deep Water 1992, Be Yourself 2003; libretti: Hello Life! 2004, Tinsel 2004; contrib. to Puffin Post. *Honours:* Hon. DLitt; Guardian Award for Children's Fiction, UK 1981, Int. Reading Asscn Children's Award, USA 1982, American Library Asscn Notable Children's Books 1982, American Library Asscn Best Book for Young Adults 1982, American Library Asscn Young Adult Reviewers' Choice 1982, Western Australia Young Readers Book Award 1983, 1987, BAFTA Award 1999, Costa (Whitbread) Children's Book Award 2009. *Literary Agent:* c/o Patricia White, Rogers, Coleridge & White Ltd, 20 Powis Mews, London, W11 1JN, England. *Telephone:* (20) 7221-3717. *Fax:* (20) 7229-9084. *E-mail:* patw@rcwlitagency.co.uk. *Website:* www.rcwlitagency.co.uk; www.michellemagorian.com.

MAGRIS, Claudio; Italian journalist, writer and academic; *Professor Emeritus of German Language and Literature, University of Trieste*; b. 10 April 1939, Trieste; s. of Duilio Magris and Pia de Grisogono Magris; m. Marisa Madieri 1964; two s. *Education:* Univ. of Turin. *Career:* Lecturer in German Language and Literature, Univ. of Trieste 1968–70, Turin 1970–78, Trieste 1978–, now Prof. Emer.; mem. Deutsche Akad. für Sprache und Dichtung (Darmstadt), Österreichische Akad. der Wissenschaften, Accad. delle Scienze di Torino, Ateneo Veneto, Akad. der Wissenschaften (Göttingen). *Plays:* Stadelmann 1988, Le Voci 1999, La Mostra 2001. *Publications include:* Il Mito absburgico nella letteratura austriaca moderna 1963, 1988, Wilhelm Heinse 1968, Tre studi su Hoffman 1969, Lontano da dove 1971, Joseph Roth e la tradizione ebraico-orientale 1971, Dietro le parole 1978, L'altra ragione. Tre saggi su Hoffman 1978, Dietro le parole 1978, Itaca e oltre 1982, Trieste. Un'identità di frontiera 1982, 1987, L'anello di Clarisse 1984, Illazioni su una sciabola 1984, Danubio 1986 (trans. in numerous languages), Stadelmann 1988, Un altro mare 1991, Microcosmi 1997, Utopia e disincanto 1999, Telling Tales (contrib. to charity anthology) 2004, Alla cieca 2005, L'infinito viaggiare 2005, Lei dunque capirà 2006, La storia non è finita 2006, Davanti alla legge. Due Saggi 2006, Alfabeti 2008; numerous essays and book reviews in Corriere della Sera and other European newspapers and periodicals; trans. Ibsen, Kleist, Schnitzler, Büchner. *Honours:* Debenedetti 1972, Val di Comino 1978, Goethe Medaille 1980, Aquileia 1983, Premiolino 1983, San Giusto d'Oro 1984, Musil Medaille der Stadt Klagenfurt 1984, Bagutta 1987, Accad. dei Lincei 1987, Marotta 1987, Città di Modena 1987, Antico Fattore 1988, Juan Carlos I 1989, Premio Strega 1997, Premio Chiara alla Carriera 1999, Premio Würth per la Cultura Europea 1999, Premio Grinzane Piemonte 1999, Medaglia d'Oro della Cultura della Scuola e dell' Arte 1999, Premio Sikken 2000, Premio Nietsche 2000, Premium Erasmianum 2001, Leipziger Buchpreis zur Europäischen Verständigung 2001, Osterreichisches Ehrenkreuz für Wissenschaft und Kunst (First Class), Premio Príncipe de Asturias for Literature 2004, Österreichischem Staatpreis für Europäische literatur 2006, Friedenspreis des Deutschen Buchhandels 2009. *Address:* Department of Anglo-German Literature, University of Trieste, Via Lazzaretto Vecchio 8, III Piano, Stanza 309, 34123 Trieste, Italy (office). *Telephone:* (040) 5587252 (office). *Fax:* (040) 6763093 (office).

MAGRS, Paul, BA, MA, PhD; British writer and academic; *Senior Lecturer in Creative Writing, Manchester Metropolitan University*; b. 12 Nov. 1969, Jarrow, Tyne and Wear, England. *Education:* Univ. of Lancaster. *Career:* teacher of creative writing from 1993; fmr Lecturer and creative writing organizer, Univ. of East Anglia, Norwich seven years; currently Sr Lecturer in Creative Writing, Manchester Metropolitan Univ. *Publications:* fiction: Marked for Life 1995, Playing Out (short stories) 1997, Does it Show? 1997, Could it be Magic? 1998, Dr Who: The Scarlet Empress 1998, Dr Who: The Blue Angel 1999, Modern Love 2000, Dr Who: Verdigris 2000, All the Rage 2001, Dr Who: Mad Dogs and Englishmen 2002, Strange Boy 2002, Aisles 2003, Hands Up! 2003, To the Devil: A Diva! 2004, The Good, the Bat and the Ugly 2004, Exchange 2006, Never the Bride 2006, Twin Freaks 2007, Something Borrowed 2007, Conjugal Rights 2008, The Diary of a Dr Who Addict 2010. *Address:* Department of English, Manchester Metropolitan University, Geoffrey Manton Building Room 116, Rosamond Street West (off Oxford Road), Manchester, M15 6LL, England (office). *Telephone:* (161) 247-1715 (office). *E-mail:* p.magrs@mmu.ac.uk (office).

MAHADEVA, Devanur, MA; Indian writer; b. 1948. *Career:* Kannada writer; co-f. Sarvodaya Karnataka political party 2005–; fmr Writer-in-Residence,

Univ. of Iowa. *Publications include:* Dyavanooru 1973, Odalala 1979, Kusumabale (Sahitya Akademi Award) 1990.

MAHAPATRA, Jayanta, BSc, MSc, LLD; Indian poet, writer and editor; b. 22 Oct. 1928, Cuttack, Orissa; m. Jyotsna Rani Das 1951; one s. *Education:* Univ. of Cambridge, Utkal Univ., Patna Univ. *Career:* Lecturer and Reader in Physics, Ravenshaw Coll., Cuttack 1950–86; Poet-in-Residence, Rockefeller Foundation Conference Center, Bellagio, Italy 1986; Poetry Ed. The Telegraph, Kolkata 1994–98; Ed. Lipi 1998; Ed. Chandrabhaga magazine, Cuttack 2000–; Visiting Writer, Int. Writing Program, Univ. of Iowa 1976–77; Cultural Award Visitor, Australia 1978; Visiting Fellow, Univ. of Kolhapur, Univ. of Bombay, Univ. of Hyderabad. *Publications include:* Close the Sky 1971, Svayamvara and Other Poems 1971, A Rain of Rites 1976, Waiting 1979, Relationship 1980, The False Start 1980, Life Signs 1983, Dispossessed Nests 1986, Selected Poems 1987, Burden of Waves and Fruit 1988, Temple 1989, A Whiteness of Bone 1992, The Best of Jayanta Mahapatra 1995, Shadow Space 1997, The Green Gardener (short stories) 1997, Bare Face 2000, Random Descent 2005, Door of Paper: Essays and Memoirs 2007, The Lie of Dawns: Poems 1974–2008 2009; various children's stories and translations; contribs to reviews, quarterlies and journals. *Honours:* Hon. DLit (Utkal Univ.) 2006, Hon. DLitt (Ravenshaw Univ.) 2009; awards include Jacob Glatstein Memorial Award, Chicago 1975, Japan Foundation Visitor Award 1980, Sahitya Acad. Award, Nat. Acad. of Letters 1981, El consejo nacional para la cultura y las artes, Mexico 1994, Gangadhar Nat. Award for Poetry, Sambalpur Univ. 1994, Ramakrishna Jaidayal Harmony Award 1994, Bishuva Award, Prajatantra Prachara Samiti 2007, Padma Shri 2009, Allen Tate Award, Sewanee Review 2009. *Address:* Tinkonia Bagicha, Cuttack 753 001, Orissa (home); Authorspress, E-35/103, Jawahar Park, Laxmi Nagar, Delhi 110 092, India. *Telephone:* (671) 2417434 (home). *E-mail:* authorspress@yahoo.com. *Website:* www.jayantamahapatra.com.

MAHARIDGE, Dale Dimitro; American writer and academic; *Associate Professor of Journalism, Columbia University*; b. 24 Oct. 1956, Cleveland, OH. *Education:* Cleveland State Univ., Cuyahoga Community Coll. *Career:* mem. of staff, Gazette, Medina, OH 1977–78; journalist, Sacramento Bee 1980–91; Asst Prof., Columbia Univ. 1991–92, Assoc. Prof. of Journalism 2001–; Visiting Prof., Stanford Univ. 1992–2001; mem. Sierra Club. *Publications:* Journey to Nowhere: The Saga of the New Underclass 1985, And Their Children After Them 1989, Yosemite: A Landscape of Life 1990, The Last Great American Hobo 1993, The Coming White Minority: California, Multiculturalism, and the Nation's Future 1999, Homeland (with Michael Williams) 2004, Denison, Iowa: Searching for the Soul of America through the Secrets of a Midwest Town 2005, Someplace Like America: Tales From The New Great Depression 2011; contrib. to periodicals. *Honours:* World Hunger Award, New York City 1987, Lucius W. Nieman Fellowship, Harvard Univ. 1988, Pulitzer Prize for Non-Fiction 1990, Pope Foundation Award 1994, Freedom Forum Profs' Publishing Program Grant 1995, Social Justice Journalism Award, Hunter Coll., CUNY 2001. *Address:* Columbia University Graduate School of Journalism, 2950 Broadway, New York, NY 10027, USA (office). *Telephone:* (212) 854-3854 (office). *E-mail:* dm2021@columbia.edu (office). *Website:* www.journalism.columbia.edu (office).

MAHER, Terence Anthony, FCCA; British bookseller and publisher; b. 5 Dec. 1935, Manchester; s. of the late Herbert Maher and Lillian Maher; m. Barbara Grunbaum 1960; three s. *Education:* Xaverian Coll., Manchester. *Career:* Controller, Carborundum Co. Ltd 1961–69; Dir Corp. Finance, First Nat. Finance Corpn 1969–72; f. Pentos PLC 1972, Chair. and CEO –1993; Chair. and CEO Dillons Bookstores 1977–93; Athena Int. 1980–93, Ryman 1987–93; Chair. The Chalford Publishing Co. Ltd 1994–98, Maher Booksellers Ltd 1995–2008, Race Dynamics Ltd 1998–2007; Founder Trustee, Liberal Democrats 1988–2001; mem. Advisory Council on Libraries 1997–98; Fellow, Chartered Asscn of Certified Accountants. *Achievements include:* led successful campaign to abolish price control on books in UK. *Publications:* Counterblast (co-author) 1965, Effective Politics (co-author) 1966, Against My Better Judgement (autobiog.) 1994, Unfinished Business (fiction) 2003, Grumpy Old Liberal – A Political Rant 2005, What would a Liberal Do? – A Polemic 2010. *Address:* 33 Montagu Square, London, W1H 2LJ (home); The Old House, Whichford, nr Shipston on Stour, Warwicks., CV36 5PG, England. *Telephone:* (20) 7723-4254 (London); (1608) 684-614 (Whichford).

MAHJOUB, Jamal, BSc; British/Sudanese novelist; b. 1960, London. *Education:* Comboni Coll., Sudan, Atlantic Coll., South Wales, Univ. of Sheffield, UK. *Publications:* Navigation of a Rainmaker 1989, Wings of Dust 1994, In the Hour of Signs 1996, The Carrier 1998, Travelling with Djinns 2003, Nubian Indigo 2006, The Drift Latitudes 2006. *Honours:* The Guardian/Heinemann African Story Award 1993, Pris de L'Astrolabe 2004, Premio NH Mario Vargas Llosa 2006. *Literary Agent:* c/o Euan Thorneycroft, AM Heath and Co., 6 Warwick Court, London, WC1R 5DJ, England. *Telephone:* (20) 7242-2811. *Fax:* (20) 7242-2711. *Website:* www.amheath.com; www.jamalmahjoub.com (office).

MAHON, Derek, BA; Northern Irish poet, critic and editor; b. 23 Nov. 1941, Belfast, Northern Ireland. *Education:* Belfast Institute, Trinity College, Dublin. *Career:* Drama Critic, Ed., Poetry Ed., New Statesman; Poet-in-Residencies. *Publications:* Twelve Poems 1965, Night-Crossing 1968, Lives 1972, The Man Who Built His City in Snow 1972, The Snow Party 1975, Light Music 1977, The Sea in Winter 1979, Poems 1962–1978 1979, Courtyards in Delft 1981, The Hunt by Night 1982, A Kensington Notebook 1984, Antarctica 1986, Selected Poems 1991, The Yaddo Letter 1992, The Hudson Letter 1995, Collected Poems 1999, Harbour Lights 2005, Selected Poems 2006, Life on Earth 2008, An Autumn Wind 2010; editor: Modern Irish Poetry 1972, The Penguin Book of Contemporary Irish Poetry 1990. *Honours:* Irish American Foundation Award, Lannan Foundation Award, American Ireland Fund Literary Award, Eric Gregory Award, David Cohen Prize 2007. *Address:* c/o The Gallery Press, Loughcrew, Oldcastle, Co. Meath, Ireland (office). *Website:* www.gallerypress.com (office).

MAHY, Margaret Mary, ONZ, BA; New Zealand writer; b. 21 March 1936, d. of Francis George Mahy and Helen May Penlington; two d. *Career:* Asst Librarian, Petone Public Library 1959; Asst Children's Librarian, Christchurch Public Library 1960, Children's Librarian 1977; Librarian in charge of school requests, School Library Service, Christchurch Br. 1967; writer 1980–. *Publications include:* picture books: The Dragon of an Ordinary Family 1969, Mrs Discombobulous 1969, Pillycock's Shop 1969, The Little Witch 1970, The Princes and the Clown 1971, The Boy with Two Shadows 1971, The Man Whose Mother Was a Pirate 1971, The Rare Spotted Birthday Party 1974, The Ultra-Violet Catastrophe 1975, The Wind Between the Stars 1976, The Boy Who was Followed Home 1977, Jam 1985, The Great White Maneating Shark 1989, Down the Back of the Chair 2006, Bubble Trouble (Boston Globe-Horn Book Award 2009) 2008; short stories: Nonstop Nonsense 1977, The Great Piratical Rumbustification, The Librarian and the Robbers 1978, The Chewing-Gum Rescue 1982, The Birthday Burglar and a Very Wicked Headmistress 1984, Wibble Wobble 1984, The Spider in the Shower 1984, The Downhill Crocodile Whizz 1986, The Three Wishes 1986, The Door in the Air 1988, Tick Tock Tales 1994; juvenile fiction: The Bus Under the Leaves 1975, The Pirate Uncle 1977, Raging Robots and Unruly Uncles 1981, The Adventures of a Kite 1985, Sophie's Singing Mother 1985, A Very Happy Bathday 1985, Clever Hamburger 1985, The Man Who Enjoyed Grumbling 1986, The Pop Group 1986, The Terrible Topsy-Turvy Tissy-Tossy Tangle 1986, Mr Rumfitt 1986, My Wonderful Aunt 1986, The Blood and Thunder Adventure on Hurricane Peak 1989, The Cousins Quartet (4 books) 1994, Zeralda's Horses 2005, Portable Ghosts 2005, Maddigan's Fantasia 2006, Family Surprises 2006; school books: The Crocodile's Christmas Jandals 1982, The Bubbling Crocodile 1983, Shopping with a Crocodile 1983, The Great Grumbler and the Wonder Tree 1984, Fantail Fantail 1984, The Crocodile's Christmas Thongs 1985, Horrakapotchin 1985; also books for older children and for children learning to read. *Honours:* Carnegie Medal 1982, Esther Glen Medal, Hans Christian Andersen Award 2006. *Website:* christchurchcitylibraries.com/MargaretMahy.

MAIDEN, Jennifer Margaret, BA; Australian poet and writer; b. 7 April 1949, Penrith, NSW. *Education:* Macquarie Univ. *Publications:* Tactics 1974, The Occupying Forces 1975, The Problem of Evil 1975, Birthstones 1978, The Border Loss 1979, For the Left Hand 1981, The Terms 1982, The Trust 1988, Play with Knives 1990, Selected Poems of Jennifer Maiden 1990, Acoustic Shadow 1993, Mines 1999, Friendly Fire 2005; contrib. to numerous newspapers and magazines. *Honours:* several Australia Council Fellowships and grants, Grenfell Henry Lawson Award 1979, NSW Premier's Prizes 1991, 2000, Victorian Premier's Prize 1991, Christopher Brennan Award for Lifetime Achivement 1999. *Address:* PO Box 4, Penrith, NSW 2751, Australia.

MAIER, Paul Luther, MA, MDiv, PhD; American academic; *Russell H. Seibert Professor Emeritus of Ancient History, Western Michigan University*; b. 31 May 1930, St Louis, Mo.; s. of Dr Walter A. Maier and Hulda Augusta Eickhoff; m. Joan M. Ludtke 1967; four d. *Education:* Harvard Univ., Concordia Seminary, St Louis, Univ. of Heidelberg, Germany, Univ. of Basel, Switzerland. *Career:* Campus Chaplain 1958–99, Russell H. Seibert Prof. of Ancient History, Western Michigan Univ. 1960–2011, Prof. Emer. 2011–. *Films:* DVDs: Jesus: Legend or Lord?, The Odyssey of St. Paul, Christianity – The First Three Centuries, Christianity and the Competition (four hour-four video series), Christ or Caricature?, How We Got the Bible, Christianity and the Competition. *Publications:* A Man Spoke, A World Listened: The Story of Walter A Maier 1963, Pontius Pilate 1968, First Christmas 1971, First Easter 1973, First Christians 1976, The Best of Walter A. Maier (ed.) 1980, The Flames of Rome 1981, Josephus: The Jewish War (ed.) 1982, Josephus: The Essential Writings (ed. and trans.) 1988, In the Fullness of Time 1991, A Skeleton in God's Closet 1994, Josephus: The Essential Works (ed. and trans.) 1995, Eusebius: The Church History (ed. and trans.) 1999, More Than a Skeleton 2003, The Da Vinci Code – Fact or Fiction? (with H. Hanegraaff) 2004, The Constantine Codex 2011; juvenile: The Very First Christmas 1998, The Very First Easter 2000, The Very First Christians 2001, Martin Luther – A Man Who Changed the World 2004, The Real Story of the Creation 2007, The Real Story of the Flood 2008, The Real Story of the Exodus 2009; contrib. to numerous professional journals. *Honours:* Hon. LittD (Concordia Seminary) 1995, (Concordia Univ., Irvine) 2007; Hon. LLD (Concordia Univ., Ann Arbor) 2000; Western Michigan Univ. Alumni Award for Teaching Excellence 1974, and Distinguished Faculty Scholar 1981, Outstanding Educator in America 1974–75, Council for the Advancement and Support of Education Prof. of the Year 1984, Michigan Acad. of Sciences, Arts and Letters Citation 1985, ECPA Gold Medallion Book Award 1989, 1999, Concordia Univ. Christus in Mundo Award 2001, The Wittenberg Award 2001. *Address:* Department of History, Western Michigan University, Kalamazoo, MI 49008, USA (office). *Telephone:* (269) 387-4816 (office). *Fax:* (269) 387-4651 (office). *E-mail:* maier@wmich.edu (office). *Website:* paulmaier.com.

MAILLARD, Keith; Canadian/American writer, poet and academic; *Professor of Creative Writing, University of British Columbia*; b. 28 Feb. 1942, Wheeling, W Va; m.; two d. *Education:* West Virginia Univ., Vancouver Community Coll. *Career:* Instructor, Univ. of British Columbia 1980–89, Asst Prof. 1989–94, Assoc. Prof. 1994–2002, Prof. of Creative Writing 2002–. *Publications:* novels: Two Strand River 1976, Alex Driving South 1980, The Knife in My Hands 1981, Cutting Through 1982, Motet 1989, Light in the Company of Women 1993, Hazard Zones 1995, Gloria 1999, The Clarinet Polka 2003, Difficulty at the Beginning Quartet: Running 2005, Morgantown 2006, Lyndon Johnson and the Majorettes 2006, Looking Good 2006; poetry: Dementia Americana 1994; contribs to newspapers, reviews, journals and anthology. *Honours:* Ethel Wilson Fiction Prize 1990, Gerald Lampert Prize for Best First Book of Poetry, League of Canadian Poets 1995, Literary Merit Award, West Virginia Library Asscn 2004, inducted into Wheeling W Va Hall of Fame 2004, Creative Arts Award, Polish-American Historical Asscn 2005, Dorothy Somerset Award in the Creative Arts, Univ. of British Columbia 2007. *Address:* UBC Creative Writing Program, Buchanan Room E462, 1866 Main Mall, University of British Columbia, Vancouver, BC V6T 1Z1, Canada (office). *Telephone:* (604) 822-4596 (office). *Fax:* (604) 822-3616 (office). *E-mail:* maillard@mail.ubc.ca (office). *Website:* keithmaillard.com.

MAILLET, Antonine, PC, CC, OQ, ONB, LèsL, MA, DèsL; Canadian author and dramatist; b. 10 May 1929, Bouctouche, NB. *Education:* Collège de Notre-Dame d'Acadie, Moncton, University of Moncton, University of Montréal, Université Laval. *Career:* Teacher, University of Moncton, 1965–67, Collège des Jesuites, Québec, 1968–69, Université Laval, 1971–74, University of Montréal, 1974–75; Visiting Prof., University of California at Berkeley, 1983, SUNY at Albany, 1985; mem. Académie canadienne-française; Asscn des Écrivains de Langue Française; PEN; Queen's Privy Council for Canada; Royal Society of Canada; Société des Gens de Lettres de France. *Publications:* Pointe-aux-Coques 1958, On a mangé la dune 1962, La Sagouine 1971, Don l'Original 1972, Par derrière chez mon père 1972, Mariaagélas 1973, Emmanuel a Joseph a Davit 1975, La Cordes-de-bois 1977, Pélagie-la-Charrette (trans. as Pélagie: The Return to a Homeland) 1979, Cent ans dans les bois 1981, La Gribouille 1982, Crache-a-Pic (trans. as The Devil is Loose) 1984, Le Huitième jour (trans. as On the Eighth Day) 1986, L'Oursiade 1990, Les Confessions de Jeanne de Valois 1992, Le Foire de la Saint-Barthélmy (trans. from Ben Jonson) 1994, L'Ile-sux-Puces 1996, Le Chemin St-Jacques (novel) 1996, Chronique d'une sorcière de vent (novel) 1999, Madame Perfecta 2001; many plays. *Honours:* Governor-General's Award for Fiction 1972, Prix France-Canada 1975, Prix Goncourt, France 1979; Officer des Palmes académiques françaises 1980, Officier, Ordre des Arts et des Lettres, France 1985, Commdr, Ordre du mérite culturel de Monaco 1993; several hon. doctorates. *Address:* 735 Antonine Maillet Avenue, Montréal, QC H2V 2Y4, Canada.

MAIR, (Alexander) Craig, BA; Scottish educator and writer; b. 3 May 1948, Glasgow; m. Anne Olizar 1970; two s. one d. *Education:* Stirling Univ. *Career:* mem. Scottish Society of Antiquaries, fellow; Educational Institute of Scotland; various local history groups. *Publications:* A Time in Turkey, 1973; A Star for Seamen, 1978; The Lighthouse Boy, 1981; Britain at War 1914–18, 1982; Mercat Cross and Tolbooth, 1988; David Angus, 1989; Stirling, The Royal Burgh, 1990; The Incorporation of Glasgow Maltmen: A History, 1990.

MAIRS, Nancy Pedrick, AB, MFA, PhD, DHL; American writer; b. (Nancy Pedrick Smith), 23 July 1943, Long Beach, Calif.; d. of John Eldredge Smith Jr and Anne Pedrick; m. George Anthony Mairs 1963; one s. one d. *Education:* Wheaton Coll., Mass, Univ. of Arizona. *Career:* currently Sirow Scholar, Southwest Inst. for Research on Women; mem. Authors' Guild, Poets and Writers, Nat. Women's Studies Asscn. *Publications:* Instead it is Winter 1977, In All the Rooms of the Yellow House 1984, Plaintext 1986, Remembering the Bone House 1989, Carnal Acts 1990, Ordinary Time 1993, Voice Lessons 1994, Waist High in the World 1996, A Troubled Guest 2001, A Dynamic God 2007. *Honours:* Western States Book Award 1984, Nat. Endowment for the Arts Fellowship 1991, Soros Foundation Award 1999, Arizona Literary Treasure 2008. *Address:* 579 S Third Avenue, Tucson, AZ 85701, USA (home). *E-mail:* nancymairs@msn.com (home). *Website:* www.nancymairs.com.

MAJA-PEARCE, Adewale, BA, MA; British researcher, writer and poet; b. 3 June 1953, London, England. *Education:* University of Wales, Swansea and SOAS, London. *Career:* Researcher, Index on Censorship, London, 1986–; Consultant, Heinemann International, Oxford, 1986–94; mem. PEN; Society of Authors. *Publications:* Christopher Okigbo: Collected Poems (ed.), 1986; In My Father's Country: A Nigerian Journey (non-fiction), 1987; Loyalties (short stories), 1987; How Many Miles to Babylon? (non-fiction), 1990; The Heinemann Book of African Poetry in English (ed.), 1990; Who's Afraid of Wole Soyinka?: Essays on Censorship, 1991; A Mask Dancing: Nigerian Novelists of the Eighties, 1992. Contributions: various periodicals.

MAJDALANI, Charif; French/Lebanese writer; b. 1960, Beirut. *Education:* Université de Aix-en-Provence, France. *Career:* literary critic, L'Orient-Express 1995–98; fmrly taught at Univ. of Balamand; Chair of Dept of French Literature, Univ. Saint-Joseph, Beirut, Lebanon 1999–. *Publications:* Petit traité des mélanges 2002, Histoire de la grande maison (novel) 2005. *Address:* Université Saint Joseph, rue de Damas, BP 17-5208, Mar Mikhaël, Beirut 1104 2020, Lebanon (office).

MAJOR, André; Canadian writer and poet; b. 22 April 1942, Montréal; m. Ginette Lepage 1970; one s. one d. *Education:* Collège de Montréal, Collège des Eudistes. *Publications include:* fiction: Nouvelles, 1963; Le Cabochon, 1964; La chair de poule, 1965; Le Vent du diable, 1968; L'Épouvantail, 1974 (trans. as The Scarecrows of Saint-Emmanuel 1977); L'Épidéme 1975 (English trans. as Inspector Therrien 19800; Les Rescapés, 1976 (English trans. as Man on the Run 1984); La folle d'Elvis 1983 (English trans. as Hooked on Elvis 1983); L'hiver au coeur, 1987 (English trans. as The Winter of the Heart 1989); La vie provisoire, 1995 (English trans. as A Provisional Life 1997); poetry: Le froid se meurt, 1961; Holocauste à 2 voix, 1961; Poèmes pour durer, 1969; other: Journal: Le Sourire d'Anton ou l'adieu au roman (1975–92) 2001. *Honours:* Gov.-Gen.'s Literary Award 1977, Prix Canada-Communauté française de Belgique 1991, Prix Études françaises 2001.

MAJOR, Clarence, BS, PhD; American poet, painter, novelist and academic; *Professor Emeritus of English, University of California, Davis*; b. 31 Dec. 1936, Atlanta, Ga; s. of Clarence Major and Inez Huff; m. Pamela Ritter 1980. *Education:* Union Inst. and Univ., Yellow Springs and Cincinnati, Ohio, State Univ. of NY, Albany. *Career:* Prof. of English, Univ. of California, Davis 1989–2010, Prof. Emer. 2010–; various appointments at Sara Lawrence Coll., Brooklyn Coll., Queens Coll., New York Univ., Temple Univ., Washington Univ., Univ. of California, San Diego, State Univ. of NY, Binghamton; has given lectures in USA, Europe and in N and W Africa. *Exhibitions include:* Kresge Art Museum, East Lansing, Mich. Natsoulas Art Gallery, Davis, Calif., Gayles Art Gallery Chicago, Sarah Lawrence Coll., NY, First Nat. Bank, Boulder, Colo, Schacknow Museum of Art, Plantation Florida, Exploding Head Gallery and Phoenix Gallery, Sacramento, Calif., Hamilton Club Art Gallery, Paterson, NJ, John Natsoulas Art Gallery, Davis, Calif., Main Street Gallery, Winters, Calif., Pierre Menard Gallery, Harvard Square, Cambridge, Univ. Art Gallery, Indiana State Univ., Terre Haute, Ind.; online galleries: art-avisen-avk, Denmark, Saatchi Gallery, London, artvitae, yourart. *Publications:* novels: All-Night Visitors 1969, NO 1973, Reflex and Bone Structure 1975, Emergency Exit 1979, My Amputations (Western States Book Award for Fiction) 1986, Such Was the Season 1987, Painted Turtle: Woman with Guitar 1988; short stories: Fun and Games 1990, Calling the Wind: Twentieth Century African-American Short Stories 1993, Dirty Bird Blues 1996, All-Night Visitors (new version) 1998; poetry: Swallow the Lake 1970, Symptoms and Madness 1971, Private Line 1971, The Cotton Club 1972, The Syncopated Cakewalk 1974, Inside Diameter: The France Poems 1985, Surfaces and Masks 1987, Some Observations of a Stranger at Zuni in the Latter Part of the Century 1989, The Garden Thrives, Twentieth Century African-American Poetry 1995, Configurations: New and Selected Poems 1958–98, 1998, Waiting for Sweet Baby 2002; non-fiction: Dictionary of Afro-American Slang 1970, The Dark and Feeling: Black American Writers and their Work 1974, Juba to Jive: A Dictionary of African-American Slang 1994, Necessary Distance: Essays and Criticism 2001, Come by Here: My Mother's Life 2002, Conversations with Clarence Major, Clarence Major and His Art; numerous works in anthologies and periodicals. *Honours:* Fulbright Fellowship, Pushcart Prize, Nat. Council on the Arts Award, Int. Writers' Hall of Fame, Gwendolyn Brooks Foundation Award, Chicago State Univ., Western States Book Award, Sister Circle Book Award, Stephen Henderson Poetry Award for Outstanding Achievement, Bronze Medal as Finalist for Nat. Book Award. *Address:* Department of English, Voorhies Hall, University of California, Davis, CA 95616, USA (office). *E-mail:* clmajor@ucdavis.edu (office). *Website:* english.ucdavis.edu/people/directory/cmajor (office); www.clarencemajor.com.

MAJOR, Devorah; American poet, novelist, performer, lecturer and editor; *Adjunct Professor, California College of the Arts*; b. San Francisco; one s. one d. *Career:* Poet-in-Residence, San Francisco Fine Arts Museum; Mediator, California Lawyer for the Arts; Poet Laureate of San Francisco; composer (with Guillermo Galindo), Trade Routes 2005; Adjunct Prof., Calif. Coll. of the Arts 2004–; poetry performances with jazz music as 'Daughters of Yam'; tours of England and Wales, Italy, France and Bosnia. *Publications:* novels: An Open Weave 1995, Brown Glass Windows 2002; poetry: Travelling Women (with Opal Palmer Adisa) 1989, Street Smarts 1996; other: Where River Meets Ocean 2003, With More Than Tongue 2003, The Other Side of the Postcard (ed.) 2005. *Honours:* inducted into San Francisco State Univ. Hall of Fame 2004; PEN Oakland/Josephine Miles Award 1997, First Novelist Award from American Library Asscn Black Caucus 1997. *Address:* POB 423634, San Francisco, CA 94142, USA (home). *E-mail:* devmajor@pacbell.net (home). *Website:* www.daughtersofyam.com (home).

MAJOR, Kevin Gerald, BSc; Canadian writer; b. 12 Sept. 1949, Stephenville, NF; m. Anne Crawford 1982, two s. *Education:* Memorial University, St John's, NF. *Career:* mem. Writers' Union of Canada. *Publications:* Far from Shore 1980, Thirty-Six Exposures 1984, Dear Bruce Springsteen 1987, Blood Red Ochre 1989, Eating Between the Lines 1991, Diana: My Autobiography 1993, No Man's Land 1995, Gaffer: A Novel of Newfoundland 1997, The House of Wooden Santas 1997, Eh? to Zed: A Canadian Abecedarium 2000, As Near to Heaven by Sea: A History of Newfoundland and Labrador 2001, Ann and Seamus 2003. *Honours:* Book of the Year Award, Canadian Asscn of Children's Librarians 1978, Canada Council Award for Children's Literature 1978, Canadian Young Adult Book Award 1980, Book of the Year Award for Children, Canadian Library Asscn 1991, Vicky Metcalf Award 1992, Mr Christie Award 1998. *Address:* 27 Poplar Avenue, St John's, NF A1B 1C7, Canada.

MAKANIN, Vladimir Semenovich; Russian writer; b. 13 March 1937, Orsk, Orenburg Region. *Education:* Moscow Univ., Higher Workshop for Scenario Writers and Film Dirs. *Career:* started writing 1965. *Publications include:* Straight Line 1965, Air-Vent, Portrait and Around (novel) 1976, Story about an Old Settlement (collection of short stories) 1974, Voices 1982, River with a Fast Current 1983, Where the Skies Meet the Hills 1987, One and One 1987, Subject of Averaging 1992, The Loss: A Novella and Two Stories (Writings from an Unbound Europe), Baize-Covered Table with Decanter 1993, Quasi 1993, Captives 1996, Escape Hatch and The Long Road Ahead: Two Novellas 1998, Underground, or a Hero of Our Time 1998, Letter A 2000, A Good Love Story 2000. *Honours:* Russian Booker Prize 1993, Pushkin Prize 1998, Penne Prize, Italy 1999, Russian State Prize 2000. *Address:* Novinski Boulevard 16, Apartment 14, 121069 Moscow, Russia. *Telephone:* (495) 291-92-53. *Fax:* (495) 781-01-82. *E-mail:* vmakanin@hotmail.com.

MAKARA, Mpho 'Mampeke, BA, MA; Lesotho author, teacher and student guidance counsellor; *Acting Head Machabeng College – International School of Lesotho;* b. 28 Oct. 1954, Quthing; d. of the late Tefo Stephen Moroeng and Malesia Maria Moroeng (née Masilo); m. Thabo Makara 1977; two d. one s. *Education:* Morija Girls' Training Coll., Nat. Univ. of Lesotho and Univ. of Bath (UK). *Career:* primary school teacher 1974–77; Asst Teacher, Machabeng Coll. –Int. School of Lesotho 1982–85, Deputy Head 1987, Teacher, Counsellor of the Lower School 1987, Co-ordinator Middle Years Programme 2000–05, Deputy Headteacher 2007–11, Acting Head 2011–. *Publications:* plays: Mali A Llelana 1986, Ke Fahliloe 1990, Sehaeso I 1991, II 1993, III 1994; novels: Mohanuoa 1996, Lintsing Tsa Selomo 2007; short stories: Sepetlele, Materaseng 1997; Poetry: U Etsang Uena? 2002; has also written language courses. *Honours:* Vodacom Lesotho Hall of Fame Contemporary Literature Award. *Address:* AO49/50 Thetsane West, Maseru (home); PO Box 15291, Maseru 100 (home); PO Box 1570, Maseru 100, Lesotho (office). *Telephone:* 22315480 (home); 22313224 (office). *Fax:* 22316109 (office). *E-mail:* mmakara@machcoll.co.ls (home); mphothabo@leo.co.ls (home); machbhm@lesoff.co.za (office). *Website:* www.lesoff.co.za/machab (office); machcoll.co.ls (office).

MAKINE, Andreï; French/Russian writer; b. 1957, Siberia; s. of Maria Stepanovna Dolina. *Career:* worked as teacher of literature in Novgorod; emigrated from USSR to France 1987, writes in French. *Play:* Le Monde selon Gabriel 2007. *Publications:* fiction: La Fille d'un Héros (trans. as A Hero's Daughter) 1990, Confession d'un Porte-Drapeau Déchu (trans. as Confessions of a Fallen Standard-Bearer) 1992, Au Temps du Fleuve Amour (trans. as Once Upon the River Love) 1994, Le Testament Français (trans. as Dreams of My Russian Summers; Prix Goncourt, Prix Médicis Étranger, Prix Goncourt des Lycéens, Eeva Joenpelto Prize, Finland) 1995, Le Crime d'Olga Arbelina (trans. as The Crime of Olga Arbelina 1998, Requiem pour l'Est (trans. as Requiem for a Lost Empire 2001, La Musique d'un Vie (trans. as A Life's Music; Prix RTL-Lire) 2001, La Terre et le ciel de Jacques Dorme (trans. as The Earth and Sky of Jacques Dorme) 2003, La Femme qui Attendait (trans. as The Woman Who Waited; Prix Lanterna Magica 2005) 2004, L'Amour Humain (trans. as Human Love) 2006, La Vie d'un Homme Inconnu (trans. as The Life of an Unknown Man) 2009; non-fiction: St Pétersbourg (with Ferrante Ferranti) 2002, Cette France qu'on oublie d'aimer 2006. *Honours:* Priz de la Fondation Prince Pierre de Monaco 2005. *Address:* c/o Editions du Seuil, 25 boulevard Romain Rolland, 75993 Paris, France (office). *Website:* www.editionsduseuil.fr (office); andreimakine.com.

MAKINSON, John, BA; British publishing executive; *Chairman and Chief Executive,* Penguin Group; m.; two c. *Education:* Univ. of Cambridge. *Career:* journalist Reuters (London, Paris and Frankfurt offices) 1976–79; journalist, later Ed. Lex column Financial Times 1979–86; Vice-Chair. Saatchi & Saatchi US holding co. 1986–89; co-founder and head of consultancy Makinson Cowell 1989–94; Man. Dir Financial Times 1994–96; Chief Financial Officer, Pearson Group 1996–2002, mem. bd of dirs 2002–; Chair. Penguin Group 2001–, also CEO 2002–; Dir and Co-Chair. International Rescue Cttee (UK); Chair., Interactive Data Corporation; Non-Exec. Dir George Weston Ltd, Canada, and Recoletos Grupo de Comunicacion SA, Spain. *Address:* Penguin Group, 80 Strand, London, WC2R 0RL, England. *Website:* www.penguin.com.

MALASHENKO, Igor Yevgenyevich, CandPhilSc; Russian journalist; b. 2 Oct. 1954, Moscow; m. Yelena Pivovarova; two d. *Education:* Moscow State Univ. *Career:* jr, sr researcher, Inst. of USA and Canada USSR Acad. of Sciences 1980–89, research in problems of the concept of nuclear deterrence and public opinion; staff-mem. Int. Div. Cen. Cttee CPSU, admin. of Pres. Gorbachev March–Dec. 1991; political Dir TV & Radio Co. Ostankino 1992–93; Pres. and Dir-Gen. Ind. TV Co. NTV 1993–, Pres. NTV-Telemost Holding 1998; First Deputy Chair. Bd of Dirs Media-Most Co. 1998–2001; adviser to Pres. of Russia on public relations problems, mem. election campaign staff of Boris Yeltsin 1996. *Honours:* Prize of Russian Union of Journalists 1994. *Address:* NTV-Telemost, Academica Koroleva str. 19, 127427 Moscow, Russia. *Telephone:* (495) 215-15-88 (office).

MALHERBE, René Cornelis; Dutch publisher; b. 22 Aug. 1942, 's-Hertogenbosch; s. of G. Malherbe and R. Algra; m. Renate Emma van de Venne 1966; two s. one d. *Career:* qualified as electro-tech. engineer; with Philips Medical Equipment 1960–62, with Smeets Printing Weert 1964–66, Cargill Marketing, London and Eindhoven 1966–68, Marketing & Promotion, Eindhoven 1968–74, M & P Publishing Weert 1974–86; Dir Malherbe Group Publishing Weert 1986–.

MALIK, Zubeida, BA, MA; British journalist; *Correspondent,* Today Programme, BBC Radio 4. *Career:* Reporter, Today Programme, BBC Radio 4 1997–; first British broadcaster and only woman to interview the Taliban during war on terrorism; one of first journalists to uncover training camps in UK; reported from Nigeria, Israel and Saudi Arabia; first woman journalist for the BBC to report on the Haaj from inside Mecca and Medina. *Honours:* Foreign Press Asscn Young Journalist of the Year 2000, Best Radio News Journalist, Ethnic Multicultural Media Awards (EMMAs) 2001, 2002, Asian Women of Achievement Media Personality of the Year Award 2002, Radio and TV Media Personality, Carlton Multicultural Achievement Awards 2003, Muslim News Award for Journalism 2007. *Address:* c/o Today Programme, BBC Radio 4, Room 9630, Stage Six, Television Centre, Wood Lane, London, W12 7RJ, England (office). *Telephone:* (20) 8624-9644 (office).

MALLET-JORIS, Françoise; French novelist; b. (Françoise Lilar), 6 July 1930, Antwerp, Belgium; d. of M. Lilar and Suzanne Lilar. *Education:* Bryn Mawr Coll., Pennsylvania, Sorbonne, University of Paris. *Career:* reader, Grasset Publishers 1965; mem. Académie Goncourt 1971–. *Publications:* The Illusionist 1951, Into the Labyrinth 1951, The Red Room 1955, Cordelia and Other Stories 1956, House of Lies 1956, Café Celeste 1958, The Favourite 1961, A Letter to Myself 1963, The Uncompromising Heart 1964, Signs and Wonders 1966, The Witches: Three Tales of Sorcery 1968, The Paper House 1970, The Underground Game 1973, Allegra 1976, Le Rire de Laura 1985, La Tristesse du cerf-volant 1988, Adriana Sposa 1989, Divine 1991; other: French version of Shelagh Delaney's play A Taste of Honey 1960, A Letter to Myself 1964, The Paper House 1970, Juliette Greco 1975, Marie-Paule Belle 1987. *Honours:* Ordre National du Mérite 1986; Prix des Libraires 1957, Prix Fémina 1958, Prix Prince de Monaco 1964.

MALLON, Maurus Edward, BEd, MA; British teacher, writer and dramatist; b. 10 July 1932, Greenock, Scotland; s. of Peter and Agnes Mallon. *Education:* Univ. of Glasgow, Univ. of Manitoba, Winnipeg. *Career:* mem. Living Authors' Soc., Nat. Writers' Asscn (USA), PEN Canada. *Publications:* Basileus 1971, The Opal 1973, Pegaso 1975, Way of the Magus 1978, Anogia 1980, Bammer McPhie 1984, Treasure Mountain 1986, Postcards 1991, Ex Novo Mundo (short stories) 1992, Compendulum 1993, A Matter of Conscience (play) 1994. *Address:* PO Box 331, Deep River, ON K0J 1P0, Canada (home). *Telephone:* (613) 584-3293 (home).

MALLON, Thomas, BA, MA, PhD; American writer and academic; b. 2 Nov. 1951, Glen Cove, NY; s. of Arthur Mallon and Caroline Mallon (née Moruzzi); pnr William Bodenschatz. *Education:* Brown Univ., Harvard Univ. *Career:* fmr Literary Ed., GQ; fmr Prof. of English, Vassar Coll.; fmr Deputy Chair. Nat. Endowment for the Humanities; Visiting Scholar, St Edmund's Coll., Cambridge, England; currently Adjunct Prof. of English, The George Washington Univ. *Publications:* Edmund Blunden 1983, A Book of One's Own: People and Their Diaries 1984, Arts and Sciences: A Seventies Seduction 1988, Stolen Words: Forays into the Origins and Ravages of Plagarism 1989, Aurora 7 1991, Rockets and Rodeos and Other American Spectacles 1993, Henry and Clara 1994, Dewey Defeats Truman 1997, Two Moons 2001, Mrs Paine's Garage 2002, Bandbox 2004, Fellow Travelers 2007, Yours Ever: People and Their Letters 2009; contrib. to GQ, Atlantic Monthly, The New Yorker, American Scholar, Yale Review Architectural Digest, New York Times Book Review, The Washington Post Book World. *Honours:* Rockefeller Fellowship 1986, Guggenheim Fellowship 2000, Ingram Merrill Award 1994, Nat. Book Critics Circle Award for Reviewing 1998. *Address:* c/o Pantheon, Random House Inc., 1745 Broadway, New York, NY 10019, USA (office). *E-mail:* tvmallon@aol.com (home).

MALMSTEN, Bodil; Swedish poet and writer; b. 1944, Jämtland. *Education:* Acad. of Fine Arts, Stockholm. *Career:* writer for children, for TV and radio; moved to Brittany, France 2000; involved in art educ., translating, directing plays for the stage. *Publications:* Dvärgen Gustaf (poems) 1977, Damen, det brinner! (poems) 1984, Paddan & branden (poems) 1987, B-ställningar 1987, Ett bloss för Bodil Malmsten, dikter 1977–1987 (poems) 1988, Svartvita bilder 1988, Nåd & onåd (poems) 1989, Nefertiti i Berlin 1990, Det är ingen ordning på mina papper 1991, Landet utan lov 1991, Inte med den eld jag har nu. dikt för annan dam 1993, Den dagen kastanjerna slår ut är jag långt härifrån 1994, Dikter 1977–1990 (poems) 1991, Samlade dikter (poems) 1995, En julsaga 1993 1993, Tulipomani (novella) 1995, Nåsta som rör mig 1996, Undergångarens sånger (novella) 1998, Det finns inga lyckopiller 2000, Priset på vatten i Finistère (trans. as The Price of Water in Finistère) 2001, Det är fortfarande ingen ordning på mina papper 2003, Mitt första liv (autobiog.) 2004, Press Star (play) 2005, För att Lämna röstmeddelandele Tryck Syjärna (novel) 2005. *Honours:* winner of around 20 Swedish literary awards, including Tilldelad Aniara Prize 1996, Ivar Lo Prize 2006. *Address:* c/o The Harvill Press, Random House, 20 Vauxhall Bridge Road, London, SW1V 2SA, England. *E-mail:* bodil@wanadoo.fr. *Website:* www.finistere.se.

MALOUF, David George Joseph, AO, BA; Australian writer and poet; b. 20 March 1934, Brisbane, Qld; s. of G. Malouf. *Education:* Brisbane Grammar School and Univ. of Queensland. *Publications include:* poetry: Bicycle and other poems 1970, Neighbours in a Thicket 1974, First Things Last 1981, Selected Poems 1991, Poems 1959–89 1992, Typewriter Music 2007, Revolving Days: selected poems 2008; novels: Johnno 1975, An Imaginary Life 1978, Child's Play 1982, Fly Away Peter 1982, Harland's Half Acre 1984, 12 Edmondstone Street 1985, The Great World 1990, Remembering Babylon 1993, The Conversations at Curlow Creek 1996, Ransom 2009; short stories:

Antipodes 1983, Dream Stuff 2000, Every Move You Make 2006, The Complete Stories 2007; play: Blood Relations 1987; opera librettos: Voss 1986, Mer de Glace 1991, Baa Baa Black Sheep 1993, Jane Eyre 2000. *Honours:* Hon. Fellow, Australian Acad. of the Humanities; Gold Medal, Australian Literature Soc. 1974, 1982, 2009, Age Book of the Year, NSW Premier's Award for Fiction, Vance Palmer Award, Pascal Prize, Commonwealth Writers' Prize and Prix Femina Etranger, for The Great World 1991, inaugural IMPAC Dublin Literary Award 1993, Neustadt Int. Prize for Literature 2000, Criticos Prize 2010, many other awards. *Literary Agent:* c/o Rogers, Coleridge & White, 20 Powis Mews, London, W11 1JN, England. *Telephone:* (20) 7221-3717. *Fax:* (20) 7229-9084. *Address:* c/o Barbara Mobbs, 35A Sutherland Crescent, Darling Point, Sydney, NSW 2027 (office); 53 Myrtle Street, Chippendale, NSW 2008, Australia (home).

MALZBERG, Barry Norman, AB; American writer; b. 24 July 1939, New York, NY. *Education:* Syracuse Univ. *Career:* pseudonyms include Mike Barry, Francine de Natale, Claudine Dumas, Mel Johnson, Lew W. Mason, K. M. O'Donnell, Gerrold Watkins. *Publications:* Screen 1968, Oracle of the Thousand Hands 1968, The Empty People 1969, Final War and Other Fantasies 1969, Dwellers of the Deep 1970, Confessions of Westchester County 1971, The Falling Astronauts 1971, Gather in the Hall of the Planets 1971, In My Parents' Bedroom 1971, In the Pocket and Other SF Stories 1971, Universe Day 1971, Beyond Apollo (John W. Campbell Memorial Award for Best Novel 1973) 1972, Overlay 1972, The Men Inside 1972, Revelations 1972, Phase IV 1973, Herovit's World 1973, In the Enclosure 1973, Tactics of Conquest 1973, The Destruction of the Temple 1974, On a Planet Alien 1974, The Sodom and Gomorrah Business 1974, Guernica Night 1974, The Day of the Burning 1974, Underlay 1974, Out from Ganymede 1974, The Many Worlds of Barry Malzberg 1975, The Best of Barry N. Malzberg 1975, The Gamesman 1975, Galaxies 1975, Conversations 1975, Down Here in the Dream Quarter 1976, The Running of Beasts (with Bill Pronzini) 1976, Chorale 1976, Scop 1976, The Last Transaction 1977, Acts of Mercy (with Bill Pronzini) 1977, Night of Screams (with Bill Pronzini) 1979, Malzberg at Large 1979, Prose Bowl (with Bill Pronzini) 1980, The Man Who Loved the Midnight Lady: A Collection 1980, The Cross of Fire 1982, The Engines of the Night: Science Fiction in the Eighties (essays) 1982, The Remaking of Sigmund Freud 1985, The Passage of the Light: The Recursive Science Fiction of Barry N. Malzberg (with Tony Lewis and Mike Resnick) 1994, In the Stone House 2000, Shiva and Other Stories 2001, Problems Solved (with Bill Pronzini) 2003, Breakfast in the Ruins 2007; contrib. short stories to numerous magazines and anthologies.

MAMONOVA, Tatyana; Russian author, academic, poet and activist; *President, Woman and Earth*; b. St Petersburg; m. Gennday Shikarioff; one s. *Education:* Harvard Univ. *Career:* literary journalist, critic for Aurora Publications; post-doctoral fellow, Bunting Inst., Harvard Univ.; founder, Woman & Russia Almanac and org. 1979, currently Pres.; Ed.-in-Chief, Succès d'Estime 2000–; Dir Women around the World (seminar series). *Television:* Tatyana Mamonova Presents (Manhattan Network) 1988–2010. *Publications:* non-fiction: Women and Russia 1984, Russian Women's Studies: Essays on Sexism in Soviet Culture 1989, Woman and Earth 1990–2010, Women's Glasnost versus Glasnost: Stopping Russian Backlash 1994, Succès d'estime 2000–10, Album Around the World 2005–10, Woman and Earth Almanac 2000–10. *Honours:* Diamond Homer Trophy for Famous Poet 1998, Living Legacy Award by Int. Women's Centre of San Diego 2002, Heart of Danko (St Petersburg) 2006. *Address:* Woman & Earth, 467 Central Park West, Suite 7F, New York, NY 10025, USA (office); Woman and Earth aka Woman and Russia, Dekabristov Street 7–12, St Petersburg 190000, Russia. *Telephone:* (212) 866-8130 (office); (812) 314-59-80 (home). *Fax:* (212) 866-8130 (office). *E-mail:* womearth@yahoo.com (office). *Website:* www.dorsai.org/~womearth (office); www.womanandearth.com (office).

MAMET, David Alan, BA; American playwright, screenwriter and director; b. 30 Nov. 1947, Chicago; s. of Bernard Morris Mamet and Lenore June Mamet (née Silver); m. 1st Lindsay Crouse 1977 (divorced); m. 2nd Rebecca Pidgeon 1991. *Education:* Goddard Coll., Plainfield, Vt. *Career:* Artist-in-Residence, Goddard Coll. 1971–73; Artistic Dir St Nicholas Theatre Co., Chicago 1973–75; Guest Lecturer, Univ. of Chicago 1975, 1979, NY Univ. 1981; Assoc. Artistic Dir Goodman Theatre, Chicago 1978; Assoc. Prof. of Film, Columbia Univ. 1988. *Films directed:* House of Games 1986, Things Change 1987, Homicide 1991, Oleanna 1994, The Spanish Prisoner 1997, The Winslow Boy 1999, Catastrophe 2000, State and Main 2000, Heist 2001, Spartan 2004, Redbelt 2008. *Films written include:* The Postman Always Rings Twice 1981, The Verdict 1982, About Last Night 1986, The Untouchables 1987, House of Games 1987, Things Change 1988, We're No Angels 1989, Homicide 1991, Glengarry Glen Ross 1992, Hoffa 1992, Oleanna 1994, American Buffalo 1996, The Edge 1997, The Spanish Prisoner 1997, Wag the Dog 1997, Ronin 1998, State and Main 2000, Hannibal 2001, Heist 2001, Spartan 2004, Edmond 2005, Redbelt 2008. *Works include:* The Duck Variations 1971, Sexual Perversity in Chicago 1973 (Village Voice Obie Award 1976), The Reunion 1973, Squirrels 1974, American Buffalo (Village Voice Obie Award 1976) 1976, (New York Drama Critics Circle Award 1977), A Life in the Theatre 1976, The Water Engine 1976, The Woods 1977, Lone Canoe 1978, Prairie du Chien 1978, Lakeboat 1980, Donny March 1981, Edmond 1982 (Village Voice Obie Award 1983), The Disappearance of the Jews 1983, The Shawl 1985, Glengarry Glen Ross (Pulitzer Prize for Drama, New York Drama Critics Circle award) 1984, Speed-the-Plow 1987, Bobby, Gould in Hell 1989, The Old Neighborhood 1991, Oleanna 1992, Ricky Jay and his 52 Assistants 1994, The Village (novel) 1994, Death Defying Acts 1996, Boston Marriage 1999, The Wicked Son 2006, Race 2009; screenplays: The Postman Always Rings Twice 1979, The Verdict 1980, The Untouchables 1986, House of Games 1986, Things Change (with Shel Silverstein) 1987, We're No Angels 1987, A Life in the Theatre (also dir) 1989, Oh Hell! 1991, Homicide 1991, Hoffa 1991, Glengarry Glen Ross 1992, The Rising Sun 1992, Oleanna 1994, The Edge 1996, The Spanish Prisoner 1996, Wag the Dog 1997, State and Main 2000, The Winslow Bo 1999, Boston Marriage 2001, Heist 2001, Hannibal 2001, Spartan 2004; children's books: Mr Warm and Cold 1985, The Owl (with Lindsay Crouse) 1987, The Winslow Bay 1999; essays: Writing in Restaurants 1986, Some Freaks 1989, On Directing Film 1990, The Hero Pony 1990, The Cabin 1992, A Whore's Profession (also screenplay adaptation) 1993, The Cryptogram 1994, Passover 1995, Make-Believe Town: Essays and Remembrances 1996, Plays 1996, Plays 2 1996, The Duck and the Goat 1996, The Old Religion 1996, True and False 1996, The Old Neighborhood 1998, Jafsie and John Henry 2000, Bambi vs Godzilla (non-fiction) 2007. *Honours:* Hon. DLitt (Dartmouth Coll.) 1996; Outer Critics Circle Award for contrib. to American theatre 1978, PEN/Laura Pels Foundation Award for Drama 2010. *Literary Agent:* Abrams Artists Agency, 275 Seventh Avenue, 25th Floor, New York, NY 10001, USA. *Telephone:* (646) 486-4600. *E-mail:* vincent.devito@abramsart.com. *Website:* www.abramsartists.com.

MAMLEYEV, Yuri; Russian writer, playwright, poet and philosopher; b. 11 Dec. 1931, Moscow; m. Farida Mamleyev 1973. *Education:* Forestry Inst., Moscow. *Career:* mem. French PEN Centre, Russian PEN Centre, Russian Union of Writers, Russian Union of Playwrights. *Publications:* The Sky Above Hell 1980, Iznanka Gogena 1982, Chatouny 1986, Zhivaja Smert 1986, Derniere Comedie 1988, Golos iz Nichto 1990, Utopi Moyu Golovu 1990, Vechnyi dom 1991, Der Murder aus dem Nichts 1992, Izbzannoe 1993, Die Letzte Komödie 1994, Shatuny 1996, Union Mistice 1997, Chernoe zerkalo 1998, J. M. Chatouny 1998, Der Tod des Erotomanen 1999, Moskovski Gambit 1999, Bluzhdajusheje Vremia 2001, Chernoe zerkalo 2001, Bunt luny 2001, Mir i khokhot 2003, Les Couluirs du Temps 2004, Drougoi 2006, Plat' romanov 2008, Soud'la lytia 2006, Byvoet 2007, Zivoie Kladlishche 2007, Le Monde et le Rire 2007, Zapiski povara 2009, Imperia doucha 200, Posle kontsa, Destin de l'Etre 2012; contrib. to periodicals. *Honours:* Int. Pushkin Award of Alfred Töpfer, Hamburg, Germany 2000, Andrei Belyi Prize 2001. *Address:* 142 rue Legendre, 75017 Paris, France; Apt 132, Michuzinski Prospect 37, Poccur Mockba, Moscow 117607, Russia. *Telephone:* 1-53-31-08-53 (home).

MANA, Samira Al, BA; British (b. Iraqi) writer, teacher and librarian; b. 25 Dec. 1935, Basra, Iraq; m. Salah Niazi 1959; two d. *Education:* Univ. of Baghdad, Ealing Tech. Coll., UK (Postgraduate Dipl. in Librarianship). *Career:* Asst Ed. Alightrab Al-Adabi (Literature of the Exiled) 1985–2002; teaches Arabic in Iraq and UK. *Play:* Only a Half 1984 (read on stage, sponsored by Int. Women Playwrights Centre and Baffalo State Univ., NY, USA 1990). *Publications:* novels: The Forerunners and the Newcomers 1972, A London Sequel 1979, The Umbilical Cord 1990 (English trans. 2005), The Oppressors 1997, Look at Me... Look at Me Only 2002, Knowing Not What They Want 2010; short story collections: The Song 1976, The Soul and Other Stories 1999; contrib. many short stories to Arabic magazines, some trans. into Dutch and English anthologies of Arabic fiction, including Contemporary Iraqi Fiction 2008. *Address:* 46 Tudor Drive, Kingston-upon-Thames, Surrey, KT2 5PZ, England (home). *Telephone:* (20) 8549-0894 (office). *E-mail:* lulaaa999@yahoo.co.uk (home). *Website:* alightirab.cjb.net (office).

MANCHESTER, Rt Rev. Seán; British author and prelate; *Bishop of Glastonbury*; b. Nottinghamshire, England. *Education:* Doctor of Pastoral Ministry, Coll. David's Coll. *Career:* diaconated 1990, ordained priest 1990, consecrated Bishop 1991; founder and Pres. Vampire Research Soc. 1970; Superior Gen. Ordo Sancti Graal 1973; Chair. Soc. of St George 1990; Primate Ecclesia Apostolica Jesu Christi 1991; Bishop of Glastonbury 1993; Presiding Bishop, Traditional Old Catholic Movement 2000; Founder Sacerdotal Soc. of the Precious Blood 2002. *Publications:* From Satan to Christ: A Story of Salvation 1988, The Highgate Vampire: The Infernal World of the Undead Unearthed at London's Highgate Cemetery 1991, Mad, Bad and Dangerous to Know: The Life of Lady Caroline Lamb 1992, The Grail Church: Its Ancient Tradition and Renewed Flowering 1995, The Vampire Hunter's Handbook: A Concise Vampirological Guide 1997, Carmel: A Vampire Tale 2000. *Honours:* Kt Commdr, Order of St George, Companion, Holy Order of St Michael and St George, Companion, Order of the Sangreal. *Website:* seanmanchester.blogspot.com (office); www.holygrail-church.fsnet.co.uk (office).

MANDANIPUR, Shahriar; Iranian writer and academic; b. 15 Feb. 1957, Shiraz; m.; two c. *Education:* Univ. of Tehran. *Career:* served in army 1981–82; fmr Dir Hafiz Research Centre; prohibited from publishing his stories in Iran 1992–97; Ed. in Chief Asr-e Pandjshanbeh (literary journal) 1999–; moved to USA 2006; Fellow, Int. Writers Project, Brown Univ. 2005–07, Visiting Lecturer in Literary Arts 2011–; Writer-in-Residence, Harvard Univ. 207–08, Boston Coll. 2009. *Publications include:* short story collections: Sâyehâ-ye Qar (Shadows of the Cave) 1989, Hashtomin Ruz-e Zamin (The Eighth Day of the Earth) 1992, Mumiyâ va Asal (Mummy and Honey) 1996, Mâh-e Nimruz (Midday Moon) 1997, Sharq-e Banafsheh (Violent Orient) 1998, Ultramarine Blue 2003; novels: Del-e Deldâdegi (The Courage of Love) 1998, Censoring an Iranian Love Story (in trans.) 2009; other: Shahrzad's Ghosts (essays on creative writing) 2004; contrib. articles and literary criticism to magazines and newspapers. *Honours:* Golden Tablet

Award for Best Fiction in Iran during the previous two decades 1998, Mehregan Award for Best Iranian children's novel 2004. *Address:* Brown University, Room 228, 70 Brown Street, Providence, RI 02912, USA (office). *E-mail:* shahriar_mondanipour@brown.edu (office). *Website:* www.mandanipour.net.

MANDEL, Oscar, BA, MA, PhD; American writer, dramatist, poet, translator and art historian and academic; *Professor Emeritus, California Institute of Technology*; b. 24 Aug. 1926, Antwerp, Belgium; m. Adriana Schizzano 1960. *Education:* New York Univ., Columbia Univ., Ohio State Univ. *Career:* mem. Faculty, Univ. of Nebraska 1955–60; Fulbright Lecturer, Univ. of Amsterdam 1960–61; Assoc. Prof., California Inst. of Tech., Pasadena 1961–65, Prof. of Humanities 1965, now Prof. Emer.; mem. Dramatists' Guild, Modern Language Asscn, Soc. des Auteurs et Compositeurs Dramatiques. *Publications:* poetry: Simplicities 1974, Collected Lyrics and Epigrams 1981, Where is the light? – Poems 1955–2005, Cette Guépe me Regarde de Travers: Poémes en Deux Langues 2010; plays: The Fatal French Dentist 1967, Collected Plays (Vols One and Two) 1970, 1972, Amphitryon (adaptation of Molière's comedy) 1976, The Rebels of Nantucket: A Romantic Comedy of the American Revolution 1976, The Kukkurrik Fables: 43 mini-plays for all media 1987, revised and augmented edn 2004, Sigismund, Prince of Poland: A Baroque Entertainment 1988, The Virgin and the Unicorn: Four Plays by Oscar Mandel 1993, Reinventions: Four Plays After Homer, Cervantes, Calderon and Marivaux 2002, L'Arc de Philocète 2002, Amphitryon, ou le cocu béni 2003, Le Triomphe d'Agamemnon 2003; fiction: Chi Po and the Sorcerer: A Chinese Tale for Children and Philosophers 1964, The Gobble-Up Stories (fables) 1967, Cho Po et le Sorcier: Conte Chinois 2004, La Reine de Patagonie et son Caniche 2007; non-fiction: A Definition of Tragedy (literary theory) 1961, The Theater of Don Juan (thematic history, anthology) 1963, Annotations to Vanity Fair (notes) 1981, Philoctetes and the Fall of Troy: Plays, Documents, Iconography, Interpretations 1982, The Book of Elaborations (essays) 1985, August von Kotzebue: The Comedy, the Man 1990, The Art of Alessandro Magnasco: An Essay in the Recovery of Meaning 1994, The Cheerfulness of Dutch Art: A Rescue Operation 1996, Fundamentals and the Art of Poetry 1997; translations: Seven Comedies by Marivaux 1968, Five Comedies of Medieval France 1970, The Land of Upside Down by Ludwig Tieck 1978, Thomas Corneille's Ariadne 1982, The Theatre of Don Juan: A Collection of Plays and Views, 1630–1963 1986, Prosper Mérimée: Plays on Hispanic Themes (with annotations) 2003; contrib. to scholarly journals. *Address:* Division of Humanities and Social Sciences, California Institute of Technology, Pasadena, CA 91125, USA (office). *Telephone:* (626) 395-4078 (office). *Fax:* (626) 432-1726 (office). *E-mail:* om@hss.caltech.edu (office). *Website:* www.oscarmandel.com.

MANDELA, Nelson Rolihlahla; South African politician, lawyer, international affairs consultant and fmr head of state; b. 1918, Umtata, Transkei; s. of Chief of Tembu tribe; m. 1st Evelyn Mandela 1944 (divorced 1957, died 2004); four c. (three deceased); m. 2nd Winnie Mandela 1958 (divorced 1996); two d.; m. 3rd Graca Machel (widow of the late Pres. Machel of Mozambique) 1998. *Education:* Univ. Coll. of Fort Hare, Univ. of the Witwatersrand. *Career:* legal practice, Johannesburg 1952; Nat. organizer African Nat. Congress (ANC) on trial for treason 1956–61 (acquitted 1961); arrested 1962, sentenced to five years' imprisonment Nov. 1962; on trial for further charges 1963–64, sentenced to life imprisonment June 1964; released Feb. 1990; Deputy Pres. ANC 1990–91, Pres. 1991–97, mem. Nat. Exec. Cttee 1991–; Pres. of South Africa 1994–99; Chancellor Univ. of the North 1992–; Jt Pres. United World Colls 1995–. *Publications:* No Easy Walk to Freedom 1965, How Far We Slaves Have Come: South Africa and Cuba in Today's World (with Fidel Castro) 1991, Nelson Mandela Speaks: Forging a Non-Racial Democratic South Africa 1993, Long Walk to Freedom 1994, Conversations with Myself 2010. *Honours:* Hon. Fellow Magdalene Coll., Cambridge 2001; Hon. Freeman of London; Freedom of City of Glasgow 1981; Hon. Citizen of Rome 1983; Freeman of Dublin 1988; Hon. Bencher Lincoln's Inn 1994; Hon. QC 2000; Foreign Hon. Fellow, American Acad. of Arts and Sciences 2009; Order of the Niger 1990; Hon. LLD (Nat. Univ. of Lesotho) 1979, (City Coll. of City Univ. of New York) 1983, (Lancaster) 1984, (Strathclyde) 1985, (Calcutta) 1986, (Harare) 1987, (Kent) 1992, Hon. DLitt (Texas Southern Univ.) 1991; Dr hc (Complutense) 1991; Hon. DCL (Oxford) 1996, Cambridge (1996); Hon. LLD (London) 1996, Bristol (1996), (Nottingham) 1996, (Warwick) 1996, (De Montfort) 1996, (Glasgow Caledonian) 1996; Jawaharlal Nehru Award (India) 1979, Bruno Kreisky Prize for Human Rights 1981, Simon Bolivar Int. Prize (UNESCO) 1983, Third World Prize 1985, Sakharov Prize 1988, Gaddafi Human Rights Prize 1989, Bharat Ratna (India) 1990, Jt winner Houphouët Prize (UNESCO) 1991, Nishan-e-Pakistan 1992, Asturias Prize 1992, Liberty Medal (USA) 1993; shared Nobel Prize for Peace 1993; Mandela-Fulbright Prize 1993, Tun Abdul Razak Award 1994, Anne Frank Medal 1994, Int. Freedom Award 2000, Johannesburg Freedom of the City Award 2004, Amnesty Int. Amb. of Conscience Award 2006. *Address:* c/o ANC, 51 Plein Street, Johannesburg 2001, South Africa (office). *Telephone:* (11) 3307000 (office). *Fax:* (11) 3360302 (office). *E-mail:* info@anc.org.za (office).

MANDLER, Peter, BA, PhD; American historian; b. 29 Jan. 1958, Boston, Mass; m. Ruth Ehrlich 1987; one s. one d. *Education:* Magdalen College, Oxford, Harvard University. *Career:* Asst Prof., Princeton University, 1984–91; Senior Lecturer, 1991–95, Reader, 1995–97, Prof., 1997–, London Guildhall University; mem. Royal Historical Society, hon. sec., 1998–. *Publications:* Aristocratic Government in the Age of Reform, 1990; The Uses of Charity (ed.), 1990; After the Victorians (co-ed.), 1994; The Fall and Rise of the Stately Home, 1997. Contributions: journals, magazines and newspapers.

MANEA, Norman, MS; American writer and academic; *Frances Flournoy Professor of European Culture, Bard College*; b. 19 July 1936, Suceava, Romania; m. Josette-Cella Boiangiu 1969. *Education:* Inst. of Construction, Faculty of Hydrotechnology, Bucharest. *Career:* Int. Acad. Fellow, Bard Coll. 1989–92, Frances Flournoy Prof. of European Culture 1992–, currently Writer-in-Residence; numerous lectures; mem. Berlin Acad. of Art 2006. *Publications:* fiction: Noaptea pe latura lunga 1969, Captivi 1970, Atrium 1974, Primele porti 1975, Cartea fiului 1976, Zilele si jocul 1977, Octombrie, ora opt (trans. as October, Eight O'Clock) 1981, Plicul Negru (trans. as The Black Envelope) 1986, Compulsory Happiness 1993; other: Anii de ucenicie ai lui August Prostul 1979, Pe contur 1984, On Clowns: The Dictator and the Artist 1992, Casa melcului 1999, Le Retour du Hooligan (The Hooligan's Return, Prix Medicis Etranger 2006) 2003; contrib. to anthologies, periodicals and television. *Honours:* Literary Prize Asscn of Bucharest Writers 1979, Deutscher Akademischer Austauschdienst grant, Berlin 1987, Fulbright Scholarship 1988, Bard Coll. Int. Acad. for Scholarship and the Arts Fellowship 1989–92, Guggenheim Fellowship 1992, John D. and Catherine T. MacArthur Foundation Fellowship 1992, Nat. Jewish Book Award Jewish Book Council/Jewish Welfare Board 1993, New York Public Library Literary Lion Award 1993, Int. Nonino Prize for Literature 2001, Napoli Prize for Int. Fiction 2004. *Address:* Bard College, Annandale-on-Hudson, NY 12504, USA (office).

MANES, Christopher, BA, MA, JD; American writer; b. 24 May 1957, Chicago, IL; one d. *Education:* University of California, University of Wisconsin. *Career:* mem. California State Bar Asscn; Writers Guild. *Publications:* Place of the Wild, 1994; Post Modernism and Environmental Philosophy, 1994. Contributions: Reference works, books, journals and magazines.

MANFREDI, Valerio Massimo; Italian archaeologist, academic and writer; *Professor of Archaeology, Bocconi University*; b. 1943. *Career:* specialist in topography of the ancient world; has taken part in many archaeological excavations in Italy and abroad; has taught at Università Cattolica, Milan, Venice Univ., Loyola Univ., Chicago and Ecole Pratique des Hautes Etudes, Paris, currently Prof. of Archaeology Bocconi Univ., Milan; corresp. on antiquities for publs Panorama and Il Messaggero. *Television:* Stargate (LA7–TV). *Publications include:* Xenophon's Anabasis (translator), Lo Scudo di Talos, Palladion, Il Faraone delle Sabbie, L'Oracolo, Le Paludi di Hesperia, La Torre della Solitudine, Alexandros: Child of a Dream, Alexander: The Sands of Amon, Alexander: The Ends of the Earth, Chimaira Akropolis 2001, L'ultima Legione (The Last Legion: Spartan) 2002, Il Tiranno (trans. as Tyrant) 2003, L'impero dei draghi 2005, Zeus e altro racconti 2006, L'armata Perduta 2007, Idi di Marzo 2008. *Honours:* Commendatore della Repubblica; Premio Rhegium Julii, Premio Hemingway 2004. *Address:* Laura Grandi (Agent), Via Caradosso 12, 20123, Milan (office); Via delle Grazie 31, 41010, Piumazzo, Modema, Italy (home). *Telephone:* 059-931519 (home). *Fax:* 059-931519 (home). *E-mail:* toilos@tim.it (home).

MANGUEL, Alberto; Canadian (b. Argentine) writer, editor and translator; b. 13 March 1948, Buenos Aires, Argentina. *Career:* Fellow, Simon Guggenheim Foundation, S. Fischer Stiftung. *Publications:* (in English) novels: News from a Foreign Country Came (McKitterick Prize 1992) 1991, Stevenson Under the Palm Trees 2002, The Return 2006, The Overdiscriminating Lover 2006, At the Mad Hatter's Table 2006, The Library at Night 2008, All Men Are Liars 2010; collections: In Another Part of the Forest: The Flamingo Anthology of Gay Literature (with Craig Stephenson) 1968, The Gates of Paradise: The Flamingo Anthology of Erotic Literature 1969, Black Water: The Flamingo Anthology of Fantastic Literature 1990; non-fiction: The Dictionary of Imaginary Places 1980, Into the Looking-Glass Wood: Essays on Books, Reading and the World 1985, A History of Reading (TLS Int. Book of the Year, Prix Médicis 1998) 1996, Reading Pictures 2001, A Reading Diary 2005, With Borges 2006, Homer's The Iliad and The Odyssey: A Biography 2007, The City of Words 2008, A Reader on Reading 2010; ed. of numerous anthologies, many trans. *Honours:* Officier, Ordre des Arts et des Lettres; Dr hc (Univ. of Liège, Anglia Ruskin Univ., Cambridge); Premio La Nacion 1971, Harbourfront Festival Prize 1992, Canadian Authors' Asscn Prize 1992, Prix France-Culture 2000, Premio German Sánchez Ruiperez 2002, Prix Poitou-Charentes 2004, Prix Roger Caillois 2004, Premio Grinzane Cavour 2004. *Literary Agent:* c/o Guillermo Schavelzon Agency, Calle Muntaner 339 5, 08021 Barcelona, Spain. *Telephone:* (93) 2011310. *Fax:* (93) 2006886. *E-mail:* info@schavelzon.com. *Website:* www.schavelzon.com; www.alberto.manguel.com.

MANHIRE, William (Bill), BA, MLitt, MPhil; New Zealand poet, writer and academic; *Professor of Creative Writing and English Literature, Victoria University of Wellington*; b. 27 Dec. 1946, Invercargill; s. of Jack Manhire and Madeline Mary Manhire; m. Barbara Marion McLeod 1970; one s. one d. *Education:* S Otago Dist High School, Otago Boys' High School, Univ. of Otago at Dunedin, Univ. Coll., London, UK. *Career:* Lecturer in English, Vic. Univ., Wellington 1973, f. creative writing programme 1976, Prof. of Creative Writing and English Literature 1997–; Dir Int. Inst. of Modern Letters 2001–; Fiction Ed. Victoria Univ. Press 1976–96; Fulbright Visiting Prof. in NZ Studies, Georgetown Univ., USA Jan.–June 1999; inaugural Te Mata Estate New Zealand Poet Laureate 1997–99; Nuffield Fellowship 1981. *Publications:*

Malady 1970, The Elaboration 1972, Song Cycle 1975, How to Take Your Clothes Off at the Picnic 1977, Dawn/Water 1980, Good Looks 1982, Locating the Beloved and Other Stories 1983, Zoetropes: Poems 1972–82 1984, Maurice Gee 1986, The Brain of Katherine Mansfield 1988, The New Land: A Picture Book 1990, The Old Man's Example 1990, Milky Way Bar 1991, An Amazing Week in New Zealand 1993, Fault 1994, South Pacific 1994, Hoosh 1995, My Sunshine 1996, Songs of My Life 1996, Sheet Music: Poems 1967–1982 1996, Mutes and Earthquakes 1997, What to Call Your Child 1999, Doubtful Sounds: Essays and Interviews 2000, Collected Poems 2001, Under the Influence (memoir) 2003, Lifted (poems) 2005, Pine 2005; editor: New Zealand Listener Short Stories Vol. 1 1977, Vol. 2 1978, Some Other Country: New Zealand's Best Short Stories (with Marion McLeod) 1984, Six by Six 1989, Soho Square 1991, 100 New Zealand Poems 1994, Denis Glover: Selected Poems 1995, Spectacular Babies (with Karen Anderson) 2001, The Wide White Page: Writers Imagine Antarctica 2004, 121 New Zealand Poems 2006, The Goose Bath 2006, Still Shines When You Think of It (with Peter Whiteford) 2007. *Honours:* Companion NZ Order of Merit; Hon. DLitt (Otago); NZ Book Award 1977, 1984, 1992, 1996, Montana Book Award 1994, Katherine Mansfield Fellowship 2004, NZAF Arts Laureate 2005, Montana NZ Book Award 2006, Prime Minister's Award for Poetry. *Address:* Creative Writing Programme, International Institute of Modern Letters, Victoria University of Wellington, PO Box 600, Wellington, New Zealand (office). *Telephone:* (4) 463-6808 (office). *Fax:* (4) 463-6865 (office). *E-mail:* bill.manhire@vuw.ac.nz (office). *Website:* www.vuw.ac.nz/modernletters (office).

MANJI, Irshad, BA; Canadian writer and broadcaster. *Education:* Univ. of British Columbia. *Career:* fmr aide to an MP, press sec. to Ontario Minister for Women's Issues, and speechwriter for first female leader of a Canadian political party; fmrly nat. affairs editorialist Ottawa Citizen newspaper; prod./host Queer Television (Toronto's Citytv) (Gemini Award for Best Edited Information Show) 1998–2001; hosts Big Ideas (TV Ontario); Pres. VERB TV channel; fmrly writer-in-residence Univ. of Toronto's Hart House; Dir Moral Courage Project, New York Univ. 2007–; Visiting Fellow, Yale Univ. 2005–06; Sr Fellow, European Foundation for Democracy; mem. inter-faith ed bd Seventeen magazine. *Publications:* Risking Utopia: On the Edge of a New Democracy 1997, The Trouble with Islam Today: A Muslim's Call for Reform in her Faith 2005. *Honours:* Gov.-Gen.'s Award 1990, MS Magazine Feminist for the 21st Century. *E-mail:* comments@irshadmanji.com (office). *Website:* www.irshadmanji.com.

MANKELL, Henning; Swedish playwright and writer; b. 3 Feb. 1948, Stockholm; m. 3rd Eva Bergman 1998; four s. *Career:* merchant seaman 1964–66; Dir Teatro Avenida, Maputo, Mozambique 1987–; co-f. Leopard publishing house 2001–. *Plays include:* The Amusement Park 1968, Tale on the Beach of Time 1997, Labyrinten (trans. as The Labyrinth) 2000. *Publications include:* fiction: Bergsprängaren (trans. as The Rock Blaster) 1973, Vettvillingen (trans. as The Mad Man) 1978, Fångvårdskolonin som försvann (trans. as The Prison Colony that Disappeared) 1979, Dödsbrickan (trans. as The Death Badge) 1980, En seglares död (trans. as The Death of a Sailor) 1981, Daisy Sisters 1982, Sagan om Isidor (trans. as The Tale of Isidor) 1984, Leopardens Öga (trans. as The Eye of the Leopard) 1990, Comédia infantil 1995, Vindens Son (trans. as Daniel) 2000, Tea-bag 2001, Djup (trans. as Depth) 2004, Italienska Skor (trans. as Italian Shoes) 2006; crime fiction: Mördare utan ansikte (trans. as Faceless Killers; Acad. of Swedish Crime Writers' Prize 1991, Scandinavian Crime Soc. Prize 1991) 1991, Hundarna i Rīga (trans. as The Dogs of Rīga) 1992, Den vita lejoninnan (trans. as The White Lioness) 1993, Mannen som log (trans. as The Man Who Smiled) 1994, Villospår (trans. as Sidetracked) 1995, Den femte kvinnan (trans. as The Fifth Woman) 1996, Steget efter (trans. as One Step Behind) 1997, Brandvägg (trans. as Firewall) 1998, Pyramiden (trans. as The Pyramid) 1999, Danslärarens återkomst (trans. as The Return of the Dancing Master) 1999, Innan Frosten (trans. as Before the Frost) 2002, Kennedys Hjärna (trans. as Kennedy's Brain) 2005, Kinesen (trans. as The Man from Beijing) 2006, Den orolige mannen (trans. as The Troubled Man) 2009; juvenile fiction: Sandmålaren (trans. as The Sand Painter) 1974, Hunden som sprang mot en stjärna (trans. as The Dog that ran towards a star) 1990, Skuggorna Växer i Skymningen (trans. as The Shadows grow in the Dark) 1991, Katten som Älskade Regn 1992, Eldens Hemlighet (trans. as Secrets in the Fire) 1995, Pojken som sov med snö i sin säng (trans. as The Boy who slept with snow in his bed) 1996, A Bridge to the Stars 1998; short stories: Anton och det Gripenstedtska sommarnöjet (trans. as Anton and the Summerhouse of Gripenstedtessays) 1974; essays: Jag dör, men minnet lever, I sand och i lera 1999. *Honours:* German Crime Prize 1999, Macallan CWA Golden Dagger Award 2001, Author of the Year, Germany 2002, Premio Pepe Carvalho, Spain 2007. *Address:* c/o Leopard förlag AB, S:t Paulsgatan 11, 118 46 Stockholm, Sweden (office). *E-mail:* info@henningmankell.com (office). *Website:* www.henningmankell.com.

MANLOW, James; British poet and novelist; b. 1978, Hertfordshire, England. *Education:* Univ. of East Anglia. *Publication:* Attraction (novel) 2004. *Literary Agent:* c/o John Murray Ltd, Hodder Headline, 338 Euston Road, London, NW1 3BH, England. *Website:* www.johnmurray.co.uk.

MANN, Anthony Phillip, MA; British writer and theatre director; b. 7 Aug. 1942, Northallerton, Yorks., England; m. Nonnita Rees; one s. one d. *Education:* Univ. of Manchester, Humboldt State Univ., Calif., USA. *Career:* Trustee, New Zealand Players 1992; mem. NZSA (PEN), New Zealand, British Soc. of Dowsers, New Zealand Asscn for Drama in Educ. *Publications:* Eye of the Queen 1982, Master of Paxwax 1986, Fall of the Families 1987, Pioneers 1988, Wulfsyarn – A Mosaic 1990, A Land Fit For Heroes, Vol. 1, Into the Wild Wood 1993, Vol. 2, Stand Alone Stan 1994, Vol. 3, The Dragon Wakes 1995, Vol. 4, The Burning Forest 1996; contributions: books. *Honours:* Personal Chair in Drama, Victoria Univ. of Wellington 1997. *Address:* 22 Bruce Avenue, Brooklyn, Wellington, New Zealand (home).

MANN, Christopher (Chris) Michael Zithulele, BA, MA; South African poet, writer, dramatist and administrator; *Ad Hominem Professor of Poetry, Rhodes University*; b. 6 April 1948, Port Elizabeth; s. of Norman Bertram Fleetwood Mann and Daphne Eva Mann; m. Julia Georgina Skeen 1981; one s. one d. *Education:* Univ. of the Witwatersrand, Univ. of Oxford, SOAS, London. *Career:* Dir, The Valley Trust 1980–92; Deputy CEO, Grahamstown Foundation 1992–95; Research Assoc. Inst. for the Study of English in Africa, Rhodes Univ., Grahamstown 1995–; Convenor, Wordfest 1999–; Ad Hominem Prof. of Poetry 2005–. *Recording:* Walking on Gravity 2004. *Plays:* Thuthula 2003. *Publications:* First Poems 1977, A New Book of South African Verse (ed. with Guy Butler) 1979, New Shades 1982, Kites 1990, Mann Alive (video and book) 1992, South Africans: A Series of Portrait Poems 1995, Heartlands: A Series of Place Poems 2002, In Praise of the Shades 2003, Lifelines 2005; plays: The Sand Labyrinth 2001, Mahoon's Testimony 1995, The Horn of Plenty: A Series of Painting-Poems (with Julia Skeen, artist) 1997, Frail Care: A Play in Verse 1997, The Roman Centurion's Good Friday, Cathedral of St Michael and St George 1999, Walking on Gravity 2004; contrib. to numerous journals and magazines. *Honours:* Newdigate Prize, Olive Schreiner Award, South African Performing Arts Council Playwright Award, Eastern Cape Premier's Award for Literature 2002, Thomas Pringle Award for Poetry (for Seahorse) 2007; Hon. DLitt (Univ. of Durban-Westville) 1993. *Address:* 19 Frances Street, Grahamstown, 6140 (home); c/o Institute for the Study of English in Africa, Rhodes University, Grahamstown, 6139, South Africa (office). *Telephone:* (46) 622-6093 (office). *Fax:* (46) 603-8566 (office). *E-mail:* c.mann@ru.ac.za (office). *Website:* www.chrismann.co.za.

MANN, Emily Betsy, BA, MFA; American writer, theatre director and playwright; *Artistic Director, McCarter Theatre*; b. 12 April 1952, Boston, Mass; d. of Arthur Mann and Sylvia Mann (née Blut); m. Gary Mailman; one s. from previous m. *Education:* Harvard Univ., Univ. of Minnesota. *Career:* Resident Dir Guthrie Theater, Minneapolis 1976–79; Dir Brooklyn Acad. of Music Theater Co., Brooklyn, NY 1980–81; freelance writer and dir, New York 1981–90; Artistic Dir McCarter Theatre, Princeton, NJ 1990–; mem. Soc. of Stage Dirs and Choreographers, Theater Communications Group, New Dramatists, PEN, Writer's Guild; mem. Exec. Bd Dramatists' Guild. *Plays directed include:* Suddenly Last Summer, Loeb Drama Center 1971, The Bull Gets the Matador Once in a Lifetime, Agassiz Theater 1972, Macbeth, Loeb Drama Center 1973, Matrix, Guthrie Theater 1975, The Birthday Party, Guthrie Theater 1975, Cold, Guthrie Theater 1976, Ashes, Guthrie 2 Theater 1977, Cincinnati Playhouse 1980, Annulla, Guthrie Theater 1977, New Theater of Brooklyn 1989, Dark Pony and Reunion, Guthrie Theater 1978, The Farm, Actors Theater of St Paul 1978, On Mount Chimborazo, Guthrie 2 Theater, 1978, Surprise Surprise, Guthrie 2 Theater 1978, The Roads in Germany, Theater in the Round 1978, The Glass Menagerie, Guthrie Theater 1979, McCarter Theatre 1990, He and She, Brooklyn Acad. of Music 1980, Still Life (Obie Award), Goodman Theater 1980, American Place Theater 1981, Dwarfman Master of a Million Shapes, Goodman Theater 1981, A Doll's House, Oregon Contemporary Theater 1982, Hartford Stage Co. 1986, Through the Leaves, Empty Space Theater 1983, A Weekend Near Madison, Astor Place Theater 1983, The Value of Names, Hartford Stage Co. 1984, Execution of Justice, Guthrie Theater 1985, Virginia Theater (Broadway) 1986, Hedda Gabbler, La Jolla Playhouse 1987, Betsey Brown, American Music Theater Festival 1989, McCarter Theatre 1991, Miss Julie, McCarter Theatre 1992, Three Sisters, McCarter Theatre 1992, Cat on a Hot Tin Roof, McCarter Theatre 1992, Twilight: Los Angeles 1992 (LA Nat. Asscn for the Advancement of Colored People (NAACP) Award for Best Dir), Mark Taper Forum/McCarter Theatre 1993, The Perfectionist, McCarter Theatre 1993, The Matchmaker, McCarter Theatre 1994, Having our Say, McCarter Theatre 1995, Booth Theater (Broadway) 1995, The Mai, McCarter Theatre 1996, Greensboro (A Requiem) 1996, Betrayal, McCarter Theatre 1997, The House of Bernarda Alba, McCarter Theatre 1997, Safe as Houses, McCarter Theatre 1998, Meshugah, McCarter Theatre 1998, Fool for Love, McCarter Theatre 1999, The Cherry Orchard, McCarter Theatre 2000, Romeo and Juliet, McCarter Theatre 2001, Because He Can, McCarter Theatre 2001, All Over, McCarter Theatre and Roundabout Theater Co. 2002, The Tempest, McCarter Theatre 2003, Anna in the Tropics, McCarter Theatre/Broadway 2003, Last of the Boys, McCarter Theatre 2004, The Bells, McCarter Theatre 2005, Miss Witherspoon, McCarter Theatre/Playwright's Horizons 2005, The Birthday Party, McCarter Theatre 2006, Mrs. Packard, McCarter Theatre/Kennedy Center 2007, Me, Myself & I, McCarter Theatre 2008, A Seagull in the Hamptons, McCarter Theatre 2008. *Plays translated and adapted include:* Nights and Days (Les nuits et les jours, Pierre Laville) 1985, Miss Julie 1992, Having Our Say 1995, Greensboro (A Requiem) 1996, The House of Bernarda Alba 1997, Meshugah 1998, The Cherry Orchard 2000, Uncle Vanya 2003, Mrs. Packard 2007, A Seagull in the Hamptons 2008. *Plays included in publications:* New Plays USA 1, New Plays 3, Coming to Terms: American Plays and the Vietnam War 1985, The Ten Best Plays of 1986, Out Front 1988, Testimonies: Four Plays by Emily Mann (Theater Communications Group Inc.) 1997. *Publications include:* plays: Annulla Allen: The Autobiography of a Survivor 1977, Still Life (six Obie Awards 1981, Fringe First Award 1985)

1982, Execution of Justice (Helen Hayes Award, Bay Area Theater Critics Circle Award, HBO/USA Award, Playwriting Award Women's Cttee Dramatists Guild for Dramatizing Issues of Conscience) 1986, Having Our Say: The Delaney Sisters' First 100 Years (LA NAACP Award for Best Play) 1994, Greensboro: A Requiem 1996; musicals: Betsey Brown: A Rhythm and Blues Musical (co-author with Ntozake Shange); screenplays: Fanny Kelly (unproduced) 1981, You Strike a Woman, You Strike a Rock: The Story of Winnie Mandela (unproduced mini-series) 1988, The Greensboro Massacre (unproduced) 1992, Having Our Say (Christopher Award, Peabody Award) 1999, Political Stages (co-ed.) 2002. *Honours:* Hon. Dr of Arts (Princeton Univ.) 2002; BUSH Fellowship 1975–76, Obie Awards for Directing 1981, 2002, Obie Award for Playwriting 1981, New Drama Forum Asscn Rosamond Gilder Award 1983, Nat. Endowment for the Arts (NEA) Asscns Grant 1984, Tony Award for Outstanding Regional Theater 1984, Guggenheim Fellowship 1985, McKnight Fellowship 1985, CAPS Award 1985, NEA Playwrights Fellowship 1986, Brandeis Univ. Women of Achievement Award 1995, Douglass Coll. of NJ Woman of Achievement Award 1996, Rosamond Gilder Award for Outstanding Achievement in the Theater 1999, Harvard Univ. Alumnae Recognition Award 1999, Nat. Conf. for Community and Justice Award 2004, Leader of the Year Award, Princeton Regional Chamber of Commerce 2005. *Address:* McCarter Theatre, 91 University Place, Princeton, NJ 08540-5121, USA (office). *Telephone:* (609) 258-6502 (office). *Fax:* (609) 497-0369 (office). *E-mail:* emann@mccarter.org (office). *Website:* www.mccarter.org (office).

MANN, James, BA; American political analyst and journalist; *Author-in-Residence, Paul H. Nitze School of Advanced International Studies, Johns Hopkins University*. *Education:* Harvard Univ. *Career:* Supreme Court corresp. Los Angeles Times 1978, Chief of Beijing Bureau 1984–87, fmr diplomatic corresp. and foreign affairs columnist –2001; fmr Guest Scholar, Woodrow Wilson Int. Center for Scholars and Sr Writer-in-Residence, Int. Security Program, Center for Strategic and Int. Studies (CSIS); currently Author-in-Residence School of Advanced Int. Studies, Johns Hopkins Univ. and Fellow Foreign Policy Inst.; commentator All Things Considered radio program PBS; contrib. LA Times; mem. Council on Foreign Relations. *Publications:* Beijing Jeep 1989, About Face: A History of America's Curious Relationship with China from Nixon to Clinton (New York Public Library Helen Bernstein Award 2000, Asia-Pacific Prize) 1999, Rise of the Vulcans: The History of Bush's War Cabinet 2004, The China Fantasy: How Our Leaders Explain Away Chinese Repression 2007, The Rebellion of Ronald Reagan: A History of the End of the Cold War 2009. *Honours:* Edwin M. Hood Award 1993, 1999, Edward Weintal Prize 1999. *Address:* Paul H. Nitze School of Advanced International Studies, Foreign Policy Institute, Johns Hopkins University, Rome Building, Room 405, 1619 Massachusetts Avenue, NW, Washington, DC 20036, USA (office). *Telephone:* (202) 587-3217 (office). *Fax:* (202) 663-5656 (office). *E-mail:* jmann12@jhu.edu (office). *Website:* www.sais-jhu.edu/faculty/directory/bios/m/mann.htm (office).

MANNING, Maurice, MFA; American poet and academic; *Associate Professor and Associate Chair of Creative Writing, Department of English, Indiana University*; b. 1966, Danville, Ky. *Education:* Univ. of Alabama. *Career:* currently Assoc. Prof. and Assoc. Chair of Creative Writing, Indiana Univ. *Publications:* Lawrence Booth's Book of Visions (Yale Series of Younger Poets Award) 2001, A Companion for Owls: Being the Commonplace Book of D. Boone, Lone Hunter, Back Woodsman, &c. 2004, Bucolics 2007, The Common Man 2010; contrib. poems to The New Yorker, Shenandoah, Southern Review, Washington Square, Green Mountains Review, Hayden's Ferry Review, The Spoon River Poetry Review, Wind, Hunger Mountains, Black Warrior Review, Virginia Quarterly Review and others. *Honours:* Fellow, Fine Art Work Center, Provincetown. *Address:* Department of English, University of Indiana, Ballantine Hall 442, 1020 East Kirkwood Avenue, Bloomington, IN 47405-7103, USA (office). *Telephone:* (812) 855-8224 (office). *E-mail:* maumanni@indiana.edu (office). *Website:* www.indiana.edu/~engweb (office).

MANNING, Ned, BA, DipEd; Australian writer, actor, teacher and script consultant; b. 25 Oct. 1950, Coonabarabran, NSW; s. of Alan Manning and Margot Body. *Education:* Univ. of Newcastle. *Plays:* Actors at Work (Bell Shakespeare) (ten plays), The Bridge is Down, The Flash Stockman, Belonging, Women of Troy (adaptation). *Plays as writer:* Us or Them 1984, Kenny's Coming Home 1987, Close to the Bone 1994, Milo, Kingaroy (with Martin Buzacott) 1996, Luck of the Draw 2000, Last One Standing 2008, Alice Dreaming 2010. *Films:* Dead End Drive In, Looking for Alibrandi. *Television appearances:* Young Ramsay 1980, Prisoner: Cell Block H 1981, A Country Practice 1990, The Brides of Christ 1991, Heartbreak High 1994. *Radio:* Women of Troy (adaptation for ABC Radio). *Publication:* Playground Duty. *Literary Agent:* c/o RGM Associates, Level 2, Suite 202, 64–76 Kippax Street, Surry Hills, NSW 2010, Australia. *Telephone:* (2) 9281-3911. *Fax:* (20) 9281-4705. *E-mail:* info@rgm.com.au. *Website:* www.rgm.com.au. *E-mail:* nedmanningwriteractor@gmail.com (office). *Website:* www.nedmanning.com.

MANNING, Phillip, BS, PhD; American science writer; b. 8 July 1936, Atlanta, Ga; m. Diane Karraker 1960; one s. one d. *Education:* The Citadel, Univ. of North Carolina at Chapel Hill. *Career:* mem. Nat. Asscn of Science Writers, Nat. Book Critics Circle. *Publications:* Afoot in the South 1993, Palmetto Journal 1995, Orange Blossom Trails 1997, Islands of Hope 1999; contrib. of more than 150 articles to Backpacker, Field & Stream, and others. *Honours:* Nat. Outdoor Book Award 1999. *Address:* 315 East Rosemary Street, Chapel Hill, NC 27514, USA (home). *E-mail:* pvmanning@mindspring.com (home). *Website:* www.scibooks.org.

MANNING, Robert Joseph; American journalist and publisher; *President and Editor-in-Chief, Bobcat Books Inc.*; b. 25 Dec. 1919, Binghamton, NY; s. of Joseph James Manning and Agnes Pauline Brown; m. 1st Margaret Marinda Raymond 1944 (died 1984); three s.; m. 2nd Theresa Slomkowski 1987. *Career:* served in US Army 1942–43; State Dept and White House Corresp. United Press 1944–46, Chief UN Corresp. United Press 1946–49; Writer, Time magazine 1949–55, Senior Ed. 1955–58, Chief, London Bureau, Time, Life, Fortune, Sports Illustrated magazines 1958–61; Sunday Ed. New York Herald Tribune 1961–62; Asst Sec. of State for Public Affairs, US Dept of State, Washington, DC 1962–64; Exec. Ed. Atlantic Monthly 1964–66, Ed.-in-Chief 1966–80, Vice-Pres. Atlantic Monthly Co. 1966–80; Ed.-in-Chief Boston Publishing Co. 1981–87; Pres. and Ed.-in-Chief Bobcat Books Inc., Boston 1987–; Nieman Fellow, Harvard Univ. 1945–46; Fellow, Kennedy Inst. of Politics, Harvard Univ. 1980; mem. AAAS. *Publications include:* Who We Are 1976, The Swamp Root Chronicle 1992, The Vietnam Experience (25 vols). *Honours:* Dr hc (Tufts Univ.), (St Lawrence Univ.). *Address:* 1200 Washington Street, Apt 507, Boston, MA 02118, USA. *E-mail:* bobcat1225@rcn.com (office).

MANOTTI, Dominique; French novelist; b. 1942, Paris. *Career:* fmr teacher of history in schools; currently teacher of economic history, Université de Paris VIII—Vincennes à St-Denis. *Publications:* Sombre Sentier (Premier roman 1995) 1995, A nos chevaux! 1997, Kop 1998, Nos fantastiques années fric (Prix Mystère de la Critique 2002, Prix du roman noir du Festival de Cognac 2002) 2001, Le corps noir 2004, Lorraine Connection 2007. *Address:* Université de Paris VIII—Vincennes à St-Denis, 2 rue de la Liberté, 93526 St Denis Cedex 02, France (office).

MANSBACH, Adam; American author and fmr editor and DJ; b. 1976. *Career:* Founding ed., hip hop journal Elementary 1990s; fmr Artistic Consultant to Columbia Univ. Center for Jazz Studies; New Voices Prof. of Fiction, Rutgers Univ.-Camden 2009–11; contrib., New Yorker, New York Times Book Review, Esquire, The Times, Los Angeles Times, Boston Globe, The Believer, Granta and others. *Publications include:* poetry: Genius B-Boy Cynics Getting Weeded in the Garden of Delights 2001; novels: Shackling Water 2003, Angry Black White Boy 2005, The End of the Jews (California Book Award 2008) 2008, Go the Fuck to Sleep 2011, Seriously, Just Go to Sleep 2012; graphic novel: Nature of the Beast: A Graphic Novel (co-author) 2012; as co-ed.: A Fictional History of the United States (with Huge Chunks Missing) 2006. *Address:* c/o Akashic Books, 232 Third Street, Suite A115, Brooklyn, NY 11215, USA (office). *Telephone:* (718) 643-9193 (office). *Fax:* (718) 643-9195 (office). *E-mail:* info@akashicbooks.com (office); adam.mansbach@gmail.com (home). *Website:* www.akashicbooks.com (office); www.adammansbach.com (home).

MANSEL, Philip Robert Rhys, MA, PhD, FRHistS, FRAsiaticS, FRLitS; British writer and historian; *Fellow, Institute of Historical Research*; b. 19 Oct. 1951, London, England; s. of John Mansel and Damaris Mansel. *Education:* Balliol Coll., Oxford, Univ. Coll. London. *Career:* co-f. Soc. for Court Studies 1995, Ed. The Court Historian 1995–; Fellow, Inst. of Historical Research, London 2001, Comité d'honneur, Centre de Recherche, Chateau de Versailles 2005; Founding Trustee, Levantine Heritage Foundation 2011; frequent appearances on TV and radio in UK, France and Turkey; Fellow, Royal Asiatic Soc. of GB and Ireland, Royal Literary Soc. *Publications:* Louis XVIII 1981, Pillars of Monarchy 1984, The Eagle in Splendour: Napoleon I and his Court 1987, Sultans in Splendour: The Last Years of the Ottoman World 1988, The Court of France 1789–1830 1989, Le Prince de Ligne: Le Charmeur de l'Europe 1992, Constantinople: City of the World's Desire 1453–1924 1995, The French Emigres in Europe and the Struggle against Revolution 1789–1814 1999, Paris Between Empires 1814–1852 2001, Prince of Europe: The Life of Charles-Joseph de Ligne 1735–1814 2003, Dressed to Rule 2005, Levant: Splendour and Catastrophe on the Mediterranean 2010; contrib. to Apollo, History Today, International Herald Tribune, Spectator, TLS, Guardian and exhbn catalogues on Winterhalter, Zonaro, Thomas Hope, At the Sublime Porte. *Honours:* Chevalier des Arts et des Lettres 2010. *Address:* 13 Prince of Wales Terrace, London, W8 5PG, England (home). *E-mail:* philipmansel@compuserve.com (home). *Website:* www.philipmansel.com.

MANSELL, Chris, BEc; Australian poet, writer and publisher; *Publisher, PressPress*; b. 1 March 1953, Sydney, NSW; m. Steven G. Sturgess (deceased) 1986; one s. one d. *Education:* Univ. of Sydney. *Career:* residencies include Curtin Univ. 1985, Univ. of Southern Queensland 1990, K. S. Prichard Centre 1992, Bundanon 1996; Lecturer, Univ. of Wollongong 1987–89, Univ. of Western Sydney 1989–91; Publr, PressPress publishing house; mem. Australian Soc. of Authors, Poets Union. *Publications:* Delta 1978, Head, Heart and Stone 1982, Redshift/Blueshift 1988, Shining Like a Jinx 1992, Day Easy Sunlight Fine 1995, Fickle Brat 2002, Stalking the Rainbow 2002, Mortifications & Lies 2005, Love Poems 2006, Letters 2009, Spine Lingo: New and Selected Poems 2011, Schadenvale Road 2011; contribs to numerous reviews, quarterlies and magazines. *Honours:* Amelia Chapbook Award 1987, Queensland Premier's Prize for Poetry 1993. *Address:* PO Box 94, Berry, NSW 2535, Australia (home). *E-mail:* info@chrismansell.com (office). *Website:* www.chrismansell.com; www.presspress.com.au.

MANSER, Martin Hugh, BA, MPhil; British editor and language trainer; b. 11 Jan. 1952, Bromley; m. Yusandra Tun 1979; one s. one d. *Education:* Univ. of York, CNAA. *Career:* Part-time Tutor, London Coll. of Communication 2006–; Visiting Lecturer, Bucks. New Univ. 2008–. *Publications include:* Concise Book of Bible Quotations 1982, A Dictionary of Everyday Idioms 1983,

Listening to God 1984, Pocket Thesaurus of English Words 1984, Children's Dictionary 1984, Macmillan Student's Dictionary 1985, Penguin Wordmaster Dictionary 1987, Guinness Book of Words 1988, Dictionary of Eponyms 1988, Visual Dictionary, Bloomsbury Good Word Guide 1988, Printing and Publishing Terms 1988, Marketing Terms 1988, Guinness Book of Words 1988, Bible Promises: Outlines for Christian Living 1989, Oxford Learner's Pocket Dictionary, Get To the Roots: A Dictionary of Words and Phrase Origins 1992, The Lion Book of Bible Quotations 1992, Oxford Learner's Pocket Dictionary with Illustrations 1992, Chambers Compact Thesaurus 1994, Bloomsbury Key to English Usage 1994, Collins Gem Daily Guidance 1995, NIV Thematic Study Bible 1996, Chambers English Thesaurus 1997, Dictionary of Bible Themes 1997, NIV Shorter Concordance 1997, Guide to English Grammar 1998, Crash Course in Christian Teaching 1998, Dictionary of the Bible 1998, Christian Prayer 1998, Bible Stories 1999, Millennium Quiz Book (ed.) 1999, I Never Knew That Was in the Bible 1999, Lion Bible Quotation Collection 1999, New Penguin English Thesaurus (joint ed.) 2000, The Westminster Collection of Christian Quotations (compiler) 2001, Heinemann English Dictionary (man. ed.), fifth edn 2001, NIV Comprehensive Concordance (consultant ed.) 2001, Writer's Manual (joint ed.) 2002, Dictionary of Foreign Words and Phrases 2002, Dictionary of Proverbs 2002, Eagle Handbook of Bible Prayers (joint ed.) 2002, Holy Bible: NRSV Cross-Reference Edition (man. ed.) 2003, A Treasury of Psalms (compiler) 2003, Dictionary of Classical and Biblical Allusions (ed.) 2003, The Joy of Christmas (co-author) 2003, Bible A–Z (co-author) 2004, The Chambers Thesaurus (ed.) 2004, 2009, The Really Useful Concise English Dictionary (ed.) 2004, Dictionary of Saints (ed.) 2004, Best Loved Christmas Carols, Readings and Poetry (compiler) 2005, Collins Dictionary of the Bible (compiler) 2005, Walking with God: 365 Promises and Prayers from the Bible for Every Day of the Year (compiler) 2005, Facts on File Guide to Good Writing (co-author) 2005, Facts on File Guide to Style (co-author) 2006, Wordsworth Book of Hymns (compiler) 2006, Collins Dictionary for Writers and Editors (jt ed.) 2006, Wordsworth Thesaurus (ed.) 2006, Wordsworth Dictionary of Proverbs (ed.) 2006, Wordsworth Dictionary of Idioms (ed.) 2006, Pocket Writer's Handbook (ed.) 2006, Facts on File Dictionary of Proverbs (ed.) 2007, Good Word Guide (ed.) 2007, Buttering Parsnips Twocking Chavs (ed.) 2007, New Book of Business Quotations (compiler) 2007, Prayers for Good Times and Grim (compiler) 2008, Best Loved Prayers and Words of Wisdom (compiler) 2009, Christian Christian Names (compiler) 2009, An A–Z of Effective Vocabulary 2009, Facts on File Dictionary of Allusions (ed.) 2009, Critical Companion to the Bible (ed.) 2009, Christianity for Blockheads (co-author) 2009, Collins Bible Companion (ed.) 2009, Scapegoats, Shambles & Shibboleths 2009, The New Matthew Henry Commentary (ed.) 2010, 1001 Words You Need to Know and Use: an A-Z of effective vocabulary 2010, Lion Bible Guide (co-author) 2010, Business Secrets: Time Management 2010, Business Secrets: Presenting 2010, Business Secrets: Mindpower 2010. *Address:* 102 Northern Road, Aylesbury, Bucks HP19 9QY, England (home). *Website:* www.martinmanser.com.

MANSFIELD, Sir Peter, Kt, BSc, PhD, FRS; British physicist and academic; *Professor Emeritus in Residence, University of Nottingham*; b. 9 Oct. 1933, London, England; s. of the late S. G. Mansfield and R. L. Mansfield; m. Jean M. Kibble 1962; two d. *Education:* William Penn School, Peckham and Queen Mary Coll., London, Univ. of London. *Career:* Research Assoc. Dept of Physics, Univ. of Ill. 1962; lecturer, Univ. of Nottingham 1964, Sr Lecturer 1967, Reader 1970, Prof. of Physics 1979–94, Prof. Emer. in Residence 1995–; MRC Professorial Fellow 1983–88; Sr Visitor, Max Planck Inst. for Medical Research, Heidelberg 1972–73; Fellow, Queen Mary Coll. 1985; Pres. Soc. of Magnetic Resonance in Medicine 1987–88. *Publications:* NMR Imaging in Biomedicine 1982, NMR Imaging (co-ed.) 1990, MRI in Medicine 1995; some 200 scientific publs in learned journals. *Honours:* Hon. FRCR 1992; Hon. FInstP 1996; Hon. mem. British Inst. of Radiology (BIR) 1993; Hon. DrMed (Strasbourg) 1995; Hon. DSc (Univ. of Kent at Canterbury) 1996; Royal Soc. Wellcome Foundation Gold Medal and Prize 1985, Duddell Medal, Inst. of Physics 1988, Royal Soc. Mullard Medal 1990, ISMAR Prize 1992, Barclay Medal, BJR 1993, Gold Medal, European Asscn of Radiology 1995, Garmisch-Partenkirchen Prize for MRI 1995, Rank Prize 1997, Nobel Laureate in Physiology or Medicine (jtly with Paul C. Lauterbur) 2003, several other awards. *Address:* Sir Peter Mansfield Magnetic Resonance Centre, Department of Physics and Astronomy, University of Nottingham, NG7 2RD, England (office). *Telephone:* (115) 951-4740 (office). *Fax:* (115) 951-5166 (office). *E-mail:* pamela.davies@nottingham.ac.uk (office). *Website:* www.magres.nottingham.ac.uk (office).

MANTEL, Hilary Mary, CBE, BJur, FRSL; British writer; b. 6 July 1952, Hadfield, Derbyshire; d. of Henry Thompson and Margaret Mary Thompson; m. Gerald McEwen 1973. *Education:* Harrytown Convent, Cheshire, London School of Econs, Sheffield Univ. *Radio:* The Giant, O'Brien (drama) 2002, Learning to Talk (5 plays) 2003, The Price of Light (drama) 2005. *Publications:* Every Day is Mother's Day 1985, Vacant Possession 1986, Eight Months on Ghazzah Street 1988, Fludd (Winifred Holtby Memorial Award, Southern Arts Literature Prize, Cheltenham Festival Prize) 1989, A Place of Greater Safety (Sunday Express Book of the Year Award 1993) 1992, A Change of Climate 1994, An Experiment in Love (Hawthornden Prize 1996) 1995, The Giant, O'Brien 1998, Giving up the Ghost (MIND Book of the Year 2004) 2003, Learning to Talk 2003, Beyond Black (Yorks. Post Fiction Award 2005) 2005, Wolf Hall (Man Booker Prize 2009, Nat. Book Critics' Circle Award for Fiction 2009, Walter Scott Prize for Historical Fiction 2009, Galaxy Nat. Book Awards UK Author of the Year 2010, Ind. Booksellers' Book of the Year 2010) 2009, Bring Up the Bodies 2012. *Honours:* Dr hc (Sheffield) 2002, (Hallam) 2004, (Royal Holloway Coll.) 2009, (Bedford) 2009, (Kingston) 2010, (Exeter) 2011. *Literary Agent:* A. M. Heath & Co., 6 Warwick Court, London, WC1R 5DJ, England. *Telephone:* (20) 7242-2811. *Fax:* (20) 7242-2711. *Website:* www.amheath.com.

MANWARING, Randle Gilbert, MA; British poet and writer; b. 3 May 1912, London, England; m. Betty Violet Rout 1941; three s. one d. *Education:* University of Keele. *Career:* mem. Downland Poets, chair., 1981–83; Kent and Sussex Poetry Society; Society of Authors; Society of Sussex Authors. *Publications:* The Heart of This People, 1954; Satires and Salvation, 1960; Christian Guide to Daily Work, 1963; Under the Magnolia Tree, 1965; Slave to No Sect and Other Poems, 1966; Crossroads of the Year, 1975; Insurance, 1976; From the Four Winds, 1976; In a Time of Unbelief, 1977; The Swifts of Maggiore, 1981; The Run of the Downs, 1984; Collected Poems, 1986; A Study of Hymn Writing and Hymn-singing in the Christian Church, 1990; Some Late Lark Singing, 1992; Love So Amazing, 1995; The Swallow, The Fox and the Cuckoo, 1997; Trade Winds, 2001; From Controversy to Co-Existence, 2002. Contributions: reviews, quarterlies, and magazines.

MAPLE, Gordon Extra, FRSL; British writer and dramatist; b. 6 Aug. 1932, Jersey, Channel Islands; m. Mabel Atkinson-Frayn 1953, one s. one d. *Career:* mem. BPM, Oxford Yec. *Publications:* Limeade, 1963; Here's a Funny Thing, 1964; Dog, 1967; Elephant, 1968; Tortoise, 1974; Singo, 1975; Napoleon Has Feet, 1977; Pink Circle, 1984; Chateau Schloss, 1985; Popeye, 1985; Keeping in Front (memoirs), 1986; Sour Grapes (with Miles Whittier), 1986; Yet Another Falklands Film, 1987. *Honours:* Evening Standard Awards, 1964, 1973; SWEAT Award, 1986.

MARAINI, Dacia; Italian writer and poet; b. 13 Nov. 1936, Fiesole; d. of Fosco Maraini and Alliata Topazia. *Education:* Collegio S.S. Annunziata, Florence and Rome. *Plays include:* La famiglia normale 1967, Centocelle gli anni del fascismo 1971, Dialogo di una prostituta con un solo cliente 1973, Da Roma a Milano 1975, Don Juan 1976, Due Donne di Provincia 1978, Erzbeth Bartory 1980, Donna Lionora giacubina 1981, I Sogni di Clitennestra 1981, Dramma d/amore al circo Bagno Balò 1981, Lezioni d'Amore 1982, Bianca Garofani 1982, Delitto 1987, Charlotte Corday 1989, Celia Carli 1990, Commedia Femminile 1994, Camille 1995. *Publications:* La Vacanza 1962, L'Età del Malessere 1962, Crudeltà All' Aria Aperta 1966, A Memoria 1967, Mio Marito 1968, Memoirs of a Female Thief 1973, Donne mie 1974, Donna in Guerra 1975, Mangiami Pure 1978, Lettere a Marina 1981, Dimenticato di Dimenticare 1983, Il treno per Helsinki 1984, Isolina 1985, Devour me too 1987, La Bionda, la bruna e l'asino 1987, La Lunga Vita di Marianna Ucria 1990, L'Uomo tatuato 1990, Viaggiando con passo de volpe 1991, Bagheria 1993, Voci 1994, La ragazza con la treccia 1994, Mutino, Orlov e il gatto che si crede pantera 1995, Dolce per sé 1997, Se amando troppo 1998, Buio 1999, La nave per Kobe 2001, Colomba 2004, Il gioco dell'universo 2007, Il treno dell'ultima notte 2008, La Ragazza di via Maqueda 2009. *Honours:* Prix Formentor for L'Età del Malessere (The Age of Discontent) 1962. *Address:* c/o Rizzoli, RCS Libri, Via Mecenate 91, 20138 Milan (office); Via Beccaria 18, 00196 Rome, Italy (home). *Telephone:* 3611795 (home). *Website:* www.rcslibri.it (office); www.daciamaraini.it.

MARANGOU, Niki; Cypriot writer; b. 23 May 1948, Limassol; d. of George Marangos and Kaety Chasapis; m. 1st Michael Attalides 1970 (divorced 1975); one d.; m. 2nd Constantin Candounas 1999. *Education:* studied in Nicosia and Free Univ., Berlin. *Career:* Dramaturgist Nicosia State Theatre 1975–85; Dir Kochlias Bookshop, Nicosia 1980–2008; regular newspaper columnist; seven exhibitions of painting; participated in Biennale of Graphic Arts, Ljubljana 1993, Alexandria 1996; State Prize for Poetry 1981, 1987, State Prize for Prose 1990, Cavafy Prize for Poetry in Alexandria 1998, Biannual State Prize for Prose 2000; her poem Roses was chosen to be hung in waiting rooms in NHS hospitals in UK; mem. Hellenic Authors Soc., Cyprus Writers Asscn. *Publications:* Ta Apo Kipon 1981, Arhi Indiktou 1987, Mia Strosi Ammou 1991, Paramythia tis Kyprou (Fairy Tales from Cyprus) 1994, Is the Panther Alive? 1998, Recipes for Katerina 2000, Und sie feierten Hochzeit, Romisini 2000, Selections from the Divan 2001, Doctor from Vienna 2003, Seven Tales from Cyprus 2003, Divan (Nana Kontou Prize, Acad. of Athens 2007) 2005, Doctor of Bneha, Sofia 2005, Din Famagusta la Vienna 2005, O Tsangaris ne o vasilias 2005, The Boy and the Goblet 2006, Nicosienses 2006, A night with Alexis 2007, The Daemon of Lust (short stories) 2007, Gezoul 2010, Magosa'dan Viyana'ya 2011, Statuja (poetry selection) 2011; contrib. poems to European Constitution in Verse, Brussels Poetry Collective 2009 and Nachrichten von der Poesie (CD). *Address:* Ioanni Metaxa 14, 2368 Ayios Dometios, Nicosia, Cyprus (home). *Telephone:* (22) 775772 (home). *E-mail:* nikimarangou@cytanet.com.cy (home). *Website:* www.marangou.com.

MARANI, Diego; Italian author, translator, newspaper columnist and interpreter; b. 1959, Ferrara. *Education:* Liceo Ludovico Ariosto, Ferrara, Univ. of Trieste. *Career:* fmrly worked for Council of EU; fmrly worked in Multilingualism Policy Unit, currently Policy Officer, Directorate-General for Interpretation, EC; columnist, Il Fatto Quotidiano, La Nuova Ferrara, Il Sole 24 Ore; inventor of Europanto language 1996. *Publications include:* novels: Caprice des Dieux 1994, Zanzare 1995, Nuova grammatical finlandese (trans. as New Finnish Grammar 2011) 2000, L'ultimo dei Vostiach (The Last of the Vostiaks) 2002, L'interprete 2004, Il Compagno di scuola 2005, Enciclopedia tresigallese 2006, Sentieri partigiani in Italia 2006, La bicicleta incantata

2007, Darfur – geografia di una crisi 2008, L'amico delle donne 2008, Germania in bicicleta 2010, Il cane di Dio 2012; short stories: Las Adventures des Inspector Cabillot 1998, A Trieste con Svevo 2003, Come ho imparato le lingue 2005. *Address:* c/o Frida Sciolla, Bompiani Editore, RCS MediaGroup S.p.A., via Angelo Rizzoli 8, 20132 Milan, Italy (office); c/o Dedalus Books Limited, Langford Lodge, St. Judith's Lane, Sawtry, Cambs., PE28 5XE, England (office). *Telephone:* (02) 2584-2535 (Milan) (office); (1487) 832382 (Cambs.) (office). *Fax:* (1487) 832382 (Cambs.) (office). *E-mail:* frida.sciolla@rcs.it (office); info@dedalusbooks.com (office). *Website:* bompiani.rcslibri.corriere.it (office); www.dedalusbooks.com (office).

MARBER, Patrick; British writer and director; b. 19 Sept. 1964, London; s. of Brian Marber and Angela Benjamin; m. Debra Gillett; one s. *Education:* Wadham Coll., Oxford. *Plays directed and/or written include:* Dealer's Choice 1995, Blue Remembered Hills 1996, '1953' 1996, Closer 1997, The Old Neighbourhood 1998, The Caretaker 2000, Howard Katz 2001. *Television work includes:* The Day Today, Paul Calf Video Diary, Knowing Me Knowing You, 3 Fights 2 Weddings and a Funeral, The Curator, After Miss Julie. *Publications include:* Dealer's Choice 1995, After Miss Julie 1996, Closer 1997, Howard Katz 2001. *Honours:* Evening Standard Award for Best Comedy 1995, Writers' Guild Award for Best West End Play 1995 (both for Dealer's Choice), Evening Standard Best Comedy Award 1997, Critics' Circle Award for Best Play 1997, Olivier Award 1998, New York Drama Critics' Award 1999 (all four for Closer). *Literary Agent:* c/o Judy Daish Associates Ltd, 2 St Charles Place, London, W10 6EG, England. *Telephone:* (20) 8964-8811. *Fax:* (20) 8964-8966.

MARCH, Jessica (see Africano, Lillian)

MARCUS, Emilie, BA, PhD; American editor; *Editor, Cell;* b. 1960. *Education:* Wesleyan Univ., Univ. of Yale, Salk Inst., CA. *Career:* fmr Ed., Neuron; Ed., Cell 2003–. *Address:* Cell, Cell Press, 600 Technology Square, Fifth Floor, Cambridge, MA 02139, USA (office). *E-mail:* emarcus@cell.com. *Website:* www.cell.com.

MARCUS, Steven, AB, PhD; American academic and writer; b. 13 Dec. 1928, New York, NY; m. Gertrud Lenzer 1966; one s. *Education:* Columbia Univ. *Career:* Prof. of English, Columbia Univ. 1966–, George Delacorte Prof. of Humanities 1976–, Chair Dept of English and Comparative Literature 1977–80, 1985–90, Vice-Pres. School of Arts and Sciences 1993–95, Dean Columbia Coll. 1993–95; Fellow Center for Advanced Studies in the Behavioural Sciences 1972–73; Dir of Planning, Nat. Humanities Center 1974–76, Chair of the Exec. Cttee, Bd of Dirs 1976–80; Chair Lionel Trilling Seminars 1976–80; Fellow Acad. of Literary Studies, American Acad. of Arts and Sciences; mem. American Acad. of Psychoanalysis, American Psychoanalytic Asscn, Inst. for Psychoanalytic Teaching and Research. *Publications:* Dickens: From Pickwick to Dombey, 1965; Other Victorians, 1966; Engels, Manchester and the Working Class, 1974; Representations: Essays on Literature and Society, 1976; Doing Good (with others), 1978; Freud and the Culture of Psychoanalysis, 1984. Editor: The Life and Work of Sigmund Freud (with Lionel Trilling), 1960; The World of Modern Fiction, 2 vols, 1968; The Continental Op, 1974; Medicine and Western Civilization (with David Rothman), 1995. Contributions: Professional journals and to general periodicals. *Honours:* Guggenheim Fellowship, 1967–68; Rockefeller Foundation Fellowship, 1980–81; National Humanities Center Fellowship, 1980–82; Fulbright Fellowship, 1982–84; Hon. DHL, Clark University, 1985. *Address:* c/o Department of English and Comparative Literature, Columbia University, New York, NY 10027, USA.

MARDELL, Mark Ian, BA; British journalist; *Europe Editor, BBC News;* b. 10 Sept. 1957, s. of Donald Mardell and Maureen Mardell; m. Joanne Veale 1990; two s. one d. *Education:* Priory School, Banstead, Epsom Coll. and Univ. of Kent at Canterbury. *Career:* journalist Radio Tees, Teesside 1980–82, Radio Aire, Leeds 1982; Industrial Ed. Independent Radio News, London 1983–87; reporter Sharp End (Channel 4) 1987–89; worked for BBC from 1988, Political Correspondent 1988–93, Political Ed. Newsnight 1993–2000, Political Correspondent BBC News at Six 2000–03, Chief Political Correspondent BBC News 2003–05, Europe Ed. 2005–10, North America Ed. 2010–. *Television programmes:* presenter This Week (BBC 1). *Radio programmes:* Judgement Day (Radio 4 short story) 2004, occasional presenter World at One, Broadcasting House (both BBC Radio 4). *Publication:* How to Get On in TV (juvenile) 2001. *Address:* BBC TV Centre, Wood Lane, London, W12 7RJ, England (office). *Website:* www.bbc.co.uk/blogs/thereporters/markmardell (office).

MARFEY, Anne, PhD; Danish writer and academic; b. 19 Feb. 1927, Copenhagen; m. Dr Peter Marfey 1964 (deceased); one s. one d. *Education:* Danish Teachers' Coll., Copenhagen, Columbia Univ., Pacific Western Univ., HI. *Career:* Adjunct Lecturer in Danish, SUNY at Albany; Lecturer, NY State Conf. for Early Childhood; Rep. for Danes Worldwide, Albany Area; mem. Danish Writers Guild; Bd Mem., UN Albany, US-China Friendship Asscn, Albany, New York Acad. of Sciences 1997, American Asscn of Univ. Women 1998. *Publications:* Learning to Write, 1961; Vejen til hurtigere Laesning, 1962; Svante, 1965; Las Bedre, 1966; Amerikanere, 1967; Telefontraden, 1968; Skal Skal ikke, 1969; How Parents Can Help Their Child with Reading, 1976; Rose's Adventure, 1989; Moderne Dansk, 1989; The Duckboat, The Pump, The Pine Tree, 1994; The Chipmunk, 1994; The Miracle of Learning, 1997; The Ugly Carrot, 2002, Callaway The Cat, Callaway The Cat Disappears, Poems in the National Library of Poetry. *Address:* 9 Tudor Road, Albany, NY 12203, USA. *Telephone:* (518) 482-6145.

MARGOLIN, Phillip Michael, BA, JD; American lawyer and writer; b. 20 April 1944, New York, NY; m. Doreen Stamm 1968, one s. one d. *Education:* American University, New York University. *Career:* Law Clerk to the Chief Judge, Oregon Court of Appeals 1970–71; Deputy District Attorney and Special Agent for Multnomah County, OR 1971–72; Partner, Nash & Margolin 1974–80, Margolin & Margolin, 1986–96, Portland, OR; mem. MWA, National Asscn of Criminal Defense Lawyers, Oregon Criminal Defense Lawyers Asscn, Oregon State Bar Asscn. *Publications:* Heartstone 1978, The Last Innocent Man 1981, Gone, but Not Forgotten 1993, After Dark 1995, The Burning Man 1996, The Undertaker's Widow 1998, Wild Justice 2000, The Associate 2002, Ties That Bind 2003, Sleeping Beauty 2004, Lost Lake 2005, Proof Positive 2006, Executive Privilege 2008, Fugitive 2009, Supreme Justice 2010; contributions: professional journals, anthologies and periodicals. *Address:* c/o Author Mail, 7th Floor, HarperCollins Publishers, 10 East 53rd Street, New York, NY 10022, USA (office). *Website:* www.phillipmargolin.com.

MARGOSHES, Dave, BA, MFA; Canadian writer and poet; b. 8 July 1941, New Brunswick, NJ, USA. *Education:* Univ. of Iowa. *Career:* instructor, numerous writers' workshops and creative writing courses; Writer-in-Residence, Univ. of Winnipeg 1995–96, Saskatoon Public Library 2001–02. *Publications:* Third Impressions (short stories with Barry Dempster and Don Dickinson) 1982, Small Regrets (short stories) 1986, Walking at Brighton (poems) 1988, Northwest Passage (poems) 1990, Nine Lives (short stories) 1991, Saskatchewan 1992, Long Distance Calls (short stories) 1996, Fables of Creation (short stories) 1997, Tommy Douglas: Building the New Society (biog.) 1999, We Who Seek: A Love Story (novella) 1999, I'm Frankie Sterne (novel) 2000, Purity of Absence (poems) 2001, Drowning Man (novel) 2003, Bix's Trumpet and other stories 2007, The Horse Knows the Way (poems) 2009, Dimensions of an Orchard (poems) 2010, A Book of Great Worth (stories) 2012; contrib. to numerous anthologies, journals and magazines. *Honours:* Canadian Author and Bookman Poem of the Year Award 1980, Saskatchewan Writers' Guild Long Manuscript Award 1990, Second Prize, League of Canadian Poets' Nat. Poetry Contest 1991, Stephen Leacock Award for Poetry 1996, John V. Hicks Award for Fiction 2001, City of Regina Writing Award 2004, 2007, Saskatchewan Book Awards Book of the Year 2007, City of Regina Writing Award 2010, Anne Szumigalski Poetry Award 2010. *Address:* R.R. 2, Site 201, Box 131, Saskatoon, SK S7K 3J5, Canada (home). *Telephone:* (306) 283-4405 (office). *E-mail:* davemargoshes@gmail.com (home).

MARIANI, Paul Louis, BA, MA, PhD; American academic, writer, biographer, poet and critic; *University Professor of English, Boston College;* b. 29 Feb. 1940, New York, NY; s. of the late Paul Patrick Mariani and Harriet Green Mariani; m. Eileen Spinosa 1963; three s. *Education:* Manhattan Coll., Colgate Univ., Grad. School and Univ. Center, CUNY. *Career:* Asst Prof., John Jay Coll. of Criminal Justice, CUNY 1967–68; Asst Prof., Univ. of Massachusetts, Amherst 1968–71, Assoc. Prof. 1971–75, Prof. 1975–85, Distinguished Univ. Prof. 1985–; Univ. Prof. of English, Boston Coll. 2000–, Chair. Dept of English Sept. 2000; Robert Frost Fellow, Bread Loaf Writers' Conf. 1980, Faculty 1982–96, Robert Frost Prof. 1983, Visiting Lecturer 1986, School of English Staff 1981–84; Dir The Glen, Colorado Springs 1995, 1996, 1998, The Image Conf., Santa Fe 2004, 2005, 2006; Ed. William Carlos Williams and Contemporary Poetry: University Microfilms 1985–90; Poetry Ed. America Magazine 1999–2006; Assoc. Ed. The William Carlos Williams Review, The Hopkins Quarterly, Sagetribe, Twentieth Century Literature, Editorial Committee: Religion & the Arts; mem. Seton Hall Seminars 2004, Nat. Endowment for the Humanities panels on Literature and Film 1980–2005; mem. Acad. of American Poets, Poetry Soc. of America; Glen/Image workshops, St John's Coll., Santa Fe, NM 2004, 2005, 2006; Whidbey Island workshops, Seattle Pacific Univ. 2006, 2007. *Publications:* poetry: Timing Devices 1979, Crossing Cocytus 1982, Prime Mover 1985, Salvage Operations: New and Selected Poems 1990, The Great Wheel 1996, Deaths and Transfigurations: Poems (designed and illustrated by Barry Moser) 2005; prose: Commentary on the Complete Poems of Gerard Manley Hopkins 1970, William Carlos Williams: A New World Naked 1981, Dream Song: The Life of John Berryman 1990, Lost Puritan: A Life of Robert Lowell 1994, The Broken Tower: A Life of Hart Crane (Ohioana Award for Best Book about an Ohioan 2000) (optioned and made into a film, directed by and starring James Franco, screened at Cannes Film Festival 2011) 1999, Thirty Days: On Retreat with the Exercises of St Ignatius (Catholic Press Asscn First Place Award 2003) 2002, God and the Imagination: On Poets, Poetry and the Ineffable 2002, Gerard Manley Hopkins: A Life 2008; contrib. to books and journals. *Honours:* Hon. DHL (Manhattan Coll.) 1998, (The Elms Coll.) 2001; Nat. Endowment for the Humanities Fellowships 1972–73, 1981–82, New Jersey Writers' Award 1982, New York Times Notable Books 1982, 1994, 1999, Univ. of Massachusetts Chancellor's Medal 1984, Nat. Endowment for the Arts Fellowship 1984, Prairie Schooner Choice Awards 1989, 1995, Ohioana Award 2000, Catholic Press Asscn Award for Popular Presentation of the Catholic Faith 2003, Keynote Address, Hopkins Int. Soc., Oriel Coll. Oxford 2004, Address to Hopkins Int. Soc., Denver, Colo, 2006, Keynote Address, Hopkins Int. Soc., Milltown Park, Dublin 2007, John Ciardi Lifetime Award for Poetry 2009. *Literary Agent:* c/o The Kneerim & Williams Agency, 90 Canal Street, Boston, MA 02114, USA. *Telephone:* (617) 303-1654. *E-mail:* jill@kwlit.com. *Website:* www.kwlit.com. *Address:* PO Box M, Montague, MA 01351, USA (home). *Telephone:* (413) 367-2820 (home); (617) 552-3177 (office). *Fax:* (413) 367-0358 (home). *E-mail:* pmariani@english.umass.edu (office); paul.mariani@bc.edu (office).

MARÍAS FRANCO, Javier; Spanish writer and translator; b. 20 Sept. 1951, Madrid; s. of Julián Marías Aguilera and the late Dolores Franco Manera. *Education:* Institución Libre de Enseñanza, Colegio Estudio, Universidad Complutense de Madrid. *Career:* trans. and writer of film screenplays 1969–; Ed. Alfaguara 1974; lecturer at various univs worldwide; mem. Int. Parliament of Writers (exec. council 2001–). *Publications:* novels: Los dominios del lobo 1971, Travesía del horizonte 1972, El Monarca del tiempo 1978, El hombre sentimental (Premio Herralde de Novela, Premio Ennio Flaiano 2000) 1986, El Siglo 1982, Todas las almas (Premio Ciudad de Barcelona) 1989, Corazón tan blanco (Premio de la Crítica 1993, Prix L'Oeil et la Lettre 1993, Int. IMPAC Prize 1997) 1992, Mañana en la batalla piensa en mí (Premio Fastenrath de la Real Academia Española de la Lengua 1995, Premio Internacional de Novela Rómulo Gallegos 1995, Prix Fémina Étranger, France 1996, Premio Arzobispo Juan de San Clemente 1995, Premio Letterario Internazionale Mondello-Città di Palermo 1998) 1994, Negra espalda del tiempo 1998, Tu rostro mañana 1. Fiebre y lanza (Premio Salambó 2003) 2002, Tu rostro mañana 2: Baile y sueño 2006, Tu rostro mañana 3. Veneno y sombra y adiós 2007; other fiction: Gospel (screenplay) 1969, Mientras ellas duermen (short stories) 1990, Cuando fui mortal (short stories) 1996, Mala índole (short story) 1998; non-fiction: Pasiones pasadas (articles and essays) 1991, Vidas escritas (articles) 1992, Literatura y fantasma (articles and essays) 1993, Vida del fantasma (articles) 1995, Si yo amaneciera otra vez (articles and poems) 1997, Miramientos (articles) 1997, Mano de sombra (articles) 1997, Desde que te vi morir (articles and poems) 1999, Seré amado cuando falte (articles) 1999, Salvajes y sentimentales (articles) 2000, A veces un caballero (articles) 2001, While the Women Are Sleeping (in trans., short stories) 2010; numerous translations; contrib. to anthologies, including Cuentos únicos 1989, El hombre que parecia no querer nada 1996; contrib. to journals and newspapers, including El País, El Diario de Barcelona, Hiperión, Revista de Occidente. *Honours:* Chevalier, Ordre des Arts et des Lettres, Premio Comunidad de Madrid 1998; Premio Nacional de Traducción (for translation of Tristram Shandy) 1979, Alberto Moravia Int. Prize, Rome 2000, Grinzane Cavour prize, Turin 2000. *Address:* Mercedes Casanovas Agencia Literaria, Iradier 24, 08017 Barcelona, Spain (office). *E-mail:* webmaster@javiermarias.es (office). *Website:* www.javiermarias.es.

MARINEAU, Michele, BA; Canadian writer and translator; b. 12 Aug. 1955, Montréal, QC; m. (divorced); one s. one d. *Education:* University of Montréal. *Career:* mem. Union des écrivaines et des écrivains québécois; Corporation Professionnelle des Traducteurs et Interprétes Agréés du Québec; Asscn des Traducteurs Litteraires du Canada; Communication-Jeunesse. *Publications:* Cassiopée ou L'été Polonais, 1988; L'été des Baleines, 1989; L'Homme du Cheshire, 1990; Pourquoi pas Istambul?, 1991; La Route de Chlifa, 1992. *Honours:* Prix du Gouverneur Général, 1988, 1993; Prix, Brive-Montréal, 1993; Prix, Alvine-Bélisle, 1993. *Address:* 4405 rue de Brebeuf, Montréal, QC H2J 3K8, Canada.

MARININA, Col. Aleksandra Borisovna, PhD; Russian writer and fmr criminologist; b. (Marina Anatolyevna Alekseyeva), 16 June 1957, Lviv, Ukraine; m. Col Sergey Zatochny. *Education:* Moscow State Univ. *Career:* fmr mem. of staff, Acad. of Internal Affairs; began writing detective stories 1991–; mem. of staff, Moscow Inst. of Justice, Ministry of Internal Affairs 1994–97. *Films for television:* Kamenskaya (48 episodes). *Publications:* Death and Some Love, Ghost of Music, Stolen Dream, I Died Yesterday, Men's Game, Forced Murderer, Black List, Requiem, When Gods Laugh, He Who Knows (vols 1–2), and numerous others. *Address:* COP Literary Agency, Zhukovskogo str. 4, Apt 29, 103062 Moscow (office); Verhnaya Krasnoselskaya str. 9, Apt 44, 107140 Moscow, Russia (home). *Telephone:* (495) 628-84-56 (office); (495) 628-84-56 (home). *Fax:* (495) 628-84-56 (office). *E-mail:* alexandra@marinina.ru (office). *Website:* www.marinina.ru (home).

MARINOS, Ioannis, (Kritovoulos, Popolaros, W.), BA; Greek journalist and politician; *Chairman, Structural Reforms Committee, Ministry of Economy and Finance*; b. 20 July 1930, Hermoupolis. *Education:* School of Law, Univ. of Athens. *Career:* journalist, To Vima (daily political journal) 1953–65, columnist 1992–; journalist, Economicos Tachydromos, Ed.-in-Chief 1956, Ed. and Dir 1964–96, consultant/columnist 1996–; political commentator in Ta Nea (daily) 1972–75; commentator for many radio and TV stations in Greece; mem. European Parl., European Popular Party 1999–2004; currently Chair., Structural Reforms Cttee, Ministry of Economy and Finance; mem. Bd Music Hall of Athens, Red Cross, Amnesty Int. *Publications:* The Palestinian Problem and Cyprus 1975, For a Change Towards Better 1983, Greece in Crisis 1987, Common Sense 1993, Constitutional Reform: Ideas & Proposals (co-author) 2007. *Honours:* Hon. PhD (Aristotelian Univ. Salonika) 1999; more than 30 awards, including Best European Journalist of 1989 (EC Comm. and Asscn of European Journalists) and awards from UN and Athens Acad. *Address:* 26 Nikis Street, Athens 105 57 (office); 2 Kontziadon Street, Piraeus 185 37, Greece (home). *Telephone:* (210) 321-0280 (office); (210) 452-6823 (home). *Fax:* (210) 321-0281 (office). *E-mail:* jmarinos@dolnet.gr (office).

MARIZ, Linda Catherine French, (Linda French), BA, MA; American novelist; b. 27 Nov. 1948, New Orleans, LA; m. George Eric Mariz 1970; one s. one d. *Education:* Univ. of Missouri, Columbia, Western Washington Univs. *Career:* apptd Creative Writing Instructor, Western Washington Univ. 1994; mem. Sisters in Crime, International Asscn of Crime Writers, Washington Comm. for the Humanities. *Publications:* as Linda Mariz: Body English 1992, Snake Dance 1992; as Linda French: Talking Rain 1998, Coffee to Die For 1998, Steeped in Murder 1999, The Lilac Room 2010; contribs to Cash Buyer (story) in Reader, I Murdered Him Too (anthology) 1995.

MARKHAM, Jehane; British poet and playwright; b. 12 Feb. 1949, Sussex, England; d. of David Markham and Olive Dehn; m.; three s. *Education:* Cen. School of Art, Univ. of North London. *Career:* mem. Poetry Book Soc., Highgate Literary and Scientific Soc., Poetry Soc. *Publications:* poetry: The Captain's Death 1975, Ten Poems 1993, Virago New Poets 1993, Twenty Poems 1999, My Mother, Myself (audio) 2001, Between Sessions and Beyond the Couch 2002, In the Company of Poets 2003; radio plays: More Cherry Cake 1980, Thanksgiving 1984, The Bell Jar, Frost in May, A Child of the Sun, Lawrence and Frieda; television play: Nina 1978; theatre plays: One White Day 1976, The Birth of Pleasure 1997, Hermes 2006; contribs to Women's Press, Longmans Study, Sunday Times, BBC 2 Epilogue, Bananas Literary Magazine, Camden Voices, Independent, Observer, Acorn, Ambit, New Statesman, Cork Literary Review, Wild Cards (anthology) 1999, Between Sessions and On the Couch 2002. *Honours:* winner BBC Radio 4 Open Book Paradelle Competition 2002. *Address:* 56 Lady Somerset Road, London, NW5 1TU, England (home). *Website:* www.roughwinds.co.uk.

MARKHAM, Marion Margaret, BS; American writer; b. 12 June 1929, Chicago, IL; m. Robert Bailey Markham 1955, two d. *Education:* Northwestern University. *Career:* mem. Society of Midland Authors, MWA, Authors' Guild of America, Society of Children's Book Writers. *Publications:* Escape from Velos, 1981; The Halloween Candy Mystery, 1982; The Christmas Present Mystery, 1984; The Thanksgiving Day Parade Mystery, 1986; The Birthday Party Mystery, 1989; The April Fool's Day Mystery, 1991; The Valentine's Day Mystery, 1992.

MARKISH, David; Russian/Israeli writer; b. 24 Sept. 1938, Moscow, Russia; m. Nathalie Markish-Laskin 1990; two s. *Education:* Gorky Literary Inst., Moscow. *Publications:* Five Close to the Sky 1966, A New World for Simon Ashkenazy 1976, The Cock 1980, Forward 1980, Jesters 1983, The Dog 1984, In the Shadow of a Big Stone 1986, The Field 1989, The Garnet Shaft 1990, My Enemy Cat 1991, To Be Like Others 2000, To Become Lutov 2001, The White Circle 2004, To Kill Marco Polo 2008, Knight Tubplar 2012. *Honours:* seven Israeli Literary Awards, British Book League Award, Int. Literary Award of Ukraine, Machabeli Literary Award of Georgia. *Address:* Erez 65, Or-Ehuda, Israel (home). *E-mail:* markishd@gmail.com (office).

MARKOVIĆ, Predrag; Serbian politician and publisher; b. 7 Dec. 1955, Cepure. *Education:* Univ. of Belgrade. *Career:* Ed. Student, Vreme (newspapers), Vidici (magazine); Owner Stubovi kulture publishing house 1993–; Pres. G17 PLUS Man. Bd 2000–01, Pres. Political Council, mem. Exec. Bd 2001–02, Vice-Pres. G17 PLUS party 2003–; Pres. Nat. Ass. of Serbia 2004–; Acting Pres. of Serbia March–July 2004; fmr Pres. Asscn of Publrs of Serbia and Montenegro; mem. PEN, Serbian Literary Soc. *Publications:* Morali su doći nasmejani lavovi 1983, Otemenost duše 1989. *Address:* G17 PLUS, Trg Republike 5, 11000 Belgrade, Serbia (office). *Telephone:* (11) 3344930 (office). *Fax:* (11) 3344459 (office). *Website:* www.g17plus.org.yu (office).

MARKS, Stanley, AO; Australian writer; b. 1929, London, England; m. Eva Mass; one s. one d. (deceased). *Education:* Univ. of Melbourne (did not complete course). *Career:* journalist and foreign corresp. in Australia, UK, USA, Canada; Originator-Writer, MS cartoon series, Australian and NZ newspapers 1975–80; Ed. Journal of Melbourne Holocaust Centre; fmr Supervisor of Publicity and Public Relations, Australian Broadcasting Corpn; fmr Public Relations Man. Australian Tourist Comm.; mem. Australian Soc. of Authors. *Publications include:* God Gave You One Face 1964, Graham is an Aboriginal Boy 1968, Fifty Years of Achievement 1972, Animal Olympics 1972, Rarua Lives in Papua New Guinea 1974, Ketut Lives in Bali 1976, St Kilda Sketchbook 1980, Malvern Sketchbook 1981, Welcome to Australia 1981, Out and About in Melbourne 1988, Holocaust Ten Year History 1994, St Kilda Heritage Sketchbook 1995, Reflections 2004; essay in anthology Memory Guide My Hand 1994; contribs to int. newspapers and journals. *Honours:* Australia Day Citizen of the Year for the large municipality of Glen Eira 2003, Distinguished Service Award for Neighbourhood Watch Services, B'nai B'nai Menorah Award 2003, Australia Day Award 2007. *Telephone:* (3) 9578-6697 (home). *Fax:* (3) 9578-5197 (home). *E-mail:* smar4858@bigpond.net.au.

MARKWORT, Helmut; German journalist, publisher, editor and presenter; *Editor, Focus Magazine*; b. 8 Dec. 1936, Darmstadt; s. of August Markwort and Else Markwort (née Volz). *Career:* started in journalism 1956, various posts in local media –1966; founder Ed.-in-Chief of several magazines and radio stations; Publr and Ed.-in-Chief Focus Magazine 1993–2010, Ed. 2010–; Man. Focus TV 1996–; Publr Focus Money 2000–; Head of Bd Tomorrow Focus AG 2001–, Playboy Publishing Deutschland AG 2002–; presenter, Bookmark 2004–, Der Sonntags Stammtisch 2007–; Dir, Hubert Burda Media Holding GmbH 1991–2010. *Honours:* Nat. Merit Cross (First Class) 1999; 'Horizont Mann der Medien' Award 1983, 1993, Advertising Age 'Marketing Superstar' 1994, Hildegard von Bingen Award for Journalism, BDS Mittelstandspreis Award, Bavarian's Merit Medal 1996, Premio Capo Circeo 2004, Reinhold Maier Medal 2007, Karl Carstens Award 2007. *Address:* Focus Magazine, Arabella str. 23, 81925 Munich, Germany (office). *Website:* www.focus.de (office).

MARLANTES, Karl A.; American author; b. 24 Dec. 1944, Seaside, Ore.; five c. *Education:* Yale Univ., Univ. Coll., Oxford Univ., UK. *Career:* served as US

Marine in Vietnam War as First Lt, Exec. Officer of Company C, First Battalion, Fourth Marines, Third Marine Division (Reinforced), Fleet Marine Force 1968–69; later worked as energy consultant. *Publications include:* Matterhorn: a Novel of the Vietnam War (Washington State Book Award for Fiction 2011) 2010, What It Is Like to Go to War 2011. *Honours:* Navy Cross 1969, two Navy Commendation Medals for Valor, two Purple Hearts, ten Air Medals. *Address:* c/o Grove/Atlantic, Inc., 841 Broadway, 4th Floor, New York, NY 10003, USA (office). *Telephone:* (212) 614-7850 (office). *Fax:* (212) 614-7886 (office). *E-mail:* info@groveatlantic.com (office). *Website:* www.groveatlantic.com (office).

MARLATT, Daphne Shirley, OC, BA, MA; Canadian poet and writer; b. 1942, Melbourne, Vic., Australia; m. Gordon Alan Marlatt 1963 (divorced 1970); one s. *Education:* Univ. of British Columbia, Indiana Univ., USA. *Career:* Co-Ed. Tessera (Journal) 1983–91; Special Lecturer in Creative Writing, Univ. of Saskatchewan 1998–99; Faculty mem. Banff Centre for the Arts Writing Studio 2000, 2005, 2010–12; Writer-in-Residence, Univ. of Windsor 2001–02, Simon Fraser Univ. 2004–05, McMaster Univ. 2007; Markin-Flanagan Distinguished Visiting Writer, Univ. of Calgary 2007; mem. Writers' Union of Canada. *Plays:* The Gull, Pangaea Arts 2006, Shadow Catch, Vancouver Pro Musica 2011. *Recording:* Like Light Off Water 2008. *Film:* screenplay: The Portside 2009. *Publications:* Frames of a Story 1968, Leaf/Leaf/s 1969, Rings 1971, Vancouver Poems 1972, Steveston 1974, Our Lives 1975, Steveston Recollected: A Japanese-Canadian History (with M. Koizumi) 1975, Zócalo 1977, Opening Doors: Vancouver's East End (with Carole Itter) 1979, What Matters 1980, Selected Writing: Net Work 1980, How Hug a Stone 1983, Touch to My Tongue 1984, Double Negative (with Betsy Warland) 1988, Ana Historic 1988, Salvage 1991, Ghost Works 1993, Taken 1996, Readings from the Labyrinth 1998, This Tremor Love Is 2001, Seven Glass Bowls 2003, The Given (Dorothy Livesay Award for Poetry 2009) 2008, Between Brush Strokes 2008, At the River's Mouth: Writing Migrations 2009, The Gull (Uchimura Naoya Prize) 2009. *Honours:* Hon. DLitt (Western Ontario) 1996, Hon. DHumLitt (Mount St Vincent Univ.) 2004; Mayor's Arts Award, Literary Arts 2008, BC Book Prize (Dorothy Livesay Poetry Award) 2009. *E-mail:* otterbay@lostsound.com*Address:* The Writers' Union of Canada, 200-90 Richmond Street East, Toronto, ON M5C 1P1, Canada (office). *Telephone:* (416) 703-8982 (office). *Fax:* (416) 504-9090 (office). *E-mail:* info@writersunion.ca (office). *Website:* www.abcbookworld.com/view_author.php?id=834 (office).

MARLIN, Henry (see Giggal, Kenneth)

MARLOW, Joyce; British author; b. 27 Dec. 1929, Manchester, England. *Education:* Whalley Range High School, Manchester. *Career:* professional actress 1950–65; author 1964–. *Publications:* The Man with the Glove 1964, A Time to Die 1966, Billy Goes to War 1967, The House on the Cliffs 1968, The Peterloo Massacre 1969, The Tolpuddle Martyrs 1971, Captain Boycott and the Irish 1973, The Life and Times of George I 1973, The Uncrowned Queen of Ireland 1975, Mr and Mrs Gladstone 1977, Kings and Queens of Britain 1977, Kessie 1985, Sarah 1987, Anne 1989, Industrial Tribunals and Appeals 1991, Virago Book of Women of the Great War 1998, Virago Book of Votes for Women 2000. *Literary Agent:* c/o Sara Menguc (literary agent). *E-mail:* saramenguc@aol.com. *Address:* 3 Spring Bank, New Mills, High Peak, SK22 4AS, England (home). *Telephone:* (1663) 742600 (home). *E-mail:* joyce.marlow@firenet.uk.net (home).

MARLOWE, Hugh (see Patterson, Harry)

MARMOT, Sir Michael Gideon, Kt, MBBS, PhD, FFPHM, FRCP, FAcMedSci; British academic and director of health research; *Director, International Institute for Society and Health and Professor of Epidemiology and Public Health, University College London;* b. 26 Jan. 1945, s. of Nathan Marmot and Alice Marmot (née Weiner); m. Alexandra Naomi Ferster 1971; two s. one d. *Education:* Univ. of Sydney and Univ. of California, Berkeley. *Career:* Resident Medical Officer, Royal Prince Alfred Hosp. 1969–70; Fellowship in Thoracic Medicine 1970–71; Resident Fellow and Lecturer Univ. of Calif., Berkeley 1971–76 (fellowships from Berkeley and American Heart Asscn); Lecturer then Sr Lecturer in Epidemiology, London School of Hygiene and Tropical Medicine, Univ. Coll. London 1976–85; Prof. of Epidemiology and Public Health Medicine 1985–; Dir Int. Centre for Health and Society, Univ. Coll. London 1994–; Hon. Consultant in Public Health Medicine, Bloomsbury and Islington Dist Health Authority 1985–; Visiting Prof. Royal Soc. of Medicine 1987; MRC Research Professorship 1995; Chair. Comm. on Social Determinants of Health, WHO 2004–; mem. Faculty of Community Medicine; Foreign Assoc. mem. Inst. of Medicine (Nat. Acads of Sciences). *Publications:* Status Syndrome (Bloomsbury and Times Holt) 2004; numerous articles in learned journals. *Honours:* Hon. MD (Univ. of Sydney) 2006; Balzan Prize for Epidemiology 2004, Harveian Oration 2006. *Address:* Department of Epidemiology and Public Health, University College London, 1–19 Torrington Place, London, WC1E 6BT (office); Wildwood Cottage, 17 North End, London, NW3 7HK, England (home). *Telephone:* (20) 7679-1717 (office). *Fax:* (20) 7813-0242 (office). *E-mail:* m.marmot@ucl.ac.uk (office). *Website:* www.ucl.ac.uk/epidemiology/staff/marmot (office); www.ucl.ac.uk/iish (office).

MARNY, Dominique Antoinette Nicole; French novelist, screenwriter and journalist; b. 21 Feb. 1948, Neuilly; m. Michel Marny 1970 (divorced); one d. *Career:* mem. PEN Club. *Publications:* Crystal Palace, 1985; Les orages desirés, 1988; Les fous de lumière, 1991; Les desirs et les jours, 1993; Les courtisanes, 1994; Les belles de Cocteau, 1995. Contributions: Madame Figaro; Vogue; Marie France. *Honours:* Prix Madame Europe 1993.

MAROWITZ, Charles, MA, MFA; American writer and director; b. 26 Jan. 1934, New York; m. Jane Elizabeth Allsop 1980; one s. *Education:* Univ. Coll. London, UK. *Career:* Artistic Dir, Malibu Stage Co 2000–, Texas Stage Co; West Coast Correspondent, Theatre Week Magazine; Senior Ed., Matzoh Ball Gazette; Theatre Critic, Los Angeles Village View; Guest Artist-in-Residence, California State Univ., Long Beach, CA, 1997; Columnist Swans.com 2004–; mem. Dramatists Guild, Writers Guild, Asscn of Literary Scholars and Critics. *Plays:* The Marowitz Shakespeare, Sherlock's Last Case 1996, Caesar 1999, Murdering Marlowe 2002, Silent Partners 2006. *Publications:* The Method as Means 1961, The Marowitz Hamlet 1966, The Shrew 1972 (LA Weekly Award 1988), Artaud at Rodez 1975, Confessions of a Counterfeit Critic 1976, The Marowitz Shakespeare 1980, Act of Being 1980, Sex Wars 1983, Sherlock's Last Case 1984, Prospero's Staff 1986, Potboilers 1986, Recycling Shakespeare 1990, Burnt Bridges 1991, Directing the Action 1992, Cyrano de Bergerac (trans.) 1995, Alarums and Excursions 1996, The Other Way: An Alternative Approach to Acting and Directing 1998, Boulevard Comedies 2000, Stage Dust 2001, Roar of the Canon, Kott and Marowitz on Shakespeare (with Jan Kott) 2002, The Other Chekhov: A Biography of Michael Chekhov 2004, How to Stage a Play 2005; contributions: newspapers, journals and magazines. *Honours:* Order of Purple Sash, 1965; Whitbread Award, 1967; First Prize, Louis B. Mayer Award, 1984. *Address:* 3058 Sequit Drive, Malibu, CA 90265, USA (office). *Telephone:* (310) 456-5060 (office). *Fax:* (310) 456-8170 (office). *E-mail:* winomar@mac.com (office). *Website:* www.marowitztheater.com (office).

MARQUAND, David Ian, FBA, FRHistS, FRSA; British academic, author and fmr politician; *Visiting Fellow, Department of Politics, University of Oxford;* b. 20 Sept. 1934, Cardiff, Wales; s. of Rt Hon. Hilary Marquand and Rachel Marquand; m. Judith M. Reed 1959; one s. one d. *Education:* Emanuel School, Magdalen Coll., Oxford, St Antony's Coll., Oxford, Univ. of California, Berkeley, USA. *Career:* Sr Scholar, St Antony's Coll. Oxford 1957–58; Teaching Asst, Univ. of California 1958–59; editorial writer, The Guardian 1959–61; Research Fellow, St Antony's Coll. Oxford 1962–64, Hon. Fellow 2003–; Lecturer in Politics, Univ. of Sussex 1964–66; MP (Labour) for Ashfield, Notts. 1966–77; del. to Council of Europe and WEU assemblies 1970–73; Opposition Spokesman on Treasury Affairs 1971–72; Chief Adviser, Sec.-Gen. EC 1977–78; Prof. of Contemporary History and Politics, Univ. of Salford 1978–91; Prof. of Politics, Univ. of Sheffield 1991–96, Dir Political Economy Research Centre 1993–96, Hon. Prof. 1997–; Prin. Mansfield Coll. Oxford 1996–2002, Hon. Fellow; Visiting Fellow, Dept of Politics, Univ. of Oxford 2002–; Jt Ed. The Political Quarterly 1987–96. *Publications:* Ramsay Macdonald 1973, Parliament for Europe 1979, The Unprincipled Society 1988, The Progressive Dilemma 1991, The New Reckoning 1997, Religion and Democracy 2000, Decline of the Public 2004, Britain Since 1918 2008. *Honours:* Hon. DLitt (Salford, Sheffield), Hon. Dr of Political Science (Bologna); George Orwell Memorial Prize 1979, Isaiah Berlin Prize for Lifetime Achievement in Political Studies. *Address:* Department of Politics and International Relations, Manor Road, University of Oxford, Oxford, OX1 3UQ (office); Mansfield College, Oxford, OX1 3TF, England (office). *Telephone:* (1865) 751026 (office). *Fax:* (1865) 278725 (office). *E-mail:* david.marquand@politics.ox.ac.uk (office); david.marquand@mansfield.ox.ac.uk (office). *Website:* www.politics.ox.ac.uk (office).

MÁRQUEZ, Gabriel García (see GARCÍA MÁRQUEZ, Gabriel)

MARR, Andrew William Stevenson, BA; British journalist; b. 31 July 1959, Glasgow, Scotland; s. of Donald Marr and Valerie Marr; m. Jackie Ashley 1987; one s. two d. *Education:* Dundee High School, Craigflower School, Loretto School, Trinity Hall, Cambridge. *Career:* gen. reporter, business reporter The Scotsman 1982–84, Parl. Corresp. 1984–86, Political Ed. 1988; Political Ed. The Economist 1988–92; Political Corresp. The Independent 1986–88, Chief Commentator 1992–96, Ed. 1996–98, Ed.-in-Chief 1998; columnist The Express and The Observer 1998; Political Ed. BBC 2000–05; presenter Start the Week, BBC Radio 4 2002–; presenter morning interview programme, Sunday AM (BBC One) 2005–07, The Andrew Marr Show (BBC One) 2007–; Chair. Jury Bd Samuel Johnson Prize for Non-Fiction 2001. *Publications:* The Battle for Scotland 1992, Ruling Britannia 1996, The Day Britain Died 2000, My Trade: A Short History of British Journalism 2004, A History of Modern Britain (also TV series; winner, British Documentary Award for Best Series 2008) 2007, The Making of Modern Britain (Galaxy Nat. Book Awards Non-Fiction Book of the Year 2010) 2009. *Honours:* What The Papers Say Award for Columnist of the Year 1995, British Press Award for Columnist of the Year 1995, Creative Freedom Award for Journalist of the Year 2000, Channel 4 Political Awards Journalist Award 2001, Royal Television Soc. Television Journalism Award for specialist journalism 2001, Voice of the Listener and Viewer Award for Best Individual Contributor on TV 2002, BAFTA Richard Dimbleby Award 2004. *Address:* Room 3200, BBC Television Centre, Wood Lane, London, W12 7RJ, England (office). *Website:* www.bbc.co.uk (office).

MARR, David; Australian journalist, writer and television producer; *Features Writer, Sydney Morning Herald.* *Education:* Univ. of Sydney. *Career:* Ed. National Times 1981–82; worked on TV programme, Four Corners (ABC) 1985, 1990–91; presenter, Arts Today radio programme 1994–96; feature writer, Sydney Morning Herald. *Publications:* Barwick 1981, The Ivanov Trail; Patrick White—A Life 1991, Patrick White—Letters 1994, The High Price of Heaven (essays) 1999, Dark Victory: The Story of The Tampa (with Marian Wilkinson) 2002. *Honours:* NSW Premier's Literary Award 1981, numerous literary awards. *Literary Agent:* Australian Literary Management, 2–4 Booth Street, Balmain, NSW 2041, Australia. *Telephone:* (2) 9818-8557. *E-mail:* alpha@austlit.com. *Website:* www.austlit.com.

MARR, William Wei-Yi, (Fei Ma), MS, PhD; American/Chinese fmr engineer, poet, editor and artist; b. 3 Sept. 1936, China; s. of Jie-Ying Marr; m. Jane Jy Chyun Liu 1962; two s. *Education:* Taipei Inst. of Technology (Taipei Univ. of Technology), Marquette Univ. and Univ. of Wisconsin, USA. *Career:* fmr researcher, Argonne Nat. Lab., Chicago; Editorial Adviser Chinese Poetry International, New World Poetry; adviser, Chinese Writers Asscn of Greater Chicago, Asscn of Modern Chinese Literature and Arts of N America; mem. Chinese Artists Asscn of N America, Illinois State Poetry Soc. (Pres. 1993–95), Li Poetry Soc., New Poetry, Beijing (Vice-Pres. 1994–2000), Poets' Club of Chicago. *Exhibitions:* several solo and group exhbns of artworks (paintings and sculptures) in Chicago area and Beijing, China; also on internet. *Publications include:* In the Windy City 1975, Selected Poems 1983, White Horse 1984, Selected Poems of Fei Ma 1985, The Galloping Hoofs 1986, Road 1987, Selected Short Poems 1991, Fly Spirit 1992, Selected Poems 1994, Autumn Window 1995, A Microscopic World 1998, Not All Flowers Need to Bear Fruit 2000, The Collected Poems of Fei Ma 2000, Selected Poems of William Marr 2003, The Awakening of Worldly Desires (Selected Essays) 2005, Poetry of Fei Ma 2009, Between Heaven and Earth 2010, Will Never Write a Dirge for a Cat 2011, You Are That Wind 2011; poems have been included in more than 100 anthologies and textbooks and translated into over ten languages; contrib. to periodicals and magazines. *Honours:* Wu Cho Liu Poetry Award 1982, Li Poetry Trans. Award 1982, and Poetry Award 1984, Illinois State Poetry Soc. Award 1993, 1994, Chicago Poets and Patrons Award 1993, 1995. *E-mail:* marrfei@yahoo.com (home). *Website:* wmarr9.home.comcast.net/bmz.htm.

MARS-JONES, Adam, FRSL; British novelist and critic; b. 26 Oct. 1954, London, England; s. of the late Sir William Mars-Jones; partner Keith King. *Education:* Westminster School, Trinity Hall, Cambridge and Univ. of Virginia, USA. *Career:* film critic, The Independent 1989–97, The Times 1999–2001; regular contrib. to The Guardian, The Observer, The Times Literary Supplement, and BBC TV's Newsnight Review. *Publications:* Lantern Lecture (short stories) (Somerset Maugham Award 1982) 1981, Mae West is Dead 1983, The Darker Proof: Stories from a Crisis (with Edmund White) 1987, Monopolies of Loss 1992, The Waters of Thirst (novel) 1993, Blind Bitter Happiness (essays) 1997, Pilcrow (novel) 2008, Cedilla (novel) 2011, Noriko Smiling (film study) 2011. *Honours:* Hatchet Job of the Year Award 2012. *Address:* 38 Oakbank Grove, Herne Hill, London, SE24 0AJ, England.

MARSDEN, George M., BA, BD, MA, PhD; American academic and writer; *Francis A. McAnaney Professor of History, University of Notre Dame*; b. 25 Feb. 1939, Harrisburg, Pennyslvania; m. Lucie Commeret, 30 March 1969, one s. one d. *Education:* Haverford Coll., Westminster Theological Seminary, Yale Univ. *Career:* instructor, Asst. and Assoc. Prof. 1965–74, Prof. 1974–86, Calvin Coll., Grand Rapids; Assoc. Ed., Christian Scholar's Review 1970–77; Visiting Prof. of Church History, Trinity Evangelical Divinty School, Deerfield, IL 1976–77; Ed., The Reformed Journal 1980–90; Visiting Prof. of History, Univ. of California at Berkeley 1986, 1990; Prof. of the History of Christianity in America, Divinity School, Duke Univ. 1986–92; Francis A. McAnaney Prof. of History, Univ. of Notre Dame 1992–; mem. American Soc. of Church History (pres. 1992), Inst. for the Study of American Evangelicals (advisory council). *Publications:* The Evangelical Mind and the New School Presbyterian Experience 1970, A Christian View of History? (ed. with Frank Roberts) 1975, Fundamentalism and American Culture: The Shaping of Twentieth-Century Evangelicalism, 1870–1925 1980, Eerdman's Handbook to the History of Christianity in America (co-ed.) 1983, The Search for Christian America (with Mark A. Noll and Nathan O. Hatch) 1983, Evangelicalism and Modern America (ed.) 1984, Reforming Fundamentalism: Fuller Seminary and the New Evangelicalism 1987, Religion and American Culture 1990, Understanding Fundamentalism and Evangelicalism 1991, The Secularization of the Academy (ed. with Bradley J. Longfield) 1992, The Soul of the American University 1994, The Outrageous Idea of Christian Scholarship 1997, Jonathan Edwards: A Life (Soc. for Eighteenth Century Studies Annibel Jenkins Prize 2002–04, Bancroft Prize 2004, Org. of American Historians Merle Curti Award 2004, Historical Soc. Eugene Genovese Prize 2004, John Pollock Award for Christian Biography 2004, Christianity Today Book Award for History and Biography 2004) 2003; contrib. to many scholarly books and journals. *Honours:* Younger Humanists Fellowship, Nat. Endowment for the Humanities 1971–72, Fellow, Calvin Center for Christian Scholarship 1979–80, Book of the Year Citations, Eternity magazine 1981, 1988, Calvin Research Fellowship 1982–83, J. Howard Pew Freedom Trust Grant 1988–92, Guggenheim Fellowship 1995. *Address:* c/o Department of History, University of Notre Dame, Notre Dame, IN 46556, USA.

MARSDEN, Peter Richard Valentine, FSA; British archaeologist and writer; b. 29 April 1940, Twickenham, Middlesex, England; m. Frances Elizabeth Mager 1979, two s. one d. *Education:* Kilburn Polytechnic, University of Oxford. *Career:* mem. Institute of Field Archaeologists. *Publications:* Londinium, 1971; The Wreck of the Amsterdam, 1974; Roman London, 1980; The Marsden Family of Paythorne and Nelson, 1981; The Roman Forum Site in London, 1987; The Historic Shipwrecks of South-East England, 1987. *Contributions:* Geographical Magazine; Independent; TLS; Illustrated London News; Telegraph Colour Magazine; various academic journals.

MARSDEN, Sir Simon Neville Llewelyn, Bt; British writer and photographer; b. 1 Dec. 1948, Lincoln, England; m. Caroline Stanton 1984; one s. one d. *Education:* Ampleforth Coll., Yorkshire, Sorbonne, Univ. of Paris. *Career:* mem. Chelsea Arts Club, Arthur Machen Soc. *Film:* The Twilight Hour (drama/documentary). *Publications:* In Ruins 1980, The Haunted Realm 1986, Visions of Poe 1988, Phantoms of the Isles 1990, The Journal of a Ghost Hunter 1994, Beyond the Wall: The Lost World of East Germany 1999, Venice, City of Haunting Dreams 2001, The Twilight Hour 2003, This Spectred Isle 2005, Ghosthunter: A Journey through Haunted France 2006, Memento Mori: Churches & Churchyards of England 2007, Vampires: The Twilight World 2011. *Honours:* Arts Council of Great Britain Awards 1975, 1976. *Address:* The Presbytery, Hainton, Market Rasen, Lincs., LN8 6LR, England (home). *Telephone:* (1507) 313646 (office). *Fax:* (1507) 313646 (office). *E-mail:* info@marsdenarchive.com (office). *Website:* www.simonmarsden.co.uk; www.marsdenarchive.com.

MARSÉ, Juan Faneca Roca; Spanish writer; b. 8 Jan. 1933, Barcelona. *Publications include:* Encerrados con un solo juguete 1961, Esta cara de la luna 1962, Últimas tardes con Teresa 1966, La oscura historia de la prima Montse 1970, Si te dicen que caí (Premio Internacional de Novela México) 1973, Confidencias de un chorizo 1977, La muchacha de las bragas de oro (Premio Planeta) 1978, Un día volveré (trans. as One Day I Will Return) 1982, La ronda de Guinardó 1984, La fuga del Rio Lobo (trans. as The Flight of Wolf River) 1985, Teniente Bravo 1987, El amante bilingüe (Premio Ateneo) 1990, El embrujo de Shangai (trans. as The Bewitchment of Shanghai) 1993, Las mujeres de Juanito Marés 1997, Rabos de Lagartija (trans. as Lizard Tails) 2000, Amor de un Gladiador 2003, La gran Desilusión 2004, Canciones de Amor en Lolita's Club 2005; contrib. to Dietario de Posguerra 1998. *Honours:* Premio Sésamo 1959, Planeta Prize 1978, European Literature Prize 1994, Premio Juan Rolfo 1997, Premio Internacional Unión Latina 1998, Premio Cervantes 2008. *Address:* c/o Editorial Lumen, Random House Mondadori, Travessera de Grácia 47–49, 08021 Barcelona, Spain (office). *Website:* www.editoriallumen.com (office).

MARSHALL, Jack; American writer and poet; b. 25 Feb. 1937, New York, NY. *Education:* Brooklyn Public Schools. *Publications:* The Darkest Continent, 1967; Bearings, 1970; Floats, 1972; Bits of Thirst, 1974; Bits of Thirst and Other Poems and Translations, 1976; Arriving on the Playing Fields of Paradise, 1983; Arabian Nights, 1986; Sesame, 1993.

MARSHALL, Owen, DipEd, MA; New Zealand writer; b. (Owen Marshall Jones), 17 Aug. 1941, Te Kuiti; m. Jacqueline Hill 1965; two d. *Education:* Univ. of Canterbury, Christchurch Teachers' Coll. *Career:* Adjunct Prof., Univ. of Canterbury 2005–. *Publications:* Supper Waltz Wilson 1979, The Master of Big Jingles 1982, The Day Hemingway Died 1984, The Lynx Hunter 1987, The Divided World 1989, Tomorrow We Save the Orphans 1991, A Many Coated Man 1995, Coming Home in the Dark 1995, The Best of Owen Marshall 1997, Harlequin Rex 1999, When Gravity Snaps 2002, Essential New Zealand Short Stories (ed.) 2002, Watch of Gryphons 2005; contrib. to numerous magazines and journals. *Honours:* Hon. DLitt (Univ. of Canterbury) 2002; New Zealand Literary Fund Scholarship in Letters 1988, Robert Burns Fellowship 1992, ONZM 2000, Creative New Zealand Arts Fellowship. *Address:* 10 Morgans Road, Timaru, New Zealand (home).

MARSHALL, Paule, BA; American writer; b. 9 April 1929, New York, NY; m. 1st Kenneth E. Marshall 1957 (divorced 1963); one s.; m. 2nd Nourry Menard 1970. *Education:* Brooklyn College, CUNY. *Career:* staff mem., Our World magazine 1953–56. *Publications:* Brown Girl, Brownstones 1959, Soul Clap Hands and Sing 1962, The Chosen Place, The Timeless People 1969, Praisesong for the Widows 1983, Reena and Other Stories 1983, Daughters 1991, The Fisher King 2000, Triangular Road 2009; contributions: anthologies and periodicals. *Honours:* Guggenheim Fellowship 1961, John D. and Catherine T. MacArthur Foundation Fellowship 1992. *Address:* c/o Basic Civitas Books, 387 Park Avenue South, New York, NY 10016, USA (office). *Website:* www.perseusbooksgroup.com/civitas (office).

MARSHALL, Penelope, BA; British journalist; b. 7 Nov. 1962, Addlestone, Surrey, England; d. of the late Alan Marshall and of Mary Marshall (née Hanlin); m. Tim Ewart 1991; three d. *Education:* London School of Econs. *Career:* Foreign Corresp. for ITN (Ind. TV News), Moscow coverage 1990, Bosnia coverage 1992, Defence and Diplomatic Corresp. 1994–, S Africa Corresp. 1999–2001; Visiting Prof., City Univ., London. *Honours:* BAFTA Award 1992, Royal TV Soc. Award, Gold, Silver and Bronze Medals, New York. *Address:* City University, Northampton Square, London, EC1V 0HB, England (office). *E-mail:* penny.marshall@itn.co.uk (office).

MARTEL, Yann; Canadian writer; b. 1963, Salamanca, Spain. *Education:* Trent Univ. *Career:* grew up in Alaska, BC, Costa Rica, France, Ont. and Mexico; fmr tree planter, dishwasher, security guard; became professional writer 1990. *Publications:* Facts Behind the Helsinki Roccamatios (short stories) (Journey Prize) 1993, Self (novel) 1996, Life of Pi (novel) (Hugh MacLennan Prize for Fiction 2001, Man Booker Prize 2002, Boeke Prize 2003) 2001, We Ate the Children Last (short stories) 2004, Beatrice and Virgil 2010. *Address:* c/o Knopf Canada, Random House of Canada Ltd, One Toronto Street, Unit 300, Toronto, ON M5C 2VC, Canada (office). *Telephone:* (416)

364-4449 (office). *Fax:* (416) 364-6863 (office). *Website:* www.randomhouse.ca (office).

MARTELL, Owen; Welsh novelist; b. 1976, Exeter, England. *Career:* writer-in-residence School of Welsh, Cardiff Univ. *Publications:* Cadw dy ffydd, brawd (novel, Gomer First Novel Prize, Arts Council of Wales Book of the Year 2001) 2000, Dyn yr Eiliad (novel) 2003. *E-mail:* owen@thisisom.com (office). *Website:* www.thisisom.com.

MARTELLA, Maureen; Irish writer; b. 28 Jan. 1947, Dublin; three s. one d. *Education:* St Brigid's Coll., Co. Dublin. *Publications:* Are You the Other Listener? (poems), Bugger Bucharest (novel) 1995, Maddy Goes to Holywood (novel) 1999, Annie's New Life (novel) 2000, A Perfect Partnership (novel) 2004, Friends & Lovers (novel) 2007; contribs to Woman's Way (Dublin), radio documentaries (RTÉ Radio), Sunday Miscellany (RTÉ Radio), The Sunday Times (UK). *Address:* Nunsland, Naas, Co. Kildare, Ireland (home). *E-mail:* info@maureenmartella.com (office). *Website:* www.maureenmartella.com.

MARTI, René; Swiss writer, poet and journalist; b. 7 Nov. 1926, Frauenfeld; m. Elizabeth Wahrenberger 1955; one s. two d. *Education:* Commercial School, Lausanne, Cambridge Proficiency Class, Polytechnic School, London, Univ. of Konstanz. *Career:* mem. PEN of Switzerland and other literary organizations; Regensburger Schriftstellergruppe intern., Turmbund Innsbruck, Verband Kath. Schriftsteller Oesterreichs, PEN German-speaking Writers Abroad, London, Freier deutscher Autorenverband, Autoren der Schweiz, Interessengemeinschaft deutschsprachiger Autoren (IGdA), Zürcher Schriftstelleryerband, Berner Schriftstellerverband, Präsidium des Internat, Bodenseeclubs, Konstanz. *Publications:* Das unauslöschliche Licht 1954, Dom des Herzens 1967, Die fünf Unbekannten (with others) 1970, Der unsichtbare Kreis 1975, Weg an Weg 1979, Besuche dich in der Natur (with Lili Keller) 1983, Gedichte zum Verschenken (with Lili Keller) 1984, Stationen 1986, Die verbrannten Schreie 1989, Gib allem ein bisschen Zeit (with Brigitta Weiss) 1993, Rückblicke 1996, Spatenstich für die Rose (with Magdalena Obergfell) 2001, Atrium: 28 poems set to music by eight composers 2006; contribs to more than 200 anthologies, to newspapers, magazines and for radio. *Honours:* several publishing grants, AWMM Lyric Poetry Prize, Luxembourg 1985, Lyrikpreis der Nationalbibliothek des deutschsprachigen Gedichts in München für ein unter Tausenden von Einsendungen hervorragendes Gedicht, welches in einzigartigem Einfallsreichtum ein herausragendes Sprachkunstwerk darstelle (Gedicht 'Zum blauen Abschied'), Ehrenpräsident der IGdA, Anerkennungspreis für Literatur der Stadt Frauenfeld 2006. *Address:* Haus am Herterberg, Haldenstrasse 5, 8500 Frauenfeld, Switzerland. *Telephone:* 721 43 74 (office).

MARTIN, Alexander George, MA, DipArts; American writer; b. 8 Nov. 1953, Baltimore, MD; m. 1979, two s. *Education:* University of Cambridge, University College, Cardiff. *Career:* mem. Society of Authors. *Publications:* Boris the Tomato, 1984; Snow on the Stinker, 1988; The General Interruptor, 1989; Modern Poetry, 1990; Modern Short Stories, 1991. *Honours:* Betty Trask Award 1988.

MARTIN, Rev. David Alfred, DipEd, BSc, PhD, FBA; British sociologist, academic, writer and priest; *Professor of Sociology Emeritus, London School of Economics and Political Science*; b. 30 June 1929, London, England; s. of Frederick Martin and Miriam Martin; m. 1st Daphne Sylvia Treherne 1953; one s.; m. 2nd Bernice Thompson 1962; two s. one d. *Education:* Westminster Coll., Univ. of London, London School of Econs. *Career:* Asst Lecturer, Univ. of Sheffield 1961–62; Lecturer, LSE 1962–67; Reader 1967–71, Prof. of Sociology 1971–89, Prof. Emer. 1989–; Ordained Deacon 1983, Priest 1984; Scurlock Prof. of Human Values, Southern Methodist Univ., Dallas, Tex., USA 1986–90; Sr Professorial Fellow, later Int. Fellow, Inst. for the Study of Econ. Culture, Boston Univ., USA 1990–; Hon. Prof., Lancaster Univ. 1993–2006; Adjunct Prof., Liverpool Hope Univ. 2006–; various visiting lectureships; mem. Int. Conf. of the Sociology of Religion (Pres. 1975–83). *Publications:* Pacifism 1965, A Sociology of English Religion 1967, The Religious and the Secular 1969, Tracts Against the Times 1973, A General Theory of Secularisation 1978, Dilemmas of Contemporary Religion 1978, Crisis for Cranmer and King James (ed.) 1978, The Breaking of the Image 1980, Theology and Sociology (co-ed.) 1980, No Alternative (co-ed.) 1981, Unholy Warfare (co-ed.) 1983, Divinity in a Grain of Bread 1989, Tongues of Fire 1990, The Forbidden Revolution 1996, Reflections on Sociology and Theology 1997, Does Christianity Cause Wars? 1997, Pentecostalism: The World their Parish 2002, Christian Language in the Secular City 2002, Christian Language and its Mutations 2002, Christian Language in the Secular City 2002, On Secularization 2005, Sacred History and Sacred Geography 2008, The Future of Christianity 2011; contribs to journals. *Honours:* Hon. Asst Priest, Guildford Cathedral 1983–; Hon. DTheol (Univ. of Helsinki) 2000. *Address:* Cripplegate Cottage, 174 St John's Road, Woking, Surrey, GU21 7PQ, England. *Telephone:* (1483) 762134.

MARTIN, George Whitney, BA, LLB; American writer; b. 25 Jan. 1926, New York. *Education:* Harvard Coll., Trinity Coll., Cambridge, Univ. of Virginia Law School. *Career:* practised law 1955–59; writer 1959–. *Publications:* The Damrosch Dynasty, America's First Family of Music 1983, Verdi, His Music, Life and Times (fourth edn) 1992, Aspects of Verdi (second edn) 1993, Verdi at The Golden Gate, Opera and San Francisco in the Gold Rush Years 1993, The Opera Companion (sixth edn) 2008, Twentieth Century Opera, A Guide 1999, CCB: The Life and Century of Charles C. Burlingham, New York's First Citizen 1858–1959 (US Supreme Court Historical Soc. Erwin N. Griswold Award 2006) 2005; contrib. numerous articles on Verdi and his operas in The Opera Quarterly. *Address:* 53 Crosslands Drive, Kennett Square, PA 19348, USA (office). *Telephone:* (610) 388-0529 (office). *Website:* www.georgewmartin .com.

MARTIN, Jay Herbert, BA, MA, PhD; American psychoanalyst, academic, author and editor; *Edward S. Gould Professor of Humanities and Professor of Government, Claremont McKenna College*; b. 30 Oct. 1935, Newark, NJ; m. Helen Bernadette Saldini 1956, one s. two d. *Education:* Columbia Univ., Ohio State Univ., Southern California Psychoanalytic Inst. *Career:* Instructor in English, Pennsylvania State Univ. 1957–58; Instructor in English and American Studies, Yale Univ. 1960–64, Asst Prof. 1964–67, Assoc. Prof. 1967–68; Prof. of English, American Studies and Comparative Culture, Univ. of California at Irvine 1968–79, Lecturer and Clinical Supervisor in Psychiatry and Human Behaviour 1978–95; Leo S. Bing Prof. of English and American Literature, Univ. of Southern California at Los Angeles 1979–96; Edward S. Gould Prof. of Humanities and Prof. of Govt, Claremont McKenna Coll. and Claremont Graduate Univ., CA 1996–; Dai Ho Chun Distinguished Visiting Prof., Univ. of Hawaii (Honolulu) 2000–01; mem. American Psychoanalytic Asscn, Authors' Guild, Int. Psychoanalytic Asscn, MLA. *Publications:* Winfield Townley Scott (ed) 1961, Conrad Aiken: A Life of His Art 1962, Harvests of Change: American Literature 1865–1914 1967, A Collection of Critical Essays on 'The Waste Land' (ed.) 1968, Nathanael West: The Art of His Life 1970, Robert Lowell 1970, Twentieth-Century Views of Nathanael West: A Collection of Critical Essays (ed.) 1972, A Singer in the Dawn: Reinterpretations of Paul Laurance Dunbar 1975, A Dunbar Reader (ed. with Gossie H. Hudson) 1975, Always Merry and Bright: The Life of Henry Miller: An Unauthorized Biography 1978, Winter Dreams: An American in Moscow 1979, Economic Depression and American Humor (ed.) 1984, Who Am I This Time?: Uncovering the Fictive Personality 1988, A Corresponding Leap of Love: Henry Miller, Lying and Dying 1996, Henry Miller's Dream Song 1996, Swallowing Tigers Whole: Conceptions of the Desirable in American Life and Education 1997, Journey to Heavenly Mountain 2002, The Education of John Dewey 2003, Baseball and Other Games 2005; Contributions: scholarly books, professional journals and literary periodicals. *Honours:* American Philosophical Society Fellowship 1966, Guggenheim Fellowship 1966–67, Rockefeller Foundation Senior Fellowship in the Humanities 1977–78, National Endowment for the Humanities Senior Research Grant 1983–84, Research Fellow Rockefeller Study Center Bellagio Italy 1985–86, Burlington Northern Foundation Award for Outstanding Scholarship 1989, Durfee Fellowship to China 2000, University of Southern California at Los Angeles Distinguished Emer. Prof. Award 2001, Research Fellow Bogliasco (Italy) Foundation 2004. *Address:* 748 Via Santo Tomas, Claremont, CA 91711 (home); Claremont McKenna College, 850 N Columbia Avenue, Claremont, CA 91711, USA (office). *Telephone:* (909) 398-0193 (home); (909) 607-3184 (office). *Fax:* (909) 398-1352 (home); (909) 621-8419 (office). *E-mail:* helenjay@comcast.net (home); jmartin@claremontmckenna.edu (office). *Website:* www.mckenna.edu (office).

MARTIN, Sir Laurence Woodward, Kt, MA, PhD, DL; British academic; *Professor Emeritus, Newcastle University*; b. 30 July 1928, St Austell, Cornwall, England; s. of Leonard Martin and Florence Mary Woodward; m. Betty Parnall 1951; one s. one d. *Education:* St Austell Grammar School, Christ's Coll., Cambridge, Yale Univ., USA. *Career:* RAF Flying Officer 1948–51; Asst Prof., MIT, USA 1956–61; Assoc. Prof., Johns Hopkins Univ., USA 1961–64; Prof., Univ. of Wales 1964–68; King's Coll. London 1968–78, Fellow, London 1984; Vice-Chancellor Newcastle Univ. 1978–90, Prof. Emer. 1991–; Arleigh Burke Chair in Strategy, Center for Strategic and Int. Studies, Washington, DC, USA 1998–2000; Visiting Prof., Univ. of Wales 1985–90; Dir Royal Inst. of Int. Affairs 1991–96; Bodichon Fellow, Girton Coll. Cambridge 2010. *Radio:* Reith Lecturer (BBC) 1981. *Publications:* Peace Without Victory 1958, The Sea in Modern Strategy 1967, Arms and Strategy 1973, The Two Edged Sword 1982, The Changing Face of Nuclear War 1987, British Foreign Policy (co-author) 1997. *Honours:* Hon. DCL (Newcastle) 1991; Lees Knowles Lecturer, Cambridge. *Address:* 35 Witley Court, Coram Street, London, WC1N 1HP, England (home). *E-mail:* lw.martin@hirundo.co.uk (office).

MARTIN, (Roy) Peter, (James Melville), MBE, BA, MA; British writer; b. 5 Jan. 1931, London, England; two s. *Education:* Birkbeck Coll., London, Tübingen Univ., Germany. *Career:* crime fiction reviewer, Hampstead, Highgate Express 1983–2000; mem. CWA, Detection Club. *Publications:* 13 Superintendent Otani mysteries, The Imperial Way 1986, A Tarnished Phoenix 1990, The Chrysanthemum Throne 1997.

MARTIN, Philip John Talbot, BA; Australian lecturer (retd) and poet; b. 28 March 1931, Melbourne, Vic. *Education:* University of Melbourne. *Career:* Tutor to Senior Tutor in English, University of Melbourne 1960–62; Lecturer in English, Australian National University 1963; Lecturer to Senior Lecturer, Monash University 1964–88. *Publications:* poetry: Voice Unaccompanied 1970, A Bone Flute 1974, From Sweden 1979, A Flag for the Wind 1982, New and Selected Poems 1988; other: Shakespeare's Sonnets: Self Love and Art (criticism) 1972, Lars Gustafsson: The Stillness of the World Before Bach (trans.) 1988; contributions: seven anthologies 1986–98, Age, Australian, Carleton Miscellany, Helix, Meanjin, New Hungarian Quarterly, Poetry USA, Quadrant, Southerly, TLS. *Address:* 25/9 Nicholson Street, Balmain 2041, NSW, Australia (home).

MARTIN, Ralph Guy, BJ; American writer; b. 4 March 1920, Chicago, IL; m. Marjorie Jean Pastel 1944, one s. two d. *Education:* University of Missouri. *Career:* Managing Ed., Box Elder News Journal, Brigham, Utah 1941; Assoc. Ed., The New Republic, New York City 1945–48, Newsweek magazine, New York City 1953–55; Exec. Ed., House Beautiful, New York City 1955–57; mem. Authors' Guild, Century Asscn, Dramatists Guild, Overseas Press Club. *Publications:* Boy from Nebraska 1946, The Best is None too Good 1948, Eleanor Roosevelt: Her Life in Pictures (with Richard Harrity) 1958, The Human Side of FDR (with Richard Harrity) 1959, Front Runner, Dark Horse (with Ed Plaut) 1960, Money, Money, Money (with Morton Stone) 1961, Man of Destiny: Charles de Gaulle (with Richard Harrity) 1962, World War II: From D-Day to VE-Day (with Richard Harrity) 1962, The Three Lives of Helen Keller (with Richard Harrity) 1962, Ballots and Bandwagons 1964, The Bosses 1964, President from Missouri 1964, Skin Deep 1964, World War II: Pearl Harbor to VJ-Day 1965, Wizard of Wall Street 1965, The GI War: 1941–1945 1967, A Man for All People: Hubert H. Humphrey 1968, Jennie: The Life of Lady Randolph Churchill (two vols) 1969, 1971, Lincoln Center for the Performing Arts 1971, The Woman He Loved: The Story of the Duke and Duchess of Windsor 1973, Cissy: The Life of Eleanor Medill Patterson 1979, A Hero of Our Time: An Intimate Study of the Kennedy Years 1983, Charles and Diana 1985, Golda: Golda Meir, the Romantic Years 1988, Henry and Clare: An Intimate Portrait of the Luces 1991, Seeds of Destruction: Joe Kennedy and His Sons 1995; contributions: books and periodicals.

MARTIN, Rhona Madeline; British writer and artist; b. 3 June 1922, London, England; m. 1st Peter Wilfrid Alcock 1941 (divorced); two d.; m. 2nd Thomas Edward Neighbour (divorced). *Career:* part-time Tutor in Creative Writing, Univ. of Sussex 1986–91; mem. Romantic Novelists Asscn, Soc. of Authors, PEN, Friends of the Arvon Foundation, Soc. of Limners. *Publications:* Gallows Wedding 1978, Mango Walk 1981, The Unicorn Summer 1984, Goodbye Sally 1987, Writing Historical Fiction 1988; contrib. to London Evening News, South East Arts Review, Cosmopolitan, Prima. *Honours:* Georgette Heyer Historical Novel Award 1978.

MARTIN, Valerie; American writer; b. 1948, Missouri. *Publications:* Love: Short Stories 1976, Set in Motion (novel) 1978, Alexandra (novel) 1980, A Recent Martyr (novel) 1987, The Consolation of Nature and Other Stories 1988, Mary Reilly (novel) 1990, The Great Divorce (novel) 1994, Italian Fever (novel) 1999, Salvation: Scenes from the Life of St Francis (biog.) 2001, Property (novel) (Orange Prize for Fiction) 2003, The Unfinished Novel and Other Stories 2006, Trespass 2007, The Confessions of Edward Day 2009. *Address:* c/o Doubleday Publicity, 1745 Broadway, New York, NY 10019, USA (office). *Website:* doubleday.knopfdoubleday.com (office).

MARTIN, Victoria Carolyn; British writer; b. 22 May 1945, Windsor, Berks.; d. of Lancelot Arthur Martin and Jean Yvonne Slocock; m. Tom Storey 1969; four d. *Education:* Winkfield Place, Berks., Byam Shaw School of Art. *Career:* cook (Cordon Bleu), antique dealer, farmer. *Publications:* September Song 1970, Windmill Years 1975, Seeds of the Sun 1980, Opposite House 1984, Tigers of the Night 1985, Obey the Moon 1987; contrib. to Woman, Woman's Own, Woman's Realm, Woman's Journal, Good Housekeeping, Woman's Weekly, Redbook, Honey 1967–87. *Address:* Newells Farm House, Lower Beeding, Horsham, Sussex, RH13 6LN, England (home). *Telephone:* (1403) 891326 (home). *Fax:* (1403) 891530 (home). *E-mail:* vicky.storey@btinternet.com (home).

MARTINAC, Paula, BA, MA; American writer and editor; b. 30 July 1954, Pittsburgh, PA; pnr Katie Hogan. *Education:* Chatham College, Pittsburgh, College of William and Mary. *Career:* Asst Curator, West Virginia State Museum, Charleston, 1979–82; Production Ed., Prentice-Hall Inc, Englewood Cliffs, NJ, 1982–85; Mem., Editorial Collective, Womanews, 1982–85; Production Dir, Feminist Press, CUNY, 1985–94; Ed., 1988–90, Mem., Editorial Board, 1990–92, Conditions magazine, New York; Curator, In Our Own Write reading series, New York City Lesbian and Gay Community Services Center, 1988–90; Panelist, Cultural Council Foundation, New York City, 1991. *Publications:* The One You Call Sister: New Women's Fiction (ed., contributor), 1989; Out of Time (novel), 1990; Home Movies, 1993; k d lang, 1996; Chicken (novel), 1997; The Queerest Places: A National Guide to Gay and Lesbian Historic Sites, 1997; The Lesbian and Gay Book of Love and Marriage: Creating the Stories of Our Lives, 1998. Contributions: books and periodicals including: Focus: A Journal for Lesbians; Conditions; Binnewater Tides; Sinister Wisdom; Queer City; Art and Understanding; Blithe House Quarterly. *Honours:* Lambda Literary Award for Lesbian Fiction, 1990; Puffin Foundation Grant, 1990; Best Book for Teens Citation, New York Public Library, 1997.

MARTÍNEZ, Guillermo, PhD; Argentine writer; b. (Néstor Guillermo Martínez), 29 July 1962, Bahía Blanca. *Education:* Univ. Nacional del Sur, Bahía Blanca, Univ. of Buenos Aires, Univ. of Oxford, UK. *Career:* graduate asst (Jefe de Trabajos Prácticos), Univ. of Buenos Aires 1985–91, Prof. of Math. 1991–; reviewer, literary collaborator Radar, Página 12 1997, Clarín and La Nación 1998–; Visiting Lecturer, St Antony's Coll. Oxford, Literary Week, Hamburg, Univ. del Nordeste, Chaco, literary festival in Segovia, Spain, book fair in Buenos Aires; Latin American Eminent Scholar Chair, Columbus State Univ. *Publications:* La jungla sin bestias (Nat. Roberto Arlt Short Story Prize) 1982, Infierno Grande (short stories, trans. as Vast Hell) (Fondo Nacional de las Artes First Prize 1988) 1989, Acerca de Roderer (novel, trans. as Regarding Roderer) 1993, La mujer del maestro (novel, trans. as The Woman of the Master) 1998, Borges y la matemática (essays) 2003, Crímenes imperceptibles (novel, published in Spain as Los crímenes de Oxford, trans. as The Oxford Murders) (Premio Planeta) 2003, La fórmula de la inmortalidad (essays and articles) 2005, La Muerte lenta de Luciana B. (novel) 2007, Gödel para todos (essays) (with Gustavo Pineiro) 2009, Yo también tuve una novia bisexual (novel) 2011; contrib. numerous articles, essays and reviews to anthologies and periodicals, including Vast Hell (published in The New Yorker) April 2009. *Honours:* Distinguished Citizen of Bahía Blanca; Fondo Nacional de las Artes 1988, Bienal de Arte Joven Short Story Award 1989, Premio Planeta Argentina 2003, Premio Mandarache 2006; numerous grants. *Literary Agent:* c/o Carmen Balcells Agency, Diagonal 580, Barcelona, Spain. *E-mail:* infogmartinez@yahoo.com.ar (office). *Website:* www.guillermo-martinez.net.

MARTÍNEZ-GÓMEZ, Raquel, PhD; Spanish writer and novelist; b. 1973, La Mancha. *Education:* Complutense Univ., Madrid. *Career:* taught at Instituto Technológico, Monterrey, Mexico; lives in England; works for Inter Press Service (news agency). *Publications include:* three novels: Sombras de unicornio (Shadows of the Unicorn) (EU Prize for Literature 2010) 2007; also short stories and poetry. *Address:* c/o Algaida Editores, Avenida de San Francisco Javier 22, 41018 Sevilla, Spain (office). *Telephone:* (95) 4652311 (office). *Fax:* (95) 4656254 (office). *E-mail:* algaida@algaida.es (office). *Website:* www.algaida.es (office).

MARTONE, Michael, AB, MA; American academic, writer and poet; *Professor, University of Alabama*; b. 22 Aug. 1955, Fort Wayne, Ind.; m. Theresa Pappas 1984. *Education:* Butler Univ., Indianapolis, Indiana Univ., Johns Hopkins Univ. *Career:* Asst Prof., Iowa State Univ. 1980–83, Assoc. Prof. 1983–87; Ed., Poet and Critic magazine 1981–86; Contributing Ed., North American Review 1984–; Briggs-Copeland Lecturer on Fiction, Harvard Univ. 1987–89, Briggs-Copeland Asst Prof. on Fiction 1989–91; Assoc. Prof. of English, Syracuse Univ 1991–96; Prof. and Dir Program for Creative Writing, Univ. of Alabama 1996–; mem. Associated Writing Programs, Nat. Writers' Union, PEN. *Publications:* fiction: Alive and Dead in Indiana 1984, Safety Patrol 1988, Fort Wayne is Seventh on Hitler's List 1990, Pensées: The Thoughts of Dan Quayle 1994, Seeing Eye 1995, The Blue Guide to Indiana 2001, Extreme 2004, Michael Martone 2005, Double-wide 2007; prose poems: At a Loss 1977, Return to Powers 1985, The Sex Lives of the Fantastic Four; other: The Flatness and Other Landscapes (essays) 1999, Unconventions (essays) 2006, Racing in Place (essays) 2008; editor: A Place of Sense: Essays in Search of the Midwest 1988, Townships: Pieces of the Midwest 1992, The Scribner Anthology of Contemporary Short Fiction 1999, Michael Martone 2005, Unconventions 2005, Rules of Thumb (ed.) 2006, The Touchstone Anthology of Contemporary Creative Nonfiction (co-ed.) 2007; contrib. to various books and journals. *Honours:* Nat. Endowment for the Arts Fellowship 1983, 1988, Black Ice magazine Margaret Jones Fiction Prize 1987, Ingram Merrill Foundation Award 1989, Pushcart Prize 1990, second place Thin Air Fiction Contest 1998, honorable mention 32 Pages Chapbook Contest 1998, Associated Writing Programs Award for Non-Fiction 1998, Best American Essays 2005. *Address:* PO Box 21179, Tuscaloosa, AL 35402 (office); 29 Country Club Hills, Tuscaloosa, AL 35401, USA (home). *Telephone:* (205) 348-8495 (office); (205) 344-5059 (home). *E-mail:* mmartone@english.ac.ua.edu (office).

MARTY, Martin E., MDiv, PhD, STM; American academic and ecclesiastic; *Fairfax M. Cone Distinguished Service Professor Emeritus of the History of Modern Christianity, Divinity School, University of Chicago*; b. 5 Feb. 1928, West Point, Neb.; s. of Emil A. Marty and Anne Louise Wuerdemann Marty; m. 1st Elsa Schumacher 1952 (died 1981); seven c.; m. 2nd Harriet Lindemann 1982. *Education:* Concordia Seminary, St Louis, Lutheran School of Theology, Chicago and Univ. of Chicago. *Career:* Lutheran Minister 1952–63; Prof. of History of Modern Christianity Univ. of Chicago 1963–, Fairfax M. Cone Distinguished Service Prof. 1978–98, now Emer.; Assoc. Ed. The Christian Century 1956–85, Sr Ed. 1985–98; Sr Scholar in Residence, Park Ridge Center 1985, Pres. 1985–89; Pres. American Soc. of Church History 1971, American Catholic History Asscn 1981, American Acad. of Religion 1988; Dir Fundamentalism project American Acad. of Arts and Sciences 1988–, The Public Religion Project 1996–99; Fellow, AAAS, Soc. of American Historians. *Publications:* many books and numerous articles on religious history, theology and cultural criticism. *Honours:* more than 70 hon. degrees; Nat. Book Award for Righteous Empire 1972, Nat. Medal Humanities 1997. *Address:* 175 East Delaware #85081, Chicago, IL 60611, USA (home). *Telephone:* (312) 640-1558 (office). *E-mail:* memarty@aol.com (home). *Website:* www.illuminos.com (office).

MARX, Michael William, BA, MFA, MA; American writer, publisher and teacher; b. 11 Jan. 1951, Philadelphia, PA; m. Ilsun Kang, one s. two d. *Education:* Hobart and William Smith Colleges, New York, New York University, Indiana State University. *Career:* Teacher, Indiana State University, 1999–, Lake Land College, Danville, IL, 2000–, Ivy Tech State College, Terre Haute, Indiana, 2001–. *Publications:* A War Ends, 1985; Eric Greenfield – Middle American, 1987; Justus – A Upopia, 1999. Contributions: newspapers, magazines and journals. *E-mail:* michael@michaelmarx.com.

MASCHLER, Thomas Michael; British publisher; *Managing Director and Publisher, Jonathan Cape Ltd*; b. 16 Aug. 1933, Berlin; s. of Kurt Leo Maschler and Rita Masseron; m. 1st Fay Coventry 1970 (divorced 1987); one s. two d.; m. 2nd Regina Kulinicz 1988. *Education:* Leighton Park School,

Reading. *Career:* Production Asst, André Deutsch 1955–56; Ed., MacGibbon and Kee 1956–58; Fiction Ed., Penguin Books 1958–60; Editorial Dir, Jonathan Cape Ltd 1960–70, Man. Dir 1960–, Chair. 1970–91, Publr 1991–; Dir Random House 1987. *Film:* The French Lieutenant's Woman (assoc. producer) 1981. *Publications:* Declarations (ed.) 1957, New English Dramatists series (ed.) 1959–63, Publisher (memoir) 2005. *Address:* Jonathan Cape Ltd, Random House, 20 Vauxhall Bridge Road, London, SW1V 2SA, England (office). *Telephone:* (20) 7840-8400 (office). *Fax:* (20) 7233-6117 (office). *Website:* www.randomhouse.co.uk (office).

MASŁOWSKA, Dorota; Polish writer; b. 3 July 1983, Wejcherowo; one d. *Plays:* Dwoje biednych Rumunów mówiących po polsku (trans. as A Couple of Poor, Polish-Speaking Romanians) 2006, Miedzy Nami dobrze Jest (trans. as All OK Between Us) 2009. *Publications:* Wojna polsko-ruska pod flagą biało-czerwoną (novel, trans. as White and Red) (Polityka Prize) 2003, Paw Królowej (novel) 2005. *Honours:* NKE Literary Award 2006. *Literary Agent:* Syndykat Autorów, 08–450 Łaskarzew, ul. Lewikow 7B, Poland. *E-mail:* info@syndykatautorow.com.pl. *Website:* www.syndykatautorow.com.pl.

MASON, Bobbie Ann, PhD; American writer; *Writer in Residence, University of Kentucky;* b. 1 May 1940, Mayfield, Ky; d. of Wilburn Arnett and Christy Lee Mason; m. Roger Rawlings 1969. *Education:* Univs of Kentucky and Connecticut and Binghamton Univ., NY. *Career:* short stories have appeared in numerous journals including The New Yorker, Harper's, The North American Review, The Washington Post Magazine, The Atlantic, The Boston Globe Magazine, The Paris Review, Oxford American, DoubleTake; contrib. to journals Esquire and Vanity Fair; Prof., Mansfield Coll., Pa 1972–79; Grantee, Nat. Endowment for the Arts 1983, Pennsylvania Arts Council 1983, 1989; Guggenheim Fellow 1984; Writer in Residence, Univ. of Kentucky 2001–. *Publications include:* Shiloh and Other Stories (Ernest Hemingway Foundation Award 1982, Award of American Acad. and Inst. for Arts and Letters 1984) 1982, In Country (Award for Cultural Contrib. to the Arts, Vietnam Veterans of America 1989, made into feature film 1989) 1985, Spence + Lila 1988, Love Life 1989, Feather Crowns (Southern Book Award) 1993, Midnight Magic 1998, Clear Springs (shortlisted for Pulitzer Prize) 1999, Zigzagging Down A Wild Trail (Southern Book Award) 2001, Elvis Presley (Kentucky Literary Award) 2003, An Atomic Romance 2005, Nancy Culpepper 2006. *Honours:* several short story awards 1981–; Appalachian Medallion Award, Univ. of Charleston 1991, Corrington Award 2005. *Literary Agent:* c/o Amanda Urban, International Creative Management, 825 Eighth Avenue, New York, NY 10019, USA. *Telephone:* (212) 556-5764. *E-mail:* aurban@icmtalent.com. *Website:* www.icmtalent.com. *Address:* Department of English, University of Kentucky, 1239 Patterson Office Tower, Lexington, KY 40506-0027, USA (office). *E-mail:* bamaso2@uky.edu (home). *Website:* www.as.uky.edu/academics (office).

MASON, Connie; American writer; b. 22 April 1930, Niles, MI; m. Lewis G. Mason 1950; one s. two d. *Education:* Buchanan Michigan High School. *Career:* author of historical romance fiction. *Publications:* Tender Fury 1984, Caress and Conquer 1985, For Honor's Sake 1985, Promised Splendour 1986, My Lady Vixen 1986, Desert Ecstasy 1987, Wild is my Heart 1987, Bold Land, Bold Love 1988, Tempt the Devil 1988, Beyond the Horizon 1989, Love me with Fury 1989, Wild Love, Wild Land 1989, Promise Me Forever 1990, Brave Land, Brave Love 1990, Surrender to the Fury 1990, A Frontier Christmas 1990, Ice and Rapture 1991, A Promise of Thunder 1991, Lord of the Night 1991, Treasures of the Heart 1992, Wilderness Christmas 1992, Tears Like Rain 1993, Wind Rider 1993, Their First Noel 1993, Sierra 1994, Christmas Miracle 1994, The Lion's Bride 1994, Taken by You 1996, Pure Temptation 1996, A Love to Cherish 1996, Flame 1997, Shadow Walker 1997, To Love a Stranger 1997, Sheik 1998, Viking 1998, Swept Away 1998, To Tame a Renegade 1998, Pirate 1998, Gunslinger 1999, To Tempt a Rogue 1999, The Outlaws: Rafe 2000, A Taste of Sin 2000, The Outlaws: Jess 2000, A Breath of Scandal 2001, The Outlaws: Sam 2001, The Dragon Lord 2001, A Touch so Wicked 2002, The Rogue and the Hellion 2002, Lionheart 2002, Seduced by a Rogue 2003, The Laird of Stonehaven 2003, The Last Rogue 2004, The Pirate Prince 2004, Gypsy Lover 2005, A Knight's Honor 2005, A Taste of Paradise 2006, Highland Warrior 2007, The Price of Pleasure 2007, Viking Warrior. *Honours:* Career Storyteller of the Year 1992, Romantic Times Achievement Award 1994. *Literary Agent:* Natasha Kern Literary Agency, PO Box 1069, White Salmon, WA 98672, USA. *Telephone:* (509) 493-3803. *Fax:* (509) 493-3826. *E-mail:* natashakern@natashakern.com. *Website:* www.natashakern.com; www.conniemason.com.

MASON, David James, BA, MA, PhD; American academic, poet, critic and writer; *Professor of English, The Colorado College;* b. 11 Dec. 1954, Bellingham, Wash.; s. of James Cameron Mason and Evelyn Mae Peterson; m. Anne Lennox 1988; one step-d. *Education:* Colorado Coll., Univ. of Rochester, NY. *Career:* Visiting Instructor, Colorado Coll. 1983, 1987, Visiting Prof. 1986, 1987, 1988, 1994, Assoc. Prof. 1998–2000, 2002–08, Prof. 2008–; instructor, Univ. of Rochester 1986–88; Asst Prof., Moorhead State Univ. 1989–93, Assoc. Prof. 1993–98. *Publications:* Blackened Peaches 1989, Small Elegies 1990, The Buried Houses 1991, Questions at Christmas 1994, Three Characters from a Lost Home 1995, The Country I Remember 1996, Land Without Grief 1996, Rebel Angels: 25 Poets of the New Formalism (ed. with Mark Jarman) 1996, Kalamitsi 1997, The Poetry of Life and the Life of Poetry (essays) 2000, Western Wind: An Introduction to Poetry (co-ed.) 2000, Twentieth Century American Poetry (co-ed.) 2004, Twentieth Century American Poetics (co-ed.) 2004, Arrivals (poems) 2004, Ludlow: A Verse Novel 2007; News from the Village (memoir) 2010; contrib. to books, reviews, quarterlies and journals. *Honours:* Hon. DHL (Colorado Coll.) 1996; Nicholas Roerich Poetry Prize 1991, Poetry Soc. of America Alice Fay Di Castagnola Award 1993, Minnesota Prof. of the Year, Carnegie Foundation for the Advancement of Teaching and Council for Advancement and Support of Educ. 1994, Fulbright Artist-in-Residence Fellowship (Greece) 1997, Thatcher Hoffman Smith Creativity in Motion Prize 2009. *Address:* 516 Laurel Street, Colorado Springs, CO 80904, USA (home). *Telephone:* (719) 389-6502 (office); (719) 686-1191 (home). *Fax:* (719) 389-6833 (office). *E-mail:* dmason@coloradocollege.edu (office).

MASON, Francis Kenneth, FRHistS; British editor, writer, archivist and researcher; b. 4 Sept. 1928, London, England. *Education:* Royal Air Force Coll., Cranwell. *Career:* Ed., Flying Review Int. 1963–64; Managing Dir, Profile Publications Ltd 1964–67, Alban Book Services Ltd, Watton, Norfolk; Managing Ed., Guinness Superlatives Ltd, Enfield, Middlesex 1968–71. *Publications:* author 91 books and ed. of numerous others 1961–96; contrib. to radio and television. *Honours:* Int. History Diploma, Aero Club of France, Paris 1973, Founder Fellowship, Canadian Guild of Authors 1988. *Address:* 68 Hunter's Oak, Watton, Thetford, Norfolk IP25 6HL, England. *E-mail:* alanfoster@con-brio.com.

MASON, Haydn Trevor, BA, AM, DPhil; British academic and writer; *Professor Emeritus and Senior Research Fellow, University of Bristol;* b. 12 Jan. 1929, Saundersfoot, Pembrokeshire, Wales; s. of Herbert Mason and Margaret Mason; m. 1st Gretchen Reger 1955 (divorced 1982); one s., one d.; m. 2nd Adrienne Mary Barnes 1982. *Education:* Univ. Coll. of Wales, Middlebury Coll., Vermont, Jesus Coll., Oxford. *Career:* instructor, Princeton Univ., USA 1954–57; Lecturer, Univ. of Reading 1964–65, Reader 1965–67; Prof. of European Literature, Univ. of East Anglia 1967–79; Ed. Studies on Voltaire and the Eighteenth Century 1977–95; Prof. of French Literature, Univ. of Paris III 1979–81; Prof. of French, Univ. of Bristol 1981–94, Prof. Emer. and Sr Research Fellow 1994–; Scholar-in-Residence, Univ. of Maryland 1986; Gen. Ed. Complete Works of Voltaire 1998–2001; Pres. Modern Humanities Research Assen 1999; mem. Asscn of Univ. Profs of French (Chair. 1981–82), Soc. for French Studies (Pres. 1982–84), British Soc. for Eighteenth-Century Studies (Pres. 1984–86), Int. Soc. for Eighteenth-Century Studies (Pres. 1991–95), Voltaire Foundation (Dir 1977–97, Chair. 1989–93). *Publications:* Pierre Bayle and Voltaire 1963, Marivaux: Les Fausses Confidences (ed.) 1964, Leibniz-Arnauld Correspondence (trans. and ed.) 1967, Voltaire: Zadig and Other Stories (ed.) 1971, Voltaire 1974, Voltaire: A Life 1981, French Writers and Their Society 1715–1800 1982, Cyrano de Bergerac: L'Autre Monde 1984, Voltaire: Discours en vers sur l'homme (ed.) 1991, Candide: Optimism Demolished 1992, Candide (ed.) 1995, Voltaire: Micromégas and Other Short Fictions 2002, Le Mondain (ed.) 2003, Zadig (ed.) 2004. *Honours:* Hon. Fellow, British Soc. for Eighteenth-Century Studies 2006; Médaille d'Argent de la Ville de Paris 1989, Jt Prizewinner, European Humanities Research Centre Philosophical Dialogue Competition 1998; Officier, Ordre des Palmes académiques 1985. *Address:* 11 Goldney Avenue, Bristol, BS8 4RA, England (home).

MASON, Sarah J., (Hamilton Crane), MA; British novelist; b. 18 Dec. 1949, Bishop's Stortford, Herts., England; m. William G. Welland 1976. *Education:* St Andrews Univ., Scotland. *Career:* mem. CWA, Soc. of Authors. *Publications:* Let's Talk of Wills 1985, Murder in the Maze (Trewley and Stone series) 1993, Frozen Stiff (Trewley and Stone series) 1993, Corpse in the Kitchen (Trewley and Stone series) 1993, Dying Breath (Trewley and Stone series) 1994, Sew Easy to Kill (Trewley and Stone series) 1996, Seeing is Deceiving (Trewley and Stone series) 1997, Death on her Doorstep 2003; as Hamilton Crane: Miss Seeton Cracks the Case 1991, Miss Seeton Paints the Town 1991, Hands Up, Miss Seeton 1992, Miss Seeton by Moonlight 1992, Miss Seeton Rocks the Cradle 1992, Miss Seeton Goes to Bat 1993, Miss Seeton Plants Suspicion 1993, Miss Seeton Rules 1994, Starring Miss Seeton 1994, Miss Seeton Undercover 1994, Sold to Miss Seeton 1995, Sweet Miss Seeton 1996, Bonjour Miss Seeton 1997, Miss Seeton's Finest Hour 1999. *Literary Agent:* c/o Curtis Brown Ltd, Haymarket House, 28–29 Haymarket, London, SW1Y 4SP, England. *Telephone:* (20) 7393-4400. *E-mail:* cb@curtisbrown.co.uk. *Website:* www.curtisbrown.co.uk. *E-mail:* sarahjmason@waitrose.com.

MASON, Stanley Allen, MA; Canadian editor, translator, poet and dramatist; b. 16 April 1917, Blairmore, Alberta; m. Cloris Ielmini 1944; one d. *Education:* Oriel College, Oxford, UK. *Career:* Technical Trans., 1943–63; Literary Ed., Graphis Magazine, 1963–83; Ed., Elements, Dow Chemical Europe house organ, 1969–75. *Publications:* Modern English Structures (with Ronald Ridout), four vols 1968–72; A Necklace of Words (poems) 1975; A Reef of Honours (poems) 1983; Send Out the Dove (play) 1986; The Alps, by Albrecht von Haller (trans.) 1987; The Everlasting Snow (poems) 1993; Collected Poems 1993; A German Treasury (anthology, trans.) 1993–95; contributions: numerous publications. *Honours:* Borestone Mountain Poetry Award, Living Playwright Award.

MASSIE, Allan Johnstone, BA, FRSL; British author; b. 19 Oct. 1938, Singapore; m. Alison Agnes Graham Langlands 1973; two s. one d. *Education:* Trinity Coll., Glenalmond and Trinity Coll., Cambridge. *Career:* fiction reviewer, The Scotsman 1976–; Creative Writing Fellow, Univ. of Edinburgh 1982–84; Univ. of Glasgow and Univ. of Strathclyde 1985–86; Columnist, Glasgow Herald 1985–88, Sunday Times Scotland 1987–, Daily Telegraph 1991–; mem. Scottish Arts Council. *Publications:* fiction: Change and Decay in

All Around I See 1978, The Last Peacock 1980, The Death of Men 1981, One Night in Winter 1984, Augustus: The Memoirs of the Emperor 1986, A Question of Loyalties 1989, The Hanging Tree 1990, Tiberius: The Memoirs of an Emperor 1991, The Sins of the Father 1991, These Enchanted Woods 1993, Caesar 1993, The Ragged Lion 1994, King David 1995, Arthur the King 2003, Caligula 2003, The Thistle and the Rose 2005, Charlemagne and Roland 2007, Surviving 2009, Death in Bordeaux 2010; other: Muriel Spark 1979, Ill Met by Gaslight: Five Edinburgh Murders 1980, The Caesars 1983, Edinburgh and the Borders: In Verse (ed.) 1983, A Portrait of Scottish Rugby 1984, Eisenstadt: Aberdeen, Portrait of a City 1984, Colette: The Woman, the Writer and the Myth 1986, 101 Great Scots 1987, PEN New Fiction: Thirty-Two Short Stories (ed.) 1987, How Should Health Services be Financed? A Patient's View 1988, The Novelist's View of the Market Economy 1988, Byron's Travels 1988, Glasgow: Portraits of a City 1989, The Novel Today: A Critical Guide to the British Novel, 1970–1989 1990, Edinburgh 1994, Scottish Cultural Identity 2006; contributions: periodicals. *Honours:* Niven Award 1981, Scottish Arts Council Award 1982. *Literary Agent:* Curtis Brown Group Ltd, Haymarket House, 28–29 Haymarket, London SW1Y 4SP, England. *Telephone:* (20) 7293-4400. *Fax:* (20) 7393-4401. *E-mail:* info@curtisbrown.co.uk. *Website:* www.curtisbrown.co.uk. *Address:* Thirladean House, Selkirk TD7 5LU, Scotland (home).

MASSIE, Robert Kinloch, BA; American writer; b. 5 Jan. 1929, Lexington, Ky; m. 1st Suzanne L. Rohrbach 1954 (divorced 1990); one s. two d.; m. 2nd Deborah L. Karl 1992; one s. two d. *Education:* Yale Univ., Univ. of Oxford, UK. *Career:* reporter, Collier's magazine, New York 1955–56; writer, Newsweek magazine, New York 1956–62, USA-1 magazine, New York 1962, Saturday Evening Post, New York 1962–65; Ferris Prof. of Journalism, Princeton Univ. 1977, 1985; Mellon Prof. in the Humanities, Tulane Univ. 1981; mem. Authors' Guild of America (Pres. 1987–91), PEN, Soc. of American Historians. *Publications include:* Nicholas and Alexandra 1967, Journey 1976, Peter the Great: His Life and World (Pulitzer Prize for Biography 1981) 1980, Dreadnought: Britain, Germany and the Coming of the Great War 1991, The Romanovs: The Final Chapter 1995, Castles of Steel: Britain, Germany and the Winning of the Great War at Sea 2004, Catherine the Great: Portrait of a Woman 2011; contrib. to periodicals. *Honours:* Christopher Award 1976. *Address:* 60 West Clinton Avenue, Irvington, NY 10533, USA.

MASSON, Jeffrey Moussaieff, BA, PhD; American writer, editor and translator; b. (Jeffrey Lloyd Masson), 28 March 1941, Chicago, Ill.; m. 1st; one d.; m. 2nd Leila Siller; two s. *Education:* Harvard Univ. *Career:* Instructor in Religious Studies, Brown Univ. 1967–68; Asst Prof. of Sanskrit and Indian Studies, Univ. of Toronto 1969–70, Assoc. Prof. 1970–75, Prof. 1976–80; Visiting Prof. of Sanskrit, Univ. of California, Berkeley 1978–79, Research Assoc., Dept of South and Southeast Asian Studies 1981–92, Visiting Lecturer, Graduate School of Journalism 1994; Projects Dir, Sigmund Freud Archives, New York 1980–81; Visiting Part-time Lecturer in Journalism, Univ. of Michigan 1993. *Publications:* Santarasa and Abhinvagupta's Philosophy of Aesthetics (with M. V. Patwardhan) 1969, Avimaraka: Love's Enchanted World (with D. D. Kosambi) 1970, Aesthetic Rapture: The Rasadhyaya of the Natyasastra (with M. V. Patwardhan), two vols 1970, The Oceanic Feeling: The Origins of Religious Sentiment in Ancient India 1980, Love Poems from the Ancient Sanskrit (with W. S. Merwin) 1981, revised edn as The Peacock's Egg 1983, The Assault on Truth: Freud's Suppression of the Seduction Theory 1984, Complete Letters of Sigmund Freud to Wilhelm Fuess, 1887–1904 (ed. and translator) 1985, A Dark Science: Women, Sexuality and Psychiatry in the Nineteenth Century 1987, Against Therapy: Emotional Tyranny and the Myth of Psychological Healing 1988, The Dhvanyaloka of Anandavardhana with the Locana of Abhinavagupta (co-ed. and co-translator) 1990, Final Analysis: The Making and Unmaking of a Psychoanalyst 1991, My Father's Guru: A Journey Through Spirituality and Disillusion 1992, When Elephants Weep: The Emotional Lives of Animals (with Susan McCarthy) 1994, Lost Prince: The Unsolved Mystery of Kaspar Hauser 1996, Dogs Never Lie About Love: The Emotional World of Dogs 1997, The Emperor's Embrace: The Evolution of Fatherhood 1999, Dogs Have the Strangest Friends and Other True Stories of Animal Feelings 1999, The Nine Emotional Lives of Cats 2002, The Pig Who Sang to the Moon: The Emotional World of Farm Animals 2003, The Cat Who Came in From the Cold 2004, Raising the Peaceable Kingdom 2005, Altruistic Armadillos, Zenlike Zebras 2006, The Face on Your Plate: The Truth about Food 2009, The Dog Who Couldn't Stop Loving 2010; contrib. of articles to Atlantic Monthly, International Journal of Psycho-Analysis, New York Times. *Honours:* Hon. Fellow, Dept of Philosophy, Univ. of Auckland, NZ . *Address:* c/o W.W. Norton & Co. Inc., 500 Fifth Avenue, New York, NY 10110, USA (office). *Website:* www.jeffreymasson.com.

MASTER, Simon Harcourt; British publisher; b. 10 April 1944, Caterham; s. of Humphrey R. Master and Rachel B. Plumbly; m. Georgina M. C. Batsford 1969; two s. *Education:* Ardingly Coll. Sussex. *Career:* Publishing Dir Pan Books Ltd 1973–80, Man. Dir 1980–87; Chief Exec. Random House UK and Exec. Vice-Pres. Random House Int. Group 1987–89, Group Man. Dir Random Century Group 1989–90, Group Deputy Chair. 1989–2006, Chair., CEO Gen. Books Div., Random House UK 1992–2006; Chair., Arrow Books 1990–92; Dir (non-exec.) HMSO 1990–95; mem. Council Publrs Asscn 1989–95 (Vice-Pres. 1995–96, 2000–2001, Pres. 1996–97, 2001–02); mem. Advisory Panel, London Book Fair 2008.

MASTERS, Hilary Thomas, AB; American writer and academic; *Professor of English and Creative Writing, Carnegie Mellon University;* b. 3 Feb. 1928, Kansas City, MO; m. 1st Polly Jo McCulloch 1955 (divorced 1986); one s. two d.; m. 2nd Kathleen E. George 1994. *Education:* Davidson Coll., Brown Univ. *Career:* Ed. and Publisher Hyde Park Record newspaper, New York 1956–59; Prof. of English and Creative Writing, Carnegie Mellon Univ. 1983–; several visiting univ. positions; mem. Associated Writing Programs, Authors' Guild, Authors' League of America, PEN Center New York. *Publications:* The Common Pasture 1967, An American Marriage 1969, Palace of Strangers 1971, Last Stands: Notes from Memory 1982, Clemmons 1985, Hammertown Tales 1986, Cooper 1987, Manuscript for Murder 1987, Strickland 1989, Success: New and Selected Stories 1992, Home is the Exile 1996, In Montaigne's Tower 2000, Shadows on a Wall 2005, Elegy for Sam Emerson 2006, In Rooms of Memory (essays) 2009, How the Indians Buried their Dead (short stories) (Ind. Publrs Award for Fiction 2010) 2009, Post, a Fable 2011; contrib. to anthologies and periodicals. *Honours:* Yaddo Fellowships 1980, 1982, 2000, Fulbright Lecturer to Finland 1983, Time magazine Ed.'s Choice 1984, Los Angeles Times Notable Novel 1990, Sewanee Review Monroe Spears Prize 1997, Balch Prize for Fiction 1998, Anchor Best Essays 1998, Best American Essays 1999, American Acad. of Arts and Letters Award for Literature 2003. *Address:* c/o Department of English, Carnegie Mellon University, Pittsburgh, PA 15213, USA (office). *E-mail:* hm05@andrew.cmu.edu (office).

MASTORAKI, Jenny; Greek poet and translator; b. 1949, Athens. *Education:* Athens Univ. *Publications:* The Legend of Saint Youth 1971, Tolls 1972, Kin 1979, Tales of the Deep 1983, With a Crown of Life 1989; contrib. to The Rehearsal of Misunderstanding: Three Collections by Contemporary Greek Women Poets 1998.

MATAR, Hisham; Libyan writer; b. 1970, New York, NY, USA. *Publications:* Amorous/Amatory: Poems 1998, In the Country of Men (novel) (Commonwealth Writers' Prize Best First Book – Europe and South Asia 2007, Ondaatje Prize 2007) 2006. *Address:* c/o Penguin Books Ltd, 80 Strand, London, WC2R 0RL, England (office).

MATAR, Salim; Iraqi writer and journalist; b. 1956, Baghdad. *Career:* left Iraq 1978; has lived in Syria and Italy, now in Geneva, Switzerland; Ed. Mesopotamia review 2004–. *Publications include (in translation):* The Woman of the Flask (novel) (al-Naqid Award) 1990, The Lost Twin 2000, The Dialogue of Identities. *Website:* www.salim-matar.com.

MATAS, Carol Rosaline, BA; Canadian writer; b. 14 Nov. 1949, Winnipeg, Man.; d. of Roy Matas and Ruth Matas; m. Per K. Brask 1977; one s. one d. *Education:* Univ. of Western Ontario, Actors' Lab, London, UK. *Career:* Visiting Prof., Bemidji State Univ. Minnesota; Creative Writing Instructor, Continuing Educ. Div., Univ. of Winnipeg; mem. Manitoba Writers Guild, Soc. of Children's Book Writers and Illustrators, Writer's Union of Canada. *Publications:* The D.N.A Dimension 1982, The Fusion Factor 1986, Zanu 1986, Me, Myself and I 1987, Lisa (aka Lisa's War) 1987, Jesper (aka Code Name Kris) 1989, Adventure in Legoland 1991, The Race 1991, Sworn Enemies 1993, Safari Adventure in Legoland 1993, Daniel's Story 1993, The Lost Locket 1994, The Burning Time 1994, Of Two Minds (with Perry Nodelman) 1994, The Primrose Path 1995, After the War 1996, More Minds (with Perry Nodelman) 1996, The Freak 1997, The Garden 1997, Greater Than Angels 1998, Telling 1998, Out of Their Minds 1998, Cloning Miranda 1999, In My Enemy's House 1999, Meeting of Minds 1999, Rebecca 2000, The War Within 2001, The Second Clone 2001, Sparks Fly Upwards 2001, Gotcha! Rosie in New York City 2003, Playball! Rosie in Chicago 2003, Action! Rosie in LA 2004, Turned Away 2005, The Dark Clone 2005, Turned Away 2005, Past Crimes 2006, Visions 2007, The Whirlwind 2007, The Proof that Ghosts Exist (with Perry Nodelman) 2008, Far 2008, The Curse of The Evening Eye (with Perry Nodelman) 2009, Tales of a Reluctant Psychic 2009, The Hunt for The Haunted Elephant (with Perry Nodelman) 2010. *Honours:* many awards and citations for young people's literature. *Literary Agent:* c/o David Bennett, TLA Inc., 72 Glengowan Road, Toronto, ON M4N 1G4, Canada. *Telephone:* (416) 488-9214. *Fax:* (416) 488-4531. *E-mail:* david@tla1.com. *Website:* www.tla1.com; www.carolmatas.com.

MATESIS, Pavlos; Greek novelist, playwright and translator; b. 7 Dec. 1935, Lampia, Arcadia; s. of Vassilios and Euphrosyme Matesis; single. *Career:* drama teacher, Stavrakos Drama School, Athens 1966–74; Asst to Art Counsellor, Nat. Theatre of Greece 1974–76; mem. Artistic Council, Nat. Theatre of Greece 1994–96. *Plays:* 13 full-length plays produced including The Ceremony 1967 (State Theatre Prize 1967), The Ghost of Ramon Novaro Esq 1973, Exile 1984, Nurseryman 1989 (Karolos Koun City of Athens Award 1989), Towards Eleusis 1995, Guardian Angel for Rent 2003; eight plays by Aristophanes translated into modern Greek, as well as plays by Shakespeare, Molière, Beckett, Pinter, Ionesco, Genet, etc. *Publications:* fiction: Mother of the Dog (Grecophonie Prize 1999, Giuseppe Acerbi Prize 2002), The Ancient of the Days, Always Well, Sylvan Substances, Dark Gerryman, The Daughter (Greek Critics Award) 1990, Myrtos, Contemporary Greek Theatre Vol. 2 (four plays) 2002; translations of novels by Ackroyd, Faulkner, Alain Fournier, Artaud etc. *Address:* c/o Arcadia Books, 15-16 Nassau Street, London, W1W 7AB, England (office); E. Benaki 146A, 11473 Athens, Greece (home). *Telephone:* (210) 3304024 (also fax) (home). *E-mail:* pavlos.matessis@yahoo.gr (home).

MATHESON, Alex (see Mackay, James Alexander)

MATHESON, Richard Burton, BA; American writer and dramatist; b. 20 Feb. 1926, Allendale, NJ; m. Ruth Ann Woodson 1952, two s. two d. *Education:* University of Missouri. *Career:* mem. Dramatists' Guild, Writers' Guild. *Publications include:* novels: Someone is Bleeding 1953, Fury on Sunday 1953, I Am Legend 1954, The Shrinking Man 1956, A Stir of Echoes 1958, Ride the Nightmare 1959, The Beardless Warriors 1960, Hell House 1971, Bid Time Return 1975, What Dreams May Come 1978, Earthbound 1982, Through Channels 1989, Journal of the Gun Years 1991, The Gunfight 1993, 7 Steps to Midnight 1993, Shadow on the Sun 1994, The Memoirs of Wild Bill Hickock 1995, Now You See It… 1995, Passion Play 2000, Hunger and Thirst 2000, Hunted Past Reason 2002, Woman 2006; other: Born of Man and Woman: Tales of Science Fiction and Fantasy 1954, The Shores of Space 1957, Shock: Thirteen Tales to Thrill and Terrify 1961, Shock II 1964, Shock III 1966, Shock Waves 1970, By the Gun: Six from Richard Matheson 1993, Shadow on the Sun 1993, By the Gun 1993, The Path 1993, The Memoirs of Wild Bill Harris 1996, The Twilight Zone Scripts of Richard Matheson 1998, Nightmare at 20,000 Feet 2000, Hunger and Thirst 2000, Camp Pleasant 2001, ABU and the 7 Marvels 2002, A Primer of Reality 2002, Duel 2002, Offbeat 2002, Darker Places 2004, Unrealized Dreams 2004, Duel and The Distributor 2005, Button, Button: Uncanny Stories 2008, Uncollected Matheson: Vol. 1 2008, Uncollected Matheson: Vol. 2 2010; non-fiction: The Path: Metaphysics for the '90s 1993, Robert Bloch: Appreciations of the Master (ed. with Ricia Mainhardt) 1995, Mediums Rare 2000; other: many screenplays. *Honours:* Hugo Award, World Science Fiction Convention, 1958; Writers' Guild Awards, 1960, 1974; World Fantasy Award, 1976, and Life Achievement Award, 1984; Bram Stoker Award, 1990. *Address:* Gauntlet Press, Inc., 5307 Arroyo Street, Colorado Springs, CO 80922, USA (office). *Telephone:* (719) 591-5566 (office). *E-mail:* info@gauntletpress.com (office). *Website:* www.gauntletpress.com (office).

MATHEWS, Harry, BA; American writer, poet, editor and translator; b. (Henry Burchell Mathews), 14 Feb. 1930, New York, NY; m. Marie Chaix; one s. *Education:* Princeton Univ., Harvard Univ., L'École Normale de Musique, Paris. *Career:* writes under pseudonym, Harry Mathews; faculty mem., Bennington Coll.; Visiting Lecturer, Temple Univ., New School, Brown Univ.; mem. Ouvroir de Littérature Potentielle (Oulipo), France. *Publications:* prose: The Conversions 1962, The Tlooth 1966, The Sinking of the Odradek Stadium and Other Novels 1975, Selected Declarations of Dependence 1977, Country Cooking and Other Stories 1980, Cigarettes 1987, The Orchard (memoirs) 1988, Twenty Lines a Day 1988, Singular Pleasures 1988, The American Experience 1991, Immeasurable Distances (criticism) 1991, The Journalist 1994, Oulipo Compendium (co-ed.) 1998, Sainte Catherine 2000, The Human Country 2002, The Case of the Persevering Maltese: Collected Essays 2003, My Life in CIA: A Chronicle of 1973 2005; poetry: The Planisphere 1974, Trial Impressions 1977, Armenian Papers 1987, Out of Bounds 1989, A Mid-Season Sky 1992; contrib. to numerous anthologies, reviews, quarterlies and journals. *Honours:* Chevalier, Ordre des Arts et des Lettres; Nat. Endowment for the Arts grant 1982, American Acad. and Inst. of Arts and Letters Award 1991, Award for Fiction Writing, American Acad. of Arts and Letters. *Literary Agent:* c/o Melanie Jackson, 41 West 72nd Street, Suite 3F, New York, NY 10023, USA. *Telephone:* (212) 873-3373. *E-mail:* m.jackson@mjalit.com. *Address:* 619 Grinnell Street, Key West, FL 33040, USA (office); 67, rue de Grenelle, 75007 Paris, France (office). *E-mail:* hmathews2@cs.com (office).

MATHIS-EDDY, Darlene, PhD; American poet and academic; *Professor Emerita, Ball State University*; b. 19 March 1937, Elkhart, Ind.; d. of the late William Eugene Mathis and Fern Roose Paulmer Mathis; m. Spencer Livingston Eddy, Jr 1964 (died 1971). *Education:* Goshen Coll. and Rutgers Univ. *Career:* Instructor in English, Douglass Coll. 1962–64; Instructor in English, Rutgers Univ. 1964, 1965, Rutgers Univ. Coll. (Adult Educ.) 1967; Asst Prof. in English, Ball State Univ. 1967–71, Assoc. Prof. 1971–75, Prof. 1975–99, Poet-in-Residence 1989–93, Prof. Emer., English and Humanities 1999–, Ralph S. Whitinger Lecturer, Ball State Univ. Honors Coll. 1998–99; Adjunct Prof., Core Program and Coll. Seminar Program, Univ. of Notre Dame, South Bend, Ind. 2001–06; Consulting Ed. Blue Unicorn 1995–; Founding Ed. The Hedge Row Press 1995–; mem. Comm. on Women for the Nat. Council of Teachers of English 1976–79; Poetry Ed. BSU Forum; Vice-Pres. of Programs, American Asscn of Univ. Women, Elkhart Br.; Pres. American Asscn of Univ. Women 2008–. *Publications:* Leaf Threads, Wind Rhymes 1986, The Worlds of King Lear 1971, Weathering 1992, Reflections: Studies in Light 1993; Contributing Ed. Snowy Egret 1988–90; numerous poems in literary reviews; book reviews and essays in numerous journals; articles in American Literature, English Language Notes, etc. *Honours:* Woodrow Wilson Nat. Fellow 1959–62, Rutgers Univ. Grad. Honors and Honors Dissertation Fellow 1964–65, 1966–67, Notable Woodrow Wilson Nat. Fellow 1991; numerous creative arts, creative teaching, research grants and awards. *Address:* 1840 West Cobblestone Boulevard, Elkhart, IN 46514-4961, USA (home). *Telephone:* (574) 266-4394 (home).

MATRAY, James Irving, BA, MA, PhD; American academic and writer; *Professor of History, California State University, Chico*; b. 6 Dec. 1948, Chicago, IL; m. Mary Karin Heine 1971; one s. one d. *Education:* Lake Forest Coll., Univ. of Virginia. *Career:* Visiting Asst Prof. 1980–82, Asst Prof. 1982–87, Assoc. Prof. 1987–92, Prof. of History 1992–2002, New Mexico State Univ.; Visiting Assoc. Prof. of History, Univ. of Southern California 1988–89; Distinguished Visiting Scholar, Kyung Hee Univ., Seoul 1990; Dept Chair, Prof. of History, California State Univ., Chico 2002–; mem. American Historical Asscn, Soc. for Historians of American Foreign Relations; mem. Bd of Eds, Diplomatic History 2005–07. *Publications:* The Reluctant Crusade: American Foreign Policy in Korea 1941–1950 1985, Historical Dictionary of the Korean War 1991, Korea and the Cold War: Division, Destruction, and Disarmament (ed. with Kim Chull-Baum) 1993, Japan's Emergence as a Global Power 2000, East Asia and the United States: An Encyclopedia of Relations Since 1784, Korea Divided: The 38th Parallel and the DMZ; contrib. to many scholarly books and journals. *Honours:* several research grants, Soc. for Historians of American Relations Stuart L. Bernath Article Award (co-recipient) 1980, Best Reference Book Award, Library Journal 1992, Outstanding Academic Book Award, Choice 1992 recipient Bautzer Advancement 2003. *Address:* 246 Eagle Nest Drive, Chico, CA 95928, USA.

MATSON, Clive, MFA; American writer and teacher; *CEO, WordSwell*; b. 13 March 1941, Los Angeles; s. of Randolph Matson and Evelyn Ghia Vincent; m. Gail Ford 1993 (divorced); one s. *Education:* Univ. of Chicago, Columbia Univ., New York. *Career:* poetry readings 1964–; Instructor in Creative Writing, Univ. of California extension at Berkeley 1985–2009, John F. Kennedy Univ., Orinda, Calif. 1993–95; has taught more than 3,000 creative writing workshops; Founder and CEO WordSwell (non-profit org.), revived 2010. *Plays:* Cactus (first workshop production, 42nd Street, New York 1990), Nobody's Business (first workshop production, Marin Theatre Co., Calif. 1995). *Publications:* Mainline to the Heart 1966 (reissued 2009), Space Age 1969, Heroin 1972, On the Inside 1982, Equal in Desire 1983, Hourglass 1987, Breath of Inspiration (essay) 1987, Let the Crazy Child Write 1998, Squish Boots 2002, An Eye for an Eye Makes the Whole World Blind: Poets on 9/11 (co-ed. with Allen Cohen) 2002, Chalcedony's First Ten Songs 2007, Chalcedony's Second Ten Songs 2010; contrib. to anthologies and journals. *Honours:* Columbia Univ. Grad. Writing Fellowship 1987–88, PEN Oakland Josephine Miles Nat. Literary Award 2003. *Address:* 472 44th Street, Oakland, CA 94609, USA (office). *Telephone:* (510) 654-6495 (office). *E-mail:* clive@matsonpoet.com (office). *Website:* www.matsonpoet.com.

MATSUURA, Rieko; Japanese author; b. 7 Aug. 1958, Matsuyama, Ehime. *Education:* Aoyama Gakuin Univ. *Publications include:* The Day of the Funeral (Bungakuki New Writers Award 1978) 1980, Sebastian 1981, Natural Woman 1987, Apprenticeship of Big Toe P (Women Writers Prize 1994) 1993, Drowning Counseling Service 1998, Opposite Version 2007, Kenshin 2007; several essays. *Address:* c/o Kodansha Europe Limited, 40 Stockwell Street, Greenwich, London, SE10 8EY (office); c/o Asahi Shimbun Publishing, The Asahi Shimbun Company, 6th Floor, Halton House, 20–23 Holborn, London, EC1N 2JD, England (office). *Telephone:* (20) 8293-0111 (Kodansha) (office); (20) 7831-0033 (Asahi Shimbun) (office). *Fax:* (20) 7430-1597 (office). *E-mail:* info@kodansha.eu (office); adsales@asahi.uk.com (office). *Website:* www.kodansha.eu (office); adv.asahi.com/english/contact.html (office).

MATTESON, Stefanie Newton, BA; American writer; b. 9 Oct. 1946, Hackensack, NJ; m. 1st David Bruce Matteson 1971 (divorced 1994); one s. one d.; m. 2nd Richard Leon Grocholski 1994 (divorced 2002). *Education:* Skidmore Coll., Saratoga Springs, NY, Boston Univ., School of Public Communications. *Career:* mem. MWA (dir New York chapter 1996–97), Sisters in Crime. *Publications:* Murder at the Spa 1990, Murder at Teatime 1991, Murder on the Cliff 1991, Murder on the Silk Road 1992, Murder at the Falls 1993, Murder on High 1994, Murder Among the Angels 1996, Murder Under the Palms 1997. *Address:* Dominick Abel Literary Agency, 146 W 82nd Street, No. 1B, New York, NY 10024, USA (office). *Telephone:* (908) 955-4767 (home).

MATTHEW, Christopher Charles Forrest, MA (Hons) (Oxon.); British novelist, journalist and broadcaster; b. 8 May 1939, London; m. Wendy Mary Matthew 1979; two s. one d. *Education:* King's School, Canterbury (King's Scholar), St Peter's Coll., Oxford. *Career:* Ed. Times Travel Guide 1972–73; columnist, Punch 1983–88; restaurant critic, Vogue (UK) 1983–86; book and TV reviewer, Daily Mail 1997–2009; columns in Daily Telegraph, Observer; Chair./presenter for BBC Radio 4: Sound Archive Features 1972–74, Something to Declare 1977–82, Points of Departure 1980–82, Invaders 1982–83, The Travelling Show 1982–85, Fourth Column 1990–93, Plain Tales from the Rhododendrons 1991, Cold Print 1992, A Nest of Singing Birds 1996, Freedom Pass with Alan Coren 2003–06, Touchline Tales with Des Lynam 2010–; mem. Soc. of Authors, Chelsea Arts Club. *Stage play:* Summoned by Betjeman, with Robert Daws 2002–. *Radio:* plays: A Portrait of Richard Hillary 1980, Madonna's Plumber 2003, A Nightingale Sang in Fernhurst Road 2007; short stories for BBC Radio 4 2005–. *Television:* Three More Men in a Boat 1983, A Perfect Hero (adapted from The Long-Haired Boy) 1991, The Good Guys 1992–93. *Publications:* A Different World: Stories of Great Hotels 1976, Diary of a Somebody 1978, Loosely Engaged 1980, The Long Haired Boy 1980, The Crisp Report 1981, Three Men in a Boat (annotated edn with Benny Green) 1982, The Junket Man 1983, How to Survive Middle Age 1983, Family Matters 1987, The Amber Room 1995, A Nightingale Sang in Fernhurst Road 1998, Now We Are Sixty 1999, Knocking On 2001, Now We Are Sixty (And a Bit) 2003, Summoned by Balls 2005, When We Were Fifty 2007; contrib. to newspapers, magazines and TV. *Address:* 4 Fleming House, 20 Danvers Street, London, SW3 5AT, England (home). *Telephone:* (20) 7244-7004 (office). *E-mail:* cmatt@onetel.com (home).

MATTHIAS, John Edward, BA, MA; American academic, poet, writer and translator; *Professor Emeritus, University of Notre Dame*; b. 5 Sept. 1941, Columbus, OH; m. Dianna Clare Jocelyn 1967; two c. *Education:* Ohio State

Univ., Stanford Univ., Univ. of London. *Career:* Asst Prof., Univ. of Notre Dame 1967–73, Assoc. Prof. 1973–80, Prof. 1980–2005, Emer. 2005–; Visiting Fellow in Poetry, Clare Hall, Cambridge 1976–77, Assoc. 1977–80; Visiting Prof., Skidmore Coll. 1978, Univ. of Chicago 1980; mem. American Literary Trans Asscn, PEN American Center, Poetry Soc. of America. *Publications:* Bucyrus 1971, 23 Modern Poets (ed.) 1971, Turns 1975, Crossing 1979, Five American Poets (ed.) 1979, Contemporary Swedish Poetry (trans. with Goran Printz-Pahlson) 1979, Barthory and Lermontov 1980, Northern Summer: New and Selected Poems 1984, David Jones: Man and Poet 1989, Tva Dikter 1989, A Gathering of Ways 1991, Reading Old Friends 1992, Selected Works of David Jones 1993, Swimming at Midnight: Selected Shorter Poems 1995, Beltane at Aphelion: Collected Longer Poems 1995, Pages: New Poems and Cuttings 2000, Working Progress, Working Title 2002, New Selected Poems 2004, Kedging 2006, Trigons 2010; contrib. to numerous anthologies, reviews, quarterlies and journals. *Honours:* Fulbright Grant 1966, Swedish Inst. Trans. Award 1977–78, Columbia Univ. Trans. Award 1978, Ingram Merrill Foundation Awards 1984, 1990, Soc. of Midland Authors Poetry Award 1986, Soc. for the Study of Midwestern Literature Poetry Prize 1986, Slobodan Janovic Literary Prize 1989, Poetry Soc. of America George Bogin Memorial Award 1990, Lilly Endowment grant 1991–92, Ohio Library Asscn Poetry Award 1996. *Address:* 840 Park Avenue, South Bend, IN 46616-1338 (home); c/o Department of English, University of Notre Dame, 201 Decio Faculty Hall, Notre Dame, IN 46556, USA (office). *Telephone:* (574) 287-0735 (home). *E-mail:* matthias.1@nd.edu (office).

MATTHIESSEN, Peter, BA; American writer and editor; *Founding Editor, The Paris Review*; b. 22 May 1927, New York; s. of Erard A. Matthiessen and Elizabeth Matthiessen (née Carey); m. 1st Patricia Southgate 1951 (divorced); m. 2nd Deborah Love 1963 (died 1972); three s. one d.; m. 3rd Maria Eckhart 1980. *Education:* Sorbonne, Paris, Yale Univ. *Career:* Co-founder and now Founding Ed. The Paris Review 1953–; ordained a Zen Monk 1981; fmr corresp., New Yorker; Trustee, New York Zoological Soc. 1965–78; mem. American Acad. of Arts and Letters 1974–, Nat. Inst. of Arts and Science 1986–. *Publications:* Race Rock 1954, Partisans 1955, Wildlife in America 1959, Raditzer 1960, The Cloud Forest 1961, Under the Mountain Wall 1963, At Play in the Fields of the Lord 1965, The Shore Birds of North America 1967, Oomingmak: The Expedition to the Musk Ox Island in the Bering Sea 1967, Sal si puedes 1969, Blue Meridian 1971, The Tree Where Man Was Born 1972, The Wind Birds 1973, Far Tortuga 1975, The Snow Leopard 1978, Sand Rivers 1981, In the Spirit of the Crazy Horse 1983, Indian Country 1984, Midnight Turning Grey 1984, Nine-Headed Dragon River 1986, Men's Lives 1986, Partisans 1987, On the River Styx 1989, Killing Mr Watson 1990, African Silences 1991, Baikal 1992, Shadows of Africa 1992, East of Lo Monthang: In the Land of Mustang 1995, Lost Man's River 1997, Bone by Bone (novel) 1999, Tigers in the Snow 2000, Peter Matthiessen Reader: Non Fiction 1959-1991 2000, An African Trilogy 2000, Sal si Puedes – Cesar Chávez and the New American Revolution 2000, Birds of Heaven: Travels with Cranes 2001, Ends of the Earth: Voyages to Antarctica 2003, Shadow Country: A New Rendering of the Watson Legend (Nat. Book Award for Fiction) 2008. *Honours:* Atlantic Prize 1950, American Acad. of Arts and Letters Award 1963, National Book Award 1978, John Burroughs Medal 1981, African Wildlife Leadership Foundation Award 1982, Gold Medal for Distinction in Natural History 1985, Orion-John Hay Award 1999, Soc. of Conservation Biologists Award 1999, Heinz Award for Arts and Humanities 2000, Lannan Lifetime Achievement Award 2002, Harvard Nat. History Museum Roger Tory Peterson Medal 2003. *Address:* The Paris Review, 62 White Street, New York, NY 10013, USA (office). *Website:* www.parisreview.com (office).

MATTINGLEY, Christobel Rosemary, AM, BA, DUnivSA, ALAA; Australian writer; b. (Christobel Rosemary Shepley), 26 Oct. 1931, Adelaide, S Australia; d. of Arthur Raymond Shepley and Isabelle Margaret Mary Shepley; m. Cecil David Mattingley 1953; two s. one d. *Education:* Presbyterian Ladies' Coll., Pymble, NSW, The Friends' School, Hobart, Tasmania, Univ. of Tasmania Library Training School, State Library of Victoria. *Career:* librarian 1951–57, 1966–74; freelance writer, lecturer, ed., researcher 1975–; Assoc., Library Asscn of Australia 1971; Patron Soc. of Women Writers SA 1998–. *Film scripts:* Children's Libraries 1979, Woman Artists of Australia 1980. *Publications include:* The Picnic Dog 1970, Windmill at Magpie Creek 1971, Worm Weather 1971, Emu Kite 1972, Queen of the Wheat Castles 1973, The Surprise Mouse 1974, Tiger's Milk 1974, The Battle of the Galah Trees 1974, Show and Tell 1974, Lizard Log 1975, The Great Ballagundi Damper Bake 1975, The Long Walk 1976, New Patches for Old 1977, The Special Present 1977, The Big Swim 1977, Budgerigar Blue 1978, The Jetty 1978, Black Dog 1979, Rummage 1981, Brave with Ben 1982, Lexl and the Lion Party 1982, The Magic Saddle 1983, Duck Boy 1983, Southerly Buster 1983, The Angel with a Mouth Organ 1984, Ghost Sitter 1984, The Miracle Tree 1985, McGruer and the Goat 1987, Survival in Our Own Land: Aboriginal Experiences in South Australia since 1836 1988, The Butcher, the Beagle and the Dog Catcher 1990, Tucker's Mob 1992, The Sack 1993, No Gun for Asmir 1993, The Race 1995, Asmir in Vienna 1995, Escape from Sarajevo 1996, Ginger 1997, Daniel's Secret 1997, Work Wanted 1998, Hurry up Alice 1998, Cockawun and Cockatoo 1999, First Friend 2000, King of the Wilderness 2001, Ruby of Trowutta 2003, Nest Egg 2005, Battle Order 204 2007, Chelonia Green, Champion of Turtles 2008; contrib. to Australian Library Journal, New Zealand Libraries, Landfall, Reading Time, Classroom, Magpies, Something About the Author Autobiography Series, National Library of Australia News, Word of Mouth; also writes poetry. *Honours:* Hon. DUniv (South Australia) 1995; Christobel Mattingley Young Writers' Award inaugurated by City of S Perth, WA 1987, Advance Australia Award 1990, Pheme Tanner Award, La Trobe Univ. 1999, Lifetime Recognition Award 2004. *Literary Agent:* c/o Curtis Brown, 2 Boundary Street, Paddington, NSW 2021, Australia. *Telephone:* (2) 9331-5301. *E-mail:* fiona@curtisbrown.com.au. *Website:* www.curtisbrown.com.au. *Address:* 10 Rosebank Terrace, Stonyfell, S Australia 5066, Australia (home).

MATURA, Mustapha; Trinidadian/British playwright; b. (Noel Mathura), 17 Dec. 1939, Trinidad; m. Ingrid Selberg. *Education:* Belmont Boys Intermediate School, Trinidad. *Career:* moved to England 1961. *Plays:* Black Pieces (ICA, London) 1970, As Time Goes By (Traverse Theatre, Edinburgh) 1971, Bakerloo Line (Almost Free, London) 1972, Nice (Almost Free, London) 1973, Play Mas (Royal Court, London) 1974, Black Slaves, White Chains (Royal Court Theatre Upstairs, London) 1975, Bread (Young Vic, London) 1976, Rum An' Coca Cola (Royal Court, London) 1976, Another Tuesday (ICA, London) 1978, More, More (ICA, London) 1978, Independence (Bush Theatre, London) 1979, Welcome Home Jacko (Factory, London) 1979, A Dying Business (Riverside Studios, London) 1980, Meetings (Phoenix Theatre, New York) 1981, One Rule (Riverside Studios, London) 1981, The Playboy of the West Indies (Oxford) 1984, The Trinidad Sisters (Donmar Warehouse, London) 1988, The Coup: A Play of Revolutionary Dreams (London) 1991, A Small World (Southwark Playhouse, London) 1996, Three Sisters (regional tour) 2007. *Television writing:* No Problem (sitcom, Channel 4) 1983. *Honours:* George Deveine Award 1971, John Whiting Award 1971, Evening Standard Most Promising Playwright Award 1974, Helen Hayes Award 1994. *Literary Agent:* Judy Daish Associates Ltd, 2 St Charles Place, London, W10 6EG, England. *Telephone:* (20) 8964-8811. *Fax:* (20) 8964-8966. *E-mail:* judy@judydaish.demon.co.uk. *E-mail:* info@mustaphamatura.com (office). *Website:* www.mustaphamatura.com.

MATURA, Thaddée, LicTh, LicSS; French/Canadian Franciscan monk, theologian and scholar; b. 24 Oct. 1922, Zalesie Wielkie, Poland. *Education:* Pontificio Ateneo Antoniano, Rome, Studio Biblico Francescano, Jerusalem. *Career:* entered Franciscan Order 1940; mem. Tantur Ecumenical Inst., Jerusalem 1973–75; religious counsellor, all cloistered monasteries, France 1981–90. *Publications:* Célibat et communauté: Les Fondements évangéliques de la vie religieuse (trans. as Celibacy and Community: The Gospel Foundation for Religious Life) 1967, La Vie religieuse au tournant (trans. as The Crisis of Religious Life) 1971, Readings in Franciscanism (ed. with Dacian Francis Bluma) 1972, La Naissance d'un charisme (trans. as The Birth of a Movement) 1973, Le Projet évangélique de François d'Assise aujourd-hui (trans. as The Gospel Life of Francis of Assisi Today) 1977, Le Radicalisme évangélique (trans. as Gospel Radicalism) 1978, Franz von Assisi (with Anton Rotzetter, trans. as Gospel Living: Francis of Assisi Yesterday and Today) 1981, François d'Assise, Ecrits (with Theophile Desbonnets) 1981, Suivre Jésus 1983, Claire d'Assise, Ecrits (with Marie-France Becker) 1985, Une Absence ardente 1988, Dieu le Père trés saint 1990, Chants de terre étrangere 1991, Prier 15 jours avec François d'Assise (trans. as A Dwelling Place for the Most High) 1994, François d'Assise 'auteur spirituel' (trans. as Francis of Assisi: The Message in his Writings) 1996, François d'Assise, maître de vie spirituelle (trans. as Francis of Assisi, Writer and Spiritual Master) 2000, François d'Assise, héritage et héritiers huit siècles après 2008. *Address:* 33 rue de la Porte-Evèque, 84000 Avignon, France (home). *Telephone:* (4) 32-76-86-55 (home). *E-mail:* thaddee.matura@wanadoo.fr (home).

MATVEJEVIC, Predrag, PhD; Croatian writer; b. 1932, Mostar. *Education:* Sarajevo. Univ., Zagreb Univ., Univ. of Paris, Sorbonne. *Career:* moved to France 1991; currently lives in Rome, Italy; fmr Prof. of French Literature, Zagreb Univ., Prof. of Comparative Literatures, Sorbonne, Paris, Catholic Univ., Prof. of Slavic Studies, La Sapienza Univ., Rome; Vice-Pres., Int. PEN, London; Pres., Foundation Laboratori Mediterraneo, Naples; f. mem. Sarajevo Asscn (Paris and Rome). *Publications:* Ces Moulins à vent 1977, Pour une poétique de l'événement 1979, La Yougoslavité d'aujourd'hui 1982, Lettres Ouvertes - exercices de morale 1985, Bréviaire Méditerranéen (Prix Européen Ch. Veillon à Genève, Prix Malaparte à Capri) 1987, Epistolaire asile et exil 1995, Sarajevo Motta 1995, Ex Jugoslavia. Diario di una guerra 1995, Le Monde Ex1996, Tra asilo ed esilio 1998, Il Mediterraneo e l'Europa lezioni al College de France 1998, I signori della guerra 1999, Isolario mediterraneo 2000, L'Autre Venise 2004. *Honours:* Légion d'honneur; European Essay Prize 1992, French European Book Prize 1993. *Address:* 10000 Zagreb, Jurisiceva 1A, Croatia (office). *E-mail:* matvejevic@mclink.it (office). *Website:* giardini.sm/matvejevic.

MATVEYEVA, Novella Nikolaevna; Russian poet and chansonnier; b. 7 Oct. 1934, Pushkin, nr Leningrad; d. of Nikolai Nikolaevich Matveye-Bodryi and Nadejda Timofeevna Matveyeva (Orleneva); m. Ivan Semyonovich Kiuru 1963. *Recordings:* A Gipsy Girl 1966, What a Strong Wind! 1966, Poems and Songs 1973, A Princess on a Peascod 1980, A Trail is my Home 1982, (with Ivan Kiuru) The Music of Light 1984, My Small Raven 1985, Ballads 1985, A Red-haired Girl 1986, The Unseverable Circle 1991, (with I. Kiuru) The Poetic Dialogue 1993, (with I. Kiuru) Hosanna to Skhodnya 1993, Sonnets to Dashkova 1994, Minuet 1994. *Publications:* Lirika 1961, Little Ship 1963, Selected Lyrics 1964, The Soul of Things 1966, Reflection of a Sunbeam 1966, School for Swallows 1973, River 1978, The Song's Law 1983, The Land of the Surf 1983, Rabbit's Village 1984, Selected Works 1986, Praising the Labour 1987, An Unseverable Circle 1988, Poems 1988; (play) The Foretelling of an

Eagle (in Theatre magazine) 1988. *Address:* 103009 Moscow, Kammergerski per. 2, Apt. 42, Russia (office). *Telephone:* (495) 292-33-61 (office).

MAUGARLONNE, Mathurin (see George, François)

MAUPIN, Armistead Jones, Jr; American writer; b. 13 May 1944, s. of Armistead Jones Maupin and the late Diana Jane (née Barton) Maupin. *Education:* Univ. of North Carolina. *Career:* reporter, News and Courier, Charleston, SC 1970–71; Associated Press, San Francisco 1971–72; Account Exec. Lowry Russom and Leeper Public Relations 1973; columnist, Pacific Sun Magazine 1974; publicist, San Francisco Opera 1975; serialist, San Francisco Chronicle 1976–77, 1981, 1983; Commentator K.R.O.N.-TV San Francisco 1979; serialist, San Francisco Examiner 1986; Exec. Producer Armistead Maupin's Tales of the City 1993; contrib. to New York Times, Los Angeles Times and others. *Film:* The Night Listener (adapted from his book, exec. prod.) 2006. *Publications:* Tales of the City (Big Gay Read Award 2006) 1978, More Tales of the City 1980, Further Tales of the City 1982, Babycakes 1984, Significant Others 1987, Sure of You 1989, 28 Barbary Lane 1990, Back to Barbary Lane 1991, Maybe the Moon 1992, The Essential Clive Baker (co-author) 1999, The Night Listener 2000, Michael Tolliver Lives 2007, Mary Ann in Autumn 2010; as librettist: Heart's Desire 1990. *Honours:* numerous awards, including: Freedom Leadership Award, Freedoms Foundation 1972, Communications Award, Metropolitan Elections Comm., LA 1989, Exceptional Achievement Award, American Libraries Asscn 1990, Outstanding Miniseries Award, Gay and Lesbian Alliance Against Defamation 1994. *Address:* c/o Literary Bent, PO Box 4109990, Suite 528, San Francisco, CA 94141 (office); c/o Amanda Urban, 40 West 57th Street, Floor 16, New York, NY 10019, USA. *E-mail:* inquiries@literarybent.cor (office).

MAVOR, Elizabeth Osborne; British author; b. 17 Dec. 1927, Glasgow, Scotland. *Education:* St Andrews, and St Leonard's and St Anne's Colleges, Oxford. *Publications:* Summer in the Greenhouse, 1959; The Temple of Flora, 1961; The Virgin Mistress: A Biography of the Duchess of Kingston (aka The Virgin Mistress: A Study in Survival: The Life of the Duchess of Kingston) 1964; The Redoubt, 1967; The Ladies of Llangollen: A Study in Romantic Friendship, 1971; A Green Equinox, 1973; Life with the Ladies of Llangollen, 1984; The Grand Tour of William Beckford, 1986; The White Solitaire, 1988; The American Journals of Fanny Kemble, 1990; The Grand Tours of Katherine Wilmot, France 1801–3 and Russia 1805–7, 1992; The Captain's Wife, The South American Journals of Maria Graham 1821–23, 1993. *Literary Agent:* Curtis Brown Ltd, Haymarket House, 28–29 Haymarket, London, SW1Y 4SP, England. *Telephone:* (20) 7393-4400. *Fax:* (20) 7393-4401. *E-mail:* info@curtisbrown.co.uk. *Website:* www.curtisbrown.co.uk.

MAXWELL, Catherine (Cathy) Fern, BA; American writer; b. 17 July 1953, Memphis, TN; m. Kevin M. Maxwell 1979; one s. two d. *Education:* Washington Univ. *Publications:* All Things Beautiful 1994, Treasured Vows 1996, You and No Other 1996, Falling in Love Again 1997. *Honours:* co-recipient first place award Reader's Voice Best Read of 1994, Romantic Times Award for Best Historical Love and Laughter 1996. *Literary Agent:* Rowland-Axelrod, 510 E 23rd Street, Suite 8-G, New York, NY 10010-5020, USA. *Address:* PO Box 1532, Midlothian, VA 23113, USA. *E-mail:* CathyMaxwell@msn.com.

MAXWELL, Douglas; British playwright; b. 1974, Girvan, Scotland. *Plays:* The Chameleon's Play 1997, The Crusader 1998, Helmet 1999, Our Bad Magnet 2000, Decky Does a Bronco 2001, Variety 2002, If Destroyed True 2005, Mancub 2005, The Backpacker Blues 2005, Melody 2006, Blood Country 2007, The Ballad of James II 2007, The Mother Ship 2008. *Honours:* Fringe First, Edinburgh Festival. *Literary Agent:* United Agents, 12–26 Lexington Street, London, W1F 0LE, England. *Telephone:* (20) 3214-0800. *Fax:* (20) 3214-0801. *E-mail:* info@unitedagents.co.uk. *Website:* unitedagents.co.uk.

MAXWELL, Glyn Meurig, BA, MA, FRSL; British poet, writer and editor; b. 7 Nov. 1962, Welwyn Garden City, Hertfordshire, England. *Education:* Worcester Coll., Oxford, Boston Univ., USA. *Career:* Editorial Asst, W.H. Allen, London 1989–90; Fiction Reviewer, Vogue 1990–94; Visiting Writer, Nanyang Tech. Univ., Singapore 1995, Warwick Univ. 1996–97, Amherst Coll., USA 1996–2000, The New School, New York 2002–03; Adjunct Faculty mem. Columbia Univ., New York 2002–, Princeton Univ. 2003–04, New York Univ. 2005–06; Poetry Ed., The New Republic 2001–; Fellow, Welsh Acad. 2000; mem. PEN, Poetry Soc. *Plays:* Gnyss the Magnificent: Three Verse Plays 1993, Plays One: The Lifeblood, Wolfpit, The Only Girl in the World 2005, Plays Two: Broken Journey, Best Man Speech, The Last Valentine 2006. *Publications:* poetry: Tale of the Mayor's Son 1990, Out of the Rain 1992, Rest for the Wicked 1995, The Breakage 1998, The Boy's at Twilight: Poems 1990–95 2000, Time's Fool 2001, The Nerve (Geoffrey Faber Memorial Prize 2004) 2002, The Sugar Mile 2005, Hide Now 2008; fiction: Blue Burneau 1994, The Girl who was Going to Die 2008; non-fiction: Moon Country (with Simon Armitage) 1996; contrib. to reviews, journals and magazines. *Honours:* Eric Gregory Award 1992, Somerset Maugham Prize 1992, E.M. Forster Prize, American Acad. of Arts and Letters 1997, British Theatre Guide's Best Play on the Fringe, Edinburgh Festival (for Lifeblood) 2004. *Literary Agent:* c/o Antony Harwood, Antony Harwood Ltd, 109 Riverbank House, 1 Putney Bridge Approach, London SW6 3JD, England. *Telephone:* (20) 7384-9209. *Fax:* (20) 7384-9206. *E-mail:* ant@antonyharwood.com. *Website:* www.antonyharwood.com; www.glynmaxwell.com.

MAXWELL, Gordon Stirling, MA, FRSA; British archaeologist; b. 21 March 1938, Edinburgh, Scotland; m. Kathleen Mary King 1961, two d. *Education:* University of St Andrews. *Career:* Curatorial Officer, Royal Commission for Ancient and Historical Monuments, Scotland, 1964–; Fellow Soc. of Antiquaries of London, Soc. of Antiquaries of Scotland. *Publications:* The Impact of Aerial Reconnaissance on Archaeology (ed.), 1983; Rome's Northwest Frontier: The Antonine Wall, 1983; The Romans in Scotland, 1989; A Battle Lost: Romans and Caledonians at Mons Graupius, 1990. *Contributions:* Britannia; Proceedings of the Society of Antiquaries of Scotland; Glasgow Archaeological Journal.

MAXWELL, Ian, MA; British/French publisher; b. 15 June 1956, Maisons-Laffitte, France; s. of the late (Ian) Robert Maxwell and of Elisabeth Meynard; brother of Kevin Maxwell; m. 1st Laura Plumb 1991 (divorced 1998); m. 2nd Tara Dudley Smith 1999. *Education:* Marlborough Coll. and Balliol Coll., Oxford. *Career:* Man. Dir Pergamon Press France 1980–81; Jt Man. Dir Pergamon Pres. GmbH 1980; Marketing Dir Pergamon Press Inc. 1982–83; Dir Sales Devt BPCC PLC 1985–86; Dir Group Marketing BPCC PLC (now Maxwell Communication Corpn PLC) 1986; Chair. Agence Centrale de Presse, Paris 1986–89; Dir TFI TV station, Paris 1987–89; CEO Maxwell Pergamon Publrs 1988–89; Jt Man. Dir Maxwell Communication Corpn 1988–91; Acting Chair. Mirror Group Newspapers 1991; Dir New York Daily News –1991, Telemonde Holdings 1997–; publishing consultant Westbourne Communications Ltd 1993; Publr Maximov Publs Ltd. 1995–; Chair. Derby Co. Football Club 1984–87, Vice-Chair. 1987–91; mem. Nat. Theatre Devt Council 1986; Pres. Club d'Investissement Media 1988.

MAXWELL, John (see Freemantle, Brian Harry)

MAXWELL, Patricia Anne, (Jennifer Blake, Maxine Patrick, Patricia Ponder, Elizabeth Trehearne); American writer and poet; b. 9 March 1942, Winn Parish, La; m. Jerry R. Maxwell 1957; two s. two d. *Career:* Writer-in-Residence, Univ. of Northeastern Louisiana; mem. Nat. League of American Pen Women, Romance Writers of America. *Publications include:* as Patricia Maxwell: The Secret of the Mirror House 1970, Stranger at Plantation Inn 1971, The Bewitching Grace 1973, The Court of the Thorn Tree 1973, Dark Masquerade 1974, Bride of a Stranger 1974, Love's Wild Desire 1977, The Notorious Angel 1977, Sweet Piracy 1978, Night of the Candles 1978; as Elizabeth Trehearne: Storm at Midnight 1973; as Patricia Ponder: Haven of Fear 1974, Murder for Charity 1974; as Maxine Patrick: The Abducted Heart 1978, Bayou Bride 1978, The Hired Wife 1978, Snowbound Heart 1979, Captive Kisses 1980, Love at Sea 1980, April of Enchantment 1981; as Jennifer Blake: Tender Betrayal 1979, The Storm and the Splendor 1979, Golden Fancy 1980, Embrace and Conquer 1981, Midnight Waltz (Maggie Award, Georgia Romance Writers 1985) 1984, Surrender in Moonlight 1984, Fierce Eden 1985, Prisoner of Desire 1986, Louisiana Dawn 1987, Southern Rapture (Maggie Award, Georgia Romance Writers 1987, Silver Plume Award, Affaire de Coeur 1988) 1987, Perfume of Paradise 1988, Love and Smoke 1989, Spanish Serenade 1990, Joy and Anger 1991, Wildest Dreams (Reviewer's Choice Certificate of Excellence, Romantic Times) 1992, Arrow to the Heart (Reviewer's Choice Certificate of Excellence, Romantic Times) 1993, Shameless (Reviewer's Choice Award, Affaire de Coeur, Reviewer's Choice Certificate of Excellence, Romantic Times) 1994, Silver-Tongued Devil (Holt Medallion) 1995, Tigress 1996, Garden of Scandal 1997, Roan 2000, With a Southern Touch (co-author) 2002, Dawn Encounter 2006, By His Majesty's Grace 2011, By Grace Possessed 2011, Seduced by Grace 2011, The Rent-A-Groom 2012; contribs to anthologies and periodicals. *Honours:* Hon. mem. Romance Writers of America 1988, Coeur de Louisiane Inc. Writers Club 1995,; Best Historical Romance Novelist of the Year 1985, Reviewer's Choices 1984, 1995, Climbing Rose Award, North Louisiana Romance Authors 1995, Romantic Times, Golden Treasure Award, Romance Writers of America 1987, Romance Hall of Fame, Affaire de Coeur 1995, Frank Waters Award for Writing Excellence 1997. *Literary Agent:* c/o Richard Curtis Associates Inc., 171 East 74th Street, Second Floor, New York, NY 10021, USA. *Website:* www.curtisagency.com. *E-mail:* help@steelmagnoliapress.com. *Website:* www.jenniferblake.com.

MAY, Derwent James, MA; British writer and journalist; b. 29 April 1930, Eastbourne, Sussex; m. Yolanta Izabella Sypniewska; one s. one d. *Education:* Lincoln Coll., Oxford. *Career:* theatre and film critic, Continental Daily Mail, Paris 1952–53; Lecturer in English, Univ. of Indonesia 1955–58; Sr Lecturer in English, Univs of Łódź and Warsaw 1959–63; chief leader writer, TLS 1963–65; Literary Ed., The Listener 1965–86; Literary and Arts Ed., Sunday Telegraph 1986–90, The European 1990–91; European Arts Ed., The Times 1992–; Literary Consultant, The London Magazine 2010; mem. Booker Prize jury 1978, Hawthornden Prize cttee 1987–; mem. Beefsteak Club, Garrick Club. *Publications:* fiction: The Professionals 1964, Dear Parson 1969, The Laughter in Djakarta 1973, A Revenger's Comedy 1979; non-fiction: Proust 1983, The Times Nature Diary 1983, Hannah Arendt 1986, The New Times Nature Diary 1993, Feather Reports 1996, Critical Times: The History of the Times Literary Supplement 2001, How To Attract Birds to Your Garden 2001, The Times: A Year in Nature Notes 2004; contrib. to Encounter, Hudson Review, Standpoint. *Address:* 45 Burghley Road, London, NW5 1UH, England (home).

MAY, Gita, MA, PhD; American academic and writer; b. 16 Sept. 1929, Brussels, Belgium; m. Irving May 1947. *Education:* Hunter Coll., CUNY, Columbia Univ. *Career:* Prof. of French and Chair Dept of French, Columbia

Univ. 1968–94; Pres. American Soc. for 18th Century Studies 1985–86; Gen. Ed., The Age of Revolution and Romanticism 1990–; mem. Société Française d'Étude du 18e Siècle, Société Diderot, North American Soc. for the Study of Rousseau, MLA (exec. council 1980–83); mem. editorial bds, including Romanic Review 1959–, French Review 1975–86, 1998–, Women in French Studies 2000–. *Publications:* Diderot Studies III (ed. with O. Fellows) 1961, Madame Roland and the Age of Revolution 1970, Stendhal and the Age of Napoleon 1977, Diderot: Essais sur la peinture, Vol. XIV of his complete works (ed.) 1984, Pensées détachées sur la peinture 1995, Rebecca West 1996, Anita Brookner 1997, Graham Swift 1999; contrib. to Dictionary of Literary Biography 2003, Voltaire's Candide 2003, Elisabeth Vigée Le Brun: The Odyssey of an Artist in an Age of Revolution 2005; other books and professional journals. *Honours:* Guggenheim Fellowship 1964, Officier, Ordre des Palmes Académiques 1981, Nat. Endowment for the Humanities Sr Fellow 1971, Columbia Univ. Van Amringe Distinguished Book Award 1971, named Outstanding Mentor by Women in French Studies 2003, honoured by American Soc. for 18th Century Studies as one of its great teachers. *Address:* c/o Department of French, Columbia University, 516 Philosophy Hall, New York, NY 10027, USA (office). *Telephone:* (212) 854-3905 (office); (212) 864-5997 (home). *Fax:* (212) 854-5863 (office). *E-mail:* gm9@columbia.edu (office).

MAY, Julian, (Lee N. Falconer, Ian Thorne); American writer and editor; b. 10 July 1931, Chicago, IL; m. Thaddeus E. Ditky 1953 (died 1991); two s. one d. *Career:* Science Ed. for a Chicago encyclopedia publisher 1953–57; co-founder (with Ted Ditky) Publication Associates 1957–. *Publications include:* Dune Roller (short story) 1951, Star of Wonder (short story) 1953, Robots and Thinking Machines (non-fiction) 1961, Land Beneath the Sea 1972, The Many Colored Land (Pliocene Exiles series) 1981, The Golden Torc (Pliocene Exiles series) 1982, The Nonborn King (Pliocene Exiles series) 1983, The Adversary (Pliocene Exiles series) 1984, Intervention (Intervention series) 1987, The Surveillance (Intervention series) 1988, Metaconcert (Intervention series) 1988, Black Trillium (with Marion Zimmer Bradley and Andre Norton) 1990, Jack the Bodiless (Galactic Milieu series) 1991, Blood Trillium (with Marion Zimmer Bradley and Andre Norton) 1992, Golden Trillium (with Marion Zimmer Bradley and Andre Norton) 1993, Diamond Mask (Galactic Milieu series) 1994, Magnificat (Galactic Milieu series) 1996, Sky Trillium 1997, Perseus Spur (Rampart World series) 1998, Orion Arm (Rampart World series) 1999, Sagittarius Whorl (Rampart World series) 2001, Conqueror's Moon (Boreal Moon series) 2003, Ironcrown Moon (Boreal Moon series) 2004, Ironcrown Moon (Boreal Moon series) 2005, Sorcerer's Moon (Boreal Moon series) 2006; as Lee N. Falconer: The Gazetteer of the Hyborian World of Conan 1977; as Ian Thorne (adaptations): Frankenstein 1977, King Kong 1977, The Wolf Man 1977, Godzilla 1977, Dracula 1977, Mad Scientists 1977, The Loch Ness Monster 1978, Murders in the Rue Morgue 1978, Bigfoot 1978, Bermuda Triangle (with Howard Schroeder) 1978, Ancient Astronauts (co-author) 1978, Monster Tales of Native Americans (with Barbara Howell Furan) 1978, UFOs 1978, Creature from the Black Lagoon 1981, The Mummy 1982, Frankenstein Meets Wolfman 1982, Deadly Mantis 1982, The Blob 1982, It Came from Outer Space 1982, Phantom of the Opera 1987, Invisible Man 1987. *Address:* PO Box 851, Mercer Island, WA 98040, USA.

MAY, Naomi Young, DFA; British novelist, journalist and painter; b. 27 March 1934, Glasgow, Scotland; m. Nigel May 1964; two s. one d. *Education:* Slade School of Fine Art, London and Univ. of London. *Career:* mem. PEN. *Publications:* At Home 1969, radio adaptation 1987, The Adventurer 1970, Troubles 1976; contrib. to anthologies, newspapers and magazines. *Honours:* Slade School of Fine Art History of Art Prize. *Address:* 6 Lion Gate Gardens, Richmond, Surrey TW9 2DF, England.

MAY, Sarah, BA; British writer; b. (Sarah Hutchinson), 1972, Northumberland; m.; two s. *Education:* Univs of London and Lancaster. *Plays:* The Butterfly Club 2008. *Publications:* novels: The Nudist Colony 1999, Spanish City 2002, The Internationals 2003, The Rise and Fall of the Queen of Suburbia 2006, The Rise and Fall of a Domestic Diva 2008, The Rise and Fall of the Wonder Girls 2009. *Honours:* Amazon.co.uk Writers' Bursary 2001. *Address:* c/o Random House, 20 Vauxhall Bridge Road, London SW1V 2SA (office); 9 Stories Mews, London SE5 8JJ, England. *Website:* www.randomhouse.com.

MAY, Stephen James, (Julian Poole), BA, MA, DLitt; American writer and academic; b. 10 Sept. 1946, Toronto, Ont., Canada; m. Caroline Casteel 1972; one s. *Education:* El Camino Coll., California State Univ. at Carson, Int. Univ., Mumbai. *Career:* Instructor in English, Colorado Northwestern Coll. 1992–98; Visiting Prof. of English, Univ. of Northern Colorado 1999–; currently Visiting Prof. of English and Literature, Front Range Community Coll., Fort Collins, Colo; mem. Colorado Authors' League, James Michener Soc., Soc. of Southwestern Authors, Western Writers of America, World Literary Acad., Zane Grey Soc. *Publications:* Pilgrimage: A Journey Through Colorado's History and Culture 1987, Intruders in the Dust 1988, Fire from the Skies 1990, Footloose on the Santa Fe Trail 1992, A Land Observed 1993, Zane Grey: Romancing the West 1997, Maverick Heart: The Further Adventures of Zane Grey 2000, Rascals 2001, James A. Michener: A Writer's Journey 2005, Michener's South Pacific 2011; contrib. to Denver Post, Frontier Rocky Mountain News, Southwest Art, Artists of the Rockies, National Geographic. *Honours:* Western Writers of America Non-Fiction Award 2001, Colorado Authors' League Non-Fiction Award 2001. *Address:* 731 Peregrine Run, Fort Collins, CO 80524, USA. *E-mail:* stepkm@msn.com (home).

MAY OF OXFORD, Baron (Life Peer), cr. 2001, of Oxford in the County of Oxfordshire; **Robert McCredie May**, Kt, OM, AC, PhD, PRS, FAAS; Australian/British biologist and academic; *Professor, University of Oxford*; b. 1 Aug. 1936, Sydney, NSW, Australia; s. of Henry W. May and Kathleen M. McCredie; m. Judith Feiner 1962; one d. *Education:* Sydney Boys' High School, Univ. of Sydney. *Career:* Gordon MacKay Lecturer in Applied Math., Harvard Univ., USA 1959–61; at Univ. of Sydney 1962–73, Sr Lecturer in Theoretical Physics 1962–64, Reader 1964–69, Personal Chair 1969–73; Class of 1877 Prof. of Biology, Princeton Univ., USA 1973–88, Chair. Univ. Research Bd 1977–88; Royal Soc. Research Prof., Dept of Zoology, Univ. of Oxford and Imperial Coll., London, UK 1988–95, currently Prof. and Fellow, Merton Coll., Oxford 1988–; Chief Scientific Adviser to UK Govt and Head, Office of Science and Tech. 1995–2000; Pres. Royal Soc. 2000–05, British Ecological Soc. 2000–05; Crossbench Peer in House of Lords 2001–, mem. Science and Tech. Select Cttee 2006–, Science and Cttee Sub-cttees: I (Scientific Aspects of Ageing) 2005, I (Allergy/Waste Reduction) 2007–08, Systematics and Taxonomy Enquiry 2008, Draft Climate Change Bill Jt Cttee 2007; fmr Ind. mem. Jt Nature Conservancy Councils; Overseas mem. Australian Acad. of Sciences 1991–; Foreign mem. NAS 1992–; mem. Academia Europaea 1994–; Foreign mem. NAS 1992–; fmr Chair. Bd of Trustees, Natural History Museum, London; Trustee, British Museum 1989–, Royal Botanic Gardens, Kew 1991–95, WWF (UK) 1990–94, Nuffield Foundation (Exec. Trustee) 1993–, BAAS (now the British Science Asscn) 2006– (also Hon. Fellow, Pres.-Elect 2010). *Publications:* Stability and Complexity in Model Ecosystems 1973, Exploitation of Marine Communities (ed.) 1974, Theoretical Ecology: Principles and Applications (ed.) 1976, Population Biology of Infectious Diseases (ed.) 1982, Exploitation of Marine Ecosystems (ed.) 1984, Perspectives in Ecological Theory (ed.) 1989, Population Regulation and Dynamics (ed.) 1990, Infectious Diseases of Humans: Transmission and Control (with R. M. Anderson) 1991, Large Scale Ecology and Conservation Biology 1994, Extinction Rates 1995, Evolution of Biological Diversity 1999, Virus Dynamics: the Mathematical Foundations of Immunology and Virology (with Martin Nowak) 2000. *Honours:* hon. degrees from univs including Uppsala (1990), Yale (1993), Sydney (1995); Princeton (1996), (ETH) 2003; Croonian Lecturer, Hitchcock Lecturer, John M. Prather Lecturer, Weldon Memorial Prize, Univ. of Oxford 1980, Medal of Linnean Soc. of London 1991, Marsh Christian Prize 1992, Frink Medal, Zoological Soc. of London 1995, Crafoord Prize 1996, Balzan Prize 1998, Blue Planet Prize 2001, Copley Medal, Royal Soc. 2007. *Address:* Department of Zoology, University of Oxford, The Tinbergen Building, South Parks Road, Oxford, OX1 3PS (office); House of Lords, Westminster, London, SW1A 0PW, England. *Telephone:* (1865) 271276 (office). *E-mail:* robert.may@zoo.ox.ac.uk (office). *Website:* www.zoo.ox.ac.uk/staff/academics/may_r.htm (office); www.parliament.uk/biographies/lords/robert-may/26570.

MAYER, Bernadette; American poet and writer; b. 12 May 1945, New York, NY; one s. two d. *Education:* New School for Social Research, New York. *Career:* Resident Dir, St Mark's Poetry Project, Greenwich Village, 1980–84; various workshops. *Publications:* Ceremony Latin, 1964; Story, 1968; Moving, 1971; The Basketball Article (with Anne Waldman), 1975; Memory, 1975; Studying Hunger, 1975; Poetry, 1976; Eruditio Ex Memoria, 1977; The Golden Book of Words, 1978; Midwinter Day, 1982; Incidents Reports Sonnets, 1984; Utopia, 1984; Mutual Aid, 1985; The Art of Science Writing (with Dales Worsley), 1989; Sonnets, 1989; The Formal Field of Kissing, 1990; A Bernadette Mayer Reader, 1992; The Desires of Mothers to Please Others in Letters, 1994. Contributions: anthologies.

MAYER, Peter, BA, MA; American/British book publisher; *President, Overlook Press, New York; Gerald Duckworth Publishers, London*; b. 28 March 1936, Hampstead, London, England; s. of Alfred Mayer and Lee Mayer; one d. *Education:* Columbia Univ., New York, Christ Church, Oxford. *Career:* Grad. Fellow, Indiana Univ.; Fulbright Fellow, Freie Universität Berlin 1959; worked with Orion Press before joining Avon books for 14 years; Publr and Pres. Pocketbooks 1976–78; Chief. Exec. Penguin Books Ltd, London 1978–96, later Chair. Penguin USA; exec. positions with The Overlook Press (co-f. with his father 1970) 1996–, acquired Ardis Publrs 2001, Duckworth Publrs 2003, Nonesuch Press 2005; mem. Bd Asscn of American Publrs –2003, Bd Frankfurt Bookfair Fellowship, Bd Nat. Book Foundation –2003), New York Univ. Publrs Advisory Bd, Scholastic Bd of Dirs, German Book Office. *Publications:* An Idea is Like a Bird 1963, The Pacifist Conscience (ed.) 1966. *Honours:* Chevalier and Officier, Ordre des Arts et des Lettres 1996; Most Distinguished Publr of the Year 1995, Foundation of Publrs' and Booksellers' Asscn's in India Award for Oustanding Contrib. to Int. Publishing 1996, London Book Fair/Trilogy Lifetime Achievement Award 2008. *Address:* Duckworth Publishers, 90–93 Cowcross Street, London, EC1M 6BF, England (office); The Overlook Press, 141 Wooster Street, New York, NY 10012, USA. *Telephone:* (20) 7490-7300 (London) (office); (212) 673-2223 (New York) (office). *Fax:* (20) 7490-0080 (London) (office); (212) 673-2296 (New York) (office). *E-mail:* info@duckworth-publishers.co.uk (office); sales@overlookpress.com (office). *Website:* www.ducknet.co.uk (office); www.overlookpress.com (office).

MAYER, Robert, BA, MS; American writer; b. 24 Feb. 1939, New York, NY; m. La Donna Cocilovo 1989; one step-d. *Education:* City College, CUNY, Columbia University. *Career:* reporter and columnist, Newsday, 1961–71; Managing Ed., Santa Fe Reporter, 1988–90. *Publications:* Superfolks, 1977; The Execution, 1979; Midge and Decker, 1982; Sweet Salt, 1984; The Grace of

Shortstops, 1984; The Search, 1986; The Dreams of Ada, 1987; I, JFK, 1989. Contributions: Vanity Fair; New York Magazine; Travel and Leisure; Rocky Mountain Magazine; New Mexico Magazine; Santa Fe Reporter; Newsday. *Honours:* National Headliner Award, 1968; Mike Berger Awards, 1969, 1971.

MAYER-KOENIG, Wolfgang; Austrian poet, writer, editor and academic; *Editor, LOG literary magazine*; b. 28 March 1946, Vienna. *Education:* Univs of Vienna, Saarbrücken and Los Angeles. *Career:* univ. Prof. 1987–; Ed. int. literary magazine, LOG; mem. Acad. Tiberina, Acad. Burckhardt St Gallen, Acad. Consentina, Acad. Europa; mem. Austrian Writers' Asscn (bd mem.), PEN, Robert-Musil Archive Asscn (vice-pres. 1975–), Europa Literaturkreis Kapfenberg. *Publications:* Sichtbare Pavilions 1969, Stichmarken 1970, Texte und Bilder 1972, Sprache-Politik-Aggression 1975, Texte und Zeichnungen 1975, Psychologie und Literatursprache 1976, Language-Politics-Agression 1977, Italienreisen Goethes 1978, Robert Musils Moglichkeitsstil 1979, In den Armen unseres Waerters 1980, Chagrin non dechiffré 1986, A Hatalom bonyolult Angyala 1988, Underestimated Deep 1989, A Complicated Angel 1989, Responsibility of Writing: Contributions to a Modern Grammar 1990, Risks of Writing 1991, Verzögerung des Vertrauens 1995, Colloquios nel Cuarto 1996, Fire and Ice 1996, Mirror Wading 1996, Verkannte Tiefe 1996, Grammatik der Modernen Poesie 1996, Behind Desires Deficits 1997, Confessions of an Angry Loving European 1999, Another Place for Victory 2000, Visiting 2001, The Three Dolphins 2004, The Necessary Doubt 2005, The Adoption 2005; contrib. to various publications. *Honours:* Officer Order of Merit, Egypt 1974, Commander Order of St Agatha, San Marino 1982, Ordre du Mérite Africain 1983, Chevalier, Ordre des Arts et des Lettres 1987, Golden Cross Order of Eagle of Tyrol 1988, Papal Lateran Cross first class, Grand Cross of Honour, Govt of Carinthia 1993, Cross of merit first class of Lilienfeld 1984, Cross of Merit of Greek Orthodox Papal Patriarch of Alexandria, Egypt, Star of Peace, Rome, Italy; Theodor Körner Prize for Poetry 1974, Austrian Cross of Honour for Science and Arts 1976, Cross of Honour, Lower Austria 1982, Int. ARC Golden medal of merit 1983, Premio Prometeo Aureo Lazio, Vienna Art Foundation Prize, New Century Award, Int. Peace Prize 2005. *Address:* Hernalser Guertel 41, 1170 Vienna (office); Haubenbiglstrasse 1A, 1190 Vienna, Austria (home). *Telephone:* 223652306 (office); 6643570361 (home). *Fax:* 13707620 (home). *E-mail:* univ.prof.mayer-koenig@aon.at (home).

MAYNE, Seymour, BA, MA, PhD; Canadian poet, writer, editor, translator and academic; *Professor of English, University of Ottawa*; b. Montreal. *Education:* McGill Univ., Univ. of British Columbia. *Career:* Lecturer, Univ. of British Columbia 1972; Lecturer, Univ. of Ottawa 1973, Asst Prof. 1973–78, Assoc. Prof. 1978–85, Prof. of English 1985–; Visiting Prof., Hebrew Univ. of Jerusalem 1979–80, Visiting Prof. and Scholar 1983–84, 1992, Writer-in-Residence 1987–88; Visiting Prof., Concordia Univ., Montréal 1982–83, Univ. of La Laguna, Spain 1993; Adjunct Research Prof., Carleton Univ. 2002–05; Contributing Ed. Viewpoints 1982–90, Poetry Ed. 1990–95; Contributing Ed. Tel-Aviv Review 1989–96, Poet Lore 1992–2000, Jerusalem Review 1997–2001; Founder and Consulting Ed. Bywords 1990–2001, Graffito 1994–2000; Guest Ed. Shirim 2012; Faculty mem. and Adviser, Canadian Yeshiva and Rabbinical School, Toronto School of Theology, Univ. of Toronto 2008–; Guest Prof., Nat. Univ. of La Plata, Argentina 2008. *Music:* Hail 2006. *Publications:* That Monocycle the Moon 1964, Tiptoeing on the Mount 1965, From the Portals of Mouseholes 1966, Manimals 1969, Mouth 1970, For Stems of Light 1971, Face 1971, Name 1975, Diasporas 1977, The Impossible Promised Land: Poems New and Selected 1981, Children of Abel 1986, Diversions 1987, Six Ottawa Poets (with others) 1990, Killing Time 1992, The Song of Moses and Other Poems 1995, Five-O'Clock Shadows (with others) 1996, Dragon Trees 1997, City of the Hidden 1998, Carbon Filter 1999, Light Industry 2000, Hail: Word Sonnets 2002, Cinque Foil (with others) 2003, Ricochet: Word Sonnets 2004, El Viejo Sofá Azul 2004, Foreplay: An Anthology of Word Sonnets (co-ed .) 2004, September Rain 2005, Hail/Granzo 2006, A Dream of Birds: Word Sonnets, (co-author) 2007, Reflejos. Sonetos de una palabra 2008, Les pluies de Septembre: poèmes choisis 1980–2005, 2008, Fly Off into the Strongest Light: Selected Poems 2009, Ricochet: Word Sonnets/ Sonnets d'un mot 2011; ed. or co-ed. of 17 other books 1968–97; trans. or co-trans. of eight books 1974–98; contrib. to anthologies, books, journals, reviews and quarterlies. *Honours:* Chester Macnaghten First Prize in Creative Writing 1962, J. I. Segal Prize in English-French Literature 1974, York Poetry Workshop Award 1975, American Literary Trans Asscn Poetry Trans. Award 1990, Jewish Book Cttee Prize 1994, Louis L. Lockshin Memorial Award 1997, Fuerstenberg-Aaron Prize 2000, Capital Educators' Award 2003, Excellence in Educ. Prize 2005, Louis L. Lockshin and Brenda Freedman Memorial Award in Poetry 2007, Louis Rosenberg Canadian Jewish Studies Distinguished Service Award 2009, Prof. of the Year Award, Faculty of Arts, Univ. of Ottawa 2010; numerous grants and fellowships. *Address:* Department of English, Faculty of Arts, University of Ottawa, Ottawa, ON K1N 6N5, Canada (office). *Telephone:* (613) 562-5764 (office). *Fax:* (613) 562-5990 (office). *Website:* www.english.uottawa.ca/faculty/smayne.html.

MAYO, Wendell, Jr, BS, BA, MFA, PhD; American academic and writer; *Professor of English, Bowling Green State University*; b. 16 Aug. 1953, Corpus Christi, Tex.; s. of Wendell Mayo and Blanche Soledad Durant; m. Deborah Masonis 1982. *Education:* Ohio State Univ., Ohio Univ., Univ. of Toledo, Vermont Coll. *Career:* Asst Prof. of English, Indiana Univ., Purdue Univ., Fort Wayne 1991–94; Asst Prof. of Creative Writing and Literature, Univ. of Southwestern Louisiana, Lafayette 1994–96; Asst Prof. of Creative Writing and Literature, then Assoc. Prof., then Prof. of English, Bowling Green State Univ., OH 1996–; mem. Bd Dirs American Professional Partnership for Lithuanian Educ. (APPLE) 1999–2001, Div. Chair. Language Arts, APPLE 1995–; mem. Associated Writing Programs; Fellow, Millay Colony for the Arts 1992, Master Fellow, Indiana Arts Comm. 1992, Yado Fellow 1992, 1994, 1996, Fellow, Edward F. Albee Foundation 1993. *Publications:* Centaur of the North (short stories) 1996, In Lithuanian Wood (novel), B Horror and Other Stories 1999, Vilko Valanda (short stories); contrib. to various reviews, quarterlies and magazines, including Harvard Review, Prairie Schooner, Missouri Review, The Yale Review, Threepenny Review, and to anthologies, including City Wilds, 100% Pure Florida Fiction. *Honours:* First Prize for Fiction, Mississippi Valley Review 1995, New Delta Review 1996, Univ. of New Mexico Premio Aztlan 1997, Nat. Endowment for the Arts grant 2001, Fulbright grant 2002. *Address:* Department of English, Creative Writing Program, Bowling Green State University, Bowling Green, OH 43403 (office). *Telephone:* (419) 823-7005 (office). *E-mail:* wmayo@bgsu.edu (office). *Website:* personal.bgsu.edu/~wmayo (home).

MAYRÖCKER, Friederike; Austrian writer and poet; b. 20 Dec. 1924, Vienna; d. of Franz and Friederike Mayröcker. *Education:* secondary school and teacher training Coll., Vienna. *Career:* English teacher 1946–68; first book published 1956; freelance writer 1969–; about 100 publications (prose, poetry, radio plays and children's books). *Recordings:* Sprech Klavier, Umarmungen, etc. *Publications include:* Larifari 1956, Die Abschiede, Gute Nacht, guten Morgen, Magische Blätter (five vols), Reise durch die Nacht, Das Herzzerreißende der Dinge, Winterglück, Mein Herz mein Zimmer mein Name, Gesammelte Prosa, Stilleben, Das besessere Alter, Ausgewählte Gedichte 1944–78, Lektion, Notizen auf einem Kamel (poetry) 1996, five vols of Magische Blätter, mein Arbeitstirol, Die kommunizierenden Gefäsze 2003, Requiem für Ernst Jandl, Gesammelte Gedichte, Und ich schüttelte einen Liebling, Liebesgedichte, Paloma 2008, Scardanelli (poetry) 2009, Dieses Jäckchen (nämlich) des Vogel Greif: Gedichte 2004–2009 (poetry) 2009, Ich bin in der Anstalt 2010; play: Nada–Nichts. *Honours:* Dr hc; Österreichischer Würdigungspreis für Literatur 1975, Literature Prize (City of Vienna) 1977, Großer Österreichischen Staatspreis für Literatur, Roswitha-von-Gandersheim Preis, Austrian Insignia for Arts and Letters, Friedrich-Hölderlin-Preis 1993, Manuskripte-Preis 1994, Großer Literaturpreis der Bayerischen Akad. der Schönen Künste 1996, Georg-Büchner-Preis 2001, Premio Internazionale, Camaiore, Italy 2003, Hermann Leux Preis 2009, Peter Huchel Preis 2009, Bremer Literaturpreis 2010. *Address:* Zentagasse 16/40, 1050 Vienna, Austria (home). *Telephone:* (1) 545-66-60 (home). *Fax:* (1) 545-66-60 (home).

MAYSON, Marina (see Rogers, Rosemary)

MAZLISH, Bruce, MA, PhD; American historian and writer; *Professor of History Emeritus, Massachusetts Institute of Technology*; b. 15 Sept. 1923, New York, NY; m. 1st; three s., one d.; m. 2nd Neva Goodwin 1988. *Education:* Columbia Univ. *Career:* Instructor, Univ. of Maine 1946–48, Columbia Univ. 1949–50; Instructor, MIT 1950–53, Faculty 1955–, Prof. of History 1965–2004, Chair. History Section 1965–70, Head Dept of Humanities 1974–79, now Prof. of History Emer.; Dir American School, Madrid 1953–55; mem. American Acad. of Arts and Sciences, fellow; mem. bd of dirs, Rockefeller Family Fund 1987–97, Toynbee Prize Foundation (Pres. 1999–). *Publications:* The Western Intellectual Tradition (with J. Bronowski) 1960, The Riddle of History 1966, In Search of Nixon 1972, James and John Stuart Mill: Father and Son in the 19th Century 1975, The Revolutionary Ascetic 1976, Kissinger: The European Mind in American Policy 1976, The Meaning of Karl Marx 1984, A New Science: The Breakdown of Connections and the Birth of Sociology 1989, The Leader, the Led and the Psyche 1990, The Fourth Discontinuity: The Co-Evolution of Humans and Machines 1993, The Uncertain Sciences 1998, Civilization and Its Contexts 2004; editor: Psychoanalysis and History 1963, The Railroad and the Space Program: An Exploration in Historical Analogy 1965, Conceptualizing Global History (with Ralph Bultjens) 1993, Progress: Fact or Illusion? (with Leo Marx) 1996, The Global History Reader (with Akira Iriye) 2005; contrib. to professional journals. *Honours:* Clement Staff Essay Award 1968, Toynbee Prize 1986–87. *Address:* 11 Lowell Street, Cambridge, MA 02138, USA.

MAZOWER, Mark, BA, MA, PhD; British historian, academic and writer; *Professor of History, Columbia University*. *Education:* Univ. of Oxford, UK and Johns Hopkins Univ., USA. *Career:* fmr Prof. of History, Birkbeck Coll., London; currently Prof. of History and Dir Center for Int. History, Columbia Univ.; Visiting Scholar Minda de Gunzburg Center for European Studies, Harvard Univ. *Publications:* Greece and the Inter-War Economic Crisis 1991, Inside Hitler's Greece: The Experience of Occupation 1941–44 (Fraenkel Prize in Contemporary History, Longman/History Today Book of the Year) 1993, The Policing of Politics in the Twentieth Century (ed.) 1997, Dark Continent: Europe's 20th Century 1998, After the War was Over: Reconstructing the Family, Nation and State in Greece 1943–60 2000, The Balkans 2000, Ideologies and National Identities: The Case of Twentieth-Century South-Eastern Europe (co-ed.) 2003, Salonica, City of Ghosts (Runciman Award, Duff Cooper Prize) 2005, Hitler's Empire: Nazi Rule in Occupied Europe 2008, No Enchanted Palace: The End of Empire and the Ideological Origins of the United Nations 2009; contrib. to The Nation, Financial Times. *Address:* Department of History, Columbia University, 503 Fayerweather Hall, 1180 Amsterdam Avenue, New York, NY 10027, USA (office). *Telephone:* (212)

854–4646 (office). *Fax:* (212) 932–0602 (office). *E-mail:* mm2669@columbia.edu (office). *Website:* www.columbia.edu (office); mazower.com.

MAZUR, Grace Dane, BA, MFA, PhD; American writer; b. 22 April 1944, Boston, MA; m. Barry C. Mazur; one s. *Education:* Harvard Coll., Harvard Univ., Warren Wilson Coll. *Career:* Lecturer, Harvard Univ. 1996–; faculty mem., MFA Program for Writers, Warren Wilson Coll.; Fiction Ed., Tupelo Press. *Publications:* Silk (short stories) 1996, Trespass (novel) 1998; contrib. to reviews and journals. *Honours:* Bread Loaf Literary Fellowship. *E-mail:* gracedanemazur@gmail.com (office).

MAZZANTINI, Margaret; Italian writer and actress; b. 27 Oct. 1961, Dublin, Ireland; m. Sergio Castellitto; three c. *Education:* Accademia di Arte Drammatica, Rome. *Films as actress:* Un caso di coscienza 1983, Lucas 1988, Nulla ci può fermare 1988, L'assassina 1989, Una fredda mattina di maggio 1990, Quando le montagne finiscono 1994, Paesaggio con figure 1995, Il cielo è sempre più blu 1995, Festival 1996, Il barbiere di rio 1996, Libero burro 1998. *Television as actress:* Antropophagus 1980, La voce 1982, Un delitto 1983, Venezia salvata 1985, Cheri 1985, Sentimental 1987, Cuore di mamma 1987, Duel of Love 1990, Cane sciolto II 1990, Eurocops 1990, Kaminsky, un flic a Moscou (series) 1991, Promo 1992. *Plays as actress:* Ifigenia 1982, Venezia salvata 1982–83, Le tre sorelle 1984–85, L'onesto Jago 1984–85, L'Alcade di Zalamea 1984–85, La signora Giulia 1985–86, Antigone 1986, Faust 1987, Mon Faust 1987, Bambino 1988, Praga magica-Valeria 1989, A piedi nudi nel parco 1992–93, Colpi bassi 1994, Manola 1994, 1995, 1996, 1998. *Publications:* Il catino di zinco (novel) (Premio Selezione Campiello, Premio Opera Prima Rapallo-Carige) 1994, Manola (play) 1994, Libero burro (screenplay) 1999, Non ti muovere (novel) (Premio Città di Bari-Costiera del Lavante-Pinuccio Tatarella 2001, Premio Strega 2002, Premio Rapallo-Carige 2002, Premio Grinzane-Cavour 2002) 2001, Zorro: Un eremita sul marciapiede (novel) 2002. *Honours:* Premio UBU for Best Young Actress 1984, Maschera d'oro IDI 1985, Premio Biglietto d'oro 1994. *E-mail:* margaret_mazzantini@yahoo.it. *Website:* www.margaretmazzantini.com.

MAZZARELLA, David; American newspaper editor; b. 1938. *Career:* with Assoc. Press, Lisbon, New York, Rome 1962–70; with Daily American, Rome 1971–75, Gannett News, Washington, DC 1976–77, The Bridgewater, Bridgewater, NJ 1977–83; Ed., Sr Vice-Pres. USA Today –1999; Ombudsman Stars and Stripes (newspaper for American mil. services) 2000–01, 2007–, Ed. Dir 2001–07. *Address:* Stars and Stripes, 529 14th Street NW, Suite 350, Washington, DC 20450, USA. *Telephone:* (202) 761-0900. *Fax:* (202) 761-089. *E-mail:* mazzarellad@stripes.osd.mil. *Website:* www.stripes.com.

MAZZARO, Jerome Louis, AB, MA, PhD; American academic, poet, writer and editor; b. 25 Nov. 1934, Detroit, Michigan. *Education:* Wayne University, University of Iowa, Wayne State University. *Career:* Instructor, University of Detroit 1958–61; Ed., Fresco 1960–61, Modern Poetry Studies 1970–79; Asst Prof., SUNY at Cortland 1962–64; Asst Ed., North American Review 1963–65, Noetics 1964–65; Prof. of English and Comparative Literature, SUNY at Buffalo1964–96; Contributing Ed., Salmagundi 1967–97, American Poetry Review 1972–, Italian-American 1974–88; Poetry Ed., Helios 1977–79; mem. Dante Society of America, Mark Twain Society. *Publications:* The Achievement of Robert Lowell, 1939–1959 1960, Juvenal: Satires (trans.) 1965, The Poetic Themes of Robert Lowell 1965, Changing the Windows (poems) 1966, Modern American Poetry (ed.) 1970, Transformation in the Renaissance English Lyric 1970, Profile of Robert Lowell (ed.) 1971, Profile of William Carlos Williams (ed.) 1971, William Carlos Williams: The Later Poetry 1973, Postmodern American Poetry 1980, The Figure of Dante: An Essay on the 'Vita Nuova' 1981, The Caves of Love (poems) 1985, Rubbings (poems) 1985, John Logan: The Collected Poems (ed. with Al Poulin) 1989, John Logan: The Collected Fiction (ed.) 1991, Mind Plays: Luigi Pirandello's Theatre 2000, Robert Lowell and Ovid 2001, War Games (fiction) 2001, Robert Lowell and America 2002, Weathering the Changes (poems) 2002, Memory and Making 2003; contributions: reference works, books and journals. *Honours:* Guggenheim Fellowship 1964–65, Hadley Fellowship 1979–80. *Address:* 392 Central Park W, Apartment 11J, New York, NY 10025, USA (home).

MAZZIERI, Julie, DèsL; Canadian writer; b. 1975, Saint-Paul-de-Chester, Québec. *Education:* Univ. of Montréal, McGill Univ. *Career:* taught translation at McGill Univ.; now lives in Corsica. *Publications:* Le Discours sur la tombe de l'idiot (novel) (Gov.-Gen.'s Literary Award for Fiction) 2009; articles and criticism for literary journals. *Address:* c/o Éditions José Corti, 60 rue Monsieur-Le-Prince, 75006 Paris, France (office). *E-mail:* librairie-corti@orange.fr (office). *Website:* www.jose-corti.fr (office).

MAZZUCCO, Melania Gaia; Italian writer and screenwriter; b. 1966, Rome; d. of Ruberto Mazzucco and Andreina Mazzucco. *Education:* Univ. of Rome, La Sapienza, Centro Sperimentale di Cinematografia. *Publications:* Il bacio della Medusa 1996, La camera di Baltus 1998, Lei così amata 2000, Vita (Premio Strega) 2003, Un giorno perfetto 2005, Un giorno da cani 2007; has written numerous scripts for film, theatre and radio. *Address:* c/o Rizzoli, RCS Libri, SpA, Via Mecenate 91, 20138 Milan, Italy (office). *Website:* www.rcslibri.it (office).

MDA, Zanemvula Kizito Gatyeni (Zakes), PhD; South African playwright, novelist, poet and painter; *Professor of Creative Writing, Ohio University*; b. 1948, Herschel District, Eastern Cape Province; s. of the late Ashby Peter Solomzi Mda and Nompumelelo Rose Mda. *Education:* Ohio Univ., Univ. of Capetown. *Career:* lived with family in exile in Basotholand Protectorate (later became Lesotho) 1964–80; wrote first plays in English while still at high school; worked as teacher, bank clerk and in marketing during law studies; studied theatre in USA then returned to Lesotho 1985; worked with Lesotho Nat. Broadcasting Corpn Television Project; also Dir Theatre-for-Development Project, Univ. of Lesotho; f. Marotholi Travelling Theatre; Lecturer in English, Nat. Univ. of Lesotho, Full Prof. and Head of English Dept 1991; taught at US univs 1991–94; writer-in-residence Univ. of Durham, UK 1991; research fellow Yale Univ. 1992; Visiting Prof. School of Dramatic Art, Witwatersrand Univ., S Africa 1995; now Prof. of Creative Writing Ohio Univ.; Dir Southern African Multimedia AIDS Trust, Johannesburg. *Publications:* plays: We Shall Sing for the Fatherland and Other Plays (Amstel Playwright of the Year Award) 1980, The Road (Christina Crawford Award of American Theatre Asscn 1984) 1982, The Plays of Zakes Mda 1990, The Nun's Romantic Story 1991, The Dying Screams of the Moon 1992, Four Works (Joys of War, And the Girls in their Sunday Dresses, Banned, The Final Dance) 1993; novels: Ways of Dying 1995, She Plays with the Darkness 1995, The Heart of Redness 2001, The Madonna of Excelsior 2002, The Whale Caller 2005, Black Diamond 2010; prose: When People Play People (development communication through theatre) 1993, Melville 67 (novella) 1998, Penny and Puffy (juvenile, with Mpapa Mokhoane) 2000, Fools, Bells and the Habit of Eating (three satires); poetry: Bits of Debris 1986; contrib. short stories to anthologies and articles to academic journals and newspapers. *Honours:* American Library Asscn Notable Book 2005, Commonwealth Writers' Prize (Africa region) 2005, Zora Neale Hurston/Richard Wright Legacy Award 2005. *Literary Agent:* Blake Friedmann Literary, Film and Television Agency, 122 Arlington Road, London, NW1 7HP, England. *Telephone:* (20) 7284-0408. *Fax:* (20) 7284-0442. *Address:* Department of English, University of Ohio, 365 Ellis Hall, Athens, OH 45701, USA (office). *Telephone:* (740) 593-9940 (office). *E-mail:* mda@ohio.edu (office). *Website:* www.english.ohiou.edu (office).

MEAD, Matthew; British poet and translator; b. 12 Sept. 1924, Buckinghamshire, England. *Career:* Ed., Satis Magazine, Edinburgh 1960–62. *Publications:* A Poem in Nine Parts 1960, Identities 1964, Kleinigkeiten 1966, Identities and Other Poems 1967, Penguin Modern Poets 16 (with Harry Guest and J. Beeching) 1970, In the Eyes of the People 1973, Minusland 1977, The Midday Muse 1979, A Roman in Cologne 1986, A Sestina at the End of Socialism 1996, A Dozen Villanelles 1999, The Sentences of Death 2000, Walking Out of the World 2003; also numerous trans. from German (with Ruth Mead). *Address:* c/o Anvil Press, Neptune House, 70 Royal Hill, London, SE10 8RF, England.

MEADES, Jonathan Turner; British journalist, writer and broadcaster; b. 21 Jan. 1947, Salisbury, Wilts., England; s. of John William Meades and Margery Agnes Meades; m. 1st Sally Dorothee Renee Brown 1980 (divorced); two d.; m. 2nd Frances Anne Bentley 1988 (divorced); two d.; m. 3rd Colette Claudine Forder 2003. *Education:* King's Coll., Taunton, Royal Acad. of Dramatic Art, London, Univ. of Bordeaux, France. *Career:* Ed. Event 1981–82; Features Ed. Tatler 1982–85; restaurant critic, The Times 1986–2001, columnist 2002–05. *Film:* L'Atlantide (script) 1992. *Television:* The Victorian House, Abroad in Britain, Further Abroad, Jerry Building, Even Further Abroad, Travels with Pevsner: Worcestershire, Meades Eats, Heart Bypass, Victoria Died in 1901 and is Still Alive Today, tvSSFBM, Abroad Again (i), Joe Building, Abroad Again (ii), Magnetic North, Off Kilter, Jonathan Meades on France. *Publications:* This is Their Life 1979, An Illustrated Atlas of the World's Great Buildings 1980, Filthy English 1984, Peter Knows What Dick Likes 1989, Pompey 1993, The Fowler Family Business 2001, Incest and Morris Dancing 2002, Museum without Walls 2012; contrib. to The Times, Sunday Times, Observer, Independent, Economist etc. *Honours:* Essay Prize, Paris Int. Art Film Festival 1994, Glenfiddich Awards 1986, 1990, 1996. *Literary Agent:* c/o Capel & Land, 24 Wardour Street, London, W1D 6PS, England. *Telephone:* (20) 7734-2414. *E-mail:* georgina@capelland.co.uk (office). *E-mail:* jtm.juvarra@orange.fr (home).

MEARS, Gillian, BA; Australian writer; b. 21 July 1964, Lismore, NSW. *Career:* mem. Australian Society of Authors. *Publications:* Ride a Cock Horse (short stories) 1989, Fineflour (short stories) 1990, The Mint Lawn 1991, The Grass Sister 1995, Collected Stories 1997, Paradise Is a Place (essay) 1997, A Map of the Gardens (short stories) 2002; contrib. to periodicals. *Honours:* Commonwealth Writers Regional First Book Prize 1989, Regional Best Book Prize 1996, Australian/Vogel Award 1991, Steele Rudd Award 2003. *Literary Agent:* Barbara Mobbs, PO Box 126, Edgecliff, NSW 2027, Australia. *E-mail:* bmobbs@pogo.com.au.

MEASHAM, Donald Charles, BA, MPhil; British teacher (retd), writer and editor; b. 19 Jan. 1932, Birmingham; m. Joan Doreen Barry 1954; one s. one d. *Education:* Birmingham Univ., Nottingham Univ. *Career:* Founding Ed. 1983, Company Secretary, Co-Ed. 1988–2001, Staple New Writing. *Publications:* Leaving 1965, Fourteen 1965, English Now and Then 1965, Larger Than Life 1967, Quattordicenni 1967, The Personal Element 1967, Lawrence and the Real England 1985, Ruskin: The Last Chapter 1989, Twenty Years of Twentieth Century Poetry 2001, Jane Austen out of the Blue 2006, Jane Austen and the Polite Puzzle 2007, Fourteen Revisited 2008, A Dream of Fair Women (John Ruskin) 2009. *Honours:* Companion, Ruskin's Guild of St George 2010. *Address:* Tor Cottage, 81 Cavendish Road, Matlock, Derbyshire DE4 3HD, England (home).

MECKEL, Christoph; German author, poet and graphic artist; b. 12 June 1935, Berlin. *Education:* studied in Freiburg, Paris and Munich. *Career:* mem.

Acad. of Science and Literature, Mainz; Akademie für Sprache und Dichtung eV, Darmstadt; PEN. *Publications:* Manifest der Toten, 1960; Im Land der Umbramauten, 1961; Wildnisse, 1962; Die Drummheit liefert uns ans Messer: Zeitgespräch in zehn Sonetten (with Volker von Törne), 1967; Bockshorn, 1973; Wen es angeht, 1974; Komödie der Hölle, 3 vols, 1979, 1984, 1987; Suchbild: Über meinen Vater, 1980; Ein roter Faden, 1983; Das Buch Jubal, 1987; Das Buch Shiralee, 1989; Von den Luftgeschäften der Poesie, 1989; Die Messingstadt, 1991; Gesang vom unterbrochenen Satz, 1995. *Honours:* Rainer Maria Rilke Prize, 1979; Georg Trakl Prize, 1982; Literature Prize, Kassel, 1993.

MEDDEB, Abdelwahab; Tunisian poet, novelist and translator; *Professor of Comparative Literature, Université de Paris X (Paris-Nanterre);* b. 1946, Tunis. *Career:* Prof. of Comparative Literature, Université de Paris X (Paris-Nanterre); fmr Visiting Prof. Yale Univ.; Ed. Dédale literary journal; curator West by East exhibition, Centre for Contemporary Culture, Barcelona 2005. *Publications:* Talismano (novel) 1976, Tombeau d'Ibn Arabi (poems) 1987, Phantasia (novel) 1989, Le Dits de Bistami 1989, Récit de l'exil occidental 1993, Les 99 stations de Yale (poems) 1995, Aya dans les villes 1999, Matière des oiseaux 2001, La Maladie de l'Islam (non-fiction) 2002, Ibn Arabis Grab 2004; contrib. to Banipal magazine. *Address:* Université de Paris X (Paris-Nanterre), 200 avenue de la République, Paris 92001, Nanterre Cedex, France (office). *Telephone:* 1-40-97-56-30 (office). *E-mail:* Abdelwahab.Meddeb@u-paris10.fr (office). *Website:* www.u-paris10.fr.

MEDEIROS, Teresa, AA; American writer; b. 26 Oct. 1962, Heidelberg, Germany; m. Michael Medeiros 1984. *Education:* Madisonville Community Coll. *Career:* mem. Kentucky Romance Writers, Novelists Inc, Romance Writers of America. *Publications:* Lady of Conquest 1989, Shadows and Lace 1990, Heather and Velvet 1991, Once an Angel 1993, A Whisper of Roses 1993, Thief of Hearts 1994, Fairest of Them All 1995, Breath of Magic 1996, Touch of Enchantment 1997, Nobody's Darling 1998, Charming the Prince 1999, The Bride and the Beast 2000, A Kiss to Remember 2002, One Night of Scandal 2003, Yours until Dawn 2004, After Midnight 2005, The Vampire who Loved Me 2006, Some Like it Wicked 2008. *E-mail:* teresa@teresamedeiros.com (office). *Website:* www.teresamedeiros.com.

MEDINA, Dante, BA, MA, DLitt; Mexican poet, writer, translator and academic; b. 1954, Jilotlán de los Dolores, Jalisco. *Education:* Universidad Paul Valéry de Montpellier, France. *Career:* Founder and Dir Dept of Literary Studies, Universidad de Guadalajara 1985; Guggenheim Fellowship 1994. *Publications include:* fiction: La delicuescencia del lenguaje 1987 and 2004, Niñoserías 1989, Cosas de cualquier familia 1990, Léérere, Manual para hispanoandantes 1992, Tola, La Dama de la Gardenia 1992, Sólo los viajeros saben que al sur está el verano 1993, Cómo perder amigos (Premio Casa de las Américas) 1994, Maneras de describir a Ana/el agua, la luna, la montaña y los puentes 1995, Yo soy Don Juan, para servir a usted 1996 and 1998, Ciudades de por sí 1997, Vivir 1989, Feminus 2000, Del amor que te di 2000, Libreta de poemas para enamorar a la amada 2000, Te ve, mi amor, TV (Premio Casa de las Américas) 2001, A la bisconversa 2002, Ir, volver y... qué darse 2003, Doktor Psiquiatra 2003, Culito y Lugubrio 2004, La Musa Fea 2006, Mundus Novus: Américo 2006, Dibujos al carbón de la flor y la abeja para Amy 2007; translation: Djinn o la cita, de Alain Robbe-Grillet 1991, René Char 1993, Henri Michaux. De aquí y de otras partes 2004, Perspectiva de templos de Jalisco 2004, En la línea/Standing in line 2006. *Honours:* Chevalier de Tir Douzil, France; Juan Rulfo Award (Radio France Int.) 1984, Jalisco de las Artes 2002. *E-mail:* dantemedina@cybercable.net.mx. *Website:* www.dantemedina.com.

MEDOFF, Mark Howard, BA, MA; American dramatist and screenwriter; b. 18 March 1940, Mount Carmel, IL; m. Stephanie Thorne, three d. *Education:* University of Miami, Coral Gables, Stanford University. *Career:* mem. Actors Equity Asscn; Screen Actors Guild; Writers Guild of America. *Publications:* Plays: When You Comin' Back, Red Ryder?, 1973; Children of a Lesser God, 1979; The Majestic Kid, 1981; The Hands of Its Enemy, 1984; The Heart Outright, 1986; Big Mary, 1989; Stumps, 1989; Stephanie Hero, 1990; Kringle's Window, 1991. Film Scripts: Good Guys Wear Black, 1977; When You Comin' Back, Red Ryder?, 1978; Off Beat, 1985; Apology, 1986; Children of a Lesser God, 1987; Clara's Heart, 1988; City of Joy, 1992. Contributions: periodicals. *Honours:* Obie Award, 1974; Drama Desk Awards, 1974, 1980; New York Outer Critics Circle Awards, 1974, 1980; Guggenheim Fellowship, 1974–75; Antoinette Perry Award, 1980; Governor's Award for Excellence in the Arts, State of New Mexico, 1980; Distinguished Alumnus, University of Miami, 1987; California Media Access Award, 1988.

MEDVED, Michael, BA, MFA; American film critic, writer and broadcaster; b. 3 Oct. 1948, Philadelphia, Pennsylvania; m. 1st Nancy Harris Herman 1972 (divorced 1983); m. 2nd Diane Elvenstar 1985; one s. two d. *Education:* Yale Univ., California State Univ. at San Francisco. *Career:* political speech writer 1970–73; Creative Dir, Advertising, Anrick Inc, Oakland, CA 1973–74; Co-Founder and Pres., Pacific Jewish Center, Venice, CA 1977–94; On-Air Film Critic, People Now, Cable News Network 1980–83; Pres., Emanuel Streisand School, Venice, CA 1980–85; On-Air Film Critic and Co-Host, Sneak Previews, PBS-TV 1985–96; Chief Film Critic, New York Post 1993–98; radio talk show host, Seattle, Washington 1996–; nationally syndicated radio host, SRN Radio Network 1998–; mem. American Federation of Television and Radio Artists, Writers Guild of America. *Publications:* What Really Happened to the Class of '65? 1976, The 50 Worst Films of All Time (with Harry Medved) 1978, The Shadow Presidents 1979, The Golden Turkey Awards (with Harry Medved) 1980, Hospital 1983, The Hollywood Hall of Shame (with Harry Medved) 1984, Son of Golden Turkey Awards (with Harry Medved) 1986, Hollywood vs America 1992, Saving Childhood (with Diane Medved) 1998, Right Turns: Unconventional Lessons from a Controversial Life 2005, The 10 Big Lies About America 2008, The 5 Big Lies About American Business 2009; contributions: periodicals. *Website:* www.michaelmedved.com.

MEDVEDEV, Roy Aleksandrovich, PhD; Russian historian and sociologist; b. 14 Nov. 1925, Tbilisi; s. of Aleksandr Romanovich Medvedev and Yulia Medvedeva (née Reiman); twin brother of Zhores Medvedev (q.v.); m. Galina A. Gaidina 1956; one s. *Education:* Leningrad State Univ., Acad. of Pedagogical Sciences of USSR. *Career:* mem. CPSU –1969, 1989–91; worker at mil. factory 1943–46; teacher of history, Ural Secondary School 1951–53; Dir of Secondary School in Leningrad region 1954–56; Deputy to Ed.-in-Chief of Publishing House of Pedagogical Literature, Moscow 1957–59; Head of Dept, Research Inst. of Vocational Educ., Acad. of Pedagogical Sciences of USSR 1960–70, Senior Scientist 1970–71; freelance author 1972–; People's Deputy of USSR, mem. Supreme Soviet of USSR 1989–91; mem. Cen. Cttee CPSU 1990–91; Co-Chair. Socialist Party of Labour 1991–2003. *Publications:* Vocational Education in Secondary School 1960, Faut-il réhabiliter Staline? 1969, A Question of Madness (with Zhores Medvedev) 1971, Let History Judge 1972, On Socialist Democracy 1975, Qui a écrit le 'Don Paisible? 1975, La Révolution d'octobre était-elle inéluctable? 1975, Solschenizyn und die Sowjetische Linke 1976, Khrushchev–The Years in Power (with Zhores Medvedev) 1976, Political Essays 1976, Problems in the Literary Biography of Mikhail Sholokhov 1977, Samizdat Register 1978, Philip Mironov and the Russian Civil War (with S. Starikov) 1978, The October Revolution 1979, On Stalin and Stalinism 1979, On Soviet Dissent 1980, Nikolai Bukharin–The Last Years 1980, Leninism and Western Socialism 1981, An End to Silence 1982, Khrushchev 1983, All Stalin's Men 1984, China and Superpowers 1986, L'URSS che cambia (with G. Chiesa) 1987, Time of Change (with G. Chiesa) 1990, Brezhnev: A Political Biography 1991, Gensek s Lybianki: A Political Portrait of Andropov 1993, 1917. The Russian Revolution 1997, Capitalism in Russia? 1998, The Unknown Andropov 1998, Post-Soviet Russia 2000, The Unknown Stalin (with Zhores Medvedev) 2004, Putin 2004, Solzhenitsyn and Sakharov (with Zhores Medvedev) 2004, Moscow Model of Yuri Luzhkov 2005, Putin 2007, Divided Ukraine 2007, Nursaltan Nazarbayev 2008, The Soviet Union. The Last Years 2009, Boris Yeltsyn 2010; and over 400 professional and general articles. *Address:* c/o Z. A. Medvedev, 4 Osborn Gardens, London, NW7 1DY, England (home); Pos.Novo-Ivanovskoye 129, Post Box 16, P/O Nemchinovka, Odintsovky district, 143025 Moscow, Russia (home). *Telephone:* (495) 597-6120 (Moscow) (home).

MEDVEDEV, Zhores Aleksandrovich, PhD; British/Russian biologist (retd); b. 14 Nov. 1925, Tbilisi; s. of Aleksandr Romanovich Medvedev and Yulia Medvedeva (née Reiman); twin brother of Roy Medvedev (q.v.); m. Margarita Nikolayevna Buzina 1951; two s. *Education:* Timiriazev Acad. of Agricultural Sciences, Moscow, Inst. of Plant Physiology, USSR Acad. of Sciences. *Career:* joined Soviet Army 1943, served at front as a pvt.; Scientist, later Sr Scientist, Dept of Agrochemistry and Biochemistry, Timiriazev Acad. 1951–62; Head of Lab., Molecular Radiobiology, Inst. of Medical Radiology, Obninsk 1963–69; Sr Scientist All-Union Scientific Research Inst. of Physiology and Biochemistry of Farm Animals, Borovsk 1970–72; Sr Scientist, Nat. Inst. for Medical Research, London 1973–92; mem. American Gerontological Soc., Biochemical Soc., Genetic Soc.; Soviet citizenship restored 1990. *Publications:* Protein Biosynthesis and Problems of Heredity, Development and Ageing 1963, Molecular-Genetic Mechanisms of Development 1968, The Rise and Fall of T. D. Lysenko 1969, The Medvedev Papers 1970, A Question of Madness (with Roy Medvedev) 1971, Ten Years After 1973, Khrushchev – The Years in Power (with Roy Medvedev) 1976, Soviet Science 1978, The Nuclear Disaster in the Urals 1979, Andropov 1983, Gorbachev 1986, Soviet Agriculture 1987, The Legacy of Chernobyl 1990, The Unknown Stalin (with Roy Medvedev) 2001, Stalin and the Jewish Problem 2003, Solzhenitsyn and Sakharov (with Roy Medvedev) 2004, Nutrition and Longevity 2007, Polonii v Londone 2008; more than 400 papers and articles on gerontology, genetics, biochemistry, environment, history and other topics. *Honours:* Book Award, Moscow Naturalist Soc. 1965, Aging Research Award of US Aging Asscn 1984, René Schubert Preis in Gerontology 1985. *Address:* 4 Osborn Gardens, London, NW7 1DY, England (home). *Telephone:* (20) 8346-4158 (home). *E-mail:* zhmedvedev@yahoo.co.uk (home).

MEEK, James; British writer and journalist; b. 7 Dec. 1962, London. *Career:* newspaper reporter 1985–2006; writer for The Guardian, in Russia and Ukraine 1991–99, in London 1999–2006. *Publications:* novels: Mcfarlane Boils the Sea 1989, Drivetime 1995, The People's Act of Love (RSL Ondaatje Prize 2006, Scottish Arts Council Book of the Year 2006) 2005, We Are Now Beginning our Descent 2008; short story collections: Last Orders 1992, The Museum of Doubt 2000; contrib. to LRB, Granta. *Honours:* British Press Awards Foreign Reporter of the Year 2004. *Literary Agent:* c/o AP Watt Ltd, 20 John Street, London, WC1N 2DR, England. *Telephone:* (20) 7405-6774. *Fax:* (20) 7831-2154. *E-mail:* apw@apwatt.co.uk. *Website:* www.apwatt.co.uk. *Address:* c/o Canongate Books, 14 High Street, Edinburgh, EH1 1TE, Scotland (office). *E-mail:* customerservices@canongate.co.uk (office). *Website:* www.canongate.co.uk (office).

MEEK, Jay, BA, MA; American academic and poet; *Professor Emeritus, University of North Dakota;* b. 23 Aug. 1937, Grand Rapids, Mich.; m. Martha

George 1966; one d. *Education:* Univ. of Michigan, Syracuse Univ. *Career:* Faculty mem., Wake Forest Univ. 1977–80, Sarah Lawrence Coll. 1980–82; Assoc. Prof., MIT 1982–83; Writer-in-Residence, Memphis State Univ. 1984; Prof., Univ. of North Dakota 1985–2004, Prof. Emer. 2004–. *Publications:* The Week the Dirigible Came 1976, Drawing on the Walls 1980, Earthly Purposes 1984, Stations 1989, Windows 1994, Headlands: New and Selected Poems 1997, The Memphis Letters (novel) 2002, Trains in Winter 2004; contrib. to journals and magazines. *Honours:* NEA Award 1972–73, Guggenheim Fellowship 1985–86, Bush Artist Fellowship 1989. *Address:* 3149 34th Avenue South, Minneapolis, MN 55406, USA (home). *Telephone:* (612) 729-0260 (home).

MEGGED, Aharon; Israeli (b. Polish) writer; b. 10 Aug. 1920, Wloclawek; m. Eda Zoritte 1946; two s. *Career:* Ed. MASSA 1953–55; Literary Ed. Lamerchav Daily 1955–68; Cultural Attaché, Israel Embassy, London 1968–71; columnist, Davar Daily 1971–85; mem. Israel PEN Centre (Pres. 1980–87), Hebrew Acad. 1982–. *Plays include:* Hedva and I 1955, Hannah Senesh 1963, Genesis 1965, The High Season 1968. *Publications include:* Hedva and I 1953, Fortunes of a Fool 1960, Living on the Dead 1965, The Short Life 1971, The Bat 1975, Asahel 1978, Heinz, His Son and the Evil Spirit 1979, Journey in the Month of Av 1980, The Flying Camel and the Golden Hump 1982, The Turbulent Zone (essays) 1985, Foiglmann 1987, The Writing Desk (literary essays) 1988, Anat's Day of Illumination 1992, Longing for Olga 1994, Iniquity 1996, Love-Flowers from the Holy Land 1998, Persephone Remembers 2000, Until Evening 2001, Beautiful Milisinda 2002, Yotam's Vengeance 2003, Three of Them 2006, Flies 2008, The Ten Days of Awe; contribs to Atlantic Monthly, Encounter, Midstream, Listener, Moment, Present Tense, Partisan Review, Ariel. *Honours:* Dr hc (Bar-Ilan Univ.) 2008; Brenner Prize 1960, Bialik Prize 1973, Present Tense, New York 1983, Agnon Prize 1997, Wizo-Paris Prize 1998, Prime Minister's Prize 1998, 2007, Pres.'s Prize 2001, Koret Prize 2003, Israel Prize for Literature 2003. *Literary Agent:* c/o Lipman AG, Marienberg Str. 23, PO Box 572, 8044 Zürich, Switzerland. *Address:* 8 Pa'amoni Street, Tel-Aviv 62918, Israel (home). *Telephone:* (3) 6021680 (home). *Fax:* (3) 6022408 (home). *E-mail:* meged1@zahav.net.il.

MEGUID, Ibrahim Abdel, BA; Egyptian novelist; b. 1946, Alexandria. *Education:* Alexandria Univ. *Career:* Consultant for Cultural Matters, Popular Culture Council. *Publications include:* al-Balda al-oukhra (trans. as The Other Place 1997) (Naguib Mahfouz Medal for Literature 1996), La ahad yanam fi al-iskandaria (trans. as No One Sleeps in Alexandria 1999), Tujur al-'anbar (trans. as Birds of Amber 2005), Bayt al-yasmin (trans. as La Maison de Jasmin), Burj al-azra' (The Virgo Sign), Distant Train (in trans.) 2008. *Address:* c/o American University in Cairo Press, 113 Kasr el Aini Street, POB 2511, Cairo 11511, Egypt (office). *Telephone:* (2) 2797-6926 (office). *Fax:* (2) 2794-1440 (office). *E-mail:* aucpress@aucegypt.edu (office). *Website:* www .aucpress.com.

MEHREN, Stein; Norwegian poet, novelist and playwright; b. 16 May 1935, Oslo. *Education:* Univ. of Oslo. *Career:* also renowned as a painter. *Publications include:* poetry: Gjennom stillheten en natt (Through the Silence One Night) 1960, Mot en verden av lys (Norwegian Critics' Prize for Literature) 1963, Gobelin Europa (Goblin Europe) 1965, Den store søndagsfrikosten (The Great Sunday Breakfast) 1976, Evighet, vårt flyktigste stoff 1994, Hotell Memory 1996, Kjærlighetsdikt 1997, Nattmaskin (Nightmachine) 1998, Utvalgte dikt 1999, Ark 2000, Den siste ildlender 2002, Imperiet lukker seg 2005, Nye bilder, tidlige dikt (New Paintings, Early Poems) 2005, Call from a Dark Star 2006. *Honours:* Dagbladets lyrikkpris i 1966, Kulturrådets bokpris 1966, 1969, Doublougprisen 1971, Nordic Council Literature Prize 1971, 1978, 1982, 1984, 1993, 2005, Fritt Ord-prisen 1978, Det norske Akademi for Sprog og Litteraturs pris 1987, Anders Jahres Pris 1993. *Literary Agent:* Aschehoug Agency, POB 363 Sentrum, 0102 Oslo, Norway.

MEHROTRA, Sriram, MA, PhD; Indian writer and educator; b. 23 June 1931, Anantram, Etawah, UP; m. Eva Mehrotra 1957. *Education:* Univ. of Allahabad, Univ. of London. *Career:* Lecturer, Univ. of London 1962; Fellow, Indian Inst. of Advanced Study, Shimla 1971–79; Prof., Himachal Pradesh Univ. 1972; Visiting Prof., Univ. of Wisconsin 1974; Visiting Fellow, St John's Coll., Cambridge 1983–84; Nehru Prof., MD Univ. 1992–96; mem. Indian Inst. of Public Admin. *Publications:* India and the Commonwealth, 1885–1929 1965, The Emergence of the Indian National Congress 1971, The Commonwealth and the Nation 1978, Towards India's Freedom and Partition 1979, A History of the Indian National Congress, Vol. 1 1885–1918 1995, Selected Writings of Allan Octavian Hume (1829–1867) Vol. 1 (co-ed.) 2004; contrib. to scholarly journals. *Address:* Seva, Kenfield Estate, Ambedkar Chowk, Shimla 171 004, India (home). *Telephone:* (177) 2656615 (home); 9816 136171 (mobile). *E-mail:* srirammehrotra@yahoo.com (home).

MEHTA, Ajai Singh (Sonny); American (b. Indian) publishing company executive; *Chairman and Editor-in-Chief, Knopf Publishing Group;* b. 1942, India; m. Gita Mehta; one s. *Education:* Lawrence School, Sanawar, and St Catherine's Coll., Univ. of Cambridge. *Career:* fmrly with Paladin, Pan and Picador Publs, UK; Pres. Alfred A. Knopf Div. of Random House (now Knopf Publishing Group, New York) 1987–, now Chair. and Ed.-in-Chief. *Honours:* Lifetime Achievement Award, Asian American Writers Workshop 2009. *Address:* Alfred A. Knopf Inc., 1745 Broadway, New York, NY 10019, USA (office). *E-mail:* knopfpublicity@randomhouse.com (office). *Website:* www .randomhouse.com/knopf (office).

MEHTA, Gita; Indian writer; b. 1943, Delhi; d. of the late Biju Patnaik and Gyan Patnaik; m. Ajai Singh 'Sonny' Mehta; one s. *Education:* Univ. of Cambridge. *Career:* Dir, documentaries about India for BBC, NBC. *Publications:* Karma Cola: Marketing The Mystic East 1979, Raj (novel) 1989, A River Sutra (novel) 1993, Snakes and Ladders: Glimpses of Modern India (essays) 1997, Mountain Sutra 1999; contrib. essay 'Unborn', in Clemente 1999. *Address:* c/o Random House Publicity Department, 1745 Broadway, New York, NY 10019, USA (office). *Website:* www.randomhouse.com (office).

MEHTA, Suketu; Indian writer and journalist; *Associate Professor of Journalism, New York University;* b. 1963, Calcutta; m.; two c. *Education:* New York Univ., Univ. of Iowa. *Career:* currently Assoc. Prof. of Journalism, New York Univ. *Films:* screenplays: The Goddess, Mission Kashmir. *Publications:* Maximum City: Bombay Lost and Found (Kiriyama Prize 2005, Hutch Crossword Prize) 2004; contribs to New York Times, Granta, Harper's, Time Condé Nast Traveler, The Village Voice. *Honours:* Whiting Writers Award 1997, O. Henry Prize 1997, New York Foundation for the Arts Fellowship, Guggenheim Fellowship 2007. *Address:* c/o Russell Perreault, Random House, 1745 Broadway, New York, NY 10019, USA (office). *E-mail:* rperreault@ randomhouse.com (office); suketu@suketu.com (office). *Website:* www .suketumehta.com.

MEHTA, Ved (Parkash), MA, FRSL; American (naturalized) writer and academic; b. 21 March 1934, Lahore, Pakistan (fmrly British India); s. of Dr. Amolak Ram and Shanti Mehta (née Mehra); m. Linn Cary 1983; two d. *Education:* Arkansas School for the Blind, Pomona Coll., Calif., Balliol Coll., Oxford, UK, Harvard Univ. *Career:* staff writer, New Yorker magazine 1961–94; Visiting Scholar, Case Western Reserve 1974; Visiting Prof. of Literature, Bard Coll. 1985, 1986; Noble Foundation Visiting Coll. of Art and Cultural History, Sarah Lawrence Coll. 1988; Fellow, New York Inst. for the Humanities 1988–92; Visiting Fellow (Literature), Balliol Coll., Oxford 1988–89; Visiting Prof. of English, New York Univ. 1989–90; Rosenkrantz Chair in Writing, Yale Univ. 1990–93, Lecturer in History 1990, 1991, 1992, Lecturer in English 1991–93; Assoc. Fellow, Berkeley Coll. (a constituent of Yale Coll.) 1988–89, Residential Fellow 1990–93; Arnold Bernhard Visiting Prof. of English and History, Williams Coll. 1994; Randolph Visiting Distinguished Prof. of English and History, Vassar Coll., New York 1994–96; Sr Fellow, Freedom Forum, Media Studies Center and Visiting Scholar, Columbia Univ., New York 1996–97; Fellow, Center for Advanced Study in Behavioral Sciences 1997–98; mem. Council on Foreign Relations 1979–, Usage Panel, American Heritage Dictionary 1982. *Television:* writer and narrator of documentary film, Chachaji: My Poor Relation (DuPont Columbia Award for Excellence in Broadcast Journalism 1977–78) (PBS) 1978, (BBC) 1980. *Publications:* Face to Face (Secondary Educ. Annual Book Award 1958, serial reading on BBC Light Programme 1958, dramatization on BBC Home Programme 1959) 1957, Walking the Indian Streets 1960, Fly and the Fly Bottle 1963, Delinquent Chacha (novel) 1967, Portrait of India 1970, John Is Easy to Please 1971, Mahatma Gandhi and His Apostles 1977, The New India 1978, Photographs of Chachaji 1980, A Family Affair: India Under Three Prime Ministers 1982, Three Stories of the Raj (fiction) 1986, Rajiv Gandhi and Rama's Kingdom 1995, A Ved Mehta Reader: The Craft of the Essay 1998, Continents of Exile (autobiography): Daddyji 1972, Mamaji 1979, Vedi 1982 (serial reading on BBC Book at Bedtime 1990), The Ledge Between the Streams 1984, Sound-Shadows of the New World 1986, The Stolen Light 1989, Up at Oxford 1993, Remembering Mr. Shawn's New Yorker 1998, All For Love 2001, Dark Harbor 2003, The Red Letters (concluding volume) 2004, Veritas 2012. *Honours:* Hon. Fellow, Balliol Coll. Oxford 1999; Hon. DLtrs (Pomona Coll.) 1972, (Williams Coll.) 1986; Hon. DLitt (Bard Coll.) 1982; Hon. DUniv (Stirling, Scotland) 1988; Hon. LHD (Bowdoin) 1995; Hazen Fellow 1956–59, Harvard Prize Fellow 1959–60, Residential Fellow, Eliot House 1959–61, Guggenheim Fellow 1971–72, 1977–78, Ford Foundation Travel and Study Grantee 1971–76, and Public Policy Grantee 1979–82, MacArthur Prize Fellow 1982–87, Asscn of Indians in America Award 1978, Signet Medal, Harvard Univ. 1983, Distinguished Service Award, Asian/Pacific American Library Asscn 1986, New York City Mayor's Liberty Medal 1986, Centenary Barrows Award, Pomona Coll. 1987, New York Public Library Literary Lion Medal 1990, and Literary Lion Centennial Medal 1996, New York State Asian-American Heritage Month Award 1991, South Asian Literary Asscn Lifetime Achievement Award 2004. *Address:* 139 East 79th Street, New York, NY 10075, USA (home). *Fax:* (212) 472-7220 (home). *E-mail:* mehta.ved@ gmail.com (home). *Website:* www.vedmehta.com.

MEIGHAN, Roland, DSocSc, PhD, FRSA; British writer, publisher and consultant; b. 29 May 1937, Sutton Coldfield; m. Janet Meighan; one s. two step-s. *Career:* various school teaching positions; Lecturer, then Sr Lecturer in Educ., Univ. of Birmingham; Special Prof. of Educ., Univ. of Nottingham; ind. writer and consultant; Founder and Dir Educational Heretics Press; Dir and Trustee Centre for Personalised Educ. Trust. *Publications:* Flexischooling 1988, Theory and Practice of Regressive Education 1993, The Freethinkers' Guide to the Educational Universe 1994, John Holt: Personalised Education and the Reconstruction of Schooling 1995, The Next Learning System 1997, The Next Learning System: Pieces of the Jigsaw 2000, Learning Unlimited 2001, Natural Learning and the Natural Curriculum 2001, John Holt: Personalised Learning Instead of Uninvited Teaching 2002, Damage Limitation: Trying to Reduce the Harm Schools do to Children 2004, Comparing Learning Systems: The Good, the Bad, the Ugly and the Counterproductive 2005, A Sociology of Educating (fifth edn) 2007; contrib. to Natural Parent

Magazine, Observer, Yorkshire Post, Times Educational Supplement. *Address:* 113 Arundel Drive, Bramcote, Nottingham, NG9 3FQ, England (office). *Telephone:* (115) 925-7261 (office). *Website:* www.edheretics.gn.apc.org (office).

MEINER, Richard; German publisher; b. 8 April 1918, Dresden; s. of Felix Meiner and Elisabeth Meiner (née Gensel); m. Ursula Ehlert 1947; one s. one d. *Career:* mil. service 1937–45; f. Richard Meiner Verlag, Hamburg 1948–64; Dir Verlage Felix Meiner 1964–81, Felix Meiner Verlag GmbH, Hamburg 1981–98. *Publications include:* Verlegerische Betreuung der Philosophischen Bibliothek, Corpus Philosophorum Teutonicorum Medii Aevi, G.W.F. Hegel, Gesammelte Werke. Krit. Ausgabe, G.W.F. Hegel, Vorlesungen, Kant-Forschungen, Nicolai de Cusa Opera omnia. Krit. Ausgabe, Handbuch PRAGMATIK, Studien zum achtzehnten Jahrhundert und weitere philosophische Reihen und Einzelmonographien. *Honours:* Hon. Fellow, German Soc. for Philosophy in Germany 1988; Bundesverdienstkreuz I. Klasse 1989; Mil. Medal, Gold Medal of Union of German Booksellers 1983, Medal of Honour of German Bücherei Leipzig 1987. *Address:* c/o Felix Meiner Verlag GmbH, Richardstrasse 47, 22081 Hamburg, Germany.

MEINKE, Peter, AB, MA, PhD; American fmr academic, poet and writer; *Professor Emeritus, Eckerd College;* b. (James Peter Meinke), 29 Dec. 1932, Brooklyn, NY; s. of Harry Meinke and Kathleen McDonald; m. Jeanne Clark 1957; two s. two d. *Education:* Hamilton Coll., Univ. of Michigan, Univ. of Minnesota. *Career:* Asst Prof., Hamline Univ., St Paul, Minn. 1961–66; Prof. of Literature and Dir of the Writing Workshop, Eckerd Coll., St Petersburg, Fla 1966–93, Prof. Emer. 1993–; Fulbright Sr Lecturer, Univ. of Warsaw 1978–79; Visiting Distinguished Writer, Univ. of Hawaii 1993, Univ. of North Carolina, Greensboro 1996; Fellow, Le Château de Lavigny, Switzerland 1998; Darden Chair in Creative Writing, Old Dominion Univ., Norfolk, Va 2003–05; Distinguished Poet-in-Residence, Wichita State Univ. 2008; Writer-in-Residence, Hamilton Coll. 2008, Univ. of Southern Florida, Tampa 2010; Distinguished Writer-in-Residence, Converse Coll. 2010; Poet Laureate, St Petersburg, Fla 2009–; joined faculty of MFA A in Creative Writing (low residency program), Univ. of Tampa, FL 2012; mem. Acad. of American Poets, Poetry Soc. of America. *Publications:* Lines from Neuchâtel 1974, The Night Train and the Golden Bird 1977, The Rat Poems 1978, Trying to Surprise God 1981, The Piano Tuner 1986, Underneath the Lantern 1987, Night Watch on the Chesapeake 1987, Far from Home 1988, Liquid Paper: New and Selected Poems 1991, Scars 1996, Campocorto 1996, The Shape of Poetry 1999, Zinc Fingers 2000, Greatest Hits 2001, The Contracted World 2006, Unheard Music 2007, 35th Anniversary Edn of Lines from Neuchatel (Award of Excellence, Southeastern Library Asscn 2009) 2009, Lassing Park 2011; contrib. to periodicals. *Honours:* Hon. DHumLitt (Eckerd Coll.) 2007; First Prize, Olivet Sonnet Competition 1966, Nat. Endowment for the Arts Fellowships 1974, 1989, Gustav Davidson Memorial Award, Poetry Soc. of America 1976, Lucille Medwick Memorial Award, Poetry Soc. of America 1984, Flannery O'Connor Award 1986, Emily Dickinson Award, Poetry Soc. of America 1992, Paumanok Poetry Award 1993, Master Artist's Fellowship, Fine Arts Work Center, Provincetown 1995, Award for Poetry, Southeast Booksellers Asscn 2000. *Address:* 147 Wildwood Lane SE, St Petersburg, FL 33705, USA (home). *Telephone:* (727) 896-1862 (home). *E-mail:* meinkep@eckerd.edu (home). *Website:* www.petermeinke.com.

MELCHETT, Sonia (see Sinclair, Sonia Elizabeth)

MELCHIOR, Ib Jorgen; American writer, dramatist and director; b. 17 Sept. 1917, Copenhagen, Denmark; s. of Lauritz and Inger Melchior; m. 1st Kate Hathaway 1942 (divorced 1960); one s.; m. 2nd Cleo Baldon 1964; one step.s. *Education:* Stenhus Coll., Univ. of Copenhagen. *Career:* writer, dir, over 500 live and filmed TV episodes, 12 feature films, 60 documentary films 1959–76; mem. Authors' Guild, Dirs Guild of America, Manuscript Soc., Writers' Guild of America, Acad. of Science Fiction. *Films include:* Live Fast, Die Young (writer) 1958, The Angry Red Planet (writer and dir) 1960, Reptilicus (writer) 1961, Journey to the Seventh Planet (writer) 1962, Robinson Crusoe on Mars (writer) 1964, The Time Travelers (writer and dir) 1964, Terrore nello spazio (writer) 1965, Ambush Bay (writer) 1966, Death Race 2000 (writer) 1975. *Television includes:* The Perry Como Show (series dir) 1948, The March of Medicine (series dir) 1958, Men Into Space (series writer) 1959, The Outer Limits (series writer) 1963. *Publications:* Order of Battle 1972, Sleeper Agent 1975, The Haigerloch Project 1977, The Watchdogs of Abaddon 1979, The Marcus Device 1980, Hour of Vengeance (stage play, Shakespeare Soc. of America Hamlet Award 1982) 1982, Eva 1984, V-3 1985, Code Name: Grand Guignol 1987, Steps and Stairways 1989, Quest 1990, Hitler's Werewolves 1991, Case by Case 1993, Reflections on the Pool 1997, Lauritz Melchior: The Golden Years of Bayreuth 2003. *Honours:* Golden Scroll 1976, Outstanding American-Scandinavian 1995, Bronze Star, King Christian X Medal, Denmark, Knight Commander, Militant Order of St Brigitte, Sweden. *Address:* 8228 Marmont Lane, Los Angeles, CA 90069, USA (home). *E-mail:* ijmelchior@aol.com (office).

MELEAGROU, Evie (Ivi), BA; Cypriot writer; b. 27 May 1928, Nicosia; d. of Efstathios Hadjidemetriou and Euridice Akritas; m. Ioannis Meleagros 1952; two d. one s. *Education:* Pancyprian Gymnasium (Nicosia), Athenerum Inst. (Athens), Ecole de St Joseph (Nicosia) and Univ. of London (UK). *Career:* Secondary school teacher of English and French 1947–52; broadcaster 1952–55; Ed. Cyprus Chronicles literary magazine 1960–72, George Seferis' works 1969–72; Pres. Pancyprian Women's Asscn 1974–81; Official Rep. World Writers' Conf. 1965, Panhellenic Congress on the Status of Women 1975, TV discussion on Cyprus, Greece 1984; public speaker on Cyprus in many countries; numerous TV appearances in UK, USA, Norway, Lebanon, France, etc; First Prize Pancyprian Short Story Competition 1952, Pancyprian Novella Competition 1957, Cyprus Nat. Novel Award 1970, 1981, Hellenic Nat. Novel Award 1981. *Publications:* Solomos Family 1957, Anonymous City (short stories) 1963, Eastern Mediterranean 1969, Conversation With Che 1970, Penultimate Era 1980, Persona is the Unknown Cypriot Woman (essays and poetry) 1994, The Virgin Plunge in the Ocean Depths (short stories and novellas) 1996; short stories have been translated into English, German, Russian and Hungarian. *Address:* 22 Mesolongi St, Nicosia 100, Cyprus. *Telephone:* (2) 463507.

MELECKI, Maciej; Polish poet and screenwriter; b. 1969. *Career:* works at the Mikołów Institute; co-ed., Arcadia journal. *Publications:* poetry: Zachodzenie za siebie (Behind the Self), 1993; Te sprawy (Such Things), 1995; Niebezpiecznie blisko (Dangerously Close), 1996; Dalsze zajecia (Further Goings Behind), 1998; Zimni ogrodnicy (Mid-May Cold Spell), 1999; Przypadki i odmiany (Cases and Declensions), 2001. Screenplays: Wojaczek (co-writer), 1997; Autsajder, 2000; Dzien Oszusta, 2000. Contributions: Chicago Review; anthologies: Inny Swit, 1994; Macie swoich poetów, 1995, 1997; Dlugie pozegnanie, 1997; Antologia współczesnej poezji polskiej, 2000; 14, 44, 2000.

MELFI, Mary, BA, MLS; Canadian author, poet and dramatist; b. 10 June 1951, near Rome, Italy; m. George Nemeth 1975; two s. *Education:* Loyola College, Concordia University, McGill University. *Publications:* The Dance, the Cage and the Horse (poems), 1976; A Queen Is Holding a Mummified Cat (poems), 1982; A Bride in Three Acts (poems), 1983; A Dialogue with Masks (novella), 1985; The O Canada Poems, 1986; A Season in Beware (poems), 1989; Infertility Rites (novel), 1991; Ubu: The Witch Who Would Be Rich (children's novel), 1994; Sex Therapy (play), 1996; Painting Moments, Art, AIDS and Nick Palazzo (ed.), 1998; Stages: Selected Poems, 1998; Office Politics (poems), 1999. Contributions: many reviews, quarterlies and journals. *Honours:* Canada Council Arts Grants, 1981–82, 1982–83; Québec Arts Council Grants, 1993–94, 1996–97; Canadian Heritage Grant, 1995. *Address:* c/o Guernica Editions, PO Box 117, Station P, Toronto, ON M5S 2S6, Canada.

MELINESCU, Gabriela; Romanian poet, editor, essayist and translator; b. 16 Aug. 1942, Bucharest. *Education:* Univ. of Philology, Bucharest. *Career:* began career as Ed. Femeia and Luceafarul magazines; based in Sweden 1975–; trans. of works by Swedenborg, Strindberg, Brigitta Trotzig, Goran Sonevi. *Publications:* poetry: Ceremonie de iarna 1965, Fiintele abstracte 1967, Interiorul legii 1968, Boala de origine divina 1970, Juramantul de saracie, castitate si supunere (Writers' Union Prize) 1972, Inginarea lumiir 1972, Impotriva celui drag 1975, Zeul fecunditatii 1977, Oglinda femeii 1986, Lumina spre lumina 1993; prose: Jurnal suedez Vols I–III, Bobinocarii 1969, Catargul cu doua corabii (juvenile) 1969, Viata cere viata (jtly) (non-fiction) 1975, Copiii rabdarii 1979, Lupii urca in cer 1981, Vrajitorul din Gallipoli 1986, Regina strazii 1988, Omul pasare (Swedish Acad. De Nio Prize) 1991; contrib. to Crossing Boundaries: An International Anthology of Women's Experiences in Sport 1999. *Honours:* Albert Bonniers Prize 2002, Nichita Stanescu Prize 2002, Inst. of Romanian Culture Prize 2004. *Address:* c/o Editura Polirom, Bd. Copou nr. 4, 700506 Iași, Romania. *E-mail:* office@polirom.ro.

MELLAH, Fawzi; Tunisian writer and sociologist; b. 1946. *Career:* based in Geneva, Switzerland; has acted as legal consultant to immigrants. *Plays:* Néron, ou Les oiseaux de passage 1973, Palais de non-retour 1975. *Publications:* novels: Elissa la reine vagabonde 1988, Le Conclave des pleureuses 1997, Entre chien et loup 1997; non-fiction: De lunité arabe: essai d'interprétation critique 1985, Clandestins en méditerranée 2001. *Address:* c/o Éditions Cérès, 6 rue Alain Savary, Le Belvédère, Tunis 1002, Tunisia. *E-mail:* info@ceres-editions.com.

MELLING, John Kennedy, FRSA, FCA; English drama critic, editor, writer, lecturer and broadcaster and chartered accountant; b. 11 Jan. 1927, Westcliff-on-Sea, Essex; s. of John Robert Melling and Ivy Edith May Melling (née Woolmer). *Education:* Thirsk School, Westcliff High School for Boys. *Career:* drama critic The Stage 1957–90; theatre correspondent Essex Countryside 1966–77; drama critic Fur Weekly News 1968–73; Ed. The Liveryman Magazine 1970–75; Antiques Correspondent, Evening Echo 1971–74; Ed. Chivers Black Dagger Series of Crime Classics 1986–91; radio crime book critic BBC London 1984–85, BBC Essex 1987; Fellow Inst. of Taxation; Fellow Faculty of Building; mem. BAFTA, CWA (cttee mem. 1985–88), Cookery and Food Asscn, Marylebone Rifle and Pistol Club, City Livery Club, American Federation of Police (int. life vice-pres.); conducted masterclasses for Arts Council 2004–; lectured on crime fiction on liner QEII. *Radio:* conducted interview with Alfred Hitchcock (BBC) 1966. *Play:* The Gilbertian Consequences of Mr Sullivan 1971. *Publications:* Discovering Lost Theatres 1969, Southend Playhouses from 1793 1969, Discovering London's Guilds and Liveries 1973, Discovering Theatre Ephemera 1974, She Shall Have Murder 1987, Murder in the Library (ed.) 1987, Crime Writers' Handbook of Practical Information (ed.) 1989, Gwendoline Butler: Inventor of the Women's Police Procedural 1993, Alchemy of Murder 1993, Murder Done to Death 1996, Scaling the High C's (with John L. Brecknock) 1996, A Little Manual of Etiquette for Gentlemen 2004, The Constructors – Genesis and Growth 2004, A Little Manual of Etiquette for Ladies 2006; plays: George... From Caroline 1971, The Toast Is... (series) 1979–84, Old Christmas, Diarists' Pleasures

1982, Murder at St Dunstan's 1983; contrib. to newspapers, journals and audiobooks; regular columnist Crime Time 1996–2002. *Honours:* elected Livery Worshipful Cos of Bakers 1975, of Farriers 1980, of Constructors 2004; Master Worshipful Company of Poulters 1980–81; Hon. Chief of Police (USA) 1989; Knight Grand Cross, Order of St Michael, Knight Order of St Basil 1984; CWA Award for Outstanding Services 1989, American Law Enforcement Officers Asscn Medal of Honor 1984. *Address:* 44A Tranquil Vale, Blackheath, London, SE3 0BD (home); 85 Chalkwell Avenue, Westcliff-on-Sea, Essex SS0 8NL, England (home). *Telephone:* (20) 8852-9230 (home); (1702) 476012 (home). *Fax:* (20) 8852-9230 (home).

MELLOR, David Hugh, MA, MEng, MS, PhD, ScD; British philosopher and academic; *Professor Emeritus of Philosophy, University of Cambridge*; b. 10 July 1938, London, England; s. of S. D. Mellor and E. N. Mellor (née Hughes). *Education:* Newcastle Royal Grammar School, Manchester Grammar School and Pembroke Coll., Cambridge. *Career:* Harkness Fellowship in Chem. Eng, Univ. of Minnesota, USA 1960–62, MIT School of Chem. Eng Practice 1962; Tech. Officer, ICI 1962–63; research student in philosophy 1963–68; Fellow, Pembroke Coll., Cambridge 1964–70; Fellow, Darwin Coll., Cambridge 1971–2005, Vice-Master 1983–87; Asst Lecturer in Philosophy, Univ. of Cambridge 1965–70, Lecturer 1970–83, Reader in Metaphysics 1983–86, Prof. of Philosophy 1986–99, Prof. Emer. 1999–, Pro-Vice-Chancellor 2000–01; Visiting Fellow in Philosophy, ANU 1975; Radcliffe Fellow in Philosophy 1978–80; Visiting Prof., Auckland Univ., NZ 1985; Pres. British Soc. for the Philosophy of Science 1985–87, Aristotelian Soc. 1992–93; Fellow, British Acad. 1983–2008. *Publications:* The Matter of Chance 1971, Real Time 1981, Matters of Metaphysics 1991, The Facts of Causation 1995, Real Time II 1998, Probability: A Philosophical Introduction 2005, Mind, Meaning and Reality 2012; numerous articles on philosophy of science, metaphysics and philosophy of mind. *Honours:* Hon. Prof. of Philosophy, Univ. of Keele 1989–92; Hon. PhD (Lund) 1997. *Address:* 25 Orchard Street, Cambridge, CB1 1JS, England (home). *Telephone:* 7815-687505 (mobile). *E-mail:* dhm11@cam.ac.uk (home). *Website:* people.pwf.cam.ac.uk/dhm11 (office).

MELO, Patrícia; Brazilian playwright, writer and screenwriter; b. 1962, Assis, São Paulo. *Screenplays:* Colônia Cecília (TV film) 1989, Traição (with others) 1998, Bufo & Spallanzani 2001, O Xangô de Baker Street 2001, O Homem do Ano 2003. *Publications:* novels: Acqua Toffana 1994, O Matador (trans. as The Killer) (Deux Océans Prize, France 1997, Deutscher Krimi Prize, Germany) 1995, Elogio da Mentira (trans. as In Praise of Lies) 1998, Inferno 2000, Valsa Negra (trans. as Black Waltz) 2003, Mundo Perdido (trans. as Lost World) 2006, Jonas, o Copromanta 2008. *Address:* c/o Departamento Editorial, Editoria Companhia das Letras, Rua Bandeira Paulista 702, cj. 32, São Paulo, SP 04532-002, Brazil. *Website:* www.companhiadasletras.com.br.

MELTZER, David; American poet, writer, teacher, editor and musician; b. 17 Feb. 1937, Rochester, NY; m. Christina Meyer 1958; one s. three d. *Education:* Los Angeles City College, University of California at Los Angeles. *Career:* Ed., Maya, 1966–71, Tree magazine and Tree Books, 1970–; Faculty, Graduate Poetics Program, 1980–, Chair, Undergraduate Writing and Literature Program, Humanities, 1988–, New College of California, San Francisco. *Publications:* Poetry: Poems (with Donald Schenker), 1957; Ragas, 1959; The Clown, 1960; Station, 1964; The Blackest Rose, 1964; Oyez!, 1965; The Process, 1965; In Hope I Offer a Fire Wheel, 1965; The Dark Continent, 1967; Nature Poem, 1967; Santamaya (with Jack Shoemaker), 1968; Round the Poem Box: Rustic and Domestic Home Movies for Stan and Jane Brakhage, 1969; Yesod, 1969; From Eden Book, 1969; Abulafia Song, 1969; Greenspeech, 1970; Luna, 1970; Letters and Numbers, 1970; Bronx Lil/Head of Lilian S.A.C., 1970; 32 Beams of Light, 1970; Knots, 1971; Bark: A Polemic, 1973; Hero/Lil, 1973; Tens: Selected Poems 1961–1971, 1973; The Eyes, the Blood, 1973; French Broom, 1973; Blue Rags, 1974; Harps, 1975; Six, 1976; Bolero, 1976; The Art, the Veil, 1981; The Name: Selected Poetry 1973–1983, 1984; Arrows: Selected Poetry 1957–1992, 1994; No Eyes: Lester Young, 2001. Fiction: Orf, 1968; The Agency, 1968; The Agent, 1968; How Many Blocks in the Pile?, 1968; Lovely, 1969; Healer, 1969; Out, 1969; Glue Factory, 1969; The Martyr, 1969; Star, 1970; The Agency Trilogy, 1994; Under, 2000. Other: We All Have Something to Say to Each Other: Being an Essay Entitled 'Patchen' and Four Poems, 1962; Introduction to the Outsiders, 1962; Bazascope Mother, 1964; Journal of the Birth, 1967; Isla Vista Notes: Fragmentary, Apocalyptic, Didactic Contradictions, 1970; Two-way Mirror: A Poetry Note-Book, 1977; San Francisco Beat: Talking With the Poets, 2002. Editor: Journal for the Protection of All Beings 1 and 3 (with Lawrence Ferlinghetti and Michael McClure), 2 vols, 1961, 1969; The San Francisco Poets, 1971, revised as Golden Gate, 1976; Birth: An Anthology, 1973; The Secret Garden: An Anthology in the Kabbalah, 1976; Death, 1984; Reading Jazz: The White Invention of Jazz, 1993; Writing Jazz, 1997. *Honours:* Council of Literary Magazine Grants, 1972, 1981; National Endowment for the Arts Grants, 1974, 1975; Tombstone Award for Poetry, James Ryan Morris Memorial Foundation, 1992.

MELVILLE, James (see Martin, (Roy) Peter)

MELVILLE, Jennie (see Butler, Gwendoline Williams)

MEMMI, Albert; French writer; b. 15 Dec. 1920, Tunis; s. of François Memmi and Marguerite née Sarfati; m. Germaine Dubach 1946; three c. *Education:* Lycée Carnot, Tunis, Univ. of Algiers and Univ. de Paris à la Sorbonne. *Career:* Teacher, Lycée Carnot, Tunis 1953, Teacher of Philosophy, Tunis 1955; Dir Psychological Centre, Tunis 1953–57; moved to France 1956; attached to Centre Nat. de la Recherche Scientifique (CNRS) 1957, Researcher, CNRS, Paris 1959–; Chargé de conférences, Ecole pratique des hautes études 1958, Asst Prof. 1959–66, Prof. 1966–70; Prof., Inst. de Psychanalyse, Paris 1968–; Prof., Univ. of Paris 1970–, Dir, Social Sciences Dept 1973–76, Dir, Anthropological Lab.; mem. Acad. des Sciences d'Outre-mer; Vice-Pres., Pen-Club 1976-79; Managing Agent, Syndicat des Écrivains de Langue Française (SELF) 1981; Vice-Pres., Comité Nat. Laïcité-République 1991; mem. Comité de patronage du MRAP; mem. Ligue Internationale Contre le Racisme et l'Anti-sémitisme (LICRA); Hon. Cttee Mem. l'Union Rationaliste, Comité Culturel Tunisien en France 1995; Scientific Cttee Mem. Cahiers Francophones d'Europe Centre-Orientale 1996; Cttee Mem. sponsoring Association des Anciens Elèves du Lycée Carnot de Tunis 1996; Hon. Mem. Association des Etudes Françaises en Afrique Australe 1996; Advisory mem., Institut des Études Transrégionales du Centre d'Études, Int. Study Centre, Princeton Univ. 1995; mem. l' Acad. des Sciences d'Outremer, l'Accademia Internazionale, l' Acad. de la Méditerranée. *Publications include:* novels: Le Statue de Sel (trans. as The Pillar of Salt) 1953, Strangers 1955, Agar 1955, Le Scorpion 1969, Le Désert 1977, Le Pharaon 1988; poems: Le Mirliton du ciel 1990, short stories: Le nomade immobile 2000, Térésa et autre femmes 2004; non-fiction: Portrait du colonisé 1957, Portrait d'un Juif 1962, Anthologie des écrivains Maghrebins 1964, 1969, Anthologie des écrivains nord-africains 1965, Les français et le racisme 1965, The Liberation of the Jew 1966, Dominated Man 1968, Decolonisation 1970, Juifs et Arabes 1974, Entretien 1975, La terre intérieure 1976, La dependance 1979, Le racisme 1982, Ce que je crois 1984, Les écrivains francophones du Maghreb 1985, L'Écriture colorée 1986, Testament insolent 1990, Bonheurs 1992, A contre-courants 1993, Ah, quel bonheur 1995, Le Juif et l'autre 1995, L'Exercice du bonheur 1996, Le Buveur et l'amoureux 1996, Feu sur 40 idées recues 1999, Dictionnaire à l'usage des incrédules 2002, Portrait du décolonisé, arabo-musulman et de quelques autres 2004; contrib. to Le onde 1989–94, Le Figaro 1995, New York Times, L'Action. *Honours:* Officier Légion d'honneur; Commdr Ordre de Nichan Iftikhar; Officier des Palmes académiques, Officier des Arts et des Lettres, Officier Ordre de la République Tunisienne; Chevalier des affaires culturelles du Burkina Faso; Dr hc (Ben Gurion) 1999, (Beer Schéba); Hon. Prof. Walker Aims Univ., Washington Univ., l'école des H.E.C.; Prix de Carthage 1953, Prix Fénéon 1953, Prix Simba 1978, Prix de l'Union Rationaliste 1994, Grand Prix Littéraire de l'Afrique du Nord, Grand Prix Littéraire du Maghreb 1995, Prix littéraire Tunisie-France 1999, Chalom du Crif 2000, Grand Prix de la ville de Bari 2000, Prix de l'Afrique méditeranéenne 2002, Prix de la Fondation Ignacio Silone 2003, Grand Prix de la Francophonie décerné par l'Académie Française 2004. *Address:* 5 rue Saint Merri, 75004 Paris, France. *Telephone:* 1-40-29-08-31. *Fax:* 1-42-74-25-22. *E-mail:* albert.memmi@yahoo.fr.

MEMMOTT, David R., BA; American editor, writer and poet; *Managing Editor, Phantom Drift*; b. 10 Dec. 1948, Grand Rapids, Mich.; m. Susan A. Memmott 1974; one d. *Education:* Eastern Oregon Univ. *Career:* Man. Ed. Ice River: Magazine of Speculative Writing 1986–90, Contributing Ed. 1990, 1997; Ed. Wordcraft of Oregon LLC 1988–; currently Man. Ed. Phantom Drift; mem. Council for Literature of the Fantastic, Council of Literary Magazines and Presses, Science Fiction Poetry Asscn. *Exhibitions:* Wallowa Valley Festival of the Arts 2010, Artists of Eastern Oregon Arts Show 2010. *Publications:* Alpha Gallery: Selections from the Fantastic Small Press (poetry ed.) 1991, House on Fire: Poetry and Collage 1992, The Larger Earth: Descending Notes of a Grounded Astronaut (poems) 1996, Within the Walls of Jericho (poems) 1998, Shadow Bones (short stories) 1999, Watermarked (poems) 2004, Primetime (postcyberpunk novel) 2007, Giving It Away (poems) 2009, Where the Yellow Brick Road Turns West (long poem) 2010. *Honours:* Co-ordinating Council of Literary Magazines Grant 1988, Oregon Arts Comm. Grants 1988, 1989, Fishtrap Fellow 1990, Rhysling Award 1990, Literary Arts Inc. Fellowships 1995, 2000, 2006. *Address:* 1003 Y Avenue, PO Box 3235, La Grande, OR 97850, USA (home). *Telephone:* (541) 912-8261 (office). *Fax:* (541) 963-0723 (office). *E-mail:* editor@wordcraftoforegon.com (office). *Website:* www.wordcraftoforegon.com (office).

MÉNARD, Jean-François; French writer and translator; b. 1948, Paris. *Career:* translator 1980–, including J.K. Rowling's Harry Potter series, Eoin Colfer's Artemis Fowl series, and other authors' works, including Martin Amis, Malcolm J. Bosse, Roald Dahl, Jerome K. Jerome. *Publications include:* Le Voleur de chapeaux et autres contes pour la semaine 1980, Quinze millions pour un fantôme 1980, Calebasse d'étoiles, Haïti Blues: echo poèmes, De l'autre bord de l'eau 1994, Fromage ou dessin 1994, Jimmy Lalouette 1995, Le Vagabond du Middle West 1995, D'écume au vent la vie 1996, La Belle anglaise a disparu 1996, La Ville du désert et de l'eau 1997, La Sorcière Mangetout (with Alex Sanders) 1998, L'Oiseau de malheur 1998, Le Soleil sur l'ardoise 1999, Du balai la sorcière (with Alex Sanders) 1999, Les Pieds de la sorcière (with Alex Sanders) 1999, Léger goût d'orange sure 2000, Dehors la sorcière (juvenile) 2001, Brumes en lumière 2002. *Address:* c/o Éditions Gallimard-Jeunesse, 5 rue Sébastien-Bottin, 75328 Paris, cedex 07, France. *E-mail:* litterature@gallimard-jeunesse.fr.

MENASSA, May; Lebanese journalist, writer and translator; b. 1939, Beirut. *Career:* began career as TV journalist 1959–68; critic for An-Nahar newspaper 1969–; Chief Ed., Jamalouki (women's magazine) 1985–; mem. The Odyssee Cttee. *Publications:* five novels including Walking in the Dust (novel) 2006; children's fiction: Dans le Jardin de Sarah 2006. *Address:* c/o Riad el Rayyes

Books, PO Box 113/5796, Sanayeh Union Building. Fourth Floor, Beirut, Lebanon (office). *Telephone:* (1) 743640 (office). *Fax:* (1) 743641. *E-mail:* elrayyes@sodotel.net.lb (office); may@maymenassa.com (office). *Website:* maymenassa.com.

MENASSE, Robert, PhD; Austrian writer and translator; b. 21 June 1954, Vienna; m. *Career:* lecturer, Inst. of Literature Theory, Univ. of São Paulo, Brazil 1981–88. *Plays:* Das Paradies der Ungeliebten 2006. *Publications:* fiction: Sinnliche Gewissheit (trans. as Meaningful Certainty 1988) Selige Zeiten, brüchige Welt (trans. as Wings of Stone) 1991, Schubumkehr (trans. as Reverse Thrust) 1995, Die Vertreibung aus der Hölle 2001, Don Juan de La Mancha Oder die Erziehung der Lust 2007; non-fiction: Phänomenologie der Entgeisterung 1995, Das Land ohne Eigenschaften 1995, Überbau und Underground 1997, Die Letze Märchenprinzessin (jtly) 1997, Erklär mir Österreich 2000, Das war Österreich 2005, Gesammelte Essays zum Land ohne Eigenschaften (with Eva Schörkhuber) 2005, Die Zerstörung der Welt als Wille und Vorstellung 2006. *Honours:* Heimito von Doderer Prize 1990, Alexander Sacher Masoch Prize 1994, Österreichischer Staatspreis für Kulturpublizistik 1998, Joseph Breitbach Prize 2002, Friedrich Hölderlin Prize 2002, Lion Feuchtwanger Prize 2002, Marie Luise Kaschnitz Prize 2002, Erich Fried Prize 2003. *Address:* c/o Suhrkamp Verlag, Postfach 101945, 60019 Frankfurt am Main, Germany (office). *E-mail:* geschaeftsleitung@suhrkamp.de (office). *Website:* www.suhrkamp.de (office).

MENDES, David (Bob); Belgian writer and poet; b. 15 May 1928, Antwerp. *Career:* mem. Flemish Writers' Guild; PEN Club. *Publications include:* Day of Shame, 1988; The Chunnel Syndrome, 1989; The Fourth Sura, 1990; The Fraud Hunters, 1991; Vengeance, 1992; Races/Riots, 1993; Link, 1994; Merciless, 1995; The Power of Fire, 1996; The Power of Ice, 1998; Taste of Freedom, 1999; Dirty Dancing, 2000; Blood Feud, 2001. *Honours:* Golden Noose Awards, 1993, 1997; Dutch Award for Best Thriller (twice); Cultural Award, Schoten, 2000. *Literary Agent:* Dan Wright, Ann Wright Literary Agency, 136 E 56th Street, New York, NY 10022, USA. *Address:* Wezelsebaan 191, 2900 Schoten, Belgium. *E-mail:* bob.mendes@pandora.be. *Website:* www.mendes.be.

MENDOZA, Eduardo; Spanish writer; b. 11 Jan. 1943, Barcelona. *Education:* Hermanos Maristas school, studied law. *Career:* lawyer in Barcelona 1968–72; translator UN, New York 1973–78; Lecturer in Faculty of Translation and Interpretation, Universidad Pompeu Fabra, Barcelona 1995–96. *Publications:* La verdad sobre el caso Savolta (Premio de la Crítica) 1975, El misterio de la cripta embrujada (novel) 1978, El laberinto de las aceitunas (novel) 1982, La ciudad de los prodigios (novel) (Premio Ciudad de Barcelona 1987, Lire magazine Book of the Year, France 1988) 1986, Nueva York 1986, La isla inaudita 1989, Barcelona modernista (with Cristina Mendoza) 1989, Sin noticias de Gurb (originally serialised in El País; trans. as No Word from Gurb) 1990, Restauració (play) 1990, El año del diluvio 1992, Una comedia ligera (Prix du meilleur livre étranger, France 1998) 1996, La aventura del tocador de señoras (novel) (Gremio de Libreros de Madrid Premio al Mejor Libro del Año 2002) 2001, Baroja, la contradicción (biog.) 2001, El último trayecto de Horacio Dos (novel, originally serialised in El País) 2002, Mauricio o la elecciones primarias 2006. *Address:* c/o Editorial Seix Barral, Avda Diagonal 662–664, 7°, Barcelona 08034, Spain (office). *E-mail:* editorial@seix-barral.es. *Website:* www.clubcultura.com/clubliteratura/clubescritores/mendoza.

MENDOZA, Élmer; Mexican writer, playwright and academic; *Professor of Literature, Universidad Autónoma de Sinaloa;* b. 6 Dec. 1949, Culiacan, Sinaloa. *Education:* Nat. Polytechnic Inst., Universidad Autónoma de México. *Career:* currently Prof. of Literature, Universidad Autónoma de Sinaloa. *Publications:* Mucho qué reconocer 1978, Trancapalanca 1989, El amor es un perro sin dueño 1992, Cada respiro que tomas 1992, Buenos muchachos 1995, El Amante De Janis Joplin (XVII Premio Nacional de Literatura José Fuentes Mares) 2001, Efecto tequila 2004; novels: Un asesino solitario 1999, Cóbraselo caro 2005, Balas de Plata (Premio Tusquets de Novela 2007) 2008, Firmado con un klínex 2009, La prueba del ácido 2010. *Honours:* Premio Nacional de Literatura José Fuentes Mares 2002. *Address:* c/o Tusquets Editores, SA, Col. Hipódromo Condesa, Campeche 280, Desp. 301–302, 06100 México DF, México. *Website:* www.tusquetseditores.com.

MENDOZA, Mario, BA, MA; Colombian novelist; b. 1964, Bogotá. *Education:* Univ. of Bogotá, Fundación José Ortega y Gasset, Toledo, Spain. *Publications:* La ciudad de los umbrales 1992, La travesía del vidente (short stories) 1995, Scorpio City 1998, Relato de un asesino 2001, Satanás 2003. *Honours:* Premio Nacional de Literatura, Instituto Distrital de Cultura y Turismo 1995. *Address:* c/o Seix Barral, Avda Diagonal 662–664, 7°, Barcelona 08034, Spain (office).

MENGESTU, Dinaw, BA, MFA; American/Ethiopian writer; b. 1978, Addis Ababa. *Education:* Georgetown Univ, Columbia Univ. *Publications:* novel: The Beautiful Things that Heaven Bears (UK title: Children of the Revolution) (Guardian First Book Award, Los Angeles Times Book Prize, Prix du Meilleur Premier Roman Etranger, France) 2007, How to Read the Air 2010; contrib. to The New Statesman, Rolling Stone, Harper's, Jane Magazine. *Honours:* Lannan Literary Fellowship 2007, Nat. Book Foundation's '5 under 35' Award, New York Foundation for the Arts Fellowship in Fiction 2006. *Literary Agent:* McCormick and Williams, 37 West 20th Street, New York, NY 10011, USA. *Telephone:* (212) 691-9726. *E-mail:* pm@mccormickwilliams.com. *Website:* www.mccormickwilliams.com.

MENKES-SPANIER, Suzy Peta, OBE, MA; British journalist and writer; *Fashion Editor, International Herald Tribune;* b. 24 Dec. 1943, Beaconsfield; d. of Edouard Menkes and Betty Curtis Menkes (née Lightfoot); m. David Spanier (died 2000); three s. one d. (deceased). *Education:* Brighton and Hove High School and Newnham Coll., Cambridge. *Career:* jr reporter The Times 1966–69, Fashion Ed. 1979–87; Fashion Ed. The Evening Standard 1968–77; Women's Ed. Daily Express 1977–79; Fashion Ed. The Independent 1987–88, Int. Herald Tribune 1988–; writes column in the Tribune. *Publications include:* The Royal Jewels 1985, The Windsor Style 1987, Queen and Country 1992. *Honours:* Freedom, City of Milan 1986, City of London 1987; British Press Awards Commendations 1983, 1984, Eugenia Sheppard Award for Fashion Journalism, Council of Fashion Designers of America; Chevalier, Legion d'Honneur 2005. *Address:* c/o International Herald Tribune, 6 bis rue des Graviers, 92521 Neuilly Cedex, France (office). *Telephone:* 1-41-43-94-28 (office). *Fax:* 1-41-43-93-38 (office). *E-mail:* smenkes@iht.com (office). *Website:* iht.com (office).

MERCHANT, Carolyn, MA, PhD; American environmental historian and academic; *Professor of Environmental History, Philosophy and Ethics, University of California, Berkeley;* b. 12 July 1936, Rochester, NY. *Education:* Vassar Coll., Univ. of Wisconsin. *Career:* fmr Chair. Dept of Conservation and Resource Studies, now Prof. of Environmental History, Philosophy and Ethics, Univ. of California at Berkeley; Ecofeminist Scholar, Murdoch Univ., Western Australia 1991; various consultantships, lectureships; Pres. American Soc. for Environmental History 2001–03; has served on exec. and advisory bds of the History of Science Soc., Asscn for the Study of Literature and the Environment, and the journals: Environmental History, Environmental Ethics, Ethics and the Environment, International Journal of Ecoforestry, Organization and Environment; Fellow, Center for Advanced Study in the Behavioural Sciences, Stanford 1978, American Council of Learned Socs 1978, Inst. for Advanced Study, Princeton 2012. *Publications:* The Death of Nature: Women, Ecology and the Scientific Revolution 1980, Ecological Revolutions: Nature, Gender, and Science in New England 1989, Radical Ecology: The Search for a Livable World 1992, Major Problems in American Environmental History: Documents and Essays (ed.) 1993, Key Concepts in Critical Theory: Ecology (ed.) 1994, Earthcare: Women and the Environment 1996, Green Versus Gold: Sources in California's Environmental History (ed.) 1998, Columbia Guide to American Environmental History 2002, Reinventing Eden: The Fate of Nature in Western Culture 2003, Encyclopedia of World Environmental History (co-ed with John McNeill and Shepard Krech III) 2004; numerous papers in scholarly journals. *Honours:* Dr hc (Umeå Univ., Sweden) 1995; NSF grants 1976–78, Nat. Endowment for the Humanities grants 1977, 1981–83, ACLS Fellowship 1978, Fulbright Sr Scholar, Umeå, Sweden 1984, Guggenheim Fellowship 1995, MacArthur Fellow in Ecological Humanities, Nat. Humanities Center 2001, Distinguished Scholar Award, American Soc. for Environmental History 2010, AAAS Fellow 2011. *Address:* Department of Environmental Science Policy and Management, University of California, 138 Giannini Hall, Berkeley, CA 94720-3312, USA (office). *Telephone:* (510) 642-0326 (office). *Fax:* (510) 643-4361 (office). *E-mail:* merchant@berkeley.edu (office). *Website:* nature.berkeley.edu/merchant (office); ecohhistory.org (office).

MEREDITH, Christopher Laurence, BA, PGCE; Welsh novelist, poet, academic and translator; *Professor of Creative Writing, University of Glamorgan;* b. 15 Dec. 1954, Tredegar, Wales; s. of Emrys Meredith and Joyce Meredith; m. V. Smythe 1981; two s. *Education:* Univ. Coll. Wales, Aberystwyth, Swansea Univ. *Career:* fmrly steelworker, then schoolteacher; Sr Lecturer in Creative Writing, Univ. of Glamorgan 1993–, awarded personal chair 2007; Fellow, Yr Academi Gymreig (English language section), Soc. of Authors. *Exhibition:* Bog-Mawnog Exhbn (with Elizabeth Adeline, Lin Charlston, Kirsty Claxton, Deborah Aguirre-Jones and Pip Woolf), Brecknock Museum and Art Gallery 2011. *Play:* The Carved Chair (first performed, Sherman Arena, Cardiff). *Publications:* poetry: This 1984, Snaring Heaven 1990, The Meaning of Flight 2005, Black Mountains 2011; novels: Shifts 1988, Griffri 1991, Sidereal Time 1998, The Book of Idiots 2012; non-fiction: Cefn Golau 1996; for children: Nadolig bob Dydd 2000, Christmas Every Day 2006; translation from Welsh: Melog by Mihangel Morgan 2005; edited books: Five Essays on Translation (with Katja Krebs) 2005, Moment of Earth: Poems and Essays in Honour of Jeremy Hooker 2007; contrib. to literary magazines in Wales, England and the USA. *Honours:* Eric Gregory Award 1984, Welsh Arts Council Young Writer's Prize 1985, and Fiction Prize 1989, Arts Council Bursaries 1988, 1995. *Address:* c/o Seren Books, 57 Nolton Street, Bridgend, Mid Glamorgan, CF31 3AE, Wales (office). *E-mail:* info@serenbooks.com (office). *Website:* www.serenbooks.com (office); www.geocities.com/christophermeredith.

MERNISSI, Fatema, PhD; Moroccan sociologist and writer; b. 1941, Fez. *Education:* Univ. of Paris (Sorbonne) and in the USA. *Career:* sociologist, feminist and expert in the Koran; Prof. Univ. Mohammed V, Rabat. *Publications include:* The Veil and the Male Elite: A Feminist Interpretation of Women's Rights in Islam 1992, Islam and Democracy: Fear of the Modern World 1994, The Forgotten Queens of Islam 1994, Dreams of Trespass: Tales of a Harem Girlhood 1994, Fear of Modernity or The Political Harem, Women's Rebellion and Islamic Memory 1996, Dreams on the Threshold, Les Ait Débrouille 1997, Scheherazade Goes West 2001, Beyond the Veil: Male-Female Dynamics in Muslim Society 2003, Les Sindbads Marocains: Voyage dans le Maroc civique 2004. *E-mail:* fatema@mernissi.net (office). *Website:* www.mernissi.net.

MERRILL, Christopher Lyall, BA, MA; American poet, writer, editor, translator and academic; *Director of the International Writing Program, University of Iowa*; b. 24 Feb. 1957, Northampton, Mass; m. Lisa Ellen Gowdy 1983; two d. *Education:* Middlebury Coll., Univ. of Washington at Seattle. *Career:* Dir Santa Fe Writers' Conference 1987–90; Founder-Dir Taos Conference on Writing and the Natural World 1987–92, Santa Fe Literary Center 1988–92; General Ed. Peregrine Smith Poetry Series 1987–; Poetry Ed. Orion Magazine 1993–; freelance journalist 1987–95; William H. Jenks Chair in Contemporary Letters, Coll. of the Holy Cross 1995–2000; Visiting Lecturer, Chatham Coll. 1999–2000; Prof. of English, Univ. of Iowa 2000–, Dir Int. Writing Program 2000–; literary critic, The World (Public Radio International) 2000–10; mem. Acad. of American Poets, Authors' Guild, PEN American Center. *Publications:* Workbook (poems) 1988, Fevers and Tides (poems) 1989, The Forgotten Language: Contemporary Poets and Nature (ed.) 1991, From the Faraway Nearby: Georgia O'Keefe as Icon (co-ed. with Ellen Bradbury) 1992, The Grass of Another Country: A Journey Through the World of Soccer 1993, Watch Fire (poems) 1994, Anxious Moments, by Aleš Debeljak (trans.) 1994, The Old Bridge: The Third Balkan War and the Age of the Refugee 1995, What Will Suffice: Contemporary American Poets on the Art of Poetry (co-ed. with Christopher Buckley) 1995, The Forest of Speaking Trees: An Essay on Poetry 1996, Your Final Pleasure: An Essay on Reading 1996, The Four Questions of Melancholy: New and Selected Poems of Tomaz Šalamun (ed.) 1996, The Way to the Salt Marsh: A John Hay Reader (ed.) 1998, Only the Nails Remain: Scenes from the Balkan Wars 1999, Brilliant Water (poems) 2001, The City and the Child, by Aleš Debeljak (trans.) 2003, Things of the Hidden God: Journey to the Holy Mountain 2005, Because of the Rain: An Anthology of Korean Zen Poetry (ed.) 2006, Seven Poets, Four Days, One Book (co-author) 2009; contrib. to many periodicals. *Honours:* Chevalier, Ordre des Arts et des Lettres 2006; Univ. of Utah Sherman Brown Neff Fellowship 1986–87, Bread Loaf Writers' Conf. John Ciardi Fellow in Poetry 1989, Pushcart Prize in Poetry 1990, Ingram Merrill Foundation Award in Poetry 1991, Prairie Schooner Readers' Choice Award in Poetry 1992, Acad. of American Poets Peter I. B. Lavan Younger Poets Award 1993, Slovenian Ministry of Culture Trans. Award 1997, The Bosnian Stecak Writers' Asscn of Bosnia-Herzegovina Annual Literary Award 2001, Kostas Kyrzias Foundation Hon. Int. Literary Award 2005. *Address:* International Writing Program, Shambaugh House, University of Iowa, 430 N Clinton Street, Iowa City, IA 52242-2020 (office). *Telephone:* (319) 335-2609 (office). *Fax:* (319) 335-3843 (office). *E-mail:* christopher-merrill@uiowa.edu (office). *Website:* www.christophermerrillbooks.com.

MERRIN, Jeredith, BS, MA, PhD; American academic, writer and poet; *Professor of English, Ohio State University*; b. 9 April 1944, California; one d. *Education:* Iowa State University, San Jose State University, University of California, Berkeley. *Career:* Instructor, Gifted Program, University of California, Berkeley 1983–85; Asst Prof., Ohio State University 1987–93, Assoc. Prof. 1993–97, Prof. of English 1997–; MacDowell Artists Colony residencies 1999, 2001; Fellow, Skidmore College, 1993; presenter, workshops and poetry readings. *Publications include:* An Enabling Humility: Marianne Moore, Elizabeth Bishop, and the Uses of Tradition, 1990; Shift (poems), 1996; Bat Ode (poems), 2001; contributions: books, anthologies, reviews, quarterlies and journals. *Honours:* Lilly Foundation Fellow, 1988–89; Regdale Artists Colony Residencies, 1990, 1991, 1996; Elizabeth Gee Award for Research on Women, 1993; National Endowment for the Humanities Grant, 1995, 1997, Ohio Arts Council Grant for Poetry 2005. *Address:* Department of English, Ohio State University, 164 West 17th Avenue, Columbus, OH 43210, USA. *E-mail:* merrin.1@osu.edu (office). *Website:* www.jeredithmerrin.com.

MERTZ, Barbara Louise Gross, (Barbara Michaels, Elizabeth Peters), PhD; American writer; b. 29 Sept. 1927, Canton, IL; m. (divorced); one s. one d. *Education:* Univ. of Chicago. *Career:* mem. ACWL (pres. 1991–94); mem. advisory bd, KMT: A Modern Journal of Ancient Egypt; mem. advisory bd, The Writer. *Publications:* Temples Tombs & Hieroglyphs 1964, Red Land Black Land 1966, The Master of Blacktower 1966, Sons of the Wolf 1967, The Jackal's Head 1968, Ammie Come Home 1968, Prince of Darkness 1969, The Camelot Caper 1969, The Dark on the Other Side 1970, The Crying Child 1971, The Night of 400 Rabbits 197l, Greygallows 1972, The Seventh Sinner 1972, Witch 1973, Borrower of the Night 1973, House of Many Shadows 1974, Murders of Richard III 1974, Sea King's Daughter 1975, Crocodile on the Sandbank 1975, Patriot's Dream 1976, Legend in Green Velvet 1976, Wings of the Falcon 1977, Devil-May-Care 1977, Wait For What Will Come 1978, Street of the Five Moons 1978, The Walker in the Shadows 1979, Summer of the Dragon 1979, The Wizard's Daughter 1980, The Love Talker 1980, The Curse of the Pharaohs 1981, Someone in the House 1981, The Copenhagen Connection 1982, Black Rainbow 1982, Silhouette in Scarlet 1983, Here I Stay 1983, Die for Love 1984, The Grey Beginning 1984, The Mummy Case 1985, Be Buried in the Rain 1985, Lion in the Valley 1986, Shattered Silk 1986, Trojan Gold 1987, Search the Shadows 1987, Deeds of the Disturber 1988, Naked Once More 1989, Smoke and Mirrors 1989, Into the Darkness 1990, The Last Camel Died at Noon 1991, Vanish with the Rose 1992, Houses of Stone 1993, The Snake the Crocodile and the Dog 1992, Night Train to Memphis 1994, Stitches in Time 1995, The Hippopotamus Pool 1996, The Dancing Floor 1997, Seeing a Large Cat 1997, The Ape Who Guards the Balance 1998, Other Worlds 1999, The Falcon at the Portal 1999, He Shall Thunder in the Sky 2000, Lord of the Silent 2001, The Golden One 2002, Children of the Storm 2003, Amelia Peabody's Egypt: A Compendium 2003, Guardian of the Horizon 2004, The Serpent on the Crown 2005, Tomb of the Golden Bird 2006, The Laughter of the Dead Kings 2008, A River in the Sky 2010; contrib. to reference works and periodicals, The Writing Life. *Honours:* Hon. DHumLitt (Hood Coll.) 1992; Lifetime Achievement Award, Bouchercon 1986, Agatha Best Novel 1992, MWA Grand Master Award 1998, Agatha Best Non-Fiction 2003, Lifetime Achievement Award, Malice Domestic 2003, Univ. of Chicago Professional Achievement Award 2004. *Address:* c/o Dominick Abel, 146 W 82nd Street, No. 1B, New York, NY 10024, USA (office). *Website:* www.mpmbooks.com (office); www.ameliapeabody.com.

MERVILLON, Pol-Jean (see Nadaus, Roland)

MERWIN, William Stanley (W.S.), AB; American poet, dramatist, writer and translator; b. 30 Sept. 1927, New York City; m. Paula Schwartz 1983. *Education:* Princeton Univ. *Career:* Playwright-in-Residence, Poet's Theatre, Cambridge, Mass 1956–57; Poetry Ed. The Nation 1962; Assoc., Théâtre de la Cité, Lyons 1964–65; Special Consultant in Poetry, Library of Congress, Washington, DC 1999–2000; Poet Laureate of USA 2010–11; Acad. of American Poets Fellowship 1973; mem. Acad. of American Poets, American Acad. of Arts and Letters. *Publications:* poetry: A Mask for Janus 1952, The Dancing Bears 1954, Green with Beasts 1956, The Drunk in the Furnace 1960, The Moving Target 1963, The Lice 1967, Three Poems 1968, Animae 1969, The Carrier of Ladders 1970, Signs 1971, Writings to an Unfinished Accompaniment 1973, The First Four Books of Poems 1975, Three Poems 1975, The Compass Flower 1977, Feathers from the Hill 1978, Finding the Islands 1982, Opening the Hand 1983, The Rain in the Trees 1988, Selected Poems 1988, Travels 1993, The Vixen 1996, The Folding Cliffs 1998, Migration: New and Selected Poems (Nat. Book Award for Poetry) 2005, Present Company 2007, The Shadow of Sirius (Pulitzer Prize for Poetry 2009) 2008; plays: Darkling Child (with Dido Milroy) 1956, Favor Island 1957, The Gilded West 1961, adaptations of five other plays; other: A New Right Arm, West Wind: Supplement of American Poetry (ed.) 1961, The Miner's Pale Children 1970, Houses and Travellers 1977, Unframed Originals: Recollections 1982, Regions of Memory: Uncollected Prose 1949–1982 1987, The Essential Wyatt (ed.) 1989, The Lost Upland 1993, The Ends of the Earth (essays) 2005, Summer Doorways (memoir) 2005, The Book of Fables 2007; translator: Selected Translations 1948–1968 1968, Selected Translations 1968–1978 1979, Sir Gawain and the Green Knight: A New Verse Translation 2004. *Honours:* Yale Series of Younger Poets Award 1952, Bess Hokin Prize 1962, Ford Foundation grant 1964, Harriet Monroe Memorial Prize 1967, PEN Translation Prize 1969, Rockefeller Foundation grant 1969, Pulitzer Prize in Poetry 1971, Shelley Memorial Award 1974, NEA grant 1978, Bollingen Prize 1979, Aiken Taylor Award 1990, Maurice English Award 1990, Dorothea Tanning Prize 1994, Lenore Marshall Award 1994, Ruth Lilly Poetry Prize 1998. *Literary Agent:* Steven Barclay Agency, 12 Western Avenue, Petaluma, CA 94952, USA. *Telephone:* (707) 773-0654. *Fax:* (707) 778-1868. *Website:* www.barclayagency.com.

MESERVE, Walter Joseph, AB, MA, PhD; American academic, editor and writer; b. 10 March 1923, Portland, Maine; m. 1st; two s. two d.; m. 2nd Mollie Ann Lacey 1981. *Education:* Portland Junior Coll., Bates Coll. Lewiston, Maine, Boston Univ., Univ. of Washington. *Career:* Instructor to Prof., Univ. of Kansas 1951–68; Visiting Lecturer, Manchester Univ., UK 1959–60; Prof. of Dramatic Literature and Theory, Indiana Univ. 1968–88, Assoc. Dean, Research and Graduate Devt 1980–83, Dir Inst. for American Theatre Studies 1983–88; Vice-Pres., Feedback Services, New York City, Brooklin, Maine 1983–; Ed.-in-Chief, Feedback Theatrebooks 1985–; Distinguished Prof., Graduate School and Univ. Center, PhD Programs in Theatre and English, CUNY 1988–93, Distinguished Prof. Emer. 1993–; Co-Ed., American Drama and Theatre journal 1989–93; mem. Cosmos Club. *Publications:* The Complete Plays of W. D. Howells (ed.) 1960, Outline History of American Drama 1965, American Satiric Comedies (co-ed.) 1969, Robert E. Sherwood 1970, Modern Drama from Communist China (co-ed.) 1970, Studies in Death of a Salesman (ed.) 1972, Modern Literature from China (co-ed.) 1974, An Emerging Entertainment: The Drama of the American People to 1828 1977, The Revels History of Drama in English, Vol. VIII: American Drama (co-author) 1977, American Drama to 1900 1980, Cry Woolf (co-author) 1982, Heralds of Promise: The Drama of the American People During the Age of Jackson 1829–1849 1986, Who's Where in the American Theatre (co-ed.) 1990, A Chronological Outline of World Theatre (co-author) 1992, The Theatre Lover's Cookbook (co-ed.) 1992, Musical Theatre Cookbook (co-ed.) 1993, On Stage, America! 1996, When Conscience Trod the Stage (co-ed.) 1998, Fateful Lightning (co-ed.) 2000. *Honours:* National Endowment for the Humanities Fellowships, 1974–75, 1983–84, 1988–89; Rockefeller Foundation Fellowship, 1979; Guggenheim Fellowship, 1984–85. *Address:* PO Box 174, Brooklin, ME 04616, USA. *Telephone:* (207) 359-2781 (office). *Fax:* (207) 359-5532 (office). *E-mail:* info@feedbacktheatrebooks.com (office). *Website:* www.feedbacktheatrebooks.com (office).

MESSENT, Peter Browning, BA, MA, PhD; British academic; *Professor of Modern American Literature, University of Nottingham*; b. 24 Oct. 1946, Wimbledon, England; m. 1st Brenda 1972 (divorced); one s. one d.; m. 2nd Carin 1994. *Education:* Univ. of Manchester, Univ. of Nottingham. *Career:* temporary lecturer, Univ. of Manchester 1972–73; Lecturer, Univ. of Nottingham 1973–94, Sr Lecturer in American and Canadian Studies 1994–95, Reader in Modern American Literature 1995–99, Prof. of Modern

American Literature 1999–, Head, School of American and Canadian Studies 2008–; mem. British Asscn for American Studies, Mark Twain Circle, Hemingway Soc. *Publications:* Twentieth Century Views: Literature of the Occult (ed.) 1981, New Readings of the American Novel 1990, Ernest Hemingway 1992, Henry James: Selected Tales (ed.) 1992, Mark Twain 1997, Criminal Proceedings (ed.) 1997, The Short Works of Mark Twain: A Critical Study 2001, A Companion to Mark Twain (co-ed.) 2005, The Civil War Letters of Joseph Hopkins Twichell (co-ed.) 2005, Cambridge Introduction to Mark Twain 2007, Mark Twain and Male Friendship (British Asscn for American Studies Book Prize 2010, European Asscn for American Studies Book Prize (jt winner) 2010) 2009; contrib. to books, journals and magazines. *Address:* School of American and Canadian Studies, University of Nottingham, Nottingham, NG7 2RD, England (office). *Telephone:* (115) 951-4265 (office). *Fax:* (115) 951-4270 (office). *E-mail:* peter.messent@nottingham.ac.uk (office). *Website:* www.nottingham.ac.uk/american (office).

MESSER, Thomas Maria, BA, MA; American museum director; *Director Emeritus, Solomon R. Guggenheim Museum*; b. 9 Feb. 1920, Bratislava, Czechoslovakia; s. of Richard Messer and Agatha Messer (née Albrecht); m. Remedios García Villa 1948 (died 2002). *Education:* Thiel Coll., Greenville, Pa, Boston and Harvard Univs, Univ. of the Sorbonne, Paris. *Career:* Dir Roswell Museum, New Mexico 1949–52; Dir American Fed. of Arts, New York 1952–56, Trustee and First Vice-Pres. 1972–75; Dir Inst. of Contemporary Art, Boston 1956–61; Dir Solomon R. Guggenheim Museum, New York 1961–88, Dir Emer. 1988–; Pres. Asscn of Art Museum Dirs 1974–75 (Hon. mem. 1988–); Chair. Int. Cttee for Museums and Collections of Modern Art, Int. Council of Museums 1974–77, Hon. Chair. 1977–; Chair. Int. Exhbns Cttee 1976–78, US/ICOM (Nat. Cttee of Int. Council of Museums) 1979–81; Adjunct Prof. of Art History, Harvard Univ. 1960; Barnard Coll. 1965, 1971; Sr Fellow, Center for Advanced Studies, Wesleyan Univ. 1966; Trustee Center for Inter-American Relations (now Americas Soc.) 1974–, Exec. Council Int. Council of Museums 1983–85; Vice-Chair. US Int. Council of Museums Cttee of American Asscn of Museums, Washington, DC 1979–81; Pres. MacDowell Colony Inc. 1977–80; Dir Solomon R. Guggenheim Foundation 1980–90, Trustee 1985–90, Dir Emer. 1988–; mem. Advisory Bd, Palazzo Grassi Venice 1986–97; Trustee Fontana Foundation, Milan 1988–; Chair. Arts Int., Inst. of Int. Educ. 1988–90; Trustee, Inst. of Int. Educ. 1991–99, Hon. Trustee 1999–, Fontana Foundation 1996–; Curatorships Schirn Kunsthalle, Frankfurt 1988–99, Sr Adviser La Caixa Foundation, Barcelona 1990–94; Visiting Prof. Frankfurt Goethe Univ. 1991–; fmr mem. Museum Advisory Panel of Nat. Endowment for the Arts, Art Advisory Panel to Commr of Internal Revenue Service 1974–77; mem. Council Nat. Gallery of the Czech Repub. 1994–99; Trustee Isamo Noguchi Foundation, New York and Tokyo 1998–. *Major retrospective exhibitions at the Guggenheim Museum include:* Edvard Munch, Vasily Kandinsky, Egon Schiele, Paul Klee and Alberto Giacometti. *Publications:* The Emergent Decade: Latin American Painters and Paintings in the 1960s 1966, Edvard Munch 1973, Vasily Kandinsky 1997; museum catalogues on Vasily Kandinsky, Paul Klee, Edvard Munch, Egon Schiele, etc.; articles and contribs to numerous art journals. *Honours:* Hon. mem. Inst. of Int. Educ. 1999–; Kt, Royal Order of St Olav (Norway), Cross of Merit (FRG) 1975, Officer, Order of Leopold II (Belgium) 1978, Austrian Cross of Merit 1980, Royal Danish Kt Order 1983, Orden de Isabel la Católica 1984, Great Cross of Merit (FRG) 1986, Officier, Légion d'honneur 1989; Hon. DFA (Univ. of Massachusetts); Goethe Medal 1990. *Address:* 303 E 57th Street, New York, NY 10022 (office); 35 Sutton Place, New York, NY 10022, USA (home). *Telephone:* (212) 486-1393 (office); (212) 355-8611 (home). *E-mail:* tmmesser@aol.com (office).

MESSUD, Claire; American novelist; b. 1966; m. James Wood; two c. *Education:* Yale Univ., Univ. of Cambridge, UK. *Career:* grew up in Australia and Canada, returned to USA as a teenager; has taught creative writing at Amherst Coll., in the MFA programme at Warren Wilson Coll. in N Carolina, and in the Grad. Writing programme at Johns Hopkins Univ.; Fellow, Radcliffe Inst. for Advanced Study, Harvard Univ. 2004–05; Zale Writer-in-Residence, Newcomb Coll. Center for Research on Women, Tulane Univ. 2008–. *Publications:* When the World Was Steady 1994, The Last Life 1999, The Hunters (two novellas) 2001, The Professor's History (novella) 2006, The Emperor's Children 2006. *Honours:* Guggenheim Fellowship 2002, Strauss Living Award, American Acad. of Arts and Letters 2002, Metcalf Award, American Acad. of Arts and Letters 2003. *Address:* Newcomb College Center for Research on Women, 200 Caroline Richardson Hall, Tulane University, New Orleans, LA 70118, USA (office). *Telephone:* (504) 865-5238 (office). *Fax:* (504) 862-8948 (office). *E-mail:* nccrow@tulane.edu (office). *Website:* newcomb.tulane.edu (office).

MESTAS, Jean-Paul, BA, LLB; French poet, writer and translator; b. 15 Nov. 1925, Paris; m. Christiane Schoubrenner 1977; two s. one d. *Education:* Institute of Political Studies, Paris. *Career:* mem. International Acad., Chennai, fellow; International Poetry, Republic of Korea; International Writers and Artists, board of research. *Publications:* various poems, essays and translations 1965–95; contrib. to many anthologies and periodicals. *Honours:* Excellence in Poetry, International Poet, New York, 1982; Premio de la Cultura, Palermo, 1991; Prix Marcel Beguey, Bergerac, 1992.

MESTRE, Juan Carlos; Spanish poet and artist; b. 15 April 1957, Villafranca de Bierzo, León. *Education:* Autonomous Univ. of Barcelona. *Career:* Fellow, Acad. of Spain 1999; recorded works with artists and musicians including Amancio Prada, Luis Delgado and Jose Zarate. *Exhibitions include:* solo: Galería de arte el Caballo Verde, Chile 1988, 1999, Galería Brita Prinz, Madrid 1992, 1996, Sala de Columnas. Circulo de Bellas Artes, Madrid 1993, Musée de Guétary, France 1993, Galería Siena, León 1993, 1996, 1999, 2005, Exposición Itinerante. Sala de las Carnicerias de León y Centros Culturales de caja España de Ponferrada, Zamora, Palencia, Valladolid y la Bañeza 1996, 1997, Galería de la Universidad de Concepcion, Chile 1999, Galería Fontanar, Segovia 1999, 2006, Centro Internacional de la Estampa Contemporanea, A Coruña 2002, Galería Acanto, Almería 2004, Galería Artra, A Coruña 2005, 2007; collective: Galería de arte el Caballo Verde, Chile 1987, 1997, Museo Del Teatro de Almagro 1989, Palacio Moztezuma, Cáceres 1989, Quinto Salon Internacional de arte Primitivo, Francia 1990, Galería af, Madrid 1990, Galería Margerit, Madrid 1990, Galería Torculo, Madrid 1991, Galería Brita Prinz, Madrid 1991, 1993, 1997, 2000, 2001, Galería Fontanar, Madrid 1992, Kunstausstellung, Germany 1992, Soho Graphic Arts Workshop, New York 1992, Museo Municipal de Orense, Muestra Internacional de Grabado 1992, Galería Duna, Barcelona 1993, Galería el Progreso, Madrid 1994, Sala de Exposiciones de la Estacion Maritima de la Coruna, Menéndez Pelayo 1995, Palacio Revillagigedo, Asturias 1995, Sala Provincia, León 1996, Casa de la Cultura, Ponferrada 1996, Fontanar Espacio de arte, Segovia 1996, Calcografia nacional, Madrid 1996, Palacio de Exposiciones, La Coruña 1996, Sala de Exposiciones del Centro Cultural, Granada 1996, Feria Internacional de arte Contemporaneo, Granada 1996, Convento de la Concepcion, Premio de Grabado Ciudad de Borja, Zaragoza 1996, Grafica 97, Segovia 1997, Obra Social Caja de Madrid, IV Certamen Nacional de Grabado, Madrid 1977, Galería Cervantes, Rome 1998, Conventino Dei Serviti Di Maria, Italy 1998, Instituto Cervantes, Milán 1998, Real Academia De Bellas Artes De San Fernando, Madrid 1998, Galeria Cruce, Madrid 1998, Museo Postal y Telegráfico, Madrid 1998, Palacio De Sastago, Zaragoza 2000, Museo De Navarra, Pamplona 2000, Universidad De Cantabria, Santander 2000, Ayuntamiento De Logroño 2000, Museu d'Art Jaume Morera, Lleida 2000, Centro De Arte Lía Bermúdez, Venezuela 2000, Museo De La Estampa y Del Diseño Carlos Cruz Díez, Venezuela 2000, Centro Cultural De España, Perú 2000, Museo De Arte De La Universidad Nacional, Colombia 2000, Centro Cultural De España, Santiago de Chile 2001, Arte Aquí, Las Rozas 2001, Museo Nacional De Arte, Bolivia 2001, Centro De Formación De La Agencia Española De Cooperación, Bolivia 2001, Centro Cultural Recoleta, Argentina 2001, Centro Cultural De España, Paraguay 2001, Museo Torres García, Uruguay 2001, Aula De Cultura Caixanova, VII Bienal Internacional De Grabado, Orense 2002, Galeria El Caballo Verde, Chile 2002, 2003, Fundación Antonio Pérez, Cuenca 2002, Fundación Rodríguez-Acosta, Granada 2002, Galería Orán, Valladolid 2003, Centromunicipal De Arte Y Exposiciones De Avilés, Asturias 2003, VII Bienal Internacional De Grabado, Orense 2003, Sala De Exposiciones, Pontevedra 2003, Sala De Exposiciones Del Museo Provincial, Lugo 2003, Sala De Exposiciones De La Autoridad Portuaria, A Coruña 2003, Auditorio De La Casa De La Cultura, A Coruña 2003, Dearte contemponareo. Feria de Galerias Españolas, Madrid 2004, Galeria El Caballo Verde. Centenario Neruda, Chile 2004, Galeria Siena, Ponferrada 2004, Centro Cultural De España, Santiago de Chile 2005, VIII Bienal Internacional De Grabado Caixanova, Orense 2005, Sala De Exposiciones Del Centro Cultural De Caixanova, Pontevedra 2005, Sala De Exposiciones De La Autoridad Portuaria, A Coruña 2005, Sala De Exposiciones Del Museo Provincial, Lugo 2005, Sala De Exposiciones De Caixanova, A Estrada, Pontevedra 2005, IX Bienal Internacional De Grabado Caixanova, Orense 2006, Visión Del Frío, Antonio Gamoneda Premio Cervantes 2006, Sala De Exposiciones Del Centro Cultural, Vigo 2007, Sala De Exposiciones De Caixanova, Pontevedra 2007, Sala De Exposiciones Do Porto, A Coruña 2007, Sala De Exposiciones Del Centro Social Caixanova, Pontevedra 2007, Sala De Exposiciones Angel Botello, Cangas, Pontevedra 2007. *Publications:* Siete poemas escritos junto a la lluvia 1982, La visita de Safo 1983, Antífona del Otoño en el Valle del Bierzo (Adonais Prize) 1985, Las páginas del fuego 1987, La poesía ha caído en desgracia (Premio Jaime Gil de Viedma) 1992, La tumba de Keats (Jaén Prize for Poetry) 1999, Cuaderno de Roma 2005, Las estrellas para quien las trabaja 2007, El universo está en la noche 2006, Piedra de Alma (co-author José María Parreño) 2000, Crónica de amor de una muchacha albina (co-author Rafael Pérez Estrada) 2000, Emboscados (co-author Amancio Prada) 2000, Bestiario apócrifo (co-author Alvaro Delgado) 2000, Enea y los gatos (co-author Javier Fernandez de Molina) 2002, El Adepto (co-author Bruno Ceccobelli) 2005, Arde la oscuridad (co-author Alfredo Erias) 2007, Los sepulcros de Cronos (co-author Evaristo Bellotti) 2007, La casa roja (National Prize for Poetry 2009) 2008. *Honours:* Honorable Mention, Nat. Engraving Prize 1999, Honorable Mention, VII Int. Print Biennial Orense 2002, Botillo Gold, El Bierzo. *Address:* Leon SA Editions, Luzar Cuesta Way, S/N (Trobajo Road), San Andres Del Rabanedo, 24010 Leon, Spain. *Telephone:* (98) 7800905. *E-mail:* mestre@juancarlosmestre.com (home). *Website:* www.juancarlosmestre.com.

MESTROVIC, Stjepan Gabriel, BA, EdM, MTS, PhD; American academic, writer and editor; *Professor of Sociology, Texas A&M University*; b. 12 March 1955, Croatia; two d. *Education:* Harvard Univ., Syracuse Univ. *Career:* Prof. of Sociology, Texas A&M Univ., College Station, USA 1990–; Series Ed. Postmodern Social Futures, Eastern Europe, Classical and Contemporary Social Theory; mem. American Sociological Asscn, Schopenhauer Soc. *Publications:* Emile Durkheim and the Reformation of Sociology 1988, The Coming Fin de Siècle: An Application of Durkheim's Sociology to Modernity and Postmodernity 1991, Durkheim and Postmodern Culture 1992, The Road from Paradise: The Possibility of Democracy in Eastern Europe 1993, Habits of the

Balkan Heart: Social Character and the Fall of Communism 1993, The Barbarian Temperament: Towards a Postmodern Critical Theory 1993, The Balkanization of the West: The Confluence of Postmodernism with Postcommunism 1994, Genocide after Emotion: The Postemotional Balkan War 1996, This Time We Knew: Western Responses to Genocide in Bosnia (co-ed.) 1996, The Conceit of Innocence: How the Conscience of the West Was Lost in the War against Bosnia 1997, Postemotional Society 1997, Anthony Giddens: The Last Modernist 1998, Veblen on Theory, Culture and Society 2004, The Trials of Abu Ghraib 2006, Rules of Engagement? A Social Anatomy of an American War Crime 2008, The Good Soldier on Trial: A Sociological Study of Misconduct by the US Military Pertaining to Operation Iron Triangle, Iraq 2009. *Honours:* Fellow, Nat. Endowment for the Humanities 1986–87, Fulbright Fellow in Croatia 1992–93. *Address:* Department of Sociology, Texas A&M University, College Station, TX 77843-4351, USA (office). *E-mail:* mestrovic@neo.tamu.edu (office). *Website:* sociweb.tamu.edu (office).

METCALF, John Wesley, BA, CM; Canadian author and editor; *Editor, Canadian Notes and Queries*; b. 12 Nov. 1938, Carlisle, UK; s. of Thomas Metcalf and Gladys Moore; m. Myrna Teitelbaum 1975; three s. three d. *Education:* Beckenham and Penge Grammar School and Univ. of Bristol. *Career:* emigrated to Canada 1962; Writer-in-Residence, Univs of NB 1972–73, Loyola of Montreal 1976, Ottawa 1977, Concordia Univ. Montreal 1980–81, Univ. of Bologna 1985; Sr Ed. Porcupine's Quill Press 1989–, Ed. Canadian Notes and Queries (literary magazine) 1997–; Sr Ed. Biblioasis Press 2005–. *Publications:* The Lady Who Sold Furniture 1970, The Teeth of My Father 1975, Girl in Gingham 1978, Selected Stories 1982, Kicking Against the Pricks 1982, Adult Entertainment 1986, What is a Canadian Literature? 1988, Volleys 1990, How Stories Mean 1992, Shooting the Stars 1992, Freedom from Culture: Selected Essays 1982–1992 1994, Acts of Kindness and of Love (jtly) 1995, Forde Abroad 2003, An Aesthetic Underground 2003, Standing Stones: The Best Stories of John Metcalf 2004, Shut Up He Explained 2007. *Address:* 253 Botanica Private, Suite 5, Ottawa, ON K1Y 4P8, Canada. *Telephone:* (613) 761-6031 (office); (613) 761-6031 (home). *Website:* www.biblioasis.com.

MÉTELLUS, Jean, MD, PhD; Haitian poet, writer, dramatist and neurologist; b. 30 April 1937, Jacmel; m.; three c. *Education:* Université de Paris. *Career:* teacher, Collège de Médecine des Hôpitaux de Paris; neurologist, Hôpital Emile Roux, Limeil-Brévannes. *Plays:* Anacaona 1986, Le Pont Rouge 1991, Colomb 1992, Toussaint Louverture 2003, Henri le cacique 2005. *Publications:* poetry: Au pipirite chantant 1978, Tous ces chants sereins 1980, Hommes de plein vent 1981, Voyance 1984, Jacmel 1991, Voix Nègres 1992, Au pipirite chantant et autres poèmes 1995, Filtro amaro 1996, Les dieux pèlerins 1997, Voix Nègres, Voix Rebelles 2000, Empreintes 1: Poèmes de Jean Métellus 2005, Empreintes 2: Poèmes de Jean Métellus 2005, Alliance: Textes poétiques de Jean Métellus 2005, La Peau et autres poèmes 2006, Voix nègres, voix rebelles, voix fraternelles 2007, Jacmel, toujours 2007, Visages de Femmes 2008, Eléments 2008; novels: Jacmel au Crépuscule 1981, La Famille Vortex 1982, Une Eau-Forte 1983, La Parole Prisonnière 1986, L'Année Dessalines 1986, Les Cacos 1989, Charles Honoré Bonnefoy 1990, Louis Vortex 1992, L'Archevêque 1999, La Vie en Partage 2000, Toussaint Louverture Le Précurseur 2004; essays: Haïti, une nation pathétique 1987, Voyage à travers le langage 1996, De l'esclavage aux abolitions: XVIIe–XXe siècle 1998, Sous la dictée du vrai 1999, Vive la dyslexie 2002, Des maux du langage à l'art des mots 2004; numerous scientific articles. *Honours:* Grand Prix de Poésie de la Société des Gens De Lettres (SGDL), Grand Prix International de Poésie de langue française. *E-mail:* ammetellus@wanadoo.fr (home). *Website:* www.jeanmetellus.com.

METZGER, Deena, BA, MA, PhD; American writer, poet, playwright, teacher and healer; b. 17 Sept. 1936, New York, NY; m. 1st H. Reed Metzger 1957; m. 2nd Michael Ortiz Hill 1987; two s. *Education:* Brooklyn College, CUNY, University of California, International College, Los Angeles. *Career:* Prof., Los Angeles Valley College 1966–69, 1973–74, 1975–79; Faculty, California Institute of the Arts 1970–75; International Lecturer, Teacher of Writing, Supervision and Training of Healers in the Ethical, Creative and Spiritual Aspects of Healing 1997–. *Plays:* Not as Sleepwalkers, Dreams Against the State. *Radio:* Her Raven Tresses, The Book of Hags. *Publications:* Skin Shadows/Silence 1976, Dark Milk 1978, The Book of Hags 1978, The Axis Mundi Poems 1981, What Dinah Thought 1989, Looking for the Face of God 1989, A Sabbath Among the Ruins 1992, Writing for Your Life: A Guide and Companion to the Inner Worlds 1992, Tree: Essays and Pieces (co-ed.) 1997, Intimate Nature: Women's Bond with Animals (co-ed.) 1998, The Other Hand 1999, Entering the Ghost River: Meditations on the Theory and Practice of Healing 2001, Doors: A Fiction for Jazz Horn 2004, Dreams Against the State (play) 2005, From Grief into Vision: A Council 2006. *Address:* PO Box 186, Topanga, CA 90290, USA (office). *Telephone:* (310) 455-1089 (office). *Fax:* (310) 455-1089 (office). *E-mail:* deenametzger@deenametzger.com (office). *Website:* www.deenametzger.com.

METZGER, Henry, AB, MD, FAAS; American (b. German) scientific researcher; b. 23 March 1932, Mainz, Germany; s. of Paul Alfred Metzger and Anne (Daniel) Metzger; m. Deborah Stashower 1957; two s. one d. *Education:* Univ. of Rochester, Columbia Univ. *Career:* emigrated to USA 1938; Intern, then Asst Resident, Col-Presbyterian Medical Center 1957–59; Research Assoc., NIAMD, NIH 1959–61, Medical Officer, Arthritis and Rheumatism Branch, Bethesda, MD 1963–73, Chief, Section on Chemical Immunology 1973–, Chief, Arthritis and Rheumatism Branch, Nat. Inst. of Arthritis and Musculoskeletal and Skin Diseases 1983–94, Dir Intramural Research Program 1987–98; Fellow Helen Hay Whitney Foundation, Dept of Biology, Univ. of Calif., San Diego 1961–63; Pres. American Asscn of Immunologists 1991–92; Pres. Int. Union of Immunological Socs 1992–95; mem. Health Research Council BMFT, German Govt 1994–97; mem. NAS. *Publications:* over 200 scientific papers and contribs to scientific journals. *Honours:* Hon. mem. Chilean and French Socs of Immunology; several awards. *Address:* 3410 Taylor Street, Chevy Chase, MD 20815, USA (home).

MEWSHAW, Michael, MA, PhD; American author and poet; b. 19 Feb. 1943, Washington, DC; m. Linda Kirby 1967; two s. *Education:* Univ. of Virginia. *Career:* Instructor, Univ. of Virginia 1970, Visiting Writer 1989–91; Asst Prof. of English, Univ. of Massachusetts 1970–71; Asst Prof. to Assoc. Prof. of English, Univ. of Texas, Austin 1973–83; Visiting Artist, American Acad., Rome 1975–76, Writer-in-Residence 1977–78; mem. PEN, Soc. of Fellows of the American Acad. in Rome, Texas Inst. of Letters, US Tennis Writers Asscn. *Publications:* fiction: Man in Motion 1970, Waking Slow 1972, The Troll 1974, Earthly Bread 1976, Land Without Shadow 1979, Year of the Gun 1984, Blackballed 1986, True Crime 1991, Shelter from the Storm 2003, Island Tempest 2004, Lying with the Dead 2009; non-fiction: Life for Death 1980, Short Circuit 1983, Money to Burn: The True Story of the Benson Family Murders 1987, Playing Away: Roman Holidays and Other Mediterranean Encounters 1988, Ladies of the Court: Grace and Disgrace on the Women's Tennis Tour 1993, Do I Owe You Something? A Memoir of Literary Life 2003, If You Could See Me Now 2006; contributions: newspapers and magazines. *Honours:* Fulbright Fellowship 1968–69, William Rainey Fellowship 1970, National Endowment for the Arts Fellowship 1974–75, Carr Collins Awards for Best Book of Non-Fiction 1980, 1983, Guggenheim Fellowship 1981–82, Book of the Year Award, Tennis Week 1993. *Address:* c/o Other Press, 2 Park Avenue, 24th Floor, New York, NY 10016, USA (office). *Website:* www.otherpress.com (office).

MEYER, Kai; German novelist; b. 1969. *Career:* fmr journalist; freelance author 1995–, writing mainly for young adults; co-creator of fantasy roleplaying game, Engel. *Publications:* Der schwarze Storch (trans. as The Black Stork) 1999, Die Rückkehr des Hexenmeisters (trans. as The Wizard's Return) 1999, Die Katakomben des Damiano (trans. as Damiano's Catacombs) 1999, Der Dornenmann (trans. as The Thorn Man) 1999, Jenseits des Jahrtausands (trans. as Beyond the Millennium) 1999, Teuflisches Halloween (trans. as A Diabolic Halloween) 2000, Dämonen der Tiefe (trans. as Demons of the Depth) 2000, Die Nacht der lebenden Scheuchen (trans. as The Night of the Living Scarecrows) 2000, Schattenengel (trans. as Shadow Angel) 2000, Tor Zwischen den Welten (trans. as Gateway Between Two Worlds) 2001, Die Fliessende Königin (trans. as The Flowing Queen 2005) (Marsh Award for Children's Literature in Translation 2007) 2001, Mondwanderer (trans. as Moon Wanderer) 2002, Das Steinerne Licht (trans. as The Stone Light) 2002, Das Gläserne Wort (trans. as The Glass Word) 2002, Die Wellenläufer (trans. as The Wave Runners) 2003, Die Muschelmagier (trans. as The Shell Magicians) 2004, Die Wasserweber (trans. as The Water Weavers) 2004, Das Buch Von Eden (The Book of Eden) 2004, Frostfeuer (trans. as Frostfire) (Corine Award for Books for Children and Adolescents) 2005, Seide und Schwert (trans. as Silk and Sword) 2006, Lanze und Licht (trans. as Lance and Light) 2007, Drache und Diamant 2007; also Pandoramicum (comic book), screenplays. *Address:* c/o Egmont Books, 239 Kensington High Street, London, W8 6SA, England (office). *E-mail:* info@egmont.co.uk. *Website:* www.kaimeyer.com.

MEYER, Lynn (see Slavitt, David Rytman)

MEYER, Philipp, BA, MFA; American writer; b. 1 May 1974, New York City, NY. *Education:* Cornell Univ., Michener Center for Writers, Austin, Tex. *Career:* fmr motorbike mechanic, construction worker, derivatives trader, UBS, New York. *Publications:* fiction: American Rust 2009; contribs to The New Yorker, Esquire, The Iowa Review, McSweeney's. *Honours:* Guggenheim Foundation Fellowship 2010. *Literary Agent:* c/o Eric Simonoff, William Morris Endeavor, 1325 Avenue of the Americas, New York, NY 10019, USA. *Telephone:* (212) 903-1100. *Website:* www.wma.com. *E-mail:* reader@philippmeyer.net (office). *Website:* www.philippmeyer.net.

MEYER, Stephenie, BA; American author; b. 24 Dec. 1973, Hartford, Conn.; d. of Stephen Morgan and Candy Morgan; m. Christian Meyer 1994; three s. *Education:* Chaparral High School, Scottsdale, Ariz., Brigham Young Univ., Provo, Utah. *Career:* grew up in Phoenix, Ariz.; held only one job, as a receptionist in an Ariz. property co., before penning Twilight series, has sold more than 116 million copies world-wide in 37 languages; teamed up with skateboard and clothing co. Hobo Skate Company to produce own clothing line related to her science-fiction novel The Host 2009. *Publications include:* Twilight series: Twilight (Publishers Weekly Best Book of the Year, Amazon Best Book of the Decade. . . So Far, American Library Asscn Top Ten Best Book for Young Adults, New York Times Editor's Choice) 2005, New Moon 2006, Eclipse (British Book Award) 2007, Breaking Dawn 2008; other books: Prom Nights from Hell (section) 2007, The Host (science-fiction novel, spent 26 weeks as a best-seller) 2008, The Short Second Life of Bree Tanner (novella) 2010. *Honours:* named amongst one of Time magazine's Most Influential People 2007, (49th) 2008, included in the Forbes Celebrity 100 list of the world's most powerful celebrities (26th) 2009, (59th) 2010, ranked by Forbes magazine amongst The World's 100 Most Powerful Women (49th) 2010. *Literary Agent:* c/o Jodi Reamer, Writers House, 21 West 26th Street, New

York, NY 10010, USA. *Telephone:* (212) 685-2400. *Fax:* (212) 685-1781. *Website:* www.writershouse.com; www.stepheniemeyer.com; www.thetwilightsaga.com.

MEYERS, Carol, AB, MA, PhD; American archaeologist, academic and writer; *Mary Grace Wilson Professor, Duke University*; b. (Carol Lyons), 26 Nov. 1942, Wilkes-Barre, PA; d. of Dr Harry J. Lyons and Irene W. Lyons; m. Eric Meyers 1964; two d. *Education:* Wellesley Coll., Hebrew Union Coll. Biblical and Archaeological School, Jerusalem, Hebrew Univ. of Jerusalem, Israel, Brandeis Univ. *Career:* Lecturer, Univ. of North Carolina at Chapel Hill 1975, part-time Lecturer 1976–77, Visiting Asst Prof. 1979; Asst Prof., Duke Univ. 1977–84, Assoc. Prof. 1984–90, Prof. 1990–, Mary Grace Wilson Prof. of Religion 2002–; Assoc. Dir Meiron Excavation Project 1978–; Co-Dir Jt Sepphoris Project 1984–, Sepphoris Regional Project 1992–, Sr Advisor, Sepphoris Acropolis Project 1999–; Visiting Faculty, MA Program in Judaic Studies, Univ. of Connecticut 1994–; mem. Center of Theological Inquiry, Princeton 1991–, American Schools of Oriental Research, Archaeological Inst. of America, Asscn for Jewish Studies, British School of Archaeology in Jerusalem, Catholic Biblical Asscn, Center for Cross-Cultural Research on Women, Oxford, UK, Israel Exploration Soc., Palestine Exploration Soc., Soc. for Values in Higher Educ., Soc. of Biblical Literature, Wellesley Coll. Center for Research on Women; Assoc. Ed. Semeia 1990–96, Bulletin of the American Schools of Oriental Research 1997–2006; Consulting Ed. (on Genesis and Exodus, for gender language) Contemporary Torah: A Gender-Sensitive Adaptation of the JPS Translation, for Dictionary of the Bible, for Jesus and His World: An Archaeological and Cultural Dictionary; mem. Editorial Bd and Consulting Ed. The Torah: A Women's Commentary; mem. Editorial Bd Jewish Women: A Comprehensive Historical Encyclopedia, Library of Hebrew Bible/Old Testament Studies (fmr Journal for the Study of the Old Testament Supplement); mem. Editorial Advisory Bd Journal of Ancient Judaism; many consultant positions. *Television:* documentaries on archaeology and the Bible. *Publications:* The Tabernacle Menorah: A Synthetic Study of a Symbol from the Biblical Cult 1976, Excavations at Ancient Meiron: Upper Galilee, Israel 1971–72, 1974–75, 1977 (with E. M. Meyers and J. F. Strange) 1981, The Word of the Lord Shall Go Forth (co-ed. with M. O'Connor) 1983, Haggai, Zechariah 1–8 (with E. Meyers) 1987, Discovering Eve: Ancient Israelite Women in Context 1988, Excavations at the Ancient Synagogue of Gush Halav (with E. Meyers) 1990, Sepphoris (with E. Netzer and E. Meyers) 1992, Zechariah 9–14 (with E. Meyers) 1993, Ethics and Politics in the Hebrew Bible (co-ed. with D. A. Knight) 1995, Community, Identity, and Ideology: Social Science Approaches to the Hebrew Bible (co-ed. with C. W. Carter) 1996, Sepphoris in Galilee: Cross-Currents of Culture (co-ed. with R. Nagy, E. M. Meyers and Z. Weiss) 1996, Families in Ancient Israel (with L. G. Perdue, J. Blenkinsopp and J. J. Collins) 1997, Women in Scripture: A Dictionary of Named and Unnamed Women in the Hebrew Bible, the Apocryphal/Deuterocanonical Books, and the New Testament (co-ed. with T. Craven and R. S. Kraemer) 2000, Households and Holiness: The Religious Culture of Israelite Women 2005, Exodus (trans.) 2009, Excavations at Ancient Nabratein: Synagogue and Environs (with E. M. Meyers) 2009; contribs to scholarly books and professional journals. *Honours:* various grants; Thayer Fellow, Albright Inst. 1975–76, Nat. Endowment for the Humanities Fellowships 1982–83, 1990–91, Howard Foundation Fellowship 1985–86, Int. Corresp. Fellow, Ingeborg Rennert Center for Jerusalem Studies, Bar Ilan Univ., Israel 1998–, Severinghaus Award 1991, Wellesley Coll. Alumnae Achievement Award 1999, Educ. Endowment Award, Women's Inst. for Continuing Jewish Educ. 2001, Award for Outstanding Service in Mentoring, Soc. of Biblical Literature 2008. *Address:* Department of Religion, Duke University, Box 90964, Durham, NC 27708-0964, USA (office). *Telephone:* (919) 660-3514 (office). *Fax:* (919) 660-3530 (office). *E-mail:* carol@duke.edu (office). *Website:* www.duke.edu/religion (office).

MEYERS, Jeffrey, MA, PhD, FRSL; American writer; b. 1 April 1939, New York, NY. *Education:* Univ. of Michigan, Univ. of California at Berkeley. *Publications:* Fiction and the Colonial Experience 1973, The Wounded Spirit: A Study of Seven Pillars of Wisdom 1973, T. E. Lawrence: A Bibliography 1975, A Reader's Guide to George Orwell 1975, George Orwell: The Critical Heritage 1975, Painting and the Novel 1975, A Fever at the Core 1976, George Orwell: An Annotated Bibliography of Criticism 1977, Married to Genius 1977, Homosexuality and Literature, 1890–1930 1977, Katherine Mansfield: A Biography 1978, The Enemy: A Biography of Wyndham Lewis 1980, Wyndham Lewis: A Revaluation 1980, D. H. Lawrence and the Experience of Italy 1982, Hemingway: The Critical Heritage 1982, Disease and the Novel, 1860–1960 1984, Hemingway: A Biography 1985, D. H. Lawrence and Tradition 1985, The Craft of Literary Biography 1985, The Legacy of D. H. Lawrence 1987, Manic Power: Robert Lowell and his Circle 1987, Robert Lowell: Interviews and Memoirs 1988, The Biographer's Art 1989, The Spirit of Biography 1989, T. E. Lawrence: Soldier, Writer, Legend 1989, Graham Greene: A Revaluation 1989, D. H. Lawrence: A Biography 1990, Joseph Conrad: A Biography 1991, Edgar Allan Poe: His Life and Legacy 1992, Scott Fitzgerald: A Biography 1994, Edmund Wilson: A Biography 1995, Robert Frost: A Biography 1996, Bogart: A Life in Hollywood 1997, Gary Cooper: American Hero 1998, Orwell: Wintry Conscience of a Generation 2000, Privileged Moments: Encounters with Writers 2000, Hemingway: Life into Art 2000, The Sir Arthur Conan Doyle Reader 2002, Inherited Risk: Errol and Sean Flynn in Hollywood and Vietnam 2002, Somerset Maugham: A Life 2004, The Somerset Maugham Reader 2004, Impressionist Quartet: The Intimate Genius of Manet and Morisot, Degas and Cassatt 2005, Married to Genius 2005, Modigliani: A Life 2006, Samuel Johnson: The Struggle 2009. *Honours:* awards from American Council of Learned Socs, Huntington Library; Fulbright Fellowship, Guggenheim Fellowship. *Address:* 84 Stratford Road, Kensington, CA 94707, USA (home). *E-mail:* vjmeyers@nothingbutnet.net (home).

MEYNELL, Hugo Anthony, BA, PhD; British/Canadian professor of religious studies and writer; b. 23 March 1936, Derbyshire, England; m. Jenifer Routledge 1969; three d. one adopted s. *Education:* King's Coll., Cambridge. *Career:* Lecturer, Univ. of Leeds 1961–81; Visiting Prof., Emory Univ. 1978; Prof. of Religious Studies, Univ. of Calgary 1981–98; mem. Canadian Philosophical Asscn, Canadian Soc. for Religious Studies, RSC. *Publications include:* Sense, Nonsense and Christianity 1964, Grace versus Nature 1966, The New Theology and Modern Theologians 1967, God and the World 1971, An Introduction to the Philosophy of Bernard Lonergan 1976, Freud, Marx and Morals 1981, The Intelligible Universe: A Cosmological Argument 1982, The Nature of Aesthetic Value 1986, The Theology of Bernard Lonergan 1986, The Art of Handel's Operas 1986, Is Christianity True? 1994, Redirecting Philosophy 1998, Postmodernism and the New Enlightenment 2001; contribs to scholarly journals. *Address:* # 309, 1320 Eighth Avenue SE, Calgary, AB T2G 0M9, Canada (home). *Telephone:* (403) 283-3320 (home). *E-mail:* hugomeynell@shaw.ca.

MHLANGA, Cont; Zimbabwean playwright and writer; b. 16 March 1958. *Career:* political satirist whose work has frequently been banned because it challenged Mugabe regime; f. Amakhosi Productions 1980; f. Amakhosi Performing Arts Acad. 1987; f. and spearheaded building of Amakhosi Township Square Cultural Center, Bulawayo 1995; f. www.amakhosi.org, www.voicesfromzimbabwe.com, www.inxusaculturalexpo.org. *Plays:* 21 as writer, including The Good President (Artventure Freedom to Create Prize 2008), The End, Vikela, Sinjalo, Children On Fire, Games and Bombs, The Members; as dir: Bamqgibela Ephila, Omunye Umngcwabo. *Television:* creator, Amakorokoza (soap opera). *Radio:* creator, Ngokwako Sigadula (soap opera). *Publications:* three books. *Address:* c/o Amakhosi Cultural Training Centre, POB 7030, Mzilikazi, Bulawayo, Zimbabwe (office). *Telephone:* (9) 885097 (office). *Fax:* (9) 76673 (office). *E-mail:* info@amakhosi.org (office). *Website:* www.amakhosi.org (office); www.voicesfromzimbabwe.com (office).

MIALL, Robert (see Burke, John Frederick)

MIAN MIAN; Chinese writer; b. 1970, Shanghai. *Career:* started writing aged 16; DJ, Cotton Club, Shanghai 1996; music promoter and dance party organizer 1997–; contributor of short stories and novellas to Chinese literary magazines, including Xiaoshuo Jie 1997–; books banned in China 2000–02; columnist for Hong Kong independent newspaper, Apple Daily, and for fashion magazines 2002–. *Publications:* La La La (short stories) 1997, Candy (novel) 2000, Every Good Child Deserves Candy (short stories) 2000, Acid Lover (short stories) 2000, Social Dance (short stories) 2002, Panda Sex (novel) 2005. *E-mail:* nanawang@mianmian.com. *Website:* www.modernsky.com; www.mianmian.com.

MICHAEL, Ib; Danish novelist and poet; b. (Ib Michael Rasmussen), 17 Jan. 1945, Roskilde. *Education:* Univ. of Copenhagen. *Publications include:* novels: En hidtil uset drøm om skibe (A Previously Unseen Dream of Ships) 1970, Den flyvende kalkundræber (The Flying Turkey Hunter) 1971, Hjortefod (Stag's Hoof) 1974, Rejsen tilbage (The Journey Back) 1977, Kejserfortællingen (The Tiger's Tale) 1981, Troubadurens læring (The Minstrel's Apprentice) 1984, Kilroy, Kilroy 1989, Vanillepigen (The Vanilla Girl) 1991, Den tolvte rytter (The Midnight Soldier) 1993, Brev til månen (Letter to the Moon) 1995, Prins (Prince) 1997, Kejserens atlas (The Emperor's Atlas) 2001, Paven af Indien (The Pope of India) 2003, Grill 2005, Orbit 2010; travelogue: Mayalandet (The Land of the Maya) 1973; poetry: Himmelbegravelse: Digte fra Tibet (Sky Burial: Poems from Tibet) 1986, Vinden i metroen (The Wind in the Metro) 1990; short stories: Atkinson's biograf (Atkinson's Cinema) 1998. *Honours:* Booksellers Club Golden Laurel for Author of the Year 1990, Danish Author Asscn Peace Prize 1991, Danish Acad. Prize 1994. *Address:* c/o Gyldendal Publishing, Klareboderne 3, 1001 Copenhagen, Denmark (office). *Telephone:* 58200115 (office). *Website:* www.gyldendal.dk/forfattere/ib-michael (office).

MICHAELS, Anne, BA; Canadian poet, novelist, writer and teacher; *Professor of Creative Writing, University of Toronto*; b. 15 April 1958, Toronto, Ont. *Education:* Univ. of Toronto. *Career:* many workshops and guest residencies; Prof. of Creative Writing, Univ. of Toronto 1988–; mem. League of Canadian Poets, Writers' Union of Canada, PEN Canada. *Film:* Fugitive Pieces (and radio). *Play:* Vanishing Points. *Publications:* poetry: The Weight of Oranges (Commonwealth Poetry Prize for the Americas) 1986, Miner's Pond (Canadian Authors' Asscn Award for Poetry) 1991, Skin Divers 1999; fiction: Fugitive Pieces (several awards including Trillium Award, Beatrice and Martin Fischer Award, Orange Prize for Fiction, Guardian Fiction Award, Orange Prize Youth Panel Award 2010) 1997, The Winter Vault 2009; fiction translated into over 30 languages; contrib. to numerous anthologies, reviews and magazines. *Honours:* Epstein Award for Poetry 1980, Canadian Author's Asscn Award 1991, Nat. Magazine Award for Poetry 1991, Chapter/Books in Canada First Novel Award 1997, Lannan Prize 1997, H. H. Wingate Award 1997, Harry Ribalow Award 1998, Acerbi Prize 2001. *Address:* c/o McClelland and Stewart Inc., 75 Sherbourne Street, 5th floor, Toronto, ON M5A 2P9, Canada (office); c/o Bloomsbury Publishing, 38 Soho Square, London, W1D 3HB, England (office).

MICHAELS, Barbara (see Mertz, Barbara Louise Gross)

MICHAELS, Kristin (see Williams, Jeanne)

MICHEL, Caroline; British literary agent and fmr publisher; *CEO, PFD Group Ltd*; m. Matthew Evans (later Lord Evans of Temple Guiting) 1991; two s. one d. *Education:* Univ. of Edinburgh. *Career:* worked at poetry magazine, Agenda; Publicity Dept Chatto & Windus from 1981; founder and Dir Bloomsbury Publishing; Man. Dir Granta Books; worked at Orion; Deputy Man. Dir and Deputy Publisher of CCV division of Random House, and Publisher Vintage (Random House imprint) 1993–2003; Man. Dir and Publisher HarperPress (division of HarperCollins Publishers) 2003–05; Man. Dir William Morris Agency (UK) Ltd 2005–07; CEO PFD Group Ltd 2007–; Gov. British Film Inst.; mem. exec. cttee English PEN 2006; fmr mem. Man Booker Prize cttee. *Address:* PFD, Drury House, 34–43 Russell Street, London, WC2B 5HA, England (office). *Telephone:* (20) 7344-1000 (office). *Website:* www.pfd.co.uk (office).

MICHEL, Pauline, Bacc. Pédagogie, LèsL; Canadian author, poet, scenarist, songwriter and performer; b. 17 May 1944, Asbestos, PQ. *Education:* École normale Marguerite Bourgeois, Univ. of Sherbrooke, Laval Univ., Québec City. *Career:* fmr Prof., Cegep de Sherbrooke, Univ. du Québec à Montréal; numerous poetry and song tours and recitals in Canada, Africa, France; scenarist for TV and films; Parl. Poet Laureate of Canada 2004–06; mem. Union des écrivaines et des écrivains du Québec (UNEQ), Writers' Union of Canada, League of Canadian Poets, Soc. of Composers, Authors and Music Publrs of Canada (SOCAN), Soc. for Reproduction Rights of Authors, Composers and Publrs in Canada (SODRAC), Soc. des auteurs, compositeurs et éditeurs de musique (SACEM), Centre des auteurs dramatiques (CEAD) and others. *Plays:* Farfelu ou Les sens ensorceleurs, Au fil de l'autre, On perd la boule. *Films:* as co-scenarist, actress, singer in La Caresse d'une ride (documentary), Les héritières d'Esther Blondin; consultant for Les Cheveux en quatre (documentary). *Recordings:* albums: Animagerie, Au coeur d'la vie 1979, Contrastes 1980, Hello moineau 1985, Le tour du monde 2000. *Music:* Sors de ta cage (comedy musical). *Radio:* À deux voix, Le jardin des ombres. *Writing for television:* scenarist for L'animagerie, You-hou (Radio-Canada), Le Château des enfants, Télé-Métropole, Télé-Ressources, Passe-Partout (consultant) (Télé-Québec), À la Claire Fontaine (TV Ontario), Hello Moineau (coproduction for Francophone countries), La Maison de Ouimzie/Wimzie's House (broadcast in 100 countries), Dossi, Rémi et compagnie (France). *Publications include:* novels: Les yeux d'eau 1975, 2002, Mirage 1978, 2004, Le papillon de Vénus 1999, Eyes of Water 2006, Venus Butterfly 2010; short stories: Frissons d'enfants/Haunted Childhoods 2006; play: Au fil de l'autre 2004; poetry: L'oeil sauvage 1988, Funambule/Tightrope 2006; children's book: Cannelle et pruneau dans les feuilles de thé 1992; songbooks: Le tour du monde 2000, Hello Moineau 1985, Demeurez dans mon amour 1987, Voyez comme ils s'aiment 1988; contrib. of novellas and poems to numerous anthologies. *Honours:* Winner, Québec en chansons, Prix Adate, Ministry of Cultural Affairs grant, Canadian Embassy in Paris bursary 1980. *Address:* 3315 Ridgewood Avenue, Apt 6, Montréal, PQ H3V 1BY, Canada (home). *Telephone:* (514) 344-0588 (home). *E-mail:* pauline_michel@videotron.ca (home).

MICHEL, Sandra Seaton, BA; American writer, poet, editor and teacher; b. (Sandra Seaton), 30 Jan. 1935, Hancock, Mich.; d. of Donald W. Seaton and Mary Lucille Finlayson; m. Philip R. Michel 1956; three s. one d. *Education:* Stanford Univ. *Career:* Ed., Lenape Publishing 1973–78; teacher, Coast Episcopal Schools 1982–84; Delaware State Arts Council and Nat. Endowment for the Arts Residency Artist in Creative Writing 1974–79, 1984–2004; Ed., Highland Publishing House 1996–2002; mem. Bd Dirs Mobius, The Poetry Magazine 1998–2005; mem. Nat. League of American Pen Women (Nat. Historian 2004–06, 2010–12, Vice-Pres. 2006–08, 2008–10), Soc. of Children's Book Writers and Illustrators, Nat. Fed. of Press Women, Delaware Press Asscn. *Publications:* books: My Name is Jaybird 1972, No More Someday 1973, From the Peninsula South 1980, Thomas, My Brother 1981, Visions to Keep 1990. *Honours:* First State Writers Nat. Bicentennial Poetry Award 1976, First Place, Contra Costa County Fair Nat. Poetry Contest 1979, Distinguished Service Award, Lutheran Community Services Bd, Wilmington 1994–95, First Place, Nat. League of American Pen Women Children's Short Story Award 1998. *Address:* 3 Lanark Drive, Wilmington, DE 19803, USA (home). *E-mail:* sandramichel@verizon.net (home).

MICKLETHWAIT, John; British journalist and writer; *Editor-in-Chief, The Economist.* *Education:* Magdalen Coll., Oxford. *Career:* fmrly with Chase Manhattan Bank; joined The Economist 1987, as Media Correspondent, then established Los Angeles office 1990–93, Ed. business section 1993–97, New York Bureau Chief 1997–99, US Ed. 1999–2006, Ed.-in-Chief 2006–. *Publications:* The Witch Doctors (with Adrian Wooldridge) (Financial Times/Booz Allen Global Business Book Award 1995) 1996, A Future Perfect: The Challenge and Hidden Promise of Globalisation (with Adrian Wooldridge) 2000, The Company: A Short History of a Revolutionary Idea (with Adrian Wooldridge) 2003, The Right Nation (with Adrian Wooldridge) 2004, God is Back (with Adrian Wooldridge) 2009; contrib. articles to the New York Times, Los Angeles Times, Wall Street Journal, Guardian, Spectator and the New Statesman, Boston Globe. *Honours:* Harold Wincott Press Award for Young Financial Journalist 1989. *Address:* The Economist, 25 St James's Street, London, SW1A 1HG, England (office). *Website:* www.economist.com (office).

MIDDLETON, (John) Christopher, MA, DPhil; British academic; *David J. Bruton Centennial Professor Emeritus of Modern Languages, University of Texas*; b. 10 June 1926, Truro; s. of Hubert S. Middleton and Dorothy M. Miller; m. 1953 (divorced); one s. two d. *Education:* Felsted School and Merton Coll. Oxford. *Career:* Lektor in English, Univ. of Zürich 1952–55; Asst Lecturer in German, King's Coll. Univ. of London 1955–57, Lecturer 1957–66; Prof. of Germanic Languages and Literature Univ. of Texas 1966–98, David J. Bruton Centennial Emer. Prof. 1998–. *Publications:* Torse 3, poems 1948–61 1962, Nonsequences/Selfpoems 1965, Our Flowers and Nice Bones 1969, The Lonely Suppers of W.V. Balloon 1975, Carminalenia 1980, 111 Poems 1983, Two-Horse Wagon Going By 1986, Selected Writings 1989, The Balcony Tree 1992, Some Dogs 1993, Andalusian Poems 1993, Intimate Chronicles 1996, The Swallow Diver 1997, Twenty Tropes for Doctor Dark 2000, The Word Pavilion and Selected Poems 2001, Of the Mortal Fire 2003, The Anti-Basilisk 2005, The Tenor on Horseback 2007, Collected Poems 2008, Poems 2006–2009 2010, A Company of Ghosts 2011, Just Look at the Dancers 2012; prose: Pataxanadu and Other Prose 1977, Serpentine 1985, In the Mirror of the Eighth King 1999, Crypto-Topographia 2002, Depictions of Blaff 2010; trans: Ohne Hass und Fahne (with W. Deppe and H. Schönherr) 1958, Modern German Poetry 1910–60 (with M. Hamburger) 1962, Germany Writing Today 1967, Selected Poems, by Georg Trakl 1968, Selected Letters, by Friedrich Nietzsche 1969, Selected Poems, by Friedrich Hölderlin and Eduard Mörike 1972, Selected Poems of Goethe 1983, Slected Stories, by Robert Walser 1983, Andalusian Poems (with Leticia Garza-Falcón) 1993, Faint Harps and Silver Voices: Selected Translations 2000; essays and other writings. *Honours:* Sir Geoffrey Faber Memorial Prize 1964, Guggenheim Poetry Fellowship 1974–75, Nat. Endowment for Humanities Poetry Fellowship 1980, Tieck-Schlegel Trans Prize 1985, Max Geilinger Stiftung Prize 1987, Soeurette Diehl Fraser Award for Trans, Texas Inst. of Letters 1993, Camargo Foundation Fellow 1999, American Acad. of Arts and Letters Award for Literature 2012. *Address:* 1112 W 11th Street, Apt 201, Austin, TX 78703 (home); Department of Germanic Studies, University of Texas, Austin, TX 78712, USA (office). *Telephone:* (512) 471-4123 (office). *Website:* www.utexas.edu/depts/german/faculty/middleton.html (office).

MIELI, Paolo; Italian journalist; *Director, Corriere della Sera*; b. 25 Feb. 1949, Milan; two s. *Education:* classical lycée, La Sapienza Univ., Rome. *Career:* Asst to Chair of History of Political Parties, Univ. of Rome; Corresp., Political Commentator at Home, Head of Cultural Desk and then Cen. Man. Ed., Espresso (weekly) 1967–85; worked for La Repubblica 1985–86; Leader Writer, La Stampa 1986–90, Ed.-in-Chief 1990–92; Ed. Corriere della Sera 1992–97, Dir 2004–; apptd Pres. RAI (Radiotelevisione Italiana) March 2003 (resgnd after five days); Prof. of Contemporary History, Univ. of Milan; mem. Bd Govs Storia Illustrata, Pagina and has collaborated with Tempi Moderni, Questi Istituzioni, Mondo operaio. *Publications:* Litigo a Sinistra, Il Socialismo Diviso, Storia del Partito Socialista Negli Anni della Repubblica, Le Storie – La Storia 1999, Storia e Politica: Risorgimento, fascismo e comunismo 2001, La goccia cinese 2002. *Honours:* Premio Spoleto 1990; Premio Mediterraneo 1991, Premio Alfio Russo 1995. *E-mail:* pmieli@corriere.it (office). *Address:* Corriere della Sera, Via Solferino 28, 20121 Milan (office); Via Medaglie d'Oro 391, 00136 Rome, Italy (home). *Telephone:* (02) 2827979 (office). *Fax:* (02) 29009705 (office).

MIÉVILLE, China, BA, MA, PhD; British writer; b. 6 Sept. 1972, London. *Education:* Univ. of Cambridge, LSE. *Career:* fmrly taught English in Egypt; Frank Knox Fellowship, Harvard Univ. *Publications:* novels: King Rat 1998, Perdido Street Station (Arthur C. Clarke Award 2001, British Fantasy Award 2001) 2000, The Scar 2002, The Tain 2002, Iron Council (Arthur C. Clarke Award 2005) 2004, Looking for Jake: Stories 2005, Un Lun Dun (for children) 2007, The City & the City (Arthur C. Clarke Award 2010) 2009, Kraken 2010, Embassytown (Locus Award for Best Science Fiction Novel 2012) 2011. *Address:* c/o Pan Macmillan, 20 New Wharf Road, London, N1 9RR, England (office). *Website:* www.panmacmillan.com (office).

MIHAILOVICH, Vasa D., MA, PhD; American academic (retd), writer and poet; b. 12 Aug. 1926, Prokuplje, Yugoslavia; m. Branka 1957 (died 2006); two s. *Education:* Wayne State Univ., Univ. of California, Berkeley. *Career:* Instructor, Univ. of North Carolina, Chapel Hill 1961–63, Asst Prof. 1963–68, Assoc. Prof. 1968–75, Prof. of Slavic Languages and Literatures 1975–95; mem. Asscn of Writers of Serbia. *Publications:* Library of Literary Criticism: Modern Slavic Literatures, two vols 1972, 1976, Introduction to Yugoslav Literature 1973, A Comprehensive Bibliography of Yugoslav Literature in English 1976, Contemporary Yugoslav Poetry 1977, Stari i Novi Vilajet 1977, Bdenja 1980, Emigranti i Druge Price 1980, Krugovi na Vodi 1982, U Tudjem Pristanistu 1988, Serbian Poetry From the Beginnings to the Present 1988, Litija Malih Praznika 1990, Na Brisanom Prostoru 1994, Bozic u Starom Kraju 1994, Dictionary of Literary Biography: South Slavic Writers, two vols 1994, 1997, Songs of the Serbian People: From the Collections of Vuk St Karadzic 1997, Rasejano Slovo/The Scattered Word 1997, Braca i Druge Price 1997, Darovi: Sna 2001, Sesta Rukovet 2002, Elze i Druge Price 2002, Vrane na Snegu 2002, Jagnje i Vuk 2003, Tango, Poems in Prose 2004, Belly Dancer and Other Stories 2004, Anthology of Serbian Literature 2004, Skitnica i druge price 2008, Korifeji/Coryphaei 2008, Sumi suma 2008, Granice nemerljive 2009; contribs to Books Abroad/World Literature Today, Saturday Review, Serbian Studies, Slavic and East European Journal, Slavic Review. *Honours:* Serbian PEN Center 1988, Zlatni Prsten 1994, Vukova Zaduzbina 1997, Povelja Rastko Petrovic 1998, Vukova nagrada 2003, Povelja Arsenije

Carnojevic 2004. *Address:* 1864 Summer Street, Stamford, CT 06905, USA (home). *Telephone:* (203) 973-0775 (home). *E-mail:* vamih@aol.com (home).

MIKHAIL, Dunya, MA; Iraqi writer and poet; *Teacher of Arabic, Wayne State University*; b. 1965. *Education:* Univ. of Baghdad, Wayne State Univ. *Career:* Literary Ed. The Baghdad Observer 1988–95; Man. Dir Al-Mashreq Co. for Press, Amman, Jordan 1995–96; facing increasing threats from Iraqi authorities for her writing, fled to USA in late 1990s; currently teacher of Arabic, Wayne State Univ.; Dir Iraqi American Center humanitarian org. *Publications in translation include:* poetry: Bleeding of the Sea 1986, The Songs of Absence 1993, Almost Music 1997, Diary of a Wave Outside the Sea 1999, The War Works Hard 2000; contrib. poems to anthologies, magazines and newspapers, including Le Poème Arabe Moderne, Iraqi Poetry Today, The Post-Gibran Anthology of New Arab-American Writing, New Arab Poetry, The Poetry of Arab Women: A Contemporary Anthology, Poetry International, Modern Poetry in Translation, The Times. *Honours:* UN Human Rights Award for Freedom of Writing 2001. *E-mail:* DMik139729@aol.com. *Website:* www.dunyamikhail.com.

MIKHAIL, Edward Halim, BA, BEd, DES, PhD; Canadian academic and writer; *Professor Emeritus of English, University of Lethbridge*; b. 29 June 1926, Cairo, Egypt. *Education:* Univ. of Cairo, Trinity Coll., Dublin, Univ. of Sheffield. *Career:* Lecturer to Asst Prof., Univ. of Cairo 1949–66; Assoc. Prof. Univ. of Lethbridge 1966–72, Prof. of English Literature 1972–, now Emer. *Publications:* The Social and Cultural Setting of the 1890s 1969, John Galsworthy the Dramatist 1971, Comedy and Tragedy: A Bibliography of Criticism 1972, Sean O'Casey: A Bibliography of Criticism 1972, A Bibliography of Modern Irish Drama 1899–1970 1972, Dissertations on Anglo-Irish Drama 1973, The Sting and the Twinkle: Conversations with Sean O'Casey (co-ed.) 1974, J. M. Synge: A Bibliography of Criticism 1975, Contemporary British Drama 1950–1976: An Annotated Critical Bibliography 1976, W. B. Yeats: Interviews and Recollections 1977, J. M. Synge: Interviews and Recollections 1977, English Drama 1900–1950 1977, Lady Gregory: Interviews and Recollections 1977, Oscar Wilde: An Annotated Bibliography of Criticism 1978, A Research Guide to Modern Irish Dramatists 1979, Oscar Wilde: Interviews and Recollections 1979, The Art of Brendan Behan 1979, Brendan Behan: An Annotated Bibliography of Criticism 1980, An Annotated Bibliography of Modern Anglo-Irish Drama 1982, Brendan Behan: Interviews and Recollections 1982, Lady Gregory: An Annotated Bibliography of Criticism 1982, Sean O'Casey and His Critics 1985, The Abbey Theatre 1987, Sheridan: Interviews and Recollections 1989, James Joyce: Interviews and Recollections 1990, The Letters of Brendan Behan 1991, Goldsmith: Interviews and Recollections 1993, Dictionary of Appropriate Adjectives 1994; contrib. to journals. *Honours:* several awards from Canada Council and Social Sciences and Humanities Research Council of Canada 1966–86. *Address:* No. 115, 100-2 Avenue S, Lethbridge, AB T1J OB5, Canada (home).

MIKHAYLOVA, Lilyana; Bulgarian screenwriter and author; b. 11 May 1939, Plovdiv; m. Mladen Denew 1968; one s. *Education:* Univ. of Sofia. *Career:* teacher 1962–68; journalist 1968–74; Chief Ed. in a publishing house 1974–90. *Films include:* Solistat (The Soloist) 1980, Otkoga te chakam (It's Nice to See You) 1984, Grehat na Maltitza (Sin of Maltitza) 1985. *Television includes:* Dom za nashite deca (Home for Our Children) 1987, Neizchezvashtite (People, Who Never Disappear) 1988, Bashti i sinove (Fathers and Sons) 1990, Yosif i Mariya (Joseph and Maria) 1995. *Honours:* First Prize Varna Int. Film Festival 1974, 1984, Nat. Award for Contemporary Literature 1984, Sofia Award for Literature 1986. *Address:* Brest 11, Sofia 1126, Bulgaria (home). *Telephone:* (2) 66-32-32 (home).

MIKI, Taku; Japanese novelist and poet; b. 13 May 1935, Tokyo. *Career:* involved in publication of Han (Inundation) and Shi soshiki (Poetry Organization) magazines. *Publications:* poetry: Tokyô gozen sanji (3am in Tokyo) 1959, Wa ga kidirando (My Kiddyland) 1971; novels: Hiwa (The Siskin) (Akutagawa Award) 1972, Furueru shita (With Quivering Tongue) 1974, Karera ga hashirinuketa hi (The Day They Went the Distance) 1978, Gyosha no aki (The Charioteer in Autumn) 1985, Koguma-za no otoko (The Man from the Little Dipper) 1989, Hadashi to kaigara (Naked Feet and Seashell) (Yomiuri Prize) 1999; prose: Tokyo bishiteki hokô (Microscopic Strolls Through Tokyo, essays) 1975, Kotoba no suru shigoto (The Work Words Do, criticism) 1975, Potapota (Drip, Drip, juvenile) 1984, Roji (Alley, short stories) (Tanizaki Jun'ichiro Prize) 1997. *Address:* c/o Shueisha Incorporated, 5–10, 2 Chome, Hitotsubashi, Chiyoda-ku, Tokyo 101 50, Japan.

MIKLOWITZ, Gloria, BA; American writer; b. 18 May 1927, New York, NY; m. Julius Miklowitz 1948; two s. *Education:* Hunter Coll., CUNY, Univ. of Michigan, New York Univ. *Career:* Instructor, Pasadena City Coll. 1970–80; mem. Soc. of Children's Book Writers and Illustrators. *Publications:* some 70 books for children 1964–; contrib. to newspapers, journals and magazines. *Honours:* Western Australia Young Book Award 1984, Bucks Herald for Teens Publrs' Award 1990, Wyoming Soaring Eagle Award 1993, Sugarman Family Award for Best Book for Children on a Jewish Theme 1999. *Address:* 5255 Vista Miguel Drive, La Canada, CA 91011, USA (home). *Telephone:* (818) 952-3382 (home). *E-mail:* glow7@aol.com (home).

MILES, John (Jack) Russiano, LittB, PhB, PhD; American journalist, critic and religious scholar; *Distinguished Professor of English and Religious Studies, University of California, Irvine*; b. 30 July 1942, Chicago, IL; m. Jacqueline Russiano 1980; one d. *Education:* Xavier Univ., Cincinnati, Pontifical Gregorian Univ., Rome, Hebrew Univ., Jerusalem, Harvard Univ. *Career:* Asst Prof., Loyola Univ., Chicago 1970–74; Asst Dir, Scholars Press, Missoula, MT 1974–75; Post-doctoral Fellow, Univ. of Chicago 1975–76; Ed., Doubleday & Co., New York 1976–78; Exec. Ed., Univ. of California Press at Berkeley 1978–85; Book Ed. 1985–91, mem. editorial bd 1991–95, Los Angeles Times; Dir, Humanities Center, Claremont Graduate School, CA 1995–97; Visiting Prof. Calif. Inst. of Tech. 1997–98; Distinguished Prof. of English and Religious Studies, Univ. of California, Irvine 2007–; Sr Adviser to the Pres. J. Paul Getty Trust 1998–2006; mem. American Acad. of Religion, Amnesty Int., Nat. Books Critics Circle (pres. 1990–92), PEN. *Publications:* Retroversion and Text Criticism 1984, God: A Biography 1995, Christ: A Crisis in the Life of God 2001; contrib. to many periodicals. *Honours:* Guggenheim Fellowship 1990–91, Pulitzer Prize in Biography 1996, MacArthur Fellow 2003–07, Getty Research Fellowship 2006–07. *Address:* University of California, 435 HIB, Irvine, CA 92697-2650, USA (office). *Telephone:* (949) 824-1919 (office). *Fax:* (949) 824-6834 (office). *E-mail:* milesj@uci.edu (office). *Website:* www.JackMiles.com.

MILLAR, Sir Ronald Graeme; British dramatist, screenwriter and author; b. 12 Nov. 1919, Reading, England. *Education:* King's Coll., Cambridge. *Career:* screenwriter in Hollywood, USA 1948–54. *Publications:* Plays: Frieda, 1946; Champagne for Delilah, 1948; Waiting for Gillian, 1954; The Bride and the Bachelor, 1956; The More the Merrier, 1960; The Bride Comes Back, 1960; The Affair (after C. P. Snow), 1961; The New Men (after C. P. Snow), 1962; The Masters (after C. P. Snow), 1963; Number 10, 1967; Abelard and Heloise, 1970; The Case in Question (after C. P. Snow), 1975; A Coat of Varnish (after C. P. Snow), 1982. Musicals: Robert and Elizabeth, 1964; On the Level, 1966. Autobiography: A View from the Wings, 1993.

MILLÁS, Juan José; Spanish writer, journalist and academic; b. 1946, Valencia; m.; two c. *Education:* Francoist Univ. *Career:* columnist, El Sol, El Pais and Prensa Ibérica group; fmr Prof., School of Arts. *Publications:* novel: Cerbero son las sombras (Premio Sésamo 1974) 1975, Visión del ahogado 1977, El jardín vacío 1981, Papel mojado 1983, Letra muerta 1984, El desorden de tu nombre 1987, La soledad era esto (Premio Nadal) 1990, Volver a casa 1990, Tonto, muerto, bastardo e invisible 1995, Trilogía de la soledad 1996, El orden alfabético 1998, El orden alfabético (Premio de la crítica de la Asociación de escritores y críticos de Valencia) 1999, No mires debajo de la cama 1999, Dos mujeres en Praga (Premio Primavera de Novela) 2002, Laura y Julio 2006, El mundo (Premio Planeta, Premio Nacional de Narrativa 2008) 2007, Lo que sé de los hombrecillos 2010; stories: Primavera de luto y otros cuentos 1989, Cuentos de adúlteros desorientados 2003, Los objetos nos llaman 2008; monologue: Ella imagina (Teatro de Rojas) 1994; art history: Los suenos se cumplen 2002; reports: Ciego por un día (XII Tiflos de periodismo) 1998, María y Mercedes 2005, El ojo de la cerradura 2006; articles: Algo que te concierne 1995, Lo real (Mariano de Cavia 1999) 1998, En el vientre de la ballena (Continente de periodismo) 1998, Cuerpo y prótesis 2000, Articuentos 2001, Numeros pares,impares e idiotas 2001, Errores (Premio Nacional de Periodismo Miguel Delibes) 2002, Hay algo que no es como me dicen 2004, Todo son preguntas 2005, Sombras sobre sombras 2006, Un adverbio se le ocurre a cualquiera (Don Quijote Award for Journalism) 2010; radio: Acércate al Quijote (Concostrina Nieves by the King of Spain) 2009. *Honours:* Acebo de honor, Ediciones Azucel 1993; Dr hc (Universidad de Turín) 2006, (Universidad de Oviedo) 2007; I Premio de Lectura Sánchez-Ruipérez 2000, Premio de Periodismo Francisco Cerecedo 2005. *Address:* Editorial Seix Barral, 7 Avenida Diagonal 662–64, 08034 Barcelona, Spain. *Telephone:* (49) 3928913; (49) 4928913. *Fax:* (49) 4967004. *Website:* www.planetadelibros.com/editorial-seix-barral-9.

MILLER, Alexander (Alex) McPhee, BA, DipEd; Australian author; b. 27 Dec. 1936, London, England, UK; m. 1st Anne Roslyn Neil 1962 (divorced 1983); one s. one d.; m. 2nd Stephanie Ann Pullin 1983. *Education:* Univ. of Melbourne, Hawthorn Inst. *Career:* Visiting Fellow, La Trobe Univ. 1994–; mem. Australian Soc. of Authors, Fellowship of Australian Writers. *Publications:* Watching the Climbers on the Mountain 1988, The Tivington Nott 1989, The Ancestor Game (Miles Franklin Award, Commonwealth Writers Prize 1993) 1992, The Sitters 1995, Conditions of Faith (Christina Stead Prize for Fiction 2001) 2000, Journey to the Stone Country (Miles Franklin Award 2003) 2002, Prochownik's Dream 2005, Landscape of a Farewell 2007, Lovesong (The Age Book of the Year Award 2010) 2009; plays: Kitty Howard 1978, The Exiles 1981; contrib. to newspapers, journals and periodicals. *Honours:* Centenary Medal; Braille Book of the Year Award 1990, Barbara Ramsden Award, Fellowship of Australian Writers 1993, Manning Clark Cultural Award 2008, Miles Franklin Literary Award 1993, 2003, Commonwealth Writers' Prize 1993, Christina Stead Prize for Fiction, NSW Premier's Award 2001, The Age Literary Award 2011, The Age Book of the Year Award 2011. *Address:* c/o Allen and Unwin, PO Box 8500, St Leonards, NSW 1590, Australia.

MILLER, Andrew, PhD; British writer; b. 29 April 1960, Bristol, England. *Education:* Univ. of East Anglia, Lancaster Univ. *Publications:* Ingenious Pain (James Tait Black Memorial Prize for Fiction 1997, Grinzane Cavour Prize, Italy, Int. IMPAC Dublin Literary Award 1999) 1997, Casanova 1998, Oxygen 2001, The Optimists 2005, One Morning Like A Bird 2008, Pure 2011. *Literary Agent:* Sheil Land Associates, 43 Doughty Street, London, WC1N 2LF, England.

MILLER, Anesa, BA, MA, PhD; American writer, poet, editor, translator and educator; b. 8 June 1954, Wichita, Kan.; m. 1st Timothy Pogacar 1980 (divorced 1990); m. 2nd Jack Panksepp 1991; two d. *Education:* Occidental College, University of Kansas. *Career:* Instructor in Russian Language and Literature, University of Kansas, 1979–83, Bowling Green State University, Ohio, 1986–94; Ed., Memorial Foundation for Lost Children, 1994–. *Publications:* After the Future: Paradoxes of Postmodernism and Contemporary Russian Culture (trans. and ed.), 1995; Re-Entering the Sign: Articulating New Russian Culture (co-ed.), 1995; A Road Beyond Loss: Three Cycles of Poems and an Epilogue, 1995; contributions: periodicals.

MILLER, Arthur I., BS, PhD; American/British academic and writer; *Emeritus Professor of History and Philosophy of Science, University College London. Education:* City Coll. of New York and Massachusetts Inst. of Technology. *Career:* Visiting Prof., École Pratique des Hautes Études, Paris 1977; fmr Assoc. Ed., American Journal of Physics; Vice-Chair. Division of History of Physics, American Physical Soc. 1983–84 Chair. 1984–85; Prof. of History and Philosophy of Science, Univ. Coll. London, now Emeritus Prof.; Dir Int. History of Physics School, Ettore Majorana Centre for Scientific Culture, Erice, Sicily; Fellow American Physical Soc.; Corresponding Fellow Académie Internationale d'Histoire des Sciences; mem. Int. Acad. of the History of Science. *Television:* presenter Einstein (WGBH Nova production). *Publications:* Albert Einstein's Special Theory of Relativity: Emergence (1905) and Early Interpretation (1905–1911) 1981, Imagery in Scientific Thought: Creating 20th-Century Physics 1984, Frontiers of Physics: 1900–1911 1986, Sixty-Two Years of Uncertainty: Historical, Philosophical and Physical Inquiries into the Foundations of Quantum Mechanics (ed.) 1990, Early Quantum Electrodynamics: A Source Book 1994, Insights of Genius: Imagery and Creativity in Science and Art 1996, Einstein and Picasso: Space, Time and the Beauty that Causes Havoc 2001, Empire of the Stars: Friendship, Obsession and Betrayal in the Quest for Black Holes 2005. *Honours:* fellowships and grants from American Council of Learned Socs, American Philosophical Soc., Centre Nat. de la Recherche Scientifique, Fritz Thyssen Stiftung, John Simon Guggenheim Memorial Foundation, Nat. Endowment for the Humanities, Nat. Science Foundation. *Address:* Department of Science and Technology Studies, University College London, Gower Street, London, WC1E 6BT, England (office). *E-mail:* a.miller@ucl.ac.uk (office).

MILLER, Edmund, BA, MA, PhD; American academic, poet and writer; *Senior Professor, C. W. Post Campus, Long Island University;* b. 18 July 1943, Queens, NY; s. of Edmund Miller Jr and Eugenia Marie Miller (née Andreani). *Education:* C. W. Post Campus, Long Island Univ., Ohio State Univ., State Univ. of NY at Stony Brook. *Career:* Lecturer, Ohio State Univ. 1968–69; Instructor, Rockhurst Coll. 1969–71; Asst Prof., Temple Univ. 1977–78, Illinois State Univ. 1979–80; Assoc. Prof., Hofstra Univ. 1980–81; Asst Prof., C. W. Post Campus, Long Island Univ. 1981–86, Assoc. Prof. 1986–90, Prof. 1990–2008, Sr Prof. 2008–, Chair. Dept of English 1993–2011; mem. Conf. on Christianity and Literature, Lewis Carroll Soc. of N America (Life Mem.), Milton Soc. of America, Modern Language Asscn. *Play:* The Greeks Have A Word: A Satyr Play in Five Scenes with All the Ambiguities 2011. *Publications:* poetry: Fucking Animals: A Book of Poems 1973, The Nadine Poems 1973, Winter 1975, A Rider of Currents 1986, The Happiness Cure and Other Poems 1993, Leavings 1995, The Go-Go Boy Sonnets: Men of the New York Club Scene 2005, A Rider of Currents 2009, Eye Brushes 2010, Cornered 2011, I Shouldn't Have Waited 2011; non-fiction: Drudgerie Divine: The Rhetoric of God and Man in George Herbert 1979, Exercises in Style 1980, Like Season'd Timber: New Essays on George Herbert (co-ed. with Robert DiYanni) 1987, George Herbert's Kinships: An Ahnentafel with Annotations 1993; fiction: Night Times 2000; contrib. to books and journals. *Address:* Department of English, C. W. Post Campus, Long Island University, Brookville, NY 11548, USA (office). *Telephone:* (516) 299-2391 (office). *Fax:* (516) 299-3325 (office). *E-mail:* edmund.miller@liu.edu (office). *Website:* www.go-goboysonnets.com.

MILLER, Hugh; British writer; b. 27 April 1937, Wishaw, Lanarkshire, Scotland. *Education:* Univ. of Glasgow; Stow Coll.; London Polytechnic. *Publications:* A Pocketful of Miracles, 1969; Secrets of Gambling, 1970; Professional Presentations, 1971; The Open City, 1973; Levels, 1973; Drop Out, 1973; Short Circuit, 1973; Koran's Legacy, 1973; Kingpin, 1974; Double Deal, 1974; Feedback, 1974; Ambulance, 1975; The Dissector, 1976; A Soft Breeze from Hell, 1976; The Saviour, 1977; The Rejuvenators, Terminal 3, 1978; Olympic Bronze, 1979; Head of State, 1979; District Nurse, 1984; Honour a Physician, 1985; Eastenders, 1986; Teen Eastenders, 1986; Snow on the Wind, 1987; Silent Witnesses, 1988; The Paradise Club, 1989; An Echo of Justice, 1990; Home Ground, 1990; Skin Deep, 1992; Scotland Yard (co-author), 1993; Unquiet Minds, 1994; Proclaimed in Blood, 1995; Prime Target, 1996; Ballykissangel, 1997; Borrowed Time, 1997; Forensic Fingerprints, 1998; Charlie's Case Notes, 1999; Secrets of the Dead, 2000; Crimewatch Solved, 2001; What the Corpse Revealed, 2002, Mindset 2003. *Literary Agent:* Lucas Alexander Whitley Ltd, 14 Vernon Street, London, W14 0RJ, England.

MILLER, Ian (see MILNE, John Frederick)

MILLER, Sir Jonathan Wolfe, Kt, CBE, MB, BCh, FRA, FRCP; British stage director, film director, physician and writer; b. 21 July 1934, London; s. of the late Emanuel Miller; m. Helen Rachel Collet 1956; two s. one d. *Education:* St Paul's School, St John's Coll., Cambridge and Univ. Coll. Hosp. Medical School, London. *Career:* co-author of and appeared in Beyond the Fringe 1961–64; Dir John Osborne's Under Plain Cover, Royal Court Theatre 1962, Robert Lowell's The Old Glory, New York 1964 and Prometheus Bound, Yale Drama School 1967; Dir at Nottingham Playhouse 1968–69; Dir Oxford and Cambridge Shakespeare Co. production of Twelfth Night on tour in USA 1969; Research Fellow in the History of Medicine, Univ. Coll., London 1970–73; Assoc. Dir Nat. Theatre 1973–75; mem. Arts Council 1975–76; Visiting Prof. in Drama, Westfield Coll., Univ. of London 1977–; Exec. Producer Shakespeare TV series 1979–81; Artistic Dir Old Vic 1988–90; Research Fellow in Neuropsychology, Univ. of Sussex; Fellow, Univ. Coll. London 1981–, Royal Coll. of Physicians; mem. American Acad. of Arts and Sciences. *Productions:* for Nat. Theatre, London: The Merchant of Venice 1970, Danton's Death 1971, The School for Scandal 1972, The Marriage of Figaro 1974; other productions The Tempest, London 1970, Prometheus Bound, London 1971, The Taming of the Shrew, Chichester 1972, The Seagull, Chichester 1973, The Malcontent, Nottingham 1973, Arden Must Die (opera) 1973, The Family in Love, Greenwich Season 1974, The Importance of Being Earnest 1975, The Cunning Little Vixen (opera) 1975, All's Well That Ends Well, Measure For Measure, Greenwich Season 1975, Three Sisters 1977, The Marriage of Figaro (ENO) 1978, Arabella (opera) 1980, Falstaff (opera) 1980, 1981, Otello (opera) 1982, Rigoletto (opera) 1982, 1984, Fidelio (opera) 1982, 1983, Don Giovanni (opera) 1985, The Mikado (opera) 1986, Tosca (opera) 1986, Long Day's Journey into Night 1986, Taming of the Shrew 1987, The Tempest 1988, Turn of the Screw 1989, King Lear 1989, The Liar 1989, La Fanciulla del West (opera) 1991, Marriage of Figaro (opera), Manon Lescaut (opera), Die Gezeichneten (opera) 1992, Maria Stuarda (opera), Capriccio (opera), Fedora (opera), Bach's St Matthew Passion 1993, Der Rosenkavalier (opera), Anna Bolena (opera), Falstaff (opera), L'Incoronazione di Poppea (opera), La Bohème (opera) 1994, Così fan Tutte (opera) 1995, Carmen (opera) 1995, Pelléas et Mélisande (opera) 1995, She Stoops to Conquer, London 1995, A Midsummer Night's Dream, London 1996, The Rake's Progress, New York 1997, Ariadne auf Naxos, Maggio Musicale, Florence 1997, Falstaff, Berlin State Opera 1998, The Beggar's Opera 1999, Tamerlano, Sadler's Wells, Paris and Halle 2001, Jenufa, Glimmerglass Opera 2006, The Cherry Orchard, Sheffield Crucible 2007, La Bohème, ENO, London 2009. *Films:* Alice in Wonderland 1966, Take a Girl Like You 1969 and several films for television including Whistle and I'll Come to You 1967, The Body in Question (series) 1978, States of Mind (series) 1983, The Emperor 1987, Jonathan Miller's Opera Works (series) 1997, Brief History of Disbelief (series) 2005. *Art exhibition:* Mirror Image, National Gallery, London 1998. *Publications:* McLuhan 1971, Freud: The Man, his World, his Influence (ed.) 1972, The Body in Question 1978, Subsequent Performances 1986, The Don Giovanni Book: Myths of Seduction and Betrayal (ed.) 1990, On Reflection 1998, Nowhere in Particular 2001. *Honours:* Hon. Fellow, St John's Coll. Cambridge, Royal Coll. of Physicians (Edin.) 1998; Dr hc (Open Univ.) 1983, Hon. DLitt (Leicester) 1981, (Kent) 1985, (Leeds) 1996, (Cambridge) 1996; Royal Television Soc. Silver Medal 1981, Royal Soc. of Arts Albert Medal 1992.

MILLER, Karl Fergus Connor, BA, MA, FRSL; British academic, writer and editor; b. 2 Aug. 1931, s. of William Miller and Marion Miller; m. Jane Elisabeth Collet 1956; two s. one d. *Education:* Royal High School, Edinburgh and Downing Coll., Cambridge. *Career:* Asst Prin., HM Treasury 1956–57; BBC TV producer 1957–58; Literary Ed., The Spectator 1958–61, New Statesman 1961–67; Ed., The Listener 1967–73; Lord Northcliffe Prof. of Modern English Literature, Univ. Coll., London 1974–92; Ed., London Review of Books 1979–89, Co-Ed. 1989–92; currently freelance. *Publications:* Poetry from Cambridge 1952–54 (ed.) 1955, Writing in England Today: The Last Fifteen Years (ed.) 1968, Memoirs of a Modern Scotland (ed.) 1970, A Listener Anthology, August 1967–June 1970 (ed.) 1970, A Second Listener Anthology (ed.) 1973, Cockburn's Millennium 1975, Robert Burns (ed.) 1981, Doubles: Studies in Literary History 1985, Authors 1989, Rebecca's Vest (autobiog.) 1993, Boswell and Hyde 1995, Dark Horses (autobiog.) 1998, Electric Shepherd: A Likeness of James Hogg 2003, Tretower to Clyro (selected essays) 2011. *Honours:* James Tait Black Prize 1975, Scottish Arts Council Book Award 1993. *Address:* 26 Limerston Street, London, SW10 0HH, England (home). *Telephone:* (20) 7351-1994 (home).

MILLER, Leslie Adrienne, BA, MA, MFA, PhD; American poet and academic; *Professor of English, University of St Thomas;* b. 22 Oct. 1956, Medina, OH; d. of Ray G. Miller and Martha Ann Ferguson. *Education:* Stephens Coll., Univ. of Missouri, Univ. of Iowa, Univ. of Houston. *Career:* Dir, Creative Writing Program, Stephens College 1983–87; Visiting Writer, University of Oregon 1990; Prof. of English, Univ. of St Thomas 1991–; mem. Associated Writing Programs, MLA, Poetry Soc. of America, Poets and Writers. *Publications:* Hanging on the Sunburned Arm of Some Homeboy (with Matthew Graham) 1982, No River 1987, Staying Up for Love 1990, Ungodliness 1994, Yesterday Had a Man In It 1998, Eat Quite Everything you See 2002, The Resurrection Trade 2007; contributions to anthologies, reviews, quarterlies, and journals. *Honours:* Nat. Endowment for the Arts Fellowship, John and Becky Moores Fellowship, Univ. of Houston, Goethe-Institut Cultural Exchange Fellowship, Berlin, Loft-McKnight Award in Poetry and Award of Distinction, Edward Stanley Award, Nebraska Review Poetry Award, Strousse Award, Billee Murray Denny Poetry Award, Stanley Young Fellowship in Poetry, Pen Southwest Discovery Award, Ann Stanford Prize in Poetry, Writers at Work Poetry Fellowships, Stanley Hanks Chapbook Award. *Address:* Department of English, Mail # JRC 333, University of St Thomas, St Paul, MN 55105-1096, USA (office). *Telephone:* (651) 962-5604 (office). *E-mail:* lamiller@stthomas.edu (office). *Website:* www.lesliemillerpoet.com.

MILLER, Madeline, BA, MA; American author and teacher; b. Boston. *Education:* Brown Univ., Univ. of Chicago, Yale School of Drama. *Career:*

teaches Latin, Greek and Shakespeare to high school students. *Publications:* The Song of Achilles (Orange Prize for Fiction 2012) 2011. *Literary Agent:* Julie Barer, Barer Literary LLC, 20 West 20th Street, Suite 601, New York, NY 10011, USA. *Telephone:* (212) 691-3513. *Website:* www.barerliterary.com. *Address:* c/o Katie Bond, Bloomsbury Publishing PLC, 50 Bedford Square, London, WC1B 3DP, England (office). *Telephone:* (20) 7631-5730 (office). *E-mail:* katie.bond@bloosmbury.com (office); *Website:* www.bloomsbury.com (office); www.madelinemiller.com.

MILLER, Marc William, BS; American writer; b. 29 Aug. 1947, Annapolis, MD; m. Darlene File 1981, one s. one d. *Education:* University of Illinois. *Career:* Contributing Ed., Fire and Movement Magazine, 1977–84; Staff, Grenadier Magazine, 1977–79, Journal of the Traveller's Aid Society, 1979–85, Challenge Magazine, 1986–92; mem. Acad. of Adventure Gaming Arts and Sciences; Game Designer's Guild; SFWA. *Publications:* Traveller, 1977; Imperium, 1977; 2300 AD, 1986; Mega Traveller, 1988; Mega Traveller II, Quest for the Ancients, 1991; Spellbound, 1992. Contributions: journals.

MILLER, Sue, BA, MA; American writer; b. 29 Nov. 1943; m. 1st (divorced); one s.; m. 2nd Doug Bauer (divorced 2001). *Education:* Radcliffe Coll., Harvard Univ., Boston Univ., Wesleyan Univ. *Career:* mem. PEN, PEN New England (chair. 1999–2003). *Publications:* The Good Mother 1986, Inventing the Abbotts and Other Stories 1987, Family Pictures: A Novel 1990, For Love 1993, The Distinguished Guest 1995, While I Was Gone: A Novel 1999, The World Below 2001, The Story of My Father 2003, Lost in the Forest 2005, The Senator's Wife 2008, The Lake Shore Limited 2010. *Honours:* MacDowell Colony Fellowship, Guggenheim Fellowship, Radcliffe Inst. of Advanced Study 2001. *Literary Agent:* Maxine Groffsky Literary Agency, 853 Broadway, Suite 708, New York, NY 10003, USA.

MILLET, Lydia, BA, MSc; American novelist; b. 5 Dec. 1968, Boston, Mass. *Education:* Univ. of North Carolina at Chapel Hill, Duke Univ. *Career:* worked for Natural Resources Defense Council, New York 1996–98; staff writer, Center for Biological Diversity 1999–. *Publications:* novels: Omnivores 1996, George Bush: Dark Prince of Love 2000, My Happy Life (PEN-USA Award for Fiction 2003) 2002, Everyone's Pretty 2005, Oh Pure and Radiant Heart 2005, How the Dead Dream 2008, Ghost Lights 2011; other: Love in Infant Monkeys (short stories) 2010; contrib. stories and essays to anthologies and journals. *Literary Agent:* Lippincott Massie McQuilkin. *E-mail:* maria@lmqlit.com. *E-mail:* lydiamillet@yahoo.com (home). *Website:* www.lydiamillet.net.

MILLETT, Katherine (Kate) Murray, PhD; American artist and writer; b. 14 Sept. 1934, St Paul, Minn.; m. Fumio Yoshimura 1965. *Education:* Univ. of Minnesota, St Hilda's Coll., Univ. of Oxford, UK and Columbia Univ. *Career:* Sculptor, Tokyo 1961–63; teacher, Barnard Coll. 1964–68; Distinguished Visiting Prof., Sacramento State Coll., Calif. 1973–; f. Women's Art Colony Farm (now Millett Farm), Poughkeepsie, NY; mem. Congress of Racial Equality 1965–. *Exhibitions include:* Minami Gallery, Tokyo, Judson Gallery 1967, Soho Gallery, New York 1976, 1978 1980, 1982, 1984, 1986, Women's Bldg, Los Angeles 1977, Andre Wanters Gallery, New York 1977, Chuck Levitan Gallery, New York, deVille Galerie, New Orleans, Emmy Gallery, Berlin 1977. *Publications include:* Sexual Politics 1970, The Prostitution Papers 1973, Flying 1974, Sita 1977, The Basement 1979, Going to Iran 1982, The Loony Bin Trip 1990, The Politics of Cruelty 1994, AD 1995, Mother Millett 2001. *Address:* Millett Farm, 20 Old Overlook Road, Poughkeepsie, NY 12603; Apt 5E, 59 East 4th Street, New York, NY 10003–7104, USA (office). *Telephone:* (845) 473-9267. *Website:* www.katemillett.com.

MILLHAUSER, Steven, BA; American author; b. 3 Aug. 1943, NY; m. Cathy Allis 1986; one s. one d. *Education:* Columbia College, Brown Univ. *Publications:* Edwin Mullhouse: The Life and Death of an American Writer 1972, Portrait of a Romantic 1976, In the Penny Arcade 1986, From the Realm of Morpheus 1986, The Barnum Museum 1990, Little Kingdoms 1993, Martin Dressler: The Tale of an American Dreamer (Pulitzer Prize 1997) 1996, The Knife Thrower and Other Stories 1998, Enchanted Night 1999, The King in the Tree 2003, Dangerous Laughter 2008, We Others: New and Selected Stories 2011. *Honours:* Prix Médicis Étranger 1975, Award in Literature 1987. *Address:* c/o Knopf Publishing/Author Mail, 1745 Broadway, New York, NY 10019, USA.

MILLHISER, Marlys Joy, BA, MA; American writer; b. 27 May 1938, Charles City, IA; m. David Millhiser 1960, one s. one d. *Education:* University of Iowa, University of Colorado. *Career:* mem. Authors' Guild; Colorado Authors League; MWA; Sisters in Crime; Western Writers of America. *Publications:* Michael's Wife, 1972; Nella Waits, 1974; Willing Hostage, 1976; The Mirror, 1978; Nightmare Country, 1981; The Threshold, 1984; Murder at Moot Point, 1992; Death of the Office Witch, 1993; Murder in a Hot Flash, 1995. Contributions: Magazines. *Honours:* Top Hand Awards 1975, 1985.

MILLINGTON, Barry John, BA; British music journalist and writer; b. 1 Nov. 1951, Hadleigh, Suffolk, England; m. Deborah Jane Calland 1996. *Education:* Clare Coll., Cambridge. *Career:* editorial staff mem. The New Grove Dictionary of Music and Musicians 1975–76; criticism for Musical Times and newspapers, notably The Times 1977–82, 1988–2001; Reviews Ed. for BBC Music Magazine 1992–2002; Chief Music Critic, Evening Standard 2002–; Founder and Artistic Dir Hampstead and Highgate Festival 1999–2003; dramaturgical adviser on new production of Lohengrin at Bayreuth Festival 1999; Ed. The Wagner Journal 2007–; mem. Royal Musical Asscn, Critics Circle. *Publications:* Wagner 1984, Selected Letters of Richard Wagner (trans. and co-ed. with S. Spencer) 1987, The Wagner Compendium: A Guide to Wagner's Life and Music (ed.) 1992, Wagner in Performance (co-ed. with S. Spencer) 1992, Wagner's Ring of the Nibelung: A Companion (co-ed. with S. Spencer) 1993, The New Grove Wagner 2002; contrib. to Oxford Illustrated History of Opera 1994, The New Grove Dictionary of Opera 1992, The New Grove Dictionary of Music and Musicians (revised edn) 2001, The New Grove Guide to Wagner and his Operas 2006; numerous other pubs in newspapers and periodicals. *Address:* 50 Denman Drive South, London, NW11 6RH, England (home). *E-mail:* milcal@btinternet.com (office). *Website:* www.thewagnerjournal.co.uk (office).

MILLS, Kyle; American novelist; b. 1966. *Publications:* Rising Phoenix 1997, Storming Heaven 1998, Free Fall 2000, Burn Factor 2001, Sphere of Influence 2002, Smoke Screen 2003, Fade 2006, The Second Horseman 2006, Darkness Falls 2007, Lords of Corruption 2009. *Address:* PO Box 8036, Jackson, WY, 83002 USA (home). *E-mail:* author@kylemills.com (home). *Website:* www.kylemills.com.

MILLS, Magnus; British writer; b. 1954, Birmingham. *Education:* Wolverhampton Polytechnic. *Publications:* novels: The Restraint of Beasts 1998, All Quiet on the Orient Express 1999, Three to See the King 2001, The Scheme for Full Employment 2003, Explorers of the New Century 2005, The Maintenance of Headway 2009; short story collections: Only When the Sun Shines Brightly 1999, Once in a Blue Moon 2003, Screwtop Thompson 2010; contrib. to The Independent, The Verb (BBC Radio 3), Front Row (BBC Radio 4). *Literary Agent:* Rogers, Coleridge and White, 20 Powis Mews, London, W11 1JN, England. *Telephone:* (20) 7221-3717. *Fax:* (20) 7229-9084. *E-mail:* info@rcwlitagency.com. *Website:* www.rcwlitagency.com.

MILLS, Ralph Joseph, Jr, MA, PhD; American academic, poet and writer; *Professor Emeritus of English, University of Illinois at Chicago*; b. 16 Dec. 1931, Chicago; m. Helen Daggett Harvey 1959; one s. two d. *Education:* Lake Forest Coll., Northwestern Univ., Univ. of Oxford. *Career:* Instructor, University of Chicago 1959–61, Asst Prof. 1962–65; Assoc. Prof., University of Illinois at Chicago 1965–67, Prof. of English 1967–97, Prof. Emer. 1997–. *Publications:* poetry: Door to the Sun, 1974; A Man to His Shadow, 1975; Night Road, 1978; Living with Distance, 1979; With No Answer, 1980; March Light, 1983; For a Day, 1985; Each Branch: Poems 1976–1985, 1986; A While, 1989; A Window in Air, 1993; In Wind's Edge, 1997; Grasses Standing: Selected Poems, 2000. other: Contemporary American Poetry, 1965; On the Poet and His Craft: Selected Prose of Theodore Roethke (ed.), 1965; Edith Sitwell: A Critical Essay, 1966; Kathleen Raine: A Critical Essay, 1967; Creation's Very Self: On the Personal Element in Recent American Poetry, 1969; Cry of the Human: Essays on Contemporary American Poetry, 1975; Essays on Poetry 2004; contributions: books and journals. *Honours:* English-Speaking Union Fellowship, 1956–57; Illinois Arts Council Awards for Poetry, 1979, 1983, 1984; Society of Midland Authors Prize for Poetry, 1980; Carl Sandburg Prize for Poetry, 1984; William Carlos Williams Prize, Poetry Society of America, 2002. *Address:* 110 South Fairview Avenue, Park Ridge, IL 60068 (home); 1451 North Astor Street, Chicago, IL 60610, USA.

MILNE, John, (Ian Miller, Tom Bowling), BA; British writer, scriptwriter and lecturer; *Principal Lecturer in Creative Writing, Sheffield Hallam University*; b. 20 Sept. 1952, Bermondsey, South London, England; s. of Alexander Milne and Sheila Milne; m. Sarah Laetitia Beresford Verity 1983, two s. *Education:* St Joseph's Acad., Blackheath, Chelsea School of Art, Ravensbourne School of Art. *Career:* book reviewer and feature writer for the Daily Telegraph and Time Out; currently Prin. Lecturer in Creative Writing, Sheffield Hallam Univ. *Television:* Waking the Dead (BBC 1), The Bill (ITV), Bergerac (BBC 1), Silent Witness (BBC 1), Maisie Raine (BBC 1), Pie in the Sky (BBC 1), Heartbeat (ITV1), Lovejoy (BBC 1). *Publications:* as John Milne: Tyro 1981, London Fields 1982, Dead Birds 1984, Out of the Blue 1985, Shadow Play 1986, Daddy's Girl 1988, Alive and Kicking 1998; as Ian Miller: Wet Wickets and Dusty Balls 1982; as Tom Bowling: Pirate and Privateers 2008, The Antigallican 2008. *Honours:* John Llewellyn Rhys Prize 1985, Writers' Guild Award 1991, Edgar Award, Mystery Writers of America 1998. *Literary Agent:* c/o The Agency, 24 Pottery Lane, Holland Park, London, W11 4LZ, England. *Telephone:* (20) 7727-1346. *E-mail:* info@theagency.co.uk. *Website:* www.theagency.co.uk. *E-mail:* john.milne@shu.ac.uk (office).

MILTNER, Robert F., BA, MEd, PhD; American writer, poet and educator; b. 25 Feb. 1949, Cleveland, OH; m. 1st Linda Smith 1975 (divorced 1996); m. 2nd Mari Artzner Wolf 1996 (divorced 2002); one s. one d. *Education:* Xavier University, John Carroll University, Kent State University. *Career:* English Teacher, private religious high schools, Denver, CO, 1975–77, including Dept Head, Parma, Ohio, 1977–87; Co-ordinator for Developmental Education, 1987–93, 1993–95, Instructor in English, 1987–95, Dir, Writing Center, 1990–92, 1995–97, Asst Prof. of English, 1998–, Kent State University, Stark Campus, Canton, Ohio; Instructor in English, Walsh University, Canton, 1993–94; mem. Associated Writing Programs; American Asscn of University Profs. *Publications:* The Seamless Serial Hour (poems), 1993; Against the Simple (poems), 1995; On the Off Ramp (poems), 1996; Ghost of a Chance (poems), 2002; Four Crows on a Phone Line (poems), 2002; A Box of Light (prose poems), 2002; Curriculum materials. Contributions: New York Quarterly; English Journal; Chiron Review; Ohioana Quarterly; Mid-American Review; Birmingham Poetry Review. *Honours:* Wick Poetry Chapbook Award, 1994. *E-mail:* rmiltner@stark.kent.edu.

MIN, Anchee, BFA, MFA; Chinese novelist; b. 1957, Shanghai; m.; one d. *Education:* Univ. of Illinois, Chicago Inst. of Arts. *Career:* born and raised in Communist China, during the Cultural Revolution; fmly worked as a peasant in the rural areas of the country, later in the Chinese film industry; moved to USA in 1984. *Publications:* Red Azalea (memoir) (New York Times Notable Book 1995) 1994, Katherine (novel) 1995, Becoming Madame Mao (novel) 2000, Wild Ginger (novel) 2002, Empress Orchid (novel) 2004, The Last Empress 2007, Pearl of China (novel) 2010. *Literary Agent:* Steven Barclay Agency, 12 Western Avenue, Petaluma, CA 94952, USA. *Telephone:* (707) 773-0654. *Fax:* (707) 778-1868. *Website:* www.barclayagency.com; ancheemin.com.

MINA, Hanna; Syrian novelist; b. 1924, Latakia. *Publications:* novels: Al Shams fi Youm Gha'em (trans. as Sun on a Cloudy Day 1997) 1973, Al Marsad 1980, al-Qissah wa-al-dalalah al-fikriyah, al-Fam al-karazi: Riwayah 1999, Harat Al Shahhadeen 2000, Siraa' Imra'tin 2001, Al Bahar wal Safina wahi (The Sail and the Storm) 2002, Al Yatar 2004, Shrif Kata' trik 2004, Black Wolf 2005, Nihaya Rajol Shoja'a 2007, Al Nar Bayna Asabi' Imra'a 2007, Al Rabia' wal Khari 2008, A'ahrah wa Nisf Majnoun 2008, Imra' Tajhalu Anaha Imra'a 2009; other: Fragments of Memory: A Story of a Syrian Family (autobiog., in trans.) 1993. *Honours:* Sultan Bin Ali Al Owais Award, Cairo Arab Novel Award 2005, Assilah Int. Forum Mohamed Zafzaf Prize for Arabic Literature 2010. *Address:* c/o Dar Al Adab Publishers, Berlin Street - Saqaiet Al Ganzir, Beirut 114123, Lebanon; c/o Interlink Publishing, 46 Crosby Street, Northampton, MA 01060-1804, USA. *E-mail:* info@interlinkbooks.com.

MINARIK, John Paul, BS, BA; American poet, writer and engineer; b. 6 Nov. 1947, McKeesport, Pa; s. of Rudolph Andrew and Pauline Anne Minarik; m. 1st Marcia Margaret Tarasovic 1978 (divorced 1987); two d.; m. 2nd Susan Kay Minarik 1988 (divorced 2005); one s. *Education:* Carnegie Mellon Univ., Univ. of Pittsburgh. *Career:* engineer, United Steel Corpn 1966–71; Instructor, Community Coll. of Allegheny County 1977–83; teaching consultant, Univ. of Pittsburgh 1978–96; Poet-in-the-Schools, Pennsylvania Council on the Arts 1979–83; project engineer-consultant, Economy Industrial Corpn 1981–82; Chief Engineer, New Directions 1989–96; Founder-Ed., Acad. of Prison Arts; Advisory Ed., Greenfield Review Press; poetry readings; mem. American Soc. of Mechanical Engineers, Authors' Guild. *Publications include:* Patterns in the Dusk 1978, Past the Unknown, Remembered Gate 1981, Kicking Their Heels with Freedom (ed.) 1982; contrib. to over 100 newspapers in the USA and journals including American Ethnic, Ars Interpres (Sweden), Backspace, Caprice, Carnegie Mellon Magazine, Confrontation, Gravida, Greenfield Review, Happiness Holding Tank, Hyacinths and Biscuits, Interstate, Joint Conference, Journal of Popular Culture, Mill Hunk Herald, New Orleans Review, Nitty-Gritty, Old Main, Painted Bride Quarterly, Pittsburgh and Tri-State Area Poets, Prison Writing Review, Poetry Society of America Bulletin, Small Pond, Sunday Clothes; poems read on Monitoradio, Voice of America, WQED-FM and WYEP, and at Three Rivers Arts Festival and American Wind Symphony. *Honours:* hon. mention PEN Writing Award 1976–77, Carnegie Magazine Best Book of the Year Citation 1982, poetry and prose writing contest winner, Pennsylvania Dept of Corrections 1985, 1988. *Address:* 1600 Walters Mill Road, APO-580, Somerset, PA 15510-0005, USA (home).

MINATOYA, Lydia, BA, MA, PhD; American writer; b. 8 Nov. 1950, New York, NY; one s. *Education:* Saint Lawrence University, George Washington University, University of Maryland. *Publications:* Talking to High Monks in the Snow, 1992; The Strangeness of Beauty, 1999. *Honours:* PEN Jerard Fund Award, 1991; American Library Asscn Notable Book, 1992; New York Public Library Notable Book, 1992; Pacific Northwest Booksellers Award, 1993.

MINEAR, Richard Hoffman, MA, PhD; American academic and writer; *Professor of History, University of Massachusetts*; b. 31 Dec. 1938, Evanston, Ill.; m. Edith Christian 1962; two s. *Education:* Yale and Harvard Univs. *Career:* Asst Prof., Ohio State Univ. 1967–70; Assoc. Prof. of History, Univ. of Massachusetts 1970–75, Prof. 1975–2008. *Publications:* Japanese Tradition and Western Law 1970, Victors' Justice 1971, Through Japanese Eyes 1974, Requiem for Battleship Yamato by Yoshida Mitsuru (ed. and trans.) 1985, Hiroshima: Three Witnesses 1990, Black Eggs by Kurihara Sadako (ed. and trans.) 1994, When we say 'Hiroshima' 1999, Dr Seuss Goes to War 1999, Japan's Past, Japan's Future: One Historian's Odyssey by Ienaga Saburo (ed. and trans.) 2000, The Scars of War: Tokyo during World War II, Writings of Takeyama Michio (ed. and trans.) 2007, Hiroshima: The Autobiography of Barefoot Gen (ed. and trans.) 2010, War and Conscience in Japan: Nambara Shigeru and the Asia-Pacific War ed. and trans.) 2011, The Day the Sun Rose in the West: Bikini, The Lucky Dragon, and I (ed. and trans.) 2011; contrib. to professional journals and general magazines. *Address:* Department of History, University of Massachusetts, Amherst, MA 01003, USA.

MINOGUE, Valerie Pearson, BA, MLitt; British academic (retd), writer, editor and translator; b. (Valerie Pearson Hallett), 26 April 1931, Llanelli, S Wales; d. of Frederick George Hallett and Martha Hallett; m. Kenneth Robert Minogue 1954 (divorced 2000); one s. one d. *Education:* Girton Coll., Cambridge. *Career:* Asst Lecturer, Univ. Coll., Cardiff 1952–53; contrib. to Cambridge Italian Dictionary 1956–61; Lecturer, Queen Mary Coll., London 1963–74, Sr Lecturer 1975–81; Prof., Univ. of Wales, Swansea 1981–88, Research Prof. 1988–96, Prof. Emer. 1996–; Founding Ed. Romance Studies 1982–98, Gen. Ed. 1998–2003; mem. Modern Humanities Research Asscn, Soc. for French Studies, Romance Studies Inst., Émile Zola Soc. (Pres.), Soc. des Dix-Neuviémistes. *Publications:* Proust: Du Côté de chez Swann 1973, Nathalie Sarraute: The War of the Words 1981, Zola: L'Assommoir 1991, Eight texts, Pléiade Oeuvres complètes of Nathalie Sarraute (ed., with notes and critical essays) 1996; contributions to Quadrant, Literary Review, Modern Language Review, French Studies, Romance Studies, Forum for Modern Language Studies, New Novel Review, Revue des Sciences Humaines, Times Literary Supplement, Esprit Créateur, Theatre Research International, Critique, Littératura, Roman 20–50, The Literary Encyclopaedia; numerous chapters in books. *Honours:* Officier, Ordre des Palmes académiques; Mary Elizabeth Ponsonby Prize for French Literature 1952, Maria Degani Scholarship 1953. *Address:* 23 Richford Street, London, W6 7HJ, England (home). *E-mail:* valerie@valminogue.com (home).

MINOT, Susan Anderson, BA, MFA; American writer; b. 7 Dec. 1956, Boston, MA; m. Davis McHenry 1988 (divorced). *Education:* Brown Univ., Columbia Univ. *Publications:* Monkeys, 1986; Lost & Other Stories, 1989; Folly, 1992; Evening, 1998; Rapture, 2002. Contributions: New Yorker; Grand Street; Paris Review; Mademoiselle; Harper's; GQ; New England Monthly; Conde Nasts Traveler; Esquire; New York Times Magazine; Atlantic Monthly. *Honours:* Prix Fémina Étranger 1987.

MINTER, David Lee, BA, MA, BD, PhD; American academic and writer; b. 20 March 1935, Midland, TX. *Education:* North Texas State University, Yale University. *Career:* Lecturer, University of Hamburg, 1965–66, Yale University, 1966–67; Asst Prof., 1967–69, Assoc. Prof. 1969–74, Prof., 1974–80, 1991–, Rice University; Prof., Dean of Emory College, Vice-Pres. for Arts and Sciences, Emory University, 1981–90. *Publications:* The Interpreted Design as a Structural Principle in American Prose, 1969; William Faulkner: His Life and Work, 1980; The Harper American Literature, 1986; The Norton Critical Edn of The Sound and the Fury, 1987; A Cultural History of the American Novel: Henry James to William Faulkner, 1994; Faulkner's Questioning Narratives: Fiction of His Major Phase 1929–1942, 2001. Contributions: Professional journals.

MIOT, Jean Louis Yves Marie; French journalist; b. 30 July 1939, Châteauroux (Indre); s. of René Miot and Madeleine Moreau; two s. three d. *Education:* Lycée Jean Giraudoux de Châteauroux and Univ. de Poitiers. *Career:* Ed. Centre Presse, Poitiers 1964–68; journalist, French Antilles 1968–70; Ed.-in-Chief, later Political Dir Havre-Presse 1970–74; Man. Dir France Antilles Martinique Guadeloupe, launched France-Guyane (weekly) 1974–76; Head, Legis. Elections Service, Le Figaro 1977–78; Man. Dir Berry Républicain, Bourges 1978; Dir Groupe de Presse Robert Hersant 1978–79; Political corresp. L'Aurore 1979–80; mem. Man. Bd Société de Gestion et Assoc. Dir Le Figaro 1980–93; Pres. Advisory Bd Le Figaro 1993–96; Pres. Syndicat de la Presse Parisienne 1986–96; Pres. Féd. Nat. de la Presse Française 1993–96; Pres. Agence-France-Presse (AFP) 1996–99, Syndicat des agences de presse de nouvelles (SANOV) 1996–99; Pres.-Dir Gen. Codalie, Financière-CDP and CD-Presse 1999–; mem. Conseil Econ. et Social 1993–96, Comm. de réflexion sur la justice 1997; Dir Société Financière de Radio-Diffusion (SOFIRAD) 1995. *Honours:* Chevalier, Légion d'honneur, Officier de l'Etoile Civique, Officer, Order of Lion (Senegal). *Address:* SARL Codalie, 59 avenue Victor Hugo, 75116 Paris (office); CD-Presse, 3 chemin du Clos, 95650 Puiseux-Pontoise (office); 10 rue Maître Albert, 75005 Paris, France (home). *Telephone:* 1-46-34-70-21 (office). *Fax:* 1-46-34-70-21 (office). *E-mail:* janmio@wanadoo.fr (home).

MIRABELLI, Eugene, BA, MA, PhD; American writer and academic; *Professor Emeritus, State University of New York at Albany*; b. 3 Feb. 1931, Arlington, Mass; s. of Eugene Mirabelli and Josephine Mirabelli; m. Margaret Anne Black 1959; one s. two d. *Education:* Harvard Univ., Johns Hopkins Univ. *Career:* Faculty, Williams Coll. 1960–64, State Univ. of NY at Albany 1965–95; Founder, mem. Bd and Officer, non-profit Alternative Literary Programs; mem. Authors' Guild, PEN American Center. *Play:* Right in the Oval Office (political puppet play). *Publications:* The Burning Air 1959, The Way In 1968, No Resting Place 1972, The World at Noon 1994, The Language Nobody Speaks 1999, The Passion of Terri Heart 2004, Cheap Poems 2004, The Queen of the Rain Was in Love with the Prince of the Sky 2008, The Goddess in Love with a Horse 2008, Renato, the Painter 2011; various short stories, book reviews and political opinion pieces. *Honours:* Rockefeller Foundation Grant 1969. *Literary Agent:* c/o McPherson & Co., PO Box 1126, Kingston, NY 12402, USA. *Telephone:* (845) 331-5807. *Fax:* (845) 331-5807. *E-mail:* bmcphersonco@gmail.com. *Website:* members.authorsguild.net/mirabelli; www.criticalpages.com.

MISHRA, Jaishree, MA; Indian author; b. 1961, New Delhi; m.; one d. *Education:* Kerala Univ., Univ. of London, UK. *Career:* fmrly taught adults with special needs; fmrly worked in Child Care Dept of Social Services, Bucks., England; fmr journalist, BBC Radio; film classifier, British Board of Film Classification 2002–09; returned to New Delhi 2009; helped to found residential home for adults with learning disabilities. *Publications include:* novels: Ancient Promises 1999, The Little Book of Romance 2001, Accidents Like Love and Marriage 2001, Afterwards 2004, Rani 2007, Secrets and Lies 2009, Secrets and Sins 2010, A Scandalous Secret 2011. *Honours:* Part-Scholarship, Charles Wallace for India Trust. *Address:* c/o Avon, HarperCollins, 77–85 Fulham Palace Road, Hammersmith, London, W6 8JB, England (office). *Telephone:* (20) 8741-7070 (office). *Fax:* (20) 8307-4440 (office). *E-mail:* enquiries@harpercollins.co.uk (office). *Website:* www.harpercollins.co.uk (office); www.jaishreemisra.com.

MISRA, Jaishree, MA; Indian writer; b. 1961, New Delhi; m.; one d. *Education:* Kerala Univ., Inst. of Educ., London, UK. *Career:* moved to UK 1990; fmrly worked in Special Educ., Social Services and for BBC; currently film classifier, British Bd of Film Classification. *Publications include:* Ancient Promises 2000, The Little Book of Romance 2001, Accidents like Love and Marriage 2002, Afterwards 2004, Rani 2007, Secrets and Lies 2009. *E-mail:* jaishreemisra@googlemail.com (office). *Website:* www.jaishreemisra.com.

MISTRY, Rohinton, BA, BSc; Canadian author; b. 3 July 1952, Bombay (now Mumbai), India; m. Freny Elavia 1975. *Education:* St Xavier's High School, Bombay, Univ. of Bombay, Univ. of Toronto and York Univ., Canada. *Career:* moved to Canada 1975; bank clerk, Toronto 1975–85; began writing short stories 1982; writings have been translated into more than 25 languages. *Publications include:* Tales from Firozsha Baag (short stories) 1987, Such a Long Journey (novel) 1991, A Fine Balance (novel) 1995, Family Matters (novel) 2002, The Scream 2008; essays and articles in various languages and periodicals. *Honours:* Hon. PhD (Ottawa) 1996, (Toronto) 1999, (York) 2003; Gov.-Gen.'s Award for Fiction 1991, Commonwealth Writers' Prize for Best Book 1992, 1996, First Novel Award, W. H. Smith/Books in Canada 1992, Giller Prize 1995, Winifred Holtby Prize, RSL 1996, Los Angeles Times Fiction Prize 1997, ALOA Prize for Asscn Fiction (Denmark) 1997, Kiriyama Pacific Rim Book Prize for Fiction 2002, Canadian Authors' Asscn Award for Fiction 2003, Guggenheim Fellowship 2005, Neustadt Int. Prize for Literature 2012. *Literary Agent:* c/o Bruce Westwood, Westwood Creative Artists Ltd, 94 Harbord Street, Toronto, ON M5S 1G6, Canada. *Telephone:* (416) 964-3302. *Fax:* (406) 975-9209. *E-mail:* wca_office@wcaltd.com. *Website:* www.wcaltd.com.

MITCHARD, Jacquelyn, BA; American writer; b. 10 Dec. 1953, Chicago, IL; m. Dan Allegretti 1981 (died 1993); five c. *Education:* Rockford Coll. *Career:* reporter, Man. Ed., Pioneer Press, Chicago 1976–79; Metro reporter and columnist, Milwaukee Journal 1984–88; syndicated columnist. *Publications:* non-fiction: Mother Less Child: The Love Story of a Family 1985, Jane Addams: Pioneer in Social Reform and Activist for World Peace 1991, Jane Addams: Peace Activist (co-author) 1992; novels: The Deep End of the Ocean 1996, The Most Wanted 1998, A Theory of Relativity 2001, Christmas, Present 2003, Twelve Times Blessed 2003, The Breakdown Lane 2005, Cage of Stars 2006, Still Summer 2007, No Time to Wave Goodbye 2009; also books for children and young adults; other: screenplays. *Honours:* Maggie Awards for Public Service Magazine Journalism 1993, 1994, Parenting Network Public Awareness Award 1997, Milwaukee Press Club Headliner Award 1997; Anne Powers Award for Fiction, Council of Wisconsin Writers 1997. *E-mail:* jackie@jackiemitchard.com (office). *Website:* www.jackiemitchard.com.

MITCHELL, Chris, BA; Australian journalist and editor; *Editor-in-Chief, The Australian*; b. 13 Oct. 1956, Brisbane; divorced; two s.; one s. one d. from previous m. *Education:* Padua Coll., Brisbane, Univ. of Queensland. *Career:* journalist with The Telegraph, Brisbane 1973–79, The Townsville Bulletin 1979–81, The Daily Telegraph, Sydney 1981, The Australian Financial Review; Chief Sub-Ed., Night Ed., Deputy Ed., The Australian 1984–92, Ed. 1992–95, Ed.-in-Chief 2002–; Ed.-in-Chief, The Courier Mail and The Sunday Mail, Queensland 1995–2002; fmr Ed.-in-Chief, Queensland Newspapers. *Address:* The Australian, PO Box 4245, Sydney, NSW 2001, Australia (office). *Telephone:* (2) 9288-2302 (office). *Fax:* (2) 9288-2912 (office). *Website:* www.theaustralian.com.au (office).

MITCHELL, David, MA; British writer; b. Jan. 1969, Southport; m. Keiko Mitchell; one d. *Education:* Univ. of Kent. *Career:* worked in Waterstone's, Canterbury 1990–91; taught English in Japan 1994–2002. *Publications:* Ghostwritten (Mail on Sunday/John Llewellyn Rhys Prize, James Tait Black Memorial Prize) 1999, Number9Dream 2001, Cloud Atlas (British Book Awards for Richard & Judy Best Read of the Year 2005, South Bank Show Literary Fiction Award, Geoffrey Faber Memorial Prize 2005) 2004, Black Swan Green 2006, The Thousand Autumns of Jacob de Zoet 2010. *Honours:* one of Granta's Best of Young British Novelists 2003. *Address:* c/o Sceptre, Hodder Headline Ltd, 338 Euston Road, London, NW1 3BH, England.

MITCHELL, David John, MA; British writer; b. 24 Jan. 1924, London; m. 1955; one s. *Education:* Bradfield Coll., Berkshire, Trinity Coll., Oxford. *Career:* staff writer Picture Post 1947–52; mem. Soc. of Authors. *Publications:* Women on the Warpath 1966, The Fighting Pankhursts 1967, 1919 Red Mirage 1970, Pirates 1976, Queen Christabel 1977, The Jesuits: A History 1980, The Spanish Civil War 1982, Travellers in Spain 1990, The Spanish Attraction (ed.) 2001; contrib. to newspapers and magazines. *Honours:* Civil List Pension for services to literature 1998. *Address:* 20 Mountacre Close, Sydenham Hill, London, SE26 6SX, England (home). *Telephone:* (20) 8670-5992 (home).

MITCHELL, Jerome, MA, PhD; American academic and writer; b. 7 Oct. 1935, Chattanooga, Tenn. *Education:* Emory Univ., Univ. of Bonn, Germany, Duke Univ. *Career:* Asst Prof., Univ. of Illinois 1965–67; Assoc. Prof., Univ. of Georgia 1967–72, Prof. 1972–97; Fulbright Guest Prof., Univ. of Bonn 1972–73; Visiting Exchange Prof., Univ. of Erlangen 1975; Richard Merton Guest Prof., Univ. of Regensburg 1978–79. *Publications:* Thomas Hoccleve: A Study in Early 15th Century English Poetic 1968, Hoccleve's Works: The Minor Poems 1970, Chaucer: The Love Poet 1973, The Walter Scott Operas 1977, Scott, Chaucer and Medieval Romance 1987, Old and Middle English Literature 1994, More Scott Operas 1996; contributions: various scholarly journals. *Address:* PO Box 1268, Athens, GA 30603, USA (home).

MITCHELL, Julian, BA, FRSL, FSA; British author; b. 1 May 1935, Epping, Essex; s. of the late William Moncur Mitchell and Christine Mitchell (née Browne). *Education:* Winchester and Wadham Coll., Oxford. *Career:* mem. Literature Panel, Arts Council 1966–69, Welsh Arts Council 1988–92. *Publications:* novels: Imaginary Toys 1961, A Disturbing Influence 1962, As Far As You Can Go 1963, The White Father 1964, A Circle of Friends 1966, The Undiscovered Country 1968; biography: Jennie: Lady Randolph Churchill (with Peregrine Churchill), A Disgraceful Anomaly 2003; plays: Half Life 1977, The Enemy Within 1980, Another Country 1981 (SWET Award 1982, filmed 1984), Francis 1983, After Aida (or Verdi's Messiah) 1986, Falling over England 1994, August 1994 (adapted from Uncle Vanya, filmed 1995), The Good Soldier (adapted from Ford Madox Ford) 2010, Family Business 2011. *Art exhibition:* Curator, Joshua Gosselin in Wales, Chepstow 2003, The Wye Tour and its Artists, Chepstow 2010. *Films:* Arabesque 1965, Vincent and Theo 1990, Wilde 1997; television plays and adaptations; translation of Pirandello's Henry IV. *Television:* more than 50 TV plays. *Honours:* John Llewellyn Rhys Prize 1965; Somerset Maugham Award 1966. *Address:* 25 Rylott Road, London, W12 9SS, England (home). *Telephone:* (20) 8740-5036 (home). *E-mail:* julian.mitchell606@btinternet.com (home).

MITCHELL, Kenneth Ronald, OC, BA, MA; Canadian academic, writer and dramatist; b. 13 Dec. 1940, Moose Jaw, Sask.; m. Jeanne Shami 1983; four s. one d. *Education:* Univ. of Saskatchewan. *Career:* instructor, Univ. of Regina 1967–70, Prof. 1984–2005; Visiting Prof., Univ. of Beijing 1980–81, Foreign Affairs Coll., Beijing 1986–87; mem. Canadian Asscn of Univ. Teachers, Playwrights' Union of Canada. *Publications:* Wandering Rafferty 1972, The Meadowlark Connection 1975, Everybody Gets Something Here 1977, Cruel Tears (co-author) 1977, Horizon: Writings of the Canadian Prairie (ed.) 1977, The Con Man 1979, Davin 1979, Sinclair Ross 1981, Ken Mitchell Country 1984, Gone the Burning Sun 1985, Through the Nan Da Gate 1986, Witches and Idiots 1990, The Plainsman 1992, Stones of the Dalai Lama 1993, The Heroic Adventures of Donny Coyote 2003, The Jazz Province 2005. *Honours:* Ottawa Little Theatre Prize 1971, Canadian Authors' Asscn Award for Best Canadian Play 1985. *Address:* 209 Angus Crescent, Regina, SK S4T 6N3, Canada (home).

MITCHELL, Roger Sherman, AB, MA, PhD; American poet and teacher; b. 8 Feb. 1935, Boston, Mass; two d. *Education:* Harvard College, University of Colorado, Manchester University. *Career:* Ed., Minnesota Review, 1973–81; Dir, Writers Conferences, Indiana University 1975–85, Creative Writing Program 1978–96; mem. Associated Writing Programs. *Publications include:* Letters from Siberia, 1971; Moving, 1976; A Clear Space on a Cold Day, 1986; Adirondack, 1988; Clear Pond, 1991; The Word for Everything, 1996; Braid, 1997; Savage Baggage, 2001; contributions: periodicals. *Honours:* Abby M. Copps Award 1971, Midland Poetry Award 1972, Borestone Mountain Award 1973, PEN Award 1977, Arvon Foundation Award 1985, 1987, National Endowment for the Arts Fellowship 1986, 2001, Chester H. Jones Award 1987.

MITCHELL, Susanna Ryland; British writer; b. 8 April 1941, Newry, Northern Ireland; m. Charles Donald Mitchell 1965, two d. *Education:* University of Cambridge. *Publications:* The Token, 1984; The Christening, 1986; The Colour of His Hair, 1994. *Literary Agent:* Curtis Brown Ltd, Haymarket House, 28–29 Haymarket, London, SW1Y 4SP, England. *Telephone:* (20) 7393-4400. *Fax:* (20) 7393-4401. *E-mail:* info@curtisbrown.co.uk. *Website:* www.curtisbrown.co.uk. *Address:* 63 Cloudesley Road, London N1 0EL, England (home).

MITCHELL, William John Thomas, BA, MA, PhD; American academic, editor and writer; *Gaylord Donnelley Distinguished Service Professor, University of Chicago*; b. 24 March 1942, Anaheim, CA; m. Janice Misurell 1968; one s. one d. *Education:* Michigan State Univ., Johns Hopkins Univ. *Career:* Ed., Critical Inquiry 1979–; Prof. of English and Art History, Chair Dept of English Univ. of Chicago 1989–92; Fairchild Distinguished Scholar, Cal Tech 1994; Berg Prof., New York Univ. 1998, 2000; Maclean Visiting Prof., Colorado Coll. 2001; Hawke Prof., Univ. of South Australia 2001; mem. Acad. of Literary Studies, MLA, PEN. *Publications:* Blake's Composite Art 1977, The Language of Images 1980, The Politics of Interpretation 1983, Against Theory 1983, Iconology 1986, Art and the Public Sphere 1993, Landscape and Power 1993, Picture Theory 1994, The Last Dinosaur Book: The Life and Times of a Cultural Icon 1998, What Do Pictures Want? 2005; contrib. to professional journals and general periodicals. *Honours:* American Philosophical Soc. Essay Prize 1968, Nat. Endowment for the Humanities Fellowships 1978, 1986, Guggenheim Fellowship 1983, Gaylord Donnelley Distinguished Service Professorship 1989, Coll. Art Asscn's Charles Rufus Morey Prize for Distinguished Book in Art History 1996, Univ. of Chicago Press Laing Prize for Picture Theory 1997, American Acad. in Berlin Berlin Prize Fellow 2002, Hon. Fellow Wissenschaftskolleg zu Berlin 2004–05, Leverhulme Prof., UK 2006. *Address:* c/o Dept of English and Art History, University of Chicago, 1050 E 59th Street, Chicago, IL 60637, USA (office). *Telephone:* (773) 702-8475 (office). *Fax:* (772) 702-3397 (office). *E-mail:* wjtm@uchicago.edu (office).

MITSON, Eileen Nora; British writer; b. 22 Sept. 1930, Langley, Essex; m. Arthur Samuel Mitson 1951; two d. (one deceased). *Education:* Cambridge Technical Coll. and School of Art. *Career:* columnist, Christian Woman magazine, later Woman Alive Magazine 1982–94. *Publications:* Stairway of Surprises 1964, The Door in the Way 1964, His Bright Designs 1968, Beyond the Shadows 1968, Amazon Adventure 1969, House of Strangers 1971, The Inside Room 1973, A Kind of Freedom 1976, Reaching for God 1978, Creativity (co-author) 1985, Songs of Freedom 2005, Pathways to Joy 2007. *Address:* 39 Oaklands, Hamilton Road, Reading, Berkshire RG1 5RN, England (home). *Telephone:* (118) 926-4144 (home).

MITTMAN, Stephanie, (Stevi Mittman), BA; American writer and artist; b. 15 April 1950, New York, NY; m. Alan Mittman 1969; one s. one d. *Education:* Ithaca Coll. *Career:* mem. Authors' Guild, Novelists Inc., Romance Writers of America. *Publications:* as Stephanie Mittman: Bridge to Yesterday 1995, A Taste of Honey 1995, The Marriage Bed 1996, A Christmas Miracle 1996, Sweeter than Wine 1997, Outlaw Love 1997, The Courtship 1998, A Kiss to Dream On 1999, Head Over Heels 1999, A Heart Full of Miracles 2000; as Stevi Mittman: What Goes with Blood Red, Anyway? 2006, Who Makes up these Rules, Anyway? 2006, Why is Murder on the Menu, Anyway? 2007, Whose Number is Up, Anyway? 2007, Who Creamed Peaches, Anyway? 2008; contributions: anthologies. *Honours:* Best Sweet Historical Award, American Online Romance Reader Awards 1995, Reviewer's Choice Certificate of Excellence, Romantic Times 1996, Best Americana Historical Romance Award, Romantic Times 1997, Career Achievement Award, Romantic Times 1997. *E-mail:* stevi@stevimittman.com (office). *Website:* www.stevimittman.com.

MIYAMOTO, Teru; Japanese novelist; b. 6 March 1947, Kobe. *Education:* Otemon Gakuin Univ. *Career:* began career as advertising copywriter. *Publications:* Doro no Kawa (River of Mud) (Dazai Osamu Prize) 1977, Hoterugawa (Firefly River) (Akutagawa Prize) 1978, Maborosi no Hikari (Illusory Light) 1979, Kinshu (trans. as Kinshu: Autumn Brocade) 1982, Yumemidori no hitobito (The People of Dream Street) 1989. *Address:* c/o New Directions Publishing Corporation, 80 Eighth Avenue, New York, NY 10011, USA. *E-mail:* editorial@ndbooks.com.

MIZUMURA, Minae, BA, MA, MPh; Japanese novelist and critic; b. Tokyo; d. of Naosuke Mizumura and Setsuko Mizumura; m. Katsuhito Iwai. *Education:* Yale Coll. and Yale Univ., USA. *Career:* Lecturer, Princeton Univ., USA 1987–91; Visiting Asst Prof., Univ. of Michigan, USA 1991; Visiting Prof., Stanford Univ., USA 1998; mem. Int. Writing Program at Univ. of Iowa, USA 2003; participating novelist, PEN World Voices: The New York Festival of Int. Literature 2005; featured novelist, Book Festival and Symposium, 'The Text of Asia and a Real Novel', Aix-en-Provence, France 2009. *Publications:* Zoku Meian (trans. as Light and Darkness Continued) 1990, Shishosetsu from Left to Right (trans. as An I-Novel from Left to Right) 1995, Tegami - Shiori wo Souete (trans. as Letters with Bookmarks Attached) 1998, Honkaku Shosetsu (trans. as A Real Novel) 2002, Nihongo ga Horobiru Toki - Eigo no Seiki no Nakade (trans. as The Fall of the Japanese), Nihongo de Yomutoiukoto (trans. as To Read in the Japanese Language) 2009, Nihongo de Kakutoiukoto (trans. as To Write in the Japanese Language) 2009, Shinbun Shosetsu, Haha no Isan (trans. as Inheritance from Mother, A Newspaper Novel) 2011, Honkaku Shosetsu translated into Traditional Chinese, Korean, Spanish and French. *Honours:* Japan Foundation Fellowship 1984–85; Ministry of Educ. Award for New Artists 1991, Noma New Author Award 1995, Yomiuri Literature Award 2003, Kobayashi Hideo Award 2009. *Literary Agent:* c/o Yurika Yokota Yoshida, Japan Foreign-Rights Centre, Sun Mall No. 3, Room 201, 1-19-10 Shinjuku, Shinjuku-ku, Tokyo 160-0022, Japan. *Telephone:* (3) 3226-2711. *Fax:* (3) 3226-2714. *E-mail:* yurika@jfc-tokyo.co.jp. *Address:* c/o Shinchosha Publishing Co. Ltd, 71 Yaraicho, Shinjukuku, Tokyo 162-8711, Japan (office). *Telephone:* (3) 3266-5371 (office). *Fax:* (3) 3266-5460 (office). *E-mail:* y-yano@shinchosha.co.jp (office). *Website:* www.shinchosha.co.jp/writer/2893 (office); mizumuraminae.com.

MLECHIN, Leonid M.; Russian journalist and writer; b. 12 June 1957; m.; one s. *Education:* Moscow State Univ. *Career:* staff, head of division, Deputy Ed.-in-Chief weekly Novoye Vremya 1979–93; Deputy Ed.-in-Chief newspaper Izvestia 1993–96; political reviewer All-Russian State Cttee on Radio and Television 1996–97; writer and narrator Particular Dossier (TV-Tsentr) 1997–. *Publications include:* more than 20 books, including detective stories, novels, historical non-fiction, and biographies of Yevgeny Primakov and the chairmen of the KGB. *Address:* TV-Tsentr, ul. B. Tatarskaya 33/1, Moscow 113184, Russia (office). *Telephone:* (495) 215-18-12 (office); (495) 217-75-50 (office).

MNATSAKANOVA, Jelisaveta Arkad'evna, (Elisabeth Netzkowa); Austrian poet and teacher; b. (Jelisaweta Mnatsakanjan), 31 May 1922, Baku, Azerbaijan; d. of Dr Arcady Mnatsakanov and Dr Anna Mnatsakanova; one s. *Education:* Moscow Conservatory, Moscow State Univ. *Career:* teacher of Russian Literature and Literary Translation, Wiener Universität, Austria. *Art exhibitions:* Albertina, Vienna 2001, Symposium at Harvard Univ. 2004, Lamont Library, Harvard Univ. 2004–05, Mihail Chemiakin Foundation, St Petersburg 2006, jt internet Conf. exhbn, Moscow Univ. and Univ. of Vienna 2008. *Publications include:* Autumn in the Lazaretto of Innocent Sisters 1977, Velikoe tikhoe more (The Great Quiet Sea: 10 poems in memory of Anne N. Segodnia) 1977, Shagi i vzdokhi: Chetyre knigi stikhov 1982, Das Buch Sabeth 1988, Metamorphosen 1989, Vita breve 1994, Arcadia 2006. *Honours:* W.H. Auden Literary Prize 1985, Staatlicher Preis für Übersetzungen österreichischer Lyrik 1987, Andrei Bely Prize 2004. *Address:* c/o Universität Wien, Institut f. Slawistik, Universität Kampus, Spitalgasse 2, 1090 Vienna, Austria (office). *Telephone:* (1) 427-742-802 (office). *E-mail:* elisabeth.netzkowa@chello.at (office); elisabeth.mnatsakanjan@univie.ac.at (office).

MO, Timothy; British author; b. 30 Dec. 1950, Hong Kong; s. of Peter Mo Wan Lung and Barbara Helena Falkingham. *Education:* Mill Hill School and St John's Coll., Univ. of Oxford. *Career:* fmrly worked for Times Educational Supplement and New Statesman; fmr reporter for Boxing News and PAYE clerk. *Publications include:* The Monkey King 1979 (Geoffrey Faber Memorial Prize 1979), Sour Sweet 1982, An Insular Possession 1986, The Redundancy of Courage 1991 (E. M. Forster Award 1992), Brownout on Breadfruit Boulevard 1995, Renegade or Halo 2 1999 (James Tait Black Memorial Prize 1999), Pure 2012. *Honours:* Hawthornden Prize 1983. *Website:* www.timothymo.co.uk.

MO, Yan; Chinese novelist; b. (Guan Moye), 1955, Gaomi, Shandong Prov. *Education:* PLA Acad. of Arts, Beijing Normal Univ. *Career:* joined PLA 1976. *Publications:* Red Sorghum, Thirteen Steps, The Herbivora Family, Jiuguo, The Republic of Wine 1992, Garlic Ballads 1995, Big Breasts and Wide Hips 1996, Shifu You'll Do Anything for a Laugh 2001, Life and Death Are Wearing Me Out 2008. *Address:* c/o Arcade Publishing, 116 John Street, #2810, New York, NY 10038, USA (office). *Website:* www.arcadepub.com (office).

MOAT, John, MA; British author and poet; b. 11 Sept. 1936, India; m. 1962; one s. one d. *Education:* Univ. of Oxford. *Publications:* 6d per Annum 1966, Heorot (novel) 1968, A Standard of Verse 1969, Thunder of Grass 1970, The Tugen and the Toot (novel) 1973, The Ballad of the Leat 1974, Bartonwood (children's) 1978, Fiesta and the Fox Reviews and His Prophecy 1979, The Way to Write (with John Fairfax) 1981, Skeleton Key 1982, Mai's Wedding (novel) 1983, Welcombe Overtunes 1987, The Missing Moon 1988, Firewater and the Miraculous Mandarin 1990, Practice 1994, The Valley (poems and drawings) 1998, 100 Poems 1998, Rain (short stories) 2000, Hermes & Magdalen (poetry and related prints) 2004, The Founding of Arvon (memoir) 2006, The Best of Didymus 2007, Blanche (novel) 2010, The Fabrication of Gold (novel) 2011. *Address:* Crenham Mill, Hartland, North Devon, EX39 6HN, England (home). *Website:* www.johnmoat.co.uk.

MODIANO, Patrick Jean; French novelist; b. 30 July 1945, Boulogne-Billancourt; s. of Albert Modiano and Luisa Colpyn; m. Dominique Zehrfuss 1970; two d. *Education:* schools in Biarritz, Chamonix, Deauville, Thônes, Barbizon, coll. in Paris. *Publications:* La place de l'étoile 1968, La ronde de nuit 1969, Les boulevards de ceinture 1972, Lacombe Lucien (screenplay) 1973, La polka (play) 1974, Villa triste (novel) 1975, Interrogatoire d'Emmanuel Berl 1976, Livret de famille (novel) 1977, Rue des boutiques obscures 1978, Une jeunesse 1981, Memory Lane 1981, De si braves garçons (novel) 1982, Poupée blonde 1983, Quartier perdu 1985, Dimanches d'août 1986, Une aventure de Choura 1986, La fiancée de Choura 1987, Remise de peine (novel) 1988, Catherine Certitude 1988, Vestiaire de l'enfance (novel) 1989, Voyage de noces 1990, Fleurs de ruine (novel) 1991, Un cirque passe (novel) 1992, Chien de printemps 1993, Du plus loin de l'oubli 1995, Dora Bruder 1997, Des inconnues 1999, La petite bijou 2001, Accident nocturne 2003, Un pedigree 2005. *Honours:* Chevalier des Arts et des Lettres; Prix Roger Nimier 1968, Prix Felix Fénéon 1969, Grand Prix de l'Académie française 1972, Prix Goncourt 1978, Prix Pierre de Monaco 1984, Grand Prix du Roman de la Ville de Paris 1994, Grand Prix de Littérature Paul Morand de l'Académie française 2000. *Address:* c/o Editions Gallimard, 5 rue Sébastien Bottin, 75007 Paris, France.

MOFFAT, Gwen; British writer; b. 3 July 1924, Brighton, Sussex; m. 1st Gordon Moffat 1948; one d.; m. 2nd John Rodney Lees 1956. *Education:* Hove Co. Grammar School. *Career:* mem. Crime Writers' Asscn, Soc. of Authors, Pinnacle Club. *Radio:* short stories and talks. *Publications:* Space Below My Feet 1961, Two Star Red 1964, On My Home Ground 1968, Survival Count 1972, Lady With a Cool Eye 1973, Deviant Death 1973, The Corpse Road 1974, Hard Option 1975, Miss Pink at the Edge of the World 1975, Over the Sea to Death 1976, A Short Time to Live 1976, Persons Unknown 1978, Hard Road West 1981, The Buckskin Girl 1982, Die Like a Dog 1982, Last Chance Country 1983, Grizzly Tail 1984, Snare 1987, The Stone Hawk 1989, The Storm Seekers 1989, Rage 1990, The Raptor Zone 1990, Pit Bull 1991, Veronica's Sisters 1992, The Outside Edge 1993, Cue the Battered Wife 1994, The Lost Girls 1998, A Wreath of Dead Moths 1998, Running Dogs 1999, Private Sins 1999, Quicksand 2001, Retribution 2002, Man Trap 2003, Dying for Love 2005; contribs: short stories, features and series for newspapers and magazines; reviews for Shots E magazine. *Address:* c/o Juliet Burton Literary Agency, 2 Clifton Avenue, London, W12 9DR, England. *Telephone:* (20) 8762-0148. *Fax:* (20) 8743-8765. *E-mail:* juliet.burton@btinternet.com. *Website:* www.twbooks.co.uk/authors/gmoffat.html.

MOFFEIT, Tony A., BSc, MLS; American librarian and poet; b. 14 March 1942, Claremont, Okla. *Education:* Oklahoma State University, University of Oklahoma. *Career:* Asst Dir, Library, University of Southern Colorado 1980–, Poet-in-Residence 1986–95; Dir, Pueblo Poetry Project 1980–; mem. American Library Asscn. *Publications include:* La Nortenita, 1983; Outlaw Blues, 1983; Shooting Chant, 1984; Coyote Blues, 1985; Hank Williams Blues, 1985; The Spider Who Walked Underground, 1985; Black Cat Bone, 1986; Dancing With the Ghosts of the Dead, 1986; Pueblo Blues, 1986; Boogie Alley, 1989; Luminous Animal, 1989; Poetry is Dangerous, the Poet is an Outlaw, 1995; contributions: journals and magazines. *Honours:* Jack Kerouac Award 1986, National Endowment for the Arts Fellowship 1992.

MOFFETT, Judith, BA, MA, PhD; American poet, writer and teacher; b. 30 Aug. 1942, Louisville, Ky; m. Edward B. Irving 1983. *Education:* Hanover College, Colorado State University, University of Wisconsin at Madison, University of Pennsylvania. *Career:* Fulbright Lecturer, University of Lund, Sweden 1967–68; Asst Prof., Behrend College, Pennsylvania State University 1971–75; Visiting Lecturer, University of Iowa 1977–78; Visiting Lecturer,

University of Pennsylvania 1978–79, Asst Prof. 1979–86, Adjunct Asst Prof. 1986–88, Adjunct Assoc. Prof. 1988–93, Adjunct Prof. of English 1993–94. *Publications include:* poetry: Keeping Time 1976, Whinny Moor Crossing 1984; fiction: Pennterra 1987, The Ragged World 1991, Time, Like an Ever-Rolling Stream 1992, Two That Came True 1992; other: James Merrill: An Introduction to the Poetry 1984, Homestead Year: Back to the Land in Suburbia 1995. *Honours:* Fulbright Grant 1967, 1973, American Philosophical Society Grant 1973, Eunice Tiejens Memorial Prize 1973, Borestone Mountain Poetry Prize 1976, Levinson Prize 1976, Ingram Merrill Foundation Grant 1977, 1980, 1989, Columbia University Trans. Prize 1978, Bread Loaf Writers Conference Tennessee Williams Fellowship 1978, Swedish Acad. Trans. Prize 1982, National Endowment for the Humanities Trans. Fellowship 1983, National Endowment for the Arts Fellowship, 1984, Swedish Acad. Trans. Grant 1993.

MOGGACH, Deborah, BA, DipEd, FRSL; British writer; b. 28 June 1948, London; d. of Richard Hough and Helen Charlotte Hough; m. Anthony Moggach 1971 (divorced); one s. one d. *Education:* Camden School for Girls, Univ. of Bristol, Univ. of London. *Career:* Chair. Soc. of Authors 1999–2001; mem. PEN. *Television:* (dramas) To Have and To Hold 1986, Stolen 1990, Goggle-Eyes (adaptation) 1993 (Writers' Guild Award for Best Adapted TV Serial), Seesaw 1998, Close Relations 1998, Love in a Cold Climate (adaptation) 2001, Final Demand 2003, The Diary of Anne Frank 2009. *Film:* Pride and Prejudice (adaptation) 2005. *Play:* Double Take. *Publications:* novels: You Must Be Sisters 1978, Close to Home 1979, A Quiet Drink 1980, Hot Water Man 1982, Porky 1983, To Have and To Hold 1986, Driving in the Dark 1988, Stolen 1990, The Stand-in 1991, The Ex-Wives 1993, Seesaw 1996, Close Relations 1997, Tulip Fever 1999, Final Demand 2001, These Foolish Things 2004, In the Dark 2007; short stories: Smile 1987, Changing Babies 1995. *Literary Agent:* Curtis Brown Group Limited, Haymarket House, 28–29 Haymarket, London, SW1Y 4SP, England. *Telephone:* (20) 7393-4400. *Fax:* (20) 7393-4401. *E-mail:* cb@curtisbrown.co.uk. *Website:* www.curtisbrown.co.uk.

MOHAIMEED, Yousef al-; Saudi Arabian writer; b. 1964, Riyadh. *Education:* King Saud Univ., Norwich Coll., UK. *Career:* Cultural Ed. literary journal, Al-Yamama. *Publications include:* novels: The Dead's Gossip 2003, Traps of Scent 2003, The Bottle 2004, The Dolphin's Excursion 2006, Pigeons Don't Fly in Buraydah (Abu al-Qasim Ashabbi 2011) 2009; contrib. to journals, including Banipal. *Literary Agent:* The Colchie Agency, 324 85th Street, Brooklyn, NY 10209, USA. *Telephone:* (718) 921-7468. *E-mail:* colchielit@earthlink.net. *Address:* PO Box 90521, Riyadh 11623, Saudi Arabia (home); c/o Riad El-Rayyes Books, Sanayeh, Union Bldg, Beirut, Lebanon (office). *E-mail:* info@elrayyesbooks.com (office). *Website:* www.al-mohaimeed.net.

MOHAN, Dominic, BA; *Editor, The Sun;* b. 1969; m.; three c. *Education:* Southampton Univ. *Career:* fmr reporter, News of the World; columnist, Bizarre showbiz column, The Sun 1996–98, Ed. Bizarre column 1998–2002, Asst Ed. 2002–04, Assoc. Ed. 2004–07, Deputy Ed. 2007–09, Ed. 2009–. *Address:* The Sun, 1 Virginia Street, London, E98 1SN, England (office). *Telephone:* (20) 7782-4000 (office). *Fax:* (20) 7782-4108 (office). *Website:* www.thesun.co.uk (office).

MOI, Toril, DArt; Norwegian academic and writer; *James B. Duke Professor of Literature and Romance Studies, Duke University*; b. 28 Nov. 1953, Farsund; d. of Georg Seval Moi and Nora Moi; m. David Leon Paletz 1999. *Education:* Bergen Univ. *Career:* fmr teacher at Univ. of Bergen and Univ. of Oxford, UK; James B. Duke Prof. of Literature and Romance Studies, Prof. of English and Theater Studies, Duke Univ., Durham, NC; mem. Norwegian Acad. of Sciences. *Publications include:* Sexual/Textual Politics: Feminist Literary Theory 1985, Simone de Beauvoir: The Making of an Intellectual Woman 1994, What is a Woman? and Other Essays 1999, Henrik Ibsen and the Birth of Modernisim 2006; editor: The Kristeva Reader 1986, French Feminist Thought 1987; articles on feminist theory, psychoanalytic theory, French phenomenology and ordinary language philosophy. *Honours:* Guggenheim Fellowship 2001, The Modern Language Asscn's Aldo and Jeanne Scaglione Prize for Best Book in Comparative Literature 2007. *Address:* Literature Program, Duke University, Box 90670, Durham, NC 27708-0670, USA (office). *Telephone:* (919) 681-4971 (office). *Fax:* (919) 684-3598 (office). *Website:* fds.duke.edu/db/aas/Literature/faculty/toril (office).

MOJTABAI, Ann Grace, MA, MS; American author and educator; b. 8 June 1937, Brooklyn, NY; d. of Robert Alpher and Naomi Friedman; m. Fathollah Motabai 1960 (divorced 1966); one s. one d. *Education:* Antioch Coll., Columbia Univ. *Career:* Lecturer in Philosophy, Hunter Coll., CUNY 1966–68; Briggs-Copeland Lecturer on English, Harvard Univ. 1978–83; Writer-in-Residence, Univ. of Tulsa 1983–; mem. Mark Twain Soc., PEN . Texas Inst. of Letters. *Publications:* Mundome 1974, The 400 Eels of Sigmund Freud 1976, A Stopping Place 1979, Autumn 1982, Blessed Assurance 1986, Ordinary Time 1989, Called Out 1994, Soon 1998, All that Road Going 2008; contributions: New York Times Book Review, New Republic, Philosophy Today, Philosophical Journal. *Honours:* Radcliffe Institute Fellow 1976–78, Guggenheim Fellowship 1981–82, Richard and Hinda Rosenthal Award, American Acad. and Inst. of Arts and Letters 1983, Lillian Smith Award, Southern Regional Council 1986, Award in Literature, American Acad. of Arts and Letters 1993. *Address:* 2329 Woodside, Amarillo, TX 79124-1036, USA (home). *Telephone:* (806) 457-8647. *E-mail:* agmojtabai@aol.com (home).

MOKEDDEM, Malika; Algerian novelist and physician; b. 1949, Kenadsa. *Education:* studied medicine in France. *Career:* currently based in France, worked as general practitioner focusing on health needs of immigrant North African community, Montpellier. *Publications:* novels: Le Siècle des sauterelles (Century of Locusts) (ADELF Prix Afrique–Méditerranée) 1992, L'Interdite (The Forbidden Women) (Prix Méditerranée, Perpignan) 1994, Des rêves et des assassins (Of Dreams and Assassins) 1995, Les Hommes qui marchent 1997, La Nuit de la lézarde 1998, N'zid 2001, La Transe des insoumis 2003, Mes hommes 2005. *Address:* c/o Éditions Grasset & Fasquelle, 61 rue des Saints-Pères, Paris 75006, France. *E-mail:* dfanelli@grasset.fr.

MOKYR, Joel, BA, PhD; Dutch/American academic and writer; *Robert H. Strotz Professor of Arts and Sciences, Northwestern University;* b. 26 July 1946, Leyden, The Netherlands; m. Margalit B. Moky 1969; two d. *Education:* Hebrew Univ., Yale Univ. *Career:* Robert H. Strotz Prof. of Arts and Sciences, NW Univ.; Sackler Prof., Eitan Berglas School of Econs., Tel Aviv Univ.; Fellow, American Acad. of Arts and Sciences, 1996; Pres. Economic History Asscn 2003–04; Foreign Mem. Royal Dutch Acad. of Sciences 2001–, Accademia Nazionale dei Lincei (Social Science Section) 2004–. *Publications:* Industrialization in the Low Countries, 1976; Why Ireland Starved, 1983; The Lever of Riches, 1990; The British Industrial Revolution, 1993; The Gifts of Athena, 2002; Oxford Encyclopedia of Economic History (Ed.-in-Chief), 2003. *Address:* Department of Economics, Northwestern University, 2003 Sheridan Road, Evanston, IL 60208, USA (office). *Telephone:* (847) 491-5693 (office). *Fax:* (847) 491-7001 (office). *Website:* www.faculty.econ.northwestern.edu/facullty/mokyr (office).

MOLCHANOV, Vladimir Kyrillovich; Russian journalist; b. 7 Oct. 1950, Moscow; s. of Kyrill Molchanov; m. Consuella Segura; one d. *Education:* Moscow State Univ. *Career:* with Press Agency Novosti 1973–86; observer USSR State Cttee for TV and Radio 1987–91; artistic Dir studio of independent co. REN-TV 1991–, Observer Reuter-TV 1994–; regular appearances in his own TV programmes Before and After Midnight 1987–93, Before and After 1994–, Panorama 2000–, Longer than Age 2000–; mem. Acad. of Russian TV, Acad. of Natural Sciences. *Publications:* TV films: Remembrance, I, You, He and She, People and Years, Zone, I Still Have More Addresses, Tied with One Chain, August of 1991 (screenplays), Retribution Must Come (M. Gorky Prize 1982). *Honours:* Prize of Journalists' Union as the Best TV Journalist 1990 and other awards. *Address:* REN-TV, Zubovsky blvd 17, Moscow, Russia. *Telephone:* (495) 255-90-77 (office).

MOLE, John Douglas, MA; British poet and critic; b. 12 Oct. 1941, Taunton, Somerset, England; m. Mary Norman 1968; two s. *Education:* Magdalene Coll., Cambridge. *Career:* teacher, Haberdashers' School, Elstree 1964–73; Exchange Teacher, Riverdale School, New York 1969–70; Head, Dept of English, Verulam School 1973–81, St Albans School 1981–98; Poet-in-Residence, Magdalene Coll. Cambridge 1996; Visiting Poet, Univ. of Hertfordshire 1998–2003; Poet to the City of London 1999–; Pres. Ver Poets, Toddington Poetry Soc.; mem. Soc. of Authors. *Publications:* poetry: Feeding the Lake 1981, In and Out of the Apple 1984, Homing 1987, Boo to a Goose 1987, The Mad Parrot's Countdown 1989, Catching the Spider 1990, The Conjuror's Rabbit 1992, Depending on the Light 1993, Selected Poems 1995, Hot Air 1996, Copy Cat (for children) 1997, The Dummy's Dilemma 1999, For the Moment 2000, The Wonder Dish 2002, Counting the Chimes: New & Selected Poems 2004, This is the Blackbird (for children) 2007, The Other Day 2007, All the Frogs (for children) 2011, The Point of Loss 2011; other: Passing Judgements: Poetry in the Eighties 1989, Poetry (ed.) 1945–80, Figures of Speech (ed.) 2000, librettist for 'Alban' (community opera first performed in St Albans Cathedral) 2010; contribs to newspapers, reviews, and magazines. *Honours:* Hon. DLitt (Hertfordshire) 2004; Eric Gregory Award 1970, Signal Award for Outstanding Contrib. to Children's Poetry 1988, Cholmondeley Award 1994. *Address:* 11 Hill Street, St Albans, Herts., AL3 4QS, England (home). *Telephone:* (1727) 857153 (home). *E-mail:* jdmole@hotmail.com (home).

MOLINA, Silvia; Mexican novelist; b. 11 Oct. 1946, México. *Education:* Nat. Autonomous Univ. of Mexico. *Career:* has lived in France, England, Belgium and USA; Fellow, Mexican Center of Writers 1979–80, International Writing Program, Univ. of Iowa, USA 1991. *Play:* Circuito cerrado 1995. *Publications:* novels: La mañana debe seguir gris (Gray Skies Tomorrow) (Xavier Villarrutia Prize 1977) 1977, Ascención Tunn 1981, La familia vino del norte 1987, Imagen de Héctor 1990, El amor que me juraste (The Love You Promised Me; Sor Juana Inés de la Cruz Prize) 1999, Muchacha en azul 2001; short stories: Lides de estaño 1984, Dicen que me caso yo 1989, Un Hombre Cerca 1992, Recomenzar 1999; children's fiction: El papel 1985, El algodón 1987, Los cuatro hermanos 1988, La leyenda del sol y la luna 1991, La creación del hombre 1991, Los tres corazones 1992, El misterioso caso de la perra extraviada 1992, Mi familia y la Bella Durmiente cien años después 1993, Las dos iguanas 1993, El abuelo ya no duerme en el armario 1996, Marina y el pirata 1998, El topo y la codorniz 1999, Quiero ser la que será 2000, Las aventuras de don Sebas y Campeona 2000, Mi abuelita tiene ruedas 2000, Martín Martán fuera del gallinero 2003, Le comieron la lengua los ratones 2005, Hasta el ratón y el gato pueden tener un buen trato 2006; non-fiction: Leyendo en la tortuga 1981, Encuentros y reflexiones 1998. *E-mail:* contacto@silviamolina.com (office). *Website:* www.silviamolina.com.

MOLINA SÁNCHEZ, César Antonio, LicenDer; Spanish writer and politician; *Minister of Culture*; b. 1952, La Coruña. *Career:* fmr Prof. of Literary

Theory and Criticism, Complutense Univ., Prof. of Humanities and Journalism, Univ. Carlos III; worked for Cambio 16 (magazine) and Diario 16 (newspaper) 1985–96, becoming Deputy Dir; Man. Dir Círculo de Bellas Artes 1996–2004; Dir Cervantes Inst. 2004–07; Minister of Culture 2007–; Deputy (Spanish Socialist Workers' Party–PSOE) for A Coruña 2008–. *Publications:* Épica 1974, Proyecto preliminar para una arqueología de campo (poetry) 1978, Últimas horas en Lisca Blanca 1979, La estancia saqueada (poetry) 1983, La revista Alfar y la prensa literaria de su época (1920-1930) 1984, Antología de la poesía Gallega contemporánea 1984, Gobierno de un jardín 1986, Derivas 1987, El fin de Finisterre 1988, Prensa literaria en Galicia (1809-1920) 1989, Prensa literaria en Galicia (1920-1960) 1989, Medio siglo de Prensa literaria española (1900-1950) 1990, Sobre el iberismo y otros escritos de literatura portuguesa 1990, Las ruinas del mundo 1991, El fin de Finisterre 1992, Para no ir a parte alguna 1994, Sobre la inutilidad de la poesía 1995, Nostalgia de la nada perdida; ensayo sobre narrativa contemporánea 1996, Vivir sin ser visto 2000, A fin de Fisterra (poetry) 2001, A Coruña, agua y luz 2001, Olas en la noche 2001, Regresar a donde no estuvimos 2003, Viaje a la Costa da morte 2003, En el mar de Ánforas 2005, En honor de Hermes 2005, Fuga del amor 2005, El rumor del tiempo 2006, Custode delle antiche forme (poetry) 2007, Eume 2007, Esperando a los años que no vuelven 2007. *Address:* Ministry of Culture, Plaza del Rey 1, 28071 Madrid, Spain (office). *Telephone:* (91) 7017000 (office). *Fax:* (91) 7017352 (office). *E-mail:* contacte@mcu.es (office). *Website:* www.mcu.es (office).

MOLLENKOTT, Virginia Ramey, MA, PhD; American academic, writer and editor; *Professor Emerita of English, William Paterson University*; b. 28 Jan. 1932, Philadelphia, PA; d. of Robert Franklin Ramey and May Lotz; m. Friedrich H. Mollenkott 1954 (divorced 1973); one s. *Education:* Bob Jones Univ., Temple Univ., New York Univ. *Career:* Chair. Dept of English, Shelton Coll. 1955–63, Nyack Coll. 1963–67; Assoc. Prof., William Paterson Univ. 1967–74, Prof. of English 1974–97, Chair. Dept of English 1972–76, Prof. Emer. 1997–; Life mem. Milton Soc. of America, Modern Language Assen, Evangelical and Ecumenical Women's Caucus. *Publications:* Adamant and Stone Chips: A Christian Humanist Approach to Knowledge 1967, In Search of Balance 1969, Adam Among the Television Trees: An Anthology of Verse by Contemporary Christian Poets (ed.) 1971, Women, Men and the Bible 1976, Speech, Silence, Action 1980, Is the Homosexual My Neighbor? (with L. D. Scanzoni) 1978, The Divine Feminine: Biblical Imagery of God as Female 1983, Views from the Intersection (with Catherine Barry) 1984, Women of Faith in Dialogue (ed.) 1987, Sensuous Spirituality: Out from Fundamentalism 1992, Omnigender: A Trans-Religious Approach 2001, Transgender Journeys (with V. Sheridan) 2003; contrib. to numerous journals and reviews; The Witness (contributing ed.) 1994–. *Honours:* Hon. Dr of Ministry (Samaritan Coll.) 1989; Penfield Fellow 1973, Andiron Award 1964, Founders Day Award 1964, New York Univ., New Jersey Lesbian and Gay Coalition Achievement Award 1992, SAGE (Sr Action in a Gay Environment) Lifetime Achievement Award 1999, Lambda Literary Award 2002. *Address:* 11 Yearling Trail, Hewitt, NJ 07421, USA. *Telephone:* (973) 853-4281 (office). *E-mail:* jstvrm@warwick.net (home). *Website:* www.virginiarameymollenkott .com.

MOLLOY, Michael John; British journalist, editor and writer; b. 22 Dec. 1940, England; m. Sandra June Foley 1964, three d. *Education:* Ealing School of Art. *Career:* staff, 1962–70, Asst Ed., 1970–75, Deputy Ed., 1975, Ed., 1975–85, Daily Mirror; Dir, 1976–90, Ed.-in-Chief, 1985–90, Mirror Group Newspapers; Ed., Sunday Mirror, 1986–88. *Publications:* The Black Dwarf, 1985; The Kid from Riga, 1987; The Harlot of Jericho, 1989; The Century, 1990; The Gallery, 1991; Sweet Sixteen, 1992; Cat's Paw, 1993; Home Before Dark, 1994; Dogsbody, 1995.

MOLTMANN, Jürgen, DTheol; German theologian and academic; *Professor and Rector, Wuppertal Church University*; b. 8 April 1926, Hamburg; m. Dr. Elisabeth Moltmann-Wendel; four d. *Career:* POW during Second World War; with Dept of Theology, Univ. of Göttingen 1948–52, Prof. of Theology 1957–; fmr Minister, Bremen; Prof. and Rector Wuppertal Church Univ. 1958–; co-ed. Deutsch-Polnische Hefte 1959–68; Visiting Prof. in USA 1967–68; Dir CONCILIUM 1979–94. *Publications:* Christliche Petzel und das Calvinismus in Bremen 1958, Prädestination und Perseveranz 1961, Anfänge Dialektische Theologie 1963, Theologie der Hoffnung (Theology of Hope) (Isle of Elba Literary Prize) 1964, Mensch 1971, Der gekreuzigte Gott (The Crucified God) 1972, Der Sprache der Befreiung 1972, Das Experiment Hoffnung 1974, Kirche in der Kraft des Geistes 1975, Zukunft der Schöpfung 1977, Trinität und Reich Gottes 1980, Gott in der Schöpfung (God in Creation) 1985, Das Weg Jesu Christi (The Way of Jesus Christ) 1989, Der Geist des Lebens (The Spirit of Life) 1991, Das Kommen Gottes (The Coming of God) (Grawemeyer Religion Award) 1995, Experiences in Theology 1999, Science and Wisdom 2002, In the End – the Beginning: The Life of Hope 2004. *Honours:* Italian Prize of Literature, Isle of Elba 1971, Amos Comenius Medal, Bethlehem, Pa 1992, Ernst Bloch Prize of the City of Ludwigshafen 1995, Grawemeyer Award on Religion, Louisville, Ky 2000 Dr hc (Duke Univ.), (Bethlehem Theological Seminary), (Kalamazoo Coll.), (Raday Kolleg, Budapest), (St Andrews Univ.), (Emory Univ.), (Univ. of Leuven), (Univ. of Iasi), (Nottingham Univ.), (Managua, Nicaragua). *Address:* Liebermeister Strasse 12, 72076 Tübingen, Germany.

MOMADAY, N(avarre) Scott, BA, MA, PhD; American writer, painter and academic; b. 27 Feb. 1934, Lawton, Oklahoma; m. Regina Heitzer 1978; four d. *Education:* Univ. of New Mexico, Univ. of Massachusetts, Stanford Univ. *Career:* Visiting Prof., Columbia Univ., Princeton Univ. 1979; Writer-in-Residence, Southeastern Univ. 1985, Aspen Writers Conference 1986; mem. PEN; Okla. Poet Laureate 2007–. *Publications:* House Made of Dawn (Pulitzer Prize for Fiction 1969), 1968, The Way to Rainy Mountain 1969, The Names 1976, The Gourd Dancer 1976, The Ancient Child 1989, In the Presence of the Sun 1992, Enchanted Circle 1993, The Native Americans (with Linda Hozan) 1993, The Man Made of Words 1997. *Honours:* numerous hon. degrees; Premio Mondello, Italy, 1979, Nat. Medal of Arts 2007. *Literary Agent:* Julian Bach Literary Agency, 22 East 71st Street, New York, NY 10021, USA.

MOMEN, Wendi, PhD, JP; British publisher and religious organization official; *Representative, Office of External Affairs, UK Bahá'í Community*; b. (Wendy Wirtshafter), 21 Oct. 1950, Hollywood, Calif., USA; d. of Robert Wirtshafter and Carol Allen (née Morris); m. Moojan Momen 1971; one s. one d. *Education:* London School of Econs. *Career:* Ed. George Ronald publishing co., Oxford 1979–; editorial services OneWorld Publications, Oxford 1989–95, Intellect Books, Oxford 1991–2000; Chair. Man. Exec. Bahá'í Publishing Trust (UK) 1989–94, Ed. 1991–2005, Asst Ed. The Bahá'í Encyclopedia, Bahá'í Publishing Trust, USA 1991–94; mem. Nat. Spiritual Ass. of the Bahá'ís of the UK 1982–2004, Treas. 1984–90, 2001–04, Chair. 1990–2000, Asst Sec. 2000–01, now Rep. Office of External Affairs, UK Bahá'í Community and Office for the Advancement of Women 2005–; Pres. European Bahá'ís Business Forum 1991–2002, Chair. 2003–09, Sec.-Gen. 2009–; JP Biggleswade (now Bedford) Petty Sessional Div. 1982–, Court Chair. 1994–; Dir (non-exec.) Beds. Family Health Services Authority 1990–94, 1999–2001, Beds. Heartlands Primary Care Trust 2003–05, NHS Bedfordshire 2007–; mem. Int. Steering Cttee Global Women sector of Global Forum 1994, Bedford Council of Faiths 2002– (Chair. 2007–); Trustee, One World Trust 1997–2007 (Chair. 2002–07), BASED-UK 1997–2010 (Chair. 1997–2010), Multi-Faith Centre (Derby Univ.) 2000–, Bedfordshire and Luton Community Foundation (Vice-Chair. 2009–); Sec. UNIFEM UK Nat. Cttee 2007–11; Gov., LSE 2010–. *Television:* programmes for Broomsticks Productions, Tonga 1994–96, 2009. *Publications:* Call Me Ridvan 1982, Family Worship 1989, A Basic Bahá'í Dictionary 1989, Jewels (series) 1994, Meditation 1996, I'm a Bahá'í 1996, Basic Bahá'í Chronology (with Glenn Cameron) 1996, To Be a Mother 1999, Paradise Created (with Brenton Edwards) 2001, To Be a Father 2002, The Devotional Meeting 2003, Understanding the Bahá'í Faith (with Moojan Momen) 2005; numerous conf. papers. *Address:* Wixamtree, Sand Lane, Northill, nr Biggleswade, Beds., SG18 9AD, England (home). *Telephone:* (1767) 627626 (home). *Fax:* (1767) 627626 (home). *E-mail:* wendi@northill .demon.co.uk (home). *Website:* www.northill.demon.co.uk (home); www .wendimomen.com (home).

MOMI, Balbir Singh, MA, PhD; Indian teacher (retd), writer, dramatist, editor and translator; b. 20 Nov. 1935, Amagarh; m. Baldev Kaur 1954, four d. *Education:* Panjab Univ., Chandigarh. *Career:* Lecturer and Research Asst, GND Univ., Amritsar 1974–76; Literary Ed., Perdesi Canafi Ajit Punjab, Toronto 1982–97; Ed., Nagara; mem. Int. Cultural Forum, India and Canada, Sr Int. Vice-Pres. 1993. *Publications include:* novels: Jija ji, Pila Gulab, Ik Phul Mera Vee, Alvida Hindustan; short stories: Masale Wala Ghora, Je Main Mar Jawan, Sheeshe da Samundar, Phul Khire Han, Man Janat Sabh Baat, Sar da Bujha, Kauri-giri; plays: Naukriyan hi Naukriyan; Laudha Vela; contrib. to many publications. *Honours:* various literary awards.

MOMPLE, Lilia, BA; Mozambican writer; b. 1935; m. *Education:* studied social work in Portugal. *Career:* Sec.-Gen., Mozambique Writers' Assen, 1995–2001, Pres., 1997–99; mem., UNESCO Exec. Council. *Publications:* No One Killed Suhara 1988, The Eyes of the Green Cobra 1997, Muhupitit Alima (screenplay) 1988, Neighbours: The Story of a Murder 1995, Celina's Banquet (novel) 2001.

MONACO, James Frederick, BA, MA; American writer and publisher; b. 15 Nov. 1942, New York, NY; s. of George C. Monaco and Susanne Monaco (née Hirschland); m. Susan R. Schenker 1976; two s. one d. *Education:* Muhlenberg Coll., Columbia Univ. *Career:* Fellow, Inst. of Directors, London; Publisher, Harbor Electronic Publishing; mem. Bd Dirs Copyright Clearance Center Inc. 2002–; mem. Authors' Guild, Writers' Guild. *Publications:* How to Read a Film 1977 (multimedia edn) 2000, American Film Now 1979, The New Wave 1976, Media Culture 1977, Celebrity 1977, Connoisseur's Guide to the Movies 1985, The International Encyclopedia of Film 1991, The Movie Guide 1992, Cinemania: Interactive Movie Guide 1992, Dictionary of New Media 1999; contrib. to numerous pubs. *Address:* UNET 2 Corporation, 80 East 11th Street, New York, NY 10003, USA (office). *E-mail:* jmonaco@unet.net (office). *Website:* jamesmonaco.com.

MONÉNEMBO, Tierno, DrSc; Guinean writer; b. (Thierno Saïdou Diallo), 21 July 1947, Porédaka. *Education:* Univ. of Lyon. *Career:* has lived in Senegal, Algeria, Morocco; living in France 1973–; taught biochemistry in France, Algeria and Morocco; now full-time writer, living in France 1973–; writer-in-residence Chateau La Napoule 1992. *Publications:* novels: Les Crapauds-brousse (The Bush Toads) 1979, Un Rêve utile 1991, Un Attiéké pour Elgass 1993, Pelourinho 1995, Cinéma 1997, Les Écailles du ciel 1997, L'Aîné des orphelins (The Oldest Orphan) 2000, Peuls 2004, Le Roi de Kahel (Prix Renaudot) 2008; contrib. to Notre Librairie, Forum for Modern Language Studies. *Address:* c/o Éditions du Seuil, 27 rue Jacob, 75261 Paris, France (office). *Website:* www.editionsduseuil.fr (office).

MONETTE, Hélène; Canadian poet, writer and artist; b. 11 June 1960, Saint-Philippe de Laprairie, Quebec. *Education:* Université du Québec à

Montréal, Université Concordia. *Career:* fmrly worked as ed., event co-ordinator, librarian; co-founder, Ciel Variable magazine; mem. Band de poètes (performance group of five poets and two musicians) 2002–06. *Publications:* fiction: Le Goudron et les Plumes (Grand Prix du Livre de Montréal) 1993, Unless 1995; poetry: Le Blanc des Yeux 1999, Il y a quelqu'un? 2004, Thérèse pour joie et orchestre (Gov.-Gen.'s Literary Award for Poetry 2009) 2008; stories: Plaisirs et Paysages Kitsch 1997, Crimes et Chatouillements 2000, Un Jardin dans la Nuit 2001. *Address:* c/o Les Éditions du Boréal, 4447 rue Saint-Denis, Montréal, QC H2J 2L2, Canada (office). *Website:* www.editionsboreal.qc.ca (office).

MONETTE, Madeleine, MA; Canadian writer and translator; b. 3 Oct. 1951, Montréal, QC; d. of Ernest Monette and Yvette Monette; m. William R. Leggio 1979. *Education:* Univ. of Québec. *Career:* mem. Acad. des lettres du Québec, Québec Writers Union, PEN. *Radio:* book reviewer for American literature, Société Radio-Canada 2008–09. *Publications:* Le Double suspect 1980, English trans. as Doubly Suspect 2000, Petites Violences 1982, Fuites et Poursuites 1982, Plages 1986, L'Aventure, la mésaventure 1987, Amandes et melon 1991, Nouvelles de Montréal 1992, La Femme furieuse 1997, Nouvelles d'Amérique 1998, Ligne de métro 2002, Les Rouleurs 2007; contribs to periodicals. *Honours:* Robert-Cliche Award 1980, grants from Canadian Council of Arts, Conseil des Arts et des Lettres du Québec, Fonds Gabrielle-Roy, Writer's Residency, Chateau de Lavigny, Fondation Ledig-Rowohlt. *Address:* 2 Charlton Street, 11K, New York, NY 10014, USA (home). *E-mail:* mmonet@aol.com (home); madeleinemonette@gmail.com (home). *Website:* www.madeleinemonette.com.

MONEY, David Charles, BSc, FRGS; British teacher (retd) and writer; b. 5 Oct. 1918, Oxford, England; m. Madge Matthews 1945, one s. *Education:* St John's College, Oxford. *Career:* mem. Farmer's Club. *Publications:* Human Geography, 1954; Climate, Soils and Vegetation, 1965; The Earth's Surface, 1970; Patterns of Settlement, 1972; Environmental Systems (series), 1978–82; Foundations of Geography, 1987; Climate and Environmental Systems, 1988; China – The Land and the People, 1984; China Today, 1987; Australia Today, 1988; Environmental Issues – The Global Consequences, 1994; China in Change, 1996; The Vocation of Bachan Singh, 1997; Weather and Climate, 2000. *Honours:* hon. mem. Geographical Asscn.

MONEY, Keith; New Zealand author, artist and photographer; b. 1934, Auckland. *Publications:* Salute the Horse 1960, The Horseman in Our Midst 1963, The Equestrian World 1963, The Art of the Royal Ballet 1964, The Art of Margot Fonteyn 1965, The Royal Ballet Today 1968, Fonteyn: The Making of a Legend 1973, John Curry 1978, Anna Pavlova: Her Life and Art 1982, The Bedside Book of Old Fashioned Roses 1985, Some Other Sea: The Life of Rupert Brooke 1988–89, Margot, assoluta 1993, Fonteyn and Nureyev: The Great Years 1994; Other: Screenplays. Contributions: anthologies, journals, and magazines. *E-mail:* fairprospectimprint@ihug.co.nz. *Website:* www.fairprospect.co.nz.

MONGRAIN, Serg; Canadian writer, poet and photographer; b. 15 Jan. 1948, Trois Rivières, PQ. *Education:* Mathematical Université du Québec. *Career:* mem. Union des écrivaines et des écrivains québécois. *Publications:* L'Oeil du l'idée, 1988; Le calcul des heures, 1993; L'objet des sens, 1996; Brouillard, 1999; Le Poème déshabillé, 2000; Gladys, 2001; as photographer: Lis: écris, 1981; L'image titre, 1981; Agrestes, 1988; Québec Kerouak Blues, 1998; other: many exhibition catalogues in art; contributions: periodicals.

MONK, Lorraine Althea Constance, OC, MA, LLD, DLitt, FDCA, FOCA, ESFIAP; Canadian writer, curator and producer of photographic books and exhibitions; *Founder, Photographers for Peace;* b. Montréal, PQ; d. of Edwin and Eileen Marion (née Nurse) Spurrell; m. John McCaughan Monk; two s. two d. *Education:* McGill Univ. *Career:* Founder, Photographers for Peace Foundation; Exec. Dir Canadian Museum of Photography; Exec. Dir Still Photography Div., Nat. Film Bd of Canada. *Publications include:* A Year of the Land 1967, Ces visages qui sont en pays 1967, Stones of History 1967, Call Them Canadians 1968, A Time To Dream – Reveries en couleurs 1971, The Female Eye 1975, Between Friends (Gold Medal Int. Book Fair, Leipzig, Germany) 1977, Robert Bourdeau Monograph 1979, Image (series), Signature (series), Canada With Love 1982, Celebrate our City 1983, Ontario: A Loving Look 1984, Photographs That Changed the World 1989, Canada: Romancing the Land 1996, These Things We Hold Dear – An Album of Photographic Memories (producer) 2000, Moritz Liebling 2002, Hannah: A Story about the Journey of a Lifetime 2003. *Honours:* first Hon. mem. Canadian Photographic Historical Soc. 1984; Order of Ontario 2008; Chester Macnaughton Prize, McGill Univ. 1945, Centennial Medal 1967, Fed. Int. de l'art photographique Excellence of Service Award, Nat. Asscn of Photographic Art Gold Medal, Leipzig Book Fair Silver Medal 1975, First Prize, Int. Craftsman Guild 1983. *Address:* 176 Balmoral Avenue, Toronto, Ontario, M4V 1J6, Canada (home). *Telephone:* (416) 929-9357 (also fax) (home). *E-mail:* lorrainemonk@hotmail.com (home). *Website:* lorrainemonk.com (home); www.photographersforpeace.com (home).

MONNIER, Claude Michel, PhD; Swiss journalist (retd); b. 23 March 1938, Rwankéri, Rwanda; s. of Henri Monnier and Olga Pavlov; m. Estela Troncoso Balandrán 1958 (died 2005); two s. *Education:* Univs of Geneva and Mexico, Grad. Inst. of Int. Studies, Geneva. *Career:* educational tour in Asia and America 1956–58; Research Fellow, Swiss Nat. Fund for Scientific Research, Tokyo 1963–66; Tokyo Corresp. Journal de Genève 1963–66, Foreign Ed. 1966–70, Ed.-in-Chief 1970–80; Ed. Le Temps Stratégique, Genève 1982–2001; mem. Bd French-speaking Swiss TV and radio 1989–2000; mem. Academic Council, Univ. of Lausanne 1998–2005, Bd Médias et Société Foundation, Geneva; Adviser to Gen. Man., Edipresse Suisse SA 2001–09. *Publications:* Les Américains et sa Majesté l'Empereur: Etude du conflit culturel d'où naquit la constitution japonaise de 1946 1967, Alerte, citoyens! 1989, L'année du Big-Bang 1990, La terre en a marre 1991, La déprime, ça suffit! 1992, Dieu, que la crise est jolie! 1993, Les Rouges nous manquent 1994, La bonté qui tue 1995, Envie de bouffer du lion 1996, Programme d'un agitateur 1997, Le temps des règlements de compte 1998, Le Culte suspect de l'action 1999, La trahison de l'an 2000 2000, Morts de trouille 2001, Il faut nous faire soigner! 2002, Où est ta victoire, George W.? 2003, La Suisse devient folle 2004, Et maintenant, on fait quoi? 2005, Les Helvètes auraient-ils la potion magique? 2006, Vous êtes viré? Bravo! 2007, Panique planétaire 2008, Ce coup-ci, les riches ont aussi la trouille 2009, Nous sommes gouvernés par des Martiens 2010. *Address:* Chemin de Saussac 2, 1256 Troinex, Geneva, Switzerland (home). *Telephone:* (22) 322-34-92 (office); (22) 343-95-55 (home). *E-mail:* claude.monnier@edipresse.ch (office).

MONTAG, Tom, BA; American poet, writer, editor and publisher; b. 31 Aug. 1947, Fort Dodge, Ia; m. Mary Montag; two d. *Education:* Dominican Coll. of Racine. *Career:* Ed. and Publr Monday Morning Press, Milwaukee 1977–79, Margins Books 1974–79, Wisconsin Poet's Calendar 1982–84, MWPH Books 1980–; poet and blogger, The Middlewesterner. *Music:* Dr. Finnegan's All-American Medicine Show, with Doug Burk; Somewhere There's a Jukebox, with Doc Abbick in Trinity. *Publications include:* Wooden Nickel 1972, Twelve Poems 1972, Measurers 1972, To Leave This Place 1972, Making Hay 1973, The Urban Ecosystem: A Holistic Approach (ed. with F. Stearns) 1974, Making Hay and Other Poems 1975, Ninety Notes Toward Partial Images and Lover Prints 1976, Concerns: Essays and Reviews 1977, Letters Home 1978, The Essential Ben Zen 1992, Ben Zen: The More I Know 2000, Curlew: Home 2001, Kissing Poetry's Sister 2002, The Sweet Bite of Morning 2003, The Big Book of Ben Zen 2004. *Honours:* Runner-up, Wisconsin Poet Laureate 2004. *Address:* 314 Washington Street, PO Box 8, Fairwater, WI 52931, USA (office). *Telephone:* (920) 539-5071 (office). *E-mail:* tmmontag@centurylink.net (office). *Website:* middlewesterner.com (office).

MONTAGUE, John Patrick, BA, MA, MFA; Irish poet, writer and lecturer; b. 28 Feb. 1929, New York City, USA. *Education:* Univ. Coll., Dublin, Yale Univ. and Univ. of Iowa, USA. *Career:* Lecturer in Poetry, Univ. Coll., Cork. *Publications:* Forms of Exile 1958, The Old People 1960, Poisoned Lands and Other Poems 1961, The Dolmen Miscellany of Irish Writing (ed.) 1962, Death of a Chieftain and Other Stories 1964, All Legendary Obstacles 1966, Patriotic Suite 1966, A Tribute to Austin Clarke on his Seventieth Birthday, 9th May 1966 (ed. with Liam Miller) 1966, Home Again 1967, A Chosen Light 1967, Hymn to the New Omagh Road 1968, The Bread God: A Lecture, with illustrations in Verse 1968, A New Siege 1969, The Planter and the Gael (with J. Hewitt) 1970, Tides 1970, Small Secrets 1972, The Rough Field (play) 1972, The Cave of Night 1974, O'Riada's Farewell 1974, The Faber Book of Irish Verse (ed.) 1974, A Slow Dance 1975, The Great Cloak (Alice Hunt Bartlett Award) 1978, Selected Poems 1982, The Dead Kingdom 1984, Mount Eagle 1989, Smashing the Piano (poems) 1999, Time in Armagh 2002, Drunken Sailor (poems) 2004, The Pear is Ripe 2008, A Ball of Fire (stories) 2009, In My Grandfather's Mansion 2010, Speech Lessons 2011. *Honours:* Hon. DLit (Univ. of Ulster, Coleraine) 2009; Award of the Irish American Cultural Inst. 1976, Marten Toonder Award 1977, The Vincent Buckley Poetry Prize 2000. *Address:* c/o The Gallery Press, Loughcrew, Oldcastle, County Meath, Ireland.

MONTAZAM, Mir Ali Asghar, MA, PhD; Iranian/British academic, historian and writer; *Head, Centre for Advice on Islam-related Causes of International Concern;* b. 25 Sept. 1935, Tabriz; s. of Sayyid Hassan Mousavi-Harzandi and Ismat; m. Zakieh 1974; two d. *Education:* Middle East Coll., Beirut, American Univ. of Beirut, Lebanon and Univ. of Tehran. *Career:* Islamologist and life-long activist in advocating reform of Islam; Head, Centre for Advice on Islam-related Issues of International Concern 2004–; Chair. The Reformation of Islam Foundation 2009–. *Publications include:* non-fiction: Politics of Religion in the Middle East 1988, The Life and Times of Ayatollah Khomeini 1994, Islam and Mullahcracy in Iran 2000, Islam in Iran: The Background to the Rule of Anarchy and Despotism in the Country's Islamic Past and Present: Egalitarian Principles of Islamic Government, Islam's Pagan Code of Punishments, Historical Roots of Despotism in Muslim Communities 2007, The Life and Legacy of Prophet Muhammad: A Solution to the Dilemma: 'War on Terror' 2007, The Long Shadow of the Safavid Fascistic Shi'ism 2009, The Turban Revolution: The Return of Iran's Safavid Fascistic Shi'ism 2010, The Life and True Legacy of Prophet Muhammad: Did the Martyrdom of Hussein Mark the End of Islam? 2012, Drama of the Ages: 1350 Years of Quest for Reformation of Islam: The Islamist Shopkeepers' Age-long Despotic Rule over the Lives of Muslims, A History of the Mullahcracy in Iran 2012, The Life and True Legacy of Prophet Muhammad 2012; historical novel: The Strange Death of a Dream: On the Verge of Israel's Lebanon War 2012. *Address:* 5 Elsie Lane Court, Westbourne Park Villas, London, W2 5EF, England (office). *Fax:* (20) 7727-7388 (office). *E-mail:* montazam100@hotmail.co.uk (office). *Website:* montazam-islam.tripod.com (office); heretic-islam.webs.com (office).

MONTEJO, Victor D., MA, PhD; Guatemalan/American writer, anthropologist and academic; *Professor Emeritus of Native American Studies, University of California at Davis;* b. (Victor Dionicio Montejo Esteban), 9 Oct. 1951, s. of Eusebio Montejo and Juana Esteban Mendez; m. Mercedes Montejo; two s. one d. *Education:* State Univ. of New York at Albany, Univ. of Connecticut.

Career: fmr Prof. of Native American Studies, Univ. of California, Davis, now Emer.; mem. Congreso de la República (Guatemalan Congress) 2004–08. *Publications include:* El Q'Anil: El Hombre Rayo (trans. as Man of Lightning) 1984, 1991, Testimony: Death of a Guatemalan Village 1987, Sculpted Stories 1988, The Bird Who Cleans the World 1992, Las Aventuras de Mister Puttison Among the Mayas 1995, Voices from Exile: Violence and Survival in Modern Maya History (Nat. Prize in Ethnic Studies) 1999, Popol Vuh: A Sacred Book of the Maya 1999, Oxlanh Baktun 2003, Maya Intellectual Renaissance 2004, Blanca Flor: A Maya Princess 2005. *Telephone:* (530) 754-6128 (office). *Fax:* (530) 752-7097 (office). *E-mail:* vmontejo@ucdavis.edu (office). *Website:* nas.ucdavis.edu/site/people/faculty/vmontejo.html (office).

MONTELEONE, Thomas Francis, BS, MA; American writer and dramatist; b. 14 April 1946, Baltimore, MD; m. Elizabeth; two s. one d. *Education:* Univ. of Maryland. *Career:* writes for television; mem. SFWA, Horror Writers of America. *Publications:* fiction: Seeds of Change 1975, The Time Connection 1976, The Time-Swept City 1977, The Secret Sea 1979, Dragonstar (with David F. Bischoff) 1980, Guardian 1980, Night Things 1980, Ozymandias 1981, Dark Stars and Other Illuminations (short stories) 1981, Day of the Dragonstar (with David F. Bischoff) 1983, Night Trains 1984, Random Access Messages of the Computer Age 1984, Microworlds 1985, Night of the Dragonstar (with David F. Bischoff) 1985, The Crooked House (with John DeChancie) 1987, Fantasma 1987, Lyrica: A Novel of Horror and Desire 1987, The Magnificent Gallery 1987, Borderlands (ed.) 1988, Dragonstar Destiny (with David F. Bischoff) 1989, Borderlands 2 (ed.) 1991, Borderlands 3 (ed.) 1992, The Blood of the Lamb (Bram Stoker Award 1993) 1992, Borderlands 4 (ed., with Elizabeth Monteleone) 1993, The Resurrectionist 1995, Between Floors 1997, Night of Broken Souls 1997, The Reckoning 1999, Eyes of the Virgin 2002, Rough Beasts and Other Mutations (short stories) 2003, From the Borderlands (ed.) 2004, Fearful Symmetries 2004, Serpentine 2007; non-fiction: The Arts and Beyond: Visions of Man's Aesthetic Future 1977, The Mothers and Fathers Italian Association 2003, The Complete Idiot's Guide to Writing a Novel 2004; contrib. to anthologies and magazines. *Honours:* Nebula Awards 1976, 1977, Gabriel Award 1984, Int. Film and TV Festival Bronze Award, New York 1984. *Literary Agent:* Howard Morhaim Literary Agency, 11 John Street, Suite 407, New York, NY 10038, USA.

MONTERO, Mayra; Puerto Rican journalist and writer; b. 1952, Havana, Cuba. *Career:* fmr newspaper corresp. in Cen. America and the Caribbean; currently columnist, El Nuevo Dia newspaper. *Publications:* Veintitrés y una tortuga (trans. as Twenty-Three and a Turtle) (short stories), La trenza de la hermosa luna (trans. as The Braid of the Beautiful Moon) 1987, La última noche que pasé contigo (trans. as The Last Night I Spent With You) 1991, Del rojo de su sombra (trans. as The Red of His Shadow) 1993, Tú, la oscuridad (trans. as In the Palm of Darkness) 1995, Como un mensajero tuyo (trans. as The messenger) 1998, Púrpura profundo (trans. as Deep Purple) 2000, Vana ilusión 2002, El capitán de los dormidos (trans. as Captain of the Sleepers) 2002, Son de Almendra (trans. as Dancing to 'Almendra') 2005. *Address:* c/o Alfaguara, Avenida Roosevelt, 1506, Guaynabo 00968, Puerto Rico (office). *Website:* www.alfaguara.com (office).

MONTGOMERY, David John, BA; British newspaper executive; b. 6 Nov. 1948, Bangor, Northern Ireland; s. of William John Montgomery and Margaret Jean Montgomery; m. 1st Susan Frances Buchanan Russell 1971 (divorced 1987); m. 2nd Heidi Kingstone 1989 (divorced 1997); m. 3rd Sophie, Countess of Woolton 1997. *Education:* Queen's Univ., Belfast. *Career:* Sub-Ed., Daily Mirror London, Manchester 1973–76, Asst Chief Sub-Ed. 1976–80; Chief Sub-Ed. The Sun 1980; Asst Ed. Sunday People 1982; Asst Ed. News of the World 1984, Ed. 1985–87; Ed. Today 1987–91 (Newspaper of the Year 1988); Man. Dir News UK 1987–91; Chief Exec. London Live TV 1991–92, Dir 1991–92; Chief Exec. Mirror Group 1992–99; Dir Satellite Television PLC 1986–91, News Group Newspapers 1986–91, Donohue Inc. 1992–95, Newspaper Publishing 1994–98, Scottish Media Group 1995–99, Press Asscn 1996–99; Founder and Exec. Chair. Mecom Group plc 2000–09, CEO 2009–11; Chair. Tri-Mex Group PLC 1999–2008, Yava 2000–02, Africa Lakes PLC 2000–07, Integrated Educ. Fund Devt Bd, NI 2000–, Espresso 2001–07; with other investors acquired Berliner Verlag (Berliner Zeitung and Berliner Kurier newspapers), Germany, Chair. Supervisory Bd 2005–. *Address:* c/o Mecom Group plc, 5th Floor, 70 Jermyn Street, London, SW1Y 6NY (office); 15 Collingham Gardens, London, SW5 0HS, England (home). *Telephone:* (20) 7373-1982 (home).

MONTGOMERY, Marion H., Jr, AB, MA; American academic, writer and poet; *Emeritus Professor of English, University of Georgia*; b. 16 April 1925, Thomaston, Ga; m. Dorothy Carlisle 1952; one s., four d. *Education:* Univ. of Georgia, Creative Writing Workshop, Univ. of Iowa. *Career:* Asst Dir, Univ. of Georgia Press 1950–52; Business Man., Georgia Review 1951–53; Instructor, Darlington School for Boys 1953–54; Instructor, Univ. of Georgia 1954–60, Asst Prof. 1960–67, Assoc. Prof. 1967–70, Prof. of English 1970, now Prof. Emer.; Writer-in-Residence, Converse Coll. 1963. *Publications:* fiction: The Wandering of Desire 1962, Darrell 1964, Ye Olde Bluebird 1967, Fugitive 1974; poetry: Dry Lightening 1960, Stones from the Rubble 1965, The Gull and Other Georgia Scenes 1969; non-fiction: Ezra Pound: A Critical Essay 1970, T. S. Eliot: An Essay on the American Magus 1970, The Reflective Journey Toward Order: Essays on Dante, Wordsworth, Eliot and Others 1973, Eliot's Reflective Journey to the Garden 1978, The Prophetic Poet and the Spirit of the Age, Vol. 1, Why Flannery O'Connor Stayed Home 1980, Vol. II, Why Poe Drank Liquor 1983, Vol. III, Why Hawthorne Was Melancholy 1984, Possum, and Other Receipts for the Recovery of 'Southern' Being 1987, The Trouble with You Innerleckchuls 1988, The Men I Have Chosen for Fathers: Literary and Philosophical Passages 1990, Liberal Arts and Community: The Feeding of the Larger Body 1990, Virtue and Modern Shadows of Turning: Preliminary Agitations 1990, Romantic Confusions of the Good: Beauty as Truth, Truth Beauty 1997, Concerning Intellectual Philandering: Poets and Philosophers, Priests and Politicians 1998, Making: The Proper Habit of Our Being 1999, The Truth of Things: Liberal Arts and the Recovery of Reality 1999, Romancing Reality: Homo Viator and the Scandal of Beauty 2000, John Crowe Ransom and Allen Tate: At Odds About the Ends of History and the Mystery of Nature 2003, Eudora Welty and Walker Percy: The Concept of Home in Their Lives and Literature 2004, On Matters Southern: Essays About Literature and Culture 1964–2000 (ed. Michael Jordan) 2005, Hillbilly Thomist: Flannery O'Connor, St Thomas and the Limits of Art (two vols) 2006, With Walker Percy at the Tupperware Party, In Company with Flannery O'Connor, T. S. Eliot and Others 2009; contrib. to anthologies and magazines. *Honours:* Eugene Saxton Memorial Award 1960, Georgia Writers' Asscn Literary Achievement Award in Fiction 1964, Georgia Writers' Asscn Literary Achievement Award in Poetry 1970, Earhart Foundation Fellowship 1973–74, Stanley W. Lindberg Award 2001, Intercollegiate Studies Inst. Gerhart Niemeyer Award 2003. *Address:* PO Box 115, Crawford, GA 30630, USA (home).

MOODY, Rick, BA, MFA; American writer and editor; b. (Hiram F. Moody III), 18 Oct. 1961, New York, NY. *Education:* Brown Univ., Columbia Univ. *Career:* founder mem., The Wingdale Community Singers; collaboration with experimental group, One Ring Zero. *Recording:* The Wingdale Community Singers (album) 2005. *Publications:* Garden State: A Novel 1991, The Ice Storm 1994, The Ring of Brightest Angels Around Heaven (short stories) 1995, Demonology 2001, The Black Veil (memoir) 2002, The Diviners 2006, Right Livelihoods: Three Novellas 2007, The Omega Force 2008, The Four Fingers of Death 2010; contrib. to various periodicals. *Honours:* Ed.'s Book Award, Pushcart Press 1991. *Address:* c/o Little, Brown & Co., 1271 Avenue of the Americas, New York, NY 10020, USA (office).

MOONEY, Bel, BA; British writer and broadcaster; b. (Beryl Ann Mooney), 8 Oct. 1946, Liverpool; d. of Edward Mooney and Gladys Mooney; m. 1st Jonathan Dimbleby 1968 (divorced 2006); one s. one d.; m. 2nd Robin Allison-Smith 2007. *Education:* Univ. Coll. London. *Career:* columnist, Daily Mirror 1979–80, Sunday Times 1982–83, The Listener 1984–86, The Times 2005–, Daily Mail 2007–; TV interview series, TV films and radio programmes; Gov. Bristol Polytechnic 1989–91, Theatre Royal, Bath 2009–; Fellow, Univ. Coll. London 1994, Liverpool John Moores Univ. 2002. *Radio:* presenter of Devout Sceptics, BBC Radio 4 (Sandford St Martin Award for religious broadcasting). *Publications:* fiction: The Windsurf Boy 1983, The Anderson Question 1985, The Fourth of July 1988, Lost Footsteps 1993, Intimate Letters 1997, The Invasion of Sand 2005; children's books: Liza's Yellow Boat 1980, I Don't Want To! 1985, The Stove Haunting 1986, I Can't Find It! 1988, It's Not Fair! 1989, A Flower of Jet 1990, But You Promised! 1990, Why Not? 1990, I Know! 1991, The Voices of Silence 1994, I'm Scared! 1994, I Wish! 1995, The Mouse with Many Rooms 1995, Why Me? 1996, I'm Bored! 1997, Joining the Rainbow 1997, The Green Man 1997, It's not my Fault 1999, So What! 2002, Kitty's Friends 2003, Mr Tubs is Lost 2004, the Bonnie series (six books) 2005–10, Who Loves Mr Tibs 2006, Like Mother, Like Daughter (ed.) 2006; other: The Year of the Child 1979, Differences of Opinion 1984, Father Kissmass and Mother Claws (with Gerald Scarfe) 1985, Bel Mooney's Somerset 1989, From this Day Forward 1989, Perspectives for Living 1992, Devout Sceptics 2003, Small Dogs Can Save your Life 2010. *Honours:* Hon. DLitt (Bath Univ.) 1998. *Address:* The Daily Mail, 2 Derry Street, London, W8 5TS, England (office). *Telephone:* (20) 7938-6000 (office). *Website:* www.belmooney.co.uk.

MOORCOCK, Michael John, (Edward P. Bradbury, Desmond Read); British novelist; b. 18 Dec. 1939, London; s. of Arthur Moorcock and June Moorcock; m. 1st Hilary Bailey 1963 (divorced 1978); one s. two d.; m. 2nd Jill Riches 1978 (divorced 1983); m. 3rd Linda M. Steele 1983. *Education:* Michael Hall School, Sussex. *Career:* worked as musician and journalist; Ed. Outlaws Own 1951–53, Tarzan Adventures 1957–59, Sexton Blake Library 1959–61, Current Topics 1961–62; Ed. New Worlds 1964–71, 1976–96, Consulting Ed. 1996–. *Films:* The Final Programme 1973, The Land that Time Forgot 1975. *Records:* Warrior on the Edge of Time (Hawkwind) 1975, The New World's Fair 1975, The Brothel in Rosenstrasse 1982, Roller Coaster Holiday 2004. *Publications include:* The Eternal Champion sequence 1963–98, Behold the Man (Nebula Award 1967) 1966, The Knight of the Swords (August Derleth Fantasy Award 1972, 1973) 1971, The Jade Man's Eyes (British Fantasy Award) 1974, The Sword and the Stallion (August Derleth Fantasy Award 1975) 1974, The Hollow Lands (August Derleth Fantasy Award 1976) 1974, Condition of Muzak (Guardian Fiction Prize, Guardian Fiction Award 1977) 1976, Gloriana (World Fantasy Award 1979) 1977, Gloriana (John W. Campbell Memorial Award, World Fantasy Award 1979) 1978, Byzantium Endures 1981, The Laughter of Carthage 1984, Mother London 1988, Jerusalem Commands 1992, Blood 1994, The War Amongst Angels 1996, Tales from the Texas Woods 1997, King of the City 2000, Silverheart (co-author) 2000, London Bone 2001, The Dreamthief's Daughter 2001, Firing the Cathedral 2002, The Skrayling Tree 2003, The Lives and Times of Jerry Cornelius 2004, Wizardry and Wild Romance 2004, The White Wolf's Son 2005, The Vengeance of Rome 2006, The Metatemporal Detective 2007, The Best of Michael Moorcock 2009, The Coming of the Terraphiles 2010, Modem

Times 2.0 2011, The Sunday Books 2011, London Peculiar and Other Nonfiction (co-ed.) 2012. *Honours:* British Fantasy Award 1993, August Derleith Prize, World Fantasy Lifetime Achievement Award 2000, Science Fiction Hall of Fame 2002, Priz Utopiales 2004, Bram Stoker Lifetime Achievement Award 2004, named Damon Knight Grand Master, Science Fiction and Fantasy Writers of America 2008. *Literary Agent:* c/o Howard Morhaim Literary Agency, 30 Pierrepont Street, Brooklyn, NY 11201, USA. *Telephone:* (718) 222-8400. *Fax:* (718) 222-5056. *E-mail:* howard@morhaimliterary.com. *Address:* PO Box 1230, Bastrop, TX 78602, USA (home). *Website:* www.multiverse.org.

MOORE, Ann S., BSc, MBA; American publisher and media executive; b. 29 May 1950, McLean, Va; m. Donovan Moore; one s. *Education:* Vanderbilt Univ., Nashville, Harvard Univ. Business School. *Career:* financial analyst, Time Inc. 1978, served in various exec. positions including Publr and Pres. People magazine (est. spin-offs Teen People, Instyle, Real Simple, People en Español 2001), cr. Sports Illustrated for Kids 1989, Exec. Vice-Pres. Time Inc. 2001–02, Chair. and CEO 2002–10, responsible for Time magazine, People, Fortune, Money, Entertainment Weekly and 135 other titles (first woman in position); mem. Bd of Dirs Avon Products Inc., Wallace Foundation 2004–. *Honours:* Adweek's Publishing Exec. of the Year 1998, MIN Magazine's Consumer Magazine Player of the Year 1999, named one of Advertising Age's Women to Watch 2001, ranked by Fortune magazine amongst the 50 Most Powerful Women in Business in the US 1998–2001, (11th) 2002, (13th) 2003–05, (15th) 2006, (19th) 2007, (20th) 2008, (21st) 2009, first Annual AOL Time Warner Civic Leadership Award 2003, ranked by Forbes magazine amongst The World's 100 Most Powerful Women (20th) 2004, (38th) 2005, (53rd) 2006, (57th) 2007, (93rd) 2008, (87th) 2009. *Address:* c/o Wallace Foundation, 5 Penn Plaza, 7th Floor, New York, NY 10001, USA (office). *Telephone:* (212) 251-9700 (office). *Fax:* (212) 679-6990 (office). *Website:* www.wallacefoundation.org (office).

MOORE, Charles Hilary, MA; British journalist; *Group Consulting Editor, The Daily Telegraph (UK)*; b. 31 Oct. 1956, Hastings; s. of Richard Moore and Ann Moore; m. Caroline Baxter 1981; twin s. and d. *Education:* Eton Coll. and Trinity Coll. Cambridge. *Career:* editorial staff, Daily Telegraph 1979–81; leader writer 1981–83; Asst Ed. and Political Columnist, The Spectator 1983–84, Ed. 1984–90, fortnightly columnist ('Another Voice') 1990–95; weekly columnist, Daily Express 1987–90; Deputy Ed. Daily Telegraph 1990–92; Ed. Sunday Telegraph 1992–95, Daily Telegraph 1995–2003, Group Consulting Ed. Daily Telegraph (UK) 2003–; Chair. Policy Exchange; Trustee T. E. Utley Memorial Fund, Benenden Council, ShareGift. *Publications:* 1936 (co-ed. with C. Hawtree) 1986, The Church in Crisis (with A. N. Wilson and G. Stamp) 1986, A Tory Seer: The Selected Journalism of T. E. Utley (co-ed. with S. Heffer) 1986. *Address:* c/o Daily Telegraph, 11 Buckingham Palace Road, London, SW1W 0DT, England (office).

MOORE, Christopher Hugh, BA, MA; Canadian historian and writer; b. 9 June 1950, Stoke-on-Trent, England; m. Louise Brophy 1977. *Education:* Univ. of British Columbia, Univ. of Ottawa. *Career:* mem. Writers' Union of Canada, Canadian Historical Asscn, Ontario Historical Soc., Heritage Canada Foundation. *Publications:* Louisbourg Portraits 1982, The Loyalists 1984, The Illustrated History of Canada (co-author) 1987; also school texts, historical guidebooks, educational software programmes and radio documentaries; contrib. to numerous scholarly journals and magazines. *Honours:* Governor-General's Award for Non-Fiction 1982, Canadian Historical Assen Award of Merit 1984, Secretary of State's Prize for Excellence in Canadian Studies 1985. *E-mail:* cmed@sympatico.ca. *Website:* www.christophermoore.ca.

MOORE, Eric (see Bruton, Eric)

MOORE, Capt. John Evelyn, RN, FRGS; British editor, author and naval officer (retd); b. 1 Nov. 1921, Sant' Ilario, Italy; s. of William John Moore and Evelyn Elizabeth (née Hooper); m. 1st Joan Pardoe 1945; one s. two d.; m. 2nd Barbara Kerry. *Education:* Sherborne School, Dorset. *Career:* entered RN 1939, specialized in hydrographic surveying, then submarines: commanded HM Submarines Totem, Alaric, Tradewind, Tactician, Telemachus; RN staff course 1950–51; Commdr 1957; attached to Turkish Naval Staff 1958–60; subsequently Plans Div., Admiralty, 1st Submarine Squadron, then 7th Submarine Squadron in command; Capt. 1967; served as Chief of Staff, C-in-C Naval Home Command; Defence Intelligence Staff; retd list at own request 1972; Ed., Jane's Fighting Ships 1972–87; Ed., Jane's Naval Review 1982–87. *Publications:* Jane's Major Warships 1973, The Soviet Navy Today 1975, Submarine Development 1976, Soviet War Machine (jtly) 1976, Encyclopaedia of World's Warships 1978, World War 3 1978, Seapower and Politics 1979, Warships of the Royal Navy 1979, Warships of the Soviet Navy 1981, Submarine Warfare: Today and Tomorrow (jtly) 1986; ed. The Impact of Polaris 1999. *Honours:* Hon. Prof. of Int. Relations, Aberdeen Univ. 1987–90, St Andrews Univ. 1990–92. *Address:* 1 Ridgelands Close, Eastbourne, East Sussex, BN20 8EP, England (home). *Telephone:* (1323) 638836 (home).

MOORE, Lorrie, BA, MFA; American academic and writer; *Professor of English, University of Wisconsin at Madison*; b. 13 Jan. 1957, Glens Falls, NY. *Education:* St Lawrence Univ., Cornell Univ. *Career:* Lecturer in English, Cornell Univ. 1982–84; Asst Prof., Univ. of Wisconsin at Madison 1984–87, Assoc. Prof. 1987–91, Prof. of English 1991–, currently Delmore Schwartz Prof. in the Humanities; mem. Associated Writing Programs (AWP), Authors' Guild, PEN. *Publications:* Self-Help 1985, Anagrams 1986, The Forgotten Helper 1987, Like Life 1990, I Know Some Things: Stories About Childhood by Contemporary Writers (ed.) 1992, Birds of America 1998, Collected Stories 2008, A Gate at the Stairs 2009; contributions: periodicals including New Yorker, New York Review of Books. *Honours:* Guggenheim Fellowship 1991, Irish Times Int. Prize for Literature 1999, Nat. Book Critics' Circle Nominee 1999, Rea Prize for the Short Story 2004. *Address:* Department of English, University of Wisconsin at Madison, 7187 Helen C. White Hall, 600 North Park Street, Madison, WI 53706, USA (office). *Telephone:* (608) 263-3613 (office). *Fax:* (608) 263-3709 (office). *E-mail:* english100@english.wisc.edu (office). *Website:* www.english.wisc.edu (office).

MOORE, Michael Francis; American writer and filmmaker; b. 23 April 1954, Davison, Mich.; m. Kathleen Glynn 1991. *Education:* Davison High School. *Career:* elected to Davison, Mich. school bd aged 18; active in student politics; began career as journalist with The Flint Voice, later Ed., expanded into The Mich. Voice; Ed. Mother Jones magazine, San Francisco 1986–88; Founder and mem. bd of Dir Traverse City (Mich.) Film Festival. *Television includes:* Pets or Meat: The Return to Flint 1992, TV Nation (NBC series) 1994–95, 1997, And Justice for All (dir) 1998, The Awful Truth (series) 1999. *Films:* Roger and Me (writer, dir, producer) 1989, Canadian Bacon (writer, producer, dir) 1994, The Big One (dir) 1997, Bowling for Columbine (screenwriter, dir, producer; Jury Award, Cannes Film Festival 2003, Acad. Award for Best Documentary 2003) 2002, Fahrenheit 9/11 (dir; Palme d'Or, Cannes Film Festival, US People's Choice Award for Best Film 2005) 2004, Sicko 2007, Capitalism: A Love Story 2009. *Film appearances:* Lucky Number 1999, EdTV 1999. *Publications:* Downsize This!: Random Threats from an Unarmed America 1996, Stupid White Men (Book of the Year, British Book Awards 2003) 2001, Adventures in a TV Nation (with Kathleen Glynn) 2002, Dude, Where's My Country? 2003, Will They Ever Trust Us Again?: Letters from the War Zone 2004, The Official Fahrenheit 9/11 Reader 2004, Mike's Election Guide 2008 2008, Here Comes Trouble: Stories from My Life 2011, I Am Moore 2011. *Address:* c/o Random House Inc., 1745 Broadway, Suite B1, New York, NY 10019-4305, USA. *E-mail:* mike@michaelmoore.com. *Website:* www.michaelmoore.com.

MOORE, Sir Patrick Alfred Caldwell-, Kt (see Caldwell-Moore, Sir Patrick Alfred, Kt)

MOORE, Susanna; American writer; *Lecturer in Creative Writing, Princeton University*; b. 9 Dec. 1948, Bryn Mawr, PA; m., one d. *Education:* Punahou School, Honolulu, HI. *Career:* Lecturer in Creative Writing, Univ. of Princeton 2007–11. *Publications:* My Old Sweetheart 1982, The Whiteness of Bones 1989, Sleeping Beauties 1993, In the Cut 1995, One Last Look 2003, I Myself Have Seen It 2003, The Big Girls 2007. *Honours:* PEN/Ernest Hemingway Citation, American Acad. of Arts and Letters Sue Kaufman Prize 1983, American Acad. of Arts and Letters Prize for Literary Achievement 1999, Fellowship in Literature, American Acad. in Berlin 2006. *Address:* The Gernert Company, 136 East 57th Street, New York, NY 10022, USA (office). *Telephone:* (212) 838-3402 (office).

MOOREHEAD, Caroline Mary, OBE, BA, FRSL; British journalist and writer; b. 28 Oct. 1944, London, England. *Education:* Univ. of London. *Career:* reporter, Time magazine, Rome 1968–69; feature writer, Telegraph Magazine, London 1969–70, The Times, London 1973–88; Features Ed., Times Educational Supplement 1970–73; human rights columnist, The Independent 1988–93. *Publications:* Myths and Legends of Britain (ed. and trans.) 1968, Helping: A Guide to Voluntary Work 1975, Fortune's Hostages 1980, Sidney Bernstein: A Biography 1983, Freya Stark: A Biography 1985, Troublesome People: Enemies of War 1916–1986 1987, Over the Rim of the World: The Letters of Freya Stark (ed.) 1988, Betrayed: Children in the Modern World 1988, Bertrand Russell: A Life 1992, The Lost Treasures of Troy 1996, 6 Dunant's Dream: War, Switzerland and the Red Crown 1998, Iris Origo: A Life 1999, Martha Gellhorn: A Life 2003, Human Cargo 2005, Letters of Martha Gellhorn (ed.) 2006, Dancing to the Edge of the Precipice: Lucie de la Tour du Pin and the French Revolution 2009; contrib. to newspapers and magazines. *Address:* 89 Gloucester Avenue, London, NW1 8LB, England. *E-mail:* cmmoorehead@clara.co.uk (home).

MOORHOUSE, Frank; Australian writer; b. 21 Dec. 1938, Nowra, Qld. *Education:* University of Queensland, WEA. *Career:* Pres., Australian Society of Authors 1979–82; Chair. Copyright Council of Australia 1985; mem. Groucho Club, London; AM. *Publications:* Futility and Other Animals 1969, The Americans, Baby 1972, The Electrical Experience 1974, Conference-Ville 1976, Tales of Mystery and Romance 1977, Days of Wine and Rage 1980, Room Service 1986, Forty-Seventeen 1988, Lateshows 1990, Dark Palace 2000, Satanic Killings 2006; contrib. to Bulletin. *Honours:* Henry Lawson Short Story Prize 1970, National Award for Fiction 1975, Awgie Award 1976, Gold Medal for Literature, Australian Literary 1989, Miles Franklin Award 2001.

MORAVCOVÁ, Jana, PhD; Czech writer and translator; b. 8 May 1937, Černčice; d. of Jindřich and Anna Moravec; m. Bohumil Neumann 1959; one d. *Education:* Charles Univ., Prague. *Career:* writer and trans. from Russian and Spanish; publishing house Ed. 1959–; Ed.-in-Chief Int. Asscn of Crime Writers' Czech Section; has written over 30 novels and collections of poetry; numerous awards for literature. *Radio:* Interview with Butterfly (drama) 2003. *Publications include:* Club of Unmistakables 1973, Snow Circle 1974, Still Life With Citadel 1978, Silent Cormorant 1979, Second Glass 1990, Fear Has Long Legs 1992, Holidays With Monica 1994, Fixdictionary 1996, J. Petrovická (biog.) 1999, Cases of a Kind Detective 2000, Thirteen Colours of Love 2000, Killer 2002, Murder in Spa Luhacovice 2004, Death Doesn't Wear

Glasses 2005, Pekingese of the Baskervilles 2007, Traps of Intellect 2008, Crime for Miss Poirot 2008, Thirteenth Comet 2009, Angels to Watch over You 2010, Murder with Polar Gloriole 2010. *Address:* Podolská 1487, 147 00 Prague 4, Czech Republic (home). *Telephone:* (2) 44460015 (home).

MORENCY, Pierre, OC, BA, LèsL; Canadian poet, writer and dramatist; b. 8 May 1942, Lauzon, PQ; m. Renée Dupuis. *Education:* Collège de Lévis, Université Laval, Québec. *Career:* broadcaster; Co-founder, Estuaire poetry journal; mem. PEN Club, Union des écrivaines et des écrivains québécois. *Publications:* Lieu de naissance 1973, Le temps des oiseaux 1975, Torrentiel 1978, Effets personnels 1978, L'oeil américain: Histoires naturelles du Nouveau Monde 1989, Lumière des oiseaux: Histoires naturelles du Nouveau Monde 1992, Les paroles qui marchent dans la nuit 1994, La vie entière 1996, A l'heure du loup 2004, Poèmes (1966–1986) 2004, Chez les oiseaux 2004, Amouraska 2008. *Honours:* Chevalier, Ordre des Arts et des Lettres, Officier, Ordre du Canada 2003, Chevalier, Ordre National du Québec 2005; Prix Alain Grandbois 1987, Prix Québec-Paris 1988, Prix Ludger Duvernay 1991, Prix France Québec 1992, Prix Athanase-David 2000, Prix Guillevic 2003. *Address:* 41 chemin de l'Eglise, RR3, Sainte-Pétronille, PQ G0A 4C0, Canada (office). *E-mail:* p.morency@globetrotter.net (home).

MORENO, Armando, LM, LL, PhD; Portuguese academic, physician, writer, poet and dramatist; b. 19 Dec. 1932, Porto; m. Maria Guinot Moreno 1987. *Education:* Faculdade Medicina, Porto. *Career:* academic, physician –2005 (retd); mem. many professional and literary organizations. *Publications:* A Chamada (short stories) 1982, As Carreiras 1982, O Bojador 1982, Historias Quase Clinicas (short stories, three vols) 1982, 1984, 1988, Cais do Sodre (short stories) 1988, O Animal Que deupla Mente 1993, Contos Oeirenses (short stories) 1994, A Governaçao pela Competencia 1995, O Mundo Fascinante da Medicina (12 vols, illustrated) 1997, Disseram que Já É Tarde (short stories) 2003, Glória e Suicídio (literary study) 2003, As Fezes (literary study) 2003, História da Ortopedia Portuguesa 2003, Ética em Tecnologias da Saúde (literary study) 2004, Fingindo Poesia (poems) 2004, Ética em Medicina (literary study) 2005, O Terceiro Túnel (romance) 2006; also medical books, poetry, plays and television series; contrib. to periodicals. *Honours:* drama and fiction awards. *Address:* Rua Almirante Matos Moreira 7, 2775 Carcavelos, Portugal (home). *Telephone:* 214578739. *Fax:* 214578739.

MORETON, John (see Cohen, Morton Norton)

MORGAN, Abi; British playwright; b. 1969, Cardiff, S Glamorgan, Wales. *Film:* screenplays: Brick Lane 2007. *Plays:* Skinned 1998, Sleeping Around 1998, Fast Food 1999, Splendour 2000, Tender 2001, Tiny Dynamite 2002, Fugee 2008, 27 2011. *Television drama:* My Fragile Heart 2000, Murder 2002, Sex Traffic (serial for Granada TV/Channel 4) (BAFTA Award for Best Drama Serial 2005) 2004, Life Isn't all Ha Ha Hee Hee 2005, Tsunami: The Aftermath 2006, White Girl 2008, The Hour 2011. *Literary Agent:* Independent, Oxford House, 76 Oxford Street, London, W1D 1BS, England. *Website:* www.independenttalent.com.

MORGAN, C. E., MTS; American writer; b. 23 June 1976, Cincinnati, Ohio. *Education:* Berea Coll., Harvard Divinity School. *Publications:* fiction: All the Living: A Novel 2009. *Address:* c/o Farrar, Strauss & Giroux, 18 West 18th Street, New York, NY 10011, USA (office). *Website:* us.macmillan.com/fsg.aspx (office).

MORGAN, Edmund Sears, AB, PhD; American historian and academic; *Sterling Professor Emeritus, Yale University;* b. 17 Jan. 1916, Minneapolis; s. of Edmund Morris Morgan and Elsie Sears Smith; m. 1st Helen Theresa Mayer 1939; two d.; m. 2nd Marie Caskey 1983. *Education:* Harvard Univ. *Career:* radiation laboratory instrument maker, Massachusetts Inst. of Technology 1942–45; Instructor, Univ. of Chicago 1945–46; Asst Prof., Brown Univ. 1946–49, Assoc. Prof. 1949–51, Prof. 1951–55, Acting Dean of the Graduate School 1951–52; Research Fellow, Huntington Library 1952–53; Prof., Yale Univ. 1955–65, Sterling Prof. 1965–86, Sterling Professor Emeritus 1986–; Johnson Research Prof., Univ. of Wisconsin 1968–69; Trustee, Smith Coll. 1984–89; mem. editorial bd, New England Quarterly, The Benjamin Franklin Papers; mem. American Acad. of Arts and Sciences, American Antiquarian Soc., American Philosophical Soc., British Acad., Colonial Soc. of Massachusetts, Massachusetts Historical Soc., Organization of American Historians (pres. 1971–72), Royal Historical Soc. *Publications:* The Puritan Family 1942, Virginians at Home 1953, The Stamp Act Crisis (with Helen M. Morgan) 1953, The Birth of the Republic 1956, The Puritan Dilemma 1958, The Gentle Puritan 1962, Visible Saints 1963, Roger Williams 1967, So What About History 1969, American Slavery, American Freedom (Soc. of American Historians Francis Parkman Prize, Southern Historical Asscn Charles S. Sydnor Prize, American Historical Asscn Albert J. Beveridge Award) 1975, The Challenge of the American Revolution 1976, The Meaning of Independence 1976, The Genius of George Washington 1980, Inventing the People: The Rise of Popular Sovereignty in England and America (Columbia Univ. Bancroft Prize in American History 1989) 1988, Benjamin Franklin 2002, The Genuine Article 2004. *Honours:* Yale Chapter of Phi Beta Kappa William Clyde DeVane Medal 1971, Douglas Adair Memorial Award for scholarship in early American history 1972, American Historical Asscn Distinguished Scholar Award 1986, Nat. Humanities Medal 2000, Pulitzer Special Citation 2006, American Acad. of Arts and Letters Gold Medal 2008. *Address:* c/o Department of History, Yale University, PO Box 208324, New Haven, CT 06520-8324, USA (office). *E-mail:* edmund.morgan@yale.edu (office).

MORGAN, Mihangel (see Morgan-Finch, Mihangel Ioan)

MORGAN, Peter, BA; British scriptwriter, screenwriter and producer; b. 10 April 1963, London; s. of the late Arthur Morgenthau and Inga Morgenthau; m. Lila Morgan; three s. one d. *Education:* Downside School, Leeds Univ. *Play:* Frost/Nixon (Donmar Warehouse, London) 2006. *Films:* as writer: Martha, Meet Frank, Daniel And Laurence 1998, The Queen (Best Screenplay Award, Venice Film Festival) 2006; screenplays: The Last King of Scotland 2006, The Other Boleyn Girl 2007, Frost/Nixon (also exec. producer) 2008, The Damned United (also exec. producer) 2009. *Television:* as writer: Micky Love 1993, Metropolis (mini-series) 2000, The Jury (mini-series) (also exec. producer) 2002, Henry VIII (also exec. producer) (Emmy Award for Best Drama 2004) 2003, The Deal (screenplay) 2003, Colditz 2005, Longford (also exec. producer) 2006. *Address:* c/o Working Title Films, 5th Floor, Oxford House, 76 Oxford Street, London, W1D 1BS, England (office). *Website:* www.workingtitlefilms.com (office).

MORGAN, Piers Stefan; British broadcaster, writer and fmr journalist; b. (Piers Stefan O'Meara), 30 March 1965, Guildford; s. of Anthony Pughe-Morgan and Gabrielle Oliver; m. 1st Marion E. Shalloe 1991 (divorced); three s.; m. 2nd Celia Walden 2010; one d. *Education:* Cumnor House Preparatory School, Chailey School, Sussex, Lewes Priory Sixth Form Coll. and Harlow Journalism Coll. *Career:* reporter, Surrey and S London newspapers 1987–89; Showbusiness Ed. The Sun newspaper 1989–94; Ed. The News of the World newspaper 1994–95, Daily Mirror (later The Mirror) 1995–2004; Co-founder Press Gazette Ltd, Owner, Press Gazette 2005–07; Editorial Dir First News (newspaper for children) 2006. *Television:* presenter: The Importance of Being Famous (Channel 4) 2004, Morgan & Platell (Channel 4) 2005–06, You Can't Fire Me, I'm Famous (BBC1) 2006–07, Piers Morgan on Sandbanks (ITV 1) 2008, Piers Morgan's Life Stories 2009–10; judge: America's Got Talent (NBC) 2006–08, Britain's Got Talent (ITV 1) 2007–09, Piers Morgan's Life Stories 2009–, Piers Morgan On 2010, Piers Morgan Tonight (CNN) 2011–. *Publications include:* Private Lives of the Stars 1990, Secret Lives of the Stars 1991, Phillip Schofield, To Dream a Dream 1992, Take That, Our Story 1993, Take That: On the Road 1994, The Insider (memoir) 2005, Don't You Know Who I Am? 2007, God Bless America 2009. *Honours:* Atex Award for Nat. Newspaper Ed. of Year 1994, What the Papers Say Newspaper of the Year Award 2001, GQ Ed. of the Year 2002, British Press Awards Newspaper of the Year 2002, Magazine Design and Journalism Awards Columnist of the Year Award (Live Magazine) 2007. *Literary Agent:* c/o James Grant Media, 94 Strand on the Green, Chiswick, London, W4 3NN, England. *Telephone:* (20) 8742-4950. *Fax:* (20) 8742-4951. *E-mail:* tracey@jamesgrant.co.uk. *Website:* www.jamesgrantmedia.co.uk.

MORGAN, Robert Ray, BA, MFA, LittD; American professor of english, poet and writer; *Kappa Alpha Professor of English, Cornell University;* b. 3 Oct. 1944, Hendersonville, NC; m. Nancy K. Bullock 1965; one s. two d. *Education:* Emory Coll., Oxford, North Carolina State Univ., Raleigh, Univ. of North Carolina, Chapel Hill, Univ. of North Carolina, Greensboro. *Career:* Instructor, Salem Coll., Winston-Salem, NC 1968–69; Lecturer, Cornell Univ. 1971–73, Asst Prof. 1973–78, Assoc. Prof. 1978–84, Prof. 1984–92, Kappa Alpha Prof. of English 1992–. *Publications:* poetry: Zirconia Poems 1969, The Voice in the Crosshairs 1971, Red Owl 1972, Land Diving 1976, Trunk & Thicket 1978, Groundwork 1979, Bronze Age 1981, At the Edge of the Orchard Country 1987, Sigodlin 1990, Green River: New and Selected Poems 1991, Wild Peavines: Poems 1996; fiction: The Blue Valleys: A Collection of Stories 1989, The Mountains Won't Remember Us and Other Stories 1992, The Hinterlands: A Mountain Tale in Three Parts 1994, The Truest Pleasure 1995, Gap Creek 1999, The Balm of Gilead Trec: New and Selected Stories 1999, Topsoil Road 2000, This Rock 2001, Brave Enemies: A Novel of the American Revolution 2003, The Strange Attractor: New and Selected Poems 2004; non-fiction: Good Measure: Essays, Interviews and Notes on Poetry 1993. *Honours:* Nat. Endowment for the Arts Fellowships 1968, 1974, 1981, 1987, Southern Poetry Review Prize 1975, Eunice Tietjins Award 1979, Jacaranda Review Fiction Prize 1988, Guggenheim Fellowship 1988–89, Amon Liner Prize 1989, James G. Hanes Poetry Prize 1991, North Carolina Award in Literature 1991, Southern Book Award 2000, Fellowship of Southern Writers 2005–, Award in Literature, American Acad. of Arts and Letters 2007, Thomas Wolfe Prize 2008, North Carolina Literary Hall of Fame 2010, Frances Hobson Prize 2011. *Address:* 1608 Hanshaw Road, Ithaca, NY 14850 (home); Department of English, 363 Goldwin Smith Hall, Cornell University, Ithaca, NY 14853, USA (office). *Telephone:* (607) 255-3503 (office). *Fax:* (607) 255-6661 (office). *E-mail:* rrm4@cornell.edu (office). *Website:* www.arts.cornell.edu/english/people/morgan (office); robert-morgan.com.

MORGAN, Robin Evonne; American author and book and magazine editor; *Global Editor, Ms. Magazine;* b. 29 Jan. 1941, Lake Worth, Fla; one c. *Education:* Columbia Univ., New York. *Career:* freelance book ed 1961–69; Ed. Grove Press 1967–70; Ed. and Columnist, World Ms. Magazine, New York 1974–87, Ed.-in-Chief 1990–93, Global Ed. 1993–; Visiting Chair. and Guest Prof., New Coll., Sarasota, FL 1973; Distinguished Visiting Scholar and Lecturer, Centre for Critical Analysis of Contemporary Culture, Rutgers Univ. 1987; Distinguished Visiting Scholar, Univ. of Denver 1995; Special Adviser to Gen. Ass. Conf. on Gender, UN Int. School 1985–86; Special Consultant UN Cttee, UN Convention to End All Forms of Discrimination Against Women, Brazil 1987; organized first feminist demonstration against Miss America Pageant 1968; Co-founder and mem. Bd of Dirs Feminist Women's Health Network, Nat. Battered Women's Refuge Network, Nat.

Network Rape Crisis Centers, Women's Media Center; f. Sisterhood Is Global (think-tank) 1984, Officer 1989–97, Chair. Advisory Bd 1997–; Founding mem. Nat. Museum of Women in Arts; mem. advisory bd Equality Now; co-f. and bd mem., The Women's Media Center 2005; co-f. GlobalSister.org; mem. Bd of Dirs Women's Foreign Policy Council; mem. Feminist Writers' Guild, Media Women, Women's Action Alliance, N America Feminist Coalition, Pan Arab Feminist Solidarity Asscn; Grantee Writer-in-Residence Yaddo 1980, Nat. Endowment for Arts 1979–80, Ford Foundation 1982, 1983, 1984. *Publications include:* poetry: Monster 1972, Lady of the Beasts 1976, Death Benefits 1981, Depth Perception 1982, Upstairs in the Garden 1990, A Hot January 1999; non-fiction: Sisterhood is Powerful: An Anthology of Writings from the Women's Liberation Movement (compiler and ed.) 1970, Going Too Far: The Personal Chronicle of a Feminist 1978, The Anatomy of Freedom: Feminism, Physics and Global Politics 1982, Sisterhood is Global: The International Women's Movement Anthology (compiler and ed.) 1984, The Demon Lover: The Roots of Terrorism 1989, The Word of a Woman 1994, A Woman's Creed 1995, Saturday's Child: A Memoir 2000, Sisterhood is Forever: The Women's Anthology for A New Millennium 2003, Fighting Words: A Tool Kit for Combating the Religious Right 2006; fiction: Dry Your Smile: A Novel 1987, The Mer-Child: A Legend for Children and Other Adults 1991, The Burning Time 2006. *Honours:* Hon. DHL (Connecticut) 1992; Front Page Journalism Award, National Endowment for the Arts Prize (Poetry), Equality Now Human Rights Award, and numerous other awards. *E-mail:* carolnewton@robinmorgan.us (office); info@robinmorgan.us (office). *Website:* www.robinmorgan.us.

MORGAN, Robin Richard; British journalist, editor and writer; *CEO, Robin Morgan Media Ltd;* b. 16 Sept. 1953, Stourbridge, West Midlands, England; two s. one d. *Career:* Ed.-in-Chief Sunday Express 1989–91; Editorial Dir designate, The Readers Digest 1993–94; Ed. The Sunday Times Magazine 1995–2009; CEO Robin Morgan Media Ltd 2009–. *Publications:* The Falklands War (co-author) 1982, Bullion (co-author) 1983, Rainbow Warrior (co-author) 1986, Manpower (ed.) 1986, Ambush (co-author) 1988, Book of Movie Biographies (co-ed.) 1997, Sinatra: Frank and Friendly 2007, Eltonography 2008, Cliffhistory 2010. *Honours:* Campaigning Journalist of the Year 1982, 1983. *Address:* 19 South Audley Street, London, W1K 2NU, England (office). *Telephone:* (20) 7493-1900 (office). *E-mail:* morganrr@me.com (office).

MORGAN, Rozanne (see Gentle, Mary Rosalyn)

MORGAN, Susan Margaret, MA; British journalist; b. 7 Feb. 1944, Exeter; d. of Frederick Morgan and H. M. Morgan. *Education:* Redland High School for Girls, Univ. Coll. of Wales, Aberystwyth and Univ. of Essex. *Career:* teacher, Univ. of Qusqo, Cuzco, Peru 1966–68; Simultaneous Interpreter, Geneva 1968–70; freelance journalist and writer, Cen. America, N Africa, Middle East, UK 1970–. *Publication:* In Search of the Assassin (also film documentary 1988) 1991. *Address:* Garden Flat, 22 Belsize Gardens, London NW3 4LH, England. *Telephone:* (20) 7483-2817.

MORGAN-FINCH, Mihangel Ioan, (Mihangel Morgan), BA, PhD; British academic, writer and poet; b. 7 Dec. 1959, Aberdare, Wales. *Education:* University of Wales. *Career:* mem. Gorsedd Beirdd, Ynys Prydain. *Publications:* poetry: Diflaniad Fy Fi 1988, Beth Yw Rhif Ffon Duw 1991; fiction: Hen Lwybr A Storiau Eraill 1992, Saith Pechod Marwol 1993, Dirgel Ddyn 1993, Te Gyda'r Frenhines 1994, Tair Ochr y Geiniog 1996, Melog 1997, Dan Gadam Goncrit 1999, Cathod a Chwn 2000, Y Ddynes Ddirgel 2001, Pan Oeddwn Fachgen 2002, Croniclau pentre Simon 2003, Saith Pechod Marwol 2004, Digon o Fwydod 2005, Cesyll yn y Cymylau 2007; contributions: several publications. *Honours:* Prose Medal, Eisteddfod 1993. *Address:* c/o Y Lolfa, Talybont, Ceredigion SY24 5AP, Wales (office). *E-mail:* ylolfa@ylolfa.com (office). *Website:* www.ylolfa.com (office).

MORIARTY, Marilyn Frances, BA, MA, PhD; American academic and writer; *Professor of English, Hollins University;* b. 6 Jan. 1953, Fort Jackson, SC. *Education:* University of Edinburgh, University of Florida, University of California at Irvine. *Career:* Instructor in Rhetoric and Composition, Saddleback Community College, Mission Viejo, CA 1985–86; Fellow, University of California at Irvine 1991, National Humanities Center 1994; Asst Prof., Hollins University, Roanoke, 1992–98, Assoc. Prof. of English 1998–2007, Prof. of English 2007–. *Publications:* Critical Architecture and Contemporary Culture (co-ed.) 1994, Writing Science Through Critical Thinking 1997, Moses Unchained 1998; contributions: periodicals. *Honours:* First Place Award, University of Utah Novella Contest 1987, Katherine Anne Porter Prize for Fiction, Arts and Humanities Council, Tulsa 1990, Creative Non-Fiction Prize, Associated Writing Programs 1996, Peregrine Prize for Short Fiction, Amherst Writers and Artists Press 1997. *Address:* PO Box 9535, Hollins University, Roanoke, VA 24020, USA (office). *Telephone:* (540) 362-6277 (office). *E-mail:* mmoriarty@hollins.edu (office).

MÖRING, Marcel; Dutch novelist; b. 5 Sept. 1957, Enschede. *Publications:* Mendels erfenis 1990, Betaaldag 1991, Het grote verlangen (The Great Longing) 1992, De Kotzker 1993, Bederf is de weg van alle vlees (Decay is the Way of All Flesh, novella) 1994, Het derde testament 1995, In Babylon 1997, Nachtzwemmen 1998, Modelvliegen (The Dream Room) 2001, Dis (In a Dark Wood) 2006. *Honours:* Geertjan Lubberhuizen Prize for Best Debut 1990, AKO Prize 1992, two Golden Owl awards 1998, Aga Khan Prize 2000, Bordewijk Prize 2007. *Literary Agent:* c/o AP Watt Ltd, 20 John Street, London, WC1N 2DR, England. *Website:* www.marcelmoring.com.

MORITS, Yunna Petrovna; Russian poet; b. 2 June 1937, Kiev, Ukraine; m. Yuri Grigor'yevich Vasil'yev; one s. *Education:* Gorky Literary Inst. *Career:* began publishing poetry 1954; has participated in int. poetry festivals London, Cambridge, Toronto, Rotterdam, other locations; has made recordings of recitations of her poetry; mem. Russian PEN, Exec. Cttee, Russian Acad. of Natural Sciences. *Publications:* eleven collections of poetry (trans. in many languages), including The Vine 1970, With Unbleached Thread 1974, By Light of Life 1977, The Third Eye 1980, Selected Poems 1982, The Blue Flame 1985, On This High Shore 1987, In the Den of Vice 1990, The Face 2000, In This Way 2000, By the Law to the Postman Hello 2005, and six books for children including The Great Secret for a Small Company 1987, A Bunch of Cats 1997, Move Your Ears 2003; poems appeared in journal Oktyabr 1993–97; also short stories, essays, scripts for animated cartoons. *Honours:* Golden Rose, Italy 1996, Triumph Prize, Russia 2000, A. D. Sakharov Prize for Civil Courage of Writer 2004. *Address:* 129010 Moscow, Astrakhansky per. 5, Apt 76, Russia (home). *Telephone:* (495) 680-08-16 (home). *E-mail:* morits@owl.ru (home). *Website:* morits.ru.

MORITZ, Albert Frank, BA, MA, PhD; Canadian poet and writer; *Senior Lecturer, Victoria University at the University of Toronto;* b. 15 April 1947, Niles, Ohio, USA; s. of Albert Frank Moritz and Mary Elizabeth Moritz; m. Theresa Carrothers; one s. *Education:* Marquette Univ. *Career:* Asst Prof. of English, Univ. of Toronto 1986–90, Northrop Frye Visiting Lecturer in Poetry 1993–94; currently Sr Lecturer, Victoria Univ. at the Univ. of Toronto. *Publications:* Here 1975, Signs and Certainties 1979, Music and Exile 1980, Black Orchid 1982, The Pocket Canada (with Theresa Moritz) 1982, Canada Illustrated: The Art of Nineteenth-Century Engraving 1982, Between the Root and the Flower 1982, The Visitation 1983, America the Picturesque: The Art of Nineteenth-Century Engraving 1983, Stephen Leacock: A Biography (with Theresa Moritz) 1985, The Oxford Literary Guide to Canada (with Theresa Moritz) 1987, The Tradition 1986, Song of Fear 1991, Phantoms in the Ark 1992, The Ruined Cottage 1992, Mahoning 1994, A Houseboat on the Styx 1998, Conflicting Desire 1999, Rest on the Flight into Egypt 1999, The End of the Age 2000, The World's Most Dangerous Woman: A New Biography of Emma Goldman (with Theresa Moritz) 2002, Early Poems 2002, Stephen Leacock: An Extraordinary Life (with Theresa Moritz) 2002, Night Street Repairs (ReLit Award 2005) 2004, Now That You Revive 2007, The Sentinel (Griffin Prize for Poetry 2009) 2008; contribs to periodicals. *Honours:* Ingram Merrill Foundation Fellowship 1983–84, selected for Princeton Series of Contemporary Poets 1984, Guggenheim Fellowship 1990, American Acad. of Arts and Letters Award in Literature 1991, Bess Hokin Prize for Poetry 2004. *Address:* Northrop Frye Hall, Room 206, Victoria University in the University of Toronto, 73 Queens Park Crescent, Toronto, ON M5S 1K7, Canada (office). *Telephone:* (416) 585-4531 (office). *E-mail:* albert.moritz@utoronto.ca (office). *Website:* www.vicu.utoronto.ca (office).

MORLAND, Dick (see Hill, Reginald Charles)

MORLEY, Patricia Marlow, BA, MA, PhD; Canadian writer and educator; b. 25 May 1929, Toronto, ON; m. Lawrence W. Morley (divorced); three s. one d. *Education:* University of Toronto, Carleton University, University of Ottawa. *Career:* Asst Prof. of English, 1972–75, Assoc. Prof., 1975–80, Fellow, 1979–89, Prof. of English and Canadian Studies, 1980–89, Lifetime Hon. Fellow, 1989–, Simone de Beauvoir Institute, Concordia University, Montréal; mem. Writer's Union of Canada. *Publications:* The Mystery of Unity: Theme and Technique in the Novels of Patrick White, 1972; The Immoral Moralists: Hugh MacLennan and Leonard Cohen, 1972; Robertson Davies: Profiles in Canadian Drama, 1977; The Comedians: Hugh Hood and Rudy Wiebe, 1977; Morley Callaghan, 1978; Kurelek: A Biography, 1986; Margaret Laurence: The Long Journey Home, 1991; As Though Life Mattered: Leo Kennedy's Story, 1994; The Mountain is Moving: Japanese Women's Lives, 1999. Contributions: Professional and mainstream journals. *Honours:* Ottawa-Carleton Literary Award, 1988; Hon. Doctor of Sacred Letters, Thorneloe College, Laurentian University, 1992.

MORPURGO, Michael, OBE; British writer; b. 5 Oct. 1943, St Albans, Hertfordshire; m. Clare Morpurgo. *Career:* co-f., Farms for City Children project; Children's Laureate 2003–05; Writer-in-Residence, The Savoy Hotel, London 2007. *Publications include:* Beyond the Rainbow Warrior, Billy the Kid, Black Queen, Colly's Barn, Conker, Dear Olly, Escape from Shangri-La, Farm Boy, Friend or Foe, From Hearabout Hill, Grania O'Malley, Joan of Arc, Kensuke's Kingdom, King of the Cloud Forests, Long Way Home, Marble Crusher, Mr Nobody's Eyes, My Friend Walter, Out of the Ashes, Red Eyes at Night, Sam's Duck, Snakes and Ladders, The Butterfly Lion, The Nine Lives of Montezuma, The Rainbow Bear, The Sleeping Sword, The War of Jenkins' Ear, The White Horse of Zennor, The Wreck of the Zanzibar, Toro! Toro!, Twist of Gold, Waiting for Anya, War Horse, Wartman, Who's a Big Bully Then?, Why the Whales Came, Wombat Goes Walkabout, The Last Wolf 2002, Private Peaceful (Prix Sorcières for children's novel, France, Blue Peter Book Award 2005) 2003, The Amazing Story of Adolphus Tips 2005, Alone on a Wide Wide Sea 2006, On Angel Wings 2006, Born to Run 2007, Kaspar Prince of Cats 2008, Running Wild 2009, Not Bad for a Bad Lad 2010, An Elephant in the Garden 2010, Shadow 2010. *Honours:* Whitbread Children's Book Award 1995, Smarties Book Prize 1996, Bronze Prize in 6–8 years group 2003, Children's Book Awards 1996, 2000, 2002. *Literary Agent:* c/o Laura West, David Higham Associates, 5–8 Lower John Street, Golden Square, London, W1R 4HA, England. *Website:* www.davidhigham.co.uk. *Address:* c/o Harper-Collins Publishers, 77–85 Fulham Palace Road, Hammersmith, London W6

8JB, England (office). *Website:* www.harpercollins.co.uk (office); www.michaelmorpurgo.com.

MORRALL, Clare, BMus, DLit; British writer and music teacher; b. (Clare Portman), 29 July 1952, Exeter, Devon, England; two c. *Education:* Univ. of Birmingham. *Publications:* Astonishing Splashes of Colour 2003, Natural Flights of the Human Mind 2006, The Language of Others 2008, The Man who Disappeared (TV Book Club choice 2010) 2010. *Literary Agent:* c/o Laura Longrigg, MBA, 62 Grafton Way, London, W1P 5LD, England. *Telephone:* (20) 7387-2076. *E-mail:* laura@mbalit.co.uk.

MORRELL, David, BA, MA, PhD; Canadian writer; b. 24 April 1943, Kitchener, ON; m. Donna Maziarz 1965; one s. (deceased) one d. *Education:* Univ. of Waterloo, Pennsylvania State Univ. *Career:* Asst Prof. 1970–74, Assoc. Prof. 1974–77, Prof. of American Literature 1977–86, Univ. of Iowa; mem. Horror Writers of America, Writers' Guild of America, Int. Thriller Writers organization (co-pres.). *Publications:* fiction: First Blood 1972, Testament 1975, Last Reveille 1977, The Totem 1979, Blood Oath 1982, The Hundred-Year Christmas 1983, The Brotherhood of the Rose 1984, The Fraternity of the Stone 1985, Rambo (First Blood Part II) 1985, The League of Night and Fog 1987, Rambo III 1988, The Fifth Profession 1990, The Covenant of the Flame 1991, Assumed Identity 1993, Desperate Measures 1994, Extreme Denial 1996, Double Image 1998, Black Evening 1999, Burnt Sienna 2000, Long Lost 2002, The Protector 2003, Nightscape 2004, Creepers 2005, Scavenger 2006, The Spy Who Came for Christmas 2008, The Shimmer 2009; non-fiction: John Barth: An Introduction 1976, Fireflies: A Father's Tale of Love and Loss 1988, American Fiction, American Myth: Essays by Philip Young 2000, Lessons from a Lifetime of Writing: A Novelist Looks at his Craft 2002; contrib. to journals and magazines. *Honours:* hon. life mem. Special Operations Asscn, Asscn of Former Intelligence Officers; Friends of American Writers Distinguished Recognition Award 1972, Horror Writers of America Best Novella Awards 1989, 1991. *Address:* c/o Henry Morrison, PO Box 235, Beford Hills, NY 10507, USA. *Website:* www.davidmorrell.net.

MORRILL, Rev. John Stephen, DPhil, FBA; British historian and academic; *Professor of British and Irish History, University of Cambridge*; b. 12 June 1946, Manchester; s. of William Henry Morrill and Marjorie Morrill (née Ashton); m. Frances Mead 1968 (died 2007); four d. *Education:* Altrincham Grammar School, Trinity Coll., Oxford. *Career:* Research Fellow, Trinity Coll. Oxford 1970–74, Hon. Fellow 2006–; Lecturer in History, Univ. of Stirling 1974–75; Fellow, Selwyn Coll. Cambridge 1975–, Sr Tutor 1989–92, Vice-Master 1994–2005; Lecturer in History, Cambridge Univ. 1975–92, Reader in Early Modern History 1992–98, Prof. of British and Irish History 1998–; mem. Council, Royal Historical Soc. 1988–92, Vice-Pres. 1992–96; Chair. Communications and Activities Cttee, British Acad. 1998–, mem. Council 1998–, Vice-Pres. 2000–02; mem. and Trustee Arts and Humanities Research Council 2000–04, Chair. Rescue Cttee 2001–04; ordained Perm. Deacon, RC Diocese of East Anglia 1996; mem. Acad. of Finland 2001. *Publications:* Cheshire 1630–1660 1974, The Revolt of the Provinces 1976, Reactions to the English Civil War 1981, Oliver Cromwell and the English Revolution 1989, The Impact of the English Civil War 1991, Revolution and Restoration 1992, The Nature of the English Revolution 1992, The British Problem 1534–1707 1996, The Oxford Illustrated History of Tudor and Stuart Britain 1996, Revolt in the Provinces 1998, Soldiers and Statesmen of the English Revolution (co-author) 1998; 40 articles in learned journals. *Honours:* Hon. DLitt (Univ. of East Anglia) 2001; Hon. DUniv (Surrey) 2001. *Address:* Selwyn College, Cambridge, CB3 9DQ (office); 1 Bradford's Close, Bottisham, Cambridge, CB25 9DW, England (home). *Telephone:* (1223) 335895 (office); (1223) 811822 (home). *Fax:* (1223) 335837 (office). *E-mail:* jsm1000@cam.ac.uk (office).

MORRIS, Desmond John, BSc, DPhil; British zoologist; b. 24 Jan. 1928, Purton, Wilts., England; s. of Capt. Harry Howe Morris and Marjorie Morris (née Hunt); m. Ramona Joy Baulch 1952; one s. *Education:* Dauntsey's School, Wilts., Univs of Birmingham and Oxford. *Career:* zoological research worker Univ. of Oxford 1954–56; Head of Granada TV/Film Unit Zoological Soc. of London 1956–59, Curator of Mammals 1959–67; Dir Inst. of Contemporary Arts, London 1967–68; Research Fellow, Wolfson Coll., Oxford 1973–81; privately engaged in writing books on animal and human behaviour 1968–73, 1981–2011 and making TV programmes; artist; Scientific Fellow, Zoological Soc. of London. *Solo exhibitions include:* Swindon Museum and Art Gallery 1976, Galerie D'Eendt Amsterdam 1978, Mayor Gallery, London 1987, 1989, 1991, 1994, 1997, 1999, Keitelman Gallery, Brussels, 1998, Jessy Van der Velde Gallery, Antwerp 1998, Museum of Modern Art, Antwerp 2002, Solomon Gallery, Dublin 2004, Madrid 2005 and many others. *Television:* Zootime (Granada) 1956–67, Life in the Animal World (BBC) 1965–67, The Human Race (Thames TV) 1982, The Animals Roadshow (BBC) 1987–89, The Animal Contract 1989, Animal Country 1991–95, The Human Animal 1994, The Human Sexes 1997. *Publications include:* The Reproductive Behaviour of the Ten-spined Stickleback 1958, The Story of Congo 1958, Curious Creatures 1961, The Biology of Art 1962, Apes and Monkeys 1964, The Mammals: A Guide to the Living Species 1965, The Big Cats 1965, Men and Snakes (with Ramona Morris) 1965, Zootime 1966, Men and Apes (with Ramona Morris) 1966, Men and Pandas (with Ramona Morris) 1966, Primate Ethology (Ed.) 1967, The Naked Ape 1967, The Human Zoo 1969, Intimate Behaviour 1971, Manwatching: A Field-Guide to Human Behaviour 1977, Gestures, Their Origins and Distribution 1979, Animal Days (autobiography) 1979, The Giant Panda 1981, The Soccer Tribe 1981, Inrock (fiction) 1983, Bodywatching 1985, The Illustrated Naked Ape 1986, Dogwatching 1986, Catwatching 1986, The Secret Surrealist 1987, The Human Nestbuilders 1988, The Animals Roadshow 1988, Horsewatching 1988, The Animal Contract 1990, Animal-Watching 1990, Babywatching 1991, Christmas Watching 1992, The World of Animals 1993, The Naked Ape Trilogy 1994, The Human Animal 1994, Body Talk: A World Guide to Gestures 1994, The Illustrated Catwatching 1994, Illustrated Babywatching 1995, Catworld: A Feline Encyclopedia 1996, Illustrated Dogwatching 1996, The Human Sexes 1997, Illustrated Horsewatching 1998, Cool Cats: The 100 Cat Breeds of the World 1999, Cosmetic Behaviour and the Naked Ape 1999, The Naked Eye 2000, Dogs, a Dictionary of Dog Breeds 2001, People-Watching 2002, The Silent Language 2004, The Nature of Happiness 2004, The Naked Woman: A Study of the Female Body 2004, Watching: Encounters with Humans and Other Animals (autobiography) 2006, The Naked Man 2008, Baby, The Story of a Baby's First Two Years 2008, Planet Ape (with Steve Parker) 2009. *Honours:* Hon. FLS; Hon. DSc (Reading) 1998. *Address:* c/o Jonathan Cape, 20 Vauxhall Bridge Road, London, SW1V 2SA, England. *Fax:* (1865) 512103 (home). *E-mail:* dmorris@ukstudio.org (office). *Website:* www.desmond-morris.com (home).

MORRIS, Dick, BA; American political strategist, consultant and journalist; *President, Vote.com*; b. 28 Nov. 1948, New York; s. of Eugene Morris; m. Eileen McGann. *Education:* Stuyvesant High School, New York, Columbia Univ. *Career:* freelance consultant/adviser to politicians; organized poll for Bill Clinton in governorship election, Arkansas 1978; worked for Clinton's election campaigns 1980–96; political analyst, FOX News and newspaper columnist NY Post; Pres. Vote.com (polling web site). *Publications include:* Behind the Oval Office 1997, The New Prince: Machiavelli Updated for the Twenty-First Century 1999, Vote.com 1999, Power Plays 2002, Off With Their Heads 2004, Rewriting History 2004, Because He Could 2005, Condi vs. Hilary 2008, Fleeced 2008, Catastrophe 2009, 2010 Take Back America 2010. *E-mail:* dickmorris@dickmorris.com (office); comments@vote.com (office). *Website:* www.dickmorris.com; www.vote.com.

MORRIS, Edmund; American writer; b. 27 May 1940, Nairobi, Kenya; m. Sylvia Jukes Morris. *Education:* Rhodes Univ. *Publications:* The Rise of Theodore Roosevelt (Pulitzer Prize in Biography 1980) 1979, Dutch: A Memoir of Ronald Reagan 1999, Theodore Rex 2001, Beethoven: The Universal Composer 2005, Colonel Roosevelt 2010. *Honours:* Pulitzer Prize 1980, American Book Award 1980, Los Angeles Times Book Award for Biography 2002. *Address:* 222 Central Park S, New York, NY 10019-1408, USA (home).

MORRIS, James Humphry (see Morris, Jan)

MORRIS, Jan, (James Humphry Morris), CBE, MA, FRSL; British writer; b. 2 Oct. 1926, Somerset, England. *Education:* Christ Church Coll., Oxford. *Career:* editorial staff, The Times 1951–56, The Guardian 1957–62; Commonwealth Fellowship, USA 1954; mem. Yr Academi Gymreig, Gorsedd of Bards, Welsh Nat. Eisteddfod. *Publications:* as James Morris: Coast to Coast (aka I Saw the USA) 1956, Sultan in Oman 1957, The Market of Seleukia (aka Islam Inflamed: A Middle East Picture) 1957, Coronation Everest 1958, South African Winter 1958, The Hashemite Kings 1959, Venice 1960, South America 1961, The Upstairs Donkey (juvenile) 1962, The World Bank: A Prospect (aka The Road to Huddersfield: A Journey to Five Continents) 1963, Cities 1963, The Outriders: A Liberal View of Britain 1963, The Presence of Spain 1964, Oxford 1965, Pax Britannica: The Climax of an Empire 1968, The Great Port: A Passage through New York 1969, Places 1972, Heaven's Command: An Imperial Progress 1973, Farewell the Trumpets: An Imperial Retreat 1978; as Jan Morris: Conundrum 1974, Travels 1976, The Oxford Book of Oxford 1978, Destinations: Essays from 'Rolling Stone' 1980, The Venetian Empire: A Sea Voyage 1980, My Favourite Stories of Wales 1980, The Small Oxford Book of Wales, Wales The First Place, A Venetian Bestiary 1982, The Spectacle of Empire 1982, Stones of Empire: The Buildings of the Raj 1983, Journeys 1984, The Matter of Wales: Epic Views of a Small Country 1984, Among the Cities 1985, Last Letters from Hav: Notes from a Lost City 1985, Stones of Empire: The Buildings of the Raj 1986, Scotland, The Place of Visions 1986, Manhattan, '45 1987, Hong Kong: Xianggang 1988, Pleasures of a Tangled Life 1989, Ireland Your Only Place 1990, City to City 1990, O Canada 1992, Sydney 1992, Locations 1992, Travels with Virginia Woolf (ed.) 1993, A Machynlleth Triad 1994, Fisher's Face 1995, The Princeship of Wales 1995, The World of Venice 1995, 50 Years of Europe 1997, Hong Kong: Epilogue to an Empire 1997, Lincoln: A Foreigner's Quest 1999, Our First Leader 2000, A Writer's House in Wales 2001, Trieste and the Meaning of Nowhere 2001, A Writer's World: Travels 1950–2000 2003, Hav (fiction) 2006, Portmeirion (with others) 2006, Contact! A Book of Glimpses 2009, Hav 2011. *Honours:* Hon. Fellow, Univ. Coll. Wales, Univ. of Wales, Bangor; Hon. FRIBA; Hon. Student, Christ Church Oxon.; Dr hc (Univ. of Wales) 1993, (Univ. of Glamorgan) 1996. *Literary Agent:* c/o AP Watt Ltd, 20 John Street, London, WC1N 2DR, England. *Telephone:* (20) 7405-6774. *Fax:* (20) 7831-2154. *E-mail:* apw@apwatt.co.uk. *Website:* www.apwatt.co.uk. *Address:* Trefan Morys, Llanystumdwy, Gwynedd, LL52 0LP, Wales (home). *Telephone:* (1766) 522222 (home). *E-mail:* janmorris1@msn.com (home).

MORRIS, Janet Ellen, (Casey Prescott, Daniel Stryker); American writer; b. 25 May 1946, Boston, MA; m. 31 Oct. 1970. *Career:* mem. SFWA; MWA; New York Acad. of Science; National Intelligence Study Center; Asscn of Old Crows. *Publications:* Silistra Quartet, 1976–78, 1983–84; Dream Dance Trilogy, 1980–83; I the Sun, 1984; Heroes in Hell, 10 vols, 1984–88; Beyond Sanctuary, 3 vols, 1985–86; Warlord, 1986; The Little Helliad, 1986; Outpassage, 1987; Kill Ratio, 1987; City at the Edge of Time, 1988; Tempus

Vabound, 1989; Target (with David Drake), 1989; Warrior's Edge, 1990; Threshold, 1991; Trust Territory, 1992; American Warrior, 1992; The Stalk, 1994. Contributions: various publications. *Honours:* Hellva Award for Best Novel, 1985.

MORRIS, Mark, (J. M. Morris), BA; British writer; b. 15 June 1963, Bolsover, Derbyshire; m. Nel Whatmore 1990; one s. one d. *Education:* Trinity and All Saints Coll., Horsforth, Leeds. *Career:* full-time writer 1988–; mem. British Fantasy Soc. *Publications:* fiction: Toady 1989, Stitch 1991, The Immaculate 1993, The Secret of Anatomy 1994, Close to the Bone (short stories) 1995, Mr Bad Face 1996, Longbarrow 1997, Doctor Who: The Bodysnatchers 1997, Genesis 1999, Doctor Who: Deep Blue 1999, The Dogs 2001, The Uglimen 2002, Fiddleback (as J. M. Morris) 2002, Nowhere Near An Angel 2005, Stumps 2005, Doctor Who: Forever Summer 2007, The Deluge 2007; non-fiction: Cinema Macabre 2006; works included in numerous anthologies; contrib. to several magazines including Fear, Interzone, Million, SFX, The Third Alternative, The Dark Side, Me, Skeleton Crew, Beyond, Subterranean. *E-mail:* mark@markmorriswriter.com (office). *Website:* www.markmorriswriter.com.

MORRIS, Mary, BA, MA, MPhil; American writer; *Professor, Sarah Lawrence College;* b. 14 May 1947, Chicago, Ill.; m. Larry O'Connor 1989; one d. *Education:* Tufts Coll., Columbia Univ. *Career:* teacher, Princeton Univ. 1980–87, 1991–94, New York Univ. 1988–94, Sarah Lawrence Coll. 1994–; mem. American PEN, Authors' Guild, Friends of the American Acad. in Rome. *Publications:* Vanishing Animals 1978, The Bus of Dreams 1985, Nothing to Declare: Memoirs of a Woman Travelling Alone 1989, The Waiting Room 1991, Wall to Wall: From Beijing to Berlin by Rail 1992, A Mother's Love 1993, Maiden Voyages 1993, House Arrest 1996, The Lifeguard 1997, Angels and Aliens 1998, Acts of God 2000, Revenge 2004; contribs to periodicals. *Honours:* Guggenheim Fellowship 1980, Rome Prize 1981. *Literary Agent:* Ellen Levine, Trident Media Group, 41 Madison Avenue, New York, NY 10010, USA. *E-mail:* mmorris348@yahoo.com. *Website:* www.marymorris.net.

MORRIS, Mary Joan McGarry; American writer; b. 1943, Meriden, CT; m. Michael Morris 1962; one s. four d. *Education:* Univ. of Vermont, Univ. of Massachusetts. *Publications:* Vanished 1988, A Dangerous Woman 1991, Songs in Ordinary Time 1995, Fiona Range 2000, A Hole in the Universe 2004, The Lost Mother 2005, The Last Secret 2009; contrib. to periodicals. *E-mail:* mary@marymcgarrymorris.com (office). *Website:* www.marymcgarrymorris.com.

MORRIS, Sara (see Burke, John Frederick)

MORRIS, Stephen; British artist, poet and writer; b. 14 Aug. 1935, Smethwick; m. 1963 (divorced 1989); one s. two d. *Education:* Moseley Art School, Fircroft Coll., Marie Borgs Folk High School, Univs of Cardiff and Leicester. *Career:* ed. student newspaper, Univ. of Cardiff 1961–62; Asst Lecturer, Univ. of Wolverhampton 1967–69, Lecturer 1969–72, Sr Lecturer 1972–86; full-time artist 1986–; commissioned by British Art Medal Soc. to produce a medal 2003. *Film:* To Forgive the Unforgivable 1996. *Exhibitions:* 70 solo exhbns of painting and sculpture. *Publications:* poetry: The Revolutionary 1972, The Kingfisher Catcher 1974, Death of a Clown 1976, The Moment of Truth 1978, Too Long at the Circus 1980, Rolling Dice 1986, To Forgive the Unforgivable 1997, Twelve 1998, Limbus of the Moon 2005, Thingy Magigs 2009, Nil Carborundum 2010; other: Lord of Death (play) 1963; contribs to Guardian, Observer, Peace News, Rolling Stone, Sunday Times, Tribune. *Honours:* elected to be a Companion of the Guild of St George 2001. *Address:* 4 rue Las Cours, Aspiran, L'Herault 34800, France (home). *E-mail:* palehorse-publishing@hotmail.com (office), morris.stephen@wanadoo.fr (home). *Website:* www.stephen-morris.net.

MORRISON, Dorothy Jean Allison, MA, DipEd, FSA; Scottish author and lecturer; b. 17 Feb. 1933, Glasgow; m. James F. T. Morrison 1955; one s. one d. *Education:* Univ. of Glasgow. *Career:* Principal Teacher of History, Montrose Acad., 1968–73; Lecturer in History, Dundee Coll. of Educ., 1973–83; Adviser to Scottish History series, History at Hand series, Scotland's War series, Scottish TV; mem. Church and Nation Cttee, Church of Scotland, 1996–; Netherbow Council for the Arts, Church of Scotland, 2000. *Publications:* Old Age, 1972; Young People, 1973; Health and Hospitals, 1973; The Civilian War (with M. Cuthbert), 1975; Travelling in China, 1977; The Romans in Britain, 1978; Billy Leaves Home, 1979; Story of Scotland (with J. Halliday), I, 1979, 1980, II, 1982; The Great War, 1914–18, 1981; Historical Sources for Schools, I Agriculture, 1982; History Around You, 1983; People of Scotland, I, 1983, II, 1985; Ancient Greeks (with John Morrison), 1984; Handbook on Money Management, 1985; Modern China, 1987; The Rise of Modern China, 1988; Montrose Old Church – A History, 1991; Scotland's War, 1992; A Sense of History – Castles, 1994; Ancient Scotland, 1996; The Wars of Independence, 1996; Changed Days in Montrose (with Isobel Reynolds), 1999; The Lifeboat: 200 Years of Service, 2000; Rural Schools in Angus (with Isobel Reynolds), 2003. *Address:* Craigview House, Usan, Montrose, Angus, DD10 9SD, Scotland. *Telephone:* (1674) 672639 (home). *Fax:* (1674) 672639 (home). *E-mail:* d.j.morrison@talk21.com (home).

MORRISON, (Philip) Blake, BA, MA, PhD, FRSL; British author, poet and dramatist; *Professor of Creative and Life Writing, Goldsmith's College;* b. 8 Oct. 1950, Burnley, Lancs.; m. Katherine Ann Drake 1976; two s. one d. *Education:* Univ. of Nottingham, McMaster Univ., Canada, Univ. Coll., London. *Career:* Poetry and Fiction Ed. Times Literary Supplement 1978–81; Deputy Literary Ed. The Observer 1981–86, Literary Ed. 1987–89; Literary Ed. The Independent on Sunday 1990–94; Prof. of Creative and Life Writing, Goldsmiths Coll., London 2003–. *Publications:* The Movement: English Poetry and Fiction of the 1950s 1980, Seamus Heaney 1982, Penguin Book of Contemporary British Poetry (ed. with Andrew Motion) 1982, Dark Glasses (poems) 1984, The Ballad of the Yorkshire Ripper and Other Poems 1987, The Yellow House (juvenile) 1987, And When Did You Last See Your Father? (memoir) 1993, The Cracked Pot: A Play, after Heinrich von Kleist 1996, As If: A Crime, a Trial, a Question of Childhood 1997, Too True (essays and stories) 1998, Dr Ox's Experiment (libretto) 1998, Selected Poems 1999, The Justification of Johann Gutenberg (novel) 2000, Things My Mother Never Told Me (memoir) 2002, Oedipus/Antigone (drama) 2003, South of the River 2008, The Last Weekend 2010, We Are Three Sisters (play) 2011. *Honours:* Eric Gregory Award 1980, Somerset Maugham Award 1984, Dylan Thomas Prize 1985, E. M. Forster Award 1988, J. R. Ackerley Prize 1994. *Address:* 54 Blackheath Park, London, SE3 9SJ, England (office). *Telephone:* (20) 7919-7514 (office). *E-mail:* blakemorr@aol.com (office).

MORRISON, Sally, BSc; Australian writer; b. 29 June 1946, Sydney, NSW; one s. *Education:* Australian National University. *Career:* mem. Fellowship of Australian Writers; Australian Society of Authors; Victorian Writers Centre. *Publications:* Who's Taking You to the Dance? (novel), 1979; I Am a Boat (short stories), 1989; Mad Meg (novel), 1994. Contributions: Bulletin; Australian Literary Supplement; Overland; Quadrant; Island; Sydney Morning Herald; Age Monthly Review. *Honours:* Project Assistance Grants, Victorian Ministry of the Arts, 1988, 1993, 1994; Writer's Grants, Australia Council Literary Board, 1990, 1991, 1992; National Book Council Banjo Award for Fiction, 1995.

MORRISON, Toni, MA; American novelist and academic; *Goheen Professor in the Humanities Emerita, Princeton University;* b. (Chloe Anthony Wofford), 18 Feb. 1931, Lorain, Ohio; d. of George Wofford and Ella Ramah (Willis) Wofford; m. Harold Morrison 1958 (divorced 1964); two c. *Education:* Lorain High School, Howard Univ., Cornell Univ. *Career:* taught English and Humanities, Tex. Southern Univ. 1955–57, Howard Univ. 1957–64; Ed., then Sr Ed. Random House, New York 1965–85; Assoc. Prof. of English, State Univ. of New York 1971–72, Schweitzer Prof. of the Humanities 1984–89; Robert F. Goheen Prof. of the Humanities, Princeton Univ. 1989–, now Emer.; Visiting Lecturer Yale Univ. 1976–77, Bard Coll. 1986–88; Clark Lecturer Trinity Cambridge 1990; Massey Lecturer Harvard Univ. 1990; mem. Council, Authors Guild, American Acad. of Arts and Sciences, American Acad. of Arts and Letters, Authors League of America, Nat. Council on the Arts. *Publications:* The Bluest Eye 1970, Sula 1974, The Black Book (ed) 1974, Song of Solomon 1977, Tar Baby 1983, Dreaming Emmett (play) 1986, Beloved 1987 (Pulitzer Prize and Robert F. Kennedy Book Award 1988), Jazz 1992, Playing in the Dark: Whiteness and the Literary Imagination (lectures) 1992, Race-ing Justice, En-gendering Power (ed, essays) 1992, Honey and Rue (song cycle) 1993, Nobel Prize Speech 1994, Birth of a Nation'hood: Gaze, Script and Spectacle in the O. J. Simpson Trial 1997, Paradise 1998, Collected Essays of James Baldwin (ed) 1998, Love 2003, A Mercy 2008, Home 2011; co-author, for children: The Big Box (poems) 1999, The Book of Mean People 2002, The Ant or the Grasshopper, The Lion or the Mouse 2003, Beloved 2004, Sula 2004, Peeny Butter Fudge 2009, Little Cloud and Lady Wind 2010. *Honours:* Commdr Ordre des Arts et des Lettres; Ohioana Book Award 1975, American Acad. and Inst. of Arts and Letters Award 1977, Nat. Book Critics Circle Awards 1977, 1997, NY State Gov.'s Arts Award 1987, Nobel Prize for Literature 1993, Nat. Book Foundation Medal 1995, Nat. Humanities Medal 2000, Presidential Medal of Freedom 2012. *Address:* Program in Creative Writing, Princeton University, Room 305, 185 Nassau Street, Princeton, NJ 08544, USA (office). *Telephone:* (609) 258-1071 (office). *Fax:* (609) 258-1454 (office). *Website:* www.princeton.edu (office).

MORRISON, Anthony (Tony) James, BSc; British writer; *Director, South American Pictures;* b. 5 July 1936, Gosport; m. Elizabeth Marion Davies 1965; one s. one d. *Education:* Univ. of Bristol. *Career:* Partner, South American Pictures; Dir, Nonesuch Expeditions Ltd. *Publications:* Steps to a Fortune (co-author) 1967, Animal Migration 1973, Land Above the Clouds 1974, The Andes 1976, Pathways to the Gods 1978, Lizzie: A Victorian Lady's Amazon Adventure (co-ed.) 1985, The Mystery of the Nasca Lines 1987, Margaret Mee: In Search of Flowers of the Amazon (ed.) 1988, QOSQO: Navel of the World 1995, Peru: Country of Contrasts 2001. *Address:* 48 Station Road, Woodbridge, Suffolk IP12 4AT, England (home). *Telephone:* (1394) 383963 (office). *E-mail:* info@nonesuchexpeditions.com (office). *Website:* www.nonesuchexpeditions.com (office).

MORTIER, Erwin; Belgian writer and poet; b. 28 Nov. 1965, Nevele, Ghent. *Education:* Ghent Univ. *Career:* research asst, Museum of the History of Psychiatry, Ghent 1991–99; Poet Laureate, City of Ghent 2005–07; regular columnist for newspapers including De Morgen, De Volkskrant, and literary journals De Gids, De Revisor, Tzum. *Publications:* novels: Marcel (Van Der Hoogt Prize) 1999, Mijn tweede huid (trans. as My Second Skin) 2000, Sluitertijd (trans. as Shutter Speed) 2002, Alle dagen samen 2004, Godenslaap 2008; poetry: Vergeten licht 2001, Uit één vinger valt men niet 2005, Voor de stand en de wereld. Alle gedichten tot dusver 2009. *Honours:* Gerard Walschapprijs 1999, Vlaamse Debuutprijs 2000, Vanderhoogtprijs 2000, Academia Debutantenprijs 2000, Gouden Ezelsoor 2000, Cees Buddingh'prijs 2001, Ako Literatuurprijs 2009. *Address:* c/o Uitgeverij De Bezige Bij bv, Van Miereveldstraat 1, 1071 DW Amsterdam, Netherlands (office). *E-mail:* info@

debezigebij.nl (office). *Website:* www.debezigebij.nl (office); www.erwinmortier.be.

MORTON, Colin Todd, MA; Canadian novelist, poet and editor; b. 26 July 1948, Toronto; m. Mary Lee Bragg 1969; one s. *Education:* Univs of Calgary and Alberta. *Career:* Creative Writing Instructor, Algonquin Coll. 1993–94; Writer-in-Residence, Concordia Coll. 1995–96, Connecticut Coll. 1997; mem. League of Canadian Poets (Vice-Pres. 2000–01). *Play:* The Cabbage of Paradise 1988. *Film:* Primiti Too Taa 1987. *Publications:* poetry: In Transit 1981, This Won't Last Forever 1985, Word/Music (cassette with First Draft) 1986, North/South (with A. McClure and S. McMaster) 1987, The Merzbook: Kurt Schwitters Poems 1987, Two Decades: From A Century of Inventions 1987, How to Be Born Again 1992, Coastlines of the Archipelago 2000, Dance, Misery 2003, The Cabbage of Paradise 2007; novel: Oceans Apart 1995; contribs to reviews and journals; anthologies, including Capital Poets 1989, In the Clear 1998, Vintage '94 1995, Waging Peace 2002, In Fine Form 2005. *Honours:* Third Prize, CBC Radio Literary Competition 1984, Archibald Lampman Award 1986, Best Soundtrack, ASIFA East Film Festival, New York 1988, Bronze Apple, Nat. Educational Film and Video Festival 1988, Second Prizes for prose poem, Short Grain Contest 1989, postcard fiction 1990, Archibald Lampman Award for Poetry 2001. *Address:* 40 Grove Avenue, Ottawa, ON K1S 3A6, Canada. *E-mail:* cmorton@sympatico.ca (home). *Website:* www3.sympatico.ca/cmorton.

MORTON, Frederic, BS, MA; American/Austrian author; b. 5 Oct. 1924, Vienna, Austria; m. Marcia Colman 1957; one d. *Education:* Coll. of the City of New York, New School for Social Research, New York. *Career:* Contributing Ed., Vanity Fair 2003–; mem. Authors' Guild, PEN Club. *Publications:* The Rothschilds (also Broadway musical 1972) 1962, A Nervous Splendour (also musical, premiered in Budapest 2006) 1978, The Forever Street 1987, Thunder at Twilight 1991, Runaway Waltz 2005; contributions: newspapers and journals. *Honours:* Author of the Year Award, Anti Defamation League, USA 1963; City of Vienna Gold Medal of Honour 2001; Cross of Honour in Arts and Letters, Repub. of Austria 2003. *Literary Agent:* Gersh Agency, 41 Madison Avenue, 33rd Floor, New York, NY 10010, USA. *Telephone:* (212) 997-1818. *Website:* www.gershagency.com.

MORTON, G. L. (see Fryer, Jonathan)

MORTON, Henry (Harry) Albert, BA, BEd, MA, PhD; New Zealand academic (retd) and writer; b. 20 July 1925, Gladstone, MB, Canada. *Education:* University of Manitoba, University of Cambridge, University of Otago, New Zealand. *Career:* mem. Blenheim Club; New Zealand Society of Authors; Royal New Zealand Airforce Asscn. *Publications:* And Now New Zealand, 1969; The Wind Commands, 1975; Which Way New Zealand, 1975; Why Not Together?, 1978; The Whale's Wake, 1982; The Farthest Corner, 1988. *Honours:* Sir James Wattie Award, Book of the Year, 1976.

MOSEBACH, Martin; German writer and journalist; b. 1951, Frankfurt am Main. *Career:* regular contributor, Frankfurter Allgemeine Zeitung newspaper. *Publications:* novels: Das Bett 1983, Ruppertshain 1985, 1992, Stilleben mit wildem Tier 1995, Das Grab der Pulcinellen 1996, Die schöne Gewohnheit zu leben 1997, Die Türkin 1999, Eine lange Nacht 2000, Der Nebelfürst 2001, Das Beben 2005, Der Mond und das Mädchen 2007; other: Blaubart: Drama giocoso 1985, Rotkäppchen und der Wolf (verse drama) 1988, Das Kissenbuch 1995, Oberon (libretto for opera by Weber) 1997, Du sollst dir ein Bild machen (essays) 2005, Schöne Literatur (essays) 2006, Häresie der Formlosigkeit (trans. as The Heresy of Formlessness: The Roman Liturgy and Its Enemy) 2007, Ultima ratio regis 2007, Stadt der wilden Hunde 2008. *Honours:* Heimito von Doderer prize 1999, Heinrich von Kleist Prize 2002, Georg Büchner Prize 2007. *Address:* c/o Carl Hanser Verlag GmbH & Co. KG, Kolbergerstrasse 22, 81679 Munich, Germany (office). *Telephone:* (89) 99830-0 (office). *Fax:* (89) 99830-460 (office). *E-mail:* info@hanser.de (office). *Website:* www.hanser.de (office); www.martin-mosebach.de.

MOSES, Daniel David, BA, MFA; Canadian writer, dramatist and poet; b. 18 Feb. 1952, Ohsweken, Ont. *Education:* York University, University of British Columbia. *Career:* Instructor in Creative Writing, University of British Columbia 1990; Instructor in Playwrighting, Graduate Drama Centre, University of Toronto 1992; Resident Artist, Banff Centre for the Arts 1993; Writer-in-Residence, University of Western Ontario 1994, University of Windsor 1995–96; mem. League of Canadian Poets, Playwrights Union of Canada, Writers' Guild of Canada, Writers' Union of Canada. *Publications:* Plays: The Dreaming Beauty, 1989; Coyote City, 1991; Almighty Voice and His Wife, 1992; The Indian Medicine Shows, 1995. Poetry: Delicate Bodies, 1980; The White Line; other: An Anthology of Canadian Native Literature in English (co-ed.) 1992. *Honours:* First Prize, Theatre Canada National Playwrighting Competition 1990, Winner, New Play Centre Playwrighting Competition 1994.

MOSLEY, Nicholas (see Ravensdale, 3rd Baron)

MOSLEY, Walter; American writer; b. 1952, Los Angeles; m. Joy Kellman 1987 (divorced). *Education:* Goddard Coll., Johnson State Coll., City Coll. CUNY. *Career:* Artist-in-Residence Africana Studies Inst., New York Univ. 1996; mem. Bd of Dirs Nat. Book Awards, Poetry Soc. of America –2007; Past Pres. Mystery Writers of America. *Publications include:* Devil in a Blue Dress (Shamus Award) 1990, A Red Death 1991, White Butterfly 1992, Black Betty 1994, RL's Dream 1995, A Little Yellow Dog 1996, Gone Fishin' 1997, Always Outnumbered, Always Outgunned 1997, Blue Light 1998, Walkin' the Dog 1999, Fearless Jones 2001, Futureland: Nine Stories of an Imminent Future 2001, Bad Boy Brawly Brown 2002, Fear Itself 2003, Six Easy Pieces (short stories) 2003, What Next: An African American Initiative Toward World Peace 2003, The Man in My Basement 2004, Little Scarlet 2004, Cinnamon Kiss 2005, 47 (for young adults) 2006, Fortunate Son 2006, Killing Johnny Fry 2007, This Year You Write Your Novel 2007, Blonde Faith 2007, Diablerie 2008, The Long Fall 2009, Known to Evil 2010, The Last Days of Ptolemy Grey 2010; contribs to New York Times, Library of Contemporary Thought, New Yorker, GQ, Esquire, USA Weekend, Los Angeles Times Magazine, Savoy. *Honours:* American Library Asscn Literary Award 1996, O. Henry Award 1996, Anisfield Wolf Award 1996, TransAfrica Int. Literary Prize 1998. *Address:* c/o W. W. Norton, 500 Fifth Avenue, Floor 6, New York, NY 10110, USA (office). *Website:* www.waltermosley.com.

MOSS, Norman Bernard; British writer and journalist; b. 30 Sept. 1928, London; m. Hilary Sesta 1963; two s. *Education:* Hamilton Coll., New York. *Career:* Staff Journalist with newspapers, news agencies and radio networks; mem. Int. Inst. of Strategic Studies, Soc. of Authors. *Publications:* Men Who Play God – The Story of the Hydrogen Bomb 1968, A British-American Dictionary 1972, The Pleasures of Deception 1976, The Politics of Uranium 1982, Klaus Fuchs: The Man Who Stole the Atom Bomb 1987, Managing the Planet 2000, 19 Weeks: America, Britain and the Fateful Summer of 1940 2003, Picking Up the Reins: America, Britain and the Postwar World 2009. *Honours:* Magazine Writer of the Year, Periodical Publishers Asscn 1982. *Address:* 21 Rylett Crescent, London, W12 9RP, England. *E-mail:* norman.moss@homecall.co.uk (office).

MOSSE, Kate, BA, MA, FRSA; British writer and broadcaster; *Co-founder, Orange Prize for Fiction;* m. Greg Mosse; two c. *Education:* Chichester High School for Girls, New Coll., Oxford. *Career:* fmr publisher, Random House; Deputy Dir, Chichester Festival Theatre, W Sussex 1998–2001; co-founder and Hon. Dir, Orange Prize for Fiction 1996–; Chair., Orange Futures initiative; creator and writer-in-residence of creative writing and reading website, www.labyrinth.co.uk; Co-Dir, Mosse Associates, provider of creative writing workshops; judge of numerous literary competitions and awards; Trustee, Arts & Business; mem. Inst. of Dirs, South West Sussex Arts Group, Arts Council of England South East (council mem.). *Radio:* The Business of the Arts (series, BBC Radio 4), guest presenter Saturday Review (BBC Radio 4). *Television:* presenter Readers and Writers Roadshow (BBC4). *Publications:* fiction: Eskimo Kissing 1996, Crucifix Lane 1998, Labyrinth (British Book Awards Richard and Judy Best Read of the Year 2006) 2005, Sepulchre 2007, The Winter Ghosts 2010; non-fiction: Becoming a Mother 1993, The House: Behind the Scenes at the Royal Opera House, Covent Garden 1995; contrib. short stories and articles to magazines and newspapers. *Honours:* Hon. MA (Chichester) 2006; European Woman of Achievement for contribution to the arts 2000. *Website:* www.katemosse.com; www.orangeprize.co.uk.

MOSTEGHANEMI, Ahlam, BA, PhD; Algerian poet and novelist; b. 13 April 1953, Algiers; d. of Mohammed Chérif; m.; three c. *Education:* Univ. of Algiers, Sorbonne Univ., Paris, France. *Career:* worked for Centre Arabe de Documentation et d'Information, Paris, France; broadcast daily programme on poetry on Algerian radio; wrote for the Ech-Chaâb newspaper. *Publications:* Aâla marfaâ el-ayam (poems, trans. as Au hâvre des jours) 1973, Kitaba fi lahdat ouâr (poems, trans. as L'Écriture dans un moment de nudité) 1976, Femmes et écritures (essays) 1985, Zakirat al-jassed (novel, trans. as Memory in the Flesh) (Naguib Mahfouz Medal for Literature) 1985, Faoud al-hawess (novel, trans. as Chaos of the Senses) 1997, Akhadib samaka (poems, trans. as Mensonges d'un poisson) 1993, Aber Sereer (novel) 2003. *Honours:* Damascus Medal of Honour, Syria 2000, Pioneers of Lebanon Committee Medal 2004, Algerian Medal of Honour 2006, Forbes Magazine Most Successful Arabic Writer 2008, Shield of Beirut 2009. *Address:* POB 113, 5734 Beirut, Lebanon. *E-mail:* ahlem2@mosteghanemi.com.

MOTION, Sir Andrew Peter, Kt, MLitt, FRSA; British biographer and poet; b. 26 Oct. 1952, London, England; s. of Andrew R. Motion and Catherine G. Motion; m. 1st Joanna J. Powell 1973 (divorced 1983); m. 2nd Janet Elisabeth Dalley 1985; two s. one d. *Education:* Radley Coll. and Univ. Coll., Oxford. *Career:* Lecturer in English, Univ. of Hull 1977–81; Ed. Poetry Review 1981–83; Poetry Ed. Chatto & Windus 1983–89, Editorial Dir 1985–87; Prof. of Creative Writing Univ. of E Anglia, Norwich 1995–2003; Chair. Literature Advisory Panel Arts Council of England 1986–98; Poet Laureate 1999–2009; Chair of Creative Writing, Royal Holloway Coll., Univ. Coll. London 2003–; Chair., Museums, Libraries and Archives Council 2008–; Chair. Man Booker Prize jury 2010; mem. Poetry Soc. (Vice-Pres.). *Publications:* poetry collections: The Pleasure Steamers 1978, Independence 1981, The Penguin Book of Contemporary British Poetry (ed., anthology) 1982, Secret Narratives 1983, Dangerous Play (Rhys Memorial Prize) 1984, Natural Causes 1987, Love in a Life 1991, The Price of Everything 1994, Salt Water 1997, Selected Poems 1996–97 1998, Public Property 2001, Here to Eternity: An Anthology of Poetry (ed.) 2001, The Cinder Path 2009; poems as Poet Laureate: Remember This: An Elegy on the Death of HM Queen Elizabeth The Queen Mother 2002, A Hymn for the Golden Jubilee 2002, On the Record (for Prince William's 21st birthday) 2003, Spring Wedding (for the wedding of Prince Charles and Camilla Parker Bowles) 2005, The Golden Rule (anthem for 80th birthday of HM Queen Elizabeth II, with music by Sir Peter Maxwell-Davies) 2006, Diamond Wedding (for the Diamond Wedding Anniversary of HM Queen Elizabeth II and HR Duke of Edinburgh) 2007; non-fiction: The Poetry of Edward Thomas 1981, Philip Larkin 1982, The Lamberts (Somerset

Maugham Award 1987) 1986, Philip Larkin: A Writer's Life 1993, William Barnes Selected Poems (ed.) 1994, Keats 1997, Wainewright the Poisoner 2000, In the Blood: A Memoir of my Childhood 2006, Ways of Life: Selected Essays and Reviews, 1994–2006 2008; fiction: The Pale Companion 1989, Famous for the Creatures 1991, The Invention of Dr Cake 2003; other: additional texts for a performance of Haydn's Seven Last Words of Our Saviour on the Cross 2003. *Honours:* Hon. DLitt (Hull) 1996, (Exeter) 1999, (Brunel) 2000, (A.P.U.) 2001, (Open Univ.) 2002; Arvon/Observer Prize 1982, Dylan Thomas Award 1987, Whitbread Biography Award 1993. *Address:* c/o Faber & Faber, Bloomsbury House, 74–77 Great Russell Street, London, WC1B 3DA, England. *Website:* www.faber.co.uk.

MOTT, Michael Charles Alston, BA; British academic, writer and poet; *Professor Emeritus, Bowling Green State University;* b. 8 Dec. 1930, London; m. 1st Margaret Ann Watt 1961 (died 1990); two d.; m. 2nd Emma Lou Powers 1992. *Education:* Central School of Arts and Crafts, London, Law Soc., London, Univ. of London, Courtauld Inst. and Warburg Inst., London. *Career:* Ed., Air Freight 1954–59, Thames and Hudson Publrs 1961–64; Asst Ed., Adam International Review 1956–66, The Geographical Magazine 1964–66; Poetry Ed., The Kenyon Review 1966–70; Visiting Prof. and Writer-in-Residence, Kenyon Coll. 1966–70, SUNY at Buffalo 1968, Concordia Univ., Montréal, QC, Canada 1970, 1974, Emory Univ. 1970–77, Coll. of William and Mary 1978–79, 1985–86; Prof. of English, Bowling Green State Univ. 1980–92, Prof. Emer. 1992–; mem. Amnesty Int., Kilvert Soc., RGS. *Publications:* fiction: The Notebooks of Susan Berry 1962, Master Entrick 1964, Helmet and Wasps 1964, The Blind Cross 1968; poetry: Absence of Unicorns, Presence of Lions 1977, Counting the Grasses 1980, Corday 1986, Piero di Cosimo: The World of Infinite Possibility 1990, Taino 1992, Woman and the Sea: Selected Poems 1999; The World of Richard Dadd, 2005; non-fiction: The Seven Mountains of Thomas Merton 1984; contrib. to journals and newspapers, including TLS. *Honours:* Hon. DLitt (St Mary's Coll., Notre Dame) 1983; Governor's Award in Fine Arts, State of Georgia 1974, Guggenheim Fellowship 1979–80, Christopher Award 1984, Ohioana Book Award 1985, Olscamp Research Award 1985, Nancy Dasher Book Award 1985, Fortsam Award 1999, Allen Tate Award in Poetry 2002, Robert E. Lee and Ruth I. Wilson Poetry Book Award 2004. *Address:* 122 The Colony, Williamsburg, VA 23185, USA (office). *Telephone:* (757) 220-1042 (office).

MOTTA, Federico; Italian publisher; *Managing Director, Federico Motta Editore;* b. Milan. *Career:* Man. Dir Federico Motta Editore; Pres. Associazione Italiana Editori. *Honours:* Officier, Ordre des Arts et des Lettres 2003. *Address:* Gruppo Editoriale Motta, Via Branda Castiglioni 7, 20156 Milan, Italy (office). *Telephone:* (02) 300761 (office). *Fax:* (02) 38010046 (office). *E-mail:* info@mottaeditore.it (office). *Website:* www.mottaeditore.it (office).

MOUGEOTTE, Etienne Pierre Albert; French journalist; *Editor-in-Chief, Le Figaro Magazine;* b. 1 March 1940, La Rochefoucauld; s. of Jean Mougeotte and Marcelle Thonon; m. Françoise Duprilot 1972; one s. two d. *Education:* Lycée Buffon, Lycée Henri-IV, Paris, Inst. d'études politiques de Paris, Inst. Français de presse. *Career:* reporter, France-Inter 1965-66, Beirut Corresp. 1966–67; Ed. Europe Numéro 1 1968–69; Chief Reporter, Asst Ed.-in-Chief Information Première (TV) 1969–72; Producer l'Actualité en question 1972; journalist Radio-Télé Luxembourg 1972–73; Ed.-in-Chief Europe 1 1973, News Dir 1974–81; monthly contrib. Paradoxes 1974–; Editorial Dir Journal du Dimanche 1981–83, Télé 7 Jours 1983–87; Dir Gen. Broadcasting TF1 1987–89, Dir Gen. 1987–89, Vice-Pres. Broadcasting 1989–; Vice-Pres. French Fed. of Press Agencies 1975–81; mem. Interprofessional communication group (Gic) 1985–87; Pres. Nat. Videocommunication Syndicate 1982–87, TF1 Films, Tricom; Dir TF1 1991–2007; Pres. TF1 Films Productions; Dir TF1 Films 1991–2007, Pres. TF1 Films and TF1 Digital 2000–07; Assoc. Prof. École de Journalisme, Univ. of Paris Sciences Po 2004–; Ed.-in-Chief Le Figaro Magazine 2007–. *Honours:* Officier Légion d'honneur, Ordre nat. du Mérite. *Address:* Société du Figaro SA, 14 boulevard Haussman, 75009 Paris, France (office). *Website:* www.lefigaro.fr/lefigaromagazine (office).

MOUNT, (William Robert) Ferdinand, MA, FRSL, FSA; British writer and journalist; b. 2 July 1939, London; s. of the late Robert Mount and Julia Mount; m. Julia Margaret Lucas 1968; two s. (one deceased), one d. *Education:* Eton Coll., Christ Church, Oxford. *Career:* Political Ed., The Spectator 1977–82, 1985, Literary Ed. 1984–85; Head, Prime Minister's Policy Unit 1982–84; Dir, Centre for Policy Studies 1984–91; Political Columnist, The Standard 1980–82, The Times 1984–85, Daily Telegraph 1985–90; Ed., Times Literary Supplement 1991–2002; Sr Columnist, The Sunday Times 2002–04; Vice-Chair., Power Comm. 2004–05; mem. RSL (mem. of Council 2002–05). *Publications:* Very Like a Whale 1967, The Theatre of Politics 1972, The Man Who Rode Ampersand 1975, The Clique 1978, The Subversive Family 1982, The Selkirk Strip 1987, Of Love and Asthma 1991 (Hawthornden Prize 1992), The British Constitution Now 1992, Communism 1992, Umbrella 1994, The Liquidator 1995, Jem (and Sam) 1998, Fairness 2001, Mind the Gap: The New Class Divide in Britain 2004, Heads You Win 2004, The Condor's Head 2007, Cold Cream: My Early Life and Other Mistakes 2008, Full Circle: How the Classical World Came Back to Us 2010. *Honours:* Hon. Fellow (Univ. of Wales, Lampeter) 2002. *Address:* 17 Ripplevale Grove, London, N1 1HS, England (home). *Telephone:* (20) 7607-5398 (home).

MOWAT, Farley McGill, OC, BA; Canadian writer; b. 12 May 1921, Belleville, Ont.; s. of Angus Mowat and Helen Mowat (née Thomson); m. 1st Frances Mowat 1947; two s.; m. 2nd Claire Mowat 1963. *Education:* Toronto Univ. *Career:* served in the Canadian Army 1939–45; Arctic exploration 1947–49; full-time writer 1950–. *Publications:* People of The Deer 1952, The Regiment 1955, Lost in The Barrens 1956, The Dog Who Wouldn't Be 1957, Coppermine Journey 1958, The Grey Seas Under 1958, The Desperate People 1959, Ordeal by Ice 1960, Owls in the Family 1961, The Serpent's Coil 1961, The Black Joke 1962, Never Cry Wolf 1963, Westviking 1965, The Curse of the Viking Grave 1966, Canada North 1967, The Polar Passion 1967, This Rock Within the Sea 1968, The Boat Who Wouldn't Float 1969, Sibir 1970, A Whale for the Killing 1972, Tundra 1973, Wake of the Great Sealers (with David Blackwood) 1973, The Snow Walker 1975, Canada North Now 1976, And No Birds Sang 1979, The World of Farley Mowat 1980, Sea of Slaughter 1984, My Discovery of America 1985, Virunga (Woman in the Mist, USA) 1987, The New Founde Land 1989, Rescue the Earth 1990, My Father's Son 1992, Born Naked 1993, Aftermath 1995, A Farley Mowat Reader 1997; TV documentary: Sea of Slaughter 1990, The Farfarers 1998, Walking on the Land 2000, High Latitudes 2002, No Man's River 2004, Bay of Spirits 2006, Otherwise 2008. *Honours:* Hon. DLitt (Laurentian Univ.) 1970, (Univ. of Victoria) 1982, (Lakehead Univ.) 1986, (Univ. Coll. of Cape Breton) 1996; Hon. DLaws (Lethbridge, Toronto, Prince Edward Island, Queen's Univ.); Hon. DH (McMaster Univ., Hamilton) 1994; Hon. LLD (Queen's Univ.) 1995; Gov.-Gen.'s Award, Canadian Centennial Medal, Leacock Medal for Humour, Hans Christian Andersen Award, Anisfield Wolf Award, Mark Twain Award, Gemini Award (Best Documentary Script), Award of Excellence (Atlantic Film Festival) 1990, Canadian Achievers Award, Take Back the Nation Award, Council of Canadians 1991, Author's Award, Author of the Year, Foundation for Advancement of Canadian Letters 1993, Fourth Nat. Prize for Foreign Literature Books, Beiyue Literature and Art Publishing House, People's Repub. of China 1999, Jubilee Commemorative Medal 2002, Nat. Outdoor Book Award for Lifetime Achievement 2005. *Address:* 18 King Street, Port Hope, ON, L1A 2R4, Canada.

MOYERS, William (Bill) D., FAAS; American journalist and broadcaster; *Executive Editor, Public Affairs Television, Inc.;* b. 5 June 1934, Hugo, Okla; s. of Henry Moyers and Ruby Johnson; m. Judith Davidson 1954; two s. one d. *Education:* Univ. of Texas, Edinburgh Univ. and Southwestern Baptist Theological Seminary. *Career:* Exec. Asst to Senator Lyndon Johnson 1959–60; Assoc. Dir US Peace Corps 1961–63, Deputy Dir 1963; Special Asst to Pres. Johnson 1963–66, Press Sec. to Pres. 1965–66; Publr of Newsday, Long Island, NY 1966–70; host of This Week, weekly current affairs TV programme 1970; Ed.-in-Chief Bill Moyers Journal, Public Broadcasting Service 1971–76, 1978–81; Contrib. Newsweek 1974–76; Chief Corresp. CBS Reports 1976–78, Sr News Analyst, CBS News 1981–86; Exec. Ed. Public Affairs TV Inc. 1987–; news analyst, NBC News 1995–; Pres. Florence and John Schumann Foundation 1991–; mem. American Philosophical Soc. *Publications:* Listening to America 1971, The Secret Government 1988, Joseph Campbell and the Power of Myth 1988, A World of Ideas 1989, Healing and the Mind 1993, Genesis: A Living Conversion 1996, Fooling with Words 1999. *Honours:* Emmy Awards 1983–90, Gold Baton Award 1991, 1999, American Jewish Cttee Religious Liberty Award 1995, Walter Cronkite Award 1995, Fred Friendly First Amendment Award 1995, Charles Frankel Prize 1997, George Peabody Award 2000. *Address:* Public Affairs Television Inc., 450 West 33rd Street, New York, NY 10001, USA.

MOYES, Jojo, BA, MA; British writer and journalist; b. 1969, London; m. Charles Arthur; three c. *Education:* Royal Holloway and New Bedford Coll., London, City Univ. *Career:* fmr arts and media correspondent, The Independent newspaper; contrib. to Woman's Hour (BBC Radio 4). *Publications:* Sheltering Rain 2002, Foreign Fruit (aka Windfallen) (RNA Novel of the Year 2004) 2003, The Peacock Emporium 2004, The Ship of Brides 2005, Silver Bay 2007, Night Music 2008, The Horse Dancer 2009, The Last Letter from Your Lover 2010. *Literary Agent:* c/o Sheila Crowley, Curtis Brown, Haymarket House, 28–29 Haymarket, London, SW1Y 4SP, England. *Telephone:* (20) 7393-4400. *Fax:* (20) 7393-4401. *E-mail:* cb@curtisbrown.co.uk. *Website:* www.curtisbrown.co.uk; www.jojomoyes.com.

MTSHALI, Oswald (Joseph) Mbuyiseni; South African poet and journalist; b. 1940, KwaBhanya, N Natal. *Education:* Columbia Univ., USA. *Career:* travelled to Johannesburg aged 18 to enrol at the Univ. of Witwatersrand, but was refused because of separate univs legislation; worked as messenger in Soweto; studied in USA, returning to S Africa 1980; fmr Vice-Principal, Pace Coll., Soweto; fmr Adjunct Prof., New York City Coll. of Tech., teaching African folklore and modern African history. *Publications:* Sounds of a Cowhide Drum (poems) 1971, Poems: The Soweto I Love 1977, Fireflames (poems) 1980; contrib. to journals, newspapers and anthologies, including The Classic, New Coin, The Purple Renoster, Ophir. *Honours:* Poetry Int. Award, London 1973, Olive Schreiner Prize for Literature 1975.

MU XIN; Chinese writer, poet and artist; b. (Sun Pu), 1927, Wuzhen, Zhejiang Prov. *Education:* Shanghai Fine Arts Inst. *Career:* imprisoned three times during Cultural Revolution; many manuscripts and paintings destroyed by authorities; moved to USA 1982. *Exhibitions:* The Art of Mu Xin: Landscape Paintings and Prison Notes (toured galleries including Smart Museum of Art, Chicago 2002, Asia Soc., New York 2003, Yale Univ. Art Gallery, Harvard Univ. Art Gallery), other exhbns at World Econ. Forum, China Business Summit 2004. *Publications:* Sanwen Yiji 1983, Qionmeika Suixianglu 1986, Wensha Muyuan (short stories) 1988, Xibanya Sankeshu (poems) 1988, Jixing Panduan (essays) 1988, Suli Zhi Wang (prose poems) 1994, Balong (poems) 1998, Wo fenfen de qingyu (poems) 1998, Hui wu zhong (poems) 1998, Malage

Jihua (essays) 1999, Tongqing zhongduanlu (short stories) 1999. *Address:* c/o Elizabeth Wang Gallery, 800 Fifth Avenue, New York, NY 10065-7216, USA (office). *E-mail:* ewanggallery@aol.com (office). *Website:* www.elizabethwanggallery.com (office).

MUAMBA, Muepu; Democratic Republic of the Congo journalist, writer and poet; b. 23 Nov. 1946, Tshilundu. *Education:* Institut St Ferdinand, Jernappes, Belgium. *Career:* mem. Maison Africaine de la Poesie Internationale, Dakar; Royal African Society, London; Société Française des Gens de Lettres, Paris; Union Internale des Journalistes et de la Presse de la Langue Française, Paris. *Publications:* Afrika in eigener Sache (essays with Jochen Klicker and Klaus Paysan), 1980; Devoir d'ingerence, 1988; Moi Qui T'Amour, 1997; Ma Terre d'O, 1999. Contributions: various anthologies and periodicals.

MUBARAK, Rabia'; Moroccan writer; *Professor, Université Mohammed V Souissi*; b. 1940. *Career:* currently Prof., Université Mohammed V Souissi, Rabat. *Publications include:* Attayyibun (The Good Ones) 1972, Dar wa Dukhkhan (A House and Smoke) 1975, Rufqata Assilah'i wa Lqamar (In the Company of Weapons and the Moon) 1976, Arrih' Ashshatwiyya (The Winter Rain) 1977, Rih'alat Al-H'asad wa Al-H'ubb (Voyage of Harvest and Love) 1983, Badru Zamanihi (Full Moon of his Time) 1984, Burju Assua'ud (Tower of Fortunes) 1990; other: short stories, plays, novels, children's books, psychological studies on childhood. *Address:* c/o Université Mohammed V Souissi, BP 8007, N. U. Agdal, Rabat, Morocco.

MUDIMBE, Valentin-Yves, (Hermano Mateo); American academic and writer; *Newman Ivey White Professor of Literature, Duke University*; b. 8 Dec. 1941, Likasi Jadotville, Belgian Congo (now the Democratic Repub. of the Congo). *Education:* Univ. of Lovanium, Belgian Congo, Catholic Univ. of Louvain, Belgium, Univ. of Besançon and Univ. of Paris, France. *Career:* specialist in phenomenology and structuralism; fmr Lecturer, Univs of Louvain, Paris-Nanterre, Zaïre, Haverford Coll., Stanford Univ.; Assoc. Dir of Studies, Ecole des Hautes-Etudes, Paris 1988–99; Louis H. Jordan Lecturer, SOAS, Univ. of London, UK; Samuel Fischer Prof., Free Univ. of Berlin, Germany; Commonwealth Prof., Univ. of Cambridge, UK; currently Newman Ivey White Prof. of Literature, Duke Univ., NC; Visiting Prof., El Colegio de Mexico, Univ. of Antioquia, Colombia, Univ. of Cologne, Germany, Univ. of Warwick, UK; Gen.-Sec. Soc. for African Philosophy in N America (SAPINA) 1988–99; Chair. Int. African Inst., Univ. of London; Corresp. mem. Belgian Acad. of Overseas Sciences 1978–2006, Hon. Corresp. mem. 2006–. *Publications include:* L'odeur du père 1982, The Invention of Africa 1988, Parables and Fables 1991, Le corps glorieux des mots et des êtres 1994, The Idea of Africa 1994, Tales of Faith 1997; editor: The Surreptitious Speech 1992, Nations, Identities, Cultures 1997, Diaspora and Immigration (with Sabine Engel) 1999, Cheminements 1999, The Normal & Its Orders (with Gode Iwele and Laura Kerr) 2006; co-editor: Africa and the Disciplines (with Robert H. Bates and Jean O'Barr) 1993; 70 articles; three collections of poetry, four novels. *Honours:* Chevalier de la Pléiade, Ordre de la Francophonie et du Dialogue des Cultures 1997; Dr hc (Université de Paris VII-Denis Diderot), (La Chancellerie des Universités de Paris, Sorbonne) 1997, (Katholieke Universiteit Leuven) 2006. *Address:* Duke University, Literature Program, 101 Friedl Bldg, Box 90670, Durham, NC 27708, USA (office). *Telephone:* (919) 684-4240 (office). *Fax:* (919) 684-3598 (office). *E-mail:* mwr079@gmail.com (office).

MUEENUDDIN, Daniyal, MFA; Pakistani/American lawyer and writer; b. April 1963, Los Angeles; s. of Ghulam Mueenuddin and Barbara Mueenuddin; m. 1st Rachel Jeanne Harris 1999; m. 2nd Cecilie Brenden Mueenuddin. *Education:* Dartmouth Coll., Yale Univ. Law School, Univ. of Arizona at Tucson. *Career:* grew up in Lahore, Pakistan and Elroy, Wis., USA; practised law with Debevoise & Plimpton, New York 1998–2001; now lives on family farm in southern Punjab, Pakistan. *Publications:* short story collection: In Other Rooms, Other Wonders (short stories) (The Story Prize 2009, Commonwealth Writers' Prize for Best First Book, Europe and South Asia 2010) 2009; short stories include: Our Lady of Paris 2006, Nawabdin Electrician 2007, A Spoiled Man 2008, Provide, Provide 2008; contrib. stories to Granta, Zoetrope, The New Yorker, Best American Short Stories of 2008 (selected by Salman Rushdie), PEN/O. Henry Prize Stories 2010. *Honours:* Fulbright Scholarship, Norway, American Acad. of Arts and Letters Rosenthal Family Foundation Award 2010. *Literary Agent:* c/o Bill Clegg, William Morris Agency, 1325 Avenue of the Americas, New York, NY 10019, USA. *E-mail:* bc@wma.com. *E-mail:* inotherrooms@gmail.com (home). *Website:* inotherrooms.com.

MUEHL, Lois Baker, BA, MA; American academic (retd), writer and poet; b. 29 April 1920, Oak Park, IL; m. Siegmar Muehl 1944; two s. two d. *Education:* Oberlin Coll., Univ. of Iowa. *Career:* fmr Assoc. Prof. of Rhetoric; mem. Iowa Poetry Asscn, Univ. Women's Writers Group. *Publications:* My Name is... 1959, Worst Room in the School 1961, The Hidden Year of Devlin Bates 1967, Winter Holiday Brainteasers 1979, A Reading Approach to Rhetoric 1983, Trading Cultures in the Classroom (with Siegmar Muehl) 1993, Talkable Tales 1993; poems; contrib. to scholarly journals and general magazines. *Honours:* Old Gold Creative Fellowship 1970, Community Service Commendation, Merced, California 1984, grand prize Poetry Guild Contest 1997, Lyrical Iowa Poetry Prize for humour 2005. *Address:* 701 Oaknoll Drive, Iowa City, IA 52246, USA.

MUELLER, Lisel, BA; American poet, writer and translator; b. 8 Feb. 1924, Hamburg, Germany; m. Paul E. Mueller 1943; two d. *Education:* Univ. of Evansville, Indiana Univ. *Career:* instructor in poetry, Elmhurst Coll. 1969–72; associated with poets in the schools programme 1972–77; Visiting Prof., Goddard Coll. and Warren Wilson Coll. 1977–86. *Publications:* poetry: Dependencies 1965, Life of a Queen 1970, The Private Life 1976, Voices from the Forest 1977, The Need to Hold Still 1980, Second Language 1986, Waving from Shore 1989, Learning to Play by Ear (essays and poetry) 1990, Alive Together (Pulitzer Prize for Poetry 1997) 1996; contrib. to anthologies and journals. *Honours:* Dr hc (Lake Forest Coll.) 1985; Friends of Literature Robert M. Ferguson Memorial Award 1966, Helen Bullis Awards 1974, 1977, Lamont Poetry Selection 1975, Emily Clark Balch Award 1976, Nat. Book Award 1981, Nat. Endowment for the Arts Fellowship 1990, Carl Sandburg Award 1990, Ruth Lilly Poetry Prize 2002. *Address:* c/o Louisiana State University Press, PO Box 25053, Baton Rouge, LA 70894-5053, USA.

MUGGESON, Margaret Elizabeth, (Margaret Dickinson, Everatt Jackson); British writer; b. 30 April 1942, Gainsborough, Lincolnshire, England; m. Dennis Muggeson 1964, two d. *Education:* Lincoln College of Technology. *Career:* mem. Romantic Novelists Asscn. *Publications:* Pride of the Courtneys 1968, Brackenbeck 1969, Portrait of Jonathan 1970, The Road to Hell (as Everatt Jackson) 1975, Abbeyford Trilogy 1981, Lifeboat! 1983, Beloved Enemy 1984, Plough the Furrow 1994, Sow the Seed 1995, Reap the Harvest 1996, The Miller's Daughter 1997, Chaff Upon the Wind 1998, The Fisher Lass 1999, The Tulip Girl 2000, The River Folk 2001, Tangled Threads 2002, Twisted Strands 2003, Red Sky in the Morning 2004, Without Sun 2005, Wish Me Luck 2007, Sing As We Go 2008, Suffragette Girl 2009. *Address:* 17 Seacroft Drive, Skegness, Lincolnshire PE25 3AP, England (home).

MUHLSTEIN, Anka; French author and biographer; b. 1935, Paris; m. Louis Begley 1974. *Career:* settled in New York 1974; author of biographies on Queen Victoria, James de Rothschild, Queen Elizabeth I, Mary Stuart and others. *Publications include:* Par les yeux de Marcel Proust 1971, La Femme Soleil 1976, Victoria 1978, Baron James: The Rise of the French Rothschilds 1983, Manhattan 1986, A Taste for Freedom: The Life of Astolphe de Custine (Goncourt Prize for Biography 1996) 1996, Reines éphémères, Mères perpètuelles 2001, Les Périls du Mariage (aka Elizabeth I and Mary Stuart: On the Perils of Marriage) 2004, Napoléon à Moscou 2007, Garcon, un cent d'huîtres (aka Balzac's Omelette) 2011; with Louis Begley: Venice for Lovers (essays) 2005. *Honours:* two History Prizes, Académie Française. *Address:* c/o Editions Odile Jacob, 15 rue Soufflot, 75240 Paris, cedex 05, France (office). *Telephone:* (1) 44-61-64-84 (office). *Website:* www.odilejacob.fr (office).

MUIR, Richard, MA, PhD; British writer, photographer, lecturer, editor and researcher; b. 18 June 1943, Yorkshire; m.; one s. *Education:* Univ. of Aberdeen. *Career:* Ed. Nat. Trust Regional Histories and Countryside Comm. Nat. Park Series; founder LANDSCAPES Journal 2000; Hon. Research Fellow in Geography and Environment, Univ. of Aberdeen; self-employed landscape historian and archaeologist. *Publications include:* Modern Political Geography 1975, Hedgerows: Their History and Wildlife (with N. Muir) 1987, Old Yorkshire 1987, The Countryside Encyclopaedia 1988, Fields (with Nina Muir) 1989, Portraits of the Past 1989, The Dales of Yorkshire 1991, The Villages of England 1992, The Coastlines of Britain 1993, Political Geography: A New Introduction 1997, The Yorkshire Countryside: A Landscape History 1997, Approaches to Landscape 1999, The New Reading the Landscape 2000, Landscape Detective 2001, Landscape Encyclopaedia 2004, Ancient Trees, Living Landscapes 2005, Valley of Ghosts 2006; contrib. to academic journals and general periodicals. *Honours:* Yorkshire Arts Literary Prize 1982–83, hon. life mem. Yorkshire Dales Soc. 2004–. *Address:* 20 Stray Walk, Harrogate, Yorkshire, HG2 8HU, England (home). *Telephone:* (1423) 529343 (home). *E-mail:* richard.muir1@btinternet.com (home). *Website:* www.richardmuir.net.

MUJAHID, Jamila; Afghan journalist and broadcaster; *President, Afghanistan Women in Media Network*; b. Kabul; m. Sayed Amin; five c. *Education:* in Afghanistan. *Career:* broadcaster with Radio-Television Afghanistan from 1980, evening news broadcaster on TV and radio 1985–96; worked for NGOs during Taleban regime; first female broadcaster to appear on Radio-Television Afghanistan announcing the departure of the Taleban 2001; Pres., Afghanistan Women in Media Network, Kabul 2002–, publishing monthly magazine, Hefat and running 'The Voice of Afghan Women' radio station (Dir of radio station 2003, relaunched 2005–); Ed., Malalai women's magazine 2003–. *Address:* Afghanistan Women in Media Network, Afghan Media and Culture Centre, Behind Ministry of Planning, Malik Ashgar Crossroads, Kabul, Kabul Province, Afghanistan (office). *E-mail:* ainakabul@ainaworld.org (office).

MUJICA, Barbara, AB, MA, PhD; American academic and writer; *Professor of Spanish, Georgetown University*; b. 25 Dec. 1943, Los Angeles, Calif.; m. Mauro E. Mujica 1966; one s. two d. *Education:* Univ. of California, Los Angeles, Middlebury Grad. School, Paris, New York Univ. *Career:* Teacher of French, UCLA Extension Div. 1963–64; Assoc. Ed. of Modern Languages, Harcourt Brace Jovanovich, New York City 1966–73; Instructor, Baruch College, CUNY 1973–74, Asst Prof. of Romance Languages 1974; Asst Prof., Georgetown Univ. 1974–79, Assoc. Prof. 1979–91, Prof. of Spanish 1991–; Ed.-in-Chief Comedia Performance; mem. American Asscn of Teachers of Spanish and Portuguese, American Asscn of Univ. Profs, American Council on the Teaching of Foreign Languages, Asscn for Hispanic Classical Theater (Pres. Emer.), Feministas Unidas, Modern Language Asscn, Washington Ind. Writers, Writer's Center, S Atlantic Modern Language Asscn, Golden Age Division (Sec. 1999, Pres. 2000), PEN International, Nat. Writers Union,

Asociación de Escritoras de España y las Américas. *Publications:* scholarly: Readings in Spanish Literature (co-ed. with Anthony Zahareas) 1975, Calderón's Characters: An Existential Point of View 1983, Expanding the Curriculum in Foreign Language Classes: Spanish and Contemporary Affairs (with William Cressey and Mark Goldin) 1983, Iberian Pastoral Characters 1986, Texto y espectáculo: Selected Proceedings of the Symposium on Spanish Golden Age Theater 1987, 1989, Texto y vida: Introducción a la literatura española 1990, Antología de literatura española, Vol. I, La Edad Media (with Amanda Curry) 1991, Vol. II, Renacimiento y Siglo de Oro 1991, Vol. III, Siglos XVIII y XIX (with Eva Florensa) 1999, Et in Arcadia Ego: Essays on Death in the Pastoral Novel (with Bruno Damiani) 1990, Texto y vida: Introducción a la literatura hispanoamericana 1992, Looking at the Comedia in the Year of the Quincentennial (co-ed. with Sharon Voros) 1993, Premio Nóbel: Once grandes escritores del mundo hispánico (ed.) 1997, Books of the Americas: Reviews and Interviews from Americas Magazine 1990–1991 1997, El texto puesto en escena (ed. with Anita Stoll) 2000, Hispanomundo 2001, Early Modern Spanish Women Writers 2004, Teresa de Jesús: Espiritualidad y feminismo 2006, Teresa de Avila: Lettered Woman 2009, Texts and Playtexts: A New Anthology of Early Modern Spanish Theater 2010; other: The Deaths of Don Bernardo (novel) 1990, Sanchez across the Street (short stories) 1997, Far from My Mother's Home (short stories) 1999, Frida (novel) (Trailblazers Award, Dialogue on Diversity Award 2004) 2001, Affirmative Actions (novel) 2006, Sister Teresa 2007; contrib. to anthologies, scholarly publs and the popular press. *Honours:* Poets and Writers Recognition for Fiction, New York 1984, One of Best Fifty Op Ed Pieces of the Decade, New York Times 1990, Winner, E. L. Doctorow Int. Fiction Contest 1992, Pangolin Prize for Best Short Story of 1998, Theodore Christian Hoepfner Award for Short Fiction 2002. *Literary Agent:* c/o Anna Ghosh, Scovil, Galen, Ghosh Literary Agency, 276 Fifth Avenue, Suite 708, New York, NY 10001, USA. *Telephone:* (212) 679-8686. *Fax:* (212) 679-6710. *E-mail:* annaghosh@sgglit.com. *Website:* www.sgglit.com. *Address:* Department of Spanish and Portuguese, Georgetown University, Box 571039, Washington, DC 20057, USA (office). *Telephone:* (202) 687-5778 (office). *Fax:* (301) 365-0502 (office). *E-mail:* mujica@georgetown.edu (office). *Website:* www.barbaramujica.com.

MUKHERJEE, Bharati, BA, MA, MFA, PhD; American (b. Indian) academic and writer; *Professor, English Department, University of California, Berkeley*; b. 27 July 1940, Kolkata; d. of Sudhir Lal Mukherjee and Bina Banerjee; m. Clark Blaise 1963; two s. *Education:* Univs of Calcutta, Baroda and Iowa. *Career:* fmr Prof. of English, McGill Univ., Montréal, Lecturer, Skidmore Coll.; Lecturer in Literature and Creative Writing, Queen's Coll., New York; Prof., Univ. of Calif., Berkeley 1990–. *Publications:* The Tiger's Daughter 1971, The Tiger's Daughter and Wife 1975, Days and Nights in Calcutta (with Clark Blaise) 1977, Darkness 1985, The Sorrow and the Terror (with Clark Blaise) 1987, The Middleman and Other Stories (Nat. Book Critics Circle Award for Fiction 1988) 1988, Jasmine 1989, The Holder of the World 1993, Leave it to Me 1996, Desirable Daughters 2002, The Tree Bride 2004. *Address:* English Department, University of California, 334 Wheeler Hall, Berkeley, CA 94720 (office); 130 Rivoli Street, San Francisco, CA 94117, USA. *Telephone:* (510) 642-2765 (office); (415) 681-0345. *Fax:* (415) 759-9810. *E-mail:* mukhster@aol.com. *Website:* english.berkeley.edu (office).

MUKHERJEE, Mani Sankar, (Sankar); Indian writer; b. Bongaon. *Education:* Univ. of Calcutta. *Career:* Bengali writer. *Publications include:* novels (in Bengali): Kato Ajanare 1954, Chowringhee 1962, Swarga Martya Patal (short stories), Gharer Madhye Ghar, Nagar Andini, Bamlara Meye, Simanta Sambada, Kamana Basana, Purohit Darpan, Sri Sri Ramkrishner Rahsyamrito, Mane Pare, Samrat O Sundari, Carana Chumye Yai, Yabara Belaya, Mathar Opor Cchadh, Patabhumi, Rasabati, Kamana Basana, Shonar Sansar, Cchayacchabi, Muktir Swadh, Charan Chunye Jai (vols one and two); also biographies, travelogues. *Address:* c/o Marketing and Promotions Department, Penguin Books India Pvt. Ltd, 11 Community Centre, Panchsheel Park, New Delhi 110 017, India (office).

MUKHERJEE, Siddhartha; American (b. Indian) physician, academic and writer; *Assistant Professor of Medicine, Columbia University*; b. 1970, New Delhi, India; m. Sarah Sze; two d. *Education:* Stanford Univ., Harvard Medical School, Oxford Univ., UK. *Career:* Asst Prof. of Medicine, Columbia Univ., Staff Cancer Physician, Columbia Univ. Medical Center. *Publications:* The Emperor of All Maladies: A Biography of Cancer (Pulitzer Prize for Nonfiction 2011, Guardian First Book Award 2011) 2010; contrib. articles in Nature, The New England Journal of Medicine, The New York Times and The New Republic. *Address:* c/o Scribner Publicity Department, Simon & Schuster, 1230 Avenue of the Americas, New York, NY 10020, USA (office).

MUKUNDAN, M.; Indian short story writer and novelist; b. 10 Sept. 1942, Mayyazhi, Mahe, Kerala. *Career:* Malayalam writer; Deputy Cultural Attaché, French Embassy in New Delhi, India; Pres. Kerala Sahitya Akademi. *Publications include:* novels and collections of short stories: Delhi (novel) 1969, Mayyazhi Puzhayude Theerangalil (trans. as On the Banks of the Mayyazhi) (M P Paul Award, Muttath Varkey Award), Daivathinte Vikrithikal (trans. as God's Mischief) (Kendra Sahithya Acad. Award, N.V. Prize), Appam Chudunna Kunkiyamma, Lesli Achante Kadangal, Ee Lokam Athiloru Manushyan, Nrittam (trans. as Dance) (Kerala Sahitya Akademi Award), Adithyanum Radhayum Mattu Chilarum, Oru Dalit Yuvathiyude Kadanakatha, Nirtham, Haridwaril Manikal Muzhangunnu (trans. as The Bells are Tolling in Haridwar), Kesavante Vilapanghal, Pravasam, Unnikatha (Katha Award 2003). *Honours:* Chevalier, Ordre des Arts et des Lettres 1998; Crossword Award, Kerala State Award. *Address:* Kerala Sahitya Akademi, Thrissur 680 020, India (office). *Telephone:* (487) 2331069 (office). *Fax:* (487) 2331069 (office). *Website:* www.keralasahityaakademi.org (office).

MULDOON, Paul Benedict, BA, FRSL; Irish poet, academic and editor; *Howard G. B. Clark '21 University Professor in the Humanities and Professor of Creative Writing, Princeton University*; b. 20 June 1951, Portadown, Northern Ireland; s. of Patrick Muldoon and Brigid Regan; m. Jean Hanff Korelitz 1987; one s. one d. *Education:* St Patrick's Coll., Armagh, Queen's Univ., Belfast. *Career:* radio and TV producer, BBC NI 1973–86; has taught at Univs of Cambridge, East Anglia, Columbia Univ., New York, Univ. of California, Berkeley, Univ. of Massachusetts, Univ. of St Andrews, Univ. of Ulster; Lecturer, Princeton Univ., NJ 1987–88, 1990–95, Dir Creative Writing Program 19932–2002, Prof. 1995–, Howard G. B. Clark '21 Prof. in the Humanities and Prof. of Creative Writing 1998–; Founding Chair. Lewis Center for the Arts 2006–12; Founder Princeton Poetry Festival 2009–; Visiting Prof., Bread Loaf School of English 1997–2010; Poetry Ed. The New Yorker 2007–; mem. Aosdána, American Acad. of Arts and Sciences 2000–, American Acad. of Arts and Letters 2008–. *Publications:* poetry: Knowing My Place 1971, New Weather 1973, Spirit of Dawn 1975, Mules 1977, Names and Addresses 1978, Immram 1980, Why Brownlee Left 1980, Out of Siberia 1982, Quoof 1983, The Wishbone 1984, Selected Poems 1968–83 1986, Meeting the British 1987, Madoc: A Mystery 1990, Incantata 1994, The Prince of the Quotidian 1994, The Annals of Chile (T. S. Eliot Prize) 1995, Kerry Slides 1996, New Selected Poems 1968–1994 1996, Hopewell Haiku 1997, The Bangle (Slight Return) 1998, Hay (poems) 1999, Poems 1968–1998 2001, Horse Latitudes 2006, Plan B (with Norman McBeath) 2009, Wayside Shrines 2009, Maggot 2010; for children: The O-O's Party 1981, The Last Thesaurus 1995, The Noctuary of Narcissus Batt 1997; other: Monkeys (TV play) 1989, Shining Brow (opera libretto) 1993, Six Honest Serving Men (play) 1995, Bandanna (opera libretto) 1999, To Ireland, I (essays) 2000; ed.: The Scrake of Dawn 1979, The Faber Book of Contemporary Irish Poetry 1986, The Essential Byron 1989, Moy Sand and Gravel (Pulitzer Prize for Poetry) 2002; trans.: The Astrakhan Cloak, by Nuala Ni Dhomhnaill 1993, The Birds, by Aristophanes (with Richard Martin) 1999. *Honours:* Hon. Prof. of Poetry, Univ. of Oxford 1999–2004; Eric Gregory Award 1972, Sir Geoffrey Faber Memorial Awards 1980, 1991, Guggenheim Fellowship 1990, American Acad. of Arts and Letters Award for Literature 1996, Irish Times Poetry Prize 1997, Pulitzer Prize for Poetry 2003, Griffin Prize 2003, American Ireland Fund Literary Award 2004, Shakespeare Prize 2004, Aspen Prize for Poetry 2005, European Prize for Poetry 2006, John William Corrington Award 2009. *Address:* Creative Writing Program, Room 122, Lewis Center for the Arts, 185 Nassau Street, Princeton University, Princeton, NJ 08544, USA (office). *Telephone:* (609) 258-4708 (office). *E-mail:* muldoon@princeton.edu (office). *Website:* www.paulmuldoon.net.

MÜLLER, Herta; German (b. Romanian) writer; b. 17 Aug. 1953, Nitzkydorf, Banat, Romania; m. Richard Wagner. *Education:* Univ. of Timişoara. *Career:* as a student, involved with Aktionsgruppe Banat (authors' group opposed to Nicolae Ceauşescu's rule of Romania); worked as translator in a machine factory 1977–79; emigrated to Germany 1987; Heiner-Müller Guest Prof., Freie Universität Berlin 2005; has lectured in Germany, UK and USA; mem. German Acad. for Language and Poetry 1995–. *Publications:* Niederungen 1982, Drückender Tango: Erzählungen 1984, Der Mensch ist ein grosser Fasan auf der Welt 1986, Barfüssiger Februar: Prosa 1987, Reisende auf einem Bein 1989, Der Teufel sitzt im Spiegel 1991, Der Fuchs war damals schon der Jäger 1992, Eine warme Kartoffel ist ein warmes Bett 1992, Der Wächter nimmt seinen Kamm: vom Weggehen und Ausscheren 1993, Herztier: Roman 1994, Hunger und Seide: Essays 1995, In der Falle 1996, Heute wär ich mir lieber nicht begegnet 1997, Der fremde Blick oder Das Leben ist ein Furz in der Laterne 1999, Im Haarknoten wohnt eine Dame 2000, Heimat ist das, was gesprochen wird 2001, Der König verneigt sich und tötet 2003, Die blassen Herren mit den Mokkatassen 2005, Atemschaukel 2009 (translated as The Hunger Angel 2012). *Honours:* Kleist Preis 1994, Aristeion Prize 1995, Int. IMPAC Dublin Literary Award 1998, Franz Kafka Preis 1999, Literature Prize, Konrad Adenauer Foundation 2004, Berliner Literaturpreis 2005, Würth Preis 2005, Nobel Prize for Literature 2009, Hoffmann-von-Fallersleben-Preis 2010. *Address:* c/o Carl Hanser Verlag, Kolbergerstrasse 22, 81679 Munich, Germany (office). *E-mail:* info@hanser.de (office). *Website:* www.hanser-literaturverlage.de (office).

MULLER, Marcia, BA, MA; American writer and editor; b. 28 Sept. 1944, Detroit, MI; m. 1st Frederick T. Guilson Jr 1967 (divorced 1981); m. 2nd Bill Pronzini 1992. *Education:* Univ. of Michigan. *Publications:* Edwin of the Iron Shoes 1977, Ask the Cards a Question 1982, The Cheshire Cat's Eye 1983, The Tree of Death 1983, Games to Keep the Dark Away 1984, Leave a Message for Willie 1984, Double (with Bill Pronzini) 1984, The Legend of Slain Soldiers 1985, There's Nothing to Be Afraid of 1985, Beyond the Grave (with Bill Pronzini) 1986, The Cavalier in White 1986, The Lighthouse (with Bill Pronzini) 1987, Eye of the Storm (with Bill Prozini) 1988, There Hangs the Knife 1988, Dark Star 1989, The Shape of Dread 1989, There's Something in a Sunday 1989, Trophies and Dead Things 1990, Deceptions 1991, Where Echoes Live 1991, Pennies on a Dead Woman's Eyes 1992, The Wall 1993, Wolf in the Shadows 1993, Till the Butchers Cut Him Down 1994, A Wild and Lonely Place 1995, The McCone Files: The Complete Sharon McCone Stories 1995, The Broken Promise Land 1996, Both Ends of the Night 1997, While Other People Sleep 1998, Duo (with Bill Pronzini) 1998, A Walk Through the

Fire 1999, Listen to the Silence 2000, McCone and Friends 2000, Point Deception 2001, Dead Midnight 2002, Cyanide Wells 2003, The Dangerous Hour 2004, Cape Perdido 2005, Vanishing Point 2006, The Ever-Running Man 2007, Burn Out 2008, Locked In 2009, Coming Back 2010; editor: several anthologies. *Honours:* American Mystery Award 1989, Shamus Award 1991, Life Achievement Award, Private Eye Writers of America 1993, Anthony Boucher Awards 1994, 1996, Lifetime Achievement in Suspense Award, Romantic Times 1999, Grand Master, Mystery Writers of America 2005. *Address:* c/o Grand Central Publishing, 237 Park Avenue, New York, NY 10017, USA (office). *Website:* www.marciamuller.com.

MULLIN, Christopher John, LLB; British politician and writer; b. 12 Dec. 1947, Chelmsford, Essex, England; s. of Leslie Mullin and Teresa Mullin; m. Nguyen Thi Ngoc 1987; two d. *Education:* Univ. of Hull. *Career:* sub-ed., BBC World Service 1974–78; Ed. Tribune 1982–84; MP (Labour), Sunderland S 1987–2010; Chair. Home Affairs Select Cttee 1997–99, 2001–03; Under-Sec., Dept of the Environment 1999–2001, Dept of Int. Devt 2001, Foreign Office 2003–05, Standards and Privileges Cttee 2006–10; Chair. Heritage Lottery Fund (North East); Council mem. Churchill Memorial Trust; Trustee, North of England Civic Trust; judge, Man Booker Prize 2011. *Television:* A Very British Coup (Channel 4) 1988, Who Bombed Birmingham (Granada TV) 1991. *Publications:* fiction: A Very British Coup 1982, The Last Man Out of Saigon 1986, The Year of the Fire Monkey 1991; non-fiction: Error of Judgement: The Truth About the Birmingham Bombings 1986, 1997, A View from the Foothills, Diaries 1999–2005, Decline and Fall: Diaries 2005–2010 2010. *Honours:* hon. degrees from Univs of Essex, Hull, Newcastle, Sunderland and City Univ.. *Literary Agent:* c/o United Agents, 12–26 Lexington Street, London, W1F 0LE, England. *Telephone:* (20) 3214-0800. *Fax:* (20) 3214-0801. *E-mail:* info@unitedagents.co.uk. *Website:* unitedagents.co.uk. *E-mail:* chris@chrismullinexmp.com (office). *Website:* www.chrismullinexmp.com.

MUNGOSHI, Charles Muzuva; Zimbabwean writer, poet and playwright; b. 2 Dec. 1947, Chivhu; m. Jesesi Jaboon 1976; four s. one d. *Education:* secondary school. *Career:* clerk in bookshop, Harare 1969–74; Ed. with the Literature Bureau 1974–81; Dir and Ed. publisher in Zimbabwe 1981–88; Writer-in-Residence, Univ. of Zimbabwe 1985–87; Visiting Arts Fellow, Univ. of Durham 1990; Writer-in-Residence Univ. of Florida, Gainesville (USA) 2000. *Film:* The Axe (writer and Dir) 1999. *Publications:* (novels) Makunun'unu Maodzamwoyo (in Shona) 1970, Waiting for the Rain 1975, Ndiko Kupindana Kzamawuzve (in Shona) 1975, Kunyarara Hakusi Kutaura? (in Shona) 1983; (short stories) Coming of the Dry Season 1972, Some Kinds of Wounds 1980, Setting Sun and Rolling World 1987, One Day Long Ago: Tales from a Shona Childhood (folk tales) 1991, Walking Still 1997; (poetry) The Milkman Doesn't Only Deliver Milk 1981. *Honours:* Hon. DLitt (Zimbabwe) 2004; Noma Award for Publishing in Africa, Book Centre/PEN Award, Commonwealth Writers Award (Africa Region). *Address:* P.O. Box 1688, Harare (office); 47/6156 Uta Crescent, Zengeza 1, Chitungwiza, Zimbabwe. *E-mail:* muzuva47@yahoo.com.

MUNONYE, John Okechukwu, ON, CertEd; Nigerian novelist; b. 22 April 1929, Akokwa; m. Regina Nwokeji 1957, one s. one d. *Education:* University of London. *Career:* Chief Inspector of Education, East Central State, 1973–76, Imo State, 1976–77. *Publications:* The Only Son, 1966; Obi, 1969; Oil Man of Obange, 1971; A Wreath for Maidens, 1973; A Dancer of Fortune, 1974; Bridge to a Wedding, 1978. Short Stories: Silent Child, 1973; Pack Pack Pack, 1977; Man of Wealth, 1981; On a Sunday Morning, 1982; Rogues, 1985.

MUNRO, Alice, BA; Canadian writer; b. 10 July 1931, Wingham, Ont.; d. of Robert E. Laidlaw and Anne Chamney; m. 1st James A. Munro 1951 (divorced 1976); three d.; m. 2nd Gerald Fremlin 1976. *Education:* Univ. of Western Ontario. *Publications:* Dance of the Happy Shades 1968 (Gov.-Gen.'s Award for Literature 1968), A Place for Everything 1970, Lives of Girls and Women 1971, Something I've Been Meaning to Tell You 1974, Who Do You Think You Are? (aka The Beggar Maid) 1978, The Moons of Jupiter 1982, The Progress of Love 1986, Friend of My Youth 1990, Open Secrets 1994, Selected Stories 1996, The Love of A Good Woman 1998, Hateship, Friendship, Courtship, Loveship, Marriage 2001, Runaway (short stories) 2005, The View from Castle Rock 2006, Too Much Happiness 2009. *Honours:* Gov.-Gen.'s Award for Literature 1978, 1986, Canadian Booksellers' Award 1972, Marian Engel Award 1986, Canada-Australia Literary Prize 1994, Lannan Literary Award 1995, WH Smith Literary Award 1996, Fiction Prize, Nat. Book Critics Circle 1999, Giller Prize 1999, O. Henry Award 2001, Man Booker Int. Prize 2009. *Address:* William Morris Agency, 1325 Avenue of the Americas, Floor 16, New York, NY 10019, USA (office); PO Box 1133, Clinton, ON, N0M 1L0, Canada (home).

MUNRO, David Mackenzie, BSc, PhD, FRGS, FRSA; British geographer, editor and writer; *Director and Secretary, Royal Scottish Geographical Society;* b. 28 May 1950, Glasgow, Scotland. *Education:* Univ. of Edinburgh. *Career:* Research Assoc., then Research Fellow, Univ. of Edinburgh 1979–96; Dir and Sec., Royal Scottish Geographical Soc. 1996–; consultant, Times Atlas of the World 2000; Fellow Soc. of Antiquaries of Scotland; Trustee, South Georgia Heritage Trust; UK Rep., UN Group of Experts on Geographical Names; mem. Michael Bruce Trust (Chair.), Nat. Trust for Scotland (council mem.), Permanent Cttee on Geographical Names for British Official Use (Chair.). *Publications:* Chambers World Gazetteer (ed.) 1988, Ecology and Environment in Belize (ed.) 1989, A World Record of Major Conflict Areas (with Alan J. Day) 1990, The Hutchinson Guide to the World (assoc. ed.) 1990, Loch Leven and the River Leven: A Landscape Transformed 1994, The Oxford Dictionary of the World (ed.) 1995, Scotland, An Encyclopedia of Places and Landscape (with B. Gittings) 2006; contrib. to reference works and journals. *Honours:* Hon. Prof., Univ. of Dundee 2007; Scotia Centenary Medal 2005. *Address:* c/o Royal Scottish Geographical Society, 40 George Street, Glasgow, G1 1QE, Scotland (office). *Telephone:* (141) 552-3330 (office). *Fax:* (141) 552-3331 (office). *E-mail:* rsgs@strath.ac.uk (office). *Website:* www.rsgs.org.uk (office).

MUNRO, J. Richard, BA; American publishing executive; b. 26 Jan. 1931, Syracuse, NY; m. Carol Munro; three s. *Education:* Colgate, Columbia and New York Univs. *Career:* joined Time Inc. 1957; Pres. Pioneer Press Inc. (Time subsidiary) 1969; Publr Sports Illustrated 1969–71; Vice-Pres. Time Inc. 1971–75, Group Vice-Pres. for Video 1975–79, Exec. Vice-Pres. 1979–80, Pres. 1980–86, CEO 1980–90, Chair. 1986–90, Chair. Exec. Comm. 1990–96, also Dir; Chair. Genentech Inc. 1997; mem. Bd of Chancellors Juvenile Diabetes Research Foundation Int. (JDRF); fmr Dir IBM Corpn; Trustee RAND Corpn 1984-1994. *Honours:* Hon. LittD (Richmond Univ.) 1983; Purple Heart with two Clusters.

MUNRO, John Murchison, BA, PhD; American university administrator and writer; b. 29 Aug. 1932, Wallasey, Cheshire, England; m. Hertha Ingrid Bertha Lipp 1956, two s. two d. *Education:* University of Durham, Washington University, St Louis. *Career:* part-time Instructor of English, Washington University, St Louis, 1956–60; Instructor, University of North Carolina, 1960–63; Asst Prof., University of Toronto, Canada, 1963–65; Prof., American University of Beirut, Lebanon, 1965–87; Dir, Outreach Services, Prof. of Mass Communications, 1987–, Assoc. Dean for External Affairs, 1990–97, American University, Cairo, Egypt; Contributing Ed., Cairo Times, 1997–; Media Consultant, NSCE, Cairo, 1998–. *Publications:* English Poetry in Transition, 1968; Arthur Symons, 1969; The Decadent Poets of the 1890s, 1970; Selected Poems of Theo Marzials, 1974; James Elroy Flecker, 1976; A Mutual Concern: The Story of the American University of Beirut, 1977; Cyprus: Between Venus and Mars (with Z. Khuri), 1984; Selected Letters of Arthur Symons (with Karl Beckson), 1988; Theatre of the Absurd: Lebanon, 1982–88, 1989. Contributions: scholarly journals and general periodicals. *Honours:* Fulbright Research Award, University of California, Los Angeles, 1987.

MUNRO, Rona, MA; British playwright; b. 7 Sept. 1959, Aberdeen, Scotland. *Education:* Univ. of Edinburgh. *Career:* Literary Assoc., Hampstead Theatre, London 1996. *Plays include:* Stick Granny on the Roofrack, The Band and the Whimper (Stage Traffic Theatre Co.) 1982, The Salesman (Stage Traffic Theatre) 1982, Fugue (Traverse Theatre, Edinburgh) 1983, Touchwood (Guizer Theatre) 1984, The Bus (Scottish Youth Theatre) 1984, Ghost Story (Thron Theatre, Glasgow) 1985, Watching Waiters (Offstage Theatre) 1985, Piper's Cave (Soho Poly Theatre, London) 1985, Dust and Dreams 1986, The Biggest Party in the World 1986, The Way to Go Home (The Upstairs, London) 1987, Winners 1987, Off the Road 1988, Saturday at the Commodore (Sabhal Mor Ostaig, Isle of Skye) 1989, Bold Girls (Hampstead Theatre, London) 1990, Your Turn to Clean the Stair (Traverse Theatre, Edinburgh) 1992, The Maiden Stone (Hampstead Theatre, London) 1996, Haunted (Traverse Theatre, Edinburgh) 1999, Snake (Hampstead Theatre, London) 1999, Iron (Traverse Theatre, Edinburgh) 2002, Gilt (Tron Theatre, Glasgow) 2003, Catch a Falling Star! (Theatre Royal) 2004, Women on the Verge of a T Junction (Theatre Royal) 2004, Strawberries in January 2006, The Last Witch 2009, Little Eagles 2011. *Screenplays include:* Ladybird Ladybird 1994, Aimée & Jaguar 1999, I'm the Father 2002, Almost Adult 2006, Oranges and Sunshine 2010. *Honours:* Evening Standard Award 1991. *Literary Agent:* Independent Talent Group Ltd, Oxford House, 76 Oxford Street, London, W1D 1BS, England.

MURA, David Alan, BA, MFA; American poet, writer and teacher; b. 17 June 1952, Great Lakes, Ill.; m. Susan Sencer 1983; one d. *Education:* Grinnell Coll., Univ. of Minnesota, Vermont Coll. *Career:* Instructor 1979–85, Assoc. Dir of the Literature Program 1982–84, Writers and Artists-in-the-Schools, St Paul, Minnesota; Faculty mem. The Loft, St Paul, Minnesota 1984–; Instructor, St Olaf Coll. 1990–91; Visiting Prof., Univ. of Oregon 1991; various poetry readings; mem. Asian-American Renaissance Conference, Center for Arts Criticism (Pres. 1991–92), Jerome Foundation, Playwrights' Center. *Publications:* A Male Grief: Notes on Pornography and Addiction 1987, After We Lost Our Way (poems) 1989, Turning Japanese 1991, The Colors of Desire (poems) 1995, Where the Body Meets Memory 1996; contrib. to anthologies and magazines. *Honours:* Hon. DHumLitt (Cornell Coll.) 1997; Fanny Fay Wood Memorial Prize, Acad. of American Poets 1977, US/Japan Creative Artist Fellow 1984, Nat. Endowment for the Arts Fellowship 1985, 1993, Discovery/Nation Award 1987, Nat. Poetry Series Contest 1988, Pushcart Prize 1990, Minnesota State Arts Board Grant and Fellowship 1991, New York Times Notable Book of the Year 1991, Loft McKnight Award of Distinction 1992, Lila Wallace Reader's Digest Writers' Award 1995. *Address:* 1920 East River Terrace, Minneapolis, MN 55414, USA.

MURAKAMI, Haruki, BA; Japanese writer; b. 12 Jan. 1949, Kyoto; m. Yoko Takahashi 1971. *Education:* Kobe High School, Waseda Univ. *Career:* Owner, Peter Cat jazz club, Tokyo 1974–81; began writing in 1978, lived in Europe 1986–89, USA 1991–95; Visiting Scholar, Princeton Univ. 1991–93; Una's Lecturer in the Humanities, Univ. of Calif., Berkeley 1992; Writer-in-Residence, Tufts Univ. 1993–95, Harvard Univ. 2005–06. *Publications:* fiction: Hear the Wind Sing (Gunzo Literature Prize) 1979, Pinball 1980, A

Wild Sheep Chase (Noma Literary Award for New Writers) 1982, Hard-Boiled Wonderland and The End of the World (Junichi Tanizaki Award) 1985, Norwegian Wood 1987, Dance Dance Dance 1988, South of the Border, West of the Sun 1992, Wind-Up Bird Chronicle (Yomiuri Literary Award 1996) 1994–95, Sputnik Sweetheart 1999, Kafka on the Shore 2002, After Dark 2004, 1Q84 2009; short stories: Slow Boat to China 1983, A Perfect day for Kangaloos 1983, Dead Heat 1985, The Elephant Vanishes 1986, TV People 1990, Phantoms of Lexington 1998, After the Quake 2000, Blind Willow, Sleeping Woman (Frank O'Connor Int. Short Story Award, Kiriyama Prize 2007) 2006; non-fiction: Underground 1997, The Place That was Promised (Kuwahara Takeo Award) 1998, What I Talk About When I Talk About Running 2008; essays: A Young Reader's Guide to Short Fiction 1997; has translated works by F. Scott Fitzgerald, Raymond Carver, Truman Capote, Paul Theroux, John Irving, J. D. Salinger. *Honours:* Franz Kafka Prize 2006, Jerusalem Prize 2009. *Literary Agent:* ICM, 40 West 57th Street, New York, NY 10019, USA. *Telephone:* (212) 556-5600. *Website:* www.icmtalent.com; www.randomhouse.com/features/murakami/site.php.

MURAKAMI, Ryunosuke (Ryū); Japanese writer and film director; b. 19 Feb. 1952, Sasebo City, Nagasaki; m. Tazuko Takahashi 1976. *Career:* fmr rock band drummer, TV talk show host; writer and film-maker 1976–. *Films:* adaptations of many of his novels, including Almost Transparent Blue (writer and dir) 1978, Daijôbu, mai furendo (writer and dir) 1983, Raffles Hotel (writer and dir) 1989, Topâzu (writer and dir) 1992, Ôdishon (writer) 1999, Kyoko (writer and dir) 2000, Hashire! Ichiro (from novel Hashire! Takahashi) 2001, Shōwa kayō daizenshū 2003, Shikusutinain 2004, Popular! 2006, Koinrokkā Beibīzu 2008. *Publications:* novels: Kagirinaku tōmei ni chikai burrū (trans. as Almost Transparent Blue) (Akutagawa Prize, Gunzou Prize) 1976, Hashire! Takahashi, Ôdishon, Topâzu (trans. as Tokyo Decadence), Raffles Hotel, Daijôbu, mai furendo (trans. as All Right, My Friend), Kyoko (trans. as Because of You), 69 1987, Coin Locker Babies 1995, In the Miso Soup (Yomiuri Literary Award 1998) 1997, Exodus (serialised) 1998–99, Piercing 2007, Audition 2009, Popular Hits of the Showa Era 2011; non-fiction: Ano kane de nani ga kaeta ka 2003. *Address:* c/o Kodansha International Ltd, Otowa YK Building, 1-17-14 Otowa, Bunkyo-ku, Tokyo 112-8652, Japan (office).

MURDOCH, (Keith) Rupert, AC; American (b. Australian) publisher, broadcaster and media business developer; *Chairman and CEO, News Corporation;* b. 11 March 1931, Melbourne, Vic., Australia; s. of the late Sir Keith Murdoch and of Dame Elisabeth Murdoch; m. 1st Patricia Booker (divorced); one d.; m. 2nd Anna Maria Torv 1967 (divorced); two s. one d.; m. 3rd Wendi Deng 1999; two d. *Education:* Geelong Grammar School, Vic., Worcester Coll., Oxford, UK. *Career:* inherited Adelaide News 1954; has since built up News Corporation (Group CEO 1979–, Chair. 1991–); has acquired newspapers, broadcasting and other interests in Australia, UK, USA, Latin America, Europe and Asia, including: Australia – newspapers: The Australian (nat.), Daily Telegraph, Sunday Telegraph, Daily Mirror (Sydney), Sunday Sun (Brisbane), The News and Sunday Mail (Adelaide), The Sunday Times (Perth); USA – New York Post; UK – newspapers: Sun, News of the World (nat., acquired 1969); acquired Times Newspapers Ltd 1981, group includes The Times, The Sunday Times, The Times Literary Supplement, The Times Educational Supplement, The Times Higher Education Supplement; Dir Times Newspapers Holdings 1981–, Chair. 1982–90, 1994–; magazines: Weekly Standard (US politics); film: Fox Film Entertainment; TV: British Sky Broadcasting (UK), STAR (Asia), Fox Broadcasting Co., Fox Cable Networks; other interests include lifestyle portal MySpace.com, book publr HarperCollins and ownership of 35 US TV stations; Chair. and CEO Fox Entertainment Group USA 1992–; mem. Bd of Dirs Associated Press 2008–. *Honours:* Commdr of the White Rose (First Class) 1985, Kt, Order of St Gregory the Great 1998; ranked by Forbes magazine amongst The World's Most Powerful People (seventh) 2009, (13th) 2010, (24th) 2011. *Address:* News Corporation, 1211 Avenue of the Americas, New York, NY 10036, USA (office); News Corporation Ltd, 2 Holt Street, Surry Hills, Sydney, NSW 2010, Australia (office). *Telephone:* (212) 852-7017 (New York) (office); (2) 9288-3000 (Sydney) (office). *Fax:* (212) 852-7145 (New York) (office); (2) 9288-3292 (Sydney) (office). *Website:* www.newscorp.com (office).

MURÍN, Gustáv, PhD; Slovak writer; b. 9 April 1959, Bratislava; s. of Augustín Murín and Filoména Murínová; m. Jana Murín; two d. *Education:* Comenius Univ., Bratislava. *Career:* founder samizdat Voice of the Boiler Room 1989–92; founder and Pres. Circle for Young Writers; mem. Slovak PEN Centre (sec. 1995–97), chair. Trans. and Linguistic Rights Cttee 2006, pres. 2000–04, 2009–), Slovak Syndicate of Journalists, World Innovation Foundation. *Film:* Vyrástol z prostého Ľudu. *Radio:* 12 radio dramas. *Television:* presenter, numerous scientific programmes. *Publications in translation include:* The Case of a Buried Cemetery (novella) 1986, Summer Favors Lovers (short stories) 1990, Comebacks from Light (short stories) 1990, Substitutional End of the World (essays) 1992, Instinct Contra Culture (essay) 1994, Orgasmodromes (essays and articles) 1997, Proppe and others (fiction in electronic form) 1997, How Are You (novel) 1998, Animals, Me and Other (Prose) (short stories) 1998, Just Like the Gods (essay) 2001, And You Will Become Gods (essays) 2002, Mafia v. Bratislava 2008, The Mafia in Slovakia 2009; co-author of nine story collections; contrib. over 990 articles in newspapers and magazines. *Honours:* Hon. Fellow in Writing Univ. of Iowa 1995; Best Slovak Story 1979, Best Czech and Slovak Story 1981, Best Czech and Slovak Novella 1986, Special Prize in Slovak Radio Drama 1988, Slovenské pohľady magazine Best Essay of the Year 1996, E. E. Kisch Award 2003, Fifik's Children Jury Award 2005. *Address:* J. Hagaru 17, 83151 Bratislava, Slovakia (home). *Telephone:* (2) 2070-6635 (home); (2) 5441-5603 (office). *Fax:* (2) 5441-5603 (office). *E-mail:* gmurin@fns.uniba.sk (office); gustavmurin@yahoo.com (home). *Website:* gustavmurin.webgarden.cz.

MURISON, Krissi; Briitsh journalist. *Career:* joined NME (New Musical Express) as staff writer 2003, then New Music Ed., Features Ed., Deputy Ed. 2003–09, Ed. 2009–12; Music Dir, Nylon magazine Feb.–Sept. 2009. *Honours:* Breaking Music Writer 2005. *Address:* c/o NME, IPC Music Magazines, Blue Fin Building, 110 Southwark Street, London SE1 0SU, England.

MURNANE, Gerald, BA; Australian writer; b. 1939, Melbourne, Vic.; three s. *Education:* Univ. of Melbourne. *Career:* Lecturer, Victoria Coll., Melbourne; Senior Lecturer, Deakin Univ., Melbourne. *Publications:* Tamarisk Row 1974, A Lifetime on Clouds 1976, The Plains 1982, Landscape with Landscape 1985, Inland 1988, Velvet Waters (short stories) 1990, Emerald Blue (short stories) 1995, Invisible Yet Enduring Lilacs (essays) 2005, Barley Patch 2009. *Honours:* Patrick White Literary Award 1999, Australia Council Emer. Fellowship 2008, Melbourne Prize for Literature 2009. *Literary Agent:* Golvan Arts, PO Box 766, Kew, Vic. 3101, Australia. *Address:* PO Box 40, Goroke, Vic. 3412, Australia (home). *Telephone:* (3) 5386-1271 (home).

MURPHEY, Rhoads, AB, MA, PhD; American academic and writer; b. 13 Aug. 1919, Philadelphia, PA; m. 1st Katherine Elizabeth Quinn 1942 (died 1950); one s. one d.; m. 2nd Eleanor Taylor Albertson 1952; one s. one d. *Education:* Harvard University. *Career:* Asst Prof. of Geography, Ohio State University, 1950–51; Asst Prof. to Prof. of Geography, University of Washington, 1952–64; Prof. of Asian Studies and History, University of Michigan, Ann Arbor, 1964–; mem. Asscn of American Geographers; Asscn for Asian Studies, pres., 1987–88; American Historical Asscn. *Publications:* Shanghai: Key to Modern China, 1953; A New China Policy (with others), 1967; An Introduction to Geography, 1969; The Scope of Geography, 1969; The Treaty Ports and China's Modernization, 1970; China Meets the West, 1975; The Mozartian Historian (with others), 1976; The Outsiders, 1977; The Fading of the Maoist Vision, 1980; Civilizations of the World (with others), 1990; A History of Asia, 1992; East Asia: A New History, 1996. Contributions: scholarly books and journals. *Honours:* Ford Foundation Fellowship, 1955–56; Guggenheim Fellowship, 1966–67; National Endowment for the Humanities Fellowship, 1972–73; Hons Award, Asscn of American Geographers, 1980.

MURPHY, Caryle Marie, BA; American journalist; b. 16 Nov. 1946, Hartford, Conn.; d. of Thomas Joseph Murphy and Muriel Kathryn Murphy (née McCarthy). *Education:* Jeanne d'Arc Acad. High School, Milton, Mass, Trinity Coll. and Johns Hopkins School for Advanced Int. Studies. *Career:* English and history teacher, Nyeri, Kenya 1968–70; Staff Reporter, Brockton Enterprise, Brockton, Mass 1972–73; Freelance Foreign Corresp., Angola 1974–76; joined Washington Post 1976, Foreign Corresp. for S Africa 1977–82, Staff Reporter, Washington, DC 1982–89, Middle East Corresp. 1989–2006; Edward R Murrow Fellow, Council on Foreign Relations 1994–95; currently Saudi Arabia Corresp., GlobalPost; currently lives in Riyadh, Saudi Arabia. *Publication:* Passion for Islam: Shaping the Modern Middle East: The Egyptian Experience 2002. *Honours:* awards for reporting from Kuwait following its invasion by Iraqi troops 1990 include Int. Women's Media Foundation Award for Courage in Journalism 1990, George Polk Award for Foreign Reporting, Long Island Univ. 1990, Pulitzer Prize for Int. Reporting 1991, Edward Weintal Journalism Prize for Diplomatic Reporting 1991. *Website:* www.globalpost.com/bio/caryle-murphy (office); www.carylemurphy.com.

MURPHY, Clive, BA, LLB, ARSL; Irish writer, poet and editor; b. 28 Nov. 1935, Liverpool, England. *Education:* Trinity Coll., Dublin. *Career:* Solicitor, Incorporated Law Soc. of Ireland 1958; mem. PEN, Soc. of Authors. *Publications:* novels: Freedom for Mr Mildew 1975, Nigel Someone 1975, Summer Overtures 1976; poetry: Sour Grapes 2000, Cave Canem 2002, Orts and All 2003, Lust and Malice 2005, Sodomy is not Enough! 2008, Heavenly Blue 2009; compiler and ed. of 10 autobiographies 1978–94; contrib. to anthologies and magazines. *Honours:* co-winner Adam Int. Review First Novel Competition 1968. *Address:* 132 Brick Lane, London, E1 6RU, England (office). *Telephone:* (20) 7247-6626 (office). *Website:* www.clivemurphy.org.

MURPHY, Dervla Mary; Irish author and critic; b. 28 Nov. 1931, Cappoquin; d. of Fergus Murphy and Kathleen Rochfort-Dowling; one d. *Education:* Ursuline Convent, Waterford. *Publications:* Full Tilt 1965, Tibetan Foothold 1966, The Waiting Land 1967, In Ethiopia with a Mule 1968, On a Shoestring to Coorg 1976, Where the Indus is Young 1977, A Place Apart 1978, Wheels Within Wheels 1979, Race to the Finish? 1981, Eight Feet in the Andes 1983, Muddling Through in Madagascar 1985, Ireland 1985, Tales from Two Cities 1987, Cameroon with Egbert 1989, Transylvania and Beyond 1992, The Ukimwi Road 1993, South from the Limpopo 1997, Visiting Rwanda 1998, One Foot in Laos 1999, Through the Embers of Chaos: Balkan Journeys 2002, Through Siberia by Accident 2005, Silverland: A Winter Journey Beyond the Urals 2006, The Island That Dared 2008. *Honours:* American Irish Foundation Literary Award 1975, Ewart-Biggs Memorial Prize 1978, Irish American Cultural Inst. Literary Award 1985. *Address:* Lismore, Co. Waterford, Ireland.

MURPHY, Jill; British writer and illustrator; b. 1949, Wimbledon, London; one s. *Education:* Chelsea Coll. of Art, Croydon and Camberwell Schools of

Art. *Career:* fmr nanny, now writer of jr fiction and illustrator. *Publications include:* My Teddy 1973, The Worst Witch 1975, Peace at Last 1980, The Worst Witch Strikes Again 1981, A Bad Spell for the Worst Witch 1982, On the Way Home 1982, Whatever Next! 1983, Geoffrey Strangeways 1985, Baby Bear's Press-out Book 1985, Five Minutes' Peace 1986, All in One Piece 1987, Worlds Apart 1989, A Piece of Cake 1989, The Christmas Babies 1992, The Worst Witch All at Sea 1993, A Quiet Night In 1993, The Last Noo-noo 1995, Whatever Next 1997, All For One 2002, The Worst Witch Saves the Day 2005, Mr Large in Charge 2005, The Worst Witch to the Rescue 2007. *Address:* c/o Images of Delight, 3 Hurle Crescent, Bristol, BS8 2SX, England (office). *Website:* www.imagesofdelight.com (office).

MURPHY, Richard, BA, MA, FRSL; Irish poet and author; b. 6 Aug. 1927, Co. Mayo; s. of the late Sir William Murphy; m. Patricia Avis 1955 (divorced 1959); one d. *Education:* Magdalen Coll., Oxford, Univ. of Paris (Sorbonne). *Career:* various visiting positions, including Univ. of Virginia, USA 1965, Univ. of Reading, UK 1968, Bard Coll., Annandale-on-Hudson, New York 1972–74, Princeton Univ., USA 1974–75, Univ. of Iowa, USA 1976–77, Syracuse Univ., USA 1977–78, Catholic Univ. of America, Washington, DC 1983, Pacific Lutheran Univ., Tacoma, Wash., USA 1985, Wichita State Univ., USA 1987; Compton Lecturer in Poetry, Univ. of Hull, UK 1969; O'Connor Prof. of Literature, Colgate Univ., , USA 1971; Distinguished Visiting Poet, Univ. of Tulsa, USA 1992–95; mem. Aosdána, Ireland. *Publications include:* The Archaeology of Love 1955, Sailing to an Island 1963, The Battle of Aughrim 1968, High Island 1974, The Price of Stone 1985, The Mirror Wall 1989, New Selected Poems 1989, Collected Poems 2000, The Kick: A Memoir 2002, The Kick: a Life among Writers 2003; contrib. to various periodicals. *Address:* c/o Aosdána, The Arts Council, 70 Merrion Square, Dublin 2, Ireland.

MURPHY, Thomas (Tom); Irish playwright and theatre director; b. 23 Feb. 1935, Tuam, Co. Galway; s. of John (Jack) Murphy and Winifred Shaughnessy; m. Jane Brennan. *Education:* Tuam Vocational School, Vocational Teachers' Training Coll., Dublin. *Career:* metalwork teacher 1957–62; playwright and theatre Dir 1962–; Writer-in-Asscn Druid Theatre Co., Galway 1983–86, Abbey Theatre 1986–89; Tom Murphy at the Abbey (Irish Nat. Theatre), six-play season 2001; Mem. Irish Acad. of Letters, Aosdána. *Stage plays:* On the Outside 1959, A Whistle in the Dark 1961, A Crucial Week in the Life of a Grocer's Assistant 1966, The Orphans 1968, Famine 1968, The Morning After Optimism 1971, The White House 1972, The Vicar of Wakefield (adaptation) 1974, On the Inside 1974, The Sanctuary Lamp 1975, The J. Arthur Maginnis Story 1976, The Blue Macushla 1980, The Informer (adaptation) 1981, The Gigli Concert 1983, Conversations on a Homecoming 1985, Bailegangaire 1985, A Thief of a Christmas 1986, Too Late for Logic 1989, The Patriot Game 1991, She Stoops to Folly 1995, The Wake 1998, The House 2000, The Cherry Orchard 2003, The Drunkard 2003, Alice Trilogy 2005, The Last Days of a Reluctant Tyrant 2009. *Publications:* The Seduction of Morality (novel) 1994. *Honours:* Hon. DLitt (Trinity Coll., Dublin) 1998, (Nat. Univ. of Ireland, Galway) 2000; Irish Acad. of Letters Award 1972, Harveys Award 1983, 1985, Sunday Tribune Arts Award 1985, Independent Newspapers Award 1983, 1989, Drama-Logue Critics' Award 1995, Irish Times ESB Theatre Awards Special Tribute 1997, 2000, Irish Times Theatre Award for Best Play 2005. *Literary Agent:* c/o Alexandra Cann Representation, 52 Beauchamp Place, London, SW3 1NY, England. *Telephone:* (20) 7584-9047. *E-mail:* alex@alexandracann.co.uk.

MURRAY, Brian; American publishing executive; *President and CEO, HarperCollins Worldwide. Career:* fmr media consultant, Booz Allen and Hamilton; Dir of Finance and Strategy, Gen. Books Group, HarperCollins 1997–99, Sr Vice-Pres. and Man. Dir, Gen. Books Group 1999–2001, CEO HarperCollins Australia/NewZealand 2001–04, Group Pres. USA 2004–07, Pres. HarperCollins Worldwide 2007–, CEO 2008–. *Address:* HarperCollins Publishers, 10 East 53rd Street, New York, NY 10022, USA (office). *Telephone:* (212) 207-7000 (office). *Website:* www.harpercollins.com (office).

MURRAY, Denis James, OBE; British journalist; b. 7 May 1951, s. of the late James Murray and Helen Murray; m. Joyce Linehan 1978; two s. two d. *Education:* St Malachy's Coll. Belfast, Trinity Coll. Dublin, Queen's Univ. Belfast. *Career:* grad. trainee, Belfast Telegraph 1975–77, also reporter; Belfast Reporter, Radio Telefís Éireann 1977–82; Dublin Corresp. BBC 1982–84, NI Political Corresp. 1984–88, Ireland Corresp. 1988–2008 (retd). *Address:* c/o BBC, Broadcasting House, Ormeau Avenue, Belfast, BT2 8HQ, Northern Ireland.

MURRAY, Douglas; British journalist and biographer; b. 1979. *Education:* Eton Public School, Magdalen Coll., Oxford. *Publications:* Bosie: A Biography of Lord Alfred Douglas 2000, Neo-Conservatism: Why We Need It 2006. *Literary Agent:* c/o Hodder and Stoughton General, 338 Euston Road, London, NW1 3BH, England. *Website:* www.hodderheadline.co.uk.

MURRAY, Frances (see Booth, Rosemary)

MURRAY, John; British novelist; b. 1950, Cumbria; m.; one d. *Career:* founder and co-ed., Panurge 1984. *Publications:* novels: Samarkand 1985, Kin 1986, Radio Activity 1993, John Dory 2001, Jazz, etc. 2003, Murphy's Favourite Channels 2004, The Legend of Liz and Joe 2009; short story collection: Pleasure 1987. *Honours:* Dylan Thomas Award 1988, winner of creative category Lakeland Book of the Year 2002. *Address:* c/o Independent Northern Publishers, Flambard Press, PO Box 990, Newcastle upon Tyne, NE99 2US, England (office). *E-mail:* info@northernpublishers.co.uk (office). *Website:* www.flambardpress.co.uk (office).

MURRAY, John R.; British publisher and author. *Education:* Univ. of Oxford. *Career:* fmr Chair. John Murray (Publrs) Ltd (bought by Hodder Headline 2002). *Publications include:* A Gentleman Publisher's Commonplace Book 1996, Old Chestnuts Warmed Up (ed.) 2002, Above Eye Level: Glimpses of the Unexpected 2007. *Address:* c/o 50 Albemarle Street, London, W1S 4BD, England (office).

MURRAY, Leslie (Les) Allan, BA, AO; Australian poet; b. 17 Oct. 1938, Nabiac, NSW; s. of the late Cecil Allan Murray and Miriam Pauline Murray (née Arnall); m. Valerie Gina Morelli 1962; three s. two d. *Education:* Univ. of Sydney. *Career:* translator, Australian Nat. Univ. 1963–67; in Prime Minister's Dept 1970–71; Acting Ed., Poetry Australia 1973–80; Ed., New Oxford Book of Australian Verse 1985–97; Literary Ed., Quadrant 1989–. *Publications:* The Ilex Tree (with Geoffrey Lehmann) 1965, The Weatherboard Cathedral 1969, Poems Against Economics 1972, Collected Poems 1976, Selected Poems: The Vernacular Republic 1979, The Boys Who Stole the Funeral (verse novel) 1980, Selected Poems 1986, Dog Fox Field 1990, The Paperbark Tree (selected prose) 1991, Translations from the Natural World 1992, Fivefathers (ed.) 1995, Subhuman Redneck Poems 1996, A Working Forest (prose) 1997, Fredy Neptune (verse novel) 1998, Conscious & Verbal 1999, Learning Human – New Selected Poems 2001, Poems the Size of Photographs 2002, New Collected Poems 2003, The Best Australian Poems (ed.) 2004, The Biplane Houses 2006, Taller When Prone 2010. *Honours:* Petrarca Prize (Germany) 1995, T. S. Eliot Prize 1997, Queen's Gold Medal for Poetry 1999, Mondello Prize (Italy) 2004. *Literary Agent:* Margaret Connolly & Associates, 16 Winton Street, Warrawee, NSW 2074, Australia.

MURRAY, Paul, MA; Irish novelist; b. 1975, Dublin. *Education:* Trinity Coll., Dublin, Univ. of East Anglia, UK. *Career:* fmr bookseller. *Publications:* An Evening of Long Goodbyes 2003, Skippy Dies 2010. *Literary Agent:* c/o Natasha Fairweather, AP Watt Ltd, 20 John Street, London, WC1N 2DR, England. *Website:* www.apwatt.co.uk.

MURRELL, John, OC, BFA, BEd; Canadian dramatist and translator; *Executive Artistic Director, The Banff Centre;* b. 15 Oct. 1945, Lubbock, TX, USA. *Education:* Southwestern University, Georgetown, Texas, University of Calgary. *Career:* Playwright-in-Residence, Alberta Theatre Project 1975–76; Assoc. Dir, Stratford Festival 1977–78; Dramaturg, Theatre Calgary 1981–82; Head, Playwright's Colony, Banff Centre School of Fine Art 1986, Theatre Section, Canada Council 1988–92; Artistic Dir and Exec. Producer of Theatre Arts, Banff Centre 1999–2005, Exec. Artistic Dir 2005–. *Libretti:* Filumena 2003, Frobisher 2006. *Publications:* Haydn's Head 1973, Power in the Blood 1975, Teaser (with Kenneth Dyba) 1975, Arena 1975, A Great Noise, a Great Light 1976, Memoir 1977, Waiting for the Parade 1980, Farther West 1986, New World 1986, October 1988, Democracy 1992, Faraway Nearby 1995, Death in New Orleans 1998. *Honours:* Alberta Order of Excellence 2002; Clifford E. Lee Playwrighting Award 1975, Walter Carsen Prize for Excellency in the Performing Arts 2002. *Address:* Theatre Arts Department, The Banff Centre, Box 1020, Banff, Alberta, T1L 1H5, Canada (office). *Telephone:* (403) 762-6100 (office). *Fax:* (403) 762-6444 (office). *E-mail:* arts_info@banffcentre .ca (office). *Website:* www.banffcentre.ca (office).

MURTAGH, Peter, BA; Irish journalist; *Managing Editor, The Irish Times;* b. 9 April 1953, Dublin; s. of Thomas Murtagh and Olive de Lacy; m. Moira Gutteridge 1988; one s. one d. *Education:* The High School, Dublin, Trinity Coll., Dublin, Scandinavian Int. Man. Inst., Copenhagen, Denmark. *Career:* reporter, The Irish Times 1981–84, Foreign Ed., Opinion Ed., Managing Ed. 1997–; Ed. Insight, The Sunday Times, London 1985; reporter, Deputy Foreign Ed. and News Ed. The Guardian, London 1986–94; Ed. The Sunday Tribune, Dublin 1994–96. *Publications:* The Boss: Charles J. Haughey in Government (with J. Joyce) 1983, Blind Justice: The Sallins Mail Train Robbery (with J. Joyce) 1984, The Rape of Greece 1994, Irish Times Book of the Year 1999–2009. *Honours:* Journalist of the Year, Ireland 1983, Reporter of the Year, UK 1986. *Address:* The Irish Times, Tara Street, Dublin 2 (office); Somerby Road, Greystones, Co. Wicklow, Ireland (home). *Telephone:* (1) 6758000 (office). *Fax:* (1) 6615302 (office). *E-mail:* pmurtagh@irishtimes.com (office). *Website:* www.irishtimes.com (office).

MUSCHG, Adolf, PhD; Swiss writer, dramatist and academic; b. 13 May 1934, Zollikon. *Education:* Zürich, Cambridge, England. *Career:* Prof., Eidgenössische Technische Hochschule, Zürich 1970–1999; Pres. Akademie der Künste, Berlin 2003–06. *Publications:* Im Sommer des Hasen 1965, Fremdkörper 1968, Das Kerbelgericht 1969, Die Aufgeregten von Goethe 1971, Liebesgeschichten 1972, Albissers Grund 1974, Kellers Abend 1975, Gottfried Keller 1977, Baiyun oder die Freundschaftsgesellschaft 1980, Literatur als Therapie? 1981, Das Licht und der Schlüssel 1984, Der rote Ritter 1993, Nur ausziehen wollte sie sich nicht 1995, Goethe bis an die Sterne weit? 1999, Sutters Glück 2001, Eikan, du bist spät 2004, Was ist europäisch? 2005, Sax 2010. *Honours:* Order of Merit (Germany); Hermann Hesse Prize 1974, Literature Prize, Zürich 1984, Carl Zuckmayer Medal 1990, Georg Büchner Prize 1994, Grimmelshausen Prize. *Address:* Hasenacker str. 24, 8708 Männedorf, Switzerland; Knesebecker str. 76, 10623 Berlin, Germany.

MUSGRAVE, Susan; Canadian writer; b. 12 March 1951, Santa Cruz, Calif.; d. of Edward Lindsay Musgrave and Judith Bradfield Musgrave (née Stevens); m. Stephen Douglas Reid 1982; two d. *Career:* writer since the age of 16; Bi-weekly Columnist Toronto Star, Vancouver Sun; book reviewer CBC Journal; Writer-in-Residence Univ. of Waterloo 1983–85, Univ. of New Brunswick 1985, Univ. of Western Ontario 1992–93; teacher of English Arvon Foundation 1975, 1980, Univ. of Waterloo 1983–84, Kootenay School of Writing 1986, Camosun Coll., Victoria 1988–91; Ralph Gustafson Chair of Poetry, Malaspina Coll., Fall 2000; Adjunct Prof., Univ. of British Columbia Optional-Residency MFA in Creative Writing Programme 2005–; frequent judge and jury mem. of poetry competitions; Toronto Univ. Presidential Writer-in-Residence Fellowship 1995. *Publications include:* Poetry: Songs of the Sea-Witch 1970, Entrance of the Celebrant 1972, Grave-Dirt and Selected Strawberries 1973, Gullband 1974, The Impstone 1976, Kiskatinaw Songs 1977, Selected Strawberries and Other Poems 1977, Becky Swan's Book 1978, A Man to Marry, A Man to Bury 1979, Tarts and Muggers: Poems New and Selected 1982, Cocktails at the Mausoleum 1985, Kestrel and Leonardo 1990, In The Small Hours of the Rain 1991, The Embalmer's Art 1992, Forcing the Narcissus 1994, Things That Keep and Do Not Change 1999, What the Small Day Cannot Hold 2000; Novels: The Charcoal Burners 1980, Hag Head 1980, The Dancing Chicken 1987, Dreams Are More Real than Bathtubs 1998, Cargo of Orchids 2000; Essays: Great Musgrave 1989, Musgrave Landing 1994, You're in Canada Now 2005; has written numerous articles and poems for periodicals and anthologies. *Honours:* Nat. Magazine Award (Silver) 1981, b. p. nichol Poetry Chapbook Award 1991, CBC/Tilden Award for Poetry 1996, Vicky Metcalf Short Story Editors Award 1996. *Address:* PO Box 2421, Station Main, Sidney, BC V8L 3Y3; c/o Denise Bukowski, The Bukowski Agency, 14 Prince Arthur Avenue, Suite 202, Toronto, ON M5R 1A9, Canada. *Telephone:* (416) 928-6728 (Toronto). *Website:* www.susanmusgrave.com.

MUSGROVE, Frank, BA, PhD, FRSA; British academic and writer; *Sarah Fielden Professor of Education Emeritus, University of Manchester*; b. 16 Dec. 1922, Nottingham; m. Dorothy Ellen Nicholls; one d. *Education:* Magdalen Coll., Oxford, Univ. of Nottingham. *Career:* Lecturer Univ. of Leicester 1957–62; Sr Lecturer Univ. of Leeds 1963–65; Prof. of Research in Education Univ. of Bradford 1965–70; Sarah Fielden Prof. of Education 1970–82, Prof. Emeritus 1982–, Univ. of Manchester; Co-Ed. Research in Education 1971–76; various guest lectureships; mem. Royal Anthropological Inst. *Publications:* The Migratory Elite 1963, Youth and the Social Order 1964, The Family, Education and Society 1966, Society and the Teacher's Role (with P. H. Taylor) 1969, Patterns of Power and Authority in English Education 1971, Ecstasy and Holiness 1974, Margins of the Mind 1977, School and the Social Order 1979, Education and Anthropology 1982, The North of England: A History from Roman Times to the Present 1990, Dresden and the Heavy Bombers 2005; contrib. to professional journals. *Honours:* Hon. DLitt (Open Univ.) 1982; Chancellor's Lecturer, Univ. of Wellington, NZ 1970, Hon. Prof. Univ. of Hull 1985–88. *Address:* Dib Scar, The Cedar Grove, Beverley, East Yorkshire, HU17 7EP, England (home). *Telephone:* (1482) 868799 (home).

MUSHKETIK, Yuri Mikhailovich; Ukrainian writer; b. 21 March 1929, Verkiivka, Chernigiv Region; s. of Mikhail Petrovich Mushketik and Uliana Onufriivna Mushketik; m. Lina Sergiivna Mushketik (née Lushnikova); two d. *Education:* Kiev State Univ. *Career:* mem. CPSU 1951–91; Chair. Bd Union of Writers of Ukraine 1987–; Ed.-in- Chief Dripro journal; Chair. Nat. Cttee of UNESCO; first works published 1952. *Publications include:* Fires in the Middle of the Night 1959, Black Bread 1960, The Heart and the Stone 1961, Drop of Blood 1964, A Bridge Across the Night 1975, White Shadow 1975, Position 1979, Pain 1981, The Boundary 1987, Selected Works (2 vols) 1989, Hetman's Treasure (novel) 1993, Brother Against Brother (novel) 1995. *Honours:* T. Shevchenko Ukrainian State Prize 1980. *Address:* Suvorova Str. 3, Apt. 10, 252010 Kiev, Ukraine. *Telephone:* (44) 290-80-04.

MUSICANT, Ivan Martin, BA; American naval historian; b. 18 Dec. 1943, New York, NY; m. Gretchen Granlund Musicant 1982, one s. *Education:* Bemidji State University. *Publications:* United States Armored Cruisers: A Design and Operational History, 1985; Battleship At War: The Epic Story of the USS Washington, 1986; The Banana Wars: United States Military Intervention in Latin America, 1990; Divided Waters: The Naval History of the Civil War, 1995; Empire by Default: The Spanish-American War, 1998. Contributions: journals, reviews, periodicals and quarterlies. *Honours:* Samuel Eliot Morison Awards for Naval Literature, 1987, 1998.

MUSKE-DUKES, Carol Anne, BA, MA; American poet, writer and academic; *Poet Laureate of California*; b. 17 Dec. 1945, St Paul, Minn.; m. David Dukes 1983 (died 2000); one step-s. one d. *Education:* Creighton Univ., Omaha, California State Univ. *Career:* Founder-Writing Program Dir, Art Without Walls, New York 1971–84; Lecturer, New School for Social Research, New York City 1975; Asst Prof., Univ. of New Hampshire 1978–79; Visiting Writer, Univ. of California at Irvine 1978, Visiting Poet 1983, 1993; Adjunct Prof., Columbia Univ. 1979–81; Visiting Poet, Iowa Writers' Workshop 1980; Jenny McKean Moore Lecturer, George Washington Univ. 1980–81; Writer-in-Residence, Univ. of Virginia 1981; Lecturer, Univ. of Southern California, Los Angeles 1984–88, Asst Prof. 1989–91, Assoc. Prof. 1991–93, Prof. 1993–, Founder-Dir, PhD Program in Creative Writing and Literature 1999–; Visiting Fiction Writer, Univ. of California, Los Angeles 1989; Poet Laureate of California 2008–; mem. Poetry Society of America. *Publications:* poetry: Camouflage 1975, Skylight 1981, Wyndmere 1985, Applause 1989, Red Trousseau 1993, An Octave Above Thunder: Selected and New Poems 1997, Sparrow 2004; fiction: Dear Digby 1989, Saving St Germ 1993, Life After Death 2001, Channeling Mark Twain 2007; non-fiction: Women and Poetry (essays) 1997, Married to the Icepick Killer: A Poet in Hollywood 2002; contributions: numerous anthologies and journals. *Honours:* Dylan Thomas Poetry Award 1973, Pushcart Prizes 1978, 1988–89, 1992–93, 1998, Alice Fay di Castagnola Award, Poetry Society of America 1979, Guggenheim Fellowship 1981, National Endowment for the Arts Grant 1984, Ingram Merrill Foundation Fellowship 1988, New York Times Most Notable Book Citation 1993, Alumni Achievement Award, Creighton Univ. 1996, Witter Bynner Award, Library of Congress, Washington, DC 1997–98. *Address:* c/o Dept of English, University of Southern California, Los Angeles, CA 90095, USA (office). *E-mail:* cmd@carolmuskedukes.com (office). *Website:* www.carolmuskedukes.com.

MUSSO, Guillaume; French writer; b. 1974, Antibes, Alpes-Maritimes. *Education:* Univ. of Nice, Univ. of Montpellier. *Career:* teacher of economics in Lorraine and at Centre Int. de Valbonne 1999–2008. *Publications:* Et Après... 2004, Sauve-moi 2005, Seras-tu là? 2006, Parce que je t'aime 2007, Je reviens te chercher 2008, Que serais-je sans toi? 2009. *Address:* c/o XO Editions, 33 avenue du Maine, BP 142, 75755 Paris cédex 15, France (office). *E-mail:* press@xoeditions.com (office). *Website:* www.xoeditions.com (office); www.guillaumemusso.com.

MUSTAFAJ, Besnik; Albanian writer, academic and politician; b. 23 Sept. 1958, Bajram Curri City; m.; two c. *Education:* Univ. of Tirana. *Career:* Prof. of Foreign Literature, Faculty of History and Philology, Univ. of Tirana 1983–91; Founding mem. Democratic Party of Albania 1990–, Sec. for Int. Relations 1999–2005; elected MP 1991, Deputy Chair. Foreign Relations Comm. 2001–05, Deputy Chair. of Perm. Del. to European Parl. 2001–05; Amb. to France and Perm. Rep. to UNESCO, Paris 1992–97; Minister of Foreign Affairs 2005–07 (resgnd); Co-founder Albanian Helsinki Cttee 1990; Founding Chair. Albanian Writers' Pen Club. *Publications:* Vera pa kthim (The Summer of no Return) 1989, Gjinkallat e vapës (The Cicadas of the Heat) 1994, Një sagë e vogël (A Little Saga) 1995, Daullja prej letre (The Paper Drum) 1996, Boshti (The Void) 1998; several books and papers on poetry and aesthetics.

MUTAFCHIEVA, Vera, PhD; Bulgarian writer, historian and academic; b. 28 March 1929, Sofia; d. of Petar and Nadia (née Tritonova) Mutafchiev; m. 1st Jossif Krapchev 1950 (divorced 1956); m. 2nd Atanas Slavov 1961 (divorced 1967); two d. *Education:* Univ. of Sofia. *Career:* Sr Researcher in Ottoman History, Inst. of History, Sofia 1958–63, Inst. of Balkan Studies 1963–79; Prof. Inst. of Literature 1979–91, Inst. of Demographic Studies, Acad. of Sciences 1991, Univ. of Sofia 1991; Dir Language and Ancient Civilization Centre 1979–80, Bulgarian Inst. of Research, Austria 1980–82; Sec. Union of Bulgarian Writers 1982–86. *Publications include:* over 30 novels, several plays, numerous essays, monographs and translations; has published 67 scientific studies 1952–92. *Honours:* Dr hc (New Bulgarian Univ.) 2000; Gottfried von Herder Preis, Hamburg, Vienna 1980, State Prize 1982, Paissii Hilendarsky Award 2000. *Address:* c/o Balkani Publishers, 47 A Tsarigradsko Chaussee, Block B, Floor 2, Sofia 1124, Bulgaria (office). *E-mail:* balkani@cablebg.net (office). *Website:* www.balkani.eu (office).

MUTIS, Alvaro; Colombian poet and novelist; b. 25 Aug. 1923, Bogotá; m. Mireya Durán; three s. *Publications:* poetry: La balanza 1948, Los elementos del desastre 1953, Reseñas de los Hospitales de Ultramar 1955, Los Trabajos Perdidos 1965, Summa de Maqroll el Gaviero 1973, Caravansary 1981, Los emisarios 1984, Crónica regia y alabanza del reino 1985, Un homenaje y siete nocturnos 1986; novels: Diario de Lecumberri 1960, La mansión de Araucaíma 1973, La verdadera historia del flautista de Hammelin 1982, La Nieve del Almirante, Ilona llega con la lluvia 1987, Un bel morir 1989, La última escala del Tramp Steamer 1989, La muerte del estratega 1990, Amirbar 1990, Abdul Bashur, soñador de navíos 1991, Tríptico de mar y tierra 1993; essays: Contextos para Maqroll 1997, De lecturas y algo del mundo 1999, Caminos y encuentros de Maqroll el Gaviero 2001. *Honours:* Comendador de la Orden del Águila Azteca, Mexico 1988, Commdr., Ordre des Arts et des Lettres, France 1989, Ordre nat. du Mérite, France 1993, Gran Cruz de la Orden de Boyacá 1993, Gran Cruz de la Orden de Alfonso X el Sabio, Spain 1996; Dr hc, Universidad del Valle, Colombia 1988; Premio Nacional de Letras 1974, Premio Nacional de Poesía 1983, Premio de la Crítica 'Los Abriles' 1985, Premio Xavier Villaurrutia, Mexico 1988, Prix Médicis Étranger, France 1989, Nonino Prize, Italy 1990, Roger Caillois Prize, France 1993, Grinzane-Cavour Prize, Italy 1997, Premio Príncipe de Asturias de las Letras, Spain 1997, Premio Reina Sofía de Poesía Iberoamericana, Spain 1997, Rossone d'Oro Prize, Italy 1997, Trieste Poetry Prize, Italy 2000, Premio Cervantes, Spain 2001, Neustadt Int. Prize for Literature 2002.

MUTSAERS, Charlotte; Dutch writer, painter and illustrator; b. 2 Nov. 1942, Utrecht; d. of the late Barend Mutsaers; m. Jan Fontijn. *Education:* Gerrit Rietveld Academie. *Career:* stood for House of Reps (Partij voor de Dieren) 2006. *Art exhibitions:* Galerie Clement, Amsterdam, Frans Hals Museum, Haarlem, Museum of Modern Art, Arnhem, Nieuwe Kerk, Amsterdam, Beiaard, Breda. *Publications:* novels: De Markiezin 1988, Rachels rokje 1994, Koetsier Herfst 2008; essays: Hazepeper 1985, Kersebloed (Jan Greshoff Prize 1992) 1990, Paardejam 1996, Pedante pendules en andere wekkers 2010; juvenile: Mijnheer Donselaer zoekt een vrouw 1986, Hanegeschrei 1988, Bont 2002, Cheese! 2003; other: Het circus van de geest (emblems) 1983, Zeepijn (short stories) (Busken Huet Prize) 2000, Feestvarkens en andere jarigen (short stories). *Honours:* Constantijn Huygens Prize 2000, Jacobus van Looy Prize 2000, P.C. Hooft Prijs 2010. *Address:* c/o Uitgeverij De Bezige Bij, Van Miereveldstraat 1, 1071 DW Amsterdam, Netherlands (office).

E-mail: info@debezigebij.nl (office); charlottemutsaers304@hotmail.com (home). *Website:* www.debezigebij.nl (office); www.charlottemutsaers.nl.

MWANGI, Meja; Kenyan novelist; b. 1948, Nanyuki. *Education:* Kenyatta Coll. *Career:* soundman, TV ORTF 1972–73; film librarian, British Council 1974–75; Fellow in Writing, Iowa Univ. 1975–76; also film dir, casting agent and location manager. *Publications:* Kill Me Quick 1973, Carcase for Hounds 1974, Going Down River Road 1976, The Cockroach Dance 1979, The Bushtrackers 1980, Bread of Sorrow 1987, Weapon for Hunger 1989, The Return of Shaka 1990, Striving for the Wind 1990, The Last Plague 2000; also children's books, plays. *Honours:* Jomo Kenyatta Prize 1974.

MYAMBO, Melissa Tandiwe; Zimbabwean author. *Career:* work appears in numerous journals including Prick of the Spindle, Chelsea Station, Montreal Review, Journal of African Travel Writing, 34th Parallel. *Publications include:* short stories: Jacaranda Journals 2004; features in several anthologies including: African Violet: The 2012 Caine Prize Anthology (includes story La Salle de Départ) 2012. *Address:* c/o Macmillan South Africa, 2nd Floor, 34 Whiteley Road, Melrose Arch Piazza, 2116 Johannesburg, South Africa (office). *Telephone:* (11) 731-3300 (office). *Fax:* (11) 731-3535 (office). *Website:* www.macmillan.co.za (office); www.jacarandajournals.com (home).

MYERS, (Margaret Jane) Dee Dee, BS; American broadcaster, magazine editor and fmr government official; *President, Dee Dee Myers & Associates*; b. 1 Sept. 1961, Quonset Point, RI; d. of Stephen George Myers and Judith Ann Burleigh; one d. *Education:* Univ. of Santa Clara. *Career:* Press Asst Mondale for Pres. Campaign, LA 1984, to deputy Senator Art Torres, LA 1985; Deputy Press Sec. to Mayor Tom Bradley, LA 1985–87, Tom Bradley for Gov. Campaign 1986; Calif. Press Sec. Dukakis for Pres. Campaign, LA 1988; Press Sec. Feinstein for Gov. Campaign, LA and San Francisco 1989–90; Campaign Dir Jordan for Mayor Campaign, San Francisco 1991; Press Sec. Clinton for Pres. Campaign, Little Rock 1991–92, White House, Washington, DC 1993–94; Co-Host Equal Time, CNBC, Washington, DC 1995–97; Contributing Ed. Vanity Fair magazine, Washington, DC 1995–; Founder and Pres. Dee Dee Myers & Associates; mem. Bd Trustees, Calif. State Univ. 1999–2004 (Vice-Chair. 2000–01); lecturer on politics, current affairs and women's issues; consultant to NBC TV drama The West Wing. *Publication:* Why Women Should Rule the World 2008. *Honours:* Robert F. Kennedy Award, Emerson Coll., Boston 1993. *Address:* 5146 Klingle Street, NW, Washington, DC 20016-2655; c/o Vanity Fair, Condé Nast Publications, 4 Times Square, 17th Floor, New York, NY 10036, USA (office). *Website:* www.vanityfair.com (office).

MYERS, Jack Elliot, BA, MFA; American academic, poet and writer; b. 29 Nov. 1941, Lynn, Mass; m. 1st Nancy 1967; m. 2nd Willa 1981; m. 3rd Thea 1993, three s. one d. *Education:* University of Massachusetts, Boston, University of Iowa. *Career:* Asst Prof., Southern Methodist University, Dallas 1975–81, Assoc. Prof. 1982–88, Prof. of English 1988–, Dir Creative Writing Program 1990–94; Poetry Ed., Fiction International 1978–80, Cimarron Review 1989–91; Faculty mem., MFA Program in Writing, Vermont College 1981–; Distinguished Poet-in-Residence, Wichita State University 1992; Distinguished Visiting Writer, University of Idaho 1993; Distinguished Writer-in-Residence, Northeast Louisiana University 1995; mem. Associated Writing Programs, PEN, Texas Asscn of Creative Writing Teachers, Texas Institute of Letters. *Publications:* poetry: Black Sun Abraxas, 1970; Will It Burn, 1974; The Family War, 1977; I'm Amazed That You're Still Singing, 1981; Coming to the Surface, 1984; As Long as You're Happy, 1986; Blindsided, 1993; Human Being, 1997; other: A Trout in the Milk: A Composite Portrait of Richard Hugo, 1980; New American Poets of the 80s (ed. with Roger Weingarten), 1984; The Longman Dictionary of Poetic Terms, 1985; A Profile of Twentieth-Century American Poetry (ed. with David Wojahn), 1991; New American Poets of the 90s (ed. with Roger Weingarten), 1991; Leaning House Poets, Vol. 1 (ed. with Mark Elliott), 1996; One On One, 1999; contributions: anthologies, reviews, quarterlies, journals, and magazines. *Honours:* Acad. of American Poets Award 1972; Texas Institute of Letters Poetry Award 1978, 1993, Yaddo Fellowship, 1978, National Endowment for the Arts Fellowship 1982–83, 1986–87, Winner, National Poetry Series Open Competition 1985, Southern Methodist University Author's Award 1987.

MYERSON, Julie, BA; British writer and journalist; b. 2 June 1960, Nottingham, England; m. Jonathan Myerson; three c. *Education:* Univ. of Bristol. *Career:* publicist, Royal Nat. Theatre, London, Walker Books; novelist, columnist, broadcaster, panellist on Newsnight Review (BBC 2). *Publications include:* novels: Sleepwalking 1994, The Touch 1996, Me and the Fatman 1998, Laura Blundy 2000, Something Might Happen 2003, The Story of You 2006, Out of Breath 2008, Then 2011; non-fiction: Home: The Story of Everyone Who Ever Lived in Our House 2004, Not a Games Person 2005, The Lost Child 2009. *Honours:* Elle talent contest 1993. *Literary Agent:* c/o Rogers, Coleridge & White, 20 Powis Mews, London, W11 1JN, England. *Telephone:* (20) 7221-3717. *Fax:* (20) 7229-9084. *E-mail:* info@rcwlitagency.com. *Website:* www.rcwlitagency.co.uk.

MYNERS, Baron (Life Peer), cr. 2008, of Truro in the County of Cornwall; **Paul Myners,** CBE, FRSA; British publishing executive and government official; *Financial Services Secretary and Minister for the City*; b. 1 April 1948; m. Alison Myners; one s. four d. *Education:* Univ. of London. *Career:* teacher with Inner London Educ. Authority 1971–72; finance writer, Daily Telegraph 1972–75; with N. M. Rothschild (merchant bank) 1974–85; CEO Gartmore Investment Man. 1985–87, Chair. 1987–2001; Deputy Chair. Powergen 1999–2001; Exec. Dir Nat. Westminster Bank 1999–2000; Chair. Guardian Media Group 2001–08, also Publisher The Guardian and The Observer newspapers; Financial Services Sec. and Minister for the City, HM Treasury 2008–, also Govt Spokesperson for HM Treasury in House of Lords; mem. Financial Reporting Council 1995–2004, Company Law Review Consultative Cttee 1998–2000; Court of Dirs of Bank of England 2005–; Chair. Low Pay Comm. 2006–; fmr mem. Bd of Dirs (non-exec.) mmO_2 2001–, Bank of NY, Marks & Spencer 2002 (interim Chair. 2004); Chair. Tate Galleries –2009; Visiting Fellow, Nuffield Coll., Oxford; mem. Royal Acad. Trust, United Response. *Honours:* Dr hc (Univ. of Exeter). *Address:* House of Lords, London, SW1A 0PW, England (office). *Telephone:* (20) 7219-5353 (House of Lords) (office); (20) 7270-5696 (office). *E-mail:* fsst.action@hm-treasury.gsi.gov.uk (office). *Website:* www.hm-treasury.gov.uk (office).

MYRDAL, Jan; Swedish writer; b. 19 July 1927, Stockholm; s. of the late Gunnar Myrdal and Alva Reimer; m. 1st Nadja Wiking 1948; m. 2nd Maj Liedberg 1953; m. 3rd Gun Kessle 1956 (died 2007); m. 4th Andrea Gaytan Vegaone 2008; s. one d. *Career:* Sunday columnist (politics, culture) Stockholms-Tidningen 1963–66, Aftonbladet 1966–72; Chair. and Publr Folket i Bild/Kulturfront 1971–72, columnist 1972–. *Works include:* films: Myglaren 1966, Hjalparen 1968, Balzac or The Triumphs of Realism 1975, Mexico: Art and Revolution 1991; TV documentaries: Democratic Kampuchea 1978–79, Guerilla Base Area of Democratic Kampuchea 1979, China 1979, 20 films on history of political caricature and posters 1975–87. *Publications include:* (in Swedish) novels: Hemkomst 1954, Jubelvår 1955, Att bli och vara 1956, Badrumskranen 1957, Karriär 1975, Barndom 1982, En annan värld 1984; drama: Folkets Hus 1953, Moraliteter 1967, Garderingar 1969, B. Olsen 1972; travel: Resa i Afghanistan 1960, Bortom berg och öknar 1962, Turkmenistan 1966, Sidenvägen 1977, Indien väntar 1980; politics: Kina: Revolutionen går vidare 1970, Albansk utmaning 1970, Ett 50-tal 1972, lag utan ordning, Kinesiska frågor, Tyska frågor 1976, Kina efter Mao Tse-tung 1977, Kampuchea och kriget 1978, Kampuchea hösten 1979, Den albanska utmaningen 1968–86, 1987, Mexico, Dröm och längtan 1996; essays: Söndagsmorgon 1965, Skriftställning 1968, Skriftställning II 1969, III 1970, IV 1973, V 1975, Klartexter 1978, Skriftställning X 1978, Balzac und der Realismus (in German) 1978, Strindberg och Balzac 1981, Ord och Avsikt 1986, Det nya Stor, Tyskland 1992, När Västerlandet trädde fram 1992, Inför nedräkningen 1993, När morgondagarna sjöng 1994, En fest i Liu Lin 1994, När morgondagarna sjöng 1994, Rölvag as an example 1995, Maj, en kärlek 1998, Om vin 1999, Det odelbara ordet 2002, Gubbsjuka 2002, Meccano 2005, Sälja krig som margarin 2005; autobiography: Rescontra 1962, Samtida bekännelser 1964, Inför nedräkningen 1993, När morgondagarna sjöng 1994, En kärlek 1998, Maj: En kärlek 1998; art: Ansikte av sten, Angkor 1968, Ondskan tar form 1976; Dussinet fullt 1981, Den trettonde 1983, Franska revolutionens bilder 1989, 5 ar av frihet 1830–35 1991, När Västerlandet tradde fram 1992, André Gill 1995, Drömmen om det goda samhallet; Kinesiska affischer 1966–1976 1996; wine: Jan Myrdal on vin 1999; biography: August Strindberg and Ole Edvart Roelvag 1997, Johan August Strindberg 2000; (in English) Report from a Chinese Village 1965, Chinese Journey 1965, Confessions of a Disloyal European 1968, Angkor: an essay on art and imperialism 1970, Gates to Asia 1971, Albania Defiant 1976, The Silk Road 1979, China Notebook 1975–78 1979, Return to a Chinese Village 1984, India Waits 1984, Childhood 1991, Another World 1993, 12 Going on 13 1995. *Honours:* Hon. DLit (Upsala Coll., NJ) 1980; Hon. PhD (Nankai Univ., China) 1993. *Address:* Kalvängen 70 D, 739 91 Skinnskatteberg, Sweden (home). *Telephone:* (223) 51-012 (home). *Fax:* (223) 51-007 (home). *E-mail:* myrdal@myrdal.pp.se (home). *Website:* www.myrdal-kessle.se (home).

N

NAAMANI, Houda an-, LLB; Lebanese poet; b. Damascus, Syria; two s. *Education:* Lycée-Français, Franciscan School, Univ. of Damascus and Cornell Univ., New York, USA. *Career:* fmr lawyer; writer 1970–. *Publications include:* Ilayka 1970, Anamili… Laa 1971, Qasidat Hub 1973, Adhkuru Kuntu Nuqtah Kuntu Da'ira 1978, Haa Tatadahraju 'ala al'Thalj 1982, Ru'ya 'ala 'Arsh 1989, Huda… Ana al-Haq 1990, I Was a Point. I Was a Circle (trans.) 1993. *E-mail:* naamanih@terra.net.lb (home).

NÁDAS, Péter; Hungarian novelist, essayist and playwright; b. 1942, Budapest. *Publications:* A biblia (short stories) 1967, Kulcskereso játék (short stories) 1969, Takarítás 1977, Egy családregény vége (The End of a Family Story, novel) 1977, Takarítás (play) 1977, Találkozás (play) 1979, Leírás 1979, Temetés 1980, Színtér 1982, Nézotér 1983, Emlékiratok kónyve (A Book of Memories) 1986, Játéktér 1988, A Biblia és más régi történetek 1988, Évkönyv 1989, Égi és földi szerelem 1991, Talált cetli 1992, Párbeszéd 1992, Esszék 1995, Vonulás 1995, Drámák 1996, Minotaurus 1997, Emlékiratok könyve 1998, Egy családregény vége 1999, Vonulás 2001, Saját halál 2004, Párhuzamos történetek 2005. *Honours:* Prize for Hungarian Art 1989, Austrian State Prize for European Literature 1991, Kossuth Prize 1992, Vilenica International Prize for Literature 1998, Franz Kafka Prize 2003. *Address:* c/o Twisted Spoon Press, Preslova 12, 150 00 Prague 5, Czech Republic (office). *E-mail:* info@twistedspoon.com (office). *Website:* www.traktor.cz/twisted/nadas (office).

NADAUS, Roland, (Pol-Jean Mervillon); French writer and poet; b. 28 Nov. 1945, Paris; m. Simone Moris 1967, one d. *Career:* mem. PEN Club of France. *Publications:* Maison de Paroles 1969, Journal: Vrac 1981, Je ne Tutoie que Dieu et ma femme (poems) 1992, Dictionnaire initiatique de l'orant 1993, L'homme que tuèrent les mouches 1996; contributions: journals. *Honours:* Prix Gustave Gasser 1993. *E-mail:* roland.nadaus@wanadoo.fr (office). *Website:* rolandnadaus.monsite.wanadoo.fr.

NADER, Ralph, AB, LLB; American lawyer, author and consumer advocate; b. 27 Feb. 1934, Winsted, Conn.; s. of Nadra Nader and Rose Bouziane. *Education:* Princeton and Harvard Univs. *Career:* admitted to Conn. Bar 1958, Mass Bar 1959, also US Supreme Court; US Army 1959; law practice in Hartford, Conn. 1959–; Lecturer in History and Govt, Univ. of Hartford 1961–63; Founder and fmr Head of Public Citizen Inc. 1980; Lecturer, Princeton Univ. 1967–68; Co-founder Princeton Project 55 1989; launched political movt Democracy Rising 2001; Green Party cand. for presidential election 1996, 2000, ind. cand. 2004, 2008; mem. ABA; f. Clean Water Action Project, Disability Rights Center, Public Interest Research Groups (PIRGs), Center for Study of Responsive Law, Center for Auto Safety, Pension Rights Center, Project for Corp. Responsibility; Contributing Ed. Ladies Home Journal 1973–81, syndicated columnist, In the Public Interest 1972–; f. The Multinational Monitor (monthly magazine). *Film appearance:* (as himself) Fun with Dick and Jane 2005. *Publications:* Unsafe at Any Speed 1965, Who Runs Congress? 1972, The Consumer and Corporate Accountability 1974, Taming the Giant Corporation (co-author) 1976, The Menace of Atomic Energy (with John Abbotts) 1979, The Lemon Book 1980, Who's Poisoning America? 1981, The Big Boys 1986, Winning the Insurance Game (co-author) 1990, Good Works 1993, No Contest: Corporate Lawyers and the Perversion of Justice in America 1996, The Ralph Nader Reader 2000, Crashing the Party 2002, Civic Arousal 2004, It Happened in the Kitchen: Recipes for Food and Thought, Why Women Pay More (with Frances Cerra Whittelsley), Children First! A Parent's Guide to Fighting Corporate Predators, The Seventeen Traditions 2007, Only the Super-Rich Can Save Us! 2009. *Honours:* Nieman Fellows Award 1965–66, named one of ten Outstanding Young Men of Year by the US Jr Chamber of Commerce 1967, Woodrow Wilson Award, Princeton Univ. 1972. *Address:* Democracy Rising, PO Box 18485, Washington, DC 20036; PO Box 19312, Washington, DC 20036, USA. *E-mail:* info@nader.org. *Website:* www.democracyrising.us; www.nader.org.

NADJ ABONJI, Melinda, MA; Swiss author, singer and musician; b. 22 June 1968, Bečej, Serbia. *Education:* Univ. of Zürich. *Career:* emigrated with parents to Switzerland; singer and violinist, collaborating with rapper/lyricist Jurczok 1001 1998–; Lecturer, Zürich Teachers' Coll. 2003–09; runS writing workshop 2007–. *Recordings:* albums: with Jurczok 1001: Voice Beatbox Violin 2006. *Publications include:* novels: Im Schaufenster im Frühling (In the Shop Window in Spring) 2004, Tauben fliegen auf (Pigeons Fly Away) (German Book Prize 2010, Swiss Book Prize 2010) 2010. *Honours:* Hermann Ganz Prize 2001, Border Crossers Stipend awarded by Robert Bosch Stiftung 2006. *Address:* c/o Dr. Jochen Jung, Jung und Jung Verlag GmbH, Hubert-Sattler-Gasse 1, 5020 Salzburg, Austria (office); c/o Masterplanet, Idastrasse 48, 8003 Zürich, Switzerland (office). *E-mail:* office@jungundjung.at (office); info@masterplanet.ch (office). *Website:* www.jungundjung.at (office); www.masterplanet.ch (office).

NADOLNY, Sten, DPhil; German writer; b. 29 July 1942, Zehdenick/Havel. *Publications:* Netzkarte 1981, Die Entdeckung der Langsamkeit 1983, Selim oder die Gabe der Rede 1990, Das Erzählen und die guten Absichten 1990, Ein Gott auf der Frechheit 1994, Er oder ich 1999, Ullsteinroman 2003, Deustoche Gestalten 2004. *Honours:* Ingeborg Bachmann Prize 1980, Hans Fallada Prize 1985, Vallombrosa Prize, Florence 1986, Ernst Hoferichter Prize 1995.

Literary Agent: Agence Hoffman, Bechsteinstrasse 2, 80804 Munich, Germany. *Telephone:* (89) 308 48 07. *Fax:* (89) 308 21 08. *E-mail:* u.bender@agencehoffman.de. *Website:* www.agencehoffman.de.

NAFISI, Azar, PhD; Iranian writer and academic; *Director, Dialogue Project, School of Advanced International Studies, Johns Hopkins University*; b. 1962; m.; one d. *Education:* Oklahoma Univ., USA. *Career:* fmrly teacher, Tehran Univ., Allemeh Tabatabai Univ.; fmrly visiting fellow, Oxford Univ.; currently Dir of the Dialogue Project, School of Advanced Int. Studies, Johns Hopkins Univ., Washington, DC, USA. *Publications:* Anti-Terra: A Study of Vladimir Nabokov's Novels 1994, Reading 'Lolita' in Tehran: A Memoir in Books 2003, La Voce Verde 2006, Things I've Been Silent About 2009; contrib. numerous chapters and articles on promotion of democracy, human rights in Muslim societies, women's rights, literature, culture. *Literary Agent:* Steven Barclay Agency, 12 Western Avenue, Petaluma, CA 94952, USA. *Telephone:* (707) 773-0654. *Fax:* (707) 778-1868. *E-mail:* steven@barclayagency.com. *Website:* www.barclayagency.com/nafisi.html. *Address:* The Paul H. Nitze School of Advanced International Studies, Johns Hopkins University, The Rome Building, Room 731, 1619 Massachusetts Avenue, Washington, DC 20036, USA (office). *Telephone:* (202) 663-5785 (office). *E-mail:* anafisi@jhu.edu (office); info@azarnafisi.com (office). *Website:* www.sais-jhu.edu (office); www.azarnafisi.com.

NAFTALI, Ben (see Offen, Yehuda)

NAGARKAR, Kiran; Indian writer and playwright; b. 1942, Bombay (now Mumbai). *Education:* Ferguson Coll., Pune, S.I.E.S. Coll., Bombay. *Career:* writer in Marathi and English; has been an Asst Prof. journalist, screenplay writer, and in advertising industry; fmr teacher, S.I.E.S. Coll., Bombay. *Plays:* Bedtime Story 1978, Kabirache Kay Karayache. *Publications:* Saat Sakkam Trechalis (trans. as Seven Sixes are Forty Three) (H. N. Apte Award 1975) 1974, Ravan and Eddie 1994, Cuckold (Sahitya Akademi Award 2001) 2000, God's Little Soldier 2006. *Honours:* Fellow, Rockefeller Foundation; Dalmia Award 1996, German Academic Exchange Service Scholarship 2008–09. *Address:* c/o HarperCollins Publishers India, A 53, Sector 57, Noida, Uttar Pradesh, India (office).

NAGATSUKA, Ryuji; Japanese academic and writer; b. 20 April 1924, Nagoya; m. 1949. *Education:* Univ. of Tokyo. *Career:* Prof., Nihon Univ. 1968–; mem. Asscn Internationale des Critiques Littéraires, Paris. *Publications:* Napoleon tel qu'il était 1969, J'étais un kamikaze 1972, George Sand, sa vie et ses oeuvres 1977, Napoleon (two vols) 1986, Talleyrand 1990; contrib. to Yomiuri Shimbun. *Honours:* Prix Pierre Mille 1972, Prix Senghor 1973. *Address:* 7-6-37 Oizumigakuen-cho, Nerima-ku, Tokyo, Japan.

NAGEL, Paul Chester, BA, MA, PhD; American historian and writer; b. 14 Aug. 1926, Independence, MO; s. of Paul Conrad Nagel and Freda Sabrowsky; m. Joan Peterson 1948; three s. *Education:* Univ. of Minnesota. *Career:* historian, Strategic Air Command, US Air Force, Omaha, 1951–53; Asst Prof., Augustana Coll., Sioux Falls, SD 1953–54; Asst Prof. to Assoc. Prof., Eastern Kentucky Univ., Richmond 1954–61; Visiting Prof., Amherst Coll. 1957–58, Vanderbilt Univ. 1959, Univ. of Minnesota 1964; Faculty, Univ. of Kentucky 1961–65, Prof. of History 1965–69, Dean, Coll. of Arts and Sciences 1965–69; Special Asst to Pres. for Academic Affairs, Univ. of Missouri 1969–71, Prof. of History 1969–78, Vice-Pres. for Academic Affairs 1971–74; Prof. of History and Head of Dept of History, Univ. of Georgia 1978–80; Dir, Virginia Historical Soc., Richmond 1981–85; Distinguished Lee Scholar, Lee Memorial Foundation 1986–90; Visiting Scholar, Duke Univ. 1991–92, Univ. of Minnesota 1992–, Carleton Coll. 1993–; mem. Colonial Williamsburg Foundation (Trustee 1983–95), Mass Historical Soc., Pilgrim Soc., Soc. of American Historians, Southern Historical Asscn (Pres. 1984–85). *Publications:* One Nation Indivisible: The Union in American Thought 1776–1861 1964, This Sacred Trust: American Nationality 1798–1898 1971, American: A History 1977, Descent from Glory: Four Generations of the John Adams Family 1983, Extraordinary Lives: The Art and Craft of American Biography (co-author) 1986, The Adams Women: Abigail and Louisa Adams, Their Sisters and Daughters 1987, George Caleb Bingham (co-author) 1989, The Lees of Virginia: Seven Generations of an American Family 1990, Massachusetts and the New Nation (co-author) 1992, John Quincy Adams: A Public Life, A Private Life 1997, The German Migration to Missouri 2002, George Caleb Bingham: Missouri's Famed Painter and Forgotten Politician 2005; contribs to professional journals and general publications. *Honours:* Best Book Award 1977, Book of the Month Club Main Selection 1983, Laureate of Virginia 1988, American Soc. of Colonial Dames Book Award 1998, Best Biography Award 1999. *Address:* 1314 Marquette Avenue, Apt. 1206, Minneapolis, MN 55403, USA (home).

NAGEL, Thomas, BA, BPhil, PhD; American academic; *Professor of Philosophy and Law, School of Law, New York University*; b. 4 July 1937, Belgrade, Serbia; s. of Walter Nagel and Carolyn Baer Nagel; m. 1st Doris Blum 1968 (divorced 1972); m. 2nd Anne Hollander 1979. *Education:* Cornell and Harvard Univs and Univ. of Oxford, UK. *Career:* Asst Prof. of Philosophy, Univ. of Calif., Berkeley 1963–66; Asst Prof. of Philosophy, Princeton Univ. 1966–69, Assoc. Prof. 1969–72, Prof. 1972–80; Prof. of Philosophy, New York Univ. 1980–, Prof. of Philosophy and Law 1986–, Fiorello LaGuardia Prof. of

Law 2001–03, Univ. Prof. 2002–; Fellow, American Acad. of Arts and Sciences, British Acad. *Publications:* The Possibility of Altruism 1970, Mortal Questions 1979, The View from Nowhere 1986, What Does It All Mean? 1987, Equality and Partiality 1991, Other Minds 1995, The Last Word 1997, The Myth of Ownership (with Liam Murphy) 2002, Concealment and Exposure and other essays 2002. *Honours:* Rolf Schock Prize in Logic and Philosophy, Royal Swedish Acad. of Sciences 2008. *Address:* School of Law, New York University, 40 Washington Square South, 418, New York, NY 10012, USA (office). *Telephone:* (212) 998-6225 (office). *Fax:* (212) 995-4179 (office). *E-mail:* nagelt@juris.law.nyu.edu (office). *Website:* philosophy.fas.nyu.edu (office).

NAGY, Paul, BA, DipArts; Hungarian writer; b. 23 Aug. 1934. *Education:* studied in Hungary and at Sorbonne, Univ. of Paris. *Career:* co-founder, Atelier Hongrois 1962, p'ART video review 1987; mem. Union des écrivains français, Union des écrivains hongrois. *Publications:* Les faineants de Hampstead 1969, Sadisfactions 1977, Journal in-time, I 1984, II 1994, Points de Repères 'Postmodernes': Lyotard, Habermas, Derrida 1993, Les genres nouveaux de la littérature 1995, Sacrés Grecs! 1998, Le texte inaccessible 1999, Recueil d'essais 2005; contrib. to several publications. *Honours:* Prix Attila József, Budapest 2000. *Address:* 141 avenue Jean Jaurès, 92120 Montrouge, France (home). *E-mail:* nagypal@free.fr (home).

NAGY, Phyllis; American/British playwright, filmmaker and theatre director; b. 7 Nov. 1962, New York, NY, USA. *Career:* Writer-in-Residence, Royal Court Theatre, London 1994–95; currently commissioned to write plays for Royal Court Theatre, Royal Nat. Theatre, RSC; playwriting fellowships from Nat. Endowment of the Arts, McKnight Foundation, New York State Council for the Arts. *Plays include:* Weldon Rising, Entering Queens, Butterfly Kiss, The Scarlet Letter, Trip's Crinch, The Strip, Disappeared, The Talented Mr Ripley, Never Land. *Screenplays include:* Mrs. Harris (also dir) 2006. *Radio:* The Strip, Delores. *Honours:* Writers' Guild of GB Award, Eileen Anderson Playwriting Prize, Susan Smith Blackburn Prize, Gracie Allen Award for Outstanding Direction, PEN USA Prize, Mobil Int. Playwriting Prize. *Literary Agent:* c/o Mel Kenyon, Casarotto Ramsay Ltd, Waverley House, 7–12 Noel Street, London, W1F 8GQ, England. *Telephone:* (20) 7287-4450 (office). *Fax:* (20) 7287-9128 (office). *E-mail:* mel@casarotto.co.uk (office). *Website:* www.casarotto.co.uk (office).

NAHAL, Chaman Lal, MA, PhD; Indian writer; b. 2 Aug. 1927, Sialkot. *Education:* Univ. of Delhi, Univ. of Nottingham. *Career:* Lecturer at various univs 1949–62; Reader, Rajasthan Univ. 1962–63; Reader, Univ. of Delhi 1963–80, Prof. 1980–92, mem. 1963; Visiting Fulbright Fellow, Princeton Univ. 1967–70; Fellow, Churchill Coll., Cambridge 1991; visiting lecturer at several univs; columnist, Talking About Books, The Indian Express newspaper 1966–73; Assoc. Prof. of English, Long Island Univ., NY, USA 1968–70. *Publications:* The Weird Dances (short stories) 1965, A Conversation with J. Kristnamurti 1965, D. H. Lawrence: An Eastern View 1970, Drugs and the Other Self (ed.) 1971, The Narrative Pattern in Ernest Hemingway's Fiction 1971, The New Literatures in English 1985, The Bhagavad-Gita: A New Rendering 1987; fiction: My True Faces 1973, Azadi 1975, Into Another Dawn 1977, The English Queens 1979, The Crown and the Loincloth 1982, Sunrise in Fiji 1988, The Salt of Life 1990, The Triumph of the Tricolour 1993, The Ghandi Quartet 1993, Silent Life: Memoirs of a Writer 2005. *Honours:* Sahitya Acad. Award 1977, Fed. of Indian Publrs Award 1977. *Address:* c/o Roli Books Private Ltd, M-75, Greater Kailash, New Delhi 110 048, India.

NAIDOO, Beverley, PhD; South African/British author and educationalist; b. (Beverley Trewhela), 21 May 1943, Johannesburg, South Africa; d. of Ralph Henry Trewhela and Evelyn Levison; m. Nandhagopaul Naidoo 1969; one s. one d. *Education:* Univs of Witwatersrand, York and Southampton. *Career:* NGO worker, SA 1964; detained without trial, SA 1964; teacher, London then Dorset, UK 1969–89; educ. adviser on English and cultural diversity, Dorset 1990–97; writer 1985–; int. writers' workshops and readings 1991–. *Play:* The Playground, Polka Theatre, London 2004. *Radio:* The Other Side of Truth (BBC) 2003. *Publications:* Censoring Reality: An Examination of Non-fiction Books on South Africa 1985, Journey to Jo'burg 1985, Chain of Fire 1989, Through Whose Eyes? Exploring Racism: Reader, Text and Context 1992, Letang and Julie (series – illustrator Petra Rohr-Rouendaal) 1994, No Turning Back 1995, Where is Zami? (illustrator Petra Rohr-Rouendaal) 1998, The Other Side of Truth 2000, Out of Bounds 2001, Baba's Gift (with Maya Naidoo, illustrator Karin Littlewood) 2003, The Great Tug of War and Other Stories 2003, Web of Lies 2004, Burn My Heart 2007, Call of the Deep 2008, S is for South Africa (with photographer Prodeepta Das) 2011, Aesop's Fables (illustrator Piet Grobler). *Honours:* Hon. Visiting Fellow, School of Educ., Univ. of Southampton 1992–2006; Hon. DLitt (Southampton) 2002, (Exeter) 2007; Hon. DUniv (Open Univ.) 2003; The Other Award (UK) 1985, Child Study Children's Book Cttee Award (USA) 1986, 1998, Vlag en Wimpel Award (Netherlands) 1991, African Studies Asscn Africana Children's Book Award (USA) 1998, 2004, 2010, 2011, Arts Council Writer's Award (UK) 1999, Smarties Silver Medal for Children's Books (UK) 2000, Carnegie Medal for Children's Literature (UK) 2000, Jane Addams Book Award (USA) 2002, 2004, Sankei Children's Book Award (Japan) 2003, Parents' Choice Silver Award (USA) 2011. *Literary Agent:* c/o Hilary Delamere, The Agency, 24 Pottery Lane, London, W11 4LZ, England. *Telephone:* (20) 7727-1346. *Fax:* (20) 7727-9037. *E-mail:* info@theagency.co.uk. *Website:* www.theagency.co.uk; www.beverleynaidoo.com.

NAIFEH, Steven Woodward, AB, MA, JD; American writer; b. 19 June 1952, Tehran, Iran. *Education:* Princeton University, Harvard University. *Publications:* Culture Making: Money, Success, and the New York Art World 1976, Moving Up in Style (with Gregory White Smith) 1980, Gene Davis 1981, How to Make Love to a Woman 1982, What Every Client Needs to Know About Using a Lawyer 1982, The Bargain Hunter's Guide to Art Collecting 1982, Why Can't Men Open Up?: Overcoming Men's Fear of Intimacy 1984, The Mormon Murders: A True Story of Greed, Forgery, Deceit, and Death 1988, Jackson Pollack: An American Saga 1989 (Pulitzer Prize for Biography 1991), The Best Lawyers in America (ed. with Gregory White Smith) 1990, The Best Doctors in America (ed. with Gregory White Smith) 1992, Final Justice: The True Story of the Richest Man Ever Tried for Murder 1993, A Stranger in the Family: A True Story of Murder, Madness, and Unconditional Love 1995, On a Street Called Easy, In a Cottage Called Joye 1996, Making Miracles Happen 1997, Vincent van Gogh (with Gregory White Smith) 2011. *Address:* Woodward/White, Inc., 129 First Avenue, SW, Aiken, SC 29801, USA. *E-mail:* info@bestlawyers.com.

NAIPAUL, Sir V(idiadhar) S(urajprasad), Kt, CLit, BA, FRSL; Trinidadian-born writer; b. 17 Aug. 1932, Chaguanas; m. 1st Patricia Ann Hale 1955 (died 1996); m. 2nd Nadira Khannum Alvi 1996; one d. (adopted). *Education:* Queen's Royal Coll., Port-of-Spain and Univ. Coll. Oxford. *Career:* for two years freelance broadcaster with the BBC, producing programmes for the Caribbean area; fiction reviewer on New Statesman 1958–61; grant from Trinidad Govt to travel in Caribbean and S America 1961; in India 1962–63, 1975, 1988–89, in Uganda 1965–66, in USA 1969, 1978–79, 1987–88, in Argentina 1972, 1973–74, 1977, 1991, in Venezuela 1977, 1985, in Iran, Pakistan, Malaysia and Indonesia 1979–80, 1995; mem. Soc. of Authors. *Publications:* The Mystic Masseur 1957, The Suffrage of Elvira 1958, Miguel Street 1959, A House for Mr Biswas 1961, The Middle Passage 1962, Mr Stone and the Knights Companion 1963, An Area of Darkness 1964, The Mimic Men 1967, A Flag on the Island 1967 (collection of short stories), The Loss of El Dorado 1969, In a Free State 1971, The Overcrowded Barracoon (essays) 1972, Guerrillas 1975, India: A Wounded Civilization 1977, A Bend in the River 1979, A Congo Diary 1980, The Return of Eva Perón 1980, Among the Believers 1981, Finding the Centre 1984, The Enigma of Arrival 1987, A Turn In The South 1989, India: A Million Mutinies Now 1990, A Way in the World 1994, Beyond Belief 1998, Letters Between a Father and Son 1999, Reading and Writing: a Personal Account 2000, Half a Life 2001, Literary Occasions 2004, Magic Seeds 2004, A Writer's People 2007, The Masque of Africa: Glimpses of African Belief 2010. *Honours:* Hon. DLitt (Univ. of the W Indies, St Augustine) 1975, (St Andrews) 1979, (Columbia) 1981, (Cambridge) 1983, (London) 1988, (Oxford) 1992; John Llewellyn Rhys Memorial Prize 1958, Somerset Maugham Award 1961, Phoenix Trust Award 1962, Hawthornden Prize 1964, W. H. Smith Award 1968, Booker Prize 1971, Jerusalem Prize 1983, Ingersoll Prize 1986, David Cohen British Literature Prize 1993, Nobel Prize for Literature 2001. *Address:* The Wylie Agency, 17 Bedford Square, London, WC1B 3JA, England. *Telephone:* (20) 7908-5900. *Fax:* (20) 7908-5901. *E-mail:* mail@wylieagency.co.uk. *Website:* www.wylieagency.com.

NAIR, Anita, BA; Indian writer; b. 26 Jan. 1966, Shoranur, Kerala; m.; one s. *Education:* NSS Ottapalam Coll., Kerala. *Career:* fmrly worked in advertising; columnist Mid Day newspaper. *Publications:* Satyr of the Subway and Eleven Other Stories 1997, Malabar Mind 1997, The Better Man 2000, Ladies Coupé 2001, Where the Rain is Born (ed.) 2003, Mistress 2005, Adventures of Nonu, the Skating Squirrel 2006, Living Next Door to Alise 2007, Magical Indian Myths 2008, Goodnight and God Bless 2008, Lessons in Forgetting 2010. *Honours:* Women Achievers Award for Literature, Fed. of Indian Chambers of Commerce and Industry Ladies Org. 2008. *Literary Agent:* c/o The Marsh Agency, 50 Ablemarle Street, London, W1S 4BD, England. *Telephone:* (20) 7493-4361. *Fax:* (20) 7495-8961. *Website:* www.marsh-agency.co.uk. *E-mail:* info@anitanair.net (office). *Website:* www.anitanair.net.

NAIR, M. T. Vasudevan; Indian writer and scriptwriter; b. 15 July 1933, Kudallur, Palakkad Dist, Kerala; m. Kalamandalam Saraswathi. *Career:* Malayalam writer; Ed., Mathrubhoomi Weekly; fmr mem. Faculty, Film and TV Inst., Pune; fmr President, Kerala Sahitya Akademi; fmr Chair. Tunchan Memorial Trust. *Films:* Nirmalyam 1973, Edavazhiyile Poocha Mindapoocha 1979, Oppol 1980, Vikkandu Swapnangal 1980, Valarthu Mrugangal 1981, Thrishna 1981, Manju 1983, Aaroodam 1983, Uyarangalil 1984, Aksharangal 1984, Adiyozhukkukal 1984, Aalkottathil Thaniye 1984, Anu Bandham 1985, Panchagni 1986, Nakhakshatangal 1986, Amritam Gamaya 1987, Vaishali 1988, Aranyakam 1988, Oru Vadakkan Veeragatha 1989, Utharam 1989, Thazhvaram 1990, Perumthachan 1990, Midhya 1990, Venal Kinavukal 1991, Kadavu 1991, Sadhyam 1992, Parinayam 1994, Parinayam 1994, Sukrutham 1994, Ennu Swantham Janakikutty 1998, Daya 1998, Theerthadanam 2001. *Publications:* novels: Naluketthu (Kerala Sahitya Akademi Award 1959) 1958, Asuravithu 1962, Manju 1964, Kaalam (Kendra Sahitya Akademi Award 1970) 1969, Gopura Nadayil (Kerala Sahitya Akademi Award 1982) 1981, Swargam Thurakkunna Samayam (Kerala Sahitya Akademi Award 1986) 1985, Bandhanam, Varikuzhi and Kadavu, Randamoozham 1997. *Honours:* Hon. DLit (Univ. of Calicut) 1996; four-time winner, Nat. Award for Best Screenplay, Jnanpith Award 1995, Best Lifetime Achievement Award, Asianet Film Awards 2003, Padma Bhushan 2005. *Website:* www.mtvasudevannair.com.

NAIRN, Tom, BA, MA; British academic and writer; *Research Fellow, Department of Politics, Durham University;* b. (Thomas Cunningham Nairn),

2 June 1932, Freuchie, Fife, Scotland; s. of David Robertson Nairn and Catherine Herd Cunningham; m. Millicent Petrie. *Education:* Univs of Edinburgh and Oxford, Univ. of Rome, Italy. *Career:* taught at Univ. of Birmingham and Hornsey Coll. of Art, London 1960s; Sr Research Fellow, Transnational Inst., Amsterdam, Netherlands 1973–79; worked for Scottish TV as writer-producer with Agenda Productions 1990–98 before returning to academic life; worked with Ernest Gellner at Central European Univ., Prague, Czechoslovakia; f. Nationalism Studies degree at Grad. School, Univ. of Edinburgh 1995–2000; taught at Monash Univ., Australia 2001–02; Innovation Prof. of Nationalism and Cultural Diversity, Globalism Research Centre, Royal Melbourne Inst. of Tech. (RMIT Univ.) 2002–09; currently Research Fellow, Dept of Politics, Durham Univ.; Fellow, Acad. of the Social Sciences in Australia 2009–; Co-Ed. International Journal of the Humanities. *Publications include:* The Left Against Europe 1973, The Enchanted Glass: Britain and its Monarchy 1988, Faces of Nationalism: Janus Revisited 1997, The Break-Up of Britain: Crisis and Neo-Nationalism 1977, Pariah: Misfortunes of the British Kingdom 2002, After Britain: New Labour and the Return of Scotland 2000, Global Matrix: Nationalism, Socialism and State-Terror (with Paul James) 2005. *Address:* c/o Globalism Research Centre, Royal Melbourne Institute of Technology, GPO Box 2476V, 411 Swanston Street, Melbourne, Vic. 3001, Australia (office). *E-mail:* tom.nairn@yahoo.co.uk (home).

NAJJAR, Alexandre; Lebanese writer and poet; b. 5 Feb. 1967, Beirut; s. of Roger Najjar. *Career:* lawyer; literary critic for two French-language magazines. *Publications:* narratives: La Honte du survivant 1989, Comme un aigle en dérive 1993, L'École de la guerre 1999; novels: Les Exilés du Caucase 1995, L'Astronome 1997, Athina 2000, Lady Virus 2002, Le Roman de Beyrouth 2005, Saint Jean-Baptiste 2005, La Passion de lire 2005, Awraq Jubbrania 2006, Le Silence du Ténor 2006, Phénicia 2008; non-fiction: Pérennité de la littérature libanaise d'expression française, L'Administration de la Société Anonyme Libanaise 1998, Le Procureur de l'Empire: Ernest Pinard (1822–1909) 2001, Le Crapaud 2001, Kahlil Gibran, L'auteur du Prophète (biog.) 2002, De Gaulle et le Liban, Vers l'Orient compliqué (1929–1931) 2002, De Gaulle et le Liban, de la Guerre à l'Indépendance (1941–1943) 2004, Le Mousquetaire 2004; poetry: A quoi rêvent les statues? 1989, Khiam 2000, A quoi rêvent les statues? 1989. *Honours:* Chevalier, Ordre des Arts et des Lettres 2001; Bourse de l'Ecrivain Fondation Hachette 1990, Prix de Poésie de la Ville de Paris 1990, Prix du Palais littéraire 1994, Prix littéraire de l'Asie French-speaking Writers' Asscn 1996, France-Liban Prize 1998, Amsterdam Prize 1999. *E-mail:* alexandre@najjar.org (office). *Website:* www.najjar.org.

NAKAE, Toshitada; Japanese journalist; b. 4 Oct. 1929, Chiba City; m. Yohko Nakae 1959; three s. *Education:* Tokyo Univ. *Career:* local reporter Asahi Shimbun 1953–58, econ. reporter 1958–72, Econ. Ed. 1972–76, Asst Man. Ed. 1976–78, Man. Ed. 1978–83, Dir 1982–97, Pres. 1989–96, Special Adviser 1996–; Pres. Japan Newspaper Publrs' and Eds' Asscn 1991–95. *Publications:* (in English trans.) Cities 1966, The Pulitzer Prize Story 1970, The News Media 1971, The Economy of Cities 1971. *Honours:* Commdr des Arts et des Lettres 1994; Newspaper Culture Award 2007. *Address:* 1-11-1-401 Hamadayama, Suginami-ku, Tokyo, Japan. *Telephone:* (3) 3302-7087. *Fax:* (3) 3302-7087 (home).

NAMBISAN, Kavery, (Kaveri Bhatt), FRCS; Indian writer, essayist and surgeon; b. Karnataka; m. Vijay Nambisan; one d. (from previous m.). *Education:* St John's Medical Coll., Bangalore. *Career:* worked as a surgeon at hosps including Tata Coffee Hosp. in Kodagu, Karnataka; now runs a medical centre for migrant labour; began literary career writing for children's magazines. *Publications:* novels: The Scent of Pepper 1996, Pig on the Run 1998, Mango-Coloured Fish 1998, The Truth (Almost) About Bharat 2002, On Wings of Butterflies 2002, The Hills of Angheri 2005, The Story that Must Not be Told 2008; books for children; contrib. essays on literature and health care to newspapers and magazines. *Address:* c/o Marketing and Promotions Department, Penguin Books India Pvt. Ltd, 11 Community Centre, Panchsheel Park, New Delhi 110 017, India (office). *E-mail:* publicity@in.penguingroup.com (office). *E-mail:* kavery.nambisan@gmail.com (home). *Website:* www.penguinbooksindia.com (office).

NAMJOSHI, Suniti, MBA, PhD; Canadian/British/Indian writer; b. 20 April 1941, Bombay (now Mumbai), India; d. of Manohar Namjoshi and Sarojini Namjoshi (née Naik Nimbalkar); pnr Gillian Hanscombe. *Education:* Univ. of Pune, India, Univ. of Missouri and McGill Univ., Montréal. *Career:* fmr civil servant; fmr Lecturer, Univ. of Toronto; fmr Research Fellow, Exeter Univ., England; lives and writes in Devon. *Publications:* Feminist Fables 1981, 1994, The Conversations of Cow 1985, The Mothers of Maya Diip 1989, Saint Suniti and the Dragon 1994, Building Babel 1996, Goja 2000, Sycorax 2006, several 'Aditi' children's books. *Telephone:* (1297) 443422 (home). *E-mail:* suniti@freeuk.com (home); S.M.Namjoshi@ex.ac.uk. *Website:* people.exeter.ac.uk/smnamjos/welcome.html.

NANDA, Bal Ram, MA; Indian historian and writer; b. 11 Oct. 1917, Rawalpindi; m. Janak Khosla 1946; two s. *Education:* Univ. of Punjab, Lahore. *Career:* Dir, Nehru Memorial Museum and Library, New Delhi 1965–79; mem. Institute for Defence Studies and Analyses, New Delhi, Authors' Guild of India, Indian International Centre. *Publications:* Mahatma Gandhi: A Biography 1958, The Nehrus, Motilal and Jawaharlal 1962, Gandhi: A Pictorial Biography 1972, Gokhale: The Indian Moderates and the British Raj 1977, Jawaharlal Nehru: A Pictorial Biography 1980, Gandhi and His Critics 1986, Gandhi, Pan-Islamism, Imperialism and Nationalism in India 1989, In Gandhi's Footsteps: Life and Times of Jamnalal Bajaj 1990, Jawaharal Nehru: Rebel and Statesman 1996, The Making of a Nation: India's Road to Independence 1998, In Search of Gandhi 2002, Witness to Partition 2003; editor: Socialism in India 1972, Indian Foreign Policy: The Nehru Years 1975, Science and Technology in India 1977, Essays in Modern Indian History 1980, Selected Works of Gobind Ballabh Pant, Vols 1–18, 1993–2002; Mahatma Gandhi: 125 Years 1995, Road to Pakistan: The Life and Times of Mohammad Ali Jinnah 2010; contributions: numerous newspapers, magazines and journals. *Honours:* Rockefeller Fellowship 1964, National Fellowship, Indian Council of Social Science Research, New Delhi 1979, Dadabhai Naoroji Memorial Prize 1981, Padma Vibhushan 2003. *Address:* S-174 Panchshila Park, New Delhi 110 017, India (home).

NAPELS, Stella (see Van De Laar, Waltherus Antonius Bernardinus)

NAPIER, William (Bill) McDonald, PhD, FRAS; British astronomer and writer; b. 29 June 1940, Perth, Scotland; m. Nancy Miller Baillie 1965; one s. one d. *Education:* Univ. of Glasgow. *Career:* mem. Int. Astronomical Union; Founding mem. Spaceguard UK. *Publications:* The Cosmic Serpent 1982, The Cosmic Winter 1990, The Origin of Comets 1990, Nemesis (novel) 1998, Revelation (novel) 2000, The Lure (novel) 2002, Shattered Icon (novel) 2004, The Furies (novel) 2009; contrib. to New Scientist, Astronomy Today. *Honours:* Hon. Prof., Cardiff Univ. 2001–, Univ. of Buckingham 2011–; Arthur Beer Memorial Prize (co-recipient) 1986–87. *Website:* www.bill-napier.com.

NARANG, Gopi Chand, MA, PhD; Indian academic and writer; *Professor Emeritus, University of Delhi*; b. 11 Feb. 1931, Dukki; s. of Dharam Chand Narang and Tekan Bai; m. Manorma Narang; two s. *Education:* Univ. of Delhi, Indiana Univ. *Career:* Urdu writer; Lecturer, St Stephen's Coll., Delhi 1957–58; Lecturer, Univ. of Delhi 1959–61, Reader of Urdu 1961–74, Prof. of Urdu 1985–2005, Prof. Emer. 2005–; Fellow, Royal Asiatic Soc., London, UK 1963–72; Prof. and Head, Jamia Millia Islamia Univ. 1974–85, Acting Vice-Chancellor 1981–82; Visiting Prof., Univ. of Wisconsin at Madison, USA 1963–65, Univ. of Minnesota 1968–70, Univ. of Oslo, Norway 1997; Vice-Pres. Sahitya Akademi 1998–2002, Pres. 2003–07; mem. Nat. Book Trust 1997–2007; mem. Advisory Bd T.V. Urdu Channel, Doordarshan 2008–; mem. Advisory Cttee on Culture, Govt of India 2008–; mem. Cen. Advisory Bd of Educ., Govt of India 2009–. *Publications:* in Urdu: Hindustani Qisson se Makhuz Urdu Mansnawiyan 1959, 2002, Imla Nama 1974, Puranon ki Kahaniyan 1976, Wazahati Kitabiyat 1976, Safar Ashna 1982, Iqbal ka Fan 1983, Usloobiyat-e-Mir 1985, Naya Urdu Afsana 1986, Saniha-e-Karbala bataur She'ri Isti'ara 1986, Amir Khusrau ka Hindavi Kalaam 1987, Urdu ki Nai Kitab 1989, Adabi Tanqeed aur Usloobiyaat 1989, Qaari Asaas Tanqeed 1992, Saakhtiyaat, Pas-Saakhtiyaat aur Mashriqi She'riyaat 1995, Urdu Maba'd-e-Jadidiyat par Mukalama 1998, Urdu Ghazal aur Hindustani Zehn-o-Tahzib 2002, Hindustan ki Tehreek-e-Azadi aur Urdu Shairi 2004, Taraqqi Pasandi Jadidiyat Ma'bad Jadidiyat 2004, Jadidiat ke Baad 2005, Anis-o-Dabir 2005, Wali Dakni 2005, Urdu Zaban aur Lisaniyaat 2006, Sheriyat Tashkeel o Tanqeed 2009, Dekhna Taqreer ki Lazzat 2010, Khwaja Ahmad Faruqi ke Khutoot Gopi Chand Narang ke Naam 2010; in English: as ed.: Karkhandari Dialect of Delhi 1961, Readings in Literary Urdu Prose 1967, Anthology of Modern Urdu Poetry 1981, Contribution of Writers to Indian Freedom Movement 1985, Rajinder Singh Bedi: Selected Short Stories 1989, Krishnan Chander: Selected Short Stories 1990, Balwant Singh: Selected Short Stories 1996, Urdu Language and Literature: Critical Perspectives 1991, Encyclopedia of Indian Literature (four vols) 1987–94, Masterpieces of Indian Literature (three vols) 1997, Let's Learn Urdu 2000. *Honours:* Padma Shri 1991, Padma Bhushan 2004; Hon. DLitt (Central Univ. of Hyderabad) 2007, (Aligarh Muslim Univ.) 2009, (Manulana Azad Nat. Urdu Univ.) 2009; Ghalib Award 1962, 1985, Nat. Award 1977, Iqbal Centenary Gold Medal 1977, Mir Award 1977, Urdu-Hindi Sahitya Cttee Award 1985, Amir Khusrau Award 1987, Canadian Acad. of Urdu Language and Literature Award 1987, Rajiv Gandhi Award 1994, Sahitya Akademi Award 1995, Rockefeller Foundation Fellowship 1997, Khwaja Ashkar Husain Award 2000, Indira Gandhi Memorial Fellowship 2002–04, Bapu Reddy Jaatheeya Sahiti Puraskaram 2003, Zainabia Trust Award 2003, Mazzini Gold Medal, Italian Govt 2005, Sahir Ludhianvi Award 2005. *Address:* D-252 Sarvodaya Enclave, New Delhi 110 017, India (home). *Telephone:* (11) 26511460 (home); (11) 26568956 (home). *E-mail:* narang_5@yahoo.co.in (home). *Website:* gopichandnarang.com.

NARAYAMA, Fujio; Japanese writer and poet; b. 13 June 1948, Iwate. *Education:* Toho Gakuen Junior College, Tokyo. *Career:* mem. Japan Writers Asscn; MWA; Mystery Writers of Japan; Sino-Japanese Cultural Exchange Society. *Publications:* Manhattan Ballad, 1977; Sanctuary of Evil, 1979; Lay Traps in the Winter, 1981; The Scarred Bullet, 1989; Neverending Night, 1992. *Honours:* Iwate Arts Festival Awards, 1967, 1969; All Yomimono New Writer's Award, 1975.

NASAW, David, PhD; American writer and historian; *Distinguished Professor of History, City University of New York*. *Education:* Columbia Univ. *Career:* Distinguished Prof. of History, Graduate Center, City Univ. of New York; historical consultant for television documentaries. *Publications:* Schooled to Order: A Social History of Public Schooling in United States 1979, Children of the City: At Work and at Play 1985, Going Out: The Rise and Fall of Public Amusements 1993, The Chief: The Life of William Randolph

Hearst 2000, Andrew Carnegie 2006; articles include: Learning to go to the Movies, in American Heritage (Nov. 1993), Teaching Cultural History to Graduate Students, in Radical History Review (Fall 1996), Cities of Light, Landscapes of Pleasure, in Landscapes of Modernity (ed. by Oliver Zunz and David Ward) 1992; contrib. to New Yorker, The Nation, Traveler and other periodicals. *Honours:* Bancroft Prize 2000, J. Anthony Lucas Prize 2000, American History Book Prize 2006. *Address:* The Graduate Center, The City University of New York, 365 Fifth Avenue, New York, NY 10016-4309, USA (office). *Telephone:* (212) 817-8431 (office). *E-mail:* dnasaw@gc.cuny.edu (office).

NASH, Gary Baring, BA, PhD; American academic and writer; *Director, National Center for History in the Schools, UCLA*; b. 27 July 1933, Philadelphia, PA; m. 1st Mary Workum 1955 (divorced); one s. three d.; m. 2nd Cynthia Shelton 1981. *Education:* Princeton Univ. *Career:* Asst to the Dean, Graduate School, Princeton Univ. 1959–61, Instructor 1964–65, Asst Prof. 1965–66; Asst Prof., Univ. of California at Los Angeles 1966–68, Assoc. Prof. 1969–72, Prof. of History 1972–, Dean, Undergraduate Curriculum Development 1984–91, Assoc. Dir, National Center for History in the Schools 1988–94, Dir 1994–; Co-Chair., National History Studies Project 1992–96; mem. American Antiquarian Soc., American Historical Asscn, Inst. of Early American History and Culture, Organization of American Historians (pres., 1994–95), Soc. of American Historians, American Philosophical Soc., American Acad. of Arts and Sciences. *Publications:* Quakers and Politics: Pennsylvania, 1681–1726 1968, Class and Society in Early America 1970, The Great Fear: Race in the Mind of America (ed. with Richard Weiss) 1970, Red, White, and Black; The Peoples of Early America 1974, The Urban Crucible: Social Change, Political Consciousness, and the Origins of the American Revolution 1979, Struggle and Survival in Colonial America (ed. with David Sweet) 1980, The Private Side of American History (co-ed.), 2 vols 1975, 1979, The American People: Creating a Nation and a Society (with J. R. Jeffrey), 2 vols 1985, 1989, Retracing the Past, 2 vols 1985, 1989, Race, Class and Politics: Essays on American Colonial and Revolutionary Society 1986, Forging Freedom: The Formation of Philadelphia's Black Community, 1720–1840 1988, Race and Revolution 1990, Freedom by Degrees: Emancipation and Its Aftermath in Pennsylvania (with Jean R. Soderlund) 1991, American Odyssey: The United States in the 20th Century 1991, History on Trial: Culture Wars and the Teaching of the Past (with Charlotte Crabtree and Ross Dunn) 1997, Forbidden Love: The Secret History of Mixed-Race America 1999, First City: Philadelphia and the Forging of Historical Memory 2002, Landmarks of the American Revolution 2003, African American Lives: The Struggle for Freedom (co-author) 2005, The Unknown American Revolution: The Unruly Birth of Democracy and the Struggle to Create America 2005, The Forgotten Fifth: African Americans in the Age of Revolution 2006, Friends of Liberty: Thomas Jefferson, Tadeusz Kosciuszko, and Agrippa Hull 2008, The Liberty Bell: An American Icon 2009; contrib. to professional journals. *Honours:* Guggenheim Fellowship 1969–70, ACLS Fellowship 1973–74. *Address:* 1336 Las Canoas Road, Pacific Palisades, CA 90272, USA (home). *Telephone:* (310) 825-4702 (office); (310) 454-5824 (home). *Fax:* (310) 454-1808 (home). *E-mail:* gnash@ucla.edu (home).

NASHASHIBI, Nassiriddin; Palestinian journalist; b. 1924. *Education:* American Univ. of Beirut. *Career:* Arab Office, Jerusalem 1945–47; Chief Chamberlain, Amman, Jordan 1951; Dir Gen. Hashemite Broadcasting 1952; Ed. Akhbar al Youm, Cairo; Chief Ed. Al-Gumhuriyah, 1959–65; Rep. of the Arab League 1965–67; Diplomatic Ed. Al-Ahram; freelance journalist in Europe and the Middle East; Diplomatic Commentator, Jordanian, Israeli and other Middle Eastern TV stations. *Publications:* What Happened in the Middle East 1958, Political Short Stories 1959, Return Ticket to Palestine 1960, Some Sand 1962, An Arab in China 1964, Roving Ambassador 1970, The Ink is Very Black 1976 and 40 other books. *Honours:* Order of Independence, Jordan; Order of the Jordanian Star. *Address:* 55 Avenue de Champel, Geneva, Switzerland; PO Box 1897, Jerusalem 91017, Israel; 26 Lowndes Street, London, SW1X 9JD, England. *Telephone:* (22) 3463763 (Geneva) (office); (20) 7235-1427 (London) (office).

NASIR, Agha, MA; Pakistani television executive and playwright; *Executive Director, Geo TV Network*; b. 9 Feb. 1937, Meerut, UP, India; s. of Ali Ahmad Khan and Ghafari Begum; m. Safia Sultana 1957; one s. two d. *Education:* Karachi Univ. *Career:* Programmes Man. Pakistani TV 1967–68, Additional Gen. Man. 1967, Gen. Man. 1969–72, Dir Programmes Admin. 1972–86, Deputy Man. Dir 1986–87, Man. Dir 1987–88; Man. Dir Nat. Film Devt Corpn 1979; Dir-Gen. Pakistan Broadcasting Corpn 1989–92; Chief Exec. Shalimar Recording and Broadcasting Co. 1992–97; media consultant 1997–; Exec. Dir Geo TV Network 1998–. *Radio:* has written numerous features and plays for radio and produced more than 500 programmes. *Television:* has written more than 20 plays for TV and has produced about 100. *Publications:* Saat Dramay (plays), Television Dramey (TV plays), Gumshuda Log (collection of articles), Gulshan-e-Yaad, Hum Jeetay Jee Masroof Rahey (collection and comments on poet Faiz Ahmad Faiz), This is PTV (history or Pakistan Television). *Honours:* recipient of numerous awards for radio and TV plays; Pride of Performance Award from Pres. of Pakistan for services in field of broadcasting 1993. *Address:* Geo TV Network, 40 Blue Area, Fazal-ul-huq Road, Islamabad (office); House No. 23, Street No. 3, F-8/3, Islamabad, Pakistan (home). *Telephone:* (51) 2263685 (home); (51) 2852619 (home). *Fax:* (51) 2827396 (office); (51) 2263685 (home). *E-mail:* agha.nasir@geo.tv (office). *Website:* www .geo.tv (office).

NASIRI, Buthaina al; Iraqi short story writer and publisher; b. 1947. *Education:* Univ. of Baghdad Coll. of Arts. *Career:* moved to Cairo, Egypt 1979, where she runs a publishing house specializing in the works of Iraqi writers under UN sanctions. *Publications:* five short story collections in Arabic; Final Night (in trans.) 2003. *Address:* c/o The American University in Cairo Press, 113 Sharia Kasr el Aini Street, Cairo, Egypt. *E-mail:* aucpress@ aucegypt.edu. *Website:* www.aucpress.com.

NASR, Ramsey; Dutch poet, writer, actor and musical theatre director; *Poet Laureate*; b. 28 Jan. 1974, Rotterdam. *Education:* Studio Herman Teirlinck, Antwerp. *Career:* actor, Het Zuidelijk Toneel 1995–90; leading parts in several films and TV series; also dir of musical theatre productions, including Mozart's The Abduction from the Seraglio; numerous poetry performances at int. festivals; Poet Laureate of the Netherlands 2009–(13). *Plays:* theatrical monologues (as writer and actor): De doorspeler – Geen lied (Taalunie Toneelschrijfprijs—Playwright's Prize for Best Theatre Text) 2000); other: Leven in Hel – de operette (libretto writer, actor, singer, director), Il Re Pastore, opera by Mozart (trans./adaptation, dir), Een totale Entführung (adaptation/trans., dir of new adaptation of Mozart's The Abduction from the Seraglio). *Films include:* as actor: De man met de hond 1998, Mariken 2000, Liefje 2001, Magonia 2001, Het Echte Leven 2008. *Television:* actor in series De Enclave – Overspel. *Publications:* poetry collections: 27 gedichten & Geen lied 2000, onhandig bloesemend (Hugues C. Pernath Prize) 2004, onze-lieve-vrouwe-zeppelin 2006, tussen lelie en waterstofbom 2009, anthology of poetry in English: Heavenly Life (trans. David Colmer) 2010; prose: Kapitein Zeiksnor & De Twee Culturen (novella) 2001; music theatre: Twee libretto's 2002; essays and opinion articles: Van de vijand en de muzikant 2006; travel diaries: Homo safaricus 2009, In de gouden buik van Boeddha (Burma/ Myanmar) 2010; contrib. of articles to newspapers and journals. *Honours:* City Poet of Antwerp 2005; Dr hc (Antwerp); Mary Dresselhuys Prize for outstanding acting performance 2000, Hugues C. Pernath Prize (biennial prize for best volume of poetry) 2004, Journalist for Peace, Humanistic Peace Council 2006, Humanistic Peace Council Journalist for Peace 2006, Poet of the Fatherland 2009. *Address:* c/o Uitgeverij De Bezige Bij, Van Miereveldstraat 1, 1071 Amsterdam, Netherlands (office). *Telephone:* (20) 305-9810 (office). *E-mail:* info@debezigebij.nl (office). *Website:* www.ramseynasr.nl.

NASRALLAH, Emily, BA; Lebanese writer, journalist and translator; b. (Emily Abi Rashed), 6 July 1931, Kfeir; d. of Daoud Abi Rashed and Lutfa Abou Nasr; m. Philip Nasrallah 1957; two s. two d. *Education:* Shoueifat Nat. Coll., Beirut Univ. Coll. and American Univ. of Beirut. *Career:* mem. writing staff Al-Sayyad magazine and Al-Anwar newspaper 1955–70; Cultural and Public Relations Consultant Beirut Univ. Coll. 1973–75; Feature Writer and Ed. Fayruz Magazine 1981–87; ECWA Del. to UN Women's Forum on Population and Devt, New York, USA 1974; writer and women's rights activist, one of the Beirut Decentrist women writers; participated in Olympics Authors' Festival, Calgary, Canada 1988; panellist and guest reader PEN Int. Congress, Toronto and Montréal, Canada 1989; currently short story writer, Sayyidaty magazine. *Publications:* novels: Toyour Ayloui (trans. as Birds of September; Laureate Best Novel, Said Akl Prize, Friends of the Book Prize) 1962, Shajarat ad-Dufia (trans. as The Oleander Tree) 1968, Ar-Rahina (trans. as The Bondaged) 1974, Tilka az-Zikrayat (trans. as Those Memories) 1980, Al Iklaa aks az-Zaman (trans. as Flight Against Time) 1981, Al Jamr ak-Ghafi (trans. as Sleeping Ember) 1995, Ma Hadatha fi Jozor Tamaya (trans. as What Happened in Tamaya Islands) 2006; short story collections: Jazirat al-Wahm (trans. as Island of Illusion) 1973, Al Younbouh (trans. as The Source) 1978, Al Mara'a Fi saba't Ashar Qissah (trans. as The Woman in Seventeen Stories) 1983, Al Tahouna al Daiaa (trans. as The Lost Mill) 1984, Khoubzouna al-Yawmi (trans. as Our Daily Bread) 1990, Awraq Mansiya (trans. as Forgotten Papers) 1992, Mahattat ar-Rahil (trans. as Stations of Departure) 1996, Al-Layali al-Ghajariyyah (trans. as Gypsy Nights) 1998, Aswad wa Abiyad (trans. as Black and White) 2001, Ryah Janoubia (trans. as Southern Winds) 2005; children's books: Al-Bahira (trans. as The Resplendent Flower) 1975, Shadi al-Saghir (trans. as Little Shadi) 1977, Yawmiyyat Hirr (trans. as A Cat's Diary; IBBY Children's Book Prize 1998) 1997, Rawat li al-Ayyam (trans as Time Has Told Me) 1997, Al'Ghazaleh (trans. as The Deer) 1998, Anda al-Khawta (trans. as Crazy Anda) 2000, Aina Tazhab Anda (trans as Where does Anda Go?) 2002; non-fiction: Fil-Bal (memoirs) 2000, Nisaa Raidat (trans. as Biographies of Pioneer Women, six vols) 2001. *Honours:* Khalil Gibran Prize, Arab Heritage Union, Australia 1991. *Fax:* (1) 862483 (home). *E-mail:* pnsralah@cyberia.net.lb (home). *Website:* www.emilynasrallah.com (home).

NASRALLAH, Ibrahim; Palestinian poet, writer, painter and photographer; *Vice President, Darat al-Fun Cultural Centre*; b. 1954, Amman, Jordan. *Career:* born and grew up in Al-Wihdat refugee camp; trained as a teacher in United Nations Relief and Works Agency inst.; taught in Saudi Arabia 1976–78; returned to Jordan 1978; journalist, Dostur, Afaq and Hasad newspapers 1978–2005; full-time writer 2005–; Dir of Cultural Affairs, Darat al-Funun arts centre, Amman 1996–2002, now Vice Pres.; mem. Sakakini Gen. Ass. *Publications:* 15 poetry collections, 11 novels including: Barari Al-Humma (trans. as Prairies of Fever 1998) (novel) 1985, Inside the Night 1992 (novel, in trans.) 2007, Rain Inside (poetry, in trans.) 2009. *Honours:* Award for Best Poetry Collection published in Jordan, Arar Literary Award for body of work 1991, Jordanian Writers Soc. Hon. Prize (three times) for poetry collections, Sultan Oweiss Award 1987, Al-Uweis Literary Award (UAE) 1997. *Literary Agent:* Pontas Agency, Sèneca 31, 08006 Barcelona, Spain. *Tele-*

phone: (93) 2182212. *Fax:* (93) 2182212. *E-mail:* anna@pontas-agency.com. *Website:* www.pontas-agency.com.

NASREEN, Taslima, BS, MD, MB; Bangladeshi/Swedish feminist, writer and doctor; *Research Scholar, New York University*; b. 25 Aug. 1962, Mymensingh, East Pakistan (now Bangladesh); d. of Rajab Ali and Edul Wara; m. 1st Rudra Mohammad Shahidullah 1982 (divorced 1986); m. 2nd Nayeemul Islam Khan (divorced 1991); m. 3rd Minar Mahmood 1991 (divorced 1992). *Education:* Mymensingh Medical Coll., Dhaka Univ. *Career:* practised as a gynaecologist and anaesthesiologist 1986–93; columnist, Khoborer Kagoj 1989; books banned in Bangladesh and Indian state of West Bengal 1993–2004, first fatwa (death threat) pronounced against her 1993; forced to leave Bangladesh for Sweden 1994, later in Germany, USA, France and India; further fatwas issued against her in India 2004–08, forced to leave there 2008; currently Research Scholar, New York Univ., USA; lectures on human rights worldwide. *Publications include:* Shikore Bipul Khudha 1986, Nirbashito bahire Ontore 1989, Amar Kichu Jay Ashe Ne 1990, Atole Ontorin 1991, Nirbachito Kolam 1991, Nosto meyer nosto goddo 1992, Oporpokkho 1992, Shodh 1992, Balikar Gollachut 1992, Nimontron 1993, Laija (novel) 1993, Phera 1993, Choto choto dukkho kotha (selected columns) 1994, Bhromor koio gia 1994, Nirbashito Narir Kobita 1996, Amar Meyebela (autobiog.) 1999, Jolopodyo 2000, Utal Hawa (autobiog.) 2002, Forashi Premik 2002, Dwihkandita (autobiog.) 2003, Ko 2003, Sei Sob Ondhokar (autobiog.) 2004, Khali Khali Lage 2004, Kicchukhan Thako 2005, Ami bhalo nei, tumi bhalo theko prio desh (autobiog.) 2006, Minu (short stories) 2007, Narir Kono Desh Nei 2007, Bhalobaso? Cchai Baso 2008, Bondini 2008, Shorom 2009, Nei, kichu nei 2010 (autobiog.). *Honours:* Hon. Citizen, Esch, Luxembourg, Metz, France, Thionville, France 2011; Dr hc (Ghent Univ., Belgium) 1995, (American Univ. in Paris) 2005, (Université Catholique de Louvain, Belgium) 2010; Ananda Puroshkar, India 1992, Kurt Tukholsky Prize, Sweden 1994, Feminist of the Year, USA 1994, Human Rights Award, French Govt 1994, Edit de Nantes Award, France 1994, Monismanien Prize, Sweden 1995, Sakharov Prize, European Parl. 1995, Int. Humanist Award, Int. Humanist and Ethical Union 1996, Erwin Fischer Award 2002, UNESCO Prize 2004, Grand Prix International Condorcet-Aron 2005, Prix Simone de Beauvoir 2008, Citoyenne d'honneur, France 2008, Woodrow Wilson Fellowship, USA, Crossing Border Award 2009, Prins Global Scholars Fellowship, New York Univ., USA 2009, Medal of Honour, City of Lyon, France 2009. *Telephone:* (718) 419-4713 (New York). *E-mail:* taslima.nasrin@gmail.com; email@taslimanasrin.com. *Website:* taslimanasrin.com.

NASSAR, Eugene Paul, BA, MA, PhD; American academic, writer and poet; b. 20 June 1935, Utica, NY; m. Karen Nocian 1969; one s. two d. *Education:* Kenyon Coll., Worcester Coll., Oxford, Cornell Univ. *Career:* Instructor in English, Hamilton Coll. 1962–64; Asst Prof., Utica Coll., Syracuse Univ. 1964–66, Assoc. Prof. 1966–71, Prof. of English 1971–; Dir, Ethnic Heritage Studies Center. *Publications:* Wallace Stevens: An Anatomy of Figuration 1965, The Rape of Cinderella: Essays in Literary Continuity 1970, Selections from a Prose Poem: East Utica 1971, The Cantos of Ezra Pound: The Lyric Mode 1975, Wind of the Land: Two Prose Poems 1979, Essays: Critical and Metacritical 1983, Illustrations to Dante's Inferno 1994, A Walk Around the Block: Literary Texts and Social Contexts 1999; editor: several books; contributions: various publications. *Honours:* NEH Fellowship 1972. *Address:* 918 Arthur Street, Utica, NY 13501, USA (home).

NASSER, Amjad; Jordanian poet and journalist; *Arts Editor and Associate Editor, Al-Quds Al-Arabi newspaper*; b. 1955, al-Turra. *Career:* worked as tv journalist in Jordan; fmr journalist, Al-Hadaf, Beirut, Lebanon; fmr Arts Ed., Al-Ufq magazine, Cyprus; based in London 1987–; co-founder, Arts Ed. and Assoc. Ed., Al-Quds Al-Arabi newspaper 1987–; co-founding ed, Banipal magazine; jury mem. Lettre Ulysses Award 2006. *Publications:* Flight of Wings (travel writing) 1998, Under More than One Sky (travel writing) 2002; several poetry collections. *Address:* Al-Quds Al-Arabi, 164-166 King Street, London W6 0QU, England (office). *Telephone:* (20) 8741-8008 (office). *Fax:* (20) 8741-8902 (office). *E-mail:* alquds@alquds.co.uk (office). *Website:* www.alquds.co.uk (office).

NASTA, Susheila, MBE, MA, DLitt, FRSA; British literary critic, teacher, broadcaster and editor; *Editor, Wasafiri*; b. (Sheila Nasta), 16 Oct. 1953, Wallington, Surrey, England; d. of Kanayalal Nasta and Winnifred Nasta; m.; one s. one d. *Education:* Univ. of Kent, Univ. of London. *Career:* lived in India, Holland and Germany before returning to Great Britain 1960s; held academic posts at Univ. of Cambridge; Sr Lecturer, School of English and Drama Queen Mary, Univ. of London –1998, founding-course dir MA in Nat. and Int. Literatures in English Inst. of English Studies –1998, currently Sr Visiting Research Fellow and Assoc. Fellow Inst. of English Studies; Prof. of Modern Literature, Open Univ. 1998–, Founding Ed. Wasafiri literary journal; mem. exec. cttee Commonwealth Writers Prize; judge for many literary prizes, including British Book Awards Nibbies Prize. *Radio:* plays: Highway in the Sun, El Dorado: West One. *Publications include:* Critical Perspectives on Sam Selvon 1988, Motherlands: Women's Writing from Africa, the Caribbean and South Asia (ed.) 1991, Tiger's Triumph 1995, Reading the 'New' Literatures in a Postcolonial Era (ed.) 2000, Home Truths: Fictions of the South Asian Diaspora in Britain 2002, Writing Across Worlds (ed.) 2004. *Address:* Literature Department, Faculty of Arts, The Open University, Walton Hall, Milton Keynes, MK7 6AA (office); Wasafiri: The Open University in London, 1–11 Hawley Crescent, London, NW1 8NP, England (office). *Telephone:* (1908) 652092 (Milton Keynes) (office). *E-mail:* s.m.nasta@open.ac.uk (office); wasafiri@open.ac.uk (office). *Website:* www.wasafiri.org (office).

NATHAN, Robert Stuart, BA; American writer; b. 13 Aug. 1948, Johnstown, PA. *Education:* Amherst College. *Career:* Producer, Law and Order series, NBC-TV. *Publications:* Amusement Park, 1977; Rising Higher, 1981; The Religion, 1982; The Legend, 1986; The White Tiger, 1988; In the Deep Woods, 1989. Other: In the Deep Woods (television film), 1992. Contributions: periodicals and national public radio.

NATSUKI, Shizuko; Japanese novelist; b. (Shizuko Idemitsu), 21 Dec. 1938, Tokyo; m. Yoshihide Idemitsu 1963; one s. one d. *Education:* Keio Univ. *Career:* screenplay for Only I Know (Japanese TV); followed by numerous novels, short stories and screenplays. *Films:* Tragedy of W 1984. *Plays:* novels adapted for the stage: Tragedy of W 1993, Actress X 1994. *Works adapted for television include:* The Angel Vanishes 1972 and more than 200 others. *Publications:* 39 novels including The Angel Vanishes 1970, Disappearance 1973, Murder at Mt. Fuji 1984, Dome 1986, The Third Lady 1987, The Obituary arrives at Two O'Clock 1988, Portal of the Wind 1990, Marianne 1997, Mariko 1999, The Punishment 2001, and about 240 novelettes and short stories. *Honours:* Mystery Writers of Japan Prize 1973, Prix du Roman d'Aventures (France) 1989, Nishinippon Shinsbeen Cultural Award 1999, Fukuoka Prefecture Cultural Award 2001. *Address:* 2-6-1 Ooike, Minami-ku, Fukuoka-shi 815-0073, Japan. *Telephone:* (92) 553-1893. *Fax:* (92) 552-0181.

NATSUME, Fusanosuke; Japanese Manga researcher and critic; b. 18 Aug. 1950, Tokyo. *Education:* Aoyama Gakuin Univ. *Career:* fmrly worked in publishing; Manga critic and historian; gives lectures worldwide; columnist Shunkan Asahi magazine 1982–91; currently Prof. of Literature, Gakushuin Univ., Tokyo; also Guest Prof., Hanazono Univ., Kyoto. *Television:* Natsume Fusanosuke's 'Class' - Manga wa Naze Omoshiroinoka (Why is Manga Interesting?) (weekly programme, NHK TV) 1987–89, Manga Yawa (NHK BS2 TV) 1996–2009. *Publications:* Natsume Fusanosuke no mangagaku (Natsume Fusanosuke's Mangalogy) 1985, Tezuka Osamu wa doko ni iru (Where is Tezuka Osamu?) 1992, Tezuka Osamu no Bouken (The Adventure of Tezuka Osamu) 1995, Manga no Yomikata (How to Read and Understand Manga) 1995, Manga/Sekai/Senryaku 2001, Manga no Fukayomi Otonoayomi (Profound and Mature Reading of Manga) 2004.

NATUSCH, Sheila Ellen, MA; British/New Zealand writer and illustrator; b. 14 Feb. 1926, Invercargill, New Zealand; m. Gilbert G. Natusch 1950 (died 2005). *Education:* Otago Univ. *Career:* worked in Nat. Library of NZ, old Dominion Museum, New Zealand Correspondence School; produces her own paperbacks (Nestegg Books); has produced numerous illustrations for her own and others' books 1980s–. *Publications:* Stewart Island (with N. S. Seaward) 1951, Native Plants 1956, Native Rock 1959, Animals of New Zealand 1967, A Bunch of Wild Orchids 1968, New Zealand Mosses 1969, Brother Wohlers: A Biography 1969, On the Edge of the Bush: Women in Early Southland 1976, Hell and High Water: A German Occupation of the Chatham Islands 1843–1910 1977, The Cruise of the Acheron: Her Majesty's Steam Vessel on Survey in New Zealand Waters 1848–1851 1978, The Roaring Forties 1978, Fortnight in Iceland 1979, Wild Fare for Wilderness Foragers 1979, Pop Kelp and Poha Bags 1980, A Pocketful of Pebbles 1983, Southward Ho!: The Search for a Southern Edinburgh 1844 1985, Granny Gurton's Garden (with Lois Chambers) 1987, William Swainson: The Anatomy of a Nineteenth-Century Naturalist 1987, Roy Traill of Stewart Island 1991, An Island Called Home 1992, The Natural World of the Traills: An Investigation into Some of the 19th Century Naturalists of a Particular Family in Scotland and the Colonies 1996, Ruapuke Visited 1998, My Dear Friend Tuckett, Vol. I 1998, Vol. II 1999, Wellington Awash 2000, Pop Kelp 2000, Rugged Shores 2001, Out of Our Tree 2001, The Salty Shore 2003, Letters from Jean 2004, Journal on the Wing: May–August 1975 2007, Round the World in '83 2007, So Far So Good: an Autobibliography 2007, Emily and Dorothea: two Southland artists 2007; Erinnerungen by J.F.H Wohlers (illustrations) 2007; contrib. to books, periodicals and dictionaries of biog. *Honours:* NZ Order of Merit 2007; Hubert Church Award, PEN New Zealand 1969. *Address:* 46 Owhiro Bay Parade, Wellington 6023, New Zealand (home). *Telephone:* (4) 3836645 (home).

NAUGHTIE, (Alexander) James, MA; British journalist; b. 9 Aug. 1951, Aberdeen, Scotland; s. of Alexander Naughtie and Isabella Naughtie; m. Eleanor Updale 1986; one s. two d. *Education:* Univ. of Aberdeen and Syracuse Univ., USA. *Career:* journalist, The Scotsman (newspaper) 1977–84, The Guardian 1984–88, also Chief Political Corresp.; Presenter The World at One, BBC Radio 1988–94, The Promes, BBC Radio and TV 1991–, Today, BBC Radio 4 1994–, Book Club BBC Radio 4 1998–; mem. Council Gresham Coll. 1997–. *Publications:* The Rivals 2001, The Accidental American: Tony Blair and the Presidency 2004, The Making of Music: A Journey with Notes 2007. *Honours:* Hon. LLD (Aberdeen), (St Andrews); Hon. DUniv (Stirling). *Address:* BBC News Centre, London, W12 8QT, England. *Telephone:* (20) 8624-9644. *Website:* www.bbc.co.uk/radio4/today.

NAUMANN, Michael, DPhil; German publisher; b. 8 Dec. 1941, Köthen; s. of Eduard Naumann and Ursula Naumann (née Schönfeld); m. Christa Wessel 1969 (divorced); one s. one d. *Education:* Univ. of Munich and Queen's Coll., Oxford, UK. *Career:* Asst Prof., Univ. of Bochum 1971–76; Florey Scholar, Queen's Coll. Oxford 1976–78; Ed., Foreign Corresp. Die Zeit, Hamburg 1978–82; Sr Foreign Ed. Der Spiegel, Hamburg 1982–84; Publr Rowohlt Verlag, Reinbek 1984–95; Pres. and CEO Henry Holt and Co., New York

1996–98; Minister of State for Culture 1998–2000; Chief Ed. and Publisher, Die Zeit 2001–07; SPD cand. for Hamburg mayoral elections 2008. *Publications:* Der Abbau einer Verkehrten Welt 1969, Amerika liegt in Kalifornien 1983, Strukturwandel des Heroismus 1984, Die Geschichte ist offen 1990, Die schönste Form der Freiheit 2001. *Honours:* Commdr Légion d'honneur. *Address:* Kurt-Schumacher-Allee 10, 20097 Hamburg, Germany (office). *Telephone:* (40) 2808480 (office). *Fax:* (40) 28084818 (office). *Website:* www.naumann-hamburg.de (office).

NAUMOFF, Lawrence Jay, BA; American author; *Professor of Creative Writing, University of North Carolina at Chapel Hill*; b. 23 July 1946, Charlotte, NC; m. (divorced); one s. *Education:* Univ. of N Carolina at Chapel Hill. *Career:* Prof. of Creative Writing, Univ. of N Carolina at Chapel Hill 2000–. *Publications:* The Night of the Weeping Women 1988, Rootie Kazootie 1990, Taller Women 1992, Silk Hope, NC 1994, A Plan for Women 1997, A Southern Tragedy, in Crimson and Yellow 2005; contribs to various literary magazines, short stories. *Honours:* Thomas Wolfe Memorial Award 1969, Nat. Endowment for the Arts Grant, 1970, Whiting Foundation Writers' Award 1990. *Address:* 1240 Epps Clark Road, Siler City, NC 27344, USA.

NAVASKY, Victor Saul, AB, LLB, JD; American writer, editor and academic; *Chairman, Columbia Journalism Review*; b. 5 July 1932, New York, NY; s. of Macy Navasky and Esther Goldberg; m. Anne Landey Strongin 1966; one s. two d. *Education:* Swarthmore Coll., Yale Univ. Law School. *Career:* Special Asst to Gov. G. Mennen Williams, Mich. 1959–60; Founding Ed. and Publr Monocle quarterly 1961–65; Ed. New York Times Magazine 1970–72, wrote monthly column (In Cold Print) for The New York Times Book Review; Ed.-in-Chief The Nation magazine 1978–94, Editorial Dir and Publr 1995–2007, Publr Emer. 2007–; George Delacorte Prof. of Magazine Journalism, Grad. School of Journalism, Columbia Univ. 1999–, Dir Delacorte Center of Magazines, Chair. Columbia Journalism Review; Visiting Scholar, Russell Sage Foundation 1975–76; Ferris Visiting Prof. of Journalism, Princeton Univ. 1976–77; Visiting Prof. of Social Change, Swarthmore Coll. 1982; Fellow, John F. Kennedy School of Govt, Harvard Univ. 1994, Freedom Forum Media Studies Center 1995; has taught at numerous colls and univs; mem. Man. Bd Swarthmore Coll. 1991–94; fmr mem. Bd Authors' Guild, Cttee to Protect Journalists, Bd of Govs New School for Social Research; fmr Vice-Pres. PEN; mem. American Acad. of Arts and Sciences. *Play:* Starr's Last Tape (with Richard R. Lingeman) 1999. *Publications include:* Kennedy Justice, Naming Names (Nat. Book Award), The Experts Speak: The Definitive Compendium of Authoritative Misinformation, A Matter of Opinion (George Polk Book Award 2005, Ann M. Sperber Prize 2006) 2005, Mission Accomplished: The Experts Speak About Iraq (with Christopher Cerf) 2008; numerous articles and reviews published in magazines and journals of opinion. *Honours:* numerous hon. degrees; Guggenheim Fellow 1975–76, Carey McWilliams Award, American Political Science Asscn 2001. *Address:* Room 802, Columbia Graduate School of Journalism, 2950 Broadway, New York, NY 10027 (office); The Nation, 33 Irving Place, 8th Floor, New York, NY 10003 (office); 33 W 67th Street, New York, NY 10023, USA (home). *Telephone:* (212) 854-5751 (Columbia Grad. School) (office); (212) 209-5411 (The Nation) (office). *Fax:* (212) 982-9000 (The Nation) (office). *E-mail:* vic@thenation.com (office). *Website:* thenation.com (office).

NAVON, Robert, BA, MS, MA, PhD; American editor, poet, writer and philosopher; b. 18 May 1954, New York, NY. *Education:* Lehman College, CUNY, SUNY at Geneseo, New School for Social Research, New York City, University of New Mexico. *Career:* mem. Society of Ancient Greek Philosophy; American Philosophical Asscn. *Publications:* Patterns of the Universe, 1977; Autumn Songs: Poems, 1983; The Pythagorean Writings, 1986; Healing of Man and Woman, 1989; Harmony of the Spheres, 1991; Cosmic Patterns, Vol. I, 1993; Great Works of Philosophy, 7 vols (ed.). *Honours:* New York State Regents Scholar, 1971; Intern, Platform Asscn, 1980.

NAYLOR, Gloria, BA, MA; American author; b. 25 Jan. 1950, New York, NY. *Education:* Brooklyn College, CUNY, Yale University. *Career:* Writer-in-Residence, Cummington Community of the Arts, 1983; Visiting Prof., George Washington University, 1983–84, Princeton University, 1986–87, Boston University, 1987; United States Information Agency Cultural Exchange Lecturer, India, 1985; Visiting Writer, New York University, 1986; Fannie Hurst Visiting Prof., Brandeis University, 1988; Senior Fellow, Society for the Humanities, Cornell University, 1988; Pres., One Way Productions, New York City, 1990–. *Publications:* The Women of Brewster Place: A Novel in Seven Stories, 1982; Lindin Hills, 1985; Mama Day, 1988; Bailey's Cafe, 1992; Children of the Night: The Best Short Stories by Black Writers, 1967 to the Present (ed.), 1995; The Men of Brewster Place, 1998; contributions: magazines. *Honours:* National Book Award for Best First Novel 1983, Distinguished Writer Award, Mid-Atlantic Writers Asscn 1983, National Endowment for the Arts Fellowship 1985, Candace Award, National Coalition of 100 Black Women 1986, Guggenheim Fellowship 1988, Lillian Smith Award 1989.

NAYLOR, Phyllis, BA; American writer; b. 4 Jan. 1933, Anderson, IN. *Education:* Joliet Junior College, American University. *Publications:* over 134 books for adults or children 1965–. *Honours:* American Library Asscn Newbery Medal 1992, Edgar Allan Poe Mystery Writers Award, Christopher Award, Mark Twain Award and others. *Address:* 401 Russell Avenue, Apartment 713, Gaithersburg, MD 20877, USA (home).

NAYLOR, Thomas Herbert, BS, MBA, PhD; American academic and writer; *Founder, Second Vermont Republic*; b. 30 May 1936, Jackson, Miss.; m. Magdalena Raczkowska 1985; one s. one d. *Education:* Millsaps Coll., Columbia Univ., New York, Indiana Univ., Tulane Univ. *Career:* Instructor, Tulane Univ. 1961–63; Asst Prof., Duke Univ. 1964–66, Assoc. Prof. 1966–68, Prof. of Econs 1968–93, Prof. Emer. 1994–; Visiting Prof., Univ. of Wisconsin, 1969–70, Middlebury Coll. 1993–94, Univ. of Vermont, 1994–96; Pres. Social Systems Inc. 1971–80; Man. Dir Naylor Group 1980; Founder Second Vermont Repub. (Vermont's independence movt). *Publications:* Linear Programming (with Eugene Byrne) 1963, Computer Simulation Techniques (with Joseph L. Balintfy, Donald S. Burdick and King Chu) 1966, Microeconomics and Decision Models of the Firm (with John Vernon) 1969, Computer Simulation Experiments with Models of Economic Systems 1971, Corporate Planning Models 1979, Strategic Planning Management 1980, Managerial Economics: Corporate Economics and Strategy (with John M. Vernon and Kenneth Wertz) 1983, The Corporate Strategy Matrix 1986, The Gorbachev Strategy 1988, The Cold War Legacy 1991, The Search for Meaning 1994, The Abandoned Generation: Rethinking Higher Education (with William H. Willimon) 1995, The Search for Meaning in the Workplace (with Rolf Osterberg and William H. Willimon) 1996, Downsizing the USA 1997, Affluenza 2001, The Vermont Manifesto 2003, Secession 2008; contrib. to scholarly books and journals. *Address:* 202 Stockbridge Road, Charlotte, VT 05445, USA (office). *Telephone:* (802) 425-4133 (office). *Website:* www.vermontrepublic.org (office).

NDEBELE, Njabulo Simakahle, PhD; South African academic, writer and university administrator; *Vice-Chancellor and Principal, University of Cape Town*; b. 4 July 1948, Johannesburg; m. Kathleen Mpho; one s. two d. *Education:* Univs of Botswana, Lesotho and Swaziland, Univ. of Cambridge, UK, Univ. of Denver, USA. *Career:* Head of Dept, Nat. Univ. of Lesotho, Dean of Humanities Faculty 1987, Pro-Vice-Chancellor 1988; Chair. and Head of Dept of African Literature, Wits Univ.; Vice-Rector, Univ. of the Western Cape; Vice-Chancellor and Prin. Univ. of the North, Scholar in Residence, Ford Foundation; Vice-Chancellor and Prin. Univ. of Cape Town 2000–; Chair. S African Broadcasting Policy Project, Ministry of Post, Telecommunications and Broadcasting, S African Univs Vice-Chancellors' Asscn –2000; mem. Exec. Bd AA4, AC4. *Publications:* Fools and Other Stories 1983, Bonolo and the Peach Tree 1991, Rediscovery of the Ordinary 1991, The Prophetess 1992, Sarah, Rings and I 1993, South African Literature and Culture: Rediscovery of the Ordinary 1994, Death of a Son 1996, The Cry of Winnie Mandela (novel) 2004, Telling Tales (contrib. to charity anthology) 2004, Fine Lines from the Box 2007. *Honours:* Dr hc (Natal Univ., Chicago State Univ., Vrije Univ. Amsterdam, Soka Univ. Japan, Wesleyan Univ., Univ. of Cambridge, Univ. Coll. London); Lincoln Univ. President's Award, Nat. Univ. of Lesotho Fiftieth Anniversary Distinguished Service Award, NOMA Award for Publishing in Africa 1984, Sanlam Award for Outstanding Fiction, Pringle Prize for Outstanding Criticism. *Address:* University of Cape Town, Private Bag, Rondebosch 7701, Cape Town (office); Glenara, Burg Road, Rondebosch 7700, Cape Town, South Africa (home). *Telephone:* (21) 6502105 (office); (21) 6502106 (office). *Fax:* (21) 6505100 (office). *E-mail:* vc@uct.ac.za (office). *Website:* www.uct.ac.za (office).

NDIAYE, Marie; French writer; b. 4 June 1967, Pithiviers; m. Jean-Yves Cendrey; three c. *Education:* Sorbonne, Univ. of Paris. *Plays:* Hilda (Grand Prix de la Critique 2001) 1999, Providence 2001, Papa doit manger 2003, Les Serpents 2004, Rien d'humain 2004, Puzzle 2007. *Publications:* Quant au riche avenir (novel) 1985, Comédie classique (novel) 1987, La Femme changée en bûche (novel) 1989, En famille (novel) 1991, Un Temps de saison (novel) 1994, La Sorcière (novel) 1996, La Naufragée (text to pictures by J. M. W. Turner) 1999, Rosie Carpe (novel) (Prix Fémina) 2001, Papa doit manger 2003, Tous mes amis (short stories) 2004, Autoportrait en vert 2005, Mon Coeur à l'Étroit (novel) 2007, Trois Femmes Puissantes (novel) (Prix Goncourt) 2009; also children's fiction. *Honours:* Académie de France grant for residency at Villa Médicis, Rome. *Address:* c/o Les Éditions Gallimard, 5 rue Sébastian Bottin, 75328 Paris, France (office). *Website:* www.gallimard.fr (office).

NDIBE, Okey A.; Nigerian poet and writer; b. 1960, Yola; m. Sheri Fafunwa-Ndibe; three c. *Career:* fmr magazine ed.; moved to USA, 1988; f. ed., African Commentary magazine; Visiting Writer-in-Residence, Asst Prof. of English, Connecticut College; weekly column, Nigerian newspaper, Guardian. *Publications:* Arrows of Rain, 2000. Contributions: An Anthology of New West African Poets; essays in numerous magazines.

NEATE, Patrick; British writer and journalist; b. London, England; one d. *Publications:* Musungu Jim and the Great Chief Tuloko 2000, Twelve Bar Blues 2001, The London Pigeon Wars 2003, Where You're At: Notes from the Frontline of a Hip Hop Planet 2004, City of Tiny Lights 2005, Culture is our Weapon 2006, Jerusalem 2009; contrib. to Q, The Face, Mixmag, Sky, The Washington Post, Building, Hospital Doctor, Doctor, Minx, The Times, The Telegraph, Marie-Claire, The Sunday Times, The Guardian, Harpers and Queen, The Sunday Tribune, The Standard, Time Out, Tatler. *Honours:* Whitbread Novel Award 2001. *Address:* c/o Simon Trewin, United Agents, 12–26 Lexington Street, London, W1F 0LE, England. *Telephone:* (20) 3214-0800. *Fax:* (20) 3214-0801. *E-mail:* info@unitedagents.co.uk. *Website:* unitedagents.co.uk. *Address:* c/o Penguin Books Ltd, 80 Strand, London, WC2R 0RL, England (office). *Website:* www.patrickneate.com.

NEEDLE, Jan, BA; British author; b. 8 Feb. 1943, Holybourne, Hants., England. *Education:* Victoria Univ. of Manchester. *Publications:* fiction for adults: Wild Wood (illustrated by William Rushton) 1981, A Fine Boy for Killing 2002, The Wicked Trade 2003, The Spithead Nymph 2004, Undertaker's Wind 2006, Killing Time at Catterick 2010, Panopticon Burning 2011, Dracula Lives 2011; fiction for young adults: Piggy in the Middle 1982, Dracula 2005, Hunchback of Notre Dame 2006, Moby Dick 2008, Woman in White 2009; fiction for children: Albeson and the Germans 1977, My Mate Shofiq 1978, Rottenteeth (illustrated by Roy Bentley) 1979, A Sense of Shame and Other Stories 1980, The Bee Rustlers (illustrated by Paul Wright) 1980, The Size Spies (illustrated by Roy Bentley) 1980, Losers Weepers (illustrated by Jane Bottomley) 1981, Another Fine Mess (illustrated by Roy Bentley) 1982, Going Out 1983, A Pitiful Place and Other Stories 1984, Tucker's Luck 1984, A Game of Soldiers 1985, Behind the Bike Sheds 1985, Great Days at Grange Hill 1985, Tucker in Control 1985, Skeleton at School (illustrated by Robert Bartelt) 1987, Uncle in the Attic (illustrated by Robert Bartelt) 1987, Wagstaffe the Wind-Up Boy (illustrated by Roy Bentley) 1987, In the Doghouse (illustrated by Robert Bartelt) 1988, The Sleeping Party (illustrated by Robert Bartelt) 1988, The Thief 1989, Mad Scramble (illustrated by Kate Aldous) 1990, The War of the Worms (illustrated by Kay Widdowson) 1992, Wagstaffe and the Life of Crime (illustrated by Roy Bentley) 1992, Bogeymen (illustrated by Liz Tofts) 1992, The Bully 1993. *Address:* Rye Top, Knowl Top Lane, Uppermill, Oldham, OL3 6LQ, England (home). *Telephone:* 7754-777011 (mobile). *E-mail:* jan@janneedle.com (office). *Website:* www.janneedle.com.

NEEDLEMAN, Jacob, PhD; American philosopher and academic; *Professor of Philosophy, San Francisco State University*; b. 6 Oct. 1934, Philadelphia, Pa; s. of Benjamin Needleman and Ida Needleman; m. 1st Carla Satzman 1959 (divorced 1989); one s. one d.; m. 2nd Gail Anderson 1990. *Education:* Research Assoc., Rockefeller Inst., New York 1960–61, Harvard Coll., Yale Univ. *Career:* Assoc. Prof. of Philosophy, San Francisco State Univ. 1962–66, Prof. 1967–; Dir Center for the Study of New Religions, Grad. Theological Union, Berkeley, Calif. 1977–83; Vice-Pres. Audio Literature Co. 1987–; Rockefeller Humanities Fellow, Fulbright Scholar. *Publications:* The New Religions 1970, A Sense of the Cosmos 1975, Lost Christianity 1980, The Heart of Philosophy 1982, The Way of the Physician 1985, Sorcerers 1986, Money and the Meaning of Life 1991, A Little Book on Love 1996, Time and the Soul 1998, The American Soul 2002, The Wisdom of Love 2005, Why Can't We Be Good 2007, What Is God? 2009. *Address:* San Francisco State University, Department of Philosophy, 1600 Holloway Avenue, San Francisco, CA 94132, USA (office). *Telephone:* (415) 338-1596 (office). *E-mail:* jneedle@sfsu.edu (office). *Website:* www.jacobneedleman.com.

NEELY, Mark Edward, Jr, BA, PhD; American writer, editor and academic; b. 10 Nov. 1944, Amarillo, TX; m. Sylvia Eakes 1966. *Education:* Yale University. *Career:* Dir, Louis A Warren Lincoln Library and Museum, Fort Wayne, Indiana; Visiting Instructor, Iowa State University, 1971–72; Ed., Lincoln Lore, 1973–; Prof., St Louis University; mem. Abraham Lincoln Asscn; Indiana Asscn of Historians, pres., 1987–88; Society of Indiana Archivists, pres., 1980–81. *Publications:* The Abraham Lincoln Encyclopedia, 1981; The Lincoln Image: Abraham Lincoln and the Popular Print (with Harold Holzer and Gabor S. Boritt), 1984; The Insanity File: The Case of Mary Todd Lincoln (with R. Gerald McMurty), 1986; The Confederate Image: Prints of the Lost Cause, 1987; The Lincoln Family Album: Photographs from the Personal Collection of a Historic American Family, 1990; The Fate of Liberty: Abraham Lincoln and Civil Liberties, 1991; The Last Best Hope on Earth: Abraham Lincoln and the Promise of America, 1993; Mine Eyes Have Seen the Glory: The Civil War in American Art (with Harold Holzer), 1993. *Honours:* Pulitzer Prize for History, 1992. *Address:* c/o Dept of History, St Louis University, 221 N Grand Avenue, St Louis, MO 63103, USA.

NEESER, Andreas, DipEd; Swiss teacher, writer and poet; b. 25 Jan. 1964, Schlossrued. *Education:* Univ. of Zürich. *Career:* mem. PEN Switzerland, Swiss Writers' Union, Zürich. *Publications:* Schattensprünge (novel) 1995, Treibholz (poems) 1997. *Honours:* grants.

NEGRI, Antonio; Italian political philosopher and writer; b. 1933. *Career:* fmrly Lecturer in Political Science Univ. of Paris, Prof. of Political Science Univ. of Padua. *Publications include (in translation):* Revolution Retrieved: Selected Writings on Marx, Keynes, Capitalist Crisis and New Social Subjects 1967–1983 1988, Marx beyond Marx 1979, The Savage Anomaly 1981, Communists Like Us (with Felix Guattari) 1985, The Politics of Subversion 1986, Labor of Dionysus (with Michael Hardt) 1994, Empire 2000, Time for Revolution 2003, Subversive Spinoza: (Un)contemporary Variations 2004, Negri on Negri 2004, Political Descartes 2007, The Porcelain Workshop 2008, Commonwealth (with Michael Hardt) 2009; contrib. essays to numerous publications. *Address:* c/o Penguin Books Ltd, 80 Strand, London, WC2R 0RL, England (office). *Website:* www.antonionegri.com.

NEHAMAS, Alexander, BA, PhD; Spanish/American academic and writer; *Edmund N. Carpenter II Class of 1943 Professor in the Humanities, Princeton University*; b. 22 March 1946, Athens, Greece; s. of Albert Nehamas and Christine Nehamas; m. Susan Glimcher 1983; one s. *Education:* Swarthmore Coll., Princeton Univ. *Career:* Asst Prof., Univ. of Pittsburgh 1971–76, Assoc. Prof. 1976–81, Prof. of Philosophy 1981–86; Visiting Fellow, Princeton Univ. 1978–79, Prof. of Philosophy 1988, 1990, Edmund N. Carpenter II Class of 1943 Prof. in the Humanities 1989–, Prof. of Comparative Literature 1990–; Mills Prof. of Philosophy, Univ. of California, Berkeley 1983, Sather Prof. of Classical Literature 1993; Visiting Scholar, Univ. of Pennsylvania 1983–84, Prof. of Philosophy 1986–90; Tanner Lecturer, Yale Univ. 2000; mem. American Acad. of Arts and Sciences, American Soc. for Aesthetics, Modern Greek Studies Asscn, North American Nietzsche Soc., American Philosophical Asscn, British Soc. for Aesthetics. *Art exhibition:* contrib. to This Progress, Guggenheim Museum New York 2010. *Publications:* Nietzsche: Life as Literature 1985, Plato's 'Symposium' (trans. and ed. with Paul Woodruff) 1989, Aristotle's 'Rhetoric': Philosophical Essays (co-ed. with D. J. Furley) 1994, Plato's 'Phaedrus' (trans. and ed. with Paul Woodruff) 1995, The Art of Living: Socratic Reflections from Plato to Foucault 1998, Virtues of Authenticity: Essays on Plato and Socrates 1999, Only a Promise of Happiness: The Place of Beauty in a World of Art 2007; contribs to books and professional journals. *Honours:* Hon. DPhil (Univ. of Athens) 1993; Nat. Endowment for the Humanities Fellowship 1978–79, Guggenheim Fellowship 1983–84, Romanell-Phi Beta Kappa Prof. in Philosophy 1990–91, Phi Beta Kappa Visiting Scholar 1995, Howard T. Behrman Award for Distinguished Achievement in the Humanities, Princeton Univ. 1999, Award for Distinguished Achievement, Acad. of Athens 2000, Int. Nietzsche Prize 2001, Mellon Distinguished Achievement in the Humanities Award 2001, Gifford Lecturer, Univ. of Edinburgh, UK 2008. *Address:* Department of Philosophy, 1879 Hall, Princeton University, Princeton, NJ 08544-1006, USA (office). *Telephone:* (609) 258-4309 (office). *Fax:* (609) 258-1502 (office). *E-mail:* nehamas@princeton.edu (office). *Website:* philosophy.princeton.edu (office).

NEIL, Andrew Ferguson, MA, FRSA; British publisher, broadcaster, editor and business executive; *Chairman and Publisher, Spectator Magazine Group*; b. 21 May 1949, Paisley, Renfrewshire, Scotland; s. of James Neil and Mary Ferguson. *Education:* Paisley Grammar School, Univ. of Glasgow. *Career:* with Conservative Party Research Dept 1971–73; with The Economist 1973–83, Ulster Political then Industrial Corresp. 1973–79, American Corresp. 1979–82, UK Ed. 1982–83; Ed. The Sunday Times 1983–94; Exec. Ed. Fox TV News, USA 1994; Exec. Chair. Sky TV 1988–90; Publr The Scotsman, Scotland on Sunday, Edinburgh Evening News 1996–2006; Publr, The Business 1999–2007; regular anchorman and TV commentator UK and USA; anchorman, The Daily Politics (BBC 2) 2003–, This Week (BBC 1) 2003–, Straight Talk with Andrew Neil (BBC News Channel) 2004–09, Sunday Politics (BBC 1) 2012–; Contrib. Ed. Vanity Fair, New York 1994–2007; Chief Exec., then Chair. The Spectator and Apollo magazines 2004–; Chair. World Media Rights (WMR) 2005–, ITP Magazines (Dubai) 2005–, Peters Fraser & Dunlop (talent agency) 2008–10; Lord Rector Univ. of St Andrews 1999–2002. *Publications:* The Cable Revolution 1982, Britain's Free Press: Does It Have One? 1989, Full Disclosure 1996, British Excellence 1999, 2000, 2001. *Honours:* Hon. DLit (Napier Univ.) 1998; Hon. DUniv (Paisley) 2001; Hon. LLD (St Andrews) 2002. *Address:* Glenburn Enterprises, Flat 3, 53 Onslow Gardens, London, SW7 3QY (office); c/o 22 Old Queen Street, London, SW1H 9HP, England (office). *Telephone:* (20) 7244-9968 (office); (20) 7581-1655 (home). *E-mail:* afneil@aol.com (office).

NEILSON, Anthony; Scottish playwright and theatre director. *Plays:* Welfare My Lovely (Traverse Theatre, Edinburgh), Heredity (Royal Court Theatre, London), White Trash (Nat. Theatre Studio, London), Normal (Edinburgh Festival) 1991, Penetrator (Traverse Theatre, Edinburgh) 1993, The Year of the Family (Finborough Theatre, London) 1994, The Night Before Christmas (Finborough Theatre Red Room, London) 1995, Hoover Bag (Young Vic Theatre, London) 1996, The Censor (Finborough Theatre Red Room, London) (Writers' Guild Award for Best Fringe Play) 1997, Edward Gant's Amazing Feats of Loneliness (Theatre Royal, Plymouth) 2002, Stitching (Traverse Theatre, Edinburgh) 2002, The Lying Kind (Royal Court Theatre Downstairs) 2002, Twisted (theatre workshop, Edinburgh Festival) 2003, The Wonderful World of Dissocia (Tron, Glasgow) 2004, The Menu (work in progress, Nat. Theatre, London) 2006, Home (Edinburgh Queens Hall) 2006. *Other Productions include:* The Death of Klinghoffer (by John Adams; dir, Edinburgh Int. Festival and Scottish Opera) 2005. *Television includes:* Deeper Still (ten-minute film for Channel 4, also dir), A Terrible Coldness (for Granada), 'Bible John' (episode of In Suspicious Circumstances). *Film:* The Debt Collector 1999. *Radio plays include:* The Colours of the King's Rose (BBC Scotland Radio) 1988, A Fluttering of Wings. *Literary Agent:* Julia Tyrrell Management, 57 Greenham Road, London, N10 1LN, England. *Telephone:* (20) 8374-0575. *Fax:* (20) 8374-5800. *E-mail:* julia@jtmanagement.co.uk. *Website:* www.jtmanagement.co.uk.

NEIMAN, Susan, AB, AM, PhD; American philosopher and writer; *Director, Einstein Forum*; b. 1955, Atlanta, Ga; m. Felix de Mendelssohn; three c. *Education:* Harvard Univ., Freie Universität Berlin. *Career:* Asst, then Assoc. Prof. of Philosophy, Yale Univ. 1989–96; Assoc. Prof. of Philosophy, Tel-Aviv Univ. 1996–2000; Dir Einstein Forum 2000–; mem. Berlin Brandenburg Akad. der Wissenschaften. *Publications:* Slow Fire: Jewish Notes from Berlin 1992, The Unity of Reason: Rereading Kant 1994, Evil in Modern Thought: An Alternative History of Philosophy 2002, Moral Clarity: A Guide for Grown-Up Idealists 2008. *Honours:* Fulbright Fellowship 1982, 1983, Carrier Dissertation Prize 1987, Morse Fellowship, Yale Univ. 1992, American Asscn of Publishers Scholarly and Professional Award for Philosophy 2002, American Acad. of Religion Award for Excellence 2003, Tanner Lecturer 2009, Margherita von Brentano Prize 2010. *Address:* Einstein Forum, Am Neuen Markt 7, 14467 Potsdam, Germany (office). *Telephone:* (331) 271780 (office).

Fax: (331) 2717827 (office). *E-mail:* susan.neiman@einsteinforum.de (office). *Website:* www.einsteinforum.de (office); www.susan-neiman.de.

NELSON, Antonya, BA, MFA; American writer and academic; *Associate Professor, New Mexico State University*; b. 6 Jan. 1961, Wichita, KS; m. Robert L. Boswell 1984; two s. *Education:* Univ. of Kansas, Univ. of Arizona. *Career:* Asst Prof., New Mexico State Univ. 1989–95, Assoc. Prof. of English 1995–. *Publications:* The Expendables 1990, In the Land of Men 1992, Family Terrorists: A Novella and Seven Stories 1994, Talking in Bed 1996, Nobody's Girl: A Novel 1998, Living to Tell: A Novel 2000, Some Fun: Stories and a Novella 2006, Nothing Right: Short Stories 2009, Bound 2010; contrib. to anthologies and periodicals. *Honours:* Nelson Algren Award 1988, Flannery O'Connor Award 1990, Heartland Award, Chicago Tribune 1996, American Library Asscn Award 2000, Guggenheim Fellowship 2000–01. *Address:* Department of English, New Mexico State University, PO Box 30001, MSC 3E, Las Cruces, NM 88003, USA (office). *Telephone:* (505) 646-3536 (office). *Fax:* (505) 646-7725 (office). *E-mail:* annelson@nmsu.edu (office). *Website:* www.nmsu.edu/~english/faculty/nelson.html (office).

NELSON, Fraser; British journalist; *Editor, The Spectator*; b. 1973, Scotland; m.; one s. *Education:* Univ. of Glasgow. *Career:* began career as business corresp., The Times; fmr Political Ed., The Scotsman; columnist, News of the World; Political Ed., The Spectator 2006–09, Ed. 2009–. *Address:* The Spectator, 22 Old Queen Street, London, SW1H 9HP, England (office). *Telephone:* (20) 7961-0200 (office). *Fax:* (20) 7961-0058 (office). *E-mail:* editor@spectator.co.uk (office). *Website:* www.spectator.co.uk (office).

NELSON, Marilyn, (Marilyn Nelson Waniek), BA, MA, PhD; American academic, poet and translator; *Professor Emerita of English, University of Connecticut*; b. 26 April 1946, Cleveland, OH; d. of Melvin M. Nelson Sr and Johnnie Mitchell Nelson; one s. one d. *Education:* Univ. of California at Davis, Univ. of Pennsylvania, Univ. of Minnesota. *Career:* Visiting Asst Prof., Reed Coll., Portland, OR 1971–72; Asst Prof., St Olaf Coll., Northfield, MN 1973–78; Instructor, Univ. of Hamburg, Germany 1977; Asst Prof. to Prof. of English, Univ. of Connecticut at Storrs 1978–2002, Prof. Emer. 2002–; faculty, MFA Program, New York Univ. 1988, 1994, Vermont Coll. 1991; Elliston Poet-in-Residence, Univ. of Cincinnati 1994; Writer-in-Residence, Vanderbilt Univ. 1999; Visiting Prof., US Mil. Acad., West Point 2000; Connecticut Poet Laureate 2001–06; Prof., Univ. of Delaware 2002–04; f. writers' colony, Soul Mountain Retreat 2004; mem. Associated Writing Programs, Poetry Soc. of America, Soc. for the Study of Multi-Ethnic Literature of the USA, Soc. for Values in Higher Educ. *Publications:* For the Body 1978, The Cat Walked Through the Casserole (with Pamela Espeland) 1984, Mama's Promises 1985, The Homeplace (Annisfield-Wolf Award 1992) 1990, Partial Truth 1992, Magnificat 1995, The Fields of Praise: New and Selected Poems (The Poets Prize 1998) 1997, Carver: A Life in Poems 2001, Triolets for Triolet (chapbook), Fortune's Bones 2004, A Wreath for Emmett Till 2005, The Cachoiera Tales 2005, The Thirteenth Month (trans of the poems of Danish poet Inge Pedersen) 2006, The Ladder (trans. of a verse narrative for children by Danish poet Halfdan Rasmussen) 2006, The Freedom Business 2006, Miss Crandall's School for Young Ladies and Little Misses of Color 2007; contribs to books and journals. *Honours:* Commdr's Award for Public Service, Dept of the Army; Kent Fellowship 1976, National Endowment for the Arts Fellowships 1981, 1990, Danish Ministry of Culture Grant 1984, Connecticut Arts Award 1990, Individual Artist Grant, Connecticut Commission for the Arts 1990, Fulbright Teaching Fellow 1995, Contemplative Practices Fellowship 1999, Guggenheim Fellowship 2001, Boston Globe/Horn Book Award 2001, Newbery Honor Book 2002, Coretta Scott King Honor Book 2002, Flora Stieglitz Strauss Award 2002. *Literary Agent:* Blue Flower Arts, PO Box 1361, Millbrook, NY 12545, USA. *E-mail:* alison@blueflowerarts.com. *Website:* blueflowerarts.com. *Address:* Soul Mountain Retreat, PO Box 1071, Old Lyme, CT 06371, USA (home). *E-mail:* soulmountainretreat@yahoo.com (home); marilyn.nelson@uconn.edu (office). *Website:* web.uconn.edu/mnelson/mainframe/index.html (office); www.soulmountainretreat.com (office).

NELSON, Martha, BA; American editor; *Editor, Time, Inc.*; b. 13 Aug. 1952, Pierre, South Dakota. *Education:* Barnard Coll. *Career:* fmrly staff ed., Ms magazine, Man. Ed. Signs: Journal of Women in Culture & Society, Ed.-in-Chief Women's Sports & Fitness, Ed.-in-Chief Savvy magazine; joined Time Inc. as Consulting Ed. Who Weekly, Sydney, Australia 1992, then Asst Man. Ed. People Magazine; left to co-found InStyle magazine 1994–2002; returned to Time Inc. as Man. Ed. People Magazine 2002–06, Ed. People Group 2006–08; Ed. Time Inc. Style & Entertainment Group 2008–. *Honours:* Corporate Citizen Award, The Actors' Fund 2003, ranked by Forbes magazine amongst 100 Most Powerful Women (92nd) 2004, (92nd) 2005, (98th) 2006. *Address:* Time Inc., 1271 Avenue of the Americas, New York, NY 10020-1393, USA (office). *Telephone:* (212) 522-1212 (office). *Fax:* (212) 467-0979 (office). *Website:* www.people.com (office).

NELSON, Richard, BA; American dramatist and screenwriter; b. 17 Oct. 1950, Chicago, IL. *Education:* Hamilton College. *Career:* Literary Man., BAM Theatre Co, Brooklyn, 1979–81; Assoc. Dir, Goodman Theatre, Chicago, 1980–83; Dramaturg, Guthrie Theatre, Minneapolis, 1981–82. *Publications:* The Vienna Notes (in Word Plays I), 1980; II Campiello (adaptation), 1981; An American Comedy and Other Plays, 1984; Between East and West (in New Plays USA 3), 1986; Principia Scriptoriae, 1986; Strictly Dishonorable and Other Lost American Plays (ed.), 1986; Rip Van Winkle, 1986; Jungle Coup (in Plays from Playwrights Horizons), 1987; Accidental Death of an Anarchist (adaptation), 1987.

NEMADE, Bhalchandra, PhD; Indian writer and academic; b. (Bhagavat Nemade), 5 May 1938, Sangavi, Maharashtra; s. of Vana Dharma Nemade and Girija Nemade; m. Pratibha Nemade; two s. *Education:* Fergusson Coll. and Deccan Coll., Pune, Univ. of Mumbai, Dr B.A. Marathwada Univ., Aurangabad. *Career:* Marathi writer; taught at Ahmednagar Coll. 1964, SSVP Coll., Dhulia 1965, S.B. Coll., Aurangabad 1966–71, School of Oriental and African Studies, London 1971–72, Dr B.A. Marathwada Univ., Aurangabad 1973–87, Goa Univ. 1987–91; Prof., Gurudev Tagore Chair of Comparative Literature, Univ. of Mumbai 1991–98; mem. Exec. Bd Sahitya Akademi 1998–2002; Ed Vacha (Marathi magazine). *Publications include:* fiction: Kosala 1963, Bidhar 1975, Hool 1975, Jarila 1977, Jhool 1979, Hindu 2010; non-fiction: Tukaram 1980, Sahityachi Bhasha 1987, Teekasvayamvara (Sahitya Akademi Award 1991) 1990, The Influence of English on Nineteenth-century Marathi 1990, Sola Bhashane 2008, Nivadak Mulakhati 2008, Nativism Desivad 2009; poetry: Melody 1970, Dekhani 1991. *Honours:* Hon. DLit (North Maharashtra Univ., Jalgaon) 1993; Maharashtra Foundation Award 2001, Labhsetwar Award 2003, Nat. Fellow, Indian Inst. of Advanced Study, Shimla 2008–10, Padma Shri 2011. *Address:* B401 Nilesh Apartments, Mithagar Road, Kandarpada, Dahisar (West), Mumbai 400 068, India (home). *Telephone:* (22) 28932809 (office). *E-mail:* jnemade@hotmail.com (office).

NESBØ, Jo, MBA; Norwegian singer, songwriter and writer; b. Molde. *Career:* fmr freelance journalist; fmr mem. De Tusen Hjem, Di Derre; numerous concerts; currently crime writer, creator of Harry Hold series of detective novels. *Recordings:* albums: with Di Derre: Den Derre 1992, Jenter and Sånn 1994. *Publications:* Harry Hole novels: Flaggermusmannen (The Bat) (Riverton Prize for Best Norwegian Crime Novel of the Year 1997, Glass Key Award for Best Nordic Crime Novel of the Year 1998) 1997, Kakerlakkene (The Cockroaches) 1998, Rødstrupe (The Redbreast) (Norwegian Booksellers' Prize for Best Novel of the Year 2000, Norwegian Book Clubs' Award for Best Norwegian Crime Novel Ever Written 2004) 2000, Sorgenfri (Nemesis) (Mads Wiel Nygaards Bursary 2002) 2002, Marekors (The Devil's Star) (Finnish Acad. of Crime Writers Special Commendation for Excellence in Foreign Crime Writing 2007) 2003, Frelseren (The Redeemer) 2005, Snømannen (The Snowman) (Norwegian Booksellers' Prize for Best Novel of the Yeaer 2007, Norwegian Book Club Prize for Best Novel of the Year 2008) 2007, Panserhjeerte (The Leopard) 2009, Gjenferd (Phantom) 2011; Doktor Proktor novels: Doktor Proktors prompepulver (trans. as Doctor Proctor's Fart Powder) 2007, Doktor Proktors Tidsbadekar (trans. as Doktor Proktor's Time Bathtub) 2008, Doctor Proctor and the Armageddon: Maybe 2010; other stand-alone novels: Stemmer fra Balkan (trans. as Figures in the Balkans) 1999, Det hvite hotellet (trans. as The White Hotel) 2007, Hodejegerne (trans. as Headhunters) 2008; short stories: Karusellmusikk 2001. *Literary Agent:* Solomonsson Agency, Svartensgatan 4, 116 20 Stockholm, Sweden. *Telephone:* (8) 22-32-11. *E-mail:* info@salomonssonagency.com. *Website:* www.salomonssonagency.com; www.jonesbo.com.

NESS, Patrick; American/British writer; b. Fort Belvoir, Va. *Education:* Univ. of Southern California. *Career:* fmr corp. writer; moved to London, UK 1999; has taught creative writing, Univ. of Oxford; Booktrust Writer in Residence 2009. *Publications:* fiction: for adults: The Crash of Hennington 2003, Topics About Which I Know Nothing (short stories) 2004; for young adults: The Knife of Never Letting Go (Guardian Children's Fiction Prize, Booktrust Teenage Prize) 2008, The Ask and the Answer 2009, Monsters of Men 2010, A Monster Calls (Galaxy Nat. Book Award for Children's Book of the Year 2011). *Literary Agent:* Michelle Kass Associates, 85 Charing Cross Road, London, WC2H 0AA, England. *Telephone:* (20) 7439-1624. *E-mail:* office@michellekass.co.uk. *Address:* c/o Walker Books, 87 Vauxhall Walk, London SE11 5HU, England (office). *E-mail:* alice.burden@walker.co.uk (office). *Website:* www.walker.co.uk (office); www.patrickness.com.

NETTL, Bruno, BA, MA, PhD; American musicologist and writer; *Professor of Music and Anthropology Emeritus, University of Illinois*; b. 14 March 1930, Prague, Czechoslovakia; m. Wanda Maria White 1952; two d. *Education:* Indiana Univ., Univ. of Michigan Ann Arbor. *Career:* instructor in music 1953–54, Asst Prof. of Music 1954–56, 1959–64, Music Librarian 1958–64, Wayne State Univ., Detroit; Ed., Ethnomusicology 1961–65, 1988–2002, Yearbook of the Int. Folk Music Council 1975–77; Assoc. Prof. of Music 1965–67, Prof. of Music and Anthropology 1967–92, Prof. Emeritus 1992–, Chair Division of Musicology 1967–72, 1975–77, 1982–85, Univ. of Illinois, Urbana; numerous visiting lectureships and professorships, including Visiting Prof. of Music Harvard Univ. 1990, Distinguished Albert Seay Prof. of Music Colorado Coll. 1992, Visiting Hill Prof. of Music Univ. of Minnesota 1995, Benedict Distinguished Visiting Prof. of Music Carleton Coll. 1996; mem. American Acad. of Arts and Sciences, Coll. Music Soc., Int. Council for Traditional Music, Int. Musicological Soc., Soc. of Ethnomusicology (pres. 1969–71, hon. mem. 2001). *Publications:* North American Indian Musical Styles 1954, Music in Primitive Culture 1956, An Introduction to Folk Music in the United States (third edn, revised by H. Myers, as Folk Music in the United States: An Introduction 1976) 1960, Cheremis Musical Styles 1960, Reference Materials in Ethnomusicology 1961, Theory and Method in Ethnomusicology 1964, Folk and Traditional Music of the Western Continents 1965, Daramad of Chahargah: A Study in the Performance Practice of Persian Music (with B. Foltin Jr) 1972, Contemporary Music and Music Cultures (with C. Hamm and R. Byrnside) 1975, Eight Urban Musical Cultures: Tradition and Change (ed.) 1978, The Study of Ethnomusicology: 29 Issues and Concepts 1983, The Western Impact on World Music: Change, Adaptation, and Survival 1985, The Radif of Persian Music: Studies of Structure and Cultural Context 1987, Blackfoot Musical Thought: Comparative Perspectives 1989, Comparative Musicology and Anthropology in Music: Essays on the History of Ethnomusicology (ed. with P. Bohlman) 1991, Excursions in World Music (with others) 1992, Community of Music: An Ethnographical Seminar in Champaign-Urbana (ed. with others) 1993, Heartland Excursions: Ethnomusicological Reflections on Schools of Music 1995, In the Course of Performance: Studies in the World of Musical Improvisation (ed. with M. Russell) 1998, Encounters in Ethnomusicology 2002. *Honours:* Hon. LHD (Univ. of Chicago) 1993, (Univ. of Illinois) 1996, (Carleton Coll.) 2000, (Kenyon Coll.) 2002;hon. mem. American Musicological Soc. 1995; Koizumi Prize in Ethnomusicology, Tokyo 1994. *Address:* c/o University of Illinois, Department for Performing Arts, EPASW Bldg, 1040 W Harrison Street, MC-255, Chicago, IL 60607; 1423 Cambridge Drive, Champaign, IL 61821, USA.

NEUBERGER, Baroness (Life Peer), cr. 2004, of Primrose Hill in the London Borough of Camden; **Rabbi Julia Babette Sarah Neuberger,** DBE, MA; British rabbi, author, broadcaster and politician; *Senior Rabbi, West London Synagogue;* b. 27 Feb. 1950, London, England; d. of the late Walter Schwab and Alice Schwab; m. Anthony John Neuberger 1973; one s. one d. *Education:* South Hampstead High School, Newnham Coll. Cambridge and Leo Baeck Coll. London. *Career:* Rabbi, South London Liberal Synagogue 1977–89, currently Sr Rabbi, West London Synagogue; Lecturer and Assoc. Fellow, Leo Baeck Coll. 1979–97; Assoc. Newnham Coll. Cambridge 1983–96; Sec. and Chief Exec. The King's Fund 1997–2004; Chancellor Univ. of Ulster 1994–2000; Chair. Rabbinic Conf. Union of Liberal and Progressive Synagogues 1983–85; Camden and Islington Community Health Services Nat. Health Service (NHS) Trust 1993–97; mem. Policy Planning Group, Inst. of Jewish Affairs 1986–90, NHS Complaints Review 1993–94, Gen. Medical Council 1993–2001, Council, Univ. Coll. London 1993–97, MRC 1995–2000, Council, Save the Children Fund 1995–96; Visiting Fellow, King's Fund Inst. 1989–91; Chair. Patients Asscn 1988–91, Royal Coll. of Nursing Comm. on Health Service; mem. Nat. Cttee Social Democratic Party 1982–88, Funding Review of BBC 1999, Cttee on Standards in Public Life 2001–04; Civil Service Commr 2001–02; mem. Bd of Visitors, Memorial Church, Harvard Univ. 1994–2000, Bloomberg Prof. of Philanthropy and Public Policy, Divinity School 2006; Prime Minister's Champion for Volunteering 2007–09; Chair. Liberal Judaism –2011, One Housing Group, Advisory Panel Judicial Diversity –2010; other public and charitable appointments; Harkness Fellow, Commonwealth Fund of New York; Visiting Fellow, Harvard Medical School 1991–92; Chair. Responsible Gambling Strategy Bd –2011, Responsible Gambling Fund –2011; Trustee, Runnymede Trust 1990–97; fmr Trustee, Imperial War Museum, British Council, Booker Prize Foundation, Jewish Care; Chair. W & L Schwab Charitable Trust; mem. House of Lords (Liberal Democrat) 2004–11, (Crossbench) 2011–. *Radio:* Pause for Thought (BBC Radio 2). *Television:* Presenter, Choices (BBC) 1986, 1987. *Publications:* The Story of Judaism 1986, Days of Decision (ed., four vols) 1987, Caring for Dying Patients of Different Faiths 1987, Whatever's Happening to Women? 1991, A Necessary End (co-ed. with John White) 1991, Ethics and Healthcare: The Role of Research Ethics Committees in the UK 1992, The Things That Matter 1993, On Being Jewish 1995, Dying Well: A Health Professional's Guide to Enabling a Better Death 1999, Hidden Assets: Values and Decision-Making in the NHS Today (co-ed. with Bill New) 2002, The Moral State We're In 2005, Not Dead Yet: A Manifesto for Old Age 2008, Is That All There Is? Thoughts on Leaving a Legacy 2011; contribs to various books on cultural, religious and ethical factors in nursing; contribs journals and newspapers, including Nursing Times, Jewish Chronicle, Times, Irish Times, The Independent, Guardian, Telegraph, Sunday Express, Mail on Sunday, Evening Standard. *Honours:* Hon. FRCP 2004; Hon. Fellow, Royal Coll. of Gen. Practitioners, Royal Coll. of Psychiatrists, City and Guilds Inst.; Hon. Fellow, Mansfield Coll. Oxford; Dr hc (Open Univ., City Univ. London, Humberside, Ulster, Stirling, Oxford Brookes, Teesside, Nottingham, Queen's Belfast, Aberdeen). *Address:* House of Lords, Westminster, London, SW1 0PW, England (office). *Telephone:* (20) 7219-2716 (office); (20) 7535-0255 (office). *E-mail:* paolachurchill@googlemail.com (office); paola.churchill@wls.org.uk (office).

NEUGEBOREN, Jay Michael, BA, MA; American writer and academic; b. (Jacob Mordecai Neugeboren), 30 May 1938, Brooklyn, NY; s. of David Neugeboren and Anne Nassofer Neugeboren; m. 1st Betsey Bendorf 1964 (divorced); two s. one d.; m. 2nd Judy Karasik 1985 (divorced 1987); m. 3rd Kathleen Reilly 2007 (divorced 2011). *Education:* Columbia Univ., New York, Indiana Univ. *Career:* Preceptor in English, Columbia Univ. 1964–66; Visiting Writer, Stanford Univ., Calif. 1966–67; Asst Prof., State Univ. of NY at Old Westbury 1969–70; Prof. and Writer-in-Residence, Univ. of Massachusetts, Amherst 1971–2001; mem. Authors' Guild, PEN, Writers' Guild. *Plays:* The Edict, Jewish Repertory Theatre. *Radio:* The Stolen Jew (NPR). *Television:* The Hollow Boy (film, PBS) 1991. *Publications:* Big Man 1966, Listen Ruben Fontanez 1968, Corky's Brother 1969, Parentheses: An Autobiographical Journey 1970, Sam's Legacy 1974, An Orphan's Tale 1976, The Stolen Jew 1981, Before My Life Began 1985, Poli: A Mexican Boy in Early Texas 1989, Don't Worry About the Kids: Stories 1997, Imagining Robert: My Brother, Madness, and Survival: A Memoir 1997, Transforming Madness: New Lives for People Living With Mental Illness 1999, Open Heart: A Patient's Story of Life-Saving Medicine and Life-Giving Friendship 2003, News from the New American Diaspora and Other Tales of Exile 2005, 1940 2008, You Are My Heart 2011; contribs to many anthologies and periodicals. *Honours:* Transatlantic Review Novella Award 1967, Nat. Endowment for the Arts Fellowships 1972–73, 1989–90, Guggenheim Fellowship 1978–79, Kenneth B. Smilen/Present Tense Award for Best Novel 1982, Edward Lewis Wallant Prize for Best Novel 1985, Ken Book Award, National Alliance for the Mentally Ill 2000. *Literary Agent:* c/o Richard Parks, PO Box 692, Salem, NY 12865, USA. *E-mail:* rp@richardparksagency.com. *Address:* 532 West 111th Street #65, New York, NY 10025, USA (home). *E-mail:* jneug@earthlink.net (home). *Website:* www.jayneugeboren.com.

NEUHÄUSER CANUTO, Mary Helen; American artist, playwright and author; b. 17 Feb. 1943, San Antonio, Tex.; d. of Gotthelf Friedrich and Edna Earl Ritter Neuhäuser (née Walling); m. Federico Andrea Canuto 1972 (divorced 1981). *Education:* Bethesda-Chevy Chase High School, Md, Catholic Univ., Washington, DC, Carnegie Mellon Univ., Pa, Studio Nera Simi and Univ. of Florence, Italy. *Career:* group and one-woman exhbns include Potters House Gallery, Washington, DC, Martha Washington Library, Alexandria, Va, Nat. Cathedral, Washington, DC, Nat. Museum of Fine Arts, Washington, DC, Smithsonian Inst., Washington, DC, Corcoran Gallery of Art, Veerhoff Galleries, Washington, DC, Capricorn Galleries, Bethesda, Md, Lorenz Gallery, Bethesda, Art and Design Gallery, Chantilly, Va, Seloff Art Gallery, Brownsville, Tex., Dellinger Gallery, Alexandria, VA, Thirty-Year Retrospective, Friendship Gallery, Chevy Chase, Md 1989; official portrait comms include FBI Bldg, House of Reps Bldg, Trinity Univ., Sidwell Friends School, Washington, DC; portrait of poet Robert Frost at J. F. Kennedy inauguration; portraits of J. Edgar Hoover, Patricia Nixon; contribs to newspapers including The Washington Post, The Evening Star, Capitol Hill Roll Call; poet and writer for Democratic Presidential Campaign 1988; First Place The Washington Post (Portraits) 1961, 1964. *Plays:* The Great Sin 1993, Awkwright and Murgatroyd 1994, Threatened by Hitler – My Father's Crusade Against Nazi Subversion in America 2002, Crusade (screenplay) 2005. *Honours:* numerous awards for portraits and abstract paintings 1961–76.

NEUHOFF, Eric; French writer and journalist; b. 1956. *Publications:* Des gens impossibles 1986, Lettre ouverte à François Truffaut 1987, Les Hanches de Laetitia 1989, Actualités françaises 1992, Comme hier 1993, Pas trop près de l'écran 1993, Michel Déon 1994, Barbe à Papa 1996, La Petite française (Prix Interallié) 1997, Champagne! 1998, La Séance du mercredi à 14 heures 1998, Précautions d'usage 2001, Un Bien fou (Grand Prix du Roman) 2001, Rendez-vous à Samarra 2005, Folie dans la famille 2005, Histoire de Franck 2005. *Address:* c/o Albin Michel, 22 rue Huyghers, 75680 Paris Cédex 14, France.

NEUMEYER, Peter Florian, BA, MA, PhD; American professor of English and writer; *Professor Emeritus, San Diego State University*; b. 4 Aug. 1929, Munich, Germany; m. Helen Wight Snell 1952; three s. *Education:* Univ. of California at Berkeley. *Career:* Asst Prof., Harvard Univ. 1963–69; Assoc. Prof., State Univ. of New York at Stony Brook 1969–75; Prof. and Chair Dept of English, West Virginia Univ. 1975–78; Prof. 1978–95, Prof. Emeritus 1995–, San Diego State Univ. *Publications:* Kafka's The Castle 1969, Donald and the... 1969, Donald Has a Difficulty 1970, The Faithful Fish 1971, Elements of Fiction (co-ed.) 1974, Homage to John Clare 1980, Image and Maker (co-ed.) 1984, The Phantom of the Opera (adaptation) 1988, The Annotated Charlotte's Web 1994, Floating Worlds: The Letters of Edward Gorey & Peter F. Neumeyer (ed.) 2011; contribs to journals. *Address:* 45 Marguerita Road, Kensington, CA 94707, USA. *Telephone:* (510) 526-3746. *Fax:* (510) 526-3746. *E-mail:* Neum1400@aol.com.

NEVILLE, Robert Cummings, BA, MA, PhD, DD; American philosopher, academic and author; *Professor of Philosophy, Religion and Theology, Boston University*; b. 1 May 1939, St Louis, Mo.; s. of Richard Perry Neville and Rose Naomi Cummings Neville; m. Elizabeth Egan Neville 1963; three d. *Education:* Yale Univ., Lelhigh Univ., Russian Acad. of Sciences. *Career:* Instructor, Yale Univ. 1963–65; Visiting Lecturer and Instructor, Wesleyan Univ. 1964–65; Asst Prof., Fordham Univ. 1965–68, Assoc. Prof. 1968–73; Assoc. for the Behavioral Sciences, Inst. of Society, Ethics, and the Life Sciences, Hastings-on-Hudson, NY 1971–73; Assoc. Prof., State Univ. of NY (SUNY) at Purchase 1971–74, Prof. of Philosophy 1974–77; Adjunct Prof. of Religious Studies and Research Prof., SUNY at Stony Brook 1977–78, Prof. of Philosophy and Prof. of Religious Studies 1978–87; Prof., Depts of Religion and Philosophy and School of Theology, Boston Univ. 1987–, Dean School of Theology 1988–2003, Dean of Marsh Chapel and Univ. Chaplain 2003–06, Exec. Dir The Danielsen Inst. 2005–09; Dir Inst. for the Biocultural Study of Religion 2008–; mem. American Acad. of Religion (Pres. 1992), American Philosophical Asscn, American Theological Soc. (Pres. 2005–06), Boston Theological Soc., Inst. of Society, Ethics, and the Life Sciences, Soc. for Studies of Process Philosophies, Soc. of Philosophers in America, Int. Soc. for Chinese Philosophy (Pres. 1993), Metaphysical Soc. of America (Pres. 1989), Highlands Inst. for American Religious and Philosophical Thought (Pres. 2008–). *Publications:* God the Creator: On the Transcendence and Presence of God 1968, The Cosmology of Freedom 1974, Soldier, Sage, Saint 1978, Creativity and God: A Challenge to Process Theology 1980, Reconstruction of Thinking 1981, The Tao and the Daimon: Segments of a Religious Enquiry 1982, The Puritan Smile 1987, Recovery of the Measure 1989, Behind the Masks of God 1991, A Theology Primer 1991, The Highroad Around Modernism 1992, Eternity's and Time's Flow 1993, Normative Cultures 1995, The Truth of Broken Symbols 1996, The God Who Beckons 1999, Boston Confucianism 2000, Symbols of Jesus 2001, Religion in Late Modernity 2002,

Preaching the Gospel without Easy Answers 2005, The Scope and Truth of Theology 2006, Ritual and Deference 2008, Realism in Religion 2009; editor: Operating on the Mind: The Psychosurgery Conflict (with Willard Gaylin and Joel Meister) 1975, Encyclopedia of Bioethics (assoc. ed.) 1978, New Essays in Metaphysics 1987, The Recovery of Philosophy in America (with Thomas Kasulis) 1997, The Human Condition 2001, Ultimate Realities 2001, Religious Truth 2001; contribs: books, professional journals, and periodicals. *Honours:* Dr hc (Russian Acad. of Sciences). *Address:* 5 Cliff Road, Milton, MA 02186, USA (home). *Telephone:* (617) 358-3384 (office). *E-mail:* rneville@bu.edu (office).

NEVINS, Francis Michael, Jr, AB, JD; American academic and writer; *Professor Emeritus, St Louis University School of Law*; b. 6 Jan. 1943, Bayonne, NJ; s. of Francis Michael Nevins and Rosemary Konzelmann; m. 1st Muriel Walter 1966 (divorced 1978); m. 2nd Patricia Brooks 1982 (died 2011). *Education:* St Peter's Coll., New York Univ. *Career:* admitted to NJ Bar 1967; Asst Prof., St Louis Univ. School of Law 1971–75, Assoc. Prof. 1975–78, Prof. 1978–2005, Prof. Emer. 2005–. *Publications:* fiction: Publish and Perish 1975, Corrupt and Ensnare 1978, The 120-Hour Clock 1986, The Ninety Million Dollar Mouse 1987, Into the Same River Twice 1996, Beneficiaries' Requiem 2000, Night of Silken Snow and Other Stories 2001, Leap Day and Other Stories 2003, Night Forms 2010; non-fiction: Detectionary (co-author) 1971, Royal Bloodline: Ellery Queen, Author and Detective 1974, Missouri Probate: Intestacy, Wills and Basic Administration 1983, The Films of Hopalong Cassidy 1988, Cornell Woolrich: First You Dream, Then You Die 1988, Bar-20: The Life of Clarence E. Mulford, Creator of Hopalong Cassidy 1993, Joseph H. Lewis: Overview, Interview and Filmography 1998, The Films of the Cisco Kid 1998, Paul Landres: A Director's Stories 2000, The Sound of Detection 2001, The Cisco Kid: American Hero, Hispanic Roots 2008, Cornucopia of Crime 2010; editor/co-editor (fiction): Nightwebs 1971, The Good Old Stuff 1983, Exeunt Murderers 1983, Buffet for Unwelcome Guests 1983, More Good Old Stuff 1985, Carnival of Crime 1985, Hitchcock in Prime Time 1985, The Best of Ellery Queen 1985, Leopold's Way 1985, The Adventures of Henry Turnbuckle 1987, Better Mousetraps 1988, Mr President – Private Eye 1988, Death on Television 1989, Little Boxes of Bewilderment 1989, The Night My Friend 1991, Night and Fear 2003, Tonight, Somewhere in New York 2005, Love and Night 2007; editor/co-editor (non-fiction): The Mystery Writer's Art 1970, Mutiplying Villainies 1973, The Anthony Boucher Chronicles (three vols) 2001–02 (one vol. edn) 2005, The Keeler Keyhole Collection 2005. *Honours:* MWA Edgar Awards 1975, 1989. *Address:* 7045 Cornell, University City, MO 63130, USA (office). *E-mail:* nevinsfm@slu.edu (office).

NEWBERY, Linda; British writer and children's writer; b. 12 Aug. 1952, Romford, Essex, England; m. *Publications include:* Run with the Hare 1988, Hard and Fast 1990, Some Other War 1990, The Kind Ghosts 1991, The Wearing of the Green 1992, Riddle Me This 1993, Smoke Cat 1995, The Shouting Wind 1995, A Fear of Heights 1996, The Cliff Path 1996, Whistling Jack 1997, The Nowhere Girl 1999, Flightsend 1999, The Cat with Two Names 2000, The Little Mermaid 2001, The Damage Done 2001, Windfall 2002, Break Time 2002, The Shell House 2002, Sisterland 2003, Polly's March 2004, At the Firefly Gate 2004, Lost Boy 2005, Set in Stone (Costa Book Award for Children's Book of the Year 2006) 2006, Catcall (Silver Medal, Nestle Book Awards 2007) 2006, Nevermore 2008, Flightsend 2008, Rain Cat 2008, Shop Cat 2009, The Sandfather (IBBY Honour List 2010) 2009, The Cat Who Wasn't There 2010, Lob 2010 (published as 'Lucy and the Green Man' in USA). *Literary Agent:* c/o Felicity Bryan Literary Agency, 2A North Parade, Banbury Road, Oxford, OX2 6LX, England. *Telephone:* (1865) 513816. *E-mail:* agency@felicitybryan.com. *E-mail:* lindanewbery@hotmail.co.uk (office). *Website:* www.lindanewbery.co.uk.

NEWBOULD, Brian Raby, BA, BMus, MA; British writer, musicologist and academic; *Professor Emeritus of Music, University of Hull*; b. 26 Feb. 1936, Kettering, Northants., England; m. 1st Anne Leicester 1960; one s. one d.; m. 2nd Ann Airton 1976; one d. *Education:* Univ. of Bristol. *Career:* Lecturer, Royal Scottish Acad. of Music, Glasgow 1960–65, Univ. of Leeds 1965–79; Prof. of Music, Univ. of Hull 1979–2001, Prof. Emer. 2001–; numerous talks/discussions on nat. radio, lectures with live illustrations by Allegri String Quartet, Chilingirian String Quartet, the Lindsays, London Mozart Trio, Jyväskylä Sinfonia. *Artistic achievements:* realizations of Schubert's Symphonies No. 7 in E 1979, No. 10 in D 1981, completion of Schubert's Symphony No. 8 in B minor 1982, orchestration of Schubert's other symphonic fragments, completions of Schubert's String Trio String Trio in B flat 2000, Piano Sonata in C 2003; Patrick for narrator and small orchestra, completion of fragmentary Klavierstück 1995, transcription for clarinet and string quartet of Arpeggione Sonata 1996. *Publications:* Musical Analysis in the Sixth Form, Music to an Unpurged Ear 1981, Schubert and the Symphony: A New Perspective 1992, Schubert: The Music and the Man 1997, Schubert Studies (ed.) 1998, Schubert the Progressive (ed.) 2003; contrib. to Musical Times, Music & Letters, 19th-Century Music, Current Musicology Music Review, Musiktheorie, Schubert-Jahrbuch, Schubert durch die Brille, The Schubertian, BBC Music Magazine, The Guardian, The Scotsman, Glasgow Herald, Daily Telegraph, Radio Times, Jewish Echo, Classic CD, Classical Music, Ovation, Journal of the Conductors' Guild, Beethoven Newsletter, Nieuwsbrief Franz-Schubert Stichting, Meddelelse Franz Schubert Selskabet Danmark, Music Teacher. *Honours:* Hon. Vice-Pres. Schubert Inst. (UK), Hon. Pres. Sheffield Gramophone Soc., Scunthorpe and North Lincolnshire Concert Soc. *Address:* c/o Department of Music, University of Hull, Hull, HU6 7RX, England (office). *E-mail:* B.R.Newbould@hull.ac.uk (office). *Website:* www.briannewbould.co.uk.

NEWCOMER, James William; American academic, writer and poet; b. 14 March 1912, Gibsonburg, OH; m. 1946; one s. two d. *Education:* PhB, Kenyon College; MA, University of Michigan; PhD, University of Iowa. *Publications:* Non-Fiction: Maria Edgeworth the Novelist, 1967; Maria Edgeworth, 1973; The Grand Duchy of Luxembourg, 1984; Lady Morgan the Novelist, 1990; Luxembourg, 1995; The Nationhood of Luxembourg, 1996. Poetry: The Merton Barn Poems, 1979; The Resonance of Grace, 1984. Contributions: journals and periodicals. *Honours:* Commander, Order of Merit, Hon. Mem., L'Institut Grand-Ducal, Grand Duchy of Luxembourg. *Address:* 1100 Elizabeth Blvd, Fort Worth, TX 76110, USA.

NEWHOUSE, Samuel I., Jr; American publishing executive; *Chairman and CEO, Advance Publications, Inc.*; b. 8 Nov. 1927, s. of the late Samuel Irving Newhouse and Mitzi Newhouse (née Epstein); m. 1st Jane Franke (divorced); three c.; m. 2nd Victoria Newhouse. *Career:* took over father's Staten Island Advance co. 1922 and built newspaper and magazine chain; Publr Vogue magazine 1964; Chair. Condé Nast Publs Inc., New York 1975–, also Chair. and CEO Advance Publs Inc., New York 1979–; fmr mem. Bd NY Museum of Modern Art. *Honours:* Henry Johnson Fisher Award, Magazine Publishers' Asscn 1985. *Address:* Advance Publications, Inc. 950 Fingerboard Road, Staten Island, NY 10305, USA (office). *Telephone:* (212) 286-2860 (office). *Fax:* (212) 981-1456 (office). *Website:* www.advance.net (office).

NEWLAND, Courttia; British writer and playwright; b. 1973, London. *Career:* resident playwright, Post Office Theatre 2000–. *Plays:* Euripides' Women of Troy 1999, The Far Side 2000, Mother's Day 2002, B Is For Black 2003. *Publications:* novels: The Scholar 1998, Society Within 1999, IC3 (co-ed.) 2000, Snakeskin 2002, The Dying Wish; short stories: Music for the Off Key 2006; contrib. to Disco 2000, New Writers 8, Afrobeat, Time Out Book of Short Stories Vol. 2, England Calling, Voices for Peace. *Address:* c/o Little, Brown and Co. Ltd, Time Warner Books, Brettenham House, Lancaster Place, London, WC2E 7EN, England (office). *E-mail:* urbanfactor2000@yahoo.co.uk (office). *Website:* www.courttianewland.com.

NEWMAN, Andrea, BA, MA; British writer; b. 7 Feb. 1938, Dover, England; m. (divorced). *Education:* Univ. of London. *Career:* mem. PEN, Writers' Guild. *Publications:* A Share of the World 1964, Mirage 1965, The Cage 1966, Three Into Two Won't Go 1967, Alexa 1968, A Bouquet of Barbed Wire 1969, Another Bouquet 1977, An Evil Streak 1977, Mackenzie 1980, A Sense of Guilt 1988, Triangles 1990, A Gift of Poison 1991, Imogen's Face (TV script) 1998, Pretending to be Judith (TV script) 2001; contributions: magazines and television. *Address:* c/o Serpent's Tail, 3A Exmouth Market, Pine Street, London, EC1R 0JH, England (office). *Website:* www.serpentstail.com (office).

NEWMAN, Aubrey Norris, BA, MA, DPhil; British academic and writer; *Professor Emeritus of Modern History, University of Leicester*; b. 14 Dec. 1927, London, England. *Education:* Univ. of Glasgow, Wadham Coll., Oxford. *Career:* Research Fellow, Bedford College, Univ. of London, 1954–55; Prof. Emer. of Modern History, Univ. of Leicester, Founding Dir Stanley Burton Centre for Holocaust Studies; mem. Jewish Historical Soc. of England (pres. 1977–79, 1992–93). *Publications:* The Parliamentary Diary of Sir Edward Knatchbull, 1722–1730 1963, The Stanhopes of Chevening: A Family Biography 1969, The United Synagogue, 1870–1970 1977, The Jewish East End, 1840–1939 1981, The Board of Deputies, 1760–1985: A Brief Survey 1987, The World Turned Inside Out: New Views on George II 1988, The Holocaust 2001, A History of the Masonic Province of Leicestershire and Rutland 2010. *Address:* School of Historical Studies, University of Leicester, University Road, Leicester, LE1 7RH, England (office). *Telephone:* (116) 252-2804 (office); (116) 270-4065 (home). *Fax:* (116) 252-3986 (office). *E-mail:* new@le.ac.uk (office).

NEWMAN, Gordon F.; British writer, dramatist, producer and director; b. 19 May 1947; two s. *Career:* Man. Dir, One-Eyed Dog Ltd, DramaX Ltd; mem. Writers' Guild. *Plays:* Operation Bad Apple 1982, An Honourable Trade 1986, The Testing Ground 1989; screenplay: Number One 1984. *Television:* Law and Order 1978, Billy 1979, The Nation's Health 1983, Here Is the News 1989, Black and Blue 1992, The Healer 1994, Judge John Deed (series) 2000–06, New Street Law (series) 2006. *Publications:* Sir, You Bastard 1970, Billy: A Family Tragedy 1971, You Nice Bastard 1972, The Player and the Guest 1972, The Split 1973, Three Professional Ladies 1973, The Price 1974, The Streetfighter 1975, The Guvnor 1977, The List 1980, The Obsession 1980, Charlie and Joanna 1981, The Men With the Guns 1982, Law and Order 1983, Set a Thief 1986, The Testing Ground 1987, Trading the Future 1992, Circle of Poison 1995, Crime and Punishment 2009. *Honours:* Writer's Awards, BAFTA 1992, Best Drama 1995, Golden Knight 1999. *Literary Agent:* c/o Independent Talent, Oxford House, 76 Oxford Street, London, W1D 1BS, England. *Telephone:* (20) 7636-6561. *E-mail:* cathyking@independenttalent.com. *Address:* 67 George Street, Edinburgh, EH2 2JG, Scotland (office). *Telephone:* (131) 225-8999 (office). *E-mail:* gf.newman@one-eyed-dog.co.uk (office). *Website:* www.one-eyed-dog.co.uk (office); www.gfnewman.com.

NEWMAN, John Kevin, BA, MA, PhD; British/American writer and academic; *Professor Emeritus of Classics, University of Illinois, Urbana-Champaign*; b. 17 Aug. 1928, Bradford, Yorks., England; m. Frances M. Stickney 1970; one s. two d. *Education:* St Bede's Grammar School, Bradford, Univs of Oxford and Bristol. *Career:* Classics Master, St Francis Xavier Coll., Liverpool 1952–54,

Downside School, Somerset 1955–69; Faculty mem. Univ. of Illinois, Urbana-Champaign 1969–, Prof. of Classics 1980–2000, Prof. Emer. 2000–; Ed. Illinois Classical Studies 1982–87. *Publications:* Augustus and the New Poetry 1967, The Concept of Vates in Augustan Poetry 1967, Latin Compositions 1976, Golden Violence 1976, Dislocated: An American Carnival 1977, Pindar's Art 1984, The Classical Epic Tradition 1986, Roman Catullus 1990, Lelio Guidiccioni, Latin Poems 1992, Horace-Bénédict de Saussure (with A. V. Carozzi) 1995, Augustan Propertius 1997, de Saussure on Geography (with A. V. Carozzi) 2003, Troy's Children: Lost Generations in Virgil's Aeneid (with F. S. Newman) 2005, Horace as Outsider 2011. *Honours:* Silver Medals for original poems in Latin, Vatican City 1960, 1962, 1965, 1997. *Address:* 703 West Delaware Avenue, Urbana, IL 61801, USA (home). *E-mail:* j-newman@uiuc.edu (home).

NEWMAN, Lesléa, BS; American writer, poet and teacher; b. 5 Nov. 1955, New York, NY. *Education:* University of Vermont, Naropa Institute. *Career:* teacher, women's writing workshops; mem. Authors' Guild; Authors League of America; Poets and Writers. *Publications:* Good Enough to Eat, 1986; Love Me Like You Mean It, 1987; A Letter to Harvey Milk, 1988; Heather Has Two Mommies, 1989; Bubbe Meisehs by Shayneh Maidelehs, 1989; Secrets, 1990; In Every Laugh a Tear, 1992; Writing from the Heart, 1992; Every Woman's Dream, 1994; Fat Chance, 1994; Too Far Away to Touch, 1995; A Loving Testimony: Remembering Loved Ones Lost to AIDS, 1995; The Femme Mystique, 1995; Remember That, 1996; My Lover is a Woman: Contemporary Lesbian Love Poems, 1996; Out of the Closet and Nothing to Wear, 1997; Matzo Ball Moon, 1998; Still Life With Buddy, 1998; Girls Will Be Girls, 2000; Signs of Love, 2000; Cats, Cats, Cats!, 2001; She Loves Me, She Loves Me Not (short stories), 2002; Dogs, Dogs, Dogs!, 2002; Runaway Dreidel, 2002; Felicia's Favourite Story, 2002. Contributions: Magazines. *Honours:* Massachusetts Artists Fellowship in Poetry, 1989; National Endowment for the Arts Fellowship, 1997. *Address:* PO Box 815, Northampton, MA 01061, USA.

NEWMAN, Paul Nigel; British author, poet and editor; *Editor, Abraxas;* b. 12 Oct. 1945, Bristol. *Education:* Weston Super-Mare Tech. Coll., St Paul's Coll., Cheltenham. *Career:* founder and Ed. Abraxas: A Journal of Literature, Philosophy and Ideas 1991–. *Publications:* Channel Passage 1975, The Hill of the Dragon 1979, Channel Portraits 1980, Grandeur and Decay 1981, Somerset Villages 1986, Bath 1986, Bristol 1987, Gods and Graven Images 1987, Spiders and Outsiders 1989, The Meads of Love 1994, Murder as an Antidote for Boredom 1996, In Many Ways Frogs (poems with A. R. Lamb) 1997, Lost Gods of Albion 1998, A History of Terror 2000, That Summer in Lamorna (script commissioned by Cornwall Film Fund) 2003, Galahad (novel) (Peninsula Prize 2003) 2004, Aleister Crowley and the Cult of Pan (critical study) 2004, The Tregerthen Horror: Aleister Crowley, D.H. Lawrence and Peter Warlock in Cornwall 2005, entries on terror and literary history in Scribner's World Dictionary of Ideas 2005; contribs to Time Out travel guides, Writers' Monthly, 3rd Stone, British Archaeology, South West Arts, Westwords, Cornish Review, Psychopoetica, The Journal, Ramraid Extraordinaire, Story Cellar, Dreams from a Stranger's Café, The Cerne Giant: Antiquity on Trial, The Dreamt Sea: An Anthology of Anglo-Cornish Poetry 1928–2004. *Address:* 57 Eastbourne Road, St Austell, Cornwall, England.

NEWMAN, Peter Charles, CC, CD; Canadian author and journalist; b. 10 May 1929, Vienna, Austria; s. of Oscar Newman and Wanda Newman; m. 1st Christina McCall (divorced); m. 2nd Camilla J. Turner 1978; two d.; m. 3rd Alvy Björklund 1992. *Education:* Upper Canada Coll., Toronto, Univ. of Toronto and McGill Univ. *Career:* Asst Ed. The Financial Post 1951–55; Ottawa Ed. Maclean's 1955–64; Ottawa Ed. Toronto Daily Star 1964–69, Ed.-in-Chief 1969–71; Ed.-in-Chief, Maclean's 1971–82, Sr Contributing Ed. 1982–; Dir Maclean Hunter Ltd 1972–83, Key Radio Ltd 1983–; Prof. Creative Writing, Univ. of Victoria 1985–90; Prof. Creative Writing, Univ. of British Columbia. *Publications:* Flame of Power 1959, Renegade in Power 1963, The Distemper of Our Times 1968, Home Country 1973, The Canadian Establishment: Vol. I 1975, Bronfman Dynasty 1978, The Acquisitors – The Canadian Establishment: Vol. II 1981, The Establishment Man 1982, True North – Not Strong and Free 1983, Debrett's Illustrated Guide to the Canadian Establishment 1983, Company of Adventurers 1985, Caesars of the Wilderness 1987, Sometimes A Great Nation 1988, Empire of Bay 1989, Merchant Princes 1991, The Canadian Revolution 1995, Defining Moments 1996, Titans: How the New Canadian Establishment Seized Power 1998, Sometimes a Great Nation – Will Canada belong to the 21st Century? 1998, Here be Dragons: Telling Tales of People, Passion and Power 2004, The Secret Mulroney Tapes: Unguarded Confessions of a Prime Minister 2005. *Honours:* several honours and awards including Kt Commdr Order of St Lazarus; Hon. LLD (Brock) 1974, (Wilfrid Laurier) 1983, (Royal Mil. Coll.) 1986, (Queens) 1986; Hon. DLitt (York) 1975, (British Columbia) 1998. *Address:* One Mount Pleasant Road, Toronto, M4Y 2Y5, Canada. *Telephone:* (604) 222-8274 (office); (604) 222-8274 (home). *Fax:* (604) 222-8275 (office). *E-mail:* petercnewman@home.com (home).

NEWMAN, Rachel, BA; American magazine editor; b. 1 May 1938, Walden, Mass; d. of Maurice Newman and Eythe Brenda Newman (née Techell); m. Herbert Bleiweiss 1973. *Education:* Pennsylvania State Univ. and New School of Interior Design. *Career:* Accessories Ed. Women's Wear Daily, New York 1964–65; Designer and Publicist, Grandoe Glove Corpn, New York 1965–67; Assoc. Ed. McCall's Sportswear and Dress Merchandiser magazine, New York 1967, Man. Ed. McCall's You-Do-It Home Decorating 1968–70; Man. Ed. Ladies Home Journal Needle and Craft magazine, New York 1970–72; Ed.-in-Chief American Home Crafts, New York 1972–77; Fashion Dir Good Housekeeping, New York 1977–78, Dir of Home Bldg and Decorating 1978–82; Ed. Country Living 1979–1998; Founding Ed. Country Cooking 1985–90, Dream Homes 1989–2000, Country Kitchens 1990–93, Country Living Gardener 1993–2000, Healthy Living 1996–2000; mem. American Soc. of Magazine Editors; Fellow, Pennsylvania State Univ. Alumni 1986; mem. Editorial Advisory Bd The Green Guide. *Publications:* Living with Folk Art, Country Look and How to Get It, Country Gardens, Country Quilts, Country Decorating, Country Kitchens, Country Christmas, New Country Kitchens. *Honours:* Distinguished Alumni Pennsylvania State Univ. 1988.

NEYREY, Jerome Henry, BA, MA, PhL, MDiv, MTh, PhD, STL; American writer, academic, editor and priest; b. 5 Jan. 1940, New Orleans, LA; s. of Henry G. Neyrey and Olga Lux Neyrey. *Education:* St Louis University, Regis College, Toronto, Yale University, Weston School of Theology. *Career:* Ordained Roman Catholic Priest 1970; Faculty, Weston School of Theology 1977–92; Assoc. Ed., New Testament Abstracts 1977–81, Catholic Biblical Quarterly 1983–91, 1994–, Biblical Theology Bulletin 1986–, Hervormde Teologiese Studies 1995–, Journal for the Study of the New Testament 1997–; Visiting Prof., Pontifical Biblical Institute, Rome 1989; Prof., University of Notre Dame, IN 1992–2007; mem. Catholic Biblical Asscn (Pres. 2007–08), Society of Biblical Literature, The Context Group: Project on the Bible in Its Cultural Environment, charter mem. 1989–. *Publications:* First Timothy, Second Timothy, Titus, James, First Peter, Second Peter, Jude, Vol. Nine, Collegeville Bible Commentary 1983, Christ is Community 1985, The Passion Narrative in St Luke 1985, The Resurrection Stories 1988, Calling Jesus Names (with Bruce Malina) 1988, An Ideology of Revolt: John's Christology in Social-Science Perspective 1988, Paul, In Other Words: A Cultural Reading of His Letters 1990, The Social World of Luke–Acts: Models for Interpretation (ed.) 1991, Peter and Jude, Anchor Bible Commentary 1993, Portraits of Paul: An Archaeology of Ancient Personality (with Bruce Malina) 1996, Honor and Shame in the Gospel of Matthew 1998, Render to God 2004, The Gospel of John 2007, Give God the Glory 2007, The Social World of the New Testament (ed. with Eric Stewart) 2008; contributions: Catholic Biblical Quarterly, Journal of Biblical Literature, Biblica, Novum Testamentum, New Testament Studies, Journal for the Study of the New Testament, Journal for the Study of Judaism. *Honours:* Bannan Fellowship, Santa Clara University 1984–85, Young Scholars Grant 1984, ATS Grant 1989, Lilly Foundation 1989, Plowshares 1990. *Address:* PO Box D, Grand Coteau, LA 70541, USA (office). *Telephone:* (337) 662-5410 (office). *E-mail:* neyrey.1@nd.edu (office).

NGANANG, Patrice, PhD; Cameroonian writer; *Assistant Professor of Literary Theory, State University of New York at Stony Brook;* b. 17 March 1970, Yaoundé. *Education:* Univ. of Yaoundé, Univ. of Frankfurt, Germany. *Career:* Assoc. Prof. of French and German, Shippensburg Univ. 2000–07; Distinguished Visiting Assoc. Prof. of German and Africana Studies, Vassar Coll. 2006–; Asst Prof. of Literary Theory, State Univ. of New York at Stony Brook 2007–. *Publications:* Histoire d'un enfant Quatr' Z'yeux (short story, Prix CREPLA 1986), elobi (poetry collection) 1995, Promesse des fleurs (novel) 1997, Interkulturalität und Bearbeitung: Untersuchung zu Soyinka und Brecht (literary criticism) 1998, Temps de chien (novel) (Grand Prix Littéraire de l'Afrique Noire 2003) 2001, La joie de vivre (novel) 2003, L'Invention du beau regard 2005, Le principe dissident (essay) 2005, La chanson du joggeur (novel, serialised in Le Messager newspaper) 2005, Apologie du vandale (poetry) 2006, Manifeste d'une nouvelle litterature africaine (essay) 2007; short stories, essays and articles on African literature and film. *Honours:* Prix Marguerite Yourcenar for Francophone writers living in the USA . *Address:* Department of CLCS, University of New York at Stony Brook, 2124 Humanities Building, Stony Brook, NY 11794-5355, USA (office). *Telephone:* (631) 632-9475 (office). *E-mail:* patrice.nganang@stonybrook.edu (office). *Website:* www.stonybrook.edu/complit/new/nganang.html (office).

NGEMA, Mbongeni; South African writer, producer and composer; b. 1955, Hlabisa; m. Leleti Khumalo (separated). *Career:* mem. Gibson Kente's acting co., f. Cttee Artists; est. S African struggle theatre on London and New York stages 1981. *Plays:* Woza Albert! (with Percy Mtwa and Barney Simon) 1981, Asinamali 1986, Sarafina! 1987, Township Fever 1989, Sarafina 2! 1996, The Zulu 2000. *Recordings:* Sarafina! 1990, Time to Unite 1990, Woza My Fohlaza 1998, AmaNyida 2002, Best of Mbongeni Ngema 2002. *Publications:* Voices of Sarafina! Songs of Hope and Freedom 1988; contrib. to Woza Afrika!: A Collection of South African Plays 1986, Where is the Way: Song and Struggle in South Africa 1990. *Address:* c/o Skotaville Publishers, PO Box 32483, Braamfontein, South Africa.

NGUYEN, Duy; Vietnamese poet, writer and dramatist; b. (Nguyen Duy Nhue), 12 Dec. 1948, Dong Ve, Thanh Hoa. *Education:* Univ. of Hanoi. *Career:* served as militia squad leader defending Ham Rong-Thanh Hoa 1965–67; staff mem., Van Nghe Giai Phong (Liberation Literature and Arts) newspaper 1967–77; rep. of Van Nghe (Literature and Arts) in the South 1977–; has given several lectures at univs in USA. *Publications:* ten poetry collections, including Anh trang (Moonlight), Qua Tang (The Gift), Ve (Returning), Distant Road: Selected Poems 1999; also three memoir collections, one novel. *Honours:* Van Nghe Poetry Prize 1973, Viet Nam Writers' Asscn Poetry Prize 1985, Grand Prize for Poetry, Inst. of the Romanian Acad. 2010. *Address:* c/o Van Nghe, 17 Tran Quoc Toan, Hanoi, Viet Nam.

NGUYEN, Huu Thinh; Vietnamese writer and editor; *Editor-in-Chief, Van Nghe (Literary Arts) Newspaper;* b. 15 Feb. 1942, Phu Vinh, Duy Phien, Tam

Duong, Vinh Phuc. *Education:* Nguyen Du Inst., Cultural Coll. *Career:* fmr soldier, served in the 202nd Regt as a tank driver, squad leader and journalist 1963–75; Head, Poetry Council, Ed.-in-Chief, Van Nghe Quan Doi 1982–90; Ed.-in-Chief, Van Nghe (Literary Arts) Newspaper 1990–; mem. Viet Nam Writers' Asscn (mem. Bd of Dirs, Exec. Cttee), Deputy Gen. Sec. Viet Nam Writers' Asscn. *Publications include:* poetry: Duong toi thanh pho (trans. as On the Way to the City), Tu chien hao toi thanh pho (trans. as From the Trench to the City), Troung ca bien (trans. as Song of the Sea), The Time Tree: Selected Poems 2003; juvenile: Khi be Hoa ra doi (trans. as When Little Hoa was Born); contrib. to Am vang chien hao (anthology, Echo from the Trench). *Honours:* Van Nghe Prizes 1973, 1976, Viet Nam Writers' Asscn Poetry Awards 1980, 1995. *Address:* Van Nghe (Literary Arts) Newspaper, 17 Tran Quoc Toan, Quan Hoan Kiem, Hanoi, Viet Nam (office). *Telephone:* (4) 8229895 (office); 91-3208160 (mobile). *Fax:* (4) 8263926 (office). *E-mail:* vannghe@fpt.vn (office).

NGUYEN, Huy Thiep; Vietnamese writer and playwright; b. 1950, Hanoi. *Education:* Teachers' Coll., Hanoi. *Career:* spent most of his childhood in rural areas of northwestern Viet Nam; returned to Hanoi 1960; then taught remedial education to CP officials in S?n La Prov. for many years; returned to Hanoi and worked as a labourer; succeeded as a writer under the more liberal policies of Doi moi (Renovation) initiated in 1987; his 1987 short story, Tuong ve huu (The General Retires) established him as a major force in Vietnamese literature; opened a popular restaurant, Hoa Ban, on a bank of the Red River in Hanoi. *Publications include:* The Winds of Hua Tat (short stories) 1989, The General Retires (short stories) 1989, Works and Critical Responses (stories with essays on him) 1990, The Water Nymph (short stories) 1992, Red Spring (play) 1994, Like Gusts of Wind (collected works, including several plays) 1995, Selected Works 1996, Tuoi hai muoi yeu dau (novel), Tieu long nu (novel), Crossing the River 2003; edns of his stories have appeared in French and English translations, including The General Retires and Other Stories (Oxford University Press, USA 1993), translated by Greg Lockhart, and Crossing the River: Short Fiction by Nguyen Huy Thiep (Curbstone Press, 2002), edited by Dana Sachs and Nguyen Nguyet Cam, also published in numerous anthologies, including one story in Night, Again: Contemporary Fiction from Vietnam (Seven Stories Press 1996), edited by Linh Dinh, also has four stories in Vietnam: A Traveler's Literary Companion, edited by John Balaban and Nguyen Qui Duc; contribs to Today, Sung Huong, Bao Van Nghe, Libération. *Website:* nguyenhuythiep.free.fr.

NÍ CHUILLEANÁIN, Eiléan, BLitt, MA; Irish poet and lecturer; Associate Professor of English, Trinity College, Dublin; b. 28 Nov. 1942, Cork; d. of Cormac Ó Cuilleanáin and Eilis Dillon; m. Macdara Woods 1978; one s. *Education:* Univ. Coll. Cork and Lady Margaret Hall, Oxford. *Career:* Lecturer, Trinity Coll., Dublin 1966–, then Assoc. Prof. in English, Fellow; Co-founder Cyphers literary magazine 1975–; mem. Aosdána. *Publications include:* Irish Women: Image and Achievement 1985; poems: The Second Voyage (2nd edn) 1986, The Magdalene Sermon 1989, The Brazen Serpent 1994, The Girl Who Married the Reindeer 2001, Selected Poems 2008, The Sun-Fish 2009. *Honours:* Irish Times Poetry Prize 1966, Patrick Kavanagh Prize 1973, O'Shaughnessy Prize for Poetry 1993, Griffin Int. Prize for Poetry 2010. *Address:* Room 4023, School of English, Arts Building, Trinity College, Dublin 2, Ireland (office). *Telephone:* (1) 8961360 (office). *Fax:* (1) 6717114 (office).

NÍ DHOMHNAILL, Nuala, BA; Irish poet; b. 16 Feb. 1952, St Helens, Lancs., England; d. of Séamus Ó Dhomhnaill and Eibhlín Ní Fhiannachta; m. Dogan Leflef 1973; one s. three d. *Education:* Laurel Hill Convent, Limerick and Univ. Coll., Cork. *Career:* travel overseas 1973–80; writer-in-residence Univ. Coll., Cork 1992–93; Visiting Prof. New York Univ., 1998, Villanova Univ. 2001; Ireland Prof. of Poetry 2002–04; mem. Aosdána, Irish Writers' Union, Poetry Ireland. *Publications:* An Dealg Droighinn 1981, Feár Suaithinseach 1984, Raven Introductions (with others) 1984, Selected Poems/Rogha Danta 1986, Pharoah's Daughter 1990, Feís 1991, The Astrakhan Cloak 1992, Jumping Off Shadows: Selected Contemporary Irish Poets (ed. with Greg Delanty) 1995, Cead Aighnis 1998, In the Heart of Europe: Poems for Bosnia 1998, The Water Horse 1999, The Fifty Minute Mermaid: Poems in Irish 2007; contribs to many anthologies and magazines. *Honours:* Oireachtas Poetry Awards, 1982, 1989, 1990, 1998; Irish Arts Council Awards, 1985, 1988; Irish American O'Shaughnessy Award 1988, Ireland Fund Literary Prize 1991. *Website:* www.nualanidhomhnaill.com.

NIALL, Brenda, (Elinor Doyle), AO, MA; Australian biographer, literary critic and journalist; b. (Brenda Mary Niall), 25 Nov. 1930, St Kilda, Vic. *Education:* Genazzano FCJ Coll., Kew, Univ. of Melbourne, ANU. *Career:* Teaching Fellow, English Dept, Monash Univ. 1964–75, Sr Lecturer 1975–94, apptd Reader 1994–; visiting fellowships at Univ. of Michigan and Yale Univ., USA; regular reviewer for the Age, Sydney Morning Herald, Australian Book Review. *Publications:* Martin Boyd 1974, Seven Little Billabongs: The World of Ethel Turner and Mary Grant Bruce 1979, Australia through the Looking-Glass: Children's Fiction 1830–1980 1984, Martin Boyd, A Life 1988, Georgiana: A Biography of Georgiana McCrae, Painter, Diarist, Pioneer (Fellowship of Australian Writers Australian Unity Award; Victorian Premier's Literary Award for Non-Fiction 1995) 1994, The Oxford Book of Australian Schooldays (co-ed) 1997, The Oxford Book of Australian Letters (co-ed) 1998, The Boyds: A Family Biography (Queensland Premier's Literary Award for Non-Fiction) 2002, Brenda Niall on Arthur Boyd 2005, Judy Cassab: A Portrait 2005, Life Class: The Education of a Biographer 2007, The Riddle of Father Hackett: A Life in Ireland and Australia 2009. *Honours:* Soc. of Women Writers' Alice Award 2008. *Address:* c/o Melbourne University Publishing, 187 Grattan Street, Carlton, Vic. 3053, Australia (office). *Website:* www.mup.com.au (office).

NIAZI, Mohammad Munir Khan, BA; Pakistani poet; b. 1928, Khanpur. *Education:* SE Coll., Bahawalpur, Diyal Singh Coll., Lahore. *Career:* writes poems in Urdu and Punjabi; founder Saat Rang weekly publ., Sahiwal 1949, al-Misal 1960; wrote songs for films 1960s; has worked for Lahore TV. *Publications:* Urdu poetry: Taiz Hawa Aur Tanha Phool, Jungle mein Dhanak, Dushmanoon Kai Darmiyan Sham, Mah-e-Munir, Ek Musalsal; Punjabi poetry: Safar di Raat, Char Chup Cheezan, Rasta Dasan Walay Tarey; poetry in trans.: A Cry in the Wilderness 2001; contrib. to Selected New Punjabi Literature in English Translation. *Honours:* Pres.'s Award for Pride of Performance 1992, Sitara-i-Imtiaz 1998, 2005, Kamal-e-fun Award 2002, al-Muftah Award 2003. *Address:* 43-B Block 1, Sector B-i, Lahore Township, Lahore, Pakistan (home).

NICHOLLS, Christine Stephanie, BA, MA, DPhil; British editor and writer; b. 23 Jan. 1943, Bury, Lancs.; d. of Christopher James Metcalfe and Olive Metcalfe (née Kennedy); m. Anthony James Nicholls 1966; one s. two d. *Education:* Kenya High School, Lady Margaret Hall, Oxford, St Antony's Coll., Oxford. *Career:* Henry Charles Chapman Research Fellow Inst. of Commonwealth Studies, Univ. of London 1968–69; freelance writer for BBC 1970–74, Research Asst 1975–76; Jt Ed., Dictionary of Nat. Biography 1977–89, Ed. 1989–95; Ed. Sutton Pocket Biographies 1996–; Assoc. Fellow, St Antony's Coll., Oxford 1990–. *Publications:* The Swahili Coast 1971, Cataract (with Philip Awdry) 1985, Power: A Political History of the 20th Century 1990, Dictionary of National Biography Missing Persons 1986–90 (ed.) 1993, 1996, The Hutchinson Encyclopedia of Biography 1996, David Livingstone 1998, The History of St Antony's College, Oxford 1950–2000 2000, Elspeth Huxley: A Biography 2002, Red Strangers – The Whites of Kenya 2005, A Kenya Childhood 2011. *Address:* 27 Davenant Road, Oxford, OX2 8BU, England (home). *Telephone:* (1865) 511320 (home). *E-mail:* cs.nicholls@tiscali.co.uk (home).

NICHOLLS, David, (David Holdaway), BA; British novelist, screenwriter and actor; b. 30 Nov. 1966, Eastleigh, Hants.; pnr Hannah; two c. *Education:* Bristol Univ., American Musical and Dramatic Acad., New York. *Career:* acted in plays at Battersea Arts Centre, the Finborough, West Yorkshire Playhouse and Birmingham Rep.; fmr bookseller, Waterstones; fmr actor, Royal Nat. Theatre; fmr script reader/researcher, BBC Radio Drama; script editing jobs at London Weekend Television and Tiger Aspect Productions. *Films include:* Simpatico (co-writer) 1999, And When Did You Last See Your Father? (screenplay) 2007. *Television includes:* Cold Feet (four episodes) 2001, I Saw You (Best Single Play, BANFF TV Festival) 2001, 2002, Shakespeare Retold: Much Ado About Nothing 2004, Tess of the D'Urbervilles 2008. *Plays:* as actor at Royal Nat. Theatre: Arcadia, Machinal, Inadmissable Evidence, The Seagull; as writer: After Sun (also adapted for TV) 2006. *Publications:* novels: Starter for Ten (also film) 2003, The Understudy 2005, One Day (also film) (Galaxy Nat. Book Awards Popular Fiction Book of the Year and Overall Book of the Year 2010) 2009. *Literary Agent:* c/o Curtis Brown Group, 5th Floor, Haymarket House, 28-29 Haymarket, London, SW1Y 4SP, England. *E-mail:* gelleroffice@curtisbrown.co.uk (office). *E-mail:* david@davidnichollswriter.com. *Website:* www.davidnichollswriter.com.

NICHOLS, Grace; Guyanese writer and poet; b. 18 Jan. 1950, d. of the late Iris Nichols; pnr John Agard; two d. *Education:* Univ. of Guyana, Georgetown. *Career:* moved to UK 1976; poet-in-residence Tate Britain, London 2002–. *Publications:* Trust You, Wriggly 1980, I is a Long Memoried Woman (Commonwealth Poetry Prize) 1983, Leslyn in London 1984, The Fat Black Woman's Poems 1984, The Discovery 1986, Whole of a Morning Sky 1986, Come on into my Tropical Garden 1988, Black Poetry (ed.) 1988, Lazy Thoughts of a Lazy Woman and Other Poems 1989, Can I Buy a Slice of Sky? (ed.) 1991, No Hickory Dickory Dock (with John Agard) 1991, Give Yourself a Hug 1994, A Caribbean Dozen (ed.) 1994, Sunris 1996, Asana and the Animals 1997, The Poet Cat (children's book) 2000, Paint Me a Poem 2004, Startling the Flying Fish 2006. *Honours:* Arts Council Bursary 1988, Guyana Prize for Poetry 1996. *Literary Agent:* Curtis Brown Ltd, Haymarket House, 28–29 Haymarket, London, SW1Y 4SP, England.

NICHOLS, John Treadwell, BA; American writer; b. 23 July 1940, Berkeley, CA; m. (divorced); one s. one d. *Education:* Hamilton College. *Career:* Visiting Prof., University of New Mexico, 1992, 1993. *Publications:* The Sterile Cuckoo 1965, The Wizard of Loneliness 1966, The Milagro Beanfield War 1974, The Magic Journey 1978, If Mountains Die 1979, A Ghost in the Music 1979, The Nirvana Blues 1981, The Last Beautiful Days of Autumn 1982, In Praise of Mountain Lions (with Edward Abbey) 1984, On the Mesa 1986, American Blood 1987, A Fragile Beauty: John Nichol's Milagro Country 1987, The Sky's the Limit: A Defense of the Earth 1990, An Elegy for September 1992, Keep It Simple: A Defense of the Earth 1992, Conjugal Bliss: A Comedy of Marital Arts 1994, Dancing on the Stones: Selected Essays 2000, An American Child Supreme: The Education of a Liberation Ecologist 2001, The Voice of the Butterfly: A Novel 2001, The Empanada Brotherhood 2007; contrib. to periodicals. *Honours:* Hon. doctorates (Colo Coll.) 1989, (Hamilton Coll.) 2000, Univ. of New Mexico) 2000; New Mexico Gov.'s Award 1981, Frank Waters Award 2003, Wallace Stegner Award 2004. *Address:* PO Box 1165, Taos, NM 87571, USA (home).

NICHOLS, Leigh (see Koontz, Dean Ray)

NICHOLS, Peter Richard, FRSL; British playwright; b. 31 July 1927, Bristol; s. of the late Richard G. Nichols and of Violet A. Poole; m. Thelma Reed 1960; one s. two d. (and one d. deceased). *Education:* Bristol Grammar School, Bristol Old Vic School and Trent Park Training Coll. *Career:* actor, mostly in repertory 1950–55; schoolteacher 1958–60; mem. Arts Council Drama Panel 1973–75; Playwright-in-Residence, Guthrie Theatre, Minneapolis; Visiting Writer, Nanyang Coll., Singapore 1994; directed revivals of Joe Egg and Forget-me-not Lane (Greenwich), National Health (Guthrie, Minneapolis) and first productions of Born in the Gardens (Bristol), A Piece of My Mind (Southampton), Blue Murder (Bristol), Nicholodeon (Bristol). *Plays:* A Day in the Death of Joe Egg 1967, The National Health 1969, Forget-me-Not Lane 1971, Chez Nous 1973, The Freeway 1974, Privates on Parade 1977, Born in the Gardens 1979, Passion Play 1980, Poppy (musical) 1982, A Piece of My Mind 1986, Blue Murder 1995, So Long Life 2000, Nicholodeon 2000. *Films:* Catch Us If You Can 1965, Georgy Girl 1967, Joe Egg 1971, The National Health 1973, Privates on Parade 1983. *Television:* plays include Walk on the Grass 1959, Promenade 1960, Ben Spray 1961, The Reception 1961, The Big Boys 1961, Continuity Man 1963, Ben Again 1963, The Heart of the Country 1963, The Hooded Terror 1963, When the Wind Blows 1964, The Brick Umbrella 1968, Daddy Kiss It Better 1968, The Gorge 1968, Hearts and Flowers 1971, The Common 1973 and Greeks Bearing Gifts (in the Inspector Morse series). *Radio:* Something In The Air, Jam Yesterday. *Publications:* Feeling You're Behind (memoirs) 1984, Nichols: Plays One and Two 1991, Diary 1969–71, Diary Selection 2000; all listed plays published separately; archive now available in Manuscripts Dept, British Library. *Honours:* Tony Award, New York 1985; several SWET and four Evening Standard Drama Awards, Ivor Novello Award for Best Musical 1977. *Literary Agent:* Alan Brodie Representation, Fairgate House, 6th Floor, 78 New Oxford Street, London, WC1A 1HB, England. *Address:* 22 Belsize Park Gardens, London, NW3 4LH, England. *Telephone:* (20) 7079-7990 (office). *E-mail:* info@alanbrodie.com (office).

NICHOLS, Roger David Edward, MA; British writer, broadcaster and pianist; b. 6 April 1939, Ely, Cambs., England; m. Sarah Edwards 1964; two s. one d. *Education:* Worcester Coll., Oxford. *Career:* Master, St Michael's Coll., Tenbury, 1966–73; Lecturer, Open Univ. 1974–80, Univ. of Birmingham 1974–80. *Publications:* Debussy 1973, Through Greek Eyes (with Kenneth McLeish) 1974, Messiaen 1975, Through Roman Eyes (with Kenneth McLeish) 1976, Ravel 1977, Greek Everyday Life (with Sarah Nichols) 1978, Ravel Remembered 1987, Debussy: Letters (ed. and trans.) 1987, Claude Debussy: Pelléas et Mélisande (with Richard Langham Smith) 1989, Debussy Remembered 1992, The Life of Debussy 1998, The Harlequin Years: Music in Paris 1917–1929 2002, Camille Saint-Saëns on Music and Musicians (ed. and trans.) 2008, Ravel 2011. *Honours:* Chevalier de la Légion d'honneur 2006. *Address:* The School House, The Square, Kington, Herefords., HR5 3BA, England (home). *Telephone:* (1544) 231742 (office). *E-mail:* roger@nicholsnet.org (home). *Website:* www.rogernichols.org.

NICHOLS, (Joanna) Ruth, BA, MA, PhD; Canadian theologian and writer; b. 4 March 1948, Toronto, ON; m. W. N. Houston 1974. *Education:* University of British Columbia, McMaster University. *Publications:* Ceremony of Innocence 1969, A Walk Out of the World 1969, The Marrow of the World 1972, Song of the Pearl 1976, The Left-handed Spirit 1978, The Burning of the Rose 1989, What Dangers Deep: A Story of Philip Sidney 1992. *Honours:* Shankar International Literary Contest Awards 1963, 1965, Woodrow Wilson Fellowship 1968, Fellow 1971–72, Research Fellow 1978, Canada Council, Gold Medal, Canadian Asscn of Children's Librarians 1972.

NICHOLSON, Christina (see Nicole, Christopher Robin)

NICHOLSON, Geoffrey (Geoff) Joseph, BA, MA; British writer; b. 4 March 1953, Sheffield, Yorks., England; m. Dian Hanson. *Education:* Gonville and Caius Coll., Cambridge, Univ. of Essex. *Publications:* Street Sleeper 1987, The Knot Garden 1989, What We Did On Our Holidays 1990, Hunters and Gatherers 1991, Big Noises 1991, The Food Chain 1992, Day Trips to the Desert 1992, The Errol Flynn Novel 1993, Still Life with Volkswagens 1994, Everything and More 1994, Footsucker 1995, Bleeding London 1997, Flesh Guitar 1998, Female Ruins 1999, Bedlam Burning 2000, Frank Lloyd Wright, A Beginner's Guide 2002, Andy Warhol, A Beginner's Guide 2002, The Hollywood Dodo 2004, Sex Collectors 2006, The Lost Art of Walking 2008, Gravity's Volkswagen 2009; contrib. to Ambit magazine, Grand Street, Night, Twenty Under 35, A Book of Two Halves, The Guardian, Independent, Village Voice, New York Times Book Review, Salon.Com, Slake, Black Clock, Los Angeles Review of Books, Gastronomica. *Literary Agent:* c/o Trena Keating, Keating Literary LLC, 80 Fifth Avenue, Suite 1101, New York, NY 10011, USA. *Telephone:* (212) 255-2112. *Fax:* (212) 675-1381. *E-mail:* info@keatingliterary.com. *Website:* www.keatingliterary.com.

NICHOLSON, Michael Thomas, OBE, MA; British foreign correspondent and writer; b. 9 Jan. 1937, Romford, Essex, England; m. Diana Margaret Slater 1968, two s. two d. *Education:* Univ. of Leicester. *Publications:* Partridge Kite, 1978; Red Joker, 1979; December Ultimatum, 1981; Across the Limpoto, 1985; Pilgrims Rest, 1987; Measure of Danger, 1991; Natasha's Story, 1993.

NICHOLSON, Robin (see Nicole, Christopher Robin)

NICHOLSON, William; British author and screenwriter; b. 1948; m.; three c. *Education:* Univ. of Cambridge. *Career:* documentary maker and producer, BBC Television, mid-1970s to mid-1980s; screenwriter for television and film. *Television screenplays:* Shadowlands 1985, Sweet as You Are 1987, Life Story 1987, A Private Matter 1992, Crime of the Century 1996. *Film screenplays:* The Vision 1987, Sarafina! 1992, Shadowlands 1993, Nell 1994, First Knight 1995, Firelight 1997, Gladiator 2000. *Publications:* novels: The Seventh Level 1979, The Society of Others 2004, The Trial of True Love 2005, The Secret Intensity of Everyday Life 2009, Rich and Mad 2009, All the Hopeful Lovers 2010; juvenile novels: The Wind Singer (Wind on Fire trilogy, book one) (Nestlé Smarties Book Prize) 2000, Slaves of the Mastery (Wind on Fire trilogy, book two) 2001, Firesong (Wind on Fire trilogy, book three) 2002, Seeker (Noble Warriors trilogy, book one) 2005, Jango (Noble Warriors trilogy, book two) 2006, Noman (Noble Warriors trilogy, book three) 2007. *Literary Agent:* United Agents, 12–26 Lexington Street, London, W1F 0LE, England. *Telephone:* (20) 3214-0800. *Fax:* (20) 3214-0801. *E-mail:* info@unitedagents.co.uk. *Website:* unitedagents.co.uk; www.williamnicholson.com.

NICOL, Michael George, BA; South African writer, poet and journalist; b. 17 Nov. 1951, Cape Town; one s. one d. *Education:* University of South Africa. *Career:* reporter, To The Point, Johannesburg, 1974–76, The Star, Johannesburg, 1976–79; Ed., African Wildlife, Johannesburg, 1979–81; Freelance Journalist, 1981–85; Asst to the Ed., Leadership, Cape Town, 1986–88; Writer, Journalist, 1989–. *Publications:* Among the Souvenirs (poems), 1979; The Powers That Be (novel), 1989; A Good-Looking Corpse (history), 1991; This Day and Age (novel), 1992; This Sad Place (poems), 1993; Horseman (novel), 1994; The Waiting Country (memoir), 1995; The Ibis Tapestry (novel), 1998; Bra Henry (novella for young adults), 1998; The Invisible Line: The Life and Photography of Ken Oosterbroek (biog.), 1998. Contributions: The Guardian; New Statesman; London Magazine. *Honours:* Ingrid Jonker Award 1980.

NICOLE, Christopher Robin, (Daniel Adams, Leslie Arlen, Robin Cade, Peter Grange, Nicholas Grant, Caroline Gray, Mark Logan, Simon MacKay, Max Marlow, Christina Nicholson, Robin Nicholson, Alan Savage, Alison York, Andrew York); British novelist; b. 7 Dec. 1930, Georgetown, British Guiana (now Guyana); m. Diana Bachmann 1982; four s. three d. *Education:* Harrison Coll., Barbados, Queen's Coll., Guyana. *Career:* mem. Soc. of Authors, Literary Guild of America, Mark Twain Soc.; Fellow, Canadian Bankers Asscn. *Publications:* as Christopher Nicole: West Indian Cricket 1957, Off White 1958, Shadows in the Jungle 1961, Ratoon 1962, Dark Noon 1963, Amyot's Cay 1964, Blood Amyot 1964, The Amyot Crime 1965, The West Indies 1965, White Boy 1966, The Self Lovers 1968, The Thunder and the Shouting 1969, The Longest Pleasure, 1970, The Face of Evil 1971, Heroes 1972, A Beginner's Guide to Chess 1973, Lord of the Golden Fan 1973, Caribee 1974, The Devil's Own 1975, Mistress of Darkness 1976, Black Dawn 1977, Sunset 1978, The Secret Memoirs of Lord Byron 1979, Haggard 1980, Haggard's Inheritance 1981, The Young Haggards 1982, The Crimson Pagoda 1983, The Sun Rises 1983, The Scarlet Princess 1984, The Sun in Splendour 1984, Black Majesty 1984, Red Dawn 1985, The Sun on Fire 1985, Days of Wine and Roses 1986, The Ship With No Name 1986, Old Glory 1986, The Sea and the Sand 1986, The Titans 1987, The Regiment 1987, Iron Ships, Iron Men 1987, Wind of Destiny 1987, The High Country 1987, The Command 1988, Resumption 1988, Raging Sea, Searing Sky 1988, The Happy Valley 1988, Singpura 1988, The Last Battle 1989, The Triumph 1989, The Passion and the Glory 1989, Dragon's Blood 1989, Sword of Fortune 1990, Dark Sun 1990, Sword of Empire 1991, Bloody Sunrise 1993, Bloody Sunset 1994, Courtesan 1995, The Seeds of Power 1995, The Masters 1995, The Crimson Tide 1995, A Woman of Her Time 1996, The Red Gods 1996, The Scarlet Generation 1997, Death of a Tyrant 1997, The Trade 1997, Shadows in the Sun 1998, Guns in the Desert 1998, Prelude to War 1999, To All Eternity 1999, The Quest 1999, Be Not Afraid 2000, Commando 2000, The Cause 2001, The Tiger 2001, The Search 2001, Ransom Island 2001, Poor Darling 2002, The Pursuit 2002, Demon 2003 The Voyage 2003, The Followers 2004, A Fearful Thing 2005, The Falls of Death 2005, Cold Country, Hot Sun 2005, Them That Sleep 2005, The Angel from Hell 2006, Angel in Red 2006, Angel of Vengeance 2007, Angel in Jeopardy 2007, Angel of Doom 2008, Angel Rising 2008, Angel of Destruction 2009, Angel of Darkness 2009, Dawn of a Legend 2010, Twilight of a Goddess 2010; as Daniel Adams: Brothers and Enemies 1982, Defiant Loves 1983; as Leslie Arlen: Love and Honour 1980, War and Passion 1981, Fate and Dreams 1982, Hope and Glory 1983, Rage and Desire 1984, Fortune and Fury 1985; as Robin Cade: The Fear Dealers 1974; as Peter Grange: King Creols 1966, The Devil's Emissary 1968, The Tumult at the Gate 1971, The Golden Goddess 1973; as Nicholas Grant: Khan 1993, Siblings 1995; as Alan Savage: Ottoman 1990, The Eight Banners 1991, Mogul 1991, The Last Bannerman 1992, Queen of Night 1992, Eleanor of Aquitaine 1995, Queen of Love 1995, The Sword and the Scalpel 1996, The Sword and the Jungle 1996, The Sword and the Prison 1997, Stop Rommel 1997, Afrika Crops 1998, The Traitor Within 1998, Queen of Fury 2000, Queen of Destiny 2001, Partisan 2001, Murder's Art 2002, Battleground 2002, Queen of the Sun (in German) 2002, The Killing Ground 2003, Queen of Warriors (in German) 2003, Queen of Mountains (in German) 2003, Resistance 2003, The Game of Treachery 2004, The Legacy of Hate 2004, Queen of Lovers 2004, The Brightest Day 2005, Blue Yonder 2005, Death in the Sky 2006, The Whirlwind 2006, Storm Warning 2007, The Flowing Tide 2008, The Calm and the Storm 2008, The Vortex 2009; as Caroline Gray: First Class 1984, So Grand 1984, White Rani 1986, Victoria's Walk 1986, The Third Life 1988, Shadow of Death 1989, Blue

Water, Black Death 1991, Spares 1993, The Daughter 1992, Golden Girl 1992, Spawn of the Devil 1993, Sword of the Devil 1994, Death of the Devil 1995, Crossbow 1996, Masquerade 1997, The Promised Lane 1997, The Phoenix 1997, The Torrent 1998, The Inheritance 1998; as Mark Logan: Tricolour 1976, Guillotine 1977, Brumaire 1978; as Simon MacKay: The Seas of Fortune 1983, The Rivals 1984; as Robin Nicholson: The Power and the Passion 1977, The Savage Sands 1978, The Queen of Paris 1978, Hitler's Woman 1981; as Andrew York: The Eliminator 1966, The Co-Ordinator 1967, The Predator 1968, Operation Destruct 1969, The Deviator 1969, The Dominator 1969, Operation Manhunt 1970, Where the Cavern Ends 1971, The Infiltrator 1971, Operation Neptune 1971, The Expurgator 1972, The Captivator 1973, The Fascinator 1975, Dark Passage 1976, Tallant for Trouble 1977, Tallant for Disaster 1978, The Fire and the Rope 1979, The Scented Sword 1980, Tallant for Terror 1995, Tallant for Democracy 1996; as Max Marlow with Diana Bachmann: Her Name will be Faith 1988, The Red Death 1990, Arctic Peril 1990, Meltdown 1990, The Growth 1993, Where the River Rises 1994, Shadow at Evening 1994, The Burning Rocks 1996, Children of Hell 1996, Dry 1996, The Trench 1999; other: Refugees (drama) 1987; contribs to numerous journals and magazines. *Address:* 25 Les Blancs Bois, Castel, Guernsey, GY5 7SY, Channel Islands (home). *Telephone:* (1481) 252570 (home). *E-mail:* nicoles@cwgsy.net (home).

NICOLOPULOS, Thania; Brazilian poet and writer; b. 12 Jan. 1924, Pernambuco; d. of Elias Nicolopulos Pablopulos and Georgina (née Joanides) Reissis; m. Ricardo Farias Rosas 1942; one s. one d. *Education:* La Prensa, Mexico. *Career:* freelance writer 1960–; founder and Ed. Centro Editorial Mexicano Osiris 1974; Fellow Altrusas, Red Cross, Fed. of Int. Volunteers; mem. Asscn Escritores Poetas Mexicanos, Soc. Autores Compositores, Anthropology Museum of Mexico. *Publications:* Interpretación de los Sueños 1965, El Mágico Lenguaje de los Sueños 1967, Antologí del Pensamiento 1973, Tlaltelolco Presente 1974, El Despertar de los Sentidos 1975, Metáforas y Paradijas 1975, Un album de poesie musicale 1979, Interpretación de las Manos 1980, Sebastiana la Medium 1981, El Verano de la Vida 1982, La Ofrenda 1983, Remonicencias 1983, Poesía Haiku en español 1990. *Address:* Sierra Ventana 545, 11000 México, DF, Mexico.

NICOLSON, Adam, MA, FRSL, FSA; British writer and journalist; b. 12 Sept. 1957, s. of Nigel Nicolson and Philippa Tennyson d'Eyncourt; m. 1st Olivia Fane 1982 (divorced 1992); three s.; m. 2nd Sarah Raven 1993; two d. *Education:* Eton Coll., Magdalene Coll., Cambridge. *Career:* fmr columnist, Daily Telegraph, Sunday Telegraph. *Publications:* The National Trust Book of Long Walks 1981, Long Walks in France 1983, Frontiers (Somerset Maugham Award) 1985, Wetland: Life in the Somerset Levels (British Topography Prize) 1997, Two Roads to Dodge City 1988, Prospects of England 1990, Restoration (British Book Award for Illustrated Book 1998) 1997, Perch Hill 1999, Regeneration: The Story of the Dome 1999, The Hated Wife 2000, Sea Room 2001, Power and Glory (Royal Soc. of Literature Heinemann Prize 2004) 2003, Seamanship 2004, Men of Honour 2005, Earls of Paradise 2008, Sissinghurst: an Unfinished History (Royal Soc. of Literature Ondaatje Prize 2009) 2008. *Literary Agent:* c/o Georgina Capel, Capel and Land, 29 Wardour Street, London, W1D 6PS, England. *Telephone:* (20) 7734-2414. *Fax:* (20) 7734-8101. *E-mail:* georgina@capelland.co.uk. *Website:* www.capelland.com.

NIEMI, Mikael; Swedish writer and poet; b. 1959. *Plays:* Man måste kunna försvara sig (Radioteater) 1988, Ulosveisu (Tornedalsteatern) 1991, Specialaren (Lule Stasteater) 1992, Ska hon vara snygg eller oneurotisk (Radioteater) 1993, Kuppari (Tornedalsteatern) 1994, Innan det rasar (Teater Normlösa) 1994, Ulkojärvi cabaré (Radioteater) 1995–96, Elsa Laula (Sydsamisk Teater) 1996, Bondånger (comedy series for SvT) 1997, Samerevy (Dolgi Teater, Kiruna) 1997, Konsten att begrava en kärring (Upsala Stadsteater) 1998, Kalla tjejer och varma killar (Tornedalsteatern) 2000, Hej Hitler (Lule Stassteater) 2000, Min pappa är knivjonglör (ToTe, Kiruna) 2000, Dansa din djävul (Tornedalsteatern) 2001, En ö i Valhall (S. Ölands Musikteater) 2001, Tahto rautanen on (Tornedalsteatern) 2002. *Publications:* Näsblod under högmässan (poems) 1988, Mitt i skallen! (non-fiction) 1988, Änglar med mausergevär (poems) 1989, Med rötter häruppe (non-fiction) 1989, Kyrkdjävulen (juvenile fiction) 1994, Blodsugarna (juvenile fiction) 1997, Populärmusik från Vittula (novel, Popular Music from Vittula, aka Popular Music) (Augustpriset) 2000, Svålhålet (short stories) 2004, Astrotruckers (short stories) 2007. *Honours:* Tidningen Vis litteraturpris 2000, Årets Norrbottning 2000, Din bok - vårt val 2000, Årets Bok, Månadens boks pris 2002, Piratenpriset 2002. *Address:* c/o Norstedts, PO Box 2052, 103 12 Stockholm, Sweden.

NIFFENEGGER, Audrey, BFA, MFA; American novelist and visual artist; b. 13 June 1963, South Haven, MI. *Education:* School of the Art Inst. of Chicago, Northwestern Univ. *Career:* Prof., Columbia Coll., Chicago Centre (Interdisciplinary Book Arts, MFA program); Ragdale Foundation Fellowship 1996–2003, Illinois Art Council Fellowship in Prose 2000. *Publications:* The Time Traveler's Wife (novel) (British Book Awards Sainsbury's Popular Fiction Award 2006) 2003, The Three Incestuous Sisters 2005, The Adventures 2006, Her Fearful Symmetry 2009. *Literary Agent:* c/o Joseph Regal, Regal Literary Agency, 52 Warfield Street, Montclair, NJ 07043, USA. *Telephone:* (973) 509-5767. *E-mail:* office@regal-literary.com. *Website:* www.regal-literary.com; www.audreyniffenegger.com.

NIGG, Joseph Eugene, (John Topsell), BA, MFA, PhD; American editor and writer; b. 27 Oct. 1938, Davenport, Ia; s. of Joseph John Nigg and Hollis Ellen Nigg; m. 1st Gayle Madsen 1960 (divorced 1979); two s. (one deceased); m. 2nd Esther Muzzillo 1989. *Education:* Kent State Univ., Iowa Writers' Workshop, Univ. of Denver. *Career:* teacher, Nunda Central School, New York, West Street Coll. of Colorado, Univ. of Denver, Arapahoe Junior Coll., Littleton, Metropolitan Street Coll., Denver, Univ. of Colorado, Denver 1964–1980; Asst Ed. Essays in Literature 1974–75; Fiction Ed. Pendragon 1981–84, Wayland Press 1985–92; Assoc. Ed., then Ed., then Exec. Ed. RE/MAX International 1980–2005; Ed. The Wildlife Experience 2000–05; mem. Colorado Authors' League (Pres. 1980), Authors' Guild (Pres. 2005). *Television:* participant and historical consultant, Ancient Mysteries' Dragons segment 1997; on Myths and Legends DVD 2001. *Publications:* The Book of Gryphons 1982, The Strength of Lions and the Flight of Eagles 1982, A Guide to the Imaginary Birds of the World 1984, Winegold 1985, The Great Balloon Festival 1989, Wonder Beasts 1995, The Book of Fabulous Beasts 1998, The Book of Dragons and Other Mythical Beasts 2002, How to Raise and Keep a Dragon 2006, Sea Monsters 2012; contribs to various journals and magazines, including Bloomsbury Press, Cricket, Epoch, IKON, Short Story International. *Honours:* Non-Fiction Book of the Year Awards, Colorado Authors League 1983, 1985, 1989, 1996, 2003, 2007, Mary Chase Author of the Year, Rocky Mountain Writers' Guild 1984. *Address:* 1114 Clayton Street, Denver, CO 80206, USA (home). *Telephone:* (303) 322-2175 (home). *E-mail:* jegryphon@aol.com (home); joe@josephnigg.com (home). *Website:* www.josephnigg.com.

NIGHTINGALE, (William) Benedict Herbert, BA; British writer and theatre critic; b. 14 May 1939, London; s. of R. E. Nightingale and Hon. Mrs Nightingale (née Gardner); m. Anne B. Redmon 1964; two s. one d. *Education:* Charterhouse School, Magdalene Coll., Cambridge and Univ. of Pennsylvania. *Career:* gen. writer, The Guardian 1963–66; Literary Ed. New Society 1966–67; Theatre Critic, New Statesman 1968–86; Prof. of English, Theatre and Drama Univ. of Mich. 1986–89; Chief Drama Critic The Times 1990–2010 (retd); Sunday Theatre Critic, New York Times 1983–84. *Publications:* Charities 1972, Fifty British Plays 1982, Fifth Row Center 1986, The Future of the Theatre 1998; numerous articles on cultural and theatrical matters in British and American journals. *Address:* 40 Broomhouse Road, London, SW6 3QX, England.

NIKLANDER, Hannu, MA; Finnish poet, writer and critic; b. 16 March 1951, Helsinki; s. of Karl Veio Niklander and Maija-Liisa Tuulikki Suomalainen; m. Kirsti Salmi-Niklander; one s. one d. *Education:* Univ. of Helsinki. *Career:* mem. Bd Union of Finnish Writers 2001–03, 2005– (Vice-Pres.), Bd European Writers' Council 2011–, Bd Baltic Writers' Center, Visby, Sweden 2012–; Deputy mem. Writers' Centre of Three Seas, Rhodes, Greece. *Publications:* poetry: Kotiinpäin 1974, Maakuntalaulu 1979, Kauniisti Niiaava Tytär 1983, Suksien Surujuhla 1985, Muodonmuutoksia 1987, Vackert Nigande Dotter 1989, Hopeatornien maa 2008; fiction: Kenkää enolle (short stories, with Anja Kauranen and Kosti Sironen) 1983, Öinen Kävely (short stories) 1989, Sairaskertomuksia (short stories) 1994, Aurinko Katsoo Taakseen (novel) 1999, Leskimiehen Kevät (short stories) 2000, Radan varrella varjo (novel) 2003, Kuu jättää jäljen (novel) 2006, Ansionsa mukaan (short stories) 2009; non-fiction: Kössi Kaatran Elämää Ja Lohjalaisvaiheita (essays) 1982, Kahvilavieraan Muistiinpanot (essays) 1987, Tuokiokuvia Euroopasta (essays) 1990, Vaahteranlehti Ja Vaakunalilja 1996; contrib. to Länsi-Uusimaa, Karkkilan Seutu, Karkkilan Tienoo, Kul Hunrivihkot, Helsingin Sanomat, Etelä-Suomen Sanomat, Suomenmaa, Kirjastolehti, Suomen Luonto, Parnasso, Kanava, Kaltio. *Honours:* Poetry Prize of NVL 1971, Nuoren Voiman Liitto Poetry Award 1971, State Award for Literature 1999. *Address:* c/o Atena Kustannus Oy, Pl 436, 40101 Jyväskylä (office); Fagerkulla 75, 03600 Karkkila, Finland (home). *E-mail:* hannu.niklander@kolumbus.fi (home).

NIMIER, Marie; French writer; b. 1957, Paris. *Plays:* A quoi tu penses? 2007, Peine, Pénis, Penne 2007, La Confusion, Les Siamoises 2009, Joyeux Noël 2009, Adoptez un écrivain, Papa au Paradis. *Dance:* Texte de "A quoi tu penses", chorégraphie Dominique Boivin. *Publications:* novels: Sirène 1985, La Girafe 1987, Anatomie d'in choeur, L'Hypnotisme à la portée de tous (trans. as Hypnotism Made Easy) 1992, La caresse 1994, Celui qui court derrière loiseau 1996, Sabine Weiss: Des enfants 1997, Domino 1998, La Nouvelle pornographie 2000, La Reine du Silence (Prix Médicis) 2004, Vous dansez? 2005, Les inséparables (Prix Georges Brassens 2009, Prix des Lycéens 2009) 2008; children's fiction: Comment l'éléphant a perdu ses ailes 1997, Une Mémoire D'éléphant 1997, Les Trois Soeurs Casseroles 2000, Charivari à Cot-Cot city 2001, Le Monde de Nounouille 2001, Etna, la fille du volcan 2003, Les Trompes d'Eustache 2005, Un enfant disparaît 2005, La Kangouroute 2007; contrib. to fictions contemporaines au féminin 2002. *Honours:* Prix Médicis 2004. *Address:* c/o Gallimard, 5 rue Sébastian Bottin, 75007 Paris, France (office). *Website:* www.marienimier.com.

NISBET, Jim; American writer and poet; b. 20 Jan. 1947. *Publications:* Poems for a Lady 1978, Gnachos for Bishop Berkeley 1980, The Gourmet (novel) 1980, Morpho (with Alastair Johnston) 1982, The Visitor 1984, Lethal Injection (novel) 1987, Death Puppet (novel) 1989, Laminating the Conic Frustum 1991, Small Apt 1992, Ulysses' Dog 1993, Sous le Signe de la Razoir 1994, Across the Tasman Sea 1997, Prelude to a Scream 1997, The Octopus on My Head 2007, Windward Passage 2010, A Moment of Doubt 2010. *Address:* 571 Icy Street, San Francisco, CA 94102, USA (office). *Telephone:* (415) 626-4395 (office). *E-mail:* psifuncthe@gmail.com (office). *Website:* www.noirconeville.com.

NISBET, Robin George Murdoch, MA, FBA; British classical scholar; b. 21 May 1925, Glasgow; s. of Robert George Nisbet and Agnes Thomson Husband; m. Anne Wood 1969 (died 2004). *Education:* Glasgow Acad., Glasgow Univ. and Balliol Coll. Oxford. *Career:* Fellow and Tutor in Classics, Corpus Christi Coll. Oxford 1952–70, Prof. of Latin 1970–92. *Publications:* Commentary on Cicero, In Pisonem 1961, Horace, Odes I, II (with M. Hubbard) 1970, 1978, III (with N. Rudd) 2004, Collected Papers on Latin Literature 1995. *Honours:* Hon. Fellow, Balliol Coll. 1989, Corpus Christi Coll. 1992; Kenyon Medal, British Acad. 1997. *Address:* 80 Abingdon Road, Cumnor, Oxon., OX2 9QW, England (home). *Telephone:* (1865) 862482 (home).

NISH, Ian Hill, CBE; British academic and writer; b. 3 June 1926, Edinburgh, Scotland; m. Rona Margaret Speirs 1965; two d. *Education:* Univ. of Edinburgh, Univ. of London. *Career:* Univ. of Sydney, NSW, Australia 1957–62, LSE, England 1962–91; mem. European Asscn of Japanese Studies (Pres. 1985–88), British Asscn of Japanese Studies (Pres. 1978). *Publications:* Anglo-Japanese Alliance 1966, The Story of Japan 1968, Alliance in Decline 1972, Japanese Foreign Policy 1978, Anglo-Japanese Alienation 1919–52 1982, Origins of the Russo-Japanese War 1986, Contemporary European Writing on Japan 1988, Japan's Struggle with Internationalism, 1931–33 1993, The Iwakura Mission in America and Europe 1998, Collected Writings, Part I 2001, Part II 2002, Japanese Foreign Policy in the Interwar Period 2002, The Japanese in War and Peace 1942–48: Selected Documents from a Translator's In-tray 2011. *Honours:* Hon. mem. Japan Acad. 2007; Order of the Rising Sun, Japan 1991; Japan Foundation Award 1991. *Address:* Oakdene, 33 Charlwood Drive, Oxshott, Surrey, KT22 0HB, England (home).

NISSABOURI, Mostafa; Moroccan poet and editor; b. 1943, Casablanca. *Career:* Co-founder and Ed. of journals, Poésie Toute 1964, Eaux Vives 1965, Souffles, Intégral; Dir Éditions Archimédia; mem. Bd House of Poetry, Morocco; mem. The Book of Hope and World Healing Book. *Publications:* Plus haute mémoire 1968, La Mille et deuxieme nuit 1975, Approaching the Wilderness 2001; contrib. to Aufgabe, Banipal. *Address:* c/o Editions al-Manar, Art Point France, Catherine Plassart, 6 rue Gimelli, 83000 Toulon, France.

NITCHIE, George Wilson, BA, MA, PhD; American academic, writer and poet; b. 19 May 1921, Chicago; m. Laura Margaret Woodard 1947; three d. *Education:* Middlebury College, Columbia University. *Career:* Instructor, Simmons College 1947–50, Asst Prof. 1950–59, Assoc. Prof. 1959–66, Prof. of English 1966–86, Chair. Dept of English 1972–79, Prof. Emer. 1986–; mem. American Asscn of University Profs. *Publications:* Human Values in the Poetry of Robert Frost 1960, Marianne Moore: An Introduction to the Poetry 1969; contributions: various critical essays in scholarly journals and poems in many publications.

NIU, Han; Chinese poet; b. (Shi Chenghan), 23 Oct. 1923, Dingxiang, Shanxi Prov.; s. of Niu Yingfeng and Shi Buchan; m. Wu Ping; one s. one d. *Education:* Northwest Univ. *Career:* fmrly Sec. Research Dept Renmin Univ.; Dir Cultural and Educational Office, Political Dept of Northeast Air Force; Exec. Assoc. Chief Ed. Chinese Literature; Chief Ed. Historical Records of New Literature Movt; Dir Editorial Office of May 4th Literature; Sr Ed. People's Publishing House; mem. Nat. Cttee, Chinese Writers' Asscn. *Publications:* Motherland, In Front of the Motherland, Coloured Life, Hot Spring, Love and Songs, Earthworm and Feather, Selected Lyric Poems of Niu Han, Notes Taken While Learning to Write Poems, A Sonambulist's Talk on Poetry 2001, Spaciousness Afar-off 2005. *Honours:* Creative Literary Works Award 1981–82, Literary Stick Prize for Nation's Best New Poem (Macedonia) 2003, China Central TV Poet of the Year 2006, Zhongkun Int. Poetry Award 2011. *Address:* 203 Gate 6 Building 309, Balizhuang Beili, Beijing 100025 (home); People's Literature Publishing House, 166 Chaoyangmen Nei Dajie, Beijing 100705, People's Republic of China (office). *Telephone:* (10) 85836410 (home); (10) 65138394 (office). *Fax:* (10) 65138394 (office). *E-mail:* fangjia2001@yahoo.com.cn.

NIVEDITA, Charu; Indian author and critic; b. (K. Avirvazhagan), Nagore, Tamil Nadu; m. *Publications include:* novels: Existentialisamum Fancy Baniyanum, Raasa Leela, Zero Degree 1998, Kaamarooba Kadhaigal 2005, Exile 2011. *Address:* c/o Kizhakku Publishing, New Horizon Media Private Limited, 177/103 First Floor, Ambal's Building, Lloyds Road, Royapettah, Chennai, 600 014 (office); c/o Blaft Publications Private Limited, 4/192 Elliamman Koil Street, Neelankarai, Chennai, 600 014, India (office). *Telephone:* (44) 42009601 (office). *Fax:* (44) 43009701 (office). *E-mail:* support@nhm.in (office); blaft@blaft.com (office); charu.nivedita.india@gmail.com (home). *Website:* www.nhm.in (office); www.blaft.com (office); www.charuonline.com.

NIVEN, Larry, BA, DLitt; American science fiction writer; b. (Laurence Van Cott Niven), 30 April 1938, Los Angeles, Calif.; s. of Waldemar Van Cott Niven and Lucy Estelle Doheny; m. Marilyn Joyce Wisowaty 1969. *Education:* Washburn Univ., Kan. *Career:* first published story, The Coldest Place, appeared in Dec. 1964 issue, World of If. *Publications include:* The World of Ptavvs 1966, Neutron Star (Hugo Award for Best Short Story 1967) 1966, A Gift From Earth 1968, The Shape of Space (short story collection) 1969, Ringworld (Nebula Award for Best Novel 1970, Hugo Award for Best Novel 1971, Locus Award for Best Novel 1970, Ditmar Award, Australia 1972) 1970, All the Myriad Ways (short story collection) 1971, Inconstant Moon (Hugo Award for Best Short Story 1972) 1971, Protector (originally published in Galaxy Magazine as 'The Adults') (Ditmar Award, Australia) 1973, Tales of Known Space (short story collection) 1975, The Long Arm of Gil Hamilton (short story collection) 1976, The Convergent Series (short story collection) (Locus Award for single author collection 1980) 1979, The Ringworld Engineers 1980, The Patchwork Girl (short story collection) 1980, Niven's Laws (short story collection) 1984, Limits (short story collection) 1985, N-Space (short story collection) 1990, Playgrounds of the Mind (short story collection) 1991, Bridging the Galaxies (short story collection) 1993, Crashlander (short story collection) 1994, The Ringworld Throne 1996, Ringworld's Children 2004, Fleet of Worlds (with Edward Lerner) 2007, Juggler of Worlds (with Edward Lerner) 2008, Destroyer of Worlds (with Edward Lerner) 2009, Stars and Gods (short story collection) 2010; other books: The Flying Sorcerers (with David Gerrold) 1971, The Flight of the Horse 1973, The Hole Man (Hugo Award for Best Short Story 1975) 1974, A Hole in Space 1974, The Mote In God's Eye (with Jerry Pournelle) 1974, Inferno (with Jerry Pournelle) 1975, The Borderland of Sol (Hugo Award for Best Short Story 1976) 1975, A World Out of Time 1976, The Magic Goes Away 1977, Lucifer's Hammer (with Jerry Pournelle) 1977, Dream Park (with Steven Barnes) 1981, Oath of Fealty (with Jerry Pournelle) 1981, The Descent of Anansi (with Steven Barnes) 1982, The Integral Trees (Locus Award for Best Novel) 1984, Footfall (with Jerry Pournelle) 1985, The Legacy of Heorot (with Jerry Pournelle and Steven Barnes) 1987, The Smoke Ring 1987, The Barsoom Project (with Steven Barnes) 1989, Achilles' Choice (with Steven Barnes) 1991, Dream Park: The Voodoo Game (aka The California Voodoo Game) (with Steven Barnes) 1991, Fallen Angels (with Jerry Pournelle and Michael Flynn) (Prometheus Award for Best Novel 1992, Seiun Award, Japan 1998) 1991, The Gripping Hand (aka The Moat Around Murcheson's Eye) (with Jerry Pournelle) 1993, Rainbow Mars 1999, Saturn's Race (with Steven Barnes) 2000, The Burning City (with Jerry Pournelle) 2000, The Missing Mass (Locus Award for Best Short Story) 2001, The Moon Maze Game (with Steven Barnes) 2011, Small Wonder (with Matthew Joseph Harrington) 2011, The Secret of Black Ship Island (with Jerry Pournelle and Steven Barnes) 2011; contrib. numerous short stories to books and magazines. *Honours:* Hon. DLitt (Washburn Univ.) 1984; Edward E. Smith Memorial Award for Imaginative Fiction (Skylark Award), New England Science Fiction Asscn 1973, San Diego Comic Convention Inkpot Award 1979, five Science Fiction Achievement Awards, Nebula Award, Heinlein Life Achievement Award. *Literary Agent:* Spectrum Literary Agency, 320 Central Park West, Suite 1–D, New York, NY 10025, USA. *Telephone:* (818) 718-7419. *Website:* www.spectrumliteraryagency.com. *Telephone:* (818) 718-4029. *E-mail:* organlegger@earthlink.net.

NIXON, Colin Harry; British poet and writer; b. 9 March 1939, London, England; m. Betty Morgan 1967; three d. *Education:* Univ. of London. *Career:* civil servant 1960–99; Disablement Resettlement Officer 1974–83; Conciliation Officer, Advisory, Conciliation and Arbitration Service 1983–99. *Publications:* Roads 1975, Geography of Love 1977, With All Angles Equal 1980, The Bright Idea 1983; contributions: anthologies, including: Spongers 1984, Affirming Flame 1989, Poetry Street 3 1991, Red Candle Treasury, 1948–1998 1998, The Art of Haiku 2000 2000; periodicals, including: Outposts, Tribune, Countryman, Cricketer. *Honours:* George Camp Memorial Poetry Prizes 1975, 1983, First Prize Civil Service Poetry 1978. *Address:* 72 Barmouth Road, Wandsworth Common, London, SW18 2DS, England.

NOBBS, David Gordon, BA; British writer; b. 13 March 1935, Orpington, Kent, England; m. 1st Mary Jane Goddard 1968 (divorced 1998); two step-s. one step-d.; m. 2nd Susan Sutcliffe 1998; one step-d. *Education:* Marlborough Coll., St John's Coll., Cambridge. *Television:* The Fall and Rise of Reginald Perrin, A Bit of a Do, Fairly Secret Army, Love on a Branch Line, Gentlemen's Relish, Stalag Luft, Cupid's Darts, Dogfood Dan and the Carmarthen Cowboy; contribs to That Was the Week, That Was, The Frost Report, The Two Ronnies. *Radio:* Three Large Beers: The Maltby Collection. *Publications:* The Itinerant Lodger 1965, Ostrich Country 1967, A Piece of the Sky is Missing 1968, The Fall and Rise of Reginald Perrin 1975, The Return of Reginald Perrin 1977, The Better World of Reginald Perrin 1978, Second From Last in the Sack Race 1983, A Bit of a Do 1986, Pratt of the Argus 1988, Fair Dos 1990, The Cucumber Man 1994, The Legacy of Reginald Perrin 1995, Going Gently 2000, I Didn't Get Where I Am Today (autobiog.) 2003, Sex and Other Changes 2004, Pratt a Manager 2006, Cupid's Dart 2007, Obstacles to Young Love 2010, It Had To Be You 2011. *Literary Agent:* c/o Jonathan Clowes Ltd, Literary Agents, 10 Iron Bridge House, Bridge Approach, London, NW1 8BD, England. *Telephone:* (20) 7722-7674. *Fax:* (20) 7722-7677. *E-mail:* admin@jonathanclowes.co.uk. *Website:* www.jonathanclowes.co.uk.

NOBLE, Denis, CBE, PhD, FRS; British scientist and academic; *Director of Computational Physiology, University of Oxford*; b. 16 Nov. 1936, London, England; s. of George Noble and Ethel Rutherford; m. Susan Jennifer Barfield 1965; one s. (adopted) one d. *Education:* Emanuel School and Univ. Coll. London. *Career:* Asst Lecturer, Univ. Coll. London 1961–63; Fellow, Lecturer and Tutor in Physiology, Balliol Coll. Oxford 1963–84, Praefectus, Balliol Grad. Centre 1971–89, Burdon Sanderson Prof. of Cardiovascular Physiology, Univ. of Oxford 1984–2004, Professorial Fellow 1984–2004, currently Dir of Computational Physiology, Univ. of Oxford; Visiting Prof., Univ. of Alberta 1969–70; Ed., Progress in Biophysics 1967–; Founder-Dir, Oxsoft Ltd 1984–, Physiome Sciences Inc. 1994–; Chair., Jt Dental Cttee 1984–90; Pres. Medical Section, British Asscn 1992, Int. Union of Physiological Sciences 2009–; Gen.-Sec., Int. Union of Physiological Sciences 1993–2001; Pres. Int. Union of Physiological Sciences 2009–13; Hon. Sec. Physiological Soc. 1974–80, Foreign Sec. 1986–92; Fellow, Univ. Coll., London 1986; Adjunct Prof., Xi'an Jiaotong

Univ., China 2003–07; Visiting Prof., Osaka Univ., Japan 2006–11; Founder-Fellow, Acad. of Medical Sciences 1998; Founder and performer, Oxford Trobadors. *Publications:* Initiation of the Heartbeat 1975, Electric Current Flow in Excitable Cells 1975, Electrophysiology of Single Cardiac Cells 1987, Goals, No Goals and Own Goals 1989, Sodium-Calcium Exchange 1989, Logic of Life 1993, Ionic Channels and the Effect of Taurine on the Heart 1993, Ethics of Life 1997, The Music of Life 2006, The Selected Papers of Denis Noble CBE, FRS, A Journey in Physiology towards Enlightenment 2012; scientific papers mostly in Journal of Physiology. *Honours:* Hon. FRCP; Hon. mem. Acad. de Medécine de Belgique, American Physiological Soc., Academia Europaea 1989, Japanese Physiological Soc. 1998, The Physiological Soc. 1999; Hon. DSc (Sheffield) 2004, (Warwick) 2008, Dr hc (Bordeaux) 2005; Darwin Lecturer, British Asscn 1966, Scientific Medal, Zoological Soc. 1970, Nahum Lecturer, Yale Univ. 1977, British Heart Foundation Gold Medal and Prize 1985, Lloyd Roberts Lecturer 1987, Bowden Lecturer 1988, Alderdale Wyld Lecturer 1988, Pierre Rijlant Prize, Belgian Royal Acad. 1991, Baly Medal, Royal Coll. of Physicians 1993, Pavlov Medal Russian Acad. of Science 2004, Hodgkin-Huxley-Katz Prize, Physiological Soc. 2004, Mackenzie Prize, British Cardiac Soc. 2005, Gordon Moe Lecturer, Cardiac Electrophysiology Soc. 2010. *Address:* Department of Physiology, Anatomy and Genetics, Parks Road, Oxford, OX1 3PT (office); 49 Old Road, Oxford, OX3 7JZ, England (home). *Telephone:* (1865) 272533 (office); (1865) 762237 (home). *Fax:* (1865) 272554 (office). *E-mail:* denis.noble@dpag.ox.ac.uk (office). *Website:* www.physiol.ox.ac.uk (office); www.musicoflife.co.uk.

NOEL, Lise, BA, LèsL, MA, PhD; Canadian writer and columnist; b. 19 April 1944, Montréal, QC. *Education:* University of Montréal, University of Aix-en-Provence, France. *Publications:* Intolerance: A General Survey 1994, Le Devoir, Mariage Homosexuel: Les Termes du Débat 2003; contributions to Critère, Liberté, Possibles, Service Social. *Honours:* Hachette-Larousse 1967, Governor-General's Award for Non-Fiction 1989, Myers Centre Award for the Study of Human Rights in North America 1994. *Address:* 2608 Chemin Cote Sainte Catherine, Montréal, QC H3T 1B4, Canada (home). *E-mail:* lise@videotron.ca (home).

NOËL-HUME, Ivor, (Richard Akerman), OBE; British archaeologist and writer; b. 1927, London. *Education:* St Lawrence College, Kent. *Career:* archaeologist, Guildhall Museum Corp, London, 1949–57; Chief Archaeologist, 1957–64, Dir, Dept of Archaeology, 1964–72, Resident Archaeologist, 1972–87, Colonial Williamsburg; Research Assoc., Smithsonian Institution, Washington, DC, 1959–; Guest Curator, Steuben Glass Co, 1990; Dir, Roanoke Project, 1991–93; Chair., Jamestown Rediscovery Advisory Board, 1994–95; mem. American Antiquarian Society; Society of Antiquaries, London, fellow; Society of Historical Archaeology; Society for Post-Medieval Archaeology; Virginia Archeological Society. *Publications:* Archaeology in Britain, 1953; Tortoises, Terrapins and Turtles (with Audrey Noël-Hume), 1954; Treasure in the Thames, 1956; Great Moments in Archaeology, 1957; Here Lies Virginia, 1963; 1775: Another Part of the Field, 1966; Historical Archaeology, 1969; Artifacts of Early America, 1970; All the Best Rubbish, 1974; Early English Delftware, 1977; Martin's Hundred, 1982; The Virginia Adventure, 1994; Shipwreck: History from the Bermuda Reeds, 1995; In Search of This and That, 1995; If These Pots Could Talk, 2001, Civilized Men 2006, Something from the Cellar 2006. Films: Doorway to the Past, 1968; The Williamsburg File, 1976; Search for a Century, 1981. Contributions: Professional journals. *Honours:* Award for Historical Archaeology, University of South Carolina, 1975; Hon. Doctor of Humane Letters, University of Pennsylvania, 1976, College of William and Mary, Williamsberg, VA, 1983; Achievement Award, National Society of the Daughters of the Founders and Patriots of America, 1989, National Society of the Daughters of the American Colonists, 1990. *Address:* 2 West Circle, Williamsburg, VA 23185, USA. *E-mail:* thamesis1@msn.com.

NOLAN, Patrick, MA, PhD; American academic, writer and dramatist; b. 2 Jan. 1933, New York, NY; three s. *Education:* Univ. of Detroit, Bryn Mawr Coll. *Career:* instructor, Univ. of Detroit; Prof., Villanova Univ.; mem. Writers' Guild of America (West), Dramatists' Guild. *Film screenplays:* Hourglass Moment 1969, Jericho Mile 1978. *Plays:* Chameleons 1981, Midnight Rainbows 1991. *Honours:* Emmy Award 1979, Philadelphia Magazine citation for teaching excellence 1980. *Address:* c/o Department of English, Villanova University, Villanova, PA 19085, USA.

NOLAN, William Francis, (Frank Anmar, Mike Cahill, F. E. Edwards, Michael Phillips); American writer and poet; b. 6 March 1928, Kansas City, Mo. *Education:* Kansas City Art Inst., San Diego State Coll., Los Angeles City Coll. *Television:* Brain Wave, One Step Beyond 1959, Vanishing Act, Wanted: Dead or Alive 1959, Black Belt, Wanted: Dead or Alive 1960, The Joy of Living 1971, The Norliss Tapes 1973, The Turn of the Screw 1974, Trilogy of Terror 1975, Sky Heist 1975, The Kansas City Massacre 1975, Logan's Run 1977, First Loss 1981, The Partnership, Darkroom 1981, Terror at London Bridge 1985, Trilogy of Terror II (The Graveyard Rats; He Who Kills) 1996. *Films:* as screenwriter: Burnt Offerings (1976); as actor: The Intruder 1962, Charles Beaumont: The Life of Twilight Zone's Magic Man 2010, The Ackermonster Chronicles 2010. *Publications include:* Barney Oldfield 1961, Phil Hall: Yankee Champion 1962, Impact 20 (short stories) 1963, John Huston: King Rebel 1965, Sinners and Superman 1965, Logan's Run 1967, Death is for Losers 1968, The White Card Cross-Up 1969, Dashiell Hammett: A Casebook 1969, Space for Hire 1971, Alien Horizons (short stories) 1974, Hemingway: Last Days of the Lion 1974, Wonderworlds (short stories) 1977, Logan's World 1977, Logan's Search 1980, Hammett: A Life on the Edge 1983, Things Beyond Midnight (short stories) 1984, Look Out for Space 1985, Dark Encounters (poems) 1986, Logan: A Trilogy 1986, Pirate's Moon 1987, How to Write Horror Fiction 1990, 3 for Space 1992, Six in Darkness (short stories) 1993, Night Shapes (short stories) 1993, The Black Mask Murder's 1994, The Marble Orchard 1996, The Brothers Challis 1996, Sharks Never Sleep 1998, The Winchester Horror 1998, Logan's Return 2001, A Life Beyond Thursday 2004, Demon! 2005, Wild Galaxy: Selected Science Fiction Stories 2005, The Bleeding Edge: Dark Barriers, Dark Frontiers (with Jason V. Brock) 2009, Dark Dimensions (short stories) 2010, Logan's Run: LastDay 2010. *Honours:* Hon. Author Emer., Science Fiction and Fantasy Writers of America Inc.; Lifetime Achievement Stoker Award, Horror Writers Asscn 2010. *Address:* c/o Fairwood Press, 21528 104th Street, Ct E, Bonney Lake, WA 98391, USA. *Website:* www.williamfnolan.com.

NONHEBEL, Clare, BA (Hons); British social worker, public relations executive, journalist and writer; b. (Clare Jonnart), 7 Nov. 1953, London, England; m. Robin Nonhebel 1975. *Education:* Univ. of Warwick. *Career:* social work for Jewish Blind Soc.; public relations exec., Patrick Deuchar Assocs; freelance journalism for women's magazines, business magazines, Christian publs, nat. daily newspapers; mem. MENSA. *Publications:* Cold Showers 1985, The Partisan 1986, Incentives 1988, Healed and Souled 1988, Child's Play 1991, Eldred Jones, Lulubelle and the Most High (novel) 1998, Don't Ask Me to Believe (non-fiction) 1998, Far From Home (non-fiction) 1999, Healing for Life (non-fiction) 2000, Finding Oasis (non-fiction) 2010; contribs to newspapers and magazines. *Honours:* Jt Winner, Betty Trask Award 1984. *Website:* clarenonhebel.com.

NOONAN, Peggy, BA; American writer; b. 7 Sept. 1950, Brooklyn, NY; d. of James J. Noonan and Mary Jane Noonan (née Byrne); m. Richard Rahn 1985 (divorced); one s. *Education:* Fairleigh Dickson Univ., Rutherford, NJ. *Career:* Adjuster, Aetna Insurance Co., Newark, NJ until 1970; scriptwriter, producer and later Editorial Dir WEEI (CBS), Boston; Writer and Ed. CBS 1977–81, writer, radio commentaries 1981–84; Adjunct Prof. of Journalism, New York Univ. 1978–79; speech writer and special asst to Pres. Ronald Reagan 1984–86; chief speech writer for Pres. George Bush 1988; advisor, Bush–Quayle 1992 presidential campaign; columnist, Mirabella Magazine, New York Times, Forbes Magazine, Newsweek 1990–92; currently columnist, Wall Street Journal, Time magazine, Good Housekeeping magazine; mem. Bd of Dirs Manhattan Inst. *Publications:* I Am Often Booed Because of Who My Friends Are, What I Saw at the Revolution: A Political Life in the Reagan Era 1990, Life, Liberty and the Pursuit of Happiness 1994, The Case Against Hillary Clinton 2000, When Character was King: A Story of Ronald Reagan 2001, A Heart, a Cross and a Flag 2003, John Paul the Great: Remembering a Spiritual Father 2005, Patriotic Grace 2008. *Honours:* Dr hc (Fairleigh Dickinson) 1990, (Adelphi Univ.), (St. John Fisher Coll.); Esquire Magazine Achievement Award 1984, Republican Nat. Women's Club Award for Journalism 1992. *Address:* The Wall Street Journal, 200 Liberty Street, New York, NY 10281, USA (office). *Telephone:* (212) 416-2000 (office). *Website:* online.wsj.com/public/page/peggy-noonan.html (office); www.peggynoonan.com.

NOORT, Saskia; Dutch writer and journalist; b. 13 April 1967, Bergen; partner; one s. one d. *Career:* has written articles and columns for Marie Claire, Playboy, Viva, TopSanté, Ouders van Nu, LINDA. *Publications:* novels: Terug naar de kust (trans. as Back to the Coast) 2003, De eetclub (trans. as The Dinner Club) 2004, Nieuwe buren (trans. as New Neighbours) 2006, Afgunst & Een goed huwelijk 2007, 40 2007, Babykoorts 2008, Aan de goede kant van 30 2008, De verbouwing 2009. *Honours:* Prix SNCF du Polar. *Address:* c/o Ambo Anthos, Herengracht 499, 1017 BT Amsterdam, Netherlands (office). *E-mail:* info@amboanthos.nl (office). *Website:* www.amboanthos.nl (office); www.saskianoort.nl.

NOOTEBOOM, Cornelis (Cees) Johannes Jacobus Maria; Dutch writer and poet; b. 31 July 1933, The Hague. *Publications:* fiction: Philip en de anderen (Anne Frank-prijs 1957) 1954, De verliefde gevangene 1958, De koning is dood 1961, De ridder is gestorven (Lucy B. en C. W. van der Hoogtprijs 1963) 1963, Rituelen (F. Bordewijkprijs 1981, Mobil Pegasus Literatuurprijs 1982) 1980, Een lied van schijn en wezen 1981, Mokusei 1982, In Nederland (Multatuliprijs 1985) 1984, De Boeddha achter de schutting. Aan de oever van de Chaophraya 1986, Ina Rilke 1991, Allerzielen 1998, Paradijs Verloren 2004, 's Nachts kommen de vossen 2009; plays: De zwanen van de Theems (ANV-Visser Neerlandia-prijs 1960) 1959, Gyges en Kandaules. Een koningsdrama 1982; poetry: De doden zoeben een huis 1956, Koude gedichten 1959, Het zwarte gedicht 1960, Ibicenzer gedicht (Poëzieprijs van de gemeente Amsterdam) 1960, Gesloten gedichten (Poëzieprijs van de gemeente Amsterdam 1965) 1964, Gemaakte gedichten 1970, Open als een schelp – dicht als een steen (Jan Campertprijs 1978) 1978, Aas 1982, Vuurtijd, Ijstijd. Gedichten 1955–1983 1984, Het gezicht van het oog 1989, Zo kon het zijn (Gedichtendagprijzen 2000) 1999, Bitterzoet, honderd gedichten van vroeger en zeventien nieuwe 2000, Met andere woorden 2004, Die schlafenden Götter 2005; non-fiction: Een middag in Bruay 1963, Een nacht in Tunesië 1965, Een ochtend in Bahia 1968, De Parijse beroerte 1968, Bitter Bolivia, Maanland Mali 1971, Een avond in Isfahan 1978, Waar je gevallen bent, blijf je 1983, De zucht naar het Westen 1985, De wereld een reiziger 1989, Berlijnse notities 1990, Vreemd water 1991, Het volgende verhaal 1991, De omweg naar Santiago (Preis für Reiseliteratur des Landes Tirol 1996) 1992, Zurbaránk 1992, De ontvoering van Europa (essay) 1993, De koning van Suriname 1993, Van de lente de dauw. Oosterse reizen 1995, De filosoof zonder ogen: Europese reizen 1997, Terugkeer naar Berlijn 1997, Nootebooms Hotel 2002, Het geluid van Aijn naam. Reizen door de Islamitische wereld 2005, Rode regen 2007, Verleden als eigenschap. Kronieken 1961/1968 2008, Berlin 1989/2009 2009, Het raadsel van het licht 2009, Scheepsjournaal 2010. *Honours:* hon. mem. Modern Language Asscn, USA 1997; Chevalier, Légion d'honneur 1991, Commdr, Ordre des Arts et des Lettres; Hon. DLitt (Katholieke Universiteit Brussel) 1998; Dr hc (Freie Universität Berlin) 2008; Prijs van de dagbladjournalistiek 1969, Cestoda-prijs 1982, Preis zum 3 Oktober 1990, Constantijn Huygensprijs 1992, Hugo Ball Preis 1993, Aristeion Prijs 1993, Premio Grinzane Cavour 1994, Dirk Martens-prijs 1994, Goethe-prijs 2002, Oostenrijkse staatsprijs 2002, P. C. Hooftprijs 2004. *Address:* c/o Arbeiderspers, Herengracht 370-372, 1016 CH Amsterdam, The Netherlands (office). *Website:* www.ceesnooteboom.com.

NORÉN, Lars; Swedish playwright and director; b. 9 May 1944, Stockholm; s. of Matti Norén and Britt Norén; m. 1st Titti Mörk 1979; m. 2nd Charlott Neuhauser 1993; two d. *Career:* started career as a poet; wrote first play 1968; has written 55 plays, performed world-wide. *Plays include:* Courage to Kill 1978, Munich-Athens 1981, Night is Day's Mother 1982, Comedians 1985, Hebriana 1987, Autumn and Winter 1987, And Give Us the Shadows 1988, Trick or Treat 1989, Lost and Found 1991, The Shadow Boys 1991, Leaves in Vallombrosa 1992, Blood 1994, Some Kind of Hades 1994, The Clinic 1995, Personkrets 3:1 1997, 7:3 1998, Autumn and Winter 1997, Blood 2003, War 2008. *Honours:* De Nio's Pris 1985, Expressens Reviewers' Prize 1993, Pilot Prize 1994 and many other prizes and awards. *Address:* Östermalmsgatan 33, S-11426 Stockholm, Sweden, (home).

NORFOLK, Lawrence; British writer; b. 1963, London, England. *Education:* King's Coll., London. *Career:* worked briefly as a teacher; fmr freelance writer for reference book publisher. *Publications:* novels: Lemprière's Dictionary (Somerset Maugham Award 1992) 1991, The Pope's Rhinoceros 1997, In the Shape of a Boar 2000; ed. of anthologies.

NORFOLK, Mark; British playwright and filmmaker; b. Croydon, Surrey, England. *Education:* Univ. of Wales, Cardiff, Postgraduate Diploma in Film Studies. *Career:* Co-founder Prussia Lane Productions Ltd; Writer-in-Residence, HM's Prison High Down 2006–10, London Borough of Newham 2008–09. *Plays:* Fair as the Dark Get 1998, Buy Your Leave 1998, Knock Down Ginger 2003, Wrong Place 2003, Fess Up 2003, Dear Mama 2005, A Walk in the Park 2008, Naked Soldiers 2010, Where the Flowers Grow 2011. *Films:* Love is Not Enough (also screenplay) 2001, Crossing Bridges (also screenplay) 2004, Jewish Mothers and Daughters (archive) 2006, Ham & The Piper (also screenplay) 2011. *Radio:* Medium Risk (BBC Radio 3) 2005, City Speaks (BBC Radio 4). *Publications:* contrib. to Black Filmmaker Magazine 2001–05, New Statesman 2006, London Evening Standard 2010, 2011. *Honours:* Production Award, London Film and Video Development Agency 1999, Tidy Britain Campaign Award 2001, Champion of Culture Award 2003, Best Editing Award, Cyprus Int. Film Festival 2007, Independent Spirit Award, Screen Nation Film and Television 2007, Audience Award, Corinthian Film Festival 2008. *Literary Agent:* c/o Prussia Lane Productions Ltd, 1 Upper Brockley Road, London, SE4 1SY, England. *Telephone:* (20) 8694-8821. *Fax:* (20) 8694-8821. *E-mail:* prussialane@gmail.com. *Website:* www.pruzz.com; www.marknorfolk.co.uk.

NORMAN, Barry Leslie, CBE; British author and broadcaster; b. 21 Aug. 1933, London, England; s. of Leslie Norman and Elizabeth Norman; m. Diana Narracott 1957; two d. *Education:* Highgate School, London. *Career:* Entertainment Ed., Daily Mail, London 1969–71; weekly columnist, The Guardian 1971–80; Writer and Presenter of BBC 1 Film 1973–81, 1983–98, The Hollywood Greats 1977–79, 1984, The British Greats 1980, Omnibus 1982, Film Greats 1985, Talking Pictures 1988, Barry Norman's Film Night, BSkyB 1998–2001, Radio 4 Today 1974–76, The News Quiz 1978–79, Going Places 1977–81, Breakaway 1979–80; Barry Norman's Film Night, Sky 1998–2001. *Publications:* novels: The Matter of Mandrake 1967, The Hounds of Sparta 1968, End Product 1975, A Series of Defeats 1977, To Nick a Good Body 1978, Have a Nice Day 1981, Sticky Wicket 1984, The Birddog Tape 1992, The Mickey Mouse Affair 1995, Death on Sunset 1998; non-fiction: Tales of the Redundance Kid 1975, The Hollywood Greats 1979, The Movie Greats 1981, The Film Greats 1985, Talking Pictures 1987, The Good Night In Guide 1992, 100 Best Films of the Century 1992, And Why Not? (autobiography) 2002, Barry Norman's Book of Cricket 2009. *Honours:* Hon. DLitt (E Anglia) 1991, (Herts.) 1996; Richard Dimbleby Award, BAFTA 1981, Columnist of the Year Award 1990. *Telephone:* (1438) 812087 (office). *E-mail:* barry@datchworth.org (office). *Literary Agent:* c/o Curtis Brown Group Ltd, Haymarket House, 28–29 Haymarket, London, SW1Y 4SP, England. *Telephone:* (20) 7396-4400. *Fax:* (20) 7393-4401. *E-mail:* presenters@curtisbrown.co.uk. *Website:* www.curtisbrown.co.uk.

NORMAN, Geraldine Lucia, (Geraldine Keen, Florence Place), MA; British journalist and writer; *UK Representative, State Hermitage Museum, St Petersburg;* b. (Geraldine Lucia Keen), 13 May 1940, Wales; m. Frank Norman 1971. *Education:* St Anne's Coll., Oxford, Univ. of California at Los Angeles, USA. *Career:* Sale Room Corresp., The Times 1969–87; Art Market Corresp., The Independent 1987–95; UK Rep., State Hermitage Museum, St Petersburg 2001–, Ed. Hermitage Magazine 2002–05. *Publications:* The Sale of Works of Art (as Geraldine Keen) 1971, 19th Century Painters and Paintings: A Dictionary 1977, The Fake's Progress (co-author) 1977, The Tom Keating Catalogue (ed.) 1977, Mrs Harper's Niece (as Florence Place) 1982, Biedermeier Painting 1987, Top Collectors of the World (co-author) 1993, The Hermitage: The Biography of a Great Museum 1997; contrib. to newspapers. *Honours:* Russian State Medal 'In memory of St Petersburg's 300th Anniversary'; News Reporter of the Year 1976. *Address:* 5 Seaford Court, 220 Great Portland Street, London, W1W 5QP, England (home). *Telephone:* (20) 7387-6067 (office). *Fax:* (20) 7383-3470 (office).

NORMAN, John; American academic, writer and poet; b. 20 July 1912, Syracuse, NY; m. Mary Lynott 1948; four d. *Education:* BA, 1935, MA, 1938, Syracuse Univ.; PhD, Clark Univ., 1942. *Publications:* Edward Gibbon Wakefield: A Political Reappraisal, 1963; Labor and Politics in Libya and Arab Africa, 1965; Life Lines: A Volume of Verse, 1997. Contributions: anthologies, reference books, and journals. *Honours:* World Poetry Prize, 1991. *Address:* 94 Cooper Road, John's Pond, Ridgefield, CT 06877, USA.

NORMAN, Marsha, BA, MAT; American playwright and writer; b. 21 Sept. 1947, Louisville, Ky; d. of Billie Williams and Bertha Conley; m. 1st Michael Norman (divorced 1974); m. 2nd Dann C. Byck Jr 1978 (divorced); m. 3rd Timothy Dykman; one s. one d. *Education:* Agnes Scott Coll. and Univ. of Louisville. *Career:* Rockefeller playwright-in-residence grantee 1979–80; American Acad. and Inst. for Arts and Letters grantee. *Plays:* Getting Out 1977, Third and Oak 1978, Circus Valentine 1979, Merry Christmas 1979, The Holdup 1980, 'Night, Mother 1982, Traveler in the Dark 1984, The Fortune Teller 1987, Sarah and Abraham 1987, The Secret Garden (musical) 1991, D. Boone 1991–92, Loving Daniel Boone 1992, The Red Shoes 1992, Trudy Blues 1995, Love's Fire 1998, 140 1998, Last Dance 2003, The Color Purple 2005. *Television plays:* It's the Willingness 1978, In Trouble at Fifteen 1980, The Laundromat 1985, The Pool Hall 1989, Face of a Stranger 1991. *Publications:* The Fortune Teller (novel) 1987; books of lyrics; plays. *Honours:* Pulitzer Prize for Drama 1983; Tony Award 1991; many other awards and prizes. *Literary Agent:* The Gersh Agency, 41 Madison Avenue, 33rd Floor, New York, NY 10010, USA. *Telephone:* (212) 997-1818. *Fax:* (212) 997-1818. *E-mail:* info@gershla.com. *Website:* www.gershagency.com.

NORMANBY, Marquis of Constantine Edmund Walter Phipps, MA; British company director and writer; b. 24 Feb. 1954, Whitby, North Yorkshire, England; m. Nicola St Aubyn (née Shulman) 1990; two s. two d. *Education:* Worcester Coll., Oxford, City Univ., London. *Publications:* Careful with the Sharks 1985, Among the Thin Ghosts 1989; other: The Day's Work by Rudyard Kipling (ed.) 1988. *Address:* Mulgrave Castle, Whitby, YO21 3RJ, England (home).

NORRELL, Gregory T., BS, PhD; American writer, poet and publisher; b. 24 Nov. 1960, Tallahassee, Fla; m. Karen Norrell 1980 (divorced 1995); one s. one d. *Education:* State University of West Georgia, SUNY at Albany. *Career:* Publisher, Dandelion Press and Dandelion Media, Idaho Falls 1955–; Owner, Dandelion Studios, Dandelion Multimedia Recording Division; mem. Acad. of American Poets, Web Poets Society. *Publications:* 'Til Death Do Us Part (short stories), 1997; 95 Windows: An Unofficial Poetry Collection from the Microsoft Network, 1997; Amongst the Shadows (poems), 1997; The River of No Return (novel), 1998; Impact (novel), 1999. *Address:* 1935 East 113 South Street, Idaho Falls, ID 83404, USA. *E-mail:* dandelion@dandelion-multimedia.com.

NORRIS, Bruce; American actor and playwright; b. 16 May 1960, Tex. *Education:* Northwestern Univ. *Career:* work produced at Steppenwolf Theater, Chicago, Lookingglass Theater, Chicago, Philadelphia Theater Co., Woolly Mammoth Theater, Washington, DC, The Royal Court Theatre, London, Staatstheater Mainz, Germany. *Plays:* as playwright: The Actor Retires 1992, The Vanishing Twin 1996, The Infidel 2002, Purple Heart 2002, We All Went Down to Amsterdam (Joseph Jefferson Award for Best New Work) 2003, The Pain and the Itch (Joseph Jefferson Award for Best New Work) 2004, The Unmentionables 2006, Clybourne Park (Pulitzer Prize for Drama 2011, Tony Award for Best Play 2012) 2009, A Parallelogram 2010; as actor: Wrong Mountain, An American Daughter, Biloxi Blues, Closer, Picasso at the Lapin. *Film appearance:* All Good Things 2010. *Honours:* Whiting Foundation Prize for Drama, Honorable Mention, Kesselring Prize, Steinberg Distinguished Playwright Award 2009. *Literary Agent:* c/o Harden-Curtis Associates, 850 Seventh Avenue, Suite 405, New York, NY 10019, USA. *Telephone:* (212) 977-8502. *E-mail:* info@hardencurtis.com. *Website:* www.hardencurtis.com. *Address:* c/o Steppenwolf Theater Ensemble, 758W North Avenue, 4th floor, Chicago, IL 60610, USA (office). *Telephone:* (312) 335-1888 (office). *Fax:* (312) 335-0808 (office).

NORRIS, Geoffrey, BA, ARCM; British critic and musicologist; *Chief Music Critic, The Daily Telegraph;* b. 19 Sept. 1947, London. *Education:* Univ. of Durham, Univ. of Liverpool, Inst. of Theatre, Music and Cinematography, Leningrad. *Career:* music critic, The Daily Telegraph 1983, chief music critic 1995–, also for The Times; Lecturer in Music History, Royal Northern Coll. of Music 1975–77; Commissioning Ed., New Oxford Companion to Music 1977–83; Prof., Rachmaninoff Music Inst., Tambov, Russia 2005–; mem Critics' Circle, The Arts Club. *Publications include:* Encyclopedia of Opera (co-author) 1976, Rachmaninoff 1976, 2nd edn 2001, Shostakovich: The Man and his Music (co-author) 1982, A Catalogue of the Compositions of S. Rachmaninov (co-author) 1982; contrib. to New Grove Dictionary of Music and Musicians 1980, 2001, Musical Times, Music Quarterly, Tempo, Music and Letters, BBC broadcasts. *Address:* The Daily Telegraph, 1 Canada Square, Canary Wharf, London, E14 5DT, England (office).

NORRIS, Kathleen, BA; American poet and writer; b. 27 July 1947, Washington, DC; m. David J. Dwyer. *Education:* Bennington Coll. *Career:* Poet-in-Residence, North Dakota Arts Council 1979–92; Oblate, Benedictine Order 1986–; mem. National Book Critics Circle, Poetry Society of America. *Publications:* poetry: Falling Off 1971, From South Dakota: Four Poems 1978, The Middle of the World 1981, How I Came to Drink My Grandmother's Piano: Some Benedictine Poems 1989, The Year of Common Things 1990, The Astronomy of Love 1994, Little Girls in Church 1995, Journey: New and Selected Poems 1969–1999 2001; other: Dakota: A Spiritual Geography 1993, The Cloister Walk 1996, Amazing Grace: A Vocabulary of Faith 1998, The Quotidian Mysteries 1998, The Holy Twins 2001, The Virgin of Bennington 2002, Acedia and Me: A Marriage, Monks and a Writer's Life 2008; editor: Leaving New York: Writers Look Back 1995; contributions: anthologies and periodicals. *Honours:* Big Table Poetry Series Younger Poets Award 1971, Creative Artists Public Service Programme Grant, New York State 1972, Fine Arts Work Centre Fellowship, Provincetown, Massachusetts 1972, Bush Foundation Grant 1993, Guggenheim Foundation Grant 1994, Western Libraries Asscn Award 1995. *Literary Agent:* Steven Barclay Agency, 12 Western Avenue, Petaluma, CA 94952, USA. *Telephone:* (707) 773-0654. *Fax:* (707) 778-1868. *Website:* www.barclayagency.com. *Address:* PO Box 570, Lemmon, SD 57638, USA.

NORRIS, Ken, BA, MA, PhD; American academic and poet; b. 3 April 1951, New York, NY; two d. *Education:* SUNY at Stony Brook, Concordia University, McGill University. *Career:* Prof. of Canadian Literature, University of Maine, 1985–; mem. League of Canadian Poets; Writers' Union of Canada. *Publications:* Vegetables, 1975; The Perfect Accident, 1978; Autokinesis, 1980; Whirlwinds, 1983; The Better Part of Heaven, 1984; Islands, 1986; Report: Books 1–4, 1988, 8–11, 1993; In the House of No, 1991; Full Sun: Selected Poems, 1992; The Music, 1995; Odes, 1997; Limbo Road, 1998. Contributions: various reviews, journals, and periodicals. *Honours:* Third Prize, CBC Literary Competition 1986.

NORTH, Anthony (see Koontz, Dean Ray)

NORTH, Kate (see Lloyd, Kathleen Annie)

NORTHCUTT, Wayne, MA, PhD; American academic and writer; b. 5 July 1944, New Orleans, LA; s. of Bernard Northcutt and Claire Northcutt; m. Renee Northcutt. *Education:* California State Univ., Long Beach, Univ. of California, Irvine. *Career:* teaching asst, Univ. of California, Irvine 1969–72, Teaching Assoc. 1973–74, 1979–80, Lecturer 1972–73, Asst Prof. 1975–78, Monterey Inst. of Int. Studies, Calif.; Lecturer, Schiller Coll., Paris, France 1978; Asst Prof., Niagara Univ. 1980–83, Assoc. Prof. 1983–88, Prof. of History 1988–2007 (retd); Foreign Expert, Chinese People's Univ., Beijing 1983; Adjunct Prof. of History, State Univ. of New York at Buffalo 1993. *Publications:* The French Socialist and Communist Party Under the Fifth Republic 1958–1981: From Opposition to Power 1985, Historical Dictionary of the French Fourth and Fifth Republics 1946–1991 (ed.-in-chief) 1992, Mitterrand: A Political Biography 1992, The Regions of France: A Reference Guide to History and Culture 1996; contribs to scholarly books and journals. *Honours:* numerous research grants and fellowships. *E-mail:* waynenorthcutt44@aol.com (office).

NORTHROP, Peggy, BA; American publishing and media executive and editor; *Vice-President and Global Editor-in-Chief, Reader's Digest Magazine*. *Education:* Univ. of California, Berkeley. *Career:* began career in newspapers, including The San Francisco Examiner; held sr editorial positions at Vogue, Glamour, Redbook, Real Simple and Health magazines; Ed.-in-Chief Organic Style magazine –2004; Ed.-in-Chief MORE magazine 2004–09; mem. Exec. Cttee, Vice-Pres. and US Ed.-in-Chief Reader's Digest magazine 2007–09, Global Ed.-in-Chief (responsible for all 50 edns printed in 21 languages and sold in more than 60 countries) 2009–; regular contrib. to The Today Show, CBS Early Show and PBS's To The Contrary, as well as XM radio show MoreTime; mem. Bd of Dirs American Soc. of Magazine Eds; fmr mem. Bd Observer Publishing Co., Washington, Pa; mem. Advisory Bd Develop – Don't Destroy – Brooklyn; active with int. humanitarian org. CARE. *Honours:* named by MIN to its "21 Most Intriguing People" list 2003, inaugural Women Who Get it Right Award, Nat. Breast Cancer Coalition 2006, Nat. Magazine Award for General Excellence 2009. *Address:* The Reader's Digest Association Inc., New York, NY 10017, USA (office). *Telephone:* (646) 293-6363 (office). *Fax:* (646) 293-6255 (office). *E-mail:* peggy_northrop@rd.com (office). *Website:* www.rd.com (office).

NORTON, Augustus Richard, BA, MA, PhD; American academic and writer; *Professor of Anthropology and International Relations, Boston University*; b. New York, NY. *Education:* Univ. of Miami, Defense Language Inst., Monterey, Calif., Univ. of Chicago 1984. *Career:* Asst Prof. of Mil. Science, Univ. of Illinois-Chicago Circle Campus 1974–78, Adjunct Asst Prof. of Political Science 1975–77; Adjunct Asst Prof. of Political Science, Old Dominion Univ. 1979–80; Asst Prof., US Mil. Acad., West Point, NY 1981–84, Assoc. Prof. of Int. Studies 1984, Perm. Assoc. Prof. of Comparative Politics 1984–90, Prof. of Political Science 1990–93; Visiting Assoc. Prof. of Political Science, Univ. of Texas at Austin 1986; Visiting Research Prof., New York Univ. 1992–95; Prof. of Anthropology and Int. Relations, Boston Univ. 1993–; Distinguished Visiting Fellow, Oxford Centre for Islamic Studies 2000; Distinguished Visiting Scholar, al-Ahram Center for Strategic Studies, Cairo, Egypt 2006–07; Advisor, Baker-Hamilton Comm., Iraq Study Group 2006; mem. American Political Science Asscn, Boston Forum on the Middle East, Council on Foreign Relations, Middle East Studies Asscn. *Publications:* Studies in Nuclear Terrorism (sr ed. and contrib.) 1979, International Terrorism: An Annotated Bibliography and Research Guide (sr ed.) 1980, The Emergence of a New Lebanon: Fantasy or Reality? (co-author) 1984, NATO: A Bibliography and Resource Guide (sr ed.) 1985, Touring Nam: The Vietnam War Reader (co-ed. and contrib.) 1985, Amal and the Shi'a: Struggle for the Soul of Lebanon 1987, The International Relations of the Palestine Liberation Organization (sr ed. and contrib.) 1989, UN Peacekeepers: Soldiers with a Difference 1990, Political Tides in the Arab World 1992, Civil Society in the Middle East (ed., two vols) 1995–96, 2005, Al-Amn fi al-sharq al-awsat: Tujahat jdida (ed. and contrib.) 1999, Hizballah: Extremist Ideals vs Mundane Politics 2000, Hezbollah: A Short History 2007; contrib. to reference works, scholarly books, professional journals and non-specialist publs, including Survival, Foreign Policy, Current History, International Spectator, The Nation, New Outlook, New Leader, Middle East Journal. *Honours:* Legion of Merit, Purple Heart, Cross of Gallantry, Bronze Star, Combat Infantryman Badge; various grants and fellowships; Outstanding Academic Book Citation, Choice 1980. *Address:* Department of International Relations, Boston University, 152 Bay State Road, Boston, MA 02215, USA (office). *Telephone:* (617) 353-9279 (office). *Fax:* (617) 353-9290 (office); (508) 653-9258 (home). *E-mail:* arn@bu.edu (office). *Website:* www.people.bu.edu/arn (office).

NORTON, Rictor Carl, BA, MA, PhD; American editor and writer; b. 25 June 1945, Friendship, NY; s. of Arnold C. Norton and Marion Norton (née Anderson); partner, David W. Allen. *Education:* Florida Southern Coll., Florida State Univ. *Career:* Instructor, Florida State Univ. 1970–72; Research Ed. Gay News, London 1974–78; Foreign Rights Man. Western Publishing Co., London, 1979–90; freelance since 1990; mem. Int. William Beckford Soc., Nat. Trust, Royal Horticultural Soc., London Natural History Soc., Royal Soc. for the Protection of Birds, The Art Fund, Camping and Caravan Club. *Publications:* The Homosexual Literary Tradition: An Interpretation 1974, College English 36 (co-ed.) 1974, Mother Clap's Molly House: The Gay Subculture in England, 1700–1830 1992, revised 2nd edn 2006, The Myth of the Modern Homosexual: Queer History and the Search for Cultural Unity 1997, My Dear Boy: Gay Love Letters Through the Centuries (ed.) 1998, The Mistress of Udolpho: The Life of Ann Radcliffe 1999, Gothic Readings 2000, Eighteenth-Century British Erotica (ed.) 2002 2004; contribs to The Male Homosexual in Literature: A Bibliography, Oxford Dictionary of National Biography, Essays to Gay Roots, Vols 1 and 2, A Cultural History of Sexuality (Vols 1–6 by Julie Peakman) 2010, The Ontic Return (by James Ford) 2012; contrib. of articles to scholarly journals and periodicals, including American Imago, Renascence, Yearbook of Comparative and General Literature, London Journal, Gay News, Gay Sunshine, Advocate; columns and book reviews to periodicals. *Address:* 29 Huddleston Road, Tufnell Park, London, N7 0AD, England (home). *Telephone:* (20) 7607-2035 (office). *E-mail:* rictor_norton@yahoo.co.uk (home). *Website:* rictornorton.co.uk.

NORWICH, 2nd Viscount, cr. 1952, of Aldwick; **John Julius Cooper,** CVO, FRSL, FRGS; British author and broadcaster; b. 15 Sept. 1929, London; s. of 1st Viscount Norwich, PC, GCMG, DSO and of the late Lady Diana Cooper; m. 1st Anne Clifford 1952 (divorced 1985); one s. one d.; m. 2nd Mollie Philipps 1989. *Education:* Upper Canada Coll. Toronto, Eton Coll., Univ. of Strasbourg, France and New Coll., Oxford. *Career:* entered Foreign Office 1952; Third Sec. Belgrade 1955–57; Second Sec. Beirut 1957–60; Foreign Office and British del. to Disarmament Conf., Geneva 1961–63; Chair. British Theatre Museum 1966–71, Venice in Peril Fund 1970–99, World Monuments Fund in Britain 1994–2009; mem. Exec. Cttee Nat. Trust 1969–95; mem. Franco-British Council 1972–79; mem. Bd ENO 1977–81. *Television:* has made over 30 documentary films for TV, mainly on history and architecture. *Publications:* as John Julius Norwich: Mount Athos (with R. Sitwell) 1966, The Normans in the South 1967, Sahara 1968, The Kingdom in the Sun 1970, Great Architecture of the World (ed.) 1975, A History of Venice Vol. I 1977, Vol. II 1981, Christmas Crackers 1970–79 1980, Britain's Heritage (ed.) 1982, The Italian World (ed.) 1983, Fifty Years of Glyndebourne 1985, A Taste for Travel (anthology) 1985, The Architecture of Southern England 1985, Byzantium, the Early Centuries 1988, More Christmas Crackers 1980–89 1990, Venice: a Traveller's Companion 1990, The Oxford Illustrated Encyclopaedia of the Arts, Vol. V (ed.) 1990, Byzantium: The Apogee 1991, Byzantium: Decline and Fall 1995, The Twelve Days of Christmas 1998, Shakespeare's Kings 1999, Still More Christmas Crackers 1990–99 2000, Paradise of Cities 2003, The Middle Sea 2007, Great Cities in History (ed.) 2009, The Popes: A History 2011, A History of England in 100 Places 2011. *Honours:* Commendatore, Ordine al Merito della Repubblica Italiana; Commendatore della Solidarità Italiana; Hadrian Award, World Monuments Fund, New York 2005. *Address:* 24 Blomfield Road, London, W9 1AD, England. *Telephone:* (20) 7286-5050; 7799-625598 (mobile). *E-mail:* jjnorwich@dial.pipex.com (home).

NOTHOMB, Amélie; Belgian writer; b. 13 Aug. 1967, Kobe, Japan; d. of Patrick Nothomb. *Education:* Université Libre de Bruxelles. *Publications include:* Hygiène de l'assassin (trans. as Hygiene and the Assassin) 1992, Le Sabotage amoureux 1993, Les Combustibles 1994, Les Catallinaires 1995, Péplum 1996, Attentat 1997, Mercure 1998, Stupeur et tremblements (Grand Prix du Roman, Acad. française) (trans. as Fear and Trembling) 1999, Métaphysique des tubes (trans. as The Character of Rain) 2000, Cosmétique de l'ennemi 2001, Robert des noms propres (trans. as The Book of Proper

Names) 2002, Biographie de la faim (trans. as The Life of Hunger) 2004, Acide Sulfurique (trans. as Sulphuric Acid) 2005, Journal d'Hirondelle 2006, Ni d'Eve, Ni d'Adam (trans. as Tokyo Fiancée) (Prix de Flore) 2007, Les Champignons de Paris 2007, Le Fait du Prince 2008, Le Voyage d'Hiver 2009, Une forme de vie 2010. *Honours:* Prix Rene-Fallet, Prix Alain Fournier (two times), Grand Prix Giono 2008. *Website:* www.albin-michel.fr/auteur-Amelie-Nothomb-09208.

NOTLEY, Alice, BA, MFA; American poet and writer; b. 8 Nov. 1945, Bisbee, Ariz.; m. 1st Ted Berrigan 1972 (died 1983); two s.; m. 2nd Douglas Oliver 1988 (died 2000). *Education:* Barnard College, Univ. of Iowa. *Career:* Co-ed. (with Douglas Oliver) Gare du Nord magazine, Paris 1998–99. *Publications:* poetry: 165 Meeting House Lane 1971, Phoebe Light 1973, Incidentals in the Day World 1973, For Frank O'Hara's Birthday 1976, Alice Ordered Me to be Made: Poems 1975 1976, A Diamond Necklace 1977, Songs for the Unborn Second Baby 1979, When I Was Alive 1980, Waltzing Matilda 1981, How Spring Comes (San Francisco Poetry Award 1982) 1981, Three Zero, Turning Thirty (with Andrei Codrescu) 1982, Sorrento 1984, Margaret and Dusty 1985, Parts of a Wedding 1986, At Night the States 1988, Homer's Art 1990, The Scarlet Cabinet (with Douglas Oliver) 1992, Selected Poems of Alice Notley 1993, To Say You 1994, Désamère 1995, Closer to me & Closer... (The Language of Heaven) 1995, The Descent of Alette 1996, Mysteries of Small Houses 1998, Disobedience (Int. Griffin Poetry Prize 2002) 2001, Grave of Light: New and Selected Poems 1970–2005 (Lenore Marshall Prize, Acad. of American Poets 2007) 2007, In the Pines 2007, Reason and Other Women 2010, Culture of One 2011, Songs and Stories of the Ghouls (Wesleyan Poetry Series) 2011; other: Doctor Williams' Heiresses: A Lecture 1980, Tell Me Again 1981, The Collected Poems of Ted Berrigan (co-ed.) 2005, The Selected Poems of Ted Berrigan (co-ed.) 2011. *Honours:* Nat. Endowment for the Arts grant 1979, Poetry Center Award 1981, General Electric Foundation Award 1983, Fund for Poetry Awards 1987, 1989, Los Angeles Times Book Award for Poetry, Acad. Award in Literature, American Acad. of Arts and Letters 2001, Shelley Memorial Award, Poetry Soc. of America 2001.

NOTTAGE, Lynn; American playwright; b. 2 Nov. 1964, Brooklyn; m. Tony Gerber. *Education:* Brown Univ., Yale School of Drama. *Career:* Visiting Lecturer, Yale School of Drama; bd mem. BRIC Arts/Media/Brooklyn, Voice and Vision. *Plays:* Poof! (Heideman Award) 1993, Crumbs from the Table of Joy 1995, Mud, River, Stone 1998, Becoming American 2002, Snapshot 2002, Las Meninas (AT&T OnStage Award) 2002, Intimate Apparel (New York Drama Critics' Circle Award for Best Play 2004, AT&T OnStage Award) 2003, A Walk Through Time (children's musical), Por'Knockers, Fabulation (Obie Award for Playwriting 2005) 2003, Give Again? 2006, Point of Revue 2006, A Stone's Throw, Ruined (Manhattan Theatre Club, NY) (Pulitzer Prize for Drama) 2009. *Publications:* Poof! 1993, Crumbs From the Table of Joy 1998, Mud, River, Stone 1999, Las Meninas 2004, Intimate Apparel/Fabulation 2006, Ruined 2009. *Honours:* NEA/TCG residency grant 1999, Manhattan Theatre Club Fellowship, New Dramatists Fellowship, New York Foundation for the Arts Fellowship 2000, 2004, Audelco Award for Best Production of the Year and Best Playwright 2004, American Theatre Critics'/Steinberg New Play Award 2004, PEN/Laura Pels Award for Drama 2004, John Gassner Award for Best Playwright 2004, Outer Critic Circle Award for Best Play 2004, Guggenheim Foundation Fellowship 2005, National Black Theatre Festival August Wilson Playwriting Award 2005, Lucille Lortel Foundation Fellowship 2007, MacArthur Genius Award 2007, Obie Award for Playwriting 2009, Outer Critics Award 2009, Lucille Lortel Award 2009, New York Drama Critics Circle Award 2009, Jeff Award 2009, Audelco 2009. *Literary Agent:* c/o Oliver Sultan, Creative Artists Agency, 162 Fifth Avenue, 6th Floor, New York, NY 10010, USA. *Telephone:* (212) 277-9000. *Fax:* (212) 277-9099. *E-mail:* osultan@caa.com. *Website:* www.caa.com. *E-mail:* info@lynnnottage.net (home). *Website:* www.lynnnottage.net.

NOVA, Craig, BA, MFA; American writer; b. 5 July 1945, Los Angeles, CA; m. Christina Barnes 1977, two c. *Education:* Univ. of California at Berkeley, Columbia Univ. *Career:* Class of 1949 Distinguished Prof. of Humanities, Univ. of North Carolina at Greensboro 2005–. *Publications:* Turkey Hash 1972, The Geek 1975, Incandescence 1978, The Good Son 1982, The Congressman's Daughter 1986, Tornado Alley 1989, Trombone 1992, The Book of Dreams 1994, The Universal Door 1997, Brook Trout and the Writing Life 1999, Wetware 2002, Cruisers 2004, The Informer 2010. *Honours:* National Endowment for the Arts Fellowships 1973, 1975, 1985, Guggenheim Fellowship 1977. *E-mail:* craig@craignova.com (office). *Website:* www.craignova.com.

NOVÁK, Jan, MA; American (b. Czechoslovakian) author; b. 4 April 1953, Kolín, Czechoslovakia. *Education:* Univ. of Chicago. *Career:* moved to USA aged 17. *Film screenplays:* Valmont (script consultant), Septej (Whisper) 1996, Bájecná léta pod psa (The Wonderful Years That Sucked) 1997, Ax Murder in St Petersburg (Astorka Theatre, Bratislava) 2001, 3x12 (documentary, also prod.) 2004, Citizen Václav Havel Goes on Vacation (documentary, also prod.) 2005. *Publications:* Zatím dobrý (So Far So Good) (Book of the Year Magnesia Litera Awards 2005) 2004, The Willys Dream Kit (fiction) (Sandburg Prize for Chicago's Book of the Year), Commies, Spooks, Gypsies, Crooks & Poets (non-fiction) (Sandburg Prize for Chicago's Book of the Year) 1995, The Grand Life (novel), Turnaround (autobiog. of Milos Forman, co-author); also trans.

NOVAK, Maximillian Erwin, PhD, DPhil; American professor of English, writer and editor; *Distinguished Professor Emeritus of English, University of California, Los Angeles*; b. 26 March 1930, New York, NY; s. of George Novak and Elsie Novak; m. Estelle Gershgoren 1966, two s. one d. *Education:* Univ. of California, Los Angeles, St John's Coll., Oxford, UK. *Career:* Asst Prof. of English, Univ. of Michigan, 1958–62; Prof. of English, UCLA 1962–2001, Prof. Emer. 2001–; Pres.'s Fellow, Univ. of California 1991–, Huntington Library Fellow 1991–, Beinecke Library Fellow 1991, Clark Literary Prof. 2003–04; mem. American Soc. of 18th Century Studies, Modern Language Asscn. *Publications:* Economics and the Fiction of Daniel Defoe 1962, Defoe and the Nature of Man 1963, Congreve 1970, Realism, Myth and History in the Fiction of Daniel Defoe 1983, Eighteenth-Century English Literature 1983, The Stoke Newington Defoe, Vol. 1 1999, Vol. 2 2000, Daniel Defoe, Master of Fictions 2001; Ed.: The Works of John Dryden, Vol. X 1971, Vol. XIII 1984, The Wild Man Within 1972, English Literature in the Age of Disguise 1977, Passionate Encounters 2000, Enchanted Ground 2004, Approaches to Robinson Crusoe 2005, The Age of Projects 2008; contribs to scholarly books and journals. *Honours:* Fulbright Fellowship 1955–57, Guggenheim Fellowships 1965–66, 1985–86, American Philosophical Soc. Fellowship 1979, Nat. Endowment for the Humanities Fellowship 1980–81. *Address:* 451 S El Camino Drive, Beverly Hills, CA 90212, USA (home). *Telephone:* (310) 825-4173 (office); (310) 552-0433 (home). *Fax:* (310) 552-3709 (home). *E-mail:* novak@humnet.ucla.edu (office).

NOVAK, Michael, BT, MA; American theologian and writer; *George Frederick Jewett Scholar in Religion, Philosophy and Public Policy, American Enterprise Institute*; b. 9 Sept. 1933, Johnstown, Pa; s. of Michael J. Novak and Irene Sakmar; m. Karen R. Laub 1963; one s. two d. *Education:* Stonehill Coll., North Easton, Mass. and Gregorian Univ., Rome. *Career:* Teaching Fellow, Harvard Univ. 1961–63; Asst Prof. of Humanities, Stanford Univ. 1965–68; Assoc. Prof. of Philosophy and Religious Studies, State Univ. of NY, Old Westbury 1969–71; Assoc. Dir Humanities, Rockefeller Foundation 1973–74; Ledden-Watson Distinguished Prof. of Religion, Syracuse Univ. 1976–78; Resident Scholar American Enterprise Inst. 1978–, George Frederick Jewett Prof. of Religion, Philosophy, and Public Policy 1983–, Dir Social and Political Studies 1987–; Visiting Prof., Univ. of Notre Dame 1987–88; columnist, The Nat. Review 1979–86, Forbes Magazine 1989–; f., Publr Crisis 1982–95, Ed.-in-Chief 1993–95; mem. Bd for Int. Broadcasting 1983; Judge, Nat. Book Awards, DuPont Awards in Broadcast Journalism; Head, US Del. to UN Human Rights Comm., Geneva 1981, 1982, to CSCE, Berne 1996; other public appointments. *Publications include:* Belief and Unbelief 1965, The Rise of the Unmeltable Ethnics 1972, Choosing Our King 1974, The Spirit of Democratic Capitalism 1982, Freedom with Justice: Catholic Social Thought and Liberal Institutions 1984, Taking Glasnost Seriously 1988, Free Persons and the Common Good 1989, This Hemisphere of Liberty 1990, The Catholic Ethic and the Spirit of Capitalism 1993, Business as a Calling 1996, The Experience of Nothingness 1998, Tell Me Why 1998, On Cultivating Liberty 1999, A Free Society Reader (ed.) 2000, Three in One 2001, On Two Wings 2002, The Universal Hunger for Liberty 2004, Washington's God 2006 and more than 500 articles in journals. *Honours:* Kt of Malta; several hon. degrees; Freedom Award, Coalition for a Democratic Majority 1979, George Washington Honor Medal, Freedom Foundation 1984, Angel Award 1985, Ellis Island Medal of Honor 1986, Templeton Prize 1994, Bratislava Medal 1998, Boyer Award 1999, Masaryk Medal 2000, Econs Medal, Inst. of Italian Mans and Entrepreneurs 2000. *Address:* American Enterprise Institute, 1150 17th Street, NW, Washington, DC 20036, USA. *Telephone:* (202) 862-5839. *Fax:* (202) 862-5821 (office). *E-mail:* mnovak@aei.org (office). *Website:* www.aei.org (office).

NOWRA, Louis; Australian writer and scriptwriter; b. 12 Dec. 1950; m. Mandy Sayer. *Radio:* Albert Names Edward 1975, The Song Room 1980, The Widows 1984, Summer of the Aliens 1989, Sydney 1993, Moon of the Exploding Trees 1995, The Divine Hammer 2001, Jez 2006, Far North 2008. *Publications:* The Misery of Beauty 1976, The Cheated 1978, Albert Names Edward 1975, Inner Voices 1978, Visions 1979, Inside The Island/The Precious Woman 1981, The Song Room 1982, Sunrise 1983, The Golden Age 1985, Palu 1987, Capricornia 1988, The Watchtower 1992, Summer of the Aliens 1992, Cosi 1992, Radiance 1993, The Temple 1993, Crow 1994, The Incorruptible 1995, Cosi (Australian Film Inst. Award for Best Adapted Screenplay 1996) 1996, Red Nights 1997, The Jungle 1998, Language of the Gods 1999, The Twelfth of Never 1999, Byzantine Flowers 2000, Radiance 2000, In the Gutter... Looking at the Stars (anthology, co-ed.) 2000, Abaza 2001, Warne's World 2002, Walkabout 2003, Shooting the Moon 2004, Chihuahuas, Women and Me 2005, Bad Dreaming 2007, The Boyce Trilogy Includes: The Woman with Dog's Eyes, The Marvellous Boy, The Emperor of Sydney 2007, Ice 2008. *Honours:* Dr hc (Griffiths Univ.) 1996; Literature Board Grants 1975, 1977, 1979, 1980, 1981, 1982; Prix Italia 1990, NSW Premier's Literary Prize 1992, Victoria Premier's Prize 1994, Australian Literary Soc. Gold Medal 1994, The Australia/Canada Award 1994, The Green Room Award for Best New Play 1995, Courier-Mail Book of the Year 2000. *Literary Agent:* c/o HLA Management, PO Box 1536, Strawberry Hills, NSW 2012, Australia. *Telephone:* (2) 9549-3000. *Fax:* (2) 9310-4113. *E-mail:* hla@hlamgt.com.au. *Website:* www.hlamgt.com.au.

NOYES, Stanley Tinning, AB, MA; American writer, poet and teacher; b. 7 April 1924, San Francisco; s. of James Goodman Noyes and Winnifred Tinning Noyes; m. Nancy Black 1949; two s. one d. *Education:* Univ. of California, Berkeley. *Career:* taught English in UC Berkeley Extension Program, at California Coll. of Arts and Crafts, Oakland (also Dean of Men), and Coll. of

Santa Fe; fmrly Literary arts coordinator, New Mexico Arts Div.; mem. PEN American Center. *Publications:* No Flowers for a Clown (novel) 1961, Shadowbox (novel) 1970, Faces and Spirits (poems) 1974, Beyond the Mountains (poems) 1979, The Commander of Dead Leaves (poems) 1984, Annus Mirabilis: A Peripatetic Calendar (poems) 2003, Alles Kaputt: Poems of World War II 2007; non-fiction: Los Comanches: The Horse People, 1751–1845, 1993, Comanches in the New West: Historic Photographs, 1895–1908, 1999; contributions: reviews and quarterlies. *Honours:* MacDowell Fellow 1967. *Address:* 634 East Garcia, Santa Fe, NM 87505, USA (home). *Telephone:* (505) 982-4067 (home).

NUDELSTEJER, Sergio; Mexican journalist and writer; b. 24 Feb. 1924, Warsaw, Poland; m. Tosia Malamud. *Education:* National University of Mexico. *Publications:* Theodor Herzl: Prophet of Our Times, 1961; The Rebellion of Silence, 1971; Albert Einstein: A Man in His Time, 1980; Franz Kafka: Conscience of an Era, 1983; Rosario Castellanos: The Voice, the Word, the Memory (anthology), 1984; Borges: Getting Near to His Literary Work, 1987; Elias Canetti: The Language of Passion, 1990; Spies of God: Authors at the End of the Century, 1992; Stefan Zweig: The Conscience of Man, 1992; Everlasting Voices: Latin American Writers, 1996; Jerusalem: 3000 Years of History, 1997. Contributions: periodicals.

NUMMI, Lassi; Finnish writer, poet and journalist; b. 9 Oct. 1928, Helsinki; m. Pirkko Aho 1959; two s. *Education:* Univ. of Helsinki. *Career:* State Prof. of Art 1990–95; mem. Finnish Writers' Union (pres. 1969–72, hon. mem. 1982–), PEN Centre Finland (pres. 1983–88). *Publications include:* Collected Poems 1978, 1998, Requiem 1990, Grandfather's Poems 1999, Mediterranean 2000, Existing for Each Other 2003. *Honours:* Hon. PhD 1986, Hon. DTh 2000; State Literary Prizes 1950, 1964, 1968, 1978, 1983, Pro Finlandia Medal 1972, Savonia Prize 1990, Suometar Journalist Prize 1990. *Address:* Ulvilantie 11 BA, 00350 Helsinki, Finland (home). *Telephone:* (9) 553494 (home). *Fax:* (9) 506 2905 (home).

NUNN, Frederick McKinley, BA, MA, PhD; American academic and writer; b. 29 Oct. 1937, Portland, OR; m. 1st Tey Diana Rebolledo 1960 (divorced 1973); one d.; m. 2nd Susan Karant Boles 1974, one d. *Education:* University of Oregon, University of New Mexico. *Career:* Asst Prof., 1965–67, Assoc. Prof., 1967–72, Prof. of History, 1972–, Portland State University, Oregon. *Publications:* Chilean Politics, 1920–31: The Honorable Mission of the Armed Forces, 1970; The Military in Chilean History: Essays on Civil-Military Relations, 1810–1973, 1976; Yesterday's Soldiers: European Military Professionalism in South America, 1890–1940, 1983; The Time of the Generals: Latin American Professional Militarism in World Perspective, 1992. Contributions: professional journals.

NUNN, Malla, BA, MA; South African author and screenwriter; b. Swaziland; m.; two c. *Education:* Univ. of Western Australia, Villanova Univ., Philadelphia, USA. *Career:* moved to Australia with family in 1970s; worked on film sets and wrote screenplays in New York; devised Detective Emmanuel Cooper series of novels. *Films include:* Fade to White 1991, Sweetbreeze 1992, Servant of the Ancestors 1998. *Publications include:* novels: A Beautiful Place to Die (Sisters in Crime Davitt Award for Best Adult Crime Novel by an Australian Female Author 2009) 2008, Let the Dead Lie 2011, Silent Valley 2012. *Literary Agent:* c/o Cameron's Management, Locked Bag 848, Surry Hills, NSW 2010, Australia. *Telephone:* (2) 9319-7199. *Fax:* (2) 9319-6866. *E-mail:* info@cameronsmanagement.com.au. *Website:* camersons .dreamhosters.com/home.

NUSSBAUM, Martha Craven, MA, PhD; American academic; *Ernst Freund Distinguished Service Professor of Law and Ethics, University of Chicago*; b. 6 May 1947, New York, NY; d. of George Craven and Betty Craven; m. Alan J. Nussbaum 1969 (divorced 1987); one d. *Education:* New York and Harvard Univs. *Career:* Jr Fellow, Soc. of Fellows, Harvard Univ. 1972–75, Asst Prof. of Philosophy and Classics 1975–80, Assoc. Prof. 1980–83; Assoc. Prof. of Philosophy and Classics, Brown Univ. 1984–85, Prof. of Philosophy, Classics and Comparative Literature 1985–87, David Benedict Prof. 1987–89, Prof. 1989–95; Visiting Prof. of Law, Univ. of Chicago 1994, Prof. of Law and Ethics 1995–96, Prof. of Philosophy 1995–, Prof. of Divinity 1995–, Ernst Freund Prof. of Law and Ethics 1996–, Assoc. mem. Classics Dept 1996–, Assoc. mem. Dept of Political Science 2003–, Founder and Coordinator, Center for Comparative Constitutionalism 2002–; Visiting Prof., Jawaharlal Nehru Univ., New Delhi, India 2004; Fellow, American Acad. of Arts and Science; mem. American Philosophical Assen (Chair. Cttee on Status of Women 1994–97). *Publications:* Aristotle's De Motu Animalium 1978, Language and Logic (ed.) 1983, The Fragility of Goodness 1986, Love's Knowledge 1990, Essays on Aristotle's De Anima (ed. with A. Rorty) 1992, The Therapy of Desire 1994, The Quality of Life (ed. with A. Sen) 1993, Passions and Perceptions (ed. with J. Brunschwig) 1993, Women, Culture and Development (ed. with J. Glover) 1995, Poetic Justice 1996, For Love of Country 1996, Cultivating Humanity 1997, Sex and Social Justice 1998, Hiding from Humanity: Disgust, Shame and the Law 2004, Liberty of Conscience 2008, From Disgust to Humanity: Sexual Orientation and Constitutional Law 2010, Not for Profit: Why Democracy Needs the Humanities 2010. *Honours:* Brandeis Creative Arts Award 1990, PEN Spielvogel-Diamondstein Award 1991, NY Univ. Distinguished Alumni Award 2000, Grawemeyer Award in Educ. 2002, Barnard Medal of Distinction 2003; many other awards. *Address:* 520 Law Quad, Law School, University of Chicago, 1111 East 60th Street, Chicago, IL 60637, USA (office). *Telephone:* (773) 702-3470 (office). *Fax:* (773) 702-0730 (office). *E-mail:* martha_nussbaum@law.uchicago.edu (office). *Website:* www.law .uchicago.edu/faculty/nussbaum (office).

NYE, Joseph Samuel, Jr, BA, PhD, FBA; American political scientist, academic and fmr government official; *University Distinguished Service Professor, Harvard University*; b. 19 Jan. 1937, NJ; s. of Joseph Nye and Else Ashwell; m. Molly Harding 1961; three s. *Education:* Princeton and Harvard Univs, Univ. of Oxford, UK. *Career:* Prof. of Govt, Harvard Univ. 1969–, also Dir Centre for Int. Affairs 1989–93, Dean and Don K. Price Prof. of Public Policy, John F. Kennedy School of Govt 1995–2004, Univ. Distinguished Service Prof. 2004–; Deputy Under-Sec. Dept of State, Washington, DC 1977–79, Chair. Nat. Intelligence Council 1992–; Asst Sec. of Defense for Int. Security Affairs 1994–95; mem. Trilateral Comm.; mem. Council, Int. Inst. of Strategic Studies; mem. Council on Foreign Relations; Fellow, American Acad. of Arts and Sciences, American Acad. of Diplomacy, Aspen Inst. *Publications include:* Power and Independence (co-author) 1977, The Making of America's Soviet Policy (ed. and co-author) 1984, Hawks, Doves and Owls (co-author and ed.) 1985, Nuclear Ethics 1986, Fateful Visions (co-ed.) 1988, Bound to Lead: The Changing Nature of American Power (co-ed.) 1990, Understanding International Conflicts: An Introduction to Theory and History 1993 (fourth edn) 2002, Governance in a Globalizing World 2000, The Paradox of American Power 2002, Soft Power: The Means to Success in World Politics 2004, Power in a Global Information Age 2004, The Power Game (novel) 2004, The Powers to Lead 2008, The Future of Power 2011. *Honours:* Dept of State Distinguished Honor Award 1979, Intelligence Distinguished Service Award 1994, Dept of Defense Distinguished Service Medal 1995, Charles E. Merriman Award, American Political Science Asscn 2003, Woodrow Wilson Award, Princeton Univ. 2004. *Address:* Harvard University, John F. Kennedy School of Government, Mailbox 124, 79 John F. Kennedy Street, Cambridge, MA 02138-5801, USA (office). *Telephone:* (617) 495-1123 (office). *Fax:* (617) 496-3337 (office). *E-mail:* joseph_nye@harvard .edu (office). *Website:* www.hks.harvard.edu/about/faculty-staff-directory/ joseph-nye (office).

NYE, Naomi Shihab, BA; Palestinian/American poet and writer; b. 1952, St Louis, Mo.; m. Michael Nye; one s. *Education:* Trinity Univ., San Antonio. *Career:* has travelled twice to Middle East and Asia for the US Information Agency promoting int. goodwill through the arts; fmr Lannan Fellow, Guggenheim Fellow, Wittner Bynner Fellow; columnist, Organica. *Publications:* poetry: Different Ways to Pray 1980, On the Edge of the Sky 1981, Hugging the Jukebox 1982, Yellow Glove 1986, Travel Alarm 1993, The Children of Nigh 1993, Red Suitcase 1994, Words Under the Words 1995, Fuel 1998, What Have You Lost? 1999, Come with Me: Poems for a Journey (juvenile) 2000, 19 Varieties of Gazelle: Poems of the Middle East 2002, You and Yours (Isabella Gardner Award) 2005, A Maze Me: Poems for Girls 2005; juvenile fiction: Sitti's Secrets 1994, Benito's Dream Bottle 1995, Lullaby Raft 1997, Habibi 2001, Baby Radar 2003, Going Going 2005; editor: This Same Sky 1992, The Tree is Older Than You Are: A Bilingual Gathering of Poems and Stories from Mexico (co-ed.) 1995, I Feel a Little Jumpy Around You 1996, Salting the Ocean: 100 Poems by Young Poets 2001, The Flag of Childhood: Poems from the Middle East 2002, Is This Forever or What? 2004; other prose: Never in a Hurry (essays) 1996, Mint Snowball (short stories) 2001. *Honours:* Texas Inst. of Letters Prize, Carity Randall Prize, Int. Poetry Forum Award. *Literary Agent:* Steven Barclay Agency, 12 Western Avenue, Petaluma, CA 94952, USA. *Telephone:* (707) 773-0654. *Fax:* (707) 778-1868. *E-mail:* steven@barclayagency.com. *Website:* www .barclayagency.com.

NYE, Robert, FRSL; British poet, novelist and critic; b. 15 March 1939, London; s. of Oswald William Nye and Frances Dorothy Weller; m. 1st Judith Pratt 1959 (divorced 1967); three s.; m. 2nd Aileen Campbell 1968; one d. one step-s. one step-d. *Education:* Southend High School. *Career:* freelance writer 1961–; Chief Book Reviewer, The Scotsman 1965–2000; contributes critical articles and reviews to British periodicals, including The Times and The Scotsman; Poetry Critic, The Times 1971–96. *Publications include:* poetry: Juvenilia 1 1961, Juvenilia 2 1963, Darker Ends 1969, Agnus Dei 1973, Two Prayers 1974, Five Dreams 1974, Divisions on a Ground 1976, A Collection of Poems 1955–1988 1989, 14 Poems 1994, Henry James and Other Poems 1995, Collected Poems 1995, 1998, The Rain and the Glass: 99 Poems, New and Selected 2005, Sixteen Poems 2005, One or Two Swallows 2008, An Almost Dancer 2012; novels: Doubtfire 1967, Falstaff 1976, Merlin 1978, Faust 1980, The Voyage of the Destiny 1982, The Facts of Life and Other Fictions 1983, The Memoirs of Lord Byron 1989, The Life and Death of My Lord Gilles de Rais 1990, Mrs. Shakespeare: The Complete Works 1993, The Late Mr. Shakespeare 1998, and several children's books; plays: ed.: A Choice of Sir Walter Raleigh's Verse 1972, William Barnes of Dorset: A Selection of his Poems 1973, A Choice of Swinburne's Verse 1973, The English Sermon 1750–1850 1976, The Faber Book of Sonnets 1976, PEN New Poetry I 1986, First Awakenings: The Early Poems of Laura Riding (co-ed.) 1992, A Selection of the Poems of Laura Riding 1993, Some Poems by Ernest Dowson 2006, Some Poems by Thomas Chatterton 2007, Some Poems by Clere Parsons 2008, The Liquid Rhinoceros and other uncollected poems by Martin Seymour-Smith 2009, Some Poems by James Reeves 2009. *Honours:* Eric Gregory Award 1963, Scottish Arts Council Bursary 1969, James Kennaway Memorial Award 1970, Guardian Fiction Prize 1976, Hawthornden Prize 1977, Soc. of Authors Travelling Scholarship 1991, Authors' Foundation Award 2003, 2007,

Cholmondeley Award 2007. *Literary Agent:* c/o Curtis Brown Ltd, 28–29 Haymarket, London, SW1Y 4SP, England. *Telephone:* (20) 7393-4400. *Fax:* (20) 7393-4401. *E-mail:* cb@curtisbrown.co.uk. *Website:* www.curtisbrown.co.uk.

NYSTROM, Debra, BA, MFA; American poet, writer and academic; *Professor of English, University of Virginia*; b. 12 July 1954, Pierre, SD. *Education:* Univ. of South Dakota, Boston Univ., Goddard Coll., Univ. of Virginia. *Career:* Faculty in Creative Writing, Univ. of Virginia 1984–, now Prof.; mem. PEN, Associated Writing Programs, Poetry Soc. of America. *Publications:* A Quarter Turn 1991, Torn Sky 2003, Bad River Road 2009; contributions: various anthologies, reviews, quarterlies, and journals. *Honours:* Virginia Commission for the Arts Prizes for Poetry 1987, 1997, Balch Prize for Poetry, Virginia Quarterly Review 1991, James Boatwright Prizes for Poetry, Shenandoah 1994, 2000, Borders Books/HEART Prize 2002, Library of Virginia Prize 2004, 2009, James Dickey Prize 2007. *Address:* University of Virginia, Department of English, 219 Bryan Hall, PO Box 400121, Charlottesville, VA 22904-4121, USA (office).

O

OAKLEY, Ann, BA, MA, PhD; British sociologist, academic and writer; *Professor of Social Policy and Founding Director, Social Science Research Unit, Institute of Education, University of London*; b. 17 Jan. 1944, London, England; d. of the late Richard Titmuss and Kay Titmuss; m. Robin Oakley; three c. *Education:* Chiswick Polytechnic, Somerville Coll., Oxford, Bedford Coll., London. *Career:* Research Fellow, Bedford Coll., Univ. of London 1974–79, Univ. of Oxford 1979–84; Deputy Dir Thomas Coram Research Unit, Univ. of London 1985–90; Prof. of Social Policy and Dir Social Science Research Unit, Inst. of Educ., Univ. of London 1991–2005, Founding Dir Social Science Research Unit 2005–. *Publications include:* novels: The Men's Room (adapted for TV 1991) 1988; as Rosamund Clay: Only Angels Forget 1990; as Ann Oakley: Matilda's Mistake 1991, The Secret Lives of Eleanor Jenkinson 1992, Scenes Orginating in the Garden of Eden 1993, A Proper Holiday 1996, Overheads 1999; two short stories; non-fiction: Sex, Gender and Society 1972, Housewife 1974, The Sociology of Housework 1974, The Rights and Wrongs of Women (co-ed. with J. Mitchell) 1976, Becoming a Mother (also published as From Here to Maternity 1981) 1979, Women Confined: Towards a Sociology of Childbirth 1980, Subject Women 1981, Miscarriage (with A. McPherson and H. Roberts) 1984, The Captured Womb: A History of the Medical Care of Pregnant Women 1984, Taking it Like a Woman 1984, What is Feminism? (co-ed. with J. Mitchell) 1986, Telling the Truth About Jerusalem: Selected Essays 1986, Helpers in Childbirth: Midwifery Today (with S. Houd) 1990, Social Support and Motherhood: The Natural History of a Research Project 1992, Essays on Women, Medicine and Health 1993, Young People, Health and Family Life (with others) 1994, The Politics of the Welfare State (co-ed. with A. S. Williams) 1994, Evaluating Social Interventions: A Report on Two Workshops (co-ed. with H. Roberts) 1996, Man and Wife: Richard and Kay Titmus, My Parents' Early Years 1996, Who's Afraid of Feminism? (co-ed. with J. Mitchell) 1997, The Gift Relationship: From Human Blood to Social Policy (co-ed. with J. Ashton) 1997, Welfare Research: A Critical Review (co-ed. with F. Williams and J. Popay) 1998, Experiments in Knowing: Gender and Method in the Social Sciences 2000, Welfare and Being: Richard Titmuss's Contribution to Social Policy (co-ed. with P. Alcock and H. Glennerster) 2001, Gender on Planet Earth 2002, The Ann Oakley Reader 2005. *Honours:* Hon. Prof., Univ. Coll. London 1996–; Hon. Fellow, Somerville Coll., Oxford 2001–; Hon. DLitt (Salford) 1995. *Address:* Social Science Research Unit, Institute of Education, University of London, Room 102, 18 Woburn Square, London, WC1H 0NR (office); c/o The Sayle Literary Agency, 1 Petersfield, Cambridge, CB1 1BB, England. *Telephone:* (20) 7612-6380 (office). *Fax:* (20) 7612-6400 (office). *E-mail:* a.oakley@ioe.ac.uk (office). *Website:* www.ioe.ac.uk/SSRU (office); www.annoakley.co.uk (home).

OATES, Joyce Carol, (Rosamond Smith, Lauren Kelly), MA; American writer, poet, publisher and academic; *Roger S. Berlind '52 Professor in the Humanities, Princeton University*; b. 16 June 1938, Lockport, NY; d. of Frederic J. Oates and Caroline Bush; m. Raymond J. Smith 1961. *Education:* Syracuse Univ. and Univ. of Wisconsin. *Career:* instructor, Univ. of Detroit 1961–65, Asst Prof. of English 1965–67; Faculty mem. Dept of English, Univ. of Windsor, Ont. 1967–78; publr (with Raymond Joseph Smith) Ontario Review 1974–; Writer-in-Residence, Princeton Univ. 1978–81, Prof. 1987–, currently Roger S. Berlind '52 Prof. in the Humanities; mem. American Acad., Inst. of Arts and Letters; Guggenheim Fellow 1967–68. *Plays:* Three Plays: Ontological Proof of My Existence, Miracle Play, The Triumph of the Spider Monkey 1980, Twelve Plays 1991, The Perfectionist and Other Plays 1995. *Publications:* novels: With Shuddering Fall 1964, A Garden of Earthly Delights 1967, Expensive People 1968, Them 1969, Wonderland 1971, Do With Me What You Will 1973, The Assassins: A Book of Hours 1975, Childwold 1976, Son of the Morning 1978, Unholy Loves 1979, Cybele 1979, Bellefleur 1980, A Sentimental Education 1981, Angel of Light 1981, A Bloodsmoor Romance 1982, Mysteries of Winterthurn 1984, Solstice 1985, Marya: A Life 1986, You Must Remember This 1987, American Appetites 1989, Because it is Bitter and Because it is my Heart 1990, Black Water 1992, Foxfire 1993, What I Lived For 1994, Zombie 1995, First Love: A Gothic Tale 1996, We Were the Mulvaneys 1996, Man Crazy 1997, My Heart Laid Bare 1998, Come Meet Muffin 1998, The Collector of Hearts 1999, Broke Heart Blues 1999, Blonde: A Novel 2000, Middle Age: A Romance 2002, I'll Take You There 2002, Big Mouth and Ugly Girl 2002, The Tattooed Girl 2004, Rape: A Love Story 2004, I Am No One You Know 2004, The Falls 2004, Mother, Missing 2005, The Gravedigger's Daughter 2007, My Sister, My Love: The Intimate Story of Skyler Rampike 2008, Little Bird of Heaven 2009, A Fair Maiden 2010, Blonde 2011; short story collections: By the North Gate 1963, Upon the Sweeping Flood and Other Stories 1966, The Wheel of Love 1970, Cupid and Psyche 1970, Marriages and Infidelities 1972, A Posthumous Sketch 1973, The Girl 1974, Plagiarized Material 1974, The Goddess and Other Women 1974, Where Are You Going, Where Have You Been?: Stories of Young America 1974, The Hungry Ghosts: Seven Allusive Comedies 1974, The Seduction and Other Stories 1975, The Poisoned Kiss and Other Stories from the Portuguese 1975, The Triumph of the Spider Monkey 1976, Crossing the Border 1976, Night-Side 1977, The Step-Father 1978, All the Good People I've Left Behind 1979, Queen of the Night 1979, The Lamb of Abyssalia 1979, A Middle-Class Education 1980, A Sentimental Education 1980, Last Day 1984, Wild Saturday and Other Stories 1984, Wild Nights 1985, Raven's Wing 1986, The Assignation 1988, Heat and Other Stories 1991, Where Is Here? 1992, Haunted Tales of the Grotesque 1994, Faithless: Tales of Transgression 2001, The Female of the Species 2006, High Lonesome: New & Selected Stories 1966–2006 2006, Wild Nights! 2008, Museum of Doctor Moses 2008, Sourland 2010, Give Me Your Heart 2011, The Corn Maiden and Other Nightmares 2011; poetry: Women in Love and Other Poems 1968, Anonymous Sins and Other Poems 1969, Them (Nat. Book Award 1970) 1969, Love and its Derangements 1970, Wooded Forms 1972, Angel Fire 1973, Dreaming America and Other Poems 1973, The Fabulous Beasts 1975, Seasons of Peril 1977, Women Whose Lives are Food, Men Whose Lives are Money 1978, Celestial Timepiece 1980, Nightless Nights: Nine Poems 1981, Invisible Women: New and Selected Poems 1970–1982 1982, Luxury of Sin 1984, The Time Traveller: Poems 1983–1989 1989; non-fiction: The Edge of Impossibility: Tragic Forms in Literature 1972, The Hostile Sun: The Poetry of D. H. Lawrence 1973, New Heaven, New Earth: The Visionary Experience in Literature 1974, The Stone Orchard 1980, Contraries: Essays 1981, The Profane Art: Essays and Reviews 1983, Funland 1983, On Boxing 1987, (Woman) Writer: Occasions and Opportunities 1988, George Bellows: American Artist (biog.) 1995, The Faith of a Writer: Life, Craft, Art 2004, Black Girl/White Girl 2006, The Journals of Joyce Carol Oates, 1973–1982 2007, In Rough Country: Essays and Reviews 2010; editor: Scenes from American Life: Contemporary Short Fiction 1973, The Best American Short Stories 1979 (with Shannon Ravenel) 1979, Night Walks: A Bedside Companion 1982, First Person Singular: Writers on Their Craft 1983, Story: Fictions Past and Present (with Boyd Litzinger) 1985, Reading the Fights (with Daniel Halpern) 1988, The Oxford Book of American Short Stories 1993, The Best American Mystery Stories 2006; as Rosamond Smith: The Lives of the Twins 1987, Kindred Passions 1988, Soul-Mate 1989, Nemesis 1990, Snake Eyes 1992, You Can't Catch Me 1995, Double Delight 1997, Starr Bright Will Be With You Soon 1999, The Barrens 2001, Beasts 2003; fiction in nat. magazines. *Honours:* O. Henry Prize Story Award 1967, 1968, Rea Award for Short Story 1990, Elmer Holmes Bukst Award 1990, Ivan Sandrof Lifetime Achievement Award, Nat. Book Critics' Circle 2009. *Address:* Department of Creative Writing, Princeton University, 185 Nassau Street, Princeton, NJ 08544 (office); c/o John Hawkins, 71 West 23rd Street, Suite 1600, New York, NY 10010, USA. *Website:* www.princeton.edu/~visarts/cwr.

OATES, Stephen Baery, BA, MA, PhD; American academic and writer; *Paul Murray Kendall Professor Emeritus of Biography and Professor Emeritus of History, University of Massachusetts at Amherst*; b. 5 Jan. 1936, Pampa, TX; m. 1st; one s. one d.; m. 2nd Marie Philips. *Education:* Univ. of Texas at Austin. *Career:* instructor 1964–67, Asst Prof. 1967–68, Arlington State Coll.; Asst Prof. 1968–70, Assoc. Prof. 1970–71, Prof. of History 1971–80, Adjunct Prof. of English 1980–85, Paul Murray Kendall Prof. of Biography 1985–, Univ. of Massachusetts at Amherst; various guest lectureships; Fellow Texas State Historical Asscn 1968; Fellow Texas Inst. of Letters 1969; mem. American Antiquarian Soc., Soc. of American Historians. *Publications:* Confederate Cavalry West of the River 1961, John Salmon Ford: Rip Ford's Texas (ed.) 1963, The Republic of Texas (gen. ed.) 1968, Visions of Glory, Texas on the Southwestern Frontier 1970, To Purge This Land with Blood: A Biography of John Brown 1970, Portrait of America (ed.): Vol. I From the European Discovery to the End of Reconstruction, Vol. II From Reconstruction to the Present 1973, The Fires of Jubilee: Nat Turner's Fierce Rebellion 1975, With Malice Toward None: The Life of Abraham Lincoln 1977, Our Fiery Trial: Abraham Lincoln, John Brown, and the Civil War Era 1979, Let the Trumpet Sound: The Life of Martin Luther King Jr 1982, Abraham Lincoln: The Man Behind the Myths 1984, Biography as High Adventure: Life-Writers Speak on Their Art (ed.) 1986, William Faulkner: The Man and the Artist, a Biography 1987, A Woman of Valor: Clara Barton and the Civil War 1994, The Approaching Fury: Voices of the Storm, 1820–1861 1997, The Whirlwind of War: Voices of the Storm, 1861–1865 1998; contrib. to professional journals. *Honours:* Guggenheim Fellowship 1972, Christopher Awards 1977, 1982, New York Civil War Round Table Baroness/Lincoln Award 1978, Nat. Endowment for the Humanities Fellow 1978, Robert F. Kennedy Memorial Book Award 1983, Inst. for Advanced Studies in the Humanities Fellow 1984, New England History Teachers Asscn Kidger Award 1992, Chicago Civil War Round Table Nevins-Freeman Award 1993. *Address:* 10 Bridle Path, Amherst, MA 01002, USA.

O'BALANCE, Edgar; Irish writer; b. 17 July 1918, Dalkey, County Dublin; m. 1st Mary Edington-Gee 1949 (died 1969); two s. one d.; m. 2nd Kathleen Barbara Tanner 1972. *Education:* studied in Ireland. *Career:* mem. Military Commentators Circle. *Publications:* The Arab-Israeli War, 1956; The Sinai Campaign, 1956; The Story of the French Foreign Legion, 1961; The Red Army of China, 1962; The Indo-China War 1945–1954, 1964; The Red Army of Russia, 1964; The Greek Civil War 1948–1960, 1966; The Algerian Insurrection 1954–1962, 1967; The Third Arab-Israeli War 1967, 1972; The Kurdish Revolt 1961–1970, 1973; Arab Guerrilla Power, 1974; The Electronic War in the Middle East 1968–1970, 1974; The Wars in Vietnam 1954–1972, 1975; The Secret War in the Sudan 1955–1972, 1977; No Victor, No Vanquished, 1978; The Language of Violence, 1979; Terror in Ireland, 1979; The Tracks of the Bear, 1982; The Gulf War, 1988; The Cyanide War, 1989; Terrorism in the 1980s, 1989; Wars in Afghanistan: 1839–1990, 1991; Civil War in Bosnia:

1992–1994; The Kurdish Struggle: 1920–94, 1995; Islamic Fundamentalist Terrorism, 1996; Wars in the Caucasus: 1990–95, 1996.

OBREHT, Téa, BA, MFA; American writer; b. (Téa Bajraktarevic), 30 Sept. 1985, Belgrade, Serbia. *Education:* Univ. of Southern California, Cornell Univ. *Career:* spent childhood in Cyprus and Egypt; moved to USA 1997; Lecturer in Creative Writing, Cornell Univ. 2008–09. *Publications:* fiction: The Tiger's Wife (Orange Prize for Fiction 2011) 2011; contribs to The New Yorker, The Atlantic Monthly, The Best American Short Stories, The Best American Nonrequired Reading. *Literary Agent:* c/o Seth Fishman, Sterling, Lord Literistic, 65 Bleecker Street, New York, NY 10012, USA. *Telephone:* (212) 780-6050. *Fax:* (212) 780-6095. *E-mail:* seth@sll.com. *Website:* www.sll.com. *E-mail:* tea@teaobreht.com (office). *Website:* www.teaobreht.com.

O'BRIEN, Alison D., AB, PhD; American scientist and writer; *Professor, Uniformed Services University of the Health Sciences. Education:* Univ. of California at Davis, Ohio State Univ. *Career:* Prof. and Chair of Dept of Microbiology and Immunology, Uniformed Services Univ. of the Health Sciences. *Publications include:* co-author: Bacterial Toxins: Friends or Foes? 1999, Microbiology: A Centenary Perspective 1999; co-editor: Escherichia coli and Other Shiga Toxins Producing E.coli 1998, Comparative Pathogenicity of E.coli 2003. *Address:* Department of Microbiology and Immunology, Uniformed Services University of the Health Sciences, 4301 Jones Bridge Road, Bethesda, MD 20814, USA (office). *Fax:* (301) 295-3773 (office). *E-mail:* aobrien@usuhs.mil (office). *Website:* www.usuhs.mil (office).

O'BRIEN, Edna; Irish writer; b. Tuamgraney, Co. Clare; d. of Michael O'Brien and Lena Cleary; m. Ernest Géblev 1954 (divorced 1964); two s. *Education:* convents, Pharmaceutical Coll. of Ireland. *Career:* engaged in writing from an early age. *Publications include:* The Country Girls 1960 (film 1983), The Lonely Girl 1962, Girls in Their Married Bliss 1963, August is a Wicked Month 1964, Casualties of Peace 1966, The Love Object 1968, A Pagan Place 1970 (play 1971), Night 1972, A Scandalous Woman (short stories) 1974, Mother Ireland 1976, Johnny I Hardly Knew You (novel) 1977, Arabian Days 1977, Mrs. Reinhardt and other stories 1978, Virginia (play) 1979, Mrs. Reinhardt (adapted for TV) 1981, The Dazzle (children's book), Returning: A Collection of New Tales 1982, A Christmas Treat 1982, A Fanatic Heart (Selected Stories) 1985, Madame Bovary (play) 1987, Vanishing Ireland 1987, Tales for the Telling (children's book) 1987, The High Road (novel) 1988, On the Bone (poetry) 1989, Scandalous Woman and Other Stories 1990, Lantern Slides (stories) 1990, Time and Tide (novel) 1992, House of Splendid Isolation (novel) 1994, Down By the River (novel) 1997, Maud Gonne (screenplay) 1996, James Joyce 1999, Wild Decembers 1999, In the Forest (novel) 2002, Iphigenia (play) 2003, Triptych (play) 2004, The Light of Evening (novel) 2006, Byron in Love (biography) 2009. *Honours:* Hon. DLitt (Queen's) 1999; Yorkshire Post Novel Award 1971, Kingsley Amis Award, Writers' Guild of GB Award 1993, European Prize for Literature 1995, American Nat. Arts Gold Medal, Bob Hughes Lifetime Achievement Award, Irish Book Awards 2009. *Literary Agent:* ICM, 66 Charlotte Street, London, W1T 4QE, England. *Telephone:* (20) 7851-4853. *Website:* www.icmtalent.com.

O'BRIEN, Michael, PhD, FBA; British historian, academic and author; *Professor of American Intellectual History and Fellow of Jesus College, University of Cambridge*; b. 13 April 1948, Plymouth, Devon, England; s. of John McCarthy O'Brien and Lilian Isabella O'Brien (née Collicott); m. Patricia Caroline Mary Bacon. *Education:* Univ. of Cambridge. *Career:* taught in USA at Univs of Michigan and Arkansas and Miami Univ., Ohio; Prof. of American Intellectual History and Fellow of Jesus Coll., Univ. of Cambridge 2002–. *Publications:* The Idea of the American South 1920–1941 1979, All Clever Men, Who Make Their Way (critical discourse) 1982, A Character of Hugh Legaré 1985, Intellectual Life in Antebellum Charleston (co-ed) 1986, Rethinking the South (essays) 1988, An Evening When Alone: Four Journals of Single Women in the South 1827–67 (ed) 1993, Conjectures of Order: Intellectual Life and the American South 1810–1860, Vols 1 and 2 2004, abridged version (Bancroft Prize, Columbia Univ.) 2010, Henry Adams and the Southern Question 2005, Placing the South 2007, Mrs Adams in Winter: A Journey in the Last Days of Napoleon 2010. *Honours:* Merle Curti Award 2005, Southern Historical Asscn Frank L. and Harriet C. Owsley Award, Soc. for the Study of Southern Literature C. Hugh Holman Award, American Studies Network Book Prize. *Address:* Jesus College, Cambridge, CB5 8BL, England (office). *Telephone:* (1223) 339317 (office). *Fax:* (1223) 324910 (office). *E-mail:* mo10003@hermes.cam.ac.uk (office). *Website:* www.hist.cam.ac.uk (office).

O'BRIEN, Sean Patrick, BA, MA, PGCE, FRSL; British writer and poet; *Professor of Creative Writing, Newcastle University*; b. 19 Dec. 1952, London, England. *Education:* Selwyn Coll., Cambridge, Univ. of Birmingham, Univ. of Hull, Univ. of Leeds. *Career:* Fellow in Creative Writing, Univ. of Dundee 1989–91; Northern Arts Literary Fellow 1992–94; Visiting Writer, Univ. of Odense, Denmark 1996, Hokudai Univ., Sapporo, Japan 1997; Lecturer in Writing, then Prof. of Poetry, Sheffield Hallam Univ. 1998–2006; Writer-in-Residence, Univ. of Leeds 1999; Prof. of Creative Writing, Newcastle Univ. 2006–; Vice-Pres. The Poetry Soc. *Publications:* poetry: The Indoor Park 1983, The Frighteners 1987, Boundary Beach 1989, HMS Glasshouse 1991, Ghost Train (Forward Prize for Best Collection) 1995, The Deregulated Muse: Essays on Contemporary Poetry in Britain and Ireland 1998, The Firebox: Poetry in Britain and Ireland after 1945 (ed.) 1998, Downriver (Forward Prize for Best Collection) 2001, Cousin Coat: Selected Poems 1976–2001 2002, Inferno: A Verse Version of Dante's Inferno 2006, The Drowned Book (Forward Prize for Best Collection, T.S. Eliot Prize) 2007, Night Train 2009, November 2011; plays: The Birds: A New Verse Version of Aristophanes' Birds 2002, Keepers of the Flame 2003, Laughter When We're Dead, My Last Barmaid; short stories: The Silence Room 2008; fiction: Afterlife 2009; contrib. to anthologies, newspapers, reviews and radio. *Honours:* Eric Gregory Award 1979, Somerset Maugham Award 1984, Cholmondeley Award 1988, Arts Council Writer's Bursary 1992, E. M. Forster Award 1993, Northern Writer of the Year Award 2001, Forward Prize for Best Poem (for Fantasia on a Theme of James Wright) 2006, Northern Rock Foundation Award 2007. *Literary Agent:* TriplePA, 15 Connaught Gardens, Forest Hall, Newcastle, NE12 8AT, England. *Telephone:* (191) 266-2225. *Fax:* (191) 266-2225. *E-mail:* triplepa@blueyonder.co.uk. *Address:* School of English Literature, Language and Linguistics, Percy Building, University of Newcastle upon Tyne, Newcastle, NE1 7RU, England (office). *Telephone:* (191) 222-3875 (office). *Fax:* (191) 222-8708 (office). *E-mail:* s.p.o'brien@ncl.ac.uk (office). *Website:* www.ncl.ac.uk/elll (office).

O'BRIEN, (William) Timothy (Tim), BA; American writer; b. 1 Oct. 1946, Austin, MN; m. Anne O'Brien. *Education:* Macalester Coll., Harvard Univ. *Career:* currently faculty mem. Dept of English, Texas State Univ. at San Marcos. *Publications:* If I Die in a Combat Zone, Box Me Up and Ship Me Home 1973, Northern Lights 1975, Going After Cacciato 1978, The Nuclear Age 1981, The Things They Carried: A Work of Fiction (Prix du Meilleur Livre Étranger, France 1993, Soc. of American Historians James Fenimore Cooper Prize) 1990, In the Lake of Woods 1994, Tomcat in Love 1998, July July 2002; contrib. short stories to Esquire, Harper's, Atlantic, Playboy, Granta, GQ and The New Yorker. *Honours:* O. Henry Memorial Awards 1976, 1978, Nat. Book Award 1979, Vietnam Veterans of America Award 1987, Chicago Tribune Heartland Prize 1990, Guggenheim Foundation fellowship, NEA fellowship. *Address:* Department of English, Texas State University, 601 University Drive, San Marcos, TX 78666, USA (office). *E-mail:* mfinearts@txstate.edu (office).

OBSTFELD, Raymond, (Pike Bishop, Jason Frost, Don Pendleton, Carl Stevens), BA, MA; American academic, writer, poet, dramatist and screenwriter; b. 22 Jan. 1952, Williamsport, Pa; s. of Ludwig Obstfeld and Ilse Obstfeld; m. Loretta Obstfeld; one s. *Education:* Johnston Coll., Univ. of Redlands, Univ. of California, Davis. *Career:* Lecturer to Asst Prof. of English, Orange Coast Coll. 1976–; mem. Bd of Dirs Orange County Screenwriters Asscn; mem. MWA. *Publications:* poetry: The Cat with Half a Face 1978; as Raymond Obstfeld: The Golden Fleece 1979, Dead-End Option 1980, Dead Heat 1981, Dead Bolt 1982, The Remington Factor 1985, Masked Dog 1986, Redtooth 1987, Brainchild 1987, The Whippin Boy 1988, Earth Angel 1995, Twang!: The Ultimate Book of Country Music Quotations 1997, Jabberrock! The Ultimate Book of Rock 'n' Roll Quotations (co-author with Patricia Fitzgerald) 1997, Novelists Essential Guide to Crafting Sciences 2000, Napoleon Bonaparte (co-author with Loretta Obstfeld) 2000, Fiction First Aid: Instant Remediies for Novels 2001, Careers For Your Characters 2002, The Renaissance 2002, Moby-Dick: Critical Essays 2003, On the Shoulders of Giants: My Journey Through the Harlem Renaissance (co-author with Kareem Abdul-Jabbar) 2007, Anatomy Lesson 2008, What Color Is My World?: The Lost History of African-American Inventors (co-author with Kareem Abdul-Jabbar) 2012, Nations in Transition: India; as Pike Bishop: Diamondback 1983; Judgement at Poisoned Well 1983; as Jason Frost: Warlord series 1983–85; Invasion USA 1985; as Don Pendleton: Bloodsport 1982, Flesh Wounds 1983, Savannah Swingsaw 1985, The Fire Eaters 1986; as Carl Stevens: The Centaur Conspiracy 1983, Ride of the Razorback 1984; contribs to anthologies and other publs.

OCKRENT, Christine; Belgian journalist; b. 24 April 1944, Brussels, Belgium; d. of Roger Ockrent and Greta Bastenie; m. Bernard Kouchner; one s. *Education:* Collège Sévigné, Paris, Cambridge Univ., England and Institut d'Etudes Politiques de Paris. *Career:* journalist, Information Office, EEC 1965–66; researcher, NBC News, USA 1967–68; producer and journalist, CBS News, USA 1968–77; journalist and producer, FR3, France 1976–80; Ed. and Anchor, news programme on Antenne 2 1980–85; Chief Ed. RTL 1985–86; Deputy Dir-Gen. TF1 1986–87; Ed., anchor and producer, news programmes on Antenne 2 1988–92, on France 3 1992–95; Chief Ed. L'Express 1995–96; Deputy Dir BFM 1996–2000; currently with The Guardian newspaper, London; Ed.-in-Chief Dimanche Soir programme France 3 1996–98; Ed.-in-Chief and Presenter France Europe Express 1997; Pres. BFMbiz.com; columnist, La Provence, Dimanche CH. *Publications include:* Dans le secret des princes 1986, Duel 1988, Les uns et les autres 1993, Portraits d'ici et d'ailleurs 1994, La Mémoire du cœur 1997, Les Grands patrons (jtly) 1998, L'Europe racontée à mon fils, de Jules César à l'euro 1999, La double vie d'Hillary Clinton 2000, Françoise 2003. *Honours:* Chevalier de la Légion d'honneur 2000. *Address:* The Guardian, Kings Place, 90 York Way, London, N1 9GU, England. *E-mail:* christine.ockrent@guardian.co.uk. *Website:* www.guardian.co.uk/profile/christine-ockrent.

O'CONNELL, Richard James, BS, MA; American academic, poet and translator; *Professor Emeritus, Temple University*; b. 25 Oct. 1928, New York, NY. *Education:* Temple Univ., Johns Hopkins Univ. *Career:* Instructor, Temple Univ. 1957–61, Asst Prof. 1961–69, Assoc. Prof. 1969–86, Sr Assoc. Prof. 1986–93, Prof. Emer. 1993–; Fulbright Lecturer, Univ. of Brazil, Rio de Janeiro 1960, Univ. of Navarre, Pamplona, Spain 1962–63; Guest Lecturer, Johns Hopkins Univ. 1961–74; Poet-in-the-Schools, Pennsylvania Council for the Arts 1971–73; mem. Associated Writing Programs, Modern Language Asscn, PEN. *Play:* System Klam 2000 (first performed at Off-Broadway Theatre, Fort Lauderdale, Fla 1988). *Publications:* From an Interior Silence 1961, Cries of Flesh and Stone 1962, New Poems and Translations 1963, Brazilian Happenings 1966, Terrane 1967, Thirty Epigrams 1971, Hudson's Fourth Voyage 1978, Temple Poems 1985, Hanging Tough 1986, Battle Poems 1987, Selected Epigrams 1990, Lives of the Poets 1990, The Caliban Poems 1992, RetroWorlds 1993, Simulations 1993, Voyages 1995, The Bright Tower 1997, American Obits 2001, Fractals 2002, Dawn Crossing 2003; translator: various works, including: Irish Monastic Poems 1975, Middle English Poems 1976, More Irish Poems 1976, Epigrams from Martial 1976, The Epigrams of Luxorius 1984, New Epigrams from Martial 1991. *Honours:* Contemporary Poetry Press Prize 1972. *Address:* 1147 Hillsboro Mile, Suite 510, Hillsboro Beach, FL 33062, USA (home). *Telephone:* (954) 426-8906 (home). *Fax:* (954) 426-8906 (home). *E-mail:* rocon100@comcast.net (home).

O'CONNOR, Joseph, BA, MA; Irish writer, playwright and critic; b. 20 Sept. 1963, Glenageary, Co. Dublin. *Education:* Univ. Coll., Dublin, Univ. of Oxford, Univ. of Leeds. *Plays:* Red Roses and Petrol 1995. *Publications:* novels: Cowboys and Indians 1991, Desperadoes 1995, The Salesman 1998, Inishowen 2000, The Last of the Irish Males 2001, Star of the Sea (Irish Post Literature Award 2004) 2002, Redemption Falls 2007, Ghost Light 2010; biography: Even the Olives are Bleeding: The Life and Times of Charles Donnelly 1992; contrib. and columnist for The Sunday Tribune. *Honours:* Hennessy Award. *Literary Agent:* c/o Carole Blake, Blake Friedmann Agency, 122 Arlington Road, London NW1 7HP, England. *Telephone:* (20) 7284-0408. *Fax:* (20) 7284-0442. *Website:* www.blakefriedmann.co.uk. *Address:* c/o Harvill Secker, Random House UK Ltd, 20 Vauxhall Bridge Road, London, SW1V 2SA, England (office). *E-mail:* samaradivakara@randomhouse.co.uk (office). *Website:* www.josephoconnorauthor.com.

Ó CURRAOIN, Seán, NT, BA, MA, MPhil, LLB; Irish fmr parliamentary translator, teacher and poet; b. Connemara, Co. Galway; s. of James Curran and Mary Barnacle. *Education:* St Patrick's Training Coll, Drumcondra. *Career:* fmr Chief Translator, Irish Parl.; linguistic researcher and Asst Ed. on Ó Dónaill's Irish-English Dictionary; fmr Asst Ed. Béaloideas (Journal of the Folklore of Ireland Soc.); fmr Prin. Glenicmurrin Nat. School, Connemara, Colehill Nat. School and Colehill Boys' Nat. School, Colehill, Co. Westmeath-Longford border; fmr teacher Suckeen Nat. School, Galway and St Peter's Nat. School, Walkinstown, Dublin; mem. Irish Trans' Asscn, Folklore of Ireland Soc. *Publications:* Soilse ar na Dumhchannaí 1985, Beairtle 1985, Tinte Sionnaigh (short stories) 1985, De Ghlaschloch an Oileáin (biog. of Máirtín O'Cadhain) (co-author) 1987, Iascairín Chloch na Cora 2000, Cloch na Cainte (poems) 2003, Boscaí (short stories) 2003; contrib. to Comhar, Feasta, Inntí. *Honours:* Michael Hartnett Poetry Award 2004. *Address:* Apartment 7, Bailey Point, Salthill, Galway, Ireland (home).

ODDOUL, Haggag Hassan; Egyptian writer; b. 1944, Alexandria. *Career:* fmr construction worker on the Aswan High Dam; fmrly served in the armed forces. *Publications include:* Nights of Musk (State Prize for Short Stories 1990). *Honours:* Sawiris Foundation Award for Best Egyptian Novel 2005. *Address:* c/o BANIPAL, 1 Gough Square, London, EC4A 3DE, England (office).

ØDEGÅRD, Knut, LittD; Norwegian poet, writer, critic and diplomatist; *Consul General, Republic of Macedonia;* b. 6 Nov. 1945, Molde; m. Thorgerdur Ingólfsdóttir 1981; two d. *Education:* Univ. of Oslo. *Career:* poetry critic Aftenposten newspaper 1968–2009, Vårt Land 2009–; Publr Noregs Boklag 1975–77; Cinema and Cultural Dir, Kristiansund Municipality 1977–78; Cultural Dir Sør-Trøndelag Co. 1978–84; Man. Dir Scandinavian Centre, Nordens Hus, Reykjavík 1984–89; Founder and Pres. Bjornson Festivalen, Norwegian Festival of Int. Literature 1992–2002; Consul Republic of Slovakia 1995–97; Consul Gen. Republic of Macedonia 1997–; Pres. Bjornstjerne Bjornson Acad., Norwegian Acad. of Literature and Freedom of Expression 2003–; mem. Icelandic Soc. of Authors, Literary Acad. of Romania, Norwegian Soc. of Authors, European Acad. of Poetry (Sec. Gen. 2009–). *Publications include:* poetry: Bee-buzz, Salmon Leap 1968, Cinema Operator 1991, Ventriloquy 1994, Selected Poems 1995, Missa 1998, The Stephensen House 2003, Look-out 2005, It Flowered So Insane 2009; books of prose and essays, a play, two non-fiction books about Iceland 1992, 1998 and a book about St Olaf 2011; works trans. into 29 languages. *Honours:* Norwegian State Scholar for Life 1989–; knighted by Pres. of Iceland 1987, Grand Kt Commdr, Order of the Icelandic Falcon 1993, Int. Order of Merit 1993, Kt, Norwegian Order of Literature 1995, knighted by King of Norway 1998, Kt, Equestrial Order of Holy Sepulchre of Jerusalem (Vatican) 2009; Jan Smrek International Poetry Award, Slovakia 2008, Bastian Prize 1984, Anders Jahre Cultural Prize 2001, Dobloug Prize, Swedish Acad. 2010. *Address:* Postboks 326, 6401 Molde, Norway. *Telephone:* 71-21-59-91 (office); 91-83-86-67 (office). *E-mail:* knutode@mimer.no (office).

ODELL, Peter Randon, BA, MA, PhD, FRSA, FRGS, FEI; British academic and writer; *Professor Emeritus, Erasmus University, Rotterdam;* b. 1 July 1930, Coalville, England; m. Jean Mary McKintosh 1957; two s. two d. *Education:* Univ. of Birmingham, Fletcher School of Law and Diplomacy, Cambridge, USA. *Career:* Economist, Shell International Petroleum Co. 1958–61; Lecturer 1961–65, Senior Lecturer 1965–68, Visiting Prof. 1983–2001, LSE; Prof. of Economic Geography 1968–81, Dir, Centre for Int. Energy Studies 1981–91, Prof. Emeritus 1991–, Erasmus Univ., Rotterdam; Stamp Memorial Lecturer, Univ. of London 1975; Prof., Coll. of Europe, Bruges 1983–90; Scholar-in-Residence, Rockefeller Centre, Bellagio, Italy 1984; European Ed., Energy Journal 1988–90; Killam Visiting Scholar, Univ. of Calgary, Canada 1989; Visiting Scholar, Univ. of Plymouth 1996–2003; Fellow, Inst. of Energy 1973–. *Publications:* An Economic Geography of Oil 1963, Oil: The New Commanding Height 1966, Natural Gas in Western Europe: A Case Study in the Economic Geography of Energy Resources 1969, Oil and World Power: A Geographical Interpretation 1970, Economies and Societies in Latin America (with D. A. Preston) 1973, Energy: Needs and Resources 1974, The North Sea Oil Province (with K. E. Rosing) 1975, The West European Energy Economy: The Case for Self-Sufficiency 1976, The Optimal Development of the North Sea Oilfields (with K. E. Rosing) 1976, The Pressures of Oil: A Strategy for Economic Revival (with L. Vallenilla) 1978, British Offshore Oil Policy: A Radical Alternative 1980, The Future of Oil 1980–2080 (with K. E. Rosing) 1980, Energie: Geen Probleem? (with J. A. van Reijn) 1981, The International Oil Industry: An Interdisciplinary Perspective (ed. with J. Rees) 1986, Energy in Europe: Resources and Choices 1990, Global and Regional Energy Supplies: Recent Fictions and Fallacies Revisited 1991, The New Europe: Energy Resources and Choices 1998, Fossil Fuel Reserves in the 21st Century 1999, Oil and Gas: Crises and Controversies 1961–2000, Vol. 1: Global Issues 2001, Vol. 2: Europe's Entanglement 2002, Why Carbon Fuels Will Dominate the 21st Century's Global Energy Economy 2004. *Honours:* Canadian Council Fellow 1978, Int. Asscn for Energy Economics Prize 1991, Royal Scottish Geographical Soc. Centenary Medal 1993. *Address:* 22A Compton Road, London, N1 2PB, England. *Telephone:* (20) 7359-8199. *E-mail:* peter@odell.u-net.com.

ODELL, Robin Ian; British writer; b. 19 Dec. 1935, Totton, Hants.; m. Joan Bartholomew, 19 Sept. 1959. *Career:* mem. Paternosters, Our Society. *Publications:* Jack the Ripper in Fact and Fiction 1965, Exhumation of a Murder 1975, Jack the Ripper: Summing-up and Verdict (with Colin Wilson) 1977, The Murderers' Who's Who (with J. H. H. Gaute) 1979, Lady Killers 1980, Murder Whatdunit 1982, Murder Whereabouts 1986, Dad Help Me Please (with Christopher Berry-Dee) 1990, A Question of Evidence 1992, The Long Drop 1993, Landmarks in Twentieth Century Murder 1995, The International Murderer's Who's Who 1996, Ripperology 2006, Murderer's Row (with Wilf Gregg) 2006; contributions: Crimes and Punishment, The Criminologist. *Honours:* Hon. Fellow, Chartered Inst. of Water and Environmental Man. 2003; FCC Watts Memorial Prize 1957, Edgar Award, MWA 1980, 2007, Gold Medal, Independent Publishers Book Awards 2007. *Address:* 11 Red House Drive, Sonning Common, Reading, RG4 9NT, England (office). *Telephone:* (118) 972-3532 (office). *E-mail:* bobodell1888@aol.com (office).

ODONE, Cristina, MA; Italian journalist and writer; b. 11 Nov. 1960, Nairobi, Kenya; d. of Augusto Odone and Ulla Sjöström. *Education:* Oxford Univ. *Career:* Vice-Pres. Odone Assocs (consultancy), Washington, DC; Ed. The Catholic Herald, UK 1992–96; Diary journalist The Times 1991; TV reviewer Daily Telegraph 1996–98, fmr Posh but Poor columnist, now contrib.; Deputy Ed. The New Statesman 1998–; currently writing articles for The Guardian, Observer, Daily Telegraph, The Times. *Publications:* The Shrine 1996, Renewal 1997, A Perfect Wife 1997, A Married Man 1997, The Dilemmas of Harriet Carew 2007. *Literary Agent:* Capel & Land, 29 Wardour Street, London, W10 6PS, England. *Telephone:* (20) 7734-2414.

O'DONNELL, Donat (see O'Brien, Conor Cruise)

O'DONNELL, M. R. (see Ross-Macdonald, Malcolm John)

O'DONNELL, Mary Elizabeth Eugenie, BA, DipHigherEd; Irish writer, poet, critic, lecturer and broadcaster and essayist; b. 3 April 1954, Monaghan; m. Martin Nugent 1977; one d. *Education:* Maynooth Univ. *Career:* Writer-in-Residence, Univ. Coll., Dublin, and Co. Laois 1995; teacher of creative writing, Univ. of Iowa Summer Writing Programme, USA, Trinity Coll., Dublin 1998–2000; poetry mentor for MFA in Creative Writing, Carlow Coll., Pittsburgh; mem. Poetry Ireland, Aosdána (the Irish 'Acad.'). *Radio:* Plays: The Deathday Party, A Genuine Woman. *Publications:* Reading the Sunflowers in September (poems) 1990, Strong Pagans and Other Stories 1991, The Light-Makers (novel) (Best New Irish Novel, Sunday Tribune Award) 1992, Spiderwoman's Third Avenue Rhapsody (poems) 1993, Virgin and the Boy (novel) 1996, Unlegendary Heroes (poems) 1998, The Elysium Testament (novel) 1999, September Elegies (poems) 2003, The Place of Miracles (new and selected poems) 2005, New Island 2006, Storm Over Belfast (short stories) 2008; contribs to anthologies, reviews, quarterlies and periodicals. *Honours:* Second Prize, Patrick Kavanagh Poetry Award 1986, Second Prize, Bloodaxe Nat. Poetry Competition 1986, Allingham Poetry Award 1988, Jameson Short Story Award, Listowel 1990, prize-winner, V. S. Pritchett Short Story Award 2000. *Address:* Rook Hollow, Newtownmacabe, Maynooth, Co. Kildare, Ireland (home). *Telephone:* (1) 6272204 (office). *E-mail:* maryelizabeth@eircom.net (home); maryodonnell4@gmail.com (home). *Website:* www.maryodonnell.com.

O'DONOGHUE, (James) Bernard, MA, BPhil, FRSL; Irish academic and poet; *Fellow in English, Wadham College Oxford;* b. 14 Dec. 1945, Cullen, Co. Cork; s. of Batt O'Donoghue and Maureen McNulty; m. Heather MacKinnon 1977; one s. two d. *Education:* Lincoln Coll., Oxford. *Career:* Lecturer and Tutor in English, Magdalen Coll. Oxford 1971–95; Fellow in English, Wadham Coll. Oxford 1995–; Poetry Reviewer, TLS, Irish Times; mem. Poetry Soc., London 1984–; Fellow, English Soc. 1999. *Publications:* Selected Poems of Thomas Hoccleve 1982, The Courtly Love Tradition (Medieval European Love-Poetry) 1984, Razorblades and Pencils 1984, Poaching Rights 1987, The

Weakness (Southern Arts Literature Prize 1991) 1991, Gunpowder (poetry) (Whitbread Prize for Poetry 1995) 1995, Seamus Heaney and the Language of Poetry 1995, Here Nor There 1999, Oxford Irish Quotations 1999, Outliving (poetry) 2003, Sir Gawain and the Green Knight (trans.) 2006, Selected Poems 2008, Farmers Cross (poetry) 2011. *Honours:* Hon. DLitt (Sunderland) 2006; Cholmondeley Award for Poets (co-recipient) 2009. *Address:* Wadham College, Oxford, OX1 3PN, England (office). *E-mail:* bernard.odonoghue@wadh.ox.ac.uk (office). *Website:* www.english.ox.ac.uk (office); www.wadham.ox.ac.uk/fellows-staff/staff/bernard-odonoghue.html (office).

O'DONOHOE, Nick; American writer and academic; b. 31 Oct. 1952, Charles City, IA; m. Lynn Anne Evans 1978. *Education:* BA, Carleton College, 1975; PhD, Syracuse University, 1983. *Career:* Instructor, 1981–83, Asst Prof., 1983–, Virginia Polytechnic Institute and State University, Blacksburg; mem. MWA. *Publications:* April Snow, 1984; Wind Chill, 1985; Open Season, 1986; Too, Too Solid Flesh, 1989; The Magic and the Healing, 1994; Under the Healing Sign, 1995; The Healing of Crossroads, 1996. *Address:* c/o Ace Books, 375 Hudson Street, New York, NY 10014, USA.

O'DRISCOLL, Dennis; Irish editor, poet and critic; b. 1 Jan. 1954, Thurles, Co. Tipperary; m. Julie O'Callaghan 1985. *Education:* Inst. of Public Admin, Univ. Coll., Dublin. *Career:* civil servant, Revenue Commrs, Dublin 1970–2009; Literary Organizer, Dublin Arts Festival 1977–79; Ed. Poetry Ireland Review 1986–87. *Publications:* poetry: Kist 1982, Hidden Extras 1987, Long Story Short 1993, The Bottom Line 1994, Quality Time 1997, Weather Permitting (Lannan Literary Award 1999) 1999, Exemplary Damages 2002, New and Selected Poems 2004, Fifty O'Clock 2005, Reality Check 2007, All the Living 2008, Dear Life 2012; prose: The First Ten Years: Dublin Arts Festival Poetry (co-ed.) 1979, As The Poet Said (selection of columns) 1997, Troubled Thoughts, Majestic Dreams: Selected Prose Writings 2001, The Bloodaxe Book of Poetry Quotations 2006, Quote Poet Unquote 2008, Stepping Stones: Interviews with Seamus Heaney 2008. *Honours:* Hon. mem. Royal Hibernian Acad. 2008–; Hon. DLitt (Univ. Coll. Dublin) 2009; Arts Council Literature Bursaries 1985, 1996, 2004, 2009, E.M. Forster Award, American Acad. of Arts and Letters 2005, O'Shaughnessy Award for Poetry 2006, Argosy Irish Non-Fiction Book of the Year Award 2009. *Address:* c/o Anvil Press Poetry Ltd, Neptune House, 70 Royal Hill, London, SE10 8RF, England. *Website:* www.dennisodriscoll.com.

ŌE, Kenzaburō, BA; Japanese writer; b. 31 Jan. 1935, Ehime, Shikoku; m. Yukari Itami 1960; two s. one d. *Education:* Tokyo Univ. *Career:* first stories published 1957; first full-length novel Pluck The Flowers, Gun The Kids 1958; represented young Japanese writers at Peking (now Beijing) 1960; travelled to Russia and Western Europe writing a series of essays on Youth in the West 1961. *Publications:* fiction: Shisha no ogori (trans. as The Catch) (Japanese Soc. for the Promotion of Literature Akutagawa Prize) 1958, Memushiri kouchi (trans. as Nip the Buds, Shoot the Kids) 1958, Miru mae ni tobe 1958, Our Age (in trans.) 1959, Screams (in trans.) 1962, The Perverts (in trans.) 1963, Nichijo seikatsu no boken 1963, Kojinteki na taiken (trans. as A Personal Matter) 1964, Adventures in Daily Life (in trans.) 1964, Man'en gannen no futtoburu (trans. as The Silent Cry) 1967, Football in The First Year of Mannen (in trans.) 1967, Pinchi ranna chosho (trans. as The Pinch Runner Memorandum) 1976, Warera no kyoki o iki nobiru michi o 1969, Shosetsu no hoho 1978, Natsukashii toshi e no tegami 1986, M/T to mori no fushigi no monogatari 1986, A Healing Family (in trans.) 1996, A Quiet Life (in trans.) 1998, Rouse Up, O Young Men of the New Age (in trans.) 2002, Somersault (in trans.) 2003, Telling Tales (contrib. to charity anthology) 2004, Torikaeko (trans. as The Changeling) 2000, Jibun no Ki'no Sitade (trans. as Under My Tree) 2000, Sakokushiteha Naranai 2001, Iigataki Nagekimote 2001, Ureigao no Douij 2002, Bouryoku ni Sakaratte kaku (trans. as Writing Against Violence) 2003, Atarasii hito' no houe 2003, Nihyakunen no kodomo 2003, Sayounara, Watashi no Hon yo! 2005, Routashi Anaberu rī souke dachitu mimakaritu (trans. as The Beautiful Annabel Lee was Chilled and Killed) 2007, Sui Si 2009; non-fiction: Hiroshima noto (trans. as Hiroshima Notes) 1963, Okinawa noto 1970, Chiryo noto 1990, Japan, the Ambiguous and Myself (the Nobel Prize speech and other lectures) 1995. *Honours:* Commdr, Légion d'Honneur 2002; Hon. DLit (Harvard) 2000; Shinchosha Literary Prize 1964, Tanizaka Prize 1967, Europelia Arts Festival Literary Prize 1989, Nobel Prize for Literature 1994. *Address:* 585 Seijo-machi, Setagaya-ku, Tokyo, Japan (home). *Telephone:* 482-7192 (home).

O'FAOLÁIN, Julia, MA, FRSL; Irish writer; b. 1932, London; d. of Sean and Eileen (née Gould) O'Faoláin; m. Lauro R. Martines 1957; one s. *Education:* Sacred Heart Convent, Monkstown, Co. Dublin, Univs of Dublin, Paris (Sorbonne) and Rome. *Career:* writer and translator since 1968; Dir Susan Smith Blackburn Prize; mem. Aosdána, Soc. of Authors. *Publications include:* We Might See Sights! and Other Stories 1968, Godded and Codded, Man in the Cellar, Women in the Wall, No Country for Young Men 1980, The Obedient Wife, The Irish Signorina, Daughters of Passion 1982, The Judas Cloth 1992, Not in God's Image (co-ed.), Are You Somebody? The Accidental Memoir of a Dublin Woman 1996, Women in History from the Greeks to the Victorians (co-ed.), Ercoli e il Guardiano Nolluno 1999, My Dream of You 2001, Almost There: The Onward Journey of a Dublin Woman 2003, The Story of Chicago May (Prix Femina 2006) 2006. *Literary Agent:* c/o Rogers, Coleridge and White Ltd, 20 Powis Mews, London W11 1JN, England. *Telephone:* (20) 7221-3717. *E-mail:* info@rcwlitagency.com. *Website:* www.rcwlitagency.com.

O'FARRELL, John; British scriptwriter and writer; b. 27 March 1962, Maidenhead, Berkshire, England; m.; two c. *Education:* Univ. of Exeter. *Career:* newspaper columnist, The Independent, The Guardian. *Writing for radio:* Week Ending (BBC Radio 4) 1987–92, Peter Dickson's Nightcap (BBC Radio 2) 1987–89, A Look Back at the Nineties (BBC Radio 4) 1992–93. *Radio:* as performer: The News Quiz (BBC Radio 4), We've Been Here Before (BBC Radio 4). *Writing for television:* Spitting Image (ITV) 1989–95, Brian Conley: This Way Up (ITV) 1990, Smith and Jones (TalkBack/BBC1) 1990–93, Clive Anderson Talks Back (Hat Trick/Channel 4) 1993–95, Room 101 (Hat Trick/BBC2) 1994–97, Have I Got News For You (Hat Trick/BBC2) 1994–99, The Peter Principle (Hat Trick/BBC1) 1995–2000, Never Mind The Horrocks (Hat Trick/Channel 4) 1996, The Best Show in the World... Probably (BBC1) 1998. *Television appearances:* The 11 O'Clock Show (TalkBack/Channel 4) 2000, Grumpy Old Men (BBC2) 2003. *Publications:* non-fiction: Things Can Only Get Better 1998, Global Village Idiot 2001, I Blame the Scapegoats 2003, An Utterly Impartial History of Britain (Or 2000 Years of Upper Class Idiots in Charge) 2007; fiction: The Best A Man Can Get 2000, This is Your Life 2002, May Contain Nuts 2005, The Man Who Forgot His Wife 2012. *Address:* c/o Random House UK Ltd, 20 Vauxhall Bridge Road, London, SW1V 2SA, England. *Website:* www.randomhouse.co.uk.

O'FARRELL, Maggie, BA; Northern Irish novelist; b. 1972; pnr William Sutcliffe; one s. *Education:* Univ. of Cambridge. *Career:* fmr journalist. *Publications:* After You'd Gone (Betty Trask Prize 2001) 2000, My Lover's Lover 2002, The Distance Between Us (Soc. of Authors Somerset Maugham Award 2005) 2004, The Vanishing Act of Esme Lennox 2006, The Hand that First Held Mine (Costa Novel Award) 2010. *Address:* c/o Hodder Headline Ltd, 338 Euston Road, London, NW1 3BH, England (office). *E-mail:* enquiries@headline.co.uk (office). *Website:* www.maggieofarrell.com.

OFFEN, Yehuda, (Huri Halim, Ben Naftali), BA, MA; Israeli writer and poet; b. 4 April 1922, Altona, Germany; m. Tova Arbisser 1946; one d. *Education:* Univ. of London, Hebrew Univ. of Jerusalem. *Career:* Sr Ed., Al Hamishmar, Daily Guardian 1960–80; mem. ACUM (Soc. of Authors, Composers and Editors in Israel), Hebrew Writers Asscn (Israel), Int. Acad. of Poets (USA), Int. Federation of Journalists (Brussels), Nat. Federation of Israeli Journalists, PEN Centre (Israel). *Publications:* L'Lo L'An 1961, Har Vakhol 1963, Lo Agadat Khoref 1969, Nofim P'nima 1979, B'Magal Sagur (short stories) 1979, N'Vilat Vered 1983, Shirim Bir'hov Ayaif 1984, P'Gishot Me'ever Lazman 1986, Massekhet Av 1986, Stoning on the Cross Road (short stories) 1988, Who Once Begot a Star 1990, Silly Soil 1992, Back to Germany 1994. *Honours:* ACUM Prizes for Literature 1961, 1979, 1984, Talpir Prize for Literature 1979, Efrat Prize for Poetry 1989. *Address:* c/o Acum Ltd, 9 Tuval Street, POB 1704, Ramat-Gan 52117, Israel.

Ó FIANNACHTA, Pádraig, BA, MA, PhD, MRIA; Irish academic, poet, writer, editor and publisher; *Chairperson, Díseart Institute of Education and Celtic Culture;* b. 20 Feb. 1927, Co. Kerry. *Education:* St Patrick's Coll., Maynooth, Nat. Univ. of Ireland, Univ. College, Cork, Pontifical Univ., Maynooth. *Career:* Lecturer, St Patrick's Coll., Maynooth 1959–60, Prof. of Early Irish and Lecturer in Welsh 1960–81, Prof. of Modern Irish 1981–92; est. An Díseart, Ireland 1996; mem. staff, RIADIC; mem. Cumann na Sagart, Oireachtas (also Pres.) 1985, Poetry Ireland. *Publications:* Ponc (poetry) 1966, Ruin 1969, Feoirlingi Fileata 1972, Donn Bo 1976, An Bíobla Naofa (ed. ed. and trans.) 1981, Spaisteoireacht 1982, Deora Dé (poetry) 1987, Léim An Dá Míle (Jesus in Dingle) 1999, An Dá Shaol 2004; Series Ed.: Irisleabhair Má Nuad, Dán agus Tallann; contribs to various publs. *Honours:* Monsignor 1998; Hon. DPh (Maynooth) 1995, Hon. DLittHum (SHU) 2004; Douglas Hyde Prize for Literature 1969. *Address:* An Sagart, Dingle, Ireland (office). *Telephone:* (66) 9150000 (home). *E-mail:* pof@ansagart.ie (office). *Website:* www.ansagart.ie (office).

O'FLAHERTY, Patrick Augustine, BA, MA, PhD; Canadian academic and writer; *Professor Emeritus, Memorial University;* b. 6 Oct. 1939, Long Beach, NF. *Education:* Memorial Univ., St John's, NF, Univ. of London. *Career:* Prof. 1965–95, Head Dept of English 1981–86, Prof. Emeritus 1997–, Memorial Univ.; mem. Writers' Union of Canada. *Publications:* The Rock Observed 1979, Part of the Main: An Illustrated History of Newfoundland and Labrador (with Peter Neary) 1983, Summer of the Greater Yellowlags 1987, Priest of God 1989, A Small Place in the Sun 1989, Come Near at Your Peril: A Visitor's Guide to the Island of Newfoundland 1992, Benny's Island 1994, Reminiscences of J. P. Howley: Selected Years (co-ed.) 1997, Old Newfoundland: A History to 1843 1999, Lost Country: The Rise and Fall of Newfoundland 1843–1933 2005; contrib. to numerous publications. *Address:* 4 King's Brdg Court, St John's, NL A1A 0A1, Canada (home). *Telephone:* (709) 722-0784 (home).

OGAWA, Yoko; Japanese writer; b. 30 March 1962, Okayama; m.; one s. *Education:* Waseda Univ. *Publications:* over 20 works of fiction and non-fiction including novels: Agehacho ga kowareru toki (Kaien Prize) 1988, Ninshin karendaa (Akutagawa Prize) 1990, Hisoyaka na kesshō 1994, Gibusu o uru hito 1998, Koritsui ta kaori 1998, Hakase no aishita sushiki (novel, trans. as The Housekeeper and the Professor 2009) (Yomiuri Prize 2004) 2003, Burafuman no maisō (Izumi Prize 2004) 2003, Mīna no kōshin (Tanizaki Prize) 2006, Kusuriyubi no hyōhon (also film as L'Annulaire), Hoteru Airisu (trans. as Hotel Iris 2010); other: An Introduction to the World's Most Elegant Mathematics (essay) (co-author) 2006; contrib. stories to The New Yorker, A Public Space, Zoetrope. *Address:* c/o Harvill Secker, Random House, 20

Vauxhall Bridge Road, London, SW1V 2SA, England (office). *Website:* www.randomhouse.co.uk/harvill (office).

OGDEN, Margaret Astrid Lindholm, (Megan Lindholm, Robin Hobb); American writer; b. 1952, Oakland, CA; m.; four c. *Education:* Univ. of Denver. *Publications:* as Megan Lindholm: Harpy's Flight 1983, The Windsingers 1984, The Limbreth Gate 1984, The Wizard of the Pigeons 1986, The Reindeer People 1988, Wolf's Brother 1988, Luck of the Wheels 1989, Cloven Hooves 1991, Gypsy (with Steven Brust) 1992, Alien Earth 1992; as Robin Hobb: The Assassin's Apprentice 1995, Royal Assassin 1996, Assassin's Quest 1997, Ship of Magic 1998, The Mad Ship 1999, Ship of Destiny 2000, Fool's Fate 2003, Shaman's Crossing 2005, Forest Mage 2006, Renegade's Magic 2007, The Dragon Keeper 2010; contrib. to anthologies and periodicals. *Website:* www.meganlindholm.com; www.robinhobb.com.

OGG, Wilson Reid, AB, JD; American social scientist, philosopher, lawyer and poet, lyricist, educator and judge; *Curator in Residence, Pinebrook and CEO, Pinebrook Press*; b. 26 Feb. 1928, Alhambra, Calif.; s. of James Brooks Ogg and Mary Newton Wilson. *Education:* Univ. of California. *Career:* mem. California State Bar; Psychology Instructor, US Armed Forces Inst., Taegu, Repub. of Korea 1953–54; English Instructor, Taegu English Language Inst. 1954; Trustee Sec. First Unitarian Church of Berkeley 1957–58; Research Attorney, Continuing Educ. of the Bar, Univ. of California 1958–63; Vice-Pres. International House Asscn 1961–62; Pres. Bd and Chair. California Soc. for Physical Study 1963–65; pvt. law practice 1955–; Dir of Admissions, Int. Soc. for Philosophical Enquiry 1981–84; currently Curator in Residence, Pinebrook, CEO Pinebrook Press; mem. San Francisco Bar Asscn, American Mensa, ASCAP, International Acad. of Law and Sciences, World Diplomatic Acad., Scientific Faculty, Cambridge, UK, Faculty Club, Univ. of California at Berkeley, New York Acad. of Sciences. *Publications:* The Enfolding Universe 1995, Constitutional Law, Constitutional Crisis Facing American Democracy 2005, Collective Essay 2005; contrib. poems to various anthologies and articles in journals. *Honours:* Cultural Doctorate (World Univ.); Hon. DD (Univ. of Life Church) 1969; Dr hc in Religious Humanities 1970; Commendation Ribbon W. Medal Pendant. *Address:* Pinebrook at Bret Harte Way, 8 Bret Harte Way, Berkeley, CA 94708; 1104 Keith Avenue, Berkeley, CA 94708, USA (home). *Telephone:* (510) 845-7155 (home). *Fax:* (510) 540-6052 (home). *E-mail:* wilsonogg@cal.berkeley.edu (office); wilsonogg@comcast.net (home). *Website:* wilsonogg.com.

O'GRADY, Desmond James Bernard, MA, PhD; Irish poet, writer, translator and academic; b. 27 Aug. 1935, Limerick City; one s. two d. *Education:* Jesuit Coll., Limerick, Cistercian Coll., Roscrea, Univ. Coll., Dublin, Harvard Univ., USA. *Career:* secondary school teacher, univ. prof. 1955–82; poetry readings in Ireland, UK, France, Italy, Germany, Greece, Egypt, Sweden, Hungary, Czechoslovakia, Yugoslavia, USA, Canada; selected poems translated into Croatian, Hebrew, German, Italian, Spanish; Distinguished Visiting Prof. and Poet-in-Residence, American Univ., Cairo, Egypt, Univ. of Alexandria, Egypt; Distinguished Visiting Poet, Stockholm, Sweden; Founding mem. and Fellow, Aosdána; mem. Irish Acad. of Arts and Letters. *Publications:* Chords and Orchestrations 1956, Reilly 1961, Prof. Kelleher and the Charles River 1964, Separazioni 1965, The Dark Edge of Europe 1967, The Dying Gaul 1968, Off Licence (trans.) 1968, Hellas 1971, Separations 1973, Stations 1976, Sing Me Creation 1977, The Gododdin (trans.) 1977, A Limerick Rake (trans.) 1978, The Headgear of the Tribe 1979, His Skaldcrane's Nest 1979, Grecian Glances (trans.) 1981, Alexandria Notebook 1989, The Seven Arab Odes (trans.) 1990, Tipperary 1991, Ten Modern Arab Poets (trans.) 1992, My Fields This Springtime 1993, Alternative Manners (trans.) 1993, Trawling Tradition: Collected Translations 1954–1994 1994, Il Galata Morente 1996, The Road Taken: Poems 1956–1996 1996, The Golden Odes of Love (trans.) 1997, C. P. Cavafy: Selected Poems (trans.) 1998, The Wandering Celt 2001, The Battle of Kinsale 1601 2002, The Song of Songs (trans.) 2002, The Wide World (a casebook) 2003, Croatia My Love (trans.) 2003, Summer Harvest: a poem with Matthew Garden 2004, Pegasus 2005, Kurdish Poems of Love and Liberty (trans.) 2005, On My Way, Poems 2006, My Alexandria, Poems and Prose Diary 2006; prose memoirs: Ezra Pound, Patrick Kavanagh, Samuel Beckett, Olga Rudge, Anna Akhmatova; essays: on poetry, poets, translating poetry; contrib. to The Norton Anthology of Modern Poetry 1973, The Norton World Poetry 1998, Archeology of Literature 2004, all anthologies of modern Irish poetry, numerous magazines. *Honours:* Patrick and Catherine Kavanagh Fellowship Award 2004. *Address:* Rincurran Cottage, Kinsale, Co. Cork, Ireland. *Telephone:* (21) 4772898 (office). *E-mail:* bandonbooks@eircom.ie (office).

O'GRADY, Tom, BA, MA; American poet, writer, dramatist, translator and editor and vintner; b. 26 Aug. 1943, Baltimore, Md; s. of Thomas Joseph Grady and Sallie Mapp Dennis; m. Bronwyn Southworth; two s. *Education:* Univ. of Baltimore, Johns Hopkins Univ., Univ. of Delaware. *Career:* teacher of writing and literature, various colls and univs 1966–96; founder and dir, The Rose Bower Vineyard and Winery 1972–2002; Adjunct Prof. of English and Poet-in-Residence, Hampden-Sydney Coll. 1974–2008; Founder-Ed. The Hampden-Sydney Poetry Review 1975–2008; numerous lectures and poetry readings. *Publications:* poetry: Unicorn Evils 1973, Establishing a Vineyard 1977, Photo-Graphs 1980, The Farmville Elegies 1981, In the Room of the Just Born 1989, Carvings of the Moon 1992, Sun, Moon, and Stars 1996; prose: Shaking the Tree: A Book of Works and Days 1993, The Same Earth, The Same Sky: New and Selected Poems and Translations 2002; plays: The Gardens of November 1996, Remote Controls 1997; editor: The Hampden-Sydney Poetry Anthology 1990; contribs to anthologies, newspapers, journals and magazines; also trans. stage and TV plays. *Honours:* Leache Prize for Poetry 1975, Co-ordinating Council of Literary Magazine Ed.'s Award 1977, Merit Award 1977, Mettauer Research Award 1984, Trustees Award 1986, Hampden-Sydney Coll. Virginia Prize for Poetry 1989, Nat. Foundation for Advancement in the Arts Teacher of the Arts Award 1989–90, Virginia Center for the Arts Fellowship residency 1995, Henrico Theater Co. Prize 1997, Virginia Comm. for the Arts Poetry Fellowship 2001–02. *Address:* 121 The O'Grady Way, Farmville, VA 23901; Rose Bower Vineyard, PO Box 126, Hampden-Sydney, VA 23943, USA (home). *Telephone:* (434) 223-8209 (home). *E-mail:* togrady@hsc.edu (office).

O'HAGAN, Andrew, BA; British writer; b. 25 May 1968, Glasgow, Scotland; s. of Gerald O'Hagan and Agnes O'Hagan; one d. *Education:* Univ. of Strathclyde. *Career:* Dir, London Review of Books; Ed.-at-Large, Esquire; Film Critic, London Evening Standard 2009–; Amb. for UNICEF. *Television:* writer and presenter, The World According to Robert Burns (BBC). *Publications:* The Missing (non-fiction) 1995, Calling Bible John (TV adaptation of an excerpt from The Missing) 1996, Our Fathers (novel) 1999, The End of British Farming (non-fiction) 2001, New Writing 11 (ed.) 2002, Personality (novel) (James Tait Black Memorial Prize for Fiction 2004) 2003, Be Near Me (novel) 2006, The Atlantic Ocean (non-fiction) 2008, The Life and Opinions of Maf the Dog, and of his friend Marilyn Monroe (novel) 2010; contrib. to London Review of Books, New York Review of Books, The New Yorker, The Weekenders (anthology) 2001. *Honours:* Hon. DLitt (Strathclyde) 2009; Winifred Holtby Memorial Prize 1999, BAFTA Award 1996, E.M. Forster Award, American Acad. of Arts and Letters, LA Times Book Award 2008. *Literary Agent:* AP Watt Ltd, 20 John Street, London, WC1N 2DR, England. *E-mail:* edit@lrb.co.uk (office).

OHLSSON, Bengt; Swedish writer, playwright and journalist; b. 1963, Stockholm. *Publications:* Dö som en man, sa jag 1984, Rida på en gris 1985, Jazz är farligt 1988, Solo 1992, Den där lilla stunden av närhet 1994, Se till mig som liten är 2000, Gregorius (August Prize) 2004, Benke@swipnet.se 2005, Hennes mjukaste röst 2007, Syster 2009, Kolka 2010, Rekviem för John Cummings 2011. *Honours:* City of Stockholm Hon. Award 2001, Eyvind Johnson Prize 2008. *Address:* c/o Albert Bonniers Förlag, Sveavägen 56, Box 3159, 103 63 Stockholm, Sweden (office). *E-mail:* info@abforlag.bonnier.se (office). *Website:* www.albertbonniersforlag.se (office).

OHLSSON, Per Evald Torbjörn; Swedish journalist and author; *Senior Columnist, Sydvenska Dagbladet*; b. 3 March 1958, Malmö; s. of Ulla Ohlsson and Torsten Ohlsson; m. Maria Rydqvist-Ohlsson 1989; one s. *Education:* Univ. of Lund. *Career:* Ed. Lundagard 1980–81; editorial writer, Expressen, Stockholm 1981–85; New York Corresp., Sydvenska Dagbladet 1985–88, Ed.-in-Chief 1990–2005, Sr Columnist 2005–. *Publications:* Over There – Banden Över Atlanten 1992, Gudarnas Ö 1993, 100 År Av Tillväxt 1994. *Honours:* Soderberg Foundation Prize for Journalism 1998. *Address:* Sydvenska Dagbladet, 205 05 Malmö, Sweden (office). *Telephone:* 40-28-12-00 (office). *Fax:* 40-28-13-86 (office). *E-mail:* per.t.ohlsson@sydsvenskan.se (office).

OHNEMUS, Günter; German writer, translator and critic; b. 1946. *Publications include:* Siebenundsechzig Ansichten einer Frau 1995, Der Tiger auf deiner Schulter (trans. as The Tiger on your Shoulder) 1998, Reise in die Angst (trans. as The Russian Passenger) 2002, Ein MAcho auf der Suche nach seinem Stuntman 2003, Als die richtige Zeit verschwand 2005. *Honours:* Tukan-Award, Alfred Kerr Award. *Address:* c/o Bitter Lemon Press, 37 Arundel Gardens, London, W11 2LW, England. *E-mail:* fvh@bitterlemonpress.com. *Website:* www.bitterlemonpress.com.

OJAIDE, Tanure, BA, MA, PhD; Nigerian poet, writer and academic; *Professor of Africana Studies, University of North Carolina at Charlotte*; b. 24 April 1948, Okpara Inland; s. of Dafetanure Ojaide and Avwerhoke Ojaide; m. Anne Numuoja 1976; five c. *Education:* Fed. Govt Coll., Warri, Univ. of Ibadan, Syracuse Univ., USA. *Career:* Teacher of English, Fed. Govt Coll., Warri 1973–75; Lecturer in English and Communication, Petroleum Training Inst., Effurun 1975–77; Lecturer, Univ. of Maiduguri 1977–85, Sr Lecturer 1985–87, Reader 1987–89; Visiting Johnston Prof. of Third World Literatures, Whitman Coll., Walla Walla, WA 1989–90; Asst Prof., Univ. of North Carolina, Charlotte 1990–93, Assoc. Prof. 1993–98, Prof. of Africana Studies 1998–; Nat. Endowment for the Humanities Prof., Albright Coll., Reading, Pa 1996–97; Frank Porter Graham Endowed Prof. 2006–; mem. African Literature Asscn, African Studies Asscn, Associated Writing Programs, Asscn of Nigerian Authors, Int. Asscn of Univ. Profs of English, Int. Black Writers, Charlotte, NC, MLA, N Carolina Writers' Network; Fellow, Headlands Center for the Arts, Sausalito, Calif. 1994. *Publications:* poetry: Children of Iroko and Other Poems 1973, Labyrinths of the Delta 1986, The Eagle's Vision 1987, Poems 1988, The Endless Song 1989, The Fate of Vultures and Other Poems 1990, The Blood of Peace 1991, Daydream of Ants 1997, Delta Blues and Home Songs 1998, Invoking the Warrior Spirit: New and Selected Poems 1999, Cannons for the Brave 1999, When It No Longer Matters Where You Live 1999, In the Kingdom of Songs: A Trilogy of Poems, 1995–2000 2001, I Want to Dance and Other Poems 2003, In the House of Words 2005, The Tale of the Harmattan 2007, Waiting for the Hatching of a Cockeral 2008, The Beauty I Have Seen 2010; fiction: God's Medicine Men and Other Stories 2004, Sovereign Body 2004, The Activist 2006, The Debt-Collector and Other Stories 2009, Matters of the Moment 2009; other: Yono Urhobo: Obe Rerha (with S. S. Ugheteni) 1981, The Poetry of Wole Soyinka 1994, Poetic Imagination in Black

Africa: Essays on African Poetry 1996, Great Boys: An African Childhood 1998, The New African Poetry: An Anthology (ed. with Tijan M. Sallah) 1999, Texts and Contexts: Culture, Society, and Politics in Modern African Literature (with Joseph Obi) 2001, God and his Medicine Men: Short Stories 2002; contributions: books, anthologies, magazines and journals. *Honours:* Africa Regional Winner, Commonwealth Poetry Prize 1987, Overall Winner, BBC Arts and Africa Poetry Award 1988, Asscn of Nigerian Authors' Poetry Prizes 1988, 1994, 2004, All-Africa Okigbo Prizes for Poetry 1988, 1997, Nat. Endowment for the Humanities Fellowship 1999–2000, Residency, Bellagio Center for Scholars and Artists 1989, 2001, Fulbright Scholar 2003–04, First Citizen's Scholar Medal 2005. *Address:* Department of Africana Studies, University of North Carolina at Charlotte, 138 Garinger, Charlotte, NC 28223-0001, USA (office). *Telephone:* (704) 687-2665 (office). *Fax:* (704) 687-3888 (office). *E-mail:* tojaide@uncc.edu (office). *Website:* www.tanureojaide.com.

OKAI, Atukwei; Ghanaian poet and academic; b. 1941, Accra; m.; one d. *Education:* Gorky Literary Inst., Moscow, Univ. of London. *Career:* teacher in Russian literature, Univ. of Ghana; faculty mem., Inst. of African Studies, Legon; exec., Pan-African Writers' Asscn (PAWA). *Publications:* poetry: Flowerfall 1969, The Oath of the Fontomfrom and Other Poems 1971, Lorgorligi Logarithms 1974, The Anthill in the Sea 1988. *Literary Agent:* c/o Pan-African Writers' Association, PAWA House, Roman Ridge, POB C456, Accra, Ghana. *Telephone:* (21) 773 062. *Fax:* (21) 773 042. *E-mail:* pawa@ghana.com.

O'KANE, Margaret (Maggie) Mary, BA (Hons); Irish journalist; *Editorial Director, Guardian Films*; b. 8 June 1962, Ardglas, Co. Down, Northern Ireland; d. of Peter O'Kane and Maura McNeil; m. John Mullin 1995; one s. two d. *Education:* Loreto Convent (Balbriggan, Co. Dublin), Univ. Coll., Dublin, Coll. de Journalistes en Europe, Paris and Coll. of Commerce, Dublin. *Career:* reporter on Irish TV 1982–84, for Sunday Tribune newspaper 1984–87; reporter, TV Producer and Presenter 1987–89; Foreign Corresp. and Feature Writer, The Guardian 1989–2003; has reported from world trouble spots: Eastern Europe 1989–91, Baghdad 1991, Kurdistan 1991–92, Yugoslavia 1992–94, Bosnia, Haiti, Cuba 1994–96, Afghanistan, Cambodia, Kosovo, Yugoslavia 2000 etc.; Editorial Dir Guardian Films 2003–; writer and presenter of various TV documentaries. *Films:* (documentaries) Milosevic: Puppet Master of the Balkans (Channel 4) (Royal TV Soc. (RTS) Documentary of the Year 1993), Bloody Bosnia (RTS Documentary of the Year 1994), Looking for Karadzic (Guardian Films) (European Journalist of the Year 2002, RTS Best Documentary 2004, International Emmy 2008), Baghdad: A Doctor's Story (Best News Award 2009, Zimbabwe Emmy Award 2008) 2008. *Publications:* A Woman's World: Beyond the Headlines 1996, Mozambique. *Honours:* hon. degree from Bradford Univ.; Journalist of the Year 1992, Foreign Corresp. of the Year 1992, Reporter of the Year (commended) (jt award) 1994, Amnesty Int. Foreign Corresp. of the Year 1993, James Cameron Award for Journalism 1996, European Journalist of the Year 2002, 2003. *Address:* The Guardian, Kings Place, 90 York Way, London, N1 9GU, England (office). *Telephone:* (20) 3353-2000 (office). *E-mail:* maggie.okane@guardian.co.uk (office). *Website:* www.guardian.co.uk/guardianfilms (office).

OKAWA, Ryuho; Japanese religious leader; *Leader, Kofuku-no-Kagaku*; b. 7 July 1956, Tokushima Pref. *Education:* Univ. of Tokyo, Graduate Center, City Univ. of New York, USA. *Career:* attained enlightenment 23 March 1981, realized his identity as El Cantare, saviour of humanity; f. Kofuku-no-Kagaku (Inst. for Research in Human Happiness) 1986; holds numerous open lecture sessions with large audiences that are broadcast by satellite throughout Japan. *Publications:* more than 400 books including The Starting Point of Happiness – A Practical and Intuitive Guide to Discovering Love, Wisdom, and Faith, Love, Nurture, and Forgive – A Handbook on Adding New Richness in Your Life, An Unshakeable Mind – How to Cope with Life's Difficulties and Turn Them into Food for Your Soul 2002, A Revolution of Happiness – The Power of Thought to Change the Future, The 'Inability to Attain Happiness' Syndrome – Say Good-bye to a Life of Gloom, Work and Love – Become a True Leader in the Business World, Invincible Thinking – Become a Master of Your Own Destiny. *Address:* Kofuku-no-Kagaku, 1–2–38 Higashi Gotanda, Shinagawa-ku, Tokyo, 141-0022, Japan (office). *Telephone:* (3) 5437-2777 (office). *Fax:* (3) 5437-2806 (office). *E-mail:* inquiry@happy-science.org (office). *Website:* www.kofuku-no-kagaku.or.jp (office).

OKRI, Ben, OBE, FRSL, FRSA; Nigerian/British author and poet; b. 15 March 1959, Minna; s. of Silver Okri and Grace Okri. *Education:* John Donne's School, Peckham, London, Children's Home School, Sapele, Nigeria, Christ High School, Ibadan, Urhobo Coll., Warri and Univ. of Essex, UK. *Career:* staff writer and librarian, Afriscope magazine 1978; Poetry Ed. West Africa magazine 1983–86; broadcaster with BBC 1983–85; Fellow Commoner in Creative Arts, Trinity Coll. Cambridge 1991–93; Visiting Prof. School of English, Univ. of Leicester 2012–; mem. Int. PEN, a Vice-Pres. English Centre of Int. PEN 1997–; mem. Bd Royal Nat. Theatre of GB 1999–2006; mem. Soc. of Authors, RSL (mem. of Council 1999–2004). *Plays:* In Exilus (The Studio, Royal Nat. Theatre of GB) 2001, The Heart's Tent is Broken (Tristam Bates Theatre) 2011. *Television:* Great Railway Journey: London to Arcadia 1996. *Publications:* Flowers and Shadows 1980, The Landscapes Within 1982, Incidents at the Shrine 1986, Stars of the New Curfew 1988, The Famished Road (Booker Prize) 1991, An African Elegy (vol. of poems) 1992, Songs of Enchantment 1993, Astonishing the Gods 1995, Birds of Heaven (essays) 1996, Dangerous Love (novel) 1996, A Way of Being Free (non-fiction) 1997, Infinite Riches (novel) 1998, Mental Fight (epic poem) 1999, In Arcadia (novel) 2002, Starbook (novel) 2007, Tales of Freedom 2009, A Time for New Dreams (poetic essays) 2011, Wild (vol. of poems) 2012; poems, essays, short stories. *Honours:* Hon. DLitt (Westminster) 1997, (Essex) 2002, (Exeter) 2004, (SOAS, London) 2010; Dr hc (Universiteit voor het Algemeen Belang, Belgium) 2009; Hon. Dr of Arts (Bedfordshire) 2010; Commonwealth Prize for Africa 1987, Paris Review Aga Khan Prize for Fiction 1987, Premio Letterario Internazionale, Chianti Ruffino-Antico Fattore 1992, Premio Grinzane Cavour 1994, The Crystal Award (World Econ. Forum, Switzerland) 1995, Premio Palmi 2000, Grinzane for Africa Mainstream Prize 2008, Int. Literary Award of Novi Sad, Serbia 2008. *Literary Agent:* The Marsh Agency, 50 Albemarle Street, London, W1S 4BD, England. *Website:* www.marsh-agency.co.uk.

OKSANEN, Sofi; Finnish/Estonian writer and essayist; b. 7 Jan. 1977, Jyväskylä. *Education:* Theatre Acad., Helsinki. *Career:* Christina of the Year (Univ. of Helsinki) 2008. *Plays include:* Puhdistus (Finnish Nat. Theatre 2007). *Publications:* novels: Stalinin lehmät (trans. as Stalin's Cows) 2003, Baby Jane 2005, Puhdistus (trans. as Purge) (Mika Waltari Award 2008, SSKR/The Great Finnish Book Club Prize 2008, Varjo-Runeberg Award 2008, Kalevi Jäntti Prize 2008, Varjo-Finlandia Award 2008, Finlandia Award 2008, Runeberg Prize 2009, Nordic Council Literature Prize 2010) 2008; other: Kaiken takana oli pelko (essays) (co-ed. and contrib.) 2009. *Literary Agent:* c/o Szilvia Molnar, Salomonsson Agency, Svartensgatan 4, 116 20 Stockholm, Sweden. *Telephone:* (8) 22-32-11. *E-mail:* szilvia@salomonssonagency.com. *Website:* www.salomonssonagency.com; www.sofioksanen.com.

OLAFSSON, Olaf, BSc; Icelandic writer and media executive; *Executive Vice-President, Time Warner*; b. 1962, Reykjavík. *Education:* Brandeis Univ. *Career:* various positions at Sony Corpn 1985–91, founder, Pres. and CEO Sony Interactive Entertainment 1991–97; mem. of bd Advanta Corpn 1997–99, Pres. 1998–99; Vice-Chair. Time Warner Digital Media 1999–2001, Exec. Vice Pres., Time Warner 2003–. *Publications:* Absolution 1994, The Journey Home 2000, Walking into the Night 2003. *Address:* Time Warner Inc., One Time Warner Center, New York, NY 10019-8016, USA (office). *Telephone:* (212) 484-8000 (office). *Website:* www.timewarner.com (office).

OLASKY, Marvin, BA, MA, PhD; American writer, editor and academic; *Editor-in-Chief, World magazine*; b. 12 June 1950, Malden, Mass; s. of Eli Olasky and Ida Olasky; m. Susan Northway 1976; four s. *Education:* Yale Univ., Univ. of Michigan. *Career:* reporter and corresp., Boston Globe 1970–71, 1973; reporter, Bulletin, Bend, Ore. 1971–72; Lecturer, San Diego State Univ. 1976–77; Academic Affairs Co-ordinator and Speechwriter, Du Pont Co., Wilmington, Del. 1978–83; Asst Prof., Univ. of Texas at Austin 1983–88, Assoc. Prof. 1988–93, Prof. of Journalism 1993–2008; Bradley Resident Scholar, Heritage Foundation 1989–90; Resident Scholar, Americans United for Life 1990–91; Ed. Philanthropy, Culture and Society 1991–94; Ed.-at-Large, World magazine 1991–94, Ed. 1994–2001 Ed.-in-Chief 2001–; Provost, The King's Coll., New York 2007–10; Sr Fellow, Acton Inst. 1999–; mem. Nat. Asscn of Scholars. *Publications:* Corporate Public Relations: A New Historical Perspective 1987, Patterns of Corporate Philanthropy: Public Affairs and the Forbes 100 1987, Turning Point: A Christian Worldview Declaration (with Herbert Schlossberg) 1987, Prodigal Press: The Anti-Christian Bias of the News Media 1988, The Press and Abortion, 1838–1988 1988, More Than Kindness: A Compassionate Approach to Childbearing (with Susan Olasky) 1990, Central Ideas in the Development of American Journalism 1991, The Tragedy of American Compassion 1992, Abortion Rites: A Social History of Abortion in America 1992, Philanthropically Correct: The Story of the Council on Foundations 1993, Loving Your Neighbor: A Principled Guide to Charity 1995, Fighting for Liberty and Virtue: Political and Cultural Wars in Eighteenth-Century America 1995, Renewing American Compassion 1996, Telling the Truth: How to Revitalize Christian Journalism 1996, Whirled Views: Tracking Today's Culture Storms (with Joel Belz) 1997, The American Leadership Tradition: Moral Vision from Washington to Clinton 1999, revised edn as The American Leadership Tradition: The Inevitable Impact of a Leader's Faith on a Nation's Destiny 2000, Compassionate Conservatism: What It Is, What It Does, and How It Can Transform America 2000, Standing for Christ in a Modern Babylon 2003, The Religions Next Door 2004, Monkey Business (with John Perry) 2005, Scimitar's Edge 2006, The Politics of Disaster 2006, 2048: A Story of America's Future 2009, Echoes of Eden 2011, The Madame 2011; contrib. to periodicals. *Address:* World, PO Box 20002, Asheville, NC 28802 (office). *Telephone:* (800) 951-6397 (office). *E-mail:* molasky@worldmag.com (office). *Website:* www.worldmag.com (office).

OLDKNOW, Antony, BA, PhD; American poet, writer, literary translator and academic; *Professor of Literature, Eastern New Mexico University*; b. 15 Aug. 1939, Peterborough, England. *Education:* Univ. of Leeds, Univ. of Edinburgh, Univ. of North Dakota, USA. *Career:* Ed., Publisher, Scopcraeft Press Inc 1966–; travelling writer, The Plains Book Bus 1979–81; writer-in-residence, Wisconsin Arts Board 1980–83; poetry staff, Cottonwood 1984–87; Prof. of Literature, Eastern New Mexico Univ. 1987–; Assoc. Ed., Blackwater Quarterly 1993. *Publications:* Lost Allegory 1967, Tomcats and Tigertails 1968, The Road of the Lord 1969, Anthem for Rusty Saw and Blue Sky 1975, Consolations for Beggars 1978, Miniature Clouds 1982, Ten Small Songs 1985, Clara d'Ellébeuse (trans.) 1992, The Villages and Other Poems (trans.) 1993, The Passion Play and Nine Other Ghost Stories 2006; contrib. short stories and articles to anthologies, reviews, journals and magazines. *Address:* Department of Languages and Literature, Eastern New Mexico University, Portales, NM 88130 (office); POB 1091, Portales, NM 88130-1091, USA (home). *Telephone:* (505) 562-2688 (office); (505) 359-0901 (home). *Fax:* (505) 562-2142 (home). *E-mail:* antony.oldknow@enmu.edu (office); oldknowa@msn.com (home).

OLDS, Sharon, BA, PhD; American poet and academic; b. 19 Nov. 1942, San Francisco. *Education:* Stanford Univ., Columbia Univ. *Career:* Lecturer-in-Residence on Poetry, Theodor Herzl Inst., New York 1976–80; Adjunct Prof. 1983–90, Dir 1988–91, Assoc. Prof. 1990, Graduate Program in Creative Writing, New York Univ., now Erich Maria Remarque Prof.; Fanny Hurst Chair in Literature, Brandeis Univ. 1986–87; New York State Poet Laureate 1998–2000. *Publications:* Satan Says 1980, The Dead and the Living (National Book Critics Circle Award 1985) 1984, The Gold Cell 1987, The Matter of This World: New and Selected Poems 1987, The Sign of Saturn 1991, The Father 1992, The Wellspring 1996, Blood, Tin, Straw 1999, The Unswept Room 2002, Strike Sparks: Selected Poems 2006, One Secret Thing 2009. *Honours:* Creative Arts Public Service Award 1978, Madeline Sadin Award 1978, Guggenheim Fellowship 1981–82, NEA Fellowship 1982–83, Lamont Prize 1984, Lila Wallace-Reader's Digest Fellowship 1993–96, Harriet Monroe Poetry Award 1997. *Address:* c/o Department of English, New York University, 19 University Place, New York, NY 10003, USA.

OLDSEY, Bernard Stanley, BA, MA, PhD; American academic (retd), editor and writer; b. 18 Feb. 1923, Wilkes-Barre, PA; m. Ann Marie Re 1946; one s. one d. *Education:* Pennsylvania State University. *Career:* Instructor to Assoc. Prof. of English, Pennsylvania State University, 1951–69; Senior Fulbright Prof. of American Literature, Universidad de Zaragoza, Spain, 1964–65; Prof. of English, West Chester University of Pennsylvania, 1969–90; Ed., College Literature, 1974–90; Prof., University of Innsbruck, Austria, 1986; mem. Authors' Guild. *Publications:* From Fact to Judgment, 1957; The Art of William Golding, 1967; The Spanish Season (novel), 1970; Hemingway's Hidden Craft, 1979; Ernest Hemingway: Papers of a Writer (ed.), 1981; British Novelists, 1930–1960, 1983; Critical Essays on George Orwell, 1985; The Mayfield Story, 1999; The Snows of Yesteryear (novel), 2001. *Address:* 520 William Ebbs Lane, West Chester, PA 19380, USA. *Telephone:* (610) 436-4223. *E-mail:* oldbern@aol.com.

O'LEARY, Patsy Baker, BS, MA; American writer, poet and teacher; b. 23 Sept. 1937, NC; m. Denis L. O'Leary 1962 (divorced 1979); one d. *Education:* East Carolina College, California State University at Northridge. *Career:* Instructor in Creative Writing, Pitt Community College, 1980–; Lecturer in English, 1980–81, and Communications, 1990–95, East Carolina University; mem. National Writers' Union; Poets and Writers; North Carolina Writers Network; Southeastern Writers Asscn. *Publications:* With Wings as Eagles (novel), 1997; Phoenix (poem); A Voice Heard in Ramah (short story). *Honours:* First Place Awards for article, 1981, 1982, for novel-in-progress, 1981, 1982, for inspirational poem, 1983, Council of Authors and Journalists; First Place Award for short story, Tar Heel Writer's Roundtable, 1984; Award established in her honour, Pitt Community College, 1989. *Address:* 310 Baytree Drive, Greenville, NC 27858, USA.

OLIVER, Douglas Dunlop, BA, MA; British poet, novelist and prosodist; b. 14 Sept. 1937, Southampton, England; m. 1st Janet Hughes 1962; m. 2nd Alice Notley 1988; two d. two step-s. *Education:* University of Essex. *Career:* Journalist, newspapers in England, Agence France-Presse, Paris, 1959–72; University Lecturer, Literature, English, various, 1975–; Editorial Board, Franco-British Studies; Co-Ed., Gare du Nord Magazine. *Publications:* Oppo Hectic, 1969; The Harmless Building, 1973; In the Cave of Succession, 1974; The Diagram Poems, 1979; The Infant and the Pearl, 1985; Kind, 1987; Poetry and Narrative in Performance, 1989; Three Variations on the Theme of Harm, 1990; Penniless Politics, 1991; The Scarlet Cabinet (with Alice Notley), 1992; Selected Poems, 1996; Penguin Modern Poets 10, 1996. Contributions: anthologies including: A Various Art, 1987; The New British Poetry 1968–1988, 1988; numerous poems, articles, fiction, to magazines and journals. *Honours:* Eastern Arts Grant, 1977; South-East Arts Grant, 1987; Fund for Poetry Grants, 1990, 1991; Judith E. Wilson Lecturer, University of Cambridge, 1995.

OLIVER, Mary; American poet and educator; b. 10 Sept. 1935, Cleveland, OH. *Education:* Ohio State Univ., Vassar Coll. *Career:* Mather Visiting Prof., Case Western Reserve Univ. 1980, 1982; Poet-in-Residence, Bucknell Univ. 1986; Elliston Visiting Prof., Univ. of Cincinnati 1986; Margaret Banister Writer-in-Residence, Sweet Briar Coll. 1991–95; William Blackburn Visiting Prof. of Creative Writing, Duke Univ. 1995; Catharine Osgood Foster Prof., Bennington Coll. 1996–; mem. PEN. *Publications:* No Voyage, and Other Poems 1963, The River Styx, Ohio, and Other Poems 1972, The Night Traveler 1978, Twelve Moons 1978, Sleeping in the Forest 1979, American Primitive (Pulitzer Prize in Poetry 1984) 1983, Dream Work 1986, Provincetown 1987, House of Light 1990, New and Selected Poems 1992, A Poetry Handbook 1994, White Pine: Poems and Prose Poems 1994, Blue Pastures 1995, West Wind 1997, Rules for the Dance 1998, Winter Hours 1999, The Leaf and the Cloud 2000, What Do We Know 2002, Owls and Other Fantasies 2003, Long Life 2004, Why I Wake Early 2004, Blue Iris 2004, Thirst 2006, Evidence 2010, Swan 2010, The Truro Bear and Other Adventures 2010; contrib. to periodicals in the USA and UK. *Honours:* Poetry Soc. of America First Prize 1962, Devil's Advocate Award 1968, Shelley Memorial Award 1972, National Endowment for the Arts Fellowship 1972–73, Alice Fay di Castagnola Award 1973, Guggenheim Fellowship 1980–81, American Acad. and Inst. of Arts and Letters Award 1983, Christopher Award 1991, L. L. Winship Award 1991, Nat. Book Award for Poetry 1992, Lannan Literary Award 1998. *Literary Agent:* Steven Barclay Agency, 12 Western Avenue, Petaluma, CA 94952, USA. *Telephone:* (707) 773-0654. *Fax:* (707) 778-1868. *Website:* www.barclayagency.com.

OLIVER, Roland Anthony, PhD, FBA; British writer and Africanist; b. 30 March 1923, Srinagar, Kashmir; s. of Douglas Gifford Oliver and Lorimer Janet Donaldson; m. 1st Caroline Linehan 1947 (died 1983); one d.; m. 2nd Suzanne Miers 1990. *Education:* Univ. of Cambridge. *Career:* Lecturer, SOAS, Univ. of London 1948–49, 1950–57, Reader 1958–63, Prof. of African History 1963–86, Hon. Fellow 1992; organized first confs on history and archaeology of Africa, London Univ. 1953, 1957, 1961; founder and Ed. Journal of African History 1960–73; Pres. British Inst. in E Africa 1981–93; Chair. Minority Rights Group 1976–92. *Publications:* The Missionary Factor in East Africa 1952, Sir Harry Johnston and the Scramble for Africa 1957, The Dawn of African History 1961, Short History of Africa (with J. D. Fage) 1962, History of East Africa (with G. Mathew) 1963, Africa Since 1800 (with A. Atmore) 1967, Africa in the Iron Age (with B. M. Fagan) 1975, The African Middle Ages 1400–1800 (with A. Atmore) 1980, The African Experience 1991, The Realms of Gold 1997, Medieval Africa (with A. Atmore) 2001; Gen. Ed. Cambridge History of Africa (eight vols) 1975–86. *Honours:* Distinguished Africanist Award, American African Studies Asscn 1989, African Studies Asscn of the UK 2004. *Address:* Frilsham Woodhouse, School Lane, near Thatcham, Berkshire, RG18 9XB, England (home). *Telephone:* (1635) 201407 (home). *Fax:* (1635) 202716 (home).

OLMSTEAD, Andrea, BM, MA; American musicologist; *Faculty Member, New England Conservatory of Music;* b. 5 Sept. 1948, Dayton, OH; d. of Dr Edwin Guy Olmstead and Mary Alice Olmstead; m. Larry Thomas Bell 1982. *Education:* Hartt Coll. of Music, New York Univ., Juilliard School, New York. *Career:* Faculty mem., The Juilliard School 1972–80, Boston Conservatory 1981–2004; Christopher Hogwood Research Fellow, Handel and Haydn Soc. 2005–07; Faculty mem. New England Conservatory of Music 2007–, Boston Univ. (online faculty mem.) 2007–, Univ. of Massachusetts, Amherst 2009–10. *Libretto:* wrote opera libretto for Holy Ghosts by Larry Bell and based on the play by Romulus Linney. *Publications:* Roger Sessions and His Music 1985, Conversations with Roger Sessions 1987, The New Grove 20th Century American Masters 1987, The Correspondence of Roger Sessions 1992, Juilliard: A History 1999, Roger Sessions: A Biography 2008, Cultivating the Past: A Celebration of Hadley's 350th Anniversary 2009; contrib. to Journal of the Arnold Schoenberg Institute, American Music, Musical Quarterly, Tempo, Musical America, Perspectives of New Music, Music Library Association Notes, Journal of Musicology. *Honours:* three Nat. Endowment for the Humanities grants 1989, 1992, 2000, Outstanding Academic Book, Choice 1986, Outstanding Teacher of the Year Boston Conservatory 2000, 2004, six Visiting Scholar residencies, American Acad., Rome, four residencies at Virginia Center for the Creative Arts. *Address:* 73 Hemenway Street, Apt 501, Boston, MA 02115, USA (home). *Telephone:* (617) 262-1775 (home). *E-mail:* andrea.olmstead@gmail.com (home). *Website:* www.andreaolmstead.com; www.holyghoststheopera.com.

OLSEN, Lance, BA, MFA, MA, PhD; American writer, academic and critic; *Professor of Innovative Narrative Theory and Practice, University of Utah;* b. 14 Oct. 1956, Englewood, New Jersey; m. Andrea Hirsch 1981. *Education:* Univs of Wisconsin, Iowa and Virginia. *Career:* Prof. of Creative Writing and Contemporary Fiction, Univ. of Idaho 1996–2001; Writer-in-Residence, State of Idaho 1996–98; Fulbright Scholar, Turku, Finland 2000; Prof. of Innovative Narrative Theory and Practice, Univ. of Utah 2007–; Chair. Bd of Dirs Fiction Collective Two 2001–; Assoc. Ed., American Book Review 2006–; Fiction Ed., Western Humanities Review 2007–. *Publications:* Ellipse of Uncertainty 1987, Circus of the Mind in Motion 1990, Live From Earth 1991, William Gibson 1992, My Dates With Franz 1993, Natural Selections (poems with Jeff Worley) 1993, Scherzi I Believe 1994, Tonguing the Zeitgeist 1994, Lolita 1995, Burnt 1996, Time Famine 1996, Rebel Yell: A Short Guide to Fiction Writing 1998, Sewing Shut My Eyes 2000, Freaknest 2000, Girl Imagined By Chance 2002, Hideous Beauties 2003, 10:01 2005, Nietzsche's Kisses 2006, Anxious Pleasures: A Novel after Kafka 2007, Head in Flames 2009, Calendar of Regrets 2010; contrib. to journals and magazines. *Honours:* Fullbright Scholarship (Finland) 2000, Nat. Endowment of the Arts 2006. *Website:* www.lanceolsen.com.

OLSEN, Theodore Victor, (Joshua Stark, Christopher Storm, Cass Willoughby), BSc; American writer; b. 25 April 1932, Rhinelander, Wisconsin; m. Beverly Butler 1976. *Education:* University of Wisconsin. *Career:* mem. Western Writers of America. *Publications:* Haven of the Hunted, 1956; The Rhinelander Story, 1957; The Man from Nowhere, 1959; McGivern, 1960; High Lawless, 1960; Gunswift, 1960; Ramrod Rider, 1960; Brand of the Star, 1961; Brothers of the Sword, 1962; Savage Sierra, 1962; The Young Duke, 1963; Break the Young Land, 1964; The Sex Rebels, 1964; A Man Called Brazos, 1964; Canyon of the Gun, 1965; Campus Motel, 1965; The Stalking Moon, 1965; The Hard Men, 1966; Autumn Passion, 1966; Bitter Grass, 1967; The Lockhart Breed, 1967; Blizzard Pass, 1968; Arrow in the Sun, 1969; Keno, 1970; A Man Named Yuma, 1971; Eye of the Wolf, 1971; There Was a Season, 1973; Mission to the West, 1973; Run to the Mountain, 1974; Track the Man Down, 1975; Day of the Buzzard, 1976; Westward They Rode, 1976; Bonner's Stallion, 1977; Rattlesnake, 1979; Roots of the North, 1979; Allegories for One Man's Moods, 1979; Our First Hundred Years, 1981; Blood of the Breed, 1982; Birth of a City, 1983; Red is the River, 1983; Lazlo's Strike, 1983; Lonesome

Gun, 1985; Blood Rage, 1987; A Killer is Waiting, 1988; Under the Gun, 1989; The Burning Sky, 1991; The Golden Chance, 1992. Contributions: 20 short stories in Ranch Romances, 1956–57. *Honours:* Award of Merit, State Historical Society of Wisconsin, 1983; Western Writers of America Spur Award for Best Western Paperback Novel, 1992.

OLSON, Peter, AB, MBA, JD; American publishing executive; b. 1 May 1950, Chicago, Ill.; m. 1st (divorced); three c.; m. 2nd Candice Carpenter 2001. *Education:* Harvard Univ., Cambridge, Mass, Harvard Business School, Harvard Law School. *Career:* Assoc. Attorney, Baker & Botts (law firm), Washington, DC 1976–77; Assoc. Attorney, Hamada & Matsumoto (law firm), Tokyo, Japan 1977–79; Officer, Int. Div. Dresdner Bank, Frankfurt am Main, Germany 1979–81, Deputy Man. Corp. Business Dept, Tokyo Br. 1981–84, Man. Credit Dept, Tokyo Br. 1984–87, Vice-Pres. Planning Dept, Treasury Div., Frankfurt 1987–88; Man. Bertelsmann AG Corp. Office, Gütersloh, Germany 1988–89; Sr Vice-Pres. Doubleday Book & Music Clubs, Inc., Garden City, NY, USA 1989–90, Pres. Bertelsmann, Inc., New York, USA 1990–92; Exec. Vice-Pres. and Chief Financial Officer Bantam Doubleday Dell Publishing Group, New York 1992–94; Chair. and CEO Bertelsmann Book Group North America, New York 1994–98 (mem. Bertelsmann Book AG Exec. Bd); Chair. and CEO Random House, Inc., New York 1998–2008 (mem. Bertelsmann Book AG Exec. Bd), mem. Bd Bertelsmann AG 2001–. *Honours:* Detur Prize; Phi Beta Kappa. *Address:* c/o Random House, Inc., 1745 Broadway, New York, NY 10019, USA (office).

OLSON, Toby, BA, MA; American academic (retd), writer and poet; *Professor Emeritus, Temple University*; b. 17 Aug. 1937, Berwyn, Ill.; s. of Merle Olson and Elizabeth Skowbo; m. Miriam Meltzer Olson. *Education:* Occidental Coll., Los Angeles, Long Island Univ. *Career:* Assoc. Dir Aspen Writers' Workshop 1964–67; Asst Prof., Long Island Univ. 1966–74; Faculty, New School for Social Research, New York City 1967–75; Prof. of English, Temple Univ., Phila 1975–2000, Prof. Emer. 2000–. *Compositions:* librettos: Dorit, Chihuahua. *Publications:* fiction: The Life of Jesus 1976, Seaview 1982, The Woman Who Escaped From Shame 1986, Utah 1987, Dorit in Lesbos 1990, The Pool 1991, Reading 1992, At Sea 1993, Write Letter to Billy 2000, The Blond Box 2003, The Bitter Half 2006, Tampico 2008; poetry: Maps 1969, Worms Into Nails 1969, The Hawk-Foot Poems 1969, The Brand 1969, Pig's Book 1970, Vectors 1972, Fishing 1973, The Wrestler and Other Poems 1974, City 1974, Changing Appearances: Poems 1965–1975 1975, Home 1976, Three and One 1976, Doctor Miriam 1977, Aesthetics 1978, The Florence Poems 1978, Birdsongs 1980, Two Standards 1982, Still/Quiet 1982, Sitting in Gusevik 1983, We Are the Fire 1984, Unfinished Building 1993, Human Nature 2000, Darklight 2007; editor: Writing Talks: Views on Teaching Writing from Across the Professions (with Muffy E. A. Siegel) 1983; opera libretti: Dorit 1994, Chihuahua 1999, contribs to numerous anthologies, newspapers, and magazines. *Honours:* CAPS Award in Poetry, New York State 1974, Pennsylvania Council on the Arts Fellowship 1983, PEN/Faulkner Award for Fiction 1983, Guggenheim Fellowship 1985, Nat. Endowment for the Arts Fellowship 1985, Yaddo Fellowships 1985, 1986, Rockefeller Foundation Fellowship, Bellagio, Italy 1987, Creative Achievement Award, Temple Univ. 1990, PENN/Book Philadelphia Award for Fiction 1990. *Address:* 275 S 19th Street, Philadelphia, PA 19103 (home); Box 807, 10 Priest Street, North Truro, MA 02652, USA (home). *Telephone:* (215) 732-8296 (office); (508) 487-0882 (office). *E-mail:* toby.olson@verizon.net (office).

OLUDHE-MACGOYE, Marjorie Phyllis, BA, MA; Kenyan writer and poet; b. 21 Oct. 1928, Southampton, England; m. D. G. W. Oludhe-Macgoye 1960 (died 1990); three s. one d. *Education:* Univ. of London. *Publications:* Growing Up at Lina School (children's) 1971, Murder in Majengo (novel) 1972, Song of Nyarloka and Other Poems 1977, Coming to Birth (novel) 1986, The Story of Kenya (history) 1986, The Present Moment (novel) 1987, Street Life (novella) 1988, Victoria and Murder in Majengo 1993, Homing In (novel) 1994, Moral Issues in Kenya 1996, Chira (novel) 1997, The Black Hand Gang (children's) 1997, Make It Sing and Other Poems 1998, A Farm Called Kishinev (novel) 2005, Further Adventures of the Black Hand Gang (children's) 2005, The Black Hand Gang Grow Up (children's) 2006, The Composition of Poetry (non-fiction) 2009, Creative Writing in Prose (non-fiction) 2009; contribs to anthologies, reviews, and journals. *Honours:* BBC Arts in Africa Poetry Award 1982, Sinclair Prize for Fiction 1986, First Prize, Jomo Kenyatta Prize for Literature 2007. *Address:* PO Box 70344, Nairobi 00400, Kenya (home).

O'MALLEY, Mary; British playwright; b. 19 March 1941, Bushey, Hertfordshire, England. *Career:* Writer-in-Residence, Royal Court Theatre 1977. *Publications:* Superscum, 1972; A 'Nevolent Society, 1974; Oh If Ever a Man Suffered, 1975; Once a Catholic, 1977; Look out, Here Comes Trouble, 1978; Talk of the Devil, 1986. *Honours:* Evening Standard Award 1978.

OMOTOSO, Kole, BA, PhD; Nigerian writer. *Education:* Univ. of Ibadau, Univ. of Edinburgh, Scotland. *Career:* Lecturer, Dept of Arabic and Islamic Studies, Univ. of Ibadau, 1972–76; Senior Lecturer, Head of Dept of Dramatic Arts, Dir of the Univ. of Ife Theatre, Univ. of Ife, Ile-Ife, 1976–88; Visiting Prof., Dept of English Studies, Univ. of Stirling, Scotland, 1989–90; Visiting Prof., Dept of English, National Univ. of Lesotho Roma, Lesotho, Aug.–Dec. 1990; worked with Tawala Theatre, London, England, 1991; Prof. of English, Univ. of the Western Cape, Cape Town, 1991–2000; Second Prof. and Researcher of Drama, Univ. of Stellenbosch, 2001–. *Publications:* Fiction: The Edifice, 1972; The Combat, 1972; Just Before Dawn, 1988. Non-Fiction: The Theatrical into Theatre: A Study of Drama in the English-speaking Caribbean, 1982; Achebe or Soyinka?: A Re-interpretation and a Study in Contrasts, 1995. Other: Short story collection, plays, historical narratives. Contributions: numerous articles. *Address:* University of Stellenbosch, Private Bag XI, Matieland 7602, South Africa. *E-mail:* bankole@yebo.co.za.

ONDAATJE, Michael, OC, BA, MA; Canadian (b. Sri Lankan) writer, poet and filmmaker; b. 12 Sept. 1943, Colombo, Sri Lanka; s. of Philip Mervyn Ondaatje and Enid Doris Gratiaen; m. Linda Spalding; two s. *Education:* Dulwich Coll. London, Bishop's Univ., Queen's Univ. and Univ. of Toronto. *Career:* has taught at Univ. of Western Ontario, York Univ., Univ. of Hawaii at Manoa, Brown Univ., Univ. of Toronto; Founding Trustee, Griffin Trust For Excellence In Poetry. *Films include:* Sons of Captain Poetry 1970, Carry on Crime and Punishment 1970, The Clinton Special: A Film About The Farm Show 1974. *Publications include:* poetry: The Dainty Monsters 1967, The Man with Seven Toes 1968, The Collected Works of Billy the Kid (Gov.-Gen.'s Award) 1970, There's a Trick with a Knife I'm Learning to Do (Gov.-Gen.'s Award) 1979, Secular Love 1984, The Cinnamon Peeler 1991, Handwriting 1998; fiction: In the Skin of a Lion (City of Toronto Book Award) 1988, The English Patient (shared the Booker Prize for Fiction, Gov.-Gen.'s Award) 1992, Running in the Family 1993, The Collected Works of Billy the Kid 1996, Coming Through Slaughter 1996, Anil's Ghost (Prix Médicis, Giller Prize, Gov.-Gen.'s Award, Kiriyama Pacific Rim Book Prize) 2000, The Conversations 2004, The Story 2005, Divisadero (Gov.-Gen.'s Literary Award) 2007, Divisadero 2008, The Cat's Table 2011. *Honours:* Foreign Hon. mem., American Acad. of Arts and Letters. *Address:* c/o Trident Media Group LLC, 41 Madison Avenue, 36th Floor, New York, NY 10010, USA; 2275 Bayview Avenue, Toronto, ON N4N 3M6, Canada.

ONDERDONK, Andrew Bruce, BA, MS, PhD; American medical scientist and academic; *Editor-in-Chief, Journal of Clinical Microbiology*; b. 5 July 1947, Hartfod, Conn.; m. Juliet Onderdonk; one s. two d. *Education:* MacMurray Coll., Univ. of Missouri. *Career:* Prof. of Pathology, Harvard Medical School; Dir of Clinical Microbiology, Channing Lab. at Brigham and Women's Hosp.; Pres. Int. Soc. for Anaerobic Bacteria; Ed.-in-Chief, Journal of Clinical Microbiology. *Television:* programme on Lyme Disease, NBC Today Show 1986. *Publications:* 20 book chapters, three medical educ. movies, three patents and more than 160 peer-reviewed publs. *Honours:* Hon. MS (Harvard); Distinquished Alumni Award, MacMurray Coll., Phalen Award, Crohn's and Colitis Foundation of America. *Address:* Journal of Clinical Microbiology, American Society for Microbiology, 1752 N Street NW, Washington, DC 20036-2904, USA (office). *Telephone:* (617) 732-7372 (office). *Fax:* (617) 731-1541 (office). *E-mail:* aonderdonk@partners.org (office); onderdonk@aol.com (home). *Website:* jcm.asm.org (office).

O'NEILL, Joseph, BA; Irish writer and barrister; b. 23 Feb. 1964, Cork; m. Sally Singer 1994. *Education:* Girton College, Cambridge. *Career:* barrister 1990–. *Publications:* This is the Life 1991, The Breezes 1995, Blood-Dark Track 2001, Netherland (PEN/Faulkner Award for Fiction 2009) 2008; contributions: reviews and articles in TLS, Spectator, Literary Review. *Address:* c/o Pantheon Publicity, Random House, 1745 Broadway, New York NY 10019, USA (office). *Website:* www.randomhouse.com/pantheon (office).

O'NEILL, Michael Stephen Charles, BA, DPhil; British academic, writer, poet and editor; *Professor of English, University of Durham*; b. 2 Sept. 1953, Aldershot, Hants., England; m. Rosemary Ann McKendrick 1977; one s. one d. *Education:* Exeter Coll., Oxford. *Career:* Lecturer, Univ. of Durham 1979–91, Sr Lecturer 1991–93, Reader 1993–95, Prof. of English 1995–, Head, Dept of English 1997–2000, 2002–05, Dir, Inst. of Advanced Study 2006–12; Co-founder and Ed. Poetry Durham 1982–94; Fellow, English Asscn 2000–. *Publications:* The Human Mind's Imaginings: Conflict and Achievement in Shelley's Poetry 1989, Percy Bysshe Shelley: A Literary Life 1989, The Stripped Bed (poems) 1990, Auden, MacNeice, Spender: The Thirties Poetry (with Gareth Reeves) 1992, Percy Bysshe Shelley (ed.) 1993, The 'Defence of Poetry' Fair Copies (ed.) 1994, Keats: Bicentenary Readings (ed.) 1997, Fair-Copy Manuscripts of Shelley's Poems in American and European Libraries (co-ed. with Donald H. Reiman) 1997, Romanticism and the Self-Conscious Poem 1997, Literature of the Romantic Period: A Bibliographical Guide (ed.) 1998, Shelley: The Major Works (co-ed. with Zachary Leader) 2003, A Routledge Literary Sourcebook on the Poems of W. B. Yeats (ed.) 2004, Romanticism: Critical Concepts (four vols) (co-ed. with Mark Sandy) 2006, The All-Sustaining Air: Romantic Legacies and Renewals in British, American and Irish Poetry Since 1900 2007, Dante Rediscovered: From Blake to Rodin (with David Bindman and Stephen Hebron) 2007, Romantic Poetry: An Annotated Anthology (co-ed. with Charles Mahoney) 2007, Wheel (Poems) 2008, Thinking About Almost Everything (co-ed. with Ash Amin) 2009, The Cambridge History of English Poetry (ed.) 2010, Twentieth-Century British and Irish Poetry (co-ed. with Madeleine Callaghan) 2011; contribs to books and journals. *Honours:* Eric Gregory Award 1983, Cholmondeley Award for Poets 1990. *Address:* Department of English Studies, University of Durham, Hallgarth House, 77 Hallgarth Street, Durham, DH1 3AY, England (office). *E-mail:* m.s.oneill@durham.ac.uk (office).

O'NEILL, Paul; Canadian author; b. 26 Oct. 1928, St John's, NF. *Education:* National Acad. of Theatre Arts, New York. *Career:* mem. Canadian Authors Asscn; Canadian Radio Producers Asscn; Newfoundland and Labrador Arts Council, chair., 1988–89; Newfoundland Writers Guild; Writers Union of Canada. *Publications:* Spindrift and Morning Light, 1968; The City in Your Pocket, 1974; The Oldest City, 1975; Seaport Legacy, 1976; Legends of a Lost

Tribe, 1976; Breakers, 1982; The Seat Imperial, 1983; A Sound of Seagulls, 1984; Upon This Rock, 1984. Other: Radio and stage plays; Television and film scripts. Contributions: many periodicals. *Honours:* Literary Heritage Award, Newfoundland Historical Society; Robert Weaver Award, National Radio Producers Asscn of Canada, 1986; Hon. Doctor of Laws, Memorial University of Newfoundland, 1988; Order of Canada, 1990; Newfoundland and Labrador Arts Hall of Honour, 1991; Canada Commemorative Medal, 1992.

O'NEILL, Robert John, AO, MA, BE, DPhil, FASSA; Australian historian, academic and army officer (retd); *Honorary Professor, University of Sydney*; b. 5 Nov. 1936, Melbourne, Vic.; s. of Joseph Henry O'Neill and Janet Gibbon O'Neill; m. Sally Margaret Burnard 1965; two d. *Education:* Scotch Coll. Melbourne, Royal Mil. Coll. of Australia, Melbourne Univ., Brasenose Coll. Oxford. *Career:* served in Australian army 1955–68, Fifth Bn Royal Australian Regt, Vietnam (despatches) 1966–67, Maj. 1967–68 (resgnd); Rhodes scholar, Vic. 1961; Official Australian Historian for the Korean War 1969–82; Head of Strategic and Defence Studies Centre, ANU 1971–82; Dir IISS, London 1982–87, Chair. Council 1996–2001; Chichele Prof. of the History of War, Univ. of Oxford 1987–2001; Dir Grad. Studies Modern History Faculty, Oxford 1990–92; Fellow, All Souls Coll. Oxford 1987–2001; Sr Fellow in Int. Relations, ANU 1969–77, Professorial Fellow 1977–82; Trustee, Imperial War Museum 1990–2001, Deputy Chair. 1996–98, Chair. 1998–2001; Gov. Ditchley Foundation 1989–2001, Int. Peace Acad. 1990–2001; Chair. Bd Centre for Defence Studies and Bd Centre for Australian Studies, Univ. of London 1990–95; Chair. Council of Australian Strategic Policy Inst. 2001–05; Deputy Chair., Grad. School of Govt, Univ. of Sydney 2001–05, Planning Dir, US Studies Centre 2006–07; Dir The Shell Transport and Trading Co. 1992–2002 and two mutual funds of Capital Group, LA 1992–, The Lowy Inst. 2001–; mem. Advisory Bd Investment Co. of America 1988–2010; mem. Commonwealth War Graves Comm. 1990–2001, The Rhodes Trust 1995–2001; Fellow, Australian Inst. of Int. Affairs 2008. *Publications:* The German Army and the Nazi Party 1933–39 1966, Vietnam Task 1966, General Giap: politician and strategist 1969, (ed.) The Strategic Nuclear Balance 1975, (ed.) The Defence of Australia: fundamental new aspects 1977, (ed.) Insecurity: the spread of weapons in the Indian and Pacific Oceans 1978, (co-ed.) Australian Dictionary of Biography Vols 7–12, 1891–1939, 1979–91, (co-ed.) New Directions in Strategic Thinking 1981, Australia in the Korean War 1950–53: Vol. I Strategy and Diplomacy 1981, Vol. II Combat Operations 1985, (co-ed.) Australian Defence Policy for the 1980s 1982, (ed.) Security in East Asia 1984, (ed.) The Conduct of East–West Relations in the 1980s 1985, (ed.) New Technology and Western Security Policy 1985, (ed.) Doctrine, the Alliance and Arms Control 1986, (ed.) East Asia, the West and International Security 1987, (ed.) Security in the Mediterranean 1989, (co-ed.) The West and the Third World 1990, (co-ed.) Securing Peace in Europe 1945–62 1992, (co-ed.) War, Strategy and International Politics 1992, Alternative Nuclear Futures 1999; articles in numerous journals. *Honours:* Hon. Fellow, Brasenose Coll. Oxford; Hon. Col 5th (V) Bn, The Royal Greenjackets 1993–99; mentioned in despatches, Viet Nam 1967; Hon. DLitt (ANU) 2001. *Address:* The Lowy Institute for International Affairs, 31 Bligh Street, Sydney, NSW 2000, Australia (office). *E-mail:* director@lowyinstitute.org (office). *Website:* www .lowyinstitute.org (office).

ONG, Han; Philippine playwright and novelist; b. 1968. *Career:* moved to USA 1984–. *Plays:* The LA Plays: In A Lonely Country and A Short List of Alternate Places (Almeida, London) 1993, Middle Finger 2001, The Suitcase Trilogy 2006. *Publications:* Fixer Chao (novel) 2001, The Disinherited (novel) 2004. *Honours:* MacArthur Fellowship 1997, Guggenheim Fellowship 2005. *Literary Agent:* c/o Susan Bergholz Literary Services, 17 West 10th Street #5, New York, NY 10011, USA.

ONWUEME, Osonye Tess, (Tess Akaeke Onwueme, Tess Osonye Onwueme); Nigerian dramatist, novelist and academic; b. 8 Sept. 1955; m. Obika Gray 1998; two s. three d. *Education:* BA, Education, 1979, MA, Literature, 1982, University of Ife; PhD, African Drama, University of Benin, 1988. *Career:* Lecturer, University of Ife, 1980–82; Asst Prof., Federal University of Technology, Owerri, 1982–87; Assoc. Prof. and Head, Performing Arts Dept, Imo State University, 1986–88; Assoc. Prof., Montclair State University, NJ, 1990–92, Wayne State University, Detroit, 1990–98; Prof. of English and Africana Studies, Vassar College, 1992–93; Distinguished Prof. of Cultural Diversity and Prof. of English, University of Wisconsin at Eau Claire, 1994–; mem. African Literature Asscn; African Studies Asscn; Asscn of Nigerian Authors; International Women Playwrights Asscn; Organization of Women Writers of African Descent; PEN International. *Publications:* A Hen Too Soon, 1983; The Broken Calabash, 1984; The Desert Encroaches, 1985; Ban Empty Barn, 1986; A Scent of Onions, 1986; Mirror for Campus, 1987; The Reign of Wazobia, 1988; Legacies, 1989; Riot in Heaven, 1996; The Missing Face, 1997; Tell it to Women, 1997; Shakara: Dance Hall Queen, 2000; Why the Elephant Has No Butt, 2000; Then She Said It: An Epic Drama, 2002; What Mama Said, 2003. Contributions: periodicals. *Honours:* Drama Prizes, Asscn of Nigerian Authors, 1985, 1995, 2001; Distinguished Authors Award, Ife International Bookfair, 1988; Ford Foundation Award, 2000. *Literary Agent:* Kimberly Crank, 1019 Huebsh Street, Eau Claire, WI 54701, USA. *Address:* c/o Dept of English, University of Wisconsin at Eau Claire, Eau Claire, WI 54701, USA.

ONYEAMA, Charles Dillibe Ejiofor; Nigerian publisher, writer and journalist; *CEO, Delta Publications (Nigeria) Limited*; b. 6 Jan. 1951, Enugu; s. of Judge Charles Dadi Onyeama and Susannah Uzoamaka Onyeama; m. 1st Ethel Ekwueme 1984; four s.; m. 2nd Nneka Okwu; two d. *Education:* Eton Coll. and Premier School of Journalism, London, UK (Diploma in Journalism). *Career:* mem. Bd of Dirs Star Printing and Publishing Co. Ltd 1992–94; Man. Dir Delta Publications (Nigeria) Ltd; Pres. Delta Book Club 1981–; Chair. Asscn of Nigerian Authors, Enugu chapter 2003–05; mem. Local Govt Caretaker Cttee, Udi, Enugu State 1994–96. *Publications:* Nigger at Eton 1972, John Bull's Nigger 1974, Sex is a Nigger's Game 1975, The Book of Black Man's Humour 1975, I'm the Greatest 1975, Juju 1976, Secret Society 1977, Revenge of the Medicine Man 1978, The Return 1978, Night Demon 1979, Female Target 1980, The Rules of the Game 1980, The Story of an African God 1982, Modern Messiah 1983, Godfathers of Voodoo 1985, African Legend 1985, Correct English 1986, Beauty & Hair Care (ed.) 1986, Notes of a So-Called Afro-Saxon 1988, A Message to My Compatriots 1997, The Boomerang 1998, The Joys of African Humour 2000, The New Man 2002, The Joys of Ibo Humour 2003, And The Last Shall Be First 2006, Anti-Christ 2008; contrib. to Books and Bookmen, Spectator, The Times, Daily Express, Sunday Express, Drum, West Africa, Roots, The Guardian, Evening News. *Honours:* Most Outstanding Publr of the Year Award 2010. *Address:* 8B Byron Onyeama Close, New Haven, PO Box 1172, Enugu, Enugu State, Nigeria (home). *Telephone:* (802) 8862786 (home). *E-mail:* dillibeonyeama@yahoo.com (home); thefirstliterature@yahoo.com (home).

ONYEFULU, Ifeoma, DipMan.; British/Nigerian author and photographer; b. 30 March 1959, Onitsha; two s. *Education:* Seven Sisters Coll., London. *Photographic exhibitions:* Hornimann Museum 2001, Bristol Museum 2006, Liverpool Museum 2006. *Publications:* A is for Africa 1993, Emeka's Gift 1994, Chidi Only Likes Blue 1997, One Big Family 1996, My Grandfather is a Magician 1998, Ebele's Favourite 1999, A Triangle for Adaora 2000, And Saying Goodbye 2001, Welcome Dede 2003, Here Comes the Bride 2004, African Christmas 2005, Ikenna Goes to Nigeria 2007. *Honours:* Notable Book Award (USA), Children's Africana Book Award 2005, Children's African Book Award 2008. *Address:* 15 Bickerton Road, London, N19 5JU, England (home). *E-mail:* onyefulu_ifeoma@hotmail.com (office). *Website:* www.ifeomaonyefulu .co.uk.

OOKA, Makoto; Japanese poet, writer and academic; b. 16 Feb. 1931, Mishima City; s. of Hiroshi Ooka and Ayako Ooka; m. Kaneko Aizawa 1957; one s. one d. *Education:* Tokyo Nat. Univ. *Career:* journalist with Yomiuri (newspaper), foreign news section 1953–63; Asst Prof., Meiji Univ., Tokyo 1965–70, Prof. 1970–87; Pres. Japan Poets' Asscn 1979–81; Prof., Nat. Univ. for Fine Arts and Music 1988–93; Soshitsu Sen XV Distinguished Lecturer in Japanese Culture and Visiting Fellow, Donald Keene Center of Japanese Culture, Columbia Univ. 2000; Pres. Japan PEN Club 1989–93; mem. Int. Advisory Bd of Poetry Int., Rotterdam; mem. Japan Art Acad. 1995–. *Publications:* poetry: Memories and the Present 1956, For a Girl in Springtime 1978, City of Water 1981, Odes to the Waters of my Hometown 1989, The Afternoon in the Earthly Paradise 1992, The Last Will of Fire 1995; Criticism: The Banquet and the Solitary Mind, Aesthetics of Japanese Poetry 1978; English translations: Japanese Poetry; Past and Present, A Poet's Anthology 1979–, an anthological series for the newspaper Asahi, A String Around Autumn 1982, A Play of Mirrors: Eight Major Poets of Modern Japan (co-ed) 1987, Elegy and Benediction 1991, The Colours of Poetry – Essays on Classic Japanese Verse 1991, What the Kite Thinks, a linked poem with three American poets 1994, The Range of Japanese Poetry 1994, Beneath the Sleepless Tossing of the Planets 1995, The Poetry and Poetics of Ancient Japan 1997, Love Songs from the Man'yoshu: Selections from a Japanese Classic 2000; French translations: Poèmes de tous les jours 1993, Propos sur le vent et autres poèmes 1995, Poésie et Poétique du Japon Ancien 1995, Dans l'Océan du Silence 1998, Citadelle de Lumière 2002. *Honours:* Officier des Arts et Lettres; Order of Cultural Merit 2003; Yomiuri Prize for Literature, Kikuchi Kan Prize, Hanatsubaki Prize for Poetry, Golden Wreath Prize, Struga Poetry Evenings Macedonia 1996, Asahi Prize 1996, Japanese Art Acad. Imperial Award 1996, Person of Cultural Merit 1997, Japan Foundation Prize 2002. *Address:* 2-18-1-2606, Iidabashi, Chiyoda-ku, Tokyo 102-0072, Japan.

OPIE, Iona Margaret Balfour, CBE, FBA; British writer and folklorist; b. 13 Oct. 1923, d. of the late Sir Robert Archibald and Olive Cant; m. Peter Mason Opie 1943 (died 1982); two s. one d. *Education:* Sandecotes School (Parkstone). *Career:* served with meteorological section of Women's Auxiliary Air Force (WAAF) 1941–43; writer and folklorist 1947–; Hon. mem. Folklore Soc. 1974. *Publications:* I Saw Esau (jtly) 1947, The Oxford Dictionary of Nursery Rhymes (jtly) 1951, The Oxford Nursery Rhyme Book (jtly) 1955, Christmas Party Games (jtly) 1957, The Lore and Language of Schoolchildren (jtly) 1959, Puffin Book of Nursery Rhymes (jtly, European Prize City of Caorle, Italy) 1963, Children's Games in Street and Playground (jtly, Chicago Folklore Prize) 1969, The Oxford Book of Children's Verse (jtly) 1973, The Classic Fairy Tales (jtly) 1974, A Nursery Companion (jtly) 1980, The Oxford Book of Narrative Verse 1983, The Singing Game (Katharine Briggs Folklore Award, Rose Mary Crawshay Prize, Children's Literature Asscn Book Award) 1985, Tail Feathers From Mother Goose 1988, The Treasures of Childhood (co-ed) 1989, A Dictionary of Superstitions 1989, Babies: an unsentimental anthology (jtly) 1990, The People in the Playground 1993, My Very First Mother Goose 1996, Here Comes Mother Goose 1999. *Honours:* Hon. MA (Oxon) 1962, (Open) 1987, Hon. DLitt (Southampton) 1987, (Nottingham) 1991 Jt recipient Coote-Lake Medal 1960. *Address:* Mells House, Farnham Road, West Liss, Hants. GU33 6JQ, England (home). *Telephone:* (1730) 893309 (home).

O'REILLY, Kenneth, BA, MA, PhD; American historian and writer; b. 24 Oct. 1951, New York, NY; m. Maureen Alice Moore 1976, three s. *Education:* University of Detroit, Central Michigan University, Marquette University. *Career:* Prof. of History, University of Alaska, Anchorage, 1983–; Writer. *Publications:* Hoover and the Un-Americans: The FBI, HUAC, and the Red Menace, 1983; 'Racial Matters': The FBI's Secret File on Black America, 1960–1972, 1989; Black Americans: The FBI Files, 1994; Nixon's Piano: Presidents and Racial Politics from Washington to Clinton, 1995. *Address:* 18728 Snowy Plover, Anchorage, AK 99516, USA.

ORFALEA, Gregory Michael, AB, MFA; American academic; *Assistant Professor and Director, Center for Writing, Pitzer College*; b. 9 Aug. 1949, Los Angeles, Calif.; m. Eileen Rogers 1984; three s. *Education:* Georgetown University, University of Alaska. *Career:* Reporter, Northern Virginia Sun, 1971–72; Prof., Santa Barbara City College, Calif., 1974–76; Ed., Political Focus, 1979–81, Small Business Administration, 1985–91, Resolution Trust Corporation, 1991–95, Federal Deposit Insurance Corporation, 1995–96, Comptroller of the Currency, 1996–97, Freddie Mac, 1997–, Substance Abuse and Mental Health Services 1998–2004; Asst Prof. and Dir Center for Writing, Pitzer Coll. 2004–; mem. American PEN. *Publications:* Before the Flames, 1988; The Capital of Solitude, 1988; Grape Leaves, 1988; Imagining America: Stories of the Promised Land, 1991; Messengers of the Lost Battalion, 1997, Up All Night 2004, The Arab Americans 2005. Contributions: Washington Post; TriQuarterly; Cleveland Plain-Dealer; Christian Science Monitor, Los Angeles Times. *Honours:* California Arts Council Award, 1976; American Middle East Peace Research Award, 1983; District of Columbia Commission on the Arts and Humanities Awards, 1991, 1993. *Address:* Pitzer College, 1050 N Mills Avenue, Claremont, CA 91711, USA (office). *Telephone:* (909) 607-3766 (office). *Fax:* (909) 607-7880 (office). *E-mail:* gregory-orfalea@pitzer.edu (office). *Website:* www.pitzer.edu (office).

ORGEL, Doris, BA; American children's writer; b. (Doris Adelberg), 15 Feb. 1929, Vienna, Austria; m. Shelley Orgel 1949; two s. one d. *Education:* Barnard College. *Career:* Sr Staff Writer, Ed., Publications and Media Group, Bank Sheer College of Education 1961–. *Publications include:* Sarah's Room 1963, The Devil in Vienna 1978, My War with Mrs Galloway 1985, Whiskers Once and Always 1986, Midnight Soup and a Witch's Hat 1987, Starring Becky Suslow 1989, Nobodies and Somebodies 1991, Next Time I Will 1993, The Mouse Who Wanted To Marry 1993, Ariadne, Awake 1994; young adult fiction: Risking Love 1985, Crack in the Heart 1989; other: some 30 works; contributions: cricket magazine. *Address:* 140 East 81th Street, Apartment 11B, New York, NY 10028-1876, USA (home).

O'RIORDAN, Marie, BA, MA; British magazine editor; b. 1960, Dublin, Ireland. *Education:* Univ. Coll., Dublin. *Career:* fmr Ed. More!; Ed. Elle magazine 1996–99; Group Publishing Dir EMAP Elan 1999–2001; Ed. Marie Claire 2001–08. *Honours:* EMAP Editor of the Year 1996, IPC Editor of the Year 2003. *Address:* c/o Marie Claire, European Magazines Ltd, 13th Floor, King's Reach Tower, Stamford Street, London, SE1 9LS, England (office).

ORLANDERSMITH, Dael; American playwright and performer; b. Harlem, NY. *Stage appearances:* Macbeth, Romeo and Juliet, Raisin in the Sun, Goin' for Dolo, US, European and Australian tours with the Nuyorican Poets' Cafe, Leftover Life to Kill (solo show). *Plays written:* Beauty's Daughter (Obie Award) 1993, Liar Liar 1994, Monster, The Gimmick 1997, Yellowman 2002. *Publications:* Lone Dancer Underground (novel). *Honours:* OBIE Award 1994, New York Foundation for the Arts Fellowship, Helen Merrill Award for Emerging Playwrights, Whiting Writers' Award 2008. *Literary Agent:* c/o Judy Boals, 307 West 38th Street, Suite 812, New York, NY 10001, USA. *Telephone:* (212) 500-1424. *Fax:* (212) 500-1426. *E-mail:* info@judyboals.com. *Website:* www.judyboals.com. *Address:* c/o Random House Inc, 1745 Broadway, Third Floor, New York, NY 10019, USA. *Website:* www.randomhouse.com.

ORLEAN, Susan; American author and journalist; b. 31 Oct. 1955, Cleveland, Ohio; m.; one s. *Education:* Univ. of Michigan. *Career:* fmr staff writer, Williamette Week, Portland, Ore., Boston Phoenix; fmr contrib. Boston Globe Sunday Magazine; staff writer, New Yorker 1992–; Nieman Fellow, Harvard Univ. 2003. *Publications include:* Red Sox and Bluefish 1987, Saturday Night 1990, The Orchid Thief 1998, The Bullfighter Checks Her Makeup: My Encounters with Extraordinary People 2001, My Kind of Place: Travel Stories from a Woman Who's Been Everywhere 2004, Throw Me a Bone (co-author) 2007, Lazy Little Loafers 2008, Rin Tin Tin: the Life and the Legend 2011, Animalish 2011; as ed.: Best American Essays 2005, Best American Travel Writing 2007; contrib. Esquire, Rolling Stone, Vogue, Spy, Outside. *Literary Agent:* c/o Richard Pine, InkWell Management, 521 Fifth Avenue, 26th Floor, New York, NY 10175, USA. *Telephone:* (212) 922-3500. *Fax:* (212) 922-0535. *E-mail:* Richard@inkwellmanagement.com. *Website:* www.inkwellmanagement.com; susanorlean.com.

ORLEDGE, Robert Francis Nicholas, MA, PhD; British academic, author, editor and orchestrator; *Professor Emeritus of Music, University of Liverpool*; b. 5 Jan. 1948, Bath, Somerset. *Education:* Assoc., Royal Coll. of Organists 1964; Clare Coll., Cambridge; Univ. of Cambridge. *Career:* Prof. of Music, Univ. of Liverpool –2004, Prof. Emer. 2004–; mem. Royal Musical Assn, Centre de Documentation Claude Debussy, Asscn des Amis de Charles Koechlin, Fondation Erik Satie. *Music:* completion and orchestration of Debussy's opera The Fall of the House of Usher and Debussy's ballet No-ja-li ou Le Palais du Silence. *Publications:* Gabriel Fauré 1979, Debussy and the Theatre 1982, Charles Koechlin (1867–1950): His Life and Works 1989, Satie the Composer 1990, Satie Remembered 1995; contrib. to Music and Letters, Musical Quarterly, Musical Times, Music Review, Current Musicology, Journal of the Royal Musical Association. *Address:* 6 Dorset Gardens, Brighton, BN2 1RL, England (home). *Telephone:* (1273) 698384 (home). *E-mail:* robertorledge@aol.com (home).

ORMEROD, Roger; British author; b. 17 April 1920, Wolverhampton, Staffordshire, England. *Publications:* Time to Kill, 1974; The Silence of the Night, 1974; Full Fury, 1975; A Spoonful of Luger, 1975; Sealed with a Loving Kill, 1976; The Colour of Fear, 1976; A Glimpse of Death, 1976; Too Late for the Funeral, 1977; The Murder Come to Mind, 1977; A Dip into Murder, 1978; The Weight of Evidence, 1978; The Bright Face of Danger, 1979; The Amnesia Trap, 1979; Cart Before the Hearse, 1979; More Dead than Alive, 1980; Double Take, 1980; One Breathless Hour, 1981; Face Value, 1983; Seeing Red, 1984; The Hanging Doll Murder, 1984; Dead Ringer, 1985; Still Life with Pistol, 1986; A Death to Remember, 1986; An Alibi Too Soon, 1987; The Second Jeopardy, 1987; An Open Window, 1988; By Death Possessed, 1988; Guilt on the Lily, 1989; Death of an Innocent, 1989; No Sign of Life, 1990; Hung in the Blance, 1990; Farewell Gesture, 1990.

ORMESSON, Comte Jean d'; French writer, journalist and international official; b. 16 June 1925, s. of Marquis d'Ormesson; nephew of late Comte Wladimir d'Ormesson; m. Françoise Béghin 1962; one d. *Education:* Ecole Normale Supérieure. *Career:* Deputy Sec.-Gen. Int. Council for Philosophy and Humanistic studies (UNESCO) 1950–71, Sec.-Gen. 1971; staff of various Govt ministers 1958–66; Deputy Ed. Diogène (int. journal) 1952–72, mem. Man. Cttee 1971–; mem. Council ORTF 1960–62, Programme Cttee 1973; mem. Control Comm. of Cinema 1962–69; mem. Editorial Cttee Editions Gallimard 1972–74; Ed.-in-Chief, Columnist, Le Figaro 1974–77, Dir-Gen. 1976, leader writer, columnist 1977–; mem. Acad. Française 1973; Pres., Soc. des amis de Jules Romains 1974–. *Publications:* L'amour est un plaisir 1956, Du côté de chez Jean 1959, Un amour pour rien 1960, Au revoir et merci 1966, Les illusions de la mer 1968, La gloire de l'empire (Grand Prix du Roman (Acad. Française) 1971, Au plaisir de Dieu 1974, Le vagabond qui passe sous une ombrelle trouée 1978, Dieu, sa vie, son oeuvre 1981, Mon dernier rêve sera pour vous 1982, Jean qui grogne et Jean qui rit 1984, Le vent du soir 1985, Tous les hommes en sont fous 1985, Bonheur à San Miniato 1987, Garçon de quoi écrire (jtly.) 1989 (prix de Mémorial 1990), Histoire du juif errant 1991, Tant que vous penserez à moi, entretien avec Emmanuel Berl 1992, La Douane de mer 1994, Presque rien sur presque tout 1996, Casimir mène la grande vie 1997, Une autre histoire de la littérature française 1997, Le rapport Gabriel (Prix Jean Giono) 1999, Voyez comme on danse 2001, C'était bien 2003, Une Fête en Larmes 2005, La Création du Monde 2006, Odeur du Temps 2007, La Vie ne Suffit Pas 2007, Qu'ai-je donc fait 2008, Saveur du Temps 2009; numerous articles in Le Figaro, Le Monde, France-Soir, Paris Match, etc. *Honours:* Officier, Légion d'honneur, Commdr des Arts et Lettres, Officier, Ordre nat. du Mérite, Chevalier des Palmes académiques. *Address:* 10 avenue du Parc-Saint-James, 92200 Neuilly-sur-Seine, France (home). *Telephone:* 1-46-24-27-92 (home).

ORMSBY, Frank, BA, MA; Northern Irish poet, writer and editor; b. 30 Oct. 1947, Enniskillen, Co. Fermanagh. *Education:* Queen's Univ., Belfast. *Career:* Ed., The Honest Ulsterman 1969–89. *Publications:* A Store of Candles 1977, Poets from the North of Ireland (ed.) 1979, A Northern Spring 1986, Northern Windows: An Anthology of Ulster Autobiography (ed.) 1987, The Long Embrace: Twentieth Century Irish Love Poems (ed.) 1987, Thine in Storm and Calm: An Amanda McKittrick Ros Reader (ed.) 1988, The Collected Poems of John Hewitt (ed.) 1991, A Rage for Order: Poetry of the Northern Ireland Troubles (ed.) 1992, The Ghost Train 1995, The Hip Flask: Short Poems from Ireland (ed.) 2000, The Blackbird's Nest: An Anthology of Poetry from Queen's University Belfast (ed.) 2006, John Hewitt: Selected Poems (ed. with Michael Longley) 2007, Fireflies 2009. *Address:* 33 North Circular Road, Belfast, BT15 5HD, Northern Ireland (home).

O'ROURKE, Patrick Jake, BA, MA; American writer and editor; b. 14 Nov. 1947, Toledo, OH; m. 1st Amy Lumet 1990 (divorced 1992); m. 2nd Christina Mallon 1995; one s. two d. *Education:* Miami Univ., Oxford, OH, Johns Hopkins Univ., Baltimore, Md. *Career:* writer, National Lampoon 1972–81, Ed.-in-Chief 1978–81; Correspondent, Rolling Stone 1985–2001, Atlantic Monthly 2001–. *Publications:* Modern Manners 1983, The Bachelor Home Companion 1987, Republican Party Reptile 1987, Holidays in Hell 1989, Parliament of Whores 1991, Give War a Chance 1992, All the Trouble in the World 1994, Age and Guile 1995, Eat the Rich 1998, The CEO of the Sofa 2001, Peace Kills (essays) 2004, On 'The Wealth of Nations' 2007, Driving Like Crazy 2009, Don't Vote: It Just Encourages the Bastards 2010; contribs to periodicals. *Address:* c/o Atlantic Monthly, 77 N Washington Street, Boston, MA 02114, USA.

ORR, Gregory Simpson, BA, MFA; American academic, poet and writer; *Professor of English, University of Virginia*; b. 3 Feb. 1947, Albany, NY; m. Trisha Winer 1973; two d. *Education:* Antioch Coll., Columbia Univ. *Career:* Asst Prof., Univ. of Virginia 1975–80, Assoc. Prof. 1980–88, Prof. of English 1988–; Poetry Consultant, Virginia Quarterly Review 1976–78, Poetry Ed. 1978–2003; Visiting Writer, University of Hawaii at Manoa 1982. *Publications:* poetry: Burning the Empty Nests 1973, Gathering the Bones Together 1975, Salt Wings 1980, The Red House 1980, We Must Make a Kingdom of It 1986, New and Selected Poems 1988, City of Salt 1995, Orpheus and Eurydice

2001, The Caged Owl: New and Selected Poems 2002, Concerning the Book that is the Body of the Beloved 2005, How Beautiful the Beloved 2009; non-fiction: Stanley Kunitz: An Introduction to the Poetry 1985, Richer Entanglements: Essays and Notes on Poetry and Poems 1993, Poetry as Survival 2002, The Blessing (memoir) 2002. *Honours:* Acad. of American Poets Prize 1970, YM-YWHA Discovery Award 1970, Bread Loaf Writers Conference Transatlantic Review Award 1976, Guggenheim Fellowship 1977, National Endowment for the Arts Fellowships 1978, 1989, Fulbright Grant 1983, Literature Award, American Acad. of Arts and Letters 2003. *Address:* Department of English, University of Virginia, 431 Bryan Hall, PO Box 400121, Charlottesville, VA 22904-4121, USA (office). *Telephone:* (434) 924-6668 (office). *E-mail:* gso@virginia.edu (office). *Website:* www.engl.virginia.edu (office).

ORSENNA, Erik (see Arnoult, Erik)

ORSZÁG-LAND, Thomas, (Thomas Land); Hungarian/British poet and foreign correspondent; b. 12 Jan. 1938, Budapest, Hungary. *Career:* mem. Foreign Press Asscn, Royal Inst. of Int. Affairs, Soc. of Authors; Fellow, International PEN. *Publications:* Berlin Proposal 1990, Free Women 1991, Tales of Matriarchy 1998; translations: Bluebeard's Castle, by Balázs/Bartók 1988, Splendid Stags, by Bartók 1992, 33 Poems by Radnoti 1992, Holocaust Testimony, by Mezei 1995; contribs to newspapers and reviews. *Address:* PO Box 1213, London, N6 5HZ, England (office). *E-mail:* thomland111@hotmail.com (office).

ORTIZ, Simon Joseph; American poet and writer; b. 27 May 1941, Albuquerque, NM; m. Marlene Foster 1981 (divorced 1984); three c. *Education:* Fort Lewis College, University of New Mexico, University of Iowa. *Career:* Instructor, San Diego State University, 1974, Institute of American Arts, Santa Fe, New Mexico, 1974, Navajo Community College, Tsaile, AZ, 1975–77, College of Marin, Kentfield, CA, 1976–79, University of New Mexico, Albuquerque, 1979–81, Sinte Gleska College, Mission, SD, 1985–86, Lewis and Clark College, Portland, Oregon, 1990; Consulting Ed., Navajo Comunity College Press, Tsaile, 1982–83; Pueblo of Acoma Press, Acoma, New Mexico, 1982–84; Arts Co-ordinator, Metropolitan Arts Commission, Portland, Oregon, 1990. *Publications:* Naked in the Wind (poems), 1971; Going for the Rain (poems), 1976; A Good Journey (poems), 1977; Howbah Indians (short stories), 1978; Song, Poetry, Language (essays), 1978; Fight Back: For the Sake of the People, For the Sake of the Land (poems and prose), 1980; From Sand Creek: Rising in This Heart Which is Our America (poems), 1981; A Poem is a Journey, 1981; The Importance of Childhood, 1982; Fightin': New and Collected Stories, 1983; Woven Stone: A 3-in-1 Volume of Poetry and Prose, 1991; After and Before the Lightning (poems), 1994. Editor: Califa: The California Poetry (co-ed.), 1978; A Ceremony of Brotherhood (co-ed.), 1980; Earth Power Coming (anthology of Native American short fiction), 1983. Contributions: various anthologies and textbooks. *Honours:* National Endowment for the Arts Discovery Award, 1969, and Fellowship, 1981; Honored Poet, White House Salute to Poetry and American Poets, 1980; New Mexico Humanities Council Humanitarian Award for Literary Achievement, 1989.

OSBORN, Karen, BA, MFA; American novelist and poet; b. 26 April 1954, Chicago, IL; m. Michael Jenkins 1983; two d. *Education:* Hollins College, University of Arkansas at Fayetteville. *Career:* poet, Arkansas Poetry in the Schools 1979–83, Dir 1982–83; Instructor of English, Clemson University, 1983–87; part-time Instructor of English, University of Kentucky 1988–93; various workshops and readings. *Publications:* Patchwork, 1991; Between Earth and Sky, 1996; The River Road, 2003. Contributions: numerous anthologies, including: Jumping Pond: Poems and Stories from the Ozarks; Cardinal: A Contemporary Anthology; Hollins Anthology; Poems to numerous periodicals, including: Artemis; Mid American Review; Seattle Review; Tar River Poetry; Embers; Southern Review; Kansas Quarterly; Poet Lore; Passages North; Montana Review; Centennial Review; Wisconsin Review. *Honours:* Hollins Literary Festival Awards for Poetry, for Fiction, 1979; Nancy Thorp Prize for Poetry, 1979; Mary Vincent Long Award, Distinguished Literary Achievement, 1979; Kentucky Foundation for Women Grant, 1991; Al Smith Artists Fellowship Award for Fiction, Kentucky Arts Council, 1991; New York Times Notable Book, 1991.

OSBORNE, Charles Thomas, FRSL; Australian/British writer, critic and poet; *Opera Critic, Jewish Chronicle*; b. 24 Nov. 1927, Brisbane, Qld; partner, Kenneth Thomson 2006. *Education:* Griffith Univ., studied with Archie Day, Irene Fletcher, Vido Luppi and Browning Mummery. *Career:* Asst Ed., London Magazine 1957–66; Asst Literary Dir, Arts Council of GB 1966–71, Literary Dir 1971–86; Opera Critic, Jewish Chronicle 1985–; Chief Theatre Critic, Daily Telegraph 1986–92; mem. Editorial Bd Opera magazine; mem. Critics' Circle, PEN. *Publications:* The Gentle Planet 1957, Opera 66 1966, Swansong 1968, The Complete Operas of Verdi 1969, Letters of Giuseppe Verdi (ed.) 1971, The Concert Song Companion 1974, Wagner and his World 1977, The Complete Operas of Mozart 1978, W. H. Auden: The Life of a Poet 1980, The Dictionary of Opera 1983, Letter to W. H. Auden and Other Poems 1984, Giving It Way 1986, The Operas of Richard Strauss 1988, The Complete Operas of Richard Wagner 1990, The Bel Canto Operas of Rossini, Donizetti and Verdi 1994, The Pink Danube 1998, The Opera Lover's Companion 2004; contribs to anthologies, newspapers and journals, including Opera, London Magazine, Spectator, Times Literary Supplement, Encounter, New Statesman, Observer, Sunday Times. *Honours:* Hon. DUniv.; Gold Medal 1993. *Address:* 125 St George's Road, London, SE1 6HY, England (home). *Telephone:* (20) 7928-1534 (home). *Fax:* (20) 7401-9099 (home).

OSBORNE, Margaret (Maggie) Ellen; American writer; b. 10 June 1941, Los Angeles, CA; m. George M. Osborne II 1972, one s. *Publications:* Alexa, 1980; Salem's Daughter, 1981; Portrait in Passion, 1981; Yankee Princess, 1982; Rage to Love, 1983; Flight of Fancy, 1984; Castles and Fairy Tales, 1986; Winter Magic, 1986; The Heart Club, 1987; Where There's Smoke, 1987; Chase the Heart, 1987; Heart's Desire, 1988; Dear Santa, 1989; Partners (with Carolyn Bransford), 1989; Jigsaw, 1990; American Pie, 1990; Lady Reluctant, 1991; Emerald Rain, 1991; Happy New Year Darling, 1992; Murder By the Book, 1992; The Pirate and His Lady, 1992; Cache Poor, 1993; A Wish and a Kiss, 1993; The Accidental Princess, 1994; The Drop in Bride, 1994; The Wives of Bowie Stone, 1994; Silver Lining, 2000; I Do, I Do, I Do, 2000.

OSBORNE, Mary Pope, BA; American writer; b. 20 May 1949, Fort Sill, OK; m. Will Osborne 1976. *Education:* University of North Carolina. *Career:* mem. Pres., Authors' Guild Inc., 1993–97. *Publications:* Run, Run, As Fast As You Can, 1982; Love Always, Blue, 1983; Best Wishes, Joe Brady, 1984; Mo to the Rescue, 1985; Last One Home, 1986; Beauty and the Beast, 1987; Christopher Columbus, Admiral of the Ocean Sea, 1987; Pandora's Box, 1987; Jason and the Argonauts, 1988; The Deadly Power of Medusa (with Will Osborne), 1988; Favorite Greek Myths, 1989; A Visit to Sleep's House, 1989; Mo and His Friends, 1989; American Tall Tales, 1990; Moonhorse, 1991; Spider Kane Series, 1992; Magic Tree House Series 1993–2004; Mermaid Tales, 1993; Molly and the Prince, 1994; Haunted Waters, 1994; Favourite Norse Myths, 1996; One World, Many Religions, 1996; Rockinghorse Christmas, 1997; Favourite Medieval Tales, 1998; Standing in the Light, 1998; The Life of Jesus, 1998, Adaline Falling Star 2000, My Secret War 2001, My Brother's Keeper 2001, After the Rain 2001, Kate and the Beanstalk 2001, The Brave Little Seamstress 2002, New York's Bravest 2002, Happy Birthday, America 2003, Tales from the Odyssey Series 2002–2005. *Honours:* Distinguished Alumnus Award, University of North Carolina, 1994. *Literary Agent:* Brandt & Hochman Literary Agents Inc., 1501 Broadway, New York, NY 10036, USA.

OSHINSKY, David M., PhD; American historian and writer; *Professor and Jack S. Blanton Chair in History*, *University of Texas at Austin*. *Education:* Brandeis Univ., Cornell Univ. *Publications:* non-fiction: Senator Joseph McCarthy and the American Labor Movement 1976, A Conspiracy So Immense: The World of Joe McCarthy (Hardeman Prize) 1983, The Case of the Nazi Professor (with R. P. McCormic) 1989, Worse Than Slavery: Parchman Farm and the Ordeal of Jim Crow Justice (Robert Kennedy Prize) 1997, American Passages: A History of the United States, two vols (jtly) 1999, Polio: An American Story (Pulitzer Prize 2006) 2005, The Oxford Companion to United States History (co-ed.); contrib. to New York Times, Washington Post, Chronicle of Higher Education. *Address:* Department of History, University of Texas at Austin, 1 Univ Sta B7000, Austin, TX 78712-0220, USA (office). *Telephone:* (512) 475-7230 (office). *E-mail:* oshinsky@mail.utexas.edu (office). *Website:* www.utexas.edu/cola/depts/history (office).

O'SIADHAIL, Micheal, BA, MLitt; Irish poet and writer; b. 12 Jan. 1947, Dublin; m. Brid Carroll 1970. *Education:* Trinity Coll., Dublin, Univ. of Oslo, Norway. *Career:* Lecturer, Trinity Coll., Dublin 1969–73; Prof., Dublin Inst. for Advanced Studies, 1974–87; Visiting Prof., Univ. of Iceland 1982; Ed. Poetry Ireland Review 1989–91; mem. Ireland's Advisory Cttee on Cultural Relations 1990–97; Founder-mem. Aosdána 1982–; mem. Arts Council of Ireland 1988–93, Bd Dublin Int. Writers' Festival; Founder-Chair. Ireland Literary Exchange 1992–99. *Publications:* poetry: Springnight 1983, The Image Wheel 1985, The Naked Flame (song cycle) 1987, The Chosen Garden 1990, Hail! Madam Jazz: New and Selected Poems 1992, Summerfest (song cycle) 1993, A Fragile City 1995, Our Double Time 1998, Poems 1975–1995 1999, Earlsfort Suite (three poems) 2000, The Gossamer Wall: Poems in Witness to the Holocaust 2002, Dublin Spring (song cycle) 2002, Love Life 2005, Globe 2007, At Night a Song is with Me (cycle of ballads and psalms) 2010, Tongues 2010; other: Learning Irish 1980, Modern Irish 1989. *Honours:* Irish-American Cultural Prize for Poetry 1982, Poetry Book of the Year, Sunday Tribune 1992, Marten Toonder Prize for Literature 1998, Wingate Jewish Quarterly Literary Award Special Recommendation 2003. *Address:* 5 Trimleston Avenue, Booterstown, Co. Dublin, Ireland (home). *Website:* www.osiadhail.com.

OSONDU, E. C., MFA; Nigerian writer. *Education:* Syracuse Univ. *Career:* fmr advertising copywriter in Lagos; moved to New York to study; fmr Lecturer in English and Creative Writing, Univ. of Maryland; currently Asst Prof. of English, Providence Coll., Rhode Island 2009–. *Publications:* short stories include: A Letter from Home 2006, Jimmy Carter's Eyes, Waiting (Caine Prize for African Writing 2009), Voice of America 2010; contrib. to Gods and Soldiers: The Penguin Anthology of Contemporary African Writing 2009, Africa's Best Stories, and magazines including Agni, Guernica, Vice, Fiction, The Atlantic. *Honours:* Allen and Nirelle Galso Prize for Fiction. *Address:* Department of English, Providence College, Phillips Memorial Library, Room LL10, Providence, RI 02918-0001, USA (office). *Telephone:* (401) 865-2467 (office). *E-mail:* eosondu@providence.edu (office). *Website:* www.providence.edu (office).

OSPINA, William; Colombian writer, poet and translator; b. 1954, Padua, Tolima; s. of Luis Ospina Ismenia Buitrago; one d. *Education:* Universidad Santiago de Cali. *Career:* Founding mem. and contrib., Número magazine 1993–. *Publications:* non-fiction: Aurelio Arturo 1991, Es tarde para el hombre 1994, Esos extraños prófugos de Occidente 1994, Los dones y los méritos 1995, Un álgebra embrujada 1996, Dónde está la franja amarilla? 1997, Las auroras de sangre 1999, Los Nuevos Centros de la esfera (Premio de Ensayo Ezequiel Martínez Estrada de Casa de la Américas 2003) 2001, La Decadencia de los dragones 2002, América mestiza 2004, La Escuela de la Noche 2008, En busca de Bolivar 2010; poetry: Hilo de Arena 1986, La Luna del Dragón 1992, El País del Viento 1992, Con quién habla Virginia caminando hacia el agua? 1995, África 1999, Poesía 1974–2004 2007; fiction: Ursúa 2005, El País de la Canela (Premio Rómulo Gallegos 2009) 2008. *Honours:* Hon. DH (Latinoamericana Univ., Medellín) 1999, (Universidad del Tolima) 2005, Dr hc (Universidad Santiago de Cali) 2009; Premio Nacional de Poesía, Instituto Colombiano de Cultura 1992, Premio de Ensayo Ezequiel Martínez Estrada. Casa de las Américas. La Habana. 2002 Premio Internacional de Novela Romulo Gallegos 2009. *Address:* Número, Carrera 19B, No. 85-40, Bogotá, Colombia (office). *Telephone:* (1) 635-8012 (office). *Fax:* (1) 635-8013 (office). *E-mail:* numero@revistanumero.com (office). *Website:* www.revistanumero.com (office).

OSTEN, Suzanne Carlota; Swedish playwright and theatre and film director; b. 20 June 1944, Stockholm; d. of Carl Otto Osten and Gud Osten; m.; one d. *Education:* Lund Univ. *Career:* started directing while a student 1963; ran Fickteatern fringe theatre group performing in schools, prisons, public areas, etc. 1967–71; joined City Theatre, Stockholm 1971; f. and Artistic Dir, Unga Klara Stadsteatern ind. repertory co. 1975–; has written and directed over 30 plays, numerous radio and TV productions; began directing films 1980; Prof. of Directing, Dramatic Inst., Stockholm 1995–. *Plays:* as writer and dir: Medea's Children 1975, The Haga-Princesses 1976, The Hunt for Snores 1976, Lazarillo 1977, Prince Carefree 1977, The Children from Mount Frostmo 1978, The Pork Horses 1981, The Frontier 2000; as dir: The Vampire 1975, The Sweaty Tiger 1978, Unga Klara tells Life 1982, The Smile of Hades 1982, A Clean Girl 1983, Hitler's Childhood 1 1984, Hitler's Childhood 2 1984, The Danton Affair 1986, Everybody – But Me 1987, The Toad Aquarium 1988, In the Summer House 1988, R 1990, The Piggle 1991, The Dolphin 1992, Preparation for Suicide 1994, Mirad 1994, Money 1994, Lilacs 1914 1996, Irina's New Life 1996, The Girl, the Mother and the Trash 1998, Difficult People 1999, Time of Darkness 2002, The Main Thing 2002. *Films include:* Ei inspelat, Mamma 1982, Bröderna Mozart (Guldbagge Award for Direction 1986) 1986, Livsfarlig film 1988, Skyddsängeln 1990, Tala det är så mörkt 1992, Bara du och jag 1994, Bengbulan 1996, Besvärliga Människor 2001. *Honours:* Nat. Theatre Critics Prize 1982, Paris-Creteil Prize 1993, Expressens Theatre Prize 2002, Assitej Int. Prize 2002, Berns Prize, Swedish PEN 2002, numerous other awards and prizes. *Address:* Unga Klara, Stockholms Stadsteater, Box 16412, 103 27 Stockholm, Sweden (office). *Telephone:* (8) 506-20-100 (office). *E-mail:* maja.svae@stadsteatern.stockholm.se (office). *Website:* www.stadsteatern.stockholm.se (office); www.suzanneosten.nu.

OSTLER, Catherine; British journalist and editor; *Editor, Tatler*; m. Albert Read. *Education:* St Hilda's Coll., Oxford. *Career:* asst, restaurant and travel sections, then Features Ed., Tatler 1991–94; Features Writer, Mail on Sunday 1994–96; Ed., Saturday Express magazine 1996–99; Ed., weekend section, The Times 1999–2000; Ed., peoplenews.com 2000; Features Writer, Daily Mail 2001–02; Ed., ES Magazine, London Evening Standard 2002–09; Ed., Tatler 2009–. *Address:* Tatler, Condé Nast Publications, Vogue House, Hanover Square, London, W1S 1JU, England (office). *Telephone:* (20) 7499-9080 (office). *Fax:* (20) 7409-0451 (office). *Website:* www.tatler.co.uk (office).

OSTRIKER, Alicia Suskin, BA, MA, PhD; American academic, poet and writer; *Faculty Member, New England College Poetry MFA Program*; b. 11 Nov. 1937, New York, NY; d. of David Suskin and Beatrice Suskin; m. Jeremiah P. Ostriker 1958; one s. two d. *Education:* Brandeis Univ., Univ. of Wisconsin. *Career:* Asst Prof., Rutgers Univ. 1965–68, Assoc. Prof. 1968–72, Prof. of English and Creative Writing 1972–2004; mem. Faculty, New England Coll. low-residency Poetry MFA Program 2004–; mem. Modern Language Asscn, PEN, Bd Govs Poetry Soc. of America 1988–91. *Publications:* poetry: Songs 1969, Once More Out of Darkness and Other Poems 1974, A Dream of Springtime: Poems, 1970–77 1978, The Mother-Child Papers 1980, A Woman Under the Surface 1983, The Imaginary Lover 1986, Green Age 1989, The Crack in Everything 1996, The Little Space: Poems Selected and New 1968–1998 1998, The Volcano Sequence 2002, No Heaven 2005; criticism: Vision and Verse in William Blake 1965, Writing Like a Woman 1982, Stealing the Language 1986, Feminist Revision and the Bible 1993, The Nakedness of the Fathers: Biblical Visions and Revisions 1994, Dancing at the Devil's Party: Essays on Poetry, Politics and the Erotic 2000, For the Love of God: The Bible as an Open Book 2007; contrib. to professional journals and general publs. *Honours:* National Endowment for the Arts Fellowship 1977, Guggenheim Fellowship 1984–85, William Carlos Williams Prize, Poetry Society of America 1986, Strousse Poetry Prize, Prairie Schooner 1987, Anna Rosenberg Poetry Award 1994, Paterson Poetry Prize 1996, San Francisco State Poetry Center Award 1997, Bookman News Book of the Year 1998, Reader's Choice Award, Prairie Schooner 1998, Larry Levis Prize, Prairie Schooner 2002. *Address:* 33 Philip Drive, Princeton, NJ 08540, USA (home). *E-mail:* ostriker@rci.rutgers.edu (home).

OSTROM, Hans Ansgar, BA, MA, PhD; American academic, writer and poet; b. 29 Jan. 1954, Grass Valley, Calif.; m. Jacquelyn Bacon 1983; one s. *Education:* University of California, Davis. *Career:* Faculty mem., University of California, Davis 1977–80, 1981–83; Visiting Lecturer in American Studies, Johannes Gutenberg University, Mainz 1980–81; Prof. of English, University of Puget Sound, Tacoma, Washington 1983–; Fulbright Senior Lecturer, University of Uppsala 1994; mem. American Asscn of University Profs, Conference on College Composition and Communication, MLA, National Book Critics Circle, National Council of Teachers of English. *Publications:* The Living Language: A Reader (co-ed.), 1984; Leigh Hunt: A Reference Guide (with Tim Lulofs), 1985; Spectrum: A Reader (co-ed.), 1987; Lives and Moments: An Introduction to Short Fiction, 1991; Three to Get Ready (novel), 1991; Langston Hughes: A Study of the Short Fiction, 1993; Colors of a Different Horse (ed. with Wendy Bishop), 1994; Water's Night (poems with Wendy Bishop), 1994; Genres of Writing: Mapping the Territories of Discourse (ed. with Wendy Bishop), 1997; The Coast Starlight (poems), 1998; contributions: books, journals, reviews, and magazines. *Honours:* First Prize, Harvest Awards, University of Houston, 1978; Grand Prize, Ina Coolbrith Memorial Award, 1979; First Prize, Warren Eyster Competition, New Delta Review, 1985; Second Prize, Redbook Magazine Annual Fiction Contest, 1985; John Lantz Fellowship, University of Puget Sound, 1996–97.

O'SULLIVAN, John, CBE, BA; British editor and journalist; *Executive Editor, Radio Free Europe / Radio Liberty*; b. 25 April 1942, Liverpool; s. of Alfred M. O'Sullivan and Margaret (née Corner) O'Sullivan; m. Melissa Matthews O'Sullivan. *Education:* Queen Mary Coll., Bedford Coll., Univ. of London. *Career:* jr tutor, Swinton Conservative Coll. 1965–67, Sr Tutor 1967–69; Conservative parl. cand. 1970; Ed. Swinton Journal 1967–69; London Corresp. Irish Radio and TV 1970–72; editorial writer and parl. sketchwriter, Daily Telegraph 1972–79; Ed. Policy Review 1979–83; Asst Ed. Daily Telegraph 1983–84; columnist, The Times 1984–86, Assoc. Ed. 1986–87; Editorial Page Ed. New York Post 1984–86; Ed.-in-Chief Nat. Review 1988–97, Ed.-at-Large 1998–; columnist, Sunday Telegraph 1988–, Independent on Sunday 1990–91; Editorial Consultant, Hollinger 1998–2001; Ed.-in-Chief, United Press International 2001–04; Ed., The National Interest 2004–06; Exec. Ed. Radio Free Europe/Radio Liberty 2008–; Dir of Studies Heritage Foundation 1979–83; Special Adviser to the Prime Minister 1987–88; Founder, Co-Chair. The New Atlantic Initiative 1996–; mem. Exec. Advisory Bd Margaret Thatcher Foundation, Advisory Council Social Affairs Unit, Hon. Bd Civic Inst., Prague; Fellow Inst. of Politics, Harvard Univ. 1983. *Publication:* The President, the Pope, and the Prime Minister: Three Who Changed the World. *Honours:* Hon. LLB (Lewis and Clark Coll.).

O'SULLIVAN, Sally Angela, BA; British magazine editor; b. 26 July 1949, d. of Lorraine and Joan Connell; m. 1st Thaddeus O'Sullivan 1973 (divorced); m. 2nd Charles Wilson 1980 (divorced); one s. one d. *Education:* Ancaster House School and Trinity Coll. Dublin. *Career:* Deputy Ed. Woman's World 1977–78; Women's Ed. Daily Record 1980, Sunday Standard 1981; Ed. Options 1982–88; Launch Ed. Country Homes & Interiors 1986; Ed. She 1989, Harpers & Queen 1989–91, Good Housekeeping 1991–95; Ed.-in-Chief Ideal Home, Homes and Ideas, Women and Home, Homes and Gardens, Country Homes and Interiors, Beautiful Homes, Living, etc. magazines 1996–98; Chief Exec. Cabal Communications 1998–2003; Editorial Dir Highbury House PLC 2003–06; Chair. August Media 2005–; Dir (non-exec.) London Transport 1995–2001, Anglian Water 1996–2001; mem. Broadcasting Standards Council 1994–, Nuffield Council of Bioethics 1995–99; Gov. Univ. of East London 2004–. *Honours:* Magazine Ed. of the Year 1986, 1994. *Address:* August Media, Zetland House, Scrutton Street, London, EC2A 4HJ, England (office). *Telephone:* (20) 7749-3300 (office). *Website:* www.augustmedia.com (office).

O'SULLIVAN, Vincent Gerard, BLitt, MA; New Zealand poet, writer, dramatist and editor; b. 28 Sept. 1937, Auckland. *Education:* University of Auckland, Lincoln College, Oxford. *Publications:* In Quiet, 1956; Opinions: Chapters on Gissing, Rolfe, Wilde, Unicorn, 1959; Our Burning Time, 1965; Revenants, 1969; An Anthology of Twentieth Century New Zealand Poetry (ed.), 1970; Bearings, 1973; New Zealand Poetry in the Sixties, 1973; Katherine Mansfield's New Zealand, 1975; New Zealand Short Stories (ed.), 1975; From the Indian Funeral, 1976; James K. Baxter, 1976; Miracle: A Romance, 1976; Butcher & Co, 1977; The Boy, the Bridge, the River, 1978; Brother Jonathan, Brother Kafka, 1980; Dandy Edison for Lunch and Other Stories, 1981; The Rose Ballroom and Other Poems, 1982; The Butcher Papers, 1982; The Oxford Book of New Zealand Writing Since 1945 (ed. with MacDonald P. Jackson), 1983; The Collected Letters of Katherine Mansfield (ed. with Margaret Scott), three vols, 1984–96; Shuriken (play), 1985; Survivals, 1986; The Pilate Tapes, 1986; Poems of Katherine Mansfield (ed.), 1988; Jones and Jones (play), 1989; Billy, 1990; The Snow in Spain, 1990; Palms and Minarets: Selected Stories, 1992; Selected Poems, 1992; The Oxford Book of New Zealand Short Stories (ed.), 1994; Believers to the Bright Coast, 1998. *Honours:* Jessie Mackay Award, 1965; Farmers Poetry Prize, 1967; New Zealand Book Award, 1981.

OSWALD, Debra; Australian playwright and writer; two s. *Education:* Australian Nat. Univ., Australian Film and Television School. *Plays:* Going Under 1983, Dags 1986, Lumps 1993, Gary's House 1996, Sweet Road 2000, Mr Bailey's Minder (Griffin Award, Queensland Premier's Literary Award for Drama) 2004, The Peach Season (Seaborn Playwright's Prize) 2007, Stories in the Dark 2007. *Writing for television:* Police Rescue, Palace of Dreams, Bananas in Pyjamas, Sweet and Sour, Dancing Daze, The Secret Life of Us. *Publications include:* juvenile fiction: Me and Berry Terrific 1987, The Return of the Baked Bean 1990, Nathan and the Ice Rockets 1998, Frank and the Emergency Joke 2000, The Redback Leftovers 2000, The Fifth Quest 2002, Frank and the Secret Club 2005, Getting Air 2007. *Literary Agent:* RGM Associates, PO Box 128, Surry Hills, NSW 2010, Australia. *Telephone:* (2) 9281-3911. *Fax:* (2) 9281-4705. *E-mail:* info@rgm.com.au. *Website:* www.rgm.com.au.

OTCHAKOVSKY-LAURENS, Paul, LenD; French publisher; *President Director-General, Editions P.O.L.*; b. 10 Oct. 1944, Valreas, Vaucluse; s. of Zelman Otchakovsky and Odette Labaume; adopted s. of Berthe Laurens; m. Monique Pierret 1970; one s. one d. *Education:* Coll. and Lycée de Sablé sur Sarthe, Coll. Montalembert de Courbevoie, Coll. St Croix de Neuilly and Faculté de Droit, Paris. *Career:* Reader, Editions Christian Bourgois 1969–70; Dir of Collection, Editions Flammarion 1970–77; Dir of Collections, then Dir of Dept Editions Hachette 1977–82; Pres. Dir-Gen. Editions P.O.L. 1983–. *Films:* Sablé-sur-Sarthe, Sarthe 2007. *Honours:* Commdr, Ordre des Arts et des Lettres, Chevalier, Légion d'honneur. *Address:* Editions P.O.L., 33 rue Saint-André-des-Arts, 75006 Paris, France (office). *Telephone:* 1-43-54-21-20 (office). *E-mail:* otchakov@pol-editeur.fr (office). *Website:* www.pol-editeur.com (office).

OTOIU, Adrian, PhD; Romanian writer and poet; *Lecturer in English and American Literature, North University of Baia Mare*. *Education:* Baia Mare Coll. of Arts, Baia Mare Univ., Babes-Bolyai Univ., Cluj-Napoca. *Career:* school teacher Oradea 1981–87; children's theatre instructor 1987–1990, teacher of English Baia Mare 1990–92; Asst Lecturer North Univ. of Baia Mare 1992–95, Lecturer in English and American Literature 1995–; has participated in numerous conferences, seminars and symposia worldwide; numerous grants; mem. Writers' Union of Romania, European Soc. for the Study of English, Asscn of Professional Writers of Romania (ASPRO). *Publications:* Coaja lucrurilor sau Dansînd cu Jupuita (novel, The Skin of the Matter or Dancing with the Flayed) (Writers' Union of Romania Award for Debut in Prose, ASPRO Best Book of the Year, The Typewriter Nat. Award, Baia Mare City Council Book of the Year) 1996, Chei fierbinti pentru ferestre moi (short stories, Hot Keys for Soft Windows) (Maramures Co. Council Book of Fiction) 1998, Tourism in Maramures (co-author) 1998, Stingacii si enormitati (short stories, Enormities and Left-handed Stuff) 1999, Trafic de frontiera (critical essay, Frontier Traffic) 2000, Ochiul bifurcat, limba sasie (critical essay, The Forked Eye, the Squinting Tongue) 2003, Under Eastern Eyes: Cross-Cultural Refractions (essays) 2003; translation: At Swim-Two-Birds by Flann O'Brien (Ireland Literature Exchange Translation Bursary) 2005; contrib. to anthologies, journals and magazines. *Address:* Universitatea de Nord din Baia Mare, Catedra de Limbi Moderne, 430083 Baia Mare, Maramures, str. Victorei, nr. 76, Romania (office). *Telephone:* (262) 276305 (office). *Fax:* (262) 275436 (home). *E-mail:* decanat-litere@ubm.ro (office); litereunbm@yahoo.com (office). *Website:* litere.ubm.ro.

OTOMO, Katsuhiro; Japanese animator and manga artist; b. 14 April 1954, Tome-gun, Miyagi Pref.; m. Yoko Otomo. *Education:* Sanuma High School. *Career:* following high school, moved to Tokyo to work in manga industry, wrote short strips for Action comics, including Prosper Merimee's short novel Mateo Falcone (retitled A Gun Report) 1973; began Fireball series (unfinished) introducing themes that later became his trademark 1979; serialization of Domu (A Child's Dream) graphic novel was his first major success, selling over half a million copies 1980–82, won Science Fiction Grand Prix 1983 (first ever manga recipient); began work on his masterpiece Akira which took 10 years and over 2,000 pages to complete, animated film version released in 1988 (greatest box office success in Japan that year). *Films:* genre filmography: Koko Erotopia: Akai seifuku (scriptwriter) 1979, Shuffle (comic strip Run) 1981, Jiyu o warera (dir) 1982, Crusher Joe (special character designer) 1983, Harmagedon: Genam taisen (Armageddon: The Great Battle with Genma) (animator, character designer) 1983, Meikyu monogatari (Labyrinth Tales) (segment scriptwriter, dir and character designer) 1987, Roboto kanibauru (segment dir) 1987, Akira (scriptwriter, dir) 1988, Akira Production Report (performed as himself) 1988, Fushigi monogatari: Hachi neko wa yoku asagata kaette kuru (scriptwriter) 1988, Rojin Z (Oldman Z) (scriptwriter) 1991, Warudo apaatoment hora (World Apartment Horror) (dir) 1991, Memories (exec. producer, scriptwriter, dir, art dir) 1995, Perfect Blue (supervisor) 1997, Spriggan (gen. supervisor) 1998, Metoroporisu (Metropolis) (scriptwriter, storyboard artist) 2001, Animax Special: The Making of Metropolis (performed as himself) 2002, Steamboy (dir) 2004, Mushishi (scriptwriter and dir) 2006; non-genre filmography: Give Us Guns (dir) 1981, So What (scriptwriter) 1988. *Address:* c/o Toho Co. Ltd, 1-2-1 Yurako-cho, Chiyoda-ku, Tokyo 100-8415, Japan (office).

.OTSUKA, Julie, MFA; American author; b. 15 May 1962, Palo Alto, Calif. *Education:* Yale Univ., Columbia Univ. *Career:* initially worked as a painter; began writing fiction aged 30; writing contribs include Powells.com, Granta, Harper's. *Publications include:* When the Emperor Was Divine 2003, The Buddha in the Attic (PEN/Faulkner Award for Fiction 2011) 2012. *Literary Agent:* c/o Nicole Aragi, Aragi Inc., 143 West 27th Street, #4F, New York, NY 10001, USA. *Telephone:* (215) 675-8353. *E-mail:* queries@aragi.net. *Website:* www.aragi.net; www.julieotsuka.com.

OTTEN, Charlotte Fennema, AB, MA, PhD; American academic (retd), poet and writer; b. 1 March 1926, Chicago; m. Robert T. Otten 1948; two s. *Education:* Calvin College, Michigan State University. *Career:* Assoc. Prof. of English, Grand Valley State University, Allendale, Michigan 1971–77; Lecturer on Women and Literature, University of Michigan Extension Center 1972; Prof. of English, Calvin College, Grand Rapids 1977–91; mem. Milton Society of America, MLA, Shakespeare Asscn of America, Society for Literature and Science, Society for Textual Scholarship, Society of Children's Book Writers and Illustrators. *Publications:* Environ'd with Eternity: God, Poems, and Plants in Sixteenth and Seventeenth Century England 1985, A Lycanthropy Reader: Werewolves in Western Culture 1986, The Voice of the Narrator in Children's Literature (ed. with Gary D. Schmidt) 1989, English Women's Voices 1540–1700 1992, The Virago Book of Birth Poetry 1993, The Book of Birth Poetry 1995, January Rides the Wind 1997, The Literary Werewolf: An Anthology 2002, Something Sweeter than Honey 2002, Home in a Wildermere Fort 2006; contrib. to scholarly books and journals and poetry journals. *Honours:* several grants and fellowships; Editors' Choice, Booklist 1997. *Address:* c/o Department of English, Calvin College, 3201 Burton Street, SE, Grand Rapids, MI 49546, USA (office).

OUELLETTE, (Marie Léonne) Francine, DFA; Canadian writer; b. 11 March 1947, Montréal, Québec; one d. *Career:* mem. Union des écrivaines et des écrivains québécois, Asoc. des écrivains de langue Française. *Publications:* Au Nom du Père et du Fils 1984, Le Sorcier 1985, Sire Gaby du Lac 1989, Les Ailes du Destin 1992, Le Grand Blanc 1993, L'Oiseau Invisible 1994, Bip: Fantasie Philosophique 2001, Feu: La Rivière Profanée Vol. 1 2004, Feu: L'Etranger Vol. 2 2005, Feu: Fleur d'Lys Vol. 3 2007. *Honours:* France-Québec, Jean Hamelin 1986, Prix, Du Grand Public 1993, Signet d'Or 2003. *Address:* PO Box 30, 1044 ch Presquîle, Lac des Iles, QC J0W 1J0, Canada. *Telephone:* (819) 597-2597 (home). *Fax:* (819) 597-2597 (home).

OUOLOGUEM, Yambo, (Utto Rodolph), DScS; Malian writer and poet; b. 1940, Bandiagary, Dogon, French Sudan (now Mali). *Career:* teacher, Lycée de Charenton, Paris 1964–66. *Publications:* Le Devoir de violence (Bound to Violence), 1968; Lettre ouverte à la France-nègre, 1969; Les Milles et un bibles du sexe (as Utto Rodolph), 1969; Terres du Soleil (with others), 1971. Contributions: Nouvelle somme. *Honours:* Prix Théophraste-Renaudot 1968.

OUŘEDNÍK, Patrik; Czech poet and author; b. 23 April 1957, Prague. *Career:* fmr bookseller, warehouseman, postman and medical orderly; moved to France 1984; fmr reader Robert Laffont publishing house; Visiting Lecturer on Czech Literature, Univs of Toulouse, Rennes, Carcassonne 1988–93; literary ed. L'Autre Europe (quarterly) 1986–. *Publications include:* Šmírbuch jazyka českého: Slovník nekonvenční češtiny (non-fiction, Rough-book of the Czech Language: A Dictionary of Unconventional Czech) 1988, Anebo (poems) 1992, Aniž jest co nového pod sluncem: Slova, rčení a úsloví biblického původu (non-fiction, No New Thing Under the Sun: Words, Phrases and Sayings of Biblical Origin) 1994, Pojednání o případném pití vína (Treatise on the appropriate drinking of wine) 1995, Rok čtyřiadvacet (novel, Year Twenty-Four) 1995, Neřkuli (poems, Let Alone) 1996, Europeana: Stručné dějiny dvacátého věku (novel, Europeana: A brief history of the 20th century) (Lidové Noviny Book of the Year) 2001; also translations of works of François Rabelais, Samuel Beckett and others; contrib. to Encyclopaedia Universalis, Dictionnaire des auteurs, Dictionnaire des oeuvres littéraires. *Honours:* Czech Literary Fund Award.

OUTERS, Jean-Luc; Belgian writer; b. 5 March 1949. *Publications:* L'ordre du jour (novel) 1987, Avec le temps (essay) 1993, Corps de métier (novel) 1993, La place du mort (novel) 1995, La compagnie des eaux (novel) 2001, Le bureau de l'heure (novel) 2004, Le Voyage de Luca (novel) 2008, Lettres du plat pays (correspondance with Kristien Hemmerechts) 2010; contrib. to numerous articles in Le Soir, La Libre Belgique, Libération, Le Monde. *Honours:* Prix Rossel 1993, Prix AT&T 1995, Prix Rossel des Jeunes 2008. *Address:* Actes Sud, BP 38, 13633 Arles Cedex, France (home). *E-mail:* jean-luc.outers@cfwb.be (office).

OUTRAM, Richard Daley, BA; Canadian poet and publisher; b. 9 April 1930, Oshawa, Ont.; m. Barbara Howard 1957. *Education:* Victoria Coll., Univ. of Toronto. *Career:* co-founder (with Barbara Howard), The Gauntlet Press 1959; reading and exhibition of published work, Nat. Library of Canada 1986; mem. PEN Canada, Arts and Letters Club of Toronto. *Publications:* Eight Poems, 1959; Exsulate, Jubilate, 1966; Creatures, 1972; Seer, 1973; Thresholds, 1974; Locus, 1974; Turns and Other Poems, 1975; Arbor, 1976; The Promise of Light, 1979; Selected Poems 1960–1980, 1984; Man in Love, 1985; Benedict Abroad, 1988; Hiram and Jenny, 1989; Mogul Recollected, 1993; Around and About the Toronto Islands, 1993; Peripatetics, 1994; Tradecraft, 1994; Eros Descending, 1995. *Honours:* City of Toronto Book Award 1999. *Address:* 226 Roslin Avenue, Toronto, ON M4N 1Z6, Canada.

OVADIA, Salomone (Moni); Italian playwright, singer and actor; *Artistic Director, Mittelfest*; b. 1946, Plovdiv, Bulgaria. *Education:* Milan Univ. *Career:* fmr mem. of band, Almanacco Popolare; founder mem., Gruppo Folk Internazionale 1972; founder mem., Theather Orchestra 1990–; Artistic Dir, Mittelfest, Cividale del Friuli 2004–. *Stage productions include:* Oylem Goylem 1990, Dybbuk 1995, Taibele e il suo demone 1995, Diario ironico dall'esilio 1995, Ballata di fine millennio 1996, Pallida madre, tenera sorella 1996, Il Caso Kafka 1997, Trieste, ebrei e dintorni 1998, Mame, mamele, mamma, mamà... 1998, Joss Rakover si rivolge a Dio 1999, Il Banchiere errante 2001, L'Armata a cavallo 2003. *Publications:* Perché no? 1996, Oylem Goylem 1998, L'ebreo che ride 1998, La porta di sion 1999, Ballata di fine millennio 1999, Speriamo che tenga 2001, Le Baladin du monde yiddish 2002, Vai a te stesso 2002, Contro l'idolatria 2005, Lavoratori di tutto il mondo ridete 2007. *Address:* c/o Oylem Goylem Produzioni, via Savona 52, 20154 Milan, Italy (office). *E-mail:* oylemgoylem@tiscali.it. *Website:* www.moniovadia.it.

OVALDÉ, Véronique; French novelist; b. 1972. *Publications:* novels: Le Sommeil des poissons 2000, Toutes choses scintillant 2002, Les hommes en général me plaisent beaucoup 2003, Déloger l'animal 2005, La Très Petite Zébuline (with Joëlle Jolivet) 2006, Et mon cœur transparent (Prix France Culture/Télérama 2008) 2008, Ce que je sais de Vera Candida (Prix Renaudot des Lycéens 2009, Prix France Télévisions 2009, Grand Prix des lectrices de Elle 2010) 2009, La Salle de bains du Titanic 2009, Des vies d'oiseaux 2011; novels have been translated into numerous languages, including Italian, Spanish, German, Romanian, Portuguese, English, Korean, Chinese and Finnish. *Address:* c/o Éditions de l'Olivier, 96 boulevard du Montparnasse, 75014 Paris, France. *Telephone:* 1-41-48-84-76. *Website:* www .editionsdelolivier.fr.

OVENDEN, Graham Stuart, MA, ARCA, ARCM; British art historian, artist and poet; b. 11 Feb. 1943, Alresford, Hants.; s. of the late Henry Ovenden and Gwendoline D. Hill; m. Ann D. Gilmore 1969; one s. one d. *Education:* Alresford Dames School, Itchen Grammar School, Southampton, Southampton Coll. of Art, Royal Coll. of Music and Royal Coll. of Art. *Career:* corresp. and critic, Architecture Design Magazine; Founder mem. South West Acad. of Fine and Applied Art. *Publications:* Illustrators of Alice 1971, Victorian Children 1972, Clementina, Lady Harwarden 1973, Pre-Raphaelite Photography 1972, Victorian Erotic Photography 1973, Aspects of Lolita 1975, A Victorian Album (with Lord David Cecil) 1976, Satirical Poems and Others 1983, The Marble Mirror (poems) 1984, Lewis Carroll Photographer 1984; Graham Ovenden... A Monograph with Essays by Laurie Lee, etc. 1987, Sold With All Faults (poems) 1991; photographs: Alphonse Mucha 1973, Hill & Adamson 1973, Graham Ovenden – Childhood Streets (Photographs 1956–64) 1998; contribs on art to numerous journals. *Address:* Barleysplatt Chapel, Panters Bridge, Mount, nr Bodmin, Cornwall, PL30 3DP, England (home).

OVERY, Richard James, PhD, FRHistS, FBA, FRSA; British historian and academic; *Professor of History, University of Exeter*; b. 23 Dec. 1947, London; s. of James Herbert Overy and Margaret Grace Overy (née Sutherland); m. 1st Tessa Coles 1969 (divorced 1976); m. 2nd Jane Giddens 1979 (divorced 1992); m. 3rd Kim Turner 1992 (divorced 2004); one s. four d. *Education:* Sexey's Blackford Grammar School, Somerset, Gonville and Caius Coll., Cambridge. *Career:* Research Fellow, Churchill Coll., Cambridge 1972–73; Fellow and Coll. Lecturer, Queen's Coll., Cambridge 1973–79; Asst Univ. Lecturer, Univ. of Cambridge 1976–79; Lecturer in History, King's Coll., London 1980–88, Reader in History 1988–92, Prof. of Modern History 1992–2004, Fellow 2003–; Prof. of History, Univ. of Exeter 2004–. *Publications:* William Morris, Viscount Nuffield 1976, The Air War 1939–1945 1980, The Nazi Economic Recovery 1982, Goering: The Iron Man 1984, The Origins of the Second World War 1987, The Road to War 1989, War and Economy in the Third Reich 1994, The Interwar Crisis 1919–1939 1994, Why the Allies Won 1995, The Penguin Atlas of the Third Reich 1996, The Times Atlas of the Twentieth Century 1996, Bomber Command 1939–1945 1997, Russia's War 1998, The Times History of the World (Gen. Ed.) 1999, The Battle 2000, Interrogations: The Nazi Elite in Allied Lands 1945 2001, The Dictators: Hitler's Germany and Stalin's Russia (Second Prize, Wolfson Prize for History 2004, Hessell-Tiltman Prize for History (jtly) 2005) 2004, What Britain Has Done: September 1939–May 1945 A Selection of Outstanding Facts and Figures 2007, The Morbid Age 2009, 1939: Countdown to War 2009, The Battle of Britain Experience 2010, Goering: Hitler's Iron Knight 2011; contrib. to scholarly books and professional journals. *Honours:* T.S. Ashton Prize 1983, Cass Prize for Business History 1987, Samuel Eliot Morison Prize for lifetime contrib. to mil. history, Soc. for Mil. History 2001. *Address:* School of Humanities and Social Science, Amory Building, Rennes Drive, Exeter, Devon, EX4 4RJ, England (office). *Fax:* (1392) 263291 (office). *E-mail:* r.overy@exeter.ac.uk (office). *Website:* humanities.exeter.ac.uk/history/staff/overy (office).

OVESEN, Ellis, MA; American poet, writer, artist and composer; b. 18 July 1923, New Effington, SD; m. Thor Lowe Smith 1949; two s. *Education:* University of Wisconsin, San Jose State University. *Career:* Teacher of English, University of Wisconsin, 1946–48, San Jose State University, 1962–63; Teaching Poetry, 1963–90; mem. National Writers Club; California Writers Club; Poetry Society of America; California State Poetry Society. *Publications:* Gloried Grass, 1970; Haloed Paths, 1973; To Those Who Love, 1974; The Last Hour: Lives Touch, 1975; A Time for Singing, 1977; A Book of Praises, 1977; Beloved I, 1980, II, 1990; The Green Madonna, 1984; The Flowers of God, 1985; The Keeper of the Word, 1985; The Wing Brush, 1986; The Year of the Snake, 1989; The Year of the Horse, 1990. Contributions: Poet India; Los Altos Town Crier; Paisley Moon; Fresh Hot Bread; Samvedana; Plowman. *Honours:* Los Altos Hills Poet, 1976–90; Hon. Doctorate, World Acad. of Arts and Culture, 1986; Dame of Merit, Knights of Malta, 1988; Golden Poet Awards, 1988, 1989, 1991; Research Fellow, 1992.

OWEN, Deborah; American/British literary agent; *Founder and Literary Agent, Deborah Owen Ltd*; b. 8 July 1942, NY; d. of the late Kyrill Schabert and Mary Babcock Smith; m. David Anthony Llewellyn Owen (now Lord Owen) 1968; two s. one d. *Career:* Founder and Literary Agent Deborah Owen Ltd 1971; Vice-Pres. Cttee Asscn of Authors' Agents 1991–94; mem. Bd of Dirs Viva radio 1993, Advisory Bd London Symphony Orchestra, Fulbright Comm. *Address:* Deborah Owen Ltd, 78 Narrow Street, Limehouse, London, E14 8BP, England (office). *Telephone:* (20) 7987-5119 (office).

OWEN, Sir Geoffrey David, Kt, MA; British newspaper editor and academic; b. 16 April 1934, s. of L. G. Owen; m. 1st Dorothy J. Owen 1961 (died 1991); two s. one d.; m. 2nd Miriam Marianna Gross 1993. *Education:* Rugby School and Balliol Coll., Oxford. *Career:* joined Financial Times as feature writer and Industrial Corresp. 1958, US Corresp. 1961, industrial 1967; Exec. Industrial Reorganization Corpn 1967–69; Dir of Admin, Overseas Div. of British Leyland Int. 1969, Dir of Personnel and Admin 1972; Deputy Ed. Financial Times 1974–80, Ed. 1981–90; Dir Business Policy Programme, Centre for Econ. Performance, LSE 1991–98, Sr Fellow Inter-disciplinary Inst. of Man. 1998–; mem. Council Foundation for Mfg and Industries 1993–; Chair. Wincott Foundation 1998–; Dir Laird Group 2000–. *Publications:* Industry in the USA 1966, From Empire to Europe 1999. *Address:* London School of Economics and Political Science, Houghton Street, London, WC2A 2AE, England. *Telephone:* (20) 7405-7686. *Fax:* (20) 7242-0392. *Website:* www.lse.ac .uk (office).

OWEN, Jan Jarrold, BA, ALAA; Australian poet and writer; b. 18 Aug. 1940, Adelaide, SA; two s. one d. *Education:* University of Adelaide. *Career:* Writer-in-Residence, Venice Studio of the Literature Board of the Australian Council, 1989, Tasmanian State Institute of Technology, 1990, Brisbane Grammar School, 1993, Tasmanian Writers Union, 1993, B. R. Whiting Library, Rome, 1994, Rimbun Dahan, Kuala Lumpur, 1997–98; mem. South Australian Writers' Centre. *Publications:* Boy With a Telescope, 1986; Fingerprints on Light, 1990; Blackberry Season, 1993; Night Rainbows, 1994. Contributions: newspapers and magazines. *Honours:* Ian Mudie Prize, 1982; Jessie Litchfield Prize, 1984; Grenfell Henry Lawson Prize, 1985; Harri Jones Memorial Prize, 1986; Anne Elder Award, 1987; Mary Gilmore Prize, 1987; Wesley Michel Wright Poetry Prize, 1992.

OWEN, Ursula Margaret, OBE, MA; British publishing executive, writer and editor; b. 21 Jan. 1937, Oxford; d. of Werner and Emma Sachs; m. Roger Owen 1960 (divorced 1977); one d.; partner Frank Kermode (died 2010). *Education:* Putney High School, St Hugh's Coll., Oxford and Bedford Coll., Univ. of London. *Career:* social worker and researcher into social issues 1960–69; Ed. Frank Cass 1971–73, Barrie and Jenkins Ltd publrs 1973–75; Founder-Dir Virago Press 1973, Editorial Dir and Jt Man. Dir 1974–90, Non-Exec. Dir 1990–95; Cultural Policy Adviser to Lab. Party, Dir Hamlyn Fund 1990–92; Ed. in Chief and CEO Index on Censorship 1993–2006; Founder Free Word 2003–09, Founding Trustee 2009–; mem. Bd New Statesman magazine 1985–90, Cttee Royal Literary Fund 1990–94; Chair. Educ. Extra 1992–2000; Vice-Pres. Hay on Wye Festival of Literature; Gov., Parliament Hill School 1993–2003, South Bank Centre 2003–; Trustee, English Touring Opera 2005–, World Film Collective 2009–, Carcanet Press 2012–. *Publications:* Fathers: Reflections by Daughters (ed.) 1984, Whose Cities? (co-ed.) 1990, An Apprenticeship in Assimilation (essay) 1993. *E-mail:* umo@ursulaowen.com.

OWENS, Agnes; British writer; b. 24 May 1926, Milngavie, Scotland; m. Patrick Owens 1964, three s. four d. *Career:* mem. Scottish PEN Centre. *Publications:* Gentlemen of the West 1985, Lean Tales 1985, Like Birds in the Wildnerness 1986, A Working Mother 1994, People Like That 1996, For the Love of Willie 1998, Bad Attitudes 2003, The Complete Short Stories 2008. *Address:* c/o Polygon Books, Birlinn Ltd, West Newington House, 10 Newington Road, Edinburgh EH9 1QS, Scotland (office). *Website:* polygon .birlinn.co.uk (office).

OWENS, John E., BA, PhD, FRSA; British political scientist and academic; *Professor of United States Government and Politics, University of Westminster, London*; b. 13 June 1948, Widnes, Cheshire, England; s. of William Thomas Owens and Catherine Owens; m. Margaret Owens 1971; one s. one d. *Education:* Univ. of Reading, Univ. of Warwick, Univ. of Essex. *Career:* Lecturer, Central London Polytechnic 1978–85, Univ. of Essex 1985–86; Senior Lecturer, Univ. of Westminster, London 1986–98, Reader, 1998–2002, Prof. of United States Govt and Politics 2002–; Faculty Fellow, Center for Congressional and Presidential Studies, American Univ., Washington DC; Assoc. Fellow, Inst. for the Study of the Americas, Univ. of London; mem., Editorial Boards, Congress and the Presidency, Presidential Studies Quarterly, Journal of Legislative Studies, Politics and Policy (Assoc. Ed.); mem. Political Studies Asscn, UK; Legislative Studies Section, American Political Science Asscn; International Political Science Asscn; British Asscn of American Studies. *Publications:* After Full Employment (with John Keane) 1986, Congress and the Presidency: Institutional Politics in a Separated System (with Michael Foley) 1996, The Republican Takeover of Congress (with Dean McSweeney) 1998, Political Leadership in Context (with Erwin C. Hargrove) 2003, America's War on Terrorism: New Dimensions in US Government and National Security (with John W. Dumbrell) 2008, The 'War on Terror' and the Growth of the Executive Power? A Comparative Analysis (with Riccardo Pelizzo) 2010; numerous book chapters and short articles; contribs to American Review of Politics, British Journal of Political Science, Journal of Legislative Studies, Political Studies, Politics and Policy, Roll Call, Times Higher Educational Supplement. *Address:* Centre for the Study of Democracy, University of Westminster, 32–38 Wells Street, London, W1T 3UW, England (office). *Telephone:* (20) 7911-5000 (office). *Fax:* (20) 7911-5164 (office). *E-mail:* owensj@westminster.ac.uk (office). *Website:* www .westminster.ac.uk/about-us/directory/owens,-john (office).

OWENS, Rochelle; American poet, dramatist, critic, academic and translator; b. 2 April 1936, New York, NY; m. 1st David Owens 1956 (divorced 1959); m. 2nd George Economou 1962. *Education:* New School for Social Research, New York, Univ. of Montréal, Alliance Française, Paris, New York. *Career:* Visiting Lecturer, Univ. of California at San Diego 1982; writer-in-residence, Brown Univ. 1989; Adjunct Prof., Univ. of Oklahoma at Norman 1993; poet-and playwright-in-residence, Deep South Writers Conference, Univ. of Southwestern Louisiana 1997; mem. ASCAP, Dramatists' Guild. *Publications:* poetry: Not Be Essence That Cannot Be 1961, Four Young Lady Poets (with others) 1962, Salt and Core 1968, I Am the Babe of Joseph Stalin's

Daughter: Poems 1961–1971 1972, Poems From Joe's Garage 1973, The Joe 82 Creation Poems 1974, The Joe Chronicles, Part 2 1979, Shemuel 1979, French Light 1984, Constructs 1985, W. C. Fields in French Light 1986, How Much Paint Does the Painting Need 1988, Black Chalk 1992, Rubbed Stones and Other Poems 1994, New and Selected Poems, 1961–1996 1997, Luca: Discourse on Life and Death 2001; plays: Futz and What Came After 1968, The Karl Marx Play and Others 1974, Emma Instigated Me 1976, The Widow and the Colonel 1977, Mountain Rites 1978, Chucky's Hunch 1982, The Passers by Liliane Atlan (trans.) 1993, Plays by Rochelle Owens: Collection of 4 Plays 2000; editor: Spontaneous Combustion: Eight New American Plays 1972; contrib. to anthologies and journals. *Honours:* Rockefeller Grants 1965, 1976, Obie Awards 1965, 1967, 1982, Yale School of Drama Fellowship 1968, American Broadcasting Corporation Fellowship 1968, Guggenheim Fellowship 1971, Nat. Endowment for the Arts Award 1976, Villager Award 1982, Franco-Anglais Festival de Poésie, Paris 1991, Rockefeller Foundation Resident Scholar, Bellagio, Italy 1993, Oklahoma Centre for the Book Award 1998. *Literary Agent:* Farber Literary Agency, 14 East 75th Street, New York, NY 10021, USA. *Telephone:* (212) 861-7075. *Fax:* (212) 861-7976. *E-mail:* farberlit@aol.com.

OWUOR, Yvonne Adhiambo, MA; Kenyan writer; b. 7 June 1968, Nairobi. *Education:* Kenyatta Univ., Nairobi, Univ. of Reading, UK. *Career:* Exec. Dir Zanzibar Int. Film Festival 2003–05; academic planner and programme specialist, Aga Khan Univ. 2007–11; Creative Industry Devt Specialist, Africa Creative Economy 2011–. *Publications:* short stories: Weight of Whispers (Caine Prize for African Writing) 2003, My Mother, My Muse 2004, Trial of Terremotto 2004, Dressing the Dirge 2004, The State of Tides 2005, The Knife Grinder's Tale 2005 (also film); contrib. Kwani (literary journal). *Honours:* Eve Woman of the Year Award (Arts) 2004. *Literary Agent:* c/o The Wylie Agency, 250 West 57th Street, Suite 2114, New York, NY 10107, USA. *Telephone:* (212) 246-0069. *Fax:* (212) 586-8953. *E-mail:* mail@wylieagency.com. *Website:* www.wylieagency.com. *Address:* c/o Kwani, PO Box 2895-00100, Nairobi, Kenya. *Website:* www.kwani.org.

OXLEY, William, FCA; British poet, writer, philosopher, translator and accountant; b. 29 April 1939, Manchester; s. of Harry Oxley and Catherine Oxley; m. Patricia Holmes 1963; two d. *Education:* Manchester Coll. of Commerce. *Career:* accountant, part-time gardener and actor 1956–76; freelance poet and writer 1976–; fmr mem. Gen. Council Poetry Soc.; Founder Long Poem Group (co-ed. of its newsletter); dubbed 'Britain's first Europoet' 1980s; consultant ed. Acumen magazine; Poet-in-Residence for Torbay 2000–01; co-f. Torbay Poetry Festival 2001–. *Publications:* The Dark Structures 1967, New Workings 1969, Passages from Time: Poems from a Life 1971, The Icon Poems 1972, Sixteen Days in Autumn (travel) 1972, Opera Vetera 1973, Mirrors of the Sea 1973, Eve Free 1974, Mundane Shell 1975, Superficies 1976, The Exile 1979, The Notebook of Hephaestus and Other Poems 1981, Poems of a Black Orpheus 1981, The Synopthegms of a Prophet 1981, The Idea and Its Imminence 1982, Of Human Consciousness 1982, The Cauldron of Inspiration 1983, A Map of Time 1984, The Triviad and Other Satires 1984, The Inner Tapestry 1985, Vitalism and Celebration 1987, The Mansands Trilogy 1988, Mad Tom on Tower Hill 1988, The Patient Reconstruction of Paradise 1991, Forest Sequence 1991, In the Drift of Words 1992, The Playboy 1992, Cardboard Troy 1993, The Hallsands Tragedy 1993, Collected Longer Poems 1994, Completing the Picture (ed.) 1995, The Green Crayon Man 1997, No Accounting for Paradise (autobiog.) 1999, Firework Planet (children's) 2000, Reclaiming the Lyre: New and Selected Poems 2001, Modern Poets of Europe (co-ed.) 2003, Namaste: Nepal Poems 2004, London Visions 2005, Poems Antibes 2006, Working Backwards (prose) 2008; contrib. to anthologies, magazines and journals including The Scotsman, New Statesman, The London Magazine, Stand, The Independent, The Spectator, The Observer in the UK and Sparrow, The Formalist in the USA. *Honours:* Millennium Year of the Artist Poet-in-Residence for Torbay, S Devon 2000–01, Echoes of Gilgamesh magazine Award for online long poem (Over the Hills of Hampstead) 2002, Torbay Arts Base Award for Literature 2008. *Address:* 6 The Mount, Furzeham, Brixham, South Devon, TQ5 8QY, England (home). *Telephone:* (1803) 851098 (home). *E-mail:* pwoxley@aol.com (home). *Website:* www.acumen-poetry.co.uk.

OYEYEMI, Helen, BA; British writer; b. 10 Dec. 1984, Nigeria. *Education:* Univ. of Cambridge. *Career:* moved to London aged four; wrote first novel whilst at school; signed first publishing deal aged 18. *Plays:* Juniper's Whitening 2005, Victimese 2005. *Publications:* The Icarus Girl 2005, The Opposite House 2007, White is for Witching 2009, Mr Fox 2011. *Literary Agent:* c/o Tracy Bohan, The Wylie Agency, 17 Bedford Square, London, WC1B 3JA, England. *Telephone:* (20) 7908-5900. *Fax:* (20) 7908-5901. *E-mail:* mail@wylieagency.co.uk. *Website:* www.wylieagency.co.uk.

OZ, Amos, BA; Israeli writer; b. 4 May 1939, Jerusalem; m. Nily Zuckermann 1960; one s. two d. *Education:* Hebrew Univ. Jerusalem. *Career:* Kibbutz Hulda 1957–86; teacher of literature and philosophy, Hulda High School and Givat Brenner Regional High School 1963–86; Visiting Fellow, St Cross Coll. Oxford 1969–70; Writer-in-residence Hebrew Univ. Jerusalem 1975; Visiting Prof. Univ. of Calif. at LA (Berkeley); Writer-in-Residence and Prof. of Literature Colorado Coll., Colorado Springs 1984–85; Prof. of Hebrew Literature, Ben Gurion Univ. 1987–, Agnon Chair in Modern Hebrew 1990–; Visiting Prof. of Literature, Writer in Residence, Boston Univ. 1987; Writer-in-Residence, Hebrew Univ. 1990– and Prof of Literature, Princeton Univ. 1997, Weidenfeld Visiting Prof. of European Comparative Literature St Anne's Coll., Oxford 1998. *Publications:* novels: Elsewhere, Perhaps 1966, My Michael 1968, Touch the Water, Touch the Wind 1973, A Perfect Peace 1982, Black Box 1987, To Know a Woman 1989, The Third Condition (Fima) 1991, The Same Sea 1991, Don't Call It Night 1994, Panther in the Basement 1995, The Same Sea 1999, The Silence of Heaven 2000, Suddenly in the Depths of the Forest 2005, Rhyming Life and Death 2007; novellas and short stories: Where the Jackals Howl 1965, Unto Death 1971, Different People (selected anthology) 1974, The Hill of Evil Counsel 1976, Soumchi (children's story) 1978, Telling Tales (contrib. to charity anthology) 2004, Scenes From Village Life 2011; essays: Under this Blazing Light 1979, In the Land of Israel 1983, The Slopes of Lebanon 1987, Report of the Situation (in German) 1992, Israel, Palestine and Peace 1994, A Story Begins 1996, All Our Hopes 1998, But These Are Two Different Wars 2002, How to Cure a Fanatic 2006, Suddenly in the Depths of the Forest 2010; other: A Tale of Love and Darkness (memoir) (The Jewish Quarterly Wingate Literary Prize for non-fiction 2005) 2002. *Honours:* Officier, Ordre des Arts et des Lettres; Kt's Cross, Légion d'honneur 1997; Dr hc (Hebrew Union Coll., Cincinnati, OH and Jerusalem) 1988, (Western New England Coll.) 1988, (Tel-Aviv) 1992; Holon Prize 1965, Brenner Prize 1976, Zeev Award for Children's Books 1978, Bernstein Prize 1983, Bialik Prize 1986, Wingate Prize, London 1988, Prix Femina, Paris 1989 (for novel Black Box), German Publrs' Int. Peace Prize 1992, Luchs Prize for Children's Books (Germany) 1993, Hamore Prize 1993, Israeli Prize for Literature 1998, Freedom of Speech Prize, Writers' Union of Norway 2002, Int. Medal of Tolerance, Polish Ecumenical Council 2002, Goethe Cultural Prize, Frankfurt, Germany 2005, Premio Príncipe de Asturias (for literature) 2007, Dan David Prize 2008. *Address:* Ben Gurion University of the Negev, PO Box 653, Beersheva 84105, Israel. *Telephone:* (8) 6461111. *Fax:* (8) 6237682. *E-mail:* acsec@bgumail.bgu.ac.il (office). *Website:* www.bgu.ac.il (office).

ÖZDAMAR, Sevgi Emine; Turkish actor, writer and dramatist; b. 1946, Malatya. *Education:* studied acting in Istanbul and with Benno Besson at the Volksbühne, E Berlin. *Career:* emigrated to Germany, pursued a career in theatre; fmr mem. Bochumer Schauspielhaus ensemble; has acted on stage and in films; first play Karagöz in Alamania premiered Frankfurter Schauspielhaus 1986; writer in residence, Bergen-Enkheim 2003; mem. Deutsche Akademie für Sprache und Dichtung 2007–. *Films:* Yasemin 1988, Süperseks 2004. *Plays:* as actor: Yasemin by Hark Bohm, Happy Birthday, Türke by Dorris Dörrie; writer: Karagöz in Alamania 1982, Keleoğlan in Alamania 1991. *Publications:* novels: Das Leben ist eine Karawanserei hat zwei Türen aus einer kam ich rein aus der anderen ging ich raus 1992, Die Brücke vom Goldenen Horn (trans. as The Bridge of the Golden Horn) 1998, Seltsame Sterne starren zur Erde 2003; short stories: Mutterzunge 1990, Der Hof im Spiegel 2001. *Honours:* Ingeborg Bachmann Prize 1991, Walter-Hasenclever-Preis 1993, New York Scholarship des Literaturfonds Darmstadt 1995, Adelbert-von-Chamisso-Preis 1999, Künstlerinnenpreis des Landes NRW 2001, Kleist Prize 2004. *Address:* c/o Verlag Kiepenheuer & Witsch GmbH & Co KG, Rondorfer Str. 5, 50968 Cologne, Germany. *E-mail:* verlag@kiwi-verlag.de (office). *Website:* www.kiwi-verlag.de (office).

OZICK, Cynthia, MA; American writer and poet; b. 17 April 1928, New York, NY; d. of William Ozick and Celia Regelson; m. Bernard Hallote 1952; one d. *Education:* New York Univ. and Ohio State Univ. *Career:* mem. PEN, Authors' League, American Acad. of Arts and Sciences, American Acad. of Arts and Letters; Founder-mem. Acad. Universelle des Cultures; Guggenheim Fellow 1982. *Publications:* Trust 1966, The Pagan Rabbi and Other Stories 1971, Bloodshed and Three Novellas 1976, Levitation: Five Fictions 1982, Art & Ardor: Essays 1983, The Cannibal Galaxy 1983, The Messiah of Stockholm 1987, Metaphor & Memory: Essays 1989, The Shawl 1989, Epodes: First Poems 1992, What Henry James Knew, and Other Essays on Writers 1993, Blue Light (play) 1994, Portrait of the Artist as a Bad Character and Other Essays on Writing 1995, The Shawl (novel) 1996, Fame & Folly: Essays 1996, The Puttermesser Papers (novel) 1997, The Best American Essays (ed.) 1998, Quarrel & Quandary (essays) 2000, Heir to the Glimmering World (novel published as The Bear Boy in UK) 2004, Collected Stories 2006, A Din in the Head: Essays 2006, Dictation: A Quartet 2008, Foreign Bodies 2010; contrib. of fiction to numerous periodicals and anthologies, including New Criterion, New Yorker, Harper's, Partisan Review, Yale Review, New York Times Magazine, Best American Short Stories, O. Henry Prize Stories, Best American Essays, The Oxford Book of Jewish Short Stories, The Norton Anthology of Jewish American Literature. *Honours:* hon. degrees (Yeshiva) 1984, (Hebrew Union Coll.) 1984, (Williams Coll.) 1986, (Hunter Coll.) 1987, (Jewish Theological Seminary) 1988, (Adelphi) 1988, (State Univ. of NY) 1989, (Brandeis) 1990, (Bard Coll.) 1991, (Spertus Coll.) 1991, (Seton Hall Univ.) 1999, (Rutgers Univ.) 1999, (Asheville) 2000, (New York) 2001, (Bar-Ilan) 2002, (Baltimore Hebrew Univ.) 2004, (Georgetown) 2007; Mildred and Harold Strauss Living Award, American Acad. of Arts and Letters 1983; Rea Award for short story 1986, PEN/Spiegel-Diamonstein Award for the Art of the Essay 1997, Harold Washington Literary Award, City of Chicago 1997, John Cheever Award 1999, Lotos Club Medal of Merit 2000, Lannan Foundation Award 2000, Nat. Critics' Circle Award for criticism 2001, Koret Foundation Award for Literary Studies 2001, Mary McCarthy Award, Bard Coll. 2007, Nat. Humanities Medal 2007, PEN/Malamud Prize 2008, PEN/Nabokov Prize 2008. *Fax:* (914) 654-6583.

P

PACHECO, José Emilio; Mexican writer and poet; b. 30 June 1939, Mexico City. *Education:* Universidad Nacional Autónoma de México. *Career:* asst ed., Estaciones magazine 1957–58, Revista de la Universidad de Mexico 1959–60; Assoc. Ed., México en la Cultura; has taught literature at Univ. of Essex, UK, Univ. of Maryland, USA; mem. Colegio Nacional de Mexico 1986–. *Publications include:* fiction: La Sangre de Medusa 1958, El Viento Distante 1963, El Principio del placer 1972, Las batallas en el desierto 1981; poetry: Los Elementos de la noche 1963, El reposo del fuego 1966, No me preguntes cómo pasa el tiempo 1969, Irás y no volveras 1973, Islas a la deriva 1976, Desde entonces 1980, Los Trabajos del mar 1983, El silencio de la luna 1996, Voz Viva de México 1996, Álbum de zoología 1998, La edad de las tinieblas 2009, Como la lluvia: poemas 2001–2008 2009. *Honours:* Premio Nacional de Poesía 1969, Premio Nacional de Periodismo Literario, Premio Xavier Villarrutia, Premio Magda Donato, Premio Nacional de Ciencias y Artes 1992, Premio José Asunción Silva 1996, Premio Mazatlán 1998, Premio Iberamericano de Letras José Donoso, Universidad de Talca, Chile 2000, Premio Octavio Paz 2003, Premio Federico García Lorca 2005, Premio Iberamericano de Poesía 2009, Premio Cervantes 2009, Miguel de Cervantes Prize 2009. *Address:* c/o El Colegio Nacional, Luis González Obregón 23, Centro Histórico, 06020 México, Mexico (office). *Telephone:* (52) 5789-4330 (office). *E-mail:* contacto@colegionacional.org.mx (office). *Website:* www.colegionacional.org.mx (office).

PACK, Robert, BA, MA; American academic, poet and writer; *Distinguished Senior Professor, Honors College, University of Montana, Missoula*; b. 29 May 1929, New York, NY; m. 1st Isabelle Miller 1950; m. 2nd Patricia Powell 1961; two s. one d. *Education:* Dartmouth Coll., Columbia Univ. *Career:* teacher, Barnard Coll. 1957–64; Coll. Prof. of Literature and Creative Writing, Middlebury Coll., Vt 1964–94; Dir Bread Loaf Writers Confs 1973–94; currently Distinguished Sr Prof., Honors Coll., Univ. of Montana, Missoula. *Publications:* poetry: The Irony of Joy 1955, A Stranger's Privilege 1959, Guarded by Women 1963, Selected Poems 1964, Home from the Cemetery 1969, Nothing But Light 1972, Keeping Watch 1976, Waking to My Name: New and Selected Poems 1980, Faces in a Single Tree: A Cycle of Monologues 1984, Clayfield Rejoices, Clayfield Laments: A Sequence of Poems 1987, Before It Vanishes: A Packet for Prof. Pagels 1989, Fathering the Map: New and Selected Later Poems 1993, Minding the Sun 1996, Rounding it Out 1999, Elk in Winter 2003; other: Wallace Stevens: An Approach to his Poetry and Thought 1958, Affirming Limits: Essays on Morality, Choice and Poetic Form 1985, The Long View: Essays on the Discipline of Hope and Poetic Craft 1991; editor: The New Poets of England and America (with Donald Hall and Louis Simpson) 1957, Poems of Doubt and Belief: An Anthology of Modern Religious Poetry (with Tom Driver) 1964, Literature for Composition on the Theme of Innocence and Experience (with Marcus Klein) 1966, Short Stories: Classic, Modern, Contemporary (with Marcus Klein) 1967, Keats: Selected Letters 1974, The Bread Loaf Anthology of Contemporary American Poetry (with Sydney Lea and Jay Parini) 1985, The Bread Loaf Anthology of Contemporary American Short Stories (with Jay Parini, two vols) 1987, 1989, Poems for a Small Planet: An Anthology of Nature Poetry (with Jay Parini) 1993, Rounding It Out (poetry) 1999, Minding the Sun (poetry) 2003, Composing Voices (poetry) 2007, Elk In Winter (poetry) 2008, Willing to Choose: Shakespeare's Later Plays 2008, Still Here, Still Now (poetry) 2009, Laughter Before Sleep (poetry) 2010. *Honours:* Dr hc (Rocky Mountain Coll., Montana) 2001; Fulbright Fellowship 1956, American Acad. of Arts and Letters grant 1957, Borestone Mountain Poetry Award 1964, Nat. Endowment for the Arts grant 1968, Medal for Lifetime Achievement, Dartmouth Coll. 1994, Presidential Medal for Distinguished Teaching, Univ. of Montana 2006. *Address:* English Department, LA 133, University of Montana, Missoula, MT 59812, USA (office). *E-mail:* cnd3199@blackfoot.net (home). *Website:* www.cas.umt.edu/english (office).

PACKER, Zuwena Z., BA, MA, MFA; American writer; b. 12 Jan. 1973, Chicago. *Education:* Yale Univ., Johns Hopkins Univ. *Career:* fmr teacher of English and Creative Writing in Baltimore; fmr Stegner Fellow and Jones Lecturer, Stanford Univ.; fmr Sr Visiting Prof. of Creative Writing, Calif. Coll. of the Arts. *Publications:* Drinking Coffee Elsewhere (short stories) 2003. *Honours:* Whiting Writer's Award, Rona Jaffe Foundation Writers Award, Ms Giles Whiting Award, Billingham Review Award; Guggenheim Fellowship 2005. *Address:* 3500 Werner Avenue, Austin, TX 78722, USA (home). *E-mail:* julia.fleischaker@us.penguingroup.com (office).

PADEL, Ruth, BA, PhD, FRSL; British poet, writer and journalist; b. 8 May 1946, London, England; one d. *Education:* Univ. of Oxford. *Career:* Poet-in-Residence, Somerset House, London 2008–; mem. PEN, Royal Zoological Soc., Soc. of Authors. *Publications:* poetry: Alibi 1985, Summer Snow 1990, Angel 1993, Fusewire 1996, Rembrandt Would Have Loved You 1998, Voodoo Shop 2002, The Soho Leopard 2004, Darwin: A Life in Poems 2009; non-fiction: In and Out of the Mind 1992, Whom Gods Destroy 1995, I'm a Man 2000, 52 Ways of Looking at a Poem 2002, Tigers in Red Weather 2005, The Poem and the Journey: And Sixty Poems to Read Along the Way 2007; fiction: Where the Serpent Lives 2010. *Honours:* Nat. Poetry Competition First Prize 1996, Poetry Book Soc. Recommendation 1993, 2002, Choice 1998, 2004, Cholmondeley Award 2004. *Literary Agent:* c/o Patrick Walsh, Conville and Walsh, 2 Ganton Street, London, W1F 7GL, England. *Telephone:* (20) 7287-4545. *E-mail:* patrick@convilleandwalsh.com. *Website:* www.convilleandwalsh.com. *E-mail:* mail@ruthpadel.com (office). *Website:* www.ruthpadel.com.

PADFIELD, Peter Lawrence Notton; British author and historian; b. 3 April 1932, Kolkata, India; m. Jean Yarwood 1960, one s. two d. *Education:* Christ's Hosp. School, Thames Nautical Training Coll., HMS, Worcester. *Publications:* The Sea is a Magic Carpet 1960, The Titanic and the Californian 1965, An Agony of Collisions 1966, Aim Straight: A Biography of Admiral Sir Percy Scott 1966, Broke and the Shannon: A Biography of Admiral Sir Philip Broke 1968, The Battleship Era 1972, Guns at Sea: A History of Naval Gunnery 1973, The Great Naval Race: Anglo-German Naval Rivalry 1900–1914 1974, Nelson's War 1978, Tide of Empires: Decisive Naval Campaigns in the Rise of the West, Vol. I 1481–1654 1979, Vol. II 1654–1763 1982, Rule Britannia: The Victorian and Edwardian Navy 1981, Beneath the Houseflag of the P & O 1982, Dönitz, The Last Führer 1984, Armada 1988, Himmler, Reichsführer SS 1990, Hess: Flight for the Führer 1991, revised edn as Hess: The Führer's Disciple 1993, War Beneath the Sea: Submarine Conflict 1939–1945 1995, Maritime Supremacy and the Opening of the Western Mind: Naval Campaigns that Shaped the Modern World 1588–1782 1999, Maritime Power and the Struggle for Freedom: Naval Campaigns that shaped the Modern World 1788–1851 2003, Maritime Dominion and the Triumph of the Free World: Naval Campaigns that Shaped the Modern World 1852–2001 2009; fiction: The Lion's Claw 1978, The Unquiet Gods 1980, Gold Chains of Empire 1982, Salt and Steel 1986. *Honours:* Mountbatten Maritime Prize 2003. *Literary Agent:* c/o The Andrew Lownie Literary Agency Ltd, 36 Great Smith Street, London, SW1P 3BU, England. *E-mail:* mail@andrewlownie.co.uk.

PADGAONKAR, Dileep, PhD; Indian journalist; *Consulting Editor and Columnist, Times of India*; b. 1 May 1944, Pune; s. of Vasant Padgaonkar and Shakuntala Padgaonkar (née Kattakar); m. Latika Tawadey 1968; two s. *Education:* Fergusson Coll. Pune, Institut des Hautes Etudes Cinématographiques, Sorbonne, France. *Career:* Paris Corresp. The Times of India 1968–73, Asst Ed. Bombay and Delhi 1973–78, Assoc. Ed. and Exec. Ed. The Times of India Group 1986–88, Ed. 1988–94, Dir (Corp.) and Exec. Man. Ed. 1998–2002, Consulting Ed. and Columnist 2002–; f. Asia Pacific Communication Assocs 1994; Information Chief for Asia and Pacific, UNESCO 1978–81; Deputy Dir Office of Public Information, Paris 1981–85, Acting Dir 1985–86, Acting Dir Communication Sector 1986; Presenter Question Time India, BBC World. *Television:* presenter, BBC World's Question Time India panel discussion programme. *Publications include:* When Bombay Burned (ed.) 1993, Under Her Spell: Roberto Rossellini in India 2008. *Honours:* Chevalier, Legion d'honneur 2001. *Address:* The Times of India, Times House, 7 Bahadur Shah Zafar Marg, New Delhi 110 002 (office); C-313, Defence Colony, New Delhi 110 024, India (home). *Telephone:* (11) 3312277 (office); (11) 4697949 (home). *Fax:* (11) 3323346 (office). *Website:* www.timesofindia.com (office).

PADILLA, Ignacio, BA, MA, DLit; Mexican writer, novelist, academic and diplomatist; b. 1968, Mexico City; m.; two c. *Education:* Universidad Iberoamericana, Univ. of Edinburgh, UK, Univ. of Salamanca, Spain. *Career:* currently Prof. of Spanish Literature, Universidad de Puebla, Mexico City; Cultural Attache, Embassy in London 2001–03; Dir Nat. Library of Mexico 2007; mem. Querétaro de Academia Mexicana de la Lengua 2011. *Publications include:* La catedral de los ahogados (Premio Juan Rulfo para Primera Novela 1994) 1995, Si volviesen sus majestades 1996, Amphitryon (Premio Primavera de Novela) 2000, Crónicas africanas. Espejismo y utopía en el reino de Swazilandia 2001, Espiral de artillería 2003, La gruta del Toscano (Premio Mazatlán de Literatura 2007) 2006; fiction: Subterráneos (Premio Nacional de las Juventudes Alfonso Reyes 1989) 1990, Trenes de humo bajoalfombra 1993, El año de los gatos amurallados (Premio Kalpa de Ciencia Ficción) 1994, Imposibilidad de los cuervos (Tres bosquejos del mal) 1994, Las antípodas y el siglo (Micropedia I) (Premio de Cuento Gilberto Owen 1999) 2001, El androide y las quimeras (Micropedia II) 2008, Los anacrónicos y otros cuentos (Premio Internacional Juan Rulfo de cuento 2008) 2010; children's books: Los papeles del dragón típico 1991 and 2001, Las tormentas del mar embotellado (Premio Juan La Cabada 1994) 1994 and 2000, Por un tornillo 2009, Todos los osos son zurdos 2010. *Address:* c/o Fondo De Cultura Economica, Matrix House, Picacho-Ajusco Rt 227, Col. Bosques del Pedregal, CP 14738 Deleg., Tlalpan, México DF, Mexico. *Website:* www.fondodeculturaeconomica.com.

PADMANABHAN, Neela, BSc, BSc (Eng), FIE; Indian engineer (retd), poet and writer; b. 26 April 1938, Trivandrum; s. of Neelakanta Pillai and Janaki Ammal; m. U. Krishnammal 1963; one s. three d. *Education:* Kerala Univ. *Career:* joined Kerala State Electricity Bd as Jr Engineer 1963, retd as Deputy Chief Eng. 1993; mem. Bd of Studies Kerala Univ. 1985–89; mem. Authors' Guild of India, PEN, Poetry Soc. of India, Sahitya Akademi (mem. Exec. Cttee 1998–2002). *Films:* film on Neela Padmanabhan, Sahitya Akademi Delhi 2003, Makizchi (adaptation of Talaimuraikal novel) 2011. *Publications include:* Talaimuraikal (novel, trans. as Generations) 1968, Pallikondapuram (novel, trans. as The City Where God Sleeps) 1970, Filekal (novel) 1973, Bothayil Karainthavarkal, Uravugal (novel, trans. as Relations) (Rajah Sir Annamalai Chettiar Award 1977) 1975, Neela Padmanabhan Kavithaikal (poems) 1975, Min ulakam (novel, trans. as World of Power) 1976,

Anubhavankal (novel, trans. as Experiences) 1977, Samar (novel, trans. as Agitation) 1977, Vattathin Veliye (novel, trans. as Beyond the Circle) 1980, Surrender and Other Poems 1982, Naa Kaakka (poems) 1984, Therodum Veedhi (novel) (Government of Tamilnadu Award) 1987, Peyarilenna (poems) 1993, Vellam (short stories) (Lily Deva Sikhamoni Award) 1994, Koondinul Pakshikal (novel) (Thiruppur Tamil Sangham Award) (trans. as Birds in the Cage 2009) 1995, Neela Padmanabhan 148 Kavithaikal (poems) 2003, Ilai Uthir Kaalam (novel) (Sahitya Akademi Award 2007, Rangammal Award, Kasturi Srinivasan Trust, Coimbatore) 2005, Arkande Koanil (short story) (Basha Bharathi Award, Central Inst. of Indian Languages, Mysore 2006); 12 short story collections, 10 essay collections; contrib. to numerous publications. *Honours:* Hon. Fellow, Inst. of Engineers, Kolkata; Tamilannai Prize 1987, Ulloor Parameswaraiyer Poetry Award 2001, Sahitya Akademi Award for Translation 2003. *Address:* Nilakant 39/1870 Kuriyathi Bypass Road, Manacaud PO, Thiruvanantha Puram 695 009, India (home). *Telephone:* (471) 2476060 (home). *E-mail:* neelapadmanabham1@rediffmail.com (home). *Website:* www.neelapadmanabhan.com; neelapadmam.blogspot.com.

PADOVANO, Anthony Thomas, BA, MA, PhL, PhD, STD; American academic and writer; *Distinguished Professor of Literature and Philosophy, Ramapo College of New Jersey;* b. 18 Sept. 1934, Harrison, NJ; m. Theresa P. Lackamp 1974; three s. one d. *Education:* Seton Hall Univ., Pontifical Gregorian Univ., Rome, St Thomas Pontifical Int. Univ., Rome, New York Univ., Fordham Univ. *Career:* Prof. of Systematic Theology, Darlington School of Theology, Mahwah, NJ 1962–74; Prof. of Literature and Philosophy, Ramapo Coll. of New Jersey 1971–, now Distinguished Prof.; various visiting professorships; mem. Catholic Theological Soc. of America, Int. Fed. of Married Priests, Int. Thomas Merton Soc., Priests for Equality. *Publications:* The Cross of Christ, The Measure of the World 1962, The Estranged God 1966, Who Is Christ? 1967, Belief in Human Life 1969, American Culture and the Quest for Christ 1970, Dawn Without Darkness 1971, Free to Be Faithful 1972, Eden and Easter 1974, A Case for Worship 1975, Presence and Structure 1975, America: Its People, Its Promise 1975, The Human Journey: Thomas Merton, Symbol of a Century 1982, Trilogy 1982, Contemplation and Compassion 1984, Winter Rain: A Play in One Act and Six Scenes 1985, His Name is John: A Play in Four Acts 1986, Christmas to Calvary 1987, Love and Destiny 1987, Summer Lightning: A Play in Four Acts and Four Seasons 1988, Conscience and Conflict 1989, Reform and Renewal: Essays on Authority, Ministry and Social Justice 1990, A Celebration of Life 1990, The Church Today: Belonging and Believing 1990, Scripture in the Street 1992, A Retreat with Thomas Merton: Biography as Spiritual Journey 1995, Hope is a Dialogue 1998, Resistance and Renewal 2002, Life Choices 2004; contrib. to books and periodicals. *Honours:* awards and citations; all professional and personal papers retained in the archives of the Univ. of Notre Dame, Ind. *Address:* School of American and International Studies, Ramapo College of New Jersey, Mahwah, NJ 07430 (office); 9 Millstone Drive, Morris Plains, NJ 07950, USA (home). *Telephone:* (201) 684-7430 (office). *E-mail:* apadovan@ramapo.edu (office); tpadovan@optonline.net (home). *Website:* apadovano.com.

PADURA FUENTES, Leonardo, BA; Cuban novelist, essayist and critic; b. 1955, Havana. *Education:* Havana Univ. *Career:* fmr investigative journalist. *Publications include:* Con la espada y la pluma: Comentarios al Inca Garcilaso (literary criticism), Lo real maravilloso: creación y realidad (literary criticism), El viaje más largo, La cultura y la revolucion cubana: conversaciones en La Habana, La novela de mi vida, La puerta de Alcalá y otras cacerías, Pasado perfecto (vol. one of Las cuatro estaciones quartet) 1991, Vientos de cuaresma (vol. two of Las cuatro estaciones quartet) 1994, Máscaras (vol. three of Las cuatro estaciones quartet) (Premio Café Gijón) 1997, Paisaje de otoño (vol. four of Las cuatro estaciones quartet) (Int. Asscn of Crime Writers Premio Hammett 1998) 1998, La Novela de mi Vida 2002, Adios Hemingway (novella) 2005, La neblina del ayer 2005, El Hombre que amaba a los perros 2009. *Address:* c/o Tsuquets Editores, Cesare Cantù 8, 08023 Barcelona, Spain (office). *Website:* www.tusquetseditores.com (office).

PAGANO, Emmanuelle; French writer; b. Sept. 1969, Aveyron; three c. *Publications:* novels: À goutte (aka Pour être chez moi) 1992, La Rivière, la Rivière (aka Pas devant les gens), Le Tiroir à cheveux 2005, Les Adolescents troglodytes (EU Prize for Literature 2009, Prix Rhône-Alpes de l'adaptation cinématographique d'une œuvre littéraire contemporaine) 2007, Les Mains gamines (Prix Wepler Fondation La Poste 2008, Prix Rhône-Alpes du Livre 2009) 2008, L'Absence d'oiseaux d'eau 2010; novella: Le guide automatique 2008; contrib. essays and short stories to numerous publications. *Address:* c/o Éditions POL, 33 rue Saint-André-des-Arts, 75006 Paris, France (office). *E-mail:* emmanuelle.pagano@lescorpsempeches.net (home). *Website:* www.pol-editeur.fr (office); lescorpsempeches.net.

PAGE, Bruce; British journalist; b. 1 Dec. 1936, London; s. of Roger Page and Amy B. Page; m. 1st Anne Gillison 1964 (divorced 1969); m. 2nd Anne L. Darnborough 1969; one s. one d. *Education:* Melbourne High School and Melbourne Univ., Australia. *Career:* trained as journalist, Melbourne Herald 1956–60; Evening Standard, London 1960–62; Daily Herald, London 1962–64; various exec. posts, Sunday Times, London 1964–76; Assoc. Ed. Daily Express 1977; Ed. New Statesman 1978–82; Dir Direct Image Systems and Communications 1992–95; various awards for journalism. *Publications:* co-author: Philby, the Spy who Betrayed a Generation, An American Melodrama, Do You Sincerely Want to be Rich?, Destination Disaster, Ulster (contrib.), The Yom Kippur War, The British Press; author: The Murdoch Archipelago 2003. *Honours:* British Newspaper Hall of Fame 2005. *Address:* c/o PFD Limited, Drury House, 34–43 Russell Street, London WC2B 5HA (office); Beach House, Shingle Streeet, Shottisham, Suffolk, IP12 3BE, England (home). *Telephone:* (1394) 411427 (home); (7771) 641018 (mobile). *E-mail:* bruce@pages2.ads24.co.uk (office).

PAGE, Clarence, BS; American journalist and columnist; b. 2 June 1947, Dayton, OH; m. Lisa Johnson Cole 1987. *Education:* Ohio University. *Career:* reporter and Asst City Ed., Chicago Tribune 1969–80, columnist and editorial bd mem. 1984–; Dir Dept of Community Affairs, WBBM-TV 1980–82; syndicated columnist; many television appearances. *Publications:* contrib. to various periodicals. *Honours:* James P. McGuire Award 1987, Pulitzer Prize for Commentary 1989.

PAGE, Geoffrey (Geoff) Donald, BA (Hons), DipEd; Australian poet, writer and educator; b. 7 July 1940, Grafton, NSW; partner; one s. *Education:* Univ. of New England, Armidale, NSW. *Career:* Head, Dept of English, Narrabundah Coll., Canberra 1974–2001; Writer-in-Residence, Univ. of Wollongong, NSW 1982, Curtin Univ. 1990, Edith Cowan Univ. 1993; mem. Australian Soc. of Authors. *Publications:* The Question 1971, Smalltown Memorials 1975, Collecting the Weather 1978, Cassandra Paddocks 1980, Clairvoyant in Autumn 1983, Shadows from Wire: Poems and Photographs of Australians in the Great War Australian War Memorial (ed.) 1983, Benton's Conviction 1985, Century of Clouds: Selected Poems of Guillaume Apollinaire (co-trans. with Wendy Coutts) 1985, Collected Lives 1986, Smiling in English, Smoking in French 1987, Footwork 1988, Winter Vision 1989, Invisible Histories 1990, Selected Poems 1991, Gravel Corners 1992, On the Move (ed.) 1992, Human Interest 1994, Reader's Guide to Contemporary Australian Poetry 1995, The Great Forgetting 1996, The Secret 1997, Bernie McGann: A Life in Jazz 1998, Collateral Damage 1999, The Scarring 1999, Darker and Lighter 2001, Day after Day: Selected Poems of Salvatore Quasimodo (co-trans. with R. F. Brissenden and Loredana Nardi-Ford) 2002, Drumming on Water 2003, The Indigo Book of Modern Australian Sonnets 2003, My Mother's God 2003, Cartes Postales 2004, Freehold 2005, Europe 101 2006, Agnostic Skies 2006, Eighty Great Poems from Chaucer to Now 2007, Bahn Dance 2008, Seriatim 2008, 60 Classic Australian Poems 2009, Coffee with Miles (poetry CD) 2010; contrib. to newspapers and magazines. *Honours:* Hon. Visiting Fellow, Australian Defence Force Acad., Univ. of New South Wales; Australia Council Literature Board Grants 1974, 1983, 1987, 1989, 1992, 1997, 2000, Queensland Premier's Prize 1990, Patrick White Literary Award 2001, ACT Poetry Award 2004. *Address:* 8/40 Leahy Close, Narrabundah, ACT 2604, Australia (home). *Telephone:* (2) 6239-4027 (office). *E-mail:* gpage40@bigpond.net.au (home). *Website:* www.geoffpage.info.

PAGE, Jeremy Neil, BA, MA, DipRSA; British educator, poet and editor; *Deputy Director, Sussex Centre for Language Studies, University of Sussex;* b. 23 Feb. 1958, Folkestone, Kent, England; s. of Harold Percy Page and Doris Irene Hawker; m. Alexandra Loske; three s. three d. *Education:* Univs of Warwick, Bristol and Sussex. *Career:* Ed. The Frogmore Papers 1983–; teacher and trainer, International House, London 1984–95, Dir of Studies 1995–2003; Founder Frogmore Poetry Prize 1987; teacher, Accad. Britannica, Arezzo, Italy 1987–88; Series Ed., Crabflower Pamphlets 1990–98; Deputy Dir Sussex Centre for Language Studies, Univ. of Sussex 2003–. *Play:* Loving Psyche. *Publications:* Bliss (poems) 1989, Secret Dormitories (poems) 1993, Think Ahead To First Certificate Workbook (with Jon Naunton) 1993, Poetry South East 2000 (ed.) 2000, The Alternative Version (poems) 2001, Search (with Janet Hardy-Gould) 2002, The Norwood Mystery (adaptation) 2006, The Sign of Four (adaptation) 2008, In and Out of The Dark Wood (poems) 2010, Poetry South East 2010 (co-ed.) 2010, The Cost of All Desire (poems) 2011. *Honours:* Acad. of Paraphysical Science Grand Transcendent Kt Salamander 1992. *Address:* Sussex Centre for Language Studies, University of Sussex, Falmer, Brighton, East Sussex, BN1 9SH, England (office). *E-mail:* J.N.Page@sussex.ac.uk (office).

PAGE, Katherine Hall, AB, EdM, DEd; American writer; b. 9 July 1947, New Jersey, USA; m. Alan Hein 1975; one s. *Education:* Wellesley College, Tufts University, Harvard University. *Career:* mem. Mystery Readers International; MWA; Authors' Guild; Sisters in Crime; American Crime Writers League; Society of Children's Bookwriters and Illustrators; International Asscn of Crime Writers; Boston Author's Club; Brontë Society; Agatha Christie Society. *Publications:* The Body in the Belfry (Agatha Award for Best First Mystery) 1990, The Body in the Bouillon 1991, The Body in the Kelp 1991, The Body in the Vestibule 1992, The Body in the Cast 1993, The Body in the Basement 1994, The Body in the Bog 1996, The Body in the Fjord 1997, The Body in the Bookcase 1998, The Body in the Big Apple 1999, The Body in the Moonlight 2001, The Body in the Bonfire 2002, The Body in the Lighthouse 2003, The Body in the Attic 2004, The Body in the Snowdrift (Agatha Award for Best Mystery Novel) 2005, The Body in the Ivy 2006, The Body in the Gallery 2008, The Body in the Sleigh 2009; children's fiction: Christie and Company, 1996; Christie and Company Down East, 1997; Christie and Company in the Year of the Dragon, 1998; Bon Voyage Christie and Company, 1999. *Honours:* Agatha for Best First Domestic Mystery 1991, Agatha for Best Short Story 2002. *Literary Agent:* Sanford J. Greenburger Associates Inc, 55 Fifth Avenue, New York, NY 10003, USA. *Website:* www.katherine-hall-page.org.

PAGE, Louise, BA; British playwright; b. 7 March 1955, London, England. *Education:* University of Birmingham. *Career:* Resident Playwright, Royal Court Theatre, 1982–83. *Publications:* Want Ad, 1977; Glasshouse, 1977;

Tissue, 1978; Lucy, 1979; Hearing, 1979; Flaws, 1980; House Wives, 1981; Salonika, 1982; Real Estate, 1984; Golden Girls, 1984; Beauty and the Beast, 1985; Diplomatic Wives, 1989; Adam Wasxa Gardener, 1991; Like to Live, 1992; Hawks and Doves, 1992. Other: Radio and television plays. *Honours:* George Devine Award 1982.

PAGE, Norman; British academic and writer; b. 8 May 1930, Kettering, Northamptonshire, England; m. Jean Hampton 1958; three s. one d. *Education:* BA, 1951, MA, 1955, Emmanuel College, Cambridge; PhD, University of Leeds, 1968. *Career:* Principal Lecturer in English, Ripon College of Education, Yorkshire, 1960–69; Asst Prof., 1969–70, Assoc. Prof., 1970–75, Prof. of English, 1975–85, University of Alberta; Prof. of Modern English Literature, University of Nottingham, 1985–; mem. Royal Society of Canada, fellow; Thomas Hardy Society; Vice-Pres., Newstead Abbey Byron Society; Vice-Pres., Tennyson Society. *Publications:* The Language of Jane Austen, 1972; Speech in the English Novel, 1973; Thomas Hardy, 1977; A. E. Housman: A Critical Biography, 1983; A Kipling Companion, 1984; E. M. Forster, 1988; Tennyson: An Illustrated Life, 1992; Auden and Isherwood: The Berlin Years, 1998; Oxford Reader's Companion to Hardy, 2000. Contributions: London Magazine; London Review of Books; Literary Review. *Honours:* Guggenheim Fellowship, 1979; University of Alberta Research Prize, 1983. *Address:* 23 Braunston Road, Oakham, Rutland LE15 6LD, England.

PAGE, Robin; British writer; b. 3 May 1943, Cambridgeshire, England. *Publications:* Down with the Poor, 1971; The Benefits Racket, 1972; Down Among the Dossers, 1973; The Decline of an English Village, 1974; The Hunter and the Hunted, 1977; Weather Forecasting: The Country Way, 1977; Cures and Remedies: The Country, 1978; Weeds: The Country Way, 1979; Animal Cures: The Country Way, 1979; The Journal of a Country Parish, 1980; Journeys into Britain, 1982; The Country Way of Love, 1983; The Wildlife of the Royal Estates, 1984; Count One to Ten, 1986; The Fox's Tale, 1986; The Duchy of Cornwall, 1987; The Fox and the Orchid, 1987; The Twitcher's Guide to British Birds, 1989. *Address:* Bird's Farm, Barton, Cambridgeshire, England.

PAGE, S. M. (see McMaster, Susan)

PAGE, Stephen; British publisher; *CEO and Publisher, Faber and Faber Ltd*; b. 1965. *Education:* Bristol Univ. *Career:* bookseller Sherratt & Hughes, Croydon 1987–88; marketing exec. Longman 1988–90; retail sales manager Transworld 1990–94; Sales Dir Fourth Estate 1994–2000, Man. Dir, then (after takeover by Harper Collins) group sales and marketing dir Harper Collins 2000; CEO Faber & Faber Ltd 2001–04, CEO and Publisher 2004–; Pres. Publishers Asscn 2006–. *Address:* Faber and Faber Ltd, Bloomsbury House, 74–77 Great Russell Street, London, WC1B 3DA, England. *Telephone:* (20) 7927-3800 (office). *Fax:* (20) 7927-3801 (office). *E-mail:* contact@faber.co.uk (office). *Website:* www.faber.co.uk (office).

PAGELS, Elaine Hiesey, PhD; American writer and academic; *Harrington Spear Paine Professor of Religion, Princeton University*; b. 13 Feb. 1943, Palo Alto, Calif.; m 1st Heinz R. Pagels 1969 (died 1988); two s. (one died 1987) one d.; m. 2nd Kent Greenawalt 1995. *Education:* Stanford and Harvard Univs. *Career:* Asst Prof., Barnard Coll., Columbia Univ. 1970–74, then Assoc. Prof., later Prof. of Religion and Head of Dept of Religion 1974–82; Harrington Spear Paine Prof. of Religion, Princeton Univ. 1982–; mem. American Acad. of Religion, Biblical Theologians Club, Soc. of Biblical Literature; Aspen Inst. of Humanistic Studies Mellon Fellow 1974, Hazen Fellow 1975, Rockefeller Foundation Fellowship 1978, Guggenheim Fellowship 1979, John D. and Catherine T. MacArthur Foundation Fellowship 1981. *Publications:* The Johannine Gospel in Gnostic Exegesis: Heracleon's Commentary on John 1973, The Gnostic Paul: Gnostic Exegesis of the Pauline Letters 1975, The Gnostic Gospels (Nat. Book Critics' Circle Award, Nat. Book Award 1980) 1979, The Gnostic Jesus and Early Christian Politics 1981, Adam, Eve and the Serpent 1988, The Origin of Satan: The New Testament Origins of Christianity's Demonization of Jews, Pagans and Heretics 1995, Beyond Belief: The Secret Gospel of Thomas 2003, Reading Judas: The Gospel of Judas and the Shaping of Christianity (with Karen L. King) 2007; contrib. to various scholarly books and journals. *Honours:* National Endowment for the Humanities grant 1972. *Address:* Princeton University, Department of Religion, 1879 Hall, Room 240, Princeton, NJ 08544-1007, USA (office). *Telephone:* (609) 258-4484 (office). *E-mail:* epagels@princeton.edu (office). *Website:* www.princeton.edu/~religion (office).

PAGLIA, Camille, BA, MPhil, PhD; American academic and writer; *University Professor of Humanities and Media Studies, University of the Arts*; b. 2 April 1947, Endicott, NY; d. of Pasquale Paglia and Lydia Paglia. *Education:* State Univ. of New York at Binghamton, Yale Univ. *Career:* Faculty mem., Bennington Coll. 1972–80; Visiting Lecturer, Wesleyan Univ. 1980, Yale Univ. 1980–84; Asst Prof., Philadelphia Coll. of Performing Arts (now Univ. of the Arts) 1984–87, Assoc. Prof. 1987–91, Prof. of Humanities 1991–2000; Univ. Prof. of Humanities and Media Studies 2000–; columnist, Salon.com 1995–2001, 2007–; Contributing Ed. Interview magazine 2001–. *Publications:* Sexual Personae: Art and Decadence from Nefertiti to Emily Dickinson 1990, Sex, Art and American Culture: Essays 1992, Vamps and Tramps: New Essays 1994, Alfred Hitchcock's The Birds 1998, Break, Blow, Burn: Camille Paglia Reads Forty-Three of the World's Best Poems 2005. *Address:* University of the Arts, 320 South Broad Street, Philadelphia, PA 19102, USA (office). *Telephone:* (212) 421-1700 (agent) (office); (215) 717-6265 (office). *Fax:* (212) 980-3671 (agent). *Website:* www.uarts.edu (office).

PAHOR, Boris; Italian writer; b. 28 Aug. 1913, Trieste. *Education:* Capodistria Seminary Coll., Univ. of Padua. *Career:* promoted Slovene culture and democratic principles throughout lifetime; published first short stories in Yugoslavia under pseudonym Jožko Ambrožič; spent time in German concentration camps during World War II; teacher of Italian literature in a Slovene-language school, Trieste 1953–75; co-founder Zaliv magazine (with Alojz Rebula) to promote democracy and culture 1966, magazine banned in Yugoslavia and Pahor banned from entering country –1981; fmr mem. Association internationale des langues et cultures minoritaires (AIDLCM). *Publications:* Moj tržaški naslov (My Trieste Address) 1948, Mesto v zalivu (The City in the Bay) 1955, Vila ob jezeru (The Villa by the Lake) 1955, Nomadi brez oaze (Nomads without an Oasis) 1956, Kres v pristanu (The Bonfire in the Quay) 1959, Onkraj pekla so ljudje (There Are People Beyond Hell) 1961, Nekropola (trans. as Pilgrim Among the Shadows) 1967, Varno naročje (In a Safe Haven) 1975, Zatemnitev (Twilight) 1975, Edvard Kocbek: pričevalec našega časa (Edvard Kocbek: the Witness of Our Epoch) (with Alojz Rebula) 1975, Spopad s pomladjo (Struggling with Spring) 1978, V labirintu (In the Labirinth) 1984, Ta ocean strašnó odprt (This Ocean So Terribly Opened) 1989, Zibelka sveta (The Craddle of the World) 1999, Dihanje morja (The Breathing of the Sea) 2001, Notranji odmevi (Inner Echoes) 2003, Trg Oberdan (Oberdan Square) 2006, Srečko Kosovel: pričevalec zaznamovanega stoletja (Srečko Kosovel: the Witness of a Stigmatized Century) 2008, Necropoli 2008. *Honours:* Chevalier, Legion d'honneur (France) 2007; Dr hc (Ljubljana, Koper); Prešeren Award 1992, Besten Liste (Germany) 2001. *Address:* c/o Fazi Editore, Via Isonzo 42/c, 00198 Rome (office); Salita a Contovello 71, 34136 Trieste, Italy (home). *Telephone:* 40425048 (home). *E-mail:* info@fazieditore.it (office); b.pahor@yahoo.it (home). *Website:* www.fazieditore.it (office).

PAIGE, Richard (see Koontz, Dean Ray)

PAIGE, Robin (see Albert, Susan Wittig)

PAINTER, Rev. John, ThL, ThSchol, BD, PhD, FAHA; Australian theologian, academic and writer; *Biblical Research Scholar and Professor of Theology, St Mark's National Theological Centre, Charles Sturt University*; b. (Jack Painter), 22 Sept. 1935, Bellingen, NSW; s. of Edward Vincent Painter and Gladys Lucy Painter; m. Gillian Gray 1963; two d. *Education:* Australian Coll. of Theology, Univs of London and Durham, UK. *Career:* Tutor, St John's Coll., Durham 1965–68; Precentor, St Andrew's Cathedral, Sydney 1968–70; Assoc. Prof., Univ. of Cape Town, SA 1971–76; Assoc. Prof. and Reader, Latrobe Univ., Melbourne 1977–97; Biblical Research Scholar and Prof. of Theology, St Mark's Nat. Theological Centre, Charles Sturt Univ., Canberra 1997–. *Publications:* John: Witness and Theologian 1975 (and subsequent edns), Theology as Hermeneutics: Rudolf Bultmann's Interpretation of the History of Jesus 1987, The Quest for the Messiah 1991 (second revised and expanded edn 1993), Mark: Worlds in Conflict 1997, Just James, The Brother of Jesus in History and Tradition 1997 (second revised and expanded edn 2004), 1, 2, and 3 John 2002; more than 100 articles and chapters in monographs and journals including New Testament Studies, Journal for the Study of the New Testament, Scottish Journal of Theology, Interpretation, Journal of Theological Studies, Novum Testamentum. *Honours:* Centenary Medal 2003. *Address:* St Mark's National Theological Centre, Charles Sturt University, 15 Blackhall Street, Barton, ACT 2600 (office); PO Box 321, Jamison Centre, Macquarie, ACT 2614, Australia (home). *Telephone:* (2) 6272-6211 (office); (2) 6273-1572 (office); (2) 6272-6252 (office). *Fax:* (2) 6273-4067 (office). *E-mail:* jpainter@csu.edu.au (office). *Website:* www.csu.edu.au/faculty/arts/theology/staff/profiles/academic-staff/john-painter (office); www.stmarksntc.org.au/thl/staff/default.htm.

PAKENHAM, Thomas Francis Dermot, BA; British historian and writer; b. 14 Aug. 1933, s. of 7th Earl of Longford and Elizabeth, Countess of Longford (succeeded father as 8th Earl of Longford 2001, but does not use title); m. Valerie 1964; two s. two d. *Education:* Dragon School, Oxford, Belvedere Coll., Dublin, Ampleforth Coll., York, Magdalen Coll., Oxford. *Career:* travelled in Nr East and Ethiopia 1955–56; freelance writer 1956–58; editorial staff mem., Times Educational Supplement 1958–60, Sunday Telegraph 1961, The Observer 1961–64; Chair. Ladbroke Asscn 1988–91; mem., Victorian Soc. (co-founder 1958–, cttee mem. 1958–64) Historic Irish Tourist Houses and Gardens Asscn (co-founder, cttee mem. 1968–72), British-Irish Asscn (treas. 1972–2002, chair. 2002–), Christopher Ewart-Biggs Memorial Trust (sec., co-founder 1976–), Irish Tree Soc. (founder and chair. 1990–); sr assoc. mem. St Antony's Coll., Oxford 1979–81. *Publications:* non-fiction: The Mountains of Rasselas: an Ethiopian Adventure 1959, The Year of Liberty: History of the Great Irish Rebellion of 1798 1969, The Boer War (Cheltenham Prize 1980) 1979, Dublin: A Traveller's Companion (with Valerie Pakenham) 1988, The Scramble for Africa (Alan Paton Memorial Prize 1992, WHSmith Award 1992) 1991, Meetings with Remarkable Trees 1996, Remarkable Trees of the World 2002, Mythic Woods: The World's Most Remarkable Forests 2004, Remarkable Baobab 2004, In Search of Remarkable Trees 2007. *Honours:* Hon. DLitt (Ulster) 1992. *Address:* 111 Elgin Crescent, London, W11 2JF, England; Tullynally, Castlepollard, Westmeath, Ireland.

PALAHNIUK, Chuck; American novelist and essayist; b. 21 Feb. 1962, Pasco, Wash. *Education:* Univ. of Oregon. *Publications:* novels: Fight Club 1996, Invisible Monsters 1999, Survivor 2000, Lullaby 2002, Nana 2003, Diary 2003, Haunted: a Novel in Stories 2005, Rant 2007, Snuff 2008, Pygmy 2009, Tell-All 2010, Damned 2011; short story collections: Choke 2001, Fugitives and Refugees: A Walk through Portland, Oregon 2003, Stranger than Fiction: True Stories 2004, Non-Fiction 2004; contrib. to Bikini, Black Book, Gear, The Guardian, The Stranger. *Address:* ChuckPalahniuk.net, 3657 Mentone Avenue, Suite 4, Los Angeles, CA 90034-5638, USA (office); c/o Doubleday Publicity, Random House, 1745 Broadway, New York, NY 10019, USA (office). *E-mail:* tdoughty@randomhouse.com (office). *Website:* www.chuckpalahniuk.net.

PALČINSKAITE, Violeta; Lithuanian writer; b. 20 Nov. 1943, Kaunas; m. (divorced). *Education:* Univ. of Vilnius. *Career:* first book of poetry published 1961; first children's play performed by Lithuanian State Youth Theatre 1966. *Plays:* I Am Going after Summer, The Iron Princess, Andrius, Kristian Andersen's Rose. *Film scripts include:* Andrius, Train to Bulzibar, The Iron Princess. *Publications include:* Stairs (poetry) 1985, The Dolls of the Old City (children's poetry) 1987, I am Going After Summer (plays) 1988, A Spotted Snail of Dreamland 1997, Window-Sills Over an Alley (collection of poetry and plays for children) 2003; books for children: The King Forgot the ABC..., The Magic Flute of Mozart, Music for Troll. *Honours:* Gold Medal Int. Children's Film Festival, Italy 1982, Int. Bd on Books for Young People Honours List 1988, WIPO Creativity Award 2009. *Address:* Antakalnio 8-3, 10308 Vilnius, Lithuania (home). *Telephone:* (5) 2625628 (home). *E-mail:* violpalc@gmail.com (home).

PALEI, Marina Anatolevna; Dutch (b. Russian) writer and physician; b. (Marina Anatolevna Spivak), 1955, Leningrad (now St Petersburg); m. (divorced); one s. *Education:* State Medical Acad., Leningrad, Inst. of Literature, Moscow. *Career:* model at the Mukhina Fine Arts Inst., Leningrad; joined amateur theatre group; lecturer and speaker across Europe 1992–; writer-in-residence Italy, Germany, USA, Sweden, Scotland, Greece; mem. Russian Soc. of Authors, Russian PEN, Netherlands Soc. of Authors. *Publications include:* Pominovenie (translated as Remembrance) 1990, Evgesha i Annushka (translated as Evgesha and Annushka) 1990, Kabiriia s Obvodnogo kanala (translated as Cabiria of the Obvodny Canal) 1991; short story collections: Otdelenie propashchikh (translated as The Lost Souls' Division) 1991, Die Cabiria vom Umleitungskanal 1992, Iz zhizni avtoovetchikov (translated as From the Life of Answering Machines) 1993, Herinnerd huis 1995, Cabiria di Pietroburgo 1996, Rückwärtsgang der Sonne 1997, The Wind-Field 1998, The Long Distance, or the Slavic Accent 2000, The Lunch 2000; contrib. to numerous nat. and int. journals and anthologies. *Honours:* Rockefeller Foundation Grant, awards from Limbus Press (Russia), The Prince Bernhard Foundation (The Netherlands), Graz – The Cultural Capital of Europe 2003. *Literary Agent:* Bettina Nibbe, Nibbe & Wiedling Literary Agency, Rumfordstrasse 10, 80469, Munich, Germany. *Telephone:* (89) 290-840-12. *Fax:* (89) 290-840-50. *E-mail:* nibbe@nibbe-wiedling.de. *Website:* www.nibbe-wiedling.de. *E-mail:* marinapalei@yahoo.co.uk (home). *Website:* www.marinapalei.com.

PALIN, Michael Edward, CBE, BA; British actor, writer and traveller; b. 5 May 1943, Sheffield, Yorks.; s. of the late Edward Palin and Mary Palin; m. Helen M. Gibbins 1966; two s. one d. *Education:* Birkdale School, Sheffield, Shrewsbury School, Brasenose Coll. Oxford. *Career:* Pres. Transport 2000, Royal Geographical Soc. 2009–. *Television:* actor and writer: Monty Python's Flying Circus, BBC TV 1969–74, Ripping Yarns, BBC TV 1976–79; actor: Three Men in a Boat, BBC 1975: writer: East of Ipswich, BBC TV 1987, Number 27, BBC TV, The Weekend (play for stage) 1994; TV series: contrib. to Great Railway Journeys of the World, BBC TV 1980, 1993; presenter Around the World in 80 Days 1989, Pole to Pole 1992, Palin's Column 1994, Full Circle 1997, Michael Palin's Hemingway Adventure 1999, Sahara 2002, Himalaya with Michael Palin 2004, Michael Palin's New Europe 2007; art documentaries (presenter): Palin on Redpath 1997, The Bright Side of Life 2000, The Ladies Who Loved Matisse 2003, Michael Palin and the Mystery of Hammershoi 2005. *Musical theatre:* Monty Python's Spamalot 2006. *Films:* actor and co-author: And Now for Something Completely Different 1970, Monty Python and the Holy Grail 1974, Monty Python's Life of Brian 1979, Time Bandits 1980, Monty Python's 'The Meaning of Life' 1982; actor, writer and co-producer: The Missionary 1982; actor, co-scriptwriter: American Friends 1991; actor: Jabberwocky 1976, A Private Function 1984, Brazil 1985, A Fish Called Wanda 1988 (Best Supporting Film Actor, BAFTA Award 1988), GBH (Channel 4 TV) 1991, Fierce Creatures 1997. *Publications include:* Monty Python's Big Red Book 1970, Monty Python's Brand New Book 1973, Montypythonscrapbook 1979, Dr Fegg's Encyclopaedia of All World Knowledge 1984, Limericks 1985, Around the World in 80 Days 1989, Pole to Pole 1992, Hemingway's Chair 1995, Full Circle 1997, Michael Palin's Hemingway Adventure 1999, Sahara 2002, The Pythons Autobiography (co-author) 2003, Himalaya (British Book Award for TV & Film Book of the Year 2005) 2004, Diaries 1969–1979: The Python Years 2006, New Europe 2007, Halfway to Hollywood: Diaries 1980–88 2009; for children: Small Harry and the Toothache Pills 1981, The Mirrorstone 1986, The Cyril Stories 1986. *Honours:* Dr hc (Sheffield) 1992, (Queen's, Belfast) 2000; Michael Balcon Award for outstanding contrib. to cinema (with Monty Python), BAFTA 1987, Travel Writer of the Year, British Book Awards 1993, Lifetime Achievement Award, British Comedy Awards 2002, BCA Illustrated Book of the Year Award 2002, BAFTA Special Award for Outstanding Contrib. to TV 2005, British Book Award for Outstanding Achievement 2009. *Literary Agent:* Mayday Management, 34 Tavistock Street, London, WC2E 7PB, England. *Telephone:* (20) 7497-1100. *Fax:* (20) 7497-1133. *Website:* www.palinstravels.co.uk.

PALING, Chris, BA; British writer and radio producer; b. 7 Dec. 1956, Derby, England; m. Julie Fiona 1979; one s. one d. *Education:* Sussex Univ. *Publications:* After the Raid, Deserters, Morning All Day, The Silent Sentry, Newton's Swing 2000, The Repentant Morning 2003, A Town by the Sea 2005, Minding 2007, Nimrod's Shadow 2010; contrib. to Literary Review, The Times, Punch, Independent Magazine, Spectator. *Literary Agent:* Rogers, Coleridge & White Ltd, 20 Powis Mews, London, W11 1JN, England. *Telephone:* (20) 7221-3717. *Website:* www.rcwlitagency.com.

PALLEY, Julian, BA, MA, PhD; American academic, poet and translator; b. 16 Sept. 1925, Atlantic City, NJ; m. Shirley Wilson 1950; four s. *Education:* Mexico City College, University of Arizona, University of New Mexico. *Career:* Instructor, Rutgers University, 1956–59; Assoc. Prof., Arizona State University, 1959–62, University of Oregon, 1962–66; Prof. of Spanish Literature, University of California at Irvine, 1966–; mem. California State Poetry Society. *Publications:* Spinoza's Stone, 1976; Bestiary, 1987; Pictures at an Exhibition, 1989; Family Portraits, 1994. Other: several trans. Contributions: reviews, quarterlies, and journals. *Honours:* Arizona Quarterly Poetry Prize, 1956; Jefferson Poetry Prize, 1976.

PALMA, Milagros, DèsL; French (b. Nicaraguan) anthropologist, writer and publisher; *Professor, University of Caen;* b. 26 March 1949, León, Nicaragua; d. of Alicia Guzmán. *Education:* León, Paris and Univ. of Paris X (Paris-Nanterre). *Career:* Ed. Indigo and Côté-Femmes Publrs 1989–. *Publications:* Palabra mítica de la Gente del Agua 1983, El Cóndor, dimensión mítica del Ave Sagrada (2nd edn) 1984, Los viajeros de la Gran Anaconda, Le ventre de la grande femme de l'Amazonie 1986, La mujer es puro cuento 1987, Senderos Míticos de Nicaragua, Revolución tranquila de Santos, Diablos y Diablitos 1988, Nicaragua: Once mil. vírgenes 1988, Bodas de cenizas (novel) 1990, Le ver et le fruit ou L'apprentissage de la féminité en Amérique latine 1991, Desencanto al amanecer (novel) 1995, Le pacte 1998, Un Latino-américain à Paris (novel) 2005, El Mito de Paris, Veinte entrevistas con escritores de América Latina en Francia 2005, Le Paris Latino-Américains, El Paris Latinoamericano, Anthologie d'écrivains latino-américains à Paris 2006, Ecriture de femmes d'Amérique latine en France du XIX siècle à nos jours 2007. *Honours:* Maison des Ecrivains grant for foreign writers 1987, Prix José Marti UNESCO 1998. *Address:* Côté-Femmes, 55 rue des Petites Ecuries, 75010 Paris, France (office). *Telephone:* 9-61-24-33-54 (office). *Fax:* 1-43-79-46-87 (home). *E-mail:* indigo-cf@wanadoo.fr (office). *Website:* indigo-cf.com (office).

PALMER, Alan Warwick, MA, MLitt, FRSL; British writer; b. 28 Sept. 1926, Ilford, Essex, England; m. Veronica Mary Cordell 1951. *Education:* Oriel Coll., Oxford. *Career:* Asst Master Highgate School, London 1951–53, Sr History Master 1953–69. *Publications:* A Dictionary of Modern History, 1789–1945 1962, Independent Eastern Europe: A History (with C. A. Macartney) 1962, Yugoslavia 1964, The Gardeners of Salonika 1965, Napoleon in Russia 1967, The Lands Between: A History of East Central Europe Since the Congress of Vienna 1970, Metternich 1972, The Life and Times of George VI 1972, Russia in War and Peace 1972, Alexander I: Tsar of War and Peace 1974, Age of Optimism 1974, Nations and Empires (ed.) 1974, Frederick the Great 1974, Bismark 1976, Kings and Queens of England 1976, Quotations in History: A Dictionary of Historical Quotations, c. 800 AD to the Present (with Victoria Palmer) 1976, The Kaiser: Warlord of the Second Reich 1978, Princes of Wales 1979, The Facts on File Dictionary of 20th Century History 1979, The Penguin Dictionary of Twentieth-Century History 1979, Who's Who in Modern History 1980, Who's Who in Shakespeare's England (with Veronica Palmer) 1981, The Chancelleries of Europe 1983, Royal England: A Historical Gazetteer (with Veronica Palmer) 1983, An Encyclopaedia of Napoleon's Europe 1984, Crowned Cousins: The Anglo-German Royal Connection 1985, The Banner of Battle: The Story of the Crimean War 1987, Who's Who in Bloomsbury (with Veronica Palmer) 1987, The East End: Four Centuries of London Life 1989, The Chronology of British History (with Veronica Palmer) 1992, The Decline and Fall of the Ottoman Empire 1992, Twilight of the Habsburgs: The Life and Times of Emperor Francis Joseph 1995, Dictionary of the British Empire and Commonwealth 1996, The Pimlico Chronology of British History: From 250,000 BC to the Present (with Veronica Palmer) 1996, Who's Who in World Politics: From 1860 to the Present Day 1996, Victory 1918 2000, Fictional Minds 2005; contribs to journals. *Address:* c/o Carroll & Graf Publishers, 245 West 17th Street, 11th floor, New York, NY 10011-5300, USA. *Telephone:* (212) 981-9919. *Fax:* (646) 375-2571.

PALMER, Diana (see Kyle, Susan Eloise Spaeth)

PALMER, Frank Robert, MA, DLitt, FBA; British academic; *Professor Emeritus of Linguistic Science, University of Reading;* b. 9 April 1922, Westerleigh, Glos., England; s. of George Samuel Palmer and Gertrude Lilian Palmer (née Newman); m. Jean Elisabeth Moore 1948; three s. two d. *Education:* Bristol Grammar School, New Coll., Oxford, Merton Coll., Oxford. *Career:* Lecturer in Linguistics, SOAS, Univ. of London 1950–60; Prof. of Linguistics, Univ. Coll. of North Wales, Bangor 1960–65; Prof. of Linguistic Science, Univ. of Reading 1965–87, Dean, Faculty of Letters and Social Sciences 1969–72, Prof. Emer. 1987–; Vice-Pres., Philological Soc.; Chair. Linguistics Asscn (GB) 1965–68, Ed. Journal of Linguistics 1969–79, Linguistic Soc. of America Prof., Buffalo, USA 1971; Distinguished Visiting Prof., Univ. of Delaware, Newark, USA 1982; mem. Academia Europaea 1992. *Publications:* The Morphology of the Tigre Noun 1962, A Linguistic Study of the English Verb 1965, Selected Papers of J. R. Firth (1951–58) (ed.) 1968,

Prosodic Analysis (ed.) 1970, Grammar 1971, 1984, The English Verb 1974, 1987, Semantics 1976, 1981, Modality and the English Modals 1979, 1990, Mood and Modality 1986, 2001, Studies in the History of Western Linguistics in Honour of R. H. Robins (co-ed.) 1986, Grammatical Roles and Relations 1994, Grammar and Meaning: Essays in Honour of Sir John Lyons (ed.) 1995, Modality in Contemporary English (co-ed.) 2003, English Modality in Perspective (co-ed.) 2004. *Honours:* Hon. DLitt 1997. *Address:* 'Whitethorns', Roundabout Lane, Winnersh, Wokingham, Berks., RG41 5AD, England (home). *Telephone:* (118) 978-6214 (home). *E-mail:* llspalmf@reading.ac.uk (home).

PALMER, John, BA; Canadian playwright, teacher, screenwriter and theatre and film director; *Course Instructor, Ryerson University, Toronto*; b. (Murray John Palmer), 13 May 1943, Sydney, NS. *Education:* Carleton Univ., Ottawa. *Career:* early career in writing radio shows for CBC; Artistic Dir, Le Hibou Theatre, Ottawa 1965, Woodstock Little Theatre 1968; Co-founder, Artistic Dir, Canadian Place Theatre, Stratford 1969; Assoc. Dir dramaturg Factory Theatre, Toronto 1970–73, resident playwright 1997–98; founder and Co-Chair., Playwrights Union of Canada 1971; Literary Co-founder, Co-Artistic Dir and Literary Man. Toronto Free Theatre 1972–76; teacher/dir/playwright Juilliard School, New York 1979–81; resident playwright, Canadian Rep Theatre 1983–87; Resident Playwright, Nat. Theatre School of Canada, Montreal 1983–87; teacher Nat. Theatre School of Canada 1993–2003, Humber Coll. 1996–97, Course Dir York Univ., Toronto 1991–93, Directing Course Instructor, Ryerson Univ., Toronto 2003–06, also Brooklyn Acad. of Music, Smith Coll., Massachusetts, Glasgow School of Art, Arcadia Univ., Yale School of Drama. *Films:* Monkeys in the Attic 1973, Me 1975, SUGAR (writer, dir) (Best Feature, Toronto Lesbian and Gay Film Festival) 2004, Lockpick Pornography 2010. *Plays:* Singapore, Lillian's Lament, Making Brownies Like we Used to, A Day at the Beach, How it all Began, Memories for my Brother, Out to Breakfast, A Touch of God in the Golden Age, Bland Hysteria, Henrik Ibsen on the Necessity of Producing Norwegian Drama, The Pits, Anthem, Confessions of a Necrophile, Diary of a Madman, I'm Going to Pin my Medal on the Girl I left behind, Visions of an Unseemly Youth, Vesuvius Goes to Market. *Publications:* many of his plays. *Address:* 32 Monteith Street, Toronto, ON M4Y 1K7, Canada (home). *Telephone:* (416) 967-7455 (home). *E-mail:* jpadd09@sympatico.ca (home).

PALMER, (George) Michael, BA, MA; American poet, writer and translator; b. 11 May 1943, New York; m. Cathy Simon 1972; one d. *Education:* Harvard Univ. *Career:* has lectured at colls and univs in USA and Europe; collaborates on dance works and with numerous composers and performance artists; contributing ed. Facture magazine; Visiting Prof. Cardiff Univ. 2004; chancellor American Acad. of Poets. *Publications:* Plan of the City of O 1971, Blake's Newton 1972, C's Songs 1973, The Circular Gates 1974, Without Music 1977, Transparency of the Mirror 1980, Alogon 1980, Notes for Echo Lake 1981, Code of Signals: Recent Writings in Poetics (ed.) 1983, First Figure 1984, Songs for Sarah 1987, Sun 1988, For a Reading 1988, An Alphabet Underground 1993, At Passages (America Award for Poetry) 1995, The Lion Bridge 1998, The Danish Notebook 1998, The Promises of Glass 2000, Codes Appearing: Poems 1979–1988 2001, Company of Moths (poems) 2005, Active Boundaries (Selected Essays) 2008; other: trans, ed. of books; contributions to many anthologies, books and journals. *Honours:* two Nat. Endowment for the Arts Fellowships, Guggenheim Fellowship, Lila Wallace Readers Digest Fund Writer's Award 1992–94, Shelley Memorial Award of the Poetry Soc. of America 2001, Wallace Stevens Prize, Acad. of American Poets 2006. *Address:* 265 Jersey Street, San Francisco, CA 94114, USA (home).

PAMUK, Orhan; Turkish novelist and academic; *Robert Yik-Fong Tam Professor of the Humanities, Columbia University*; b. 7 June 1952, Istanbul; m. Aylin Turegen 1982 (divorced 2001); one d. *Education:* Robert Coll., Istanbul Technical Univ., Inst. of Journalism at Istanbul Univ. *Career:* jury mem. Cannes Film Festival 2007; mem. American Acad. of Arts and Sciences 2008–, Chinese Acad. for Social Sciences 2008–; currently Robert Yik-Fong Tam Prof. of the Humanities, Columbia Univ., USA. *Publications:* Cevdet Bey ve Ogullari (Cevdet Bey and His Sons) 1983, Sessiz Ev (The Quiet House) (Madarali Novel Prize, Turkey 1984) 1983, Beyaz Kale (trans. as The White Castle) (Independent Foreign Fiction Prize 1990) 1985, Kara Kitap (trans. as The Black Book) (Prix France Culture 1995) 1990, Gizli Yuz (screenplay of Kara Kitap) 1992, Yeni Hayat (trans. as The New Life) 1995, My Name is Red (trans.) (Prix du Meilleur Livre Etranger, France 2002, Premio Grinzane Cavour, Italy 2002, Int. IMPAC Dublin Literary Award 2003) 2000, Istanbul 2003, Snow (trans.) (Prix Médicis Etranger, France 2005) 2004, Istanbul: Memories of a City 2006, Istanbul: City of a Hundred Names 2007, Other Colours (essays) 2007, Masumiyet Müzesi (trans. as The Museum of Innocence) 2008, Manzaradan Parçalar 'Hayat, Sokaklar, Edebiyat' 2010, The Naive and the Sentimental Novelist 2011; contrib. to various newspapers and magazines. *Honours:* Dr hc (American Univ. of Beirut) 2003, (Georgetown Univ.) 2007, Bogaziçi Univ.) 2007, (Tilburg Univ.) 2007, (Free Univ. of Berlin) 2007, (Univ. of Bucharest) 2008, (Madrid Univ.) 2008; Milliyet Press Novel Contest, first prize 1979, Orhan Kemal Novel Prize 1983, Prix de la Découverte Européenne 1991, Ricardo-Huch Prize 2005, Nobel Prize in Literature 2006, Distinguished Humanist Award, Washington Univ. 2006, Puterbaugh Award 2006, Ovid Award 2008, Norman Mailer Lifetime Achievement Award 2010. *Address:* 415 Dodge Hall, School of the Arts, Columbia University, 2960 Broadway, New York, NY 10027, USA (office). *Website:* arts.columbia.edu (office); www.orhanpamuk.net.

PANDE, Mrinal; Indian journalist, editor and broadcasting executive; *Chairman of Prasar Bharati*; b. 1946, Tikamgarh, Madhya Pradesh; d. of the late Gaura Pant Shivani; m.; two d. *Education:* Allahabad Univ. *Career:* taught at Univs of Allahabad, Delhi and Bhopal; Ed. Vama (women's magazine) 1984–87; Editor-Anchor (Hindi news), Star News and Doordarshan; Chief Ed. Hindustan (Hindi daily) 2000–09; Chair. Prasar Bharati (public service broadcaster) 2010–; fmr Sec. Gen. Eds Guild of India; Founder-Pres. Indian Women's Press Corps. *Television:* Baaton Baaton Mein (host). *Publications include:* The Subject is Woman 1991, Daughter's Daughter 1993, That Which Ram Hath Ordained 1993, Devi, Tales of the Goddess in Our Time 2000, My Own Witness 2001. *Honours:* Padmashree 2006. *Address:* Prasar Bharati, 2nd Floor, PTI Building, Sansad Marg, New Delhi 110 001, India (office). *Telephone:* (11) 23753687 (office). *Fax:* (11) 23737589 (office). *Website:* prasarbharati.gov.in.

PANKIN, Boris Dmitriyevich; Russian diplomatist (retd) and essayist; b. 20 Feb. 1931, Frunze (now Bishkek); m.; two s. one d. *Education:* Moscow State Univ. *Career:* journalist and literary critic 1957–; Ed. Komsomolskaya Pravda 1965–73; Chair. Bd USSR Copyright Agency 1973–82; USSR Amb. to Sweden 1982–90, to Czechoslovakia 1990–91; Foreign Minister Aug.–Dec. 1991; Russian Amb. to UK 1991–94; now living in Sweden. *Publications:* Severe Literature, Time and Word, Boundaries and Books, The Last 100 Days of the Soviet Union, Four I of Konstantin Simonov. *Honours:* USSR State Prize 1982. *Telephone:* (46) 880-7871.

PANNENBERG, Wolfhart Ulrich, DTheol, FBA; German academic; *Professor Emeritus, University of Munich*; b. 2 Oct. 1928, Stettin; s. of Kurt B.S. Pannenberg and Irmgard Pannenberg; m. Hilke Sabine Schütte 1954. *Education:* Univ. of Heidelberg. *Career:* ordained as Lutheran Minister 1956; Privatdozent, Heidelberg 1955–58; Prof. of Systematic Theology, Univ. of Wuppertal 1958–61; Prof., Univ. of Mainz 1961–67; Prof., Univ. of Munich 1967–94, Prof. Emer. 1994–, fmr Head, Inst. of Ecumenical Theology; mem. Bavarian Acad. of Sciences. *Publications:* Offenbarung als Geschichte (translated as Revelation as History) 1961, Was ist der Mensch?: Die Anthropologie der Gegenwart im Lichte der Theologie (translated as What is Man?) 1962, Grundzüge der Christologie (translated as Jesus: God and Man) 1964, Grundfragen systematischer Theologie (two vols, translated as Basic Questions in Theology) 1967, 1980, Theology and the Kingdom of God 1969, Spirit, Faith and Church (with Carl E. Braaten and Avery Dulles) 1970, Thesen zur Theologie der Kirche 1970, Das Glaubensbekenntnis (translated as The Apostles' Creed in the Light of Today's Questions) 1972, Gottesgedanke und menschliche Freiheit (translated as The Idea of God and Human Freedom) 1972, Wissenschaftstheorie und Theologie (translated as Theology and the Philosophy of Science) 1973, Glaube und Wirklichkeit (translated as Faith and Reality) 1975, Ethik und Ekklesiologie 1977, Human Nature, Election and History 1977, Anthropologie in Theologischer Perspektive (translated as Anthropology in Theological Perspective) 1983, Christian Spirituality 1983, Christentum in Einer Säkularisierten Welt (translated as Christianity in a Secularized World) 1988, Systematische Theologie (three vols, translated as Systematic Theology) 1988–93, Metaphysik und Gottesgedanke (translated as Metaphysics and the Idea of God) 1988, An Introduction to Systematic Theology 1991, Toward a Theology of Nature: Essays on Science and Faith 1993, Grundlagen der Ethik 1996, Theologie und Philosophie 1996, Problemgeschichte der neueren Evangelischen Theologie in Deutschland 1997, Beiträge zur systematischen Theologie (three vols) 1999–2000, Beiträge zur Ethik 2004, Analogie und Offenbarung 2007. *Honours:* Hon. DD (Glasgow) 1972, (Manchester) 1977, (Trinity Coll. Dublin) 1979, (St Andrews) 1993, (Cambridge) 1997, (Comillas, Madrid) 1999. *Telephone:* (89) 21803482 (office); (89) 855915 (home).

PANYCH, Morris Stephen, BFA; Canadian dramatist, writer, actor and director; b. 30 June 1952, Calgary, AB. *Education:* NAIT, Edmonton, Univ. of British Columbia. *Publications:* Last Call 1983, 7 Stories 1990, The Ends of the Earth 1993, Other Schools of Thought 1994, Vigil 1995, Lawrence and Holloman 1998, Girl in the Goldfish Bowl 2002, Earshot 2004, The Dishwashers 2005, What Lies Before Us 2007, Benevolence 2007. *Honours:* six Jessie Awards, Vancouver Theatre, five Dora Mavor Moore Awards, Toronto Theatre, two Gov.-Gen.'s Awards for English Drama 1994, 2004. *Literary Agent:* c/o Gary Goddard Agency, 305 10 St Mary Street, Toronto, ON M4Y 1P9, Canada. *Telephone:* (416) 928-0299. *Fax:* (416) 924-9593. *E-mail:* goddard@canadafilm.com. *Website:* 2X2ltd.com.

PAOLINI, Christopher; American children's writer; b. 17 Nov. 1983, California. *Publications:* Inheritance Trilogy: Book I: Eragon 2002, Book II: Eldest (Quill Book Award for Young Adult/Teen 2006) 2005, Book III: Brisingr 2008. *Literary Agent:* Simon Lipskar, Writers' House, 21 W 26th Street, New York, NY 10010, USA. *Telephone:* (212) 685-2400. *Fax:* (212) 685-1781. *Website:* writershouse.com. *Address:* c/o Children's Publishing Publicity Department, Random House, 1745 Broadway, New York, NY 10019, USA (office). *Website:* www.alagaesia.com.

PAOLUCCI, Anne, BA, MA, PhD; American academic (retd), poet, writer, dramatist and editor; *President, Council on National Literatures*; b. Rome, Italy; m. Henry Paolucci (deceased). *Education:* Barnard Coll., Columbia Univ. *Career:* Instructor, City College CUNY 1959–61, Asst Prof. 1961–69; Fulbright Lecturer in American Drama, Univ. of Naples 1965–67; Distinguished Research Prof., St John's Univ., Jamaica, New York 1969–75, Prof. of English 1969–97, Chair Dept of English 1974–75, 1982–91, Dir Doctor of Arts

Degree Program in English 1982–96; Founder, Publisher, and Ed.-in-Chief, Review of National Literatures 1970–2001; Founder-Pres. Council on National Literatures 1975–; mem. Nat. Council on the Humanities 1986–93; mem. American Comparative Literature Asscn; CUNY board of trustees 1996–, chair. 1997–99; Dante Society of America; Dramatists Guild; Hon. mem. MLA. *Film:* Admiral of the Ocean Sea (screenplay) 2009. *Publications:* poetry: Poems Written for Sbek's Mummies, Marie Menken, and Other Important People, Places, and Things 1977, Riding the Mast Where It Swings 1980, Gorbachev in Concert (and Other Poems) 1991, Queensboro Bridge (and Other Poems) 1995; fiction: Eight Short Stories 1977, Sepia Tones: Seven Short Stories 1985, Terminal Degrees (novella) 1997, Do Me A Favor (and Other Stories) 2002, In Wolf's Clothing (novel) 2003, Slow Dance to Samara (mystery novel) 2007, Where the Sun is Silent (novel) 2010; non-fiction: Hegel on Tragedy (with Henry Paolucci) 1962, A Short History of American Drama 1966, Eugene O'Neill, Arthur Miller, Edward Albee 1967, From Tension to Tonic: The Plays of Edward Albee 1972, Pirandello's Theater: The Recovery of the Stage for Dramatic Art 1974, Dante and the 'Quest for Eloquence' in the Vernacular Languages of India (with Henry Paolucci) 1984, The Women in Dante's Divine Comedy and Spenser's Faerie Queene 2005, Edward Albee (The Later Plays) 2009, Selected Essays on Luigi Pirandello 2009; plays: The Short Season, Minions of the Race 1978 (video 2003), Cipango! 1986 (video 1990); editor: Dante's Influence on American Writers 1977; trans.: Selected Poems of Giacomo Leopardi 2004; contrib. to numerous books, reviews and journals. *Honours:* Commendatore Order of Merit, Italy 1992; Hon. Degree in Humane Letters, Lehman Coll., CUNY 1995; Fulbright Scholarship, Univ. of Rome, Italy 1951–52, Woodbridge Hon. Fellowship, Columbia Univ. 1961–62, Writer-in-Residence, Yaddo 1965, ACLS Grant 1978, Gold Medal, Canada 1991, Lifetime Achievement Award, New York State Senate. *Address:* CNL/ Anne and Henry Paolucci International Conference Center, 68–02 Metropolitan Avenue, Middle Village, NY 11379, USA (office). *Telephone:* (718) 821-3916 (office); (718) 767-8380 (home). *Website:* www.annehenrypaolucci.com.

PAPALEO, Joseph, BA, MA; American academic and writer; b. 13 Jan. 1926, New York, NY; m., four s. *Education:* Sarah Lawrence College, University of Florence, Italy, Columbia University. *Career:* Teacher, Fieldston Prep School, 1952–60; Prof. of Literature and Writing, Sarah Lawrence College, 1960–68, 1969–92; Guest Prof., Laboratorio de Cibernetica, Naples, Italy, 1968–69; mem. Authors' Guild; Italian American Writers Asscn; American Asscn of University Profs. *Publications:* All the Comforts (novel), 1968; Out of Place (novel), 1971; Picasso at Ninety One, 1988; several short stories; contrib. to journals and magazines. *Honours:* Guggenheim Fellowship, 1974; Ramapo College Poetry Prize, 1986.

PAPINEAU, David Calder, BA, BSc, PhD; British philosopher, academic and writer; *Professor, King's College, London*; b. 30 Sept. 1947, Como, Italy; m. Rose Wild 1986; one s. one d. *Education:* Univ. of Natal, Univ. of Cambridge. *Career:* Prof., King's College, London 1990–; mem. British Soc. for the Philosophy of Science, Pres. 1993–95. *Publications:* For Science in the Social Sciences 1978, Theory and Meaning 1979, Reality and Representation 1987, Philosophical Naturalism 1993, Introducing Consciousness 2000, Thinking About Consciousness 2002, The Roots of Reason. *Address:* Department of Philosophy, King's College, Strand, London, WC2R 2LS, England (office). *Website:* www.kcl.ac.uk/philosophy (office).

PARES, Marion, (Judith Campbell, Anthony Grant); British writer; b. 7 Nov. 1914, West Farleigh, Kent, England; m. Humphrey Pares 1937, four d. *Publications:* Family Pony 1962, The Queen Rides 1965, Horses in the Sun 1966, Police Horse 1967, World of Horses 1969, World of Ponies, 1970, Anne: Portrait of a Princess 1970, Family on Horseback (with N. Toyne) 1971, Princess Anne and Her Horses 1971, Elizabeth and Philip 1972, The Campions 1973, Royalty on Horseback 1974, The World of Horses 1975, Anne and Mark 1976, Queen Elizabeth II 1979, The Mutant 1980, Charles: A Prince of His Time 1980, The Royal Partners 1982, Royal Horses 1983. *E-mail:* enquiries@janebadgerbooks.co.uk.

PARETSKY, Sara N., MBA, PhD; American writer; b. 8 June 1947, Ames, Ia; d. of David Paretsky and Mary E. Edwards; m. Courtenay Wright 1976; three c. *Education:* Univs of Kansas and Chicago. *Career:* Man. Urban Research Center, Chicago, Ill. 1971–74, CNA Insurance Co., Chicago 1977–85; writer of crime novels 1982–; Pres. Sisters in Crime, Chicago 1986–88; Dir Nat. Abortion Rights Action League, Ill. 1987–90; mem. Crime Writers' Asscn. *Publications include:* Indemnity Only 1982, Deadlock (Friends of American Writers Prize 1985) 1984, Killing Orders 1986, Bitter Medicine 1987, Toxic Shock (British Crime Writers' Asscn Silver Dagger for Fiction 1988) 1987, Blood Shot 1988, Burn Marks 1990, Guardian Angel 1992, A Woman's Eye (ed.) 1992, Tunnel Vision 1994, Women on the Case 1997, Hard Time 2000, Total Recall 2002, Blacklist 2003 (British Crime Writers' Asscn Gold Dagger for Fiction 2004), Fire Sale 2006, Writing in an Age of Silence 2007, Bleeding Kansas 2008, Hardball 2009, Body Work 2010; numerous short stories and articles. *Honours:* four hon. degrees; Ms Magazine Woman of the Year 1987, CWA Silver Dagger Award 1988, Diamond Dagger for Lifetime Achievement, British Crime Writers Asscn 2002. *Literary Agent:* c/o Dominick Abel Literary Agency, Inc., 146 West 82nd Street, Apartment 1A, New York, NY 10024, USA. *Telephone:* (212) 877-0710. *E-mail:* dominick@dalainc.com. *E-mail:* viwarshawski@mindspring.com (office). *Website:* www.saraparetsky.com.

PARINI, Jay, AB, BPhil, PhD, DLitt, LLD; American writer, poet, literary critic and academic; *D.E. Axinn Professor of English and Creative Writing, Middlebury College*; b. 2 April 1948, Pittston, Pa; m. Devon Stacey Jersild 1981; three s. *Education:* Lafayette Coll., Univ. of St Andrews, UK. *Career:* Faculty, Dartmouth Coll. 1975–82; Co-founder New England Review 1976; Prof. of English, Middlebury Coll. 1982–, D.E. Axinn Prof. of English and Creative Writing, currently also Dir Creative Writing Programme; Fowler Hamilton Fellow, Christ Church Coll. Oxford, UK 1993–94; Fellow, Inst. for Advanced Studies, Univ. of London 2004–05. *Film:* The Last Station 2009. *Publications:* fiction: The Love Run 1980, The Patch Boys 1986, The Last Station 1990, Bay of Arrows 1992, Benjamin's Crossing 1997, The Apprentice Lover 2002, The Passages of H.M 2010; poetry: Singing in Time 1972, Anthracite Country 1982, Town Life 1988, House of Days 1988; non-fiction: Theodore Roethke: An American Romantic 1979, An Invitation to Poetry 1988, John Steinbeck: A Biography 1995, Some Necessary Angels (essays) 1998, Robert Frost 1999, One Matchless Time: A Life of William Faulkner 2005, Why Poetry Matters 2008; editor: Gore Vidal: Writer Against the Grain 1992, The Columbia History of American Poetry 1993, The Columbia Anthology of American Poetry 1995, The Norton Book of American Autobiography 1999, Promised Land: Thirteen Books That Changed America 2009, The Passages of H.M. (novel) 2010. *Honours:* Dr hc (Lafayette Coll., Univ. of Scranton); Guggenheim Fellowship 1993–94. *Address:* English Department, Middlebury College, Middlebury, VT 05753, USA (office). *Telephone:* (802) 443-5042 (office). *E-mail:* parini@middlebury.edu (office). *Website:* www.middlebury.edu (office).

PARIS, Bernard Jay, AB, PhD; American academic (retd) and writer; *Professor Emeritus of English, University of Florida*; b. 19 Aug. 1931, Baltimore, Md; s. of Albert Paris and Anna Paris; m. Shirley Helen Freedman 1949, one s. one d. *Education:* Johns Hopkins Univ. *Career:* Instructor, Lehigh Univ. 1956–60; Asst Prof., Michigan State Univ. 1960–64, Assoc. Prof. 1964–67, Prof. 1967–81; Prof. of English, Univ. of Florida 1981–96, Prof. Emer. 1996–; Dir Inst. for Psychological Study of the Arts 1985–92, Int. Karen Horney Soc. 1991–; mem. Modern Language Asscn of America. *Publications:* Experiments in Life: George Eliot's Quest for Values 1965, A Psychological Approach to Fiction: Studies in Thackeray, Stendhal, George Eliot, Dostoevsky and Conrad 1974, Character and Conflict in Jane Austen's Novels 1978, Third Force Psychology and the Study of Literature (ed.) 1986, Shakespeare's Personality (co-ed.) 1989, Bargains with Fate: Psychological Crises and Conflicts in Shakespeare and His Plays 1991, Character as a Subversive Force in Shakespeare: The History and the Roman Plays 1991, Karen Horney: A Psychoanalyst's Search for Self-Understanding 1994, Imagined Human Beings: A Psychological Approach to Character and Conflict in Literature 1997, The Therapeutic Process, by Karen Horney (ed.) 1999, The Unknown Karen Horney, by Karen Horney (ed.) 2000, Rereading George Eliot: Changing Responses to Her Experiments in Life 2003, Conrad's Charlie Marlow: A New Approach to Heart of Darkness and Lord Jim 2005, Dostoevsky's Greatest Characters: A New Approach to Notes from Underground, Crime and Punishment, and The Brothers Karamazov 2008, Heaven and Its Discontents: Milton's Characters in Paradise Lost 2010; contrib. to numerous scholarly and literary journals. *Honours:* Hon. mem. American Inst. for Psychoanalysis, Asscn for the Advancement of Psychoanalysis; Nat. Endowment for the Humanities Fellow 1969, Guggenheim Fellowship 1974. *Address:* 1430 NW 94th Street, Gainesville, FL 32606, USA (home). *Telephone:* (353) 331-6605 (home). *E-mail:* bjparis@ufl.edu (office). *Website:* grove.ufl.edu/~bjparis (office); plaza.ufl.edu/bjparis (office).

PARISI, Joseph Anthony, BA, MA, PhD; American editor, writer, poet and consultant; b. 18 Nov. 1944, Duluth, Minn. *Education:* Coll. of St Thomas, St Paul, Minn., Univ. of Chicago. *Career:* Instructor to Asst Prof. of English, Roosevelt Univ., Chicago 1969–78; Assoc. Ed., Poetry Magazine, Chicago 1976–83, Acting Ed. 1983–85, Ed. 1985–2003; Visiting and Adjunct Asst Prof. of English, Univ. of Illinois at Chicago 1978–87; consultant, American Library Asscn 1980–; Chair., Ruth Lilly Poetry Prize 1986–2003, and Fellowships 1989–2003; producer, writer and host, Poets in Person, Nat. Public Radio 1991; Exec. Dir Modern Poetry Asscn (now The Poetry Foundation) 1996–2003; Fellow, Churchill Coll., Cambridge 2002. *Publications:* The Poetry Anthology 1912–1977: Sixty-five Years of America's Most Distinguished Verse Magazine (ed. with Daryl Hine) 1978, Voices & Visions: Viewer's Guide 1987, Marianne Moore: The Art of a Modernist (ed.) 1989, Poets in Person: Listener's Guide 1992, Dear Editor: A History of Poetry in Letters: The First Fifty Years 1912–1962 (co-ed.) 2002, The Poetry Anthology 1912–2002 (co-ed.) 2002; contributions to reference books, scholarly journals and literary publications. *Honours:* Everett Helm Travelling Fellowship 1999, Guggenheim Fellowship 2000,. *Address:* 3440 North Lake Shore Drive, Chicago, IL 60657, USA. *Telephone:* (773) 525-3116 (home).

PARK, Linda Sue, MA; American writer; b. 25 March 1960, Urbana, Ill.; d. of Ed Park and Susie Park; m. 1983; one s. one d. *Education:* Stanford Univ., Trinity Coll. Dublin, Ireland, Univ. of London. *Career:* worked as writer in public-relations dept of Amoco Oil Co. 1981–83; taught English as second language, London, UK 1984–86, Brooklyn Coll. 1990, Rochester Inst. of Tech.'s English Language Center 1993; began writing children's books 1997. *Publications include:* Seesaw Girl 1999, The Kite Fighters 2000, A Single Shard (American Library Asscn John Newbery Medal 2002) 2001, When My Name Was Keoko (Jane Addams Children's Book Award) 2002, Project Mulberry (Chicago Tribune Young Adult Fiction Prize 2005) 2005, Archer's Quest 2006, Keeping Score 2008, The 39 Clues: Storm Warning 2010, A Long Walk to Water 2010; picture books: Mung-Mong 2004, The Firekeeper's Son

2004, What Does Bunny See? 2005, Bee-bim Bop! 2005, Yom! Yuck! 2006, Tap Dancing on the Roof 2007; contribs to Cricket, Contemporary Poetry, Alsop Review, Click,. *Address:* c/o Clarion Books, 215 Park Avenue South, New York, NY 10003, USA (office). *Website:* www.lspark.com.

PARK, Yongsoo; South Korean/American filmmaker and novelist; m. *Career:* lives in New York, USA. *Film:* Free Country the Movie (writer, dir) 1996, Antigone 5000. *Play:* Free Country (Asian American Theater Co.) 1997. *Publications:* novels: Boy Genius (Kiriyama Prize notable book) 2002, Las Cucarachas 2004. *Honours:* Asian American Writers' Workshop Van Lier Fellowship. *Address:* c/o Akashic Books, PO Box 1456, New York, NY 10009, USA (office).

PARKER, Rev. David C., MTheol, DipTh, ThD, FSA; British theologian and educator; *Edward Cadbury Professor of Theology, University of Birmingham*; b. 4 July 1953, Boston, Lincolnshire; s. of Rev. Dr T. H. L. Parker and Mary Parker; m. Karen Parker, two s. two d. *Education:* Univs of St Andrews and Cambridge and Univ. of Leiden, Netherlands. *Career:* curate, Christian churches, London 1977–80, Oxon. 1980–85; Theological Coll. Tutor, Birmingham, 1985–93; Lecturer and Reader, Univ. of Birmingham, Prof. in Theology, Dir Inst. for Textual Criticism and Electronic Editing 2002–, Edward Cadbury Prof of Theology 2005–; Co-Ed., Int. Greek New Testament Project; mem. Studiorum Novi Testamenti Societas, Soc. of Biblical Literature. *Publications:* Codex Bezae: An Early Christian Manuscript and Its Text 1992, The Gospel of John: The Papyri 1995, The Living Text of the Gospels 1997, Calvin: Commentary on Romans (with T. H. L. Parker) 1999, The Gospel of John: The Majuscule Manuscripts 2007, An Introduction to the New Testament Manuscripts and their Texts 2008, Codex Sinaiticus: The Story of the World's Oldest Bible 2009. *Address:* Institute for Textual Scholarship and Electronic Editing, Graduate Institute for Technology and Religion, University of Birmingham, Elmfield House, Bristol Road, Birmingham, B29 6LQ, England (office). *Telephone:* (121) 415-8341 (office). *E-mail:* d.c.parker@bham.ac.uk (office). *Website:* www.itsee.bham.ac.uk (office).

PARKER, Gordon; British author and playwright; b. 28 Feb. 1940, Newcastle upon Tyne, England. *Education:* Newcastle Polytechnic (HND in Mechanical Eng). *Career:* book reviewer, BBC Radio and ITV. *Publications:* The Darkness of the Morning 1975, Lightning in May 1976, The Pool 1978, Action of the Tiger 1981, A Waking of Rooks 2011; radio plays: The Seance 1978, God Protect the Lonely Widow 1982. *Address:* 14 Thornhill Close, Seaton Delaval, Northumberland, NE25 0JS, England (home). *Telephone:* (191) 237-7333 (home). *E-mail:* delavallad14@aol.com (home).

PARKER, Gwendolyn McDougald, BA, JD, LLM; American writer; b. 9 June 1950, Durham, NC. *Education:* Radcliffe College, New York Univ. School of Law. *Publications:* These Same Long Bones, 1994; Trespassing, My Sojourn in the Halls of Privilege, 1997. *Honours:* New York Times Notable Book of the Year citation 1994.

PARKER, Peter Robert Nevill, BA, FRSL; British writer; b. 2 June 1954, Hereford, Herefords., England. *Education:* Univ. Coll., London. *Career:* mem. Exec. Cttee English PEN 1994–97; Trustee, PEN Literary Foundation 1994–2009, Chair. 1998–2000; Assoc. Ed. Oxford Dictionary of National Biography 1996–2004, Advisory Ed. 2006–; mem. Cttee London Library 1999–2003, Trustee 2004–07; mem. Council, Royal Soc. of Literature 2004, Vice-Chair. 2008–; mem. Lindley Library Advisory Cttee, Royal Horticultural Soc. 2008–, Chair. 2009–; mem. Editorial Bd London Library Magazine 2008–; judge, J.R. Ackerley Prize 1990– (Chair. 2007–), Encore Award 2005–. *Film:* My Dog Tulip (additional writing and adviser to the producers) 2010. *Publications:* The Old Lie 1987, Ackerley 1989, The Reader's Companion to the Twentieth-Century Novel (ed.) 1994, The Reader's Companion to Twentieth-Century Writers (ed.) 1995, Isherwood: A Life 2004, The Last Veteran: Harry Patch and the Legacy of War 2009; contrib. to Daily Telegraph, Independent, Sunday Times, Hortus, Spectator, Times Literary Supplement. *Literary Agent:* c/o Rogers, Coleridge & White Literary Agency, 20 Powis Mews, London, W11 1JN, England. *Telephone:* (20) 7221-3717. *Fax:* (20) 7229-9084. *E-mail:* info@rcwlitagency.co.uk. *Website:* www.rcwlitagency.co.uk.

PARKER, Robert M., Jr, BA, LLB; American writer and wine critic; *Publisher, The Wine Advocate*; b. 23 July 1947, Baltimore, Md; m. Patricia Parker 1969; one d. *Education:* Univ. of Maryland. *Career:* attorney, Sr Attorney and later Asst Gen. Counsel for Farm Credits, Bank of Baltimore 1973–84; Founder, Writer and Publr The Wine Advocate 1978–; Contributing Ed. Food and Wine Magazine; wine critic for L'Express magazine (first non-French holder of post). *Publications include:* Bordeaux (Glenfiddich Award 1986, Int. Asscn of Cooking Professionals Award for second edn 1992, Goldene Feder Award (Germany) for third edn 1993, Moët-Hennessy Wine and Vine Communication Award for French edn 1993) 1985, Parker's Wine Buyer's Guide 1987, The Wines of the Rhône Valley and Provence (Tastemaker's Award, USA 1989, Wine Guild's Wine Book of the Year Award, UK 1989) 1987, Burgundy (Moët-Hennessy Wine and Vine Communication Award for French edn 1993) 1990; contribs to The Field. *Honours:* Hon. Citizen of Châteauneuf du Pape 1995; Chevalier, Ordre nat. du Mérite 1993, Chevalier, Légion d'honneur 1999; Loyola Coll. Marylander of the Year Award 1992, James Beard Foundation Wine and Spirits Professional of 1997. *Address:* The Wine Advocate, Inc., PO Box 311, Monkton, MD 21111, USA (office). *Telephone:* (410) 329-6477 (office). *Fax:* (410) 357-4504 (office). *E-mail:* wineadvocate@erobertparker.com (office). *Website:* www.erobertparker.com.

PARKER, Trey; American screenwriter, film director and producer; b. (Randolph Severn Parker III), 19 Oct. 1969, Conifer, Colo. *Career:* collaborated with Matt Stone on short animation, Jesus vs Frosty 1992, later remade as animated Christmas card for FoxLab, titled The Spirit of Christmas 1995; Co-creator and Exec. Producer, South Park animation (with Matt Stone) 1997–, and other films and TV series. *Films include:* Jesus vs Frosty (writer, dir, producer) 1992, American History (writer, dir) (Student Acad. Award) 1992, Your Studio and You (writer, dir) 1995, The Spirit of Christmas (writer, dir, producer) 1995, For Goodness Sake II (dir) 1996, Alferd Packer: The Musical (aka Cannibal! The Musical) (writer, dir, producer) 1996, Orgazmo (writer, dir, producer) 1997, South Park: Bigger Longer & Uncut (writer, dir, producer) (Los Angeles Film Critics Award, New York Film Critics Award, MTV Movie Award) 1999, How's Your News? (exec. producer) 1999, Team America: World Police (writer, dir, producer) 2004. *Film appearances include:* BASEketball 1998, provides voices for many characters in his animation films and television series. *Television includes:* South Park (series writer, dir, producer) 1997–, That's My Bush! (series writer, dir, producer) 2001, Kenny vs. Spenny (producer) 2007. *Recordings include:* albums: Chef Aid: The South Park Album, South Park: Bigger, Longer and Uncut (soundtrack), Mr Hankey's Christmas Classics, Timmy and the Lords of the Underworld, The Book of Mormon (Grammy Award for Best Musical Theater Album 2012) 2011. *Play:* The Book of Mormon (Tony Award for Best Musical 2011) 2011. *Address:* c/o Paramount Studios, 5555 Melrose Avenue, Hollywood, CA 90038, USA. *E-mail:* news@southparkstudios.com. *Website:* www.southparkstudios.com.

PARKES, Nii Ayikwei, BSc, MA; Ghanaian writer and poet; b. 1974, UK. *Education:* Manchester Metropolitan Univ., Birkbeck Coll. *Career:* raised in Ghana; regular Ed. X magazine; has performed poetry world-wide on stages including NuYorican, New York, Royal Festival Hall, London, Java, Paris, Paradiso, Amsterdam and at festivals including Lancaster Literature Festival, Austin Int. Poetry Festival, Texas, USA; US tour 2002; commissions include poems for the V&A museum's summer reading series 2003, mural for Lewisham High Street, London, reading for the Mayor of London's vigil (in response to the London bombings) 14 July 2005; featured face for poetry Time Out London Guide 2004; assoc. writer-in-residence BBC Radio 3 2005; writer-in-residence Calif. State Univ., USA 2007; poet-in-residence Poetry Café, Covent Garden, London 2003, now runs its African Writers' Evening series; Booktrust online Writer-in-Residence 2009–. *Publications:* poetry chapbooks: eyes of a boy, lips of a man 1999, M is for Madrigal 2004, shorter 2005; other: The Cost of Red Eyes (novel) (Arts Council Award) 2003, Tell Tales Vol. I (short stories) (co-ed.) 2005, Tail of the Blue Bird (novel) 2009; contrib. to anthologies, magazines and literary journals including The New Writer, The Interpreter's House, The Accra Mail, The Map of Austin Poetry Journal, Dreamcatcher, Sable, Wasafiri. *Address:* c/o the tall-lighthouse, Stark Gallery, 384 Lee High Road, Lee Green, London, SE12 8RW (office); 21 Tugela Street, London, SE6 4DQ, England. *E-mail:* info@tall-lighthouse.co.uk (office). *Website:* www.niiparkes.com.

PARKHOMENKO, Sergey Borisovich; Russian journalist; b. 13 March 1964, Moscow; m.; two s. *Education:* Moscow State Univ. *Career:* Head of Div. Teatre (magazine) 1985–90; political observer Nezavisimaya Gazeta 1990–92; mem. Bd Segodnya (newspaper) 1993–95; co-founder Moscow Charter for Journalists 1994; Ed.-in-Chief Itogi (magazine) 1996–2001, IT Weekly (journal) 2002, Real Itogi 2002, now ind. journalist.

PARKIN, Andrew Terence Leonard, (Jiang An Dao), BA, MA, PhD; British/Canadian poet and critic; *Professor Emeritus and Honorary Senior Tutor, Shaw College, Chinese University of Hong Kong*; b. (Terence Leonard Parkin), 30 June 1937, Birmingham, England; s. of F. S. Parkin and M. P. M. Stansfield; m. 1st Christine George 1959; one s., m. 2nd Françoise Lentsch 1990. *Education:* Pembroke Coll., Cambridge, Univ. of Bristol. *Career:* Ed. Canadian Journal of Irish Studies 1974–89; Prof. of English, Univ. of British Columbia; Prof. of English, Chinese Univ. of Hong Kong, Prof. Emer. and Hon. Sr Tutor, Shaw Coll. 2001–; Distinguished Research Assoc., Faculty of Int. Affairs, Le Havre Univ., France, South East Asia Research, Univ. of Caen, France; mem. Canadian Asscn for Irish Studies (Hon. Life mem.), League of Canadian Poets, Cambridge Club of Paris, Writers' Union of Canada, Soc. des Anglicistes de l'Enseignement Supérieure, Paris Asscn for Decorative and Fine Arts (Chair.); read poems accompanied by pianist Isabelle Le Goux at Institut Polonais, Paris 2006; has read at Yale, Cambridge, Oxford, London, Toronto, Hong Kong, Japan, Taiwan and in China. *Exhibition:* suite of 12 poems read with Chinese trans. at Opening of Art Exhbn of Chan Hang 2006, poems relating to his paintings, at Chinese Univ. of Hong Kong. *Radio:* two series of Poetry on the Air for RTHK 1987. *Publications:* Stage One: A Canadian Scenebook 1973, The Dramatic Imagination of W. B. Yeats 1978, Shaw's Caesar and Cleopatra 1980, Dion Boucicault: Selected Plays 1987, Dancers in a Web 1987, Yeats's Herne's Egg 1991, Yokohama Days, Kyoto Nights 1991, File on Nichols 1993, Hong Kong Poems (with L. Wong) 1997, The Humanities (ed.) 2001, Shakespeare Global/Local: The Hong Kong Imaginary in Transcultural Production (co-ed. with K. K. Tam and Terry Yip) 2002, The Rendez-Vous: Poems of Multicultural Experience 2003, Shaw Sights and Sounds: A Collection of Painting and Poetry (with C. Hang and L. Wong) 2006, Star of a Hundred Years: A Scenariode to Celebrate Achievements of Sir Run Run Shaw, At the Hawk's Well 2010, The Cat and the Moon Manuscript Materials by W.B. Yeats (ed.) 2010; contribs; more than 100 essays and reviews in scholarly journals; more than 30 radio broadcasts; two TV interviews; 200 poems; poems anthologized in VS: 12 Hong Kong Poets

1993, Tolo Lights 1993, Tolo Lights 1994, First Hong Kong International Poetry Festival anthology 1997, Pembroke Poets, Cambridge 1997, City Voices 2003, Hong Kong: Poems/Gedichte 2006. *Honours:* Hon. Adviser, Chinese Acad. of Social Sciences, Beijing 2000–, Chinese Canadian Writers' Asscn; First Prize, Martini Rossi Sonnet Competition 1985, Most Distinguished Ed. of a Learned Journal 1989, Award for services to China-Canada literary relations 2010. *Address:* 52 rue du Rendez-vous, 75012 Paris, France (home). *Telephone:* 1-40-04-96-91 (home). *Fax:* 1-40-04-96-91 (office). *E-mail:* andrew.parkin@wanadoo.fr (home).

PARKS, Suzan-Lori, BA; American playwright; b. 10 May 1963, Fort Knox, Ky; m. Paul Oscher. *Education:* John Carroll School, Mount Holyoke Coll. *Career:* Guggenheim Foundation Fellow 2000; Master Writer Chair., Public Theater, New York 2008–; Visiting Arts Prof., Tisch School of the Arts, New York Univ. 2008–. *Plays include:* The Sinner's Place 1984, Imperceptible Mutabilities in the Third Kingdom (OBIE Award for Best New American Play) 1989, Betting on the Dust Commander 1990, The Death of the Last Black Man in the Whole Entire World 1990, Devotees in the Garden of Love 1992, The America Play 1994, Venus 1996, In the Blood 1999, Fucking A 2000, Topdog/Underdog (Pulitzer Prize for Drama 2002) 2001, 365 Days/365 Plays 2006, Ray Charles Live! A New Musical 2007. *Plays for radio:* Pickling 1990, Third Kingdom 1990, Locomotive 1991. *Screenplays:* Girl 6 1996, Their Eyes Were Watching God 2005, The Great Debaters (co-writer) 2007. *Publication:* Getting Mother's Body: A Novel 2003. *Honours:* MacArthur Foundation Award 2001, Eugene McDermott Award in the Arts, Council for the Arts at MIT 2006. *Address:* The Public Theater, 425 Lafayette Street, New York, NY 10003, USA (office). *Telephone:* (212) 539-8500 (home). *E-mail:* press@publictheater.org (office). *Website:* www.publictheater.org (office).

PARKS, Timothy Harold, BA, MA; British writer, educator and translator; *Professor of English Literature, Università IULM, Milan*; b. 19 Dec. 1954, Manchester, England; m. Rita Baldassare; three d. *Education:* Univ. of Cambridge and Harvard Univ., USA. *Career:* teacher of trans. studies, Università IULM, Milan, Prof. of English Literature 2006–; mem. Authors' Soc. *Publications:* novels: Tongues of Flame 1985, Loving Roger 1986, Home Thoughts 1987, Family Planning 1989, Cara Massimina 1990, Goodness 1991, Italian Neighbours 1992, Juggling the Stars 1993, Shear 1993, Mimi's Ghost 1995, An Italian Education 1996, Europa 1997, Adultery and Other Diversions 1999, Destiny 2000, A Season with Verona 2002, Judge Savage 2003, Rapids 2005, Cleaver 2006, Dreams of Rivers and Seas 2008; short stories: Keeping Distance 1988, The Room 1992; non-fiction: Translating Style: The English Modernists and their Italian Translations 1999, Hell and Back: Reflections on Writers and Writing from Dante to Rushdie 2001, Medici Money: Banking, Metaphysics and Art in Fifteenth-Century Florence 2005, The Fighter 2007, Teach Us to Sit Still 2010; numerous translations from Italian; contrib. of numerous articles, reviews and talks to BBC Radio 3. *Honours:* Somerset Maugham Award 1986, Betty Trask Prize 1986, Rhys Prize 1986, John Floria Prize for Best Translation from Italian. *Address:* Istituto di Anglistica, Università IULM, Via Carlo Bo, 20143 Milan, Italy (office). *Website:* tim-parks.com.

PARMET, Herbert Samuel, BS, MA; American academic and writer; b. 28 Sept. 1929, New York, NY; m. Joan Kronish 1948, one d. *Education:* SUNY at Oswego, Queens College, CUNY, Columbia University. *Career:* Prof. of History, 1968–83, Distinguished Prof. of History, 1983–95, Prof. Emeritus, 1995–, Graduate School and University Center, CUNY; Consultant, ABC-TV, New York City, 1983, KERA-TV, Dallas, 1986–91, WGBH-TV, Boston, 1988–91; mem. American Historical Asscn; Authors' Guild; Authors League; Organization of American Historians; Society of American Historians, fellow. *Publications:* Aaron Burr: Portrait of an Ambitious Man, 1967; Never Again: A President Runs for a Third Term, 1968; Eisenhower and the American Crusades, 1972; The Democrats: The Years after FDR, 1976; Jack: The Struggles of John F. Kennedy, 1980; JFK: The Presidency of John F. Kennedy, 1983; Richard Nixon and His America, 1990; George Bush: The Life of a Lone Star Yankee, 1997; Presidential Power: From the New Deal to the New Right, 2002. Contributions: Professional journals. *Honours:* National Endowment for the Humanities grant 1987.

PARODI, Anton Gaetano; Italian journalist and playwright; b. 19 May 1923, Castanzaro Lido (Calabria); s. of Luigi Parodi and Grazia Scicchitano; m. Piera Somino 1952; two c. *Education:* Università degli Studi, Turin and Genoa. *Career:* journalist 1945–; professional journalist 1947–; corresp. of Unità, Budapest 1964–. *Plays include:* Il gatto, Il nostro scandalo quotidiano, L'ex-maggiore Hermann Grotz, Adolfo o della nagia, Filippo l'Impostore, Una corda per il figlio di Abele, Quel pomeriggio di domenica, Dialoghi intorno ad un'uovo, Una storia della notte, Pioggia d'estate, Cielo di pietra, I giorni dell'Arca, Quello che dicono. *Honours:* Premio nazionale di teatro Riccione 1959, 1965, Premio nazionale di teatro dei giovani 1947 and numerous other prizes.

PARQUE, Richard Anthony, BA, MA; American writer, poet and teacher; b. 8 Oct. 1935, Los Angeles; m. Vo Thi Lan 1975; three s. *Education:* California State University, Los Angeles, University of Redlands. *Career:* mem. Authors' Guild, Acad. of American Poets. *Publications:* Sweet Vietnam, 1984; Hellbound, 1986; Firefight, 1987; Flight of the Phantom, 1988; A Distant Thunder, 1989; contributions: journals, magazines and newspapers. *Honours:* Bay Area Poets Award, 1989; Viet Nam novels have been placed in the Colorado State University Vietnam War Collection.

PARRA, Nicanor; Chilean poet; b. 5 Sept. 1914, San Fabián; s. of Nicanor P. Parra and Clara S. Navarrete; m. 1st Ana Troncoso 1948; m. 2nd Inga Palmen; seven c. *Education:* Univ. de Chile, Brown Univ., USA and Oxford. *Career:* Prof. of Theoretical Mechanics, Univ. de Chile 1964–; has given poetry readings in LA, Moscow, Leningrad, Havana, Lima, Ayacucho, Cuzco. *Publications:* poetry: Cancionero sin nombre 1937, Poemas y antipoemas 1954, La cueca larga 1958, Antipoems 1958, Versos de salón 1962, Discursos (with Pablo Neruda) 1962, Manifiesto 1963, Deux Poèmes (bilingual) 1964, Antología (also in Russian) 1965, Antología de la Poesía Soviética Rusa (bilingual) 1965, Canciones Rusas 1967, Defensa de Violeta Parra 1967, Artefactos 1972, Sermones y prédicas del Cristo de Elqui 1977, Nuevos sermones y prédicas del Cristo de Elqui 1979, El anti-Lázaro 1981, Poema y antipoema de Eduardo Frei 1982, Cachureos, ecopoemas, guatapiques, últimas prédicas 1983, Chistes para desorientar a la policía 1983, Coplas de Navidad 1983, Poesía política 1983, Hojas de Parra 1985, Poemas para combatir la calvicie 1993, Páginas en blanco 2001, Lear Rey & Mendigo 2004, Discursos de Sobremesa 2006; scientific works: La Evolución del Concepto de Masa 1958, Fundamentos de la Física (trans. of Foundation of Physics by Profs Lindsay and Margenau) 1967, Obra Gruesa 1969, Los profesores, 1971. *Honours:* Premio Municipal de Poesía, Santiago 1937, 1954, Premio Nacional de Literatura 1969, Miguel de Cervantes Prize 2011. *Address:* Julia Bernstein, Parcela 272, Lareina, Santiago, Chile. *Website:* www.nicanorparra.uchile.cl.

PARRINDER, (John) Patrick, MA, PhD; British academic, literary critic and historian; *Professor Emeritus, University of Reading*; b. 11 Oct. 1944, Wadebridge, Cornwall, England; s. of Eric Reginald Parrinder and Eileen Dorothy Skeffington-White; m. 1st Ewa Christina Wildte; two d.; m. 2nd Janet Christina Bourne Taylor. *Education:* Christ's Coll. and Darwin Coll., Cambridge. *Career:* Fellow, King's Coll. Cambridge 1967–74; Lecturer, Univ. of Reading 1974–80, Reader 1980–86, Prof. of English 1986–2008, Prof. Emer. 2008–; Gen. Ed., Oxford History of the Novel in English; mem. H.G. Wells Soc., Science Fiction Foundation, Soc. of Authors; Fellow, English Asscn 2001. *Publications:* H. G. Wells 1970, Authors and Authority 1977, Science Fiction: Its Criticism and Teaching 1980, James Joyce 1984, The Failure of Theory 1987, Shadows of the Future 1995; ed.: H. G. Wells: The Critical Heritage 1972, Science Fiction: A Critical Guide 1979, Learning from Other Worlds 2000, Nation and Novel: The English Novel from its Origins to the Present Day 2006, The Reinvention of the British and Irish Novel 1880–1940 (co-ed.) 2011; contribs to London Review of Books and many academic journals. *Honours:* Pres.'s Award, World Science Fiction 1987, Leverhulme Major Research Fellowship 2001–04. *Address:* Department of English Language and Literature, University of Reading, PO Box 218, Reading, Berks., RG6 6AA (office); 82 Hillfield Avenue, Crouch End, London, N8 7DN, England (home). *Telephone:* (118) 378-8360 (office); (20) 8340-6355 (home). *E-mail:* j.p.parrinder@reading.ac.uk (office).

PARRIS, Matthew Francis, BA, MA; British author, broadcaster and fmr politician; b. 7 Aug. 1949, Johannesburg, S Africa; s. of Leslie F. Parris and Theresa E. Parris (née Littler); civil partnership with Julian Glover. *Education:* Waterford School, Swaziland, Clare Coll., Cambridge and Yale Univ. *Career:* FCO 1974–76; with Conservative Research Dept 1976–79; MP (Conservative) for W Derbyshire 1979–86; Parl. Sketch Writer for The Times 1988–2001; columnist, The Times 1988–, The Spectator 1992–; mem. Broadcasting Standards Council 1992–97. *Radio:* presenter, Great Lives series (BBC Radio 4) 2007–. *Television:* presenter, Weekend World (LWT) 1986–88. *Publications:* Inca Kola (travel) 1990, Chance Witness (memoir) 2001, Great Parliamentary Scandals (with Kevin Maguire) 2004, A Castle in Spain 2005, Mission Accomplished (with Phil Mason) 2007, Scorn 2008, Parting Shots (with Andrew Bryson) 2010, The Spanish Ambassador's Suitcase, and Other Stories (with Andrew Bryson) 2012; various books about politics, insult and scandal; various collections of journalism. *Honours:* various awards for writing and journalism. *Address:* The Spout, Gratton, Bakewell, Derbyshire, DE45 1LN; c/o The Times, Pennington Street, London, E1 9XN, England. *Telephone:* (20) 7219-4078 (office). *E-mail:* wrighte@parliament.uk (office).

PARROTT, Jasper William, BA; British impresario and agent; b. 8 Sept. 1944, Stockholm, Sweden; s. of the late Prof. Sir Cecil Parrott and of Lady Parrott; m. Cristina Ortiz; two d. *Education:* Tonbridge School, Peterhouse Cambridge. *Career:* joined Ibbs & Tillett Ltd 1965–69; f. Harrison Parrott Ltd 1969, Chair. and Man. Dir 1987–; Dir Japan Festival 1991, Swiss Festival in UK 1991; Dir Rambert Dance Co. 1993–98; Hon. Trustee Kew Foundation, Royal Botanical Gardens 1991–; Co-Dir Simdi Now, Turkish Festival of Arts, Berlin 2004; Int. Adviser, Sakip Sabanci Museum, Istanbul 2005–07; Dir Polyarts UK 2004–; consultant, The Icelandic Nat. Concert and Conf. Centre 2007–11. *Publication:* Beyond Frontiers: Vladimir Ashkenazy. *Address:* Harrison Parrott, 5–6 Albion Court, Albion Place, London, W6 0QT, England (office). *Telephone:* (20) 7313-3527 (office). *Fax:* (20) 7221-5042 (office). *E-mail:* sb@harrisonparrott.co.uk (office). *Website:* www.harrisonparrott.com (office).

PARRY, Graham, MA, PhD, FSA; British academic and author; *Professor Emeritus of English, University of York*; b. 5 Jan. 1940, Sutton Coldfield; m. Barbara Henry, 4 Nov. 1967. *Education:* Pembroke Coll., Cambridge, Columbia Univ., New York, USA. *Career:* Preceptor, Columbia Univ. 1962–65; Asst Prof., Univ. of British Columbia, Canada 1965–67, Visiting Prof. 1993–94; Lecturer in English, Univ. of Leeds 1967–76; Visiting Prof., Université de Toulouse, France 1972–73, City Coll., CUNY 1975–76, Doshisha Univ., Japan 1981–82, 1997–98; Lecturer in English 1977, then Prof. of

Renaissance Literature, Univ. of York, now Prof. Emer. *Publications:* Lady Mary Wroth's Urania 1975, The Pre-Raphaelite Image: Style and Subject 1848–56 1978, Hollar's England: A Mid-Seventeenth Century View 1980, The Golden Age Restor'd: The Culture of the Stuart Court 1603–1642 1981, Seventeenth-Century Poetry: The Social Context 1985, The Seventeenth Century: The Intellectual and Cultural Context of English Literature 1603–1700 1989, The Trophies of Time: English Antiquarians of the Seventeenth Century 1995, The Life and Letters of John Talman 1997, Milton and the Terms of Liberty (ed. with J. Raymond) 2002, Glory, Laud and Honour: the Arts of the Anglican Counter-Reformation 2006. *Address:* Department of English and Related Literature, University of York, Heslington, York, YO10 5DD, Yorks. (office); 28 Micklefield Lane, Rawdon, Leeds, England (home). *Telephone:* (1904) 433330. *E-mail:* gp8@york.ac.uk (office).

PARSONS, Nigel; British media executive; *CEO, Continental Broadcasting Ltd*; b. 27 May 1951, England; Lt Col and Mrs F. A. Parsons; m. Zoulfia Parsons; four c. *Education:* Framlingham Coll., Suffolk, Portsmouth Univ. (Certificate of Journalism). *Career:* previous roles as journalist/producer at BBC Radios 1–4, BBC World Service Radio and TV and WTN (Worldwide Television News), conceived and oversaw launch of global broadcaster Al Jazeera English, also managed TV start-up news network teams, EBC in Switzerland, Middle East Broadcasting and Telecampione in Italy; Vice-Pres. (Eastern European and fmr USSR markets), WTN; Dir of Associated Press TV News (APTN, cr. when Associated Press bought WTN); Man. Dir Al Jazeera English, Doha, Qatar 2004–09; Sr Partner, NZN Media Consultants 2009–11; CEO Continental Broadcasting Ltd, Lagos, Nigeria 2011–. *Address:* 456 Merton Road, London, SW18 5AE, England (office). *Telephone:* 7768-728234 (mobile) (office). *E-mail:* nigel.parsons@gmail.com (home).

PARSONS, Tony; British writer. *Publications include:* Man and Boy 1999, One for My Baby 2001, Man and Wife 2002, The Family Way 2004, Stories We Could Tell 2005, My Favourite Wife 2007, Starting Over 2009, Men from the Boys 2010, Catching the Sun 2012. *Honours:* Butler and Tanner Book of the Year 2001, Nielsen BookScan and the Times Platinum Book Award, British Book Awards 2002.

PASCHEN, Elise Maria, BA, MPhil, DPhil; American arts administrator and poet; b. 4 Jan. 1959, Chicago, IL. *Education:* Harvard University, University of Oxford. *Career:* Exec. Dir, Poetry Society of America; mem. National Arts Club. *Publications:* Houses: Coasts, 1985; Infidelities, 1996. Contributions: Reviews, journals, and magazines. *Honours:* Lloyd McKim Garrison Medal for Poetry, Harvard University, 1982; Joan Grey Untermyer Poetry Prize, Harvard University/Radcliffe College, 1982; Richard Selig Prize for Poetry, Magdalen College, Oxford, 1984; Nicholas Roerich Poetry Prize, 1996.

PATCHETT, Ann, BA, MFA; American writer; b. 2 Dec. 1963, Los Angeles. *Education:* Sarah Lawrence Coll. and Univ. of Iowa Writers' Workshop. *Career:* writer-in-residence Allegheny Coll. 1989–90; Yaddo Fellow 1990; Millay Fellow 1990; Resident Fellow, Fine Arts Work Center, Provincetown 1990–91; Visiting Asst Prof. Murray State Univ. 1992; Bunting Fellow, Mary Ingram Bunting Inst., Radcliffe Coll. 1993; Guggenheim Fellowship 1994. *Publications:* The Patron Saint of Liars (Univ. of Iowa James A. Michener/Copernicus Award for a book in progress 1989, American Library Asscn Notable Book 1992) 1992, Taft (Janet Heidinger Kafka Prize) 1994, The Magician's Assistant 1997, Bel Canto (PEN/Faulkner Award 2002, Orange Prize 2002) 2001, Truth and Beauty (biog.) 2004, Run 2007, What Now? 2008, State of Wonder 2011; contrib. to anthologies and to periodicals, including The New York Times Magazine, Chicago Tribune, Boston Globe, Vogue, GQ, Elle, Gourmet. *Honours:* Nashville Banner Tenn. Writer of the Year Award 1994. *Address:* c/o Author Mail, 11th Floor, Harper Collins Publishers, 10 East 53rd Street, New York, NY 10022, USA (office). *Website:* www.annpatchett.com (office).

PATERSON, Alistair Ian, (Ian Hughes), BA, DipEd; New Zealand poet, writer and educational consultant; b. 28 Feb. 1929, Nelson; m. 1984; two s. three d. *Education:* University of New Zealand, University of Auckland. *Career:* Royal New Zealand Navy, 1954–74; Dean of General Studies, New Zealand Police, 1974–78; Tertiary Inspector, New Zealand Dept of Education, 1979–89; Educational Consultant, 1990–; mem. PEN, Wellington Poetry Society. *Publications:* Caves in the Hills, 1965; Birds Flying, 1973; Cities and Strangers, 1976; The Toledo Room: A Poem for Voices, 1978; 15 Contemporary New Zealand Poets (ed.), 1980; Qu'appelle, 1982; The New Poetry, 1982; Incantations for Warriors, 1982; Oedipus Rex, 1986; Short Stories from New Zealand (ed.), 1988; How to be a Millionaire by Next Wednesday (novel), 1994. Contributions: various publications. *Honours:* Fulbright Fellowship, 1977; John Cowie Reid Award, University of Auckland, 1982; Katherine Mansfield Award for Fiction, 1993; New Zealand Creative Writing Grant, 1995.

PATERSON, Donald (Don), OBE; British poet, editor and musician; b. 30 Oct. 1963, Dundee, Scotland. *Career:* writer-in-residence, Dundee Univ. 1993–95; Poetry Ed. Picador Ltd; Lecturer in School of English, Univ. of St Andrew's. *Publications:* Nil Nil (Forward Prize for Best First Collection) 1993, God's Gift to Women (T. S. Eliot Prize) 1997, The Eyes 1999, The White Lie: New and Selected Poetry 2001, Landing Light (T. S. Eliot Prize, Whitbread Award for Poetry) 2003, The Book of Shadows 2004, Orpheus (trans.) 2006, The Blind Eye 2007, Best Thoughts, Worst Thoughts 2008, Rain (Forward Prize for Best Collection) 2009, Reading Shakespeare's Sonnets: A New Commentary 2010; ed. of numerous anthologies and collections. *Honours:* Eric Gregory Trust Fund Award 1990, Arvon/Observer International Poetry Competition 1993, Scottish Arts Council Book Awards 1993, 1997, 1999, Geoffrey Faber Memorial Prize 1998, Forward Prize for Best Single Poem (for Love Poem for Natalie 'Tujsa' Beridze) 2008, Queen's Gold Medal for Poetry 2010. *Address:* c/o Faber and Faber, Bloomsbury House, 74–77 Great Russell Street, London, WC1B 3DA, England (office). *Website:* www.faber.co.uk (office).

PATERSON, Katherine Womeldorf; American children's writer; b. 31 Oct. 1932, Qing Jiang, People's Republic of China; m. John Paterson 1962; four c. *Education:* King Coll., Bristol, TN and Union Theological Seminary, New York. *Career:* Nat. Amb. to Young People's Literature, Library of Congress 2010–. *Publications:* novels: Bread and Roses, Too, Bridge to Terabithia (Newbery Medal 1978, Lewis Carroll Shelf Award 1978, Janusz Korczak Medal, Poland 1981, Silver Pencil Award, Netherlands 1981, Grand Prix des Jeunes Lecturs, France 1986, Colorado Blue Spruce Young Adult Book Award 1986), Come Sing, Jimmy Jo, The Day of the Pelican, Flip-Flop Girl, The Great Gilly Hopkins (Nat. Book Award 1979, Newbery Honor Award 1979, Jane Addams Children's Book Award 1979, Christopher Award 1979), Jacob Have I Loved (Newbery Medal 1981), Jip, his Story (Scott O'Dell Award for Historical Fiction 1997), Lyddie (Int. Bd of Books for Young People Honor Book 1994, IBBY Honor Book), The Master Puppeteer (Nat. Book Award for Children's Literature 1977, MWA Edgar Allen Poe Special Award 1977), Of Nightingales that Weep (Children's Literature Asscn Phoenix Award 1994), Park's Quest, Preacher's Boy (Jefferson Cup of Virginia Library Asscn), Rebels of the Heavenly Kingdom, The Same Stuff as Stars (Paterson Prize 2003, Jane Addams Award 2003, Judy Lopez Memorial Award 2003), Sign of the Chrysanthemum; picture books: The Angel and the Donkey, Blueberries for the Queen, Celia and the Sweet, Sweet Water, The King's Equal, The Tale of the Mandarin Ducks (Boston Globe/Horn Book Picture Book Award 1991), The Wide-Awake Princess; non-fiction: Consider the Lilies, Gates of Excellence, Images of God, The Invisible Child, A Sense of Wonder, The Spying Heart, Who Am I?. *Honours:* Dr hc (St Mary of the Woods, IN), (Univ. of Maryland), (Hope Coll., Holland, MI), (Otterbein Coll., OH), (Presbyterian Coll., SC), (King Coll., TN), (Norwich Univ., VT), (St Michael's Coll., VT), (Shenandoah Coll. and Conservatory, VA), (Washington and Lee Univ., VA), (Mount Saint Vincent Univ., Halifax, Canada); Union Theological Seminary Union Medal, New York, Univ. of Southern Mississippi Medallion 1983, Univ. of Minnesota Kerlan Award 1983, Keene State Coll. Children's Literature Award 1987, Catholic Library Asscn Regina Medal 1988, New England Book Award 1992, Tulsa Public Library Anne V. Zarrow Award 1993, Education Press Friend of Education Award 1993, Hans Christian Andersen Medal for Writing 1998, New York Public Library Lion 1998, Library of Congress Living Legend Award 2000, Boston Public Library Literary Light 2000, Astrid Lindgren Memorial Award 2006. *Address:* c/o Clarion Books, 215 Park Avenue S, New York, NY 10003, USA (office). *Website:* www.terabithia.com

PATERSON, Stuart A.; British writer, poet and editor; b. 31 Jan. 1966, Truro, Cornwall, England. *Education:* Stirling Univ. *Career:* Founder-Ed., Spectrum review, 1990–96; Scottish Arts Council Writer-in-Residence, Dumfries and Galloway Region, 1996–98; mem. Kilmarnock North West Writers Group, Artists for Independence, Scottish Poetry Library, Scottish National Party. *Publications:* Mulaney of Larne and Other Poems, 1991; Saving Graces, 1997; contributions: anthologies, reviews, newspapers and journals. *Honours:* Eric Gregory Award 1992, Scottish Arts Council Writer's Bursary 1993.

PATON WALSH, Jill, CBE, MA, DipEd, FRSL; British writer; b. 29 April 1937, d. of John Llewelyn Bliss and Patricia Paula DuBern; m. 1st Anthony Paton Walsh 1961 (deceased); two d. one s; m. 2nd John Townsend. *Education:* St Michael's Coll., Finchley and St Anne's Coll., Oxford. *Career:* teacher 1959–62; Arts Council Creative Writing Fellow, Brighton Polytechnic 1976–78; Gertrude Clark Whitall Memorial Lecturer, Library of Congress, USA 1978; Visiting Faculty mem., Center for Children's Literature, Simmons Coll. Boston, MA, USA; Judge Whitbread Literary Award 1984; Chair. Cambridge Cttee, Children's Writers' and Illustrators' Group; Adjunct British Bd of Children's Literature, New England. *Publications include:* general fiction: Farewell, Great King 1972, Lapsing 1986, A School for Lovers 1989, The Wyndham Case 1993, Knowledge of Angels 1994, A Piece of Justice 1995, A Desert in Bohemia 2001, A Presumption of Death 2003, Debts of Dishonour 2006, The Bad Quarto 2007, The Attenbury Emeralds 2010; children's books: Hengest's Tale 1966, The Dolphin Crossing 1967, Wordhoard (jtly) 1969, Fireweed (Book World Festival Award) 1970, Goldengrove 1972, Toolmaker 1973, The Dawnstone 1973, The Emperor's Winding Sheet (jtly, Whitbread Prize) 1974, The Butty Boy 1975, The Island Sunrise: pre-historic Britain (non-fiction) 1975, Unleaving (Boston Globe/Horn Book Award) 1976, Crossing to Salamis, The Walls of Athens, and Persian Gold 1977–78, A Chance Child 1978, The Green Book 1981, Babylon 1982, Lost and Found 1984, A Parcel of Patterns (Universe Prize) 1984, Gaffer Samson's Luck (Smarties Prize Grand Prix 1984) 1985, Five Tides 1986, Torch 1987, Birdy and the Ghosties 1989, Can I Play? (series of four titles) 1990, Grace 1992, When Grandma Came 1992, Little Pepi and the Secret Names 1994, Connie Came to Play 1995, Thomas and the Tinners 1995, When I Was Little Like You 1997. *Literary Agent:* David Higham Associates, 5–8 Lower John Street, Golden Square, London, W1R 4HA, England. *Telephone:* (20) 7434-5900. *Fax:* (20) 7437-1072. *E-mail:* dha@davidhigham.co.uk. *Website:* www.davidhigham.co.uk.

PATRICK, Maxine (see Maxwell, Patricia Anne)

PATRICK, Susan (see Clark, Patricia Denise)

PATTEN, Brian, FRSL; British poet and author; b. 7 Feb. 1946, Liverpool, Merseyside, England; s. of Ireen Stella Bevan. *Career:* Regents Lecturer, Univ. of California, San Diego; performance work and lectures worldwide for British Council. *Radio:* various, including History of 20th-Century Poetry for Children, BBC Radio 2000, The Dittisham Nativity, BBC Radio 2005, Lost Voices, BBC Radio 2009, 2010, 2011. *Publications include:* poetry: The Mersey Sound 1967, Little Johnny's Confession 1967, The Home Coming 1969, Notes to the Hurrying Man 1969, At Four O'Clock in the Morning 1971, Walking Out: The Early Poems of Brian Patten 1971, Love Poems 1981, New Volume 1983, Gargling With Jelly 1985, Storm Damage 1988, Grinning Jack: Selected Poems 1990, Thawing Frozen Frogs 1990, Armada 1996; (ed) Clare's Countryside: A Book of John Clare 1981, Selected Poems 2007, New Collected Love Poems 2007, View From The Boathouse Window 2010; children's fiction: Grizzelda Frizzle and Other Stories 1992, The Magic Bicycle 1993, Impossible Parents 1994, Frognapped! and Other Stories 1994, The Utter Nutters 1995, The Blue and Green Ark 1999, Juggling with Gerbils 2000, Little Hotchpotch 2000, The Impossible Parents Go Green 2001, View From The Boathouse Window 2009, The Big Snuggle-up 2011; (ed) The Puffin Book of 20th Century Children's Verse 1991, The Story Giant 2001, Ben's Magic Telescope 2003, The Puffin Book of Modern Children's Verse 2006, The Big Snuggle-Up 2011. *Honours:* Freedom of the City of Liverpool 2000; Hon. Fellow, John Moores Univ. 2002; Hon. DLitt (Liverpool) 2006; Cholmondeley Award for Poetry 2002. *Literary Agent:* c/o Rogers, Coleridge & White Literary Agency, 20 Powis Mews, London, W11 1JN, England. *Telephone:* (20) 7221-3717. *Fax:* (20) 7229-9084. *E-mail:* info@rcwlitagency.co.uk. *Website:* www.rcwlitagency.co.uk. *E-mail:* happydaze@uku.co.uk (office). *Website:* www.brianpatten.co.uk.

PATTEN OF BARNES, Baron (Life Peer), cr. 2005, of Barnes in the London Borough of Richmond; **Christopher Francis Patten**, CH, PC; British politician and government official; *Chairman, BBC Trust;* b. 12 May 1944, s. of the late Francis Joseph Patten and Joan McCarthy; m. Mary Lavender Thornton 1971; three d. *Education:* St Benedict's School, Ealing, Balliol Coll., Oxford. *Career:* worked in Conservative Party Research Dept 1966–70, Dir 1974–79; seconded to Cabinet Office 1970; at Home Office, then personal asst to Lord Carrington, Party Chair. 1972–74; MP for Bath 1979–92; Parl. Pvt. Sec. (PPS) to Leader of the House 1979–81, to Social Services Sec. 1981–83; Parl. Under-Sec. for Northern Ireland 1983–85; Minister of State for Educ. 1985–86; Overseas Devt Minister 1986–89; Sec. of State for the Environment 1989–90; Chancellor of the Duchy of Lancaster and Chair. of the Conservative Party 1990–92; Gov. of Hong Kong 1992–97; Chair. Comm. charged with reform of Royal Ulster Constabulary 1998–99; EU Commr for External Relations 1999–2004; Chancellor, Newcastle Univ. 1999–2009, Univ. of Oxford 2003–; Chair. BBC Trust 2011–; Co-Chair. UK-India Round Table, Int. Crisis Group 2004–11; Pres. Medical Aid for Palestinians 2010–11; mem. Bd of Dirs Russell Reynolds Associates; mem. Int. Advisory Bd BP; mem. European Advisory Bd Bridgepoint; European Adviser, Hutchinson Whampoa Ltd; Int. Adviser to Praemium Imperiale, Japan Art Asscn; mem. Bd of Overseers, Sabanci Univ. *Publications:* The Tory Case 1983, East and West 1998, Not Quite the Diplomat: Home Truths About World Affairs 2005, What Next? Surviving the 21st Century 2008. *Honours:* Hon. FRCP (Edin.) 1994; Hon. Fellow, Balliol Coll., Oxford 1999; several hon. degrees from British and foreign univs including Hon. DCL (Newcastle) 1999; Coolidge Travelling Scholarship, USA 1965. *Address:* House of Lords, London, SW1A 0PW, England. *Telephone:* (20) 7219-3000. *Website:* www.bbc.co.uk/bbctrust.

PATTERSON, Glenn, BA, MA; Northern Irish writer; *Creative Writing Fellow, Seamus Heaney Centre for Poetry, Queen's University Belfast;* b. 9 Aug. 1961, Belfast; m. Ali Fitzgibbon 1995. *Education:* Univ. of East Anglia. *Career:* writer-in-the-community, Arts Council, Northern Ireland 1989–91; Creative Writing Fellow, Univ. of East Anglia 1992; writer-in-residence, Univ. Coll., Cork 1993–94, Queen's Univ., Belfast 1994–97; currently Creative Writing Fellow Seamus Heaney Centre for Poetry, Queen's Univ., Belfast; mem. Arts Council Northern Ireland (bd mem. 1996–2000), Soc. of Authors, Tyrone Guthrie Centre (bd mem. 2004–). *Publications:* novels: Burning Your Own 1988, Fat Lad 1992, Black Night at Big Thunder Mountain 1995, The International 1999, Number 5 2003, That Which Was 2004, Lapsed Protestant 2006, The Third Party 2007; non-fiction: Once Upon a Hill: Love in Troubled Times 2008. *Honours:* Betty Trask Prize 1988, Rooney Prize for Irish Literature 1988, Lannan Literary Foundation Fellowship 2008. *Address:* c/o Hamish Hamilton, Penguin Books Ltd, 80 Strand, London, WC2R 0RL, England.

PATTERSON, Henry (Harry), (Martin Fallon, James Graham, Jack Higgins, Hugh Marlowe), BSc (Soc.), FRSA; British/Irish novelist; b. 27 July 1929, Newcastle upon Tyne; s. of Henry Patterson and Rita Higgins Bell; m. 1st Amy Margaret Hewitt 1958 (divorced 1984); one s. three d.; m. 2nd Denise Leslie Ann Palmer 1985. *Education:* Roundhay School, Leeds, Beckett Park Coll. for Teachers, London School of Econs. *Career:* NCO, The Blues 1947–50, tried numerous jobs including clerk and circus tent hand 1950–58; schoolmaster, lecturer in liberal studies, Leeds Polytechnic, Sr Lecturer in Educ., James Graham Coll. and Tutor in School Practice, Leeds Univ. 1958–72; full-time writer from age of 41. *Publications:* as Martin Fallon: The Testament of Caspar Schultz 1962, Year of the Tiger 1963, The Keys to Hell 1965, Midnight Never Comes 1966, Dark Side of the Street 1967, A Fine Night for Dying 1969, Day of Judgement 1979; as Hugh Marlowe: Seven Pillars to Hell 1963, Passage by Night 1964, A Candle for the Dead (aka The Violent Enemy) 1966; as James Graham: A Game for Heroes 1970, The Wrath of God 1971, The Khufra Run 1972, The Run to Morning 1974; as Harry Patterson: Sad Wind from the Sea 1959, Cry of the Hunter 1960, The Thousand Faces of Night 1961, Comes the Dark Stranger 1962, Wrath of the Lion 1963, Pay the Devil 1963, The Dark Side of the Island 1963, A Phoenix in Blood 1964, Thunder at Noon (aka Dillinger) 1964, The Graveyard Shift 1965, Iron Tiger 1966, Brought in Dead 1967, Hell is Always Today 1968, Toll for the Brave 1971, To Catch a King (aka The Judas Gate) 1979; as Jack Higgins: East of Desolation 1968, In the Hour Before Midnight 1969, Night Judgement at Sinos 1970, The Last Place God Made 1971, The Savage Day 1972, The Eagle has Landed 1975, Storm Warning 1976, The Valhalla Exchange 1976, A Prayer for the Dying 1977, Solo (aka The Cretan Lover) 1980, Luciano's Luck 1981, Touch the Devil 1982, Exocet 1983, Confessional 1985, Night of the Fox 1986, Walking Wounded (play) 1987, Memoirs of a Dance Hall Romeo 1989, A Season in Hell 1989, Cold Harbour 1989, The Eagle Has Flown 1990, Eye of the Storm (aka Midnight Man) 1992, Thunder Point 1993, On Dangerous Ground 1994, Angel of Death 1995, Sheba 1995, Drink With the Devil 1996, The President's Daughter 1996, The Violent Enemy 1997, Flight of Eagles 1998, The White House Connection 1999, Day of Reckoning 1999, Midnight Runner 2001, Edge of Danger 2001, The Keys of Hell 2002, Bad Company 2003, Without Mercy 2005, Death Run (with Justin Richards) 2007, Sure Fire (juvenile, with Justin Richards) 2007, The Killing Ground 2008, Rough Justice 2008, A Darker Place 2009, Wolf at the Door 2009. *Honours:* Hon. DUniv (Leeds Metropolitan Univ.) 1995. *Literary Agent:* Ed Victor Ltd, 6 Bayley Street, London, WC1B 3HB, England.

PATTERSON, James, BA, MA; American writer and fmr advertising executive; b. 22 March 1947, Newburgh, NY; m.; one s. *Education:* Manhattan Coll., Vanderbilt Univ. *Career:* wrote first novel 1976; joined J. Walter Thompson as jr copywriter 1971, subsequently Exec. Creative Dir, CEO, Chair. 1990–96. *Publications:* The Thomas Berryman Number (MWA Edgar Award) 1976, The Season of the Machete 1977, The Jericho Commandment (aka See How They Run) 1979, Virgin 1980, Black Market 1986, The Midnight Club 1989, The Day America Told the Truth: What People Really Believe About Everything that Matters (non-fiction, with Peter Kim) 1991, Along Came a Spider 1993, The Second American Revolution 1994, Kiss the Girls 1995, Hide & Seek 1996, Jack & Jill 1996, Miracle on the 17th Green (with Peter de Jonge) 1996, Cat & Mouse 1997, When the Wind Blows 1998, Pop Goes the Weasel 1999, Cradle and All (revised version of Virgin) 2000, Roses are Red 2000, Suzanne's Diary for Nicholas 2001, 1st to Die 2001, Violets are Blue 2001, 2nd Chance (with Andrew Gross) 2002, Four Blind Mice 2002, The Beach House (with Peter de Jonge) 2002, The Jester 2003, The Lake House 2003, The Big Bad Wolf 2003, 3rd Degree 2003, Sam's Letters to Jennifer 2004, London Bridges 2004, Honeymoon 2005, 4th of July 2005, Mary Mary 2005, Maximum Ride: The Angel 2005, The 5th Horseman (with Maxine Paetro) 2006, Judge and Jury 2006, Lifeguard (with Andrew Gross) 2006, Thriller (short stories) (ed) 2006, Maximum Ride: School's Out Forever (with Peter De Jonge) 2006, Cross 2006, Step on a Crack (with Michael Ledwidge) 2007, The Beach Road (with Peter De Jonge) 2007, The 6th Target (with Maxine Paetro) 2007, Maximum Ride: Saving the World and Other Extreme Sports (children's fiction) 2007, The Quickie (with Michael Ledwidge) 2007, Double Cross 2007, You've Been Warned 2007, 7th Heaven 2008, Maximum Ride: The Final Warning 2008, Sundays at Tiffany's 2008, Sail 2008, The Dangerous Days of Daniel X 2008, Against All Odds (non-fiction), Cross Country 2008, 8th Confession (with Maxine Paetro) 2009, Max: A Maximum Ride Novel 2009, Swimsuit 2009, Alex Cross's Trial 2009, Run for Your Life 2009, The Murder of King Tut (with Martin Dugard) 2009, I, Alex Cross 2009, Worst Case 2010, 9th Judgement (with Maxine Paetro) 2010, Private (with Maxine Paetro) 2010, Daniel X: Demons and Druids 2010, The Postcard Killers (with Liza Marklund) 2010, Don't Blink 2010, The Gift (with Ned Rust) 2010, Tick Tock 2011, The Christmas Wedding 2011, Kill Alex Cross 2011. *Address:* c/o Author Mail, Hachette Book Group USA, 237 Park Avenue, New York, NY 10017, USA (office). *Website:* www.jamespatterson.com.

PATTERSON, (Horace) Orlando Lloyd; Jamaican academic and writer; *John Cowles Professor of Sociology, Harvard University;* b. 5 June 1940. *Education:* BSc, University of the West Indies 1962; PhD, LSE 1965. *Career:* Prof. of Sociology 1971–, John Cowles Prof. of Sociology 1993, Harvard University; Assoc. Ed., American Sociological Review 1989–92; mem. American Acad. of Arts and Sciences, fellow; American Sociological Asscn. *Publications:* fiction: The Children of Sisyphus 1964, An Absence of Ruins 1967, Die the Long Day 1972; non-fiction: The Sociology of Slavery: Jamaica 1655–1838 1967, Ethnic Chauvinism: The Reactionary Impulse 1977, Slavery and Social Death: A Comparative Study 1982, Freedom 1991, The Ordeal of Integration: Progress and Resentment in America's 'Racial' Crisis 1997, Rituals of Blood: The Consequences of Slavery in Two American Centuries 1999; contributions to books and professional journals. *Honours:* Hon. DHumLitt (The New School) 2000, (Northwestern) 2001, (Chicago) 2002, (La Trobe) 2006; Best Novel in English Award, Dakar Festival of Negro Arts 1965, Co-Winner, Ralph Bunche Award, American Political Science Asscn 1983, Distinguished Contribution to Scholarship Award, American Sociological Asscn 1983, Walter Channing Cabot Faculty Prizes, Harvard University 1983, 1997, National Book Award for Non-Fiction 1991, University of California at Los Angeles Medal 1992; Order of Distinction, Government of Jamaica 1999. *Address:* Department of Sociology, Harvard University, 520 William James Hall, 33 Kirkland Street, Cambridge, MA 02138, USA (office). *Telephone:* (617) 495-

3707 (office). *Fax:* (617) 496-5794 (office). *E-mail:* opatters@fas.harvard.edu (office). *Website:* www.wjh.harvard.edu (office).

PATTERSON, Richard North, BA, JD; American novelist; b. 22 Feb. 1947, Berkeley, CA; m. Nancy Clair Patterson; three s. two d. *Education:* Ohio Wesleyan Univ., Case Western Reserve Law School. *Career:* fmr Asst Attorney, state of Ohio, fmr trial attorney, SEC, Washington, DC; fmr partner, Bingham-McCutchen; Chair., Common Cause; mem. bd of dirs, Nat. Partnership for Women and Families, Family Violence Prevention Fund, PEN Center West, Brady Campaign to Prevent Gun Violence. *Publications:* The Lasko Tangent 1979, The Outside Man 1981, Escape the Night 1983, Private Screening 1985, Degree of Guilt 1993, Eyes of a Child 1995, The Final Judgement 1995, Silent Witness 1997, No Safe Place 1997, When the Wind Blows 1998, Dark Lady 1999, Protect and Defend 2000, Balance of Power 2003, Conviction 2005, Exile 2007, Eclipse 2009, The Race 2007, The Spire 2009, In the Name of Honor 2010; contrib. to magazines, journals and newspapers. *Honours:* Edgar Allan Poe Award 1979, French Grand Prix de Littérature Policière 1995, Case Western Reserve Univ. Pres.'s Award to Distinguished Alumni 1997. *Literary Agent:* Hill Nadell Literary Agency, 8999 Beverly Boulevard, Suite 805, Los Angeles, CA 90048, USA. *Telephone:* (310) 860-9605. *Fax:* (310) 860-9672. *Website:* www.hillnadell.com; richardnorthpattersonbooks.com.

PATTISON, Robert, AB, MA, PhD; American academic and writer; *Professor of English, Long Island University, Brooklyn*; b. 28 Oct. 1945, Orange, NJ. *Education:* Yale and Columbia Univs, Univ. of Sussex, UK. *Career:* Adjunct Lecturer, Richmond Coll., CUNY 1974, Adjunct Instructor, Queensborough Community Coll., CUNY 1974–75; Instructor of English, St Vincent's Coll., St John's Univ., New York 1975–77; Prof. of English, Southampton Coll., Long Island Univ., New York 1978–2004, Co-ordinator of the English and Writing Programme 1992–2004; Prof. of English, Long Island Univ., Brooklyn 2005–; Pres. Southampton Coll. Fed. of Teachers 1981–83, 1985–86, 1996–2001, 2003–04. *Publications:* The Child Figure in English Literature 1978, Tennyson and Tradition 1980, On Literacy 1982, The Triumph of Vulgarity 1987, The Great Dissent: John Henry Newman and the Liberal Heresy 1991; contrib. to Nation, ADE Bulletin, University of Toronto Quarterly, Mosaic, New York Times, Dickens Studies Newsletter; various edited vols. *Honours:* Long Island Univ. Trustees Awards for Scholarship 1979, 1985, Rockefeller Foundation Fellowship 1980–81, Guggenheim Fellowship 1986–87. *Address:* Department of English, Long Island University, 1 University Place, Brooklyn, NY 11201, USA (office). *Telephone:* (718) 488-1000 (office). *E-mail:* robert.pattison@liu.edu (office).

PAULIN, Thomas (Tom) Neilson, BA, BLitt; British poet, critic and academic; *G. M. Young Lecturer in English Literature, Hertford College, University of Oxford*; b. 25 Jan. 1949, Leeds, Yorkshire; m. Munjiet Kaut Khosa 1973; two s. *Education:* Univ. of Hull, Lincoln Coll., Oxford. *Career:* Lecturer, Univ. of Nottingham 1972–89, Reader in Poetry 1989–94; G. M. Young Lecturer in English Literature, Hertford Coll., Univ. of Oxford 1994–; Fellow, Hertford Coll., Oxford 1994–; Co-founder Field Day Theatre Co., Derry. *Television:* panel mem. Newsnight Review (BBC 2). *Publications:* poetry: Theoretical Locations 1975, A State of Justice (Somerset Maugham Award 1978) 1977, Personal Column 1978, The Strange Museum 1980, The Book of Juniper 1981, Liberty Tree 1983, The Argument at Great Tew 1985, Fivemiletown 1987, Selected Poems 1972–90 1993, Walking a Line 1994, The Wind Dog 1999, The Invasion Handbook 2002, The Road to Inver 2004; non-fiction: Thomas Hardy: The Poetry of Perception 1975, Ireland and the English Crisis 1984, The Faber Book of Political Verse (ed.) 1986, Hard Lines 3 (co-ed.) 1987, Minotaur: Poetry and the Nation State 1992, Writing to the Moment: Selected Critical Essays 1996, The Day Star of Liberty: William Hazlitt's Radical Style (biog.) 1998, Crusoe's Secret: The Aesthetics of Dissent 2005, The Secret Life of Poems 2008. *Honours:* Eric Gregory Award 1978, Faber Memorial Prize 1982, Fulbright Scholarship 1983–84. *Address:* Hertford College, Catte Street, Oxford, OX1 3BW (office); c/o Faber and Faber, Bloomsbury House, 74–77 Great Russell Street, London, WC1B 3DA, England (office). *Website:* www.faber.co.uk (office).

PAULS, Alan; Argentine writer; b. 1959, Buenos Aires. *Career:* has worked as univ. lecturer, scriptwriter, film critic and journalist. *Films:* scriptwriter: Los Enemigos 1983, La Era del ñandú 1986, Sinfin 1988, El Censor 1995, Vidas privadas 2001, Los Rubios 2003, Imposible 2004, Arizona sur 2007. *Publications:* El pudor del pornógrafo 1984, Manuel Puig: La traición de Rita Hayworth 1986, El coloquio 1990, Wasabi 1994, Lino Palacio: la infancia de la risa 1995, Cómo se escribe: El diario íntimo 1996, El factor Borges: Nueve ensayos ilustrados con imágenes de Nicolás Helft 1996, El Pasado (trans. as The Past) (Herralde Prize) 2003, La vida descalzo 2006, Historia del llanto 2007. *Address:* c/o Editorial Anagrama, Pedro de la Creu 58, Barcelona 08034, Spain (office). *E-mail:* anagrama@anagrama-ed.es (office). *Website:* www.anagrama-ed.es (office).

PAULSEN, Nancy; American publishing executive; *President and Publisher, G.P. Putnam's Sons Children's Books*. *Career:* fmr Ed.-in-Chief Puffin Books, Publr 1991–94; fmr Sr Ed. Viking Children's Books; Pres. and Publr G.P. Putnam's Sons Children's Books 1994–, Dial Books for Young Readers 1998–. *Publications include:* All That You Are (co-author) 2000, Miracle's Boys (co-author) 2000, Belly Button Boy 2000, Forging Freedom 2000, Hope Was Here 2000. *Address:* G.P. Putnam's Sons Children's Books, Penguin USA, 375 Hudson Street, New York, NY 10014, USA (office). *Website:* us.penguingroup.com (office).

PAULSON, Ronald Howard, BA, PhD; American writer and academic; *Mayer Professor Emeritus of Humanities, Johns Hopkins University*; b. 27 May 1930, Bottineau, ND; s. of Howard Clarence Paulson and Ethel Florence Tvete; m. Barbara Lee Appleton 1957 (divorced 1982); one s. one d. *Education:* Yale Univ. *Career:* Instructor, Univ. of Illinois 1958–59, Asst Prof. 1959–62, Assoc. Prof. 1962–63; Prof. of English, Johns Hopkins Univ. 1967–75, Chair. Dept of English 1968–75, Andrew W. Mellon Prof. of Humanities 1973–75, Mayer Prof. of Humanities 1984–2005, Mayer Prof. Emer. 2005–, Chair. Dept of Humanities 1985–91; Prof. of English, Yale Univ. 1975–84; mem. American Soc. of 18th Century Studies, Pres. 1986–87; Fellow, American Acad. of Arts and Sciences. *Publications:* Theme and Structure in Swift's Tale of a Tub 1960, Fielding: The Critical Heritage (ed. with Thomas Lockwood) 1962, Fielding: 20th Century Views (ed.) 1962, Hogarth's Graphic Works 1965, The Fictions of Satire 1967, Satire and the Novel 1967, Satire: Modern Essays in Criticism 1971, Hogarth: His Life, Art and Times 1971, Rowlandson: A New Interpretation 1972, Emblem and Expression: Meaning in Eighteenth Century English Art 1975, The Art of Hogarth 1975, Popular and Polite Art in the Age of Hogarth and Fielding 1979, Literary Landscape: Turner and Constable 1982, Book and Painting: Shakespeare, Milton and the Bible 1983, Representations of Revolution 1983, Breaking and Remaking 1989, Figure and Abstraction in Contemporary Painting 1990, Hogarth: Vol. I, The Making of the Modern Moral Subject 1991, Vol. II, High Art and Low 1992, Vol. III, Art and Politics 1993, The Beautiful, Novel and Strange: Aesthetics and Heterodoxy 1996, The Analysis of Beauty (ed.) 1997, Don Quixote in England: The Aesthetics of Laughter 1998, The Life of Henry Fielding: A Critical Biography 2000, Hogarth's Harlot: Parody in Enlightenment England 2003, Sin and Evil: Moral Values in Literature 2007, The Art of Riot in England and America 2010; contrib. to professional journals. *Honours:* Guggenheim Fellowships 1965–66, 1986–87, Nat. Endowment for the Humanities Fellow 1977–78. *Address:* 2722 St Paul Street, Baltimore, MD 21218, USA (home). *Telephone:* (410) 366-7454 (home). *E-mail:* pauls_r@jhu.edu (home).

PAVLYCHKO, Dmytro Vasylovych; Ukrainian poet and politician; *President, Ukrainian World Coordinating Council*; b. 28 Sept. 1929, Ivano-Frankivsk; s. of Vasyl Pavlychko and Paraska Bojchuk. *Education:* Lviv Univ. *Career:* started publishing in early 1950s; mem. CPSU 1954–88; keen advocate of de-Stalinization from 1962; f. Taras Shevchenko Ukrainian Language Soc. 1988, for protection of language; Chair. Inaugural Congress of the Popular Movt of the Ukraine for Perestroika (Rukh); Deputy to Ukrainian Supreme Soviet 1990–95; Chair., Parl. Cttee for Int. Affairs 1991–95; Amb. to Slovakia 1995–98, to Poland 1999–2003; Pres., Ukrainian World Coordinating Council 2006–. *Publications include:* poems: My Land 1955, The Day 1960, Bread and Banner 1968, Sonnets 1978, Turned to the Future 1986, Repentance Psalms 1994, Nostalgia 1998, Thimble 2002, Memory 2004, Three Verses 2007, Autodaphe 2008; trans.: C. Baudelaire, Poems 2001, José Martí, Poesías 2001, W. Shakespeare, Sonnets 2001; contrib. to anthologies. *Address:* c/o Ministry of Foreign Affairs, pl. Mykhailivska 1, 01018 Kiev (office); Khreshchatyk str. 13, Apt 42, 01001 Kiev, Ukraine (home). *Telephone:* (44) 287-22-41 (office); (44) 278-79-75 (home). *Fax:* (44) 287-22-41 (office). *E-mail:* uvkr@ipteleocm.net.ua (office). *Website:* www.uvkr.ua (office).

PAXMAN, Jeremy Dickson, MA; British broadcast journalist and writer; *Presenter, Newsnight*; b. 11 May 1950, Leeds; s. of Arthur Keith Paxman and Joan McKay Dickson; one s. two d. *Education:* Malvern Coll., St Catharine's Coll., Cambridge. *Career:* journalist, NI 1973–77; reporter, BBC TV Tonight and Panorama programmes 1977–85, presenter, BBC TV Breakfast Time 1986–89, Newsnight 1989–, Univ. Challenge 1994–, Start the Week, Radio 4, 1998–2002; Fellow, St Edmund Hall, Oxford, St Catharine's Coll. Cambridge 2001; Vice-Pres. The Wild Trout Trust 2004–, The London Library. *Publications:* A Higher Form of Killing (co-author) 1982, Through the Volcanoes 1985, Friends in High Places 1990, Fish, Fishing and the Meaning of Life 1994, The Compleat Angler 1996, The English 1998, The Political Animal 2002, On Royalty 2006, The Victorians: Britain Through the Paintings of the Age 2009, Empire 2011; numerous articles in newspapers and magazines. *Honours:* Dr hc (Leeds, Bradford) 1999, (Open Univ.) 2006; TV Soc. Award for Int. Reporting, Richard Dimbleby Award, BAFTA 1996, 2000, Royal TV Soc. Interview of the Year 1997, Presenter of the Year 2001, 2007, Voice of the Viewer and Listener Presenter of the Year 1994, 1997, 2005, Variety Club Media Personality of the Year 1999. *Address:* c/o Capel & Land, 29 Wardour Street, London, W1V 6PS, England (office). *Website:* news.bbc.co.uk/1/hi/programmes/newsnight.

PAXSON, Diana Lucile, BA, MA; American author and editor; b. 20 Feb. 1943, Detroit, Mich.; d. of Edwin Woolman Paxson and Mary Herrington Paxson; m. Donald C. Studebaker 1968; two s. *Education:* Mills Coll., Univ. of California, Berkeley. *Career:* ordained Minister, Fellowship of the Spiral Path 1982; Elder, The Troth, Covenant of the Goddess; Ed. Idunna journal 1996–; mem. Science Fiction and Fantasy Writers of America. *Publications:* fiction: Lady of Light 1982, Lady of Darkness 1983, Brisingamen 1984, Silverhaird the Wanderer 1986, White Mare, Red Stallion 1986, The Earthstone 1987, The Paradise Tree 1987, The Sea Star 1988, The White Raven 1988, The Wind Crystal 1990, Lady of Darkness 1990, The Serpent's Tooth 1991, The Wolf and the Raven 1993, Master of Earth and Water 1993, The Shield Between the Worlds 1994, Sword of Fire and Shadow 1995, The Dragons of the Rhine 1995, The Lord of Horses 1996, Priestess of Avalon 2000, The Hallowed Isle 2001,

Ancestors of Avalon 2004, The Golden Hills of Westria 2006, Ravens of Avalon 2007, Sword of Avalon 2009; non-fiction: Celestial Wisdom 2003, Taking Up the Runes 2005, Essential Asatru 2006, Trance-Portation 2008, Seeing for the People 2012; contrib. of articles to Sagewoman magazine, short stories in various publs. *Address:* PO Box 472, Berkeley, CA 94701, USA (home). *Telephone:* (510) 658-6033. *E-mail:* diana@westria.org (home). *Website:* www.westria.org; www.seidh.org; www.avalonbooks.net.

PAXTON, Lois (see Low, Lois Dorothea)

PAYNE, Alexander, BA, MFA; American film director and screenwriter; b. 10 Feb. 1961, Omaha, Neb.; s. of George Payne and Peggy Payne (née Constantine); m. Sandra Oh 2003. *Education:* Stanford Univ. and Univ. of California, Los Angeles. *Career:* began making films aged six; employee Universal Pictures; completed several shorts for Propaganda Films and screened on Playboy Channel; feature film debut with Citizen Ruth (co-wrote screenplay with Jim Taylor) 1996. *Films include:* The Passion of Martin (thesis film, dir) 1989, Inside Out (dir and screenwriter) 1992, Citizen Ruth (dir and screenwriter) (First Prize, Munich Film Festival) 1996, Election (dir and co-screenwriter with Jim Taylor) (Best Screenplay Award: WGA, New York Film Critics' Circle and Ind. Spirit, Best Film and Best Dir, Ind. Spirit Awards) 1999, Jurassic Park III (screenplay) 2001, About Schmidt (dir and co-screenwriter with Jim Taylor) (Best Movie of the Year, Los Angeles Film Critics' Asscn 2002, Golden Globe for Best Screenplay 2003) 2002, Sideways (dir) (Los Angeles Film Critics' Asscn Best Movie of the Year, Golden Globe Award for Best Screenplay 2005, BAFTA Award for Best Adapted Screenplay 2005, Writers' Guild of America Award for best adapted screenplay 2005, Acad. Award for Best Writing, Adapted Screenplay2005), Independent Spirit Awards for Best Dir, Best Screenplay 2005) 2004, Paris, je t'aime (segment) 2006, I Now Pronounce You Chuck and Larry (co-screenwriter) 2007, The Descendants (dir) (Dallas-Fort Worth Film Critics Asscn Award for Best Dir and Best Screenplay 2011, Florida Film Critics Circle Award for Best Adapted Screenplay 2011, Acad. Award for Best Writing, Adapted Screenplay 2012) 2011. *Television includes:* Hung 2009. *Address:* c/o David Lonner, WME, 9601 Wilshire Boulevard, Beverly Hills, CA 90210, USA (office).

PAYNE, (William) David; American writer; b. 13 April 1955, Henderson, NC. *Publications:* Confessions of a Taoist on Wall Street: A Chinese American Romance 1984, Early from the Dance 1989, Ruin Creek 1993, Gravesend Light 2000, Back to Wando Passo 2006. *Honours:* Houghton Mifflin Company Fellowship 1984. *Literary Agent:* Janklow & Nesbit Associates, 445 Park Avenue, New York, NY 10022, USA.

PAZ MARTÍNEZ, (Arsenio) Senel, BA; Cuban writer and screenwriter; b. 1950, Fomento. *Education:* Universidad de La Habana. *Publications include:* El niño aquel (short stories), Entre sus cuentos figuran ese niño 1980, El rey en el jardín (novel) (Premio de la Crítica Literaria 1985) 1983, Mentiras adorables (play), El lobo, el bosque y el hombre nuevo (novel) 1991, Fresa y chocolate (screenplay, from El lobo, el bosque y el hombre nuevo) 1994, Las Hermanas, En el cielo con diamantes (novel) 2007. *Honours:* Premio Juan Rulfo de Literatura, Medalla Alejo Carpentier 1999.

PEACE, David; British writer; b. 1967, Ossett, W Yorks.; m.; two c. *Education:* Manchester Polytechnic. *Career:* taught English in Istanbul and Tokyo 1993–2001. *Publications:* novels: Red Riding quartet: Nineteen Seventy-Four 1999, Nineteen Seventy-Seven 2000, Nineteen Eighty 2001, Nineteen Eighty-Three 2002, GB84 (James Tait Black Prize for Fiction 2005) 2004, The Damned Utd 2006, Tokyo Year Zero 2007, Tokyo Occupied City 2009. *Honours:* one of Granta magazine's 20 Best of Young British Novelists 2003. *Address:* c/o Faber and Faber Ltd, Bloomsbury House, 74–77 Great Russell Street, London, WC1B 3DA, England (office). *Website:* www.faber.co.uk (office).

PEACOCK, Molly, BA, MA; American/Canadian writer and poet; *Member, Graduate Faculty, Brief Residency Master of Fine Arts Program, Spalding University;* b. (Mary Peacock), 30 June 1947, Buffalo, NY; d. of Edward Frank Peacock and Pauline Ruth Wright; m. Michael Groden 1992. *Education:* Harpur Coll., State Univ. of New York (SUNY) at Binghamton, Johns Hopkins Univ. *Career:* Lecturer, SUNY at Binghamton 1975–76, Univ. of Delaware 1978–79; Writer-in-Residence, Delaware State Arts Council 1978–81, Univ. of Western Ontario 1995–96, English Faculty, Friends Seminary, New York 1981–87; Visiting Poet, Hofstra Univ. 1986, Columbia Univ. 1986, 1992, Carlow Coll. 1993; Poet-in-Residence, Bucknell Univ. 1993, Bennington Coll. 2001, American Poets' Corner, Cathedral of St John the Divine, New York 2000–05; mem. Grad. Faculty, Spalding Univ. 2002–; Contributing Writer, House & Garden, 1996–2001; Regents Lecturer, Univ. of California at Riverside 1998; mem. Acad. of American Poets, Associated Writing Programs, PEN, Poetry Soc. of America (Pres. 1989–95). *Works include:* The Shimmering Verge: A One-Woman Show in Poems 2003. *Publications:* poetry: And Live Apart 1980, Raw Heaven 1984, Take Heart 1989, Original Love 1995, Cornucopia 2002, The Second Blush 2008; other: Paradise, Piece by Piece (literary memoir) 1998, How to Read a Poem . . . and Start a Poetry Circle 1999, The Paper Garden: Mrs. Delany Begins Her Life's Work at 72 (biog.) 2010; ed.: Poetry in Motion: 100 Poems from the Subways and Buses (with Elise Paschen and Neil Neches) 1996, The Private I: Privacy in a Public Age (essays) 2001; contribs to anthologies, reviews, quarterlies, journals, and magazines. *Honours:* MacDowell Colony Fellowships 1975–76, 1979, 1982, 1985, 1989, Danforth Foundation Fellowships 1976–77, Yaddo Fellowships 1980, 1982, Ingram Merrill Foundation Awards 1981, 1986, New Virginia Review Fellowship 1983; PEN/Nat. Endowment for the Arts Fiction Award 1984, New York Foundation for the Arts Grant 1985, 1989, Nat. Endowment for the Arts Grant 1990, Woodrow Wilson Fellowships 1993–99, Leon Levy Fellowship 2008. *Address:* 109 Front Street E, No. 1041, Toronto, ON M5A 4P7, Canada (home). *Telephone:* (212) 677-3535 (office); (414) 866-8779 (home); (416) 774-8779 (mobile). *Fax:* (414) 866-8780 (home). *E-mail:* molly@mollypeacock.org (office). *Website:* www.mollypeacock.org (home).

PEARCE, Mary Emily; British writer; b. 7 Dec. 1932, London, England. *Career:* mem. Society of Authors. *Publications:* Apple Tree Lean Down, 1973; Jack Mercybright, 1974; The Sorrowing Wind, 1975; Cast a Long Shadow, 1977; The Land Endures, 1978; Seedtime and Harvest, 1980; Polsinney Harbour, 1983; The Two Farms, 1985; The Old House at Railes, 1993.

PEARLMAN, Daniel D., BA, MA, PhD; American academic and writer; *Professor Emeritus, University of Rhode Island;* b. 22 July 1935, New York, NY; one d. *Education:* Brooklyn Coll., CUNY, Columbia Univ., New York. *Career:* positions at Brooklyn Coll., Univ. of Ariz., Monmouth Coll., NJ, Univ. of Seville, Lehman Coll. 1958–76; Dept Chair. Univ. of Idaho 1976–80; Prof., Univ. of Rhode Island 1980–2005, Dept Chair. 1980–83, Prof. Emer. 2005–. *Publications:* The Barb of Time: On the Unity of Ezra Pound's Cantos 1969, Guide to Rapid Revision (eighth edn) 2002, Letter Perfect: An ABC for Business Writers 1985, The Final Dream and Other Fictions 1995, Black Flames (novel) 1997, The Best Known Man in the World (short stories) 2001, Memini (novel) 2003; contrib. to science fiction magazines and anthologies, including Amazing Stories, Synergy, Semiotext SF, Simulations: 15 Tales of Virtual Reality, Imaginings: An Anthology of Long Short Fiction, short stories to literary journals, including Florida Review, New England Review/Bread Loaf Quarterly, Quarterly West. *Address:* c/o Department of English, University of Rhode Island, Kingston, RI 02881, USA.

PEARLMAN, Edith; American writer; m.; two c. *Education:* Radcliffe Coll. *Career:* has worked in computer firm and soup kitchen and has served in the Town Meeting of Brookline, Mass. *Publications:* short stories collections: Vaquita and Other Stories (Drue Heinz Literature Prize 1996) 1996, Love Among the Greats (Spokane Annual Fiction Prize) 2002, How to Fall (Mary McCarthy Prize in Short Fiction 2005) 2005, Binocular Vision: New & Selected Stories 2011; has published more than 250 works of short fiction and short non-fiction in nat. magazines, literary journals, anthologies and on-line publs; work has appeared in Best American Short Stories, The O. Henry Prize Collection, New Stories from the South and The Pushcart Prize Collection – Best of the Small Presses; short essays have appeared in The Atlantic Monthly, Smithsonian Magazine, Preservation, Yankee Magazine and Ascent; travel writing – about the Cotswolds, Budapest, Jerusalem, Paris and Tokyo – has been published in the New York Times and elsewhere. *Honours:* Syndicated Fiction Awards 1991, 1987, 1991, Distinguished Fiction Award, Antioch Review 1999, Prize Stories: The O. Henry Collection 1978, 1984, 2003, Best American Short Stories 1998, 2000, 2006, PEN/Malamud Award for Short Story Fiction 2011. *Literary Agent:* c/o Jill Kneerim, Kneerim & Williams, 90 Canal Street, Boston, MA 02114, USA. *Telephone:* (617) 521-7084. *E-mail:* info@kwlit.com. *Website:* www.kwlit.com; www.edithpearlman.com.

PEARLSTINE, Norman, LLB; American journalist and organization official; *President and CEO, The American Academy in Berlin; Chief Content Officer, Bloomberg L.P;* b. 4 Oct. 1942, Philadelphia; s. of Raymond Pearlstine and Gladys Pearlstine (née Cohen); m. Nancy Colbert Friday 1988. *Education:* Haverford Coll., Univ. of Pennsylvania. *Career:* staff reporter, Wall Street Journal, Dallas, Detroit, LA 1968–73, Tokyo Bureau Chief 1973–76, Man. Ed. Asian Wall Street Journal, Hong Kong 1976–78; Exec. Ed. Forbes Magazine, LA 1978–80; Nat. News Ed. Wall Street Journal, New York 1980–82, Ed. and Publr Wall Street Journal Europe, Brussels 1982–83, Man. Ed. and Vice-Pres. Wall Street Journal, New York 1983–91, Exec. Ed. 1991–92; Pres. and CEO Friday Holdings L.P., New York 1993–94; Ed.-in-Chief Time Inc. 1995–2006, now Sr Advisor to Time Warner; Sr Advisor to global telecommunications and media team, The Carlyle Group 2006–; Pres. and CEO The American Acad. in Berlin 2007–; Chief Content Officer, Bloomberg L.P. 2008–; mem. New York Historical Soc., Council on Foreign Relations. *Publication:* Off the Record 2007. *Honours:* Ed. of Year Award, Nat. Press Foundation 1989, American Soc. of Magazine Editors Lifetime Achievement Award. *Address:* The American Academy in Berlin, Hans Arnhold Center, Am Sandwerder 17-19, 14109 Berlin, Germany (office); Bloomberg L.P., 731 Lexington Avenue, New York, NY 10022, USA (office). *Telephone:* (30) 804830 (Berlin) (office); (212) 318-2000 (New York) (office). *Fax:* (30) 80483111 (Berlin) (office); (917) 369-5000 (New York) (office). *E-mail:* mailbox@americanacademy.de (office). *Website:* www.americanacademy.de (office); www.bloomberg.com (office).

PEARS, Tim; British author; b. 11 Nov. 1956, Tunbridge Wells, Kent; m. Hania Pears; two c. *Education:* Nat. Film and Television School. *Career:* writer of features, Observer Sports Monthly; Writer-in-Residence, Cheltenham Festival of Literature 2002–03; currently Writer-in-Residence, First Story charity; Royal Literary Fund Fellow, Oxford Brookes Univ. 2006–. *Film:* as screenwriter: Loop 1999. *Publications include:* novels: In the Place of Fallen Leaves (Ruth Hadden Memorial Award 1993, Hawthornden Prize 1994) 1993, In a Land of Plenty 2000, A Revolution of the Sun 2000, Wake Up 2002, Blenheim Orchard 2007, Landed (MJA Open Book Award 2011) 2010. *Honours:* Lannan Literary Award, USA 1996. *Address:* c/o Victoria Hobbs, A.M. Heath & Company Limited, 6 Warwick Court, Holborn, London, WC1R

5DJ, England. *Telephone:* (20) 7242-2811. *Fax:* (20) 7242-2711. *E-mail:* Victoria.Hobbs@amheath.com. *Website:* www.amheath.com. *Address:* c/o William Heinemann, Random House Group Limited, 20 Vauxhall Bridge Road, London, SW1V 2SA, England (office). *Telephone:* (20) 7840-8400 (office). *Fax:* (20) 7840-8778 (office). *E-mail:* heinemannpublicity@randomhouse.co.uk (office). *Website:* www.randomhouse.co.uk (office); www.timpears.com.

PEARSALL, Derek Albert, MA; British academic and writer; *Gurney Professor Emeritus of English, Harvard University*; b. 28 Aug. 1931, Birmingham, England; m. Rosemary Elvidge 1952; two s. three d. *Education:* Univ. of Birmingham. *Career:* Asst Lecturer, then Lecturer, King's Coll. London 1959–65; Lecturer, then Sr Lecturer, then Reader, Univ. of York 1965–76, Prof. 1976–87; Visiting Prof., Harvard Univ., USA 1985–87, Gurney Prof. of English 1987–2000, Prof. Emer. 2000–; Pres. New Chaucer Soc. 1988–90; mem. Early English Text Soc. (Council mem.), Modern Humanities Research Assen (Pres. 2004–05); Fellow, Medieval Acad. of America, American Acad. of Arts and Sciences. *Publications:* John Lydgate 1970, Landscapes and Seasons of the Medieval World (with Elizabeth Salter) 1973, Old English and Middle English Poetry 1977, Langland's Piers Plowman: An Edition of the C-Text 1978, The Canterbury Tales: A Critical Study 1985, The Life of Geoffrey Chaucer: A Critical Biography 1992, John Lydgate (1371–1449): A Bio-bibliography 1997, Chaucer to Spenser: An Anthology of Writings in English 1375–1575 1999, Gothic Europe 1200–1450 2001, Arthurian Romance: A Short Introduction 2003. *Address:* 4 Clifton Dale, York, YO30 6LJ, England (home). *E-mail:* derek@apearsall.fsnet.co.uk (home).

PEARSE, Lesley Margaret; British novelist; b. (Lesley Sargent), 24 Feb. 1945, Rochester, Kent; three d. *Education:* Northbrook School, Lee, London. *Career:* mem. Romantic Writers Assen, RNA, West Country Writers Assen. *Publications:* Georgia 1993, Tara 1994, Charity 1995, Ellie 1996, Camellia 1997, Rosie 1998, Charlie 1999, Never Look Back 2000, Trust Me 2001, Father Unknown 2002, Till We Meet Again 2002, Remember Me 2003, Secrets 2004, A Lesser Evil 2005, Hope 2006, Faith 2008, Gypsy 2009, Stolen 2010, Belle 2011. *Address:* c/o Penguin Books Ltd, 80 Strand, London, WC2R 0RL, England (office).

PEARSON, Ridley; American author; b. 13 March 1953, Glen Cove, NY; m. Marcelle Pearson; two d. *Education:* Univ. of Kansas, Brown Univ. *Career:* mem. Writers Guild of America, MWA, Authors' Guild, International Assen of Crime Writers. *Publications:* Never Look Back 1985, Blood of the Albatross 1986, The Seizing of Yankee Green Mall 1987, Undercurrents 1988, Probable Cause 1990, Hard Fall 1992, The Angel Maker 1993, No Witnesses 1994, Chain of Evidence 1995, Beyond Recognition 1997, The Pied Piper 1998, The First Victim 1999, Middle of Nowhere 2000, Parallel Lies 2001, The Art of Deception 2002, The Body of David Hayes 2004, Dead Aim (as Wendell McCall) 2007, Killer Weekend 2007, Killer View 2008, Killer Summer 2009, In Harm's Way 2010. *Honours:* Fulbright Fellow 1990–91. *Literary Agent:* c/o Amy Berkower, Writers House, 21 West 26th Street, New York, NY 10010, USA. *Telephone:* (212) 685-2400. *Fax:* (212) 685-1781. *Website:* www.writershouse.com. *E-mail:* nancy@ridleypearson.com (office). *Website:* www.ridleypearson.com.

PEARSON, Thomas Reid, BA, MA; American writer; b. 27 March 1956, Winston-Salem, NC. *Education:* North Carolina State Univ., Pennsylvania State Univ. *Publications:* A Short History of a Small Place 1985, Off for the Sweet Hereafter 1986, The Last of How It Was 1987, Call and Response 1989, Gospel Hour 1991, Cry Me a River 1993, Blue Ridge 2000, True Cross 2004. *Literary Agent:* Young Agency, 156 Fifth Avenue, New York, NY 10010, USA.

PECK, Dale; American writer and critic; b. 1967, Long Island, NY. *Education:* Drew Univ., NJ and Columbia Univ. *Career:* book reviewer, Village Voice Literary Supplement, London Book Review, New York Times; currently creative writing teacher, New School, New York. *Publications:* Fucking Martin (novel, aka Martin and John) 1993, The Law of Enclosures (novel) 1996, Now It's Time to Say Goodbye (novel) 1998, What We Lost (memoir) 2003, A Story of my Father's Childhood 2003, Hatchet Jobs (criticism) 2004; juvenile: Drift House: The First Voyage 2005, The Lost Cities: A Drift House Voyage 2007. *Honours:* Guggenheim Fellowship. *Address:* c/o Houghton Mifflin Publishing, 222 Berkeley Street, Boston, MA 02116, USA.

PECKER, David J., CPA; American publishing executive; *Chairman and CEO, American Media, Inc.*; b. 24 Sept. 1951; m. Karen Balan 1987. *Education:* Pace and New York Univs. *Career:* fmrly Sr Auditor Price Waterhouse & Co.; fmrly Man. Financial Reporting Diamandis Communications Inc., also Dir Financial Reporting, Dir Accounting, Asst Controller; Exec. Vice-Pres. Hachette Magazines Inc. 1990–91, Pres. 1991–92, Pres., CEO 1992–99, Chair. and CEO American Media Inc. 1999–; mem. Fashion Group's Int. Advisory Bd, NY City Partnership Cttee, American Man. Asscn; mem. Bd Dirs Pace Univ., Drug Enforcement Agents Foundation 1995–. *Address:* American Media Inc., 1000 American Media Way, Boca Raton, FL 33431-1000, USA (office). *Telephone:* (561) 997-7733 (office). *Fax:* (561) 272-8411 (office). *Website:* www.nationalenquirer.com (office).

PEDEN, W(illiam) Creighton, BA, BD, MA, PhD; American academic, author and editor; *Fuller E. Callaway Professor Emeritus of Philosophy, Augusta State University*; b. 25 July 1935, Concord, NC; m. 2nd Harriet McKnight Peden 1978 (died 2007); two d. one step-s. *Education:* Davidson Coll., NC, Univ. of Chicago, St Andrews Univ., UK. *Career:* Founding Faculty mem. Florida Presbyterian Coll. 1960–61; Asst Prof., St Andrews Coll. 1964–65; Prof., Radford Coll., Va 1965–68; Chair. Dept of Philosophy, Millikin Univ., Decatur, Ill. 1968–69; Visiting Prof., Iliff School of Theology 1969, 1973, 1978, Univ. of Glasgow, UK 1982–83, Vrije Univ., Amsterdam, The Netherlands 1991; Fuller E. Callaway Prof. of Philosophy, Augusta Coll., later Augusta State Univ., Ga 1969–93, Prof. Emer. 1993–; Founding Ed. Journal of Social Philosophy 1970–83; Founding Co-Ed. American Journal of Theology and Philosophy 1980–91; Exec. Dir Highlands Inst. of American Religious and Philosophical Thought 1987–92, Pres. 1992–2008, Pres. Emer. 2008–; Scholar-in-Residence, Univ. of Copenhagen, Denmark 1988; mem. American Acad. of Religion, American Philosophical Asscn, North American Soc. for Social Philosophy, Social Philosophy Research Inst., Soc. for the Advancement of American Philosophy, Soc. of Religious Humanism; Fellow, Soc. of Philosophers in America. *Publications:* Wieman's Empirical Process Philosophy 1977, Whitehead's View of Reality (with Charles Hartshorne) 1981, The Chicago School: Voices of Liberal Religious Thought 1987, The Philosopher of Free Religion: Francis Ellingwood Abbot, 1836–1903 1992, Civil War Pulpit to World's Parliament of Religion: The Thought of William James Potter, 1829–1893 1996, A Good Life in a World Made Good, Albert Eustace Haydon, 1880–1975 2006, Pragmatism and the Rise of Religious Humanism, The Writings of Albert Eustace Haydon, 1880-1975, Vols I, II, III 2006, Intellectual Biography of David Atwood Wasson, 1823–1887: A Transcendentalist 2008, Evolutionary Theist: An Intellectual Biography of Minot Judson Savage, 1841–1918 2009, Empirical Tradition in American Liberal Religious Thought 1860–1960 2010; editor: Philosophical Reflections on Education and Society (with Donald Chapman) 1978, Critical Issues in Philosophy of Education (with Donald Chapman) 1979, Philosophy for a Changing Society 1983, Philosophical Essays on Ideas of a Good Society 1988, Freedom, Equality and Social Change 1989, God, Values and Empiricism 1989, Revolution, Violence and Equality 1990, Terrorism, Justice and Social Values 1990, The American Constitutional Experiment 1991, Communitarianism, Liberalism and Social Responsibility 1991, Rights, Justice and Community 1992, The Bill of Rights: Bicentennial Reflections 1993, Freedom, Dharma and Rights 1993, New Essays in Religious Naturalism (with Larry E. Axel) 1993, Essays and Sermons of William James Potter (1829–1893), Unitarian Minister and Freethinker (with Everett J. Tarbox Jr, two vols) 1993, The Chicago School of Theology: Pioneers in Religious Inquiry (with J. Stone, two vols) 1996, The Collected Essays of Francis Ellingwood Abbot (1836–1903): American Philosopher and Free Religionist (with Everett J. Tarbox Jr, four vols) 1996, Essays and Sermons of William James Potter (1929–1893): Unitarian Minister and Freethinker (with Everett J. Tarbox Jr, two vols) 2003, A Good Person in a World Made Good: Albert Eustace Haydon 1880–1975 2005, Works of Albert Eustace Haydon 1880–1975 (three vols, co-ed.) 2006, Meditations on Man 2006, Intellectual Biography of David Atwood Wasson, 1823–1887: A Transcendentalist 2008, Evolutionary Theist: An Intellectual Biography of Minot Judson Savage, 1841–1918 2009, Empirical Tradition in American Liberal Religious Thought, 1860–1960 2010, Life and Thought of Henry Nelson Wieman, 1884–1975, with an "Intellectual Autobiography of H. N. Wieman" 2010, (republication with new sections) Whitehead's View of Reality (with Charles Hartshorne) 2010, Life and Thought of Bernard Eugene Meland, American Constructive Theologian, 1899–1993 2010; contrib. to Dictionary of Modern American Philosophers 1860–1960 2005, scholarly books and journals. *Address:* 295 Bonnie Drive, Highlands, NC 28741, USA (home). *Telephone:* (828) 526-4038 (office).

PEDRAM, Abdul Latif; Afghan poet, writer and journalist; b. 1963, Badakhstan. *Career:* taught journalism 1989–91; Deputy Ed.-in-Chief, Haghighat-e Enghelab-e Sor, Ed.-in-Chief, Theoretical supplement 1982–85; f. and Ed.-in-Chief, Shora journal 1988–89; Deputy Dir, Hakim Nasser Khosrow Balki Foundation Library, Baghlan (Ed.-in-Chief, Hojjat foundation journal, f., foundation newsletter, Kian) 1996–98; Lecturer of Literary Critique, Thought and Poetry, Univ. of Baghlan, Pol-i Khomri 1996–98; founder National Congress Party of Afghanistan 2004 (ran for Pres. 2004); mem. bd of eds, Peyvand journal. *Publications:* poetry: Naqshi dar abgineh va baran (A Figure in Crystal and Rain) 1979, Lahzehay-e massloub (Crucified Moments) 1983, She'rhay-e enzeva (Poems of Solitude) 1984, Khatabeh az sakouyeh hendo-koush (A Letter from the Hend and Koush) 1988, Mo'alegh-e-ye hashtom (The Eighth Moalegheh) 1988, Ta'reef-e talkh-e mandan 1999; prose: Delavaraneh kuhestan (The Brave Men from the Mountains) 1979, Safarnomeyeh Czechoslovaqui (My Travels in Czechoslovakia) 1980, Chand nokteh beh sheeveyeh tarh (A Few Points Told in Rough) 1983, Darssyahey journalism (Lessons in Journalism, two vols) 1988, Chahar magholeyeh falsafi (Four Philosophical Essays) 1990, Afateh ideology (The Evil of Ideology) 1996, Dar zarurateh jodayee deen az siasat (About the Necessity of Separation of Religion from Politics) 1996; contrib. numerous articles in newspapers and journals, including Erfan, Avaz, Jowandun, Iness, Hevad. *Honours:* hon. mem. Int. Parliament of Writers, Asscn of the Persian Speakers of the World Peyvand; Reporters sans Frontières grant 1998, Human Rights Watch Hellman-Helmet Prize 1999.

PEDRETTI, Erica; Swiss writer and artist; b. Feb. 1930, Šternberk (Czechoslovakia, now Czech Repub.); m. Gian Pedretti 1952; five c. *Education:* Schule für Gestaltung, Zürich. *Career:* lived in Czechoslovakia 1930–45, Switzerland 1946–50, USA 1950–52, Switzerland 1952–; Corresp. mem. Deutschen Akad. für Sprache und Dichtung, Darmstadt 1998–. *Publications:* Harmloses, bitte 1970, Heiliger Sebastian, Valerie oder das Unerzogene Auge 1986, Engste Heimat 1995, Zerhümmerung 1996, Kuckuckskind 1998, Heute

Ein Tagebuch 2002, Szenenwechsel: Tagebuchblätter/ Change of scene: a Venetian Diary 2005, Fremd Genug 2010. *Honours:* Bachmann-Preis 1984, Großer Literatur-Preis des Kantons Bern 1990, Berliner-Preis, Bobrowski-Medaille 1994, M. L. Kaschnitz-Preis 1996, Kunstpreis der Stadt Biel 1996, Mitteleuropäischer Literaturpreis Vilenica, Slowenien 1999, Kunstpreis des Kantons Graubünden 1999. *Address:* 4 chemin de Beausite, 2520 La Neuveville, Switzerland (home). *Telephone:* (32) 7513561 (home). *E-mail:* e_pedretti@hotmail.com (home).

PEERY, Janet, BA, MFA; American writer and teacher; *Professor, Old Dominion University*; b. (Janet Sawhill), 18 July 1948, Wichita, Kan.; d. of Walter A. Sawhill and Joyce E. Sawhill; m. William Peery 1976 (divorced 1988); three d. *Education:* Wichita State Univ. *Career:* Prof., Old Dominion Univ. 1993–. *Publications:* Alligator Dance (short stories) 1993, The River Beyond the World (novel) 1996, What the Thunder Said (novella and stories) 2007; contribs to New Virginia Review, American Short Fiction, Shenandoah, Black Warrior Review, Chattahoochee Review, Kansas Quarterly, Southwest Review, Quarterly West, Los Angeles Times, Washington Post Book World, 64 Magazine, Image, Southern Review, Kenyon Review, Blackbird. *Honours:* Writers at Work Fellowship 1990, Nat. Endowment for the Arts Fellowship 1990, Goodheart Prizes, Washington and Lee Univ. 1991, 1992, Pushcart Prize 1991, 1992, Best American Short Stories Award 1993, Seaton Award, State of Kansas 1992, KAQ Award, Kansas Quarterly 1992, Whiting Writers' Award 1993, Rosenthal Award, American Acad. of Arts and Letters 1994, Distinguished Alumnus Award, Wichita State Univ. 1997, Guggenheim Fellowship 1998, Outstanding Faculty Award, State Council of Higher Educ., Virginia 2002, Willa Award for Contemporary Fiction 2008, Library of Virginia Literary Award for Fiction 2008. *Address:* Old Dominion University, Department of English, Norfolk, VA 23529, USA (office). *Telephone:* (757) 683-3991 (office). *E-mail:* jpeery@odu.edu (office).

PEET, Mal; British children's writer; m. Elspeth Graham; three c. *Publications include:* novels: Keeper (Branford-Boase Award 2004) 2003, Tamar (Carnegie Medal 2006) 2005, The Penalty 2006, Exposure (Guardian Children's Fiction Prize 2009) 2008. *Literary Agent:* Lucas Alexander Whitley Ltd, 14 Vernon Street, London W14 0RJ, England. *Telephone:* (20) 7471-7900. *Fax:* (20) 7471-7910. *Website:* www.lawagency.co.uk. *Address:* c/o Walker Books, 87 Vauxhall Walk, London, SE11 5HJ, England. *Website:* www.walkerbooks.co.uk.

PEIXOTO, José Luis, BA; Portuguese writer and journalist; b. 1974, Galveias. *Education:* Universidade Nova de Lisboa. *Publications:* fiction: Morreste-me (Prémio Jovens Criadores) 2000, Nenhum Olhar (Prémio José Saramago), Uma Casa na Escuridão 2002, Antidoto 2003, Cemitério de Pianos 2006; poetry: A Criança em Ruínas 2001, A Casa, A Escuridão 2002. *Address:* c/o Quetzal Editores, Rua Prof. Jorge da Silva Horta 1, 1500-499 Lisbon, Portugal (office). *Website:* www.joseluispeixoto.net.

PELECANOS, George Peter; American journalist, writer and screenwriter; b. 18 Feb. 1957, Washington, DC; m.; three c. *Television:* The Wire (writer, story ed., producer, HBO), The Pacific (writer, producer, HBO) Treme (writer, HBO). *Publications:* novels: A Firing Offense 1992, Nick's Trip 1993, Shoedog 1994, Down by the River 1995, The Big Blowdown 1996, The Sweet Forever 1999, King Suckerman 2000, Shame the Devil 2000, Right as Rain 2001, Hell to Pay 2002, Soul Circus 2003, Hard Revolution 2004, Drama City 2005, The Night Gardener 2006, The Turnaround 2008, The Way Home 2009, Hell to Pay 2011, The Cut 2012; contrib. to Esquire, GQ, The Washington Post. *Honours:* Los Angeles Times Book Award 2003, 2004, Int. Crime Novel of the Year in France, Germany and Japan, Edgar Award 2006, Hammett Award for Literary Excellence 2008, Writers' Guild of America Award 2008. *Address:* c/o Little, Brown and Company, 237 Park Avenue, New York, 10017, USA. *Website:* www.hachettebookgroupusa.com.

PELEVIN, Viktor Olegovich; Russian writer; b. 27 Nov. 1962, Moscow. *Education:* Moscow Power Engineering Inst., Gorky Inst. of Literature, Moscow. *Career:* army service; corresp. Face-to-Face journal 1989–90; journal Science and Religion; author of numerous novels and stories. *Publications include:* (most in trans.) Omon Ra (novel) 1996, Vera Pavlovna's Ninth Dream, Reconstructor, Prince of Gosplan, The Yellow Arrow (novella) 1996, Ivan Kublakhanov, Generation, Babylon, The Blue Lantern (short stories) (Russian Booker Prize 1997), The Life of Insects 1998, Crystal World, A Werewolf Problem in Central Russia (short stories) 1998, Chapayev and Pustota (Buddha's Little Finger, aka Babylon) 2000, The Clay Machine-Gun (novel), Generation P 1999, Homo Zapiens (aka Generation P) 2002, Dialectic for the Transitional Phase From Nowhere to Nowhere 2003, The Sacred Book of the Werewolf 2006. *Honours:* Wanderer Prize 1995, Nonino Literary Prize 2001, Robert Schönefeld Prize 2000, 2001, Grigoriev Prize 2004. *Literary Agent:* c/o Aragi Inc., 143 West 27th Street, #4F, New York, NY 10001, USA. *E-mail:* queries@aragi.net (office).

PELLETIER, Chantal; French writer and screenwriter; b. 1949, Lyon. *Career:* mem. Les Trois Jeanne trio 1976–86. *Writing for television:* En cas de bonheur (TF1) 1989, Divisé par deux (adaptation, Antenne 2) 1990, Carré d'as (FR2) 1992, Le prix d'une femme (FR3) 1994, Les malheurs du Sophie 1997, Danger d'aimer (FR3) 1998, L'Inconnu du Val perdu 2001, Agrippine 2001. *Publications include:* novels: L'Octobre 1976, Supermarché rayon bonheur 1990, Le fils d'Ariadne 1992, Le squatt 1996, Lavande tuera 1997, Éros et Thalasso 1998, Le Chant du bouc 2000, Les otages de Gutenberg (with Claude Pujade Renaud and Daniel Zimmermann) 2000, Le Bout du Monde 2001, Troubles fêtes 2001, More is Less (in trans.) 2002, La visite 2003, L'Enfer des Anges 2005, Paradis Andalous 2007, Tirez sur le Caviste 2007. *Address:* c/o Éditions Gallimard, 5 rue Sébastien-Bottin, 75328 Paris, France (office). *Website:* www.gallimard.fr (office); chantalpelletier.free.fr.

PEMBERTON, Margaret, (Rebecca Dean, Maggie Hudson), BA (Hons); British writer; b. (Kathleen Margaret Hudson), 10 April 1943, Bradford, Yorks., England; d. of George Arthur Hudson and Kathleen May Dean; m. Mike Pemberton; one s. four d. *Career:* Chair. Romantic Novelists' Assen; mem. Crime Writers' Asscn, PEN, Soc. of Authors. *Publications:* 35 novels, including Harlot 1981, Lion of Languedoc 1981, The Flower Garden 1982, Silver Shadows, Golden Dreams 1985, Never Leave Me 1986, Multitude of Sins 1988, White Christmas in Saigon 1990, An Embarrassment of Riches 1992, Zadruga 1993, Moonflower Madness 1993, Tapestry of Fear 1994, The Londoners 1995, Magnolia Square 1996, Yorkshire Rose 1996, Coronation Summer 1997, A Many Splendoured Thing 2002, The Four of Us 2004; as Maggie Hudson: Tell Me No Secrets 1998, Fast Women 1999, Looking for Mr Big 2000, Nowhere to Run 2001; as Rebecca Dean: Enemies of the Heart 2008, Palace Circle 2009, The Golden Prince 2010, Wallis 2012, The Shadow Queen 2012. *Literary Agent:* c/o Curtis Brown, Haymarket House, 28–29 Haymarket, London, SW1Y 4SP, England. *Telephone:* (20) 7393-4400. *Fax:* (20) 7393-4401. *E-mail:* cb@curtisbrown.co.uk. *Website:* www.curtisbrown.co.uk.

PENCHEVA, Stanka Michaylova; Bulgarian writer; b. 9 July 1929, Sliven; d. of Michael Penchev and Maria Pencheva; m. 1st Kliment Tzachev 1951 (divorced 1965); m. 2nd Georgy Bourmov 1984 (died 1991); one d. *Education:* Univ. of Sofia. *Career:* Journalist and Literary Ed. Bulgarsko Radio 1950–55, Septemvri magazine 1959–75, Otechestvo magazine 1975–86; trans. three books of poetry; writer of 26 anthologies of poetry, an autobiographical novel, a short novel for children and three books of essays, including one on the contemporary Bulgarian woman 1952–2004; mem. Union of Bulgarian Writers. *Publications include:* 25 poetry collections, three essay collections, including A Baker's Dozen (ed, anthology of 13 Bulgarian women poets) 1990, Tuk sum 2008. *Honours:* Union of Bulgarian Writers award for poetry 1970, 2002. *Address:* 1113 Sofia, 20-3 Tintyava Str, Entr G, Bulgaria (home). *Telephone:* (2) 72-86-01 (home).

PENDLETON, Don (see Obstfeld, Raymond)

PENHALL, Joe; British playwright; b. 1968, Thames Ditton. *Career:* Chief Reporter, Hammersmith Guardian 1992–94; Writer in Residence Royal Nat. Theatre 1995. *Plays:* Some Voices 1994, Pale Horse 1995, Love and Understanding 1997, The Bullet 1998, Blue/Orange 2000, Dumb Show 2004, Landscape with Weapon 2006. *Film:* Some Voices (screenplay) 2000, Enduring Love (screen adaptation) 2004, The Undertaker (screenplay) 2005, The Road (screen adaptation) 2009. *Television:* The Long Firm (screen adaptation for BBC). *Publications:* Methuen Plays I. *Honours:* John Whiting Award 1995, Evening Standard Award Best Play 2000, Critics Circle Best Play 2001, Olivier Award Best Play 2001. *Address:* c/o Methuen Publishing Ltd, 8 Artillery Row, London, SW1P 1RZ, England (office). *Website:* www.methuen.co.uk (office).

PENNAC, Daniel, MA; French novelist; b. (Daniel Pennacchioni), 1 Dec. 1944, Casablanca, Morocco. *Education:* Univ. of Nice. *Career:* teacher in secondary schools in Soissons and Paris 1969–95. *Publications:* juvenile fiction: Le Grand Rex 1980, Cabot caboche 1982, L'Oeil du loup 1984, Au bonheur des ogres 1985, La Fée carabine 1987, La Petite marchande de prose (Prix Inter 1990) 1989, Kamo et moi 1992, Kamo, l'agnece Babel 1992, Kamo, l'idée du siècle 1993, Sang pour sang, le réveil des vampires 1993, Miro: le tour du ciel Pennac 1994, Monsieur Malaussène 1995, Monsieur Malaussène au théatre 1996, Vercors d'en haut 1996, La Réserve naturelle des Hauts Plateaux 1996, Messieurs les enfants 1997, Des chrétiens et des maures 1999, Lévasion Kamo 1997, Aux fruits de la passion 2000, Le Dictateur et le hamac (trans. as The Dictator and the Hammock) 2003, Merci 2004); non-fiction: Comme un roman (essay) 1992, Nemo par Pennac 2006, Chagrin d'école 2007. *Address:* c/o Éditions Gallimard-Jeunesse, 5 rue Sébastien-Bottin, 75328 Paris cedex 07, France (office).

PENNEY, Stef; British filmmaker and writer; b. 1969, Edinburgh. *Education:* Bristol Univ., Bournemouth Coll. of Art. *Short Films:* writer/dir: The Messenger, You Drive Me, The Dying Day, The Knowledge. *Films:* The Passion of Alice (adaption), Was (adaption), Nova Scotia (screenplay), The Seed (adaption). *Publications:* The Tenderness of Wolves (novel) (Costa Awards for Best First Novel, for Best Novel 2007, Theakston's Crime Novel of the Year Award 2008) 2006. *Literary Agent:* MBA Literary Agents Ltd, 62 Grafton Way, London, W1T 5DW, England. *Telephone:* (20) 7387-2076. *Fax:* (20) 7387-2042. *E-mail:* meg@mbalit.co.uk. *Website:* www.mbalit.co.uk.

PENROSE, Sir Roger, Kt, OM, PhD, FRS; British mathematician and academic; *Professor Emeritus of Mathematics, University of Oxford*; b. 8 Aug. 1931, Colchester; s. of Lionel Sharples Penrose; m. 1st Joan Wedge 1959 (divorced 1981), three s.; m. 2nd Vanessa Thomas 1988; one s. *Education:* Univ. Coll. School, Univ. Coll. London and St John's Coll. Cambridge. *Career:* Asst Lecturer, Bedford Coll. London 1956–57; Research Fellow, St John's Coll. Cambridge 1957–60; NATO Research Fellow, Princeton and Syracuse Univs 1959–61; Research Assoc., King's Coll. London 1961–63; Visiting Assoc. Prof., Univ. of Tex. Austin 1963–64; Reader, Birkbeck Coll. London 1964–66, Prof. of Applied Math. 1966–73; Rouse Ball Prof. of Math., Univ. of Oxford 1973–98, Prof. Emer. 1998–, Emer. Fellow, Wadham Coll.; Gresham Prof. of Geometry,

Gresham Coll. 1998–2001; Fellow, Univ. Coll. London 1975; Visiting Prof. Yeshiva, Princeton and Cornell Univs 1966–67, 1969; Lovett Prof. Rice Univ. Houston 1983–87; Distinguished Prof. of Physics and Math. Syracuse Univ. 1987–93, Francis and Helen Pentz Distinguished Prof. of Physics and Math., Pa State Univ. 1993–; mem. London Math. Soc., Cambridge Philosophical Soc., Inst. for Math. and its Applications, Int. Soc. for Gen. Relativity and Gravitation; Fellow, Birkbeck Coll. 1998, Inst. of Physics 1999; Foreign mem. Polish Acad. of Science, Accademia Nazionale dei Lincei; Foreign Assoc. Nat. Acad. of Sciences, USA 1998. *Publications:* Techniques of Differential Topology in Relativity 1973, Spinors and Space-time (with W. Rindler), (Vol. I) 1984, (Vol. II) 1986, The Emperor's New Mind 1989, The Nature of Space and Time (with S. W. Hawking) 1996, The Large, the Small and the Human Mind 1997, White Mars (with B. Aldiss) 1999, The Road to Reality: A Complete Guide to the Laws of the Universe 2004, Cycles of Time: An Extraordinary New View of the Universe 2010; articles in scientific journals. *Honours:* Hon. mem. Royal Irish Acad. of Science 2001; Dr hc, (New Brunswick) 1992, (Surrey) 1993, (Bath) 1994, (London) 1995, (Glasgow) 1996, (Essex) 1996, (St Andrew's) 1997, (Santiniketon) 1998, Hon. DUniv (Open Univ.) 1998, (Southampton) 2002, (Waterloo, Ontario) 2003, (Leiden) 2004, (Athens) 2005, (York) 2006; Hon. Fellow, St John's Coll. Cambridge 1987; Adams Prize (Cambridge Univ.) 1966–67, Dannie Heinemann Prize (American Physics Soc. and American Inst. of Physics) 1971, Eddington Medal (with S. W. Hawking) (Royal Astronomical Soc.) 1975, Royal Medal (Royal Soc.) 1985, Wolf Foundation Prize for Physics (with S. W. Hawking) 1988, Dirac Medal and Prize, Inst. of Physics 1989, Einstein Medal 1990, Science Book Prize 1990, Naylor Prize, London Math. Soc. 1991, DeMorgan Medal 2004, Copley Medal 2008. *Address:* Mathematical Institute, 24–29 St Giles', Oxford, OX1 3LB, England (office). *Telephone:* (1865) 273525 (office). *Fax:* (1865) 273583 (office). *E-mail:* rouse@maths.ox.ac.uk (office). *Website:* www.maths.ox.ac.uk (office).

PEONIDOU, Elli; Cypriot writer; b. 21 Nov. 1940; m. Panos Peonides 1963; one s. one d. *Education:* Charokopios Coll., Athens. *Career:* has written nine books of poetry, 16 children's books, three novels and several other works; works published in Bulgaria, Czech Repub., Slovenia, Slovakia, France, Poland, Hungary, Russia, Yugoslavia, Germany and Portugal; two children's plays staged in Cyprus and abroad; mem. of jury, Neustadt Literary Prize; mem. Hon. List IBBY, Basel (Switzerland) 2002. *Honours:* Repub. of Cyprus Awards 1978, 1980, 1984, 1997, 2001, 2004, Asscn of Children's Books Awards 1987, 1991, 1992, 1993, 2000, awards for books 1994, 1996, for plays 1994, State Prize for Novel 1997, 2001, 2004. *Address:* 14 M Parides Street, 3091 Limassol, Cyprus (home). *Telephone:* (5) 354142 (home). *E-mail:* peonide@cytanet.com.cy (home).

PEPETELA; Angolan novelist; b. (Artur Carlos Mauricio Pestana), 1941, Benguela. *Career:* co-f. Centre of Angolan Studies, Algeria; trained as sociologist and Movimento Popular de Libertação de Angola (MPLA) operative, Algeria 1960s; guerilla fighter for seven years, rising to regional commdr in defence of Angola against first S African invasion 1975; Deputy Minister of Education, Angola 1976–82; mem. Angolan Writers' Union. *Play:* A Revolta da casa dos ídolos 1980. *Publications:* A revolta da casa dos ídolos, As aventuras de Ngunga, Muana Puó 1978, Mayombe 1980, O cão e os calús 1985, Yaka 1984, Lueji, o nascimento dum império 1990, A geração da utopia 1992, O desejo de Kianda (trans. as The Return of the Water Spirit) 1995, Parábola do cágado velho 1996, A gloriosa família 1997, Jaime Bunda, agente secreto 2001, Jaime Bunda e a morte do agente americano 2003, Predadores 2005, O Terrorista de Berkeley, Califórnia 2007. *Honours:* Nat. Literature Prize 1986, Camões Prize 1997, Rio Branco Order 2002. *Literary Agent:* Literarische Agentur Mertin, Taunusstrasse 38, 60329 Frankfurt am Main, Germany. *Telephone:* (69) 27108966. *Fax:* (69) 27108967. *E-mail:* info@mertin-litag.de. *Website:* www.mertin-litag.de.

PEPPE, Rodney Darrell; British writer and artist; b. 24 June 1934, Eastbourne, E Sussex; m. Tatjana Tekkel 1960; two s. *Education:* Eastbourne School of Art, London Co. Council Cen. School of Art, NDD, Illustration (special subject) and Cen. School Diploma. *Career:* mem. Soc. of Authors. *Television:* Huxley Pig (26 episodes for ITV) 1989, Angelmouse (26 episodes for BBC) 1999. *Publications:* The Alphabet Book 1968, Circus Numbers 1969, The House That Jack Built 1970, Hey Riddle Diddle! 1971, Simple Simon 1972, Cat and Mouse 1973, Odd One Out 1974, Henry series 1975–84, Rodney Peppe's Moving Toys 1980, The Mice Who Lived in a Shoe 1981, Run Rabbit Run! 1982, The Kettleship Pirates 1983, The Mice and the Flying Basket 1985, The Mice and the Clockwork Bus 1986, Huxley Pig series 1989, The Mice on the Moon 1992, The Mice and the Travel Machine 1993, The Magic Toybox 1996, Gus and Nipper 1996, Hippo Plays Hide and Seek 1997, Angelmouse series 2000, Automata and Mechanical Toys 2002, Toys and Models 2003, Making Mechanical Toys 2005; contribs to periodicals. *Address:* Stoneleigh House, 6 Stoneleigh Drive, Livermead, Torquay, Devon TQ2 6TR, England (home). *Telephone:* (1803) 690794 (home).

PERALTA, Bertalicia; Panamanian poet and writer; b. 1 March 1940, Panama City. *Education:* Universidad de Panamá, Instituto Nacional de Música. *Career:* fmr secondary school teacher; worked in Radio y Televisión Educativa del Ministerio de Educación de Panamá; f. co-Ed. of literary magazine, El Pez Original 1961–68. *Publications:* poetry: Canto de esperanza filial 1962, Sendas fugitivas 1962, Dos poemas 1964, Atrincherado amor 1965, Los Retornos: poesía 1966, Crecimiento (anthology) 1970, Un lugar en la esfera terrestre 1971, Libro de las fábulas 1972, Himno a la alegría 1973, Ragul 1976, Casa Flotante: poesía 1979, Piel de Gallina 1982, Frisos 1983, En tu cuerpo cubierto de flores 1985, Zona de silencio 1987, Invasión USA 1989, Leit Motiv 1989, La única mujer, Concurso de Belleza, Dos Amigos; short stories: Largo en crescendo 1967, Barcarola y otras fantasías incorregibles (Premio Universidad) 1973, Muerto en enero (Instituto Nacional de Cultura Premio Itinerario del Cuento) 1974, Encore y Guayacán de marzo (Instituto Nacional de Cultura Premio Itinerario del Cuento) 1980; juvenile: Puros cuentos 1986, Historia de una nube blanca; contrib. to anthologies and journals.

PERELMAN, Robert (Bob), MA, MFA, PhD; American poet, writer and academic; *Professor, University of Pennsylvania*; b. 2 Dec. 1947, Youngstown, OH; m. Francie Shaw 1975; two s. *Education:* University of Michigan, University of Iowa, University of California. *Career:* Ed., Hills magazine 1973–80; Asst Prof. University of Pennsylvania 1990–95, Assoc. Prof. 1995–2001, Prof. 2001–. *Publications:* Braille, 1975; Seven Works, 1978; aka, 1979; Primer, 1981; To the Reader, 1984; The First World, 1986; Writing/Talks (ed.), 1985; Face Value, 1988; Captive Audience, 1988; Virtual Reality, 1993; The Trouble with Genius: Reading Pound, Joyce, Stein, and Zukovsky, 1994; The Marginalization of Poetry: Language Writings and Literary History, 1996; The Future of Memory 1998, Ten to One 1999, Playing Bodies 2003.

PERES DA COSTA, Suneeta, BA, MFA; Australian playwright and novelist; b. 1976, Sydney, NSW. *Education:* Univ. of Technology, Sydney, Sarah Lawrence Coll., New York, USA, Univ. of Sydney. *Radio plays:* Watermark (ABC Radio), Angelina's Song (ABC Radio), Children See Everything (ABC Radio), Fire and Water (ABC Radio). *Plays:* I am an Island 1995, Free Men 1996, Blood is Blue 1996, The Art of Straying 1998, Klactoveesedstene 2001. *Publication:* Homework (novel) 1999. *Honours:* Sydney Theatre Co.-ICI Young Playwrights' Award 1995, 1996, NSW Ministry for the Arts Philip Parsons Young Playwrights' Award 1996, Ian Reed Foundation Prize for Radio Drama 1998. *Literary Agent:* Tifanny Loehnis, Janklow & Nesbit (UK) Ltd, 33 Drayson Mews, London, W8 4LY, England; RGM Associates, PO Box 128, Surry Hills, NSW 2010, Australia. *Telephone:* (20) 7376-2733 (England); (2) 9281-3911 (Aus.). *Fax:* (20) 7376-2915 (England); (2) 9281-4705 (Aus.). *E-mail:* tifloehnis@janklow.co.uk; info@rgm.com.au. *Website:* www.rgm.com.au.

PÉREZ-REVERTE, Arturo; Spanish journalist and writer; b. 1951, Cartagena, Murcia. *Career:* fmr journalist, war corresp., Pueblo; war corresp., Spanish nat. TV; now writes fiction full-time; elected to Spanish Royal Acad. 2003. *Films include:* El Maestro de Esgrima 1992, La Tabla de Flandes 1994, Cachito 1995, Territorio Comanche 1997, La Novena Puerta 1999, Gitano 2000, Alatriste 2006, La Carta Esférica 2007. *Publications include:* El Húsar 1986, El maestro de esgrima (trans. as The Fencing Master) 1988, La tabla de Flandes (trans. as The Flanders Panel) 1990, El club Dumas (trans. as The Dumas Club) 1993, La sombra del águila 1993, Territorio comanche 1994, Un asunto de honor 1995, Obra breve 1995, La piel del tambor (trans. as The Seville Communion; Jean Monnet Prize for European Literature 1997) 1995, El capitán Alatriste (trans. as Captain Alatriste) 1996, Limpieza de sangre (trans. as Purity of Blood) 1997, El sol de Breda (trans. as The Sun Over Breda) 1998, Patente de corso 1998, La carta esférica (trans. as The Nautical Chart) (Prix Beau Livre, Acad. de Marine Française) 2000, El oro del rey (trans. as The King's Gold) 2000, Con ánimo de ofender 2001, La Reina del Sur (translated as The Queen of the South) 2002, El caballero del jubón amarillo (trans. as The Man in the Yellow Doublet) 2003, Cabo Trafalgar 2004, No me cogeréis vivo 2005, El pintor de batallas (trans. as The Painter of Battles) (Premio Vallombrosa-Gregor von Rezzori 2008) 2006, Corsarios de Levante 2006, Un Día de Cólera 2007, Ojos Azules 2009, Cuando éramos honrados mercenarios 2009, El asedio 2010, El puente de los Asesinos 2011; contrib. to Spanish periodicals, including XL Semanal (weekly article). *Honours:* Chevalier, Ordre des Arts et des Lettres 1998, Gran Cruz del Mérito Naval 2005, Chevalier, Ordre nat. du Mérite 2008; Grand Prix for Detective Literature (France) 1993, Asturias Prize for Journalism for his coverage of the war in the fmr Yugoslavia for TV 1993, Ondas Prize for Radio de España's La Ley de la Calle 1993. *Literary Agent:* c/o RDC Agencia Literaria, Fernando VI 13–15, 3° derecha, 28004 Madrid, Spain. *Telephone:* (91) 3085585; (91) 3912034. *Fax:* (91) 3085600. *E-mail:* rdc@rdclitera.com; RDCprom@rdclitera.com. *Website:* www.perezreverte.com; www.perez-reverte.com.

PERILLO, Lucia, MA; American poet; b. 1958; m. James Rudy. *Education:* McGill Univ., Canada, Syracuse Univ. *Career:* worked as park ranger at Mount Rainier National Park and as naturalist at San Francisco Bay National Wildlife Refuge; taught creative writing at Syracuse Univ., St Martins Coll., Olympia, Wash., Warren Wilson Coll.; apptd Assoc. Prof. of English, Southern Illinois Univ. 1991. *Publications:* poetry collections: Dangerous Life (Poetry Soc. of America Norma Farber Award, Samuel French Morse Poetry Prize) 1989, The Body Mutinies (PEN/Revson Foundation Poetry Prize, Claremont Univ. Kate Tufts Prize) 1996, The Oldest Map With the Name America 1999, Luck is Luck (Claremont Univ. Kingsley Tufts Prize) 2005, Inseminating the Elephant (Bobbitt Nat. Prize for Poetry 2010) 2009; other: I've Heard the Vultures Singing (essays) 2009; contrib. to The New Yorker, Atlantic Monthly, Kenyon Review. *Honours:* MacArthur Fellowship 2000. *Address:* 1910 East 4th Avenue, PMB #29, Olympia, WA 98516-4632, USA (home). *Website:* www.luciaperillo.com.

PERKINS, Emily; New Zealand novelist; b. 1970, Christchurch; m. Karl Maughan; three c. *Education:* New Zealand Drama School, Victoria Univ. *Career:* fmr TV actor. *Publications:* novels: Leave Before You Go 1998, The

Picnic Virgin (ed.) 2000, The New Girl 2001, Novel about my Wife (Montana New Zealand Book Award for Fiction 2009) 2008; short stories: Not her Real Name (Geoffrey Faber Memorial Prize for Fiction) 1996. *Literary Agent:* c/o Georgia Garrett, AP Watt Ltd, 20 John Street, London, WC1N 2DR, England. *Telephone:* (20) 7405-6774. *Fax:* (20) 7831-2154. *E-mail:* apw@apwatt.co.uk. *Website:* www.apwatt.co.uk.

PERKINS, George Burton, AB, MA, PhD; American academic (retd), editor and writer; b. 16 Aug. 1930, Lowell, Mass; m. Barbara Miller 1964; three d. *Education:* Tufts Coll., Duke Univ., Cornell Univ. *Career:* Duke Univ. Fellow 1953–54, Cornell Univ. Fellow 1954–55; Teaching Asst, Cornell Univ. 1955–57; Asst Prof., Washington Univ. 1957–60, Baldwin-Wallace Coll. 1960–63, Farleigh Dickinson Univ. 1963–66; Lecturer in American Literature, Univ. of Edinburgh 1966–67, Fellow, Inst. for Advanced Studies in the Humanities 1981; Prof., Eastern Michigan Univ. 1967–2001; lectures at Peking Univ., Zhengzhou Univ., The Chinese Univ. of Hong Kong, and at various Australian univs; Gen. Ed. Journal of Narrative Technique 1970–92; mem. Soc. for the Study of Narrative Literature, The Authors Guild, Nat. Book Critics Circle. *Publications:* (often with Barbara Perkins): Writing Clear Prose 1964, The Theory of the American Novel 1970, Realistic American Short Fiction 1972, American Poetic Theory 1972, The American Tradition in Literature (with B. Perkins, 12th edn 2009), The Practical Imagination (with Frye and Baker) 1985, Contemporary American Literature (with B. Perkins) 1991, A Season in New Sourh Wales 1996, Harper Collins Reader's Encyclopedia of American Literature (with Perkins and Leininger) 2002, Kaleidoscope (with B. Perkins) 1993, Women's Work (with Perkins and Warhol) 1994, The Harper Handbook to Literature (with Frye, Baker and Perkins) 1997, A Season in New South Wales 1998, Stones Stand, Waters Flow: A New England Story (memoir) 2008, Rare Days in Lost Valley: The Bellwether University Book of Universal Truths 2008, Around the World on the QE2 2010; contribs to professional journals. *Honours:* Distinguished Faculty Award, Eastern Michigan Univ. 1978, Sr Fulbright Scholar, Univ. of Newcastle, Australia 1989. *Address:* 1316 King George Blvd, Ann Arbor, MI 48108, USA (home). *Telephone:* (734) 971-1893 (home). *E-mail:* gperkins@emich.edu (home). *Website:* www.georgeperkins.net.

PERKINS, Michael; American writer and editor; b. 3 Nov. 1942, Lansing, Mich.; m. 1st Renie (Shoemaker) McCune 1968; one s. two d.; 2nd Sondra Howell 2004. *Education:* New School for Social Research, New York, Ohio Univ., Athens, City Coll., CUNY. *Career:* Ed., Tompkins Square Press 1966–68, Croton Press Ltd 1969–72, Ulster Arts Magazine 1978–79; Program Dir, Woodstock Guild 1985–95, Woodstock Library 1985–; Sr Ed., Masquerade Books, New York 1992–98; panellist, Thayer/Ross Prize, State Univ. of NY 1987–; mem. Advisory Bd and contrib., Encyclopedia of Erotic Literature 2007; mem. Authors' Guild, Nat. Book Critics Circle, Poets and Writers. *Publications:* Evil Companions 1968, Down Here 1969, The Secret Record 1977, The Persistence of Desire 1977, The Good Parts 1994, Gift of Choice 1994, Dark Matter 1996, Coming Up (ed.) 1996, Burn 2002, I Could Walk All Day 2002, Praise in the Ears of Clouds 2005, Closer to the Bone 2007, Walking Woodstock 2009; contrib. to reviews and periodicals. *Honours:* Leydig Trust Writer of the Year in the UK 2002, Obelisk Lifetime Achievement Award 2007. *Address:* 750 Ohayo Mountt Road, Glenford, NY 12433, USA. *Telephone:* (845) 657-6439.

PERLIS, Vivian, BMus, MMus; American musicologist, musician and writer; *Director, Oral History of American Music, Yale University Library;* b. (Vivian Goldberger), 26 April 1928, New York, NY. *Education:* University of Michigan, Philadelphia Acad. of Music, Columbia University. *Career:* Reference Librarian, Music Library 1967–72, Senior Research Assoc. and Founder, Oral History, American Music Project, School of Music, Yale University 1972–; Lecturer, University of Southern California at Los Angeles 1974–75; Visiting Senior Research Fellow, Brooklyn College, CUNY 1976–77; Visiting Lecturer, Wesleyan University 1992–93. *Publications:* Charles Ives Remembered: An Oral History 1974, An Ives Celebration: Papers and Panels of the Charles Ives Centennial Festival-Conference (with H. Wiley Hitchcock) 1977, Two Men for Modern Music 1978, The Charles Ives Papers 1983, Copland: 1900 through 1942 (with Aaron Copland) 1984, Copland: Since 1943 (with Aaron Copland) 1989, Composers' Voices from Ives to Ellington (with Libby Van Cleve) 2005; contributions: many publications and television documentaries. *Honours:* Hon. mem. American Musicological Soc. 2008; Charles Ives Award, National Institute of Arts and Letters 1971, Otto Kinkeldey Award, American Musicological Society 1975, ASCAP-Deems Taylor Award 1985, Guggenheim Fellowship 1987, Irving Lowens Award, Sonneck Society 1991, ASCAP Special Recognition Award 2006, Lifetime Achievement Award, Soc. of American Music 2007, Musical America Award for Educator of the Year 2011. *Address:* 139 Goodill Road, Weston, CT 06883, USA (home). *E-mail:* vperlis@optonline.net (home).

PERRETT, Bryan, (R. Eldworth); British author and military historian; b. 9 July 1934, Liverpool, England; m. Anne Catherine Trench 1966. *Education:* Liverpool Coll. *Career:* served in regular and territorial regts, Royal Armoured Corps 1952–71; Defence Corresp. to Liverpool Echo during Falklands War and Gulf War; mem. Rotary Club of Ormskirk. *Television:* scripts for Fighting the Iron Fist (series). *Publications:* The Czar's British Squadron (with A. Lord) 1981, A History of Blitzkrieg 1983, Knights of the Black Cross: Hitler's Panzerwaffe and its Leaders 1986, Desert Warfare 1988, Encyclopaedia of the Second World War (with Ian Hogg) 1989, Canopy of War 1990, Liverpool: A City at War 1990, Last Stand: Famous Battles Against the Odds 1991, The Battle Book: Crucial Conflicts in History from 1469 BC to the Present 1992, At All Costs: Stories of Impossible Victories 1993, Seize and Hold: Master Strokes of the Battlefield 1994, Iron Fist: Crucial Armoured Engagements 1995, Against All Odds! More Dramatic Last Stand Actions 1995, Impossible Victories: Ten Unlikely Battlefield Successes 1996, The Real Hornblower: The Life and Times of Admiral Sir James Gordon, GCB 1998, The Taste of Battle 2000, The Changing Face of Battle 2000, Gunboat! 2000, Last Convoy 2000, Beach Assault 2000, Heroes of the Hour 2001, My Story: Trafalgar 2002, My Story: The Crimea 2002, My Story: Waterloo 2003, For Valour: Victoria Cross and Medal of Honour Battles 2003, My Story: D Day 2004, My Story: U-Boat Hunter 2005; contrib. to War Monthly, Military History, World War Investigator, War in Peace (partwork), The Elite (partwork), Battleground Geography and the History of Warfare, British Military Greats. *Honours:* Territorial decoration. *Address:* 7 Maple Avenue, Burscough, Ormskirk, Lancs., L40 5SL, England. *Telephone:* (1704) 892598. *E-mail:* bbperrett@aol.com.

PERRIAM, Wendy Angela, BA, MA; British writer, poet and novelist; *Creative Writing Tutor, Morley College;* b. 23 Feb. 1940, London; d. of Edward Brech and Irene Thompson; m. 1st 1964; one d.; m. 2nd John Alan Perriam 1974. *Education:* St Anne's Coll., Oxford, Univ. of Oxford, London School of Econs. *Career:* advertising copywriter 1962–73; Creative Writing Tutor, Morley Coll., Lambeth 2003–; mem. British Actors Equity Asscn, PEN, Soc. of Authors. *Publications:* Absinthe for Elevenses 1980, Cuckoo 1981, After Purple 1982, Born of Woman 1983, The Stillness The Dancing 1985, Sin City 1987, Devils, for a Change 1989, Fifty-Minute Hour 1990, Bird Inside 1992, Michael, Michael 1993, Breaking and Entering 1994, Coupling 1996, Second Skin 1998, Lying 2000, Dreams, Demons and Desire 2001, Tread Softly 2002, Virgin in the Gym and Other Stories 2004, Laughter Class and Other Stories 2006, The Biggest Female in the World and Other Stories 2007, Little Marvel and Other Stories 2008, The Queen's Margarine and Other Stories 2009, Broken Places 2010, "I'm on the Train!" and Other Stories 2012; contribs to anthologies, newspapers and magazines. *Literary Agent:* Curtis Brown Ltd, Haymarket House, 28–29 Haymarket, London, SW1Y 4SP, England. *Telephone:* (20) 7393-4400. *Fax:* (20) 7393-4401. *E-mail:* info@curtisbrown.co.uk. *Website:* www.curtisbrown.co.uk; www.wendyperriam.com.

PERRICK, Penny; British novelist, critic and biographer; b. 30 June 1941, London; m. Clive Labovitch 1962 (divorced 1973); one s. one d. *Education:* S Hampstead High School, London, Alliance Française, Paris. *Career:* feature writer, Vogue magazine 1959–62; columnist, The Sun 1974–79, The Times 1983–89; Fiction Ed., The Sunday Times 1989–95; mem. Society of Authors, RSL, English PEN. *Publications:* Malina 1993, Impossible Things 1995, Evermore 1997, Something to Hide 2007; contrib. to Times, Sunday Times, Country Homes and Interiors, You Magazine, The Irish Times, The Irish Tatler, Gardens Illustrated. *Address:* Parnells, The Quay, Roundstone, Connemara, Co. Galway, Ireland (home).

PERRIE, Walter, MA, MPhil; British poet, author and critic; b. 5 June 1949, Lanarkshire, Scotland; s. of James Perrie and Jean Gray Perrie. *Education:* Univs of Edinburgh and Stirling. *Career:* Ed. Chapman 1970–75; Scottish-Canadian Exchange Fellow, Univ. of British Columbia, Canada 1984–85; Man. Ed. Margin: International Arts Quarterly, 1985–90; Ed. FRAS Publications 2004–, Co-Ed. FRAS: A Scottish Literary Magazine 2004; part-time Lecturer in Philosophy and Creative Writing Perth Coll. 2000–; Stirling Writing Fellow, Univ. of Stirling 1991. *Publications:* Metaphysics and Poetry (with Hugh MacDiarmid) 1974, Poem on a Winter Night 1976, A Lamentation for the Children 1977, By Moon and Sun 1980, Out of Conflict 1982, Concerning the Dragon 1984, Roads that Move: A Journey Through Eastern Europe 1991, Thirteen Lucky Poems 1991, From Milady's Wood and Other Poems 1997, The Light in Strathearn (poems) 2000, Caravanserai: Poems 2004, Decagon: Selected Poems 1995–2005 2005, Rhapsody of the Red Cliff (poems) 2006, As Far As Thales – Beginning Philosophy 2006, The King of France is Bald: Philosophy and Meaning 2007, Twelve Fables of Jean de la Fontaine (trans. into Scots) 2007, Lyrics and Tales in Twa Tongues 2011; contribs to journals and periodicals. *Honours:* Scottish Arts Council Bursaries 1976, 1983, 1994, 1999, and Book Awards 1976, 1983, Eric Gregory Award 1978, Ingram Merrill Foundation Award 1987, Soc. of Authors Travelling Scholarship 2000. *Address:* 10 Croft Place, Dunning, Perthshire, PH2 0SB, Scotland (home).

PERROTTA, Tom, BA, MA; American writer; b. 13 Aug. 1961, Garwood, NJ; m. Mary Granfield 1991; two c. *Education:* Yale and Syracuse Univs. *Career:* fmr creative writing tutor, Yale Univ. *Film:* Little Children (co-writer) 2006. *Publications:* Bad Haircut: Stories of the Seventies (short stories) 1994, The Wishbones 1997, Election 1998, Joe College 2000, Little Children 2004, The Abstinence Teacher 2007, The Leftovers 2011; contrib. to GQ, Rolling Stone. *Literary Agent:* Maria Massie, Lippincott, Massie, McQuilkin, 80 Fifth Avenue, Suite 1101, New York, NY 10011, USA. *Telephone:* (212) 352-2055. *E-mail:* maria@lmqlit.com. *Website:* www.lmqlit.com. *E-mail:* tom@tomperrotta.net (office). *Website:* www.tomperrotta.net.

PERRY, John Curtis, BA, MA, PhD; American academic and writer; b. 18 July 1930, Orange, NJ; m. Sarah Hollis French 1957, five c. *Education:* Yale University, Harvard University. *Career:* Instructor, 1962–64, Asst Prof. of History, 1964–66, Connecticut College; Asst Prof., 1966–68, Assoc. Prof., 1968–74, Prof. of History, 1974–80, Acting Dir, College Library, 1975–76, Carleton College; Visiting Research Assoc., Fairbank Center, 1976–79, Japan

Institute, 1979–80, Assoc. in Research, 1980–, Harvard University; Henry Willard Denison Prof. of History, 1981–, Organizer-Dir, Fletcher North Pacific Seminars, 1985–97, Fletcher School of Law and Diplomacy, Tufts University; mem. American Historical Asscn; Asscn for Asian Studies; Japan Society. *Publications:* Beneath the Eagle's Wings: Americans in Occupied Japan, 1980; Sentimental Imperialists: The American East Asian Experience (with James C. Thomson Jr and Peter W. Stanley), 1981; Facing West: Americans and the Opening of the Pacific, 1994; The Flight of the Romanovs: A Family Saga (with Constantine Pleshakov), 1999. Contributions: scholarly books, journals, newspapers, radio and television. *Honours:* Research Grants, NIRA, 1986–87, Nippon Foundation, 1998–2001, Japan Economic Foundation, 2000–; Order of the Sacred Treasure, Japan, 1991.

PERRY, Ritchie, (John Allen), BA; British teacher and author; b. 7 Jan. 1942, King's Lynn, Norfolk, England. *Education:* St John's College, Oxford. *Publications:* The Fall Guy, 1972; Nowhere Man, US edn as A Hard Man to Kill, 1973; Ticket to Ride, 1973; Holiday with a Vengeance, 1974; Your Money and Your Wife, 1975; One Good Death Deserves Another, 1976; Dead End, 1977; Brazil: The Land and Its People, 1977; Copacabana Stud (as John Allen), 1977; Dutch Courage, 1978; Bishop's Pawn, 1979; Up Tight (as John Allen), 1979; Grand Slam, 1980; Fool's Mate, 1981; Foul Up, 1982; MacAllister, 1984; Kolwezi, 1985; Presumed Dead, 1988; Comeback, 1991. Children's Books: George H. Ghastly, 1982; George H. Ghastly to the Rescue, 1982; George H. Ghastly and the Little Horror, 1985; Fenella Fang, 1986; Fenella Fang and the Great Escape, 1987; Fenella Fang and the Wicked Witch, 1989; The Creepy Tale, 1989; Fenalla Fang and the Time Machine, 1991; The Runton Werewolf, 1994.

PERUTZ, Kathrin, BA, MA; American author; b. 1 July 1939, New York, NY. *Education:* Barnard College, New York University. *Career:* Exec. Dir, Contact Program Inc.; mem. PEN, Authors' Guild. *Publications:* The Garden, 1962; A House on the Sound, 1964; The Ghosts, 1966; Mother is a Country: A Popular Fantasy, 1968; Beyond the Looking Glass: America's Beauty Culture, 1970; Marriage is Hell: The Marriage Fallacy, 1972; Reigning Passions, 1978; Writing for Love and Money, 1991. Also as Johanna Kingsley: Scents, 1985; Faces, 1987.

PESETSKY, Bette, BA, MFA; American writer and academic; *Writer-in-Residence, New College of Florida, Florida State University, Sarasota*; b. 16 Nov. 1932, Milwaukee, Wis.; m. Irwin Pesetsky 1956; one s. *Education:* Washington Univ., Univ. of Iowa. *Career:* Visiting Prof., Writers Workshop, Univ. of Iowa 1990–91, Dept of English and Comparative Studies, Univ. of California, Irvine 1992–93, Dept of English, St Lawrence Univ., Canton, NY; Distinguished Visiting Writer, Wichita (Kan.) State Univ. 1994; Distinguished Visiting Prof., English Dept, Univ. of Miami 1997; Priaker Visiting Prof., Dept of English, Gen. Literature and Rhetoric, State Univ. of NY, Binghamton 2002; Writer-in-Residence, New Coll. of Florida, Florida State Univ., Sarasota 2004–. *Publications include:* Stories Up to a Point (New York Times Notable Books 1982) 1982, Author from a Savage People (New York Times Notable Books) 1983, Digs 1985, Midnight Sweets (New York Times Notable Books) 1988, Confessions of a Bad Girl (New York Times Notable Books) 1989, Late Night Muse (New York Times Notable Books) 1991, Cast a Spell (New York Times Notable Books) 1993; contribs to New Yorker, Vanity Fair, Ms, Vogue, Paris Review, Ontario Review, Stand. *Honours:* Creative Writing Fellowship, Nat. Endowment for the Arts 1979–80, Creative Writing Public Service Award, New York Council for the Arts 1980–81. *Address:* Hilltop Park, Dobbs Ferry, NY 10522-1410, USA.

PESSL, Marisha; American novelist; b. 1977; m. *Education:* Northwestern Univ., Chicago and Columbia Univ., New York. *Publications:* Special Topics in Calamity Physics (novel) (one of New York Times Ed.'s Choice five best works of fiction) 2006. *Address:* c/o Penguin Publicity, 80 Strand, London, WC2R 0RL, England (office). *Website:* www.marishapessl.com.

PETERFREUND, Stuart Samuel, BA, MFA, PhD; American academic and poet; *Professor of English, Northeastern University*; b. 30 June 1945, New York, NY; m. 1st Carol Jean Litzler 1981 (divorced 1997); one d.; m. 2nd Christina Sieber 2001. *Education:* Cornell Univ., Univ. of California at Irvine, Columbia Univ., Univ. of Washington. *Career:* Lecturer, Univ. of Puget Sound 1975; Asst Prof., Univ. of Arkansas at Little Rock 1975–78; Asst Prof., Dept of English, Northeastern Univ. 1978–82, Assoc. Prof. 1982–91, Prof. of English and Chair. 1991–99, Prof. of English 1999–, Assoc. Dean for Curriculum and Faculty Affairs, Div. of Adult and Continuing Educ. 2005–11, Acting Chair. Dept of Communications Studies 2011–; mem. American Soc. for Eighteenth-Century Studies, British Soc. for History of Science, Byron Soc., History of Science Soc., Interdisciplinary Nineteenth-Century Studies, Int. Asscn for Philosophy and Literature, Keats-Shelley Asscn of America, Modern Language Asscn, Poets and Writers, Soc. for Literature and Science (Pres. 1995–97), Wordsworth-Coleridge Asscn. *Publications:* poetry: The Hanged Knife and Other Poems 1970, Harder than Rain 1977, Interstatements 1986; other: William Blake in the Age of Newton: Essays on Literature as Art and Science 1998, Shelley Among Others: The Play of the Intertext and the Idea of Language 2002; ed.: Critical Theory and the Teaching of Literature 1985, Culture/Criticism/Ideology 1986, Literature and Science: Theory and Practice 1990; contribs to scholarly books, professional journals, poetry anthologies and reviews. *Honours:* grants; fellowships; First Prize in Poetry, Writers' Digest Competition, 1970; Poet-in-Residence, Southern Literary Festival, 1977; First Prize, Worcester County Poetry Asscn Contest, 1989; Third Prize, Abiko Journal Poetry Contest, 1994; Third Prize, Anna Davidson Rosenberg Award for Poems on the Jewish Experience, 1996. *Address:* Department of English, Northeastern University, 405 Lake Hall, 360 Huntington Avenue, Boston, MA 02115, USA (office). *Telephone:* (617) 373-7013 (office); (617) 864-0053 (home). *Fax:* (617) 373-2509 (office). *E-mail:* s.peterfreund@neu.edu (office). *Website:* www.northeastern.edu/english/people/faculty-members/stuart-s-peterfreund (office).

PETERS, Andrew Fusek; British/Czech children's author; b. (Andrew Frederick Peters), 2 July 1965, Hildesheim, Germany; m. Polly Peters; two c. *Education:* Corpus Christi Coll., Oxford. *Career:* grew up in London; twenty years working as performer in schools and media; author and editor of more than 75 books for children. *Plays:* with Polly Peters: Twisted, Much Ado About Clubbing, Angelcake, Dragon Chaser, Kick Off, Flipside, Crash, Impact. *Radio:* Poetry Please, Talking Poetry. *Television:* Heart of the Country (ITV), Wham Bam Strawberry Jam (BBC), Poetry Pie (BBC). *Publications include:* When I Come to the Dark Country 1997, The Moon is on the Microphone 1997, The Barefoot Book of Strange and Spooky Stories 1997, May the Angels be With Us: Poems of Life, Love, AIDS and Death 1999, Sheep Don't go to School 1999, Sadderday and Funday (with Polly Peters) 2001, Plays with Attitude (collection of plays, with Polly Peters) 2002, Poems with Attitude: Uncensored 2002, Ed and the Witchblood 2003, Dragon and Mousie 2003, Hubble Bubble 2003, Monkey's Clever Tale 2003, The Tiger and the Wise Man 2004, Crash (juvenile novel; with Polly Peters) 2004, The Dog Ate my Bus Pass 2004, Ed and the River of the Damned 2005, Turtle and Bear and the Great Lake Race 2005, The Ding-Dong Bag 2006, Spies Unlimited, Ghosts Unlimited 2006, Roar! Bull! Roar! 2006, Mad, Bad and Dangerously Haddock 2006, Here's a Little Poem (ALA Notable Award) 2006, Animals Aboard 2007, Story Thief 2007, Dragon and Mousie and the Snow Factory 2007, The Ant and the Big Bad Bully Goat 2007, It's Raining, It's Pouring, We're Exploring 2007, Skateboard Detectives 2008, Priceless and Diamonds are for Evil 2008, Poems with Attitude+Uncensored (with Polly Peters) 2008, Falcons Fury 2008, The No-No Bird 2008, Dingo Dog and the Invisible Storm 2009, Mae In The Middle 2010, Ravenwood (fantasy novel) 2011; editor: Sheep Don't Go To School 1999, The Upside Down Frown 1999, The Unidentified Frying Omelette 2000, Out of Order 2002, The Dog Ate My Bus Pass (co-ed.) 2004, Love, Hate and My Best Mate (co-ed.) 2004, Poems About Earth 2006, Poems About Air, Poems About Fire, Poems About Water, The Chinese Dragon and other festival poems 2009, Poems About Seasons 2010, Switching On The Moon 2010 (co-ed.). *Honours:* Claudia Lewis Poetry Award. *Literary Agent:* c/o Uli Rushby-Smith Literary Agency, 72 Plimsoll Road, London N4 2EE, England. *Telephone:* (20) 7354-2718. *E-mail:* uli.rushby-smith@btconnect.com. *Address:* The Old Chapel, Lydbury North, Shropshire, SY7 8AU, England (home). *E-mail:* verytallpoet@aol.com (office). *Website:* www.tallpoet.com (office).

PETERS, Catherine Lisette, MA; British academic and writer; b. 30 Sept. 1930, London, England; m. 1st John Glyn Barton 1952, four s. (one deceased); m. 2nd Anthony Storr 1970. *Education:* Univ. of Oxford. *Career:* Ed., Jonathan Cape 1960–74; Lecturer in English, Somerville College, Oxford 1981–92; mem. Wilkie Collins Society, Society of Authors, FRSL, International PEN. *Publications:* Thackeray's Universe 1987, The King of Inventors: A Life of Wilkie Collins 1991, Charles Dickens 1998, Byron 2000; contributions: books and journals. *Literary Agent:* PFD, Drury House, 34–43 Russell Street, London, WC2B 5HA, England. *Address:* 4 Murray Court, 80 Banbury Road, Oxford, OX2 6LQ, England (home). *E-mail:* catherine.peters@ell.ox.ac.uk (home).

PETERS, Elizabeth (see Mertz, Barbara Louise Gross)

PETERS, Janis; Latvian writer, poet, essayist, publicist and fmr diplomatist; b. 30 June 1939, Liepāja Region; s. of Janis Peters and Zelma Peters; m. Baiba Kalniņa 1969; one s. *Education:* Rīga 25 secondary school. *Career:* started as journalist in Latvian newspapers, later freelance; Chair. Bd of Latvian Writers' Union 1985–89; led historic Latvian Writers' Union conf. against censorship and for freedom of speech 1st and 2nd June 1988; participant democratic movt for independence; Chair. Org. Cttee People's Front of Latvia 1988; signed petition to Pres. of Communist Czechoslovakia to free dissident Vaczlav Havel in Copenhagen (with Danish PEN Club members) 1990; USSR People's Deputy 1989–90; Perm. Rep. of Council of Ministers of Latvia to Russia 1990–91, then first Amb. of Repub. of Latvia to Russian Fed. after regaining independence 1992–97; mem. govt del. to negotiations with Russia. *Publications:* more than 20 books of poetry, prose and essays in Latvian, Russian, English, Ukrainian; poems translated also into Lithuanian, Estonian, Finnish, Georgian, Spanish, Bulgarian, German, Danish, etc. *Honours:* Hon. mem. Latvian Acad. of Sciences 1990–, Latvian Univ. 1991–; Cavaliere di San Marco 1993. *Address:* Vesetas Str. 8, Apt 12, 1013 Rīga, Latvia (home). *Telephone:* 6733-9350 (home). *E-mail:* peters@apollo.lv (office).

PETERS, Lance; Australian author, dramatist and screenwriter; b. 8 May 1934, Auckland, New Zealand; m. Laura Chiang 1981, two s. two d. *Career:* hon. life mem. Australian Writers' Guild (pres. 1970–72); mem. Australian Soc. of Authors, Writers' Guild of Great Britain, BAFTA. *Publications:* Carry On Emmannuelle, 1978; The Dirty Half Mile, 1981; Cut-Throat Alley, 1982; Enemy Territory, 1988; God's Executioner, 1988; The Civilian War Zone, 1989; The Red Collar Gang, 1989; The Dirty Half Mile (Again), 1989; Gross Misconduct, 1993; Savior in the Grave, 1994. Other: Assault with a Deadly

Weapon (play); 5 screenplays; many television comedies, documentaries. Contributions: numerous popular magazines.

PETERS, Margot McCullough, BA, MA, PhD; American academic and writer; *Professor Emerita, University of Wisconsin at Whitewater*; b. 13 May 1933, Wausau, Wisconsin; m. Peter Ridgway Jordan 1981; one s. one d. *Education:* Univ. of Wisconsin at Madison. *Career:* Asst Prof. of English Northland Coll., Ashland, Wisconsin 1963–66; Asst Prof. 1969–74, Assoc. Prof. 1974–77, Prof. of English 1977–91, Prof. Emerita 1991–, Univ. of Wisconsin at Whitewater; Kathe Tappe Vernon Prof. of Biography, Dartmouth Coll. 1978; mem. Brontë Soc., Mark Twain Soc., Bernard Shaw Soc., Wisconsin Center for the Book, Int. Shaw Soc. *Publications:* Charlotte Brontë: Style in the Novel 1973, Unquiet Soul: A Biography of Charlotte Brontë 1975, Bernard Shaw and the Actresses 1980, Mrs Pat: The Life of Mrs Patrick Campbell 1984, The House of Barrymore 1990, Wild Justice (as Margret Pierce) 1995, May Sarton: A Biography 1997, Design for Living: Alfred Lunt and Lynn Fontanne 2003; contributions to professional journals, newspapers, reviews and periodicals. *Honours:* Friends of American Writers Award for Best Prose Work 1975, ACLS Fellow 1976–77, George R. Freedley Memorial Awards 1980, 1984, Banta Awards 1981, 1985, Guggenheim Fellowship 1988–89, Wisconsin Institute for Research in the Humanities Grant 1988–89, English-Speaking Union Ambassador Award 1991, Wisconsin Library Asscn Distinguished Achievement Awards 1991, 1998 Outstanding Achievement Award 2004, Triangle Book Publishers Judy Gran Award 1998. *Address:* 511 College Street, Lake Mills, WI 53551, USA (home). *E-mail:* margo.peters@charter.net (home).

PETERS, Michael Adrian, BA, DipEd, MA, PhD, FRSA, FRSNZ; New Zealand academic and writer; *Professor of Policy, Cultural and Social Studies in Education, University of Waikato*; b. 4 Sept. 1948, Wellington; s. of Warren Manual Peters and Joan Elizabeth Collinson; m. Christine Athlone Besley 1996; two s. *Education:* Victoria Univ. of Wellington, Christchurch Coll. of Educ., Univ. of Canterbury, Univ. of Auckland. *Career:* secondary teacher, Linwood High School 1973–78; Head of Geography, Longbay High School 1979–80; pvt. consultant 1981–89; Lecturer in Educ., Univ. of Canterbury 1990–92; Sr Lecturer, Univ. of Auckland 1993–95, Assoc. Prof. 1996–2000, Prof. 2000–05; Research Prof., Univ. of Glasgow, UK 2000–05; Adjunct Prof. of Communication Studies, Auckland Univ. of Tech. 2001–05; Research Prof., Univ. of Illinois at Urbana-Champaign, USA 2005–11, Prof. Emer. 2011–, Dir of Global Studies in Educ., Sr Scholar 2008, Distinguished Sr Scholar 2011–; Prof. of Policy, Cultural and Social Studies in Educ., Univ. of Waikato 2011–; Adjunct Prof., Guangzhou Univ., People's Repub. of China, School of Art, School of Art, Royal Melbourne Inst. of Tech.; Ed. Education, Philosophy & Theory, policy futures in educ., e-learning online journals; mem. Humanities Soc. of NZ (Council 1997–98), RSA; Fellow, Philosophy of Educ. Soc. of Australasia Inc., NZ Acad. of the Humanities. *Publications:* Education and the Postmodern Condition 1995, Poststructuralism, Politics and Education 1996, Critical Theory, Poststructuralism and the Social Context 1996, Cultural Politics and the University 1997, Virtual Technologies and Tertiary Education 1998, Naming the Multiple: Poststructuralism and Education 1998, Wittgenstein: Philosophy, Postmodernism, Pedagogy (with James Marshall) 1999, Individualism and Community: Education and Social Policy in the Postmodern Condition (with James Marshall) 1999, University Futures and the Politics of Reform (with Peter Roberts) 1999, Nietzsche's Legacy for Education: Past and Present Values (with James Marshall and Paul Smeyers) 2001, Postructuralism, Marxism and Neoliberalism: Between Politics and Theory 2001, Richard Rorty: Education, Philosophy and Politics (with Paulo Ghiraldelli), Heidegger, Education and Modernity 2002, Critical Theory and the Human Condition: Founders and Praxis (with Colin Lankshear and Mark Olssen) 2003, Derrida, Deconstruction and Education: Ethics of Pedagogy and Research (with Peter Trifonas) 2004, Deconstructing Derrida, Tasks for the New Humanities (with Peter Trifonas) 2005, Education, Globalisation and the State in the Age of Terrorism 2006, Building Knowledge Cultures (with Tina Besley) 2006, Edutopias: New Utopian Thinking in Education (with John Freeman-Moir) 2006, Postfoundationalist Themes in Philosophy of Education (with Paul Smeyers) 2006, Why Foucault? New Directions in Educational Research (with Tina Besley) 2007, Subjectivity and Truth: Foucault, Education and the Culture of Self (with Tina Besley) 2007, Global Knowledge Cultures (with Cushla Kapitzke), Knowledge Economy, Development and the Future of Higher Education 2007, Derrida, Politics and Pedagogy (with Gert Biesta) 2008, Environmental Education Today (with Edgar Gonzalez-Gaudiano) 2008, Military Pedagogies and Why They Matter (with T. Kvernbekk and Harold Simpson) 2008; Global Citizenship Education (with Harry Blee & Alan Britton) 2008, Saying and Doing: Wittgenstein as a Pedagogical Philosopher (with N. Burbules & P. Smeyers) 2008, Governmentality Studies in Education (with T. Belsey, M. Olssen, S. Maurer, S. Weber) 2009, Creativity and the Global Knowledge Economy (with S. Marginson, P. Murphy) 2009, Derrida, Politics and Pedagogy: Deconstructing the Humanities (with G. Biesta) 2009, Academic Writing, Genres and Philosophy 2009, Imagination: Three Models of Imagination in the Age of the Knowledge Economy (with P. Murphy and S. Marginson) 2010, Global Creation: Space, Connection and Synchrony in the Age of the Knowledge Economy (with P. Murphy, S. Marginson) 2010, Re-Reading Education Policies: Studying the Policy Agenda of the 21st Century (with M. Simons, M. Olssen) 2010, Education in the Creative Economy (with D. Araya) 2010, The Last Book of Postmodernism: Apocalyptic Thinking, Philosophy and Education in the Twenty-First Century 2011, Neoliberalism and After? – Education, Social Policy and the Crisis of Capitalism 2011, Leo Strauss, Political Philosophy and Education (with J. York) 2011, The Virtues of Openness (with P. Roberts) 2011, Subjects in Process (with A. de Alba) 2011, Bakhtin and Educational Thought (with J. White) 2011; contribs to journals. *Honours:* Hon. mem. Royal Soc. of NZ 2009; Hon. DLitt (State Univ. of NY) 2012; Postgraduate Scholarship, Univ. of Auckland 1981, Macmillan Brown Lecturer, Univ. of Canterbury 2000, Lifetime Achievement Award, Soc. for Research into Higher Educ. 2010, AESA Critics Book Award 2004, 2009, 2010. *Address:* Faculty of Education, PO Box 3105, University of Waikato, Hamilton 3240, New Zealand (office). *Telephone:* (7) 838-4466 (ext. 7841) (office). *E-mail:* mpeters@waikato.ac.nz (office). *Website:* education.waikato.ac.nz/about/faculty-staff/?user=mpeters (office); www.michaeladrianpeters.com.

PETERS, Robert Louis, BA, MA, PhD; American academic, poet and writer; b. 20 Oct. 1924, Eagle River, Wis.; m. (divorced); three s. one d. *Education:* University of Wisconsin at Madison. *Career:* Instructor, University of Idaho, 1952–53, Boston University, 1953–55; Asst Prof., Ohio Wesleyan University, 1955–58; Assoc. Prof., Wayne State University, 1958–63; Prof. of English, University of California, Riverside, 1963–68, University of California, Irvine, 1968–94; mem. American Society for Aesthetics, PEN, Writer's Guild. *Publications:* The Drowned Man to the Fish, 1978; Picnic in the Snow: Ludwig of Bavaria, 1982; What Dillinger Meant to Me, 1983; Hawker, 1984; Kane, 1985; Ludwig of Bavaria: Poems and a Play, 1986; The Blood Countess: Poems and a Play, 1987; Haydon, 1988; Brueghel's Pigs, 1989; Poems: Selected and New, 1992; Goodnight Paul: Poems, 1992; Snapshots for a Serial Killer: A Fiction and Play, 1992; Zapped: 3 Novellas, 1993; Nell: A Woman from Eagle River, 1994; Lili Marlene: A Memoir of World War II, 1995; Familial Love: Poems, 2001. Other: Victorians in Literature and Art, 1961; The Crowns of Apollo: Swinburne's Principles of Literature and Art, 1965; The Letters of John Addington Symonds (co-ed., 3 vols) 1967–69; Letter to a Tutor: The Tennyson Family Letters to Henry Graham Dakyns (ed.), 1988; contributions: professional journals. *Honours:* Guggenheim Fellowship, 1966–67; Yaddo, MacDowell Colony, and Ossabaw Island Project Fellowships, 1973–74; National Endowment for the Arts Grant, 1974.

PETERSEN, Peter James, AB, MA, PhD; American writer and teacher; b. 23 Oct. 1941, Santa Rosa, CA; m. Marian Braun 1964; two d. *Education:* Stanford Univ., San Francisco State Univ., Univ. of New Mexico. *Career:* English Instructor, Shasta Coll.; mem. Soc. of Children's Bookwriters and Illustrators. *Publications:* Would You Settle for Improbable 1981, Nobody Else Can Walk It for You 1982, Going for the Big One 1986, Good-bye to Good Ol'Charlie 1987, The Freshman Detective Blues 1987, I Hate Camping 1991, Liars 1992, The Sub 1993, I Hate Company 1994, White Water 1997, Can You Keep A Secret 1997, My Worst Friend 1998, I Hate Weddings 2000, Rising Water 2002, rob&sara.com 2004, Wild River 2009. *Honours:* Nat. Endowment for the Humanities Fellowship 1976–77, William Allen White Award, Children's Crown Award. *Address:* 1243 Pueblo Court, Redding, CA 96001, USA (home). *E-mail:* pjpetersen@charter.net (home).

PETERSON, Robert, BA, MA; American writer and poet; b. 2 June 1924, Denver, Colo; one d. *Education:* Univ. of California, Berkeley, San Francisco State Coll. *Career:* Writer-in-Residence, Reed Coll., Portland, Oregon 1969–71; mem. Marin Poetry Soc. *Publications include:* Home for the Night 1962, The Binnacle 1967, Wondering Where You Are 1969, Lone Rider 1976, Under Sealed Orders 1976, Leaving Taos 1981, The Only Piano Player in La Paz 1985, Waiting for Garbo: 44 Ghazals 1987, All The Time in the World 1996. *Honours:* Nat. Endowment for the Arts grant 1967, Amy Lowell Travelling Fellowship 1972–73.

PETKOVA, Wania, (Katidja Sadik), DLit; Bulgarian poet and journalist; b. 10 July 1954, Sofia; m.; one d. one s. *Education:* Cuba, Bulgaria and Inst. Gamal Abdel Nasser, Dar es Salaam. *Career:* fmr diplomat, postings included Sudan; journalist Trud (newspaper); interpreter and poet. *Publications include:* Salt Winds, Sinner, The Black Dove, Bullets in the Sand; 32 books of poetry, short stories and essays published. *Honours:* numerous Bulgarian and int. awards for poetry including two Pres. Awards, Bulgaria 2005, Union of Bulgarian Writers Award 2005. *Address:* Complex Hippodroma, Block 134, entry 5, Sofia (office); Complex 'Goze Delchev', Block 109, Entry 1, 2nd Floor, 1404 Sofia, Bulgaria (home). *Telephone:* (2) 859-37-82 (home). *Fax:* (2) 859-63-54 (home).

PETRAKIS, Harry Mark; American writer; b. 5 June 1923, St Louis, MO,; m. Diane Perparos 1945; three s. *Education:* University of Illinois. *Career:* teacher, writing workshops; McGuffey Visiting Lecturer, Ohio University, 1971; Writer-in-Residence, Chicago Public Library, 1976–77, Chicago Board of Education, 1978–79; Kazantzakis Prof., San Francisco State University, 1992; mem. Authors' Guild; PEN; Writers Guild of America, West. *Publications:* Lion at My Heart, 1959; The Odyssey of Kostas Volakis, 1963; Pericles on 31st Street, 1965; The Founder's Touch, 1965; A Dream of Kings, 1966; The Waves of Night, 1969; Stelmark: A Family Recollection, 1970; In the Land of Morning, 1973; The Hour of the Bell, 1976; A Petrakis Reader: 28 Stories, 1978; Nick the Greek, 1979; Days of Vengeance, 1983; Reflections on a Writer's Life and Work, 1983; Collected Stories, 1986; Ghost of the Sun, 1990; Tales of the Heart, 1999; Twilight of the Ice, 2002. Contributions: various magazines. *Honours:* Carl Sandburg Award; Ellis Island Medal of Honour, 1995. *Address:* 80 East Road, Dune Acres, Chesterton, IN 46304, USA.

PETREU, Marta; Romanian editor, essayist and poet; *Professor of Philosophy, Babes-Bolyai University of Cluj*; b. (Rodica Marta Vartic), 1955. *Education:* Univ. Babes-Bolyai, Cluj, Univ. of Bucharest. *Career:* teacher of philosophy Emil Racovita school, Cluj 1980–90; Ed. Steaua magazine 1990; Ed. Apostrof magazine 1990–; Lecturer in Philosophy Babes-Bolyai Univ. of Cluj 1992–2001, Prof. of Philosophy 2001–; residency Ledig House Int. Writers' Colony Ghent, New York 1998; mem. Echinox literary group, Writers' Union of Romania, Apostrof Cultural Foundation (f. mem.). *Publications:* Aduceti verbele (poems) (Premiul Uniunii Scriitorilor) 1981, Dimineata tinerelor doamne (poems) 1983, Loc psihic (poems) 1991, Teze neterminate (essays) 1991, Poeme nerusinate (poems) 1993, Jocurile manierismului logic (essay) 1995, Cartea miniei (poems) 1997, Apocalipsa dupa Marta (poems) 1999, Un trecut deocheat sau Schimbarea la fata a Romaniei 1999, Ionescu in tara tatalui (Centrul Cultural Francez Premiul Henri Jacquier) 2001, Falanga (poems) 2001, Filosofia lui Caragiale 2003; editor of numerous vols; contrib. poems to anthologies and journals, including Sulfur, Partisan Review, Compost, Mississippi Review, The Bitter Oleander, Salt Hill, The Alembic, The Literary Review, Transylvanian Voices, Massachusetts Review, Beacons, Paper Street, and essays and articles to journals and other publs. *Honours:* Poesis magazine prize 1993, Premiul Salonului de Carte Oradea 1993, Contemporanul magazine Premiul George Bacovia 1993, Premiul Uniunii Scriitorilor 1997, Premiul Nichita Stanescu 1998, Premiul Salonului Nat. de Carte, Cluj 1998, Kenneth Rexroth Memorial Trans. Prize 1999, Human Rights Watch Hellman/Hammett grant 2001. *Address:* Catedra de Istorie si Filosofie, Universitatea Babeş-Bolyai, Str. M. Kogălniceanu 1, etaj I, sala 131, 3400 Cluj-Napoca, Romania (office). *E-mail:* fam@hiphi.ubbcluj.ro (office). *Website:* hiphi.ubbcluj.ro/fam/membri/mpetreu (office).

PETRIE, Paul James, BA, MA, PhD; American academic (retd) and poet; b. 1 July 1928, Detroit, Mich.; m. Sylvia Spencer 1954; one s. two d. *Education:* Wayne State Univ., Univ. of Iowa. *Career:* Assoc. Prof., Peru State University, Neb. 1958–59; Instructor to Prof. of English, University of Rhode Island 1959–90. *Publications:* Confessions of a Non-Conformist, 1963; The Race With Time and the Devil, 1965; From Under the Hill of Night, 1969; The Academy of Goodbye, 1974; Light From the Furnace Rising, 1978; Not Seeing is Believing, 1983; Strange Gravity, 1985; The Runners, 1988, Rooms of Grace: New and Selected Poems 2005; contrib. to newspapers, reviews, quarterlies, journals, and magazines. *Honours:* Scholarly Achievement Award, University of Rhode Island, 1983; Catholic Press Award, 1985; Arts Achievement Award, Wayne State University, 1990. *Address:* 200 Dendron Road, Peace Dale, RI 02879, USA (home). *Telephone:* (401) 783-8644 (home).

PETROBELLI, Pierluigi, BLitt, MFA; Italian musicologist, academic and writer; b. 18 Oct. 1932, Padua; s. of Giuseppe Petrobelli and Carolina Talpo. *Education:* Univ. of Rome, Princeton Univ., Harvard Univ. Summer School, Univ. of California, Berkeley, USA. *Career:* Ed. Rivista Italiana di Musicologia 1968–71, Studi verdiani 1981–; teaching asst, Univ. of Parma 1968–70, Assoc. Prof. of Music History 1970–72; librarian and teacher of music history, Rossini Conservatory, Pesaro 1970–73; Lecturer in Music, King's Coll., London, UK 1973–77; Reader in Musicology, Univ. of London 1978–80; Dir Istituto di Studi Verdiani, Parma 1980–89, Istituto Nazionale di Studi Verdiani, Parma 1989–; Prof. of Music History, Univ. of Perugia 1981–83, Univ. of Rome 'La Sapienza' 1983–2005; Chair of Italian Culture, Univ. of California at Berkeley 1988; Lauro de Bosis Lecturer in the History of Italian Civilization, Harvard Univ. 1996; Visitante distinguido, Univ. of Cordoba, Argentina 1996; mem. External Advisory Bd, Faculty of Music, Univ. of Oxford, UK, Advisory Bd, Forschungsinstitut für Musiktheater, Univ. of Bayreuth, Thurnau, Germany 1989–2008; mem. Akad. für Mozartforschung, Salzburg 1989; Corresp. mem. Accad. Naz. dei Lincei (Nat. mem. 2007), American Musicological Soc. 1989, Academia Europaea 1990; Foreign Hon. mem. Royal Musical Asscn, UK. *Publications:* Thematic Catalog of an 18th-Century Collection of Italian Instrumental Music (held in the Music Library, Univ. of California at Berkeley, with V. Duckles and M. Elmer) 1963, Giuseppe Tartini: le fonti biografiche 1968, Mozart's Il re pastore (critical edn, with Wolfgang Rehm) 1985, Carteggio Verdi-Ricordi 1880–1881 (co-ed.) 1988, Tartini, le sue idee e il suo tempo 1992, Music in the Theater: Essays on Verdi and Other Composers 1994, Italian edn 1998; contribs to scholarly books and professional journals. *Honours:* Hon. mem. Int. Musicological Soc. 2009, Mozart Soc. of America 2010. *Address:* 34 via di San Anselmo, 00153 Rome (home); Giudecca 786, 30133 Venice, Italy (home). *Telephone:* (0521) 285273 (office); (06) 5750433 (home); (041) 5224924. *Fax:* (0521) 287949 (office). *E-mail:* direzione@studiverdiani.it (office); petrobel@rmcisadu.let.uniromat.it (office). *Website:* www.studiverdiani.it (office).

PETROSKI, Catherine, BA, MA; American writer; b. (Catherine Groom), 1939, St Louis, Mo.; m. Henry Petroski 1966; one s. one d. *Education:* MacMurray Coll., Bread Loaf School of English, Middlebury Coll., Univ. of Illinois. *Career:* mem. Authors' Guild, Nat. Book Critics' Circle, Soc. for American Baseball Research. *Publications:* Gravity and Other Stories 1981, Beautiful My Mane is the Wind 1983, The Summer That Lasted Forever 1984, A Bride's Passage: Susan Hathorn's Year Under Sail 1997; contrib. to reviews, quarterlies and periodicals. *Honours:* Hon. DLitt (MacMurray Coll.) 1984; Nat. Endowment for the Arts Fellowships 1978–79, 1983–84, Berlin Prize 1960, Texas Inst. of Letters Prize 1976, PEN Syndicated Fiction Prizes 1983–85, 1988, O. Henry Award 1989, John Lyman Book Award 1997. *Address:* 3910 Plymouth Road, Durham, NC 27707, USA (home).

PETROSKI, Henry, BME, MS, PhD; American academic, engineer, historian and writer; *Vesic Professor of Civil Engineering and Professor of History, Duke University*; b. 6 Feb. 1942, New York, USA; s. of Henry Frank Petroski and Victoria Rose Petroski; m. Catherine Ann Groom 1966; one s. one d. *Education:* Manhattan Coll., Univ. of Illinois. *Career:* Instructor, Univ. of Illinois 1965–68; Asst Prof., Univ. of Texas at Austin 1968–74; Engineer, Argonne Nat. Lab. 1975–80; Assoc. Prof. of Civil Eng, Duke Univ. 1980–87, Dir Grad. Studies 1981–86, Prof. 1987–93, Chair. Dept of Civil and Environmental Eng 1991–2000, Aleksandar S. Vesic Prof. 1993–, Prof. of History 1995–; Distinguished Mem. American Soc. of Civil Engineers; mem. Nat. Acad. of Eng, American Acad. of Arts and Sciences, American Philosophical Soc.; Fellow, ASME. *Television:* writer and presenter of To Engineer is Human (50-minute documentary for BBC) 1987. *Publications:* To Engineer is Human 1985, Beyond Engineering 1986, The Pencil 1990, The Evolution of Useful Things 1992, Design Paradigms 1994, Engineers of Dreams 1995, Invention by Design 1996, Remaking the World 1997, The Book on the Bookshelf 1999, Paperboy: Confessions of a Future Engineer (memoir) 2002, Small Things Considered 2003, Pushing the Limits 2004, Success Through Failure 2006, The Toothpick: Technology and Culture 2007, The Essential Engineer: Why Science Alone Will Not Solve our Global Problems 2010, An Engineer's Alphabet: Gleanings from the Softer Side of a Profession 2011, To Forgive Design: Understanding Failure 2012; contribs to professional journals; columnist for American Scientist, ASEE Prism, Design News. *Honours:* Dr hc (Clarkson Univ.) 1990, (Trinity Coll.) 1997, (Valparaiso Univ.) 1999, (Manhattan Coll.) 2003, (Missouri S&T) 2011; Nat. Endowment for the Humanities Fellowship 1987–88, Guggenheim Fellowship 1990–91, Best Book Award in Eng, American Asscn of Univ. Presses 1994. *Address:* School of Engineering, Duke University, PO Box 90287, Durham, NC 27708, USA (office). *Telephone:* (919) 660-5203 (office). *Fax:* (919) 660-5219 (office). *E-mail:* petroski@duke.edu (office).

PETRUSHEVSKAYA, Liudmila Stefanovna; Russian author, playwright and poet; b. 26 May 1938, Moscow; d. of Stefan Antonovitsh Petrushevskij and Valentina Nikolaevna Jakovleva; m. 1st Evgenij Kharatian; one s.; m. 2nd Boris Pavlov; one s. one d. *Education:* Moscow Univ. *Career:* newspaper and radio journalist 1957–73; started writing short stories 1968, plays and folk tales 1971; stage productions and publ. of works were forbidden for many years; first underground performance 1975, first official performance, Tallinn 1979; mem. Bayerische Akad. der Schönen Kunste 1997. *Plays include:* Two Windows 1971, Music Lessons 1973, Cinzano 1973, Love 1974, The Landing 1974, Andante 1975, The Execution, A Glass of Water, Smirnova's Birthday 1977–78, Three Girls in Blue 1980, Colombina's Flat 1981, Moscow Choir 1984, The Golden Goddess 1986, The Wedding Night 1990, The Men's Quarters 1992; co-author of screenplay Tale of Tales (prize for best animated film of all time, Los Angeles 1980). *Publications include:* Immortal Love 1988, Songs of the 20th Century 1988, On the Way to the God Eros 1993, The Mystery of the House 1993; (children's books) Vasilli's Treatment 1991, Once Upon a Time There Was a Trrrr! 1994, Real Fairy Tales 1997, The Alphabet's Tale 1997; Complete Works (5 vols) 1996, The Girl's House 1998, Find Me, My Dream 2000, There Once Lived a Woman Who Tried to Kill Her Neighbor's Baby 2009. *Honours:* Int. A. Pushkin Prize (Germany) 1991, Triumph Award for Lifetime Achievement 2002, Russian State Prize for Arts 2004, Stanislavsky Award 2005, Triumph Prize 2006; prizes for the best short story of the year from Ogoniok 1988, 1989 and Oktiabr 1993, 1996, Grand Prize for play The Time: Night, Annual All-Russian Theatre Festival of Solo Theatre, Perm 1995, Moscow-Penne Prize (Russia/Italy) 1996. *Address:* 107113 Moscow, Staroslobodsky per. 2A, Apt 20, Russia. *Telephone:* (495) 269-74-48. *Fax:* (495) 269-74-48.

PETTERSON, Per; Norwegian writer; b. 18 July 1952, Hemnes. *Career:* fmr librarian, bookseller, translator. *Publications:* Aske i munnen, sand i skoa (short stories; trans. as Ashes in my Mouth, Sand in my Shoes) 1987, Ekkoland (novel; trans. as Echoland) 1989, Det er greit for meg (novel; trans. as It's Fine by Me) 1992, Til Sibir (novel, trans. as To Siberia) 1996, I kjølvannet (novel, trans. as In the Wake) (Brage Prize 2000) 2000, Ut og stjæle hester (novel; trans. as Out Stealing Horses) (Norwegian Critics' Prize 2003, Norwegian Booksellers' Prize 2003, Independent Foreign Fiction Prize 2006, Le Prix Mille Pages 2006, Impac Award (jtly) 2007) 2003, Månen over Porten (novel, trans. as The Moon above the Gate) 2004, Jeg forbanner tidens elv (novel, trans. as I Curse the River of Time) (Nordic Council Literary Prize 2009) 2008. *Address:* c/o Forlaget Oktober AS, Postboks 6848, St Olavs plass, 0130 Oslo, Norway (office). *E-mail:* oktober@oktober.no (office). *Website:* www.oktober.no (office).

PETTIFER, Julian, OBE, MA; British writer and broadcaster; b. 21 July 1935, Malmesbury. *Education:* St John's Coll., Cambridge. *Career:* TV Reporter, Writer, Presenter, Southern TV 1958–62; Tonight 1962–64, 24 Hours 1964–69, Panorama 1969–75, BBC; Presenter, Cuba – 25 Years of Revolution, series 1984, Host, Busman's Holiday 1985–86, ITV; numerous TV documentaries including: Vietnam War Without End 1970, The World About Us 1976, The Spirit of 76 1976, Diamonds in the Sky 1979, Nature Watch, 5 series 1981–90, Automania 1984, The Living Isles 1986, Africawatch 1989, Missionaries 1990, BBC Crossing Continents 2001–; BBC Assignment 1993–94; BBC Correspondent 1994–95; mem. Royal Soc. for Nature Conservation (Vice-Pres. 1992–), RSPB (Pres. 1994–2000, 2004–09). *Publications:* Diamonds in the Sky: A Social History of Air Travel (co-author) 1979, Nature Watch (co-author) 1981, Automania (co-author) 1984, The Nature Watchers (co-author) 1985, Missionaries (co-author) 1990, Nature Watch (co-author) 1994. *Honours:* Reporter of the Year Award, Guild of Television Dirs and Producers 1968, Royal Geographical Soc. Cherry Kearton Award for Wildlife Films 1990, Royal Scottish Geographical Soc. Mungo Park Award 1995.

Literary Agent: Curtis Brown, Haymarket House, 28–29 Haymarket, London SW1Y 4SP, England. *Telephone:* (20) 7393-4400. *Fax:* (20) 7393-4401. *Website:* www.curtisbrown.co.uk.

PETTIT, Philip Noel, PhD, FAHA, FASSA; Irish/Australian philosopher and academic; *L.S. Rockefeller University Professor of Politics and Human Values, Princeton University*; b. 20 Dec. 1945, Ballinasloe, Co. Galway, Ireland; s. of Michael A. Pettit and Bridget C. Molony; m. Victoria McGeer; two s. *Education:* Maynooth Coll., Nat. Univ. of Ireland, Queen's Univ. Belfast, Northern Ireland. *Career:* Lecturer, Univ. Coll. Dublin 1968–72, 1975–77; Research Fellow, Trinity Hall Cambridge, UK 1972–75; Prof. of Philosophy, Univ. of Bradford, UK 1977–83; Professorial Fellow, Research School of Social Sciences, ANU, Canberra, Australia 1983–89, Prof. of Social and Political Theory 1989–2002; Visiting Prof. of Philosophy, Columbia Univ., New York, USA 1997–2001; William Nelson Cromwell Prof. of Politics, Princeton Univ., USA 2002, currently L.S. Rockefeller Univ. Prof. of Politics and Human Values; Assoc. Faculty mem. Dept of Philosophy; Fellow, American Acad. of Arts and Sciences. *Publications:* Concept of Structuralism 1975, Judging Justice 1980, Semantics and Social Science (with G. Macdonald) 1981, Not Just Deserts: A Republican Theory of Criminal Justice (with J. Braithwaite) 1990, The Common Mind: An Essay on Psychology, Society and Politics 1992, Republicanism: A Theory of Freedom and Government 1997, A Theory of Freedom: From the Psychology to the Politics of Agency 2001, Rules, Reasons and Norms: Selected Essays 2002, Penser en Société 2003, Mind, Morality, and Explanation: Selected Collaborations (co-author) 2004, The Economy of Esteem (with Geoffrey Brennan) 2004, Made with Words: Hobbes on Language, Thought and Mind 2008, Examen a Zapatero 2008. *Honours:* Hon. mem. Italian Soc. for Analytical Philosophy, Hon. MRIA; Hon. DLitt (Nat. Univ. of Ireland) 2000, (Queen's Univ., Belfast), Hon. PhD (Univ. of Crete) 2005, (Univ. of Montreal), Hon. DPhil (Lund Univ.) 2008; Univ. Medal, Univ. of Helsinki 1992. *Address:* UCHV, 308 Marx Hall, Princeton University, Princeton, NJ 08544-1012 (office); 16 College Road, Princeton, NJ 08540, USA (home). *Telephone:* (609) 258-4759 (office); (609) 924-3664 (home). *E-mail:* ppettit@princeton.edu (office). *Website:* www.princeton.edu/~ppettit (office).

PETTY, William Henry, CBE, BSc, MA, DLitt; British educator (retd) and poet; b. 7 Sept. 1921, Bradford, Yorks., England; m. Margaret Elaine Bastow 1948; one s. two d. *Education:* Peterhouse, Cambridge, Univs of London and Kent. *Career:* admin., teaching and lecturing posts, London, Doncaster, N and W Ridings of Yorks., Kent 1945–73; Chief Educ. Officer, Kent 1973–84; Chair. Govs Christ Church Univ. Coll., Canterbury 1992–94; mem. Poetry Soc., English Asscn, Soc. of Educ. Officers (Pres. 1981–82). *Publications:* No Bold Comfort 1957, Conquest 1967, Educational Administration (co-author) 1980, Executive Summaries (booklets) 1984–90, Springfield: Pieces of the Past 1994, Genius Loci (with Robert Roberts) 1995, The Louvre Imperial 1997, Interpretations of History 2000, No-one Listening 2002, Breaking Time 2005, Hi-jacked in China with Jane Austen 2006, But Someone Liked Them 2008; contrib. to various anthologies, reviews, quarterlies and journals. *Honours:* Cheltenham Festival of Literature Prize 1968, Camden Festival of Music and the Arts Prize 1969, Greenwood Prize, Poetry Soc. 1978, Lake Aske Memorial Award 1980, Swanage Festival of Literature Prize 1995, Ali Competition Prize 1995, Kent Fed. of Writers Prize 1995, White Cliffs Prize 2000, Envoi Prize 2004, Ottaker/Faber local prize 2004, Essex Literary Festival Prize 2006, Newark Poetry Prize 2007. *Address:* Willow Bank, Moat Road, Headcorn, Kent, TN27 9NT, England (home). *Telephone:* (1622) 890087 (home).

PEYTON, Kathleen Wendy, (Kathleen Herald, K. M. Peyton); British writer; b. 2 Aug. 1929, Birmingham, England; d. of William Joseph and Ivy Kathleen Herald; m. Michael Peyton 1950; two d. *Education:* Wimbledon High School and Manchester School of Art. *Career:* art teacher, Northampton 1953–55; writer 1947–. *Publications:* as Kathleen Herald: Sabre, the Horse from the Sea 1947, The Mandrake 1949, Crab the Roan 1953; as K. M. Peyton: North to Adventure 1959, Stormcock Meets Trouble 1961, The Hard Way Home 1962, Windfall 1963, Brownsea Silver 1964, The Maplin Bird (New York Herald Tribune Award 1965) 1964, The Plan for Birdsmarsh 1965, Thunder in the Sky 1966, Flambards Trilogy (Guardian Award 1970), Vol. I: Flambards 1967, Vol. II: The Edge of the Cloud (Carnegie Medal) 1969, Vol. III: Flambards in Summer 1969, Fly-by-Night 1968, Pennington's Seventeenth Summer 1970, The Beethoven Medal 1971, The Pattern of Roses 1972, Pennington's Heir 1973, The Team 1975, The Right-Hand Man 1977, Prove Yourself a Hero 1977, A Midsummer Night's Death 1978, Marion's Angels 1979, Flambards Divided 1981, Dear Fred 1981, Going Home 1983, Who Sir? Me Sir? 1983, The Last Ditch 1984, Froggett's Revenge 1985, The Sound of Distant Cheering 1986, Downhill All the Way 1988, Darkling 1989, Skylark 1989, No Roses Round the Door 1990, Poor Badger 1991, Late to Smile 1992, The Boy Who Wasn't There 1992, The Wild Boy and Queen Moon 1993, Snowfall 1994, The Swallow Tale 1995, Swallow Summer 1995, Unquiet Spirits 1997, Firehead 1998, Swallow the Star 1998, Blind Beauty 1999, Small Gains 2003, Greater Gains 2005, Blue Skies ad Gunfire 2006, Minna's Ride 2007, No Turning Back 2008, Far from Home 2009, Paradise House 2011. *Honours:* Carnegie Medal 1969, Guardian Award 1970. *Address:* Rookery Cottage, North Fambridge, Chelmsford, Essex, CM3 6LP, England (home). *Telephone:* (1621) 828545 (home). *E-mail:* mikeandkath.anon@virgin.net.

PFAFF, William W., III; American author and journalist; b. 29 Dec. 1928, Council Bluffs, Iowa; s. of William W. Pfaff, Jr and Adele Keeline Pfaff; m. Carolyn Cleary; one s. one d. *Education:* Univ. of Notre Dame, Ind. *Career:* Asst Ed. Commonweal magazine, New York 1949–55; Writer, ABC News 1955–57; Exec. Free Europe Cttee 1957–61; Sr mem. Hudson Inst., New York 1961–75, Deputy Dir Hudson Research Europe, Paris 1971–78; freelance writer 1978–; syndicated columnist, International Herald Tribune 1978–2003; contrib. to The New Yorker magazine 1971–92, also New York Review of Books, Harper's Magazine, Foreign Affairs, The National Interest, The Observer (London), Commentaire (Paris) and others. *Publications include:* The New Politics (with Edmund Stillman) 1960, The Politics of Hysteria (with Edmund Stillman) 1964, Power and Impotence (with Edmund Stillman) 1966, Condemned to Freedom 1971, Barbarian Sentiments: How the American Century Ends (Prix Jean-Jacques Rousseau for Best Political Book of 1990, Geneva) 1989, The Wrath of Nations 1993, Barbarian Sentiments: America in the New Century 2000, Fear Anger and Failure 2004, The Bullet's Song: Romantic Violence and Utopia 2004, The Irony of Manifest Destiny 2010; published in Best American Essays: The Lay Intellectual (autobiographical essay) 1987. *Honours:* Hon. LLD (Univ. of Notre Dame) 1992; Rockefeller Foundation Grant 1962, Prix de l'Annuaire Français de Relations Internationales 2004, Arthur Ross Award for Distinguished Commentary, American Acad. of Diplomacy 2006. *Address:* 23/25 rue de Lisbonne, 7608 Paris Cedex, France (office). *Telephone:* 1-43-59-05-66 (office). *E-mail:* wpfaff@orange.fr (office). *Website:* www.williampfaff.com (office).

PHELAN, Thomas (Tom) J., BA, MA; Irish novelist; b. 1940, Mountmellick, Co. Laois; s. of John J. Phelan and Anne Hayes; m. Patricia Mansfield 1991; two s. *Education:* St Patrick's Seminary, Carlow, Seattle Univ., USA. *Career:* farmer; priest; insurance clerk; Asst Prof. of English, Harriman Coll., NY. *Publications:* fiction: In the Season of the Daisies (chosen for Barnes & Noble Discover Great New Writers Series 1996) 1993, Iscariot 1995, Derrycloney 1999, The Canal Bridge 2005, Nailer 2011; short stories: In the Vatican Museum 1998; essays: My Life as a Priest 2004, Ireland's Forgotten Heroes 2005, A Place Where Childhood Died 2009, Frank McCourt Was a Lyrical Truth-Teller 2009, A Former Priest Looks at the Hierarchy 2010. *Honours:* Christopher Isherwood Foundation Fellow 2008. *E-mail:* glanvil3@aol.com (office). *Website:* www.tomphelan.net.

PHILIP, Marlene Nourbese, BSc, MA, LLB; Trinidad and Tobago/Canadian poet, writer and lawyer; b. 3 Feb. 1947, Tobago; m. Paul Chamberlain 1978; three c. *Education:* University of the West Indies, University of Western Ontario. *Publications:* Thorns, 1980; Salmon Courage, 1983; Harriet's Daughter, 1988; She Tries Her Tongue, Her Silence Softly Breaks, 1989; Looking for Livingstone: An Odyssey of Silence, 1991; Frontiers: Essays and Writings on Racism and Culture, 1992; Showing Grit: Showboating North of the 44th Parallel, 1993. *Honours:* Casa de las Americas Prize for Poetry, 1988; Toronto Book Award for Fiction, 1990; Max and Greta Abel Award for Multicultural Literature, 1990; Guggenheim Fellowship, 1990; Toronto Arts Award, 1995. *E-mail:* nourbese@nourbese.com. *Website:* www.nourbese.com.

PHILIPPE, Cécile; French novelist and playwright. *Plays include:* Ruptures, Qui est cette femme?, Dis leur, C'est trop, La Mémoire longue, Le bonheur va bien, Audition, Zapping, Non-lieu, Bavardages. *Publications include:* Petites histoires horizontales 1997, Nouvelles histoires horizontales 1999, Don Juan, père et fils 1999, Je ne suis là pour personne (Prix Charles Exbrayat 2003) 2002, Le Magané 2003, Salut Lulu! 2003, Tous les hommes sont des pères Noël 2004. *Address:* c/o Editions Mercure de France, 26 rue de Condé, 75006 Paris, France.

PHILLIPS, Adam; British psychoanalyst and writer. *Career:* fmr Principal Child Psychotherapist, Charing Cross Hospital, London; Visiting Prof., English Dept, Univ. of York; Series Ed., Penguin translations of Sigmund Freud's work. *Publications:* On Kissing, Tickling and Being Bored: Psychoanalytic Essays on the Unexamined Life 1993, On Flirtation 1994, Terrors and Experts 1995, Monogamy 1996, The Beast in the Nursery 1998, Darwin's Worms: On Life Stories and Death Stories 2000, Promises Promises: Essays on Psychoanalysis and Literature 2000, Houdini's Box: The Art of Escape 2001, Psychoanalysis 2001, Equals 2002, Going Sane 2005, Side Effects 2006, Imtimacies (with Leo Bersani) 2008, On Kindness (with Barbara Taylor) 2009, On Balance 2010. *Address:* c/o Faber and Faber Ltd, Bloomsbury House, 74–77 Great Russell Street, London, WC1B 3DA, England (office). *Website:* www.faber.co.uk (office).

PHILLIPS, Carl, BA, MAT, MA; American academic, poet and writer; *Professor of English, African Studies and Afro-American Studies, Washington University, St Louis*; b. 23 July 1959, Everett, Wash. *Education:* Harvard Univ., Univ. of Massachusetts at Amherst, Boston Univ. *Career:* Poet-in-Residence 1993–94, Washington Univ., St Louis, Asst Prof. 1994–96, Assoc. Prof. 1996–2000, Dir Writing Program 1996–98, 2000–, Prof. of English, African Studies and Afro-American Studies 2000–; Visiting Asst Prof., Harvard Univ. 1995–96; Faculty mem. Warren Wilson Coll. 1997–; Visiting Writer-in-Residence, Univ. of Iowa 1998; mem. Acad. of American Poets, Associated Writing Programs, MLA, PEN American Center, Poetry Soc. of America. *Publications:* In the Blood (Samuel French Morse Poetry Prize) 1992, Cortège 1995, From the Devotions 1998, Pastoral (Lambda Literary Award) 2000, The Tether (Kingsley Tufts Poetry Prize 2002) 2001, Rock Harbor 2002, The Rest of Love (Theodore Roethke Memorial Foundation Prize, Thom Gunn Award) 2004, Riding Westward 2006, Quiver of Arrows: Selected Poems 1986–2006 2007, Speak Low 2009; contrib. to many anthologies, reviews, quarterlies and journals. *Honours:* Acad. of American Poets Prize 1993, Guggenheim Fellowship 1997–98, Witter Bynner Fellowship

1997–98, Pushcart Prizes 1998, 2001, Lambda Literary Award in Poetry 2001, American Acad. of Arts and Letters Award in Literature 2001, Acad. of American Poets Fellowship 2006. *Address:* University of Washington, Campus Box 1122, 1 Brookings Drive, St Louis, MO 63130-4899, USA (office). *Telephone:* (314) 935-7133 (office). *E-mail:* cphillips@wustl.edu (office). *Website:* artsci.wustl.edu/faculty/phillips-carl (office).

PHILLIPS, Caryl, BA, FRSL, FRSA; British/Saint Christopher and Nevis writer and academic; *Professor of English, Yale University*; b. 13 March 1958, St Kitts, West Indies. *Education:* The Queen's Coll., Oxford. *Career:* Writer-in-Residence, The Factory Arts Centre, London 1980–82, Univ. of Mysore, India 1987, Univ. of Stockholm 1989; visiting writer, Amherst Coll., Mass., USA 1990–92, Writer-in-Residence and Co-Dir Creative Writing Center 1992–94, Prof. of English 1994–97, Prof. of English and Writer-in-Residence 1997–98; Prof. of English and Henry R. Luce Prof. of Migration and Social Order, Barnard Coll., Columbia Univ., New York 1998–2005, Dir of Initiatives in the Humanities 2003–05; Prof. of English, Yale Univ. 2005–; Visiting Prof. of English, Dartmouth Coll., NH 2008, Univ. of Oxford 2009; Writing Instructor, Arvon Foundation, UK 1983–; Visiting Prof. of Humanities, Univ. of the West Indies, Barbados 1999–2000; Exec. Sec., N American Network of Cities of Asylum 2005–09; Consultant Ed., Faber Inc., Boston 1992–94, Graywolf Press, Minneapolis 1994–; Contributing Ed., Bomb Magazine, New York 1993–; Dir Heartland Productions Ltd 1994–2000; Advisory Ed. Wasifiri Magazine, London 1995–; Series Ed. Faber and Faber, London 1996–2000; mem. Arts Council of GB Drama Panel 1982–85, British Film Inst. Production Bd 1985–88, Bd, The Bush Theatre, London 1985–89; mem. English PEN 1997, Writers' Guild of GB 1997, American PEN (Council mem.) 1998; Fellow. New York Public Library 2002–03. *Films:* Playing Away 1986, The Mystic Masseur 2001. *Plays:* Strange Fruit 1980, Where There is Darkness 1982, The Shelter 1983, Rough Crossings 2007. *Radio:* plays: The Wasted Years (BBC Giles Cooper Award for Best Radio Play of the Year) 1984, Crossing the River 1985, The Prince of Africa 1987, Writing Fiction 1991, A Kind of Home 2004, Hotel Cristobel 2005, Dinner with Friends 2011; several documentaries. *Television:* The Final Passage (Channel 4) 1996. *Publications:* fiction: The Final Passage (Malcolm X Prize for Literature) 1985, A State of Independence 1986, Higher Ground 1989, Cambridge (Sunday Times Young Writer of the Year Award) 1991, Crossing the River (James Tait Black Memorial Prize) 1993, The Nature of Blood 1997, A Distant Shore (Commonwealth Writers Prize 2004) 2003, Dancing in the Dark 2005, In the Falling Snow 2009; non-fiction: The European Tribe (Martin Luther King Memorial Prize) 1987, The Atlantic Sound 2000, A New World Order: Selected Essays 2001, Foreigners: Three English Lives 2007, Colour Me English: Selected Essays 2011; editor: Extravagant Strangers 1997, The Right Set: A Tennis Anthology 1999. *Honours:* Hon. Sr mem. Univ. of Kent 1988–; Hon. AM (Amherst Coll.) 1995; Hon. DUniv (Leeds Metropolitan) 1997, (York) 2003; Hon. DLitt (Leeds) 2003, (Univ. of the West Indies) 2010; Hon. MA (Yale) 2006; British Council 50th Anniversary Fellowship 1984, Guggenheim Fellowship 1992, Lannan Literary Award 1994. *Literary Agent:* c/o Georgia Garrett, Rogers, Coleridge & White Literary Agency, 20 Powis Mews, London, W11 1JN, England. *Telephone:* (20) 7221-3717. *Fax:* (20) 7229-9084. *E-mail:* georgia@rcwlitagency.co.uk. *Website:* www.rcwlitagency.co.uk; www.carylphillips.com.

PHILLIPS, Edward O., BA, LLL, AMT, MA; Canadian teacher and writer; b. 26 Nov. 1931, Montréal, QC. *Education:* McGill University, University of Montréal, Harvard University, Boston University. *Career:* mem. Canadian Writers Union; PEN. *Publications:* Sunday's Child, 1981; Where There's a Will, 1984; Buried on Sunday, 1986; Hope Springs Eternal, 1988; Sunday Best, 1990; The Landlady's Niece, 1992; The Mice Will Play, 1996; Working on Sunday, 1998; No Early Birds, 2001. Contributions: Short stories to various Canadian journals. *Honours:* Arthur Ellis Award 1986.

PHILLIPS, Jayne Anne, BA, MFA; American writer; *Professor of English and Director, MFA Program in Creative Writing, Rutgers University*; b. 19 July 1952, Buckhannon, WV; m. Mark Brian Stockman 1985; one s. two step-s. *Education:* West Virginia University, University of Iowa. *Career:* Adjunct Assoc. Prof. of English, Boston Univ. 1982–86; Fanny Howe Chair of Letters, Brandeis Univ. 1986–87; also taught at Harvard Univ., Williams Coll.; currently Prof. of English and Dir, MFA Creative Writing Program, Rutgers Univ.; mem. Authors' Guild; Authors League of America, PEN. *Publications:* Sweethearts 1976, Counting 1978, Black Tickets 1979, How Mickey Made It 1981, Machine Dreams 1984, Fast Lanes 1987, Shelter 1994, Motherkind 2000, Lark and Termite 2009. *Honours:* Pushcart Prize 1977, 1979, 1983, Fels Award in Fiction, Co-ordinating Council of Literary Magazines 1978, Nat. Endowment for the Arts Fellowships 1978, 1985, St Lawrence Award for Fiction 1979, Sue Kaufman Award for Fiction, American Acad. and Institute of Arts and Letters 1980, O. Henry Award 1980, Bunting Institute Fellowship, Radcliffe College 1981, Notable Book Citation, American Library Asscn 1984, Best Book Citation, New York Times 1984. *Address:* Department of English, Rutgers University-Newark, Hill Hall Room 504, 360 Dr Martin Luther King, Jr Boulevard, Newark, NJ 07102-1801, USA (office). *Telephone:* (973) 353-1107 (office). *Fax:* (973) 353-1450 (office). *E-mail:* aphillips@andromeda.rutgers.edu (office). *Website:* mfa.newark.rutgers.edu (office); www.jayneannephillips.com.

PHILLIPS, Kate, BA, MA, PhD; American writer; b. 30 July 1966, Pomona, CA; m., two c. *Education:* Dartmouth College, Harvard University. *Career:* Teacher, Beijing Normal University, People's Republic of China, 1988–89; Grant Writer, Newsletter Ed., Irish Immigration Center, Boston, 1992–95. *Publications:* White Rabbit, 1996; Helen Hunt Jackson: A Literary Life, 2003.

PHILLIPS, Louis, BA, MA; American academic, writer, dramatist and poet; b. 15 June 1942, Lowell, Mass; m. Patricia L. Ranard 1971; two s. *Education:* Stetson University, University of North Carolina at Chapel Hill, CUNY. *Career:* Prof. of Humanities, School of Visual Arts, New York, 1977–. *Publications:* The Man Who Stole the Atlantic Ocean, 1971; Theodore Jonathon Wainwright is Going to Bomb the Pentagon, 1973; The Time, the Hour, the Solitariness of the Place, 1986; A Dream of Countries Where No One Dare Live, 1994; The Hot Corner, 1997; contributions: The Georgia Review; Massachusetts Review; Chicago Review; Regular Columnist for The Armchair Detective; Shakespeare Bulletin. *Address:* 375 Riverside Drive, Apt 14C, New York, NY 10025, USA.

PHILLIPS, Michael (see Nolan, William Francis)

PHILLIPS, Mike, (Joe Canzius), OBE, BA, PhD, FRSA, FRSL; British novelist, broadcaster and historian; *Cross Cultural Consultant, Tate Britain*; b. (Michael Angus Phillips), Georgetown, Guyana; s. of George Milton Phillips and Marjorie Phillips; two s. *Education:* Univ. of London, Univ. of Essex, Goldsmiths Coll., London. *Career:* journalist and broadcaster BBC 1972–83; fmr Lecturer in Media Studies Univ. of Westminster; full-time writer 1992–; Curator Tate Britain 2005–06, Cross Cultural Consultant 2006–; Consultant, Culturmakelaar's Office, Tilburg 2006–; mem. Bd and Trustee, Nat. Heritage Memorial Fund 2001–07; mem. jury, European Cultural Foundation Princess Margaret Routes Award 2008–; Fellow, Goldsmiths Coll., London 2008–. *Music:* Shadowball (with Julian Joseph), Hackney Music Devt Trust 2009. *Opera:* Bridgetower (with Julian Joseph), City of London Festival 2007. *Television:* Windrush (BBC) 1998. *Publications include:* Community Work and Racism (non-fiction) 1982, Blood Rights (novel, also adapted for TV) 1989, The Late Candidate (novel) (CWA Macallan Silver Dagger for Fiction) 1990, Boyz 'n' the Hood 1991, Notting Hill in the Sixties (non-fiction) 1991, Point of Darkness (novel) 1994, An Image to Die For (novel) 1995, Fast Road to Nowhere (as Joe Canzius) (novel) 1996, The Dancing Face (novel) 1997, Windrush: The Irresistible Rise of Multi-Racial Britain (non-fiction, co-author) 1998, A Shadow of Myself (novel) 2000, London Crossings: A Biography of Black Britain (essays and stories) 2001, The Name You Once Gave Me 2006. *Honours:* Hon. DUniv (Middlesex); Crime Writers' Asscn Silver Dagger Award 1990, Arts Foundation Fellowship 1998. *Literary Agent:* c/o ProFusion International Creative Consultancy, 18 Fitzhardinge Street, London, W1H 6EQ, England. *Address:* Expert Panel, HLF, 7 Holbein Place, London, SW1W 8NR, England (office). *E-mail:* mpushkin2@aol.com (home).

PHILLIPS, Robert Schaeffer, BA, MA; American academic, poet and writer; b. 2 Feb. 1938, Milford, Del.; m. Judith Anne Bloomingdale 1962; one s. *Education:* Syracuse University. *Career:* Instructor, New School for Social Research, New York City, 1966–68, Belle Levine Arts Center, 1968–69; Poetry Review Ed., Modern Poetry Studies, 1969–73; Prof. of English, 1991–, Dir, Creative Writing Program, 1991–96, John and Rebecca Moores University Scholar, 1998–2006, University of Houston; Poetry Reviewer, Houston Post, 1992–95, Houston Chronicle, 1995–; mem. Acad. of American Poets; American PEN Center, board of dirs; Asscn of Literary Scholars and Critics; English-Speaking Union; Friends of Poets and Writers; National Book Critics Circle; Poetry Society of America; South Central MLA; Texas Institute of Letters, councillor; The Poets' Prize, chair. *Publications:* poetry: Inner Weather, 1966; The Pregnant Man, 1978; Running on Empty, 1981; Personal Accounts: New and Selected Poems, 1966–1986, 1986; The Wounded Angel, 1987; Face to Face, 1993; Breakdown Lane, 1994; Spinach Days, 2000; Interviews: The Madness of Art, 2003; fiction: The Land of the Lost Content, 1970; Public Landing Revisited, 1992; News About People You Know, 2002; criticism: Aspects of Alice (ed.), 1971; The Confessional Poets, 1973; Denton Welch, 1974; William Goyen, 1978, Are Those Real Poems, or Did You Write Them Yourself? (essays) 2005; contributions: many anthologies, reviews, quarterlies, and journals. *Honours:* American Acad. and Institute of Arts and Letters Award, 1987; Arents Pioneer Medal, Syracuse University, 1988; Greenwood Award, 1993; New York Times Notable Book of the Year Citations, 1994, 2000; Fort Concho Literary Festival Fiction Prize, 1994. *Address:* 1903 Banks Street, Houston, TX 77098 (home); c/o Creative Writing Program, Department of English, University of Houston, Houston, TX 77204, USA (office). *Telephone:* (713) 526-6263 (home); (713) 743-2951 (office). *E-mail:* cwbobphillips@yahoo.com.

PHILLIPS, Warren Henry, BA; American publisher and newspaper executive; b. 28 June 1926, New York City; s. of Abraham Phillips and Juliette Phillips; m. Barbara Anne Thomas 1951; three d. *Education:* Queens Coll. *Career:* Copyreader, Wall Street Journal 1947–48, Foreign Corresp., Germany 1949–50, Chief, London Bureau 1950–51, Foreign Ed. 1951–53, News Ed. 1953–54, Man. Ed. Midwest Edition 1954–57, Man. Ed. Wall Street Journal 1957–65, Publr 1975–88; Exec. Ed. Dow Jones & Co. 1965–70; Vice-Pres. and Gen. Man. Dow Jones & Co. Inc. 1970–71; Editorial Dir 1971–88, Exec. Vice-Pres. 1972, Pres. 1972–79, CEO 1975–90, Chair. 1978–91, mem. Bd of Dirs 1972–97, Dir Emer. 1997–; Pres. American Council on Educ. for Journalism 1971–73; Co-Publr Bridge Works Publishing Co. 1992–; mem. Bd of Dirs Public Broadcasting Service 1991–97; Pres. American Soc. of Newspaper Eds 1975–76; mem. Pulitzer Prizes Bd 1977–87; Trustee, Columbia Univ. 1980–93, Trustee Emer. 1993–; mem. Visitors' Cttee Kennedy School of Govt, Harvard Univ. 1984–90, 1992–97; mem. Corp. Advisory Bd Queens Coll. 1986–90,

Foundation Bd of Trustees 1990–97. *Publication:* China: Behind the Mask (with Robert Keatley) 1973. *Honours:* Hon. LHD (Pace) 1982, (Queens Coll.) 1987, (Long Island) 1987, Hon. JD (Portland) 1973. *Address:* Bridge Works Publishing, PO Box 1798, Bridgehampton, NY 11932, USA (office). *Telephone:* (631) 537-3418 (office). *Fax:* (631) 537-5092 (office).

PHILLIPS, Will (see Williamson, Philip G.)

PICANO, Felice, BA; American publisher, writer and poet; b. 22 Feb. 1944, New York, NY. *Education:* Queens College, CUNY. *Career:* founder SeaHorse Press 1977; founding mem. Gay Presses of New York 1981; mem. PEN Club; Writers Guild of America; Authors' Guild; Publishing Triangle. *Plays:* One O'Clock Jump 1985, Immortal 1986, The Bombay Trunk 2002, Universal Donor 2003, Perfect Setting 2004, Very Large Array 2004. *Publications:* Smart as the Devil 1975, Eyes 1976, Deformity Lover and Other Poems 1977, The Mesmerist 1977, The Lure 1979, Late in the Season 1980, An Asian Minor 1981, Slashed to Ribbons in Defense of Love and Other Stories 1982, House of Cards 1984, Ambidextrous 1985, Dryland's End 1985, Window Elegies 1986, Men Who Loved Me 1989, To the Seventh Power 1989, The New Joy of Gay Sex 1993, Dryland's End 1995, A House on the Ocean, A House on the Bay 1997, Like People in History 1995, Looking Glass Lives 1997, The Book of Lies 1998, The New York Years: An Asian Minor 2000, Onyx 2001, Art and Sex in Greenwich Village 2007; Contribs: Men on Men, Violet Quill Reader, numerous magazines and journals. *Honours:* PEN Syndicated Short Fiction Award; Chapbook Award, Poetry Society of America. *Address:* Carroll and Graf Publishers, 245 W. 17th Street, 11th Floor, New York, NY 10011-5300, USA (office). *Website:* www.carrollandgraf.com (office); www.felicepicano.com (home).

PICARD, Barbara Leonie; British author; b. 4 Dec. 1917, Richmond, Surrey, England. *Publications:* Ransom for a Knight, 1956; Lost John, 1962; One is One, 1965; The Young Pretenders, 1966; Twice Seven Tales, 1968; Three Ancient Kings, 1972; Tales of Ancient Persia, revised edn, 1993; The Iliad, 1991; The Odyssey, 1991; French Legends, Tales and Fairy Stories, 1992; German Hero-sagas and Folk-tales, 1993; Tales of the Norse Gods, 1994; Selected Fairy Tales, 1994; The Deceivers, 1996; The Midsummer Bride, 1999.

PICARD, Robert George, BA, MA, PhD; American writer; b. 15 July 1951, Pasadena, CA; m. Elizabeth Carpelan 1979, two d. one s. *Education:* Loma Linda University, California State University, Fullerton, University of Missouri. *Career:* Ed., Journal of Media Economics, 1988–97; Assoc. Ed., Political Communication and Persuasion, 1989–91. *Publications:* The Press and the Decline of Democracy, 1985; Press Concentration and Monopoly, 1988; The Ravens of Odin: The Press in the Nordic Nations, 1988; In the Camera's Eye: News Coverage of Terrorist Events, 1991; Media Portrayals of Terrorism: Functions and Meaning of News Coverage, 1993; The Cable Networks Handbook, 1993; Joint Operating Agreements: The Newspaper Preservation Act and its Application, 1993; The Newspaper Publishing Industry, 1997.

PICHASKE, David Richard, BA, MA, PhD; American academic, poet, writer and editor; *Professor of English, Southwest State University;* b. 2 Sept. 1943, Kenmore, NY; m. 1st Elaine Ezekian 1968 (divorced 1988); one s. one d.; m. 2nd Michelle Payne 1991. *Education:* Wittenberg Univ., Ohio Univ. *Career:* Assoc. Prof. of English, Bradley Polytechnical Institute, Peoria, IL 1970–80; Ed., Spoon River Quarterly 1977–; Prof. of English, Southwest State University, Marshall, MN 1980–; Sr Fulbright Lecturer, Łódź, Poland 1989–91, Rīga, Latvia 1997–98, Ulaanbaatar, Mongolia 2003; Publisher-Ed. Spoon River Poetry Press, Plains Press, Ellis Press 1976–. *Publications:* Beowulf to Beatles: Approaches to Poetry, 1972; Writing Sense: A Handbook of Composition, 1975; Chaucer's Literary Pilgrimage: Movement in the Canterbury Tales, 1978; A Generation in Motion: Popular Music and Culture in the 1960s, 1979; Beowulf to Beatles and Beyond: The Varieties of Poetry, 1980; The Poetry of Rock, 1981; The Jubilee Diary: April 10 1980–April 19 1981, 1982; Salem/Peoria, 1883–1982, 1982; Bringing the Humanities to the Countryside: Access to the Humanities in Western Minnesota (ed. with Gerrit Groen), 1985; Tales from Two Rivers (ed. with John E. Halwas), Vol. 4, 1987; Visiting the Father and Other Poems, 1987; Late Harvest: Rural American Writing (ed.), 1991; Poland in Transition, 1989–1991, 1994; Exercises Against Retirement (poems), 1995; Southwest Minnesota: The Land and the People, 2000; UB03 2003, A Place Called Home 2003, Harassment: A Novel of Ideas 2003, Hallelujah Anyway 2004, Rooted: Six Midwest Writers of Place 2006; contrib. to reviews, quarterlies and journals. *Address:* c/o Department of English, Southwest State University, Marshall, MN 56258, USA (office). *Telephone:* (507) 537-6463 (office); (320) 564-2424 (home). *E-mail:* pichasked@hotmail.com (home).

PICKARD, Tom; British writer, poet, photographer and documentary filmmaker; b. 7 Jan. 1946, Newcastle upon Tyne, England; m. 1st (divorced 1976); one s. one d.; m. 2nd (divorced 1986); one s.; m. 3rd (divorced 2002). *Career:* Co-founder Morden Tower 1963–72; C.D. Lewis Fellowship 1976; Writer-in-Residence, Univ. of Warwick 1979–80; freelance TV dir/producer of documentaries 1983–94. *Exhibitions:* photographic exhbn of Sunderland shipyards, Sunderland Art Gallery 1986, photo exhbn of Fiends Fell, Woodland Pattern Book Center, Milwaukee 2011. *Libretto:* The Ballad of Jamie Allan, for composer John Harle, performed and commissioned by Sage Gateshead 2005, recorded 2007, City Solstice, words for choral work by John Harle commissioned by Choir of King's Coll., Cambridge 2010. *Film:* Squire (BBC 2) (writer) 1974. *Television:* Word of Mouth (series ed./dir film inserts for int. poetry series for Border Television and Arts Council of GB) (Gold Medal, New York Int. Film and TV Festival for Best Performing Arts Series 1990) 1989–90. *Publications:* High on the Walls 1967, The Order of Chance 1971, Guttersnipe 1972, Dancing Under Fire 1973, Hero Dust: New and Selected Poems 1979, OK Tree 1980, The Jarrow March 1982, Custom and Exile 1985, We Make Ships 1989, Tiepin Eros: New and Selected Poems 1994, Fuckwind: New Poems and Songs 1999, Hole in the Wall: New and Selected Poems 2001, The Dark Months of May 2004, Ballad of Jamie Allan 2007, More Pricks Than Prizes 2010; other: TV plays and documentaries; contribs to Chicago Review, London Magazine, Northern Review, Sniper Logic, David Jones Journal, Salzburg Review, Dodgem Logic, Poetry. *Honours:* Creative Writing Fellowship, Univ. of Warwick 1979–80, George Oppen Memorial Lecturer 2004, Runner Up, Royal Television Soc. Awards, Bess Hokin Prize for poem Lark and Merlin 2011. *Literary Agent:* c/o Judy Daish Associates Ltd, 2 St Charles Place, London, W10 6EG, England. *Telephone:* (20) 8964-8811. *Fax:* (20) 8964-8966. *Website:* www.judydaish.com.

PICKERING, Paul Granville, BA; British novelist and playwright; b. 9 May 1952, Rotherham, England; m. Alison Beckett 1983, one d. *Education:* Leicester Univ. *Career:* mem. Society of Authors. *Publications:* Wild About Harry 1985, Perfect English 1986, The Blue Gate of Babylon 1989, Charlie Peace 1991, Plays: After Hamlet 1994, Walk Her Home 1999, Bad Man 2008; contributions: Times,; Sunday Times, Independent, Anthologies. *Literary Agent:* c/o Caroline Wood, Felicity Bryan Associates, 2a North Parade, Banbury Road, Oxford, OX2 6LX, England. *Telephone:* (1865) 513816. *E-mail:* ryetrip@aol.com (home).

PICOULT, Jodi, AB, MA; American writer; b. 1967, Long Island, NY; m. Tim Van Leer; three c. *Education:* Univ. of Princeton. *Publications:* novels: Songs of the Humpback Whale: A Novel in Five Voices 1992, Harvesting the Heart 1993, Picture Perfect 1995, Mercy 1996, Keeping Faith 1999, Pact: A Love Story 1999, Plain Truth 2000, Salem Falls 2001, Second Glance 2003, Falling to Earth 2004, My Sister's Keeper 2004, Vanishing Acts 2005, Perfect Match 2005, The Tenth Circle 2006, Mercy 2006, Nineteen Minutes 2007, Second Glance 2007, Change of Heart 2008, Handle with Care 2009, House Rules 2010, Lone Wolf 2012; author of 5 issues of Wonder Woman comic 2007. *Honours:* New England Bookseller Award for Fiction 2003. *Address:* c/o Hodder Headline, 338 Euston Road, London, NW1 3BH, England. *Website:* www.jodipicoult.com.

PIELMEIER, John, BA, MFA; American dramatist and actor; b. 3 Feb. 1949, Altoona, PA; m. Irene O'Brian 1982. *Education:* Catholic University of America, Pennsylvania State University. *Career:* mem. Writers Guild of America; Dramatists Guild; American Federation of Television and Radio Artists; Actors Equity Asscn. *Publications:* Agnes of God, 1983; Haunted Lives (A Witches Brew, A Ghost Story, A Gothic Tale), 1984. *Honours:* Christopher Award, 1984; Humanitas Award, 1984.

PIERARD, Richard Victor, BA, MA, PhD; American academic and writer; b. 29 May 1934, Chicago, IL; m. Charlene Burdett 1957; one s. one d. *Education:* California State Univ., Los Angeles, Univ. of Hamburg, Univ. of Iowa. *Career:* instructor, Univ. of Iowa 1964; Asst Prof. 1964–67, Assoc. Prof. 1967–72, Prof. of History 1972–2000, Indiana State Univ., Terre Haute; Research Fellow, Univ. of Aberdeen 1978; Fulbright Prof., Univ. of Frankfurt 1984–85, Univ. of Halle 1989–90; mem. American Historical Soc., American Soc. of Church History, American Soc. of Missiology, Baptist World Alliance (Baptist Heritage study cttee 1990–2000), Evangelical Theological Soc. (pres. 1985), Greater Terre Haute Church Federation (pres. 1987–88), Int. Asscn of Mission Studies, American Baptist Historical Soc. (bd of mans). *Publications:* Protest and Politics: Christianity and Contemporary Affairs (with Robert G. Clouse and Robert D. Linder), 1968; The Unequal Yoke: Evangelical Christianity and Political Conservatism, 1970; The Cross and the Flag (ed. with Robert G. Clouse and Robert D. Linder), 1972; Politics: A Case for Christian Action (with Robert D. Linder), 1973; The Twilight of the Saints: Christianity and Civil Religion in Modern America (with Robert D. Linder), 1977; Streams of Civilization, Vol. II (with Robert G. Clouse), 1980; Bibliography on the Religious Right in America, 1986; Civil Religion and the Presidency (with Robert D. Linder), 1988; Two Kingdoms: The Church and Culture Through the Ages (with Robert G. Clouse and E. M. Yamauchi), 1993; The Revolution of the Candles (with Joerg Swoboda), 1996; The New Millennium Manual (with Robert G. Clouse and Robert N. Hosdck), 1999. Contributions: many books, reference works, and professional journals. *Honours:* Research and Creativity Award, Indiana State Univ. 1994.

PIERCE, Meredith Ann, AA, BA, MA; American writer; b. 5 July 1958, Seattle, WA. *Education:* University of Florida. *Career:* mem. Authors' Guild; SFWA. *Publications:* The Darkangel, 1982; A Gathering of Gargoyles, 1984; The Woman Who Loved Reindeer, 1985; Birth of the Firebringer, 1985; Where the Wild Geese Go, 1988; Rampion, 1989; The Pearl of the Soul of the World, 1990. Contributions: magazines. *Honours:* several citations and awards for children's and young adult literature.

PIERCY, Marge, MA; American novelist, poet and essayist; b. 31 March 1936, Detroit, Mich.; d. of Robert Douglas Piercy and Bert Bernice Piercy (née Bunnin); m. Ira Wood 1982. *Education:* Univ. of Mich. and Northwestern Univ. *Career:* instructor, Gary Extension, Indiana Univ. 1960–62; Poet-in-Residence, Univ. of Kansas 1971; Distinguished Visiting Lecturer, Thomas Jefferson Coll., Grand Valley State Coll. 1975, 1976, 1978, 1980; mem. staff, Fine Arts Work Center, Provincetown, Mass 1976–77; Visiting Faculty,

Women's Writers' Conf., Cazenovia, NY 1976, 1978, 1980; Fiction Writer-in-Residence, Holy Cross Univ., Worcester, Mass 1976; Purdue Univ. Summer Write-In 1977; Butler Chair of Letters, State Univ. of NY at Buffalo 1977; poetry and fiction workshops at Writers' Conf., Univ. of Indiana, Bloomington 1977, 1980; poetry, Writers' Conf., Vanderbilt Univ., Nashville, Tenn. 1981; Visiting Faculty, Women's Writers' Conf., Hartwick Coll. 1979, 1981, 1984; poetry and fiction, Lake Superior Writers' Conf. 1984; Fiction Writer-in Residence, Ohio State Univ. 1986; Elliston Poetry Fellow, Univ. of Cincinnati 1986; master-class in poetry, Omega Inst. for Holistic Studies 1990, 1991, 1994; DeRoy Distinguished Visiting Prof., Univ. of Michigan 1992; Thunder Bay Writers' Conf. 1994; Univ. of N Dakota Writers' Conf. 1995; Florida Suncoast Writers' Conf. 1996; Hassayampa Summer Inst. for Creative Writing, Prescott, Ariz. 1998, 2000, 2002, 2004, 2006; Washington Library Association Conf., Spokane, Wash. 2001; Bilgray Scholar-in-Residence, Temple Emmanuel Residency, Univ. of Arizona 2001; Residency and Silver Memorial Lecture, Temple Israel, Duluth, Minn. 2002; mini-residency, Trinity Coll., San Antonio, Tex. 2003; Writers in Residence, World Fellowship Center, Conway, NH 2005; mem. Advisory Bd Eastern Massachusetts Abortion Fund 1999–, Advisory Bd FEMSPEC: An Interdisciplinary Feminist Journal 1998–2004, Advisory Bd The Poetry Center at Passaic Co. Community Coll. 2004–, Advisory Bd Carrie A. Seaman Animal Shelter 2005–, Artists Grants Panel in Poetry 2006; Ed. Leapfrog Press 1997–; Poetry Ed. Lilith 2000–; Fiction Ed. Seattle Review 2003–. *Recording:* Louder We Can't Hear You (Yet!): The Political Poems of Marge Piercy 2004. *Publications:* Breaking Camp 1968, Hard Loving 1969, Going Down Fast 1969, Dance the Eagle to Sleep 1970, Small Changes 1973, To Be of Use 1973, Living in the Open 1976, Woman on the Edge of Time 1976, The High Cost of Living 1978, Vida 1980, The Moon is Always Female 1980, Braided Lives 1982, Circles on the Water 1982, Stone, Paper, Knife 1983, My Mother's Body 1985, Gone to Soldiers 1988, Available Light (May Sarton Award 1991) 1988, Summer People 1989, He, She and It 1991, Body of Glass (Arthur C. Clarke Award 1993) 1991, Mars and Her Children 1992, The Longings of Women 1994, Eight Chambers of the Heart 1995, City of Darkness, City of Light 1996, What Are Big Girls Made Of? 1997, Storm Tide 1998, Early Grrrl 1999, The Art of Blessing the Day 1999, Three Women 1999, So You Want to Write: How to Master the Craft of Writing Fiction and the Personal Narrative (with Ira Wood) 2001, 2005, Sleeping with Cats, A Memoir 2002, The Third Child 2003, Colors Passing Through Us 2003, Sex Wars 2005, The Crooked Inheritance 2006, Pesach for the Rest of Us 2007. *Honours:* Hon. DLitt (Lesley Coll.), (Bridgewater State Coll.); Hon. DHumLitt (Hebrew Union Coll.) 2004, (Eastern Connecticut State Univ.) 2005; Rhode Island School of Design Faculty Asscn Medal, Borestone Mountain Poetry Award (twice), Avery Hopwood Contest, Orion Scott Award in Humanities, Lucinda Goodrich Downs Scholar, James B. Angell Scholar, Sheaffer-PEN/New England Award for Literary Excellence, Calapooya Coll. 1986, 1990, Carolyn Kizer Poetry Prize, Literary Award, Gov. of Mass Comm. on Status of Women 1974, Nat. Endowment for the Arts Award 1978, Golden Rose Poetry Prize 1990, The Golden Rose, New England Poetry Club 1990, May Sarton Award, New England Poetry Club 1991, Barbara Bradley Award, New England Poetry Club 1992, Brit ha-Dorot Award, The Shalom Center 1992, Arthur C. Clarke Award for Best Science Fiction Novel published in UK 1993, American Library Asscn Notable Book Award 1997, Paterson Poetry Prize 2000, Paterson Award for Literary Achievement 2004. *Address:* PO Box 1473, Wellfleet, MA 02667, USA (home). *Telephone:* (508) 349-3163 (office). *E-mail:* hagolem@c4.net (office). *Website:* www.margepiercy.com (office).

PIERPOINT, Katherine, BA; British writer and poet; b. 1961, Northampton. *Education:* Univ. of Exeter. *Publications:* Truffle Beds 1995, Moon Apple 2001. *Honours:* Somerset Maugham Award 1996, Sunday Times Young Writer of the Year 1996, Royal Literary Fund Writing Fellowship 2004–06, Arts Council Writers' Award 2004. *Website:* www.faber.co.uk.

PIERRE, D. B. C. (Dirty But Clean); British novelist; b. (Peter Finlay), 18 June 1961, Australia; s. of Dr Keith W. Finlay and Lilian Mary Tate. *Career:* allegorist, cartoonist, photographer, designer, filmmaker. *Television:* Imagine, with Antony Yentob (biographical; BBC) 2004, The Last Aztec (Channel 4 two-hour special on the Spanish conquest of Mexico) 2006. *Publications:* Vernon God Little (Man Booker Prize, Bollinger Everyman Woodhouse Award, Whitbread Prize for first novel) 2003, Ludmila's Broken English 2006, Lights Out in Wonderland 2010. *Honours:* James Joyce Award, Literary & Historical Soc., Univ. Coll., Dublin 2005. *Literary Agent:* c/o Conville & Walsh Ltd, 2 Ganton Street, London, W1F 7QL, England. *Telephone:* (20) 7287-3030. *Fax:* (20) 7287-4545. *E-mail:* info@convilleandwalsh.com. *Website:* www.convilleandwalsh.com. *Address:* c/o Faber and Faber Ltd, Bloomsbury House, 74–77 Great Russell Street, London, WC1B 3DA, England. *Telephone:* (20) 7927-3800. *Fax:* (20) 7927-3801. *Website:* www.faber.co.uk; www.dbcpierre.com.

PIGLIA, Ricardo; Argentine writer and academic; *Walter S. Carpenter Professor of Language, Literature and Civilization of Spain and Professor of Spanish and Portuguese Languages and Cultures, Princeton University;* b. 1941, Adrogué, Buenos Aires. *Career:* Prof. of Romance Literatures, Princeton Univ., USA, currently Walter S. Carpenter Prof. of Language, Literature and Civilization of Spain and Prof. of Spanish and Portuguese Languages and Cultures. *Publications:* La invasión 1967, Crítica y ficción 1986, Artificial Respiration 1994, Assumed Name 1996, Formas breves 1999, Absent City 2000, Money to Burn 2003, El Ultimo Lector 2005, Prisión perpetua 2007. *Literary Agent:* c/o Guillermo Schavelzon & Associates, Muntaner 339, 5°, Barcelona 08021, Spain. *Telephone:* (93) 2011310. *Fax:* (93) 2006886. *E-mail:* info@schavelzon.com. *Website:* www.schavelzon.com. *Address:* Department of Spanish, 346 East Pyne, Princeton University, Princeton, NJ 08544-5264, USA (office).

PIGOTT, Mark, (David Riggs), BA, PhD; American biographer and academic; m. *Education:* Univ. of Harvard. *Career:* Asst Prof., Stanford Univ. 1970–85; Prof., School of Humanities and Sciences, Stanford Univ. 1985–. *Publications:* as David Riggs: Ben Jonson: A Life 1989, The World of Christopher Marlowe 2004. *Honours:* Frank Knox Fellowship 1963–64, Nat. Endowment for the Humanities and Stanford Humanities Centre Fellowships, Guggenheim Foundation Fellowship. *Address:* School of Humanities and Sciences, Stanford University, Stanford, CA 94305, USA.

PIGUET, Suzanne, (Suzanne Deriex), LicMathSc, Semi-licTheol; Swiss writer; b. (Suzanne Cuendet), 16 April 1926, Yverdon; m. Jean-François Piguet 1949; three s. *Education:* Univ. of Lausanne. *Publications:* Corinne 1961, San Domenico 1964, L'enfant et la Mort 1968, Pour dormir sans rêves 1980, L'homme n'est jamais seul 1983, Les sept vies de Louise Croisier née Moraz 1986, Un Arbre de Vie (Vol. I) 1995, Exils (Vol. II) 1997, La Tourmente (Vol. III) 2001, Graines de ciel 2004. *Honours:* Jubilé de Lyceum Club de Suisse Prize 1963, Prix Veillon 1969, Prix Pro Helvetia 1983, Prix Alpes-Jura 1988, Prix des Murailles 1988, Prix du Livre Vaudois 1990. *Address:* Rte de Lausanne 11, 1096 Cully, Switzerland (home). *Telephone:* (21) 799-15-03 (home). *Fax:* (21) 799-41-47 (home).

PIKE, Charles R. (see Harknett, Terry)

PILCHER, Rosamunde, (Jane Fraser), OBE; British writer; b. 22 Sept. 1924, Lelant, Cornwall; m. Graham Pilcher 1946; four c. *Education:* St Clare's School, Penzance, Howell's School, Llandaff. *Publications:* A Secret to Tell 1955, April 1957, On My Own 1965, Sleeping Tiger 1967, Another View 1969, The End of the Summer 1971, Snow in April 1972, The Empty House 1973, The Day of the Storm 1975, Under Gemini 1976, Wild Mountain Thyme 1979, The Carousel 1982, Voices in Summer 1984, The Blue Bedroom and Other Stories 1985, The Shell Seekers 1987, September 1990, Blackberry Days 1991, Flowers in the Rain and Other Stories 1991, Coming Home (Romantic Novelists Asscn Novelist of the Year 1996) 1995, Winter Solstice 2000, Eisblumen 2008; as Jane Fraser: Halfway to the Moon 1949, The Brown Fields 1951, Dangerous Intruder 1951, Young Bar 1952, A Day Like Spring 1953, Dear Tom 1954, Bridge of Corvie 1956, A Family Affair 1958, A Long Way from Home 1963, The Keeper's House 1963; contrib. to Woman and Home, Good Housekeeping. *Honours:* Hon. Fellow, Univ. Coll. Falmouth 2009; Deutscher Videopreis 1996, Bunte magazine Bambi Award 1997, Goldene Kamera Award, Hörzu 1998.

PILGER, John Richard; Australian journalist, filmmaker and writer; b. Sydney, NSW; s. of Claude Pilger and Elsie Pilger (née Marheine); m. (divorced); one s. one d. *Education:* Sydney High School, Journalism Cadet Training, Australian Consolidated Press. *Career:* journalist, Sydney Daily/Sunday Telegraph 1958–62, Reuters, London 1962; feature writer, columnist and Foreign Corresp. (latterly Chief Foreign Corresp.), Daily Mirror, London 1963–86; columnist, New Statesman, London 1991–; freelance contrib., The Guardian, London, The Independent, London, New York Times, Melbourne Age, The Nation, New York, South China Morning Post, Hong Kong, Aftonbladet, Sweden; documentary filmmaker, Granada TV, UK 1969–71, Associated Television 1972–80, Central/Carlton/Granada Television, UK 1980–; credited with alerting much of int. community to horrors of Pol Pot régime in Cambodia, also occupation of Timor-Leste; Visiting Fellow, Deakin Univ., Australia 1995; Frank H. T. Rhodes Visiting Prof., Cornell Univ., USA 2003–. *Exhibitions:* Reporting the World: John Pilger's Great Eyewitness Photographers, The Barbican Summer Exhbn 2001. *Feature film:* The Last Day 1983. *Documentary films include:* Cambodia: Year Zero 1979 (and four other films on Cambodia), The Quiet Mutiny 1970, Japan Behind the Mask 1986, The Last Dream 1988, Death of a Nation 1994, Flying the Flag: Arming the World 1994, Inside Burma 1996, Breaking The Mirror: The Murdoch Effect 1997, Apartheid Did Not Die 1998, Welcome to Australia 1999, Paying the Price: Killing the Children of Iraq 2000, The New Rulers of the World 2001, Palestine Is Still The Issue 2002, Breaking the Silence: Truth and Lies in the War on Terror 2003, Stealing a Nation 2004, The War on Democracy 2007. *Publications:* The Last Day 1975, Aftermath: The Struggle of Cambodia and Vietnam 1981, The Outsiders 1983, Heroes 1986, A Secret Country 1989, Distant Voices 1992, Hidden Agendas 1998, Reporting the World: John Pilger's Great Eyewitness Photographers 2001, The New Rulers of the World 2002, Tell Me No Lies: Investigative Journalism and its Triumphs (ed) 2004, Freedom Next Time 2006. *Honours:* Hon. DLitt (Staffordshire Univ.) 1994, (Lincoln) 2008; Hon. PhD (Dublin City Univ.) 1995, (Kingston) 1999, (Open Univ.); Hon. DArts (Oxford Brookes Univ.) 1997; Hon. DrIur (St Andrews) 1999; Hon. DUniv (Open Univ.) 2001, Hon. DrLaw (Rhodes, SA) 2008; Descriptive Writer of the Year, UK 1966, Journalist of the Year, UK 1967, 1979, Int. Reporter of the Year, UK 1970, Reporter of the Year, UK 1974, BAFTA Richard Dimbleby Award 1991, US Acad. Award (Emmy) 1991, Reporteurs sans frontières, France 1993, George Foster Peabody Award, USA 1992, Sophie Prize for Human Rights 2003, Royal TV Soc. Award 2005, One World Award for Best Documentary 2008, Sydney Peace Prize 2009. *Address:* 57 Hambalt Road, London, SW4 9EQ, England (home). *Telephone:* (20) 8673-2848 (home). *Fax:* (20) 8772-0235 (home). *E-mail:* jpilger2003@yahoo.co.uk (home). *Website:* www.johnpilger.com.

PILIKIAN, Hovhanness Israel, BSc, MA; British theatre director, writer, composer, academic and filmmaker; *Group Executive Director, SHE Management*; b. 15 April 1942, Nineveh-Mosul, Iraq; s. of Israel and Tefarik Pilikian; m. 1st Gail Rademacher (divorced 1992, died 2000); two s. one d.; m. 2nd Clarice Stephens 1993; one s. two d. *Education:* Univ. of Munich, Univ. of London, Royal Acad. of Dramatic Art, Open Univ., American Univ. of Beirut. *Career:* has directed more than 40 plays (specializing in classical Greek drama); cr. Hanano Mask Theatre Co. 1970, Cervantes Players (first all-black actors' co. in Europe), London 1971; f. Spice of Life Theatre Club 1980, Bloomsbury Theatre Club 1982; Consultant, Cheltenham Int. Guitar Music Festival 2001; mem. Acad. Bd City Lit Inst. 2000–; Group Exec. Dir SHE Management, London 2004–; Fellow, Royal Anthropological Inst., Deutscher Akademischer Austauschdienst; life mem. Swedenborg Soc. of GB, Univ. of London Convocation Governing Bd; mem. Turner Soc.; Visiting Prof., State Univ. of Yerevan, Dutch Drama Center, Slade School of Art, Cen. School of Art and Design, Yerevan Inst. of Literature, Armenian Acad. of Sciences; regular columnist, Gibrahayer weekly internet magazine 2005–. *Films:* The New Supremes in London 1986, A King of Arabia 1987. *Plays directed include:* Euripides' Electra (Greenwich Theatre, London) 1971, Euripides' Medea (Yvonne Arnaud Theatre) 1971, William Alfred's Agamemnon (McCarthur Theater, Princeton Univ.) 1973, Sophocles' Oedipus Tyrannus (Chichester Festival Theatre) 1974, Schiller's Die Räuber (Roundhouse) 1975, King Lear (Nat. Theatre of Iceland) 1977, Fat Hamlet (Shaw Theatre, London) 1993. *Music:* Clarice de Lune 2003, Katya's Baby Or Lenin's Revolution 2005. *Achievements:* organized and produced first ever season of Armenian Cinema for the Nat. Film Theatre, London 1981; Armenian Cinema weeks in Venice 1983, Paris 1986, Montreal 2000. *Publications include:* My Hamlet 1961, An Armenian Symphony and Other Poems 1980, Armenian Cinema, A Source Book 1981, Flower of Japanese Theatre 1984, Aspects of Armenian History 1986; contrib. to Society Matters (Open Univ. newspaper), Encyclopedia Britannica. *Honours:* Adamian Award for Lifetime Achievement, Ministry of Culture of Armenian SSR 1985, Calouste Gulbenkian Foundation Scholar (LSE) 1990, Wandsworth Council Business Award 2004. *E-mail:* profpilikian@hotmail.com. *Website:* pilikian.blogspot.com.

PILLING, Christopher Robert, BA; British writer, poet, translator and playwright; b. 20 April 1936, Birmingham; m. Sylvia Hill 1960; one s. two d. *Education:* Univ. of Poitiers, France, Univ. of Leeds, Loughborough Coll. *Career:* English Asst, École Normale, Moulins, France 1957–58; teacher of French and Physical Educ., Wirral Grammar School, Cheshire, 1959–61; King Edward's School for Boys, Birmingham, 1961–62; teacher of French and athletics, and House Master, Ackworth School, Yorkshire, 1962–73; reviewer, Times Literary Supplement 1973–74; Head of Modern Languages and Housemaster, Knottingley High School, West Yorkshire, 1973–78; Tutor, Dept of Adult Educ., Univ. of Newcastle upon Tyne 1978–80; Head of French, Keswick School, Cumbria 1980–88; mem. Cumbrian Poets (Co-founder and Sec.), Soc. of Authors, Translators' Asscn, Cercle Édouard et Tristan Corbière, North Cumbria Playwrights, Les Amis de Max Jacob, Slate (New Writing Cumbria), Cumbria Cultural Skills Partnership. *Plays:* Torquemada (Kate Collingwood Award) 1983, The Ghosts of Greta Hall (with Colin Fleming) at Theatre by the Lake, Keswick 2001, Emperor on a Lady's Bicycle at Theatre by the Lake, Keswick 2001. *Publications:* Snakes and Girls 1970, In All the Spaces on All the Lines 1971, Foreign Bodies 1992, Cross Your Legs and Wish 1994, These Jaundiced Loves, by Tristan Corbière (trans.) 1995, Dialogue Imaginaire avec Tristan Corbière 1996, The Lobster Can Wait 1998, In the Pink 1999, The Dice Cup, by Max Jacob (translated with David Kennedy) 2000, The Ghosts of Greta Hall (with Colin Fleming) 2001, Tree Time 2003, Emperor on a Lady's Bicycle 2003, Love at the Full, by Lucien Becker (trans.) 2003, Life Classes 2004, Alive in Cumbria (with photos by Stuart Holmes) 2005, Defying Fate, by Maurice Carême (trans.) 2009, Springing from Catullus (trans.) 2009, Coming Ready or Not 2009, A Splendid Specimen 2009; contribs to books, anthologies, reviews, quarterlies, journals and newspapers. *Honours:* New Poets Award 1970, Arts Council Grants 1971, 1977, Kate Collingwood Award 1983, Northern Arts Writers' Award 1985, and Tyrone Guthrie Centre Residency 1994, Lauréat du Concours Européen de Création Littéraire, Centre Culturel du Brabant Wallon, Belgium 1992, European Poetry Trans' Network Residencies 1995, 1998, European Comm. Residency, Collège Int. des Traducteurs Littéraires, Arles 1996, Hawthornden Fellowship 1998, Translator Residency, British Centre for Literary Trans., Univ. of East Anglia 2000. *Address:* 25 High Hill, Keswick, Cumbria, CA12 5NY, England (home).

PILON, Jean-Guy, OC, LLB, CQ; Canadian poet; b. 12 Nov. 1930, St Polycarpe; s. of Arthur Pilon and Alida Besner; m. 2nd Denise Viens 1988; two s. from 1st marriage. *Education:* Univ. de Montréal. *Career:* f. Liberté (review) 1959, Ed. 1959–79; Head of Cultural Programmes and Producer Radio-Canada 1970–88; with Les Ecrits (literary review); mem. Académie des lettres du Québec 1982, Royal Soc. of Canada 1967–. *Publications:* poetry: La fiancée du matin 1953, Les cloîtres de l'été 1954, L'homme et le jour 1957, La mouette et le large 1960, Recours au pays 1961, Pour saluer une ville 1963, Comme eau retenue 1969 (enlarged edn 1985), Saisons pour la continuelle 1969, Silences pour une souveraine 1972. *Honours:* Ordre du Canada 1986, Chevalier Ordre Nat. du Québec 1987, Officier Ordre des Arts et des Lettres 1992; Prix de Poésie du Québec 1956, Louise Labé (Paris) 1969, France-Canada 1969, van Lerberghe (Paris) 1969, du Gouverneur gén. du Canada 1970, Athanase-David 1984, Prix littéraire int. de la Paix (PEN Club Québec) 1991. *Address:* 5724 Côte St-Antoine, Montréal, PQ, H4A 1R9, Canada (home).

PINCHER, (Henry) Chapman, BSc; British writer; b. 29 March 1914, Ambala, India; m. 1st; one d. one s.; m. 2nd Constance Wolstenholme 1965. *Career:* Defence, Science and Medical Ed., Daily Express 1946–73; Chief Defence Correspondent, Beaverbrook Newspapers 1972–79; freelance journalist and author; Fellow King's Coll. London 1979; elected Prof. Moscow Acad. for Defence, Security and Law Enforcement 2005–. *Publications:* non-fiction: Breeding of Farm Animals 1946, A Study of Fishes 1947, Into the Atomic Age 1947, Spotlight on Animals 1950, Evolution 1950, It's Fun Finding Out (with Bernard Wicksteed) 1950, Sleep and How to Get More of It 1954, Sex in Our Time 1973, Inside Story 1978, Their Trade is Treachery 1981, Too Secret Too Long 1984, The Secret Offensive 1985, Traitors: The Labyrinth of Treason 1987, A Web of Deception 1987, The Truth about Dirty Tricks 1991, One Dog and her Man 1991, Pastoral Symphony 1993, A Box of Chocolates 1993, Life's a Bitch! 1996, Tight Lines! 1997, Treachery: Betrayals, Blunders and Cover-Ups 2009; fiction: Not with a Bang 1965, The Giantkiller 1967, The Penthouse Conspirators 1970, The Skeleton at the Villa Wolkonsky 1975, The Eye of the Tornado 1976, The Four Horses 1978, Dirty Tricks 1980, The Private World of St John Terrapin 1982, Contamination 1989. *Honours:* Order of the Great Victory (Russia) 2006; Hon. DLitt (Univ. of Newcastle upon Tyne) 1979; Granada Award for Journalist of the Year 1964, Reporter of the Decade 1966. *Address:* The Church House, 16 Church Street, Kintbury, Near Hungerford, Berkshire, RG7 9TR, England (home). *Telephone:* (1488) 658397 (office).

PINCIO, Tommaso; Italian writer; b. 1963, Rome. *Publications:* novels: M 1999, Lo Spazio Sfinito 2000, Un amore dell'Altro Mondo (trans. as Love Shaped Story) 2002, La ragazza che non era lei 2005; non-fiction: Gli Alieni: come e perché sono giunti fra noi 2006; contrib. to Il Manifesto, Nuovi Argomenti. *E-mail:* info@tommasopincio.com (office). *Website:* www.tommasopincio.com.

PINEAU, Gisèle; French writer; b. 18 May 1956, Paris. *Education:* Université de Nanterre, Centre Hospitalier de Villejuif. *Career:* also psychiatric nurse; currently Ed. Mercure de France. *Publications:* Un papillon dans la cité 1992, La Grande drive des esprits 1993, L'espérance-macadam 1995, L'exil selon Julia 1996, L'âme prêtée aux oiseaux 1998, Guadeloupe: Découverte 1998, Caraïbes sur Seine 2000, C'est la règle 2002, Chair piment (Prix des hémisphères Chantal Lapicque 2003) 2002, Les colères du Volcan 2004, Case mensonge, numéro 153 2004, Guadeloupe d'Antan 2005, Fleur de Barbarie (Prix Rosine Perrier 2006) 2005, Mes Quatre Femmes, Morne Câpresse 2008; many essays and short stories; contrib. to various publications. *Honours:* Chevalier, Ordre des Arts et des Lettres; Prix Écritures d'Iles 1987, Prix Carbet de la Caraïbe 1993, Grand Prix des Lectrices de Elle 1994, Oscar Littérature du Conseil de la Guadeloupe 1996, Prix RFO Radio Télévision Française 1996, Grande Prix du Livre de Jeunesse de la Martinique 1996. *Address:* c/o Editions Mercure de France, 26 rue de Condé, 75006 Paris (office); c/o Éditions Gallimard, 5 rue Sébastien-Bottin, 75328 Paris, Cédex 07 (office); Hall 18, 3 rue du Général Séré de Rivières, 75014 Paris, France (home). *Telephone:* 6-19-59-89-02 (office); 1-45-42-62-08 (home). *E-mail:* giselepineau@yahoo.fr (home).

PINGEL, Martha Mary, (Velande Regnia), BA, MA, PhD; American academic (retd), writer, poet, composer and artist; b. (Martha Mary Pingel), 10 Sept. 1923, New York, NY; d. of Regnar S. A. (von) Pingel and Ella Charlotte Pries; m. Bert Raymond Taylor Jr 1961 (died 2003). *Career:* Instructor, Paul Smiths Coll., New York 1946–47; Asst Prof., East Carolina Univ., NC 1947–58; Prof. and Head of Div. of Humanities, Colorado Woman's Coll. 1958–66; Visiting Prof., St Mary's Univ., TX 1966–69; Prof., Middle Georgia Coll. 1969–72; Prof. and Writer-in-Residence, Hong Kong Baptist Coll. 1974–84; Retreat Facilitator in Poetry and Fiction, WordCraft by Lan 1984–2007; recently began series of workshops and retreats in meditation techniques and grief ministry; mem. American Philosophical Asscn, Nat. Authors' Registry. *Music:* Pale Violet & Gold (song) 1961, Hemisphere Happenings: San Antonio Commemorative Suite for organ 1968, Night Passage (song) 1968, Seasons (song) 1975, Impressions, eight tone-poems for piano 2000–05. *Art:* numerous works in various media. *Publications:* An American Utilitarian 1948, Catalyst 1951, Mood Montage 1968, Immortal Dancer 1968, Mode and Muse in a New Generation 1979, Homilies in the Marketplace 1996, Copper Flowers 1996, Walking Songs 1997, Zbyx 1997, Tales from the Archetypal World 1998, Flowing Water, Singing Sand 1999, Between the Lines 1999, The Zodiac Affair 2000, Gallery 2001, The Shining Kingdom (trans. of Sollyse Egne, by Helga P. Marstrand) 2004, Inner Worlds: Meditations 2005, A Metaphysical Approach to Meditation (Exploring Inner Space) 2009; contrib. to anthologies, periodicals, radio and TV. *Honours:* Int. Mark Twain Soc. Certificate 1947, Order of the Dannebrog Miniature Medal 1951, Gold Medal, Freedoms Foundation 1953, Writer's Digest Rhymed Poetry Contest Certificate 1994. *Address:* 910 Marion Street, No. 505, Seattle, WA 98104-1272, USA. *Telephone:* (206) 621-1376.

PINKER, Steven, BA, PhD; Canadian/American psychologist, scientist, writer and academic; *Harvard College Professor and Johnstone Family Professor of Psycholog, Harvard University*; b. 18 Sept. 1954, Montreal, Canada; s. of Harry Pinker and Roslyn Pinker; m. 1st Nancy Etcoff 1980 (divorced 1992); m. 2nd Ilavenil Subbiah 1995 (divorced). *Education:* McGill Univ., Canada, Harvard Univ. *Career:* Asst Prof., Harvard Univ. 1980–81,

Harvard College Prof. and Johnstone Family Prof. of Psychology 2003–; Asst Prof., Stanford Univ. 1981–82; Asst Prof., MIT 1982–85, Assoc. Prof., Dept of Brain and Cognitive Sciences 1985–89, Prof. 1989–, Peter de Florez Prof. 2000–03, Margaret MacVicar Fellow 2000–, Co-Dir Center for Cognitive Science 1985–94, Dir McDonnell-Pew Center for Cognitive Neuroscience 1994–99; Assoc. Ed. Cognition. *Publications include:* Language Learnability and Language Development 1984, Visual Cognition (ed.) 1985, Connections and Symbols (ed. with J. Mehler) 1988, Learnability and Cognition: The Acquisition of Argument Structure 1989, The Language Instinct 1994 (William James Book Prize, American Psychological Asscn 1995), How the Mind Works 1997 (William James Book Prize, American Psychological Asscn 1999), Words and Rules: The Ingredients of Language 1999, The Blank Slate: The Modern Denial of Human Nature (Troland Award 2003, Walter P. Kistler Book Award 2005) 2002, The Stuff of Thought: Language as a Window into Human Nature 2007, The Better Angels of our Nature 2011; contribs to Animal Learning and Behavior, Annals of the New York Academy of Sciences, Behavioral and Brain Sciences, Canadian Journal of Psychology, Child Development, Cognition, Cognitive Psychology, Cognitive Science, Communication and Cognition, Journal of Child Language, Journal of Cognitive Neuroscience, Journal of Experimental Psychology, Journal of Mental Imagery, Journal of Psycholinguistic Research, Journal of Verbal Learning and Verbal Behavior, Language and Cognitive Processes, Language, Lingua, Memory and Cognition, Monographs of the Society for Research in Child Development, Nature, New York Times, The New Yorker, Papers and Reports in Child Language, Psychological Science, Science, Slate, Time, Trends in Cognitive Science, Trends in Neurosciences, Visual Cognition. *Honours:* Hon. DSc (McGill) 1999; Hon. DPhil (Tel-Aviv) 2003; Hon. DUniv (Surrey) 2003; Distinguished Scientific Award for Early Career Contribution to Psychology, American Psychological Asscn 1984, Boyd R. McCandless Young Scientist Award, Div. of Developmental Psychology, American Psychological Asscn 1986, Troland Research Award NAS 1993, Linguistics, Language and the Public Interest Award, Linguistics Soc. of America 1997, Los Angeles Times Book Prize in Science and Technology 1998, Golden Plate Award, American Acad. of Achievement 1999, Humanist Laureate Int. Acad. of Humanism 2001, Henry Dale Prize 2004, Humanist of the Year 2006, George Miller Prize 2010. *Literary Agent:* The Lavin Agency, 872 Massachusetts Avenue, Cambridge, MA 02139, USA. *Address:* Department of Psychology, Harvard University, William James Hall, 33 Kirkland Street, Cambridge, MA 02138, USA (office). *Website:* pinker.wjh.harvard.edu (office); stevenpinker.com.

PINNER, David John; British writer and dramatist; b. 6 Oct. 1940, Peterborough, England; m. Catherine 1965, one s. one d. *Education:* RADA. *Publications:* plays: Dickon, 1965; Fanghorn, 1966; The Drums of Snow, 1969; Corgi, 1969; The Potsdam Quartet, 1973; An Evening with the GLC, 1974; The Last Englishman, 1975; Lucifer's Fair, 1979; Screwball, 1985; The Teddy Bears' Picnic, 1988; Cartoon; Hereward the Wake; Shakebag; Revelations; The Sins of the Mother; Lenin in Love, 2000. Television Plays: Juliet and Romeo, 1975; 2 Crown Courts, 1978; The Potsdam Quartet, 1980; The Sea Horse. Novels: Ritual, 1967; With My Body, 1968; There'll Always Be an England, 1984. Non-Fiction: Newton's Darkness: Two Dramatic Views (with Carl Djerassi), 2003.

PINNEY, Lucy Catherine, BA; British writer and journalist; b. 25 July 1952, London; d. of Christopher William Wentworth Dilke; m. Charles Pinney 1975 (divorced 2000); two s. one d. *Education:* York Univ. *Career:* columnist, The Times. *Publications:* The Pink Stallion 1988, Tender Moth 1994, A Country Wife 2004; contrib. to Sunday Times, Observer, Daily Mail, Telegraph, Company, Cosmopolitan, Country Living, The Express, She. *Address:* Egremont Farm, Payhembury, Honiton, Devon, EX14 3JA, England (home). *E-mail:* lucy@egremontfarm.wanadoo.co.uk (home).

PINNOCK, Winsome, BA, MA; British playwright and academic; *Senior Lecturer in Creative Writing, English Literature and Drama, Kingston University*; b. 26 Aug. 1961, London, England. *Education:* Goldsmiths Coll., London, Birkbeck Coll., London. *Career:* Playwright-in-Residence, Tricycle Theatre, Kilburn 1990, Royal Court Theatre, London 1991, Clean Break Theatre Co. 1994; Visiting Lecturer in Scriptwriting, Royal Holloway, Univ. of London 1996–97; Sr Visiting Fellow, Univ. of Cambridge 1997–98; Script Ed., BBC TV, Cardiff 1998–2000; Lecturer in Creative Writing, Bath Spa Univ. 2000–01; Sr Lecturer in Creative Writing, London Metropolitan Univ. 2002–; currently also Sr Lecturer in Creative Writing, English Literature and Drama, Kingston Univ.; Chair. Alfred Fagon Awards. *Plays:* The Wind of Change 1987, Leave Taking (Liverpool Playhouse) 1988, Picture Palace 1988, A Rock in Water 1989, A Hero's Welcome 1989, Talking in Tongues 1991, Mules 1996, Can You Keep a Secret? 1999, Water 2001, One Under (Tricycle, London) 2005, IDP 2006. *Film screenplay:* Bitter Harvest. *Radio plays:* Let them call it Jazz 1998, Her Father's Daughter 1999, Water 2002, Something Borrowed 2004, Indiana 2004. *Television plays:* episodes in South of the Border and Chalkface Series. *Honours:* Thames TV Award 1991, George Devine Award 1991. *Literary Agent:* c/o Mel Kenyon (Agent), Casarotto Ramsay & Associates Ltd, Waverley House, 7–12 Noel Street, London, W1F 8GQ, England. *Telephone:* (20) 7287-4450. *Fax:* (20) 7287-9128. *Website:* www.casarotto.co.uk. *Address:* Department of Creative Writing, Faculty of Arts and Social Sciences, Kingston University, Penrhyn Road, London, KT1 2EE, England (office). *Telephone:* (20) 8547-2000 (office). *E-mail:* w.pinnock@kingston.ac.uk (office). *Website:* fass.kingston.ac.uk (office).

PIÑON, Nélida, BPhil; Brazilian writer, journalist and academic; b. 3 May 1937, Vila Isabel, Rio de Janeiro; d. of Lino Piñon Muiños and Olívia Carmen Cuiñas Piñon. *Education:* Pontificia Universidade Católica, Rio de Janeiro, Columbia Univ., New York, USA. *Career:* Chair. in Creative Writing, Fed. Univ. of Rio de Janeiro 1970, Dr Henry King Stanford Chair in Humanities, Univ. of Miami 1990–2003; visiting writer, Columbia Univ. 1978, Johns Hopkins Univ. 1988, Georgetown Univ., Washington, DC 1999, Harvard Univ. 2001; has lectured at univs in France, Spain and Peru; mem. Brazilian Acad. of Letters (Chair. 1996–97) 1989–; Corresp. mem. Acad. of Sciences of Lisbon; mem. Brazilian Acad. of Philosophy 2004–. *Publications:* Guia-mapa de Gabriel Arcanjo (novel, trans. as Guide Map of Archangel Gabriel) 1961, Madeira feita cruz (novel) 1963, Tempo das frutas (short stories, trans. as Season of Fruit) 1966, Fundador (novel, trans. as Founder, Walmap Prize) 1969, A casa da paixão (novel, trans. as The House of Passion, Mario Andrade Prize) 1972, Sala de armas (short stories, trans. as Weapons Room) 1973, Tebas do meu coração (novel, trans. as Thebes of my Heart) 1974, A força do destino (novel, trans. as The Force of Destiny) 1977, O calor das coisas (short stories) 1980, A república dos sonhos (novel, trans. as The Republic of Dreams) (Asscn of Art Critics' Award) 1984, A doce canção de Caetana (novel) (trans. as Caetana's Sweet Song) 1987, O pão de cada dia (articles) 1994, A roda do vento (juvenile novel) 1996, Até amanhã, outra vez (short stories) 1999, O cortejo do divino, O ritual da arte (literary criticism), O Presumível Coração da América (articles) 2002, Vozes do Deserto (Prêmio Jabuti 2005) (trans. as Voices of the Desert) 2004. *Honours:* Order of Río Branco, Cruzeiro do Sul, Medalha Mérito Cultural, Brazil, Aguila Medal, Mexico, Dom Afonso Henriques Medal, Portugal, Lazo de Dama Medal, Spain, Gabriela Mistral Medal and Grand Officer, Order of Cultural Merit, Chile, Chevalier des Arts et des Lettres, France, Order of Feminine Merit, Brazil 2004; Dr hc (Florida Atlantic Univ.) 1996, (Univ. of Poitiers, France) 1997, (Univ. of Santiago de Compostela) 1998, (Rutgers Univ., USA) 1998, (Univ. of Montréal, Canada) 2004; Pen Club Award, Juan Rulfo Literary Award 1995, Don Alfonso Enrique Medal, Portugal, Gabriella Mistral Medal, Chile, Isabel la Católica Award 2000, Jorge Isaacs Ibero-American Narrative Award 2001, Rosalía de Castro Award 2002, Menéndez Pelayo Int. Prize 2003, Puterbaugh Felow 2004, Prince of Asturias Award for Literature 2005. *Address:* Av. Epitácio Pessoa, no. 4956, ap. 801, Lagoa, CEP 22471-001 (home); c/o Editora Record, Rua Argentina 171, São Cristóvão, Rio de Janeiro, RJ CEP 20921-380, Brazil (office). *Telephone:* (21) 2537-2996 (home); (21) 2535-3385 (office). *Fax:* (21) 2537-1108 (home). *E-mail:* pinonproducoes@terra.com.br (office). *Website:* www.nelidapinon.com.br.

PINSKER, Sanford, BA, PhD; American academic, writer and poet; *Shadek Professor of Humanities, Franklin and Marshall College*; b. 28 Sept. 1941, Washington, Pennsylvania; m. Ann Getson 1968; one s. one d. *Education:* Washington and Jefferson Coll., Univ. of Washington. *Career:* Asst Prof. 1967–74, Assoc. Prof. 1974–84, Prof. 1984–88, Shadek Prof. of Humanities 1988–, Franklin and Marshall Coll.; Visiting Prof., Univ. of California at Riverside 1973, 1975; Fulbright Sr Lecturer, Belgium 1984–85, Spain 1990–91; Pennsylvania Humanist 1985–87, 1990–91, 1996–97; Ed., Academic Questions 1995–; mem. Nat. Book Critics Circle. *Publications:* The Schlemiel as Metaphor: Studies in the Yiddish and American-Jewish Novel, 1971; The Comedy That 'Hoits': An Essay on the Fiction of Philip Roth, 1975; Still Life and Other Poems, 1975; The Languages of Joseph Conrad, 1978; Between Two Worlds: The American Novel in the 1960s, 1978; Philip Roth: Critical Essays, 1982; Memory Breaks Off and Other Poems, 1984; Conversations with Contemporary American Writers, 1985; Whales at Play and Other Poems of Travel, 1986; Three Pacific Northwest Poets: Stafford, Hugo, and Wagoner, 1987; The Uncompromising Fictions of Cynthia Ozick, 1987; Bearing the Bad News: Contemporary American Literature and Culture, 1990; Understanding Joseph Heller, 1991; Jewish-American Literature and Culture: An Encyclopedia (ed. with Jack Fischel), 1992; Jewish-American Fiction, 1917–1987, 1992; Sketches of Spain (poems), 1992; The Catcher in the Rye: Innocence Under Pressure, 1993; Oedipus Meets the Press and Other Tragi-Comedies of Our Time, 1996. Contributions: Articles, stories, poems, and reviews in numerous publications. *Address:* 700 N Pine Street, Lancaster, PA 17603, USA.

PINSKY, Robert Neal, PhD; American poet and academic; *Professor of Creative Writing, Boston University*; b. 20 Oct. 1940, Long Branch, NJ; s. of Milford Simon Pinsky and Sylvia Pinsky (née Eisenberg); m. Ellen Jane Bailey 1961; three d. *Education:* Rutgers Univ., Stanford Univ. *Career:* taught English at Univ. of Chicago 1967–68, Wellesley Coll. 1968–80; Prof. of English, Univ. of Calif., Berkeley 1980–89; Prof., Boston Univ. 1980–89, Prof. of Creative Writing 1989–; Poet Laureate of USA 1997–2000; f. Favorite Poem Project; Visiting Lecturer, Harvard Univ.; Hurst Prof., Washington Univ., St Louis; Poetry Ed. New Republic magazine 1978, Slate Magazine 1994–; Guggenheim Fellow 1980; mem. AAAL (Sec. 2003–06); Chancellor, Acad. of American Poets. *Publications:* Landor's Poetry 1968, Sadness and Happiness 1975, The Situation of Poetry 1977, An Explanation of America 1980, History of My Heart 1980, Poetry and the World 1988, The Want Bone 1990, The Inferno of Dante (trans.; Howard Morton Landon Trans. Prize) 1994, The Figured Wheel: New and Collected Poems 1966–96 (Lenore Marshall Award, Amb. Book Award, English Speaking Union) 1996, The Sounds of Poetry 1998, The Handbook of Heartbreak 1998, Americans' Favorite Poems (co-ed.) 1999, Jersey Rain 2000, Democracy, Culture, and the Voice of Poetry 2002, Poems to Read (co-ed.) 2002, Invitation to Poetry (co-ed.) 2004, First Things to Hand 2006, Gulf Music 2007, The Life of David (Jewish Encounters) 2008, Thousands of Broadways: Dreams and Nightmares of the American Small

Town 2009, Essential Pleasures: A New Anthology of Poems to Read Aloud 2009, Death and the Powers (libretto) 2010, Selected Poems 2011. *Honours:* Artist's Award, American Acad. of Arts and Letters 1979, Saxifrage Prize 1980, William Carlos Williams Prize 1984, Shelley Memorial Award 1996, Harold Washington Literary Award 1999, Manhae Foundation Prize 2006, Jewish Cultural Foundation Achievement Award 2006, Theodore Roethke Prize 2008. *Literary Agent:* Steven Barclay Agency, 12 Western Avenue, Petaluma, CA 94952, USA. *Telephone:* (707) 773-0654. *Fax:* (707) 778-1868. *E-mail:* steven@barclayagency.com. *Website:* www.barclayagency.com. *Address:* Department of English, Boston University, 236 Bay State Road, Boston, MA 02215, USA (office). *Telephone:* (617) 353-2506 (office). *E-mail:* rpinsky@bu.edu (office). *Website:* www.bu.edu/english (office).

PINTER, Frances Mercedes Judith, PhD; American/British publisher; *Publisher, Bloomsbury Academic;* b. 13 June 1949, Venezuela; d. of George Pinter and Vera Hirschenhauser Pinter; m. David Percy 1985. *Education:* Univ. Coll., London. *Career:* Research Officer, Centre for Criminological Research, Univ. of Oxford, UK 1976–79; Man. Dir Pinter Publrs 1979–94; Chair. Ind. Publrs Guild 1979–82, Publrs Asscn E European Task Force 1990–; Man. Dir Cen. European Univ. Press 1994–96; Chair. Bd of Trustees, Int. House 2001, CEO Int. House Trust 2002–06; Deputy Chair. Book Devt Council 1985–89; Publr, Bloomsbury Academic 2008–; mem. Bd UK Publrs Asscn 1987–92, IBIS Information Services 1988–90, Libra Books 1991–; Exec. Dir Centre for Publishing Devt 1994–, Open Soc. Inst. 1994–99; Visiting Fellow, LSE 2000–01, 2006–. *Address:* 1 Belsize Avenue, London, NW3 4BL, England (home). *Telephone:* (20) 7431-7849 (office). *E-mail:* frances@pinter.org.uk (office). *Website:* www.pinter.org.uk.

PINTO CORREIA, Clara, PhD; Portuguese writer and scientist; b. 30 Jan. 1960, Lisbon. *Education:* Portugal and USA. *Career:* journalist; researcher on developmental biology; writes for various newspapers and magazine; contributes to various radio and television programmes. *Publications:* Agrião 1984, Adeus Princesa (Goodbye Princess) 1987, The Ovary of Eve, Secondary Messengers 1999, Return of the Crazy Bird: The Sad, Strange Tale of the Dodo 2003; numerous other publs including short stories, children's books, histories of science and an opera libretto. *Address:* c/o University of Chicago Press, 1427 East 60th Street, Chicago, IL 60637, USA.

PIPER, Christa, MA; German painter and writer. *Education:* Kunst Schüle Westerd, Frankfurt am Main. *Career:* paintings and drawings exhibited in Germany, fmr GDR, Austria, Switzerland, Israel, People's Repub. of China, Monaco, Norway; Producer lyric/sound/dance collage Wieviel Erde braucht das Mensch 1984. *Publications include:* illustrated poems: Alltag 1969, Der Übermensch (Persiflage auf die Menschen im Jahr 3000) 1970, Spiel zu zweit 1976; novels: Trotzdem Christine 1984, Im Zeichen der Rose 1984, Nimm dir dein Leben 1986, Die Wolke und der Regenbogen 1991, Wenn Dr Wieder 'Anion' Sagst 1998; work featured in calendars and catalogues. *Honours:* Study Prize Heussenstammschen Stiftung, Frankfurt 1984. *Address:* Koselstr 19, 60318 Frankfurt am Main, Germany. *Telephone:* (69) 557899.

PIPES, Richard Edgar, BA, MA, PhD; American historian, academic and writer; *Frank B. Baird Jr Professor Emeritus of History, Harvard University;* b. 11 July 1923, Cieszyn, Poland; s. of Mark Pipes and Sophia Pipes; m. Irene Eugenia Roth 1946; two s. *Education:* Muskingum Coll., Cornell Univ., Harvard Univ. *Career:* Faculty, Harvard Univ. 1950–, Prof. of History 1958–96, Assoc. Dir Russian Research Center 1962–64, Dir 1968–73, Frank B. Baird Jr Prof. of History 1975–96, Walter Channing Cabot Fellow 1990–91, Frank B. Baird Jr Prof. Emer. of History 1996–; Visiting Asst Prof. of History, Univ. of California, Berkeley 1955–56; Fellow, Center for Advanced Study in the Behavioural Sciences, Stanford, Calif. 1969–70; Sr Consultant, Stanford Research Inst. 1973–78; Dir East European and Soviet Affairs, Nat. Security Council 1981–82; mem. Council on Foreign Relations; Foreign mem. Polish Acad. of Learning (PAU) 1996–; Fellow, American Acad. of Arts and Sciences 1965–, American Council of Learned Socs 1965–. *Publications:* Formation of the Soviet Union 1954, Karamzin's Memoir on Ancient and Modern Russia 1959, The Russian Intelligentsia (ed.) 1961, Social Democracy and the St Petersburg Labor Movement 1963, Of the Russe Commonwealth (1591), by Giles Fletcher (ed. with John Fine) 1966, Revolutionary Russia (ed.) 1968, Europe Since 1815 1970, Struve: Liberal on the Left 1870–1905 1970, P. B. Struve: Collected Works in Fifteen Vols (ed.) 1973, Russia Under the Old Regime 1974, Soviet Strategy in Europe (ed.) 1976, Struve: Liberal on the Right, 1905–1944 1980, U.S.–Soviet Relations in the Era of Détente 1981, Survival is Not Enough 1984, Russia Observed 1989, The Russian Revolution 1990, Communism: The Vanished Specter 1993, Russia Under the Bolshevik Regime 1994, A Concise History of the Russian Revolution 1995, The Unknown Lenin: From the Secret Archive (ed.) 1996, Three 'Whys' of the Russian Revolution 1996, Property & Freedom 1999, Land-Tenure in Pre-Roman Antiquity and its Political Consequences 2001, Communism: A History 2001, The Degaev Affair 2003, Vixi: Memoirs of a Non-Belonger 2003, Russian Conservatism and its Critics 2006; contributions: scholarly books and journals. *Honours:* Hon. Citizen, Georgia 1997, Hon. Consul, Georgia 1997–; Commdr's Cross of Merit (Poland) 1996; Dr hc (Adelphi Coll.) 1991, (Muskingum Coll.) 1998, (Univ. of Silesia) 1994, (Univ. of Szczecin) 2008, (Univ. of Warsaw) 2010; George Louis Beer Prize, American Historical Asscn 1955, Guggenheim Fellowships 1956, 1965, Nat. Humanities Medal 2007. *Address:* 17 Berkeley Street, Cambridge, MA 02138, USA. *Telephone:* (617) 492-0727. *E-mail:* rpipes23@aol.com.

PIRIE, David Tarbat; British dramatist and writer; b. 4 Dec. 1946, Dundee, Scotland; m. Judith Harris 1983, one s. one d. *Education:* Univ. of York, Univ. of London. *Career:* tutor; film critic and Ed., Time Out Magazine 1980–84; mem. Soho House, London 1990. *Film screenplays:* Rainy Day Women 1984, Wild Things 1988, Black Easter 1993, Element of Doubt 1996. *Television screenplays:* Never Come Back (BBC serial) 1989, Ashenden (BBC serial) 1990, Natural Lies (serial) 1991, The Woman in White (adaptation) 1997, Murder Rooms: The Dark Beginnings of Sherlock Holmes 2000, Murder Rooms 2: The Safe House 2002. *Publications:* Heritage of Horror 1974, Mystery Story 1980, Anatomy of the Movies 1981, The Patient's Eyes 2001, The Night Calls 2002; contrib. to various journals. *Honours:* New York Festival Drama Prize 1985, Chicago Film Festival Best TV Network Series Prize 1990 and Best TV Feature Film Prize 1996, Crimescene/Sherlock Holmes Magazine/NFT Award for Best TV Detective Series 2002. *Literary Agent:* The Agency, 24 Pottery Lane, Holland Park, London, W11 4LZ, England.

PIRSIG, Robert Maynard, BA, MA; American author; b. 6 Sept. 1928, Minneapolis, MN; m. 1st Nancy Ann James 1954 (divorced 1978); two s.; m. 2nd Wendy Kimball 1978; one d. *Education:* Univ. of Minnesota. *Publications:* Zen and the Art of Motorcycle Maintenance: An Inquiry into Values 1974, Lila: An Inquiry into Morals 1991. *Honours:* Guggenheim Fellowship 1974, AAAL Award 1979.

PIŠŤANEK, Peter; Slovak writer. *Publications:* novels: Rivers of Babylon 1991, The Wooden Village, The End of Freddy. *Address:* c/o The Garnett Press, Department of Russian, School of Languages, Linguistics and Film, Queen Mary, University of London, Mile End Road, London, E1 4NS, England (office). *E-mail:* sllf@qmul.ac.uk. *Website:* www.sllf.qmul.ac.uk/research/russian/garnett/.

PITCHER, Harvey John, BA; British writer; b. 26 Aug. 1936, London, England. *Education:* Univ. of Oxford. *Publications:* Understanding the Russians 1964, The Chekhov Play: A New Interpretation 1973, When Miss Emmie was in Russia 1977, Chekhov's Leading Lady 1979, Chekhov: The Early Stories, 1883–1888 (with Patrick Miles) 1982, The Smiths of Moscow 1984, Lily: An Anglo-Russian Romance 1987, Muir and Mirrielees: The Scottish Partnership that Became a Household Name in Russia 1994, Witnesses of the Russian Revolution 1994, Chekhov: The Comic Stories 1998, If Only We Could Know: An Interpretation of Chekhov, by Vladimir Kataev (ed. and trans.) 2002; contrib. to magazines and journals, including TLS. *Address:* 37 Bernard Road, Cromer, Norfolk, NR27 9AW, England.

PITMAN, Jennifer (Jenny) Susan, OBE; British consultant and fmr race horse trainer and writer; b. (Jennifer Susan Harvey), 11 June 1946, Leicester; d. of George Harvey and Mary Harvey; m. 1st Richard Pitman 1965 (annulled); two s.; m. 2nd David Stait 1997. *Education:* Sarson Secondary Girls' School. *Career:* Nat. Hunt trainer 1975–99; Dir Jenny Pitman Racing Ltd 1975–99; Racing and Media Consultant, DJS Racing 1999–; winners include: Watafella (Midlands Nat. 1977), Bueche Giorod (Ferguson Gold Cup 1980), Corbiere (Welsh Nat. 1982, Grand Nat. 1983), Burrough Hill Lad (Anthony Mildmay Peter Cazalet Gold Cup 1983, Welsh Nat. 1983, Cheltenham Gold Cup 1984, King George VI Gold Cup 1984, Hennessy Gold Cup 1984), Smith's Man (Whitbread Trophy 1985), Stears By (Anthony Mildmay Peter Cazalet Gold Cup 1986, Welsh Nat. 1986), Gainsay (Ritz Club Chase 1987, Sporting Life Weekend Chase 1987), Willsford (Midlands Nat. 1990), Crumpet Delite (Philip Cornes Saddle of Gold Final 1988), Garrison Savannah (Sun Alliance Chase 1990, Cheltenham Gold Cup 1991), Wonder Man (Welsh Champion Hurdle 1991), Don Valentino (Welsh Champion Hurdle 1992), Superior Finish (Anthony Mildmay Peter Cazalet Gold Cup 1993), Royal Athlete (Grand Nat. 1995), Willsford (County Hurdle 1989, Scottish Nat. 1995), Mudahim (Irish Nat. 1995), Nathen Lad (Sun Alliance Chase 1996), Indefence (Supreme Novice Hurdler 1996), Master Tribe (Ladbroke Hurdler Leopardstown 1997), Princeful (Stayers Hurdle Cheltenham 1998), Smiths Cracker (Philip Cornes Saddle of Gold Final 1998); first woman to train Grand Nat. winner 1983. *Publications:* Glorious Uncertainty (autobiog.) 1984, Jenny Pitman: The Autobiography 1999; novels: On the Edge 2002, Double Deal 2002, The Dilemma 2003, The Vendetta 2004, The Inheritance 2005. *Honours:* numerous awards including Racing Personality of the Year, Golden Spurs 1983, Commonwealth Sports Award 1983, 1984, Piper Heidsieck Trainer of the Year 1983–84, 1989–90, Variety Club of GB Sportswoman of the Year 1984, BBC East Midlands Lifetime Achievement Award 2005. *Address:* Owls Barn, Kintbury, Hungerford, Berks., RG17 9SX, England (office). *Telephone:* (1488) 668774 (office); (1488) 669191 (home). *Fax:* (1488) 668999 (office). *E-mail:* jpr@owlsbarn.fsbusiness.co.uk (office).

PITOL, Sergio; Mexican writer and fmr diplomatist; b. 18 March 1933, Puebla. *Career:* cultural attaché, Paris, Warsaw, Budapest, Moscow 1969–72; Amb. to Czechoslovakia 1983–88; Prof., Bristol Univ., Universidad de Veracruz 1993–. *Publications:* Victoriano Ferri cuenta un cuento 1958, Tiempo cercado 1959, Infierno de todos 1964, Los climas 1966, No hay tal lugar 1967, Del encuentro nupcial 1970, El tañido de la flauta 1972, Asimetria 1980, Nocturno de Bujara 1981, Juegos florales 1982, Cementerio de tordos 1982, El vals de Mefisto 1984, El desfile del amor 1984, Domar a la divina garza 1988, Cuerpo Presente 1990, La vida conyugal 1991, El arte de la fuga 1997, Soñar la realidad 1998, Tríptico de carnaval 1999, El viaje 2001, Obras reunidas 2003, El mago de Viena 2005, Los mejores cuentos 2005. *Honours:* Premio Nacional de Novela de México 1973, Premio Xabier Villarrutia 1981,

Premio Nacional de Literatura de México 1983, Premio Herralde de Novela 1985, Premio Nacional de las Artes y Letras 1994, Premio Nacional Francisco Javier Clavijero 2002, Premio Miguel de Cervantes 2005. *Address:* c/o Fondo de Cultura Económico, Carretera Picacho-Ajusco, Piso 7, 227, Col. Bosques del Ped, México, DF 14728, Mexico (office). *E-mail:* gerente.editorial@fondodeculturaeconomica.com (office). *Website:* www.fondodeculturaeconomica.com.

PITT, David George, BA, MA, PhD; Canadian academic (retd) and writer; b. 12 Dec. 1921, Musgravetown, NF; m. Marion Woolfrey 1946, one s. one d. *Education:* Mt Allison Univ., Univ. of Toronto. *Career:* Prof. of English Literature, Memorial Univ. of Newfoundland 1949–83; mem. Asscn of Canadian Univ. Teachers of English, Humanities Asscn of Canada. *Publications:* Elements of Literacy 1964, Windows of Agates 1966, Critical Views on Canadian Writers: E. J. Pratt 1969, Toward the First Spike: The Evolution of a Poet 1982, Goodly Heritage 1984, E. J. Pratt: The Truant Years 1984, E. J. Pratt: The Master Years 1987, Tales from the Outer Fringe 1990. *Honours:* Hon. LLD (Mt Allison Univ.) 1989, Hon. DLitt (Memorial Univ.) 2005; Univ. of British Columbia Medal for Biography 1984, Newfoundland Arts Council Artist of the Year 1988. *Address:* 7 Chestnut Place, St John's, NL A1B 2T1, Canada (home).

PITT-KETHLEY, (Helen) Fiona, BA; British writer and poet; b. 21 Nov. 1954, Edgware, Middlesex, England; m. James Plaskett; one s. *Education:* Chelsea School of Art. *Publications:* London, 1984; Rome, 1985; The Tower of Glass, 1985; Gesta, 1986; Sky Ray Lolly, 1986; Private Parts, 1987; Journeys to the Underworld, 1988; The Perfect Man, 1989; The Misfortunes of Nigel, 1991; The Literary Companion to Sex, 1992; The Maiden's Progress, 1992; Too Hot to Handle, 1992; Dogs, 1993; The Pan Principle, 1994; The Literary Companion to Low Life, 1995; Double Act, 1996; Memo from a Muse, 1999; Red Light Districts of the World, 2000; Baker's Dozen, 2000; My Schooling (autobiog.), 2000. Contributions: numerous newspapers and magazines. *Honours:* Calouste Gulbenkian Award 1995.

PITTOCK, Murray George Hornby, MA, DPhil, FRSE, FRSA, FEA FRHistS, FSAScot; British academic, writer and editor; *Bradley Professor of Literature, University of Glasgow*; b. 5 Jan. 1962; m. Anne Grace Thornton Martin 1989; two d. *Education:* Univs of Glasgow and Oxford. *Career:* British Acad. Postdoctoral Fellow, Univ. of Aberdeen 1988–89; Lecturer and Reader, Dept of English Literature, Univ. of Edinburgh 1994–96; Prof. in Literature, Univ. of Strathclyde 1996–2003, Head, Dept of Literature 1997–2000; Prof. of Scottish and Romantic Literature, Univ. of Manchester 2003–07, Chair. Dept of English and American Studies 2003–04, Deputy Head School of Arts, Histories and Cultures 2004–07; Bradley Prof. of Literature and Head of Coll. of Arts, Univ. of Glasgow 2010–; Co-Ed. Scottish Studies Review 2000–; Assoc. Ed. New Dictionary of National Biography. *Publications include:* The Invention of Scotland 1991, Spectrum of Decadence: The Literature of the 1890s 1993, Poetry and Jacobite Politics in Eighteenth-Century Britain and Ireland 1994, The Myth of the Jacobite Clans 1995, Inventing and Resisting Britain 1997, Jacobitism 1998, Celtic Identity and the British Image 1999, Scottish Nationality 2001, The Jacobite Relics of Scotland 2002, 2003, A New History of Scotland 2003, The Edinburgh History of Scottish Literature (co-ed.) 2006; contribs scholarly books and journals. *Honours:* various research grants; Royal Soc. of Edinburgh BP Humanities Research Prize, 1992–93, Chatterton Lecturer, British Acad. 2002. *Address:* School of Critical Studies, University of Glasgow, 4 University Gardens, Glasgow, G12 8QQ, Scotland (office). *Telephone:* (141) 330-2000 (office). *E-mail:* Murray.Pittock@glasgow.ac.uk (office); criticalstudies@arts.gla.ac.uk (office). *Website:* www.gla.ac.uk/schools/critical (office).

PITTS, Leonard, Jr.; American writer, commentator and journalist; b. 11 Oct. 1957, Orange, Calif. *Career:* freelance writer for Soul (entertainment tabloid), then Ed.; worked as music critic at Miami Herald newspaper, now columnist on social issues, popular culture and family life. *Radio includes:* Who We Are (documentary) 1988. *Publications include:* Becoming Dad: Black Men and the Journey to Fatherhood 2006, Forward From this Moment 2009, Before I Forget 2009, Freeman 2012. *Honours:* Columnist of the Year, Nat. Soc. of Newspaper Columnists 2002, Pulitzer Prize for Commentary 2004, four American Asscn of Sunday and Feature Editors Award for Excellence in Commentary, five Nat. Headliners Awards, Press Club of Atlantic City, six Green Eyeshade Awards, Soc. of Professional Journalists. *Address:* c/o Zach Rudin, Agate Publishing, Inc., 1328 Greenleaf Street, Evanston, IL 60202, USA. *E-mail:* lpitts@MiamiHerald.com. *Website:* www.leonardpittsjr.com.

PIVOT, Bernard; French journalist; b. 5 May 1935, Lyons; s. of Charles Pivot and Marie-Louise Pivot (née Dumas); m. Monique Dupuis 1959; two d. *Education:* Centre de formation des Journalistes. *Career:* on staff of Figaro littéraire, then Literary Ed.; Figaro 1958–74; Chronique pour sourire, on Europe 1 1970–73; Columnist, Le Point 1974–77; producer and presenter of Ouvrez les guillemets 1973–74, Apostrophes, France 2 1975–90, Bouillon de culture 1991–2001, Double Je 2002–05; Ed. Lire 1975–93; Dir Sofica Créations 1986–; mem. Conseil supérieur de la langue française 1989–; Pres. Grévin Acad. 2001–; mem. Académie Goncourt 2004–. *Publications:* L'Amour en vogue (novel) 1959, La vie oh là là! 1966, Les critiques littéraires 1968, Beaujolaises 1978, Le Football en vert 1980, Le Métier de lire. Réponses à Pierre Nora 1990, Remontrances à la ménagère de moins de cinquante ans (essay) 1998. *Honours:* Chevalier du Mérite agricole; Grand Prix de la Critique l' Acad. française 1983, Prix Louise Weiss, Bibliothèque Nat. 1989, Prix de la langue française décerne à la Foire 2000. *Address:* c/o France 2, 7 esplanade Henri de France, 75907 Paris Cedex 15; Les Jonnerys, 69430 Quincié-en-Beaujolais, France (home).

PIZZEY, Erin Patria Margaret; British writer and campaigner; b. 19 Feb. 1939, China; d. of Cyril Edward Antony Carney and Ruth Patricia Carney (née Balfour-Last); m. John Leo Pizzey 1961 (divorced 1979); one s. one d. *Education:* Leweston Manor, Dorset. *Career:* protests on behalf of women and children's rights led to several court appearances; Founder first Shelter for Battered Wives and their children 1971; toured USA to help set up shelters 1974, NZ 1978; now writer; has translated 18 books into Japanese, Russian, Greek, Portuguese, Polish, Latvian, Hebrew, Italian; resident expert on family violence on Phil Donahue Show, TV 1982; gave evidence to Attorney-Gen.'s Task Force on Family Violence, USA 1984; Guest of Honour at confs of Int. Supreme Court Judges, Rome 1994; Lunch of Honour on Capitol Hill, Washington, DC, sponsored by Congresswomen; lecture tours, NZ 1978, USA 1979; has opened refugee shelter in Bahrain. *Publications:* non-fiction: Scream Quietly or the Neighbours Will Hear (also film 1979) 1974, Infernal Child (autobiog.) 1978, The Slut's Cookbook (co-author) 1981, Prone to Violence 1982, Erin Pizzey Collects 1983, This Way to the Revolution 2011; fiction: The Watershed 1983, In the Shadow 1984, The Pleasure Palace 1986, First Lady 1987, The Consul General's Daughter 1988, The Snow Leopard of Shanghai 1989, Other Lovers 1991, Swimming with Dolphins, For the Love of a Stranger, Kisses, The Wicked World of Women 1996, The Fame Game 1999; short stories: The Man in the Blue Van, The Frangipani Tree, Addictions, Dancing, Sand; contribs to The New Statesman, The Sunday Times, Cosmopolitan and to other int. magazines. *Honours:* numerous awards, including Diploma of Honour, Int. Order of Volunteers for Peace, Italy 1981, Nancy Astor Award for Journalism 1983, Distinguished Leadership Award, World Congress of Victimology 1987, St Valentino Palm d'Oro Int. Award for Literature, Italy 1994. *Address:* Flat 5, 29 Lebanon Park, Twickenham, TW1 3DH, England. *Telephone:* (20) 8241-6541. *E-mail:* erin.pizzey@blueyonder.co.uk. *Website:* www.erinpizzey.com.

PLACE, Florence (see Norman, Geraldine Lucia)

PLAICE, Stephen James, BA, MPhil; British writer, poet and librettist; b. 9 Sept. 1951, Watford, Herts.; m. Marcia Bellamy; three c. *Education:* Univ. of Sussex, Univ. of Marburg, Germany, Univ. of Zürich, Switzerland. *Career:* Writer-in-Residence, HM Prison, Lewes 1987–94; Artistic Dir Alarmist Theatre 1987–2002; Ed. Printer's Devil 1990–2002. *Plays:* Trunks 1993, The Last Post 1994, Home Truths 1995, Nemesis 2006. *Opera libretti:* Misper 1997, Zoë 2000, The Io Passion 2004, Tangier Tattoo 2005, School4Lovers 2006, Daddy Cool 2006, The Finnish Prisoner 2007. *Films:* The Last Post 1996, Zoë 2000. *Television:* The Bill, Dream Team, Ballykissangel. *Publications:* Rumours of Cousins 1983, Over the Rollers 1992. *Literary Agent:* c/o Gavin Plumley, Macnaughton Lord 2000 Ltd, Unit 10, The Broomhouse Studios, 50 Sulivan Road, London, SW6 3DX, England. *Telephone:* (20) 7384-9517. *Fax:* (20) 7371-7563. *E-mail:* gavin@mlrep.com. *Website:* www.ml200.org.uk. *Address:* 83 Stanford Road, Brighton, East Sussex, BN1 5PR, England (home). *Telephone:* (1273) 700849 (home). *E-mail:* cultureshock@ntlworld.com (home). *Website:* www.stephenplaice.co.uk (home).

PLANTE, David Robert, BA, FRSL; American/British author and academic; *Professor Emeritus of Creative Writing, Columbia University*; b. 4 March 1940, Providence, RI. *Education:* Univ. of Louvain, Belgium, Boston Coll. *Career:* Writer-in-Residence, Univ. of Tulsa 1979–82; Visiting Fellow, Univ. of Cambridge 1984–85, L'Université de Québec à Montréal 1990, Gorky Inst. of Literature, Moscow 1991; Prof. of Creative Writing, Columbia Univ. 1998–2010, Prof. Emer. 2010–. *Publications:* fiction: The Ghost of Henry James 1970, Slides 1971, Relatives 1974, The Darkness of the Body 1974, Figures in Bright Air 1976, The Family 1978, The Country 1981, The Woods 1982, The Foreigner 1984, The Catholic 1986, The Native 1988, The Accident 1991, Annunciation 1994, The Age of Terror 1999, American Ghosts 2005, ABC 2007; non-fiction: Difficult Women: A Memoir of Three 1983, The Pure Lover: A Memoir of Grief 2009; contributions: anthologies and magazines. *Honours:* Henfield Fellow, Univ. of East Anglia 1975, British Arts Council Grant 1977, Guggenheim Fellowship 1983, American Acad. and Inst. of Arts and Letters Award 1983, Sr mem. King's Coll. Cambridge, New York Inst. of the Humanities, GLBT Amb.,New York Public Library. *Address:* Writing Program, Department of English, Columbia University, 617 Kent Hall, New York, NY 10027, USA (office). *E-mail:* drp14@columbia.edu (office). *Website:* www.columbia.edu/cu/writing (office).

PLANTINGA, Alvin, AB, MA, PhD; American academic and writer; *John A. O'Brien Professor of Philosophy, University of Notre Dame*; b. 15 Nov. 1932, Ann Arbor, MI; m. Kathleen Ann DeBoer 1955; two s. two d. *Education:* Calvin Coll., Grand Rapids, Univ. of Michigan and Yale Univ. *Career:* Instructor, Yale Univ. 1957–58; Assoc. Prof., Wayne State Univ. 1958–63; Prof., Calvin Coll. 1963–82; Fellow, Center for Advanced Study in the Behavioral Sciences 1968–69; Visiting Fellow, Balliol Coll., Oxford 1975–76; John A. O'Brien Prof. of Philosophy 1982–, Dir Center for Philosophy of Religion 1983–, Univ. of Notre Dame, IN; Gifford Lecturer, Aberdeen Univ. 1987; Fellow American Acad. of Arts and Sciences 1975; Gifford Lecturer 2005; mem. American Philosophical Asscn, Soc. of Christian Philosophers (pres. 1983–86). *Publications:* God and Other Minds 1967, The Nature of Necessity 1974, God, Freedom, and Evil 1974, Does God Have a Nature? 1980, Faith and Rationality 1983, Warrant: The Current Debate 1993, Warrant and Proper

Function 1993, The Analytic Theist 1998, Warranted Christian Belief 2000, Essays in the Metaphysics of Modality 2003. *Honours:* Guggenheim Fellowship 1971–72, Nat. Endowment for the Humanities Fellowships 1975–76, 1987, 1995–96, hon. doctorates. *Address:* c/o Department of Philosophy, University of Notre Dame, Notre Dame, IN 46556, USA (office).

PLANTINGA, Leon Brooks, BA, MMus, PhD; American musicologist, academic and writer; *Professor Emeritus of Music, Yale University*; b. 25 March 1935, Ann Arbor, MI. *Education:* Calvin Coll., Michigan State Univ., Yale Univ. *Career:* Faculty, Yale Univ. 1963–74, Prof. of Music 1974–2005, Prof. Emer., Acting Chair Dept of Music 1978–79, Chair Dept of Music 1979–86, Dir Division of Humanities 1991–97; mem. American Musicological Soc. *Publications:* Schumann as Critic 1967, Muzio Clementi: His Life and Music 1977, Romantic Music: A History of Musical Style in Nineteenth-Century Europe 1984, Anthology of Romantic Music 1984, Beethoven's Concertos: History, Style, Performance 1999; contrib. to scholarly books and journals. *Honours:* ASCAP-Deems Taylor Award 1985. *Address:* c/o Department of Music, Yale University, PO Box 208310, New Haven, CT 06520-8310, USA (office).

PLATELL, Amanda, BA; Australian writer and fmr newspaper executive. *Career:* fmr mem. staff Perth Daily News; moved to London 1986; joined Today newspaper, later Features Production Ed., then Deputy Ed.; fmr mem. staff London Daily News; Group Man. Dir Mirror Group Newspapers (MGN) 1995–96, Head of Promotions for MGN Titles, mem. subsidiary MGN Bd, Group Man. Dir and Acting Ed. Sunday Mirror 1996–97; Ed. Sunday Express 1998–99; Head of Media, Conservative Party 1999–2001 (resgnd); currently columnist Daily Mail. *Television:* Littlejohn (series) 2003, Morgan & Platell 2004. *Publication:* Scandal 1999. *Address:* c/o Daily Mail, Northcliffe House, 2 Derry Street, London, W8 5TT, England (office). *Website:* www.dailymail.co.uk (office).

PLATH, James Walter, BA, MA, PhD; American writer, academic and film critic; *Professor of English, Illinois Wesleyan University*; b. 29 Oct. 1950, Chicago, Ill.; s. of Norman Plath and Audrey Kuester; three s. three d. *Education:* California State Univ. at Chico, Univ. of Wisconsin-Milwaukee. *Career:* Prof. of English, Illinois Wesleyan Univ.; Man. Ed., Moviemet.com website; Pres. John Updike Soc.; mem. Acad. of American Poets, Fitzgerald Soc., Fulbright Asscn, John Updike Soc., Hemingway Soc., Illinois College Press Asscn, Int. Raymond Carver Soc., Soc. of Midland Authors, Online Film Critics Soc. *Publications:* Conversations With John Updike 1994, Courbet, On the Rocks 1994, Remembering Ernest Hemingway 1999, Historic Photos of Ernest Hemingway 2009; contribs to anthologies, reviews, periodicals, journals, quarterlies, magazines and newspapers. *Honours:* Fulbright Scholar, Ed.'s Award, Council of Literary Magazines and Presses 1990, Pantagraph Award for Teaching Excellence 2004. *Address:* Department of English, Illinois Wesleyan University, PO Box 2900, Bloomington, IL 61702-2900, USA (office). *Telephone:* (309) 556-3352 (office); (309) 556-3333 (office). *Fax:* (309) 556-3545 (office). *E-mail:* jplath@iwu.edu (office). *Website:* www.iwu.edu/english (office); www.iwu.edu/~jplath (office).

PLATT, Charles Michael, (Aston Cantwell, Robert Clarke, Charlotte Prentiss); British writer; b. 26 April 1945, London, England; one d. *Education:* Univ. of Cambridge, London Coll. of Printing. *Publications:* fiction: Garbage World 1967, The Gas 1968, The City Dwellers (aka Twilight of the City) 1970, Highway Sandwiches (collection, with T. M. Disch and M. Hacker) 1970, Planet of the Voles 1971, The Power and the Pain 1971, The Image Job 1971, Outdoor Survival 1976, Sweet Evil 1977, Love's Savage Embrace (as Charlotte Prentiss) 1981, Double Delight (as Aston Cantwell) 1983, Tease for Two (as Aston Cantwell) 1983, Less Than Human (as Robert Clarke) 1986, Plasm 1987, Free Zone 1988, Soma 1989, The Silicon Man 1991, Children of the Ice (as Charlotte Prentiss) 1993, People of the Mesa (as Charlotte Prentiss) 1994, Children of the Sun (as Charlotte Prentiss) 1995, Protektor 1996, The Island Tribe (as Charlotte Prentiss) 1997, The Ocean Tribe (as Charlotte Prentiss) 1999, Loose Canon 2001; editor: New Worlds 6 (ed. with M. Moorcock) 1973, New Worlds 7 (ed. with H. Bailey) 1974; non-fiction: Who Writes Science Fiction? (aka The Dream Makers) 1976, Dream Makers: The Uncommon People Who Write Science Fiction 1980, Micromania 1984, How to be a Happy Cat (with Gray Joliffe) 1986, When You Can Live Twice as Long, What Will You Do? 1989, Anarchy Online: Netsex / Netcrime 1996, Loose Canon 2001, Make: Elektronik 2010. *E-mail:* other@platt.us. *Website:* www.davidpascal.com/charlesplatt.

PLATT, Stephen (Steve), BSc (Econ); British journalist, writer and editor; b. 29 Sept. 1954, Stoke-on-Trent, Staffs., England; s. of Kenneth Platt and Joyce Pritchard; one d. with Diane Louise Paice. *Education:* Longton High School, Stoke On Trent, Wade Deacon School, Widnes and London School of Econs. *Career:* teacher, Moss Brook Special School, Widnes 1972–73; Dir Self Help Housing Resource Library, Polytechnic of N London 1977–80; co-ordinator, Islington Community Housing 1980–83; freelance writer and journalist 1983–; News Ed., subsequently Acting Ed. New Society 1986–88; Ed. Midweek 1988–89, Enjoying the Countryside 1988–91; Ed. New Statesman and Society 1991–96; Contributing Ed. Channel 4 TV 1996–; Website and Contributing Ed., Time Team 1999–2010 (BAFTA Award for Interactive Entertainment 2002); Dispatches Website Ed. 1999–2010; freelance writer, ed. and consultant 1996–. *Honours:* UKGLO Award for Outstanding Achievement 1999. *Address:* 46 Tufnell Park Road, London, N7 0DT, England. *Telephone:* (20) 7263-4185. *E-mail:* mail@steveplatt.net. *Website:* www.steveplatt.net.

PLENEL, Edwy; French journalist; b. 31 Aug. 1952, Nantes; s. of Alain Plenel and Michèle Bertreux; m. Nicole Lapierre; one d. *Education:* Institut d'études politiques, Paris. *Career:* journalist Rouge 1976–78, Matin de Paris 1980; joined Le Monde 1980, Educ. Ed. 1980–82, Legal columnist 1982–90, Reporter 1991, Head Legal Dept 1992–94, Chief Ed. 1994–95, Asst Editorial Dir 1995–96, Ed. 1996–2000, Ed.-in-Chief 2000–04 (resgnd). *Publications:* L'Effet Le Pen 1984, La République inachevée: l'État et l'école en France 1985, Mourir à Ouvéa: le tournant calédonien 1988, Voyage avec Colomb 1991, La République menacée: dix ans d'effet Le Pen 1992, La Part d'ombre 1992, Un temps de chien 1994, Les Mots volés 1997, L'Epreuve 1999, Secrets de jeunesse 2001, La Découverte du monde 2002, Procès 2006. *Address:* c/o Le Monde, 21 bis rue Claude Bernard, 75242 Paris Cedex, France (office).

PLUMLY, Stanley Ross, BA, MA, PhD; American poet and academic; *Distinguished University Professor and Director, Creative Writing Program, University of Maryland*; b. 23 May 1939, Barnesville, Ohio; s. of Herman Plumly and Esther Plumly. *Education:* Wilmington Coll., Ohio Univ. *Career:* Instructor in Creative Writing, Louisiana State Univ. 1968–70; Ed. Ohio Review 1970–75, Iowa Review 1976–78; Prof. of English, Ohio Univ. 1970–74; also taught at Princeton Univ., Columbia Univ., Univs of Iowa, Houston and Michigan; currently Prof. of Literature and Dir Creative Writing Program, Univ. of Maryland; mem. American Acad. of Arts and Sciences 2010. *Publications:* poetry: In the Outer Dark 1970, How the Plains Indians Got Horses 1973, Giraffe 1973, Out-of-the-Body Travel (William Carlos Williams Award) 1977, Summer Celestial 1983, Boy on the Step 1989, The Marriage in the Trees 1998, The New Bread Loaf Anthology of Contemporary American Poetry (co-ed. with Michael Collier) 1999, Now That My Father Lies Down Beside Me: New and Selected Poems, 1970–2000 2000, Old Heart 2007, Posthumous Keats 2008; non-fiction: Argument & Song: Sources and Silences in Poetry 2003; contribs to periodicals. *Honours:* Delmore Schwartz Memorial Award 1973, Guggenheim Fellowship 1973, Nat. Endowment for the Arts Grant 1977. *Address:* Department of English, University of Maryland, 2119 Tawes Hall, College Park, MD 20742, USA (office). *Telephone:* (301) 405-3815 (office). *E-mail:* splumly@umd.edu (office). *Website:* www.english.umd.edu/profiles/splumly (office).

PODHORETZ, John, AB; American writer and editor; *Editor, Commentary*; b. 18 April 1961, New York; s. of Norman Podhoretz (q.v.) and Midge Podhoretz (née Rosenthal); m. 1st Elisabeth Hickey 1996 (divorced); m. 2nd Ayala Cohen; two d. *Education:* Univ. of Chicago. *Career:* Exec. News Ed. Insight Magazine 1985–87; contrib. US News and World Report 1987–88; speechwriter to Pres. of USA 1988–89; Asst Man. Ed. Washington Times 1989–91; Sr Fellow, Hudson Inst. 1991–94; TV critic New York Post 1994–95, then political columnist; Deputy Ed. The Weekly Standard 1995–97, then movie critic; Editorial Dir Commentary (magazine) 2007–09, Ed. 2009–. *Publication:* Hell of a Ride: Backstage at the White House Follies 1989–93 1993. *Honours:* J.C. Penney/Mo. Award for Excellence in Feature Sections 1990. *Address:* Commentary, 165 East 56th Street, New York, NY 10022, USA (office). *E-mail:* letters@commentarymagazine.com. *Website:* www.commentarymagazine.com (office).

PODHORETZ, Norman, BA, MA, BHL; American writer and editor; b. 16 Jan. 1930, Brooklyn, NY; s. of Julius Podhoretz and Helen Podhoretz (née Woliner); m. Midge R. Decter 1956; one s. (John Podhoretz) three d. *Education:* Columbia Univ., Jewish Theological Seminary and Univ. of Cambridge. *Career:* Assoc. Ed. Commentary 1956–58, Ed.-in-Chief 1960–95, Ed.-at-Large 1995–2008; Ed.-in-Chief, Looking Glass Library 1959–60; Chair. New Directions Advisory Comm. US Information Agency 1981–87; Sr Fellow, Hudson Inst. 1995–2003; Fulbright Fellow 1950–51; Kellett Fellow 1950–53. *Publications:* Doings and Undoings: The Fifties and After in American Writing 1964, Making It 1968, Breaking Ranks: A Political Memoir 1979, The Present Danger 1980, Why We Were in Vietnam 1982, The Bloody Crossroads: Where Literature and Politics Meet 1986, Ex-Friends 1999, My Love Affair with America 2000, The Prophets: Who They Were, What They Are 2002, The Norman Podhoretz Reader 2004, World War IV 2007, Why Are Jews Liberal? 2009. *Honours:* Hon. LLD (Jewish Theological Seminary); Hon. LHD (Hamilton Coll.), (Boston) 1995, (Adelphi) 1996; Hon. DHumLitt (Yeshiva) 1991; Presidential Medal of Freedom 2004. *Address:* c/o Commentary, 165 East 56th Street, New York, NY 10022, USA (office). *Telephone:* (212) 891-6735 (office). *Fax:* (212) 891-6700 (office). *E-mail:* nhp30@hotmail.com (office).

POHL, Frederik James MacCreigh; American writer and editor; b. 26 Nov. 1919, New York, NY. *Career:* Book Ed. and Assoc. Circulation Man., Popular Science Co, New York City 1946–49; Literary Agent, New York City 1949–53; Ed., Galaxy Publishing Co, New York City 1960–69; Exec. Ed., Ace Books, New York City 1971–72; Science Fiction Ed., Bantam Books, New York City 1973–79; mem. Authors' Guild; SFWA, pres. 1974–76; World Science Fiction, pres. 1980–82. *Publications:* author or ed. of over 45 books 1953–98; The Boy Who Would Live Forever 2004. *Address:* c/o World, 855 S Harvard Drive, Palatine, IL 60067, USA.

POIVRE D'ARVOR, Patrick, LenD; French journalist and radio and television presenter; b. 20 Sept. 1947, Reims (Marne); s. of Jacques Poivre and Madeleine France Jeuge; m. Véronique Courcoux 1971; six c. (two deceased). *Education:* Lycée Georges-Clemenceau, Reims, Instituts d'études politiques, Strasbourg and Paris, Faculties of Law, Strasbourg, Paris and Reims, Ecole des langues orientales vivantes. *Career:* Special Corresp., France-Inter 1971, journalist 1971–74, Head Political Dept 1975–76, Deputy

Chief Ed., Antenne 2 1976–83, Presenter, evening news programme 1976–83, 1987–2008, Deputy Dir News 1989–; Leader-writer Paris-Match, Journal du Dimanche 1983–91; Producer and Compère, A nous deux, Antenne 2 1983–86, A la folie, TF1 1986–88; Compère, Tous en Scène, Canal Plus 1984–85; Compère and Producer Ex libris 1988–99; Compère Vol de nuit 1999–; Presenter and Producer magazine programme Le Droit de savoir, TF1 1990–94. *Publications:* Mai 68-Mai 78 1978, Les Enfants de l'aube 1982, Deux amants 1984, Le Roman de Virginie 1985, Les Derniers trains de rêve 1986, La Traversée du miroir 1986, Rencontres 1987, Les Femmes de ma vie 1988, L'Homme d'images 1992, Lettres à l'absente 1993, Les Loups et la bergerie 1994, Elle n'était pas d'ici 1995, Anthologie des plus beaux poèmes d'amour 1995, Un héros de passage 1996, Lettre ouverte aux violeurs de vie privée 1997, Une trahison amoureuse 1997, La fin du monde (collection) 1998, Petit homme 1999, Les rats de garde (collection) 2000, L'Irrésolu 2000 (Prix Interallié), Un enfant 2001, Courriers de nuit (collection) 2002, J'ai aimé une reine 2003, Coureurs des morts (collection) 2003, La Mort de don Juan (Prix Maurice-Genevoix 2205) 2004, Les Plus Beaux Poèmes d'amour 2004, Chasseurs de trésors et autres flibustiers 2005, Pirates et corsaires 2005, Coureurs des mers 2005, Le Monde selon Jules Verne 2005, Confessions 2005, Disparaître 2006, Rêveurs des Mers 2007, J'ai tant rêvé de toi 2007. *Honours:* Commdr de l'Ordre des Arts et des Lettres, Chevalier de l'Ordre National du Mérite, Chevalier de la Légion d'Honneur; Prix Interallié 2000, Prix des Lettres du Livre de Poche 2003, Prix Cyrano 2004. *Address:* TF1, 1 quai du Point du Jour, 92656 Boulogne-Billancourt Cedex, France (office). *Telephone:* 1-41-41-23-28 (office). *Fax:* 1-41-41-19-63 (office). *Website:* tf1.lci.fr (office).

POKHRIYAL, Ramesh (Nishank), MA, PhD; Indian journalist, poet and politician; b. 15 Aug. 1959, Pinani, Pauri dist; s. of Parmanand Pokhriyal and Vishwambhari Devi; m. Kusum Kanta; three d. *Career:* fmr teacher; started political career Ram Mandir Movt; elected mem. Vidhan Sabha (Legis. Ass.) of Uttar Pradesh from Karnpryag 1991, re-elected 1993, 1996, elected from Thalisain constituency 2007; fmr Minister of Culture, Arts and Religion, Minister of Uttaranchal Devt 1998, Minister of Finance 2000, Minister of Health 2007–09; Chief Minister of Uttarakhand 2009–11; mem. Bharatiya Janata Party; Chief Ed. Seemant Varta. *Publications include:* has written more than 20 books including several collections of poems, among them Samarpan 1983, Navankur 1984, Mujhe Vidhata Banna Hai 1985, Tum Bhee Mera Saath Chalo 1986, Desh Hum Jalne Na Denge 1988, Koi Mushkil Naheen 2005, Ae Vatan Tere Liye 2006, Ek aur Kahani 2007, Nishant 2008, Sangharsh Jaari Hai 2009, Apna Paraya 2010. *Honours:* Dr hc (International Open Univ., Colombo) 2007, Hon. DLitt (International Open Univ., Colombo) 2009; honoured for his literary work by Univ. of Hamburg, Germany 2008. *Address:* 37/1, Vijay Colony, Rabindranath Tagore Marg, Dehradun 248 001, India (home). *E-mail:* nishankramesh@gmail.com. *Website:* www.rameshpokhriyalnishank.com.

POLAND, Dorothy Elizabeth Hayward, (Alison Farely, Jane Hammond); British writer; b. 3 May 1937, Barry, Wales. *Publications:* as Alison Farely: The Shadows of Evil 1963, Plunder Island 1964, High Treason 1966, Throne of Wrath 1967, Crown of Splendour 1968, The Lion and the Wolf 1969, Last Roar of the Lion 1969, Leopard From Anjou 1970, King Wolf 1974, Kingdom under Tyranny 1974, Last Howl of the Wolf 1975, The Cardinal's Nieces 1976, The Tempestuous Countess 1976, Archduchess Arrogance 1980, Scheming Spanish Queen 1981, Spain for Mariana 1982; as Jane Hammond: The Hell Raisers of Wycombe 1970, Fire and the Sword 1971, The Golden Courtesan 1975, Shadow of the Headsman 1975, The Doomtower 1975, Witch of the White House 1976, Gunpowder Treason 1976, The Red Queen 1976, The Queen's Assassin 1977, The Silver Madonna 1977, Conspirator's Moonlight 1977, Woman of Vengeance 1977, The Admiral's Lady 1978, The Secret of Petherick 1982, The Massingham Topaz 1983, Beware the King's Enchantress 1983, Moon in Aries 1984, Eagle's Talon 1984, Death in the New Forest 1984, One Voyage Too Far 2003, Bitch in Black 2009. *E-mail:* polandangelcake@aol.com (office).

POLIAKOFF, Stephen, CBE; British playwright and film director; b. 1 Dec. 1952, London; s. of the late Alexander Poliakoff and Ina Montagu; m. Sandy Welch 1983; one s. one d. *Education:* Westminster School and Univ. of Cambridge. *Theatre:* Clever Soldiers 1974, The Carnation Gang 1974, Hitting Town 1975, City Sugar 1976, Strawberry Fields (Nat. Theatre) 1978, Shout Across the River (RSC) 1978, The Summer Party 1980, Favourite Nights 1981, Breaking the Silence (RSC) 1984, Coming in to Land (Nat. Theatre) 1987, Playing with Trains (RSC) 1989, Siena Red 1992, Sweet Panic (Hampstead) 1996, Blinded by the Sun (Nat. Theatre) 1996 (Critics' Circle Best Play Award), Talk of the City (RSC) 1998, Remember This (Nat. Theatre) 1999, My City 2011. *Films:* Runners (original story and screenplay) 1983, Hidden City 1988, Close My Eyes (Best British Film Award, Evening Standard) 1991, Century 1993, Glorious 39 2009. *Television:* Stronger Than the Sun 1977, Bloody Kids (aka One Joke Too Many, USA) 1979, Caught on a Train (BAFTA for Best Single Drama) 1980, Soft Targets 1982, She's Been Away (Venice Film Festival Prize) 1989, Frontiers 1996, Food of Love 1998, The Tribe 1998, Shooting the Past (Prix Italia for Best Drama, RTS Award for Best Drama) 1999, Perfect Strangers/Almost Strangers (RTS Award for Best Drama and Best Writer, BAFTA Dennis Potter Award, Peabody Award for Drama) 2001, The Lost Prince (Primetime Emmy for Outstanding Miniseries, Best Costume and Best Production Design) 2004, Friends and Crocodiles 2006, Gideon's Daughter (Peabody Award for Drama) 2007, Joe's Palace 2007, A Real Summer 2007, Capturing Mary 2007. *Publications:* Plays One 1989, Plays Two 1994, Plays Three 1998, Sweet Panic and Blinded by the Sun, Talk of the City, Shooting the Past, Remember This. *Honours:* Hon. degree (Tavistock Inst.). *Address:* Ruby Films, 26 Lloyd Baker St, London, WC1X 9AW, England (office). *Telephone:* (20) 7833-9990 (office).

POLING-KEMPES, Lesley Ann, BA; American writer; b. 9 March 1954, Batavia, NY; m. James Kempes 1976, one s. one d. *Education:* University of New Mexico. *Publications:* Harvey Girls: Women Who Opened the West, 1989; Canyon of Remembering, 1996; Valley of Shining Stone: The Story of Abiquiu, 1997, Ghost Ranch: A History 2005. Contributions: Puerta del Sol; Writer's Forum 16; Best of the West 3; Higher Elevations; New Mexico Magazine. *Honours:* Zia Award for Excellence, New Mexico Press Women, 1991. *Address:* PO Box 36, Abiquiu, NM 87510, USA. *Telephone:* (505) 685-4579.

POLITO, Robert, BA, PhD; American writer and poet; *Director, Creative Writing Program, The New School;* b. 27 Oct. 1951, Boston, Mass; m. Kristine M. Harris 1987. *Education:* Boston Coll., Harvard Univ. *Career:* Faculty mem., Harvard University 1976–81, Wellesley College 1981–89, New York University 1990–92; Dir, Creative Writing Program, The New School, New York City 1992–. *Publications:* poetry: Doubles 1995, Hollywood and God 2009; non-fiction: Fireworks: The Lost Writings of Jim Thompson (ed.) 1988, A Reader's Guide to James Morrill's The Changing Light at Sandover 1994, Savage Art: A Biography of Jim Thompson (Nat. Book Critics Circle Award) 1995, At the Titan's Breakfast: Three Essays on Byron's Poetry, The Complete Film Writings of Manny Farber 2009; contributions: newspapers and magazines. *Honours:* National Book Critics Circle Award 1995. *Address:* Creative Writing Program, The New School, 66 West 12th Street, Room 507, New York, NY 10011, USA (office). *Telephone:* (212) 229-5611 (office). *E-mail:* politor@newschool.edu (office). *Website:* www.newschool.edu/writing (office).

POLKINGHORNE, Rev. Canon John Charlton, Kt, KBE, MA, PhD, ScD, FRS; British fmr ecclesiastic and physicist; b. 16 Oct. 1930, Weston-super-Mare; s. of George B. Polkinghorne and Dorothy E. Charlton; m. Ruth I. Martin 1955; two s. one d. *Education:* Perse School, Cambridge, Trinity Coll. Cambridge and Westcott House, Cambridge. *Career:* Commonwealth Fund Fellow Calif. Inst. of Tech. 1955–56; Lecturer, Univ. of Edin. 1956–58; Lecturer, Univ. of Cambridge 1958–65, Reader 1965–68, Prof. of Math. Physics 1968–79; Fellow, Trinity Coll. Cambridge 1954–86; ordained deacon 1981, priest 1982; Curate, St Andrew's, Chesterton 1981–82, St Michael & All Angels, Bedminster 1982–84; Vicar of St Cosmus and St Damian in the Blean 1984–86; Fellow and Dean, Trinity Hall, Cambridge 1986–89, Hon. Fellow 1989–; Pres. Queens' Coll. Cambridge 1989–96, Fellow 1996–, Hon. Fellow 1996–; Canon Theologian, Liverpool Cathedral 1994–2005; Six Preacher, Canterbury Cathedral 1996–2006; mem. Church of England Doctrine Comm. 1989–95, General Synod 1990–2000, Human Genetics Advisory Comm. 1996–99, Human Genetics Comm. 2000–02; Hon. Fellow, St Edmund's Coll., Cambridge 2002. *Publications:* The Analytic S-Matrix (jointly) 1966, The Particle Play 1979, Models of High Energy Processes 1980, The Way the World Is 1983, The Quantum World 1984, One World 1986, Science and Creation 1988, Science and Providence 1989, Rochester Roundabout 1989, Reason and Reality 1991, Science and Christian Belief 1994, Quarks, Chaos and Christianity 1994, Serious Talk 1995, Scientists as Theologians 1996, Beyond Science 1996, Searching for Truth 1996, Belief in God in an Age of Science 1998, Science and Theology 1998, Faith, Science and Understanding 2000, The End of the World and the Ends of God (ed with M. Welker) 2000, Faith in the Living God (with M. Welker) 2001, The Work of Love (ed.) 2001, The God of Hope and the End of the World 2002, Quantum Theory: A Very Short Introduction 2002, Living with Hope 2003, Science and the Trinity 2004, Exploring Reality 2005, Quantum Physics and Theology 2007, From Physicist to Priest 2007, Theology in the Context of Science 2008, Questions of Truth (with N. Beale) 2009, Encountering Scripture 2010, Science and Theology in Quest of Truth 2011. *Honours:* Hon. Prof. of Theoretical Physics, Univ. of Kent 1984–89; Hon. DD (Kent) 1994, (Durham) 1999, (Gen. Theological Seminary) 2010; Hon. DSc (Exeter) 1994, (Leicester) 1995, (Marquette) 2003; Hon. DHum (Hong Kong Baptist) 2006; Templeton Prize 2002. *Address:* Queens' College, Cambridge, CB3 9ET, England (office).

POLKINHORN, Harry, BA, MA, PhD; American writer, poet, editor and translator; b. 3 March 1945, Calexico, Calif.; m. Armida Romero 1986 (divorced 1991); one d. *Education:* University of California, Berkeley, San Diego State University, New York University. *Publications:* Excisions (poems), 1976; Radix Zero (poems), 1981; Volvox (poems), 1981; El Libro de Calo: Pachuco Slang Dictionary, 1983, revised edn as El Libro de Calo: Chicano Slang Dictionary (co-author), 1986; Travelling with Women (fiction), 1983; Anaesthesia (poems), 1985; Bridges of Skin Money (visual poems), 1986; Summary Dissolution (visual poems), 1988; Jerome Rothenberg: A Descriptive Bibliography, 1988; Lorenia La Rosa: A Travelogue (fiction), 1989; Begging for Remission (poems), 1989; Teraphim (visual poems), 1995; Mount Soledad (poems), 1996; Throat Shadow (poems), 1997; Blueshift (poems), 1998; other: Ed. or co-ed. of several publications; contributions: periodicals, including: American Book Review; Afterimage; Poetics Journal; Photostatic; Moody Street Irregulars; Smile; Uno Más Uno; Score; Tempus Fugit; La Poire d'Angoisse; Sink; Kaldron. *Address:* PO Box 927428, San Diego, CA 92192, USA. *E-mail:* hpolkinh@mail.sdsu.edu.

POLLAND, Madelaine Angela, (Frances Adrian); Irish writer; b. 31 May 1918, Kinsale, County Cork. *Publications:* Children of the Red King, 1961; Beorn the Proud, 1962; The White Twilight, 1962; Chuiraquimba and the

Black Robes, 1962; City of the Golden House, 1963; The Queen's Blessing, 1963; Flame over Tara, 1964; Thicker Than Water, 1964; Mission to Cathay, 1965; Queen Without Crown, 1965; Deirdre, 1967; The Little Spot of Bother, 1967, US edn as Minutes of a Murder; To Tell My People, 1968; Stranger in the Hills, 1968; Random Army, 1969, US edn as Shattered Summer; To Kill a King, 1970; Alhambra, 1970; A Family Affair, 1971; Package to Spain, 1971; Daughter to Poseidon, 1972, US edn as Daughter of the Sea; Prince of the Double Axe, 1976; Double Shadow (as Francis Adrian), 1977; Sabrina, 1979; All Their Kingdoms, 1981; The Heart Speaks Many Ways, 1982; No Price Too High, 1984; As It Was in the Beginning, 1987; Rich Man's Flowers, 1990; The Pomegranate House, 1992.

POLLARD, Eve, OBE; British newspaper editor; b. 25 Dec. 1945, d. of Ivor Pollard and Mimi Pollard; m. 1st Barry L. D. Winkleman 1968 (divorced 1978); one d.; m. 2nd Sir Nicholas M. Lloyd 1978; one s. *Career:* Fashion Ed. Honey 1967–68; Fashion Ed. Daily Mirror Magazine 1968–69, top feature writer 1969–70, Women's Ed. Sunday Mirror 1971–81, Ed. (and responsible for launch of Sunday Mirror Magazine) 1988–91; Women's Ed. Observer Magazine 1970–71; Asst Ed. Sunday People 1981–83; Features Ed., Presenter TV-AM 1983–85; Ed., Elle USA (and launched magazine, New York) 1985–86, Sunday magazine, News of the World 1986, You magazine, Mail on Sunday 1986–88, Sunday Express and Sunday Express Magazine 1991–94; f. Wedding Magazine 1999; TV Presenter The Truth About Women; Founder and fmr Chair. Women in Journalism 1995 (now Hon. Pres.); Vice-Chair. WOW (Wellbeing of Women) 2003–; Visiting Fellow, Bournemouth Univ. 1995–; mem. English Tourism Council (fmrly English Tourist Bd) 1993–2000, Competition Comm. Newspaper Takevover Panel 2001–; Ed. of the Year, Focus Awards 1991. *Publications:* Jackie: Biography of Mrs J. K. Onassis 1971, Splash! 1995, Best of Enemies 1996, Double Trouble 1997, Unfinished Business 1998. *Address:* c/o Wellbeing of Women, 27 Sussex Place, Regent's Park, London, NW1 4SP, England.

POLLARD, Jane, (Jane Jackson, Dana James); British writer; b. 22 Nov. 1944, Goole, Yorks., England; m. 3rd Michael Pollard 1992; two s. one d. *Career:* mem. Romantic Novelists Asscn. *Publications include:* Harlyn Tremayne 1984, Doctor in The Andes 1984, Desert Flower 1986, Doctor in New Guinea 1986, Rough Waters 1986, The Marati Legacy 1986, The Eagle and the Sun 1986, The Consul's Daughter 1986, Heart of Glass 1987, Snowfire 1988, Pool of Dreaming 1988, Dark Moon Rising 1989, Love's Ransom 1989, A Tempting Shore 1992, Bay of Rainbows 1993, A Place of Birds 1997, The Iron Road 1999, Eye of the Wind 2001, Tide of Fortune 2004, Dangerous Waters 2006, The Chain Garden 2006, Devil's Prize 2008, Bonded Heart 2009, Heart of Stone 2009; contrib. to periodicals, radio and TV. *Address:* 32 Cogos Park, Comfort Road, Mylor, Falmouth, Cornwall, TR11 5SF, England (home). *Website:* www.janejackson.net (home).

POLLARD, John Richard Thornhill, TD, MA, MLitt; British academic and writer; b. 5 April 1914, Exeter, Devon, England; m. Shirley Holt 1952; one s. three d. *Education:* Hereford High School, The King's School, Ottery-St-Mary, Univ. Coll., Exeter and Exeter Coll., Oxford. *Career:* Classics Master, Herne Bay Coll. 1938–39; Capt., Devonshire Regt and King's African Rifles 1939–45; Asst in Classics, St Andrews Univ. 1948–49; Lecturer in Classics, Univ. Coll. of N Wales, Bangor 1949–66, Sr Lecturer in Classics 1966–88 (retd). *Publications:* Journey to the Styx 1955, Adventure Begins in Kenya 1957, Africa for Adventure 1961, Horace the Minstrel 1961, African Zoo Man 1963, Wolves and Werewolves 1964, Helen of Troy 1965, Seers, Shrines and Sirens 1965, The Long Safari 1967, Virgil: The Aeneid Appreciation (with C. Day-Lewis) 1969, Gilbert Harding by His Friends (contrib.) 1969, Birds in Greek Life and Myth 1977, Divination and Oracles: Greece, Civilization of the Ancient Mediterranean 1988, No County to Compare 1994; contrib. Greek Mythology and Greek Religion, in Encyclopaedia Britannica.

POLLEY, Jacob, MA; British poet, writer and screenwriter; *Lecturer in Creative Writing, University of St Andrews*; b. 1975, Carlisle, Cumbria, England. *Education:* Univ. of Lancaster. *Career:* Writer-in-Residence, The Wordsworth Trust 2002; Visiting Fellow Commoner in Creative Arts, Trinity Coll., Cambridge 2005–07; Lecturer in Creative Writing, Univ. of St Andrews 2010–. *Film:* Flickerman and the Ivory-Skinned Woman (co-author). *Publications:* poetry: Salvage 2000, The Brink 2003, Little Gods 2006; prose: Talk of the Town (Somerset Maugham Award, Soc. of Authors 2010) 2009. *Honours:* Arts Council of England/BBC Radio 4 First Verse Award 2002, Eric Gregory Award, Soc. of Authors 2002, 2010. *Literary Agent:* c/o Peter Straus, Rogers, Coleridge & White Ltd, 20 Powis Mews, London, W11 1JN, England. *Telephone:* (20) 7221-3717. *Fax:* (20) 7229-9084. *Website:* www.rcwlitagency.com. *E-mail:* jake@jacobpolley.com (office). *Website:* jacobpolley.com.

POLLEY, Judith Anne, (Helen Kent, Valentina Luellen, Judith Stewart); British author; b. 15 Sept. 1938, London, England; m. Roy Edward Polley 1959; one s. *Education:* High School, Belgravia and Maida Vale, London. *Career:* founding mem. English Romantic Novelists' Asscn. *Publications include:* To Touch the Stars 1980, Beloved Enemy 1980, Don't Run From Love 1981, Moonshadow 1981, Prince of Deception 1981, Beloved Adversary 1981, Shadow of the Eagle 1982, Silver Salamander 1982, The Wind of Change 1982, The Measure of Love 1983, The Peaceful Homecoming 1983, The Valley of Tears 1984, Moonflower 1984, Elusive Flame of Love 1984, Mistress of Tanglewood 1984, Black Ravenswood 1985, The Lord of Darkness 1985, Devil of Talland 1985, Passionate Pirate 1986, Where the Heart Leads 1986, Love the Avenger 1986, The Devil's Touch 1987, My Lady Melisande 1987, Dark Star 1988, Love and Pride (Book 1) 1988, The Web of Love (Book 2) 1989, Winter Embers, Summer Fire 1991, To Please a Lady 1992, One Love 1993, Hostage of Love 1994; many foreign edns and trans; contributions: Woman's Weekly Library, Woman's Realm, Woman's Weekly Fiction series, Museum of Peace and Solidarity, Samarkand, Uzbekistan.

POLLITT, Katha, BA, MFA; American writer, poet and editor; b. 14 Oct. 1949, New York, NY; m. 1st (divorced); one c.; m. 2nd Steven Lukes 2006. *Education:* Harvard Univ., Columbia Univ. *Career:* Literary Ed., The Nation 1982–84, Contributing Ed. 1986–92, Assoc. Ed. 1992–2001, currently regular columnist; Jr Fellow Council of Humanities, Princeton Univ. 1984; Lecturer, New School for Social Research, New York 1986–90, Poetry Center, 92nd Street YMHA and WYHA, New York 1986–95; contribs to The New Yorker, The Atlantic, The New Republic, Harper's, Glamour, Mother Jones, The New York Times, London Review of Books. *Publications:* Antarctic Traveller (National Book Critics Circle Award 1983) (poetry) 1982, Reasonable Creatures: Essays on Women and Feminism 1994, Subject to Debate: Sense and Dissents on Women, Politics and Culture 2001, Virginity or Death! And Other Social and Political Issues of our Time 2006, Learning to Drive and Other Life Stories 2007, The Mind-Body Problem (poetry) 2009; contrib. to journals and periodicals. *Honours:* Acad. of American Poets I. B. Lavan Younger Poet's Award 1984, NEA grant 1984, Guggenheim Fellowship 1987, Whiting Fellowship 1993, Nat. Magazine Award for Essays and Criticism 1993, for Columns and Commentary 2003. *Address:* The Nation, 33 Irving Place, New York, NY 10003, USA (office). *Telephone:* (212) 209-5400 (office). *Website:* www.thenation.com (office); www.kathapollitt.com.

POLLOCK, Rev. John Charles, BA, MA; British clergyman and writer; b. 9 Oct. 1923, London, England; m. Anne Barrett-Lennard 1949. *Education:* Trinity Coll., Cambridge. *Career:* Asst Master, Wellington Coll., Berkshire 1947–49; Ordained Anglican Deacon 1951, Priest 1952; Curate St Paul's Church, Portman Square, London 1951–53; Rector Horsington, Somerset 1953–58; Chaplain to High Sheriff of Devon 1990–91; Ed. The Churchman (quarterly) 1953–58; mem. English Speaking Union Club. *Publications:* Candidate for Truth 1950, A Cambridge Movement 1953, The Cambridge Seven 1955, Way to Glory: The Life of Havelock of Lucknow 1957, Shadows Fall Apart 1958, The Good Seed 1959, Earth's Remotest End 1960, Hudson Taylor and Maria 1962, Moody Without Sankey 1963, The Keswick Story 1964, The Christians from Siberia 1964, Billy Graham 1966, The Apostle: A Life of Paul (revised edn as Paul the Apostle and The Apostle: a Life of St. Paul) 1969, Victims of the Long March 1970, A Foreign Devil in China: The Life of Nelson Bell 1971 (revised edn 1988), George Whitefield 1972 (revised edns 1982, 2008), Wilberforce (revised edn as Wilberforce: God's Statesman) (Clapham Prize) 1977, Billy Graham: Evangelist to the World 1979, The Siberian Seven 1979, Amazing Grace: John Newton's Story (revised edn as Newton: The Liberator) 1981, The Master: A Life of Jesus (revised edn as Jesus: The Master) 1984, Billy Graham: Highlights of the Story 1984, Shaftesbury: The Poor Man's Earl (revised edn as Shaftesbury: The Reformer) 1985, A Fistful of Heroes: Great Reformers and Evangelists 1988, John Wesley (revised edn as Wesley: The Preacher) 1989, On Fire for God: Great Missionary Pioneers 1990, Fear No Foe: A Brother's Story 1992, Gordon: The Man Behind the Legend 1993, Kitchener: The Road to Omdurman 1998, Kitchener: Saviour of the Nation 2000, Kitchener (comprising The Road to Omdurman and Saviour of the Nation) 2001, The Billy Graham Story 2004, Abolition! Newton the Ex-Slave Trader and Wilberforce the Little Liberator 2007; contrib. to reference works incl. Oxford DNB and religious periodicals. *Honours:* Hon. DLitt (Samford Univ., USA) 2002; Samford Univ. created the John Pollock Award for Christian Biography in his name 1999, Gordon Coll. Clapham Prize, USA 2002. *Address:* 8 Deans Park, South Molton, Devon EX36 3DY, England (home). *Telephone:* (1769) 572104 (home).

POLONSKY, Antony Barry, BA, MA, DPhil; British/American (b. South African) academic and writer; *Albert Abramson Professor of Holocaust Studies, Brandeis University and the United States Holocaust Memorial Museum*; b. 23 Sept. 1940, Johannesburg, S Africa; m. Arlene Polonsky; two c. *Education:* Univ. of the Witwatersrand, Worcester Coll. and St Antony's Coll., Univ. of Oxford, UK. *Career:* Lecturer in East European History, Univ. of Glasgow, UK 1968–70; Lecturer in Int. History, LSE, Univ. of London, UK 1970–89, Prof. 1989–93; Visiting Prof. of East European Jewish History, Brandeis Univ., Waltham, Mass, USA 1992–93, Walter Stern Hilborn Chair in Judaic and Social Studies 1993–99, Chair. Dept of Near Eastern and Judaic Studies 1995–98, Albert Abramson Prof. of Holocaust Studies (held jointly at US Holocaust Memorial Museum and Brandeis Univ.) 1999–; Skirball Visiting Fellow, Oxford Centre for Hebrew and Jewish Studies 1997–98; fmr Visiting Prof., Univ. of Warsaw, Inst. for the Human Sciences, Vienna, Univ. of Cape Town; fmr Sr Assoc. mem. St Antony's Coll., Oxford; Founder Inst. for Polish-Jewish Studies at Oxford; Vice-Pres. American Asscn for Polish-Jewish Studies; fmr mem. Int. Council of the State Museum at Auschwitz; mem. Bd Board of Deputies of British Jews for six years, fmr mem. of its Yad Vashem Holocaust Memorial Cttee and Chair. Academic and Educational Sub-cttee; mem. Int. Advisory Bd Mordekhai Anielewicz Centre for Jewish Studies, Univ. of Warsaw, Jewish Univ. in Moscow, Int. Advisory Council of Sefer, the Center for Univ. Teaching of Jewish Civilization in Moscow; mem. Exec. Cttee Nat. Polish American-Jewish American Task Force; Assoc., Ukrainian Research Inst., Harvard Univ.; Jt Chair. Cttee to publish in English the post-war testimonies collected by the Jewish Historical Comm. in Poland; Ed.-in-Chief of Polin: Studies in Polish Jewry; Ed. The Library of Holocaust

Testimonies; mem. Editorial Advisory Bd Simon Dubnow Inst. Yearbook; mem. Editorial Bd of Cen. Europe; fmr mem. Inter-university film consortium, London; has appeared frequently on radio and TV as a commentator on Polish and Jewish matters. *Films:* producer and director of a 55 minute documentary on Fascism, consultant for documentary series, The Struggles for Poland. *Publications:* Politics in Independent Poland 1972, The Little Dictators – A History of Eastern Europe since 1918 1975 (Japanese edn 1993), The Great Powers and the Polish Question 1941–1945 1976, The History of Poland since 1863 (co-author) 1981, The Beginnings of Communist Rule in Poland 1981; editor: Abraham Lewin's A Cup of Tears: A Diary of the Warsaw Ghetto (Joseph and Edith Sunlight Literary Prize 1989, Prize of the Jewish Book Council of America in the Holocaust section 1990) 1988 , 'My Brother's Keeper?' Recent Polish Debates about the Holocaust 1990, Jews in Eastern Poland and the USSR (co-ed. with Norman Davies) 1991, From Shtetl to Socialism: Studies from Polin 1994, Contemporary Jewish Writing in Poland: An Anthology 2001, The Neighbours Respond: The Controversy over the Jedwabne Massacre in Poland (with Joanna Michlic) 2004, The Jews in Russia and Poland, Vol. 1 2009, Vol. 2 2010, Polin: Studies in Polish Jewry (Ed.-in-Chief of 22 vols, Vol. 17 won Nat. Jewish Book Award in the category of Eastern European Studies 1999, subsequent vol. was runner-up in same section 2006); numerous articles on Polish and Jewish history. *Honours:* Hon. Research Fellow, Univ. Coll., London; Kt's Cross, Order of Merit (Poland) for "outstanding services to studies in Polish Jewry" 1999, Officer's Cross 2011; Officer's Cross, Order of Ind. Lithuania 2011; Dr hc (Univ. of Warsaw) 2010; Charles Payne History Prize 1958, Abe Bailey Memorial Essay Prize 1959, Rhodes Scholarship (Transvaal) 1960, Rafael Scharf Award for outstanding achievement in preserving and making known the heritage of Polish Jewry 2006, Ina Levine Invitational Fellowship, US Holocaust Memorial Museum 2007, Gantz-Zahler Prize in Nonfiction Publishing, Foundation of Jewish Culture 2007, Oskar Halecki Prize, Polish American Historical Asscn 2008, Kulczycki Prize, Asscn of Slavic, Eastern European and Eurasian Studeis 2011. *Address:* Brandeis University, Lown 308, 415 South Street, Waltham, MA 02454-9110, USA (office). *Telephone:* (781) 736-2980 (office). *Fax:* (781) 736-2070 (office). *E-mail:* polonsky@brandeis.edu (office). *Website:* www.brandeis.edu (office).

PONDER, Patricia (see Maxwell, Patricia Anne)

PONIATOWSKA, Elena; Mexican writer and journalist; b. 19 May 1932, Paris, France. *Career:* mem. exec. bd, Int. Center for Writing and Translation, Univ. of California at Irvine. *Publications include:* Hasta no verte Jesús mío 1969, Ay vida, no me mereces de noche vienes 1974, Quendo Diego te Abreza Quiela 1978, Fuerte es el silencio 1982, Lilus Kikus 1982, Domingo siete 1983, Dear Diego 1986, Nada, nadie: Las voces del temblor 1988, Compañeros de México: Women Photograph Women 1990, Todo México 1990, Frida Kahlo: The Camera Seduced 1992, Luz y luna, las lunitas 1996, Tinisima 1996, Guerrero vieja 1997, Todo empezó el domingo 1998, Octavio Paz, las palabras del árbol 1998, Paseo de la Reforma 1998, El Niño: Children of the Streets, Mexico City 1999, La casa en Mango Street 1999, Cuentos Méxicanos 1999, La noche de Tlatelolco 1999, Las soldaderas 2000, La piel del cielo 2001, Here's To You Jesusa 2001, Cartas de Alvaro Mutis a Elena Poniatowska 2002, Tlapaleria 2003, El tren pasa primero 2006, Amanecer en el Zócano: Los 50 días que confrontaram a México 2007. *Honours:* Nat. Mexican Award for Journalism 1979, Premio Alfguara 2001, Lifetime Achievement Award, Int. Women's Media Foundation 2006, Premio Rómulo Gallegos 2007. *Address:* International Center for Writing and Translation, School of Humanities, 172 Humanities Instruction Building, University of California, Irvine, CA 92697-3380, USA (office).

PONOMAREVA, Ksenya Yuryevna; Russian journalist; b. 19 Sept. 1961, Moscow; m.; one s. one d. *Education:* Moscow State Univ. *Career:* school-teacher 1984–86, teacher of Slavic languages, Diplomatic Acad. 1986–88; on staff, Kommersant Publrs 1988–95, Deputy Ed. Kommersaut Daily 1992–93; Ed.-in-Chief Revisor (magazine) 1993–95; First Deputy Dir Information and Political Broadcasting, Russian Public TV 1995–96, concurrently gen. producer of information programmes 1996–97, mem. Bd of Dirs Russian Public TV 1996–, Dir-Gen. 1997–98, resigned in protest against political activity of broadcaster S. Dorenko; Deputy Head of election campaign of Vladimir Putin. *Address:* Akademika Koroleva str. 12, 127000 Moscow, Russia (office). *Telephone:* (495) 217-98-38 (office); (495) 215-18-95 (office).

POOLE, Josephine (see Helyar, Jane Penelope Josephine)

POOLE, Julian (see May, Stephen James)

POOLE, Margaret (Peggy) Barbara, (Terry Roche, Margaret Thornton); British broadcaster, poet and writer; b. 8 March 1925, Petham, Kent, England; m. Reginald Poole 1949 (died 1994); three d. *Education:* Benenden School. *Career:* co-organizer Jabberwocky 1968–86; Producer-Presenter First Heard poetry programme, BBC Radio Merseyside 1976–88; Poetry Consultant, BBC Network Northwest 1988–96; contributor, Writers' News; tutor, Writers' News Home Study Poetry Course; adjudicator, Writers' News Competitions, Southport Open Poetry Competition 2004; mem. Poetry Soc., Soc. of Women Writers and Journalists. *Recordings include:* album: Polishing Pans 2003. *Publications:* Never a Put-up Job 1970, Cherry Stones and Other Poems 1983, No Wilderness in Them 1984, Midnight Walk 1986, Hesitations 1990, Trusting the Rainbow 1994, From the Tide's Edge 1999, Polishing Pans 2001, Selected Poems 2003; editor (anthologies): Windfall (co-ed.) 1994, Poet's England: Cumbria 1995, Marigolds Grow Wild on Platforms 1996, Perceptions 2000; contrib. to various anthologies, children's anthologies, other publs. *Honours:* first prize Waltham Forest Competition 1987, winner Lancaster Litfest 1987, 1991, 2002, first prize Southport Open 1989, winner LACE Competition 1992, winner Sandburg-Livesey Award 1999. *Address:* 36 Hilbre Court, West Kirby, Wirral, Merseyside CH48 3JU, England (home). *Telephone:* (151) 625-8957. *E-mail:* peggypoole@hilbrecourt.fsnet.co.uk.

POOLE, Richard Arthur, MA; British novelist, poet, translator and literary critic; b. 1 Jan. 1945, Yorks., England; m. Sandra Pauline Smart 1970; one s. *Education:* Univ. Coll. of N Wales. *Career:* Tutor in English Literature, Coleg Harlech 1970–2001; Ed. Poetry Wales, 1992–96; Fellow, Welsh Acad. *Publications:* Goings and Other Poems 1978, Words Before Midnight 1981, Richard Hughes, Novelist (literary biog.) 1987, Natural Histories 1989, Autobiographies and Explorations 1994, That Fool July 2003, Jewel and Thorn (novel) 2005, The Brass Key (novel) 2006, The Iron Angel (novel) 2007; contrib. to many reviews and journals. *Honours:* Fellow, Welsh Acad. *Website:* www.richardpoole.net.

POPE, Pamela Mary Alison; British writer; b. 26 April 1931, Lowestoft, Suffolk, England; m. Ronald Pope 1954; two d. *Career:* mem. Romantic Novelists Asscn; Society of Women Writers and Journalists. *Publications:* The Magnolia Seige, 1982; The Candleberry Tree, 1982; Eden's Law, 1983; The Wind in the East, 1989; The Rich Pass By, 1990; Neither Angels Nor Demons, 1992; A Collar of Jewels, 1994. Contributions: Good Housekeeping; Woman; Woman's Realm; Vanity Fair; True; Loving; Hampshire Magazine; Hampshire Life; London Evening News.

POPESCU, Dumitru Radu; Romanian writer and editor; *Director General, Editura Academiei Române;* b. 19 Aug. 1935, Păusa Village, Bihor Co. *Education:* Colls of Medicine and Philology, Cluj. *Career:* reporter, literary magazine Steaua 1956–69; Ed.-in-Chief literary magazine Tribuna 1969–82, Contemporanul 1982; Dir Gen., Editurii Academiei Române 2006–; Alt. mem. Cen. Cttee Romanian CP 1968–89, mem. 1979–90; Chair. Romanian Writers' Union 1980–90; Corresp. mem. Romanian Acad. 1997–; in custody Jan. 1990. *Publications:* collections of short stories: Fuga (Flight) 1958, Fata de la miazăzi (A Girl from the South) 1964, Somnul pământului (The Earth's Sleep) 1965, Dor (Longing) 1966, Umbrela de soare (The Parasol) 1967, Prea mic pentru un război așa de mare (Too Little for Such a Big War) 1969, Duios Anastasia trecea (Tenderly Anastasia Passed) 1967, Leul albastru (The Blue Lion) 1981, The Ice Bridge 1980, the Lame Hare 1981, God in the Kitchen 1994, Truman Capote and Nicolae 1995; novels: Zilele săptămînii (Weekdays) 1959, Vara oltenilor (The Oltenians' Summer) 1964, F 1964, Vînătoarea regală (Royal Hunt) 1973, O bere pentru calul meu (A Beer for My Horse) 1974, Ploile de dincolo de vreme (Rains beyond Time) 1976, Împăratul norilor (Emperor of the Clouds) 1976; plays: Vara imposibilei iubiri (The Summer of Impossible Love) 1966, Vis (Dream) 1968, Acești îngeri triști (Those Sad Angels) 1969, Pisica în noaptea Anului nou (Cat on the New Year's Eve) 1970, Pasărea Shakespeare (The Shakespeare Bird) 1973, Rezervația de pelicani (The Pelican Reservation) 1983, Iepurele schiop (The Lame Rabbit) 1980, Orasul îngerilor (The Angel's City) 1985, Powder Mill 1989, The Bride with False Eyelashes 1994, Love is like a Scab 1995; poems: Cîinele de fosfor (The Phosphorus Dog) 1981; essays: Virgule (Commas) 1978, Galaxy 1994, Ophelia's Complex 1998. *Honours:* Prize of the Writers' Union 1964, 1969, 1974, 1977, 1980, Prize of the Romanian Acad. 1970, Grand Prize for Balkan Writers 1998, Writers' Union Prize 1994, Writers' Asscn of Bucharest Prize 1997, Grand Prize Camil Petrescu 1995. *Address:* Editura Academiei Române, 050711 Bucharest 5, Calea 13 Septembrie nr. 13, Romania (office). *Telephone:* (21) 3188146 (office). *Fax:* (21) 3182444 (office). *Website:* www.ear.ro (office).

PORAD, Francine Joy, BFA; American poet and painter; b. 3 Sept. 1929, Seattle, Wash.; m. Bernard L. Porad 1949; three s. three d. *Education:* University of Washington. *Career:* Ed., Brussels Sprout haiku journal, 1988–95, Red Moon Anthologies, 1996; mem. Asscn of International Renku, Haiku Society of America (Pres. 1993–95), National League of American Pen Women. *Publications:* many poetry books, including: Pen and Inklings, 1986; After Autumn Rain, 1987; Free of Clouds, 1989; Round Renga Round, 1990; A Mural of Leaves, 1991; Joy is My Middle Name, 1993; Waterways, 1995; Extended Wings, 1996; Fog Lifting, 1997; Let's Count the Trees (edited by Le Roy Gorman), 1998; Cur*rent, Linked Haiku, 1998; Other Rens, 2000; The Perfect Worry-stone, 2000; Other Rens, Book 2 plus Book 3, 2000; Trio of Wrens, 2000; To Find the Words (anthology, co-ed.); contributions: Haiku journals world-wide. *Honours:* Cicada Chapbook Award 1990, International Tanka Award 1991, 1992, 1993, First Prize, Poetry Society of Japan International Tanka Competition 1993, Haiku Society of America Merit Book Award 1994, 2000, Haiku Oregon Pen Women Award 1995. *Address:* 6944 SE 33rd, Mercer Island, WA 98040, USA. *E-mail:* poradf@aol.com.

PORRITT, Sir Jonathon Espie, 2nd Bt, cr. 1963, CBE, BA; British environmentalist and writer; *Founding Director, Forum for the Future;* b. 6 July 1950, London; s. of the late Lord Porritt, 11th Gov.-Gen. of NZ; m. Sarah Staniforth 1986; two d. *Education:* Eton Coll. and Magdalen Coll. Oxford. *Career:* trained as a barrister; English teacher, St Clement Danes Grammar School (later Burlington Danes School), Shepherd's Bush, West London 1975–84; Head of English, Burlington Danes School, London 1980–84; Chair. Ecology Party 1979–80, 1982–84; parl. cand. at gen. elections in 1979, 1983; Dir Friends of the Earth 1984–90; Founder Dir Forum for the Future 1996–; Chair. UK Sustainable Devt Comm. 2000–09; Co-Dir Prince of Wales Business and Environment Programme; mem. Bd South West Regional Devt Agency

2000, Wessex Water; adviser to many bodies on environmental matters, as well as to individuals, including Prince Charles and Chief Exec. of Marks & Spencer; Chancellor, Keele Univ. 2012–; mem. Advisory Bd BBC Wildlife magazine; Patron Optimum Population Trust. *Publications:* Seeing Green: The Politics of Ecology Explained 1984, Friends of the Earth Handbook 1987, The Coming of the Greens 1988, Save the Earth (ed.) 1990, Where on Earth are We Going? 1991, Captain Eco (for children) 1991, The 'Reader's Digest' Good Beach Guide 1994, Liberty and Sustainability: Where One Person's Freedom is Another's Nuisance 1995, Playing Safe: Science and the Environment (Prospects for Tomorrow) 2000, Making the Net Work: Sustainable Development in a Digital Society 2004, Capitalism: As if the World Matters 2005 (revised edn 2007). *Address:* 9 Imperial Square, Cheltenham, Glos., GL50 1QB; 9 Lypiatt Terrace, Cheltenham, Glos., GL50 2SX, England (home). *Telephone:* (1242) 262737 (office). *Fax:* (1242) 262757 (office). *E-mail:* a.paintin@forumforthefuture.org (office). *Website:* www.jonathonporritt.com.

PORTER, Andrew Brian, MA; British music critic; b. 26 Aug. 1928, Cape Town, South Africa; s. of Andrew Ferdinand and Vera Sybil Porter (née Bloxham). *Education:* Diocesan Coll., Rondebosch, Cape Town, Univ. Coll., Oxford. *Career:* music critic, The Financial Times 1950–74; Ed. The Musical Times 1960–67; music critic, The New Yorker 1972–92, The Observer 1992–97, Times Literary Supplement 1997–2010; Visiting Fellow, All Souls Coll., Oxford 1973–74; Bloch Prof., Univ. of Calif., Berkeley 1981; Corresp. mem. American Musicological Soc. 1993. *Opera:* librettos for The Tempest 1985, The Song of Majnun 1991 and numerous trans. *Publications:* A Musical Season 1974, Wagner's Ring 1976, Music of Three Seasons 1974–77 1978, Music of Three More Seasons 1977–80 1981, Musical Events: A Chronicle 1980–1983 1987, Musical Events: A Chronicle 1983–1986 1989, Verdi's Macbeth: A Sourcebook (ed. with David Rosen) 1984, A Music Critic Remembers 2000; contrib. to Music and Letters, Musical Quarterly, Musical Times, Proceedings of the Royal Musical Association, Atti del Congresso Internazionale di Studi Verdiani. *Honours:* ASCAP–Deems Taylor Award 1975, 1978, 1982, Nat. Music Theater Award 1988, Words on Music: Essays in Honour of Andrew Porter on the Occasion of His 75th Birthday (co-ed. by David Rosen and Claire Brook) 2003. *Address:* 9 Pembroke Walk, London, W8 6PQ, England (home).

PORTER, Anna Maria, OC, MA; Canadian (b. Hungarian) publishing executive; b. (Anna Szigethy), Budapest; d. of Steven and Maria (née Racz) Szigethy; m. Julian Porter 1971; two d. *Education:* Univ. of Canterbury, Christchurch, NZ. *Career:* mem. staff Cassell and Co., UK, Collier Macmillan Ltd, London 1967–69, Toronto 1970; Pres. and Publr McClelland-Bantam Ltd (Seal Books) until 1982, Pres. 1987–92; Publr, CEO and Dir Key Porter Books Ltd 1982–2005; Chair. Doubleday Canada 1986–91; Dir Key Publrs, Alliance Communications Ltd, Young Naturalists Foundation, Imperial Life Assurance Co., People's Jewelry Ltd, Conf. Bd of Canada, WWF—World Wide Fund for Nature, Canada; mem. Advisory Bd Schulich School of Business; mem. Soulpepper Theatre Company Advisory Council, Interval House Capital Campaign Cttee; mem. Bd of Govs York Univ. 2004–; mem. Asscn of Canadian Publrs, Asscn for Export of Canadian Books, UNICEF (advisory), Information Highway Council. *Publications:* Hidden Agenda 1985, Mortal Sins 1987, The Bookfair Murders 1997, The Storyteller (Canadian Authors' Asscn/Birks Family Foundation Award) 2001, Kasztner's Train 2007. *Honours:* Order of Ontario 2003; Dr hc (Ryerson Univ.) (St. Mary's Univ.), (Univ. of Toronto), (Law Soc. of Upper Canada). *Address:* c/o Douglas and McIntyre, Suite 500, 720 Bathurst Street, Toronto, ON M5S 2R4, Canada (office). *Website:* www.dmplbooks.com (office).

PORTER, Bernard John, MA, PhD; British historian and writer; *Professor Emeritus of Modern History, University of Newcastle*; b. 5 Feb. 1941, Essex, England; m. Deirdre O'Hara 1972 (divorced 1996); one s. two d.; partner, Kajsa Ohrlander. *Education:* Corpus Christi Coll., Cambridge. *Career:* Fellow, Corpus Christi Coll., Cambridge 1966–68; Lecturer, Univ. of Hull 1968–78, Sr Lecturer 1978–87, Reader 1987–92; Prof. of Modern History, Univ. of Newcastle 1992–2002, Prof. Emer. 2002–; Visiting Prof., Yale Univ., USA 1999–2000, Univ. of Sydney, Australia 2006. *Publications:* Critics of Empire: British Radical Attitudes to Colonialism in Africa 1896–1914 1968, The Lion's Share: A Short History of British Imperialism 1850–1970 1976, The Refugee Question in Mid-Victorian Politics 1979, Britain, Europe and the World 1850–1982: Delusions of Grandeur 1983, The Origins of the Vigilant State: The London Metropolitan Police Special Branch Before the First World War 1987, Plots and Paranoia: A History of Political Espionage in Britain 1790–1988 1989, Britannia's Burden: The Political Development of Britain 1857–1990 1994, The Absent-Minded Imperialists 2004, Empire and Super-empire 2006, The Battle of the Styles 2011; contrib. to London Review of Books and to professional journals. *Honours:* Morris D. Forkosch Prize, American Historical Asscn 2005. *Address:* 29 Salisbury Street, Hull, HU5 3HA, England (home); Kantarellvägen 26, 12263 Enskede, Sweden (home). *Telephone:* (1482) 494415 (Hull) (home); (8) 649-4379 (Enskede) (home). *E-mail:* bernard.porter@kajsa.karoo.co.uk (home).

PORTER, Brian Ernest, BSc, PhD, FRHistS; British academic and writer; b. 5 Feb. 1928, Seasalter, Kent, England. *Education:* LSE. *Career:* Lecturer in Political Science, University of Khartoum, 1963–65; Lecturer, 1965–71, Senior Lecturer in International Politics, 1971–85, University College, Aberystwyth; Acting Vice-Counsel, Muscat, 1967; Hon. Lecturer in International Relations, University of Kent, Canterbury, 1984–; mem. Royal Institute of International Affairs. *Publications:* Britain and the Rise of Communist China, 1967; The Aberystwyth Papers: International Politics 1919–1969 (ed.), 1972; The Reason of States (co-author), 1982; Home Fires and Foreign Fields: British Social and Military Experience in the First World War (co-author), 1985; The Condition of States (co-author), 1991; Martin Wight's International Theory: The Three Traditions (co-ed.), 1991. *Honours:* Gladstone Memorial Essay Prize, 1956; Mrs Foster Watson Memorial Prize, 1962–67.

PORTER, Burton Frederick, BA, PhD; American academic and writer; *Professor of Philosophy, Western New England College, Springfield*; b. 22 June 1936, New York, NY; m. 1st Susan Jane Porter 1966 (divorced 1974); one d.; m. 2nd Barbara Taylor Metcalf 1980; one s. one step-d. *Education:* Univ. of Maryland, Univ. of Oxford, England and St Andrews Univ., Scotland. *Career:* Asst Prof., Univ. of Maryland Overseas Division, London 1966–69; Assoc. Prof., King's Coll., Wilkes-Barre, PA 1969–71; Dept Chair and Prof. of Philosophy, Russell Sage Coll., Troy, NY 1971–87; Head Humanities and Communications Dept, Drexel Univ. 1987–91; Dean of Arts and Sciences 1991–99, Western New England Coll., Springfield, MA, Prof. of Philosophy 1999–; mem. American Philosophical Asscn. *Publications:* Deity and Morality 1968, Philosophy: A Literary and Conceptual Approach 1974, Personal Philosophy: Perspectives on Living 1976, The Good Life: Alternatives in Ethics 1980, Reasons for Living: A Basic Ethics 1988, Religion and Reason 1993, The Voice of Reason 2001, Philosophy Through Fiction and Film 2003, The Head and the Heart 2006; contrib. to professional journals. *Honours:* Outstanding Educator of America 1973. *Address:* c/o Department of Communications and Humanities, Western New England College, Springfield, MA 01119 (office); 72 Belchertown Road, Amherst, MA 01002, USA (home). *Telephone:* (413) 782-1760 (office); (413) 256-4524 (home). *E-mail:* bporter@wnec.edu (office); bfporter@rcn.com (home).

PORTER, Joshua Roy; British theologian and writer; b. 1921, England. *Career:* Fellow, Chaplain and Tutor, Oriel Coll., Oxford and Univ. Lecturer in Theology, Univ. of Oxford 1949–62; Canon and Prebendary of Wightring, Chichester Cathedral and Theological Lecturer 1965–88, mem. Wiccamical Canon and Prebendary of Exceit 1988–2001; Prof. of Theology and Head of Dept, Univ. of Exeter 1962–86, Dean, Faculty of Arts 1968–71; mem. Soc. for Old Testament Study (Pres. 1983), Soc. of Biblical Literature, Folklore Soc. (Pres. 1976–79), Prayer Book Soc. (Vice-Chair. 1987–96). *Publications:* Eight Oxford Poets (with J. Heath-Stubbs and S. Keyes) 1941, Poetry from Oxford in War-Time (with W. Bell) 1944, World in the Heart 1944, Promise and Fulfilment (with F.F. Bruce) 1963, Moses and Monarchy 1963, The Extended Family in the Old Testament 1967, A Source Book of the Bible for Teachers (with R.C. Walton) 1970, Proclamation and Presence (ed. with J.I. Durham) 1970, The Non-Juring Bishops 1973, The Journey to the Other World (with H.R.E. Davidson) 1975, The Book of Leviticus 1976, Animals in Folklore (ed. with W.D.M. Russell) 1978, The Monarchy, the Crown and the Church 1978, Tradition and Interpretation (with G.W. Anderson) 1979, A Basic Introduction to the Old Testament (with R.C. Walton) 1980, Folklore Studies in the Twentieth Century (co-ed.) 1980, Divination and Oracles (with M. Loewe and C. Blacker) 1981, The Folklore of Ghosts (with H.R.E. Davidson) 1981, Israel's Prophetic Tradition (co-author) 1982, Tracts for Our Times (co-author) 1983, The Hero in Tradition and Folklore (with C. Blacker) 1984, Arabia and the Gulf: From Traditional Society to Modern States (with I. Netton) 1986, Schöpfung und Befreiung (co-author) 1989, Synodical Government in the Church of England 1990, Christianity and Conservatism (co-author) 1990, Oil of Gladness 1993, Boundaries and Thresholds (with H.R.E. Davidson) 1993, World Mythology 1993, The Illustrated Guide to the Bible 1995, Jesus Christ: The Jesus of History, the Christ of Faith 1999, The First and Second Prayer Books of Edward VI (ed.) 1999, The Lost Bible 2001, Supernatural Enemies (with H.R.E. Davidson) 2001, The New Illustrated Companion to the Bible 2003, Bell of Chichester (with Paul Foster) 2004. *Address:* 36 Theberton Street, Barnsbury, London, N1 OQX, England (home).

PORTIS, Charles McColl, BA; American writer; b. 28 Dec. 1933, El Dorado, AR. *Education:* Univ. of Arkansas. *Publications:* fiction: Norwood 1966, True Grit 1968, The Dog of the South 1979, Masters of Atlantis 1985, Gringos 1991. *Address:* 7417 Kingwood, Little Rock, AR 72207, USA (home).

PORTWOOD, Nigel, BEng, MBA; British publishing executive; *CEO, Oxford University Press*; m.; two c. *Education:* Cambridge Univ., INSEAD. *Career:* joined Strategy & Devt Group, Pearson plc 1995, Dir of Strategy and Development 1997–99, Pres. and CEO, Pearson Education Europe, Middle East and Africa 1999–2002, Chief Financial Officer, Penguin Group 2003–08, Exec. Vice Pres., Global Operations 2008–09; CEO, Oxford University Press 2009–. *Address:* Oxford University Press, Great Clarendon Street, Oxford, OX2 6DP, England (office). *Telephone:* (1865) 556767 (office). *Fax:* (1865) 556646 (office). *Website:* www.oup.co.uk (office).

POSNER, Gerald, BA, JD; American attorney and writer; b. 20 May 1954, San Francisco, CA; m. Trisha D. Levene 1984. *Education:* Univ. of California at Berkeley, Hastings College of Law. *Career:* Chief Investigative Reporter, The Daily Beast; mem. National Writers Union, Authors' Guild, PEN. *Publications:* Mengele: The Complete Story 1986, Warlords of Crime 1988, Bio-Assassins 1989, Hitler's Children 1991, Case Closed (Pulitzer Prize for History 1994) 1993, Citizen Perot 1996, Killing the Dream 1998, Motown 2002, Why America Slept: The Failure to Prevent 9/11 2003, Secrets of the Kingdom: The Inside Story of the Saudi-U.S. Connection 2005, Miami Babylon: Crime, Wealth, and Power—A Dispatch from the Beach 2009;

contributions: New York Times, New Yorker, Chicago Tribune, US News & World Report, Talk Magazine. *E-mail:* feedback@posner.com (office). *Website:* www.thedailybeast.com/author/gerald-posner; www.posner.com.

POSTE, George, CBE, BVSC, PhD, FRS, FRCVS, FRCPath; American (b. British) research scientist, business executive and academic; *Del E. Webb Distinguished Professor of Biology, Regents Professor and Director, Biodesign Institute, Arizona State University*; b. 30 April 1944, Polegate, Sussex, England; s. of the late John H. Poste and of Kathleen B. Poste; m. Linda Suhler 1992; one s. two d. *Education:* Bristol Univ. *Career:* Lecturer, Royal Postgraduate Medical School, Univ. of London 1969–72; Sr Lecturer 1974; Assoc. Prof. of Experimental Pathology, State Univ. of New York (SUNY), Buffalo 1972–74, Prin. Cancer Research Scientist and Prof. of Cell and Molecular Biology 1975–80; Vice-Pres. and Dir of Research, Smith Kline & French Labs, Philadelphia, Pa 1980–83, Vice-Pres. Research and Devt Technologies 1983–86, Vice-Pres. Worldwide Research and Preclinical Devt 1987–88, Pres. Research and Devt 1988–89, Exec. Vice-Pres. Research and Devt SmithKline Beecham Pharmaceuticals 1989–91, Pres. Research and Devt 1991–97, Chief Science and Tech. Officer 1997–99; CEO Health Tech. Networks 2000–; Partner, Care Capital, Princeton, NJ 2000–; Research Prof., Univ. of Pennsylvania 1981–, Univ. of Texas Medical Center 1986–; Fleming Fellow, Lincoln Coll. Oxford 1995; William Pitt Fellow, Pembroke Coll. Cambridge 1996–; Distinguished Visiting Fellow, Hoover Inst., Stanford Univ. 2000–; Del E. Webb Distinguished Prof. of Biology and Dir Biodesign Inst., Arizona State Univ. 2003–, Regents Prof. 2006–; Chair. (non-exec.) Orchid Biosciences, Princeton NJ; mem. Bd of Dirs Exelixis, Monsanto; mem. Defense Science Bd of US Dept of Defense, Chair. Task Force on Bioterrorism; mem. NAS Working Group on Defense Against Bioweapons; mem. Human Genetics Advisory Cttee 1996–; mem. Bd of Govs Center for Molecular Medicine and Genetics, Stanford Univ. 1992–; mem. Alliance for Ageing 1992–97; Jt Ed. Cell Surface Reviews 1976–83, New Horizons in Therapeutics 1984–; mem. Council on Foreign Relations 2004–; Fellow, Royal Coll. of Veterinary Surgeons. *Publications:* numerous reviews and papers in learned journals. *Honours:* Hon. FRCP 1993; Hon. Fellow, Univ. Coll. London 1993; Hon. DSc 1987, (Sussex) 1999; Hon. LLD (Bristol) 1995, (Dundee) 1998; Albert Einstein Award, Global Business Leadership Council 2006, SCRIP Lifetime Achievement Award 2009. *Address:* The Biodesign Institute, Arizona State University, PO Box 875001, Tempe, AZ 85287-5001, USA (office). *Telephone:* (480) 727-8662 (office). *Fax:* (480) 965-2765 (office). *E-mail:* george.poste@asu.edu (office). *Website:* www.biodesign.org (office).

POSTER, Jem, MA, PhD; British poet, novelist, professor of creative writing and fmr archaeologist; *Professor of Creative Writing, University of Aberystwyth*; b. 3 Nov. 1949, Cambridge, England; m.; two c. *Education:* Univs of Cambridge and Nottingham. *Career:* Prof. of Creative Writing, Univ. of Aberystwyth 2003–; mem. Welsh Acad. *Publications:* poetry: Brought to Light 2001; novels: Courting Shadows 2002, Rifling Paradise 2006; criticism: The Thirties Poets 1993. *Address:* Department of English, University of Aberystwyth, Aberystwyth, Ceredigion, SY23 3DY, Wales (office). *Telephone:* (1970) 621578 (office). *E-mail:* jem.poster@aber.ac.uk (office).

POTAPOV, Alexander Serafimovich, CandPhil; Russian journalist; *Editor-in-Chief, Trud;* b. 6 Feb. 1936, Oktyabry, Kharkov Region, Ukraine; m.; one s. *Education:* Vilnius State Univ., Lithuania. *Career:* contrib. Leninskaya Smena (newspaper) 1958–66; Head of Dept, Deputy Ed.-in-Chief Belgorodskaya Pravda (newspaper) 1966–73; Head of Dept Belgorod Regional Exec. CPSU Cttee 1973–75; Ed. Belgorodskaya Pravda 1975–76; instructor CPSU Cen. Cttee 1976–78, 1981–85; Ed.-in-Chief Trud (Labour) newspaper 1985–; People's Deputy of Russian Fed., mem. Cttee of Supreme Soviet of Russian Fed. on Problems of Glasnost and Human Rights –1993. *Address:* Trud, Nastas'yinsky per. 4, 103792 Moscow, Russia (office). *Telephone:* (495) 299-39-06 (office). *Fax:* (495) 299-47-40 (office). *E-mail:* letter@trud.ru (office). *Website:* www.trud.ru (office).

POTTER, Jeremy Ronald, MA; British writer and publisher; b. 25 April 1922, London, England; m. 1950, one s. one d. *Education:* Queen's College, Oxford. *Publications:* Good King Richard?, 1983; Pretenders, 1986; Independent Television in Britain, Vol. 3: Politics and Control 1968–80, 1989 and Vol. 4: Companies and Programmes 1968–80, 1990; Tennis and Oxford, 1994. Fiction: Hazard Chase, 1964; Death in Office, 1965; Foul Play, 1967; The Dance of Death, 1968; A Trail of Blood, 1970; Going West, 1972; Disgrace and Favour, 1975; Death in the Forest, 1977; The Primrose Hill Murder, 1992; The Mystery of the Campden Wonder, 1995.

POTTS, Robert; British writer. *Education:* Univ. of Oxford. *Career:* fmrly Politics Ed. TLS; Poetry Critic, The Guardian; judge, Geoffrey Faber Memorial Prize 1998; Jt Ed. Poetry Review 2002–05. *Publications:* contrib. to The Times, The Observer, Atlantic Monthly, London Magazine, Literary Review, Scribners' British Writers' Series, BBC Radio London. *Address:* c/o The Guardian, Kings Place, 90 York Way, London, N1 9GU, England. *E-mail:* review@observer.co.uk. *Website:* www.guardian.co.uk.

POULIN, Gabrielle, MA, DLitt; Canadian writer and poet; b. 21 June 1929, St Prosper, PQ. *Education:* University of Montréal, University of Sherbrooke. *Career:* Writer-in-Residence, Ottawa Public Library 1988; mem. Union des écrivaines et des écrivains québécois. *Publications:* Les Miroirs d'un poète: Image et reflets de Paul Éluard 1969, Cogne la caboche 1979, English trans. as All the Way Home 1984, L'age de l'interrogation 1937–52 1980, Un cri trop grand (novel) 1980, Les Mensonges d'Isabelle (novel) 1983, La couronne d'oubli (novel) 1990, Petites fugues pour une saison sèche (poems) 1991, Nocturnes de l'oeil (poems) 1993, Le livre de déraison (novel) 1994, Mon père aussi était horloger (poems) 1996, Qu'est-ce qui passe ici si tard? (novel) 1998, La vie l'écriture (memoir) 2000, Ombres et lueurs (poems) 2003; contributions: periodicals. *Honours:* Swiss Embassy Prize 1967, 11 Arts Council of Canada Grant 1968–83, 1985, Champlain Literary Prize 1979, Carleton Literary Prize, Ottawa 1983, Alliance Française Literary Prize 1984, Salon du Livre de Toronto Literary Prize 1994. *Address:* 1997 Avenue Quincy, Ottawa, ON K1J 6B4, Canada. *E-mail:* gabriellepoilin@rogers.com (home).

POULIN, Jacques; Canadian writer; b. 23 Sept. 1937, Saint-Gédéon-de-Beauce, QC. *Education:* Université Laval. *Career:* mem. Union des écrivaines et des écrivains québécois. *Publications:* Mon cheval pour un royaume (trans. as My Horse for a Kingdom) 1967, Jimmy 1969, La Coeur de la baleine bleue (trans. as The Heart of the Blue Whale) 1970, Faites de beaux rêves 1974, Les Grandes marées (trans. as Spring Tides) 1978, La Tournée d'automne 1993. *Honours:* Prix de La Presse 1974, Gov.-Gen.'s Literary Award 1978, Prix Athanase-David 1995.

POURNELLE, Jerry Eugene, (Wade Curtis), BS, MS, PhD; American writer and academic; b. 7 Aug. 1933, Shreveport, LA. *Education:* Univs of Iowa, Washington. *Career:* mem. Operations Research Soc. of America; Fellow, American Asscn for the Advancement of Science; Pres. SFWA 1974; fmr Pres. Science Fiction and Fantasy Writers of America. *Publications:* Red Heroin (as Wade Curtis) 1969, The Strategy of Technology: Winning the Decisive War (with Stefan Possony) 1970, Red Dragon (as Wade Curtis) 1971, A Spaceship for the King 1973, Escape From the Planet of the Apes (novelization of screenplay) 1973, The Mote in God's Eye (with Larry Niven) 1974, 20/20 Vision (ed.) 1974, Birth of Fire 1976, Inferno (with Larry Niven) 1976, West of Honor 1976, High Justice (short stories) 1977, The Mercenary 1977, Lucifer's Hammer (with Larry Niven) 1977, Exiles to Glory 1978, Black Holes (ed.) 1979, A Step Further Out (non-fiction) 1980, Janisseries 1980, Oath of Fealty (with Larry Niven) 1981, Clan and Crown (with Roland Green) 1982, There Will Be War (co-ed.) 1983, Mutual Assured Survival (with Dean Ing) 1984, Men of War (co-ed.) 1984, Blood and Iron (co-ed.) 1984, Day of the Tyrant (co-ed.) 1985, Footfall (with Larry Niven) 1985, Warriors (co-ed.) 1986, Imperial Stars: The Stars at War, Republic and Empire (co-ed.) 2 vols 1986–87, Guns of Darkness (co-ed.) 1987, Storms of Victory (with Roland Green) 1987, Legacy of Hereot (with Larry Niven) 1987, Prince of Mercenaries 1989, Fallen Angels (with Larry Niven, Michael Flynn) (Prometheus Award 1992, Seiun Award 1998) 1991, The Gripping Hand (with Larry Niven) 1993, The Burning City (with Larry Niven) 2000, Starswarm 2003, PC Hardware: The Definitive Guide (with Bob Thompson) 2003, 1001 Computer Words You Need to Know 2004, Burning Tower (with Larry Niven) 2005, Escape from Hell (with Larry Niven) 2009, The Secret of Black Ship Island (with Steven Barnes and Larry Niven). *Honours:* Bronze Medal, American Security Council 1964, John W. Campbell Award 1973, Heinlein Soc. Award (with Larry Niven) 2005.

POWELL, Neil Ashton, BA, MPhil; British writer and poet; b. 11 Feb. 1948, London, England; s. of Ian Otho James Powell and Dulcie Delia Powell (née Lloyd). *Education:* Sevenoaks School, Univ. of Warwick. *Career:* teacher Kimbolton School 1971–74, St Christopher School, Letchworth 1974–78, Head of English 1978–86; bookshop owner 1986–90; writer and editor 1990–; mem. Soc. of Authors. *Publications:* Suffolk Poems 1975, At the Edge 1977, Carpenters of Light 1979, Out of Time 1979, A Season of Calm Weather 1982, Selected Poems of Fulke Greville (ed.) 1990, True Colours: New and Selected Poems 1991, Unreal City 1992, The Stones on Thorpeness Beach 1994, Roy Fuller: Writer and Society 1995, Gay Love Poetry (ed.) 1997, The Language of Jazz 1997, Selected Poems 1998, George Crabbe: An English Life 2004, A Halfway House 2004, Amis and Son: Two Literary Generations 2008, Proof of Identity (2012); contrib. to anthologies, newspapers, reviews and journals. *Honours:* Eric Gregory Award 1969. *Literary Agent:* c/o Natasha Fairweather, AP Watt Ltd, 20 John Street, London, WC1N 2DR, England. *Telephone:* (20) 7405-6774. *E-mail:* nfairweather@apwatt.co.uk (office).

POWELL, Padgett, BA, MA; American academic and writer; *Professor of Creative Writing, University of Florida, Gainesville*; b. 25 April 1952, Gainesville, Fla; two d. *Education:* Coll. of Charleston, Univ. of Houston. *Career:* Prof. of Creative Writing, Univ. of Florida, Gainesville 1984–; mem. PEN, Authors' Guild, Writers' Guild of America (East). *Publications:* Edisto (novel) 1984, A Woman Named Drown (novel) 1987, Typical (short stories) 1991, Edisto Revisited (novel) 1996, Aliens of Affection (short stories) 1998, Mrs Hollingsworth's Men (novel) 2000, The Interrogative Mood (novel) 2009, You & I (novel) 2011, You & Me (novel) 2012; contrib. to periodicals, including Harper's Magazine, New Yorker, Paris Review, Travel and Leisure, Esquire. *Honours:* Time Magazine Best Book Citation 1984, Whiting Foundation Writers' Award 1986, Prix de Rome 1987. *Literary Agent:* c/o Cynthia Cannell, Cannell Literary Agency, 833 Madison Avenue, New York, NY 10021, USA. *Telephone:* (212) 396-9595. *Fax:* (212) 396-9797. *E-mail:* cannell@cannellagency.com. *Website:* cannellagency.com. *Address:* Turlington Hall 4211E, Department of English, University of Florida, Gainesville, FL 32611, USA (office). *Telephone:* (352) 392-0860 (office). *E-mail:* padgettpowell@yahoo.com (home).

POWER, Susan, JD, MFA; American writer; b. 12 Oct. 1961, Chicago, IL. *Education:* Radcliffe College, Harvard University Law School, University of Iowa Writers' Workshop. *Career:* mem. Standing Rock Sioux Reservation. *Publications:* Fiction: The Grass Dancer, 1994; Strong Heart Society, 1997.

Contributions: journals including: Atlantic Monthly; Paris Review; Ploughshares; Story; Short stories to anthologies. *Honours:* Award for First Fiction, Ernest Hemingway Foundation, 1995; Iowa Arts Fellowship; James Michener Fellowship; Bunting Institute Fellowship; Alfred Hodder Fellowship; Other fellowships.

POWERS, Richard; American writer; b. 1957; m. Jane Powers. *Career:* Swanlund Chair in English, Univ. of Illinois 1996–. *Publications:* Three Farmers on Their Way to a Dance (Richard and Hinda Rosenthal Foundation Award, American Acad. and Inst. of Arts and Letters, PEN/Hemingway Foundation special citation) 1985, Prisoner's Dilemma 1988, The Gold Bug Variations 1991, Operation Wandering Soul 1993, Galatea 2.2 1995, Gain (American Soc. of Historians James Fenimore Cooper Prize 1999) 1998, Plowing the Dark (American Acad. and Inst. of Arts and Letters Vursell Prize) 2000, The Time of Our Singing (WHSmith Literary Award 2004) 2003, The Echo Maker (Nat. Book Award for Fiction) 2006, Generosity: An Enhancement 2009; contrib. to journals and magazines. *Honours:* John D. and Catherine T. MacArthur Foundation grant 1989. *Address:* Department of English, University of Illinois, 608 South Wright Street, Urbana, IL 61801, USA (office). *Telephone:* (217) 244-4958 (office). *E-mail:* rpowers@illinois.edu (office). *Website:* www.english.illinois.edu/people/rpowers (office); www.richardpowers.net.

POWERS, Thomas Moore, BA; American writer and editor; b. 12 Dec. 1940, New York, NY; m. Candace Molloy 1965; three d. *Education:* Yale University. *Career:* reporter, Rome Daily American 1965–67, United Press International 1967–70; Ed.-Founding Partner, Steerforth Press, South Royalton, Vermont 1993–; mem. Council on Foreign Relations, PEN American Center. *Publications:* Diana: The Making of a Terrorist 1971, The War at Home 1973, The Man Who Kept the Secrets: Richard Helms and the CIA 1979, Thinking About the Next War 1982, Total War: What It Is, How It Got That Way 1988, Heisenberg's War: The Secret History of the German Bomb 1993, The Confirmation 2000, Intelligence Wars: American Secret History from Hitler to Al Qaeda 2003, The Military Error: Baghdad and Beyond in America's War of Choice 2008, The Killing of Crazy Horse 2010; contributions: New York Review of Books, London Review of Books. *Honours:* Pulitzer Prize for National Reporting, 1971. *Address:* 216 Chelsea Street, South Royalton, VT 05068, USA (office). *Telephone:* (802) 763-8585 (office).

POWNALL, David, BA, FRSL; British author and dramatist; b. 19 May 1938, Liverpool, England; m. 1st Glenys Elsie Jones 1961 (divorced); one s.; m. 2nd Mary Ellen Ray 1981; one s.; m. 3rd Alex Sutton 1993; one s. *Education:* Univ. of Keele. *Career:* Resident Writer, Century Theatre 1970–72; Resident Playwright, Duke's Playhouse, Lancaster 1972–75; Founder-Resident Writer, Paines Plough Theatre, London 1975–80. *Publications:* fiction: The Raining Tree War 1974, African Horse 1975, The Dream of Chief Crazy Horse 1975, God Perkins 1977, Light on a Honeycomb 1978, Beloved Latitudes 1981, The White Cutter 1989, The Gardener 1990, Stagg and His Mother 1991, The Sphinx and the Sybarites 1994, The Catalogue of Men 1999, The Ruling Passion 2008, The Archivist 2010; plays: more than 25 stage plays 1969–98, including Master Class, Beef, An Audience Called Edouard; radio and TV plays. *Honours:* Hon. DLitt (Keele) 2001; Edinburgh Festival Fringe Awards 1976, 1977, Giles Cooper Awards 1981, 1985, John Whiting Award, Arts Council of GB 1982, Sony Gold and Silver Awards for Original Radio Drama 1994, 1995, 1996. *Literary Agent:* Johnson & Alcock Ltd, Clerkenwell House, 45–47 Clerkenwell Green, London, EC1R 0HT, England.

POYER, Joseph (Joe) John, BA; American author, editor and publisher; *Publisher, North Cape Publications Inc.*; b. 30 Nov. 1939, Battle Creek, Mich.; s. of Joseph Poyer and Eileen Poyer (née Powell); m. Bonnie Prichard 1987. *Education:* Michigan State Univ. *Career:* Publr and Ed., Safe and Secure Living, International Military Review, International Naval Review 1990–93; currently Publr North Cape Publs Inc. *Publications:* fiction: North Cape 1968, Balkan Assignment 1971, Chinese Agenda 1972, Shooting of the Green 1973, Operation Mabeca 1976, The Contract 1978, Tunnel War 1979, Vengeance 10 1980, Devoted Friends 1982, Time of War (two vols) 1983, 1985; non-fiction: The 45–70 Springfield 1991, US Winchester Trench and Riot Guns 1993, Pocket Guide 45–70 Springfield 1994, The M1 Garand, 1936 to 1957 1995, The SKS Carbine 1997, The M14-type Rifles 1997, The SAFN Battle Rifle 1998, The Swedish Mauser Rifles 1999, The M16/AR15 Rifles 2000, The Model 1903 Springfield Rifle and its Variations 2001, The American Krag Rifle and Carbine 2002, Swiss Magazine Loading Rifles 1869–1958 2003, The AK-47 and AK-74 Rifles and Their Variations 2004, The Model 1911 and Model 1911A1 Military and Commercial Pistols 2008; contrib. to journals. *Address:* PO Box 1027, Tustin, CA 92681, USA (office). *E-mail:* ncape@ix.netcom.com (office). *Website:* www.northcapepubs.com (office).

PRABHJOT KAUR; Indian poet and politician; b. (Matia), 6 July 1924, Langaryal; d. of Nidhan Singh Sachar and Rajinder Kaur; m. Col Narenderpal Singh 1948; two d. *Education:* Khalsa Coll. for Women, Lahore and Punjab Univ. *Career:* first collected poems published 1943 (aged sixteen); represented India at numerous int. literary confs; mem. Legis. Council, Punjab 1966; Ed. Vikendrit; mem. Sahitya Akademi (Nat. Acad. of Letters), Exec. Bd 1978; mem. Cen. Comm. for UNESCO, Nat. Writers Cttee of India; Fellow Emer., Govt of India. *Television:* Ishak Shara Kee Nata (musical play). *Publications:* 50 books, including: poetry: Supne Sadhran 1949, Do Rang 1951, Pankheru 1956, Lala (in Persian) 1958, Bankapasi 1958, Pabbi 1962, Khari 1967, Plateau (French) 1968, Wad-darshi Sheesha 1972, Madhiantar 1974, Chandra Yug 1978, Dreams Die Young 1979, Shadows and Light (Bulgarian) 1980, Him Hans 1982, Samrup 1982, Ishq Shara Ki Nata 1983, Shadows (English and Danish) 1985, Charam Serma, Men Tapu Mukhatab Han–Manas Man the Gagan Mokla (collected poems in four vols); short stories: Kinke 1952, Aman de Na 1956, Zindgi de Kujh Pal 1982, Main Amanat Naheen (Hindi), Kuntith, Casket (English); autobiog.: Jeena vi ek Ada Hai (two vols). *Honours:* Sahitya Shiromani 1964, Rajya Kavi (Poet Laureate) conferred by Punjab Govt 1964, Sahitya Akademi Award 1964, Golden Laurel Leaves, United Poets Int., Philippines 1967, Padma Shri 1967, Grand Prix de la Rose de la France 1968, Most Distinguished Order of Poetry, World Poetry Soc. Intercontinental, USA 1974; Woman of the Year, UPLI, Philippines 1975, Sewa Sifti Award 1980, NIF Cultural Award 1982, Josh Kenya Award 1982, Delhi State Award 1983, Safdar Hashmi Award. *Address:* D-203, Defence Colony, New Delhi 110 024, India (home). *Telephone:* (11) 4622756 (home).

PRADO, Benjamin; Spanish writer and poet; b. 1961, Madrid. *Publications:* poetry: Un caso sencilio 1986, El corazón azul del alumbrado 1991, Asuntos Personales 1992, Cobijo contra la tormenta (Hiperión Prize) 1995, Todos nosotros 1998, Ecuador poesía 1986–2001 2002, Iceberg 2002, Marea humana 2006; novels: Raro 1995, Dónde crees que vas y quién te crees que eres 1996, Nunca le des la mano a un pistolero zurdo (trans. as Never Shake Hands with a Left-handed Gunman) 1996, Alguien se acerca 1998, No sólo el fuego (trans. as Not Only Fire) (Premio Andalucía de Novela) 1999, La nieve está vacía (trans. as Snow is Silent) 2000, Los nombres de Antígona (biog.) 2001, Mala gente que camina 2006. *Address:* c/o Alfaguara, Santillana Ediciones Generales, Calle Torrelaguna 60, 28043 Madrid, Spain (office). *E-mail:* alfaguara@santillana.es (office). *Website:* www.alfaguara.santillana.es (office).

PRADO FREITAS, Adélia Luzia; Brazilian poet and writer; b. 13 Dec. 1935, Divinópolis, Minas Gerais; d. of João do Prado Filho and Ana Clotilde Corrêa; m. José Assunção de Freitas; three s. two d. *Education:* Faculty of Philosophy, Science and Letters, Divinópolis. *Career:* teacher of religious education and philosophy in schools and colls 1955–79; full-time writer aged 40; Head of Cultural Division, Municipal Office of Education and Culture, Divinópolis 1983–88. *Publications:* poetry: Bagagem 1976, O coração disparado (Prêmio Jabuti da Câmara Brasileira do Livro) 1978, Terra de Santa Cruz 1981, O pelicano 1987, A faca no peito 1988, Oráculos de maio 1999; prose: Solte os cachorros 1979, Cacos para um vitral 1980, Os componentes da banda 1984, O homem da mão seca 1994, Manuscritos de Felipa 1999, Filandras 2001, Quero Minha Mãe 2005; contrib. to anthologies and journals.

PRALL, Stuart Edward, BA, MA, PhD, FRHistS; American academic and writer; *Professor Emeritus of History, City University of New York*; b. 2 June 1929, Saginaw, MI; m. Naomi Shafer 1958; one s. one d. *Education:* Michigan State Univ., Univ. of Rhode Island, Univ. of Manchester, England and Columbia Univ. *Career:* Queens Coll. and Graduate School and Univ. Center, CUNY 1955–58, 1960–2001; Newark State Coll., NJ 1958–60; Exec. Officer PhD Program in History, Graduate School and Univ. Center, CUNY 1988–94, Prof. Emer. 2001–; mem. North American Conference on British Studies; mem. Phi Beta Kappa. *Publications:* The Agitation for Law Reform during the Puritan Revolution, 1640–1660 1966, The Puritan Revolution: A Documentary History 1968, The Bloodless Revolution: England, 1688 1972, A History of England 1991, Church and State in Tudor and Stuart England 1993, The Puritan Revolution and the English Civil War 2002; contrib. to The Development of Equity in Tudor England, American Journal of Legal History. *Honours:* Univ. of Manchester Fulbright Scholar 1953–54. *Address:* 7050 Owl's Nest Terrace, Bradenton, FL 34203, USA (home); 27 Wildwood Lane, Bethel, NB E5C 3W1, Canada (home). *Telephone:* (941) 739-0198 (USA) (home); (506) 755-9197 (Canada) (home). *E-mail:* prall34203@yahoo.com (home).

PRANTERA, Amanda; British author; b. 23 April 1942, England. *Publications:* Strange Loop, 1984; The Cabalist, 1985; Conversations with Lord Byron on Perversion, 163 Years After His Lordship's Death, 1987; The Side of the Moon, 1991; Pronto-Zoe, 1992; The Young Italians, 1993; Spoiler, 2003.

PRASHAD, Vijay, PhD; Indian/American writer and journalist; *Professor of International Studies and George and Martha Kellner Chair of South Asian History, Trinity College, Hartford*; b. Kolkata, India. *Education:* Ponoma Coll., Univ. of Chicago, USA. *Career:* Visiting Asst Prof. of History, Syracuse Univ., Cornell Univ. 1995–96, New York Univ. 2001; Asst Prof. of Int. Studies, Trinity Coll., Hartford, Conn. 1996–2000, Dir Int. Studies Program 2000–03, Assoc. Prof. of Int. Studies 2000–06, Prof. of Int. Studies and George and Martha Kellner Chair of South Asian History 2006–; Fellow, Univ. of Chicago 1990–91, MacArthur Foundation 1991–92, American Inst. of Indian Studies 1992–93, Mellon Foundation 1993–94, Trinity Coll. 1998–2001; Ed. Amerasia Journal; mem. Center for Third World Organizing (bd mem.), Forum of Indian Leftists (Co-founder). *Publications:* The Karma of Brown Folk 2000, Untouchable Freedom: A Social History of a Dalit Community 2000, Everybody was Kung Fu Fighting: Afro-Asian Connections and the Myth of Cultural Purity 2002, The American Scheme: Three Essays 2002, War Against the Planet: The Fifth Afghan War, Imperialism and Other Assorted Fundamentalism 2002, Fat Cats and Running Dogs: The Enron Stage of Capitalism 2002, Keeping Up with the Dow Joneses: Stocks, Jails, Welfare 2003, Namaste Sharon: Hindutva and Sharonism Under US Hegemony 2003, The Darker Nations: A People's History of the Third World (Muzaffar Ahmed Book Award 2009) 2008; contributions: Colorlines, Himal South Asia, Frontline, Z Magazine,

ColorLines Magazine, The Indian American, Naked Punch, Counterpunch, www.truthindia.com, Little India, ZNET. *Honours:* Dean Arthur H. Hughes Award, Trinity College 2000. *Address:* Department of History, Trinity College, 300 Summit Street, Hartford, CT 06106-3100, USA (office). *Telephone:* (870) 297-2518 (office). *E-mail:* vijay.prashad@trincoll.edu (office). *Website:* www.trincoll.edu (office).

PRATCHETT, Sir Terence (Terry) David John, Kt, OBE; British writer; b. 28 April 1948, Beaconsfield, Bucks.; m. Lyn Marian Purves 1968; one d. *Career:* journalist 1965–80; Press Officer Cen. Electricity Generating Bd 1980–87; Chair. Soc. of Authors 1994–95. *Television:* Terry Pratchett: Choosing to Die (documentary) (BAFTA Award for Best Single Documentary 2012) 2011. *Publications:* Discworld series: The Colour of Magic 1983, The Light Fantastic 1986, Equal Rites 1987, Mort 1987, Sourcery 1989, Wyrd Sisters 1988, Pyramids 1989, Eric (illustrated by Josh Kirby) 1989, Guards! Guards! 1989, Moving Pictures 1990, Reaper Man 1991, Witches Abroad 1991, Small Gods 1992, Lords and Ladies 1993, Men at Arms 1993, The Streets of Ankh-Morpork (with Stephen Briggs) 1993, Soul Music 1994, Interesting Times 1994, The Discworld Companion (with Stephen Briggs) 1994, Maskerade 1995, Discworld Mapp (with Stephen Briggs) 1995, Feet of Clay 1996, Hogfather 1996, The Pratchett Portfolio (with Paul Kidby) 1996, Jingo 1997, The Last Continent 1998, Carpe Jugulum 1998, A Tourist Guide to Lancre (with Stephen Briggs and Paul Kidby) 1998, The Fifth Elephant 1999, The Science of Discworld (with Ian Stewart and Jack Cohen) 1999, Death's Domain (with Paul Kidby) 1999, The Truth 2000, Nanny Ogg's Cookbook (with Stephen Briggs, Tina Hannan and Paul Kidby) 2000, The Last Hero (illustrated by Paul Kidby) 2001, Thief of Time 2001, Night Watch 2002, The Science of the Discworld II (with Ian Stewart and Jack Cohen) 2002, Monstrous Regiment 2003, The Wee Free Men 2003, A Hat Full of Sky 2004, The Science of Discworld III: Darwin's Watch (with Ian Stewart and Jack Cohen) 2005, Going Postal 2004, Thud! 2005, Where's My Cow 2005, Wintersmith 2006, Making Money 2007, The Folklore of Discworld (with Jacqueline Simpson) 2008, Unseen Academicals 2009, I Shall Wear Midnight 2010, Snuff 2011; other fiction: The Carpet People 1971, The Dark Side of the Sun 1976, Strata 1981, The Unadulterated Cat (illustrated by Gray Jolliffe) 1989, Truckers 1989, Diggers 1990, Wings 1990, Good Omens: The Nice and Accurate Predictions of Agnes Nutter, Witch (with Neil Gaiman) 1990, Only You Can Save Mankind 1992, Johnny and the Dead 1993, Johnny and the Bomb 1996, The Amazing Maurice and his Educated Rodents (Carnegie Medal) 2001, Nation (Boston Globe-Horn Book Award 2009) 2008; screenplay: Terry Pratchett's Hogfather (BAFTA Award 2007) 2006; other: short stories. *Honours:* Hon. DLitt (Portsmouth) 2001, (Bath) 2003, (Bristol) 2004, (Warwick) 1999, (Bradford) 2009, (Winchester) 2009; Hon. LittD (Dublin) 2008; Dr hc (Bucks New) 2008; Galaxy Nat. Book Award for Outstanding Achievement 2010. *Literary Agent:* c/o Colin Smythe Ltd, 38 Mill Lane, Gerrards Cross, Bucks., SL9 8BA, England. *Telephone:* (1753) 886000. *Fax:* (1753) 886469. *Website:* www.terrypratchett.co.uk; www.terrypratchettbooks.com.

PRAWER, Siegbert Salomon, MA, DLitt, PhD, LittD, FBA; British university teacher (retd) and author; b. 15 Feb. 1925, Cologne, Germany; s. of Marcus Prawer and Eleonora Prawer; brother of Ruth Prawer Jhabvala (q.v.); m. Helga Alice Schaefer 1949; one s. two d. (and one s. deceased). *Education:* King Henry VIII School, Coventry, Jesus Coll., Christ's Coll. Cambridge. *Career:* Adelaide Stoll Research Student, Christ's Coll. Cambridge 1947–48; Asst Lecturer, then Lecturer, then Sr Lecturer, Univ. of Birmingham 1948–63; Prof. of German, Westfield Coll., London Univ. 1964–69; Taylor Prof. of German Language and Literature, Oxford 1969–86, Prof. Emer. 1986–; Co-editor, Oxford Germanic Studies 1971–75, Anglica Germanica 1973–79; Fulbright Exchange Scholar, Columbia Univ. 1956; Visiting Prof. City Coll., New York 1956–57, Univ. of Chicago 1963–64, Harvard Univ. 1968, Hamburg Univ. 1969, Univ. of Calif., Irvine 1975, Otago Univ., NZ 1976, Univ. of Pittsburgh 1977, ANU Canberra 1980, Brandeis Univ. 1981–82; Resident Fellow, Knox Coll., Dunedin, NZ 1976, Russell Sage Foundation, New York 1988; Fellow, Queen's Coll. Oxford 1969–86, Supernumerary Fellow 1986–90, Hon. Fellow 1990–, Dean of Degrees 1976–93; Pres. British Comparative Literature Asscn 1984–87, Hon. Fellow 1989; Corresp. Fellow, German Acad. of Literature 1989; Pres. English Goethe Soc. 1992–95, Vice-Pres. 1995–. *Exhibitions:* drawings on exhbn Queen's Coll. and St Edmund Hall, Oxford and other insts . *Publications:* German Lyrical Poetry 1952, Mörike und seine Leser 1960, Heine's Buch der Lieder: A Critical Study 1960, Heine: The Tragic Satirist 1962, The Penguin Book of Lieder 1964, The Uncanny in Literature (inaugural lecture) 1965, Heine's Shakespeare, a Study in Contexts (inaugural lecture) 1970, Comparative Literary Studies: An Introduction 1973, Karl Marx and World Literature 1976, Caligari's Children: The Film as Tale of Terror 1980, Heine's Jewish Comedy: A Study of His Portraits of Jews and Judaism 1983, Coalsmoke and Englishmen 1984, A. N. Stencl–Poet of Whitechapel 1984, Frankenstein's Island–England and the English in the Writings of Heinrich Heine 1986, Israel at Vanity Fair: Jews and Judaism in the Writings of W. M. Thackeray 1992, Breeches and Metaphysics, Thackeray's German Discourse 1997, W. M. Thackeray's European Sketch Books: A Study of Literary and Graphic Portraiture 2000, The Blue Angel 2002, Werner Herzog's Nosferatu 2004, Between Two Worlds: The Jewish Presence in German and Austrian Film 1910–1933 2005, A Cultural Citizen of the World: Sigmund Freud's Knowledge and Use of British and American Writings 2009; edited: The Penguin Book of Lieder 1964, Essays in German Language, Culture and Society (with R. H. Thomas and L. W. Forster) 1969, The Romantic Period in Germany 1970, Seventeen Modern German Poets 1971; screenplay: Das Kabinett des Dr Caligari (ed and introduction); numerous articles on German, English and comparative literature. *Honours:* Hon. Dir London Univ. Inst. of Germanic Studies 1965–68, Hon. Fellow 1986; Hon. mem. Modern Languages Asscn of America 1986; Hon. Fellow, Jesus Coll. Cambridge 1996–; Hon. DPhil (Cologne) 1985; Hon. DLitt (Birmingham) 1988; Goethe Medal 1973, Gold Medal, German Goethe Soc. 1995; Isaac Deutscher Memorial Prize 1977, Gundolf-Prize of the German Acad. 1986. *Address:* The Queen's College, Oxford, OX1 4AW, England (office); 9 Hawkswell Gardens, Oxford, OX2 7EX, England (home). *Telephone:* (1865) 279121 (office); (1865) 557614 (home).

PRENTISS, Charlotte (see Platt, Charles Michael)

PRESCOTT, Casey (see Morris, Janet Ellen)

PRESCOTT, Richard Chambers; American poet and writer; b. 1 April 1952, Houston, Tex.; m. Sarah Elisabeth Grace 1981. *Publications:* The Sage 1975, Moonstar 1975, Neuf Songes (Nine Dreams) 1976, The Carouse of Soma 1977, Lions and Kings 1977, Allah Wake Up 1978, Night Reaper 1979, Dragon Tales 1983, Dragon Dreams 1986, Dragon Prayers 1988, Dragon Songs 1988, Dragon Maker 1989, Dragon Thoughts 1990, Tales of Recognition 1991, Kings and Sages 1991, Dragon Sight: A Cremation Poem 1992, Three Waves 1992, Years of Wonder 1992, Dream Appearances 1992, Remembrance, Recognition and Return 1992, Spare Advice 1992, The Imperishable 1993, The Dark Deitess 1993, Disturbing Delights: Waves of the Great Goddess 1993, The Immortal: Racopa and the Rooms of Light 1993, Hanging Baskets 1993, Writer's Block and Other Gray Matters 1993, The Resurrection of Quantum Joe 1993, The Horse and the Carriage 1993, Kalee Bhava: The Goddess and Her Moods 1995, Because of Atma 1995, The Skills of Kalee 1995, Measuring Sky without Ground 1996, Kalee: The Allayer of Sorrows 1996, The Goddess and the God Man 1996, Living Sakti: Attempting Quick Knowing in Perpetual Perception and Continuous Becoming 1997, The Mirage and the Mirror 1998, Inherent Solutions to Spiritual Obscurations 1999, The Ancient Method 1999, Quantum Kamakala 2000, Mortal Grounding: Cosmology and Consciousness 2008; contrib. of articles and essays to professional publs. *Address:* 8617 188th Street SW, Edmonds, WA 98026, USA.

PRESNYAKOV, Oleg; Russian playwright; b. Sverdlovsk, Siberia. *Career:* taught literary theory and psychology, Ekaterinburg; co-f., Gorky Urals State Univ. youth theatre; writes and produces plays with brother, Vladimir Presnyakov; connected with New Writing Project, Russia. *Publications:* with Vladimir Presnyakov: Set-2, We Shall Overcome 2002, Terrorism 2002, Plenniye Dukhi (Captive Spirits) 2003, Playing the Victim 2003. *Literary Agent:* Judy Daish Associates Ltd, 2 St Charles Place, London, W10 6EG, England. *Telephone:* (20) 8964-8811. *Fax:* (20) 8964-8966.

PRESNYAKOV, Vladimir; Russian playwright; b. Sverdlovsk, Siberia. *Career:* taught literary theory and psychology, Ekaterinburg; co-f., Gorky Urals State Univ. youth theatre; writes and produces plays with brother, Oleg Presnyakov; connected with New Writing Project, Russia. *Publications:* with Oleg Presnyakov: Set-2, We Shall Overcome 2002, Terrorism 2002, Plenniye Dukhi (Captive Spirits) 2003, Playing the Victim 2003. *Literary Agent:* Judy Daish Associates Ltd, 2 St Charles Place, London, W10 6EG, England. *Telephone:* (20) 8964-8811. *Fax:* (20) 8964-8966.

PRESTON, Ivy Alice Kinross; New Zealand writer; b. 11 Nov. 1913, Timaru, Canterbury; m. Percival Edward James Preston 1937, two s. two d. *Career:* mem. South Canterbury Writers Guild; New Zealand Women Writers Society; South Island Writers Asscn; Romance Writers of America; Romantic Novelists Asscn, London. *Publications:* The Silver Stream (autobiog.), 1958; Hospital on the Hill, 1967; Voyage of Destiny, 1974; The House Above the Bay, 1976; Fair Accuser, 1985; Stranger From the Sea, 1987. Other: 40 romance novels. Contributions: many publications.

PRESTON, Paul, CBE, MA, DPhil, FRHistS, FBA; British historian, academic and author; *Prince of Asturias Professor of Contemporary Spanish History, London School of Economics*; b. 21 July 1946, Liverpool, England; s. of Charles R. Preston and Alice Hoskisson; m. Gabrielle P. Ashford-Hodges 1983; two s. *Education:* St Edward's Coll. Liverpool, Oriel Coll. Oxford and Univ. of Reading. *Career:* Research Fellow, Centre for Mediterranean Studies, Rome 1973–74; Lecturer in History, Univ. of Reading 1974–75; Lecturer in Modern History, Queen Mary Coll. London 1975–79, Reader 1979–85, Prof. of History 1985–91; Prof. of Int. History, LSE 1991–94, Prince of Asturias Prof. of Contemporary Spanish History 1994–; regular contrib. to Times Literary Supplement; columnist in ABC, Diario 16 and El País, Madrid. *Publications:* The Coming of the Spanish Civil War 1978, The Triumph of Democracy in Spain 1986, The Spanish Civil War 1986, The Politics of Revenge 1990, Franco: A Biography 1993, Comrades: Portraits from the Spanish Civil War 1999, Doves of War: Four Women of Spain 2003, Juan Carlos: A People's King 2004, We Saw Spain Die 2008, The Spanish Holocaust 2011. *Honours:* Comendador, Orden del Mérito Civil (Spain) 1987, Caballero Gran Cruz de la Orden de Isabel la Católica 2006; Yorkshire Post Book of the Year 1994, Así fue – La Historia rescatada Prize 1998, Premi Internacional Ramon Llull, Catalan Govt 2005, Trias Fargas Non-Fiction Prize 2006, Marcel Proust Chair of European Acad. 2006. *Address:* Department of International History, London School of Economics, Houghton Street, London, WC2A 2AE, England (office). *Telephone:* (20) 7955-6508 (office). *Fax:* (20) 7955-6757 (office). *E-mail:*

p.preston@lse.ac.uk (office). *Website:* www2.lse.ac.uk/europeanInstitute/research/canadaBlanch/home.aspx (office).

PRESTON, Peter John, MA; British journalist; b. 23 May 1938, Barrow-upon-Soar, Leicestershire; s. of John Whittle Preston and Kathlyn Preston (née Chell); m. Jean Mary Burrell 1962; two s. two d. *Education:* Loughborough Grammar School and St John's Coll. Oxford. *Career:* editorial trainee, Liverpool Daily Post 1960–63; Political Reporter, The Guardian 1963–64, Educ. Corresp. 1965–66, Diary Ed. 1966–68, Features Ed. 1968–72, Production Ed. 1972–75, Ed. The Guardian 1975–95, Ed.-in-Chief 1995, Ed.-in-Chief The Observer 1995–96, Editorial Dir Guardian Media Group 1996–98; Co-Dir Guardian Foundation 1997–; mem. Scott Trust 1976–; Chair. Int. Press Inst. 1995–97, Asscn of British Eds 1996–99; mem. UNESCO Advisory Group on Press Freedom 2000–04; Gov. British Asscn for Cen. and Eastern Europe 2000–. *Publications:* Dunblane: Reflecting Tragedy 1996, The 51st State 1998, Bess 1999. *Honours:* Hon. Fellow, St John's Coll. Oxford 2003; Hon. DLitt (Loughborough) 1982, (E Anglia), (City Univ.) 1997, (Leicester) 2003; What the Papers Say Award for Lifetime Achievement 2006. *Address:* The Guardian, Kings Place, 90 York Way, London, N1 9GU, England (office). *Telephone:* (20) 3353-2000 (office). *Website:* www.guardian.co.uk (office).

PRESTON, Richard McCann, BA, PhD; American writer; b. 5 Aug. 1954, Cambridge, MA; m. 1985. *Education:* Pomona Coll., Princeton Univ. *Career:* Lecturer in English, Princeton Univ. 1983; Visiting Fellow, Princeton Univ. Council of the Humanities 1994–95; mem. Authors' Guild. *Publications:* First Light 1987, American Steel 1991, The Hot Zone 1994, The Cobra Event 1998, The Demon in the Freezer 2003, The Boat of Dreams 2003, The Wild Trees: A Story of Passion and Daring 2007; contrib. to newspapers and magazines. *Honours:* American Inst. of Physics Science Writing Award 1988, Asteroid 3686 named 'Preston' 1989, AAAS Westinghouse Award 1992, MIT McDermott Award 1993. *Address:* c/o Author mail, Random House, 20 Vauxhall Bridge Road, London, SW1V 2SA, England (office). *Website:* www.richardpreston.net.

PREUSS, Paul F., BA; American writer; b. 7 March 1942, Albany, GA; m. 1st Marsha May Pettit 1963, one d.; m. 2nd Karen Reiser 1973; m. 3rd Debra Turner 1993. *Education:* Yale Univ. *Career:* mem. Northern California Science Writers Asscn; SFWA; Bay Area Book Reviewers' Asscn. *Publications:* The Gates of Heaven, 1980; Re-entry, 1981; Broken Symmetries, 1983; Human Error, 1985; Venus Prime series (with Arthur C. Clarke), 1987–91; Starfire, 1988; The Ultimate Dinosaur, 1992; Core, 1993; Secret Passages, 1997. Contributions: books and newspapers; New York Review of Science Fiction.

PRICE, (Alan) Anthony, MA; British writer and journalist; b. 16 Aug. 1928, Herts., England; m. Yvonne Ann Stone 1953; two s. one d. *Education:* The King's School, Canterbury, Merton Coll., Oxford. *Career:* Ed. The Oxford Times 1972–88. *Publications:* The Labryinth Makers 1970, The Alamut Ambush 1971, Colonel Butler's Wolf 1972, October Men 1973, Other Paths to Glory 1974, Our Man in Camelot 1975, War Game 1976, The '44 Vintage 1978, Tomorrow's Ghost 1979, The Hour of the Donkey 1980, Soldier No More 1981, The Old Vengeful 1982, Gunner Kelly 1983, Sion Crossing 1984, Here Be Monsters 1985, For the Good of the State 1986, A New Kind of War 1987, A Prospect of Vengeance 1988, The Memory Trap 1989, The Eyes of the Fleet 1990. *Honours:* CWA Silver Dagger 1970, Gold Dagger 1974, Swedish Acad. of Detection Prize 1978. *Address:* Wayside Cottage, Horton cum Studley, Oxford, OX33 1AW, England (home). *Telephone:* (1865) 351326 (home).

PRICE, Glanville, BA, MA, DUniv; British academic and writer; *Professor Emeritus, University of Wales Aberystwyth*; b. 16 June 1928, Rhaeadr, Wales; m. Christine Winifred Thurston 1954; three s. one d. *Education:* Univ. of Wales Bangor, Université de Paris, France. *Career:* Prof. of French, Univ. of Stirling 1967–72; Prof. of French, Univ. of Wales Aberystwyth 1972–92, Research Prof. 1992–95, Prof. Emer. 1995–; mem. Modern Humanities Research Asscn (Chair. 1979–90), Philological Soc. *Publications:* The Present Position of Minority Languages in Western Europe 1969, The French Language, Present and Past 1971, The Year's Work in Modern Language Studies (co-ed.) 1972–92, William, Count of Orange: Four Old French Epics (ed.) 1975, Romance Linguistics and the Romance Languages (with Kathryn F. Bach) 1977, The Languages of Britain 1984, Ireland and the Celtic Connection 1987, An Introduction to French Pronunciation 1991, (second edn) 2005, The Celtic Connection (ed.) 1992, Hommages offerts à Maria Manoliu (co-ed. with Coman Lupu) 1994, Encyclopedia of the Languages of Europe (ed.) 1998, Languages in Britain and Ireland 2000, A Comprehensive French Grammar 2008; contrib. to professional journals. *Address:* Department of European Languages, Aberystwyth University, Aberystwyth, Ceredigion, SY23 3DY, Wales (office).

PRICE, Richard, PhD; British poet, librarian, editor and writer; *Head of Modern British Collections, British Library*; b. 15 Aug. 1966, Reading, England; m. Jacqueline Canning 1990 (divorced 2006); two d. *Education:* Univ. of Strathclyde, Glasgow. *Career:* Head of Modern British Collections, British Library, London 2003–; mem. Poetry Soc. (Council 1998–2002). *Publications:* poetry: Sense and a Minor Fever 1993, Tube Shelter Perspective 1993, Marks & Sparks 1995, Eftirs/Afters (trans of Apollinaire, with Donny O'Rourke) 1996, Hand Held 1997, Perfume and Petrol Fumes 1999, Renfrewshire in Old Photographs (with Raymond Friel) 2000, Frosted, Melted 2002, Lucky Day 2005, Greenfields 2007, Rays 2009; prose: The Fabulous Matter of Fact: The Poetics of Neil M. Gunn 1991, La Nouvelle alliance: Influences francophones sur la littérature écossaise (ed. with David Kinloch) 2000, The Star You Steer By: Basil Bunting and 'British' Modernism (ed. with James McGonigal) 2000, A Boy in Summer (short stories) 2002, British Poetry Magazines: A Bibliography and History of the Little Magazine (with David Miller) 2006; artists' books: Gifthorse (with Ron King) 1999, The Mechanical Word (with Karen Bleitz) 2005, Little But Often (with Ron King) 2007, Folded (with Julie Johnstone) 2008; contrib. to Scotland on Sunday, Poetry Review, PN Review, Object Permanence, TLS. *Address:* Modern British Collections, British Library, 96 Euston Road, London, NW1 2DB, England (office). *E-mail:* info@hydrohotel.net (office). *Website:* www.hydrohotel.net.

PRICE, Richard; American writer and screenwriter; b. 12 Oct. 1949, New York, NY. *Career:* mem. American Acad. of Arts and Letters 2009–. *Screenplays include:* The Wanderers 1979, The Color of Money 1986, New York Stories 1989, Sea of Love 1989, Night and the City 1992, Mad Dog and Glory 1993, Kiss of Death 1995, Clockers 1995, Ransom 1996, Shaft 2000, Freedomland 2004. *Television:* The Wire (series writer) 2002. *Publications:* novels: The Wanderers 1975, Bloodbrothers 1978, The Breaks 1983, Clockers 1992, Freedomland 1998, Samaritan 2003, Lush Life 2008. *Honours:* Edgar Award 2007. *Address:* c/o Farrar, Strauss and Giroux, 18 West 18th Street, New York, NY 10011, USA (office). *Telephone:* (212) 741-6900 (office). *Website:* www.fsgbooks.com (office).

PRICE, Roger David, BA, DLitt, FRHistS; British historian and writer; *Professor Emeritus of Modern History, Aberystwyth University*; b. 7 Jan. 1944, Port Talbot, S Wales; s. of Godfrey Price and Martha Price; m. Heather Price; one s. three d. *Education:* Univ. of Wales, Univ. Coll. of Swansea. *Career:* Lecturer, Univ. of East Anglia 1968–82, Sr Lecturer 1982–83, Reader in Social History 1984–91, Prof. of European History 1991–94; Prof. of Modern History, Univ. of Wales, Aberystwyth (Aberystwyth Univ. since 2007) 1993–2011, Prof. Emer. 2011–. *Publications:* The French Second Republic: A Social History 1972, The Economic Modernization of France 1975, Revolution and Reaction: 1848 and the Second French Republic (ed. and contrib.) 1975, 1848 in France 1975, An Economic History of Modern France 1981, The Modernization of Rural France: Communications Networks and Agricultural Market Structures in 19th Century France 1983, A Social History of 19th Century France 1987, The Revolutions of 1848 1989, A Concise History of France 1993, 2005, Documents on the French Revolution of 1848 1996, Napoleon III and the French Second Empire 1997, The French Second Empire: An Anatomy of Political Power 2001, People and Politics in France 1848–1870 2004; contrib. to numerous magazines and journals. *Address:* Department of History and Welsh History, Aberystwyth University, Aberystwyth, Ceredigion, SY23 3DY, Wales (office). *Telephone:* (1970) 627212 (office). *E-mail:* rdp@aber.ac.uk (office).

PRICE, Stanley, MA; British writer and dramatist; b. 12 Aug. 1931, London, England; m. Judy Fenton 1957, one s. *Education:* University of Cambridge. *Career:* mem. Writer's Guild; Dramatists Club. *Publications:* Fiction: Crusading for Kronk, 1960; A World of Difference, 1961; Just for the Record, 1962; The Biggest Picture, 1964. Stage Plays: Horizontal Hold, 1967; The Starving Rich, 1972; The Two of Me, 1975; Moving, 1980; Why Me?, 1985. Screenplays: Arabesque, 1968; Gold, 1974; Shout at the Devil, 1975. Television Plays: All Things Being Equal, 1970; Exit Laughing, 1971; Minder, 1980; The Kindness of Mrs Radcliffe, 1981; Moving, 1985; Star Quality, series, 1986; Close Relations, 1986–87; The Bretts, 1990. Contributions: Observer; Sunday Telegraph; New York Times; Los Angeles Times; Punch; Plays and Players; New Statesman; Independent; Town.

PRICE, Susan; British children's author; b. 8 July 1955, Brades Row. *Career:* mem. Soc. of Authors. *Publications include:* Devil's Piper 1973, Twopence a Tub 1975, Sticks and Stones 1976, Home from Home 1977, Christopher Uptake 1981, The Carpenter (short stories) 1981, In a Nutshell 1983, From Where I Stand 1984, Ghosts at Large 1984, Odin's Monster 1986, The Ghost Drum 1987, The Bone Dog 1989, Forbidden Doors 1990, The Sterkarm Handshake 1998, A Sterkarm Kiss 2004, Odin's Voice 2005, Odin's Queen 2006, Odin's Son 2007, Feasting the Wolf 2007. *Honours:* The Other Award 1975, Carnegie Medal 1987, The Guardian Children's Fiction Award 1999. *Literary Agent:* c/o Sarah Molly, A. M. Heath & Co, 6 Warwick Court, London, WC1R 5DJ, England. *Website:* www.susanpriceauthor.com.

PRICE, Victor, BA; Northern Irish writer and poet; b. 10 April 1930, Newcastle, County Down. *Education:* Queen's Univ., Belfast. *Career:* with the BBC, 1956–90, ending as Head of German Language Service. *Publications:* The Death of Achilles, 1963; The Other Kingdom, 1964; Caliban's Wooing, 1966; The Plays of Georg Büchner, 1971; Two Parts Water (poems), 1980. Contributions: Financial Times; Scotsman; BBC World Service; Deutschland Rundfunk; Channel Four.

PRIEST, Christopher McKenzie; British writer; b. 14 July 1943, Cheadle, Cheshire; m. Laura Priest; one s. one d. *Career:* professional writer 1968–. *Publications include:* Indoctrinaire 1970, Fugue for a Darkening Island 1972, Real-Time World (short stories) 1974, Inverted World 1974, The Space Machine 1976, A Dream of Wessex 1977, An Infinite Summer 1979, The Affirmation 1981, The Glamour 1984, The Book on the Edge of Forever (non-fiction) 1984, The Quiet Woman 1990, The Prestige 1995, The Extremes 1998, The Dream Archipelago 1999, The Separation 2002, The Islanders 2011; short stories, TV plays; contrib. to Impulse, New Worlds, New Writings in SF, various anthologies. *Honours:* John W. Campbell Jr Memorial Award for Outstanding British Novel 1972, BSFA Awards for Best Novel 1974, 1999,

2003, for Best Short Story 1979, Ditmar Awards for Best Int. Novel 1977, 1982, Kurd Lasswitz Award for Best Foreign Novel 1988, James Tait Black Memorial Prize for Fiction 1995, World Fantasy Award 1996, Prix Utopia Lifetime Achievement Award 2001, Grand Prix de l'Imaginaire 2001, 2006, Arthur C. Clarke Award 2003. *Literary Agent:* c/o United Agents, 12–26 Lexington Street, London, W1F 0LE, England. *Telephone:* (20) 3214-0800. *Fax:* (20) 3214-0801. *E-mail:* info@unitedagents.co.uk. *Website:* unitedagents.co.uk. *E-mail:* cp@christopher-priest.co.uk. *Website:* www.christopher-priest.co.uk.

PRIGENT, Michel; French editor; b. 29 Sept. 1950, Paris; s. of Jean Prigent and Germaine Morvan; m. Elisabeth Depierre 1974; two s. *Education:* Lycées Henri IV and Louis-le-Grand, Ecole Normale Supérieure and Sorbonne, Paris. *Career:* joined Presses Universitaires de France 1974, Sec. to Bd of Dirs 1978, Editorial Dir 1985; Président du Directoire 1994; Pres. Editeurs de Sciences Humaines et Sociales 1984–90; Admin., Cercle de la Librairie 1997–2003, 2006; mem. Admin. Council, Ecole Normale Supérieure 1988–91. *Publications:* La liberté à refaire 1984, Le héros et l'Etat dans la tragédie de Pierre Corneille 1986. *Honours:* Officier, Ordre nat. du Mérite. *Address:* c/o Presses Universitaires de France, 108 boulevard Saint-Germain, 75006 Paris (office); 17 rue de Tournon, 75006 Paris, France (home). *Telephone:* 1-46-34-12-01 (office). *Website:* www.puf.com (office).

PRINCE, Alison Mary, DFA, DipEd; British writer, poet and journalist; b. 26 March 1931, Kent, England; m. Goronwy Siriol Parry 1957; two s. one d. *Education:* Beckenham Grammar School, Univ. of London, Slade School of Fine Art, Goldsmiths Coll. *Career:* fmr art teacher and TV scriptwriter; Fellow in Creative Writing, Jordanhill Coll., Glasgow 1988–90; currently writing children's books, poetry and journalism; mem. Scottish PEN, Soc. of Authors; Fellow, Inst. of Contemporary Scotland. *Play:* Balloons (musical). *Television:* Trumpton (writer, TV series) 1966–67. *Publications:* adult fiction: The Doubting Kind 1974; adult non-fiction: The Necessary Goat (essays) 1992, Kenneth Grahame: An Innocent in the Wild Wood (biog.) 1994, Hans Christian: The Fan Dancer (biog.) 1998, Poetry: Having Been in the City 1994, The Whifflet Train 2003; juvenile: The House on the Common 1969, The Red Alfa 1970, The Doubting Kind 1977, The Turkey's Nest 1979, The Night I Sold My Boots 1979, Who Wants Pets 1980, The Good Pets Guide, 1981, The Type One Super Robot 1981, Haunted Children 1982, The Sinister Airfield 1982, Night Landings, 1983, Goodbye Summer 1983, Scramble 1984, The Ghost Within 1984, Nick's October 1986, How's Business 1985, The Blue Moon Day 1989, The Sherwood Hero (Guardian Children's Fiction Award) 1996, Magic Dad 1997, Fergus, Fabulous Ferret 1997, Screw Loose 1998, Cat Number Three 1999, Dear Del 1999, Second Chance 2000, A Nation Again 2000, Bird Boy 2000, Bumble 2001, Oranges and Murder 2001, The Fortune Teller 2001, My Tudor Queen 2001, Boojer 2002, Turnaround 2002, Spud 2003, Three Blind Eyes 2003, Anne Boleyn and Me 2004, Luck 2004, The Summerhouse 2005, Tower-Block Pony 2004, Smoke 2005, Help 2006, Speed 2006, Doodlebug Summer 2007, Jacoby's Game 2008, Outbreak 2008, Tudor Stories for Girls 2009, Web 2010. *Honours:* Hon. DLitt (Leicester) 2005; Scottish Arts Council Awards for Children's Literature, Literary Review Grand Poetry Prize 2001, 2007. *Address:* Burnfoot, Whiting Bay, Isle of Arran, KA27 8QL, Scotland (home). *Telephone:* (1770) 700574 (home). *Fax:* (1770) 700204 (home). *E-mail:* alison.prince1@virgin.net (office). *Website:* www.alisonprince.co.uk.

PRINCE, Mona; Egyptian novelist. *Publications:* Three Suitcases for Departure (in Arabic) 2003. *Address:* c/o American University in Cairo, POB 2511, 113 Sharia Kasr El-Aini, Cairo, Egypt.

PRINCE, Peter Alan, BA, MA; British writer and screenwriter; b. 10 May 1942, Bromley, England. *Education:* Univ. of Pennsylvania, Columbia Univ. *Television plays include:* Oppenheimer 1980. *Publications:* Play Things (Soc. of Authors Somerset Maugham Award 1973) 1972, Dogcatcher 1974, Agents of a Foreign Power 1977, The Good Father 1983, Death of a Soap Queen 1990, The Great Circle 1997, Waterloo Story 1999, Adam Runaway 2005; contrib. to periodicals. *Honours:* BAFTA Award 1980, Writers' Guild of Great Britain Award, MWA Special Award. *Address:* c/o Bloomsbury Publishing Plc, 36 Soho Square, London, W1D 3QY (office). *Website:* www.bloomsbury.com (office).

PRINGLE, Heather Anne, BA, MA; Canadian writer; b. 8 Dec. 1952, Edmonton, AB; m. Geoff. *Education:* Univ. of Alberta, Univ. of British Columbia. *Publications:* In Search of Ancient North America 1996, The Mummy Congress 2001, The Master Plan: Himmler's Scholars and the Holocaust (Hubert Evans Non–Fiction Prize 2007) 2006; contribs to Science, Discover, Stern, Geo, New Scientist, National Geographic Traveler, Islands, Saturday Night, Canadian Geographic. *Honours:* American Asscn for the Advancement of Science Excellence in Science Journalism Award for Magazines 2001, Nat. Magazine Award 1988, Authors' Award 1992. *E-mail:* pringle@heatherpringle.com (office). *Website:* www.heatherpringle.com.

PRITCHARD, R(obert) John, AB, MA, PhD, LLB, FRHistS; American historian; b. 30 Nov. 1945, Los Angeles, CA; m. 1st Sonia Magbanna Zaide 1969 (divorced 1984); one s. one d.; m. 2nd Lady Selina Elaine Antonia FitzAlan-Howard Lodge 1989. *Education:* University of California, LSE, University of Kent at Canterbury, Inns of Court School of Law, London. *Career:* Lecturer in History, University of Kent, 1990–93; Fellow in War Studies, King's College, London, 1990–93; Simon Senior Research Fellow in History, University of Manchester, 1993–94; Dir, Historical Enterprises, 1993–; Dir, Robert M. Kempner Collegium, 1996–2000; Lecturer in Law, Business Studies and History, Stafford House College, Canterbury 2001–; mem. Middle Temple, 1995–. *Publications:* Reichstag Fire: Ashes of Democracy 1972, Cry Sabotage (co-author) 1972, The Tokyo War Crimes Trial: An International Symposium (co-author) 1984, General History of the Philippines Vol. 1: The American Half-Century 1898–1946 (co-author) 1984, Far Eastern Influences on British Strategy Towards the Great Powers 1937–39 1987, Overview of the Historical Importance of the Tokyo War Trial 1987, Total War: Causes & Courses of the Second World War (co-author) 1989, 1995, Japan and the Second World War (with Lady Toskiko Marks) 1989, Unit 731: The Japanese Army's Secret of Secrets (co-author) 1989, From Pearl Harbour to Hiroshima (co-author), 1993, The Cambridge Encyclopedia of Japan (co-author) 1993, La Déportation: La Système Concentrationnaire Nazi (co-author) 1995, Wada umi no Koe wo Kiku: senso sekinin to Ningen no Tsumi; to no Ma (Harken to the Cries at Our Birth: The Intervals Separating War Responsibility and Crimes of Humanity) (co-author) 1996, The Tokyo Major War Crimes Trial: The Records of the International Military Tribunal for the Far East with an Authoritative Commentary and Comprehensive Guide 1998–, World War II in Asia and the Pacific and the War's Aftermath, with General Themes: A Handbook of Literature and Research (co-author) 1998, Showa Japan: Political, Economic and Social History 1926–1989, II: 1941–1952, Section I: Politics & Economics (co-author) 1999, 1945: War and Peace in the Pacific, Selected Essays (co-author) 1999, The Penguin History of the Second World War 1999, International Criminal Law, III: Enforcement (co-author) 1999, A History of Anglo-Japanese Relations, III: The Military Dimension (co-author) 2003, International Humanitarian Law: Origins, Challenges, Prospects (with John N. Carey and William V. Dunlap), 3 vols, 2003, Encyclopedia of Genocide and Crimes against Humanity (co-author) 2004. *Honours:* many grants and fellowships. *Address:* 11 Charlotte Square, Margate, Kent, CT9 1LR, England.

PRITCHARD, William Harrison, BA, MA, PhD; American academic and author; b. 12 Nov. 1932, Binghamton, NY; m. Marietta Pritchard 1957, three s. *Education:* Amherst Coll., Columbia Univ., Harvard Univ. *Career:* Instructor 1958–61, Asst Prof. 1961–65, Assoc. Prof. 1965–70, Prof. 1970–, later Henry Clay Folger Prof. of English, Amherst Coll.; mem. Editorial Bd, Hudson Review; mem. Asscn of Literary Scholars and Critics, American Acad. of Arts and Sciences. *Publications:* Wyndham Lewis 1968, Wyndham Lewis: Profiles in Literature 1972, W. B. Yeats (ed.) 1972, Seeing Through Everything: English Writers 1918–1940 1977, Lives of the Modern Poets 1980, Frost: A Literary Life Reconsidered 1984, Randall Jarrell: A Literary Life 1990, Selected Poems of Randall Jarrell (ed.) 1990, Playing It By Ear: Literary Essays and Reviews 1994, English Papers: A Teaching Life 1995, Talking Back to Emily Dickinson and Other Essays 1998, Updike: America's Man of Letters 2000, Shelf Life: Literary Essays and Reviews 2003, On Poets and Poetry 2009; contrib. to Boston Sunday Globe, Hudson Review, New York Times Book Review, and numerous others. *Honours:* ACLS Junior Fellowship 1963–64, and Fellowship 1977–78, Guggenheim Fellowship 1973–74, Nat. Endowment for the Humanities Fellowships 1977–78, 1986, Under Criticism (essays) published in his honour 1998. *Address:* Department of English, Amherst College, Amherst, MA 01002 (office); 62 Orchard Street, Amherst, MA 01002, USA (home). *E-mail:* whpritchard@amherst.edu (office).

PROCHÁZKOVÁ, Petra; Czech journalist and humanitarian worker; b. 20 Oct. 1964, Césky Brod. *Education:* Charles Univ., Prague. *Career:* reporter Lidové Noviny newspaper 1989–97, foreign corresp. 1992–97; f. (with Jaromír Štetina) of war reporting agency, Epicentrum 1994; covered events in war zones including Georgia, Afghanistan and Grozny, Chechnya; also reported for Tyden and for Slovak newspaper, SME; began to organize relief efforts for war-ravaged families 2000–, est. shelter for orphans in Grozny; f. humanitarian org., Berkat to bring aid to Chechnya and Afghanistan; now freelance journalist and documentary maker. *Television:* Dark Side of the World (documentary) (Johns Hopkins Univ. SAIS-Novartis Prize for Excellence in Int. Journalism, Washington) 2000. *Publication:* Aluminiová Královna: ruskocecenská válka ocima žen (The Aluminium Queen: The Russian-Chechen War through the Eyes of Women) 2003. *Honours:* Ferdinand Peroutka Award 1998, K. H. Borovský Prize for extraordinary journalism activities 1999, 2000, Medal of Merit for humanitarian work in Chechnya 2000, Woman of Europe 2001, SVU Andrew Elias Humanitarian and Tolerance Award 2006. *Address:* c/o Berkat, Rumunská 24, 12000 Prague 2, Czech Republic.

PROCTER, Jane Hilary Elizabeth; British journalist; b. London; d. of Gordon H. Procter and Florence Bibby Procter; m. Thomas C. Goldstaub 1985; one s. one d. *Education:* Queen's Coll. Harley St London. *Career:* Fashion Asst Vogue 1974–75; Asst Fashion Ed. Good Housekeeping 1975–77; Acting Fashion Ed. Woman's Journal 1977–78; Fashion Writer Country Life 1978–80; Freelance Fashion Ed. The Times, Daily Express 1980–87; Ed. Tatler 1990–99, Ed. Dir PeopleNews Network 1999–2002. *Publication:* Dress Your Best 1983.

PROKHANOV, Aleksandr Andreevich; Russian writer, journalist and publisher; b. 1938, Moscow. *Education:* Moscow Institute of Aviation. *Career:* fmr correspondent, various Moscow newspapers, publisher, newspaper, Den; Ed., nationalist newspaper, Zavtra. *Publications:* Idu v moi put (I'm Entering My Way, prose), 1971; Kochuiushchaia roza (A Wandering Rose, novel), 1976; Vremia polden (The Time is Noon, novel), 1977; Mesto deistviia (A Place of Action, novel), 1980; Vechnyi gorod (Eternal Town, novel), 1981; Derevo v tsentre Kabula (The Tree in Kabul Downtown, novel), 1982; Risunki batalista (The Sketches of the Battle-pieces Painter, novel), 1985; Angel proletel (An Angel Has Flown, novel), 1991; Poslednii soldat imperii (The Last Soldier of the Empire, novel), 1992; Dvorets (The Palace, novel), 1994; Mr Hexagon, 2001. Contributions: various journals and magazines incl.: Znamia, Lunost, Oktiabr, Nash sovremennik. *Honours:* National Bestseller Prize 2002.

PROSE, Francine, BA, MA; American writer and academic; b. 1 April 1947, New York, NY; m. Howard Michels 1976; two s. *Education:* Radcliffe Coll., Harvard Univ. *Career:* teacher of creative writing, Harvard Univ. 1971–72; Visiting Lecturer in Fiction, Univ. of Arizona at Tucson 1982–84; instructor, Bread Loaf Writers' Conference 1984; fmr faculty mem., MFA Program, Warren Wilson Coll. 1984; Guggenheim and Fulbright fellowships; mem. Associated Writing Programs, PEN. *Publications:* Judah the Pious 1973, The Glorious Ones 1974, Stories From Our Living Past 1974, Marie Laveau 1977, Animal Magnetism 1978, Household Saints 1981, Hungry Hearts 1983, Bigfoot Dreams 1986, Women and Children First and Other Stories 1988, Primitive People 1992, A Peaceable Kingdom 1993, Hunters & Gatherers 1995, Guided Tours of Hell: Novellas 1997, The Demon's Mistake: A Story from Chelm 2000, Blue Angel: A Novel 2000, On Writing Short Stories (with others) 2000, The Lives of the Muses: Nine Women and the Artists They Inspired (non-fiction) 2002, Gluttony (non-fiction) 2003, After (juvenile) 2003, Best New American Voices (ed., anthology) 2005, A Changed Man 2005, Leopold, the Liar of Leipzig (juvenile) 2005, Reading Like a Writer 2006, Goldengrove 2008, Anne Frank: The Book, the Life, the Afterlife 2009; contrib. to periodicals, including Harper's and the Wall Street Journal. *Honours:* Dir's Fellow, Center for Scholars and Writers at the New York Public Library; Jewish Book Council Award 1973, Mademoiselle MLLE Award 1975, Hartford Jewish Community Center Edgar Lewis Wallant Memorial Award 1984. *Address:* c/o HarperCollins Publishers Inc., 10 E 53rd Street, New York, NY 10022, USA. *Website:* www.francineprose.com.

PROUD, Linda Helena; British writer; b. 9 July 1949, Broxbourne, Herts.; d. of William Wilfred Proud and Sybil Grace Proud; m. David Smith. *Education:* Coll. of Distributive Trades, London (Diploma in Display and Exhbn). *Career:* mem. Soc. of Authors. *Publications include:* Consider England 1994, Knights of the Grail 1995, Tabernacle for the Sun 1997, 2000 Years 1999, Icons: A Sacred Art 2000, Angels 2001, Pallas and the Centaur 2004, The Rebirth of Venus 2008. *Honours:* Southern Arts Bursary Fund 1995. *Address:* Godstow Press, 60 Godstow Road, Wolvercote, Oxford, OX2 8NY, England (office). *Telephone:* (1865) 556215 (office). *E-mail:* info@godstowpress.co.uk (office). *Website:* www.godstowpress.co.uk (office); www.lindaproud.com (home).

PROULX, (Edna) Annie, MA; American writer; b. 22 Aug. 1935, Norwich, Conn.; d. of George Napoleon Proulx and Lois Nellie Gill; m. 1st H. Ridgeley Bullock 1955 (divorced); one d.; m. 2nd James Hamilton Lang 1969 (divorced 1990); three s. *Education:* Univ. of Vermont and Sir George Williams (now Concordia) Univ., Montréal. *Career:* freelance journalist, Vt 1975–87; f. Vershire Behind the Times newspaper, Vershire, Vt; short stories appeared in Blair & Ketchums Country Journal, Esquire, etc.; Vt Council Arts Fellowship 1989, Ucross Foundation Residency, Wyo. 1990, 1992; mem. PEN; Guggenheim Fellow 1993; active anti-illiteracy campaigner. *Publications:* Heart Songs and Other Stories 1988, Postcards (novel) (PEN/Faulkner Award for Fiction 1993) 1992, The Shipping News (Chicago Tribune Heartland Prize for Fiction, Irish Times Int. Fiction Prize, Nat. Book Award for Fiction, Pulitzer Prize for Fiction 1994) 1993, Accordion Crimes 1996, Best American Short Stories (ed.) 1997, Brokeback Mountain (short story, Nat.Magazine Award 1998, O. Henry Awards Prize 1998) 1998, Close Range: Wyoming Stories (New Yorker Book Award Best Fiction 1999, English-Speaking Union's Amb. Book Award 2000, Borders Original Voices Award in Fiction 2000) 1998, That Old Ace in the Hole (Best Foreign Language Novels of 2002/Best American Novel Award, Chinese Publishing Asscn and Peoples' Literature Publishing House 2002) 2002, Bad Dirt: Wyoming Stories 2 2004, Fine Just the Way It Is: Wyoming Stories 3 2008, Bird Cloud: A Memoir 2011. *Honours:* Hon. DHumLitt (Maine) 1994; Alumni Achievement Award, Univ. of Vt 1994, New York Public Library Literary Lion 1994, Dos Passos Prize for Literature 1996, American Acad. of Achievement Award 1998. *Address:* PO Box 230, Centennial, WY 82055; c/o Simon & Schuster Inc., 1230 Avenue of the Americas, New York, NY 10020, USA (office). *Fax:* (307) 742-6159.

PRUNTY, Wyatt, BA, MA, PhD; American poet and editor; b. 15 May 1947, Humbolt, Tenn.; m. Barbara Heather Stell 1973; one s. one d. *Education:* Sewanee, Univ. of the South, Johns Hopkins Univ., Louisiana State Univ. *Career:* Instructor in English, Louisiana State Univ. 1978–79; Asst Prof. to Prof. of English, Virginia Polytechnic Inst. and State Univ., 1978–89; Visiting Writer, Washington and Lee Univ., 1982–83; Visiting Assoc. and Prof., Johns Hopkins Univ. 1987–89, Elliot Coleman Prof. 1988; Carlton Prof. of English, Univ. of the South 1989–; Distinct., Univ. of Cincinnati 1986; Founding Dir Sewanee Writers' Conf.; f. and ed Sewanee Writers' Series; Dir Tennessee Williams Fellowships; mem. Associated Writing Programs, Coll. English Asscn, English Inst., MLA. *Publications:* poetry: Domestic of the Outer Banks, 1980; The Times Between, 1982; What Women Know, What Men Believe, 1986; Balance as Belief, 1989; The Run of the House, 1993; Since the Noon Mail Stopped, 1997; Unarmed and Dangerous: New and Selected Poems, 1999; other: Fallen from the Symboled World: Precedents for the New Formalism, 1990, The Lovers' Guide to Trapping 2009; edited: Sewanee Writers on Writing, 2001, Just Let me Say This About That, How Animals Mate, Siam, The Determined Days, The Last of the Thorntons, The Aerialist, Errors in the Script, The King of Limbo, Starting from Sleep: New and Selected Poems, All Saints' Day, Ecstatic in the Poison, The Carpetbaggers' Children, The Actor, Boomtown; contributions: anthologies, reviews, quarterlies and journals. *Honours:* Poetry Prize, Sewanee Review 1969; Fellow, Bread Loaf Writers' Conference 1982, Brown Foundation Fellow 1986, Guggenheim Fellowship 2001–02, The Poet's Prize 2001, Rockefeller Foundation residency 2002, Fellowship of Southern Writers 2005. *Address:* Sewanee Writers' Conference, University of the South, Sewanee, TN 37383, USA.

PRYCE-JONES, David, BA, MA; British writer; *Senior Editor, National Review;* b. 15 Feb. 1936, Vienna, Austria; s. of Alan Pryce-Jones and Thérèse Fould-Springer; m. 1959, one s. two d. *Education:* Magdalen College, Oxford. *Career:* Literary Ed., Time & Tide 1961, Spectator 1964; Senior Ed., National Review, New York 1999–; mem. RSL. *Publications:* Owls & Satyrs 1961, The Sands of Summer 1963, Next Generation 1964, Quondam 1965, The Stranger's View 1967, The Hungarian Revolution 1969, Running Away 1969, The Face of Defeat 1971, The England Commune 1973, Unity Mitford 1976, Vienna 1978, Shirley's Guild 1981, Paris in the Third Reich 1983, Cyril Connolly 1984, The Afternoon Sun 1986, The Closed Circle 1989, Inheritance 1992, You Can't Be Too Careful 1993, The War That Never Was 1995, Betrayal 2006, Safe Houses 2007, Treason of the Heart 2011; contrib. to numerous journals and magazines. *Honours:* Wingate Prize 1986, Sunlight Literary Prize 1989, Steinberg Award 2010. *Address:* Lower Pentwyn, Gwenddwr, Powys LD2 3LQ, Wales (home).

PRYOR, Boori Monty; Australian writer; b. 12 July 1950, Townsville, Qld. *Publications:* Maybe Tomorrow (with Meme McDonald), 1998; My Girragundji (with Meme McDonald), 1998; The Binna Binna Man (with Meme McDonald), 1999; Reconcilliation, 2000. Contributions: Australian Bookseller and Publisher, 1999; The Bulletin, 2000. *Honours:* Children's Book Council of Australia Book of the Year Award for Younger Readers, 1999; NSW State Literary Award for Younger Readers, 2000, and Book of the Year, 2000, and Ethnic Affairs Commission Award, 2000; Australian Audio Book Awards, Author/Narrator Category winner and Overall Narration Book Winner. *Address:* c/o Penguin Group (Australia), 250 Camberwell Road, Camberwell, Vic. 3124, Australia (office).

PU, Nai-fu; Taiwanese writer; b. Nanjing; m. *Education:* Beijing Russian-Language Jr Coll. *Career:* imprisoned for various periods in labour-reform camps during anti-intellectual campaigns in China; moved to Hong Kong, subsequently to Taiwan 1983. *Publications include:* Romance in the Arctic, The Woman in the Pagoda, Books Without Names (six vols), The Scourge of the Sea, Red in Tooth and Claw.

PULKKINEN, Riikka; Finnish author; b. 8 July 1980, Tampere. *Education:* Univ. of Helsinki. *Publications include:* novels: Raja (Border) 2006, Totta (True) 2010. *Honours:* Kaarle Prize 2007, Laila Hirvisaari Prize 2007. *Address:* c/o Otava Publishing Company Limited, Uudenmaankatu 10, 00120 Helsinki, Finland (office). *Telephone:* (9) 19961 (office). *Fax:* (9) 643136 (office). *E-mail:* name.surname@otava.fi (office). *Website:* www.otava.fi/en_GB (office).

PULLINGER, Kate; Canadian writer; *Reader in Creative Writing and New Media, De Montfort University;* b. Cranbrook, British Columbia; m.; two c. *Career:* currently lives in London, UK; Reader in Creative Writing and New Media, De Montfort Univ. 2007–; mem. Soc. of Authors. *Publications:* Tiny Lies (short stories) 1988, When the Monster Dies (novel) 1989, Where Does Kissing End? (novel) 1992, The Piano (co-writer) 1994, Forcibly Bewitched (short stories) 1996, The Last Time I Saw Jane (novel) 1996, My Life as a Girl in a Men's Prison (short stories) 1997, Weird Sister (novel) 1999, A Little Stranger (novel) 2004, The Mistress of Nothing (novel) (Gov.-Gen.'s Literary Award for Fiction) 2009; digital fiction: Inanimate Alice, Flight Paths: A Networked Novel; numerous short story contribs to various anthologies. *Literary Agent:* Anne McDermid and Associates, 83 Willcocks Street, Toronto, ON M5S 1C9, Canada. *Telephone:* (416) 324-8845. *E-mail:* info@mcdermidagency.com. *Website:* www.katepullinger.com. *Address:* Department of English and Creative Writing, Faculty of Humanities, Clephan Building, De Montfort University, The Gateway, Leicester, LE1 9BH, England (office). *E-mail:* hello@katepullinger.com (office). *Website:* www.katepullinger.com.

PULLMAN, Philip, CBE, BA, FRSL; British writer; b. 19 Oct. 1946, Norwich, Norfolk; m. Jude Speller 1970; two s. *Education:* Exeter Coll., Oxford. *Career:* teacher in Oxford 1972–86; part-time Lecturer, Westminster Coll., Oxford 1986–96. *Publications:* Count Karlstein 1982, The Ruby in the Smoke (Sally Lockhart series) 1985, The Shadow in the Plate 1986, The Shadow in the North (Sally Lockhart series) 1987, Spring-Heeled Jack 1989, The Tiger in the Well (Sally Lockhart series) 1990, The Broken Bridge 1990, The White Mercedes 1992, The Tin Princess (Sally Lockhart series) 1994, The New Cut Gang: Thunderbolt's Waxwork 1994, The New Cut Gang: The Gas-fitter's Ball 1995, The Wonderful Story of Aladdin and the Enchanted Lamp 1995, The Firework-Maker's Daughter 1995, Northern Lights (aka The Golden Compass, Vol. I, His Dark Materials trilogy) (Carnegie Medal 1996, Guardian Children's Fiction Prize 1996, British Book Awards Children's Book of the Year 1996, CILIP Carnegie Medal 2007) 1995, Clockwork 1996, The Subtle Knife (Vol. II, His Dark Materials trilogy) 1997, The Butterfly Tattoo 1998, Mossycoat 1998, Detective Stories (ed.) 1998, I Was a Rat! 1999, The Amber Spyglass (Vol. III, His Dark Materials trilogy) (British Book Awards WH Smith Children's Book of the Year, Whitbread Children's Book of the Year Prize 2001, Whitbread Book of the Year Award 2001) 2000, Puss-in-Boots 2000, Sherlock Holmes and the Limehouse Horror 2001, Lyra's Oxford 2003,

The Scarecrow and his Servant 2004, A Word or Two About Myths 2005, The Good Man Jesus and the Scoundrel Christ 2010; contrib. reviews to Times Educational Supplement, The Guardian. *Honours:* Hon. Fellow Univ. of Wales, Bangor; Hon. DLitt (Univ. of East Anglia), (Oxford Brookes Univ.), (Oxford Univ.) 2009, (Exeter Univ.) 2010, Hon. DUniv (Univ. of Surrey Roehampton); Booksellers' Asscn/Book Data Author of the Year Award 2001, Booksellers' Asscn Author of the Year 2001, 2002, British Book Awards Author of the Year Award 2002, Whitbread Book of the Year Award 2002. *Literary Agent:* c/o Caradoc King, A. P. Watt Ltd, 20 John Street, London, WC1N 2DR, England. *Telephone:* (20) 7405-6774. *Fax:* (20) 7831-2154. *Website:* www.philip-pullman.com.

PUNTER, David Godfrey, BA, MA, PhD, FRSA, FSA; British professor of english, writer and poet; *Professor of English, University of Bristol*; b. 19 Nov. 1949, London, England; s. of Douglas Herbert Punter and Hilda Mary Punter; m. Caroline Case 1988; one s. two d. *Education:* Univ. of Cambridge. *Career:* Lecturer in English, Univ. of East Anglia, 1973–86; Prof. and Head of Dept, Chinese Univ. of Hong Kong 1986–88; Prof. of English, Univ. of Stirling 1988–2000; Prof. of English, Univ. of Bristol 2000–, Research Dean of Arts 2004–08; Fellow, English Asscn (UK), Higher Educ. Acad.; Founding Fellow, Inst. of Contemporary Scotland. *Publications:* The Literature of Terror 1980, Blake, Hegel and Dialectic 1981, Romanticism and Ideology 1982, China and Class 1985, The Hidden Script 1985, Introduction to Contemporary Cultural Studies (ed.) 1986, Lost in the Supermarket 1987, Blake: Selected Poetry and Prose (ed.) 1988, The Romantic Unconscious 1989, Selected Poems of Philip Larkin (ed.) 1991, Asleep at the Wheel 1997, Gothic Pathologies 1998, Spectral Readings (ed.) 1999, Selected Short Stories 1999, Companion to the Gothic (ed.) 2000, Writing the Passions 2000, Postcolonial Imaginings 2000, The Influence of Postmodernism on Contemporary Writing 2005, Metaphor 2007, Modernity 2007, Rapture: Literature, Addiction, Secrecy 2009; contribs: hundreds of articles, essays, and poems in various publs. *Honours:* Hon. DLitt (Stirling) 1999; Scottish Arts Council Award. *Address:* The Coach House, Church Lane, Backwell, Bristol, BS48 3JJ, England (home). *Telephone:* (117) 928-8082 (office). *E-mail:* david.punter@bristol.ac.uk (office).

PURPURA, Lia, BA, MFA; American poet and teacher; b. 22 Feb. 1964, Long Island, NY; m. Jed Gaylin 1992; one s. *Education:* Oberlin Coll., Iowa Writers' Workshop. *Career:* Dept of Writing and Media, Loyola College, Baltimore, MD, 1990. *Publications:* The Brighter the Veil, 1996; Taste of Ash and Berliner Tagebuch-Poems of Grzegorz Musial, in press; Trans., poems by Katarzyna Borun-Jagodzinska and Krzysztof Piechowicz. Contributions: poems to numerous journals including: American Poetry Review; Antioch Review; Denver Quarterly; Ploughshares; Essays and reviews to several journals including: Willow Springs; Verse. *Honours:* Acad. of American Poets Award, 1986; Teaching and Writing Fellowship, University of Iowa Writers Workshop, 1988–90; Fulbright Fellowship, 1991–92; Blue Mountain Center Residency, 1995; First Prize, Visions International Trans. Prize, 1996; Millay Colony Resident Fellow, 1996.

PURSER, Philip John, MA; British journalist and author; b. 28 Aug. 1925, Letchworth, Herts.; m. Ann Elizabeth Goodman 1957; one s. two d. *Education:* St Andrews Univ. *Career:* mem. staff, Daily Mail 1951–57; TV Critic, Sunday Telegraph 1961–87; mem. Writers Guild of Great Britain, BAFTA. *Plays:* Calf Love (BBC TV) 1966, Hawks and Doves (A-R TV) 1967, Hazard (episode of A Family at War, Granada TV) 1970, Dr Glas (play, from novel by Hjalmar Soderberg, Derby Playhouse) 1970 (also on BBC Radio 3), Heydays Hotel (Granada TV) 1976, The One & Only Phyllis Dixey (Thames TV) 1978, Backfischliebe (WDR/NDR, Germany) 1985, Ceremonies of War (BBC Radio 4) 1985. *Publications:* Peregrination 22 1962, Four Days to the Fireworks 1964, The Twentymen 1967, Night of Glass 1968, The Holy Father's Navy 1971, The Last Great Tram Race 1974, Where is He Now? 1978, A Small Explosion 1979, The One and Only Phyllis Dixey 1978, Halliwell's Television Companion (with Leslie Halliwell) 1982, 1986, Shooting the Hero 1990, Poeted: The Final Quest of Edward James 1991, Done Viewing 1992, Lights in the Sky 2005; contribs to numerous magazines and journals. *Honours:* Critic of the Year, British Press Awards 1965. *Address:* 10 The Green, Blakesley, Towcester, Northants., NN12 8RD, England (home). *Telephone:* (1327) 860274 (home). *E-mail:* annphil.purser@btinternet.com.

PURVES, Elizabeth (Libby) Mary, OBE, MA; British writer and broadcaster; b. 2 Feb. 1950, London; d. of James Grant and Mary (née Tinsley) Purves; m. Paul Heiney 1980; one s. (deceased) one d. *Education:* Convent of the Sacred Heart, Tunbridge Wells and St Anne's Coll., Oxford. *Career:* BBC local radio, Oxford 1972–76; Reporter Today Programme BBC Radio 4 1976–79, Presenter 1979–81, currently Presenter on Radio 4 and BBC World Service; Presenter, BBC TV Choices 1982, BBC Radio Midweek 1984–; Ed. Tatler magazine 1983; columnist, The Times 1990–, Theatre Critic 2010–; Pres. Council for Nat. Parks 2000–01; writer for newspapers and magazines including The Times and Good Housekeeping. *Publications include:* Sailing Weekend Book 1985, Where Did You Leave the Admiral 1987, The English and their Horses (jtly) 1988, How Not to be a Perfect Mother 1988, One Summer's Grace 1990, How Not to Raise a Perfect Child 1991, Casting Off (novel) 1995, A Long Walk in Wintertime (novel) 1996, Grumpers' Farm (with Paul Heiney) 1996, Home Leave (novel) 1997, Holy Smoke 1998, More Lives than One (novel) 1998, How Not to be a Perfect Family 1999, Regatta (novel) 1999, Nature's Masterpiece: A Family Survival Book 2000, Passing Go (novel) 2000, Regatta 2002, Radio: A Love Story 2003, Continental Drift 2003, Mother Country 2003, Acting Up 2005, Love Songs and Lies (novel) 2007, Shadow Child (novel) 2009. *Literary Agent:* Lisa Eveleigh Literary Agency, 3rd Floor, 11-12 Dover Street, London, W1S 4LJ, England. *Telephone:* (20) 7399-2803. *Fax:* (20) 7399-2801. *E-mail:* eveleigh@dial.pipex.com.

PUTNAM, Hilary, PhD; American philosopher, mathematician and academic; *Cogan University Professor Emeritus, Department of Philosophy, Harvard University*; b. 31 July 1926, Chicago, Ill.; s. of Samuel Putnam and Riva Sampson; m. 1st Erna Diesendruck 1948 (divorced 1962); one d.; m. 2nd Ruth A. Hall 1962; two s. one d. *Education:* Cen. High School of Philadelphia, Univ. of Pennsylvania, Harvard Univ. and Univ. of California, Los Angeles. *Career:* Asst Prof. of Philosophy, Princeton Univ. 1953–60, Assoc. Prof. of Philosophy and of Math. 1960–61; Prof. of Philosophy of Science, MIT 1961–65; Prof. of Philosophy, Harvard Univ. 1965, Walter Beverly Pearson Prof. of Mathematical Logic and Modern Math. 1976–, then Cogan Univ. Prof., Emer. 2000–; Corresp. mem. British Acad., Acad. des Sciences Morales et Politiques; many other fellowships. *Publications:* Meaning and the Moral Sciences 1978, Reason, Truth and History 1981, Philosophical Papers (three vols) 1975–83, The Many Faces of Realism 1987, Representation and Reality 1989, Realism with a Human Face 1990, Renewing Philosophy 1992, Words and Life 1994, Pragmatism: an Open Question 1995, The Threefold Cord 1999, Enlightenment and Pragmatism 2001, The Collapse of the Fact/Value Dichotomy 2002, Ethics without Ontology 2004, Philosophy in an Age of Science 2012. *Honours:* ten hon. degrees; Guggenheim Fellow 1960–61, Rolf Schock Prize in Logic and Philosophy 2011. *Address:* Department of Philosophy, Emerson 207, Harvard University, Cambridge, MA 02138 (office); 31 Cleveland Street, Arlington, MA 02174, USA (home). *Telephone:* (617) 495-2191 (office). *Fax:* (617) 495-2192 (office). *E-mail:* hputnam@fas.harvard.edu (office). *Website:* www.fas.harvard.edu/~phildept/putnam.html (office).

PYBUS, Rodney, BA, MA; British writer and poet; b. 5 June 1938, Newcastle upon Tyne, England; m. Ellen Johnson 1961; two s. *Education:* Gonville and Caius Coll., Cambridge. *Career:* Lecturer, Macquarie Univ., Australia 1976–79; Literature Officer, Cumbria 1979–81; mem. Soc. of Authors. *Performance:* In Memoriam Milena poems set to music by Jacques Michon and performed Toulouse 2001, Paris 2004. *Publications:* In Memoriam Milena 1973, Bridging Loans 1976, At the Stone Junction 1978, The Loveless Letters 1981, Talitha Cumi 1985, Cicadas in Their Summers: New and Selected Poems 1988, Flying Blues 1994, In Memoriam Milena 1995 (bilingual edn, French trans. by Françoise Trichet), Darkness Inside Out 2012; contrib. to numerous publs. *Honours:* Poetry Soc. Alice Hunt Bartlett Award 1974, Arts Council Writer's Fellowships 1982–85, Nat. Poetry Competition Awards 1984, 1985, 1988, Hawthornden Fellowship 1988, First Prize, Peterloo Poetry Competition 1989, major prizewinner, Arvon Int. Poetry Competition 2006. *Address:* 21 Plough Lane, Sudbury, Suffolk, CO10 2AU, England (home). *E-mail:* rodneypybus@gmail.com (home). *Website:* www.rodneypybus.co.uk.

PYLKKÄNEN, Alison, BA, MA; British magazine editor; *Editor-Publisher, Zest magazine*; b. 1963, Maltby, South Yorkshire; d. of Michael Green and Betty Green; m. Jussi Pylkkänen 1986; one s. one d. *Education:* Lady Margaret Hall, Oxford. *Career:* Sub-Ed., Good Housekeeping 1987, Deputy Ed. 1991; Ed. Good Housekeeping's Wedding magazine 1995; Ed. She magazine 1995–2001; Ed. Zest magazine 2001–05, Ed.-Publisher 2005–. *Address:* Zest magazine, National Magazine House, 72 Broadwick Street, London, W1F 9EP, England (office). *Website:* www.zest.co.uk (office).

PYNCHON, Thomas Ruggles, Jr, BA; American novelist; b. 8 May 1937, Glen Cove, NY; s. of Thomas R. Pynchon. *Education:* Cornell Univ. *Career:* fmr editorial writer, Boeing Aircraft Co.; Fellow, American Acad. of Arts and Sciences 2009–. *Publications:* V (Faulkner Prize for Best First Novel) 1963, The Crying of Lot 49 (Rosenthal Foundation Award 1967) 1965, Gravity's Rainbow (Nat. Book Award) 1973, Mortality and Mercy in Vienna 1976, Low-Lands 1978, Slow Learner (short stories) 1984, In the Rocket's Red Glare 1986, Vineland 1989, Deadly Sins 1994, Mason & Dixon 1996, Against the Day 2006, Inherent Vice 2009; contrib. short stories to various publs, including Saturday Evening Post. *Honours:* John D. and Catherine T. MacArthur Foundation Fellowship 1988; American Acad. of Arts and Letters Howells Medal 1975. *Literary Agent:* Melanie Jackson Agency, 250 West 57th Street, Suite 1119, New York, NY 10019, USA. *Address:* c/o Penguin Books, 250 Madison Avenue, New York, NY 10016, USA (office).

Q

QAEED, Yousef al-; Egyptian novelist and writer; b. 1944, Al-Bihera. *Career:* his novel War in the Land of Egypt was banned in Egypt until 1985; mem. Hizb al-Tagammu' al-Watani al-Taqadomi al-Wahdawi (National Progressive Unionist Party). *Publications:* short story collections and 11 novels including: Alhidad 1969, Akhbar Izbat al-Minisi 1970, Man yakaf Kamb David, wa qismat Al gurama, Laban al-'usfur 1994, Atlal al-Nihar 1997, Adab al-rihlat 1998, Alharb fe Barri misr (trans. as War in the Land of Egypt 1997, also film), Muhammad Hasanayn Haykal yatadhakkar: Abd al-Nasir wa-al-muthaqqafun wa-al-thaqafah 2003; stories published in Banipal. *Address:* c/o Hizb al-Tagammu' al-Watani al-Taqadomi al-Wahdawi (National Progressive Unionist Party), 1 Sharia Karim el-Dawlah, Cairo, Egypt.

QIAN, Xinbo; Chinese journalist; b. (Jiarui Qian), 14 Jan. 1923, Jiading Co., Jiangsu Prov.; m. Chen Meixia 1953; one s. one d. *Education:* Yanjing Univ. *Career:* Council mem. of New China News Agency 1982–; Vice-Pres. and Sec.-Gen. of Fed. Journalism Soc. 1984–90; Deputy Dir of Journalism Inst. Acad. of Social Sciences 1982–90. *Publications:* On News' Role of Guidance, Five Historical Periods of Development of Chinese Journalism. *Address:* 6-1-502 Tuanjiehu Beili, Beijing 100026, People's Republic of China. *Telephone:* (10) 85989648.

QUANDT, William Bauer, BA, PhD; American political scientist, academic and writer; *Edward R. Stettinius, Jr Professor of Politics, University of Virginia*; b. 23 Nov. 1941, Los Angeles, Calif.; m. 1st Anna Spitzer 1964 (divorced 1980); m. 2nd Helena Cobban 1984, one d. *Education:* Stanford Univ., Massachusetts Inst. of Tech. *Career:* researcher, RAND Corpn, Santa Monica, Calif. 1967–72; staff mem., Nat. Security Council, Washington, DC 1972–74, sr staff mem. 1977–79; Assoc. Prof., Univ. of Pennsylvania 1974–76; Sr Fellow, Brookings Inst., Washington, DC 1979–94; Sr Assoc., Cambridge Energy Research Assocs, Mass 1983–90; Edward R. Stettinius, Jr Prof. of Politics, Univ. of Virginia 1994–; mem. Council on Foreign Relations, Middle East Inst., Middle East Studies Assn (Pres. 1987–88), American Acad. of Arts and Sciences. *Publications include:* Revolution and Political Leadership: Algeria 1954–68 1969, The Politics of Palestinian Nationalism 1973, Decade of Decisions 1977, Saudi Arabia in the 1980s 1981, Camp David: Peacemaking and Politics 1986, The Middle East: Ten Years After Camp David 1988, The United States and Egypt 1990, Peace Process: American Diplomacy and the Arab–Israeli Conflict Since 1967 (third edn 2005), The Algerian Crisis (with Andrew Pierre) 1996, Between Ballots and Bullets: Algeria's Transition from Authoritarianism 1998; contribs to professional journals. *Honours:* Nat. Defense Educ. Act Fellow 1963, Social Science Research Council Fellow 1966, Council on Foreign Relations Fellow 1972. *Address:* Department of Politics, University of Virginia, PO Box 400787, 164 Gibson Hall, Charlottesville, VA 22904-4787, USA (office). *Telephone:* (434) 924-7896 (office). *Fax:* (434) 971-1810 (office). *E-mail:* quandt@virginia.edu (office). *Website:* www.people.virginia.edu/~wbq8f (office).

QUARTON, Marjorie; Irish writer and fmr farmer, horse dealer and dog breeder; *Writer, Public Relations, Publicity, Editor, Volunteer Welfare, National Council for the Blind of Ireland*; b. (Marjorie Smithwick), 25 Oct. 1930, Nenagh, Tipperary; m. John Quarton; one d. *Education:* educated at home and at Knockrabo School, Co. Dublin. *Career:* mem. Irish PEN, Writers' Union; writer, public relations, publicity, editor, volunteer welfare, Nat. Council for the Blind of Ireland. *Radio:* RTÉ1 and BBC Radio 4, prov. radio stations in Ireland. *Television:* TV1 (Ireland). *Publications include:* Corporal Jack (novel) 1987, No Harp Like My Own (novel) 1988, Breakfast The Night Before (memoir) 1989 (revised edn 2000), The Cow Watched the Battle (juvenile) 1990, The Other Side of the Island (juvenile) 1991, Renegade (novel) 1991, Saturday's Child (memoir) 1993; non-fiction: The Working Border Collie 1986 (revised edn 1998), One Dog, His Man and His Trials 1994, Part Time Writer: Notes and Reflections 2010, Mary Cannon's Commonplace Book 2010, Foxhunting in North Tipperary 2010, Oil and Water 2011. *Address:* 1 Casement Terrace, Dublin Road, Nenagh, Co. Tipperary, Ireland (home). *Telephone:* 87-2670152 (mobile) (office). *E-mail:* mquarton@eircom.net (home). *Website:* ncbi.ie (office).

QUEFFÉLEC, Yann; French writer; b. 4 Sept. 1949, Paris; s. of Henri Queffélec. *Publications include:* Béla Bartok 1881–1945 (biog.) 1981, Le Charme noir 1983, Les Noces barbares (Prix Goncourt) 1985, La Femme sous l'horizon 1988, Le Maître des chimères 1990, Prends garde au loup 1992, Disparue dans la nuit 1994, Bretagne, le soleil se lève à l'ouest 1994, Et la force d'aimer 1996, Happy Birthday Sara 1998, Trente jours à tuer (online interactive novel) 1998, Noir animal, ou la menace 1999, Osmose 2000, Boris après l'amour 2002, Nellys Lachen 2002, La Dégustation 2003, Vert cruel 2003, Moi et toi 2004, Les Affamés 2004, Dora 2004, Vents et marées 2005, Eloge de l'alcool 2005, Ma première femme 2005, L'Amante 2006, Mineure 2006, Le plus heureux des hommes 2007, L'Amour est Fou 2007, Passions Criminelles 2008, Barbaque 2008, Tabarly 2008, Adieu au Bugaled Breizh 2009, La Puissance des Corps 2009, Le Piano de ma Mère 2009, Les Sables du Jubaland 2010. *Address:* c/o Editions Plon, 76 rue Bonaparte, 75284 Paris, France (office). *Website:* www.plon.fr (office).

QUERRY, Ronald (Ron) Burns, BA, MA, PhD; American novelist; b. (Ronald Downer Burns), 22 March 1943, Washington, DC; m. Elaine Stribling Querry; one d. *Education:* Central State Univ., Oklahoma, New Mexico Highlands Univ., Univ. of New Mexico. *Career:* Asst Prof., New Mexico Highlands Univ. 1975–77; Assoc. Prof., Lake Erie Coll. 1979–83; Instructor, Univ. of Oklahoma 1979–83, Visiting Assoc. Prof. and Writer-in-Residence 1993; mem. PEN, Native Writers Circle of the Americas, Tucson-Pima Co. Arts Comm. *Publications:* Growing Old at Willie Nelson's Picnic 1983, I See By My Get-Up 1987, Native Americans Struggle for Equality 1992, The Death of Bernadette Lefthand 1993, Bad Medicine 1998. *Honours:* Mountains & Plains Booksellers Award, Southwest Book Award, Border Regional Library Assn. *Address:* 1015 Third Street, Las Vegas, NM 87701-4417, USA (home). *E-mail:* rquerry@gmail.com (office).

QUICK, Barbara Susan, BA (Hons); American novelist, poet, screenwriter and essayist; b. 28 May 1954, Los Angeles, CA; d. of Harold C. Tritel and Edith Tritel (née Shepard); m. John Antony Quick 1988 (divorced 2010); one s.; m. Wayne Roden 2011. *Education:* Univ. of California, Santa Cruz. *Films:* screenplay: Saving Puccini. *Publications:* Northern Edge: A Novel 1990, Vivaldi's Virgins 2007 (15 translations worldwide), A Golden Web 2010; contrib. to Ms, New York Times Book Review, Newsweek, People magazine. *Honours:* Second Place, Ina Coolbrith Poetry Prize 1977, Discover: Great New Writers Prize 1990, Ed.'s Choice, Historical Novel Society 2007. *Literary Agent:* c/o Felicia Eth Literary Representation, 555 Bryant Street, Suite 350, Palo Alto, CA 94301, USA. *Telephone:* (650) 375-1276. *Fax:* (650) 375-1276. *E-mail:* feliciaeth@aol.com. *E-mail:* barbara@barbaraquick.com (office). *Website:* www.barbaraquick.com.

QUIGNARD, Pascal Charles Edmond, LicenFil; French writer; b. 23 April 1948, Verneuil-sur-Avre, Eure; s. of Jacques Quignard and Anne Quignard (née Bruneau); one s. *Education:* Lycée de Havre, Lycée de Sèvres and Faculté des Lettres de Nanterre. *Career:* lecturer 1969–77; mem. Cttee of Lecturing 1977–94; Sec.-Gen. for Editorial Devt, Editions Gallimard; Pres. Int. Festival of Opera and Baroque Theatre, Château de Versailles 1990–94; Pres. Concert des Nations 1990–93. *Publications include:* L'être du balbutiement 1969, Alexandra de Lycophron 1971, La parole de la Délie 1974, Michel Deguy 1975, Echo 1975, Sang 1976, Le lecteur 1976, Hiems 1977, Sarx 1977, Inter aerias fagos 1977, Sur le défaut de terre 1979, Carus 1979, Le secret du domaine 1980, Petits traités (tome I à VIII) 1990, Les tablettes de buis d'Apronenia Avitia 1984, Le vœu de silence (essay) 1985, Une gêne technique à l'égard des fragments 1986, Ethelrude et Wolframm 1986, Le salon de Wurtemberg 1986, La leçon de musique 1987, Les escaliers de Chambord 1989, La raison 1990, Albucius 1990, Tous les matins du monde 1991, Georges de La Tour 1991, La Frontière 1992, Le nom sur le bout de la langue 1993, Le sexe et l'effroi 1994, L'occupation américaine 1994, Rhétorique spéculative 1995, L'amour conjugal 1995, Les septante 1995, La haine de la musique 1996, Vie secrète 1998, Terrasse à Rome (Grand Prix du roman de l' Acad. française 2000) 2000, Albucius 2001, Les ombres errantes (Prix Goncourt 2002) 2002, Sur le jadis 2002, Abîmes 2002, Les Paradisiaques 2005, Sordidissimes 2005, Écrits de l'éphémère 2005, Pour trouver les Enfers 2005, Villa Amalia 2006, L'Enfant au visage couleur de la mort 2006, Triomphe du temps 2006, Ethelrude et Wolframm 2006, Le Petit Cupidon 2006, Requiem 2006, La Nuit sexuelle 2007, Boutès 2008, La Barque Silencieuse 2009, Assises du roman 2009. *Honours:* Chevalier, Légion d'honneur; Prix de la Soc. des gens de lettres for his collected works 1998, Grand prix du roman de la Ville de Paris 1998, Prix de la fondation Prince Pierre de Monaco for his collected works 2000. *Address:* c/o Éditions du Seuil, 25 boulevard Romain Rolland, 75993 Paris, France (office). *Website:* www.seuil.com (office).

QUINN, Julia, (Julia Pottinger), BA; American writer; b. (Julie Pottinger), 1970; m. Paul Pottinger. *Education:* Harvard Univ. *Career:* historical romance writer. *Publications:* Splendid 1995, Dancing at Midnight 1995, Minx 1996, Everything and the Moon 1997, Brighter than the Sun 1997, To Catch an Heiress 1998, How to Marry a Marquis 1999, The Duke and I 2000, The Viscount Who Loved Me 2000, An Offer from a Gentleman 2001, Romancing Mister Bridgerton 2002, To Sir Phillip, With Love 2003, When He Was Wicked 2004, It's In His Kiss 2005, On the Way to the Wedding (Romance Writers of America RITA Award for Best Long Historical Romance 2007) 2006, The Secret Diaries of Miss Miranda Cheever (Romance Writers of America RITA Award for Best Regency Historical Romance 2008) 2007, The Lost Duke of Wyndham 2008, Mr Cavendish, I Presume 2008, What Happens in London 2009. *Address:* c/o Author Mail, 7th Floor, HarperCollins Publishers, 10 East 53rd Street, New York, NY 10022, USA (office). *E-mail:* jq@juliaquinn.com (office). *Website:* www.juliaquinn.com.

QUINNEY, Richard, BS, MA, PhD; American author, photographer and academic; *Professor Emeritus, Northern Illinois University*; b. 16 May 1934, Elkhorn, Wis.; s. of Floyd Quinney and Alice Quinney (née Holloway); m. Solveig Quinney; two d. *Education:* Carroll Coll., Northwestern Univ., Univ. of Wisconsin. *Career:* Instructor, St Lawrence Univ. 1960–62; Asst Prof., Univ. of Kentucky 1962–65; Assoc. Prof., New York Univ. 1965–70, Prof. 1970–73; Visiting Prof., CUNY 1974–75, Boston Univ. 1975; Visiting Prof., Brown Univ. 1975–78, Adjunct Prof. 1978–83; Assoc. Ed. Victimology 1976–82, Contemporary Crises 1977–90, California Sociologist 1977–, Critical Sociology 1978–, Western Sociological Review 1982–, Journal of Political and Military Sociology 1984–, Visual Sociology 1991–, Contemporary Justice Review 1997–; Distinguished Visiting Prof., Boston Coll. 1978–79, Adjunct Prof. 1980–83; Prof., Univ. of Wisconsin, Milwaukee 1980; Prof. of Sociology, Northern Illinois Univ. 1983–97, Prof. Emer. 1998–; Founder Borderland Books (ind. publr) 2005–; Fellow, American Soc. of Criminology 1995; mem. American Sociological Asscn. *Publications include:* Criminal Behavior Systems: A Typology (with Marshall B. Clinard) 1967, The Problem of Crime 1970, The Social Reality of Crime 1970, Criminal Justice in America: A Critical Understanding (ed.) 1974, Critique of Legal Order: Crime Control in Capitalist Society 1974, Criminology: Analysis and Critique of Crime in America 1975, Class, State, and Crime: On the Theory and Practice of Criminal Justice 1977, Capitalist Society: Readings for a Critical Sociology (ed.) 1979, Providence: The Reconstruction of Social and Moral Order 1980, Marxism and Law (co-ed. with Piers Beirne) 1982, Social Existence: Metaphysics, Marxism and the Social Sciences 1982, Criminology as Peacemaking (co-ed. with Harold E. Pepinsky) 1991, Journey to a Far Place: Autobiographical Reflections 1991, For the Time Being: Ethnography of Everyday Life 1998, Eric Fromm and Critical Criminology 2000, Bearing Witness to Crime and Social Justice 2000, Borderland: A Midwest Journal 2001, Storytelling Sociology 2004, Where Yet the Sweet Birds Sing 2006, Once Again the Wonder 2006, Of Time and Place 2006, Things Once Seen 2008, Field Notes 2008. *Honours:* Edwin Sutherland Award, American Soc. of Criminology 1984, Fulbright Lecture and Research Award, Univ. Coll., Galway, Ireland 1986, Pres.'s Award, Western Soc. of Criminology 1992, Canterbury Visiting Fellowship, Univ. of Canterbury, New Zealand 1993. *Address:* 33 Frederick Circle, Madison, WI 53711, USA (home). *Telephone:* (608) 232-0135 (office). *E-mail:* rquinney@earthlink.net (home). *Website:* www.borderlandbooks.net (office).

QUINTANA, Leroy V., BA, MA; American poet and writer; *Professor of English, San Diego Mesa College*; b. 1944, Alberquerque, NM. *Education:* Univ. of New Mexico, Univ. of Denver, New Mexico State Univ. *Career:* served in Viet Nam war 1967–68; Prof. of English, San Diego Mesa Coll. *Publications include:* Hijo del Pueblo 1976, Sangre 1981, Interrogations 1990, The History of Home 1993, My Hair Turning Gray Among Strangers 1996, The Great Whirl of Exile 1999, La Promesa and other stories 2002. *Honours:* American Book Awards 1981, 1992, Southwest Book Award 1981. *Address:* English Department, San Diego Mesa College, G-248, 7250 Mesa College Drive, San Diego, CA 92111-4998, USA (office). *Telephone:* (619) 388-2366 (office). *E-mail:* lquintan@sdccd.edu (office). *Website:* www.sdmesa.edu (office).

QUIRK, Baron (Life Peer), cr. 1994, of Bloomsbury in the London Borough of Camden; **(Charles) Randolph Quirk,** Kt, CBE, PhD, DLitt, LLD, FBA; British academic; b. 12 July 1920, Isle of Man; s. of the late Thomas Quirk and Amy Randolph Quirk; m. 1st Jean Williams 1946; two s.; m. 2nd Gabriele Stein 1984. *Education:* Cronk y Voddy School, Douglas High School, Isle of Man, Univ. Coll., London. *Career:* served in RAF 1940–45; Lecturer in English, Univ. Coll. London 1947–54; Commonwealth Fund Fellow, Yale Univ. and Univ. of Mich., USA 1951–52; Reader in English Language and Literature, Univ. of Durham 1954–58, Prof. of English Language 1958–60; Quain Prof. of English, Univ. Coll. London 1960–81; Dir, Univ. of London Summer School of English 1962–67; Survey of English Usage 1959–83; mem. Senate, Univ. of London 1970–85 (Chair. Academic Council 1972–75), Court 1972–85; Vice-Chancellor, Univ. of London 1981–85; Pres., Inst. of Linguists 1983–86, British Acad. 1985–89, Coll. of Speech Therapists 1987–91; Gov., British Inst. of Recorded Sound, English-Speaking Union; Chair., Cttee of Enquiry into Speech Therapy Services, British Council English Cttee 1976–80, Hornby Educational Trust 1979–93; mem. BBC Archives Cttee 1975–79, British Council 1983–91; Trustee, Wolfson Foundation 1987–; Lee Kwan Yew Fellow, Singapore 1985–86; Vice-Pres., Foundation of Science and Tech. 1986–90; mem. House of Lords Select Cttee on Science and Tech. 1999–2002; Fellow, King's Coll. London, Queen Mary Coll. London, Univ. Coll. London, Imperial Coll. London, Academia Europaea; Foreign Fellow, Royal Belgian Acad. Sciences 1975, Royal Swedish Acad. 1986, Finnish Acad. of Sciences 1992, American Acad. of Arts and Sciences 1995. *Publications:* The Concessive Relation in Old English Poetry 1954, Studies in Communication (with A. J. Ayer and others) 1955, An Old English Grammar (with C. L. Wrenn) 1955, Charles Dickens and Appropriate Language 1959, The Teaching of English (with A. H. Smith) 1959, The Study of the Mother-Tongue 1961, The Use of English (with supplements by A. C. Gimson and J. Warburg) 1962, Prosodic and Paralinguistic Features in English (with D. Crystal) 1964, A Common Language (with A. H. Marckwardt) 1964, Investigating Linguistic Acceptability (with J. Svartvik) 1966, Essays on the English Language–Medieval and Modern 1968, Elicitation Experiments in English (with S. Greenbaum) 1970, A Grammar of Contemporary English 1972 (with S. Greenbaum, G. Leech, J. Svartvik) 1972, The English Language and Images of Matter 1972, A University Grammar of English (with S. Greenbaum) 1973, The Linguist and the English Language 1974, Old English Literature: A Practical Introduction (with V. Adams, D. Davy) 1975, A Corpus of English Conversation 1980; contrib. to many others including Charles Dickens (ed. S. Wall) 1970, A New Companion to Shakespeare Studies 1971, The State of the Language (with J. Svartvik) 1980, Style and Communication in the English Language 1982, A Comprehensive Grammar of the English Language (with S. Greenbaum, G. Leech and J. Svartvik) 1985, Words at Work: Lectures on Textual Structure 1986, English in Use (with Gabriele Stein) 1990, A Student's Grammar of the English Language (with S. Greenbaum) 1990, Grammatical and Lexical Variance in English 1995, Cronk y Voddy (with V. Cottle) 2010; papers in linguistic and literary journals. *Honours:* Hon. Fellow, Coll. of Speech Therapists, Inst. of Linguists, Hon. Master, Gray's Inn Bench 1983; numerous hon. degrees (Lund, Uppsala, Poznań, Nijmegen, Paris, Liège, Helsinki, Prague, Reading, Leicester, Salford, London, Newcastle, Bath, Durham, Essex, Open Univ., Glasgow, Bar-Ilan, Brunel, Bucharest, Sheffield, Richmond Coll., Aston, Copenhagen, Queen Margaret); Jubilee Medal, Inst. of Linguists 1973. *Address:* University College London, Gower Street, London, WC1E 6BT, England (office). *Telephone:* (20) 7219-2226 (office). *Fax:* (20) 7219-5979 (office).

R

RAAB, Lawrence Edward, BA, MA; American academic, poet and writer; *Morris Professor of Rhetoric, Williams College*; b. 8 May 1946, Pittsfield, Mass; m. Judith Ann Michaels 1968; one d. *Education:* Middlebury Coll., Syracuse Univ. *Career:* Instructor, American Univ. 1970–71; Lecturer, Univ. of Michigan 1974; Prof. of English, Williams Coll. 1976–, currently Morris Prof. of Rhetoric; staff, Bread Loaf School of English 1979–81, Bennington Writer's Conf. 1988, Bread Loaf Writer's Conf. 1994. *Publications:* poetry: Mysteries of the Horizon 1972, The Collector of Cold Weather 1976, Other Children 1986, What We Don't Know About Each Other 1993, The Probable World 2000, Visible Signs: New and Selected Poems 2003, The History of Forgetting 2009; contribs to numerous anthologies, scholarly journals and periodicals. *Honours:* Acad. of American Poets Prize 1972, Nat. Endowment for the Arts Fellowships 1972, 1984, Robert Frost Fellowship, Bread Loaf Writer's Conf. 1973, Yaddo Residencies 1979–80, 1982, 1984, 1986–90, 1994, 1996, 1998, Bess Hokin Prize, Poetry Magazine 1983, Nat. Poetry Series Winner 1992, MacDowell Colony Residencies 1993, 1995, 1997, 2000, Mellon Foundation Fellowship 2003, Guggenheim Fellowship 2007. *Address:* Department of English, Williams College, Hollander Hall, Room 209, 85 Mission Park Drive, Williamstown, MA 01267-0687, USA (office). *Telephone:* (413) 597-2560 (office). *E-mail:* lawrence.e.raab@williams.edu (office). *Website:* english.williams.edu/profile/lraab (office).

RABAN, Jonathan Mark Hamilton Priaulx, BA, FRSL; British author and critic; b. 14 June 1942, Fakenham, Norfolk; s. of Rev. Peter J. C. P. Raban and Monica Sandison; m. 1st Bridget Johnson (divorced 1970s); m. 2nd Caroline Cuthbert 1985 (divorced 1992); m. 3rd Jean Cara Lenihan 1992 (divorced 1997); one d. *Education:* King's School, Worcester, Peter Symonds School, Winchester, Brockenhurst Grammar, Univ. of Hull. *Career:* Asst Lecturer, Univ. Coll. of Wales, Aberystwyth 1965–67; Lecturer in English and American Literature, Univ. of E Anglia 1967–69; professional writer 1969–; emigrated to USA 1990. *Publications:* The Technique of Modern Fiction 1969, Mark Twain: Huckleberry Finn 1969, The Society of the Poem 1971, Soft City 1973, Robert Lowell's Poems (ed.) 1974, Arabia Through the Looking Glass 1979, Old Glory (RSL Heinemann Award and Thomas Cook Award 1982) 1981, Foreign Land (novel) 1985, Coasting 1986, For Love and Money 1987, God, Man & Mrs Thatcher 1989, Hunting Mister Heartbreak (Thomas Cook Award 1991) 1990, The Oxford Book of the Sea (ed.) 1992, Bad Land: An American Romance (Nat. Book Critics Circle Award and PEN/West Creative Nonfiction Award 1997) 1996, Passage to Juneau 1999, Waxwings (novel) 2003, My Holy War: Dispatches from the Home Front 2005, Surveillance (novel) 2006, Driving Home: An American Journey 2011; contribs to Harper's, Esquire, New Republic, Atlantic Monthly, New York Review of Books, London Review of Books, Outside, Granta, New York Times Book Review, Vogue, The Guardian, Independent, Financial Times, Wall Street Journal. *Honours:* Hon. DLitt (Univ. of Hull); Thomas Cook Award, Pacific Northwest Booksellers Asscn Award, Murray Morgan Prize, Gov.'s Award of the State of Washington, Nat. Book Critics' Circle Award, Heinemann Award, Royal Soc. of Literature, PEN/West Award for Creative Nonfiction. *Literary Agent:* c/o Aitken Alexander Associates Ltd, 18–21 Cavaye Place, London, SW10 9PT, England. *Telephone:* (20) 7373-8672. *Fax:* (20) 7373-6002. *E-mail:* reception@aitkenalexander.co.uk. *Website:* www.aitkenalexander.co.uk.

RABE, Berniece, BSEd, MA; American author; b. 11 Jan. 1928, Parma, MO; m. 1946, three s. one d. *Education:* National College, Northern Illinois University, Roosevelt University, Columbia College, Chicago. *Career:* Writing Instructor, Columbia College, Chicago; Consultant, Missouri Council of the Arts; mem. Society of Midland Authors; Off Campus Writers; Fox Valley Writers. *Publications:* Rass, 1973; Naomi, 1975; The Girl Who Had No Name, 1977; The Orphans, 1978; Who's Afraid, 1980; Margaret's Moves, 1987; A Smooth Move, 1987; Rehearsal for the Bigtime, 1988; Where's Chimpy, 1988; Tall Enough to Own the World, 1988; Magic Comes In It's Time, 1993; The Legend of the First Candy Cares, 1994. Other: Two film scripts; Picture books for children. Contributions: Short stories and articles. *Honours:* Honor Book, 1975, Golden Kite Award, 1977, National Society of Children's Book Writers; Midland Author's Award, 1978; Notable Book of the Year, American Library Asscn, 1982; National Children's Choice Award, 1987.

RABE, David William, BA, MA; American dramatist, screenwriter and author; b. 10 March 1940, Dubuque, IA; m. 1st Elizabeth Pan 1969 (divorced); one c.; m. 2nd Jill Clayburgh 1979. *Education:* Loras Coll., Villanova Univ. *Career:* feature writer, Register, New Haven 1969–70; Asst Prof., Villanova Univ. 1970–72. *Publications:* plays: The Basic Training of Pavlo Hummel 1971, Sticks and Bones 1971, The Orphan 1973, In the Boom Boom Room 1973, Burning 1974, Streamers 1976, Goose and Tomtom 1976, Hurlyburly 1984, Those the River Keeps 1990, Crossing Guard 1994, A Question of Mercy 1997; screenplays: I'm Dancing as Fast as I Can 1982, Streamers 1983, Casualties of War 1989, State of Grace 1990, The Firm 1993; novels: Recital of the Dog 1992, A Primitive Heart 2005, Dinosaurs on the Roof 2008, Girl by the Road at Night 2010. *Honours:* Rockefeller Foundation grant 1969, Associated Press Award 1970, Drama Desk Award 1971, Drama Guild Award 1971, Dramatists' Guild Elizabeth Hull-Kate Warriner Award 1971, Obie Award 1971, Outer Critics' Circle Award 1972, Tony Award 1972, American Acad. of Arts and Letters Awards 1974, 1976, Guggenheim Fellowship 1976, New York Drama Critics' Circle Award 1976. *Address:* c/o Simon and Schuster, Publicity Department, 1230 Avenue of the Americas, New York, NY 10020, USA (office). *Website:* www.simonsays.com (office).

RABEE, Hayder K. Gafar, BA; Iraqi teacher of calligraphy; b. 22 Feb. 1962, Najaf; m. Ahalam A. al-Zahawi 1986; two s. one d. *Education:* Inst. of Fine Arts. *Career:* calligrapher, Baghdad TV 1982–88; worked as designer, newspapers and magazines 1989–91; teacher, Inst. of Fine Arts, Baghdad 1992–, Head, Calligraphy Dept (evening classes) 1995–; teacher of Arabic Calligraphy, Jordanian Calligraphers' Soc. 1998; Gen. Sec. Iraqi Calligraphers' Soc. 1998–99; mem. Iraqi Plastic Arts Soc. 1996–2002, Iraqi Union of Artists, Iraqi Soc. for Calligraphy Jordanian Calligraphers' Soc., Egyptian Calligraphers' Soc. *Exhibitions:* Breezes from Baghdad, Italy 2001, 2004, Postal Card Fair, Sharijah Art Museum 2004. *Publication:* Proposed Alphabetic Study for Arabic Calligraphy in Printing 1989. *Honours:* State Trophy for Plastic Arts and Calligraphy 1989, 1999, Gold Medal, 2nd World Festival 1992, Third World Festival 1993, Gold Medal for Creativity, Dar Es-Salaam 1st Nat. Festival 1993, Appreciation Prize, 4th Baghdad Nat. Festival 1998, Appreciation Prize in 5th Int. Competition for Calligraphy, Turkey 2001, a main prizewinner, Int. Meeting for Calligraphy of the Islam World, Tehran 2002. *Address:* al-Waziria, Sec. 301, St. 13 Ho. 50, Baghdad (home); Department of Calligraphy, Institute of Fine Arts, al-Mansur, Baghdad, Iraq (office).

RABINOWICH, Julya; Russian novelist and playwright; b. 1970, Leningrad (now St Petersburg); one d. *Education:* Vienna Dolmetschuniversität, University of Applied Arts, Vienna. *Career:* moved to Vienna, Austria 1977; studied translation, philosophy and art; works as interpreter in psychotherapy and psychiatry sessions with refugees, Vienna Integrationshaus (House for Integration) 2006–. *Plays include:* Nach der Grenze 2007, Romeo + Julia 2008, Orpheus im Nestroyhof 2008, Fluchtarien 2009, Stück ohne Juden (A Play Without Jews) 2010, Auftauchen 2010. *Publications include:* novels: Spaltkopf (Splithead) (Rauriser Literaturpreis 2009) 2008, Herznovelle 2011. *Honours:* Vienna Wortstätten Fellowship 2004, MiA Award 2009, Elias Canetti Scholarship 2010. *Literary Agent:* c/o Anna Webber, United Agents, 12–26 Lexington Street, London, W1F 0LE, England. *Telephone:* (20) 3214-0876. *Fax:* (20) 3214-0801. *E-mail:* awebber@unitedagents.co.uk. *Website:* www.unitedagents.co.uk. *E-mail:* julya.rabinowich@gmail.com (home). *Website:* www.julya-rabinowich.com (home).

RACHLIN, Nahid, BA; Iranian/American writer and teacher; b. 6 June 1944, Abadan, Iran; m. Howard Rachlin, one d. *Education:* Lindenwood Coll., St Charles, MO and Columbia Univ. *Career:* teacher in New York Univ., School of Continuing Education 1978–90, Marymount Manhattan Coll. 1986–87, Hofstra Univ. 1988–90, Yale Univ. 1989–90, Hunter Coll., CUNY 1990, Barnard Coll. 1991–; mem. PEN. *Publications:* Foreigner 1978, John Murray 1978, Married to a Stranger 1983, Veils 1992; contrib. to reviews, journals and magazines. *Honours:* Doubleday-Columbia Fellowship, Stanford Univ. Stegner Fellowship, NEA grant, Bennet Certificate, PEN Syndicated Fiction Project. *E-mail:* nahidr@rcn.com. *Website:* nahidrachlin.com.

RACIONERO GRAU, Luis; Spanish librarian, academic and writer; b. 1940, Seu d'Urgell, Lleida. *Education:* Univ. of Calif., Berkeley, USA, Churchill Coll., Cambridge, UK. *Career:* industrial engineer, Barcelona 1965; Prof. of Micro Econs, Faculty of Econ. Sciences and Urban Studies, School of Architecture, Barcelona; fmr Dir Spanish Coll., Paris; Dir-Gen. Biblioteca Nacional, Madrid 2001–04. *Publications include:* Taoista textos de estética 1991, Atenas de Pericles 1993, El arte de escribir 1995, La sonrisa de la Gioconda: Memorias de Leonardo 1999, Filosofias del Underground 2000, El pecado original 2001, Oriente y Occidente 2001, El progreso decadente (Espasa de Ensayo Prize) 2001, El alquimista trouador 2003. *Address:* c/o Editorial Planeta, Córcega 273-277, 08008 Barcelona, Spain.

RADAKOVIĆ, Borivoj; Serbian playwright and writer; b. 1951. *Career:* f. Festival of Alternative Culture, network of new writers and publishers (invites UK and US writers to perform); currently full-time writer Zagreb, Croatia. *Publications:* Sjaj epohe (novel) 1990, Dobro dosli uplavi pakao (play) 1996, Jako, Croatian Nights (ed., anthology) 2005; two collections of short stories, trans. *Address:* c/o Rende, Hadži Đerina 7, II sprat, stan br. 8, 11000 Belgrade, Serbia. *E-mail:* info@rende.co.yu. *Website:* www.rende.co.yu.

RADDEN, Jennifer H., BA, BPhil, DPhil; Australian/American academic and writer; b. 10 Sept. 1943, Melbourne, Vic., Australia. *Education:* Univ. of Melbourne, Univ. of Oxford, UK. *Career:* psychiatric social worker, Melbourne 1966–67, Greenfield, Mass, USA 1971–72; Lecturer in Philosophy, Tufts Univ., Medford, Mass 1972–74; Lecturer, Univ. of Massachusetts, Boston 1975–84, Asst Prof. 1984–89, Assoc. Prof. 1990–97, Prof. of Philosophy 1997–2010, Chair. of Dept 2002–07; Guest Lecturer in Australia 1995, 1996, England 1995, 1999, 2006, Sweden 1996, Denmark 1997; mem. Forensic Psychiatry Group 1992–99, Human Rights Cttee 1996–2000, Massachusetts Mental Health Center and Harvard Medical School; mem. Ethics Cttee, McLean Hosp. 1996–; Fellow, Harvard Univ. 1991; mem. American Philosophical Asscn, Soc. for Women in Philosophy, Asscn for the Advancement of Philosophy and Psychiatry (Exec. Bd 1992–2002, Pres. 1997–), Soc. for Practical and Professional Ethics. *Publications:* Madness and Reason 1985,

Divided Minds and Successive Selves: Ethical Issues in Disorders of Identity and Personality 1996, The Nature of Melancholy (ed.) 2000, The Philosophy of Psychiatry: A Companion (ed.) 2004, Moody Minds Distempered: Essays on Melancholy and Depression 2009, The Virtuous Psychiatrist: Character Ethics in Psychiatric Practice (with John Z. Sadler) 2010, On Delusion 2011; contrib. to Philosophical Studies, Current Opinion in Psychiatry, Philosophy and Phenomenological Research, Bioethics, Journal of Social Theory and Practice, Dialogue, Philosophy, Psychiatry and Psychology Review, Harvard Review of Psychiatry. *Address:* Department of Philosophy, University of Massachusetts, Boston, MA 02125 (office); 10 Beaumont Street, Boston, MA 02124, USA (home). *Telephone:* (617) 436-5011 (home). *E-mail:* jennifer .radden@umb.edu.

RADLEY, Sheila (see Robinson, Sheila Mary)

RĂDULESCU, Răzvan; Romanian novelist and screenwriter; b. 23 Oct. 1969, Bucharest. *Career:* mem. Letters (training centre for young writers); fmr Art Dir, Elle Romania. *Screenplays:* Goods and Money 2001, Niki Ardelean, Colonel in Reserve 2001, Feed for Small Fry 2004, Offset 2004, The Death of Mr Lăzărescu 2005, The Paper will be Blue 2005. *Publications include:* Viaţa şi faptele lui Ilie Cazane (The Life and Deeds of Elijah Cazane) (novel) (Romanian Writers' Union Debut Prize) 1997, Theodosie cel Mic (Theodosius the Small) (novel) 2006; contrib. to anthologies and journals including Dilema, 22, Cotidianul. *Address:* c/o Polirom, PO Box 266, 700506 Iasi, Romania (office). *Telephone:* (232) 214100 (office). *Fax:* (232) 214111 (office). *E-mail:* office@polirom.ro (office). *Website:* www.polirom.ro.

RADZINSKY, Edvard Stanislavovich; Russian dramatist; b. 23 Sept. 1936, Moscow; s. of Stanislav Radzinsky and Sofia Radzinsky; m. 2nd Yelena Timofeyevna Denisova. *Education:* Inst. of History and Archival Science, Moscow. *Plays include:* My Dream is India 1960, You're All of Twenty-Two, you Old Men! 1962, One Hundred and Four Pages on Love 1964, Kolobashkin the Seducer 1967, Socrates 1977, Lunin 1980, I Stand at the Restaurant 1982, Theatre of the Time of Nero and Seneca 1984, Elderly Actress in the Role of Dostoevsky's Wife 1986, Sporting Scenes 1987, Our Decameron 1989. *Television:* author and narrator of TV series Mysteries of History 1997–. *Publications:* novels: The Last of the Romanovs 1989, Our Decameron 1990; non-fiction: The Last Tsar: The Life and Death of Nicholas II 1992, God Save and Restrain Russia 1993, Stalin 1996, Mysteries of History 1997, Mysteries of Love 1998, Fall of Gallant Century 1998, Collected Works (7 Vols) 1998–99, Rasputin 1999, The Theatrical Novel (memoirs) 1999, Alexander II, The Last Great Tsar 2005. *Address:* Usiyevicha Street 8, Apt 96, 125319 Moscow, Russia (home). *E-mail:* edvard@radzinski.ru (office). *Website:* www.radzinski .ru (office).

RAE, Hugh Crauford, (James Albany, Robert Crawford, R. B. Houston, Stuart Stern, Jessica Stirling); British novelist; b. 22 Nov. 1935, Glasgow, Scotland; m. Elizabeth Dunn 1960, one d. *Career:* mem. Scottish Asscn of Writers. *Publications:* Skinner 1965, Night Pillow 1966, A Few Small Bones 1968, The Saturday Epic 1970, Harkfast 1976, Sullivan 1978, Haunting at Waverley Falls 1980, Privileged Strangers 1982; as Jessica Stirling: The Spoiled Earth 1974, The Hiring Fair 1976, The Dark Pasture 1978, The Deep Well at Noon 1980, The Blue Evening Gone 1982, The Gates at Midnight 1983, Treasures on Earth 1985, Creature Comforts 1986, Hearts of Gold 1987, The Good Provider 1988, The Asking Price 1989, The Wise Child 1990, The Welcome Light 1991, Lantern for the Dark 1992, Shadows on the Shore 1993, The Penny Wedding 1994, The Marrying Kind 1995, The Workhouse Girl 1996, The Island Wife 1997, Prized Possessions 2001; as James Albany: Warrior Caste 1982, Mailed Fist 1982, Deacon's Dagger 1982, Close Combat 1983, Matching Fire 1983, Last Bastion 1984, Borneo Story 1984.

RAE, Simon; British poet, biographer, broadcaster and playwright; b. 1952. *Career:* Poet-in-Residence, Warwickshire County Cricket Club/Midlands Arts Centre 1999; Founder mem., Top Edge Theatre Productions. *Radio:* Poetry Please (presenter, BBC Radio 4), 20,000 Frenchmen under the Sea (writer) 1993, A Memory Lost (writer) 1994, Who Shall Bind the Infinite? (writer) 1995, Not at Dorking (writer) 1996. *Plays:* A Quiet Night In 1999, Grass 2001, Rose 2003. *Publications:* poetry: Faber Introduction 5 1982, Great Tew 1989, Seren Poets 2 1990, Calendar 1990, Soft Targets 1991, Thatcher's Inferno 1992, Listening to the Lake 1993, Allotment 1996, Rapid Response: Poems from The Guardian 1991–1996, The Face of War 1999, Empires 2001, Caught On Paper: Cricket Poems 2002, Gift Horses 2006; biography: W.G. Grace: A Life 1998, It's Not Cricket: A History of Skulduggery, Sharp Practice and Downright Cheating in the Noble Game 2001; editor: The Orange Dove of Fiji: Poems for the World Wide Fund for Nature 1989, The Faber Book of Drink, Drinkers and Drinking 1991, The Faber Book of Murder 1994, The Faber Book of Christmas 1996, News That Stays News: The Twentieth Century in Poems 1999; contrib. poetry to anthologies, including Give Me Shelter 1991, Klaonica: Poems for Bosnia 1993, Bearing Witness 1995, The Gift: New Writing for the NHS 2002; contrib. to The Guardian, TLS, The Observer, New Statesman, Poetry Review, London Magazine, Leviathan. *Honours:* Royal Literary Fund Fellow, Warwick Univ. 1999–2001, Oxford Brookes Univ. 2003; Nat. Poetry Competition winner 1999, Southern Arts Literature Bursary, Gregory Award. *Address:* Top Edge Productions, 4 High Street, Bampton, Oxon., OX18 2JR, England (office). *Telephone:* (1993) 850581 (office). *Website:* www.topedge.biz (office).

RAE-ELLIS, Vivienne, (Antonia Bell), FRGS; Australian writer; b. 23 July 1930, Tasmania, Australia; m. W.F. Ellis 1952; one s. one d. *Career:* worked as newspaper columnist, radio scriptwriter, public relations officer; also worked as actress and mem. Launceston Players Theatre Co.; began writing in the 1960s; mem. Australian TTT Soc. of Authors, RSL, Soc. of Authors, London. *Publications:* Lively Libraries 1975, Trucanini: Queen or Traitor? 1976, Queen Trucanini (with Nancy Cato) 1976, Menace at Oyster Bay 1978, The Tribe With No Feet 1978, Louisa Anne Meredith: A Tigress in Exile 1979, The Cavendish Affair 1980, Black Robinson 1988, True Ghost Stories 1990; contrib. to books, newspapers, journals, radio and TV. *Address:* Gainsborough's House, 17 The Circus, Bath, BA1 2ET, England (home). *E-mail:* vraellis@gifford.co.uk.

RAFFEL, Burton Nathan; American academic, lawyer, writer, poet and editor and translator; b. 27 April 1928, New York, NY; m. Elizabeth Clare Wilson 1974; three s. three d. *Education:* BA, Brooklyn College, CUNY, 1948; MA, Ohio State Univ., 1949; JD, Yale Univ., 1958. *Career:* Lecturer, Brooklyn College, CUNY, 1950–51; Ed., Foundation News, 1960–63; Instructor, 1964–65, Asst Prof., 1965–66, State Univ. of New York at Stony Brook; Assoc. Prof., State Univ. of New York at Buffalo, 1966–68; Visiting Prof., Haifa Univ., 1968–69, York Univ., Toronto, 1972–75, Emory Univ., 1974; Prof. of English and Classics, Univ. of Texas at Austin, 1969–71; Sr Tutor (Dean), Ontario College of Art, Toronto, 1971–72; Prof. of English, 1975–87, Lecturer in Law, 1986–87, Univ. of Denver; Ed.-in-Chief, Denver Quarterly, 1976–77; Contributing Ed., Humanities Education, 1983–87; Dir, Adirondack Mountain Foundation, 1987–89; Advisory Ed., The Literary Review, 1987–2003; Distinguished Prof. of Humanities and Prof. of English, Univ. of Louisiana at Lafayette, 1989–2003; mem. National Faculty. *Publications:* Non-Fiction: The Development of Modern Indonesian Poetry, 1967; The Forked Tongue: A Study of the Translation Process, 1971; Introduction to Poetry, 1971; Why Re-Create?, 1973; Robert Lowell, 1981; T. S. Eliot, 1982; American Victorians: Explorations in Emotional History, 1984; How to Read a Poem, 1984; Ezra Pound: The Prime Minister of Poetry, 1985; Politicians, Poets and Con Men, 1986; The Art of Translating Poetry, 1988; Artists All: Creativity, the University, and the World, 1991; From Stress to Stress: An Autobiography of English Prosody, 1992; The Art of Translating Prose, 1994; The Annotated Milton, 1999. Fiction: After Such Ignorance, 1986; Founder's Fury (with Elizabeth Raffel), 1988; Founder's Fortune (with Elizabeth Raffel), 1989. Poetry: Mia Poems, 1968; Four Humours, 1979; Changing the Angle of the Sun-Dial, 1984; Grice, 1985; Evenly Distributed Rubble, 1985; Man as a Social Animal, 1986; Beethoven in Denver, and other poems, 1999. Other: numerous trans.; annotated version of Hamlet, 2003. Contributions: professional journals. *Honours:* Frances Steloff Prize for Fiction, 1978; American-French Foundation Trans. Prize, 1991; several grants. *Address:* 203 S Mannering Avenue, Lafayette, LA 70508, USA. *E-mail:* bnraffel@cox-internet.com.

RAGAN, James, BA, PhD, LittD; American poet, dramatist, screenwriter and academic; *Professor and Director Emeritus of Professional Writing Program, University of Southern California*; b. 19 Dec. 1944, Pa; m. Debora Ann Skovranko 1982; one s. two d. *Education:* St Vincent Coll., Ohio Univ. *Career:* Prof. and Dir Professional Writing Program, Univ. of Southern California 1981–2007, Emer. 2007–; Visiting Prof., California Inst. of Tech. (Caltech) 1989–92; Distinguished Visiting Poet, Charles Univ., Prague, Czech Repub. 1993–; Distinguished Visiting Prof., Univ. of Oklahoma 2007–09; Arts & Sciences Distinguished Visiting Prof., Bowling Green State Univ. 2009–10; mem. Associated Writing Programs, MLA, Modern Poetry Asscn, PEN, Poetry Soc. of America, Writers' Guild of America, West. *Music:* Tokyo Special: Kimiko Kasai, Lyrics, CBS/Sony, Tokyo 1977, 'Lyric Recovery' Performance, Carnegie Hall, Poetry Lyrics 2000, 2002. *Plays produced:* The Landlord, Ohio Univ. 1971, Saints, Los Angeles 1972, Commedia, San Francisco 1984 (Moscow 1987, 2008, Athens 2008, Beijing 2008). *Films:* Exile (writer-dir) (USA) 1981, The House (script ed./consultant) (Slovakia) 2011. *Television:* host/writer, Poet's Corner, BHTV, Beverly Hills, Calif. (Telly Award 1996) 1995. *Publications:* In the Talking Hours 1979, Womb-Weary 1990, Yevgeny Yevtushenko: The Collected Poems (ed.) 1991, The Hunger Wall 1995, Lusions 1996, Selected Poems 2005, Too Long a Solitude 2009, The World Shouldering I 2012; contrib. to anthologies, reviews, quarterlies, journals and magazines. *Honours:* Hon. mem. Russian Acad. of Natural Sciences 1997; Hon. DHumLitt (St Vincent Coll.) 1990, (Richmond Univ., London) 2001; Emerson Poetry Prize 1971, Swan Foundation Humanitarian Award, Pittsburgh 1972, Nat. Endowment for the Arts grant 1972, Fulbright Fellow 1985, 1988, citation, Poetry Soc. of America Gertrude Claytor Award 1987, Ohio Univ. Medal of Merit for Poetry 1990, St Vincent Coll. Phi Kappa Phi Nat. Creative Artist Award 1999, and Presidential Medal 2003. *Address:* 1516 Beverwil Drive, Los Angeles, CA 90035-2911, USA (home). *Telephone:* (310) 277-1914 (home). *E-mail:* jjragan@yahoo.com (home).

RAHIMI, Atiq, PhD; Afghan novelist and film-maker; b. 1962, Kabul; m. *Education:* Univ. of Kabul, Sorbonne, France. *Career:* political asylum in France 1985–. *Publications:* Terre et Cendres (trans. as Earth and Ashes) 2001, Les Mille Maisons du Rêve et de la Terreur (trans. as A Thousand Rooms of Dream and Fear) 2002, Le Retour Imaginaire 2005, Syngué Sabour (trans. as The Patience Stone) (Prix Goncourt) 2008. *Address:* c/o Editions P.O.L., 33 rue Saint-André-des-Arts, 75006 Paris, France (office). *Website:* www.pol -editeur.fr (office).

RAINE, Craig Anthony, BA, BPhil; British writer; b. 3 Dec. 1944, Shildon, Co. Durham; s. of Norman Edward and Olive Marie Raine; m. Ann Pasternak Slater 1972; three s. one d. *Education:* Exeter Coll., Oxford. *Career:* Lecturer, Exeter Coll., Oxford 1971–72, 1975–76, Lincoln Coll. 1974–75, Christ Church

1976–79; Books Ed. New Review 1977–78; Ed. Quarto 1979–80; Poetry Ed. New Statesman 1981; Poetry Ed. Faber and Faber Ltd 1981–91; Fellow in English, New Coll. Oxford 1991–2010; Ed. Areté 1999–. *Publications:* The Onion, Memory 1978, A Martian Sends a Postcard Home 1979, A Free Translation 1981, Rich 1984, The Electrification of the Soviet Union (opera) 1986, A Choice of Kipling's Prose (ed.) 1987, The Prophetic Book 1988, '1953' (play) 1990, Haydn and the Valve Trumpet: Literary Essays 1990, Rudyard Kipling: Selected Poetry (ed.) 1992, History: The Home Movie 1994, Clay. Whereabouts Unknown 1996, New Writing 7 1998, A la recherche du temps perdu 1999, In Defence of T.S. Eliot: Literary Essays (Vol. 2) 2000, Collected Poems 1978–1999 2000, Rudyard Kipling: The Wish House and Other Stories (ed.) 2002, T.S. Eliot 2006, Heartbreak (novel) 2010, How Snow Falls (poems) 2010, The Divine Comedy (novel) 2012, More Dynamite (essays) 2012. *Honours:* Kelus Prize 1979, Southern Arts Literature Award 1979, Cholmondeley Poetry Award 1983, Sunday Times Award for Literary Excellence 1998. *Address:* New College, Oxford, OX1 3BN, England (office).

RAINES, Howell, MA; American journalist and editor. *Education:* Birmingham-Southern Coll. and Univ. of Alabama. *Career:* journalist, Birmingham Post-Herald 1964, Birmingham (Ala) News 1970; Political Ed. Atlanta Constitution 1971–76, St Petersburg (Fla) Times 1976–78; Nat. Corresp. in Atlanta, NY Times 1978, Atlanta Bureau Chief 1979–81, White House Corresp. 1981–84, Nat. Political Corresp. 1984, Deputy Washington Ed. 1985–87, London Bureau Chief 1987–88, Washington Bureau Chief 1988–93, Editorial Page Ed. 1993–2001, Exec. Ed. 2001–03 (resgnd); currently columnist The Guardian (UK). *Publications:* My Soul Is Rested 1977, Whiskey Man 1977, Fly Fishing Through the Midlife Crisis 1993, The One That Got Away 2006. *Honours:* Pulitzer Prize for feature writing 1992. *Address:* c/o The New York Times, 229 West 43rd Street, New York, NY 10036, USA (office).

RAJAN, Tilottama, BA, MA, PhD, FRSC; American academic, writer and poet; *Canada Research Chair in English and Theory, University of Western Ontario*; b. 1 Feb. 1951, New York, NY. *Education:* Trinity Coll., Toronto, Univ. of Toronto. *Career:* Asst Prof., Huron Coll., Univ. of Western Ontario 1977–80; Asst Prof. 1980–83, Assoc. Prof. 1983–85, Queen's Univ.; Prof., Univ. of Wisconsin at Madison 1985–90; Prof. 1990–, Dir Centre for the Study of Theory and Criticism 1995–2001, Canada Research Chair in English and Theory 2001–, Univ. of Western Ontario; mem. Canadian Comparative Literature Asscn, Univ. of Teachers of English, Keats-Shelley Asscn, MLA of America, North American Soc. for the Study of Romanticism, Wordsworth-Coleridge Asscn. *Publications:* Myth in a Metal Mirror 1967, Dark Interpreter: The Discourse of Romanticism 1980, The Supplement of Reading 1990, Intersections: Nineteenth Century Philosophy and Contemporary Theory 1995, Romanticism, History and the Possibilities of Genre 1998, Deconstruction and the Remainders of Phenomenology: Sartre, Derrida, Foucault, Baudrillard 2002, After Poststructuralism: Writing the Intellectual History of Theory 2002, Idealism Without Absolutes: Philosophy and Romantic Culture (with Arkady Plotnitsky) 2004; contrib. to professional journals. *Honours:* Guggenheim Fellowship 1987–88, Keats-Shelley Asscn of America Distinguished Lifetime Award 2005. *Address:* Department of English, University of Western Ontario, London, ON N6A 5B8, Canada (office). *Telephone:* (519) 661-2211 (office). *E-mail:* trajan@uwo.ca.

RAJIC, Négovan, BEng, DipEng; Canadian writer; b. 24 June 1923, Belgrade, Yugoslavia; s. of Vladimir Rajic and Zagorka Rajic (née Vuletic); m. Mirjana Knezevic 1970; one s. one d. *Education:* Gymnasium of Belgrade, Univ. of Belgrade, Conservatoire des Arts et Metiers, France. *Career:* fought with Resistance during World War II; settled in France 1947; research engineer, physics laboratory, École Polytechnique de Paris 1956–63; electronics teacher, France 1963–69; settled in Canada 1969; Prof. of Mathematics, Collège de Trois-Rivières –1987; mem. Int. PEN, Asscn of Writers of Québec. *Publications:* Les Hommes-Taupes (trans. as The Mole Men) 1978, Propos d'un vieux radoteur (trans. as The Master of Srappado) 1982, Sept Roses pour une boulangère (trans. as Seven Roses for a Baker) 1987, Service pénitentiaire national (trans. as The Shady Business) 1988, Vers l'autre rive: Adieu Belgrade (novel) (Grand prix culturel de Trois-Rivières 2001) 2000, Le Puits ou histoire sans queue ni tête (play); contrib. numerous articles and short stories to publications. *Honours:* hon. mem. Asscn of Serbian Writers, Belgrade; Prix Esso du Cercle du Livre de France 1978, Prix Air Canada for best short story 1980, Prix Slobodan Yovanovitch, Asscn des écrivains et artistes serbes en éxil 1984, Prix littéraire de Trois-Rivières 1988, Franz Kafka Medal, European Circle, Prague 2000. *Address:* 300 rue Dunant, Trois-Rivières, QC G8Y 2W9, Canada (home).

RAKOVSZKY, Zsuzsa; Hungarian writer, poet and translator; b. 4 Dec. 1950, Sopron; d. of Tibor Rakovszky and Zsuzsa Szűcs; one s. *Education:* Eötvös Univ., Budapest. *Career:* mem. Hungarian PEN, Hungarian Writers' Asscn. *Publications:* Joslatok es hataridok 1981, Tovabb egy hazzal 1987, Feher-fekete 1991, A kigyo arnyeka (novel) 2002, A hullocsillag eve (novel) 2005, Visszaút az időben (collected poems) 2007, A Hold a hetedik házban (short stories) 2009; contrib. to Kortars, Jelenkor, Alfold, Holmi, 2000, New Hungarian Quarterly. *Honours:* Graves Prize 1980, Dery Prize 1986, József Attila Prize 1986, Magyar Köztársaság Babérkoszorúja Prize 1997. *Address:* Torna u 22, Sopron, Hungary (home).

RAKOWSKI, Andrzej, MA, MSc, PhD, DSc; Polish musicologist and acoustician; *Professor Emeritus, Fryderyk Chopin Academy of Music*; b. 16 June 1931, Warsaw; m. Magdalena Jakobczyk 1972; one s. two d. *Education:* Univ. of Durham, UK, Warsaw Univ. of Technology, Warsaw Univ., State Coll. of Music in Warsaw. *Career:* Prof. of Musical Acoustics, Fryderyk Chopin Acad. of Music, Warsaw 1963–2001, Prof. Emer. 2001–; Pres. 1981–87; part-time Prof., Inst. of Musicology, Warsaw Univ. 1987–2003; Chair. of Musicology, A. Mickiewicz Univ. 1997–2009; Visiting Prof., Central Inst. for the Deaf, St Louis, Mo., USA 1977–78, McGill Univ., Montreal, Canada 1985, Hebrew Univ., Jerusalem, Israel 1991, Univ. Nova de Lisboa, Portugal 2004; mem. Polish Music Council (Vice-Pres. 1984–89), Union of Polish Composers, Polish Acad. of Sciences (Pres. Acoustical Cttee 1996–2007), European Soc. for Cognitive Sciences of Music (Pres. 2000–03); Fellow, Acoustical Soc. of America 2001–. *Publications:* Categorical Perception of Pitch in Music 1978, The Access of Children and Youth to Musical Culture 1984, Studies on Pitch and Timbre of Sound in Music (ed.) 1999, Creation and Perception of Sound Sequences in Music (ed.) 2002; contrib. over 100 articles on music perception and music acoustics to int. journals. *Honours:* Golden Cross of Merit 1973, Bachelor's Cross, Order of Polonia Restituta 1983, Officer's Cross 2002. *Address:* Fryderyk Chopin Academy of Music, Okolnik 2, 00-368 Warsaw (office); Pogonowskiego 20, 01-564 Warsaw, Poland (home). *Telephone:* (22) 827-8303 (office); (22) 839-9456 (home). *Fax:* (22) 827-8310 (office). *E-mail:* rakowski@chopin.edu.pl. *Website:* www.chopin.edu.pl/angielskie/osobowe/rakowski.html (office).

RAMA, Carlos M., PhD; Uruguayan writer, lawyer, academic and editor; b. 26 Oct. 1921, Montevideo; s. of Manuel Rama and Carolina Facal; m. Judith Dellepiane 1943; one s. one d. *Education:* Univ. de la República and Univ. de Paris. *Career:* journalist 1940–48, 1972–; Exec. Sec. of Uruguayan Bar Asscn 1940–49; Prof. of Universal History in secondary schools 1944–48; Ed. Nuestro Tiempo 1954–56, Gacetilla Austral 1961–73; Prof. of Sociology and Social Research, Prof. of Contemporary History, Prof. of Theory and Methodology of History, Univ. de la República 1950–72; Prof. of Latin American History, Univ. Autónoma de Barcelona 1973–; Pres. PEN Club Latinoamericano en España; Sec. Gen. Grupo de Estudios Latinoamericanos de Barcelona. *Publications:* La Historia y la Novela 1947, 1963, 1970, 1974, Las ideas socialistas en el siglo XIX 1947, 1949, 1963, 1967, 1976, Ensayo de Sociología Uruguaya 1956, Teoría de la Historia 1959, 1968, 1974, 1980, Las clases sociales en el Uruguay 1960, La Crisis española del siglo XX 1960, 1962, 1976, Itinerario español 1961, 1977, Revolución social y fascismo en el siglo XX 1962, Sociología del Uruguay 1965, 1973, Historia del movimiento obrero y social latinoamericano contemporáneo 1967, 1969, 1976, Los afrouruguayos 1967, 1968, 1969, 1970, Garibaldi y el Uruguay 1968, Uruguay en Crisis 1969, Sociología de América Latina 1970, 1977, Chile, mil días entre la revolución y el fascismo 1974, España, crónica entrañable 1973–77, 1978, Historia de América Latina 1978, Fascismo y anarquismo en la España contemporánea 1979. *Honours:* Commdr, Order of Liberation (Spain), Officier des Palmes académiques (France). *Address:* c/o Monte de Orsá 7, Vallvidrera, Barcelona 17, Spain.

RAMADAN, Tariq, MA, PhD; Swiss academic; *Professor of Contemporary Islamic Studies, St Antony's College, University of Oxford*; b. 26 Aug. 1962, Geneva. *Education:* Univ. of Geneva. *Career:* fmr Prof. of Islamic Studies and Philosophy, Freiburg Univ.; Prof. of Islamic Studies and Luce Prof. of Religion Conflict and Peacebuilding, Kroc Inst., Univ. of Notre Dame, USA Aug.–Dec. 2004 (visa revoked); Sr Research Fellow, Lokahi Foundation 2004–, Doshisha Univ., Kyoto 2007–; Prof. of Contemporary Islamic Studies, St Antony's Coll., Oxford, UK 2004–; Chair Citizenship and Identity, Erasmus Univ., Rotterdam, Netherlands 2007–; Chair. European Muslim Network, Brussels. *Publications:* Islam, le face à face des civilisations, Quel projet pour quelle modernité? 1995, Les Musulmans dans la Laïcité, responsabilités et droits des musulmans dans les sociétés occidentales 1994, To be a European Muslim 1999, Muslims in France: The Way Towards Coexistence 1999, Islam, the West, and the Challenges of Modernity 2001, Jihad, Violence, War and Peace in Islam (in French) 2002, Western Muslims and the Future of Islam 2004, Globalisation: Muslim Resistances 2004, Radical Reform, In the Footsteps of the Prophet 2007, Radical Ijtihad 2008, The Quest for Meaning: Developing a Philosophy of Pluralism 2010; contrib. of more than 850 articles, reviews and chapters in books and magazines. *Honours:* One of the Seven Innovators of the 21st Century, Time magazine 2000, One of the 100 People of the Year 2004, European of the Year, European Voice 2006, The Muslim News Special Award for Excellence (Faith and Action) for academic and intellectual contrib. to Islamic thought 2007. *Address:* St Antony's College, 62 Woodstock Road, Oxford, OX2 6JF, England (office); 39 rue de la boulangerie, 93200 Saint Denis, France (home). *Telephone:* (1865) 612302 (Oxford) (office); 1-49-22-01-12 (Saint Denis) (home). *Fax:* (1865) 612844 (Oxford) (office); 1-49-22-00-39 (Saint Denis) (home). *E-mail:* office@tariqramadan.com (office); cisoq@sant.ox.ac.uk (office). *Website:* www.tariqramadan.com (office).

RAMBAUD, Patrick; French writer; b. 21 April 1946, Paris; s. of François Rambaud and Madeleine de Magondeau; m. Pham-thi Tieu Hong 1988. *Career:* mil. service with French AF 1968–69; co-f. Actual magazine 1970–84; mem. Acad. Goncourt 2008–. *Plays:* Fregoli (with Bernard Haller) (Théâtre nat. de Chaillot 1991. *Publications:* La Saignée 1970, Les Aventures communautaires de Wao-le-Laid (with Michel-Antoine Burnier) 1973, Les Complots de la liberté: 1832 (with Michel-Antoine Burnier) (Prix Alexandre Dumas) 1976, Parodies (with Michel-Antoine Burnier) 1977, 1848 (with Michel-Antoine Burnier) 1977, Le Roland Barthes sans peine (with Michel-Antoine Burnier) 1978, Comme des rats 1980, La Farce des choses et autres parodies (with Michel-Antoine Burnier) 1982, Fric-Frac 1984, La Mort d'un ministre 1985, Frontière suisse (with Jean-Marie Stoerkel) 1986, Comment se tuer sans en avoir l'air 1987, Virginie Q (Prix de l'Insolent) 1988, Le Visage parle (with Bernard Haller) 1988, Bernard Pivot reçoit… 1989, Le Dernier voyage de San Marco 1990, Ubu Président ou L'Imposteur 1990, Les Carnets secrets d'Elena Ceaucescu (with Francis Szpiner) 1990, Les Mirobolantes aventures de Frégoli 1991, Mururoa mon amour 1996, Le Gros secret 1996, Oraisons funèbres des dignitaires politiques qui ont fait leur temps et feignent de l'ignorer (with André Balland) 1996, La Bataille (Grand Prix du Roman de l' Acad. française 1997, Prix Goncourt 1997, Napoleonic Soc. of America Literary Award 2000) 1997, Le Journalisme sans peine (with Michel-Antoine Burnier) 1997, Les Aventures de Mai 1998, Il neigeait (Prix Ciné-Roman 2001) 2000, L'Absent 2003, L'Idiot du village (Prix de la dédicace sonore 2005) 2004, Le Chat botté 2006, La Grammaire en s'amusant 2007, Chronique du règne de Nicolas I 2008, Deuxième Chronique du règne de Nicolas I 2009, Troisième Chronique du règne de Nicolas I 2010, Quatrième Chronique du règne de Nicolas I 2011, Cinquième Chronique du règne de Nicolas I 2012. *Honours:* Prix Alexandre Dumas 1976, Prix Lamartine 1981, Prix de l'Insolent 1988, Grand Prix du roman, Acad. Française 1997, Prix Goncourt 1997, Napoleonic Soc. of America Literary Award 2000, Prix Cine-Roman 2001, Prix Rabelais 2005. *Address:* c/o Editions Grasset, 61 rue des Saints-Pères, 75006 Paris, France. *Telephone:* (06) 03-97-72-52 (home).

RAMDIN, Ronald Andrew, DipArts, BSc, DLitt, FRHistS, FRSA; Trinidad and Tobago historian, biographer, novelist and academic; b. 20 June 1942, Marabella; m. Irma de Freitas 1969, one s. *Education:* New Era Acad. of Drama and Music, Univ. of Middlesex, LSE. *Career:* First Sec., Whitley Council, British Library 1973–75; Section Exec. Mem., Museums and Galleries Commission; mem. Society of Authors. *Publications:* From Chattel Slave to Wage Earner 1982, Introductory Text: The Black Triangle 1984, The Making of the Black Working Class in Britain 1987, Paul Robeson: The Man and His Mission 1987, World in View: The West Indies 1990, Reimaging Britain: 500 Years of Black and Asian History, The Other Middle Passage 1995, Arising From Bondage: A History of the Indo-Caribbean People 2000, Martin Luther King, Jr: Life and Times 2004, Rama's Voyage 2004, Mary Seacole (Life and Times) 2005, The Griot's Tale 2009; essays: 'Multicultural Britain' in Fragments of British Culture 1998, 'The English Test: Post-War Immigration' in England 1945–2000 2000; contributions to Anglo-British Review, City Limits, Dragon's Teeth, Race Today, Caribbean Times, West Indian Digest, History Workshop Journal, Wasafiri, Dalit Voice, The Hindu. *Honours:* Scarlet Ibis Medal, Gold Award, Trinidad and Tobago High Commission 1990, Hansib, Caribbean Times Community Award 1990, Outstanding Achievement Award, Trinidad and Tobago High Commission 2006. *E-mail:* ron@ramdin.wanadoo.co.uk (office). *Website:* www.ronramdin.com.

RAMÍREZ CODINA, Pedro Jeta; Spanish journalist and newspaper executive; *Director, El Mundo (del Siglo Veintiuno)*; b. 26 March 1952, Logroño; m. 1st Rocío Fernández Iglesias; m. 2nd Agatha Ruíz de la Prada; one s. one d. *Education:* Univ. of Navarre. *Career:* Prof. of Contemporary Spanish Literature, Lebanon Valley Coll., Pa, USA 1973–74; with La Actualidad Económica 1974–76; wrote a weekly column for ABC newspaper; corresp. for El Noticiero Universal, Madrid; Dir of Diario 16 1980; Co-founder, with Alfonso de Salas, Balbino Fraga and Juan González, El Mundo (del Siglo Veinte, now Veintiuno) 1989, Publr and Ed. 1989–. *Address:* El Mundo, Pradillo 42, 28002 Madrid, Spain (office). *Telephone:* (91) 5864800 (office). *Fax:* (91) 5864848 (office). *E-mail:* editor@elmundo.es (office). *Website:* www.elmundo.es (office).

RAMÍREZ MERCADO, Sergio; Nicaraguan politician and author; b. 5 Aug. 1942, Masatepe, Masaya; s. of late Pedro Ramírez Gutiérrez and Luisa Mercado Gutiérrez; m. Gertrudis Guerrero Mayorga 1964; one s. two d. *Education:* Univ. Autónoma de Nicaragua, León. *Career:* was active in revolutionary student movt and founding mem. of Frente Estudiantil Revolucionario 1962; mem. Cen. American Univ. Supreme Council (CSUCA), Costa Rica 1964, Pres. 1968; mem. Int. Comm. of FSLN (Sandinista Liberation Front) 1975; undertook tasks on diplomatic front, propaganda and int. work on behalf of FSLN leading to overthrow of regime 1979; mem. Junta of Nat. Reconstruction Govt 1979; Vice-Pres. of Nicaragua 1984–90; minority leader, Speaker, Nat. Ass. 1990–94; Pres. Movimiento de Renovación Sandinista (MRS) 1994, MRS pre-cand. for presidency 1996; Co-founder literary journal Ventana; mem. Nicaraguan Acad. of Language; Corresp. mem. Royal Spanish Acad.; columnist for numerous newspapers and journals including El País, Madrid, La Jornada, Mexico, El Tiempo, Bogotá, El Nacional of Caracas, Listín Diario of Santo Domingo, La Opinion, Los Angeles, La Nacion, San Jose, El Tiempo, Tegucigalpa, La Prensa Gráfica, San Salvador, El Periodico in Guatemala and La Prensa, Managua. *Publications include:* Cuentos 1963, El cuento centroamericano 1974, Charles Atlas también muere 1976, El cuento nicaragüense 1976, ¿Te dio miedo la sangre? (Premio Latinoamericano de Cuento, revista Imagen, Caracas) 1978, Castigo divino (Premio Dashiel Hammett 1990) 1988, Confesión de amor 1991, Clave de sol 1992, Cuentos 1994, Oficios compartidos 1994, Un baile de máscaras (Premio Laure Bataillon for Best Foreign Book translated in France 1998) 1995, Margarita, Está Linda la Mar (Premio Internacional de Novela Alfaguara 1998, Premio Latinoamericano de Novela José María Arguedas 2000) 1998, Adiós muchachos 1999, Mentiras Verdaderas 2001, Catalina y Catalina 2001, Sombras nada más 2002, El viajo arte de menir 2004, Mil y una muertes 2004, El reino animal 2006, Tambor Olvidado 2007, Juego perfecto 2008, El cielo llora por mi 2008, Cuando todos hablamos 2008, Perdón y olvido: Antología de cuentos (1960–2009) 2009, Casa de las Américas (Premio Iberoamericano de Letras José Donoso) 2011, La Fugitiva 2011. *Honours:* Hon. Prof., Faculty of Humanities, Universidad Pedagógica Francisco Morazán, Honduras 2007; Chevalier des Arts et des Lettres 1993, Orden Mariano Fiallos Gil del Consejo Nacional de Universidades de Nicaragua 1994, Medalla Presidencial del centenario de Pablo Neruda, otorgada por el gobierno de Chile 2004, Order of Merit, First Class (Germany) 2007; Dr hc (Universidad Central del Ecuador) 1984, (Université Blaise Pascal de Clermont-Ferrand, France) 2000, (Universidad der Catamarca, Argentina) 2007, (Universidad Latina, Panamá) 2011; De Tropeles y Tropelías 1971, Premio Bruno Kreisky a los Derechos Humanos, Vienna 1988, Premio Rafael Heliodoro Valle (Honduras) 2007, Simon Guggenheim Foundation Scholarship 2008. *Address:* Apdo. Postal LM-280, Managua, Nicaragua (office). *Telephone:* (22) 771718 (office). *Fax:* (22) 660548 (office). *E-mail:* srm@ibw.com.ni (office); sergioramirezm@gmail.com (office). *Website:* www.sergioramirez.org.ni (office); www.sergioramirez.com (office).

RAMKE, Bin, MA, PhD; American professor of English, editor and poet; *Evans Professor and Phipps Chair, University of Denver*; b. 19 Feb. 1947, Port Neches, Tex.; m. 1967; one s. *Education:* Louisiana State Univ., Univ. of New Orleans, Ohio Univ. *Career:* Prof. of English, Columbus Univ., Ga 1976–85; Prof. of English, Univ. of Denver 1985–, currently Evans Prof. and Phipps Chair; Ed. Contemporary Poetry Series, University of Georgia Press 1984–2005; Poetry Ed., The Denver Quarterly 1985–94, Ed. 1994–; mem. Associated Writing Programs, Nat. Book Critics Circle, PEN American Centre. *Publications:* The Difference Between Night and Day 1978, White Monkeys 1981, The Language Student 1987, The Erotic Light of Gardens 1989, Massacre of the Innocents 1995, Wake 1999, Airs, Waters, Places 2001, Matter 2004, Tendril 2007, Theory of Mind: New and Selected Poems 2009; contribs to reviews, quarterlies and journals. *Honours:* Yale Younger Poets Award 1977, Texas Inst. of Arts and Letters Award for Poetry 1978, Iowa Poetry Award 1995. *Address:* Sturm Hall, Room 384, University of Denver, 2000 E Asbury Avenue, Denver, CO 80208, USA (office). *E-mail:* bramke@du.edu (office). *Website:* portfolio.du.edu/bramke (office).

RAMNEFALK, (Sylvia) Marie Louise, DLitt; Swedish poet, essayist and literary critic; b. 21 March 1941, Stockholm. *Education:* Univ. of Stockholm. *Career:* literary critic for several newspapers and magazines, now especially Svenska Dagbladet; mem. Bd Swedish Writers' Union 1979–83, 2006–, Swedish PEN. *Writing for music performance:* Love Love Love (opera libretto after poems by Robert Graves, music by Eskil Hemberg; premiered Rotunda of the Royal Opera, Stockholm) 1973, Någon har jag sett (opera libretto, music by Karólína Eiríksdóttir; premiered Vadstena Acad.) 1988, Det är du (mass, with music by Johannes Johansson; premiered Uppsala Cathedral) 2000, also texts for choral music and solo singing. *Publications:* Modern dramatik, tio analyser (with Gösta Kjellin) 1971, Tre lärodiktare. Studier i Harry Martinsons, Gunnar Ekelöfs och Karl Vennbergs lyrik (diss.) 1974, Enskilt liv pågår (poems) 1975, Robert Graves: Poems, interpretations 1976, Verkligheten gör dig den äran (poems) 1978, Någon har jag sett (poems) 1979, Kungsådra (poems) 1981, Kvinnornas litteraturhistoria (ed. with Anna Westberg) 1981, Sorg (poems) 1982, Levnadskonster. Lyrisk polemik om det Rätta, det Sanna, det Sköna (poems) 1983, Adam i Paradiset (narrative poetry) 1984, Det behövs något underjordiskt som kärlek och musik (selected poems) 1987, Julian såg Gud (narrative poetry) 1992, Älska mig nu! Dikter om kärlek och relationer av ungdomar (poems, ed. with Tom Hedlund) 1994, Författaren, världen, språket. Essäer om litteratur och skrivande (essays) 1996, Mystik – en kärlekshistoria. Richard Rolle, Walter Hilton, Julian av Norwich och Margery Kempe I senmedeltidens England (essays) 1997, Tusen och en natt I–II (stories) 1999, Lugna ner sig till det gråa (poems) 2001, Skönhet, odjur, häxor, prinsar, sagor återberättade (fairy tales); also writes for TV drama, subjects including Esaias Tegnér; contrib. to various periodicals. *Honours:* several scholarships. *Address:* Vastra Valhallavagen 25A, 182 66 Djursholm, Sweden.

RAMOS ROSA, António; Portuguese poet and literary critic; b. 17 Oct. 1924, Faro; m. Agripina Costa Marques 1962; one d. *Career:* Dir literary reviews, Árvore 1951–53, Cassiopeia 1955, Cadernos do Meio-Dia 1958–60. *Publications include:* poetry: Delta seguido de Pela Primeira Vez 1996, Nomes de Ninguém 1997, À Mesa do Vento seguido de As Espirais de Dioniso 1997, A Imobilidade Fulminante 1998; essays: Poesia, Liberdade Livre 1962, A Poesia Moderna e a Interrogação do Real 1979, Incisões Oblíquas 1987, A Parede Azul 1991, As Palavras 2001, Génese 2005. *Honours:* Grand Oficial, Order of Santiago da Espada; Great Cross, Order of Infante Dom Henrique; Prize of Portuguese Centre of Int. Asscn of Literary Critics 1980, PEN Club's Poetry Prize 1980, 2006, Portuguese Asscn of Writers' Grand Prize 1989, Pessoa Prize 1988, International Poetry Prize of Liège Poetry Biennial 1991, European Poet of the Decade (Collège de l'Europe) 1991, Jean Malrieu Prize (Marseille) 1992, Luís Miguel Nava Poetry Prize 2006. *Address:* c/o Roma Editora, Avenida Roma, 129 r/c Esq., 1700-346 Lisbon, Portugal.

RAMPERSAD, Arnold, BA, MA, AM, PhD; American academic and writer; *Sara Hart Kimball Professor Emeritus in the Humanities Emeritus, Stanford University*; b. 13 Nov. 1941, Trinidad; m. 1985, one c. *Education:* Bowling Green State Univ., Harvard Univ. *Career:* Faculty mem. Dept of English, Univ. of Virginia 1973–74, Stanford Univ. 1974–83, Rutgers Univ. 1983–88, Columbia Univ. 1988–90; Faculty mem. Dept of English, Princeton Univ. 1990–98, Sara Hart Kimball Prof. in the Humanities 1998–2008, Emer. 2008–; mem. American Acad. of Arts and Sciences, American Philosophical Soc.

Publications: Melville's Israel Potter: A Pilgrimage and Progress 1969, The Art and Imagination of W. E. B. DuBois 1976, Life of Langston Hughes Vol. I 1902–1941: I Too Sing America 1986, Vol. II 1941–1967: I Dream a World 1988, Slavery and the Literary Imagination (co-ed.) 1989, Days of Grace: A Memoir (with Arthur Ashe) 1993, Jackie Robinson: A Biography 1997, Ralph Ellison: A Biography 2007. *Honours:* Dr hc (Univ. of the West Indies) 2009, (Bloomfield Coll., Bowling Green State Univ.); Cleveland Foundation Anisfield Wolf Book Award in Race Relations 1987, Phelps Stokes Fund Clarence L. Holte Prize 1988, MacArthur Foundation Fellowship 1991. *Address:* Department of English, Stanford University, Building 460, Margaret Jacks Hall, Stanford, CA 94305, USA (office). *E-mail:* rampersad@stanford.edu (office).

RAMPLING, Anne (see Rice, Anne)

RAMSAY-BROWN, John Andrew, (Jay Ramsay), BA; British poet, writer, editor and translator; b. 20 April 1958, Guildford, Surrey, England. *Education:* Pembroke College, Oxford, London Institute. *Career:* mem. College of Psychic Studies, London; Poetry Society; Psychosynthesis Education and Trust, London. *Publications:* Psychic Poetry: A Manifesto, 1985; Angels of Fire (co-ed.), 1986; New Spiritual: Selected Poems, 1986; Trwyn Meditations, 1987; The White Poem, 1988; Transformation: The Poetry of Spiritual Consciousness (ed.), 1988; The Great Return, books 1 to 5, 2 vols, 1988; Transmissions, 1989; Strange Days, 1990; Journey to Eden (with Jenny Davis), 1991; For Now (with Geoffrey Godbert), 1991; The Rain, the Rain, 1992; St Patrick's Breastplate, 1992; Tao Te Ching: A New Translation, 1993; I Ching, 1995; Kuan Yin, 1995; Chuang Tzu (with Martin Palmer), 1996; Alchemy: The Art of Transformation, 1996; Earth Ascending: An Anthology of New and Living Poetry (ed.), 1996; Kingdom of the Edge: New and Selected Poems 1980–1998, 1998. Contributions: periodicals.

RAMSEY, Jarold William, BA, PhD; American academic, poet, writer and dramatist; *Professor Emeritus, University of Rochester*; b. 1 Sept. 1937, Bend, Ore.; m. Dorothy Ann Quinn 1959; one s. two d. *Education:* Univ. of Oregon, Univ. of Washington. *Career:* acting instructor, Univ. of Washington 1962–65; Asst Prof., Univ. of Rochester 1965–70, Assoc. Prof. 1970–80, Prof. 1980–97, Prof. Emer. 1997–; Visiting Prof. of English, Univ. of Victoria, BC 1974, 1975–76; mem. Modern Language Asscn. *Publications:* poetry: The Space Between Us 1970, Love in an Earthquake 1973, Dermographia 1983, Hand-Shadows 1989, The Bones of the Heart: Uncollected Poems 2011, Thinking Like a Canyon: New and Selected Poems 1973–2010; plays and libretti: Coyote Goes Upriver (play) 1981, The Lodge of Shadows (cantata with Samuel Adler) 1974; non-fiction: Coyote Was Going There: Indian Literature of the Oregon Country 1977, Reading the Fire: Essays in the Traditional Indian Literature of the Far West 1983; editor: Elizabeth and Melville Jacobs, Nehalem Tillamook Tales 1990, The Stories We Tell: Anthology of Oregon Folk Literature (with Suzi Jones) 1994, New Era: Reflections on the Human and Natural History of Central Oregon 2003, The Piper of Cloone: Father Keegan and the Early Gaelic Revival (with Dorothy Quinn Ramsey) 2005, In Beauty I Walk: The Literary Roots of Native American Writing (with Lori Burlingame) 2008; contrib. to anthologies, reviews, quarterlies and journals. *Honours:* Nat. Endowment for the Arts grant 1974, and Fellowship 1975, Ingram Merrill Foundation grant 1975, Don Walker Award for Best Essay on Western Literature 1978, Helen Bullis Award for Poetry 1984, Inst. of Int. Poetry Prize, Quarterly Review 1989. *Address:* 5884 NW Highway, No. 26, Madras, OR 97741, USA. *Telephone:* (541) 475-5390. *E-mail:* ramseyjarold@yahoo.com.

RAMSLAND, Morten; Danish writer; b. 1971, Naesby på Fyn. *Education:* Aarhus Univ. *Publications:* novels: Akaciedrømme 1998, Hundehoved (trans. as Doghead) (Author of the Year, Book of the Year, Reader's Prize, Golden Laurel Prize) 2005; children's: Da Bernard skød hul I himlen 2004, Pedes uhyrer 2005, Onkel Pedro kommer hjem 2005, Tarvelige Tom 2006, Havmanden 2006; poetry: Når fuglene driver bort 1993. *Address:* c/o Rosinante Publishers, Købmagergade 62, POB 2252, 1019 Copenhagen, Denmark (office). *E-mail:* rosinante@rosinante.dk (office). *Website:* www .rosinante.dk (office).

RAND, Peter, MA; American writer; b. 23 Feb. 1942, San Francisco, CA; m. Bliss Inui 1976, one s. *Education:* Johns Hopkins University. *Career:* Fiction Ed., Antaeus, 1970–72; Ed., Washington Monthly, 1973–74; Teaching Fellow, Johns Hopkins University, 1975; Lecturer in English, Columbia University, 1976–91; mem. PEN; Authors' Guild; Poets and Writers; East Asian Institute, Columbia University; Research Assoc., Fairbank Center, Harvard University. *Publications:* Firestorm, 1969; The Time of the Emergency, 1977; The Private Rich, 1984; Gold From Heaven, 1988; Deng Xiaoping: Chronicle of an Empire, by Ruth Ming (ed. and trans. with Nancy Liu and Lawrence R. Sullivan), 1994; China Hands, 1995. Contributions: periodicals. *Honours:* CAPS 1977.

RANDALL, Jeff William, BA; British journalist; *Editor-at-Large, The Daily Telegraph*; b. 3 Oct. 1954, London; s. of Jeffrey Charles Randall and Grace Annie Randall (née Hawkridge); m. Susan Diane Fidler 1986; one d. *Education:* Royal Liberty Grammar School, Romford, Univ. of Nottingham, Univ. of Florida, USA. *Career:* with Hawkins Publrs 1982–85; Asst Ed. Financial Weekly 1985–86; City Corresp. Sunday Telegraph 1986–88; Deputy City Ed. The Sunday Times 1988–89, City Ed. 1989–94, City and Business Ed. 1994–95, Asst Ed. and Sports Ed. 1996–97; Ed. Sunday Business 1997–2001; Business Ed. BBC 2001–05; Ed.-at-Large The Daily Telegraph 2005–; host Jeff Randall Live (Sky News) 2007–; freelance contrib. Daily Telegraph, Euromoney; Dir Times Newspapers 1994–95; Deputy Chair. Financial Dynamics Ltd 1995–96. *Publications:* The Day That Shook the World (co-author). *Honours:* Dr hc (Anglia Ruskin Univ.) 2001, (Univ. of Nottingham) 2006; Financial Journalist of the Year, FT-Analysis 1991, Business Journalist of the Year, London Press Club 2000, Sony Gold Award 2003, Communicator of the Year 2004, Business Broadcaster of the Year, Wincott Awards 2004. *Address:* The Daily Telegraph, 111 Buckingham Palace Road, London, SW1W 0DT, England (office). *Website:* www.telegraph.co.uk (office).

RANDALL, Lisa, PhD; American physicist and academic; *Professor of Physics, Harvard University*. *Education:* Harvard Univ. *Career:* summer research at Smithsonian Astrophysical Observatory 1981, IBM Poughkeepsie 1982, FNAL 1982, Bell Laboratories 1983; Teaching Asst, Physics Dept, Harvard Univ. 1984, Physics Tutor, Adams House 1984–87, Asst Sr Tutor 1985–87; Pres.'s Fellow, Univ. of Calif., Berkeley 1987–89; Postdoctoral Fellow, Lawrence Berkeley Lab. 1989–90; Jr Fellow, Harvard Soc. of Fellows 1990–91; mem. staff MIT and Inst. for Theoretical Physics 1994, Asst Prof. of Physics, MIT 1991–95, Assoc. Prof. 1995–98, Prof. 1998–2001; Prof. of Physics, Princeton Univ. 1998–2000; Prof. of Physics, Harvard Univ. 2001–; Radcliffe Inst. Fellow 2002; Chair Radcliffe Inst. Cosmology and Theoretical Astrophysics Cluster 2003; mem. numerous conference programme and advisory cttees; Ed. Annual Review of Nuclear and Particle Science 1997–, Journal of High Energy Physics 1997–98, 2000–; Assoc. Ed. Nuclear Physics 1999–; John Harvard Scholarship, Elizabeth Cary Agassiz Scholarship; Bell Laboratories Graduate Research Fellowship for Women; Alfred P. Sloan Foundation Research Fellowship 1992; Fellow, American Acad. of Arts and Science 2004. *Publications include:* Warped Passages 2005; numerous articles in magazines and journals. *Honours:* Westinghouse Science Talent Search Winner, David J. Robbins Prize, Dept of Energy Outstanding Jr Investigator Award 1992, Nat. Science Foundation Young Investigator Award 1992, Premio Caterina Tomassoni e Felice Pietro Chisesi Award 2003, Klopsted Award, American Soc. of Physics Teachers 2006. *Address:* Jefferson 461, 17 Oxford Street, Cambridge, MA 02138, USA (office). *Telephone:* (617) 496-8188 (office). *E-mail:* randall@physics.harvard.edu (office). *Website:* randall.physics .harvard.edu (office).

RANDALL, Margaret; American writer, poet, photographer and teacher; b. 6 Dec. 1936, New York, NY; one s. three d. *Career:* Managing Ed., Frontiers: A Journal of Women's Studies, 1990–91; Distinguished Visiting Prof., University of Delaware, 1991; Visiting Prof., Trinity College, Hartford, CT, 1992. *Publications:* Giant of Tears, 1959; Ecstasy is a Number, 1961; Poems of the Glass, 1964; Small Sounds from the Brass Fiddle, 1964; October, 1965; Twenty-Five Stages of My Spine, 1967; Getting Rid of Blue Plastic, 1967; So Many Rooms Has a House But One Roof, 1967; Part of the Solution, 1972; Day's Coming, 1973; With These Hands, 1973; All My Used Parts, Shackles, Fuel, Tenderness and Stars, 1977; Carlota: Poems and Prose from Havana, 1978; We, 1978; A Poetry of Resistance, 1983; The Coming Home Poems, 1986; Albuquerque: Coming Back to the USA, 1986; This is About Incest, 1987; Memory Says Yes, 1988; The Old Cedar Bar, 1992; Dancing with the Doe, 1992; Hunger's Table: The Recipe Poems, 1997. Oral History: Cuban Women Now, 1974; Sandino's Daughters, 1981. Photography: Women Brave in the Face of Danger, 1985; Nicaragua Libre!, 1985. Contributions: anthologies, reviews, journals, and magazines. *Honours:* first prize in photography Nicaraguan Children's Asscn 1983, Creating Ourselves Nat. Art Exhibition 1992.

RANDALL, William Lowell, AB, MDiv, ThM, EdD; Canadian educator and writer; *Associate Professor, Department of Gerontology, St Thomas University*; b. 1 Dec. 1950, Black's Harbour, NB. *Education:* Harvard Univ., Emmanuel Coll., Victoria Univ., Univ. of Cambridge, Princeton Theological Seminary, Univ. of Toronto. *Career:* Minister, United Church of Canada 1979–90; English instructor, Seneca Coll. of Applied Arts and Tech., North York, Ont. 1991–95; Adjunct Lecturer, St Bonaventure Univ. 1992–94; part-time instructor, Univ. of Toronto 1993; seminar facilitator, site leader, Brock Univ. 1993–95; Visiting Chair, Dept of Gerontology, St Thomas Univ., Fredericton, NB 1995, Research Assoc. 1996–2001, Asst Prof. 2001–05, Assoc. Prof. 2005–, Project Dir, Fredericton 80+ Study 1998–2007; Co-organizer Narrative Matters Conf. 2002, 2004, 2010; mem. Harvard Club of Atlantic Canada, Canadian Asscn on Gerontology; Dir Centre for Interdisciplinary Research on Narrative; Founding mem. Atlantic Inst. on Aging; Inst. Assoc. with Taos Inst. *Publications:* Restorying Our Lives: Personal Growth through Autobiographical Reflection (co-author) 1997, The Stories We Are: An Essay on Self-Creation 1995, Ordinary Wisdom: Biographical Aging and the Journey of Life (co-author) 2001, Reading Our Lives: The Poetics of Growing Old (co-author) 2008, Storying Later Life: Issues, Investigations, & Interventions in Narrative Gerontology (co-ed.) 2011; contrib. of articles to Aging and Biography: Explorations in Adult Development 1996, Journal of Aging Studies 1999, 2006, Narrative Gerontology: Theory, Research and Practice 2001, Rural Social Work 2001, 2005, Critical Advances in Reminiscence 2002, Education and Ageing 2002, 2004, Canadian Journal on Aging 2004, Narrative Inquiry 2004, McGill Journal of Education 2005, Theory & Psychology 2007, 2010, Journal of Aging Studies 1999, 2006, 2008, Encyclopedia of Gerontology 2006, Encyclopedia of Aging 2007, Interchange 2007, Psychological Studies 2011. *Honours:* Harvard Univ. Regular Scholarship 1968–72, Emmanuel Coll., Victoria Univ. Wallace, Mitchell and Billes Postgraduate Scholarships 1973–76, United Church of Canada McLeod Scholarship 1989–91, Special Merit Award, St Thomas Univ. 2008. *Address:* Department of Gerontology, St Thomas University, Fredericton, NB E3B 5G3,

Canada (office). *Telephone:* (506) 452-0632 (office). *Fax:* (506) 452-0611 (office). *E-mail:* brandall@stu.ca (office). *Website:* www.stu.ca (office).

RANDHAWA, Ravinder, BA; British writer; b. 25 Jan. 1952, India; d. of Pakhar Singh and Kartar Kaur Randhawa; two d. *Education:* Leamington Coll. for Girls, Leamington Spa. *Career:* came to UK aged seven years; worked for women's groups establishing refuges and resource centres for Asian women 1978–84; Founder Asian Women Writers' Collective 1984; Fellow, Tonybee Hall 2000–02, Project Fellow 2002–04; Fellow, St Mary's Coll., Univ. of Surrey 2006–07; Writing Fellow, Royal Literary Fund, Queen Mary, Univ. of London 2007–08; mem. PEN Int. *Publications:* More to Life than Mr. Right (contrib.) 1986, A Wicked Old Woman 1987, Right of Way (contrib.) 1989, Hari-jan 1992, Flaming Spirit (contrib.) 1994, The Coral Strand 2001. *Honours:* Kathleen Burnett Award 1990. *E-mail:* ravi@randhawa.co.uk (office).

RANKIN, Ian James, (Jack Harvey), OBE, BA; Scottish writer; b. 1960, Cardenden, Fife; m. Miranda; two s. *Education:* Edinburgh Univ. *Career:* mem. Literary Comm., Scottish Labour Party 2008–; mem. CWA, Int. Asscn of Crime Writers. *Recording:* Jackie Leven Said (short story, put to songs by Jackie Leven) 2005. *Publications include:* The Flood 1986, Watchman 1988, Death is Not the End 1998, Beggars Banquet (short stories) 2002, Doors Open 2008, The Complaints 2009;, Impossible Dead 2011; Inspector Rebus series: Knots and Crosses 1987, Hide and Seek 1991, Tooth and Nail (aka Wolfjack) 1992, A Good Hanging and Other Stories (short stories) 1992, Strip Jack 1992, The Black Book 1993, Mortal Causes 1994, Let it Bleed 1996, Black and Blue 1997, The Hanging Garden 1998, Dead Souls 1999, Set in Darkness 2000, The Falls 2000, Resurrection Men 2001, A Question of Blood 2003, Fleshmarket Close (British Book Award for Crime Thriller of the Year 2005) 2004, The Naming of the Dead (British Book Award for Crime Thriller of the Year 2007) 2006, Exit Music 2007, Dark Entries (graphic novel; with Werther Dell'edera) 2009; as Jack Harvey: Witch Hunt 1993, Bleeding Hearts 1994, Blood Hunt 1995; contrib. to anthologies, including One City 2006. *Honours:* CWA Golden Dagger 1997, Hawthornden Fellow, Chandler-Fulbright Award in Detective Fiction, CWA Dagger for best short story 1994, CWA Cartier Diamond Dagger 2005. *Address:* c/o Orion House, 5 Upper St Martin's Lane, London, WC2H 9EA, England (office). *Website:* www.ianrankin.net.

RANKIN, Robert; British writer; b. 27 July 1949, London; m. *Publications:* The Antipope 1981, The Brentford Triangle 1982, East of Ealing 1984, The Sprouts of Wrath 1984, Armageddon: The Musical 1988, They Came and Ate Us 1991, The Suburban Book of the Dead 1992, The Book of Ultimate Truths 1993, Raiders of the Lost Car Park 1994, The Greatest Show Off Earth 1994, The Most Amazing Man Who Ever Lived 1995, The Garden of Unearthly Delights 1995, A Dog Called Demolition 1996, Nostradamus Ate My Hamster 1996, Sprout Mask Replica 1997, The Brentford Chainstore Massacre 1997, The Dance of the Voodoo Handbag 1998, Apocalypso 1998, Snuff Fiction 1999, Sex and Drugs and Sausage Rolls 1999, Waiting for Godalming 2000, Web Site Story 2001, Fandom of the Operator 2001, The Hollow Chocolate Bunnies of the Apocalypse (SFX Award for Best Book 2003) 2002, The Witches of Chiswick 2003, Knees Up Mother Earth 2004, The Brightonomicon 2004, The Toyminator 2006, The Da-da-di-da-da Code 2007, Necrophenia 2009. *Address:* Sproutlore, 211 Black Horse Avenue, Dublin 7, Ireland (office); c/o Gollancz, Orion House, 5 Upper Saint Martin's Lane, London, WC2H 9EA, England (office). *Website:* www.sproutlore.com.

RANKOV, Pavol, PhD; Slovak writer, essayist and academic; *Assistant Professor, Comenius University*; b. 16 Sept. 1964, Poprad. *Education:* Comenius Univ., Bratislava. *Career:* worked in Slovak Nat. Library, Martin 1987–90, Slovak Educational Library, Bratislava 1991–92; Asst Prof., Dept of Library and Information Science, Comenius Univ., Bratislava 1993–. *Publications:* novels: S odstupom času, My a oni/Oni a my, V tesnej blízkosti, Stalo sa prvého septembra (alebo inokedy) (EU Prize for Literature 2009) 2009. *Honours:* Ivan Krasko Prize 1995. *Literary Agent:* c/o Elpeka, Ukrajinska 10, 101 00 Prague 10, Czech Republic. *Telephone:* (602) 204111 (mobile). *Fax:* (2) 71746388. *E-mail:* elpeka@seznam.cz.

RANSFORD, Tessa, OBE, MA, Dip Ed.; British poet, writer, translator and editor; *Chairman, Scottish Pamphlet Poetry*; b. (Teresa Mary Ransford), 8 July 1938, Mumbai, India; m. 1st Iain Kay Stiven 1959 (divorced 1986); one s. three d.; m. 2nd Callum Macdonald 1989 (deceased). *Education:* Univ. of Edinburgh, Craiglockhart Coll. of Educ. *Career:* cultural activist; Founder School of Poets, Edinburgh 1981–; Founder/Dir Scottish Poetry Library 1984–99; Ed. Lines Review 1988–98; freelance poet and adviser 1999–; mem. Scottish Int. PEN (Pres. 2003–06), Soc. of Authors; Royal Literary Fund Writing Fellowship 2001–04, 2006–08; Fellow, Centre for Human Ecology 2005; currently Chair. Scottish Pamphlet Poetry. *Publications include:* Light of the Mind 1980, Fools and Angels 1984, Shadows from the Greater Hill 1987, A Dancing Innocence 1988, Seven Valleys 1991, Medusa Dozen and Other Poems 1994, Scottish Selection 1998, When it Works it Feels Like Play 1998, Indian Selection 2000, Natural Selection 2001, Noteworthy Selection 2002, The Nightingale Question 2004, Shades of Green 2005, Sonnet Selection and Five Rilke Lyrics (trans.) 2007, Not Just Moonshine, New and Selected Poems 2008; contrib. to anthologies, reviews and journals. *Honours:* Hon. Fellow, Inst. for Contemporary Scotland 2000; Hon. mem. Saltire Soc. 1993, Scottish Library Asscn 1999, Scottish Poetry Library 1999, Asscn of Scottish Literary Studies 2010; Hon. Research Fellow, Queen Margaret Univ. 2008; Hon. Pres. Scottish Poetry Library 2011; Hon. DUniv (Paisley) 2003; Scottish Arts Council Book Award 1980, Howard Sergeant Award for Services to Poetry 1989, Heritage Soc. of Scotland Annual Award 1996, Soc. of Authors Travelling Scholarship 2001, Scottish Arts Council Bursary 2010. *Address:* 31 Royal Park Terrace, Edinburgh, EH8 8JA, Scotland (home). *Telephone:* (131) 661-1277 (home). *E-mail:* wisdomfield@talk21.com. *Website:* www.wisdomfield.com (office); www.scottish-pamphlet-poetry.com (office).

RANSOM, Bill, MA; American writer and poet; b. 6 June 1945, Puyallup, WA; one d. *Education:* Univ. of Washington, Utah State Univ. *Career:* Poetry-in-the-Schools Master Poet, National Endowment for the Arts 1974–77; Founder Director Port Townsend Writers' Conf.; mem. International Asscn of Machinists and Aerospace Workers, Poetry Society of America, Poets and Writers, Poets, Essayists and Novelists, SFWA. *Publications:* fiction: The Jesus Incident 1979; The Lazarus Effect 1983; The Ascension Factor 1988; Jaguar 1990; Viravax 1993; Burn 1995; poetry: Finding True North 1974; Waving Arms at the Blind 1975; Last Rites 1979; The Single Man Looks at Winter 1983; Last Call 1984; Semaphore 1993, War Baby 2004; other: Learning the Ropes (poems, essays, and short fiction) 1995; contrib. to numerous publications. *Honours:* National Endowment for the Arts Discovery Award 1977. *Address:* 1193 Wood Lane, Grayland, WA 98547, USA.

RANSOM, Jane Reavill, BA, MA; American poet and writer; b. 28 June 1958, Boulder, Colo. *Education:* Indiana University, New York University. *Career:* Asst Ed., San Juan Star, 1981–84; National and International News Ed., New York Daily News, 1984–89; Adjunct Prof., New York University, 1991; guest lecturer in creative writing. *Publications:* Without Asking (poems), 1989; Bye-Bye (novel), 1997; Scene of the Crime: Poems, 1997; Missed (essay), 1997. *Honours:* Nicholas Roerich Poetry Prize, Story Line Press 1989, New York University Press Award 1997. *Literary Agent:* Linda Chester Literary Agency, Rockefeller Center, 630 Fifth Avenue, New York, NY 10103, USA.

RANSOM, Roberto; Mexican novelist and essayist; b. 1960, Mexico City; m.; two c. *Education:* Universidad Nacional Autónoma de México, Univ. of Virginia, USA. *Publications include:* novels: En esa otra tierra 1991, Historia de dos leones 1994, Saludos a la familia 1995, La línea del agua (Serie del volador) 1999, Desaparecidos, animales y artistas 1999, Los Días sin Bárbara 2006, João y el oso Antártica 1999 and 2006. *Address:* Editorial Santillana, Avda. Universidad, 767, 03100 Colonia del Valle, Mexico. *Telephone:* (52) 5688-7566; (52) 5688-8227. *Fax:* (52) 5604-2304. *E-mail:* mexico@santillana.com.mx. *Website:* www.santillana.com.mx.

RAO, R. Raj, PhD; Indian author and academic; *Head of English Department, University of Pune*; b. 1955, Bombay. *Education:* Univ. of Bombay, Univ. of Warwick, UK. *Career:* Prof. of English, Univ. of Pune 1988–, Head of Dept 2011–; f. Queer Studies Circle 2007. *Publications include:* Slideshow (poems) 1992, Nissim Ezekiel: The Authorized Biography 2000, One Day I Locked My Flat in Soul City (short stories) 2001, Boyfriend (novel) 2003, Hostel Room 131 (novel) 2010; as co-editor: Image of India in the Indian Novel in English 1960 – 1985 1993, Whistling in the Dark: Twenty-One Queer Interviews 2009. *Honours:* Recipient, Nehru Centenary British Fellowship. *Address:* Department of English, Arts Faculty Building, University of Pune, Pune, 411 007, Maharashtra State, India (office). *Telephone:* (20) 25690648 (office). *E-mail:* raj@unipine.ac.in (office). *Website:* www.unipune.ac.in (office).

RÂPEANU, Valeriu; Romanian literary critic, historian and editor; b. 28 Sept. 1931, Ploiestiori, Prahova Co.; s. of Gheorghe Râpeanu and Anastasia Râpeanu; m. Sanda Marinescu 1956; one s. *Education:* Univ. of Bucharest. *Career:* journalist 1954–69; Vice-Chair. of the Romanian Cttee of Radio and TV 1970–72; Dir Mihai Eminescu Publishing House, Bucharest 1972–90; Prof., Faculty of Journalism and Philosophy, Spiru Haret Univ., Bucharest; mem. Romanian Writers' Union; fmr mem. Cen. Cttee Romanian CP; mem. Int. Assoc. of Literary Critics. *Publications:* the monographs George Mihail-Zamfirescu 1958, Al. Vlahuţă 1964, Noi şi cei dinaintea noastră (Ourselves and Our Predecessors) 1966, Interferenţe spirituale (Spiritual Correspondences) 1970, Călător pe două continente (Traveller on Two Continents) 1970, Pe drumurile tradiţiei (Following Traditions) 1973, Interpretări si înţelesuri (Interpretations and Significances) 1975, Cultură si istorie (Culture and History) (two vols) 1979, 1981; Tărâmul unde nu ajungi niciodată (The Land You Could Never Reach) 1982, Scriitori dintre cele două războaie (Writers between the two World Wars) 1986, La vie de l'histoire et l'histoire d'une vie 1989, N. Iorga: Opera, Omul, Prietenii 1992, N. Iorga, Mincea Eliade, Nae Ionescu 1993, N. Iorga 1994; vols by Nicolae Iorga, Gh. Brătianu, Al. Kiriţescu, Cella Delavrancea, Marcel Mihalovici, I. G. Duca, Gh.I. Brătianu, George Enescu, C. Rădulescu-Motru, C. Brâncuşi; anthology of Romanian drama; essays on François Mauriac, Jean d'Ormesson, Marcel Proust, Aaron Copland, André Malraux, Jean Cocteau. *Address:* Universitatea Spiru Haret, Strada Ion Ghica nr. 13, Sector 3, Bucharest (office); Str. Mecet 21, Bucharest, Romania. *Telephone:* (21) 3149931 (office). *Fax:* (21) 3149932 (office). *E-mail:* info@spiruharet.ro (office). *Website:* www.spiruharet.ro (office).

RAPHAEL, Frederic Michael, MA, FRSL; American writer; b. 14 Aug. 1931, Chicago, Ill.; s. of Cedric Michael Raphael and Irene Rose Mauser; m. Sylvia Betty Glatt 1955; two s. one d. *Education:* Charterhouse, St John's Coll., Cambridge. *Publications include:* novels: Obbligato 1956, The Earlsdon Way 1958, The Limits of Love 1960, A Wild Sunrise 1961, The Graduate's Wife 1962, The Trouble with England 1962, Lindmann 1963, Orchestra and Beginners 1967, Like Men Betrayed 1970, April, June and November 1972, The Glittering Prizes 1976, Heaven and Earth 1985, After the War 1988, A Wild Surmise 1991, A Double Life 1993, Old Scores 1995, All His Sons 1999,

Fame and Fortune 2007, Final Demands 2010; short stories: Sleeps Six 1979, Oxbridge Blues 1980, Think of England 1986, The Hidden I (illustrated by Sarah Raphael) 1990, The Latin Lover and Other Stories 1994; biography: Somerset Maugham and his World 1977, Byron 1982; essays: Cracks in the Ice 1979, Of Gods and Men (illustrated by Sarah Raphael) 1992, The Necessity of Anti-Semitism 1997, Historicism and its Poverty 1998, Karl Popper 1998, Eyes Wide Open 1999, Personal Terms 2001, The Benefits of Doubt 2002, Rough Copy (Personal Terms II) 2004, Cuts and Bruises (Personal Terms III) 2006, Ticks and Crosses (Personal Terms IV) 2008; translations: Catullus (with K. McLeish) 1976, The Oresteia of Aeschylus 1978, Aeschylus (complete plays, with K. McLeish) 1991, Euripides' Medea (with K. McLeish) 1994, Euripides: Hippolytus, Bacchae (with K. McLeish) 1997, Sophocles Aias (with K. McLeish) 1998, Bacchae 1999, The Satyrica of Petronius 2009; screenplays: Nothing But the Best 1964 (Writers' Guild Best Comedy), Darling (US Acad. Award for Best Original Screenplay, Writer's Guild Best Screenplay, British Film Acad. Award) 1965, Far from the Madding Crowd 1967, Two for the Road 1968, Daisy Miller 1974, Rogue Male 1976, Richard's Things 1980, The Man in the Brooks Brothers Shirt (ACE Award 1991), Armed Response 1995, Eyes Wide Shut 1998, Gordon 2010; numerous plays for TV and radio including: The Glittering Prizes (Royal TV Soc. Writer of the Year Award) 1976, From the Greek 1979, The Daedalus Dimension (radio) 1982, Oxbridge Blues 1984, The Thought of Lydia (radio) 1988, After the War 1989, The Empty Jew (radio) 1993, Final Demands (radio) 2010, Couples (radio) 2010, Eyes Wide Open (TV) 2010. *Honours:* Lippincott Prize 1961, Prix Simone Genevois 2000. *Address:* Ed Victor Ltd, 6, Bayley Street, Bedford Square, London, WC1B 3HE, England (office).

RAPOPORT, Janis, BA; Canadian poet, writer and dramatist; b. 22 June 1946, Toronto, Ont.; m. 1st; one s. two d.; m. 2nd Douglas Donegani 1980; one d. *Education:* University of Toronto. *Career:* Assoc. Ed., Tamarack Review, 1970–82; Playwright-in-Residence, Tarragon Theatre, 1974–75; Dir, Ethos Cultural Development Foundation, 1981–; Ed., Ethos magazine, 1983–87; Part-time Instructor, Sheridan College, 1984–86; Writer-in-Residence, St Thomas Public Library, 1987, Beeton Public Library, 1988, Dundas Public Library, 1990, North York Public Library, 1991; Instructor, School of Continuing Studies, University of Toronto, 1988–; mem. League of Canadian Poets; Playwrights' Union of Canada; Writers' Guild of Canada; Writers' Union of Canada. *Publications:* Within the Whirling Moment, 1967; Foothills, 1973; Jeremy's Dream, 1974; Landscape (co-ed.), 1977; Dreamgirls, 1979; Imaginings (co-author), 1982; Upon Her Fluent Route, 1992; After Paradise, 1996; contributions: anthologies, newspapers, magazines, and radio. *Honours:* Canadian Council Arts Award, 1981–82; AIGA Certificate of Excellence, 1983; New York Dirs Club Award, 1983; Outstanding Achievement Award, American Poetry Asscn, 1986; Toronto Arts Council Research and Development Awards, 1990, 1992; Excellence in Teaching Award for Creative Writing, School of Continuing Studies, University of Toronto, 1998.

RASHID, Ahmed; Pakistani journalist and author; b. 1948, Rawalpindi; m.; two c. *Education:* Malvern Coll., UK, Government Coll., Lahore, Fitzwilliam Coll., Univ. of Cambridge, UK. *Career:* fmr Pakistan, Afghanistan and Cen. Asia Corresp. Far Eastern Economic Review; now writes regularly for Daily Telegraph, London, International Herald Tribune, New York Review of Books, BBC Online, The Nation, Lahore and other academic and foreign affairs journals as well as several Pakistani newspapers and magazines; appears on TV and radio including BBC World Service, ABC Australia, Radio France Int. and German Radio; mem. Advisory Bd Eurasia Net of the Soros Foundation; Scholar, Davos World Econ. Forum; consultant for Human Rights Watch; mem. Bd of Advisers Int. Cttee of the Red Cross, Geneva 2004–08; f. Open Media Fund for Afghanistan (charity) 2002. *Publications include:* The Resurgence of Central Asia: Islam or Nationalism, Fundamentalism Reborn: Afghanistan and the Taliban, Jihad: The Rise of Militant Islam in Central Asia, Taliban: Islam, Oil and the New Great Game in Central Asia 2000, Descent into Chaos 2008. *Honours:* Nisar Osmani Award for Courage in Journalism, Human Rights Soc. of Pakistan. *Address:* c/o The Daily Telegraph, 111 Buckingham Palace Road, London, SW1W 0DT, England (office). *Telephone:* (20) 7931-2000 (office). *Fax:* (20) 7513-2506 (office). *E-mail:* dtnews@telegraph.co.uk (office). *Website:* www.telegraph.co.uk (office); www.ahmedrashid.com.

RASPUTIN, Valentin Grigoriyevich; Russian writer; b. 15 March 1937, Ust-Uda (Irkutsk). *Education:* Irkutsk Univ. *Career:* first works published 1961; elected People's Deputy 1989; mem. Presidential Council 1990–91. *Publications:* I Forgot to Ask Lyosha 1961, A Man of This World 1965, Bearskin for Sale 1966, Vasilii and Vasilisa 1967, Deadline 1970, Live and Remember, Stories, 1974, Parting with Matera 1976, Live and Love 1982, Fire 1985, Collected Works (2 vols) 1990, Siberia, Siberia 1991. *Honours:* USSR State Prize 1977, 1987; Hero of Socialist Labour 1987. *Address:* 5th Army Street 67, Apt 68, 664000 Irkutsk, Russia. *Telephone:* (3952) 4-71-00.

RATCLIFFE, Eric Hallam; British poet, writer, editor and physicist (retd) and information scientist (retd); b. 8 Aug. 1918, Teddington, Middx. *Career:* war service 1938–45; Founder-Ed. Ore 1955–95; reviewer, New Hope Int. Online. *Publications include:* The Visitation 1952, The Chronicle of the Green Man 1960, Gleanings for a Daughter of Aeolus 1968, Leo Poems 1972, Commius 1976, Nightguard of the Quaternary 1979, Ballet Class 1986, The Runner of the Seven Valleys 1990, The Ballad of Polly McPoo 1991, Advent 1992, The Golden Heart Man 1993, Fire in the Bush: Poems, 1955–1992 1993, William Ernest Henley (1849–1903): An Introduction 1993, The Caxton of her Age: The Career and Family Background of Emily Faithfull (1835–1895) 1993, Winstanley's Walton, 1649: Events in the Civil War at Walton-on-Thames 1994, Ratcliffe's Megathesaurus 1995, Anthropos 1995, Odette 1995, Sholen 1996, The Millennium of the Magician 1996, The Brussels Griffon 1996, Strange Furlongs 1996, Wellington—A Broad Front 1998, Capabilities of the Alchemical Mind 1999, Cosmologia 2000, Loyal Women 2000, The Ghost with Nine Fathers 2001, No Jam in the Astral 2002, On Baker's Level 2002, The Divine Peter 2002, Desert Voices: A Tribute to Abu'l-Ala 2003, Going for God 2005, Unfinished Business 2005, Islandia 2005, The Ruffian on the Stair 2005; contrib. to anthologies and journals. *Honours:* Baron, Royal Order of the Bohemian Crown 1995. *Address:* 7 The Towers, Stevenage, Hertfordshire SG1 1HE, England (home). *E-mail:* octillion@ntlworld.com (home). *Website:* homepage.ntlworld.com/chessmaster/eric.

RATHER, Dan, BA; American broadcast journalist; b. Oct. 1931, Wharton, Tex.; m. Jean Goebel; one s. one d. *Education:* Sam Houston State Coll., Univ. of Houston, Tex., S Tex. School of Law. *Career:* writer and sports commentator with KSAM-TV; taught journalism for one year at Houston Chronicle; with CBS 1962; with radio station KTRH, Houston for about four years; News and Current Affairs Dir CBS Houston TV affiliate KHOU-TV late 1950s; joined CBS News 1962; Chief London Bureau 1965–66; worked in Viet Nam; White House 1966; anchorman CBS Reports 1974–75; co-anchorman 60 Minutes CBS-TV 1975–81; anchorman Dan Rather Reporting CBS Radio Network 1977–2006; co-ed. show Who's Who CBS-TV 1977; anchorman Midwest desk CBS Nat. election night 1972–80; CBS Nat. Political Consultant 1964–2006; anchorman Man. Ed. CBS Evening News with Dan Rather 1981–2005, co-anchorman 1993–2005; host Dan Rather Reports, HDNet 2006–; anchored numerous CBS News Special Programmes, including coverage of presidential campaigns in 1982 and 1984; as White House corresp. accompanied Pres. on numerous travels, including visits to Middle East, USSR, People's Repub. of China. *Publications:* The Palace Guard 1974 (with Gary Gates), The Camera Never Blinks Twice (with Mickey Herskowitz) 1977, I Remember (with Peter Wyden) 1991, The Camera Never Blinks Twice: The Further Adventures of a Television Journalist 1994. *Honours:* numerous acad. honours; ten Emmy awards; Distinguished Achievement for Broadcasting Award, Univ. of Southern Calif. Journalism Alumni Asscn, Bob Considine Award 1983. *Address:* c/o HDNet, 2909 Taylor Street, Dallas, TX 75226, USA (office). *Telephone:* (214) 651-1446 (office). *Website:* www.hd.net/danrather.html (office).

RATNER, Rochelle; American poet, writer and editor; b. 2 Dec. 1948, Atlantic City, NJ; m. Kenneth Thorp 1990. *Career:* poetry columnist, Soho Weekly News 1975–82; Co-Ed. Hand Book 1976–82; Exec. Ed., American Book Review 1978–; small press columnist, Library Journey 1985; poetry consultant, Israel Horizons 1988–97; Ed. New Jersey Online: Reading Room 1995–96; NBCC Board of Dirs 1995–2001; mem. Editorial Bd Marsh Hawk Press 2004–; mem. Authors' Guild, Hudson Valley Writers Guild, Nat. Book Critics Circle, Nat. Writers Union, PEN, Poetry Soc. of America, Poets and Writers. *Publications:* poetry: A Birthday of Waters 1971, False Trees 1973, The Mysteries 1976, Pirate's Song 1976, The Tightrope Walker 1977, Quarry 1978, Combing the Waves 1979, Sea Air in a Grave Ground Hog Turns Toward 1980, Hide and Seek 1980, Practicing to be a Woman: New and Selected Poems 1982, Someday Songs 1992, Zodiac Arrest 1995, Tellings 2003, House and Home 2003, Lady Pinball 2004, Leah 2004, Beggars at the Wall 2006; fiction: Bobby's Girl 1986, The Lion's Share 1991; non-fiction: Trying to Understand What it Means to be a Feminist: Essays on Women Writers 1984, Bearing Life: Women's Writings on Childlessness (ed.) 2000. *Honours:* Susan Koppelman Award 2000. *Address:* 609 Columbus Avenue, Apt 16F, New York, NY 10024, USA. *E-mail:* rochelleratner@mindspring.com. *Website:* www.rochelleratner.com.

RATUSHINSKAYA, Irina Borisovna; Russian poet; b. 4 March 1954; m. Igor Gerashchenko 1979. *Education:* Odessa Pedagogical Inst. *Career:* teacher Odessa Pedagogical Inst. 1976–83; arrested with husband, Moscow 1981; lost job, arrested again, 17 Sept. 1982, convicted of 'subverting the Soviet regime' and sentenced 5 March 1983 to seven years' hard labour; strict regime prison camp Aug. 1983, released Sept. 1986; settled in UK 1986; f. Democracy and Independence Group April 1989–; poetry appeared in samizdat publs, West European Russian language journals, trans. in American and British press and in USSR 1989–. *Publications include:* Poems (trilingual text) 1984, No, I'm Not Afraid 1986, Off Limits (in Russian) 1986, I Shall Live to See It (in Russian) 1986, Grey Is the Colour of Hope 1989, In the Beginning 1990, The Odessans 1992, Fictions and Lies 1998. *Address:* c/o Vargius Publishing House, Kazakova str. 18, 107005 Moscow, Russia. *Telephone:* (495) 785-09-62.

RAUSING, Sigrid, BA, MSc, PhD; Swedish anthropologist, philanthropist and publisher; b. 1962, Lund; d. of Hans Anders Rausing and Märit Rausing; m. 1st Dennis Hotz; one s.; m. 2nd Eric Abraham 2003. *Education:* Univ. of York, Univ. Coll. London, UK. *Career:* wealth derived from family-owned co. Tetra-Pak (manufacturer of drink cartons); f. Ruben and Elisabeth Rausing Trust 1995 (changed name to Sigrid Rausing Trust 2003); co-f. Portobello Books 2005; acquired Granta (magazine and publishing house) 2005; mem. Bd of Dirs Human Rights Watch, Charleston, Sussex. *Publications:* History, Memory, and Identity in Post-Soviet Estonia 2004; articles in academic journals. *Honours:* Int. Service Human Rights Award, Global Human Rights Defender Category 2004, Beacon Special Award for Philanthropy 2005, Changing Face of Philanthropy Award, Women's Funding Network 2006. *Website:* www.sigrid-rausing-trust.org (office).

RAVENSDALE, 3rd Baron, cr. 1911, 7th Baronet; **Sir Nicholas Mosley,** Bt, MC; British writer; b. 25 June 1923, London; s. of the late Sir Oswald Mosley and of Lady Cynthia Curzon; m. 1st Rosemary Salmond 1947 (divorced 1974, died 1991); three s. one d.; m. 2nd Verity Bailey (née Raymond) 1974; one s. *Education:* Eton, Balliol Coll., Oxford. *Publications:* novels: Spaces of the Dark 1951, The Rainbearers 1955, Corruption 1957, African Switchback 1958, The Life of Raymond Raynes 1961, Meeting Place 1962, Accident 1964, Assassins 1966, Impossible Object (also screenplay) 1968, Natalie, Natalia 1971, Catastrophe Practice (three plays and a novella) 1979, Imago Bird 1980, Serpent 1981, Judith 1986, Hopeful Monsters (Whitbread Book of the Year) 1990, Children of Darkness and Light 1996, The Hesperides Tree 2001, Inventing God 2003, Look at the Dark 2005, God's Hazard 2009; non-fiction: Experience and Religion: A Lay Essay in Theology 1965, The Assassination of Trotsky (also screenplay) 1972, Julian Grenfell: His Life and the Times of his Death 1988–1915 (biog.) 1976, Rules of the Game: Sir Oswald and Lady Cynthia Mosley 1896–1933 (biog.) 1982, Beyond the Pale: Sir Oswald Mosley and Family 1933–1980 (biog.) 1983, Efforts at Truth (autobiog.) 1994, Time at War: A Memoir 2006, Paradoxes of Peace 2009. *Address:* 5 Hungerford Road, London, N7 9LA, England (home). *Telephone:* (20) 7607-3579 (home).

RAVITCH, Diane Silvers, PhD; American education scholar and academic; *Research Professor of Education, New York University*; b. (Diane Silvers), 1 July 1938, Houston, Tex.; d. of Walter Cracker and Ann Celia Silvers (née Katz); m. Richard Ravitch 1960 (divorced 1986); three s. (one deceased). *Education:* Wellesley Coll., Mass, Columbia Univ., New York. *Career:* Adjunct Asst Prof. of History and Educ., Teachers' Coll., Columbia Univ. 1975–78, Assoc. Prof. 1978–83, Adjunct Prof. 1983–91; Dir Woodrow Wilson Nat. Fellowship Foundation 1987–91; Chair. Educational Excellence Network 1988–91; Asst Sec. Office of Research and Improvement, US Dept of Educ., Washington, DC 1991–93, Counsellor to Sec. of Educ. 1991–93; Visiting Fellow, Brookings Inst. 1993–94, Brown Chair in Educ. Policy 1997–; Sr Research Scholar, New York Univ. 1994–98, Research Prof. in Educ. 1998–; Sr Fellow, Progressive Policy Inst. 1998–2002, Hoover Inst.; Adjunct Fellow, Manhattan Inst. 1996–99; Trustee New York Historical Soc. 1995–98, New York Council on the Humanities 1996–2004. *Publications:* The Great School Wars: New York City 1805–1973 1974, The Revisionists Revised 1977, Educating and Urban People (co-author) 1981, The Troubled Crusade: American Education 1945–1980 1983, The School and the City (co-author) 1983, Against Mediocrity (co-author) 1984, The Schools We Deserve 1985, Challenges to the Humanities (co-author) 1985, What Do Our 17-Year-Olds Know? (with Chester E. Finn Jr) 1987, The American Reader (co-ed.) 1990, The Democracy Reader (ed. with Abigail Thernstrom) 1992, National Standards in American Education 1995, Debating the Future of American Education (ed.) 1995, Learning from the Past (ed. with Maris Vinovskis) 1995, New Schools for a New Century (ed. with Joseph Viteretti) 1997, Left Back 2000, City Schools (ed.) 2000, The Language Police 2003, Forgotten Heroes of American Education (co-ed.) 2006, The English Reader (co-ed.) 2006, Edspeak 2007, The Death and Life of the Great American School System 2010; contrib. of articles and reviews to scholarly books and professional journals. *Honours:* Hon. DHumLitt (Williams Coll.) 1984, (Reed Coll.) 1985, (Amherst Coll.) 1986, (State Univ. of New York) 1988, (Ramopo Coll.) 1990, (St Joseph's Coll., NY) 1991; Hon. LHD (Middlebury Coll.) 1997, (Union Coll.) 1998; Leadership Award, Klingenstein Inst., Teachers Coll. 1994, Horace Kidger Award, New England History Teachers Asscn 1998, Leadership Award, New York City Council of Supervisors and Admins 2004, John Dewey Award, United Fed. of Teachers of New York City 2005, Gaudium Award, Breukelein Inst. 2005, Uncommon Book Award, Hoover Inst. 2005, Kenneth J. Bialkin/Citigroup Public Service Award 2006. *Address:* New York University, 82 Washington Square East, New York, NY 10003, USA (office). *E-mail:* dr19@nyu.edu (office); gardendr@gmail.com (home). *Website:* www.dianeravitch.com (office).

RAVIZZA, Filippo; Italian poet and critic; b. 1951, Milan. *Career:* journalist, La Repubblica 1979–86; Artistic Dir, Nat. Poetry Festival at Induno Olona and Varese 1995–96; fmr theatre critic, Il Mondo. *Publications:* Le Porte 1987, Vesti nel Pomeriggio 1995, Bambini delle Onde 2000, Prigionieri del tempo 2006. *Address:* c/o Editore LietoColle, Via Principale 9, Faloppio, 22020 Italy (office). *E-mail:* filippo.ravizza@unione.milano.it (home); info@lietocolle.com (office). *Website:* www.lietocolle.com (office).

RAVVIN, Norman, BA, MA, PhD; Canadian novelist and teacher; b. 26 Aug. 1963, Calgary, AB. *Education:* University of British Columbia, University of Toronto. *Career:* Instructor, Concordia University; General Ed., Hungry I Books, 2000–; mem. Writers Guild of Alberta; Asscn of Canadian College and University Teachers of English; MLA of America. *Publications:* Café des Westens (novel) 1991, Sex, Skyscrapers and Standard Yiddish (short stories) 1997, A House of Words: Jewish Writing, Identity and Memory (essays) 1997, Great Stories of the Sea (ed.) 1999, Hidden Canada: An Intimate Travelogue 2001, Not Quite Mainstream: Canadian Jewish Short Stories (ed.) 2001, Lola by Night (novel) 2003. Contributions: anthologies: Fresh Blood: New Canadian Gothic Fiction, The Nelson Introduction to Literature; journals: Canadian Jewish Studies, Canadian Literature, English Studies in Canada, Malcolm Lowry Review, Prairie Fire, Prism International, Studies in Canadian Literature, Wascana Review, West Coast Review, Western Living. *Honours:* K.M. Hunter Emerging Artist Award, Alberta Culture and Multiculturalism New Fiction Award 1990, PhD Fellowship, Social Sciences and Humanities Research Council of Canada. *Address:* c/o Concordia University, Department of Religion, Montréal, QC H3G 1M8, Canada (office).

RAWN, Melanie Robin, BA; American writer; b. 12 June 1954, Santa Monica, CA. *Education:* Scripps College, University of Denver, California State University at Fullerton. *Career:* mem. SFWA. *Publications:* Dragon Prince 1988, The Star Scroll 1989, Sunrunner's Fire 1990, Stronghold 1990, The Dragon Token 1992, Skybowl 1993, The Ruins of Ambrai 1994, Knights of the Morningstar 1994, The Golden Key (co-author) 1996, The Mageborn Traitor 1997, Spellbinder 2006, Fire Raiser 2009. *Website:* www.melanierawn.com.

RAWNSLEY, Andrew Nicholas James, MA, FRSA; British journalist, broadcaster and author; *Associate Editor and Chief Political Commentator, The Observer*; b. 5 Jan. 1962, Leeds, Yorks., England; s. of Eric Rawnsley and Barbara Rawnsley (née Butler); m. Jane Leslie Hall 1990; three d. *Education:* Lawrence Sheriff Grammar School, Rugby, Rugby School, Sidney Sussex Coll., Cambridge. *Career:* with BBC 1983–85, The Guardian 1985–93 (political columnist 1987–93); Assoc. Ed. and Chief Political Commentator, The Observer 1993–; Ed.-in-Chief, politicshome.com (political website) 2008–09; Presenter Channel 4 TV series A Week in Politics 1989–97, ITV series The Agenda 1996, Channel 4 series Bye Bye Blues 1997, Blair's Year 1998, BBC 2 series What The Papers Say and Review of the Year 2002–07, ITV series The Sunday Edition 2006–08, BBC Radio 4 series The Westminster Hour 1998–2006, The Unauthorised Biography of the United Kingdom 1999, The Rise and Fall of Tony Blair 2007, Gordon Brown: Where Did it All Go Wrong? 2008, Crash Gordon: The Inside Story of the Financial Crisis 2009, Cameron Uncovered 2010. *Publications:* Servants of the People: The Inside Story of New Labour (Channel 4 Book of the Year 2001) 2000 (revised edn 2001), The End of the Party: The Rise and Fall of New Labour (No. 1 best-seller) 2010. *Honours:* Student Journalist of the Year, Guardian/NUS Media Awards 1983, Young Journalist of the Year, British Press Awards 1987, Columnist of the Year, What the Papers Say Award 2000, Book of the Year Award, Channel 4 Political Awards 2001, Political Journalist of the Year, Channel 4 Political Awards 2003, Commentator of the Year, Public Affairs Awards 2005, Commentator of the Year, House Magazine Awards 2008. *Address:* The Observer, Kings Place, 90 York Way, London, N1 9GU, England (office). *Telephone:* (20) 7278-2332 (office). *E-mail:* a.rawnsley@observer.co.uk (office). *Website:* www.observer.co.uk (office).

RAWORTH, Thomas Moore, MA; British poet, writer, translator and graphic artist; b. 19 July 1938, London, England; s. of Thomas Alfred Raworth and Mary Moore; m. Valarie Murphy; four s. one d. *Education:* Univ. of Essex. *Career:* Poet-in-Residence, Literature Dept, Univ. of Essex 1969, King's Coll., Cambridge 1977–78; Lecturer, Bowling Green State Univ., OH, USA 1972–73; Visiting Lecturer, Northeastern Ill. Univ. 1973–74, Univ. of Texas 1974–75, Univ. of Cape Town, SA 1991, Univ. of California, San Diego 1996; Resident Writer, New Coll. of California, San Francisco 1997; Visiting Distinguished Writer, Columbia Coll., Chicago 1999; shorter residencies at Hungarian PEN, Budapest 1974, British Council, Paris 1982, Univ. of Venice 1986, CIPM, Marseille 1990–91, 2002, Univ. of Trieste 1992, Porto dei Santi Bologna 1999, State Univ. of NY, Buffalo 2002, Audible Gallery, Chicago 2006, Miami Univ., Ohio 2007. *Exhibitions:* graphic work shown in Europe, USA and SA 1984–. *Film:* Hands 2007. *Publications:* The Relation Ship 1967, The Big Green Day 1968, A Serial Biography 1969, Lion, Lion 1970, Moving 1971, Act 1973, Ace 1974, Common Sense 1976, Logbook 1977, Sky Tails 1978, Nicht Wahr, Rosie? 1979, Writing 1982, Lèvre de Poche 1983, Heavy Light 1984, Tottering State: Selected Poems 1963–83 1984, Lazy Left Hand 1986, Visible Shivers 1987, All Fours 1991, Catacoustics 1991, Eternal Sections 1991, Survival 1991, Clean and Well Lit: Selected Poems 1987–1995 1996, Meadow 2000, Collected Poems 2003, Caller 2006, Let Baby Fall 2008, Earn Your Milk (collected prose) 2009, Windmills on Fire 2010, There Are Few People Who Put on Any Clothes 2009, Incomprehensible Things 2011, Selected Poems published in Dutch, Swedish, Spanish (Mexico and Chile) and German; cover designs for many books 1990–. *Honours:* Alice Hunt Bartlett Prize 1969, Cholmondeley Award 1971, Int. Cttee on Poetry Award, New York 1988, Poetry Skipper Gold Medal for Services to Int. Poetry, Bologna 1999, Antonio Delfini Prize for Lifetime Achievement, Modena 2007, Stanford Calderwood Fellowship, Macdowell, USA 2007–08. *Address:* Flat 3, 20 Brunswick Terrace, Hove, East Sussex, BN3 1HJ, England (home). *Telephone:* (1273) 220759. *E-mail:* raworth@gmail.com. *Website:* www.tomraworth.com.

RAWSON, Claude Julien, BA, BLitt, MA; British academic, writer and editor; *Maynard Mack Professor of English, Yale University*; b. 8 Feb. 1935, Shanghai, China; m. Judith Ann Hammond 1959; three s. two d. *Education:* Magdalen Coll., Oxford. *Career:* Lecturer in English, Newcastle Univ. 1957–65; Lecturer, then Prof., Univ. of Warwick 1965–85, Hon. Prof. 1986–; George Sherburn Prof. of English, Univ. of Illinois, USA 1985–86; George M. Bodman Prof. of English, Yale Univ., USA 1986–96, Maynard Mack Prof. of English 1996–, Sr Faculty Fellow 1991–92; Ed. Modern Language Review and Yearbook of English Studies 1974–88; Gen. Ed. Unwin Critical Library 1974–, Blackwell Critical Biographies 1985–; Visiting Prof., Univ. of Pennsylvania 1973, Univ. of California, Berkeley 1980; Life mem. Modern Humanities Research Asscn (Cttee mem. 1974–88); mem. Int. Soc. for 18th Century Studies, American Soc. for 18th-Century Studies, British Soc. for 18th-Century Studies (Pres. 1973–74); Fellow, American Acad. of Arts and Sciences. *Publications:* Henry Fielding 1968, Focus Swift 1971, Henry Fielding and the Augustan Ideal 1972, Gulliver and the Gentle Reader 1973, Fielding: A Critical Anthology 1973, The Character of Swift's Satire 1983, English Satire and the Satiric Tradition 1984, Order from Confusion

Sprung 1985, Collected Poems of Thomas Parnell (ed. with F. P. Lock) 1989, Satire and Sentiment 1660–1830 (with F. P. Lock) 1994, Jonathan Swift: A Collection of Critical Essays (ed.) 1995, Cambridge History of Literary Criticism, Vol. 4: The Eighteenth Century (with H. B. Nisbet) 1997, God, Gulliver and Genocide 2001, Basic Writings of Jonathan Swift 2002, Essential Writings of Jonathan Swift (co-author) 2009, Politics and Literature in the Age of Swift 2010, Great Shakespeareans: Dryden, Pope, Johnson, Malone 2010, Cambridge Companion to English Poets 2011; Gen. Ed., Cambridge History of Literary Criticism 1983–; Chair. and Gen. Ed. Yale edn of the Private Papers of James Boswell 1990–2001; Gen. Ed. Cambridge edn of the Works of Jonathan Swift 2001–. *Honours:* Hon. DLitt (Keele Univ.) 2007; Andrew Mellon Fellow, Clark and Huntington Library 1980, 1990, Conf. of Eds of Learned Journals Certificate of Merit for Distinguished Service 1988, Guggenheim Fellow 1991–92, Nat. Endowment of the Humanities Grant 1991. *Address:* Department of English, Yale University, PO Box 208302, New Haven, CT 06520-8302, USA (office). *E-mail:* claude.rawson@yale.edu (office). *Website:* english.yale.edu (office).

RAWSON, Michael J., PhD; American historian, author and academic; *Assistant Professor of History, Brooklyn College. Education:* Univ. of Wisconsin, Madison. *Career:* taught at Univ. of Wisconsin and Stanford Univ.; Asst Prof., Dept of History, Brooklyn Coll. 2007–. *Publications:* Eden on the Charles: The Making of Boston 2010; contrib. of articles, reviews and essays in historical journals. *Honours:* numerous awards and fellowships including Andrew W. Mellon Fellowship, Massachusetts Historical Soc. 2002, Carter Manny Award, Graham Foundation for Advanced Studies in the Fine Arts 2003, Mrs Giles Whiting Foundation Fellowship for Excellence in Teaching 2010, Feliks Gross Endowment Award for Outstanding Research, CUNY Acad. for the Humanities and Sciences 2011. *Address:* 503 Whitehead Hall, Department of History, Brooklyn College, Campus Road, Brooklyn, NY 11210, USA (office). *Telephone:* (718) 951-5000 (ext. 1166) (office). *Fax:* (718) 951-4504 (office). *E-mail:* mrawson@brooklyn.cuny.edu (office). *Website:* www.brooklyn.cuny.edu/web/academics/schools/socialsciences/undergraduate/history.php (office).

RAY, David Eugene, BA, MA; American academic, poet and writer; *Professor Emeritus of English, University of Missouri-Kansas City*; b. 20 May 1932, Sapulpa, Okla; m. Suzanne Judy Morrish 1970; one s. three d. *Education:* Univ. of Chicago. *Career:* instructor, Wright Junior Coll. 1957–58, Northern Illinois Univ. 1958–60; instructor, Cornell Univ. 1960–64; Asst Prof., Reed Coll., Portland, Ore. 1964–66; Lecturer, Univ. of Iowa 1969–70; Visiting Assoc. Prof., Bowling Green State Univ. 1970–71; Prof. of English, Univ. of Missouri, Kansas City 1971–95, Prof. Emer. 1995–; Visiting Prof., Syracuse Univ. 1978–79, Univ. of Rajasthan, India 1981–82; Exchange Prof., Univ. of Otago, NZ 1987; Visiting Fellow, Univ. of Western Australia 1991; Ed. New Letters Magazine 1971–85; mem. Acad. of American Poets, PEN, Poetry Soc. of America. *Publications:* poetry: X-Rays 1965, Dragging the Main and Other Poems 1968, A Hill in Oklahoma 1972, Gathering Firewood: New Poems and Selected 1974, Enough of Flying: Poems Inspired by the Ghazals of Ghalib 1977, The Tramp's Cup 1978, The Farm in Calabria and Other Poems 1979, The Touched Life 1982, On Wednesday I Cleaned Out My Wallet 1985, Elysium in the Halls of Hell 1986, Sam's Book 1987, The Maharani's New Wall 1989, Not Far From the River 1990, Wool Highways 1993, Kangaroo Paws 1995, Heartstones: New and Selected Poems 1998, Demons in the Diner 1999, One Thousand Years: Poems about the Holocaust 2004, The Death of Sardanapalus and Other Poems of the Iraq Wars 2004, David Ray: Greatest Hits 2004, Music of Time: Selected Poems 2006, When 2007, After Tagore: Poems Inspired by Rabindranath Tagore 2008, Hemingway: A Desperate Life 2011; prose: The Mulberries of Mingo (short stories) 1978, The Endless Search: A Memoir 2003, contrib. to journals and newspapers. *Honours:* William Carlos Williams Award 1979, 1993, PEN Syndicated Fiction Awards 1982–86, Amelia Magazine Bernice Jennings Award for Traditional Poetry 1987, Maurice English Poetry Award 1988, Nat. Poetry Award, Passaic Community Coll. 1989, First Prize, St Louis Poetry Centre Stanley Hanks Memorial Contest 1990, Daniel Varoujan Award, New England Poetry Club 1996, New Millennium Poetry Award 1997, Allen Ginsberg Poetry Award, Poetry Centre, Paterson 1997, Poetry Award, Explorations magazine 1997, Long Poem Award, Amelia Magazine 1998, Richard Snyder Memorial Prize 1999, Poetry Award, Flyway Magazine 2000, Poetry Award, Nuclear Age Peace Foundation 2001. *Address:* 2033 East 10th Street, Tucson, AZ 85719, USA. *E-mail:* djray@gainbroadband.com. *Website:* www.davidraypoet.com.

RAY, Pratibha, BSc, MEd, PhD; Indian academic, writer and poet; b. 21 Jan. 1943, Alabol, Cuttack Dist, Orissa; d. of the late Parashuram Das and the late Manorama Devi; m. Akshaya Chandra Ray; two s. one d. *Education:* Balikuda High School, Ravenshaw Coll., Cuttack. *Career:* Oriya writer; school teacher at various Orissa State Govt colls for 30 years; mem. Public Service Comm., Orissa State 1998–2004; f. Bhashyan Literary Foundation 2004; mem. Exec. Bd Sahitya Akademi. *Publications:* novels: Barsha Basanta Baishakha 1974, Aranya 1977, Nishidha Prithivi 1978, Parichaya 1979, Aparichita 1979, Punyatoya 1979, Meghamedura 1980, Ashabari 1980, Ayamarambha 1981, Nilatrishna 1981, Samudrara Swara 1982, Shilapadma (trans. as Stone Lotus, Orissa Sahitya Akademi Award 1985) 1983, Yajnaseni (Sarla Award 1990, Moorti Devi Bharatiya Jnanpath Award 1991) 1984, Dehatit 1986, Uttarmagi 1988, Aadibhoomi (trans. as Primal Land) 1993, Maha Moha 1998, Magnamati (trans. as The Tranced Earth) 2004; short stories: Samanya Kathana 1978, Gangashiuli 1979, Asamapta 1980, Aikatana 1981, Anabana 1983, Hatabaksa 1983, Ghasa o Akasha 1984, Chandrabhaga o Chadrabhaga 1984, Shrestha Galpa 1984, Abyakta 1986, Itibut 1987, Haritpatra 1989, Prithak Ishwar 1991, Bhagabanara Desha (trans. as Land of God) 1991, Manushya Swara 1992, Sasthasati 1996, Moksha 1996, Ullanghana (Sahitya Akademi Award 2000) 1998, Nivedanamidam 2000, Gandhinka 2002, Jhoti paka Kantha 2006. *Honours:* Jhankara Award 1989, Saptarshi Award, Sambalpur Univ. 1989, Katha Prize 1994, 1999, Bisuva Award for Lifetime Achievement 1995, Rastriya Ekta Puruskar 1999, Kapilash Award 2000, Katha Bharati Title 2000, Rajiv Gandhi Sacbhawana Nat. Puraskar 2002, Chitrapuri Samman 2006, Amrita Keerti Award 2006, Padma Shri 2007. *Website:* www.pratibharay.org.

RAY, Robert Henry, BA, PhD; American academic and writer; *Professor of English and Graduate Program Director, Baylor University*; b. 29 April 1940, San Saba, Tex.; m. Lynette Elizabeth Dittmar 1962, two d. *Education:* Univ. of Texas at Austin. *Career:* Asst Prof. of English, Baylor Univ. 1967–75, Assoc. Prof. of English 1975–85, Prof. of English 1985–, Grad. Program Dir; mem. Modern Language Asscn of America, John Donne Soc. *Publications:* The Herbert Allusion Book 1986, Approaches to Teaching Shakespeare's King Lear 1986, A John Donne Companion 1990, A George Herbert Companion 1995, An Andrew Marvell Companion 1998; contrib. to various publs. *Address:* Department of English, PO Box 97406, Baylor University, Waco, TX 76798, USA. *E-mail:* Robert_Ray@baylor.edu (office).

RAY, Robert J., BA, MA, PhD; American teacher and writer; b. 15 May 1935, Amarillo, TX; m. 1st Ann Allen (divorced); m. 2nd Margot M. Waale 1983. *Education:* University of Texas, Austin. *Career:* Instructor, 1963–65, Asst Prof., 1965–68, Assoc. Prof., 1968–75, Prof., 1976, Beloit College, Wisconsin; Writing Teacher, Valley College, 1984–88, University of California, Irvine, 1985–88; Adjunct Prof., Chapman College, 1988–; mem. MWA. *Publications:* The Art of Reading: A Handbook on Writing (with Ann Ray), 1968; The Heart of the Game (novel), 1975; Cage of Mirrors (novel), 1980; Small Business: An Entrepreneur's Plan (with L. A. Eckert and J. D. Ryan), 1985; Bloody Murdock (novel), 1987; Murdock for Hire (novel), 1987; The Hitman Cometh (novel), 1988; Dial M for Murder (novel), 1988; Murdock in Xanadu (novel), 1989. *Address:* c/o Random House Inc., 1745 Broadway, New York, NY 10019, USA.

RAYBAN, Chlöe (see Bear, Carolyn Ann)

RAYMOND, Patrick Ernest; British royal air force officer (retd) and writer; b. 25 Sept. 1924, Cuckfield, Sussex, England; m. Lola Pilpel 1950, one s. *Education:* Art School, Cape Town, South Africa. *Career:* Royal Air Force, rising to Group Captain 1942–77. *Publications:* A City of Scarlet and Gold, 1963; The Lordly Ones, 1965; The Sea Garden, 1970; The Last Soldier, 1974; A Matter of Assassination, 1977; The White War, 1978; The Grand Admiral, 1980; Daniel and Esther, 1989.

RAYSON, Hannie, BA; Australian playwright; b. 31 March 1957, Brighton, Melbourne, Vic. *Education:* Univ. of Melbourne, Victoria Coll. of Arts. *Career:* writer-in-residence, various insts; mem. Literature Bd Australia Council 1992–95. *Publications:* Please Return to Sender 1980, Mary 1981, Leave it Till Monday 1984, Room to Move 1985, Hotel Sorrento 1990, SLOTH (television play) 1992, Falling from Grace (Sidney Myer Award 1996) 1994, Scenes from a Separation (play) 1995, Competitive Tenderness 1996, Life After George (Victoria Premier's Literary Award 2000, Green Room Award for Best New Australian Play 2001, Helpmann Award for Best Play 2001) 2001, Inheritance (play; Helpmann Awards for Best Play and Best New Australian Work 2004) 2003, Two Brothers 2005. *Honours:* Australian Writers' Guild Awards 1986, 1991, 2001, New South Wales Premier's Literary Award. *Literary Agent:* c/o HLA Management, PO Box 1536, Strawberry Hills, NSW 2012, Australia. *Telephone:* (2) 9310-4948. *Fax:* (2) 9310-4113. *E-mail:* hla@hlamgt.com.au. *Website:* www.hlamanagement.com.au.

RAZ, Joseph, MA, MJr, DPhil, FBA; British (b. Israeli) philosopher and academic; *Thomas M. Macioce Professor of Law, Columbia University*; b. 21 March 1939. *Education:* Hebrew Univ., Jerusalem and Univ. of Oxford. *Career:* Lecturer, Faculty of Law and Dept of Philosophy, Hebrew Univ. 1967–71, Sr Lecturer 1971–72; Fellow and Tutor in Law, Balliol Coll., Oxford 1972–85, also mem. Sub-faculty of Philosophy 1977–2006; Ed. (with Prof. A. M. Honoré), The Clarendon Law Series 1984–92; Prof. of Philosophy of Law, Univ. of Oxford and Fellow, Balliol Coll. 1985–2006, Research Prof. and Fellow Emer. 2006–09; Visiting Prof., School of Law, Columbia Univ., New York 1995–2002, Thomas M. Macioce Prof. of Law 2002–; Visiting Prof. Rockefeller Univ. 1974, ANU 1979, Univ. of California, Berkeley 1984, Univ. of Toronto 1987, Yale Law School 1988, Univ. of Southern California 1989; British-Hispanic Prof., Complutensa Univ., Madrid 2007; Philosopher in residence, Univ. of Michigan 2001; Fellow, British Acad. 1987–, Humanities Research Inst., Univ. of California, Irvine 1989; Visiting Mellon Fellow, Princeton Univ. 1993. *Publications:* The Concept of a Legal System 1970, Practical Reason and Norms 1975, The Authority of Law 1979 (second edn 2009), The Morality of Freedom (W.J.M. Mackenzie Book Prize, Political Studies Asscn of the UK, Elaine and David Spitz Book Prize, Conf. for the Study of Political Thought, New York) 1986, Ethics in the Public Domain 1994, Engaging Reason 2000, Value, Respect and Attachment 2001, The Practice of Value 2003, Between Authority and Interpretation 2009, From Normativity to Responsibility 2011. *Honours:* Foreign Hon. mem. American Acad. of Arts and Sciences; Dr hc (Katholieke Univ. Brussels) 1994; Hon. DJur (King's Coll., London); first Hector Fix-Zamudio Int. Prize for Legal Research (Univ. Nacional Autonoma de Mexico) 2005. *Address:* Columbia Law School, 435

READ, Miss (see Saint, Dora Jessie)

READ, Anthony; British writer and dramatist; b. 21 April 1935, Staffs., England; m. Rosemary E. Kirby 1958; two d. *Education:* Queen Mary's Grammar School, Walsall and Central School of Speech and Drama, London. *Career:* Trustee and fmr Chair. Writers' Guild of GB; fmr Dir and Acting Chair. Authors' Licensing and Collecting Soc. *Publications:* The Theatre 1964, Operation Lucy (with David Fisher) 1980, Colonel Z (with David Fisher) 1984, The Deadly Embrace (with David Fisher) 1988, Kristallnacht (with David Fisher) 1989, Conspirator (with Ray Bearse) 1991, The Fall of Berlin (with David Fisher) 1992, Berlin: The Biography of a City (with David Fisher) 1994, The Proudest Day: India's Long Road to Independence (with David Fisher) 1997, The Devil's Disciples: The Lives and Times of Hitler's Inner Circle 2003, The Baker Street Boys: The Case of the Disappearing Detective 2005, The Baker Street Boys: The Case of the Captive Clairvoyant 2006, The Baker Street Boys: The Case of the Ranjipur Ruby 2006, The Baker Street Boys: The Case of the Limehouse Laundry 2007, The Baker Street Boys: The Case of the Stolen Sparklers 2008, The World on Fire: 1919 and the Battle with Bolshevism 2008, The Baker Street Boys: The Case of the Haunted Horrors 2009; also more than 200 TV films, plays, series and serials. *Honours:* BAFTA (SFTA) Best Drama Series Award 1966, Pye Colour TV Award 1983, Wingate Literary Prize 1989. *Address:* 7 Cedar Chase, Taplow, Bucks., SL6 0EU, England (home). *E-mail:* readwrites@msn.com (home).

READ, Desmond (see Moorcock, Michael (John))

READ, Piers Paul, MA, FRSL; British writer; b. 7 March 1941, Beaconsfield, Bucks.; s. of Herbert Edward Read and Margaret Ludwig; m. Emily Albertine Boothby 1967; two s. two d. *Education:* Ampleforth Coll., York and St John's Coll., Cambridge. *Career:* Artist-in-Residence, Ford Foundation, W Berlin 1964; Sub-Ed. Times Literary Supplement, London 1965; Harkness Fellow Commonwealth Fund, New York 1967–68; Council mem. Inst. of Contemporary Arts (ICA), London 1971–75; Cttee of Man. Soc. of Authors, London 1973–76; mem. Literature Panel Arts Council, London 1975–77; Adjunct Prof. of Writing, Columbia Univ., New York 1980; Chair. Catholic Writers' Guild 1992–97; mem. Bd Aid to the Church in Need 1991– ; Trustee Catholic Library 1997– ; mem. Council RSL 2001– . *Publications:* Game in Heaven with Tussy Marx 1966, The Junkers 1968, Monk Dawson 1969, The Professor's Daughter 1971, The Upstart 1973, Alive: The Story of the Andes Survivors 1974, Polonaise 1976, The Train Robbers 1978, A Married Man 1979, The Villa Golitsyn 1981, The Free Frenchman 1986, A Season in the West 1988, On the Third Day 1990, Quo Vadis? The Subversion of the Catholic Church 1991, Ablaze: The Story of Chernobyl 1993, A Patriot in Berlin 1995, Knights of the Cross 1997, The Templars 1999, Alice in Exile 2001, Alec Guinness: The Authorised Biography 2003, Hell and Other Essays 2006, The Death of a Pope 2009, The Misogynist 2010. *Honours:* Sir Geoffrey Faber Memorial Prize 1968, Somerset Maugham Award 1969, Hawthornden Prize 1969, Thomas More Award (USA) 1976, James Tait Black Memorial Prize 1988. *Literary Agent:* Aitken Alexander Associates, 18–21 Cavaye Place, London, SW10 9PT, England. *Telephone:* (20) 7373-8672. *Fax:* (20) 7373-6002. *Website:* www.aitkenalexander.co.uk. *Address:* 50 Portland Road, London, W11 4LG, England (home). *Telephone:* (20) 7460-2499 (office); (20) 7727-5719 (home). *E-mail:* piersread@dial.pipex.com (office).

REARDON, Katherine (Kate) Genevieve; British writer; b. 20 Nov. 1968, New York; d. of P. W. J. Reardon and J. H. A. Wood. *Education:* Cheltenham Ladies' Coll. and Stowe School, Buckingham. *Career:* worked at Vogue magazine, New York 1988–90; apptd Fashion Ed. Tatler Magazine, London 1990, later Fashion Dir; writer The Times 2004–06, Daily Mail 2008– ; Founder, Top Tips for Girls website 2007– ; also Contributing Ed. Vanity Fair. *Publication:* Top Tips for Girls 2008. *Address:* Top Tips Ltd, Curzon Directors Ltd, Ashford House, Grenadier Road, Exeter, EX1 3LH, England (office). *Website:* www.toptipsforgirls.com (office).

REBECK, Theresa, MFA, PhD; American writer, playwright and novelist; b. Kenwood, Ohio; m.; two c. *Education:* Univ. of Notre Dame, Brandeis Univ. *Career:* mem. Bd Dramatists Guild; Contrib. Ed. Harvard Review; Assoc. Artist, Roundabout Theatre Co.; has taught at Brandeis and Columbia Univs. *Plays include:* at Second Stage: The Scene, The Water's Edge, Loose Knit, The Family of Mann (Nat. Theater Conference Award) and Spike Heels; at Playwrights Horizons: Bad Dates, The Butterfly Collection and Our House; View of the Dome (New York Theater Workshop), Omnium Gatherum (co-writer, Humana Festival and Variety Arts Theater), The Bells (William Inge New Voices Playwriting Award 2003), The Understudy (Williamstown Theater Festival 2008 and Laura Pels Theater/Roundabout Theater Co. 2009–10), Mauritius (Huntington Theater, Boston) (IRNE Award for Best New Play 2007, Eliot Norton Award). *Television includes:* as writer: episodes of Dream On, Brooklyn Bridge, L.A. Law, American Dreamer, Maximum Bob, First Wave, Third Watch; as writer/producer: Canterbury's Law, Smith, Law and Order: Criminal Intent, NYPD Blue (Mystery Writers of America's Edgar Award, Writers' Guild of America Award for Episodic Drama, Hispanic Images Imagen Award, Peabody Award); feature films include Harriet the Spy, Gossip, Sunday on the Rocks, Seducing Charlie Barker. *Publications:* Theresa Rebeck: Complete Plays, Volumes I, II and III, Free Fire Zone (essays), Three Girls and Their Brother (novel) 2008, Twelve Rooms With A View (novel) 2010; contrib. articles in American Theater Magazine and excerpts of plays in the Harvard Review. *Honours:* PEN/Laura Pels Foundation Award for an American Playwright in Mid-Career 2010. *Literary Agent:* Creative Artists Agency, 162 5th Avenue, 6th Floor, New York, NY 10010, USA. *Telephone:* (212) 277-9000. *Fax:* (212) 277-9099. *E-mail:* info@theresarebeck.com (office). *Website:* www.theresarebeck.com.

REBOUL, Jacquette Suzanne Danièle, PhD; French librarian and writer; b. 5 Dec. 1937, Valence (Drome); d. of Paul Reboul and Camille Reboul (née Marchal). *Education:* Lycée de Jeunes Filles, Valence, Univ. of Paris (Sorbonne), Ecole Nat. Supérieure de Bibliothécaires. *Career:* Librarian, Univ. of Rennes Library 1966–70; Librarian, Library of the Sorbonne 1970–85, Chief Librarian 1986–98; now retd. *Publications:* Le lever de l'aurore 1969, Le vieux Roi 1972, A l'intérieur de la vue 1973, Du bon usage des bibliographies 1973, La nuit scintille 1975, L'apprentie sorcière (Prix Louis Guillaume) 1982, Les cathédrales du savoir ou les bibliothèques universitaires de recherche aux Etats-Unis 1982, La liberté pour l'ombre 1985, Face à face 1986, Critique universitaire et critique créatrice 1986, L'œil du monde 1990, Raison ardente 1992, Cristal 1996, Psyché 2001, Ta Solitude et le Monde 2002, La Mort en Inde 2003, Le Chemin 2007, Enigme de l'oracle 2010. *Honours:* Chevalier, Légion d'honneur; Officier des Palmes académiques; Prix Louis Guillaume for poetry. *Address:* c/o La Maison des Ecrivains et de la Littérature, 67 boulevard de Montmorency, 75016 Paris, France (office). *E-mail:* courrier@maison-des-ecrivains.asso.fr (office). *Website:* www.m-e-l.fr (office).

REBUCK, Dame Gail Ruth, DBE, BA, FRSA; British publishing executive; *Chairman and Chief Executive, The Random House Group Limited;* b. 10 Feb. 1952, London; d. of Gordon Rebuck and Mavis Rebuck; m. Philip Gould 1985 (died 2011); two d. *Education:* Lycée Français de Londres, Univ. of Sussex. *Career:* Production Asst, Grisewood & Dempsey (children's book packager) 1975–76; Ed., later Publr Robert Nicholson Publs London Guidebooks 1976–79; Publr Hamlyn Paperbacks 1979–82; Founder Partner Century Publishing Co. Ltd, Publishing Dir Non-Fiction 1982–85, Publr Century Hutchinson 1985–89, Chair. Random House Div., Random Century 1989–91, Chair. and Chief Exec. Random House UK Ltd (now The Random House Group Ltd) 1991– ; mem. COPUS 1995–97, Creative Industries Task Force 1997–2000, Advisory Bd Cambridge Judge Inst. 2004–08; Dir (non-exec.) Work Foundation 2001–09, BSkyB 2002– ; mem. Court Univ. of Sussex 1997– , Council RCA 1999– ; Trustee, Inst. for Public Policy Research 1993–2003. *Honours:* ranked 25th by the Financial Times amongst Top 25 Businesswomen in Europe 2005, Veuve Clicquot Businesswoman of the Year 2009, ranked ninth by the Guardian amongst top people in British books industry 2011. *Address:* The Random House Group Ltd, 20 Vauxhall Bridge Road, London, SW1V 2SA, England (office). *Telephone:* (20) 7840-8886 (office). *Fax:* (20) 7233-6120 (office). *E-mail:* grebuck@randomhouse.co.uk (office). *Website:* www.randomhouse.co.uk (office).

REDDY, T. Vasudeva, BSc, MA, PGTDE, PhD; Indian educator, writer and poet; b. 21 Dec. 1943, Mittapalem; m. 1970; two s. one d. *Career:* Nat. Fellowship, UGC, N Delhi 1998–2000; mem. Int. Poets' Acad. (Chennai), World Poetry Soc. (CA), ABI (NC). *Publications:* When Grief Rains (poems) 1982, The Vultures (novel) 1983, The Broken Rhythms (poems) 1987, Jane Austen 1987, Jane Austen: Matrix of Matrimony 1987, The Fleeting Bubbles (poems) 1989, Melting Melodies (poems) 1994, Advanced Grammar and Composition in English 1995, Pensive Memories (poems) 2005, Minor Gods 2008, Gliding Ripples: A Collection of Poems 2008; contrib. to journals and magazines. *Honours:* Hon. mem. Research Bd of Advisors, ABI, North Carolina, USA; Hon. DLitt (WAAC, Calif.) 1987; Int. Eminent Poet Award 1987, Best Teacher Award (univ. level) Govt of Andhra Pradesh 1990, Michael Madhusudan Award 1995. *Address:* Mittapalem, Narasingapuram, Chandragiri 517 102, India (home). *Telephone:* (877) 2276414 (home). *E-mail:* kumar_kvr@yahoo.com (home).

REECE, Henry Michael, MA, DPhil; British publisher; b. 10 Aug. 1953; m. Allison Jane King 1993 (divorced 2005). *Education:* Univs of Bristol and Oxford. *Career:* Tutor in History, Univ. of Exeter 1977–78; Field Sales Ed., Prentice Hall International 1979–82; Academic Sales Man., Simon and Schuster International 1982–84, UK Sales Man. 1984–85, Asst Vice-Pres. 1985–88; Exec. Ed., Allyn & Bacon, USA 1988–91; Man. Dir Pitman Publishing 1991–94; Exec. Dir Longman Group Ltd 1994–95; Exec. Dir Pearson Professional 1995–97; Man. Dir Financial Times Professional 1997–98; CEO Oxford University Press (Sec. to the Delegates and Chair. Group Strategy Cttee 1998–2009 (retd); Dir (non-exec.) Knowledge Pool 2000–01; mem. Publishers' Asscn (mem. Council 1999–2004, Pres. 2004–05. *Honours:* Fellow, Jesus Coll. Oxford 1998– . *Address:* c/o Oxford University Press, Great Clarendon Street, Oxford, OX2 6DP, England (office). *Website:* www.oup.com (office).

REED, Ishmael Scott; American writer and poet; b. 22 Feb. 1938, Chattanooga, Tenn.; s. of Bennie S. Reed and Thelma Coleman; m. 1st Priscilla Rose 1960 (divorced 1970); two s.; m. 2nd Carla Blank; one d. *Education:* Univ. of Buffalo. *Career:* Co-founder and Dir Reed, Cannon & Johnson Co. 1973– ; Assoc. Fellow, Calhoun House, Yale Univ. 1982– ; Founder (with Al Young) and ed., Quilt magazine 1981– ; Guest Lecturer, Univ. of Calif., Berkeley 1968, then Sr Lecturer, now Lectuer Emer.; mem. usage panel, American Heritage Dictionary; Assoc. Ed. American Book Review; Exec. Producer Personal Problems (video soap opera); collaborator in multimedia Bicentennial mystery, The Lost State of Franklin (winner Poetry in Public Places contest 1975); Chair. Berkeley Arts Comm.; Advisory Chair. Co-ordinating Council of Literary Magazines; Pres. Before Columbus Foundation 1976–; Nat. Endowment for Arts Writing Fellow 1974; Guggenheim Fellow 1975; mem. Authors' Guild of America, PEN; Publr Konch magazine. *Publications:* fiction: The Free-Lance Pallbearers 1967, Yellow Back Radio Broke Down 1969, Mumbo Jumbo 1972, The Last Days of Louisiana Red 1974, Flight to Canada 1976, The Terrible Twos 1982, Reckless Eyeballing 1986, Cab Calloway Stands in for the Moon 1986, The Terrible Threes 1989, Japanese By Spring 1993; poetry: Catechism of a Neoamerican Hoodoo Church 1970, Conjure: Selected Poems 1963–1970 1972, Chattanooga 1973, A Secretary to the Spirits 1978, Calafia: The California Poetry (ed.) 1979, New and Collected Poems 1988, New and Collected Poems 1964–2006 2006; non-fiction: The Rise, Fall and...? of Adam Clayton Powell (with others) 1967, 19 Necromancers from Now (ed.) 1970, Yardbird Reader (five vols, ed.) 1971–77, Yardbird Lives! (ed., with Al Young) 1978, Shrovetide in Old New Orleans 1978, Quilt 2–3 (ed., with Al Young, two vols) 1981–82, God Made Alaska for the Indians 1982, Writin' is Fightin': Thirty-Seven Years of Boxing on Paper (ed.) 1988, Ishmael Reed: An Interview 1990, The Before Columbus Foundation Fiction Anthology: Selections from the American Book Awards 1980–1990 (ed., with Kathryn Trueblood and Shawn Wong) 1992, Airin' Dirty Laundry 1993, Multi-America 1996, The Reed Reader (ed.) 2000. *Honours:* Nat. Inst. of Arts and Letters Award 1975, Rosenthal Foundation Award 1975, Michaux Award 1978, ACLU Award 1978. *Address:* c/o Penguin Putnam Inc., 375 Hudson Street, New York, NY 10014, USA. *E-mail:* uncleish@aol.com. *Website:* www.ishmaelreedpub.com.

REED, Jane Barbara, CBE, FRSA; British journalist, editor and publishing executive; *Director, Times Newspapers Ltd*; b. 31 March 1940, Letchworth, Herts., England; d. of the late William Reed and Gwendoline Reed. *Education:* Royal Masonic School. *Career:* Ed. Woman's Own 1969–79; Publr IPC Magazines Ltd Women's Monthly Magazines Group 1979–81; Ed.-in-Chief Woman magazine 1981–83; Asst Man. Dir IPC Specialist Educ. and Leisure Group 1983; Man. Dir IPC Holborn Publishing Group 1983–85; Man. Ed. Today newspaper 1985–89; Dir of Corp. Affairs, News Int. PLC 1989–2000; currently Dir Times Newspapers Ltd; fmr Pres. Media Soc.; mem. Council Nat. Literacy Trust; Dir (non-exec.) Media Trust. *Publications:* Girl About Town 1965, Kitchen Sink – or Swim? (co-author) 1981. *Honours:* Editor of the Year 1975, 1981, Mark Boxer Award for Lifetime Achievement 2002.

REED, Jeremy, BA; British poet and writer; b. 1951, Jersey, Channel Islands. *Education:* Univ. of Essex, Colchester. *Publications:* poetry: Target 1972, Saints and Psychotics: Poems 1973–74 1974, Vicissitudes 1974, Diseased Near Deceased 1975, Emerald Cat 1975, Ruby Onocentaur 1975, Blue Talaria 1976, Count Bluebeard 1976, Jack's in His Corset 1978, Walk on Through 1980, Bleecker Street 1980, No Refuge Here 1981, A Long Shot to Heaven 1982, A Man Afraid 1982, By the Fisheries 1984, Elegy for Senta 1985, Skies 1985, Border Pass 1986, Selected Poems 1987, Engaging Form 1988, The Escaped Image 1988, Nineties 1990, Diving for Pearls 1990, Red-Haired Android 1992; fiction: The Lipstick Boys 1984, Blue Rock 1987, Madness: The Price of Poetry 1990. *Honours:* Somerset Maugham Award 1985. *Address:* c/o Jonathan Cape Ltd, 20 Vauxhall Bridge Road, London, SW1V 2SA, England.

REEDER, Carolyn, BA, MEd; American writer; b. 16 Nov. 1937, Washington, DC; m. Jack Reeder 1959; one s. one d. *Education:* American Univ. *Career:* mem. Children's Book Guild of Washington, DC (fmr Treas.), Authors' Guild. *Publications:* non-fiction: Shenandoah Heritage (with Jack Reeder) 1978, Shenandoah Vestiges (with Jack Reeder) 1980, Shenandoah Secrets (with Jack Reeder) 1991, From a True Soldier and Son: The Civil War Letters of William C. H. Reeder (with Jack Reeder) 2008; juvenile fiction: Shades of Gray 1989, Grandpa's Mountain 1991, Moonshiner's Son 1993, Across the Lines 1997, Foster's War 1998, Captain Kate 1999, Before the Creeks Ran Red 2003, The Secret Project Notebook 2005. *Honours:* Scott O'Dell Award for Historical Fiction 1989, Child Study Asscn Award 1989, American Library Asscn Notable Book 1989, Honour Book for the Jane Addams' Children's Book Award 1989, Notable Trade Book in the Language Arts 1989, Jefferson Cup Award 1990, Int. Reading Asscn Young Adult Choice 1991, Joan G. Sugarman Children's Book Award 1992–93, Hedda Seisler Mason Honor Award 1995. *Address:* PO Box 419, Washington, VA 22747, USA (home). *Website:* www.reederbooks.com.

REEMAN, Douglas Edward, (Alexander Kent); British writer; b. 15 Oct. 1924, Thames Ditton, Surrey, England; m. Kimberley June Jordan 1985. *Publications include:* A Prayer for the Ship 1958, High Water 1959, Send a Gunboat 1960, Dive in the Sun 1961, The Hostile Shore 1962, The Last Raider 1963, With Blood and Iron 1964, HMS Saracen 1965, Path of the Storm 1966, The Deep Silence 1967, The Pride and the Anguish 1968, To Risks Unknown 1969, The Greatest Enemy 1970, Against the Sea 1971, Rendezvous – South Atlantic 1972, Go In and Sink! 1973, The Destroyers 1974, Winged Escort 1975, Surface with Daring 1976, Strike from the Sea 1978, A Ship Must Die 1979, Torpedo Run 1981, Badge of Glory 1982, The First to Land 1984, D-Day: A Personal Reminiscence 1984, The Volunteers 1985, The Iron Pirate 1986, In Danger's Hour 1988, The White Guns 1989, Killing Ground 1991, The Horizon 1993, Sunset 1994, A Dawn Like Thunder 1996, Battlecruiser 1997, Dust on the Sea 1999, For Valour 2000, Twelve Seconds to Live 2002, Knife Edge 2004; as Alexander Kent: To Glory We Steer 1968, Form Line of Battle 1969, Enemy in Sight! 1970, The Flag Captain 1971, Sloop of War 1972, Command a King's Ship 1974, Signal – Close Action! 1974, Richard Bolitho – Midshipman 1975, Passage to Mutiny 1976, In Gallant Company 1977, Midshipman Bolitho and the 'Avenger' 1978, Captain Richard Bolitho, RN 1978, The Inshore Squadron 1978, Stand Into Danger 1980, A Tradition of Victory 1981, Success to the Brave 1983, Colours Aloft! 1986, Honour This Day 1987, With All Despatch 1988, The Only Victor 1990, Beyond the Reef 1992, The Darkening Sea 1993, For My Country's Freedom 1995, Cross of St George 1996, Sword of Honour 1998, Second to None 1999, Relentless Pursuit 2001, Man of War 2003, Band of Brothers 2005, Heart of Oak 2007; contrib. to various journals and magazines. *E-mail:* highseas1@btconnect.com (office). *Website:* www.douglasreeman.com.

REES, Rev. D(avid) Ben(jamin), (Ceredig), BA, BD, MA, MSc, PhD, FRHistS; British writer, editor, minister of religion and academic; *Professor of Theology, North-West University, South Africa*; b. 1 Aug. 1937, Wales; s. of John Rees and Anne Rees; m. 1963; two s. *Education:* Univs of Wales, Liverpool and Salford. *Career:* minister, Presbyterian Church of Wales, Cynon Valley 1962–68, Heathfield Road, Liverpool 1968–2008; Founder-Sec. Modern Welsh Publs 1963–; part-time Lecturer, Univ. of Liverpool 1970–2001, Prof. of Theology 1998–; Prof. of Theology, North-West Univ., South Africa 2011–; Ed. Peace and Reconciliation Magazine 2000–02, Y Bont/Bridge 1997–; Vice-Pres. Wales and the World 1979, Liverpool Welsh Choral Union 2004; mem. Cymmrodorion Soc., Welsh Acad.; Founder-mem. Merseyside Welsh Heritage Soc. 1999. *Publications include:* Wales: A Cultural History 1980, Preparation for a Crisis: Adult Education in England and Wales 1945–1980 1981, Liverpool, Welsh and Their Religion 1984, Owen Thomas: A Welsh Preacher in Liverpool 1991, The Welsh of Merseyside 1997, Local and Parliamentary Politics in Liverpool from 1800 to 1911 1999, The Welsh of Merseyside in the Twentieth Century 2001, Vehicles of Grace and Hope (ed.) 2002, The Call and Contribution of Dr Robert Arthur Hughes 2004, Life and Work of Bessie Braddock MP 2011; contrib. to magazines and newspapers. *Honours:* Ellis Griffith Prize, Univ. of Wales 1979, Paul Harris Fellow 2007. *Address:* 32 Garth Drive, Liverpool, L18 6HW, England. *E-mail:* ben@garthdrive.fsnet.co.uk. *Website:* www.welshpublications.co.uk; www.lordsdaywales.co.uk.

REES, Paul, BA; British journalist; b. West Bromwich; m. Denise Jeffrey; one s. *Education:* Alsager Coll. *Career:* contrib. to Brum Beat; News Ed., Raw – 1995; News Ed., freelance writer, Ed. Kerrang! 1995–2002; Ed. Q magazine 2002–08, Ed.-in-Chief 2008–12.

REES-MOGG, Baron (Life Peer), cr. 1988, of Hinton Blewett in the County of Avon; **William Rees-Mogg;** British journalist and publisher; *Chairman, Pickering and Chatto Publishers Ltd*; b. 14 July 1928, Bristol, England; s. of the late Edmund Fletcher Rees-Mogg and Beatrice Rees-Mogg (née Warren); m. Gillian Shakespeare Morris 1962; two s. three d. *Education:* Charterhouse and Balliol Coll., Oxford. *Career:* Pres. Oxford Union 1951; Financial Times 1952–60, Chief Leader Writer 1955–60, Asst Ed. 1957–60; City Ed. Sunday Times 1960–61, Political and Econ. Ed. 1961–63, Deputy Ed. 1964–67; Ed. of The Times 1967–81, Dir The Times Ltd 1968–81; Vice-Chair. BBC 1981–86; Chair. Arts Council 1982–89; Chair. Broadcasting Standards Council 1988–93; mem. Exec. Bd Times Newspapers Ltd 1968–81, Dir 1978–81; Dir Gen. Electric Co. 1981–97; Chair. and Propr Pickering and Chatto Publishers Ltd 1983–; Chair. Sidgwick and Jackson 1985–89, Int. Business Communications PLC 1994–98, Fleet Street Publications 1995–; Dir M & G Group 1987, EFG Pvt. Bank and Trust Co. 1993–2005, Value Realization Trust PLC 1996–98, Newsmax Media, Inc., USA 2000–06; columnist, The Times 1992–, The Mail on Sunday 2004–; mem. Int. Cttee Pontifical Council for Culture 1983–87. *Publications:* The Reigning Error: the Crisis of World Inflation 1974, An Humbler Heaven 1977, How to Buy Rare Books 1985, Blood in the Streets (with James Dale Davidson) 1987, The Great Reckoning (with James Dale Davidson) 1992, Picnics on Vesuvius 1992, The Sovereign Individual (with James Dale Davidson) 1997. *Honours:* Hon. LLD (Bath) 1977, (Leeds) 1992. *Address:* Pickering & Chatto Publishers Ltd, 21 Bloomsbury Way, London, WC1A 2TH, England (office). *Telephone:* (20) 7242-2241 (office). *Fax:* (20) 7405-6216 (office). *E-mail:* amtraco@btconnect.com (office). *Website:* www.pickeringchatto.com (office).

REES OF LUDLOW, Baron (Life Peer), cr. 2005, of Ludlow in the County of Shropshire; **Martin John Rees,** OM, MA, PhD, FRS; British astronomer and academic; *Master, Trinity College Cambridge*; b. 23 June 1942, York, Yorks., England; s. of Reginald J. Rees and Joan Rees; m. Caroline Humphrey 1986. *Education:* Shrewsbury School and Trinity Coll., Cambridge. *Career:* Fellow, Jesus Coll., Cambridge 1967–69; Research Assoc. Calif. Inst. of Tech. 1967–68, 1971; mem. Inst. for Advanced Study, Princeton 1969–70, Prof. 1982–96; Visiting Prof., Harvard Univ. 1972, 1986–87; Prof., Univ. of Sussex 1972–73; Plumian Prof. of Astronomy and Experimental Philosophy, Univ. of Cambridge 1973–91, Royal Soc. Research Prof. 1992–2002, Prof. of Cosmology and Astrophysics 2004–; Astronomer Royal 1995–; Master Trinity Coll. Cambridge 2004–; Fellow, King's Coll., Cambridge 1969–72, 1973–2003; Visiting Prof., Imperial Coll., London 2001–, Univ. of Leicester 2001–; Dir Inst. of Astronomy 1977–82, 1987–91; Regents Fellow, Smithsonian Inst. 1984–88; mem. Council of Royal Soc. 1983–85, 1993–95, Pres. 2005–10; mem. Council of Royal Inst. of GB –2010; Pres. Royal Astronomical Soc. 1992–94, BAAS 1994–95; Trustee, British Museum 1996–2002, Inst. for Advanced Study, Princeton, USA 1998–, Nat. Endowment for Sciences, Tech. and Arts 1998–2001, Kennedy Memorial Trust 1999–2004, Inst. for Public Policy Research 2001; Foreign Assoc. NAS; mem. Academia Europaea 1989, Pontifical Acad. of Sciences 1990; Foreign mem. American Philosophical Soc., Royal Swedish Acad. of Science, Russian Acad. of Sciences, Norwegian Acad. of Arts and Science, Accad. Lincei (Rome),

Royal Netherlands Acad., Finnish Acad. of Arts and Sciences; mem. (Crossbench) House of Lords 2005–. *Achievement:* his studies of the distribution of quasars led to final disproof of Steady State Theory. *Television:* What We Still Don't Know (documentary series, Channel 4) 2004. *Publications:* Perspectives in Astrophysical Cosmology 1995, Gravity's Fatal Attraction (with M. Begelman) 1995, Before the Beginning 1997, Just Six Numbers 1999, Our Cosmic Habitat 2001, Our Final Century? 2003; edited books; more than 500 articles and reviews in scientific journals on the origin of the cosmic microwave background radiation, as well as on galaxy clustering and formation, and numerous gen. articles. *Honours:* Hon. Fellow, Trinity Coll., Darwin Coll. and Jesus Coll., Cambridge, Indian Acad. of Sciences, Univ. of Wales, Cardiff 1998, Inst. of Physics 2001; Foreign Hon. mem. American Acad. of Arts and Sciences; Officier, Ordre des Arts et des Lettres; Hon. DSc (Sussex) 1990, (Leicester) 1993, (Copenhagen, Keele, Uppsala, Newcastle) 1995, (Toronto) 1997, (Durham) 1999, (Oxford) 2000, (Yale) 2008, (McMaster) 2009; Heinemann Prize, American Inst. of Physics 1984, Gold Medal (Royal Astronomical Soc.) 1987, Guthrie Medal, Inst. of Physics 1989, Balzan Prize 1989, Robinson Prize for Cosmology 1990, Bruce Medal, Astronomical Soc. of Pacific 1993, Science Writing Award, American Inst. of Physics 1996, Bower Award, Franklin Inst. 1998, Rossi Prize, American Astronomical Soc. 2000, Cosmology Prize of Peter Gruber Foundation 2001, Einstein Award, World Cultural Congress 2003, Michael Faraday Prize 2004, Crafoord Prize, Royal Swedish Acad. (jtly) 2005, Niels Bohr Medal, UNESCO 2005, Caird Medal, Nat. Maritime Museum 2007, BBC Reith Lecturer 2010, Asteroid 4587 Rees named after him. *Address:* Trinity College, Cambridge, CB2 1TQ (office); Institute of Astronomy, Madingley Road, Cambridge CB3 0HA, England (office). *Telephone:* (1223) 338412 (office). *E-mail:* mjr@ast.cam.ac.uk (office). *Website:* www.ast.cam.ac.uk/IoA/staff/mjr (office); www.trin.cam.ac.uk/index.php?pageid=172 (office); www.parliament.uk/biographies/martin-rees/45773.

REEVE, Franklin Dolier, PhD; American academic, writer, poet, translator and editor; *Professor of Letters Emeritus, Wesleyan University;* b. 18 Sept. 1928, Philadelphia, Pa; m. Laura C. Stevenson; five c. *Education:* Princeton Univ., Columbia Univ. *Career:* Lecturer, Columbia Univ. 1952–61; Exchange Scholar, ACLS-USSR Acad. of Sciences 1961; Prof. of Letters, Wesleyan Univ. 1962–2002, Prof. Emer. 2002–; Visiting Prof., Univ. of Oxford, UK 1964, Columbia Univ. 1988; Visiting Lecturer, Yale Univ. 1974–86, New England Coll. MFA Program 2003–05; mem. Poetry Soc. of America 1974–94, Governing Bd 1978–80, Vice-Pres. 1980–84, Ed. Poetry Review 1982–84; mem. Poets House, mem. Governing Bd 1985–99, Sec. 1994–99; mem. Pettee Memorial Library (Trustee), Marlboro Review (Advisory Bd), New England Poetry Soc. (Bd Dir); JP 2011–. *Performances include:* Alcyone (poetic drama with music by T. L. Reed) 1997, The Urban Stampede (poetic drama with music by Andrew Gant) 2000, The Return of the Blue Cat (poems with improvised jazz trio Exit 59) 2004, The Puzzle Master (poetic drama with music by Eric Chasalow) 2007, The Blue Cat Walks the Earth (poems with music by jazz trio) 2007. *Publications include:* Five Short Novels by Turgenev (trans.) 1961, Anthology of Russian Plays (trans.) 1961, 1963, Aleksandr Blok: Between Image and Idea (non-fiction) 1962, Robert Frost in Russia (non-fiction) 1964, The Russian Novel (non-fiction) 1966, In the Silent Stones (poems) 1968, The Red Machines (fiction) 1968, Just Over the Border (fiction) 1969, The Brother (fiction) 1971, The Blue Cat (poems) 1972, White Colors (fiction) 1973, Nightway (poems) 1987, The White Monk (non-fiction) 1989, The Garden (trans.) 1990, Concrete Music (poems) 1992, The Trouble with Reason (trans.) 1993, A Few Rounds of Old Maid and Other Stories (fiction) 1995, The Moon and Other Failures (poems) 1999, A World You Haven't Seen (poems) 2001, The Urban Stampede and Other Poems 2002, The Return of the Blue Cat (poems) 2005, My Sister Life (fiction) 2005, Lions and Acrobats: Selected Poems (trans.) 2005, North River (fiction) 2006, The Blue Cat Walks the Earth (poems) 2007 (UK 2009), The Puzzle Master and Other Poems 2010, Nathaniel Purple (novella) 2012; contrib. to journals and periodicals. *Honours:* Hon. DLit (New England Coll.) 2004; American Acad. of Arts and Letters Award in Literature 1970, PEN Syndicated Fiction Awards 1985, 1986, New England Poetry Soc. Golden Rose 1994, May Sarton Award 2004, Allen Tate Award 2005. *Address:* PO Box 14, Wilmington, VT 05363, USA. *E-mail:* lcsfdr@gmail.com.

REGÀS, Rosa, BPhil; Spanish writer and journalist; b. 1933, Barcelona; m.; five c. *Education:* Barcelona Univ. *Career:* editorial staff with Seix Barral 1964–70, with Edhasa; f. and Publisher, La Gaya Ciencia 1970–, journals Arquitectura Vis, Cuadernos de la Gaya Ciencia 1976–; trans. for UN 1983–94; Head of Culture Dept of Casa de América, part of Foreign Affairs Ministry 1994–98; Gen. Dir Biblioteca Nacional de España 2004–07 (resgnd). *Publications include:* fiction: Memoria de Almator (novel) 1991, Azul (novel) (Premio Nadal) 1994, Pobre corazón (short stories) 1996, Barcelona, un día (short stories) 1998, Luna Lunera (novel) (Premio Ciudad de Barcelona) 1999, La canción de Dorotea (novel) (Premio Planeta) 2001, contrib. short stories to anthologies, including Relatos para un fin de milenio 1998, Cuentos solidarios 1999, Mujeres al alba 1999, La paz y la palabra 2003; non-fiction: La cuina de l'ampurdanet (leaflet) 1985, Ginebra (leaflet) 1988, Canciones de amor y de batalla: 1993–1995 (articles) 1995, Viaje a la luz del Cham 1995, Una revolución personal 1997, Desde el mar 1997, España: una nueva mirada (leaflet) 1997, Más canciones 1995–1998 (articles) 1998, La creación, la fantasía y la vida (essay) 1998, Sangre de mi sangre (essay) 1999, Diario de una abuela de verano (biog.) 2004, El valor de la protesta (articles) 2004; contrib. essays to collections, including Retratos literarios 1997, Ser mujer 2000, and to numerous journals and periodicals. *Honours:* Chevalier de la Legion d'Honneur 2005, Creu de Sant Jordi, Generalitat de Catalunya 2005; Premio Grandes Viajeros 2005. *Address:* c/o Biblioteca Nacional, Paseo de Recoletos 20, 28071 Madrid, Spain. *E-mail:* arcano@rosaregas.net. *Website:* www.rosaregas.net.

REGNAULT, François; French philosopher, dramatist and translator; b. Nov. 1938, Paris; s. of Jacques Regnault. *Education:* Lycée Montaigne, Lycée Louis-le-Grand. *Career:* teacher Prytanée Militaire de la Flèche, then Lycée de Reims 1964–70; teacher Dept of Philosophy, Univ. de Vincennes 1970–74, then Dept of Psychoanalysis 1974–; first involvement in theatre 1973; co-f. Compagnie Pandora 1976; Co-Dir Théâtre de la Commune/Pandora, Aubervilliers 1991–97; speech tutor Conservatoire Nat. d'Art dramatique, Paris 1994–2001. *Play:* Corneille's L'Illusion comique (actor, Théâtre de Gennevilliers) 2005. *Publications:* non-fiction: Mais on doit tout oser puisque 1981, Dieu est inconscient 1986, Le Spectateur 1986, Dire le vers (with Jean-Claude Milner) 1987, Le Théâtre et la mer 1989, La Doctrine inouï: Dix leçons sur le théâtre classique français 1996, Conférences d'esthétique lacanienne 1997, L'Une des trois unités 1999, Le Théâtre de Pandora 1999, Théâtre-Equinoxes 2001, Théâtre-Solstices 2002, Notre objet a 2003, Dire le vers 2008; translations: Wedekind's L'Eveil du printemps, Ibsen's Peer Gynt 1996, J. M. Synge's Le Baladin du monde occidental; contrib. articles and essays. *Address:* c/o Faculty of Psychology, Université de Paris VIII – Vincennes à St-Denis, 2 rue de la Liberté, 93526 St Denis Cédex, France.

REICH, Robert Bernard, BA, MA, JD; American political economist, academic and fmr government official; *Professor of Public Policy, Goldman School of Public Policy, University of California, Berkeley;* b. 24 June 1946, Scranton, Pa; s. of Edwin Saul Reich and Mildred Dorf Reich (née Freshman); m. Clare Dalton 1973; two s. *Education:* Dartmouth Coll., Univ. of Oxford, UK, Yale Univ. *Career:* Asst Solicitor-Gen., US Dept of Justice, Washington, DC 1974–76; Dir of Policy Planning Fed. Trade Comm., Washington 1976–81; mem. Faculty, John F. Kennedy School of Govt, Harvard Univ. 1981–92; fmr Econ. Adviser to Pres. Bill Clinton; Sec. of Labor 1993–97; Univ. Prof., Maurice B. Hexter Prof. of Social and Econ. Policy, Brandeis Univ. Grad. School for Advanced Studies in Social Welfare 1997–2006; Prof. of Public Policy, Goldman School of Public Policy, Univ. of Calif., Berkeley 2006–; Chair. Biotechnology Section US Office Tech. Assessment, Washington 1990–91; Co-founder and Chair. Editorial Bd The American Prospect 2002-03; mem. Nat. Governing Bd, Common Cause 1982–88; mem. Mass Comm. on Mature Industries 1985–87; mem. Bd of Dirs Business Enterprise Trust 1986–93, Econ. Policy Inst. 1988–93, 2002–03; Trustee Dartmouth Coll. 1988–93; Contributing Ed. The New Republic, Washington 1982–93; Rhodes Scholar 1968. *Publications:* The Next American Frontier 1983, Tales of a New America 1987, The Power of Public Ideas (co-author) 1987, The Work of Nations 1991, Putting People First 1997, Locked in the Cabinet 1997, The Future of Success 2001, Reason: Why Liberals Will Win the Battle for America 2004, Supercapitalism: The Transformation of Business, Democracy and Everyday Life 2007, Aftershock: The Next Economy and America's Future 2010. *Honours:* Dr hc (Dartmouth Coll.) 1994, (Univ. of New Hampshire) 1997, (Wheaton Coll.) 1998, (Emory Univ.) 1999, (Bates Coll.) 2001, (Grinnell Coll.) 2002; Mass Teachers Asscn Award for Excellence 1997, Lifetime Achievement Award, Nat. Ass. of Voluntary Health and Social Welfare Orgs 1997, Eleanor Roosevelt Award for Public Service, Americans for Democratic Action 2001, Vaclev Havel Humanitarian Prize 2003. *Address:* Richard & Rhoda Goldman School of Public Policy, 301 GSPP Main, 2607 Hearst Avenue, University of California, Berkeley, CA 94720-7320, USA (office). *Telephone:* (510) 642-0551 (office). *E-mail:* rreich@berkeley.edu (office); bob@RobertReich.org. *Website:* gspp.berkeley.edu/people/faculty/reich.htm (office); www.robertreich.org.

REICHS, Kathleen (Kathy) J., BA, MA, PhD; American writer and forensic anthropologist; *Professor Emeritus, University of North Carolina;* b. 1950, Chicago; m. Paul Reichs; two d. one s. *Education:* American Univ., Northwestern Univ. *Career:* Asst Prof., Northern Illinois Univ. 1974–78; Instructor, Stateville Correctional Facility, Joliet, Ill. 1975–78; Asst Prof., Davidson Coll. 1981–83; Lecturer, Univ. of North Carolina at Charlotte 1978–81, 1983–87, Asst Prof. 1987–88, Assoc. Prof. 1988–96, then Prof., now Prof. Emer.; works as forensic anthropologist at Office of the Chief Medical Examiner, State of North Carolina and Laboratoires des Sciences Judiciaires et de Médecine Légale, Canada; Visiting Prof., Univ. of Pittsburgh 1987, Visiting Assoc. Prof., Concordia Univ. 1988–89, McGill Univ. 1988–97 (summers); mem. American Acad. of Forensic Sciences, Sec. Physical Anthropology Section 1994–95, Chair, Physical Anthropology Section 1995–96, mem. Bd of c 1996–2002, mem. Exec. Cttee 2000–; mem. Bd of Dir American Bd of Forensic Anthropology 1986–93, Vice-Pres. 1989–93; mem. Canadian Nat. Police Services Advisory Council; producer, Bones (TV series). *Publications:* Déjà Dead (Ellis Award for Best First Novel) 1997, Death du Jour 1999, Deadly Decisions 2000, Fatal Voyage 2001, Grave Secrets 2002, Bare Bones 2003, Monday Mourning 2004, Cross Bones 2005, Bones to Ashes 2007, Devil Bones 2008, 206 Bones 2009, Spider Bones 2010, Mortal Remains 2010, Flash and Bones 2011, Virals 2011. *Honours:* named one of Canada's 100 Most Powerful Women 2004, Premio Piemonte Grinzane Noir, Vincitore Sezione Giallo Internazionale Award, Italy 2007. *Address:* c/o Simon & Schuster, Inc., 1230 Avenue of the Americas, New York, NY 10020, USA. *E-mail:* kjreichs@aol.com. *Website:* www.kathyreichs.com.

REID, Alastair, MA; British writer, translator and poet; b. 22 March 1926, Whithorn, Wigtonshire, Scotland. *Education:* Univ. of St Andrews, Scotland. *Career:* visiting lecturer at univs in the UK and USA; staff writer, correspondent, New Yorker 1959–. *Publications:* To Lighten my House 1953, Oddments, Inklings, Omens, Moments 1959, Passwords: Places, Poems, Preoccupations 1963, Mother Goose in Spanish 1967, Corgi Modern Poets in Focus 3 1971, Weathering: Poems and Translations 1978, Whereabouts: Notes on Being a Foreigner 1987, An Alastair Reid Reader 1995, OASES: Poems and Prose 1997, Inside Out 2008; stories for children and trans. from Spanish of Pablo Neruda, Jorge Luis Borges and other writers. *Honours:* Scottish Arts Council Award 1979, PEN Award for Translation 2000. *Address:* c/o Canongate Books Ltd, 14 High Street, Edinburgh, EH1 1TE, Scotland (office). *Website:* www.canongate.net (office).

REID, Barbara Jane; Canadian illustrator and writer; b. 16 Nov. 1957, Toronto, Ont.; d. of Robert Johnstone and Dora Ann Reid; m. Ian Robert Crysler 1981; two d. *Education:* Lawrence Park Coll. Inst. and Ontario Coll. of Art and Design. *Career:* author and illustrator of children's books 1980–; Writer in Residence, Toronto Dist School Bd 2010–11; mem. Canadian Soc. of Children's Authors, Illustrators and Performers (CANSCAIP), PEN Canada, Writers' Union of Canada, Children's Book Centre. *Illustrated works include:* The New Baby Calf 1984, Have You Seen Birds 1986, Sing a Song of Mother Goose 1987, Effie 1990, Two By Two 1992, Gifts 1994, The Party (Gov.-Gen.'s Award for Illustration) 1997, Fun with Modelling Clay 1998, The Golden Goose 2000, The Subway Mouse 2003, Peg and the Yeti 2004, Read Me a Book 2004, Fox Walked Alone 2006, Perfect Snow 2009. *Honours:* Illustration Award, Ind. Order of Daughters of the Empire 1986, Canadian Council Prize 1986, Ruth Schwartz Award for Children's Literature 1986, Elizabeth Cleaver Award 1987, 1993, UNICEF Ezra Jack Keats Award 1988, Mr Christie Book Award 1991, Amelia Francis Howard Gibbon Award 1995, 1997, 2010, Ruth Schwartz Award 2003, Libris Awards for Children's Author and for Children's Illustrator of the Year 2007, Int. Honour List, Int. Bd on Books for Young People (IBBY) 2008. *Address:* c/o Scholastic Canada Ltd, 604 King Street West, Toronto, ON M5V 1P1, Canada. *E-mail:* barb@barbarareid.ca (office). *Website:* www.barbarareid.ca.

REID, Christina; Northern Irish playwright; b. 12 March 1942, Belfast. *Education:* Queen's Univ., Belfast. *Career:* Writer-in-Residence, Lyric Theatre, Belfast 1983–84, Young Vic. Theatre, London 1988–89. *Plays include:* Did You Hear the One About the Irishman? 1980, Tea in a China Cup 1983, Joyriders 1986, The Last of a Dyin' Race 1986, The Belle of the Belfast City 1986, My Name, Shall I Tell You My Name? 1987, Lords, Dukes and Earls 1989, Les Miserables (after Hugo) 1992, Clowns 1996, The King of the Castle 1999, The Gift of the Gab 2004, The Understudy 2003. *Screenplays include:* The Last of a Dyin' Race 1987, Streetwise (series of 13 episodes) 1991, Pie in the Sky 1995, Mighty Belfast (based on Joyriders and the sequel, Clowns). *Publications include:* Christina Reid: Plays One 1997, The Gift of the Gab 2003; featured in anthologies Best Radio Plays of 1986, New Connections. *Honours:* Ulster TV Drama Award 1980, Giles Cooper Award 1986, George Devine Award 1986. *Literary Agent:* c/o Lisa Foster, Alan Brodie Representation, Sixth Floor, Paddock Suite, The Courtyard, 55 Charterhouse Street, London, EC1M 6HA, England. *Telephone:* (20) 7253-6226 (office). *Fax:* (20) 7183-7999 (office). *E-mail:* lisa@alanbrodie.com. *Website:* www.alanbrodie.com.

REID, Philip (see Ingrams, Richard Reid)

REID BANKS, Lynne (see Banks, Lynne Reid)

REIDY, Carolyn Kroll, AB, MA, PhD; American publishing executive; *President and CEO, Simon and Schuster, Inc.*; b. (Carolyn Judith Kroll), 2 May 1949, Washington, DC; d. of Henry Kroll and Mildred Kroll; m. Stephen K. Reidy 1974. *Education:* Middlebury Coll., Vt and Indiana Univ. *Career:* various positions, Random House, New York 1975–83; Dir of Subsidiary Rights, William Morrow & Co., New York 1983–85; Vice-Pres. Assoc. Publr, Vintage Books, Random House, New York 1985–87; Assoc. Publr, Random House (concurrent with Assoc. Publr and Publr of Vintage Books) 1987–88; Publr, Vintage Books 1987–88, Anchor Books, Doubleday, New York 1988; Pres. and Publr, Avon Books, New York 1988–92; Pres. and Publr, Simon and Schuster Trade Div. 1992–2001, Pres. Adult Publishing Div., Simon and Schuster 2001–08, Pres. and CEO 2008–; Dir NAMES Project 1994–98, New York Univ. Center for Publishing 1997–2008, Literacy Partners, Inc. 1999–2011, Nat. Book Foundation 2000–. *Honours:* Matrix Award 2002, Distinguished Alumna, Indiana Univ. 2011. *Address:* Simon and Schuster, Inc., 1230 Avenue of the Americas, New York, NY 10020, USA (office). *Telephone:* (212) 698-7323 (office). *Fax:* (212) 698-1258 (office). *E-mail:* carolyn.reidy@simonandschuster.com (office). *Website:* simonandschuster.com (office).

REIF, Stefan Clive, MA, PhD, LittD, FRAS; British academic and writer; *Professor Emeritus of Medieval Hebrew Studies and Fellow of St John's College, University of Cambridge*; b. 21 Jan. 1944, Edinburgh, Scotland; s. of Pinkas Reif and Annie Reif; m. Shulamit Stekel 1967; one s. one d. *Education:* Univs of London and Cambridge. *Career:* Ed. Cambridge University Library Genizah Series 1978–; Prof. of Medieval Hebrew Studies and Dir of Genizah Research, Univ. of Cambridge –2006, Prof. Emer. 2007–; Fellow, St John's Coll., Cambridge; Fellow, Mekize Nirdamim Soc., Jerusalem; mem. Jewish Historical Soc. of England (fmr Pres.), British Asscn for Jewish Studies (fmr Pres.), Soc. for Old Testament Study. *Publications:* Shabbethai Sofer and his Prayer-book 1979, Interpreting the Hebrew Bible 1981, Published Material from the Cambridge Genizah Collections 1988, Genizah Research after Ninety Years 1992, Judaism and Hebrew Prayer 1993, Hebrew Manuscripts at University of Cambridge Library 1997, A Jewish Archive from Old Cairo 2000, Why Medieval Hebrew Studies 2001, The Cambridge Genizah Collections: Their Contexts and Significance 2002, Problems with Prayers 2006, Charles Taylor and the Genizah Collection 2009, Ha-Tefillah Ha-Yehudit 2010; contrib. of more than 350 articles in Hebrew and Jewish studies. *Address:* Cambridge University Library, West Road, Cambridge, CB3 9DR, England (office). *Telephone:* (1223) 766370 (office). *Fax:* (1223) 333160 (office). *E-mail:* scr3@cam.ac.uk (office). *Website:* www.lib.cam.ac.uk/Taylor-Schechter (office).

REINSHAGEN, Gerlind; German writer; b. 4 May 1926, Königsberg; d. of Ekkehard Technau and Frieda Technau; m. 1949. *Education:* studies in pharmacy and art, Berlin. *Career:* freelance author of novels, theatre and radio plays, screenplays, poetry, essays and criticism; mem. German PEN; mem. Deutsche Akad. der darstellenden Künste. *Plays:* Doppelkopf 1968, Leben und Tod der Marilyn Monroe 1971, Himmel und Erde 1974, Sonntagskinder 1976, Frühlingsfest 1980, Eisenherz 1982, Die Clownin 1988, Feuerblume 1987, Tanz, Marie! 1989, Die fremde Tochter 1993, Die grüne Tür 1999. *Television:* Doppelkopf 1972, Himmel und Erde 1976, Sonntagskinder 1981. *Radio:* 12 radio plays. *Publications:* novels: Rovinato 1981, Die flüchtige Braut 1984, Zwölf Nächte 1989, Jäger am Rand der Nacht 1993, Am grossen Stern 1996, Göttergeschichte 2000, Nachts 2011; Gesammelte Stücke (collected pieces) 1986, Joint Venture 2003, Vom Feuer 2006, Die Frau und die Stadt 2007; contribs to theatrical journals and yearbooks etc. *Honours:* Fördergabe Schillerpreis, Baden Württemberg 1974, Mülheimer Dramatikerpreis 1977, Roswitha von Gandersheim Medaille 1984, Ludwig Mülheims Preis 1993, Niedersächsischer Kunstpreis 1997, Niedersächsischer Staatspreis 1999, Kritikerpris 2008. *Address:* Rheingaustrasse 2, 12161 Berlin, Germany. *Telephone:* (30) 8217171.

REISMAN, Heather; Canadian publishing executive; *CEO, Indigo Books & Music Inc.*; b. Montreal; m. Gerald Schwartz; four c. *Education:* McGill Univ. *Career:* Co-founder and Man. Dir Paradigm Consulting 1979–92; Pres. Cott Corpn 1992–96; Founder, Pres. and CEO Indigo Books, Music and Café, Inc. 1996–2001, Pres. and CEO Indigo Books & Music Inc. (following merger with Chapters Inc. 2001) 2001–; mem. Bd of Dirs Onex Corpn, Right to Play; fmr mem. Bd of Dirs Magna Int., Suncor, Rogers Communications, Inc., Williams-Sonoma Inc.; Dir and Officer Mt Sinai Hosp.; fmr Gov. McGill Univ., Toronto Stock Exchange; mem. Bilderberg Steering Cttee. *Publications include:* numerous articles on media, communications, manufacturing and retailing. *Honours:* Dr hc (Ryerson Univ.) 2006; Int. Distinguished Entrepreneur Award, Univ. of Manitoba, John Molson School of Business Award of Distinction, Concordia Univ.; inducted into Waterloo Entrepreneur Hall of Fame, Univ. of Waterloo. *Address:* Indigo Books & Music Inc., 468 King Street West, Suite 500, Toronto, ON M5V 1L8, Canada (office). *Telephone:* (416) 364-4499 (office). *Fax:* (416) 364-0355 (office). *Website:* www.chapters.indigo.ca (office).

REISS, James, MA; American academic, poet, writer and editor; *Professor of English, Miami University at Oxford, OH*; b. 11 July 1941, New York, NY; m. Barbara Eve Klevs 1964 (divorced 1995); two d. *Education:* Univ. of Chicago. *Career:* instructor, Miami Univ., Oxford, OH 1965–69, Asst Prof. of English 1969–73, Assoc. Prof. of English 1973–81, Prof. of English 1981–; Visiting Poet and Assoc. Prof. of English, Queens Coll., CUNY 1975–76; Ed., Miami Univ. Press 1992–; numerous poetry readings; mem. Acad. of American Poets, Poetry Soc. of America. *Publications:* Self-Interviews: James Dickey (co-ed.) 1970, The Breathers (poems) 1974, Express (poems) 1983, The Parable of Fire (poems) 1996, Ten Thousand Good Mornings (poems) 2001, Riff on Six: New and Selected Poems 2003, Greatest Hits: 1970–2005 2005, Facade for a Penny Arcade (novel) 2008; contrib. to many anthologies and periodicals. *Honours:* first prizes Acad. of American Poets 1960, 1962, MacDowell Colony Fellowships 1970, 1974, 1976, 1977, two Borestone Mountain Poetry Awards 1974, Poetry Soc. of America Consuelo Ford Award 1974, Poetry Soc. of America Lucille Medwick Award 1989, Nat. Endowment for the Arts Fellowship 1974–75, Bread Loaf Fellowship 1975, New York State Council on the Arts Creative Artists Public Service Awards 1975–76, Ohio Arts Council grants 1980, 1981, Coll. English Asscn of Ohio Nancy Dasher Book Award 1984, Dorland Mountain Arts Colony Fellow 1991, 1993, 1999, Acad. of American Poets James Laughlin Award 1995, Pushcart Prize 1996, Helen & Laura Krout Memorial Ohioana Poetry Award 2005. *Address:* c/o Department of English, 326 Bachelor Hall, Miami University, Oxford, OH 45056, USA (office).

REISS, Tom, BA, MA; American writer; b. 1964, New York, NY; m.; two d. *Education:* Harvard Coll., Univ. of Houston. *Career:* fmr teacher and journalist. *Publications:* Fuhrer-Ex: Memoirs of a Former Neo-Nazi (memoir, with Ingo Hasselbach) 1996, The Orientalist 2005; contrib. to magazines and newspapers, including The New Yorker, The New York Times, The Wall Street Journal. *Literary Agent:* c/o Svetlana Katz, Janklow & Nesbit Associates, 445 Park Avenue, 13th Floor, New York, NY 10022-2606, USA. *Telephone:* (212) 421-1700. *Fax:* (212) 980-3671. *E-mail:* info@janklow.com. *Website:* www.janklowandnesbit.com. *E-mail:* tom@theorientalist.info (office). *Website:* www.theorientalist.info.

REITER, David Philip, BA, MA, PhD, Dipl. Publishing; Australian (b. American) publisher, writer and multimedia artist; *Director, IP (Interactive Publications)*; b. (b. Stanley Gerald Kleinman), 30 Jan. 1947, Cleveland, Ohio, USA; m. Cherie Lorraine Reiter 1992. *Education:* Univ. of Oregon, Univ. of Alberta,

Canada, Univ. of Denver, Harvard Univ. *Career:* Lecturer, Cariboo Univ. Coll., Canada 1975–84, Univ. of British Columbia 1984, British Columbia Inst. of Tech. 1984, Univ. of Canberra, Australia 1986–90; Publishing Man., Bd of Sr Secondary School Studies 1991–93; Publishing Man., Criminal Justice Comm. 1993–97; Dir IP (Interactive Publications) 1997–. *Plays:* Piano in the Garden 2000, Paul & Vincent 2004. *Films:* Hemingway in Spain 2004, Mum: Speaking Latin with a Singlet Tan 2009. *Radio:* Paul & Vincent 2003. *Publications:* The Snow in Us 1989, Changing House 1991, The Cave After Saltwater Tide 1992, Liars and Lovers 1993, Hemingway in Spain (book 1994, film 1997), Letters We Never Sent 1995, Triangles 2000, The Gallery (multimedia) 2001, Sharpened Knife (multimedia) 2002, Kiss & Tell: Selected & New Poems 1987–2002 2003, The Greenhouse Effect 2004, Real Guns 2004, Rainshadows 2007, Global Cooling 2008, Primary Instinct 2008; contribs to Australian, Canadian, US and UK journals. *Honours:* Queensland Premier's Poetry Award 1989, Imago-QUT Short Story Competition 1990, John Bray Award, South Australian Literary Festival, Steele Rudd Short Fiction Award 1991, Runner-up, Queensland Premier's Award 1993. *Address:* 9 Kuhler Court, Carindale, Queensland 4152, Australia (home). *Telephone:* (7) 3324-9319 (office). *Fax:* (7) 3324-9319 (office). *E-mail:* reiter@ipoz.biz (home). *Website:* ipoz.biz (office); www.drdavidreiter.com.

REKAI, Catherine (Kati), OC; Canadian (b. Hungarian) journalist, writer and fmr broadcaster; b. (Katalin Elek), 20 Oct. 1921, Budapest; d. of Desider Elek and Ilona Elek (née Hajdu); m. Dr John Rekai, CM 1941; two d. *Education:* Maria Terezia Gymnazium, Budapest, Hungary. *Career:* newspaper and radio reporter; Public Relations Consultant Cen. Hosp., Toronto; Dir Canadian Ethnic Media Asscn, Hungarian-Canadian Chamber of Commerce, Russian and European Studies, Univ. of Toronto, Performing Arts Magazine, Toronto Int. Cultural Exchange Foundation; Vice-Pres. Canadian Ethnic Journalists and Writers Club; mem. Multicultural Advisory Cttee, Toronto History Bd, Writers' Union of Canada (chair. Foreign Affairs Cttee), Asscn of Children's Writers and Illustrators, PEN Int., George R. Gardiner Museum, Stratford Festival, Nat. Ballet of Canada, Canadian Opera Co., TMAC-Travel Media Asscn of Canada; weekly arts commentator for CIAO Radio, Hungarian Hour, Kanadai Magyarsag (int. newspaper), Kaleidoscope Magazine. *Puppet shows:* The Great Totem Pole Caper, Tale of Tutenkhamen, The Boy Who Forgot, Puppet Plays. *Publications include:* children's books: (travel book series in storybook form) The Adventures of Mickey, Taggy, Puppo and Cica and How They Discover… Toronto, Ottawa, Montréal, Kingston, Brockville, The Thousand Islands, The Gardiner Museum of Ceramic Art, British Columbia, Greece, Switzerland, Budapest, Vienna, The Netherlands, Italy and Mickey Taggy, Puppo and Cica Celebrate Toronto 2000, France (Prix Saint-Exupéry Francophonie Valeurs Jeunesse, Paris 1988); writer of series of guidebooks for children in storybook form, The Adventures of Mickey, Taggy, Puppo and Cica; numerous contribs to newspapers and radio programmes. *Honours:* Kt of St Ladislaus of Hungary 1980, Cross of the Order of Merit (Hungary) 1993; Certificate of Honour for Contribution to Canadian Unity 1981, Prix Saint-Exupery, Francophonie Valeurs-Jeunesse 1988, Rakoczi Foundation Award 1990, Sierhey Khamara Ziniak Award for Excellence in Multilingual Media 1996. *E-mail:* j.rekai .rickerd@gmail.com.

REMINI, Robert Vincent, BS, MA, PhD; American historian, academic and writer; *Historian to the House of Representatives*; b. 17 July 1921; m. Ruth T. Kuhner 1948, one s. two d. *Education:* Fordham Univ., Columbia Univ. *Career:* Instructor, Fordham Univ. 1947–51, Asst Prof. 1951–59, Assoc. Prof. of American History 1959–65; Prof. of History, Univ. of Illinois at Chicago 1965–91, Research Prof. of Humanities 1985–91, Prof. of History Emeritus and Research Prof. of Humanities Emeritus 1991–, Univ. Historian 1997–; Historian to the House of Representatives 2005–; mem. American Historical Asscn, Society of Amerian Historians. *Publications:* Martin Van Buren and the Making of the Democratic Party 1959, The Election of Andrew Jackson 1963, Andrew Jackson 1966, Andrew Jackson and the Bank War 1967, Freedom's Frontiers: The Story of the American People (with James I. Clark) 1975, We the People: A History of the United States (with James I. Clark) 1975, The Revolutionary Age of Jackson 1976, Andrew Jackson and the Course of American Empire, 1767–1821 1977, The Era of Good Feelings and the Age of Jackson, 1816–1841 (with Edwin A. Miles) 1979, The American People: A History (with Arthur S. Link, Stanley Coben, Douglas Greenberg and Robert McMath) 1981, Andrew Jackson and the Course of American Freedom, 1822–1833 1981, Andrew Jackson and the Course of American Democracy, 1833–1845 1984, The Legacy of Andrew Jackson: Essays on Democracy, Indian Removal and Slavery 1988, The Life of Andrew Jackson 1988, The Jacksonian Era 1989, Andrew Jackson: A Bibliography (with Robert O. Rupp) 1991, Henry Clay: Statesman for the Union 1991, Daniel Webster: The Man and His Time 1997, The Battle of New Orleans 1999, The University of Illinois at Chicago: A Pictorial History (with Fred W. Beuttler and Melvin G. Holly) 2000, Andrew Jackson and His Indian Wars 2001, John Quincy Adams 2002, Joseph Smith 2002, The House: A History of the House of Representatives 2006, A Short History of the United States 2008, The Edge of the Precipice: Henry Clay and the Compromise that Saved the Union 2010; contributions: scholarly books and journals. *Honours:* Hon. doctorates, Guggenheim Fellowship 1978–79, Rockefeller Foundation Fellowships, Bellagio, Italy 1979, 1989, George Washington Medal of Honor, Freedom Foundation 1982, National Book Award 1984, Carl Sandburg Award 1989, Society of Midland Authors Award for Biography 1992, American Historical Asscn Award for Scholarly Distinction 2001, Western Writers of America Award 2002, Chicago Historical Soc. Award for Distinguished Scholarship 2003. *Address:* Office of the Historian, U.S. House of Representatives, B-56 Cannon House Office Building, Washington, DC 20515, USA (office); c/o Department of History, University of Illinois, PO Box 4348, Chicago, IL 60680, (office). *Telephone:* (312) 355-0604 (home); (202) 226-5525 (Washington) (office). *Fax:* (212) 226-2931 (Washington) (office); (312) 355-0755 (Chicago) (office). *E-mail:* historian@mail.house.gov (office); remini@uic.edu (office). *Website:* historian.house.gov (office).

REMNICK, David J., AB; American journalist, editor and writer; *Editor-in-Chief, The New Yorker*; b. 29 Oct. 1958, Hackensack, NJ; s. of Edward C. Remnick and Barbara Remnick (née Seigel); m. Esther B. Fein; two s. one d. *Education:* Princeton Univ. *Career:* reporter, The Washington Post 1982–91; staff writer, The New Yorker 1992–, Ed.-in-Chief 1998–. *Publications:* Lenin's Tomb: The Last Days of the Soviet Empire (Pulitzer Prize for General Nonfiction 1994) 1993, The Devil Problem (and other true stories) 1996, Resurrection: The Struggle for a New Russia 1997, King of the World: Muhammad Ali and the Rise of an American Hero 1998, Life Stories: Profiles from The New Yorker (ed.) 1999, Wonderful Town: Stories from The New Yorker (ed.) 1999, Reporting: Writings from The New Yorker 2006, The Bridge: The Life and Rise of Barack Obama 2010; contrib. to newspapers and periodicals. *Honours:* Livingston Award 1991, George Polk Award 1994, Helen Bernstein Award 1994. *Address:* The New Yorker, 4 Times Square, New York, NY 10036, USA (office). *E-mail:* themail@newyorker.com (office). *Website:* www.newyorker.com (office).

RENAUD, (Ernest) Hamilton Jacques; Canadian writer, poet and translator; b. 10 Nov. 1943, Montréal; two s. one d. *Career:* critic and researcher, Radio Canada 1965–67; reporter, Metro-Express, Montréal 1966; critic, Le Devoir, Montréal 1975–78; teacher, creative writing workshop, University of Québec 1980–89; spokesman, Equality Party 1989; researcher, Senator Jacques Hebert 1990. *Publications include:* Electrodes (poems), 1962; Le Casse (short stories), 1964; Clandestines (novel), 1980; L'espace du Diable (short stories), 1989; Les Cycles du Scorpion (poems), 1989; La Constellation du Bouc Emissaire (non-fiction), 1993; contributions: various publications.

RENAUT, Alain; French philosopher, academic and writer; b. 25 Feb. 1948, Paris; m. Sylvie Mesure 1984. *Education:* École Normale Supérieure, Paris. *Career:* researcher, Institut Raymond Aron, Écoles des Hautes Études en Sciences Sociales, Paris 1984–; Prof., Univ. of Caen 1986–. *Publications:* Des droits de l'homme à l'idée républicaine 1985, Système et critique 1985, La Pensée 68: Essais sur l'individualisme contemporain 1985, Le système du droit 1986, 68–86: Itinéraires de l'individu 1987, Heidegger et les modernes 1988, L'Ère de l'individu: Contribution à une histoire de la subjectivité 1989, Philosophie du droit 1991, Sartre: Le Dernier Philosophe 1993, Les révolutions de l'université 1995, L'individu 1995, La guerre des dieux 1996, Kant aujourd'hui 1997, Libéralisme et pluralisme culturel 1999, Alter ego 1999, Philosopher à 18 ans 1999, La libération des enfants 2002, Que faire des universités? 2002, Une éducation sans autorité ni sanction? 2003, La fin de l'autorité 2004, Qu'est-ce qu'une politique juste? 2004, Débat sur l'éthique: Idéalisme ou réalisme 2004, Un débat sur la laïcité 2005, La Philosophie 2005, Qu'est-ce qu'un peuple libre? 2005, Modèle social: une chimère française? 2006; contrib. to scholarly books and journals. *Address:* Bat 134, Et Rdc Porte Droite, 134 rue Chevilly, 94240 L'Hay-les-Roses, France (home). *Telephone:* 9-51-16-92-89 (home).

RENDELL OF BABERGH, Baroness (Life Peer), cr. 1997, of Aldeburgh in the County of Suffolk; **Ruth Barbara Rendell,** (Barbara Vine), CBE, FRSL; British crime novelist; b. 17 Feb. 1930, d. of Arthur Grasemann and Ebba Kruse; m. Donald Rendell 1950 (divorced 1975), remarried 1977 (died 1999); one s. *Education:* Loughton County High School. *Publications include:* From Doon with Death 1964, To Fear a Painted Devil 1965, Vanity Dies Hard 1965, A New Lease of Death (aka Sins of the Father) 1967, Wolf to the Slaughter 1967, The Secret House of Death 1968, The Best Man to Die 1969, A Guilty Thing Surprised 1970, No More Dying Then 1971, One Across, Two Down 1971, Murder Being Once Done 1972, Some Lie and Some Die 1973, The Face of Trespass 1974, Shake Hands Forever 1975, A Demon in My View 1976, A Judgement in Stone 1976, A Sleeping Life 1978, Make Death Love Me 1979, The Lake of Darkness 1980, Put on by Cunning (aka Death Notes) 1981, Master of the Moor 1982, The Speaker of Mandarin 1983, The Killing Doll 1984, The Tree of Hands 1984, An Unkindness of Ravens 1985, Live Flesh 1986, Heartstones 1987, Talking to Strange Men 1987, The Veiled One 1988, The Bridesmaid 1989, Mysterious 1990, Going Wrong 1990, The Strawberry Tree 1990, Walking on Water 1991, Kissing the Gunner's Daughter 1992, The Crocodile Bird 1993, Simisola 1994, Blood Lines 1996, The Keys to the Street 1997, Road Rage 1997, A Sight for Sore Eyes 1998, Harm Done 1999, Babes in the Wood 2002, The Rottweiler 2003, Thirteen Steps Down 2004, End in Tears 2005, The Water's Lovely 2006, Not in the Flesh 2007, Portobello 2008, The Monster in the Box 2009, Tigerlily's Orchids 2010, The Vault 2011; as Barbara Vine: A Dark-Adapted Eye 1986, A Fatal Inversion 1987, The House of Stairs 1988, Gallowglass 1990, King Solomon's Carpet 1991, Asta's Book 1993, The Children of Men 1994, No Night is Too Long 1994, The Keys to the Street 1996, The Brimstone Wedding 1996, The Chimney Sweeper's Boy 1998, Grasshopper 2000, The Blood Doctor 2002, The Minotaur 2005, The Water's Lovely 2007, The Birthday Present 2008; short story collections: The Fallen Curtain 1976, Means of Evil 1979, The Fever Tree 1982, The New Girlfriend 1985, Collected Short Stories 1987, Undermining the Central Line (with Colin Ward) 1989, The Copper Peacock 1991, Blood Lines 1995, Piranha to Scurfy and Other Stories 2001; other: A Warning to the Curious: The Ghost Stories of M. R. James (ed.) 1987, Ruth Rendell's Suffolk 1989, The Reason Why: An Anthology of the Murderous Mind (ed.) 1995, Harm Done (ed.) 2000. *Honours:* Dr hc (Essex) 1990; Arts Council Nat. Book Award for Genre Fiction 1981, Sunday Times Award for Literary Excellence 1990 and other awards. *Address:* House of Lords, London, SW1A 0PW (office); 26 Cornwall Terrace Mews, London, NW1 5LL, England. *Telephone:* (20) 7219-2185 (office).

RENÉE, BA; New Zealand playwright and writer; b. (Renée Gertrude Taylor), 19 July 1929, Napier. *Education:* Univ. of Auckland. *Career:* Robert Burns Fellowship, University of Otago, 1989; Writers Fellowship, University of Waikato, New Zealand, 1995. *Publications:* Secrets: Two One-Woman Plays, 1982; Breaking Out, 1982; Setting the Table, 1982; What Did You Do in the War, Mummy?, 1982; Asking For It, 1983; Dancing, 1984; Wednesday to Come, 1984; Groundwork, 1985; Pass It On, 1986; Born to Clean, 1987; Jeannie Once, 1990; Touch of the Sun, 1991; Missionary Position, 1991; The Glass Box, 1992; Tiggy Tiggy Touchwood, 1992; Willy Nilly (novel), 1990; Daisy and Lily, 1993; Does This Make Sense To You?, 1995; The Snowball Waltz (novel), 1997; Let's Write Plays (textbook for schools), 1998; Yin and Tonic (humour), 1998; The Skeleton Woman (novel), 2002. Other: Television plays and short stories. *Honours:* Project Grant, 1991; Queen Elizabeth II Arts Council Scholarship in Letters, 1993.

RENFREW OF KAIMSTHORN, Baron (Life Peer), cr. 1991, of Hurlet in the District of Renfrew; **Andrew Colin Renfrew,** PhD, ScD, FBA, FSA; British archaeologist and academic; *Research Fellow, McDonald Institute for Archaeological Research, University of Cambridge*; b. 25 July 1937, Stockton-on-Tees; s. of the late Archibald Renfrew and Helena D. Renfrew; m. Jane M. Ewbank 1965; two s. one d. *Education:* St Albans School, St John's Coll., Cambridge and British School of Archaeology, Athens. *Career:* Lecturer in Prehistory and Archaeology, Univ. of Sheffield 1965–70, Sr Lecturer 1970–72, Reader in Prehistory and Archaeology 1972; Prof. of Archaeology and Head of Dept, Univ. of Southampton 1972–81; Disney Prof. of Archaeology, Univ. of Cambridge 1981–2004, Dir McDonald Inst. for Archaeological Research 1990–2004, Fellow 2004–; Fellow, St John's Coll., Cambridge 1981–86; Master Jesus Coll., Cambridge 1986–97, Professorial Fellow 1997–2004, Fellow Emer. 2004–; Foreign Assoc. Nat. Acad. of Sciences, USA; Visiting Lecturer, UCLA 1967; mem. Ancient Monuments Bd for England 1974–84, Royal Comm. on Historical Monuments 1977–87, Historic Buildings and Monuments Comm. for England 1984–86, Ancient Monuments Advisory Cttee 1984–2002, British Nat. Comm. for UNESCO 1984–86; Foreign mem. American Philosophical Asscn 2006; Trustee, British Museum 1991–2001. *Publications:* The Emergence of Civilization 1972, Before Civilization 1973, The Explanation of Culture Change (ed.) 1973, British Prehistory (ed.) 1974, Transformations: Mathematical Approaches to Culture Change 1979, Problems in European Prehistory 1979, An Island Polity 1982, Theory and Explanation in Archaeology (ed.) 1982, Approaches to Social Archaeology 1984, The Archaeology of Cult 1985, Peer, Polity Interaction and Socio-Political Change (ed.) 1986, Archaeology and Language: The Puzzle of Indo-European Origins 1987, The Idea of Prehistory (co-author) 1988, Archaeology: Theories, Methods and Practice (co-author) 1991, The Cycladic Spirit 1991, The Archaeology of Mind (co-ed. with E. Zubrow) 1994, Loot, Legitimacy and Ownership 2000, Archaeogenetics (ed.) 2000, Figuring It Out 2003, Archaeology, The Key Concepts (co-ed.) 2005; contribs to Archaeology, Scientific American, Phylogenetic Methods and the Prehistory of Languges (co-ed.) 2006. *Honours:* Hon. FSA (Scotland); Hon. FRSE 2001; Hon. LittD (Sheffield) 1990, (Southampton) 1995, (Edinburgh) 2004, (Liverpool) 2004, (St Andrews) 2006; Dr hc (Faculty of Letters, Univ. of Athens) 1991; Rivers Memorial Medal, British Anthropological Inst. 1979, Sir Joseph Larmor Award 1961, Huxley Memorial Medal, Royal Anthropological Inst. 1991, Prix Int. Fyssen, Fondation Fyssen, Paris 1997, Language and Culture Prize, Univ. of Umeå, Sweden 1998, Rivers Memorial Medal, European Science Foundation Latsis Prize 2003, Bolzan Prize 2004. *Literary Agent:* c/o Curtis Brown Ltd, Haymarket House, 28–29 Haymarket, London, SW1Y 4SP, England. *Telephone:* (20) 7393-4400. *Fax:* (20) 7393-4401. *Address:* Room 3.2, West Building, McDonald Institute for Archaeological Research, Downing Street, Cambridge, CB2 3ER, England (office). *Telephone:* (1223) 333521 (office). *Fax:* (1223) 333536 (office). *E-mail:* des25@cam.ac.uk (office). *Website:* www.mcdonald.cam.ac.uk (office).

RENRICK, D. F. (see Kerner, Fred)

RENTCHNICK, Pierre, MD; Swiss physician (retd) and editor; b. 17 July 1923, Geneva; s. of Jacques Rentchnick and Blanche (Spiegel) Rentchnick; m. Paule Adam 1948; one s. *Education:* Univs of Geneva and Paris. *Career:* Ed.-in-Chief, Médecine et Hygiène, Geneva 1956–93, Recent Results in Cancer Research; Ed. Springer, Heidelberg and New York 1962–83, Bulletin de l'Union int. contre le cancer, Geneva 1962–80; f. Kiwanis-Club, Geneva 1966, Pres. 1976–77; f. Int. Soc. for Chemotherapy 1959; Fellow, New York Acad. of Sciences, Medical Soc. of Prague, French Soc. of Infectious Pathology. *Publications:* Esculape chez les Soviets 1954, Klinik und Therapie der Nebenwirkungen 1963, Esculape chez Mao 1973, Ces malades qui nous gouvernent 1976, Les orphelins mènent-ils le monde? 1978, Ces malades qui font l'Histoire 1983, Ces nouveaux malades qui nous gouvernent 1988–96; numerous publs on antibiotics in infectious diseases, on ethical problems, euthanasia etc.; numerous pathographies. *Honours:* Prix Littré (France) 1977. *Address:* La Rose des Vents, 74160 Saint-Julien-en-Genevois, France (home). *Telephone:* (4) 50-37-85-47 (home).

RESCHER, Nicholas, PhD, FRSC; American philosopher and author; *Distinguished University Professor of Philosophy, University of Pittsburgh*; b. 15 July 1928, Hagen, Germany; s. of Erwin Hans Rescher and Meta Anna Rescher; m. 1st Frances Short 1951 (divorced 1965); one d.; m. 2nd Dorothy Henle 1968; two s. one d. *Education:* Queens Coll., New York, Princeton Univ. *Career:* Assoc. Prof. of Philosophy, Lehigh Univ. 1957–61; Distinguished Univ. Prof. of Philosophy, Univ. of Pittsburgh 1961–, Dir Center for Philosophy of Science 1982–89, Chair. 1989–; consultant, RAND Corpn 1954–66, Encyclopaedia Britannica 1963–64, North American Philosophical Publs 1980–; Ed. American Philosophical Quarterly 1964–94; Sec.-Gen. Int. Union of History and Philosophy of Science 1969–75; visiting lectureships at Univs of Oxford, Munich, Konstanz, Western Ontario and others; Pres. American Philosophical Asscn (Eastern Div.) 1989–90, American Catholic Philosophical Asscn 2003–04, American Metaphysical Soc. 2004–05; mem. Academia Europea, Institut Int. de Philosophie, Acad. Int. de Philosophie des Sciences; Guggenheim Fellow 1970–71; Fellow, American Acad. of Arts and Sciences 2009, Royal Astronomical Soc. *Publications:* more than 100 books, including The Coherence Theory of Truth 1973, Methodological Pragmatism 1977, Scientific Progress 1978, The Limits of Science 1984, Ethical Idealism 1987, Rationality 1988, A System of Pragmatic Idealism (three vols) 1992–94, Pluralism 1993, Predicting the Future 1997, Paradoxes 2001, Philosophical Reasoning 2001, Metaphysics 2005, Epistemetrics 2006, Free Will 2009; numerous articles in many areas of philosophy. *Honours:* Hon. mem. Corpus Christi Coll. Oxford; six hon. degrees; Alexander von Humboldt Prize 1983, Aquinas Medal, Cardinal Mercier Prize. *Address:* 1012 Cathedral of Learning, University of Pittsburgh, Pittsburgh, PA 15260 (office); 1033 Milton Avenue, Pittsburgh, PA 15218, USA (home). *Telephone:* (412) 624-5950 (office); (412) 243-1290 (home). *Fax:* (412) 383-7506 (office). *E-mail:* rescher@pitt.edu (office). *Website:* www.pitt.edu/~rescher (office).

RESTAK, Richard Martin, MD; American physician and writer; b. 4 Feb. 1942, Wilmington, Del.; m. Carolyn Serbent 1968; three d. *Education:* Georgetown Medical School. *Career:* Consultant, Encyclopedia of Bioethics 1978; Special Contributing Ed., Science Digest 1981–85; mem. Editorial Bd Integrative Psychiatry: An International Journal for the Synthesis of Medicine and Psychiatry 1986; mem. American Acad. of Neurology, American Acad. of Psychiatry and the Law, American Psychiatric Asscn, Behavioral Neurology Soc., New York Acad. of Sciences, Int. Neuropsychological Soc., Nat. Book Critics Circle, Int. Brotherhood of Magicians, Philosophical Soc. of Washington. *Publications:* Premeditated Man: Bioethics and the Control of Future Human Life 1975, The Brain: The Last Frontier: Explorations of the Human Mind and Our Future 1979, The Self Seekers 1982, The Brain 1984, The Infant Mind 1986, The Mind 1988, The Brain has a Mind of its Own 1991, Receptors 1994, Modular Brain 1994, Brainscopes 1995, Older and Wiser 1997, The Secret Life of the Brain 2001, Mozart's Brain and the Fighter Pilot 2001, The New Brain 2003, Poe's Heart and the Mountain Climber 2004; contrib. to anthologies, journals and periodicals. *Honours:* Nat. Endowment for the Humanities Fellowship 1976, Claude Bernard Science Journalism Award, Nat. Soc. for Medical Research 1976, Distinguished Alumni Award, Gettysburg Coll. 1985. *Address:* 1800 R Street NW, Suite C-3, Washington, DC 20009, USA (office). *Telephone:* (202) 462-0455 (office); (202) 362-6547 (home). *Fax:* (202) 462-0340 (office); (202) 686-6993 (home). *E-mail:* neurology.associates.office@gmail.com (office); braindoc97@aol.com (office). *Website:* www.richardrestak.com.

RESTON, James Barrett, Jr, BA; American writer; *Senior Scholar, Woodrow Wilson International Center for Scholars*; b. 8 March 1941, New York, NY; m. Denise Brender Leary 1971. *Education:* Univ. of Oxford, Univ. of North Carolina at Chapel Hill. *Career:* reporter, Chicago Daily News 1964–65; Lecturer in Creative Writing, Univ. of North Carolina at Chapel Hill 1971–81; Watergate adviser and strategist for David Frost in Nixon interviews 1977; Sr Scholar, Woodrow Wilson Int. Center for Scholars, Washington, DC; mem. Authors' Guild, Dramatists' Guild, PEN; US Tennis Asscn Capt. 2001–05. *Plays:* Sherman the Peacemaker 1979, Jonestown Express 1983, Man of the Millennium 1999; adviser to playwright Peter Morgan for play Frost/Nixon 2007; also radio and TV documentaries and plays. *Films:* adviser to dir Ron Howard for film Frost/Nixon 2008. *Publications include:* fiction: To Defend, To Destroy 1971, The Knock at Midnight 1975; non-fiction: The Amnesty of John David Herndon 1973, Perfectly Clear: Nixon from Whittier to Watergate (with Frank Mankiewicz) 1973, The Innocence of Joan Little: A Southern Mystery 1977, Our Father Who Art in Hell: The Life and Death of Jim Jones 1981, The Lone Star: The Life of John Connally 1989, Collision at Home Plate: The Lives of Peter Rose and Bart Giamatti 1991, The Last Apocalypse: Europe at the Year 1000 AD 1998, Warriors of God: Richard the Lionheart and Saladin in the Third Crusade 2001, Dogs of God: Columbus, the Inquisition and the Defeat of the Moors 2005, Fragile Innocence: A Father's Memoir of his Daughter's Courageous Journey 2006, The Conviction of Richard Nixon: The Untold Story 2007, Defenders of the Faith: Charles V, Suleyman the Magnificent, and the Battle for Europe, 1520–1536 2009; contrib. to various periodicals. *Honours:* Dupont-Columbia Award 1982, Prix Italia, Venice 1982, Nat. Endowment for the Arts grant 1982, Valley Forge Award 1985. *Address:* 4714 Hunt Avenue, Chevy Chase, MD 20815, USA (home). *E-mail:* jreston@erols.com (home).

RESTREPO, Laura; Colombian writer; b. 1950, Bogotá. *Education:* Univ. of the Andes. *Career:* fmr lecturer, Nat. Univ. of Colombia; left-wing political activist, spent time in Argentina, Spain and Mexico; involved in negotiations between govt and M-19 guerrilla movt 1983; Dir Inst. of Culture and Tourism, Bogotá 2004. *Publications:* Historia de Entusiasmo (trans. as Story of a Fascination) 1986, Operación Príncipe (co-author) 1988, La Isla de la Pasion (trans. as Isle of Passion) 1989, Las vacas comen espaguetis (children's) 1989, En qué momento se jodió Medellín (co-author) 1991, Del amor y del fuego (co-author) 1991, El Leopardo al Sol (trans. as Leopard in the Sun) (Arzobispo San Clemente Prize) 1993, Otros niños (co-author) 1993, Dulce Compania (trans. as The Angel of Galilea) (Sor Juana Ines de la Cruz Prize, Mexico, Prix France Culture) 1995, The Dark Bride 1999, A Tale of the Dispossessed 2001, Olor a rosas invisibles 2002, La novia oscura 2002, Delirio (trans. as Delirium) (Alfaguara Prize, Grinzane Cavour Prize, Italy) 2004, Desmasiados Heroes (trans. as No Place for Heroes) 2009. *Literary Agent:* c/o Thomas Colchie, The Colchie Agency, 324 85th Street, Brooklyn, NY 11209, USA. *E-mail:* colchielit@earthlink.net. *Address:* c/o Alfaguara, GrupoSantillana Colombia, Calle 80 No. 10–23, Bogotá, Colombia (office). *Website:* www.santillana.com.co/alfaguara (office).

RESTREPO, Luis Carlos, MPhil; Colombian psychiatrist, government official and writer; b. 1954, Filandia, Quindío. *Career:* clinical and therapeutic practitioner in fields of drug addiction, and problems involving violence; fmr psychiatrist Simón Bolívar Community Centre; fmr Prof. of Clinical Psychology, Universidad Javeriana de Bogotá; fmr Prof., Nat. Pedagogical Univ.; fmr Nat. Coordinator, Citizens' Mandate for Peace; fmr Dir Instituto SER for rehabilitation of drug addicts; has served as consultant to UNDCP, Nat. Office for Drugs, Office of the Mayor of Bogota; High Commr for Peace, Govt of Colombia 2002–09, responsible for prisoner exchange negotiations between govt and FARC guerillas, also responsible for demobilization process of AUC paramilitary groups. *Publications:* non-fiction: Libertad y locura 1983, La Fruta Prohibida: la droga como espejo de la cultura 1994, El Derecho a la Ternura 1995, La trampa de la razón 1996, Ecología humana 1996, Ética del amor 1996, El derecho a la paz 1997, Memorias de la tierra 1997, Proyecto para un arca en medio de un diluvio de plomo 1997, Ética del amor 1998, Cultura, Politica y Modernidad (jtly) 2000, Mas allá del terror: abordaje cultural de la violencia en Colombia 2002, El retorno de lo sacro 2004, Viaje al fondo del Mal 2005, Origen del concepto de espíritu 2010. *Website:* www.luiscarlosrestrepo.com.

REVAZ, Noëlle; Swiss author and teacher; b. 1968, Valais. *Education:* Univ. of Lausanne. *Career:* currently teacher of creative writing, Swiss Literature Inst., Biel; writes plays and monologues, sketches for television. *Radio:* several plays and monologues. *Publications include:* novels: Rapport aux bêtes (With the Animals) (Schiller Foundation Award, Prix Lettres Frontière, Prix Marguerite Audoux) 2002, Efina 2009; monologue: Quand Mamie 2011; several short stories. *Honours:* Pro Helvetia HALMA Grant. *Address:* Swiss Literature Institute, Bern University of the Arts, Rockhall IV, Seevorstadt 99, 2502 Biel, Switzerland (office). *Telephone:* (31) 8483900 (office). *Fax:* (31) 8483901 (office). *E-mail:* noelle.revaz@hkb.bfh.ch (office); lit@hkb.bfh.ch (office). *Website:* www.hkb.bfh.ch/en/studies/divisions/sli (office).

REVERE, Michael Rigsby; American writer, poet, musician and music teacher; b. 26 July 1951, East Point, Ga; pnr Judy Revere; one s. one d. *Education:* Southwestern Community College, Sylva, NC. *Career:* guest lectures, poetry readings and workshops. *Publications:* Spirit Happy (poems), 1974; The Milky Way Poems, 1976; Shotgun Vision (poems), 1977; Fire and Rain (poems), 1998; Lizard Man: Collected Poems 1969–2002 (with original music soundscapes CD), 2002; contributions: journals and periodicals.

REY, Alain; French lexicographer and linguist; b. 30 Aug. 1928, Pont-du-Château; m. Josette Rey-Debove. *Career:* fmr Prof., Univ. of Indiana, Univ. of Montréal; employed by Paul Robert to produce dictionaries 1952, Editorial Gen. Sec. for Le Robert publications 1956, now Ed.-in-Chief; Co-Dir of collection, Approaches to Semiotics (Berlin-New-York); Co-Dir of German journal, Lexicographie 1985–; Pres. Commission de terminologie, Ministry of Culture and Communication 1997–; two-year collaboration on production of 'Trésor de la Langue Française' for Centre National de la Recherche Scientifique. *Television:* presenter Le mot de la fin (France-Inter) 1995–. *Publications:* as editor: Dictionnaire alphabétique et analogique de la langue française (six vols) 1964, Le Petit Robert 1967, Le Micro-Robert 1971, Le Petit Robert des noms propres 1974, Dictionnaire des expressions et locutions 1979, Grand Robert de la langue française (nine vols) 1985, Dictionnaire historique de la langue française (five vols) 1992, Petit Robert de la langue française 1993, Dictionnaire historique de la langue française en petit format (three vols) 1998, Dictionnaire culturel en langue française (four vols) 2005; as writer: Littré, l'humaniste et les mots (Prix de l'Académie française) 1970, La Lexicologie: lectures 1970, Théories dusigneet du sens (two vols) 1973, La Terminologie 1979; contrib. to numerous books and journals. *Honours:* Commandeur, Ordre des Arts et des Lettres 2005. *Address:* Le Robert, 25 avenue Pierre de Coubertin, 75211 Paris cedex 13, France (office). *Website:* www.lerobert.com (office).

REYES, Carlos, BA, MA, ABD; American poet and teacher; b. 2 June 1935, Marshfield, Mo.; m. 1st Barbara Ann Hollingsworth 1958 (divorced 1973); one s. three d.; m. 2nd Karen Ann Stoner 1979 (divorced 1992); m. 3rd Elizabeth Atly 1993 (divorced 2003); m. 4th Karen Checkoway 2005. *Education:* Univ. of Oregon, Univ. of Arizona. *Career:* mem. Governor's Advisory Cttee on the Arts, Oregon 1973; Poet to the City of Portland 1978; Poet-in-Residence at various public schools in Oregon and Washington; Ed., Hubbub 1982–90, Ar Mhuin Na Muicea (journal of Irish literature, music, current events) 1995; mem. Portland Poetry Festival Inc. (bd 1974–84), PEN Northwest (co-chair. 1992–93), Mountain Writers Series (bd 1996–2000), Writers-in-Schools 2005–; Fellow, Henrich Böll Cottage, Achill Island, Ireland 2008. *Publications:* The Prisoner 1973, The Shingle Weaver's Journal 1980, At Doolin Quay 1982, Nightmarks 1990, A Suitcase Full of Crows 1995, Poemas de la Isla (trans. of Josefina de la Torre) 2000, Puertas Abiertas/Open Doors (bilingual edn of poems by Edwin Madrid) 2000, Obra Poética Completa de Jorge Carrera Andrade/Complete Poetic Works of Jorge Carrera Andrade (bilingual edn) 2004, At the Edge of the Western Wave (poems) 2004, The Book of Shadows: New and Selected Poems 2009; contrib. to various journals and magazines. *Honours:* Oregon Arts Commission Individual Artist Fellowship 1982, Yaddo Fellowship 1984, Hon. Fellow Fundación Valparaíso, Mojácar, Spain 1998, Ethel N. Fortner Writer and Community Award, St Andrews Coll. 2008. *Address:* 6034 SE Stephens Street, Portland, OR 97215, USA (home).

REYN, Evgeny Borisovich; Russian poet and writer; b. 29 Dec. 1935, Leningrad; m. Nadejda Reyn 1989; one s. *Education:* Leningrad Tech. Inst. *Career:* freelance poet published in samizdat magazine Sintaksis and émigré press abroad in magazines Grani, Kovcheg; participated in publication of almanac Metropol; literary debut in Russia 1984; Prof., Moscow M. Gorky Inst. of Literature; mem. Writers' Union, Union of Moscow Writers, Russian PEN Centre. *Television:* Kuprin 1967, The Thcukokkala 1969, The Tenth Chapter 1970, Journeys with Josef Brodsky 1993, Josef Brodsky: The Hatchings to Portrait 1996. *Publications:* The Names of Bridges 1984, Shore Line 1989, The Darkness of Mirrors 1989, Breda 1995, Irretrievable Day 1991, Counter-Clockwise 1992, Nezhnosmo 1993, Selected Poems 1993, The Prognostication 1994, The Top-booty 1995, The Others 1996, The News Stages of the Life of The Moscow Beau Monde 1997, Balkony 1998, Arch over Water 2000, The Remarks of Marathon Man: Inconclusive Memoirs 2003, The Overground Transition 2004, After Our Age 2005, My Best Addressman... 2005, The Poems, Prose, Essays 2006. *Honours:* Peterburg Prize of Arts 'Tsarskoye Selo' 1995, State Prize of Russia in Literature and Art 1996, Ind. Alexander Block Literature Award 1999, Alfred Tepfer Foundation Pushkin Prize (Hamburg, Germany) 2003, State Pushkin Prize in Literature and Art 2004, Grinzane Cavour Prize (Turin, Italy) 2004, Petropol Prize in Literature and Arts, St Peterburg 2005. *Address:* Leningradsky Prospect, 75, Apt 167, 125057 Moscow (home). *Telephone:* (499) 157-20-14 (home). *Fax:* (495) 203-46-78 (office). *E-mail:* Reyne@cnt.ru (home).

REYNOLDS, (Eva Mary) Barbara, BA, MA, PhD; British academic (retd), writer and translator; *President, Dorothy L. Sayers Society;* b. 13 June 1914, d. of the late Alfred Charles Reynolds; m. 1st Lewis Thorpe 1939 (died 1977); one s. one d.; m. 2nd Kenneth Imeson 1982 (died 1994). *Education:* St Paul's Girls' School and Univ. Coll. London. *Career:* Asst Lecturer in Italian LSE 1937–40; Asst Lecturer in Italian Univ. of Cambridge 1940–45, Lecturer in Italian Literature and Language 1945–62, mem. Senate Council 1961–62; Chief Exec. and Gen. Ed. The Cambridge Italian Dictionary 1948–81; Warden Willoughby Hall, Univ. of Nottingham 1963–69, Reader in Italian Studies 1966–78; Visiting Prof. Univ. of California at Berkeley, USA 1974–75, Wheaton Coll., IL, USA 1977–78, 1982, Trinity Coll. Dublin 1980, 1981, Hope Coll., MI, USA 1982; Hon. Reader in Italian, Univ. of Warwick 1975–80; Man. Ed. Seven Anglo-American literary review 1980–89; Pres. Dorothy L. Sayers Soc. 1995–. *Publications include:* Tredici Novelle Moderne (jtly) 1947, The Linguistic Writings of Alessandro Manzoni: a textual and chronological reconstruction 1950, The Cambridge Italian Dictionary (vol. I) 1962, (vol. II) 1981, Guido Farina, Painter of Verona (jtly) 1967, Concise Cambridge Italian Dictionary 1975, Cambridge-Signorelli Dizionario 1986, The Translator's Art (co-ed.) 1987, The Passionate Intellect: Dorothy L. Sayers' Encounter with Dante 1989, Dorothy L. Sayers: Her Life and Soul 1993, The Letters of Dorothy L. Sayers (vol. I) 1995, (vol. II) 1997, (vol. III) 1998, (vol. IV) 2000, (vol. V) 2002, Dante: The Poet, the Political Thinker, the Man 2006 (translated into Italian, Hungarian, Dutch and Portuguese); several translations of Italian works, including Orlando Furioso vol. I (Int. Literary Prize 1976) 1975, (vol. II) 1977; numerous articles in professional journals. *Honours:* Hon. DLitt (Wheaton Coll.) 1979, (Hope Coll., MI) 1982, (Durham) 1995; Edmund Gardner Prize 1964; Silver Medal, Italian Govt 1964, Silver Medal Prov. Admin. of Vicenza 1971, Cavaliere Ufficiale al Merito della Repubblica Italiana 1978. *Address:* 220 Milton Road, Cambridge, CB4 1LQ, England (home). *Telephone:* (1223) 565380 (home). *Fax:* (1223) 424894 (home). *Website:* www.sayers.org.uk (office).

REYNOLDS, David James, MA, PhD, FBA; British academic and writer; *Professor of International History, University of Cambridge;* b. 17 Feb. 1952, Orpington, Kent, England; m. Margaret Philpott Ray 1977; one s. *Education:* Univ. of Cambridge. *Career:* Choate Fellow, Harvard Univ., USA 1973–74, Warren Fellow 1980–81; Research Fellow, Gonville and Caius Coll., Cambridge 1978–80, 1981–83; Fellow, Christ's Coll., Cambridge 1983–; Asst Lecturer in History, Univ. of Cambridge 1984–88, Lecturer 1988–97, Reader in Int. History 1997–2002, Prof. of Int. History 2002–. *Radio:* writer and presenter for BBC Radio 4: America, Empire of Liberty series 2008–09. *Television:* writer and presenter for BBC 2 and BBC 4: Churchill's Forgotten Years 2005, The Improbable Mr Attlee 2005, Summits: Munich 1938, Vienna 1961, Geneva 1985 2008, Armistice 2008, Nixon in the Den 2010. *Publications:* The Creation of the Anglo-American Alliance, 1937–1941: A Study in Competitive Co-operation 1981, Lord Lothian and Anglo-American Relations, 1939–1940 1983, An Ocean Apart: The Relationship Between Britain and America in the Twentieth Century (with David Dimbleby) 1988, Britannia

Overruled: British Policy and World Power in the Twentieth Century 1991, Allies at War: The Soviet, American, and British Experience, 1939–1945 (co-ed. with Warren F. Kimball and A. O. Chubarian) 1994, The Origins of the Cold War in Europe: International Pespectives (ed.) 1994, Rich Relations: The American Occupation of Britain, 1942–1945 1995, One World Divisible: A Global History Since 1945 2000, From Munich to Pearl Harbor: Roosevelt's America and the Origins of the Second World War 2001, In Command of History: Churchill Fighting and Writing the Second World War (Wolfson Prize for History 2005) 2004, From World War to Cold War: Churchill, Roosevelt and the International History of the 1940s 2006, Summits: Six Meetings that Shaped the Twentieth Century 2007, America, Empire of Liberty 2009; contrib. to scholarly books and journals. *Honours:* Bernath Prize, Soc. for Historians of American Foreign Relations 1982, Distinguished Book Award, Soc. for Mil. History 1996, Wolfson History Prize 2005, Voice of the Viewer and Listener Award for Best New Radio Programme 2008. *Address:* Christ's College, Cambridge, CB2 3BU, England (office). *Telephone:* (1223) 334986 (office). *E-mail:* djr17@cam.ac.uk (office). *Website:* www.christs.cam.ac.uk (office).

REYNOLDS, Graham, OBE, CVO, BA, FBA; British writer and art historian; b. 10 Jan. 1914, London, England; m. Daphne Dent 1943 (died 2002). *Education:* Queens' Coll., Cambridge. *Career:* Keeper Dept of Prints and Drawings and of Paintings, Victoria & Albert Museum 1959–74. *Publications:* Nicholas Hilliard and Isaac Oliver 1947, English Portrait Miniatures 1952, Painters of the Victorian Scene 1953, Catalogue of the Constable Collection, Victoria and Albert Museum 1960, Constable, The Natural Painter 1965, Victorian Painting 1966, Turner 1969, Concise History of Watercolour Painting 1972, Catalogue of Portrait Miniatures, Wallace Collection 1980, The Later Paintings and Drawings of John Constable (two vols) 1984, English Watercolours 1988, The Earlier Paintings of John Constable (two vols) 1996, Catalogue of European Portrait Minatures, Metropolitan Museum of Art, New York 1996, The Miniatures in the Collection of HM the Queen, The Sixteenth and Seventeenth Centuries 1999, Daphne Reynolds: A Memoir 2007; contrib. to TLS, Burlington Magazine, Apollo, New Departures. *Honours:* Hon. Keeper of Miniatures, Fitzwilliam Museum, Cambridge 1994–; Mitchell Prize 1984. *Address:* The Old Manse, Bradfield St George, Bury St Edmunds, Suffolk, IP30 0AZ, England (home). *Telephone:* (1284) 386610 (home).

REYNOLDS, Keith (Kev) Ronald; British writer, photo journalist and lecturer; b. 7 Dec. 1943, Ingatestone, Essex; m. Linda Sylvia Dodsworth 1967; two d. *Career:* mem. Outdoor Writers' Guild. *Publications:* Walks and Climbs in the Pyrenees 1978, Mountains of the Pyrenees 1982, The Visitor's Guide to Kent 1985, The Weald Way and Vanguard Way 1987, Walks in the Engadine 1988, The Valais 1988, Walking in Kent 1988, Classic Walks in the Pyrenees 1989, Classic Walks in Southern England 1989, The Jura 1989, South Downs Way 1989, Eye on the Hurricane 1989, The Mountains of Europe 1990, Visitors Guide to Kent 1990, The Cotswold Way 1990, Alpine Pass Route 1990, Classic Walks in the Alps 1991, Chamonix to Zermatt 1991, The Bernese Alps 1992, Walking in Ticino 1992, Central Switzerland 1993, Annapurna: A Trekkers' Guide 1993, Walking in Kent, Vol. II 1994, Everest: A Trekkers' Guide 1995, Langtang: A Trekkers Guide 1996, Tour of the Vanoise 1996, Walking in the Alps 1998, Kangchenjunga: A Trekkers' Guide 1999, Walking in Sussex 2000, 100 Hut Walks in the Alps 2000, Manaslu: A Trekkers' Guide 2000, The South Downs Way 2001, The North Downs Way 2001, The Ecrins National Park 2001, Tour of Mont Blanc 2002, The Pyrenees 2004, Alpine Points of View 2004; contrib. to The Great Outdoors, Climber and Hill Walker, Environment Now, Trail Walker, Country Walking, High, The Alpine Journal, The Observer. *Address:* Little Court Cottage, Froghole, Crockham Hill, Edenbridge, Kent, TN8 6TD, England. *E-mail:* kev.reynolds@virgin.net. *Website:* www.kevreynolds.co.uk.

REYNOLDS, Sheri, AB, MFA; American writer; *Ruth and Perry Morgan Chair of Southern Literature, Old Dominion University*; b. 29 Aug. 1967, Conway, SC. *Education:* Davidson Coll., Virginia Commonwealth Univ. *Career:* fmrly part-time instructor of English, Virginia Commonwealth Univ., Visiting Asst Prof. of English, Coll. of William and Mary; Ruth and Perry Morgan Chair. of Southern Literature, Dept of English, Old Dominion Univ. 2002–, currently Univ. Prof. of Creative Writing; mem. Authors' Guild. *Play:* Orabelle's Wheelbarrow (Women Playwrights' Initiative Award) 2005. *Publications:* Bitterroot Landing 1994, The Rapture of Canaan 1996, A Gracious Plenty 1997, The Firefly Cloak 2006. *Honours:* Outstanding Faculty Award, Rising Star Award, State Council for Higher Educ. of Virginia 2004, Virginia Commission for the Arts Individual Artist Fellowship 2005. *Address:* c/o Department of English, BAL 204, Old Dominion University, Norfolk, VA 23529, USA (office). *Telephone:* (757) 683-4770 (office). *E-mail:* SReynold@odu.edu (office). *Website:* www.sherireynolds.com.

REYNOLDS, Vernon, MA, PhD; British academic and writer; *Professor Emeritus, University of Oxford*; b. 14 Dec. 1935, Berlin, Germany; m. Frances Glover 1960; one s. one d. *Education:* Univs of London and Oxford. *Career:* academic, primatologist, studying chimpanzees in Uganda and teaching students, principally at Univ. of Oxford; Prof. Emer., Univ. of Oxford; Fellow Emer., Magdalen Coll. Oxford. *Publications:* Budongo: A Forest and its Chimpanzees 1965, The Apes 1967, The Biology of Human Action 1976, The Biology of Religion (with R. Tanner) 1983, Primate Behaviour: Information, Social Knowledge and the Evolution of Culture (with D. Quiatt) 1993, The Chimpanzees of the Budongo Forest 2005. *Honours:* Chairman's Award, Nat. Geographic Soc. 2000, President's Award, American Soc. of Primatologists 2000. *Address:* Orchard House, West Street, Alfriston, East Sussex, BN26 5UX, England (home). *Telephone:* (1323) 871136 (office). *E-mail:* vreynolds@btopenworld.com (home). *Website:* www.budongo.org.

REZA, (Evelyne Agnès) Yasmina; French novelist, dramatist, screenwriter and actress; b. 1 May 1959, Paris; d. of Jean Reza and of Nora Reza (née Heltaï); one s. one d. *Education:* Lycée de St-Cloud, Paris Univ. X, Nanterre, Ecole Jacques Lecoq. *Stage appearances include:* Le Malade imaginaire 1977, Antigone 1977, Un Sang fort 1977, La Mort de Gaspard Hauser 1978, L'An mil 1980, Le Piège de Méduse 1983, Le Veilleur de nuit 1986, Enorme changement de dernière minute 1989, La Fausse suivante 1990. *Plays directed include:* Birds in the Night 1979, Marie la louve 1981. *Plays written include:* Conversations après un enterrement (Molière Award for Best Author, Prix des Talents nouveaux de la Soc. des auteurs et compositeurs dramatiques, Johnson Foundation prize) 1987, La Traversée de l'hiver 1989, La Métamorphose (adaptation) 1988, 'Art' 1994, L'Homme du hasard 1995, Trois versions de la vie 2000, Une pièce espagnole 2004, Le Dieu du carnage 2007, Comment Vous Racontez la Partie 2011. *Screenplays written include:* Jusqu'à la nuit (also dir) 1984, Le Goûter chez Niels 1986, A demain 1992, Le Piquenique de Lulu Kreutz 2000. *Publications:* novels: Hammerklavier 1997, Une Désolation (trans. as Desolation) 1999, Adam Haberberg 2003, Nulle part 2005, Dans la luge d'Arthur Schopenhauer 2005; non-fiction: L'aube le soir ou la nuit (trans. as Dawn, Dusk or Night) 2007. *Honours:* Chevalier, Ordre des Arts et des Lettres; Prix du jeune théâtre Beatrix Dussane-André Roussin de l'Acad. française 1991. *Address:* c/o Marta Andras (Marton Play), 14 rue des Sablons, 75116 Paris, France.

REZVANI, Serge; Russian writer and artist; b. 1928, Tehran, Iran. *Publications include:* Les Années-lumière 1967, Les Années Lula 1968, Les Américanoïaques 1970, Coma 1970, La Voie de l'Amérique 1970, Mille aujourd'hui 1972, Feu 1973, Fokoulo 1974, Le Portrait Ovale 1976, Le Canard di doute 1979, Civagation sentimentale dans les Maures 1979, La Table d'asphalte, récits 1980, Le Testament amoureux 1981, La Loi humaine 1983, Variations sur les jours et les nuits 1985, La nuit transfigurée 1986, J'avais un ami 1987, Le 8e fiéau 1989, Phénix 1990, L'anti-portrait ovale 1991, La traversée des Monts Noirs 1992, Les repentirs du peintre 1993, L'énigme 1995, Fous d'échecs 1997, Un fait divers esthétique 1999, Le vol du feu 2000, L'éclipse 2003, Venise qui bouge 2004, Au bonheur des sphères 2006; poetry: Doubles stances des amants 1995, Élégies à Lula 1996. *Literary Agent:* c/o Dedalus Ltd, Langford Lodge, St Judith's Lane, Sawtry, Cambridgeshire PE28 5XE, England. *E-mail:* info@dedalusbooks.com. *Website:* www.dedalusbooks.com.

RHEINSBERG, Anna Rose Anette; German poet and essayist; b. 24 Sept. 1956, Berlin; d. of Joachim and Anneliese Puscheck Rheinsberg; m. 1st Matthias Hoffbauer 1975 (divorced 1979); m. 2nd Mischka Krahl Rheinsberg 1980; one s. *Education:* Friedrichs Gymnasium (Kassel) and Philipps Univ. (Marburg). *Career:* writer and ed.; acted in Anna experimental film, Austria 1980. *Publications:* fiction: Hannah 1982, Alles trutschen 1983, Wolfskuss 1984, Marthe und Ruth 1987, Herzlos 1988, Schwarzkittelweg 1995, Schau mich an 2000, Basco 2004; poetry: Marlene in den Gassen 1979, Bella Donna 1981, Annakonda 1985, Narcisse noir 1990; other: Liebe Hanna, Deine Anna. *Address:* c/o Edition Nautilus, Verlag Lutz Schulenberg, Alte Holstenstrasse 22, 21031 Hamburg, Germany (office). *E-mail:* info@edition-nautilus.de (office). *Website:* www.edition-nautilus.de (office).

RHODES, Richard Lee, BA; American writer; *Associate, Center for International Security and Cooperation, Stanford University*; b. 4 July 1937, Kansas City, Kan.; s. of Arthur Rhodes and Georgia Collier Rhodes; m. Ginger Untrif 1993; two c. by previous m. *Education:* East High School, Kansas City, Yale Univ. *Career:* Trustee, Atomic Heritage Foundation 2004–, Cypress Fund 2005–; Assoc., Center for Int. Security and Cooperation, Stanford Univ. *Play:* Reykjavik 2010. *Publications:* non-fiction: The Inland Ground: An Evocation of the American Middle West 1970, The Ozarks 1974, Looking for America: A Writer's Odyssey 1979, The Making of the Atomic Bomb (Nat. Book Critics' Circle Award for Gen. Non-fiction, Nat. Book Award for Non-fiction 1987, Pulitzer Prize for Non-fiction 1988) 1987, Farm: A Year in the Life of an American Farmer 1989, A Hole in the World: An American Boyhood 1990, Making Love: An Erotic Odyssey 1992, Nuclear Renewal: Common Sense about Energy 1993, Dark Sun: The Making of the Hydrogen Bomb 1995, How To Write 1995, Trying To Get Some Dignity: Stories of Triumph Over Childhood Abuse (with Ginger Rhodes) 1996, Deadly Feasts: Tracking the Secrets of a Terrifying New Plague 1997, Visions of Technology (ed) 1999, Why They Kill 1999, Masters of Death 2001, John James Audubon: The Making of an American (biog.) 2004, The Audubon Reader (ed) 2006, Arsenals of Folly: Nuclear Weapons in the Cold War 2007, The Twilight of the Bombs 2010, Hedy's Folly 2011; fiction: The Ungodly 1973, Holy Secrets 1978, The Last Safari 1980, Sons of Earth 1981. *Honours:* Hon. mem. American Nuclear Soc. 2001, Hon. DHumLitt (Westminster Coll., Fulton, Mo.) 1988; Hon. DLitt (Colby Coll., Me); Fellowships: John Simon Guggenheim Memorial Foundation 1974–75, Nat. Endowment for the Arts 1978, Ford Foundation 1981–83, Alfred P. Sloan Foundation 1985, 1993, 1995, 2001, 2010, MacArthur Foundation Program on Peace and Int. Co-operation 1990–91, 2008–09. *Literary Agent:* c/o Janklow & Nesbit Assocs, 455 Park Avenue, New York, NY 10021, USA. *Telephone:* (212) 421-1700. *Telephone:* (650) 560-9117 (office). *E-mail:* rhodes.today@comcast.net (office). *Website:* www.richardrhodes.com.

RI, Kai-sei, (Yi Hoe-song); South Korean writer; b. 1935, Kabata Shinoka. *Education:* Waseda Univ. *Career:* lives in Japan. *Publications include:* (titles translated) Towards the Peak of Our Youth (novel) 1969, The Woman at the Washing Block (novel) (Akutagawa Prize, Japan 1972) 1971.

RIBEIRO, João Ubaldo Osório Pimentel, LLB, MS; Brazilian writer and journalist; b. 23 Jan. 1941, Itaparica, Bahia; s. of Manoel Ribeiro and Maria Felipa Osório Pimentel Ribeiro; m. 1st Maria Beatriz Moreira Caldas 1962; m. 2nd Mônica Maria Roters 1971; m. 3rd Berenice de Carvalho Batella Ribeiro 1982; one s. three d. *Education:* Fed. Univ. of Bahia Law School and School of Admin. and Univ. of Southern California, USA. *Career:* Reporter, Jornal da Bahia, Salvador 1958–59, City Ed. and Columnist 1960–63; Chief Ed. Tribuna da Bahia 1968–73; Columnist O Globo, Rio de Janeiro, O Estado de São Paulo, São Paulo; Editorial-writer Folha de São Paulo 1969–73; Prof. of Political Science, Fed. Univ. of Bahia 1965–71, Catholic Univ of Bahia 1967–71; mem. Brazilian Acad. of Letters. *Publications:* novels: Setembro Não Tem Sentido 1968, Sargento Getúlio 1971, Vila Real 1980, Viva o Povo Brasileiro 1984, O Sorriso do Lagarto 1989, O Feitiço da Ilha do Pavão 1997, Miséria e Grandeza do Amor de Benedita 2000, Diário do Farol 2002; short stories: Vencecavalo e o Outro Povo 1973, Livro de Histórias 1983, Ein Brasilianer in Berlin (autobiog.) 1994, Você me mata, Mãe gentil 2004, A gente se acostuma a tudo 2006, O rei da noite 2008. *Honours:* Jabuti Prize (Brazilian Book Chamber) 1971, 1984; Golfinho de Ouro (Govt of Rio), Premio Camões 2008, and many other awards. *Address:* c/o Academia Brasileira de Letras, Av. Presidente Wilson 203, Castelo, CEP 20030-021, Rio de Janeiro RJ; c/o Editora Nova Fronteira SA, Rua Bambina 25, 22251-050 Rio de Janeiro, R.J.; Rua General Urquiza, 147/401, 22431-040 Rio de Janeiro, R.J., Brazil (home). *Telephone:* (21) 537-8770 (office); (21) 239-8528 (home). *Fax:* (21) 286-6755. *Website:* www.academia.org.br.

RIBMAN, Ronald Burt, BBA, MLitt, PhD; American dramatist; b. 28 May 1932, New York, NY; m. Alice Rosen 1967, one s. one d. *Education:* Brooklyn College, CUNY, University of Pittsburgh. *Career:* Asst Prof. of English, Otterbein College, 1962–63; Rockefeller Playwright-in-Residence, Public Theater, 1975; mem. Dramatists Guild. *Publications:* Harry, Noon and Night, 1965; The Journey of the Fifth Horse, 1966; The Ceremony of Innocence, 1967; Passing Through from Exotic Places, 1969; Fingernails Blue as Flowers, 1971; A Break in the Skin, 1972; The Poison Tree, 1976; Cold Storage, 1977; Buck, 1982; Seize the Day, 1985; The Cannibal Masque, 1988; The Rug Merchants of Chaos, 1991; Dream of the Red Spider, 1993. Contributions: films and television. *Honours:* Obie Award, 1966; Rockefeller Foundation Grants, 1966, 1968; Guggenheim Fellowship, 1970; National Endowment for the Arts Fellowship, 1973; Straw Hat Award, 1973; Elizabeth Hull-Kate Warriner Award, 1977; Drama Critics Award, 1977; Playwrights USA Award, 1984.

RICCI, Nino, BA, MA; Canadian writer; b. 23 Aug. 1959, Leamington; s. of Virginio Ricci and Amelia Ricci (née Ingratta); m. Erika de Vasconcelos 1997. *Education:* York Univ., Toronto, Concordia Univ., Montreal. *Career:* taught Creative Writing and Canadian Literature at Concordia Univ.; Pres. Canadian Centre, Int. PEN 1995–96; Writer in Residence, Univ. of Windsor 2005–06. *Publications:* Lives of the Saints (Books in Canada First Novel Award, Gov. Gen's Award for Fiction, Betty Trask Award, Winifred Holtby Prize for Best Regional Novel, F.G. Bressani Prize) 1990, In a Glass House 1993, Where She Has Gone 1997, Testament 2003 (Trillium Book Award), The Origin of Species (Gov. Gen's Award for Fiction, Canadian Authors Asscn Award) 2008. *Honours:* Alistair MacLeod Award for Literary Achievement. *Literary Agent:* c/o Anne McDermid & Associates, 83 Willcocks Street, Toronto, ON M5S 1C9, Canada. *Telephone:* (416) 324-8845. *Fax:* (416) 324-8870. *E-mail:* info@mcdermidagency.com. *Website:* www.mcdermidagency.com. *E-mail:* author@ninoricci.com (office). *Website:* www.ninoricci.com.

RICE, Anne, (Anne Rampling, A. N. Roquelaure), BA, MA; American writer; b. 4 Oct. 1941, New Orleans, La; m. Stan Rice 1961; one s. one d. (deceased). *Education:* Texas Women's Univ., San Francisco State Coll., Univ. of California, Berkeley. *Career:* mem. Authors' Guild. *Publications:* Interview with the Vampire 1976, The Feast of All Saints 1979, Cry to Heaven 1982, The Claiming of Sleeping Beauty (as A. N. Roquelaure) 1983, Beauty's Punishment (as A. N. Roquelaure) 1984, The Vampire Lestat 1985, Exit to Eden (as Anne Rampling) 1985, Beauty's Release (as A. N. Roquelaure) 1985, Belinda (as Anne Rampling) 1986, The Queen of the Damned 1988, The Mummy, or Ramses the Damned 1989, The Witching Hour 1990, The Tale of the Body Thief 1992, Lasher 1993, Taltos 1994, Memnoch the Devil 1995, Servant of the Bones 1996, Violin 1997, Pandora 1998, Armand 1998, Vittorio the Vampire 1999, Merrick 2000, Blood and Gold 2001, The Master of Rampling Gate (short story) 2002, Blackwood Farm 2002, Blood Canticle 2003, Christ the Lord: Out of Egypt 2005, Christ the Lord: The Road to Cana 2008, Called out of Darkness: A Spiritual Confession (auto-biog.) 2008, Angel Time: The Songs of the Seraphim 2009, The Wolf Gift 2012. *Address:* c/o Alfred A. Knopf Inc., 1745 Broadway, Suite B1, New York, NY 10019-4305, USA. *Website:* www.annerice.com.

RICE, Earle Wilmont, Jr; American writer; b. 21 Oct. 1928, Lynn, Mass; m. Georgia Joy Black Wood 1958 (died 2007); one s. one d. *Education:* San Jose City Coll., Foothill Coll., Los Altos. *Career:* mem. Soc. of Children's Book Writers and Illustrators, League of World War I Aviation Historians, Air Force Asscn, Disabled American Veterans. *Publications:* fiction: Tiger, Lion, Hawk 1977, The Animals 1979, Fear on Ice 1981, More Than Macho 1981, Death Angel 1981, The Gringo Dies at Dawn 1993; non-fiction: The Cuban Revolution 1995, The Battle of Britain 1996, The Battle of Midway 1996, The Inchon Invasion 1996, The Battle of Belleau Wood 1996, The Attack on Pearl Harbor 1996, The Tet Offensive 1996, The Nuremberg Trials 1996, The Salem Witch Trials 1996, The O. J. Simpson Trial 1996, The Final Solution 1997, Nazi War Criminals 1997, The Battle of the Little Bighorn 1997, Life Among the Great Plains Indians 1997, Life During the Crusades 1997, Life During the Middle Ages 1997, Kamikazes 1999, Strategic Battles of the Pacific 2000, Strategic Battles in Europe 2000, The Bombing of Pearl Harbor 2000, The Third Reich: Demise of the Nazi Dream 2000, The Cold War: Collapse of Communism 2000, Sir Francis Drake: Navigator and Pirate 2003, Normandy 2002, First Battle of the Marne 2002, The Battle of Gettysburg 2002, Claire Chennault, Flying Tiger 2003, Manfred von Richthofen The Red Baron 2003, George S. Patton 2004, Erwin J. E. Rommel 2004, Douglas MacArthur 2004, Korea 1950: Pusan to Chosin 2004, Point of No Return: Tonkin Gulf and the Vietnam War 2004, Alexandra David-Néel: Explorer at the Roof of the World 2004, Great Military Leaders (series ed.) 2004, Ulysses S. Grant: Defender of the Union 2005, Robert E. Lee: First Soldier of the Confederacy 2005, Empire in the East: The Story of Genghis Khan 2005, Adolf Hitler and Nazi Germany 2006, The U.S. Army and Military Careers 2006, The Life and Times of Sir Walter Raleigh 2007, The Life and Times of John Cabot 2007, A Brief Political and Geographic History of Latin America 2008, Canaletto 2008, Blitzkrieg! Hitler's Lightning War 2008, Overview of the Korean War 2009, Overview of the Persian Gulf War, 1990 2009, The Life and Times of Erik the Red 2009, The Life and Times of Leif Eriksson 2009, The Brothers Custer: Galloping to Glory 2009, FDR and the New Deal 2010, Eleanor of Aquitaine 2010, Clovis, King of the Franks 2010, Attila the Hun 2010, The Battle of Marathon 2011; adaptations: Dracula 1995, All Quiet on the Western Front 1995, The Grapes of Wrath 1996; contrib. to California Today, Calliope, PSA Magazine, Pro/Am Hockey Review. *Honours:* Second Place, Children's Book Chapters Category 1993, Third Place 1994, Ninth Hon. Mention Novel Chapter 1994, All in Florida Freelance Writers' Asscn Florida State Writing Competition. *Address:* PO Box 2131, Julian, CA 92036-2131, USA (home). *Telephone:* (760) 765-2854 (office). *E-mail:* ericejr@sbcglobal.net (home).

RICH, Elaine Sommers, BA, MA; American writer and poet; b. 8 Feb. 1926, Plevna, Ind.; m. Ronald L. Rich 1953; three s. one d. *Education:* Goshen Coll., Michigan State Univ. *Career:* instructor, Goshen Coll. 1947–49, 1950–53, Bethel Coll., North Newton, KS 1953–66; Lecturer, Int. Christian Univ., Tokyo 1971–78; columnist, Mennonite Weekly Review 1973–2010; Adviser to Int. Students, Bluffton Coll., OH 1979–89; Adjunct Prof. of English, Univ. of Findlay, OH 1990–95, Owens Community Coll. 1995–97; mem. Fellowship of Reconciliation, Int. League for Peace and Freedom. *Publications:* Breaking Bread Together (ed.) 1958, Hannah Elizabeth 1964, Tomorrow, Tomorrow, Tomorrow 1966, Am I This Countryside? 1981, Mennonite Women 1683–1983: A Story of God's Faithfulness 1983, Spiritual Elegance: A Biography of Pauline Krehbiel Raid 1987, Prayers for Everyday 1990, Walking Together in Faith (ed.) 1993, Pondered in Her Heart 1998; contrib. to books and journals. *Address:* 327 S Jackson, Bluffton, OH 45817, USA.

RICH, Frank Hart, Jr, BA; American journalist and critic; b. 2 June 1949, Washington, DC; s. of Frank Hart Rich and Helene Aaronson; m. 1st Gail Winston 1976; two s.; m. 2nd Alexandra Rachelle Witchel 1991. *Education:* Harvard Univ. *Career:* Film Critic and Sr Ed. New Times Magazine 1973–75; Film Critic, New York Post 1975–77; Film and TV Critic, Time Magazine 1977–80; Chief Drama Critic, New York Times 1980–93, Op-Ed. Columnist 1994–, also Sr Adviser to Culture Ed.; Assoc. Fellow, Jonathan Edwards Coll., Yale Univ. 1998–. *Publications:* Hot Seat: Theater Criticism for the New York Times 1980–93 1998, Ghost Light 2000, The Greatest Story Ever Sold 2006. *Address:* The New York Times, 620 Eighth Avenue, New York, NY 10018, USA (office). *Website:* topics.nytimes.com/top/opinion/editorialsandoped/oped/columnists/frankrich/index.html (office).

RICH, Robert R., BA, MD; American microbiologist, immunologist and writer; *Editor-in-Chief, Journal of Immunology*. *Education:* Oberlin Coll. OH, Univ. of Kansas School of Medicine, Univ. of Washington School of Medicine, Seattle, Nat. Insts of Health, Harvard Medical School. *Career:* Asst Prof, then Assoc. Prof. 1973–78, Head of Immunology section 1977–98, Prof. 1978–95, Vice-Pres. and Dean of Research 1990–98, Distinguished Service Prof. 1995–98, Microbiology and Immunology and Medicine, Baylor Coll. of Medicine; mem. of Immunobiology Study Section, Nat. Insts of Health 1977–81; Investigator, Howard Hughes Medical Inst. 1977–91; Advisory Ed., The Journal of Experimental Medicine 1981–84; mem., Transplantation Biology and Immunology Sub-cttee 1982–86, chair. 1984–86 NIAID; Assoc. Ed., The Journal of Infectious Diseases 1983–88; mem. 1984–88, chair. 1986–88, Nat. Research Cttee for Arthritis Foundation; mem. of bd of dirs 1988–93, chair. 1991, American Board of Allergy and Immunology; editiorial bd mem., The Journal of Clinical Immunology 1989–96; mem. 1989–94, chair. 1993–94, Nat. Multiple Sclerosis Soc. Research Programs Advisory Cttee; mem. of bd of dirs, American Board of Internal Medicine 1990–93; Section Ed. and Deputy Ed. 1991–2002, Ed.-in-Chief 2003–, The Journal of Immunology; mem. of cttee on public affairs 1993–2000, chair. 1994–2000, American Asscn of Immunologists; pres., Clinical Immunology Soc. 1995; mem. of bd of dirs 1998–, pres. and chair. 2001–02, FASEB; Exec. Assoc., Dean/Research and Strategic Initiatives 1998–, Prof. of Medicine, Microbiology and Immunology 1998–, Emory Univ. School of Medicine; Vice-Pres., American Acad. of Allergy, Asthma and Immunology. *Publications:* over 200 publications (some collaborative). *Address:* Journal of Immunology, 9650 Rockville Pike, Bethesda, MD

20814-3998, USA (office). *Telephone:* (301) 634-7197 (office). *Fax:* (301) 634-7829 (office). *E-mail:* infoji@aai.org (office). *Website:* www.jimmunol.org (office).

RICHARDS, David Adams, CM, ONB; Canadian writer and academic; b. 17 Oct. 1950, Newcastle, NB. *Education:* St Thomas Univ., NB. *Career:* Artist in Residence, St Thomas Univ. 2011–. *Screenplays include:* Small Gifts, For Those Who Hunt the Wounded Down. *Publications:* The Coming of Winter 1974, Blood Ties 1976, Dancers at Night 1978, Lives of Short Duration 1981, Road to the Stilt House 1985, Nights Below Station Street (Governor-General's Award) 1988, Evening Snow Will Bring Such Peace 1990, For Those Who Hunt the Wounded Down 1993, Hockey Dreams: Memories of a Man Who Couldn't Play 1996, Lines on the Water: A Fisherman's Life on the Miramichi (Governor-General's Award) 1998, The Bay of Love and Sorrows 1998, Mercy Among the Children (Giller Prize, Canadian Booksellers Asscn Libris Award) 2000, River of the Brokenhearted 2004, The Friends of Meager Fortune 2006, The Lost Highway 2007, God Is 2009, Incidents in the Life of Markus Paul 2011, Facing the Hunter 2011. *Honours:* Canada Authors Asscn Literary Award 1991, Canada-Australian Literary Award 1992, Matt Cohen Award 2011. *Address:* George Martin Hall, Room 303 A, St Thomas University, Fredericton, NB E3B 5G3, Canada. *E-mail:* darich@stu.ca. *Website:* w3.stu.ca/stu/academic/artist_residence/default.aspx.

RICHARDS, Hubert John, STL, LSS; British academic and writer; b. 25 Dec. 1921, Weilderstadt, Germany; m. 1975, one s. one d. *Education:* Gregorian University, Rome, Biblical Institute, Rome. *Career:* mem. Norfolk Theological Society. *Publications:* The First Christmas: What Really Happened? 1973, The Miracles of Jesus: What Really Happened? 1975, The First Easter: What Really Happened? 1977, Death and After: What Will Really Happen? 1979, What Happens When You Pray? 1980, Pilgrim to the Holy Land 1985, Focus on the Bible 1990, The Gospel According to St Paul 1990, God's Diary 1991, Pilgrim to Rome 1994, Quips and Quotes 1997, Anthology for the Church Year 1998, Philosophy of Religion 1998, The Bible: What Does It Really Say? 1999, Who's Who and What's What in the Bible 1999, More Quips and Quotes 2000, Jesus: Who Did He Think He Was? 2000, The Bible: 150 Readings 2001; contrib. of regular articles and reviews in various publications. *Address:* 59 Park Lane, Norwich, Norfolk NR2 3EF, England.

RICHARDS, Leigh (see King, Laurie R.)

RICHARDSON, James, AB, PhD; American poet and academic; *Professor of English and Creative Writing, Princeton University*; b. 1 Jan. 1950, Bradenton, Fla; s. of James E. Richardson and Betty Richardson (née Behrer); m. Constance Walter Hassett; two d. *Education:* Princeton Univ., Univ. of Virginia. *Career:* joined faculty at Princeton Univ. 1980, currently Prof. of English and Creative Writing, Lewis Center for the Arts. *Publications:* poetry collections: Reservations 1977, Second Guesses 1984, As If 1992, How Things Are 2000, Vectors: Aphorisms and Ten-Second Essays 2001, Interglacial: New and Selected Poems and Aphorisms 2004, By the Numbers: Poems and Aphorisms 2010; literary criticism: Thomas Hardy: The Poetry of Necessity 1977, Vanishing Lives: Tennyson, Rossetti, Swinburne and Yeats 1988; contrib. poems and aphorisms in anthologies and journals including Slate, The New Yorker, Paris Review, Best American Poetry, Poetry Daily, 2010 Pushcart Prize Anthology and Geary's Guide to the World's Great Aphorists. *Honours:* fellowships from Nat. Endowment for the Humanities and New Jersey State Council on the Arts, American Acad. of Arts and Letters Award in Literature, Poetry Soc. of America Robert H. Winner, Cecil Hemley and Emily Dickinson Awards, Jackson Poetry Prize 2011. *Address:* Lewis Center for the Arts, New South Building, Floor 6, McCosh Hall, Princeton University, Princeton, NJ 08544, USA (office). *Telephone:* (609) 258-3775 (office). *E-mail:* jrich@princeton.edu (office). *Website:* www.princeton.edu/arts/lewis_center (office).

RICHARDSON, Keith, MA; British writer, administrator and fmr journalist; b. 14 June 1936, Wakefield, Yorks.; s. of Gilbert Richardson and Ellen Richardson; m. Sheila Carter 1958; three d. *Education:* Wakefield Grammar School, Univ. Coll., Oxford. *Career:* feature writer, The Financial Times 1960–63; Industrial Ed. and European Corresp. The Sunday Times 1964–68, 1970–83; Production Man. GKN 1969–70; Head of Group Public Affairs, BAT Industries 1983–88; Sec.-Gen. The European Round Table of Industrialists 1988–98; Trustee, Friends of Europe. *Publications:* Monopolies and Mergers 1963, Do it the Hard Way 1971, Daggers in the Forum 1978, Reshaping Europe 1991, Beating the Crisis 1993, Europe Made Simple 1998. *Address:* c/o Friends of Europe, La Maison de l'Europe at the Bibliotheque Solvay, Leipoldpark, 137 Rue Belliard, 1040 Brussels, Belgium (office).

RICHARDSON, Robert Dale, Jr, AB, PhD; American academic and writer; b. 14 June 1934, Milwaukee, WI; m. 1st Elizabeth Hall 1959 (divorced 1987); m. 2nd Annie Dillard 1988; three d. *Education:* Harvard Univ. *Career:* instructor, Harvard Univ. 1961–63; Asst Prof. 1963–68, Assoc. Prof. 1968–72, Chair Dept of English 1968–73, Prof. of English 1972–87, Assoc. Dean for Graduate Studies 1975–76, Univ. of Denver; Assoc. Ed. 1967–76, 1983–87, Book Review Ed. 1976–83, Denver Quarterly; Visiting Fellow, Huntington Library 1973–74; Visiting Prof., Queens Coll. and Graduate School and Univ. Center, CUNY 1978, Sichuan Univ., People's Republic of China 1983; Prof. of English, Univ. of Colorado 1987; Visiting Lecturer, Yale Univ. 1989; Visiting Prof. of Letters 1990, Adjunct Prof. of Letters 1993–94, Wesleyan Univ.; Assoc. Fellow, Calhoun Coll., Yale Univ. 1997–; mem. American Studies Asscn, Asscn of Literary Scholars and Critics, Authors' Guild, Emerson Soc., Melville Soc., Soc. of American Historians, Soc. for Eighteenth Century Studies, Thoreau Soc. *Publications:* Literature and Film 1969, The Rise of Modern Mythology, 1680–1860 (with B. Feldman) 1972, Myth and Literature in the American Renaissance 1978, Henry Thoreau: A Life of the Mind 1986, Ralph Waldo Emerson: Selected Essays, Lectures and Poems (ed.) 1990, Emerson: The Mind on Fire 1995, Three Centuries of American Poetry (with Allen Mandelbaum) 1999, William James: In the Maelstrom of American Modernism 2006, First we Read, Then we Write: Emerson and the Creative Process 2009; contrib. to scholarly books and journals. *Honours:* Hon. DHumLitt (Meadville Lombard Theological School) 2003, (Univ. of Denver) 2008; Melcher Prizes 1986, 1995, Guggenheim Fellowship 1990, Francis Parkman Prize 1995, Washington Irving Award for Literary Excellence 1995, Dictionary of Literary Biography Award for a Distinguished Literary Biography 1995, New York Times Book Review Notable Book Citation 1995, American Acad. of Arts and Letters Special Award in Literature 1998, Emerson Soc. Prize 2001, Thoreau Soc. Distinguished Achievement Award 2001, Bancroft Prize 2007. *Address:* 143 W Margaret Lane, Hillsborough, NC 27278, USA (home). *E-mail:* rrichardson@aol.com (home).

RICHIE, Donald Steiner, PhD; American critic and writer; *Arts Critic, The Japan Times*; b. 17 April 1924, Lima, OH; m. Mary Evans 1961 (divorced 1965). *Education:* Antioch Coll., US Maritime Acad., Columbia Univ. *Career:* film critic, Pacific Stars and Stripes, Tokyo 1947–49; arts critic, Saturday Review of Literature, New York 1950–51, The Nation, New York 1959–61, Newsweek Magazine, New York 1973–76, Time Magazine 1997; film critic, Japan Times, Tokyo 1953–69, literary critic 1972–03, arts critic 1975–; Lecturer in American Literature, Waseda Univ., Tokyo 1954–59; Curator of Film, Museum of Modern Art, New York 1968–73; Toyoda Chair, Univ. of Michigan 1993; Lecturer in Film, Temple Univ., Tokyo 1996–; directed numerous avant-garde 16mm films during 1960s. *Films:* A Donald Richie Film Anthology (films directed 1962–68, on DVD). *Publications:* Where Are the Victors? (novel) 1956, The Japanese Film: Art and Industry (with Joseph L. Anderson) 1959, The Japanese Movie: An Illustrated History 1965, The Films of Akira Kurosawa 1965, Companions of the Holiday (novel) 1968, George Stevens: An American Romantic 1970, The Inland Sea 1971, Japanese Cinema 1971, Three Modern Kyogen 1972, Ozu: The Man and his Films 1974, Ji: Signs and Symbols of Japan (with Mana Maeda) 1975, The Japanese Tattoo 1980, Zen Inklings: Some Stories, Fables, Parables, Sermons and Prints with Notes and Commentaries 1982, A Taste of Japan: Food Fact and Fable, What the People Eat, Customs and Etiquette 1985, Viewing Film 1986, Introducing Tokyo 1987, A Lateral View 1987, Different People: Pictures of Some Japanese 1987, Tokyo Nights 1988, Japanese Cinema: An Introduction 1990, The Honorable Visitors 1994, Partial Views 1995, The Temples of Kyoto 1995, Lafcadio Hearn's Japan: An Anthology of his Writings on the Country and its People (ed.) 1997, The Memoirs of the Warrior Kumagai 1999, Tokyo: A View of the City 1999, A Hundred Years of Japanese Film: A Short History and a Selective Guide to Videos and DVDs 2001, The Donald Richie Reader: Fifty Years of Writing on Japan (ed. by Arturo Silva) 2001, The Image Factory: Fads and Fashions in Japan 2003, Japanese Literature Reviewed 2003, Tokyo Story: The Script 2003, A View from the Chuo Line and Other Stories 2004, The Japan Journals 2004, A Tractate on Japanese Aesthetics 2007, Travels in the East 2008. *Honours:* Citations from Govt of Japan 1963, 1970, 1983, Citation from US Nat. Soc. of Film Critics 1970, Kawakita Memorial Foundation Award 1983, Presidential Citation New York Univ. 1989, San Francisco Film Festival Novikoff Award 1990, Tokyo Metropolitan Govt Cultural Award 1993, John D. Rockefeller III Award 1994, Japan Foundation Prize 1995, Japan Soc. Award, New York 2001, Order of the Rising Sun (Gold Rays), Japan 2004; Dr hc (Univ. of Maryland) 1999, (Bard Coll.) 2004, (Temple Univ.) 2007. *Address:* Ueno 2, 12.18 (804), Taito-ku, Tokyo 110 0005, Japan.

RICHTER, Harvena, BA, MA, PhD; American academic (retd), writer and poet; b. 13 March 1919, Reading, Pa. *Education:* University of New Mexico, New York University. *Career:* Lecturer, New York University 1955–66, University of New Mexico 1969–89; mem. Authors' Guild. *Publications:* The Human Shore 1959, Virginia Woolf: The Inward Voyage 1970, Writing to Survive: The Private Notebooks of Conrad Richter 1988, The Yaddo Elegies and Other Poems 1995, Green Girls: Poems Early and Late 1996, The Innocent Island 1999, Frozen Light: The Crystal Poems 2002, The Golden Fountains: Sources of Energy and Life 2002; contributions: magazines and newspapers. *Honours:* grants and fellowships. *Address:* 1932 Candelaria Road NW, Albuquerque, NM 87107-2855, USA (home). *Telephone:* (505) 344-6766 (home).

RICKS, Sir Christopher Bruce, Kt, BA, BLitt, MA, FBA; British academic and writer; *Warren Professor of the Humanities, Boston University*; b. 18 Sept. 1933, London; s. of James Bruce Ricks and Gabrielle Roszak; m. 1st Kirsten Jensen 1956 (divorced 1975); two s. two d.; m. 2nd Judith Aronson 1977; one s. two d. *Education:* King Alfred's School, Wantage, Oxon., Balliol Coll., Oxford. *Career:* 2nd Lt Green Howards 1952; Andrew Bradley Jr Research Fellow, Balliol Coll. Univ. of Oxford 1957, Fellow, Worcester Coll. 1958–68; Prof. of English, Bristol Univ. 1968–75; Fellow, Christ's Coll., Prof. of English, Univ. of Cambridge 1975–86, King Edward VII Prof. of English Literature 1982–86; Prof. of English, Boston Univ. 1986–98, Warren Prof. of the Humanities 1998–, Co-Dir Editorial Inst. 1999–; Prof. of Poetry, Univ. of Oxford 2004–09; Visiting Prof., Univ. of California, Berkeley and Stanford Univ. 1965, Smith Coll. 1967, Harvard Univ. 1971, Wesleyan 1974, Brandeis 1977, 1981, 1984, USA; Distinguished Visiting Fellow in Residence, Columbia Univ. 2006; Vice-

Pres. Tennyson Soc.; Fellow, American Acad. of Arts and Sciences 1991. *Publications:* Milton's Grand Style 1963, Tennyson 1972, Keats and Embarrassment 1974, The Force of Poetry 1984, T. S. Eliot and Prejudice 1988, Beckett's Dying Words 1993, Essays in Appreciation 1996, Reviewery 2002, Allusion to the Poets 2002, Decisions and Revisions in T. S. Eliot 2003, Dylan's Visions of Sin 2003, True Friendship: Geoffrey Hill, Anthony Hecht and Robert Lowell under the Sign of Eliot and Pound 2010; editor: Poems and Critics: An Anthology of Poetry and Criticism from Shakespeare to Hardy 1966, A. E. Housman: A Collection of Critical Essays 1968, Alfred Tennyson: Poems 1842 1968, John Milton: Paradise Lost and Paradise Regained 1968, The Poems of Tennyson 1969, The Brownings: Letters and Poetry 1970, English Poetry and Prose 1540–1674 1970, English Drama to 1710 1971, Selected Criticism of Matthew Arnold 1972, The State of the Language (with Leonard Michaels) 1980, The New Oxford Book of Victorian Verse 1987, Collected Poems and Selected Prose of A. E. Housman 1988, The Faber Book of America (with William Vance) 1992, Inventions of the March Hare: Poems 1909–1917 by T. S. Eliot 1996, The Oxford Book of English Verse 1999, Selected Poems of James Henry 2002, Samuel Menashe: New and Selected Poems (ed.) 2006; contribs to professional journals. *Honours:* Hon. Fellow, Balliol Coll. 1989, Worcester Coll. 1990, Christ's Coll. Cambridge 1993; Hon. DLitt (Oxford) 1998, (Bristol) 2003; George Orwell Memorial Prize 1979; Beefeater Club Prize for Literature 1980, Distinguished Achievement Award Andrew W. Mellon Foundation 2004. *Address:* 143 Bay State Road, Boston, MA 02215 (office); 39 Martin Street, Cambridge, MA 02138, USA (home); Lasborough Cottage, Lasborough Park, Tetbury, Glos., GL8 8UF, England (home). *Telephone:* (617) 358-2895 (USA) (office); (617) 354-7887 (USA) (home); (1666) 890252 (England) (home). *E-mail:* cricks@bu.edu (home).

RIDE, Sally, PhD; American scientist, academic and fmr astronaut; *Hibben Professor of Space Science, University of California, San Diego;* b. 26 May 1951, Los Angeles; d. of Dale Ride and Joyce Ride; m. Steven Hawley (divorced). *Education:* Westlake High School, Los Angeles and Stanford Univ. *Career:* astronaut trainee, NASA 1978–79, astronaut 1979–87; on-orbit capsule communicator STS-2 mission, Johnson Space Center, NASA, Houston; on-orbit capsule communicator STS-3 mission NASA, mission specialist STS-7 1983; Scientific Fellow, Stanford Univ. 1987–89; Dir Calif. Space Inst., Univ. of Calif. at San Diego 1989–96, Prof. of Physics 1989–; Pres. Space.com 1999–2000; co-founder Imaginary Lines Inc., Pres. 2000–; mem. Presidential Comm. on Space Shuttle 1986, Presidential Comm. of Advisers on Science and Tech. 1994–; mem. Bd of Dirs Apple Computer Inc. 1988–90. *Publications:* To Space and Back (with Susan Okie) 1986, Voyager: An Adventure to the Edge of the Solar System (with Tam O'Shaughnessy) 1992, The Third Planet: Exploring the Earth from Space (with Tam O'Shaughnessy) 1994, The Mystery of Mars 1999, Exploring Our Solar System (with Tam O'Shaughnessy) 2003, Space (with Mike Goldsmith) 2005. *Honours:* Jefferson Award for Public Service, von Braun Award, Lindbergh Eagle, two Nat. Space Flight Medal. *Address:* California Space Institute, 9500 Gilman Drive, Dept 0524, University of California at San Diego, La Jolla, CA 92093-0524, USA (office). *Telephone:* (619) 534-5827 (office). *Fax:* (619) 822-1277 (office). *Website:* www.calspace.ucsd.edu (office).

RIDLEY, Matt, BA, DPhil; British business executive and fmr journalist and writer; b. 1958, Newcastle upon Tyne, England; m. Anya Hurlbert; two c. *Education:* Univ. of Oxford. *Career:* Science Ed. and American Ed., The Economist 1983–92; columnist, Sunday Telegraph, Daily Telegraph 1993–2000; Chair., Int. Centre for Life, Newcastle upon Tyne 1996–2003; Chair., Northern 2 VCT 1999–2008; Chair., Northern Rock plc 2004–07; Dir, Northern Investors Co. plc 1994–2007. *Publications:* The Red Queen: Sex and the Evolution of Human Nature 1993, The Origins of Virtue: Human Instincts and the Evolution of Co-operation 1997, Genome: The Autobiography of a Species in 23 Chapters 2000, Nature via Nurture: Genes, Experience and What Makes us Human 2004, Francis Crick: Discoverer of the Genetic Code (Davis Prize, American History of Science Soc. 2007) 2006, The Rational Optimist: How Prosperity Evolves 2010; contrib. articles and book reviews in The Times, Guardian, TLS, New Statesman, TIME, Newsweek, New York Times, Wall Street Journal, Atlantic Monthly, Discover, Natural History. *Address:* c/o Fourth Estate, 77–85 Fulham Palace Road, London, W6 8JB, England (office). *Website:* www.rationaloptimist.com.

RIDPATH, Ian William, FRAS; British writer, broadcaster and lecturer; b. 1 May 1947, Ilford, Essex, England. *Career:* fmrly worked at Univ. of London Observatory; Fellow, Royal Astronomical Soc. (Council mem. 2004–07); mem. Soc. of Authors, Asscn of British Science Writers. *Publications include:* Worlds Beyond 1975, Encyclopedia of Astronomy and Space (ed.) 1976, Messages From the Stars 1978, Stars and Planets 1978, Young Astronomer's Handbook 1981, Hamlyn Encyclopedia of Space 1981, Life Off Earth 1983, Collins Guide to Stars and Planets 1984, Gem Guide to the Night Sky 1985, Secrets of the Sky 1985, A Comet Called Halley 1985, Concise Handbook of Astronomy 1986, Longman Illustrated Dictionary of Astronomy and Astronautics 1987, Monthly Sky Guide 1987, Go Skywatching 1987, Star Tales 1989, Norton's Star Atlas (ed.) 1989, Pocket Guide to Astronomy 1990, Book of the Universe 1991, Atlas of Stars and Planets 1992, Oxford Dictionary of Astronomy (ed.) 1997, Eyewitness Handbook of Stars and Planets 1998, Gem Stars 1999, Collins Encyclopedia of the Universe (Gen. Ed.) 2001, The Times Space 2002, The Times Universe 2004, Astronomy Eyewitness Companion 2006, Exploring Stars & Planets 2011. *Address:* 48 Otho Court, Brentford Dock, Brentford, Middx, TW8 8PY, England (home). *E-mail:* ian@ianridpath.com (office). *Website:* www.ianridpath.com.

RIDPATH, Michael William Gerrans; British author; b. 7 March 1961, Exeter, Devon, England; m. Barbara Nunemaker 1994; one s. two d. *Education:* Merton Coll., Oxford. *Career:* fmr credit analyst and bond trader, Saudi International Bank; joined venture capital firm, Apax Partners 1991–96; full-time writer 1996–; mem. Soc. of Authors, CWA (Vice-Chair.), People of Today. *Publications:* Free to Trade 1995, Trading Reality 1996, The Marketmaker 1998, Final Venture 2000, The Predator 2001, Fatal Error 2003, On the Edge 2005, See No Evil 2006, Where the Shadows Lie 2010, Edge of Nowhere 2011. *Literary Agent:* c/o Oliver Munson, Blake Friedmann, 122 Arlington Road, London NW1 7HP, England. *Telephone:* (20) 7284-0408. *Fax:* (20) 7284-0442. *Website:* www.blakefriedmann.co.uk. *E-mail:* comments@michaelridpath.com (office). *Website:* www.michaelridpath.com.

RIFBJERG, Klaus; Danish author; *Adjunct Professor of Languages, Copenhagen Business School;* b. 15 Dec. 1931, Copenhagen; s. of Thorvald Rifbjerg and Lilly Nielsen; m. Inge Merete Gerner 1955; one s. two d. *Education:* Princeton Univ., USA and Univ. of Copenhagen. *Career:* Literary Critic, Information 1955–57, Politiken 1959–65 (Copenhagen daily newspapers); Literary Dir Gyldendal Publrs 1984–92, mem. Bd of Dirs 1992–98; Prof. of Aesthetics, Laererhøjskole, Copenhagen 1986; Adjunct Prof. of Languages, Copenhagen Business School 2003–; Grant of Honour from the Danish Dramatists 1966, Grant of Honour from the Danish Writers' Guild 1973. *Publications include:* novels: Den Kroniske Uskyld 1958, Operaelsken 1966, Arkivet 1967, Lonni Og Karl 1968, Anna (Jeg) Anna 1970, Marts 1970 1970, Leif den Lykkelige JR. 1971, Til Spanien 1971, Lena Jorgensen, Klintevej 4, 2650 Hvidovre 1971, Brevet til Gerda 1972, R.R. 1972, Spinatfuglene 1973, Dilettanterne 1973, Du skal ikke vaere ked af det Amalia 1974, En hugorm i solen 1974, Vejen ad hvilken 1975, Tak for turen 1975, Kiks 1976, Twist 1976, Et Bortvendt Ansigt 1977, Tango 1978, Dobbeltgœnger 1978, Drengene 1978, Joker 1979, Voksdugshjertet 1979, Det sorte hul 1980, De hellige aber 1981, Maend og Kvinder 1982, Jus 1982, En omvej til Klostret 1983, Falsk Forår 1984, Borte tit 1986, Engel 1987, Rapsodi i blåt 1991, Divertimento i mol 1996, Billedet 1999, Regnvejr 2001, Nansen og Johansen 2002; short stories: Og Andre Historier 1964, Rejsende 1969, Den Syende Jomfru 1972, Sommer 1974, Det. Svage Køn 1989; non-fiction: I Medgang Og Modgang 1970, Deres Majestæt! 1977; plays: Gris Pa Gaflen 1962, Hva Skal Vi Lave 1963, Udviklinger 1965, Hvad en Mand Har Brug For 1966, Voks 1968, Ar 1970, Narrene 1971, Svaret Blaeser i Vinden 1971, Det Korte af det lange 1976; poems: Livsfrisen 1979 and several other vols of poetry; 20 radio plays, essays, several film and TV scripts. *Honours:* Dr hc (Lund) 1991, (Odense) 1996; Aarestrup Medal 1964, Danish Critics' Award 1965, Danish Acad. Award 1966, Golden Laurels 1967, Soren Gyldendal Award 1969, Nordic Council Award 1970, PH Prize 1979, Holberg Medal 1979, H. C. Andersen Prize 1988, Johannes V. Jensen Prize 1998, Prize for Nordic Writers, Swedish Acad. 1999, Danish Publicists' Award 2001, Danish Language Soc. Award 2001. *Address:* c/o Gyldendal, 3 Klareboderne, 1001 Copenhagen, Denmark (office). *E-mail:* gyldendal@gyldendal.dk (office). *Website:* www.gyldendal.dk (office).

RIGGS, David (see Pigott, Mark)

RIIS, Povl, MD, DM, FRCP; Danish physician, academic and editor; *Chairman, AgeForum;* b. 28 Dec. 1925, Copenhagen; s. of Lars Otto Riis and Eva Elisabeth Riis (née Erdmann); m. Else Harne 1954 (died 1997); one s. three d. *Education:* Univ. of Copenhagen. *Career:* specialist in internal medicine 1960, gastroenterology 1963; Head of Medical Dept B, Gentofte Univ. Hosp. 1963–76; Prof. of Internal Medicine, Univ. of Copenhagen 1974–96, Vice-Dean Faculty of Medicine 1979–82; Head of Gastroenterological Dept C, Herlev Co. Hosp. 1976–96; Asst Ed. Journal of the Danish Medical Asscn 1957–67, Chief Ed. 1967–90; Ed. Bibliothek for Laeger 1965–90, Danish Medical Bulletin 1968–90, Nordic Medicine 1984–91; mem. Bd, Danish Soc. for Internal Medicine 1962–67, Danish Anti-Cancer League 1970–75, Danish Soc. for Theoretical and Applied Therapy 1972–77, Int. Union against Cancer 1978–86; mem. Danish Medical Research Council 1968–74, Chair. 1972–74; mem. Danish Science Advisory Bd 1972–74, Co-Chair. 1974; mem. Nordic Scientific Co-ordination Cttee for Medicine 1968–72, Chair. 1970–72; Vice-Pres. European Science Foundation (ESF) 1974–77, mem. Exec. Council 1977–83; mem. Council for Int. Org. of Medical Sciences Advisory Cttee 1977; mem. Trustees Foundation of 1870 1976, Trier-Hansen Foundation 1977–, Hartmann Prize Cttee 1986–2002, Buhl Olesen Foundation 1982–, Madsen Foundation 1978–, Jakobsen Foundation 1989–, Brinch Foundation 1990–96; Chair. Danish Central Scientific-Ethical Cttee 1979–98, Nat. Medical Bd Danish Red Cross 1985–94, Int. Org. of Inflammatory Bowel Diseases 1986–89; Danish Foreign Office del. Helsinki negotiations, Hamburg 1980; mem. Nuffield Foundation Working Party on Ethics 1999–2002, Ethical Collegial Council, Ethical Collegial Council, Danish Medical Asscn 2000–03; mem. Medical Advisory Bd NetDoktor 1999–; mem. Int. Cttee of Medical Journal Eds 1980–90, Editorial Bd, Acta Medica Scandinavica, Journal Int. Medicine 1980, Ethics Bd, Danish Medical Asscn 1980–82, WHO European Advisory Cttee for Medical Research 1980–85, Scientific Bd, Danish Nat. Encyclopaedia 1991–2001, Editorial Bd JAMA 1994–; Chair. Nat. Center for First Aid and Health Promotion 1991, AeldreForum (AgeForum) 1996–, Bd Epidemiological Research, Univ. of Århus 2004–; mem. Preid. Cttee Foundation of Psychiatry 1996–. *Television:* several contribs to Danish Broadcasting System for radio and TV. *Publications include:* contrib.: Handbook of

Scientific Methodology (in Danish) 1971–, World Medical Association Helsinki Declaration 1975, We Shall All Die – But How? (in Danish) 1977; author: Handbook of Internal Medicine (in Danish) 1968, Grenzen der Forschung 1980, Community and Ethics (in Danish) 1984, Medical Ethics (in Danish) 1985, Ethical Issues in Preventive Medicine 1985, Bearing and Perspective 1988, Face Death 1989, Ethics in Health Education 1990, The Future of Medical Journals 1991, Research on Man: Ethics and Law 1991, Scientific Misconduct – Good Scientific Practice 1992, The Culture of General Education 1996, Drugs and Pharmacotherapy 1997, The Time That Followed (in Danish) 1998, Ethics and Clinical Medicine (in Danish) 1998, Can Our Nat Heritage Survive? (in Danish) 1999, Frailty in Aging (in Danish) 1999, Ethics and Evidence-based Pharmacotherapy 2000, Can We Not Do It A Little Better? 2000, In That We Believe 2001, Fraud and Misconduct in Biomedical Research 2001, The Ethics of Research Related to Health Care in Developing Countries 2002; 48 AgeForum publs 1996–2007; Council of Europe, Ethical Eye: Biomedical Research 2004; many articles in medical journals; lyrics to contemporary Danish compositions, trans of lyrics. *Honours:* Hon. mem. Icelandic Medical Asscn 1978, Swedish Medical Soc., Finnish Medical Soc., Danish Soc. of Gastroenterology 1995 and 2004; Hon. MRCP (UK) 1991; Hon. DMed (Univ. of Odense) 1996, (Gothenburg); Alfred Benzon Prize, August Krogh Prize 1974, Christensen-Ceson Prize 1976, Klein-Prize 1980, Barfred-Pedersen Prize 1980, Hagedorn Prize 1983, Nordic Gastro Prize 1983, Nordic Language Prize in Medicine 1993, Danish Prize of Honour in Research Ethics 2003, National Prize of Honour, JL-Foundation 2005, Medal of Honour, Icelandic Medical History Soc. 2005. *Address:* Alice Hansen, AeldreForum, Edisonsvej 18, 1, 5000, Odense C (office); Nerievej 7, 2900 Hellerup, Denmark (home). *Telephone:* 72423990 (office); 39629688 (home). *Fax:* 72423991 (office); 39629588 (home). *E-mail:* aef@aeldreforum.dk (office). *Website:* www.aeldreforum.dk (office).

RILEY, Denise, PhD; British poet, philosopher and translator; b. 1948, England. *Education:* University of Sussex. *Publications:* Marxism for Infants, 1977; No Fee: A Line or Two for Free, 1979; Some Poems: 1968–1978 (with Wendy Mulford), 1982; War in the Nursery: Theories of the Child and Mother, 1983; Dry Air, 1985; 'Am I That Name?': Feminism and the Category of 'Women' in History, 1988; Poets on Writing: Britain, 1970–1991 (ed.), 1992; Mop Mop Georgette: New and Selected Poems, 1993; Selected Poems, 2001; The Words of Selves: Identification, Solidarity, Irony, 2001.

RILEY, Joan; Jamaican novelist; b. 1959, St. Mary. *Education:* Univ. of Sussex, Univ. of London. *Career:* moved to UK 1976; active career in social work, on which her works draw. *Publications:* The Unbelonging (novel) 1985, Waiting in the Twilight (novel) 1987, Romance (novel) 1988, A Kindness to Children (novel) (MIND Prize 1993) 1992, Leave to Stay: Stories of Exile and Belonging (ed. with Briar Wood) 1996. *Honours:* Voice Award for Fiction 1992. *Address:* c/o The Women's Press, 27 Goodge Street, London, W1T 2LD, England.

RIMAWI, Fahid Nimer ar-, BA; Jordanian journalist; *Publisher and Editor-in-Chief, Al Majd*; b. 1942, Palestine; m.; two s. five d. *Education:* Cairo Univ., Egypt. *Career:* Ed. Difa (newspaper) 1965–67; Ed.-in-Chief, Jordan News Agency 1968–70; Sec. Editorial Bd of Afkar (magazine) 1970–73; Dir Investigating Dept of Al-Raiue (newspaper) 1975–76; writer Al-Destour (newspaper) 1978–81; Political Writer, Al-Raiue (newspaper) 1981–85; Corresp. al Talie'ah (magazine) Paris 1982–85; political writer 1985–94; Publr and Ed.-in-Chief Al Majd (weekly). *Publications:* Mawaweel Fi al Layl Al Taweel, short stories in Arabic 1982. *Address:* PO Box 926856, Amman 11190 (office); Dahiyat al-Rashid, Amman, Jordan. *Telephone:* (6) 5530553 (office); (6) 5160615 (home). *Fax:* (6) 553 0352. *E-mail:* almajd@almajd.net (office). *Website:* www.almajd.net (office).

RIMINGTON, Dame Stella, DCB, MA; British fmr civil servant and author; b. (Stella Whitehouse), 1935, London; m. John Rimington 1963; two d. *Education:* Nottingham High School for Girls, Univs of Edinburgh and Liverpool (Diploma Archive Admin). *Career:* Dir-Gen. Security Service 1992–96; Dir (non-exec.) Marks and Spencer 1997–2004, BG PLC 1997–2000, BG Group 2000–05, GKR Group (now Whitehead Mann) 1997–2001; Chair. Inst. of Cancer Research 1997–2001; Trustee Royal Marsden Hosp. 1997–2001, Refuge (charity), Int. Spy Museum, Washington, DC, USA; Gov. St Felix School, Southwold 1998–2002, Town Close House Preparatory School, Norwich 1999–2005. *Publications:* Intelligence, Security and the Law (non-fiction) 1994, Open Secret (autobiog.) 2001; novels: At Risk 2004, Secret Asset 2006, Illegal Action 2007, Dead Line 2008, Present Danger 2009. *Honours:* Hon. Air Cdre 7006 (VR) Squadron Royal Auxiliary Air Force 1997–2001; Dame Commdr of the Bath 1996; Hon. LLD (Nottingham) 1995, (Exeter) 1996, (London Metropolitan) 2004, (Liverpool) 2006, Hon. DSocS (Nottingham Trent) 2009; Spirit of Everywoman Award 2007. *Address:* PO Box 1604, London, SW1P 1XB, England.

RINALDI, Ange-Marie (Angelo); French writer and literary critic; b. 17 June 1940, Bastia; s. of Pierre-François Rinaldi and Antoinette Pietri. *Education:* Lycée de Bastia, Corsica. *Career:* journalist Nice-Matin 1961–68, Paris-Jour 1969–72; Literary Ed. L'Express 1972–98; journalist Nouvel Observateur 1998–; writer 1968–; elected mem. Acad. Française 2001. *Publications:* La Loge du gouverneur (Prix Fénéon) 1969, La Maison des Atlantes (Prix Fémina 1972) 1971, L'Education de l'oubli 1974, Les Dames de France 1977, La Dernière fête de l'empire (Prix Marcel Proust 1981) 1980, Les Jardins du consulat 1985, Les Roses de Pline (Prix Jean Freustié 1988) 1987, La Confession des collines 1990, Les jours ne s'en vont pas longtemps 1993, Dernières nouvelles de la nuit 1997, Service de presse: chroniques 1999, Tou ce que je sais de Marie 2000. *Honours:* Prix Prince Pierre de Monaco 1994, Prix de la Fondation Mumm 1995. *Address:* c/o Le Nouvel Observateur, 10 place de la Bourse, 75002 Paris, France.

RINALDI, Nicholas Michael, AB, MA, PhD; American academic, writer and poet; *Professor, Fairfield University*; b. 2 April 1934, New York, NY; m. Jacqueline Tellier 1959; three s. one d. *Education:* Shrub Oak Coll., Fordham Univ. *Career:* Instructor to Asst Prof., St John's Univ. 1960–65; Lecturer, CUNY 1966; Assoc. Prof., Columbia Univ. 1966; Asst Prof. to Prof., Prof., Fairfield Univ. 1966–; Prof., Univ. of Connecticut 1972; mem. Associated Writing Programs; Poetry Society of America. *Publications:* novels: Bridge Fall Down 1985, The Jukebox Queen of Malta 1999, Between Two Rivers 2004; poetry: The Resurrection of the Snails 1977, We Have Lost Our Fathers 1982, The Luftwaffe in Chaos 1985; contrib. to periodicals and journals, including Virginia Quarterly Review. *Honours:* Joseph P. Slomovich Memorial Award for Poetry, 1979; All Nations Poetry Awards, 1981, 1983; New York Poetry Forum Award, 1983; Eve of St Agnes Poetry Award, 1984; Charles Angoff Literary Award, 1984. *Address:* c/o English Department, Fairfield University, 1073 North Benson Road, Fairfield, CT 06824, USA (office). *Website:* www.fairfield.edu (office).

RINDO, Ronald J.; American academic and writer; b. 21 March 1959, Milwaukee, WI; m. Ellen S. Meyer, 13 Oct. 1984, one s. one d. *Education:* BA, Carroll College, 1981; MA, 1984, PhD, 1989, University of Wisconsin, Milwaukee. *Career:* Asst Prof. of English, Birmingham Southern College, AL, 1989–92, University of Wisconsin, Oshkosh, 1992–; mem. MLA; Society for the Study of Midwestern Literature; Wisconsin Council of Teachers of English. *Publications:* Suburban Metaphysics and Other Stories, 1990; Secrets Men Keep (short stories), 1995. Contributions: anthologies, books, reviews and periodicals. *Honours:* Milwaukee Small Press Award, 1989, Wisconsin Writer's Award, Wisconsin Library Asscn, 1990; Bell South Foundation Grant, 1990; Wye Fellow, Aspen Institute, 1991; Wisconsin Humanities Council Grant, 1995. *E-mail:* rindo@uwosh.edu.

RIPLEY, Michael (Mike) David, BA; British writer and critic; b. 29 Sept. 1952, Huddersfield, England. *Career:* fmr crime fiction critic, Sunday Telegraph, Daily Telegraph, Birmingham Post; co-ed., Fresh Blood anthology series. *Publications:* novels: Just Another Angel 1988, Angel Touch 1989, Angel Hunt 1990, Angel in Arms 1992, Angel City 1994, Angel Confidential 1995, Family of Angels 1996, That Angel Look 1997, Bootlegged Angel 1999, Lights, Camera, Angel 2001, Double Take 2001, Angel Underground 2002, Angel on the Inside 2003, Angel in the House 2005, Angel's Share 2006. *Honours:* CWA Last Laugh Awards 1989, 1991, Angel Literary Award for Fiction 1990, Sherlock Award 1999.

RISSET TODINI, Jacqueline Renée; French/Italian poet, writer and translator; *Professor Emeritus and President, Centro di Studi Italo-francesi, Università degli Studi di Roma Tre*; b. (Jacqueline Risset), 25 May 1936, Besançon, France; m. Umberto Todini. *Education:* École Normale Supérieure de Sèvres. *Career:* fmr Asst de Littérature comparée, Univ. of Aix en Provence, France; fmr Magistero, Lettrice di lingua madre, Sapienza – Università di Roma; Prof. 'ordinario' in Faculty of Philosophy and Literature, Università degli Studi di Roma Tre 1973–2009, Prof. Emer. and Pres. Centro di Studi Italo-francesi 2009–; Visiting Prof., Univ. of California, Berkeley, Columbia Univ., Collège de France; mem. Editorial Bd journal Tel Quel. *Exhibition:* painters on J. Risset poems at BNF, Paris 2011. *Publications:* poetry vols: Jeu 1971, Mors 1977, La Traduction commence 1978, En voyage 1980, Sept passages de la vie d'une femme 1985, L'Amour de loin 1988, Petits éléments de physique amoureuse 1991, L'anagramme du désir 1995, Puissances du sommeil 1997, Les instants 2000, Il tempo dell'istante 2011, Sleep's Powers 2011; translations into French: Dante's Divine Comedy (Prix SGDL française) 1985–90, Machiavelli's Prince 2000; essays: Dante écrivain: ou l'Intelletto d'amore 1982, Dante, une vie (biog.) 1995, Il silenzio delle sirene 2006, Traduction et memoire poetique (Prix Acad. française) 2008, Une certain Joie (Prix R. Caillois) 2009. *Honours:* Chevalier, Légion d'honneur, Ordre nat. du Mérite, Fiorino d'Oro (Florence). *Address:* Centro di Studi Italo francesi, Università degli Studi di Roma Tre, Piazza Campitelli 3, 00186 Rome, Italy (office). *E-mail:* risset@uniroma3.it (office).

RITTER, Erika, MA; Canadian dramatist and writer; b. 1948, Regina, Sask. *Education:* McGill Univ., Montreal, Univ. of Toronto. *Career:* freelancer author, playwright, journalist 1975–; host and broadcaster, CBC Radio 1981–2005; Writer-in-Residence, Concordia Univ. 1984; Playwright-in-Residence, Smith Coll. 1985, Stratford Festival 1985, Univ. of Toronto 1988–89. *Radio:* numerous radio dramas, comedies and series. *Publications:* plays: A Visitor from Charleston 1975, The Splits 1978, Winter 1671 1979, Automatic Pilot 1980, The Passing Scene 1982, Murder at McQueen 1986, The Road to Hell 1992; prose: Urban Scrawl 1984, Ritter in Residence 1987, The Hidden Life in Humans 1997, The Great Big Book of Guys: Alphabetical Encounters with Men 2004. *Honours:* Chalmers Award 1980, ACTRA Awards 1982, 1986. *Literary Agent:* c/o Shain Jaffe, Hilary McMahon, Westwood Creative Artists Ltd, 93 Harbord Avenue, Toronto, ON M5S 1G6, Canada. *Telephone:* (416) 964-3302. *Fax:* (416) 975-9209. *E-mail:* hilary@wcaltd.com. *Website:* www.wcaltd.com; www.erikaritter.com.

RIVARD, David, BA, MFA; American writer, poet and editor; b. 2 Dec. 1953, Fall River, Mass; m. Michaela Sullivan 1982; one d. *Education:* Southeastern

Massachusetts University, University of Arizona. *Career:* Faculty mem., Dept of English, Tufts University; Poetry Ed., Harvard Review. *Publications:* Torque, 1988; Wise Poison, 1996; Bewitched Playground, 2000; contributions: periodicals. *Honours:* Fine Arts Work Center Fellowships, Provincetown, Massachusetts, 1984–85, 1986–87; National Endowment for the Arts Fellowships, 1986, 1991; Agnes Lynch Starrett Poetry Prize, University of Pittsburgh, 1987; Pushcart Prize, 1994; Massachusetts Cultural Council Fellow, 1994; James Laughlin Award, Acad. of American Poets, 1996; Guggenheim Fellowship, 2001.

RIVAS, Manuel; Spanish journalist, novelist and poet; b. 1957, A Coruña. *Career:* contributor to Galician literature, co-establishing a number of Galician- and Spanish-language journals. *Publications:* poetry: Libro de Entroido 1979, Balada nas praias do Oeste 1985, Mohicania 1987, Ningún cisne 1989, El pueblo de la noche 1997; novels: Todo ben 1985, Un millión de vacas (Premio de la Crítica) 1989, Los comedores de patatas 1991, En salvaje compañía 1995, ¿Qué me quieres, amor? (Premio Nacional de Narrativa) 1996, Bala perdida 1997, El lápiz do carpinteiro 1998, Ela, maldita alma 1999, A man dos paíños 2000, La Mano del Emigrante 2001, Las llamadas perdidas 2002, Cuentos de un invierno 2005, Poesía El Pueblo de la noche y Mohicania revisitada 2005, Os libros arden mal (Premio de la Crítica Española 2006, Premio de los Libreros de Madrid 2007, Premio Antón Losada Diegue 2007, Irmandade do Libro da Federación de Libreiros de Galicia 2007) 2006; essays: El bonsái atlántico 1994, El periodismo es un cuento 1997, Toxos e flores 1999, Galicia Galicia 2001; numerous short stories; contrib. to El País, El Ideal Gallego, Diario de Galicia, La voz de Galicia. *Honours:* Amnesty International Prize (Belgian section), Premio Torrente Ballester, Premio Arcebispo Xoán de San Clemente y el de la Crítica, Premio ONCE – Galicia a la Solidaridad, Premio de Periodismo Julio Camba 2002, El Premio Cálamo Extraordinario 2006. *Literary Agent:* La Oficina del Autor, Calle Gran Via 32, 28013 Madrid, Spain. *E-mail:* gisellew@laoficinadelautor.com. *Website:* www.elboomeran.com/autor/31/manuel-rivas/.

RIVERA, Guillermo; Chilean poet; b. 30 Dec. 1958, Viña del Mar. *Career:* fmr ed. Intento (poetry magazine); lived in Stockholm, Sweden 1986–93. *Publications include:* El Tractatus y Otros Poemas 2002, Ennio Moltedo, Obra Poética 2005, Comedia de Chile 2009. *Honours:* Winner, Concurso de Poesia y Premio Critica del Jurado, Valparaiso 2002, Winner, Premio Adquisición de Libros, Consejo Nacional del Libro y la Lectura 2003, Winner, Concurso Nacional de Poesia Juegos Florales de Vicuña 2003, Winner, Beca Fondo del Libro, Consejo Nacional del Libro y la Lectura 2005, Winner, Premio Mejor Obra Nacional en Poesia Inédita 2007, Consejo Nacional del Libro y la Lectura Beca de Creación Literaria 2008. *Address:* c/o Ediciones LOM, Concha y Toro 23, Santiago, Chile (office). *Telephone:* (2) 6885273 (office). *Fax:* (2) 6966388 (office). *E-mail:* lom@lom.cl (office). *Website:* www.lom.cl/default.aspx (office).

RIVERA-GARZA, Cristina, PhD; Mexican writer, poet and historian; *Professor of Writing, University of California, San Diego*; b. 1964, Matamoros, Tamaulipas. *Education:* Nat. Autonomous Univ. of Mexico, Mexico City, Univ. of Houston, USA. *Career:* Assoc. Prof. of Mexican History, San Diego State Univ.; Head of Creative Writing Narrative Program, Centro Cultural Tijuana; currently Prof. of Writing, Univ. of California, San Diego. *Publications:* La guerra no importa 1991, Desconocer 1994, La más mia 1998, Nadie me verá llorar (trans. as No One Will See Me Cry) 2000, Cruzar al Atlántico con los ojos vendados 2001, La cresta de Ilion 2002, Ningún reloj cuenta esto 2002, Lo anterior 2004, Los Textos del Yo 2005, La Novela por los novelistas 2007, La Muerte me da (Premio Sor Juana Inés de la Cruz 2009) 2007, La Frontera más distante 2008; contrib. to Hispanic American Historical Review, Journal of the History of Medicine. *Honours:* Anna Seghers Prize 2005. *Address:* Department of Literature, University of California, 9500 Gilman Drive, La Jolla, CA 92093-0410, USA (office). *Telephone:* (858) 534-3488 (office). *E-mail:* criveragarza@gmail.com (office). *Website:* www.itesm.edu; cristinariveragarza.blogspot.com.

RIVERO CASTAÑEDA, Raúl Ramón; Cuban journalist and poet; b. 1945, Morón, Camagüey; m. Blanca Reyes Castañón. *Education:* Havana Univ. School of Journalism. *Career:* Co-founder satirical magazine Caimán Barbudo 1966; Moscow correspondent Prensa Latina (govt press agency) 1973–76, then worked for science and culture service, Cuba; independent journalist 1988–; Co-founder and Dir Cuba Press news agency 1995–2003, contributing to newspapers and journals abroad, including El Nuevo Herald, The Miami Herald, Encounter magazine; correspondent for French press agency, Reporters sans frontières; fmr regional vice-chair. for Cuba, Inter-American Press Asscn Cttee on Freedom of the Press and Information; accused of collaborating with the USA and sentenced to 20 years' imprisonment by govt April 2003, released Nov. 2004; mem. Manuel Márquez Sterling Journalists' Asscn. *Publications:* poems include: Suite de la muerte, Patria 1994, Orden de registro, Oración de septiembre, Foto en La Habana, Ensayo sobre la tiranía. *Honours:* Reporters sans frontières Fondation de France prize 1997, Inter-American Press Asscn Grand Prize for Press Freedom, Columbia Univ. Graduate School of Journalism Maria Moors Cabot Prize 1999, World Press Freedom Prize 2004. *Address:* c/o Reporters sans Frontières, 5 rue Geoffroy-Marie, 75009 Paris, France (office). *Telephone:* 1-44-83-84-84 (office). *Fax:* 1-45-23-11-51 (office). *E-mail:* rsf@rsf.org (office). *Website:* www.rsf.org (office).

RIX, Timothy John, CBE, BA, CIMgt, FRSA, FIoD; British publisher (retd); b. 4 Jan. 1934, Maidenhead, Berks., England; s. of the late Howard T. Rix and of Marguerite Selman Rix; m. 1st Wendy E. Wright 1960 (divorced 1967); m. 2nd Gillian Greenwood 1968; one s. two d. *Education:* Radley Coll., Clare Coll., Cambridge and Yale Univ., USA. *Career:* joined Longmans Green & Co. Ltd 1958, Overseas Educ. Publr 1958–61, Publishing Man. Far East and SE Asia 1961–63, Head, English Language Teaching Publishing 1964–68, Div. Man. Dir 1968–72, Jt Man. Dir 1972–76, Chief Exec. Longman Group Ltd 1976–90, Chair. 1984–90; Chair. Addison-Wesley-Longman Group Ltd 1988–89; Chair. Pitman Examinations Inst. 1987–90; mem. Bd of Dirs Pearson Longman Ltd (now Pearson PLC) 1979–83, Goldcrest Television 1981–83, Yale University Press Ltd, London 1984–2009, ECIC (Man.) Ltd 1990–92, Blackie & Son Ltd 1990–93, B.H. Blackwell Ltd 1991–95, Geddes and Grosset Ltd 1996–98, Jessica Kingsley Publrs Ltd 1997–2007, Frances Lincoln Ltd 1997–2008, Meditech Media Ltd 1997–2003, Scottish Book Source 1999–2007, Central European University Press 1999–2005; Pres. Publrs' Asscn 1981–83; Chair. Book Trust 1986–88, British Library Centre for the Book 1989–95, Book Marketing Ltd 1990–2003, Soc. of Bookmen 1990–92, British Library Publishing 1992–2003, Book Aid International 1994–2006, Bell Educational Trust 1994–2001, Nat. Book Cttee 1997–2003, Edinburgh University Press 2001–07, Advisory Bd of Centre for Publishing Studies, Univ. of Stirling 2000–08; mem. British Library Bd 1986–96, British Council Bd 1988–97, Oxford Brookes Univ. Devt Cttee 1991–96, Finance Cttee, Oxford University Press 1992–2002, Council, Ranfurly Library Service 1992–94, Health Educ. Authority Bd 1995–99, Advisory Council, Inst. of English Studies, Univ. of London 2000–08; Gov. English-Speaking Union 1998–2005. *Publications:* articles on publishing in trade journals. *Honours:* Hon. Pres. Ind. Publrs Guild 1993–2008; Hon. MA (Oxford) 1993, Hon. DUniv (Stirling) 2006. *Address:* Flat 1, 29 Barrington Road, London, N8 8QT, England (home). *Telephone:* (20) 8348-4143 (home). *E-mail:* tim@rixpublishing.co.uk (home).

ROBB, Graham Macdonald, PhD, FRSL; British writer; b. 2 June 1958, Manchester, England; m. Margaret Hambrick 1986. *Education:* Univ. of Oxford, Goldsmiths Coll., London and Vanderbilt Univ., Nashville, Tenn., USA. *Career:* British Acad. Fellowship 1987–90. *Publications include:* Le Corsaire – Satan en Silhouette 1985, Baudelaire Lecteur de Balzac 1988, Scènes de la Vie de Bohème (ed.) 1988, Baudelaire (trans.) 1989, La Poésie de Baudelaire et la Poésie Française 1993, Balzac 1994, Unlocking Mallarmé 1996, Victor Hugo: A Biography 1998, Rimbaud 2000, Strangers: Homosexual Love in the 19th Century, The Discovery of France (Duff Cooper Prize, Ondaatje Prize, Royal Soc. of Literature 2008) 2007, Parisians: An Adventure History of Paris 2010; contribs to Times Literary Supplement, Daily Telegraph, London Review of Books, Sunday Times, New York Times. *Honours:* Chevalier, Ordre des Arts et des Lettres; New York Times Book of the Year 1994, 1999 and 2001, Whitbread Biography of the Year Award 1997, R.S.L. Heinemann Award 1998. *Literary Agent:* c/o Rogers, Coleridge & White Ltd, 20 Powis Mews, London, W11 1JN, England. *Telephone:* (20) 7221-3717. *Fax:* (20) 7229-9084. *E-mail:* info@rcwlitagency.com. *Website:* www.rcwlitagency.com.

ROBB, J. D. (see Roberts, Nora)

ROBBINS, Kenneth Randall, AA, BSEd, MFA, PhD; American academic, writer and dramatist; *Director, School of the Performing Arts, Louisiana Tech University*; b. 7 Jan. 1944, Douglasville, Ga; s. of James Aubrey Robbins and Inez Graham Robbins; m. Dorothy Dodge 1988; one s. one d. *Education:* Young Harris Coll., Georgia Southern Univ., Univ. of Georgia, Southern Illinois Univ. at Carbondale. *Career:* Asst Prof., Jacksonville Univ., Fla 1974–79; Assoc. Prof., Newberry Coll., SC 1977–85, Univ. of S Dakota 1985–98; Dir School of the Performing Arts, Louisiana Tech Univ. 1998–; mem. Soc. for Study of Southern Literature, Nat. Partners of American Theatre, Asscn of Theatre in Higher Educ.; stage plays have been produced throughout the USA, Canada, Denmark and Japan. *Plays:* Atomic Field, Molly's Rock, Bar None, The Hunger Feast, One Man's Hero, The Audition, In the River, Impasse, Goober Peas, The Warwoman of Wauhatchie Creek, A Good & Dandy World, A Match for General Sherman. *Publications:* The Dallas File (play) 1982, Buttermilk Bottoms (novel) 1987, The Baptism of Howie Cobb (novel) 1995, In the Shelter of the Fold (novel) 2002, Christmas Stories from Louisiana (co-ed.) 2003, The City of Churches 2004, Christmas on the Great Plains (co-ed.) 2004, Christmas Stories from Georgia (co-ed.) 2005, Matchless, Dynamite Hill (radio play), Christmas Stories from Ohio 2010; contrib. to journals and radio. *Honours:* Toni Morrison Prize for Fiction 1986, Associated Writing Programs Novel Award 1986, Festival of Southern Theatre Awards 1987, 1990, Japan Foundation Arts Fellowship 1995, Louisiana Div. of Arts Theatre Fellowship 2002, Georgia Southern Univ. Coll. of Educ. Alumnus of the Year 2003, Fulbright Scholar to Macedonia 2003. *Address:* School of the Performing Arts, Louisiana Tech University, PO Box 8608, Ruston, LA 71272, USA (office). *Telephone:* (318) 257-2711 (office). *Fax:* (318) 257-4571 (office). *E-mail:* krobbins@latech.edu (office). *Website:* www.latech.edu (office).

ROBBINS, Richard Leroy, Jr, AB, MFA; American academic, poet, writer and editor; *Professor of English and Director, Good Thunder Reading Series, Minnesota State University, Mankato*; b. 27 Aug. 1953, Los Angeles, Calif.; s. of Richard Leroy Robbins, Sr and Irene Cecilia Annand; m. Candace L. Black 1979; two s. *Education:* San Diego State Univ., Univ. of Montana. *Career:* Co-Ed. Cafeteria 1971–81, CutBank and SmokeRoot Press 1977–79, Montana Arts Council anthologies 1979–81; Writer-in-Residence, Poet-in-the-Schools, Montana Arts Council 1979–81; instructor, Moorhead State Univ. 1981–82, Oregon State Univ. 1982–84; Prof., Minnesota State Univ., Mankato 1984–, Mankato Distinguished Faculty Scholar; Asst Ed. Mankato Poetry Review 1984–2004; mem. Asscn of Writers and Writing Programs, The Loft, Poetry

Soc. of America, Western Literature Asscn. *Publications:* Where We Are: The Montana Poets Anthology (ed. with Lex Runciman) 1978, Toward New Weather 1979, The Invisible Wedding 1984, Famous Persons We Have Known 2000, The Untested Hand 2008, Radioactive City 2009, Other Americas 2010; contrib. to 29 anthologies 1978–, 400 poems in quarterlies and journals. *Honours:* Mankato Distinguished Faculty Scholar, Minnesota State Univ., Branford P. Millar Award First Prize in Poetry, Portland Review 1978, Univ. of Montana Frontier Award 1978, Minnesota State Arts Bd Individual Artist Fellowships 1986, 1999, Robert H. Winner Memorial Award, Poetry Soc. of America 1988, Nat. Endowment for the Arts Fellowship 1992, McKnight Individual Artist grants 1993, 1996, and Fellowship 1997, Hawthornden Fellowship 1998, Loft Award of Distinction in Poetry 2000, Kay Sexton Award, Minnesota Humanities Comm. 2006, The Writer/Emily Dickinson Award, Poetry Soc. of America 2009, Louis Hammer Award, Poetry Soc. of America 2009, Bellday Poetry Prize 2009. *Address:* Department of English, Minnesota State University, 230 Armstrong Hall, Mankato, MN 56001, USA (office). *Telephone:* (507) 389-1354 (office). *Fax:* (507) 389-5362 (office). *E-mail:* richard.robbins@mnsu.edu (office). *Website:* english2.mnsu.edu/robbins (office).

ROBBINS, Tim, BA; American actor, director and screenwriter; b. 16 Oct. 1958, West Covina, Calif.; s. of folk singer Gil Robbins; fmr pnr Susan Sarandon; three c. *Education:* Univ. of California, Los Angeles. *Career:* began career as mem. Theater for the New City; Founder and Artistic Dir The Actors' Gang 1981–; Founder Havoc Inc. (production co.). *Theatre includes:* as actor: Ubu Roi 1981; as dir: A Midsummer Night's Dream 1984, The Good Woman of Setzuan 1990; as writer, with Adam Simon: Alagazam, After the Dog Wars, Violence: The Misadventures of Spike Spangle, Farmer, Carnage – A Comedy (rep. USA at Edin. Int. Festival, Scotland); as writer: Embedded 2004. *Films include:* No Small Affair 1984, Toy Soldiers 1984, The Sure Thing 1985, Fraternity Vacation 1985, Top Gun 1986, Howard the Duck 1986, Five Corners 1987, Bull Durham 1988, Tapeheads 1988, Miss Firecracker 1989, Eric the Viking 1989, Cadillac Man 1990, Twister 1990, Jacob's Ladder 1990, Jungle Fever 1991, The Player 1992, Bob Roberts (also writer and dir) 1992, Amazing Stories: Book Four 1992, Short Cuts 1993, The Hudsucker Proxy 1994, The Shawshank Redemption 1994, Prêt-à-Porter 1994, I.Q. 1994, Dead Man Walking (writer and dir) 1995, Nothing to Lose 1997, Arlington Road 1999, Cradle Will Rock (also writer and dir) 1999, Austin Powers: The Spy Who Shagged Me 1999, Mission to Mars 2000, High Fidelity 2000, Antitrust 2001, Human Nature 2001, The Truth About Charlie 2002, The Day My God Died 2003, Mystic River (Golden Globe for Best Supporting Actor 2004, Critics' Choice Award for Best Supporting Actor 2004, Screen Actors Guild Best Supporting Actor Award 2004, Acad. Award for Best Supporting Actor 2004) 2003, Code 46 2003, The Secret Life of Words 2005, War of the Worlds 2005, La Vida secreta de las palabras 2005, Zathura: A Space Adventure 2005, Catch a Fire 2006, Tenacious D: The Pick of Destiny 2006, Noise 2007, The Lucky Ones 2008, City of Ember 2008, Green Lantern 2011. *Television:* Queens Supreme (pilot episode and series dir) 2003, Cinema Verite (movie) 2011. *Literary Agent:* Havoc Inc., 16 West 19th Street, 12th Floor, New York, NY 10011; c/o Elaine Goldsmith Thomas, ICM, 40 West 57th Street, New York, NY 10019 (office); The Actors' Gang at The Ivy Substation, 9070 Venice Blvd., Culver City, CA 90232, USA. *Website:* www.theactorsgang.com.

ROBBINS, Tom, BA; American writer; b. 22 July 1936, Blowing Rock, NC; s. of George T. Robbins and Katherine Robinson Robbins; m. 1st Terrie Lunden 1967 (divorced 1972); one s., m. 2nd Alexa d'Avalon 1987. *Education:* Virginia Commonwealth Univ. and Univ. of Washington. *Career:* operated black market ring in S Korea 1956–57; int. news Times-Dispatch, Richmond, Va 1959–62; Art Critic, The Seattle Times and contrib. to Artforum and Art in America etc. 1962–65; Art Critic, Seattle Magazine 1965–67. *Films:* Even Cowgirls Get the Blues 1994. *Publications:* novels: Another Roadside Attraction 1971, Even Cowgirls Get the Blues 1976, Still Life With Woodpecker 1980, Jitterbug Perfume 1984, Skinny Legs and All 1990, Half Asleep in Frog Pajamas 1994, Fierce Invalids Home from Hot Climates 2000, Villa Incognito 2003, Wild Ducks Flying Backward 2005, B is for Beer 2009. *Honours:* Bumbershoot Golden Umbrella for Lifetime Achievement 1998, Writers' Digest 100 Best Writers of the 20th Century 2000. *Address:* PO Box 338, La Conner, WA 98257, USA (home).

RÖBEL, Udo; German editor; b. 20 Jan. 1950, Neustadt, Weinstrasse. *Career:* Restaurant Ed. for Rheinpfalz and Mil. Service Corresp. for DPA and AP 1969–71; mem. editorial staff BILD newspaper, Frankfurt, Kettwig, and Aachen-zum-Schluss 1972–82; Deputy Ed.-in-Chief Express newspaper, Cologne 1983–89; journalistic adviser Heinrich-Bauer-Verlag 1989–92; mem. Chief Editorial Staff Bild 1993–97, Ed.-in-Chief Bild 1998–2000, Ed.-in-Chief Bild.de 2001–05; Ed. Fairpress.biz 2005–. *Honours:* Wächter-Preis, Deutschen Tagespresse 1985. *Website:* www.fairpress.biz (office).

ROBERTS, Adam, (A.R.R.R. Roberts), MA, PhD; British science fiction writer; b. 1966, London; m.; two c. *Education:* Univ. of Aberdeen, Univ. of Cambridge. *Career:* Prof. of 19th-Century Literature, Royal Holloway, Univ. of London 1991–. *Publications:* novels/novellas: On 2001, Salt 2000, Park Polar 2002, Stone 2002, Jupiter Magnified 2003, Polystom 2003, The Snow 2004, Gradisil 2006, Land of the Headless 2007, Splinter 2007, Swiftly 2008, Yellow Blue Tibia 2010; parodies, as A.R.R.R. Roberts: The Soddit 2003, The Sellamillion 2004, The Va Dinci Cod 2005, Doctor Whom 2006; as A3R Roberts: Star Warped 2005; as Robertski Brothers: The McAtrix Derided 2004; non-fiction: The Palgrave History of Science Fiction 2005, Science Fiction: The New Critical Idiom 2005; short stories: Swiftly 2004. *Literary Agent:* Steve Calcutt, Anubis Literary Agency, 6 Birdhaven Close, Lighthorne, Warwick, CV35 0BE, England. *Telephone:* (1784) 443511 (Royal Holloway). *E-mail:* A.C.Roberts@rhul.ac.uk; Adam@AdamRoberts.com. *Website:* www.adamroberts.com.

ROBERTS, Andrew, MA, FRSL; British author; b. 13 Jan. 1963, London, England; s. of Simon Roberts and Katie Roberts; m. Susan Gilchrist; one s. one d. *Education:* Gonville and Caius Coll., Cambridge. *Career:* mem. Beefsteak Club, Univ. Pitt Club, Cambridge, Brooks's, Garrick, Pratt's, The Brook, New York. *Publications:* The Holy Fox: A Biography of Lord Halifax 1991, Eminent Churchillians 1994, The Aachen Memorandum 1995, Salisbury: Victorian Titan 1999, Napoleon and Wellington 2001, Hitler and Churchill: Secrets of Leadership 2003, What Might Have Been: Leading Historians on Twelve 'What Ifs' of History (ed.) 2004, Waterloo: Napoleon's Last Gamble 2004, A History of the English Speaking Peoples Since 1900 2006, Mr Disraeli's Letters to Mrs Sarah Brydges Willyams 2007, Masters and Commanders 2008, The Storm of War 2009; contrib. to Sunday Telegraph, Literary Review and more than 50 other publs. *Honours:* Hon. DHumLitt (Univ. of Westminster, Fulton, Mo.) 2000, Hon. PhD (Cambridge); Wolfson History Prize 1999, PEN Silver Pen Award 1999, Int. Churchill Soc. Emery Reves Award 2010, Canadian Inst. for Jewish Research Lion of Judah Award 2010, British Army Mil. History Book of the Year Award 2010. *Literary Agent:* c/o Capel & Land Ltd, 29 Wardour Street, London, W1D 6PS, England. *Telephone:* (20) 7734-2414. *Fax:* (20) 7734-8101. *E-mail:* georgina@capelland.co.uk. *Website:* www.capelland.com. *Address:* 22 South Eaton Place, London, SW1W 9GA, England (office); 15 Central Park West, Apt 27C, New York, NY 10023, USA (office). *E-mail:* andrew@roberts-london.fsnet.co.uk (office). *Website:* www.andrew-roberts.net.

ROBERTS, Brian, DipSoc; British writer; b. 19 March 1930, London, England. *Education:* St Mary's Coll., Twickenham, Univ. of London. *Career:* teacher of English and history 1955–65. *Publications:* Ladies in the Veld 1965, Cecil Rhodes and the Princess 1969, Churchills in Africa 1970, The Diamond Magnates 1972, The Zulu Kings 1974, Kimberley: Turbulent City 1976, The Mad Bad Line: The Family of Lord Alfred Douglas 1981, Randolph: A Study of Churchill's Son 1984, Cecil Rhodes: Flawed Colossus 1987, Those Bloody Women: Three Heroines of the Boer War 1991. *Address:* 7 The Blue House, Market Place, Frome, Somerset, BA11 1AP, England (home). *Telephone:* (1373) 471581 (home).

ROBERTS, Gregory David; Australian writer; b. 1952, Melbourne, Vic. *Publications:* Shantaram 2003. *E-mail:* info@shantaram.com (office). *Website:* www.shantaram.com.

ROBERTS, Irene, (Roberta Carr, Elizabeth Harle, I. M. Roberts, Ivor Roberts, Iris Rowland, Irene Shaw); British writer; b. 27 Sept. 1925, London, England; m. Trevor Roberts (deceased); two s. one d. *Career:* Woman's Page Ed., South Hams Review 1977–79; Tutor in Creative Writing, Kingsbridge Community Coll., Devon; Founder-mem. Romantic Novelists' Asscn. *Publications:* Let There Be Light 1950, Squirrel Walk 1961, Come Back Beloved 1962, Tangle of Gold Lace 1963, The Whisper of Sea-Bells 1964, The Mountain Sang 1965, Where Flamingoes Fly 1966, A Handful of Stars 1967, Shadows on the Moon 1968, Thunder Heights 1969, Surgeon in Tibet 1970, Birds Without Bars 1970, The Shrine of Fire 1970, Sister at Sea 1971, Gull Haven 1971, Moon Over the Temple 1972, The Golden Pagoda 1972, Desert Nurse 1976, Nurse in Nepal 1976, Stars Above Raffael 1977, Hawks Burton 1979, Symphony of Bells 1980, Nurse Moonlight 1980, Weave Me a Moonbeam 1982, Jasmine for a Nurse 1982, Sister on Leave 1982, Nurse in the Wilderness 1983, Moonpearl 1986, Sea Jade 1987, Kingdom of the Sun 1987, Song of the Nile 1987, Jezebel Street 1995, Limehouse Lady 1996, Walker Street 1997, London's Pride 1999, Kingdom of the Sun: A Novel 2002, Hatshepsut: The Feminine Pharaoh 2003; children's books: Holiday's for Hanbury 1964, Laughing is for Fun 1964; as Ivor Roberts: Jump into Hell 1960, Trial by Water 1961, Green Hell 1961; as Iris Rowland: Blue Feathers 1967, Moon Over Moncrieff 1969, Star Drift 1970, Rainbow River 1970, The Wild Summer 1970, Orange Blossom for Tara 1971, Blossoms in the Snow 1971, Sister Julia 1972, Golden Bubbles 1976, Hunter's Dawn 1977, Golden Triangle 1978, Forgotten Dreams 1978, Temptation 1983, Theresa 1985; as Roberta Carr: Sea Maiden 1965, Fire Dragon 1967, Golden Interlude 1970; as Elizabeth Harle: Golden Rain 1964, Gay Rowan 1965, Sandy 1967, Spray of Red Roses 1971, The Silver Summer 1971, The Burning Flame 1979, Come to Me Darling 1983; as Irene Shaw: Moonstone Manor 1968, US edn as Murder Mansion 1976, The Olive Branch 1968, Cosy Cottage 2006, Poetic Leisure 2008; as I. M. Roberts: The Throne of the Pharoahs 1974, Hatsheput, Queeen of the Nile 1976, Hour of the Tiger 1985, Jezebel Street 1994, Limehouse Lady 1995, More Laughter Than Tears 1996, London's Pride in Progress 1997. *Address:* c/o Kingsbridge Community College, Balkwill Road, Kingsbridge, Devon, TQ7 1PL, England.

ROBERTS, Ivor (see Roberts, Irene)

ROBERTS, Leonard (Len), BA, MA, PhD; American academic, poet and translator; *Professor of English, Northampton County College;* b. 13 March 1947, Cohoes, NY; m. 1981; two s. one d. *Education:* Siena Coll., Univ. of Dayton, Lehigh Univ. *Career:* Prof. of English, Northampton County Coll. 1974–83, 1986–87, 1989–93, 1995–; Visiting Asst Prof., Lafayette Coll. 1983–85; Visiting Prof., Univ. of Pittsburgh 1984–; Fulbright Scholar, Janus Pannonius Univ., Pécs, Hungary 1988–89, Univ. of Turku, Finland 1994; mem. MLA, Pennsylvania Council on the Arts (advisory bd 1990–), Poetry Soc. of America, Poets and Writers. *Publications:* poetry: Cohoes Theater 1980,

From the Dark 1984, Sweet Ones 1988, Black Wings 1989, Learning About the Heart 1992, Dangerous Angels 1993, The Million Branches: Selected Poems and Interview 1993, Counting the Black Angels 1994, The Trouble-Making Finch 1998, The Silent Singer: New and Selected Poems 2001; translator: The Selected Poems of Sándor Csoóri 1992, Before and After the Fall: New Poems by Sándor Csoóri 2004, The Disappearing Trick 2007; contrib. to anthologies and journals. *Honours:* Pennsylvania Council on the Arts Writing Awards in Poetry 1981, 1986, 1987, 1991, Nat. Endowment for the Arts Awards 1984, 1989, Great Lakes and Prairies Award 1988, Nat. Poetry Series Award 1988, Soros Foundation Poetry Trans. Awards 1989, 1990, 1992, 1997, Guggenheim Fellowship 1990–91, Pushcart Prize 1991, Witter Bynner Poetry Trans. Award 1991–92, winner Silverfish Review Chapbook Competition 1992, first prize Wildwood Poetry Contest 1993, Nat. Endowment for the Humanities Trans. Award 1999, Pennsylvania Council on the Arts Poetry Award 2000. *Address:* 2443 Wassergass Road, Hellertown, PA 18055, USA (office). *Telephone:* (610) 861-5393 (office).

ROBERTS, Michael Symmons; British poet and librettist; b. 1963, Preston, Lancs.; m.; three s. *Education:* Univ. of Oxford. *Career:* joined BBC as radio prod., Cardiff 1989; worked in Manchester and London, also TV scriptwriter and documentary film-maker, fmr Exec. Prod. and Head of Devt for Religion and Ethics; Creative Writing Lecturer, Manchester Metropolitan Univ. *Libretti:* with James McMillan: Chosen, Sun Dogs, Parthenogenesis 2001, The Birds of Rhiannon 2001, Raising Sparks 2002, Quickening 2002, The Sacrifice 2007, Miracle on the Estate (Premier Prize for Television, Sandford St Martin Awards) 2008. *Radio:* poetry (BBC Radio): Anno Domini 1999, A Fearful Symmetry (Sandford St Martin Prize) 2000, Behold the Man 2000, The Wounds 2001, The Hurricane 2002, Last Words 2002, Crossing the Dark Sea 2004; documentaries: The Good Book (Jerusalem Trust Premier Award 2004) 2003, The Cross 2003, Sacred Nation 2004. *Publications:* poetry: Soft Keys (Soc. of Authors Gregory Award) 1993, Raising Sparks 1999, Burning Babylon (Poetry Book Soc. Recommendation, Soc. of Authors K. Blundell Trust Award) 2001, Corpus (Whitbread Poetry Award 2005) 2004, The Half-Healed 2008; novels: Patrick's Alphabet 2006, Breath 2008. *Literary Agent:* David Godwin Associates, 55 Monmouth Street, London, WC2H 9DG, England. *Telephone:* (20) 7240-9992. *E-mail:* assistant@davidgodwinassociates.co.uk. *Website:* www.davidgodwinassociates.co.uk. *Address:* c/o Jonathan Cape, Random House, 20 Vauxhall Bridge Road, London SW1V 2SA, England. *Website:* www.symmonsroberts.com.

ROBERTS, Michèle Brigitte, MA (Oxon.), ALA, FRSL; British novelist and poet; *Professor of Creative Writing Emerita, University of East Anglia*; b. 20 May 1949, Herts.; d. of Reginald Roberts and Monique Caulle; m. 1st Howard Burns 1984 (divorced 1987); m. 2nd Jim Latter 1991 (divorced 2004); two step-s. *Education:* Convent Grammar School, Somerville Coll., Oxford and University Coll. London. *Career:* British Council Librarian, Bangkok 1973–74; Poetry Ed. Spare Rib 1974, City Limits 1981–83; Visiting Fellow Univ. of E Anglia 1992, Univ. of Nottingham Trent 1994; Visiting Prof. Univ. of Nottingham Trent 1996–2001; Prof. of Creative Writing, Univ. of E Anglia 2002–07, Emer. 2008–; Chair. Literary Cttee British Council 1998–2002; judge, Booker Prize 2001; mem. Soc. of Authors. *Plays:* The Journeywoman 1988, Child-Lover 1995. *Television film:* The Heavenly Twins (Channel 4) 1993. *Publications include:* novels: A Piece of the Night 1978, The Visitation 1983, The Wild Girl 1984, The Book of Mrs Noah 1987, In the Red Kitchen 1990, Daughters of the House 1992, Flesh and Blood 1994, Impossible Saints 1997, Fair Exchange 1999, The Looking-Glass 2000, The Mistressclass 2003, Reader, I Married Him 2005, Paper Houses (auto-biog.) 2007; Mind Readings (co-ed.) 1996; short stories: During Mother's Absence 1993, Playing Sardines 2001, Mud: Stories of Sex and Love 2010, Wooing Mr Wickham: Stories Inspired by Jane Austen and Chawton House 2011; essays: Food, Sex and God 1998; poetry: The Mirror of the Mother 1986, Psyche and the Hurricane 1991, All the Selves I Was 1995; plays: The Journeywoman 1987, Child Lover 1993. *Honours:* Chevalier, Ordre des Arts et des Lettres 2001; Hon. MA (Nene) 1999; WHSmith Literary Award 1993. *Literary Agent:* Aitken Alexander Associates Ltd, 18–21 Cavaye Place, London, SW10 9PT, England. *Telephone:* (20) 7373-8672. *Fax:* (20) 7373-6002. *E-mail:* reception@aitkenalexander.co.uk. *Website:* www.aitkenalexander.co.uk; www.micheleroberts.co.uk.

ROBERTS, Nora, (J. D. Robb); American writer; b. 10 Oct. 1950, Silver Spring, Md. *Career:* f. Nora Roberts Foundation; Co-owner, Inn BoonsBoro, Boonsboro, Md; mem. Romance Writers of America, Novelists Inc. *Publications:* Irish Thoroughbred 1981, Blithe Images 1982, Song of the West 1982, Search for Love 1982, Island of Flowers 1982, The Heart's Victory 1982, From This Day 1983, Her Mother's Keeper 1983, Reflections 1983, Once More with Feeling 1983, Untamed 1983, Dance of Dreams 1983, Tonight and Always 1983, This Magic Moment 1983, Endings and Beginnings 1984, Storm Warning 1984, Sullivan's Woman 1984, Rules of the Game 1984, Less of a Stranger 1984, A Matter of Choice 1984, The Law is a Lady 1984, First Impressions 1984, Opposites Attract 1984, Promise Me Tomorrow 1984, Partners 1985, The Right Path 1985, Boundary Lines 1985, Summer Desserts 1985, Dual Images 1985, Night Moves 1985, Playing the Odds 1985, Tempting Fate 1985, All the Possibilities 1985, One Man's Art 1985, The Art of Deception 1986, One Summer 1986, Treasures Lost, Treasures Found 1986, Risky Business 1986, Lessons Learned 1986, Second Nature 1986, A Will and a Way 1986, Home for Christmas 1986, Affaire Royale 1986, Mind Over Matter 1987, Temptation 1987, Hot Ice 1987, Sacred Sins 1987, For Now, Forever 1987, Command Performance 1987, The Playboy Prince 1987, Brazen Virtue 1988, Local Hero 1988, Irish Rose 1988, The Name of the Game 1988, Rebellion 1988, The Last Honest Woman 1988, Dance to the Piper 1988, Skin Deep 1988, Sweet Revenge 1989, Loving Jack 1989, Best Laid Plans 1989, Gabriel's Angel 1989, Lawless 1989, Public Secrets 1990, Taming Natasha 1990, Night Shadow 1991, Genuine Lies 1991, With This Ring 1991, Night Shift 1991, Without a Trace 1991, Luring a Lady 1991, Courting Catherine 1991, A Man for Amanda 1991, For the Love of Lilah 1991, Suzannah's Surrender 1991, Carnal Innocence 1992, Unfinished Business 1992, The Welcoming 1992, Honest Illusions 1992, Divine Evil 1992, Captivated 1992, Entranced 1992, Charmed 1992, Second Nature 1993, Private Scandals 1993, Falling for Rachel 1993, Time Was 1993, Times Change 1993, Boundary Lines 1994, Hidden Riches 1994, Nightshade 1994, The Best Mistake 1994, Night Smoke 1994, Born in Fire 1994, Born in Ice 1995, True Betrayals 1995, Born in Shame 1996, Montana Sky 1996, From the Heart 1997, Sanctuary 1997, Holding the Dream 1997, Daring to Dream 1997, Finding the Dream 1997, The Reef 1998, The Winning Hand 1998, Sea Swept 1998, Homeport 1999, The Perfect Neighbor 1999, Megan's Mate 1999, Enchanted 1999, Rising Tides 1999, Inner Harbor 1999, Carolina Moon 2000, The Villa 2001, Heaven and Earth 2001, Three Fates 2002, Chesapeake Blue 2002, Key of Knowledge 2003, Key of Light 2003, Once Upon a Midnight 2003, Birthright 2003, Remember When 2003, Blue Dahlia 2004, Key of Valor 2004, Northern Lights 2005, Blue Smoke (Quill Award for Romance) 2006, Angels Fall (Quill Award for Book of the Year and for Romance 2007) 2006, Heart of the Sea 2007, Divine Evil 2007, The Hollow 2008, High Noon 2008, Tribute 2008, The Pagan Stone 2008, Black Hills 2009, Vision in White 2009, Bed of Roses 2009, Hot Rocks 2010, The Search 2010, Savour the Moment 2010, Happy Ever After 2010 The Next Always 2011; as J. D. Robb: Only Survivors Tell Tales 1990, Naked in Death 1995, Glory in Death 1995, Rapture in Death 1996, Ceremony in Death 1997, Vengeance in Death 1997, Holiday in Death 1998, Immortal in Death 1998, Silent Night 1998, Loyalty in Death 1999, Conspiracy in Death 1999, Witness in Death 2000, Judgment in Death 2000, Seduction in Death 2001, Out of this World 2001, Betrayal in Death 2001, Reunion in Death 2002, Purity in Death 2002, Imitation in Death 2003, Remember When 2003, Portrait in Death 2003, Once Upon a Midnight 2003, Divided in Death 2004, Visions in Death 2004, Memory in Death 2006, Born in Death 2006, Innocent in Death 2007, Strangers in Death 2008, Creation in Death 2008, Salvation in Death 2008, Kindred in Death 2009, Fantasy in Death 2010, Indulgence in Death 2010, The Witness 2012. *Honours:* various Romance Writers of America Awards, named as one of 100 People Who Shape Our World, Time magazine 2007. *Literary Agent:* Inn BoonsBoro, 1 North Main Street, Boonsboro, MD 21713; Writers' House Inc., 21 West 26th Street, New York, NY 10010, USA (office). *Telephone:* (212) 685-2400. *Fax:* (212) 685-1781. *E-mail:* write2nora@msn.com. *Website:* www.noraroberts.com; www.innboonsboro.com.

ROBERTS, Yvonne, BA; British journalist and writer; b. 1949, Newport Pagnell; d. of John Roberts and Nancy Roberts; fmr pnr John Pilger; one d.; pnr Stephen Scott; one d. *Education:* Univ. of Warwick. *Career:* fmr Assoc. Features Ed., London Daily News; Section Ed., The Observer; has been published in New Statesman and New Society magazines, Guardian, Sunday Times and Independent newspapers. *Publications include:* Man Enough 1984, Mad About Women 1994, Every Woman Deserves an Adventure (novel) 1994, The Trouble with Single Women 1997, A History of Insects 2000, Shake 2004, Where Did Our Love Go? 2006. *Honours:* Young Journalist of the Year 1970. *Literary Agent:* c/o David Higham Associates, 5-8 Lower John Street, Golden Square, London, W1F 9HA. *Telephone:* (20) 7434-5900. *Fax:* (20) 7437-1072. *E-mail:* dha@davidhigham.co.uk. *Website:* www.davidhigham.co.uk. *E-mail:* yroberts@dial.pipex.com (home).

ROBERTSON, Barbara, BA, MA; Canadian writer; b. 20 July 1931, Toronto, ON. *Education:* University of Toronto, Queen's University, Kingston. *Publications:* The Wind Has Wings (ed. with M. A. Downie), 1968, revised edn as The New Wind Has Wings, 1984; Wilfrid Laurier: The Great Conciliator, 1971; The Well-Filled Cupboard (with M. A. Downie), 1987, revised edn as The Canadian Treasury of Cooking and Gardening, 1997; Doctor Dwarf and Other Poems for Children (ed. with M. A. Downie), 1990; Ottawa at War: The Grant Dexter Memoranda 1939–1945 (ed. with F. W. Gibson), 1994. Contributions: periodicals.

ROBERTSON, Denise; British writer and broadcaster; b. 9 June 1933, Sunderland, England; m. 1st Alexander Robertson 1960; m. 2nd John Tomlin 1973, five s. *Publications:* Year of Winter, 1986; Land of Lost Content, 1987; Blue Remembered Hills, 1987; Second Wife, 1988; None to Make You Cry, 1989; Remember the Moment, 1990. Contributions: numerous publications. *Honours:* Constable Fiction Trophy 1985.

ROBERTSON, Geoffrey Ronald, QC, BA, LLB, BCL; Australian/British judge and barrister; *Head, Doughty Street Chambers*; b. 30 Sept. 1946, Sydney; s. of Francis Robertson and Bernice Beattie; m. Kathy Lette (q.v.) 1990; one s. one d. *Education:* Epping Boys' High School and Univs of Sydney and Oxford. *Career:* Rhodes scholar; solicitor, Allen, Allen & Hemsley 1970; called to bar, Middle Temple, London 1973; QC 1988; Visiting Prof., Univ. of NSW 1979, Univ. of Warwick 1981; leader, Amnesty missions to S Africa 1983–90; consultant on Human Rights to Govt of Australia 1984; Founding mem. and Head, Doughty Street Chambers 1990–; Counsel to Royal Comm. on gun-running to Colombian drug cartels 1991; Asst Recorder 1993–99, a Recorder 1999–; Master of Bench, Middle Temple 1997–; Chief Counsel Comm. on Admin. of Justice in Trinidad and Tobago 2000; Appeal Judge, UN Special Court for War Crimes in Sierra Leone 2002–07; Chair. Staff Panel on Reform of UN Justice 2006; mem. Exec. Council Justice; Jurist mem. UN Internal Justice Council 2008–12. *Radio:* Chair. You the Jury (BBC Radio 4). *Plays:* The Trials of Oz (BBC) 1992. *TV series:* Hypotheticals, Granada TV, ABC and Channel 7 (Australia). *Publications:* Reluctant Judas 1976, Obscenity 1979, People Against the Press 1983, Geoffrey Robertson's Hypotheticals 1986, Does Dracula Have AIDS ? 1987, Freedom, The Individual and The Law 1989, The Justice Game 1998, Crimes Against Humanity 1999, Media Law (with A. Nicol) 2002, The Tyrannicide Brief 2006, The Levellers – The Putney Debates 2007, Statute of Liberty 2009, The Case of the Pope 2010. *Honours:* Hon. LLD (Sydney) 2006; Freedom of Information Award 1992. *Address:* Doughty Street Chambers, 11 Doughty Street, London, WC1N 2PL, England (office). *Telephone:* (20) 7404-1313 (office); (20) 7624-3268 (home). *Fax:* (20) 7404-2283 (office); (20) 7624-7146 (home). *E-mail:* g.robertson@doughtystreet.co.uk (office). *Website:* www.doughtystreet.co.uk (office).

ROBERTSON, James, MA, PhD; British novelist, poet, editor and publisher; b. 1958, Sevenoaks, Kent. *Education:* Edinburgh Univ. *Career:* founder of pamphlet publisher, Kettillonia 1999–; Gen. Ed. of children's book imprint, Itchy Coo; Writer-in-Residence, Brownsbank Cottage 1993–95, Scottish Parl. 2004. *Publications:* Close 1991, The Ragged Man's Complaint (short stories) 1993, A Tongue in Yer Heid (ed.) 1994, Sound Shadow (poems) 1995, I Dream of Alfred Hitchcock (poems) 1999, The Fanatic (novel) 2000, Fae the Flouers o Evil: Baudelaire in Scots 2001, Stirling Sonnets 2002, A Scots Parliament 2002, Joseph Knight (novel) (Saltire Soc. Scottish Book of the Year 2003, Scottish Arts Council Book of the Year 2004) 2003, Voyages of Intent 2005, The Testament of Gideon Mack (novel) 2006, And the Land Lay Still (novel) (Saltire Soc. Scottish Book of the Year) 2010, many children's books in Scots language (co-author). *Address:* Kettillonia, Sidlaw House, South Street, Newtyle, Angus, PH12 8UQ, Scotland (office). *E-mail:* james@kettillonia.co.uk (office). *Website:* www.scotgeog.com.

ROBERTSON, James Irvin, Jr, BA, MA, PhD, LittD; American academic; b. 18 July 1930, Danville, VA; m. Elizabeth Green 1952; two s. one d. *Education:* Randolph-Macon Coll., Emory Univ., Randolph-Macon Coll. *Career:* Assoc. Prof. of History, University of Montana, 1965–67; Prof. of History, 1967–75, C. P. Miles Prof. of History, 1976–92, Alumni Distinguished Prof. of History, 1992–, Virginia Polytechnic Institute and State University; mem. Virginia Historical Society; Organization of American Historians; Southern Historical Asscn; Confederate Memorial Society. *Publications:* The Stonewall Brigade, 1963; The Civil War Letters of General Robert McAllister, 1965; Recollections of a Maryland Confederate Soldier, 1975; Four Years in the Stonewall Brigade, 1978; The 4th Virginia Infantry, 1980; Civil War Sites in Virginia: A Tour-Guide, 1982; The 18th Virginia Infantry, 1983; Tenting Tonight: The Soldiers' View, 1984; General A. P. Hill, 1987; Soldiers Blue and Gray, 1988; Civil War: America Becomes One Nation, 1992; Jackson and Lee: Legends in Gray (with Mort Kunstler), 1995; Stonewall Jackson: The Man, The Soldier, The Legend, 1997. Contributions: More than 150 articles in historical journals and history magazines; Regular appearances in Civil War programmes on television and radio. *Honours:* Freeman-Nevins Award, 1981; Bruce Catton Award, 1983; William E. Wine Award for Teaching Excellence, 1983; A. P. Andrews Memorial Award, 1985; James Robertson Award of Achievement, 1985. *Address:* Department of History, Virginia Polytechnic Institute and State University, Blacksburg, VA 24061, USA.

ROBINETTE, Joseph Allen, BA, MA, PhD; American playwright and academic; b. 8 Feb. 1939, Rockwood, Tenn.; m. Helen M. Seitz 1965; four s. one d. *Education:* Carson-Newman Coll., Southern Illinois Univ. *Career:* fmr Prof., Dept of Theatre and Dance, Rowan Coll.; mem. American Soc. of Composers, Authors and Publrs, American Asscn for Theatre in Educ., Opera for Youth. *Publications:* The Fabulous Fable Factory 1975, Once Upon a Shoe (play) 1979, Legend of the Sun Child (musical) 1982, Charlotte's Web (dramatization) 1983, Charlotte's Web (musical with Charles Strouse) 1989, Anne of Green Gables (dramatization) 1989, The Lion, the Witch and the Wardrobe (dramatization) 1989, The Trial of Goldilocks (operetta) 1990, Dorothy Meets Alice (musical) 1991, Stuart Little (dramatization) 1992, The Trumpet of the Swan (dramatization) 1993, The Adventures of Beatrix Potter and her Friends (musical) 1994, The Littlest Angel (musical) 1994, The Jungle Book (dramatization) 1995, The Trial of the Big Bad Wolf (play) 1999, Just So Stories (play) 2001, Humpty-Dumpty is Missing (play) 2001, Sarah, Plain and Tall (American Alliance for Theatre and Educ. Award for Best Play 2004) 2003, book for musical 'A Christmas Story, The Musical!' (premiered at Kansas City Repertory Theatre) 2009; contrib. to Children's Theatre News, Opera for Youth News. *Honours:* Charlotte Chorpenning Cup, Nat. Children's Playwriting Award 1976, Lifetime Achievement Award Children's Theatre Foundation of America 2006. *Address:* PO Box 11, Richwood, NJ 08074, USA.

ROBINS, Patricia (see Clark, Patricia Denise)

ROBINSON, David Julien, BA; British film critic, festival director and writer; b. 6 Aug. 1930, England. *Education:* King's Coll., Cambridge. *Career:* Assoc. Ed., Sight and Sound, and Ed., Monthly Film Bulletin 1956–58; Programme Dir, Nat. Film Theatre 1959; film critic, Financial Times 1959–74, The Times 1974–92; Dir, Garrett Robinson Co. 1987–88, The Davids Film Co. 1988–, Channel 4 Young Film-maker of the Year Competition, Edinburgh Film Festival 1992–95, Pordenone Silent Film Festival, Italy 1997–; Guest Dir, Edinburgh Film Festival 1989–91. *Publications:* Hollywood in the Twenties 1969, Buster Keaton 1969, The Great Funnies 1972, World Cinema (aka The History of World Cinema) 1973, Chaplin: The Mirror of Opinion 1983, Chaplin: His Life and Art 1985, The Illustrated History of the Cinema (co-ed.) 1986, Music of the Shadows 1990, Masterpieces of Animation 1833–1908 1991, Richard Attenborough 1992, Georges Méliès 1993, Lantern Images: Iconography of the Magic Lantern 1440–1880 1993, Sight and Sound Chronology of the Cinema 1994–95, Musique et cinema muet 1995, Charlot: Entre rires et larmes 1995, Peepshow to Palace 1995, Light and Image: Incunabula of the Motion Picture (co-author) 1996; contrib. to newspapers and periodicals. *Address:* 19 Lansdown Crescent, Bath, BA1 5EX, England. *Telephone:* (1225) 333391. *E-mail:* robinorama@aol.com.

ROBINSON, Derek, (Dirk Robson), MA; British writer; b. 12 April 1932, Bristol, England; m. Sheila Collins 1968. *Education:* Downing Coll., Cambridge. *Career:* nat. service with RAF; advertising copywriter, London and New York; freelance writer. *Publications:* Goshawk Squadron 1971, Rotten With Honour 1973, Kramer's War 1977, The Eldorado Network 1979, Piece of Cake (also televised as mini-series) 1983, War Story 1987, Artillery of Lies 1991, A Good Clean Fight 1993, Rugby: A Player's Guide to the Laws 1995, Hornet's Sting 1999, Kentucky Blues 2002, Damned Good Show 2002, Invasion 1940 2005, Red Rag Blues 2006, Better Rugby Refereeing 2007, Hullo Russia, Goodbye England 2008, Operation Bamboozle 2010, A Splendid Little War 2012. *E-mail:* delrobster@googlemail.com (office). *Website:* www.derekrobinson.info.

ROBINSON, Jeffrey, BS; American writer; b. 19 Oct. 1945, New York, NY; m. Aline Benayoun 1985; one s. one d. *Education:* Temple Univ., Philadelphia. *Career:* mem. PEN. *Television, radio and screenplays:* The Laundrymen 1996, Same Time Next Week 2000, Tightrope 2002, Rossum's Cyber Café 2003, Sister Banjo 2003, The Real Amos 'n' Andy 2004, Bardot 2005, Notice of Claim 2005, The Confession 2006, I Je t'Aime You 2006, The Wind Off Drumcliffe Bay 2007. *Publications:* Bette Davis – Her Stage and Film Career 1983, Teamwork 1984, The Risk Takers 1985, Pietrov and Other Games (fiction) 1985, Minus Millionaires 1986, The Ginger Jar (fiction) 1986, Yamani – The Inside Story 1988, Rainier and Grace 1989, The Risk Takers – Five Years On 1990, The End of the American Century 1992, The Laundrymen 1994, Bardot – Two Lives 1994, The Margin of the Bulls (fiction) 1995, The Hotel 1996, The Monk's Disciples (fiction) 1996, The Manipulators 1997, A True and Perfect Knight (fiction) 1998, The Merger 2000, Prescription Games 2001, The Sink 2003, Standing Next to History (with Joseph Petro) 2005, Ronnie: My Life as a Rolling Stone (with Ronnie Wood) 2007, Leading from the Front: My Life (with Gerald Ronson) 2009, There's a Sucker Born Every Minute 2010, The Takedown – A Suburban Mom, A Coal Miner's Son and the Unlikely Demise of Colombia's Brutal Norte Valle Cartel 2011; contrib. of more than 700 articles and short stories to major magazines and journals world-wide. *Honours:* Overseas Press Club 1984, Benedictine After Dinner Speaker of the Year 1990. *Literary Agent:* c/o Mel Berger, William Morris Endeavor, 1325 Avenue of the Americas, New York, 10019, USA. *Website:* www.jeffreyrobinson.com.

ROBINSON, Kim Stanley, BA, MA, PhD; American author; b. 23 March 1952, Waukegan, IL. *Education:* Univ. of California at San Diego, Boston Univ. *Career:* Visiting Lecturer, Univ. of California at San Diego 1982, 1985, Univ. of California at Davis 1982–84, 1985. *Publications:* Black Air (World Fantasy Award 1983) 1982, Icehenge 1984, The Wild Shore (Locus Award 1985) 1984, The Blind Geometer (novella) (Nebula Award for Best Novella 1986) 1985, The Memory of Whiteness 1985, The Planet on the Table (short stories) 1986, Escape from Kathmandu (short stories) 1987, The Gold Coast 1988, Pacific Edge (John W. Campbell Memorial Award for Best Science Fiction Novel 1991) 1990, A Short, Sharp Shock (Locus Award 1991) 1990, Remaking History (short stories) 1991, Red Mars (Nebula Award for Best Novel 1993) 1992, Green Mars (Hugo Award for Best Novel 1994, Locus Award 1994) 1993, Blue Mars (Hugo Award for Best Novel 1997, Locus Award 1997) 1996, Antarctica 1997, Martians (Locus Award 2000) 1999, Vinland the Dream 2002, The Years of Rice and Salt (Locus Award 2003) 2002, Forty Signs of Rain 2004, Fifty Degrees Below 2005, Journey to the Center of the Earth 2006, Sixty Days and Counting 2007, Galileo's Dream 2009; other: Future Primitive (ed.) 1982, The Novels of Philip K. Dick 1984, Nebula Awards Showcase (ed.) 2002; contrib. to periodicals and anthologies. *Address:* c/o Spectra Publicity, Random House, 1745 Broadway, New York, NY 10019, USA (office).

ROBINSON, Marilynne, PhD; American novelist and essayist; b. 1947, Sandpoint, ID; d. of John J. Summers and Ellen Harris Summers; m.; two s. *Education:* Coeur d'Alene High School, Brown Univ., Univ. of Washington. *Career:* taught at Univ. de Haute Bretagne, Rennes, France 1966–67; writer-in-residence and visiting prof. at numerous colls and univs, including Univ. of Kent, England, Amherst Coll., Univ. of Massachusetts, Skidmore Coll.; mem. of faculty Writers' Workshop 1991–, Univ. of Iowa. *Publications:* Housekeeping (novel) (PEN/Hemingway Foundation Award for Best First Novel, Richard and Hilda Rosenthal Award) 1980, Mother Country: Britain, the Welfare State and Nuclear Pollution (non-fiction) 1988, The Death of Adam: Essays on Modern Thought 1998, Puritans and Prigs (non-fiction) 1999, Gilead (fiction) (Nat. Book Critics Circle Award, Pulitzer Prize for Fiction 2005) 2004, Home (Orange Prize for Fiction 2009) 2008, Absence of Mind 2010, When I Was a Child I Read Books (essays) 2012; contrib. essays and book reviews to Harper's, Paris Review, The New York Times Book Review. *Address:* c/o Farrar, Strauss and Giroux, 18 West 18th Street, New York, NY 10011, USA (office). *Website:* us.macmillan.com/fsg.aspx.

ROBINSON, Nick; British journalist; *Political Editor, BBC*; b. 5 Oct. 1963, Macclesfield, Cheshire. *Education:* Cheadle Hulme School, Univ. Coll.,

Oxford. *Career:* trainee producer on programmes, including Brass Tacks, Newsround, Crimewatch 1986, then Deputy Ed. On the Record, Panorama; fmr presenter Late Night Live and Weekend Breakfast (both on BBC Radio Five Live), Westminster Live (BBC 2); fmr Chief Political Corresp., BBC News 24, presenting Straight Talk and One to One –2002; Political Ed. ITV News 2002–05; columnist of political 'Notebook' in The Times 2003–; Political Ed. BBC 2005–. *Address:* BBC Westminster, 4 Millbank, London, SW1P 3JA, England (office). *Website:* www.bbc.co.uk/nickrobinson (office).

ROBINSON, Sheila Mary, (Sheila Radley, Hester Rowan), BA; British writer; b. 18 Nov. 1928, Cogenhoe, Northamptonshire, England. *Education:* University of London. *Publications:* Overture in Venice, 1976; The Linden Tree, 1977; Death and the Maiden, 1978; Snowfall, 1978; The Chief Inspector's Daughter, 1981; A Talent for Destruction, 1982; Blood on the Happy Highway, 1983; Fate Worse Than Death, 1985; Who Saw Him Die?, 1987; This Way Out, 1989; Cross My Heart and Hope to Die, 1992; Fair Game, 1994; New Blood from Old Bones, 1998.

ROBINSON, Spider, BA; Canadian writer and musician; b. 23 Nov. 1948, New York, NY, USA; s. of Charles Robinson and Evelyn Meade; m. Jeanne Robinson (died 2010); one d. *Education:* State Univ. of New York at Stony Brook. *Career:* book reviewer, Galaxy magazine 1974–77, Destinies magazine 1977–79, Analog magazine 1978–80; columnist, The Globe and Mail 1996–2004; Writer-in-Residence, H.R. MacMillan Space Centre, Vancouver, BC 2006; Writer-in-Residence, Vancouver Public Library 2010; Chair. Nova Dance Theatre, Halifax, NS 1981–84; Chair. Exec. Council, Writers Fed. of Nova Scotia 1981–83. *Achievements include:* invited by First Lady Laura Bush to dine with her and Pres. George W. Bush and to read aloud at the Nat. Mall during the Library of Congress's Nat. Book Festival, Washington, DC 2006. *Dance:* In their collaborative award-winning novella 'Stardance' Robinson and his wife Jeanne invented a new art form, zero gravity dance, and defined most of its basic axioms, principles and vocabulary in three subsequent novels, The Stardance Trilogy. *Recordings:* Belaboring the Obvious, On The Way To The Stars (collaboration with David Crosby), Kokura Loves Its Fog (collaboration with Todd Butler), Drowntown Brown (collaboration with Todd Butler). *Radio:* Stardance (collaboration with Jeanne Robinson, adapted by Ken Methold) (voted Best Australian Radio Drama of 1977). *Publications include:* Telempath (Hugo Award for Best Novella 1976) 1976, Callahan's Crosstime Saloon (American Library Asscn Best Book for Young Adults 1977) 1977, Stardance (with Jeanne Robinson) (Hugo Award for Best Novella 1977, Nebula Award for Best Novella 1977, Locus Award for Best Novella 1977) 1979, Antinomy 1980, Time Travelers Strictly Cash 1981, Mindkiller 1982, Melancholy Elephants (Hugo Award for Best Short Story 1984) 1983, Night of Power 1985, Callahan's Secret 1986, Time Pressure 1987, Callahan and Company 1988, Callahan's Lady 1989, Copyright Violation (novella) 1990, True Minds 1990, Starseed (with Jeanne Robinson) 1991, Kill the Editor (novella) 1991, Lady Slings the Booze 1992, The Callahan Touch 1993, Off the Wall at Callahan's 1994, Starmind 1994, Callahan's Legacy 1996, Lifehouse 1997, User Friendly 1998, Callahan's Key 2001, The Free Lunch 2001, By Any Other Name (Hugo Award for Best Novella) 2001, God is an Iron and Other Stories 2002, Callahan's Con 2003, The Crazy Years (non-fiction) 2004, Very Bad Deaths 2004, Variable Star (with Robert A. Heinlein) 2006, Very Hard Choices 2008. *Honours:* John W. Campbell Award for Best New Writer 1974, Locus Award for Best Critic 1976, Pat Terry Memorial Award for Humorous Writing, Sydney (Australia) Science Fiction Foundation 1977, E.E. Smith Memorial Award for Speculative Fiction, New England Science Fiction Asscn 1977, Canada Council for the Arts grants 1983, 1984, 1986, 1989, 1992, NS Dept of Culture, Recreation & Fitness grants 1983, 1986, BC Ministry of Municipal Affairs, Recreation & Culture grant 1991, Robert A. Heinlein Award for Lifetime Excellence 2008, Earphones Award for audiobook readings 2008. *Literary Agent:* c/o Eleanor Wood, Spectrum Literary Agency, 320 Central Park West, Suite 1-D, New York, NY 10025, USA. *Telephone:* (212) 362-4323. *Fax:* (212) 362-4562. *E-mail:* eleanorspectrum@verizon.net. *Website:* www.spectrumliteraryagency.com. *Telephone:* (604) 947-2437 (office). *E-mail:* spiderweb@shaw.ca (office). *Website:* www.spiderrobinson.com.

ROBSKI, Oksana; Russian author. *Career:* chat show host. *Publications:* titles in translation: Casual (novel) 2005, Pro Liuboff/on 2005, The Rich Russian's Guide to Sex, Shopping, and Revenge: A Novel.

ROBSON, Dirk (see Robinson, Derek)

ROCA, Juan Manuel; Colombian poet; b. 29 Dec. 1946, Medellin. *Career:* grew up in Mexico and later Paris, France; Co-founder of magazines including Clave de Sol and La Sagrada Escritura; co-ordinated Sunday magazine of El Espectador 1988–99. *Publications:* poetry: Memoria del agua 1973, Luna de ciegos (Premio Nacional de Poesia Universidad de Antioquia 1976) 1976, Los ladrones nocturnos 1977, Cartas desde el sueño 1978, Señal de cuervos 1979, Mester de caballería 1979, Fabulario real 1980, Antología poética 1983, País secreto 1987, Ciudadano de la noche 1989, Pavana con el diablo 1990, Monólogos 1994, Memoria de encuentros 1995, La farmacia del ángel 1995, Tertulia de ausentes 1998, Lugar de apariciones 2000,Los cinco entierros de Pessoa 2001, Arenga del que sueña 2002,Teatro de sombras con César Vallejo 2002, Un violín para Chagall 2003, Las hipótesis de Nadie 2005, Cantar de lejanía (anthology) (Premio Casa de las Américas de Poesía José Lezama Lima 2007) 2005, El ángel sitiado y otros poemas 2006, Testamentos 2008, Biblia de Pobres (Premio Casa de América de Poesia Americana 2009) 2009, Pasaporte del apátrida 2012; prose collections: Prosa reunida 1993, Las plagas secretas y otros cuentos 2001, Esa maldita costumbre de morir 2003; essays: Museo de encuentros 1995, Cartógrafa memoria 2003; other: Rocabulario: Antología de sus definiciones 2006, Diccionario anarquista de emergencia (co-author) 2008. *Honours:* Dr hc (Universidad del Valle); Premio Nacional de Poesía Eduardo Cote Lamus 1975, Premio Nacional de Poesía Universidad de Antioquia 1979, Premio Mejor Comentarista de Libros Cámara Colombiana del Libro 1992, Premio Nacional de Periodismo Simón Bolívar 1993, Premio Nacional de Cuento Universidad de Antioquia 2000, Premio Nacional de Poesía Ministerio de Cultura 2004. *Address:* c/o Editoria Pre-Textos, Luis Santángel 10, 1-C, 46005 Valencia, Spain (office). *Telephone:* (96) 3333226 (office). *Fax:* (96) 3955477 (office). *E-mail:* info@pre-textos.com (office). *Website:* www.pre-textos.com (office).

ROCHA URTECHO, Luis; Nicaraguan poet, essayist and journalist; b. 1942, Granada. *Career:* worked at various periodicals and literary journals; Secretary, Central American Literary Press 1976–77; CEO Nuevo Amanecer Cultural 1980–2007; fmr Founding Dir, literary supplement of El Nuevo Diario newspaper; Founding mem. and fmr Pres. Centro Nicaragüense de Escritores (Nicaraguan Center for Writers); fmr President, Instituto Nicaragüense de Cultura Hispánica; fmr Editorial Dir, Nueva Nicaragua; judge for Premio Casa de las Americas 2004. *Publications:* La vida consciente 1966, Domus Aurea 1968, Ejercicios de Composición 1974, Phocas 1983, Dichoso el árbol 1997, Un solo haz de energía ecumenical 1998, Pedro: Teniendo conocidos en el cielo 2008. *Honours:* Premio Nacional Ruben Dario 1983. *Address:* c/o Centro Nicaragüense de Escritores, Reparto los Robles, Del Hotel Seminole 2 cuadras al sur, Managua, Nicaragua (office). *Telephone:* 2267-0304 (office). *Fax:* 2278-5781 (office). *E-mail:* escritor@ibw.com.ni (office). *Website:* www.escritoresnicaragua.com (office).

ROCHE, Charlotte Grace; German writer and television presenter; b. 18 March 1978, High Wycombe, England; m.; one d. *Career:* lived in Germany from childhood; presenter, VIVA II music channel 1998–2001, VIVA 2002–05; writer and presenter of programmes and late-night talk shows, for VIVA, Arte and ZDF; currently host, Fast Forward (VIVA) and Charlotte Meets.... (ProSieben). *Publication:* Feuchtgebiete (trans. as Wetlands) 2008. *Honours:* Grimme Prize for television 2002. *Address:* c/o DuMont Buchverlag GmbH, Amsterdamer Straße 192, 50735 Cologne, Germany (office). *E-mail:* info@dumont-buchverlag.de (office). *Website:* www.dumont-buchverlag.de (office); www.charlotteroche.de.

ROCHE, Denis; French writer, photographer and editor; b. 1937, Paris. *Career:* Dir Tel Quel magazine 1962–72; Literary Dir Editions Tchou 1964–70; worked for Editions du Seuil 1971, later as mem. editorial cttee and directing Les Contemporains imprint, cr. Fiction & Cie imprint 1974–; co-f. Les Cahiers de la Photographie publisher 1980–; began exhibiting photographs 1978–. *Photography exhibitions:* solo: Galerie l'oeil, Chateauroux 2000 1978, Canon Photo Galerie, Geneva, Switzerland 1979, Galerie Déclinaisons, Rouen 1980, Centre Culturel franco-italien, Turin, Italy, Inst. Supérieur pour l'étude du langage plastique, Brussels, Belgium 1981, Menées photographiques, Galerie J. et J. Donguy, Paris 1985, Galerie Images Nouvelles, Bordeaux 1986, Musée d'Art moderne, Vienna, Austria, Fulton Co. Public Library, Atlanta, USA, Frankfurter Kunstverein, Germany 1987, Musée de Tijuana, Mexico, Musée d'Art Moderne de Mexico, L'Art des circonstances, Centre culturel français, Cairo, Egypt 1988, Le Mas de l'enfant, Barbentane, Arles, Espace photographique de Paris 1989, Galerie Le Réverbère, Lyon, Artothèque Grand Place, Grenoble 1990, Galerie Maeght, Paris 1991, Alliance française, Lima, Peru, Galerie municipale du Château d'Eau, Toulouse 1992, Artothèque, Vitré 1994, Centre régional de la photographie Nord-Pas-de-Calais, Douchy-les-Mines, Galerie Zeit-Foto Salon, Tokyo, Japan 1995, Il n'y a pas de leçon des Ténèbres, Galerie Le Réverbère, Lyon 1996, Saint-Gervais, Geneva, Switzerland, Galerie J. et J. Donguy, Paris, Encontros da Imagem, Braga, Portugal 1997, Galerie Archi typographies, Bordeaux 1997, Univ. Saint-Esprit de Kaslik, Beirut, Lebanon 1998, Florence ilenri – Denis Roche, Rencontres Int. de la Photographie, Arles 1999, Centre culturel français, Damascus, Syria 2000, Hôpitaux universitaires Belle-Idée, Geneva, Switzerland, La question que je pose, Galerie Le Réverbère, Lyon 2001, Les preuves du temps Musée Nicéphore Niepee, Chalon-sur-Saône, Maison européenne de la photographie, Paris; numerous jt exhbns. *Publications:* Forestière Amazonide 1962, Récits complets 1963, Les Idées centésimales de Miss Elanize 1964, Eros énergumène 1968, Carnac, ou les mésaventures de la narration 1969, 3 Pourrissements poétiques 1972, Le Mécrit 1972, Louve basse 1972, Notre antéfixe 1978, Antéfixe de Françoise Peyrot 1978, Dépôts de savoir et de technique 1980, A quoi sert le lynx? A rien, comme Mozart 1980, Légendes de Denis Roche 1981, La Disparition des lucioles 1982, Conversations avec le temps 1985, A Varèse 1986, Ecrits momentanés chroniques photo du magazine City 1984–87 1988, Photoalies 1988, Prose au devant d'une femme 1988, Lettre ouverte à quelques amis et à un certain nombre de jean-foutres 1988, L'Hexaméron (co-author) 1990, Ellipse et laps 1991, Dans la Maison du Sphinx 1992, La Poésie est inadmissible 1995, L'Embarquement pour Mercure (with Michel Butor) 1996, Le Boîtier de mélancolie, la photographie en 100 photographies (ed.) (Prix André Malraux) 1999. *Honours:* Grand Prix de Photographie de la Ville de Paris 1997. *Address:* c/o Editions du Seuil, 27 rue Jacob, 75006 Paris, France.

ROCHE, Terry (see Poole, Margaret Barbara)

ROCHE, William (Billy) Michael; Irish playwright and author; b. 11 Jan. 1949, Wexford. *Career:* singer, The Roach Band 1975–80; Playwright-in-Residence, Bush Theatre, London 1988; Writer in Asscn with Druid Theatre, Galway 1997, The Abbey Theatre, Dublin 2000. *Plays:* A Handful of Stars (Bush Theatre, London), Amphibians (RSC), Poor Beast in the Rain (Bush Theatre, London) (London Theatre Fringe Award 1992), Belfry (Bush Theatre, London) (Time Out Award 1992), The Cavalcaders (Abbey Theatre, Dublin, Royal Court, London), On Such As We (Abbey Theatre), Lay Me Down Softly (Abbey Theatre). *Publications:* plays: A Handful of Stars 1987, Amphibians 1987, Poor Beast in the Rain 1989, Belfry (Time Out Award 1992) 1991, The Cavalcaders 1993, On Such As We 2001, Lay Me Down Softly 2008; other: Tumbling Down (novel) 1986, Trojan Eddie (film script; San Sebastian Film Festival Prize 1997) 1997, Tales from Rain Water Pond (short stories) 2006, The Eclipse (screenplay co-written with Conor McPherson, based on short story Table Manners) (Irish Film and Television Award for Best Screenplay and Best Film) 2009. *Literary Agent:* c/o Leah Schmidt, The Agency, 24 Pottery Lane, Holland Park, London, W11 4LZ, England. *Telephone:* (20) 7727-1346. *Fax:* (20) 7727-9037. *E-mail:* info@theagency.co.uk. *Website:* www.theagency.co.uk. *Address:* 44 Pineridge, Clonard, Co. Wexford, Ireland.

RODDY, Lee, AA; American writer; b. 22 Aug. 1921, Marion County, IL; m. Cicely Price 1947, one s. one d. *Education:* Los Angeles City College. *Career:* mem. Authors' Guild of America; Authors League; National Society of Children's Book Writers. *Publications:* The Life and Times of Grizzly Adams, 1977; The Lincoln Conspiracy, 1977; Jesus, 1979; Ghost Dog of Stoney Ridge, 1985; Dooger, Grasshopper Hound, 1985; The City Bear's Adventures, 1985; The Hair Pulling Bear Dog, 1985; Secret of the Shark Pit, 1988; Secret of the Sunken Sub, 1989; The Overland Escape, 1989; The Desperate Search, 1989; Danger on Thunder Mountain, 1990; Secret of the Howland Cave, 1990; The Flaming Trap, 1990; Mystery of the Phantom Gold, 1991; The Gold Train Bandits, 1992. Other: several books made into films and television programmes.

RODGERS, Mary Columbro, MA, PhD; American university chancellor and writer; b. 17 April 1925, Autora, OH; d. of Nicola and Nancy (née DeNicola) Columbro; m. Daniel Richard Rodgers 1965; two d. one s. *Education:* Notre Dame Coll., Western Reserve Univ. and Ohio State Univ. *Career:* English teacher, Cleveland, OH 1945–62; Supervisor Ohio State Univ. 1962–64; Asst Prof. of English Univ. of Maryland 1965–66; Assoc. Prof. Trinity Coll. 1967–68; Prof. of English, DC Teachers' Coll. 1968–; Chancellor and Dean American Open Univ. 1965–; Pres. Maryland Nat. Univ. 1972–; Ind. Researcher 2002–; Fellow Catholic Scholars; mem. Poetry Soc. of America, Nat. Council of English Teachers, American Educational Research Asscn. *Publications include:* A Short Course in English Compositions 1976, Chapbook of Children's Literature 1977, Essays and Poems on Life and Literature 1979, Modes and Models: Four Lessons for Young Writers 1981, Open University Structures and Adult Learning 1982, English Pedagogy in the American Open University 1983, Design for Personalized Graduate Degrees in the Urban University 1984, Poet and Pedagogue in Moscow and Leningrad: a travel report 1989, Twelve Lectures in Literary Analysis 1990, Ten Lectures in Literary Production 1990, Analyzing Fact and Fiction 1991, Analyzing Poetry and Drama 1991, A Chapbook of Poetry and Drama Analysis 1992, Convent Poems 1943–61 1993, Catholic Marriage Poems 1962–79 1993, New Design Responses 1945–93 (10 vols) 1993, Catholic Widow with Children Poems 1979–93 1994, Journals: Reflections and Resolves 1984–95 (16 vols) 1995, Biographical Sourcebook: Mary Columbro Rodgers 1969–95 1995, Catholic Teacher Poems 1945–95 1995. *Honours:* Hon. DipEd (California Nat. Open) 1975, Hon. DLitt (California Nat. Open) 1978. *Address:* College Heights Estate, 3916 Commander Drive, Hyattsville, MD 20782, USA.

RODOLPH, Utto (see Ouologuem, Yambo)

RODRIGUES, Louis Jerome, BA, MA, MPhil, PhD; writer, poet and translator; b. 20 July 1938, Chennai, India; m. 1st Malinda Weaving (deceased); one s.; m. 2nd Josefina Bernet Soler 1984; one s. *Education:* University of Chennai, University of London, University of Barcelona. *Career:* Asst Dir, Benedict, Mannheim 1977; Dir of Studies, Inlingua, Barcelona 1978–82; Dir, Phoenix, Barcelona 1982–87; mem. International Asscn of Anglo-Saxonists, RSL, Society of Authors, exec. committee mem., 1988–91, 2003–06, Trans. Asscn, American Literary Trans. Asscn. *Publications:* A Long Time Waiting 1979, Anglo-Saxon Riddles 1990, Seven Anglo-Saxon Elegies 1991, Chiaroscuro 1991, The Battles of Maldon and Brunanburh 1991, Anglo-Saxon Verse Runes 1992, Anglo-Saxon Verse Charms, Maxims and Heroic Legends 1993, Anglo-Saxon Elegiac Verse 1994, Anglo-Saxon Didactic Verse 1995, Three Anglo-Saxon Battle Poems 1995, Salvador Espriu: Selected Poems (trans.) 1997, Beowulf and the Fight at Finnsburh, Buttercups and Daisies 2006; contrib. to various publications. *Honours:* Poetry Trans. Prize, Catholic University of America, Washington, DC 1993. *Address:* 132 Wisbech Road, Littleport, Ely, Cambridgeshire CB6 1JJ, England (home). *E-mail:* louis.rodrigues@ntlworld.com (home). *Website:* www.louisrodrigues.co.uk.

RODRÍGUEZ, Antonio Orlando; Cuban writer and editor; b. 1956, Clego de Avila. *Education:* Univ. of Havana. *Career:* has lived in Costa Rica, Colombia; currently lives in Florida, USA. *Play:* El León y la Domadora 1998. *Publications:* novels: Aprendices de brujo 2002, Chiquita (Premio Alfaguara) 2008; short stories: Strip-tease 1985, Querido Drácula 1989; non-fiction: Literatura infantil de América Latina 1993, Puertas a la lectura 1993, Panorama histórico de la literatura infantil en América Latina y el Caribe 1994, Escuela y poesía 1997. *Address:* c/o Editorial Alfaguara, Santillana Ediciones Generales, Calle Torrelaguna 60, 28043 Madrid, Spain (office). *E-mail:* alfaguara@santillana.es (office). *Website:* www.alfaguara.santillana.es (office).

RODRIGUEZ, Judith Catherine, AM, BA, MA, PGCE; Australian poet (retd), dramatist, librettist, editor and lecturer; *Teacher of Poetry Writing, Council of Adult Education, Melbourne;* b. (Judith Catherine Green), 13 Feb. 1936, Perth, WA; m. 1st Fabio Rodriguez 1964 (divorced 1981); four c.; m. 2nd Thomas Shapcott 1982. *Education:* Univ. of Queensland, Brisbane, Girton Coll., Cambridge and Univ. of London, UK. *Career:* Lecturer in External Studies, Univ. of Queensland 1959–60; Lecturer in English, Philippa Fawcett Coll. of Educ., London 1962–63, Univ. of the West Indies, Jamaica 1963–65, St Mary's Coll. of Educ., Twickenham, UK 1966–68, Macarthur Inst. of Higher Educ., Milperra, Sydney 1987–88; Lecturer in Professional Writing, Royal Melbourne Inst. of Tech. 1988–89, Victoria Coll. 1989–92; Teacher of English as a Foreign Language, St Giles School of English, London 1965–66; Lecturer, La Trobe Univ., Bundoora 1969–75, Sr Lecturer in English 1977–85; Writer-in-Residence, Rollins Coll., Fla, USA 1986; Sr Lecturer in Professional Writing, Deakin Univ. 1993–2003; Visiting Fellow, Univ. of Madras, India 2000–04; currently Teacher of Poetry Writing, Council of Adult Educ., Melbourne; mem. Australian Soc. of Authors, Melbourne PEN Centre, Victorian Writer's Centre, Melbourne Shakespeare Soc., Australian Fed. of Grad. Women. *Publications:* poetry: Four Poets 1962, Nu-Plastik Fanfare Red 1973, Water Life 1976, Shadow on Glass 1978, Mudcrab at Gambaro's 1980, Witch Heart 1982, Floridian Poems 1986, The House By Water: New and Selected Poems 1988, The Cold 1992, Terror: Poems 2002, Manatee 2007; play: Poor Johanna (with Robyn Archer) 1994; opera libretto: Lindy 1994; editor: Mrs Noah and the Minoan Queen 1982, Poems Selected from the Australian's 20th Anniversary Competition (with Andrew Taylor) 1985, Modern Swedish Poetry (with Thomas Shapcott) 1985, Collected Poems of Jennifer Rankin 1990; contrib. to numerous publs. *Honours:* Arts Council of Australia Fellowships 1974, 1978, 1983, Govt of South Australia Biennial Prize for Literature 1978, International PEN Peter Stuyvesant Prize for Poetry 1981, Fellowship of Australian Writers Christopher Brennan Award 1994. *Address:* 18 Churchill Street, Mont Albert, Vic. 3127, Australia (home). *Telephone:* 402-049487 (mobile) (home). *Fax:* (3) 9898-7889 (home). *E-mail:* rodju@tpg.com.au (home).

RODRIGUEZ, Luis J.; American poet and writer; b. 1954, El Paso, Tex. *Career:* regular speaker and poet at nat. conferences and cultural centres; Founder, Tia Chucha Press. *Publications include:* poetry: The Concrete River 1991, Poems Across the Pavement 1993, Trochemoche 1998; How to Make Sure Your Child Behaves 2000, My Nature is Hunger 2005; fiction: Music of the Mill 2004; short story collections: The Republic of East L.A. 2003; juvenile: La llaman América (trans. as America is her Name) 1998, It Doesn't Have to be This Way 1999; memoirs: Always Running: La Vida Loca: Gang Days in L.A. 1995; contrib. to The Nation, Los Angeles Weekly, America's Review. *Honours:* Carl Sandburg Award for Non-Fiction, Poetry Center Book Award from San Francisco State Univ., PEN Oakland/Josephine Miles Award for Poetry 1991, Skipping Stones Award, Paterson Prize for Books for Young People, Hispanic Heritage Award for Excellence in Literature 1998. *Literary Agent:* Steven Barclay Agency, 12 Western Avenue, Petaluma, CA 94952, USA. *Telephone:* (707) 773-0654. *Fax:* (707) 778-1868. *E-mail:* kathryn@barclayagency.com. *Website:* www.barclayagency.com. *E-mail:* luis@luisjrodriguez.com (office). *Website:* www.luisjrodriguez.com.

RODRÍGUEZ RODRÍGUEZ, Martha; Mexican poet; b. 20 Oct. 1939, Chihuahua. *Education:* studies in accountancy. *Honours:* numerous awards for poetry, including Golden Rose Award, Ciudad Juárez 1971, Silver Medal and First Prize for poem El Campesino 1984. *Address:* Calle Colima 415, Departamento 1303, Col Condesa, México, DF 06700, Mexico. *Telephone:* (5) 2112149. *Fax:* (5) 2112149.

RODRIQUEZ, Julián Isaias, PhD; Venezuelan lawyer, poet and politician; *Attorney General; Education:* Univs of Santa Maria and Zulia and Cen. Univ. of Venezuela. *Career:* legal adviser to Ministry of Agric. 1969; fmr Attorney-Gen.; Chief Attorney of Aragua 1990–91; Senator for Aragua 1998; First Vice-Pres. Nat. Constituency Ass. 1999–2000; Vice-Pres. of Venezuela 2000; Attorney Gen. 2000–; Prof., Univ. of Carabobo; regular columnist for El Siglo; consultant to Veterinary Asscn 1971; mem. Movimiento Quinta República. *Publications:* legal: New Labour Procedures 1987, Legal Stability in Labour Laws 1993; poetry: Pozo de cabrillas, Con las aspas de todos los molinos, Los tiempos de la sed; contrib. numerous articles. *Address:* c/o Ministry of the Interior and Justice, Edif. Ministerio del Interior y Justicia, esq. de Platanal, Avda Urdaneta, Caracas 1010, Venezuela. *Telephone:* (212) 506-1101. *Fax:* (212) 506-1559. *E-mail:* webmaster@mij.gov.ve. *Website:* www.mij.gov.ve.

ROEBUCK, Derek, MA, MCom; British lawyer and writer; b. 22 Jan. 1935, Stalybridge, England; m. Susanna Leonie Hoe 1981; two s. one d. *Education:* Univ. of Oxford, Victoria Univ. of Wellington, NZ. *Career:* mem. Selden Soc. *Publications include:* Credit and Security in Asia (10 vols, with D. E. Allan and M. E. Hiscock) 1973–80, Whores of War: Mercenaries Today (with Wilfred Burchett) 1976, The Background of the Common Law (second edn) 1990, Hong Kong Digest of Contract 1995, Hong Kong Digest of Criminal Law (three vols) 1995–96, Hong Kong Digest of Criminal Procedure (three vols) 1996–97, The Taking of Hong Kong: Charles and Clara Elliot in China Waters (with

Susanna Hoe) 1999, A Miscellany of Disputes 2000, Ancient Greek Arbitration 2001, The Charitable Arbitrator: How to Mediate and Arbitrate in Louis XIV's France 2002, Roman Arbitration (with Bruno de Loynes de Fumichon) 2004, Early English Arbitration 2008, Disputes and Differences: Comparisons in Law, Language and History 2010; more than 50 articles on law, history and language. *Address:* 20A Plantation Road, Oxford, OX2 6JD, England (home).

ROGERS, Evelyn, (Keller Graves), BA, MA; American writer and teacher; b. 30 Aug. 1935, Mobile, AL; m. Jay Rogers 1957; two c. *Education:* North Texas State Univ., Our Lady of the Lake Univ. *Career:* mem. Romance Writers of America, National Society of Arts and Letters, Novelists Inc, San Antonio Romance Authors, Opera Guild of San Antonio. *Publications:* Brazen Embrace (co-author) 1987, Rapture's Gamble (co-author) 1987, Desire's Fury (co-author) 1988, Velvet Vixen (co-author) 1988, Lawman's Lady (co-author) 1988, Midnight Sins 1989, Texas Kiss 1989, Wanton Slave 1990, A Love So Wild 1991, Surrender to the Night 1991, Sweet Texas Magic 1992, Desert Fire 1992, Desert Heat 1993, Flame 1994, Raven 1995, Angel 1995, Wicked 1996, The Forever Bride 1997, Betrayal 1997, Hot Temper 1997, Texas Empires: Crown of Glory 1998, Golden Man 1999, Lone Star 1999, Second Opinion 1999, Longhorn 2000, Devil in the Dark 2001, The Loner 2001, The Grotto 2002, The Ghost of Carnal Cove 2002, Dark of the Moon 2003, More than You Know 2004; novellas: Cactus and Thistle 1991, A Christmas Wagon 1993, Always Paradise 1994, Gentle Rain 1995, The Gold Digger 1997, Something Borrowed 2000. *Honours:* Prism Award for Best Light Paranormal Novel, Romance Writers of America, Fantasy, Futuristic and Paranormal Chapter 1997, Texas Gold Award, East Texas Romance Writers of America. *Literary Agent:* Evan Marshall Agency, 6 Tristan Place, Pine Brook, NJ 07058-9445, USA. *Address:* 2722 Belvoir Drive, San Antonio, TX 78230, USA (home). *Website:* www.evelynrogers.com.

ROGERS, Floyd (see Spence, William John Duncan)

ROGERS, Ingrid, PhD; German teacher and writer; b. 3 May 1951, Rinteln; m. H. Kendall Rogers 1972, one s. one d. *Education:* DUEL, Sorbonne Nouvelle, Paris, Univ. of Oxford, Philipps Univ., Marburg, Dr of Ministry Bethany Theological Seminary. *Publications:* Tennessee Williams: A Moralist's Answer to the Perils of Life, 1976; Peace Be Unto You, 1983; Swords into Plowshares, 1983; In Search of Refuge, 1984; Glimpses of Clima, 1989; Recollections of East Germany, 1996. *Honours:* Christopher Book Award 1985, Angel Award of Excellence 1985.

ROGERS, Jane Rosalind, BA, PGCE, FRSL; British writer and academic; *Professor of Writing, Sheffield Hallam University*; b. 21 July 1952, London, England; m. Michael Harris 1981; one s. one d. *Education:* New Hall, Cambridge, Univ. of Leicester. *Career:* novelist and radio dramatist; Writer-in-Residence, Northern Coll., Barnsley, S Yorkshire 1985–86, Sheffield Polytechnic 1987–88; Judith E. Wilson Fellow, Cambridge 1991; tutor for MA in Writing, Sheffield Hallam Univ. 1994–; Prof. Invitee, Univ. of the Sorbonne, Paris 2008, Visiting Fellow, Univ. of Adelaide, Australia 2007–09; mem. Soc. of Authors. *Radio:* Shirley (Classic Serial, BBC Radio 4) 2002, Island (BBC Radio 4 play) 2002, The Inland Sea (BBC Radio 4) 2005, Lorna Doone (BBC Radio 4) 2005, The Bottle Factory Outing (adaptation, BBC Radio 4) 2006, Age of Innocence (BBC Radio 4) 2008, Dear Writer (BBC Radio 4) 2008, The Custom of the Country (BBC Radio 4) 2010. *Television:* Dawn and the Candidate (Channel 4) 1989, Mr Wroe's Virgins (BBC 2). *Publications:* novels: Separate Tracks 1983, Her Living Image 1984, The Ice is Singing 1987, Mr Wroe's Virgins (also scripted BBC TV serial) 1991, Promised Lands 1995, Island 1999, The Voyage Home 2004, The Testament of Jessie Lamb (Arthur C. Clarke Award 2012) 2011; other: Dawn and the Candidate (screenplay) 1989, OUP Good Fiction Guide (ed.) 2001, Ellipsis 2 (short stories) 2006; contrib. to magazines. *Honours:* North West Arts Writers Bursary 1985, Somerset Maugham Award 1985, Samuel Beckett Award 1990, Writers' Guild Award for Best Fiction Book 1996, Arts Council Writers' Bursary 1996, ACE Overseas Writers' Fellowship 2006. *Telephone:* (1457) 834570 (office). *Literary Agent:* c/o Norman North, The Agency Ltd, 24 Pottery Lane, Holland Park, London, W11 4LZ, England. *Telephone:* (20) 7727-1346. *Fax:* (20) 7727-9037. *E-mail:* nnorth@theagency.co.uk. *Website:* www.theagency.co.uk. *E-mail:* jane.rogers@btinternet.com (home). *Website:* www.janerogers.org.

ROGERS, Linda Hall, MA; Canadian poet, writer and lecturer; b. 10 Oct. 1944, Port Alice, BC; m. Rick Van Krugel; three s. *Education:* Univ. of British Columbia. *Career:* Lecturer, Univ. of British Columbia, Univ. of Victoria, Camosum Coll., Malaspina Coll.; currently cultural columnist, Focus Magazine; mem. Federation of British Columbia Writers (pres.), League of Canadian Poets, Soc. of Canadian Composers, Writers' Union of Canada, York Univ. Writers in Electronic Residence. *Television:* host, Bookshelf. *Publications:* Some Breath 1978, Queens of the Next Hot Star 1981, I Like to Make a Mess 1985, Witness 1985, Singing Rib 1987, Worm Sandwich 1989, The Magic Flute 1990, Brown Bag Blues 1991, Letters from the Doll Hospital 1992, Hard Candy 1994, The Half Life of Radium 1994, Frankie Zapper and the Disappearing Teacher 1994, Molly Brown is Not a Clown 1996, Love in the Rainforest (selected poems) 1996, Heaven Cake 1997, The Saning 1999, The Broad Canvas: Portraits of Women Artists (non-fiction) 1999, Say My Name (novel) 2000, Rehearsing the Miracle (poems) 2001, P. K. Page: Essays on her Work (ed.) 2001, Al Purdy: Essays on his Work (ed.) 2002, Bill Bissett: Essays on his Work (ed.) 2002, The Bursting Test (poems) 2002, Friday Water (fiction) 2003, The Empress Letters 2007; contrib. to journals, magazines and newspapers. *Honours:* Aya Poetry Prize 1983, Canada Council Arts Awards 1987, 1990, British Columbia Writers Poetry Prize 1989, Cultural Services Award 1990, Alcuin Awards 1991, 2002, Gov.-Gen.'s Centennial Medal for Poetry and Performance 1993, Stephen Leacock Awards for Poetry 1994, 1996, Dorothy Livesay Award for Poetry 1995, Voices Israel Poetry Award 1995, People's Poetry Award 1996, Acorn Rukeyser Award 1999, Cardiff Poetry Prizes 1999, 2001, Canada's People's Poet 2000, Bridport Poetry Prize (UK) 2000, Millennium Award 2000, Prix Anglais (France) 2000, Petra Kenny Award 2001, Monday Award 2004, Arc Poetry Prize 2004. *Address:* 1235 Styles Street, Victoria, BC V9A 3Z6, Canada (home). *Telephone:* (250) 386-8066 (home). *E-mail:* lrogers@pacificoast.net (home).

ROGERS, Michael Alan, BA; American journalist, editor and writer; b. 29 Nov. 1950, Santa Monica, CA; m. Donna Rini 2000. *Education:* Stanford University. *Career:* Assoc. Ed., Rolling Stone Magazine, San Francisco, 1972–76; Ed.-at-Large, Outside magazine, San Francisco, 1976–78; Visiting Lecturer in Fiction, University of California at Davis, 1980; Senior Writer, Newsweek magazine, 1983–; Man. Ed., Newsweek InterActive, 1993–97; Exec. Prod., Broadband Division, Washington Post Co, 1995–96; Vice-Pres., Washingtonpost.Newsweek Interactive, 1996–; Ed. and Gen. Man., Newsweek.MSNBC.com, 1998–; mem. Authors' Guild; Sierra Club. *Publications:* Mindfogger, 1973; Biohazard, 1977; Do Not Worry About the Bear, 1979; Silicon Valley, 1982; Forbidden Sequence, 1988. Contributions: newspapers and magazines. *Honours:* Distinguished Science Writing Award, American Asscn for the Advancement of Science, 1976; Best Feature Articles Award, Computer Press Asscn, 1987.

ROGERS, Pat, BA, MA, PhD, LittD, DLitt, FBA, FEA, FRHistS, FSA; British academic and writer; *DeBartolo Chair in the Liberal Arts, University of South Florida*; b. 17 March 1938, Beverley, Yorks., England. *Education:* Fitzwilliam Coll., Cambridge. *Career:* Fellow, Sidney Sussex Coll. Cambridge 1964–69; Lecturer, King's Coll. London 1969–73; Prof. of English, Univ. Coll. of North Wales, Bangor 1973–76, Univ. of Bristol 1977–86; DeBartolo Chair in the Liberal Arts, Univ. of South Florida, Tampa 1986–. *Publications:* Daniel Defoe: A Tour Through Great Britain (ed.) 1971, Grub Street: Studies on a Sub-culture (aka Hacks and Dunces) 1972, Daniel Defoe: The Critical Heritage (ed.) 1972, The Augustan Vision 1974, An Introduction to Pope 1976, The Eighteenth Century (ed.) 1978, Henry Fielding: A Biography 1979, Robinson Crusoe 1979, Swift: Complete Poems (ed.) 1983, Literature and Popular Culture in the Eighteenth Century 1983, Eighteenth-Century Encounters 1985, The Oxford Illustrated History of English Literature (ed.) 1987, Enduring Legacy: Tercentenary Essays on Alexander Pope (co-ed.) 1988, An Outline of English Literature (ed.) 1992, Joshua Reynolds, Discourses on Art (ed.) 1992, The Blackwell Companion to the Enlightenment (co-ed.) 1992, Samuel Johnson 1993, Essays on Pope 1993, The Oxford Authors: Pope (ed.) 1993, Johnson and Boswell in Scotland (ed.) 1993, Daniel Defoe, Moll Flanders (ed.) 1993, Jane Austen, Persuasion (ed.) 1994, Johnson and Boswell: The Transit of Caledonia 1995, The Samuel Johnson Encyclopedia 1996, W.M. Thackeray, Vanity Fair (ed.) 1997, The Text of Great Britain: Theme and Design in Defoe's Tour 1998, Orthodoxy and Heresy in Eighteenth-Century Society (co-ed.) 2002, The Alexander Pope Encyclopedia 2004, The Symbolic Design of Windsor-Forest 2004, The Letters, Life and Works of John Oldmixon 2004, Pope and the Destiny of the Stuarts 2005, Jane Austen: Pride and Prejudice (ed.) 2006, Edmund Curll, Bookseller (co-author) 2007, Producing the Eighteenth Century Book (co-ed.) 2009, A Political Biography of Alexander Pope 2010, The Wiley-Blackwell Encyclopedia of Eighteenth-Century Writers and Writing (co-author) 2011, The Life and Times of Thomas, Lord Coningsby 2011. *Address:* Department of English, University of South Florida, 4202 East Fowler Avenue, CPR-107, Tampa, FL 33620-5550, USA (office). *Telephone:* (813) 974-4134 (office). *Fax:* (813) 974-2270 (office). *E-mail:* rogersp@usf.edu (office). *Website:* english.usf.edu/faculty/progers (office).

ROGERS, Rosemary, (Marina Mayson), BA; American writer; b. 7 Dec. 1932, Sri Lanka; m. 1st Summa Navaratnam 1953 (divorced); two s. two d.; m. 2nd Leroy Rogers 1957 (divorced 1964); m. 3rd Christopher M. Kadison 1984. *Career:* mem. Writers Guild of America, Authors' Guild. *Publications:* Sweet Savage Love 1974, Wildest Heart 1974, Dark Fires 1975, Wicked Loving Lies 1976, The Crowd Pleasers 1978, The Insiders 1979, Lost Love, Last Love 1980, Love Play 1981, Surrender to Love 1982, The Wanton 1984, Bound by Desire 1988, Tea Planter's Bride 1995, Dangerous Man 1996, Midnight Lady 1997, All I Desire 1998, In Your Arms 1999, Savage Desire 2000, A Reckless Encounter 2001, An Honorable Man 2002, Return to Me 2003, Jewel of My Heart 2004, Sapphire 2005, A Daring Passion 2007, Scandalous Deception 2008, Bound by Love 2009, Scoundrel's Honor 2010; contributions: Star Magazine, Good Housekeeping. *Address:* FAO: Maureen Stead, c/o Harlequin Enterprises Ltd, 225 Duncan Mill Road, Don Mills, ON M3B 3K9, Canada (office). *Website:* www.eharlequin.com (office).

ROGNET, Richard; French poet; b. 5 Nov. 1942, Val d'Ajol. *Education:* Ecole Normale d'Instituteurs de Mirecourt, Fac de Lettres, Nancy and Académie Mallarmé. *Career:* teacher 1969–. *Publications include:* (first vol. of poems) 1966, L'Épouse émiettée (Prix Charles-Vildrac) 1978, Petits poèmes en fraude 1980, L'eternel détour. Le Verbe et l'Empreinte 1983, Le Transi (Prix Louise Labé) 1985, Je suis cet homme (Prix Max Jacob) 1988, Maurice, amoroso 1991, Recours à l'abandon 1992, Chemin Bernard 1995, Lutteur sans triomphe (Prix Apollinaire) 1996, La Jambe coupée d'Arthur Rimbaud 1997, Seigneur vocabulaire 1998, L'Ouvresse de Parnasse 1998, Juste le temps de s'effacer suivi de Ni toi ni personne 2002, Belles, en moi, belle 2002, Dérive du voyageur

(Prix Théophile Gautier 2004) 2003, Le visieur délivré 2005, Le promeneur et ses ombres 2007. *Honours:* Chevalier, Ordre des Arts et des Lettres 1994, Chevalier, Ordre des Palmes Académiques 1996; Prix Louise Labé 1985, Prix Max Jacob 1989, Prix Théophile Gautier 1993, Prix Apollinaire 1997, Prix Louis Montalte 1998, Grand Prix de Poésie de la Société des Gens de Lettres 2002, Prix Alain Bosquet 2005. *Address:* c/o Éditions Gallimard, 5 rue Sébastien-Bottin, 75328 Paris, Cédex 07, France (office). *Website:* www.gallimard.fr (office).

ROHAN, Michael Scott, (Mike Scott Rohan, Michael Scot), MA; British writer and editor; b. 22 Jan. 1951, Edinburgh, Scotland; m. Deborah Rohan. *Education:* University of Oxford. *Publications:* The Hammer and the Cross (co-author), 1980; Fantastic People (co-author), 1982; First Byte: Choosing and Using a Home Computer, 1983; Run to the Stars, 1983; The BBC Micro Add-On-Guide (co-author), 1985; The Ice King (co-author, aka Burial Rites) 1986; The Anvil of Ice, 1986, The Forge in the Forest, 1987, The Hammer of the Sun, 1988; Chase the Morning, 1990, The Gates of Noon, 1992, The Horns of Tartarus (co-author), 1992; Cloud Castles, 1993; The Lord of the Middle Air, 1994; The Classical Video Guide (ed.), 1994; Maxie's Little Demon, 1997. Contributions: anthologies and periodicals. *Honours:* All-Time Great Fantasy Short Story, Gamemaster International, 1991; William F. Crawford Award for Best First Fantasy Novel, International Asscn for the Fantastic Arts, 1991.

ROHRBACH, Peter Thomas, (James Cody), BA, MA; American writer; b. 27 Feb. 1926, New York, NY; m. Sheila Sheehan 1970, one d. *Education:* Catholic University of America. *Career:* mem. Authors' Guild of America; Poets, Playwrights, Editors, Essayists and Novelists; Washington Independent Writers. *Publications:* 17 books, including: Conversation with Christ, 1981; Stagecoach East, 1983; American Issue, 1985; The Largest Event: World War II, 1993; National Issue, 1994. Contributions: Encyclopedias and periodicals.

ROITFELD, Carine; French magazine editor; *Editor-in-Chief, French Vogue*; b. Paris; d. of Jacques Roitfeld; pnr Christian Restoin; one s. one d. *Career:* fmrly writer, then a stylist for French Elle; freelance stylist, worked with Mario Testino; consultant for Ford at Gucci and YSL six years; Ed.-in-Chief French Vogue 2001–. *Address:* Vogue, 56A rue du Faubourg St Honoré, 75008 Paris, France (office). *Telephone:* 1-53-43-60-00 (office). *Fax:* 1-53-43-61-61 (office). *E-mail:* magazine@vogueparis.com (office). *Website:* www.vogue.fr (office).

ROJA, Clarita (see Aguilar, Mila D.)

ROLAND, Alex, BS, MA, PhD; American academic and writer; b. 7 April 1944, Providence, RI; m. 1979, four c. *Education:* US Naval Acad., University of Hawaii, Duke University. *Career:* Historian, National Aeronautics and Space Administration, 1973–81; Assoc. Prof., 1981–87, Prof. of History, 1987–, Chair, Dept of History, 1996–99, Duke University; Harold K. Johnson Visiting Prof. of Military History, US Army War College, 1988–89; Senior Fellow, MIT, 1994–95; mem. Society for Military History; Society for the History of Technology, pres., 1995–96. *Publications:* Underwater Warfare in the Age of Sail, 1978; Model Research: The National Advisory Committee for Aeronautics, 1915–1958, 2 vols, 1985; A Spacefaring People: Perspectives on Early Spaceflight (ed.), 1985; Men in Arms: A History of Warfare and Its Interrelationships with Western Society (with Richard A Preston and Sydney F. Wise), fifth edn, 1991; Atmospheric Flight (ed. with Peter Galison), 2000; The Military – Industrial Complex, 2001. Contributions: scholarly books and journals. *Honours:* grants and fellowships; Fellow, Dibner Institute, MIT, 1993–94.

ROLIN, Jean; French novelist, journalist and essayist; b. 14 June 1949, Boulogne-Billancourt. *Publications:* Journal de Gand aux Aléoutiennes 1982, L'Or du scaphandrier 1983, Vu sur la mer 1986, La Ligne de front (Prix Albert Londres) 1988, La Frontière belge 1989, Cyrille et Méthode 1994, Joséphine 1994, Zones 1995, L'Organisation (Prix Médicis) 1996, Chemins d'eau 1998, C'était juste cinq heures du soir (with Jean-Christian Bourcart) 1998, Traverses 1999, Campagnes 2000, La Clôture 2001, Dingos—Cherbourg-est/Cherbourg-ouest 2002, La Clôture 2002, Chrétiens 2003, Terminal Frigo 2005, L'Homme qui a vu l'ours: reportages et autres articles 1980–2005 2006. *Address:* c/o Éditions P.O.L., 33 rue Saint-André-des-Arts, 75006 Paris, France.

ROLOFF, Michael, BA, MA; American playwright, poet and writer; b. (translator), 19 Dec. 1937, Berlin, Germany. *Education:* Haverford Coll., Pennsylvania, Stanford Univ. *Film screenplays:* Feelings 1982, Darlings and Monsters 1983, Graduation Party 1984. *Plays:* My Foot my Tutor 1971, Offending the Audience 1971, Kaspar 1973, Self-Accusation 1973, The Ride across Lake Constance 1973, They are Dying Out 1975, Calling for Help 1976, Prophecy 1976, Quodlibet 1976, Screams for Help 1976, Farmyard 1981, Michi's Blood 1982, Wolves of Wyoming 1985, Palombe Blue 1985, Schizzohawk 1986, It Won't Grow Back 1988, The Wolves of Wyoming 1988, B.L.T. 1989, Walk about the Villages 1989, Balzac's Godot 1995, People Annihilation 1995, Fernando Krapp wrote me this Letter 1996. *Publications:* poetry: Headshots 1984, It Won't Grow Back 1985; fiction: Darlings and Monsters Quartet (four vols) 1986; other: numerous trans from German. *E-mail:* roloff_michael@hotmail.com (home).

ROMER, Stephen Charles Mark, PhD, FRSL; British academic and poet; *Lecturer, Université François-Rabelais, Tours*; b. 20 Aug. 1957, Bishops Stortford, Herts., England; m. Bridget Stevens 1982; one s. *Education:* Radley Coll., Trinity Hall, Cambridge, Harvard Univ., USA, British Inst., Paris, France. *Career:* Lecturer, Univ. François-Rabelais, Tours, France; Visiting Prof. in French, Colgate Univ., New York 2001, USA 2004, 2005; Visiting Fellow, Sidney Sussex Coll., Cambridge 2003, All Souls Coll., Oxford 2010. *Publications:* Islay, and other poems 1978, The Growing Dark 1981, Firebird 3 1985, Idols 1986, Plato's Ladder 1992, Tribute 1998, 20th Century French Poems (ed.) 2002, Yellow Studio 2008, Into the Deep Street: Seven Modern French Poets (co-ed. with Jennie Feldman) 2009, Robert Herrick (Faber Poet to Poet Series) 2010; contribs: academic, anthologies, journals and periodicals. *Honours:* Gregory Award for Poetry 1985. *Address:* Department of English, Université François-Rabelais, 3 rue des Tanneurs, Bâtiment F. Rez de ch., Bureau 45, 37041 Tours, France (office). *Telephone:* (2) 47-36-66-52 (office). *E-mail:* stephenromer@hotmail.com (office). *Website:* www.univ-tours.fr/romer (office); www.contemporarywriters.co.uk; www.poetryinternationalweb.org.

ROMERIL, John; Australian playwright; b. 26 Oct. 1945, Melbourne, Vic. *Education:* BA, Monash University, Clayton, 1970. *Career:* Writer-In-Residence, various Australian groups and National University, Singapore, 1974–87. *Publications:* A Nameless Concern, 1968; The Kitchen Table, 1968; The Man from Chicago, 1969; In a Place Like Somewhere Else, 1969; Chicago, Chicago, 1970; Marvellous Melbourne, 1970; Dr Karl's Kure, 1970; Whatever Happened to Realism?, 1971; Rearguard Action, 1971; Hackett Gets Ahead, 1972; Bastardy, 1972; Waltzing Matilda, 1974; The Floating World, 1974; The Golden Holden Show, 1975; The Accidental Poke, 1977; Mickey's Moomba, 1979; Centenary Dance, 1984; The Kelly Dance, 1984; Definitely Not the Last, 1985; Koori Radio, 1987; Top End, and History of Australia (co-author), 1989; Lost Weekend, 1989; Black Cargo, 1991; The Reading Boy, 1991; Working Out, 1991. Other: Television plays. *Honours:* Victorian Government Drama Fellowship, 1988. *Literary Agent:* Almost Managing, PO Box 1034, Carlton, Vic. 3053, Australia.

ROMTVEDT, David William, BA, MFA; American writer, poet and musician; *Professor of English, Creative Writing and American Studies, University of Wyoming*; b. 7 June 1950, Portland, Ore.; m. Margo Brown 1987. *Education:* Reed Coll., Iowa Writers' Workshop. *Career:* State Literature Consultant, WY 1987; mem. faculty Dept of English, Univ. of Wyoming 1995–, Assoc. Prof. of English, Creative Writing and American Studies 2001–08, Prof. 2008–; Poet Laureate of Wyoming 2004–. *Publications:* Free and Compulsory for All 1984, Moon 1984, Letters from Mexico 1987, Black Beauty and Kiev the Ukraine 1987, Crossing the River: Poets of the Western US 1987, How Many Horses 1988, A Flower Whose Name I Do Not Know 1992, Crossing Wyoming 1992, Certainty 1996, Windmill: Essays from Four Mile Ranch 1997, Deep West: A Literary Tour of Wyoming (ed.) 2003, Some Church (poems) 2005, Wyoming Fence Lines (ed.) 2007; contrib. to Paris Review, Canadian Forum, American Poetry Review, Poets and Writers Magazine. *Honours:* NEA Residency Award 1979, NEA Fellowship 1987, Pushcart Prize 1991, Nat. Poetry Series Award 1991, NEA Tri-Nat. Exchange Fellowship 1996, Wyoming Gov.'s Arts Award 2000, Best Radio Documentary, Broadcast Educ. Asscn 2005, Distinguished Service Award, Wyoming Music Educators Asscn 2008. *Address:* 457 North Main, Buffalo, WY 82834, USA (home). *E-mail:* romtvedt@uwyo.edu (office). *Website:* davidromtvedt.com.

RONAN, Frank; Irish novelist; b. 6 May 1963, New Ross. *Publications:* The Men Who Loved Evelyn Cotton 1989, A Picnic in Eden 1991, The Better Angel 1992, Dixie Chicken 1994, Handsome Men are Slightly Sunburnt (short stories) 1996, Lovely 1996, Home 2002. *Honours:* Irish Times/Aer Lingus Irish Literature Prize 1989. *Literary Agent:* Rogers, Coleridge & White Ltd, 20 Powis Mews, London W11 1JN, England. *E-mail:* a@frankronan.com (office). *Website:* www.frankronan.com.

RONCAGLIOLO, Santiago; Peruvian writer and translator; b. (Santiago Rafael Roncagliolo Lohmann), 29 March 1975, Lima; m.; two c. *Career:* has lived in Mexico, Peru and Spain. *Play:* Tus amigos nunca te harían daño. *Publications include:* Rugor, el dragón enamorado (children's fiction) 1999, Crecer es un oficio triste (short stories) 2003, Pudor (novel) 2005, Abril rojo (trans. as Red April) (novel) (Premio Alfaguara) 2006, Matías y los imposibles (children's fiction) 2006, Jet Lag (essays) 2007, La Cuarta Espada (non-fiction) 2008, Memorias de una dama (novel) 2009, Tan cerca de la vida (novel) 2010, El amante Uruguayo (non-fiction) 2012. *Honours:* Alfaguara Prize (Spain), Independent Prize of Foreign Fiction (UK). *Literary Agent:* c/o Girona 24, 4-3, 08010 Barcelona, Spain. *Telephone:* (932) 654165. *Fax:* (932) 657610. *E-mail:* paucentellas@silviabastos.com. *Address:* c/o Alfaguara, Calle Torrelaguna 60, 28043 Madrid, Spain (office). *E-mail:* alfaguara@santillana.es (office). *Website:* www.alfaguara.santillana.es (office).

ROOKE, Leon; American writer; b. 11 Sept. 1934, Roanoke Rapids, NC. *Education:* Mars Hill College, NC, University of North Carolina at Chapel Hill. *Career:* writer-in-residence, University of North Carolina, 1965–66, University of Victoria, 1972–73, University of Southwest Minnesota, 1974–75, University of Toronto, 1984–85, University of Western Ontario, 1990–91; Visiting Prof., University of Victoria, 1980–81; mem. PEN; Writers' Union of Canada. *Publications:* Fiction: Last One Home Sleeps in the Yellow Bed, 1968; Vault, 1974; The Broad Back of the Angel, 1977; The Love Parlour, 1977; Fat Woman, 1980; The Magician in Love, 1980; Death Suite, 1982; The Birth Control King of the Upper Volta, 1983; Shakespeare's Dog, 1983; Sing Me No Love Songs I'll Say You No Prayers, 1984; A Bolt of White Cloth, 1984; How I Saved the Province, 1990; The Happiness of Others, 1991; A Good Baby, 1991; Who Do You Love?, 1992; Muffins, 1995. Stage Plays: A Good Baby, 1991; The

Coming, 1991; 4 others. Contributions: About 300 short stories in leading North American journals. *Honours:* Canada and Australia Literary Prize, 1981; Best Paperback Novel of the Year, 1981; Governor-General's Award, 1984; North Carolina Award for Literature, 1990. *Website:* www.leonrooke.com.

ROOM, Adrian Richard West, DipEd, MA, FRGS; British writer; b. 27 Sept. 1933, Melksham, England. *Education:* Univ. of Oxford. *Career:* mem. English Place-Name Soc., American Name Soc. *Publications:* Placenames of the World 1974, 2006, Great Britain: A Background Studies English–Russian Dictionary 1978, Room's Dictionary of Confusibles 1979, Place-Name Changes since 1900 1980, Naming Names 1981, Room's Dictionary of Distinguishables 1981, Dictionary of Trade Name Origins 1982, Room's Classical Dictionary 1983, Dictionary of Cryptic Crossword Clues 1983, A Concise Dictionary of Modern Place-Names in Great Britain and Ireland 1983, Dictionary of Changes in Meaning 1986, Dictionary of Coin Names 1988, Dictionary of Dedications 1990, A Name for Your Baby 1992, The Street Names of England 1992, Brewer's Dictionary of Names 1992, Corporate Eponymy 1992, Place-Name Changes 1900–91 1993, The Naming of Animals 1993, African Place-Names 1994, Cassell Dictionary of Proper Names 1994, A Dictionary of Irish Place-Names 1994, Cassell Dictionary of First Names 1995, Brewer's Dictionary of Phrase and Fable (revised edn) 1995, Literally Entitled 1996, An Alphabetical Guide to the Language of Name Studies 1996, Placenames of Russia and the Former Soviet Union 1996, Placenames of the World 1997, Cassell Dictionary of Word Histories 1999, Cassell's Foreign Words and Phrases 2000, Dictionary of Art Titles 2000, Dictionary of Music Titles 2000, Brewer's Dictionary of Modern Phrase and Fable 2000, Encyclopedia of Corporate Names Worldwide 2002, Penguin Dictionary of British Place Names 2003, Dictionary of Pseudonyms 2004, Placenames of France 2004. *Address:* 12 High Street, St Martin's, Stamford, Lincs., PE9 2LF, England (home). *Telephone:* (1780) 752097 (home). *Fax:* (1780) 752097 (home). *E-mail:* adrian-room@msn.com (home).

ROORBACH, Bill, BA, MFA; American academic and writer; b. 18 Aug. 1953, Chicago, IL; m. Juliet Brigitte Karelsen 1990; one d. *Education:* Ithaca Coll., Columbia Univ. *Career:* Asst Prof. of English, Univ. of Maine at Farmington 1991–95; Asst Prof., Ohio State Univ. 1995–98, Assoc. Prof. of English, 1998–2001; Jenks Chair in Contemporary American Letters, Coll. of the Holy Cross 2004; Distinguished Visiting Writer, Ithaca Coll. 2006; mem. Associated Writing Programs, Authors' Guild, MLA of America. *Publications:* Summers with Juliet 1992, Writing Life Stories: How to Make Memories into Memoirs, Ideas into Essays, and Life into Literature 1998, The Art of Truth: A Contemporary Creative Nonfiction Reader (ed.) 2000, Big Bend: Stories 2001, The Smallest Color 2001; Contribs: anthologies, magazines, reviews, quarterlies and journals. *Honours:* Ohio Arts Council Grants, Flannery O'Connor Award 2001. *Address:* c/o Betsy Lerner, The Gernert Company, 136 East 57th St., New York, NY 10022, USA (office). *Website:* www.billroorbach.com.

ROOT, Deane Leslie, BA, MMus, PhD; American musicologist, museum curator, teacher, librarian and editor; *Editor in Chief, Grove Music, Oxford University Press*; b. 9 Aug. 1947, Wausau, Wis.; s. of Forrest K. Root and Marguerite Root; m. Doris J. Dyen 1972; two d. *Education:* New Coll., Sarasota, Fla, Univ. of Illinois. *Career:* Faculty, Univ. of Wisconsin 1973; editorial staff, New Grove Dictionary of Music and Musicians, Macmillan 1974–76, Ed.-in-Chief Grove Music, Oxford University Press 2009–; Research Assoc., Univ. of Illinois 1976–80; Visiting Research Assoc., Florida State Univ. 1981–82; Curator, Stephen Foster Memorial and Adjunct Asst Prof. in Music, Univ. of Pittsburgh 1982–96, Chair. Music Dept 2002–07, Heinz Chapel Admin. 1983–95, Dir of Cultural Resources 1990–94, Adjunct Assoc. Prof. 1992–96, Prof. of Music, Dir and Fletcher Hodges Jr Curator, Center for American Music 1998–; Pres. Sonneck Soc. for American Music 1989–93; Del., American Council of Learned Socs 1996–99; mem. American Antiquarian Soc. Fellowship panels 2005, 2008, Nat. Endowment for the Humanities Review panels 1990–. *Recordings:* Proud Traditions, Musical Tribute to Pitt 1987. *Art Exhibitions:* Pittsburgh Rhythms, Historical Soc. of Western Pa (consultant) 1990–96, perm. exhbn on Stephen Foster, Center for American Music, Univ. of Pittsburgh. *Television:* consultant, I Hear America Singing (PBS) 1996, Stephen Foster (PBS) 2001, Broadway: The American Musical (PBS) 2004. *Films:* music consultant, Gangs of New York (dir, Martin Scorsese) 2002. *Publications:* American Popular Stage Music 1860–1880, Music of Florida Historic Sites, Resources of American Music History (co-author), Music of Stephen C. Foster (co-ed.), Nineteenth Century American Musical Theater (series ed., 16 vols) 1994, Voices Across Time: American History Through Song (co-author) 2004, Emily's Songbook: Music in 1850s Albany (co-ed.) 2011; contrib. to New Grove Dictionary of Music and New Grove Dictionary of American Music, American National Biography, various journals, yearbooks, conf. proceedings, articles in journals, multi-author books. *Honours:* Woodrow Wilson Fellow 1968, Music Library Assn Book of the Year 1981, American Library Assn Choice Award 1992, Soc. for American Music Distinguished Service 2000. *Address:* Department of Music, 205 Music Building, University of Pittsburgh, Pittsburgh, PA 15260, USA (office). *Telephone:* (412) 624-4126 (office), (412) 624-7775 (office). *Fax:* (412) 624-4186 (office). *E-mail:* dir@pitt.edu (office). *Website:* www.music.pitt.edu (office).

ROOT, William Pitt, BA, MFA; American fmr academic and poet; b. 28 Dec. 1941, Austin, Tex.; m. Pamela Uschuk 1988; one d. *Education:* University of Washington, University of North Carolina at Greensboro. *Career:* Stegner Fellow, Stanford University 1967–68; Asst Prof., Michigan State University 1967–68; Visiting Writer-in-Residence, Amherst College 1971, University of Southwest Louisiana 1976, Wichita State University 1976, University of Montana 1978, 1980, 1982–85, Pacific Lutheran University 1990; Prof., Hunter College, CUNY 1986–2005; Poet Laureate of Tuscon, Ariz. 1997–2002. *Publications:* The Storm and Other Poems, 1969; Striking the Dark Air for Music, 1973; A Journey South, 1977; Reasons for Going It on Foot, 1981; In the World's Common Grasses, 1981; Invisible Guests, 1984; Faultdancing, 1986; Trace Elements from a Recurring Kingdom, 1994, A Beauty Warrior: Bruce's Book 2005; contrib. to magazines and periodicals. *Honours:* Acad. of American Poetry Prize, 1967; Rockefeller Foundation Grant, 1969–70; Guggenheim Fellowship, 1970–71; National Endowment for the Arts Grant, 1973–74; Pushcart Awards, 1977, 1980, 1985; US-UK Exchange Artist, 1978–79; Stanley Kunitz Poetry Award, 1981; Guy Owen Poetry Award, 1984. *Address:* 154 Concho Circle, Bayfield, CO 81122, USA (home). *Telephone:* (970) 884-3623 (home). *E-mail:* wprpoet@tglobal.net (home).

ROQUELAURE, A. N. (see Rice, Anne)

ROSA, Isaac; Spanish writer; b. 1974, Seville. *Play:* Adiós muchachos (Premio Caja España) 1998. *Publications:* fiction: El ruido del mundo 1998, La malamemoria 1999, El vano ayer (Premio Rómulo Gallegos, Premio Ojo Crítico, Premio Andalucía de la Crítica 2005) 2004, Otra maldita novela sobre la guerra civil! 2007, El país del miedo (Premio Fundación José Manuel Lara Hernández) 2008; non-fiction: Kosovo: La Coartada humanitaria (co-author) 2001. *Address:* c/o Editoiral Seix Barral, Avenida Diadonal 662-664, 7°, 08034 Barcelona, Spain (office). *E-mail:* editorial@seix-barral.es (office). *Website:* www.seix-barral.es (office).

ROSALES, Emili; Spanish writer and publisher; b. 1968, Sant Carles de la Ràpita. *Career:* has worked as a secondary school teacher and translator; Literary Dir (Catalan-language publications), Planeta; mem. Asscn of Catalan Language Writers. *Publications:* poetry collections: Ciutats i mar 1989, Els dies i tu 1991; novels: La casa de la platja 1995, Els amos del món 1997, Mentre Barcelona dorm 1998, La ciutat invisible (Sant Jordi Prize 2004) (trans. as The Invisible City 2009) 2005; regular contrib. to Avui and La Vanguardia newspapers. *Honours:* Premi Salvador Espriu 1989. *Address:* c/o Alma Books Ltd, London House, 243–253 Lower Mortlake Road, Richmond, Surrey, TW9 2LL, England (office). *Website:* www.almabooks.co.uk; www.escriptors.cat/autors/rosalese/pagina.php?id_sec=676.

ROSE, Andrew, MA, LLM; British barrister and author; b. 1944, England. *Education:* Trinity Coll., Cambridge. *Career:* called to Bar, Grays Inn, London 1968, barrister 1968–, Immigration Judge 1999–2008; mem. Crimes Club or 'Our Society', Biographers' Club. *Television:* contrib.: The Last Secret of Dr Crippen (Channel 4) 2004, Was Crippen Innocent? (Five) 2007, Forensic Casebook (ITV 1) 2008, Fire and Explosions (BBC World) 2009, Profile of Death (BBC World) 2009. *Publications:* Stinie: Murder on the Common 1985, Penguin True Crime 1989, Scandal at the Savoy 1991, Lethal Witness 2007. *E-mail:* andrewroseauthor@gmail.com.

ROSE, Daniel Asa, AB; American writer, essayist, poet and editor; b. 20 Nov. 1949, New York, NY; m. 1st Laura Love 1974 (divorced); two s.; m. 2nd Shelley Roth 1993; two s. *Education:* Brown Univ. *Career:* fmr travel columnist, Esquire; book reviewer, Vanity Fair 1977–85, the Providence Journal 1977–85; Book Ed. Success Magazine 1985–88; Arts and Culture Ed. The Forward 2000–03; Sr Book Reviewer, The New York Observer 2003–, New York Magazine 2004–; currently Ed.-in-Chief The Reading Room literary magazine. *Publications:* Flipping For It 1987, Small Family with Rooster 1988, Hiding Places: A Father and his Sons Retrace their Family's Escape from the Holocaust 2000, Larry's Kidney: Being the True Story of How I Found Myself in China with my Black Sheep Cousin and His Mail-Order Bride, Skirting the Law to Get Him a Transplant and Save his Life 2009; also screenplays, poems, stories, reviews and literary essays; contrib. to The New Yorker, The New York Times Magazine, GQ, Esquire, Playboy, Partisan Review, Ploughshares, etc. *Honours:* O. Henry Prize 1980, PEN Literary Awards 1987, 1988, Massachusetts Cultural Council Award 1992, Ella Baker Fellowship 2004, Nat. Endowment for the Arts Fellowship 2006. *Address:* 138 Bay State Road, Rehoboth, MA 02769, USA (home). *Telephone:* (508) 252-6315 (office). *E-mail:* rose@danielasarose.com (office). *Website:* www.danielasarose.com.

ROSE, Jacqueline, BA, PhD, Maitrise (Paris-Sorbonne), FBA; British academic and writer; *Professor, School of English and Drama, Queen Mary, University of London*; b. 1949, London; one adopted d. *Education:* St Hilda's Coll., Oxford, Univ. of Paris-Sorbonne, Univ. of London. *Career:* fmr staff mem., Univ. of Sussex; currently Prof. of English Literature, Queen Mary, Univ. of London. *Films include:* Dangerous Liaison (UK Channel 4) 2002. *Publications include:* Feminine Sexuality (co-ed. with Juliet Mitchell) 1982, The Case of Peter Pan 1984, Sexuality in the Field of Vision 1986, The Haunting of Sylvia Plath (Fawcett Prize for Non–Fiction) 1991, Why War? Psychoanalysis, Politics and the Return to Melanie Klein, The Bucknell Lectures in Literary Theory 1993, Black Hamlet (co-ed. with Saul Dubow) 1996, States of Fantasy, The Oxford Clarendon Lectures 1998, Albertine 2001, On Not Being Able To Sleep: Psychoanalysis and the Modern World 2003, The Question of Zion (Christian Gauss seminars, Princeton Univ.) 2004, The Last Resistance 2007. *Honours:* Hon. Fellow (Sussex Univ.); Dr hc (Goodenough Coll.). *Address:* School of English and Drama, Queen Mary, University of London, Mile End Road, London, E1 4NS (office). *Telephone:* (20) 7882-5014 (office). *Fax:* (20) 7882-

3357 (office). *E-mail:* j.rose@qmul.ac.uk (office). *Website:* www.english.qmul.ac.uk (office).

ROSE, Joel Steven, BA, MFA; American writer; b. 1 March 1948, Los Angeles, CA; m. Catherine Texier; two d. *Education:* Hobart College, Columbia University. *Career:* f., publisher, ed. two literary magazines, The Seneca Review and Between C and D 1988; mem. Co-ordinating Council of Literary Magazines; Poets and Writers; Writers Guild of America. *Publications include:* Kill the Poor (novel, also film) 1988, Love is Strange (co-ed.) 1993, The Big Book of Thugs 1996, Kill Kill Faster Faster 1998, New York Sawed in Half 2001, The Blackest Bird 2007; contrib. to newspapers and magazines. *Honours:* National Endowment for the Arts Award, 1986; New York State Council on the Arts Award, 1986–87. *E-mail:* joeyrose@nyc.rr.com. *Website:* www.joelrosebooks.com.

ROSE, Kenneth Vivian, CBE, MA, FRSL; British writer; b. 15 Nov. 1924, Bradford, Yorkshire, England. *Education:* Repton School, New College, Oxford. *Career:* Asst Master, Eton College, 1948; Editorial Staff, Daily Telegraph, 1952–60; Founder, Writer, Albany Column, Sunday Telegraph, 1961–97. *Publications:* Superior Person: A Portrait of Curzon and his Circle in Late Victorian England, 1969; The Later Cecils, 1975; William Harvey: A Monograph, 1978; King George V, 1983; Kings, Queens and Courtiers: Intimate Portraits of the Royal House of Windsor, 1985; Harold Nicolson, 1992; Elusive Rothschild: The Life of Victor, 3rd Baron, 2003. Contributions: Dictionary of National Biography. *Honours:* Wolfson Award for History, 1983; Whitbread Award for Biography, 1983; Yorkshire Post Biography of the Year Award, 1984.

ROSE, Marion (see Harris, Marion Rose)

ROSE, Mark Allan, AB, BLitt, PhD; American academic and writer; *Professor Emeritus, University of California at Santa Barbara*; b. 4 Aug. 1939, New York, NY; m. Ann Bermingham; one s. *Education:* Princeton Univ., Merton Coll., Harvard Univ. *Career:* Instructor to Assoc. Prof. of English, Yale Univ. 1967–74; Prof. of English, Univ. of Illinois 1974–77; Prof. of English, Univ. of California at Santa Barbara 1977–2008, Prof. Emer. 2008–, Assoc. Vice-Chancellor 2001–04; Dir Univ. of California Humanities Research Inst. 1989–94; mem. Modern Language Asscn, Renaissance Soc. of America, Shakespeare Soc. of America. *Publications:* Heroic Love 1968, Golding's Tale 1972, Shakespearean Design 1972, Spenser's Art 1975, Alien Encounters 1981, Authors and Owners 1993; editor: Twentieth Century Views of Science Fiction 1976, Twentieth Century Interpretations of Antony and Cleopatra 1977, Bridges to Science Fiction (with others) 1980, Shakespeare's Early Tragedies 1994, Norton Shakespere Workshop 1997; more than 50 essays and reviews on Shakespeare, Renaissance literature, science fiction and copyright history. *Honours:* Woodrow Wilson Fellow 1961, Henry Fellow 1961–62, Dexter Fellow 1966, Morse Fellow 1970–71, Nat. Endowment for the Humanities Fellowships 1979–80, 1990–91. *Address:* 1135 Oriole Road, Montecito, CA 93108, USA (home). *E-mail:* mrose@english.ucsb.edu (home).

ROSE, Richard, BA, DPhil, FBA; American writer, professor of public policy and consultant; *Professor of Public Policy, University of Strathclyde*; b. 9 April 1933, St Louis, Mo.; s. of Charles Imse Rose and Mary C. Rose; m. Rosemary J. Kenny 1956; two s. one d. *Education:* Clayton High School, Mo., Johns Hopkins Univ., London School of Econs, Univ. of Oxford. *Career:* worked in political public relations, Miss. Valley 1954–55; reporter, St Louis Post-Dispatch 1955–57; Lecturer in Govt, Univ. of Manchester 1961–66; Prof. of Politics, Strathclyde Univ. 1966–82, Prof. of Public Policy and Dir Centre for the Study of Public Policy 1976–2005, 2012–; Prof. of Public Policy, Univ. of Aberdeen 2005–11; Visiting Prof., European Univ. Inst., Florence; Specialist Adviser, House of Commons Public Admin Cttee 2002–03; Consultant Psephologist, The Times, ITV, Daily Telegraph, etc. 1964–; Sec. Cttee on Political Sociology, Int. Sociology Asscn 1970–85; Founding mem. European Consortium for Political Research 1970; mem. US/UK Fulbright Comm. 1971–75; Guggenheim Fellow 1974; Visiting scholar at various insts, Europe, USA, Hong Kong; mem. Home Office Working Party on Electoral Register 1975–77; Co-founder British Politics Group 1974–; Convenor Work Group on UK Politics, Political Studies Asscn 1976–88; mem. Council Int. Political Science Asscn 1976–82; Tech. Consultant OECD, UNDP, World Bank, Council of Europe, Int. IDEA; Dir SSRC Research Programme, Growth of Govt 1982–86, Scotland in the World Forum 2008–11; Ed. Journal of Public Policy 1985–2011, Chair. 1981–85; Scientific Adviser, New Democracies Barometer, Paul Lazarsfeld Soc., Vienna 1991–; Fellow, British Acad.; Sr Fellow in Governance, Oxford Internet Inst. 2003–05. *Publications:* numerous books on politics and public policy including Politics in England 1964, People in Politics: Observations Across the Atlantic 1970, Governing Without Consensus: An Irish Perspective 1971, International Almanack of Electoral History (co-author) 1974, The Problem of Party Government 1974, Northern Ireland: A Time of Choice 1976, Managing Presidential Objectives 1976, What is Governing? Purpose and Policy in Washington 1978, Can Government Go Bankrupt? (co-author) 1978, Do Parties Make A Difference 1984, Understanding Big Government 1984, Public Employment in Western Nations (co-author) 1985, Taxation by Political Inertia (co-author) 1987, Ministers and Ministries 1987, Presidents and Prime Ministers, The Postmodern President 1988, Ordinary People in Public Policy 1989, Training With Trainers? How Germany Avoids Britain's Supply-side Bottleneck (co-author) 1990, The Loyalties of Voters (co-author) 1990, Lesson-Drawing in Public Policy 1993 Inheritance in Public Policy (co-author) 1994, What is Europe? 1996, How Russia Votes (co-author) 1997, Democracy and Its Alternatives, Understanding Post-Communist Societies (co-author) 1998, A Society Transformed: Hungary in Time-Space Perspective, International Encyclopedia of Elections (co-author) 2000, The Prime Minister in a Shrinking World 2001, Elections without Order: Russia's Challenge to Vladimir Putin (co-author) 2002, Elections and Parties in New European Democracies 2003, Learning from Comparative Public Policy 2005, Russia Transformed (co-author) 2006, Parites and Elections in New European Democracies 2009, Understanding Post-Communist Transformation 2009; hundreds of papers in academic journals. *Honours:* Hon. Vice-Pres. UK Political Studies Asscn, Hon. Fellow American Acad. of Arts and Sciences, Finnish Acad. of Science and Letters, Acad. of Learned Socs in the Social Sciences 2000; Dr hc (Örebro Univ., Sweden), (European Univ. Inst., Florence); AMEX Prize in Int. Econs 1992, Lasswell Prize for Lifetime Achievement, Policy Studies Org. 1999; Lifetime Achievement Award, UK Political Studies Asscn 2000, Lifetime Achievement, Int. Council on Comparative Study of Electoral Systems 2008, Prize for European Political Sociology, ECPR Dogan Foundation 2009, Sir Isaiah Berlin Award for Lifetime Achievement in Political Studies 2009. *Address:* Centre for the Study of Public Policy, University of Strathclyde, Glasgow, G1 1XQ (office); 1 East Abercromby Street, Helensburgh, G84 7SP, Scotland (home). *Telephone:* (1436) 672164 (office). *Fax:* (1436) 673125 (home). *E-mail:* richard.rose@strath.ac.uk (office). *Website:* www.cspp.strath.ac.uk (office).

ROSE-INNES, Henrietta, BSc, MA; South African author; *Fellow, Gordon Institute for Performing and Creative Arts, University of Cape Town*; b. 14 Sept. 1971, Cape Town; d. of A.P. (Peter) Rose-Innes and Ann Rose-Innes (née Schweizer). *Education:* Univ. of Witwatersrand, Univ. of Cape Town. *Career:* Fellow in Literature, Akad. Schloss Solitude, Stuttgart 2007–08; residencies at Chateau de Lavigny, Lausanne 2004, kunst:raum sylt quelle, Sylt 2006, Univ. of Georgetown 2009, Caldera Arts Centre, Portland 2010; Writer-in-Residence, Creative Writing Centre, Univ. of Cape Town 2006–09, currently Fellow, Gordon Inst. for Performing and Creative Arts, Univ. of Cape Town. *Publications:* novels: Shark's Egg 2001, The Rock Alphabet 2004, Nineveh 2011; short stories: Homing 2010; ed.: Nice Times (miscellany) 2006. *Honours:* Southern African PEN Literary Award 2007, Caine Prize for African Writing 2008. *Literary Agent:* Isobel Dixon, Blake Friedmann Literary, Film & TV Agency, 122 Arlington Road, London, NW1 7HP, England. *Telephone:* (20) 7284-0408. *Fax:* (20) 7284-0442. *E-mail:* isobel@blakefriedmann.co.uk. *Website:* www.blakefriedmann.co.uk. *E-mail:* info@henriettarose-innes.com (home). *Website:* www.henriettarose-innes.com.

ROSEN, Charles, PhD; American pianist and writer; b. 5 May 1927, New York, NY; s. of Irwin Rosen and Anita Gerber. *Education:* Juilliard School of Music, Princeton Univ., Univ. of Southern California. *Career:* studied piano with Moriz Rosenthal and Hedwig Kanner-Rosenthal 1938–45; recital début, New York 1951; first complete recording of Debussy Etudes 1951; première of Double Concerto by Elliott Carter, New York 1961; has played recitals and as soloist with orchestras throughout America and Europe; has made over 35 recordings including Stravinsky: Movements with composer conducting 1962, Bach: Art of Fugue, Two Ricercares, Goldberg Variations 1971, Beethoven: Last Six Sonatas 1972, Boulez: Piano Music, Vol. I, Diabelli Variations, Beethoven Concerto No. 4, 1979, Schumann: The Revolutionary Masterpieces, Chopin: 24 Mazurkas 1991; Prof. of Music, State Univ. of NY 1972–90; Guggenheim Fellowship 1974; Messenger Lectures, Cornell Univ. 1975, Bloch Lectures, Univ. of Calif., Berkeley 1977, Gauss Seminars, Princeton Univ. 1978; Norton Prof. of Poetry, Harvard Univ. 1980–81; George Eastman Prof., Balliol Coll., Oxford 1987–88, Prof. of Music and Social Thought, Univ. of Chicago 1988–96; Int. Chair. of Performing and Musicology, Royal Northern Coll. of Music and Drama 2006–09. *Publications:* The Classical Style: Haydn, Mozart, Beethoven 1971, Beethoven's Last Six Sonatas 1972, Schoenberg 1975, Sonata Forms 1980, Romanticism and Realism: The Mythology of Nineteenth-Century Art (with Henri Zerner) 1984, The Musical Language of Elliott Carter 1984, Paisir de jouer, plaiser de penser 1993, The Frontiers of Meaning: Three Informal Lectures on Music 1994, The Romantic Generation 1995, Romantic Poets, Critics and Other Madmen 1998, Critical Entertainment: Music Old and New 2000, Beethoven's Piano Sonatas: A Short Companion 2001, Piano Notes 2003, Music and Sentiment 2010; contrib. to books, newspapers and journals. *Honours:* Hon. DMus (Trinity Coll., Dublin 1976, Leeds Univ. 1976, Durham Univ.); Dr hc (Cambridge) 1992; Nat. Book Award 1972, Edison Prize, Netherlands 1974, Musical America Instrumentalist of the Year 2008. *Literary Agent:* c/o Owen/White Management, Flat 6, 22 Brunswick Terrace, Hove, East Sussex BN3 1HJ, England. *Telephone:* (1273) 727127. *Fax:* (1273) 527038. *E-mail:* info@owenwhitemanagement.com. *Website:* www.owenwhitemanagement.com.

ROSEN, Michael, MA; British children's writer, poet, broadcaster and critic; b. 7 May 1946, Harrow, Middlesex, England. *Education:* Wadham Coll., Oxford, Reading Univ. *Career:* worked for BBC television, on Play School and other children's programmes, BBC radio as presenter, Treasure Islands (Radio 4), Best Worlds (Radio 3), Meridian (World Service), Word of Mouth (Radio 4); Children's Laureate 2007–09; Chair. of judges, Warwick Prize for Writing 2011; mem. Poetry Soc. (vice-pres.). *Publications include:* fiction: Backbone (play) (Sunday Times Nat. Union of Students Drama Festival Award 1968) 1969, Everybody Here (Children's Rights Workshop Other Award 1983) 1982, Hairy Tales and Nursery Crimes 1985, Smelly Jelly, Smelly Fish 1986, Under the Bed 1986, Hard-boiled Legs 1987, Spollyollydiddlytiddlyitis 1987, You're Thinking About Doughnuts 1987, Silly Stories (aka

Michael Rosen's Horribly Silly Stories) 1988, We're Going on a Bear Hunt (Smarties Best Children's Book of the Year Award 1990, Boston Globe-Horn Book Honor Award, USA 1990, School Library Journal Best Book of the Year, USA 1990, Horn Book Fanfare Title, USA 1990, Japanese Picture Book Award for an Outstanding Picture Book from Abroad 1991) 1989, The Wicked Tricks of Till Owlyglass (re-telling) 1989, The Golem of Old Prague (re-telling) 1990, Clever Cakes 1991, Walking the Bridge of Your Nose (Publishers Weekly Cuffies Award for Best Anthology or Collection, USA) 1992, Burping Bertha 1993, The Man with no Shadow (re-telling) 1994, This is Our House 1996, Snore! (Parent magazine Play and Learn Award) 1998, Mission Ziffoid 1999, Rover 1999, Lovely Old Roly 2002, Oww! 2003, Howler 2004, Michael Rosen's Sad Book 2004, William Shakespeare's Romeo and Juliet (re-telling) 2004, You're Thinking About Tomatoes 2005, Totally Wonderful Miss Plumberry 2006, Mustard, Custard, Grumble Belly and Gravy 2006, The Bear in the Cave 2007; poetry for children: Mind Your Own Business 1974, Wouldn't You Like to Know 1977, You Tell Me (with Roger McGough) 1979, You Can't Catch Me (Signal Poetry Award 1982) 1981, Quick, Let's Get Out of Here 1983, Don't Put Mustard in the Custard 1985, The Kingfisher Book of Children's Poetry (anthology ed.) 1985, A Spider Bought a Bicycle (anthology ed.) 1987, The Hypnotiser 1988, The Kingfisher Book of Funny Stories (anthology ed.) 1988, Little Rabbit Foo Foo 1990, A World of Poetry (anthology ed.) 1991, Sonsense Nongs (aka Michael Rosen's Book of Very Silly Poems, anthology ed.) 1992, Poetry for the Very Young (anthology ed.) (Nat. Asscn of Parenting Publications Best Book Award, USA) 1993, A Different Story: Poems from the Past (anthology ed.) 1994, The Zoo at Night 1996, You Wait Till I'm Older Than You (Talkies Award for the Best Poetry Audio Tape of the Year 1998) 1996, Tea in the Sugar Bowl, Potato in my Shoe 1997, Michael Rosen's Book of Nonsense 1997, Classic Poetry (anthology ed.) 1998, Night-Night, Knight (anthology ed.) 1998, Lunch Boxes Don't Fly 1999, Centrally Heated Knickers 1999, Even More Nonsense 2000, Uncle Billy Being Silly 2001, No Breathing in Class 2003, Alphabet Poem (Nat. Literacy WOW Award 2005) 2004, A-Z: The Best Children's Poetry from Agard to Zephaniah (anthology ed.) 2009; poetry for adults: The Chatto Book of Dissent (ed.) 1991, The Penguin Book of Childhood (ed.) 1994, Carrying the Elephant: A Memoir of Love and Loss 2002, This is Not My Nose 2004, In the Colonie 2005; non-fiction: Did I Hear You Write? 1989, Goodies and Daddies, an A–Z Guide to Fatherhood 1991, A Year With Poetry: Teachers Write About Teaching Poetry (co-ed.) 1997, Shakespeare: His Life and his Work 2001, William Shakespeare in his Times, for our Times 2004, Dickens 2005. *Honours:* Dr hc (Open Univ.) 2005; Glennfiddich Award for the Best Radio Programme on the subject of food (for Treasure Islands Special: Lashings of Ginger Beer) 1996, Eleanor Farjeon Award for distinguished services to children's literature 1997. *Literary Agent:* United Agents, 12–26 Lexington Street, London, W1F 0LE, England. *Telephone:* (20) 3214-0800. *Fax:* (20) 3214-0801. *E-mail:* info@unitedagents.co.uk. *Website:* unitedagents.co.uk. *E-mail:* michael@michaelrosen.co.uk (office). *Website:* www.michaelrosen.co.uk.

ROSEN, Norma, BA, MA; American writer and teacher; b. 11 Aug. 1925, New York, NY; m. Robert S. Rosen 1960, one s. one d. *Education:* Mt Holyoke College, Columbia University. *Career:* Teacher of Creative Writing, New School for Social Research, New York City, 1965–69, University of Pennsylvania, 1969, Harvard University, 1971, Yale University, 1984, New York University, 1987–95; mem. PEN; Authors' Guild. *Publications:* Joy to Levine!, 1962; Green, 1967; Touching Evil, 1969; At the Center, 1982; John and Anzia: An American Romance, 1989; Accidents of Influence: Writing as a Woman and a Jew in America (essays), 1992; Biblical Women Unbound: Counter-Tales (narratives), 1996. Contributions: anthologies and other publications.

ROSENBERG, Bruce Alan, BA, MA, PhD; American teacher and writer; b. 27 July 1934, New York, NY; m. Ann Harleman 1981, three s. *Education:* Hofstra University, Pennsylvania State University, Ohio State University. *Career:* mem. Folklore Fellows International. *Publications:* The Art of the American Folk Preacher, 1970; Custer and the Epic of Defeat, 1975; The Code of the West, 1982; The Spy Story, 1987; Can These Bones Live?, 1988; Ian Fleming, 1989; The Neutral Ground, 1995. Contributions: Over 60 professional journals. *Honours:* James Russell Lowell Prize, 1970; Chicago Folklore Prizes, 1970, 1975.

ROSENBERG, Liz, BA, MA, PhD; American academic, poet and writer; b. 3 Feb. 1956, Glen Cove, NY; m. David Bosnick 1996; one s. *Education:* Bennington College, Johns Hopkins University, SUNY at Binghamton. *Career:* Assoc. Prof. of English, SUNY at Binghamton; Guest Teacher-Poet, various venues; many poetry readings; mem. Associated Writing Programs, PEN. *Publications:* The Fire Music (poems) 1987, A Book of Days (poems) 1992, Children of Paradise (poems) 1994, Heart and Soul (novel) 1996, The Invisible Ladder (ed.) 1997, Earth-Shattering Poems (ed.) 1998, These Happy Eyes (prose poems) 1999; contributions: many newspapers, reviews, and journals. *Honours:* Kelloggs Fellow 1980–82, Pennsylvania Council of the Arts Poetry Grant 1982, Agnes Starrett Poetry Prize 1987, Claudia Lewis Poetry Prize 1997, Best Book for Teens Citation, New York Public Library 1997, Paterson Prizes for Children's Literature 1997, 1998. *Address:* c/o Department of English, General Literature, and Rhetoric, State University of New York at Binghamton, PO Box 6000, Binghamton, NY 13902, USA (office).

ROSENBERG, Nancy Taylor; American writer; b. 9 July 1946, Dallas, TX; m. 1st Calvin S. Kyrme (divorced); two s. one d.; m. 2nd Jerry Rosenberg; two d. *Education:* Gulf Park College, University of California at Los Angeles. *Career:* fmr police officer. *Publications:* Mitigating Circumstances 1993, Interest of Justice 1993, The Eyewitness 1994, First Offense 1994, California Angel 1995, Trial by Fire 1995, Abuse of Power 1997, Buried Evidence 2000, Conflict of Interest 2002, Sullivan's Law 2004, Sullivan's Justice 2005, Sullivan's Evidence 2006, Revenge of Innocents 2007, The Cheater 2009. *Address:* c/o Forge Books, Macmillan, 175 Fifth Avenue, New York, NY 10010, USA (office). *Website:* www.nancytrosenberg.com.

ROSENBERG, Peter Michael, BSc, MA; British writer; b. 11 July 1958, London, England. *Education:* Univ. of Sussex, Univ. of the Arts, London. *Publications:* The Usurper (co-author) 1988, Kissing Through a Pane of Glass 1993, Touched By a God or Something 1994, Because It Makes My Heart Beat Faster 1995, Daniel's Dream 1996; contribs to journals and magazines. *Honours:* Second Prize, Betty Trask Award 1992. *Literary Agent:* c/o Christopher Little Literary Agency, 10 Eel Brook Studios, 125 Moore Park Road, London, SW6 4PS, England. *Telephone:* (20) 7736-4455. *Fax:* (20) 7736-4490. *E-mail:* info@christopherlittle.net. *Website:* www.christopherlittle.net. *E-mail:* petermrosenberg@gmail.com (home).

ROSENBLATT, Joseph (Joe); Canadian poet, writer and artist; b. 26 Dec. 1933, Toronto, Ont.; m. Faye Smith 1970; one s. *Education:* Central Tech. School, Toronto, George Brown Coll., Toronto. *Career:* Ed. Jewish Dialog magazine 1969–83; Writer-in-Residence, Univ. of Western Ontario, London 1979–80, Univ. of Victoria, BC 1980–81, Saskatoon Public Library, Saskatchewan 1985–86; Visiting Lecturer, Univ. of Rome, Italy 1987, Univ. of Bologna, Italy 1987; writing and painting 1980–. *Art exhibitions include:* with Eastside Group: McPherson Library, Univ. of Victoria 2004, The Enormous Room: Pteros Gallery, Toronto 2004, Amelia Douglas Gallery, New West, BC 2004, Arts Building, Parksville, BC 2004, Spirit Wings (solo show), Arts Building, Parksville, BC 2005, Closing of Fran Willis Gallery Final Group Exhbn 2007, Art Auction Catalogue, Vancouver Trade & Convention Centre 2008, Leighdon Studio Gallery 2009, Synergy: Words and Images, Amelia Douglas Gallery, New Westminster Campus, Douglas Coll., BC 2010. *Publications include:* The Voyage of the Mood 1960, The LSD Leacock 1963, The Winter of the Luna Moth 1968, Greenbaum 1970, The Bumblebee Dithyramb 1972, Blind Photographer: Poems and Sketches 1973, Dream Craters 1974, Virgins and Vampires 1975, Top Soil 1976, Doctor Anaconda's Solar Fun Club: A Book of Drawings 1977, Loosely Tied Hands: An Experiment in Punk 1978, Snake Oil 1978, The Sleeping Lady 1979, Brides of the Stream 1984, Escape from the Glue Factory: A Memoir of a Paranormal Toronto Childhood in the Late Forties 1985, Poetry Hotel: Selected Poems 1963–1985 1985, The Kissing Goldfish of Siam: A Memoir of Adolescence in the Fifties 1989, Gridi nel Buio 1990, Beds and Consenting Dreamers 1994, The Joe Rosenblatt Reader 1995, The Voluptuos Gardener: The Collected Art and Writing of Joe Rosenblatt 1973–1996 1996, The Lunatic Muse 2007, Dog 2008, Dark Fish & Other Infernos 2011; contrib. to many publications. *Honours:* Canada Council Senior Arts Awards 1973, 1976, 1980, 1987, Ontario Arts Council Poetry Award 1970, Gov.-Gen.'s Award for Poetry 1976, British Columbia Book Award for Poetry 1986. *Address:* 221 Elizabeth Avenue, Qualicum Beach, BC V9K 1G8, Canada. *Telephone:* (250) 752-9297 (home). *Fax:* (250) 752-0531 (home). *E-mail:* moishe_r@telus.net.

ROSENDORFER, Herbert; German novelist and academic; b. 19 Feb. 1934, Bolzano; s. of Josef Rosendorfer and Johanna Ennsfellner; m. Julia Andreae-Rosendorfer; four c. *Education:* Ludwig-Maximilians-Universität, Munich. *Career:* fmr attorney and judge (retd), Prof. of German Literature, Univ. of Munich. *Publications include:* novels: Der Ruinenbaumeister (trans. as The Architect of Ruins) 1969, Grosses Solo für Anton (trans. as Grand Solo for Anton) 1976, Stephanie und das vorige Leben (trans. as Stephanie or a Previous Existence) 1977, Briefe in die chinesische Vergangenheit (trans. as Letters Back to Ancient China) 1983, Die Nacht der Amazonen 1989, Ein Liebhaber ungerader Zahlen 1994, Die grosse Umwendung: neue Briefe in die chinesische Vergangenheit 1997, Kadon, Ehemaliger Gott 2001, Die Kellnerin Anni 2002, Die Donnerstage des Oberstaatsanwalts 2004, Der Hilfskoch 2006, Monolog in Schwartz 2007. *Honours:* Bundesverdienstkreuz, Bayerischer Verdienstorden, Österreichisches Ehrenkreuz für Kust und Wissenschaft 1.Klasse; Jean-Paul Prize 1999, Lieraturpreis der Stadt München 2005. *Literary Agent:* c/o Dedalus Ltd, Langford Lodge, St Judith's Lane, Sawtry, Cambridgeshire PE28 5XE, England. *E-mail:* info@dedalusbooks.com. *Website:* www.dedalusbooks.com.

ROSENTHAL, Barbara Ann, BFA, MFA; American writer, artist, photographer and video artist; b. 17 Aug. 1948, New York, NY; two d. *Education:* Carnegie-Mellon University, Queens College, CUNY. *Career:* Ed.-in-Chief, Patterns, 1967–70; Adjunct Lecturer in English, College of Staten Island, CUNY, 1990–. *Publications:* Clues to Myself, 1982; Sensations, 1984; Old Address Book, 1985; Homo Futurus, 1986; In the West of Ireland, 1992; Children's Shoes, 1993; Soul and Psyche, 1999. Contributions: anthologies and journals. *Honours:* various awards and residencies.

ROSENTHAL, Thomas Gabriel, MA, PhD; British publisher, critic and broadcaster; b. 16 July 1935, s. of the late Erwin I. J. Rosenthal and Elisabeth Charlotte Marx; m. Ann Judith Warnford-Davis; two s. *Education:* Perse School, Cambridge and Pembroke Coll., Cambridge. *Career:* served in RA 1954–56; joined Thames and Hudson Ltd 1959, Man. Dir Thames and Hudson Int. 1966; joined Martin Secker and Warburg Ltd as Man. Dir 1971, Dir Heinemann Group of Publrs 1972–84, Man. Dir William Heinemann Int. Ltd 1979–84, Chair. World's Work Ltd 1979–84, Heinemann Zsolnay Ltd 1979–84,

Kaye and Ward Ltd 1980–84, William Heinemann, Australia and SA 1981–82, Pres. Heinemann Inc. 1981–84; Jt Man. Dir and Jt Chair. André Deutsch Ltd 1984, CEO 1987–96, Sole Man. Dir and Chair. 1987, Chair. 1984–98; Chair. Frew McKenzie (Antiquarian Booksellers) 1985–93, Bridgewater Press 1997–; Art Critic The Listener 1963–66; Chair. Soc. of Young Publrs 1961–62; mem. Cambridge Univ. Appointments Bd 1967–71, Exec. Cttee Nat. Book League 1971–74, Cttee of Man. Amateur Dramatic Club, Cambridge (also Trustee), Council RCA 1982–87, Exec. Council Inst. of Contemporary Arts 1987–99 (Chair. 1996–99); Trustee Phoenix Trust, Fitzwilliam Museum, Cambridge 2002–; mem. Editorial Bd Logos 1989–93. *Publications:* Monograph on Jack B. Yeats 1964, Monograph on Ivon Hitchens (with Alan Bowness) 1973; A Reader's Guide to European Art History 1962, A Reader's Guide to Modern American Fiction 1963, Monograph on Arthur Boyd (with Ursula Hoff) 1986, The Art of Jack B. Yeats 1993, Sidney Nolan 2002, Paula Rego: The Complete Graphic Works 2004, Joseph Albers: Formulation Articulation 2006, L.S. Lowry: The Art and the Artist 2010; articles in journals and newspapers. *Address:* Flat 7, Huguenot House, 19 Oxendon Street, London, SW1Y 4EH, England (home). *Telephone:* (20) 7839-3589 (home).

ROSERO, Evelio, (Evelio José Rosero, Evelio Rosero Diago); Colombian writer and journalist; b. 20 March 1958, Bogotá. *Education:* Univ. Externado de Colombia. *Publications include:* Ausentes (short story) (Nat. Short Story Award) 1979, Mateo solo (novel) 1984, Juliana los mira (novel) 1986, El incendiado (novel) (Pedro Gómez Valderrama Award for Best Colombian Novel) 1988, Papá es santo y sabio (novella) (Premio Int. de Novela Breve, Valencia, Spain) 1989, Señor que no conoce luna (novel) 1992, Plutón (novel) 2000, Los almuerzos (novel) 2001, Juega el amor (novel) 2002, En el lejero 2003, Los ejércitos (trans. as The Armies) (Premio Tusquets 2006, Ind. Foreign Fiction Prize 2009) 2006; children's books: El Aprendiz de Mago y otros cuentos de miedo (Nat. Colcultura Literature for Children Prize 1992), Cuchilla (Int. Norma-Fundalectura Prize) 2000, Pelea en el parque (trans. as Fight in the Park), La Duenda (Int. Enka Prize) 2001, El hombre que quería escribir una carta 2002, La flor que camina 2005, Los escapados 2006. *Honours:* Premio Iberoamericano de Libro de Cuentos Netzahualcóyotl (Mexico) 1982, Nat. Literature Award 2006. *Address:* c/o TusQuets Editores, Calle Cesare Cantú 8, 08023 Barcelona, Spain (office). *Website:* www.tusquets-editores.es (office).

ROSOFF, Margaret (Meg) J., BA; American writer; b. 16 Oct. 1956, Boston, Mass; d. of Chester Rosoff and Lois Goldman; one d. *Education:* Harvard Univ., St Martin's School of Art, London, UK. *Career:* worked in publishing, public relations and advertising. *Publications:* children's fiction: How I Live Now (Guardian Children's Fiction Prize 2004, Michael L Printz Award (US) 2005, Branford Boase First Novel Prize 2005, Winner, Der Luchs des Jahres 2005) 2004, Meet Wild Boars 2005, Just in Case (Carnegie Medal 2007, Deutscher Jugendliteraturpreis 2008) 2006, What I Was (Winner, Der Luchs des Jahres 2009) 2007, Jumpy Jack & Googily 2008, Wild Boars Cook 2008, The Bride's Farewell 2009, Vamoose! 2010. *Literary Agent:* c/o Catherine Clarke, Felicity Bryan Literary Agency, 2A North Parade Avenue, Oxford, OX2 6LX, England. *Telephone:* (1865) 513816. *Fax:* (1865) 310055. *E-mail:* agency@felicitybryan.com. *Website:* www.felicitybryan.com. *Address:* c/o Puffin Publicity, 80 Strand, London WC2R 0RL, England (office). *Website:* www.megrosoff.co.uk.

ROSS, Alex; American journalist and writer; b. 1968, Washington, DC; spouse Jonathan Lisecki. *Education:* St Albans School, Harvard Univ. *Career:* music critic, New York Times 1992–96, The New Yorker 1996–; McGraw Prof. in Writing, Princeton Univ. 2008. *Publications:* The Rest Is Noise: Listening to the Twentieth Century (Nat. Book Critics Circle Award, Guardian First Book Award 2008, Royal Philharmonic Soc. Award for Best Creative Communication 2009, Premio Napoli 2010, Grand Prix des Muses 2011) 2007, Listen To This (ASCAP-Deems Taylor Award) 2010, Da Capo Best Music Writing (ed.) 2011; contrib. to Studio A: The Bob Dylan Reader, Best American Essays, Da Capo Best Music Writing. *Honours:* Dr hc (Manhattan School of Music, New England Conservatory, Curtis Inst.); four ASCAP-Deems Taylor Awards for music criticism, Fellowships from American Acad., Berlin, Banff Centre, Canada and American Acad., Rome, American Music Center Letter of Distinction for contribs to the field of contemporary music, MacArthur Fellowship 2008, Arts and Letters Award, American Acad. of Arts and Letters 2011, Belmont Prize 2012. *Address:* The New Yorker, 4 Times Square, New York, NY 10036, USA (office). *Telephone:* (212) 286-5984 (office). *Website:* www.therestisnoise.com.

ROSS, Angus (see Giggal, Kenneth)

ROSS, Dennis B., PhD; American academic, diplomatist and fmr government official; *Counselor, Washington Institute for Near East Policy*; b. 26 Nov. 1948, San Francisco; m. Deborah Ross; one s. two d. *Education:* Univ. of California, Los Angeles. *Career:* Deputy Dir Office of Net Assessment, US Defense Dept, Washington, DC 1982–84, 1989–92; Exec. Dir of program on Soviet Int. Behavior sponsored by Univ. of California, Berkeley and Stanford Univ. 1984–86; Dir Near East and S Asian Affairs, Nat. Security Council (during Reagan Admin); Dir Policy Planning Office, US State Dept 1988–92, Special Middle East Co-ordinator 1992–2001, helped achieve the 1995 Interim Agreement and brokered the Hebron Accord 1997; Counsellor and Ziegler Distinguished Fellow, Washington Inst. for Near East Policy 2001–08, Counsellor (part–time) 2008–09, Counselor 2011–; Special US Envoy to Middle East, US State Dept 2009; Special Asst to the Pres. and Sr Dir for Cen. Region, Nat. Security Council 2009–10; Adjunct Lecturer, Kennedy School of Govt, Harvard Univ. 2002–04; Fred and Rita Richman Distinguished Visiting Prof., Brandeis Univ. 2003, 2005; Allis-Chalmers Distinguished Prof. of Int. Affairs, Marquette Univ. 2004–05; Adjunct Prof., Georgetown Univ. School of Foreign Service 2006–07, also Adjunct Prof. of Govt, Georgetown Univ. 2007; Bartels World Affairs Fellow, Cornell Univ. 2005; Chair. Inst. for Jewish People Policy Planning, Jerusalem; has served as Foreign Affairs Analyst for Fox News Channel. *Publications include:* The Missing Peace: The Inside Story of the Fight for Middle East Peace 2004, Statecraft: And How to Restore America's Standing in the World 2007, Myths, Illusions and Peace: Finding a New Direction for America in the Middle East (with David Makovsky) 2009; numerous articles in learned journals and newspapers. *Honours:* Hon. DHumLitt (Amherst Coll.) 2002, Dr hc (Jewish Theological Seminary, Syracuse Univ.); UCLA Alumnus of the Year; Presidential Medal for Distinguished Fed. Civilian Service, Truman Peace Prize from Harry S. Truman Research Inst. for the Advancement of Peace, Hebrew Univ. of Jerusalem 2008. *Address:* Washington Institute for Near East Policy, 1828 L Street, NW, Suite 1050, Washington, DC 20036, USA (office). *Telephone:* (202) 452-0650 (office). *Fax:* (202) 223-5364 (office). *Website:* www.washingtoninstitute.org (office).

ROSS, Helaine (see Daniels, Dorothy)

ROSS, Jonathan (see Rossiter, John)

ROSS, Malcolm (see Ross-Macdonald, Malcolm John)

ROSS-MacDONALD, Malcolm John, (Malcolm Macdonald, M. R. O'Donnell, Malcolm Ross); British writer and editor (retd) and designer (retd); b. 29 Feb. 1932, Chipping, Sodbury, Glos., England; m. Ingrid Giehr; two d. *Education:* Falmouth School of Art, Slade School, Univ. Coll., London. *Career:* Lecturer, Folk Univ., Sweden 1959–61; Exec. Ed., Aldus Books 1962–65; Visiting Lecturer, Hornsey Coll. of Art 1965–69; mem. Authors' Guild, Soc. of Authors. *Plays:* Conditional People, Kristina's Winter, World from Rough Stones trilogy. *Publications:* The Big Waves 1962, Macdonald Illustrated Encyclopaedia (exec. ed., ten vols) 1962–65, Spare Part Surgery (co-author) 1968, Machines in Medicine 1969, The Human Heart 1970, World Wildlife Guide 1971, Beyond the Horizon 1971, Every Living Thing 1973, World from Rough Stones 1974, 2009, Origin of Johnny 1975, Life in the Future 1976, The Rich are With You Always 1976, 2009, Sons of Fortune 1978, 2010, Abigail 1979, 2010, Goldeneye 1981, The Dukes 1982, Tessa'd'Arblay 1983, In Love and War 1984, Mistress of Pallas 1986, Silver Highways 1987, The Sky with Diamonds 1988, A Notorious Woman 1988, His Father's Son 1989, An Innocent Woman 1989, Hell Hath No Fury 1990, A Woman Alone 1990, The Captain's Wives 1991, A Woman Scorned 1991, A Woman Possessed 1992, All Desires Known 1993, To the End of her Days 1993, Dancing on Snowflakes 1994, For I Have Sinned 1994, Kernow and Daughter 1994, Crissy's Family 1995, Tomorrow's Tide 1996, The Carringtons of Helston 1997, Like a Diamond 1998, Tamsin Harte 2000, Rose of Nancemellin 2001, The Dower House 2011, Strange Music 2012, Promises to Keep 2012; contrib. to Sunday Times, New Scientist, Science Journal, Month, Jefferson Encyclopaedia. *Honours:* Romantic Times Historical Novel of the Year, USA 1981. *Literary Agent:* c/o David Higham Associates, 5–8 Lower John Street, Golden Square, London W1F 9HA, England. *Telephone:* (20) 7434-5900. *Fax:* (20) 7437-1072. *E-mail:* dha@davidhigham.co.uk. *Website:* www.davidhigham.co.uk. *E-mail:* mirossmac2@eircom.net (home). *Website:* www.malcolmmacdonald.org.

ROSSI, Bruno (see Levinson, Leonard)

ROSSITER, John, (Jonathan Ross); British writer; b. 2 March 1916, Devonshire, England. *Education:* preparatory and military schools, Woolwich and Bulford. *Career:* Detective Chief Superintendent, Wiltshire Constabulary 1939–69; Flight Lieutenant, RAF/VR 1943–46; columnist, Wiltshire Courier, Swindon 1963–64; mem. CWA. *Publications:* as Jonathan Ross: The Blood Running Cold 1968, Diminished by Death 1968, Dead at First Hand 1969, The Deadest Thing You Ever Saw 1969, Death's Head 1982, Dead Eye 1983, Dropped Dead 1984, Fate Accomplished 1987, Sudden Departures 1988, A Time for Dying 1989, Daphne Dead and Done For 1990, Murder be Hanged 1992, The Body of a Woman 1994, Murder! Murder! Burning Bright 1996, This Too Too Sullied Flesh 1997; as John Rossiter: The Victims 1971, A Rope for General Dietz 1972, The Manipulators 1973, The Villains 1974, The Golden Virgin 1975, The Man Who Came Back 1978, Dark Flight 1981; contrib. to Police Review. *Address:* 3 Leighton Home Farm Court, Wellhead Lane, Westbury, Wilts BA13 3PT, England. *Telephone:* (1373) 826411 (home).

ROSSITER, John (see Crozier, Brian Rossiter)

ROSTON, Murray, BA (Hons), MA, PhD; British/Israeli academic and writer; *Professor Emeritus of English, Bar-Ilan University*; b. 10 Dec. 1928, London, England; m. Faith Roston. *Education:* Queens' Coll., Cambridge, Queen Mary Coll., London. *Career:* Prof. of English, Bar-Ilan Univ., Ramat Gan, Israel 1956–, Full Prof. 1969–, Chair. Dept of English 1967–72, 1976–78, Dean of Faculty of Humanities 1988–90, now Emer.; Perm. Adjunct Prof., Univ. of California, Los Angeles, USA 1999–2011. *Publications:* Prophet and Poet: The Bible and the Growth of Romanticism 1965, Biblical Drama in England from the Middle Ages to the Present Day 1968, The Soul of Wit: A Study of John Donne 1974, Milton and the Baroque 1980, Sixteenth-Century English Literature 1982, Renaissance Perspectives in Literature and the Visual Arts 1987, Changing Perspectives in Literature and the Visual Arts, 1650–1820 1990, Victorian Contexts in Literature and the Visual Arts 1995, Modernist

Patterns in Literature and the Visual Arts 1999, The Search for Selfhood in Modern Literature 2001, Graham Greene's Narrative Strategies 2006, Tradition and Subversion in Renaissance Literature: Studies in Shakespeare, Jonson, Spenser and Donne 2007, The Comic Mode in English Literature from the Middle Ages to Today 2011; contribs to professional journals. *Address:* 613 Mediterranean Towers, Nordiya, 42954, Israel (home). *E-mail:* murrayroston@gmail.com (office).

ROTH, Gerhard Jürgen; Austrian writer and photographer; b. 24 June 1942, Graz; m. 1st Erika Wolfgruber 1963 (divorced 1986); m. 2nd Senta Thonhauser 1995; one s. two d. *Education:* Univ. of Graz Medical School. *Publications:* Die Autobiographie des Albert Einstein 1972, Der Ausbruch des Ersten Weltkriegs und andere Romane 1972, Der Wille zur Krankheit 1973, Der grosse Horizont 1974, Ein Neuer Morgen 1976, Winterreise 1978, Der stille Ozean (trans. as The Calm Ocean) 1980, Circus Saluti 1981, Die schönen Bilder beim Trabrennen 1982, Das Töten des Bussards 1982, Dorfchronik zum Landläufiger Tod 1984, Die Vergessenen 1986, Am Abgrund 1986, Der Untersuchungsrichter: Die Geschichte eines Entwurfs 1988, Die Geschichte der Dunkelheit: Ein Bericht 1991, Eine Reise in das Innere von Wien 1991, Das doppelköpfige Österreich 1995, Der See (trans. as The Lake) 1995, Der Plan 1998, Der Berg 2000, Der Strom (novel) 2002, Das Labyrinth (novel) 2005, Das Alphabet der Zeit (autobiography) 2007, Die Stadt (essays) 2009, Orkus (novel) 2011; various plays, essays, etc. *Honours:* State of Styria Literature Prizes 1972, 1973, 1976, South West German Radio Critic's Prize 1978, City of Hamburg Fellowship 1979–80, Alfrid Döblin Prize 1983, Marie Luise Kaschnitz Prize 1992, Vienna Literary Prize 1992, Peter-Rossegger Prize 1994, Austrian Booksellers Hon. Prize 1994. *Address:* Am Heumarkt 7/4/37, 1030 Vienna, Austria (home).

ROTH, Philip Milton, MA; American writer and academic; b. 19 March 1933, Newark, NJ; s. of Herman Roth and Bess Finkel Roth; m. 1st Margaret Martinson 1959 (died 1968); m. 2nd Claire Bloom 1990 (divorced 1994). *Education:* Bucknell Univ. and Univ. of Chicago. *Career:* served in US Army 1955–56; Lecturer in English, Univ. of Chicago 1956–58; Visiting Lecturer, Univ. of Iowa Writers' Workshop 1960–62; Writer-in-Residence, Princeton Univ. 1962–64, Univ. of Pennsylvania 1967–80; Distinguished Prof. of Literature, Hunter Coll. 1989–92; Visiting Lecturer, State Univ. of NY, Stony Brook 1967, 1968; Houghton Mifflin Literary Fellow 1959; mem. American Acad. of Arts and Letters 1970–. *Publications include:* Goodbye Columbus (novella and stories) 1959, Letting Go 1962, When She Was Good 1967, Portnoy's Complaint 1969, Our Gang 1971, The Breast 1972, The Great American Novel 1973, My Life as a Man 1974, Reading Myself and Others (essays) 1975, The Professor of Desire 1977, The Ghost Writer 1979, A Philip Roth Reader 1980, Zuckerman Unbound 1981, The Anatomy Lesson 1983, The Prague Orgy 1985, Zuckerman Bound 1985, The Counterlife (Nat. Book Critics' Circle Award 1987) 1986, The Facts: A Novelist's Autobiography 1988, Deception 1990, Patrimony (Nat. Book Critics' Circle Award 1992) 1991, Operation Shylock (PEN/Faulkner Award) 1993, Sabbath's Theater (Nat. Book Award for Fiction) 1995, American Pastoral (Pulitzer Prize in Fiction 1998) 1997, I Married a Communist (Ambassador Book Award of the English-Speaking Union) 1998, The Human Stain (PEN/Faulkner Award 2001, Prix Médicis Étranger 2002) 2000, The Dying Animal 2001, Shop Talk 2001, The Plot Against America (WHSmith Literary Award 2005, Soc. of American Historians' Award 2005, Sidewise Award for Alternate History 2005) 2004, Everyman (PEN/Faulkner Award 2007) 2006, Exit Ghost 2007, Indignation 2008, The Humbling 2009, Nemesis 2011. *Honours:* Dr hc (Harvard) 2003; Guggenheim Fellowship Grant 1959–60, Daroff Award of Jewish Book Council of America 1959, Nat. Inst. of Arts and Letters Award 1959, Rockefeller Grant 1965, Ford Foundation Grant 1966, Nat. Arts Club's Medal of Honor for Literature 1991, Karel Capek Prize 1994, Nat. Medal of Arts 1998, Gold Medal in Fiction, American Acad. of Arts and Letters 2002, Nat. Book Foundation Medal for Distinguished Contribution to American Letters 2002, PEN/Nabokov Award for Lifetime Achievement 2006, PEN/Saul Bellow Award for Achievement in American Fiction 2007, Nat. Humanities Medal 2011, Man Booker Int. Prize 2011. *Literary Agent:* c/o The Wylie Agency, 250 West 57th Street, Suite 2114, New York, NY 10107, USA.

ROTHE-VALLBONA, Rima Gretel (see VALLBONA, Rima Gretel Rothe)

ROTHENBERG, Jerome (Dennis), BA, MA; American poet, writer and academic; *Professor Emeritus, University of California at San Diego*; b. 11 Dec. 1931, New York, NY; s. of Morris Rothenberg and Esther Lichtenstein; m. Diane Brodatz 1952; one s. *Education:* City Coll., City Univ. of New York, Univ. of Michigan. *Career:* Prof. of English and Comparative Literature, State Univ. of NY at Binghamton 1986–88; Prof. of Visual Arts and Literature, Univ. of California, San Diego 1988–98, Prof. Emer. 1998–; mem. New Wilderness Foundation, PEN International. *Publications:* New Young German Poets 1959, White Sun Black Sun 1960, Technicians of the Sacred 1968, Poems for the Game of Silence: Selected Poems 1971, Shaking the Pumpkin 1972, America Prophecy 1973, Poland/1931 1974, Revolution of the Word 1974, A Big Jewish Book 1977, A Seneca Journal 1978, Numbers and Letters 1980, Vienna Blood 1980, Pre-Faces 1981, That Dada Strain 1983, Symposium of the Whole 1983, 15 Flower World Variations 1984, A Merz Sonata 1985, New Selected Poems, 1970–85 1986, Exiled in the Word 1989, Khurbn and Other Poems 1989, Further Sightings and Conversations 1989, The Lorca Variations 1994, Gematria 1994, An Oracle for Delfi 1995, Poems for the Millennium (three vols) 1995, 1998, 2009, Pictures of the Crucifixion 1996, Seedings and Other Poems 1996, The Book Spiritual Instrument 1996, A Paradise of Poets 1999, A Book of the Book 2000, The Case for Memory 2001, A Book of Witness: Spells and Gris-Gris (poems) 2003, María Sabina Selections 2003, A Book of Concealments 2004, 25 Caprichos (after Goya) 2004, Picasso: The Burial of the Count of Orgaz and Other Poems 2004, Writing Through: Translations and Variations 2004, The Burning Babe and Other Poems 2005, China Notes & The Treasures of Dunhuang 2006, Triptych 2007, Poetics and Polemics 2008, Gematria Complete 2009, Romantic Dadas 2009, Concealments & Caprichos 2010, Ojo del Testimonio 2010, Retrievals: Uncollected and New Poems 2011, 25 Caprichos a Partir de Lorca 2011; contrib. to various publs. *Honours:* Nat. Endowment for the Arts Fellowship 1975, Guggenheim Fellowship 1976, American Book Award 1982, PEN Center, USA West Trans. Award 1994, 2002, PEN Oakland Josephine Miles Literary Awards 1994, 1996, Alfonso el Sabio Award for Trans. 2004, PEN American Center Trans. Award 2005, San Diego Library Lifetime Achievement Award 2007, American Book Award 2010, Medalla al Mérito Literario (Chihuahua, Mexico) 2011. *Address:* Department of Visual Arts, University of California at San Diego, La Jolla, CA 92093 (office); 1026 San Abella Drive, Encinitas, CA 92024, USA (home). *Telephone:* (760) 436-9923 (home). *Fax:* (760) 436-9923 (home). *E-mail:* jrothenb@ucsd.edu (office); jrothenberg@cox.net (home). *Website:* wings.buffalo.edu/epc/authors/rothenberg (office); poemsandpoetics.blogspot.com.

ROTHERMERE, 4th Viscount, cr. 1919, of Hemsted; **Jonathan Harold Esmond Vere Harmsworth,** BA; British newspaper publisher; *Chairman, Daily Mail and General Trust PLC*; b. 3 Dec. 1967, London; s. of the late 3rd Viscount Rothermere and Patricia Evelyn Beverley Brooks; m. Claudia Clemence 1993; two s. three d. *Education:* Gordonstoun School, Scotland, Kent School, Conn., USA, Duke Univ., USA. *Career:* joined Mirror Group 1993; joined Northcliffe Newspapers Group Ltd 1995; Deputy Man. Dir, then Man. Dir Evening Standard 1997; Chair. Assoc. Newspapers Ltd 1998–; Chair. Assoc. New Media 1998, Daily Mail and Gen. Trust PLC 1998–; Pres. Newspaper Press Fund 1999–. *Address:* Daily Mail and General Trust PLC, Room 602, Northcliffe House, 2 Derry Street, London, W8 5TT, England (office). *Telephone:* (20) 7938-6613. *Fax:* (20) 7937-0043. *E-mail:* chairman@chairman.dmgt.com (office). *Website:* www.dmgt.com (office).

ROTHSCHUH TABLADA, Guillermo; Nicaraguan poet, writer and teacher; b. 1926, Juigalpa; m. Maria Elba Villanueva 1949; four c. *Education:* Escuela Normal Central de Varones Franklin Delano Roosevelt. *Career:* began teaching 1946; fmr Dir Instituto Nacional de Chontales; fmr Dir Instituto Nacional Central Ramirez Goyena; has also taught at Universidad Nacional Autónoma de Nicaragua (UNAN); fmr Dir of Cultural Extension, Ministry of Educ. (Mined), fmr Advisor to Minister's Office. *Publications:* Poemas chontaleños 1960, Cita con un árbol 1965, Escritos pedagógicos 1968, Santiago, El Cid y El Quijote, tres caballeros de España 1971, Veinte elegias al cedro 1973, Cinco pioneros y una provincial 1976, Quinteto a Don José Lezama Lima 1978, Los guerrilleros vencen al los generals 1983, El retorno del cisne 1983, Letanias a Catarrán 1984, Las uvas están verdes 1998, Mitos y mitores 2002, Tela de condors: homenaje a Oswaldo Guayasamín 2005. *Honours:* Winner, Fundacion Luisa Mercado Premio Nacional al Magisterio 2010. *Address:* c/o Fundación Luisa Mercado, Apartado Postal LM 280, Managua, Nicaragua (office). *E-mail:* premiomagisterio@gmail.com (office); funluimer@fundacionluisamercado.org (office). *Website:* www.fundacionluisamercado.org (office).

ROUDINESCO, Elisabeth, Docteur en Lettres et Sciences Humaines; French historian, psychoanalyst, academic and author; *Director of Research in History, Université Paris VII-Denis Diderot;* b. 10 Sept. 1944, Paris; d. of Alexandre Roudinesco and Jenny Aubry (née Weiss); m. Olivier Bétourné. *Education:* Sévigné Collège, Université Paris VIII-Vincennes, Habilitation à Diriger des Recherches, Université Paris VII-Denis Diderot. *Career:* mem. École Freudienne de Paris 1969–81; Dir of Research in History – Habilitée à Diriger des Recherches, Université Paris VII-Denis Diderot 1991–; Sr Reader, Ecole des Hautes Etudes en Sciences Sociales 1992–96; Dir of Studies, Ecole Pratique des Hautes Etudes, Univ. of Paris I-Panthéon-Sorbonne 2001–09; Visiting Prof., Middlesex Univ., London, UK 2006–; Pres. Soc. Internationale d'Histoire de la Psychiatrie et de la Psychanalyse; mem. Editorial Advisory Bd Revue Poétique 1969–79, L'Homme 1997–2002, Cliniques Méditerranéenne 2000–, History of Psychiatry 2003–. *Publications include:* Histoire de la Psychanalyse en France, 1885–1985 (two vols) 1982, 1986 (second vol. translated as Jacques Lacan & Co. 1990), Théroigne de Méricourt 1989 (translated as Théroigne de Méricourt, Madness and Revolution 1993), Jacques Lacan: Esquisse d'une vie Histoire d'une Systéme de Pensée 1993 (translated as Jacques Lacan 1997), Généalogies (Best Book, Soc. Française d'Histoire de la Médecine 1994) 1994, Dictionnaire de la Psychanalyse (with Michel Plon) 1997, Pourquoi la psychanalyse (translated as Why Psychoanalysis? 1999), De Quoi demain… (with Jacques Derrida, translated as For What Tomorrow: A Dialogue 2004) 2001, La Famille en désordre 2002, Philosophes dans la tourmente (translated as Philosophy in Turbulent Times: Canguilhem, Sartre, Foucault, Althusser, Deleuze, Derrida) 2005, La part obscure de nous-mêmes – Une histoire des pervers (translated as Our Dark Side – A History of Perversion) 2007, Retour sur la question juive 2009, Mais pourquoi tant de haine 2010; various papers published in academic journals and magazines; regular contrib. to French nat. newspapers, Libération 1986–96, Le Monde 1996–, and to various other publs. *Address:* Université Paris Diderot - Paris 7, UFR Géographie, Histoire, Sciences de la Société, 105 rue de Tolbiac, Case 7001, 75205 Paris Cedex 13 (office); 89 avenue Denfert-

Rochereau, 75014 Paris, France (home). *Telephone:* 1-43-26-89-67 (home). *Fax:* 1-44-07-25-78 (home). *E-mail:* elisabeth.roudinesco@wanadoo.fr. *Website:* univ-paris-diderot.academia.edu/ElisabethRoudinesco (office).

ROUNTREE, Owen (see Kittredge, William Alfred)

ROUSE, Anne Barrett, BA; American poet and writer; *Visiting Writing Fellow, St Mary's College, Queen's University, Belfast*; b. 26 Sept. 1954, Washington, DC. *Education:* Univ. of London. *Career:* Dir, Islington Mind 1992–95; Visiting Writing Fellow, Univ. of Glasgow 2000–02; mem. Poetry Soc., Writers' Guild. *Publications:* Sunset Grill 1993, Timing 1997; contrib. to periodicals. *Honours:* Poetry Book Soc. recommendations 1993, 1997. *Address:* c/o Bloodaxe Books Ltd, Highgreen, Tarset, Northumberland NE48 1RP, England. *Website:* www.annerouse.com.

ROUSSEAU, George Sebastian, BA, MA, PhD; American academic; *Co-Director, Oxford University Centre for the History of Childhood*; b. 23 Feb. 1941, New York, NY; s. of Hyman Victoire Rousseau and Esther Zacuto; partner John Francis Sturley. *Education:* Amherst Coll., Princeton Univ. *Career:* Osgood Fellow in English Literature 1965–66, Woodrow Wilson Dissertation Fellow 1966, Princeton Univ.; book reviewer, The New York Times 1967–; instructor, Harvard Univ. 1966–68; Asst Prof., UCLA 1968–69, Assoc. Prof. 1969–76, Prof. of English 1976–94; Fulbright Resident Prof., West Germany 1970; Hon. Fellow, Wolfson Coll. Cambridge 1974–75; Overseas Fellow, Univ. of Cambridge 1979; Visiting Fellow Commoner, Trinity Coll. Cambridge 1982; Sr Fulbright Resident Scholar, Sir Thomas Browne Inst., The Netherlands 1983; Visiting Exchange Prof., King's Coll. Cambridge 1984; Sr Fellow, Nat. Endowment for the Humanities 1986–87; Visiting Fellow and Waynflete Lecturer, Magdalen Coll. Oxford 1993–94; Regius Prof. of English Literature, King's Coll., Univ. of Aberdeen 1994–98; Research Prof. of Humanities, De Montfort Univ. 1999–2002; mem. Faculty of Modern History, Univ. of Oxford 2003–, currently Co-Dir Oxford Univ. Centre for the History of Childhood; mem. numerous professional orgs. *Publications include:* This Long Disease My Life: Alexander Pope and the Sciences (co-ed. with Marjorie Hope Nicolson) 1968, English Poetic Satire: Wyatt to Byron (with N. Rudenstine) 1969, Tobias Smollett: Bicentennial Essays Presented to Lewis M. Knapp (co-ed.) 1971, Organic Form: The Life of an Idea (ed.) 1972, Goldsmith: The Critical Heritage 1974, The Renaissance Man in the 18th Century 1978, The Letters and Private Papers of Sir John Hill 1981, Tobias Smollett: Essays of Two Decades 1982, Literature and Science (ed.) 1985, Science and the Imagination: The Berkeley Conference (ed.) 1985, Sexual Underworlds of the Enlightenment (co-ed. with Roy Porter) 1987, The Enduring Legacy: Alexander Pope Tercentenary Essays (co-ed. with P. Rogers) 1988, Exoticism in the Enlightenment (with Roy Porter) 1990, Perilous Enlightenment: Pre- and Post-Modern Discourses: Sexual, Historical 1991, Enlightenment Crossings: Pre- and Post-Modern Discourses: Anthropological 1991, Enlightenment Borders: Pre- and Post-Modern Discourses: Medical, Scientific 1991, Hysteria Before Freud (co-author) 1993, Framing and Imagining Disease (ed.) 2003, Marguerite Yourcenar: A Biography 2003, Nervous Acts: Essays on Literature, Culture and Sensibility 2004, Children and Sexuality 2007, The Notorious Sir John Hill: The Man Destroyed by Ambition in the Era of Celebrity 2012; contribs to professional journals and general publs. *Honours:* Dr hc (mult.); Clifford Prize 1987, Leverhulme Trust Awardee 1999–2001. *Literary Agent:* c/o Jonathan Pegg Literary Agency, 32 Batoum Gardens, London, W6 7QD, England. *Telephone:* (20) 7603-6830. *Fax:* (20) 7348-0629. *E-mail:* info@jonathanpegg.com. *Website:* www.jonathanpegg.com. *Address:* Magdalen College, University of Oxford, Oxford, OX1 4AU (office); Osterley House, Wellshead, Harwell Village, Oxon., OX11 0HD, England (home). *Telephone:* (1865) 276000 (office). *Fax:* (1235) 221223 (office). *E-mail:* george.rousseau@magd.oxford.ac.uk (office). *Website:* www.history.ox.ac.uk/research/clusters/history_childhood (office); www.georgerousseau.net.

ROUX, Jean-Louis, CC; Canadian theatre director, actor and author; b. 18 May 1923, Montreal; s. of Louis Roux and Berthe Leclerc; m. Monique Oligny 1950; one s. *Education:* Coll. Sainte-Marie and Univ. de Montréal. *Career:* mem. Les Compagnons de Saint Laurent theatrical co. 1939–42, Ludmilla Pitoëff theatrical co. 1942–46; mil. training 1942–46; founder, Théâtre d'Essai, Montreal 1951; Sec.-Gen., Théâtre du Nouveau Monde 1953–63 (co-founder 1950), Artistic Dir 1966–82; Dir-Gen. Nat. Theatre School of Canada 1982–87; has appeared in more than 200 roles (in both French and English) on stage (Montreal, Stratford, Paris), TV, cinema and radio and directed more than 50 theatrical productions; apptd to Senate 1994–96; Lt Gov. of Québec 1996; Chair. Canada Council for the Arts 1998–2003; mem. Royal Soc. of Canada 1982–; Life Gov. Nat. Theatre School of Canada. *Honours:* Ordre de la Pléiade 1995, KStJ; Chevalier, Ordre Nat. du Québec 1989; Dr hc (Laval Univ.) 1988, (Univ. of Ottawa) 1995; Hon. LLD (Concordia Univ.) 1993; numerous awards and medals including Molson Award 1977, World Theatre Award 1985. *Address:* 4145 Blueridge Crescent, Apt. 2, Montreal, PQ H3H 1S7, Canada. *Telephone:* (514) 937-2505. *Fax:* (514) 937-5975.

ROWAN, Deirdre (see Williams, Jeanne)

ROWAN, Hester (see Robinson, Sheila Mary)

ROWAN, Patricia Adrienne; British journalist; d. of the late Henry Matthew and Gladys Talintyre; m. Ivan Settle Harris Rowan 1960; one s. *Education:* Harrow Co. Grammar School for Girls. *Career:* journalist, Time and Tide 1952–56, Sunday Express 1956–57, Daily Sketch 1957–58, News Chronicle 1958–60, Granada TV 1961–62, Sunday Times 1962–66, Times Educational Supplement 1972–89, Ed. 1989–97; mem. Bd Nat. Children's Bureau 1997–2003, Research Cttee Teacher Training Agency 1997–2000; Chair. Bd of Trustees, Stroud Valleys Project 2002–. *Publications:* What Sort of Life? 1980, Education – the Wasted Years? (contrib.) 1988. *Honours:* Hon. FRSA 1989; Hon. Fellow Inst. of Educ., Univ. of London 1997. *Address:* Horsley, Stroud, Glos., GL6 0PY, England (home). *Telephone:* (1453) 833305 (home). *Fax:* (1453) 833305 (home). *E-mail:* prowan@connectfree.co.uk (home).

ROWLAND, Iris (see Roberts, Irene)

ROWLAND, Peter Kenneth, BA; British writer; b. 26 July 1938, London, England. *Education:* Univ. of Bristol. *Career:* worked for London County Council 1962–96, London Water Regulation Authority and Environment Agency 1996–98. *Publications:* The Last Liberal Governments: The Promised Land 1905–1910 1968, The Last Liberal Governments: Unfinished Business 1911–1914 1971, Lloyd George 1975, Macaulay's History of England in the 18th Century (ed.) 1980, Macaulay's History of England from 1485 to 1685 (ed.) 1985, Autobiography of Charles Dickens (ed.) 1988, The Disappearance of Edwin Drood 1991, Thomas Day 1748–1789: Virtue Almost Personified 1996, Just Stylish 1998, Raffles and his Creator 1999, What's Where in the Saturday Books 2002. *Address:* 18 Corbett Road, Wanstead, London, E11 2LD, England (home). *E-mail:* prow792188@aol.com (home).

ROWLANDS, John, (Sion Prysor), MA, DPhil; Welsh novelist, critic and editor; *Professor Emeritus of Welsh, University of Wales*; b. Trawsfynydd, Wales; m. Margaret Eluned; two s. one d. *Education:* Univ. of Wales, Univ. of Oxford. *Career:* Prof. of Welsh, Univ. of Wales, Aberystwyth –2003, Prof. Emer. 2003–. *Publications include:* Lle bo'r gwenyn: Nofel 1960, Yn ol i'w teyrnasoedd: Nofel 1963, Ienctid yw 'Mhechod: Nofel 1965, Llawer is na'r angylion: Nofel 1968, Bydded tywyllwch: Nofel 1969, Arch ym Mhrâg: Nofel 1973, Tician Tician: Nofel, T. Rowland Hughes (criticism) 1975, Saunders y Beirniad (criticism), Y Meddwl a'r Dychmyg Cymreig (gen. series ed.), Cnoi Cil Ar Lenyddiaeth 1989, Ysgrifau Ar Y Nofel 1992, Sglefrio Ar Eiriau 1992, The Bloodaxe Book of Modern Welsh Poetry (co-ed. with Menna Elfyn) 2003. *Honours:* Hon. Prof., Univ. of Wales, Bangor; Hon. Fellow, Trinity Coll., Carmarthen; Hon. mem. Gorsedd of Bards. *Address:* Y Goeden Eirin, Dolydd, Caernarfon, Gwynedd, LL54 7EF, Wales. *Telephone:* (1286) 830942. *E-mail:* john_rowlands@tiscali.co.uk. *Website:* www.ygoedeneirin.co.uk.

ROWLING, Joanne (Jo) Kathleen (J. K.), OBE, BA; British writer; b. 31 July 1965, Yate, Glos., England; d. of Peter James Rowling and Anne Rowling (née Volant); m. 1st Jorge Arantes 1992 (divorced 1995); one d.; m. 2nd Neil Murray 2001; one s. one d. *Education:* Wyedean Comprehensive School, Univ. of Exeter, Moray House Teacher Training Coll. *Publications:* Harry Potter and the Philosopher's Stone (aka Harry Potter and the Sorcerer's Stone) (Smarties Book Prize 1997, British Book Awards Children's Book of the Year 1998) 1997, Harry Potter and the Chamber of Secrets (Smarties Book Prize 1998, British Book Awards Children's Book of the Year 1999) 1998, Harry Potter and the Prisoner of Azkaban (Smarties Book Prize 1999, Whitbread Children's Book of the Year 1999) 1999, Harry Potter and the Goblet of Fire (Hugo Award for Best Novel 2001) 2000, Quidditch Through the Ages by Kennilworthy Whisp 2001, Fantastic Beasts and Where to Find Them by Newt Scamander 2001, Harry Potter and the Order of the Phoenix (Bram Stoker Award for Best Work for Young Readers 2003, WHSmith People's Choice Fiction Prize 2004) 2003, Harry Potter and the Half-Blood Prince (Quill Book Award for Book of the Year, Best Children's Book, British Book Awards, WHSmith Book of the Year 2006, Royal Mail Award for Scottish Children's Books) 2005, Harry Potter and the Deathly Hallows 2007, The Tales of Beedle the Bard 2008, The Casual Vacancy 2012. *Honours:* Freedom of the City of London 2012; Chevalier, Légion d'honneur 2009; Hon. DJur (Univ. of Aberdeen) 2006; hon. degrees from Univ. of Edinburgh, Edinburgh Napier Univ., Univ. of Exeter, Harvard Univ.; Author of the Year, British Book Awards 2000, Premio Príncipe de Asturias 2003, Variety UK Entertainment Personality Award, British Ind. Film Awards 2004, British Book Award for Oustanding Achievement 2008, ranked by Forbes magazine amongst The World's 100 Most Powerful Women (85th) 2004, (40th) 2005, (61st) 2011 and as the 48th most powerful celebrity of 2007, named by TIME magazine as a runner-up for its Person of the Year 2007, Blue Peter Badge (Gold) 2007, Outstanding Achievement, British Book Awards 2008, named Most Influential Woman in Britain by leading magazine editors 2010, inaugural winner, Hans Christian Andersen Literature Award 2010, Outstanding British Contrib. to Cinema for the Harry Potter film series, British Academy Film Awards (shared with David Heyman, cast and crew) 2011. *Literary Agent:* c/o The Blair Partnership, 1st Floor, 8–14 Vine Hill, London, EC1R 5DX, England. *Telephone:* (20) 7504-2530. *Fax:* (20) 7504-2521. *E-mail:* info@theblairpartnership.com. *Website:* www.theblairpartnership.com; www.jkrowling.com.

ROY, Arundhati; Indian writer, artist, actress and activist; b. 24 Nov. 1960, Shillong, Meghalaya; d. of Mary Roy; m. 1st Gerard Da Cunha (divorced); m. 2nd Pradeep Krishen. *Education:* School of Planning and Architecture, New Delhi. *Career:* fmrly with Nat. Inst. of Urban Affairs; judge, Cannes Film Festival 2000–; faced charges of inciting violence, attacking a court official and contempt of court for opposing Sardar Sarovar dam project in the Narmada valley 2001. *Screenplays:* In Which Annie Gives It Those Ones (TV) 1988, Electric Moon 1992, DAM/AGE 2002. *Publications:* The God of Small Things (Booker Prize) 1997, The End of Imagination (essay) 1998, The Cost of Living (essays) 1998, The Great Common Good (essay) 1999, War is Peace 2000, The

Algebra of Infinite Justice (essays) 2001, Power Politics 2002, The Ordinary Person's Guide to Empire (essays) 2004, Public Power in the Age of Empire Seven Stories 2004, Introduction to 13 December, a Reader: The Strange Case of the Attack on the Indian Parliament 2006, The Shape of the Beast: Conversations with Arundhati Roy 2008, Listening to Grasshoppers (essays) 2009; contribs to periodicals. *Honours:* Lannan Prize for Cultural Freedom 2002, Sydney Peace Prize 2004. *Address:* c/o South End Press, 7 Brookline Street, Suite 1, Cambridge, MA 02139-4146, USA; c/o India Ink Publishing Co. Pvt. Ltd, C-1, Soami Nagar, New Delhi 110 017, India.

ROYLE, Nicholas John, BA; British writer; b. 20 March 1963; m. Kate Ryan 1996; one s. one d. *Education:* Queen Mary Coll., London. *Career:* mem. Soc. of Authors. *Publications:* fiction: Counterparts 1993, Saxophone Dreams 1996, The Matter of the Heart 1997, The Director's Cut 2000, Antwerp 2004, Mortality (short stories) 2006; ed.: Darklands 1991, Darklands 2 1992, A Book of Two Halves 1996, The Tiger Garden: A Book of Writers' Dreams 1996, The Time Out Book of New York Short Stories 1997, The Agony and the Ecstasy 1998, The Ex Files 1998, Neonlit: The Time Out Book of New Writing 1998, The Time Out Book of Paris Short Stories 1999, Neonlit: The Time Out Book of New Writing Vol. 2 1999, The Time Out Book of London Short Stories Vol. 2 2000, Dreams Never End 2004; contrib. to Independent, Guardian, Time Out, New Statesman, Literary Review. *Literary Agent:* c/o John Saddler, Curtis Brown Ltd, Haymarket House, 28–29 Haymarket, London, SW1Y 4SP, England. *Telephone:* (20) 7393-4400. *Fax:* (20) 7393-4401. *E-mail:* info@curtisbrown.co.uk. *Website:* www.curtisbrown.co.uk. *Address:* 38 Belfield Road, Manchester, M20 6BH, England (home). *Website:* www.nicholasroyle.com.

RÓŻEWICZ, Tadeusz; Polish poet and playwright; b. 9 Oct. 1921, Radomsko. *Education:* Jagiellonian Univ., Kraków. *Career:* fmr factory worker and teacher; mem. Art Acad. of Leipzig; Corresp. mem. Bavarian Acad. of Fine Arts 1982–, Acad. of Arts (GDR). *Plays include:* Kartoteka (The Card Index), Grupa Laokoona (Laocoön's Group), Świadkowie albo nasza mała stabilizacja (The Witnesses), Akt przerywany (The Interrupted Act), Śmieszny staruszek (The Funny Man), Wyszedł z domu (Gone Out), Spaghetti i miecz (Spaghetti and the Sword), Maja córeczka (My Little Daughter), Stara kobieta wysiaduje (The Old Woman Broods), Na czworakach (On All Fours), Do piachu (Down to Sand), Białe małżeństwo (White Marriage), Odejście Głodomora (Starveling's Departure), Na powierzchni poematu i w środku: nowy wybór wierszy, Pułapka (The Trap), Próba rekonstrukcji (Spread Card Index), Kartoteka rozrzucona (The Card Index Scattered). *Prose includes:* Tarcza z pajęczyny, Opowiadania wybrane (Selected Stories), Na powierzchni poematu (They Came to See a Poet) 1991, Płaskorzeźba (Bas-Relief) 1991, Nasz starszy brat 1992, Historia pięciu wierszy 1993. *Publications:* 15 vols of poetry including Niepokój (Faces of Anxiety), Czerwona rękawiczka (The Red Glove), Czas, który idzie (The Time Which Goes On), Równina (The Plain), Srebrny kłos (The Silver Ear), Rozmowa z księciem (Conversation with the Prince), Zielona róża (The Green Rose), Nic w płaszczu Prospera (Nothing in Prosper's Overcoat), Twarz (The Face), Duszyczka (A Little Soul), Poezje (Poetry) 1987, Słowo po słowie (Word by Word) 1994, Zawsze fragment (Always the Fragment) 1996, Zawsze fragment: Recycling (Always the Fragment: Recycling) 1999, Matka odchodzi (The Mother Goes) 2000, Nożyk profesora (The Professor's Knife) 2001, Szara strefa 2002, Wyjściě 2004. *Honours:* Order of Banner of Labour (2nd class) 1977, Great Cross of Polonia Restituta Order 1996; Dr hc (Wrocław) 1991, (Silesian Univ., Katowice) 1999, (Jagiellonian Univ.) 2000, (Kraków) 2000, (Warsaw) 2001; State Prize for Poetry 1955, 1956, Literary Prize, City of Cracow 1959, Prize of Minister of Culture and Art 1962, State Prize 1st Class 1966, Austrian Nat. Prize for European Literature 1982, Prize of Minister of Foreign Affairs 1974, 1987, Golden Wreath Prize for Poetry (Yugoslavia) 1987, Władysław Reymont Literary Prize 1999; Home Army Cross, London 1956, Alfred Jurzykowski Foundation Award, New York 1966, Medal of 30th Anniversary of People's Poland 1974, Nike Literary Prize 2000, Premio Librex Montale, Literary Prize (Italy) 2002. *Address:* ul. Promien 16, 51-659 Wrocław, Poland (home). *Telephone:* (71) 3452126 (home). *Fax:* (71) 3452126 (home).

RUBIN, Diana Kwiatkowski, BA, MA; American poet and writer; b. 30 Dec. 1958, New York, NY; m. Paul Rubin 1986; one s. two d. *Education:* Marymount Manhattan Coll., New York Univ. *Career:* mem. Acad. of American Poets. *Publications:* Spirits in Exile 1990, Visions of Enchantment 1991, Dinosauria 1995; contrib. to Poet, Amelia, Wind, Quest, Fox Cry, Voices International. *Honours:* first prize Sparrowgrass Poetry Forum Awards 1998. *Address:* PO Box 398, Piscataway, NJ 08855, USA (home).

RUBIN, Louis Decimus, Jr, PhD; American writer, academic and publisher; *Professor Emeritus of English, University of North Carolina;* b. 19 Nov. 1923, Charleston, SC; s. of Louis Decimus Rubin, Sr and Janet Weinstein Rubin; m. Eva Maryette Redfield 1951; two s. *Education:* High School of Charleston, Coll. of Charleston, Univ. of Richmond and Johns Hopkins Univ. *Career:* U.S. Army 1943–46; instructor in English Johns Hopkins Univ. 1948–54; Exec. Sec. American Studies Asscn 1954–56 (also fmr Vice-Pres.); Assoc. Ed. News Leader, Richmond, Va 1956–57; Assoc. Prof. of English, Hollins Coll., Prof., Chair. of Dept 1960–67, Prof. of English Univ. of NC 1967–73, Univ. Distinguished Prof. 1973-89, Prof. Emer. 1989–; Visiting Prof. La. State Univ., Univ. of Calif. at Santa Barbara, Harvard Univ.; lecturer, Aix-Marseille at Nice, Kyoto Summer American Studies Seminars; USICA, Austria, Germany; Ed. Southern Literary Studies Series, Louisiana State Univ. Press 1965–90; Co-Ed. Southern Literary Journal 1968–89; Co-founder and Editorial Dir Algonquin Books, Chapel Hill 1982–91; fmr Pres. Soc. for Study of Southern Literature; fmr Chair. American Literature Section, Modern Language Asscn; mem. SC Acad. of Authors, Fellowship of Southern Writers. *Publications:* author: Thomas Wolfe: The Weather of His Youth 1955, No Place on Earth 1959, The Faraway Country 1964, The Golden Weather (novel) 1961, The Curious Death of the Novel 1967, The Teller in the Tale 1967, George W. Cable 1969, The Writer in the South 1972, William Elliott Shoots a Bear 1975, The Wary Fugitives 1978, Surfaces of a Diamond (novel) 1981, A Gallery of Southerners 1982, The Even-Tempered Angler 1984, The Edge of the Swamp: a study in the Literature and Society of the Old South 1989, The Mockingbird in the Gum Tree 1991, Small Craft Advisory 1991, The Heat of the Sun (novel) 1995, Babe Ruth's Ghost 1996, Seaports of the South 1998, A Memory of Trains 2000, An Honorable Estate 2001; editor: Southern Renascence 1953, Idea of an American Novel 1961, South 1961, Comic Imagination in American Literature 1973, The Literary South 1979, American South 1980, The History of Southern Literature 1985, An Apple for My Teacher 1986, Algonquin Literary Quiz Book 1990, A Writer's Companion 1995. *Honours:* Hon. DLitt (Richmond, Clemson, Coll. of Charleston, Univ. of the South, Univ. of NC, Ashville, Univ. of NC Chapel Hill); Richard Beale Davis Award for Lifetime Achievement in Southern Letters, Society for Study of Southern Literature 2004. *Address:* 702 Gimghoul Road, Chapel Hill, NC 27514, USA (home).

RUBINA, Dina Ilyinichna; Israeli writer; b. 19 Sept. 1953, Tashkent, Uzbekistan. *Education:* Tashkent State Conservatory. *Career:* music teacher Tashkent Inst. of Culture 1977–90; literary debut in Yunost magazine 1971; emigrated to Israel 1990; book publications, theatrical stagings, film, newspaper editing (Pyatnitza and others); Head Dept of Public and Cultural Relations, The Jewish Agency in Russia 1999–2003. *Films:* Zavtra, kak obychno 1984, Na Verhney Maslovke 2004. *Publications:* The Double-Barrelled Name (short stories) 1990, In Thy Gates 1994, An Intellectual Sat Down on the Road 1995, Here Comes the Messiah 1997, The Escort Angel 1998, The Last Wild Boar from Pontevedra Forest 1998, High Water in Venice 1999, Several Hurried Words of Love (short stories) 2003. *Honours:* Ministry of Culture Award 1982, Arye Dulchin Award (Israel) 1991, Israel Writers' Union Award 1995, Best Book of literary season, France 1996. *Address:* Et Ha'zmir, 11/8, 98491 Maale-Adumim, Israel (home). *Telephone:* 2-5352435 (home). *Fax:* 2-5352435 (home). *E-mail:* web@dinarubina.com (home). *Website:* www.dinarubina.com (home).

RUBINSTEIN, Lev; Russian poet and writer; b. 1947, Moscow. *Career:* fmr librarian; leading figure of Moscow Conceptualism literary movt; developed a unique technique in which poetic texts are written on series of note cards. *Publications:* Lichnoe Delo: Literaturno-Khudozhestvennyi Almanakh 1991, Sluchai iz iazyka 1998, Ton: Izbrannoe 2001, Catalogue of Comedic Novelties (in trans.) 2003, Pogonia Za Shliapoi: I Drugie Teksty (co-author) 2004, Here I Am (in trans.), Unnamed Events (in trans.), Spirits of Time (essays). *Honours:* Andrei Bely Prize. *Literary Agent:* c/o Ugly Duckling Presse, The Old American Can Factory, 232 Third Street, #E002, Brooklyn, NY 11215, USA. *Telephone:* (718) 852-5529. *E-mail:* info@uglyducklingpresse.org. *Website:* www.uglyducklingpresse.org.

RUBIO, Juan Carlos; Spanish writer, director, actor and academic; *Director, SC Productions;* b. 1967, Montilla. *Education:* School of Theatre de Alcorcón, Royal School of Drama and Dance, Madrid. *Career:* Prof., Colectivo de Lesbianas, Gays, Transexuales y Bisexuales de Madrid 1999–2000; Prof., TB/IGUELDO 2000; Prof., Antena 3 TV 2000; Prof., Massart 2008; Prof., El Ejido (Almería) 2008; Prof., Leganés (Madrid) 2008; Prof., Lucena (Córdoba) 2008; currently Dir SC Productions. *Films:* writer: Fin de curso 2005, El Calentito 2005, Dolly 2007, Lola, la película 2007, Bon appétit (Best Screenplay Biznaga Málaga Spanish Film Festival) 2010; film writer: El idiota 2000, Slam 2002, El calentito 2005, Fin de curso 2005, Retorno a Hansala 2008; actor: Las trampas del azar 1995, Los padres terribles 1996–97, El cerco de Numancia 1998; playwright: Esta noche no estoy para nadie (City Theatre Prize Alcorcón) 1997, Las heridas del viento (Premio Hermanos Machado 2000) 1999, Tres 2000, El bosque es mío 2001, 10 2001, ¿Dónde se esconden los sueños? (Premio teatro infantil Escuela Navarra de Teatro) 2004, Epitafio (Premio Animasur 2005) 2004, Humo (also dir) (Premio SGAE 2005, Premio telón Chivas 2008) 2005, Arizona (also dir) (Premio Raúl Moreno-Fatex, Mención Especial del Premio Lope de Vega) 2006, No quemes la vida 2007, 100 metros cuadrados 2007; dir: The Big Kahuna 2009. *Publications:* No mires a los ojos de la diosa (City of Alcorcón) 1982, Mama ¿qué es un wellspringt? (Colmenar Viejo) 1982. *Address:* SC Productions, 15 Mutis Bocaue Ave, PO 8, 14550 Montilla, Spain. *Telephone:* (95) 7651227. *E-mail:* carlosrubio06@yahoo.es; jcrguion@hotmail.com. *Website:* www.juancarlosrubio.com; www.mutisproducciones.com.

RUDKIN, (James) David, MA; British dramatist and screenwriter; *Honorary Professor, University of Wales, Aberystwyth;* b. 29 June 1936, London, England; m. Alexandra Margaret Thompson 1967; two s. (one deceased) two d. *Education:* St Catherine's Coll., Oxford. *Career:* Judith E. Wilson Fellow, Univ. of Cambridge 1984; Visiting Prof., Univ. of Middlesex 2005–09; mem. Hellenic Soc. *Plays:* Afore Night Come, The Sons of Light, Ashes, The Triumph of Death, The Saxon Shore, Red Sun, The Master and Margarita (from Bulgakov), Merlin Unchained. *Screenplays:* Testimony 1987, December Bride 1989, The Woodlanders 1997. *Radio:* Cries from Casement as his Bones are Brought to Dublin, The Love Song of Alfred J. Hitchcock 1993, The Haunting of Mahler 1994. *Television:* Penda's Fen, Artemis 81 1981, White Lady,

Publications: plays in print: Ashes 1974, The Triumph of Death 1981, The Saxon Shore 1986, Afore Night Come 2001; translations: Moses und Aron (Schoenberg, for Royal Opera) 1965, Hippolytus (Euripides) 1980, Peer Gynt (Ibsen) 1983, Rosmersholm (Ibsen) 1990, When We Dead Waken (Ibsen) 1990, Dreyer's Vampyr (monograph) 2005; opera libretti: The Grace of Todd (music by Gordon Crosse) 1969, Inquest of Love (music by Jonathan Harvey) 1993, Broken Strings (music by Param Vir) 1994, Black Feather Rising (music by Param Vir) 2008; contrib. to Drama, Tempo, Encounter, Theatre Research Journal, Vertigo. *Honours:* Hon. Prof., Univ. of Wales, Aberystwyth 2006–; Evening Standard Most Promising Dramatist Award 1962, John Whiting Drama Award 1974, Obie Award, New York 1977, New York Film Festival Gold Medal for Screenplay 1987, European Film Festival Special Award 1989, Sony Silver Radio Drama Award 1994. *Literary Agent:* c/o Casarotto Ramsay & Associates Ltd, Waverley House, 7–12 Noel Street, London, W1F 8GQ, England. *Telephone:* (20) 7287-4450. *Fax:* (20) 7287-9128. *E-mail:* info@casarotto.co.uk; agents@casarotto.co.uk. *Website:* www.casarotto.co.uk; www.davidrudkin.com.

RUDMAN, Mark, BA, MFA; American poet, critic, editor, translator and academic; b. 11 Dec. 1948, New York, NY; m. Madelaine Bates; one s. *Education:* New School for Social Research, Columbia Univ. *Career:* Poetry and Criticism Ed. 1975–, Ed.-in-Chief 1984–, Pequod Journal; writer-in-residence, Univ. of Hawaii 1978, SUNY at Buffalo 1979, Wabash Coll. 1979; Adjunct Lecturer, Queens Coll., CUNY 1980–81; Lecturer, Parsons School of Design 1983; poet-in-residence and Assoc. Prof., York Coll., CUNY 1984–88; Asst Dir and Adjunct Prof., Graduate Creative Writing Program, New York Univ. 1986–; Adjunct Prof., Columbia Univ. 1988–91, 1992–95; poet-in-residence, SUNY at Purchase 1991; Walt Whitman Poet 1998; mem. PEN, Poetry Soc. of America (bd of govs 1984–88). *Publications:* In the Neighboring Cell (poems) 1982, The Mystery in the Garden (chapbook) 1985, By Contraries and Other Poems: 1970–1984, Selected and New 1986, The Ruin Revived (chapbook) 1986, The Nowhere Steps (poems) 1990, Literature and the Visual Arts (ed.) 1990, Diverse Voices: Essays on Poetry 1993, Rider (poems) 1994, Realm of Unknowing: Meditations on Art, Suicide, Uncertainty, and Other Transformations 1995, The Millennium Hotel (poems) 1996, Provoked in Venice (poems) 1999, The Killers (poems) 2000, The Couple 2001, Sundays on the Phone (poems) 2005; translator: Square of Angels, by B. Antonych 1976, My Sister – Life, by Pasternak 1983; contrib. poems and essays to many anthologies and other publications. *Honours:* Acad. of American Poets Award 1971, PEN Trans. Fellowship 1976, Yaddo Residencies 1977, 1983, Co-ordinating Council for Literary Magazines Ed.'s Award 1981, Ingram Merrill Foundation Fellowship 1983–84, Max Hayward Award for Trans. 1984, New York Foundation of the Arts Fellowship 1988, Nat. Book Critics Circle Award in Poetry 1994, NEA Fellowship 1995, Guggenheim Fellowship 1996–97. *Address:* 817 West End Avenue, New York, NY 10025, USA.

RUDMAN, Michael P.; American publishing executive; b. 1950, New York. *Education:* Univ of Michigan and New York Univ. *Career:* Pres. and CEO Nat. Learning Corpn, also Dir; Pres. and CEO Delaney Books Inc., also Dir; Pres. Frank Merriwell Inc., also CEO, Dir; mem. Asscn of American Publishers. *Address:* National Learning Corporation, 212 Michael Drive, Syosset, NY 11791, USA. *Website:* www.passbooks.com.

RUDOLF, Anthony, BA, FRSL, FEA; British writer, poet, translator and editor; b. 6 Sept. 1942, London, England; s. of the late Henry Rudolf and Esther Rudolf (née Rosenberg); m. (divorced); one s. one d. *Education:* Trinity Coll., Cambridge, British Inst., Paris. *Career:* Co-founder and Ed. Menard Press, London 1969; Adam Lecturer, King's Coll., London 1990; Pierre Rouve Memorial Lecturer, Sofia 2001; Visiting Lecturer, Faculty of Arts and Humanities, London Metropolitan Univ. 2001–03; Royal Literary Fund Fellow, Univ. of Hertfordshire 2003–05, Univ. of Westminster 2005–08; Fellow of the English Asscn. *Publications:* The Same River Twice 1976, After the Dream: Poems 1964–79 1980, Primo Levi's War Against Oblivion 1990, Mandorla 1999, The Arithmetic of Memory 1999, Engraved in Flesh 2007, Kafka's Doll 2007, Zigzag: verse/prose sequences 2010, Silent Conversations: A Reader's Life 2012; translations of poetry; contrib. to art and literary periodicals and newspapers. *Honours:* Chevalier, Ordre des Arts et des Lettres 2004. *Address:* 8 The Oaks, Woodside Avenue, London, N12 8AR, England. *E-mail:* anthony.rudolf@virgin.net. *Website:* www.menardpress.co.uk.

RUELL, Patrick (see Hill, Reginald Charles)

RUFFILLI, Paolo, PhD; Italian writer, poet and editor; *General Editor*, *Edizioni del Leone*; b. 4 July 1949, Rieti. *Education:* Bologna Univ. *Career:* fmr Ed., Garzanti publishing house, Milan; currently Gen. Ed. Edizioni del Leone, Venice; regular contrib. to Il Resto del Carlino, la Repubblica, La Stampa, Il Giornale, Il Gazzettino. *Publications:* poetry: La Quercia delle gazze 1972, Quattro quarti di luna 1974, Notizie delle Esperidi 1976, Piccola colazione 1987, Diario di Normandia (Premio Montale) 1990, Camera oscura 1992, Nuvole 1995, La gioia e il lutto (Prix Européen) 2001, Le stanze del cielo 2008; fiction: Preparativi per la partenza 2003, Un'altra vita 2010; non-fiction: Vita di Ippolito Nievo 1991, Vita amori e meraviglie del signor Carlo Goldoni 1993. *Honours:* American Poetry Prize 1987, Premio Montale 1990, Prix Européen 2001, 2008. *Address:* Edizioni Del Leone, Gruppo Editoriale Mulitgraf, Via Negrelli 10, 30038 Spinea, Venice, Italy (office). *Telephone:* (041) 990065 (office). *Fax:* (041) 994155 (office). *E-mail:* paolo.ruffilli@alice.it (home); edizionidelleone@multigraf.it (office). *Website:* www.paoloruffilli.it.

RUFIN, Jean-Christophe, MD; French writer, physician and diplomatist; b. 28 June 1952, Bourges; s. of Marcel Rufin and Denise Bonneau; one s. two d. *Education:* Lycées Janson-de-Sailly and Claude Bernard, Paris, Pitié-Salpêtrière School of Medicine, Paris, Institut d'études politiques, Paris. *Career:* Hosp. Intern, Paris 1975–81, Dir of Clinic and Asst Hôpitaux de Paris 1981–83, attaché Hôpitaux de Paris 1983–86; Chief of Mission of Sec. of State for Human Rights 1986–88; Cultural Attaché French Embassy in Brazil 1989–90; Vice-Pres. Médécins sans Frontières 1991–93; Adviser to Minister of Defence 1993–95; Dr, Nanterre Hosp. 1994–95; Practitioner, St Antoine Hospital, Paris 1995–98; Dir French Red Cross 1994–96, Inst. Pasteur, Groupe France Télévisions, l'Office français de protection des réfugiés et apatrides 2005–; Medical Dir, then Pres. Action contre la faim 2002–07; Amb. to Senegal (also accred to Gambia) 2007–10; mem. Acad. Française 2008–. *Publications:* Le Piège humanitaire 1986, L'Empire et les nouveaux barbares 1992, La Dictature libérale (Prix Jean-Jacques Rousseau) 1994, L'Aventure humanitaire 1994, L'Abyssin (Prix Goncourt, Prix Méditerranée) 1997, Sauver Ispahan 1998, Les Causes perdues (Prix Bergot, Prix Interallié) 1999, Rouge Brésil (Prix Goncourt) 2001, Globalia 2004, La Salamandre 2005, Le Parfum d'Adam 2006, Un Léopard sur le garrot 2008, 100 Stunden 2009, Katiba 2010. *Honours:* Chevalier des Arts et des Lettres, Chevalier de la Légion d'Honneur; Dr hc (Laval Univ., Catholic Univ. of Louvain). *Address:* c/o Les Editions Gallimard, 5, rue Gaston-Gallimard, 75328 Paris cedex 07, France.

RUGARLI, Giampaolo; Italian writer; b. 5 Dec. 1932, Naples; s. of Mirko Rugarli and Rubina De Marco; m. Maria Pulci 1985; three c. *Education:* legal studies. *Career:* bank dir since 1972; a dir of Cariplo 1981–85; contrib. Messaggero and Corriere della Sera and other reviews. *Publications:* Il Superlativo assoluto, La troga, Il nido di ghiaccio, Diario di un uomo a disagio, Andromeda e la notte, L'orrore che mi hai dato 1987, Una montagna australiana 1992, Per i pesci non è un problema 1992, I camini delle fate 1993, Il manuale del romanziere (The Novelist's Handbook) 1993, L'infinito, forse 1995, Una gardenia ni capilli 1997, Il bruno dei crepuscoli (Leopardi) 1998, La Viaggiatrici del tram numero 4 2001, Il Cavaliere e la vendita della saggezza 2002, La mia Milano 2003, I giardini incantati 2005, La luna di Malcontenta 2006, Il buio di notte 2008, La galassie lontane 2010, La patria delle mezzecalzette 2010, Un bacio e l'oblio 2011. *Honours:* Premio Bagutta Opera Prima 1987; Premio Capri 1990, Premio Selezione Campiello. *Address:* Via Colle di Giano 62, Olevano Romano 00035, Italy. *Telephone:* (06) 9564518.

RUGE, Eugen; German author, playwright and mathematician; b. 24 June 1954, Soswa; s. of Wolfgang Ruge. *Career:* Research Assoc., Cen. Inst. for Geophysics, Potsdam –1985; fled to W Germany 1988; trans. numerous works into German including plays by Anton Chekhov. *Plays include:* Babelsberger Elegie (Babelsberg Elegy) 1997, Ruhestörung (Disturbance of the Peace) 1998, Restwärme (Residual Heat) 1992, Akte Böhme (The Case of Böhme) 2001. *Publications include:* Zeiten des abnehmenden Lichts (In Times of Diminishing Light) (German Book Prize 2011) 2011. *Honours:* Alfred Döblin Prize 2009. *Address:* c/o Rowohlt Berlin Verlag, Kreuzbergstr.30, 10965 Berlin, Germany (office). *Telephone:* (30) 2853840 (office). *E-mail:* info@rowohlt.de (office). *Website:* www.rowohlt.de (office).

RUHM, Gerhard; Austrian writer, poet, dramatist, composer and graphic artist; b. 12 Feb. 1930, Vienna. *Education:* Acad. of Music, Vienna. *Career:* mem. Acad. of Fine Arts, Hamburg. *Publications:* Literarisches Cabaret (with H. Artmann and K. Bayer), 1958–59; hosn rosn baa (with H. Artmann and F. Achleitner), 1959; Kinderoper (with H. Artmann and K. Bayer), 1964; Gesammelte Gedichte, 1970; Gesammelte Theaterstücke 1954–1971, 1972; Erste Folger Kurzer Hörstücker, 1973; Zweite Folge kurzer Hörstücke, 1975, 1975; wald: ein deutsches requiem, 1983; Allein, verlassen, verloren: 3 Kurzhörspiele zum Thema Angst (with R. Hughes and Marie Luise Kaschnitz), 1986; leselieder/visuelle Musik, 1986; botschaft an die zukunft: gesammelte sprechtexte, 1988; Geschlechterdings: Chansons, Romanzen, Gedichte, 1990; Theatertexte, 1990; Mit Messer und Gabel, 1995. *Honours:* Asscn of War Blind Radio Prize 1983, Great Austrian State Prize 1991.

RUIZ DE GOPEGUI, Belén, (Belén Gopegui), LLB; Spanish writer; b. 1963, Madrid. *Education:* Univ. Autónoma de Madrid. *Film screenplays:* La suerte dormida (with Ángeles González-Sinde) 2003, El principio de Arquímedes 2004. *Play:* El coloquio. *Publications:* novels: La escala de los mapas (Premio Tigre Juan 1993, Premio Iberoamericano Santiago del Nuevo Extremo 1994) 1992, Tocarnos la cara 1995, Cualladó: puntos de vista 1995, La conquista del aire 1998, Lo real 2001, El lado frío de la almohada 2004, El padre de Blancanieves 2007, El balonazo 2008, Deseo de ser punk (Premio Dulce Chacón) 2009, Acceso no autorizado 2011; short stories: En desierta playa 1995, El día que mamá perdió la paciencia 2010. *Address:* c/o Editorial Anagrama SA, Pedró de la Creu 58, 08034 Barcelona, Spain. *E-mail:* anagrama@anagrama-ed.es; clopez@rhm.es; lluevecomonunca@gmail.com. *Website:* www.rebelion.org.

RUIZ GUINAZU, Magdalena; Argentine journalist; b. 13 Feb. 1935, Buenos Aires; four c. *Career:* fmr mem. Comision Nacional por la desaparicion de Personas (National Commission on the Disappearance of People); currently host Magdalena Tempranisimo, Radio Continental and La vuelta con Magdalena (Back with Magdalena) 2002–; columnist La Nación and Pagina 12 newspapers; Co-founder and fmr Pres. Asociación para la Defensa del Periodismo Independiente (Asociación Periodistas) (press freedom org.). *Publications include:* Huésped de un verano 1994, Había una vez...la vida

1995, Qué mundo nos ha tocado! (with Father Rafael Braun) 2001, Historias de hombres, mujeres y jazmines 2002. *Honours:* Officer, Legion d'Honneur, Order of Merit (Italy); Martin Fierro de Oro (Gold Martin Fierro Award) for Lifetime Achievement 1994, Int. Women's Media Foundation Lifetime Achievement Award 2003, Diamond Konex, Communication-Journalism 2007. *Address:* c/o Asociación Periodistas, Piedras 1675 Oficina B, Secretaría de Derechos, 1140 Buenos Aires, Argentina. *E-mail:* magdalena@continental.com.ar (office). *Website:* www.continental.com.ar; www.magdalenatempranisimo.blogspot.com.

RUIZ ZAFÓN, Carlos; Spanish/American writer; b. 25 Sept. 1964, Barcelona. *Education:* Colegio San Ignacio, Barcelona, Univ. of Barcelona. *Publications:* novels: El príncipe de la niebla (trans. as The Prince of Mist) 1993, El Palacio de la Moedianoche 1995, Las Luces de Septiembre 1997, Marina 1999, La sombra del viento (trans. as The Shadow of the Wind) (Prix des Amis du Scribe, France 2005, Prix Michelet, France 2005, Nielsen Gold Book Award 2006, New York Public Library Book to remember, Livre de Poche 2006, Prix de Saint Emilion, Reader's Award, Holland, Nielsen Golden Book Award, Humus Award, Belgium 2006) 2000, El Juego del Ángel (trans. as The Angel's Game) 2008. *Honours:* Edebé Prize 1993, Borders Original Voices Award, Author of the Year, British Book Awards 2006. *Literary Agent:* Antonia Kerrigan Literary Agency, Travesera de Gracia 22, 1°, 2a, 08021 Barcelona, Spain. *E-mail:* info@antoniakerrigan.com. *Website:* www.carlosruizzafon.com.

RUMENS, Carol, PGDip, FRSL; British writer and poet; *Professor of Creative Writing, University of Hull*; b. (Carol-Ann Lumley), 10 Dec. 1944, London; m. David Rumens 1965 (divorced); two d. *Education:* Univ. of London and Arden School of Theatre, Manchester. *Career:* Writing Fellow Univ. of Kent 1983–85; Northern Arts Writing Fellow 1988–90; Writer-in-Residence, Queen's Univ., Belfast 1991–, Univ. Coll., Cork 1994, Univ. of Stockholm 1999; Creative Writing Tutor, Queen's Univ. Belfast 1995–99, Univ. of Wales, Bangor 2000–; Prof. of Creative Writing, Univ. of Hull 2005–; mem. Int. PEN, Soc. of Authors, The Welsh Academi. *Publications:* A Strange Girl in Bright Colours 1973, Unplayed Music 1981, Scenes from the Gingerbread House 1982, Star Whisper 1983, Direct Dialling 1985, Selected Poems 1987, Plato Park 1987, The Greening of the Snow Beach 1988, From Berlin to Heaven 1989, Thinking of Skins: New and Selected Poems 1993, Best China Sky 1995, The Miracle Diet (with Viv Quillin) 1997, Holding Pattern 1998, Hex 2002, Collected Poems 2004, Poems 1968–2004 2005; contrib. ed. of numerous anthologies; contrib. to periodicals; trans. poems for collections of Russian poetry. *Honours:* Alice Hunt Bartlett Prize (Jt Winner) 1981, Prudence Farmer Award 1983, Cholmondeley Award 1984, First Prize, BT Section, Nat. Poetry Competition 2002, First Prize Peterloo Poetry Competition 2003. *Address:* c/o University of Hull, Hull, HU6 7RX (office); 100A Tunis Road, London, W12 7EY, England. *Telephone:* (1482) 346311 (office); (7917) 860326 (home). *E-mail:* c.rumens@hull.ac.uk (office); carol@rumens.fslife.co.uk (office). *Website:* www.2hull.ac.uk; www.carolrumens.co.uk.

RUSBRIDGER, Alan, BA, MA; British journalist; *Editor, The Guardian and Executive Editor, The Observer*; b. 29 Dec. 1953, Lusaka, Zambia; s. of G. H. Rusbridger and B. E. Rusbridger (née Wickham); m. Lindsay Mackie 1982; two d. *Education:* Cranleigh School, Magdalene Coll., Cambridge. *Career:* reporter Cambridge Evening News 1976–79; reporter The Guardian 1979–82, diary ed. and feature writer 1982–86, special writer 1987–88, launch ed. Weekend Guardian 1988–89, Features Ed. 1989–93, Deputy Ed. 1993–95, Ed. 1995–; TV critic and feature writer The Observer 1986–, Exec. Ed. 1996–; Washington Corresp. London Daily News 1987; Chair. Photographer's Gallery 2001–; mem. Bd Guardian Newspapers Ltd 1994–, Guardian Media Group 1999–; mem. Scott Trust 1997–. *Television:* presenter of What the Papers Say (Granada TV) 1983–94, co-writer (with Ronan Bennett) of Fields of Gold (BBC TV) 2001. *Publications:* New World Order (ed.) 1991, Altered State (ed.) 1992, Guardian Year 1994, The Coldest Day in the Zoo 2004, The Wildest Day at the Zoo 2005, The Smelliest Day at the Zoo 2007. *Honours:* Ed. of the Year, What the Papers Say Awards (Granada TV) 1996, 2001, Nat. Newspaper Ed., Newspaper Industry Awards 1996, Editor's Ed., Press Gazette 1997, Judges' Award, What the Papers Say 2006, Goldsmith Career Award for Excellence in Journalism, Kennedy School of Govt, Harvard Univ. 2012. *Address:* The Guardian, Kings Place, 90 York Way, London, N1 9GU, England (office). *Telephone:* (20) 3353-2000 (office). *Fax:* (20) 7239-9997 (office). *E-mail:* alan.rusbridger@guardian.co.uk (office). *Website:* www.guardian.co.uk (office).

RUSH, Norman, BA; American writer; b. 24 Oct. 1933, San Francisco, CA; m. Elsa Scheidt; one s. one d. *Education:* Swarthmore Coll. *Career:* antiquarian book dealer 1960–78; instructor in English and history and Co-Dir of Coll. A, Rockland Community Coll., Suffern, NY 1973–78; Co-Dir US Peace Corps, Botswana 1978–83; mem. PEN American Center. *Publications:* Whites (short stories) 1986, Mating (novel) 1991, Mortals (novel) 2003; contrib. to New York Review of Books, The New Yorker and other periodicals. *Honours:* Aga Khan Prize for the Short Story, NY State Council on Arts Award, Nat. Endowment for the Arts Award, Nat. Book Award, Nat. Acad. of Arts and Letters Rosenthal Award, Rockefeller Foundation Fellowship (Bellagio Residency) 1991, Irish Times/Aer Lingus Int. Fiction Prize 1992. *Address:* 18 High Tor Road, New City, NY 10956, USA (home). *E-mail:* rush18@optonline.net (home).

RUSHDIE, Sir (Ahmed) Salman, Kt, MA, FRSL; British writer and academic; *Distinguished Writer-in-Residence, Emory University*; b. 19 June 1947, Bombay (now Mumbai), India; s. of Anis Ahmed and Negin (née Butt) Rushdie; m. 1st Clarissa Luard 1976 (divorced 1987, died 1999); one s.; m. 2nd Marianne Wiggins 1988 (divorced 1993); one step-d.; m. 3rd Elizabeth West 1997 (divorced); one s.; m. 4th Padma Lakshmi 2004 (divorced). *Education:* Cathedral and John Connon Boys' High School, Bombay, Rugby School, England, King's Coll., Cambridge. *Career:* mem. Footlights revue, Univ. of Cambridge 1965–68; actor, fringe theatre, London 1968–69; advertising copywriter 1969–73; wrote first published novel Grimus 1973–74; part-time advertising copywriter while writing second novel 1976–80; mem. Int. PEN 1981–, Soc. of Authors 1983–, Exec. Cttee Nat. Book League 1983–, Council Inst. of Contemporary Arts 1985–, British Film Inst. Production Bd 1986–, PEN American Center (pres. 2004–06); Distinguished Writer in Residence, Emory Univ., Atlanta 2007–; Exec. mem. Camden Cttee for Community Relations 1977–83; Distinguished Fellow in Literature, Univ. of East Anglia 1995. *Television film screenplays:* The Painter and the Pest 1985, The Riddle of Midnight 1988. *Film appearance:* Then She Found Me 2007. *Publications:* Grimus 1975, Midnight's Children 1981, Shame (Prix du Meilleur Livre Etranger 1984) 1983, The Jaguar Smile: A Nicaraguan Journey 1987, The Satanic Verses 1988, Is Nothing Sacred (lecture) 1990, Haroun and the Sea of Stories (novel) 1990, Imaginary Homelands: Essays and Criticism 1981–91 1991, The Wizard of Oz 1992, East, West (short stories) 1994, The Moor's Last Sigh (novel) 1995, The Vintage Book of Indian Writing 1947–97 (ed. with Elizabeth West) 1997, The Ground Beneath Her Feet 1999, Fury 2001, Step Across the Line: Collected Non-Fiction 1992–2002 2002, Telling Tales (contrib. to charity anthology) 2004, Shalimar the Clown 2005, The Enchantress of Florence 2008, Luka and the Fire of Life 2010; articles for New York Times, Washington Post, The Times and Sunday Times. *Honours:* Hon. Prof. MIT 1993; Hon. Spokesman Charter 88 1989; Hon. DLitt (Bard Coll.) 1995; Booker McConnell Prize for Fiction 1981, Arts Council Literature Bursary 1981, English Speaking Union Literary Award 1981, James Tait Black Memorial Book Prize 1981, Kurt Tucholsky Prize Sweden 1992, Prix Colette Switzerland 1993, Austrian State Prize for European Literature 1994, Whitbread Fiction Award 1996, British Book Awards Author of the Year 1996, London Int. Writers Award 2002, Booker of Bookers Prize 2008, James Joyce Award 2008, Kitty Carlisle Hart Award for Outstanding Contrib. to the Arts, Americans for the Arts 2009; Commdr., Ordre des Arts et des Lettres 1999. *Literary Agent:* English Department, Emory University, N-302 Callaway Center, 537 Kilgo Circle, Atlanta, GA 30322, USA; Wylie Agency (UK) Ltd, 4–8 Rodney Street, London, N1 9JH, England. *Telephone:* (404) 727-6420 (office). *Fax:* (404) 727-2605 (office). *E-mail:* english@emory.edu (office). *Website:* www.english.emory.edu (office).

RUSHTON, Julian Gordon, BA, MusB, MA, DPhil; British professor of music and writer; *Professor Emeritus in the School of Music, University of Leeds*; b. 22 May 1941, Cambridge, England; s. of William Rushton FRS and Marjorie Rushton; two s. *Education:* Trinity Coll., Cambridge, Magdalen Coll., Oxford. *Career:* Lecturer, Univ. of East Anglia 1968–74; Lecturer in Music and Fellow, King's Coll., Cambridge 1974–81; West Riding Prof. of Music, Univ. of Leeds 1982–2002, Prof. Emer. 2002–; Chair. Editorial Cttee, Musica Britannica 1993–; mem. Royal Musical Assn (Pres. 1994–99), American Musicological Soc. (Corresp. mem.), Royal Soc. of Musicians, Royal Philharmonic Soc., Acad. of Europe 2010. *Publications:* Berlioz: Huit Scènes de Faust, La Damnation de Faust, Cipriani Potter, Symphony in G minor (ed.), Elgar: Music for String Orchestra (ed.), Vaughan Williams Serenade (1898) for Small Orhcestra (ed.), W. A. Mozart: Don Giovanni 1981, The Musical Language of Berlioz 1983, Classical Music: A Concise History 1986, W. A. Mozart: Idomeneo 1993, Berlioz: Roméo et Juliette 1994, Elgar: Enigma Variations 1999, The Music of Berlioz 2001, The Cambridge Companion to Elgar (ed. with Daniel Grimley) 2004, Mozart, an Extraordinary Life 2005, Mozart (The Master Musicians) 2006, The New Grove Guide to Mozart and his Operas 2006, Europe, Empire, and Spectacle in Nineteenth-Century British Music (co-ed. with Rachel Cowgill) 2006, Elgar Studies (co-ed. with J. P. E. Harper-Scott) 2007, Let Beauty Awake – Elgar, Vaughan Williams, and Literature (ed.) 2010; Gen. Ed.: Cambridge Music Handbooks (with J. P. E. Harper-Scott) Music in Context; contrib. to New Grove Dictionary of Music and Musicians, New Grove Dictionary of Opera, other books and professional journals. *Honours:* Hon. Corresp. mem. American Musicological Soc. *Address:* School of Music, University of Leeds, Leeds, LS2 9JT (office); 362 Leymoor Road, Golcar, Huddersfield, West Yorks., HD7 4QF, England (home). *Telephone:* (1484) 649108 (home). *E-mail:* j.g.rushton@leeds.ac.uk (office); julianrushton@btinternet.com (home).

RUSSELL, James (see Harknett, Terry)

RUSSELL, Karen, MFA; American writer; b. 10 July 1981, Miami, Fla. *Education:* Columbia Univ. *Career:* fmr publicity asst, Persea Books; Lecturer in Creative Writing, Columbia Univ. *Publications:* St Lucy's Home for Girls Raised by Wolves (short stories) 2006, Swamplandia! 2011; contribs to The New Yorker, New York magazine, Conjunctions, Granta, Zoetrope, Oxford American. *Honours:* Transatlantic Review/Henfield Foundation Award 2005. *Address:* c/o Random House, Publicity Department, 1745 Broadway, New York, NY 10019, USA (office). *Website:* www.randomhouse.com (office).

RUSSELL, Martin James; British writer; b. 25 Sept. 1934, Bromley, Kent, England; s. of Stanley William Russell and Helen Kathleen Russell. *Education:* Bromley Grammar School. *Career:* mem. Crime Writers' Assn, Detection Club. *Publications:* No Through Road 1965, The Client 1975, Mr T 1977, Death Fuse 1980, Backlash 1981, The Search for Sara 1983, A Domestic Affair

1984, The Darker Side of Death 1985, Prime Target 1985, Dead Heat 1986, The Second Time is Easy 1987, House Arrest 1988, Dummy Run 1989, Mystery Lady 1992, Leisure Pursuit 1993. *Address:* 15 Breckonmead, Wanstead Road, Bromley, Kent, BR1 3BW, England (home). *Telephone:* (20) 8290-0459 (home).

RUSSELL, Mary Doria, BA, MA, PhD; American palaeoanthropologist and novelist; b. (Mary Rose Doria), 19 Aug. 1950, Elmhurst, Ill.; d. of Richard Doria and Louise Dewing Doria; m. Donald J. Russell 1970; one s. *Education:* Univ. of Illinois, Northeastern Univ., Univ. of Michigan, Case Western Reserve Univ. *Career:* Instructor, Northeastern Univ., Univ. of Michigan 1978–83; invited lecturer various educational insts 1981–84; Prosector, Special Lecturer, Dept of Oral Biology, School of Dentistry, Case Western Reserve Univ., Cleveland, OH 1983, Clinical Instructor 1984–86, Adjunct Prof., Dept of Anthropology 1986; Propr N Coast Tech. Writing, South Euclid, OH 1986–92; mem. Authors' Guild; mem. Bd St. Adalbert Summer Enrichment Program for Inner City Youth; Commr, City of South Euclid planning and zoning comm. *Compositions:* two operas inspired by The Sparrow and Children of God. *Publications:* The Sparrow: A Novel 1996, Children of God: A Novel 1998, A Thread of Grace: A Novel 2005, Dreamers of the Day – A Novel 2008, Eight to Five, Against 2010; contrib. to scientific journals and periodicals during career as palaeoanthropologist. *Honours:* Mildred Trotter Award for outstanding work on bone 1980, 1983, Tiptree Award 1996, BSFA Best Novel 1997, Arthur C. Clarke Award 1997, John W. Campbell Award 1998, Cleveland Arts Council Prize for Literature 1998, American Library Asscn Readers' Choice Award 1999, Kurd Lasswitz Award, Germany 2001, Spectrum Classic Award 2001. *Literary Agent:* c/o Dystel & Goderich Literary Management, 1 Union Square West, Suite 904, New York, NY 10003, USA. *Telephone:* (212) 627-9100. *Fax:* (212) 627-9313. *E-mail:* jane@dystel.com. *Website:* www.dystel.com. *E-mail:* mary@marydoriarussell.net (office). *Website:* www.marydoriarussell.net.

RUSSELL, Paul, AB, MA, MFA, PhD; American academic and writer; b. 1 July 1956, Memphis, Tenn. *Education:* Oberlin Coll., Cornell Univ. *Career:* Asst Prof., Vassar Coll. 1983–90, Assoc. Prof. 1990–96, Prof. of English 1996–; Co-founder and Ed. The Poughkeepsie Review 1987–89. *Publications:* Fiction: The Salt Point 1990, Boys of Life 1991, Sea of Tranquillity 1994, The Coming Storm 1999, War Against the Animals 2003; non-fiction: The Gay 100: A Ranking of the Most Influential Gay Men and Lesbians, Past and Present 1995; contribs to anthologies, journals, and periodicals. *Honours:* Nat. Endowment for the Arts Creative Writers Fellowship 1993, Regional Winner, GRANTA-Best of Young American Novelists 1995, Ferro-Grumley Award for Fiction 2000. *Literary Agent:* c/o Harvey Klinger, Harvey Klinger Literary Agency, 300 W. 55th Street, New York, NY 10019, USA. *E-mail:* harvey@harveyklinger.com. *Address:* Department of English, Vassar College, Poughkeepsie, NY 12604, USA (office). *E-mail:* russell@vassar.edu (office).

RUSSELL, Sharman Apt, BS, MFA; American academic and writer; b. 23 July 1954, Edwards Air Force Base, CA; m. Peter Russell 1981, one s. one d. *Education:* Univ. of California at Berkeley, Univ. of Montana. *Career:* Asst Prof. of Writing, later Prof., Western New Mexico Univ., Silver City 1981–; Faculty, MFA Program in Creative Non-Fiction, Antioch Univ., Los Angeles 1997–. *Publications:* Built to Last: An Architectural History of Silver City, New Mexico (with Susan Berry) 1986, Frederick Douglass 1987, Songs of the Fluteplayer: Seasons of Life in the Southwest (Mountain and Plains Booksellers Award 1992, New Mexico Presswomen's Zia Award 1992) 1991, Kill the Cowboy: A Battle of Mythology in the New West 1993, The Humpbacked Fluteplayer 1994, When the Land was Young: Reflections on American Archaeology 1996, The Last Matriarch 2000, Anatomy of a Rose 2001, An Obsession with Butterflies: Our Long Love Affair with a Singular Insect 2003, Hunger: An Unnatural History 2006. *Honours:* Writers at Work Fellowship Winner in Nonfiction, Park City, Utah 1989 , Henry Joseph Jackson Award for Non-Fiction, San Francisco 1989, Pushcart Prize (for essay 'Illegal Aliens') 1990, WNMU Research Award in Excellence 2001, Rockefeller Foundation Residency, Bellagio, Italy 2002. *Address:* c/o Department of Humanities, Western New Mexico University, PO Box 680, Silver City, NM 88062, USA.

RUSSELL, William (Willy) Martin; British writer; b. 23 Aug. 1947, s. of William Russell and Margery Russell; m. Ann Seagroatt 1969; one s. two d. *Education:* St Katharine's Coll. of Educ., Liverpool. *Career:* ladies hairdresser 1963–69; teacher 1973–74; Fellow in Creative Writing, Manchester Polytechnic 1977–78; Founder-mem. and Dir Quintet Films; Hon. Dir Liverpool Playhouse; work for theatre includes: Blind Scouse (three short plays) 1971, When the Reds (adaptation) 1972, John, Paul, George, Ringo and Bert (musical) 1974, Breezeblock Park 1975, One for the Road 1976, Stags and Hens 1978, Educating Rita 1979, Blood Brothers (musical) 1983, Our Day Out (musical) 1983, Shirley Valentine 1986; screenplays include: Educating Rita 1981, Shirley Valentine 1989, Dancing Through the Dark 1989; TV and radio plays. *Publications:* Breezeblock Park 1978, One for the Road 1980, Educating Rita 1981, Our Day Out 1984, Stags and Hens 1985, Blood Brothers 1985, Shirley Valentine 1989, The Wrong Boy (novel) 2000; songs and poetry. *Honours:* Hon. MA (Open Univ.) 1983; Hon. DLit (Liverpool Univ.) 1990. *Address:* c/o Casarotto Company Ltd, National House, 60–66 Wardour Street, London, W1V 3HP, England. *Telephone:* (20) 7287-4450. *Website:* www.willyrussell.com.

RUSSO, Albert, BSc; Belgian writer and poet; b. 26 Feb. 1943, Kamina, Belgian Congo (now Democratic Repub. of the Congo); one s. one d. *Education:* Athéné Royal d'Usumbura, Rwanda-Urundi-Collegium Palatinum, Heidelberg, Germany, New York Univ., USA. *Career:* Co-Ed. Paris Transcontinental and Plurilingual Europe; mem. of Jury, Prix de l'Europe 1982–, Neustadt Int. Prize for Literature 1996; mem. Asscn of French Speaking Writers, Authors' Guild of America, PEN American Center. *Publications:* Incandescences 1970, Eclats de malachite 1971, La Pointe du diable 1973, Mosaique New Yorkaise 1975, Albert Russo: An Anthology 1987, Sang Mêlé ou ton Fils Léopold 1990, Le Cap des Illusions 1991, Futureyes/Dans la nuit bleu-fauve 1992, Kaleidoscope 1993, Eclipse sur le Lac Tanganyika 1994, Venetian Thresholds 1995, Painting the Tower of Babel 1996, Zapinette 1996, Poetry and Peanuts (collection) 1997, Zapinette Video (novel) 1998, Mixed Blood (novel) 1999, Eclipse over Lake Tanganyika (novel) 1999, L'amant de mon père (novel) 2000, Zapinette à New York (novel) 2000, Short Stories: Beyond the Great Water, Unmasking Hearts, The Age of the Pearl 2001, Zany: Zapinette New York (novel) 2001, Zapinette chez le Belges (novel) (Prix Jeunesse 2003) 2002, L'amant de mon père: journal romain (novel) 2003, L'ancêtre noire (novel) 2003, Sangue misto (novel) 2003, ROMAdiva (photography and poems) 2004, Le Tour du Monde de la poésie gay (poems) 2004, Chinese Puzzle (photography and poems) 2005, La Tour Shalom (novel) 2005, AfricaSoul (photography and poems) 2005, In France (photography and poems) 2005, The Benevolent American in the Heart of Darkness (three novels) 2005, Oh Zaperetta! (novel) 2005, The Crowded World of Solitude: Vol. I The Collected Stories (Writer's Digest honorable mention) 2005, Vol. II The Collected Poems 2005, Albert Russo: A Poetic Biogaphy (two vol. biog. with photography and texts) 2006, Sardinia (photography) 2006, Body Glorious (photography) 2006, Pasion de España (photography) 2007, Italia Nostra (photography) 2007, City of Lovers/City of Wonder (photography) 2007, New York at heart (photography) 2007, Israel at Heart (photography) 2007, Granada/Costa del Sol/Ronda (photography) 2007, Sang Mêlé ou ton fils Léoplold (novel) 2007, Viennese kaleidoscope (photography) 2007, Norway to Spitzberg (photography) 2007, Shalom Tower Syndrome (novel) 2008, Sangue Misto (novel) 2008, Noel in Paris (photography) 2008, Eilat, Petra and Tel Aviv (photography) 2008, Gaytude (with Adam Donaldson Powell) (poetry) 2009, Boundaries of Exile (stories, essays and poetry, co-authored with Martin Tucker) 2009, The Black Ancestor (novel) 2009, Exils Africains (novel) 2010, Mermaids of the Baltic Sea (photography) 2010, China Forever (photography) 2010, Visions of Venice (photography) 2010, Symphony in Hands (photography) 2010, Celestial Blues (photography) 2010, In the Air/on the Ground and/on the Water (photography) 2010, Senegal Live (photography) 2010, Expressive Romans (photography) 2010, Animal Kinship (photography) 2010, Garden Delights (photography) 2010, France: Art, Humour & Nature (photography) 2010, Oriental Gems (photography) 2011, Venice/Empress of the Seas (photography) 2011, Léodine l'Africaine (novel) 2011, And There Was David Kanza (novel) 2011, Israel/Jordan/Palestine (photography and text) 2012, Rainbow Paris (photography) 2012, Israel & Palestine (photography) 2012; contribs to professional journals and BBC World Service; translated into a dozen languages and published in English and French world-wide. *Honours:* Silver Prix Colette 1971, Prix de Poésie Regain 1971, Willie Lee Martin Short Story Award 1987, Silver Medal 1985, British Diversity Award 1997, AAS Memorial Trophy for Best Overseas Entry in Poetry 1999, AAS Poetry Prize 2001, Robert Penn Warren Award Editors' Choice 2002, 2004, Azsacra Int. Poetry Award 2008, several photography, poetry and fiction awards 2008, 2009, 2010. *Address:* BP 640, 75826 Paris Cedex 17, France. *E-mail:* albert.russo@orange.fr. *Website:* www.albertrusso.eu.

RUTKIEWICZ, Ignacy Mikołaj; Polish journalist; *President, Foundation Press Centre for Central and Eastern Europe;* b. 15 April 1929, Vilna; s. of Józef Rutkiewicz and Maria Rutkiewicz (née Turkułł); m. Wilma Helena Koller 1961; two s. *Education:* Poznań Univ. *Career:* Ed., Ed.-in-Chief Wrocławski Tygodnik Katolicki (weekly) 1953–55; journalist, Zachodnia Agencja Prasowa (ZAP) 1957–66, Polska Agencja Interpress 1967–70; Ed. Odra (monthly) 1961–81, Ed.-in-Chief 1982–90, mem. Editorial Council 1991–; Co-Founder, mem. Editorial Council Więź (monthly), Warsaw 1958–; Pres.-Ed.-in-Chief Polish Press Agency (PAP), Warsaw 1990–92, 1992–94; Adviser to Prime Minister, Warsaw 1994–95; TV journalist TV Centre of Training, Polish TV (TVP) 1994–96; Sec. TV Comm. for Ethics 1996–; Ed.-in-Chief Antena (weekly) 1998; Adviser to Minister of Culture and Arts 1998–99; Sr Ed. On-line News, TVP 1999–; Co-founder and Vice-Pres. Polish-German Asscn, Warsaw 1990–2001; Vice-Pres. Alliance Européenne des Agences de Presse, Zürich 1991–92; mem. Exec. Bd, Asscn of Polish Journalists (SDP) 1980–82, Pres. 1993–95; mem. Council on Media and Information, Pres.'s Office 1993–95; mem. Euroatlantic Asscn 1995–; mem. Bd Foundation Press Centre for Cen. and Eastern Europe 1996–, (Pres. 2001–), Programme Bd Nat. Club of Friends of Lithuania 1996–; Programme Bd Polish Press Agency 1998–2002; Assoc. mem. Orbicom (int. network of UNESCO Chairs in Communications) 2000–. *Publications:* author or co-author of more than 10 books; Transformation of Media and Journalism in Poland 1989–1996 (author and co-ed.), How to be Fair in the Media: Guidelines not only for TV journalists. *Honours:* Kt, Order of Polonia Restituta 1981; City of Wrocław Award 1963, B. Prus Award of SDP 1990, Phil epistémoni Award, Jagiellonian Univ., Kraków 1991. *Address:* Ośrodek Nowe Media TVP, ul. Woronicza 17, 00-999 Warsaw (office); Al. Jerozolimskie 42/55, 00-024 Warsaw, Poland (home). *Telephone:* (22) 5477082 (office); (22) 8275813 (home). *E-mail:* ignacy.rutkiewicz@waw.tvp.pl (office). *Website:* www.wiadomosci.tvp.pl (office).

RUTSALA, Vern, BA, MFA; American writer, poet and teacher; b. 5 Feb. 1934, McCall, Ida; m. Joan Colby 1957; two s. one d. *Education:* Reed Coll., Univ. of Iowa. *Career:* mem. PEN, Poetry Soc. of America, Associated Writing Programs. *Publications:* The Window 1964, Small Songs 1969, The Harmful State 1971, Laments 1975, The Journey Begins 1976, Paragraphs 1978, The New Life 1978, Walking Home from the Icehouse 1981, Backtracking 1985, The Mystery of Lost Shoes 1985, Ruined Cities 1987, Selected Poems 1991, Little-Known Sports 1994, Greatest Hits: 1964–2002 2002, A Handbook for Writers 2004, The Moment's Equation 2004, How We Spent Our Time 2006; contrib. to New Yorker, Esquire, Poetry, Hudson Review, Harper's, Atlantic, American Poetry Review, Paris Review, Times Literary Supplement, New Statesman. *Honours:* NEA Fellowships 1974, 1979, Northwest Poetry Prize 1976, Guggenheim Fellowship 1982, Carolyn Kizer Poetry Prizes 1988, 1997, Oregon Arts Commission Masters Fellowship 1990, Hazel Hall Award 1992, Juniper Prize 1993, Arvon Foundation Duncan Lawrie Prize 1994, Richard Snyder Prize 2004, Akron Poetry Prize 2005, Kenneth O. Hanson Prize 2007, Mississippi Review Poetry Prize 2009. *Address:* 2404 NE 24th Avenue, Portland, OR 97212, USA (home). *Telephone:* (503) 281-5872 (home).

RUTTER, Sir Michael Llewellyn, Kt, CBE, MD, FRS, FRCP, FRCPsych; British academic; *Research Professor, Institute of Psychiatry, King's College London*; b. 15 Aug. 1933, s. of Llewellyn Charles Rutter and Winifred Olive Rutter; m. Marjorie Heys 1958; one s. two d. *Education:* Univ. of Birmingham Medical School, training in paediatrics, neurology and internal medicine 1955–58. *Career:* practised at Maudsley Hosp. 1958–61; Nuffield Medical Travelling Fellow, Albert Einstein Coll. of Medicine, New York 1961–62; scientist with MRC Social Psychology Research Unit 1962–65; Sr Lecturer, then Reader, Univ. of London Inst. of Psychiatry 1966–73, Prof. of Child Psychiatry 1973–98, Research Prof. 1998–, Dir MRC Research Centre for Social, Genetic and Developmental Psychiatry 1994–98; Hon. Dir MRC Child Psychiatry Unit 1984–98; Fellow, Center for Advanced Study in Behavioral Sciences, Stanford Univ. 1979–80; guest lecturer at many insts in Britain and America; Pres. Soc. for Research in Child Devt 1999–2001 (Pres. elect 1997–99); Clinical Vice-Pres. Acad. of Medical Sciences 2004–07. *Publications:* Children of Sick Parents 1966: A Neuropsychiatric Study in Childhood (jtly) 1970, Education, Health and Behaviour (ed. jtly) 1970, Infantile Autism (ed.) 1971, Maternal Deprivation Reassessed (ed.) 1981, The Child with Delayed Speech (jtly) 1972, Helping Troubled Children (jtly) 1975, Cycles of Disadvantage (jtly) 1976; Child Psychiatry (ed. jtly) 1976, (2nd edn as Child and Adolescent Psychiatry 1985), Autism (ed. jtly) 1978, Changing Youth in a Changing Society (jtly) 1979, Fifteen Thousand Hours: Secondary Schools and Their Effect on Children 1979, Scientific Foundations of Developmental Psychiatry (ed.)1981, A Measure of Our Values: Goals and Dilemmas in the Upbringing of Children (jtly) 1983, Lead versus Health (jtly) 1983, Juvenile Delinquency 1983, Developmental Neuropsychiatry (ed.) 1983, Stress, Coping and Development (ed. jtly) 1983, Depression and Young People (ed. jtly) 1986, Studies of Psychosocial Risk: The Power of Longitudinal Data (ed.) 1988, Parenting Breakdown: The Making and Breaking of Inter-generational Links (jtly) 1988, Straight and Devious Pathways from Childhood to Adulthood (ed. jtly) 1990, Biological Risk Factors for Psychosocial Disorders (ed. jtly) 1991, Developing Minds (jtly) 1993, Development Through Life: A Handbook for Clinicians (ed. jtly) 1994, Stress, Risk and Resilience in Children and Adolescents (ed. jtly) 1994, Psychological Disorders in Young People 1995, Antisocial Behaviour by Young People (jtly) 1998, Genes and Behaviour: Nature-Nurture Interplay Explained 2006. *Honours:* Hon. Fellow, British Psychological Soc. 1978, American Acad. of Pediatrics 1981, Royal Soc. of Medicine 1996; Hon. doctorates (Leiden) 1985, (Catholic Univ. of Leuven) 1990, (Birmingham) 1990, (Edin.) 1990, (Chicago) 1991, (Minnesota) 1993, (Jyväskylä) 1996, (Warwick) 1999, (E. Anglia) 2000. *Address:* Institute of Psychiatry, King's College London, Box P080, De Crespigny Park, London SE5 8AF (office); 190 Court Lane, Dulwich, London, SE21 7ED, England (home). *Telephone:* (20) 7848-0882 (office). *Fax:* j.wickham@iop.kcl.ac.uk (office). *Website:* www.iop.kcl.ac.uk/iopweb/departments/home/?locator=10 (office).

RUY-SÁNCHEZ, Alberto, PhD; Mexican poet and essayist; b. 7 Dec. 1951, Mexico City; s. of María Antonieta Lacy. *Education:* Univ. of Paris, France. *Career:* Ed.-in-Chief Artes de México 1988–; Visiting Tinker Scholar, Stanford Univ., USA; Chair. Creative Non-Fiction Program, Banff Centre for Arts, Canada; Guggenheim Foundation Fellowship 1988. *Publications include:* novels: Los nombres del aire (Premio Xavier Villaurrutia) 1987, Los demonios de la lengua 1987, En los labios del agua (Prix des Trois Continents for French translation by Gabriel Iaculli 2000) 1996, Los jardines secretos de Mogador: Voces de tierra (Premio Cálamo la Otra Mirada 2003) 2001, Nueve veces el asombro 2005, La mano del fuego 2007; other works: Limulus. Visiones del fósil viviente 2004, Nueve veces el asombro 2005; short stories: Los demonios de la lengua 1987, Cuentos de Mogador 1994, De cómo llegó a Mogador la melancholia 1999, La huella del grito 2001; poetry: La inaccessible 1990. *Honours:* Hon. Citizen of Louisville, Ky; Hon. Capt. Belle of Louisville (steamship); Officier de l'Ordre des Arts et des Lettres 2000, Gran Orden de Honor Nacional al Mérito Autoral 2005; Premio a la Excelencia de lo Nuestro, Fundación México Unido 2006, Premio Juan Pablos al Mérito Editorial, Cámara Nacional de la Industria Editorial Mexicana 2006. *E-mail:* albertoruy@yahoo.com.mx. *Website:* www.albertoruysanchez.com.

RYAN, Peter Allen, BA, MM; Australian writer and publisher; b. 4 Sept. 1923, Melbourne; s. of Emmett F. Ryan and Alice D. Ryan; m. Gladys A. Davidson 1947; one s. one d. *Education:* Malvern Grammar School, Melbourne and Univ. of Melbourne. *Career:* mil. service 1942–45; Dir United Service Publicity Pty Ltd 1953–57; Public Relations Man., Imperial Chemical Industries of Australia and New Zealand Ltd 1957–61; Asst to Vice-Chancellor, Univ. of Melbourne 1962; Dir Melbourne Univ. Press 1962–88; mem. Solicitors Disciplinary Tribunal 1984–88; Sec. Bd of Examiners for Barristers and Solicitors 1988–; Exec. Officer Vic. Council of Legal Educ. and Admin. Officer Vic. Council of Law Reporting 1989–; columnist, Quadrant magazine 1994–. *Publications:* Fear Drive My Feet 1959, The Preparation of Manuscripts 1966, Encyclopedia of Papua and New Guinea (gen. ed.) 1972, Redmond Barry 1973, William Macmahon Ball: A Memoir 1989, Black Bonanza, A Landslide of Gold 1991, Lines of Fire: Manning Clark and Other Writings 1997. *Address:* Quadrant Magazine Co. Inc., PO Box 82, Balmain, NSW 2041, Australia (office). *Telephone:* (2) 9818-1155 (office). *Fax:* (2) 9818-1422 (office). *Website:* www.quadrant.org.au (office).

RYCKMANS, Pierre, (Simon Leys), PhD; Belgian/Australian academic and writer; b. 28 Sept. 1935, Brussels; m. Chang Han-fang; three s. one d. *Education:* Univ. of Louvain. *Career:* taught Chinese Literature, ANU 1970–86; Prof. of Chinese Studies, Univ. of Sydney 1987–93; Fellow, Australian Acad of Humanities; mem. Acad. Royale de Littérature Française (Brussels) 1991–. *Film:* The Emperor's New Clothes (Dir Alan Taylor, Producer U. Pasolini) 2001, adapted from Simon Leys' The Death of Napoleon. *Publications:* (under pen-name Simon Leys) The Chairman's New Clothes: Mao and the Cultural Revolution 1977, Chinese Shadows 1977, The Burning Forest 1985, La Mort de Napoléon 1986 (English trans. 1991), Les Entretiens de Confucius 1989, L'humeur, l'honneur, l'horreur 1991, The Analects of Confucius 1996, Essais sur la Chine 1998, The View from the Bridge 1996, The Angel and the Octopus 1999, Protée et autres essais 2001, Les Naufragés du Batavia 2003, La Mer dans la littérature française 2003, Les idées des autres 2005 (trans. as Other People's Thoughts 2007), The Wreck of the Batavia 2005, Le Bonheur des petits poissons 2008, With Stendhal 2010, The Hall of Uselessness 2011; (under own name Pierre Ryckmans) Les Propos sur la peinture de Shitao 1969, La Vie et l'oeuvre de Su Renshan, rebelle, peintre et fou 1970. *Honours:* Officer Ordre de Léopold, Commdr Ordre des Arts et Lettres 1999; Prix Stanislas-Julien (Institut de France), Prix Jean Walter (Acad. Française), The Independent (UK) Foreign Fiction Award 1992, Christina Stead Prize for Fiction (NSW) 1992, Prix Bernheim 1999, Prix Renaudot 2001, Prix Henri Gal (Acad. Française) 2001, Prix Guizot 2004, Prix Femina (100th anniversary) 2004, Prix del Duca (Acad. Française) 2005. *Address:* 6 Bonwick Place, Garran, ACT 2605, Australia. *Fax:* (2) 6281-4887.

S

SAADAWI, Nawal el-, MA, MD; Egyptian physician and writer; b. 27 Oct. 1931, Kafr Tahla; m. 1st Ahmed Helmi (divorced); m. 2nd (divorced); m. 3rd Sherif Hetata 1964; one s. one d. *Education:* Cairo Univ., Columbia Univ., New York, USA. *Career:* physician at University Hospital and Ministry of Health 1955–65; Dir-Gen. of Health Educ. Dept, Ministry of Health 1966–72; Researcher, Faculty of Medicine, Ain Shams Univ., Cairo 1973–78, also writer, High Inst. of Literature and Science; Head of Women's programme, UN Econ. Comm. for Africa, Addis Ababa 1978–79, UN Econ. Comm. for Africa, Beirut 1978–80; arrested and detained in Egypt for three months 1981; Founder, Arab Women's Solidarity Assen 1982, Pres. 1982–91 (prohibited by Egyptian govt); fled to USA 1991 after name appeared on fundamentalist death list, returned to Egypt 1996; Distinguished Visiting Prof., Duke Univ. 1993–96, taught at Univ. of Washington 1995, Univ. of Illinois, Chicago 1998, Florida Atlantic Univ. 1999 Montclair Univ. 2001–02, Univ. of Southern Maine 2003 Univ. of Autonoma, Barcelona 2004 Smith Coll., 2004 Claremont Univ. 2005, Spelman Coll. (Cosby Chair) 2007–09; formally charged with apostasy 2007, court dismissed all charges; fmr Ed.-in-Chief, Health magazine; fmr Asst Gen.-Sec. Medical Assen. *Publications include:* Memoirs of a Woman Doctor 1958, Two Women in One 1968, Women and Sex 1971, She Has No Place in Paradise (short story) 1972, Woman at Point Zero 1975, God Dies by the Nile 1976, The Hidden Face of Eve: Women in the Arab World (non-fiction) 1977, The Circling Song 1977, The Veil (short story) 1978, Death of an Ex-Minister 1979, Memoirs from the Women's Prison 1983, My Travels Around the World 1986, The Fall of the Imam 1987, The Innocence of the Devil 1992, Nawal el-Saadawi in the Dock 1993, The Well of Life and The Thread: Two Short Novels 1993, The Nawal el-Saadawi Reader 1997, A Daughter of Isis: The Autobiography of Nawal el-Saadawi 1999, Love in the Kingdom of Oil 2001, Walking Through Fire: A Life of Nawal el-Saadawi 2002, The Novel 2005, God Resigns in the Summit Meeting 2007, Zeina 2009; contrib. to newspapers and magazines. *Honours:* First Degree Decoration of the Republic of Libya 1989; Hon. DUniv (York) 1994, (Univ. of Illinois, Chicago) 1996, (Univ. of St Andrews, Scotland) 1997, (Univ. of Tromso, Norway) 2003, Dr hc (Université libre de Bruxelles) 2007, (Flemish Univ.) 2007, (French Univ.) 2007, (Mexico Univ.) 2010; High Council of Literature Award 1974, Short Story Award 1974, Franco-Arab Literary Award 1982, Literary Award of Gubran 1988, XV Premi Int. Catalunia Award 2003, North South Prize, Council of Europe 2004, Inana Int. Prize 2005, African Literature Assen Award, Univ. of West Virginia 2007, Pan African Writers Assen Literary Award 2009. *Address:* 19 Maahad Nasser Street, Bldg 1, Shoubra Gardens, 11241, Cairo, Egypt. *Telephone:* 2022279. *Fax:* 2035001. *E-mail:* shns@tedata.net.eg; nawalalsaadawi@yahoo.com. *Website:* www.nawalsaadawi.net.

SAALBACH, Astrid; Danish author and dramatist; b. 29 Nov. 1955, Elsinore; m. Jens Kaas 1987; two s. *Education:* Nat. School of Theatre, Copenhagen. *Career:* actress at different theatres until 1985; first radio play, Spor I Sandet 1981, first screenplay, En Verden Blegner 1984, first stage play, Den Usynlige By 1986; plays produced in most European countries, Canada and USA; mem. Danish Acad. *Publications include:* plays: Fading Colours (TV) 1980, Footprints in the Sand 1982, The Hidden City 1985, Myung (TV) 1989, Morning and Evening 1993, Blessed Child 1996, Ashes to Ashes, Dust to Dust 1998, The Cold Heart 2001, End of the World (Nordic Theatre Union Nordic Drama Award, Reumert Award for Best Drama) 2004, Pietá 2007, Red and Green 2009; novels: Who She Is 2000, Fingeren i Flammen (Finger in the Fire) 2005, The Displacement 2011; short stories: The Face of the Moon 1985. *Literary Agent:* c/o Nordiska ApS, Åbenrå 5, 4. sal, 1124 Copenhagen K, Denmark. *Telephone:* 33-11-68-83. *Fax:* 33-14-44-28. *E-mail:* info@nordiska.dk. *Website:* www.nordiska.dk. *Address:* Holsteinsgade 9, 3 tv, 2100 Copenhagen Ø, Denmark (home). *Telephone:* 35-38-18-83 (home). *E-mail:* astrid.saalbach@mail.dk (office). *Website:* www.astridsaalbach.dk.

SABATO, Haim; Israeli writer and rabbi; b. Cairo, Egypt. *Career:* forced to leave Egypt 1957; settled in Jersalem, Israel; served in tank corps, Yom Kippur War 1973; founder and Rabbi, Yeshivat Birkat Moshe, Maaleh Adumim. *Publications:* Emet me-aretz Titzmach (trans. as Aleppo Tales) 1997, Ti'um Kavanot (trans. as Adjusting Sights) (Sapir Prize) 2000, Ke-afapei Shahar (trans. as The Dawning of the Day: A Jerusalem Tale) 2006, Bo'ee HaRuach (trans. as From the Four Winds) 2008. *Address:* Yeshivat Birkat Moshe, Mitzpeh Nevo, Maaleh Adumim 98410, Israel (office). *Telephone:* 2-5353655 (office). *E-mail:* webmaster@birkatmoshe.org.il (office). *Website:* www.birkatmoshe.org.il.

SABUROV, Yevgeny Fedorovich, DEconSc; Russian economist and poet; b. 13 Feb. 1946, Crimea; m. Tatiana Petrovna; three d. *Education:* Moscow State Univ. *Career:* Researcher, econ. inst. in Moscow –1990; Deputy Minister of Educ. 1990–91; Project Leader, Programme of Econ. Reform in Russia April–Aug. 1991; Deputy Prime Minister, Minister of Econ. Aug.–Nov. 1991; Dir Centre for Information and Social Tech. 1991–94; Deputy Head of Govt Repub. of Crimea Feb.–Oct. 1994; Prof., Acad. of Econs; Dir Inst. for Investment Studies 1995, now Chair Bd of Trustees; Chief Consultant, Menatep Bank 1995; Chair. Bd of Guardians, Inst. for Urban Econs 1996–; Chair. Confidential and Investment Bank 1999–2000, Deputy Chair. 2000–; mem. Acad. of Information, Acad. of Social Sciences; columnist, NZ magazine. *Publications include:* Gunpowder Conspiracy (poems) 1996, On the Edge of the Lake (selected poems); over 100 articles on problems of econ. reform in Russia; numerous verses in periodicals. *Address:* Board of Trustees, Institute for Urban Economics, Moscow 125009, 0/1, Tverskaya Street, Russia. *Telephone:* (495) 363-50-47. *Fax:* (495) 787-45-20. *E-mail:* mailbox@urbaneconomics.ru. *Website:* www.urbaneconomics.ru.

SACHAR, Louis; American children's writer; b. 20 March 1954, East Meadow, NY; m. Carla 1985; one d. *Education:* Univ. of California at Berkeley, Hastings Coll. of Law in San Francisco. *Career:* fmr lawyer. *Publications include:* Marvin Redpost series: Kidnapped at Birth?, Why Pick on Me?, Is He A Girl?, Alone in His Teacher's House, Class President, A Flying Birthday Cake?, Super Fast Out of Control!, A Magic Crystal?; Wayside School series: Sideways Stories from Wayside School (Int. Reading Assen Children's Choice 1979, Children's Book Council Children's Choice 1979) 1977, Wayside School is Falling Down 1989, Wayside School Gets a Little Stranger 1995, Sideways Arithmetic from Wayside School, More Sideways Arithmetic from Wayside School; Johnny's in the Basement 1983, Someday, Angeline 1983, Sixth Grade Secrets 1987, There's a Boy in the Girls' Bathroom (Young Reader's Choice Award 1990) 1987, Dogs Don't Tell Jokes 1991, Monkey Soup 1992, The Boy Who Lost his Face 1997, Holes (Nat. Book Award, New York Times Book Review Notable Children's Book of the Year, New York Times Outstanding Book of the Year, School Library Journal Best Book of the Year, Horn Book Fanfare Honor List, Bulletin Blue Ribbon Book, Publishers Weekly Best Book of the Year, Newbery Award) 1998, Stanley Yelnats' Survival Guide to Camp Green Lake, Small Steps 2006, The Cardturner 2010. *Honours:* Parents' Choice Award 1987. *Address:* c/o Scholastic, 557 Broadway, New York, NY 10012, USA (office). *Website:* www.louissachar.com.

SACHS, Jeffrey David, BA, MA, PhD; American economist, writer and academic; *Special Adviser to the Secretary-General on Millennium Development Goals, United Nations*; b. 5 Nov. 1954, Detroit, Mich.; s. of Theodore Sachs and Joan Sachs; m. Sonia Ehrlich; one s. two d. *Education:* Harvard Univ. *Career:* Research Assoc. Nat. Bureau of Econ. Research, Cambridge, Mass. 1980–85; Asst Prof. of Econs, Harvard Univ. 1980–82, Assoc. Prof. 1982–83, Galen L. Stone Prof. of International Trade 1984–2001, Dir Harvard Inst. for International Devt 1995–2002, Center for International Devt –2002; Quetelet Prof. of Sustainable Devt and Prof. of Health Policy and Man. and Dir The Earth Inst., Columbia Univ. 2002–; Adviser, Brookings Inst., Washington, DC 1982–; Special Adviser to UN Sec.-Gen. on Millennium Devt Goals 2002–, Dir Millennium Project 2002–06; Founder Millennium Villages Project; Founder and Co-Pres. Millennium Promise Alliance; Founder and Chair. Exec. Cttee Inst. of Econ. Analysis, Moscow 1993–; Chair. Comm. on Macroeconomics and Health, WHO 2000–01; Co-Chair. Advisory Bd The Global Competitiveness Report; mem. International Financial Insts Advisory Comm., US Congress 1999–2000; econ. adviser to various govts in Latin America, Eastern Europe, the fmr Soviet Union, Asia and Africa, Jubilee 2000 movt; fmr consultant to IMF, World Bank, OECD and UNDP; Adviser to Pres. of Bolivia 1986–90; Fellow, World Econometric Soc.; Research Assoc. Nat. Bureau of Econ. Research; syndicated newspaper column appears in more than 50 countries; mem. American Acad. of Arts and Sciences, Harvard Soc. of Fellows, Brookings Panel of Economists, Bd of Advisers, Inst. of Medicine, Fellows of the World Econometric Soc., Nat. Bureau of Econ. Research, Bd of Advisors Chinese Economists Soc., among other international orgs; Distinguished Visiting Lecturer, LSE, Univ. of Oxford, Tel-Aviv, Jakarta, Yale Univs. *Publications include:* Economics of Worldwide Stagflation (with Michael Bruno) 1985, Developing Country Debt and the Economic Performance (ed.) 1989, Global Linkages: Macroeconomic Interdependence and Cooperation in the World Economy (with Warwick McKibbin) 1991, Peru's Path to Recovery (with Carlos Paredes) 1991, Macroeconomics in the Global Economy (with Felipe Larrain) 1993, Poland's Jump to the Market Economy 1993, The Transition in Eastern Europe (with Olivier Blanchard and Kenneth Froot) 1994, Russia and the Market Economy (in Russian) 1995, Economic Reform and the Process of Global Integration (with A. Warner) 1995, The Collapse of the Mexican Peso: What Have We Learned? (co-author) 1995, Natural Resource Abundance and Economic Growth (with A. Warner) 1996, The Rule of Law and Economic Reform in Russia (co-ed.) 1997, Economies in Transition (co-ed.) 1997, The End of Poverty 2005, Common Wealth: Economics for a Crowded Planet 2008, The Price of Civilization 2011; more than 200 scholarly articles. *Honours:* Hon. Prof., Universidad del Pacifico, Peru; Commdr's Cross, Order of Merit (Poland) 1999; Hon. PhD (St Gallen, Switzerland) 1990, (Universidad del Pacífico, Peru) 1997, (Lingnan Coll., Hong Kong) 1998, (Varna Econs Univ., Bulgaria) 2000, (Iona Coll., New York) 2000; hon. degrees from Pace Univ., State Univ. of New York, Kraków Univ. of Econs, Ursinus Coll., Whitman Coll., Mount Sinai School of Medicine, Ohio Wesleyan Univ., Coll. of the Atlantic, Southern Methodist Univ., Simon Fraser Univ., McGill Univ., Southern New Hampshire Univ., St John's Univ.; Frank E. Seidman Award in Political Econ. 1991, cited in New York Times Magazine as "probably the most important economist in the world" 1993, named by TIME magazine as "the world's best-known economist" 1994, cited by Le Nouvel Observateur magazine as "one of the world's 50 most important leaders on globalization" 1997, Berhard Harms Prize (Germany) 2000, Distinguished Public Service Award, Sec. of State's Open Forum 2002, named by TIME magazine as one of the 100 Most Influential People in the World

2004, 2005, Sargent Shriver Award for Equal Justice 2005, named by the World Affairs Councils of America as one of the "500 Most Influential People in the Field of Foreign Policy" 2007, Padma Bhushan, Govt of India 2007, Cardozo Journal of Conflict Resolution International Advocate for Peace Award 2007, Centennial Medal, Harvard Grad. School of Arts and Sciences for his contribs to society 2007, BBC Reith Lecturer 2007, first holder of Royal Prof. Ungku Aziz Chair in Poverty Studies, Centre for Poverty and Devt Studies, Univ. of Malaya, Kuala Lumpur, Malaysia 2007–09, ranked 98th by Vanity Fair magazine on its list of 100 members of the New Establishment 2008, gave commencement address to Lehigh Univ.'s Class of 2009. *Address:* The Earth Institute at Columbia University, 405 Low Library, 535 West 116th Street, MC 4335, New York, NY 10027, USA (office). *Telephone:* (212) 854-8704 (office). *Fax:* (212) 854-8702 (office). *Website:* www.earth.columbia.edu/about/director (office); www.un.org/millenniumgoals (office).

SACKS, Sir Jonathan Henry, PhD; British rabbi; *Chief Rabbi, United Hebrew Congregations of the Commonwealth*; b. 8 March 1948, London; s. of Louis Sacks and Louisa Sacks (née Frumkin); m. Elaine Taylor 1970; one s. two d. *Education:* Christ's Coll. Finchley, Gonville & Caius Coll., Cambridge, New Coll., Oxford, London Univ., Jews' Coll., London and Yeshivat Etz Hayyim, London. *Career:* Lecturer in Moral Philosophy, Middlesex Polytechnic 1971–73; Lecturer in Jewish Philosophy, Jews' Coll., London 1973–76, in Talmud and Jewish Philosophy 1976–82, Chief Rabbi Lord Jakobovits Prof. (first incumbent) in Modern Jewish Thought 1982–, Dir Rabbinic Faculty 1983–90, Prin. 1984–90; Chief Rabbi of the United Hebrew Congregations of the British Commonwealth of Nations 1991–; Assoc. Pres. Conf. of European Rabbis 2000–; Visiting Prof. of Philosophy, Univ. of Essex 1989–90; currently Visiting Prof. of Philosophy, Hebrew Univ., Jerusalem and of Theology and Religious Studies King's Coll., London; Rabbi Golders Green Synagogue, London 1978–82, Marble Arch Synagogue, London 1983–90; Ed. Le'ela (journal) 1985–90; mem. CRAC; Presentation Fellow, King's Coll., London 1993;. *Publications:* Torah Studies 1986, Tradition and Transition (essays) 1986, Traditional Alternatives 1989, Tradition in an Untraditional Age 1990, The Persistence of Faith (Reith Lecture) 1991, Orthodoxy Confronts Modernity (Ed.) 1991, Crisis and Covenant 1992, One People?: Tradition, Modernity and Jewish Unity 1993, Will We Have Jewish Grandchildren? 1994, Faith in the Future 1995, Community of Faith 1995, The Politics of Hope 1997, Morals and Markets 1999, Celebrating Life 2000, Radical Then Radical Now 2001, The Dignity of Difference: How To Avoid the Clash of Civilizations 2002, The Chief Rabbi's Hagadah 2003, To Heal a Fractured World 2005. *Honours:* Hon. Fellow Gonville and Caius Coll., Cambridge 1993; Hon. DD (Cantab.) 1993, (Archbishop of Canterbury) 2001; Dr hc (Middx Univ.) 1993, (Haifa Univ., Israel) 1996, (Yeshiva Univ., NY) 1997, (St Andrews Univ.) 1998; Hon. LLD (Univ. of Liverpool) 1997; Sherman Lecturer, Manchester Univ. 1989, Reith Lecturer 1990, Jerusalem Prize 1995, Cook Lecturer 1997. *Address:* Adler House, 735 High Road, London, N12 0US, England (office). *Telephone:* (20) 8343-6301 (office). *Fax:* (20) 8343-6310 (office). *E-mail:* info@chiefrabbi.org (office). *Website:* www.chiefrabbi.org (office).

SACKS, Oliver Wolf, MD, FRCP, CBE; British neurologist, writer and academic; *Professor of Neurology and Psychiatry and University Artist, Columbia University*; b. 9 July 1933, London; s. of Dr Samuel Sacks and Dr Muriel Elsie Sacks (née Landau). *Education:* St Paul's School, London and Queen's Coll., Oxford. *Career:* Research Asst, Parkinsonism Unit, Mt Zion Hospital, San Francisco 1960–61; Resident, UCLA 1962–65; Consultant Neurologist, Headache Unit, Montefiore Hosp., Bronx, New York 1966–68, Beth Abraham Hosp., Bronx 1966–2007, Bronx Psychiatric Center 1966–91, Little Sisters of the Poor, NY 1972–, Bronx Developmental Services 1974–76; Consultant Neurologist and mem. Medical Advisory Bd, Gilles de la Tourette Syndrome Asscn, New York 1974–; Asst Prof. of Neurology, Albert Einstein Coll. of Medicine, Bronx 1975–78, Assoc. Clinical Prof. 1978–85, Clinical Prof. 1985–2007; Adjunct Prof. of Psychiatry, New York Univ. (NYU) School of Medicine 1992–2007, Consulting Neurologist, NYU Comprehensive Epilepsy Center 1999–2007; Prof. of Neurology and Psychiatry, Medical Center, Columbia Univ. 2007–, Columbia Univ. Artist 2007–; mem. American Acad. of Neurology, American Fern Soc., Authors Guild, British Pteridological Soc., Bronx Co. and NY State Medical Socs, New York Mineralogical Club, New York Stereoscopic Soc., PEN, Soc. for Neuroscience. *Publications:* Migraine 1970, Awakenings (Hawthornden Prize 1974, Book of the Year, The Observer 1973, The Scriptor Award, Univ. of Southern California 1991) 1973, A Leg to Stand On 1984, The Man Who Mistook His Wife For A Hat 1985, Seeing Voices: A Journey Into The World of the Deaf (Odd Fellows Social Concern Book Award 1991, Mainichi Publishing Culture Award, Tokyo, Best Natural Science Book 1996) 1989, An Anthropologist on Mars (Esquire/Apple/Waterstone's Book of the Year) 1995, The Island of the Colourblind 1996, Uncle Tungsten (New York Times Editors' Choice, Jewish Quarterly Wingate Prize, Literature Award of the German Chemical Industry Fund 2004) 2001, Oaxaca Journal 2002, Musicophilia: Tales of Music and the Brain 2007, The Mind's Eye 2010. *Honours:* Hon. Fellow, American Acad. of Arts and Letters 1996, American Acad. of Arts and Sciences, American Neurological Asscn, Asscn of British Neurologists, Jonathan Edwards Coll., Yale Univ., New York Acad. of Sciences, New York Inst. for the Humanities, NYU, Queen's Coll., Oxford, Royal Coll. of Physicians. Univ. of California, Santa Cruz, Cowell Coll.; Hon. DHumLitt (Georgetown Univ.) 1990, (Staten Island Coll., CUNY) 1991; Hon. DSc (Tufts Univ.) 1991, (New York Medical Coll.) 1991, (Bard Coll.) 1992; Hon. DMedSc (Medical Coll. of Pennsylvania), (Karolinska Institutet, Stockholm) 2003; Hon. LLD (Gallaudet Univ.) 2005; Hon. DCL (Oxford Univ.) 2005, (Pontificia Universidad Católica del Perú) 2006; Oskar Pfister Award, American Psychiatric Asscn 1988, Harold D. Vursell Memorial Award, American Acad. and Inst. of Arts and Letters 1989, Prix Psyche' 1991, Nat. Headache Foundation Professional Support Award 1991, Presidential Citation, American Acad. of Neurology 1991, Special Presidential Award, American Neurological Asscn 1991, Communicator of the Year Award, Royal Nat. Inst. for the Deaf 1991, Award for Educ. in Neuroscience, Asscn of Neuroscience Depts and Programs 1991, Lewis Thomas Prize for the Scientist as Poet, Rockefeller Univ. 2002, Public Communication Award , NSF 2004, Mental Health Award, Coalition of Voluntary Mental Health Asscns 2004, E.A. Wood Scientific Writing Award, American Crystallographic Asscn 2004. *Address:* 2 Horatio Street, 3G, New York, NY 10014 (home); Neurological Institute, Columbia University, New York, NY 10032 USA (office). *Telephone:* (212) 633-8373 (home); (212) 305-3806 (office). *Fax:* (212) 633-8928 (home); (212) 305-1343 (office). *E-mail:* os2177@columbia.edu (office); mail@oliversacks.com (home). *Website:* www.cumc.columbia.edu/dept/ps (office); www.oliversacks.com.

SACKVILLE, Amy, MPhil, MA; British novelist and writer; b. 1981. *Education:* Leeds Univ., Exeter Coll., Oxford, Goldsmiths, Univ. of London. *Career:* worked in arts publishing before writing full-time. *Publications:* The Still Point (John Llewellyn Rhys Prize) 2010; contrib. short stories to anthologies and literary journals. *Address:* c/o Portobello Books, 12 Addison Avenue, London, W11 4QR, England (office). *Telephone:* (20) 7605-1380 (office). *Fax:* (20) 7605-1361 (office). *E-mail:* info@portobellobooks.com (office).

SADDLEMYER, (Eleanor) Ann, OC, PhD, FRSC, FRSA; Canadian academic, critic, biographer and university administrator; *Adjunct Professor, University of Victoria*; b. 28 Nov. 1932, Prince Albert; d. of Orrin Angus Saddlemyer and Elsie Sarah Saddlemyer (née Ellis). *Education:* Univ. of Saskatchewan, Queen's Univ., Kingston, ON and Bedford Coll., London. *Career:* Lecturer, Univ. of Victoria, BC 1956–57, Instructor 1960–62, Asst Prof. 1962–65, Prof. of English 1971, Adjunct Prof. 1995–; Prof. of English, Victoria Coll., Univ. of Toronto, Ont. 1971–95, Dir Grad. Centre for the Study of Drama 1972–77, 1985–86, Master of Massey Coll. 1988–95, Master Emer. and Prof. Emer. 1995–; Berg Prof., Univ. of New York, USA 1975; mem. Bd of Dirs Colin Smythe Publishers, UK 1970; Co-founder and Vice-Pres. Bd of Dirs of Theatre Plus, Toronto 1972–84; Chair. Int. Asscn for the Study of Anglo-Irish Literature 1973–76; Founder and Pres. Asscn for Canadian Theatre History 1976–77; Corresp. Scholar, Acad. of Shaw Festival Theatre 1999–; mem. Chancellor's Council Victoria Coll. 1984–; Guggenheim Fellow 1965, 1977. *Publications include:* The World of W. B. Yeats: Essays in Perspective (jtly) 1965, In Defence of Lady Gregory, Playwright 1966, The Plays of J. M. Synge (two vols) 1968, The Plays of Lady Gregory (four vols) 1971, Theatre History in Canada (co-ed) 1980–86, Theatre Business, the Letters of the First Abbey Theatre Directors 1982, The Letters of J. M. Synge (two vols) 1983, 1984, Early Stages – Theatre in Ontario 1800–1914 1990, The World's Classics J. M. Synge 1995, Later Stages: Essays on Theatre in Ontario 1800–1914 1997, Becoming George – The Life of Mrs W. B. Yeats 2002. *Honours:* Hon. LLD (Queen's) 1977; Hon. DLitt (Victoria, McGill) 1989, (Windsor) 1990, (Saskatchewan) 1991, (Toronto) 1999, (Concordia) 2000; Prov. of Ont. Distinguished Service Award 1985, British Acad. Rosemary Crawshay Award for Criticism 1986, cr. Ann Saddlemyer Book Prize for Theatre History 1989, YWCA Toronto Woman of the Year Award 1994. *Address:* 10876 Madrona Drive, Sidney, BC V8L 5N9, Canada (home). *Telephone:* (250) 656-9320 (home). *Fax:* (250) 656-9320 (home). *E-mail:* saddlemy@uvic.ca (home).

SADGROVE, Sidney Henry, (Lee Torrance); English artist, teacher and writer; b. 1920, England. *Career:* mem. Writers Guild of Great Britain. *Publications:* You've Got To Do Something 1967, A Touch of the Rabbits 1968, The Suitability Factor 1968, Stanislaus and the Princess 1969, A Few Crumbs 1971, Stanislaus and the Frog 1972, Paradis Enow 1972, Stanislaus and the Witch 1973, The Link 1975, The Bag 1977, Half Sick of Shadows 1977, Bleep 1977, All in the Mind 1977, Icary Dicary Doc 1978, Angel 1978, Filling 1979, First Night 1980, Only on Friday 1980, Hoodunnit 1984, Pawn en Prise 1985, Just for Comfort 1986, Tiger 1987, State of Play 1988, Warren 1989, Dear Mrs Comfett 1990. *Address:* Pimp Barn, Withyham, Hartfield, Sussex TN7 4BB, England (home). *Telephone:* (1892) 770486 (home).

SADUR, Nina Nikolayevna; Russian writer and playwright; b. 15 Oct. 1950, Novosibirsk; d. of Nikolai Sadur; one d. *Education:* Moscow Inst. of Culture, Moscow M. Gorky Inst. of Literature. *Career:* literary debut in Sibirskiye Ogni magazine; freelance writer; mem. USSR Writers' Union 1989. *Plays include:* Chudnaia Baba 1988, Pannočka 1989, Paradize Krasny 1990, Chichikov Brat 1999, Chardym, My Brother Chichikov, Weird Baba, Move Ahead. *Publications include:* Pronikšie 1990, New Amazons (collected stories) 1991, Witch's Tears and Other Stories 1997, Chudesnye znaki 2000, Večnaja merzlota 2004. *Honours:* Writer of the Year Award 1996. *Address:* Vagrius Publishers, Troitskaya str. 7/1, Bldg 2, 129090 Moscow, Russia (office). *Telephone:* (495) 785-09-63 (office).

ŞAFAK, Elif, PhD; Turkish writer, academic and activist; b. 1971, Strasbourg, France; one d. *Education:* Middle East Tech. Univ. *Career:* Asst Prof., Dept of Near Eastern Studies Univ. of Arizona 2004–06; Visiting Scholar in Women's Studies Univ. of Michigan 2003–04; fmrly taught at Istanbul Bilgi Univ.; activist for women's and minority rights. *Publications:* novels: Kem Gözlere Anadolu 1994, Pinhan (trans. as The Sufi) (Rumi Prize) 1997, Şehrin Aynalari 1999, Mahrem (trans. as The Gaze) (Turkish Writers' Asscn Best Novel of the

Year) 2000, Bit Palas (trans. as The Flea Palace) 2002, Araf (trans. as The Saint of Incipient Insanities) 2004, Med-Cezir 2005, Baba ve Piç (trans. as The Bastard of Istanbul) 2006, Aşk (trans. as The Forty Rules of Love) 2010; contrib. reviews to The Economist, San Francisco Chronicle, Boston Globe, The Washington Post and articles to various newspapers in Turkey. *Literary Agent:* Marly Rusoff & Associates Inc., POB 524, Bronxville, NY 10708, USA. *Telephone:* (914) 961-7939 (office); (212) 2454696 (home). *Website:* www.rusoffagency.com. *E-mail:* web@elifsafak.us (office). *Website:* www.elifsafak.us.

SAFIEVA, Gulrukhsor, MA; Tajikistani poet and politician; b. 17 Dec. 1947, d. of Nabiev Safi and Halimova Mastura; m. Rajabov Negmat; one s. *Education:* Tajik State Univ., Dushanbe. *Career:* Gen. Ed. Culture of Tajikistan 1987; mem. Supreme Soviet and Int. Comm. 1989–91; Chair. Int. Tajik Cultural Fund 1987; mem. Presidium Russian Culture Fund 1991; Pres. Int. Euro-Asian Acad. of Culture 1994–2003, Acad. of World Poetry, Moscow 1998–2003, PEN-Club of Tajikistan 2000–03. *Publications include:* more than 70 books, including Selected Poems 1983, 1984, 1985, 1987, Women of Mountains 1990, Neizvestniy Khayam (Unknown Khayam), Zan va Jang (Woman and War). *Honours:* Prize, Youth of Tajikistan 1976, Prize, Youth of USSR 1978, Helmut Hammit Award, Nat. Poet of Tajikistan Award. *Address:* Ismoili Somoni #8, Writer's Union, Dushanbe (office); Gogolstr. 18/3, Apt #7, 734001 Dushanbe, Tajikistan (home). *Telephone:* (3772) 24-56-82 (office); (3772) 215062 (home). *Fax:* (3772) 215062 (office).

SAFRANKO, Mark Peter, BA, MA; American writer, actor and songwriter; b. 23 Dec. 1950, Trenton, NJ; m. Lorrie Foster 1996; one s. *Publications:* fiction: The Favor 1987, Hopler's Statement 1998, Hating Olivia 2005, Lounge Lizard 2007, Loners 2008, Putain D'Olivia 2009, Confessions D'Un Loser 2010, God Bless America 2010, Dieu Benisse L'Amerique 2011; contrib. to South Carolina Review, North Atlantic Review, Paterson Literary Review, New Orleans Review, Ellery Queen's Mystery Magazine. *Address:* 5 Amherst Place, Montclair, NJ 07043, USA.

SAGALAYEV, Eduard Mikhailovich; Russian journalist; b. 3 Oct. 1946, Samarkand; m.; one s. one d. *Education:* Samarkand Univ., Acad. of Social Sciences Cen. Cttee CPSU. *Career:* Dir, Sr Ed. Cttee on TV and Radio Samarkand; on staff, Deputy Exec. Sec. Leninsky Put 1969–72; Exec. Sec. Komsomolets Uzbekistana Tashkent 1972–73; instructor Propaganda Div. Cen. Comsomol Cttee Moscow 1973–75; Deputy Ed.-in-Chief programmes for youth, USSR Cen. TV 1975–80, Ed.-in-Chief 1980–88; Ed.-in-Chief Information section of Cen. TV 1988–90; Dir Gen. Studio Channel IY 1990; First Deputy Chair. All-Union State Radio and TV Corpn 1991–92; Dir-Gen. TV Ostankino Jan.–July 1992; Founder and Pres. TV-6, Moscow's first ind. broadcasting co. 1992–96, 1997–; Chair. Russian TV and Broadcasting Co. (RTR) 1996–97; now Chair. Bd of Dirs and Pres. Moscow Ind. Broadcasting Corpn, Deputy Chair. Bd of Dirs ORT (Channel 1); Co-Chair. Int. TV and Radio Broadcasting Policies Comm. 1990–97; Dir-Gen. RTR Signal Co.; Chair. Bd of USSR Journalists' Union 1990–91; Chair. Confed. of Journalists' Unions of CIS 1992–97, Pres. Nat. Asscn of TV and Radio Producers of Russia 1995–; mem. Acad. of Russian TV 1995–, Fed. Tenders Comm. 2004–. *Honours:* Order of Friendship (twice); USSR State Prize 1978. *Address:* National Association of TV and Radio Producers, 101000 Moscow, Myasnitskaya str. 13/11, Russia. *Telephone:* (495) 924-24-38. *Fax:* (495) 923-23-18.

SAGER, Dirk; German broadcast journalist; *Vice-President, PEN Germany*; b. 13 Aug. 1940, Hamburg; m. Irene Dasbach-Sager; one s. one d. *Career:* fmrly with Radio RIAS Berlin; fmr corresp., ZDF TV, East Berlin, Washington DC, Chief of Moscow Office 1990–97, 1998–2004, Chief of Brandenburg Office 1997–98, Ed. Kennzeichen D. (political TV show) 1984–90; mem. PEN Germany, currently Vice-Pres. *Publications include:* Betrogenes Rubland 1996, Russlands hoher Norden 2005, Berlin-Saigon 2007, Pulverfass Russland 2008. *Honours:* Hanns-Joachim-Friedrichs-Preis 2002. *Address:* c/o Rowohlt Verlags, Hamburgerstrasse 17, 21465 Reinbek, Germany (office).

SAHGAL, Nayantara, BA; Indian journalist and novelist; b. (Nayantara Pandit), 10 May 1927, Allahabad; d. of Ranjit Sitaram Pandit and Vijaya Lakshmi Pandit; m. 1st Gautam Sahgal 1949 (divorced 1967); one s. two d.; m. 2nd E. N. Mangat Rai 1979 (died 2003). *Education:* Wellesley Coll., USA. *Career:* Adviser English Language Bd, Sahitya Akademi (Nat. Acad. of Letters), New Delhi 1972–75; Scholar-in-Residence, holding creative writing seminar, Southern Methodist Univ., Dallas, Texas 1973, 1977; mem. Indian Del. to UN Gen. Ass. 1978; Vice-Pres. Nat. Exec., People's Union for Civil Liberties 1980–85; Fellow, Radcliffe Inst. (Harvard Univ.) 1976, Wilson Int. Center for Scholars, Washington, DC 1981–82, Nat. Humanities Center, NC 1983–84; mem. jury Commonwealth Writers' Prize 1990, Chair. Eurasia Region 1991; Annie Besant Memorial Lecture (Banaras Hindu Univ.) 1992; Arthur Ravenscroft Memorial Lecture (Univ. of Leeds) 1993; mem. American Acad. of Arts and Sciences 1990. *Publications:* Prison and Chocolate Cake 1954, A Time to Be Happy 1958, From Fear Set Free 1962, This Time of Morning 1965, Storm in Chandigarh 1969, History of the Freedom Movement 1970, The Day in Shadow 1972, A Situation in New Delhi 1977, A Voice for Freedom 1977, Indira Gandhi's Emergence and Style 1978, Indira Gandhi: Her Road to Power 1982, Rich Like Us (Sinclair Prize 1985, Sahitya Akad. Award 1987) 1985, Plans for Departure 1985 (Commonwealth Writers' Prize 1987), Mistaken Identity 1988, Relationship: Extracts from a Correspondence 1994 (co-author), Point of View 1997, Before Freedom: Nehru's Letters to His Sister 1909–47 (ed.) 2000, Lesser Breeds 2003, Jawaharlal Nehru: Civilizing a Savage World 2010; contribs to newspapers and magazines including India Today. *Honours:* Foreign Hon. mem. American Acad. Arts and Sciences 1990; Hon. DLitt (Univ. of Leeds) 1997; Diploma of Honour, Int. Order of Volunteers for Peace, Salsomaggiore, Italy 1982, Sinclair Prize 1985, Doon Ratna Citizens' Council Prize 1992, Wellesley Coll. Alumni Achievement Award 2002, Pride of Doon Award 2002, Woodstock School Alumni Achievement Award 2004, Nanjanagudu Thirumalamba Award 2008, Zee TV Awadh Samman 2009. *Address:* 181B Rajpur Road, Dehra Dun 248 009 India (home). *Telephone:* (135) 2734278 (home).

SAHNI, Peush, MS; Indian surgeon and writer. *Education:* All India Inst. of Medical Sciences, New Delhi. *Career:* Assoc. Prof. Dept of Gastrointestinal Surgery and Liver Transplantation, All India Inst. of Medical Sciences; Pres. Exec. Bd, World Asscn of Medical Editors (WAME) 2004–05; Jt Sec., AIIMSONIANS;. *Publications:* co-author: Brain Death and Organ Transplantation in India 1990, Medical Books in India 1994, GI Surgery Annual (Vols II–V) 1995–98; contrib. to Diet, Digestion and Diabetes 1986, Scientific Approach to Surgery 1989, Trends in Hepatology 1990, Modern Concepts in Surgery 1992, GI Surgery Annual (Vol. I) 1994; contrib. articles to British Medical Journal, National Medical Journal of India, The Lancet, Hospital Today, British Journal of Surgery, Journal of Tropical Paediatrics. *Address:* Department of Gastrointestinal Surgery, Room 1005, PC Block, 1st Floor, Ansari Nagar, New Delhi 110 029, India (office). *E-mail:* peush_sahni@hotmail.com (home).

SAHU, N. S., MA, PhD; Indian academic and poet; b. 1 Sept. 1939; m. Shanti Sahu 1962; three s. *Career:* Lecturer in English, Dept of Education, Bhilai Steel Plant, Bhilainagar 1972–79; Lecturer 1979–92, Univ. of Gorakhpur, Reader in English 1992–98, Prof. 1998–2000; fmr Visiting Prof. Pt Ravishankar Shukla Univ., Raipur; life mem. American Studies Research Centre; mem. Int. Goodwill Soc. of India, Linguistic Soc. of India, Journal of Indian Writings in English. *Publications:* Aspects of Linguistics 1982, T. S. Eliot: The Man as a Poet, Playwright, Prophet and Critic 1988, A Study of the Works of Matthew Arnold 1988, Theatre of Protest and Anger 1988, Toponymy 1989, Christopher Marlowe and Theatre of Cruelty and Violence: A Shaping Thought 1990, An Approach to American Literature 1991, Poems 1996, Whispers at Midnight (poems) 1996, John Keats: A Sensuous Mystic 2003; contrib. to various publications. *Honours:* Gov.'s Nominee as Academician for Le Magnus Univ., Raipur 2003–05, Bharat Excellence Gold Medal and Certificate of Felicitation, Friendship Forum of India, New Delhi 2008. *Address:* Vani-Niketan, 2/955 Kota (West), Raipur 492 010, India (home). *Telephone:* (771) 2575661 (home).

SAID, Mekkaoui; Egyptian writer; b. 1955, Cairo. *Career:* has published several novels and written scripts for films and documentaries; also written for Arabic children's magazines. *Publications:* Running towards the Light (short stories) 1981, The Back Seat Passenger 2001, Taghridat al-Baga'a (novel, trans. as Cairo Swan Song) 2006. *Honours:* Egyptian State Prize for Literature 2008. *E-mail:* mekkawisaid@yahoo.com (office).

SAIL, Lawrence Richard, BA, FRSL; British poet and writer; b. 29 Oct. 1942, London, England; s. of Hellmut Sail and Barbara Wright; m. 1st Teresa Luke 1966 (divorced 1981); one s. one d.; m. 2nd Helen Bird 1994; two d. *Education:* St John's Coll., Oxford. *Career:* teacher of modern languages, Lenana School, Nairobi 1966–71, Millfield School 1973–74, Blundell's School, Devon 1975–81, Exeter School 1982–91; Ed., South West Review 1981–85; Chair. Arvon Foundation 1990–94; Programme Dir 1991, Co-Dir 1999, Cheltenham Festival of Literature; jury mem., European (Aristeion) Literature Prize 1994–96, Pres. UK jury 2011; mem. Soc. of Authors, Poetry Soc.; mem. Sr Common Room, St John's Coll., Oxford. *Publications:* Opposite Views 1974, The Drowned River 1978, The Kingdom of Atlas 1980, South West Review: A Celebration (ed.) 1985, Devotions 1987, Aquamarine 1988, First and Always (ed.) 1988, Out of Land: New and Selected Poems 1992, Building into Air 1995, The New Exeter Book of Riddles (co-ed.) 1999, The World Returning 2002, Cross-currents: Essays 2005, Light Unlocked (co-ed.) 2005, Eye-Baby 2006, Waking Dreams: New & Selected Poems 2010, Songs of the Darkness: Poems for Christmas 2010, Sift: Memories of Childhood 2010; contribs to anthologies, magazines and newspapers. *Honours:* Hawthornden Fellowship 1992, Arts Council Writer's Bursary 1993, Cholmondeley Award 2004. *Address:* Richmond Villa, 7 Wonford Road, Exeter, Devon, EX2 4LF, England. *E-mail:* lawrence@sail.eclipse.co.uk (office).

SAINT-AMAND, Pierre, BA, MA, PhD; American (b. Haitian) academic and writer; *Francis Wayland Professor, Brown University*; b. 22 Feb. 1957, Port-au-Prince, Haiti. *Career:* Asst Prof., Yale Univ. 1981–82, Stanford Univ. 1982–86; Assoc. Prof., Brown Univ. 1986–90, Prof. 1990–97, Francis Wayland Prof. 1997–; mem. Modern Language Asscn, American Soc. for Eighteenth-Century Studies. *Publications:* Diderot: Le Labyrinthe de la Relation 1984, Séduire ou la Passion des Lumières 1986, Les Lois de L'Hostilité 1992, The Libertine's Progress 1994, The Laws of Hostility 1996, The Pursuit of Laziness 2011; editor: Diderot 1984, Le Roman au dix-huitième siècle 1987, Autonomy in the Age of Enlightenment 1993, Thérèse philosophe 2000, Confession d'une jeune fille 2005. *Honours:* Chevalier, Ordre des Palmes académiques 2001; Guggenheim Fellowship 1989. *Address:* French Studies, Box 1961, Brown University, Providence, RI 02912, USA (office). *E-mail:* psa@brown.edu (office).

ST AUBIN de TERÁN, Lisa Gioconda, (Lisa Duff-Scott), FRSL; British author; *Director, Teran Foundation*; b. (Lisa Gioconda Carew), 2 Oct. 1953, London; d. of Jan Rynveld Carew and Joan Mary St Aubin; m. 1st Jaime Terán

1970 (divorced 1981); one d.; m. 2nd George Macbeth 1981 (divorced 1989, deceased); one s.; m. 3rd Robbie Duff-Scott (divorced) 1989; one d.; pnr Mees van Deth. *Education:* James Allen's Girls' School, Dulwich. *Career:* travelled widely in France and Italy 1969–71; managed sugar plantation in Venezuelan Andes 1971–78; moved to Italy 1983; fmr Vice-Pres. Umbria Film Festival, now Hon. Pres.; CEO Radiant Pictures 2002 (film production co.); f. Teran Foundation and Makua Coll. of Tourism and Agriculture, Mozambique 2004. *Screenplays:* The Slow Train to Milan (co-writer with Michael Radford), The Hacienda, The Blessing, A Woman Called Solitude, The Orange Sicilian (co-writer with Alex Macbeth, animated feature film). *Television:* wrote and presented documentaries Santos to Santa Cruz in Great Railway Journeys series (BBC) 1994, Great Railway Journeys of the World (BBC and PBS). *Radio:* adapted and read (for BBC) Off the Rails 1995, The Bay of Silence 1996. *Publications:* fiction: Keepers of the House 1982, The Slow Train to Milan 1983, The Tiger 1984, The Bay of Silence 1986, Black Idol 1987, The Marble Mountain (short stories) 1989, Joanna 1990, Nocturne 1993, Distant Landscapes (novella) 1995, The Palace 1998, The Virago Book of Wanderlust and Dreams (ed.) 1998, Southpaw (short stories) 1999, Otto: A Novel 2004, Sapa's Blessing and Other Stories 2005, Swallowing Stones 2006; poetry: The Streak 1980, The High Place 1985; memoirs: Off the Rails 1989, Venice: The Four Seasons 1992, A Valley in Italy 1994, The Hacienda 1997, My Venezuelan Years 1997, Memory Maps 2001, Mozambique Mysteries 2007. *Honours:* Somerset Maugham Award 1983, John Llewelyn Rhys Award 1983, Eric Gregory Award for Poetry 1983. *Address:* Caixa Postal 81, Ilha de Moçambique, Provincia de Nampula (home); c/o Teran Foundation, Sunset Boulevard Guest House, Mossuril Sede, Distrito Mossuril, Provincia de Nampula, Mozambique (office). *E-mail:* info@teranfoundation.org (office). *Website:* www.teranfoundation.org (office).

ST AUBYN, Edward; British writer and poet; b. 14 Jan. 1960, London, England; one s. one d. *Education:* Univ. of Oxford. *Publications:* Never Mind (Betty Trask Award 1992) 1992, Bad News 1992, Some Hope 1994, On the Edge 1998, The Patrick Melrose Trilogy (omnibus edn of first three novels) 1998, A Clue to the Exit 2000, Some Hope (trilogy) 2006, Mother's Milk (South Bank Show Annual Award for Literature 2007, Prix Femina Étranger 2007) 2006. *Literary Agent:* c/o Aitken Alexander Associates Ltd, 18–21 Cavaye Place, London, SW10 9PT, England. *Telephone:* (20) 7373-8672. *Fax:* (20) 7373-6002. *E-mail:* reception@aitkenalexander.co.uk. *Website:* www.aitkenalexander.co.uk.

ST AUBYN, Giles R., LVO, MA, FRSL; British writer; b. 11 March 1925, London. *Education:* Wellington Coll., Trinity Coll., Oxford. *Career:* head of History Dept, Eton Coll. 1961–75; mem. Soc. of Authors. *Publications:* Lord Macaulay 1952, A Victorian Eminence 1957, The Art of Argument 1957, The Royal George 1963, A World to Win 1968, Infamous Victorians 1971, Edward VII, Prince and King 1979, The Year of Three Kings 1483 1983, Queen Victoria: A Portrait 1991, Souls in Torment 2010. *Literary Agent:* Christopher Sinclair-Stevenson, 3 South Terrace, London, SW7 2TB, England. *Telephone:* (1481) 251789 (home).

ST CLAIR, William Linn, FRSL, FBA; British writer; b. 7 Dec. 1937, London, England; two d. *Education:* St John's Coll., Oxford. *Career:* fmrly, Under-Sec. Her Majesty's Treasury; Fellow Huntington Library, San Marino, CA 1985; Visiting Fellow 1981–82, Fellow All Souls Coll., Oxford 1992–96; Consultant to OECD 1992–95, to EU 1996; Visiting Fellow, Trinity Coll., Cambridge 1998–99, Fellow 1999–2006; Sr Resident Fellow, School of Advanced Study, Univ. of London 2005–, Centre for History and Econs, Univ. of Cambridge and Harvard Univ. 2008–; Chair., Open Book Publishers 2008–; mem. Council British Acad. 1996–2000; mem. Enterprise Man. Cttee, Re-Enlightenment Project 2008–. *Publications:* Lord Elgin and the Marbles 1967, That Greece Might Still Be Free 1972, Trelawny 1978, Policy Evaluation: A Guide for Managers 1988, The Godwins and the Shelleys: The Biography of a Family 1989, Executive Agencies: A Guide to Setting Targets and Judging Performance 1992, Conduct Literature for Women 1500–1640 (ed. with Irmgard Maassen) 2000, Conduct Literature for Women 1640–1710 (ed. with Irmgard Maassen) 2002, Mapping Lives: The Uses of Biography (ed. with Peter France) 2002, The Reading Nation in the Romantic Period 2004, The Political Economy of Reading 2005, The Grand Slave Emporium: Cape Coast Castle and the British Slave Trade 2006, A Gentleman of Literary Eminence: A Review Essay (co-author) 2008. *Honours:* RSL Heinemann Prize 1973, Time-Life Prize 1990, Thalassa Forum Award for Culture 2000. *Literary Agent:* c/o Deborah Rogers, Rogers, Coleridge and White, 20 Powis Mews, London, W11 1JN, England. *Website:* www.rcwlitagency.com. *Address:* 52 Eaton Place, London, SW1X 8AL, England (home). *Telephone:* (20) 7235-8329 (home). *E-mail:* ws214@cam.ac.uk (home).

SALAMEH, Nohad; Lebanese poet, writer and journalist; b. 1947, Baalbek; m. Marc Alyn. *Career:* fmr literary and arts critic, various Francophone newspapers, Lebanon; fmr Ed., culture pages, Le Réveil newspaper; moved to Paris 1989. *Publications:* poetry: L'Echo des souffles 1968, Lettres à ma muse 1971, Les enfants d'avril 1980, Folie couleur de mer 1983, L'Autre Écriture (Prix Louise Labé) 1987, Chants de l'avant-songe 1993, Les Lieux Visiteurs 1997, La Promise 2000, La Revenante 2007, Baalbek: les demeures sacrificielles (Grand Prix de Poésie Louis Montalte) 2007; novel: La Frustrée 1973. *Address:* c/o Editions du Cygne, 4, rue Vulpian, 75013 Paris, France (office). *E-mail:* editionsducygne@club-internet.fr (office). *Website:* www.editionsducygne.com (office).

SALAMON, Julie, BA, JD; American journalist, critic and writer; b. Seaman, Ohio; m. Bill Abrams; two c. *Education:* Tufts Univ., New York Univ. Law School. *Career:* fmr reporter and film critic, The Wall Street Journal; writer and TV critic, New York Times 2000–05; fmr Adjunct Prof., Tisch School of the Arts, New York Univ.; Kaiser Media Fellow 2006–07, MacDowell Colony Fellow 2010; mem. Bd of Dirs Bowery Residents Cttee. *Publications:* The Devil's Candy 1991, The Net of Dreams (Ohioana Book Award 1997) 1996, White Lies, The Christmas Tree (novella) (Audie Award/Best Inspirational Book 1997) 1996, Facing the Wind: A True Story of Tragedy and Reconciliation (Ohioana Book Award 2003) 2002, Rambam's Ladder (Ohioana Book Award 2005) 2003, Hospital 2008, Wendy and the Lost Boys 2011. *E-mail:* info@juliesalamon.com (office). *Website:* www.juliesalamon.com.

ŠALAMUN, Tomaž Franjo Rudolf, MA; Slovenian poet, writer and academic; *Visiting Professor, University of Richmond*; b. 4 July 1941, Zagreb, Yugoslavia; m. 1st Marusa Krese 1969 (divorced 1975); m. 2nd Metka Krašovec 1979; one s. one d. *Education:* Univ. of Ljubljana, Univ. of Iowa, USA, Scuola Normale Superiore, Pisa, Italy, Universidad National Autónoma de México. *Career:* Asst Curator Modern Gallery, Ljubljana 1968–70; Asst Prof., Acad. of Fine Arts, Ljubljana 1970–73; workshops Univ. of Tennessee at Chattanooga 1987–88, 1996; Visiting Writer, Vermont Coll. 1988, Berlin 2003–04, Bogliasco Foundation 2004; Consul, Slovenian Cultural Attaché, New York 1996–99; currently Distinguished Writer-in-Residence and Visiting Prof. Univ. of Richmond, USA; mem. PEN, Slovenian Writers' Asscn, Slovenian Acad. of Science and Art. *Publications:* Turbines: Twenty-One Poems 1973, Snow 1973, Pesmi (Poems) 1980, Maske (Masks) 1980, Balada za Metka Krašovec (trans. as A Ballad for Metka Krašovec) 1981, Analogije svetlobe 1982, Glas 1983, Sonet o mleku 1984, Soy realidad 1985, Ljubljanska pomlad 1986, Mera casa 1987, Ziva rana, zivi sok 1988, The Selected Poems of Tomaz Salamun 1988, Otrok in jelen 1990, Painted Desert: Poems 1991, The Shepherd, The Hunter 1992, Ambra 1994, The Four Questions of Melancholy: New and Selected Poems 1997, Crni labod 1997, Knjiga za mojega brata 1997, Homage to Hat and Uncle Guido and Eliot 1998, Morje 1999, Gozd in kelihi 2000, Feast 2000, Ballad for Metka Krašovec 2001, Table 2002, Poker 2003, Od tam 2003, Blackboards 2004, Z Arhilohom po Kikladih 2004, The Book For My Brother 2006, Woods and Chalices 2008, There's the Hand and There's the Arid Chair 2009, Levu sem zribal glavo potem sem nehal 2009, Mrzle pravljice 2010; contrib. to anthologies and periodicals. *Honours:* Mladost Prize 1969, residencies at Yaddo 1973–74, 1979, 1986, 1989, MacDowell Colony 1986, Karoly Foundation, Vence, France 1987, Maisons des écrivains étrangers, Saint-Nazaire, France 1996, Civitella Ranieri, Umbertide, Italy 1997, Bogliasco Foundation 2002, Fulbright Fellowship 1987, Jenko Prize 1988, Pushcart Prize 1994, Civitella Raneiri Fellowship 1997, Prešeren Prize 1999, Alta Marea Prize 2002, Festival Prize, Constanta 2004, Europäische Preis für Poesie, Münster (Germany) 2007, Jenko Prize 2007, Laurel Wreath, Struga Poetry Evenings, Macedonia, 2009. *Address:* Dalmatinova 11, 1000 Ljubljana, Slovenia (home). *Telephone:* (1) 2314522 (home). *E-mail:* metka.krasovec@siol.net (home); salamun.tomaz@gmail.com (home).

SALAS SOMMER, Dario, (John Baines), BA; Chilean writer, academic and philosopher; b. 4 March 1935, Santiago. *Education:* Dario Salas Coll., Santiago de Chile, Univ. of Santiago. *Career:* founder, Inst. for Hermetic Philosophy; mem. Authors' Guild of America. *Publications:* Hypsoconciencia 1965, Los Brujos Hablan 1968, El Hombre Estelar 1979, La Ciencia del Amor 1982, Existe la Mujer? 1983, El Desarrollo del Mundo Interno 1984, Moral para el Siglo XXI 1998. *Address:* Institute for Hermetic Philosophy, PO Box 8549, New York, NY 10150, USA (office). *E-mail:* ihpny@ihpny.org (office). *Website:* www.ihpny.org (office).

SALE, (John) Kirkpatrick, BA; American editor and writer; *Director, Middlebury Institute*; b. 27 June 1937, Ithaca, NY; s. of William M. Sale and Helen S. Sale; m. Faith Apfelbaum Sale 1962 (died 1999); two d. *Education:* Cornell Univ., Ithaca. *Career:* Ed. The New Leader 1959–61, New York Times Magazine 1965–68; Ed. The Nation 1981–82, Contributing Ed. 1986–2008; Dir Middlebury Inst. 2004–; mem. PEN American Center (Bd mem. 1976–97), E. F. Schumacher Soc. (Bd mem. 1980–2000). *Publications:* The Land and People of Ghana 1963, SDS 1973, Power Shift 1975, Human Scale 1980, Dwellers in the Land: The Bioregional Vision 1985, The Conquest of Paradise: Christopher Columbus and the Columbian Legacy 1990, The Green Revolution: The American Environmental Movement 1962–1992 1993, Rebels Against the Future: The Luddites and Their War on the Industrial Revolution 1995, The Fire of his Genius: Robert Fulton and the American Dream 2001, Why the Sea is Salt (poems) 2001, After Eden: The Evolution of Human Domination 2006. *Address:* 1976 Oak Tree Lane, Mount Pleasant, SC 29464, USA (home). *E-mail:* director@middleburyinstitute.org (office). *Website:* middleburyinstitute.org (office).

SALIVAROVÁ, Zdena; Canadian (b. Czechoslovakian) writer, publisher and translator; b. 21 Oct. 1933, Prague, Czechoslovakia; m. Josef Škvorecký. *Career:* fmr mem. Magic Lantern Theatre and Paravan Theatre; moved to Canada 1969; f. and Man.'68 Publishers Corpn, Toronto (Canada) 1971–94, publishing Czechoslovakian books banned in Czechoslovakia. *Publications:* Pánská jízda (three novellas, trans. as Gentlemen's Ride) 1968, Honzlová (novel, trans. as Summer in Prague) 1972, Nebe, peklo, ráj (eight novellas, trans. as Ashes, Ashes, All Fall Down) (Egon Hostovský Memorial Prize for best Czech fiction written in exile 1976) 1987, Hnuj zeme (trans. as Manure of the Earth) 1994, Krátké setkání, s vraždou (novel, with Josef Škvorecký, trans. as Brief Encounter, Including a Murder) 1999, Setkání po letech, s vraždou (novel, with Josef Škvorecký, trans. as Encounter Many Years Later, Including a Murder) 2000, Setkání na konci éry, s vraždou (novel, with Josef Škvorecký, trans. as Encounter at the End of an Era, Including a Murder) 2001. *Honours:* Hon. DLit (Toronto); Gold Medal of Masaryk Univ. 1990; Order of the White Lion 1991. *Website:* www.skvorecky.com.

SALLENAVE, Danièle; French novelist, journalist and academic; b. 28 Oct. 1940, Angers. *Career:* worked for Le Monde, Le Messager européen (review), Temps modernes; taught literature and film history at Univ. of Paris-X Nanterre 1968–2001; weekly columnist, France Culture 2009–; seventh woman since 1635 to become mem. of Acad. française (Seat 30 of Maurice Druon) April 2011. *Publications:* novels: Paysages de ruines avec personnages 1975, Le voyage d'Amsterdam ou les règles de la conversation 1977, Les Portes de Gubbio (Prix Renaudot 1980) 1980, Un printemps froid 1983, La vie fantôme 1986, Rome 1986, Conversations conjugales 1987, Adieu 1988, Le don des morts 1991, Le théâtre des idées 1991, Passages de l'Est 1991, Villes et villes 1991, Le principe de ruine 1991, Lettres mortes 1995, Les trois minutes du diable 1994, Viol 1997, À quoi sert la littérature? 1997, L'Amazone du grand Dieu 1997, Carnets de route en Palestine occupée: Gaza-Cisjordanie 1997, Stock 1998, D'amour 2002, Nos amours de la France – République, identités, régions (with Perico Legasse) 2002, dieu.com 2003, La Fraga (Grand Prix Jean Giono 2005) 2004, Quand même (Prix Marguerite Duras 2006) 2006, Castor de guerre (Prix Jean Monnet de littérature européenne du département de Charente 2008) 2008, Nous, on n'aime pas lire 2009, La vie éclaircie: Réponses à Madeleine Gobeil 2010; trans. of Italian, including The Divine Mimesis by Pier Paolo Pasolini. *Honours:* Grand prix de littérature de l' Acad. française 2005. *Address:* c/o Editions Gallimard, 5 rue Gaston-Gallimard, 75328 Paris Cedex 07, France. *Telephone:* 1-49-54-42-00. *Fax:* 1-45-44-94-03. *E-mail:* info@gallimard.fr. *Website:* www.gallimard.fr.

SALMA; Indian poet and writer; b. (Raasathi A. Rokiah), 5 May 1968, Tiruchirapalli, Trichy Dist, Tamil Nadu; m. Abdul Mallick; two s. *Career:* Tamil writer; Chair. Ponnampatti Town panchayat (village council) 2001; Chair. Tamil Nadu Social Welfare Bd 2007. *Publications include:* poetry: Oru Maalaiyum Innoru Maalaiyum (trans. as One Evening and Another Evening) 2000, Pachchai Devathai (trans. as Green Angel) 2003; fiction: Irandaam Jaamangalin Kathai (trans. as Midnight Tales) 2004. *Honours:* Amudan Adigal Literary Award 2006, Kadha Shatoria Award. *Address:* 6A/2 Muslim East Street, Thuvarankurichi, Manapparai Taluk, Tamil Nadu, India (home).

SALMON, Robert; French journalist; b. 6 April 1918, Marseille; s. of Pierre Salmon and Madeleine Blum; m. Anne-Marie Jeanprost 1942; five c. *Education:* Lycée Louis le Grand, Ecole Normale Supérieure and at the Sorbonne. *Career:* Founder Mouvement de Résistance Défense de la France; mem. Comité Parisien de Libération; Leader Paris Div., Mouvement de Libération Nationale; mem. Provisional Consultative Ass. 1944, First Constituent Ass. 1945; Founder Pres. and Dir Gen. France-Soir 1944; fmr Pres. Soc. France-Editions (Elle, Le Journal de Dimanche, Paris-Presse, etc.), Hon. Pres. 1976–; fmr Pres. Soc. de Publications Economiques (Réalités, Connaissance des Arts, Entreprise, etc.); Sec.-Gen. Fed. Nat. de la Presse 1951–77; Hon. Pres. French Cttee Int. Press Inst. 1973; mem. Admin. Council Foundation Nat. des Sciences Politiques 1973–93; Prof. Inst. d'Etudes Politiques, Univ. of Paris and Ecole Nat. d' Admin 1967–88; mem. Haut Conseil de l'audiovisuel 1973–82; fmr mem. Comm. de la République Française pour l' UNESCO. *Publications include:* Le sentiment de l'existence chez Maine de Biran 1943, Notions élémentaires de psychologie 1947, L'organisation actuelle de la presse française 1955, Information et publicité 1956, L'information économique, clé de la prospérité 1963, Chemins Faisant (two vols) 2004, La route de chaque jour me suffit 2006. *Honours:* Commdr, Légion d'honneur, Croix de guerre, Rosette de la Résistance, Médaille des évadés. *Address:* c/o Jaques André Editeur, Edition Cei, 5 Rue Bugeaud, 69006 Lyon; 4 rue Berlioz, 75116 Paris, France (home).

SALOM, Philip, BA, DipEd; Australian academic, poet and writer; b. 8 Aug. 1950, Bunbury, WA. *Education:* Curtin University. *Career:* Tutor and Lecturer, Curtin University, 1982–93; Writer-in-Residence, Singapore National University, 1989, B. R. Whiting Library/Studio, Rome, 1992; Lecturer, Murdoch University, 1994–97, Victorian College of the Arts of the University of Melbourne, 2000–01. *Publications:* The Silent Piano, 1980; The Projectionist: Sequence, 1983; Sky Poems, 1987; Barbecue of the Primitives, 1989; Playback, 1991; Tremors, 1992; Feeding the Ghost, 1993; Always Then and Now, 1993; The Rome Air Naked, 1996; New and Selected Poems, 1998; A Creative Life, 2001. *Honours:* Commonwealth Poetry Prizes, 1981, 1987; Western Australian Premier's Prize, 1984, 1988, 1992; Australia/New Zealand Literary Exchange Award, 1992; Newcastle Poetry Prize, 1996, 2000. *Address:* PO Box 273, Kerrimuir, Vic. 3129, Australia. *E-mail:* psalom@netspace.net.au.

SALTER, James, BS, MIA; American writer; b. 10 June 1925, New York, NY; m. 1st Ann Altemus 1951 (divorced 1976); two s. three d.; m. 2nd Kay Eldridge 1998. *Education:* West Point, NY, Georgetown Univ., Washington, DC. *Career:* mem. American Acad. of Arts and Letters, PEN USA; Fellow, American Acad. of Arts and Sciences 2009–. *Films:* scriptwriter: Downhill Racer, Threshold, Three. *Play:* The Death Star 1973. *Publications:* The Hunters 1957, The Arm of Flesh 1960, A Sport and a Pastime 1967, Light Years 1976, Solo Faces 1980, Dusk and Other Stories 1989, Burning the Days 1997, Cassada 2000, Bangkok (in French) 2003, Last Night 2005, Memorable Days: The Selected Letters of James Salter and Robert Phelps 2010; contribs to Paris Review, Antaeus, Grand Street, Vogue, Esquire. *Honours:* Hon. DLitt (Colorado Coll.) 2009; American Acad. of Arts and Letters Grant 1982, PEN-Faulkner Award 1989, John Steinbeck Prize 1999, Edith Wharton Prize 2000, Fadiman Medal 2003. *Address:* Box 765, Bridgehampton, NY 11932 (home); 500 North Street, Aspen, CO 81611, USA (home). *Telephone:* (631) 537-1630 (home); (970) 925-8086 (home). *E-mail:* saltereast@aol.com (home).

SALTER, Mary Jo, BA, MA; American poet, editor and academic; *Professor, The Writing Seminars, John Hopkins University*; b. (Mary Josephine Salter), 15 Aug. 1954, Grand Rapids, Mich.; d. of Albert Salter and Lormina Paradise Salter; m. Brad Leithauser 1980 (divorced 2011); two d. *Education:* Harvard Univ., Univ. of Cambridge, UK. *Career:* Instructor, Harvard Univ. 1978–79; Staff Ed. Atlantic Monthly 1978–80; Poet-in-Residence, Robert Frost Place 1981; Lecturer in English, Mount Holyoke Coll., South Hadley, Mass 1984, Emily Dickinson Lecturer in Humanities, Emily Dickinson Sr Lecturer 1995–2007; Poetry Ed., The New Republic 1992–95; lyricist for songs by Fred Hersch 2004–; Prof., The Writing Seminars, Johns Hopkins Univ. 2007–, Andrew W. Mellon Prof. in the Humanities 2009–; mem. International PEN, Poetry Soc. of America (Vice-Pres. 1995–2006) –2007. *Play:* Falling Bodies 2004. *Music:* lyricist for 'Rooms of Light', music by Fred Hersch, performed at Lincoln Center 2007. *Publications:* Henry Purcell in Japan 1985, Unfinished Painting 1989, The Moon Comes Home 1989, Sunday Skaters: Poems 1994, Norton Anthology of Poetry (co-ed. 4th edn 1996, 5th edn 2005), A Kiss in Space: Poems 1999, Open Shutters: Poems 2003, A Phone Call to the Future: New and Selected Poems 2008, Selected Poems of Amy Clampitt (ed.) 2010; contrib. to periodicals. *Honours:* Hon. DLitt (Amherst Coll.) 2010; The Nation Discovery Prize 1983, Nat. Endowment for the Arts Fellowship 1983–84, Lamont Prize in Poetry 1988, Guggenheim Fellowship 1993, Amy Lowell Scholarship 1995, Bogliasco Fellowship 1998, Rockefeller Fellowship 2006, Theodore Roethke Prize 2010. *Address:* The Writing Seminars, Johns Hopkins University, 3400 N Charles Street, Baltimore, MD 21218, USA (office). *Telephone:* (410) 516-7565 (office). *E-mail:* mjsalter@jhu.edu (office). *Website:* writingseminars.jhu.edu (office).

SALZBERG, Steven, BA, MS, MPhil, PhD; American scientist and writer; *Director, Center for Bioinformatics and Computational Biology and Horvitz Professor, University of Maryland*; m. Claudia Salzberg; two d. *Education:* Univ. of Yale, Univ. of Harvard. *Career:* research scientist and sr knowledge engineer, Applied Expert Systems Inc. 1985–87; Assoc. in Research, Harvard Business School 1988–89; Asst Prof. 1989–96, Assoc. Prof. 1996–99, Research Prof. 1999, Dept of Computer Science, jt Research Prof. 1999, Dept of Biology, Johns Hopkins Univ.; Investigator 1997, Sr Dir of Bioinformatics 1998, Inst. for Genomic Research; currently Dir Center for Bioinformatics and Computational Biology and Horvitz Prof., Univ. of Maryland. *Publications:* Learning with Nested Generalized Exemplars 1990, Computational Methods in Molecular Biology (ed.), contrib. to Science, Nucleic Acids Research. *Address:* Center for Bioinformatics and Computational Biology, 3115 Biomolecular Sciences Building 296, University of Maryland, College Park, MD 20742, USA (office). *Telephone:* (301) 405-5936 (office). *E-mail:* salzberg@umiacs.umd.edu (office). *Website:* www.cbcb.umd.edu/~salzberg (office).

SAMADOGHLU, Vagif; Azerbaijani (Azeri) poet; b. 5 June 1939, Baku; s. of the late Samad Vurghun. *Education:* Tchaikovsky Conservatory, Moscow. *Career:* mem. Azerbaijan Milli Majlis (Parl.); Nat. Poet of Azerbaijan 2000; Parl. Rep. to Council of Europe 2001–. *Publications:* poetry: Yoldan telegram 1968, Gunun baxti 1972, Man burdayam, Ilahi 1996, Uzaq Yashil Ada 1999; prose: Baxt uzuyu (drama) 1999, also essays.

SAMARAS, Zoe, BS, MA, PhD; Greek academic; b. 1935, Karpathos; d. of Constantinos Malaxos and Maria Malaxos; m. Nicholas Samaras 1960 (died 1981); one s. *Education:* Columbia Univ., NY, USA. *Career:* Lecturer in French, Columbia Univ. 1960; Lecturer, City Univ. of New York, USA 1965, Asst Prof. of French and French Literature 1968; Prof. of French Literature and Theory of Literature, Aristotle Univ. of Thessaloniki 1978, Chair. Dept of French Literature 1978–92, Chair. Grad. Program of French Literature; Visiting Prof. of Theory of Literature, Univ. of Athens 1987, 1995, 1998, Prof. Emer. 2002. *Publications include:* The Comic Element of Montaigne's Style 1971, L'Enfant du Taygète 1974, Le Règne de Cronos 1983, Text Perspectives (in Greek) 1987, Montaigne: Espace Voyage Ecriture (ed.) 1995, Approaches bachelardienne des œuvres littéraires (ed.) 1996, Simulation of Theatrical Discourse (in Greek) 1996, Miltos Sahtouris (in Greek) 1997; poetry (in Greek): For Maria 1991, Days of Dryness 1994, The Passage of Eurydice 1997, The Sanctuary of the Sign (in Greek; Best Book Prize) 2002, Le discours spéculaire 2003; numerous contrib. to professional journals. *Honours:* Officier de l'Ordre nat. du Mérite (France) 1988; Silver Medal of the City of Paris 1988, Montaigne Int. Award 1992, La Verbe et la Scène: Etudes sur la Littérature et le Théâtre en l'Honneur de Zoe Samara, Paris, Champion 2005. *Address:* Aristotle University of Thessaloniki, Faculty of Philosophy, 54124 Thessaloniki (office); Vassilikou 10, 54636 Thessaloniki, Greece (home). *Telephone:* (2310) 997491 (office); (2310) 212418 (home). *Fax:* (2310) 997491 (office). *E-mail:* zsamara@frl.auth.gr (office). *Website:* www.frl.auth.gr (office).

SAMBROOK, (Arthur) James, BA, MA, PhD; British academic and writer; b. 5 Sept. 1931, Nuneaton, Warwicks.; m. Patience Ann Crawford 1961; four s. *Education:* Worcester Coll., Oxford, Univ. of Nottingham. *Career:* Lecturer, St David's Coll., Lampeter, Wales 1957–64; Lecturer, Univ. of Southampton 1964–71, Sr Lecturer 1971–75, Reader 1975–81, Prof. of English 1981–92, Prof. Emer. 1992–. *Publications:* A Poet Hidden: The Life of R. W. Dixon 1962,

The Scribleriad, etc (ed.) 1967, William Cobbett 1973, James Thomson: The Seasons (ed.) 1981, English Pastoral Poetry 1983, The Eighteenth Century: The Intellectual and Cultural Context of English Literature 1700–1789 1986, Liberty, the Castle of Indolence and Other Poems 1986, James Thomson 1700–1748: A Life: Biographical, Critical 1992, William Cowper: The Task and Other Poems (ed.) 1994, With the Rank and Pay of a Sapper 1998; contrib. to reference books, including the Oxford Dictionary of National Biography, professional journals and general periodicals. *Address:* 36 Bursledon Road, Hedge End, Southampton, SO30 0BX, England (home). *Telephone:* (1489) 782552 (office). *E-mail:* jamessambrook@hotmail.com (office).

SAMMAN, Ghada al-, MA; Syrian writer, novelist and poet; b. 1942, al-Shamiya, Damascus; d. of the late Dr Ahmed al-Samman; m. Bashir Al Daouq; one s. *Education:* Syrian Univ. (now Damascus Univ.), American Univ. of Beirut, Lebanon. *Career:* left Damascus in 1963; worked as journalist in Beirut and Europe; works written in Arabic and trans. into English, French, Italian, Spanish, Russian, Polish, German, Japanese and Farsi; f. Ghada Samman publishing house. *Publications:* short story collections: Your Eyes are My Destiny 1962, No Sea in Beirut 1965, Foreigners' Nights 1966, The Departure of Old Ports 1973, Al Qamar Al Marb'a (trans. as Square Moon: Supernatural Tails 1999); novels: Al 'Shiqa fi Muhabra, Al Bahru Yuhakimu Samaka, Al Houb min al Warid Ila Warid, Al Qalb Nawaris Wahid, Al Rowayat Al Mathiliya, Al Shadu 'Aks Al Rih, Al Sibaha fi Bahar Al Shaytan, Ghurba Tahet Al Sfer, I'itaqal Li Hadha Hariba, Ila Badia Li Hadha Houb, Laylat al Milyar, Ra'sha Al Huria, Safaara Anzaar Rahkhil Rasi, Sahra Tankoriat Lil Mouti, Shahwa Janati, Task'a Rakhl Jarh, Beirut 75 (in trans.) 1974, Beirut Nightmares (in trans.) 1977, The Eve of Night of the First Billion (in trans.) 1986, Al-Riwaya al-Mustahila: Fusayfisa Dimashqiya (The Impossible Novel: A Damascene Mosaic) (autobiog.) 1997; other: The Unfinished Works (articles), Love (poems) 1973, I Declare Love Upon You (poems) 1976, Rasa'elul Hanin Ilal Yasmin (Letters of Longing for Jasmine, poems) 1996, A Costume Party for the Dead 2003, also literary criticism; contrib. to newspapers and magazines including al-Usbu' al Arabi, al-Hawadith. *Address:* c/o Quartet Books, 27 Goodge Street, London, W1T 2LD, England. *Telephone:* (20) 7636-3992. *E-mail:* info@quartetbooks.co.uk.

SAMPSON, Fiona Ruth, ARCM, FRSL, MA, PhD; British poet and editor; *Editor, Poetry Review*; b. London, England. *Education:* Royal Acad. of Music, Salzburg Mozarteum, Univ. of Oxford and Univ. of Nijmegen, The Netherlands. *Career:* series of residencies pioneering writing in health care in UK from 1988; AHRC Research Fellow, Oxford Brookes Univ. 2002–05; contributing poetry critic for The Irish Times, The Guardian, The Independent, Times Literary Supplement; judge, Foyle Young Poet of the Year 2004, Irish Times Poetry Award 2006, Ind. Foreign Fiction Prize 2009; Founder-Ed. Orient Express 2002–; Ed. Poetry Review 2005–; Fellow in Performance and Creativity, Univ. of Warwick 2008–09; Distinguished Writer, Kingston Univ. 2009–. *Publications:* BirthChart (chapbook) 1992, Picasso's Men 1994, The Self on the Page (with C. Hunt) 1998, The Healing Word 1999, Folding the Real 2001, Travel Diary 2004, Creative Writing in Health and Social Care 2004, Evening Brings Everything Back (trans. of Jaan Kaplinski) 2004, A Fine Line (co-ed with A. Buchler and J. Boase-Beier) 2004, Hotel Casino (chapbook) 2004, The Distance Between Us 2005, Writing: Self and Reflexivity (with C. Hunt) 2005, Setting the Echo (chapbook) 2005, Day (trans. of Amir Or) 2006, Common Prayer 2007, On Listening 2007, A Century of Poetry Review 2009, Poetry Writing 2009, Rough Music 2010. *Honours:* Newdigate Prize 1998, Zlaten Prsten (Macedonia) 2004, Charles Angoff Award 2006, Cholmondeley Award for Poetry 2009. *Address:* Poetry Review, Poetry Society, 22 Betterton Street, London, WC2H 9BX, England (office). *Telephone:* (20) 7420-9883 (office). *E-mail:* fsampson@poetrysociety.org.uk (office). *Website:* www.poetrysociety.org.uk (office).

SANCHEZ, Clara; Spanish writer; b. 1955, Guadalajara. *Education:* Universidad Complutense, Madrid. *Career:* fmr univ. lecturer; broadcaster; columnist, El País. *Publications:* Piedras preciosas 1989, No es distinta la noche 1990, El palacio verado 1993, Desde el mirador 1996, El misterio de todos los días 1999, Últimas noticias del paraíso (Premio Alfaguara de Novela) 2000, Un millón de luces 2004, Presentimientos 2008, Lo que esconde tu nombre (Premio Nadal 2010) 2009. *Honours:* Premio Germán Sánchez Ruipérez. *Address:* c/o Santillana Ediciones S.L., Calle Torrelaguna 60, 28043 Madrid, Spain (office). *E-mail:* alfarguara@santillana.es (office); contacto@clarasanchez.com (office). *Website:* www.alfaguara.com (office); www.clarasanchez.com.

SANCHEZ, Lavinia (see Elmslie, Kenward Gray)

SANCHEZ, Sonia, BA, PhD; American poet, dramatist, writer and academic; b. (Wilsonia Benita Driver), 9 Sept. 1934, Birmingham, Ala; m. Etheridge Knight (divorced); two s. one d. *Education:* Hunter Coll., City Univ. of New York, New York Univ., Wilberforce Univ. *Career:* Instructor, San Francisco State Coll. 1967–69; Lecturer, Univ. of Pittsburgh 1969–70, Rutgers Univ. 1970–71, Manhattan Community Coll. 1971–73, CUNY 1972; Assoc. Prof., Amherst Coll. 1972–73, Univ. of Pennsylvania, 1976–77; Assoc. Prof., Temple Univ. 1977–79, Prof. of English, then Laura Carnell Chair. in English 1979–99 (retd). *Publications:* poetry: Homecoming 1969, WE a BaddDDD People 1970, Liberation Poem 1970, It's a New Day: Poems for Young Brothas and Sistuhs 1971, Ima Talken bout the Nation of Islam 1971, Love Poems 1973, A Blues Book for Blue Black Magical Women 1974, I've Been a Woman: New and Selected Poems 1978, Homegirls and Handgrenades 1984, Under a Soprano Sky 1987, Wounded in the House of a Friend 1995, Does Your House Have Lions? 1995, Like the Singing Coming Off the Drums: Love Poems 1998, Shake Loose my Skin: New and Selected Poems 1999, Ash 2001, Morning Haiku 2009; plays: Sister Son/ji 1969, The Bronx is Next 1970, Dirty Hearts '72 1973, Uh, Uh: But How Do it Free Us? 1974, Malcolm Man/Don't Live Here no Mo' 1979, I'm Black When I'm Singing, I'm Blue When I Ain't 1982, Black Cats and Uneasy Landings 1995; juvenile fiction: The Adventures of Fat Head, Small Head and Square Head 1973, A Sound Investment 1979; other: Crisis in Culture 1983; editor: Three Hundred Sixty Degrees of Blackness Comin' at You 1972, We Be Word Sorcerers: 25 Stories by Black Americans 1973. *Honours:* PEN Award 1969, American Acad. of Arts and Letters Award 1970, Nat. Endowment for the Arts Award 1978, Smith Coll. Tribute to Black Women Award 1982, Lucretia Mott Award 1984, Before Columbus Foundation Award 1985, PEN Fellow 1993, Robert Frost Medal 2001. *Address:* c/o Beacon Press, 25 Beacon Street, Boston, MA 02108, USA (office). *Website:* www.beacon.org (office).

SÁNCHEZ PIÑOL, Albert; Spanish anthropologist and writer; b. 1965, Barcelona. *Education:* Univ. of Barcelona. *Publications:* short stories: Pallassos i monstres 2000, Les edats d'or 2001; novels: La pell freda (trans. as Cold Skin) (Premio Ojo Critico Narrativa) 2002, Pandora en el Congo (Premio Serra d'Or 2006) 2005. *Address:* c/o Isabel Martí, Edicions La Campana, Muntaner 248, 1r 2a, 08021 Barcelona, Spain. *E-mail:* campana@edicionslacampana.cat. *Website:* www.edicionslacampana.cat.

SÁNCHEZ VIDAL, Agustín, BPhil, DPhil; Spanish essayist, screenwriter, novelist and academic; *Professor of Film History, Universidad De Zaragoza*; b. 1948, Cilleros of Bastida, Salamanca. *Education:* Univ. of Zaragoza. *Career:* taught Spanish literature at Universidad De Zaragoza, Prof. of Film History 1991–; published several studies related to Spanish avant-garde movements. *Publications:* Vida y opiniones de Luis Buñuel 1985, Buñuel, Lorca, Dalí: el enigma sin fin (Premio Espejo de España) 1988, El cine de Carlos Saura 1988, Borau 1990, El cine de Florián Rey 1991, El cine de Segundo de Chomón 1992, Luis Buñuel 1992, Retrato de Carlos Saura 1993, El mundo de Luis Buñuel 1993 and 2000, Los Jimeno y los orígenes del cine en Zaragoza 1994, El Siglo de la Luz 1997, Historia del cine 1998, El rabo por desollar 1999, La llave maestra 2005, Nudo de Sangre (Premio Primavera de Novela) 2008, Esclava de nadie 2010. *Address:* Universidad De Zaragoza, 12 Pedro Cerbuna, 50009 Zaragoza, Spain (office). *Telephone:* (97) 6761000 (office). *Fax:* (97) 6761005 (office). *E-mail:* relint@unizar.es (office). *Website:* www.unizar.es (office).

SANDEMO, Margit; Norwegian writer; b. (Margit Underdal), 23 April 1924, Lena, Østre Toten, Valdres; d. of the late Anders Underdal and the late Elsa Reuterskiöld; m. Asbjørn Sandemo; three c. *Career:* has written over 170 novels, mostly in historical fantasy genre including several series. *Publications:* novels: Historien om en fjelldal (trilogy) 1992–98, Legenden om den øde skogen 1993, Drømmen om en venn 1997, Tessa 1997, Ensom i verden 1998, I nattens tystnad 1998, Skattejakten 1999, Vargens lilla lamm 2000, Den mörka sanningen 2001; Sandemo series: 40 vols (originally published in women's magazines) 1990–94; Sagaen om Isfolket series: 47 vols including Trollbundet, Heksejakten, Avgrunnen, Dødssynden, Lengsel, Den onde arven, Galgeblomsten, Dødens have, Et streif av ømhet, Demonenes fjell, Den onde dagen, Legenden om Marco, Det svarte vannet, Er det noen der ute? 1982–89; Heksemesteren series: Trolldom 1991, Lyset i dine øyne 1991, Når mørket faller på 1992, Ondskapens ansikt 1992, Ildprøven 1992, Alvelys 1992, Vergeløs 1993, Rittet mot vest 1993, Ildsverdet 1993, Dvergemål 1993, Skammens Hus 1993, Sagn om glemte riker 1993, Klosteret i Tårenes Dal 1994, Frostens datter 1994, Inn i det ukjente 1994; Sagnet om Lysets rike series: 20 vols including Bak portene, Móri og Isfolket, Piken som ikke kunne si nei, Mannen fra Tåkedalen, Johannesnatten, Skrømt, Det bevende hjerte, Ond saga, Fra toppen og popover, Så dyp en lengsel, Drepende uskyld, Et hav av kjærlighet 1995–99; De svarte ridderne series: I skyggen av et tegn 2000, Dit ingen går 2000, Vindens klage 2001, Trollmannens merke 2002, Skygger 2002, Tistel blant roser 2002, Amulettene 2002, Jernjomfruen 2003, Demonens vinger 2003, Det ukjente 2003, Steinenes stillhet 2003, Vinterdrøm 2003; Blålys series: Alarm, Anrop, Vänskap?, Nödsignaler, Stjärnstoft, Glimt av evigheten 2004; Trollruner series: Skogen bortenfor dagen 2005, Sandhammaren 2005, Der vinden får hvile 2006, Blind mane 2006, Måneheksen 2006, Svartalver 2006, Den blå jorden 2006, Steinulven 2007, Den de glemte 2007, Kom nærmere 2007, Dagen gryr 2007; Legend of the Ice People series (in English trans.): Spellbound, Witch-Hunt, Depths of Darkness, Yearning, Mortal Sin, Evil Inheritance 2008. *Address:* c/o The Tagman Press, Media House, Burrel Road, St Ives, Cambs., PE27 3LE, England (office). *Telephone:* (845) 644-4186 (office). *E-mail:* chrissy@tagmanpress.co.uk (office). *Website:* www.tagmanpress.co.uk (office); www.margitsandemo.co.uk.

SANDERS, (James) Edward, BA; American poet, writer, singer and lecturer; b. 17 Aug. 1939, Kansas City, Mo.; m. Miriam Kittell 1961; one c. *Education:* New York Univ. *Career:* Ed. and Publisher, Fuck You/A Magazine of the Arts 1962–65; Founder and lead singer, The Fugs, satiric folk-rock-theatre group 1964–69, 1985–; Owner, Peace Eye Bookstore, New York City 1964–70; Visiting Prof. of Language and Literature, Bard Coll., New York 1979, 1983; Founder and Ed., Woodstock Journal; lectures, readings, performances throughout the US and Europe; mem. New York Foundation for the Arts, PEN. *Compositions:* musical drama: The Municipal Power Cantata 1977, The Karen Silkwood Cantata 1979, Star Peace 1986, Cassandra 1992. *Recordings:* albums: with The Fugs: The Village Fugs 1965, The Fugs 1966, Virgin Fugs 1967, Tenderness Junction 1968, It Crawled into my Hand,

Honest 1968, Belle of Avenue A 1969, Golden Filth 1970, Refuse to be Burnt Out 1984, No More Slavery 1985, Star Peace 1986, The Fugs Final CD 2003, Be Free 2010; solo: Sanders' Truckstop 1969, Beer Cans on the Moon 1972, Songs in Ancient Greek 1990, American Bard 1996. *Publications include:* poetry: Poem from Jail 1963, Peace Eye 1966, Egyptian Hieroglyphics 1973, 20,000 A.D. 1976, Hymn to Maple Syrup and Other Poems 1985, Poems for Robin 1987, The Ocean Étude and Other Poems 1990, Thirsting for Peace in a Raging Century: Selected Poems 1961–1985 1987, Hymn to the Rebel Cafe: Poems 1987–1991 1993, Cracks of Grace 1994, Chekhov: A Biography in Verse 1995, 1968: A History in Verse 1997, America: A History in Verse, nine vols 2000–, The Poetry and Life of Allen Ginsberg 2000, Stanzas for Social Change 2004, Poems for New Orleans 2007, This Morning's Joy 2008, Revs of the Morrow 2008; fiction: Shards of God: A Novel of the Yippies 1970, Tales of Beatnik Glory, four vols 1975–2003, Fame and Love in New York 1980; non-fiction: The Family: The Story of Charles Manson's Dune Buggy Attack Battalion 1971, Vote! (with Abbie Hoffman and Jerry Rubin) 1972, Investigative Poetry 1976, The Z-D Generation 1980, The Family: The Manson Group and Aftermath 1990. *Honours:* Frank O'Hara Prize, Modern Poetry Asscn 1967, National Endowment for the Arts Awards 1966, 1970, Fellowship 1987–88, Guggenheim Fellowship 1983–84, American Book Award 1988. *Address:* PO Box 729, Woodstock, NY 12498, USA (office). *Telephone:* (845) 679-6556 (office). *Fax:* (845) 679-3290 (office). *E-mail:* info@woodstockjournal.com (office); info@thefugs.com (office). *Website:* www.woodstockjournal.com (office); www.thefugs.com.

SANDERS, Louis; French novelist; b. 1964. *Education:* Sorbonne, Univ. of Paris, Univ. of Cambridge, UK. *Publications include:* Death in the Dordogne 1999, The Englishman's Wife 2000, Comme des hommes 2000, An Ignoble Profession 2002, Rivages Noir 2004, La lecture du feu 2011. *Address:* c/o Editions Payot & Rivages, 106, boulevard Saint-Germain, 75006 Paris, France. *E-mail:* editions@payotrivages.com.

SANDERS, Noah (see Blount Jr, Roy Alton)

SANDERS, Scott Russell, BA, PhD; American academic and writer; *Distinguished Professor Emeritus, Indiana University*; b. 26 Oct. 1945, Memphis, Tenn.; m. Ruth Ann McClure 1967, one s. one d. *Education:* Brown Univ., Univ. of Cambridge, UK. *Career:* Literary Ed. Cambridge Reviews 1969–70, Contributing Ed. 1970–71; Fiction Ed. Minnesota Review 1976–80; Fiction Columnist, Chicago Sun-Times 1977–84; Contributing Ed. North American Review 1982–; Asst Prof. of English, Indiana Univ. 1971–1995, Distinguished Prof. of English 1995–2009, now Distinguished Prof. Emer.; Woodrow Wilson Fellowship 1967–68, Nat. Endowment for the Arts Fellowship 1983–84, Indiana Arts Comm. Master Fellowship 1984, 1990–91, Lilly Endowment Open Fellowship 1986–87, Guggenheim Fellowship 1992–93;. *Publications:* Fiction: Wilderness Plots: Tales About the Settlement of the American Land, 1983, Fetching the Dead (short stories) 1984, Wonders Hidden: Audubon's Early Years (novella) 1984, Terrarium (novel) 1985, Hear the Wind Blow (short stories) 1985, Bad Man Ballad (novel) 1986, The Engineer of Beasts (novel) 1988, The Invisible Country (novel) 1989; other: D. H. Lawrence: The World of the Major Novels 1974, Stone Country 1985 (revised edn as In Limestone Country 1991), Audubon Reader: The Best Writings of John James Audubon 1986, The Paradise of Bombs (essays) 1987, Secrets of the Universe (essays) 1991, Staying Put: Making a Home in a Restless World 1993, Writing from the Center (essays) 1995, Hunting for Hope 1998, The Force of Spirit 2001, A Private History of Awe 2006, A Conservationist Manifesto 2009; children's books: Aurora Means Dawn 2007, Warm as Wool 2007, The Floating House 2011; contribs: anthologies, journals, and magazines. *Honours:* Associated Writing Programs Award for Non-Fiction 1987, PEN Syndicated Fiction Award 1988; Kenyon Review Award for Literary Excellence 1991, Ohioana Book Award in Non-Fiction 1994, Lannan Literary Award in Non-Fiction 1995. *Address:* Department of English, Indiana University, Bloomington, IN 47405-7103, USA. *E-mail:* sanders1@indiana.edu. *Website:* www.scottrussellsanders.com.

SANDERSON, Anne Hilary, BA, MA, MLitt; British poet and writer; b. 13 Jan. 1944, Brighton, England; m. Michael Sanderson 1976. *Education:* St Anne's College, Oxford. *Career:* English Lectrice, École Normale Supérieure de Jeunes Filles, University of Paris, 1969–71; Lecturer in European Literature, University of East Anglia, 1972–98; mem. Asscn of Christian Writers; Norwich Writers' Circle; Norwich Poetry Group; Playwrights East. *Publications:* contrib. to anthologies and periodicals, including poems in Poetry Now, Peace & Freedom, Purple Patch, The Poetry Church, Advance! Isthmus, Triumph Herald, Reflections, Tree Spirit, The Firing Squad, All Year Round; articles in Studies on Voltaire & the 18th Century, Jeunesse de Racine, Norwich Papers. *Honours:* Prix Racine 1969, third prize Hilton House Nat. Open Poetry Awards for Collections 1998, 1999.

SANDERSON, John Michael, MA, PhD; British academic and writer; *Professor Emeritus of Economic and Social History, University of East Anglia*; b. 23 Jan. 1939, Glasgow, Scotland. *Education:* Queens' College, Cambridge. *Career:* Prof. of Economic and Social History, Univ. of East Anglia, now Prof. Emer.; General Ed., Cambridge Univ. Press Economic History Society Studies in Economic and Social History Series 1992–98; Council, Economic History Society 1994–2000; mem. Economic History Society. *Publications:* The Universities and British Industry, 1850–1970 1972, The Universities in the 19th Century 1975, Education, Economic Change and Society in England, 1780–1870 1983, From Irving to Olivier, A Social History of the Acting Profession in England, 1880–1983 1984, Educational Opportunity and Social Change in England, 1900–1980s 1987, The Missing Stratum, Technical School Education in England, 1900–1990s 1994, Education and Economic Decline, 1870–1990s 1999, The History of the University of East Anglia, Norwich 2002; contributions: Economic History Review, Journal of Contemporary History, Contemporary Record, Business History, Northern History, Past and Present, History of Education. *Address:* School of History, University of East Anglia, Norwich NR4 7TJ, England (office).

SANDOR, Anna, BA; Canadian (b. Hungarian) screenwriter; b. Budapest, Hungary; d. of Paul and Agnes Elizabeth (née Laszlo) Sandor; m. (divorced); one d. *Education:* Harbord Coll. Inst., Toronto and Univ. of Windsor. *Career:* has lived in USA since 1989; Lecturer in Writing for TV Summer Inst. of Film, Ottawa; held screenwriting workshops; Co-Chair. Crime Writers of Canada 1985–86; mem. Asscn of Canadian TV and Radio Artists (ACTRA) Writers' Council 1985, Acad. of TV Arts and Sciences, Writers' Guild of America and Canada. *TV productions:* films: A Population of One 1980, Charlie Grant's War 1985, The Marriage Bed 1986, Mama's Going to Buy You a Mockingbird 1987–88, Martha, Ruth and Edie 1988, Two Men (Edgar Dale Award for Excellence in Screenwriting 1989) 1988, Tarzan in Manhattan (jtly) 1989, Stolen: One Husband (jtly) 1990, Miss Rose White (Hallmark Hall of Fame) 1992, Family of Strangers (jtly) 1993, For the Love of My Child – The Anissa Ayala Story 1993, Amelia Earhart: The Final Flight 1994, Gift of Love – The Daniel Huffman Story 1999, My Louisiana Sky 2001, Tiger Cruise (jtly) 2004, Felicity 2005, Molly 2006, Mom, Dad and Her 2008, Accidental Friendships 2008, A Kiss at Midnight 2008; series: Running Man 1982–83, High Card 1982–83, Seeing Things (jtly) 1983–85, Danger Bay (Gold Medal, New York Int. Film and TV Festival) 1986–88, On the Record, Tarzan (Exec. Producer) 1991; sitcoms: King of Kensington 1975–80, Flappers, Hangin' In. *Honours:* Prix Anik 1981, 1985, 1986, 1989, ACTRA for Best Writer Original Drama Award 1986, Margaret Collier Award for Lifetime Achievement, Canadian Acad. 1986, Chris Plaque for Best Script (Columbus Film Festival) 1989, Humanitas Award 1993, 2002, Writers' Guild of America Award 2001. *Literary Agent:* c/o Steve Weiss, William Morris Agency, One William Morris Place, Beverly Hills, CA 90212, USA. *Telephone:* (310) 859-4000. *Website:* www.wma.com.

SANDOZ, (George) Ellis, Jr, BA, MA, PhD; American political scientist, professor of political science and writer; *Hermann Moyse Jr Distinguished Professor of Political Science and Director, Eric Voeglin Institute for American Renaissance Studies, Louisiana State University*; b. 10 Feb. 1931, New Orleans, La; s. of George Ellis Sandoz and Ruby Odom Sandoz; m. Therese Alverne Hubley 1957; two s. two d. *Education:* Louisiana State Univ., Univ. of North Carolina, Georgetown Univ., Univs. of Heidelberg and Munich, Germany. *Career:* Instructor to Prof., Louisiana Polytechnic Inst. 1959–68; Prof. and Head of Dept of Political Science, East Texas State Univ. 1968–78; Prof. of Political Science 1978–, Dir Eric Voegelin Inst. for American Renaissance Studies 1987–, Hermann Moyse Jr Distinguished Prof. of Political Science, Louisiana State Univ.; Fellow, Germanistic Soc. of America 1964–65; Henry E. Huntington Library Fellow 1986–87; mem. American Historical Asscn, American Political Science Asscn, Federalist Soc., Org. of American Historians, Philadelphia Soc., Southern Political Science Asscn, Southwestern Political and Social Science Asscns, Eric Voegelin Soc. (Founder-Sec. 1985–). *Publications include:* Political Apocalypse: A Study of Dostoevsky's Grand Inquisitor 1971, Conceived in Liberty: American Individual Rights Today 1978, A Tide of Discontent: The 1980 Elections and Their Meaning (ed.) 1981, The Voegelianian Revolution: A Biographical Introduction 1981, Eric Voegelin's Thought: A Critical Appraisal (ed.) 1982, Election '84: Landslide Without a Mandate? (co-ed. with Cecil V. Crabb, Jr) 1985, A Government of Laws: Political Theory, Religion and the American Founding 1990, Political Sermons of the American Founding Era, 1730–1805 (ed.) 1991, index 1996, Eric Voegelin's Significance for the Modern Mind (ed.) 1991, The Roots of Liberty: Magna Carta, Ancient Constitution, and the Anglo-American Tradition of Rule of Law (ed.) 1993, Politics of Truth and Other Untimely Essays: The Crisis of Civic Consciousness 1999, Republicanism, Religion and the Soul of America 2006; contrib. and volume ed. to The Collected Works of Eric Voegelin (gen. ed. of series, 34 vols) 1986–2009, and to scholarly books and professional journals. *Honours:* Hon. PhD (Palacky Univ., Olomouc, Czech Repub.) 1995, Dr en Ciencias Politicas (Univ. Francisco Marroquin, Guatemala) 2002; Fulbright Scholar 1964–65, Fulbright 40th Anniversary Distinguished American Scholar, Italy 1987, Distinguished Research Master and Univ. Gold Medal, Louisiana State Univ. 1993, Medal and Rector's Certificate 1994. *Address:* c/o Eric Voegelin Institute for American Renaissance Studies, Louisiana State University, 240 Stubbs Hall, Baton Rouge, LA 70803 (office); 2843 Valcour Aime Avenue, Baton Rouge, LA 70820, USA (home). *Telephone:* (225) 578-2141 (office). *Fax:* (225) 578-4766 (office). *E-mail:* esandoz@lsu.edu (home). *Website:* www.ericvoegelin.org.

SANDS, Martin (see Burke, John Frederick)

SANDS, Sarah; British editor and writer; *Editor, London Evening Standard*; b. (Sarah Harvey), 3 May 1961, Cambridge; m. 1st Julian Sands; one s.; m. 2nd Kim Fletcher; two c. *Education:* Goldsmiths Coll., London. *Career:* worked at Kent and Sussex Courier 1983–86; worked at Evening Standard, London, as diary reporter, Ed. of the Londoner's Diary, later Features Ed., then Assoc. Ed. 1986–95; Deputy Ed. The Daily Telegraph 1996–2005, responsible for The Daily Telegraph Saturday edn, Ed. The Sunday Telegraph 2005–06; Consulting Ed. The Daily Mail 2006–08; Ed.-in-Chief Reader's Digest UK 2008–09;

Deputy Ed., London Evening Standard 2009–12, Editor 2012–. *Publications:* novels: Playing the Game 2003, Hothouse 2005, Chiswick Wives 2006. *Address:* London Evening Standard, Northcliffe House, 2 Derry Street, London, W8 5TT, England (office). *Telephone:* (20) 7938-6000 (office). *Fax:* (20) 7937-2648 (office). *E-mail:* editor@standard.co.uk (office). *Website:* www.standard.co.uk (office).

SANDY, Stephen, BA, MA, PhD; American poet, writer, translator and fmr college teacher; b. 2 Aug. 1934, Minneapolis, Minn.; m. Virginia Scoville 1969; one s. one d. *Education:* Yale Univ., Harvard Univ. *Career:* Instructor in English, Harvard Univ. 1963–67, Visiting Prof. 1986, 1987, 1988; Visiting Prof. of English, Tokyo Univ. of Foreign Studies 1967–68, Brown Univ. 1968–69; Visiting Prof. of American Literature, Univ. of Tokyo 1967–68; Lecturer in English, Univ. of Rhode Island 1969; mem. Literature Faculty, Bennington Coll. 1969–2001; NEA Poet-in-Residence, Y Poetry Center, Philadelphia 1985; McGee Prof. of Writing, Davidson Coll. 1994; Sr Fellow in Literature, Fine Arts Work Center, Provincetown 1998; Ingram Merrill Foundation Fellowship 1985, Vermont Coll. on the Arts Fellowship 1988, NEA Creative Writing Fellowship 1988, Chubb Life America Fellow, MacDowell Colony 1993, Reader's Digest Residency for Distinguished Writers 1997, Howard Moss Residency for Poetry, Yaddo 1998, Rockefeller Foundation Residency, Bellagio Study and Conference Center 2001, Fulbright Lectureship; mem. jury, Wallace Stevens Award Jury; mem. Acad. of American Poets, Dept of Educ. Javits Fellows Programme, Arts Panel Wesleyan Writers Conf., Marymount Manhattan Writers Conf. *Publications:* Stresses in the Peaceable Kingdom 1967, Roofs 1971, End of the Picaro 1974, The Ravelling of the Novel: Studies in Romantic Fiction from Walpole to Scott 1980, Flight of Steps 1982, Riding to Greylock 1983, To a Mantis 1987, Man in the Open Air 1988, The Epoch 1990, Thanksgiving Over the Water 1992, Vale of Academe: A Prose Poem for Bernard Malamud 1996, Marrow Spoon 1997, The Thread: New and Selected Poems 1998, Black Box 1999, Surface Impressions 2002, Weathers Permitting 2005, Netsuke Days 2008, Overlook 2010; contrib. to numerous anthologies, including The Poetry Anthology 1912–2002, New Yorker Book of Poems, New York Times Book of Verse, Poets for Life, Poets Respond to AIDS, Best American Poetry 1995, 1998, Norton Treasury World Poetry; contrib. to numerous journals, including Agenda, Agni, Atlantic Monthly, APR, Boulevard, Grand St, Green Mountains Review, Harpers, The Nation, New Republic, New Yorker, New York Times, Poetry, Poetry London, Salmagundi, Times Literary Supplement, Hudson, Paris, Partisan, Southwest, Virginia Quarterly, Western Humanities, Yale Reviews. *Address:* PO Box 276, Shaftsbury, VT 05262, USA. *E-mail:* ssandy@saver.net (home). *Website:* www.stephensandy.com.

SANDYS, Elspeth Somerville, ONZM, BA, MA, LTCL, FTCL; New Zealand/British writer, dramatist and teacher; b. (Elspeth Sandilands Somerville), 18 March 1940, Timaru, New Zealand; d. of Thomas Somerville and Alice Alley; one s. one d. *Education:* Univ. of Auckland, Univ. of Otago. *Career:* fmr actress in NZ and UK; full-time writer; occasional creative writing teacher and ed.; Frank Sargeson Fellow, Auckland 1992; Burns Fellow, Otago Univ. 1995; Writer-in-Residence, Waikato Univ. 1998, Tasmanian Writer-in-Residence 2004; mem. Writers Guild, Soc. of Authors, New Zealand Studies Asscn (PEN NZ). *Play:* Century's Turn (selected for 20th London Int. Playwriting Festival) 2005. *Radio:* numerous original plays and adaptations broadcast on BBC and Radio NZ. *Publications:* Catch a Falling Star 1978, The Broken Tree 1981, Love and War 1982, Finding Out 1991 (also published in France as Descouvertes), Best Friends (short stories) 1993, River Lines 1995, Riding to Jerusalem 1996, Enemy Territory 1997, A Passing Guest (novel) 2002, Standing in Line (short stories) (Elena Garro Prize, PEN International Short Story Competion, Mexico 2003) 2003. *Honours:* Sarah Hosking Arts Trust Residency in the UK 2005–06. *Literary Agent:* c/o MBA Literary Agents Ltd, 62 Grafton Way, London, W1T 5DW, England. *Telephone:* (20) 7387-2076. *Fax:* (20) 7387-2042. *Website:* www.mbalit.co.uk. *Address:* PO Box 12674, Thorndon, Wellington 6144, New Zealand (office). *E-mail:* diana@mbalit.co.uk (office); elsp@xtra.co.nz (home).

SANEA, Rajaa al-; Saudi Arabian writer; b. 1981, Riyadh. *Education:* King Saud Univ. *Career:* studied dentistry, working at Nat. Guard Hospital, King Faisal Specialist Hospital, King Khalid Univ. Hospital 2005–06; currently dental grad. student. *Publication:* novel: Banat al-Riyadh 2005 (Girls of Riyadh 2007). *Address:* c/o Penguin Books, Penguin Group Inc., 375 Hudson Street, New York, NY 10014, USA (office). *Telephone:* (212) 366-2372 (office). *Fax:* (212) 366-2933 (office). *E-mail:* online@us.penguingroup.com (office). *Website:* us.penguingroup.com (office); www.rajaa.net (home).

SANER, Reginald (Reg) Anthony, BA, MA, PhD; American poet, writer and academic; b. (Reginald Alva Francis Saner), 30 Dec. 1931, Jacksonville, Ill.; s. of Reginald A. Saner and Marie C. Saner; m. Anne Costigan 1958; two s. *Education:* St Norbert Coll., Wis., Univ. of Illinois at Urbana, Università per Stranieri, Perugia and Università di Firenze, Florence, Italy. *Career:* Asst Instructor, Univ. of Illinois, Urbana 1956–60, Instructor in English 1961–62; Asst Prof., Univ. of Colorado, Boulder 1962–67, Assoc. Prof. 1967–72, Prof. of English 1972–98, Distinguished Research Lecturer 1983; mem. Dante Soc., PEN, Renaissance Soc., Shakespeare Asscn; Poet Laureate of Boulder, Colo 1999. *Publications include:* poetry: Climbing into the Roots 1976, So This is the Map 1981, Essay on Air 1984, Red Letters 1989; non-fiction: The Four-Cornered Falcon: Essays on the Interior West and the Natural Scene 1993, Reaching Keet Seel: Ruin's Echo and the Anasazi 1998, The Dawn Collector: On My Way to the Natural World 2005, Living Large in Nature: A Writer's Idea of Creationism 2010; contribs: poems and essays in 62 anthologies and other publs. *Honours:* Bronze Battle Star, UN Medal; Fulbright Scholar to Florence, Italy 1960–61, Borestone Mountain Poetry Awards 1971, 1973, Walt Whitman Award 1975, Nat. Endowment for the Arts Creative Writing Fellowship 1976, Pushcart Prize II 1977–78, Creede Repertory Theatre Poetry Competition 1980, Nat. Poetry Series Winner 1981, Colorado Gov.'s Award for Excellence in the Arts 1983, Quarterly Review of Literature Award 1989, Rockefeller Foundation Resident Scholar, Bellagio, Italy 1990, Hazel Barnes Award, Univ. of Colorado 1993, Wallace Stegner Award, Centre of the American West 1997. *Address:* 1925 Vassar, Boulder, CO 80305, USA (home). *Telephone:* (303) 494-8951 (home). *E-mail:* sanerreg@msn.com (office).

SANSOM, Ann; British poet and tutor; b. 1951, Doncaster, S Yorkshire; m. Peter Sansom. *Education:* Univ. of Cambridge. *Career:* playwright and writing tutor, Doncaster Women's Centre 1989–; playwright, Yorkshire Women Theatre; residencies for Arvon Foundation and Aldeburgh Poetry Festival. *Publications:* Romance 1994, In Praise of Men and Other People 2003. *Honours:* Arts Council Writer's Award. *Address:* c/o Bloodaxe Books Ltd, Highgreen, Tarset, Northumberland NE48 1RP, England (office). *Website:* www.bloodaxebooks.com.

SANSOM, C. J., BA, PhD; British writer; b. 1952. *Education:* Univ. of Birmingham. *Career:* fmr solicitor; author of Shardlake series of novels, set during reign of King Henry VIII; author of Winter in Madrid, set in 1940 at the end of Spanish Civil War. *Publications:* novels: Dissolution 2003, Dark Fire (Ellis Peters Historical Dagger, Crime Writers' Asscn 2005) 2004, Sovereign 2006, Winter in Madrid 2006, Revelation 2008, The Lost Prophecies (with The Medieval Murderers) 2008, Heartstone 2010. *Literary Agent:* c/o Greene and Heaton, 37 Goldhawk Road, London, W12 8QQ, England. *Telephone:* (20) 8749-0315. *Fax:* (20) 8749-0318. *E-mail:* info@greeneheaton.co.uk. *Website:* www.greeneheaton.co.uk.

SANTOS, Helen (see Griffiths, Helen)

SANTOS, Sherod, BA, MA, MFA, PhD; American poet, essayist, playwright, translator and fmr academic; b. 9 Sept. 1948, Greenville, SC; m. Lynne Marie McMahon 1976; two s. *Education:* San Diego State Univ., Univ. of California, Irvine, Univ. of Utah. *Career:* Asst Prof., California State Univ., San Bernardino 1982–83; Poetry Ed., Missouri Review 1983–90; Asst Prof., Univ. of Missouri 1983–86, Assoc. Prof. 1986–92, Curators' Distinguished Prof. of English 2001–05; Robert Frost Poet and Poet-in-Residence, Robert Frost House, Franconia, NH 1984; external examiner and poet-in-residence, Poets' House, Islandmagee, NI summers 1991–98; poetry readings, lectures and seminars in UK and USA. *Publications:* Begin, Distance 1981, Accidental Weather 1982, The New Days 1986, The Southern Reaches 1989, The Unsheltering Ground 1990, The City of Women 1993, The Pilot Star Elegies 1998, The Perishing 2003; trans.: Greek Lyric Poetry: A New Translation (Umhoefer Prize for Achievement in the Humanities 2006) 2005, The Intricated Soul: New and Selected Poems 2010. *Honours:* Discovery/The Nation Award 1978, Pushcart Prizes in Poetry 1980 and in the Essay 1994, Poetry magazine Oscar Blumenthal Prize 1981, Ingram Merrill Foundation grant 1982, Delmore Schwartz Memorial Award 1983, Guggenheim Fellowship 1984–85, Nat. Endowment for the Arts grant 1987, British Arts Council Int. Travel Grant to NI 1995, American Acad. of Arts and Letters Award in Literature 1999, Theodore Roethke Memorial Prize in Poetry 2002, John Frederick Nims Memorial Prize (for translations of the early Greek lyric poets), Poetry magazine 2004. *E-mail:* sherodsantos@gmail.com (office).

SANTOS-FEBRE, Mayra, BA, MA, PhD; Puerto Rican academic, writer and poet; *Professor of Literature, University of Puerto Rico-Río Piedras*; b. 1966, Carolina. *Education:* Universidad de Puerto Rico, Cornell Univ. *Career:* fmr Visiting Prof., univs in Europe, Latin America and USA; currently Prof. of Literature, University of Puerto Rico-Río Piedras. *Publications:* novels: Sirena Selena vestida de pena 2000, Cualquer miércoles soy tuya 2003; poetry: Anamú y manigua 1991, El orden escapado 1991, Tercer mundo 2000; short stories: Pez de vidrio 1995, El cuerpo correcto 1997. *Honours:* Premio Letras de Oro 1994. *Address:* Departamento de Estusios Hispánicos, Facultad de Humanidades, UPR-RP, Apartado 23342, San Juan, PR 00931-3342, Puerto Rico (office). *Telephone:* (787) 764-0000 (office). *E-mail:* esthisp@rrpac.upr.clu.edu (office). *Website:* humanidades.uprrp.edu/estudios_hispanicos (office); mayrasantosfebres.blogspot.com.

SAPIA, Yvonne, AA, BA, MA, PhD; American academic, poet and writer; b. 10 April 1946, New York, NY. *Education:* Miami-Dade Community College, Florida Atlantic University, University of Florida, Florida State University. *Career:* reporter and Ed., The Village Post newspaper, Miami, 1971–73; Editorial Asst, University of Florida, 1974–76; Resident Poet and Prof. of English, Lake City Community College, FL 1976–. *Publications:* The Fertile Crescent (poems), 1983; Valentino's Hair (poems), 1987; Valentino's Hair (novel), 1991. Contributions: anthologies, reviews, and journals. *Honours:* First Place, Anhinga Press Poetry Chapbook Award, 1983; Third Place, Eve of St Agnes Poetry Competition, 1983; National Endowment for the Arts Fellowship, 1986–87; First Place, Morse Poetry Prize, 1987; Second Prize, Cincinnati Poetry Review Poetry Competition, 1989; Third Place, Apalaches Quarterly Long Poem Contest, 1989; First Place, Nilon Award for Excellence in Minority Fiction, 1991.

SAPOLSKY, Robert M., AB, PhD; American biologist, neuroscientist and writer; *John A. and Cynthia Fry Gunn Professor of Biological Sciences and*

Professor of Neurology and Neurological Sciences, Stanford University; b. 1957. *Education:* Harvard Univ., Rockefeller Univ. *Career:* mem. editorial bd of journals, including Journal of Neuroscience, Psychoneuroendocrinology, Stress; Contributing Ed., The Sciences; John A. and Cynthia Fry Gunn Prof. of Biological Sciences and Prof. of Neurology and Neurological Sciences, Stanford Univ.; also Research Assoc. Inst. of Primate Research, Nat. Museum of Kenya. *Publications:* Stress, the Aging Brain and the Mechanisms of Neuron Death 1992, Why Zebras Don't Get Ulcers: An Updated Guide to Stress, Stress-Related Diseases and Coping 1994, The Trouble with Testosterone, and other essays on the biology of the human predicament 1997, A Primate's Memoir (Bay Area Book Reviewers' Award in Non-fiction 2001) 2001, Monkeyluv and Other Essays on Our Lives as Animals 2005; contrib. articles to numerous journals, including American Journal of Physical Anthropology, American Journal of Primatology, Annals of Neurology, Annals of the New York Academy of Sciences, Biological Psychiatry, Brain Research, Endocrinology, Hippocampus, Journal of Cerebral Blood Flow and Metabolism, Journal of Neurochemistry, Journal of Neurophysiology, Journal of Neuroscience, Journal of Neurovirology, Methods in Molecular Medicine, Neuroendocrinology, Neurology, Neurotoxicology, Proceedings of the National Academies of Science, Science, Scientific American, Stress, Stroke, Trends in Neuroscience. *Honours:* Nat. Science Foundation Presidential Young Investigator Award, Soc. for Neuroscience Young Investigator of the Year Award, Biological Psychiatry Soc. Young Investigator of the Year Award, Int. Soc. for Psychoneuro-Endocrinology Young Investigator of the Year Award, Alfred P. Sloan Fellowship, Klingenstein Fellowship in Neuroscience, MacArthur Fellow, Stanford Univ. Bing Award for Teaching Excellence. *Literary Agent:* The Steven Barclay Agency, 12 Western Avenue, Petaluma, CA 94952, USA. *Telephone:* (707) 773-0654. *Fax:* (707) 778-1868. *Website:* www.barclayagency.com

SARAH, Robyn, BA, MA; American/Canadian poet, writer and editor; *Poetry Editor, Cormorant Books*; b. 6 Oct. 1949, New York, NY. *Education:* McGill Univ., Conservatoire de Musique du Québec. *Publications:* poetry: Shadowplay 1978, The Space Between Sleep and Waking 1981, Three Sestinas 1984, Anyone Skating on that Middle Ground 1984, Becoming Light 1987, The Touchstone: Poems New and Selected 1992, Questions About the Stars 1998, A Day's Grace 2003, Le tamis des jours (selected poems in French trans., parallel English text) 2007, Pause for Breath 2009; fiction: A Nice Gazebo (short stories) 1992, Promise of Shelter (short stories) 1997; non-fiction: Little Eurekas: A Decade's Thoughts on Poetry (literary criticism) 2007. *Address:* c/o Véhicule Press, PO Box 125, place du Parc Station, Montréal, QC H2W 2M9, Canada (office).

SARAOGI, Alka, MA, PhD; Indian writer; b. 1960, Calcutta (now Kolkata); m.; two c. *Education:* Calcutta (now Kolkata) Univ. *Career:* Hindi writer. *Publications:* Kahaniki Talash Mein (short stories) 1996, Kali-Katha Via Bypass (novel, Sahitya Akademi Award 2001) 1998, Doosri Kahani (short stories) (trans. as The Second Story) 2000, Shesh Kadambari (novel) (trans. as Over to You, Kadambari) 2002, Koi Baat Bahin (novel) (trans. as Never Mind, It's Okay) 2004, The Tale Retold (short stories) 2009. *Honours:* Shrikant Verma Award 1998. *Address:* c/o Marketing and Promotions Department, Penguin Books India Pvt., 11 Community Centre, Panchsheet Park, New Delhi 110 017, India (office). *E-mail:* publicity@in.penguingroup.com (office). *Website:* www.penguinbooksindia.com (office).

SARDAR, Ziauddin, BSc, MSc, PhD; British (b. Pakistani) writer; *Editor, Futures journal*; b. 31 Oct. 1951, Dipalpur, Pakistan; m.; three c. *Education:* City Univ., London, UK. *Career:* moved to London as a child; fmr information scientist, Hajj Research Centre of King Abdul Aziz Univ., Jeddah, Saudi Arabia 1975–80; Consulting Ed., Inquiry magazine; reporter, London Weekend Television; established Centre for Future Studies, East-West Univ., Chicago early 1990s; Visiting Prof. of Science and Tech. Policy, Univ. of Middlesex 1994–98; Visiting Prof. of Postcolonial Studies, Dept of Cultural Policy and Man., City Univ., London; freelance programmer and writer 1985–; Ed. monthly journal of policy, planning and futures studies, Futures 1999–; Co-Ed. critical journal, Third Text 1998–2008; columnist, New Statesman 2005–09; Commr, Equality and Human Rights Comm. 2006–09; mem. Interim Nat. Security Forum 2009–10. *Radio:* featured on Today, Broadcast House, PM, Nightline, Belief, Five Live, Start the Week, Nightwaves, Thinking Aloud. *Television:* Encounters with Islam (series of four programmes, BBC) 1985, Islamic Conversations (series of six interviews, Channel 4) 1994, Battle for Islam (90-minute documentary, BBC 2) 2005, Between the Mullahs and the Military (Dispatches, Channel 4) 2007; numerous appearances on Hard Talk, Last Word and other shows. *Publications:* Science, Technology and Development in the Muslim World 1977, Islam: Outline of a Classification Scheme 1979, The Future of Muslim Civilisation 1979, The Touch of Midas: Science, Values and Environment in Islam and the West 1982, Islamic Futures: The Shape of Ideas to Come 1986, The Revenge of Athena: Science, Exploitation and the Third World 1988, Information and the Muslim World 1988, Distorted Imagination: Lessons from the Rushdie Affair (with Merryl Wyn Davies) 1990, Introducing Islam 1992, Barbaric Others: A Manifesto on Western Racism (with Ashis Nandy, Claude Alvarez and Merryl Wyn Davies) 1993, Postmodernism and the Other: New Imperialism of Western Culture 1997, Orientalism 1999, Rescuing All Our Futures: The Future of Futures Studies 1999, Thomas Kuhn and the Science Wars 2000, The A to Z of Postmodern Life: Essays on Global Culture in the Noughties 2002, Aliens R Us: The Other in Science Fiction Cinema (co-ed. with Sean Cubitt) 2002, Why Do People Hate America? (with Merryl Wyn Davies) 2003, Islam, Postmodernism and Other Futures: A Ziauddin Sardar Reader 2004, American Dream, Global Nightmare (with Merryl Wyn Davies) 2004, Desperately Seeking Paradise: Journeys of a Sceptical Muslim 2004, How Do You Know: Reading Ziauddin Sardar on Islam, Science and Cultural Relations 2006, What Do Muslims Believe? 2006, Balti Britain: A Journey through the British Asian Experience 2008, Reading the Qur'an 2011; contrib. to New Statesman, The Independent, The Guardian, The Observer, The Times, Nature, New Scientist. *E-mail:* mail@ziasardar.com. *Website:* www.ziauddinsardar.com.

SARI, Mohamed; Algerian writer and academic; b. 1958, Ménacer. *Career:* Prof. of Arabic Literature, Univ. of Algiers. *Publications:* novels: As-Sa'ir 1986, 'Ala Djibel ad-Dahra (The Mountains of Dara) 1988, Le Labyrinthe 2001. *Address:* c/o Éditions Marsa, 103 boulevard MacDonald, Paris 75019, France.

SARID, Yishai; Israeli author, journalist and lawyer; b. 1965, Tel-Aviv. *Education:* Hebrew Univ. of Jerusalem, Harvard Univ., USA. *Career:* worked as lawyer in Tel-Aviv District Attorney office, then at Dr. J. Weinroth and Partners; works full-time as attorney, currently as pvt. prosecutor; Co-founder and Partner, Chet, Sarid, Sapir-Hen, Lavron Law Office 2004–; mem. Bar Asscn 1994–. *Publications include:* novels: The Investigation of Captain Erez 2000, Limassol (Best Int. Crime Novel at Grand Prix de Littérature Policière 2011) 2009. *Address:* c/o Chet, Sarid, Sapir-Hen, Lavron Law Office, Azrieli Center 5, Squaer Tower 24, Tel-Aviv (office); Am Oved Publishing Limited, POB 470, Tel-Aviv, 61003, Israel (office). *Telephone:* (3) 6088444 (law office) (office); (3) 6288500 (Am Oved) (office). *Fax:* (3) 6088455 (law office) (office); (3) 6298911 (Am Oved) (office). *E-mail:* office@csglaw.co.il (office); info@am-oved.co.il (office). *Website:* www.csglaw.co.il (office); www.am-oved.co.il (office).

SARIF, Shamim; British novelist, screenwriter and film director; b. 24 Sept. 1969, London; pnr Hanan Kattan; two c. *Education:* Univ. of London, Boston Univ., USA. *Career:* Co-f. Enlightenment Productions. *Screenplays include:* I Can't Think Straight 2008, The World Unseen 2008. *Publications:* novels: The World Unseen (Betty Trask Award, Pendleton May First Novel Award) 2001, Despite the Falling Snow 2004, I Can't Think Straight 2008; contrib. to You magazine, American Way. *Honours:* Best Director Award, Phoenix Int. Film Festival, Best Director Award, Clip Festival. *E-mail:* shamim@shamimsarif.com (home). *Website:* www.enlightenment-productions.com (office) www.shamimsarif.com.

SARKAR, Anil Kumar, MA, PhD, DLitt; Indian academic and writer; b. 1 Aug. 1912, Ranchi, India; m. Aruna Sarkar 1941 (deceased); one s. three d. *Education:* Patna Univ. *Career:* Prof., Rajendra Coll. 1940–44; Sr Lecturer, Univs of Ceylon, Colombo and Perdeniya 1944–64; Visiting Prof., Univ. of New Mexico, Albuquerque 1964–65; Full Prof. of Philosophy and West-East Philosophy, California State Univ., Hayward 1965–82; Research Dir and Prof. of Asian Studies, California Inst. of Integral Studies, San Francisco 1968–80, Prof. Emeritus 1980–. *Publications:* An Outline of Whitehead's Philosophy 1940, Changing Phases of Buddhist Thought 1968, Whitehead's Four Principles From West-East Perspectives 1974, Dynamic Facets of Indian Thought, Vol. 1 1980, Vols 2–4 1987–88, Experience in Change and Prospect: Pathways from War to Peace 1989, Sri Aurobindo's Vision of the Super Mind – Its Indian and Non-Indian Interpreters 1989, Buddhism and Whitehead's Process Philosophy 1990, Zero: Its Role and Prospects in Indian Thought and its Impact on Post-Einsteinian Astrophysics 1992, The Mysteries of Vajrayana Buddhism: From Atisha to Dalai Lama 1993, Triadic Avenues of India's Cultural Prospects: Philosophy, Physics and Politics 1995, Shaping of Euro-Indian Philosophy 1995; contributions: Indian, US and other journals.

SARKÖZY DE NAGY BOCSA, Nicolas Paul Stéphane, LLM; French politician, barrister, civil servant and fmr head of state; b. 28 Jan. 1955, Paris; s. of Paul Sarközy de Nagy Bocsa and Andrée Mallah; m. 1st Marie-Dominique Culioli 1982 (divorced 1996); two s.; m. 2nd Cecilia Ciganer-Albeniz 1996 (divorced 2007); one s.; m. 3rd Carla Bruni 2008; one d. *Education:* Inst. of Political Studies, Paris, Paris Univ. *Career:* barrister, Paris 1981–87; Assoc., Leibovici Claude Sarközy 1987; mem. Neuilly-sur-Seine Municipal Couincil 1977–83, Mayor of Neuilly-sur-Seine 1983–2002; Vice-Chair. Hauts-de-Seine Gen. Council, responsible for Educ. and Culture 1986–88, Chair. 2004; RPR Deputy to Nat. Ass. from Hauts-de-Seine 1988–2002; Govt Spokesman 1993–95; Minister of the Budget 1993–95, of Communications 1994–95, of the Interior, Internal Security and Local Freedoms 2002–04, of the Economy, Finance and Industry 2004, of the Interior and Town and Country Planning 2005–07 (resgnd); Pres. of France 2007–12, Co-Prince of Andorra 2007–12; Nat. Sec. RPR responsible for Youth and Training 1988, for Activities, Youth and Training 1989, Deputy Gen.-Sec. responsible for local brs 1992–93, mem. Political Bureau 1993, Gen. Sec. RPR 1998, Interim Pres. April–Oct. 1999, Pres. RPR Regional Cttee of Hauts-de-Seine 2000; Leader RPR-DL List, European Elections 1999; Pres. Union pour un Mouvement Populaire (UMP) 2004–07. *Publications include:* Georges Mandel, moine de la politique 1994, Au bout de la passion, l'équilibre (co-author) 1995, Libre 2001, La République, les Religions, l'Espérance 2004, Témoignage 2006. *Honours:* Chevalier, Légion d'honneur 2004, Grand'Croix, Légion d'honneur 2007, Grand'Croix, Ordre nat. du Mérite 2007, Stara Planina (Bulgaria) 2007, Commdr, Ordre de Léopold (Belgium); ranked by Forbes magazine amongst The World's Most Powerful People (56th) 2009, (19th) 2010, (13th) 2011. *Address:* c/o Office of the President, Palais de l'Elysée, 55–57 rue du Faubourg Saint Honoré, 75008 Paris, France.

SARNA, Jonathan Daniel, BA, MA, MPh, PhD; American historian, professor of american jewish history and writer; *Joseph H. and Belle R. Braun Professor of American Jewish History, Brandeis University*; b. 10 Jan. 1955, Philadelphia, Pa; s. of the late Nahum M. Sarna and Helen H. Sarna; m. Ruth Langer 1986; one s. one d. *Education:* Hebrew Coll., Boston, Brandeis Univ., Yale Univ. *Career:* Visiting Lecturer, Hebrew Union Coll.-Jewish Inst. of Religion 1979–80, Asst Prof. to Prof. of American Jewish History 1980–90; Dir American Jewish Experience Curriculum Project, Center for the Study of the American Jewish Experience 1986–90, Boston Jewish History Project 1992–95; Visiting Asst Prof., Univ. of Cincinnati 1983–84; Visiting Assoc. Prof., Hebrew Univ., Jerusalem, Israel 1986–87; Joseph H. and Belle R. Braun Prof. of American Jewish History, Brandeis Univ. 1990–; Chief Historian, Nat. Museum of American Jewish History 2000–; mem. American Acad. of Religion, American Historical Asscn, American Jewish Historical Soc., Asscn for Jewish Studies, Org. of American Historians; Fellow, American Acad. of Arts and Sciences 2009–, American Acad. of Jewish Research. *Publications:* Jews in New Haven (ed.) 1978, Mordecai Manuel Noah: Jacksonian Politician and American Jewish Communal Leader 1979, Jacksonian Jew: The Two Worlds of Mordecai Noah 1981, Jews and the Founding of the Republic (co-ed.) 1985, The American Jewish Experience: A Reader (ed.) 1986, American Synagogue History: A Bibliography and State-of-the-Field Survey (with Alexandra S. Korros) 1988, JPS: The Americanization of Jewish Culture: A History of the Jewish Publication Society 1888–1988 1989, The Jews of Cincinnati (with Nancy H. Klein) 1989, A Double Bond: The Constitutional Documents of American Jewry (co-ed. with Daniel J. Elazar and Rela Geffen Monson) 1992, Ethnic Diversity and Civic Identity: Patterns of Conflict and Cohesion in Cincinnati Since 1820 (with Henry D. Shapiro) 1992, Yuhude Artsot Ha-Berit (with Lloyd Gartner) 1992, Observing America's Jews (co-ed. with Marshall Sklare) 1993, The Jews of Boston (with Ellen Smith) 1995, Abba Hillel Silver and American Zionism (with Mark A. Raider and Ronald W. Zweig) 1997, Minority Faiths and the American Protestant Mainstream 1997, Religion and State in the American Jewish Experience (with David G. Dalin) 1997, Women and American Judaism: Historical Perspectives (with Pamela S. Nadel) 2001, American Judaism – A History 2004, A Time to Every Purpose: Letters to a Young Jew 2008, Jews and the Civil War (co-ed. with Adam Mendelsohn) 2010; contribs to scholarly books, professional journals and general periodicals. *Honours:* Dr hc (Gratz Coll.) 2009, (Boston Hebrew Coll.) 2011; Outstanding Academic Book, Choice 1998, Benjamin J. Shevach Memorial Prize for Distinguished Leadership in Jewish Educ. 2000, Everett Family Foundation Book of the Year Award, Jewish Book Council 2004, named on Forward List of 50 Most Influential American Jews 2004, Martin E. Marty Award for the Public Understanding of Religion. *Address:* Department of Near Eastern and Judaic Studies, Brandeis University, Waltham, MA 02454, USA (office). *Telephone:* (781) 736-2977 (office). *Fax:* (781) 736-2070 (office). *E-mail:* sarna@brandeis.edu (office). *Website:* www.brandeis.edu/departments/nejs (office).

SAROYAN, Aram; American writer, poet, dramatist and academic; *Lecturer, Master of Professional Writing Program, University of Southern California*; b. 25 Sept. 1943, New York, NY; m. Gailyn McClanahan 1968; one s. two d. *Education:* Univ. of Chicago, New York Univ., Columbia Univ. *Play:* At the Beach House (premiere, Los Angeles) 2005. *Publications:* Aram Saroyan 1968, Pages 1969, Words and Photographs 1970, The Street: An Autobiographical Novel 1974, Genesis Angels: The Saga of Lew Welch and the Beat Generation 1979, Last Rites: The Death of William Saroyan 1982, William Saroyan 1983, Trio: Portrait of an Intimate Friendship 1985, The Romantic 1988, Friends in the World: The Education of a Writer 1992, Rancho Mirage: An American Tragedy of Manners, Madness and Murder 1993, Day and Night: Bolinas Poems 1972–81 1998, Starting Out in the Sixties (essays) 2001, Artists in Trouble: New Stories 2001, Day by Day 2002, Complete Minimal Poems 2007, Door to the River: Essays and Review from the 1960s into the Digital Age 2010; contrib. to New York Times Book Review, Los Angeles Times Book Review, The Nation, Village Voice, Mother Jones, Paris Review, Shambhala Sun magazine, American Poetry Review. *Honours:* Nat. Endowment for the Arts Poetry Awards 1967, 1968, William Carlos Williams Award, Poetry Soc. of America 2008. *Literary Agent:* c/o Jane Dystel, Dystel & Goderich Literary Management, One Union Square West, Suite 904, New York, NY 10003, USA. *Telephone:* (212) 627-9100. *Fax:* (212) 627-9313. *E-mail:* info@dystel.com. *Website:* www.dystel.com. *Address:* 5482 Village Green, Los Angeles, CA 90016, USA. *Website:* www.aramsaroyan.com.

SASO, Akira; Japanese writer, illustrator and academic; b. 9 Feb. 1961, Takarazuka, Hyogo Pref. *Education:* Ikeda High School, Osaka Kyoiku Univ. and Waseda Univ. *Career:* writer and illustrator of manga comics; Assoc. Prof., Dept of Manga, Kyoto Seika Univ. 2006–. *Publications include:* Shiroi Shiroi Natsuyanen (Grand Chiba Tetsuya Prize 1984), Ai ni Isogasii (Busy Love), Oretachi ni Asu ha Naissu (There is No Tomorrow for Us), Shindo (Child Prodigy), Fuji-san. *Honours:* Japan Media Arts Festival Excellence Prize 1998, Tezuka Osamu Cultural Prize 1999. *Address:* Department of Manga, Kyoto Seika University, c/o International Office, 137 Kino-cho, Iwakura, Sakyo-ku, Kyoto 606-8588, Japan. *Website:* www.kyoto-seika.ac.jp/eng/edu/manga.

SATCHIDANANDAN, Koyamparambath, BA, MA, PhD; Indian poet and writer; b. 28 May 1946, Pullut, Thrissur Dist, Kerala; m.; two d. *Education:* Univ. of Kerala, Univ. of Calicut. *Career:* writer in Malayalam and English; Lecturer, then Prof. of English, Christ Coll., Kerala 1977–92; Ed. Indian Literature journal 1992–96; Pres. Sahitya Akademi 1996–2003; fmr consultant, India Dept of Higher Educ., Nat. Trans. Mission. *Plays:* Saktan Thampuran 1983, Gandhi 1995. *Publications include:* poetry: Anchu Sooryan 1971, Atmagita 1974, Kavita 1977, Indian Sketchukal 1978, Ezhuthachan Ezhutumbol 1979, Peedana Kalam 1981, Venal Mazha 1982, Randu Deergha Kavyangal 1983, Satchidandante Kavithakal 1962–82 1983, Socrateesum Kozhiyum 1984, Ivanekkoodi 1987, Veedumattam 1988, Kayattam 1990, Kavibuddhan 1992, Ente Satchidanandan Kavitakal 1993, Desatanam 1994, Malayalam 1996, Apoornam 1998, Theranjedutha 1999, Sambhashanathinu Oru Sramam 2000, Vikku 2002, Sakshyangal 2004, Satchidanandante Kavitakal 1965–2005 2006, Onaam Padham 2006, Anantam 2007, Ente Kavita 2008; non-fiction: Kurukshetram 1970, Janatayum Kavitayum 1982, Marxian Soundarya Sadtram 1983, Thiranjedutha Lekhanangal 1985, Samvadangal 1986, Sameepanangal 1986, Samskarathinte Rashtreeyam 1989, Sambhashanangal 1989, Brechtinte Kala 1989, Padavukal 1990, Kazhchakal, Kazhachappadukal 1991, Anveshanangal 1991, Veenduvicharangal 1992, Soundaryavum Adhikaravum 1993, Muhurtangal 1996, Pala Lokam, Pala Kalam 1998, Kalayum Nishedhavum 1999, Moonnu Yatra 2004, Kizhakkum Padinjarum 2005, Adithattukal 2006, Mukjamukham 2006; prose: Kurukshetram 1970, Janatayum Kavitayum 1982, Marxian Soundarya Sastram 1983, Thiranjedutha Lekhanangal 1985, Pablo Neruda 1985, Samvadangal 1986, Sameepanangal 1986, Samskarathinte Rashtreeyam 1989, Sambhashanangal 1989, Brechtinte Kala 1989, Padavukal 1990, Kazhchakal, Kazhachappadukal 1991, Anveshanangal 1991, Veenduvicharangal 1992, Soundaryavum Adhikaravum 1993, Muhurtangal 1996, Pala Lokam, Pala Kalam 1998, Kalayum Nishedhavum 1999, Bharateeya Kavitayile Pratirodha Paramparyam 2002, Moonnu Yatra 2004, Kizhakkum Padinjarum 2005, Adithattukal 2006, Mukhamukham 2006, Indian Literature: Positions and Propositions 1999, Indian Literature: Paradigms and Praxis 2008, Indian Literature and Beyond 2009. *Honours:* Cavaliere, Ordine al Merito della Repubblica Italiana; Kerala Sahitya Akademi Award 1984, 1989, 1999, 2001, Oman Cultural Centre Award, UAE 1993, Mahakavi Ulloor Award 1996, Mahakavi P.Kunhiraman Nair Award 1997, Bharatiya Bhasha Parishad Samvatsar Award 1998, Kumaran Asan Award 2000, Odakkuzhal Award 2001, Baharain Kerala Samaj Award, UAE 2002, Gangadhar Meher Nat. Award, Sambalpur Univ., Orissa 2002, Pandalam Kerala Verma Award 2005, Bappureddy Nat. Award 2005, Vayalar Award 2005, India-Poland Friendship Medal, Govt of Poland 2005, K.Kuttikrishnan Memorial Award 2007, Subrahmanya Shenoi Memorial Award 2008, NTR Nat. Literary Award 2009. *E-mail:* satchida@gmail.com (home). *Website:* satchidanandan.blogspot.com.

SATRAPI, Marjane, MA; Iranian writer, illustrator and film director; b. (Marjan Ebrahimi-Ripa), 22 Sept. 1969, Rasht. *Education:* Visual Communication School of Fine Arts, Tehran, École des Arts Decoratifs de Strasbourg, France. *Film:* Persepolis (dir and writer with Vincent Paronnaud) (Sutherland Trophy, British Film Inst. Awards 2007, Jury Prize, Cannes Film Festival 2007, Special Jury Prize, Cinemanila Int. Film Festival 2007, César Award for Best First Work 2007, Audience Award, Rotterdam Int. Film Festival 2008, Audience Award, São Paulo Int. Film Festival 2007, Most Popular Film, Vancouver Int. Film Festival 2007) 2007, Poulet aux prunes 2011. *Publications include:* Persepolis: The Story of a Childhood (four vols) (Angoulême Coup de Coeur Award 2001, Angoulême Prize 2002) 1999–2002, Persepolis 2: The Story of a Return (adapted as screenplay 2007) 2005, Embroideries 2005, Chicken with Plums (Angoulême Best Comic Book Award) 2006; several children's books; contrib. illustrations to French magazines and periodicals. *Honours:* Dr hc (Katholieke Universiteit Leuven, Université catholique de Louvain) 2009; Gat Perich Award. *Address:* 13 rue de Thorigny, 75003 Paris, France (home). *Telephone:* 6-64-99-04-52 (home). *Fax:* 1-42-72-65-15 (home). *E-mail:* marjanesatrapi@yahoo.fr (home).

SATTERTHWAIT, Walter; American writer; b. 23 March 1946, Philadelphia; one d. *Education:* Reed Coll. *Career:* mem. Mystery Writers of America, Private Eye Writers of America. *Publications:* Cocaine Blues 1980, The Aegean Affair 1981, Wall of Glass 1987, Miss Lizzie 1989, At Ease With the Dead 1990, Wilde West 1991, A Flower In the Desert 1992, The Hanged Man 1994, Escapade 1995, Accustomed to the Dark 1996, Masquerade 1998, The Sunken Sailor (jtly) 2004, Cavalcade 2005, Perfection 2006, Dead Horse 2007; contribs: Alfred Hitchcock's Mystery Magazine; Santa Fe Reporter. *Honours:* Prix du Roman d'Aventures, France 1996. *Address:* c/o Dominick Abel Literary Agency, Inc., 146 West 82nd Street, 1A, New York, NY 10024, USA.

SAUL, John Ralston, CC, PhD; Canadian essayist, writer and philosopher; *President, International PEN*; b. 19 June 1947, Ottawa; m. Adrienne Clarkson 1999. *Education:* McGill Univ., King's Coll., London. *Career:* Gen. Ed., Penguin Extraordinary Canadians project; Pres. Canadian PEN 1990–92, co-creator, Canadian PEN Writers In Exile Network 2004, Pres. Int. PEN 2009–; co-Chair Inst. for Canadian Citizenship; founder and Hon. Chair. Le français pour l'avenir/French for the Future, LaFontaine-Baldwin symposium; Patron, PLAN; mem. Centre québécois du PEN international; mem. Council of Writers and Experts, Int. Cities of Refuge Network (ICORN), Norway. *Publications:* non-fiction: Voltaire's Bastards: The Dictatorship of Reason in the West 1992, The Doubter's Companion: A Dictionary of Aggressive Common Sense 1994, The Unconscious Civilization (Gov. Gen.'s Literary Award for Non-Fiction 1996, Gordon Montador Award for Best Canadian Book on Social Issues 1996)

1995, Le citoyen dans un cul-de-sac?: Anatomie d'une société en crise 1995, Reflections of a Siamese Twin 1997, On Equilibrium: Six Qualities of the New Humanism 2001, The Collapse of Globalism and the Reinvention of the World 2005, Joseph Howe and the Battle for the Freedom of Speech 2006, A Fair Country: Telling Truths about Canada 2008; fiction: The Paradise Eater (Premio Lettarario Internazionale, Italy), The Birds of Prey 1977, Baraka or The Lives, Fortunes and Sacred Honor of Anthony Smith 1983, The Next Best Thing 1986, The Paradise Eater 1988, De Si Bons Americains 1994; contrib. articles and essays to magazines and anthologies. *Honours:* Chevalier, Ordre des Arts et des Lettres; 14 hon. degrees including McGill Univ., Herzen State Pedagogical Univ., St Petersburg (Russia); Pablo Neruda Medal, Chile, Manhae Grand Prize for Literature, South Korea 2010. *Literary Agent:* c/o Natasha Daneman, Westwood Creative Artists, 94 Harbord Street, Toronto, Ont. M5B 1G6, Canada. *Telephone:* (416) 964-3302. *Fax:* (416) 975-9209. *E-mail:* wca_office@wcaltd.com. *Website:* www.wcaltd.com; www.johnralstonsaul.com.

SAUNDERS, Ann Loreille, (Ann Cox-Johnson), MBE, BA, PhD, FSA; British historian; b. 23 May 1930, London; m. Bruce Kemp Saunders 1960; one s. one d. (deceased). *Education:* Queen's Coll., London (Plumptre Scholar), Univ. Coll. London, Univ. of Leicester. *Career:* Deputy Librarian, Lambeth Palace 1952–55; Archivist, Marylebone Public Library, London 1956–63; Fellow, Univ. Coll. London 1992; mem. Costume Soc. (Hon. Ed. 1967–2008, Ed. Emer. 2008–), London Topographical Soc. (Hon. Ed. 1975–). *Publications:* London, North of the Thames 1972, London, City and Westminster 1975, Art and Architecture of London 1984, St Martin-in-the-Fields 1989, The Royal Exchange 1991, The Royal Exchange (ed. and co-author) 1997, St Paul's: The History of the Cathedral 2001, The History of the Merchant Taylor's Company (with Matthew Davies) 2004, Historic Views of London, from the collection of B.E.C. Howarth-Loomes 2008; contrib. to magazines. *Honours:* Prize for Best Specialist Guide Book of the Year, British Tourist Bd 1984. *Address:* 3 Meadway Gate, London, NW11 7LA, England (home). *Telephone:* (20) 8455-2171 (home).

SAUNDERS, George, BSc, MA; American writer and academic; *Associate Professor, Syracuse University*; b. 2 Dec. 1958, Amarillo, Tex. *Education:* Colorado School of Mines, Syracuse Univ., NY. *Career:* Visiting Prof. of Creative Writing, Syracuse Univ. 1996–97, Asst Prof. 1997–2001, Assoc. Prof. 2001–. *Publications:* CivilWarLand in Bad Decline (stories) 1996, Pastoralia: Stories 2000, The Very Persistent Gappers of Frip (juvenile) 2000, The Brief and Frightening World of Phil 2005, In Persuasion Nation 2006, The Brief and Frightening Reign of Phil 2006, The Braindead Megaphone: Essays 2007, Tenth of December (stories) 2012; various stories in Best American Short Stories; contrib. to books and periodicals, including The New Yorker and GQ (travel pieces). *Honours:* Nat. Magazine Awards 1994, 1996, 1999, 2003, New York Times Notable Book of the Year Citation 1996, 2000, Lannen Fellowship 2001–02, Guggenheim Fellowship 2006, MacArthur Fellowship 2006. *Literary Agent:* International Creative Management, 750 Fifth Avenue, New York, NY 10019, USA. *Telephone:* (212) 556-5600. *Fax:* (212) 556-5677. *Website:* www.icmtalent.com.

SAUR, Klaus Gerhard, DHumLitt; German publisher; *CEO and Partner, Walter de Gruyter Publishing House GmbH*; b. 27 July 1941, Pullach; s. of Karl-Otto Saur and Veronika Saur; m. Lilo Stangel 1977; one s. one d. *Education:* High School, Icking and Commercial High School, Munich. *Career:* Marketing Man. Vulkan-Verlag, Essen 1962; Publishing Man. KG Saur, Munich 1963, Publishing Dir 1966; Pres. KG Saur New York and KG Saur, London 1977–2003; Man. Dir KG Saur Munich 1988–2004, Chair. Bd –2004; CEO and Pnr, Walter de Gruyter Publishing House GmbH, Berlin and New York 2005–; Founder, World Guide to Libraries, Publrs Int. Directory; mem. Bd F.A. Brockhaus Bibliographical Inst., Mannheim; Vice-Pres. Goethe-Institut, Germany. *Publications:* World Biographical Information System, Pressehandbuch für Exportwerbung, World Guide to Libraries. *Honours:* Hon. Prof., Univ. of Glasgow, Humboldt-Univ. Berlin; Hon. Fellow, Tech. Univ. of Graz; Hon. mem. Austrian Library Asscn 1998, German Library Asscn, Bavarian Acad. of Belle Arts; Senator hc (Ludwig Maximilians Univ., Munich) 1992, (Leipzig) 2001, (Friedrich Alexander Univ., Erlangen) 2007; Bundesverdienstkreuz der Bundesrepublik Deutschland, Officier Ordre des Arts et Lettres (France), Sächsischer Verdienstordern 2002, Bayerischer Verdienstordern 2002; Hon. DPhil (Marburg) 1985, (Ishevsk, Russia) 1997, (Pisa, Italy) 1998, (Simmons Coll., Mass.) 1992; Hon. Medal City of Munich 1988, Hon. Bene Merenti Medal, Bavarian Acad. of Sciences 1997, Helmut-Sontag Award, Asscn of German Libraries 1999, Großes Österreichisches Verdienstkreuz der Wessenschaftund Künste 2003, Max-Hermann-Award, German State Library. *Address:* Verlag Walter de Gruyter, Genthinerstr. 13, 10785 Berlin (office); Beuerbergerstr. 9, 81479 Munich, Germany (home). *Telephone:* (30) 26005312 (office); (89) 74994651 (home). *Fax:* (30) 26005369 (office); (89) 74994652 (home). *E-mail:* klaus.saur@degruyter.com (office). *Website:* www.degruyter.com (office).

SAUVAIN, Philip Arthur, MA, PGCE; British writer; b. 28 March 1933, Burton on Trent, Staffs., England; s. of Alan Sauvain and Norah Sauvain; m. June Maureen Spenceley 1963; one s. one d. *Education:* Univs of Cambridge and London. *Career:* Sr Lecturer in Geography, James Graham Coll., Leeds 1963–68; Head of Environmental Studies Dept, Charlotte Mason Coll. of Educ., Ambleside 1968–74. *Publications:* A Map Reading Companion 1961, A Geographical Field Study Companion 1964, Exploring Britain (series) 1966, Discovery (series) 1970, Hulton's Practical Geography (series) 1970, Hulton's Lively History (series) 1970, The First Men on the Moon 1972, The Great Wall of China 1972, First Look Book (series) 1973, Breakaway (series) 1973, Exploring the World of Man (series) 1973, Environmental Books (series) 1974, Looking Around Town and Country 1975, A First Look Series (five vols) 1975–78, Imagining the Past: First Series (six vols) 1976, Second Series (six vols) 1979, The British Isles 1980, The Story of Britain Series (four vols) 1980, Britain's Living Heritage 1982, The History of Britain (four vols) 1982, Theatre 1983, Macmillan Junior Geography (four vols) 1983, Hulton New Geographies (five vols) 1983, History Map Books (two vols) 1983, 1985, Hulton New Histories (five vols) 1984–85, France and the French 1985, European and World History, 1815–1919 1985, Modern World History, 1919 Onwards 1985, How History Began 1985, Castles and Crusaders 1986, What to Look For (four vols) 1986, British Economic and Social History (two vols) 1987, Exploring Energy (four vols) 1987, GCSE History Companion Series (three vols) 1988, How We Build (three vols) 1989, The World of Work (three vols) 1989, Skills for Geography 1989, Skills for Standard Grade History 1990, Exploring the Past: Old World 1991, The Way it Works (three vols) 1991, Changing World 1992, Breakthrough: Communications 1992, History Detectives (three vols) 1992–93, Great Battles and Sieges (four vols) 1992–93, Expanding World 1993, The Era of the Second World War 1993, Robert Scott in the Antarctic 1993, Target Geography (14 vols) 1994–95, The Tudors and Stuarts 1995, Britain Since 1930 (four vols) 1995, Geography Detective (four vols) 1995–96, Famous Lives (two vols) 1996, Key Themes of the Twentieth Century 1996, Key Themes of the Twentieth Century: Teacher's Guide 1996, Germany in the Twentieth Century 1997, Vietnam 1997, Easter 1997. *Address:* 70 Finborough Road, Stowmarket, Suffolk, IP14 1PU, England (home).

SAVAGE, Alan (see Nicole, Christopher Robin)

SAVAGE, Thomas (Tom), BA, MLS; American poet, writer, critic and editor; b. 14 July 1948, New York, NY. *Education:* Brooklyn Coll., City Univ. of New York, Columbia Univ. School of Library Science. *Career:* Teaching Asst, Naropa Inst. School of Poetics 1975; Ed., Roof Magazine 1976–78, Gandhabba Magazine 1981–93; teacher, Words, Music, Words for Poets and Composers, St Mark's Poetry Project 1983–85; teacher, The Poetry Project workshop, Tribes Gallery, New York 2003–04; mem. Co-ordinating Council of Literary Magazines; PEN Grant 1978; Co-ordinating Council of Literary Magazines Grant 1981–82; two Fund For Poetry grants. *Publications:* Personalities 1978, Filling Spaces 1980, Slow Waltz on a Glass Harmonica 1980, Housing Preservation and Development 1988, Processed Words 1990, Out of the World 1991, Political Conditions and Physical States 1993, Brain Surgery (poems) 1999; contributions to magazines and journals. *Address:* 622 East 11th Street, No. 14, New York, NY 10009, USA.

SAVATER, Fernando, (Fernando Fernández-Savater Martín), PhD; Spanish philosopher and essayist; *Professor of Philosophy, Universidad Complutense de Madrid*; b. 21 June 1947, San Sebastián. *Education:* Universidad Complutense de Madrid. *Career:* Asst Prof. in faculty of political science, Universidad Autónoma de Madrid –1971; faculty mem. Dept of Ethics, Universidad del País Vasco 1975; Prof. of Philosophy, Universidad Complutense de Madrid 1995; co-Ed. of journal, Claves de Razón Práctica; mem. various peace organizations, including Basta Ya, which recieved the Premio Sajarov for the defence of human rights 2000. *Publications include:* Nihilismo y acción 1970, La filosofía tachada 1970, Apología del sofista y otros sofismas 1973, Ensayo sobre Cioran 1974, Escritos politeístas 1975, De los dioses y del mundo 1975, La infancia recuperada 1976, La filosofía como anhelo de la revolución 1976, Apóstatas razonables 1976, Para la anarquía y otros enfrentamientos 1977, La piedad apasionada 1977, Panfleto contra el Todo 1978, Nietzsche y su obra 1979, El estado y sus criaturas 1979, Criaturas del aire 1979, Caronte aguarda 1981, La tarea del héroe (Premio Nacional de Ensayo 1982) 1981, Impertinencias y desafíos 1981, Invitación a la ética 1982, Sobre vivir 1983, Las razones del antimilitarismo y otras razones 1984, El contenido de la felicidad 1986, Ética como amor propio 1988, Último desembarco: el vente de Sinapia 1988, Humanismo impenitente 1990, La escuela de Platón 1991, Ética para Amador 1991, Política para Amador 1992, Sin contemplaciones 1993, El jardín de las dudas 1993, El contenido de la felicidad 1994, Semearentzako Etika 1996, Ética para o seu fillo 1996, La voluntad disculpada 1996, El valor de educar (essay) 1997, Malos y malditos 1997, Despierta y lee 1998, Diccioanrio filosófico 1999, Las preguntas de la vida 1999, La aventura africana 1999, Idea de Nietzsche 2000, Ética per el meu fill 2000, A rienda suelta 2000, Perdonen las molestias: Crónica de una batalla sin armas contra las armas (collection of essays and articles) 2001, A caballo entre milenios 2001, Caronte aguarda 2001, El dialecto de la vida 2002, Pensamientos arriesgados 2002, El contenido de la felicidad 2002, Palabras cruzadas: una invitación a la filosofía 2003, Mira por dónde: autobiografía razonada 2003, Las preguntas de la vida 2003, Los caminos para la libertad: ética y educación 2003, El gran fraude: sobre terrorismo, nacionalismo y progresismo 2004, Los diez mandamientos en el siglo XX 2004, La libertad como destino 2004, El valor de escollir 2004, Criaturas del aire 2004, El gran laberinto 2005, Jorge Luis Borges (biog.) 2005, La Hermandad de la Buena Suerte (Premio Planeta) 2008. *Honours:* Premio Anagrama, Premio Fernando Abril Martorell, Premio Ortega y Gasset for journalism 2000. *Address:* Departamento de Filosofía IV, Facultad de Filosofía, Ciudad Universitaria, 28040 Madrid, Spain (office). *Telephone:* (91) 3945385 (office). *Fax:* (91) 3945397 (office). *Website:* www.savater.org.

SAVIANO, Roberto; Italian journalist and writer; b. 1979, Naples. *Education:* Univ. of Naples, 'Federico II'. *Career:* granted perm. police protection as a result of his writing and research on the Camorra (Neapolitan organized-crime network). *Play:* Gomorra. *Publications:* Gomorra (Premio Viareggio) 2006, La Bellezza e l'Inferno (essays) 2009, La Parola Contro la Camorra 2010; contrib. to L'Espresso, La Repubblica, Nuovi Argomenti, Lo Straniero, Nazione Indiana, Sud. *Honours:* Premio Giancarlo Siani, Dedalus Prize, Lo Straniero prize, Letterario Edoardo Kihlgren Opera Prima, Tropea, Vittorini per l'impegno civile il Guido Dorso per la Letteratura, PEN Pinter Prize 2011. *Address:* c/o Mondadori Editore, via Mondadori 1, 20090 Segrate, Milan, Italy (office). *E-mail:* info@robertosaviano.it (office). *Website:* www.robertosaviano.it.

SAVILLE, Diana; British writer; b. 15 Feb. 1943, London, England; m. 1974. *Education:* St Hugh's College, Oxford. *Publications:* The Observer's Book of British Gardens, 1982; Walled Gardens: Their Planning and Design, 1982; The Illustrated Garden Planter, 1984; Gardens for Small Country Houses, 1984; Colour, 1992; Walls and Screens, 1993; Green and Pleasant Land: A Thousand Years of Poetry (ed.), 1993; The Marriage Bed, 1995; The Honey Makers, 1996; The Hawk Dancer, 1997.

SAVOY, Deirdre, BBA; American author; b. 31 Oct. 1960, New York, NY; m. Carmelo (Frank) La Mantia 1988, one s. one d. *Education:* Baruch College, CUNY. *Publications:* Spellbound, 1999; Always, 2000. *Address:* PO Box 233, New York, NY 10469, USA.

SAWYER, Diane, BA; American broadcast journalist; *Anchor*, ABC World News with Diane Sawyer; b. 22 Dec. 1945, Glasgow, Ky; d. of Erbon Powers 'Tom' Sawyer and Jean W. Sawyer (née Dunagan); m. Mike Nichols 1988. *Education:* Seneca High School, Louisville, Ky, Wellesley Coll., Mass, Univ. of Louisville (one semester). *Career:* toured country as America's Junior Miss to promote Coca-Cola Pavilion at 1964–65 New York World's Fair 1962–65; reporter, WLKY-TV, Louisville, Ky 1967–70; Admin. White House Press Office 1970–74; mem. Nixon-Ford transition team 1974–75; Asst to Richard Nixon (fmr US Pres.) 1974, 1975; Gen. Reporter, later State Dept Corresp., CBS News 1978–81, apptd Co-Anchor Morning News 1981, Co-Anchor Early Morning News 1982–84, Corresp. and Co-Ed. 60 Minutes 1984–89; Co-Anchor PrimeTime Live (now Primetime Thursday), ABC News 1989–99, Good Morning America 1999–2009, Anchor, ABC World News with Diane Sawyer 2009–. *Honours:* won America's Junior Miss scholarship pageant as rep. from State of Kentucky, nine Emmy awards, Nat. Headliner Awards, George Foster Peabody Award for Public Service, Robert F. Kennedy Journalism Award, Special Dupont Award, Ohio State Award, IRTS Lifetime Achievement Award, inducted TV Acad. of Fame 1997, named by the Ladies' Home Journal as one of the 30 most powerful women in America 2001, ranked by Forbes magazine amongst The World's 100 Most Powerful Women (26th) 2004, (55th) 2005, (60th) 2006, (62nd) 2007, (65th) 2008, (46th) 2010, (47th) 2011, Peabody Award for work on A Hidden America: Children of the Mountains 2009. *Address:* Good Morning America, 147 Columbus Avenue, New York, NY 10023-5900, USA (office). *Telephone:* (212) 456-2060 (office). *Fax:* (212) 456-1246 (office). *Website:* abcnews.go.com/GMA (office).

SAWYER, Robert James, BAA; Canadian writer; b. 29 April 1960, Ottawa, Ont.; m. Carolyn Joan Clink 1984. *Education:* Ryerson Polytechnical Institute. *Career:* fmr mem. creative writing faculties Univ. of Toronto, Ryerson Univ., Humber Coll, Banff Centre; mem. Crime Writers of Canada, MWA, SFWA, Writers Union of Canada. *Publications:* Golden Fleece (Aurora Award) 1990, Far-Seer 1992, Fossil Hunter 1993, Foreigner 1994, End of an Era 1994, The Terminal Experiment (Nebula Award, Aurora Award) 1995, Starplex (Aurora Award) 1996, Illegal Alien 1997, Frameshift (Seiun Award) 1997, Factoring Humanity (Premio UPC de Ciencia Ficción), 1998, Flashforward (Aurora Award, Premio UPC de Ciencia Ficción) 1999, Calculating God 2000, Hominids (Hugo Award) 2002, Humans 2003, Hybrids 2003, Relativity (essays and stories, Aurora Award) 2004, Identity Theft Premio UPC de Ciencia Ficción) 2004, Mindscan (John W. Campbell Memorial Award for Best Science Fiction Novel of the Year) 2005, Rollback 2007, Identuty Theft 2008, Wake 2008, Watch 2008, Wonder 2008, Distant Early Warnings: Canada's Best Science Fiction 2009. *Honours:* Dr hc (Laurentian Univ.) 2007; Aurora Award, Canadian Science Fiction and Fantasy Asscn, 1992; Homer Awards, 1992, 1993; Writer's Reserve Grant, Ontario Arts Council, 1993, Toronto Public Library Celebrates Reading Award 2007, Galaxy Prize, Chengdu Int. Science Fiction and Fantasy Festival 2007. *Address:* c/o Ralph Vicinanza, 303 West 18th Street, New York, NY 10011, USA. *Telephone:* (212) 924-7090. *Fax:* (212) 691-9644. *E-mail:* sawyerrj@sfwriter.com. *Website:* www.sfwriter.com; www.sfwriter.com/blog.htm.

SAWYER, Roger Martyn, BA, DipEd, PhD, FRGS; British historian; b. 15 Dec. 1931, Gloucestershire; s. of Charles F. Sawyer and Winifred A. Sawyer (née Martin); m. Daisy Harte 1952; two s. *Education:* University of Wales, University of Southampton. *Career:* Housemaster, Blue Coat School, Edgbaston 1958–60; Deputy Head then Headmaster, Bembridge Prep. School 1960–83; Gov. Wycliffe Coll.; Research Fellow, The Airey Neave Trust; mem. Anti-Slavery Int. (Council mem. 1984–98), Bembridge Sailing Club, Independent Asscn of Preparatory Schools, Old Wycliffian Soc. *Publications:* Casement: The Flawed Hero 1984, Slavery in the Twentieth Century 1986, Children Enslaved 1988, The Island from Within (ed.) 1990, 'We are but Women': Women in Ireland's History 1993, Roger Casement's Diaries 1910: The Black and The White (ed.) 1997, The Symbolism of Womanhood 1998; contrib. to Anti-Slavery Reporter, BBC History Magazine, Immigrants and Minorities, South, UN Development Forum. *Honours:* T. G. James Prize in Educ. 1957, Airey Neave Award 1985. *Address:* Ducie House, Darts Lane, Bembridge, Isle of Wight, PO35 5YH, England (home). *Telephone:* (1983) 873384 (home).

SAYER, Ian Keith Terence; British writer; b. 30 Oct. 1945, Norwich, Norfolk, England; three s. three d. *Publications:* Nazi Gold: The Story of the World's Greatest Robbery 1984, America's Secret Army: The Untold Story of the Counter Intelligence Corps 1989, Hitler's Last General: The Case Against Wilhelm Mohnke 1989, Hitler's Bastard: Through Hell and Back in Nazi Germany and Stalin's Russia (ed.) 2003, Hitler and Women: The Love Life of Adolf Hitler 2004; contrib. to Freight News (columnist), Express Magazine (columnist), Sunday Times Magazine. *Address:* Westerlands, Sherbourne Drive, Sunningdale, Berks., SL5 0LG, England (home). *E-mail:* ian@sayer.net (home).

SAYLE, Alexei David; British writer, actor, presenter and comedian; b. 7 Aug. 1952, Liverpool, England; s. of Joseph Henry Sayle and Molly (Malka) Sayle (née Mendelson); m. Linda Rawsthorn 1974. *Education:* Alsop Grammar School, Southport Coll. of Art, Chelsea School of Art, Garnett Coll. Roehampton. *Career:* stand-up comedian 1980s; has written, co-written and performed in numerous comedy shows, films, and series; MC, Comedy Store, London 1979–80, Comic Strip Club 1980–81; columnist, Time Out, Sunday Mirror, The Independent. *Films:* as actor: Gorky Park 1983, The Supergrass 1985, The Bride 1985, Indiana Jones and the Last Crusade 1989, Carry On Columbus 1992, Swing 1999, The Thief Lord 2006. *Radio:* series: Alexei Sayle and the Fish People (Capital Radio) 1979, Alexei Sayle and the Dutch Lieutenant's Trousers (Capital Radio) 1980, Sorry About Last Night (BBC Radio 4) 1999, Chopwell Soviet (BBC Radio 4) 2006, Alexei Sayle's Alternative Take (BBC Radio 2) 2007, Where Did all the Money Go? (Smooth Network) 2008; documentaries: Migrant Music (BBC Radio 2) 2008. *Television:* as writer and/or actor: The Comic Strip Presents (Channel 4) 1982–2005, Whoops Apocalypse (series) 1982, The Private Life of the Ford Cortina (documentary) (BBC 2) 1982, The Young Ones (series) 1982, 1984, Alexei Sayle's Stuff (series) (Int. Emmy Award) 1988, 1989, 1991, Itch (film) 1990, Selling Hitler (drama series) 1991, Sex Drugs and Dinner (documentary) (BBC 2) 2004 (Best Network Programme, One World Awards) 1993, The All New Alexei Sayle Show 1994, 1995, Sorry About Last Night (film) 1995, Great Railway Journeys of the World: Aleppo to Aquaba (documentary) 1996, Alexei Sayle's Merry-Go-Round (series) 1998, Arabian Nights (film) 2000, Lose Weight...Ask Me How (film) 2001, Tipping the Velvet (drama series) 2002, Keen Eddie (Fox TV) 2003, Alexei Sayle's Liverpool (BBC 2 documentary series) 2008. *Publications:* Geoffrey The Tube Train And The Fat Comedian (graphic novel) 1987, Train to Hell (novel) (co-author) 1984, Barcelona Plates (short stories) 2000, The Dog Catcher (short stories) 2001, Overtaken (novel) 2003, End of Story (short story) 2004, The Weeping Women Hotel (novel) 2006, Mister Roberts (novel) 2008, Stalin ate my Homework (memoir) 2010; contrib. to the Observer, Independent, Car magazine, Time Out, Sunday Times. *Literary Agent:* Deborah Rogers, Rogers, Coleridge & White Ltd, 20 Powis Mews, London, W11 1JN, England. *Telephone:* (20) 7221-3717. *Fax:* (20) 7229-9084. *E-mail:* info@rcwlitagency.com; www.rcwlitagency.com. *Website:* www.alexeisayle.me.

SAYLOR, Steven Warren, (Aaron Travis), BA; American writer; b. 23 March 1956, Port Lavaca, TX; s. of Lyman Harrison Saylor and Lucy Lee Reeves Saylor; pnr Richard K. Solomon (registered 1991, m. 2008). *Education:* Univ. of Texas at Austin. *Publications:* Roman Blood 1991, Arms of Nemesis 1992, Catilina's Riddle 1993, The Venus Throw 1995, A Murder on the Appian Way 1996, House of the Vestals 1997, Rubicon 1999, A Twist at the End (aka Honour the Dead) 2000, Last Seen in Massilia 2000, A Mist of Prophecies 2002, Have You Seen Dawn? 2003, The Judgement of Caesar 2004, A Gladiator Dies Only Once 2005, Roma 2007, The Triumph of Caesar 2008, Empire: The Novel of Imperial Rome 2010; as Aaron Travis: Slaves of the Empire 1985, Big Shots 1993, Beast of Burden 1993, Exposed 1993, The Flesh Fables 1994, In the Blood 1995, Tag Team Studs 1997; contrib. to books and periodicals. *Honours:* MWA Robert L. Fish Memorial Award 1993, Lambda Literary Award 1994. *Address:* c/o Constable & Robinson Ltd, 3 The Lanchester, 162 Fulham Palace Road, London, W6 9ER, England (office). *E-mail:* steven@stevensaylor.com (office). *Website:* www.stevensaylor.com.

SCAGLIONE, Aldo Domenico, DLitt; Italian writer and academic; b. 10 Jan. 1925, Turin; m. 1st Jeanne M. Daman 1952 (died 1986); m. 2nd Marie M. Burns 1992. *Education:* Univ. of Turin. *Career:* mem. Faculty, Univ. of California, Berkeley 1952–68; W. R. Kenan Prof., Univ. of North Carolina 1969–87; Prof., New York University 1987–91, Erich Maria Remarque Prof. of Literature 1991–; Fulbright Scholar 1951; Guggenheim Fellowship 1958; Newbery Fellow 1964; Fellow, Univ. of Wisconsin Inst. for the Humanities 1981; mem. American Asscn for Italian Studies (Hon. Pres. 1989), Boccaccio Asscn of America (Pres. 1980–83), Medieval Acad. of America. *Publications:* Nature and Love in the Late Middle Ages 1963, Ars Grammatica 1970, The Classical Theory of Composition 1972, The Theory of German Word Order 1981, The Liberal Arts and the Jesuit College System 1986, Knights at Court 1991, Essays on the Art of Discourse 1998; contributions: professional journals. *Honours:* Knight of the Order of Merit, Republic of Italy.

SCALES-TRENT, Judy, BA, MA, JD; American academic, writer and poet; b. 1 Oct. 1940, Winston-Salem, NC; one s. *Education:* Oberlin College, Middlebury College, Northwestern University School of Law. *Career:* Adjunct Faculty, Catholic University Law School 1983; Prof. of Law, SUNY at Buffalo

1984–; Visiting Prof. of Law, Univ. Cheikh Anta Diop de Dakar 1990–91, St Mary's University School of Law 1994. *Publications:* Notes of a White Black Woman: Race, Color, Community 1995. Contributions: anthologies, literary periodicals and law journals. *Honours:* Fulbright Award 1990–91, Baldy Center for Law and Social Policy Award, SUNY at Buffalo 1986, 1991–93, William J. Magavern Fellowship 1993. *Address:* 352 Old Meadow Road, East Amherst, NY 14051, USA.

SCALFARI, Eugenio, DIur; Italian editor and journalist; b. 6 April 1924, Civitavecchia; m. Simonetta de Benedetti 1959; two d. *Career:* Dir L'Europeo (news magazine) 1945–54, Ed.-in-Chief –1963; Promoter Partito Radicale 1958, L'Espresso 1955–, Ed.-in-Chief 1963–68, Man. Dir 1970–75; Promoter La Repubblica 1976–, Ed.-in-Chief 1976–96, Dir 1988–; Deputy to Parl. 1968–72; currently columnist, La Repubblica and L'Espresso. *Publications include:* Incontro con Io 1994, Alla ricerca della morale perduta 1995, Il Labirinto 1998, La ruga sulla fronte 2001, La Ruga Sulla Fronte 2001, Le Prince inconstant (co-author) 2003, L'uomo che non credeva in Dio 2008, La Sera Andavamo in Via Veneto 2009, Per l'alto mare aperto 2010, Scuote l'anima mia Eros 2011, Rapporto sul Neocapitalismo Italiano, Il Potere Economico in URSS, L'Autunno della Repubblica, Razza Padrona, Interviste ai Potenti, L'Anno di Craxi. *Honours:* Siena Award 1985, Journalist of the Year Award 1986, Premio Ischia alla Carriera 1996, Premio St Vincent alla Carriera. *Address:* c/o La Repubblica, Via Cristoforo Colombo 90, 00147 Rome, Italy. *Telephone:* (06) 49821.

SCAMMACCA, Nat, BA, MA; American academic (retd), writer and poet; b. 20 July 1924, Brooklyn, New York; m. Nina Scammacca 1948; one s. two d. *Education:* Long Island Univ., New York Univ., Univ. of Perugia. *Career:* served as pilot in USAF in India-Burma-China theatre during World War II; social worker, Italian Bd of Guardians; Prof. of English, British College, Palermo (retd); Ed. Third Page, Trapani Nuova (newspaper); mem. Poets and Writers, New York City. *Publications include:* Two Worlds (novel) 1980, Schammachanat (Italian and English) 1985, Bye Bye America (short stories) 1986, Cricepeo (Italian and English) (three vols) 1990, Sikano L'Amerikano! (short stories) 1991, Due Poeti Americani (Italian and English, co-author) 1994, The Hump (World War II stories and poems) 1994; contributions: anthologies and periodicals. *Honours:* Air Medal, Bronze Star, USAF, Taormina City Poetry Prize 1978, Premio Letterario Sikania Prize 1988, VII Premio di Poesia Petrosino Prize 1991. *Website:* www.natscammacca.com.

SCAMMELL, Michael, BA, PhD; British/American writer, translator and academic; *Professor Emeritus, Columbia University*; b. 16 Jan. 1935, Lyndhurst, Hants., England; s. of Frederick George Talbot Scammell and Estelle Constance Scammell (née Ayling); m. 1st Erika Roettges; one s. three d.; m. 2nd Rosemary Nossiff. *Education:* Univ. of Nottingham, Columbia Univ., New York. *Career:* Lecturer in English, Ljubljana Univ., Yugoslavia 1958–59; Columbia Univ. Fellow 1959–61; Lecturer in Russian, Hunter Coll., CUNY 1961–62; Language Supervisor, Programme Asst, BBC, London 1965–67; Ed. Index on Censorship, London 1971–80; Dir Writers and Scholars Educational Trust, London 1971–80; Sr Visiting Fellow, Russian Inst. 1976–84; Fellow, New York Inst. for the Humanities 1982–84; Chair. Writers in Prison Cttee, International PEN 1976–84; Prof. of Russian Literature, Cornell Univ., Ithaca, NY 1987–94; Prof. of Creative Writing, Columbia Univ. 1994–; Pres. American PEN Center 1998–2001; Vice-Pres. International PEN 1986–; mem. Soc. of Authors (Vice-Chair. 1976–79), Translation Asscn, English PEN Centre; Fellow, American Acad. of Arts and Sciences. *Publications:* Blue Guide to Yugoslavia 1969, Russia's Other Writers (ed.) 1970, Alexander Solzhenitsyn 1971, Unofficial Art from the Soviet Union (ed.) 1977, Solzhenitsyn: A Biography 1984, The Solzhenitsyn Files: Secret Soviet Documents Reveal One Man's Fight Against the Monolith (ed.) 1995; translator: Cities and Years 1962, Crime and Punishment 1963, The Gift 1963, The Defense 1964, Childhood, Boyhood and Youth 1964, My Testimony 1969, Nothing is Lost: Selected Poems by Edvard Kochek (with Veno Taufer) 2004, Koestler: The Indispensable Intellectual (PEN/Jacqueline Bograd Weld Award for Biography 2010, Spears Magazine Award for Biography 2010) 2009; contrib. to periodicals including TLS, The Observer, The Times, Daily Telegraph, London, Sunday Telegraph, London, New York Times Book Review, New York Review of Books, New Republic, Harpers, USA, Los Angeles Times. *Honours:* Los Angeles Times Book Prize for Biography 1985. *Literary Agent:* c/o ICM, 825 Eighth Avenue, New York, NY 10019, USA; c/o AP Watt Ltd, 20 John Street, London, WC1N 2DR, England. *Telephone:* (20) 7405-6774 (London). *Fax:* (20) 7831-2154 (London). *E-mail:* Urban@icmtalent .com; apw@apwatt.co.uk. *Website:* www.apwatt.co.uk. *Address:* 605 West 113 Street, Apt 32, New York, NY 10025 (home); 82 Gulf Road, Dover, NH 03820, USA (home). *Telephone:* (212) 854-4391 (office). *E-mail:* ms474@columbia.edu (office). *Website:* michaelscammell.com.

SCARDINO, Dame Marjorie Morris, DBE, BA, JD; American/British journalist, lawyer and business executive; *CEO, Pearson PLC*; b. 25 Jan. 1947, Flagstaff, Ariz.; d. of Robert Weldon Morris and Beth Lamb Morris; m. Albert James Scardino 1974; two s. one d. *Education:* Baylor Univ., Univ. of San Francisco. *Career:* started career as reporter, Associated Press; Partner, Brannen, Wessels & Searcy law firm, Savannah, Ga 1975–85; Co-founder (with husband) and Publr The Georgia Gazette Co. (won Pulitzer Prize) 1978–85; Pres. The Economist Newspaper Group Inc., New York 1985–93, Chief Exec. The Economist Group, London 1993–97, mem. Bd of Dirs and CEO Pearson PLC 1997–; Dir (non-exec.) Nokia Corpn 2001–, Vice-Chair. 2007–, Chair. Corp. Governance and Nomination Cttee, mem. Personnel Cttee; mem. Bd of Trustees The MacArthur Foundation, Carter Center, Victoria & Albert Museum. *Honours:* Hon. Fellow, London Business School, City and Guilds of London Inst., RSA; Hon. LLD (Univ. of Exeter); Hon. DHumLitt (New School Univ.); Dr hc (Heriot-Watt Univ., Brunel Univ.); Veuve Clicquot Businesswoman of the Year Award 1998, Benjamin Franklin Medal, RSA 2001, ranked by Fortune magazine amongst the 50 Most Powerful Women in Business outside the US (first) 2001–03, (third) 2004–05, (fifth) 2006, (third) 2007, (fifth) 2008, (third) 2009–11, ranked by Forbes magazine amongst The World's 100 Most Powerful Women (59th) 2004, (18th) 2005, (31st) 2006, (17th) 2007, (20th) 2008, (19th) 2009, (63rd) 2010, (94th) 2011. *Address:* Pearson PLC, 80 Strand, London, WC2R 0RL, England (office). *Telephone:* (20) 7010-2300 (office). *Fax:* (20) 7010-6601 (office). *E-mail:* marjorie.scardino@pearson.com (office). *Website:* www.pearson.com (office).

SCARF, Margaret (Maggie), BA; American writer; b. 13 May 1932, Philadelphia; m. Herbert Eli Scarf 1953; three d. *Education:* South Connecticut State Univ. *Career:* Contributing Ed., The New Republic 1975–; Fellow, Center for Advanced Study, Stanford, CA 1977–78, 1985–86; Writer-in-Residence, Jonathan Edwards Coll., Yale Univ. 1992–; mem. Connecticut Soc. of Psychoanalytic Psychologists, PEN. *Publications:* Body, Mind, Behavior 1976, Unfinished Business 1980, Intimate Partners 1987, Intimate Worlds: Life Inside the Family 1995, Secrets, Lies, Betrayals 2005, September Songs 2009; contributions: magazines and journals. *Honours:* Nat. Media Award, American Psychological Foundation 1973, Ford Foundation Fellow 1973–74, Nieman Fellow, Harvard University 1975–76, Alicia Patterson Fellow 1978–79, Smith Richardson Foundation grants 1991, 1992, 1993, 1994. *Literary Agent:* c/o Camille McDuffie, Goldberg McDuffie Communications, 444 Madison Avenue, Suite 3300, New York, NY 10022, USA. *Telephone:* (212) 446-5106. *E-mail:* cmcduffie@goldbergmcduffie.com. *Website:* www.goldbergmcduffie.com. *E-mail:* maggie@maggiescarf.com (office). *Website:* www.maggiescarf.com.

SCARFE, Allan John, BA, DipEd, TPTC; Australian teacher and writer; b. 30 March 1931, Caulfield, Vic.; m. Wendy Scarfe 1955; four c. *Education:* Univ. of Melbourne. *Publications include:* A Corpse in Calcutta 2000, The Dissident Guru 2004, The Scourge of Termite-ists 2009; with Wendy Scarfe: A Mouthful of Petals 1967, 1972, 2011, Tiger on a Rein 1969, People of India 1972, The Black Australians 1974, Victims or Bludgers?: Case Studies in Poverty in Australia 1974, J. P: his Biography 1975, 1997, Victims or Bludgers?: A Poverty Inquiry for Schools 1978, Labor's Titan: The Story of Percy Brookfield 1878–1921 1983, All That Grief: Migrant Recollections of Greek Resistance to Facism 1941–49 1994, Remembering Jayaprakash 1997, No Taste for Carnage: Alex Sheppard – A Portrait 1913–1997 1998; contrib. to Overland, Australian Short Stories, Dislocations, Chance Encounters, Borderland, Mattoid Grange/Deakin Univ. anthology 2008, 2009. *Honours:* Australia Literature Boards Grants (with Wendy Scarfe) 1980, 1988. *Address:* 8 Bostock Street, Warrnambool, Vic. 3280, Australia.

SCARFE, Gerald A., CBE; British cartoonist; b. 1 June 1936, London; m. Jane Asher; two s. one d. *Career:* joined Daily Mail as political cartoonist 1966; political cartoonist London Sunday Times 1967–; contributed cartoons to Punch 1960–, Private Eye 1961–, Time 1967–; animation and film directing BBC 1969–; designer and dir of animation for Pink Floyd The Wall concerts and film 1975–78; consultant designer and character design for film Hercules 1997. *Exhibitions include:* Waddell Gallery, New York 1968, 1970, Vincent Price Gallery, Chicago 1969, Grosvenor Gallery 1969, 1970, Pavillion d'Humour, Montreal 1969, Expo 1970, Osaka 1970, Nat. Portrait Gallery 1971, Royal Festival Hall 1983, Langton Gallery 1986, Chris Beetles Gallery 1989, Nat. Portrait Gallery 1998–99, Comic Art Gallery, Melbourne, Gerald Scarfe in Southwark 2001, Fine Arts Soc., London 2005, Halle, Germany 2009, Wilhelm Busch Gallery, Germany 2010. *Television includes:* dir and presenter Scarfe on Art 1991, Scarfe on Sex 1991, Scarfe on Class 1992, Scarfe in Paradise 1992; subject of Scarfe and His Work with Disney (South Bank Special). *Theatre design:* Ubu Roi (Traverse Theatre) 1957, What the Butler Saw (Oxford Playhouse) 1980, No End of Blame (Royal Court, London) 1981, Orpheus in the Underworld (English ENO, Coliseum) 1985, Who's a Lucky Boy (Royal Exchange, Manchester) 1985, Born Again 1990, The Magic Flute (Los Angeles Opera) 1992, An Absolute Turkey 1993, Mind Millie for Me (Haymarket, London) 1996, Fantastic Mr. Fox (Los Angeles Opera) 1998, Peter and the Wolf (Holiday on Ice, Paris and world tour) 2000, The Nutcracker 2002,. *Publications include:* Gerald Scarfe's People 1966, Indecent Exposure 1973, Expletive Deleted: The Life and Times of Richard Nixon 1974, Gerald Scarfe 1982, Father Kissmass and Mother Claus 1985, Scarfe by Scarfe (autobiog.) 1986, Gerald Scarfe's Seven Deadly Sins 1987, Line of Attack 1988, Scarfeland 1989, Scarfe on Stage 1992, Scarfe Face 1993, Hades: The Truth at Last 1997, Heroes & Villains 2003, Drawing Blood: Forty-five Years of Scarfe Uncensored 2005, Monsters: How George Bush Saved The World & Other Tall Stories 2008, The Making of Pink Floyd's The Wall 2010. *Honours:* Hon. Fellow, London Inst. 2001; Hon. LLD (Liverpool) 2001, (Dundee) 2007; Zagreb Prize for BBC film Long Drawn Out Trip 1973, BAFTA Award for Scarfe on Scarfe 1987, Olivier Award for Absolute Turkey 1993, Cartoonist of the Year, British Press Awards 2006. *Literary Agent:* c/o Simpson Fox Associates, Shaftesbury Mansions, 52 Shaftsbury Avenue, London, W1D 6LP, England. *Telephone:* (20) 7434-9167. *Website:* www.geraldscarfe.com.

SCARFE, Norman, MBE, MA, FSA; British writer; b. 1 May 1923, Felixstowe. *Education:* Univ. of Oxford. *Career:* served as subaltern, 76th (Highland) Field Regt, RA 1943–46, experienced active service during Normandy landing 1944;

Lecturer, Dept of History, Univ. of Leicester 1949–63; Chair., Centre of East Anglia Studies, Univ. of East Anglia, 1989–96; mem. Int. PEN, Suffolk Book League (founder-chair. 1982), Suffolk Records Soc. (founder, hon. gen. ed. 1958–92, pres. 2002). *Publications:* Suffolk, A Shell Guide 1960, Essex, A Shell Guide 1968, The Suffolk Landscape 1972, Cambridgeshire, A Shell Guide 1983, Suffolk in the Middle Ages 1986, A Frenchman's Year in Suffolk (1784) 1988, Innocent Espionage: The La Rochefoucauld Brothers' Tour of England in 1785 1995, Jocelin of Brakelond 1997, To the Highlands in 1786: The Inquisitive Journey of a Young French Aristocrat 2001, Assault Division: A History of the 3rd Division from the Invasion of Normandy to the Surrender of Germany 2004; contribs to Proceedings, Suffolk Institute of Archaeology, Aldeburgh Festival Annual Programme Book, Country Life, The Book Collector, Dictionary of National Biography, The Impact of the Railways on Society in Britain: Essays in Honour of Jack Simmons 2003. *Honours:* Citoyen d'Honneur, Colleville Montgomery 1994; Hon. LittD (Univ. of East Anglia) 1989; East Anglia's History: Studies in Honour of Norman Scarfe (ed by Christopher Harper-Bill, Carole Rawcliffe, Richard Wilson) 2002. *Address:* The Garden Cottage, 3 Burkitt Road, Woodbridge, Suffolk, IP12 4JJ, England (home). *Telephone:* (1394) 387058 (home).

SCARFE, Wendy Elizabeth, BA, BLitt, ATTC; Australian writer, teacher and poet; b. (Wendy Elizabeth Roper), 21 Nov. 1933, Adelaide, S Australia; m. Allan Scarfe 1955; four c. *Education:* Univ. of Melbourne. *Publications:* fiction: The Lotus Throne 1976, Neither Here Nor There 1978, Laura My Alter Ego 1988, The Day They Shot Edward 1991, 1992, 2003, Miranda 1998, Fishing for Strawberries 2001, Jerusha Braddon, Painter 2005, An Original Talent 2010; poetry: Shadow and Flowers 1964, 1984, Dragonflies and Edges (with Jeffrey Ronald Keith) 2004; with Allan Scarfe: A Mouthful of Petals 1967, 1972, 2011, Tiger on a Rein 1969, People of India 1972, The Black Australians 1974, Victims or Bludgers?: Case Studies in Poverty in Australia 1974, J. P: His Biography 1975, 1997, Victims or Bludgers?: A Poverty Inquiry for Schools 1978, Labor's Titan: The Story of Percy Brookfield, 1878–1921 (ed.) 1983, All That Grief: Migrant Recollections of Greek Resistance to Fascism, 1941–1949 1994, Remembering Jayaprakash 1997, No Taste for Carnage: Alex Sheppard – A Portrait 1913–1997 1998; contrib. to Overland, Australian Short Stories, Chance Encounters, Borderland, Mattoid Grange/Deakin Univ. anthology 2008, 2009. *Honours:* Australia Literature Board Grants (with Allan Scarfe) 1980, 1988. *Address:* 8 Bostock Street, Warrnambool, Vic. 3280, Australia.

SCARPA, Tiziano; Italian writer, playwright and poet; b. 16 May 1963, Venice. *Plays include:* Il professor Manganelli e l'ingegner Gadda 2005, Comuni mortali 2005, Gli straccioni 2005, La custode 2006, L'ultima casa 2007, L'inseguitore 2008. *Radio:* Pop Com (Prix Italia 1997), La visita 2006, La musica nascosta 2008. *Publications:* novels: Occhi sulla Graticola 1996, Kamikaze d'Occidente 2003, Stabat Mater (Premio Strega, Premio Super-Mondello) 2009, Le cose fondamentali 2010; short stories: Amore, cosa voglio da te 1998, Cosa voglio da te 2003, Amami (co-author) 2007; essays: Cos'è questo fracasso? 2000, Batticuore fuorilegge 2006; poetry: Nelle galassie oggi come oggi (co-author) 2001, Groppi d'amore nella scuraglia 2005, Discorso di una guida turistica di fronte al tramonto 2008; other: Venezia è un pesce (travel guide) 2000, Corpo (aphorisms) 2004; regular contrib. to nat. newspapers. *Address:* c/o Serpent's Tail, 3A Exmouth House, Pine Street, London, EC1R 0JH, England (office). *Website:* www.serpentstail.com (office).

SCHALLER, George Beals, PhD; American zoologist, academic and author; *Vice-President, Science and Exploration Program, Wildlife Conservation Society*; b. 26 May 1933, Berlin, Germany; s. of George Ludwig Schaller and Bettina Iwersen (née Byrd); m. Kay Suzanne Morgan 1957; two s. *Education:* Univ. of Alaska, Univ. of Wisconsin-Madison. *Career:* moved to USA in his teens; Fellow, Dept of Behavioral Sciences, Stanford Univ. 1962–63; Research Assoc., Johns Hopkins Univ., Baltimore 1963–66; Adjunct Assoc. Prof., Rockefeller Univ., New York 1966–72; Research Zoologist, Wildlife Conservation Soc. 1966–, Dir Int. Conservation Program, New York Zoological Soc. 1979–88, now Vice-Pres. Science and Exploration Program and Ella Millbank Foshay Chair in Wildlife Conservation; Adjunct Prof., Peking (now Beijing) Univ.; Research Assoc., American Museum of Natural History; Fellow, Guggenheim Foundation 1971. *Achievements include:* recognized as one of the world's leading field biologists, studying wildlife throughout Africa, Asia and S America. *Publications:* The Mountain Gorilla 1963, The Year of the Gorilla 1964, The Deer and the Tiger 1967, The Serengeti Lion (Nat. Book Award 1973) 1972, Mountain Monarchs 1977, Stones of Silence 1980, The Giant Pandas of Wolong (co-author) 1985, The Last Panda 1993, Tibet's Hidden Wilderness 1997, Wildlife of the Tibetan Steppe 1998, Antelopes, Deer and Relatives (co-ed.) 2000. *Honours:* Hon. Dir Explorers' Club 1991; Order of Golden Ark (Netherlands) 1978; Int. Cosmos Prize (Japan) 1996, Tyler Prize for Environmental Achievement 1997, Gold Medal, World Wildlife Fund 1980, Beebe Fellowship, Wildlife Conservation Soc. 2006, Lifetime Achievement Award, Nat. Geographic Soc. 2007, Indianapolis Prize 2008. *Address:* Wildlife Conservation Society, 2300 Southern Boulevard, Bronx, New York, NY 10460, USA (office). *Telephone:* (718) 220-6807 (office). *Fax:* (718) 364-4275 (office). *E-mail:* asiaprogram@wcs.org (office). *Website:* www.wcs.org (office).

SCHAMA, Simon Michael, CBE, MA; British historian, academic, writer and art critic; *University Professor, Department of History, Columbia University*; b. 13 Feb. 1945, London; s. of the late Arthur Schama and of Gertrude Steinberg; m. Virginia Papaioannou 1983; one s. one d. *Education:* Christ's Coll., Cambridge. *Career:* Fellow and Dir of Studies in History, Christ's Coll., Cambridge 1966–76; Fellow and Tutor in Modern History, Brasenose Coll., Oxford 1976–80; Prof. of History (Mellon Prof. of the Social Sciences), Harvard Univ. 1980; Univ. Prof., Columbia Univ. 1997–; art critic, New Yorker 1995–; Contributing Ed., Financial Times 2009–; Vice-Pres. Poetry Soc. *Television:* Rembrandt: The Public Eye and the Private Gaze (film for BBC) 1992, A History of Britain (series) 2000–01, The Power of Art (series) 2006, The American Future: A History (series) 2008. *Publications:* Patriots and Liberators: Revolution in the Netherlands 1780–1813 1977, Two Rothschilds and the Land of Israel 1979, The Embarrassment of Riches: An Interpretation of Dutch Culture in the Golden Age 1987, Citizens: A Chronicle of the French Revolution 1989, Dead Certainties (Unwarranted Speculations) 1991, Landscape and Memory 1995, Rembrandt's Eyes 1999, A History of Britain Vol. 1: At the Edge of the World? 3000 BC–AD 1603 2000, Vol. 2: The British Wars 1603–1776 2001, Vol. 3: The Fate of Empire 1776–2001 2002, Hang-Ups: Essays on Painting 2004, Rough Crossings: Britain, the Slaves and the American Revolution 2005, Power of Art 2006, The American Future: A History 2008, Scribble, Scribble, Scribble 2010. *Honours:* Wolfson Prize 1977, Leo Gershoy Prize, American Historical Asscn 1978, Nat. Cash Register Book Prize for Non-Fiction (for Citizens) 1990. *Address:* Department of History, 522 Fayerweather Hall, Columbia University, New York, NY 10027, USA (office). *Telephone:* (212) 854-4593 (office). *E-mail:* sms53@columbia.edu (office). *Website:* www.columbia.edu/cu/history (office).

SCHANBERG, Sydney H., BA; American journalist, academic and author; b. 17 Jan. 1934, Clinton, Mass; s. of Louis Schanberg and Freda Schanberg; m. Jane Freiman Schanberg; two d. *Education:* Harvard Univ. *Career:* joined New York Times 1959, reporter 1960, Bureau Chief, Albany, New York 1967–69, New Delhi, India 1969–73, SE Asia Corresp., Singapore 1973–75, City Ed. 1977–80, Columnist 1981–85; Assoc. Ed., Columnist Newsday newspaper, New York 1986–95; Chief of Investigative Unit, APBnews.com 2000–01; columnist for Village Voice, New York 2002–06; Adjunct Prof., Dept of Communication and Media, State Univ. of New York, New Paltz, first Fellow apptd to the James H. Ottaway Sr Visiting Professorship 2002. *Film:* Academy Award-winning film 'The Killing Fields' based on his experiences covering the war in Cambodia for The New York Times. *Publications:* The Death and Life of Dith Pran 1985, Beyond the Killing Fields – War Writings 2010. *Honours:* numerous awards including Page One Award for Reporting 1972, George Polk Memorial Award 1972, Overseas Press Club Award 1972, Bob Considine Memorial Award 1975, Pulitzer Prize 1975, Elijah Parish Lovejoy Award, Colby Coll. 1992, Bart Richards Award for Outstanding Media Criticism 2005. *Address:* Box 236, Rifton, NY 12471, USA (office). *Telephone:* (212) 769-0960 (office). *E-mail:* sydneyschanberg@yahoo.com. *Website:* www.beyondthekillingfields.com.

SCHÄTZING, Frank; German writer; b. 1957, Cologne. *Publications:* Tod und Teufel 1995, Mordshunger 1996, Die dunkle Seite 1997, Keine Angst (short stories) 1997, lauTlos 2000, KölnKrimiSpiel 2001, Der Schwarm 2004, Der Puppenspieler 2005, Nachrichten aus einem unbekannten Universum 2007, Limit 2009. *Address:* c/o Verlag Kiepenheuer & Witsch, Rondorferstrasse 5, 50968 Cologne, Germany (office). *Website:* www.kiwi-verlag.de (office); www.frank-schaetzing.com.

SCHEIBER, Harry Noel, AB, MA, PhD; American academic, writer and editor; *Stefan A. Riesenfeld Professor of Law and History and Director, Earl Warren Institute for Legal Research, University of California, Berkeley*; b. 1935, New York, NY. *Education:* Columbia Univ., New York, Cornell Univ. *Career:* Instructor to Assoc. Prof., Dartmouth Coll. 1960–68, Prof. of History 1968–71; Fellow, Centre for Advanced Study in the Behavioural Sciences, Stanford 1967, 1971; Prof. of American History, Univ. of California, San Diego, 1971–80, Prof. of Law, Univ. of California, Berkeley 1980–, Assoc. Dean 1990–93, 1996–99, Stefan A. Riesenfeld Prof. of Law and History 1991–, Dir Center for the Study of Law and Society 2000–01, Earl Warren Inst. for Legal Research 2002–, Sho Sato Program in Japanese and US Law; Fulbright Distinguished Sr Lecturer, Australia 1983; Ed. Yearbook of the California Supreme Court Historical Society 1994–; Visiting Research Prof., Univ. of Uppsala, Sweden 1995; mem. American Historical Asscn, California Supreme Court Historical Soc., Economic History Asscn, Law and Society Asscn, Org. of American Historians, American Acad. of Arts and Sciences 2003–, American Soc. for Legal History (Pres. 2003–05); mem. Bd of Advisors, National Sea Grant Legal Center 2004–; mem. Scientific Advisory Bd, Joint Ocean Commission Initiative 2007–; Fellow, Japan Soc. for the Promotion of Science 2001. *Publications:* The Wilson Administration and Civil Liberties 1960, United States Economic History 1964, America: Purpose and Power (co-author) 1965, The Condition of American Federalism 1966, The Frontier in American Development (co-ed.) 1969, The Old Northwest 1969, The Ohio Canal Era 1820–1861 1969, Black Labor in American History 1972, Agriculture in the Development of the Far West 1975, American Economic History (co-author) 1976, American Law and the Consitutional Order 1978, Perspectives on Federalism (ed.) 1987, Power Divided (co-ed.) 1989, Federalism and the Judicial Mind (ed.) 1993, Legal Culture and the Legal Profession (co-author) 1995, The State and Freedom of Contract 1998, Law of the Sea: The Common Heritage and Emerging Challenges 2000, Inter-Allied Conflicts and Ocean Law, 1945–1952 2001; contribs to professional journals. *Honours:* Hon. MA (Dartmouth Coll.) 1965; Hon. DJur (Uppsala) 1998; Guggenheim Fellowships 1971, 1988, Rockefeller Foundation Fellowship 1979, Nat. Endowment for the Humanities Fellowship 1985–86. *Address:* School of Law, 442 Boalt Hall (North Addition), University of California, Berkeley, CA 94720, USA (office). *Telephone:* (510) 643-9788 (office). *Fax:* (510) 642-2951 (office). E-mail: hscheiber@law.berkeley.edu (office). Website: www.law.berkeley.edu (office).

SCHELL, Jonathan, BA; American journalist and academic; b. 21 Aug. 1943, New York; s. of Orville Hickock Schell Jr and Marjorie Bertha; m. Elspeth Schell; two s. one d. *Education:* Putney School, Vt, Harvard Univ. and Int. Christian Univ., Tokyo. *Career:* mem. staff, New Yorker 1968–87; Fellow, Inst. of Politics, Kennedy School of Govt 1987, Shorenstein Center on the Press, Politics, and Public Policy 2002; Visiting Prof., Inst. of Liberal Arts, Emory Univ. Atlanta, Ga 1987, New York Univ. School of Journalism 1988; Ferris Prof., Princeton Univ. 1989; columnist, Newsday and New York Newsday 1990–96; Distinguished Visiting Writer, Wesleyan Univ. 1997–2002; Senior Fellow, Center for the Study of Globalization, Yale Univ. 2003, Distinguished Visiting Fellow 2005, now Visiting Lecturer, Yale Univ.; Harold Willens Peace Fellow, Nation Inst. 1998–, also Peace and Disarmament Correspondent for The Nation magazine; mem. New York Inst. for the Humanities, New York Univ. 1991–. *Publications:* The Village of Ben Suc 1967, The Military Half: An Account of Destruction in Quang Ngai and Quang Tin 1968, The Time of Illusion 1976, The Fate of the Earth (Melcher Book Award 1982) 1982, The Abolition, History in Sherman Park 1987, Observing the Nixon Years: Notes & Comment from the New Yorker on the Vietnam War and the Watergate Crisis 1969–75 1989, The Unconquerable World: Power, Nonviolence and the Will of the People 2004, A Hole in the World 2004, The Seventh Decade 2007. *Honours:* Lannan Award for Literary Non-fiction 2000. *Address:* The Nation Institute, 116 East 16th Street, 8th Floor, New York, NY 10003, USA (office). *Telephone:* (212) 822-0250 (office). *Fax:* (212) 253-5356 (office). *E-mail:* jonathan.schell@yale.edu (office). *Website:* www.nationinstitute.org (office).

SCHELL, Orville Hickok, BA, MA, PhD; American journalist, writer and academic; *Senior Fellow, Center on Communication Leadership, Annenberg School for Communication, University of Southern California*; b. 20 May 1940, New York, NY; m.; three s. *Education:* Stanford Univ., National Taiwan Univ., Harvard Univ., Univ. of California, Berkeley. *Career:* Overseas Development Training Associate Fellowship, Ford Foundation, Jakarta, Indonesia 1964–66; Foreign Area Training Fellowship, Center for Chinese Studies, Univ. of California 1967–68; Co-Dir Bay Area Institute 1968–71; Founder and Ed.-in-Chief, Pacific News Service 1970–71; China Correspondent, New Yorker Magazine 1975; Research Assoc. Univ. of California, Berkeley 1986, Regents' Lecturer 1990, Dean, Graduate School of Journalism 1996–2007; Sr Fellow, Center on Communication Leadership, Annenberg School for Communication, Univ. of Southern California 2007–; Arthur Ross Director, Center on US-China Relations, Asia Soc. 2007–; Visiting Distinguished Prof., Chico State Univ. 1987; Moderator, Issues and Perspectives on China, Voice of America 1995–97; Editor, Project Syndicate China column 2000–; Sr Fellow, Freedom Forum Media Studies Center, Columbia Univ. 1995; mem. Bd of Dirs World Affairs Council of San Francisco 1999–, Current Media 2005–, Homelands Productions; mem. Media Council, Davos World Economic Forum 1998–; mem. Authors' Guild, Council on Foreign Relations 1992–, Global Business Network, Human Rights Watch Board, Pacific Council, PEN, National Committee on US-China Relations 1984–. *Publications include:* The China Reader (with Frederick Crews) 1970, Modern China: The Story of a Revolution 1972, The Town That Fought to Save Itself 1976, In the People's Republic 1976, Brown 1978, Watch Out for the Foreign Guests: China Encounters the West 1981, Modern Meat: Antibiotics, Hormones and the Pharmaceutical Farm 1983, To Get Rich is Glorious: China in the 1980s 1984, Discos and Democracy: China in the Throes of Reform 1988, Mandate of Heaven: A New Generation of Entrepreneurs, Dissidents, Technocrats, and Bohemiams Grasp for Power in China 1994, The China Reader: The Reform Years (ed. with David Shambaugh) 1999, Virtual Tibet: The West's Fascination with the Roof of the World 1999; contributions: numerous books, reviews, and journals. *Honours:* Dr hc (Dominican Univ.) 2001; Alicia Patterson Foundation Journalism Fellowship 1981, MacDowell Colony Fellowship 1983, 1986, Guggenheim Fellowship 1989–90, Emmy Award (for 60 Minutes report Made In China) 1992, Overseas Press Club of American Award 1993, George Foster Peabody Award (as producer of WGBH-Frontline documentary The Gate of Heavenly Peace) 1997, Shorenstein Journalism Award for Covering Asia, Shorenstein Center on the Press, Politics and Public Policy and Stanford Univ. Asia-Pacific Research Center 2003, Fred Cody Lifetime Achievement Award, Northern California Book Awards 2005. *Address:* Center on Communication Leadership and Policy, 350 South Grand Avenue, Suite 3350, Los Angeles, CA 90071, USA (office). *Telephone:* (213) 337-3100 (office). *E-mail:* commlead@usc.edu (office). *Website:* communicationleadership.usc.edu (office); orvilleschell.com.

SCHELLING, Andrew, BA; American poet, writer, translator, ecology activist and academic; *Professor of Poetry and Translation, Naropa University*; b. 14 Jan. 1953, Washington, DC; s. of Thomas C. Schelling and Corinne Saposs Schelling; m. Kristina Loften 1980 (divorced 1993); one d. *Education:* Univ. of California at Santa Cruz. *Career:* has taught at Naropa Univ., Boulder, Colo since 1990, now Prof. of Poetry and Translation; Arts Faculty, Deer Park Inst., Himachal Pradesh, India. *Publications:* Claw Moraine (poetry) 1987, Dropping the Bow: Poems from Ancient India (trans.) (Harold Morton Landon Translation Award, Acad. of American Poets 1992) 1991, Ktaadn's Lamp (poetry) 1991, For Love of the Dark One: Songs of Mirabai (trans.) 1993, Moon is a Piece of Tea (poetry) 1993, The India Book: Essays and Translations from Indian Asia 1993, Twilight Speech: Essays on Sanskrit and Buddhist Poetics 1993, Two Immortals (essays) 1994, Disembodied Poetics: Annals of the Jack Kerouac School (co-ed.) 1994, Old Growth: Selected Poems and Notebooks, 1986–1994 1995, Songs of the Sons and Daughters of Buddha (co-trans.) 1996, The Road to Ocosingo 1998, The Cane Groves of Narmada River: Erotic Poems from Old India (trans.) 1998, Tea Shack Interior: New and Selected Poetry 2002, Wild Form, Savage Grammar (essays) 2003, Erotic Love Poems from India (trans.) 2004, Two Elk: A High Country Notebook 2005, The Wisdom Anthology of North American Buddhist Poetry (ed.) 2005, Old Tale Road (poetry) 2008, Kamini 2008, From the Arapaho Songbook (poetry) 2011, The Oxford Anthology of Bhakti Literature (ed.) 2011; contribs to numerous anthologies and periodicals. *Honours:* Acad. of American Poets Trans. Prize 1992, Witter Bynner Foundation for Poetry trans. grants 1996, 2001, Pres.'s Award and Faculty Award, Naropa Univ. *Address:* 1483 Old Tale Road, Boulder, CO 80303, USA (home). *Telephone:* (303) 546-3508 (office). *E-mail:* schell@ecentral.com (home). *Website:* www.naropa.edu/academics/graduate/writingpoetics/mfa/faculty.cfm (office).

SCHENKEL, Andrea Maria; German writer; b. 21 March 1962, Regensburg; m.; three c. *Publications:* novels: Tannöd (trans. as The Murder Farm) (Deutsche Krimi-Preis, Friedrich-Glauser-Preis, Corine Internationaler Buchpreis 2007, Martin Beck Award 2008) 2006, Kalteis (trans. as Ice Cold) (Deutsche Krimi-Preis 2008) 2007. *Literary Agent:* c/o Ira Scheidig, Im Hollergrund 203, 28357 Bremen, Germany. *Telephone:* (42) 3783056. *Fax:* (42) 3783057. *E-mail:* info@agentur-scheidig.de. *Website:* www.agentur-scheidig.de; www.andreaschenkel.de.

SCHERER, Peter Julian; New Zealand journalist; b. 15 Aug. 1937, Stratford; s. of Arnold F. Scherer and Constance M. White; m. Gaelyn P. Morgan 1964; one s. one d. *Education:* Browns Bay School and Takapuna Grammar School. *Career:* joined New Zealand Herald 1955; mem. later Chief, Wellington Bureau 1960–71; Chair. Parl. Press Gallery 1965; leader-writer, Duty Ed., Business News Ed. 1973–76, Editorial Man. 1977–83, Asst Ed. 1977–85; Ed. New Zealand Herald 1985–96; Dir Community Newspapers Ltd 1972–73, Wilson & Horton Group 1989–96, New Zealand Press Asscn 1991–96; Chair. New Zealand Associated Press 1985–90, New Zealand section, Commonwealth Press Union (CPU) 1989–94; Chair. Planning Cttee, North Health Medical Workforce 1996–97; Councillor, CPU, London 1989–94; mem. New Zealand Press Council 1988–97, Communications and Media Law Asscn 1990–97; mem. Communications Advisory Council New Zealand Comm. for UNESCO 1989–94; mem. Bd of Control, Newspaper Publishers Asscn of New Zealand 1991–96; mem. New Zealand Nat. Cttee for Security Co-operation in Asia-Pacific 1994–96, New Zealand Div., Inst. of Dirs 1989–96; other professional appointments; CPU Fellowship 1963. *Honours:* Cowan Prize 1959. *Address:* Apartment C, 25 Ring Terrace, St Mary's Bay, Auckland 1001 (home); 267 School Road, Tomarata, RD4 Wellsford 1242, New Zealand (home). *Telephone:* (9) 378-9184 (Auckland) (home); (9) 431-5244 (Wellsford) (home). *Fax:* (9) 431-5244 (Wellsford) (home); (9) 378-9184 (Auckland) (home). *E-mail:* gandpscherer@xtra.co.nz (home).

SCHERMBRUCKER, William (Bill) Gerald, BA, PGCE, MA, PhD; Canadian writer, editor and fmr educator; *Instructor Emeritus, Capilano College*; b. 23 July 1938, Eldoret, Kenya; m. 1st Janet I. Lewis 1959 (divorced); m. 2nd Joanne C. Oben 1972 (divorced); m. 3rd Sharon F. Sawatsky 1984; three s. one d. *Education:* Univ. of Cape Town, Univ. of London, Univ. of British Columbia. *Career:* part-time Lecturer, Univ. of East Africa 1963–64; Instructor in English, Capilano Coll., North Vancouver 1968–2000, Instructor Emeritus 2000–; Lecturer, Genessee Community Coll. 1972–73; Ed., The Capilano Review 1977–82; mem. Writers' Union of Canada (nat. council 1999–2003). *Publications:* The Aims and Strategies of Good Writing 1976, Readings for Canadian Writing Students (ed.) 1976, revised edn as The Capilano Reader 1984, Chameleon, and Other Stories 1983, Mimosa (Ethel Wilson Fiction Prize 1988, BC Book Prize 1988) 1988, Motortherapy and Other Stories 1993; contrib. to periodicals. *Honours:* Second Prize, CBC Literary Competition 1980. *Address:* 362 East Point Road, PO Box 53, Saturna, BC V0N 2Y0, Canada (home). *E-mail:* bscherm@capcollege.bc.ca.

SCHICKLER, David, MFA; American writer; m.; one s. *Education:* Georgetown Univ., Columbia Univ. *Career:* fmr teacher, The Harley School in Rochester, NY. *Publications:* fiction: Kissing in Manhattan (novel) 2001, The Smoker (short story for The New Yorker) 2003, Sweet and Vicious (novel) 2004; contrib. to Tin House, Zoetrope. *Address:* c/o Jennifer Carlson, Dunow, Carlson & Lerner Literary Agency, 27 West 20th Street, Suite 1107, New York, NY 10011, USA. *E-mail:* david@davidschickler.com. *Website:* www.davidschickler.com.

SCHIFF, James Andrew, AB, MA, PhD; American academic and writer; *Associate Professor, University of Cincinnati*; b. 6 Dec. 1958, Cincinnati, Ohio; m. 1989; three s. *Education:* Duke Univ., New York Univ. *Career:* Adjunct Asst Prof., Univ. of Cincinnati 1997–2000, Asst Prof. 2000–07, Assoc. Prof. 2007–; Ed. The John Updike Review; Consulting Ed. Critique; mem. Nat. Book Critics Circle, Modern Language Asscn. *Publications:* Updike's Version: Rewriting The Scarlet Letter 1992, Understanding Reynolds Price 1996, John Updike Revisited 1998, Critical Essays on Reynolds Price 1998, Updike in Cincinnati 2007; contrib. to Southern Review, American Literature, South Atlantic Review, Tin House, Studies in American Fiction, Critique, Boulevard, Missouri Review. *Address:* 2 Forest Hill Drive, Cincinnati, OH 45208, USA (home). *Telephone:* (513) 556-0930 (office); (513) 871-8219 (home). *Fax:* (513) 556-5960 (office). *E-mail:* james.schiff@uc.edu (office).

SCHIFFRIN, André, MA; American editor and publisher; *Director and Editor-at-Large, The New Press*; b. 12 June 1935, Paris, France; s. of Jacques Schiffrin and Simone Heymann; m. Maria Elena de la Iglesia 1961; two d. *Education:* Yale Univ. and Univ. of Cambridge. *Career:* with New American Library 1959–63; with Pantheon Books, New York 1962–90, Ed., Ed.-in-Chief, Man. Dir 1969–90; Publr Schocken Books (subsidiary of Pantheon Books Inc.) 1987–90; Pres. Fund for Ind. Publishing 1990–; Founder, Dir and Ed.-in-Chief The New Press, New York 1990–, currrently Ed.-at-Large; Visiting Fellow, Davenport Coll. 1977–79; Visiting Lecturer, Yale Univ. 1977, 1979; mem. Council Smithsonian Inst.; mem. Bd of Dirs New York Council for Humanities; mem. Special Cttee American Centre, Paris 1994–; mem. Visting Cttee of Grad. Faculty The New York School 1995–; other professional appts and affiliations. *Publications include:* L'Edition sans Editeurs 1999, The Business of Books 2000, Words and Money 2010; contribs to professional journals. *Honours:* Hon. Fellow, Trumbull Coll. Yale Univ.; Grinzane Cavour Prize, Italy 2003. *Address:* The New Press, 38 Greene Street, 4th Floor, New York, NY 10013 (office); 250 West 94th Street, New York, NY 10025, USA (home). *Telephone:* (212) 629-8802 (office). *Website:* www.thenewpress.com (office).

SCHIFRES, Michel Maurice Réné; French journalist; *Vice-President, Editorial Committee, Le Figaro*; b. 1 May 1946, Orléans; s. of Jacques Schifres and Paulette Mauduit; m. Josiane Gasnier (divorced); two c. *Education:* Lycée du Mans, Lycée de Caen, Faculté des Lettres de Caen, Centre de Formation des Journalistes. *Career:* journalist with Combat 1970–72, with Monde 1972–74; Head of Political Affairs Quotidien de Paris 1974–76; Asst Head of Political Affairs France-Soir 1976; Head of Political Affairs Journal du Dimanche 1977, Deputy Ed. 1979–82, Ed. 1982–86, Deputy Editorial Dir 1985–89; mem. Comm. on quality of radio and TV broadcasts 1977–79; Editorial Dir France-Soir 1989–92, Asst Dir-Gen. 1992; Asst Editorial Dir Le Figaro (newspaper) 1992–98, Man. Dir 1998–2000, Man. Ed. Le Figaro magazine 2005–07, Vice-Pres. Editorial Cttee 2000–; mem. Editorial Cttee La Revue de l'Intelligent 2003–. *Television:* L'Elysée 1988, Ville de Chiens 1989, Un Siecle d'Ecrivain: Jules Romains 1998. *Publications include:* La CFDT des militants 1972, D'une France à l'autre 1974, L'enaklatura 1987, L'Elysée de Mitterrand 1987, La désertion des énarques 1999. *Honours:* Chevalier, Ordre nat. du Mérite. *Address:* Le Figaro, 14 blvd Haussmann, 75009 Paris (office); 150 avenue Emile Zola, 75015 Paris, France (home). *Telephone:* 1-42-21-29-73 (office); 1-40-58-16-64 (home); 6-07-59-40-91 (mobile). *Fax:* 1-42-21-63-82 (office). *E-mail:* mschifres@lefigaro.fr (office); mschifres@noos.fr (home).

SCHLAGMAN, Richard Edward, FRSA; British publisher; *Chairman and Publisher, Phaidon Press Ltd*; b. 11 Nov. 1953, London, England; s. of Jack Schlagman and the late Shirley Schlagman (née Goldston); m. Mia Hagg. *Education:* Univ. Coll. School, Hampstead, Brunel Univ. *Career:* Co-Founder, Jt Chair., Man. Dir Interstate Electronics Ltd 1973–86; purchased Bush from Rank Org., renamed IEL Bush Radio Ltd 1981, floated on London Stock Exchange 1984, sold as Bush Radio PLC 1986; acquired Phaidon Press Ltd 1990, Chair. and Publr 1990–; mem. Exec. Cttee Patrons of New Art, Tate Gallery 1994–97, Royal Opera House Trust, Glyndebourne Festival Soc., Designers and Arts Dirs Asscn of UK; Patron Bayreuther Festspiele, Salzburger Festspiele, Schubertiades; Pres. Judd Foundation, MARFA, Tex. 1999–2001, mem. Bd 2001–. *Address:* Phaidon Press Ltd, Regent's Wharf, All Saints Street, London, N1 9PA, England (office). *Telephone:* (20) 7843-1100 (office). *Fax:* (20) 7843-1212 (office). *E-mail:* richard@phaidon.com (office). *Website:* www.phaidon.com (office).

SCHLINK, Bernhard; German judge, academic and writer; *Professor Emeritus of Public Law and Legal Philosophy, Humboldt University of Berlin*; b. 1944, Grossdornberg, North Rhine-Westphalia; s. of the late Prof. Dr Edmund Schlink. *Education:* Heidelberg, Berlin, Darmstadt, Bielefeld and Freiburg Univs. *Career:* Prof., Bonn Univ. 1981–91; Judge, Constitutional Law Court of North Rhine-Westphalia, Münster 1987–2005; Prof., Frankfurt Univ. 1991–92; Prof., Humboldt Univ. of Berlin 1992–; Visiting Prof. of Law, Benjamin Cardozo School of Law, Yeshiva Univ., New York 1994–; qualified as masseur in Calif.; began writing fiction in 1980s. *Publications:* fiction: Selbs Justiz (with Walter Popp, trans. as Self's Punishment) 1987, Die Gordische Schleife 1988, Selbs Betrug (trans. as Self's Betrayal) 1992, Der Vorleser (trans. as The Reader) 1995, Liebesfluchten (short stories; trans. as Flights of Love) 2001, Selbs Mord (trans. as Self's Murder) 2005, Die Heimkehr (trans. as Homecoming) 2006, Das Wochenende (trans. as The Weekend) 2008, Guilt About the Past 2009; non-fiction: Weimar: A Jurisprudence of Crisis (with Arthur Jacobson), several books on constitutional law, fundamental separation of powers and admin. law. *E-mail:* schlink@rewi.hu-berlin.de (office). *Website:* schlink.rewi.hu-berlin.de (office).

SCHLOSSER, Eric; American journalist and writer; b. 1959, New York City; m. Shauna Redford; two c. *Education:* Princeton Univ. and Oriel Coll., Oxford, UK. *Career:* contributor, The Atlantic (fmly Atlantic Monthly) 1994–. *Play:* Americans 1985. *Publications:* Fast Food Nation 2001, Reefer Madness and Other Tales from the American Underworld (Nat. Magazine Award) 2003, Cogs in the Great Machine (collection of articles) 2005, Chew on This 2006, Fast Food Nation 2007; contrib. to numerous magazines. *Address:* c/o Atlantic Media Company, 600 New Hampshire Avenue, NW, Washington, DC 20037, USA.

SCHMATZ, Pat, BS, MA; American writer; b. Michigan. *Education:* Michigan State Univ., Univ. of California, Berkeley. *Career:* Administrator, Legal Aid Soc. of Minneapolis; mem. staff, Michigan Womyn's Music Festival. *Publications:* juvenile: Mrs. Estronsky and the U.F.O. 2001, Circle the Truth 2007, Mousetraps (Council for Wisconsin Writers Award for Children's Fiction) 2008, Bluefish (PEN/Phyllis Naylor Working Writer Fellowship 2010) 2011. *Address:* c/o Candlewick Press, 99 Dover Street, Somerville, MA 02144, USA (office). *E-mail:* pschmatz5@yahoo.com (office). *Website:* www.patschmatz .com.

SCHMIDMAN, Jo Ann, BFA; American theatre director and playwright; b. 18 April 1948, Omaha, NE. *Education:* Boston Univ. *Career:* Producing Artistic Dir, Omaha Magic Theatre, 1968–; Team Mem., Artist-in-Schools, Nebraska Arts Council, 1994. *Plays:* various unpublished but produced plays 1978–93. *Publications:* plays: This Sleep Among Women, 1974; Running Gag, 1980; Astro Bride, 1985; Velveeta Meltdown, 1985; Right Brain (ed. with M. Terry and S. Kimberlain), 1992; Body Leaks (with M. Terry and S. Kimberlain), 1995.

SCHMIDT, Helmut; German politician, economist and publisher; *Co-Publisher, Die Zeit*; b. 23 Dec. 1918, Hamburg; s. of Gustav Schmidt and Ludovica Schmidt; m. Hannelore Glaser 1942 (died 2010); one d. *Education:* Lichtwarkschule and Univ. Hamburg. *Career:* Man. Transport Admin. of State of Hamburg 1949–53; mem. Social Democrat Party 1946–; mem. Bundestag 1953–61, 1965–87; Chair. Social Democrat (SPD) Parl. Party in Bundestag 1967–69; Vice-Chair. SPD 1968–84; Senator (Minister) for Domestic Affairs in Hamburg 1961–65; Minister of Defence 1969–72, for Econ. and Finance July–Dec. 1972, of Finance 1972–74; Fed. Chancellor 1974–82; Co-Publr Die Zeit (weekly newspaper), Hamburg 1983–; Co-founder Inter Action Councils 1983. *Publications:* Defence or Retaliation 1962, Beiträge 1967, Strategie des Gleichgewichts (trans. as Balance of Power) 1969, Kontinuität und Konzentration 1976, Als Christ in der politischen Entscheidung 1976, Der Kurs heisst Frieden 1979, Pflicht zur Menschlichkeit 1981, Kunst im Kanzleramt 1982, Freiheit verantworten 1983, Die Weltwirtschaft ist unser Schicksal 1983, Eine Strategie für den Westen (trans. as A Grand Strategy for the West) (Adolphe Bentinck Prize) 1986, Vom deutschen Stolz: Bekenntnisse zur Erfahrung von Kunst 1986, Menschen und Mächte (trans. as Men and Powers) 1987, Die Deutschen und ihre Nachbarn 1990, Mit Augenmass und Weitblick 1990, Einfügen in die Gemeinschaft der Völker 1990, Kindheit und Jugend unter Hitler 1992, Ein Manifest – Weil das Land sich ändern muss (co-author) 1992, Handeln für Deutschland 1993, Jahr der Entscheidung 1994, Was wird aus Deutschland? 1994, Weggefährten 1996, Jahrhundertwende 1998, Allgemeine Erklärung der Menschenpflichten 1998, Globalisierung 1998, Auf der Suche nach einer öffentlichen Moral 1998, Die Selbstbehauptung Europas 2000, Hand aufs Herz 2002, Die Mächte der Zukunft 2005. *Honours:* Hon. DCL (Oxford) 1979; Dr hc (Newberry Coll.) 1973, (Johns Hopkins) 1976, (Cambridge) 1976, (Harvard) 1979, (Sorbonne) 1981, (Louvain) 1984, (Georgetown) 1986, (Bergamo) 1989, (Tokyo) 1991, (Haifa) 2000, (Potsdam) 2000 and others; European Prize for Statesmanship (FUS Foundation) 1979, Nahum Goldmann Silver Medal 1980, Athinai Prize 1986. *Address:* Die Zeit, Speersort 1, Pressehaus, 20095 Hamburg (office); Bundeskanzler a.D., Deutscher Bundestag, Platz der Republik 1, 11011 Berlin, Germany. *Telephone:* (40) 32800 (office); (30) 22771580. *Fax:* (40) 327111 (office); (30) 22770571. *Website:* www.zeit.de (office).

SCHMIDT, Kathrin; German poet and novelist; b. 12 March 1958, Gotha; m.; five c. *Education:* Univ. of Jena, Literaturinstitut Johannes R. Becher, Leipzig. *Career:* worked as univ. scientific asst, child psychologist, magazine editor, research asst, now freelance writer. *Publications:* poetry: Kathrin Schmidt 1982, Ein Engel fliegt durch die Tapetenfabrik 1987, Flußbild mit Engel 1995, Go-In der Belladonnen 2000, Totentänze 2001, Blinde Bienen 2010; novels: Die Gunnar-Lennefsen-Expedition (Förderpreis des Heimito-von-Doderer-Preises) 1998, Sticky ends (stories) 2001, Koenigs Kinder 2002, Seebachs schwarze Katzen 2005, Du stirbst nicht (Deutscher Buchpreis) 2009; other: Drei Karpfen blau (short stories) 2000, Finito. Schwamm drüber (short stories) 2011. *Honours:* Anna Seghers Prize 1988, Leonce-und-Lena Prize 1993, Meraner Lyric Prize 1994, GEDOK Literaturförderpreis 1998, Deutscher Kritikerpreis 2001, Droste-Preis der Stadt Meersburg 2003, Preis der SWR-Bestenliste 2009, Deutscher Buchpreis 2009. *Address:* Kiepenheuer & Witsch GmbH, Postfach 10 20 62, 50460 Köln, Germany (office). *Website:* www.kiwi-verlag.de.

SCHMIDT-BLEIBTREU, Ellen, (Ellen Conradi-Bléibtreu); German writer; b. 11 June 1929, Heidelberg; d. of Hans and Ellen (née Nass) Kesseler; m. Bruno Schmidt-Bleibtreu 1956; one d. one s. *Education:* Univ. of Mainz-Germersheim. *Career:* European Rep. for Arts, Letters and Music, Conseil Int. des Femmes. *Publications:* Jahre m FJ 1950, Kraniche (poems) 1970, Fragmente (poems) 1973, Anthologie de la poésie féminine mondiale (co-ed.) 1973, Ruhestörung (short stories) 1975, Unter dem Windsegel (poems) 1978, Im Schatten der Genius 1981, Kinder aus 14 Ländern (short stories) 1982, Zeitzeichen I (poems) 1983, Deutsche Komponistinnen des 20 Jahrhunderts 1984, Die Schillers, Schillers Lebem (novel) 1986, Klimawechsel (poems) 1989, Begegnung über Grenzen hinweg (short stories) 1993, Zeitzeichen II (poems) 1999, Die Kuhlmanns im Wandel der Zeiten (novel, two vols) 2000, Die Kuhlmanns im Wandel der Zeiten (novel) 2003, Die Zeitzeichen III 2006, Words as Reflector of Time (co-author) (prose) 2007; contrib. to newspapers and periodicals. *Honours:* Prof. hc (Istituto Europeo di Cultura) 1989; Urban Prize 1976, Literary Union Hon. Prize 1977, Accad. Italia World Culture Prize 1984. *Address:* Pregelstrasse 5, 53127 Bonn, Germany (home).

SCHMIDT-DECKER, Petra; German songwriter, record producer and writer; b. Berlin; d. of Felix-Peter Schmidt-Decker and Ingeborg Schmidt-Decker (née Lohse). *Education:* acting classes. *Career:* actress on stage, TV and in films for 13 years; songwriter, then Producer of children's records; produced 150 records, including 30 records for Disney and 25 recorded biographies of composers from Vivaldi to Ravel (with Karlheinz Böhm) 1976–92; writer of TV and theatre scripts; leading companion of START Wort-Ton-Bild Verlags GmbH Hamburg, Germany; has worked on Jungle Book and Sesame Street productions. *Achievements include:* one Double Platinum CD, six Platinum CDs, one Triple Gold CD, eighteen Gold CDs. *Publications:* novels: Die jungen Bosse, Unternehmer Portraits 1984, Das große Buch des guten Benehmens 1985, Die Seherin 1996, Der Schildkröteninstinkt, Motivationsbuch 2003; plays: In Between (TV), Casanova bevorzugt (theatre) 1998; short stories: Der Verlorene Blitz 2005, 52 Verträge mit mir selbst 2010, L'Istinto della Tartaruga (also published as Scelte di Vita) 2010. *Address:* Papenhuder Str. 42, 22087 Hamburg-Uhlenhorst, Germany (home). *Telephone:* (40) 2202203 (home).

SCHMITTER, Elke; German writer and critic; b. 1961, Krefeld. *Education:* Univ. of Munich. *Career:* Ed. for S. Fischer, Frankfurt/Main; Ed.-in-Chief, Die Tageszeitüng; freelance critic for various papers; critic, Der Spiegel, Hamburg 2001–. *Publications:* Und grüsse mich nicht unter den Linden 1998, Frau Sartoris (trans. as Mrs Sartoris) 2000, Leichte Verfehlungen 2002, Kein Spaniel 2005, Veras Tochter 2006;. *Honours:* Niederrheinischer literaturpreis 2000. *Address:* c/o Berlin Verlag/Bloomsbury Greifswalder Sh. 207, 10405, Berlin, Germany (office).

SCHMITZ, Dennis Mathew, BA, MA; American academic and poet; b. 11 Aug. 1937, Dubuque, Ia; m. Loretta D'Agostino 1960; two s. three d. *Education:* Loras College, University of Chicago. *Career:* Instructor, Illinois Institute of Technology, Chicago, 1961–62, University of Wisconsin at Milwaukee, 1962–66; Asst Prof., California State University at Sacramento 1966–69, Poet-in-Residence 1966–, Assoc. Prof. 1969–74, Prof. of English 1974, now Prof. Emer.; Sacramento Poet Laureate (jtly) 2000–02; National Endowment for the Arts Fellowship 1976, 1985, 1992; Guggenheim Fellowship 1978. *Publications:* We Weep for Our Strangeness 1969, Double Exposures 1971, Goodwill, Inc. 1976, String 1980, Singing 1985, Eden 1989, About Night: Selected and New Poems 1993, The Truth Squad 2002. *Honours:* New York Poetry Center Discovery Award 1968, di Castagnola Award 1986, Shelley Memorial Award 1988. *Address:* c/o English Department, California State University, 6000 J Street, Sacramento, CA 95819, USA.

SCHNACKENBERG, Gjertrud, BA; American poet and writer; b. 27 Aug. 1953, Tacoma, Wash.; d. of Walter Charles Schnackenberg and Doris Ione Schnackenberg (née Strom); m. Robert Nozick 1987 (died 2002). *Education:* Mount Holyoke Coll. *Career:* Fellow in Poetry, The Radcliffe Inst. 1979–80; Christensen Fellow, Saint Catherine's Coll., Oxford 1997; Visiting Scholar, Getty Research Inst., J. Paul Getty Museum 2000; Fellow, American Acad. of Arts and Sciences 1996. *Publications:* Portraits and Elegies 1982, The Lamplit Answer 1985, A Gilded Lapse of Time 1992, The Throne of Labdacus 2000, Supernatural Love: Poems 1976–1992 2000, Heavenly Questions 2010; contrib. to books and journals. *Honours:* Dr hc (Mount Holyoke Coll.) 1985; Glascock Award for Poetry 1973, 1974, Acad. of American Poets Lavan Younger Poets Award 1983, American Acad. and Inst. of Arts and Letters Rome Prize 1983–84, Amy Lowell Traveling Prize 1984–85, Nat. Endowment for the Arts grant 1986–87, Guggenheim Fellowship 1987–88, American Acad. of Arts and Letters Award in Literature 1998, Los Angeles Times Book Prize in Poetry 2001, Daimler Chrysler Berlin Prize Fellow, American Acad., Berlin 2004, Griffin Int. Poetry Prize 2011. *Literary Agent:* c/o Farrar, Straus & Giroux Inc., 18 West 18th Street, New York, NY 10011, USA. *Telephone:* (212) 741-6900. *Website:* us.macmillan.com/FSG.aspx.

SCHNAPPER, Dominique, DSc; French sociologist and writer; b. 9 Nov. 1934, Paris; d. of Raymond Aron and Suzanne Gauchon; m. Antoine Schnapper 1958; three c. *Education:* Institut d'Etudes Politiques de Paris, Sorbonne, Université Paris V. *Career:* Prof. Dir of Studies Ecole des Hautes Etudes en Sciences Sociales (Paris) 1980–; mem. Comm. Marceau Long on the reform of the nation 1987, Comm. 2000 1989, Comm. on Drugs Henrion 1994, Comm. on Educ. Fauroux 1995–96; mem. Steering Cttee of French Soc. of Sociology 1991–95, Pres. 1995–99; mem. Conseil Constitutionnel (French Supreme Court) 2001–10. *Publications include:* La Communauté des citoyens 1994, La Rélation a l'autre 1998, Qu'est ce que la citoyénneté? 2000, La Démocratie providentielle 2002, Diasporas et nations 2006, Qu'est ce que l'intégration? 2007, La condition juive en France 2009, Une sociologue au Conseil constitutionnel 2010. *Honours:* Chevalier de la Légion d'honneur, Officier des Arts et des lettres; Prix de l'Assemblée Nat. 1994, Balzan Prize for Sociology 2002. *Address:* Maison des Sciences de l'Homme, 105 blvd Raspail, 75007 Paris, France. *Telephone:* 1-53-63-51-51. *E-mail:* schnappe@ehess.fr (office).

SCHNECK, Peter; Austrian editor. *Career:* Ed. Philologie im Netz; Vice Pres. Int. Bd on Books for Young People 1998–2002, Pres. 2002–06; responsible for children's literature at the Austrian Federal Chancellery's division of literature; Pres., Hans Christian Andersen Awards Jury 1996, 1998; Chair. Austrian Children's Book Award jury. *Address:* c/o International Institute for Children's Literature and Reading Research, Mayerhofgasse 6, 1040 Vienna, Austria (office).

SCHOEMPERLEN, Diane Mavis, BA; Canadian writer; b. 9 July 1954, Thunder Bay Ont.; one s. *Education:* Lakehead Univ., Ont. *Career:* teacher Kingston School of Writing Queen's Univ. Ontario 1986–93 St Lawrence Coll. Kingston 1987–93 Univ. of Toronto Summer Writers' Workshop 1992; Ed. Coming Attractions, Oberon Press 1994–96. *Publications:* Double Exposures 1984, Frogs and Other Stories 1986, Hockey Night in Canada 1987, The Man of My Dreams 1990, Hockey Night in Canada and Other Stories 1991, In the Language of Love 1994, Forms of Devotion 1998, Our Lady of the Lost and Found 2001, Red Plaid Shirt 2002, Names of the Dead – An Elegy for the Victims of September 11 2004, At a Loss for Words 2008; contribs to anthologies. *Honours:* WGA Award for Short Fiction 1987 Silver Nat. Magazine Award 1989 Gov.-Gen.'s Award for English Fiction 1998, Lakehead Univ. Alumni Honour Award 1999, Marian Engel Award 2008. *Address:* 32 Dunlop Street, Kingston, Ont., K7L 1L2, Canada (home). *E-mail:* dianes@kingston.net (home).

SCHOLEY, Arthur Edward; British children's writer, playwright, librettist and lyric writer; b. 17 June 1932, Sheffield, Yorks. *Publications:* The Song of Caedmon (with Donald Swann) 1971, Christmas Plays and Ideas for Worship 1973, The Discontented Dervishes 1977, Sallinka and the Golden Bird 1978, Twelve Tales for a Christmas Night 1978, Wacky and His Fuddlejig (with Donald Swann) 1978, Singalive (with Donald Swann) 1978, Herod and the Rooster (with Ronald Chamberlain) 1979, The Dickens Christmas Carol Show 1979, Baboushka (with Donald Swann) 1979, Candletree (with Donald Swann) 1981, Five Plays for Christmas 1981, Four Plays About People 1983, Martin the Cobbler 1983, The Hosanna Kids 1985, Make a Model Christmas Crib 1988, Who'll Be Brother Donkey? 1990, Brendan Ahoy! (with Donald Swann) 1994, The Journey of the Christmas Creatures (with Karen Bradley) 1998, Babaushka 2001, The Paragon Parrot 2002, The Discontented Dervishes 2002, Candles in the Window 2008. *Address:* 10 Chiltern Court, Pages Hill, London, N10 1EN, England (home). *E-mail:* arthurscholey@onetel.com (home). *Website:* www.arthurscholey.co.uk.

SCHOM, Alan Morris, BA, PhD; American writer, historian and academic; b. 9 May 1937, Sterling, Ill.; m. Juliana Leslie Hill 1963 (divorced 1984); two d. *Education:* Univ. of California, Berkeley, Durham Univ., UK. *Career:* Assoc., Dept of History, Univ. of California, Riverside 1968–69; Asst Prof. of Modern French and European History, Southern Connecticut State Univ. 1969–76; Founder French Colonial Historical Soc. (Pres. 1974–76), also Founder and first Ed. French Colonial Studies (journal); Fellow, Hoover Inst. on War, Revolution, and Peace 1984; mem. American Historical Asscn, Authors Guild, IISS, The Naval Club, London, The Travellers, Paris; Historical Consultant, Simon Wiesenthal Center, Los Angeles. *Publications:* Lyautey in Morocco: Protectorate Administration, 1912–1925 1970, Émile Zola: A Bourgeois Rebel 1988, Trafalgar: Countdown to Battle 1803–1805 1989, One Hundred Days: Napoleon's Road to Waterloo 1992, Napoleon Bonaparte 1997, The Eagle and the Rising Sun—The Japanese-American War 1941-1943 2004; contributions: scholarly journals. *Address:* PO Box 8511, Portland, OR 97207, USA. *Website:* alanschom.com.

SCHRAG, Peter, BA; American journalist and editor; b. 24 July 1931, Karlsruhe, Germany. *Education:* Amherst Coll. and Univ. of Massachusetts. *Career:* reporter, El Paso Herald Post, Texas 1953–55; Asst Sec., Amherst Coll. 1956–66; Assoc. Education Ed. 1966–68, Exec. Ed. 1968–73, Saturday Review, New York; Ed., Change, New York 1969–70; Lecturer, Univ. of Massachusetts 1970–72, Univ. of California at Berkeley 1990–; Ed. editorial page, Sacramento Bee, CA 1978–; Contributing Ed., The American Prospect; contrib. The Nation; mem. Nat. Conference of Editorial Writers; Guggenheim Fellowship 1971–72. *Publications:* Voices in the Classroom 1965, Village School Downtown 1967, Out of Place in America 1970, The Decline of the WASP (US edn as The Vanishing American) 1972, The End of the American Future 1973, Test of Loyalty 1974, The Myths of the Hyperative Child (with Diane Divorky) 1975, Mind Control 1978, Paradise Lost: California's Experience, America's Future 1998, Final Test: The Battle for Adequacy in America's Schools 2004, California: America's High-Stakes Experiment 2006, Not Fit for our Society: Immigration and Nativism in America 2010; contrib. to newspapers and magazines. *Address:* PO Box 15779, Sacramento, CA 95852-0779, USA (office). *E-mail:* pschrag@sacbee.com (office).

SCHREIBER, Claudia, (Claudia Siebert); German journalist and writer; b. (Claudia Siebert), 1958, Grebenstein-Schachten, Landkreis Kassel. *Education:* univs of Göttingen and Mainz. *Career:* fmr ed., reporter and presenter for Südwestfunk (SWF) and Zweites Deutsches Fernsehen (ZDF); has lived and worked in Moscow and Brussels. *Publications:* as Claudia Siebert: Moskau ist anders (non-fiction) 1994, Der Auslandskorrespondent (novel) 1997; as Claudia Schreiber: Emmas Glück (trans. as Emma's Luck) (novel) (Euregio-Schüler-Literaturpreis 2006) 2003, Sultan und Kotzbrocken (children's fiction) 2004, Ihr ständiger Begleiter (novel) 2007. *Honours:* German Pres.'s Journalistenpreis Entwicklungspolitik, Fed. Ministry for Econ. Cooperation and Devt 1989. *Address:* c/o Piper Verlag GmbH, Georgenstraße 4, 80799 Munich, Germany (office). *E-mail:* info@piper.de (office). *Website:* www.piper-verlag.de (office); www.schreiber-werkstatt.de.

SCHREINER, Samuel Agnew, Jr, AB; American author; b. 6 June 1921, Mt Lebanon, PA; m. Doris Moon 1945; two d. *Education:* Princeton Univ. *Publications:* Thine is the Glory 1975, The Condensed World of the Reader's Digest 1977, Pleasant Places 1977, Angelica 1978, The Possessors and the Possessed 1980, The Van Alens 1981, A Place Called Princeton 1984, The

Trials of Mrs Lincoln 1987, Cycles 1990, Mayday! Mayday! 1990, Code of Conduct (with Everett Alvarez) 1992, Henry Clay Frick: The Gospel of Greed 1995, The Passionate Beechers 2004, The Concord Quartet 2006, The World According to Cycles: How Recurring Forces Can Predict the Future and Change Your Life 2009; contributions: Reader's Digest, Woman's Day, McCalls, Redbook, Parade. *Address:* c/o Skyhorse Publishing, Inc., 555 Eighth Avenue, Suite 903, New York, NY 10018, USA (office). *Website:* www.skyhorsepublishing.com (office).

SCHROEDER, Andreas Peter, BA, MA, PhD; Canadian writer, poet and translator; *Rogers Communications Chair, University of British Columbia;* b. 26 Nov. 1946, Hoheneggelsen, Germany; m. Sharon Elizabeth Brown; two d. *Education:* Univ. of British Columbia, Univ. of Toronto. *Career:* literary critic and columnist, Vancouver Province newspaper 1968–72; Co-founder and Ed.-in-Chief Contemporary Literature in Translation 1968–83; Lecturer in Creative Writing, Univ. of Victoria 1974–75, Simon Fraser Univ. 1989–90; Writer-in-Residence, Regina Public Library 1980–81, Univ. of Winnipeg 1983–84, Fraser Valley Coll. 1987; Lecturer in Creative Writing 1985–87, Prof., Maclean Hunter Chair in Creative Non-Fiction 1993, then Rogers Communications Chair, Univ. of British Columbia; mem. Writers' Union of Canada, Alliance of Canadian Cinema, Television and Radio Artists, Fed. of British Columbia Writers, PEN Club, Saskatchewan Writers' Guild. *Publications:* The Ozone Minotaur 1969, File of Uncertainties (poems) 1971, UNIverse 1971, The Late Man (short stories) 1972, Stories From Pacific and Arctic Canada (co-ed.) 1974, Shaking it Rough (memoir) 1976, Toccata in 'D' (novella) 1984, Dust-Ship Glory (novel) 1986, Word for Word: The Business of Writing in Alberta 1988, The Eleventh Commandment (trans., with Jack Thiessen) 1990, The Mennonites in Canada: A Photographic History 1990, Carved From Wood: Mission, B.C. 1891–1992 1992, Scams, Scandals and Skullduggery 1996, Cheats, Charlatans and Chicanery 1998, Fakes, Frauds and Flimflammery 1999, Scams! 2004, Thieves! 2005, Renovating Heaven 2008; contribs to numerous anthologies, newspapers and magazines. *Honours:* Hon. DLitt (Univ. of the Fraser Valley, BC); Woodward Memorial Prize for Prose 1969, Canada Council Grants 1969, 1971, 1975, 1979, 1986, 1991, Nat. Film Board of Canada Scriptwriting Prize 1971, Canadian Asscn of Journalists Award for Best Investigative Journalism 1990, Red Maple Award for Young Adult Nonfiction 2005, 2007, World Storytelling Award 2005. *Address:* University of British Columbia Creative Writing Program, Buchanan Room E462, 1866 Main Mall, Vancouver, BC V6T 1Z1, Canada (office). *Telephone:* (604) 822-6564 (office). *E-mail:* apschroeder@dccnet.com (home); aps@interchange.ubc.ca (office). *Website:* www.creativewriting.ubc.ca (office).

SCHUBIGER, Jürg, PhD; Swiss psychotherapist and writer; b. 1936, Zürich. *Education:* Univ. of Zürich. *Career:* travelled and worked in South Africa, Corsica, Spain; fmr advertising copywriter, Zürich, later worked in publishing; currently psychotherapist and freelance author based in Zürich; publs include many books for children. *Publications:* fiction: Barbara 1956, Guten Morgen 1958, Die vorgezeigten Dinge (short stories) 1972, Dieser Hund heißt Himmel 1978, Haus der Nonna: Eine Kindheit in Tessin 1980, Unerwartet grün 1983, Hin-und Hergeschichten (with Franz Hohler) 1986, Das Löwengebrüll 1988, Hinterlassene Schuhe 1989, Lange Seelen (with Erich Sahli) 1999, Haller und Helen (novel) (ZKB Schillerpreis) 2003, Die kleine Liebe (novel) 2008, Als der Tod zu uns kam 2011; children's fiction: Als die Welt noch jung war (trans. as When the World Was New) (German Children's Literature Prize 1996) 1996, Mutter, Vater, ich und sie 2001, Seltsame Abenteuer des Don Quijote 2003, Wo ist das Meer? 2003, Die Geschichte von Wilhelm Tell (Schweizer Kinder-und Jugendmedienpreis 2005) 2006, Aller Anfang 2006, Der weiße und der schwarze Bär 2007. *Honours:* Hans Christian Andersen Author Award 2008. *Address:* Neptunstrasse 29, 8032 Zurich, Switzerland. *E-mail:* jschubiger@bluemail.ch.

SCHUHL, Jean-Jacques; French writer; b. 9 Oct. 1941, Marseille. *Publications:* Rose poussière 1972, Telex No. 1 1976, Ingrid Caven (Goncourt Prize for Literature 2000) 2000, Entrée des fantômes 2010. *Address:* c/o Editions Gallimard, 5 rue Sébastien Bottin, 75007 Paris, France. *Website:* schuhl.free.fr.

SCHULER, Robert Jordan, BA, MA, PhD; American academic and poet; b. 25 June 1939, Calif.; s. of Edward Schuler and Georgia Ruth Schuler; m. Carol Forbis 1963; two s. one d. *Education:* Stanford Univ., Univ. of California, Berkeley, Univ. of Minnesota. *Career:* Instructor in English, Menlo Coll. 1965–67; Instructor in Humanities, Shimer Coll. 1967–77; Prof. of English, Univ. of Wisconsin-Stout 1978–2010 (retd); mem. Land Use Comm., Town of Menomonie; Land Use Planner, Dunn Co., Wis.; mem. Phi Kappa Phi Honours Soc.; poetry readings and/or lectures given at Univ. of Chicago, American Literature Asscn, Univ. of Illinois, Champaign-Urbana, Michigan State Univ., Shimer Coll., Univ. of Nebraska, Lincoln, Moorhead State, Saint Catherine's, several brs of Univ. of Wisconsin, Univ. of Manitoba, St Olaf Coll., Midwest Modern Language Asscn, Wisconsin Writers Conf., Wisconsin Book Festival, many other venues, libraries, bookstores, churches etc. *Publications:* Axle of the Oak 1978, Seasonings 1978, Where is Dancers' Hill? 1979, Morning Raga 1980, Red Cedar Scroll 1981, Origins 1981, Floating Out of Stone 1982, Music for Monet 1984, Grace: A Book of Days 1995, Journeys Toward the Original Mind 1995, The Red Cedar Suite 1999, In Search of Green Dolphin Street 2003, Dance into Heaven 2005, Songs of Love 2006, Collection: Ekphrastic Poems (with Janet Butler) 2007, The Book of Jeweled Visions 2010; contribs: anthologies and periodicals, including Caliban, Northeast, Tar River Poetry, Longhouse, Dacotah Territory, Wisconsin Academy Review, Wisconsin Review, North Stone Review, Wisconsin Poetry 1991 Transactions, Hummingbird, Abraxas, Lake Street Review, Inheriting the Earth, Mississippi Valley Review, Coal City Review, Free Verse, Breviies, Chiron Review, Gypsy, Imagining Home 1995, Ekphrasis, Mid-America Poetry Review, The Blueline Anthology, Minotaur, Tiger's Eye, Urban Spaghetti, The Revolutionary Poet in the United States: The Poetry of Thomas McGrath, University of Missouri Press 1988, The Illinois Review, Hollow Spring Review, etc. *Honours:* Danforth Fellow, Yale 1969–70, Hormel Professorship 1995, Fellowship for Poetry, Wisconsin Arts Bd 1997, recipient of grants from Illinois Arts Council, Illinois Humanities Comm., Wisconsin Arts Bd, Wisconsin Humanities Council, Nat. Endowment for the Arts. *Address:* E4549 479th Avenue, Menomonie, WI 54751, USA (home). *Telephone:* (715) 235-6525 (home). *E-mail:* robertschuler88@gmail.com (office); schulerr@uwstout.edu (office).

SCHULLER, Gunther Alexander; American composer, conductor, music educator and record producer; b. 22 Nov. 1925, New York, NY; s. of Arthur E. Schuller and Elsie Schuller (née Bernartz); m. Marjorie Black 1948 (died 1992); two s. *Education:* St Thomas Choir School, New York, Manhattan School of Music. *Career:* Principal French horn, Cincinnati Symphony Orchestra 1943–45, Metropolitan Opera Orchestra 1945–59; teacher, Manhattan School of Music 1950–63, Yale Univ. 1964–67; Head Composition Dept, Tanglewood 1963–84; Music Dir First Int. Jazz Festival, Washington, DC 1962; active as conductor since mid-1960s with maj. orchestras in Europe and USA; reconstructed and orchestrated Der Gelbe Klang by De Hartmann/Kandinsky; Pres. New England Conservatory of Music 1967–77; Pres. Nat. Music Council 1979–81; Artistic Co-Dir, then Artistic Dir Summer Activities, Boston Symphony Orchestra, Berkshire Music Center, Tanglewood 1969–84, Festival at Sandpoint 1985–98; Founder and Pres. Margun Music Inc. 1975–2000, GM Recordings 1981–; mem. American Acad. of Arts and Sciences, American Acad. of Arts and Letters. *Compositions include:* Horn Concerto No. 1 1945, Vertige d'Eros 1946, Concerto for cello and orchestra 1946, Jumpin' in the Future 1946, Quartet for Four Brasses 1947, Oboe Sonata 1947, Duo Concertante for cello and piano 1947, Symphonic Study (Meditation) 1948, Trio for Oboe, Horn, Viola 1948, Symphony for brass and percussion 1950, Fantasy for Unaccompanied Cello 1951, Recitative and Rondo for violin and piano 1953, Dramatic Overture 1951, Five Pieces for Five Horns 1952, Adagio for flute, string trio 1952, Music for Violin, Piano and Percussion 1957, Symbiosis for violin, piano, percussion 1957, String Quartet No. 1 1957, Contours 1958, Woodwind Quintet 1958, Spectra 1958, Concertino for jazz quartet and orchestra 1959, Seven Studies on Themes of Paul Klee 1959, Conversations 1960, Lines and Contrasts for 16 horns 1960, Abstraction for jazz ensemble 1960, Variants on a Theme of Thelonious Monk 1960, Music for Brass Quintet 1960, Contrasts for woodwind quintet and orchestra 1961, Variants (ballet with choreography by Balanchine) 1961, Double Quintet for woodwind and brass quintets 1961, Meditation for concert band 1961, Concerto for piano and orchestra 1962, Journey into Jazz 1962, Fantasy Quartet for four cellos 1963, Threnos for oboe and orchestra 1963, Composition in Three Parts 1963, Five Bagatelles for Orchestra 1964, Five Etudes for orchestra 1964, The Power Within Us 1964, Five Shakespearean Songs for baritone and orchestra 1964, String Quartet No. 2 1965, Symphony 1965, American Triptych (on paintings of Pollock, Davis and Calder) 1965, Sacred Cantata 1966, Gala Music concerto for orchestra 1966, The Visitation (opera) 1966, Movements for flute and strings, Six Renaissance Lyrics, Triplum I 1967, Study in Textures for concert band 1967, Diptych for brass quintet and orchestra 1967, Shapes and Designs 1968, Concerto for double bass and orchestra 1968, Consequents for orchestra 1969, Fisherman and his Wife (opera) 1970, Concerto da Camera No. 1 1971, Capriccio Stravagante 1972, Tre Invenzioni 1972, Three Nocturnes 1973, Five Moods for tuba quartet 1973, Four Soundscapes 1974, Triplum II 1975, Violin Concerto 1976, Concerto No. 2 for horn and orchestra 1976, Diptych for organ 1976, Concerto No. 2 for orchestra 1977, Concerto for contrabassoon and orchestra 1978, Deaï for three orchestras 1978, Sonata Serenata 1978, Octet 1979, Concerto for trumpet and orchestra 1979, Eine Kleine Posaunenmusik 1980, In Praise of Winds symphony for large wind orchestra 1981, Concerto No. 2 for piano and orchestra 1981, Symphony for organ 1981, Concerto Quaternio 1984, Concerto for alto saxophone 1983, Duologue for violin and piano 1983, On Light Wings piano quartet 1984, Piano Trio 1984, Concerto for viola and orchestra 1985, Concerto for bassoon and orchestra 1985, Farbenspiel Concerto No. 3 for orchestra 1985, String Quartet No. 3 1986, Chimeric Images 1988, Concerto for string quartet and orchestra 1988, Concerto for flute and orchestra 1988, Horn Sonata 1988, On Winged Flight: A Divertimento for Band 1989, Chamber Symphony 1989, Five Impromptus for English horn and string quartet 1989, Impromptus and Cadenzas for chamber sextet 1990, Song and Dance for violin and concert band 1990, Concerto for piano three hands 1990, Violin Concerto No. 2 1991, Brass Quintet No. 2 1993, Reminiscences and Reflections 1993, The Past is the Present for orchestra 1994, Sextet for left-hand piano and woodwind quintet 1994, Concerto for organ and orchestra 1994, Mondrian's Vision 1994, Lament for M 1994, Blue Dawn into White Heat concert band 1995, An Arc Ascending 1996, Ohio River Reflections 1998, A Bouquet for Collage 1988, Fantasia Impromptu for flute and harpsichord 2000, Quod Libet for violin, cello, oboe, horn and harp 2001, String Quartet No. 4 2002, Concerto da Camera No. 2 2002, String Trio 2003, Encounters for jazz orchestra and symphony orchestra 2003, Where the World Ends 2008. *Publications:* Horn Technique 1962, Early Jazz: Its Roots and Musical Development, Vol. I 1968, Musings: The Musical Worlds of Gunther Schuller 1985, The Swing Era: The Development of Jazz 1930–45 1989, The Compleat

Conductor 1997. *Honours:* Order of Merit (Germany) 1997; Hon. DMus (Northeastern Univ.) 1967, (Colby Coll.) 1969, (Univ. of Illinois) 1970, (Williams Coll.) 1975, (Rutgers Univ.) 1980, (Oberlin Coll.) 1989, (Florida State Univ.) 1991; Creative Arts Award, Brandeis Univ. 1960, Nat. Inst. Arts and Letters Award 1960, Guggenheim Grant 1962, 1963, ASCAP Deems Taylor Award 1970, Rogers and Hammerstein Award 1971, William Schuman Award, Columbia Univ. 1989, McArthur Foundation Fellowship 1991, McArthur Genius Award 1994, Gold Medal, American Acad. of Arts and Letters 1996, Max Rudolf Award 1998, Pulitzer Prize in Music 1999. *Address:* GM Recordings, 167 Dudley Road, Newton Center, MA 02459, USA. *Telephone:* (617) 332-6328. *Fax:* (617) 969-1079. *E-mail:* contact@gmrecordings.com. *Website:* www.gmrecordings.com.

SCHULTZ, Philip; American poet, writer and educator; *Founder and Director, The Writers Studio;* b. 1945, Rochester, NY; m. Monica Banks; two s. *Career:* taught at various insts including Tufts Univ., Kalamazoo Coll., Univ. of Massachusetts at Boston, Columbia Univ.; fmr Dir Graduate Creative Writing program, New York Univ.; Founder and Dir The Writers Studio, New York City 1987–. *Publications:* poetry: Like Wings (American Acad. and Inst. of Arts and Letters Award) 1978, Deep Within the Ravine (Acad. of American Poets' Lamont Prize) 1984, My Guardian Angel Stein 1986, The Holy Worm of Praise 2002, Living in the Past (New York Public Library List 2005) 2004, Failure (Pulitzer Prize for Poetry 2008) 2007, The God of Loneliness, Selected and New Poems 2010; non-fiction: My Dyslexia (memoir) 2011; contrib. to magazines and journals including The New Yorker, Partisan Review, The New Republic, The Paris Review, Slate. *Honours:* Nat. Endowment for the Arts Fellowship in Poetry 1981, New York Foundation for the Arts Fellowship in Poetry 1985, Fulbright Fellowship in Poetry to Israel, Guggenheim Fellowship 2005, Levinson Prize, Poetry magazine. *Address:* The Writers Studio, 78 Charles Street, #2R, New York, NY 10014, USA (office). *Telephone:* (212) 255-7075 (office). *E-mail:* info@writerstudio.com (office). *Website:* www.writerstudio.com (office).

SCHULZ, Kathryn, BA; American author and journalist; b. Shaker Heights, Ohio. *Education:* Brown Univ. *Career:* fmr writer for Feed online magazine; fmr reporter and ed. Santiago Times; ed., online environmental magazine Grist 2001–06; contrib. to New York Times, Rolling Stone, Boston Globe, The Nation, Foreign Policy, Slate magazine, Huffington Post. *Publications include:* Being Wrong: Adventures in the Margin of Error 2010. *Honours:* Pew Fellowship in Int. Journalism 2004, Nat. Book Critic Circle's Nona Balakian Prize for Excellence in Reviewing 2012. *Literary Agent:* Alexis Hurley or Kimberly Witherspoon, InkWell Management, 521 Fifth Avenue, 26th Floor, New York, NY 10175, USA. *Telephone:* (212) 922-3500. *Fax:* (212) 922-0535. *E-mail:* alexis@inkwellmanagement.com; kim@inkwellmanagement.com. *Website:* www.inkwellmanagement.com; www.beingwrongbook.com.

SCHULZ, Max Frederick, AB, MA, PhD; American art curator and writer; *Distinguished Professor Emeritus of English, University of Southern California;* b. 15 Sept. 1923, Cleveland, Ohio. *Education:* Univs of Chicago, Pittsburgh and Minnesota, Wayne State Univ. *Career:* Prof. of English, Univ. of Southern California at Los Angeles 1963–94, Chair. Dept of English 1968–80, Distinguished Prof. Emer. of English 1994–, Curator of Exhbns, Fisher Gallery (now USC Fisher Museum of Art) 1993–; Fulbright Prof., Univ. of Graz, Austria 1965–66, Univ. of Vienna 1977–78; Resident Scholar, Rockefeller Foundation Study Center, Bellagio, Italy 1978, 1989; Assoc. Ed. Critique Magazine 1971–85; Sr Fellow, Nat. Endowment for the Humanities 1985–86. *Publications:* The Poetic Voices of Coleridge 1963, Radical Sophistication: Studies in Contemporary Jewish-American Novelists 1969, Bruce Jay Friedman 1973, Black Humor Fiction of the Sixties: A Pluralistic Definition of Man and his World 1973, Paradise Preserved: Recreations of Eden in 18th and 19th Century England 1985, The Muses of John Barth: Tradition and Metafiction from Lost in the Funhouse to the Tidewater Tales 1990, Edgar Ewing: The Classical Connection 1993, The Mythic Present of Chagoya, Valdez and Gronk 1995, Crossing Boundaries 1999, Family Pictures/Ecumenical Icons 2001, Human Conditions: Manfred Müller 2003, Albert Contreras: Luminous Scapes and Environments 2005, Contemporary Soliloquies on the Natural World 2005, The Bone and Bird Art of Joyce Cutler-Shaw and Sarah Perry 2007. *Address:* USC Fisher Museum of Art, University of Southern California, 126 Harris Hall, 823 Exposition Blvd, Los Angeles, CA 90089 (office); 2413 Palm Avenue, Manhattan Beach, CA 90266, USA (home). *Telephone:* (213) 740-4561 (office). *Fax:* (213) 740-7676 (office). *E-mail:* schulz@usc.edu (office). *Website:* fisher.usc.edu (office).

SCHULZE, Ingo; German writer; b. 15 Dec. 1962, Dresden, East Germany; s. of Christa Schulze; m. Natalia Schulze; two d. *Education:* Univ. of Jena. *Career:* Dramatic Producer, Theatre of Altenburg 1988–90; Founder weekly newspaper in Altenburg 1990–92, weekly newspaper in St Petersburg 1993; writer in Berlin 1993–; mem. Akad. der Künste, Berlin, Akad. für Deutsche Sprache und Dichtung, Darmstadt, Sächsische Akad., Dresden. *Publications:* 33 Augenblicke des Glücks (Aspekte-Literatur Prize for best debut) 1995, Simple Storys: Ein Roman aus der ostdeutschen Provinz 1998, Von Nasen, Faxen und Ariadnefäden, Fax-Briefe (with Zeichnungen von Helmar Penndorf) 2000, Telling Tales (contrib. to charity anthology) 2004, Neue Leben (novel) 2005, Handy – 13 Geschichten in alter Manier 2007, Adam und Evelyn (novel) 2008, Der Herr Augustin (with Julia Penndorf), Tausend Geschichten sind nicht genug (essays), Was Wollen Wir (essays) 2009; contrib. to Granta 100 (anthology) 2008. *Honours:* Ernst Willner Prize 1995, Aspekte Literatur Prize 1995, Berlin Literature Prize 1998, Johannes Bobrowski Medal 1998, Joseph Breitbach Prize 2001, Peter Weiss Prize 2006, Thuringia Literature Prize 2007, Leipzig Book Fair Prize 2007, Premio Grinzane Cavour 2008. *Address:* c/o Berlin Verlag, Greifswalder Str. 207, 10405 Berlin, Germany. *Telephone:* (30) 4438-4515. *Fax:* (30) 4438-4595. *E-mail:* sabine.oswald@bloomsbury.com. *Website:* www.berlinverlag.de; www.ingoschulze.com.

SCHÜTZ, Helga; German writer; b. 2 Oct. 1937, Falkenhain/Goldberg; one s. one d. (deceased). *Education:* secondary school, Dresden, Arbeiter und Bauernfakultät (ABF) and Hochschule für Film und Fernsehen, Potsdam (Diplom Dramaturgin). *Career:* gardener, Dresden 1951–55; writer of novels, stories and screenplays 1964–. *Publications include:* Vorgeschichten oder Schöne Gegend Probstein 1970, Jette in Dresden 1977, Julia oder Erziehung zum Chorgesang 1980, In Annas Namen 1986, Vom Glanz der Elbe 1995, Grenze zum Gestrigen Tag 2000, Dahlien im Sand: Mein Märkischer Garten 2002, Knietief im Paradies 2005. *Honours:* Heinrich Mann Preis, Akad. der Künste, Berlin, Theodor Fontane Preis, Potsdam, Stadtschreiber-Preis, Mainz 1991, Literaturpreis, Brandenburg 1992, Preis der Deutschen Schillerstiftung 1996, Hermann Hesse Stipendium der Stadt Calw 2003. *Address:* Jägersteig 4, 14482 Potsdam, Germany (home). *Telephone:* (331) 708656 (home). *E-mail:* helschuetz@t-online.de (office).

SCHWAB, George D., BA, MA, PhD; American political scientist, editor and academic; *President, National Committee on American Foreign Policy;* b. 25 Nov. 1931, s. of Arkady Schwab and Klara Schwab (née Jacobson); m. Eleonora Storch 1965 (died 1998); three s. *Education:* City Univ. of New York, Columbia Univ., New York. *Career:* began teaching career at Columbia Coll., Columbia Univ., New York 1959; Lecturer, Dept of History, City Coll., CUNY 1960–68, Asst Prof. of History 1968–72, Assoc. Prof. 1973–79, Prof. 1980–2000, Prof. Emer. (City Coll. and Grad. Center) 2001–; Co-founder Nat. Cttee on American Foreign Policy, later Vice-Pres. and Sr Vice-Pres., Pres. 1993–, Ed. American Foreign Policy Interests (its journal) 1976–, Global Perspectives in History and Politics series; mem. Council on Foreign Relations, German Studies Asscn, CUNY Acad. of Humanities and Sciences, Columbia Univ.'s Seminar on the History of Legal and Political Thought and Insts, United States Holocaust Memorial Museum's Cttee on Conscience, Washington, DC, Latvian Pres.'s Comm. of Int. Historians; has lectured widely on his concept of The Open-Society Bloc at Univ. of Freiburg, Bundeswehrhochschule, Hamburg, Germany and other insts. *Publications include:* Dayez: Beyond Abstract Art 1967, Enemy oder Foe 1968 (ed. English version Telos, No. 72, 1987), The Challenge of the Exception: An Introduction to the Political Ideas of Carl Schmitt 1970, 1989, Appeasement and Détente, Détente in Historical Perspective (ed. and contrib.) 1975, 1981, Ideology and Foreign Policy (ed. and contrib.) 1978, 1981, State and Nation: Towards a Further Clarification, Nationalism: Essays in Honor of Louis L. Snyder, Michael Palumbo and William O. Shausban 1981, Eurocommunism: The Ideological and Political Theoretical Foundations (ed. and contrib.) 1981, Detente in Historical Perspective 1981, Toward a New Foreign Policy, United States Foreign Policy at the Crossroads (ed. and contrib.) 1982, 1988, A Decade of the National Committee on American Foreign Policy, Power and Policy in Transition 1984, The Destruction of a Family 1987, Elie Wiesel: Between Jerusalem and New York 1990, Thoughts of a Collector 1991, Journey to Belfast and London (co-author) 1999, Carl Schmitt, a Note on a Qualitative Authoritarian Bourgeois Liberal 2000; trans.: The Leviathan in the State Theory of Thomas Hobbes 1996, The Concept of the Political 1996, Carl Schmitt's Political Theology: Four Chapters on the Concept of Sovereignty 2005; numerous articles in professional journals. *Honours:* Order of the Three Stars (Latvia) 2002; Ellis Island Medal of Honor 1998. *Address:* National Committee on American Foreign Policy, 320 Park Avenue, Eighth Floor, New York, NY 10022-6839, USA (office). *Telephone:* (212) 224-1120 (office). *Fax:* (212) 224-2524 (office). *E-mail:* george.schwab@ncafp.org (office). *Website:* www.ncafp.org (office); www.tandf.co.uk/journals/titles/10803920.asp.

SCHWANDT, Stephen William, BA, BS, MA; American educator and writer; b. 5 April 1947, Chippewa Falls, Wis.; m. Karen Sambo 1970, two s. *Education:* Valparaiso Univ., St Cloud State Univ., Univ. of Minnesota, Twin Cities. *Career:* teacher of composition and American literature, Irondale High School, New Brighton, Minn. 1974–; Instructor, Concordia Coll., St Paul 1975–80, Normandale Community Coll. 1983–; mem. National Education Asscn, Authors Guild, Book Critics Circle, National Council for Teachers of English, The Loft. *Publications:* The Last Goodie 1985, A Risky Game 1986, Holding Steady 1988, Guilt Trip 1990, Funnybone 1992, Siren Song: A Suspense Novel 2004. *Address:* Irondale High School, 2425 Long Lake Road, New Brighton, MN 55112, USA.

SCHWARTZ, Elliott Shelling, AB, MA, EdD; American composer, writer and academic; *Professor of Music Emeritus, Bowdoin College;* b. 19 Jan. 1936, Brooklyn, NY; m. Dorothy Rose Feldman 1960; one s. one d. *Education:* Columbia Univ. *Career:* Instructor, Univ. of Massachusetts 1960–64; Asst Prof. 1964–70, Assoc. Prof. 1970–75, Prof. of Music and Dept Chair from 1975, Bowdoin Coll., Brunswick, ME, now Prof. of Music Emer.; Prof. of Composition, Ohio State Univ. 1985–86, 1988–91; visiting appointments, Trinity Coll. of Music, London (UK) 1967–, Univ. of California, San Diego 1978–79, Robinson Coll., Cambridge (UK) 1993–94, 1998–99, 2007; NEA grants 1978–83, Rockefeller Foundation residencies, Bellagio, Italy 1980, 1989; mem. American Soc. of Univ. Composers, Coll. Music Soc. (past pres.),

American Composers' Alliance. *Compositions:* Timepiece 1794 for chamber orchestra 1994, Rainbow for orchestra 1996, Alto Prisms for eight violas 1997, Mehitadel's Serenade for saxophone and orchestra 2001, Rainforest with Birds 2001, Voyager for orchestra 2002, Riverscape 2003, Summer's Journey for concert bands 2005. *Recordings:* Grand Concerto, Extended Piano, Mirrors, Texture for Chamber Orchestras, Concert Piece for Ten Players, Chamber Concerto, Cycles and Gongs, Extended Clarinet, Dream Music with Variations, Celebrations/Reflections for Orchestra, Memorial in Two Parts, Chiaroscuro, Elan, Aerie for six flutes, Equinox for orchestra, Voyager for orchestra, Timepiece 1794 for chamber orchestra. *Publications:* The Symphonies of Ralph Vaughan Williams 1964, Contemporary Composers on Contemporary Music (ed. with Barney Childs) 1967, Electronic Music: A Listener's Guide 1973, Music: Ways of Listening 1982, Music Since 1945: Issues, Materials and Literature (with Daniel Godfrey) 1993; contrib. to professional journals. *Honours:* Gaudeamus Prize (Netherlands) 1970, Maine State Award in the Arts and Humanities 1970. *Address:* PO Box 451, South Freeport, ME 04078, USA (home). *Telephone:* (207) 725-3320 (office); (207) 865-3722 (home). *Fax:* (207) 725-3748 (office); (207) 865-6652 (home). *E-mail:* eschwart@bowdoin.edu (home). *Website:* www.schwartzmusic.com (home).

SCHWARTZ, John Burnham, BA; American writer; b. 8 May 1965, New York; m. Aleksandra Crapanzano; one s. *Education:* Harvard Univ. *Career:* taught fiction writing at Harvard Univ., Univ. of Iowa Writers Workshop, Sarah Lawrence Coll.; Literary Dir Sun Valley Writers Conf.; mem. Authors Guild. *Publications:* Bicycle Days 1989, Reservation Road 1998, Claire Marvel 2002, The Commoner 2008, Northwest Corner 2011; contribs: periodicals, including: New Yorker, New York Times Book Review. *Honours:* Lyndhurst Prize 1991. *Address:* c/o Amanda Urban, International Creative Management, 825 Eighth Avenue, New York, NY 10019, USA. *E-mail:* jbs@johnburnhamschwartz.com. *Website:* www.johnburnhamschwartz.com.

SCHWARTZ, Lloyd, BA, MA, PhD; American academic, music critic and poet; *Frederick S. Troy Professor of English, University of Massachusetts*; b. 29 Nov. 1941, New York, NY. *Education:* Queens College, City Univ. of New York, Harvard Univ. *Career:* Classical Music Ed., Boston Phoenix 1977–; Assoc. Prof. of English, Univ. of Massachusetts, Boston 1982–86, Dir of Creative Writing 1982–92, Prof. of English 1986–94, Frederick S. Troy Prof. of English 1994–; Classical Music Critic, Fresh Air, National Public Radio 1987–; Poetry Commentator, TomPaine.com 2001–; mem. New England Poetry Club, PEN New England (mem. Exec. Cttee 1983–98, Exec. Council, 1998–), Poetry Society of America. *Publications:* These People 1981, Elizabeth Bishop and Her Art (ed.) 1983, Goodnight, Gracie 1992, Cairo Traffic 2000, Elizabeth Bishop: Poems, Prose, and Letters 2008, Essential Pleasures: Poems to Read Aloud 2009; contributions: American Review, Best American Poetry 1991, 1994, Harvard Magazine, New Republic, New York Times, Partisan Review, Pequod, Ploughshares, Poetry, New Yorker, Slate, The Handbook of Heartbreak, Boulevard, Southwest Review, Atlantic Monthly. *Honours:* ASCAP-Deems Taylor Award 1980, 1987, 1990, Daniel Varoujan Prize 1987, Pushcart Prize 1987, Somerville Arts Council Grant 1987, 1989, National Endowment for the Arts Fellowship 1990, Pulitzer Prize in Criticism 1994. *Address:* College of Liberal Arts, University of Massachusetts, 100 Morrissey Blvd., Boston, MA 02125-3393, USA (office). *Telephone:* (617) 287-6719 (office). *E-mail:* lloyd.schwartz@umb.edu (office). *Website:* www.umb.edu/academics/cla (office).

SCHWARTZ, Lynne Sharon, BA, MA; American author, poet and translator; b. 19 March 1939, New York, NY; d. of Jack Sharon and Sarah Sharon; m. Harry Schwartz 1957; two d. *Education:* Barnard Coll., Bryn Mawr Coll., New York Univ. *Career:* currently Faculty mem., Bennington Coll. Writing Seminars; mem. Authors Guild, Nat. Book Critics Circle, Nat. Writers Union, PEN American Centre, American Acad. of Arts and Sciences. *Publications include:* Rough Strife 1980, Balancing Acts 1981, Disturbances in the Field 1983, Acquainted with the Night (short stories) 1984, We Are Talking About Homes (short stories) 1985, The Melting Pot and Other Subversive Stories 1987, Leaving Brooklyn 1989, Smoke Over Birkenau by Liana Millu (trans.) 1990, A Lynne Sharon Schwartz Reader: Selected Prose and Poetry 1992, The Fatigue Artist 1995, Ruined by Reading: A Life in Books 1996, In the Family Way 1999, Face to Face: A Reader in the World 2000, In Solitary (poems) 2002, A Place to Live and Other Selected Essays of Natalia Ginzburg (trans.) 2002, Referred Pain and Other Stories 2004, The Writing on the Wall 2005, The Emergence of Memory: Conversations with W.G. Sebald (ed.) 2007, Not Now, Voyager 2009, See You in the Dark (poems) 2012, Two-Part Inventions (novel) 2012; contrib. to periodicals. *Honours:* Nat. Endowment for the Arts Fellowships 1984, 2002, Guggenheim Fellowship 1985, New York State Foundation for the Arts Fellowship 1986. *Literary Agent:* c/o Peter Matson, Sterling Lord Literistic, 65 Bleecker Street, New York, NY 10012, USA. *E-mail:* peter@sll.com. *Website:* lynnesharonschwartz.com.

SCHWARTZMAN, Adam; South African poet and writer; b. 1973, Johannesburg; m.; one d. *Education:* Univ. of Oxford, UK. *Career:* held positions in the South African Nat. Treasury, World Bank, Int. Finance Corpn; currently Assoc., Centre for African Studies, Univ. of Cape Town. *Publications:* poetry: The Good Life, The Dirty Life, and Other Stories 1995, Merrie Afrika! 1997, Book of Stones 2003; other: Ten South African Poets (co-ed.) 1999, Eddie Signwriter (novel) 2010. *Address:* c/o Random House UK Limited, Random House, 20 Vauxhall Bridge Road, London, SW1V 2SA, England (office).

SCHWARZ, Daniel Roger, BA, MA, PhD; American academic, author and poet; *Frederic J. Whiton Professor of English Literature and Stephen H. Weiss Presidential Fellow, Cornell University*; b. 12 May 1941, Rockville Centre, NY; s. of the late Joseph A. Schwarz and Florence Schwarz; m. 1st Marcia Mitson 1963 (divorced 1986); two s.; m. 2nd Marcia Jacobson 1998. *Education:* Union Coll., Brown Univ. *Career:* Asst Prof., Cornell Univ. 1968–74, Assoc. Prof. 1974–80, Prof. of English 1980–, Stephen H. Weiss Presidential Fellow 1999–, Frederic J. Whiton Prof. of English Literature 2007–; Distinguished Visiting Cooper Prof., Univ. of Arkansas at Little Rock 1988; Citizen's Chair in Literature, Univ. of Hawaii 1992–93; Visiting Eminent Scholar, Univ. of Alabama, Huntsville 1996; Dir, 9 National Endowment for the Humanities Summer Seminars for College and High School Teachers Grants, 1984–93; mem. Int. Asscn of Univ. Profs of English, Soc. for the Study of Narrative Literature (Past Pres.), Modern Language Asscn. *Publications:* Disraeli's Fiction 1979, Conrad: Almayer's Folly to Under Western Eyes 1980, Conrad: The Later Fiction 1982, The Humanistic Heritage: Critical Theories of the English Novel from James to Hillis Miller 1986, Reading Joyce's Ulysses 1987, The Transformation of the English Novel 1890–1930: Studies in Hardy, Conrad, Joyce, Lawrence, Forster and Woolf 1989, The Case for a Humanistic Poetics 1991, Narrative and Representation in the Poetry of Wallace Stevens 1993, Narrative and Culture (co-ed. with Janice Carlise) 1994, James Joyce's The Dead (ed.) 1994, Joseph Conrad's The Secret Sharer (ed.) 1997, Reconfiguring Modernism: Explorations in the Relationship Between Modern Art and Modern Literature 1997, Imagining the Holocaust 1999, Rereading Conrad 2001, Broadway Boogie Woogie: Damon Runyon and the Making of New York City Culture 2002, Reading the Modern British and Irish Novel, 1890–1940 2005, In Defense of Reading, Teaching Literature in the Twenty-First Century 2008, Endtimes? Crisis and Turmoil at the New York Times: 1999–2009 2012; other: more than 75 poems, short story, travel writing; contribs to journals and collections. *Honours:* American Philosophical Soc. Grant 1981, US Information Agency Lecturer and Academic Specialist Lecturer, Australia 1993, Cyprus 1999, Italy 2003, 2004, Cornell Univ. Russell Distinguished Teaching Award 1998, Weiss Distinguished Teaching Award, 1999, Paley Lecturer, Hebrew Univ., Israel 2009. *Address:* Department of English, 242 Goldwin Smith Hall, Cornell University, Ithaca, NY 14853 (office); 925 Mitchell Street #3, Ithaca, NY 14850, USA (home). *Telephone:* (607) 255-9313 (office); (607) 273-5735 (office). *Fax:* (607) 255-6661 (home). *E-mail:* drs6@cornell.edu (office). *Website:* courses.cit.cornell.edu/drs6 (office).

SCHWEIZER, Karl Wolfgang, MA, PhD, FRHistS, FRSA; American writer and historian; *Professor, Department of History, New Jersey Institute of Technology*; b. 30 June 1946, Mannheim, Germany; m. Pamela Schweizer; one s. *Education:* Wilfrid Laurier Univ., Univ. of Waterloo, Peterhouse Coll., Cambridge, UK. *Career:* Prof., Bishop's Univ., Lennoxville, Quebec 1976–88; Mellon Fellow, Harvard Univ. 1978; Visiting Lecturer, Univ. of Guelph 1973–74; Research Assoc., Russian Research Center, Ill. 1979–80, 1999; Academic Visitor, LSE 1986, 1994; Visiting Scholar, Queen's Univ., Ont. 1986–87; Visiting Fellow, Darwin Coll., Cambridge 1987, 1994, 2003, Yale Univ. 1994–95, Princeton Univ. 1994–95; Sr Research Assoc., Peterhouse Coll., Cambridge 2004; Chair. Dept of Humanities 1988–93, Prof., Dept of Social Science 1993–2000, Prof. and Chair. Dept of Humanities and Social Science 2000–02, currently Prof., Dept of History, New Jersey Inst. of Tech.; Grad. Faculty, Rutgers, The State Univ. of New Jersey at Newark 1993–; Pres. Republican Task Force 2006–08; Life Fellow, Int. Biographical Asscn; Assoc., Center for Global Change and Governance 1995–. *Publications:* The Devonshire Political Diary 1757–1763 (ed.) 1982, Diplomatic Thought 1648–1815 (ed.) 1983, François de Callières: The Art of Diplomacy 1983, Warfare and Tactics in the Eighteenth Century (ed.) 1984, Essays in European History 1648–1815, in Honour of Ragnhild Hatton (ed. with J. Black) 1985, The Origins of War in Early Modern Europe (co-author) 1987, Lord Bute: Essays in Re-Interpretation 1988, Intellectual History: New Perspectives (ed.) 1988, Politics and the Press in Hanoverian Britain (co-ed. with J. Black) 1989, England, Prussia and the Seven Years War 1989, Cobbett in his Times 1990, Frederick the Great, William Pitt and Lord Bute: Anglo-Prussian Relations 1756–1763 1991, Lord Chatham 1993, François de Callières: Diplomat and Man of Letters 1995, Herbert Butterfield: Essays on the History of Science (ed.) 1998, Hanoverian Britain and Empire (co-author) 1998, British Prime Ministers (co-author) 1999, Seeds of Evil: The Gray/Snyder Murder Case 2001, War, Diplomacy and Politics: The Anglo-Prussian Alliance 1756–1763 2001, Statesmen, Diplomats and the Press: Essays on 18th Century Britain 2003, Influence of Australia's Constitutional Monarchy (ed.) 2003, Parliament and the Press 1688–1939 (ed.) 2006, The International Thought of Herbert Butterfield (co-ed.) 2007, The Seven Years War: A Transatlantic History 2008; contrib. to reference works and scholarly books and journals. *Honours:* Congressional Order of Merit 2007; Adelle Mellen Prize for Distinguished Contributions to Scholarship 1990, New Jersey Writer's Conference Award 1993, Outstanding Academic Book Citations, Choice 1994, 1998, NJIT Teaching Award 2000. *Address:* New Jersey Institute of Technology, Department of History, University Heights, Newark, NJ 07102 (office); 120 Mt Hermon Way, Ocean Grove, NJ 07756, USA (home). *E-mail:* schweizer@adm.njit.edu (office).

SCIBONA, Salvatore, MFA; American writer; b. 2 June 1975, Cleveland, Ohio. *Education:* Iowa Writers' Workshop. *Career:* has taught at Harvard Summer School; currently Writing Co-ordinator, Fine Arts Work Center, Provincetown, Mass. *Publications:* The End (Young Lions Fiction Award, New

York Public Library 2009, Norman Mailer Cape Cod Award for Exceptional Writing 2009) 2008; contribs to The Pushcart Book of Short Stories, Best New American Voices, The Threepenny Review, The New York Times, The New Yorker. *Honours:* Fellowship, Fine Arts Work Center, Provincetown, Mass 2001–02, 2002–03, Whiting Writers' Award 2009, Guggenheim Fellowship 2010. *Address:* Fine Arts Work Center, 24 Pearl Street, Provincetown, MA 02657, USA (office). *E-mail:* sscibona@fawc.org (office). *Website:* www.fawc.org (office); www.theendnovel.com.

SCOBIE, Stephen Arthur Cross, MA, PhD, FRSC; Canadian academic, poet and writer; b. 31 Dec. 1943, Carnoustie, Scotland; m. Sharon Maureen 1967. *Education:* University of St Andrews, University of British Columbia. *Career:* faculty mem., University of Alberta 1969–80, Prof. 1980–81; Prof. of English, University of Victoria 1981–; Guest Prof. of Canadian Studies, Christian-Albrechts-Universität, Kiel 1990; mem. League of Canadian Poets (vice-pres. 1972–74, 1986–88), Victoria Literary Arts Festival Society (fmr pres.). *Publications:* poetry: Babylondromat, 1966; In the Silence of the Year, 1971; The Birken Tree, 1973; Stone Poems, 1974; The Rooms We Air, 1975; Airloom, 1975; Les toiles n'ont peur de rien, 1979; McAlmon's Chinese Opera, 1980; A Grand Memory for Forgetting, 1981; Expecting Rain, 1985; The Ballad of Isabel Gunn, 1987; Dunino, 1988; Remains, 1990; Ghosts: A Glossary of the Intertext, 1990; Gospel, 1994; Slowly Into Autumn, 1995; Willow, 1995; Taking the Gate: Journey Through Scotland, 1996. Other: Leonard Cohen, 1978; The Maple Laugh Forever: An Anthology of Canadian Comic Poetry (co-ed.), 1981; Alias Bob Dylan, 1991. Contributions: journals and magazines. *Honours:* Governor-General's Award for Poetry 1980.

SCOFIELD, Sandra; American writer; b. (Sandra Hupp), 5 Aug. 1943, Wichita Falls, Tex.; m. Bill Ferguson; one d. *Publications:* Gringa (New American Fiction Award) 1989, Beyond Deserving (American Book Award, New American Fiction Award) 1991, Walking Dunes 1992, More than Allies 1993, Opal on Dry Ground 1994, A Chance to See Egypt (Texas Inst. of Letters Fiction Award) 1996, Plain Seeing 1999, Occasions of Sin: A Memoir 2004. *Honours:* Nat. Endowment for the Arts Creative Writing Fellowship. *Address:* 107 Bentley Park Loop, Missoula, MT 59801, USA.

SCOT, Michael (see Rohan, Michael Scott)

SCOTT, Gail, BA; Canadian writer; b. 20 Jan. 1945, Ottawa, Ontario; one d. *Education:* Queen's University, Kingston, Ontario, University of Grenoble. *Career:* Journalist, Montréal Gazette, The Globe and Mail, 1970–79; Writing Instructor, 1981–90; Writer-in-Residence, Concordia University, Montréal, 1991–92, University of Alberta, Edmonton, 1994–95; mem. Union des écrivaines et des écrivains québécois; Writer's Union of Canada. *Publications:* Spare Parts, 1982; Heroine, 1987; La Theorie, un Dimanche, 1988; Spaces Like Stairs, 1989; Serious Hysterics (anthology), 1992; Resurgences (anthology), 1992; Main Brides, 1994. Contributions: journals and other publications.

SCOTT, John A., BA, DipEd; Australian academic, poet and writer; b. 23 April 1948, Littlehampton, Sussex, England. *Education:* Monash University, Vic., Australia. *Career:* Lecturer, Swinburne Institute 1975–80, Canberra College of Advanced Education 1980–89, University of Wollongong, NSW 1989–. *Publications:* The Barbarous Sideshow, 1976; From the Flooded City, 1981; Smoking, 1983; The Quarrel with Ourselves, 1984; Confession, 1984; St Clair, 1986; Blair, 1988; Singles: Shorter Works 1981–1986, 1989; Translation, 1990; What I Have Written, 1993. *Honours:* Poetry Society of Australia Award, 1970; Mattara Poetry Prize, 1984; Wesley Michel Wright Awards, 1985, 1988; Victorian Premier's Prize for Poetry, 1986; ANA Award, Fellowship of Australian Writers, 1990.

SCOTT, John Peter, BSc, PhD, AcSS, FRSA, FBA; British sociologist, academic and writer; *Professor of Sociology, University of Plymouth*; b. 8 April 1949, London, England; m. Jill Wheatley 1971, one s. one d. *Education:* Kingston Coll. of Tech., Univ. of London, London School of Econs, Univ. of Strathclyde. *Career:* Lecturer, Univ. of Strathclyde 1972–76; Lecturer, Univ. of Leicester 1976–87, Reader 1987–91, Prof. of Sociology 1991–94; Ed. Network Newsletter, British Sociological Asscn 1985–89, Social Studies Review, later Sociology Review 1986–; Prof. of Sociology, Univ. of Essex 1994–2008; Adjunct Prof., Univ. of Bergen, Norway 1997–2006; Prof. of Sociology, Univ. of Plymouth 2008–; mem. British Sociological Asscn (Sec. 1991–92, Chair. 1992–93, Treas. 1997–99, Pres. 2001–09, Hon. Vice-Pres. 2009–), Acad. of Social Sciences. *Publications:* Corporations, Classes and Capitalism 1979, The Upper Classes 1982, The Anatomy of Scottish Capital (with M. Hughes) 1982, Directors of Industry (with C. Griff) 1984, Networks of Corporate Power (co-ed.) 1985, Capitalist Property and Financial Power 1986, A Matter of Record 1990, The Sociology of Elites (ed., three vols) 1990, Who Rules Britain 1991, Social Network Analysis 1992, Power (ed., three vols) 1994, Poverty and Wealth 1994, Sociological Theory 1995, Stratification and Power 1996, Corporate Business and Capitalist Classes 1997, Class (ed., four vols) 1997, Sociology (with James Fulcher) 1999, Renewing Class Analysis (co-ed. with R. Crompton, F. Devine and M. Savage) 2000, Social Structure (with José López) 2000, Power 2001, Critical Concepts: Social Networks (ed., four vols) 2002, Rethinking Class: Culture, Identities, and Lifestyle (co-ed. with R. Crompton, F. Devine, M. Savage) 2004, Models and Methods in Social Network Analysis (co-ed. with P. Carrington and S. Wasserman) 2005, Oxford Dictionary of Sociology (co-ed. with G. Marshall) 2005, Social Theory: Central Issues in Sociology 2006, Documentary Research (ed., four vols) 2006, Sociology: The Key Concepts (ed.) 2006, Fifty Key Sociologists: The Formative Theorists (ed.) 2007, Fifty Key Sociologists: The Contemporary Theorists (ed.) 2007; contrib. to professional journals and general periodicals. *Honours:* Choice Outstanding Sociology Book of the Year 1995, Harrison White Outstanding Book Award, Math. Sociology Section of American Sociological Asscn 2006. *Address:* School of Social Science and Social Work, University of Plymouth, 10 Portland Villas, Drake Circus, Plymouth, Devon, PL4 8AA, England (office).

SCOTT, Jonathan Henry, BA, PhD; New Zealand historian, writer and poet; b. 22 Jan. 1958, Auckland; m. 1st Sara Bennett 1980 (divorced); m. 2nd Lindsey Bridget Shaw 1986 (divorced 1991); m. 3rd Anne Hanson Pelzel 1995; one s. one d. *Education:* Victoria University of Wellington, Trinity College, Cambridge. *Career:* Research Fellow, Magdalene College, Cambridge, 1985–87; Lecturer in History, Victoria University of Wellington, 1987–88, University of Sheffield, 1989–91; Fellow and Dir of Studies in History, Downing College, Cambridge, 1991–2002; Carroll Amundson Prof. of British History, Univ. of Pittsburgh, 2002–. *Publications:* Algernon Sidney and the English Republic, 1623–1677, 1988; Algernon Sidney and the Restoration Crisis, 1677–1683, 1991; Harry's Absence: Looking for My Father on the Mountain, 1997; England's Troubles: Seventeenth Century English Political Instability in European Context, 2000, Commonwealth Principles: Republican Writing of the English Revolution 2004; contribs to scholarly books and journals, and literary periodicals. *Address:* 3K38 Posvar Hall, University of Pittsburgh, Pittsburgh, PA 15260, USA.

SCOTT, Paul Henderson, MA, MLitt, CMG; British essayist, historian, critic and fmr diplomatist; b. 7 Nov. 1920, Edinburgh, Scotland. *Education:* Univ. of Edinburgh. *Career:* fmr Pres., Scottish PEN, Saltire Soc.; fmr Vice-Pres., Scottish Nat. Party; council mem., Asscn for Scottish Literary Studies. *Publications:* 1707: The Union of Scotland and England 1979, Walter Scott and Scotland 1981, John Galt 1985, Towards Independence: Essays on Scotland 1991, Scotland in Europe 1992, Andrew Fletcher and the Treaty of Union 1992, Scotland: A Concise Cultural History (ed.) 1993, Defoe in Edinburgh 1994, Scotland: An Unwon Cause 1997, Still in Bed with an Elephant 1998, The Boasted Advantages 1999, A Twentieth-Century Life 2002, Scotland Resurgent 2003, Spirits of the Age (ed.) 2005, The Unions of 1707: Why and How 2006, The Age of Liberation 2008, The New Scotland 2008; contrib. to newspapers and journals. *Honours:* Andrew Fletcher Award 1993, Oliver Award 2000. *Address:* 33 Drumsheugh Gardens, Edinburgh, EH3 7RN, Scotland (home). *Telephone:* (131) 225-1038 (home). *Fax:* (131) 225-1038 (home). *E-mail:* scott.fiore@virgin.net (home).

SCOTT, Peter Dale, BA, PhD; Canadian academic and poet; b. 11 Jan. 1929, Montréal; s. of Francis Reginald Scott and Marian Mildred Scott; m. Ronna Kabatznick 1993; two s. one d. *Education:* McGill Univ., Institut d'Etudes Politiques, Paris, Univ. College, Oxford. *Career:* Lecturer, McGill Univ. 1955–56; Canadian Foreign Service, Ottawa and Poland 1957–61; Prof. of Speech, Univ. of California, Berkeley 1961–66, Prof. of English 1966–94. *Publications:* poetry: Poems 1952, Rumors of No Law 1981, Coming to Jakarta 1988, Listening to the Candle 1992, Crossing Borders 1994, Minding the Darkness 2000; prose: Deep Politics and the Death of JFK 1993, Drugs, Oil and War 2003, The Road to 9/11 2007, The War Conspiracy 2008, American War Machine 2010; contributions: reviews, quarterlies, and periodicals. *Honours:* Dia Art Foundation 1989, Lannan Poetry Award 2002. *Address:* Department of English, University of California, Berkeley, CA 94720, USA (office). *E-mail:* pdscottweb@hotmail.com (home). *Website:* www.peterdalescott.net.

SCOTT, Rosie Judy, BA, MA, DCA; New Zealand/Australian writer; b. 22 March 1948, Wellington, New Zealand; d. of Dick and Elsie Scott; m. Danny Vendramini 1987; two d. *Education:* Univ. of Auckland, Victoria Univ. (Wellington), Univ. of Western Sydney, Grad. Diploma of Counselling, Inst. of Counselling, Sydney, Grad. Diploma of Drama, Univ. of Auckland. *Career:* numerous jobs including actress, social worker, counsellor, publr, waitress, editor, factory and home worker; now internationally published novelist, essayist and short story writer; fmr Chair. Australian Soc. of Authors, now mem. Perm. Council; fmr Vice-Pres. Sydney PEN; active in various political campaigns. *Publications include:* novels: Glory Days, Nights with Grace, Feral City, Lives on Fire, Movie Dreams, Faith Singer 2001; poetry: Flesh and Blood; short stories: Queen of Love; play: Say Thankyou to the Lady; non-fiction: The Red Heart 1999, Another Country (anthology). *Honours:* Bruce Mason Nat. Times Play Award 1985, Sydney PEN Award, finalist in many nat. literary awards in NZ and Australia. *Address:* 5/9 Cook Street, Glebe, NSW 2037, Australia. *Telephone:* (2) 9552-1427. *E-mail:* rosie@amaze.net.au. *Website:* www.thesecondevolution.com/rosie.

SCRUTON, Roger, BA, PhD, FRSL, FBA; British philosopher and writer; b. 27 Feb. 1944, Buslingthorpe; s. of John Scruton and Beryl C. Haines; m. 1st Danielle Laffitte 1975 (divorced 1983); m. 2nd Sophie Jeffreys 1996. *Education:* High Wycombe Royal Grammar School, Jesus Coll. Cambridge and Inner Temple, London. *Career:* Fellow, Peterhouse, Cambridge 1969–71; Lecturer in Philosophy, Birkbeck Coll. London 1971–79, Reader 1979–86, Prof. of Aesthetics 1986–92; Prof. of Philosophy, Boston Univ. 1992–95; Founder and Dir The Claridge Press 1987–2004; Ed. The Salisbury Review 1982–2000, now on Editorial Bd; currently Adjunct Prof., Inst. for the Psychological Sciences; unpaid research prof., Buckingham Univ.; currently Visiting Prof. of Philosophy, Oxford Univ., Visiting Research Prof. of Philosophy, St . Andrews Univ., Visiting Scholar, American Enterprise Inst., Washington; mem. Editorial Bd British Journal of Aesthetics, Arka (Kraków). *Compositions:* The Minister (opera in one act) 1994, Violet (opera in two acts) 2006.

Publications: Art and Imagination 1974, The Aesthetics of Architecture 1979, The Meaning of Conservatism 1980, The Politics of Culture and Other Essays 1981, Fortnight's Anger (novel) 1981, A Short History of Modern Philosophy 1982, A Dictionary of Political Thought 1982, The Aesthetic Understanding 1983, Kant 1983, Untimely Tracts 1985, Thinkers of the New Left 1986, Sexual Desire 1986, Spinoza 1987, A Land Held Hostage: Lebanon and the West 1987, The Philosopher on Dover Beach (essays) 1989, Francesca (novel) 1991, A Dove Descending (stories) 1991, Conservative Texts: An Anthology 1991, The Xanthippic Dialogues 1993, Modern Philosophy 1993, The Classical Vernacular 1994, Modern Philosophy 1996, Animal Rights and Wrongs 1996, An Intelligent Person's Guide to Philosophy 1997, The Aesthetics of Music 1997, On Hunting 1998, Town and Country (co-ed.) 1998, An Intelligent Person's Guide To Modern Culture 1998, On Hunting 1999, Perictione in Colophon 2000, England: An Elegy 2000, The West and the Rest: Globalization and the Terrorist Threat 2002, Death-Devoted Heart: Sex and the Sacred in Wagner's Tristan and Isolde 2004, News from Somewhere: On Settling 2004, Gentle Regrets (autobiog.) 2005, A Political Philosophy 2006, Culture Counts: Faith and Feeling in a World Besieged 2007, Beauty 2009, Understanding Music: Philosophy and Interpretation 2009, I Drink Therefore I Am 2009, The Uses of Pessimism and the Danger of False Hope 2010. *Honours:* Hon. doctorates (Adelphi Univ.) 1995, (Masaryk Univ., Brno, Czech Repub.) 1998; Medal of Merit, First Class (Czech Repub.). *Address:* Sunday Hill Farm, Brinkworth, Wilts., SN15 5AS, England. *Website:* www.roger-scruton.com.

SCULLY, Vincent Joseph, Jr, BA, PhD; American art historian, academic and writer; b. 21 Aug. 1920, New Haven, Conn.; m. Catherine Lynn 1980; four c. *Education:* Yale Univ. *Career:* Instructor, Yale Univ., Asst Prof., Assoc. Prof. 1947–61, Col John Trumbull Prof. of Art History 1961–83, Sterling Prof. of History of Art 1983–91, Sterling Prof. Emer. 1991–; Host, New World Visions: American Art and the Metropolitan Museum 1650–1914, PBS-TV 1983; Visiting Prof., Univ. of Miami at Coral Gables 1992–2009; Mellon Visiting Prof. of History, California Inst. of Tech. 1995; Trustee, Nat. Trust for Historic Preservation. *Publications:* The Architectural Heritage of Newport, Rhode Island (with Antoinette Forrester Downing) 1952, The Shingle Style: Architectural Theory and Design from Richardson to the Origins of Wright 1955, revised edn as The Shingle Style and the Stick Style: Architectural Theory and Design from Downing to the Origins of Wright 1971, Frank Lloyd Wright 1960, Modern Archiecture: The Architecture of Democracy 1961, Louis I Kahn 1962, The Earth, the Temple and the Gods: Greek Sacred Architecture 1962, American Architecture and Urbanism 1969, Pueblo Architecture of the Southwest 1971, The Shingle Style Today: or, The Historian's Revenge 1974, Pueblo: Mountain, Village, Dance 1975, Robert Stern (with David Dunster) 1981, Wesleyan: Photographs 1982, Michael Graves, Buildings and Projects, 1966–1981 1982, The Villas of Palladio 1986, The Architecture of the American Summer: The Flowering of the Shingle Style 1987, New World Visions of Household Gods and Sacred Places: American Art and the Metropolitan Museum 1650–1914 1988, The Architecture of Robert Venturi (with others) 1989, The Great Dinosaur Mural at Yale: The Age of Reptiles (with others) 1990, Architecture: The Natural and the Manmade 1991, French Royal Gardens: The Design of André Le Notre (with Jeannie Baubion-Maclere) 1992, Robert A. M. Stern, Buildings and Projects 1987–1992 1992, Mother's House: The Evolution of Vanna Venturi's House in Chestnut Hill (with Robert Venturi) 1992, Between Two Towers: The Drawings of The School of Miami (with George Hernandez, Catherine Lynn and Teofilo Victoria) 1996, Modern Architecture and Other Essays by Vincent Scully (ed by Neil Levine) 2003, Yale in New Haven: Architecture and Urbanism (with Catherine Lynn, Erik Vogt, Paul Goldberger) 2004; book of essays (selected by Neil Levine). *Honours:* Hon. mem. AIA; Hon. FRIBA; several hon. doctorates; Nat. Endowment for the Humanities Sr Fellowship 1972–73, AIA Medal 1976, Thomas Jefferson Medal, Univ. of Virginia 1982, Topaz Award, Asscn of Collegiate Schools of Architecture/AIA 1986, Literary Lion, New York Public Library 1992, Gov.'s Arts Awards Medal, State of Conn. 1993, American Acad. in Rome Award 1994, Thomas Jefferson Lecturer, Nat. Endowment for the Humanities 1995, chaired professorship est. in his name at Yale Univ. 1997, first recipient of Vincent Scully Prize cr. by Nat. Building Museum, Washington, DC 1999, Vincent J. Scully Jr Visiting Professorship in Architectural History est. at Yale Univ. 2003, Urban Land Inst. J.C. Nichols Prize for Visionary Urban Devt 2003, Nat. Medal of Arts 2004. *Address:* 252 Lawrence Street, New Haven, CT 06511, USA.

SCUPHAM, John Peter, BA, FRSL; British writer and poet; b. 24 Feb. 1933, Liverpool, England; m. Carola Nance Braunholtz 1957; three s. one d. *Education:* Emmanuel Coll., Cambridge. *Career:* Founder-Publr The Mandeville Press. *Publications:* The Snowing Globe 1972, Prehistories 1975, The Hinterland 1977, Summer Places 1980, Winter Quarters 1983, Out Late 1986, The Air Show 1989, Watching the Perseids 1990, Selected Poems 1990, The Ark 1994, Night Watch 1999, Collected Poems 2002, Borrowed Landscapes 2011; contribs to anthologies and magazines. *Honours:* Cholmondeley Award for Poetry. *Address:* Old Hall, Norwich Road, South Burlingham, Norfolk, NR13 4EY, England (home). *Telephone:* (1493) 750804 (home). *E-mail:* margaret@moonshinecat.fsnet.co.uk (home).

SEAGRAVE, Sterling; American writer; b. 15 April 1937, Columbus, OH; m. 1st Wendy Law-Yone 1967; m. 2nd Peggy Sawyer 1982, one s. one d. *Education:* University of Miami, University of Mexico, University of Venezuela. *Career:* mem. Authors' Guild. *Publications:* Yellow Rain 1981, Soldiers of Fortune 1981, The Soong Dynasty 1985, The Marcos Dynasty 1988, Dragon Lady 1992, Lords of the Rim 1995, The Yamato Dynasty (with Peggy Seagrave) 1999, Gold Warriors (with Peggy Seagrave) 2002; contributions to Atlantic, Far Eastern Economic Review, Esquire, Time, Smithsonian. *Website:* www.bowstring.net.

SEAL, Basil (see BARNES, Julian Patrick)

SEALY, (Irwin) Allan, BA, MA, PhD; Indian writer; b. 1951, Allahabad; m. Cushla Sealy; one d. *Education:* La Martiniere School, St Stephen's Coll., Univ. of Delhi, Western Michigan Univ., USA, Univ. of British Columbia, Canada. *Publications include:* The Trotter-Nama: A Chronicle (Commonwealth Best Book Award 1989) 1988, Hero: A Fable 1990, From Yukon to Yucatan: a western journey 1995, The Everest Hotel: A Calendar 1998, The Brainfever Bird 2002, Red 2006. *Honours:* Padma Shri 2012; Sahitya Akademi Award 1991, Crossword Book Award 1998. *Address:* D-101 Race Course, Dehradun, Uttarkhand, India (home). *Telephone:* (135) 2626450 (home).

SEARLE, Elizabeth, BA, MA; American writer and teacher; b. 13 Jan. 1962, Philadelphia, PA; m. John Hodgkinson 1984. *Education:* Arizona State University, Oberlin College, Brown University. *Career:* Adjunct Lecturer, Oberlin College, 1983–84, Brown University, 1988–89; Instructor, Suffolk University, Boston, 1990–91, University of Massachusetts at Lowell, summers 1990–92; Emerson College, Boston, 1991; mem. PEN, New England; Poets and Writers. *Publications:* My Body to You, 1993; A Four-Sided Bed, 1998. Contributions: anthologies, reviews and periodicals. *Honours:* Roberts Writing Award, 1990; Chelsea Fiction Prize, 1991; Iowa Short Fiction Prize, 1992. *Address:* 18 College Avenue, Arlington, MA 02174, USA. *E-mail:* jhodgkinson@mediaone.net.

SEARLE, John R., BA, MA, DPhil; American academic; *Willis S. and Marion Slusser Professor of Philosophy of the Mind and Language, University of California, Berkeley*; b. 1932, Denver, Colo; s. of George W. Searle and Hester Beck Searle; m. Dagmar Carboch 1958; two s. *Education:* Univ. of Wisconsin, Univ. of Oxford, UK. *Career:* Asst Prof. of Philosophy Univ. of California, Berkeley 1959–64, Assoc. Prof. 1964–67, Prof. 1967–, later Slusser Prof. of Philosophy, Chair. Dept of Philosophy 1973–75, Special Asst to Chancellor for Student Affairs 1965–67; mem. Scholar Council, Library of Congress 2000–; mem. Editorial Bd Journal of Psycholinguistic Research, Linguistics and Philosophy, Philosophy and Artificial Intelligence, Journal of Consciousness Studies, Cognitive Science Series, Harvard Univ.Press; mem. American Acad. of Arts and Sciences 1976–, Cognitive Science Group, Univ. of California, Berkeley 1981–, European Acad. of Science and Art 1993–, Scientific Bd, Vilem Mathesius Centre, Charles Univ., Prague 1994–, Nat. Council of Nat. Endowment of Humanities 1992–96; mem. Bd of Dirs American Council of Learned Socs 1979–87; mem. Bd of Trustees Nat. Humanities Center 1976–90; Fellow and Lecturer, World Econ. Forum, Davos 1991, 1995, 1998, 2001; Educ. TV series in Calif. 1960–74; Advisor to Pres.'s Comm. on Student Unrest (Scranton Comm.) 1970. *Publications include:* Speech Acts 1969, The Campus War 1972, Expression and Meaning 1979, Intentionality 1983, Minds, Brains and Science 1984, The Foundations of Illocutionary Logic (with D. Vanderveken) 1985, The Rediscovery of the Mind 1992, (On) Searle on Conversation 1992, The Construction of Social Reality 1995, Mystery of Consciousness 1997, Mind, Language and Society 1998, Conversations with John Searle 2001, La Universidad Desafiada 2002, Consciousness and Language 2002, Liberté et Neurobiologie (trans. as Freedom and Neurology) 2004, Mind, A Brief Introduction 2004, Making the Social World 2010, Thinking About the Real World 2011. *Honours:* Hon. Prof., Tsinghua Univ., Beijing 2007, East China Normal Univ., Shanghai 2007; Dr hc (Adelphi) 1993, (Wisconsin) 1994, (Bucharest) 2000, (Torino) 2000, (Lucano) 2003; Rhodes Scholar 1952, Reith Lecturer 1984, Tasan Award, South Korean 2000, Jean Nicod Prize 2000, Jovellanos Prize 2000, Nat. Humanities Medal 2005, Mind and Brain Prize, Torino, Italy 2006, Puffendorf Medal, Sweden 2006. *Address:* Department of Philosophy, 314 Moses Hall 2390, University of California, Berkeley, CA 94720-2390, USA (office). *Telephone:* (510) 642-3173 (office). *Fax:* (510) 642-5160 (office). *Website:* philosophy.berkeley.edu (office).

SEBAG-MONTEFIORE, Simon Jonathan Sebag, MA, FRSL; British writer and historian; b. 27 June 1965, London; m. Santa Montefiore; one s., one d. *Education:* Harrow School, Gonville and Caius Coll., Univ. of Cambridge. *Publications:* novels: King's Parade 1991, My Affair with Stalin 1997; non-fiction: Prince of Princes: The Life of Potemkin 2000, Stalin: The Court of the Red Tsar 2003 (History Book of the Year Prize, British Book Awards 2004), Young Stalin (Costa Book Award for Biography) 2007, Catherine the Great & Potemkin 2007, 101 World Heroes, Sashenka 2008. *Literary Agent:* Georgina Capel, Capel & Land, 29 Wardour Street, London, W1D 6PS, England. *Telephone:* (20) 7734-2414. *E-mail:* georgina@capelland.co.uk. *Website:* www.capelland.com; www.simonsebagmontefiore.com.

SEBBAR, Leïla, DèsL; French writer; b. Aflou, Algeria; two s. *Education:* Sorbonne Univ., Paris. *Career:* moved to France aged 19; teacher, Lycée Rodin, Paris; Literary Critic, France Culture. *Publications:* novels: Fatima ou les Algériennes au square 1981, Shérazade: 17 ans, brune, frisée, les yeux verts 1982, Le Chinois vert d'Afrique 1984, Parle mon fils, parle à ta mère 1984, Les Carnets de Shérazade 1985, J. H. cherche âme-soeur 1987, Le Fou de Shérazade 1991, Le Silence des rives 1993, La Seine était rouge 1999, Marguerite 2002, Le Chinois vert d'Afrique 2002, Les femmes au bain 2006, Les Femmes au bain 2006, Mon cher fils 2009; short stories: Le Baiser 1997, Litérratur Soldats 1999, La Jeune fille au balcon 2001, Sept filles 2003, Isabelle l'algérien 2006, L'habit vert 2006, Le ravin de la femme sauvage 2007,

Métro 2007, Le peintre et son modèle 2007, Louisa le vagabond 2008, La noire et la blanche 2009, Noyant d'Allier 2009; non-fiction: On tue les petites filles 1978, Le Pédophile et la maman 1980, Lettres parisiennes, histoires d'exil with Nancy Huston 1986, J'ai lu 1999, Je ne parle pas la langue de mon père 2003, Mes algéries en France (text and images) 2004, Journal de mes Algéries en France (text and images) 2005, L'Arabe comme un chant secret 2007, Voyage en Algéries autour de ma chambre, abécédaire (text and images) 2008; editor and author of collective books: Une enfance algérienne 1999, Une enfance d'ailleurs: 17 écrivains racontent (co-ed. with Nancy Huston) 2002, Femmes d'Afrique du Nord: cartes postales (1885–1930) (with Jean-Michel Belorgey and Christelle Taraud) 2002, Les algériens au café 2003, Une enfance outremer 2004, Mon père 2007, C'était leur France 2007, Ma mère 2009; children's novels: juvenile: Ismaël dans la jungle des villes 1986, Lorient-Québec 1991, J'étais enfant en Algérie: Juin 1962, 2001. *Honours:* Chevalier, Légion d'honneur, Ordre des Arts et des Lettres. *Address:* c/o Éditions Bleu Autour, 11 avenue Pasteur, Saint-Pourçain-sur-Sioule 03500 (office); c/o Al Manar, Alain Gorius, 96 boulevard Maurice Barrès, 92200 Neuilly (office); 13 rue Vergniaud, 75013 Paris, France (home). *Telephone:* 1-45-89-03-32 (home). *E-mail:* dominique.pignon@free.fr (home). *Website:* clicnet.swarthmore.edu/leila_sebbar.

SEBOLD, Alice, MFA; American author; b. Madison, WI; m. Glen David Gould. *Education:* Syracuse Univ., Univ. of Houston, Univ. of California at Irvine. *Career:* teacher and lecturer 1984–; Ed. Tonga Books 2010–. *Publications:* Lucky (memoir) 1999, The Lovely Bones (novel; Book of the Year, American Booksellers' Asscn 2003) 2002, The Almost Moon (novel) 2007. *Literary Agent:* Steven Barclay Agency, 12 Western Avenue, Petaluma, CA 94952, USA. *Telephone:* (707) 773-0654. *Fax:* (707) 778-1868. *Address:* c/o Tonga Books, Europa Editions, 116 East 16th Street, New York, NY 10003, USA (office). *Telephone:* (212) 477-8242 (office). *E-mail:* info@europaeditions.com (office).

SECOR, James L., BA, MS, PhD; American writer, dramatist and poet; b. 11 June 1947, Ft Clayton Air Force Base, Panama; one s. *Education:* Towson State Univ., Johns Hopkins Univ., Univ. of Kansas, Bunraku Nat. Puppet Theatre, Osaka. *Career:* teacher, Aoyama Univ. 1990–92, Japan Coll. of the Arts 1992; Tutor, Univ. of Kansas, 1994–99, Johnson County Community Coll. 1995; Ed., Into the Eye 1996–97; mem. Japan Language Teachers' Asscn 1990–92, Lawrence Community Theatre 1997, Acad. of American Poets. *Publications:* Sapl and Nicholas Ferguson: The Legend, 1992; Tanka, Sweetheart, 1996; Tangled in the Net of Ruin, 1996; Statesmanship, 1996; Saving Grace, 1996; A Different Thing to Do, 1996; Tanka, Reflections of Yesterday, 1996; The Crippled Heart of Man, 1997; Social Puissance, 1997; Votive, 1997; Sex Ed, 1997; Tanka, Ages and Stages, 1997; several plays.

SEDAKOVA, Olga Aleksandrovna; Russian poet, translator and essayist; b. 1949, Moscow. *Education:* Moscow State Univ. *Career:* teacher, Inst. of Theory and History of World Culture, A.M. Gorky Institute of World Literature 1991–; Visiting Lecturer, Stanford Univ. 2006. *Publications include:* Gates, Windows and Arches 1985, Vrata, okna, arki: Izbrannye stikhotvoreni, a 1986, Kitaiskoe puteshestvie: Stely i nadpisi: Starye pesni 1990, Stikhi 1994, Poems and Elegies 2004; contrib. to Silk of Time: Bilingual Selected Poems 1994. *Honours:* European Prize for Poetry 1996. *Address:* A.M. Gorky Institute of World Literature, 121069 Moscow, ul. Vorovskogo 25a, Russia (office).

SEDARIS, David; American playwright and writer; b. 1956, New York, NY. *Career:* made comic debut reading his Santa Land Diaries on Nat. Public Radio's Morning Edn; writes for This American Life (Public Radio Int.). *Plays:* with Amy Sedaris, as The Talent Family: Stump the Host, Stitches, One Woman Shoe (Obie Award), Incident at Cobbler's Knob, The Book of Liz. *Publications include:* Barrel Fever, Children Playing Before a Statue of Hercules: An Anthology of Outstanding Stories, Holidays on Ice 1997, Naked (essays) 1997, Me Talk Pretty One Day (essays) 2000, Dress Your Family in Corduroy and Denim 2004, When you are Engulfed in Flames 2008, Holidays on Ice 2008, Squirrel Seeks Chipmunk 2010; contrib. essays to Esquire and The New Yorker. *Honours:* Thurber Prize for American Humor 2001, Time magazine Humorist of the Year 2001. *Literary Agent:* The Steven Barclay Agency, 12 Western Avenue, Petaluma, CA 94952, USA. *Telephone:* (707) 773-0654. *Fax:* (707) 778-1868. *E-mail:* steven@barclayagency.com. *Website:* www.barclayagency.com.

SEDGWICK, Fred, MA; British academic and poet; b. 20 Jan. 1945, Dublin, Ireland; s. of Fred and Gladys Sedgwick; one s. *Education:* St Luke's College, Exeter, University of East Anglia at Norwich. *Career:* Head of Downing Primary School, Suffolk 1984–90; freelance writer 1990–. *Publications:* The Living Daylights, 1986; Lighting Up Time: On Children's Writing, 1990, The Expressive Arts 1993, Drawing to Learn 1993, Personal, Social and Moral Education 1994, Art Across the Curriculum 1996, Learning Together: Enhance Your Child's Creativity 1996, Read My Mind: Young Children, Poetry and Learning 1997, Thinking About Literacy: Young Children and Their Language 1999, Shakespeare and the Young Writer 1999, Writing to Learn: Poetry and Literacy Across the Primary Curriculum 2000, Themes for Poetry 2000, Forms of Poetry 1 2000, Forms of Poetry 2 2000, The Ammonite's Revenge (co-author) 2000, Teaching Literacy: a Creative Approach 2001, Will There Really Be a Nothing? (anthology) 2002, Enabling Children's Learning Through Drawing 2002, How to Write Poetry and Get It Published 2002, Teaching Poetry 2003, Stone and Other Poems 2004, How to Teach with a Hangover: a Practical Guide to Overcoming Classroom Crises 2005, 101 Essential Lists for Primary School Teachers 2006, 100 Primary School Assemblies 2006, So You Want to Be a Teacher 2008, 100 Ways of Teaching Thinking in the Primary School 2008, Where Words Come From: a Dictionary of Word Origins 2009, 100 Ideas for Teaching Literacy 2009; poems: The Living Daylights 1986, This Way, That Way (anthology for schools; ed.) 1989, Hey! (co-author) 1990, The Biggest Riddle in the World (co-author) 1990, Lies 1991, Pizza, Curry, Fish and Chips 1994, Blind Date 1997, Jenny Kissed Me (ed.) 2000. *Address:* c/o Society of Authors, 84 Drayton Gardens, London SW10 9SB, England.

SEDLEY, Kate (see Clarke, Brenda Margaret Lilian)

SEDLEY, Rt Hon. Sir Stephen John, Kt, PC, BA; British judge and writer; b. 9 Oct. 1939, s. of William Sedley and Rachel Sedley; m. 1st Ann Tate 1968 (divorced 1995); one s. two d.; m. 2nd Teresa Chaddock 1996. *Education:* Mill Hill School, Queens' Coll., Cambridge. *Career:* writer, musician, trans. 1961–64; called to Bar, Inner Temple 1964, Bencher 1989, QC 1983, Lord Justice of Appeal 1999–2011; mem. Int. Comm. on Mercenaries, Angola 1976; Visiting Professorial Fellow, Univ. of Warwick 1981; Pres. Nat. Reference Tribunals for the Coalmining Industry 1983–88; Visiting Fellow, Osgoode Hall Law School, Canada 1987, Visiting Prof. 1997; Dir Public Law Project 1989–93; Chair. Sex Discrimination Cttee, Bar Council 1992–95; Judge of the High Court of Justice, Queen's Bench Div. 1992–99; Distinguished Visitor, Hong Kong Univ. 1992; Hon. Prof., Univ. of Wales, Cardiff 1993–, Univ. of Warwick 1994–; Visiting Fellow, Victoria Univ. of Wellington, NZ 1998; Judicial Visitor, Univ. Coll. London 1999–; Pres. British Inst. of Human Rights 2000–, British Tinnitus Asscn 2006–; Chair. British Council Advisory Cttee on Governance 2002–05; mem. Admin. Law Bar Asscn (Hon. Vice-Pres. 1992–), Haldane Soc. (Sec. 1964–69). *Publications include:* Whose Child? 1987, The Making and Remaking of the British Constitution (with Lord Nolan) 1997, Freedom, Law and Justice 1999, Human Rights: A New World or Business as Usual 2000; editor: Seeds of Love (anthology) 1967, A Spark in the Ashes 1992; translator: From Burgos Jail, by Marcos Ana and Vidal de Nicolas 1964; contrib. essays to numerous books, including Freedom of Expression and Freedom of Information 2000, Judicial Review in International Perspective 2000, Discriminating Lawyers 2000; contrib. to periodicals and journals, including Civil Justice Quarterly, Industrial Law Journal, Journal of Law and Society, Journal of Legal Ethics, Law Quarterly Review, London Review of Books, Modern Law Review, Public Law. *Honours:* Hon. Fellow, Inst. for Advanced Legal Studies 1997; Dr hc (North London) 1996; Hon. LLD (Nottingham Trent) 1997, (Bristol) 1999, (Warwick) 1999, (Durham) 2001, (Hull) 2002, (Southampton) 2003, (Exeter) 2004, (Essex) 2007. *Address:* Cloisters, Temple, London, EC4Y 7AA, England (office).

SEE, Carolyn, (Monica Highland), PhD; American writer; *Professor Emerita, University of California at Los Angeles*; b. 13 Jan. 1934, Pasadena, CA; m. 1st Richard See 1954; m. 2nd Tom Sturak 1960; two d. *Education:* Univ. of California at Los Angeles. *Career:* fmr Prof. of English, UCLA, now Prof. Emer.; mem. PEN Center USA West (pres. 1993–94). *Publications:* as Carolyn See: The Rest is Done with Mirrors 1970, Blue Money 1974, Mothers, Daughters 1977, Rhine Maidens 1980, Golden Days 1985, When Knaves Meet 1988, The Mirrored Hall in the Hollywood Dance Hall 1991, Dreaming: Hard Luck and Good Times in America 1995, The Handyman 1999, There Will Never Be Another You 2006; as Monica Highland: Lotus Land 1983, 1-10 Shanghai Road 1985, Greetings From Southern California 1987, Two Schools of Thought (with John Espey) 1991, Making a Literary Life 2002, Jerusalem 2005; contrib. to newspapers and magazines. *Honours:* Samuel Goldwyn Award 1963, Sidney Hillman Award 1969, NEA grant 1974, Nat. Women's Political Caucus Bread and Roses Award 1988, Vesta Award 1989, Guggenheim Fellowship 1989, Lila Wallace Grant 1993, PEN Center USA West Lifetime Achievement Award 1998. *Address:* 1833 12 Street, Apartment A, Santa Monica, CA 90404-4625, USA (home). *Telephone:* (310) 454-7724 (office). *Fax:* (310) 459-8524 (office). *E-mail:* carolyn@carolynsee.com (office). *Website:* www.carolynsee.com.

SEED, Cecile Eugenie (Jenny); South African author; b. 18 May 1930, Cape Town; m. Edward (Ted) Robert Seed 1953, three s. one d. *Publications:* The Great Thirst, 1985; The Great Elephant, 1985; Place Among the Stones, 1987; Hurry, Hurry, Sibusiso, 1988; The Broken Spear, 1989; The Prince of the Bay, 1989; The Big Pumpkin, 1990; Old Grandfather Mantis, 1992; The Hungry People, 1993; A Time to Scatter Stones, 1993; Lucky Boy, 1995; The Strange Large Egg, 1996. *Honours:* MER Award 1987.

SEFTON, Catherine (see Martin Waddell)

SEGAL, Lore, BA; American (b. Austrian) writer and teacher; b. (Lore Groszmann), 8 March 1928, Vienna, Austria; d. of Ignatz Groszmann and Franziska Groszmann; m. David I. Segal 1960 (deceased); one s. one d. *Education:* Bedford Coll., Univ. of London, UK. *Career:* Prof., Writing Div., School of Arts, Columbia Univ., Princeton Univ., Sarah Lawrence Coll., Bennington Coll.; Prof. of English, Univ. of Illinois, Ohio State Univ., retd 1996; mem. American Acad. of Arts and Sciences, PEN. *Film:* participant in My Knees Were Shaking. *Publications:* fiction: Other People's Houses 1964, Lucinella 1976, Her First American 1985, Shakespeare's Kitchen (short stories) 2007; children's books: Tell Me a Mitzi 1970, All the Way Home 1973, Tell Me a Trudy 1977, The Story of Mrs Brubeck and How She Looked for Trouble and Where She Found Him 1981, The Story of Mrs Lovewright and Purrless Her Cat 1985, Morris the Artist 2003, Why Mole Shouted 2004, More

Mole Stories and Little Gopher Too 2005; translator: Gallows Songs (with W. D. Snodgrass) 1968, The Juniper Tree and Other Tales from Grimm 1973; contrib. to periodicals. *Honours:* Guggenheim Fellowship 1965–66, Nat. Endowment for the Arts grant 1982, Nat. Endowment for the Humanities grant 1983, Acad. of Arts and Letters Award 1986, Ohio Arts Council grant 1996, Fellowship, Dorothy and Lewis B. Cullman Center for Scholars and Writers, New York Public Library 2008–09. *Address:* 280 Riverside Drive, Apt 12K, New York, NY 10025, USA. *Telephone:* (212) 663-1524. *Fax:* (212) 663-1524. *E-mail:* Lore@usa.net. *Website:* www.loresegal.net.

SEIDMAN, Hugh, BS, MS, MFA; American writer, poet and teacher; b. 1 Aug. 1940, New York, NY; s. of Monas Seidman and Susan Seidman; m. Jayne Holsinger 1990. *Education:* Polytechnic Inst. of Brooklyn, Univ. of Minnesota, Columbia Univ. *Career:* Faculty mem. New School for Social Research 1976–98; Asst Prof. and Sophie Kerr Poetry Lecturer, Washington Coll. 1979; Visiting Lecturer, Bd of Cooperative Educational Services 1969, 1970, Univ. of Wisconsin 1981, Columbia Univ. 1985; Visiting Poet, South Carolina, Connecticut, New York City Public Schools 1970–72, Yale Univ. 1971, 1973, Writer's Voice, New York City 1988; Participating Poet, New York State Poets-in-the-Schools 1978–81, Virginia Poets-in-the-Schools 1982; Poet-in-Residence, City Coll. of CUNY 1972–75, Wilkes Coll. 1975, Aspen Writers Conf. 1979, Coll. of William and Mary 1982; Distinguished Poet-in-Residence, Wichita State Univ. 1978a. *Publications:* Collecting Evidence (Yale Series of Younger Poets Prize, Yale Univ. Press 1969) 1970, Blood Lord 1974, Throne/Falcon/Eye 1982, People Live, They Have Lives (Winner Camden Poetry Award, Walt Whitman Center for the Arts, Camden, NJ 1990) 1992, Selected Poems: 1965–1995 (cited by The Village Voice as one of the 25 Best Books of the Year 1995, cited by Critics' Choice: 1995–96 (compiled by the San Francisco Review of Books) as one of the 11 Best Poetry Books of the Year 1996) 1995, Somebody Stand Up and Sing (Green Rose Prize 2004) 2005. *Honours:* Nat. Endowment for the Arts Discovery Grant 1970, and Creative Writing Fellowships 1972, 1985, Creative Artists Public Service Program (NY State) grant 1971, Yaddo Resident Fellow 1972, 1976, 1988, MacDowell Colony Resident Fellow 1974, 1975, 1989, Writer's Digest Poetry Prize 1982, New York Foundation for the Arts Poetry Creative Writing Fellowship 1990, 2003, included in The Best American Poetry 1993, 2002. *Address:* 463 West Street, No. H822, New York, NY 10014, USA (home). *Website:* www.hughseidman.com.

SEIERSTAD, Åsne; Norwegian journalist and writer; b. 10 Feb. 1970, Oslo. *Education:* Univ. of Oslo. *Career:* staff, ITAR-TASS news agency, Moscow; covered wars in Chechnya, Kosovo, Afghanistan, Iraq for several Scandinavian newspapers 1994–2004; correspondent, Norwegian television news 1998–2000. *Publications:* non-fiction: With Their Backs to the World 2000, The Bookseller of Kabul 2002, A Hundred and One Days: A Baghdad Journal 2004, Angel of Grozny: Inside Chechnya 2008. *Honours:* award for television reporting from Kosovo, Chechnya and Afghanistan, Gullruten Award 1999, Fritt Ord Honorary Award 2001, Årets Frilanser Award 2002, Journalist of the Year, Norway 2003, EMMA Award, London 2004, Bookseller's Prize, France 2004. *Address:* Virago Press, Little, Brown Book Group, 100 Victoria Embankment, London, EC4Y 0DY, England; Tidemands gt. 20, 0260 Oslo, Norway (home). *Telephone:* (20) 7911-8000. *Fax:* (20) 7911-8100. *E-mail:* virago.press@littlebrown.co.uk; aaseie@frisurf.no. *Website:* www.virago.co.uk (office).

SEIFFERT, Rachel, BA, MLitt; British writer and teacher; b. 1971, Oxford, England; one s. *Education:* Univs of Bristol and Glasgow. *Career:* fmr Lecturer in English, Univ. of Glasgow. *Publications:* Blue (short story) 1999, The Crossing (short story) 2001, The Dark Room (novel) (LA Times First Fiction Award 2002) 2001, Field Study (short stories) 2004, Afterwards (novel) 2007. *Honours:* PEN David T. K. Wong Award 2001, Betty Trask Prize 2002. *Literary Agent:* c/o Toby Eady Associates Ltd, Third Floor, 9 Orme Court, London, W2 4RL, England. *Telephone:* (20) 7792-0092. *Fax:* (20) 7792-0879. *E-mail:* toby@tobyeadyassociates.co.uk. *Website:* www.tobyeadyassociates.co.uk.

SELBERG, Ingrid Maria, BA; American publishing executive; *Publishing Director, Children's Division, Simon & Schuster UK Limited;* b. 13 March 1950, Princeton, NJ; d. of Atle Selberg and Hedvig Selberg (née Liebermann); m. Mustapha Matura; one s. one d. *Education:* Univ. of Columbia, New York. *Career:* Ed. Collins Publs 1978–84; Editorial Dir Bantam (UK) 1984–85; Publr Heinemann Young Books, William Heinemann and Methuen Children's Books, London 1986–1995; Man. Dir Dorling Kindersley –1998, Pleasant Co. International, HIT Entertainment and Reed Consumer Books; Vice-Pres. UK and Int. Publishing Gullane Entertainment –2002; Publishing Dir, Children's Div., Simon & Schuster UK Ltd 2003–. *Publications:* Trees and Leaves 1977, Our Changing World 1981, Nature's Hidden World 1983. *Address:* Simon & Schuster UK Ltd, 1st Floor, 222 Gray's Inn Road, London, WC1X 8HB, England (office). *Telephone:* (20) 7316-1900 (office). *Fax:* (20) 7316-0332 (office). *E-mail:* enquiries@simonandschuster.co.uk (office). *Website:* www.simonandschuster.net (office).

SELBOURNE, David, BA, MA; British writer and playwright; b. 4 June 1937, London, England. *Education:* Balliol Coll., Oxford, Inner Temple, London. *Career:* mem. Acad. of Savignano (Italy). *Publications:* The Play of William Cooper and Edmund Dew-Nevett 1968, The Two-Backed Beast 1969, Dorabella 1970, Samson and Alison Mary Fagan 1971, The Damned 1971, Class Play 1973, Brook's Dream: The Politics of Theatre 1974, What's Acting? and Think of a Story Quickly! 1977, An Eye to India 1977, An Eye to China 1978, Through the Indian Looking Glass 1982, The Making of a Midsummer Night's Dream 1983, Against Socialist Illusion: A Radical Argument 1985, In Theory and In Practice: Essays on the Politics of Jayaprakash Narayan 1986, Left Behind: Journeys into British Politics 1987, A Doctor's Life: The Diaries of Hugh Selbourne MD 1960–63 1989, Death of the Dark Hero: Eastern Europe 1987–90 1990, The Spirit of the Age 1993, Not an Englishman: Conversations With Lord Goodman 1993, The Principle of Duty 1994, The City of Light 1997, One Year On: The 'New' Politics and Labour 1998, Moral Evasion 1998, The Losing Battle with Islam 2005; trans.: The City of Light, by Jacob d'Ancona 1997. *Honours:* Officer, Order of Merit of Italian Repub. 2001. *Literary Agent:* c/o Christopher Sinclair-Stevenson, 3 South Terrace, London, SW7 2TB, England. *Telephone:* (20) 7581-2550.

SELBY, Stephen, BA (Phil.), BA (Soc. Sci.); British playwright, director and horticulturalist; b. 5 June 1952, Darley Dale, Derbyshire; s. of Noel Selby and Jean Selby; m. Ann Spence 1982; one d. *Education:* Nottingham Trent Univ., Bolton Inst. *Career:* writer, dir, producer, Noc On Theatre 1987–, Hurdles of Time Theatre 1991–; Dramaturgo, La Edad de Oro Theatre Co.; mem. Theatre Writers Union, Camagüey Theatre Dirs Asscn. *Plays:* Better Looking Corpses 1989, Contentious Work 1990, Archie Pearson The One-Legged Shoemaker 1991, Erewash Giants 1993, The Concrete Silver Band 1995, Tontos Sabios y Ladrones Honestos 1996, Dead Letters 2000. *Publication:* Hurdles of Time 1993. *Address:* 53 Percival Road, Sherwood, Nottingham, Notts., NG5 2FA, England (home). *Telephone:* (115) 910-9116 (office). *E-mail:* jam53p@ntlworld.com (office).

SELF, William (Will) Woodward, MA; British writer and cartoonist; *Columnist, The Independent;* b. 26 Sept. 1961, London; s. of Peter John Otter Self and Elaine Rosenbloom; m. 1st Katharine Sylvia Anthony Chancellor 1989 (divorced 1996); one s. one d.; m. 2nd Deborah Jane Orr 1997; two s. *Education:* Christ's Coll., Exeter Coll., Oxford. *Career:* cartoon illustrations appeared in New Statesman and City Limits 1982–88; Publishing Dir Cathedral Publishing 1988–90; Contributing Ed. London Evening Standard magazine 1993–95; columnist, The Observer 1995–97, The Times 1997–99, Ind. on Sunday 2000–, Evening Standard 2002–, The Independent 2003–. *Publications:* short stories: Quantity Theory of Insanity 1991, Grey Area 1994, A Story for Europe 1996, Tough Tough Toys for Tough Tough Boys 1998, Dr Mukti and Other Tales of Woe 2003, Liver 2008; novellas: Cock and Bull 1992, The Sweet Smell of Psychosis 1996; novels: My Idea of Fun 1993, Great Apes 1997, How the Dead Live 2000, Perfidious Man 2000, Feeding Frenzy 2001, Dorian 2002, Dr Mukti 2004, The Book of Dave 2006, Umbrella 2012; non-fiction: Junk Mail (selected journalism) 1995, Sore Sites (collected journalism) 2000, Psychogeography (collected journalism) 2007, The Butt 2008, Psycho Too (with Ralph Steadman) 2009, Walking to Hollywood 2010; collected cartoons 1985. *Honours:* Geoffrey Faber Memorial Prize 1992. *Literary Agent:* The Wylie Agency, 17 Bedford Square, London, WC1B 3BA, England. *Telephone:* (20) 7908-5900.

SELMI, Habib; Tunisian writer; b. 1951, Kairouan. *Career:* lives in Paris 1985–. *Publications:* novels: Jabal al-'Anz (trans. as Goat Mountain) 1985, Surat Badawi Mayyit 1990, Matahat al-Raml 1994, Hufar Dafi'aa 1999, Ushaq Bayya (trans. as Bayya's Lovers) 2002, Asrar Abdallah 2004, Rawa'ih Marie-Claire 2008; also short stories, poems. *Address:* c/o Dar El-Adab, 3rd floor, Bayham Building, after old Libancell Building, Sakiet El Jenzir, Beirut, Lebanon (office).

SELTZER, Joanne, BA, MA; American writer and poet; b. (Joanne Zellman), 21 Nov. 1929, Detroit, Mich.; d. of the late Samuel Zellman and Ethel Goldstein; m. Stanley Seltzer 1951 (died 2005); one s. three d. *Education:* Univ. of Michigan, Coll. of St Rose. *Career:* mem. American Literary Translators Asscn, Associated Writing Programs, Poetry Soc. of America, Poets & Writers, The Authors Guild. *Publications:* Adirondack Lake Poems 1985, Suburban Landscape 1988, Inside Invisible Walls 1989, Women Born During Tornadoes 2009; contribs to journals and magazines and to anthologies including When I Am an Old Woman I Shall Wear Purple. *Honours:* All Nations Poetry Contest Award 1978, World Order of Narrative and Formalist Poets Competitions Prizes 1986, 1988, 1990, 1992, 1993, 1994, 1997, 1998, 2000, Tucumari Literary Review Poetry Contest Award 1989, Amelia Islander Magazine Literary Contest Poetry Prize 1999. *Address:* 2481 McGovern Drive, Schenectady, NY 12309, USA. *E-mail:* Joseltzer@nycap.rr.com. *Website:* www.joseltzer.com.

SELVADURAI, Shyam, BFA; Sri Lankan writer; b. 1965, Colombo. *Education:* York Univ., Canada. *Career:* moved with family to Canada aged 19 after 1983 riots in Colombo; writer for TV. *Publications:* Funny Boy (novel) (WHSmith/Books in Canada First Novel Award, Lambda Literary Award for Best Gay Men's Fiction, USA) 1994, Cinnamon Gardens (novel) 1998, Swimming in the Monsoon Sea 2005; contrib. fiction and essays to journals and anthologies. *Address:* c/o Tundra Books, 75 Sherbourne Street, 5th Floor, Toronto, ON M5A 2P9, Canada (office). *E-mail:* tundra@mcclelland.com (home). *Website:* www.tundrabooks.com (office).

SELVIDGE, Marla Jean, BA, MA, PhD; American academic and writer; b. 11 Nov. 1948, Grosse Pointe, MI; m. 1st Stephen P. Schierling (divorced 1981); m. 2nd Thomas C. Hemling 1982. *Education:* Fort Wayne Bible College, Wheaton College, IL, St Louis University. *Career:* several college and university positions, 1973–89; Assoc. Ed., Explorations: A Journal for Adventurous Thought, 1986–; Contributing Ed., Spotlight on Teaching, 1993–; Asst Prof. of

Religious Studies and Philosophy, Marist College, Poughkeepsie, New York, 1989–90; Assoc. Prof., 1990–94, Dir, Center for Religious Studies, 1990–, Prof. of Religious Studies, 1994–, Central Michigan State University, Warrensburg; Vice-Pres., American Schools of Oriental Research, 1997–; mem. American Acad. of Religion; Society of Biblical Literature; Catholic Biblical Asscn; Central States Society of Biblical Literature, Chair, Sections on New Testament, 1992–94, Chair, Gender Issues, 1994–96; Missouri State Teachers Asscn, Vice-Pres. and Board of Dirs, 1997–. *Publications:* Fundamentalism Today: What Makes It So Attractive? (ed.), 1984; Daughters of Jerusalem, 1987; Woman, Cult, and Miracle Recital, 1990; Discovering Women, 1995; Notorious Voices: The Roots of Feminist Biblical Interpretation, 1996; Violence, Women, and the Bible, 1996; A Feminist Companion to the Bible: The Old Testament in the New Testament (contributor), 1996; Notorious Voices: A Reader, 1997; The New Testament: A Timeless Book for All Peoples, 1998. Contributions: Religious Studies News; Journal of Religious Studies; Marist Working Papers; Journal of Biblical Literature; Catholic Biblical Quarterly; Journal of Theology for Southern Africa; Missouri Chautauqua: Varieties of American Religious Experience. *Honours:* Society of Biblical Literature Award, 1982–83; Grants, William R. Kenan Fund and National Endowment for the Humanities, 1984–87; Educational Communications Award, Connecticut Asscn of Boards of Education, 1988–89; American Mirror Lecturer, 1991–93, Grant, 1992–94, Missouri Humanities Council.

SEM-SANDBERG, Steve; Swedish writer, literary critic and journalist; b. 16 Aug. 1958, Oslo, Norway. *Career:* wrote for Svenska Dagbladet 1988–2008, Deputy Cultural Ed. 1995–98. *Publications:* De ansiktlösa (novel) 1987, I en annan del av staden (essays) 1990, En lektion i pardans (novel) 1993, Theres (novel) (Aftonbladet's Literature Prize) 1996, Allt fögängligt är bara en bild (novel) 1999, Prag (No Exit) (essays) 2002, Ravensbrück (novel) 2003, Härifrån till Allmänningen (novel) 2005, De fattiga i Łódź (novel) (August-priset) 2009; also trans.; contrib. articles and criticism to magazines and cultural journals including Eurozine. *Honours:* Doblougska Prize 2005, Sorescu Prize 2007, Karl Vennbergs Prize 2008, De Nios Stora Prize 2009. *Literary Agent:* Nordin Agency, PO Box 4022, SE- 102 61 Stockholm, Sweden. *Telephone:* (8) 57168525. *E-mail:* info@nordinagency.com. *Website:* www.nordinagency.se. *Address:* c/o Albert Bonniers Förlag, PO Box 3159, 103 63 Stockholm, Sweden (office). *E-mail:* info@abforlag.bonnier.se (office). *Website:* www.albertbonniersforlag.se (office).

SEMEL, Nava, MA; Israeli author, playwright and translator; b. 15 Sept. 1954; m. Noam Semel; two s. one d. *Education:* Tel-Aviv Univ. *Career:* mem. Israeli Playwright Asscn, Hebrew Writers' Asscn, PEN Int. Writers, Writers' Asscn. *Publications include:* Hat of Glass 1985, Becoming Gershona 1990, Flying Lessons 1995, Night Games 1994, Little Rose of the Mediterranean 1994, Bride on Paper 1996, Liluna 1998, Who Stole the Show? 1999, Awake in my Sleep 2000, And the Rat Laughed (novel; opera version, composed by Ella Milch-Sheriff 2005) 2004, 1000 Calories a Day (screenplay, Israeli TV) 2002, The Courage to be Afraid (poetry for children) 2004, Isra-Island (novel) 2005, Beginner's Love (YA book) 2006, Australian Wedding (autobiographical fiction) 2009, Whereabouts Unknown (TV drama) 2010; plays: An Old Lady 1984, The Child Behind the Eyes 1986, Hunger 1989, An Old Man 2004, Flying Lessons (opera libretto) 2010. *Honours:* Inst. for Holocaust Studies Award 1988, Haifa Award 1988, Nat. Jewish Book Award 1990, Israeli Prime Minister's Award for Literature 1996, Best Illustrated Book of the Year, Israel Museum Award 1998, Women's Literature Award of the Mediterranean 1994, Woman of the Year in Literature of the City of Tel-Aviv 2006. *Address:* 56 Weitzman Street, #13, Tel-Aviv 62155, Israel (home). *Telephone:* (3) 5460514 (home). *Fax:* (3) 5440398 (home). *E-mail:* semel@012.net.il (home). *Website:* www.navasemel.com (home).

SEMMLER, Clement William, MA; Australian broadcaster and writer; b. 23 Dec. 1914, Eastern Well, SA; m. 1st (divorced); one s. one d.; m. 2nd Catherine Helena Wilson 1974; one d. *Education:* University of Adelaide. *Career:* Fellow, College of Fine Arts, University of New South Wales. *Publications:* For the Uncanny Man (essays), 1963; Barcroft Boake, 1965; Literary Australia (ed.), 1965; The Banjo of the Bush, 1966; Kenneth Slessor, 1966; Twentieth Century Australian Literary Criticism (ed.), 1967; The Art of Brian James, 1972; Douglas Stewart, 1974; The ABC-Aunt Sally and the Sacred Cow, 1981; A Frank Hardy Swag (ed.), 1982; The War Diaries of Kenneth Slessor, 1985; The War Dispatches of Kenneth Slessor, 1987; Pictures on the Margin (memoirs), 1991. Contributions: periodicals and journals. *Honours:* DLitt, University of New England, Armidale, 1968; OBE, 1972; AM, 1988.

SEN, Amartya Kumar, BA, PhD, FBA; Indian economist and academic; *Thomas W. Lamont University Professor Emeritus and Professor of Economics and Philosophy, Harvard University*; b. 3 Nov. 1933, Santiniketan, Bengal; s. of the late Ashutosh Sen and of Amita Sen; m. 1st Nabaneeta Dev 1960 (divorced 1975); two d.; m. 2nd Eva Colorni 1978 (died 1985); one s. one d.; m. 3rd Emma Rothschild. *Education:* Presidency Coll., Calcutta and Trinity Coll., Cambridge. *Career:* Prof. of Econs, Jadavpur Univ., Calcutta 1956–58; Fellow, Trinity Coll., Cambridge 1957–63; Prof. of Econs, Univ. of Delhi 1963–71, Chair. Dept of Econs 1966–68; Hon. Dir Agricultural Econs Research Centre, Delhi 1966–68, 1969–71; Prof. of Econs, LSE 1971–77, Univ. of Oxford 1977–80, Drummond Prof. of Political Economy 1980–88; Thomas W. Lamont Univ. Prof., Harvard Univ. 1987–98, 2004–, Prof. Emer. 1998–2004, Prof. of Econs and Philosophy 2004–; Master Trinity Coll., Cambridge 1998–2003; Visiting Prof., Univ. of Calif., Berkeley 1964–65, Harvard Univ. 1968–69; Andrew D. White Prof.-at-Large, Cornell Univ. 1978–84; Pres. Int. Econ. Asscn 1986–89; Fellow, Econometric Soc., Pres. 1984. *Publications include:* Choice of Techniques: An Aspect of Planned Economic Development 1960, Growth Economics 1970, Collective Choice and Social Welfare 1970, On Economic Inequality 1973, Employment, Technology and Development 1975, Poverty and Famines 1981, Utilitarianism and Beyond (jtly with Bernard Williams) 1982, Choice, Welfare and Measurement 1982, Resources, Values and Development 1984, Commodities and Capabilities 1985, On Ethics and Economics 1987, The Standard of Living 1988, Hunger and Public Action (with Jean Drèze) 1989, Social Security in Developing Countries (jtly) 1991, Inequality Re-examined 1992, The Quality of Life (jtly) 1993, Development as Freedom 1999, The Argumentative Indian: Writings on Indian History, Culture and Identity 2005, Identity and Violence: The Illusion of Destiny 2006, The Idea of Justice 2009; articles in various journals in econs, philosophy and political science. *Honours:* Hon. Prof., Delhi Univ.; Foreign Hon. mem. American Acad. of Arts and Sciences; Hon. Fellow, Inst. of Social Studies, The Hague, Hon. Fellow LSE, Inst. of Devt Studies; Hon. CH 2000; Grand Cross, Order of Scientific Merit (Brazil) 2000; Hon. DLitt (Univ. of Saskatchewan, Canada) 1979, (Visva-Bharati Univ., India) 1983, (Oxford) 1996; Hon. DUniv (Essex) 1984, (Caen) 1987; Hon. DSc (Bath) 1984, (Bologna) 1988; Dr hc (Univ. Catholique de Louvain) 1989, (Padua) 1998, numerous others; Senator Giovanni Agnelli Inst. Prize for Ethics 1989, Nobel Prize for Econs 1998, UN Econ. and Social Comm. for Asia and the Pacific (UNESCAP) Lifetime Achievement Award 2007. *Address:* Department of Economics, 1805 Cambridge Street, Littauer 205, Harvard University, Cambridge, MA 02138, USA (office). *Telephone:* (617) 495-1871 (office). *Fax:* (617) 496-5942 (office). *E-mail:* asen@fas.harvard.edu (office). *Website:* www.economics.harvard.edu/faculty/sen (office).

SENCIÓN, Viriato; Dominican Republic writer; b. 1941, San José de Ocoa. *Education:* Seminary Santo Tomás de Aquino, Santo Domingo, Crown Inst of Costa Rica, Lehman Coll., CUNY. *Publications:* Los que falsifican la firma de Dios (trans. as They Forged the Signature of God) 1992, La enema Celania y otros cuentos 1994, Los ojos de la montaña 1997. *Address:* c/o Curbstone Press, 321 Jackson Street, Willimantic, CT 06226-1738, USA. *E-mail:* info@curbstone.org. *Website:* www.curbstone.org.

SENNETT, Richard, FRSA, FRSL; British sociologist, writer and academic; *Professor of Social and Cultural Theory, London School of Economics and Political Science*; b. 1 Jan. 1943, Chicago, IL, USA; m. Saskia Sassen 1987; one step-s. *Education:* Breck School, Univ. of Chicago, Juilliard Conservatory New York, Harvard Univ. *Career:* Lecturer, Yale Univ. 1968–70; Asst Prof., Brandeis Univ. 1970–72; Prof., New York Univ. 1972–98, Prof. of Sociology 2006–; Founder New York Inst. of the Humanities; Prof. of Social and Cultural Theory, LSE 1999–; Bemis Prof. of Sociology, MIT 2005–07; Fellow, American Acad. of Arts and Sciences 1996–. *Publications:* non-fiction: The Uses of Disorder: Personal Identity and City Life 1970, Families Against the City 1970, The Fall of Public Man 1974, Hidden Injuries of Class (with Jonathan Cobb) 1977, The Psychology of Society 1977, Authority 1980, The Conscience of the Eye 1990, Flesh and Stone: The Body and the City in Western Civilisation 1994, The Corrosion of Character 1998, Respect: The Formation of Character in an Age of Inequality 2003; editor: 19th Century Cities: Essays in the New Urban History (with Stephan Thernstrom) 1969, Classic Essays on the Culture of Cities 1969, The Culture of the New Capitalism 2006, The Craftsman 2008; memoir: Respect 2003; novels: The Frog Who Dared to Croak 1982, An Evening of Brahms 1984, Palais Royal 1986. *Honours:* Chevalier, Légion d'honneur 1997; Dr hc (Loyola Univ. of America) 2003; Ebert Prize for Sociology 1999, Amalti Prize 2000, American Technological Asscn Lynd Prize 2004, Hegel Prize 2006. *Address:* London School of Economics and Political Science, Houghton Street, London, WC2A 2AE, England (office). *Telephone:* (20) 7955-6076 (office). *Fax:* (20) 7955-7697 (office). *E-mail:* r.sennett@lse.ac.uk (office). *Website:* www.lse.ac.uk (office).

SERHANE, Abdelhak; Moroccan writer and poet; b. 1950. *Career:* psychology teacher, Université Ibn Tofaïl, Kénitra. *Publications:* novels: Messaouda (Prix Littéraire des Radios Libres 1984) 1983, Les Enfants des rues étroites 1986, Le Soleil des obscurs (Prix Français du Monde Arabe 1993) 1992, Le Deuil des chiens 1998; poetry: L'Ivre poème 1989, Chant d'ortie 1993, La Nuit du secret 1992; non-fiction: L'Amour circoncis 1995, Les Prolétaires de la haine 1995, Le Temps noir 2002; contrib. to Autrement, Libregment, Horizons maghrébins, Lamalif, Oualili, Actes du Colloque de Montpellier. *Address:* Université Ibn Tofaïl, BP 242, Kénitra 14000, Morocco (office). *Website:* www.univ-ibntofail.ac.ma.

SERVADIO, Gaia Cecilia, (Gualtiero Maldè); British (b. Italian) writer, journalist and broadcaster; b. 13 Sept. 1938, Padua, Italy; two s. one d. *Education:* St Martin's School of Art, London, Camberwell School of Typography. *Career:* Lecturer, ACI 1970, Manchester Museum 1982; Consultant Ed., Italy 1987; Dir of Debates and Literary Talks, Accad. Italiana 1988–94; Italian Foreign Minister, Australia 1992, India 1995, Canada 2001; corresp., La Stampa 1978–90, Il Corriere della Sera 1990–2000; apptd responsible for External Relations Teatro Massimo Opera House Palermo; Vice-Pres. Foreign Press Asscn 1989–94; Gen. Sec. Abbado's Mahler and Second School of Vienna Festival 1981–82; mem. Soc. of Authors, Associazione Culturale Italiana. *Play:* La Signora Verdi, Teatro Nuovo, Milan. *Radio:* Garibaldi, La faccia al sole. *TV documentaries for BBC:* Murder by Neglect, Verdi 1992, Damn Nation 2001. *Publications:* Melinda 1968, Don Juan/Salome 1969, Il Metodo 1971, Mafioso 1972, A Siberian Encounter 1972, A Profile of a Mafia Boss 1973, Insider Outsider 1977, To a Different World: La donna nel Rinascimento

1979, Luchino Visconti: A Biography 1981, Il Lamento di Arianna 1985, Una infanzia diversa 1989, The Story of R 1991, Edward Lear's Italian Letters (ed.) 1990, La Vallata 1990, Incontri (essays) 1992, The Real Traviata 1994, La mia Umbria (ed.) 1994, Motya, Uncovering a Lost Civilisation 2000, Rossini: A Life 2003, Woman in the Renaissance 2004, E i Morti non sanno 2005, Il rinascimento allo specchio 2008, Ancient Syrian Writings 2008, Incoronata Pazza 2010; contrib. to The Observer, The Times, Sunday Times, Sunday Telegraph, Daily Telegraph. *Honours:* Cavaliere Ufficiale della Republica Italiana 1985. *Address:* 31 Bloomfield Terrace, London, SW1W 8RE, England (home). *Telephone:* (20) 7730-4378 (home). *E-mail:* kdd39@dial.pipex.com (office); gaia@gaiaservadio.info (home). *Website:* www.gaiaservadio.info.

SERVAN-SCHREIBER, Jean-Claude, LenD; French media executive and journalist; b. 11 April 1918, Paris; s. of the late Robert Servan-Schreiber and Suzanne Crémieux; m. 1st Christiane Laroche 1947 (divorced); m. 2nd Jacqueline Guix de Pinos 1955 (divorced); two s. three d.; m. 3rd Paule Guinet 1983 (divorced). *Education:* Exeter Coll., Oxford and Sorbonne. *Career:* served World War II in Flanders 1940, in Resistance 1941–42, in N Africa 1943, France 1944, Germany 1945; with Les Echos 1946–65, Gen. Man. 1957, Dir 1963–65; Deputy for Paris, Nat. Ass. 1965–67; Asst Sec.-Gen. UNR-UDT 1965; Pres. Rassemblement français pour Israël 1967; Dir-Gen. Régie française de publicité 1968–78; mem. Haut Conseil de l'audiovisuel 1973–81; Pres. Groupe Européen des Régisseurs de Publicité Télévisée 1975–78; mem. Conseil politique, RPR 1977–81; Conseiller du Groupe de Presse L'Expansion 1980–93; Special Adviser Mitsubishi Electric (Europe) 1992–2000; Pres. Inst. Arthur Vernes (Medical and Surgical Center) 1993–. *Honours:* Commdr, Légion d'honneur; Médaille mil.; Commdr Ordre nat. du Mérite; Croix de guerre; Croix du Combattant volontaire de la Résistance; Legion of Merit (USA), etc. *Address:* 147 bis rue d'Alésia, 75014 Paris, France. *Telephone:* 1-45-39-96-11. *E-mail:* jcss@orange.fr.

SERVICE, Robert John, MA, PhD, FBA; British historian, academic and writer; *Professor of Russian History, University of Oxford;* b. 29 Oct. 1947, Northampton, Northants., England. *Education:* Univ. of Cambridge, Univ. of Essex, Univ. of Leningrad, Russia. *Career:* taught at Keele Univ. and School of Slavonic and East European Studies, Univ. Coll. London; joined Univ. of Oxford 1998–, currently Prof. of Russian History and Fellow, St Antony's Coll., Oxford. *Publications:* The Bolshevik Party in Revolution 1917–23: A Study in Organizational Change 1979, A History of Twentieth-Century Russia 1997, The Russian Revolution 1900–1927 1999, Lenin: A Biography 2000, Russia: Experiment With A People 2002, A History of Modern Russia: From Nicholas II to Putin 2003, Stalin: A Biography 2004, Comrades: A World History of Communism 2007, Trotsky: A Biography (Duff Cooper Prize) 2009, A History of Modern Russia: From Tsarism to the Twenty-First Century 2009. *Address:* St Antony's College, 62 Woodstock Road, Oxford, OX2 6JF, England (office). *Telephone:* (1865) 284700 (office). *E-mail:* robert.service@sant.ox.ac.uk (office). *Website:* www.history.ox.ac.uk/staff/postholder/service_rj.htm (office).

SETH, Vikram, CBE, MA, PhD; Indian author and poet; b. 20 June 1952, Calcutta (now Kolkata); s. of Premnath Seth and Leila Seth. *Education:* Doon School, India, Tonbridge School, UK, Corpus Christi Coll., Oxford, Stanford Univ., USA, Nanjing Univ., People's Repub. of China. *Publications:* Mappings 1980, From Heaven Lake: Travels Through Sinkiang and Tibet (non-fiction) (Thomas Cook Travel Book Award) 1983, The Humble Administrator's Garden (Commonwealth Poetry Prize) 1985, All You Who Sleep Tonight (trans.) 1985, The Golden Gate: A Novel in Verse 1986, Three Chinese Poets (trans.) 1992, A Suitable Boy (novel) (W. H. Smith Literary Prize 1994, Commonwealth Writers Prize 1994) 1993, Arion and the Dolphin (libretto) 1994, Beastly Tales (animal fables) 1994, An Equal Music (novel) (EMMA BT Ethnic and Multicultural Media Award 2001) 1999, Two Lives (biog.) 2005; several vols of poetry. *Honours:* Hon. Fellow, Corpus Christi Coll., Oxford 1994; Chevalier des Arts et des Lettres 2001; Pravasi Bharatiya Samman 2005, Padma Shri 2007. *Literary Agent:* c/o Jonny Geller, Curtis Brown, Haymarket House, 28–29 Haymarket, London, SW1Y 4SP, England. *Telephone:* (20) 7393-4400. *Fax:* (20) 7393-4401. *E-mail:* cb@curtisbrown.co.uk. *Website:* www.vikramseth.co.uk.

SEVERIN, (Giles) Tim, MA, BLitt; British traveller and writer; b. 25 Sept. 1940, Jorhat, Assam, India; s. of Maurice Watkins and Inge Severin; m. Dorothy Virginia Sherman 1966 (divorced 1979); one d. *Education:* Tonbridge School, Keble Coll., Oxford. *Career:* Commonwealth Fellow, USA 1964–66; expeditions: led motorcycle team along Marco Polo's route 1961, canoe and launch down River Mississippi 1965, Brendan Voyage from W Ireland to N America 1977, Sindbad Voyage from Oman to China 1980–81, Jason Voyage from Greece to Soviet Georgia 1984, Ulysses Voyage, Troy to Ithaca 1985, Crusade: on horseback from Belgium to Jerusalem 1987–88, Travels on horseback in Mongolia 1990, China Voyage: bamboo sailing raft Hong Kong-Japan-Pacific 1993, Spice Islands Voyage in Moluccas, E Indonesia 1996, Pacific travels in search of Moby Dick 1998, Latin America travels seeking Robinson Crusoe sources 2000; historical novelist 2005–. *Publications:* Tracking Marco Polo 1964, Explorers of the Mississippi 1967, The Golden Antilles 1970, The African Adventure 1973, Vanishing Primitive Man 1973, The Oriental Adventure 1976, The Brendan Voyage 1978, The Sindbad Voyage 1982, The Jason Voyage 1984, The Ulysses Voyage 1987, Crusader 1989, In Search of Genghis Khan 1991, The China Voyage 1994, The Spice Islands Voyage 1997, In Search of Moby Dick 1999, Seeking Robinson Crusoe 2002, Viking: Odinn's Child (novel) 2004, Viking: Sworn Brother 2005, Viking: King's Man 2005, Corsair 2007, Buccaneer 2008, Sea Robber 2009. *Honours:* Hon. DLitt (Trinity Coll., Dublin) 1996, (Nat. Univ. of Ireland) 2003; Royal Geographical Soc. Gold Medal, Royal Scottish Geographical Soc. Livingstone Medal. *Address:* Inchy Bridge, Timoleague, Co. Cork, Ireland. *Telephone:* (23) 88446127. *E-mail:* severin.tim@gmail.com. *Website:* www.timseverin.net.

SEWARD, Desmond, BA; British writer and historian; b. 22 May 1935, Paris, France. *Education:* St Catharine's Coll., Cambridge. *Publications:* The First Bourbon: Henry IV, King of France and Navarre 1971, The Monks of War: The Military Religious Orders (aka The Monks of War: The First Religious Orders) 1972, The Bourbon Kings of France 1976, Prince of the Renaissance: The Life of François I (aka Prince of the Renaissance: The Golden Life of François I) 1973, Eleanor of Aquitaine: The Mother Queen (aka Eleanor of Aquitaine) 1978, The Hundred Years War: The English in France 1337–1453 1978, Monks and Wine 1979, Marie Antoinette 1981, Richard III: England's Black Legend 1983, Napoleon's Family 1986, Italy's Knights of St George: The Constantinian Order 1986, Henry V as Warlord (aka Henry V: The Scourge of God) 1987, Napoleon and Hitler: A Comparative Biography 1988, Byzantium (co-author) 1989, Brooks's: A Social History (co-ed. with Philip Ziegler) 1991, Metternich: The First European 1991, The Dancing Sun: Journeys to the Miracle Shrines 1993, The War of the Roses through the Lives of Five Men and Women of the Fifteenth Century 1995, Sussex 1995, Caravaggio 1998, Eugénie 2004, The Burning of the Vanities: Savonarola and the Borgia Pope 2006, Jerusalem's Traitor: Josephus, Masada and the Fall of Judea 2009, Wings over the Desert: In Action with an RFC Pilot in Palestine 1916–18 2009, Old Puglia 2009, The Last White Rose 2010; contrib. to periodicals, including History Today; BBC History Magazine. *Honours:* Kt of Malta 1978. *Literary Agent:* c/o The Marsh Agency, 50 Ablemarle Street, London, W1S 4BD, England. *Telephone:* (1488) 684900. *Fax:* (20) 7495-8961. *Website:* www.marsh-agency.co.uk. *E-mail:* desmond.seward@uwclub.net.

SEWELL, Stephen, BS; Australian playwright; b. 1953, Sydney, NSW. *Education:* University of Sydney. *Career:* Chair., Australian National Playwrights Centre. *Publications:* The Father We Loved on a Beach by the Sea, 1976; Traitors, 1979; Welcome the Wright World, 1983; The Blind Giant is Dancing, 1983; Burn Victim (with others), 1983; Dreams in an Empty City, 1986; Hate, 1988; Miranda, 1989; Sisters, 1991; King Golgrutha, 1991; In the City of Grand-Daughters, 1993; Dust, 1993. *Honours:* New South Wales Premier's Award 1985. *Literary Agent:* Hilary Linstead & Associates, PO Box 1536, Strawberry Hills, NSW 2012, Australia.

SEYMOUR, Alan; Australian playwright; b. 6 June 1927, Perth, WA. *Publications:* Swamp Creatures, 1958; The One Day of the Year, 1960; The Gaiety of Nations, 1965; A Break in the Music, 1966; The Pope and the Pill, 1968; Oh Grave, Thy Victory, 1973; Structures, 1973; The Wind from the Plain, 1974; The Float, 1980; various radio and television plays. Fiction: The One Day of the Year, 1967; The Coming Self-Destruction of the United States, 1969. *Honours:* Australia Council for the Arts grant.

SEYMOUR, Arabella Charlotte Henrietta; British writer; b. 8 Dec. 1948, London; one d. *Education:* West Ham Coll. of Technology. *Career:* mem. Soc. of Authors. *Publications:* A Passion in the Blood 1985, Dangerous Deceptions 1986, The Sins of Rebeccah Russell 1988, The End of the Family 1990, No Sad Songs (as Sarah Lyon) 1990, Princess of Darkness 1991, A Woman of Pleasure 1994, Sins of the Mother 1996.

SEYMOUR, Gerald, BA; British writer and reporter; b. 1941, Guildford, Surrey. *Education:* Univ. Coll. London. *Career:* joined ITN as reporter, stories covered include the Great Train Robbery, the Munich Olympics, conflicts in Cyprus, Vietnam, Aden, Israel, Pakistan, Northern Ireland 1963–78; full-time writer 1978–. *Publications:* Harry's Game 1975, The Glory Boys 1976, Kingfisher 1977, Red Fox 1979, The Contract 1980, Archangel 1982, In Honour Bound 1984, Field of Blood 1985, A Song in the Morning 1986, At Close Quarters 1987, Home Run 1989, Condition Black 1991, The Journey-man Tailor 1992, The Fighting Man 1993, The Heart of Danger 1995, Killing Ground 1997, The Waiting Time 1998, A Line in the Sand 1999, Holding the Zero 2000, The Untouchable 2001, Traitor's Kiss 2003, The Unknown Soldier 2004, Rat Run 2005, The Walking Dead 2007, Timebomb 2008, The Collaborator 2009, The Dealer and the Deal 2010, A Deniable Death 2011. *Literary Agent:* c/o Jonathan Lloyd, Curtis Brown Group Ltd, Haymarket House, 28–29 Haymarket, London, SW1Y 4SP, England. *Telephone:* (20) 7393-4400. *Website:* www.curtisbrown.co.uk. *Address:* c/o Hodder and Stoughton, 338 Euston Road, London, NW1 3BH, England (office). *Website:* www.hodder.co.uk.

SFAR, Joann; French graphic artist and writer; b. 28 Aug. 1971, Nice; m.; two c. *Career:* graphic artist and writer for L'Association publishing house 1996–. *Publications include:* Chasseur-Cueilleur (La vallée des merveilles vol. one), L'Etoile Polaire (L'Homme-Arbre vol. one), Maison Etroite (L'Homme-Arbre vol. two), L'Atroce Abécédaire (Collection Bréal Jeunesse), Monsieur crocodile a beaucoup faim (Collection Bréal Jeunesse), Orang-outan (Collection Bréal Jeunesse), La Sorcière et la petite fille (Collection Bréal Jeunesse), Le Banquet (La Petite bibliothèque philosophique vol. one), Candide (La Petite bibliothèque philosophique vol. two), Les Carnets de Joann Sfar (five vols), Sardine de l'espace (artwork), Pourquoi cette nuit est-elle différente des autres nuits? (Les Olives noires vol. one, text), Adam Arishon (Les Olives noires vol. two, text), Tu ne mangeras pas le chevreau dans le lait de sa mère (Les Olives noires vol. three, text), Héraclès (Socrate Le Demi-Chien vol. one, text), Ulysse (Socrate Le Demi-Chien vol. two, text), L'Académie des Beaux-

Arts (Le Minuscule Mousquetaire vol. one), La Philosophie de la Baignoire (Le Minuscule Mousquetaire vol. two), Le Borgne Gauchet, L'Elficologue (Pétrus Barbygère vol. one, artwork), Le Croquemitaine d'écume (Pétrus Barbygère vol. two, artwork), Le Mexicain à deux têtes (Les Dossiers du professeur Bell vol. one), Les Poupées de Jérusalem (Les Dossiers du professeur Bell vol. two), Le Cargo du Roi Singe (Les Dossiers du professeur Bell vol. three), Promenade des anglaises (Les Dossiers du professeur Bell vol. four), Les insoumis (Troll vol. one, with Jean-David Morvan), Le dragon du Donjon (Troll vol. two, with Jean-David Morvan), Mille et un ennuis (Troll vol. three, with Jean-David Morvan), La Fille du professeur (script), Noyé le poisson, Le Livre des monstres (artwork), Pascin 1–6, La Java bleu (Pascin vol. seven), Jambon et Tartine (Merlin vol. one, script), Merlin contre le Père Noël (Merlin vol. two, script), Merlin va à la plage (Merlin vol. three, script), Merlin : Le roman de la mère de Renart (Merlin vol. four, script), Terra incognita (Les Potamoks vol. one, script), Les fontaines rouges (Les Potamoks vol. two, script), Nous et le désert (Les Potamoks vol. three, script), Donjon (with Lewis Trondheim), Donjon Zénith (with Lewis Trondheim), Donjon Crépuscule (with Lewis Trondheim), Donjon Potron-Minet (with Lewis Trondheim), Donjon Parade (script, with Lewis Trondheim), Cupidon s'en fout (Grand Vampire vol. one), Mortelles en tête (Grand Vampire vol. two), Transatlantique en solitaire (Grand Vampire vol. three), Quai des brunes (Grand Vampire vol. four), La Communauté des magiciens (Grand Vampire vol. five), Le Peuple est un Golem (Grand Vampire vol. six), Les Aventures d'Ossour Hyrsidoux 1994, Le Petit monde du Golem 1998, Petit Vampire va à l'école (Petit Vampire vol. one) 1999, Petit vampire fait du Kung Fu (Petit Vampire vol. two), La Société Protectrice des Chiens (Petit Vampire vol. three), La maison qui avait l'air normale (Petit Vampire vol. four), La soupe de caca (Petit Vampire vol. five), Les pères noel verts (Petit Vampire vol. six), Le rêve de Tokyo (Petit Vampire vol. seven), Urani (La Ville des mauvais rêves vol. one, with David B.) 2000, La Bar-Mitsva (Le Chat du rabbin vol. one) 2002, Le Malka des Lions (Le Chat du rabbin vol. two), L'Exode (Le Chat du rabbin vol. three) 2003, Le Paradis terrestre (Le Chat du rabbin vol. four) 2005, La Conquête de l'Est (Klezmer vol. one) 2005. *Honours:* Angoulême Jury Prize (for Le Chat du rabbin), Prix Goscinny du Meilleur Scénario (for La Fille du professeur), Angoulême Prix Coup de Coeur (for La Fille du professeur), Angoulême Prix de la jeunesse (for Petit Vampire) 2004. *Address:* c/o Pantheon Graphic Novels, 1745 Broadway 15-3, New York, NY 10019, USA. *E-mail:* joannsfar@pastis.org. *Website:* www.pastis.org/joann.

SHAARA, Jeff, BS; American writer; b. 21 Feb. 1952, New Brunswick, NJ; s. of Michael Shaara; m. Lynne Shaara 1992. *Education:* Florida State Univ. *Publications:* Gods and Generals 1996, The Last Full Measure 1998, Gone for Soldiers 2000, Rise to Rebellion 2001, The Glorious Cause 2002, To the Last Man 2004, Jeff Shaara's Civil War Battlefields 2006, The Rising Tide 2006, The Steel Wave 2008, No Less Than Victory 2009. *E-mail:* email@jeffshaara.com (office). *Website:* www.jeffshaara.com.

SHABAN NEJAD, Afsaneh, BA; Iranian writer and poet; b. 1963, Shahdad, Kerman; m. Shamsodin Esaie; one s. one d. *Career:* Gen. Ed., children's radio programme 1985; Gen. Ed., children's magazine 1988–91; Literary Ed., jury mem., Poetry Council of Institute for the Intellectual Development of Children and Young Adults. *Publications:* six novels, 13 collections of poetry, 15 short stories, eight short story collections; contrib. several articles in children's magazines. *Honours:* various book and press festival awards 1990–2000; Hon. diploma (Alzahra Univ.), (Ministry of Culture and Islamic Guidance). *Address:* Institute for the Intellectual Development of Children and Young Adults, 24 Khaled Slamboli Street, Tehran, Iran (office).

SHABTAI, Aharon; Israeli poet and translator; b. 1939. *Education:* Hebrew Univ., Sorbonne, Paris, France, Univ. of Cambridge, England. *Career:* currently Lecturer in Hebrew Literature, Tel-Aviv Univ. *Publications include:* poetry: Kibbutz 1973, Domestic Poem 1976, The Book of Nothing 1981, First Lecture 1985, Love 1988, Divorce 1990, Heart 1995, That Wonderful Month of May 1997, Love and Selected Poems (in trans.) 1997, J'accuse 2003, War & Love, Love & War: New and Selected Poems 2010; contrib. to Six Israeli Novellas 1999, American Poetry Review, London Review of Books, Parnassus in Review, Ha'aretz. *Honours:* Prime Minister's Prize for Translation 1993, Tchernikhovsky Prize 1999. *Address:* Department of Hebrew Literature, Tel-Aviv University, Ramat-Aviv, 69978 Tel-Aviv, Israel.

SHACHOCHIS, Robert (Bob), BA, MA, MFA; American journalist and writer; b. 9 Sept. 1951, West Pittston, Pennsylvania; m. Barbara Petersen, 1976. *Education:* University of Missouri, Columbia, University of Iowa. *Career:* columnist, GQ magazines; Contributing Ed., Outside magazine, Harper's magazine; mem. Poets and Writers. *Publications:* novel: Swimming in the Volcanos 1993; short story collections: Easy in the Islands 1985, The Next New World 1989; contrib. to many periodicals. *Honours:* Nat. Endowment for the Arts Fellowship 1982, American Book Award for First Fiction 1985, Nat. Book Award 1985, Prix de Rome, American Acad. of Arts and Letters 1989.

SHAFAK, Elif (see Şafak, Elif)

SHAFFER, Sir Peter Levin, Kt, CBE, FRSL; British playwright; b. 15 May 1926, Liverpool; s. of Jack Shaffer and Reka Shaffer (née Fredman). *Education:* St Paul's School, London, Trinity Coll., Cambridge. *Career:* with Acquisitions Dept, New York Library 1951; returned to England 1954; with Symphonic Music Dept Boosey and Hawkes 1954; Literary Critic, Truth 1956–57, Music Critic Time and Tide 1957; playwright 1957–; Cameron Mackintosh Prof. of Contemporary Theatre, St Catherine's Coll., Oxford 1994–95; mem. European Acad., Yuste 1998–. *Plays:* The Salt Land (BBC) 1954, Five Finger Exercise, London (Evening Standard Drama Award) 1958, New York 1959 (New York Drama Critics Circle Award), The Private Ear and The Public Eye, London 1962, USA 1963, The Royal Hunt of the Sun, London 1964, New York 1964, Black Comedy, London 1965, New York 1967, White Lies, New York 1967 (revised as The White Liars, London 1968 and as White Liars, London 1976), The Battle of Shrivings 1970, Equus, London (Tony Award 1975, New York Drama Critics Circle Award 1975) 1973, New York 1974, Amadeus, London (Evening Standard Drama Award, Theatre Critics Award) 1979, New York 1980, Yonadab 1985, Lettice and Lovage, London 1987, New York 1990, The Gift of the Gorgon 1992; also performed on stage, Chichester, Guildford, Malvern 1996. *Television:* several TV plays including The Salt Land 1955, Balance of Terror. *Film screenplays:* Five Finger Exercise 1962, The Public Eye 1962, The Royal Hunt of the Sun 1965, Equus 1977, Amadeus 1984 (Golden Globe Award for Best Screenplay, Oscar Award for Best Adapted Screenplay 1984). *Radio play:* Whom Do I Have the Honour of Addressing? 1989. *Honours:* Hon. DLitt (Bath) 1992, (St Andrews) 1999; New York Drama Critics' Circle Award 1959–60 (Five Finger Exercise), Antoinette Perry Award for Best Play and New York Drama Critics' Circle Award 1975 (Equus) and 1981 (Amadeus), Evening Standard Drama Award 1957 (Five Finger Exercise) and 1980 (Amadeus), London Drama Critics' Award, Acad. Award for Best Screenplay (Amadeus) 1984, Hamburg Shakespeare Prize 1987, Best Comedy, Evening Standard Award for Lettice and Lovage 1988, William Inge Award 1992. *Literary Agent:* Macnaughton Lord 2000 Ltd, 19 Margravine Gardens, London, W6 8RL, England. *Telephone:* (20) 8741-0606. *Fax:* (20) 8741-7443.

SHAH, Saira; British/Afghan journalist, writer and documentary film producer; b. 5 Oct. 1964, London; d. of the late Idries Shah and of Cynthia Kabraji; m. (divorced). *Education:* School of Oriental and African Studies, Univ. of London,. *Career:* freelance journalist in Afghanistan, covering guerrilla war against Soviet invasion 1986–89, in Baghdad, Iraq, covering Gulf War 1990–91; journalist with Channel Four News (UK) –2001. *Television:* documentary films: Beneath the Veil (Int. Documentary Asscn Courage under Fire Award) 2001, Unholy War 2001, Zarmina: Lifting the Veil 2002, Death in Gaza (with James Miller, for Frostbite Films/HBO/Channel 4) (BAFTA Award for Current Affairs 2005) 2004, The 50 Greatest Documentaries 2005; Breakfast with Frost (TV series). *Publication:* Storyteller's Daughter 2003. *Address:* Penguin Books Ltd., 80 Strand, London, WC2R 0RL, England. *Website:* www.sairashah.com.

SHAKESPEARE, Nicholas; British biographer and novelist; b. 1957, Worcester, England; m.; two s. *Publications:* The Men Who Would Be King: A Look at Royalty in Exile 1984, Londoners 1986, The Vision of Elena Silves (novel) 1989, The High Flyer (novel) 1993, The Dancer Upstairs (novel) 1995, Bruce Chatwin (biog.) 1999, Snowleg (novel) 2004, In Tasmania 2004, Secrets of the Sea (novel) 2007, Inheritance (novel) 2010. *Honours:* Somerset Maugham Award 1989, Betty Trask Award 1990, American Libraries Asscn Award 1997, BAFTA for Best Documentary 2001, Broadcasting Press Guild Award for Best Documentary 2001. *Address:* 12A St Barnabas Street, Oxford, OX2 6BG, England.

SHALEV, Zeruya, MA; Israeli poet and novelist; Chief Literary Editor, Keshet Publishing; b. 1959, Kinneret Kibbutz; m. Eyal Megged. *Career:* began writing aged 6, published collection of poems aged 15; fmr Ed. Keter Publishing House; currently Chief Literary Ed. Keshet Publishing House. *Publications include:* Rakadeti Amadeti (novel, trans. as Dancing, Standing Still) 1993, Hayei Ahavah (novel, trans. as Love Life) (ACUM Prize) 1997, Ba'al Ve Isha (novel, trans. as Husband and Wife) 2000, Yeled Shel Ima (juvenile, trans. as Mama's Best Boy) 2001, Tera (novel, trans. as Late Family) 2005; other: anthology; contrib. poems to numerous journals. *Honours:* Israeli Asscn of Publrs Gold and Platinum Book Prizes 2001, Corine Book Award (Germany) 2001, Amphi Award (France). *Address:* The Institute for the Translation of Hebrew Literature, PO Box 10051, Ramat Gan, 10051, Israel (office). *Telephone:* (3) 5796830 (office). *Fax:* (3) 5796832 (office). *E-mail:* litscene@ithl.org.il. *Website:* www.ithl.org.il (office).

SHAMSIE, Kamila, BA, MFA; Pakistani writer; b. 1973, Karachi; d. of Muneeza Shamsie. *Education:* Hamilton Coll., New York, and Univ. of Mass., Amherst, USA. *Publications include:* In the City by the Sea (Prime Minister's Award for Literature, Pakistan 1999) 1998, Salt and Saffron (Orange's list of 21 Writers for the 21st century) 2000, Kartography 2002, Broken Verses 2005, Burnt Shadows 2009. *Literary Agent:* c/o Victoria Hobbs, AM Heath & Co. Ltd, 6 Warwick Court, London, WC1R 5DJ, England.

SHAN, Sa; French writer and painter; b. 26 Oct. 1972, Beijing, China. *Career:* moved to Paris, France 1990; private sec. to painter, Balthus 1994–96. *Solo Exhibitions:* Adler-Navarra Gallery, Paris 2001, 2002, Chanel Nexis Gallery, Tokyo 2007, Takashimaya Nihonbashi Gallery, Tokyo 2007, 2008, Marlborough Gallery, New York 2008, Ricard Fondation for Contemporary Art, Paris 2009, Elisabeth de Brabant Art Centre, Shanghai 2009. *Publications:* novels: Porte de la paix céleste (Prix Goncourt du premier roman, Prix Académie Française) 1997, Les Quatre vies du saule (Prix Cazes) 1999, La Joueuse de Go (Prix Goncourt des lycéens, Kiriyama Prize 2004) 2001, Impératrice 2003, Les Conspirateurs 2005, Alexandre et Alestria 2006; poetry: four compilations of poems (in Chinese) pre-1990, Le Vent vif et le glaive rapide 2000, Le Miroir du calligraphe (illustrated) 2002, Nuages Immobiles 2009. *Honours:* winner nat. youth poetry competition, People's Republic of China 1984, Silver Sail Award,

Ministry of Educ., China 1988. *Address:* c/o Art Management, 14 rue le Verrier, 75006 Paris, France (office). *Website:* shan-sa.com.

SHANGE, Ntozake, MA; American playwright and poet; b. (Paulette Williams), 18 Oct. 1948, Trenton, NJ; d. of Paul Williams and Eloise Williams; m. David Murray 1977 (divorced); one d. *Education:* Barnard Coll. and Univ. of S Calif. *Career:* mem. Faculty, Sonoma State Univ. 1973–75, Mills Coll. 1975, City Coll. of New York 1975, Douglass Coll. 1978; fmr Artist-in-Residence, Univ. of Florida; performing mem. Sounds in Motion Dance Co.; author, An Evening with Diana Ross: The Big Event 1977; Guggenheim Fellow 1981; mem. Nat. Acad. of TV Arts and Sciences, Acad. of American Poets, PEN America etc. *Publications include:* plays: For Colored Girls Who Have Considered Suicide/When the Rainbow is Enuf 1975, A Photograph: Lovers-in-Motion 1977, Boogie Woogie Landscapes 1979, Spell #7 1979, Black and White Two Dimensional Planes 1979, Mother Courage and Her Children 1980, Three for a Full Moon 1982, Bocas 1982, Educating Rita 1982, From Okra to Greens/A Different Kinda Love Story 1983, Three Views of Mt. Fuji 1987, Daddy Says 1989; novels: Sassafrass, Cypress and Indigo 1976, Betsey Brown 1985, The Love Space Demands 1991, I Live in Music 1994, Liliane: Resurrection of the Daughter 1995, Some Sing, Some Cry (with Ifa Bayeza) 2010; poetry: Melissa and Smith 1976, Natural Disasters and Other Festive Occasions 1977, Nappy Edges 1978, Three Pieces 1981, A Daughter's Geography 1983, From Okra to Greens 1984; essays, short stories, non-fiction, adaptations; contribs to magazines and anthologies. *Honours:* recipient of numerous drama and poetry awards. *Address:* c/o St Martin's Press, 175 Fifth Avenue, New York, NY 10010, USA (office).

SHANGVI, Siddharth Dhanvant, MA, MS; Indian writer; b. 1977, Bombay (now Mumbai). *Education:* Mithibai Coll., Univ. of Westminster, London. *Career:* lives between India and USA. *Publications include:* The Last Song of Dusk (Betty Trask Award, Premio Grinzane Cavour) 2004, The Lost Flamingoes of Bombay 2009; contribs to The Sunday Times of India, Elle, San Francisco Chronicle. *Address:* c/o Marketing and Promotions Department, Penguin Books India Private Limited, 11 Community Centre, Panchsheel Park, New Delhi 110 017, India (office). *E-mail:* publicity@in.penguingroup.com (office). *Website:* www.penguinbooksindia.com (office).

SHANLEY, John Patrick; American playwright; b. 1950, Bronx, NY; m. Jayne Haynes (divorced); two s. *Plays:* Saturday Night at the War 1978, George and the Dragon (New York) 1979, Welcome to the Moon (Ensemble Studio Theater, New York) 1982, Danny and the Deep Blue Sea (Waterford, CT) 1983, Savage in Limbo (Eugene O'Neill Theater Center, Waterford, CT) 1984, Down and Out, the dreamer examines the pillow (Waterford, CT) 1985, Italian American Reconciliation (Eugene O'Neill Theater Center, Waterford, CT) 1986, Women of Manhattan (Manhattan Theater Club, New York) 1986, All for Charity (New York) 1987, The Big Funk (New York Shakespeare Festival) 1990, Cellini, Beggars in the House of Plenty (Manhattan Theater Club, New York) 1991, What is this Everything? (New York) 1992, Four Dogs and a Bone (Manhattan Theater Club) 1993, The Wild Goose, Missing Marisa (Humana Festival, Actors' Theatre of Louisville) 1995–96, Kissing Christine (Humana Festival, Actors' Theatre of Louisville) 1995–96, Let's Go Out into the Starry Night 1996, A Lonely Impulse of Delight, Out West, Psychopathia Sexualis (Seattle Repertory Theater) 1998, Where's My Money? 2001, The Red Coat, Dirty Story (Denver Center Theater Co.) 2003, Sailor's Song (Shiva Theater, New York) 2004, Doubt (Manhattan Theater Club, New York) (Pulitzer Prize for Drama 2005, Tony Award for best play 2005) 2004, Sailor's Song 2004, Defiance (Manhattan Theatre Club) 2005. *Screenplays:* Five Corners (also assoc. prod.) (Special Jury Prize for screenplay, Barcelona Film Festival) 1987, Moonstruck (Writers' Guild Award, Acad. Award for Best Screenplay 1988) 1987, January Man 1989, Joe Versus the Volcano (also dir) 1990, Danny i Roberta (TV play) 1993, Alive 1993, We're Back! A Dinosaur's Story 1993, Congo 1995, Danny and the Deep Blue Sea (book Papillons de nuit) 2002, Live from Baghdad (TV) 2002, The Waltz of the Tulips 2004, The Red Coat 2006, Doubt 2008. *Literary Agent:* Creative Artists Agency, 2000 Avenue of the Stars, Los Angeles, CA 90067, USA. *Telephone:* (310) 288-2000. *Fax:* (310) 288-2900. *Website:* www.caa.com.

SHAO, Yanxiang, (Han Yeping); Chinese poet; b. 10 June 1933, Beijing; s. of Shao Ji and Cheng Ying; m. Xie Wenxiu 1957; one s. one d. *Education:* Université Franci-Chinoise. *Career:* attached to Radio Beijing as ed. and corresp. 1949; detained in labour camp during Cultural Revolution 1966–77; rehabilitated 1978; Deputy Ed.-in-Chief Shikan magazine 1978. *Publications:* Singing of the City of Beijing 1951, Going to the Faraway Place 1955, To My Comrades 1956, The Campfire in August 1956, A Reed-Pipe 1957, Love Songs to History 1980, At the Faraway Place 1981, In Full Blossom Lake Flowers 1983, Flower Late in Blossom 1984, Collection of Long Lyrics 1985, Essays Written at Mornings and Evenings 1986, 100 Articles with Sorrows and Joys 1986, There's Joy, there's Sorrow 1988, Selected Poems 1992, Written in Little Honeycomb 1993, Catch that Butterfly 1993, Idle Talk 1993, Rewriting the Bible 1993, One's Own Cup 1993, Essay Workshop 1994, Genuine Absurdity and Sham Absurdity 1994, Multum in Parvo 1994, Selected Poems of Shao Yanxiang 1995, Collection of Works by Shao Yanxiang (three vols). *Address:* A15-3-401 Hufang Road, Beijing 100052, People's Republic of China. *Telephone:* (10) 63536604.

SHAPCOTT, Joanne (Jo) Amanda, FRSL; British poet; b. 24 March 1953, London, England. *Education:* Trinity Coll. Dublin, St Hilda's Coll. Oxford, Harvard Univ., USA. *Career:* Judith E. Wilson Fellow in Creative Writing, Univ. of Cambridge 1991, Northern Arts Literary Fellow 1998–2000; currently teaches creative writing at Royal Holloway Coll., Univ. of London; Visiting Prof. of Poetry, Univ. of Newcastle 2001–, Univ. of the Arts, London; Consulting Ed., Arc Publs; Pres. Poetry Soc. 2007–09. *Publications:* Electroplating the Baby (Commonwealth Poetry Prize for Best First Collection) 1988, Phrase Book 1992, Emergency Kit: Poems for Strange Times 1996 (co-ed. with Matthew Sweeney), My Life Asleep (Forward Poetry Prize for Best Poetry Collection of the Year) 1998, Her Book: Poems 1988–98 1998, Tender Taxes 2002, Elizabeth Bishop: Poet of the Periphery (co-ed) 2002, Poems of Farzaneh Khojandi (co-trans.) 2008, Of Mutability (Costa Book of the Year Award, Costa Poetry Award) 2010, The Transformers (lectures) 2011; contribs to The Times, Sunday Times, New Statesman, Poetry Review, Times Literary Supplement, Verse, Southern Review. *Honours:* South West Arts Literature Award 1982, First Prize, Nat. Poetry Competition 1981, 1991, Commonwealth Prize 1988, New Statesman Prudence Farmer Award 1989, Poetry Book Society Choice 1992, 1998, Cholmondeley Award 2006. *Literary Agent:* c/o TriplePA, 15 Connaught Gardens, Forest Hall, Newcastle, Tyne and Wear, NE12 8AT, England. *Telephone:* (191) 266-2225. *Fax:* (191) 266-2225. *E-mail:* triplepa@blueyonder.co.uk.

SHAPCOTT, Thomas William, AO, BA; Australian poet, novelist, writer and academic; *Professor Emeritus of Creative Writing, University of Adelaide*; b. 21 March 1935, Ipswich, Qld; s. of Harold Sutton Shapcott and Dorothy Mary Shapcott (née Gillespie); m. 1st Margaret Hodge 1960; m. 2nd Judith Rodriguez 1982; one s. three d. *Education:* Univ. of Queensland. *Career:* Dir Australia Council Literature Board 1983–90; Exec. Dir Nat. Book Council 1992–97; apptd Prof. of Creative Writing, Univ. of Adelaide 1997, now Prof. Emer. *Publications:* poetry: Time on Fire 1961, The Mankind Thing 1963, Sonnets 1960–63, 1963, A Taste of Salt Water 1967, Inwards to the Sun 1969, Fingers at Air 1969, Begin with Walking 1973, Shabbytown Calendar 1975, 7th Avenue Poems 1976, Selected Poems 1978, Make the Old Man Sing 1980, Welcome! 1983, Travel Dice 1987, Selected Poems 1956–1988 1989, In the Beginning 1990, The City of Home 1995, Chekhov's Mongoose 2001 Beginnings and Endings 2003, Adelaide Lunch Sonnets 2005, The City of Empty Rooms 2005; fiction: The Birthday Gift 1982, White Stag of Exile 1984, Hotel Bellevue 1986, The Search for Galina 1989, Mona's Gift 1993, Theatre of Darkness 1998, Spirit Wrestlers 2004; plays: The 7 Deadly Sins 1970; non-fiction: Twins in the Family: Conversations with Australian Twins 2002; editor: New Impulses in Australian Poetry (with R. Hall) 1967, Australian Poetry Now 1970, Contemporary American and Australian Poetry 1975, Poetry as a Creative Learning Process 1978, The Moment Made Marvellous (anthology) 1998, An Island on Land: Contemporary Macedonian Poetry (ed. and trans. with Ilija Casule) 1999; contribs to newspapers and journals. *Honours:* Hon. DLitt (Macquarie Univ.) 1989; Grace Leven Prize 1961, Sir Thomas White Memorial Prize 1967, Sidney Myer Charity Trust Awards 1967, 1969, Churchill Fellowship 1972, Canada-Australia Literary Prize 1978, Gold Wreath, Struga Int. Poetry Festival 1989, Christopher Brennan Award for Poetry 1994, NSW Premier's Special Literary Prize 1996, Michel Wesley Wright Award 1996, Patrick White Award 2000. *Address:* PO Box 231, Mont Albert, Vic. 3127, Australia (home). *E-mail:* thomas.shapcott@adelaide.edu.au (office).

SHAPIN, Steven, BA, MA, PhD; American writer, historian, sociologist and academic; *Franklin L. Ford Professor of the History of Science, Harvard University*; b. 11 Sept. 1943, New York, NY; m. Abigail Barrow 1989. *Education:* Reed Coll., Univ. of Pennsylvania. *Career:* fmr Reader in Science Studies, Univ. of Edinburgh, UK; fmr Prof. of Sociology, Univ. of California, San Diego; Franklin L. Ford Prof. of the History of Science, Harvard Univ. 2004–; S.T. Lee Professorial Fellow, Univ. of London 2012; Visiting Prof. of History, Columbia Univ., New York 2012; Fellow, American Acad. of Arts and Sciences 2009. *Publications:* Natural Order: Historical Studies of Scientific Cultures (co-ed.) 1979, Leviathan and the Air-Pump: Hobbes, Boyle, and the Experimental Life (co-author) 1985, A Social History of Truth: Civility and Science in Seventeenth-Century England 1994, The Scientific Revolution 1996, Science Incarnate: Historical Embodiments of Natural Knowledge (co-ed.) 1998, The Scientific Life: A Moral History of a Late Modern Vocation 2008, Never Pure: Historical Studies of Science as if It Was Produced by People with Bodies, Situated in Time, Space, Culture, and Society, and Struggling for Credibility and Authority 2010. *Honours:* Guggenheim Fellowship 1980, Center for Advanced Study in the Behavioral Sciences Fellowship 1996, Erasmus Prize 2005. *Address:* Department of History of Science, Harvard University, Science Center 371, Cambridge, MA 02138, USA (office). *Telephone:* (617) 384-7997 (office). *Fax:* (617) 495-3344 (office). *E-mail:* shapin@fas.harvard.edu (office). *Website:* www.fas.harvard.edu/~hsdept/bios/shapin.html (office).

SHAPIRO, Alan R., BA; American academic, poet, writer and translator; *William R. Kenan Professor of English, University of North Carolina at Chapel Hill*; b. 18 Feb. 1952, Boston, Mass; m. Callie Warner 2003; one s. one step-s. one d. *Education:* Brandeis Univ. *Career:* Jones Lecturer in Creative Writing, Stanford Univ. 1976–79, Visiting Asst Prof. 1981; Lecturer, Northwestern Univ. 1979–85, Assoc. Prof. 1985–88, Prof. 1988–89; Poet-in-Residence, Univ. of Chicago 1981, 1986, 1988; Visiting Asst Prof. of Creative Writing, Univ. of California, Irvine 1985, Visiting Prof. 1989; Visiting Prof. of Creative Writing, Boston Univ. 1989; Fannie Hurst Poet-in-Residence, Brandeis Univ. 1989; Prof., Univ. of North Carolina at Greensboro 1989–94; Hurst Prof. of Creative Writing, Washington Univ. 1994; Prof. of English,

Univ. of North Carolina at Chapel Hill 1995–, Gillian T. Cell Distinguished Term Prof. 2001, currently William R. Kenan Prof. of English; Richard L. Thomas Prof. of Creative Writing, Kenyon Coll. 2002. *Publications:* After the Digging (poems) 1981, The Courtesy (poems) 1983, Happy Hour (poems) 1987, Covenant (poems) 1991, In Praise of the Impure: Poetry and the Ethical Imagination: Essays (1980–1991) 1993, Mixed Company (poems) 1996, The Last Happy Occasion (memoir) 1996, Vigil (memoir) 1997, The Dead Alive and Busy (poems) 2000, Selected Poems 2000, Song and Dance (poems) 2002, The Oresteia (trans.) 2002, Tantalus in Love (poems) 2005, Old War (poems) 2008, Trojan Women (trans.) 2009; contrib. to many anthologies, reviews, quarterlies and journals. *Honours:* Wallace Stegner Creative Writing Fellowship 1975–76, Acad. of American Poets Award 1976, National Endowment for the Arts Fellowship 1984–85, 1991, Guggenheim Fellowship 1985–86, William Carlos Williams Award, Poetry Society of America 1987, Lila Wallace-Reader's Digest Writers Award 1991, Pushcart Prize 1996, Los Angeles Times Book Award in Poetry 1996, Open Society Institute Arts Fellowship 1999, Kingsley Tufts Poetry Award, Claremont Graduate University 2001. *Address:* Department of English, Greenlaw Hall, CB #3520, University of North Carolina, Chapel Hill, NC 27599-3520, USA (office). *Telephone:* (919) 962-1994 (office). *E-mail:* ashapiro@email.unc.edu (home). *Website:* english.unc.edu (office).

SHAPIRO, David Joel, BA, MA, PhD; American poet, art critic and academic; *Professor of Art History, William Paterson University, Wayne*; b. 2 Jan. 1947, Newark, NJ; m. Lindsay Stamm 1970; one c. *Education:* Columbia Univ., Clare Coll., Cambridge. *Career:* violinist in various orchestras 1963–; Instructor and Asst Prof. of English, Columbia Univ. 1972–80; Visiting Prof., Brooklyn Coll., CUNY 1979, Princeton Univ. 1982–83, Cooper Union, New York 1980–; Prof. of Art History, William Paterson Univ., Wayne, NJ 1996–; Kellett Fellow Clare Coll., Cambridge 1968–70; Milton Avery Prof., Bard Graduate School of the Arts 1996. *Film screenplays:* Regular Flavor (with Rudy Burckhardt), Mobile Homes (with Rudy Burckhardt), Daffodils (with Rudy Burckhardt). *Publications:* poetry: January: A Book of Poems 1965, Poems from Deal 1969, A Man Holding an Acoustic Panel 1971, The Page-Turner 1973, Lateness 1977, To an Idea 1984, House, Blown Apart 1988, After a Lost Original 1990, Burning Interior 2002, Inventory: New and Selected Poems: Frank Lima (ed.) 2004; prose: John Ashbery: An Introduction to the Poetry 1979, Jim Dine: Painting What One Is 1981, Jasper Johns: Drawings 1954–1984 1984, Mondrian Flowers 1990, Alfred Leslie: The Killing Cycle (with Judith Stein) 1991, Keith Haring 2005, After (with Tsibi Geva) 2005, Rabbit/Duck (with Richard Hall); also contrib. prefaces Zhiyman Long 2005, Anne Porter's Poetry 2006, Such Places as Memory. *Honours:* Bread Loaf Writers Conference Robert Frost Fellowship 1965, Ingram Merrill Foundation Fellowship 1967, Book-of-the-Month Club Fellowship 1968, Creative Artists Public Service grant 1974, Morton Dauwen Zabel Award 1977, NEA grant 1979, Nat. Endowment for the Humanities Fellowships 1980, Foundation for Contemporary Performance Arts grant 1996. *Address:* 3001 Henry Hudson Parkway, Riverdale, NY 10463, USA.

SHAPIRO, Harvey, BA, MA; American editor and poet; b. 27 Jan. 1924, Chicago; m. Edna Kaufman 1953; two s. *Education:* Yale University, Columbia University. *Career:* Staff mem. Commentary 1955–57, The New Yorker 1955–57; Staff mem. New York Times Magazine 1957–64, Deputy Ed. 1983–; Asst Ed., New York Times Book Review 1964–75, Ed. 1975–83. *Publications:* The Eye, 1953; The Book, 1955; Mountain Fire Thornbush, 1961; Battle Report, 1966; This World, 1971; Lauds, 1975; Lauds and Nightsounds, 1978; The Light Holds, 1984; National Cold Storage Company: New and Selected Poems, 1988; A Day's Portion, 1994; Selected Poems, 1997; contributions: periodicals. *Honours:* Rockefeller Grant for Poetry 1967. *Address:* The New York Times Magazine, 229 West 43rd Street, New York, NY 10036, USA.

SHAPIRO, James S., BA, MA, PhD; American writer and academic; *Larry Miller Professor of English and Comparative Literature, Columbia University*; b. 11 Sept. 1955, Brooklyn, NY; m.; one s. *Education:* Columbia Univ., New York, Univ. of Chicago. *Career:* fmrly taught at Dartmouth Coll., Goucher Coll.; Faculty mem. Columbia Univ. 1985, now Larry Miller Prof. of English and Comparative Literature; Fulbright Lecturer, Bar Ilan and Tel-Aviv Univs 1988–89; Wanamaker Fellow, The Globe Theatre, London 1998; Co-Dir two Nat. Endowment for the Humanities Insts on Shakespeare. *Publications:* Rival Playwrights: Marlowe, Jonson, Shakespeare 1991, The Columbia History of British Poetry (assoc. ed.) 1993, The Columbia Anthology of British Poetry (co-ed.) 1995, Shakespeare and the Jews (Sixteenth Century Journal Roland A. Bainton Book Prize) 1997, Oberammergau: The Troubling Story of the World's Most Famous Passion Play 2000, 1599: A Year in the Life of William Shakespeare (BBC Four Samuel Johnson Prize for Nonfiction 2006) 2005, Contested Will: Who Wrote Shakespeare? 2010. *Honours:* Nat. Endowment for the Humanities Fellowship for Univ. Teachers, Henry E. Huntington Library Research Fellowship, Memorial Foundation for Jewish Culture Research Fellowship, Hoffman Prize for Distinguished Scholarship on Marlowe, Guggenheim Fellowship, Cullman Fellowship, New York Public Library. *Address:* Department of English, Columbia University, 606B Philosophy Hall, 1150 Amsterdam Avenue, New York, NY 10027, USA (office). *Telephone:* (212) 854-6227 (office). *E-mail:* js73@columbia.edu (office). *Website:* www.columbia.edu/cu/english (office); www.jamesshapiro.net.

SHARIF, Osama ash-, BA; Jordanian/Canadian publisher, journalist, columnist and media consultant; *Chairman, Media-Arabia*; b. 14 June 1960, Jerusalem, Israel; s. of Mahmoud al-Sherif and Aida al-Sherif; m. Ghada Yasser Amr 1984; one s. one d. *Education:* Univ. of Missouri, Columbia, USA. *Career:* Chief Ed. The Jerusalem Star 1985–88; Pres. Info-Media, Jordan 1989–; Publr, Chief Ed. and weekly columnist, The Star, Jordan 1990–; Publr Arabian Communications & Publishing (ACP) 1994–97, BYTE Middle East 1994–97, Al Tiqaniyyah Wal 'Amal 1995–97; Chief Ed. and Dir General Arabia.com 1999–2002; Chief Ed. Addustour Newspaper 2003–06; Ed. Al-Ittihad daily newspaper, Abu Dhabi, UAE Jan.–June 2009; Chair. Media-Arabia 2006–; mem. Royal Cttee for the Nat. Agenda, Amman, Jordan 2005. *Address:* PO Box 9313, Amman 11191, Jordan (office). *Telephone:* (6) 5922161 (office). *Fax:* (6) 5922161 (office). *E-mail:* osama@mediaarabia.com (office). *Website:* www.mediaarabia.com (office).

SHARMA, Robin; Indian author and leadership coach; *Founder, Sharma Leadership International Inc.*; b. Uganda. *Education:* Dalhousie Univ. Law School, Halifax, NS. *Career:* Founder, Sharma Leadership Int. Inc. 1999–; Founder, Robin Sharma Foundation for Children 1999–; books published in over 60 countries. *Publications include:* Megaliving: Powerful Wisdom for Self Leadership 1994, The Monk Who Sold His Ferrari: A Fable About Fulfilling Your Dreams and Reaching Your Destiny 1997, Who Will Cry When You Die?: Life Lessons from the Monk Who Sold His Ferrari 2002, The Saint, the Surfer and the CEO: a Remarkable Story About Living Your Heart's Desires 2003, Discover Your Destiny with the Monk Who Sold His Ferrari: A Blueprint for Living Your Best Life 2005, The Greatness Guide: 101 Lessons for Making What's Good at Work and in Life Even Better 2008, Daily Inspiration from the Monk Who Sold His Ferrari 2007, The Greatness Guide: Book 2: 101 Lessons for Success and Happiness 2009, The Leader Who Had No Title: A Modern Fable on Real Success in Business and in Life 2010, The Secret Letters of the Monk Who Sold His Ferrari 2011. *Address:* Sharma Leadership International Inc., 92B Scollard Street, 2nd Floor, Toronto, ON M5R 1G2, Canada (office). *Telephone:* (416) 962-7900 (office). *E-mail:* support@robinsharma.com (office). *Website:* www.robinsharma.com (office).

SHARP, Paula, BA, JD; American writer and attorney; b. 12 Nov. 1957, San Diego, CA. *Education:* Dartmouth College, Columbia University. *Career:* mem. Asscn of the Bar of the City of New York; Authors' Guild; Lawyers' Guild; PEN. *Publications:* The Woman Who Was Not All There, 1988; The Imposter: Stories of Netta and Stanley, 1991; Lost in Jersey City, 1993; Crows Over a Wheatfield, 1996; I Loved You All, 2000. Contributions: periodicals. *Honours:* Distinguished Artist Award, New Jersey Council on the Arts, 1987; Joe Savago New Voice Award, Quality Paperback Book Club, 1988; BANTA Award, 1992; New York Times Notable Book of the Year Citations, 1993, 1996, 2000.

SHARP, Ronald Alan, BA, MA, PhD; American academic, writer and administrator; b. 19 Oct. 1945, Cleveland, OH; m. Inese Brutans 1966, two s. *Education:* Syracuse University, Kalamazoo College, Instituto Internacional, Madrid, University of Michigan, University of Edinburgh, University of Virginia. *Career:* Instructor, Western Michigan University, 1968–70; Instructor, 1970–72, Asst Prof., 1974–78, Assoc. Prof., 1978–85, Prof. of English, 1985–90, John Crowe Ransom Prof. of English, 1990–, Assoc. Provost, 1998–99, Provost, 1999–, Acting Pres., 2002–03, Kenyon College; Visiting Prof., Concordia University, 1978; Co-Ed., The Kenyon Review, 1978–82; mem. Keats-Shelley Asscn; MLA; Wordsworth-Coleridge Asscn. *Publications:* Keats, Skepticism and the Religion of Beauty, 1979; Friendship and Literature: Spirit and Form, 1986; The Norton Book of Friendship (with Eudora Welty), 1991; Reading George Steiner (with Nathan A. Scott Jr), 1994; The Persistence of Poetry: Bicentennial Essays on Keats (with Robert M. Ryan), 1998. Contributions: books and journals. *Honours:* Ford Foundation Grant, 1971; English Speaking Union Fellowship, 1973; Mellon Grant, 1980; National Endowment for the Humanities Fellowships, 1981–82, 1984, 1985, 1986–87, 1994, 1996, 1998; National Humanities Center Fellowship, 1986–87; various grants.

SHARPE, Thomas (Tom) Ridley, MA; British novelist; b. 30 March 1928, London, England; s. of Rev. George Coverdale Sharpe and Grace Egerton Sharpe; m. Nancy Anne Looper 1969; three d. *Education:* Lancing Coll., Pembroke Coll., Univ. of Cambridge. *Career:* social worker 1952; teacher 1952–56; photographer 1956–61; Lecturer in History, Cambridge Coll. of Arts and Tech. 1963–71; full-time novelist 1971–. *Publications:* Riotous Assembly 1971, Indecent Exposure 1973, Porterhouse Blue 1974, Blott on the Landscape 1975, Wilt 1976, The Great Pursuit 1977, The Throwback 1978, The Wilt Alternative 1979, Ancestral Vices 1980, Vintage Stuff 1982, Wilt on High 1984, Grantchester Grind 1995, The Midden 1996, Wilt in Nowhere 2004, The Gropes 2009, The Wilt Inheritance 2010. *Honours:* Laureat, Le Grand Prix de l'Humour Noir, Paris 1986.

SHAUQ, Shafi, MA, PhD; Indian writer, academic and translator; *Professor and Head of the Postgraduate Department of Kashmiri, University of Kashmir*; b. 1950. *Education:* Univ. of Kashmir. *Career:* writer in Kashmiri, English, Urdu and Hindi; Prof. of Kashmiri, Univ. of Kashmir, currently Head of Dept. *Publications include:* over 55 works of poetry, translation, literary criticism, linguistics and culture; poetry: Yaad Aasmaanan Hinz 2007, Remembering the Skies 2008; essays: Farshyi Pyathi Arshas Taam 1972, Keeshryi Adibuk Taveeryiekh 1992, Europeans on Kashmir 1997, Keeshryuk Grammar 2008. *Honours:* Sahitya Akademi Translation Prize 2006, Sahitya Akademi Award 2007. *Address:* Department of Kashmiri Language, University of Kashmir, Hazratbal, Srinagar 190 006, India (office). *Telephone:* (194)

2420078 (office). *E-mail:* shafi-shauq@rediffmail.com (home); info@kashmiruniversity.net (office). *Website:* www.kashmiruniversity.net (office).

SHAW, Irene (see Roberts, Irene)

SHAW, Mark, BS, JD; American author; b. 3 Oct. 1945, Auburn, IN; m. Chris R. Shaw 1989; three step-s. one step-d. *Education:* Purdue University, Indiana University School of Law. *Career:* mem. Writers' Guild. *Publications:* Down for the Count, 1992; Bury Me in a Pot Bunker, 1993; Forever Flying, 1994; The Perfect Yankee, 1995; McKlaus: A Biography, 1996; Statement to Courage, 1997; Diamonds in the Rough, 1998; Larry Legend, 1998.

SHAW, (Veronica) Patricia; Australian writer; b. 1928, Melbourne; m. (divorced); one s. one d. *Education:* Star of the Sea Convent, Melbourne, Melbourne Teachers College. *Publications:* Brother Digger: The Sullivans, 2nd AIF 1984, Valley of the Lagoons 1989, River of the Sun 1991, The Feather and the Stone 1992, Where the Willows Weep 1993, Cry of the Rain Bird 1994, Fires of Fortune 1995, The Opal Seekers 1996, The Glittering Fields 1997, Mango Hill 2007. *Address:* c/o Hachette Livre Australia, Level 17, 207 Kent Street, Sydney NSW 2000, Australia.

SHAWAR, Rashad Abu; Palestinian novelist, short story writer and journalist; b. 1942, Thikreen. *Career:* regular contrib. to Al Quds Al Arabi; lives in Amman, Jordan. *Publications:* seven collections of short stories, six novels including al-Ushshaq (Lovers) 1977, four books of essays, two children's books and one play, some in trans.; contrib. to Banipal (literary magazine) and other journals and newspapers. *Address:* c/o Banipal, 1 Gough Square, London, EC4A 3DE, England.

SHAWCROSS, William; British journalist, writer and broadcaster; b. 28 May 1946, Sussex; s. of Baron Shawcross; m. 1st Marina Warner 1972 (divorced 1980); one s.; m. 2nd Michal Levin 1981 (divorced); one d.; m. 3rd Olga Forte 1993. *Education:* Eton, Univ. Coll., Oxford. *Career:* freelance journalist in Czechoslovakia 1968–69; corresp. for The Sunday Times, London 1969–72; Chair. Article 19, Int. Centre on Censorship 1986–96; mem. Bd Int. Crisis Group 1995–, mem. Exec. Cttee 2000–; mem. Council of Disasters Emergency Cttee 1997–; mem Informal Advisory Bd UNHCR 1995–2000. *Publications:* Dubček 1970, Crime and Compromise: Janos Kadar and the Politics of Hungary Since Revolution 1974, Sideshow: Kissinger, Nixon and the Destruction of Cambodia 1979, Quality of Mercy: Cambodia, the Holocaust and Modern Conscience 1984, The Shah's Last Ride 1989, Kowtow: A Plea on Behalf of Hong Kong 1989, Murdoch 1992, Cambodia's New Deal 1994, Deliver Us from Evil: Warlords & Peacekeepers in a World of Endless Conflict 2000, Queen and Country 2002, Allies: The United States, Britain, Europe and the War in Iraq (aka Allies: The US, Britain and Europe in the Aftermath of the Iraq War) 2003, Queen Elizabeth The Queen Mother 2009; contrib. to newspapers and journals. *Literary Agent:* c/o Greene and Heaton, 37 Goldhawk Road, London, W12 8QQ, England. *Telephone:* (20) 8749-0315. *Fax:* (20) 8749-0318. *Website:* www.greeneheaton.co.uk; www.williamshawcross.com.

SHAWN, Wallace, BA; American actor and playwright; b. 12 Nov. 1943, New York; s. of William Shawn and Cecille Lyon; brother-in-law of Jamaica Kincaid (q.v.); pnr Deborah Eisenberg. *Education:* Harvard Univ., Magdalen Coll., Oxford Univ. *Films include:* My Dinner with André (also writer) 1981, Manhattan 1979, The Princess Bride 1987, The Moderns 1988, Scenes from the Class Struggle in Beverly Hills 1989, We're No Angels 1989, Shadows and Fog 1992, Mom and Dad Save the World 1992, Nickel and Dime 1992, The Cemetery Club 1993, Vanya on 42nd Street 1994, Mrs Parker and the Vicious Circle 1994, Clueless 1995, Canadian Bacon 1995, Toy Story (voice) 1995, The Wife 1995, House Arrest 1996, All Dogs Go To Heaven II (voice), Critical Care 1997, My Favorite Martian 1999, Toy Story 2 (voice) 1999, The Prime Gig 2000, Blonde 2001, The Curse of the Jade Scorpion 2002, Love Thy Neighbor 2002, Personal Velocity: Three Portraits 2002, Duplex 2003, The Haunted Mansion 2003, Teacher's Pet (voice) 2004, Melinda and Melinda 2004, The Incredibles (voice) 2004, Chicken Little (voice) 2005, Southland Tales 2006, Tom and Jerry: Shiver Me Whiskers (voice) 2006, Happily N'Ever After (voice) 2007, New York City Serenade 2007, Kit Kittredge: An American Girl 2008, Mia and the Migoo (voice) 2008, Jack and the Beanstalk 2010, Furry Vengeance 2010, Toy Story 3 (voice) 2010, Cats & Dogs: The Revenge of Kitty Galore (voice) 2010, The Speed of Thought 2011, Vamps 2012. *Television includes:* Clueless (series) 1996–1997, Blonde 2001, Crossing Jordan 2001–06, Mr. St. Nick 2002, Monte Walsh 2003, Karroll's Christmas 2004, Crossing Jordan (series) 2001–06, Gossip Girl 2008, The L Word 2008–09, Gossip Girl (series) 2008–12. *Plays:* as writer: A Thought in Three Parts 1976, Marie and Bruce 1979, Aunt Dan and Lemon 1985, The Fever 1990, The Designated Mourner 1996, Grasses of a Thousand Colours 2009. *Stage appearances include:* My Dinner with André, A Thought in Three Parts, Marie and Bruce 1979, Aunt Dan and Lemon 1985, The Fever 1991. *Literary Agent:* c/o William Morris Agency, 1325 Avenue of the Americas, New York, NY 10019, USA.

SHAYKH, Hanan ash-; Lebanese novelist and playwright; b. 1945, Beirut; m. *Education:* American Coll. for Girls, Cairo. *Career:* journalist, al-Hasna' magazine, an-Nahar newspaper 1968–75; left Lebanon 1977, moved to Saudi Arabia then London 1982–. *Publications:* Intihar rajul mayyit 1970, Faras ash-shaytan 1971, Hikayat Zahrah (The Story of Zahra) 1980, 'The Persian Carpet' in Arabic Short Stories 1983, Misk al-ghazal (Women of Sand and Myrrh) 1988, Barid Bayrut (Beirut Blues) 1992, Aknus ash-shams an as-sutuh (I Sweep the Sun off Rooftops, short stories) 1994, Dark Afternoon Tea (play) 1995, Paper Husband (play) 1997, Only in London 2000, Two Women by the Sea (novella) 2003, Hikayati Sharh Yatool (memoir of her mother) 2005, A Fly on the Wall (play) 2007, The Locust and the Bird: My Mother's Story (biog.) 2009. *Literary Agent:* c/o Deborah Rogers, Rogers, Coleridge & White, 20 Powis Mews, London, W11 1JN, England. *Telephone:* (20) 7221-3717. *Fax:* (20) 7229-9084. *E-mail:* info@rcwlitagency.com. *Website:* www.rcwlitagency.com.

SHEARER, Jill; Australian playwright; b. 14 April 1936, Melbourne, Vic. *Publications:* The Trouble with Gillian, 1974; The Foreman, 1976; The Boat, 1977; The Kite, 1977; Nocturne, 1977; Catherine, 1978; Stephen, 1980; Release Lavinia Stannard, 1980; A Woman Like That, 1986; Shimada, 1987; Comrade, 1987; The Family, 1994. *Honours:* Australia Council Grant, 1987; Arts Queensland Fellowship, 1993. *Address:* c/o The Australian Script Centre, 77 Salamanca Place, Hobart, Tasmania, Australia.

SHEEHAN, Neil, AB; American journalist and author; b. (Cornelius Mahoney Sheehan), 27 Oct. 1936, Holyoke, Mass; s. of Cornelius Sheehan and Mary O'Shea; m. Susan Margulies 1965; two d. *Education:* Harvard Univ. *Career:* Viet Nam Bureau Chief, UPI, Saigon 1962–64; reporter, New York Times, New York, Jakarta, Saigon, Washington, DC 1964–72, obtained classified Pentagon Papers from Daniel Ellsberg 1971, subsequently published in New York Times winning newspaper Pulitzer Prize; Guggenheim Fellow 1973–74; Adlai Stevenson Fellow 1973–75; Fellow, Lehrman Inst. 1975–76; Rockefeller Foundation Fellow 1976–77; Fellow, Woodrow Wilson Center for Int. Scholars 1979–80; mem. Soc. of American Historians, Acad. of Achievement. *Publications:* The Arnheiter Affair 1972, A Bright Shining Lie: John Paul Vann and America in Viet Nam (Nat. Book Award 1988, Pulitzer Prize for non-fiction 1989, J.F. Kennedy Award 1989, chosen by The Modern Library as one of 100 Best Works of Non-Fiction in 20th Century 1999) 1988, After the War Was Over: Hanoi and Saigon 1992, A Fiery Peace in a Cold War: Bernard Schriever and the Ultimate Weapon 2009; contrib. to The Pentagon Papers 1971; articles and book reviews for popular magazines. *Honours:* Hon. LittD (Columbia Coll., Chicago) 1972; Hon. LHD (American Int. Coll.) 1990, (Lowell Univ.) 1991; recipient of numerous awards for journalism. *Address:* 4505 Klingle Street, NW, Washington, DC 20016, USA (home).

SHEEHAN, Susan, BA; American writer; b. 24 Aug. 1937, Vienna, Austria; m. Neil Sheehan 1965; one s. two d. *Education:* Wellesley Coll. *Career:* Editorial Researcher, Esquire-Coronet, New York City, 1959–60; Staff, New Yorker magazine, New York City 1961–; mem. Authors' Guild, Society of American Historians. *Publications:* Ten Vietnamese 1967, A Welfare Mother 1976, A Prison and a Prisoner 1978, Is There No Place on Earth for Me? 1982, Kate Quinton's Days 1984, A Missing Plane 1986, Life for Me Ain't Been No Crystal Stair 1993; contributions: many magazines. *Honours:* Guggenheim Fellowship 1975–76, Sidney Hillman Foundation Award 1976, Gavel Award, American Bar Asscn 1978, Woodrow Wilson International Center for Scholars Fellowship 1981, Individual Reporting Award, National Mental Health Asscn 1981, Pulitzer Prize for General Non-Fiction 1983, Feature Writing Award, New York Press Club 1984, Alumnae Asscn Achievement Award, Wellesley College 1984, DHL, University of Lowell 1991, Carroll Kowal Journalism Award 1993, Public Awareness Award, National Alliance for the Mentally Ill 1995. *Address:* 4505 Klingle Street NW, Washington, DC 20016, USA (home). *Telephone:* (202) 363-3433 (home).

SHEEHY, Gail Henion, BS; American writer and journalist; b. 27 Nov. 1937, Mamaronick, NY; d. of Harold Merritt Henion and Lillian Rainey Henion (née Paquin); m. 1st Albert F. Sheehy 1960 (divorced 1967); two d. (one adopted); m. 2nd Clay Felker 1984. *Education:* Univ. of Vermont. *Career:* Home Economist, J. C. Penney & Co. 1958–60; Fashion Ed. Rochester Democrat & Chronicle 1961–63; feature writer New York Herald Tribune 1963–66; Contributing Ed. New York magazine 1968–77; Fellow, Journalism School, Columbia Univ. 1970; Political Contributing Ed. Vanity Fair 1984–; has contributed to New York Times Magazine, Parade, New Republic, Washington Point; mem. Advisory Bd Women's Health Initiative, NIH, Eminent Citizens' Comm., UN Int. Conf. on Population and Devt 1994. *Publications include:* Lovesounds 1970, Panthermania: The Clash of Black Against Black in One American City 1971, Speed is of the Essence 1971, Hustling: Prostitution in our Wide-Open Society 1973, Passages: Predictable Crises of Adult Life (trans. to 28 languages) 1976, Pathfinders 1981, Spirit of Survival 1986, Character: America's Search for Leadership 1988, Gorbachev: The Man Who Changed the World 1990, Maggie and Misha (play) 1991, The Silent Passage: Menopause 1992, New Passages 1995, Hillary's Choice 1999, Understanding Men's Passages 1999, Middletown, America 2003, Sex and the Seasoned Woman 2006. *Honours:* seven Front Page Awards, Newswomen's Club of New York; Nat. Magazine Award, Columbia Univ. 1973; Penney-Missouri Journalism Award, Univ. of Missouri 1975; Anisfield-Wolf Book Award 1986; Best Magazine Writer Award, Washington Journalism Review 1991; New York Public Library Lion 1992. *Literary Agent:* c/o Richard S. Pine, InkWell Management, 531 Fifth Avenue, 26th Floor, New York, NY 10175, USA. *Telephone:* (212) 922-3500. *Fax:* (212) 922-0535. *E-mail:* richard@inkwellmanagement.com. *Website:* www.inkwellmanagement.com; www.gailsheehy.com; www.seasonedwomansnetwork.com.

SHEERS, Owen; British writer, poet and broadcaster; b. 1974, Suva, Fiji. *Education:* New Coll., Oxford, Univ. of East Anglia. *Career:* fmr writer-in-residence, The Wordsworth Trust; arts presenter for BBC Wales; Dorothy and Lewis B. Cullman Fellow, New York Public Library 2007. *Exhibition:* Wales.

Dead Or Alive? (with Dan Llewellyn Hall) 2004. *Play:* Unicorns, Almost 2005. *Television:* presenter, A Poet's Guide to Britain (BBC 4) 2009. *Publications:* poetry: The Blue Book 2000, Skirrid Hill (Soc. of Authors Somerset Maugham Award 2006) 2005; fiction: Resistance (novel) 2007, White Ravens (novella) 2009; non-fiction: The Dust Diaries (Tir Na N-Og English Language Welsh Book of the Year 2005) 2004, A Poet's Guide to Britain 2010. *Honours:* winner Vogue Talent Contest 1999, Eric Gregory Award, Vogue Talent Contest for Young Writers, selected as a Poetry Soc. Next Generation Poet 2004. *Literary Agent:* c/o Zoe Waldie, Rogers, Coleridge and White, 20 Powis Mews, London W11 1JN, England. *Telephone:* (20) 7221-3717. *Fax:* (20) 7229-9084. *E-mail:* info@rcwlitagncy.com. *Website:* www.rcwlitagency.com. *Address:* c/o Faber and Faber Ltd, Bloomsbury House, 74–77 Great Russell Street, London, WC1B 3DA, England (office). *Website:* www.owensheers.co.uk.

SHEIKH, Ahmad ash-; broadcasting executive; *Editor-in-Chief, Aljazeera International*. *Career:* fmrly worked for BBC; fmr Chair. Dubai Sports channel; currently Ed.-in-Chief, Aljazeera International. *Address:* Aljazeera International, PO Box 23127, Doha, Qatar (office). *Website:* www.aljazeera .net.

SHELDON, Lee (see Lee, Wayne C.)

SHEN, Peng; Chinese calligrapher, poet and editor; *Honorary Chairman, Chinese Calligraphers Association*; b. Sept. 1931, Jiangyin, Jiangsu Prov. *Career:* began to learn poetry, calligraphy and art from an early age; majored in Chinese literature in coll., later studied journalism; Assoc. Ed.-in-Chief People's Fine Arts Press; fmr Vice-Chair. Chinese Calligraphers Asscn, currently Hon. Chair.; Sr Ed. and Art Counsellor, China Fine Arts Publishing Group; Adjunct Prof., Peking Univ., China Ren Min Univ.; Vice-Pres. and Deputy Chair. Nat. Book Reward Evaluation Cttee; est. Art Museum of ShenPeng Calligraphy in Jiangyin, Jiansu Prov. and Mengjin, Henan Prov.; attended China Art Museum Contemporary Famous Calligraphers Exhbn 2005; organized draft Chinese Calligraphy Devt Compendium 2001–2002; Chief Ed. numerous nat. art magazines, including Art China, Chinese Art, Friends of Chinese Fine Art, and Art Guide; Ed. The laws of the People's Republic of China, Carvings Review, Calligraphy, and 500 other magazines; visits to USA, France, Japan, Sweden, USSR, Singapore, Italy, Korea, Malaysia, Canada, Peru, Venezuela, Hong Kong, Macao and Taiwan; mem. Nat. Cttee CPPCC. *Publications:* academic thesis 'Tradition and yihua' (First Prize, Fourth Art Review Reward, China Fed. of Literary and Art Circles), Origins and Branches (Special Award, Fifth Art Review Reward) Criticism on Calligraphy and Art, Shen Peng's Talks on Calligraphy and Art, San Yu Lyrics on Grass, San Yu Lyrics Continues, Collections of San Yu Poems, Anthology of Contemporary Calligraphers – Shen Peng, Selections of Shen Peng's Calligraphy Works, Collections of Shen Peng's Calligraphy (published in Japan), Shen Peng's Calligraphy of BaiJuyi's Works, Shen Peng's Calligraphy of DuFu's Works, Shen Peng's Running Script of 'Front and Back Chibi', Collections of Running Script, Collections of Regular Script, Script of Words about Yue Yang Pavilion, Shen Peng's Script of Nineteen Ancient Poems, Collections of China Art Museum Contemporary Famous Calligraphers Exhibition. *Honours:* Hon. Commr China Fed. of Literary and Art Circles; among first group of experts honoured by State Council of China for Special Contribs, Modeling Art Creation Study Award, China Fed. of Literary and Art Circles 2006, China Calligraphy Lan Ting Lifelong Accomplishment Award, China Fed. of Literary and Art Circles and China Calligraphy Asscn 2006, World Peace and Art Authority Prize, UN Acad. *Address:* People's Fine Arts Press, Beijing, People's Republic of China. *Telephone:* (10) 65245237.

SHEPARD, James (Jim) Russell, BA, MFA; American academic and author; *J. Leland Professor of English, Williams College*; b. 29 Dec. 1956, Bridgeport, CT; s. of Albert Shepard and Ida Shepard; m. Karen Shepard; two s. one d. *Education:* Trinity Coll., Hartford, CT, Brown Univ. *Career:* Lecturer, Univ. of Michigan, Ann Arbor 1980–83; Asst Prof. of English, 1983–90, Instructor in Film, Williams Coll. 1988–95, Assoc. Prof. of English 1990–95, J. Leland Miller Prof. of English 1995–; Writer-in-Residence, Bread Loaf Writers' Conference 1982–84, 1988–93, 2002, Univ. of Tennessee at Chattanooga 1988, 1989, Vassar Coll. 1998; Fiction Faculty, MFA Program, Warren Wilson Coll. 1992–, Univ. of California at Irvine 2002; The Tin House/Sundance Conference 2003, 2006, 2007, 2009, Napa Valley Writers' Conference 2004, St Petersburg Writers' Conference 2005, the Fine Arts Work Center, Provincetown 2005, 2006, The University of Michigan 2005, the Vermont Studio Center 2005, the University of Montana 2006, the Nebraska Writers' Conference 2007, North Carolina State University 2007, New York State Writers' Inst. 2008, 2009, Sirenland Writers' Conference, Positano 2009. *Publications:* fiction: Flights 1983, Paper Doll 1986, Lights Out in the Reptile House 1990, Kiss of the Wolf 1994, Nosferatu 1998, Project X (Library of Congress/ Massachusetts Book Award for Fiction 2005, ALEX Award for Fiction, Library Services Asscn 2005) 2005; short story collections: Batting Against Castro 1996, Love and Hydrogen 2004, Like You'd Understand, Anyway (Story Prize 2008) 2007; Ed.: You've Got to Read This (with Ron Hansen) 1994, Unleashed: Poems by Writers' Dogs (with Amy Hempel) 1995, Writers at the Movies 2000; contribs: anthologies, journals, reviews and magazines. *Honours:* Transatlantic Review Award, Henfield Foundation 1980, David Sokolov Scholar in Fiction, Bread Loaf 1982, Nelson Bushnell Prize, Williams Coll. 1997, John Simon Guggenheim Memorial Award 2005, Artist's Grant, Massachusett's Cultural Council 2002, Pushcart Prize (for 'Hadrian's Wall') 2006. *Address:* Department of English, Williams College, Stetson Hall, Williamstown, MA 01267, USA (office). *Telephone:* (413) 597-2033 (office). *E-mail:* James.R.Shepard@williams.edu (office). *Website:* www .williams.edu/English/people/faculty/JShepard (office).

SHEPARD, Sam; American playwright, actor, director and screenwriter; b. (Samuel Shepard Rogers), 5 Nov. 1943, Fort Sheridan, Ill.; s. of Samuel Shepard Rogers and Jane Schook Rogers; m. O-Lan Johnson Dark 1969 (divorced); one s.; one s. one d. with Jessica Lange. *Education:* Duarte High School, Mount San Antonio Jr Coll. *Television appearances include:* Lily Dale 1996, Purgatory 1999, Hamlet 2000. *Plays include:* Cowboys and Rock Garden (double bill), Chicago, Icarus's Mother and Red Cross (triple bill; Obie Award) 1966, Melodrama Play 1966, The 4-H Club, La Turista (Obie Award) 1967, Forensic and the Navigators (Obie Award) 1968, The Unseen Hand (rock opera) 1969, Cowboy Mouth (with Patti Smith) 1971, The Mad Dog Blues 1971, The Tooth of Crime (Obie Award) 1973, Geography of a Horse Dreamer 1974, Black Dog Beast Bait, Operation Sidewinder, Shaved Splits, Rock Garden (included in Oh! Calcutta!), Curse of the Starving Class (Obie Award) 1978, Buried Child (Pulitzer Prize) 1979, True West 1980, Fool for Love 1982, A Lie of the Mind 1985 (New York Drama Critics Circle Award for Best Play 1986), States of Shock 1991, Simpatico 1994, Eyes for Consuela 1998, The Late Henry Moss 2000, The God of Hell 2004, Kicking a Dead Horse 2007, Ages of the Moon 2010. *Film appearances include:* Days of Heaven 1978, Resurrection 1980, Francis 1982, The Right Stuff 1983, Paris, Texas 1984, Country, Crimes of the Heart, Baby Boom, Defenceless 1989, Voyager 1991, Thunderheart 1992, The Pelican Brief 1994, Safe Passage 1995, The Good Old Boys 1995, Curtain Call 1997, The Only Thrill 1997, Snow Falling on Cedars 1999, One Kill 2000, All the Pretty Horses 2001, Shot in the Heart 2001, Swordfish 2001, Black Hawk Down 2001, The Pledge 2001, The Notebook 2004, Don't Come Knockin' 2005, Stealth 2005, Walker Payne 2006, Bandidas 2006, The Return 2006, Charlotte's Web (narrator) 2006, The Assassination of Jesse James by the Coward Robert Ford 2007, The Accidental Husband 2008, Brothers 2009. *Screenplay:* Zabriskie Point 1970, Paris, Texas (Palme d'Or, Cannes Film Festival 1984), Fool for Love 1985, Far North (also Dir) 1989, Silent Tongue (also Dir) 1994, Don't Come Knockin' 2005. *Publications:* Hawk Moon 1972, Motel Chronicles 1982, A Murder of Crows (novel) 1996, Cruising Paradise (autobiog.) 1996, Great Dream of Heaven (short stories) 2002, The Rolling Thunder Logbook 2005, Day Out of Days (short stories) 2010. *Address:* c/o ICM, 10250 Constellation Boulevard, Los Angeles, CA 90067, USA (office).

SHEPARD, Stephen Benjamin, BS, MS; American journalist, editor and professor of journalism; *Founding Dean, Graduate School of Journalism, City University of New York*; b. 20 July 1939, New York; s. of William Shepard and Ruth Shepard (née Tanner); m. Lynn Povich 1979; one s. one d. *Education:* City Coll., Columbia Univ. *Career:* reporter and writer, Business Week 1966–75, Exec. Ed. 1982–84, Ed.-in-Chief 1984–2005; Adjunct Prof., Grad. School of Journalism, Columbia Univ. 1971–76, also co-founder and Dir Walter Bagehot Fellowship Program in Econs and Business Journalism, mem. Bd of Visitors, Grad. School of Journalism 1998–2004; Sr Ed. Newsweek 1976–81; Ed. Saturday Review 1981–82; Founding Dean, Grad. School of Journalism, CUNY 2005–; mem. American Soc. of Magazine Eds (Vice-Pres. 1990–92, Pres. 1992–94), Council on Foreign Relations, Overseas Press Club, Century Asscn; Gov. Soc. of American Business Eds and Writers. *Honours:* Gerald Coeb Foudation Lifetime Achievement Award 1999, Henry Johnson Fisher Award for Magazine Publisher of America 2000, Pres.'s Award, Overseas Press Club 2003, Soc. of American Business Eds and Writers Distinguished Achievement Award 2005. *Address:* Graduate School of Journalism, City University of New York, 219 West 40th Street, New York, NY 10018 (office); 322 Central Park West, New York, NY 10025, USA (home). *Telephone:* (646) 758-7800 (office). *Website:* journalism.cuny.edu/about/deans -corner.php (office).

SHEPHERD, Robert James, BA, MA; British writer, journalist, television producer and director; *Managing Director, Wide Vision Productions Ltd*; b. 14 Feb. 1949, Solihull, Warwicks. *Education:* Univ. of Kent. *Career:* Leader and Features Writer, Investors Chronicle 1983; mem. Editorial Team and Producer, A Week in Politics 1983–88; Parl. Lobby Corresp. 1984–87; Producer, documentaries and BBC political programmes, Programme Ed. BBC Political Programmes 1997–; Man. Dir Wide Vision Productions Ltd 1991–; mem. Soc. of Authors, Nat. Union of Journalists. *Television:* Series Producer What Has Become of Us? (four-part history of post-War Britain, Channel 4) 1994. *Publications:* Public Opinion and European Integration 1975, A Class Divided 1988, Ireland's Fate 1990, The Power Brokers 1991, Iain Macleod 1994, Enoch Powell: A Biography 1996; contribs to Oxford Companion to 20th-Century British Politics 2002, Oxford Dictionary of National Biography 2004, Political Quarterly, New Statesman, Investors Chronicle, Marxism Today, Guardian, The Times, Irish Independent, Sunday Press, Ireland of the Welcomes, The Spectator, Contemporary History. *Honours:* Prix Stendhal 1993, Reuter Fellowship, Univ. of Oxford 1995. *Literary Agent:* c/o Jonny Pegg, Curtis Brown Ltd, Haymarket House, 28–29 Haymarket, London, SW1Y 4SP, England. *Telephone:* (20) 7393-4400. *Fax:* (20) 7393-4401. *E-mail:* info@curtisbrown.co.uk. *Website:* www.curtisbrown .co.uk.

SHER, Sir Antony, Kt, KBE; British actor, artist and author; b. 14 June 1949, Cape Town, South Africa; civil partnership with Gregory Doran 2005. *Education:* Webber Douglas Acad. of Dramatic Art. *Career:* numerous appearances at Nat. Theatre, RSC (RSC Assoc. Artist 1982–) and in West End; directorial debut with Fraser Grace's play Breakfast with Mugabe at The Other Place, Stratford-upon-Avon. *Art exhibitions* solo exhibitions at the

Barbican, Nat. Theatre, London Jewish Cultural Centre, Sheffield Crucible Theatre, Coventry Herbert Museum and Art Gallery. *Plays include:* John, Paul, Ringo and Bert (Lyric Theatre), Teeth 'n' Smiles, Cloud Nine, A Prayer for My Daughter (Royal Court Theatre), Goosepimples (Hampstead and Garrick Theatres), King Lear, Tartuffe, Richard III, Merchant of Venice, The Revenger's Tragedy, Hello and Goodbye, Singer, Tamburlaine the Great, Travesties, Cyrano de Bergerac, The Winter's Tale, Macbeth, The Roman Actor, The Malcontent, Othello, The Tempest (RSC), Torch Song Trilogy (Albery Theatre), True West, Arturo Ui, Uncle Vanya, Titus Andronicus (Royal Nat. Theatre), Stanley (Royal Nat. Theatre, Circle in the Square Theater, New York), Mahler's Conversion (Aldwych Theatre), ID (Almeida Theatre) 2003, Primo (Royal Nat. Theatre, London) 2005, (Music Box Theater, New York), (New York Drama Desk and Outer Critics' Circle Awards for Best Solo Performance 2005–06, S. Africa Fleur du Cap Award for Best Solo Performance 2005) 2005, Kean (Apollo Theatre) 2007, The Tempest (on tour) 2008, An Enemy of the People (Sheffield Crucible) 2010, Broken Glass (Kilburn Tricycle) 2010. *Films include:* Mark Gertler: Fragments of a Biography 1981, Shadey 1985, The Young Poisoner's Handbook 1995, Alive and Kicking (aka Indian Summer) 1996, Mrs. Brown 1997, Shakespeare in Love 1998, Churchill: The Hollywood Years 2004, Three and Out 2008, The Wolfman 2010. *Television includes:* ITV Playhouse – Cold Harbour , Pickersgill People – The Sheik of Pickersgill 1978, Collision Course 1979, The History Man 1981, Tartuffe 1983, Changing Step 1990, The Land of Dreams 1990, The Comic Strip Presents... – The Crying Game 1992, Genghis Cohn 1993, Moonstone 1996, Hornblower: The Frogs and the Lobsters 1999, Macbeth 2001, The Jury (mini-series) 2002, Home 2003, Murphy's Law – Jack's Back 2004, Primo 2007, God on Trial 2008, The Shadow Line 2011. *Publications:* Year of the King (theatre journal) 1986, Middlepost (novel) 1988, Characters (paintings and drawings) 1989, Changing Step (screenplay) 1989, The Indoor Boy (novel) 1991, Cheap Lives 1995, Woza Shakespeare! (theatre journal, co-written with Gregory Doran) 1996, The Feast (novel) 1998, Beside Myself (auto-biog.) 2001, I.D. (play) 2003, Primo (play) 2005, Primo Time (theatre journal) 2005, The Giant (play) 2007. *Honours:* Hon. DLitt (Liverpool) 1998 (Exeter) 2003, (Warwick) 2007, (Cape Town) 2010; Best Actor Awards from The Evening Standard Awards, for performance as Richard III (RSC) 1985, Olivier Award for Best Actor, Soc. of West End Theatres, for performances as Richard III, as Arnold in Torch Song Trilogy 1985, for Stanley 1997, Best Actor Award, Martini TMA Awards, for performance as Titus Andronicus 1996, Peter Sellers Evening Standard Film Award for performance as Disraeli in Mrs. Brown 1998. *Literary Agent:* c/o Mic Cheetham Literary Agency, 50 Albemarle Street, London, W1S 4BD, England. *Telephone:* (20) 7495-2002. *E-mail:* simon@miccheetham.com. *Website:* www.miccheetham.com.

SHER, Steven Jay, BA, MA, MFA; American writer and poet; b. 28 Sept. 1949; m. Nancy Green 1978; one s. one d. *Education:* City Coll., CUNY, Univ. of Iowa, Brooklyn Coll., CUNY. *Career:* Dir Creative Writing, Spalding Univ. 1979–81, Oregon State Univ. 1981–86, Univ. of N Carolina at Wilmington 1986–89; Visiting Writer, Western Oregon Univ. 1991–2002, Willamette Univ. 1993, Yeshiva Univ. 2003–, Fashion Inst. of Tech., State Univ. of New York 2003–; mem. Willamette Literary Guild (Pres. 1992–2002). *Publications:* Nickelodeon 1978, Persnickety 1979, Caught in the Revolving Door 1980, Trolley Lives 1985, Man With a Thousand Eyes and Other Stories 1989, Traveler's Advisory 1994, Flying Through Glass 2001, Thirty-Six 2002, At the Willamette 2003; co-editor: Northwest Variety: Personal Essays by 14 Regional Authors 1987; contrib. to anthologies and periodicals. *Honours:* All Nations Poetry Contest 1977, Weymouth Centre Residency 1988, N Carolina Writers' Network Writers and Readers Series Competition 1989, How the Ink Feels Poetry Contest 2001. *Address:* 344 W 87 Street, No. 3R, New York, NY 10024, USA. *E-mail:* ssher@yu.edu (office).

SHERKAT, Shahla, BSc; Iranian journalist, feminist and author; *Editor, Zanan magazine*; b. 30 March 1956, Isfahan. *Education:* Tehran Univ., Keyhan Inst., Tehran, Allameh Tabatabai Univ. *Career:* a pioneer of women's rights movt in Iran; Founder, Ed. and Publr Zanan (Women) magazine 1991–; has had to appear in court on several occasions when magazine's content was considered to be pushing boundaries too far; sentenced to four months in prison for attending a conf. in Berlin at which future of Iranian politics was discussed following success of reformist cands in a parl. election 2001. *Honours:* Louis Lyons Award, Nieman Foundation for Journalism, Harvard Univ., USA 2005, The Courage in Journalism Award, Int. Women's Media Foundation 2005. *E-mail:* sherkat@zanan.co.ir (office). *Website:* www.zanan .co.ir (office).

SHERMAN, Eileen Bluestone, BA, MA; American author, playwright and lyricist; b. 15 May 1951, Atlantic City, NJ; m. Neal Jonathan Sherman 1973, one s. one d. *Education:* Finch College, New York, SUNY at Albany. *Career:* faculty mem., Baker University, Overland Park, KS 1997; mem. Authors' Guild; Dramatists Guild; National League of American Pen Women; Society of Children's Book Writers. *Publications:* The Odd Potato 1984, Monday in Odessa 1986, Independence Avenue 1990, The Violin Players 1998; musicals: The Sabbath Peddler 1987, The Happiest Day in Heaven 1998, Rockwell 1999, You're Not Sandy Koufax 2000, Broadway Sings the Odd Potato 2003; other: The Magic Door (television series) 1987–90, Room 119 (drama) 1997. *Honours:* Outstanding Social Studies Trade Book Award, 1986; National Jewish Book Award for Children's Literature, 1986; Emmy Awards, 1988, 1989; Teacher's Choice Award, 1991; Jessica Cosgrave Award for Career Achievement, Finch College Asscn, 1997; Thorpe Menn Honorable Mention 1999; Sugarman Family Literature Honorable Mention, 1999; First Place, Short Story Category, National League of American Pen Women, Kansas City, 2000.

SHERMAN, Martin; American playwright; b. 1938, New Jersey. *Education:* Boston Univ. *Plays include:* A Solitary Thing 1963, Fat Tuesday 1966, Next Year in Jerusalem 1968, Night Before Paris 1969, Things Went Badly In Westphalia 1971, Passing By 1974, Soaps 1975, Cracks 1975, Rio Grande 1976, Blackout 1978, Bent 1978, Messiah 1982, When She Danced 1985, Madhouse In Goa 1989, Some Sunny Day 1996, Rose 1999, Chain Play 2001, Passage To India 2002, Absolutely! (Perhaps) 2003, Aristo 2008, Onassis 2010. *Films include:* The Clothes in the Wardrobe 1992, Indian Summer 1996, Mrs Henderson Presents 2005. *Literary Agent:* c/o Casarotto Ramsay and Associates Ltd, Waverley House, 7–12 Neal Street, London, W1F 8GQ, England. *Telephone:* (20) 7287-4450. *Website:* www.casarotto.co.uk.

SHERMAN, Susan, BA, MA; American poet, critic, editor and academic; b. 1939. *Education:* Univ. of California, Berkeley, Hunter Coll. *Career:* Founder and Ed. Ikon magazine 1965–69; currently Part Time Assoc. Teaching Prof., Eugene Lang Coll., The New School. *Publications include:* Color of the Heart: Writing from Struggle and Change 1959–1990 1990, Shango de Ima (trans.) 1996, America's Child: A Woman's Journey through the Radical Sixties (auto-biog.) 2008. *Honours:* New York Foundation for the Arts Fellowship for Poetry 1990, Puffin Foundation Grant 1992, Fellowship from the New York Foundation for the Arts for Creative Non-Fiction Literature 1997. *Address:* Eugene Lang College, The New School for Liberal Arts, 65 West 11th Street, New York, NY 10011, USA (office). *E-mail:* shermas1@newschool.edu (office). *Website:* www.newschool.edu/lang (office).

SHERMAN, William (Bill) David, (Pecos Bill, Alvaro de Campos), AB, MA, PhD; American writer, editor, publisher and lecturer; b. 24 Dec. 1940, Philadelphia, Pa; s. of Louis Sherman and Gertrude Sherman (née Benn); m. Barbara Beaumont 1970 (divorced 1978). *Education:* Temple Univ., State Univ. of New York at Buffalo, Dickinson School of Law. *Career:* Teaching Fellow, English Dept, State Univ. of New York at Buffalo 1962–64, 1965–67, Lecturer in Cinema 1967; Teacher, Inner London Educ. Authority 1964–65, 1968–69, 1979–80; Lecturer, Univ. of Maryland, UK Div. (Hendon) 1965, 1981; Lecturer in American Studies, Univ. of Hull, UK 1967–68; Lecturer, English Dept, Univ. Coll. of Wales, Aberystwyth 1969–72 (tenure granted 1971); Founder-Ed. and Publr Branch Redd Books and Branch Redd Review 1976–2002; Tutor, Open Univ. 1976–79; currently freelance lecturer and writer. *Play:* The Case of Ezra Pound (published in Anglo-Welsh Review) 1970. *Film:* Maximus To Himself (short, co-directed by Theodora Cichy, original in British Film Inst. Archives, based on Charles Olson poem, folksong excerpt from Ewan MacColl). *Publications include:* The Landscape of Contemporary Cinema (with Leon Lewis) 1967, The Cinema of Orson Welles 1967, Hydra (Broadsheet Poem) 1968, The Springbok (poems) 1973, The Hard Sidewalk (poetry collage) 1974, The Horses of Gwyddno Garanhir 1976, Mermaids, part I 1977, Heart Attack and Spanish Songs in Mandaine Land 1981, Duchamp's Door 1982, She Wants to Go to Pago-Pago 1986, Mermaids Part I (revised) and II 1986, Glimpses of India and Nepal 1988, The Tahitian Journals 1990, A Tale for Tusitala 1993, From the South Seas 1997, Mana of the Moai 2004; contrib. to anthologies, including New Poetry 3 1977, Matières d'Angleterre 1984, The Faber Book of Movie Verse 1993, The Still Horizon 2002, In the Company of Poets 2003; contribs to periodicals, including Poetry Review (London), Talus (UK), Ochre (Essex, UK), Vanessa Poetry Magazine, Fire (Oxon., UK), Spanner (Hereford, UK), Exquisite Corpse (US), American Writing: A Magazine (Philadelphia), Paper Air (Philadelphia), Chamindade Literary Review (Honolulu), Taj Mahal Review (India), Poetry Wales, Second Aeon (Cardiff), Anglo-Welsh Review and numerous other small press publs; CD (five poems/five pieces, with music by Dominic Williams) 2008; essays (uncollected; film, literature, cultural studies in a variety of publs in US and UK over 40-year time period). *Honours:* Poetry Prize, Royal Albert Hall Reading (The Return of the Reforgotten) for co-trans. of Tahitian poet, Henri Hiro 1995. *Address:* 9300 Atlantic Avenue, No. 218, Margate, NJ 08402, USA (home). *Telephone:* (609) 822-7050 (home). *E-mail:* branchredd@yahoo.com. *Website:* www.omoopart3.blogspot.com; www.omoopart4.blogspot.com; www .omoopart5.blogspot.com; www.torriano.org.

SHERRY, (Michael) Norman, BA, PhD, FRSL; British/American writer and academic; *Mitchell Distinguished Professor of Literature, Trinity University*; b. 6 July 1935, Tirana, Albania. *Education:* Univ. of Durham, UK, Univ. of Singapore. *Career:* Lecturer in English Literature, Univ. of Singapore 1961–66; Lecturer, Sr Lecturer, Univ. of Liverpool, UK 1966–70; Prof. of English, Univ. of Lancaster, UK 1970–82; Fellow, Humanities Research Center, NC, USA 1982; Mitchell Distinguished Prof. of Literature, Trinity Univ., San Antonio, Tex. 1983–; mem. Savile. *Publications:* Conrad's Eastern World 1966, Jane Austen 1966, Charlotte and Emily Brontë 1969, Conrad's Western World 1971, Conrad and his World 1972, Conrad: The Critical Heritage 1973, Conrad in Conference 1976, The Life of Graham Greene, Vol. 1 1904–39 1989, Vol. 2 1939–55 1994, Vol. 3 1955–1991 2004, Joseph Conrad 1997; ed.: An Outpost of Progress and Heart of Darkness 1973, Lord Jim 1974, Nostromo 1974, The Secret Agent 1974, The Nigger of the Narcissus, Typhoon, Falk and Other Stories 1975, Joseph Conrad: A Commemoration 1976; contrib. to Academic American Encyclopedia, Guardian, Daily Telegraph, Oxford Magazine, Modern Language Review, Review of English Studies, Notes and Queries, BBC, Times Literary Supplement, Observer. *Honours:* Edgar Allan Poe Award 1989, Guggenheim Fellowship 1989–90. *Address:*

Trinity University, 1 Trinity Place, San Antonio, TX 78212, USA (office). E-mail: nsherry@trinity.edu (office).

SHERWIN, Rabbi Byron Lee, BS, BHL, MHL, MA, PhD; American academic and author; *Distinguished Service Professor of Jewish Philosophy and Mysticism, Spertus Institute of Jewish Studies*; b. 18 Feb. 1946, New York, NY; s. of Sidney Sherwin and Jean Sherwin; m. Judith Rita Schwartz 1972, one s. *Education:* Columbia Univ., Jewish Theological Seminary, New York Univ., Univ. of Chicago. *Career:* Asst Prof., Spertus Inst. of Jewish Studies, Chicago 1970–74, Assoc. Prof. 1974–78, Prof. of Jewish Philosophy and Mysticism 1978–2000, Vice-Pres. for Academic Affairs 1984–2001, Distinguished Service Prof. of Jewish Philosophy and Mysticism 2001–; Visiting Prof., Mundelein Coll. 1974–82; Dir Holocaust Studies Project, Nat. Endowment for the Humanities 1976–78; mem. American Asscn of Univ. Profs, Rabbinical Assembly, American Philosophical Asscn, Authors' Guild. *Publications:* Judaism: The Way of Sanctification (with Samuel H. Dresner) 1978, Abraham Joshua Heschel 1979, Encountering the Holocaust: An Interdisciplinary Survey (ed. with Susan G. Ament) 1979, Garden of the Generations 1981, Jerzy Kosinski: Literary Alarmclock 1982, Mystical Theology and Social Dissent: The Life and Works of Judah Loew of Prague 1982, The Golem Legend: Origins and Implications 1985, Contexts and Content: Higher Jewish Education in the United States 1987, Thank God: Prayers of Jesus and Christians Together 1989, In Partnership with God: Contemporary Jewish Law and Ethics 1990, No Religion is an Island (with Harold Kasimov) 1991, Towards a Jewish Theology 1992, How to Be a Jew: Ethical Teachings of Judaism (with Seymour J. Cohen) 1992, The Spiritual Heritage of Polish Jews 1995, Sparks Amongst the Ashes: The Spiritual Legacy of Polish Jewry 1997, Crafting the Soul 1998, Why Be Good? 1998, John Paul II and Interreligious Dialogue (co-author) 1999, Jewish Ethics for the 21st Century 2000, Creating an Ethical Jewish Life 2001, Golems Among Us 2004, Workers of Wonders 2004, The Cubs and the Kabbalist: A Novel 2006, Kabbalah: An Introduction to Jewish Mysticism 2006, The Life Worth Living 2009, Faith Finding Meaning: A Jewish Theology 2009, The Szyk Haggadah 2011; contrib. to professional journals. *Honours:* Presidential Medal (Poland) 1995; Hon. DHL (Jewish Theological Seminary of America) 1996; Polish Council of Christians and Jews Man of Reconciliation Award 1992. *Address:* Spertus Institute of Jewish Studies, 610 S Michigan Avenue, Chicago, IL 60605, USA (office). *Telephone:* (312) 322-1738 (office). *Fax:* (312) 922-6406 (office). *E-mail:* BSherwin@spertus.edu (office). *Website:* www.spertus.edu (office).

SHIBLI, Adania; Palestinian novelist and academic; *Lecturer, School of Critical Theory and Cultural Studies, University of Nottingham*; b. 13 Aug. 1974. *Education:* Univ. of East London. *Career:* postgraduate researcher, Univ. of East London; currently Lecturer in Cultural Studies, Univ. of Nottingham; Contributing Ed. Zawaya magazine (Lebanon). *Play:* The Error, New Company Theatre, London, Golden Threads, San Francisco. *Films:* Arab (VPRO, Netherlands) 2001, Nazareth 2000 (Ikona TV, Netherlands) (co-writer). *Publications:* Masas (Touching, novel) 2002, Kulluna Ba'eed Bethat al-Meqdar an al-Hubb (We are Equally Far from Love, novel) 2004; contrib. to al-Karmel literary magazine, al-Adaab cultural magazine, Zawaya Cultural Review, Assiwar magazine, Jerusalem Quarterly, PressAsia, Babelmed. *Honours:* Feewaiver Fellowship, Univ. of East London, twice awarded A. M. Qattan Foundation Young Writers' Award. *E-mail:* adania.shibli@nottingham.ac.uk (office). *Website:* www.nottingham.ac.uk/critical-theory/staff/staff.htm#shibli.

SHIELDS, David, BA, MFA; American writer and academic; *Professor of English, University of Washington at Seattle*; b. 22 July 1956, Los Angeles, CA. *Education:* Brown Univ., Univ. of Iowa. *Career:* Visiting Lecturer in Creative Writing, Univ. of California at Los Angeles 1985; Visiting Asst Prof., St Lawrence Univ., Canton, NY 1985–86, 1987–88; Asst Prof. 1988–92, Assoc. Prof. 1992–97, Prof. of English 1997–, Univ. of Washington at Seattle; Faculty, Warren Wilson Coll., Asheville, NC 1996–; various visiting instructorships; mem. Associated Writing Programs, Authors' Guild, Int. PEN, MLA of America, Poets and Writers, Writers' Guild of America. *Publications:* Heroes: A Novel 1984, Dead Languages: A Novel 1989, Handbook for Drowning; A Novel in Stories 1992, Remote: Reflections on Life in the Shadow of Celebrity 1996, Black Planet: Facing Race During an NBA Season 1999, 'Baseball is Just Baseball': The Understated Ichiro 2004, Enough About You: Adventures in Autobiography 2004, Body Politic: The Great American Sports Machine 2004, The Thing about Life is that one day you'll be Dead 2008, Reality Hunger: A Manifesto 2010; contrib. to New York Times Magazine, Harper's, Yale Review, Village Voice, Slate, Salon, McSweeney's. *Honours:* Iowa Writers' Workshop James A. Michener Fellowship 1980–82, San Francisco Foundation James D. Phelan Award 1981, NEA Fellowships 1982, 1991, Ingram-Merrill Foundation Award 1983, PEN Syndicated Fiction Project Competitions 1985, 1988, Bread Loaf Writers' Conference William Sloane Fellowship 1986, New York Foundation for the Arts Fellowship 1988, Commonwealth Club of California Awards Silver Medal 1989, State of Washington Governor's Writers Award 1990, Artist Trust Fellowships for Literature 1991, 2003, PEN/Revson Foundation Fellowship 1992, first prize Web del Sol Creative Non-Fiction Contest 1999, John Simon Guggenheim Memorial Foundation Fellowship 2005–06, Univ. of Washington Simpson Center for Humanities Research Fellowship 2005–06. *Address:* c/o Department of English, University of Washington at Seattle, Seattle, WA 98195, USA (office). *E-mail:* dshields@davidshields.com (office). *Website:* www.davidshields.com.

SHILLITOE, Tony, BA, DipEd, BEd; Australian educator; b. 28 March 1955, Tailem Bend; m. Francesca Stropin 2001. *Education:* Flinders University, Hartley CAE. *Career:* mem. Australian Society of Authors. *Publications:* Guardians, 1992; Kingmaker, 1993; Dragon Lords, 1993; The Last Wizard, 1995; The Innkeeper, 1996; Fiction 2 – The Novel, 1996; Jammin', 1997; The Lure, 1998; The Lore Book, 1998; Joy Ride, 1999; Assassin, 1999; Honour, 1999; Introduction to Styles and Conventions, 1999; The Mother Anger, 2000; Virtual God, 2000; The Sculptor, 2000. *E-mail:* tshillitoe@concordia.sa.edu.au.

SHIMON, Samuel; Iraqi writer and editor; *Assistant Editor, Banipal magazine*; b. 1956, Al-Habbaniyah. *Career:* left Iraq 1979, lived and worked in Damascus, Amman, Beirut, Nicosia, Cairo, Tunis, before moving to Paris 1985 and later settled in London 1996–; founder Gilgamesh Editions, Paris; co-founder and Asst Ed. Banipal magazine 1998–; founding Ed. www.kikah.com Arabic literary website. *Publications:* A Crack in the Wall (poems) (co-ed.) 2000, An Iraqi in Paris (novel) 2005. *Address:* Banipal Publishing, 1 Gough Square, London EC4A 3DE, England (office). *Telephone:* (20) 7832-1350 (office). *Fax:* (20) 8568-8509 (office). *E-mail:* samuel@banipal.co.uk (office). *Website:* www.banipal.co.uk (office).

SHIN, Kyung-sook; South Korean writer; b. 1963, Jeong-eup, Jeolla Prov.; m. *Education:* Seoul Inst. of the Arts. *Publications include:* novels: Deep Sorrow 1994, A Lone Room (Manhae Literature Prize 1996, Prix de l'Inapercu 2009) 1995, The Train Departs at 7 1999, Violet 2001, Yi Jin 2007, Please Look After Mom (Man Asian Literary Prize 2012) 2009, Somewhere A Phone Is Ringing For Me, 2010; novella: Winter Fables (Munye Joongang New Author Prize) 1985; short story collections: Until It Turns into River, 1990, Where the Harmonium Once Stood, 1992, Potato Eaters, 1997, Strawberry Fields, 2000, The Sound of Bells, 2003; non-fiction: Beautiful Shade, 1995, Sleep, Sorrow, 2003. *Honours:* Today's Young Artist Award from Ministry of Culture and Sports, Dong-in Literary Award (for When Will He Come) 1997, 21st Century Literary Prize (for The Place Where He Doesn't Know) 2000, Yi Sang Literature Prize (for Buseok Temple) 2001, Oh Young-soo Literary Prize (for Linden Tree in Front of the Castle Gate) 2006. *Literary Agent:* Barbara J. Zitwer Agency, 525 West End Avenue, Suite 11H, New York, NY 10024, USA. *E-mail:* bjzitwerag@aol.com. *Website:* www.barbarajzitweragency.com.

SHINDLER, Colin, BA, MA, PhD; British film and television producer, screenwriter, academic and novelist; b. 28 June 1949, Bury, Lancs., England; m. N. Lynn White 1972 (died 2005); one s. one d. *Education:* Bury Grammar School, Univ. of Cambridge. *Publications:* Hollywood Goes to War 1979, Buster 1988, Hollywood in Crisis 1996, Manchester United Ruined My Life 1998, High on a Cliff 2000, Fathers, Sons and Football 2001, First Love Second Chance 2003, George Best and 21 Others 2004, Gilbert and Garbo in Love 2005, The Worst of Friends 2009. *Literary Agent:* LBA, 91 Great Russell Street, London, WC1, England.

SHINKAREV, Vladimir; Russian writer, geologist and artist; b. 4 March 1954, Leningrad; s. of N. F. Shinkarev and N. A. Roumiantseva; m.; one d. *Education:* Leningrad Univ. *Career:* mem. St Petersburg Union of Artists 1993–. *Paintings:* World Literature (series of paintings), Great Wall of China, Literature Itself 2000. *Exhibition:* Gloomy and Cinema Paintings, Galerie Bruno Bischofberger 2008. *Publications include:* 'Solovei i stado': Basnia 1988, Mitki 1990, Stikhi, basmi, pesni 1995, Maxim and Fyodor 2002. *Address:* Flat 4, 21/9 Bolshaja Monetnaja Ulitsa, St Petersburg 197101, Russian Federation (home). *Telephone:* (812) 232-81-56 (home). *E-mail:* vshinkarev@mail.ru (home).

SHINN, Sharon Ruth; American writer; b. 28 April 1957, Wichita, Kan.; d. of Raymond James Shinn and Carol Maile Shinn. *Education:* Northwestern Univ. *Publications:* The Shape-Changer's Wife 1995, Archangel 1996, Jovah's Angel 1997, The Alleluia Files 1998, Wrapt in Crystal 1999, Heart of Gold 2000, Summers at Castle Auburn 2001, Jenna Starborn 2002, Angelica 2003, Angel-Seeker (Reviewer's Choice Award for Best Science Fiction Novel from the Romantic Times 2005) 2004, The Safe-Keeper's Secret 2004, Fallen Angel (novella, in anthology To Weave a Web of Magic) 2004, The Sorcerer's Assassin (short story, in anthology Powers of Detection) 2004, Mystic and Rider 2005, The Truth Teller's Tale 2005, The Thirteenth House 2006, The Dream Maker's Magic 2006, Dark Moon Defender 2006, When Winter Comes (novella, in anthology The Queen in Winter) 2006, Wintermoon Wish (short story, in anthology Firebirds Rising) 2006, The Double-Edged Sword (in anthology Elemental) 2006, Reader and Raelynx 2007, General Winston's Daughter 2007, Fortune and Fate 2009, Quatrain 2009, Gateway 2009, The Wrong Bridegroom (novella, in anthology Never After) 2009, Troubled Waters 2010, Nocturne (novella, in anthology Angels of Darkness). *Honours:* Crawford Fantasy Award, Int. Asscn for the Fantastic in the Arts 1996, RT Book Reviews Career Achievement Award 2010. *Address:* PO Box 440462, Brentwood, MO 63144, USA (office). *E-mail:* sharon@sharonshinn.net (office). *Website:* www.sharonshinn.net.

SHIPLER, David Karr, AB; American journalist and writer; b. 3 Dec. 1942, Orange, NJ; m. Deborah S. Isaacs 1966; two s. one d. *Education:* Dartmouth Coll. *Career:* news clerk, The New York Times 1966–67, news summary writer 1967–68, reporter 1968–73, Foreign Corresp., Saigon 1973–75, Moscow 1975–77, Bureau Chief, Moscow 1977–79, Jerusalem 1979–84, Corresp., Washington, DC 1985–87, Chief Diplomatic Corresp. 1987–88; Guest Scholar, Brookings Inst., Washington, DC 1984–85; Sr Assoc., Carnegie Endowment for Int. Peace 1988–90; Adjunct Prof., School of Int. Service, American Univ., Washington, DC 1990; Ferris Prof. of Journalism and Public Affairs,

Princeton Univ. 1990–91; mem. Pulitzer Prize Jury for Gen. Non-Fiction 2008, Chair. 2009; Montgomery Fellow and Visiting Prof. of Govt, Dartmouth Coll. 2003. *Film documentaries:* Arab and Jew: Wounded Spirits in a Promised Land 1989, Arab and Jew: Return to the Promised Land 2002. *Publications:* Russia: Broken Idols, Solemn Dreams 1983, Arab and Jew: Wounded Spirits in a Promised Land 1986, A Country of Strangers: Blacks and Whites in America 1997, The Working Poor: Invisible in America 2004, The Rights of the People: How Our Search for Safety Invades Our Liberties 2011, Rights at Risk: The Limits of Liberty in Modern America 2012; contrib. to newspapers and journals; blogs at The Shipler Report. *Honours:* Distinguished Reporting Award, Soc. of Silurians 1971, Distinguished Public Affairs Reporting Award, American Political Science Asscn 1971, Co-winner, George Polk Award 1982, Pulitzer Prize for Gen. Non-Fiction 1987; Alfred DuPont-Columbia Univ. Award for Broadcast Journalism 1990, Outstanding Book Award, Myers Center for the Study of Bigotry and Human Rights 2005, awards from Nat. Law Center on Homelessness and Poverty 2005, New York Labor Communications Council 2005, Dist of Columbia Employment Justice Center 2005. *Address:* 4005 Thornapple Street, Chevy Chase, MD 20815, USA (home). *Telephone:* (301) 907-4758 (office). *Website:* shiplerreport.blogspot.com (office).

SHIRAISHI, Kazuko; Japanese poet; b. 1931, Vancouver, BC, Canada; m.; one d. *Career:* mem. VOU avant-garde literary group 1948–53; with Kazuo Ono mounted series of poetry/dance productions. *Publications include:* Tamago no furu machi (The City Where It Rains Eggs) 1951, Seasons of Sacred Lust (in English) 1978, Fuyû suru haha, toshi (My Floating Mother, City) 2003, Isso no canoe, mirai e modoru, Sunozoku, Moero Meiso, Hira hira hakobarete ikumono, Arawareru mono tachi wo shite, Roba no kichou na namida. *Honours:* numerous literary prizes including Yomiuri Literary Prize, Purple Ribbon Medal (Shijuhosho), Smederevo Golden Key Award, Serbia 2010.

SHMELEV, Nikolay Petrovich, DEcon; Russian economist and writer; *Director of the Institute of Europe, Russian Academy of Sciences*; b. 1936, Moscow; m.; one c. *Education:* Moscow Lomonosov State Univ. *Career:* with USSR (now Russian) Acad. of Sciences (RAN) 1958–, first at Inst. of Econs, then Inst. of World Socialist System Econs, researcher, then head of US foreign policy dept Inst. of USA and Canada Studies 1982–92, chief researcher Deputy Dir Inst. of Europe 1993, currently Dir; corresp. mem. RAN 1997, full mem. 2000–; People's Deputy 1989–92; Dir Consultative Council under the Russian Pres. 1991–93; Stockholm Inst. of Econs of the Soviet Union and Eastern Europe, Sweden 1992. *Publications:* 75 monographs and 300 scientific articles; numerous narratives including Pashkov's House, Performance in Honour of Monsieur First Minister; short stories: The Last Floor, It Serves You Right. *Honours:* Order of Honour, Order of Friendship; Medal for Valiant Labour. *Address:* c/o Institute of Europe, Russian Academy of Sciences, ul. Mokhovaya 11, Bldg 3V, 125993 Moscow, Russia.

SHNEIDMAN, Noah Norman, MPHE, MA, DipREES, PhD; Canadian academic and writer; *Professor Emeritus, University of Toronto*; b. (Noah Sznejdman), 24 Sept. 1924, Wilno, Poland; m. (divorced); two d. *Education:* Minsk, Warsaw, Univ. of Toronto. *Career:* Lecturer, Univ. of Toronto 1966–71, Asst Prof. 1971–75, Assoc. Prof. 1975–79, Prof. 1979–91, Prof. Emer. 1991–; Distinguished Visiting Prof., McMaster Univ. 1981; mem. Canadian Asscn of Slavists, American Asscn of Teachers of Slavic and East European Languages. *Publications:* Literature and Ideology in Soviet Education 1973, The Soviet Road to Olympus: Theory and Practice of Soviet Physical Culture 1978, Soviet Literature in the 1970s: Artistic Diversity and Ideological Conformity 1979, Dostoevsky and Suicide 1984, Soviet Literature in the 1980s: Decade of Transition 1989, Russian Literature 1988–1994: The End of an Era 1995, Jerusalem of Lithuania: The Rise and Fall of Jewish Vilnius 1998, The Three Tragic Heroes of the Vilnius Ghetto: Witenberg, Sheinbaum, Gens 2002, Russian Literature 1995–2002: On the Threshold of the New Millennium 2004, Double Vision: The Jew in Post-Soviet Russian Literature 2007. *Address:* Department of Slavic Languages and Literatures, University of Toronto, 121 St Joseph Street, Toronto, ON M5S 1J4, Canada (office). *E-mail:* nn.shneidman@utoronto.ca (office).

SHOAF, Richard Allen, BA, BA (Hons), MA, PhD; American academic, poet, writer and editor; *Professor of English, University of Florida at Gainesville*; b. 25 March 1948, Lexington, NC; s. of Henry Lee and Alma Lucille Shoaf; m. Judith Patricia McNamara 1975; one s. one d. *Education:* Wake Forest Univ., Univ. of East Anglia, UK, Cornell Univ. *Career:* Asst Prof. of English, Yale Univ. 1977–81, Assoc. Prof. of English 1982–85; Prof. of English, Univ. of Florida at Gainesville 1986–, Alumni Prof. of English 1990–93; Founder-Ed. Exemplaria: A Journal of Theory in Medieval and Renaissance Studies 1987–2008; Pres., Council of Eds of Learned Journals 1994–96; mem. Dante Soc. of America, Medieval Acad. of America, Modern Language Asscn of America, Milton Soc. of America. *Publications:* Dante, Chaucer, and the Currency of the Word: Money, Images, and Reference in Late Medieval Poetry 1983, The Poem as Green Girdle: 'Commercium' in Sir Gawain and the Green Knight 1984, Milton, Poet of Duality: A Study of Semiosis in the Poetry and the Prose 1985, Troilus and Criseyde (ed.) 1989, Simple Rules (poems) 1991 (reissued in augmented edn 2007), Chaucer's Troilus and Criseyde – 'Subgit to alle poesye': Essays in Criticism 1992, The Testament of Love, by Thomas Usk (ed.) 1998, Chaucer's Body: The Anxiety of Circulation in the Canterbury Tales 2001, Shakespeare's Theater of Likeness 2006, Simple Rules (poetry) 2007, Erotic Reckonings (poetry) 2011; contribs to reference works, scholarly books and literary journals; individual poems in various journals. *Honours:* Hon. Visiting Scholar, Univ. of Central Florida 1993, Univ. of Berne (Switzerland) 1999; Nat. Endowment for the Humanities Fellowships 1982–83, 1999–2000, six teaching awards, including the MLA Teaching Award for the SAMLA region in the category of doctoral institutions. *Address:* PO Box 117310, University of Florida, Gainesville, FL 32611-7310, USA (office). *Telephone:* (352) 294-2841 (office). *Fax:* (352) 392-0860 (office). *E-mail:* ras@ufl.edu (office). *Website:* www.clas.ufl.edu/users/ras (office); www .rallenshoaf.net.

SHONE, Richard, BA; British writer and editor; *Editor, The Burlington Magazine*; b. 8 May 1949, Doncaster. *Education:* Clare Coll., Cambridge. *Career:* Assoc. Ed. The Burlington Magazine 1979–2003, Ed. 2003–. *Publications include:* Bloomsbury Portraits: Vanessa Bell, Duncan Grant, and Their Circle 1976 (revised edn) 1993, The Century of Change: British Painting Since 1900 1977, Vincent van Gogh 1977, Augustus John 1979, The Post-Impressionists 1979, Walter Sickert 1988, Rodrigo Moynihan 1988, Sickert: Paintings (ed. with Wendy Baron) 1992, Sisley 1992, Sensation (co-author) 1997, Sargent to Freud: Modern Paintings in the Beaverbrook Collection (with Ian G. Lumsden) 1998, The Art of Bloomsbury 1999, The Janice H. Levin Collection of French Art 2002; contrib. to art journals and other publications. *Address:* The Burlington Magazine, 14–16 Duke's Road, London, WC1H 9SZ, England (office). *E-mail:* shone@burlington.org.uk (office).

SHREVE, Anita; American writer. *Career:* fmr high school teacher, journalist in Nairobi, Kenya and USA; teacher of writing Amherst Coll. *Publications:* non-fiction: Remaking Motherhood: How Working Mothers are Shaping Our Children's Future 1987, Women Together, Women Alone: The Legacy of the Consciousness-Raising Movement 1989; fiction: Eden Close 1989, Strange Fits of Passion 1991, Where or When 1993, Resistance 1995, The Weight of Water 1997, The Pilot's Wife 1998, Fortune's Rocks 2000, The Last Time They Met 2001, Sea Glass 2002, All He Ever Wanted 2002, Light on Snow 2004, A Wedding in December 2005, Body Surfing 2008, Testimony 2009, A Change in Altitude 2009, Rescue 2010; contrib. to Quest, US, Newsweek, New York Times Magazine. *Honours:* O. Henry Prize 1975, New York Newspaper Guild Page One Award, PEN/L. L. Winship Award 1998, New England Book Award for fiction 1998. *Address:* c/o Author Mail, Little, Brown and Company, 237 Park Avenue, New York, NY 10017, USA (office). *E-mail:* askanita@hbgusa .com (office). *Website:* www.anitashreve.com.

SHREVE, Susan Richards, MA; American writer and academic; *Professor of English Literature, George Mason University*; b. 2 May 1939, Toledo, OH; d. of Robert Richards and Helen Richards; m. 1st Porter Shreve (divorced 1987); m. 2nd Timothy Seldes 1987; two s. two d. *Education:* Univs of Pennsylvania and Virginia. *Career:* Prof. of English Literature, George Mason Univ., Fairfax, Va 1976–; Visiting Prof., Columbia Univ., New York 1982–, Princeton Univ. 1991, 1992, 1993; fmr Pres. PEN/Faulkner Foundation; producer, The American Voice for TV 1986–; Essayist, MacNeil/Lehrer Newshour. *Publications:* A Fortunate Madness 1974, A Woman Like That 1977, Children of Power 1979, Miracle Play 1981, Dreaming of Heroes 1984, Queen of Hearts 1986, A Country of Strangers 1989, Daughters of the New World 1992, The Train Home 1993, Skin Deep: Women and Race 1995, The Visiting Physician 1995, The Goalie 1996, Narratives on Justice (co-ed.) 1996, Outside the Law 1997, How We Want to Live (co-ed.) 1998, Plum and Jaggers 2000, A Student of Living Things 2006, Warm Springs: Traces of a Childhood at FDR's Polio Haven 2007; juvenile: Jonah, The Whale 1997, Ghost Cats 1999, The End of Amanda, The Good 2000. *Honours:* George Washington Univ. Jenny Moore Award 1978, Guggenheim Fellowship 1980, Nat. Endowment for the Arts Fellowship 1982. *Address:* Graduate Creative Writing Program, Department of English, George Mason University, 4400 University Drive, Fairfax, VA 22030 (office); 3319 Newark Street, NW, Washington, DC 20008, USA (home). *E-mail:* writing@gmu.edu (office). *Website:* creativewriting.gmu.edu (office); www.susanshreve.com.

SHRIGLEY, David; British cartoonist; b. 17 Sept. 1968, Macclesfield, Cheshire. *Education:* Glasgow School of Art. *Exhibitions include:* Stephen Friedman Gallery, London 1997, Surfacing – Contemporary Drawing, ICA, London 1998, Yvon Lambert Gallery, Paris 1999, 2001, 2004, 2006, Center for Curatorial Studies at Bard College, Annandale-on-Hudson, NY 2001, Anton Kern Galery, New York 2002, Galerie Nicolai Wallner, Copenhagen 2003, billboard commission at Gloucester Road Station, London 2004, CAB, Burgos, Spain 2007. *Publications:* Slug Trails 1991, Merry Eczema 1992, Blanket of Filth 1994, Enquire Within 1995, Err 1995, Drawings Done Whilst on Phone to Idiot 1996, Blank Page and Other Pages 1998, Why We Got the Sack from the Museum 1998, The Beast is Near 1999, Grip 2000, Do Not Bend 2001, Evil Thoughts 2002, Human Achievement 2002, Joy – 22 Postcards 2002, Dirt 2002, Yellow Bird with Worm 2003, Who I Am and What I Want 2003, Rules – 22 Postcards 2004, Kill Your Pets 2004, The Book of Shrigley 2005, What the Hell Are You Doing? The Essential David Shrigley 2010. *Address:* c/o Redstone Press, 7a St Lawrence Terrace, London, W10 5SU, England (office). *E-mail:* info@davidshrigley.com (office); info@redstonepress.co.uk (office). *Website:* www.davidshrigley.com; www.redstonepress.co.uk (office).

SHRIVER, Lionel, BA, MFA; American journalist and novelist; b. (Margaret Ann Shriver), 18 May 1957, Gastonia, NC; m. Jeff Williams. *Education:* Barnard Coll., Columbia Univ. *Publications include:* The Female of the Species 1987, Checker and the Derailleurs 1988, The Bleeding Heart 1990, Ordinary Decent Criminals 1992, Game Control 1994, A Perfectly Good Family 1996, Double Fault 1997, We Need to Talk About Kevin (Orange Prize

2005) 2003, The Post-Birthday World (Entertainment Weekly Best Book of the Year 2008, Time Magazine Best Book of the Year 2008) 2007, So Much for That 2010, The New Republic 2012; contrib. to the Wall Street Journal, The Economist, Philadelphia Enquirer, The Guardian. *Literary Agent:* c/o Jenne Casarotto, Casarotto Ramsay & Associates Limited, Waverley House, 7-12 Noel Street, London, W1F 8GQ, England. *Telephone:* (20) 7287-4450. *Fax:* (20) 7287-9128. *E-mail:* info@casarotto.co.uk. *Website:* www.casarotto.co.uk.

SHTEYNGART, Gary, BA, MFA; American writer; b. 5 July 1972, Leningrad, Russia. *Education:* Oberlin Coll., Hunter Coll., City Univ. of New York. *Career:* moved to USA, aged seven; fmr writer for various non-profit orgs; currently Asst Prof. of Writing, Columbia Univ.; also currently Class of 1932 Fellow in Creative Writing and Lecturer in Creative Writing, Princeton Univ. *Publications:* The Russian Debutante's Handbook (Steohen Crane Award for First Fiction, Nat. Jewish Book Award for Fiction) 2003, Absurdistan 2006, Super Sad True Love Story 2010; short story and essay contribs to The New Yorker, Granta, Esquire, GQ, New York Times Magazine. *Address:* Lewis Center for the Arts, Princeton University, 185 Nassau Street, Princeton, NJ 08544, USA (office). *E-mail:* gshteyng@princeton.edu (office). *Website:* www.princeton.edu (office).

SHU, Ting; Chinese poet and writer; b. (Gong Peiyu), 1952, Shima, Zhangzhou City, Fujian Prov.; d. of Shi Mo Gang and Xiu Zhen Yong; m. Chen Zhongyi 1981; one s. *Career:* sent to work in countryside during Cultural Revolution –1973, then worked on construction sites and in factories; published poems in Today (underground literary magazine); mem. Writers' Asscn Fujian 1983– (Vice-Chair. 1985), Council of Writers' Asscn of China 1985–; Dir Chinese Writers' Union. *Publications:* Shuangweichuan 1982, Shu Ting Shuqing Shixuan 1984, Poesiealbum Shu Ting 1989, Hui Changge de Yiweihua, Shizuniao, Selected Poems of Seven Chinese Poets 1993, Selected Poems: An Authoritative Collection 1994, Mist of my Heart: Selected Poems of Shu Ting 1995. *Honours:* Nat. Poetry Award 1981, 1983. *Address:* 13 Zhonghua Road, Gulangyu, Xiamen City, Fujian Province, 361002, People's Republic of China.

SHUBIN, Seymour, BS; American author; b. 14 Sept. 1921, Philadelphia, PA; m. Gloria Amet 1957, one s. one d. *Education:* Temple University. *Career:* mem. American Society of Authors and Journalists; Authors' Guild; MWA; PEN, American Center. *Publications:* Anyone's My Name, 1953; Manta, 1958; Wellville, USA, 1961; The Captain, 1982; Holy Secrets, 1984; Voices, 1985; Never Quite Dead, 1989; Remember Me Always, 1994; Fury's Children, 1997; My Face Among Strangers, 1999; The Good and the Dead, 2000; A Matter of Fear, 2002. Contributions: Saturday Evening Post; Reader's Digest; Redbook; Family Circle; Story; Ellery Queen's Mystery Magazine; Emergency Medicine; Official Detective Stories Magazine; Perspective in Biology and Medicine. *Honours:* Edgar Allan Poe, Special Award; Special Citation for Fiction, Athenaeum of Philadelphia; Certificate of Honor, Temple University.

SHUKAIR, Mahmoud, BA, MA; Palestinian journalist, writer and playwright; b. 1941, Jerusalem. *Education:* Damascus Univ. *Career:* jailed twice by Israeli authorities, deported to Lebanon 1975, lived in Beirut, Amman and Prague before returning to Jerusalem 1993; Cultural Affairs Ed., Al-Jihad newspaper, Jerusalem 1965–67; Occupied Territories Ed., Al-Rai Jordanian newspaper 1978–80, columnist 1991–93; Chief Ed. Attaleiaah weekly newspaper, Jerusalem 1994–96; Chief Ed., Dafater Thakafiah magazine, Palestinian Ministry of Culture 1997–2000; Cultural Affairs Ed., Sawt Al-Watan magazine, Ramallah 1997–2002; Vice-Pres. Jordanian Writers Asscn 1977–87; Bd Mem., Palestinian Writers' and Journalists' Union 1987–2004; mem. Palestinian Nat. Council. *Television:* Abd Al-Rahman Al-Kawakibi 1980, What Occurred in Al-Maamoura 1981, The Visit 1984, Ibrahim Tawqan 1985, Ways Which Don't Meet 1986, Houses in the Wind 1987. *Plays:* Democratic by Force 1996, Every Thing is on Remote Control 1999, Small Details 2000. *Publications:* short stories: Bread of Others 1975, The Palestinian Boy 1977, Rites for A Miserable Woman 1986, The Silence of Windows 1991, A Fast Passing By 2002, Shakira's Picture 2003, The Daughter of My Aunt, Condoliza 2004, A Small Place for Evening Grieves 2004, Small Probabilities 2006, Mirrors of Absence 2007, Mordechai's Moustache and his Wife's Cats 2007; short stories for children: The Soldier and The Toy 1986, The Check Point 1986, The Song of the Donkey 1988, The Profession of the Roost 1999, The Tree Has Said To Us 2004; other children's fiction: Mariam Said the Boy Said 1996, Me and Jomana 2002, A Difficult Experience 2002, The Boy Who Broke the Glass 2002, Birds On The Window 2002, The Captain (three plays for children) 2003, Alaa in the Small House 2004, The Small King 2004, Distant Planet for My Sister Queen 2007; other: Another Shadow Of The City (non-fiction) 1998, The Wood Cutter (trans.) 2002, Charming Cities and A Frivolous Wind (travel) 2005. *Honours:* Mahmoud Saif Addeen Al-Earani Award 1991, awards from Union of Jordanian Publishers and Palestinian Ministry of Culture. *Address:* POB 29027, Jerusalem, 91290 Israel (home). *Telephone:* (2) 6739104 (home). *E-mail:* info@mahmoudshukair.com (home). *Website:* mahmoudshukair.com.

SHUKLA, Vinod Kumar, MSc; Indian writer; b. 1 Jan. 1937, Rajnandgaon, Chattisgarh. *Education:* JNKVV Jabalpur. *Career:* Hindi writer; fmr Assoc. Prof., Indira Gandhi Agricultural Univ.; guest littérateur at the Nirala Srijanpeeth, Bhopal, 1994–96; currently lives in Raipur, Chattisgarh. *Publications:* novels: Naukar Ki Kameez 1979, Khilega to Dekhenge 1996, Per Par Kamra 1996, Deewar Mein Ek Khirkee Rahati Thi (Sahitya Akademi Award 1999) 1998; short stories: Per Par Kamra 1988; poetry: Lagbhag Jai Hind 1971, Vah Aadmi Chala Gaya Naya Garam Coat Pehankar Vichar ki Tarah 1981, Sab Kuch Hona Bacha Rahega 1992, Atirikt Nahin 2002. *Honours:* Dayavati Mody Kavi Shekhar Samman, Skikhar Samman, Muktibodh Fellowship. *Address:* c/o Aadhar Prakashan Pvt. Ltd, SCF 267, Sector 16, Panchkula 134113, India.

SHUKMAN, Harold, MA, DPhil, FRHistS; British academic and writer; *Fellow Emeritus, St Antony's College, Oxford;* b. (Henry Sugarman), 23 March 1931, London, England; s. of David Shukhman and Masha Shukhman of Simferopol, Russia; m. 1st Ann King Farlow 1956 (divorced 1970); two s. one d.; m. 2nd Barbara King Farlow 1973. *Education:* Univs of Nottingham and Oxford. *Career:* Fellow, St Antony's Coll., Oxford 1961–98, Fellow Emer. 1998–, Lecturer in Modern Russian History 1969–98; mem. Authors' Soc., Translators' Asscn. *Publications:* Lenin and the Russian Revolution 1966, Blackwell's Encyclopedia of the Russian Revolution (ed.) 1988, Andrei Gromyko: Memories (ed. and trans.) 1989, Stalin: Triumph and Tragedy (ed. and trans.) 1991, Lenin: His Life and Legacy (ed. and trans.) 1994, Trotsky: Eternal Revolutionary (ed. and trans.) 1996, Rasputin 1997, The Rise and Fall of the Soviet Empire (ed. and trans.) 1998, The Russian Revolution 1998, Stalin 1999, Agents for Change (ed.), The Winter War (ed.), Secret Classrooms (co-author), Redefining Stalinism (ed.) 2003, War or Revolution 2006, The Russo–Japanese War and the Trans-Siberian Railway 2007; contrib. to professional journals and general periodicals. *Address:* 11 Cunliffe Close, Oxford, OX2 7BJ, England (home). *Telephone:* (1865) 554147 (office). *E-mail:* harold.shukman@sant.ox.ac.uk (office).

SHUKMAN, Henry; British poet and writer; b. 1963, Oxford. *Career:* poet-in-residence, The Wordsworth Trust; book reviewer, New York Times; contributing ed., Conde Nast Traveller. *Publications:* Sons of the Moon: A Journey in the Andes (travel writing) 1990, Travels with my Trombone: A Caribbean Journey (travel writing) 1992, Savage Pilgrims: On the Road to Santa Fe (memoir) 1996, In Doctor No's Garden (poems) 2002, Darien Dogs (short stories) 2003, Sandstorm (novel) 2005, The Lost City (novel) 2007; contrib. to TLS, Daily Telegraph, Iowa Review, New Republic, London Review of Books. *Honours:* Daily Telegraph Arvon Prize, TLS Prize, Tabla Prize, Peterloo Prize, Arts Council Writer's Award, Aldeburgh Festival Prize, Authors Club First Novel Award, Royal Literary Fund Fellowship. *Address:* c/o The Wordsworth Trust, Dove Cottage, Grasmere, Cumbria LA22 9SH, England. *Telephone:* (1539) 435544. *Fax:* (1539) 435748. *E-mail:* enquiries@wordsworth.org.uk. *Website:* www.wordsworth.org.uk.

SHULEVITZ, Judith; American journalist, editor and critic; b. 28 Feb. 1963; m. Nicholas Lemann. *Education:* Yale Coll. *Career:* Co-ed. Lingua Franca 1991–94; fmr Culture Ed. Slate; fmr Deputy Ed. New York Magazine; columnist, New York Times Book Review 2001–03. *Publications:* The Sabbath World: Glimpses of a Different Order of Time (American Library Asscn Sophie Brody Medal for Jewish Literature 2011) 2010; contrib. New York Times Book Review, New Yorker, New Republic. *Literary Agent:* c/o Tina Bennett, Janklow & Nesbit Associates, 445 Park Avenue, New York, NY 10022-2606, USA. *Telephone:* (212) 421-1700. *Fax:* (212) 980-3671. *E-mail:* tbennett@janklow.com. *Website:* www.janklowandnesbit.com; www.judithshulevitz.com (home).

SHULMAN, Alexandra, OBE, BA; British journalist; *Editor, British Vogue*; b. 13 Nov. 1957, London; d. of Milton Shulman and Drusilla Beyfus; one s. *Education:* St Paul's Girls' School and Univ. of Sussex. *Career:* Sec. Over-21 magazine; Writer and Commissioning Ed., later Features Ed. Tatler 1982–87; Ed. Women's Page, Sunday Telegraph 1987, later Deputy Ed. 7 Days current affairs photo/reportage; Features Ed. Vogue 1988; Ed. GQ 1990; Ed. British Vogue 1992–; Dir Condé Nast Publications 1997–2002; Trustee Nat. Portrait Gallery, London 1999–2008, Arts Foundation 2001–, Royal Marsden Hospital cancer campaign 2009–. *Address:* Condé Nast Publications, Vogue House, Hanover Square, London, W1R 0AD, England (office). *Telephone:* (20) 7499-9080 (office).

SHUPE, Anson David, Jr, BA, MA, PhD; American academic and writer; b. 21 Jan. 1948, Buffalo, NY; m. Janet Ann Klicua 1970, one s. one d. *Education:* Waseda Univ., Tokyo, College of Wooster, Indiana Univ. *Career:* Asst Prof., Alfred Univ., New York 1975–76; Asst Prof., Univ. of Texas at Arlington 1976–78, Assoc. Prof. 1978–86, Prof. of Sociology 1986; Assoc. Ed., Review of Religious Research 1980, 1992–, Sociological Focus 1988–90; Visiting Faculty Lecturer, Iliff School of Theology, Denver 1985, Lecturer 1987; Prof. of Sociology and Anthropology, Indiana Univ. – Purdue Univ., Fort Wayne 1987–, Chair, Dept of Sociology and Anthropology 1987–91; mem. American Asscn of Univ. Profs; Asscn for the Scientific Study of Religion, Asscn for the Sociology of Religion, North Central Sociological Asscn, Religious Research Asscn, Society for the Scientific Study of Religion. *Publications:* 'Moonies' in America: Cult, Church, and Crusade (with David G. Bromley) 1980, Six Perspectives on New Religions: A Case Study Approach 1981, Strange Gods: The Great American Cult Scare (with David G. Bromley) 1982, Born Again Politics and the Moral Majority: What Social Surveys Really Show (with William A. Stacey) 1982, The Anti-Cult Movement in America: A Bibliography and Historical Survey (with David G. Bromley and Donna L. Stacey) 1983, Metaphor and Social Control in a Pentecostal Sect (with Tom Craig Darrand) 1984, The Mormon Corporate Empire (with John Heinerman) 1985, A Documentary History of the Anti-Cult Movement (with David G. Bromley) 1986, Violent Men, Violent Couples: The Dynamics of Family Violence (with William A. Stacey and Lonnie R. Hazelwood) 1986, Televangelism: Power and

SHUSTERMAN, Richard Marc, BA, MA, DPhil; American academic and writer; *Dorothy F. Schmidt Eminent Scholar Chair in the Humanities and Professor of Philosophy, Florida Atlantic University*; b. 3 Dec. 1949, Phila, Pa; s. of Murray H. Shusterman and Judith W. Shusterman; m. 1st Rivka Nahmani 1970 (divorced 1986); two s. one d.; m. 2nd Erica Ando 2000; one d. *Education:* Hebrew Univ. of Jerusalem, Israel, St John's Coll., Oxford, UK. *Career:* Lecturer, Bezalael Acad. of Art 1980–81; Lecturer, Ben-Gurion Univ. of the Negev, Beersheba, Israel 1980–82; Sr Lecturer in English and Philosophy 1983–87; Visiting Fellow, St John's Coll. Oxford 1984–85; Visiting Assoc. Prof., Temple Univ., Phila 1985–87, Assoc. Prof. of Philosophy 1987–91, Full Prof. 1992–, Chair. Dept of Philosophy 1998–2004; Dir of Studies, École des Hautes Études en Sciences Sociales, Paris 1990, 1993; Dorothy F. Schmidt Eminent Scholar Chair in the Humanities and Prof. of Philosophy, Florida Atlantic Univ., Boco Raton 2005–; Visiting Lecturer, Hebrew Univ. of Jerusalem 1980–82; Visiting Prof., Collège Int. de Philosophie 1990 (Dir of Studies 1995–), Hiroshima Univ., Japan 2002–03, Univ. of Paris, Sorbonne 2006, Univ. of Oslo, Norway 2006, Univ. of Paris 2010, Univ. of Rome 2011, Univ. of Lyon 2011; mem. American Philosophical Asscn, American Soc. for Aesthetics (Trustee); literary agent, Witherspoon Assocs. *Publications:* The Object of Literary Criticism 1984, T. S. Eliot and the Philosophy of Criticism 1988, Analytic Aesthetics 1989, The Interpretive Turn: Philosophy, Science, Culture (ed. with D. Hiley and J. Bohman) 1991, Pragmatist Aesthetics: Living Beauty, Rethinking Art 1992, L'Art á L'État Vif 1992, Kunst Leben 1994, Sous l'interprétation 1994, Practicing Philosophy: Pragmatism and the Philosophical Life 1997, La fin de l'éxperience esthétique 1999, Performing Live 2000, Vivre La Philosophie 2001, Philosophie als Lebenspraxis 2001, Surface and Depth 2002, The Range of Pragmatism and the Limits of Philosophy 2004, Aesthetic Experience 2007, Body Consciousness 2008. *Honours:* Chevalier, Ordre des Palmes académiques; ACLS Grant 1988, Nat. Endowment for the Humanities Grant 1988 and Fellowship 1990, Sr Fulbright Fellowship 1995–96, Alexander von Humboldt Transcoop Grant 2006–09, Japan Soc. for the Promotion of Science Fellowship 2009. *Address:* Florida Atlantic University, Boca Raton, FL 33431-0991, USA (office). *Fax:* (561) 297-0851 (office). *E-mail:* shuster1@fau.edu (office). *Website:* www .artsandletters.fau.edu/humanitieschair (office).

SHUTTLE, Penelope Diane; British writer and poet; b. 12 May 1947, Staines, Middx, England; d. of Jack Shuttle and Joan Shuttle; m. Peter Redgrove 1980 (died 2003); one d. *Career:* tutor, Poetry School, Arvon Foundation, Ty Newydd, Almasera Vella (Spain), Le Moulin, Normandy (France); judge of numerous poetry competitions and awards, including T.S. Eliot Award, The Forward Prizes, Nat. Poetry Competition, Eric Gregory Awards; has given poetry readings at all leading UK Poetry Festivals, and in Spain (Univ. of Alicante), Toronto and New York; Hawthornden Fellow. *Publications:* fiction: An Excusable Vengeance 1967, All the Usual Hours of Sleeping 1969, Wailing Monkey Embracing a Tree 1974, The Terrors of Dr Treviles (with Peter Redgrove) 1974, The Glass Cottage 1976, Rainsplitter in the Zodiac Garden 1976, The Mirror of the Giant 1979; poetry: The Hermaphrodite Album (with Peter Redgrove) 1973, The Orchard Upstairs 1980, The Child-Stealer 1983, The Lion From Rio 1986, Adventures With My Horse 1988, Taxing the Rain 1992, Building a City for Jamie 1996, Selected Poems, 1980–1996 1998, A Leaf out of his Book 1999, Redgrove's Wife 2006, Sandgrain and Hourglass 2010, Unsent: New and Selected Poems 2012; non-fiction: The Wise Wound: Menstruation and Everywoman (with Peter Redgrove) 1978, Alchemy for Women (with Peter Redgrove) 1995; numerous pamphlet collections, broadsheets, radio dramas, recordings, readings and television features; contrib. to various pubs. *Honours:* Arts Council Awards 1969, 1972, 1985, Greenwood Poetry Prize 1972, E.C. Gregory Award for Poetry 1974, Authors Foundation Grant, Cholmondeley Award 2007. *Literary Agent:* c/o David Higham Associates Ltd, 5–8 Lower John Street, Golden Square, London, W1F 9HA, England. *Telephone:* (20) 7434-5900. *Fax:* (20) 7437-1072. *E-mail:* dha@davidhigham.co.uk. *Website:* www.davidhigham.co .uk.

SHYAMALAN, M. Night, BA; Indian film director, screenwriter, actor and producer; b. (Manoj Nelliyattu Shyamalan), 6 Aug. 1970, Pondicherry, Tamil Nadu Prov.; s. of Nelliyattu C. Shyamalan and Jayalakshmi Shyamalan; m. Bhavna Vaswani 1993; two d. *Education:* New York Univ. *Career:* Co-founder M. Night Shyamalan Foundation. *Films:* Praying with Anger (writer, dir, actor, producer) 1992, Wide Awake (writer, dir) 1998, The Sixth Sense (writer, dir, actor) 1999, Stuart Little (screenplay writer) 1999, Unbreakable (writer, dir, actor, producer) 2000, Signs (writer, dir, producer) 2002, The Village (writer, dir, producer) 2004, Lady in the Water (writer, dir, producer) 2006, The Happening 2008, The Last Airbender 2010. *Publications:* juvenile: Stuart Finds His Way Home (with Kitty Richards) 1999, Stuart and the Stouts (with Greg Brooker) 2001, Stuart and Snowbell (with Greg Brooker) 2001. *Honours:* Distinguished Alumni Award, Episcopal Academy 2001, Padma Shri Award 2008. *Literary Agent:* Creative Artists Agency, 2000 Avenue of the Stars, Los Angeles, CA 90057, USA. *Telephone:* (424) 288-2000. *Fax:* (424) 288-2900. *Website:* www.caa.com; www.mnightshyamalan.com.

SIDDONS, Anne Rivers, BAA; American writer; b. 9 Jan. 1936, Atlanta, GA; m. Heyward L. Siddons 1966; four s. *Education:* Auburn Univ. *Career:* mem. Authors' Guild, Int. Woman's Forum, Woodward Acad. (Oglethorpe Univ.). *Publications include:* John Chancellor Makes Me Cry (non-fiction) 1975, Heartbreak Hotel 1976, The House Next Door 1978, Fox's Earth 1980, Homeplace 1986, Peachtree Road 1988, King's Oak 1990, Outer Banks 1991, Colony 1992, Hill Towns 1993, Downtown 1994, Fault Lines 1995, Up Island 1997, Low Country 1998, Nora, Nora 2000, Islands 2003, Sweetwater Creek 2005, Off Season 2008, Burnt Mountain 2012; contrib. to magazines. *Honours:* Hon. DLitt (Oglethorpe Univ.) 1992, (Auburn Univ.) 1997; Georgia Author of the Year Award 1988, Georgia Writers Lifetime Achievement Award 1998. *Address:* 60 Church Street, Charleston, SC 29401-2885, USA.

SIDHWA, Bapsi; American/Pakistani writer and academic; b. 11 Aug. 1939, Karachi; d. of Peshotan Bhandara and of Tehmina Bhandara; m. 1st (divorced); m. 2nd Nosher Rustam Sidhwa; two d. one s. *Education:* Kinnaird Coll. for Women, Lahore. *Career:* self-published first novel The Crow Eaters 1978; Asst Prof., Creative Writing Program, Univ. of Houston, Tex., USA 1985; Bunting Fellowship, Radcliffe Coll., Harvard Univ. 1986–87; Asst Prof., Writing Div., Columbia Univ., New York 1989; Visiting Scholar, Rockefeller Foundation Centre, Bellagio, Italy 1991; Prof. of English and Writer-in-Residence, Mount Holyoake Coll., South Hadley, Mass 1997; Fannie Hurst Writer-in-Residence, Brandeis Univ., Mass 1998–99; Postcolonial Teaching Fellowship, Univ. of Southampton, UK 2001; Chair. Commonwealth Writers' Prize 1993; mem. Advisory Cttee to Prime Minister Benazir Bhutto on Women's Devt –1996, Punjab Rep., Asian Women's Conf., Alma Ata; Sec. Destitute Women's and Children's Home, Lahore. *Plays:* Sock 'em With Honey 1993. *Films:* Earth (film of Ice-Candy-Man aka Cracking India) 1999. *Publications include:* The Crow Eaters (David Higham Award) 1978 (commercially published 1980), The Bride 1982, Ice-Candy-Man (aka Cracking India) (Notable Book of the Year, New York Times) 1991, An American Brat 1993, Bapsi Sidhwa Omnibus 2001, Water: A Novel (Premio Mondello for Foreign Authors 2007) 2006, City of Sin and Splendour: Writings on Lahore 2006, The Pakistani Bride 2008; numerous short stories and reviews. *Honours:* Sitara-I-Imtiaz 1991, Nat. Award for English Literature, Pakistan Acad. of Letters 1991, Patras Bokhari Award for Literature 1992, Lila Wallace Reader's Digest Award 1993, Excellence in Literature Award, Zoroastrian Congress 2002, South Asian Excellence Awards for Literature 2008, HCC Asian-American Legacy Award 2008. *Address:* Milkweed Editions, 1011 Washington Avenue, South Suite 300, Open Book, Minneapolis, MN 55415 (office); 5442 Cheena Drive, Houston, TX 77096, USA (home). *Telephone:* (612) 332-3192 (office); (713) 283-0811 (home). *Website:* hometown.aol.com/bsidhwa; bapsisidhwa.com.

SIEGEL, Ira Theodore, MBA; American publishing executive; b. 23 Sept. 1944, New York City; s. of David A. Siegel and Rose Minsky; m. Sharon R. Sacks 1965; three d. *Education:* New York and Long Island Univs. *Career:* Business Man. Buttenheim Publishing Co., New York 1965–72; Corp. Vice-Pres. (research) Cahners Publishing Co. (Div. Reed Publishing Co. USA, Boston) 1972–86; Pres. R.R. Bowker Publishing Co. (Div. Reed Publishing, USA, New York) 1986–91, Martindale-Hubbell Div. New Jersey 1990–91, Reed Reference Publishing 1991–95, Pres., CEO 1993–95; Pres. and CEO Lexis-Nexis 1995–97; mem. Bd of Dirs edata.com (now Seisint) 1999–2004. *Address:* 16589 Senterra Drive, Delray Beach, FL 33484, USA (home). *Telephone:* (561) 499-6457 (home).

SIEGEL, Robert Harold, BA, MA, PhD; American poet, writer and educator; *Professor Emeritus of English, University of Wisconsin at Milwaukee*; b. 18 Aug. 1939, Oak Park, Ill.; s. of Frederick William Siegel and Charlotte Lucille Chance; m. Roberta Ann Hill 1961; three d. *Education:* Wheaton Coll., Johns Hopkins Univ., Harvard Univ. *Career:* Asst Prof. of English, Dartmouth Coll. 1968–75; Lecturer in Creative Writing, Princeton Univ. 1975–76; McManes Visiting Prof., Wheaton Coll. 1976; Asst Prof., Univ. of Wisconsin, Milwaukee 1976–79, Assoc. Prof. 1979–83, Prof. of English 1983–99, Prof. Emer. 1999–; Visiting Prof., Goethe Univ., Frankfurt, Germany 1985; Nick Barker Writer-in-Residence, Covenant Coll. 2008; mem. Authors Guild, Associated Writing Programs, NAS, Asscn of Literary Scholars and Critics, Chrysostom Soc. (Pres. 2004–07). *Publications:* fiction: Alpha Centauri 1980, Whalesong 1981, The Kingdom of Wundle 1982, White Whale 1991, The Ice at the End of the World 1994; poetry: The Beasts and the Elders 1973, In a Pig's Eye 1980, The Waters Under the Earth 2005, A Pentecost of Finches: New and Selected Poems 2006; contrib. to anthologies, reviews, quarterlies and journals, including Poetry, Atlantic Monthly, Prairie Schooner, Cream City Review, Image. *Honours:* Foley Award, America magazine 1970, Poetry Magazine Glatstein Prize 1977, Cliff Dwellers Arts Foundation 1974, Prairie Schooner Poetry Prize 1977, Univ. of Wisconsin grants 1978, 1984, 1988, 1996, 1999, Nat. Endowment for the Arts Fellowship 1980, Ingram Merrill Foundation Award 1979, First Prize, Soc. of Midland Authors 1974, 1981, Gold Medallion,

ECPA, Friends of Literature Matson Award 1982, Univ. of Wisconsin at Oshkosh School of Library Science Golden Archer Award 1986, Milton Prize in Poetry 1994, EPA Poetry Prize 2003. *Address:* Department of English, University of Wisconsin, Milwaukee, WI 53201, USA (office). *E-mail:* siegelrh@uwm.edu (office). *Website:* (office); robert-siegel.com.

SIERRA, Javier; Spanish journalist; b. Aug. 1971, Teruel; m. *Education:* Universidad Complutense de Madrid. *Career:* presenter of programme on Radio Heraldo 1983; co-founder of magazine, Año Cero 1989; reporter, later Ed. of magazine, Más Allá de la Ciencia 1992–2005, Ed. at Large 2005–. *Television:* contributor: Crónicas Marcianas (Telecinco) 2000–04, Milenio 3 (Cadena SER), Herrera en la Onda (Onda Cero), La rosa de los vientos (Onda Cero); presenter: El otro lado de la realidad (Telemadrid) 2004. *Publications:* Roswell, secreto de Estado (non-fiction) 1995, La España extraña (non-fiction, with Jesús Callejo) 1997, La dama azul (novel) 1998, Las puertas templarias (novel) 2000, En busca de la Edad de Oro (non-fiction) 2000, El secreto egipcio de Napoleón (novel) 2002, La cena secreta (novel) 2004. *Address:* c/o Grupo Editorial Random House Mondadori SL, Travessera de Gràcia 47–49, 08015 Barcelona, Spain (office). *E-mail:* webmaster@randomhousemondadori.es (office). *Website:* www.javiersierra.com.

SIGAREV, Vasilii; Russian playwright; b. 1977, Nizhnii Tagil, Sverdlovsk Oblast. *Film:* Volchok (Spinning Top, in Russia) 2009. *Plays:* English-language productions include: Plasticine (Royal Court Theatre) (Evening Standard Charles Wintour Award for most promising playwright 2002) 2002; Black Milk (Royal Court Theatre) 2003, then Belfast, Chicago, Sydney, Washington and New York; Ladybird (Royal Court Theatre) 2004, then Los Angeles and Sydney; productions in the rest of the world include: Plasticine, in Russia (Playwright and Director Centre 2001), Denmark, Norway, Czech Repub., Portugal, Greece, Germany and Romania; Black Milk, in Russia (Gogol Theatre) 2002, Norway, Israel, Iceland, Germany, Poland, Belgium, Czech Repub., Hungary and Romania; Ladybird, in Germany and Romania; Phantom Pains, in Russia (Sphera Theatre/Moscow Arts Theatre) 2004–05, Poland, Latvia and Romania; Lie Detector, in Russia (Sphera Theatre/Moscow Arts Theatre) 2004–05, Czech Repub.; Goupiochka, in Russia (RAMT Theatre Group) 2006, Estonia, Slovakia, France and Belgium; Agasfer, in Slovenia and Serbia; Family of a Vampire, in Poland, France and Germany; The Pit, in Germany (reading at the Gorky Theatre). *Honours:* Anti-Booker Prize, Moscow 2001. *Literary Agent:* c/o Judy Daish Associates Ltd, 2 St Charles Place, London, W10 6EG, England. *Telephone:* (20) 8964-8811. *Fax:* (20) 8964-8966. *E-mail:* howard@judydaish.com. *Website:* www.judydaish.com.

SILBER, Joan, BA, MA; American writer and teacher; b. 14 June 1945, Millburn, NJ; d. of Samuel S. Silber and Dorothy Arlein Silber. *Education:* Sarah Lawrence Coll., New York Univ. *Career:* faculty, Sarah Lawrence Coll. 1985–; Visiting Asst Prof., Univ. of Utah 1988; Visiting Lecturer, Boston Univ. 1992; writer-in-residence, Vanderbilt Univ. 1993; mem. Authors' Guild, PEN. *Publications:* Household Words (PEN/Hemingway Award for the Best First Fiction 1981) 1980, In the City 1987, In My Other Life 2000, Lucky Us 2001, Ideas of Heaven: A Ring of Stories 2004, The Size of the World 2008; contrib. to newspapers, reviews and journals. *Honours:* Guggenheim Fellowship 1984–85, Nat. Endowment for the Arts grant 1986, New York Foundation for the Arts grant 1986, Pushcart Prizes 2000, 2003, Cohen Award (for short story The High Road) 2003, American Acad. of Arts and Letters Award in Literature 2007. *Literary Agent:* c/o Geri Thoma, Elaine Markson Agency, 44 Greenwich Avenue, New York, NY 10011, USA. *Telephone:* (212) 243-8480. *Fax:* (212) 691-9014. *E-mail:* geri@marksonagency.com. *E-mail:* jksilber@earthlink.net (home).

SILKO, Leslie Marmon, BA; American academic, writer and poet; b. 15 March 1948, Albuquerque, NM; two s. *Education:* Univ. of New Mexico. *Career:* teacher, Univ. of New Mexico; Prof. of English, Univ. of Arizona at Tucson 1978–. *Publications:* fiction: Ceremony (novel) 1977, Storyteller (short stories) 1981, Almanac of the Dead (novel) 1991, Yellow Woman and a Beauty of the Spirit (essays) 1993, Gardens in the Dunes (novel) 1999; poetry: Laguna Woman 1974; non-fiction: Leslie Silko (autobiog.) 1974, The Delicacy and Strength of Lace: Letters Between Leslie Marmon Silko and James Wright (biog.) 1986, Sacred Water: Narratives and Pictures (autobiog.) 1993, Conversations with Leslie Marmon Silko (biog.) 2000, The Turquoise Ledge: A Memoir 2010; contributions: New Mexico Quarterly. *Honours:* National Endowment for the Arts Grant 1974, Chicago Review Poetry Award 1974, Pushcart Prize 1977, MacArthur Foundation Fellowship 1983. *Address:* 7200 West El Camino Del Cerro, Tucson, AZ 85746-9298, USA (home). *Website:* literati.net/silko.

SILLIMAN, Ronald Glenn; American editor and poet; b. 8 May 1946, Pasco, Washington; m. 1st Rochelle Nameroff 1965 (divorced 1972); m. 2nd Krishna Evans 1986; two s. *Education:* Merritt College, San Francisco State College, University of California at Berkeley. *Career:* Ed., Tottel's, 1970–81; Dir of Research and Education, Committee for Prisoner Humanity and Justice, San Rafael, CA, 1972–76; Project Man., Tenderloin Ethnographic Research Project, San Francisco, 1977–78; Dir of Outreach, Central City Hospitality House, San Francisco, 1979–81; Lecturer, University of San Francisco, 1981; Visiting Lecturer, University of California at San Diego, La Jolla, 1982; Writer-in-Residence, New College of California, San Francisco, 1982; Dir of Public Relations and Development, 1982–86, Poet-in-Residence, 1983–90, California Institute of Integral Studies, San Francisco; Exec. Ed., Socialist Review, 1986–89; Managing Ed., Computer Land, 1989–. *Publications:* Poetry: Moon in the Seventh House, 1968; Three Syntactic Fictions for Dennis Schmitz, 1969; Crow, 1971; Mohawk, 1973; Nox, 1974; Sitting Up, Standing Up, Taking Steps, 1978; Ketjak, 1978; Tjanting, 1981; Bart, 1982; ABC, 1983; Paradise, 1985; The Age of Huts, 1986; Lit, 1987; What, 1988; Manifest, 1990; Demo to Ink, 1992; Toner, 1992; Jones, 1993; N/O, 1994; Xing, 1996. Other: A Symposium on Clark Coolidge (ed.), 1978; In the American Tree (ed.), 1986; The New Sentence, 1987. *Honours:* Hart Crane and Alice Crane Williams Award, 1968; Joan Lee Yang Awards, 1970, 1971; National Endowment for the Arts Fellowship, 1979; California Arts Council Grants, 1979, 1980; Poetry Center Book Award, 1985. *Address:* 1819 Curtis, Berkeley, CA 94702, USA.

SILMAN, Roberta Lynn, BA (Hons), MFA; American writer; b. 29 Dec. 1934, New York, NY; d. of Herman Karpel and Phoebe Karpel; m. Robert Silman 1956; one s. two d. *Education:* Cornell Univ., Sarah Lawrence Coll. *Career:* mem. PEN, Authors Guild. *Publications:* children's books: Somebody Else's Child 1976, Story Collection: Blood Relations 1977; novels: Boundaries 1979, The Dream Dredger 1986, Beginning the World Again 1990; contribs: book reviews and essays in The New York Times, Boston Globe and other publs; on-line book reviews for PRI World Books and The Arts Fuse; stories in New Yorker, Virginia Quarterly Review, Atlantic, American Scholar and numerous other magazines in USA and UK (also read on Nat. Public Radio). *Honours:* Nat. Magazine Award 1974, 1984, Best Children's Book Award, Child Study Asscn 1976, Pen Hemingway Hon. Mention 1978, Janet Kafka Prizes 1978, 1980, Guggenheim Fellowship 1979, Nat. Endowment for the Arts Fellowship 1983, PEN Syndicated Fiction Project Awards 1983, 1984, Washington Irving Awards 1987, 1991. *Literary Agent:* c/o Gail Hochman, Brandt & Hochman Literary Agents, Inc., 1501 Broadway, Suite 2310, New York, NY 10036, USA. *Telephone:* (212) 840-5760. *Address:* 18 Larchmont Street, Ardsley, NY 10502, USA (home). *Telephone:* (914) 693-2816 (office). *E-mail:* rsilman@verizon.net (home). *Website:* robertasilman.com.

SILVA, Lorenzo, BL; Spanish lawyer and writer; b. 7 June 1966, Carabanchel, Madrid; m.; two s. *Education:* Complutense Univ., Madrid. *Career:* worked as lawyer 1992–2002; currently writer for various media including Vocento Group, El Mundo, ABC and El Pais; has worked as radio commentator for SER and COPE. *Publications:* fiction: Noviembre violeta pecado 1995, La sustancia interior 1996, La flaqueza del bolchevique 1997, El lejano país de los estanques (Premio Ojo Crítico) 1998, El ángel oculto 1999, El urinario 1999, El alquimista impaciente (Nadal prize) 2000, El nombre de nuestro 2001, La isla del destino 2001, La niebla y la doncella 2002, Carta blanca (Premio Primavera de Novela) 2004, Nadie es mejor que otro. Cuatro cuestiones Bevilacqua 2004, La reina sin espejo 2005, Muerte en el reality show 2007, El blog del inquisidor 2008, La estrategia para el agua 2010; story: El déspota adolescente 2003; non-fiction: Literatura de viajes y literatura de viajes 2000, Rif al Yebala. Viaje al sueño y la pesadilla de Marruecos 2001, Sombra líneas. Historias de criminales y la policía 2005, En una tierra extraña, en su propia tierra. Anotaciones de viaje 2006, Y, por último, la guerra. La aventura de los soldados españoles en Irak (co-author Luis Miguel Francisco) 2006, El derecho en la obra de Kafka 2008, La flaqueza del bolchevique (co-author Manuel Martín Cuenca) 2008, Sereno en peligro. La aventura histórica de la Guardia Civil (Algaba Prize) 2010; young adult fiction: Algún día, cuando usted puede tomar a Varsovia 1997, El cazador del desierto 1998, La lluvia de París 2000, Laura y el corazón de las cosas 2002, Los amores lunáticos 2002, Pablo y el malo (co-author Violeta Monreal) 2006, Mi primer libro sobre Albéniz 2008, Albéniz, el pianista aventurero 2008, El juego al revés 2009. *Website:* www.lorenzo-silva.com (office).

SILVERS, Robert Benjamin, AB; American literary editor; *Editor, The New York Review of Books;* b. 31 Dec. 1929, Mineola, NY. *Education:* Univ. of Chicago, Sorbonne, Ecole Polytechnique, Paris, France. *Career:* Press Sec. to Gov. of Connecticut 1950; served in US Army 1950–53; Man. Ed. Paris Review 1954–58; Assoc. Ed. Harper's Magazine 1958–63; Co-founder and Co-Ed. New York Review of Books 1963–2006, Ed. 2006–; mem. Council of Foreign Relations, Century Asscn. *Honours:* Chevalier, Légion d'honneur, mem. Ordre National du Mérite; Hon. DLit (Harvard) 2007; Award for Distinguished Service to the Arts from the American Academy of Arts and Letters 2006, National Book Foundation Literarian Award 2006; Robert B. Silvers annual lectures at New York Public Library established 2002, Ivan Sandrof Lifetime Achievement Award, National Book Critics Circle 2012. *Address:* New York Review of Books, 1755 Broadway, 5th Floor, New York, NY 10019-3743, USA (office). *Telephone:* (212) 757-8070 (office). *Fax:* (212) 333-5374 (office). *E-mail:* nyrev@nybooks.com (office). *Website:* www.nybooks.com (office).

SILVIS, Randall G., BS, MEd; American novelist, playwright and screenwriter; b. 15 July 1950, Rimersburg, PA; two s. *Education:* Clarion Univ., Indiana Univ. *Career:* James Thurber Writer-in-Residence, Thurber House, Columbus, OH 1989; Visiting Writer, Mercyhurst Coll., Pennsylvania 1989–90, Ohio State Univ. 1991, 1992, Chatham Univ., Seton Hill Coll. *Film screenplays:* An Occasional Hell, Believe the Children, Mr Dream Merchant, Marguerite and the Moon Man, The Algerian. *Publications:* The Luckiest Man in the World, Excelsior, An Occasional Hell, Under the Rainbow, Dead Man Falling, On Night's Shore, Disquiet Heart, Heart So Hungry, Mysticus, In a Town Called Mundomuerto; contrib. to numerous magazines. *Honours:* Hon. DLitt' two NEA Fellowships, Drue Heinz Literature Prize, three Nat. Playwright Showcase Awards, Fulbright Sr Scholar Research grant, Screenwriting Showcase Award. *E-mail:* randallsilvis@neo.rr.com (office).

SIMIC, Charles, BA; American poet, writer and academic; *Professor of English, University of New Hampshire*; b. 9 May 1938, Belgrade, Yugoslavia (now Serbia); s. of George Simic and Helen Matijevich; m. Helen Dubin 1965; one s. one d. *Education:* Oak Park High School, Chicago, Univ. of Chicago and New York Univ. *Career:* arrived in USA 1954; army service 1961–64; worked for Chicago Sun-Times as proofreader; later business Man. Aperture Magazine 1966–69; Lecturer, Calif. State Univ., Hayward 1970–73; Assoc. Prof., later Prof. of English, Univ. of New Hampshire 1973–; first vol. of poems published 1967; elected a Chancellor of The Acad. of American Poets 2000; Poet Laureate of USA 2007–08. *Publications include:* poetry: What the Grass Says 1967, Somewhere Among Us A Stone Is Taking Notes 1969, Dismantling the Silence 1971, White 1972, Return to a Place Lit by a Glass of Milk 1974, Biography and a Lament 1976, Charon's Cosmology 1977, Brooms: Selected Poems 1978, School for Dark Thoughts 1978, Classic Ballroom Dances 1980, Shaving at Night 1982, Austerities 1982, Weather Forecast for Utopia and Vicinity: Poems 1967–82 1983, The Chicken Without a Head 1983, Selected Poems 1985, Unending Blues 1986, The World Doesn't End (prose poems) (Pulitzer Prize for Poetry 1990) 1989, In the Room We Share 1990, The Book of Gods and Devils 1990, Selected Poems: 1963–83 1990, Hotel Insomnia 1992, A Wedding in Hell 1994, Walking the Black Cat 1996, Jackstraws 1999, Night Picnic 2001, The Voice at 3:00AM 2003, Selected Poems 1963–2003 (Griffin Int. Poetry Prize) 2005, That Little Something 2008, Sixty Poems 2008, Monster Loves His Labyrinth 2008, The Renegade: Writings on Poetry and a Few Other Things 2009, Master of Disguises 2010, The Horse Has Six Legs: An Anthology of Serbian Poetry 2010, Confessions of a Poet Laureate 2010; prose: The Uncertain Certainty 1985, Wonderful Words, Silent Truth 1990, Dimestore Alchemy 1992, The Unemployed Fortune Teller 1994, Orphan Factory (essays) 1997, A Fly in the Soup 2000, The Renegade: Writings on Poetry and a Few Other Things 2009, Dime-Store Alchemy: The Art of Joseph Cornell 2011; ed.: Another Republic: 17 European and South American Writers (with Mark Strand) 1976, The Essential Campion 1988, The Best American Poetry 1992; many trans of French, Serbian, Croatian, Macedonian and Slovenian poetry. *Honours:* PEN Int. Award for Translation 1970, 1980, Guggenheim Fellowship 1972, Nat. Endowment for the Arts Fellowships 1974, 1979, Edgar Allan Poe Award 1975, American Acad. of Arts and Letters Award 1976, Harriet Monroe Poetry Award 1980, Fulbright Fellowship 1982, Ingram Merrill Foundation Fellowship 1983, John D. and Catherine T. MacArthur Foundation Fellowship 1984, Acad. of American Poets Fellowship 1998, Wallace Stevens Award 2007, Frost Medal 2011. *Address:* Department of English, University of New Hampshire, 229 Hamilton Smith Hall, PO Box 192, Durham, NH 03824, USA (office). *Telephone:* (603) 862-3991 (office). *Fax:* (603) 862-3563 (office). *E-mail:* csimic@cisunix.unh.edu (office). *Website:* www.unh.edu/english (office).

SIMIC, Goran; Bosnia and Herzegovina writer, poet and dramatist; b. 20 Oct. 1952, Vlasenica, Yugoslavia; m. Amela Simic 1982; two c. *Education:* Univ. of Sarajevo. *Career:* founder mem. PEN Bosnia-Herzegovina; mem. PEN Canada. *Publications:* poetry: A Period Next to a Circle or A Journey 1976, Vertigo 1977, Mandragora 1982, Selected Poems 1985, A Step into the Dark 1987, Fantasy Book 1989, Sorrow of Sarajevo 1994, Sprinting from the Graveyard 1997, Peace and War 1998, Walking Across the Minefield 1999, Alledaagse Adam 1999, Book of Wondering 2002, Immigrant Blues 2003; theatrical works: Wind in Uniform (comedy), A Fairy Tale About Sarajevo 1994, Europe (libretto) 1995, Three plays for puppets 1998, London Under Siege (libretto) 1999. *Honours:* several Yugoslav awards, Hellman-Hammet grant 1993, PEN Center West Freedom to Write Award, USA 1995, Canada Council grants 1996, 1998. *Address:* 226 Carlton Street, Toronto, ON M5A 2L1, Canada. *Telephone:* (416) 921-5957. *E-mail:* goransimic@aol.com. *Website:* www.angelfire.com/poetry/goransimic.

SIMMIE, Lois; Canadian writer and poet; b. 11 June 1932, Edam, Sask.; two s. two d. *Education:* Saskatchewan Business College, University of Saskatchewan. *Career:* Writer-in-Residence, Saskatoon Public Library 1987–88; instructor at community colleges; mem. Asscn of Canadian Television and Radio Artists, Canadian Children's Book Centre, Saskatchewan Writers Guild, Writers' Union of Canada. *Publications:* Ghost House, 1976; They Shouldn't Make You Promise That, 1981; Pictures, 1984; Betty Lee Bonner Lives There, 1993; The Secret Lives of Sgt John Wilson: A True Story of Love and Murder, 1995; contributions: numerous anthologies and periodicals. *Honours:* awards and grants.

SIMMONS, Michael, BA; British writer and editor; b. 17 Oct. 1935, Watford, Herts., England; m. Angela Thomson 1963; two s. *Education:* Univ. of Manchester. *Career:* East Europe Correspondent, Financial Times 1968–72; Third World Ed., The Guardian 1978–82, E Europe Corresp. 1982–92, Deputy Ed. Society 1993–97. *Publications:* Berlin: The Dispossessed City 1988; The Unloved Country: A Portrait of the GDR 1989; The Reluctant President: A Life of Václav Havel 1992; Landscapes of Poverty, 1997, On the Edge 2002, Street Credo (ed.) 1999, Getting a Life (ed.) 2001, Hearing Loss: From Stigma to Strategy 2005, Gathering 2005; contribs to various periodicals. *Literary Agent:* c/o The Sayle Agency, 86 King's Parade, Cambridge, CB2 1SJ, England. *Telephone:* (1223) 303035. *Fax:* (1223) 301638. *E-mail:* info@sayleliteraryagency.com.

SIMMONS, Richard D., AB, LLB; American newspaper publisher; b. 30 Dec. 1934, Cambridge, Mass.; m. Mary DeWitt Bleecker 1961; two s. *Education:* Harvard and Columbia Univs. *Career:* admitted to New York Bar; Assoc. Satterlee, Warfield & Stephens 1958–62; Gen. Counsel Giannini Science Corpn 1962–64; Vice-Pres. and Gen. Counsel Southeastern Publishing Service Corpn 1964–69; Counsel Dun & Bradstreet Inc., New York 1969–70, Vice-Pres. and Gen. Counsel 1970–72; Pres. Moody's Investors Service 1973–76, Dun & Bradstreet Inc. 1975–76; Exec. Vice-Pres. Dun & Bradstreet Corpn, New York 1976–78, Dir and Vice-Chair. Bd 1979–81; Pres. and COO The Washington Post Co. 1981–91, Dir 1981–; Pres. Int. Herald Tribune 1989–96. *Address:* c/o The Washington Post Company, 1150 15th Street NW, Washington, DC 20071, USA (office). *E-mail:* twcoreply@washpost.com (office). *Website:* www.washpostco.com (office).

SIMON, David, BA; American screenwriter, TV producer and fmr journalist; b. 1960, Washington, DC; m. Laura Lippman. *Education:* Bethesda-Chevy Chase High School, Univ. of Maryland. *Career:* police reporter at Baltimore Sun newspaper 1982–95; f. Blown Deadline Productions; Fellow, John D. and Catherine T. MacArthur Foundation 2010. *Television includes:* NYPD Blue (writer) 1996, Homicide: Life on the Street (producer, writer) (Writers Guild of America Award) 1993–99, The Corner (producer, writer) (three Emmy Awards) 2000, The Wire (producer, writer) 2002–08, Generation Kill (producer, writer) 2008, Treme 2010. *Publications include:* Homicide: A Year on the Killing Streets (Edgar Award 1992) 1991, The Corner: A Year in the Life of an Inner-City Neighborhood (co-author) (Notable Book of the Year, New York Times) 1997. *Address:* Blown Deadline Productions, 1801 South Clinton Street, Suite 210, Baltimore, MD 21224, USA.

SIMON, Neil; American playwright; b. 4 July 1927, New York; s. of Irving Simon and Mamie Simon; m. 1st. Joan Baim 1953 (deceased); two d.; m. 2nd Marsha Mason 1973 (divorced); m. 3rd Diane Lander 1987; one d. *Education:* New York Univ. *Career:* wrote for various TV programmes including The Tallulah Bankhead Show 1951, The Phil Silvers Show 1958–59, NBC Special, The Trouble with People 1972. *Plays:* Come Blow Your Horn 1961, Little Me (musical) 1962, Barefoot in the Park 1963, The Odd Couple 1965, Sweet Charity (musical) 1966, The Star-Spangled Girl 1966, Plaza Suite 1968, Promises, Promises (musical) 1968, Last of the Red Hot Lovers 1969, The Gingerbread Lady 1970, The Prisoner of Second Avenue 1971, The Sunshine Boys 1972, The Good Doctor 1973, God's Favorite 1974, California Suite 1976, Chapter Two 1977, They're Playing Our Song 1979, I Ought to be in Pictures 1980, Fools 1981, Little Me (revised version) 1982, Brighton Beach Memoirs 1983, Biloxi Blues 1985, The Odd Couple Female Version 1985, Broadway Bound 1986, Rumors 1988, Lost in Yonkers 1991, Jake's Women 1992, The Goodbye Girl (musical) 1993, Laughter on the 23rd Floor 1993, London Suite 1995. *Screenplays:* After the Fox 1966, Barefoot in the Park 1967, The Odd Couple 1968, The Out-of-Towners 1970, Plaza Suite 1971, The Last of the Red Hot Lovers 1972, The Heartbreak Kid 1973, The Prisoner of Second Avenue 1975, The Sunshine Boys 1975, Murder By Death 1976, The Goodbye Girl 1977, The Cheap Detective 1978, California Suite 1978, Chapter Two 1979, Seems Like Old Times 1980, Only When I Laugh 1981, I Ought to Be in Pictures 1982, Max Dugan Returns 1983, Lonely Guy (adaptation) 1984, The Slugger's Wife 1984, Brighton Beach Memoirs 1986, Biloxi Blues 1988, The Marrying Man 1991, Broadway Bound (TV film) 1992, Lost in Yonkers 1993, Jake's Women (TV film) 1996, London Suite (TV film) 1996; other motion pictures adapted from stage plays: Come Blow Your Horn 1963, Sweet Charity 1969, The Star-Spangled Girl 1971; mem. Dramatists Guild, Writers' Guild of America; many awards including Emmy Award 1957, 1959; Antoinette Perry (Tony) Awards for The Odd Couple 1965, Biloxi Blues 1985 (Best Play), Lost in Yonkers 1991 (Best Play). *Publications:* Rewrites: A Memoir 1996; individual plays. *Honours:* Hon. DHumLitt (Hofstra Univ.) 1981, (Williams Coll.) 1984; Evening Standard Award 1967, Writers' Guild Screen Award for The Odd Couple 1969, Writers' Guild Laurel Award 1979, American Comedy Award for Lifetime Achievement 1989, Pulitzer Prize (for Lost in Yonkers) 1991, Kennedy Center Mark Twain Prize for American Humor 2006. *Address:* c/o Albert DaSilva, 502 Park Avenue, New York, NY 10022, USA.

SIMON, Sheldon Weiss, BA, MA, PhD; American academic and writer; *Professor of Political Science, Arizona State University*; b. 31 Jan. 1937, St Paul, Minn.; s. of Blair Simon and Jennie Dim; m. Charlann Lilwin Scheid 1962; one s. *Education:* Univ. of Minnesota, Princeton Univ., Univ. of Geneva, Switzerland. *Career:* Visiting Prof., George Washington Univ. 1965, Univ. of British Columbia 1972–73, 1979–80, Carleton Univ. 1976, Monetary Inst. of Int. Studies 1991, 1996, American Grad. School of Int. Man. 1991–92; Asst Prof., then Prof., Univ. of Kentucky 1966–75; Prof. of Political Science, Arizona State Univ. 1975–, Chair. Dept of Political Science 1975–79, Dir Center for Asian Studies 1980–88; Sr Advisor and Chair. Southeast Asia Studies Group, Nat. Bureau of Asian Research, Seattle and Washington, DC; mem. American Political Science Asscn, Asia Soc., Asscn of Asian Studies, Int. Studies Asscn, US Council for Asia-Pacific Security; consultant to US Depts of State and Defense; Academic Assoc., US Nat. Intelligence Council; Visiting Asia Mentor Prof., US Naval War Coll. 2008–09. *Publications:* The Broken Triangle: Peking, Djakarta and the PKI 1969, War and Politics in Cambodia 1974, Asian Neutralism and US Policy 1975, The Military and Security in the Third World (ed.) 1978, The ASEAN States and Regional Security 1982, The Future of Asian-Pacific Security Collaboration 1988, East Asian Security in the Post-Cold War Era (ed.) 1993, Southeast Asian Security in the New Millennium (ed.) 1996, The Many Faces of Asian Security (ed.) 2001, Religion and Conflict in South and Southeast Asia: Disrupting Violence (ed.) 2007, China, the United States, and Southeast Asia: Contending Perspectives on Politics, Security, and Economics (ed.) 2008; contribs to scholarly books and journals. *Honours:* Outstanding Alumnus, Coll. of Liberal Arts, Univ. of

Minnesota 1958, US Inst. of Peace Grantee 2001, W. Alton Jones Grantee 2001, Earhart Foundation Grantee (several years), Outstanding Research Award, Nat. Bureau of Asian Research 2005. *Address:* Department of Political Science, Arizona State University, Tempe, AZ 85287-3802, USA (office). *Telephone:* (480) 965-1317 (office). *Fax:* (480) 965-3929 (office). *E-mail:* shells@asu.edu (office). *Website:* pgs.clas.asu.edu (office).

SIMPSON, Anne; Canadian poet, writer and artist. *Career:* fmr co-ordinator, Writing Centre, St Francis Xavier Univ., NS; Writer-in-Residence, Univ. of New Brunswick in Fredericton; mem. Writers' Union of Canada. *Publications include:* poetry: Light Falls Through You 2000, Loop (Griffin Poetry Prize 2004) 2003, Quick (Pat Lowther Memorial Award 2008) 2007; novels: Canterbury Beach 2001, Falling 2008; editor: An Orange from Portugal: Christmas Stories from the Maritimes and Newfoundland 2003. *Honours:* The Journey Prize (jtly) 1997, Lina Chartrand Award 1997, Bliss Carman Poetry Award 1999, Atlantic Poetry Award 2001, Gerard Lampert Award 2001. *Address:* c/o McLelland and Stewart Ltd, 75 Sherbourne Street, 5th Floor, Toronto, ON M5A 2P9, Canada (office).

SIMPSON, Dorothy M., BA, DipEd; British writer; b. 20 June 1933, Blaenavon, Monmouthshire, Wales; m. Keith Taylor Simpson 1961, two s. one d. *Education:* Univ. of Bristol. *Career:* teacher of English and French, Dartford Grammar School for Girls, Kent 1955–59, Erith Grammer School, Kent 1959–61; teacher of English, Senacre School, Maidstone, Kent 1961–62; mem. Soc. of Authors, CWA. *Publications:* Harbinger of Fear 1977, The Night She Died 1981, Six Feet Under 1982, Puppet for a Corpse 1983, Close Her Eyes 1984, Last Seen Alive 1985, Dead on Arrival 1986, Element of Doubt 1987, Suspicious Death 1988, Dead by Morning 1989, Doomed to Die 1991, Wake the Dead 1992, No Laughing Matter 1993, A Day for Dying 1995, Once Too Often 1998, Dead and Gone 1999. *Honours:* CWA Silver Dagger 1985. *Literary Agent:* Curtis Brown Ltd, Haymarket House, 28–29 Haymarket, London, SW1Y 4SP, England. *Telephone:* (20) 7393-4400. *Fax:* (20) 7393-4401. *E-mail:* info@curtisbrown.co.uk. *Website:* www.curtisbrown.co.uk.

SIMPSON, Joe, BA; British novelist; b. 13 Aug. 1960, Kuala Lumpur, Malaysia. *Education:* Ampleforth Public School, Yorkshire, Edinburgh Univ. *Publications:* Touching the Void 1988, The Water People 1992, This Game of Ghosts 1993, Storms of Silence 1996, Dark Shadows Falling 1997, The Beckoning Silence 2002. *Honours:* Dr hc (Edinburgh Univ.), (Sheffield Univ.), (Leeds Metropolitan Univ.), (Sheffield Hallam Univ.); Boardman-Tasker Prize 1988, NCR Non-Fiction Prize 1989, Asscn of Speakers' Clubs Speaker of the Year, Nat. Outdoor Book Awards Literary Category 2003. *Literary Agent:* c/o Vintage Publishing, Random House UK Ltd, 20 Vauxhall Bridge Road, London, SW1V 2SA, England. *Telephone:* (20) 7840-8400. *Fax:* (20) 7233-6117. *Website:* www.randomhouse.co.uk/vintage.

SIMPSON, John Andrew, BA, MA; British linguist and lexicographer; *Chief Editor, The Oxford English Dictionary*; b. 13 Oct. 1953, Cheltenham, Glos.; s. of Robert Morris Simpson and Joan Margaret Simpson (née Sersale); m. Hilary Croxford 1976; two d. *Education:* Univs of York and Reading. *Career:* Editorial Asst, Supplement to The Oxford English Dictionary 1976–79, Sr Ed. 1981–84; Ed. New Words, The Oxford English Dictionary 1984–86, Co-Ed., The Oxford English Dictionary 1986–93, Chief Ed. 1993–; Fellow Kellogg Coll., Oxford 1991–; mem. Faculty of English, Univ. of Oxford 1993–; mem. Exec. Cttee, European Fed. of Nat. Insts for Language 2003– (mem. Steering Cttee 2002–03), Advisory Bd Opera del Vocabolario Italiano 2003–05; mem. Philological Soc., Holton and Wheatley Cricket Club. *Publications:* The Concise Oxford Dictionary of Proverbs (ed.) 1982, The Oxford English Dictionary (second edn, co-ed. with Edmund Weiner) 1989, (third edn, online) 2000–, The Oxford Dictionary of Modern Slang (co-ed. with John Ayto) 1992 (second edn 2008), The Oxford English Dictionary Additions Series (two vols, co-ed. with Edmund Weiner) 1993, Gen. Edn, Vol. Three 1997; contrib. to scholarly books and journals. *Honours:* Hon. DLitt (ANU). *Address:* Oxford English Dictionary, Oxford University Press, Great Clarendon Street, Oxford, OX2 6DF (office); Chestnut Lodge, 7 St Mary's Close, Wheatley, Oxford, OX33 1YP, England (home). *Telephone:* (1865) 353728 (office). *Fax:* (1865) 353811 (office). *E-mail:* john.simpson@oup.com (office). *Website:* www.oed.com (office).

SIMPSON, John Cody Fidler-, CBE, MA, FRGS; British broadcaster and writer; *World Affairs Editor, BBC*; b. 9 Aug. 1944, Cleveleys; s. of Roy Fidler-Simpson and Joyce Leila Vivien Cody; m. 1st Diane Petteys 1965 (divorced 1996); two d.; m. 2nd Adèle Krüger 1996; one s. *Education:* St Paul's School, London, Magdalene Coll. Cambridge. *Career:* joined BBC 1966, Foreign Corresp. in Dublin, Brussels, Johannesburg 1972–78, Diplomatic Corresp., BBC TV 1978–80, Political Ed. 1980–81, Diplomatic Ed. 1982–88, Foreign Affairs Ed. (now World Affairs Ed.) 1988–; Contributing Ed. The Spectator 1991–95; columnist, Sunday Telegraph 1995–; Chancellor Roehampton Univ. 2005–. *Publications:* The Best of Granta 1966, The Disappeared 1985, Behind Iranian Lines 1988, Despatches from the Barricades 1990, From the House of War 1991, The Darkness Crumbles 1992, In the Forests of the Night 1993, Lifting the Veil: Life in Revolutionary Iran 1995, The Oxford Book of Exile 1995, Strange Places, Questionable People (autobiog.) 1998, A Mad World, My Masters 2000, News from No Man's Land: Reporting the World 2002, Days from a Different World: A Memoir of Childhood (autobiog.) 2005, Twenty Tales from the War Zone 2007, Not Quite World's End 2007, Unreliable Sources: How the 20th Century was Reported 2010. *Honours:* Hon. Fellow, Magdalene Coll., Cambridge 2000; Hon. DLitt (De Montfort) 1995, (Univ. of E Anglia) 1998; Dr hc (Nottingham) 2000; Golden Nymph Award Cannes 1979, BAFTA Reporter of the Year 1991, 2001, Royal TV Soc. Dimbleby Award 1991, Peabody Award 1998, Emmy Award (for coverage of the fall of Kabul) 2002, Bayeux War Correspondents' Prize 2002, Int. Emmy Award, New York 2002. *Address:* c/o BBC World Affairs Unit, Television Centre, Wood Lane, London, W12 7RJ, England. *Telephone:* (20) 8743-8000. *Fax:* (20) 8743-7591.

SIMPSON, Leo James Pascal; Canadian writer; b. 24 Sept. 1934, Limerick, Ireland; m. Jacqueline Anne Murphy 1964; one d. *Career:* writer-in-residence, Univ. of Ottawa 1973, Univ. of Western Ontario 1978. *Publications:* Arkwright 1971, Peacock Papers 1973, The Lady and the Travelling Salesman 1976, Kowalski's Last Chance 1980, Sailor Man 1996. *Address:* Moodie Cottage, 114 Bridge Street W, Belleville, ON K8P 1J7, Canada (home). *Telephone:* (613) 962-1737 (home).

SIMPSON, Louis Aston Marantz, PhD CD; American writer and academic; *Distinguished Professor Emeritus, State University of New York at Stony Brook*; b. 27 March 1923, Kingston, Jamaica, West Indies; s. of Aston Simpson and Rosalind (Marantz) Simpson; m. 1st Jeanne Rogers 1949 (divorced 1954); one s.; m. 2nd Dorothy Roochvarg 1955 (divorced 1979); one s. one d.; m. 3rd Miriam Bachner (née Butensky) 1985 (divorced 1998). *Education:* Munro Coll., Jamaica, Columbia Univ., New York. *Career:* Assoc. Ed. Bobbs-Merrill Publishing Co., New York 1950–55; Instructor, Asst Prof. Columbia Univ. 1955–59; Prof., Univ. of Calif. at Berkeley 1959–67; Prof. State Univ. of New York at Stony Brook 1967–91, Distinguished Prof. 1991–93, Prof. Emer. 1993–. *Publications:* poetry: The Arrivistes: Poems 1940–49 1949, Good News of Death and Other Poems 1955, The New Poets of England and America (ed.) 1957, A Dream of Governors 1959, At the End of the Open Road 1963, Selected Poems 1965, Adventures of the Letter I 1971, Searching for the Ox 1976, Armidale 1979, Out of Season 1979, Caviare at the Funeral 1980, People Live Here: Selected Poems 1949–83; The Best Hour of the Night 1983; Collected Poems 1988, Wei Wei and Other Poems 1990, In the Room We Share 1990, There You Are 1995, Nombres et poussière 1996, Modern Poets of France (trans.) 1997, Kaviar pä begravningen 1998, The Owner of the House – New Collected Poems 1940–2001 2003; prose: James Hogg: A Critical Study 1962, Riverside Drive 1962, An Introduction to Poetry (ed.) 1967, North of Jamaica 1971, Three on the Tower: The Lives and Works of Ezra Pound, T. S. Eliot and William Carlos Williams 1975, A Revolution in Taste 1978, A Company of Poets 1981, The Character of the Poet 1986, Selected Prose 1989, Ships Going Into the Blue 1994, The King My Father's Wreck 1995, François Villon – The Legacy and the Testament (trans.) 2000. *Honours:* Hon. DHL (Eastern Mich. Univ.) 1977; Hon. DL (Hampden-Sydney Coll.) 1991; Prix de Rome American Acad. of Rome 1957, Hudson Review Fellowship 1957, Edna St Vincent Millay Award 1960, Guggenheim Fellowships 1962, 1970, ACLS Grant 1963, Pulitzer Prize for Poetry 1964, Columbia Univ. Medal for Excellence 1965, Commonwealth Club of Calif. Poetry Award 1965, American Acad. of Arts and Letters Award 1976, Inst. of Jamaica Centenary Medal 1980, Jewish Book Council Award for Poetry 1981, Elmer Holmes Bobst Award for Poetry 1987, Harold Morton Landon Award for Translation 1997. *Address:* c/o English Department, Stony Brook University, Humanities Bldg., Stony Brook, NY; PO Box 119, Setauket, NY 11733, USA.

SINCLAIR, Andrew Annandale, BA, PhD, FRSL, FRSA; British writer, historian and film director; b. 21 Jan. 1935, Oxford; m. Sonia Melchett 1984; two s. *Education:* Trinity Coll., Cambridge, Harkness Fellow, Harvard Univ., ACLS Fellow, Stanford Univ. *Career:* Founding Fellow, Churchill Coll. 1961–63; Lecturer, Univ. Coll. London 1966–68; Publisher, Lorrimer Publishing 1968–89; Managing Dir, Timon Films Ltd 1968–2011; Fellow Soc. of American Historians 1970. *Films:* Under Milk Wood 1971, Dylan on Dylan 2004. *Publications:* The Breaking of Bumbo 1959, My Friend Judas 1959, Prohibition: The Era of Excess 1961, Gog 1967, Magog 1972, Jack: A Biography of Jack London 1977, The Other Victoria 1981, King Ludd 1988, War Like a Wasp 1989, The War Decade: An Anthology of the 1940s 1989, The Need to Give 1990, The Far Corners of the Earth 1991, The Naked Savage 1991, The Strength of the Hills 1991, The Sword and the Grail 1992, Francis Bacon: His Life and Violent Times 1993, In Love and Anger 1994, Jerusalem: The Endless Crusade 1995, Arts and Cultures: The History of the 50 Years of the Arts Council of Great Britain 1995, The Discovery of the Grail 1998, Death by Fame: A Life of Elisabeth, Empress of Austria 1998, Guevara 1998, Dylan the Bard: A Life of Dylan Thomas 1999, The Secret Scroll 2001, Blood and Kin 2002, An Anatomy of Terror 2003, Rosslyn 2005, Viva Che! 2005, The Grail: The Quest for a Legend 2007; contrib. to Sunday Times, Times, New York Times, Atlantic Monthly. *Honours:* Somerset Maugham Prize 1967, Venice Film Festival Award 1971. *Address:* Flat 20, Millennium House, 132 Grosvenor Road, London, SW1V 3JY, England. *Telephone:* (20) 7976-5454 (home). *Fax:* (20) 7976-6141 (home). *Website:* andrewsinclairtemplar.com (office).

SINCLAIR, Iain MacGregor, BA; British poet and writer; b. 11 June 1943, Cardiff, Wales; m. Anna Hadman 1967; one s. two d. *Education:* Cheltenham Coll., London Coll. of Film Technique, Trinity Coll., Dublin, Courtauld Inst., London. *Publications:* poetry: Back Garden Poems 1970, Muscat's Würm 1972, The Birth Rug 1973, Lud Heat 1975, Brown Clouds 1977, Suicide Bridge 1979, Fluxions 1983, Fresh Eggs and Scalp Metal 1983, Autistic Poses 1985, Significant Wreckage 1988, Selected Poems 1970–87 1989, Jack Elam's Other Eye 1992; fiction: White Chappell, Scarlet Tracings 1987, Downriver (Encore Award, James Tait Black Memorial Award 1992) 1991, Radon Daughters 1994, The Ebbing of the Kraft 1997, Slow Chocolate Autopsy 1997, Landor's Tower 2001, Dining on Stones or, The Middle Ground 2004; non-fiction: Lights

Out for the Territory 1997, Liquid City 1998, Rodinsky's Room (with Rachel Lichtenstein) 1999, London Orbital: A Walk Around the M25 2002, Edge of the Orison: In the traces of John Clare's 'Journey Out of Essex' 2005, London: City of Disappearances (ed.) 2006, Hackney, That Red Rose Empire 2009. *Address:* 28 Albion Drive, London, E8 4ET, England.

SINCLAIR, Olga Ellen, (Ellen Clare, Olga Daniels), JP; British writer; b. 23 Jan. 1923, Norfolk; m. Stanley George Sinclair 1945; three s. *Education:* The Convent, Swaffham, Norfolk. *Career:* mem. Soc. of Authors, Romantic Novelists' Asscn, Soc. of Women Journalists, Norwich Writer's Circle (also Pres.). *Publications:* Gypsies 1967, Hearts By the Tower 1968, Man of the River 1968, Bitter Sweet Summer 1970, Dancing in Britain 1970, Children's Games 1972, Toys 1974, My Dear Fugitive 1976, Never Fall in Love 1977, Master of Melthorpe 1979, Gypsy Girl 1981, Ripening Vine 1981, Lord of Leet Castle 1984, The Gretna Bride 1985, The Bride From Faraway 1987, When Wherries Sailed By 1987, The Untamed Bride 1988, Gretna Green: A Romantic History 1989, Potter Heigham: The Heart of Broadland 1989, The Arrogant Cavalier 1991, Wild Dreams 1991, A Royal Engagement 1999, An Heir for Ashingby 2004, The Countess and the Miner 2005. *Address:* 'Sycamore', 10 Norwich Road, Lingwood, Norfolk NR13 4BH, England (home). *Telephone:* (1603) 714558 (home). *E-mail:* olga.sinclair21@btinternet .com (home).

SINCLAIR, Sonia Elizabeth, (Sonia Graham, Sonia Melchett); British writer; b. 6 Sept. 1928, Nainital, India; m. 1st Julian Mond (Lord Melchett) (died 1973); one s. two d.; m. 2nd Andrew Sinclair 1984. *Education:* Queen's Secretarial College, Windsor, England. *Career:* mem. Bd of Dirs English Stage Company; fmr magistrate; fmr mem. Bd of Dirs Royal Nat. Theatre, Royal Soc. for the Prevention of Cruelty to Children. *Publications:* as Sonia Graham: Tell Me Honestly (non-fiction) 1964; as Sonia Melchett: Someone is Missing (non-fiction) 1987, Passionate Quests – Five Contemporary Women Travellers 1989, Sons and Mothers 1996; contrib. to periodicals. *Honours:* Prizewinner, Short Story Competition, Raconteur Magazine. *Address:* Flat 20, Millennium House, 132 Grosvenor Road, London SW1V 3JY, England (home).

SINDEN, Sir Donald Alfred, Kt, CBE, DLitt, DArts, FRSA; British actor and author; b. 9 Oct. 1923, Plymouth; s. of Alfred E. Sinden and Mabel A. Sinden (née Fuller); m. Diana Mahony 1948 (died 2004); two s. *Career:* entered theatrical profession with Charles F. Smith's Co., Mobile Entertainments Southern Area 1942; with Leicester Repertory Co. 1945; with Memorial Theatre Co., Stratford-upon-Avon 1946–47; with Old Vic and Bristol Old Vic 1948–50; film actor 1952–60; Chair. British Theatre Museum Asscn 1971–77, Theatre Museum Advisory Council 1973–80; Pres. Fed. of Playgoers Socs 1968–93, Royal Theatrical Fund 1983–; Vice-Pres. London Appreciation Soc. 1960–; Assoc. Artist, RSC 1967–; mem. Council, British Actors Equity Asscn 1966–77 (Trustee 1988–2004), Council, RSA 1972, Advisory Council, V&A Museum 1973–80, Arts Council Drama Panel 1973–77, Leicestershire Educ. Arts Cttee 1974–2004, BBC Archives Advisory Cttee 1975–78, Council, London Acad. of Music and Dramatic Art 1976–, Kent and E Sussex Regional Cttee, Nat. Trust 1978–82, Arts Council 1982–86. *Stage appearances include:* The Heiress 1949–50, Red Letter Day 1951, Odd Man In 1957, Peter Pan 1960, Guilty Party 1961, as Richard Plantagenet in Henry VI (The Wars of the Roses), as Price in Eh!, etc. (RSC) 1963–64, British Council tour of S. America in Dear Liar and Happy Days 1965, There's a Girl in My Soup 1966, as Lord Foppington in The Relapse (RSC) 1967, Not Now Darling 1968, as Malvolio, Henry VIII 1969, as Sir Harcourt Courtly in London Assurance 1972 RSC, (toured USA 1974), In Praise of Love 1973, as Stockmann in An Enemy of the People 1975, Habeas Corpus (USA) 1975, as Benedick in Much Ado About Nothing, King Lear (RSC) 1976–77, Shut Your Eyes and Think of England 1977, Othello (RSC) 1979–80, Present Laughter 1981, Uncle Vanya 1982, The School for Scandal 1983 (European tour 1984), Ariadne auf Naxos (ENO) 1983, Two into One 1984, The Scarlet Pimpernel 1985, Major Barbara 1988, Over My Dead Body 1989, Oscar Wilde 1990, Out of Order 1990 (Australian tour 1992), Venus Observed 1991, She Stoops to Conquer 1993, Hamlet 1994, That Good Night 1996, Quartet 1999, The Hollow Crown (tour to Australia and NZ 2002–03, Canada 2004); Dir The Importance of Being Earnest 1987. *Films:* appeared in 23 films including The Cruel Sea, Doctor in the House 1952–60. *Radio includes:* Doctor Gideon Fell (series). *Television series include:* Our Man from St Marks, Two's Company, Discovering English Churches, Never the Twain, Judge John Deed. *Publications:* A Touch of the Memoirs 1982, Laughter in the Second Act 1985, The Everyman Book of Theatrical Anecdotes (ed.) 1987, The English Country Church 1988, Famous Last Words (ed.) 1994. *Honours:* Drama Desk Award (for London Assurance) 1974, Variety Club of GB Stage Actor of 1976 (for King Lear), Evening Standard Drama Award Best Actor (for King Lear) 1977. *Address:* Rats Castle, Tenterden, TN30 7HX, England (office).

SINGER, Alan, BA, PhD; American writer and academic; *Professor of English, Temple University*; b. 18 Oct. 1948, Atlantic City, NJ; m. Nora Pomerantz 1985; two d. *Education:* Univ. of California, Los Angeles, Univ. of Washington. *Career:* Prof. of English and Dir of Grad. Creative Writing Program, Temple Univ., Philadelphia 1980–. *Publications:* The Ox-Breadth (fiction) 1978, A Metaphorics of Fiction (criticism) 1983, The Charnel Imp (fiction) 1984, The Subject as Action (criticism) 1994, Memory Wax (fiction) 1996, Aesthetic Reason (criticism) 2003, Dirtmouth (fiction) 2004, The Self-Deceiving Muse (criticism/philosophy) 2010, The Inquisitor's Tongue (fiction) 2012. *Honours:* grants, Pennsylvania Arts Council. *Address:* 10th Floor, Anderson Hall, English Department, Temple University, Philadelphia, PA 19119 (office); 117 Carpenter Lane, Philadelphia, PA 19119, USA (home). *Telephone:* (215) 870-8704 (office). *E-mail:* asinger@temple.edu (office); alansinger00@comcast.net (home).

SINGER, June Flaum; American writer; b. 17 Jan. 1932, Jersey City, NJ; m. Joseph Singer 1950; one s. three d. *Education:* Ohio State University, Columbus. *Career:* mem. Southern California Society of Women Writers; PEN West; Authors' Guild. *Publications:* The Bluffer's Guide to Interior Decorating, 1972; The Bluffer's Guide to Antiques (US ed.), 1972; The Debutantes, 1981; Star Dreams, 1982; The Movie Set, 1984; The Markoff Women, 1986; The President's Women, 1988; Sex in the Afternoon, 1990; Till the End of Time, 1991; Brilliant Divorces, 1992. *Address:* 12304 Santa Monica Blvd, Los Angeles, CA 90025-2551, USA. *E-mail:* junesinger@aol.com.

SINGER, Marilyn, BA, MA; American children's writer and poet; b. 3 Oct. 1948, New York, NY; m. Steven Aronson 1971. *Education:* Queens College, CUNY, New York University. *Career:* mem. Authors' Guild, PEN American Centre, Society of Children's Book Writers and Illustrators. *Publications:* over 80 books for children, including It Can't Hurt Forever 1978, Lizzie Silver of Sherwood Forest 1986, Tarantulas on the Brain 1982, The Lightey Club 1987, Ghost Host 1987, Mitzi Meyer, Fearless Warrior Queen 1987, Twenty Ways to Love Your Best Friend 1990, Charmed 1990, California Demon 1992, Big Wheel 1993, A Wasp is not a Bee 1995, Deal with a Ghost 1997, Prairie Dogs Kiss and Lobsters Wave 1998, Good Day, Good Night 1998, Stay True 1998, Josie to the Rescue 1999, The Circus Lunicus 2000, Face Relations 2004, Make Me Over 2005; poetry: The Morgans Dream 1995, All We Needed to Say 1996, Monster Museum 2001, Footprints on the Roof 2002, The Company of Crows 2002, Fireflies at Midnight 2003, How to Cross a Pond 2003, Creature Carnival 2004, Central Heating 2005, Monday on the Mississippi 2005; contributions: periodicals. *E-mail:* writerbabe@aol.com (office). *Website:* www .marilynsinger.net.

SINGER, Nicky Margaret; British novelist; b. 22 July 1956, Chalfont-St-Peter, Bucks., England; m. James King-Smith; two s. one d. *Education:* Univ. of Bristol. *Career:* Assoc. Dir of Talks, Inst. of Contemporary Arts 1981–83; Programme Consultant, Enigma Television 1984–85; Co-founder, Co-dir Performing Arts Labs 1987–96; Chair. Brighton Festival Literature Cttee 1988–93; mem. ACE Literary Magazines Group 1993–96; mem. Bd Printer's Devil 1993–97, South East Arts 2000–02; presenter, Labours of Eve (BBC 2) 1994–95. *Television:* Feather Boy (BBC TV adaptation) (BAFTA Children's Award for Best Drama 2004). *Play:* Feather Boy (stage musical adaptation), Nat. Theatre 2006. *Opera:* premiere of Knight Crew the opera (libretto, Nicky Singer, music, Julian Philips) at Glyndebourne 2010. *Publications:* fiction: To Still the Child 1992, To Have and To Hold 1993, What She Wanted 1996, My Mother's Daughter 1998; children's fiction: Feather Boy (Blue Peter Book of the Year) 2002, Doll 2003, The Innocent's Story 2005, GemX 2006, Knight Crew 2009; non-fiction: The Tiny Book of Time 1999, The Little Book of the Millennium 1999; contrib. to Printer's Devil, Guardian, Scotsman, Woman's Journal. *Literary Agent:* c/o Clare Conville, Conville and Walsh Ltd, 2 Ganton Street, London, W1F 7QL, England. *Telephone:* (20) 7287-3030. *Fax:* (20) 7287-4545. *E-mail:* info@convilleandwalsh.com. *Website:* www .convilleandwalsh.com; nickysinger.com.

SINGER, Peter Albert David, BPhil, MA; Australian philosopher, academic and writer; *DeCamp Professor of Bioethics, Princeton University*; b. 6 July 1946, Melbourne, Vic.; s. of Ernest Singer and Cora Oppenheim; m. Renata Diamond 1968; three d. *Education:* Scotch Coll., Univ. of Melbourne and Univ. Coll., Oxford. *Career:* Radcliffe Lecturer, Univ. Coll., Oxford 1971–73; Visiting Asst Prof., Dept of Philosophy, New York Univ. 1973–74; Sr Lecturer, Dept of Philosophy, La Trobe Univ., Bundoora, Vic., Australia 1974–76; Prof., Dept of Philosophy, Monash Univ., Clayton, Vic. 1977–99, Dir Centre for Human Bioethics 1981–91, Deputy Dir 1992–99; DeCamp Prof. of Bioethics, Princeton Univ., NJ, USA 1999–; Laureate Prof., Centre for Applied Philosophy and Public Ethics, Univ. of Melbourne 2005–; Prof., New Coll. of the Humanities, London 2011–; various visiting positions in USA, Canada and Italy. *Publications:* Democracy and Disobedience 1973, Animal Rights and Human Obligations (ed. with Thomas Regan) 1975, Animal Liberation: A New Ethics for Our Treatment of Animals 1975, Practical Ethics 1979, Marx 1980, The Expanding Circle: Ethics and Sociobiology 1981, Test-Tube Babies (ed. with William Walters) 1982, Hegel 1983, The Reproduction Revolution: New Ways of Making Babies (with Deane Wells, aka Making Babies: The New Science and Ethics of Conception) 1984, In Defence of Animals (ed.) 1985, Should the Baby Live?: The Problem of Handicapped Infants (with Helga Kuhse) 1985, Applied Ethics (ed.) 1986, Animal Liberation: A Graphic Guide (with Lori Gruen) 1987, Animal Factories (with Jim Mason) 1990, Embryo Experimentation (ed.) 1990, Companion to Ethics (ed.) 1991, How Are We to Live? 1993, The Great Ape Project: Equality Beyond Humanity (ed. with Paola Cavalieri) 1993, Rethinking Life and Death 1994, Ethics (ed.) 1994, The Greens 1996, Ethics into Action 1998, A Companion to Bioethics (with Helga Kuhse) 1998, A Darwinian Left 1999, Writings on an Ethical Life 2000, One World 2002, Pushing Time Away: My Grandfather and the Tragedy of Jewish Vienna 2003, The President of Good and Evil: Taking George W. Bush Seriously 2004, The Moral of the Story (co-ed.) 2005, Eating: What We Eat and Why it Matters (with Jim Mason) 2006, The Life You Can Save 2009. *Address:* University Center for Human Values, 5 Ivy Lane, Princeton, NJ, 08544-1013, USA (office). *Telephone:* (609) 258-2202 (office). *Fax:* (609) 258-1285 (office). *Website:* www.princeton.edu/~psinger (office); www.thelifeyoucansave.com.

SINGER, Sarah Beth, BA; American poet and writer; b. 4 July 1915, New York, NY; m. Leon E. Singer 1938; one s. one d. *Education:* New York Univ., New School for Social Research, New York. *Career:* teacher, poetry seminars and workshops 1968–74, 1981–83; Consulting Ed., Poet Lore 1976–81; mem. National League of American Penwomen, Poetry Society of America (vice-pres. 1974–78). *Publications:* After the Beginning 1975, Of Love and Shoes 1987, The Gathering 1992, Filtered Images (anthology) 1992; contributions: anthologies, newspapers and journals. *Honours:* Stephen Vincent Benét Narrative Poetry Awards 1968, 1971, five Poetry Society of America Awards 1972–76, National League of American Penwomen Awards 1976–92, Washington Poets Asscn Award 1989, Haiku Award, Brussels Sprouts 1992. *Address:* 900 University Street, Apt 6N, Seattle, WA 98101-2728, USA (home). *E-mail:* sarahsing2@aol.com (home).

SINGH, Amritjit, BA, MA, AM, PhD; American (b. Indian) writer, translator, editor and academic; *Langston Hughes Professor of English, Ohio University*; b. 20 Oct. 1945, Rawalpindi, British India; s. of Prof. Kesar Singh Uberoi and Balbir Kaur Uberoi; m. Premjit Singh (née Prem Lata Seth) 1968, one s. one d. *Education:* Panjab Univ., Kurukshetra Univ., New York Univ. *Career:* Asst Prof., Assoc. Prof., then Prof. of English, Univ. of Delhi 1965–68, CUNY 1970–71, 1973–74, New York Univ. 1972–73, 1985–86, American Studies Research Centre, Hyderabad 1974–77, Univ. of Hyderabad 1977–78, Univ. of Rajasthan 1978–83, Hofstra Univ. 1984–86, Rhode Island Coll. 1986–2006; Langston Hughes Prof. of English, Ohio Univ. 2006–; Sr Fulbright Prof., JFK Inst., Free Univ., Berlin 2002; mem. Modern Language Asscn (fmr mem. several Div. Cttees), MELUS (Pres. 1994–97), South Asian Literary Asscn (Pres. 2000–03), USACLALS (Pres. 2000–05); Mary Tucker Thorp Professorship in Arts and Sciences, Rhode Island Coll. 1991–92; Visiting Prof., Wesleyan Univ. 1984–85, New York Univ. 1985–86, Coll. of the Holy Cross 1993, Univ. of California, Berkeley 1994, Univ. of Calgary 1995; Visiting Fellow, W.E.B. Du Bois Inst., Harvard Univ. 1991–92; Fulbright Sr Specialist, Univ. of Graz, Austria 2007, Univ. of Alexandria, Egypt 2010; invited public speaker at numerous univs in Germany, Switzerland, France, Austria, Japan, India and USA. *Publications:* The Novels of the Harlem Renaissance 1976, Afro-American Poetry and Drama, 1760-1975: An Information Guide 1979, Indian Literature in English, 1827-1979: An Information Guide 1981, India: An Anthology of Contemporary Writing 1983, The Magic Circle of Henry James 1989, The Harlem Renaissance: Revaluations 1989, Memory, Narrative and Identity 1994, Conversations with Ralph Ellison 1995, Conversations with Ishmael Reed 1995, American Studies Today: Methods and Perspectives 1995, Memory and Cultural Politics 1996, Postcolonial Theory and the United States 2000, The Collected Writings of Wallace Thurman: A Harlem Renaissance Reader 2003, Interviews with Edward W. Said 2004, The Circle of Illusion, Punjabi poems by Gurcharan Rampuri (translated with Judy Ray) 2011; contribs include numerous essays and reviews in American Literature, South Asian & Postcolonial Literature, African American Studies; own poems and translations from Punjabi poetry and fiction published in Edinburgh Review, Nimrod, Chelsea, New Letters, South Asian Review, Kavya Bharati, Re-Markings, South Asian Ensemble, Toronto Review, Muse India, etc. *Honours:* Fulbright Fellowship for Grad. Study, New York Univ. 1968–69, Ford Foundation Dissertation Fellowship, New York Univ. 1972–73, American Council of Learned Socs Fellowship, Yale Univ. 1983–84, Nat. Endowment for the Humanities Fellowship, Du Bois Inst., Harvard Univ. 1991–92, Rockefeller Foundation Residency Fellowship at Bellagio Center, Italy 1994, Killam Scholar-in-Residence Fellowship, Univ. of Calgary 1995, Rhode Island Coll. Alumni Faculty Award 2003, MELUS Lifetime Achievement Award 2007, Paul Harris Service Award, Rotary Club of Athens 2009. *Address:* Department of English, Ohio University, Athens, OH 45701, USA (office). *Telephone:* (740) 593-2838 (office); (740) 593-2782 (office). *Fax:* (740) 593-2832 (office). *E-mail:* singha@ohio.edu (office). *Website:* www.english.ohiou.edu/directory/faculty_page/singha (office).

SINGH, Jaswant, BA, BSc; Indian politician and fmr army officer and writer; b. 3 Jan. 1938, Jasol, Rajasthan; s. of the late Thakur Sardar Singhji and Kunwar Baisa; m. Sheetal Kumari 1963; two s. *Education:* Mayo Coll., Ajmer, Jt Services Wing, Clement Town, Dehradun, Indian Mil. Acad., Dehradun. *Career:* commissioned Cen. India Horse 1957; resgnd his comm. and elected to Rajya Sabha 1980; Minister of Finance and Company Affairs 1996, 2002–04; Deputy Chair., Planning Comm. 1998–99; Minister of External Affairs 1999, 2001–02, of Electronics Feb.–Oct. 1999, of Surface Transport Aug.–Oct. 1999, of Defence 2000–01; Chair. Consultative Cttee for the Ministry of External Affairs 2000–01; Leader of the House, Rajya Sabha 1999–2004, Leader of the Opposition 2004; mem. Lok Sabha from Darjeeling 2009–. *Publications:* 18 books, including National Security: An Outline of Our Concerns 1996, Shauryo Tejo 1997, Defending India 1999, District Diary 2001, Khankhananama (Hindi) 2001, A Call to Honour: In Service of Emergent India 2006, Travels in Transoxiana 2006, Till Memory Serves 2007, Conflict & Diplomacy 2008, Our Republic – Post 6 December 1992 2008, Jinnah: India, Partition, Independence 2009; numerous articles on int. affairs, security and devt issues to Indian and foreign magazines, newspapers and journals. *Honours:* Outstanding Parliamentarian Award 2001. *Address:* Lok Sabha, Parliament House, New Delhi 110 001 (office). *E-mail:* jaswant@sansad.nic.in (office). *Website:* www.jaswantsingh-mp.com (office).

SINGH, Khushwant, LLB; Indian author; b. 2 Feb. 1915, s. of Sobha Singh and of Varyam Kaur; m. Kaval Malik; one s. one d. *Education:* Government Coll., Lahore, King's Coll. and Inner Temple, London, UK. *Career:* practised at High Court, Lahore 1939–47; joined Indian Ministry of External Affairs 1947; press attaché, Canada then Public Relations Officer, London 1948–51; Ministry of Information and Broadcasting; edited Yojana; Dept of Mass Communication, UNESCO 1954–56; commissioned by Rockefeller Foundation and Muslim Univ., Aligarh, to write a history of the Sikhs 1958; MP 1980–; Ed.-in-Chief The Hindustan Times, New Delhi 1980–83; Visiting Lecturer Hawaii, Oxford, Princeton, Rochester, Swarthmore; numerous TV and radio appearances; Ed. The Illustrated Weekly of India 1969–78. *Publications:* Mark of Vishnu 1949, The Sikhs 1951, Train to Pakistan 1954, Sacred Writings of the Sikhs 1960, I Shall Not Hear the Nightingale 1961, Umrao Jan Ada—Courtesan of Lucknow (trans.) 1961, History of the Sikhs (1769–1839) Vol. I 1962, Ranjit Singh: Maharaja of the Punjab 1962, Fall of the Sikh Kingdom 1962, The Skeleton (trans.) 1963, Land of the Five Rivers (trans.) 1964, History of the Sikhs (1839–Present Day) Vol. II 1965, Khushwant Singh's India 1969, Indira Gandhi Returns 1979, Editor's Page 1980, Iqbal's Dialogue with Allah (trans.) 1981, Punjab Tragedy (with Kuldip Nayar) 1984, Delhi 1990, Roots of Dissent 1992, Train to Pakistan 1998, and others. *Honours:* Grove Press Award, Mohan Singh Award, Padma Bhushan 1974, Honest Man of the Year Award, Sulabh Int. 2000, Punjab Rattan Award 2006, Padma Vibhushan 2007. *Address:* 49E Sujan Singh Park, New Delhi 110 003, India (home). *Telephone:* (11) 4620159.

SINGH, Simon Lehna, MBE, BSc, PhD; British writer, journalist and television producer; b. 19 Sept. 1964, Wellington, Somerset, England; m. Anita Anand Hari Singh. *Education:* Imperial Coll., Cambridge. *Theatre:* Theatre of Science (with Dr Richard Wiseman, Soho Theatre, London) 2005, Uncaged Monkeys (with Robin Ince, UK tour) 2011. *Radio:* Five Numbers (BBC Radio 4) 2001, The Serendipity of Science (BBC Radio 4) 2001, Another Five Numbers (BBC Radio 4) 2003. *Television:* Fermat's Last Theorem (BBC) 1996, The Science of Secrecy (Channel 4) 2000, Mind Games (BBC 4) 2003; dir and producer, Tomorrow's World (BBC 1). *Publications:* Fermat's Last Theorem 1997, The Code Book 1999, The Science of Secrecy 2000, Big Bang: the Most Important Scientific Discovery of All Time and Why You Need to Know About It 2004, Trick or Treatment? Alternative Medicine on Trial (with Edzard Ernst) 2008. *Honours:* BAFTA Award for Best Documentary 1997, Vega Award for science broadcasting 2001. *Literary Agent:* c/o Patrick Walsh, Conville and Walsh Ltd, 2 Ganton Street, London, W1F 7QL, England. *Telephone:* (20) 7287-3030. *Fax:* (20) 7287-4545. *E-mail:* patrick@convilleandwalsh.com. *Website:* www.convilleandwalsh.com. *E-mail:* simon@simonsingh.net (office). *Website:* www.simonsingh.com.

SINGH, Udaya Narayana, BA, MA, PhD; Indian poet, playwright, writer and academic; *Director, Central Institute of Indian Languages*; b. 1951. *Education:* Univ. of Delhi. *Career:* writer in Maithili and Bengali; Research Fellow in Linguistics, Univ. of Delhi 1974–79; Lecturer in Linguistics, Univ. of Baroda 1979–81; Reader in Linguistics, South Gujarat Univ. 1981–85; Reader in Theoretical Linguistics, Univ. of Delhi 1985–87; Prof. of Linguistics and Founder, Centre for Applied Linguistics and Trans. Studies 1987–2000; Dir, Central Inst. of Indian Languages, Mysore 2000–; mem. Linguistic Data Consortium for Indian Languages Project, Govt of India 2007–; Chief Ed. Indian Linguistics journal 1988–90; mem. Advisory Bd Sahitya Akademi 1995–98, Linguistic Soc. of India, Dravidian Linguistics Asscn, Indian Journal of Applied Linguistics & Language Forum, American Studies Research Centre, Hyderabad, Indian Asscn of Canadian Studies, Jijnasa Educational Foundation Calcutta, Indian Comparative Literature Asscn, Indian Asscn for Commonwealth Literature; Chief Investigator, Natural Language Processing: Teachers' Training Programme, Univ. of Hyderabad 1991–95; Gen. Ed. Longman-CIIL Dictionaries Project 2006–. *Plays include:* Naayakak naam jiivan 1971, Ek chal raajaa 1974, NaaTakak lel 1974, Pratyaavartan 1976, Anndolan 1977, Raamliilaa 1977, Janaj aa anya ekaankii 1978, Priyamvadaa 1988, No Entry: Maa Pravisha 2008. *Publications:* poetry collections: Kavayo Vadanti 1966, Amrtasya Putraah 1971, Anuttaran 1981, Ashru o Parihaas 1997, Anukriti 1999, Kham-kheyali 2003, Madhyampurush Ekvachan 2005, Second Person Singular 2006; non-fiction: Diglossia in Bangladesh and language planning 1983, A Bibliography of Bengali Linguistics 1987, India Writes: A Story of Multilingual and Pluricultural Society 2006; as trans.: Rabindranath Tagore's Raviindranaathak Baal-saahitya 1997, Contemporary Maithili Poems into Bengali 1998, Jayakanta Mishra's Maithili Sahityer Itihas 2003. *Address:* Central Institute of Indian Languages, Department of Higher Education, Language Bureau, Government of India, Manasagangothri, Hunsur Road, Mysore 570 006, India (office). *Telephone:* (821) 2345031 (office). *Fax:* (821) 2515032 (office). *E-mail:* udaya@ciil.stpmy.soft.net (office). *Website:* www.ciil.org (office).

SINGLETON, William Dean; American newspaper executive; *Vice-Chairman and CEO, MediaNews Group Inc.*; b. 1 Aug. 1951, Tex.; s. of the late William Hyde Singleton and of Florence E. Myrick Singleton; m. Adrienne Casale 1983; two s. one d. *Career:* Pres. Gloucester Co. Times, N J.; Vice-Chair. and CEO MediaNews Group, Inc. 1988–; Pres., Chair. The Houston Post 1988–95, The Denver Post; Vice-Chair. 27 daily newspapers and 55 non-daily publications including Houston Post, Denver Post, with daily circulation in excess of 1.1 million in 10 states. *Address:* MediaNews Group Inc., 101 W. Colfax Avenue, Suite 1100, Denver, CO 80202, USA (office). *Telephone:* (303) 563-6360 (office). *Fax:* (303) 954-6320 (office). *E-mail:* contact@medianewsgroup.com (office). *Website:* www.medianewsgroup.com (office).

SINHA, Indra; Indian/British writer; b. Bombay; m. Vickie Sinha; three c. *Education:* Univ. of Cambridge. *Career:* worked in advertising, positions included copywriter with Collett Dickenson Pearce; co-founder Bhopal Medical Appeal. *Publications:* The Cybergypsies (memoir) 1999, The Death of Mr Love (novel) 2002, Animal's People (novel) 2007; trans: Kama Sutra 1980, Tantra 1993. *Literary Agent:* Andrew Wylie, The Wylie Agency, 17 Bedford Square, London WC1B 3JA, England. *Telephone:* (20) 7908-5900. *Fax:* (20) 7908-5901. *E-mail:* mail@wylieagency.co.uk. *Website:* www.wylieagency.co.uk. *E-mail:* indra@indrasinha.com (office). *Website:* www.indrasinha.com.

SIPHERD, Ray, BA; American writer; b. 27 Aug. 1935, Uniontown, PA; m. Anne Marie Foran 1986. *Education:* Yale Univ. *Career:* mem. American Society of Composers, Authors and Publishers, Writers Guild of America. *Publications:* The Sesame Street Storybook 1971, The White Kite 1972, Ernie and Bert's Telephone Call 1978, The Count's Poem 1979, Down on the Farm with Grover 1980, Sherlock Hemlock and the Outer Space Creatures 1981, Big Bird's Animal Alphabet 1987, When is My Birthday? 1988, The Courtship of Peggy McCoy 1990, The Christmas Store 1993, Dance of the Scarecrows 1996, The Audubon Quartet 1998, The Devil's Hawk 2002. *Honours:* Emmy Awards 1969, 1974, 1985. *Address:* 44 Echo Valley Road, Newtown, CT 06470, USA (home).

SIROF, Harriet Toby, BA; American writer and teacher; b. 18 Oct. 1930, New York, NY; m. 1949, one s. one d. *Education:* New School for Social Research, New York. *Career:* mem. Authors' Guild, Society of Children's Book Writers. *Publications:* A New-Fashioned Love Story 1977, The IF Machine 1978, The Junior Encyclopedia of Israel 1980, Save the Dam! 1981, That Certain Smile 1981, The Real World 1985, Anything You Can Do 1986, Because She's My Friend 1993, The Road Back: Living With a Physical Disability 1993, Bring Back Yesterday 1996; contributions: Colorado Review, Descent, Inlet, Maine Review, North American Review, New Orleans Review, Sam Houston Review, San Jose Studies, Woman, Voices of Brooklyn. *Honours:* Junior Literary Guild Selection 1985. *Address:* 792 E 21st Street, Brooklyn, NY 11210-1042, USA (home). *Telephone:* (718) 859-3296 (home).

SISSAY, Lemn, MBE; British poet; b. 1967, Billinge, Manchester. *Career:* various television appearances and radio broadcasts; music collaborations with Leftfield, Izit; Writer-in-Residence, Contact (later Assoc. Artist), Southbank Centre, London 2007. *Recordings:* Blackwise 1988, Homeland (including two poems) 1988, The Flag 1996, Are You Listening 1992, Move On 1993, Earth Flower 1993, Advice For The Living 2000. *Publications:* Perceptions of the Pen 1985, Tender Fingers in a Clenched Fist 1988, Rebel Without Applause, The Fire People: a Collection of Contemporary Black British Poets (ed.) 1998, Morning Breaks in the Elevator 1999, The Emperor's Watchmaker 2000, The Listener 2008. *E-mail:* lemn@lemnsissay.com (office). *Website:* www.lemnsissay.com.

SISSON, Rosemary Anne, BA; British writer; b. 13 Oct. 1923, London. *Education:* Univ. Coll., London, Newnham Coll., Cambridge. *Career:* Jr Lecturer, Univ. of Wisconsin 1949–50; Lecturer, Univ. Coll., London 1950–53, Univ. of Birmingham 1953–54; Drama Critic, Stratford-upon-Avon Herald 1954–57; Trustee, Theatre of Comedy 1986–; mem. Dramatists Club (hon. sec.), Writers' Guild of Great Britain (Pres.), BAFTA. *Television:* The Six Wives of Henry VIII, Elizabeth R, Upstairs, Downstairs. *Publications:* The Exciseman 1972, The Killer of Horseman's Flats 1973, The Stratford Story 1975, Escape From the Dark 1976, The Queen and the Welshman 1979, The Manions of America 1981, Bury Love Deep 1985, Beneath the Visiting Moon 1986, The Bretts 1987, The Young Indiana Jones Chronicles 1993–95, Rosemary for Remembrance 1995, Footstep on the Stair 1997, First Love, Last Love 2002, We'll Meet Again 2003; contributions: newspapers and journals. *Honours:* Writers' Guild of Great Britain Laurel Award. *Literary Agent:* Andrew Mann Ltd, 1 Old Compton Street, London, W1S 5PH, England. *Telephone:* (20) 7734-4751. *Fax:* (20) 7287-9264. *E-mail:* manscript@compuserve.com.

SJÓN; Icelandic writer and poet; b. (Sigurjón Birgir Sigurðsson), 27 Aug. 1962; m.; two c. *Career:* Founding member of surrealist group Medúsa, Reykjavík; founder Children's Art Workshop, Gerðuberg Cultural Centre; helped set up Smekkleysa publishing house; collaborated with singer Björk on several compositions. *Compositions:* with Björk: Isobel, Bachelorette, Oceania, Wanderlust, I've Seen it All (from the film Dancer in the Dark). *Publications:* poetry: Sýnir 1978, Madonna 1979, Birgitta 1979, Hverning elskar maður hendur? 1981, Reiðhjól blinda mannsins 1982, Sjónhverfingabókin 1983, Oh, Isn't it Wild? 1985, Leikfangakastalar 1986, Drengurinn með röntgenaugun 1986, Ég man ekki eitthvað um skýin 1991, Night of the Lemon 1993, myrkar figúrur 1998, söngur steinasafnarans 2007, Ljóðasafn 2008; novels: Stálnótt 1987, Engill, pípuhattur og jarðarber 1989, Augu þín sáu mig (DV Newspaper Culture Prize 1995) 1994, Með titrandi tár (DV Newspaper Culture Prize 2002) 2001, Skugga-Baldur (trans. as The Blue Fox) (Nordic Council's Literature Prize 2005) 2003, Argóarflísin (trans. as The Whispering Muse) (Icelandic Bookseller's Prize for the Novel of the Year) 2005, Rökkurbýsnir (trans. as From the Mouth of the Whale) 2008. *Honours:* Icelandic Broadcasting Service Writers' Fund award 1998. *Address:* c/o Bjartur bókaforlag, Bræðraborgarstíg 9, Reykjavík, Iceland (office). *E-mail:* bjartur@bjartur.is (office). *Website:* bjartur.is (office); www.siberia.is/sjon.

SJÖWALL, Maj; Swedish writer and journalist; b. 1935, Malmö; m. Per Wahlöö 1962 (died 1975); two s. *Career:* Ed. at publishing house, Wahlström and Widstrand 1959–61. *Publications:* with Per Wahlöö: Roseanna 1965, Mannen Som Gick Upp i Rök (The Man Who Went up in Smoke) 1966, Mannen på Balkongen (The Man on the Balcony) 1967, Den Skrattande Polisen (The Laughing Policeman) 1968, Brandbilen Som Försvann (The Fire Engine that Disappeared) 1969, Polis, Polis, Potatismos (Murder at the Savoy) 1970, Den Vedervärdige Mannen Från Säffle (The Abominable Man) 1971, Det Slutna Rummet (The Locked Room) 1972, Polismördaren (Cop Killer) 1974, Terroristerna (The Terrorists) 1975, Kvinnan Som Liknade Greta Garbo (with Thomas Ross) 1990, Sista Resan Och Andra Berättelser 2007.

SKÁRMETA, Antonio, BA, MA; Chilean writer and diplomatist; b. 7 Nov. 1940, Antofagasta; m. Cecilia Boisier; two s. *Education:* Universidad de Chile, Columbia Univ., New York. *Career:* Prof. of Philosophy, Instituto Nacional 1966–68, Universidad de Chile 1968–75; escaped military dictatorship in Chile, lived in Argentina, Portugal, West Germany, Nicaragua; Distinguished Prof. of Literature and Romance Languages, Washington Univ. of St Louis, Missouri, USA 1988; Amb. to Germany 2000–03. *Radio:* Voy y Vuelo 2000. *Publications:* El entusiasmo 1967, Desnudo en el Tejado (Premio Casa de Las Americas) 1969, Tiro Libre 1973, Soné que la nieve ardía 1975, No Pasó Nada (Boccaccio Europa Prize 1986) 1980, La Insurrección 1982, Ardiente paciencia (made into film Il Postino) 1985, Match Ball 1989, La Composición (Jane Adams Prize 2001, Premio Las Américas 2001, Gustav-Heinemann Peace Prize 2004) 1998, La Boda del Poeta (Premio Altazor 2000, Grinzane Cavour Prize 2000, Prix Médicis 2001) 1999, La Chica del Trombón (Premio Elsa Morante 2002, Premio de Narrativa José María Arguedas 2003) 2001, El Baile de la Victoria (Premio Planeta 2003, Premio Municipal de Literatura de la ciudad de Santiago 2004) 2003; trans.: An American Dream, Norman Mailer 1968, The Pyramid, William Golding 1968, Typee, Herman Melville 1968, Visions of Gerard, Jack Kerouac 1969, Love, Roger, Charles Webb 1969, The Last Tycoon, F. Scott Fitzgerald 1969. *Honours:* Chevalier, Order des Arts et des Lettres (France) 1986, Commendatore dell'Ordine (Italy) 1996, Goethe Medal (Germany) 2002, Grand Cross of Merit (Germany) 2003; Fulbright Scholarship, Guggenheim Fellowship, Premio Excelencia, Universidad de Artes y Ciencias de la Comunicación 1998, Premio Neruda 2004. *E-mail:* cordillero@gmail.com (office). *Website:* www.antonio-skarmeta.com.

SKELLINGS, Edmund, BA, PhD; American academic and poet; b. 12 March 1932, Ludlow, Mass; m. Louise Skellings 1962; one d. *Education:* Univ. of Massachusetts, Univ. of Iowa. *Career:* Poet Laureate of Florida 1980–; Dir, Florida Center for Electronic Communication, Florida Atlantic Univ. *Publications:* Duels and Duets 1960, Heart Attacks 1976, Face Value 1977, Showing My Age 1978, Living Proof 1985, Collected Poems 1958–1998 1998, Personal Effects. *Honours:* Hon. DFA (International Fine Arts Coll.) 1995; Florida Governor's Award in the Arts 1979, Florida Arts Recognition Award 1997. *Address:* c/o Division of Cultural Affairs, R.A. Building, Third Floor, 500 South Bronough Street, Tallahassee, FL 32399-0250, USA (office). *Website:* www.florida-arts.org (office); www.edmundskellings.com.

SKESLIEN CHARLES, Janet; American novelist; b. 5 Aug. 1971, Shelby, Mont.; m. *Education:* Univ. of Montana, Univ. of Maryland. *Career:* taught English and creative writing in Paris for over 10 years; founded writing workshop Shakespeare & Company. *Publications:* Moonlight in Odessa (Melissa Nathan Award for Comedy Romance 2010) 2009. *Honours:* Soros Fellow, Odessa, Ukraine 1994–96. *Literary Agent:* Laura Longrigg, MBA Literary Agents Ltd., 62 Grafton Way, London, W1T 5DW, England. *Telephone:* (20) 7387-2076. *Fax:* (20) 7387-2042. *E-mail:* info@mbalit.co.uk. *Website:* www.mbalit.co.uk; www.jskesliencharles.com.

SKIBSRUD, Johanna, MA, PhD; Canadian/American writer and poet; b. 9 May 1980, New Glasgow, NS, Canada; d. of Olaf Skibsrud and Janet Shively; m. John Melillo. *Education:* Concordia Univ., Univ. of Montreal. *Publications:* poetry: Late Nights with Wild Cowboys in 2008, I Do Not Think That I Could Love a Human Being 2010; novel: The Sentimentalists (Scotiabank Giller Prize 2010, Ind. Booksellers' Choice Award, Atlantic Book Awards 2011) 2009; short fiction collection: This Will Be Difficult to Explain, and other stories 2011. *Address:* RR2, Scotsburn, NS B0K 1R0, Canada (office). *Telephone:* (520) 609-8917 (office). *E-mail:* jskibsrud@gmail.com (office). *Literary Agent:* c/o Tracy Bohan, The Wylie Agency, 17 Bedford Square, London, WC1B 3JA, England. *Telephone:* (20) 7908-5900. *Fax:* (20) 7908-5901. *E-mail:* tbohan@wylieagency.co.uk. *Website:* www.wylieagency.co.uk; johannaskibsrud.com.

SKINNER, Ainslie (see Gosling-Hare, Paula Louise)

SKINNER, Gloria Dale, (Charla Cameron, Amelia Grey); American writer; b. 4 Aug. 1951, Graceville, FL; m. Floyd D. Skinner; one s. one d. *Career:* mem. Romance Writers of America, Authors' Guild. *Publications:* Passion's Choice 1990, Georgia Fever 1992, Tender Trust 1993, Starlight 1994, Midnight Fire 1994, Bewitching 1995, Ransom 1996, Juliana 1997, Cassandra 1998, Hellion 1998; as Charla Cameron: Diamond Days 1991, Sultry Nights 1992, Glory Nights 1993; as Amelia Grey: Never a Bride 2001, A Dash of Scandal 2002, A Little Mischief 2003, A Hint of Seduction 2004, A Taste of Temptation 2005, A Duke to Die For 2009, A Marquis to Marry 2009, An Earl to Enchant 2010, Fall in Love like a Romance Writer 2011, A Gentleman Never Tells 2011. *Honours:* Romantic Times Love and Laughter Award, Georgia Romance Writers of America Maggie Award, Booksellers Best Award, Aspen Gold Award. *Address:* 2023 Thomas Drive, Panama City, FL 32408 (office); 1802 Weakfish Way, Panama City Beach, FL 32408, USA (home). *Telephone:* (850) 235-1569 (office); (850) 235-7820 (home). *Fax:* (850) 233-9815 (office). *E-mail:* gloriaskinner@comcast.net (home). *Website:* www.ameliagrey.com.

SKINNER, Quentin Robert Duthie, MA, FBA; British historian and academic; *Barber Beaumont Professor of the Humanities, Queen Mary, University of London*; b. 26 Nov. 1940, Oldham, Lancs., England; s. of Alexander Skinner and Winifred Skinner (née Duthie); m. 2nd Susan James 1979; one s. one d. *Education:* Bedford School, Gonville and Caius Coll., Cambridge. *Career:* Fellow, Christ's Coll., Cambridge 1962–2008, Vice-Master 1997–99, Hon. Fellow 2008–; Lecturer in History, Univ. of Cambridge 1967–78, Prof. of Political Science 1978–96, Regius Prof. of Modern History 1996–2008, Pro-Vice-Chancellor 1999; Barber Beaumont Prof. of the Humanities, Queen Mary, Univ. of London 2008–; mem. Inst. of Advanced Study, Princeton, NJ 1974–75, 1976–79; mem. Academia Europaea 1989; Foreign mem. American Acad. of Arts and Sciences 1986, American Philosophical Soc. 1997, Royal Irish Acad. 1999, Accad. Nazionale dei Lincei 2007, Österreichische Akad. der Wissenschaften 2009. *Publications:* The Foundations of Modern Political Thought, Vol. I The Renaissance 1978, Vol. II The Age of Reformation 1978, Machiavelli 1981, Philosophy in History (co-ed. and contrib.) 1984, The Return of Grand Theory in the Human Sciences (ed. and contrib.) 1985, The Cambridge History of Renaissance Philosophy (co-ed. and contrib.) 1988, Machiavelli: The Prince (ed. and introduction) 1988, Meaning and Context: Quentin Skinner and His Critics (ed. James Tully) 1988, Machiavelli and Republicanism (co-ed. and contrib.) 1990, Political Discourse in Early-modern Britain (co-ed. and contrib.) 1993, Milton and Republicanism (co-ed.) 1995, Reason and Rhetoric in the Philosophy of Hobbes 1996, Liberty before Liberalism 1998, Visions of Politics, Vol. I Regarding Method 2002, Vol. II Renaissance Virtues 2002, Vol. III Hobbes and Civil Science 2002, Republicanism: A Shared European Heritage (co-ed. and contrib.) Vol. I Republicanism and Constitutionalism in Early Modern Europe 2002, Vol. II The Values of Republicanism in Early Modern Europe 2002, States and Citizens (co-ed. and contrib.) 2003, Thomas Hobbes: Writings on Common Law and Hereditary Right (co-ed.) 2005, Hobbes and Republican Liberty 2008, Sovereignty in Fragments (co-ed. and contrib.) 2010. *Honours:* Hon. DLitt (Chicago) 1992, (E Anglia) 1992, (Helsinki) 1997, (Oxford) 2000, (Leuven) 2004, (St Andrews) 2005, (Harvard) 2005, (Athens) 2007, (Aberdeen) 2007, (Santiago) 2009; Hon. LittD (Oslo) 2011; Wolfson Literary Award 1979, Balzan Prize 2006, Sir Isaiah Berlin Prize 2006. *Address:* Department of History, Queen Mary, University of London, Mile End Road, London, E1 4NS, England (office). *Telephone:* (20) 7882-8325 (office). *Fax:* (20) 8980-8400 (office). *E-mail:* q.skinner@qmul.ac.uk (office). *Website:* www.history.qmul.ac.uk (office).

SKLOOT, Rebecca, BS, MFA; American writer; d. of Floyd Skloot. *Education:* Colorado State Univ., Univ. of Pittsburgh. *Career:* science writer; fmr corresp., Radiolab (WNYC), ScienceNow (PBS); Assoc. Ed., Popular Science magazine 2002–03, Contributing Ed. 2003–; Writing Instructor, Univ. of Pittsburgh 1997–2006; Adjunct Asst Prof. of Science Journalism, New York Univ. 2006–07; Asst Prof. of Creative Non-Fiction Writing, Univ. of Memphis 2007–; Vice-Pres., Nat. Book Critics Circle 2003–08. *Publications:* The Immortal Life of Henrietta Lacks (Wellcome Trust Book Prize) 2010; guest ed.: The Best American Science Writing 2011; contribs to New York Times Magazine, O, Oprah Magazine, Discover, Huffington Post. *Address:* c/o Random House, Publicity Department, 1745 Broadway, New York, NY 10019, USA (office). *E-mail:* cgreenhalgh@randomhouse.com (office); rebecca@rebeccaskloot.com (office). *Website:* rebeccaskloot.com (home).

SKOCPOL, Theda, BA, MA, PhD; American academic and writer; b. 4 May 1947, Detroit, MI; m. William John Skocpol 1967, one s. *Education:* Michigan State University, Harvard University. *Career:* Asst Prof. 1975–78, Assoc. Prof. 1978–81, Prof. of Sociology 1986–94, Prof. of Govt and Sociology 1995 97, Victor S. Thomas Prof. of Government and Sociology 1998, Dir of the Center for American Political Studies 2000–, Harvard University; Mem., Institute for Advanced Study, Princeton, NJ 1980–81; Assoc. Prof. 1981–84, Prof. of Sociology and Political Science 1984–86, Dir Center for the Study of Industrial Socs 1982–85, University of Chicago; Senior Visiting Scholar, Russell Sage Foundation 1983–84; mem. American Acad. of Arts and Sciences, fellow; American Political Science Asscn, pres. 2002–03; American Sociological Asscn; National Acad. of Social Insurance; Social Science History Asscn, pres. 1996. *Publications:* States and Social Revolutions: A Comparative Analysis of France, Russia, and China 1979, Protecting Soldiers and Mothers: The Political Origins of Social Policy in the United States 1992, Social Revolutions in the Modern World 1994, Social Policy in the United States: Future Possibilities in Historical Perspective 1995, State and Party in America's New Deal 1995, Boomerang: Clinton's Health Security Effort and the Turn Against Government in US Politics 1996, Historical, and Theoretical Perspectives (with John L. Campbell) 1994, States, Social Knowledge, and the Origins of Modern Social Policies (with Dietrich Rueschemeyer) 1996, The New Majority: Toward a Popular Progressive Politics (with Stanley B. Greenberg) 1997, Democracy, Revolution, and History 1998, Civic Engagement in American Democracy (with Morris Fiorina) 1999, The Missing Middle: Working Families and the Future of American Social Policy 2000, Diminished Democracy: From Membership to Management in American Civic Life 2003. Contributions: scholarly books and journals. Editor: Vision and Method in Historical Sociology 1984, Bringing the State Back In (with Peter Evans and Dietrich Rueschemeyer) 1985, The Politics of Social Policy in the United States (with Margaret Weir and Ann Shola Orloff) 1988, American Society and Politics: Institutional. *Honours:* Hon. degrees (Michigan) 1997, (Northwestern) 2002, (Amherst Coll.) 2004; C. Wright Mills Award, Soc. for the Study of Social Problems 1979, Award for a Distinguished Contribution to Scholarship 1980, Theory Prize 1986, American Sociological Asscn; Guggenheim Fellowship 1990; Woodrow Wilson Foundation Award 1993; J. David Greenstone Award, American Political Science Asscn 1993; Best Book Award, American Sociological Asscn 1993; Allan Sharlin Memorial Award, Social Science History Asscn 1993; Ralph Waldo Emerson Award 1993, Phi Beta Kappa 1993, Russell Sage Foundation Grant 1996–98, 2000–2001, 2002–05, John D. and Catherine T. MacArthur Foundation Grant 1997–99; Pew Charitable Trusts Grant 1997–2000, Ford Foundation Grants 1998–2000, 2000–01, 2001–05. *Address:* c/o FAS, Harvard University, Cambridge, MA 02138, USA. *Telephone:* (617) 496-0966. *Fax:* (617) 495-0438. *E-mail:* skocpol@fas.harvard.edu. *Website:* www.gov.harvard.edu/Faculty/Bios/Skocpol.

SKRZYNECKI, Peter, OAM, MLitt, MA, BA; Australian poet, writer and lecturer; *Adjunct Associate Professor, School of Humanities, University of Western Sydney*; b. 6 April 1945, Imhert, Germany; m. Kate Magrath; one s. two d. *Education:* Univ. of Sydney, Univ. of New England. *Career:* fmr Lecturer, Univ. of Western Sydney, now Adjunct Assoc. Prof., School of Humanities. *Publications:* poetry: There, Behind the Lids 1970, Headwaters 1972, Immigrant Chronicle 1975, The Aviary: Poems 1975–77, The Polish Immigrant 1982, Night Swim 1989, Easter Sunday 1993, Time's Revenge 2000, Old/New World 2007; fiction: The Wild Dogs, The Beloved Mountain 1988, Rock 'n' Roll Heroes (short stories) 1992, The Cry of the Goldfinch 1996; non-fiction: Joseph's Coat: An Anthology of Multicultural Writing 1985, Influence: Australian Voices (ed.) 1997, The Sparrow Garden (memoir) 2004. *Honours:* Order of Cultural Merit, Poland 1989; Captain Cook Bicentenary Award 1970, Grace Leven Poetry Prize 1972, Henry Lawson Short Story Award 1985. *Address:* c/o School of Humanities and Languages, University of Western Sydney, Locked Bag 1797, Penrith, South DC, NSW 1797, Australia (office). *E-mail:* p.skrzynecki@uws.edu.au (office).

SLADE, Quilla (see Lewis-Smith, Anne Elizabeth)

SLATER, Nigel; British chef and food writer; b. Wolverhampton, West Midlands. *Career:* worked in restaurants from age 16; recipe tester, cook for food photography; Food Ed., Marie Claire magazine 1988; columnist, The Observer 1993–. *Television:* presenter, Nigel Slater's Real Food (Channel 4) 1998–99, A Taste of My Life (BBC 2) 2006–08, Simple Suppers (BBC 1) 2009–. *Publications:* Marie Claire Cookbook 1992, Real Fast Food 1992, Real Fast Puddings 1993, Real Good Food: The Essential Nigel Slater 1995, 30-Minute Suppers 1996, Real Fast Desserts 1997, Real Cooking 1997, Nigel Slater's Real Food 1998, Appetite: So What Do You Want to Eat Today? 2000, Thirst 2002, Toast: The Story of a Boy's Hunger (autobiog.) 2003, The Kitchen Diaries 2005, Eating for England 2007, Tender 2009, Tender: Volume II 2010. *Honours:* Hon. MLitt (Wolverhampton) 2009; Food Writer of the Year, André Simon Cookbook of the Year Award 2001, Food Personality of the Year, BBC Food and Farming Awards 2009. *Address:* c/o Fourth Estate, 77–85 Fulham Palace Road, London, W6 8JB, England (office). *Website:* www.nigelslater.com.

SLATTA, Richard Wayne, BA, MA, PhD; American academic and writer; *Professor of History, North Carolina State University*; b. 22 Oct. 1947, Powers Lake, ND; s. of Jerome Elmer Slatta and Amy Irene Solberg Slatta; m. Maxine P. Atkinson 1982; one s. *Education:* Pacific Lutheran Univ., Tacoma, WA, Portland State Univ., Ore., Univ. of Texas at Austin. *Career:* Visiting Researcher, Instituto Torcuato di Tella, Buenos Aires 1977–78; Visiting Instructor, Univ. of Colorado at Boulder 1979–80; Asst Prof., N Carolina State Univ. 1980–85, Assoc. Prof. 1985–90, Prof. of History 1990–; staff writer, Cowboys and Indians magazine 1994–2002, Persimmon Hill magazine 1994–2001; mem. American Historical Asscn, Conf. on Latin American History, Western History Asscn, Western Writers of America. *Publications:* Gauchos and the Vanishing Frontier 1983, Bandidos: The Varieties of Latin American Banditry (ed. and contrib.) 1987, Cowboys of the Americas 1990, The Cowboy Encyclopedia 1994, Comparing Cowboys and Frontiers 1997, The Mythical West 2001, Simón Bolívar's Quest for Glory 2003, Cowboy: The Illustrated History 2006, National Cowboy Symposium & Celebration 2010; contrib. to scholarly and general publs. *Honours:* Hubert Herring Book Prize, Pacific Coast Council on Latin American Studies 1984, Western Heritage Award for Non-Fiction Literature, Nat. Cowboy & Western Heritage Museum 1991, Best Reference Source Citation, Library Journal 1992, Outstanding Reference Source Citation, American Library Asscn 1995, American Cowboy Culture Award for Writing and Publishing 2008. *Address:* Department of History, North Carolina State University, Raleigh, NC 27695-8108, USA (office). *Telephone:* (919) 513-2229 (office). *E-mail:* slatta@ncsu.edu (office). *Website:* go.ncsu.edu/slatta (office); www.cowboyprof.com.

SLAUGHTER, Audrey Cecelia; British writer and journalist; b. 17 Jan. 1930, d. of Frederick George Smith and Ethel Louise Smith; m. 1st W. A. Slaughter 1950 (divorced); m. 2nd Charles Vere Wintour 1979 (died 1999). *Education:* Chislehurst High School and Stand Grammar School, Manchester. *Career:* fashion journalist –1960; Ed. Honey magazine 1960–68; Founder Petticoat 1964; columnist Evening News 1968–69; Ed. Vanity Fair 1970–72; Founder, Dir and Ed. Over 21 1972–79; Assoc. Ed. Sunday Times 1979–81, Sunday Express magazine 1981–82; Founder, Ed. Working Woman 1984–86; Lifestyle Ed. The Independent 1986–87. *Publications:* Non-fiction: Every Man Should Have One (jtly) 1969, Getting Through… 1981, Working Woman's Handbook 1986, Your Brilliant Career 1987; Fiction: Private View 1990, Blooming 1992, Unknown Country 1994. *Honours:* Magazine Ed. of the Year 1966. *Address:* 13 Cross Street, Barnes, London, SW13 0AP, England.

SLAUGHTER, Karin; American writer; b. S Georgia. *Publications:* novels: Grant County series: Blindsighted 2001, Kisscut 2002, A Faint Cold Fear 2003, Indelible 2004, Faithless 2005; Like a Charm (ed., short stories anthology) 2004, Triptych 2006, Beyond Reach (UK edition, Skin Privilege) 2007, Fractured 2008, Undone (UK edition, Genesis) 2009, Broken 2010, Criminal 2012, Fallen 2012. *Address:* c/o Bantam Dell Publicity Department, Random House, 1745 Broadway, New York, NY 10019, USA (office). *Website:* www.karinslaughter.com.

SLAVITT, David Rytman, (David Benjamin, Henry Lazarus, Lynn Meyer, Henry Sutton), MA; American writer, poet, translator and lecturer; b. 23 March 1935, White Plains, NY; s. of Samuel Slavitt and Adele Slavitt; m. 1st Lynn Meyer 1956 (divorced 1977); two s. one d.; m. 2nd Janet Lee Abrahm 1978. *Education:* Yale and Columbia Univs. *Career:* Instructor in English, Georgia Inst. of Tech., Atlanta 1957–58; writer, Assoc. Ed., Newsweek 1958–65; Visiting Lecturer, Univ. of Maryland 1977; Visiting Assoc. Prof., Temple Univ. 1978–80; Lecturer in English and Comparative Literature, Columbia Univ. 1985–86; teacher of creative writing, Rutgers Univ. 1987; Lecturer in English and Classics, Univ. of Pennsylvania 1991–97; Visiting Lecturer in Creative Writing, Princeton Univ. 1996; Lecturer in English, Bennington Coll. 2000; Assoc. Fellow, Trumbull Coll., Yale Univ.; has lectured widely at US univs and other academic insts. *Publications include:* fiction: Rochelle, or Virtue Rewarded 1967, King Saul (play) 1967, Feel Free 1968, The Cardinal Sins (play) 1969, Anagrams 1970, ABCD 1972, The Outer Mongolian 1973, The Killing of the King 1974, King of Hearts 1976, Jo Stern 1978, Cold Comfort 1980, Ringer 1982, Alice at 80 1984, The Agent 1986, The Hussar 1987, Salazar Blinks 1988, Lives of the Saints 1990, Short Stories Are Not Real Life 1991, Turkish Delights 1993, The Cliff 1994, Get Thee to a Nunnery: Two Divertimentos from Shakespeare 1999, Aspects of the Novel: A Novel 2003, The Duke's Man 2011; as Henry Sutton: The Exhibitionist 1967, The Voyeur 1968, Vector 1970, The Liberated 1973, The Proposal 1980; as Lynn Meyer: Paperback Thriller 1975; as Henry Lazarus: That Golden Woman 1976; as David Benjamin: The Idol 1979; poetry: Suits for the Dead 1961, The Carnivore 1965, Day Sailing 1968, Child's Play 1972, Vital Signs: New and Selected Poems 1975, Rounding the Horn 1978, Dozens 1981, Big Nose 1983, Adrien Stoutenburg: Land of Superior Mirages: New and Selected Poems (ed.) 1986, The Walls of Thebes 1986, Equinox 1989, Eight Longer Poems 1990, Crossroads 1994, A Gift 1996, Epic and Epigram 1997, A New Pléiade: Seven American Poets 1998, PS3569.L3 1998, Falling from Silence: Poems 2001, Change of Address: Poems, New and Selected 2005, William Henry Harrison and Other Poems 2006, Seven Deadly Sins 2009; non-fiction: Understanding Social Life: An Introduction to Social Psychology (with Paul F. Secord and Carl W. Backman) 1976, Physicians Observed 1987, Virgil 1991, The Persians of Aeschylus 1998, Three Amusements of Ausonius 1998, The Book of Lamentations 2001, Re Verse: Essays on Poets and Poetry 2005; translator: The Eclogues of Virgil 1971, The Eclogues and the Georgics of Virgil 1972, The Tristia of Ovid 1985, Ovid's Poetry of Exile 1990, Seneca: The Tragedies 1992, The Fables of Avianus 1993, The Metamorphoses of Ovid 1994, The Twelve Minor Prophets 1999, The Voyage of the Argo of Valerius Flaccus 1999, Sonnets of Love and Death of Jean de Sponde 2001, The Elegies of Propertius 2001, The Poetry of Manuel Bandeira 2002, The Regrets of Joachim du Bellay 2004, The Phoenix and Other Translations 2004, Re Verse: Essays on Poets and Poetry 2005, Blue State Blues: A Republican in Cambridge 2006, William Henry Harrison and Other Poems 2006, Sophocles' Theban Plays 2007, De Rerum Natura of Lucretius 2008, Boethius' Consolation of Philosophy 2008, Ludovico Ariosto's Orlando Furioso 2009, George Sanders, Zsa Zsa, and Me: Essays on the Movies 2009, Dante's Vita Nuova 2010, The Latin Eclogues of Giovanni Boccaccio 2010, Poems from the Greek Anthology 2010, The Gnat and other minor poems of Virgin 2011, The Latin Poems of John Milton 2011, The Love Letters, Poems, and Remedies of Ovid 2011, The Sonnets and Short Poems of Petrarch 2012, The Poetry of Guido Cavalcanti 2012; contrib. of book reviews, articles in journals and magazines. *Honours:* Pennsylvania Council on the Arts Award 1985, Nat. Endowment for Arts Fellowship in Translation 1988, Nat. Acad. and Inst. of Arts and Letters Award 1989, Rockefeller Foundation Artist's Residence, Bellagio 1989, Umhoefer Award in the Humanities 2007, Kevin Kline Theater Award 2010. *Address:* 35 West Street, #5, Cambridge, MA 02139, USA. *Telephone:* (617) 497-1219. *E-mail:* drslavitt@comcast.net.

SLAVNIKOVA, Olga; Russian journalist, writer and editor; b. 1957, Sverdlovsk. *Education:* Ural Univ. *Career:* fmr Dir Book Club magazine; Dir Debut Prize literary award; mem. Russian Booker Prize jury 1999; mem. Bd of Dirs Novy mir Prize for short stories 2000. *Publications:* Strekoza, uvelichennaya do razmerov sobaki (A Dragon-fly the Size of a Dog) 1997, Odin v zerkale (Alone in the Mirror) (Pavel Bazhov Prize), Bessmertny (The Immortal) (Critics' Acad. Apollon Grigoriev Prize) 2001, Period, 2017 (Russian Booker Prize) 2006; contrib. to Novy mir, Znamya, Oktyabr. *Honours:* Gjenima Prize 2006–07. *Literary Agent:* c/o Bettina Nibbe, Nibbe-Wiedling, Hoehenweg 11, 82229 Seefeld, Germany. *Telephone:* (81) 52304513. *Fax:* (81) 52981877. *E-mail:* nibbe@nibbe-wiedling.de. *Website:* www.nibbe-wiedling.de.

SLOAN, Carolyn; British journalist, theatre publicist and children's writer; b. 15 April 1937, London, England; m. David Hollis 1961 (deceased); two s. *Education:* Harrogate Coll. and tutorial schools in Newcastle and Guildford. *Career:* mem. Soc. of Authors. *Publications:* Carter is a Painter's Cat 1971, Victoria and the Crowded Pocket 1973, The Penguin and the Vacuum Cleaner 1974, Shakespeare, Theatre Cat 1982, Skewer's Garden 1983, Helen Keller 1984, An Elephant for Muthu 1986, The Sea Child 1987, Don't Go Near the Water 1988, Gracie 1994, Incredible Journey 1996, The Rat 1998, Victorian Day 1999, George Goes to Town 2007, Simon's Scoop 2007, Jamie and the Chameleon 2008; contribs to newspapers and journals. *Address:* 175 Stoughton Road, Guildford, Surrey, GU1 1LQ, England (home). *E-mail:* chollis749@btinternet.com (home).

SLOTKIN, Richard Sidney, BA, PhD; American academic and writer; *Olin Professor Emeritus of American Studies and English*, Wesleyan University; b. 8 Nov. 1942, New York, NY; s. of Herman Slotkin and Roselyn Slotkin; m. Iris F. Shupack 1963; one s. *Education:* Brooklyn Coll., CUNY and Brown Univ. *Career:* Asst Prof., Wesleyan Univ., Middletown, CT 1966–73, Assoc. Prof. 1973–76, Prof. 1976–82, Olin Prof. of American Studies and English 1982–2008, Emer. 2008–; Fellow Soc. of American Historians; mem. American Asscn of Univ. Profs, American Film Inst., American Historical Asscn, American Studies Asscn, Authors' Guild, Org. of American Historians, PEN. *Publications:* Regeneration Through Violence: The Mythology of the American Frontier, 1600–1860 1973, So Dreadful a Judgement: Puritan Responses to King Philip's War, 1675–1677 (with J. Folsom) 1978, The Crater: A Novel of the Civil War 1980, The Fatal Environment: The Myth of the Frontier in the Age of Industrialization, 1800–1890 1985, The Return of Henry Starr 1988, Gunfighter Nation: The Myth of the Frontier in Twentieth Century America 1992, Abe: A Novel of the Young Lincoln 2000, Lost Battalions: The Great War and the Crisis of American Nationality 2005, No Quarter: The Battle of the Crater, 1864 2009; contrib. to professional journals. *Honours:* American Historical Asscn Albert J. Beveridge Award 1973, Nat. Endowment for the Humanities Fellowship 1973–74, Rockefeller Foundation Fellowship 1976–77, Don D. Walker Prize 1982, Little Big Horn Asscn Award 1986, American Studies Asscn Mary C. Turpie Prize 1995, Salon.com Book Award 2000, Michael Shaara Award 2001. *Address:* Center for the Americas, Wesleyan University, Middletown, CT 06459, USA (office). *Telephone:* (860) 685-3624 (office). *E-mail:* rslotkin@wesleyan.edu (office).

SLOVO, Gillian; South African/British novelist; b. 15 March 1952, Johannesburg; d. of Joe Slovo and Ruth First; one d. *Education:* Manchester Univ., England. *Career:* researcher, journalist, film producer. *Film:* Red Dust. *Play:* Guantanamo: Honor Bound to Defend Freedom (with Victoria Brittain). *Publications:* novels: Morbid Symptoms 1984, Death by Analysis 1986, Death Comes Staccato 1987, Ties of Blood 1989, The Betrayal 1991, Facade 1993, Catnap 1994, Close Call 1995, Red Dust 2000, Ice Road 2004, Black Orchids 2008, An Honourable Man 2011; memoirs: Every Secret Thing: My Family, My Country 1997. *Address:* 74 Cholmley Gardens, London, NW6 1UL, England.

SMALL, Michael Ronald, BA, BEd, MA, TESL; British teacher, writer and poet; b. 3 Jan. 1943, Croydon, Surrey, England. *Education:* Univ. of London, La Trobe Univ., Australia, Univ. of Windsor, Canada. *Career:* fmr teacher of English in England, Sweden, Canada and Australia; mem. Victorian Fellowship of Australian Writers, Melbourne Poets' Union; Teacher of English as a Second Language. *Publications:* Her Natural Life and Other Stories 1988, Film: A Resource Book for Studying Film as Text (with Brian Keyte) 1994, Unleashed: A History of Footscray Football Club (with John Lack, Chris McConville and Damien Wright) 1996, Urangeline: Voices of Carey 1923–1997 1997; contribs to numerous journals and magazines in Australia and overseas; a selection of short stories and poems can be found on issuu.com, including his collection of 50 'convict' poems entitled Slanged. *Address:* 71 Strabane Avenue, Box Hill North, Vic. 3129, Australia (home). *Telephone:* (3) 9898-4303 (home). *E-mail:* michael.small@live.com.au (office).

SMALLEY, Stephen Stewart, BA, BD, MA, PhD; British ecclesiastic and writer; *Dean Emeritus*, *Chester Cathedral*; b. 11 May 1931, London, England; m. Susan Jane Paterson 1974 (died 1995); one s. one d. *Education:* Jesus Coll., Cambridge, Eden Theological Seminary, USA. *Career:* Deacon, Ridley Hall, Cambridge 1958, Priest 1959; Asst Curate, St Paul's, Portman Square, London 1958–60; Chaplain, Peterhouse, Cambridge 1960–63, Acting Dean 1962–63; Lecturer and Sr Lecturer, Univ. of Ibadan, Nigeria 1963–69; Lecturer and Sr Lecturer, Univ. of Manchester 1970–77; Warden of St Anselm Hall 1972–77; Canon Residentiary and Precentor, Coventry Cathedral 1977–86, Vice-Provost 1986; Dean Chester Cathedral 1987–2001, Dean Emer. 2001–; Visiting Prof., Univ. of Chester 2001–; mem. Archbishops' Doctrine Comm. of the Church of England 1981–86; mem. Studiorum Novi Testamenti Societas, Chester City Club, Chester Business Club, Chesire Pitt Club. *Publications:* The Spirit's Power 1972, Christ and Spirit in the New Testament (ed.) 1973, John: Evangelist and Interpreter 1978, 1, 2, 3 John 1984, Thunder and Love: John's Revelation and John's Community 1994, The Revelation of John 2005, Hope for Ever 2005; contrib. to learned journals. *Honours:* Hon. LLD (Liverpool) 2001; Foundation and Lady Kay Scholar, Jesus Coll., Cambridge 1948, 1955, Select Preacher, Univ. of Cambridge 1963–64, Manson Memorial Lecturer, Univ. of Manchester 1986. *Address:* The Old Hall, The Folly, Longborough, Moreton-in-Marsh, Glos., GL56 0QS, England. *Telephone:* (1451) 830238 (home). *E-mail:* stephen.smalley@tiscali.co.uk (home).

SMILEVSKI, Goce; Macedonian novelist; b. 1975, Skopje. *Education:* St Cyril and Methodius Univ., Skopje, Charles Univ., Prague, Czech Repub., Central European Univ., Budapest, Hungary. *Career:* teacher, Inst. for Literature, St Cyril and Methodius Univ., Skopje. *Publications include:*

novels: Conversation with Spinoza (Macedonian Novel of the Year Award 2003), Sigmund Freud's Sister (EU Prize for Literature 2010) 2007. *Honours:* Central European Initiative Fellowship for Young European Authors 2006. *Address:* c/o Kultura, 51 No. 1/2/2 ul.Makedonija, 1000 Skopje, Macedonia (office). *Telephone:* (2) 3111332 (office). *Fax:* (2) 3111332 (office). *E-mail:* ipkultura@kultura.com.mk (office); contact@gocesmilevski.com (home). *Website:* www.kultura.com.mk (office); www.gocesmilevski.com.

SMILEY, Jane Graves, MFA, PhD; American writer and academic; b. 26 Sept. 1949, Los Angeles; d. of James La Verne Smiley and Frances Nuelle (née Graves); m. 1st John Whiston 1970 (divorced); m. 2nd William Silag 1978 (divorced); two d.; m. 3rd Stephen Mark Mortensen 1987 (divorced 1997); one s. *Education:* Vassar Coll. and Univ. of Iowa. *Career:* Asst Prof., Iowa State Univ. 1981–84, Assoc. Prof. 1984–89, Prof. 1989–90, Distinguished Prof. 1992–96; Visiting Prof., Univ. of Iowa 1981, 1987; Fulbright Grant 1976, Nat. Endowment for the Arts grants 1978, 1987. *Publications:* Barn Blind 1980, At Paradise Gate 1981, Duplicate Keys 1984, The Age of Grief 1987, Catskill Crafts: Artisans of the Catskill Mountains (non-fiction) 1987, The Greenlanders 1988, Ordinary Love and Goodwill 1989, A Thousand Acres (Pulitzer Prize in Fiction 1992, Nat. Book Critics Circle Award 1992, Midland Authors Award 1992, Heartland Prize 1992) 1991, Moo: A Novel 1995, The All-True Travels and Adventures of Lidie Newton 1998, Horse Heaven 2000, Dickens (biog.) 2002, Good Faith 2003, A Year at the Races 2004, Thirteen Ways of Looking at the Novel (non-fiction) 2006, Ten Days in the Hills 2007, The Georges and the Jewels (children's fiction) 2009, Private Life 2010, The Man Who Invented the Computer: The Biography of John Atanasoff, Digital Pioneer 2010. *Honours:* Friends of American Writers Prize 1981, O. Henry Awards 1982, 1985, 1988, Distinguished Alumni Award Univ. of Iowa 2003. *Address:* c/o Knopf Publicity, Random House, 1745 Broadway, New York, NY 10019, USA (office).

SMITH, Ali; British writer; b. 1962, Inverness, Scotland. *Education:* Univ. of Aberdeen, Univ. of Cambridge. *Career:* fmr Lecturer, Univ. of Strathclyde; gave lecture on Angela Carter, Nat. Portrait Gallery, London 2004. *Publications:* Free Love and Other Stories (Saltire First Book Award) 1995, Like (novel) 1997, Other Stories and Other Stories 1999, Hotel World (novel) (Encore Prize, Scottish Arts Council Book Award, Scottish Arts Council Book of the Year 2002) 2001, The Whole Story and Other Stories 2003, The Accidental (novel) (Whitbread Novel of the Year 2005) 2004, The Reader 2006, Girl Meets Boy (SAC Sundial Novel of the Year 2008) 2007, The First Person and other stories 2008; contrib. to TLS, The Scotsman, Guardian. *Honours:* Scottish Arts Council Award 1995; Hon. DLitt (Aberdeen) 2007, (Anglia Ruskin, Cambridge) 2008. *Address:* c/o Hamish Hamilton, c/o Penguin Books, 80 Strand, London, WC2R 0RL, England.

SMITH, Anthony Charles Hockley, MA; British writer; b. 31 Oct. 1935, Kew, Surrey, England; three c. *Education:* Univ. of Cambridge. *Career:* Literary Assoc., Royal Shakespeare Co. 1964–74; Sr Research Assoc., Univ. of Birmingham 1965–69; Dir Cheltenham Festival of Literature 1978–79, 1999; Chair., Playwrights Co. 1979–83; Visiting Prof., Emory Univ., Atlanta, Ga, USA 1986, Univ. of Texas, USA 1990–91, 1994; mem. Writers' Guild of GB. *Theatre:* Up the Feeder, Down the Mouth, Bristol Old Vic 1997, 2001, The Redcliffe Hermit, Bristol 2005, Doctor Love (musical theatre), Bristol Tobacco Factory 2008. *Publications:* The Crowd 1965, Zero Summer 1971, Orghast at Persepolis 1972, Paper Voices 1975, Treatment 1976, The Jericho Gun 1977, Edward and Mrs Simpson 1978, Extra Cover 1981, The Dark Crystal 1982, Wagner 1983, Sebastian the Navigator 1985, Lady Jane 1985, Labyrinth 1986, The Dangerous Memoir of Citizen Sade 2000; 20 plays staged; contribs to newspapers, magazines, and television. *Honours:* Arts Council Writing Awards 1970–71, 1974–75, 1980, Univ. of Bristol Drama Fellowship 1976–79. *Address:* 21 West Shrubbery, Bristol, BS6 6TA, England (home).

SMITH, Barbara Herrnstein, MA, PhD; American academic (retd), writer and lecturer; *Professor Emerita of Comparative Literature and English, Brown University and Duke University*; b. (Barbara Judith Brodo), 6 Aug. 1932, New York, NY; m. 1st R. J. Herrnstein 1951 (divorced 1961); m. 2nd T. H. Smith 1964 (divorced 1974); two d. *Education:* Brandeis Univ. *Career:* Faculty, Bennington Coll., Vt 1961–73, Univ. of Pennsylvania 1973–87; Braxton Craven Prof. of Comparative Literature and English, Duke Univ. 1987–2011, Prof. Emer. 2011–, Dir Center for Interdisciplinary Studies in Science and Cultural Theory 1999–2011; Northrop Frye Chair, Univ. of Toronto 1990; Distinguished Prof. of English, Brown Univ. 2003–11. *Publications:* Poetic Closure: A Study of How Poems End 1968, On the Margins of Discourse: The Relation of Literature to Language 1978, Contingencies of Value: Alternative Perspectives for Critical Theory 1988, The Politics of Liberal Education (co-ed.) 1991, Belief and Resistance: Dynamics of Contemporary Intellectual Controversy 1997, Mathematics, Science and Postclassical Theory (co-ed.) 1997, Scandalous Knowledge: Science, Truth and the Human 2005, Natural Reflections: Human Cognition at the Nexus of Science and Religion 2009; contribs to numerous professional journals. *Address:* Box 90015, Duke University, Durham, NC 27708-0015, USA (office). *E-mail:* bhsmith@duke.edu (office). *Website:* www.duke.edu (office).

SMITH, Bradley F., BA, MA; American writer and fmr teacher; b. 5 Oct. 1931, Seattle, Wash.; m. 1983; two d. *Education:* Univ. of California, Berkeley. *Career:* mem. Authors' Guild. *Publications:* Adolf Hitler: His Family, Childhood, and Youth 1967, Himmler Geheimreden 1974, Reaching Judgement at Nuremberg (Observer Book of the Year 1977) 1977, Operation Sunrise (with Elena Agarossi) 1979, The American Road to Nuremberg 1981, The Road to Nuremberg 1981, The Shadow Warriors 1983, The War's Long Shadow 1986, The Ultra-Magic Deals and the Special Relationship, 1940–46 1992, Sharing Secrets with Stalin: Anglo-American Intelligence Co-operation with the USSR 1941–1945 1996; contrib. dozens of articles to newspapers and journals 1959–. *Address:* 30 Madeira Road, Ventnor, HW1 8UG, Isle of Wight (home); 104 Regents Park Road, London, NW1 8UG, England (office). *Telephone:* (1983) 852653 (home).

SMITH, Bruce, MA; American poet and academic; *Professor of English, Syracuse University*; b. 1946, Philadelphia. *Education:* Bucknell Univ. *Career:* worked at Federal Penitentiary, Lewisburg; fmr teacher, Tufts Univ., Boston Univ., Harvard Univ., Portland State Univ., Lewis & Clark Coll., Univ. of Ala –2002; Prof. of English, Syracuse Univ. 2002–; fmr Co-ed. Graham House Review; fmr Contributing Ed. Born Magazine. *Publications include:* poetry collections: The Common Wages 1983, Silver and Information 1985, Mercy Seat 1994, The Other Lover 2000, Songs for Two Voices 2005, Devotions (William Carlos Williams Award, Poetry Society of America 2012) 2011; contrib. to several anthologies. *Honours:* Guggenheim Fellowship 2000, Greensboro Review Literary Award for Poetry 2001, Literature Award from American Acad. of Arts and Letters 2010, Discovery/The Nation Award, Nat. Endowment for the Arts Grant, Mass Foundation for the Arts Grant. *Address:* Department of English, College of Arts and Sciences, 207 Tolley Humanities Building, Syracuse University, Syracuse, NY 13244-5040, USA (office). *Telephone:* (315) 443-9473 (office). *E-mail:* bfsmith@syr.edu (office). *Website:* as-cascade.syr.edu/profiles/pages/smith-bruce.html (office).

SMITH, Charlie, BA, MFA; American writer, poet and academic; b. 27 June 1947, Moultrie, Ga; m. 1st Kathleen Huber 1974 (divorced 1977); m. 2nd Gretchen Mattox 1987 (divorced 1997); m. 3rd Daniela Serowinski 2003. *Education:* Duke Univ., Univ. of Iowa. *Career:* Lecturer in Humanities and Creative Writing, Princeton Univ.; Writer-in-Residence, Univ. of Alabama 2000; mem. Acad. of American Poets, International PEN, Poetry Society of America. *Publications:* fiction: Canaan 1985, Shine Hawk 1988, The Lives of the Dead 1990, Crystal River 1991, Chimney Rock 1993, Cheap Ticket to Heaven 1996, Three Delays 2010; poetry: Red Roads 1987, Indistinguishable from the Darkness 1990, The Palms 1993, Before and After: Poems 1995, Heroin and Other Poems 2000, Women of America 2004; contributions: literary journals and periodicals. *Honours:* Aga Khan Prize, Paris Review 1983, Guggenheim Fellowship 2000, National Endowment for the Arts Grant 2000. *Address:* c/o Harper Collins, 10 East 53rd Street, New York, NY 10022, USA (office).

SMITH, David (Dave) Jeddie, MA, PhD; American poet, editor and academic; *Elliot Coleman Professor of Poetry, Johns Hopkins University*; b. 19 Dec. 1942, Portsmouth, Va; m. Deloras Smith 1966; one s. two d. *Education:* Univ. of Virginia, Southern Illinois Univ., Ohio Univ. *Career:* Ed. The Back Door: A Poetry Magazine 1970–78, The Southern Review 1990–2002; Instructor in English, Western Michigan Univ. 1973–74; Asst Prof. of English, Cottey Coll. 1974–75; Asst Prof. 1976–79, Assoc. Prof. of English 1979–81, Dir of Creative Writing 1976–81, Univ. of Utah; Poetry Ed., Rocky Mountain Review 1978–79, University of Utah Press 1980–90; Visiting Prof. of English, State Univ. of New York at Binghamton 1980–81; Dir of Poetry, Bennington Writers' Conf., VT 1980–87; Assoc. Prof. of English and Dir of Creative Writing, Univ. of Florida 1981–82; Prof. of English, Virginia Commonwealth Univ. 1982–90; Prof. of English, Louisiana State Univ. 1991–97, Hopkins P. Breazeale Prof. of English 1997–98, Boyd Prof. of English 1998–2002; Elliot Coleman Prof. of Poetry and Chair. of Writing Seminars Dept, Johns Hopkins Univ. 2002–; mem. Associated Writing Programs, Fellowship of Southern Writers, Modern Language Asscn (MLA), Southern MLA. *Publications:* Bull Island 1970, Mean Rufus Throw Down 1973, The Fisherman's Whore 1974, Drunks 1975, Cumberland Station 1977, In Dark, Sudden With Light 1977, Goshawk, Antelope 1979, Blue Spruce 1981, Dream Flights 1981, Homage to Edgar Allan Poe 1981, Onliness (novel) 1981, The Travelling Photographer 1981, The Pure Clear Word: Essays on the Poetry of James Wright 1982, In the House of the Judge 1983, Southern Delights (short stories) 1984, Gray Soldiers 1984, The Morrow Anthology of Younger American Poets (ed.) 1985, The Roundhouse Voices: Selected and New Poems 1985, Local Assays: On Contemporary American Poetry 1985, Cuba Night 1990, The Essential Poe 1992, Night Pleasures: New and Selected Poems 1992, Fate's Kite: Poems 1990–1995 1996, Floating on Solitude: Three Books of Poems 1997, The Wick of Memory: New and Selected Poems 1970–2000 2000, Little Boats: Unsalvaged 2005, Hunting Men: Reflections on a Life in Poetry 2006; contrib. to anthologies, reviews, and journals. *Honours:* Bread Loaf Fellow 1975, Nat. Endowment for the Arts Fellowships 1976, 1980, American Acad. of Arts and Letters Award 1979, Guggenheim Fellowship 1981, Ohio Univ. Alumni of the Year 1985, Lyndhurst Fellowship 1987–89, Virginia Poetry Prize 1988. *Address:* The Writing Seminars, 3400 N Charles Street, Baltimore, MD 21218 (office); 14 East Bishops Road, Baltimore, MD 21218, USA (home). *Telephone:* (410) 516-3409 (office). *Fax:* (410) 516-6828 (office). *E-mail:* davesmith@jhu.edu (office).

SMITH, David Lawrence, MA, PhD, PGCE, FRHistS; British historian and academic; *Fellow, Graduate Tutor and Director of Studies in History, Selwyn College, Cambridge*; b. 3 Dec. 1963, London, England. *Education:* Eastbourne Coll., Selwyn Coll., Cambridge. *Career:* Fellow, Selwyn Coll., Cambridge 1988–, Dir of Studies in History 1992–, Admissions Tutor 1992–2003, Praelector 1996–2006, Tutor for Grad. Students 2004–; Affiliated Lecturer in History, Univ. of Cambridge 1995–; Visiting Asst Prof. of History, Univ. of Chicago 1991; Visiting Prof. of History, Kyungpook Nat. Univ., Repub. of Korea 2004; Gov. Eastbourne Coll. 1993–; Trustee, Oakham School 2000–; mem. Cambridge History Forum (Pres. 1997–). *Publications:* Oliver Cromwell 1991, Louis XIV 1992, Cambridge Perspectives in History (co-ed.) 1993–, Constitutional Royalism and the Search for Settlement 1994, The Theatrical City (co-ed.) 1995, A History of the Modern British Isles, 1603–1707: The Double Crown 1998, The Stuart Parliaments, 1603–1689 1999, The Early Stuart Kings, 1603–1642 (with Graham E. Seel) 2001, Crown and Parliaments, 1558–1689 (with Graham E. Seel) 2001, Cromwell and the Interregnum (ed.) 2003, Royalists and Royalism during the English Civil Wars (co-ed.) 2007, Parliaments and Politics during the Cromwellian Protectorate (with Patrick Little) 2007, Royalists and Royalism during the Interregnum (co-ed.) 2010, The Experience of Revolution in Stuart Britain and Ireland: Essays for John Morrill (co-ed.) 2011; contrib. to Historical Journal, Historical Research, Journal of British Studies, Transactions of the Royal Historical Society, Comparative Drama, Parliamentary History, Cromwelliana, Oxford Dictionary of National Biography (assoc. ed.) 2004. *Honours:* Royal Historical Soc. Alexander Prize 1991, Thirlwall Prize, Univ. of Cambridge 1991. *Address:* Selwyn College, Cambridge, CB3 9DQ, England (office). *Telephone:* (1223) 335881 (office); (1223) 331962 (home). *Fax:* (1223) 331720 (office). *E-mail:* dls10@cam.ac.uk (office). *Website:* www.hist.cam.ac.uk/directory/dls10@cam.ac.uk (office).

SMITH, Sir Dudley Gordon; British management consultant, former politician and writer; b. 14 Nov. 1926, Cambridge, England; m. 1st (divorced); one s. two d.; m. 2nd Catherine Amos 1976. *Career:* journalist and Sr Exec., various provincial and national newspapers 1943–66; Asst News Ed., Sunday Express 1953–59; MP for Brentford and Chiswick 1959–66, for Warwick and Leamington 1968–97; Management Consultant 1974–; UK Delegate, Council of Europe and Western European Union 1979–97; Pres., Western European Assembly 1993–96. *Publications:* They Also Served 1945, Harold Wilson: A Critical Biography 1964. *Honours:* apptd Deputy Lieutenant of Warwickshire 1988, Commander of the Order of Isabela la Católica, Spain 1994.

SMITH, Emma; British writer; b. (Elspeth Hallsmith), 21 Aug. 1923, Newquay, Cornwall, England; m. Richard Llewellyn Stewart-Jones 1951 (died 1957); one s. one d. *Publications:* Maiden's Trip 1948, The Far Cry 1949, Emily 1959, Out of Hand 1963, Emily's Voyage 1966, No Way of Telling 1972, The Opportunity of a Lifetime 1978, The Great Western Beach 2008; contributions: various magazines. *Honours:* Atlantic Award 1948, John Llewellyn Rhys Memorial Prize 1948, James Tait Black Memorial Prize 1949. *Literary Agent:* Curtis Brown Ltd, Haymarket House, 28–29 Haymarket, London, SW1Y 4SP, England. *Telephone:* (20) 7393-4400. *Fax:* (20) 7393-4401. *E-mail:* info@curtisbrown.co.uk. *Website:* www.curtisbrown.co.uk.

SMITH, Francis Barrymore, PhD, FAHA; Australian historian and academic; b. 16 May 1932, Hughesdale; s. of Francis John Smith and Bertha Smith; m. Ann Stokes 1965; two s. two d. *Education:* Univ. of Melbourne and Cambridge Univ. *Career:* Lecturer in History, Univ. of Melbourne 1962–66; Professorial Fellow in History, Inst. of Advanced Studies, ANU 1974–94, Hancock Prof. of History 1995–98; Ed. Historical Studies 1963–67; Pres. Australian Historical Asscn 1978–80. *Publications:* Making of the Second Reform Bill 1966, Radical Artisan: William James Linton 1973, The People's Health 1830–1910 1979, Florence Nightingale: Reputation and Power 1982, Retreat of Tuberculosis 1987, 'Agent Orange': The Australian Aftermath 1994, G. G. Achilli versus J. H. Newman 2000. *Address:* History Program, Research School of Social Sciences, Australian National University, Canberra 0200, Australia (office). *Telephone:* (2) 6125-2358 (office). *Fax:* (2) 6125-3969 (office).

SMITH, Gregory Blake, AB, MA, MFA; American academic and writer; *Lloyd P. Johnson Norwest Professor of English and the Liberal Arts, Carleton College*; b. 24 July 1951, Torrington, CT. *Education:* Bowdoin Coll., Boston Univ., Univ. of Iowa. *Career:* Lloyd P. Johnson Norwest Prof. of English and the Liberal Arts, Carleton Coll. 1987–. *Publications:* The Devil in the Dooryard 1986, The Divine Comedy of John Venner 1992, The Madonna of Las Vegas 2005. *Honours:* Stanford Univ. Stegner Fellowship 1985, Nat. Endowment for the Arts Fellowship 1988, Pushcart Prize 2006. *Address:* c/o Department of English, Carleton College, Northfield, MN 55057, USA.

SMITH, Hedrick Laurence, BA; British journalist, writer and academic; b. 9 July 1933, Kilmacolm, Scotland; m. 1st Ann Bickford 1957 (divorced 1985); one s. three d.; m. 2nd Susan Zox 1987. *Education:* Choate School, Williams Coll., Balliol Coll., Oxford. *Career:* staff, United Press International 1959–62; Diplomatic News Correspondent, New York Times 1962–64, 1966–71, Middle East Correspondent 1964–66, Chief, Moscow Bureau 1971–74, Washington Bureau 1976–79, Deputy National Ed. 1975–76, Washington Correspondent 1980–85; Panelist, Washington Week in Review, PBS-TV 1969–95; Visiting Journalist, American Enterprise Inst. 1985–87; Fellow, Foreign Policy Inst., School of Advanced International Studies, Johns Hopkins Univ. 1989–97; founder, Exec. Producer and Corresp., Hedrick Smith Productions 1990–; various PBS-TV documentaries; many lectures; mem. Gridiron Club. *Television:* as writer: The Power Game 1988, Surviving the Bottom Line 1998, Seeking Solutions 1999, Duke Ellington's Washington 2000, Critical Condition 2000, Juggling Work and Family 2001, Rediscovering Dave Brubeck 2001, The Wall Street Fix 2003, Tax Me If You Can 2004, Is Wal-Mart Good for America? 2004, Can You Afford to Retire 2006, Poisoned Waters 2009. *Publications:* The Pentagon Papers (co-author) 1972, The Russians 1975, Reagan the Man, the President (co-author) 1981, Beyond Reagan: The Politics of Upheaval (co-author) 1986, The Power Game: How Washington Works 1988, The New Russians 1990, Seven Days That Shook the World (co-author) 1991, The Media and the Gulf War 1992, Rethinking America 1995. *Honours:* Nieman Fellow, Harvard Univ. 1969–70, Pulitzer Prize for International Reporting 1974, Overseas Press Club Award 1976, and Citation, 1991, George Polk Award 1990, Gold Baton Award, DuPont-Columbia Univ. 1990, George Foster Peabody Award 1991, Hillman Award 1996, William Allen White Award, Univ. of Kansas 1996. *Address:* Hedrick Smith Productions, 4630 Montgomery Avenue, Suite 400, Bethesda, MD 20814, USA (office). *Telephone:* (301) 654-9848 (office). *E-mail:* HSmithProd@aol.com (office). *Website:* www.hedricksmith.com.

SMITH, Lee, BA; American academic and writer; b. 1 Nov. 1944, Grundy, Va; m. 1st James E. Seay 1967 (divorced); two c.; m. 2nd Hal Crowther 1985. *Education:* Hollins Coll., Va. *Career:* Faculty, Dept of English, N Carolina State Univ., Raleigh 1981–, now Prof. Emer.; Fellow, Center for Documentary Studies, Duke Univ. 1991–93; mem. N Carolina Writers' Network, PEN. *Publications:* The Last Day the Dogbushes Bloomed 1968, Something in the Wind 1971, Fancy Strut 1973, Black Mountain Breakdown 1980, Cakewalk (short stories) 1980, Oral History 1983, Family Linen 1985, Fair and Tender Ladies 1988, Me and My Baby View the Eclipse (short stories) 1990, The Devil's Dream 1992, Saving Grace 1994, Christmas Letters 1997, News of the Spirit (short stories) 1997, The Last Girls 2002, On Agate Hill 2006, Mrs Darcy and the Blue-Eyed Stranger (short stories) 2010. *Honours:* O. Henry Awards 1979, 1981, 1984, John Dos Passos Award 1984, Sir Walter Raleigh Award 1984, North Carolina Award for Literature 1985, Lyndhurst Prize 1990–92, Robert Penn Warren Prize 1991, Award in Literature, American Acad. of Arts and Letters 1999. *Address:* c/o MLS, PO Box 534, Efland, NC 27243, USA (office). *E-mail:* info@leesmith.com (office). *Website:* www.leesmith.com.

SMITH, Martin William Cruz, BA; American writer; b. 3 Nov. 1942, Reading, Pa; s. of John Smith and Louise Lopez; m. Emily Arnold 1968; two d. one s. *Education:* Univ. of Pennsylvania. *Career:* fmr newspaper reporter and ed. *Publications:* The Indians Won 1970, Gypsy in Amber 1971, Canto for a Gypsy 1972, Gorky Park 1972, Nightwing 1977, Analog Bullet 1981, Stallion Gate 1986, Polar Star 1989, Red Square 1992, Rose 1996, Havana Bay 1999, December 6 (aka Tokyo Station) 1999, Death by Espionage: Intriguing Stories of Betrayal and Deception 2001, Wolves Eat Dogs 2005, Stalin's Ghost 2007, Three Stations 2010. *Honours:* CWA Golden Dagger Award 1981. *Address:* c/o Publicity Department, Simon & Schuster, Inc., 1230 Avenue of the Americas, New York, NY 10020, USA (office). *Website:* literati.net/MCSmith.

SMITH, Michael Marshall, (M.M. Smith, Michael Marshall); British writer; b. 3 May 1965, Knutsford, Cheshire, England. *Education:* King's Coll., Cambridge. *Publications:* as Michael Marshall: The Straw Men 2002, The Lonely Dead 2004, Blood of Angels 2005, The Intruders 2007, Bad Things 2009, Killer Move 2011; as Michael Marshall Smith: Only Forward 1994, Spares 1996, One of Us 1998, The Servants 2007; short stories: The Vaccinator 1999, What You Make It 1999, Cat Stories 2001, More Tomorrow and other stories 2003, This is Now 2007; contribs to anthologies and periodicals. *Honours:* Philip K. Dick Award, Int. Horror Guild Award, August Derleth Award, five British Fantasy Awards. *E-mail:* contact@michaelmarshallsmith.com (office). *Website:* www.michaelmarshallsmith.com.

SMITH, Patricia Clark, BA, MA, PhD; American writer, poet and academic; *Professor of English, University of New Mexico*; b. 14 Feb. 1943, Holyoke, Mass; m. 1st Warren S. Smith 1964 (divorced 1976); two s.; m. 2nd John F. Crawford 1988. *Education:* Smith College, Yale University. *Career:* Lecturer in English, Smith College 1968–69; Asst Prof. of English, Luther College, Decorah, Ia 1969–71; Asst Prof., University of New Mexico 1971–82, Assoc. Prof. 1982–96, Prof. of English 1996–. *Publications:* Talking to the Land (poetry) 1979, Changing Your Story (poetry) 1990, Western Literature in a World Context (co-ed.), two vols 1995, As Long as the Rivers Flow: The Stories of Nine Native Americans (co-author) 1996, On the Trail of Elder Brother 2000, Weetamoo: Heart of the Pocassets 2003, Blood Dazzler (poetry) 2008; contributions: anthologies and periodicals. *Address:* Department of English Language and Literature, University of New Mexico, MSC 03 2180, Albuquerque, NM 87131-0001, USA (office). *Telephone:* (505) 277-6347 (office). *Fax:* (505) 277-0021 (office). *Website:* www.unm.edu/~English (office).

SMITH, Patti; American singer, songwriter, musician (guitar), poet and artist; b. 30 Dec. 1946, Chicago; d. of Grant Smith and Beverly Smith; m. Fred 'Sonic' Smith 1980 (died 1994); two s. *Education:* Glassboro State Teachers' Coll., NJ. *Career:* avant-garde poet, singer and artist; performed in and co-wrote Cowboy Mouth with Sam Shepard 1971; fmr rock critic for Creem, Rock, Crawdaddy and Rolling Stone magazines 1970s; solo artist 1972–, forming Patti Smith Group 1974–; nat. and int. tours of USA, Europe etc.; Artistic Dir, Meltdown Festival, South Bank Centre, London 2005. *Recordings include:* albums: Horses 1975, Radio Ethiopia 1976, Easter 1978, Wave 1979, Dream Of Life 1988, Gone Again 1996, Peace And Noise 1997, Gung Ho 2000, Land 1975–2002 2002, Twelve 2007, The Coral Sea (with Kevin Shields) 2008, Banga 2012. *Publications:* Seventh Heaven (poems) 1971, Kodak (poems) 1972, Cowboy Mouth (play, with Sam Shepard) 1972, Witt (poems) 1973, Babel 1978, Early Work 1970–1979 (poems) 1980, Woolgathering (short stories) 1993, The Coral Sea (prose poems in memory of Robert Mapplethorpe) 1996, Auguries of Innocence (poems) 2006, Just Kids (Nat. Book Award for

Non-Fiction) 2010. *Honours:* Commdr, Ordre des Arts et des Lettres 2005; ASCAP Founders Award 2010, Polar Music Prize, Royal Swedish Acad. of Music 2011. *Address:* c/o Ecco Press, HarperCollins, 10 East 53rd Street, New York, NY 10022, USA (office). *Fax:* (212) 207-7145 (office). *Website:* www.pattismith.net (home).

SMITH, Rosamond (see Oates, Joyce Carol)

SMITH, Sandra Lee, (Sandra Leesmith, Sandy Wardman), BA, MA; American writer and teacher; b. 28 June 1945, San Francisco, CA; m. Edward Leroy Smith, Jr 1967. *Publications:* Loves Miracles (fiction) 1988, Coping with Decision Making 1989, Dream Song (fiction) 1990, Value of Self Control 1990, Drug Abuse Prevention 1995, Flower for Angela (fiction) 1999, Jesus Saves 2007, God's Spirit Within Me 2008; contribs to various publs. *Honours:* Silver Pen Award 1990. *E-mail:* sandraleesmith@cox.net (office). *Website:* www.sandywardman.com.

SMITH, Sarah, BA, PhD; American writer; b. (Sarah Winthrop Smith), 9 Dec. 1947, Boston, Mass; m. 1st David Lee Robbins 1974 (divorced 1977); m. 2nd Frederick S. Perry 1979; two s. (one deceased) one d. *Education:* Radcliffe Coll., Slade Film School, Queen Mary Coll., London, UK, Harvard Univ. *Career:* Pres. Ivy Films 1970–75; Asst Prof. of English, Tufts Univ. 1976–82; Field Ed., G. K. Hall 1977–83; Man. of artificial intelligence and computer-aided software eng firms 1982–90; writer and consultant 1989–2004; with Pearson Education 2004–; mem. MWA (Founding Webmaster), Sisters in Crime (NE Chapter pres. 1999–2000), Int. Asscn of Crime Writers, PEN, Science Fiction and Fantasy Writers of America, Harvard Univ. Signet Soc. *Publications:* Colette at the Movies (non-fiction) 1980, Samuel Richardson: A Reference Guide 1984, King of Space 1991, The Vanished Child 1992, Future Boston (co-author) 1994, The Knowledge of Water 1996, Doll Street 1996, Riders 1996–97, A Citizen of the Country 2000, Chasing Shakespeares 2003, Deceived 2007, The Other Side of Dark 2010; contrib. to Bulletin of the Authors' Guild, New York Review of Science Fiction, The Third Degree, Aboriginal, F & SF, Tomorrow, Shudder Again, Best New Horror 5. *Honours:* Susan Anthony Potter Prize 1968, Fulbright Fellow 1968–69, Harvard Prize Fellow 1969–74, Frank Knox Fellow 1972–73, Bowdoin Prize 1975, Mellon Fellow 1979–80, New York Times Notable Book citations 1992, 1996, Shakespeare Fellowship. *Literary Agent:* c/o Christopher Schelling, Ralph Vicinanza Literary Agency, 303 W 18th Street, New York, NY 10011, USA. *Address:* 32 Bowker Street, Brookline, MA 02446-6955, USA (home). *E-mail:* sarahwriter@gmail.com (office). *Website:* www.sarahsmith.com.

SMITH, Steven Ross, DipArts; Canadian writer and poet; *Director of Literary Arts, The Banff Centre*; b. 25 June 1945, Toronto, Ont.; s. of Clarence Alfred Smith and Ruth Marion Smith (née McDonald); m. J. Jill Robinson; one s. *Education:* Ryerson Polytechnic Univ. *Career:* Writer-in-Residence, Weyburn Public Library 1987–88, Saskatoon 1996–97; Exec. Dir Sage Hill Writing Experience 1990–2008; Dir of Literary Arts, The Banff Centre 2008–; mem. League of Canadian Poets, Saskatchewan Writers' Guild, Writers' Union of Canada. *Publications:* fiction: Ritual Murders 1983, Lures 1997; poetry: Blind Zone 1985, Sleepwalkers (with Richard Truhlar) 1987, Transient Light 1990, Reading My Father's Book 1995, Fluttertongue Book 1: The Book of Games 1998, Fluttertongue Book 2: The Book of Emmett 2000, Pliny's Knickers 2005, Fluttertongue Book 3: Disarray 2005, Fluttertongue Book 4: Adagio for the Pressured Surround 2007, Fluttertongue 5: Everything Appears to Shine with Mossy Splendour 2011; non-fiction: Ballet of the Speech Organs: Bob Cobbing on Bob Cobbing 1998, Celebrating Saskatchewan Artists 2006; contribs to periodicals. *Honours:* Book of the Year, Saskatchewan Book Awards 2005, Chapbook of the Year 2005. *Address:* Box 5756, Stn. Main, Banff, AB T1L 1G7 (home); Department of Literary Arts, The Banff Centre, Box 1020, Banff, AB T1L 1H5, Canada (office). *Telephone:* (403) 762-6640. *E-mail:* srosssmith@gmail.com (home); steven_smith@banffcentre.ca (office). *Website:* www.banffcentre.ca (office); www.boulderpavement.ca (office); www.fluttertongue.ca.

SMITH, Tom Rob, BA; British writer and screenwriter; b. 1979. *Education:* St John's Coll., Cambridge. *Career:* fmrly Asst Story Ed., Family Affairs (Channel 5); assisted in writing Cambodia's first soap opera (BBC), Phnom Penh. *Publications:* Child 44 (Ian Fleming Steel Dagger Award for Best Thriller 2008, British Book Award for New Writer of the Year 2009) 2008, The Secret Speech 2009. *Address:* c/o Simon & Schuster, 1st Floor, 222 Gray's Inn Road, London, WC1X 8HB, England (office). *E-mail:* enquiries@simonandschuster.co.uk (office). *Website:* authors.simonandschuster.co.uk.

SMITH, Vivian Brian, MA, PhD, FAHA; Australian academic, poet and editor; b. 3 June 1933, Hobart, Tasmania; m. Sybille Gottwald 1960; one s. two d. *Education:* Univ. of Sydney. *Career:* Lecturer, Univ. of Tasmania 1955–66; Literary Ed. Quadrant magazine, Sydney 1975–90; Reader, Univ. of Sydney 1982–96; mem. Australian Soc. of Authors, PEN. *Publications:* The Other Meaning 1956, An Island South 1967, The Poetry of Robert Lowell 1975, Familiar Places 1978, Tide Country 1982, Tasmania and Australian Poetry 1984, Selected Poems 1985, New Selected Poems 1995, Late News 2000, Patrick White: A Bibliography 2004, Along the Line (poems) 2006, Windchimes: Asia in Australian Poetry (ed.) 2006; contrib. to newspapers and magazines. *Honours:* Grace Leven Prize, New South Wales Premier's Prize 1983, Patrick White Literary Award 1997, Centennial Medal for contribution to Australian literature. *Address:* 19 McLeod Street, Mosman, NSW 2088, Australia (home). *Telephone:* (2) 9969-1370 (home). *E-mail:* smith@exemail.com.au (home).

SMITH, Ward (see Goldsmith, Howard)

SMITH, Wilbur Addison, BComm; British novelist; b. 9 Jan. 1933, Zambia; m. 1st Danielle Antoinette Smith 1971 (died 1999); two s. one d.; m. 2nd Mokhiniso Rakhimova 2000. *Education:* Michaelhouse, Natal and Rhodes Univ. *Career:* business exec. 1954–58; factory owner 1958–64; professional author 1961–. *Publications:* When the Lion Feeds 1964, The Dark of the Sun 1965, The Sound of Thunder 1966, Shout at the Devil 1968, Gold Mine 1970, The Diamond Hunters 1971, The Sunbird 1972, Eagle in the Sky 1974, The Eye of the Tiger 1975, Cry Wolf 1976, A Sparrow Falls 1977, Hungry as the Sea 1978, Wild Justice 1979, A Falcon Flies 1980, Men of Men 1981, The Angels Weep 1982, The Leopard Hunts in Darkness 1984, The Burning Shore 1985, Power of the Sword 1986, Rage 1987, The Courtneys 1987, The Courtneys in Africa 1988, A Time to Die 1989, Golden Fox 1990, Elephant Song 1991, River God 1993, The Seventh Scroll 1995, Birds of Prey 1997, Monsoon 1999, Warlock 2001, Blue Horizon 2003, The Triumph of the Sun 2005, The Quest 2007, Assegai 2009, Those in Peril 2011; contrib. to numerous journals and magazines. *Literary Agent:* c/o Charles Pick Consultancy Ltd, 21 Dagmar Terrace, London, N1 2BN, England. *Telephone:* (20) 7226-2779. *Fax:* (20) 7226-2779. *Website:* www.wilbursmithbooks.com; www.wilbursmith.net.

SMITH, William Jay, BA, MA; American poet, writer and academic; *Professor Emeritus of English, Hollins College*; b. 22 April 1918, Winnfield, La; m. 1st Barbara Howes 1947 (divorced 1965); two s.; m. 2nd Sonja Haussmann 1966; one step-s. *Education:* Washington Univ., St Louis, Institut de Touraine, Tours, France, Columbia Univ., Wadham Coll., Oxford, UK, Univ. of Florence. *Career:* Instructor, Columbia Univ. 1946–47, Visiting Prof. 1973–75; Instructor, Williams Coll. 1951, Poet-in-Residence and Lecturer 1959–64, 1966–67; Writer-in-Residence, Hollins Coll. 1965–66, Prof. of English 1967–68, 1970–80, Prof. Emer. 1980–; Consultant in Poetry, Library of Congress, Washington, DC 1968–70, Hon. Consultant 1970–76; Lecturer, Salzburg Seminar in American Studies 1974; Fulbright Lecturer, Moscow State Univ. 1981; Poet-in-Residence, Cathedral of St John the Divine, New York 1985–88; mem. American Acad. of Arts and Letters (Vice-Pres. for literature 1986–89). *Publications:* poetry: Poems 1947, Celebration at Dark 1950, Snow 1953, The Stork 1954, Typewriter Birds 1954, The Bead Curtain: Calligrams 1957, The Old Man on the Isthmus 1957, Poems 1947–1957 1957, Prince Souvanna Phouma: An Exchange Between Richard Wilbur and William Jay Smith 1963, Morels 1964, The Tin Can and Other Poems 1966, New and Selected Poems 1970, A Rose for Katherine Anne Porter 1970, At Delphi: For Allen Tate on His Seventy-Fifth Birthday, 19 November 1974 1974, Venice in the Fog 1975, Verses on the Times (with Richard Wilbur) 1978, Journey to the Dead Sea 1979, The Tall Poets 1979, Mr Smith 1980, The Traveler's Tree: New and Selected Poems 1980, Oxford Doggerel 1983, Collected Translations: Italian, French, Spanish, Portuguese 1985, The Tin Can 1988, Journey to the Interior 1988, Plain Talk: Epigrams, Epitaphs, Satires, Nonsense, Occasional, Concrete and Quotidian Poems 1988, Collected Poems 1939–1989 1990, The World Below the Window: Poems 1937–1997 1998, The Cherokee Lottery: A Sequence of Poems 2000, The Girl in Glass: Love Poems 2002, Words by the Water, Poems 2008, 17 books of poetry for children 1955–90; other: The Spectra Hoax 1961, The Skies of Venice 1961, Children and Poetry: A Selective Bibliography (with Virginia Haviland) 1969, Louise Bogan: A Woman's Words 1972, The Streaks of the Tulip: Selected Criticism 1972, Green 1980, Army Brat: A Memoir 1980, Dancing in the Garden: A Bittersweet Love Affair with France 2008; editor: Herrick 1962, The Golden Journey: Poems for Young People (with Louise Bogan) 1965, Poems from France 1967, Poems from Italy 1972, A Green Place: Modern Poems 1982; contributions: journals and magazines. *Honours:* Rhodes Scholar 1947–48, Ford Foundation Fellowship 1964, Henry Bellamann Major Award 1970, National Endowment for the Arts Grant 1972, 1995, National Endowment for the Humanities Grants 1975, 1989, Gold Medal of Labor, Hungary 1978, Ingram Merrill Foundation Grant 1982, Trans. Award, Swedish Acad. 1990, Médaille de Vermeil Acad. Française 1991, Pro Cultura Hungarica Medal 1993, René Vásquez Díaz Prize, Swedish Acad. 1997. *Address:* 63 Luther Shaw Road, Cummington, MA 01026-9787, USA (home); 52–56 rue d'Alleray, 75015 Paris, France (home). *Telephone:* (413) 634-5546 (home). *Fax:* (413) 634-5546 (home).

SMITHER, Elizabeth Edwina, MNZM; New Zealand poet, novelist and short story writer; b. 15 Sept. 1941, New Plymouth; d. of Edwin Russell Harrington and Elsie Irene Bowerman; m. Michael Duncan Smither 1963; three c. *Education:* Victoria Univ., Wellington, Massey Univ., New Zealand Library School. *Career:* part-time librarian; Te Mata Estate New Zealand Poet Laureate 2001–03; mem. New Zealand Soc. of Authors. *Publications:* poetry: Here Come the Clouds 1975, You're Very Seductive William Carlos Williams 1978, The Sarah Train 1980, The Legend of Marcello Mastroianni's Wife 1981, Casanova's Ankle 1981, Shakespeare Virgins 1983, Professor Musgrove's Canary 1986, Gorilla/Guerilla 1986, Animaux 1988, A Pattern of Marching (New Zealand Book Award 1990) 1989, A Cortège of Daughters 1993, The Tudor Style: Poems New and Selected 1993, The Lark Quartet (Montana New Zealand Book Award 2000) 1999, Red Shoes 2003, A Question of Gravity 2004, The Year of Adverbs 2007, Horse playing the Accordion 2007; novels: First Blood 1983, Brother-love Sister-love 1986, The Sea Between Us 2003, Different Kinds of Pleasure 2006, Lola 2010; short story collections: Nights at the Embassy 1990, Mr Fish 1994, The Mathematics of Jane Austen 1997, Listening to the Everly Brothers 2002, The Girl who Proposed 2007; other: Tug Brothers (juvenile) 1983, The Seventies Connection (co-ed.) 1987, The

Journal Box (journals) 1996. *Honours:* Mem. NZ Order of Merit 2004; Hon. DLitt (Auckland) 2004; Scholarships in Letters 1987, 1992, Prime Minister's Award for Literary Achievement in Poetry 2008. *Address:* 19A Mt View Place, New Plymouth 4301, New Zealand (home). *Telephone:* (6) 7512398 (home). *E-mail:* elizabethsmither@xtra.co.nz (home).

SMITTEN, Richard, BA; American writer; b. 22 April 1940, New York, NY; one d. *Education:* Univ. of Western Ontario. *Career:* fmr Marketing Man., Canada Div., Vick Chemical Co.; fmr Exec. Vice-Pres., MTS International. *Publications:* Twice Killed 1987, The Man Who Made it Snow (with Max Mermelstein and Robin Moore) 1990, Godmother 1990, Bank of Death 1993, Legal Tender 1994, Kathy: A Case of Nymphomania 1994, Jesse Livermore: World's Greatest Stock Trader 1999, False Witness 2001, How to Trade in Stocks 2001. *E-mail:* info@smittenbooks.com (office). *Website:* www.smittenbooks.com.

SMYTHE, Colin Peter, BA, MA, FRSA; British editor, publisher and literary agent; *Managing Director, Colin Smythe Ltd*; b. 2 March 1942, Maidenhead, Berks., England; s. of Wing Commdr Cyril Richard Smythe and Jean Edith Smythe (née Murdoch). *Education:* Bradfield Coll., Berks., Trinity Coll., Dublin. *Career:* Man. Dir Colin Smythe Ltd 1965–; Visiting Prof., Univ. of Ulster, Coleraine 1993–2002; Sr Research Fellow, Inst. of English Studies, School of Advanced Study, Univ. of London. *Publications:* Irish Literary Studies series (gen. ed.), Lady Gregory's Writings (general ed.) 1970–, Lady Gregory 1971–, A Guide to Coole Park: Home of Lady Gregory 1973, Lady Gregory: Our Irish Theatre (ed.) 1973, Lady Gregory: Poets and Dreamers (ed.) 1974, Lady Gregory: Seventy Years 1852–1922 (ed.) 1974, The Collected Works of G. W. Russell – AE (gen. ed. with Henry Summerfield) 1978–, Robert Gregory 1881–1918 (ed.) 1981, Lady Gregory Fifty Years After (co-ed. with Ann Saddlemyer) 1986, Oxford Companion to Irish Literature (assoc. ed.) 1996. *Honours:* various orders and decorations, including Officer, Venerable Order of St John of Jerusalem 1987, Kt, Order of Polonia Restituta (Poland) 1988, Kt, Order of the Conception of Our Lady of Vila Viçosa (Portugal) 1996, Kt Commdr of Grace, S. M. Constantinian Order of St George, Bourbon/Two Sicilies 1990, Kt . Commdr, Royal Order of King Francis I 2005; Hon. LLD (Dublin) 1998. *Address:* 38 Mill Lane, Gerrards Cross, Bucks., SL9 8BA, England (office). *Telephone:* (1753) 886000 (office). *Fax:* (1753) 886469 (office). *E-mail:* cs@colinsmythe.co.uk (office). *Website:* www.colinsmythe.co.uk (office).

SNEYD, Stephen (Steve) Henry, BSc, MA; British poet and writer; *Editor on Poetry, Fantasy Commentator Magazine*; b. 20 March 1941, Maidenhead, Berkshire, England; m. Rita Ann Cockburn 1964; one s. one d. *Career:* UK Columnist, Scavenger's Newsletter, USA 1984–99; Contributing Ed. on Poetry, Fantasy Commentator magazine, USA 1992–; Ed. Data Dump genre poetry newsletter 1991–; mem. Science Fiction Poetry Asscn, Pendragon Arthurian Soc., Castle Studies Group. *Publications:* poetry: The Legerdemain of Changelings 1979, Two Humps Not One 1980, Discourteous Self-Service 1982, Prug Plac Gamma 1983, Stone Bones (with Pete Presford) 1983, Fifty-Fifty Infinity 1989, Bad News from the Stars 1991, At the Thirteenth Hour 1991, We Are Not Men 1991, What Time Has Use For 1992, A Mile Beyond the Bus 1992, In Coils of Earthen Hold 1994, A Reason for Staying 1999, Gestaltmacher, Gestaltmacher, Make Me a Gestalt 2000, NeoLithon (with John Light) 2001, The Pennine Triangle (with J. F. Haines and J. C. Hartley) 2002, Ahasuerus On Mars 2004, Three Star Chamber 2005, Icarus Rising 2008, Mistaking the Nature of the Posthuman 2009; short stories: over 500 published; contrib. to over 1,000 reviews, quarterlies, journals, magazines and websites world-wide; radio and television. *Honours:* Trend Prize for Peace Poetry 1967, Northern Star Poetry Prize 1983, Diploma di Merito, Accademia Italia 1983, Best Poet, Small Press and Magazine Awards 1986, Paterson Prize 1996, First Prize, Starlite Poetry Contest, USA 1999, Special Prize Diploma, International Cosmopoetry Festival of SARM, Romania 1999. *Address:* 4 Nowell Place, Almondbury, Huddersfield, West Yorkshire HD5 8PB, England (home).

SNICKET, Lemony (see Handler, Daniel)

SNIDER, Clifton Mark, BA, MA, PhD; American academic, poet and writer; b. 3 March 1947, Duluth, Minn.; s. of Allan George Snider and Rhoda Marion Tout; partner Mario Hernandez. *Education:* Southern California Coll. (now Vanguard Univ.), Costa Mesa, California State Univ., Long Beach, Univ. of New Mexico. *Career:* Faculty mem., California State Univ., Long Beach 1974–, Long Beach City Coll. 1975–2002. *Publications:* poetry: Jesse Comes Back 1976, Bad Smoke Good Body 1980, Jesse and his Son 1982, Edwin: A Character in Poems 1984, Blood & Bones 1988, Impervious to Piranhas 1989, The Age of the Mother 1992, The Alchemy of Opposites 2000, Aspens in the Wind 2009; other: The Stuff That Dreams are Made on: A Jungian Interpretation of Literature 1991, Loud Whisper (novel) 2000, Bare Roots (novel) 2001, Wrestling with Angels: A Tale of Two Brothers (novel) 2001; contrib. to anthologies, reviews, quarterlies and journals. *Honours:* Resident Fellow, Yaddo 1978, 1982, Helene Wurlitzer Foundation of New Mexico 1984, 1990, 1998, 2004, 2005, 2008, Michael Karolyi Memorial Foundation, Vence, France 1986, 1987, Meritorious Performance and Professional Promise Award, California State Univ. *Address:* English Department, California State University, Long Beach, 1250 Bellflower Boulevard, Long Beach, CA 90840 (office); 2719 Eucalyptus Avenue, Long Beach, CA 90806, USA (home). *E-mail:* csnider@csulb.edu (office). *Website:* www.csulb.edu/~csnider (office).

SNOW, Jonathan (Jon) George; British television journalist; b. 28 Sept. 1947, s. of Rt Rev. George Snow and Joan Snow; pnr Madeleine Colvin; two d. *Education:* St Edward's School, Oxford, Univ. of Liverpool. *Career:* Voluntary Service Overseas, Uganda 1967–68; Co-ordinator New Horizon Youth Centre, London 1970–73 (Chair. 1986–); journalist, Independent Radio News, LBC 1973–76; reporter, ITN 1977–83, Washington Corresp. 1983–86, Diplomatic Ed. 1986–89; presenter, Channel Four News 1989–; Visiting Prof. of Broadcast Journalism, Nottingham Trent Univ. 1992–2001, Univ. of Stirling 2002–; Chair. New Horizon Youth Centre 1986–, Prison Reform Trust 1992–96, Media Trust 1995–, Tate Modern Council 1999–; Trustee Noel Buxton Trust 1992–, Nat. Gallery 1999–; Chancellor Oxford Brookes Univ. 2001–. *Publications:* Atlas of Today 1987, Sons and Mothers 1996, Shooting History: A Personal Journey 2004; articles in The Guardian, Financial Times, Independent, Telegraph, New Statesman. *Honours:* Hon. DLitt (Nottingham Trent) 1994, Hon. DLitt (Open Univ.); Monte Carlo Golden Nymph Award, for Eritrea air attack reporting 1979, TV Reporter of the Year, for Afghanistan, Iran and Iraq reporting, Royal Television Soc. (RTS) 1980, Valiant for Truth Award, for El Salvador reporting 1982, Int. Award, for El Salvador reporting, RTS 1982, Home News Award, for Kegworth air crash reporting, RTS 1989, RTS Presenter of the Year 1994, 2002, BAFTA Richard Dimbleby Award 2005, RTS Journalist of the Year 2006. *Address:* Channel Four News, ITN, 200 Gray's Inn Road, London, WC1X 8HB, England. *Telephone:* (20) 7430-4237; (20) 7833-3000 (office). *Fax:* (20) 7430-4607. *E-mail:* jon.snow@itn.co.uk (office). *Website:* www.channel4.com/news (office).

SNYDER, Gary Sherman, BA; American poet, writer and fmr teacher; b. 8 May 1930, San Francisco, Calif.; m. 1st Alison Gass 1950 (divorced 1952); m. 2nd Joanne Kyger 1960 (divorced 1965); m. 3rd Masa Uehara 1967 (divorced 1987); m. 4th Carole Koda 1991; two s. two step-d. *Education:* Reed Coll., Portland, Ore., Indiana Univ., Univ. of California, Berkeley, studied Zen Buddhism and East Asian culture in Japan. *Career:* often associated with the Beat Generation and the San Francisco Renaissance; Prof. of Creative Writing, Univ. of California, Davis 1986–2001, now Prof. Emer.; mem. American Acad. of Arts and Letters, American Acad. of Arts and Sciences; often described as the 'poet laureate of Deep Ecology'. *Publications:* poetry: Riprap and Cold Mountain Poems 1959, Myths and Texts 1960, A Range of Poems 1966, Three Worlds, Three Realms, Six Roads 1966, The Back Country 1968, The Blue Sky 1969, Regarding Wave 1970, Manzanita 1971, Plute Creek 1972, The Fudo Trilogy: Spell Against Demons, Smokey the Bear Sutra, The California Water Plan 1973, Turtle Island (Pulitzer Prize for Poetry 1975) 1974, All in the Family 1975, Songs for Gaia 1979, Axe Handles 1983, Left Out in the Rain: New Poems 1947–1986 1986, No Nature: New and Selected Poems 1992, Mountains and Rivers Without End 1996, Danger on Peaks 2003, Danger on Peaks 2004, Tamalpais Walking (with Tom Killion) 2009, Pharmako Poeia 2010; prose: Earth House Hold: Technical Notes and Queries to Fellow Dharma Revolutionaries 1969, The Old Ways: Six Essays 1977, He Who Hunted Birds in His Father's Village: The Dimensions of a Haida Myth 1979, The Real Work: Interviews and Talks 1964–1979 1980, Passage Through India 1984, The Practice of the Wild 1990, A Place in Space 1995, The Gary Snyder Reader: Prose, Poetry, and Translations 1999, Back on the Fire: Essays 2007; contribs to anthologies. *Honours:* scholarship to First Zen Inst. of America 1956, American Acad. of Arts and Letters Award 1966, Bollingen Foundation grant 1966–67, Frank O'Hara Prize 1967, Levinson Prize 1968, Guggenheim Fellowship 1968–69, Bollingen Prize 1997, John Hay Award for Nature Writing 1997, Masaoka Shiki Int. Haiku Grand Prize 2004, Ruth Lilly Poetry Prize 2008. *Address:* 18442 Macnab Cypress Road, Nevada City, CA 95959, USA (home).

SNYDER, Midori; American writer; b. 1 Jan. 1954, Santa Monica, CA; m. Stephen Haessler 1979; one s. one d. *Education:* Univ. of Wisconsin. *Career:* co-dir, The Endicott Studio for Mythic Arts; co-Ed. Journal of Mythic Arts 2003–08. *Publications:* Soulstring 1987, New Moon 1989, Sadar's Keep 1991, Beldane's Fire 1993, The Flight of Michael McBride 1994, Dinotopia, Hatchling 1995, The Innamorati (Mythopoeic Award) 1998, Hannah's Garden 2005, Except the Queen (with Jane Yolen) 2010; contributions: anthologies. *Website:* www.midorisnyder.com.

SNYDER, Richard E.; American publisher; b. 6 April 1933, New York; s. of Jack Snyder and Molly Rothman; m. 1st Otilie Freund 1963 (divorced); one s. one d.; m. 2nd Laura Yorke 1992; two s. *Education:* Tufts Univ., Medford. *Career:* sales rep. Simon & Schuster 1961, Vice-Pres. Marketing 1966–69, Vice-Pres. Trade Books 1969–73, Exec. Vice-Pres. Trade and Educ. Admin 1973–75, Pres. and COO 1975–78, Pres. and CEO 1978–86, Chair. and CEO 1986–94, consultant 1994–95; Chair., CEO Golden Books Family Entertainment 1996–2001; Chair. PEN, NY Area 1988; Dir Reliance Group Holdings, Children's Blood Foundation; Trustee NY Presbyterian Hosp.; Founder-mem. Nat. Book Foundation, Nat. Book Awards; mem. Council on Foreign Relations, Wildlife Conservation Soc., Econ. Club of NY.

SNYDER, Zilpha Keatley, BA; American writer; b. 11 May 1927, Lemoore, CA; m. 1950; two s. one d. *Education:* Whittier Coll. *Publications:* Season of Ponies 1964, The Velvet Room 1965, Black and Blue Magic 1966, The Egypt Game 1967, The Changeling 1970, The Headless Cupid 1971, The Witches of Worm 1972, The Princess and the Giants 1973, The Truth About Stone Hollow 1974, The Famous Stanley Kidnapping Case 1979, Blair's Nightmare 1984, The Changing Maze 1985, And Condors Danced 1987, Squeak Saves the Day and Other Tooley Tales 1988, Janie's Private Eyes 1989, Libby on Wednesday 1990, Song of the Gargoyle 1991, Fool's Gold 1993, Cat Running 1994, The

Trespasser 1995, Castle Court Kids 1995, The Gypsy Game 1997, Gib Rides Home 1998, The Runaways 1999, Gig and the Gray Ghost 2000, Spyhole Secrets 2001, The Ghosts of Rathburn Park 2002, The Unseen 2004, The Magic Nation Thing 2005, The Treasures of Weatherby 2006, The Bronze Pen 2008, William S and the Great Escape 2009. *Honours:* Beatty Award 1995. *Address:* 52 Miller Avenue, Mill Valley, CA 94941-1920, USA (home).

SOBEL, Dava; American science writer; b. 1947; m. 1st Arthur Klein (divorced); one s. one d.; m. 2nd Alfonso Triggiani. *Education:* State Univ. of NY at Binghamton. *Career:* fmr science reporter, New York Times; reported for several journals including Audubon, Discover, Life, The New Yorker; fmr Contributing Ed. Harvard Magazine; has lectured at The Smithsonian Inst., The Explorers Club, NASA Goddard Space Flight Center, Folger Shakespeare Library, Los Angeles Public Library, NY Public Library, Royal Geographical Soc. (London); numerous radio and TV appearances; mem. American Asscn of Univ. Women, Planetary Soc.; Fellow, American Geographical Soc. *Publications:* Is Anyone Out There? The Scientific Search for Extraterrestrial Intelligence (with Frank D. Drake) 1992, Longitude (several awards including Harold D. Vursell Memorial Award American Acad. of Arts and Letters 1996, UK Book of the Year 1996, Prix Faubert du Coton, Premio del Mare Circeo) 1995, Galileo's Daughter: A Historical Memoir of Science, Faith, and Love 1999, Letters to Father 2001, The Planets 2005. *Honours:* Hon. DLit (Middlebury Coll., Vt) 2002, (Bath, UK) 2002; Nat. Media Award American Psychological Foundation 1980, Lowell Thomas Award Soc. of American Travel Writers 1992, Gold Medal Council for the Advancement and Support of Educ. 1994, Christopher Award 1999, Los Angeles Times Book Prize 2000, Nat. Science Bd Public Service Award 2001, Bradford Washburn Award Boston Museum of Science 2001, Nathaniel Bowditch Maritime Scholar 2003, Harrison Medal, Worshipful Co. of Clockmakers (UK) 2004. *Literary Agent:* c/o Michael Carlisle, InkWell Management, 521 Fifth Avenue, 26th Floor, New York, NY 10175, USA. *Telephone:* (212) 922-3500.

SOBH, Alawiya, BA; Lebanese novelist and writer; *Editor in Chief, Snob Magazine*; b. 1955, Beirut; not m. *Education:* Lebanese Nat. Univ., Beirut. *Career:* fmr high school teacher; contributor to daily Beirut newspapers, including Nida' and an-Nahar; founder and Ed.-in-Chief Snob magazine 1990–; took part in numerous cultural confs., in Beirut, Cairo, Amman, Paris, Germany. *Publications include:* novels: Mariam of the Stories (title in trans.) 2002, Donia 2006, It's Called Love (title in trans.) 2008; short stories: Slumber of the Days 1986; contribs. to many magazines and newspapers including Annahr, Assafir, Al Hayat. *Honours:* Sultan Kabous Prize for Best Arabic Novel 2006. *Address:* al-Hasnaa, al-Iktissad Wal-Aamal Group, PO Box 113-6194, Hamra, Beirut 1103 2100 (office); Baraka Building, 3rd Floor, Kuwait St, Beirut, Lebanon (home). *Telephone:* (1) 341713 (office); (1) 737629 (home). *Fax:* (1) 346800 (office). *E-mail:* snob@snobmagazine.com (office); alasobh@hotmail.com (home). *Website:* www.snobmagazine.com.

SOBOL, Joshua; Israeli playwright; b. 1939, Tel-Aviv. *Education:* Sorbonne, Paris, France. *Career:* teacher of aesthetics and dir of theatrical workshops, Tel-Aviv Univ., Kibbutz Teachers' Seminary, Belt Zvi Drama School; currently Visiting Prof. of Theater, Weslyan Univ., USA. *Plays:* The Days to Come 1971, Status Quo Vadis 1973, Sylvester 72 1974, The Joker 1975, The Night of the Twentieth 1976, Nerves 1976, Tenants 1977, Gig and Magog Show 1977, Repentance 1977, Homeward Angel 1978, Wedding Night 1979, The Last Worker 1980, Wars of the Jews 1981, Weininger's Night 1982, Ghetto 1984, Pasodoble 1984, Palestinian Girl 1985, Countdown 1986, Adam 1989, Underground 1991, Solo 1991, A&B 1991, Eye to Eye 1991, Ring Twice 1992, Nice Toni 1993, Love for a Penny 1993, Schneider and Schuster 1993, The Masked Ball 1994, Bloody Nathan 1994, The Father 1995, Village 1995, Alma 1996, Ma ni Ma Mama 1997, Strangers 1997, Gebiritg 2000, Crocodiles 2001, Real Time 2002, Eye Witness 2002, Love in Dark Times 2003, A Mentsch 2003, A Working Class Hero 2005, Kol Nidrei 2005. *Publications:* novel: Shtika (trans. as Silence) 2005. *Honours:* Evening Standard Award for Best Play 1989, Rosenblum Award 2003. *E-mail:* josobol@netvision.net.il (home).

SOBTI, Krishna; Indian writer; b. 18 Feb. 1925, Gujarat, West Punjab (now in Pakistan); d. of the late Diwan Prithvi Raj Sobti and the Late Smt Durga Devi Sobti; m. Shri Shivanath. *Education:* Fateh Chand Coll., Lahore. *Career:* Hindi writer; worked as governess to Maharaja Tej Singh of Sirohi; Ed., Adult Literacy Programme, Delhi Admin; later full-time writer; Nat. Fellow, Indian Inst. of Advanced Study 1996–99; Fellow, Sahitya Akademi 1996–, Nat. Acad. of Letters. *Publications include:* Dara se Bichuri, Mitro Marajani, Zindaginama, Ai Ladki, Dil-o-Daanish, Surajmukhi Andhere Ke, Hum Hashmat, Yaron Ke Yaar, Badalon ke Ghere, Sobti ek Sohabat, Samay Sargam, Shabdon ke Aalok Mein, Dil o Danish, Daar Se Bichhudi, Sobti Vaid Samvad. *Honours:* Sahitya Akademi Award 1980, Shiromani Award 1981, Hindi Acad. Award 1982, Katha Chudamani Award for Literary Lifetime Achievement 1999, Vyas Samman Award 2007, Shalaka Samman, Maithili Sharan Gupt Samman, Sadhbhavana Puraskar, Hutch Crossword Translation Award. *Address:* B 505 Purvasha, Anandlok Housing Society, Mayur Vihar 1, Delhi 110 091, India (home). *Telephone:* (11) 22750896 (home). *E-mail:* krishnasobti@indiatimes.com (home).

SOFER, Dalia, BA, MFA; American (b. Iranian) writer; b. 1972, Tehran. *Education:* Lycée Français de New York, New York Univ., Sarah Lawrence Coll. *Career:* emigrated to USA aged ten; fmr writer-in-residence Yaddo Community. *Publications:* The Septembers of Shiraz 2007. *Honours:* Whiting Writers' Award. *Address:* c/o Author Mail, 7th Floor, HarperCollins Publishers, 10 East 53rd Street, New York, NY 10022, USA (office). *Website:* www.harpercollins.com (office).

SOHAIL, Khalid, MB BS, FRCPC; Pakistani/Canadian psychiatrist, writer and poet; *Psychotherapist, Creative Psychotherapy Clinic*; b. 9 July 1952, Pakistan. *Education:* studied in Pakistan and Canada. *Career:* Psychotherapist, Creative Psychotherapy Clinic, Whitby, Ont.; mem. Writers' Forum of Canada, Writers' Union of Canada, Family of the Heart Canada; Fellow, Royal Coll. of Physicians and Surgeons of Canada. *Films:* documentaries on mixed marriages and domestic violence. *Television:* CBC documentary on Atheism and Humanism, Vision TV documentary on Religion and Sex. *Publications include:* Discovering New Highways in Life 1991, From One Culture to Another 1992, Literary Encounters 1992, Pages of My Heart (poems) 1993, A Broken Man (short stories) 1993, Mother Earth is Sad (fiction) 1999, Encounters With Creativity, Insanity and Spirituality 1999, The Myth of the Chosen One 2002; contributions: anthologies and journals. *Honours:* Rahul Award, Kolkata 1994. *Address:* Creative Psychotherapy Clinic, 213 Byron Street South, Whitby, ON L1N 4P7, Canada (office). *E-mail:* welcome@drsohail.com (office). *Website:* www.drsohail.com (office).

SOKOLOV, Maksim Yur'yevich; Russian journalist; b. 1959, Moscow; m. *Education:* Moscow State Univ. *Career:* worked as programmer in All-Union Centre of Transport, USSR State Cttee on Science and Tech. 1981–83; All-Union Research Inst. of Patent Information 1983–84; All-Union Research Inst. for Man. of Coal Industry 1985–87; Research Inst. of Gen. Plan of Moscow 1988–89; journalist since late 1980s; contrib. Commersant (weekly) 1989–97; political observer, Izvestiya 1998–; publs in newspapers Nezavisimaya Gazeta, Atmoda, Segodnya, magazines Vek XX i Mir, Oktyabr, Soviet Analyst (UK); broadcaster Russian Public TV Co. ORT; commentator, TV programmes; special corresp., Soviet analyst. *Honours:* Gong 94 Journalism prize; Medal for the Defence of Free Russia 1991. *Address:* Izvestiya, 103791 Moscow, Tverskaya str. 18, Russia. *Telephone:* (495) 299-21-22 (office).

SOLLERS, Philippe, (pseudonym of Philippe Joyaux); French author and critic; b. 28 Nov. 1936, Bordeaux; s. of Octave Joyaux and Marcelle Molinié; m. Julia Kristeva 1967; one s. *Education:* Lycées Montesquieu and Montaigne, Bordeaux and Ecole Sainte-Geneviève, Versailles. *Career:* co-f. and ran the avant garde journal Tel Quel (along with writer and art critic Marcelin Pleynet) 1960–82; Dir L'Infini (review) 1983–; mem. reading Cttee Editions Gallimard 1990–, Asscn of French Museums 1998–. *Publications include:* novels: Une Curieuse Solitude 1958, Le Parc 1961, Drame 1965, Nombres, Lois 1972, H 1973, Paradis, Vision à New York 1981, Femmes 1983, Portrait du joueur 1985, Paradis 2 1986, Le Coeur absolu 1987, Les Surprises de Fragonard 1987, Les Folies françaises 1988, Le Lys d'or 1989, Carnet de nuit 1989, La Fête à Venise 1991, Le Secret 1993, Venise Eternelle 1993, La Guerre du Goût 1994, Femmes, Mythologies (co-author) 1994, Les Passions de Francis Bacon 1996, Studio 1997, L'Année du Tigre, Journal de l'année 1998, 1999, L'Oeil de Proust, les dessins de Marcel Proust 1999, Passion fixe 2000, La Divine Comédie 2000, L'Etoile des amants 2002, Illuminations à travers les textes sacrés 2003, Le Saint-Ane 2004, Logique de la fiction 2006, Une Vie Divine 2007, Un vrai roman: Mémoires 2007, Les Voyageurs du temps 2009, Trésor d'Amour 2011, L'Éclaircie 2012; essays: L'Intermédiaire 1963, Logiques 1968, L'Écriture et l'Expérience des Limites 1968 ([ublished as Writing and the Experience of Limits 1982), Sur le Matérialisme 1974, Théorie des Exceptions 1985, De Kooning, vite 1988, Improvisations 1991, Sade contre l'Être suprême 1996, Les passions de Francis Bacon 1996, Picasso, le héros 1996, La Guerre du Goût 1994, Casanova l'admirable (Prix Elsa-Morante 1999) 1998, Francesca Woodman 1998, Francis Ponge 2001, Éloge de l'Infini 2001, Mystérieux Mozart 2001, Liberté du XVIIIème (Extract from La Guerre du Goût) 2002, Dictionnaire amoureux de Venise 2004, Fleurs 2006, Guerres secrètes 2007, Vers le Paradis (with DVD) 2010, Discours Parfait 2010. *Honours:* Chevalier, Légion d'honneur; Officier, Ordre nat. du Mérite, des Arts et des Lettres; Prix Médicis 1961, Grand Prix du Roman de la Ville de Paris 1988, Prix Paul-Morand (Académie française) 1992, Prix littéraire de la fondation Prince Pierre de Monaco 2006. *Address:* L'Infini, 5 rue Sébastien-Bottin, 75007 Paris, France (office). *Website:* www.philippesollers.net.

SOLOMON, Maynard Elliott, BA; American music historian and writer; b. 5 Jan. 1930, New York, NY; m. Eva Georgiana Tevan 1951; two s. one d. *Education:* Brooklyn Coll., CUNY, Columbia Univ., New England Conservatory of Music. *Career:* co-founder, co-owner, Vanguard Recording Soc. Inc 1950–86; teacher, CUNY 1979–81; Visiting Prof., SUNY at Stony Brook 1988–89, Columbia Univ. 1989–90, Harvard Univ. 1991–92, Yale Univ. 1994–95; Scholarly Adviser, Beethoven Archive, Bonn 1995–; Graduate Faculty, Juilliard School 1998–; Assoc. Ed., American Imago 1976; mem. PEN. *Publications:* Marxism and Art 1973, Beethoven 1977, 1998, Myth, Creativity and Psychoanalysis 1978, Beethoven Essays 1988, Mozart: A Life 1995, Some Romantic Images in Beethoven 1998, Late Beethoven: Music, Thought, Imagination 2003; contrib. articles to Beethoven Jahrbuch: Music and Letters, Musical Quarterly: 19th Century Music, Journal of the American Musicological Society. *Honours:* Hon. DMA; ASCAP–Deems Taylor Awards 1978, 1989, 1995, Kinkeldey Award American Musicological Soc. 1989, hon. mem. 1999, 2000. *Address:* 1 W 72nd Street, Apt 56, New York, NY 10023, USA.

SOLOW, Robert Merton, PhD; American economist and academic; *Institute Professor Emeritus, Massachusetts Institute of Technology*; b. 23 Aug. 1924, Brooklyn, NY; s. of Milton Solow and Hannah Solow; m. Barbara Lewis 1945;

two s. one d. *Education:* Harvard Univ. *Career:* Asst Prof. of Statistics, Mass. Inst. of Technology 1950–53, Assoc. Prof. of Econs 1954–57, Prof. of Econs 1958–73, Inst. Prof. 1973–95, Inst. Prof. Emer. 1995–; W. Edwards Deming Prof., New York Univ. 1996; Sr Economist, Council of Econ. Advisers 1961–62; Marshall Lecturer, Univ. of Cambridge, UK 1963–64; De Vries Lecturer, Rotterdam 1963, Wicksell Lecturer, Stockholm 1964; Eastman Visiting Prof., Univ. of Oxford, UK 1968–69; Killian Prize Lecturer, MIT 1978; Geary Lecturer, Univ. of Dublin, Ireland 1980; Overseas Fellow, Churchill Coll., Cambridge 1984; Mitsui Lecturer, Birmingham 1985; Nobel Memorial Lecture, Stockholm 1987 and numerous others in int. academic insts; mem. Nat. Comm. on Tech., Automation and Econ. Progress 1964–65, Presidential Comm. on Income Maintenance 1968–69; mem. Bd of Dirs Fed. Reserve Bank of Boston 1975–81, Chair. 1979–81; Fellow, Center for Advanced Study in Behavioral Sciences 1957–58, Trustee 1982–95; Vice-Pres. American Econ. Asscn 1968, Pres. 1979, Vice-Pres. AAAS 1970; Pres. Econometric Soc. 1964; Trustee Woods Hole Oceanographic Inst. 1988–, Alfred P. Sloan Foundation 1992–, Resources for the Future 1994–96, Urban Inst. 1994–, German Marshall Fund of US 1994–; Pres. Int. Econ. Asscn 1999–2002; mem. Nat. Science Bd 1995–2000; Fellow American Acad. of Arts and Sciences, mem. of Council, NAS 1977–80, mem. 1972–; Corresp. mem. British Acad.; mem. American Philosophical Soc.; Fellow Acad. dei Lincei (Rome); Foundation Fellow, Russell Sage Foundation 2000–. *Publications:* Linear Programming and Economic Analysis 1958, Capital Theory and the Rate of Return 1963, Sources of Unemployment in the United States 1964, Price Expectations and the Behavior of the Price Level 1970, Growth Theory: An Exposition 1970, The Labor Market as a Social Institution 1989, Learning from "Learning by Doing" 1994, A Critical Essay On Modern Macroeconomic Theory (with Frank Hahn) 1995; many journal articles. *Honours:* Orden pour le mérite, Germany 1995; Hon. LLD (Chicago) 1967, (Lehigh) 1977, (Brown) 1972, (Wesleyan) 1982; Hon. LittD (Williams Coll.) 1974, (Rensselaer Polytechnic Inst.) 2003; Dr hc (Paris) 1975, (Geneva) 1982, (Conservatoire Nat. des Arts et Métiers, Paris) 1994, (Buenos Aires) 1999, (Pompeii Fabra, Barcelona) 2008; Hon. DLitt (Warwick) 1976, (Colgate) 1990, (Glasgow) 1992, (Harvard) 1992; Hon. ScD (Tulane) 1983; Hon. DScS (Yale) 1986, (Univ. of Mass., Boston) 1989, (Helsinki) 1990, (Boston Coll.) 1990, (Chile) 1992, (Rutgers Univ.) 1994; Hon. DSc in Business Admin. (Bryant Coll.) 1988; Hon. DEng (Colorado School of Mines) 1996; Hon. DHumLitt (New York) 2006; David A. Wells Prize, Harvard Univ. 1951, John Bates Clark Medal, American Econ. Asscn 1961, Killian Award, MIT 1977, Seidman Award in Political Econ. 1983, Nobel Prize for Econs 1987, Nat. Medal of Science 2000. *Address:* 1010 Waltham Street, Apt. 328, Lexington, MA 02421-8057, USA (home). *Telephone:* (781) 538-5412 (home).

SOLWAY, David, BA, QMA, MA, MA, PhD; Canadian poet, writer, translator and academic (retd); b. 8 Dec. 1941, Montreal; s. of Samuel Solway and Sylvia Rabinovitch; m. Karin Semmler 1980; one d. *Education:* McGill Univ., Concordia Univ., Univ. of Sherbrooke, Lajos Kossuth Univ. *Career:* Lecturer in English Literature, McGill Univ. 1966–67, Dawson Coll. 1970–71, John Abbott Coll. 1971–99; Writer-in-Residence, Concordia Univ. 1999–2000; Assoc. Ed. Books in Canada 2001–; several visiting univ. lectureships; mem. International PEN, Union des écrivaines et des écrivains québécois, President's Circle, Univ. of Toronto. *Publications:* poetry: In My Own Image 1962, The Crystal Theatre 1971, Paximalia 1972, The Egyptian Airforce and Other Poems 1973, The Road to Arginos 1976, Anacrusis 1976, Mephistopheles and the Astronaut 1979, The Mulberry Men 1982, Selected Poetry 1982, Stones in Water 1983, Modern Marriage 1987, Bedrock 1993, Chess Pieces 1999, The Lover's Progress (dramatized by Rajori Theatre Ensemble, Regina, Vancouver) 2001, Franklin's Passage 2003, The Pallikari of Nesmine Rifat 2005, Reaching for Clear 2006, The Properties of Things 2007; other: Four Montréal Poets (ed.) 1973, Education Lost: Reflections on Contemporary Pedagogical Practice 1989, The Anatomy of Arcadia 1992, Lying About the Wolf: Essays in Culture and Education 1997, Random Walks: Essays in Elective Criticism 1997, Saracen Island: The Poems of Andreas Karavis (trans.) 2000, An Andreas Karavis Companion 2000, The Turtle Hypodermic of Sickenpods: Liberal Studies in the Corporate Age 2001, Director's Cut (essays) 2003, The Big Lie: On Terror, Antisemitism and Identity 2007, Le bon prof 2008, Hear, O Israel! 2009; contributions: many anthologies, reviews, quarterlies and journals including The Atlantic Monthly, International Journal of Applied Semiotics, Journal of Modern Greek Studies, Canadian Notes and Queries, Books in Canada, The Sewanee Review, Arts & Opinion, FrontPageMagazine, Pajamas Media, WorldNetDaily, American Thinker, The New Criterion, Academic Questions, The Canadian Observer. *Honours:* QSPELL Award for Poetry 1988, and for Non-Fiction 1990, Le Grand Prix du Livre de Montréal 2004, Quebec Writers' Asscn A.M. Klein Prize for Poetry, Lt Gov.'s Gold Medal, Woodrow Wilson Fellowship, various Canada Council Grants, Bourse de Carrière, Québec, Le Prix Spirale. *Address:* 143 Upper McNaughton, Hudson, PQ J0P 1H0, Canada. *Telephone:* (450) 458-8663. *E-mail:* parmenius@videotron.ca.

SOMERS, Suzanne (see Daniels, Dorothy)

SOMERS COCKS, Hon. Anna Gwenllian, (Anna Allemandi), OBE, MA, FSA; British museum curator, editor, publisher and journalist; *CEO, Umberto Allemandi Publishing Ltd*; b. 18 April 1950, Rome, Italy; d. of John Sebastian Somers Cocks and Marjorie Olive Somers Cocks (née Weller); m. 1st Martin Walker 1971 (divorced); m. 2nd John Hardy 1978 (divorced); one s. one d.; m. 3rd Umberto Allemandi. *Education:* abroad and Convent of the Sacred Heart, Woldingham, St Anne's Coll., Oxford, Courtauld Inst., London. *Career:* Asst Keeper Dept of Metalwork, Victoria and Albert Museum, London 1973–85, Dept of Ceramics 1985–87; Ed. The Art Newspaper 1990–94, 1996–2003; Group Editorial Dir The Art Newspaper and Umberto Allemandi e C. srl 2003–11, CEO Umberto Allemandi Publishing Ltd 2011–; fmr expert adviser to the Nat. Heritage Lottery Fund; Chair. Venice in Peril Fund 1999–; Trustee, Gilbert Collection 1999–, Cass Sculpture Foundation 2004–; Gov., Courtauld Inst. 2010–. *Publications:* Victoria and Albert Museum: The Making of the Collection 1980, Princely Magnificence: Court Jewels of the Renaissance (co-author) 1980, Renaissance Jewels, Gold Boxes and Objets de Vertu in the Thyssen Collection (co-author) 1985; articles in the Guardian, Daily Telegraph, New Statesman, Evening Standard, The Art Newspaper. *Honours:* Commendatore, Ordine della Stella della Solidarietà Italiana 2004; Nat. Art Collections Fund Award for Outstanding Achievement in the Arts 1992, Silver Prize, Int. Specialist Magazine, IPD Awards 1996, European Woman of the Year (Arts and Media section) 2006, Int. Inst. of Conservation Advocacy Award 2010. *Address:* c/o Umberto Allemandi e C. srl, Via Mancini 8, 10131 Turin, Italy. *Telephone:* (011) 8199111 (office). *Fax:* (011) 8193090 (office). *E-mail:* a.allemandi@theartnewspaper.com (office). *Website:* www.theartnewspaper.com.

SOMMER, Piotr, MA; Polish poet; *Editor-in-Chief, Literatura na Swiecie*; b. 13 April 1948, Walbrzych. *Education:* Univ. of Warsaw. *Career:* taught at several American insts, including Amherst Coll., Wesleyan Univ., Univ. of Notre Dame, Ind.; Ed.-in-Chief, Literatura na Swiecie 1994–. *Publications:* poetry: W krzesle 1977, Pamiatki po nas 1980, Przed snem 1981, Kolejny swiat 1983, Czynnik liryczny i inne wiersze 1988, Nowe stosunki wyrazów 1997, Piosenka pasterska 1999, Rano na ziemi. Wierse z lat 1968–1998 2009, Dni i nove 2009, Wierzse ze slów 2009; essays: Smak detalu i inne ogolniki 1995, Po stykach 2005; editor of anthologies, including Antologia nowej poezji brytyjskiej 1983, Szesciu poetów pólnocnoirlandzkich 1993, Artykuty pochodzenia zagranicznego 1996; contrib. to anthologies, including The Faber Book of Fevers and Frets 1989, Poetry with an Edge 1993; translations of poets, including John Ashbery, Douglas Dunn, D. J. Enright, Seamus Heaney, Michael Longley, Robert Lowell, Derek Mahon, Frank O'Hara, Charles Reznikoff; contrib. to: Chicago Review, Kresy, Literatura na Swiecie, Midrasz, New Yorker, Poetry, Poetry Review, Reg Publica, Threepenny Review, Times Literary Supplement. *Honours:* Iowa Int. Writing Program Fellowship 2002, Nat. Humanities Center Fellowship 2004–05; Barbara Sadowska Memorial Prize 1988, Koscielski Foundation Prize 1988, Polish PEN Prize 1997. *Address:* Literatura na Swiecie, 00-070 Warsaw, ul. Kozia 3/5 m.6, Poland (office). *Telephone:* (22) 8274791 (office). *E-mail:* litnasw@free.art.pl (office). *Website:* www.literaturanaswiecie.art.pl (office).

SOMMER, Theo, DPhil; German journalist; *Editor-at-Large, Die Zeit*; b. 10 June 1930, Constance; s. of Theo Sommer and Else Sommer; m. 1st Elda Tsilenis 1952; two s.; m. 2nd Heide Grenz 1976; two s.; m. 3rd Sabine Grewe 1989; one d. *Education:* Univ of Tübingen, Chicago and Harvard Univs. *Career:* Local Ed. Schwäbisch-Gmünd 1952–54; Foreign Ed. Die Zeit 1958, Deputy Ed. 1968, Ed.-in-Chief 1973–92, Publr 1992–, Ed.-at-Large 2000–; Lecturer in Int. Relations, Univ. of Hamburg 1967–70; Chief of Planning Staff, Ministry of Defence 1969–70; mem. Deutsche Gesellschaft für Auswärtige Politik; mem. Council IISS 1963–76, 1978–87, German Armed Forces Structure Comm. 1970–72, Int. Comm. on the Balkans 1995–96, Ind. Int. Comm. on the Balkans 1999–2000; Deputy Chair. Comm. on the Future on the Bundeswehr 1999–2000; Chair. Comm. Investigating Effects of DU Ammunitions, Radar and Asbestos on German Armed Forces 2002; mem. Indo-German Consultative Group 1992– (Co-Chair. 1996–), German-Japanese Dialogue Forum 1993–; mem. Bd Deutsche Welthungerhilfe 1992–, Max-Bauer Preis 1992–, German-Turkish Foundation 1998–; mem. German Foreign Policy Asscn, IISS, Königswinter Conf., Advisory Council, Mil. History Inst.; Contributing Ed. Newsweek Int. 1968–90; regular contrib. to American, British, Japanese and Korean publs; commentator German TV, radio and moderator of monthly programmes. *Publications:* Deutschland und Japan zwischen den Mächten (Germany and Japan Between the Powers) 1935–40 1962, Vom Antikominternpakt zum Dreimächtepakt 1962, Reise in ein fernes Land 1964, Ed. Denken an Deutschland 1966, Ed. Schweden-Report 1974, Die chinesische Karte (The Chinese Card) 1979, Allianz in Umbruch (Alliance in Disarray) 1982, Blick zurück in die Zukunft (Look Back into the Future) 1984, Reise ins andere Deutschland (Journey to the Other Germany) 1986, Europa im 21. Jahrhundert 1989, Geschichte der Bonner Republik 1949–99 1999, Der Zukunft entgegen (Toward the Future) 1999, Phoenix Europe. The European Union: Its Progress, Problems and Prospects 2000, Hamburg 2004, 1945: Biographie eines Jahres 2005. *Honours:* Hon. mem. Asscn of Anciens, NATO Defense Coll. 1971, Trilateral Comm. 1993; Fed. Order of Merit (First Class) 1998, Gold Honor Cross, German Armed Forces 2002; Hon. LLD (Univ. of Maryland, USA) 1982; Theoder-Wolf Prize 1966, Int. Communications Award, People's Repub. of China 1991, Columbus Prize 1993. *Address:* Die Zeit, Pressehaus, Speersort 1, 20079 Hamburg (office); 17 Zabelweg, 22359 Hamburg, Germany (home). *Telephone:* (40) 3280240 (office); (40) 6037300 (home). *Fax:* (40) 3280407 (office); (40) 6030044 (home). *E-mail:* sommer@zeit.de (office); tsommer01@aol.com (home). *Website:* www.zeit.de (office); www.theosommer.de.

SOMOZA, José Carlos, MD; Spanish novelist, playwright and fmr psychiatrist; b. (b. José Carlos Somoza Ortega), 13 Nov. 1959, Havana, Cuba; m.; two c. *Education:* medical studies in Córdoba, trained as a psychiatrist in

Madrid. *Plays:* Miguel Will 1997, Cuento de Ada 2003. *Radio:* Langostas 1994. *Publications:* Planos (novella) 1994, Langostas (radio play) 1994, Silencio de Blanca (novel) 1996, Miguel Will (play) 1997, La ventana pintada (novel) 1998, Cartas de un asesino insignificante (novel) 1999, Dafne desvanecida (novel) 2000, La caverna de las ideas (novel; trans. as The Athenian Murders) 2000, Clara y la penumbra (novel; trans. as The Art of Murder) 2001, La Dama Número Trece (novel) 2002, La Caja de Marfil (novel) 2003, Zigzag (novel) (first ever Spanish original sci-fi novel short-listed for John W. Campbell Memorial Award 2008) 2006, La Llave del Abismo 2007, El cebo (novel) 2010. *Honours:* Premio Gabriel Sijé 1994, Premio Margarita Xirgu 1994, Premio Sonrisa Vertical 1996, Premio Miguel de Cervantes de teatro 1997, Premio Café Gijón 1998, Premio de Novela Fernando Lara, 2001, CWA Macallan Gold Dagger 2002, Premio Hammet 2002, Premio Torrevieja de Novela 2007. *Address:* c/o Editorial Random House Mondadori, Travessera de Gracia 47–49, 08021 Barcelona, Spain. *E-mail:* jcsomoza@clubcultura.com (home). *Website:* www.josecarlossomoza.com.

SONG, Cathy, BA, MA; American poet, writer and teacher; b. 20 Aug. 1955, Honolulu, HI; m. Douglas M. Davenport 1979. *Education:* University of Hawaii at Manoa, Wellesley College, Boston University. *Career:* teacher of poetry, Hawaii 1987–; associated with Poets in the Schools programme. *Publications:* Picture Bride 1983, Frameless Windows, Squares of Light 1988, Sister Stew (ed. with Juliet S. Kono) 1991, School Figures 1994, The Land of Bliss 2001, Cloud Moving Hands 2007. Contributions: various anthologies and journals. *Honours:* Yale Series of Younger Poets Prize 1983, Frederick Book Prize for Poetry 1986, Cades Award for Literature 1988, Hawaii Award for Literature 1993, Shelley Memorial Award, Poetry Society of America 1993, Creative Writing Fellowship, Nat. Endowment for the Arts 1997, Pushcart Prize 1999, The Best American Poetry 2000. *Address:* PO Box 27262, Honolulu, HI 96827, USA.

SONG, Muwen; Chinese publishing executive; b. 1929, Yushu Co., Jilin. *Career:* Chair. Asscn of Chinese Publrs 1993–2000, Hon. Chair. 2000–; Pres. Copyright Research Society; mem. NPC Educ., Science, Culture and Public Health Cttee. *Address:* Publishers' Association of China, 85 Dongsi Nan Dajie, Beijing 100703, People's Republic of China (office). *Telephone:* (10) 65228632 (office). *Fax:* (10) 65228632 (office).

SORESTAD, Glen Allan, CM, BEd, MEd; Canadian writer and poet; b. 21 May 1937, Vancouver, BC; m. Sonia Diane Talpash 1960; three s. one d. *Education:* Univ. of Saskatchewan. *Career:* elementary school teacher 1957–69; sr English teacher 1969–81; Pres. Thistledown Press 1975–2000; First Poet Laureate of Saskatchewan 2000–04; Life mem. League of Canadian Poets, Saskatchewan Writers' Guild, Writers' Union of Canada, League of Canadian Poets. *Publications:* Hold the Rain in Your Hands: Poems Selected and New 1985, Birchbark Meditations 1996, West into Night 1991, Icons of Flesh 1998, Today I Belong to Agnes 2000, Leaving Holds Me Here: Selected Poems 1975–2000 2001, Grasses and Gravestones 2003, Blood and Bone, Ice and Stone 2005, Halo of Morning 2006, Language of Horse 2007, Road Apples 2009, What We Miss 2010, A Thief of Impeccable Taste 2011; poems translated into French, Spanish, Finnish, Norwegian, Slovene, Afrikaans; contrib. to numerous newspapers, journals, magazines and periodicals. *Honours:* Queen's Golden Jubilee Medal 2003, mem. Order of Canada 2010; SWG Founders' Award, Hilroy Fellowship. *Address:* 108–835 Heritage Green, Saskatoon, SK S7H 5S5, Canada (home). *Telephone:* (306) 374-1730 (home). *E-mail:* g.sorestad@sasktel.net (home).

SORG, Margarete; German writer and publisher; b. 4 July 1937, Bochum; m.; one d. (Margarete Sorg-Rose). *Education:* Fachhochschule, Frankfurt/Main. *Career:* freelance writer 1978–; Publr GEDOK-Journal (magazine for the arts) 1986–95, various anthologies of poetry; publishing man. 1999–; organizer literary competitions, mem. Jury, Germany 1986–; Pres. Jury Andreas Gryphius Award for Literature and Nikolaus Lenau Award for Lyric Poetry 1993–96; Pres. Literary Section of Die Künstlergilde e.V. 1993–96, Pres. Künstlergilde Hessen 1993; Pres. Kulturring HDH, Wiesbaden 1995–; Pres. GEDOK Rhein-Main-Taunus cultural man. co. for artists 1995–. *Publications:* Streiflichter (lyric poetry) (2nd edn) 1984, irgendwann der bitteren tollkirsche süße 2002; 55 publs of lyric poetry in anthologies and literary reviews. *Honours:* Verdienstkreuz am Bande des Verdienstordens der Bundesrepublik Deutschland 2004; Second GEDOK Award for Lyric Poetry 1982, Art-GEDOK-Nadel for Meritorious Artistic and Cultural Activities 1995, Pro-arte-Medaille der Künstlergilde e.V. 1998. *Address:* Henkellstr. 3, 65187 Wiesbaden, Germany (office). *Fax:* (611) 691216 (office).

SOROKIN, Vladimir Georgiyevich; Russian author, screenwriter, dramatist, librettist and painter; b. 7 Aug. 1955, Bykovo, Moscow Region; m. Irina Igorevna Sorokina; two d. *Education:* Moscow Inst. of Oil and Gas. *Career:* worked as artist and writer in Moscow underground; not published in USSR until 1987; mem. Russian PEN Centre; scholarship of Deutsche Akademische Austauschung Dienst 1992. *Plays:* wrote 12 plays 1986–2009. *Screenplays:* Moskva 1995, Kopejka 1997, The Four 2000, Cashfire 2002, The Thing 2003, Exit 2004, The Target 2010. *Libretto:* opera 'The Children of Rosenthal' by Leonid Desyatnikov (performed at Bolshoi Theatre, Moscow) 2005. *Publications include:* Thirties Love of Marina 1982–84, The Queue (novel) 1983, The Norm 1994, Obelisk (short stories) 1980–84, Roman 1989, Four Stout Hearts (novel) 1991, Blue Lard 1999, The Feast 2001, The Ice (novel) 2002, Bro 2004, Trilogy 2005. *Honours:* Andrey Beliy Prize 2003, Liberty Prize, USA 2005, Maxim Gorky Prize 2010. *Address:* 119333 Moscow, ul. Gubkina, d4 kv 47, Russia (home). *Telephone:* (499) 135-90-76 (home). *E-mail:* sornorma@mtu-net.ru (home). *Website:* www.srkn.ru (home); www.vladimirsorokin.ru (home).

SOROS, George; American (b. Hungarian) investment banker and philanthropist; *Chairman, Soros Fund Management LLC*; b. 12 Aug. 1930, Budapest; m.; five c. *Education:* London School of Econs. *Career:* moved to England 1947; with Singer & Friedlander (merchant bankers), London; moved to New York 1956; est. pvt. mutual fund, Quantum Fund, registered in Curaçao 1969; since 1991 has created other funds, including Quasar Int., Quota, Quantum Emerging Growth Fund (merged with Quantum Fund to form Quantum Endowment Fund 2000), Quantum Realty Trust; Pres. and Chair. Soros Fund Man. LLC, New York 1973–; philanthropist since 1979, provided funds to help black students attend Cape Town Univ., SA; Founder, Open Soc. Fund (currently Chair. Open Soc. Inst.) 1979, Soros Foundation, Cen. European Univ., Budapest 1992; f. Global Power Investments 1994. *Publications include:* The Alchemy of Finance 1987, Opening the Soviet System 1990, Underwriting Democracy 1991, Soros on Soros – Staying Ahead of the Curve (jtly) 1995, The Crisis of Global Capitalism – Open Society Engendered 1998, Open Society – Reforming Global Capitalism 2000, George Soros on Globalization 2002, The Bubble of American Supremacy – Correcting the Misuse of American Power 2004, Soros on Freedom 2006, Soros Lectures 2010; numerous essays on politics, society and econs in major int. newspapers and magazines. *Honours:* Dr hc (New School for Social Research, Univ. of Oxford, Budapest Univ. of Econs, Yale Univ.); Laurea hc (Univ. of Bologna) 1995. *Address:* Soros Fund Management LLC, 888 7th Avenue, 33rd Floor, New York, NY 10106 (office); Open Society Institute, 400 West 59th Street, New York, NY 10019, USA. *Telephone:* (212) 548-0600. *Website:* www.georgesoros.com; www.soros.org.

SOTO, Gary, BA, MFA; American writer, poet and academic; b. 12 April 1952, Fresno, Calif.; m. Carolyn Sadako Oda 1975; one d. *Education:* California State University, University of California, Irvine. *Career:* Asst Prof., University of California, Berkeley 1979–85, Assoc. Prof. of English and Ethnic Studies 1985–92, Part-time Senior Lecturer in English 1992–93; Elliston Prof. of Poetry, University of Cincinnati, 1988; Martin Luther King/Cesar Chavez/Rosa Park Visiting Prof. of English, Wayne State University, Detroit 1990. *Publications:* poetry: The Elements of San Joaquin, 1977; The Tale of Sunlight, 1978; Where Sparrows Work Hard, 1981; Black Hair, 1985; Who Will Know Us?, 1990; A Fire in My Hands, 1990; Home Course in Religion, 1992; Neighborhood Odes, 1992; Canto Familiar/Familiar Song, 1994; New and Selected Poems, 1995; Fearless Fernie, 2002, One Kind of Faith 2003, World's Apart (children's poetry) 2005; other: Living Up the Street: Narrative Recollections, 1985; Small Faces, 1986; Lesser Evils: Ten Quartets, 1988; California Childhood: Recollections and Stories of the Golden State (ed.), 1988; A Summer Life, 1990; Baseball in April and Other Stories, 1990; Taking Sides, 1991; Pacific Crossing, 1992; The Skirt, 1992; Pieces of the Heart: New Chicano Fiction (ed.), 1993; Local News, 1993; The Pool Party, 1993; Crazy Weekend, 1994; Jesse, 1994; Boys at Work, 1995; Chato's Kitchen, 1995; Everyday Seductions (ed.), 1995; Summer on Wheels, 1995; The Old Man and His Door, 1996; Snapshots of the Wedding, 1996; Buried Onions, 1997, Chato and the Party Animals (picture book) 1999; Nickel and Dime (novel), 2000; Poetry Lover (novel), 2001; Jessie De La Cruz: A Profile of a United Farm Worker (young adult biog.), 2002; The Effects of Knut Hamsun on a Fresno Boy (essays), 2002; If the Shoe Fits (picture book), 2002, Cesar Chavez – A Hero for Everyone (children's biography) 2003, Amnesia in a Republican (novel) 2004, The Afterlife (novel) 2004, Help Wanted (short story) 2005, Chato Goes Cruzin' (picture book) 2005; contribs to magazines. *Honours:* Discovery/The Nation Prize, 1975; United States Award, International Poetry Forum, 1976; Bess Hokin Prize for Poetry, 1978; Guggenheim Fellowship, 1979–80; National Endowment for the Arts Fellowship 1981, 1991; Levinson Award, Poetry Magazine, 1984; American Book Award, Before Columbus Foundation, 1985; California Arts Council Fellowship, 1989; Carnegie Medal, 1993; Tomas Rivera Prize, 1996; Hispanic Heritage Award, 1999; Civil Rights Award, National Education Asscn, 1999. *Address:* 43 The Crescent, Berkeley, CA 94708, USA.

SOUEIF, Ahdaf, BA, MA, PhD, FRSL; Egyptian/British writer; b. 23 March 1950, Cairo; d. of Mustapha Soueif and Fatma Moussa; m. Ian Hamilton 1981 (died 2001); two s. *Education:* Cairo Univ., American Univ. in Cairo, Univ. of Lancaster. *Career:* Assoc. Lecturer, Cairo Univ. 1971–79, Lecturer 1979–84; with Cassel Publishing, London and Cairo 1978–84; Assoc. Prof., King Saud Univ. 1987–89; with Al-Furqan Islamic Heritage Foundation, London 1989–2008; Founder and Chair., Engaged Events (PALFEST) 2008–; mem. Egyptian Writers' Union, PEN Egypt, PEN UK, Council for Advancement of Arab–British Understanding, Amnesty Int.; Fellow Lannan Foundation; Patron Palestine Solidarity Campaign. *Publications:* Aisha 1983, In the Eye of the Sun 1992, Sandpiper 1996, The Map of Love 1999, Mezzaterra 2004, I Saw Ramallah (trans.) 2004, I Think of You 2007, The Map of Love 2008; contrib. to periodicals. *Honours:* Hon. DLitt (Lancaster) 2004, (London Metropolitan) 2004, (Exeter) 2008; Cairo Int. Book Fair Award Best Collection of Short Stories 1996. *Literary Agent:* Wylie Agency, 17 Bedford Square, London, WC1B 3JA, England. *Telephone:* (20) 7908-5900. *Fax:* (20) 7908-5901. *E-mail:* mail@wylieagency.co.uk. *Website:* www.wylieagency.co.uk; www.ahdafsoueif.com.

SOULEZ-LARIVIÈRE, Daniel Joseph; French lawyer and writer; b. 19 March 1942, Angers (Maine-et-Loire); s. of Furcy Soulez-Larivière and

Suzanne Soulez-Larivière (née Larivière); m. Mathilde-Mahaut Nobecourt 1988; one s. with Michèle Abbaye. *Education:* Lycée Janson-de-Sailly, Collège Stanislas, Paris, Garden City High School, New York, USA, Faculty of Law, Paris and Institut d'Etudes Politiques, Paris. *Career:* lawyer in Paris 1965–; Chargé de mission, Ministry of Equipment and Housing 1966–67; Second Sec. Conférence du stage 1969; mem. Conseil de l'Ordre 1988–90; mem. Consultative Comm. for Revision of the Constitution 1992–93; mem. Advisory Bd Centre de prospective de la gendarmerie; Municipal Counsellor for Chambellay 1995–; mem. Soc. of French Jurists. *Publications include:* L'avocature 1982, Les juges dans la balance 1987, La réforme des professions juridiques et judiciaires, vingt propositions 1988, Justice pour la justice 1990, Du cirque médiatico-judiciaire et des moyens d'en sortir 1993, Paroles d'avocat 1994, Grand soir pour la justice 1997, Dans l'engrenage de la justice 1998, Lettres à un jeune avocat 1999, La justice à l'épreuve (with Jean-Marie Coulon) 2002, Notre justice 2002, Le temps des Victimes (with Caroline Eliacheff) 2007. *Honours:* Chevalier, Légion d'honneur, Ordre nat. du Mérite. *Address:* 22 avenue de la Grande Armée, 75858 Paris Cedex 17 (office); 6 rue des Fougères, 92140 Clamart (home); le Prieuré, 49220 Chambellay, France (home). *Telephone:* 1-47-63-37-22 (office); 1-45-34-56-50 (home). *Fax:* 1-42-67-83-05 (office); 1-46-26-23-65 (office). *E-mail:* dsl@soulezlariviere.com (office).

SOUSTER, Raymond, (John Holmes), OC; Canadian writer and poet; b. 15 Jan. 1921, Toronto, Ont.; s. of Austin Holmes Souster and Norma Rhodesia; m. Rosalia L. Geralde 1947. *Education:* Univ. of Toronto Schools, Humberside Collegiate Inst., Toronto. *Career:* Founding mem. League of Canadian Poets, Chair. 1968–72, Life mem. 1996–. *Publications:* 100 Poems of 19th Century Canada (co-ed. with D. Lochhead) 1974, Sights and Sounds (co-ed. with R. Wollatt) 1974, These Loved, These Hated Lands (co-ed. with R. Wollatt) 1974, The Poetry of W. W. Campbell (ed.) 1978, The Best-Known Poems of Archibald Lampman (ed.) 1979, Collected Poems of Raymond Souster (eight vols) 1980–93, Powassan's Drum: Selected Poems of Duncan Campbell Scott (co-ed. with D. Lochhead) 1983, Queen City: Toronto in Poems and Pictures (with Bill Brooks) 1984, Windflower: The Selected Poems of Bliss Carmen (co-ed. with D. Lochhead) 1986, Riding the Long Black Horse 1993, Old Bank Notes 1993, No Sad Songs Wanted Here 1995, Close to Home 1997, Of Time and Toronto 2000, Collected Poems 1940–2000 (ten vols) 1990–2004, Take Me Out to the Ball Game 2002, Twenty-Three New Poems 2003, Down to Earth 2006, Wondrous Wobbly World 2006, Uptown Downtown 2006, What Men Will Die For (with Les Green, ed. by Donna Dunlop) 2007, The Way It Looks from Here 2007, Sparrow Talk 2007, Good News from Nowhere 2008, Penny Whistle Blues 2008, To Live and Die in Old T.O. 2008, On the Way to the River 2008, A Little of Everything 2009, The Days That Surround Us 2009; contribs to magazines. *Honours:* Gov.-Gen.'s Award for Poetry in English 1964, Pres.'s Medal, Univ. of Western Ontario 1967, Centennial Medal 1967, City of Toronto Book Award 1980, Queen's Silver Jubilee Medal 1977, Queen's Golden Jubilee Medal 2002. *Address:* 39 Baby Point Road, Toronto, ON M6S 2G2, Canada (home). *Telephone:* (416) 762-4028 (home). *E-mail:* donna.dunlop@utoronto.ca (office).

SOWANDE, Bode, MA, PhD; Nigerian playwright and writer; b. 2 May 1948, Kaduna. *Education:* Univ. of Ife, Univ. of Dakar and Univ. of Sheffield. *Career:* Sr Lecturer, Dept of Theatre Arts, Univ. of Ibadan 1977–90. *Publications:* The Night Before 1972, Lamps in the Night 1973, Bar Beach Prelude 1976, A Sanctus for Women 1976, Afamoko – the Workhorse 1978, Farewell to Babylon 1978, Kalakuta Cross Currents 1979, The Master and the Frauds 1979, Barabas and the Master Jesus 1980, Flamingo 1982, Circus of Freedom Square 1985, Tornadoes Full of Dreams 1989, Arede Owo (after L'Avare by Molière) 1990, Mammy-Water's Wedding 1991, Ajantala-Pinocchio 1992, Superleaf 2004; fiction: Our Man the President 1981, Without a Home 1982, The Missing Bridesmaid 1988; other: My Life in the Bush of Ghosts (stage adaptation of Amos Tutuola's novel) 1995; radio and television plays. *Honours:* Chevalier, Ordre des Arts et des Lettres 1991; Asscn of Nigerian Authors Drama Award, Pan African Writers Asscn Patron of the Arts Award 1993, Rockefeller Foundation Fellowship 2000. *E-mail:* bodesowande@hotmail.com (office). *Website:* candy.in/home.php.

SOWELL, Thomas, BA, MA, PhD; American economist and writer; *Rose and Milton Friedman Senior Fellow, Stanford University;* b. 30 June 1930, Gastonia, NC; m. 1st Alma Jean Parr (divorced); m. 2nd Mary; two c. *Education:* Harvard Univ., Columbia Univ., Univ. of Chicago. *Career:* Economist, US Dept of Labor 1961–62; Instructor in Economics, Douglass Coll., Rutgers Univ. 1962–63; Lecturer in Economics, Howard Univ. 1963–64; Economic Analyst, AT&T 1964–65; Asst Prof., Cornell Univ. 1965–69; Assoc. Prof., Brandeis Univ. 1969–70; Assoc. Prof., Univ. of California at Los Angeles 1970–74, Prof. of Economics 1974–80; Fellow, Center for Advanced Study in the Behavioral Sciences, Stanford, CA, 1976–77; Visiting Prof., Amherst Coll. 1977; Senior Fellow, Hoover Institution, Stanford Univ. 1977, Rose and Milton Friedman Senior Fellow in Public Policy 1980–; mem. American Economic Asscn, National Acad. of Education. *Publications:* Economics: Analysis and Issues 1971, Black Education: Myths and Tragedies 1972, Say's Law: An Historical Analysis 1972, Classical Economics Reconsidered 1974, Affirmative Action: Was It Necessary in Academia? 1975, Race and Economics 1975, Patterns of Black Excellence 1977, Markets and Minorities 1981, Pink and Brown People, and Other Controversial Essays 1981, Knowledge and Decision 1983, Ethnic America: A History 1983, The Economics and Politics of Race: An International Perspective 1983, Compassion versus Guilt, and Other Essays 1984, Marxism: Philosophy and Economics 1985, Civil Rights: Rhetoric or Reality? 1985, Education: Assumptions versus History 1986, A Conflict of Visions: Ideological Origins of Political Struggles 1987, Judicial Activism Reconsidered 1989, Preferential Policies: An International Perspective 1990, Inside American Education: The Decline, the Deception, the Dogmas 1992, Race and Culture: A World View 1992, Is Reality Optional?, and Other Essays 1993, The Vision of the Anointed: Self-Congratulation as a Basis for Social Policy 1995, Migrations and Cultures: A World View 1996, Late-talking Children 1997, Conquests and Cultures: An International History 1998, Race, Culture, and Equality 1998, Barbarians Inside the Gates, and Other Controversial Essays 1999, The Quest for Cosmic Justice 1999, A Personal Odyssey 2000, Basic Economics: A Citizen's Guide to the Economy 2001, The Einstein Syndrome 2001, Applied Economics: Thinking Beyond Stage One 2003, Affirmative Action Around the World 2004, Black Rednecks and White Liberals 2005, On Classical Economics 2006, A Man of Letters 2007, Economic Facts and Fallacies 2008, The Housing Boom and Bust 2009, Intellectuals and Society 2009; contributions: books and newspapers. *Address:* The Hoover Institution, Stanford University, Stanford, CA 94305, USA (office). *Telephone:* (650) 723-3303 (office). *Website:* www.tsowell.com.

SOYINKA, Akinwande Oluwole (Wole), BA; Nigerian playwright and academic; *Professor Emeritus of Comparative Literature, Obafemi Awolowo University;* b. 13 July 1934, Abeokuta; s. of Ayo Soyinka and Eniola Soyinka; m.; several c. *Education:* Univ. of Ibadan, Nigeria and Univ. of Leeds, UK. *Career:* worked at Royal Court Theatre, London; Research Fellow in Drama, Univ. of Ibadan 1960–61; Lecturer in English, Univ. of Ife 1962–63; Sr Lecturer in English, Univ. of Lagos 1965–67; political prisoner 1967–69; Artistic Dir and Head, Dept of Theatre Arts, Univ. of Ibadan 1969–72; Research Prof. in Dramatic Literature, Univ. of Ife 1972, Prof. of Comparative Literature and Head of Dept of Dramatic Arts 1976–85; Goldwin Smith Prof. of Africana Studies and Theatre Cornell Univ. 1988–92; passport seized Sept. 1994, living in France; charged with treason March 1997 in absentia; Woodruff Prof. Emer. of the Arts, Emory Univ., Atlanta 2004–; Prof. Emer. of Comparative Literature, Obafemi Awolowo Univ. 2007–; founder and Chair. The Democratic Front for a People's Federation 2010–; Ed. Ch'Indaba (fmrly Transition) Accra; Artistic Dir Orisun Theatre, 1960 Masks; Literary Ed. Orisun Acting Editions; Pres. Int. Theatre Inst. 1986–; Fellow, Churchill Coll. Cambridge 1973–74; mem. American Acad. of Arts and Letters, Int. Theatre Inst., Union of Writers of the African Peoples, Nat. Liberation Council of Nigeria; Fellow, Ghana Asscn of Writers, Pan-African Writers Asscn. *Plays:* The Invention 1955, The Lion and the Jewel 1959, The Swamp Dwellers 1959, A Dance of the Forests 1960, The Trials of Brother Jero 1961, The Strong Breed 1962, The Road 1964, Kongi's Harvest 1965, Madmen and Specialists 1971, Before the Blackout 1971, Jero's Metamorphosis 1973, Camwood on the Leaves 1973, The Bacchae of Euripides 1974, Death and the King's Horsemen 1975, Opera Wonyosi 1978, A Play of Giants 1984, Six Plays 1984, Requiem for a Futurologist 1985, From Zia, with Love 1991, A Scourge of Hyacinths (radio play) 1992, The Beatification of Area Boy 1995, King Baabu 2003. *Radio:* BBC Reith Lectures 2004. *Publications:* novels: The Interpreters 1964, The Forest of a Thousand Daemons (trans.), Season of Anomy 1973; poetry: Idanre and Other Poems 1967, Poems from Prison 1969, A Shuttle in the Crypt 1972, Poems of Black Africa (ed.) 1975, Ogun Abibman 1977, Mandela's Earth and Other Poems 1988, Samarkand and Other Markets I Have Known 2002; nonfiction: The Man Died (prison memoirs) 1972, Myth, Literature and the African World (lectures) 1972, Aké, The Years of Childhood (autobiog.) 1982, Art, Dialogue and Outrage 1988, Isara: A Voyage Round Essay 1990, Continuity and Amnesia 1991, Ibadan: The Pentelemes Years (memoir) 1994, The Open Sore of a Continent, A Personal Narrative of the Nigerian Crisis 1996, The Burden of Memory, The Muse of Forgiveness 1999, Conversations with Wole Soyinka 2001, You Must Set Forth at Dawn: A Memoir 2006. *Honours:* Commdr, Légion d'honneur; Commdr, Fed. Repub. of Nigeria 1986; Commdr, Order of Merit (Italy) 1990; Hon. DLitt (Leeds) 1973, (Yale) 1981, (Morehouse), (Paul Valéry), (Bayreuth), (Ibadan), (Harvard); Hon. DScS (Edin.) 1977; Rockefeller Foundation Grant 1960, John Whiting Drama Prize 1966, Prisoner of Conscience Award, Amnesty Int., Jock Campbell-New Statesman Literary Award 1969, Nobel Prize for Literature 1986, George Benson Medal, RSL 1990, Writers Guild Lifetime Achievement Award 1996, Distinguished Scholar-in-Residence, New York Univ. 1999, and numerous other awards. *Literary Agent:* c/o Deborah Rogers, Rogers, Coleridge & White, 20 Powis Mews, London, W11 1JN, England. *E-mail:* deborahr@rcwlitagency.demon.co.uk. *Address:* c/o PO Box 935, Abeokuta, Ogun State, Nigeria.

SPACKS, Patricia Meyer, BA, MA, PhD; American academic; b. 17 Nov. 1929, San Francisco, CA; one d. *Education:* Rollins Coll., Yale Univ., Univ. of California at Berkeley. *Career:* Instructor in English, Indiana Univ. 1954–56; Instructor in Humanities, Univ. of Florida 1958–59; Instructor, Wellesley Coll. 1959–61, Asst Prof. 1961–63, Assoc. Prof. 1965–68, Prof. of English 1968–79; Prof. of English, Yale Univ. 1979–89, Chair., Dept of English 1985–88; Edgar F. Shannon Prof. of English, Univ. of Virginia 1989–, now Emer., Chair., Dept of English 1991–96; mem. MLA (pres. 1994), American Philosophical Society, ACLS (chair of board 1997), American Acad. of Arts and Sciences (pres. 2003). *Publications:* The Varied God 1959, The Insistence of Horror 1962, 18th Century Poetry (ed.) 1964, John Gay 1965, Poetry of Vision 1967, Late Augustan Prose (ed.) 1971, An Argument of Images 1971, Late Augustan Poetry (ed.) 1973, The Female Imagination 1975, Imagining a Self 1976, Contemporary Women Novelists 1977, The Adolescent Idea 1981, Gossip 1985, Desire and Truth 1990, Boredom: The Literary History of a State of Mind 1995, Privacy: Concealing the Eighteenth-Century Self 2003.

Address: c/o Department of English, University of Virginia, PO Box 400121, Bryan Hall 402, Charlottesville, VA 22904, USA (office). *Telephone:* (434) 924-6609 (office). *E-mail:* pms2b@virginia.edu (office).

SPALDING, Esta; Canadian poet and screenwriter; b. Boston, MA. *Career:* based in Vancouver, BC, Canada. *Writing for television:* Da Vinci's Inquest (CBC-TV) 1998–2001, The Zack Files (Decode Entertainment) 2000, The Eleventh Hour (also story ed., CTV Network) 2002–04. *Film screenplays:* The Republic of Love 2003, Fallen Angels 2003. *Publications:* poetry: Carrying Place 1995, Anchoress 1997, Lost August (Pat Lowther Memorial Award) 1998, Mere (with Linda Spalding) 2001, The Wife's Account 2003. *Address:* c/o House of Anansi Press, 110 Spadina Avenue, Suite 801, Toronto, ON M5V 2K4, Canada (office). *Website:* www.anansi.ca (office).

SPALDING, Frances, CBE, BA (Hons), PhD, FRSL; British art historian, critic and biographer; *Professor of Art History, Newcastle University*; b. (Catherine Frances Helen Crabtree), 16 May 1950, Woldingham, Surrey, England; d. of Hedley Stinston Crabtree and Margaret Holiday; m. Julian Spalding 1974 (divorced 1991); one s. *Education:* Farringtons School, Kent and Univ. of Nottingham. *Career:* Lecturer, Sheffield Polytechnic 1978–88; art historian, critic and biographer (freelance 1989–99), Newcastle Univ. 2000–; Paul Mellon Sr Research Fellow and Visiting Research Fellow, Newnham Coll. Cambridge 2005–06. *Radio:* various contribs to BBC radio panel discussions and documentary programmes on the arts. *Television:* various appearances in documentary programmes on the arts. *Publications include:* Roger Fry: Art and Life 1983, Vanessa Bell 1983, British Art Since 1900 1986, Stevie Smith: A Critical Biography 1988, A Dictionary of Twentieth Century British Painters and Sculpture 1990, Dance Till the Stars Come Down: A Biography of John Minton 1991, Duncan Grant: A Biography 1997, The Tate: A History 1998, Gwen Raverat: Friends, Family & Affections 2001, John Piper in the 1930s – Abstraction on the Beach (with David Fraser Jenkins) 2003, The Bloomsbury Group 2005, John Piper, Myfanwy Piper: Lives in Art 2009, Prunella Clough: Regions Unmapped 2012. *Honours:* Hon. Fellow, RCA . *Literary Agent:* c/o Rogers, Coleridge & White, 20 Powis Mews, London, W11 1JN, England. *Telephone:* (20) 7221-3717 (office). *Fax:* (20) 7229-9084 (office). *E-mail:* info@rcwlitagency.co.uk. *Website:* www.rcwlitagency.co.uk. *E-mail:* frances.spalding@ncl.ac.uk (office).

SPARKS, Minton, MEd; American poet, songwriter and author; b. (Jill Webb-Hill), 27 Feb. 1962, Murfreesboro, Tenn.; m.; two c. *Education:* Vanderbilt Univ. *Career:* fmr teacher of Women's Psychology, Middle Tenn. State Univ.; fmr Adjunct Prof. of Psychology, Tenn. State Univ.; has performed with numerous musicians and vocalists including Rodney Crowell, John Prine, Nanci Griffith. *Film:* Open Casket (documentary) 2006. *Recordings include:* albums: Middlin' Sisters 2001, This Dress (Just Plain Folk Music Spoken Word Record of the Year 2004) 2003, Sin Sick 2005. *Publications include:* Desperate Ransom: Setting Her Family Free 2007, White Lightning 2008. *Honours:* Leonard Bernstein Fellowship 1998, Fellowship of Southern Writers Spoken Word Award 2011. *Literary Agent:* c/o Allison Bishop, Silver Pear Tree Consulting, 2101 Belmont Boulevard, Suite B2, Nashville, TN 37212, USA. *Telephone:* (917) 747-3294. *E-mail:* info@silverpeartree.com. *Website:* www.silverpeartree.com. *E-mail:* minton@mintonsparks.com (home). *Website:* www.myspace.com/mintonsparks; www.mintonsparks.com.

SPARKS, Nicholas; American writer; b. 31 Dec. 1965, Omaha, NE; m. Cathy Cote 1989; three s. two d. *Education:* Univ. of Notre Dame. *Publications:* Wokini 1995, The Notebook 1996, Message in a Bottle 1998, A Walk to Remember 1999, The Rescue 2000, A Bend in the Road 2001, Nights in Rodanthe 2002, The Guardian 2003, The Wedding 2003, Three Weeks With My Brother (non-fiction) 2004, True Believer 2005, At First Sight 2005, Dear John 2006, The Choice 2007, The Lucky One 2008, The Last Song 2009, Safe Haven 2010, The Best of Me 2011. *Literary Agent:* The Park Literary Group, 270 Lafayette Street, Suite 1504, New York, NY 10012, USA. *Telephone:* (212) 691-3500. *E-mail:* info@parkliterary.com. *Website:* parkliterary.com; www.nicholassparks.com.

SPARSHOTT, Francis Edward, BA, MA, FRSC; Canadian philosopher, writer, poet and academic (retd); *University Professor Emeritus, University of Toronto*; b. 19 May 1926, Chatham, Kent; m. Kathleen Elizabeth Vaughan 1953; one d. *Education:* Corpus Christi Coll., Oxford. *Career:* Lecturer in Philosophy, Univ. of Toronto 1950–55, Asst Prof. 1955–62, Assoc. Prof. 1962–64, Prof. 1964–91, Univ. Prof. 1982–91, of Philosophy, Victoria Coll., Univ. of Toronto 1964–91, Prof. Emer. 1991–; mem. American Society for Aesthetics (Pres. 1981–82), Canadian Classical Asscn, Canadian Philosophical Asscn (Pres. 1975–76), League of Canadian Poets (Pres. 1977–78), PEN International, Canadian Centre. *Publications:* An Enquiry into Goodness and Related Concepts 1958, The Structure of Aesthetics 1963, The Concept of Criticism: An Essay 1967, Looking for Philosophy 1972, The Theory of the Arts 1982, Off the Ground: First Steps in the Philosophy of Dance 1988, Taking Life Seriously: A Study of the Argument of the Nicomachean Ethics 1994, A Measured Pace: Toward a Philosophical Understanding of the Arts of Dance 1995, The Future of Aesthetics 1998; Poetry: A Divided Voice 1965, A Cardboard Garage 1969, The Rainy Hills: Verses After a Japanese Fashion 1979, The Naming of the Beasts 1979, New Fingers for Old Dikes 1980, The Cave of Trophonius and Other Poems 1983, The Hanging Gardens of Etobicoke 1983, Storms and Screens 1986, Sculling to Byzantium 1989, Views from the Zucchini Gazebo 1994, Home from the Air 1997, The City Dwellers 2000, Scoring in Injury Time 2006; contrib. to various books and periodicals. *Honours:* Hon. DLittSac, (Victoria Univ.) 2000; Hon. LLD (Univ. of Toronto) 2000; ACLS Fellowship, 1961–62; Canada Council Fellowship, 1970–71; Killam Research Fellowship, 1977–78; First Prize for Poetry, CBC Radio Literary Competition, 1981; Centennial Medal, Royal Society of Canada, 1982; Connaught Senior Fellowship in the Humanities, 1984–85. *Address:* 50 Crescentwood Road, Scarborough, Ont. M1N 1E4, Canada (home). *Telephone:* (416) 699-1650 (home).

SPENCE, Alan; British dramatist, writer, poet and academic; *Chair in Creative Writing, Department of English, University of Aberdeen*; b. 5 Dec. 1947, Glasgow, Scotland; m. *Education:* Univ. of Glasgow. *Career:* Writer-in-Residence, Univ. of Glasgow 1975–77, Traverse Theatre, Edinburgh 1982, Univ. of Edinburgh 1989–92; Chair. in Creative Writing, Dept of English, Univ. of Aberdeen 1996–. *Plays:* Sailmaker 1982, Space Invaders 1983, Changed Days 1991, The 3 Estaites 2002. *Publications include:* fiction: It's Colours They Are Fine (short stories) 1977, The Magic Flute (novel) 1990, Stone Garden (short stories) (Scottish Writer of the Year) 1995, The Pure Land 2006; poetry: Plop (15 Haiku) 1970, Glasgow Zen 1981, Seasons of the Heart 2000, Still (with Alison Watt) 2004, Clear Light 2005, Morning Glory (with Elizabeth Blackadder) 2010. *Honours:* Scottish Arts Council Book Award 1977, 1990, 1996, People's Prize 1996, TMA Martini Prize 1996. *Address:* Department of English, School of Language and Literature, University of Aberdeen, Taylor Building, Aberdeen, AB24 3UB, Scotland (office). *Telephone:* (1224) 272540 (office). *E-mail:* a.spence@abdn.ac.uk (office). *Website:* www.abdn.ac.uk/english (office); www.alanspence.co.uk.

SPENCE, Jonathan Dermot, PhD, CMG; American historian, academic and writer; *Sterling Professor of History, Yale University*; b. 11 Aug. 1936, Surrey, England; s. of Dermot Spence and Muriel Crailsham; m. 1st Helen Alexander 1962 (divorced 1993); two s.; m. 2nd Chin Annping 1993. *Education:* Univ. of Cambridge, UK and Yale Univ. *Career:* Asst Prof. of History, Yale Univ. 1966–71, Prof. 1971–, now Sterling Prof. of History; Visiting Prof. Univ. of Beijing 1987; Pres. American Historial Asscn 2004–05; mem. Bd of Govs Yale Univ. Press 1988–; mem. American Acad. of Arts and Sciences, American Philosophical Soc.; Guggenheim Fellow 1979–80; MacArthur Fellow 1987–92. *Publications:* Ts'Ao Yin and The K'Ang-Hsi Emperor 1966, To Change China 1969, Emperor of China 1974, The Death of Woman Wang 1978, The Gate of Heavenly Peace 1981, The Memory Palace of Matteo Ricci 1984, The Question of Hu 1988, The Search for Modern China 1990, Chinese Roundabout 1992, God's Chinese Son 1996, The Chan's Great Continent 1998, Mao Zedong 1999, Return to Dragon Mountain: Memories of a Late Ming Man 2007. *Honours:* Hon. LHD (Knox Coll.) 1984, (New Haven) 1989; Hon. LittD (Wheeling Coll.) 1985, (Chinese Univ. of Hong Kong) 1996, (Gettysburg) Coll. 1996, (Union Coll.) 2000, (Beloit Coll.) 2000, (Conn. Coll.) 2000; William C. DeVane Medal, Yale Chapter of Phi Beta Kappa 1978, Los Angeles Times History Prize 1982, Vursell Prize, American Acad. and Inst. of Arts and Letters 1983, Comisso Prize (Italy) 1987; Gelber Literary Prize (Canada) 1991. *Address:* Department of History, Yale University, P.O. Box 208324, New Haven, CT 06520 (office); 691 Forest Road, New Haven, CT 06515, USA (home). *Telephone:* (203) 432-0759 (office). *E-mail:* jonathan.spence@yale.edu (office). *Website:* www.yale.edu/history/faculty/spence.html (office).

SPENCE, William (Bill) John Duncan, (Jessica Blair, Jim Bowden, Kirk Ford, Floyd Rogers); British author; b. 20 April 1923, Middlesborough, England; m. Joan Mary Rhoda Ludley 1944 (died 1999); one s. three d. *Education:* St Mary's Teachers Training Coll. *Career:* served as bomb aimer RAF, did thirty-six operational flights in Lancasters of 44 (Rhodesia) Squadron Bomber Command; mem. Soc. of Authors, Romantic Novelists' Asscn, Bomber Command Asscn, Nat. Geographic Soc., Scarborough Writers Circle. *Publications:* numerous books, including: Romantic Ryedale (with Joan Spence) 1977, Harpooned 1981, The Medieval Monasteries of Yorkshire (with Joan Spence) 1981, Stories from Yorkshire Monasteries (with Joan Spence) 1992; novels, as Jessica Blair: The Red Shawl 1993, A Distant Harbour 1993, Storm Bay 1994, The Restless Spirit 1996, The Other Side of the River 1997, The Seaweed Gatherers 1998, Portrait of Charlotte 1999, The Locket 2000, The Long Way Home 2001, The Restless Heart 2001, Time and Tide 2002, Echoes of the Past 2003, Secrets of the Sea 2004, Yesterday's Dreams 2005, Reach for Tomorrow 2006, Dangerous Shores 2007, Wings of Sorrow 2008, Stay With Me 2009, Sealed Secrets 2010, Secrets of a Whitby Girl 2011, The Road Beneath Me 2012; as Jim Bowden: Two Gun Justice 1961, Black Water Canyon 1963, Brazo Feud 1965, Gun loose 1969, Valley of Revenge 1971, Hired Gun 1976, Incident at Bison Creek 1977, Cap 1978, Gunfight at Elm Creek 1980, Pecos Trail 1983, Incident at Elm Creek 1984, Robbery at Glenrock 1992, A Man Called Abe 1993, Dollars Of Death 2008, The Return of the Sheriff 2009, Roaring Valley 2009, Trail Of Revenge 2010, Guns Along The Brazo 2010, The Shadow of Eagle Rock 2011, Hangmen's Trail 2011; as Floyd Rogers: Montana Justice 1973, Hangman's Gulch 1991, Incident At Elk River 2008, Revenge Rider 2010, The Stage Riders 2010, The Man From Cheyenne Wells 2010; as Kirk Ford: Feud Riders 1991, Trail To Sedalia 2011; other: 36 Westerns, three war novels. *E-mail:* me@jessicablair.co.uk. *Website:* www.jessicablair.co.uk.

SPENCER, Elizabeth, AB, MA; American writer; b. 19 July 1921, Carrollton, Miss.; d. of James L. Spencer and Mary James McCain; m. John A. B. Rusher 1956 (died 1998). *Education:* Belhaven Coll. and Vanderbilt Univ. *Career:* Writer-in-Residence, Univ. of N Carolina 1969, Hollins Coll. 1973, Concordia Univ. 1977–78, Adjunct Prof. 1981–86; Visiting Prof., Univ. of N Carolina, Chapel Hill 1986–92; Vice-Chancellor Fellowship of Southern Writers

1993–97; mem. American Acad. of Arts and Letters. *Film:* Light in the Piazza 1962. *Plays:* For Lease or Sale 1989, The Light in the Piazza (musical drama) 2006. *Publications:* Fire in the Morning 1948, This Crooked Way 1952, The Voice at the Back Door 1956, The Light in the Piazza 1960, Knights and Dragons 1965, No Place for an Angel 1967, Ship Island and Other Stories 1968, The Snare 1972, The Stories of Elizabeth Spencer 1981, Marilee 1981, The Salt Line 1984, Jack of Diamonds and Other Stories 1988, For Lease or Sale (play) 1989, On the Gulf 1991, The Night Travellers 1991, Landscapes of the Heart (memoir) 1998, The Southern Woman: New and Selected Fiction 2000; contrib. short stories in magazines and collections. *Honours:* Hon. LittD (Southwestern Univ., Memphis) 1968, (Concordia Univ.) 1987, (Univ. of the South) 1992, (Univ. of North Carolina) 1998, (Belhaven Coll.) 1999; Guggenheim Foundation Fellow 1953, Rosenthal Foundation Award, American Acad. of Arts and Letters 1957, McGraw-Hill Fiction Award 1960, Award of Merit for short story, American Acad. of Arts and Letters 1983, Salem Award for Literature 1992, Dos Passos Award for Fiction 1992, NC Gov.'s Award for Literature 1994, Fortner Award for Literature 1998, Mississippi State Library Asscn Award for Non-fiction 1999, Thomas Wolfe Award, Univ. of NC 2002, NC Hall of Fame 2002, William Faulkner Award for Literary Excellence 2002, Lifetime Achievement Award, MS Acad. of Arts and Letters 2009. *Address:* 402 Longleaf Drive, Chapel Hill, NC 27517, USA (home). *Telephone:* (919) 929-2115 (home). *E-mail:* elizabeth0222@earthlink.net (home). *Website:* www.elizabethspencerwriter.com (home).

SPENCER, LaVyrle; American writer; b. 17 Aug. 1943, Browerville, MN; m. Daniel F. Spencer 1962, two d. *Education:* High School, Staples, MN. *Publications:* The Fulfillment 1979, The Endearment 1982, Forsaking All Others 1982, Hummingbird 1983, A Promise to Cherish 1983, The Hellion 1984, The Gamle 1984, Spring Fancy 1984, Twice Loved 1984, Sweet Memories 1984, Separate Beds 1985, A Heart Speaks 1986, Years 1986, Vows 1988, Morning Glory 1989, Bitter Sweet 1990, Forgiving 1991, Bygones 1992, November of the Heart 1993, Family Blessings 1994, Home Song 1995, That Camden Summer 1996, Small Town Girl 1997, Then Came Heaven 1997, Sweet Memories 2010. *Honours:* Romance Writers of America Historical Romance of the Year Awards 1983, 1984, 1985. *Address:* 1530 Amundson Lane, Stillwater, MN 55082-4135, USA (home). *Telephone:* (651) 430-0115 (home).

SPENCER, Paul, BLitt, MA, DPhil; British social anthropologist and academic; b. 25 March 1932, London; m. Diane Wells; two s. *Education:* Christ's Coll., Cambridge, Wadham Coll., Oxford. *Career:* scientific officer, Tavistock Inst. of Human Relations, London 1962–71; teacher, SOAS, London 1971–97, Hon. Dir Int. African Inst. 1996–2005, currently Emeritus Prof. of African Anthropology. *Publications:* The Samburu 1965, Nomads in Alliance 1973, Society and the Dance 1985, The Maasai of Matapato 1988, Anthropology and the Riddle of the Sphinx 1990, The Pastoral Continuum 1998, Time, Space and the Unknown: Maasai Configurations of Power and Providence 2003.

SPIEGELMAN, Art; American cartoonist, editor and writer; b. 15 Feb. 1948, Stockholm, Sweden; m. Françoise Mouly 1977; two c. *Education:* High School of Art and Design, Manhattan and Harpur Coll., Binghamton, NY. *Career:* creative consultant, artist, designer, ed. and writer, Topps Chewing Gum Inc, New York 1965–87; Ed., Douglas Comix 1972; instructor, San Francisco Acad. of Art 1974–75, New York School of the Visual Arts 1979–86; Contributing Ed., Arcade, The Comics Revue 1975–76; founder-Ed., Raw comics magazine 1980–; staff artist and contributing ed., The New Yorker 1993–2003; Ed., Little Lit series of children's comics anthologies. *Publications as author and illustrator:* The Complete Mr Infinity 1970, The Viper Vicar of Vice, Villainy, and Vickedness 1972, Ace Hole, Midge Detective 1974, The Language of Comics 1974, Breakdowns: From Maus to Now: An Anthology of Strips 1977, Work and Turn 1979, Every Day Has Its Dog 1979, Two-Fisted Painters Action Adventure 1980, Maus: A Survivor's Tale (Pulitzer Prize Special Citation 1992) 1986, Read Yourself Raw (with F. Mouly) 1987, Maus II 1992, The Wild Party (illustrations to book by Joseph Moncure March) 1994, Open Me... I'm a Dog 1997, Jack Cole and Plastic Man: Forms Stretched to Their Limits 2001, In the Shadow of No Towers 2004, Breakdowns 2008. *Honours:* Playboy Editorial Award for Best Comic Strip 1982, Joel M. Cavior Award for Jewish Writing 1986, Stripschappening Award for Best Foreign Comics Album 1987, Guggenheim Fellowship 1990, Alpha Art Award, Angoulerne, France 1993. *Literary Agent:* Steven Barclay Agency, 12 Western Avenue, Petaluma, CA 94952, USA. *Telephone:* (707) 773-0654. *Fax:* (707) 778-1868. *Website:* www.barclayagency.com.

SPIOTTA, Dana; American author and academic; *Assistant Professor of English, MFA Program, Syracuse University*; b. 1966; m. Clement Coleman; one d. *Education:* Columbia Univ., Evergreen State Coll., Olympia, Wash. *Career:* moved to New York 1993; fmrly Co-Man. Ed. The Quarterly; currently Asst Prof. of English, MFA Program, Syracuse Univ. Fellow, John Simon Guggenheim Memorial Foundation 2007–08, New York Foundation for the Arts 2008. *Publications include:* Lightning Field 2001, Eat the Document 2006, Stone Arabia 2011. *Honours:* Joseph Brodsky Rome Prize for Literature 2008–09. *Address:* English Department, 210 Tolley Humanities Building, College of Arts and Sciences, Syracuse University, Syracuse, NY 13244, USA (office). *Telephone:* (315) 443-8796 (office). *E-mail:* dspiotta@syr.edu (office); dana@danaspiotta.com. *Website:* as-cascade.syr.edu/profiles/pages/spiotta-dana.html (office); www.danaspiotta.com.

SPONG, Rt Rev. John Shelby, AB, MDiv; American ecclesiastic and writer; b. 16 June 1931, Charlotte, NC; s. of John Shelby Spong and Doolie Griffith Spong; m. 1st Joan Lydia Ketner 1952 (died 1988); three d.; m. 2nd Christine Mary Bridger 1990. *Education:* Univ. of North Carolina, Virginia Theological Seminary. *Career:* Rector St Joseph's, Durham, NC 1955–57, Calvary Church, Tarboro, NC 1957–65, St John's Church, Lynchburg, Va 1965–69, St Paul's Church, Richmond, Va 1969–76, Bishop, Diocese of Newark, NJ 1976–2000; Pres. NJ Council of Churches; Quatercentenary Fellow, Emmanuel Coll. Cambridge, UK 1992; William Belden Noble Lecturer, Harvard Univ. 2000; Visiting Lecturer, Univ. of The Pacific, Stockton, Calif. 2003; mem. of Faculty, Grad. Theological Union, Berkeley, Calif.; columnist for Beliefnet.com 1999–2000, AgoraMedia 2002–, Waterfront Media 2002–. *Radio:* Play by Play sportscaster in Tarboro NC and Lynchburg, Va 1960–65. *Publications:* Honest Prayer 1973, This Hebrew Lord 1974, 1988, Dialogue: In Search of Jewish-Christian Understanding 1975, Christpower 1975, Life Approaches Death: A Dialogue on Medical Ethics 1976, The Living Commandments 1977, The Easter Moment 1980, Into the Whirlwind 1983, Beyond Moralism 1986, Consciousness and Survival 1987, Living in Sin? 1988, Rescuing the Bible from Fundamentalism 1991, Born of a Woman – A Bishop Rethinks the Virgin Birth and the Place of Women in a Male-Dominated Church 1992, Resurrection: Myth or Reality? 1994, Liberating the Gospels: Reading the Bible with Jewish Eyes 1996, Why Christianity Must Change or Die: A Bishop Speaks to Believers in Exile 1998, Here I Stand: My Struggle for a Christianity of Integrity, Love and Equality 2000, The Bishop's Voice 1999, A New Christianity for a New World 2001, Crossroads – The Sins of Scripture 2005, Eternal Life: A New Vision beyond Religion, Beyond Theism, Beyond Heaven and Hell 2009. *Honours:* Hon. DD (Virginia Theological Seminary), (St Paul's Coll.); Hon. DHL (Muhlenberg Coll.), (Holmes Inst., Chicago) 2004, (Univ. of North Carolina) 2007, (Lehigh Univ.) 2007, (Drew Univ.) 2010; Quartercentenary Scholar, Emmanuel Coll., Cambridge, UK 1992, David Frederick Strauss Award, Jesus Seminar 1999, Humanist of the Year, New York City 1999, John A. T, Robinson Award 2004, portrait hung in Hall of Honor in Martin Luther King Chapel, Morehead Coll., Atlanta, Ga for leadership in breaking the oppression of homosexual people 2010. *Literary Agent:* c/o Julie Rae Mitchell, HarperSanFrancisco, 353 Sacramento Street, Suite 500, San Francisco, CA, 94111, USA. *Address:* 24 Puddingstone Road, Morris Plains, NJ 07950, USA (home). *Telephone:* (973) 538-9825 (home). *Fax:* (973) 540-9584 (home). *E-mail:* johnsspong@aol.com (home); cmsctm@aol.com (home). *Website:* www.johnshelbyspong.com.

SPOONER, David Eugene, BA (Hons), PhD; British writer, poet and naturalist; *Member, Academic Board, London Diplomatic Academy*; b. 1 Sept. 1941, West Kirby, Wirral, England; s. of Eugene Spooner and Joyce Wright; m. Marion O'Neil 1986; one d. *Education:* Univs of Leeds, Manchester and Bristol, Dipl. in Drama with distinction. *Career:* Lecturer, Univ. of Kent 1968–73, Manchester Polytechnic 1974–75; Visiting Prof., Pennsylvania State Univ., USA 1973–74; Head of Publishing, Borderline Press 1976–85; ind. scholar 1986–; Dir Butterfly Conservation, East Scotland; mem. Welsh Acad. Assoc., Asscn Benjamin Constant, Academic Bd London Diplomatic Acad., Thoreau Soc., Nabokov Soc.; est. David Eugene Spooner Foundation for Entomology with Philosophy. *Publications:* Unmakings 1977, The Angelic Fly: The Butterfly in Art 1992, The Metaphysics of Insect Life 1995, Insect into Poem: 20th Century Hispanic Poetry 1999, Creatures of Air: Poetry 1976–2001 2001, Thoreau's Insects 2002, William Blake and Contemporary Science 2004, The Insect-Populated Mind – How Insects Have Influenced the Evolution of Consciousness 2005, Roots and Codes: the True Poetry of Languages 2009; contrib. to Iron, Interactions, Tandem, Weighbauk, Revue de Littérature Comparée, Bestia (Fable Society of America), Margin, Corbie Press, Butterfly Conservation News, Butterfly News, Field Studies, Annales Benjamin Constant. *Honours:* American Medal of Honor for Natural History 2004, American Hall of Fame 2005, listed in Great Minds of the 21st Century 2005, Congressional Medal for Literature. *Address:* 96 Halbeath Road, Dunfermline, Fife, KY12 7LR, Scotland (home). *Telephone:* (1383) 729251 (home). *E-mail:* doctorspooner@btinternet.com. *Website:* www.davidspooner.org; members.authorsguild.net/davidspooner.

SPRINGER, Nancy, BA; American writer and poet; b. 5 July 1948, Montclair, NJ; m. Joel H. Springer 1969 (divorced 1997); one s. one d. *Education:* Gettysburg Coll. *Career:* personal development plan instructor, Univ. of Pittsburgh 1983–85; Leisure Learning Instructor, York Coll., Pennsylvania 1986–91; Education Instructor, Franklin and Marshall Coll. 1988–; Instructor of Creative Writing, York Coll. of PA 1997–99; Writing Popular Fiction Masters' Degree Program, Seton Hill Coll. 1998–; mem. Society of Children's Book Writers and Illustrators, Pennwriters (pres. 1992–93). *Publications:* The Sable Moon 1981, The Black Beast 1982, The Golden Swan 1983, Wings of Flame 1985, Chains of Gold 1986, A Horse to Love 1987, Madbond 1987, Chance and Other Gestures of the Hand of Fate 1987, The Hex Witch of Seldom 1988, Not on a White Horse 1988, Apocalypse 1989, They're All Named Wildfire 1989, Red Wizard 1990, Colt 1991, The Friendship Song 1992, The Great Pony Hassle 1993, Stardark Songs (poems) 1993, Larque on the Wing 1994, The Boy on a Black Horse 1994, Metal Angel 1994, Music of Their Hooves (children's poems) 1994, Toughing It 1994, Looking for Jamie Bridger 1995, Fair Peril 1996, Secret Star 1997, I Am Mordred 1998, Sky Rider 1999, Plumage 2000, I Am Morgan Le Fay 2001, Rowan Hood: Outlaw Girl of Sherwood Forest 2001, Separate Sisters 2001, Needy Creek 2001, Lionclaw: A Tale of Rowan Hood 2002, Outlaw Princess of Sherwood 2003, Blood Trail 2003, Wild Boy 2004, Rowan Hood Returns 2005, The Case of the Missing

Marquess 2006, The Case of the Left-Handed Lady 2007, Dussie 2007, The Case of the Bizarre Bouquets 2008, The Case of the Peculiar Pink Fan 2008, The Case of the Cryptic Crinoline 2009, Somebody 2009, The Case of the Gypsy Goodbye 2010, Possessing Jessie 2010; contributions: Magazines and journals. *Honours:* Distinguished Alumna, Gettysburg Coll. 1987, International Reading Asscn Children's Choice 1988, Joan Fassler Memorial Book Award 1992, International Reading Asscn Young Adult's Choice 1993, Edgar Allan Poe Awards, MWA 1995, 1996, James Tiptree Jr Award 1995, Carolyn W. Field Award 1995, Outstanding Pennsylvania Writer Award. *Address:* c/o Holiday House, 425 Madison Avenue, New York, NY 10017, USA (office). *Website:* www.holidayhouse.com (office); www.nancyspringer.com.

SPRINKLE, Patricia Houck, AB; American writer; b. 13 Nov. 1943, Bluefield, WV; m. Robert William Sprinkle 1970, two s. *Education:* Vassar College. *Career:* mem. MWA, Penwoman, Sisters in Crime (publicity chair.). *Publications:* fiction: Murder at Markham 1988, Murder in the Charleston Manner 1990, Murder on Peachtree Street 1991, Somebody's Dead in Snellville 1992, Death of a Dunwoody Matron 1993, A Mystery Bred in Buckhead 1994, Deadly Secrets on the St Johns 1995, When Did We Lose Harriet? 1997, But Why Shoot the Magistrate? 1998, The Remember Box 2000, Carley's Song 2001, Who Invited the Dead Man? 2002, Who Left That Body in the Rain? 2002, Who Let that Killer in the House? 2003, When Will the Dead Lady Sing? 2004, Who Killed the Queen of Clubs? 2005, Did You Declare the Corpse? 2006, Death on the Family Tree 2006, Sins of the Father 2007, Guess Who's Coming to Die? 2007, What Are You Wearing to Die? 2008, Daughter of Deceit 2008, Hold Up the Sky 2010; non-fiction: Hunger: Understanding the Crisis Through Games 1980, In God's Image: Meditations for the New Mother 1988, Housewarmings: For Those Who Make a House a Home 1992, Women Who Do Too Much: Stress and the Myth of the Superwoman 1992, Children Who Do Too Little 1993, A Gift From God 1994, Women Home Alone: Learning to Thrive 1996. *E-mail:* thoroughlysouthern@earthlink.net (office). *Website:* www.patriciasprinkle.com.

SPROTT, Duncan; British writer; b. 2 Dec. 1952, Ongar, Essex, England. *Education:* Univ. of St Andrews, Fife, Scotland and Heatherley School of Art, London. *Publications:* 1784 (compiler) 1984, The Clopton Hercules (aka The Rise of Mr Warde) 1991, Our Lady of the Potatoes 1995, Sprottichronicon (genealogy) 2000, The Ptolemies: Book 1, The House of the Eagle 2004, Book 2, Daughter of the Crocodile 2006. *Honours:* Arts Council Literature Award 1995. *Literary Agent:* c/o Rogers, Coleridge & White Literary Agency, 20 Powis Mews, London, W11 1JN, England. *Telephone:* (20) 7221-3717. *Fax:* (20) 7229-9084. *E-mail:* info@rcwlitagency.co.uk. *Website:* www.rcwlitagency.co.uk. *E-mail:* duncansprott@mac.com (home).

SPUFFORD, Francis; British journalist and writer; b. 1964. *Career:* full-time writer 1990–; Fellow, Anglia Ruskin Univ. 2005–07; Sr Lecturer in Creative Writing, Goldsmiths Coll., Univ. of London 2007–. *Publications:* I May Be Some Time: Ice and the English Imagination (Writers' Guild Award for Best Non-Fiction Book 1996, Somerset Maugham Award) 1996, Cultural Babbage (ed., essay collection) 1997, The Child that Books Built 2002, Backroom Boys 2003, The Antarctic (Ed.) 2007, Red Plenty 2010; contrib. to Granta, Conde Nast Traveller. *Honours:* Somerset Maugham Award, Sunday Times Young Writer of the Year 1977, Writers' Guild Award for Best Non-Fiction Book. *Address:* Department of English and Comparative Literature, Goldsmiths College, Room 312, Warmington Tower, New Cross, London, SE14 6NW (office); 13 St. John's Street, Duxford, Cambs., CB22 4RA, England. *Telephone:* (20) 7717-2954 (office). *E-mail:* f.spufford@gold.ac.uk (office). *Website:* www.gold.ac.uk/ecl/staff/f-spufford (office).

SPURLING, (Susan) Hilary, CBE, BA; British biographer; b. 25 Dec. 1940, d. of Gilbert Alexander Forrest and Emily Maureen Forrest (née Armstrong); m. John Spurling 1961; two s. one d. *Education:* Somerville Coll., Oxford. *Career:* theatre critic, The Spectator 1964–69, Literary Ed. 1966–70; book reviewer, The Observer 1969–86, Daily Telegraph 1986–. *Publications:* Ivy When Young: The Early Life of I. Compton-Burnett 1884–1919 1974, Handbook to Anthony Powell's Music of Time 1977, Secrets of A Woman's Heart: The Later Life of I. Compton-Burnett 1920–69 (Duff Cooper Prize 1984, Heinemann Award 1984) 1984, Elinor Fettiplace's Receipt Book 1986, Paul Scott: A Life 1990, Paper Spirits 1992, The Unknown Matisse: 1869–1908 1998, La Grande Thérèse 1999, The Girl From the Fiction Department: A Portrait of Sonia Orwell 2002, Matisse the Master: 1909–1954 (Whitbread Biog. of the Year, Whitbread Book of the Year, Los Angeles Book Prize) 2005, Matisse: The Life 2009, Burying the Bones: Pearl Buck in China 2010. *Honours:* Hon. Fellow, Somerville Coll., Oxford 2006, Royal Soc. of Literature; Hon. Trustee, Royal Literary Fund; Dr hc (Anglia Ruskin Univ.) 2007; Rose Mary Crawshaw Prize 1974, Heywood Hill Literary Prize for General Achievement 2003, 2005. *Literary Agent:* David Higham Associates, 5–8 Lower John Street, Golden Square, London, W1R 4HA, England. *Telephone:* (20) 7434-5900. *Fax:* (20) 7437-1072. *E-mail:* dha@davidhigham.co.uk. *Website:* www.davidhigham.co.uk.

SPURLING, John Antony, BA; British dramatist, novelist and art critic; b. 17 July 1936, Kisumu, Kenya; s. of Antony Cuthbert Spurling and Elizabeth Frances Spurling (née Stobart); m. Hilary Forrest 1961; two s. one d. *Education:* Dragon School, Oxford, Marlborough Coll., St John's Coll., Oxford. *Career:* Nat. Service with RA 1955–57; Plebiscite Officer, Southern Cameroon 1960–61; Announcer, BBC Radio 1963–66; freelance writer 1966–; Art Critic, New Statesman 1976–88. *Plays:* MacRune's Guevara (as realised by Edward Hotel), In the Heart of the British Museum, Coming Ashore in Guadeloupe, The British Empire trilogy, The Butcher of Baghdad, Heresy. *Publications:* plays: MacRune's Guevara 1969, In the Heart of the British Museum 1971, Shades of Heathcliff and Death of Captain Doughty 1975, The British Empire Part One 1982; fiction: The Ragged End 1989, After Zenda 1995, The Ten Thousand Things; other: Beckett: A Study of His Plays (with John Fletcher) 1972, revised third edn as Beckett, the Playwright 1985, Graham Greene 1983; contrib. to books, newspapers, periodicals, theatre (17 plays produced, 1969–2004), radio (10 plays, 1976–2002) and television (4 plays, 1970–73). *Honours:* Henfield Writing Fellowship, Univ. of East Anglia 1973. *Address:* c/o Macnaughton Lord Representation, Unit 10, The Broomhouse Studios, 50 Sulivan Road, London, SW6 3DX, England. *Telephone:* (20) 7384-9517 (office). *Fax:* (20) 7371-7563 (office). *E-mail:* info@mlrep.com (office). *Website:* www.ml2000.org.uk; www.johnspurling.com.

STABENOW, Dana, BA, MFA; American writer; b. 27 March 1952, Anchorage, AK; d. of Donald Ray Stabenow and Joan Allene Perry. *Education:* Univ. of Alaska at Fairbanks and at Anchorage. *Publications include:* Second Star 1991, A Handful of Stars 1991, A Cold Day for Murder 1992, Dead in the Water 1993, A Fatal Thaw 1993, A Cold-Blooded Business 1994, Red Planet Run 1995, Play with Fire 1995, Blood Will Tell 1996, Breakup 1997, Killing Grounds 1998, Fire and Ice 1998, Hunter's Moon 1999, So Sure of Death 1999, Midnight Come Again 2000, Nothing Gold Can Stay 2000, The Singing of the Dead 2001, A Fine and Bitter Snow 2002, Better to Rest 2002, A Grave Denied 2003, A Taint in the Blood 2004, Blindfold Game 2006, A Deeper Sleep 2007, Prepared for Rage 2008, Whisper to the Blood 2009, A Night too Dark 2010, Though Not Dead 2011. *Honours:* MWA Edgar Allan Poe Award 1993. *Literary Agent:* Richard Henshaw Group, 22 West 23rd Street, Fifth Floor, New York, NY 10010, USA. *E-mail:* rhgagents@aol.com. *Website:* www.richhaddr.com; www.stabenow.com.

STAFFORD, David Alexander Tetlow, BA, PhD, FRHistS; British historian and writer; b. 10 March 1942, Newcastle upon Tyne, England; m. *Education:* Univ. of Cambridge, Univ. of London. *Career:* Third Sec., British Foreign Office, London 1967–68, Second Sec. 1968; Research Assoc., Centre of Int. Studies, LSE 1968–70; Asst Prof., Univ. of Victoria, BC 1970–76, Assoc. Prof. 1976–82, Prof. of History 1982–84; Senior Assoc. mem., St Antony's College, Oxford 1976–87; Dir of Studies, Canadian Inst. of Int. Affairs, Toronto 1985–86, Exec. Dir 1986–92; Visiting Prof., Inst. for Advanced Studies in the Humanities 1992–2000, Project Dir, Center for Second World War Studies, Univ. of Edinburgh 2000–, now Prof. Emer. *Publications:* From Anarchism to Reformism: A Study of the Political Activities of Paul Brousse, 1870–90 1971, Britain and European Resistance, 1940–1945: A Survey of the Special Operations Executive, with Documents 1980, Camp X: Canada's School for Secret Agents, 1941–1945 1986, The Silent Game: The Real World of Imaginary Spies 1988, Spy Wars: Espionage and Canada: From Gouzenko to Glasnost 1990, Security and Intelligence in a Changing World: New Perspectives for the 1990s (ed. with A. Stuart Farson and Wesley K. Ward) 1991, Churchill and Secret Service 1998, American-British-Canadian Intelligence Relations, 1939–2000 2000, Secret Agent: The True Story of the Special Operations Executive 2000, Roosevelt and Churchill: Men of Secrets 2000, Spies Beneath Berlin 2000, Ten Days to D-Day 2003, Endgame 1945: Victory, Retribution, Liberation 2007; contributions: scholarly journals and general periodicals. *Address:* Centre for Second World War Studies, University of Edinburgh, 2nd Floor, 24 Buccleuch Place, Edinburgh EH8 9LN, Scotland (office). *Telephone:* (131) 651-1389 (office). *E-mail:* david.stafford@ed.ac.uk (office). *Website:* www.shc.ed.ac.uk (office).

STAINES, David, CM, BA, AM, PhD, FRSC; Canadian academic, writer, translator and editor; *Professor of English, University of Ottawa*; b. 8 Aug. 1946, Toronto; m. Noreen Taylor. *Education:* Univ. of Toronto, Harvard Univ. *Career:* Asst Prof. of English, Harvard Univ. 1973–78; Hon. Research Fellow, Univ. Coll. London 1977–78; Assoc. Prof., Univ. of Ottawa 1978–85, Prof. of English 1985–, Dean Faculty of Arts 1996–2003; Five Coll. Prof. of Canadian Studies, Smith Coll. 1982–84. *Publications:* The Canadian Imagination: Dimensions of a Literary Culture (ed.) 1977, Reappraisals: The Callaghan Symposium (ed.) 1981, Tennyson's Camelot: The Idylls of the King and its Medieval Sources 1982, Stephen Leacock: A Reappraisal (ed.) 1986, The Forty-Ninth and Other Parallels: Contemporary Canadian Perspectives (ed.) 1986, Elements of Literature (ed.) 1987 and subsequent edns, The Complete Romances of Chrétien de Troyes (trans.) 1990, Beyond the Provinces: Literary Canada at Century's End 1995, Margaret Laurence: Critical Reflections (ed.) 2001, Northrop Frye: Essays on Canada (ed.) 2003, Marshall McLuhan: Understanding Me (ed.) 2003, The Letters of Stephen Leacock (ed.) 2006; contrib. to professional journals. *Honours:* Order of Ont.; Lorne Pierce Medal for outstanding contrib. to Canadian criticism 1998. *Address:* Department of English, University of Ottawa, Ottawa, ON K1N 6N5, Canada (office). *Telephone:* (613) 562-5800 (ext. 1182) (office). *Fax:* (613) 562-5990 (office). *E-mail:* dstaines@uottawa.ca (office).

STALLWORTHY, Jon Howie, BA, BLitt, FRSL, FBA; British professor of English, poet and writer; *Senior Research Fellow, Wolfson College, Oxford*; b. 18 Jan. 1935, London, England; m. Gillian Waldock 1960; three c. *Education:* Magdalen Coll., Oxford. *Career:* Ed., Oxford University Press 1959–71, Deputy Academic Publr 1974–77; Visiting Fellow, All Souls Coll., Oxford 1971–72; John Wendell Anderson Prof. of English Literature, Cornell Univ., Ithaca, NY 1977–86; Reader in English Literature 1986–92, Prof. of English

1992–2000, Univ. of Oxford, Sr Research Fellow, Wolfson Coll., Oxford 2000–. *Publications include:* poetry: The Earthly Paradise 1958, The Astronomy of Love 1961, Out of Bounds 1963, The Almond Tree 1967, A Day in the City 1967, Root and Branch 1969, A Dinner of Herbs 1970, Alexander Blok: The Twelve and Other Poems (trans.) 1970, The Apple Barrel: Selected Poems 1955–63 1974, A Familiar Tree 1978, The Anzac Sonata: Selected Poems 1986, The Guest from the Future 1995, Rounding the Horn: Collected Poems 1998, Body Language 2004, War Poet 2009; other: Between the Lines: Yeats's Poetry in the Making 1963, Vision and Revision in Yeats's Last Poems 1969, The Penguin Book of Love Poetry (ed.) 1973, Wilfred Owen: A Biography 1974, Poets of the First World War 1974, Boris Pasternak: Selected Poems (trans.) 1982, The Complete Poems and Fragments of Wilfred Owen (ed.) 1983, The Oxford Book of War Poetry (ed.) 1984, The Poems of Wilfred Owen (ed.) 1985, First Lines: Poems Written in Youth from Herbert to Heaney (ed.) 1987, Henry Reed: Collected Poems (ed.) 1991, Louis MacNeice 1995, Singing School: The Making of a Poet 1998, Aleksander Blok: Selected Poems (trans.) 2000, Anthem for Doomed Youth: Twelve Soldier Poets of the First World War (ed.) 2002, Survivors' Songs from Maldon to the Somme 2008, Three Poets of the First World War: Ivor Gurney, Isaac Rosenberg, Wilfred Owen (ed.) 2011; contrib. to professional journals. *Honours:* Duff Cooper Memorial Prize 1974, WHSmith Literary Award 1974, E.M. Forster Award 1975, Southern Arts Literary Prize 1995, Wilfred Owen Asscn Poetry Award 2010. *Address:* Wolfson College, Oxford, OX2 6UD, England (office). *E-mail:* jon.stallworthy@wolfson.ox.ac.uk (office).

STAMM, Peter; Swiss writer and journalist; b. 18 Jan. 1963, Weinfelden, Thurgau; two s. *Career:* worked in various professions in Paris, New York and London; freelance author and journalist 1998–; also writes stage and radio plays. *Publications:* Agnes (novel) 1998, Blitzeis 1999, Ungefähre Landschaft (novel) (trans. as Unformed Landscape) 2001, In fremden garten (short stories) (trans. as In Strange Gardens) 2003, An einem Tag wie diesem (novel) (trans. as On A Day Like This) 2006, Wir fliegen 2008, Sieben Jahre (novel) (trans. as Seven Years) 2009, Seerücken (short stories) 2011; contrib. to Neue Zürcher Zeitung, Tages-Anzeiger, Die Weltwoche, Nebelspalter. *Honours:* Rauriser Literaturpreis 1999, Rheingau Literaturpreis 2000, Alemannischer Literaturpreis 2011. *Literary Agent:* c/o Eva Koralnik, Liepman AG, Englischviertelstrasse 59, 8032 Zurich, Switzerland. *Telephone:* (1) 261-76-60. *Fax:* (1) 261-01-24. *E-mail:* info@liepmanagency.com. *Website:* www.liepmanagency.com. *E-mail:* post@peterstamm.ch (home). *Website:* www.peterstamm.ch.

STAMP, Gavin Mark, PhD, FSA; British architectural historian and writer; b. 15 March 1948, Bromley, Kent, England; s. of Barry Hartnell Stamp and Norah Clare Stamp (née Rich); m. Alexandra Artley 1982 (divorced 2006); two d. *Education:* Dulwich Coll., London, Gonville and Caius Coll., Cambridge. *Career:* freelance writer and teacher –1990; Lecturer, Mackintosh School of Architecture, Glasgow School of Art 1990–99, Sr Lecturer and Hon. Prof. 1999–2003; Mellon Sr Fellow and Bye Fellow, Gonville and Caius Coll., Cambridge 2003–04, Hon. Prof., Univ. of Cambridge 2010–; ind. scholar 2004–; Chair. The Twentieth Century Soc. (fmrly The Thirties Soc.) 1983–2007; Founder and Chair. Alexander Thomson Soc. 1991–2003. *Publications:* Robert Weir Schultz and his work for Marquesses of Bute 1981, The Great Perspectivists 1982, The Changing Metropolis 1984, The English House 1860–1914 1986, Telephone Boxes 1989, Greek Thomson (co-ed.) 1994, Alexander 'Greek' Thomson 1999, Edwin Lutyens' Country Houses 2001, An Architect of Promise: George Gilbert Scott Junior and the Late Gothic Revival 2002, Lutyens Abroad (co-ed.) 2002, The Memorial to the Missing of the Somme 2006, Britain's Lost Cities 2007, Lost Victorian Britain 2010. *Honours:* Hon. Fellow, Royal Incorporation of Architects of Scotland 1994; Hon. FRIBA 1998. *Address:* 15 Belle Vue Court, 122D Devonshire Road, London, SE23 3SY, England (home). *E-mail:* gavin.stamp@btopenworld.com (home).

STANG, Peter J., BS, PhD; American writer and academic; *Distinguished Professor of Chemistry, University of Utah*; b. 17 Nov. 1941, Nürnburg, Germany. *Education:* DePaul Univ., Chicago, Univ. of California at Berkeley. *Career:* Nat. Inst. of Health work at Princeton Univ.; Dept Chair, Univ. of Utah 1989–95, Distinguished Prof. of Chemistry 1992–, Dean of the Coll. of Science 1997–2007; Assoc. Ed. Journal of the American Chemical Soc. 1982–99, Ed. 2002–; Ed.-in-Chief, Journal of Organic Chemistry 2000–01; elected mem., Nat. Acad. of Sciences 2000; Foreign mem. Chinese Acad. of Sciences, Hungarian Acad. of Sciences; Fellow American Acad. of Arts and Sciences. *Publications include:* Metal-catalyzed Cross-Coupling Reactions 1997, Templated Organic Synthesis (co-ed.) 1999. *Honours:* JSPS Fellowship 1995, 1998, Lady Davis Fellowship in Haifa Israel 1986, 1997; Fulbright Hays Sr Scholar to Zagreb, Croatia 1988; Dr hc (Russian Acad. of Sciences), (Lomonosov Moscow State Univ.) 1992, American Chemical Soc. James Flack Norris Award in Physical Organic Chemistry 199, ACS George A. Olah Award in Hydrocarbon Chemistry 2003, Linus Pauling Medal 2006; A. von Humboldt Sr Scientist Award 1977, 1997. *Address:* Department of Chemistry, University of Utah, 315 South 1400 East, Room 2020, Salt Lake City, UT 84112-0850 (office). *Telephone:* (801) 581-8329 (office). *E-mail:* stang@chem.utah.edu (office).

STANIŠIĆ, Saša; Bosnia and Herzegovina writer, teacher and lecturer; *Lecturer, MIT-Germany*; b. 1978, Višegrad, Bosnia. *Education:* Leipzig Literature Inst. *Career:* moved from Bosnia to Heidelberg, Germany following outbreak of civil war 1992; teacher of German as a foreign language; freelance writer, photographer, journalist 2001–. *Publications:* Wie der Soldat das Grammofon repariert (trans. as How the Soldier repairs the Gramophone) (novel), Go West (play) etc. *Honours:* numerous awards. *Address:* c/o Luchterhand Literaturverlag, Verlagsgruppe Random House GmbH, Neumarkter Str. 28, 81673 Munich, Germany. *E-mail:* karsten.roesel@luchterhand-verlag.de (office). *Website:* www.randomhouse.de/luchterhand (office).

STANSKY, Peter David Lyman, BA, MA, PhD, FRHistS; American historian, academic, author and editor; *Frances and Charles Field Professor Emeritus of History, Stanford University*; b. 18 Jan. 1932, New York, NY; s. of Lyman Stansky and Ruth Macow Stansky. *Education:* Yale Univ., King's Coll., Cambridge, UK, Harvard Univ. *Career:* Instructor in History, Harvard Univ. 1961–64, Asst Prof. 1964–68; Assoc. Prof. of History, Stanford Univ. 1968–73, Prof. of History 1973–, Frances and Charles Field Prof. of History 1974–2004, Frances and Charles Field Prof. Emer. 2005–; Assoc. Ed. Journal of British Studies 1973–85; Ed. North American Conference on British Studies Bibliographical Series 1977–87; Visiting Fellow, All Souls Coll. Oxford 1979, Christensen Fellow, St Catherine's Coll. Oxford 1983; Co-Ed. Virginia Woolf Miscellany 1984–2002; Fellow, Center for Advanced Study in the Behavioral Sciences 1988–89; various guest lectureships; mem. American Historical Asscn, Nat. Book Critics' Circle (Dir 1980–85), North American Conf. on British Studies (Pres. 1974–76), Soc. for the Promotion of Science and Scholarship (Pres.), Virginia Woolf Soc., William Morris Soc.; Fellow, American Acad. of Arts and Sciences. *Publications:* Ambitions and Strategies: The Struggle for the Leadership of the Liberal Party in the 1890s 1964, Journey to the Frontier: Julian Bell and John Cornford, their Lives and the 1930s (with William Abrahams) 1966, The Unknown Orwell (with William Abrahams) 1972, England Since 1867: Continuity and Change 1973, Gladstone: A Progress in Politics 1979, Orwell: The Transformation (with William Abrahams) 1979, William Morris 1983, Redesigning the World 1985, London's Burning (with William Abrahams) 1994, On or About December 1910: Early Bloomsbury and its Intimate World 1996, Another Book that Never Was 1998, From William Morris to Sergeant Pepper 1999, Sassoon: The Worlds of Philip and Sybil 2003, The First Day of the Blitz: September 7, 1940 2007, Julian Bell: From Bloomsbury to the Spanish Civil War 2012; editor: The Left and War: The British Labour Party and the First World War 1969, John Morley Nineteenth Century Essays 1970, Conference on British Studies Biographical Series (six vols) 1970–73, Winston Churchill: A Profile 1973, The Victorian Revolution 1973, Modern British History Series (with Leslie Hume, 18 vols) 1982, On Nineteen Eighty-Four 1983, Modern European History Series (47 vols) 1987–92. *Honours:* Hon. DL (Wittenberg Univ.) 1984; Guggenheim Fellowships 1966–67, 1973–74, American Council of Learned Socs Fellow 1978–79, Nat. Endowment for the Humanities Sr Fellowships 1983, 1998–99, Award for Scholarly Distinction, American Historical Asscn 2011, Mellon Emer. Fellowship 2011–12. *Address:* Department of History, Stanford University, Stanford, CA 94305-2024, USA (office). *Telephone:* (650) 723-2663 (office). *E-mail:* stansky@stanford.edu (office).

STAPLES, Brent, BA, PhD; American writer; b. 1951, Chester, PA. *Education:* Widener Univ. and Univ. of Chicago. *Career:* reporter, Chicago Sun-Times 1982–83; editorial writer, New York Times 1983–. *Publication:* Parallel Time: Growing Up in Black and White (Anisfield Wolff Book Award) 1994, American Love Story 1999. *Honours:* Danforth Fellowship. *Address:* c/o New York Times, 620 Eighth Avenue, New York, NY 10018, USA (office). *Telephone:* (212) 556-1234 (office). *Website:* www.nytimes.com (office).

STARK, Joshua (see Olsen, Theodore Victor)

STARKEY, David Robert, CBE, MA, PhD, FSA, FRHistS; British historian, academic and broadcaster; b. 3 Jan. 1945, Kendal; s. of Robert Starkey and Elsie Lyon. *Education:* Kendal Grammar School, Fitzwilliam Coll. Cambridge. *Career:* Research Fellow, Fitzwilliam Coll. Cambridge 1970–72, Visiting Fellow 1998–2001, Bye-Fellow 2001–06, Hon. Fellow 2006–; Lecturer in History, Dept of Int. History, LSE 1972–98; Visiting Vernon Prof. of Biography, Dartmouth Coll., NH, USA 1987, 1989; British Council Specialist Visitor, Australia 1989; contribs to various newspapers; mem. Editorial Bd History Today 1980–, Commemorative Plaques Working Group, English Heritage 1993–2006; Pres., Soc. for Court Studies 1995–2005; Patron, Tory Group for Homosexual Equality 1994–; Historical Adviser to Henry VIII Exhbn, Nat. Maritime Museum, Greenwich 1991; Guest Curator, Elizabeth I Exhbn, Nat. Maritime Museum 2003, Lost Faces – Identity and Discovery in Tudor Royal Portraiture Exhbn, Philip Mould Gallery 2006, Henry VIII: Man and Monarch Exhbn, British Library 2009; mem. Fitzwilliam Soc. (Pres. 2003–04). *Radio:* panellist, The Moral Maze (BBC Radio 4) 1992–2001, presenter, Talk Radio 1995–98. *Television:* presenter/writer, This Land of England (Channel 4) 1985, Henry VIII (Channel 4) (Indie Documentary Award 2002) 1998, Elizabeth (Channel 4) 2000, The Six Wives of Henry VIII (Channel 4) (New York Festival for int. TV programming and promotion silver medal) 2001, The Unknown Tudors (Channel 4) 2002, Re-Inventing the Royals 2002, Monarchy (Channel 4) 2004–07, Starkey's Last Word (More 4) 2006, Henry VIII: Mind of a Tyrant (Channel 4) 2009. *Publications:* This Land of England (with David Souden) 1985, The Reign of Henry VIII: Personalities and Politics 1985–86, Revolution Reassessed: Revisions in the History of Tudor Government and Administration (ed. with Christopher Coleman) 1986, The English Court from the Wars of the Roses to the Civil War (ed.) 1987, Rivals in Power: the Lives and Letters of the Great Tudor Dynasties (ed.) 1990, Henry VIII: A European Court in England 1991, The Inventory of Henry VIII, Vol. 1 (with Philip Ward) 1998, Elizabeth: Apprenticeship 2000

(WHSmith Award for Biog./Autobiog. 2001), Six Wives: The Queens of Henry VIII 2003, Monarchy: the early kings 2004, The History of England: Jane Austen and Charles Dickens 2006, Monarchy: From the Middles Ages to Modernity 2006, Henry: Virtuous Prince 2008, Crown & Country 2010; numerous articles in learned journals. *Honours:* Hon. Assoc., Rationalist Press Asscn 1995–; Freeman, Worshipful Co. of Barbers 1992, Liveryman 1999; Hon. DLitt (Lancaster) 2004, (Kent) 2006; Medlicott Medal 2001. *Address:* Fitzwilliam College, Cambridge, CB3 0DG, England (office). *Telephone:* (1223) 332000 (office). *Website:* www.fitz.cam.ac.uk (office).

STARKOV, Vladislav Andreyevich; Russian journalist; *Editor, Argumenty i Fakty;* b. 28 Feb. 1940, Tomsk; s. of Andrei Nikolayevich Starkov and Maria Mikhailovna Starkova; m. Yulia Fedorovna Kuznetsova; one d. *Education:* Rostov State Univ. *Career:* researcher and computer engineer, USSR Meteorology Centre 1962–73; corresp. Radio Moscow 1973–76; Znaniye Publishing House 1976–79; Ed. Mezhdunarodnye Otnosheniya (journal) 1979–80; Ed.-in-Chief Argumenty i Fakty (weekly) 1980–, Ed. Argumenty i Fakty (weekly newspaper) 1995–; RSFSR People's Deputy 1990–93. *Address:* AiF, Myasnitskaya str. 42, 101000 Moscow, Russia. *Telephone:* (495) 921-02-34 (office). *Fax:* (495) 925-61-82 (office). *E-mail:* into@aif.ru (office). *Website:* www.aif.ru (office).

STARNES, John Kennett, BA; Canadian diplomat (retd) and writer; b. 5 Feb. 1918, Montréal, QC; m. Helen Gordon Robinson 1941; two s. *Education:* Institut Sillig, Switzerland, Trinity Coll. School, Univ. of Munich, Germany, Bishop's Univ. *Career:* Counsellor, Canadian Embassy, Bonn 1953–56; Chair. Joint Intelligence Cttee, Ottawa 1958–62; Ambassador to the Federal Republic of Germany and Head Military Mission, Berlin 1962–66; Ambassador, United Arab Republic and The Sudan 1966–67; Asst Undersecretary of State for External Affairs 1967–70; Dir-Gen., Royal Canadian Mounted Police Security Service 1970–73; mem. of the council, Int. Inst. for Strategic Studies 1977–85; life mem. Rideau Club; mem. Canadian Writers' Foundation. *Publications:* Deep Sleepers 1981, Scarab 1982, Orion's Belt 1983, The Cornish Hug 1985, Latonya (novel) 1994, Closely Guarded: A Life in Canadian Security and Intelligence (memoir) 1998; contrib. to numerous newspapers, journals and periodicals. *Honours:* hon. mem. Canadian Security Intelligence Service 1987; Centennial Medal 1967, Commemorative Medal for 125th Anniversary of the Confederation of Canada 1992; Hon. DCL (Bishop's Univ.) 1975. *Address:* 420 Mackay Street, Apt 702, Ottawa, ON K1M 2C4, Canada (home). *Telephone:* (613) 741-3169 (home). *E-mail:* jstarnes@sympatico.ca (home).

STAROBINSKI, Jean, PhD, MD; Swiss academic and writer; b. 17 Nov. 1920, Geneva; s. of Aron Starobinski and Szayndla Frydman; m. Jaqueline H. Sirman 1954; three s. *Education:* Univs of Geneva and Lausanne. *Career:* Asst Prof., Johns Hopkins Univ., Baltimore, Md, USA 1953–56, Prof. of French Literature, History of Ideas 1958–85; Pres. Rencontres Int. de Geneva 1965–; mem. Accad. dei Lincei, British Acad., American Acad. of Arts and Sciences, Deutsche Akad.; Assoc. mem. Acad. des Sciences Morales et Politiques (France), Acad. Royale de Belgique. *Publications:* Jean Jacques Rousseau: la transparence et l'obstacle 1957, The Invention of Liberty (in trans.) 1964, La Relation critique 1970, Words upon Words (in trans.) 1971, 1789: Les Emblemes de la raison 1973, Montaigne en mouvement 1983, Le Remède dans le mal 1989, La Mélancolie au miroir 1989, Largesse 1994, Action et Réaction 1999, Les Enchanteresses 2005; contrib. to newspapers and journals. *Honours:* Soc. of Fellows, Johns Hopkins Univ.; Officier, Légion d'honneur 1980; hon. degrees from Univs of Lille 1973, Brussels, Lausanne 1979, Chicago 1986, Columbia (New York) 1987, Montreal 1988, Strasbourg 1988, Neuchâtel 1990, Nantes 1992, Oslo 1994, Turin 1994, Urbino 1995, Cluj 1995, ETH, Zürich 1998, Naples 2008; Prix Européen de L'Essai 1983, Balzan Prize 1984, Monaco Prize 1988, Goethe Prize 1994, Karl-Jaspers Prize 1999, Bellas Artes Prize 2009. *Address:* 51 avenue de Champel, 1206 Geneva, Switzerland (home). *Telephone:* (22) 3209864 (home).

STARR, Paul Elliot, BA, PhD; American academic, writer and editor; *Professor of Sociology and Stuart Professor of Communications and Public Affairs, Princeton University;* b. 12 May 1949, New York, NY; m. 1st Sandra Luire Stein 1981 (died 1998); m. 2nd Ann Baynes Coiro; four c. *Education:* Columbia Univ., Harvard Univ. *Career:* Junior Fellow, Harvard Society of Fellows 1975–78; Asst Prof., Harvard Univ. 1978–82; Assoc. Prof., Princeton Univ. 1982–85, Prof. of Sociology 1985–, also Stuart Prof. of Communications and Public Affairs; Founder-Co and Ed., The American Prospect 1990–; Founder, Electronic Policy Network 1995. *Publications:* The Discarded Army: Veterans After Vietnam 1974, The Social Transformation of American Medicine 1983, The Logic of Health-Care Reform 1992, The Creation of the Media 2004, Freedom's Power: The History and Promise of Liberalism 2007; contributions: professional journals. *Honours:* Guggenheim Fellowship 1981–82, C. Wright Mills Award 1983, Pulitzer Prize in General Non-Fiction 1984, Bancroft Prize in American History 1984, Goldsmith Book Prize 2005. *Address:* Department of Sociology, Princeton University, 124 Wallace Hall, Princeton, NJ 08544, USA (office). *Telephone:* (609) 258-4533 (office). *E-mail:* starr@princeton.edu (office). *Website:* www.princeton.edu/~starr (office).

STARRATT, Thomas, BSc, MEd; American teacher, poet and writer; b. 6 Oct. 1952, Holyoke, Mass; m. Patricia Starratt 1994; three s. two d. *Education:* Plymouth State Teachers College, NH, University of New Hampshire. *Career:* mem. International Reading Asscn. *Publications include:* Nightwatch 1994, Amsterdam 1994, Summer on the Lava Plain 1994, Eye to Your Storm 1995, Passages 1995, Excess 1995, Summer Days 1995, Amsterdam Revisited 1995, Washed Up 1996; contributions: professional journals.

STASIUK, Andrzej; Polish writer, poet, playwright and publisher; b. 1960, Ukraine; m. *Career:* co-f. and owner, publishing co, Czarne 1996–. *Publications:* Mury Hebronu (The Walls of Hebron, short stories) 1992, Wiersze milosne i nie (Verses Non-)Amorous) 1994, Opowiesci galicyjskie (Tales of Galicia, short stories) 1994, Bialy kruk (The White Raven, novel) 1995, Przez rzeke (Through the River, short stories) 1996, Dukla (short stories) 1997, Dwie sztuki (telewizyjne) o smierci (Two Television Plays About Death) 1998, Jak zostalem pisarzem (proba biografii intelektualnej) (How I Became a Writer (Attempt at an Intellectual Biography) 1998, Dziewiec (Nine) 1998, Moje Europa. Dwa eseje o Europie zwanej Srodkowa (My Europe: Two essays on the place called Central Europe, with J. Andruchowicz) 2000, Tekturowy samolot (Model Aeroplane) 2000, Opowiesci wigilijne (Christmas Tales, with Olga Tokarczuk and Jerzy Pilch) 2000, Zima i inne opowiadania (Winter and Other Stories) 2001; contrib. to Gazeta Wyborcza, Tygodnik Powszechny. *Honours:* Foundation of Culture Prize 1994, Koscielski Prize 1995. *Address:* c/o Twisted Spoon Press, PO Box 21, Preslova 12, Prague 5 150-21, Czech Republic (office).

STAUDINGER, Ulrich; German publisher; b. 30 May 1935, Berlin; s. of Wilhelm Staudinger and Elfriede Poth; m. Irmengard Ehrenwirth 1960 (died 1989); one s. two d. *Education:* Volksschule and Realgymnasium. *Career:* publishing training 1954–57; Lingenbrinck Barsortiment, Hamburg 1957–58; Publicity and Sales, Ensslin & Laiblin, Jugendbuchverlag, Reutlingen 1958–59; Production, Carl Hanser Verlag, Munich 1959–60; Dawson & Sons, London 1960; Franz Ehrenwirth Verlag, Munich 1960; partner, Ehrenwirth Verlag, Munich 1964; responsible for purchase of Franz Schneekluth Verlag KG, Darmstadt by Ehrenwirth Verlag 1967 and amalgamation of two companies into single firm 1976; purchased parts of Philosophia Verlag GmbH, Düsseldorf 1978; various professional appointments. *Address:* Asgardstrasse 34, 8000 Munich 81, Germany (home). *Telephone:* (89) 98-63-67 (home).

STAVANS, Ilan; American writer, translator, editor, critic and academic; *Lewis-Sebring Professor in Latin American and Latino Culture, Amherst College;* b. 1961, Mexico. *Career:* teacher, Amherst Coll., Mass 1993–2001, Lewis-Sebring Prof. in Latin American and Latino Culture 2001–, Five College Fortieth Anniversary Prof. 2005–10; Ed.-in-Chief, Hopscotch: A Cultural Review 2000–03; Commr, Gov.'s Comm. on Latino Affairs, Mass 2008–10. *Exhibitions:* Isaac Bashevis Singer and the Lower East Side 2004, Miracles and Monsters: A Journey through Jewish Picture Books 2010, Salpica: Indigenous Artists Across Borders 2010. *Film:* My Mexican Shiva 2007. *Plays:* The Disappearance 2008, Zeta 2011. *Television:* host, Conversations with Ilan Stavans 2001–06. *Publications include:* Imagining Columbus: The Literary Voyage 1992, La pluma y la máscara 1993, Antihéroes: México y su novela political 1993, Growing Up Latino: Memoirs and Stories (co-author) 1993, La pluma mágica 1994, Bandido, Oscar Zeta Acosta and the Chicano Experience 1995, The Hispanic Condition: Reflections on Culture and Identity in America 1995, Art and Anger: Essays on Politics and the Imagination 1998, The Oxford Book of Jewish Stories 1998, The Oxford Book of Latin American Essays 1998, One-Handed Pianist and Other Stories 1998, Dictionary of Spanglish 1999, The Essential Ilan Stavans 2000, The Inveterate Dreamer: Essays and Conversations on Jewish Culture 2001, The Hispanic Condition: The Power of a People 2001, Wachale! 2001, On Borrowed Words: A Memoir of Language 2001, Riddle of the Catinflas: Essays on Hispanic Popular Culture 2001, Spanglish: The Making of a New American Language 2003, Dictionary Days 2005, The Disappearance 2006, On Love 2007, Gabriel Garcia Márquez: The Early Years 2010, A Critic's Journey 2010; editor: Tropical Synagogues: Short Stories by Jewish-Latin American Writers 1994, Prospero's Mirror 1998, Poetry of Pablo Neruda 2003, Isaac Bashevis Singer: Collected Stories 2004, Encyclopedia Latino 2005, The Schecken Book of Modern Sephardic Literature 2005, Lengua Fresca 2006, I Explain a Few Things 2007, Love and Language 2007, Cesar Chavez: An Organizer's Tale 2008, Cesar Vallejo: Spain, Take this Chalice from me 2008, Knowledge and Censorship 2008, Mr Spic Goes to Washington 2008, Resurrecting Hebrew 2008, Becoming Americans: Four Centuries of Immigrant Writing 2009, A Critic's Journey 2010, Gabriel Garcia Márquez: the Early Years 2010, The Norton Anthology of Latino Literature 2010, With All Thine Heart 2010, What Is la hispanidad? 2011, José Vasconcelos: The Prophet of Race 2011, Once@9:53 2011, The FSG Book of 20th-Century Latin American Poetry 2011. *Honours:* Latino Literature Prize, Nat. Jewish Book Award, Ruben Dario Medal, Pablo Neruda Medal, Guggenheim Fellowship, Nat. Endowment for the Humanities Award. *Address:* Amherst College, Amherst, MA 01002-5000, USA (office). *Telephone:* (513) 542-8201 (office). *Fax:* (513) 542-2759 (office). *E-mail:* istavans@amherst.edu (office). *Website:* www.amherst.edu (office).

STAVE, Bruce Martin, AB, MA, PhD; American historian and academic; *Distinguished Professor Emeritus and Director, Oral History Office, University of Connecticut;* b. 17 May 1937, New York, NY; s. of Bernard R. Stave and Mildred S. Stave; m. Sondra T. Astor 1961; one s. *Education:* Columbia Coll., Columbia Univ., New York, Univ. of Pittsburgh. *Career:* Prof., Univ. of Connecticut 1975–2000, Dir Oral History Office 1981–, Chair. Dept of History 1985–94, Bd of Trustees Distinguished Prof. 2000–02, Distinguished Prof. Emer. 2002–; Ed. Oral History Review 1996–99; mem. American Historical Asscn, Org. of American Historians, Immigration History Soc., New England Historical Asscn (Pres. 1994–95), Oral History Asscn, New England Asscn of

Oral History. *Publications:* The New Deal and the Last Hurrah 1970, Urban Bosses, Machines and Progressive Reformers (ed.) 1972, The Discontented Society (co-ed.) 1972, Socialism and the Cities (contributing ed.) 1975, The Making of Urban History 1977, Modern Industrial Cities (ed.) 1981, Talking About Connecticut (co-ed.) 1985, Mills and Meadows: A Pictorial History of Northeast Connecticut (co-author) 1991, From the Old Country: An Oral History of European Migration to America (co-author) 1994, Witnesses to Nuremberg: An Oral History of American Participants at the War Crimes Trials (co-author) 1998, Red Brick in the Land of Steady Habits: Creating the University of Connecticut 1881–2006 2006; contrib. to Journal of Urban History, Americana Magazine, International Journal of Oral History, Oral History Review. *Honours:* Fulbright Professorships, India 1968–69, Australia, NZ, Philippines 1977, People's Repub. of China 1984–85, Nat. Endowment for the Humanities Fellowship 1974, Asscn for the Study of Connecticut History Homer Babbidge Award 1995, 2007, Univ. of Hartford NEH/Harry Jack Gray Distinguished Visiting Humanist 2003. *Address:* 150 Grant Hill Road, Coventry, CT 06238, USA (home). *Telephone:* (860) 486-4578 (office); (860) 742-0200 (home). *Fax:* (860) 486-4582 (office); (860) 742-1720 (home). *E-mail:* bruce.stave@uconn.edu (office). *Website:* www.oralhistory.uconn.edu (office); www.oralhistorybythestavegroup.com (office).

STEAD, Christian Karlson (C. K.), ONZ, CBE, MA, PhD, LittD, FRSL, FEA; New Zealand writer and academic; *Professor Emeritus of English, University of Auckland*; b. 17 Oct. 1932, Auckland; s. of James Walter Ambrose Stead and Olive Ethel Stead (née Karlson); m. Kathleen Elizabeth Roberts 1955; one s. two d. *Education:* Mt Albert Grammar School, Auckland Univ. Coll. and Auckland Teachers' Coll., Univ. of Bristol, UK. *Career:* Lecturer in English, Univ. of New England, NSW, Australia 1956–57; Michael Hiatt Baker Scholar, Univ. of Bristol 1957–59; Lecturer, Sr Lecturer, Assoc. Prof., Univ. of Auckland 1960–67, Prof. of English 1967–86, Prof. Emer. 1986–; writer 1986–; Nuffield Fellow, Univ. of London 1965, Hon. Fellow, Univ. Coll. London 1977, Sr Visiting Fellow, St John's Coll. Oxford 1996–97; Chair. NZ Literary Fund Advisory Cttee 1972–75, NZ Authors' Fund Cttee 1989–91; mem. NZ PEN (Chair. Auckland br. 1986–89, Nat. Vice-Pres. 1988–90), Creative New Zealand 1999; Fellow, English Asscn. *Film:* Sleeping Dogs 1977. *Publications:* fiction: Smith's Dream 1972, All Visitors Ashore 1984, The Death of the Body 1986, Sister Hollywood 1989, The End of the Century at the End of the World 1992, The Singing Whakapapa 1994, Villa Vittoria 1997, Talking about O'Dwyer 2000, The Secret History of Modernism 2002, Mansfield: a novel 2004, My Name Was Judas 2006; poetry: Whether the Will is Free 1964, Crossing the Bar 1972, Quesada 1975, Walking Westward 1978, Geographies 1982, Poems of a Decade 1983, Paris 1984, Between 1986, Voices 1990, Straw into Gold 1997, The Right Thing 2000, Dog 2002, The Red Tram 2004, The Black River 2007, Collected Poems 1951–2006 (Montana Book Award 2009) 2008; short story collections: Five for the Symbol 1981, The Blind Blonde with Candles in Her Hair 1998; non-fiction: The New Poetic: Yeats to Eliot 1964, In the Glass Case: Essays on New Zealand Literature 1981, Pound Yeats Eliot and the Modernist Movement 1986, Answering to the Language: Essays on Modern Writers 1990, The Writer at Work 2000, Kin of Place: Essays on 20 New Zealand Writers 2002, Book Self: the reader as writer and the writer as critic 2008; editor: Oxford New Zealand Short Stories (2nd series) 1966, Measure for Measure, a Casebook 1971, Letters and Journals of Katherine Mansfield 1977, Collected Stories of Maurice Duggan 1981, The Faber Book of Contemporary South Pacific Stories 1994, Werner Forman's New Zealand 1994. *Honours:* Hon. DLetters (Bristol) 2001; Katherine Mansfield Prize 1960, Jessie Mackay Award for Poetry 1972, Katherine Mansfield Menton Fellowship 1972, New Zealand Book Award for Poetry 1976, New Zealand Book Award for Fiction 1985, 1995, Queen Elizabeth II Arts Council Scholarship in Letters 1988–89, Queen's Medal for Services to NZ Literature 1990, King's Lynn Award for poetry 2001, Michael King Fellowship 2005–06, Bogliasco Fellowship in Literature 2007, 2011, Prime Minister's Award for Literary Achievement (for fiction) 2009, Sunday Times EFG Private Bank Short Story Award 2010, Hippcrates Prize for Poetry and Medicine 2010. *Address:* 37 Tohunga Crescent, Parnell, Auckland 1052, New Zealand. *Telephone:* (9) 379-9420. *E-mail:* ckstead1@xtra.co.nz.

STEAD, Rebecca, BA; American writer; b. 16 Jan. 1968, New York; m. Sean O'Brien; two s. *Education:* Vassar Coll. *Career:* trained and worked as a lawyer; now full-time writer. *Publications:* First Light 2007, When You Reach Me (John Newbery Medal 2010) 2009. *Literary Agent:* Faye Bender, Faye Bender Literary Agency, 337 West 76th Street, #E1, New York, NY 10023, USA. *Telephone:* (212) 721-7023. *E-mail:* fayebender@fbliterary.com. *Website:* www.fbliterary.com. *Address:* c/o Wendy Lamb Books, 1745 Broadway, New York, NY 10019, USA (office). *E-mail:* rebecca@firstlightbook.com (office). *Website:* www.rebeccasteadbooks.com.

STEADMAN, Ralph Idris; British cartoonist, writer and illustrator; b. 15 May 1936, s. of Raphael Steadman and Gwendoline Steadman; m. 1st Sheila Thwaite 1959 (divorced 1971); two s. two d.; m. 2nd Anna Deverson 1972; one d. *Education:* London School of Printing and Graphic Arts. *Career:* with de Havilland Aircraft Co. 1952; cartoonist, Kemsley (Thomson) Newspapers 1956–59; freelance for Punch, Private Eye, Daily Telegraph during 1960s; political cartoonist, New Statesman 1978–80; designed set of stamps depicting Halley's Comet 1986; Artist-in-Residence, Leviathan (series of films, BBC 2) 1999; designer of set and costumes, The Crucible, Royal Ballet 2000. *Retrospective exhibitions:* Nat. Theatre 1977, Royal Festival Hall 1984, Wilhelm Busch Museum, Hanover 1988, One on One Gallery, Denver 1997, Warrington Museum 1998, William Havu Gallery, Denver 2000, Boston Art Inst. (Drawing Breath) 2006. *Written and illustrated:* Alice in Wonderland 1967, Alice Through the Looking Glass 1972, Sigmund Freud 1979, A Leg in the Wind and Other Canine Curses 1982, I, Leonardo 1983, That's My Dad 1986, The Big I Am 1988, No Room to Swing a Cat 1989, Near the Bone 1990, Tales of Weirrd 1990, Still Life with Bottle, Whisky According to Ralph Steadman 1994, Jones of Colorado 1998, Gonzo: The Art 1998, little.com 2000, The Joke's Over 2006. *Illustrator:* many books from 1961, including Friendship 1990 (in aid of John McCarthy), Adrian Mitchell, Heart on the Left, Poems 1953–84 1997, Roald Dahl, The Mildenhall Treasure 1999, Doodaa: The Balletic Art of Gavin Twinge 2002. *Publications:* Jelly Book 1968, Still Life with Raspberry: collected drawings 1969, The Little Red Computer 1970, Dogs Bodies 1971, Bumper to Bumper Book 1973, Two Donkeys and the Bridge 1974, Flowers for the Moon 1974, The Watchdog and the Lazy Dog 1974, America: drawings 1975, America: collected drawings 1977 (r.e. Scar Strangled Banger 1987), Between the Eyes 1984, Paranoids 1986, The Grapes of Ralph 1992, Teddy Where Are You? 1994, Bruised Memories: Gonzo, Hunter Thompson and Me 2006, The Joke's Over 2007, The Devil's Dictionary (with Ambrose Bierce) 2008. *Honours:* Hon. DLitt (Kent) 1995; Designers and Art Dirs' Asscn Gold Award 1977, Silver Award 1977, Lifetime Achievement Award – Milton Caniff Award, Nat. Cartoonists Soc. (USA) 2005. *Literary Agent:* c/o Nat Sobel, Sobel Weber Associates, Inc., 146 East 19th Street, New York, NY 10003-2404, USA. *Telephone:* (212) 420-8585. *Website:* www.sobelweber.com; www.ralphsteadman.com.

STEARNS, Peter Nathaniel, BA, MA, PhD; American historian, academic, writer and editor; *Professor of History and Provost, George Mason University*; b. 3 March 1936, London, England; one s. three d. *Education:* Harvard Univ. *Career:* instructor, Univ. of Chicago 1962–63, Asst Prof. 1963–66, Assoc. Prof. 1966–68; Visiting Assoc. Prof., Northwestern Univ. 1964; Ed.-in-Chief Journal of Social History 1967–; Prof. of History, Rutgers Univ. 1968–74; Visiting Prof., Sir George Williams Univ. 1970, Univ. of Houston 1978; Heinz Prof. of History, Carnegie Mellon Univ. 1974–2000, Head of Dept of History 1986–92, Dean Coll. of Humanities and Social Sciences 1992–2000; Prof. of History and Provost, George Mason Univ. 2000–; mem. American Historical Asscn, American Sociological Asscn, Nat. Council on Social Studies: Social History Asscn (UK), Soc. of French Historical Studies. *Publications:* European Society in Upheaval: Social History Since 1800 1967, Priest and Revolutionary: Lamennais and the Dilemma of French Catholicism 1967, Modern Europe 1789–1914 1969, Revolutionary Syndicalism and French Labor: A Cause Without Rebels 1971, Workers and Protest: The European Labor Movement, the Working Classes, and the Rise of Socialism 1890–1914 (with Harvey Mitchell) 1971, The European Experience Since 1815 1972, 1848: The Revolutionary Tide in Europe 1974, Lives of Labor: Work in Maturing Industrial Society 1975, Old Age in European Society 1977, Paths to Authority: Toward the Formation of the Middle Class Consciousness 1978, Be a Man!: Males in Modern Society 1979, Themes in Modern Social History (with Linda Rosenzweig) 1985, Anger: The Struggle for Emotional Control in America's History (with Carol Stearns) 1986, World History: Patterns of Change and Continuity 1987, Life and Society in the West: The Modern Centuries 1988, World History: Traditions and New Directions 1988, Emotion and Social Change: Toward a New Psychohistory (with Carol Stearns) 1988, Social History and Issues in Consciousness and Cognition (with Andrew Barnes) 1989, Jealousy: The Evolution of an Emotion in American History 1989, World Civilizations (with Michael Adas and Stuart Schwartz) 1991, Meaning Over Memory: Recasting the Teaching of Culture and History 1993, The Industrial Revolution in World History 1993, Encyclopedia of Social History (ed.) 1993, Turbulent Passage: A Global History of the 20th Century (with Michael Adas and Stuart Schwartz) 1994, American Cool: Developing the Twentieth-Century Emotional Style 1994, Discursive Psychology in Practice (with Rom Harré) 1995, Encyclopedia of the Industrial Revolution (ed. with John Hinshaw) 1996, Fat History: Bodies and Beauty in Western Society 1997, Schools and Students in Industrial Society: Japan and the West 1870–1940 1997, World History in Documents: Comparative Perspectives 1998, The Battleground of Desire: The Struggle for Self-Control in Modern America 1999, Gender in World History 2000, Encyclopedia of European Social History (ed.) 2000, Facing Up to Management Faddism (with Margaret Brindle) 2001, Consumerism in World History: The Global Transformation of Desire 2001, Encyclopedia of World History (ed., sixth edn) 2001, Cultures in Motion 2001, Anxious Parents: A History of Modern Childrearing in America 2003, Western Civilization in World History 2003, Thinking History 2004, Global Outrage: The Rise of World Opinion 2005, American Behavioral History 2005, Childhood in World History 2006, American Fear: The Causes and Consequences of High Anxiety 2006, Brief History of the World 2007, Revolutions in Sorrow: American Death Experience and Policy in Global Context 2007, Travel in World Premodern History: to 1500 (with Stephen Gosch) 2007, American History in Global Context 2008, Encyclopedia of Modern World History 2008, From Alienation to Addiction: The History of American Work in Global Context 2008, Educating Global Citizens in Colleges and Universities: Challenges and Opportunities 2009; contrib. to reference works, scholarly books and professional journals. *Honours:* Koren Prize, Soc. for French Historical Studies 1964, Newcomen Special Award, Business History Review 1965, American Philosophical Soc. grant 1967–68, Guggenheim Fellowship 1973–74, Robert Doherty Educational Leadership Award 1995. *Address:* Office of the Provost, George Mason University, MS 3A2, 101

Mason Hall, Fairfax, VA 22030, USA (office). *Telephone:* (703) 993-8776 (office). *Fax:* (703) 993-8645 (office). *E-mail:* pstearns@gmu.edu (office).

STEBEL, Sidney Leo, (Leo Bergson, Steve Toron), BA; American novelist, playwright, screenwriter and academic; *Professor Emeritus, College of Letters, Arts and Sciences, University of Southern California*; b. 28 June 1923, Iowa; s. of Abraham Stebel and Anna Wicliski; m. 1st Jan Mary Dingler 1954 (died 1999); one d.; m. 2nd Karen K. Ford 2004. *Education:* Univ. of Southern California, Los Angeles. *Career:* columnist, Los Angeles Times Sunday Book Review, Los Angeles Herald-Examiner Sunday Book Review; Exec. Script Consultant, South Australian Film Corpn; Adjunct Prof., Master of Professional Writing programme, Univ. of Southern California, Los Angeles, currently Prof. Emer.; mem. Australian Writers' Guild, Authors' Guild, PEN Centre (USA West), Writers' Guild of America, Authors' League. *Writing for theatre:* Father Against Sons (one man show for Henry Fonda), 1-4-Sex-Talk (Actors Studio production), Next in Line (adaptation of story by Ray Bradbury, Theater West, Los Angeles), Premier Ivar Theatre, Hollywood 2004–07, Breeding. *Screenplays:* Dreams of Marianne (film), Mirrors (original screenplay), Revolution of Antonio De Leon (TV movie of the week, co-author with Robert Weverka), Perilous Voyage (TV movie), Picnic at Hanging Rock, Storm Boy. *Television:* pilots: River Boy (South Australian Film Corpn, Hanna-Barbera), Winner's Circle, TV pilot for Fred Astaire. *Publications:* The Widowmaster 1967, The Collaborator 1968, The Vanishing Americans (serialized in West magazine as Main Street) 1971, The Vorovich Affair 1975, The Shoe Leather Treatment 1983, Spring Thaw 1989, The Boss's Wife 1992, Double Your Creative Power 1996, Rising Star, Setting Sun 2004. *Honours:* Short Listed Fiction Award, PEN Center West 1989. *Literary Agent:* c/o Michael Congdon, Don Congdon Associates, #823, 156 Fifth Avenue, New York, NY 10010, USA. *Telephone:* (212) 645-1229. *E-mail:* mcongdon@doncongdon.com. *Website:* www.doncongdon.com. *Address:* 1963 Mandeville Canyon Road, Los Angeles, CA 90049, USA. *Telephone:* (310) 472-0274. *E-mail:* sid@slstebel.com. *Website:* www.slstebel.com.

STEEL, Danielle Fernande Schüelein; American writer; b. 14 Aug. 1950, New York; d. of John Steel and Norma Schüelein-Steel (née Stone); m. 2nd Bill Toth 1977; m. 3rd John A. Traina Jr; four s. five d. *Education:* Lycée Français, Parsons School of Design, New York, Univ. of New York. *Career:* worked as public relations and advertising exec., Manhattan, New York; published first novel 1973, then wrote advertising copy and poems for women's magazines; wrote first bestseller, The Promise 1979. *Publications:* Going Home 1973, Passion's Promise 1977, Now and Forever 1978, Season of Passion 1978, The Promise 1979, Summer's End 1980, The Ring 1980, To Love Again 1981, Palomino 1981, Loving 1981, Remembrance 1981, Love: Poems 1981, A Perfect Stranger 1982, Once in a Lifetime 1982, Crossings 1982, Thurston House 1983, Changes 1983, Full Circle 1984, Having a Baby (contrib., nonfiction) 1984, Family Album 1985, Secrets 1985, Wanderlust 1986, Fine Things 1987, Kaleidoscope 1987, Zoya 1988, Star 1989, Daddy 1989, Heartbeat 1991, Message from Nam 1991, No Greater Love 1991, Jewels 1992, Mixed Blessings 1992, Vanished 1993, Accident 1994, The Gift 1994, Wings 1995, Lightning 1995, Five Days in Paris 1995, Malice 1995, Silent Honor 1996, The Ranch 1996, The Ghost 1997, Special Delivery 1997, His Bright Light (non-fiction) 1998, The Ranch 1998, The Long Road Home 1998, The Klone and I 1998, Mirror Image 1998, Bittersweet 1999, Granny Dan 1999, Irresistible Forces 1999, The Wedding 2000, The House on Hope Street 2000, Journey 2000, Leap of Faith 2001, The Kiss 2001, Lone Eagle 2001, The Cottage 2002, Sunset in San Tropez 2002, Answered Prayers 2002, Dating Game 2003, Johnny Angel 2003, Safe Harbour 2003, Echoes 2004, Toxic Bachelors 2005, The House 2006, Impossible 2006, Miracle 2006, Coming Out 2006, HRH 2006, Bungalow 2 2007, Amazing Grace 2007, Sisters 2007, Honor Thyself 2008, A Good Woman 2008, Rogue 2008, One Day at a Time 2009, Summer's End 2009, Matters of the Heart 2009, Southern Lights 2009, Big Girl 2010, Family Ties 2010, Legacy 2010, Happy Birthday 2011, Hotel Vendome 2011; eight children's books, one book of poetry. *Honours:* Officier, Ordre des Arts et Lettres. *Address:* c/o Random House Publicity Department, 1745 Broadway, New York, NY 10019 (office); PO Box 1637, New York, NY 10156, USA (home). *E-mail:* atrandompublicity@randomhouse.com (office). *Website:* daniellesteel.com.

STEEL, Ronald Lewis, BA, MA; American academic and writer; *Professor Emeritus of International Relations, University of Southern California at Los Angeles*; b. 25 March 1931, Morris, Ill. *Education:* Northwestern Univ., Harvard Univ. *Career:* Vice-Consul, US Foreign Service 1957–58; Ed. Scholastic Magazine 1959–62; Sr Assoc., Carnegie Endowment for Int. Peace 1962–83, Council on Foreign Relations, Washington, DC 2003–04; Visiting Fellow, Yale Univ. 1971–73; Visiting Prof., Univ. of Texas 1977, 1979, 1980, 1985, Wellesley Coll. 1978, Rutgers Univ. 1980, UCLA 1981, Dartmouth Coll. 1983, Princeton Univ. 1984, École des Hautes Études en Sciences Sociales, Paris 2001–02; Fellow, Woodrow Wilson Int. Center for Scholars 1984–85, Wissenschaftskolleg zu Berlin, Germany 1988, American Acad., Berlin 2005; Prof. of Int. Relations, Univ. of Southern California at Los Angeles 1986–2009, Prof. Emer. 2009–; Shapiro Prof. of Int. Relations, George Washington Univ. 1995–97; mem. American Historical Asscn, Soc. of American Historians. *Publications:* The End of Alliance: America and the Future of Europe 1964, Tropical Africa Today (with G. Kimble) 1966, Pax Americana 1967, Imperialists and Other Heroes 1971, Walter Lippmann and the American Century 1980, Temptations of a Superpower 1995, In Love with Night: The American Romance with Robert Kennedy 2000; contrib. to professional journals and general publications. *Honours:* Sidney Hillman Prize 1968, Guggenheim Fellowship 1973–74, Los Angeles Times Book Award 1980, Washington Monthly Book Award 1980, Nat. Book Critics' Circle Award 1981, Columbia Univ. Bancroft Prize 1981, American Book Award 1981. *Address:* School of International Relations, University of Southern California, Los Angeles, CA 90089, USA (office). *Telephone:* (213) 740-2136 (office). *E-mail:* steel@usc.edu (office).

STEELE, Shelby, MA, PhD; American academic and writer; *Robert J. and Marion E. Oster Senior Fellow, Hoover Institution, Stanford University*; b. 1 Jan. 1946, Chicago, IL; m. Rita Steele, two c. *Education:* Coe College, Iowa, Southern Illinois Univ., Univ. of Utah. *Career:* fmr Prof. of English, San Jose State Univ.; currently Robert J. and Marion E. Oster Sr Fellow, Hoover Institution, Stanford Univ. *Television:* Seven Days in Bensonhurst (Emmy Award, Writers Guild Award and San Francisco Film Festival Award for television documentary writing), PBS TV, 1991. *Publications:* The Content of Our Character: A New Vision of Race in America 1990, Essay Collection 1993, A Dream Deferred: The Second Betrayal of Black Freedom in America 1999, White Guilt: How Blacks and Whites Together Destroyed the Promise of the Civil Rights Era 2006, A Bound Man: Why we are Excited about Obama and Why he can't Win 2008; contributions: newspapers, journals, and magazines. *Honours:* National Book Critics Award 1990, Nat. Humanities Medal 2004, Bradley Prize 2006. *Address:* Hoover Institution, 434 Galvez Mall, Stanford University, Stanford, CA 94305-8010, USA (office). *Telephone:* (650) 723-1754 (office). *Fax:* (650) 723-1687 (office). *Website:* www.hoover.org/bios/steele (office).

STEFFEN, Jonathan Neil, MA; British university teacher, writer, poet and translator; b. 5 Oct. 1958, London, England. *Education:* King's College, Cambridge. *Career:* teacher, University of Heidelberg; founder, Falcon Editions Ltd. *Publications:* fiction: The Gift of Silence, In Seville 1985, Meeting the Majors 1987, Carpe Diem 1991, Cleopatra 1994, The Story of Icarus 1994, At Breakfast 1995; poetry: The Soldier and the Soldier's Son 1986, German Hunting Party 1987, The Moving Hand 1994, The Great Days of the Railway 1994, Apprentice and Master 1994, St Francis in the Slaughter 1995; contributions: reviews, quarterlies, and magazines. *Honours:* Harper-Wood Travelling Studentship 1981–82, Hawthornden Creative Writing Fellowship 1987. *Address:* Falcon Editions Ltd, Larchmont Office, Wych Hill Rise, Woking, Surrey, GU22 0ES, England (office). *Telephone:* (1483) 755176 (office). *E-mail:* jonathan.steffen@falconeditions.com (office). *Website:* www.falconeditions.com (office).

STEFFLER, John Earl, BA, MA; Canadian poet, writer and academic; b. 13 Nov. 1947, Toronto, Ont.; one s. one d. *Education:* Univ. of Toronto, Univ. of Guelph. *Career:* Prof. of English, Sir Wilfred Grenfell Coll., Memorial Univ. of Newfoundland, Corner Brook Campus 1975–2005 (retd); Parl. Poet Laureate 2006–08; Scholar-in-Residence, Concordia Univ. 2007; mem. League of Canadian Poets, PEN, Writers' Alliance of Newfoundland and Labrador. *Publications:* An Explanation of Yellow 1980, The Grey Islands 1985, The Wreckage of Play 1988, The Afterlife of George Cartwright (novel) (Smithbooks/Books in Canada First Novel Award 1992, Thomas Raddall Atlantic Fiction Award 1992) 1991, That Night We Were Ravenous (poems) (Atlantic Poetry Award) 1998, Helix 2003, Lookout 2010; contrib. to journals and periodicals. *Honours:* Newfoundland Arts Council Artist of the Year Award 1992, Joseph S. Stauffer Prize 1993, Newfoundland and Labrador Poetry Award 1998, 2003. *Address:* c/o McClelland & Stewart Ltd, 75 Sherbourne Street, 5th Floor, Toronto, ON M5A 2P9, Canada.

STEIGER, Paul E., BA; American journalist and editor; *Editor-in-Chief, President and CEO, ProPublica*; b. 15 Aug. 1942, Bronx, NY. *Education:* Yale Univ. *Career:* staff writer, LA Times 1968, Econ. Corresp., Washington, DC Bureau 1971–78, apptd Business Ed. 1978; with Wall Street Journal, reporter for San Francisco Bureau 1966–68, Asst Man. Ed. 1983–85, Deputy Man. Ed. 1985–91, Man. Ed. 1991–2007, Ed.-at-Large 2007–, also Vice-Pres. Dow Jones & Co.; Ed.-in-Chief , Pres. and CEO ProPublica (ind. non–profit newsroom) 2008–; Chair. Cttee to Protect Journalists; Trustee John S. and James L. Knight Foundation; mem. Pulitzer Prize Bd 1998–2007 (Chair. 2007), Columbia Grad. School of Journalism Bd of Visitors; Poynter Fellow, Yale Univ. 2001–02. *Publications include:* The '70s Crash and How to Survive It 1970. *Honours:* George Beveridge Ed. of the Year Award 2001, American Soc. of Newspaper Eds' Leadership Award 2002, Gerald Loeb Award 2002, John Hancock Award 2002, Columbia Journalism Award 2002, Goldsmith Career Award for Excellence in Journalism, Harvard Univ. Joan Shorenstein Center on Press, Politics and Public Policy 2008. *Address:* ProPublica, One Exchange Plaza, 55 Broadway, 23rd Floor, New York, NY 10006, USA (office). *Telephone:* (212) 514-5250 (office). *E-mail:* info@propublica.org (office). *Website:* www.propublica.org (office).

STEIN, Kevin, BS, MA, MA, PhD; American academic, writer, poet and editor; *Caterpillar Professor of English, Bradley University*; b. 1 Jan. 1954, Anderson, Ind.; s. of Joseph Stein and Mary Rita Stein; m. Debra Lang 1979; one s. one d. *Education:* Ball State Univ., Indiana Univ. *Career:* instructor, Ball State Univ. 1978–79; Assoc. Instructor, Indiana Univ. 1980–84; Asst Prof., Bradley Univ., Peoria, Ill. 1984–88, Assoc. Prof. 1988–94, Prof. of English 1994–2000, Caterpillar Prof. of English 2000–; Ed. Illinois Writers Review 1988–92; Assoc. Poetry Ed. Crazyhorse 1992–94; State of Illinois Poet Laureate 2003–; mem. Soc. of Midland Authors, Associated Writing Programs, Acad. of American Poets. *Exhibition:* Paged, Staged, and Engaged. *Publications:* A Field of Wings (poems) 1986, The Figure Our Bodies Make (poems) 1988, James Wright: The Poetry of a Grown Man 1988, A Circus of Want (poems) 1992, Bruised Paradise (poems) 1996, Private Poets: Worldly Acts: Public and Private History in Contemporary American Poetry 1996, Chance Ransom (poems) 2000, Illinois Voices: An Anthology of Twentieth-Century Poetry (co-ed. with G. E. Murray) 2001, American Ghost Roses (poems) 2005, Sufficiency of the Actual (poems) 2009, Poetry's Afterlife: Verse in the Digital Age (essays) 2010; contrib. to many reviews, quarterlies and journals. *Honours:* Illinois Arts Council Fellowship 1986, Illinois Writers Chapbook Award 1986, Stanley Hanks Chapbook Award 1988, Illinois Arts Council Award in Poetry 1987, 1991, 2001, 2007, Frederick Bock Prize for Poetry 1987, Faculty Mem. of the Year, Bradley Univ. 1989, Nat. Endowment for the Arts Fellowship 1991, Univ. of Missouri Press Devins Award for Poetry 1992, Indiana Review Poetry Prize 1998, Soc. of Midland Authors Poetry Award 2005. *Address:* Department of English, College of Liberal Arts and Sciences, Bradley University, 1501 W Bradley Avenue, Peoria, IL 61625-0258, USA (office). *Telephone:* (309) 677-2480 (office). *E-mail:* kstein@bradley.edu (office). *Website:* www.bradley.edu/poet/stein (office).

STEIN, Peter Gonville, FBA; British legal scholar and academic; *Emeritus Regius Professor of Civil Law, University of Cambridge, and Fellow, Queens' College*; b. 29 May 1926, Liverpool; s. of Walter O. Stein and Effie D. Walker; m. 1st Janet Chamberlain 1953, three d.; m. 2nd Anne Howard 1978; one step-s. *Education:* Liverpool Coll., Gonville and Caius Coll. Cambridge and Univ. of Pavia, Italy. *Career:* served RN 1944–47; admitted solicitor 1951; Prof. of Jurisprudence, Univ. of Aberdeen 1956–68; Regius Prof. of Civil Law, Univ. of Cambridge 1968–93, now Prof. Emer., and Fellow Queens' Coll., Cambridge 1968–; mem. Univ. Grants Cttee 1971–76; JP, Cambridge 1970–; Fellow, Winchester Coll. 1976–91; Pres. Soc. of Public Teachers of Law 1980–81; mem. US –UK Educational Comm. 1985–91; Fellow Academia Europaea 1989; Foreign Fellow, Accad. Nazionale dei Lincei, Accad. di Scienze Morali e Politiche di Napoli, Accad. degli Intronati di Siena, Kon. Akad. v. Wetenschappen, Brussels. *Publications:* Regulae Iuris: from juristic rules to legal maxims 1966, Legal Values in Western Society (with J. Shand) 1974, Legal Evolution 1980, Legal Institutions 1984, The Character and Influence of the Roman Civil Law: essays 1988, The Teaching of Roman Law in England around 1200 (with F. de Zulueta) 1990, Notaries Public in England since the Reformation (ed. and contrib.) 1991, Römisches Recht und Europa 1996, Roman Law in European History 1999 (trans. into Spanish, Italian, Japanese, French and Hungarian). *Honours:* Hon. Fellow, Gonville and Caius Coll., Cambridge; Hon. QC 1993; Hon. DrJur (Göttingen) 1980; Dott.Giur. hc (Ferrara) 1990, (Perugia) 2001; Hon. LLD (Aberdeen) 2000; Dr hc (Paris II) 2001. *Address:* Wimpole Cottage, 36 Wimpole Road, Great Eversden, Cambridge, CB23 1HR, England (home). *Telephone:* (1223) 262349 (home).

STEIN, Robert A., MA; American writer; b. 5 Aug. 1933, Duluth, MN; m. Betty L. Pavlik 1955; three s. *Education:* Univ. of Iowa. *Career:* Officer and Pilot, US Air Force 1956–77; Asst Prof., Univ. of Iowa 1964–66, Assoc. Prof. 1966–68, Prof. 1975–77; Faculty, Division of Writing, Kirkwood Community Coll., Iowa City and Cedar Rapids 1984–89; mem. Authors' Guild, Authors' League of America. *Publications:* fiction: Apollyon 1985, Death Defied 1988, The Chase 1988, The Black Samaritan 1997, The Vengeance Equation 2000; non-fiction: Statistical Correlations 1967, Engineers Vs. Other Students: Is There A Difference? 1967, Whatever Happened to Moe Bushkin? 1967, Quest for Viability: One Way! 1976, Threat of Emergency 1988. *Honours:* five wartime decorations; nine service awards, Outstanding Faculty Award, Univ. of Iowa 1967–68, Lifetime Achievement Award, Univ. 1999, Iowa Authors' Collection 1985, Minnesota Authors' Collection 1987, International Literary Award 1988.

STEINBACH, Meredith Lynn, BGS, MFA; American academic and writer; *Professor of English and Literary Arts, Brown University*; b. 18 March 1949, Ames, Ia; d. of Christopher Gene Steinbach and Joy Janice Steinbach (née Johnson); m. Charles Ossian Hartman 1979 (divorced 1991); one s. *Education:* Univ. of Iowa. *Career:* Teaching Fellow, Univ. of Iowa 1975–76; Writer-in-Residence, Antioch Coll. 1976–77; Lecturer, Northwestern Univ. 1977–79; Visiting Asst Prof., Univ. of Washington 1979–82; Asst Prof. to Assoc. Prof., Brown Univ. 1983–97, Prof. of English and Literary Arts 1997–; mem. PEN, Associated Writing Programs, Amnesty Int. *Publications:* novels: Zara 1982, Here Lies the Water 1990, The Birth of the World as We Know It, or Teiresias 1996, Field Notes from Provence: A Charmed Life of Flowers 2012; fiction collection: Reliable Light 1990; play: In the Realm of Which There Is No Sign; contrib. to Tri-Quarterly Magazine, Antaeus, Massachusetts Review, Antioch Review, Southwest Review, Black Warrior Review, Tuyonui, 13th Moon, Ploughshares, Post Road. *Honours:* Pushcart Prize, Best of the Small Presses 1977, Nat. Endowment for the Arts Fellowship 1978, Bunting Fellow, Bunting Summer Fellow, Mary Ingraham Bunting Inst., Radcliffe Coll., Harvard 1982–83, Rhode Island Artists Fellowship 1986–87, Rhode Island Award for Excellence in Literature, RI Council on Arts 1986–87, O. Henry Award 1990, Travel Study Grant to France and Greece 1993–94, Thomas J. Watson Travel Grantee, Thomas J. Watson Inst. for Int. Study, France and Greece 1993–94. *Address:* Graduate Program in Literary Arts, Box 1923, Brown University, Providence, RI 02912, USA (office). *Telephone:* (401) 863-3526 (office). *E-mail:* meredith_steinbach@brown.edu (office).

STEINECKERT, Gisela; German writer and journalist; b. 13 May 1931, Berlin; m. 1st Walter Steineckert 1947 (divorced); one d.; m. 2nd Wilhelm Penndorf 1971; one d. *Career:* fmr social worker, office worker and ed. in Berlin; writer of poetry, novels, essays, songs, prose and films 1957–; Cttee Pres. Demokratisches Frauenbund 1984–90, Hon. Chair. 1990–. *Publications include:* Wild auf Hoffnung, Und dennoch geht es uns gut, Presente, Für Frauen ist krieg im Land, Erster Montag im Oktober, Einefach Zuneigung, Die Schöne an den Frauen, Das Schöne an der Liebe, Der Mann mit der goldenen Nase Briefe, Ach Mama ach Tochter, Brevier für Verliebte, Die Schönen und die anderen Frauen, Die Schönste bin ich nicht, Einfach Zuneigung, Er hat gesagt, Erkundung zu zweit, Gesichter in meinem Spiegel, Poesiealbum, Ich umarme dich in Eile, Lieber September, Liebes-Gedichte, Liederbriefe, Nachricht von den Liebenden, Nebenan zu Gast, Neun-Tage-Buch, Nun leb mit mir, Unsere schöne Zeit mit dem bösen Rudi, Vor dem Wind sein, Wenn die Neugier nicht wär, Wild auf Hoffnung. *Honours:* Heinrich Heine award 1977, Nat. Preis für Kunst und Literatur 1986. *E-mail:* steineckert@onlinehome.de (home). *Website:* www.gisela-steineckert.de.

STEINEM, Gloria, BA; American writer, journalist and feminist activist; *Consulting Editor, Ms Magazine*; b. 25 March 1934, Toledo, Ohio; d. of Leo Steinem and Ruth Steinem (née Nuneviller); m. David Bale 2000. *Education:* Smith Coll. *Career:* Chester Bowles Asian Fellow, India 1957–58; Co-Dir, Dir Ind. Research Service, Cambridge, Mass. and New York 1959–60; editorial asst, contributing, ed., freelance writer various nat. and New York publs 1960–; Co-founder New York Magazine, contrib. 1968–72; co-founder Ms Magazine 1972 (Ed. 1971–87, columnist 1980–87, consulting ed. 1987–); feminist lecturer 1969–; active various civil rights and peace campaigns including United Farmworkers, Vietnam War Tax Protest, Cttee for the Legal Defense of Angela Davis and political campaigns of Adlai Stevenson, Robert Kennedy, Eugene McCarthy, Shirley Chisholm, George McGovern; co-founder and Chair Bd Women's Action Alliance 1970–; Convenor, mem. Nat. Advisory Cttee Nat. Women's Political Caucus 1971–; Co-Founder, Pres. Bd Dirs Ms Foundation for Women 1972–; founding mem. Coalition of Labor Union Women; Woodrow Wilson Int. Center for Scholars Fellow 1977, Women's Media Center 2004; mem. advisory bd Feminist.com. *Publications:* The Thousand Indias 1957, The Beach Book 1963, Outrageous Acts and Everyday Rebellions 1983, Marilyn 1986, Revolution From Within: A Book of Self-Esteem 1992, Moving Beyond Words 1994, Doing Sixty and Seventy 2006; contribs to various anthologies. *Honours:* Penney-Missouri Journalism Award 1970, Ohio Gov.'s Award for Journalism 1972, named Woman of the Year, McCall's Magazine 1972, Missouri Honor Medal for Distinguished Service in Journalism 2004. *Address:* The Women's Media Center, 350 Fifth Avenue, Suite 901, New York, NY 10118, USA (office). *E-mail:* kathy@womensmediacenter.com (office). *Website:* www.womensmediacenter.com (office).

STEINER, (Francis) George, DPhil, FBA, FRSL; American writer and scholar; b. 23 April 1929, Paris, France; s. of Dr Steiner and Mrs F. G. Steiner; m. Zara Shakow 1955; one s. one d. *Education:* Univ. of Paris, Univ. of Chicago, Harvard Univ., USA and Balliol Coll. Oxford, UK. *Career:* editorial staff, The Economist, London 1952–56; Fellow, Inst. for Advanced Study, Princeton 1956–58; Gauss Lecturer, Princeton Univ. 1959–60; Fellow and Dir of English Studies, Churchill Coll. Cambridge 1961–69, Extraordinary Fellow 1969–, Pensioner Fellow 1996–; Albert Schweitzer Visiting Prof., New York Univ. 1966–67; Visiting Prof., Yale Univ. 1970–71; Prof. of English and Comparative Literature, Univ. of Geneva 1974–94, Prof. Emer. 1994–; Visiting Prof., Collège de France 1992; First Lord Weidenfeld Visiting Prof. of Comparative Literature, Univ. of Oxford 1994–95; Charles Eliot Norton Prof. of Poetry, Harvard Univ. 2001–02; Pres. The English Asscn 1975–76; Corresp. mem. German Acad., Harvard Club, New York. *Publications:* Tolstoy or Dostoevsky: An Essay in the Old Criticism 1958, The Death of Tragedy 1960, Homer: A Collection of Critical Essays (co-ed. with Robert Flagles) 1962, Anno Domini: Three Stories 1964, The Penguin Book of Modern Verse Translation (ed.) 1966, Language and Silence 1967, Extraterritorial 1971, In Bluebeard's Castle: Some Notes Towards the Re-Definition of Culture 1971, The Sporting Scene: White Knights in Reykjavík 1973, Fields of Force 1974, A Nostalgia for the Absolute (Massey Lectures) 1974, After Babel: Aspects of Language and Translation 1975, Heidegger 1978, On Difficulty and Other Essays 1978, The Portage to San Cristóbal of A.H. 1981, Antigones 1984, George Steiner: A Reader 1984, Real Presences: Is There Anything in What We Say? 1989, Proofs and Three Parables 1992, The Deeps of the Sea 1996, Homer in English 1996, No Passion Spent 1996, Errata: An Examined Life 1998, Grammars of Creation 2001, Lessons of the Masters: The Charles Eliot Morton Lectures 2001–2002 2004, My Unwritten Books 2008. *Honours:* Hon. mem. American Acad. of Arts and Sciences 1989; Hon. RA (London) 2004; Hon. Fellow, Balliol Coll., Oxford, St Anne's Coll., Oxford; Chevalier, Légion d'honneur; Commdr, Ordre des Arts et des Lettres 2001; Hon. DLitt (East Anglia) 1976, (Louvain) 1979, (Bristol) 1989, (Glasgow, Liège) 1990, (Ulster) 1993, (Kenyon Coll., USA) 1995, (Trinity Coll. Dublin) 1995, (Rome) 1998, (Sorbonne) 1998, (Salamanca) 2002, (Athens) 2004, (London) 2006, (Bologna) 2006; O. Henry Award 1958, Jewish Chronicle Book Award 1968, Zabel Prize of Nat. Inst. of Arts and Letters 1970, Le Prix du Souvenir 1974, Massey Lecturer 1974, Ransom Memorial Lecturer 1976, King Albert Medal of the Royal Belgian Acad. 1982, F.D. Maurice Lecturer, Univ. of London 1984, Leslie Stephen Lecturer, Univ. of Cambridge 1985, Robertson Lecturer, Courtauld Inst., London 1985, W.P. Ker Lecturer, Univ. of Glasgow 1986, Page-Barbour Lecturer, Univ. of Virginia 1987, Gifford Lecturer 1990, Priestley Lecturer, Univ. of Toronto 1995, Prince of Asturias Prize 2001, 2002, Alfonso Reyes Prize (Mexico) 2007. *Address:* 32 Barrow Road, Cambridge, CB2 8AS, England.

STEINMAN, Lisa Malinowski, BA, MFA, PhD; American academic, poet, writer and editor; *Kenan Professor of English, Reed College*; b. (Lisa Malinowski), 8 April 1950, Willimantic, Conn.; d. of Zenon Malinowski and Shirley Malinowski; m. James L. Shugrue 1984. *Education:* Cornell Univ., Ithaca, NY. *Career:* Asst Prof., Reed Coll., Portland, Ore. 1976–82, Assoc. Prof. 1982–89, Prof. 1990–93, Kenan Prof. of English 1993–; Poetry Ed. Hubbub Magazine 1983–; Rockefeller Scholar-in-Residence, 92nd Street Y Poetry Center 1987; mem. Advisory Bd PMLA (Publications of the Modern Language Asscn of America) 2006–09; mem. Associated Writing Programs, Modern Language Asscn, PEN, PEN/Northwest, Poets and Writers, Wallace Stevens Soc., William Carlos Williams Soc. (Pres. 1998–2000). *Publications:* Lost Poems 1976, Made in America: Science, Technology, and American Modernist Poets 1987, All That Comes to Light 1989, A Book of Other Days 1993, Ordinary Songs 1996, Masters of Repetition: Poetry, Culture, and Work 1998, Carslaw's Sequences 2003, An Invitation to Poetry (Choice Outstanding Academic Book of 2008) 2008; contrib. to books, anthologies, reviews, quarterlies and journals. *Honours:* Scholar, Bread Loaf Writers Conf. 1981, Oregon Arts Comm. Poetry Fellow 1983, Nat. Endowment for the Arts Fellowship 1984, Pablo Neruda Award, Nimrod Magazine 1987, Rockefeller Scholar, 92nd Street Y Poetry Center 1987–88, Outstanding Academic Book, Choice 1989, 2008, Oregon Book Award, Oregon Inst. of Literary Arts 1993, Nat. Endowment for the Humanities Fellowship 1996, 2006, Oregon Arts Comm. Poetry Fellow 2011. *Address:* Department of English, Reed College, 3203 SE Woodstock Blvd, Portland, OR 97202 (office); 5344 SE 38th Avenue, Portland, OR 97202, USA (home). *Telephone:* (503) 517-7464 (office). *Fax:* (503) 777-7769 (office). *E-mail:* steinn@reed.edu (home).

STENGEL, Richard, BA; American editor; *Managing Editor, Time magazine*; b. 2 May 1955, New York, NY; m. Mary Pfaff; two c. *Education:* Princeton Univ. and Christ Church Coll., Oxford, England. *Career:* worked for MSNBC (TV); staff writer, Time magazine, New York 1981–83, Assoc. Ed. 1984–88, sr writer and essayist 1989–98; Ferris Prof. of Journalism, Princeton Univ. 1998–99; Sr Adviser and chief speechwriter for presidential candidate, Bill Bradley 1999; Man. Ed., Time.com 2000, Cultural Ed., Time magazine, then Nat. Ed. and Asst Man. Ed. –2004; Pres. and CEO, Nat. Constitutional Center, Philadelphia 2004–06; Man. Ed., Time magazine 2006–. *Film:* Mandela (prod., documentary) 1995. *Publications:* January Sun: One Day, Three Lives, a South African Town 1990, Long Walk to Freedom (with Nelson Mandela) 1993, You're Too Kind: A Brief History of Flattery 2000, Mandela's Way: Fifteen Lessons on Life, Love and Courage 2010; contrib. articles to The New Yorker, The New Republic, New York Times and others. *Address:* Time magazine, Time & Life Building, 1271 Avenue of the Americas, New York, NY 10020, USA (office). *E-mail:* letters@time.com (office). *Website:* www.time.com.

STEPHAN, John J., BA, MA, PhD; American historian and academic; *Professor Emeritus of History, University of Hawaii*; b. 8 March 1941, Chicago, Ill.; s. of the late John Stephan and Ruth Stephan; m. Barbara A. Brooks 1963. *Education:* Harvard Univ., Univ. of London, UK. *Career:* Far Eastern Ed., Harvard Review 1962; Visiting Fellow, St Antony's Coll. Oxford, UK 1977; Prof. of History, Univ. of Hawaii 1970–2001, Prof. Emer. of History 2001–; Visiting Prof. of History, Stanford Univ. 1986; Research Fellow, Kennan Inst. of Advanced Russian Studies 1987; mem. Authors' Guild, American Historical Asscn, Canadian Historical Asscn; Life mem. PEN, Int. House of Japan, American Asscn for the Advancement of Slavic Studies. *Publications:* Sakhalin: A History 1971, The Kuril Islands: Russo-Japanese Frontier in the Pacific 1974, The Russian Fascists 1978, Hawaii Under the Rising Sun 1984, Soviet-American Horizons in the Pacific (with V. P. Chichkanov) 1986, The Russian Far East: A History 1994; contributions: Washington Post, Modern Asian Studies, American Historical Review, Pacific Affairs, Pacific Community, Journal for Asian Studies, New York Times, Siberica, Pacifica, Australian Slavic and East European Studies. *Honours:* Fulbright Fellowship 1967–68, Japan Culture Trans. Prize 1973, Japan Foundation Fellowship 1977, Sanwa Distinguished Scholar, Fletcher School of Law and Diplomacy, Tufts University 1989, Distinguished Invited Speaker, Canadian Historical Asscn 1990, Kenneth W. Baldridge Prize 1996. *Address:* Department of History, University of Hawaii, 2530 Dole Street, Sakamaki Hall A203, Honolulu, HI 96822, USA (office). *Telephone:* (808) 956-8486 (office). *Fax:* (808) 947-2642 (office). *E-mail:* stephan@hawaii.edu (office).

STEPHEN, Ian, BEd; British writer, poet and artist; *Reader in Residence, Western Isles Libraries*; b. 29 April 1955, Stornoway, Isle of Lewis, Scotland; s. of John B. Stephen and Johann Smith; m. Barbara Ziehm 1984 (divorced 2010); two s. *Education:* Univ. of Aberdeen. *Career:* Inaugural Robert Louis Stevenson/Christian Salvesen Fellow, Grez-sur-Loing, France 1995; currently Reader in Residence, Western Isles Libraries; storytelling from voyage (satellite phone link to 50th Venice Biennale). *Exhibitions:* The Pier Arts Centre, Stromness, Orkney 2010, City Arts Centre, Edinburgh 2010, Is a Thing Lost?, Scottish islands tour, ECA, Highland Print Studio 2011–12. *Films:* Confluence (three films with Andy Mackinnon, Taigh Chearsabhagh comm.) 2008, A Boat Retold (co-producer) (dir Sean Martin, Louise Milne) 2011. *Music:* West of Time (lyrics and stories set to music by David P. Graham, Bonn and Cologne) 2008, Adrift – Poems with Piano Improvisations by Peter Urpeth 2009–. *Plays:* Seven Hunters (dir Gerry Mulgrew) 2003, Brazil 12 Scotland nil (dir Morven Gregor) 2004, The Sked Crew (dir Alison Peebles) 2007. *Radio:* Voyagers (series for Radio Scotland Green Waters project) 1998, Poetry of the Outdoors (with Mark Stephen) 2010. *Publications:* Malin, Hebrides, Minches 1983, Varying States of Grace 1989, Siud an T-Eilean (ed.) 1993, Providence II 1994, Broad Bay 1997, Green Waters 1998, Mackerel and Creamola (short stories) 2001, Adrift – Selected Poems (in English and Czech) 2007; other: numerous exhbns of poetry/texts with visual arts; contrib. to UK and int. publs. *Honours:* Scottish Arts Council Bursaries 1981, 1995, Creative Scotland Award 2002, two-year Bursary (prose writing) 2008. *Address:* Sail Loft 2, North Beach, Stornoway, Western Isles, HS1 2XN, Scotland (home). *Telephone:* (1851) 705320 (home). *E-mail:* ian@ianstephen.co.uk (home). *Website:* ianstephen.co.uk.

STEPHENS, Meic, BA, DLitt; Welsh journalist, poet, writer, editor and translator; *Professor Emeritus of Welsh Writing in English, University of Glamorgan*; b. 23 July 1938, Trefforest, Pontypridd, Wales; m. Ruth Wynn Meredith 1965; one s. three d. *Education:* Univ. Coll. of Wales, Aberystwyth, Univ. of Rennes, Univ. Coll. of North Wales, Bangor. *Career:* teacher of French 1962–66, journalist Western Mail 1966–67; Literature Dir, Welsh Arts Council 1967–90; Visiting Prof., Brigham Young Univ., Provo, UT 1991; Lecturer in Journalism, Univ. of Glamorgan 1994–2000, Centre for Journalism Studies, Cardiff Univ. 1998; Prof. of Welsh Writing in English, Univ. of Glamorgan 2001–03, Prof. Emer. 2003–; Literary Ed. Cambria; mem. Gorsedd of Bards, Welsh Acad. *Publications:* Linguistic Minorities in Western Europe, New Companion to the Literature of Wales, A Dictionary of Literary Quotations, The Oxford Literary Guide to Great Britain and Ireland, The Collected Poems of Harri Webb, The Complete Poems of Glyn Jones, The Collected Short Stories of Rhys Davies, The Literary Pilgrim in Wales, Welsh Names for Your Children, Illuminations: An Anthology of Welsh Short Prose, A Semester in Zion: A Journal With Memoirs, Decoding the Hare, Poetry 1900–2000 (ed); translations: Monica, Shadow of the Sickle, Return to Lleifior, The Basques, For the Sake of Wales, The Plum Tree, A White Afternoon, A Militant Muse, No Half-way House; contrib. to various anthologies, reference works and journals. *Honours:* Hon. MA (Univ. of Wales).

STEPHENS, Michael Gregory, BA, MA, MFA; American writer, poet, dramatist and academic; b. 4 March 1946. *Education:* City College, CUNY and Yale Univ. *Career:* Lecturer, Columbia Univ. 1977–91, Princeton Univ. 1986–91, New York Univ. 1989–91; Writer-in-Residence and Asst Prof., Fordham Univ. 1979–85; mem. Associated Writing Programs, PEN, Royal Asiatic Society. *Plays:* A Splendid Occasion in Spring 1974, Off-Season Rates 1978, Cloud Dream 1979, Our Father 1980, R & R 1984. *Publication include:* fiction: Season at Coole 1972, Paragraphs 1974, Still Life 1978, Shipping Out 1979, The Brooklyn Book of the Dead 1994, Conrad's List 2003; poetry: Alcohol Poems 1972, Tangun Legend 1978, After Asia 1993; other: Circles End (poems and prose) 1982, The Dramaturgy of Style 1986, Lost in Seoul: And Other Discoveries on the Korean Peninsula 1990, Jig and Reels 1992, Green Dreams: Essays Under the Influence of the Irish 1994; contributions: numerous newspapers, journals, and magazines. *Honours:* MacDowell Colony Fellowship 1968, Fletcher Pratt Fellowship, Bread Loaf Writers Conference 1971, Creative Artists Public Service Fiction Award 1978, Connecticut Commission on the Arts Grant 1979, Associated Writing Programs Award in Creative Non-Fiction 1993.

STEPHENS, Reed (see Donaldson, Stephen Reeder)

STEPHENSON, Hugh; British journalist and academic; b. 18 July 1938, Simla, India; s. of the late Sir Hugh Stephenson and Lady Stephenson; m. 1st Auriol Stevens 1962 (divorced 1987); two s. one d.; m. 2nd Diana Eden 1990. *Education:* New Coll. Oxford, Univ. of California, Berkeley, USA. *Career:* in diplomatic service, London and Bonn 1964–68; with The Times, London 1969–81, Ed., The Times Business News 1971–81; Ed. The New Statesman 1982–86; Prof. of Journalism, City Univ. 1986–2003, Prof. Emer. 2003–; Dir History Today Ltd 1981–; Dir European Journalism Centre, Maastricht 1992–2008, Chair. 1995–2002; currently crossword ed. The Guardian newspaper. *Publications include:* The Coming Clash 1972, Mrs. Thatcher's First Year 1980, Claret and Chips 1982, Libel and the Media (with others) 1997, Secrets of the Setters 2005. *Address:* c/o The Guardian, Kings Place, 90 York Way, London, N1 9GU, Englnad (office). *Telephone:* (20) 3353-2000 (office). *E-mail:* hugh.stephenson@guardian.co.uk (office). *Website:* www.guardian.co.uk/crosswords (office).

STEPHENSON, Neal, BA; American writer; b. 31 Oct. 1959, Fort Meade, MD. *Education:* Ames High School, IA, Univ. of Boston. *Publications:* novels: The Big U 1984, Zodiac: The Eco-Thriller 1988, Snow Crash 1991, Diamond Age 1995, Cryptonomicon 1999, Quicksilver (Arthur C. Clarke Award 2004) 2003, The Confusion 2004, The System of the World 2004, Anathem 2008. *Literary Agent:* Darhansoff Verrill Feldman, 236 West 26th Street, New York, NY 10001, USA. *Telephone:* (917) 305-1300. *Fax:* (917) 305-1400. *E-mail:* liz@dvagency.com. *Website:* www.dvagency.com. *E-mail:* morrowmarketing@harpercollins.com (office). *Website:* www.nealstephenson.com.

STERN, Fritz, PhD; American historian and academic; *University Professor Emeritus, Columbia University*; b. 2 Feb. 1926, Breslau, Germany; s. of Rudolf A. Stern and Catherine B. Stern; m. 1st Margaret J. Bassett 1947 (divorced 1992); one s. one d.; m. 2nd Elisabeth Niebuhr Sifton 1996. *Education:* Bentley School, New York, Columbia Univ. *Career:* Lecturer and Instructor, Columbia Univ. 1946–51; Acting Asst Prof., Cornell Univ. 1951–53; Asst Prof., Columbia Univ. 1953–57, Assoc. Prof. 1957–63, Full Prof. 1963–67, Seth Low Prof. 1967–92, Univ. Prof. 1992–96, Univ. Prof. Emer. 1997–, Provost 1980–83; Visiting Prof., Free Univ. of Berlin 1954, Yale Univ. 1963, Fondation Nationale des Sciences Politiques, Paris 1979; Perm. Visiting Prof., Konstanz

Univ. 1966–; Consultant US State Dept 1966–67; Guggenheim Fellowship 1969–70; mem. OECD team on German Educ. 1971–72; Netherlands Inst. for Advanced Study 1972–73; Trustee German Marshall Fund 1981–99, Aspen Inst. Berlin 1983–2000; Sr Advisor, US Embassy in Bonn 1993–94; mem. American Acad. of Arts and Sciences 1969–, Trilateral Comm. 1983–90, American Philosophical Soc. 1988, German-American Academic Council 1993–97; Corresp. mem. Deutsche Akad. für Dichtung und Sprache 1988; Senator, Deutsche Nationalstiftung 1993–. *Publications:* The Politics of Cultural Despair: A Study in the Rise of the Germanic Ideology 1961, Gold and Iron: Bismarck, Bleichroeder and the Building of the German Empire 1977, The Failure of Illiberalism: Essays in the Political Culture of Modern Germany 1972, Dreams and Delusions: The Drama of German History 1987; ed. The Varieties of History from Voltaire to the Present 1956, Der Nationalsozialismus als Versuchung, in Reflexionen Finsterer Zeit 1984, Verspielte Grösse: Essays zur deutschen Geschichte 1996, Das Feine Schweigen: Historische Essays 1999, Einstein's German World 1999, Grandeurs et Defaillances de l'Allemagne du XXème Siècle 2001, Five Germanys I Have Known 2006, Der Westen im 20. Jahrhundert: Selbstzerstörung, Wiederaufbau, Gefährdungen der Gegenwart 2008, Helmut Schmidt-Fritz Stern: Unser Jahrhundert, Ein Gespräch 2010. *Honours:* Hon. Senator, Deutsche Nationalstiftung 2008–; Orden pour le Mérite (Germany) 1994, Knight Commdr's Cross (Germany) 2004; Hon. DLitt (Oxford) 1985, Hon. LLD (New School for Social Research, New York) 1997, (Columbia Univ.) 1998, (Wrocław) 2002, Hon. DHumLitt (Princeton) 2007; Lionel Trilling Book Award 1977, Lucas Prize (Tübingen) 1984, Kulturpreis Schlesien (Wrocław) 1996, Peace Prize of the German Book Trade 1999, Alexander-von-Humboldt Research Prize 1999, Bruno Snell Medal, Univ. of Hamburg 2002, Lifetime Achievement Award, American Historical Asscn 2007, Jacques Barzun Prize, American Philosophical Soc. 2007, Annual Prize for Tolerance and Reconciliation, Jewish Museum, Berlin 2007, Lifetime Achievement Award, American Historical Asscn 2007. *Address:* 15 Claremont Avenue, New York, NY 10027, USA. *Telephone:* (212) 666-2891. *Fax:* (212) 316-0370. *E-mail:* fs20@columbia.edu.

STERN, Gerald, BA, MA; American poet and teacher; b. 22 Feb. 1925, Pittsburgh, Pa; m. Patricia Miller 1952 (divorced); one s. one d. *Education:* Univ. of Pittsburgh, Columbia Univ., New York. *Career:* Instructor, Temple Univ., Philadelphia 1957–63; Prof., Indiana Univ. of Pennsylvania 1963–67, Somerset Co. Coll., NJ 1968–82; Visiting Poet, Sarah Lawrence Coll. 1977; Visiting Prof., Univ. of Pittsburgh 1978, Columbia Univ. 1980, Bucknell Univ. 1988, New York Univ. 1989; Faculty Writer's Workshop, Univ. of Iowa 1982–94; Distinguished Chair, Univ. of Alabama 1984; Fanny Hurst Prof., Washington Univ., St Louis 1985; Bain Swiggert Chair, Princeton Univ. 1989; Poet-in-Residence, Bucknell Univ. 1994; NJ Poet Laureate 2000–02; Chancellor Acad. of American Poets 2006–. *Publications:* The Naming of Beasts and Other Poems 1973, Rejoicings 1973, Lucky Life 1977, The Red Coal 1981, Paradise Poems 1984, Lovesick 1987, Leaving Another Kingdom: Selected Poems 1990, Two Long Poems 1990, Bread Without Sugar 1992, Odd Mercy 1995, This Time: New and Selected Poems 1998, Last Blue 2000, American Sonnets 2002, What I Can't Bear Losing: Notes from a Life 2003, Not God After All 2004, Everything is Burning 2005, Save the Last Dance: Poems 2008, Early Collected Poems: 1965–1992 2010. *Honours:* NEA grants 1976, 1981, 1987, Lamont Poetry Selection Award 1977, Gov.'s Award, Pa 1980, Guggenheim Fellowship 1980, Bess Hokin Award 1980, Bernard F. Connor Award 1981, Melville Cane Award 1982, Jerome J. Shestack Prize 1984, Acad. of American Poets Fellowship 1993, Ruth Lilly Poetry Prize 1996, Nat. Book Award for Poetry 1998, Wallace Stevens Award 2005, Jewish Book Award 2005, Medal of Honor, American Acad. of Arts and Letters 2010. *Address:* 89 Clinton Street, Lambertville, NJ 08530-1912, USA (home). *Telephone:* (609) 397-2562 (home). *E-mail:* geraldstern2003@yahoo.com (home).

STERN, Jane, MFA; American writer; b. 24 Oct. 1946, d. of Milton Grossman and Norma Weyler; m. Michael Stern 1970. *Education:* The Pratt Inst., Brooklyn, NY and Yale Univ. *Career:* writer on popular American culture (co-author with Michael Stern); numerous appearances on radio and TV; co-writer 'Roadfood' column for Gourmet magazine. *Publications include:* Trucker: A Portrait of the Last American Cowboy 1975, Amazing America 1978, Friendly Relations 1979, Auto Ads 1979, Horror Holiday: Secrets of Vacation Survival 1981, Where to Eat in Connecticut: The Very Best Meals and the Very Best Deals 1985, Ambulance Girl: How I Saved Myself by Becoming an EMT 2003; with Michael Stern: Goodfood 1983, Roadfood 1986, Real American Food: Jane and Michael Stern's Coast-to-Coast Cookbook from Yankee Red Flannel Hash and the Ultimate Navajo Taco to Beautiful Swimme 1986, Elvis World 1987, A Taste of America 1988, Sixties People 1990, The Encyclopedia of Bad Taste 1990, American Gourmet: Classic Recipes, Deluxe Delights, Flamboyant Favorites and Swank Company Food from the 50s and 60s 1991, Jane and Michael Stern's Encyclopedia of Pop Culture: An A to Z Guide of Who's Who and What's What, from Aerobics and Bubble Gum to Valley of the Doll 1992, Way Out West 1993, Happy Trails: Our Life Story (with others) 1994, Eat Your Way Across the USA: 500 Diners, Farmland Buffets, Lobster Shacks, Pie Palaces and Other All-American Eateries 1997, Dog Eat Dog: A Very Human Book About Dogs and Dog Shows 1997, Two Puppies 1998, Chili Nation: The Ultimate Chili Cookbook with Recipes from Every State in the Nation 1999, Blue Plate Specials and Blue Ribbon Chefs: The Heart and Soul of America's Great Roadside Restaurants 2001, The Blue Willow Inn Cookbook 2001, El Charro Cafe Cookbook 2002, The Durgin-Park Cookbook: Classic Yankee Cooking in the Shadow of Faneuil Hall 2002, Roadfood: The Coast-to-Coast Guide to 500 of the Best Barbecue Joints, Lobster Shacks, Ice-Rearm Parlors, Highway Diners and Much, Much More 2002, The Louie's Backyard Cookbook 2003, The Harry Caray's Restaurant Cookbook: The Official Home Plate of the Chicago Cubs 2003, The Famous Dutch Kitchen Restaurant Cookbook: Family-Style Diner Delights from the Heart of Pennsylvania 2004, Cooking in the Lowcountry from The Old Post Office Restaurant: Spanish Moss Warm Nights and Fabulous Southern Food 2004, Southern California Cooking from The Cottage: Casual Cuisine from Old La Jolla's Favorite Beachside Bungalow 2004, Southern Country Cooking from the Loveless Cafe: Fried Chicken, Hams and Jams from Nashville's Favorite Cafe 2005, Elegant Comfort Food from Dorset Inn: Traditional Cooking from Vermont's Oldest Continuously-Operating Inn 2005, Two for the Road: Our Love Affair with American Food 2006, Roadfood Sandwiches 2007, 500 Things to Eat Before It's Too Late 2009. *Honours:* three James Beard Awards (for Roadfood column). *Address:* 28 Wayside Lane, West Redding, CT 06896-2803, USA (home). *Website:* www.roadfood.com.

STERN, Michael; American writer; m. Jane Stern 1970. *Career:* writer on popular American culture (co-author with Jane Stern); numerous appearances on radio and TV; co-writer 'Roadfood' column for Gourmet magazine. *Publications:* Stern's Guide to Disney Collectibles: Vol. 1 1989, Vol. 2 1990, Collectors' Guide to Disneyana (with David Longest) 1992; with Jane Stern: Goodfood 1983, Roadfood 1986, Real American Food: Jane and Michael Stern's Coast-to-Coast Cookbook from Yankee Red Flannel Hash and the Ultimate Navajo Taco to Beautiful Swimme 1986, Elvis World 1987, A Taste of America 1988, Sixties People 1990, The Encyclopedia of Bad Taste 1990, American Gourmet: Classic Recipes, Deluxe Delights, Flamboyant Favorites and Swank Company Food from the 50s and 60s 1991, Jane and Michael Stern's Encyclopedia of Pop Culture: An A to Z Guide of Who's Who and What's What, from Aerobics and Bubble Gum to Valley of the Doll 1992, Way Out West 1993, Happy Trails: Our Life Story (with others) 1994, Eat Your Way Across the USA: 500 Diners, Farmland Buffets, Lobster Shacks, Pie Palaces and Other All-American Eateries 1997, Dog Eat Dog: A Very Human Book About Dogs and Dog Shows 1997, Two Puppies 1998, Chili Nation: The Ultimate Chili Cookbook with Recipes from Every State in the Nation 1999, Blue Plate Specials and Blue Ribbon Chefs: The Heart and Soul of America's Great Roadside Restaurants 2001, The Blue Willow Inn Cookbook 2001, El Charro Cafe Cookbook 2002, The Durgin-Park Cookbook: Classic Yankee Cooking in the Shadow of Faneuil Hall 2002, Roadfood: The Coast-to-Coast Guide to 500 of the Best Barbecue Joints, Lobster Shacks, Ice-Rearm Parlors, Highway Diners and Much, Much More 2002, The Louie's Backyard Cookbook 2003, The Harry Caray's Restaurant Cookbook: The Official Home Plate of the Chicago Cubs 2003, The Famous Dutch Kitchen Restaurant Cookbook: Family-Style Diner Delights from the Heart of Pennsylvania 2004, Cooking in the Lowcountry from The Old Post Office Restaurant: Spanish Moss Warm Nights and Fabulous Southern Food 2004, Southern California Cooking from The Cottage: Casual Cuisine from Old La Jolla's Favorite Beachside Bungalow 2004, Southern Country Cooking from the Loveless Cafe: Fried Chicken, Hams and Jams from Nashville's Favorite Cafe 2005, Elegant Comfort Food from Dorset Inn: Traditional Cooking from Vermont's Oldest Continuously-Operating Inn 2005, Two for the Road: Our Love Affair with American Food 2006, Roadfood Sandwiches 2007, 500 Things to Eat Before It's Too Late 2009. *Honours:* three James Beard Awards (for Roadfood column). *Address:* 28 Wayside Lane, West Redding, CT 06896-2803, USA (home). *Website:* www.roadfood.com.

STERN, Richard Gustave, BA, MA, PhD; American writer and academic; b. 25 Feb. 1928, New York; m. 1st Gay Clark; m. 2nd Alane Rollings; three s. one d. *Education:* Univ. of North Carolina, Harvard Univ., Univ. of Iowa. *Career:* taught at Univ. of Chicago 1955–2004 (retd); mem. American Acad. of Arts and Sciences. *Publications include:* Golk (libretto) 1960, Europe or Up and Down with Baggish and Schreiber 1961, In Any Case 1962, Stitch 1965, Other Men's Daughters 1973, A Father's Words 1986, The Position of the Body 1986, Noble Rot Stories 1949–89 1989, Shares and Other Fictions 1992, One Person and Another 1993, Sistermony 1995, Pacific Tremors 2001, What Is What Was 2002, Almonds to Zhoof (short stories) 2004, Still on Call 2010; contribs: journals and magazines. *Honours:* Longwood Award 1954, American Acad. of Arts and Letters Award 1968, Friends of Literature Award 1968, Sandburg Award 1979, Award of Merit for the Novel, American Academy of Arts and Letters 1985, Heartland Prize 1995. *Address:* 85 Van Horne Avenue, Tybee Island, GA 31328-9726, USA.

STERN, Steve; American academic and writer; b. 21 Dec. 1947, Memphis, TN. *Education:* BA, Rhodes College, 1970; MFA, University of Arkansas, 1977. *Career:* Visiting Lecturer, University of Wisconsin, 1987; Assoc. Prof. of English, Skidmore College, Saratoga Springs, New York 1994–. *Publications:* Isaac and the Undertaker's Daughter 1983, The Moon and Ruben Shein 1984, Lazar Malkin Enters Heaven 1986, Mickey and the Golem 1986, Hershel and the Beast 1987, Harry Kaplan's Adventures Underground 1991, Plague of Dreamers 1994, The Wedding Jester (short stories) 1999, The Angel of Forgetfulness (novel) 2005, The North of God 2008, The Frozen Rabbi (novel) 2010; contrib. to magazines and journals. *Honours:* O. Henry Prize 1981, Pushcart Writers Choice Award 1984, and Prizes 1997, 2000, Edward Lewis Wallant Award 1988, National Jewish Book Award 2000, Fulbright Fellowship 2003, Guggenheim Fellowship 2006. *Address:* c/o Department of English, Skidmore College, Saratoga Springs, NY 12866, USA (office).

STERN, Stuart (see Rae, Hugh Crauford)

STERNBERG, Robert Jeffrey, BA, PhD; American psychologist, academic, writer and editor; *Provost, Senior Vice-President and Professor of Psychology, Oklahoma State University*; b. 8 Dec. 1949, Newark, NJ; m. Alejandra Campos 1991; one s. one d. *Education:* Yale Univ., Stanford Univ. *Career:* Asst Prof., Yale Univ. 1975–80, Assoc. Prof. 1980–83, Prof. 1983–86, IBM Prof. of Psychology and Education 1986–2005, Dir, Center for the Psychology of Abilities, Competencies and Expertise 2000–05; Dean, School of Arts and Sciences, Tufts Univ. 2005–10, Dir Center for the Psychology of Abilities, Competencies and Expertise 2006–10; Provost, Sr Vice-Pres. and Prof. of Psychology, Oklahama State Univ. 2010–; Ed. Psychological Bulletin 1991–96, Contemporary Psychology 1999; Distinguished Assoc., The Psychometrics Centre, Univ. of Cambridge; Ed.-in-Chief, Educational Psychology Series, Lawrence Erlbaum Assocs 1996–; mem. American Acad. of Arts and Sciences, AAAS, American Educational Research Asscn, American Psychological Soc., International Council of Psychologists, National Asscn for Gifted Children, Psychonomic Soc., Soc. for Research in Child Development, Soc. of Multivariate Experimental Psychology, American Psychological Asscn (Pres. 2003). *Publications include:* Intelligence, Information Processing, and Analogical Reasoning: The Componential Analysis of Human Abilities 1977, Beyond IQ: A Triarchic Theory of Human Intelligence 1985, Intelligence Applied: Understanding and Increasing Your Intellectual Skills 1986, What is Intelligence? (with D. K. Detterman) 1986, The Psychologist's Companion, second edn 1988, The Triangle of Love 1988, The Triarchic Mind: A New Theory of Human Intelligence 1988, Metaphors of Mind: Conceptions of the Nature of Intelligence 1990, Love the Way You Want It 1991, Tacit Knowledge Inventory for Managers (with R. K. Wagner) 1991, For Whom Does the Bell Curve Toll?: It Tolls for You 1995, In Search of the Human Mind 1995, Defying the Crowd: Cultivating Creativity in a Culture of Conformity (with T. I. Lubart) 1995, Off Track: When Poor Readers Become Learning Disabled (with L. Spear-Swerling) 1996, Cognitive Psychology 1996, Successful Intelligence 1996, Introduction to Psychology 1997, Pathways to Psychology 1997, Thinking Styles 1997, Successful Intelligence 1997, Cupid's Arrow: The Course of Love Through Time 1998, Love is a Story 1998, Perspectives on Learning Disabilities: Biological, Cognitive, Contextual (with L. Spear-Swerling) 1999, Our Labeled Children: What Every Parent and Teacher Needs to Know About Learning Disabilities (with E. L. Grigorenko) 1999, Teaching for Successful Intelligence (with E. L. Grigorenko) 2000, Psychology: In Search of the Human Mind 2001, Educational Psychology (with W. M. Williams) 2001, Dynamic Testing (with E. L. Grigorenko) 2002, Psychology 101½: The Unspoken Rules for Success in Academia 2004, The Nature of Leadership 2004, A Brief History of Intelligence 2004, Wisdom, Intelligence and Creativity Synthesized 2007; other: ed. of many books; contributions: numerous scholarly books and journals. *Honours:* Dr hc (Complutense Univ., Madrid) 1994; Distinguished Scholar Award, National Asscn for Gifted Children 1985, Outstanding Book Award, American Educational Research Asscn 1987, Sylvia Scribner Award 1996, Guggenheim Fellowship 1985–86, Award for Excellence, Mensa Education and Research Foundation 1989, G. Stanley Hall Distinguished Lecturer, American Psychological Asscn 1997, E. L. Thorndike Award for Career Achievement in Educational Psychology 2003. *Address:* Department of Psychology, Oklahoma State University, 116 North Murray, Stillwater, OK 74078-3064, USA. *Telephone:* (405) 744-6027. *Fax:* (405) 744-8067. *E-mail:* robert.sternberg@okstate.edu. *Website:* psychology.okstate.edu.

STERNLICHT, Sanford, BS, MA, PhD; American academic, literary critic and poet; *Professor of English, Syracuse University*; b. 20 Sept. 1931, New York, NY; m. Dorothy Hilkert 1956 (died 1977); two s. *Education:* State Univ. of NY (SUNY) at Oswego, Colgate Univ., Syracuse Univ. *Career:* Instructor, SUNY at Oswego 1959–60, Asst Prof. 1960–62, Assoc. Prof. 1962, Prof. of English 1962–72, Prof. of Theatre 1972–86; Leverhulme Visiting Prof. of English, Univ. of York, UK 1964–66; Prof. of English, Syracuse Univ. 1986–; Fulbright Sr Specialist and Visiting Prof. of English, Univ. of Pécs, Hungary 2004; mem. Modern Language Asscn, PEN, Shakespeare Asscn of America, American Conf. for Irish Studies; Fellow, Poetry Soc. of America. *Publications:* poetry: Gull's Way 1961, Love in Pompeii 1967; non-fiction: Uriah Philips Levy: The Blue Star Commodore 1961, The Black Devil of the Bayous: The Life and Times of the United States Steam-Sloop Hartford (with E. M. Jameson) 1970, John Webster's Imagery and the Webster Canon 1974, John Masefield 1977, McKinley's Bulldog: The Battleship Oregon 1977, C. S. Forester 1981, USF Constellation: Yankee Racehorse (with E. M. Jameson) 1981, Padraic Colum 1985, John Galsworthy 1987, R. F. Delderfield 1988, Stevie Smith 1990, Stephen Spender 1992, Siegfried Sassoon 1993, All Things Herriot: James Herriot and his Peaceable Kingdom 1995, Jean Rhys 1996, A Reader's Guide to Modern Irish Drama 1998; editor: Selected Stories of Padraic Colum 1985, Selected Plays of Padraic Colum 1989, In Search of Stevie Smith 1991, New Plays from the Abbey Theatre 1993–1995 1996, Chaim Potok: A Critical Companion 2000, New Plays from the Abbey Theatre, 1996–1998 2001, A Reader's Guide to Modern American Drama 2002, A Student's Companion to Elie Wiesel 2003, The Tenement Saga: The Lower East Side and Early Jewish American Writers 2004, A Reader's Guide to Modern British Drama 2004, Masterpieces of British and Irish Drama 2005; Masterpieces of Jewish American Literature, 2007, Modern Irish Drama: W.B. Yeats to Marina Carr 2010; contrib. to books, professional journals and general periodicals. *Honours:* prizes, fellowships and grants, including Sir Evelyn Wrench English-Speaking Union Travel/Lecture grants 1997, 1998, 1999. *Address:* English Department, Syracuse University, Syracuse, NY 13244 (office); 128 Dorset Road, Syracuse, NY 13210, USA (home). *Telephone:* (315) 443-9480 (office); (315) 472-5639 (home). *E-mail:* svsternl@syr.edu (home).

STEVENS, Carl (see Obstfeld, Raymond)

STEVENS, Sir Jocelyn Edward Greville, Kt, CVO, FRSA; British publisher; b. 14 Feb. 1932, London; s. of Major C.G.B. Stewart-Stevens and Betty Hulton; m. Jane Armyne Sheffield 1956 (dissolved 1979); one s. two d. (one s. deceased). *Education:* Eton Coll., Cambridge Univ. *Career:* mil. service Rifle Brigade 1950–52; journalist Hulton Press 1955–56; Chair. and Man. Dir Stevens Press Ltd, Ed. Queen Magazine 1957–68; Personal Asst to Chair. Beaverbrook Newspapers 1968, Dir 1971–81, Man. Dir 1974–77; Man. Dir Evening Standard Co. Ltd 1969–72, Daily Express 1972–74; Deputy Chair. and Man. Dir Express Newspapers 1974–81; Ed. and Publr The Magazine 1982–84; Dir Centaur Communications 1982–84; Gov. Imperial Coll. of Science, Tech. and Medicine 1985–92, Winchester School of Art 1986–89; Rector and Vice-Provost RCA 1984–92; Chair. The Silver Trust 1990–93, English Heritage 1992–2000; Deputy Chair. Independent TV Comm. 1991–96; Dir (non-exec.) The TV Corpn 1996–2002, Asprey & Co. –2002, Garrard & Co. –2002; Pres. The Cheyne Walk Trust 1989–93; Chair. The Prince of Wales's Phoenix Trust; Trustee Eureka! The Children's Museum 1990–2000. *Honours:* Hon. DLitt (Loughborough) 1989, (Buckingham) 1998; Hon. FCSD 1990, Sr Fellow RCA 1990.

STEVENS, Lynsey, (Lynette Desley Howard); Australian writer; b. 28 Sept. 1947, Sherwood, Qld. *Career:* mem. Queensland Writers Centre, Australian Soc. of Authors, Romance Writers of America, Romance Writers of Australia. *Publications:* Ryan's Return 1981, Terebori's Gold 1981, Race for Revenge 1981, Play Our Song Again 1981, Tropical Knight 1982, Starting Over 1982, Man of Vengeance 1982, Closest Place to Heaven 1983, Forbidden Wine 1983, The Ashby Affair 1983, Lingering Embers 1984, Leave Yesterday Behind 1986, But Never Love 1988, A Rising Passion 1990, Touched by Desire 1993, A Physical Affair 1994, Misteltoe Kisses (in Christmas Journeys) 1994, His Cousin's Wife 1996, Close Relations 1997, Male for Christmas 1998. *Honours:* Arty, Romantic Times, Worldwide Romance 1984. *Address:* PO Box 400, Red Hill, Qld 4259, Australia (office). *E-mail:* lynsey@ecn.net.au (office). *Website:* www.lynseystevens.com.

STEVENSON, Anne Katharine, MA, FRSL; American/British poet and writer; b. 3 Jan. 1933, Cambridge, England; d. of Charles Stevenson and Louise Destler; m. 1st Robin Hitchcock (divorced) 1955; one d.; m. 2nd Mark Elvin (divorced) 1963; two s.; m. 3rd Michael Farley 1979 (divorced); m. 4th Peter David Lucas 1987. *Education:* Univ. High School, Ann Arbor, Mich., Univ. of Michigan. *Career:* Literary Fellow, Lady Margaret Hall, Oxford 1973; Northern Arts Literary Fellow 1981–82; Writer-in-Residence, Univ. of Edinburgh 1989; mem. FEA, Soc. of Authors, The Welsh Acad. *Publications:* Living in America 1965, Elizabeth Bishop 1966, Reversals 1969, Travelling Behind Glass 1974, Correspondences 1974, Enough of Green 1977, Minute by Glass Minute 1982, The Fiction Makers 1985, Winter Time 1986, Selected Poems 1987, The Other House 1990, Four and a Half Dancing Men 1993, Collected Poems 1996, Bitter Fame: A Life of Sylvia Plath 1998, Five Looks at Elizabeth Bishop 1998, Between the Iceberg and the Ship (literary essays) 1998, Granny Scarecrow 2000, Hearing with My Fingers 2002, A Report from the Border 2003, Poems 1955–2005 2005, Stone Milk 2007; contrib. to reviews, journals and magazines. *Honours:* Hon. Fellow, St Chad's Coll., Durham; Hon. DLitt (Loughbrough) 1998, (Hull) 2004, (Durham) 2005, (Michigan) 2008, (Newcastle) 2010, (London) 2010; Major Hopwood Award 1954, Arts Council Award 1974, Poetry Book Soc. Choice 1985, Athena Award 1990, Soc. of Authors Cholmondeley Award 1997, Northern Rock Foundation Writers Award 2002, Poetry Foundation Neglected Masters Award 2007, Lannan Literary Award for Lifetime Achievement in Poetry 2007, Univ. of the South (Sewanee) Aiken-Taylor Award (Poet of the Year) 2007. *Address:* c/o Bloodaxe Books, Highgreen, Tarset, Northumberland, NE48 1RP, England. *Website:* www.anne-stevenson.co.uk.

STEVENSON, David, BA, PhD, DLitt, FRSE; British academic and writer; b. 30 April 1942, Largs, Ayrshire, Scotland; m. Wendy McLeod; two s. *Education:* Univ. of Dublin, Univ. of Glasgow. *Career:* taught at Univ. of Aberdeen; Prof. of Scottish History, Univ. of St Andrews 1991–94, Emer. 1994–. *Publications:* The Scottish Revolution 1973, Revolution and Counter-Revolution in Scotland 1977, Alastair MacColla and the Highland Problem 1980, Scottish Covenanters and Irish Confederates 1981, The Origins of Freemasonry 1988, The First Freemasons 1988, King or Covenant: Voices from Civil War 1996, Scotland's Last Royal Wedding 1997, Union, Revolution and Religion in 17th Century Scotland 1997, The Beggar's Benison. Sex Clubs of the Scottish Enlightenment and their Rituals 2001, The Hunt for Rob Roy (Frank Watson Prize 2005) 2003. *Address:* 5 Forgan Way, Newport-on-Tay, Fife, DD6 8JQ, Scotland (home). *E-mail:* david.stevenson@btinternet.com (home).

STEWART, Bruce Robert, BA; New Zealand writer and dramatist; b. 4 Sept. 1925, Auckland; m. Ellen Noonan 1950, three s. three d. *Education:* University of Auckland. *Career:* mem. British Film Institute, Writers' Guild of Australia, Writers' Guild of Great Britain (chair. 1979–81), Actors' Equity. *Publications:* A Disorderly Girl 1980, The Turning Tide 1980, The Hot and Copper Sky 1982, Aspects of Therese 1997, A Bloke Like Jesus 1998; other: various plays for stage, radio and television, including Me and My Shadow 1988, The Gallows in My Garden 1989, Stars in my Hair 1990, Speak Low 1993, Soeur Sourive 2000; contributions: newspapers, magazines and journals. *Honours:* MWA Edgar Allan Poe Award 1963, Charles Henry Foyle Award, UK 1968.

STEWART, Douglas Keith; New Zealand writer and critic; b. 15 Dec. 1950, Kawakana; m. Julie Joy Burgham 1972, one s. two d. *Education:* Northland College, Univ. of Auckland. *Publications:* The New Zealander's Guide to Wine 1986, The Art Award 1988, The Wine Handbook 1988, Rosa Antipodes: The History of Roses in New Zealand 1994, The Fine Wines of New Zealand 1995, Kahukura's Net: Maori Influence on Contemporary New Zealand Art 1999, Euchre (novel) 1999; contributions: newspapers and magazines.

STEWART, John, MA, MFA, PhD; American academic and writer; b. 24 Jan. 1933, Trinidad; m. Sandra MacDonald 1969; one s. one d. *Education:* Stanford Univ., Univ. of Iowa, Univ. of California at Los Angeles. *Career:* Univ. of Illinois, Ohio State Univ., Univ. of California at Davis. *Publications:* Last Cool Days (novel) 1971, Curving Road (short stories) 1975, For the Ancestors (life history) 1983, Drinkers, Drummers and Decent Folk (narrative ethnography) 1989, Looking for Josephine (short stories) 1998. *Honours:* Winifred Hoztby Memorial Prize 1971.

STEWART, Judith (see Polley, Judith Anne)

STEWART, Martha Helen Kostyra, BA; American editor, writer and business executive; b. 3 Aug. 1941, Jersey City, NJ; d. of the late Edward Kostyra and Martha Kostyra (née Ruszkowski); m. Andy Stewart 1961 (divorced 1989); one d. *Education:* Barnard Univ. *Career:* fmr model, stockbroker, caterer; Owner and Ed.-in-Chief Martha Stewart Living magazine 1990–; Founder, Chair. and CEO Martha Stewart Living Omnimedia 1997–2003, mem. Bd –2004, Founding Editorial Dir (non-exec.) March 2004–; also appears in cooking feature on NBC's Today Show; mem. Bd NY Stock Exchange June–Oct. 2002; mem. Bd Revlon Inc. –2004; under investigation for alleged insider trading June 2002, found guilty of conspiracy, making false statements and obstruction of justice March 2004, sentenced to prison and released March 2005, agreed with Securities and Exchange Comm. to settle insider trading charges and to maximum penalty of about $195,000, to a five-year bar from serving as a dir of a public co. and a five-year limitation on the scope of her service as an officer or employee of a public co. Aug. 2006; moved to cable TV's Hallmark Channel to offer eight hours of weekday programming Sept. 2010. *Television:* host of TV show Martha 2005–, starred in The Apprentice: Martha Stewart 2005. *Publications include:* (with Elizabeth Hawes) Entertaining 1982, Weddings 1987; (as sole author) Martha Stewart's Hors d'Oeuvres: The Creation and Presentation of Fabulous Finger Food 1984, Martha Stewart's Pies and Tarts 1985, Martha Stewart's Quick Cook Menus 1988, The Wedding Planner 1988, Martha Stewart's Gardening: Month by Month 1991, Martha Stewart's New Old House: Restoration, Renovation, Decoration 1992, Martha Stewart's Christmas 1993, Martha Stewart's Menus for Entertaining 1994, Holidays 1994, The Martha Rules 2005, Martha Stewart's Homekeeping Handbook 2006, Martha Stewart's Dinner at Home 2009. *Honours:* ranked by Fortune magazine amongst the 50 Most Powerful Women in Business in the US (21st) 2005, (28th) 2006, ranked by Forbes magazine amongst The World's 100 Most Powerful Women (99th) 2010. *Address:* Martha Stewart Living Omnimedia, 11 West 42nd Street, 25th Floor, New York, NY 10036 (office); Martha Stewart, 19 Newton Toke, Suite 6, Westport, CT 06880; c/o Susan Magrino Agency, 40 West 57th Street, 31st Floor, New York, NY 10019; 10 Saugatuck Avenue, Westport, CT 06880, USA (home). *Telephone:* (212) 827-8000 (office). *Fax:* (212) 827-8204 (office). *Website:* www.marthastewart.com (office); www.themarthablog.com.

STEWART, Lady Mary Florence Elinor, BA, DipEd, MA, DLitt; British writer and poet; b. 17 Sept. 1916, Sunderland; m. Sir Frederick Henry Stewart 1945 (died 2001). *Education:* St Hild's Coll., Durham Univ. *Career:* Asst Lecturer in English, Durham Univ. 1941–45, part-time Lecturer in English, St Hild's Training Coll., Durham and Durham Univ. 1948–56; mem. PEN. *Publications:* novels: Madam, Will You Talk? 1954, Wildfire at Midnight 1956, Thunder on the Right 1957, Nine Coaches Waiting 1958, My Brother Michael 1959, The Ivy Tree 1961, The Moonspinners 1962, This Rough Magic 1964, Airs Above the Ground 1965, The Gabriel Hounds 1967, The Wind off the Small Isles 1968, The Crystal Cave (Frederick Niven Prize 1971) 1970, The Hollow Hills 1973, Touch Not the Cat 1976, The Last Enchantment 1979, The Wicked Day 1983, Thornyhold 1988, Stormy Petrel 1991, The Prince and the Pilgrim 1995, Rose Cottage 1997; children's fiction: A Walk in Wolf Wood 1970, The Little Broomstick 1971, Ludo and the Star Horse (Scottish Arts Council Award) 1974; poetry: Frost on the Window and Other Poems 1990; contrib. to magazines. *Honours:* Hon. Fellow, Newnham Coll., Cambridge 1986.

STEWART, Paul, BA, MA; British writer; b. 4 June 1955, London; m. Julie Stewart; one s. one d. *Education:* Univ. of Lancaster, Univ. of East Anglia, Univ. of Heidelberg. *Publications:* Stormchaser 1999, The Blobheads (eight vols) 2000, Midnight Over Sanctaphrax 2000, Rabbit's Wish 2001, The Curse of the Gloamglozer 2001, The Last of the Sky Pirates 2002, Muddle Earth 2003, Vox 2003, Freeglader 2004, Fergus Crane (Smarties Gold Medal) 2004, Corby Flood (Smarties Silver Medal) 2005, Trek 2007; with Chris Riddell: The Stone Pilot 2006, Clash of the Sky Galleons 2006, Hugo Pepper (Nestle Silver Medal) 2006, The Lost Barkscrolls 2007, The Immortals 2009, Wyrmeweald: Returner's Wealth 2010, Bloodhoney 2011. *Literary Agent:* c/o Philippa Milnes-Smith, L. A. W. Ltd, 14 Vernon Street, London, W14 0RJ, England.

STEWART, Rory, OBE, BA, MA; British diplomatist and writer; b. politician, Hong Kong. *Education:* Balliol Coll., Oxford. *Career:* fmrly in British Army; fmr Desk Officer (Japan and Korea), FCO, London; fmr Second Sec. (Political/Economic), British Embassy in Jakarta, Indonesia; fmr British Representative in Montenegro –2000; walked from Turkey to Bangladesh 2000–02, crossing Iran, Afghanistan, Pakistan, India and Nepal; Deputy Governorate Co-ordinator (Amara/Maysan) and Sr Adviser and Deputy Governorate Co-ordinator (Nasiriyah/Dhi Qar), for the Coalition Provisional Authority, Maysan Province, Iraq 2003–04; Fellow, The Carr Center for Human Rights Policy, Harvard Univ. 2004–05, Ryan Family Prof. of Human Rights 2009–, Dir The Carr Center for Human Rights Policy 2009–; CEO Turquoise Mountain Foundation, Afghanistan 2006–08; MP (Conservative) for Penrith and the Border 2010–. *Publications:* The Places in Between (Royal Soc. of Literature Ondaatje Prize 2005) 2004, The Prince of the Marshes and Other Occupational Hazards of a Year in Iraq 2006; contrib. to Granta, LRB, New York Times Magazine. *Address:* House of Commons, London, SW1A 0AA, England (office). *Telephone:* (20) 7219-7127 (office). *E-mail:* rory@rorystewart.co.uk (office). *Website:* www.rorystewart.co.uk.

STEWART, Susan, BA, MA, PhD; American writer, poet and educator; *Annan Professor of English, Princeton University*; b. 15 March 1952, York, Pa. *Education:* Dickinson Coll., Johns Hopkins Univ., Univ. of Pennsylvania. *Career:* Asst Prof., Temple Univ. 1978–81, Assoc. Prof. 1981–85, Prof. of English 1985–97; Annan Prof. of English, Princeton Univ. 1997–; Chancellor, Acad. of American Poets 2005–; mem. American Acad. of Arts and Sciences. *Publications include:* Yellow Stars and Ice (poems) 1981, On Longing: Narratives of the Miniature, the Gigantic, the Souvenir, the Collection 1984, The Hive: Poems 1987, Nonsense: Aspects of Intertextuality in Folklore and Literature 1989, Crimes of Writing: Problems in the Containment of Representation 1991, The Forest (poems) 1995, Poetry and the Fate of the Senses (Christian Gauss Award for Literary Criticism 2002, Truman Capote Award in Literary Criticism 2004) 2002, Columbarium (poems) (Nat. Book Critics' Circle Award) 2003, The Open Studio: Essays in Art and Aesthetics 2004. *Honours:* National Endowment for the Arts Grant 1981–82, 1984, 1988, Pennsylvania Council on the Arts Grant 1984, 1988, 1989–90, Guggenheim Foundation Fellowship 1986–87, Georgia Press Second Book Award 1987, Temple Univ. Creative Achievement Award 1991, Senior Scholar, Getty Center for the History of Art and the Humanities 1995, Lila Wallace-Reader's Digest Writer's Award for Poetry 1995, Pew Fellowship 1995, Acad. Award in Literature, American Acad. of Arts and Letters 2009. *Address:* Department of English, Princeton University, McCosh Hall, Room 22, Princeton, NJ 08544-1016, USA. *Telephone:* (609) 258-4058 (office). *E-mail:* stewart1@princeton.edu (office). *Website:* english.princeton.edu (office).

STIBBE, Mark W. G., BA, MA, PhD; British writer; b. 16 Sept. 1960, London, England; m. Alison Heather Stibbe 1983; four c. *Education:* Univ. of Cambridge, Univ. of Nottingham. *Career:* founder, Father's House Trust chairty. *Publications include:* John as Storyteller 1992, The Gospel of John as Literature 1993, John: A New Biblical Commentary 1993, A Kingdom of Priests 1994, John's Gospel 1994, Explaining Baptism in the Holy Spirit 1995, O Brave New Church 1996, Times of Refreshing 1996, Know Your Spiritual Gifts 1997, A Box of Delights 2001, A Bucket of Surprises 2002, A Barrel of Fun 2003, A Bundle of Laughs 2005, Drawing Near to God 2005, Prophetic Evangelism 2005, A Basket of Gems 2009, Breakout 2010; contributions: numerous articles to Renewal; Anglicans for Renewal; various New Testament journals; Journal of Pentecostal Theology; Soul Survivor. *Honours:* Hon. MA, Hon. DipTh, Hon. PhD. *Address:* Father's House Trust, 26 The Parade, Watford, Hertfordshire, WD17 1AA, England (office). *Telephone:* (1923) 256352 (office). *Website:* www.fathershousetrust.com (office).

STIBOROVÁ, Věra; Czech writer; b. 15 Jan. 1926, Písek; m. Jaroslav Putík 1954; one d. *Education:* School of Applied Arts. *Career:* journalist, Lidové Noviny daily newspaper, Prague; journalist, translator Práce daily newspaper; collaborator with various literary magazines –1969; works prohibited in 1969, but many published through Samizdat; labourer and sales rep. 1972–89. *Publications include:* Blue Loves (Literary Award) 1963, The Minute on the Road 1968, Ikariana 1991, Forget, My River 1996, The Day of the Dames 1991, Come Back to Sorrento... 1995. *Address:* Pod Marjánkou 10, 169 00 Prague 6, Czech Republic.

STICKLAND, Caroline Amanda, BA; British writer; b. 10 Oct. 1955, Rinteln, Germany; m. William Stickland 1974; one d. *Education:* Univ. of East Anglia. *Career:* mem. Soc. of Authors, Mrs Gaskell Soc., Thomas Hardy Soc. *Publications:* The Standing Hills 1986, A House of Clay 1988, The Darkness of Corn 1990, An Ancient Hope 1993, The Darkening Leaf 1995, The Kindly Ones 2000. *Honours:* Betty Trask Award 1985. *Address:* 81 Crock Lane, Bothenhampton, Bridport, Dorset DT6 4DQ, England.

STIGLITZ, Joseph Eugene, PhD, FBA; American economist and academic; *Professor of Economics and Finance, Graduate School of Business, Columbia University*; b. 9 Feb. 1943, Gary, Ind.; s. of Nathaniel D. Stiglitz and Charlotte Fishman; m. 1st 1978; two s. two d.; m. 2nd Anya Schiffrin 2004. *Education:* Amherst Coll., Mass. Inst. of Tech. and Univ. of Cambridge (Fulbright Scholar). *Career:* Prof. of Econs, Cowles Foundation, Yale Univ. 1970–74; Visiting Fellow, St Catherine's Coll. Oxford 1973–74; Prof. of Econs, Stanford Univ. 1974–76, Sr Fellow, Hoover Inst. 1988–2001, Joan Kenney Prof. of Econs 1992–2001; Drummond Prof. of Political Econ., Univ. of Oxford 1976–79; Oskar Morgenstern Distinguished Fellow, Inst. of Advanced Studies, Princeton 1978–79; Prof. of Econs, Princeton Univ. 1979–88; Stern Visiting Prof., Columbia Univ. 2000, Prof. of Econs and Finance, Grad. School of Business 2000, Co-Founder and Pres. Initiative for Policy Dialogue 2000–, Univ. Prof. 2000–, Chair. Cttee on Global Thought 2006–; mem. Pres.'s Council of Econ. Advisers 1993–95, Chair. (mem. of cabinet) 1995–97; Special Adviser to Pres. of World Bank, Sr Vice-Pres. and Chief Economist 1997–2000; Chair. Man. Bd and Dir Grad. Summer Programs, Brooks World Poverty Inst., Univ. of Manchester 2006–; Special Adviser, Bell Communications Research, numerous consultancies in public and pvt. sector, editorial bd memberships etc.; Sr Fellow, Brookings Inst. 2000; Fellow, American Acad. of Arts and Sciences, NAS, Econometric Soc., American Philosophical Soc., Inst. for Policy Research (Sr Fellow 1991–93). *Publications include:* Globalization and its Discontents, Economics of the Public Sector 2000, Principles of Economics 1997, Rethinking the East Asia Miracle (co-ed.) 2001, The Roaring Nineties 2003, Fair Trade for All (co-author), 2005, Making Globalization Work 2006, The Three Trillion Dollar War: The True Cost of the Iraq Conflict (co-author) 2008, Freefall: America, Free Markets and the Sinking of the World Economy 2010; other books and more than 300 papers in learned journals. *Honours:* Hon. DHL (Amherst Coll.) 1974; Dr hc (Univ. of Leuven, Ben Gurion Univ.), (Oxford) 2004; Guggenheim Fellow 1969–70; John Bates Clark Award, American Econ. Asscn 1979, Int. Prize, Accad. dei Lincei, Rome 1988, UAP Scientific Prize, Paris 1989; Nobel Prize for Econs (jt recepient) 2001. *Address:* Uris Hall, Room 814, Columbia University, 3022 Broadway, New York, NY 10027, USA (office). *Telephone:* (212) 854-1481 (office). *Fax:* (212) 662-8474 (office). *E-mail:* jes322@columbia.edu (office). *Website:* www.josephstiglitz.com.

STILES, Martha Bennett (Peggy), BS; American writer; b. 30 March 1933, Manila, Philippines; d. of Forrest Hampton Wells and Jane McClintock Bennett Wells; m. Martin Stiles 1954; one s. *Education:* Univ. of Michigan. *Career:* teacher of creative writing, Univ. of Louisville 1989, Univ. of Kentucky 1989, 1990; mem. Authors Guild, King Library Assocs, Detroit Working Writers, Nature Conservancy, Historic Paris Bourbon County. *Publications:* One Among the Indians 1962, 2007, The Strange House at Newburyport 1963, Darkness Over the Land 1966, Dougal Looks for Birds 1972, James the Vine Puller 1975 (second edn 1992), The Star in the Forest 1979, Tana and the Useless Monkey 1979, Sarah the Dragon Lady 1986, Kate of Still Waters 1990, Lonesome Road 1998, Island Magic 1999, Sailing to Freedom 2011; contrib. to journals and periodicals. *Honours:* James Bryan Hope Award 1951, Avery Hopwood Awards 1956, 1958, Frankfort Arts Foundation Fiction Prizes 1984, 1986, Soc. of Children's Book Writers grant 1988, Al Smith Fellowship, Kentucky Arts Council 1992, 2003, Detroit Women Writers Millennium Contest (Children's Div.) 2000, Detroit Working Writers Creative Journalism Award 2008. *Address:* 3051 Rio Dosa Drive, No. 303, KY 40509, USA (home). *Telephone:* (859) 335-6502 (office). *E-mail:* mbsparis@msn.com (office). *Website:* www.marthabennettstiles.com.

STILES, T. J., MA, MPhil; American biographer and author; b. Foley, Minn.; m. Jessica Stiles 2006; one s. *Education:* Carleton Coll., Columbia Univ., New York. *Career:* fmrly worked for Oxford Univ. Press; mentor, Hertog Research Fellowship, Columbia Univ.'s School of the Arts; first Gilder Lehrman Fellow in American History, Dorothy and Lewis B. Cullman Center for Scholars and Writers, New York Public Library 2004–05. *Publications:* Jesse James: Last Rebel of the Civil War (Ambassador Book Award, Peter Seaborg Award for Civil War Scholarship, New York Times Notable Book) 2002, The First Tycoon: The Epic Life of Cornelius Vanderbilt (Nat. Book Award for Non-Fiction, Pulitzer Prize for Biography 2010) 2009; as editor: The Citizen's Handbook 1994, In Their Own Words (series): Civil War Commanders 1995, Warriors and Pioneers 1996, Robber Barons and Radicals 1997, The Colonizers 1998, Founding Fathers 1999; contrib. articles, book reviews and essays to New York Times Book Review, Wall Street Journal, The Atlantic online, Smithsonian, Salon.com, Washington Post, Los Angeles Times, San Francisco Chronicle, Denver Post and others. *Honours:* Guggenheim Fellowship. *E-mail:* tjstiles@tjstiles.net (home). *Website:* www.tjstiles.com.

STILLINGER, Jack Clifford, BA, MA, PhD; American writer and academic; *Professor Emeritus, University of Illinois*; b. 16 Feb. 1931, Chicago, Ill.; s. of Clifford Benjamin Stillinger and Ruth Hertzler Stillinger; m. 1st Shirley Louise Van Wormer 1952; two s. two d.; m. 2nd Nina Zippin Baym 1971. *Education:* Univ. of Texas, Northwestern Univ., Harvard Univ. *Career:* Asst Prof., Univ. of Illinois 1958–61, Assoc. Prof. 1961–64, Prof. of English 1964–2001, mem. Center for Advanced Study 1970–, Prof. Emer. 2001–; Ed. Journal of English and Germanic Philology 1961–72; mem. Byron Soc., Keats-Shelley Asscn of America, Modern Language Asscn; Fellow, American Acad. of Arts and Sciences. *Publications:* The Early Draft of John Stuart Mill's Autobiography (ed.) 1961, Anthony Munday's Zelauto (ed.) 1963, William Wordsworth: Selected Poems and Prefaces (ed.) 1965, The Letters of Charles Armitage Brown (ed.) 1966, Twentieth Century Interpretations of Keats's Odes (ed.) 1968, John Stuart Mill: Autobiography and Other Writings (ed.) 1969, The Hoodwinking of Madeline 1971, The Texts of Keats's Poems 1974, The Poems of John Keats (ed.) 1978, Mill's Autobiography and Literary Essays (ed.) 1981, John Keats: Complete Poems (ed.) 1982, The Norton Anthology of English Literature (ed.) 1986, John Keats: Poetry Manuscripts at Harvard 1990, Multiple Authorship and the Myth of Solitary Genius 1991, Coleridge and Textual Instability: The Multiple Versions of the Major Poems 1994, Reading The Eve of St Agnes: The Multiples of Complex Literary Transaction 1999, Romantic Complexity: Keats, Coleridge and Wordsworth 2006, Nina and the Balloon (poetry) 2008; contrib. to professional journals. *Honours:* Nat. Woodrow Wilson Fellow 1953–54, Guggenheim Fellowship 1964–65, Distinguished Scholar Award, Keats-Shelley Asscn of America 1986. *Address:* 806 W Indiana Avenue, Urbana, IL 61801, USA (home). *Telephone:* (217) 367-3999 (home). *E-mail:* jstill@illinois.edu (home).

STIMSON, Tess, MA; British writer and journalist; b. 17 July 1966, England; m. 1st Brent Sadler 1993 (divorced 2002); two s.; m. 2nd Erik Oliver; one d. *Education:* St Hilda's Coll., Oxford. *Career:* Producer, ITN 1987–91; Middle East reporter for CNN, BBC, NTV 1997–2000; Prof. of Creative Writing, Univ. of South Florida, USA 2002–04; columnist, Daily Mail 2004–. *Publications:* Yours Till the End (biog.) 1992, Hard News 1993, Soft Focus 1995, Pole Position 1996, The Adultery Club 2007, The Infidelity Chain 2008, The Cradle Snatcher 2009, Beat the Bitch! 2009. *Honours:* Dorothy Whitelock Award 1985, Eleanor Rooke Award 1986. *Literary Agent:* c/o Carole Blake, Blake Friedmann, 122 Arlington Road, London, NW1 7HP, England. *Telephone:* (20) 7284-0408. *E-mail:* carole@blakefriedmann.co.uk. *Website:* www.blakefriedmann.co.uk. *E-mail:* tess@tessstimson.com (office). *Website:* www.tessstimson.com.

STINE, Robert Lawrence (R. L.); American children's writer; b. 1943, Columbus, OH; m. Jane Waldhorn 1969; one s. *Education:* OH State Univ. *Career:* founder and Ed.-in-Chief juvenile magazine, Bananas, writing under pen name Jovial Bob Stine; co-founder, Parachute Press. *Publications:* fiction: Gnasty Gnomes 1981, The Forest of Enchantment: An Advanced Dungeons and Dragons Story 1983, Blind Date 1986, Spaceballs 1987, Twisted 1987, The Babysitter 1989, Phone Calls 1990, Curtains 1990, Off to Sea: A Romance 1991, The Babysitter 2 1991, The Girlfriend 1991, The Snowman 1991, Losers in Space 1991, The Hitchhiker 1992, Hit and Run 1992, Beach House 1992, The First Evil: Cheerleaders 1993, The Dead Girlfriend 1993, Halloween Night 1993, The Time Raider 1994, Call Waiting 1994, I Saw You That Night! 1994, The Beast 1994, The First Horror 1994, The Witness 1995, Superstitious 1995, The Boyfriend 1995, Deadly Experiments of Dr Eeek 1996, Summer Sizzlers 1998, I Am Your Evil Twin 1998, Revenge R Us 1998, Fright Camp 1998, When Good Ghouls Go Bad 2001, Haunted Lighthouse 2003, The Sitter 2003, Eye Candy 2004; fiction series: Fear Street (over 60 titles) 1989–, Goosebumps (over 100 titles, also Give Yourself Goosebumps and Goosebumps 2000 series) 1992–, The Nightmare Room (15 titles) 1998–, Mostly Ghostly (seven titles) 2004–, Rotten School (11 titles) 2005–, Goosebumps HorrorLand 2008–; non-fiction: The Sick of Being Sick Book 1980, Don't Stand in the Soup: The World's Funniest Guide to Manners 1982, Everything You Need to Survive: First Dates (with Jane Stine) 1983, Everything You Need to Survive: Homework (with Jane Stine) 1983, Everything You Need to Survive: Money Problems (with Jane Stine) 1983, Cool Kids' Guide to Summer Camp 1986, 101 Silly Monster Jokes 1986, 101 Vacation Jokes 1990, 101 School Cafeteria Jokes 1990, Postcard Book 1996, It Came from Ohio: My Life as a Writer 1997, 101 Wacky Kid Jokes 1997. *Honours:* Free Public Library of Philadelphia Champion of Reading Award, Nickelodeon Kids' Choice Award, Disney Adventures Kids' Choice Award. *Address:* c/o Parachute Press, 322 Eighth Avenue, #500, New York, NY 10001, USA (office). *Website:* www.rlstine.com.

STIRLING, Jessica (see Rae, Hugh Crauford)

STOCKETT, Kathryn, BA; American writer; b. Jackson, Miss.; d. of Robert Stockett Jr and Ruth Elliott Stockett; m.; one d. *Education:* Univ. of Alabama. *Career:* fmrly worked in magazine publishing and marketing. *Publications:* The Help 2009. *Literary Agent:* Susan Ramer, Don Congdon Associates, 156 Fifth Avenue, Suite 625, New York, NY 10010, USA. *Telephone:* (212) 645-1229. *E-mail:* sramer@doncongdon.com. *Address:* Amy Einhorn Books/ Putnam, Penguin Group, 375 Hudson Street, 4th Floor, New York, NY 10014, USA (office). *E-mail:* stephanie.sorensen@us.penguingroup.com (office). *Website:* www.kathrynstockett.com.

STOCKTON, 2nd Earl of; **Alexander Daniel Alan Macmillan,** FBIM, FRSA; British publisher, farmer and politician; b. 10 Oct. 1943, Oswestry; s. of the late Maurice Victor Macmillan (Viscount Macmillan of Ovenden) and of Dame Katherine Macmillan (Viscountess Macmillan of Ovenden), DBE; grandson of the late 1st Earl of Stockton (fmrly, as Harold Macmillan, Prime Minister of UK 1957–63); m. 1st Hélène Birgitte Hamilton 1970 (divorced 1991); one s. two d.; m. 2nd Miranda Elizabeth Louise Nultall 1995 (divorced 2010). *Education:* Eton Coll. and Paris and Strathclyde Univs. *Career:* Sub-Ed., Glasgow Herald 1963–65; Reporter, Daily Telegraph 1965–67, Foreign Corresp. 1967–68, Chief European Corresp., Sunday Telegraph 1968–70; Dir, Birch Grove Estates Ltd 1969–86, Chair. 1983–89; Dir, Macmillan and Co. Ltd 1970–76, Deputy Chair. 1976–80, Chair. 1984–90, Pres. 1990–; Chair., Macmillan Publrs Ltd 1980–90 (Pres. 1990–), St Martin's Press, New York 1983–88 (Dir 1974–90), Sidgwick and Jackson 1989–90; mem. (Conservative) European Parl. for SW of England 1999–2004, Vice Pres. (Defence), European Parl. Foreign Affairs Cttee 2000–04, mem. Convention on the Future of Europe (Rep. of European Peoples' Party) 2003–04; Chair., Cen. London Training & Enterprise Council 1990–95; Pres., Ludwig von Mises Institut UZW 2005–; Dir, Book Trade Benevolent Soc. 1976–88, Chair., Bookrest Appeal 1978–86; Dir, United British Artists Ltd 1984–90 (Chair. 1985–90); mem. Lindemann Fellowship Cttee 1979– (Chair. 1983–), British Inst. of Man. 1981–, Council of Publrs Asscn 1985–88, Carlton Club Political Cttee 1975–88 (Chair. 1984); Gov., Archbishop Tenison's School 1979–86, Merchant Taylor's School 1980–82, 1990–, English Speaking Union 1980–84, 1986–93; Liveryman, Worshipful Co. of Merchant Taylors 1972, Court Asst 1987, Master 1991–92; Liveryman, Worshipful Co. of Stationers 1973, Court Asst 1989. *Honours:* Hon. DLitt (De Montfort) 1993, (Westminster) 1995; Hon. DUniv

(Strathclyde) 1993; Schumann Medal 2004. *Address:* Flat M, 9 Warwick Square, London, SW1V 2AA, England (home). *Telephone:* (20) 7834-6004 (home). *E-mail:* thepriory@dbac.co.uk (home).

STOKER, Richard, FRAM, ARAM, ARCM; British composer, actor, conductor, writer and poet and painter; b. 8 Nov. 1938, Castleford, Yorks., England; s. of the late Bower Morrell Stoker and Winifred Stoker; m. Gillian Patricia Watson 1986. *Education:* Breadalbane House School, Castleford, Univ. of Huddersfield with Harold Truscott, Coll. of Art, Royal Acad. of Music and Drama, composition with Sir Lennox Berkeley, conducting with Maurice Miles, pvt. study with Nadia Boulanger in Paris (Mendelssohn Scholarship), Arthur Benjamin, Eric Fenby, Benjamin Britten. *Career:* performance debut with BBC Home Service 1953, Nat. and Int. Eisteddfods, Wales 1955–58; conducting debut 1956; Asst Librarian, London Symphony Orchestra 1962–63; Prof. of Composition, RAM 1963–87 (tutor 1970–80); composition teacher, St Paul's School 1972–74, Magdalene Coll., Cambridge 1974–76; Ed. The Composer magazine 1969–80; apptd Magistrate, Inner London Comm. 1995–2003, Crown Court 1998–2003; Adjudicator, Royal Philharmonic Soc. Composer's Award, Cyprus Orchestral Composer's Award for the Ministry of Culture 2001–, BBC Composers' Awards; mem. Composers' Guild 1962– (mem. exec. cttee 1969–80); Founder mem. RAM Guild Cttee 1994– (Hon. Treas. 1995–); Founder mem. European-Atlantic Group 1993–; mem. Byron Soc. 1993–2000, Magistrates' Asscn 1995–2003, English and Int. PEN 1996–2005; mem. and Treas. Steering Cttee Lewisham Arts Festival 1990, 1992; Founder mem. Atlantic Council 1993, RSL, Creative Rights Alliance 2001–; concert appearances as pianist including Queen Elizabeth Hall, Purcell Room, Leighton House, RAM, Pizza on the Park, Barnet Festival; mem. RAM Guild. *Art:* exhbns, various works in pvt. collections including Trinity Coll. of Music. *Compositions include:* four symphonies 1961, 1976, 1981, 1991; 12 nocturnes; two jazz preludes; overtures: Antic Hay, Feast of Fools, Heroic Overture; three string quartets, three violin sonatas, Partita for Violin and Harp or Piano, Sonatina for Guitar, two piano sonatas, three piano trios, A York Suite for piano, Piano Variations, Piano Concerto, Partita for Clarinet and Piano, Wind Quintet; organ works: Partita, Little Organ Book, Three Improvisations, Symphony; Monologue, Passacagalia, Serenade, Petite Suite, Nocturnal, Festival Suite; choral works and song cycles: Benedictus, Ecce Homo, Proverb, Psalms, Make Me a Willow Cabin, Canticle of the Rose, O Be Joyful, A Landscape of Truth; piano works: Zodiac Variations, Regency Suite, A Poet's Notebook; vocal works: Music That Brings Sweet Sleep, Aspects of Flight, Four Yeats Songs, Four Shakespeare Songs, Johnson Preserv'd (three-act opera), Thérèse Raquin (in preparation), Chinese Canticle, Birthday of the Infanta; music for film and stage includes Troilus and Cressida, Portrait of a Town, Garden Party, My Friend – My Enemy. *Recordings:* appearances on numerous CDs and records. *Films:* appearances include Red Mercury Rising, Woken, Daddy's Girl, Portrait of a Town, Lear and Goneril, The Shrink, Bedtime Story, The Usual, The End of the Line, The Queen, The Da Vinci Code, Ancient Cataclysms, Vagabond Shoes, Encounter, Bouquet, Interval, Home Guard Ron, Pirates of the Caribbean IV. *Television:* Mary Tudor (four-part series), Comment (Channel 4), Europe, Dirty Weekend in Hospital, Happiness (BBC), Troilus and Cressida. *Radio:* interviews and discussions on BBC Radio Three, Four, World Service, Radio Leeds, New York Times Radio, Radio New York, Wall Street Radio, Radio Algonquin. *Publications:* Portrait of a Town 1970, Words Without Music 1974, Strolling Players 1978, Open Window – Open Door (autobiog.) 1985, Tanglewood (novel) 1990, Between the Lines 1991, Diva (novel) 1992, Collected Short Stories 1993, Sir Thomas Armstrong: A Celebration 1998, Turn Back the Clock 1998, A Passage of Time 1999; contrib. to anthologies, including Triumph, Forward, Outposts, Spotlight, Strolling Players, American Poetry Soc. publs, reviews and articles for periodicals, including Records and Recording, Books and Bookmen, Guardian, Performance, The Magistrate, poems in numerous anthologies and internet publs; contrib. to Oxford Dictionary of Nat. Biography (nine entries) 2004, 2006 (adviser 2003–). *Honours:* BBC Music Award 1952, Eric Coates Award 1962, Dove Prize 1962, Nat. Library of Poetry (USA) Editors' Choice Award 1995, 1996, 1997. *Telephone:* 7906-843812 (mobile). *E-mail:* r_stoker@btinternet.com (home). *Website:* www.richardstoker.co.uk.

STOLTE, Dieter; German television executive, newspaper publisher and academic; b. 18 Sept. 1934, Cologne. *Education:* Univs of Tübingen and Mainz. *Career:* Head of Science Dept, Saarländischer Rundfunk 1961–62; Personal adviser to Dir-Gen. of Zweites Deutsches Fernsehen (ZDF) 1962, Controller, Programme Planning Dept 1967, Programming Dir 1976–82, Dir-Gen. ZDF March 1982–2002; publisher Die Welt and Berliner Morgenpost (newspapers) 2002–05; Dir and Deputy Dir Gen., Südwestfunk 1973; Prof. Univ. of Music and Presentation Arts, Hamburg 1980–; mem. Admin. Council, German Press Agency (dpa), Hamburg, European Broadcasting Union (EBU); Chair. Admin. Council TransTel, Cologne; Chair. Bd Dirs DeutschlandRadio, Cologne; mem. Int. Broadcast Inst., London; mem. Council, Nat. Acad. of TV Arts, New York, Int. Acad. of Arts and Sciences, New York. *Publications:* ed. and co-author of several books on programme concepts and function of television, etc.; several essays on subjects relating to the philosophy of culture and the science of communication. *Honours:* Int. Emmy Directorate Award 1997; Bundesverdienstkreuz, Officer's Cross, Golden Order of Merit (Austria), Bavarian Order of Merit, Hon. Citizen of State of Tenn., USA; Köckritz Prize 1999, Verdienstorden, Berlin 1999, Robert Geissendorfer Prize 2001. *Address:* c/o Axel Springer Verlag AG, Axel-Springer-Platz 1, 20350 Hamburg, Germany.

STOLTZFUS, Ben, BA, MA, PhD; American novelist, translator and academic; *Professor Emeritus, University of California, Riverside*; b. 15 Sept. 1927, Sofia, Bulgaria; m. 1st Elizabeth Burton 1955 (divorced 1975); two s. one d.; m. 2nd Judith Palmer 1975. *Education:* Amherst Coll., Middlebury Coll., Univ. of Paris, Univ. of Wisconsin. *Career:* instructor in French, Smith Coll. 1958–60; Asst Prof., Univ. of California, Riverside 1960–65, Assoc. Prof. 1965–66, Prof. of French, Comparative Literature and Creative Writing 1967–93, Prof. Emer. 1993–; mem. MLA of America, ACLA, ALA, Hemingway Soc., Camus Soc., D. H. Lawrence Soc., Poets and Writers, AATF, ICLA. *Publications include:* fiction: The Eye of the Needle 1967, Black Lazarus 1972, Red, White, and Blue 1989, Valley of Roses 2003; non-fiction: Alain Robbe-Grillet and the New French Novel 1964, Georges Chenneviere et l'unanimisme 1965, Gide's Eagles (MLA Award) 1969, Gide and Hemingway: Rebels Against God 1978, Alain Robbe-Grillet: The Body of the Text 1985, Alain Robbe-Grillet: Life, Work, and Criticism 1987, Postmodern Poetics: Nouveau Roman and Innovative Fiction 1987, La Belle Captive 1995, Lacan and Literature: Purloined Pretexts (NAAP Gradiva Award 1997) 1996, The Target: Alain Robbe-Grillet and Jasper Johns 2006, Hemingway and French Writers 2010; contrib. to numerous journals, quarterlies, reviews and magazines. *Honours:* Dr hc (Amherst Coll.) 1974; Fulbright Scholarships 1955–56, 1963–64, Camargo Foundation grants 1983, 1985, Distinguished Emeritus Award 2006. *Address:* c/o Department of Comparative Literature and Foreign Languages, University of California, Riverside, CA 92521, USA (office).

STONE, Joan Elizabeth, BA, MA, PhD; American academic, poet and writer; b. 22 Oct. 1930, Port Angeles, Wash.; m. James A Black 1990; four s., one d. *Education:* University of Washington. *Career:* Visiting Prof. of Poetry, University of Montana 1974; Dir, Creative Writing Workshop, University of Washington 1975; Asst Prof. of English, Colorado College 1977–. *Publications include:* The Swimmer and Other Poems 1975, Alba 1976, A Letter to Myself to Water 1981, Our Lady of the Harbor 1986; contributions: journals and magazines. *Honours:* Acad. of American Poets Award 1969, 1970, 1972, Borestone Mountain Award 1974.

STONE, Laurie, BA, MA; American writer, columnist and critic; b. 18 Oct. 1946, New York, NY. *Education:* Barnard College, Columbia College. *Career:* Instructor, Hunter and Queens Colls, CUNY 1969–75; writer, Village Voice 1975–99, columnist 1987–96; Critic-at-Large, Fresh Air, National Public Radio 1987–90; teacher in the MFA in Creative Writing programme, Fairleigh Dickinson Univ.; mem. International PEN, National Book Critics Circle, Poets and Writers. *Publications:* Starting with Serge (novel) 1990, Laughing in the Dark: A Decade of Subversive Comedy 1997, Close to the Bone: Memoirs of Hurt, Rage, and Desire 1998; contributions: periodicals, radio and television. *Honours:* Kittredge Fund grant 1984, MacDowell Colony Residencies 1984, 1989, 1990, 1991, Virginia Center for the Arts Residency 1990–91, New York Foundation for the Arts Grant 1993, Nona Balakian Prize, Excellence in Reviewing, National Book Critics Circle 1996.

STONE, Matthew (Matt) Richard; American screenwriter, film director and producer; b. 26 May 1971, Houston, Tex.; s. of the late Gerald Whitney Stone, Jr and of Sheila Lois Belasco; m. Angela Howard; one s. *Career:* collaborated with Trey Parker on short animation, Jesus vs Frosty 1992, later remade as animated Christmas card for FoxLab, titled The Spirit of Christmas 1995; Co-creator and Exec. Producer, South Park animation (with Trey Parker) 1997–, and other films and TV series. *Films include:* Jesus vs Frosty (writer, dir) 1992, Your Studio and You (writer) 1995, The Spirit of Christmas (writer, dir) 1995, Alferd Packer: The Musical (aka Cannibal! The Musical) (writer, producer) 1996, Orgazmo (writer, dir, producer) 1997, South Park: Bigger Longer & Uncut (writer, producer) (Los Angeles Film Critics Award, New York Film Critics Award, MTV Movie Award) 1999, How's Your News? (exec. producer) 1999, Team America: World Police (writer, producer) 2004. *Television includes:* South Park (series writer, dir, producer) 1997–, That's My Bush! (series writer, producer) 2001, Kenny vs. Spenny (producer) 2007. *Film appearances include:* BASEketball 1998, provides voices for many characters in his animation films and television series. *Recordings include:* albums: Chef Aid: The South Park Album, South Park: Bigger, Longer and Uncut (soundtrack), Mr Hankey's Christmas Classics, Timmy and the Lords of the Underworld, The Book of Mormon (Grammy Award for Best Musical Theater Album 2012) 2011. *Play:* The Book of Mormon (Tony Award for Best Musical 2011) 2011. *Address:* c/o Paramount Studios, 5555 Melrose Avenue, Hollywood, CA 90038, USA. *E-mail:* news@southparkstudios.com. *Website:* www.southparkstudios.com.

STONE, Robert Anthony; American writer; b. 21 Aug. 1937, New York, NY; m. Janice G. Burr 1959; one s. one d. *Education:* New York Univ. *Career:* Editorial Asst, New York Daily News 1958–60; writer, National Mirror, New York 1965–67; writer-in-residence, Princeton Univ. 1971–72; faculty mem., Amherst Coll. 1972–75, 1977–78, Stanford Univ. 1979, Univ. of Hawaii at Manoa 1979–80, Harvard Univ. 1981, Univ. of California at Irvine 1982, New York Univ. 1983, Univ. of California at San Diego 1985, Princeton Univ. 1985, Johns Hopkins Univ. 1993–94, Yale Univ. 1994–; Stegner Fellow Stanford Univ. 1962; mem. PEN. *Publications:* A Hall of Mirrors 1967, Dog Soldiers 1974, A Flag for Sunrise 1981, Images of War 1986, Children of Light 1986, Outerbridge Reach 1992, Bear and his Daughter: Stories 1997, Damascus Gate 1998, Bay of Souls 2003, Prime Green: Remembering the Sixties 2007, Fun with Problems 2010; contrib. to anthologies and periodicals. *Honours:* William Faulkner Prize 1967, Guggenheim Fellowship 1971, Nat. Book Award 1975, John Dos Passos Prize 1982, American Acad. of Arts and Letters Award

1982, and grant 1988–92, Nat. Endowment for the Humanities Fellow 1983. *Address:* c/o Houghton Mifflin Company, Trade Division, Adult Editorial, Eighth Floor, 222 Berkeley Street, Boston, MA 02116-3764, USA (office). *Website:* www.houghtonmifflinbooks.com (office).

STOPPARD, Sir Tom, Kt, OM, CBE, FRSL; British writer; b. (Thomas Straussler), 3 July 1937, Zlin, Czechoslovakia; s. of the late Dr Eugene Straussler and Martha Straussler; step-s. of Kenneth Stoppard; m. 1st Jose Ingle 1965 (divorced 1972); two s.; m. 2nd Dr Miriam Moore-Robinson 1972 (divorced 1992); two s. *Education:* Pocklington Grammar School, Yorks. *Career:* Journalist, Bristol 1954–60; freelance journalist, London 1960–64; mem. Cttee of the Free World 1981–; mem. Royal Nat. Theatre Bd 1989–. *Publications:* plays: Rosencrantz and Guildenstern are Dead 1967, The Real Inspector Hound 1968, Enter a Free Man 1968, After Magritte 1970, Dogg's Our Pet 1972, Jumpers 1972, Travesties 1975, Dirty Linen 1976, New-Found-Land 1976, Every Good Boy Deserves Favour (with music by André Previn, 1978, Night and Day 1978, Dogg's Hamlet, Cahoots Macbeth 1979, Undiscovered Country 1980, On the Razzle 1981, The Real Thing 1982, Rough Crossing 1984, Dalliance (adaption of Schnitzler's Liebelei) 1986, Hapgood 1988, Arcadia 1993 (Evening Standard Award for Best Play), Indian Ink 1995, The Invention of Love 1997, The Seagull (trans. 1997), The Coast of Utopia (trilogy: Part One: Voyage, Part Two: Shipwreck, Part Three: Salvage) (Tony Award for Best Play 2007) 2002, Rock 'N' Roll (London Critics' Circle Award for Best New Play 2006) 2006; radio plays: The Dissolution of Dominic Boot 1964, M is for Moon Among Other Things 1964, Albert's Bridge 1967, If You're Glad I'll be Frank 1968, Where Are They Now? 1970, Artist Descending a Staircase 1972, The Dog It Was That Died 1983, In the Native State 1991; short stories: Introduction 2 1963; novel: Lord Malquist and Mr Moon 1966; screenplays: The Romantic Englishwoman (co-author) 1975, Despair 1977; film scripts: The Human Factor 1979, Brazil (with Terry Gilliam, and Charles McKeown) 1984, Crown 1987, Empire of the Sun 1987, Rosencrantz and Guildenstern are Dead 1989 (also dir), Russia House 1989, Billy Bathgate 1990, Shakespeare in Love (jtly) 1998 (jt winner Acad. Award Best Original Screenplay 1999), Enigma 2001; television plays: Professional Foul 1977, Squaring the Circle 1984, The Television Plays 1965–84 1993; radio: The Plays for Radio 1964–91, 1994. *Honours:* Hon. MLitt (Bristol, Brunel Univs.); Hon. LittD (Leeds Univ.) 1979, (Sussex) 1980, (Warwick) 1981, (London) 1982; Dr hc (Kenyon Coll.) 1984, (York) 1984; John Whiting Award, Arts Council 1967, Italia Prize (radio drama) 1968, New York Drama Critics Best Play Award 1968, Antoinette Perry Awards (Tony Awards) 1968, 1976, 2007, Evening Standard Awards 1967, 1972, 1974, 1978, 1982, 1993, 1997, 2006, Sony Award 1991, Olivier Award 1993, Dan David Prize 2008, Sunday Times Award for Literary Excellence 2008, Praemium Imperiale 2009. *Literary Agent:* United Agents Ltd, 12–26 Lexington Street, London, W1F 0LE, England. *Telephone:* (20) 3214-0800. *Fax:* (20) 3214-0801. *E-mail:* info@unitedagents.co.uk. *Website:* www.unitedagents.co.uk.

STOREY, David Malcolm; British author and playwright; b. 13 July 1933, Wakefield, Yorkshire; s. of Frank Richmond Storey and Lily Storey (née Cartwright); m. Barbara Hamilton 1956; two s. two d. *Education:* Queen Elizabeth Grammar School, Wakefield, Wakefield Coll. of Art and Slade School of Art. *Career:* Fellow, Univ. Coll. London 1974. *Publications include:* novels: This Sporting Life (Macmillan Award) 1960, Flight into Camden (John Llewellyn Rhys Memorial Prize 1961, Somerset Maugham Award 1963) 1960, Radcliffe 1963, Pasmore (Faber Memorial Prize 1972) 1972, A Temporary Life 1973, Edward 1973, Saville (Booker Prize 1976) 1976, A Prodigal Child 1982, Present Times 1984, A Serious Man 1998, As It Happened 2002, Thin-Ice Skater 2004; plays: The Restoration of Arnold Middleton (Evening Standard Award 1967), In Celebration 1969 (also film), The Contractor (New York Critics' Prize 1974) 1969, Home (Evening Standard Award, New York Critics' Prize) 1970, The Changing Room (New York Critics' Prize) 1971, Cromwell 1973, The Farm 1973, Life Class 1974, Night 1976, Mother's Day 1976, Sisters 1978, Dreams of Leaving 1979, Early Days 1980, The March on Russia 1989, Stages 1992; poems: Storey's Lives: Poems 1951–1991 1992. *Honours:* Los Angeles Drama Critics Award 1969, Writer of the Year Award, Variety Club of GB 1969. *Literary Agent:* c/o A.M. Heath and Co. Ltd, 6 Warwick Court, Holborn, London, WC1R 5DJ, England.

STORM, Christopher (see Olsen, Theodore Victor)

STOTHARD, Sir Peter M., Kt, MA; British journalist and newspaper editor; *Editor, The Times Literary Supplement*; b. 28 Feb. 1951, Chelmsford, Essex; s. of Wilfred Stothard and Patricia Savage; m. Sally Ceris Emerson 1980; one s. one d. *Education:* Brentwood School, Essex and Trinity Coll. Oxford. *Career:* journalist, BBC 1974–77; Shell Petroleum 1977–79; business and political writer, Sunday Times 1979–80; Features Ed. and leader writer, The Times 1980–85; Deputy Ed. The Times 1985–92, US Ed. 1989–92, Ed. 1992–2002; Ed. The Times Literary Supplement 2002–; Chair. of judging panel for Man Booker Prize 2012; Pres. Classical Asscn –2012. *Publications:* Thirty Days: A Month at the Heart of Blair's War 2003, On the Spartacus Road: A Spectacular Journey through Ancient Italy 2010. *Honours:* Hon. Fellow, Trinity Coll. Oxford 2000–. *Address:* The Times Literary Supplement, Times House, 1 Pennington Street, London, E98 1BS, England (office). *Telephone:* (20) 7782-5000 (office). *E-mail:* editor@the-tls.co.uk (office). *Website:* www.the-tls.co.uk (office).

STOUT, Robert Joe, BA; American/Mexican writer and poet; b. 3 Feb. 1938, Scottsbluff, Neb.; s. of Charles V. Stout and Eunice Diller; divorced; two s. three d. *Education:* Mexico City Coll. *Publications:* Miss Sally 1973, The Trick 1974, Swallowing Dust 1974, Moving Out 1974, The Way to Pinal 1979, They Still Play Baseball the Old Way 1994, The Blood of the Serpent: Mexican Lives 2003, Why Immigrants come to America 2008; contrib. to The American Scholar, The Retired Officer Magazine, Notre Dame Magazine, The Beloit Poetry Journal, The South Dakota Review, America, Global Politics, International Socialist Review, New Politics. *Honours:* Gold Key as Outstanding Grad., Mexico City Coll. *Address:* Apartado Postal 361, Oaxaca, CP 68001, Mexico. *E-mail:* mexicoconamor@yahoo.com.

STRACHAN, Hew Francis Anthony, MA, PhD, FRSE; British academic and writer; *Chichele Professor of the History of War, University of Oxford*; b. 1 Sept. 1949, Edinburgh, Scotland; m. 1st Catherine Margaret Blackburn 1971 (divorced 1980); two d.; m. 2nd Pamela Dorothy Tennant 1982; one s. one step-s. one step-d. *Education:* Corpus Christi Coll., Cambridge. *Career:* Research Fellow 1975–78, Fellow 1979–, Dean of Coll. 1981–86, Admissions Tutor 1981–88, Sr Tutor 1989–92, Corpus Christi Coll., Cambridge; Sr Lecturer in War Studies, Royal Military Acad., Sandhurst 1978–79; Prof. of Modern History 1992–2001, Dir Scottish Centre for War Studies 1996–2001, Univ. of Glasgow; Lees Knowles Lecturer, Cambridge 1995; Visiting Prof., Royal Norwegian Air Force Acad. 2000–; Chichele Prof. of the History of War, Univ. of Oxford 2002–; Howard Kippenberger Visiting Prof. in Strategic Studies, Victoria Univ., Wellington, New Zealand 2009; Humanitas Visiting Prof. in War Studies, Univ. of Cambridge 2011; Fellow, All Souls Coll. Oxford; Life Fellow, Corpus Christi Coll. Cambridge 1992; DL, Tweeddale 2006. *Television:* The First World War (series, Channel 4) 2003. *Publications:* British Military Uniforms, 1768–1796 1975, History of Cambridge University Officers' Training Corps 1976, European Armies and the Conduct of War 1983, Wellington's Legacy: The Reform of the British Army 1984, From Waterloo to Balaclava: Tactics, Technology and the British Army, 1815–1854 1985, The Politics of the British Army 1997, The Oxford Illustrated History of the First World War (ed.) 1998, The British Army, Manpower and Society (ed.) 2000, The First World War, Vol. 1 To Arms 2001, Military Lives 2002, The First World War: An Illustrated History 2003, The Outbreak of War 2004, Financing the War 2004, The War in Africa 2004, Big Wars and Small Wars (ed.) 2005, Carl von Clausewitz's On War: A Biography 2007, Clausewitz in the 21st Century (ed.) 2007, The Changing Character of War (ed.) 2011; contrib. to learned books and journals. *Honours:* Hon. DUniv (Univ. of Paisley) 2005; Templer Medal 1985, Westminster Medal 1997. *Literary Agent:* David Higham Associates Ltd, 5–8 Lower John Street, Golden Square, London, W1F 9HA, England. *Telephone:* (20) 7434-5900. *Fax:* (20) 7437-1072. *E-mail:* dha@davidhigham.co.uk. *Website:* www.davidhigham.co.uk. *Address:* All Souls College, Oxford, OX1 4AL, England (office). *Telephone:* (1865) 279371 (office). *Fax:* (1865) 279299 (office). *E-mail:* hew.strachan@all-souls.ox.ac.uk (office).

STRAIGHT, Steve; American writer and lecturer; *Professor of English and Director, Poetry Program, Manchester Community College*; m. Marian Maccarone; two d. *Career:* fmr Dir of Seminar Series, Sunken Garden Poetry Festival; Prof. of English and Dir of the Poetry Program, Manchester Community Coll.; Dir, Connecticut Poetry Circuit. *Publications:* The Water Carrier (poems) 2002, In a Different Light (novel) 2005. *Address:* Faculty of Liberal Arts, Manchester Community College, Great Path, MS 19, PO Box 1046, Manchester, CT 06045-1046, USA (office). *Telephone:* (860) 512-2688 (office). *Fax:* (860) 512-3201 (office). *E-mail:* sstraight@mcc.commnet.edu (office). *Website:* www.mcc.commnet.edu (office).

STRAND, Mark, AB, BFA, MA; American poet, writer and academic; *Professor of English and Comparative Literature, Columbia University*; b. 11 April 1934, Summerside, PEI, Canada; m. 1st Antonia Ratensky 1961 (divorced 1973); one d.; m. 2nd Julia Rumsey Garretson 1976 (divorced 1998); one s. *Education:* Antioch Coll., Yale Univ., Univ. of Iowa. *Career:* instructor, Univ. of Iowa 1962–65; Fulbright Lecturer, Univ. of Brazil 1965; Asst Prof., Mount Holyoke Coll. 1966; Visiting Prof., Univ. of Washington 1967, Univ. of Virginia 1977, California State Univ. at Fresno 1977, Univ. of California, Irvine 1978, Wesleyan Univ. 1979–80; Adjunct Prof., Columbia Univ. 1968–70, Prof. of English and Comparative Literature 2005–; Visiting Lecturer, Yale Univ. 1969–70, Harvard Univ. 1980–81; Assoc. Prof., Brooklyn Coll., CUNY 1971; Bain Swiggett Lecturer, Princeton Univ. 1972; Fanny Hurst Prof. of Poetry, Brandeis Univ. 1973; Prof., Univ. of Utah 1981–86, Distinguished Prof. 1986–94; Poet Laureate of the USA 1990–91; Elliot Coleman Prof. of Poetry, Johns Hopkins Univ. 1994–97; fmr Andrew MacLeish Distinguished Service Prof., Univ. of Chicago; Writer-in-Residence, American Acad., Rome 1982; mem. American Acad. and Inst. of Arts and Letters 1980–, Nat. Acad. of Arts and Sciences 1995–. *Publications:* poetry: Sleeping With One Eye Open 1964, Reasons for Moving 1968, Darker 1970, Halty Ferguson: 18 Poems from the Quechua (trans.) 1971, Rafael Alberti: The Owl's Insomnia (trans.) 1973, The Sargentville Notebook 1973, The Story of Our Lives 1973, Carlos Drummond de Andrade: Souvenir of the Ancient World (trans.) 1976, Another Republic: 17 European and South American Writers (co-ed. with Charles Simic) 1976, The Late Hour 1978, Selected Poems 1980, Travelling in the Family: The Selected Poems of Carlos Drummond de Andrade (trans.) 1986, The Continuous Life 1990, The Best American Poetry (ed.) 1991, Dark Harbor 1993, The Golden Ecco Anthology (ed.) 1994, Blizzard of One (Pulitzer Prize in Poetry 1999) 1998, Man and Camel 2006, New Selected Poems 2007, Almost Invisible 2012; prose: The Monument 1978, The Planet of Lost Things (juvenile) 1982, The Art of the Real 1983, Mr and Mrs Baby (short stories) 1985, The Night Book (juvenile) 1985, Rembrandt Takes a Walk (juvenile) 1986, William Bailey

1987, Hopper 1994; contrib. of poems, book reviews, art reviews, essays on poetry and painting, and interviews in numerous periodicals; contribs to numerous anthologies. *Honours:* Fulbright Scholarship to Italy 1960–61, Ingram Merrill Foundation Fellowship 1966, Nat. Endowment for the Arts grants 1967–68, 1977–78, Rockefeller Fellowship 1968–69; Edgar Allan Poe Prize 1974, Guggenheim Fellowship 1974–75, Nat. Inst. of Arts and Letters Award 1975, Acad. of American Poets Fellowship 1979, John D. and Catherine T. MacArthur Foundation Fellowship 1987–92, Utah Gov.'s Award in the Arts 1992, Bobbitt Nat. Prize for Poetry 1992, Bollingen Prize for Poetry 1993, Bingham Prize for Poetry 1998, Pulitzer Prize 1999, Wallace Stevens Prize, Acad. of American Poets 2004, Gold Medal for Poetry, American Acad. for Arts and Letters 2009. *Address:* 602 Philosophy Hall, Department of English and Comparative Literature, Columbia University, New York, NY 10027 (office); 2700 Broadway (8B), New York, NY 10025, USA (home). *Telephone:* (212) 854-7468 (office); (646) 478-8704 (home). *E-mail:* ms3091@columbia.edu (office). *Website:* www.columbia.edu/cu/english (office).

STRATTON, Thomas (see De Weese, Thomas Eugene (Gene))

STRAUB, Peter Francis, BA, MA; American writer; b. 2 March 1943, Milwaukee, Wis.; s. of Gordon Straub and Elvena Nilsestuen; m. 1966; one s. one d. *Education:* Univ. of Wisconsin, Columbia Univ. *Television:* two appearances as ret. det. Pete Braust on One Life To Live 2006, a third 2008, a fourth 2011. *Publications:* Open Air (poems) 1972, Marriage 1973, Julia 1975, If You Could See Me Now 1977, Ghost Story 1979, Shadowland 1980, Floating Dragon 1983, The Talisman (with Stephen King) 1984, Koko 1988, Mystery 1989, Houses Without Doors 1990, The Throat 1993, The Hellfire Club 1996, Mr X 1999, Magic Terror 2000, Black House (with Stephen King) 2001, Conjunctions 39: The New Fabulists (ed.) 2002, Lost Boy Lost Girl 2003, In the Night Room 2004, Tales of H. P. Lovecraft (ed.) 2005, A Dark Matter 2010, The Juniper Tree and Other Blue Rose Stories 2010; contrib. to TLS, New Statesman, Washington Post. *Honours:* British Fantasy Award 1983, August Derleth Award 1983, World Fantasy Best Novel Awards 1988, 1993, Bram Stoker Awards for Best Novel 1993, 1998, 2000, 2003, 2004, 2005, named Grand Master by Horror Writers Asscn (HWA) 1998, HWA Life Achievement Award 2005, Living Legend Award, Int. Horror Guild, World Fantasy Award for Best Anthology 2010, WFC Life Achievement Award 2010. *Literary Agent:* c/o The Gernert Co., 136 East 57th Street, New York, NY 10022, USA. *Telephone:* (212) 838-7777. *Address:* 53 West 85th Street, New York, NY 10024, USA (office). *Telephone:* (212) 362-4142. *E-mail:* pstraub@nyc.rr.com (office). *Website:* www.peterstraub.net.

STRAUSS, Botho; German playwright and novelist; b. 2 Dec. 1944, Naumburg. *Education:* Cologne and Munich. *Career:* moved with family to Remscheid, Ruhr region; on staff of Theater heute, West Berlin; Dramaturg at Schaubühne Theater, West Berlin 1970–75; mem. PEN. *Plays include:* Die Hypochonder (first play, 1971, winner Hannover Dramaturgie Award), Trilogie des Wiedersehens 1976, Gross und Klein 1978, Kalldeway Farce 1981, Der Park 1983, Das Gleichgewicht 1994, Theaterstücke in zwei Banden 1994. *Publications:* Bekannte Gesichter, gemischte Gefühle (jtly) 1974, Die Widmung (novel) 1979, Rumor (novel) 1980, Paare, Passanten (novel) 1981, Der Junge Mann (novel) 1984, Diese Erinnerung an einen, der nur einen Tag zu Gast War 1985, Die Fremdenführerin 1986, Niemand Anderes (novel) 1987, Besucher 1988, Kongress: Die Kette der Demütigungen 1989, Beginnlosigkeit. Reflexionen 1992, Anschwellender 1993, Wohnen Dammern Lügen 1994, Die Fehler des Kopisten 1997, Das Partikular 2000, Der Narr und seine Frau heute abend in Pancomedia 2001, Die Nacht mit Alice, als Julia ums Haus schlich 2003, Der Untenstehende auf Zehenspitzen 2004, Mikado 2006. *Honours:* Schiller Prize Baden-Württemberg 1977, Literaturpreis, Bayerische Akademie der Schönen Künste 1981, Mülheimer Drama Prize 1982, Jean Paul Prize 1987, Georg Büchner Prize 1989. *Literary Agent:* Rowohlt Verlage, Hamburgerstrasse 17, London 21465 Reinbek, Germany. *Telephone:* (40) 72720. *Fax:* (40) 7272319. *E-mail:* info@rowohlt.de. *Website:* www.rowohlt-theaterverlag.de.

STRAUSS, Jennifer, BA, PhD; Australian academic and poet; b. 30 Jan. 1933, Heywood, Vic.; m. Werner Strauss 1958; three s. *Education:* Univ. of Melbourne, Univ. of Glasgow, Monash Univ. *Career:* Sr Lecturer 1971–92, Assoc. Prof. 1992–, Monash Univ.; mem. Premier's Literary Awards Cttee, PEN, Asscn for Study of Australian Literature, Australian Soc. of Authors. *Publications:* Children and Other Strangers 1975, Winter Driving 1981, Middle English Verse: An Anthology (co-ed.) 1985, Labour Ward 1988, Boundary Conditions: The Poetry of Gwen Harwood 1992, The Oxford Book of Australian Love Poems (ed.) 1993, Judith Wright 1995, Tierra del Fuego: New and Selected Poems 1997, Family Ties: Australian Poems of the Family (ed.) 1998, Oxford Literary History of Australia (co-ed.) 1998, Collected Verse of Mary Gilmore Vol. I 1887–1929 (ed.) 2005; contrib. to various publications. *Honours:* Hon. Sr Research Fellow, Monash Univ. 1998. *Address:* 2–12 Tollington Avenue, East Malvern, Vic. 3145, Australia (home). *Fax:* (3) 9885-8132 (office).

STRAWSON, Galen John, BA, BPhil, MA, DPhil; British philosopher and literary critic; *Professor of Philosophy, University of Reading*; b. 5 Feb. 1952, Oxford, England; s. of Peter Frederick Strawson and Grace Hall (Ann) Martin; m. 1st Jose Said 1974 (divorced 1994); one s. two d.; m. 2nd Anna Vaux 1997 (divorced 2003); two s.; m. 3rd Michelle Montague 2006. *Education:* Univ. of Cambridge, Univ. of Oxford, Ecole normale supérieure, Paris. *Career:* Asst Ed. Times Literary Supplement, London 1978–87, Consultant 1987–; Fellow, Jesus Col Oxford 1987–2000; Prof. of Philosophy, Univ. of Reading 2001–; Visiting Fellow, ANU 1993; Visiting Prof., New York Univ. 1997, Rutgers Univ. 2000; Distinguished Prof. of Philosophy, City of New York Grad. Center 2004–07; mem. Mind Asscn; Trustee, Kennedy Memorial Trust 1998–2003. *Publications:* Freedom and Belief 1986, The Secret Connexion 1989, Mental Reality 1994 (new edn 2009), The Self? (ed.) 2005, Consciousness and its Place in Nature 2006, Real Materialism and other essays 2008, Selves: An Essay in Revisionary Metaphysics 2009; contrib. to TLS, Sunday Times, Observer, Financial Times, Guardian, New York Times Book Review, The Believer, London Review of Books, Independent on Sunday, Mind, American Philosophical Quarterly, Inquiry, Journal of Consciousness Studies, Analysis, Philosophical Studies, Philosophical Topics, Ratio, Philosophical Issues, Philosophy and Phenomenological Research, many books of essays. *Honours:* R. A. Nicholson Prize for Islamic Studies, Cambridge 1971, T. H. Green Prize for Moral Philosophy, Oxford 1983. *Address:* Department of Philosophy, University of Reading, Reading, RG6 6AA, England (office). *Telephone:* (118) 378-8325 (office).

STREET, Pamela; British writer; b. 3 March 1921, Wilton, Wiltshire; m. (divorced); one d. *Education:* Salisbury and South Wiltshire College of Further Education. *Publications:* My Father, A. G. Street 1969, Portrait of Wiltshire 1971, Arthur Bryant: Portrait of a Historian 1979, Light of Evening 1981, The Stepsisters 1982, Morning Glory 1982, Portrait of Rose 1986, The Illustrated Portrait of Wiltshire 1984, Personal Relations 1987, The Mill-Race Quartet 1988, The Timeless Moment 1988, The Beneficiaries 1989, Doubtful Company 1990, Guilty Parties 1991, Late Harvest 1991, The Colonel's Son 1992, Hindsight 1993, Keeping it Dark 1994, King's Folly 1995, The General's Wife 1996; contributions: newspapers and magazines.

STREET-PORTER, Janet, FRTS; British writer, broadcaster and fmr newspaper editor; *Editor-at-Large, The Independent on Sunday*; b. (Janet Bull), 27 Dec. 1946, London, England; m. 1st Tim Street-Porter 1967 (divorced 1975); m. 2nd A. M. M. Elliott 1976 (divorced 1978); m. 3rd Frank Cvitanovich (divorced 1988, died 1995). *Education:* Lady Margaret Grammar School and Architectural Asscn. *Career:* columnist, Petticoat Magazine 1968, Daily Mail 1969–71, Evening Standard 1971–73; own show, LBC Radio 1973; presenter of youth programmes, late night talk shows and factual series, London Weekend Television 1975–83; Head of Youth and Entertainment Features, BBC TV 1988–94, Head of Ind. Production for Entertainment 1994; Head of Live TV, Mirror Group TV 1994–95; Ed. The Independent on Sunday 1999–2001, Ed.-at-Large 2001–; presenter, Bloomberg TV 2001–05; currently Columnist, Daily Mail; Pres. Ramblers' Asscn 1994–97 (now Vice-Pres.); Trustee, Science Museum 2008; Assoc. RIBA; Patron Inst. of Contemporary Arts. *Television includes:* as series presenter: London Weekend Show 1975–79, Saturday Night People 1978–80, Six O'Clock Show 1982–83, Design Awards, Travels with Pevsner, Coast to Coast, The Midnight Hour, As The Crow Flies (series), Cathedral Calls, J'Accuse, The Internet, Men Talking, Demolition, The F Word; presented two series on teaching and nursing for Channel 5 and various documentaries for Sky, The Genius of British Art, Channel 4 2009; writer and producer: The Vampire (opera for BBC 2); as producer: Network 7 (co-producer, Channel 4) 1987. *Publications:* Scandal 1980, The British Teapot 1981, Coast to Coast 1998, As the Crow Flies 1999, Baggage – My Childhood 2004, Fall Out 2006, Life's too F***ing Short 2008, Don't Let the B*****ds Get You Down 2009. *Honours:* Prix Italia 1992, BAFTA Award for Originality 1988, European Cedefop Award (twice), Food and Farming Industry Award 2008. *Literary Agent:* c/o Rosemary Scoular, United Agents, 12–26 Lexington Street, London, W1P 0LE, England. *Telephone:* (20) 3214-0893. *E-mail:* rscoular@unitedagents.co.uk. *Website:* www.janetstreetporter.com.

STRESHINSKY, Shirley, BA; American writer; b. 7 Oct. 1934, Alton, Ill.; d. of Thomas Gaghen and Edna Gaghen; m. Ted Streshinsky 1966 (deceased); one s. one d. *Education:* Univ. of Illinois. *Publications:* And I Alone Survived 1978, Hers the Kingdom 1981, A Time Between 1984, Gift of the Golden Mountain 1988, The Shores of Paradise (novel) 1991, Oats! A Book of Whimsy (with Maria Streshinsky) 1997, John James Audubon: Life and Art in the American Wilderness 1998; contribs to journals and magazines, including travel writing (several awards) and articles on Asia and the Pacific. *Honours:* Best Human Interest Article, Society Magazine Writers' Asscn 1968, Educational Press Award 1968. *Literary Agent:* c/o Dana Newman (agent), Los Angeles. *E-mail:* Danamnewman@gmail.com. *Address:* 50 Kenyon Avenue, Kensington, CA 94708, USA (home). *Telephone:* (510) 526-1976 (office). *E-mail:* streshinsky@earthlink.net (home).

STRINGER, Christopher, BSc, PhD, DSc, FRS; British anthropologist, writer and lecturer; *Research Leader in Human Origins, Natural History Museum, London*; b. 31 Dec. 1947, London, England. *Education:* Univs of London and Bristol. *Career:* Anthropologist, Prin. Researcher and Head of Human Origins Group, later Research Leader in Human Origins, Natural History Museum, London 1990–; Dir Ancient Human Occupation of Britain project; Visiting Prof., Royal Holloway, Univ. of London. *Publications:* Aspects of Human Evolution (ed.) 1981, The Human Revolution: Behavioral and Biological Perspectives on the Origins of Modern Humans (co-ed.) 1989, Human Evolution: An Illustrated Guide (co-author) 1989, In Search of Neanderthals: Solving the Puzzle of Human Origins (co-author) 1993, The Origin of Modern Humans and the Impact of Chronometric Dating: A Discussion (co-ed.) 1993, African Exodus: The Origins of Modern Humanity (co-author) 1997, The Complete World of Human Evolution (co-author) 2005, Homo britannicus 2006, The Origin of Our Species 2011. *Honours:* Hon. LLD (Univ. of Bristol)

STROHM, Reinhard, PhD, FBA; German musicologist; *Professor of Music, University of Oxford*; b. 4 Aug. 1942, Munich. *Education:* Univ. of Munich and Technical Univ., Berlin with Carl Dahlhaus. *Career:* Lecturer 1975–83, Prof. 1990–96, King's Coll. London; Prof., Yale Univ. 1983–90; Heather Prof. of Music, Univ. of Oxford 1996–2007, Prof. of Music 2007–; Visiting Prof., Institut für Musikwissenschaft, Univ. of Vienna 2009; Fellow, Wissenschaftskolleg zu Berlin 2010–11; corresponding mem. American Musicological Soc., Göttinger Akad. der Wissenschaften. *Publications:* Hasse, Scarlatti, Rolli 1975, Wagner Collected Edition (co-ed.) 1970–82, Zu Vivaldis Opern schaffen 1975, Italienische Opernarien des Frühen Settecento, 1720–1730 1976, Die Italienische Oper im 18 Jahrhundert 1979, Music in Late Medieval Bruges 1985, Essays on Handel and Italian Opera (contrib.) 1985, Music in Late Medieval Europe 1987, The Rise of European Music, 1380–1500 1993, On the Dignity and the Effects of Music: Two Fifteenth-Century Treatises (with J. D. Cullington) 1996, Dramma per musica: Italian Opera Seria in the Eighteenth Century 1997, Song Composition in the 14th and 15th Centuries: Old and New Questions 1997, The Eighteenth Century Diaspora of Italian Music and Musicians 2001, Music as Concept and Practice in the Late Middle Ages (The New Oxford History of Music, Vol. III, with B. Blackburn) 2001, The Operas of Antonio Vivaldi 2008; contrib. to learned books and journals. *Honours:* Hon. mem. Slovenian Acad. of Sciences 2009; Royal Musical Asscn Dent Medal 1977, Glarean Music Prize 2008, Leverhulme Emer. Fellowship 2008. *Address:* c/o Medieval and Modern Languages Faculty, Rom 3.17, 41 Wellington Square, Oxford, OX1 2JF, England (office). *E-mail:* reinhard.strohm@music.ox.ac.uk (office). *Website:* www.music.ox.ac.uk (office).

STRONG, Eithne, BA; Irish writer and poet; b. 23 Feb. 1923, West Limerick; m. Rupert Strong 1943; two s. seven d. *Education:* Trinity College, Dublin. *Career:* mem. Aosdána; Conradh Na Gaeilge; Irish PEN; Irish Writers Union; Poetry Ireland. *Publications:* Poetry: Songs of Living, 1965; Sarah in Passing, 1974; Circt Oibre, 1980; Fuil agus Fallat, 1983; My Darling Neighbour, 1985; Flesh the Greatest Sin, 1989; An Sagart Pinc, 1990; Aoife Faoi Ghlas, 1990; Let Live, 1990; Spatial Nosing, 1993; Nobel, 1998. Fiction: Degrees of Kindred, 1979; The Love Riddle, 1993. Short Fiction: Patterns, 1981. Contributions: anthologies, journals and magazines.

STRONG, Jonathan; American writer and teacher; *Lecturer in English, Tufts University*; b. 13 Aug. 1944, Evanston, IL. *Education:* Harvard Univ. *Career:* Lecturer in Creative Writing, Tufts Univ. 1969–78, 1989–, Harvard Univ. 1978–82, 1984–85, Univ. of Mass at Boston 1982–84, Wellesley Coll. 1985–89; mem. New England Gilbert and Sullivan Soc.; Sir Arthur Sullivan Soc. *Publications:* novels: Tike 1969, Ourselves 1971, Elsewhere 1985, Secret Words 1992, Companion Pieces 1993, An Untold Tale 1993, Offspring 1995, The Old World 1997, The Haunts of His Youth 1999, A Circle Around Her 2000, Drawn from Life 2008, Consolation 2010, More Light 2011, Hawkweed and Indian Paintbrush 2011; contributions: American Literature, journals and magazines. *Honours:* O. Henry Story Awards 1967, 1970, Rosenthal Award 1970, National Endowment for the Arts Award 1986. *Address:* Department of English, Tufts University, Room 208A, East Hall, Medford, MA 02155 (office); 7 Henderson Court, Rockport, MA 01966-1422, USA (home). *Telephone:* (617) 627-2380 (office); (978) 546-6176 (home). *Website:* jonathanwstrong.wordpress.com.

STRONG, Maggie (see Kotker, (Mary) Zane)

STRONG, Sir Roy Colin, Kt, PhD, FSA, FRSL; English historian, writer and fmr museum director; b. 23 Aug. 1935, London; s. of George Edward Clement Strong and Mabel Ada Smart; m. Julia Trevelyan Oman 1971 (died 2003). *Education:* Queen Mary Coll., Univ. of London and Warburg Inst. *Career:* Asst Keeper, Nat. Portrait Gallery, London 1959–67; Dir 1967–73; Dir, Victoria and Albert Museum, London 1974–87; Vice-Chair., South Bank Bd (now South Bank Centre) 1985–90; Dir, Oman Productions Ltd, Nordstern Fine Art Insurance 1988–2001; organizer of exhbns including The Elizabethan Image (Tate Gallery) 1969, The Destruction of the Country House (Victoria and Albert Museum) 1974, Artists of the Tudor Court (Victoria and Albert Museum) 1983; mem. Arts Council of GB 1983–87 (Chair., Arts Panel 1983–87), Council, RCA 1979–81; Patron, Pallant House, Chichester 1986–; Fellow, Queen Mary Coll., Univ. of London, Royal Soc. of Literature 1999; High Bailiff and Searcher of the Sanctuary of Westminster Abbey 2000; Pres., Garden History Soc. 2000–06. *Television:* Royal Gardens (series) 1992, The Diets Time Forgot (series) 2008, Visions of England 2010. *Radio:* numerous series. *Publications:* Portraits of Queen Elizabeth I 1963, Leicester's Triumph (with J. A. Van Dorsten) 1964, Holbein and Henry VIII 1967, Tudor and Jacobean Portraits 1969, The English Icon: Elizabethan and Jacobean Portraiture 1969, Elizabeth R (with Julia Trevelyan Oman) 1971, Van Dyck: Charles I on Horseback 1972, Inigo Jones: The Theatre of the Stuart Court (with S. Orgel) 1972, Mary Queen of Scots (with Julia Trevelyan Oman) 1972, Splendour at Court: Renaissance Spectacle and The Theatre of Power 1973, An Early Victorian Album (with Colin Ford) 1974, Nicholas Hilliard 1975, The Cult of Elizabeth: Elizabethan Portraiture and Pageantry 1977, And When Did You Last See Your Father? The Victorian Painter and British History 1978, The Renaissance Garden in England 1979, Britannia Triumphans, Inigo Jones, Rubens and Whitehall Palace 1980, Holbein 1980, The English Miniature (with J. Murdoch, J. Murrell and P. Noon) 1981, The English Year (with Julia Trevelyan Oman) 1982, The English Renaissance Miniature 1983, Artists of the Tudor Court (with J. Murrell) 1983, Glyndebourne, A Celebration (contrib.) 1984, Art and Power, Renaissance Festivals 1450–1650 1984, Strong Points 1985, Henry Prince of Wales and England's Lost Renaissance 1986, C. V. Wedgwood Festschrift (contrib.) 1986, Creating Small Gardens 1986, Gloriana, Portraits of Queen Elizabeth I 1987, The Small Garden Designers Handbook 1987, Cecil Beaton: the Royal Portraits 1988, Creating Small Formal Gardens 1989, Lost Treasures of Britain 1990, A Celebration of Gardens 1991, Small Period Gardens 1992, Royal Gardens 1992, Versace Theatre 1992, William Larkin 1994, A Country Life 1994, Successful Small Gardens 1994, The Tudor and Stuart Monarchy 1995, The Story of Britain 1996, The English Arcadia 1996, Country Life 1897–1997 1997, The Roy Strong Diaries 1967–1987 1997, On Happiness 1997, The Tudor and Stuart Monarchy 1998, The Spirit of Britain 1999, Garden Party 2000, The Artist and the Garden 2000, Ornament in the Small Garden 2001, Feast – A History of Grand Eating 2002, The Laskett – The Story of a Garden 2003, Coronation: A History of Kingship and the British Monarchy 2005, Passions Past and Present 2005, A Little History of the English Country Church 2007, Visions of England 2011; numerous articles in newspapers and periodicals. *Honours:* Hon. MA (Worcester) 2004; Hon. DLitt (Leeds) 1983, (Keele) 1984; Shakespeare Prize (FVS Foundation, Hamburg) 1980, President's Award Royal Photographic Soc. of Great Britain 2003. *Address:* The Laskett, Much Birch, Hereford, HR2 8HZ, England (home). *E-mail:* strong@ereal.net (home).

STROSS, Charles (Charlie) David George; British science fiction, horror and fantasy author; b. 18 Oct. 1964, Leeds; m. Feòrag NicBhride. *Education:* Univ. of Bradford. *Career:* contrib., articles on role-playing games for White Dwarf magazine 1970s and 1980s; fmr technical author and freelance journalist; first published short story in Interzone magazine 1987; writer for Computer Shopper magazine 1994–2004; writer of sci-fi, horror and fantasy novels 2003–; devised and wrote Laundry Files and Merchant Princes series of titles. *Publications include:* novels and novellas: Scratch Monkey 1993, Singularity Sky 2003, Iron Sunrise 2004, The Concrete Jungle (Hugo Award 2005) 2005, Accelerando (Locus Award for Best Science Fiction Novel 2006) 2005, Glasshouse (Prometheus Award 2007) 2006, Missile Gap (Locus Award 2007), The Rapture of the Nerds (co-author) 2012; Laundry Files series: The Atrocity Archives 2004, The Jennifer Morgue 2006, Down on the Farm 2008, Overtime 2009, The Fuller Memorandum 2010; Merchant Princes series: The Family Trade 2004, The Hidden Family 2005, The Clan Corporate 2006, The Merchants' War 2007, The Revolution Business 2009, The Trade of Queens 2010; short story collections: Toast: And Other Rusted Futures 2002; nonfiction: The Web Architect's Handbook 1996; work appears in numerous anthologies and story collections. *Honours:* Edward E. Smith Memorial Award, Boskone 2008. *Address:* c/o Tor Books, Tom Doherty Associates LLC, 175 Fifth Avenue, New York, NY 10010, USA (office); c/o Chloe Healy, Tor UK, Pan Macmillan, 20 New Wharf Road, London, N1 9RR, England (office). *Telephone:* (20) 7014-6186 (office). *E-mail:* questions@tor.com (office); c.healy@macmillan.co.uk (office); charlie.stross@gmail.com (home). *Website:* www.tor.com (office); www.torbooks.co.uk (office); www.accelerando.org (home); www.antipope.org (home).

STROUSE, Jean, BA; American writer and cultural administrator; *Director, Cullman Center for Scholars and Writers, New York Public Library*; b. 10 Sept. 1945, Los Angeles, Calif. *Education:* Radcliffe Coll. *Career:* Editorial Asst, New York Review of Books 1967–69; Ed. Pantheon Books 1972–75; Book Critic, Newsweek 1979–83; Phi Beta Kappa Soc. Visiting Scholar 1996–97; Ferris Prof. of Journalism, Princeton Univ. 1998; John J. Rhodes Chair in American Institutions and Public Policy, Arizona State Univ., Barrett Honors Coll. 2003; Dir Cullman Center for Scholars and Writers, The New York Public Library 2003–; various lectureships; mem. Soc. of American Historians, Pres. 2001–02, Authors' Guild, PEN. *Publications:* Women and Analysis: Dialogues on Psychoanalytic Views of Femininity (ed. and compiler) 1974, Alice James: A Biography 1980, Morgan: American Financier 1999; contributions: reviews, journals and magazines. *Honours:* Radcliffe Inst. Fellowship 1976, Nat. Endowment for the Humanities Fellowships 1976, 1992, Guggenheim Fellowships 1977, 1986, Nat. Endowment for the Arts Fellowship 1978, Bancroft Prize 1981, Ingram Merrill Foundation Grant 1989, Lila Wallace-Reader's Digest Writing Fellowship 1993–94, John D. and Catherine T. MacArthur Foundation Fellowship 2002–06, Best Book Citations, Los Angeles Times Book Review, New York Post, New York Times Book Review, Washington Post and others. *Address:* c/o Georges Borchardt Inc., 136 E 57th Street, New York, NY 10022, USA. *E-mail:* jstrouse@nypl.org (office).

STROUT, Elizabeth; American writer; b. Portland, Maine; m.; one d. *Education:* Syracuse Univ. *Career:* fmr faculty mem., Bard Coll., Warren Wilson Coll., Manhattan Community Coll.; currently faculty mem., Creative Writing Program, Queens Univ. of Charlotte. *Publications:* Amy and Isabelle (Los Angeles Times Art Siedenbaum Award for First Fiction, Chicago Tribune Heartland Prize) 1998, Abide With Me (novel) 2006, Olive Kitteridge (short stories) (Pulitzer Prize for Fiction 2009) 2008. *Address:* Creative Writing Program, Queens University of Charlotte, 1900 Selwyn Avenue, Charlotte, NC 28274, USA (office). *Telephone:* (704) 337-2499 (office). *Fax:* (704) 337-2503 (office). *Website:* www.queens.edu (office).

STRUGATSKY, Boris Natanovich, (S. Viticky); Russian writer and astronomer; b. 15 April 1933, Leningrad; s. of Natan Strugatsky; m.; one s. *Education:* Leningrad State Univ. *Career:* held astronomer's post in Pulkovo Observatory, Leningrad 1955–65; started publishing science-fiction (with his brother Arkady) 1957. *Publications include:* with A. N. Strugatsky over 25 novels including: The Land of Purple Clouds 1959, The Return 1962, Escape Attempt 1962, The Far-Away Rainbow 1964, Rapacious Things of the Century 1965, The Inhabited Island 1971, The Ugly Swans 1972, Stories 1975, The Forest 1982, The Lame Fortune 1986, One Billion Years Before the End of the World 1988, Collected Works 1991, Burdened by Evil 1988, The Search of Destination 1994, Collected Works 2001. *Honours:* Victor Hugo Prize (France). *Address:* 196070 St Petersburg, Pobeda Street 4, Apartment 186, Russia. *Telephone:* (812) 291-37-55. *E-mail:* bns@tf.ru (home).

STRYKER, Daniel (see Morris, Janet Ellen)

STUART, Dabney, AB, AM; American academic, editor, poet and writer; *Professor Emeritus of English, Washington and Lee University*; b. 4 Nov. 1937, Richmond, Va; m. 3rd Sandra Westcott 1983; two s. one d. *Education:* Davidson Coll., NC, Harvard Univ. *Career:* Instructor, Coll. of William and Mary, Williamsburg, Va 1961–65; Instructor, Washington and Lee Univ., Lexington, Va 1965–66, Asst Prof. 1966–69, Assoc. Prof. 1969–74, Prof. 1974–91, S. Blount Mason Prof. of English 1991–2002, Prof. Emer. 2002–; Poetry Ed., Shenandoah 1966–76, Ed.-in-Chief 1988–95; Visiting Prof., Middlebury Coll. 1968–69; McGuffey Chair of Creative Writing, Ohio Univ. 1972; Visiting Poet, Univ. of Virginia 1981, 1982–83; Poetry Ed., New Virginia Review 1983. *Publications:* poetry: The Diving Bell 1966, A Particular Place 1969, Corgi Modern Poets in Focus 3 1971, The Other Hand 1974, Friends of Yours, Friends of Mine 1974, Round and Round: A Triptych 1977, Rockbridge Poems 1981, Common Ground 1982, Don't Look Back 1987, Narcissus Dreaming 1990, Light Years: New and Selected Poems 1994, Second Sight: Poems for Paintings by Carol Cloar 1996, Long Gone 1996, Settlers: Poems 1999, Family Preserve 2005, Tables 2009, Open the Gates 2010, Greenbrier Forest 2012; fiction: Sweet Lucy Wine: Stories 1992, The Way to Cobbs Creek 1997, No Visible Means of Support 2001; non-fiction: Nabokov: The Dimensions of Parody 1978. *Honours:* Dylan Thomas Prize, Poetry Soc. of America 1965, Borestone Mountain Awards 1969, 1974, 1977, Nat. Endowment for the Arts Grant 1969, and Fellowships 1974, 1982, Virginia Gov.'s Award 1979, Guggenheim Fellowship 1987–88, Individual Artists Fellowship, Virginia Comm. for the Arts 1996, Residency, Rockefeller Study Centre, Bellagio, Italy 2000, Library of Virginia Poetry Prize 2006. *Address:* 30 Edmondson Avenue, Lexington, VA 24450-1904, USA (home). *Telephone:* (540) 463-5663 (home). *E-mail:* stuartd@wlu.edu (office).

STUBBS, Jean; British writer; b. (Jean Yvonne Higham), 23 Oct. 1926, Denton, Lancashire, England; m. 1st Peter Stubbs 1948; one s. one d.; m. 2nd Roy Oliver 1980. *Education:* Manchester School of Art, Loreburn Secretarial Coll., Manchester. *Career:* copywriter, Henry Melland 1964–66; reviewer, Books and Bookmen 1965–76; Writer-in-Residence for Avon 1984; mem. PEN, Soc. of Women Writers and Journalists, Detection Club, Lancashire Writers Asscn, West Country Writers, Soc. of Authors. *Publications:* The Rose Grower 1962, The Travellers 1963, Hanrahan's Colony 1964, The Straw Crown 1966, My Grand Enemy 1967, The Passing Star 1970, The Case of Kitty Ogilvie 1970, An Unknown Welshman 1972, Dear Laura 1973, The Painted Face 1974, The Golden Crucible 1976, Kit's Hill 1979, The Ironmaster 1981, The Vivian Inheritance 1982, The Northern Correspondent 1984, 100 Years Around the Lizard 1985, Great Houses of Cornwall 1987, A Lasting Spring 1987, Like We Used To Be 1989, Summer Secrets 1990, Kelly Park 1992, Charades 1994, The Witching Time 1998, I'm a Stranger Here Myself 2004; contrib. to anthologies and magazines. *Honours:* Tom Gallon Trust Award 1964, Daughter of Mark Twain 1973. *Literary Agent:* MBA Literary Agents Ltd, 62 Grafton Way, London, W1P 5LD, England.

STÜTZLE, Walther K. A., Dr rer. pol; German journalist; *Senior Distinguished Fellow. German Institute for International and Security Affairs*; b. 29 Nov. 1941, Westerland-Sylt; s. of the late Moritz Stützle and of Annemarie Ruge; m. Dr H. Kauper 1966; two s. two d. *Education:* Westerland High School and Univs of Berlin, Bordeaux and Hamburg. *Career:* researcher, Inst. for Strategic Studies, London 1967–68, Foreign Policy Inst. Bonn 1968–69; Desk Officer, Ministry of Defence, Planning Staff, Bonn 1969–72, Pvt. Sec. and Chef de Cabinet, 1973–76, Head, Planning Staff, Under-Sec. of Defence, Plans and Policy 1976–82; editorial staff, Stuttgarter Zeitung 1983–86; Dir Stockholm Int. Peace Research Inst. (SIPRI) 1986–91; Ed.-in-Chief Der Tagesspiegel 1994–98; Perm. Sec., Ministry of Defence 1998–2002, Visiting Prof., Potsdam Univ. 2004–; Sr Distinguished Fellow, German Institute for Int. and Security Affairs 2004–. *Publications:* Adenauer und Kennedy in der Berlinkrise 1961–62 1972, Politik und Kräftverhältnis 1983, Europe's Future – Europe's Choices (co-author) 1967, ABM Treaty – To Defend or Not to Defend 1987, SIPRI Yearbook (ed.) 1986–90, From Alliance to Coalition: The Future of Transatlantic Relations (contributor) 2004. *Address:* Stiftung Wissenschaft und Politik, Deutsches Institut für Internationale Politik und Sicherheit, Ludwigkirchplatz 3-4, 10719 Berlin, Germany (office). *Telephone:* (30) 880070 (office). *Fax:* (30) 88007100 (office). *E-mail:* walther.stuetzle@swp-berlin.org (office). *Website:* www.swp-berlin.org (office).

STYLIANOU, Petros Savva, PhD; Cypriot politician, journalist and writer; b. 8 June 1933, Kythrea; s. of Savvas Stylianou and Evanthia Stylianou; m. Voula Tzanetatou 1960; two d. *Education:* Pancyprian Gymnasium, Univs of Athens and Salonika. *Career:* served with Panhellenic Cttee of the Cyprus Struggle (PEKA) and Nat. Union of Cypriot Univ. Students (EFEK), Pres. EFEK 1953–54; Co-founder Dauntless Leaders of the Cypriot Fighters Org. (KARI); joined liberation Movt of Cyprus 1955; imprisoned in Kyrenia Castle 1955 and later escaped; Leader, Nat. Striking Group; sentenced to 15 years' imprisonment 1956, transferred to UK prison, released 1959; mem. Cen. Cttee United Democratic Reconstruction Front (EDMA) 1959; Deputy Sec.-Gen. Cyprus Labour Confed. (SEK) 1959, Sec.-Gen. 1960–62; f. Cyprus Democratic Labour Fed. (DEOK) 1962, Sec.-Gen. 1962–73, Hon. Pres. 1974–; mem. House of Reps 1960–70, 1985–91, Sec. 1960–62; Deputy Minister of Interior 1980–82; Special Adviser to Pres. on Cultural Affairs 1982–85; Mayor of Engomi 1992–95; Founder Pancyprian Orgs for Rehabilitation of Spastics, Rehabilitation from Kidney Disease, from Haemophilia and from Myopathy; Pres. Cyprus Historical Museum and Archives, Movement for the Salvation of Cyprus. *Publications:* numerous works on poetry, history, etc. *Honours:* numerous awards and prizes from Cyprus, Greece and USA . *Address:* Kimonos 10, Engomi, Nicosia, Cyprus (home). *Telephone:* (2) 445972 (home).

SU, Shuyang, (Su Yang, Yu Pingfu); Chinese writer; b. 1938, Baoding, Hebei Prov. *Education:* Renmin Univ. *Career:* fmr teaching asst, Dept of CCP History, Renmin Univ.; Lecturer, Beijing Teachers' Coll.; worker, Baoding Voltage Transformer Factory; Lecturer, Beijing Coll. of Chinese Medicine; currently playwright, Beijing Film Studio; Vice-Chair. China Film Asscn; mem. Bd of Dirs Chinese Writers Asscn. *Publications include:* Song of Loyal Hearts (play), Wedding, Masquerade, The Death of Lao She, The Moon Goddess, I Am a Zero, Big Family Matter, Flying Moth, Taiping Lake, Sunset Boulevard: Selected Screenplays by Su Shuyang, Homeland (novel), About Love (poetry), A Reader on China 2007, A Reader on Tibet 2009. *Address:* Chinese Writers Association, No.25, East Tucheng Road, Chaoyang District, Beijing 100013, People's Republic of China.

SU, Tong; Chinese writer; b. (Tong Zhonggui), 23 Jan. 1963, Suzhou, Jiangsu Prov. *Education:* Beijing Normal Univ. *Career:* fmrly Lecturer, Nanjing Acad. of Arts; Ed. Zhongshan Magazine; Writer-in-Residence, Univ. of Iowa Int. Writing Program 2001; mem. Jiangsu Provincial Writers' Asscn. *Publications include:* (titles in translation) The Eighth Is a Bronze Sculpture, The Escape of 1934, The Mournful Dance, The Lives of Women, Wives and Concubines 1990, Raise the Red Lantern (three novellas) 1991, Blush 1994, Rice 1995, Jasmine Woman 2004, My Life as an Emperor 2006, Binu – The Myth of Meng Jiang Nu 2007, The Boat to Redemption (Man Asian Literary Prize) 2009. *Address:* c/o Canongate Books, 14 High Street, Edinburgh, EH1 1TE, Scotland (office).

SU, Ye; Chinese writer and film editor; b. 31 Aug. 1949, Honjiang, Hunan Dist; d. of the late Sue Linxun and Wen Zhinan; m. Chen Chunnian 1980 (divorced 1991); one s. *Education:* Jiangsu Jr Coll. of Theatre and Nanjing Univ. *Career:* mem. Jiangsu Song and Dance Ensemble Chorus 1970; narrator, Nanjing Film Studio 1972–79, apptd ed. 1979; writer 1979–; mem. Chinese Writers' Union 1980. *Publications include:* Infatuation (short story) 1982, Ever Hard to Forget 1986, Paper Wild Goose 1988, Ode to the Starry Sky 1991, A Visit to La She's Tea House 1990, Only the Fan-shaped Cliff 1992, Ever Hard to Forget (collected prose) 1992. *Honours:* First Prize for Prose (Youth Magazine) 1982, Fiction Competition (Nanjing Daily) 1983, for Literature (Nanjing Municipal) 1986, Yan Wu Literary Works Solicitation 1988, Gold Cup Award, Spring Breeze Monthly 1988, Second Prize for Literature, Nanjing Municipal 1989, Creation Award, Supplement to Nanjing Daily 1989, Literary Prize, Chinese Writers' Union and China Literary Foundation 1990, Third Prize for Excellent Works, Chinese Newspapers' Supplements 1990, Jinling Full Moon Prose Competition 1991. *Address:* c/o Renditions Magazine, The Chinese University of Hong Kong, Shatin, Hong Kong Special Administrative Region, People's Republic of China.

SUÁREZ ARAÚZ, Nicomedes, (El Poeta Movima), PhD; Bolivian/American academic, poet and writer; *Director, Center for Amazonian Literature and Culture, Smith College*; b. 24 Aug. 1946, Santa Ana del Yacuma; m. Kristine Marie Cummings 1975; two s. *Education:* studied in Argentina, Exeter Univ., UK, Ohio Univ., USA. *Career:* Prof. of Spanish and Portuguese, Smith Coll. 1987–, founder and Dir, Center for Amazonian Literature and Culture 1993–; Ed. Amazonian Literary Review, Pan-Amazonia, PEN magazine, Bolivia. *Publications include:* poetry: Los escribanos de Loén 1974, El poema America (trans. as The American Poem) 1976, Caballo al anochecar 1978, Loén: Amazonía/Amnesis/América 1997, Cartas a la amnesia, Recetario Amazónico (trans. as Edible Amazonia) 2002, Literary Amazonia: Modern Writing by Amazonian Writers (ed) 2004; non-fiction: Twenty-Four Conversations with Borges 1983, Amnesis Manifesto 1984, Amnesis: The Art of Amnesia and the Lost Object 1988. *Honours:* Premio Edicion Franz Tamayo 1977, Premio Jarajorechi de Oro 2003. *Address:* Department of Spanish and Portuguese, Smith College, Hatfield Hall, Northampton, MA 01063, USA (office). *Telephone:* (413) 585-3450 (office). *E-mail:* nsuarez@smith.edu (office). *Website:* www.smith.edu/calc (office).

SUBRAMANIAM, Chitoor, (Ambai), PhD; Indian writer and researcher; *Director, Sound and Picture Archives for Research on Women*; b. (C. S. Lakshmi), 1944, Coimbatore, Tamil Nadu; m. Vishnu Mathur. *Education:* Jawaharlal Nehru Univ. *Career:* Founder and Dir Sound and Picture Archives for Research on Women (SPARROW) 1988–, Trustee. *Publications include:* Nandimalai Charalilae (novel) 1962, Andhi Malai (novel) 1966, Siragugal Muriyam (short stories) 1976, The Face Behind the Mask: Women in Tamil Literature (criticism) 1984, Veettin Moollayil Oru Samayalari (short stories)

1988, A Purple Sea: Short Stories by Ambai (Vodafone-Crossword Prize 2006) 1992, Body Blows: Women, Violence and Survival: Three Plays 2000, Kaatil Oru Maan (short stories) 2000, Seven Seas And Seven Mountains: The Singer and the Song-Conversations With Musicians 2000, Seven Seas And Seven Mountains: Mirrors and Gestures-Conversations with Women Dancers 2003, The Unhurried City (ed.) 2003, In A Forest, A Deer (short stories) 2006, Varrum Eriyin Meengal (fiction) 2007, Fish in a Dwindling Lake 2012; contribs (as C. S. Lakshmi) of articles and papers to Economic and Political Weekly, The Hindu and other journals and newspapers. *Honours:* Narayanaswamy Aiyar Prize for Fiction 1961, Iyal Virudhu (Lifetime Achievement Award), Tamil Literary Garden 2008. *Address:* SPARROW, The Nest, B-101, 201, 301, Maratha Colony Road, Dahisar, Mumbai 400 068, India (office); B-32, Jeet Nagar, J.P Road, Versova, Mumbai 400 061, India (home). *Telephone:* (22) 28280895 (office); (22) 28965019 (office). *E-mail:* sparrow1988@gmail.com (office); cslakshmi44@gmail.com. *Website:* www.sparrowonline.org (office).

SUBRAMANIAN, (Mary) Belinda, BA, MA; American poet and editor; b. 6 Sept. 1953, Statesville, NC; m. S. Ramnath 1977; two d. *Education:* Regents Coll., New York, California State Univ. *Career:* Ed., Gypsy Magazine and Vergin Press 1983–. *Publications:* Nürnberg Poems 1983, Heather and Mace 1985, Eye of the Beast 1986, Fighting Woman 1986, Body Parts 1987, Skin Divers (with Lyn Lifshin) 1988, Halloween 1989, The Jesuit Poems 1989, Elephants and Angels 1991, The Innocents 1991, A New Geography of Poets 1992, Finding Reality in Myth 1996, Notes of a Human Warehouse Engineer 1998; contributions: anthologies, journals, and magazines. *Honours:* winner, Nerve Cowboy Poetry Contest 1998. *Address:* 3286 Rain Dance Drive, El Paso, TX 79936-2319, USA (home).

SUKNASKI, Andrew; Canadian editor and poet; b. 30 July 1942, Wood Mountain, Saskatchewan. *Education:* Univ. of British Columbia, Vancouver. *Career:* Ed., Three Legged Coyote, Wood Mountain 1982–. *Publications:* This Shadow of Eden 1970, Circles 1970, Rose Wayn in the East 1972, Old Mill 1972, The Zen Pilgrimage 1972, Four Parts Sand: Concrete Poems 1972, Wood Mountain Poems 1973, Suicide Notes, Booke One 1973, These Fragments I've Gathered for Ezra 1973, Leaving 1974, Blind Man's House 1975, Leaving Wood Mountain 1975, Octomi 1976, Almighty Voice 1977, Moses Beauchamp 1978, The Ghosts Call You Poor 1978, Two for Father 1978, In the Name of Narid: New Poems 1981, Montage for an Interstellar Cry 1982, The Land They Gave Away: Selected and New Poems 1982, Silk Trail 1985. *Honours:* Canada Council Grants. *Address:* 250 Manitoba Street East, Moose Jaw, SK S6H 0A5, Canada (home). *Telephone:* (306) 693-7590 (home).

SULEIMAN, Nabil; Syrian novelist and literary critic; b. 1945. *Education:* Damascus Univ. *Career:* f. Dar Al Hiwar publishing house 1982; lectured in many Arab countries, also in Madrid, Spain, and Austin, Texas, USA. *Publications:* 16 novels including Al-Sijn (The Prison) 1972, The Cycles of the East (in 4 parts), 24 books of literary criticism. *Address:* Dar Al Hiwar, 16 Teshreen, Latakia, 1018, Syria. *E-mail:* daralhiwar@gmail.com. *Website:* www.daralhiwar.com.

SULERI GOODYEAR, Sara, BA, MA, PhD; Pakistani/American writer and academic; b. Lahore, Pakistan. *Education:* Kinnaird Coll., Lahore, Punjab Univ., Lahore, Indiana Univ. *Career:* Research Scholar and Lecturer of English, Yale Univ. 1983–; founding-ed., Yale Journal of Criticism. *Publications:* Meatless Days 1989, The Rhetoric of English India 1992, Boys Will Be Boys: A Daughter's Elegy 2003; contributions: editorial boards of YJC, The Yale Review, Transition. *Address:* Dept of English, Yale University, 63 High Street, Room 109, PO Box 208302, New Haven, CT 06520-8302, USA (office). *Telephone:* (203) 432-8827 (office). *E-mail:* sara.goodyear@yale.edu (office). *Website:* www.yale.edu/english (office).

SULLEROT, Evelyne Annie Henriette, LèsL; French sociologist, journalist and writer; b. 10 Oct. 1924, Montrouge, Seine; d. of André; and Georgette (née Roustain) Pasteur; m. François Sullerot 1946; three s. one d. *Education:* Colls of Compiègne, Royan and Uzès, Free School of Political Sciences, Univs of Paris and Aix-en-Provence. *Career:* Teacher 1947–49; f. French Family Planning Movt 1955, Sec-Gen. 1955–58, then Hon. Pres.; Researcher Centre for Mass Communications, Tech. Coll. 1960–63; teacher French Press Inst. 1963–68; Prof. Free Univ. of Brussels 1966–68; Head Faculty of Letters Univ. of Paris (Nanterre) 1967; Specialist EC 1969–92, ILO 1970; mem. Econ. and Social Council 1974–89; Founder, Pres. Retravailler (Back to Work) Centres; mem. Nat. Advisory Comm. for Human Rights 1986–99; fmr mem. French Comm. UNESCO; Corresp. mem. Acad. des sciences morales et politiques 1999. *Publications:* La presse féminine 1963, La vie des femmes 1964, Demain les femmes 1965, Aspects sociaux de la radiotélévision 1966, Histoire de la presse féminine des origines à 1848 1966, Histoire et sociologie du travail féminin 1968, Le droit de regard, La femme dans le monde moderne 1970, Les françaises aux travail 1973, Les crèches et les équipements d'accueil pour la petite enfance (jtly) 1974, Histoire et mythologie de l'amour 1976, Le fait féminin 1978, L'Aman 1981, Le statut matrimonial et ses conséquences juridiques, fiscales et sociales 1984, Pour le meilleur et sans le pire 1984, L'âge de travailler 1986, L'enveloppe 1987, Quels pères? Quels fils? 1992, Alias 1996, Le grand remue-ménage 1997, La Crise de la Famille 1997, Diderot dans l'autobus 2001, Silence 2004, Pilule, Sexe, ADN 2006; numerous research papers for UNESCO, OECD, EU, ILO. *Honours:* Grand Officier de la Légion d'Honneur; Commdr de l'Ordre Nat. du Mérite. *Address:* 95 blvd Saint-Michel, 75005 Paris, France (home).

SULLIVAN, Andrew, PhD; British journalist; b. 20 Aug. 1963, Godstone, Surrey; pnr Aaron Tone. *Education:* Magdalen Coll., Oxford Univ., Dept of Govt, Harvard Univ., USA. *Career:* intern Centre For Policy Studies, London; intern New Republic magazine 1986, returned to Harvard and taught in Govt Dept 1987, returned as Assoc. Ed. New Republic 1987, Deputy Ed. 1990, Acting Ed. 1991, Ed. 1991–96; contributing writer and columnist New York Times Magazine, contrib. New York Times Book Review –2002; weekly columnist for Sunday Times of London; est. andrewsullivan.com's Daily Dish blog 2000 at Time magazine, now with The Atlantic Monthly. *Publication:* Virtually Normal: An Argument About Homosexuality 1995, Love Undetectable: Notes on Friendship, Sex, and Survival 1999, The Conservative Soul 2006. *Address:* c/o The Atlantic Monthly Group, The Watergate, 600 New Hampshire Avenue, NW, Washington, DC 20037, USA (office). *Website:* andrewsullivan.theatlantic.com.

SULLIVAN, John Jeremiah; American author and editor; *Southern Editor, The Paris Review;* b. 1974, Louisville, Ky; s. of Mike Sullivan. *Education:* Univ. of the South, Sewanee, Tenn. *Career:* Editorial Asst, Sewanee Review 1997–98; Ed. Oxford American 1998–2000; worked in History Dept, Oxford Univ. Press, New York 2000–01; Sr Ed. Harper's 2002, currently Contrib. Ed.; currently contrib. and Southern Ed. The Paris Review. *Publications include:* Blood Horses: Notes of a Sportswriter's Son (Eclipse Award 2004) 2004, Pulphead: Essays 2011; contrib. GQ, New York Magazine, New York Times Magazine. *Honours:* Nat. Magazine Awards for Feature Writing 2003, for Essays and Criticism 2011, Whiting Writers' Award for Nonfiction 2004, Pushcart Prize 2011. *Address:* The Paris Review, 62 White Street, New York, NY 10013, USA (office). *E-mail:* queries@theparisreview.org (office). *Website:* www.theparisreview.org (office).

SULLIVAN, Rosemary, BA, MA, PhD; Canadian academic, writer and poet; *Canada Research Chair in Biography and Creative Non-Fiction, University of Toronto;* b. Montreal; d. of Michael Sullivan and Leanore Sullivan. *Education:* McGill Univ., Univ. of Connecticut, Univ. of Sussex, UK. *Career:* Faculty mem., Univ. of Dijon, France 1972–73, Univ. of Bordeaux, France 1973–74, Univ. of Victoria, BC 1974–77; Asst Prof., Univ. of Toronto, Ont. 1977–80, Assoc. Prof. 1980–91, Prof. 2001–, Canada Research Chair in Biography and Creative Non-Fiction 2001–; Maclean Hunter Chair in Literary Journalism, Banff Centre 2003–06; mem. Amnesty International, Toronto Arts Group for Human Rights (Founding mem.), Acad. of Humanities and Social Sciences, Royal Soc. of Canada 2004–. *Publications include:* The Garden Master: The Poetry of Theodore Roethke 1975, The Space a Name Makes 1986, By Heart: Elizabeth Smart, a Life 1991, Blue Panic 1991, Shadow Maker: The Life of Gwendolyn MacEwan (Gov.-Gen.'s Award for Non-Fiction 1995) 1995, The Red Shoes: Margaret Atwood Starting Out 1998, The Bone Ladder: New and Selected Poems 2000, Labyrinth of Desire: Women, Passion and Romantic Obsession 2001, Memory-Making: Selected Essays 2001, Cuba: Grace under Pressure 2003, Villa Air-Bel: World War II, Escape and a House in Marseille (Yad Vashem Award 2007) 2006, The Guthrie Road, 2009; other: ed. or co-ed. of eight books; contribs to numerous journals and magazines. *Honours:* Gerald Lampert Award for Poetry 1986, Brascan Silver Medal for Culture, Nat. Magazine Awards 1986, Guggenheim Fellowship 1992, City of Toronto Book Award 1995, Non-Fiction Prize, Canadian Authors' Asscn 1995, Pres.'s Medal for Biography, Univ. of British Columbia 1995, Killam Fellow 1996, Canada Research Chair 2000, Connaught Fellowship 2002, Camargo Fellow 2005, Canadian Jewish Books Award 2007, Jackman Humanities Fellowship 2008, Trudeau Foundation Fellow 2008–11, RSC Lorne Pierce Medal. *Address:* Department of English, University of Toronto, Jackman Humanities Building, 170 St George Street, Toronto, ON M5R 2M8, Canada (office). *Telephone:* (416) 978-6139 (office). *E-mail:* rosemary.sullivan@utoronto.ca (office); info@rosemarysullivan.com. *Website:* www.rosemarysullivan.com.

SULLIVAN, Thomas William, BA; American writer and teacher; b. 20 Nov. 1940, Highland Park, Mich.; s. of Wilson H. Sullivan and Maud E. Sullivan; one s. one d. *Career:* fmr All-American athlete in two sports, has lived in a dozen countries and been a gambler, a 'Rube Goldberg' innovator, a coach, a teacher, a city commr; currently writes full-time in Minnesota; frequent public speaker; columnist for www.storytellersunplugged.com each 16th of the month; mem. MENSA, Soc. of the Black Bull, Arcadia Mixture. *Publications:* more than 80 novels and short stories, including Diapason (novel) 1978, The Phases of Harry Moon (novel) 1988, Born Burning (novel) 1989, The Martyring (novel) 1998, Dust of Eden (novel) 2004, Second Soul (novel) 2005, The Water Wolf (novel) 2006; essays; contrib. to magazines. *Honours:* Hemingway Days Festival Literary Contest awards 1985, DADA Literary Contest 1985, 1987, listed in All-Time Top 10 Horror Stories for Writer's Digest (The Man Who Drowned Puppies), Catholic Press Journalism Award for short story (The 4th Flight Is Forever) 1996. *Address:* 15215 91st Avenue N, Maple Grove, MN 55369, USA (home). *E-mail:* mn333mn@earthlink.net (home). *Website:* www.thomassullivanauthor.com.

SULLOWAY, Frank Jones, AB, AM, PhD; American psychologist and science historian; *Adjunct Professor, Department of Psychology and Institute of Personality and Social Research, University of California, Berkeley;* b. 2 Feb. 1947, Concord, NH; s. of Alvah Woodbury Sulloway and Alison Green; one s. *Education:* Harvard Univ. *Career:* Jr Fellow, Harvard Univ. Soc. of Fellows 1974–77; mem. Inst. for Advanced Study, Princeton, NJ 1977–78; Research Fellow, Miller Inst. for Basic Research in Science 1978–80, Research Prof. 1999–2000, Visiting Prof. 2001, 2005, Visiting Scholar, Inst. of Personality and Social Research 2001–; Research Fellow, MIT 1980–81, Visiting Scholar

1989–98; Postdoctoral Fellow, Harvard Univ. 1981–82, Visiting Scholar 1984–89; Research Fellow, Univ. Coll. London, UK 1982–84; Vernon Prof. of Biography, Dartmouth Coll. 1986; Adjunct Prof., Dept of Psychology, Univ. of California, Berkeley 2011–; Fellow, Center for Advanced Study in the Behavioral Sciences, Stanford, Calif. 1998–99; Fellow, AAAS, Linnean Soc. of London; mem. American Psychological Asscn, American Psychological Soc., History of Science Soc., Human Behavior and Evolution Soc. *Publications:* Freud, Biologist of the Mind 1979, Darwin and his Finches 1982, Freud and Biology: The Hidden Legacy 1982, Darwin's Conversion 1982, Darwin and the Galapagos 1984, Darwin's Early Intellectual Development 1985, Reassessing Freud's Case Histories 1991, Born to Rebel: Birth Order, Family Dynamics and Creative Lives 1996, Birth Order, Sibling Competition, and Human Behavior 2001, The Evolution of Charles Darwin 2005, Why Darwin Rejected Intelligent Design, 2006, Psychoanalysis and Pseudoscience 2007, Birth Order and Intelligence 2007, Tantalyzing Tortoises and the Darwin-Galapagos Legend 2009, Birth Order and Risk Taking in Athletics 2010, Why Siblings Are Like Darwin's Finches 2010; contrib. to professional journals. *Honours:* Pfizer Award, History of Science Soc. 1980, Nat. Endowment for the Humanities Fellowship 1980–81, NSF Fellowship 1981–82, Guggenheim Fellowship 1982–83, John D. and Catherine T. MacArthur Foundation Fellowship 1984–89, American Acad. of Achievement Golden Plate Award 1997, Skeptics Soc. James Randi Award 1997. *Address:* Institute of Personality and Social Research, 4125 Tolman Hall, University of California, Berkeley, CA 94720-5050, USA (office). *Telephone:* (510) 642-7139 (office). *Fax:* (510) 643-9336 (office). *E-mail:* sulloway@berkeley.edu (office). *Website:* www.sulloway.org.

SULSTON, Sir John Edward, Kt, PhD, FRS; British scientist; b. 27 March 1942, Fulmer, Bucks., England; s. of the late Rev. Canon Arthur Edward Aubrey Sulston and Josephine Muriel Frearson Blocksidge; m. Daphne Edith Bate 1966; one s. one d. *Education:* Merchant Taylor's School and Pembroke Coll., Cambridge. *Career:* Postdoctoral Fellowship at the Salk Inst., Calif. 1966–69; staff scientist, MRC Lab. of Molecular Biology, Cambridge 1969–2003; Dir The Sanger Centre 1992–2000; Chair. Inst. for Science Ethics and Innovation, Univ. of Manchester 2007–; mem. Human Genetics Comm. 2001–09; mem. European Molecular Biology Org. 1989–, Academia Europaea 2001–. *Television:* Royal Inst. Christmas Lectures (Channel 4) 2001. *Publications:* The Common Thread – A Story of Science, Politics, Ethics and the Human Genome (jtly) 2002; papers in scientific journals. *Honours:* Hon. Fellow, Pembroke Coll., Cambridge 2000, Royal Soc. of Chemisty 2003, Acad. of Medical Sciences 2003, hon. mem. Biochemical Soc. 2002, Physiological Soc. 2002, Freedom of Merchant Taylors' Co. 2004; Hon. DSc (Trinity Coll., Dublin) 2000, (Essex) 2002, (Cambridge) 2003, (Royal Holloway) 2003, (Exeter) 2003, (Newcastle) 2004, (British Columbia) 2009, (Liverpool) 2009, (Manchester) 2009, Hon. LLD (Dundee) 2005; Officier, Légion d'honneur 2004; W. Alden Spencer Award (jtly) 1986, Gairdner Foundation Award (jtly) 1991, 2002, Darwin Medal, Royal Soc. 1996, Rosenstiel Award (jtly) 1998, Pfizer Prize for Innovative Science 2000, Genetics Soc. of America George W. Beadle Medal 2000, Biochemical Soc. Sir Frederick Gowland Hopkins Medal 2000, Edinburgh Medal 2001, City of Medicine Award, Durham, NC 2001, Prince of Asturias Award, Spain 2001, Robert Burns Humanitarian Award 2002, Daily Mirror Pride of Britain Award 2002, Medical Soc. of London Fothergillian Medal 2002, Tel-Aviv Univ. Dan David Prize 2002, General Motors Sloan Prize 2002, Nobel Prize in Physiology or Medicine (jtly) 2002, Dawson Prize in Genetics, Trinity Coll., Dublin 2006. *Address:* 39 Mingle Lane, Stapleford, Cambridge, CB22 5SY, England. *Telephone:* (1223) 842248. *E-mail:* jes@sanger.ac.uk (office).

SULZBERGER, Arthur Ochs; American newspaper executive; *Chairman Emeritus, New York Times Company;* b. 5 Feb. 1926, New York City; s. of Arthur Hays and Iphigene Sulzberger (née Ochs); m. 1st Barbara Grant 1948 (divorced 1956); one s. (Arthur Ochs Sulzberger Jr) one d.; m. 2nd Carol Fox 1956 (died 1995); two d.; m. 3rd Allison Stacey Cowles 1996. *Education:* Columbia Univ. *Career:* served in US Marine Corps during Second World War and Korean War; joined The New York Times Co., New York 1951, Asst Treas. 1958–63, Pres. 1963–79, Publr 1963–92, Chair., CEO 1992–97, Chair. Emer. 1997–, mem. Bd of Dirs –2002; Co-Chair. Bd Int. Herald Tribune 1983; Chair. Newspaper Pres. Asscn 1988; Dir, Times Printing Co., Chattanooga, Gapesia Pulp and Paper Co. Ltd of Canada; Trustee Columbia Univ., mem. Coll. Council, now Trustee Emer.; Trustee Metropolitan Museum of Art, Chair. Bd of Trustees 1987–99. *Honours:* Hon. LHD (Montclair State Coll.), (Tufts Univ.) 1984; Columbia Journalism Award 1992; Alexander Hamilton Medal 1982, Vermeil Medal (City of Paris) 1992. *Address:* New York Times Co., 620 Eighth Avenue, New York, NY 10018, USA (office). *Telephone:* (212) 556-1234 (office). *Fax:* (212) 556-7389 (office). *Website:* www.nytco.com (office).

SULZBERGER, Arthur Ochs, Jr, BA; American newspaper publisher; *Chairman, The New York Times Company;* b. 22 Sept. 1951, Mount Kisco, NY; s. of Arthur Ochs Sulzberger and Barbara Winslow Grant; m. Gail Gregg 1975; one s. one d. *Education:* Tufts Univ., Harvard Univ. Business School. *Career:* reporter, The Raleigh Times, N Carolina 1974–76; corresp., Associated Press, London, UK 1976–78; Washington, DC bureau corresp., The New York Times 1978–81, city hall reporter 1981, Asst Metro Ed. 1981–82, Group Man., Advertising Dept 1983–84, Sr Analyst, Corp. Planning 1985, Production Coordinator 1985–87, Asst Publr 1987–88, Deputy Publr 1988–92, Publr 1992–, Chair. The New York Times Co. 1997–; mem. Bd New York City Outward Bound Center. *Honours:* RIT Isaiah Thomas Award in Publishing 2003. *Address:* The New York Times Company, 620 Eighth Avenue, New York, NY 10018, USA (office). *Telephone:* (212) 556-1234 (office). *E-mail:* publisher@nytimes.com (office). *Website:* www.nytco.com (office).

SUMMERSCALE, Kate; British writer; b. 1965; one s. *Career:* fmr Literary Ed., The Daily Telegraph. *Publications:* The Queen of Whale Clay (Somerset Maugham Award) 1998, The Suspicions of Mr Whicher or The Murder at Road Hill House (BBC Four Samuel Johnson Prize for Non–Fiction 2008, Galaxy British Book of the Year Award 2009) 2008, Mrs. Robinson's Disgrace: The Private Diary of a Victorian Lady 2012. *Address:* c/o Bloomsbury Publishing, 36 Soho Square, London W1D 3QY, England (office). *Website:* www.bloomsbury.com (office); www.mrwhicher.com.

SUMMERTREE, Katonah (see Windsor, Patricia)

SUN, Shuyun; Chinese writer and film and television producer; b. 1963. *Education:* Beijing Univ. and Univ. of Oxford, England. *Career:* film and TV producer, making documentaries for various companies, including the BBC and Channel 4 in the UK, and int. broadcasters. *Television and radio includes:* Half the Sky (TV documentary), The Monk and the Modern Girl (radio programme) (New York Festival World Gold Medal 2004), A Year in Tibet 2008. *Publications:* Ten Thousand Miles Without a Cloud 2003, The Long March 2006, A Year in Tibet: A Voyage of Discovery 2008. *Address:* c/o HarperCollins, 77–85 Fulham Palace Road, London, W6 8JB, England (office). *E-mail:* contact@harpercollins.co.uk (office).

SÜSKIND, Patrick; German author; b. 26 March 1949, Ambach, Bavaria. *Education:* Univ. of Munich. *Career:* fmr teacher; fmr writer for TV. *Publications include:* Perfume: The Story of a Murderer (novel) 1979, The Double Bass (play), The Pigeon (novel) 1988, Three Stories and a Reflection, On Love and Death; juvenile: The Story of Mr Summer 1991. *Address:* c/o Diogenes Verlag AG, Sprecherstr. 8, 8032 Zürich, Switzerland. *Telephone:* (1) 2548511. *Fax:* (1) 2528407.

SUTHERLAND, John Andrew, PhD, FRSL; British academic and writer; *Emeritus Lord Northcliffe Professor of Modern English Literature, University College London;* b. 9 Oct. 1938, s. of Jack Sutherland and Elizabeth Sutherland (née Salter); m. Guilland Watt 1967; one s. *Education:* Colchester Royal Grammar School, Univs of Leicester and Edinburgh. *Career:* nat. service, 2nd Lt, Suffolk Regt 1958–60; Lecturer in English, Univ. of Edin. 1965–72; Lecturer in English, Univ. Coll. London 1972–84, Lord Northcliffe Prof. of Modern English Literature 1992–2004, Prof. Emer. 2004–; columnist, The Guardian. *Publications include:* Thackeray at Work 1974, Victorian Novelists and Publishers 1976, Fiction and the Fiction Industry 1978, Bestsellers 1980, Offensive Literature 1982, The Longman Companion to Victorian Fiction 1989, Mrs Humphry Ward 1992, The Life of Walter Scott: A Critical Biography 1995, Victorian Fiction: Writers, Publishers, Readers 1995, Is Heathcliffe a Murderer? 1996, Can Jane Eyre be Happy? 1997, Where Was Rebecca Shot? 1998, Who Betrays Elizabeth Bennet? 1999, Henry V, War Criminal ? 1999, Last Drink to LA 2000, The Literary Detective 2000, Literary Lives 2001, Reading the Decades 2002, Stephen Spender: The Authorised Biography 2004, How to Read a Novel: A User's Guide 2006, Bestsellers: A Very Short Introduction 2007, Curiosities of Literature 2008, Magic Moments 2008, Love, Sex, Death and Words (with Stephen Fender) 2010. *Honours:* Hon. DLitt (Leicester) 1998. *Address:* c/o Department of English, University College London, Gower Street, London, WC1E 6BT, England. *Telephone:* (20) 7387-7050.

SUTHERLAND, Margaret; New Zealand writer; b. 16 Sept. 1941, Auckland; m.; two s. two d. *Career:* registered nurse; Literary Fellow, Univ. of Auckland 1981; mem. Australian Soc. of Authors, Fed. of Australian Writers. *Publications:* The Fledgling 1974, Hello, I'm Karen (juvenile) 1974; novels: The Love Contract 1976, Getting Through (aka Dark Places, Deep Regions) 1977, The Fringe of Heaven 1984, The City Far From Home 1992, Is That Love? 1999, The Sea Between 2006, Leaving Gaza 2007, Windsong 2008, The Taj Mahal of Trundle 2009; contrib. to journals and magazines. *Honours:* Scholarship in Letters (NZ) 1984, Australia Council Writers Fellowships 1992, 1995, Nat. Short Story Award 2009. *Address:* 10 Council Street, Speers Point, NSW 2284, Australia (home). *E-mail:* chapsuth@idl.com.au (office). *Website:* www.margaretsutherland.com.

SUTHERLAND-SMITH, James Alfred, BA, MA; British poet, language teaching consultant and translator; b. 17 June 1948, Aberdeen, Scotland; m. Viera Schlosserova 1992; one d. *Education:* Univs of Leeds, Nottingham and East Anglia. *Career:* teacher 1974–85; Deputy Head of Educ., Saudi Arabian Nat. Guard Signal Corps Training School 1985–86; Head of English Language Unit, Qatar Public Telecom Corpn 1986–88; with the British Council, Lecturer, Univ. P. J. Safarik, Slovakia 1989–95, English Language Consultant, E Slovakia 1995–2002, Peacekeeping English Project Man., Serbia and Montenegro 2002–09; mem. Soc. of Authors, Asscn of Literary Translators, Royal Soc. of Literature. *Publications:* Four Poetry and Audience Poets, A Poetry Quintet, Trapped Water, A Singer from Sabiya, Naming of the Arrow, The Country of Rumour, Not Waiting for Miracles – 17 Contemporary Slovak Poets, At the Skin Resort 1999, One Hundred Years of Slovak Literature, An Album of Slovak Literature, Cranberry on Ice – Selected Poems of Ivan Laucik, Melancholy Hunter – Selected Poems of Jan Buzassy, Autumnal Furniture – Juraj Briskar, An Album of Slovak Literature 2, New Poetries III, Pomenovat' sip – Selected Poems trans. into Slovak, The Scent of the Unseen – Selected Poems of Mila Haugova, In the Country of Birds 2004, An Album of

Slovak Literature 3, And That's the Truth – Selected Poems of Milan Rufus, Salted Snow – Selected Poems of Jozef Leikert, In Search of Beauty (anthology), Popeye in Belgrade 2008, Dinner with Fish and Mirrors – Selected Poems of Ivana Milankova 2010; contrib. to PN Review, The Bow-wow Shop, BBC Radio 3, Slovak radio and TV. *Honours:* Eric Gregory Award, First Prize Peterloo Poetry Competition, Cumberland Review Poetry Competition, Prizewinner Nat. Poetry Competition of GB, TLS Cheltenham Poetry Competition, Cardiff Int. Poetry Competition, Bridport Festival Poetry Competition, Exeter Festival Poetry Competition, Stand Magazine Poetry Competition, Philips Award, San Jose Studies Poetry Award, Hviezdoslav Prize for translating Slovak poetry 2003. *Address:* c/o Carcanet Press, Alliance House, Cross Street, Manchester, M2 7AQ, England. *Website:* www.carcanet.co.uk; www.jamessutherland-smith.co.uk.

SUTTON, Henry (see Slavitt, David Rytman)

SUTTON, Penny (see Cartwright, Justin)

SUZUKI, Kôji; Japanese writer; b. 13 May 1957, Hamamatsu, Shizuoka; m.; two d. *Education:* Keio Univ. *Career:* many of his novels have been made into successful films. *Publications:* fiction: Rakuen (Paradise) (Fantasy Novel Award) 1990, Ringu (Ring) 1991, Rasen (Spiral) (Yoshikawa Eiji Young Writer Award 1996) 1995, Loop 1998, Kamigami no Promenade (The Gods' Promenade) 2003, Bâsudei (Birthday) 2004, Honogurai mizu no soko kara (Dark Water) 2004; juvenile fiction includes Namida (Tears); non-fiction: Fusei no Tanjo, Kazoku no Kizuna, Papa-ism. *Address:* c/o HarperCollins Publishers, 77–85 Fulham Palace Road, Hammersmith, London, W6 8JB England.

SVANIDZE, Nikolay Karlovich; Russian historian and broadcast journalist; b. 2 April 1955, Moscow; m. Marina Svanidze; one s. *Education:* Moscow State Univ. *Career:* Researcher, Inst. of USA and Canada, USSR (now Russian) Acad. of Sciences 1978–91; on staff, Russian TV 1992–, commentator, Vesti 1991–94, host, Zerkalo 1996–2007, Deputy Dir of Information Programmes and Head of Studio Information and Analytical Programmes 1996–97; Deputy Chair., then Chair. All Russian State TV and Radio Co. 1996–98; mem. Public Chamber. *Publication:* Medvedev 2008. *Honours:* Teffi Prize, Russian Acad. of TV. *Address:* All-Russian State Television and Radio Broadcasting Company, 125040 Moscow, ul. 5-aya Yamskogo Polya 19/21, Russia (office). *Telephone:* (495) 745-39-78 (office). *Fax:* (495) 975-26-11 (office).

SVOBODA, Terese, MFA; American poet and writer; b. 5 Sept. 1950, Ogallala, Neb.; d. of Frank B. Svoboda and Anne Marie Walsh; m. Stephen M. Bull 1981; three s. *Education:* Univ. of British Columbia, Columbia Univ. *Career:* Rare Manuscript Curator, McGill Univ. 1969; Co-Producer, PBS-TV series Voices and Visions 1980–82; Distinguished Visiting Prof., Univ. of Hawaii 1992; Prof., Sarah Lawrence Coll. 1993, New School 1996, Williams Coll. 1998, Coll. of William and Mary 2001, Bennington Coll. 2007; McGee Prof., Davidson Coll. 2008, Columbia Univ. 2010; mem. PEN, Poets and Writers, Poets' House (Founder-mem. and Advisory Bd mem. 1986–91). *Film:* Margaret Sanger: A Public Nuisance Noble Savage. *Publications:* poetry: All Aberration 1985, Laughing Africa 1990, Mere Mortal 1995, Treason 2002, Weapons Grade 2009; fiction: Cannibal (Bobst Prize, Great Lakes Colleges Asscn New Writer's Award) 1995, A Drink Called Paradise 1999, Trailer Girl (short stories) 2001 (reissue 2009), Tin God 2006, Pirate Talk or Mermalade 2010; non-fiction: Black Glasses Like Clark Kent (Graywolf Prize) 2007; contribs: poems, fiction, essays and translations to periodicals. *Honours:* New York Times Book Review Writer's Choice Column Award 1985, Jerome Foundation Fellow 1988, Iowa Prize 1990, O. Henry Prize 2006. *Literary Agent:* c/o Alison Granucci, Blue Flower Arts, LLC, PO Box 1361, Millbrook, NY 12545, USA. *Telephone:* (845) 677-8559; 914-474-1576 (mobile). *Fax:* (845) 677-6446. *E-mail:* alison@blueflowerarts.com. *Website:* blueflowerarts.com. *Address:* c/o Graywolf Press, 2402 University Avenue, Suite 203, Saint Paul, MN 55114, USA. *E-mail:* svoboda@el.net (office). *Website:* www.graywolfpress.org; www.teresesvoboda.com.

SWADOS, Elizabeth A., BA; American composer and writer; b. 5 Feb. 1951, Buffalo, NY; d. of Robert O. Swados and Sylvia Swados (née Maisel). *Education:* Bennington Coll., VT. *Career:* Composer and Music Dir Peter Brook, France, Africa, USA 1972–73; Composer-in-Residence, La Mama Experimental Theater Club, New York 1977–; mem. Faculty Carnegie-Mellon Univ., PA 1974, Bard Coll., New York 1976–77, Sarah Lawrence Coll., New York 1976–77; Creative Artists Service Program Grantee 1976. *Compositions include:* theatre scores: Elektra 1970, Medea 1972, Fragments of Trilogy 1974, Trojan Women 1974, The Good Women of Setzuan 1975, The Cherry Orchard 1977, As You Like It 1979, Haggadah 1980, Doonesbury (with Garry Trudeau) 1983, The Tower of Evil 1990, The Mermaid Wakes 1991, Spider Opera 2006, Kaspar Hauser 2007; film scores: Step By Step 1973, Sky Dance 1979, Seize the Day 1986, Family Sins 1987. *Publications include:* The Girl With the Incredible Feeling 1976, Runaways 1979, Lullaby 1980, Sky Dance 1980, The Beautiful Lady (musical) 1984, Listening Out Loud: Becoming a Composer 1988, The Four of Us 1991, The Myth Man 1994, Flamboyant (novel), At Play (textbook) 2006, The One and Only Human Galaxy (poetry) 2009; for children: Inside Out: A Musical Adventure 1990, Dreamtective: The Dreamy and Daring Adventures of Cobra Kite (Kid Genesis) 1999, Hey You! C'mere! A Poetry Slam 2002, The Animal Rescue Store 2005, My Depression: A Picture Book 2005; other: The Girl With the Incredible Feeling (audio cassette), Everyone is Different (CD). *Honours:* New York State Arts Council Playwriting Grantee 1977–, Guggenheim Fellow, Ford Fellow, Covenant Fellow, three Obie Awards, Village Voice 1972, Outer Critics' Circle Award 1977, Steven Spielberg Righteous Person Grantee. *Address:* 112 Waverly Place, New York, NY 10011, USA (home). *E-mail:* info@lizswados.com (office). *Website:* www.lizswados.com.

SWAFFORD, Jan Johnson, BA, MMA, DMA; American writer and composer; b. 10 Sept. 1946, Chattanooga, Tenn.; m. Julie Pisano 1973 (divorced 1979). *Education:* Harvard Univ., Yale School of Music, Tanglewood. *Career:* Asst Prof., Boston Univ. School for the Arts 1977–78; Visiting Asst Prof., Hampshire Coll., Amherst 1979–81, Amherst Coll. 1980–81; freelance composer and writer 1981–; Lecturer in English, Tufts Univ.; currently Instructor in Theory, Musicology and Composition, Boston Conservatory. *Compositions include:* Passage for piccolo, strings and percussion 1975, Landscape with Traveller for orchestra 1981, Shore Lines for soprano and flute 1982, Labyrinths for violin and cello 1983, Midsummer Variations for piano quintet 1985, Chamber Sinfonietta for chamber orchestra 1988, They Who Hunger for piano quartet 1989, Requiem in Winter for string trio 1991, From the Shadow of the Mountain for string orchestra 2001, They That Mourn for piano trio 2002. *Publications:* The Vintage Guide to Classical Music 1992, The New Guide to Classical Music 1993, Charles Ives: A Life with Music 1996, Johannes Brahms: A Biography 1997; contrib. articles and reviews to Symphony, New England Monthly, Musical America, Slate, Guardian Int.; programme/liner notes for Boston, Chicago and San Francisco Symphonies, and Sony, Naxos and RCA recordings. *Honours:* Massachusetts Artists' Foundation grant 1983, prizewinner, New England Composers' Competition 1984, Harvard-Mellon Fellowship 1988, Nat. Endowment for the Arts Composers Fellow 1991, L.L. Winship-PEN New England Award 1997. *Address:* English Department, Tufts University, 210 East Hall, Medford, MA 02155, USA (office). *E-mail:* JanSwaff@aol.com (home).

SWAN, Gladys, BA, MA; American writer, painter and academic; b. 15 Oct. 1934, New York, NY; m. Richard Swan 1955 (died 2008); two d. *Education:* Western New Mexico Univ., Claremont Grad. School. *Career:* Prof. of English, Franklin Coll. 1969–86; Faculty MFA Program in Creative Writing, Vermont Coll. 1981–96; Distinguished Visiting Writer-in-Residence, Univ. of Texas, El Paso 1984–85; Visiting Prof. of English, Ohio Univ. 1986–87; Assoc. Prof. of English, Univ. of Missouri-Columbia 1987–98; mem. PEN American Center, Soc. of Midland Authors. *Exhibitions:* Expressions: Paintings, Pottery, Poetry – Stephens Coll., Interior Landscapes – Boone Co. Historical Soc., Paper in Particular. *Publications:* On the Edge of the Desert 1979, Carnival for the Gods 1986, Of Memory and Desire 1989, Do You Believe in Calbega de Vaca? 1991, Ghost Dance: A Play of Voices 1992, A Visit to Strangers 1996, News From the Volcano 2000, A Garden Amid Fires 2007, The World of Carnival 2010, New & Selected Stories 2011; contrib. to Kenyon Review, Virginia Quarterly Review, Ohio Review, Writers Forum, Shenandoah, Sewanee Review. *Honours:* Hon. DHumLitt (Western New Mexico Univ.); Lilly Endowment Faculty Open Fellowship 1975–76, Fulbright Sr Lectureship 1988, Lawrence Foundation Award for Fiction 1994, Sewanee Review Tate Prize for Poetry 2001. *Address:* 2601 Lynnwood Drive, Columbia, MO 65203, USA (home). *E-mail:* swangl@missouri.edu (home). *Website:* www.gladysswan.com.

SWAN, Susan Jane, BA; Canadian novelist, writer, poet and academic; *Associate Professor of Humanities, York University*; b. 9 June 1945, Midland, Ont.; m. Barry Haywood 1969 (divorced); one d.; pnr Patrick Crean. *Education:* McGill Univ. *Career:* Assoc. Prof. of Humanities, York Univ., Toronto 1989–, Roberts Chair in Canadian Studies 1999–2000; mem. Writers' Union of Canada, PEN, Scarlet Key. *Film adaptations:* Wives of Bath, Lost and Delirious. *Publications include:* Queen of the Silver Blades 1975, Unfit for Paradise 1982, The Biggest Modern Woman of the World 1983, Tesseracts (co-author) 1985, The Last of the Golden Girls 1989, Language in Her Eye (ed.) 1990, Mothers Talk Back (co-ed.) 1991, Slow Hand 1992, The Wives of Bath 1993, Stupid Boys are Good to Relax With 1996, What Casanova Told Me 2004; contrib. many short stories, articles and poems to various publications. *Literary Agent:* InkWell Management, 521 Fifth Avenue, 26th Floor, New York, NY 10175, USA. *Telephone:* (212) 922-3500. *Fax:* (212) 922-0535. *E-mail:* info@inkwellmanagement.com. *Website:* www.inkwellmanagement.com. *Address:* 213 Brunswick Avenue, Toronto, ON M5S 2M7, Canada (home). *Telephone:* (416) 323-0870 (home). *E-mail:* sswan@yorku.ca (office). *Website:* www.susanswanonline.com.

SWARD, Robert Stuart, BA, MA; American poet, writer and university lecturer; *Poet-in-Residence, University of California, Santa Cruz*; b. 23 June 1933, Chicago, Ill.; partner Gloria K. Alford; two s. three d. *Education:* Univ. of Illinois, Univ. of Iowa, Middlebury Coll., Vermont, Univ. of Bristol, UK. *Career:* Poet-in-Residence, Cornell Univ. 1962–64, Univ. of Victoria, BC 1969–73, Univ. of California, Santa Cruz 1987–; Writer-in-Residence, Foothill Writers' Conf. summers 1988–; writer, Writing Programme, Language Arts Dept, Cabrillo Coll. 1989–2000; teaches Autobiography and Memoir workshops at Esalen Inst. and elsewhere 2010–; Contributing Ed. Blue Moon Review, Perihelion's Writers' Friendship Series, electronic chapbooks 'God is in the Cracks' and 'Rosy Cross Father', and other Internet literary pubs, including Web Del Sol, locus for literary arts; mem. League of Canadian Poets, Modern Poetry Asscn, Nat. Writers' Union (USA), Writers' Union of Canada. *Exhibition:* Lithographs at Provincial Museum, Victoria, BC. *Radio:* Producer for show Anthology (CBC) 1982–84. *Recordings:* three albums of poetry. *Publications:* Uncle Dog and Other Poems 1962, Kissing the Dancer and Other Poems 1964, Half a Life's History: New and Selected Poems 1957–83 1983, The Three Roberts (with Robert Zend and Robert Priest) 1985, Four

Incarnations: New and Selected Poems 1957–91 1991, Family (with David Swanger, Tilly Shaw and Charles Atkinson) 1994, Earthquake Collage 1995, A Much-Married Man (novel) 1996, Uncivilizing: A Collection of Poems 1997, Rosicrucian in the Basement: Selected Poems 2001, Heavenly Sex: New and Selected Poems 2002, Collected Poems 1957–2004 2004, God is in the Cracks – A Narrative in Voices 2006; contrib. to anthologies, newspapers and magazines. *Honours:* USN Korean War Veteran (combat zone); Fulbright Fellowship 1960–61, Guggenheim Fellowship 1965–66, D.H. Lawrence Fellowship 1966, Djerassi Foundation Residency 1990, Villa Montalvo Literary Arts Award for Poetry 1990, Way Cool Site Award for Editing Internet Literary Magazine 1996. *Address:* PO Box 7062, Santa Cruz, CA 95061-7062, USA (office). *Telephone:* (831) 426-5247 (office). *E-mail:* robert@robertsward.com (office); sward@cruzio.com (office). *Website:* www.robertsward.com; www.redroom.com/author/robert-sward.

SWARUP, Vikas, BA; Indian diplomatist and writer; *Deputy High Commissioner to South Africa*; b. 1963, Allahabad; m. Aparna Swarup; two s. *Education:* Allahabad Univ. *Career:* joined Indian Foreign Service 1986, posted to Turkey 1987–90, USA 1993–97, Ethiopia 1997–2000, UK 2000–03, Deputy High Commr, Pretoria, South Africa 2006–. *Publications:* Q&A (film version, Slumdog Millionaire) 2006, Six Suspects 2008. *E-mail:* vikas.swarup@gmail.com (office). *Website:* www.vikasswarup.net.

SWEDE, George, BA, MA; Canadian poet, editor, writer and educator; *Professor Emeritus of Psychology, Ryerson University*; b. (Juris Purins), 20 Nov. 1940, Riga, Latvia; s. of Janis Purins and Virginia Purins; m. 1st Bonnie Lewis 1964 (divorced 1969); m. 2nd Anita Krumins 1970; two s. *Education:* Univ. of British Columbia, Dalhousie Univ. *Career:* instructor, Vancouver City Coll. 1966–67; instructor 1968–73, Prof. of Psychology, Ryerson Univ., Toronto 1973–2006, Chair. Dept of Psychology 1998–2003, Prof. Emer. 2006–; Dir, Poetry and Things, Toronto 1969–71, Developmental Psychology, Ryerson Open Coll. 1973–75; Poetry Ed., Poetry Toronto 1980–81; Co-Ed., Cross-Canada Writer's Quarterly 1982–90; Assoc. Ed. Red Moon Press 2000–08; Ed. Frogpond: The Journal of the Haiku Society of America 2008–12; Co-founder Haiku Canada 1977 (Hon. Life mem.); mem. Haiku Soc. of America, League of Canadian Poets, PEN, Writers' Union of Canada. *Exhibitions include:* Visualog 3, Arternatives, San Luis Obispo, Calif. 1990, Visualog 4, Orange Co. Community Coll., Newburgh, NY 1991, Visualog 4, Mid-Hudson Arts & Science Centre, Poughkeepsie, NY 1991, Friends of St Bride Temporary Type Exhbns, London 2005. *Radio:* five short stories on RTE: Memories of Mexico (Quiet Quarter) 2001, poetry and interviews on CJRT, Contemporary Canadian Poets 1984, Close to Silence (BBC Radio 3) 2000, numerous shorter sessions on CBC, PBS and local stations across Canada. *Television:* interview, Romper Room (CTV) 1986, Japan Air Lines Haiku Contest, (BCTV) 1987, In Conversation With (TV Ontario) 1992, numerous shorter sessions on local stations across Canada. *Publications:* poetry: Tell-Tale Feathers 1978, A Snowman, Headless 1979, As Far as the Sea Can Eye 1979, Flaking Paint 1983, Frozen Breaths 1983, Tick Bird 1983, Bifids 1984, Night Tides 1984, Time is Flies 1984, High Wire Spider 1986, I Throw Stones at the Mountain 1988, Leaping Lizzard 1988, Holes in My Cage 1989, I Want to Lasso Time 1991, Leaving My Loneliness 1992, Five O'Clock Shadows (co-author) 1996, My Shadow Doing Something 1997, Almost Unseen 2000, First Light, First Shadows 2006, Joy In Me Still 2010, White Thoughts, Blue Mind 2010; editor: The Canadian Haiku Anthology 1979, Cicada Voices 1983, The Universe is One Poem 1990, There Will Always Be a Sky 1993, The Psychology of Art: An Experimental Approach 1994, Tanka Splendour 1998, Global Haiku: Twenty-Five Poets Worldwide (ed.) 2000; non-fiction: The Modern English Haiku 1981, Creativity: A New Psychology 1994; fiction: Moonlit Gold Dust 1979, Quilby: The Porcupine Who Lost His Quills (with Anita Krumins) 1980, Missing Heirloom 1980, Seaside Burglaries 1981, Downhill Theft 1982, Undertow 1982, Dudley and the Birdman 1985, Dudley and the Christmas Thief 1986; contrib. to magazines world-wide. *Honours:* Hon. Life mem. Canadian Psychological Asscn 2007; Hon. Curator American Haiku Archives, California State Library 2008–09; Haiku Soc. of America Book Award 1980, High/Coo Press Chapbook Competition Winner 1982, Museum of Haiku Literature Awards 1983, 1985, 1993, Canadian Children's Book Centre Our Choice Awards 1984, 1985, 1987, 1991, 1992, Third Place, Poetry Soc. of Japan Int. Tanka Contest 1990, First Prize, Mainichi Daily News Haiku in English competition 1993, Second Prize, Mainichi 125th Anniversary Haiku Contest 1997, First Prize, The Snapshot Press Tanka Collection Competition 2005, Second Prize, Mainichi Daily News Haiku in English Competition 2009, Second Prize, Foreign Language Category, 15th Kusamakura Int. Haiku Competition 2010, Grand Prize, Foreign Language Category, 16th Kusamakura Int. Haiku Competition 2011. *Address:* Box 279, Station P, Toronto, ON M5S 2S8, Canada (office). *Telephone:* (416) 534-4584 (home). *E-mail:* gswede@ryerson.ca (office). *Website:* home.primus.ca/~swede.

SWEENEY, Matthew, BA; Irish poet and writer; b. 6 Oct. 1952, Co. Donegal; m. Rosemary Barber 1979. *Education:* University College, Dublin, Polytechnic of North London. *Career:* Writer-in-Residence, Farnham College, Surrey 1984–85, South Bank Centre 1994–95; Writing Fellowship, University of East Anglia 1986; Publicist and Events Asst, Poetry Society 1988–90; Poet-in-Residence, Hereford and Worcester 1991, National Library for the Blind 1999; Writer-in-Residence on the Internet, Chadwyck-Healey 1997–98. *Publications:* A Dream of Maps 1981, A Round House 1983, The Lame Waltzer 1985, The Chinese Dressing Gown 1987, Blues Shoes 1989, The Flying Spring Onion 1992, Cacti 1992, The Snow Vulture 1992, Fatso in the Red Suit 1995, Emergency Kit: Poems for Strange Times (ed. with Jo Shapcott) 1996, Writing Poetry (with John Hartley Williams) 1997, The Bridal Suite 1997, Penguin Modern Poets 12 1997, Beyond Bedlam: Poems Written Out of Mental Distress (ed. with Ken Smith) 1997, A Smell of Fish 2000, Selected Poems 2002, Fox 2002, Sancuary 2004, Irish Poems (ed.) 2005, Stories 2006, Black Moon 2007. *Honours:* Prudence Farmer Prize 1984, Cholmondeley Award 1987, Arts Council Literature Award 1992, Arts Council of England Writer's Award 1999. *Address:* c/o Jonathan Cape Ltd., Random House UK, 20 Vauxhall Bridge Road, London SW1V 2SA, England (office). *Website:* www.randomhouse.co.uk (office).

SWICK, Marly, BA, MFA, PhD; American writer and academic; b. 26 Nov. 1949, Indianapolis, IN. *Education:* Stanford Univ., American Univ., Univ. of Iowa. *Career:* Prof. of Fiction Writing, Univ. of Nebraska 1988–; fmr teacher of creative writing, Univ. of Nebraska – Lincoln; currently Prof. in the Creative Writing Program, University of Missouri – Columbia. *Publications:* Monogamy (short stories) 1990, The Summer Before the Summer of Love (short stories) 1995, Paper Wings (novel) 1996, Evening News (novel) 1999; contrib. short stories to many magazines, including Atlantic Monthly, Gettysburg Review, Iowa Review, North American Review, Redbook. *Honours:* James Michener Award 1986, Univ. of Wisconsin Creative Writing Inst. Fellowship 1987, NEA grant 1987, Iowa Short Fiction Prize 1990, Gold Chalk Award for teaching excellence. *Address:* Creative Writing Program, University of Missouri – Columbia, 107 Tate Hall, Columbia, MO 65211-1500, USA (office). *E-mail:* marlyswick@yahoo.com (office).

SWIFT, Daniel, PhD; British, author, writer and academic; *Assistant Professor of English Literature, Skidmore College*; b. 1977. *Education:* Univ. of Oxford, Columbia Univ., USA. *Career:* Asst Prof. of English Literature, Skidmore Coll., NY. *Publications:* Bomber Country (non-fiction) 2010; contrib. essays, profiles and reviews to the Financial Times Magazine, New York Times Book Review, Daily Telegraph, The Nation, Times Literary Supplement. *Literary Agent:* David Godwin Associates Ltd, 55 Monmouth Street, London, WC2H 9DG, England. *Telephone:* (20) 7240-9992. *Fax:* (20) 7395-6110. *E-mail:* assistant@davidgodwinassociates.co.uk. *Address:* Skidmore College, Palamountain Hall 335, 815 North Broadway, Saratoga Springs, NY 12866, USA (office). *Telephone:* (518) 580-8395 (office). *E-mail:* dswift@skidmore.edu (office).

SWIFT, Graham Colin, FRSL; British writer; b. 4 May 1949, London; s. of Lionel Allan Stanley Swift and Sheila Irene Swift (née Bourne). *Education:* Dulwich Coll., Queens' Coll., Cambridge, Univ. of York. *Publications:* novels: The Sweet Shop Owner 1980, Shuttlecock 1981, Waterland 1983, Out of This World 1988, Ever After 1992, Last Orders 1996, The Light of Day 2003, Tomorrow 2007, Wish You Were Here 2011; short stories: Learning to Swim and Other Stories 1982; anthology: The Magic Wheel (co-ed. with David Profumo) 1986, Making an Elephant: Writing from Within 2009. *Honours:* Hon. Fellow, Queens' Coll. Cambridge 2005; Hon. LittD (East Anglia) 1998; Hon. DUniv (York) 1998; Hon. DLit (London) 2003; Geoffrey Faber Memorial Prize, Guardian Fiction Prize, RSL Winifred Holtby Award 1983, Premio Grinzane Cavour (Italy) 1987, Prix du meilleur livre étranger (France) 1994, Booker Prize, James Tait Black Memorial Prize 1996. *Literary Agent:* c/o AP Watt Ltd, 20 John Street, London, WC1N 2DR, England. *Telephone:* (20) 7405-6774. *Fax:* (20) 7831-2154. *E-mail:* apw@apwatt.co.uk. *Website:* www.apwatt.co.uk.

SWINBURNE, Richard Granville, MA, BPhil, FBA; British academic; *Nolloth Professor Emeritus of the Philosophy of the Christian Religion, University of Oxford*; b. 26 Dec. 1934, Smethwick, West Midlands, England; s. of William H. Swinburne and Gladys E. Swinburne; m. Monica Holmstrom 1960 (separated 1985); two d. *Education:* Univ. of Oxford. *Career:* Fereday Fellow, St John's Coll., Oxford 1958–61; Leverhulme Research Fellow in History and Philosophy of Science, Univ. of Leeds 1961–63; Lecturer in Philosophy, Univ. of Hull 1963–72; Prof. of Philosophy, Univ. of Keele 1972–84; Nolloth Prof. of the Philosophy of the Christian Religion, Univ. of Oxford 1985–2002, Prof. Emer. 2002–; Visiting Assoc. Prof., Univ. of Maryland 1969–70; Visiting Prof., Syracuse Univ. 1987, Univ. of Rome 2002, Catholic Univ. of Lublin 2002, Yale Univ. 2003, St Louis Univ. 2003. *Publications:* Space and Time 1968 (second edn) 1981, The Concept of Miracle 1971, An Introduction to Confirmation Theory 1973, The Coherence of Theism 1977 (revised edn 1993), The Existence of God 1979 (second edn) 2004, Faith and Reason 1981 (second edn) 2005, Personal Identity (with S. Shoemaker) 1984, The Evolution of the Soul 1986, revised edn 1997), Responsibility and Atonement 1989, Revelation 1991 (second edn) 2007, The Christian God 1994, Is There a God? 1996 (revised edn) 2010, Providence and the Problem of Evil 1998, Epistemic Justification 2001, The Resurrection of God Incarnate 2003, Was Jesus God? 2008. *Address:* 50 Butler Close, Oxford, OX2 6JG, England (home). *Telephone:* (1865) 514406 (home). *E-mail:* richard.swinburne@oriel.ox.ac.uk (office).

SYAL, Meera, MBE, BA; British writer and actress; b. 27 June 1963, Wolverhampton; d. of Surendra Syal and Surrinder Syal; m. 1st 1989; one d.; m. 2nd Sanjeev Bhaskar 2005; one s. *Education:* Queen Mary's High School for Girls, Walsall, Univ. of Manchester. *Career:* actress in one-woman comedy One of Us after graduation (Nat. Student Drama Award); fmr actress Royal Court Theatre, London; writer of screenplays and novels; actress and comedienne in theatre, film and on TV; contrib. to The Guardian newspaper. *Plays include:* Serious Money (London and Broadway, New York) 1987, Stitch

1990, Peer Gynt 1990, Bombay Dreams (story to musical) 2001, Rafta Rafta (Royal Nat. Theatre) 2007. *Radio includes:* Legal Affairs 1996, Goodness Gracious Me 1996–98, The World as We Know It 1999. *Film appearances include:* Sammie and Rosie Get Laid 1987, A Nice Arrangement, It's Not Unusual, Beautiful Thing 1996, Girls' Night 1997, Jhoom Barabar Jhoom 2007, Mad Sad & Bad 2009. *Television appearances include:* The Real McCoy (five series) 1990–95, My Sister Wife (BBC series) 1992, Have I Got News For You 1992, 1993, 1999, Sean's Show 1993, The Brain Drain 1993, Absolutely Fabulous 1995, Soldier Soldier 1995, Degrees of Error 1995, Band of Gold 1995, Drop the Dead Donkey 1996, Ruby 1997, Keeping Mum (BBC sitcom) 1997–98, The Book Quiz 1998, Goodness Gracious Me (first UK Asian TV comedy sketch show; co-writer) 1998–2000, Room 101 1999, The Kumars at No. 42 2002–06, Jekyll 2006, Beautiful People 2008, Holby City 2009. *Written works include:* A Nice Arrangement (short TV film) 1991, My Sister Wife (TV film; Best TV Drama Award, Comm. for Racial Equality, Awards for Best Actress and Best Screenplay, Asian Film Acad. 1993) 1992, Bhaji on the Beach (film) 1994, Anita and Me (novel and adapted for TV) (Betty Trask Award) 1996, Goodness Gracious Me (comedy sketch TV show; co-writer) 1999, Life isn't all Ha Ha Hee Hee (novel) 1999. *Honours:* Scottish Critics Award for Most Promising Performer 1984, Woman of the Year in the Performing Arts, Cosmopolitan Magazine 1994, Chair.'s Award, Asian Women of Achievement Awards 2002, Women in Film and TV Creative Originality Award 2002. *Address:* c/o Rochelle Stevens, 2 Terretts Place, Islington, London, N1 1QZ, England (office). *Telephone:* (20) 7359-3900 (office).

SYJUCO, Miguel, MFA, PhD; Philippine writer; b. 1976, Makati; s. of Augusto (Boboy) Syjuco Jr. *Education:* Ateneo de Manila Univ., Columbia Univ., USA, Univ. of Adelaide, Australia. *Career:* moved to New York 2001, has lived in Paris, Adelaide and Montréal; fmr copy editor, Montréal Gazette; co-f. and ed, Localvibe.com. *Publications:* Ilustrado (novel) (Don Carlos Palanca Memorial Award for Literature Grand Prize, Man Asian Literary Prize) 2008; contrib. poems, stories and articles to nat. and international publications including The New Yorker, Paris Review, Esquire, Time. *E-mail:* miguel.syjuco@gmail.com (home). *Website:* www.syjuco.com.

SYLVESTER, Janet, BA, MA, PhD; American poet and academic; b. 5 May 1950, Youngstown, OH; m. James Vandenberg 1973 (divorced 1980). *Education:* Goddard Coll., Univ. of Utah. *Career:* has taught at Univ. of South Carolina at Columbia, Harvard Univ., Ohio Univ., Old Dominion Univ., Wichita State Univ., Sweet Briar Coll.; currently faculty mem., Lesley Univ. *Publications:* That Mulberry Wine 1985, A Visitor at the Gate 1996, The Mark of Flesh 1997; contributions: anthologies, reviews, quarterlies and journals. *Address:* Department of Creative Writing, Lesley University, 29 Everett Street, Cambridge, MA 02138, USA (office). *Website:* www.lesley.edu (office).

SZÉCSI, Noémi, BA, MA; Hungarian novelist and translator; b. 29 March 1976, Szentes; one d. *Education:* Eötvös Loránd Univ. *Publications:* Finnugor vámpír 2002, Kommunista Monte Cristo (EU Prize for Literature 2009) 2006, Utolsó kentaur 2009, Nyughatatlanok 2011. *Honours:* József Attila State Decoration for literary achievement 2011; EU Prize for Literature 2009. *Literary Agent:* c/o Európa Kiadó, Budapest 1036, Lajos utca 74–76, Hungary. *Telephone:* (1) 3312700. *Fax:* (1) 3314162. *E-mail:* info@europakiado.hu. *Website:* www.europakiado.hu (office); www.szecsinoemi.hu.

SZEWC, Piotr; Polish writer and journalist; b. 1961, Zamościu. *Education:* Catholic Univ. of Lublin. *Career:* Ed. of periodical, Nowe Ksiazki (New Books). *Publications include:* Świadectwo 1983, Zagłada 1987, Ocalony na Wschodzie 1991, i Zmierzchy i poranki 2000, Syn kapłana 2001, Bociany nad powiatem 2005, Całkiem prywatnie 2006.

SZIRTES, George Gabor Nicholas, BA, PhD, FRSL; British (b. Hungarian) poet, writer and translator; *Reader in Creative Writing, University of East Anglia;* b. (Gábor György Miklós Szirtes), 29 Nov. 1948, Budapest, Hungary; s. of László Szirtes and the late Magdalena Nussbächer; m. Clarissa Upchurch 1970; one s. one d. *Education:* Leeds Coll. of Art, Goldsmith's Coll. of Art. *Career:* settled in UK 1956; taught in various schools 1973–91; Co-ordinator Creative Writing, Norwich School of Art and Design 1992–2007; Reader in Creative Writing, Univ. of East Anglia 2007–; Pres. Performing Right Soc.; mem. PEN, Soc. of Authors, British Centre for Literary Trans.; Fellow, English Asscn 2007–. *Publications:* poetry: The Slant Door 1979, November and May 1981, The Kissing Place 1982, Short Wave 1984, The Photographer in Winter 1986, Metro 1988, Bridge Passages 1991, Blind Field 1994, Selected Poems 1996, The Red All Over Riddle Book (juvenile) 1997, Portrait of My Father in an English Landscape 1998, The Budapest File 2000, An English Apocalypse 2001, A Modern Bestiary 2004, Reel (Poetry Book Soc. T. S. Eliot Prize 2005) 2004, New and Collected Poems 2008, English Words/Angol Szavak 2008, Shuck, Hick, Tiffey 2008, The Burning of the Books 2009, The Burning of the Books and Other Poems 2009; as editor: The Colonnade of Teeth: Modern Hungarian Poetry (co-author) 1996, The Lost Rider: Hungarian Poetry, 16th–20th Century 1998, New Writing 10 (ed. with Penelope Lively) 2001, An Island Sound: Hungarian Fiction and Poetry Before and Beyond the Iron Curtain (co-ed.) 2004, New Order, Hungarian Poets of the Post 1989 Generation 2010; criticism: Exercise of Power, The Art of Ana Maria Pacheco 2001, Fortinbras at the Fishhouses 2010; several Hungarian works translated into English, including Ottó Orbán, The Blood of the Walsungs: Selected Poems 1991, Zsuzsa Rakovsky, New Life: Selected Poems 1994, Gyula Krúdy, The Adventures of Sinbad (short stories) 1999, László Krasznahorkai, The Melancholy of Resistance 1999, The Night of Akhenaton: Selected Poems of Ágnes Nemes Nagy 2003, Sándor Márai, Conversation in Bolzano 2004, László Krasznahorkai, War and War 2005, Sándor Márai, Rebels 2007, Ferenc Karinthy, Metropole 2008, Sándor Márai, Esther's Inheritance 2008, Sándor Márai, Portraits of a Marriage 2011; own books translated into various languages; contrib. to numerous books, anthologies, journals and magazines, various introductions to books. *Honours:* Gold Star of the Hungarian Repub. 1991; Geoffrey Faber Memorial Prize 1980, Arts Council Bursary 1984, British Council Fellowship 1985, 1987, 1989, Cholmondeley Award 1987, Dery Prize for Trans. 1991, European Poetry Trans. Prize 1995, George Cushing Award 2001, Soc. of Authors Travelling Scholarship 2002, Leverhulme Research Fellowship 2003–05, Pro Cultura Hungarica Medal 2004, T.S. Eliot Prize 2004, T.S. Eliot Memorial Lecturer 2005, StAnza Lecturer 2006, Bess Hokin Prize 2008. *Address:* 16 Damgate Street, Wymondham, Norfolk, NR8 0BQ, England (home). *Telephone:* 7752-713533 (mobile) (home); (1953) 603533 (office). *E-mail:* georgeszirtes@gmail.com (office). *Website:* www.georgeszirtes.co.uk.

T

TABBERER, Margaret (Maggie) May, AM; Australian journalist, fashion executive and television presenter; b. 11 Dec. 1936, d. of A. Trigar; m. (divorced); two d. *Education:* Unley Tech. Coll. *Career:* model 1957–61; Fashion Publicity Promotions, Maggie Tabberer and Assocs 1961–80; fashion writer Sydney Daily Mirror 1965–80; host Maggie Show (Channel Seven Network) 1968–70; Fashion Ed. Australian Women's Weekly 1981–96; Dir Maggie T. Licencing; face of Fox FX Channel 2000–; patron, Melanoma Foundation. *Television:* as host: Maggie Show (Channel 7 Network) 1968–70, The Home Show (ABC-TV) 1990–93, Maggie.. At Home With (Foxtel) 2001–10. *Publication:* Maggie (autobiog.) 1998. *Honours:* Hon. Fellow, Australian Marketing Inst. 1985, Hon. Life mem., Australian Brain Foundation 1995; Gold Logie Award 1969–70; Cobb and Co. TV Woman of the Year 1970, Recognition of Excellence Award, Fashion Group of Melbourne 1986, Advance Australia Award 1988. *Address:* c/o Harry M. Miller Group, Fox Studio Australia, Mailbox 38A #38, 38 Driver Avenue, Moore Park, NSW 2021, Australia (office). *Telephone:* (2) 8353-2444 (office). *E-mail:* maggietabberer@bigpond.com (office).

TADJO, Véronique, BA, PhD; Côte d'Ivoirian writer, poet and artist; b. 1955, Paris, France. *Education:* Univ. of Abidjan, Univ. of Paris, La Sorbonne. *Career:* has lived in France, USA, UK, Kenya, Côte d'Ivoire and South Africa; Fulbright research scholar, Howard Univ., Washington, DC 1983; lecturer, English Dept, Univ. of Abidjan –1993; has conducted workshops on writing, illustrating books for children and other topics in various countries. *Exhibitions:* paintings in several solo and group exhbns. *Publications:* novels: A vol d'oiseau (trans. as As the Crow Flies) 1986, Le Royaume aveugle 1991, Champs de bataille et d'amour 1999, Reine Pokou (Grand Prix Littéraire d'Afrique Noire) 2005; poetry: Latérite 1984, À mi-chemin, Talking Drums 2000; non-fiction: L'Ombre D'Imana (trans. as The Shadow of Imana: Travels in the heart of Rwanda) 2002; children's books (illustrated by the author): La Chanson de la vie 1989, Le Seigneur de la Danse 1993, Mamy Wata et le Monstre 1993, Grand-mère Nanan 1996. *Honours:* L'Agence de Cooperation Culturelle et Technique literary prize 1983, UNICEF Prize 1993. *E-mail:* veroniqf@veroniquetadjo.com (office). *Website:* www.veroniquetadjo.com.

TAFDRUP, Pia, BA; Danish poet and writer; b. 29 May 1952, Copenhagen; d. of Finn Tafdrup and Elin Tafdrup; m. Bo Hakon Jørgensen 1978; two s. *Education:* Univ. of Copenhagen. *Career:* Chair. Art Expert Cttee for the Literary Art 1993–95; mem. Danish Literary Acad. 1989–, Danish PEN Centre, Danish Language Council 1991–99, Council of Danish Arts Foundation 2002–09, European Acad. of Poetry 2009–. *Dance:* libretto to The Town of Viso 1999. *Plays:* Døden i bjergene (Death in the Mountains) 1988, Jorden er blå (The Earth is Blue) 1991. *Film:* A Portrait Film, Thousandborn (directed by Cæcilia Holbek Trier) 2005. *Radio play:* Døden i bjergene (Death in the Mountains) 1990. *Television:* A Portrait Film, Thousandborn (directed by Cæcilia Holbek Trier) 2005. *Recording:* Morning Myth from the poem Mythic Morning, Per Nørgård: Mythic Morning. Works for Choir II 2005. *Publications:* poetry: Når der går hul på en engel (When an Angel Breaks her Silence) 1981, Konstellationer – en antologi af dansk lyrik 1976–1981 (Constellations – An Anthology of Danish Poems) (ed.) 1982, Intetfang (No Hold) 1982, Den inderste zone (The Innermost Zone) 1983, Springflod (Spring Tide) 1985, Transformationer. Poesi 1980–1985 (Transformations. Poetry 1980–1985) (ed.) 1985, Hvid feber (White Fever) 1986, Sekundernes bro (The Bridge of Moments) 1988, Over vandet går jeg. Skitse til en poetik (Walking Over Water. An Outline of a Poetics) 1991, Krystalskoven (The Crystal Forest) 1992, Territorialsang (Territorial Song) 1994, Dronningeporten (Queen's Gate) 1998, Tusindfødt (Thousand Born) 1999, Digte 1981–83 (Poems 1981–83) 1999, Digte 1984–88 (Poems 1984–88) 2000, Digte 1989–98 (Poems 1989–98) 2001, Hvalerne i Paris (The Whales in Paris) 2002, Tarkovskijs heste (Tarkovský's Horses) 2006, Springet over skyggen. Udvalgte digte 1981–2006 (Jump Across The Shadow. Selected Poems 1981–2006) 2007, The Dreamt Tree 2007, Boomerang 2008, Trækfuglens kompas (The Bird Compass) 2010; prose: Hengivelsen (Surrender, novel) 2004, Stjerne uden land (Star Without Land) 2008; translations: Spring Tide 1989, Ten Poems 1989, Dagen ditt ljus. Dikter 1981–1994 1995, Över vattnet går jag 1997, 2002, Drottningporten 2000, La Forêt de Cristal 2000, Tiché vybuchy 2000, Queen's Gate 2001, Kristaini gozd 2004, Bindooumlu 2004, Valama i Paris 2004, Ponte de Focagem do Oceano 2004, Territorial Song (in Hebrew) 2005, A gi seg bort 2005, De koninginnepoort 2006, Ge sig hän 2006, Selected Poems in Macedonian 2007, Los caballos de Tarkovski 2009 (Tarkovsky's Horses 2010); English versions of poems have appeared in literary journals in UK, USA and Canada; poems have been translated into Arabic, Bosnian, Bulgarian, Dutch, English, Estonian, Finnish, French, German, Greek, Greenlandic, Hebrew, Hungarian, Icelandic, Italian, Japanese, Latvian, Lithuanian, Macedonian, Norwegian, Polish, Portuguese, Rumanian, Russian, Serbo-Croat, Slovenian, Slovakian, Spanish, Swedish, Turkish and Vietnamese; contrib. to many journals and anthologies. *Honours:* Kt, Order of Dannebrog 2001; numerous awards, including Danish State Art Foundation Scholarship for Authors 1984–86, 12 grants 1986–97, Ragna Sidén Foundation Danish Literature Prize for Women 1997, Lifelong Artist's Grant, Danish State Art Foundation 1998, Nordic Council Literature Prize 1999, Soeren Gyldendal Award 2005, Nordic Prize, Swedish Acad. 2006, Ján Smrek Prize 2009. *Address:* c/o Gyldendal, Klarebodberne 3, 1001 Copenhagen K, Denmark (office). *Telephone:* 35-43-27-88 (home). *Fax:* 35-43-27-88 (home). *E-mail:* tafdrup@post6.tele.dk (home). *Website:* www.tafdrup.com.

TAHER, Bahaa; Egyptian writer; b. 1935, Cairo; m. Stefka Taher; two d. from previous marriage. *Education:* Univ. of Cairo. *Career:* worked for Egyptian Radio 2 culture channel –1975; mem. Gallery 68 writers' movement; left Egypt to become UN trans., Geneva, Switzerland 1981–95; later returned to Egypt. *Publications:* short stories: al-Khutuba (The Engagement) 1972, Bi-l-Amsi Halamtu Bi-K 1984, Ana al-Malik Ji'tu 1985, Zahabtu ila Shallal (I Went to a Waterfall) 1996; novels: Sharq al-Nakhila 1985, Qalat Duha 1985, Khalati Safiyya wal-Dayr (Aunt Safiyya and the Monastery) (Guiseppe Acerbi Prize, Italy 2000) 1991, Al-Hob fi al-Manfa (Love in Exile) 1995, Wahet al-Ghuroub (Sunset Oasis; Int. Prize for Arabic Fiction 2008) 2006; non-fiction: Masrahiyyat Misriyya: Ard wa-Naqd (analysis of ten Egyptian plays) 1985. *Honours:* State Award of Merit in Literature 1998. *Address:* c/o Dar El-Sharook, 8 Sibaweh Al-Masri, Cairo (Nasr City) 11371, Egypt (office). *Telephone:* (2) 24023399 (office). *Fax:* (2) 24037567 (office). *E-mail:* dar@shorouk.com (office). *Website:* www.shorouk.com (office).

TAILLANDIER, François Antoine Georges, MA; French writer; b. 20 June 1955, Chamalières; s. of Henri Taillandier and Denise Ducher; three c. *Career:* teacher 1980–83; full-time writer 1984–, also contrib. Le Figaro (newspaper), La Montagne (newspaper), L'Humanité (newspaper), L'Atelier du Roman (periodical); Admin., Soc. des Gens de Lettres de France. *Publications:* fiction: Personnages de la rue du Couteau 1984, Tott 1985, Benoît ou les contemporains obscurs 1986, Les Clandestins (Prix Jean-Freustié 1991) 1990, Les Nuits Racine 1992, Fan et le jouet qui n'existe pas (with Charles Barat) 1993, Mémoires de Monte-Cristo 1994, Des hommes qui s'éloignent 1997, Anielka (Grand Prix du roman de l'Académie française 1999) 1999, Le cas Gentile 2001, La Grande Intrigue: Vol. 1 Option Paradis 2005, Vol. 2 Telling 2006, Il n'y a personne dans les tombes 2007; non-fiction: Tous les secrets de l'avenir 1996, Aragon 1997, Journal de Marseille 1999, N6, la route de l'Italie 1999, Les Parents lâcheurs 2001, Borges, une restitution du monde 2002, Pour ou contre Jacques Chirac (with Joseph Macé-Scaron) 2002, Un Autre langue 2004, Balzac (biog.) 2005. *Honours:* Prix Roger Nimier 1992, Acad. française Prix de la critique 1997. *Address:* c/o Editions Stock, 31 rue de Fleurus, 75006 Paris, France (office).

TAIT, Arch, MA, PhD; British translator and academic; b. 6 June 1943, Glasgow, Scotland. *Education:* Trinity Hall, Cambridge. *Career:* Lecturer, Univ. of East Anglia 1970–83; Ed., Glas: New Russian Writing 1991; Sr Lecturer, Univ. of Birmingham 1997–; mem. Translators' Asscn, Soc. of Authors, British Asscn for Slavonic and East European Studies. *Publications:* Lunacharsky, The Poet Commissar 1984; translator: The Russian Style, by Evgenia Kirichenko 1991, Is Comrade Bulgakov Dead?, by Anatoly Smeliansky 1993, Baize-covered Table with Decanter, by Vladimir Makanin 1995, Skunk: A Life, by Peter Aleshkovsky 1997, Sonechka and Other Stories, by Ludmila Ulitskaya 1997, Under House Arrest, by Yevgeny Kharitonov 1998, Hurramabad, by Andrei Volos 2001, Medea and her Children, by Ludmila Ulitskaya 2002, Putin's Russia, by Anna Politkovskaya 2004, Globalisation and the Future of Mankind, by Gennady Zyuganov 2004, Sonechka: A Novella and Stories, by Ludmila Ulitskaya 2005, Another Look into Putin's Soul by Andrei Piontkovsky 2006, Lost in Translation by Lilia Shevtsova 2007, A Russian Diary by Anna Politkovskaya 2007, The Economics of Symbolic Exchange by Alexander Dolgin 2009, also numerous short stories and articles. *E-mail:* arch@russianwriting.com (office). *Website:* russianwriting.com.

TAKAGI, Nobuko; Japanese novelist and academic; *Director, Soaked in Asia Project, Asia Centre, Kyushu University*; b. (Nobuko Tsuruta), 6 April 1946, Yamaguchi Pref. *Education:* Junior Coll. of Tokyo Women's Christian Univ. (now Tokyo Women's Christian Univ.). *Career:* Special Guest Prof., Dept of Contemporary Asian Cultural Research, Kyushu Univ. Asia Centre; mem. Selection Cttee, Akutagawa Award. *Publications:* titles in trans.: That Narrow Road 1980, A Distant Friend 1981, A Following Wind 1982, To a Friend Embracing the Light (Akutagawa Prize 1984) 1983, Beyond the Shining Sea 1985, Street Corner Justice 1985, Set Sail on a Starry Night: Satsuki's Story 1986, Maze in the Heat of the Day 1988, Deep in the Forest of Swirling Blossoms: Satsuki's Story 1989, Insect Symphony 1989, Hot Letters 1989, Shades of the Land of Dreams 1989, Die the Time Blue 1990, The Tree Where Dwells the Black Noddy 1990, Foggy Meridian 1990, Flowing Elegies 1991, Southern Squall 1991, Flashback: My High Noon 1991, Afternoon of White Light 1992, Not a Confession 1992, Peak Against Colourful Clouds 1992, Forest on the Lake Bed 1993, Ice Fire 1993, Drops Falling from the Milky Way 1993, Heat 1994, The Burning Vine (Shimase Love Award 1994) 1994, Light Through Petals 1995, Parting Letters 1995, Water Veins (Women Literary Award) 1995, A Billion Nights 1995, The Season when Cherry Trees are in Leaf 1996, Swirling Blossom 1996, Love Space 1997, The Colours of the Months 1997, Darkness in Istanbul 1998, Shade of the Orchid 1998, Samoan Illusion 1998, The Translucent Trees (Tanizaki Junichiro Award) 1999, A Prophecy of a Hundred Years 2000, The Burning Tower 2001, Weird Scenery 2001, Mamiko 2001, Hundred Loves of Ephesus 2002, Flowers of Sin 2003, Devil Wind in Naples 2003, Maimai Shinko 2004, Hokkai (Minister of Education, Science and Technology Art Encouragement Prize 2006) 2005; contrib. to Inside and Other Short Fiction 2006. *Honours:* Medal of Purple

Ribbon. *Address:* Kyushu University Asia Centre, 6-10-1, Hakozaki, Higashi-ku, Fukuoka 812-8581, Japan (office). *E-mail:* asia@isc.kyushu-u.ac.jp (office).

TAKAHASHI, Genichirō; Japanese writer and critic; b. 1 Jan. 1951, Onomichi, Hiroshima. *Education:* Yokohama Nat. Univ. *Career:* participated in radical student movt 1960s and early 70s, imprisoned for six months; worked as a labourer until 1981; novelist and essayist 1982–; Visiting Fellow, Donald Keene Center of Japanese Culture, Columbia Univ., USA 2002. *Publications:* novels: Sayonara Gyangutachi (Gunzō New Writers' Award) (first novel to be translated into English, as Sayonara, Gangsters 2004) 1982, Ōbaa za reinbō (Over the Rainbow) 1984, Oyogu Otoko (The Swimming Man) 1984, Jon Renon tai kaseijin (John Lennon Versus the Martians) 1985, Yūga de kanshōteki Nihon yakkyū (Japanese Baseball: Languid and Happy) (Mishima Yukio Award 1988) 1987, Penguin mura ni hi ga Ochite (Sundown in Penguin Town) 1989, Wakusei P-13 no himitsu (The Secret of Planet 13) 1990, Gosutobasutazu (Ghostbusters) 1997; numerous collections of essays including Bungaku ga konna ni wakatte ii kashira (Is it Okay to Understand Literature So Well?) 1989. *Address:* c/o Vertical, Inc., 451 Park Avenue South, 7th Floor, New York, NY 10016, USA. *Telephone:* (212) 730-5047. *E-mail:* info@vertical-inc.com. *Website:* www.vertical-inc.com.

TAKAHASHI, Takako; Japanese writer; b. 1932, Kyoto; m. Takahashi Kazumi (died 1971). *Education:* Kyoto Univ. *Career:* writer of novels and short stories 1972–1985; trans. of French writers including Mauriac; retd from writing to become a Roman Catholic nun first in Paris, then Japan; returned to writing during 1990s. *Publications:* Sojikei (Congruent Figures) 1972, Sora no hate made (To the End of the Sky) 1973, Botsuraku Fusei (Falling Scenery) 1974, Yuwakusha (The Temptress) 1976, Ningyo no ai (Doll Love) 1976, Ronrii uuman (trans. as Lonely Woman) 1977, Ten no Mizumi 1977, Yomigaeri no ie (The House of Rebirth) 1980, Yosoi seya, waga tamashii yo (Gird up Thyself, Oh My Soul) 1982, Ikari no ko (Child of Wrath; Yomiuri Prize) 1985, Tochi no Chikara 1992, Takahashi Kazumi to iu hito: Nijugonen no nochi ni 1997, Kirei na hito 2003, Haka no hanashi 2006. *Address:* c/o Kodansha International Ltd, Otowa Building, 1-17-14 Otowa, Bunkyo-ko, Tokyo, 112-8652, Japan (office).

TALBOT, David; American author, journalist and entrepreneur; *CEO, Salon.com*; b. 22 Sept. 1951, Los Angeles; s. of Lyle Talbot; m. Camille Peri 1989; two s. *Education:* Harvard Boys School, Univ. of California, Santa Cruz. *Career:* fmr Ed. Mother Jones magazine; fmr Features Ed., San Francisco Examiner; Founder, CEO and Ed.-in-Chief, Salon.com –2005, CEO 2011–; Founder The Talbot Players media production co. 2008; has written for Time, The New Yorker, Rolling Stone, Crawdaddy. *Publications:* Brothers: the Hidden History of the Kennedy Years 2007, Devil Dog: the Amazing True Story of the Man Who Saved America 2010, Season of the Witch 2012. *Address:* c/o Salon Media Group Inc., 101 Spear Street, Suite 203, San Francisco, CA 94105, USA (office). *Telephone:* (415) 645-9200 (office). *Fax:* (415) 645-9204 (office). *E-mail:* Karen@talbotplayers.com (office). *Website:* www.salon.com (office); www.talbotplayers.com (office).

TALBOT, Michael Owen, BA, BMus, PhD, ARCM, FBA; British writer; *Professor Emeritus of Music, University of Liverpool*; b. 4 Jan. 1943, Luton, Beds.; m. Shirley Mashiane 1970; one s. one d. *Education:* Royal Coll. of Music, London, Clare Coll., Cambridge. *Career:* Lecturer, Univ. of Liverpool 1968–79, Sr Lecturer 1979–83, Reader 1983–86, James and Constance Alsop Prof. of Music 1986–2003, Emer. Prof. of Music 2003–; mem. Royal Musical Asscn, Società Italiana di Musicologia; mem. int. advisory bd, Fondazione Giorgio Cini; Corresp. Fellow, Ateneo Veneto. *Publications:* Vivaldi 1978, Albinoni: Leben und Werk 1980, Antonio Vivaldi: A Guide to Research 1988, Tomaso Albinoni: The Venetian Composer and his World 1990, Benedetto Vinaccesi: A Musician in Brescia and Venice in the Age of Corelli 1994, The Sacred Vocal Music of Antonio Vivaldi 1995, Venetian Music in the Age of Vivaldi 1999, The Musical Work: Reality or Invention (ed.) 2000, The Finale in Western Instrumental Music 2001, The Business of Music (ed.) 2002, The Chamber Cantatas of Antonio Vivaldi 2006, Vivaldi and Fugue 2009, The Vivaldi Compendium 2011; contrib. to professional journals, including Early Music, Music and Letters, Music Review, Musical Times, Journal of the Royal Musical Association, Soundings, The Consort, Note d'Archivio, Händel Jahrbuch, Informazioni e Studi Vivaldiani, Studi Vivaldiani, Journal of Eighteenth Century Music, Recercare. *Honours:* Cavaliere del Ordine al Merito (Italy) 1980; Oldman Prize 1990, Serena Medal 1999. *Address:* School of Music, The University of Liverpool, Liverpool, L69 7WW, England (office). *Fax:* (151) 794-3141 (office). *E-mail:* mtalbot@liv.ac.uk (office).

TALBOTT, Strobe; American journalist and fmr government official; *President, Brookings Institution*; b. 25 April 1946, Dayton, Ohio; s. of Nelson S. Talbott and Josephine Large; m. Brooke Lloyd Shearer 1971; two s. *Education:* Hotchkiss School, Connecticut, Yale Univ. and Univ. of Oxford, UK. *Career:* joined Time magazine; Diplomatic Corresp., White House Corresp., Eastern Europe Corresp., Washington Bureau Chief 1984–89, Ed.-at-Large 1989–94; Amb.-at-Large State Dept Feb.–Dec. 1993; Deputy Sec. of State 1994–2001; Pres. The Brookings Inst. 2002–; Rhodes Scholar, Univ. of Oxford 1969; Dir Carnegie Endowment for Int. Peace; mem. Council on Foreign Relations; Fellow, American Acad. of Arts and Sciences 2009–. *Publications:* Khrushchev Remembers 1970, Khrushchev Remembers: The Last Testament (jtly) 1974, Endgame: The Inside Story of Salt II 1979, Deadly Gambits: The Reagan Administration and the Stalemate in Nuclear Arms Control 1984, The Russians and Reagan 1984, Reagan and Gorbachev (jtly) 1987, The Master of the Game: Paul Nitze and the Nuclear Peace 1988, At the Highest Levels: The Inside Story of the End of the Cold War (jtly) 1993, The Age of Terror: America and The World After September 11 (co-ed.) 2001, The Russia Hand: A Memoir of Presidential Diplomacy 2002, Engaging India 2005, The Great Experiment 2008. *Address:* The Brookings Institution, 1775 Massachusetts Avenue, NW, Washington, DC 20036, USA (office). *Telephone:* (202) 797-6000 (office). *Fax:* (202) 797-6004 (office). *E-mail:* communications@brookings.edu (office). *Website:* www.brookings.edu (office).

TALLENT, Elizabeth Ann, BA; American writer and academic; *Professor, Stanford University*; b. 8 Aug. 1954, Washington, DC; m. Barry Smoots, 28 Sept. 1975, one s. *Education:* Illinois State Univ. at Normal. *Career:* fmrly taught literature and creative writing, Univ. of California at Irvine, Iowa Writers Workshop, Univ. of California at Davis; Dir of Creative Writing Programme, Stanford Univ. 1994–96, Prof. 1994–; mem. Poets and Writers. *Publications:* Married Men and Magic Tricks (non-fiction) 1982, In Constant Flight (short stories) 1983, Museum Pieces (novel) 1985, Time with Children (short stories) 1987, Honey (short stories) 1993; contrib. to publications, including The New Yorker, Esquire, Harper's, Grand Street, The Paris Review, The Threepenny Review, ZZYZYVA, and in The Best American Short Stories and O. Henry Award collections. *Honours:* Bay Area Book Reviewers Asscn Fiction Award, NEA Fellowship 1992. *Address:* Creative Writing Program, Department of English, Stanford University, Building 460, Margaret Jacks Hall, Stanford, CA 94305-2087, USA (office). *Telephone:* (650) 723-0031 (office). *Fax:* (650) 725-0755 (office). *E-mail:* tallent@stanford.edu (office). *Website:* english.stanford.edu (office).

TALU, Umur E., BA; Turkish journalist; b. 7 Aug. 1957, Istanbul; s. of M. Muvakkar and G. Güzin; m. Şule Talu 1987; two d. *Education:* Galatasaray High School and Bosphorus Univ. *Career:* educ. specialist, Railway Workers' Union 1977–78; Int. Econ. Cooperation Sec. Union of Municipalities 1978–80; Econ. Corresp. Günaydin (newspaper) 1980–82; Chief, Econ. Dept Günes (newspaper) 1982–83; Ed. with Cumhuriyet (newspaper) 1983–85; Chief, Econ. Dept Milliyet (newspaper) 1985–86, News Ed. 1986–87, 1988–92, Ed.-in-Chief 1992–94, columnist 1994; currently columnist, Gazete Haberturk; Ed. Hürriyet (newspaper) 1987–88. *Publications:* Social Democracy in Europe (co-author) 1985, Keynes (trans.) 1986, Mr Uguran's Post Office 1996. *Honours:* Freedom of the Press Award, Turkish Journalists' Asscn 1996. *Address:* c/o Gazete Haberturk, Abdülhakhamit Cad. No: 25, Beyoğlu, Istanbul, Turkey. *E-mail:* utalu@htgazete.com.tr. *Website:* www.haberturk.com/htyazar/umur-talu.

TAMARO, Susanna; Italian writer; b. 12 Dec. 1957, Trieste; d. of Giovanni Tamaro and Anna Tamaro. *Education:* Centro Sperimentale di Cinematografia, Rome. *Career:* fmr asst to film dir, Umberto Saba; fmr programme planner, RAI TV; columnist, Famiglia Cristiana magazine 1997–98; f. Tamaro Foundation, Zurich 2000. *Publications:* novels: La testa tra le nuvole 1989, Per voce sola (Int. PEN Prize) 1991, Va'dove ti porta il cuore 1994, Anima Mundi 1997, Cara Mathilda, non vedo l'ora che l'uomo cammini 1998, Rispondimi 2001, Più fuoco, più vento 2002, Fuori 2003, Ogni Parola è un seme 2005, Ascolta la mia voce 2006, Luisito. Una storia d'amore 2008, Il Grande Albero 2009; children's fiction: Cuore di ciccia 1992, Papirofobia 1994, Il Cerchio Magico 1994, Tobia e l'angelo 1998; non-fiction: Verso Casa 1999. *Address:* Via Cenisio 16, Milan, Italy (office). *Telephone:* (02) 48015553 (office). *E-mail:* ediper@tin.it (office). *Website:* www.susannatamaro.it.

TAMEN, Pedro, LLB; Portuguese poet and foundation executive; b. 1 Dec. 1934, Lisbon; s. of Mário Tamen and Emília Tamen; m. Maria da Graça Seabra Gomes 1975; two s. two d. *Education:* Lisbon Univ. *Career:* Dir Moraes Publishing House 1958–75; Pres. Portuguese PEN Club 1987–90, Vice Pres. 1991–2002; Trustee Calouste Gulbenkian Foundation, Lisbon 1975–2000; mem. Bd Portuguese Asscn of Writers. *Publications:* 12 books of poetry since 1958; Retábulo das Matérias (Collected Works) 2001, Analogia e Dedos (Prémio Literário Inês de Castro 2008) 2006, O Livro do Sapateiro (Poetry Prize, Portuguese Asscn of Writers 2011, Correntes de Escritas Prize 2011) 2010, Um Teatro às Escuras 2011. *Honours:* D. Diniz Prize 1981, Grand Prix for Translation 1990, Critics Award 1993, INAPA Prize for Poetry 1993, Nicola Prize for Poetry 1998, Press Poetry Prize 2000, PEN Club Poetry Prize 2000, Inês de Castro Prize 2006, Luis Miguel Nava Prize 2006. *Address:* Apartado 47, EC Palmela, 2951-901 Palmela, Portugal (home). *E-mail:* ptamen@gmail.com (home). *Website:* www.arscives.com/pedrotamen.

TAMER, Zakaria (see Tamir, Zakaria)

TAMIR, Zakaria; Syrian writer and journalist; b. 2 Jan. 1931, Damascus. *Career:* worked at Ministry of Culture 1960–63, 1980–81, Ministry of Information 1967; Ed., al-Mawqef al-Arabi 1963–65, Ed.-in-Chief 1972–75; screenwriter, Jeddah TV, KSA 1965–66; Head of Drama Dept, Syrian TV 1967–70; Ed.-in-Chief, Rafi magazine 1970–71, Osama magazine 1975–77, al-Marifah magazine 1978–80; Managing Ed., al-Dustoor magazine, UK 1981–82, al-Naquid magazine, UK 1988–93; Cultural Ed., at-Tadhamon magazine, UK 1983–88, Riyadh al-Rayes Publisher, UK 1988–93; founder mem. Syrian Writers' Union 1968– (fmr vice-pres.). *Publications:* (titles translated) short story collections: The Neighing of the White Steed 1957, Spring in the Ashes 1963, The Thunder 1970, Why the River Fell Silent 1973, Damascus Fire 1973, Tigers on the Tenth Day 1978, The Flower Spoke to the Bird 1978, Noah's Summons 1994, We Shall Laugh 1998, If! 1998, Sour Grapes 2000, Breaking the Spirit 2002, The Hedgehog 2005, Breaking Knees 2008; non-fiction: Glories, Arabs, Glories (articles) 1986, The Victim's Satire of his Killer 2003. *Honours:* Syrian Order of Merit 2002; Sultan Bin Ali al-Owais

Cultural Foundation Prize for Fiction 2001, Al Amajidi ibn Dhaher Blue Metropolis Arab Literary Prize 2009. *Address:* c/o Quartet Books, 27 Goodge Street, London, W1T 2LD, England (office).

TAMM, Peter; German publisher; *Chairman, International Maritime Museum, Hamburg;* b. 12 May 1928, Hamburg; s. of Emil Tamm; m. Ursula Weisshun 1958; one s. four d. *Education:* Univ. of Hamburg. *Career:* Shipping Ed., Hamburger Abendblatt 1948–58; Man. Dir Ullstein GmbH (Publr) Berlin 1960–62; Man. Dir Bild-Zeitung Hamburg 1962–64; Man. Dir Verlagshaus Axel Springer and Ullstein Verlag Berlin 1964–68, Chair. and CEO Axel Springer Verlag 1968–82, Chair. Bd 1982–91; Vice-Pres. Bundesverband Deutscher Zeitungsverleger 1982–91; currently Chair. of Bd Int. Maritime Museum, Hamburg, Peter Tamm Sen. Foundation. *Publication:* Maler der See 1980. *Honours:* Bayerischer Verdienstorden 1976, Bundesverdienstkreuz I. Klasse 1986, Grosses Verdienstkreuz des Verdienst-ordens der Bundesrepublik Deutschland 1993, Cavaliere Ufficiale: Orden für die Verdienste um die Italienische Republik 1994, Hamburger Bürgerpreis 1996, Vasco da Gama Naval Medal 1997, Grosses Verdienstkreuz mit Stern 1998, Seewartmedaille in Silber 1998, Bismarckmedaille in Gold 1999, Gold Ehrenkreuz der Bundeswehr 2001, Professoren-Titel durch die Stadt Hamburg 2002, Commdr Order of the White Rose of Finland 2003, Hamburg Citizen of the Year 2004. *Address:* Koreastrasse 1, 20457 Hamburg, Germany (office). *Telephone:* (30) 092300 (office). *Fax:* (30) 0923045 (office). *E-mail:* A.Reineward@peter-tamm-sen.de (office). *Website:* www.imm-hamburg.de.

TAN, Amy Ruth, MA, LHD; American writer; b. 19 Feb. 1952, Oakland, Calif.; d. of John Yuehhan and Daisy Ching Tan (née Tu); m. Louis M. DeMattei 1974. *Education:* San José State Univ., Univ. of California, Berkeley, Dominican Coll., San Rafael. *Career:* specialist in language devt, Alameda Co. Asscn for Mentally Retarded 1976–80; Project Dir MORE, San Francisco 1980–81; freelance writer 1981–88; Marian McFadden Memorial Lecturer, Indianapolis-Marion Co. Public Library 1996. *Film:* The Joy Luck Club (screenwriter, producer) 1993. *Publications:* The Joy Luck Club (Commonwealth Club and Bay Area Book Reviewers' Best Fiction Award 1990) 1989, The Kitchen God's Wife 1991, The Hundred Secret Senses 1995, The Bonesetter's Daughter 2000, Saving Fish from Drowning 2005, Rules for Virgins 2011; for children: The Moon Lady 1992, The Chinese Siamese Cat 1994; non-fiction: The Opposite of Fate: A Book of Musings (autobiog.); numerous short stories and essays. *Honours:* Best American Essays Award 1991. *Literary Agent:* Steven Barclay Agency, 12 Western Avenue, Petaluma, CA 94952, USA. *Telephone:* (707) 773-0654. *Fax:* (707) 778-1868. *Website:* www.barclayagency.com. *Address:* c/o Ballantine Publications Publicity, 201 East 50th Street, New York, NY 10022, USA. *Website:* www.amytan.net.

TAN, Hwee Hwee, MA, MFA; Singaporean writer; b. 1974. *Education:* Univs of E Anglia and Oxford, UK, New York Univ., USA. *Career:* short stories have appeared in PEN Int., New Writing; arts corresp. Business Times, Singapore 2001; sr writer Twenty4Seven Magazine 2001; Tamara S. Wanger Fellow, Nat. Univ. of Singapore; currently freelance journalist TIME, Harper's Bazaar, Elle, Far Eastern Economic Review, BBC. *Publications include:* Foreign Bodies 1996, Mammon Inc. 2001. *Honours:* New York Times Fellowship 1997, numerous awards from BBC, Nat. Univ. of Singapore; Young Artist Award from Nat. Arts Council 2003, Singapore Literature Prize 2004 (for Mammon Inc.). *E-mail:* hwee_tan@hotmail.com (office). *Website:* www.geocities.com/hweehwee_tan/index.html.

TAN, Lide; Chinese translator, literary critic and academic. *Education:* Univ. of Foreign Languages, Shanghai. *Career:* Prof., Inst. of Foreign Literature, Chinese Acad. of Social Science, Beijing; co-Ed., Critiques littéraires magazine; Sec. Gen., Chinese Asscn of Researchers in French Literature 2002; organized ceremony to celebrate Victor Hugo bicentenary, Nat. Ass. of China 2009. *Publications:* trans. of selected works of André Maurois, Marguerite Duras, Claude Anet, Françoise Sagan, Patrick Modiano, Diderot, Maupassant, Colette; also literary criticism. *Honours:* Grand Prix de la Francophonie, Acad. Française 2008. *Address:* c/o Institute of Foreign Literature, Chinese Academy of Social Science, 5 Jianguomen Nei Da Jie, Beijing 100732, China (office). *E-mail:* ldtan@sina.com (home).

TANENHAUS, Sam, MA; American editor; *Book Review Editor, The New York Times;* b. 1956; m. Kathryn Bonomi; one c. *Education:* Grinnell Coll., Iowa, Yale Univ. *Career:* fmrly with publicity Farrar, Straus and Giroux; with trade, acad. and crossover books Oxford Univ. Press, Chelsea House; Asst Ed. Op-Ed page The New York Times 1997–99, Ed. Book Review 2004–; contrib. ed. Vanity Fair 1999–2004; mem. jury on biog. Pulitzer Prize Cttee 2000; affiliated writer School of Journalism NYU 2002–03; mem. exec. bd Soc. of American Historians. *Publications:* Literature Unbound: A Guide for the Common Reader 1984, Louis Armstrong: Biography of a Musician 1989, Whittaker Chambers: A Biography (LA Times Book Prize for Biography) 1997, The Death of Conservatism 2009; contrib. to Wall Street Journal, Washington Post, Boston Globe, LA Times, New York Times Magazine, National Review, New Criterion, New York Review of Books, New Republic, American Scholar, Commentary. *Honours:* John M. Olin Foundation Award, Bradley Foundation Award, Nat. Endowment of the Humanities grant 1997, Stanford Univ. Hoover Inst. Media Fellow 2000, 2002. *Address:* The New York Times, 620 Eighth Avenue, New York, NY 10018, USA (office). *Telephone:* (212) 556-1234 (office). *Website:* www.nytimes.com (office).

TANIKAWA, Shuntaro; Japanese poet, translator, playwright and scriptwriter; b. 15 Dec. 1931, Tokyo; s. of Tanikawa Tetsuzo. *Career:* made publishing debut with poems in Bungakukai literary journal 1950; has given readings in Moscow, Leningrad, Berlin, Frankfurt, Zürich, Rotterdam, London, and under the auspices of the Japan Soc., Acad. of American Poets, Library of Congress, USA; trans. of Mother Goose and Peanuts comic strips. *Film scripts:* Tokyo orimpikku 1965, Seishun 1968, Kyoto 1969, Nihon to nihonjin 1970, Ai futatabi 1971, Matatabi 1973, Hi no tori 1978. *Publications include:* poetry: Nijuoku konen no kodoku 1952, Rokujuni no sonetto 1953, Utsumuku shonen 1971, Hibi no chizu 1983, Tanikawa Shuntaro Shishu 1995, Kotoba Asobi Uta (juvenile), Kazuki yasuo no omocha bako (with Kazuki Yasuo) 2003, Shagaru to konoha 2005; poetry in trans.: With Silence My Companion 1975, At Midnight in the Kitchen I Just Wanted to Talk to You 1980, The Selected Poems of Shuntaro Tanikawa 1983, Coca-Cola Lessons 1986, Floating the River in Melancholy 1988, Songs of Nonsense 1991, 62 Sonnets 1992, Two Billion Light-Years of Solitude 1996, Naked 1996, Map of Days 1996, Selected Poems 1998, Looking Down 2000, Les Anges de Klee, Naif, On Love, Giving People Poems. *Honours:* Saida Takashi Drama Prize, Noma, Shogakkan, Hana-Tsubaki, Yomiuri literary prizes. *Address:* c/o University of Hawaii Press, 2840 Kolowalu Street, Honolulu, HI 96822-1888, USA.

TARANTINO, Quentin; American film director, actor and screenwriter; b. 27 March 1963, Knoxville, Tenn.; s. of Tony Tarantino and Connie McHugh. *Career:* fmrly worked in Video Archives, Manhattan Beach, Calif. *Films:* My Best Friend's Birthday (actor, dir, prod.) 1987, Reservoir Dogs (actor, dir) 1992, Past Midnight (assoc. prod.) 1992, Siunin Wong Fei-hung tsi titmalau (prod.) 1993, Eddie Presley (actor) 1993, Sleep With Me (actor) 1994, Killing Zoe (exec. prod.) 1994, Somebody to Love (actor) 1994, Pulp Fiction (actor, dir) (Golden Palm, Cannes Film Festival, Acad. Award for Best Screenplay 1995) 1994, Destiny Turns on the Radio (actor) 1995, Desperado (actor) 1995, Four Rooms (actor, dir, exec. prod.) 1995, Red Rain (prod.) 1995, Girl 6 (actor) 1996, From Dusk Till Dawn (actor, exec. prod.) 1996, Curdled (actor, exec. prod.) 1996, Jackie Brown (dir) 1997, God Said, 'Ha!' (exec. prod.) 1998, 40 Lashes (dir) 2000, Little Nicky (actor) 2000, Kill Bill Vol. I (dir, prod.) 2003, Kill Bill Vol. II (dir, prod.) 2004, Daltry Calhoun (exec. prod.) 2005, Hostel (exec. prod.) 2005, Freedom's Fury (exec. prod.) 2006, Grindhouse (actor) 2007, Death Proof (writer, producer, dir, actor) 2007, Planet Terror (actor) 2007, Sukiyaki Western Django (actor) 2007, Diary of the Dead (voice) 2007, Planet Terror (prod.) 2007, Hell Ride (exec. prod.) 2008, Inglourious Basterds (dir) 2009. *Film screenplays:* My Best Friend's Birthday 1992, Reservoir Dogs 1992, True Romance 1993, Natural Born Killers 1994, Pulp Fiction 1994, Four Rooms (segment: The Man from Hollywood) 1995, From Dusk Till Dawn 1996, Jackie Brown 1997, 40 Lashes (dir) 2000, Kill Bill (also novel) 2003, Inglourious Basterds 2009. *Television:* ER (dir, episode 'Motherhood') 1994, Alias (actor, one episode) 2004, CSI: Crime Scene Investigation (dir, writer two episodes) 2005, Alias (actor, four episodes) 2006. *Honours:* Career Achievement Award, Casting Soc. of America 2004, Empire Film Award for Icon of the Decade 2005, Golden Eddie Filmmaker of the Year Award, American Cinema Eds 2007, Lifetime Achievement Award, Cinemanila Int. Film Festival 2007; Officier, Ordre des Arts et des Lettres, Order of Merit of the Hungarian Repub. 2010. *Address:* William Morris Agency, 1 William Morris Place, Beverly Hills, CA 90212; 6201 Sunset Boulevard, Suite 35, Los Angeles, CA 90028, USA.

TARN, Nathaniel, BA, MA, PhD; American poet, critic, translator, anthropologist and academic; *Professor Emeritus of Poetry, Comparative Literature and Anthropology, Rutgers University;* b. 30 June 1928, Paris, France; m. 1st (divorced); two c.; m. 2nd Janet Rodney 1981. *Education:* Univ. of Cambridge, UK, École des Hautes Études, Univ. of Paris, France, Yale Univ., Univ. of Chicago, London School of Econs and School of Oriental and African Studies, London, UK. *Career:* Visiting Prof., SUNY at Buffalo 1969–70, Princeton Univ. 1969–70, Univ. of Pennsylvania 1976, Jilin Univ., People's Repub. of China 1982; Prof. of Poetry, Comparative Literature and Anthropology, Rutgers Univ. 1970–85, Prof. Emer. 1985–. *Publications include:* poetry: Old Savage/Young City 1964, Penguin Modern Poets 7 (with Richard Murphy and Jon Silkin) 1966, Where Babylon Ends 1968, The Beautiful Contradictions 1969, October: A Sequence of Ten Poems Followed by Requiem Pro Duabus Filiis Israel 1969, The Silence 1970, A Nowhere for Vallejo: Choices, October 1971, Lyrics for the Bride of God 1975, Narrative of This Fall 1975, The House of Leaves 1976, From Alaska: The Ground of Our Great Admiration of Nature (with Janet Rodney) 1977, The Microcosm 1977, Birdscapes, with Seaside 1978, The Forest (with Janet Rodney) 1979, Atitlan/Alashka 1979, The Land Songs 1981, Weekends in Mexico 1982, The Desert Mothers 1984, At the Western Gates 1985, Palenque: Selected Poems, 1972–1984 1986, Seeing America First 1989, The Mothers of Matagalpa 1989, Flying the Body 1993, The Architextures 2000, Three Letters from the City: The St Petersburg Poems 1968–1998 2000, Selected Poems, 1950–2000 2002, Dying Trees 2003, Recollections of Being 2004, Ins and Outs of the Forest Rivers 2008, Avia 2008, The Persephones 2008; non-fiction: Views from the Weaving Mountain: Selected Essays in Poetics and Anthropology 1991, Scandals in the House of Birds 1998, The Embattled Lyric: Essays and Conversations in Poetics and Anthropology 2007. *Honours:* Guinness Prize 1963, Wenner Grenn Fellowships 1978, 1980, Commonwealth of Pennsylvania Fellowship 1984, Rockefeller Foundation Fellowship 1988. *Address:* PO Box 8187, Santa Fe, NM 87504, USA.

TARTT, Donna; American writer; b. 1963, Greenwood, Miss. *Education:* Univ. of Mississippi, Oxford, Bennington Coll., Vt. *Career:* published first sonnet in a Miss. literary review 1976. *Publications:* novels: The Secret

History 1992, The Little Friend 2002; short stories include: A Christmas Pageant (Harper's) 1993, A Garter Snake (GQ) 1995, True Crime (audio book) 1996; contrib. articles to magazines. *Honours:* WHSmith Literary Award 2003. *Literary Agent:* c/o Gill Coleridge, Rogers, Coleridge & White Ltd, 20 Powis Mews, London, W11 1JN, England. *Telephone:* (20) 7221-3717. *Fax:* (20) 7229-9084. *E-mail:* info@rcwlitagency.com. *Website:* www.rcwlitagency.com.

TARUSKIN, Richard Filler, PhD; American musicologist, critic and writer; *Professor of Musicology, University of California at Berkeley*; b. 2 April 1945, New York, NY. *Education:* Columbia Univ. *Career:* Asst Prof. 1975–81, Assoc. Prof. of Music 1981–87, Columbia Univ.; Visiting Prof., Univ. of Pennsylvania 1985; Assoc. Prof. 1986–89, Prof. 1989–, Univ. of California at Berkeley; Hanes-Willis Visiting Prof., Univ. of North Carolina at Chapel Hill 1987; music critic for Opus, New York Times; Fulbright-Hays Traveling Fellowship 1971–72; Guggenheim Fellowship 1987; mem. American Musicological Soc. *Publications include:* Opera and Drama in Russia 1981, Busnoi: The Latin-Texted Works (ed., two vols) 1990, Musorgsky: Eight Essays and an Epilogue 1993, Stravinsky and the Russian Traditions: A Biography of the Works Through Mavra (two vols) 1995, Text and Act: Essays on Music and Performance 1995, The Oxford History of Western Music (six vols) 2005; contrib. articles on Russian composers and operas in New Grove Dictionary of Opera (four vols) 1992; many articles and reviews in professional journals and general periodicals. *Honours:* Dent Medal, England 1987, ASCAP Deems Taylor Award 1989. *Address:* Department of Music, University of California at Berkeley, 216 Morrison Hall, Berkeley, CA 94720-1200, USA (office). *Telephone:* (510) 642-6185 (office). *Fax:* (510) 642-8480 (office). *E-mail:* taruskin@berkeley.edu (office). *Website:* ls.berkeley.edu/dept/music/Taruskin.html (office).

TATE, James Vincent, BA, MFA; American poet and academic; *Distinguished University Professor, University of Massachusetts at Amherst*; b. 8 Dec. 1943, Kansas City, Mo. *Education:* Univ. of Missouri, Kansas State Univ., Univ. of Iowa. *Career:* Instructor in Creative Writing, Univ. of Iowa 1966–67; Visiting Lecturer, Univ. of California, Berkeley 1967–68; Poetry Ed. Dickinson Review 1967–76; Trustee and Assoc. Ed. Pym-Randall Press 1968–80; Asst Prof. of English, Columbia Univ. 1969–71; Assoc. Prof., then Prof. of English 1971–, Univ. of Massachusetts, Amherst, currently Distinguished Univ. Prof.; Poet-in-Residence, Emerson Coll. 1970–71; Assoc. Ed. Barn Dream Press; mem. Acad. of American Poets (mem. Bd of Chancellors 2001–), American Acad. of Arts and Letters 2004–. *Publications:* poetry: Cages 1966, The Destination 1967, The Lost Pilot 1967, Notes of Woe: Poems 1968, Camping in the Valley 1968, The Torches 1968, Row with Your Hair 1969, Is There Anything? 1969, Shepherds of the Mist 1969, Amnesia People 1970, Are You Ready Mary Baker Eddy? (with Bill Knot) 1970, Deaf Girl Playing 1970, The Oblivion Ha-Ha 1970, Wrong Songs 1970, Hints to Pilgrims 1971, Absences 1972, Apology for Eating Geoffrey Movius' Hyacinth 1972, Hottentot Ossuary 1974, Viper Jazz 1976, Riven Doggeries 1979, Land of Little Sticks 1981, Constant Defender 1983, Reckoner 1986, Distance from Loved Ones 1990, Selected Poems (Pulitzer Prize 1992) 1991, Worshipful Company of Fletchers 1993, Shroud of the Gnome 1997, Memoir of the Hawk: Poems 2001, Return to the City of White Donkeys 2004, The Ghost Soldiers 2008; novels: Lucky Darryl 1977, The Route as Briefed 1999, Dreams of a Robot Dancing Bee 2001; contrib. to numerous books and periodicals. *Honours:* Yale Younger Poets Award 1966, Nat. Inst. of Arts and Letters Award 1974, Massachusetts Arts and Humanities Fellow 1975, Guggenheim Fellowship 1976, Nat. Endowment for the Arts Fellowship 1980, Nat. Book Award for Poetry 1994. *Address:* Department of English, University of Massachusetts, 466 Bartlett Hall, Amherst, MA 01003, USA (office). *Telephone:* (413) 545-5503 (office). *Fax:* (413) 545-3880 (office). *Website:* www.umass.edu/english (office).

TAVARES DIAS, Marina; Portuguese publishing executive, writer and journalist; b. 1 June 1962, Lisbon; one d. *Career:* journalist on Portugal Hoje, Diario Popular, Diario de Lisboa 1979–; writer 1987–; Publishing Dir Ibis Editores 1990–; organized 10th anniversary exhbn of Mario de Sa-Carneira's birth for UNESCO 1990. *Publications include:* Lisboa Desaparecida (Vol. 1) 1987, (Vol. 2) 1990, (Vol. 3) 1992, (Vol. 4) 1994, (Vol. 5) 1996, (Vol. 6) 1998, (Vol. 7) 2001, (Vol. 8) 2003, Photographias de Lisboa 1988, Mario Sá-Carneiro – Fotobiografia 1988, Rossio, Feira da Ladra, A Lisboa de Fernando Pessoa 1990, História de Futebol em Lisboa 2000, History of the Lisbon Trams 2001, Porto Desparecido 2002, Lisboa nos passos de Pessoa 2004, Lisboa Misteriosa 2005, Lisboa antes e Agora 2006, Lisboa Desaparecida (Vol. 9) 2007, D. Carlos 2007. *Honours:* Julio Cezar Machado Award for Journalism 1985, 1986; Julio Castilho Award for Literature 1987.

TAWADA, Yoko, MA; Japanese novelist; b. 23 March 1960, Tokyo. *Education:* Waseda Univ., Hamburg Univ. *Career:* based in Germany 1982–, writes in German and Japanese; Writer-in-Residence, Villa Aurora, Pacific Palisades, USA 1997; lectured on poetry at Univ. of Tübingen 1998; Max Kade Distinguished Visitor and Writer-in-Residence, Foreign Languages and Literatures Section, MIT 1999; Writer-in-Residence, Univ. of Kentucky 2004, Washington Univ. in St.Louis 2008, Stanford Univ. 2009, Cornell Univ. 2009. *Publications:* Nur da wo du bist da ist nichts (poems and stories) 1987, Das Bad (novel) 1989, Missing Heels (short story) 1991, Wo Europa anfaengt (Where Europe Begins, poems and stories) 1991, Sanninkankei (short stories) 1991, Inumukoiri (The Bridegroom was a Dog, short stories) (Akutagawa Prize) 1993, Ein Gast (novel) 1993, Arufabetto no kizuguchi (novel) 1993, Tintenfisch auf Reisen (short stories) 1994, Gottoharutotetsudo (short stories) 1996, Talisman (essays) 1996, Seijodensetsu (novel) 1996, Aber die Mandarinen muessen heute abend noch geraubt werden (poems) 1997, Kitunetsuki (poems) 1998, Hikon (novel) 1998, Verwandlungen (essays) 1998, Katakoto no uwagoto (essays) 1999, Hikari to zerachin no raipuchihhi (short stories) 2000, Opium fuer Ovid (novel) 2000, Hinagiku no ocha no baai (short stories) 2000, Yogisha no yakoressha 2002, Kyukeijikan 2002, Exophonie (essays) 2003, Tabi wo suru hadaka no me (novel) 2004, Uni ni otoshita namae 2006, Ameika 2006, Tokeru machi sukeru toori 2007, Students of the Snow (Noma Literary Prize) 2011. *Honours:* City of Hamburg Prize in Literature 1990, Gunzo Prize for new writers 1991, Lessing Prize 1994, Adelbert von Chamisso Prize 1996, Izumi Kyooka Literature Prize 2000, Punkamura Prix Des Deux Magots 2002, Ito Sei Literature Prize 2003, Tanizaki Junichiro Prize 2003, Goethe Medal 2005. *Address:* c/o konkursbuch Verlag Claudia Gehrke, PF 1621, 72006, Tübingen, Germany. *E-mail:* office@konkursbuch.com; tawadaoo@yahoo.co.jp. *Website:* www.konkursbuch.com/html/tawada.html; yokotawada.de.

TAWARA, Machi, BA; Japanese poet; b. 1962, Osaka. *Education:* Waseda Univ. *Career:* worked as a high school teacher 1985–89; writer of tanka poetry 1987–, over three million copies of first collection in print. *Publications:* poetry collections: Sarada kinenbi (Salad Anniversary) (Modern Japanese Poets Asscn Award 1988) 1987, Chokoreeto kakumeri (The Chocolate Revolution) 1997; translations of classic poetry into contemporary Japanese: Man'yoshu (10,000 Leaves), Taketori Monogatori (The Tale of the Bamboo Cutter), Chokoreeto-go yaku midaregami (Tangled Hair in Chocolate Language) 1998; several popular travel and photography books, numerous essays for newspapers and magazines. *Honours:* 32nd Kadokawa Tanka Award 1986. *Address:* c/o Kodansha International Limited, Otowa YK Building, Bunkyo-ku, Tokyo 112-8652, Japan (office). *Website:* www.gtpweb.net/twr/indexe.htm.

TAYLOR, Andrew John Robert, BA, MA; British writer; b. 14 Oct. 1951, Stevenage, Herts., England; m. Caroline Jane Silverwood 1979; one s. one d. *Education:* Emmanuel Coll., Cambridge, Univ. of London. *Career:* mem. Crime Writers' Asscn (CWA), Soc. of Authors. *Television:* Fallen Angel (adaptation of the Roth Trilogy) 2007. *Publications:* Caroline Minuscule 1982, Waiting for the End of the World 1984, Our Fathers' Lies 1985, An Old School Tie 1986, Freelance Death 1987, The Second Midnight 1987, Blacklist 1988, Blood Relation 1990, Toyshop 1990, The Raven on the Water 1991, The Sleeping Policeman 1992, The Barred Window 1993, Odd Man Out 1993, An Air That Kills 1994, The Mortal Sickness 1995, The Four Last Things 1997, The Lover of the Grave 1997, The Judgement of Strangers 1998, The Suffocating Night 1998, The Office of the Dead 2000, Where Roses Fade 2000, Death's Own Door 2001, Requiem for an Angel 2002, The American Boy 2003, Call the Dying 2004, Fingers to the Bone 2006, A Stain on the Silence 2006, Naked to the Hangman 2006, Bleeding Heart Square 2008, The Anatomy of Ghosts 2010; juvenile fiction: Hairline Cracks 1988, Snapshot 1989, Double Exposure 1990, Negative Image 1992, The Invader 1994; contrib. to anthologies, including Perfectly Criminal 1996, Past Crimes 1998, Crime in the City 2002, The Verdict of us All 2006. *Honours:* John Creasey Memorial Award 1982, CWA Ellis Peters Historical Dagger 2001, 2003, Audie Award 2005, CWA Cartier Diamond Dagger Award 2009, Martin Beck Award (Sweden) 2009. *Literary Agent:* c/o Sheil Land Associates, 52 Doughty Street, London, WC1N 2LS, England. *Telephone:* (20) 7405-9351. *Fax:* (20) 7831-2127. *E-mail:* info@sheilland.co.uk. *Website:* www.sheilland.co.uk; www.andrew-taylor.co.uk.

TAYLOR, Andrew MacDonald, BA, MA, DLitt; Australian academic, poet and writer; *Emeritus Professor, Edith Cowan University*; b. 19 March 1940, Warnambool, Vic.; m. Beate Josephi 1981; one s. one d. *Education:* University of Melbourne. *Career:* Lockie Fellow, University of Melbourne 1965–68; Lecturer 1971–74, Senior Lecturer 1974–91, Assoc. Prof. 1991–1992, University of Adelaide; Prof., later Emeritus Prof., School of Communication and Arts, Edith Cowan Univ. 1992–; mem. Asscn for the Study of Australian Literature; Australian Society of Authors; PEN. *Publications:* Reading Australian Poetry 1987, Selected Poems, 1960–85 1988, Folds in the Map 1991, Sandstone 1995, The Stone Threshold 2001, Götterdämmerung Café 2001, Collected Poems 2004, The Unhaunting 2009; contributions: newspapers, journals, and magazines. *Honours:* several prizes and awards, AM. *Address:* c/o School of Communication and Arts, Edith Cowan University, Mount Lawley, WA 6050, Australia (office). *E-mail:* a.taylor@ecu.edu.au (office).

TAYLOR, Beverly White, BAE, MA, PhD; American academic and writer; *Chair, Department of English & Comparative Literature, University of North Carolina—Chapel Hill*; b. 30 March 1947, Grenada, Miss. *Education:* Univ. of Mississippi, Duke Univ. *Career:* Asst Prof., Univ. of N Carolina at Chapel Hill 1977–84, Assoc. Prof. 1984–92, Prof. of English 1992–, Chair., Dept of English & Comparative Literature 2008–; mem. Victorians Inst. (Pres. 1989–90), Tennyson Soc., Browning Inst., MLA, Int. Arthurian Soc., NAVSA. *Publications:* The Return of King Arthur 1983, Arthurian Legend and Literature 1984, Francis Thompson 1987, The Cast of Consciousness 1987, Gender and Discourse in Victorian Literature and Art 1992; co-Ed.: Elizabeth Barrett Browning: Selected Poems 2009, The Works of Elizabeth Barrett Browning (5 vols) 2010 contribs to various encyclopaedias and periodicals. *Address:* Department of English, University of North Carolina, Chapel Hill, NC 27599-3520, USA (office). *E-mail:* btaylor@email.unc.edu (office).

TAYLOR, Charles, CC, OQ, BA, MA, DPhil, FRSC; Canadian academic; *Board of Trustees Professor of Law and Philosophy, Northwestern University*; b. 5 Nov.

1931, Montréal. *Education:* McGill Univ., Balliol Coll., Oxford. *Career:* Fellow, All Souls Coll., Oxford 1956–61; Asst Prof., Dept of Political Science, McGill Univ., Montréal 1961–62, Prof. 1962–97, Prof. Emer. 1998–; Bd of Trustees Prof. of Law, Northwestern Univ. 2002–; Prof., Univ. of Montréal 1962–71; Chichele Prof. of Social and Political Theory, Univ. of Oxford 1976–81; Mills Visiting Prof., Univ. of California, Berkeley 1974, 1983; Alan B. Plaunt Memorial Lecturer, Carleton Univ., Ottawa 1978; Alex Corry Lecturer, Queen's Univ., Kingston, Ont. 1980; B.N. Ganguli Lecturer, Centre for the Study of Developing Socs, Delhi 1981; Suhrkamp Lecturer, Univ. of Frankfurt 1984; Guest Prof., J.W. Goethe Univ., Frankfurt 1984; Visiting Prof. of Political Science and Philosophy, Hebrew Univ. of Jerusalem 1985; Massey Lecturer, CBC 1991; Tanner Lecturer, Stanford Univ. 1992; Max Horkheimer Lecturer, Univ. of Frankfurt 1996; Storrs Lecturer, Yale Univ. 1998. *Publications:* The Explanation of Behaviour 1964, The Pattern of Politics 1970, Erklärung und Interpretation in den Wissenschaften vom Menschen 1975, Hegel 1975, Hegel and Modern Society 1979, Social Theory As Practice 1983, Human Agency and Language: Philosophical Papers 1 1985, Philosophy and the Human Sciences: Philosophical Papers 2 1985, Negative Freiheit? Zur Kritik des neuzeitlichen Individualismus 1988, Sources of the Self: The Making of the Modern Identity 1989, The Malaise of Modernity 1991, Multiculturalism and 'The Politics of Recognition' 1992, Rapprocher les solitudes: crits sur le fédéralisme et le nationalisme au Canada 1992, Roads to Democracy: Human Rights and Democratic Development in Thailand 1994, Philosophical Arguments 1995, A Catholic Modernity? 1999, Wieviel Gemeinschaft braucht die Demokratie? Aufsätze zur politische Philosophie 2002, Varieties of Religion Today: William James Revisited 2002, Modern Social Imaginaries 2004, A Secular Age 2007. *Honours:* Templeton Prize 2007, Kyoto Prize 2008. *Address:* Department of Philosophy, Northwestern University, Kresge Hall, Campus Drive, Evanston, IL 60208-2214, USA (office). *Telephone:* (847) 491-3656 (office). *Fax:* (847) 491-2547 (office). *E-mail:* charles-taylor@law.northwestern.edu (office). *Website:* www.philosophy.northwestern.edu/people/taylor.html (office).

TAYLOR, David John, BA, FRSL; British author; b. 22 Aug. 1960, Norwich, Norfolk, England; m. Rachel Hore 1990; three s. *Education:* Univ. of Oxford. *Publications:* Great Eastern Land (novel) 1986, A Vain Conceit: British Fiction in the 1980s 1989, Other People: Portraits from the Nineties (with Marcus Berkmann) 1990, Real Life (novel) 1992, After the War: The Novel and England Since 1945 1993, English Settlement (novel) 1996, After Bathing at Baxter's (short stories) 1997, Trespass (novel) 1988, Thackeray 1999, The Comedy Man (novel) 2001, Orwell: The Life 2003, Kept: A Victorian Mystery (novel) 2006, On the Corinthian Spirit: The Decline of Amateurism in Sport 2006, Bright Young People: The Rise and Fall of a Generation 1918–1940 2007, Ask Alice (novel) 2009, At the Chime of a City Clock (novel) 2010, Derby Day (novel) 2011; contrib. to periodicals, including Independent, Guardian, Sunday Times, TLS, Spectator, Private Eye. *Honours:* Grinzane Cavour Prize (Italy) 1999, Whitbread Prize for Biography 2003. *Literary Agent:* c/o Rogers, Coleridge and White, 20 Powis Mews, London W11 1JN, England. *Telephone:* (20) 7221-3717. *Fax:* (20) 7229-9084. *E-mail:* info@rcwlitagency.com. *Website:* www.rcwlitagency.com. *Address:* Caragh House, 1 Poplar Avenue, Norwich, Norfolk, NR4 7LB, England (home).

TAYLOR, Graham P.; British children's writer; b. 1961; m.; three c. *Career:* fmr policeman; vicar at Cloughton, North Yorkshire –2004; full-time writer 2004–. *Publications:* Shadowmancer 2003, Wormwood 2004, Tersias 2005, The Curse of Salamander Street (Yorkshire Book of the Year Award 2007) 2006, Mariah Mundi: The Midas Box 2007, Mariah Mundi and the Ghost Diamonds 2008, DoppleGanger Chronicles 2008. *Address:* c/o Faber and Faber Ltd, Bloomsbury House, 74–77 Great Russell Street, London, WC1B 3DA, England (office). *Website:* www.faber.co.uk (office); www.gptaylor.info.

TAYLOR, Henry Splawn, BA, MA; American academic, poet, writer and academic; *Professor Emeritus of Creative Writing, American University*; b. 21 June 1942, Loudoun Co., Va. *Education:* Univ. of Virginia, Hollins Coll. *Career:* Instructor, Roanoke Coll. 1966–68; Asst Prof., Univ. of Utah 1968–71; Contributing Ed. Hollins Critic 1970–; Assoc. Prof., American Univ. 1971–76, Prof. of Literature 1975–2003, Prof. Emer. 2003–, Co-Dir MFA in Creative Writing 1982–2003, Dir American Studies Program 1983–85; Consulting Ed. Magill's Literary Annual 1972–1985, Poet Lore 1976–84; Writer-in-Residence, Hollins Coll. 1978; mem. Bd of Advisers, New Virginia Review 1986–, Poetry Ed. 1988–89; Distinguished Poet-in-Residence, Wichita State Univ. 1994; Poet-in-Residence, Randolph-Macon Women's Coll. 1996; Elliston Poet-in-Residence, Univ. of Cincinnati 2002. *Publications:* poetry: The Horse Show at Midnight: Poems 1966, Breakings 1971, An Afternoon of Pocket Billiards 1975, Desperado 1979, The Flying Change (Pulitzer Prize in Poetry 1986) 1985, The Horse Show at Midnight and An Afternoon of Pocket Billiards: Poems 1992, Understanding Fiction: Poems 1986–96 1996, Brief Candles: 101 Clerihews 2000, Crooked Run 2006; other: Magill's (Masterplots) Literary Annual 1972 (ed. with Frank N. Magill) 1972, Poetry: Points of Departure 1974, Magill's (Masterplots) Literary Annual 1973 (assoc. ed.) 1974, Magill's (Masterplots) Literary Annual (assoc. ed.) 1975, The Water of Light: A Miscellany in Honor of Brewster Ghiselin (ed.) 1976, Compulsory Figures: Essays on Recent American Poets 1992; contrib. to numerous books, anthologies, reviews and journals. *Honours:* Acad. of American Poets Prize 1962, 1964, Utah State Inst. of Fine Arts Poetry Prize 1969 (jtly), 1971, Nat. Endowment for the Arts Fellowships 1978, 1986, Nat. Endowment for the Humanities Research Grant 1980–81, American Acad. and Inst. of Arts and Letters Witter Bynner Prize for Poetry 1984, Virginia Cultural Laureate Award 1986, Nat. Foundation for Advancement in the Arts Teacher Recognition Award 1995–96, American Acad. of Arts and Letters Michael Braude Light Verse Prize 2002, Aiken Taylor Award in Modern Poetry 2004. *Address:* Department of Literature, American University, 237 Battelle-Tompkins, 4400 Massachusetts Avenue, NW, Washington, DC 20016-8047, USA (office).

TAYLOR, John Russell, (Charles Graham, William Hall, Brian Brooke), MA; British writer, broadcaster, editor and academic; b. 19 June 1935, Dover, Kent, England; s. of Arthur Russell Taylor and Kathleen Mary Taylor (née Picker); civil partner Ying Yeung Li. *Education:* Dover Grammar School, Jesus Coll. Cambridge, Courtauld Inst. of Art. *Career:* Sub-Ed., Times Educ. Supplement 1959–60; Editorial Asst, Times Literary Supplement 1960–62; Film Critic, The Times 1962–73; Dir of Film Studies, Tufts Univ. in London 1970–72; Prof., Div. of Cinema, Univ. of Southern Calif., USA 1972–78; Art Critic, The Times 1978–2005; Ed. Films and Filming 1983–90; Art Critic, Radio Two Arts Programme 1990–2000. *Exhibition:* Strangers in Paradise: German Emigres in California (toured US Goethe Insts 1979–80. *Film:* Charles Chaplin Makes The Countess from Hong Kong 1966. *Television:* Feet Foremost 1968, The Imposter 1969, Dracula 1969, Curse of the Mummy 1970, A Letter to David 1971, A Quiet Place in the Country 1971. *Publications:* Joseph L. Mankiewicz 1960, Anger and After 1962 (USA: The Angry Theatre 1969), Anatomy of a Television Play 1962, Cinema Eye, Cinema Ear 1964, Penguin Dictionary of the Theatre 1966, The Art Nouveau Book in Britain 1966, Art in London 1966, The Rise and Fall of the Well-Made Play 1967, The Art Dealers 1969, Harold Pinter 1969, The Hollywood Musical 1971, The Second Wave 1971, Peter Shaffer 1974, David Storey 1974, Directors and Directions 1975, The Revels History of Drama in English Vol. VII 1978, Hitch 1978, Impressionism 1981, Strangers in Paradise 1983, Ingrid Bergman 1983, Alec Guinness 1984, 2000, Vivien Leigh 1984, Hollywood 1940s 1985, Portraits of the British Cinema 1986, Orson Welles 1986, Edward Wolfe 1986, Great Movie Moments 1987, Post-War Friends 1987, Robin Tanner 1989, Bernard Meninsky 1990, John Copley 1990, Impressionist Dreams 1990, Liz Taylor 1991, Muriel Pemberton 1993, Ricardo Cinalli 1993, Igor Mitoraj 1993, Claude Monet 1995, Bill Jacklin 1997, The World of Michael Parkes 1998, Antonio Saliola 1998, The Sun is God 1999, Michael Parkes: The Stone Lithographs 2000, Peter Coker 2002, Roberto Barnardi 2002, Roboz: The Painter's Paradox 2005, One Hand, Two Fingers 2005, Philip Sutton Woodcuts 2006, The Art of Michael Parkes 2006, Adrian George 2006, The Michael Winner Collection of Donald McGill 2006, Carl Laubin 2007, The Art of Jeremy Ramsey 2007, Randy Klein: Road 2008, The Glamour of the Gods 2008, Philip Sutton 2008, Exactitude 2009, Roboz: Face to Face 2011, High Relief 2013; edited: Let the Children Write 1961, Three Plays by John Arden 1964, New English Dramatists 8 1965, Look Back in Anger: A Casebook 1968, The Pleasure Dome (USA: Graham Greene on Film) 1972, Masterworks of British Cinema 1974, The Wizard of Oz 50th Anniversary Edn 1989. *Honours:* Friend of the Festival Award, Chicago Int. Film Festival 2010. *Address:* c/o The Times, 1 Pennington Street, London, E98 1TT, England (office). *Telephone:* (20) 7782-5000 (office). *Website:* www.timesonline.co.uk (office).

TAYLOR, Mark C., BA, PhD; American academic and writer; *Cluett Professor of Humanities Emeritus, Williams College*; b. 13 Dec. 1945, Plainfield, NJ; m. Mary-Dinnis Stearns 1968; one s. one d. *Education:* Wesleyan Univ., Harvard Univ., Univ. of Copenhagen. *Career:* Instructor in Religion, Harvard Univ. 1972–73; Asst Prof. of Religion, Williams College 1973–78, Assoc. Prof. of Religion 1978–81, Prof. of Religion 1981–86, William R. Kenan Jr Prof. 1986–91, Preston S. Parish Third Century Prof. of Religion 1992–93, Preston S. Parish Prof. of Humanities 1993–97, Cluett Prof. of Humanities 1997–2009, Emer. 2009–; Visiting Lecturer in Religion, Smith College 1981; Visiting Prof. of Architecture and Religion, Columbia Univ. 1994; Visiting Prof., Univ. of Sydney 1995; William Neal Reynolds Visiting Prof. of Communication Studies, Univ. of North Carolina at Chapel Hill 1999; Visiting Prof. of Religion and Architecture, Columbia Univ. 2003–05, Chair. and Prof., Dept of Religion 2007–, Co-Dir, Inst. of Religion, Culture and Public Life 2007–; Co-Founder, Global Education Network 1999; Art exhibition, Grave Matters, Mass MOCA 2002–03; mem. American Acad. of Religion: Hegel Society of America, Society for Phenomenology and Existential Philosophy, Society for Values in Higher Education, Søren Kierkegaard Acad. *Publications:* Kierkegaard's Pseudonymous Authorship: A Study of Time and the Self 1975, Religion and the Human Image (with Carl Raschke and James Kirk) 1976, Journeys to Selfhood: Hegel and Kierkegaard 1980, Unfinished: Essays in Honor of Ray L. Hart (ed.) 1981, Deconstructing Theology 1982, Erring: A Postmodern A/theology 1984, Deconstruction in Context: Literature and Philosophy 1986, Altarity 1987, Tears 1989, Double Negative (with Michael Heizer) 1992, Disfiguring: Art, Architecture, Religion 1992, Nots 1993, Imagologies: Media Philosophy (with Esa Saarinen) 1994, Hiding 1996, Critical Terms in Religious Studies (ed.) 1998, The Picture in Question: Mark Tansey and the Ends of Representation 1999, About Religion: Economies of Faith in Virtual Cultures 1999, The Moment of Complexity: Emerging Network Culture 2002, Grave Matters 2002, Vito Acconci 2002, Confidence Games: Money and Markets in a World Without Redemption 2003, Mystic Bones 2006, After God 2007, Crisis on Campus: A Bold Plan for Reforming our Colleges and Universities 2010; contributions: numerous scholarly books and journals. *Honours:* Guggenheim Fellowship 1978–79, National Humanities Center Fellow 1982–83, Awards for Excellence, American Acad. of Religion 1988, 1994, Research Fellow, Graham Foundation for Fine Arts 1990, Rector's Medal, University of Helsinki 1993, National College Prof. of the Year,

Carnegie Foundation for the Advancement of Teaching 1995, Distinguished Alumnus Award, Wesleyan University 1998. *Address:* 309 Stetson Hall, Williams College, Williamstown, MA 01267, USA (office). *E-mail:* mark.c.taylor@williams.edu (office). *Website:* www.markctaylor.com.

TAYLOR HOUGH, Julia (Judy) Marie, MBE, FRSA; British writer; b. (Julia Ball), 12 Aug. 1932, Murton, S Wales; adopted d. of Gladys Spicer Taylor; m. Richard Hough 1980 (died 1999). *Education:* St Paul's Girls' School, London. *Career:* joined The Bodley Head publishing house 1951, Children's Book Ed. 1962–77, Dir 1967–84, Deputy Man. Dir 1971–80; mem. UNICEF Int. Arts Cttee 1968–70, 1976, 1982–83, UK UNICEF Greetings Card Cttee 1982–85; Chair. Children's Book Group 1969–72; mem. Publishers' Asscn Council 1972–78; mem. Book Devt Council 1973–76; Consultant to Penguin Books on Beatrix Potter 1981–87, 1989–92; Assoc. Dir Weston Woods Inst., USA 1984–2002; Consulting Ed. Reinhardt Books 1988–93; Trustee, Beatrix Potter Soc. 1985–2009 (Chair. 1990–97, 2000–03, 2006–09), Volunteer Reading Help 2000–04. *Play:* Beatrix (with Patrick Garland) 1996. *Publications include:* Sophie and Jack 1982, My First Year: A Beatrix Potter Baby Book 1983, Sophie and Jack in the Snow 1984, Beatrix Potter: Artist, Storyteller and Countrywoman 1986, Dudley and the Monster 1986, That Naughty Rabbit: Beatrix Potter and Peter Rabbit 1987, My Cat 1987, Dudley Bakes a Cake 1988, Sophie and Jack in the Rain 1989, Beatrix Potter's Letters: A Selection 1989, Letters to Children from Beatrix Potter 1992, Beatrix: A Play (with Patrick Garland) 1996, Sketches for Friends by Edward Ardizzone (ed.) 2000. *Address:* 31 Meadowbank, Primrose Hill Road, London, NW3 3AY, England (home). *E-mail:* taylor.hough@talk21.com (home).

TCHUKHONTSEV, Oleg Grigoryevich; Russian poet; b. 8 March 1938, Pavlov Posad, Moscow Region; m. Irina Igorevna Povolotskaya. *Education:* Moscow Pedagogical Inst. *Career:* poetry section, mem. Editorial Bd Novy Mir; published in Druzhba Narodov, Yunost, Molodaya Gvardiya, Novy Mir. *Publications:* From Three Notebooks (cycles Posad, Name, Sparrow's Night) 1976, The Dormer Window 1983, Poetry 1989, By Wind and Heat 1989, Passing Landscape 1997 and other books of poetry; translations of Goethe, Warren, Frost, Kits and numerous other poets. *Honours:* State Prize of Russia 1993. *Address:* Bolshoi Tishinsky per. 12, Apt. 10, 123557 Moscow, Russia (home). *Telephone:* (495) 253-51-95 (home).

TEJPAL, Tarun J.; Indian newspaper editor and writer; *CEO and Editor-in-Chief, Tehelka. Career:* over 20 years' experience, including reporter for The Indian Express and The Telegraph, ed. with India Today and India Express Group; has written for numerous int. publications, including The Paris Review, The Guardian, Financial Times and Prospect; co-f. India Ink publishing house; fmr Managing Ed. Outlook news magazine –2000; f., CEO and Ed.-in-Chief Tehelka newspaper 2000–, initially web-only news site, relaunched as nat. weekly newspaper 2004–. *Publications:* The Alchemy of Desire (novel) (Prix Millepages) 2005, The Story of My Assassins 2009. *Address:* Tehelka, M-76, Second Floor, M-Block Market, Greater Kallash Part 2, New Delhi 110048, India (office). *E-mail:* editor@tehelka.com (office). *Website:* www.tehelka.com (office); www.taruntejpal.com.

TEKIN, Latife; Turkish writer; b. 1 Jan. 1957, Kayseri; d. of Mustafa and Hatice Erdoğan; m. 1st Ertuğrul Tekin (divorced); one s.; m. 2nd Latif Demirci; one d. *Publications include:* Dear Shameless Death 1983, Berci Kristin Garbage Tales 1984, Night Lessons 1986, Swords By Ice 1989, Signs of Love 1995, El Panuelo Turco 2000. *Address:* Kirechane Gediği Sok 6, Arnavutköy, Istanbul, Turkey. *Telephone:* (1) 2636687. *Fax:* (1) 5139518.

TELEN, Ludmila Olegovna; Russian journalist; b. 2 Oct. 1957, Zhukovsky, Russia; d. of Oleg P. Telen and Elmira F. Telen; m. Valery Vyzhutovich 1980; one s. *Education:* Moscow M.V. Lomonosov State Univ. *Career:* journalist with Komsomolskaya Pravda newspaper 1977–85; Special Corresp. for Socialisticheskaya Industria 1985–89; analyst for Narodny Deputat magazine 1990–91; Political Columnist, Moscow News weekly newspaper 1991–, Deputy Ed.; Presenter, Political Kitchen (TV programme) 1991–93, Deputy Ed.-in-Chief, Moscow News Weekly 1995–. *Publication:* Putin's Generation 2004. *Address:* The Moscow News, 119021 Moscow, 4, Zubovsky Boulevard, Russia (office). *Telephone:* (495) 645-65-65 (office). *E-mail:* info@mnweekly.ru (office). *Website:* mnweekly.ru (office).

TELFER, Tracie (see Chaplin, Jenny)

TELLER, Janne, MSc (Econs); Danish author and fmr economist; b. 8 April 1964, Copenhagen. *Education:* Univ. of Copenhagen. *Career:* first short story published aged 14; Econ. and Political Advisor, EU and UN, specialising in conflict resolution and humanitarian issues, served in Dar-es-Salaam 1988–89, Brussels 1990–91, New York 1991–93, Mozambique 1993–94; full-time fiction writer 1995–; fmr mem. Danish Fiction Writers' Asscn, Danish PEN; fmr mem. of Bd Lettre International magazine (Danish version). *Publications include:* novels: Odins Ø (Odin's Island) 1999, Intet (Nothing) (Danish Ministry of Culture Best Children's Book Prize 2001, Le Prix Libbylit 2008, Michael L. Printz Honor Book 2011, Mildred Batchelder Honor Award 2011) 2000, Europa, All That You Lack 2004, Kattens tramp (The Trampling Cat) 2004, Hvis der var krig i Norden 2004, Kom (Come) 2008; numerous essays and short stories. *Literary Agent:* c/o Lars Ringhof, Lars Ringhof Agency Aps, Studiestræde 35A, 1455 Copenhagen K, Denmark. *Telephone:* 27-11-13-13. *E-mail:* lars@ringhof.dk. *Website:* www.ringhof.dk. *E-mail:* mail@janneteller.dk (home). *Website:* www.janneteller.dk (home).

TELLKAMP, Uwe; German writer and physician; b. 28 Oct. 1968, Dresden; m.; one s. *Career:* practising doctor –2004. *Publications:* novels: Der Hecht, die Träume und das Portugiesische Café 2000, Der Schlaf in den Uhren (Ingeborg Bachmann Prize) 2004, Der Eisvogel 2005, Zimorodek 2006, Der Turm (German Book Prize 2008, Konrad Adenauer Foundation Literature Prize 2009) 2008, Der Zitronenrabe 2009; other: Die Sandwirtschaft: Leipziger Poetikvorlesungen 2007; contrib. articles to literary journals and anthologies. *Honours:* Uwe Johnson Prize 2008, German Nat. Prize 2009. *Address:* c/o Suhrkamp Verlag, Postfach 101945, 60019 Frankfurt, Germany (office). *E-mail:* geschaeftsleitung@suhrkamp.de (office). *Website:* www.suhrkamp.de (office).

TEMPLE, Peter; Australian writer and journalist; b. 1946, South Africa; m. *Career:* fmr journalist in South Africa and Germany; moved to Australia 1980; fmr Ed. Australian Soc. journal; fmr Sr Lecturer in Editing and Publishing, Royal Melbourne Inst. of Tech.; freelance ed. and writer 1995–. *Publications:* Bad Debts (Crime Writers' Asscn of Australia's Best First Novel of the Year, Ned Kelly Award for Best First Novel 1997) 1996, An Iron Rose 1998, Black Tide 1999, Shooting Star 1999, Dead Point 2000, In the Evil Day 2002, White Dog 2003, The Broken Shore (CWA Duncan Lawrie Dagger Award 2007) 2006, Truth (Miles Franklin Literary Award 2010) 2009. *Honours:* four times winner, Ned Kelly Award for Best Novel. *Address:* c/o Text Publishing Co., Swann House, 22 William Street, Melbourne, Vic. 3000, Australia (office). *Website:* textpublishing.com.au (office).

TEMPLE, (Robert) Philip; New Zealand writer; b. 20 March 1939, Yorkshire, England; m. Daphne Evelyn Keen 1965 (divorced); one s. one d. *Career:* Ed., New Zealand Alpine Journal 1968–70, 1973, Landfall 1972–75; Assoc. Ed., Katherine Mansfield Memorial Fellowship, Menton, France 1979; Robert Burns Fellowship, University of Otago 1980; Berlin Artist's Program Fellowship 1987; Research Fellow, National Library, New Zealand 1996–97; mem. PEN, New Zealand Centre 1970–, New Zealand Society of Authors (pres. 1998–99). *Publications:* The World at Their Feet 1969, Ways to the Wilderness 1977, Beak of the Moon 1981, Sam 1984, New Zealand Explorers 1985, Kakapo 1988, Making Your Vote Count 1992, Dark of the Moon 1993, Temple's Guide to the New Zealand Parliament 1994, Kotuku 1994, The Book of the Kea 1996, To Each His Own 1998, The Last True Explorer 2002, A Sort of Conscience: The Wakefields 2002, White Shadow, Memories of Marienbad 2005, I Am Always With You 2006, Mountain: Where the Land Touches the Sky 2007. *Honours:* Arts Council Non-Fiction Bursary 1994, AIM Honour Award 1995, Prime Minister's Award for Literary Achievement 2005. *Address:* 45 Sutherland Street, Dunedin, New Zealand (home).

TEMPLE, Wayne Calhoun, AB, AM, PhD; American historian, archivist and writer; *Chief Deputy Director, Illinois State Archives;* b. 5 Feb. 1924, Richwood, OH; m. Sunderine Wilson Mohn 1979; two step-s. *Education:* Univ. of Illinois, Champaign-Urbana. *Career:* Ed.-in-Chief 1958–73, Editorial Bd 1973–, Lincoln Herald; historical consultant to sculptor, Rebecca Childers Caleel; currently Chief Deputy Dir, Ill. State Archives, Bd of Advisers, The Lincoln Forum; mem. Abraham Lincoln Asscn, Nat. Abraham Lincoln Bicentennial Comm.'s Advisory Cttee. *Publications:* Indian Villages of the Illinois Country 1958–, Campaigning with Grant 1961, Stephen A. Douglas: Freemason 1982, The Building of Lincoln's Home and its Saga 1984, Lincoln's Connections With the Illinois and Michigan Canal 1986, Illinois' Fifth Capitol (with Sunderine Temple) 1988, Abraham Lincoln: From Skeptic to Prophet 1995, Alexander Williamson: Friend of the Lincolns 1997, By Square and Compass: Saga of the Lincoln Home 2002, 'The Taste is in my Mouth a Little...': Lincoln's Victuals and Potables 2004, Abraham Lincoln and Illinois' Fifth Capitol 2006, Lincoln's Travels on the River Queen 2007; contrib. to numerous journals, including the Lincoln Herald. *Honours:* Lincoln Diploma of Honor, National Sesquicentennial Commission Lincoln Medallion, Archbishop Richard Chenevix Trench Award 1999, Lincoln Memorial Univ. Lifetime Achievement Award 2001, Red Cross of Constantine, Bicentennial Order of Lincoln, Lincoln Acad. of Illinois 2009. *Address:* Illinois State Archives, Springfield, IL 62756 (office); 1121 S Fourth Street Court, Springfield, IL 62703, USA (home). *Telephone:* (217) 782-3501 (office). *Fax:* (217) 524-3930 (office).

TEMPLETON, Edith; British writer; b. 7 April 1916, Prague; d. of Louis Gideon and Irma de Szèll; m. 1st W. S. Templeton 1938 (divorced); m. 2nd Edmund Ronald 1956 (died 1984); one s. *Education:* Lycée in Paris and Prague Medical Univ. *Career:* mem. staff, Office of Chief Surgeon, US War Office 1942–45; Conf. and Law-Court Interpreter for British Forces with rank of Capt., Germany 1945–46. *Publications:* Summer in the Country 1950, Living on Yesterday 1951, The Island of Desire 1952, Surprise of Cremona (Book Soc. Choice) 1954, This Charming Pastime 1955, Gordon 1966, Murder in Estoril 1992, The Darts of Cupid and Other Stories 2002; contrib. short stories to The New Yorker 1956–91, Holiday, Atlantic Monthly, Vogue and Harper's Magazine. *Address:* 76 corso Europa, 18012 Bordighera, Italy (home). *Telephone:* (0184) 261858 (home).

TEMPLETON, Fiona, MA; British theatre director, poet and writer; b. 23 Dec. 1951, Scotland. *Education:* Univ. of Edinburgh, New York Univ., USA. *Career:* mem. Poets and Writers, PEN; alumna, New Dramatists. *Plays:* You: The City 1988, Recognition 1995, Delirium of Interpretations 1991, L'Ile 2003, The Medead 2008. *Publications:* Elements of Performance Art 1976, London 1984, You the City 1990, Delirium of Interpretations 1997, Oops the Join 1997, Cells of Release 1997, Hi Cowboy 1997, Delirium of Interpretations 2003,

Invisible Dances 2004, Mum in Airdrie 2006, Going 2007, Medea in Aia 2008; contrib. to anthologies and journals. *Honours:* various grants, fellowships and awards. *Address:* 100 St Mark's Place, No. 7, New York, NY 10009, USA (office). *Website:* www.fionatempleton.org; www.therelationship.org.

TEN BERGE, Hans Cornelis; Dutch poet, writer and translator; b. 24 Dec. 1938. *Career:* Lecturer, Art Acad., Arnhem; Writer-in-Residence, Univ. of Texas, USA, University Coll., London, UK, Univ. of Gronigen, Netherlands; Ed. Raster literary journal; mem. PEN, Soc. of Dutch Literature. *Films:* A Poet in Texas (documentary for Flemish TV, Brussels). *Publications:* poetry: Gedichten, 3 vols 1969, White Shaman 1973, Poetry of the Aztecs 1972, Vabanque 1977, Semblance of Reality 1981, Texas Elegies 1983, Songs of Anxiety and Despair 1988, Materia Prima, Poems 1963–93, Oesters & gestoofde pot (Oysters and Pot Roast) 2001, Het vertrapte mysterie 2004, Hollandse Sermoenen (Dutch Sermons) 2008; fiction: Zelfportret met witte muts 1985, Het geheim van een oppewekt humeur 1986, The Home Loving Traveller 1995, Women, Jealousy and Other Discomforts 1996, De Jaren in Zeedorp (The Sea-Town Years) 1998, Blauwbaards Ontwaken (Bluebeard's Awakening, novel) 2003, Ontluisd verleden (The Deloused Past) 2006; prose: Exemplary Tales and Their Veiled Meanings 2009; other: The Defence of Poetry, essays 1988; Prose books; Books of myths and fables of Arctic peoples; numerous poetry translations; contribs to periodicals. *Honours:* Van der Hoogt Prize 1968, Prose Prize, City of Amsterdam 1971, Multatuli Prize 1987, Constantijn Huÿgens Prize 1996, A. Roland Holst Prize for Poetry 2003. P.C. Hooftprijs 2006. *Address:* c/o Atlas Publishers, PO Box 13, 1000 AC Amsterdam, The Netherlands (office).

TENNANT, Emma Christina, FRSL; British writer; b. 20 Oct. 1937, d. of 2nd Baron Glenconner and Elizabeth Lady Glenconner; one s. two d. *Education:* St Paul's Girls' School. *Career:* fmr freelance journalist; Founder, Ed., Bananas 1975–78; Gen. Ed., In Verse 1982–, Lives of Modern Women 1985–. *Television includes:* Frankenstein's Baby, Screen One. *Publications:* The Colour of Rain (as Catherine Aydy) 1963, The Time of the Crack 1973, The Last of the Country House Murders 1975, Hotel de Dream 1976, Bananas Anthology (ed.) 1977, Saturday Night Reader (ed.) 1978, The Bad Sister 1978, Wild Nights 1979, Alice Fell 1980, The Boggart (with M. Rayner) 1981, The Search for Treasure Island 1981, Queen of Stones 1982, Woman Beware Woman 1983, The Ghost Child 1984, Black Marina 1985, The Adventures of Robina by Herself (ed.) 1986, Cycle of the Sun: The House of Hospitalities 1987, A Wedding of Cousins 1988, The Magic Drum 1989, Two Women of London 1989, Faustine 1992, Tess 1993, Pemberley 1993, Emma in Love 1996, An Unequal Marriage 1994; Strangers: A Family Romance 1998, Girlitude 1999, Burnt Diaries 1999, The Ballad of Sylvia and Ted (contrib.) 2001, A House in Corfu 2001, Felony 2002, Corfu Banquet 2003, Heathcliff's Tale 2005, The Harp Lesson 2005, The French Dancer's Bastard 2006, The Autobiography of the Queen 2007, Diana: The Ghost Biography 2008. *Honours:* Hon. DLitt (Aberdeen) 1996. *Literary Agent:* c/o Marsh Agency, 50 Ablemarle Street, London, W1S 4BD, England. *Telephone:* (20) 7493-4361. *Fax:* (20) 7495-8961. *Website:* www.marsh-agency.co.uk.

TEPPER, Sheri S., (A.J. Orde, E.E. Horlak, B.J. Oliphant); American author of fantasy, horror and mystery novels; b. (Sheri J. Stewart), 16 July 1929, Littleton, Colo; m. Gene Tepper; two c. *Career:* began writing career creating stories for children; early poetry work published under the name Sheri S. Eberhart 1961–64; worked for Rocky Mountain Planned Parenthood 1962–86, became Exec. Dir. *Publications include:* novels: The Revenants 1984, The True Game 1985, The Chronicles of Mavin Manyshaped 1985, Marianne, the Magus and the Manticore 1985, The End of the Game 1986, Blood Heritage 1986, The Bones 1987, The Awakeners: NorthShore 1987, The Awakeners: SouthShore 1987, After Long Silence 1987, The Gate to Women's Country 1988, Marianne, the Madame and the Momentary Gods 1988, Grass 1989, Marianne, the Matchbox and the Malachite Mouse 1989, Raising the Stones 1990, Beauty (Locus Award 1992) 1991, Sideshow 1992, A Plague of Angels 1993, Shadow's End 1994, Gibbon's Decline and Fall 1996, The Family Tree 1997, Six Moon Dance 1998, Singer from the Sea 1999, The Fresco 2000, The Visitor 2002, The Companions 2003, The Margarets 2007, The Waters Rising 2010; as E.E. Horlak: Still Life 1987; as B.J. Oliphant: the Shirley McClintock Mysteries series: Dead in the Scrub 1990, The Unexpected Corpse 1990, Deservedly Dead 1992, Death and the Delinquent 1993, Death Served Up Cold 1994, A Ceremonial Death 1996, Here's to the Newly Dead 1997; as A.J. Orde: The Jason Lynx Mysteries series: A Little Neighborhood Murder 1989, Death and the Dogwalker 1990, Death for Old Time's Sake 1992, Looking for the Aardvark (aka Dead on Sunday 1994) 1993, A Long Time Dead 1994, A Death of Innocents 1996. *Address:* c/o Author Mail, 7th Floor, HarperCollins Publishers, 10 East 53rd Street, New York, NY 10022, USA (office). *Website:* sheri-s-tepper.com.

TEPPERMAN, Jonathan D., BA, MA, LLM; Canadian journalist; *Assistant Managing Editor, Newsweek International;* b. 10 Aug. 1971, Windsor, Ont.; s. of Bill and Rochelle Tepperman. *Education:* Yale Univ., Univ. of Oxford, UK, NYU School of Law. *Career:* fmr speechwriter for US Amb. to UN 1994–95; journalist writing for Forward 1996, Jerusalem Post 1997; Assoc. Ed. and Production Man. Foreign Affairs (journal of Council on Foreign Relations) 1998–2001, Sr Ed. 2001–04, Deputy Man. Ed. 2004–07; Asst Managing Ed. Newsweek International, New York 2007–. *Publications:* numerous contributions to publications including New York Times, Newsweek, LA Times, Christian Science Monitor, Wall Street Journal, New Republic. *Address:* Newsweek Inc., 251 West 57th Street, New York, NY 10019, USA (office). *Telephone:* (212) 445-5818 (office). *Fax:* (212) 445-5764 (office). *E-mail:* jonathan.tepperman@newsweek.com (office). *Website:* www.newsweekeurope.com (office).

TERRILL, Ross, BA, PhD; American/Australian writer; b. Melbourne, Vic., Australia. *Education:* Wesley Coll., Univ. of Melbourne, Harvard Univ. *Career:* Teaching Fellow, Harvard Univ. 1968–70, Lecturer 1970–74, Research Assoc. in East Asian Studies 1970–, Assoc. Prof. 1974–80; Contributing Ed., Atlantic Monthly 1970–84; Research Fellow, Asia Soc. 1978–79; Visiting Prof., Univ. of Texas 1997–2004. *Publications include:* 800,000,000: The Real China 1972, R. H. Tawney and his Times 1973, Flowers on an Iron Tree: Five Cities of China 1975, The Future of China After Mao 1978, Mao 1980, The White Boned Demon 1984, The Australians 1987, China in Our Time 1992, Madam Mao 1999, The Australians: How We Live Now 2000, The New Chinese Empire 2003; contrib. to newspapers and magazines. *Honours:* Frank Knox Memorial Fellowship 1965, Sumner Prize 1970, George Polk Memorial Award 1972, Nat. Magazine Award 1972, LA Times Book Prize 2003, Curtin-MacArthur Leadership Award 2006. *Address:* PO Box 230772, Astor Station, Boston, MA 02123-0772, USA (home). *Fax:* (617) 496-2420 (office); (617) 445-3115 (office). *E-mail:* rt5789@cs.com (home).

TERRIN, Peter; Belgian novelist; b. 1 Jan. 1968. *Education:* Univ. of Ghent. *Publications include:* novels: Kras (Crass) 2001, Blanco 2003, Vrouwen en kinderen eerst (Women and Children First) 2004, De bewaker (EU Prize for Literature 2010) (trans. as The Guard) 2009; short story collections: De code (The Code) 1998, De bijeneters (The Bee-eaters) (West Flanders Prize for Literature) 2006; short stories: For the Sake of Peace, Clean-Up or the Adventures of Abdullah and Me 2010; contrib. stories and essays to anthologies and journals. *Address:* Uitgeverij De Arbeiderspers, Herengracht 370-372, 1016 CH Amsterdam, Netherlands (office). *Telephone:* (20) 5247500 (office). *E-mail:* info@arbeiderspers.nl (office). *Website:* www.arbeiderspers.nl.

TERRY, Olufemi, MA; Sierra Leonean writer. *Education:* New York Univ., USA, Univ. of Cape Town, South Africa. *Career:* grew up Nigeria, UK and Ivory Coast; has since lived in Kenya and worked as a journalist in Somalia and Uganda; Copy Ed. The Economist 2000–03; Reports and Information Officer , Interpeace Somalia Programme Nairobi 2004–05; Ed. The World Bank 2006–09; Communication Officer, UNDP Somalia, Nairobi 2006–07; Analyst, Control Risks, Cape Town, SA 2008–; Analyst, Risk Advisory Group, Cape Town 2010. *Publications:* short stories: Digitalis Lust 2008, Stickfighting Days (Caine Prize for African Writing) 2010, Lamu Squat 2011; contrib. stories, articles and poems to various publications. *Website:* www.femiterry.net.

TESSON, Philippe, DèsSc; French journalist and publishing executive; b. 1 March 1928, Wassigny (Aisne); s. of Albert Tesson and Jeanne Ancely; m. Dr Marie-Claude Millet 1969; one s. two d. *Education:* Coll. Stanislas, Inst. of Political Studies, Paris. *Career:* Sec. of Parl. Debates 1957–60; Ed.-in-Chief, Combat 1960–74; candidate in legis. elections 1968; Diarist and Drama Critic, Canard Enchaîné 1970–83; Co-Man. and Dir Soc. d'Editions Scientifiques et Culturelles 1971, Pres. 1980; Founder, Man. Dir and Ed.-in-Chief, Quotidien de Paris 1974–94; Dir Nouvelles Littéraires 1975–83; Drama Critic, L'Express Paris 1986; Dir and Co.-Man. Quotidien du Maire 1988; Animator (TV programme with France 3) A Quel Titre 1994–96; Ed. Valeurs actuelles 1994–; Drama Critic, Revue des deux Mondes 1990–, Figaro Magazine 1995–; literary and theatre Corresp. Rive Droite/Rive Gauche (TV) 1997–2004; Dir Avant-scène Théâtre 2001–. *Publication:* De Gaulle 1er 1965, Où est passée l'autorité? 2000. *Honours:* Chevalier, Légion d'honneur 1987, Officier, Légion d'honneur 2009. *Address:* L'Avant-scène Théâtre, 75 rue des Saints-Pères, 75006 Paris, France (office). *Telephone:* 1-53-63-80-60 (office). *Fax:* 1-53-63-88-75 (office). *E-mail:* contact@avant-scene-theatre.com (office). *Website:* www.avant-scene-theatre.com (office).

TETT, Gillian, PhD; British journalist and author; *US Managing Editor, Financial Times;* b. 1967. *Education:* Clare Coll., Cambridge. *Career:* joined Financial Times 1993, worked in fmr USSR and Europe and in Econs Dept, Bureau Chief, Tokyo 1997–2003, Deputy Head of Lex column 2003, Asst Ed. and US Managing Ed. 2010–. *Publications:* Saving the Sun: How Wall Street mavericks shook up Japan's financial system and made billions 2004, Fool's Gold: How Unrestrained Greed Corrupted a Dream, Shattered Global Markets and Unleashed a Catastrophe (Spear's Book Awards Financial Book of the Year 2009) 2009. *Honours:* Wincott Prize 2007, British Business Journalist of the Year 2008, British Press Awards Journalist of the Year 2009. *Address:* The Financial Times Newspaper Group, 1330 Avenue of the Americas, New York, NY 10019-5436, USA (office). *E-mail:* gillian.tett@ft.com (office). *Website:* www.ft.com/comment/columnists/gilliantett (office).

THACKARA, James, BA; American writer; b. 7 Dec. 1944, Los Angeles, CA; m. Davina Laura Anne 1975, one d. *Education:* Harvard Univ. *Film screenplay:* Shogun 1969. *Publications:* America's Children 1984, Ahab's Daughter 1988, The Book of Kings 1999, A Land You Don't Koow. *Website:* www.jamesthackara.com.

THALER, M. N. (see Kerner, Fred)

THAROOR, Shashi, MA, MALD, PhD; Indian international organization official and writer; *Minister of State for External Affairs;* b. 9 March 1956, London, UK; s. of Chandran Tharoor and Lily Tharoor; divorced; twin s. *Education:* St Stephen's Coll., Delhi Univ., Tufts Univ. Fletcher School of Law and Diplomacy, USA. *Career:* int. civil servant and professional author; joined

UN 1978; with UNHCR, served at Geneva HQ, Head of Office in Singapore; Special Asst for UN Peace-keeping operations; Exec. Asst to UN Sec.-Gen. 1997–98, Dir Communications and Special Projects, Office of the Sec.-Gen. 1998–2000; Interim Head of Dept of Public Information 2001–02, Head and Under-Sec.-Gen. for Public Information 2002–07; mem. Lok Sabha 2009–; Minister of State for External Affairs 2009–; Chair., Afras Ventures (investment co.) 2008–; mem. Bd of Overseers Fletcher School of Law and Diplomacy, Bd of Trustees Aspen Inst. India, Advisory Bd World Policy Journal, Advisory Bd Virtue Foundation, Advisory Bd Breakthrough (human rights org.); Fellow, New York Inst. of the Humanities. *Publications:* Reasons of State 1981, The Great Indian Novel 1989, The Five Dollar Smile and Other Stories 1990, Show Business 1992, India: From Midnight to the Millennium 1997, Riot 2001, Kerala: God's Own Country 2002, Nehru: The Invention of India 2003, Bookless in Baghdad 2005, The Elephant, the Tiger and the Cellphone: Reflections on India in the 21st Century 2007. *Honours:* Hon. DLitt; Pravasi Bharatiya Samman 2004; Commonwealth Writers' Prize, several journalism and literary awards; named Global Leader of Tomorrow by World Econ. Forum, Davos, Switzerland 1998. *Address:* Ministry of External Affairs, South Block, Room 144C, New Delhi 110 011, India (office). *Telephone:* (11) 23011849 (office). *Fax:* (11) 23013387 (office). *E-mail:* asppr@mea.gov.in (office); tharoor.assistant@gmail.com (office). *Website:* meaindia.nic.in (office); www.shashitharoor.com; shashitharoor.in.

THAYER, Geraldine (see Daniels, Dorothy)

THEOPHILO, Marcia, PhD; Brazilian poet and anthropologist; b. 1941, Fortaleza. *Education:* studied in Rio de Janeiro, São Paulo and Rome, Italy. *Career:* culture and arts reporter, São Paulo 1968–71; moved to Rome 1972; returned to São Paulo 1979–81; returned to Italy 1981. *Plays:* Arapuca 1979, Diga para eles que foi Dulce quem mandou 1981. *Publications:* poetry: Somos Pensamento 1973, Basta! Que falem as vozes 1975, Canções de Outono 1977, Bahia terra marina 1980, Catuete Curupira 1983, O rio, o passaro, as nuvens 1987, Eu canto a Amazônas 1992, Os meninos Jaguar 1995, Kupahúba, árvore do Espirito Santo 2000, Floresta mio dizionario 2003, Amazônas Canta 2003, Amazônas Respiração do Mundo 2005, Amazônia Mãe d'Agua 2007; non-fiction: O massacre dos índios no Brasil de hoje 1977, Os índios do Brasil 1978. *E-mail:* marciatheophilo@yahoo.com.br (office). *Website:* www.theophilo-amazonia-e-poesia.info.

THÉORET, France, BA, MA, PhD; Canadian author, dramatist and poet; b. 1942, Montréal, QC. *Education:* Univ. of Montréal, Univ. of Sherbrooke. *Publications include:* Bloody Mary 1977, Une voix pour Odile 1978, Vertiges 1979, Nécessairement putain 1980, Nous parlerons comme on écrit 1982, Intérieurs 1984, Entre raison et déraison 1987, L'homme qui peignait Staline (trans. as The Man Who Painted Stalin) 1989, Étrangeté, l'étreinte 1992, La fiction de l'ange 1992, Journal pour mémoire 1993, Laurence 1996, Transit 2005, Une belle éducation 2006; contributions: anthologies and other publications.

THEROUX, Marcel, MA; British broadcaster and writer; b. 13 May 1968, Kampala, Uganda; s. of Paul Theroux and Anne Theroux; brother of Louis Theroux; m. *Education:* Westminster School, Clare Coll., Cambridge, Yale Univ., USA. *Career:* worked in TV news in New York and Boston. *Television:* Bering Straits 1999 (Discovery Channel), Coldest Town (Discovery Channel) 2000, All The President's Oil (MBC for Channel 4) 2000, Return to the Exclusion Zone (October Films for National Geographic TV) 2000, Arctic Pilots (October Films for National Geographic TV) 2001, Being Nice To Mr Putin (MBC for Channel 4) 2001, Our New Best Friend (MBC for Channel 4) 2001, The Talk Show (BBC 4) 2002, The State We're In for (BBC Choice) 2002, Milan in a Van (BBC 4) 2002, Mao's Children (Channel 4) 2002, The Texas Solution (Channel 4) 2003, The End of the World As We Know It (Channel 4) 2004, Death Of A Nation 2006, Oligart: The Great Russian Art Boom (Channel 4) 2008, In Search of Wabi-sabi (BBC 4) 2009. *Publications:* novels: The Stranger in The Earth 1999, The Confessions of Mycroft Holmes: A Paper Chase (Somerset Maugham Award) 2001, A Blow to the Heart 2006, Far North 2009. *Literary Agent:* c/o KBJ Management, 22 Rathbone Place, London, W1T 1LA, England. *Telephone:* (20) 7054-5999. *Fax:* (20) 7287-1191. *E-mail:* general@kbjmanagement.co.uk. *Website:* www.kbjmanagement.co.uk; www.marceltheroux.com.

THEROUX, Paul Edward, BA, FRSL, FRGS; American writer; b. 10 April 1941, Medford, Mass; s. of Albert Eugene Theroux and Anne Dittami Theroux; m. 1st Anne Castle 1967 (divorced 1993), two s.; m. 2nd Sheila Donnelly 1995. *Education:* Univ. of Massachusetts. *Career:* lecturer, Univ. of Urbino, Italy 1963, Soche Hill Coll., Malawi 1963–65, Makerere Univ., Kampala, Uganda 1965–68, Univ. of Singapore 1968–71; Writer-in-Residence, Univ. of Va 1972. *Play:* The White Man's Burden 1987. *Screenplay:* Saint Jack 1979. *Publications:* fiction: Waldo 1967, Fong and the Indians 1968, Girls at Play 1969, Murder in Mount Holly 1969, Jungle Lovers 1971, Sinning with Annie 1972, Saint Jack 1973, The Black House 1974, The Family Arsenal 1976, The Consul's File 1977, Picture Palace (Whitbread Award) 1978, A Christmas Card 1978, London Snow 1980, World's End 1980, The Mosquito Coast (James Tait Black Memorial Prize 1982, Yorkshire Post Best Novel Award 1982) 1981, The London Embassy 1982, Doctor Slaughter 1984, O-Zone 1986, My Secret History 1988, Chicago Loop 1990, Dr. DeMarr 1990, Millroy the Magician 1993, My Other Life 1996, Kowloon Tong 1997, Collected Stories 1997, Collected Short Novels 1998, Hotel Honolulu 2000, The Stranger at the Palazzo d'Oro (short stories) 2002, Telling Tales (contrib. to charity anthology) 2004, Blinding Light 2005, The Elephanta Suite 2007, A Dead Hand: A Crime in Calcutta 2009, Murder in Mount Holly 2011; non-fiction: V. S. Naipaul (criticism) 1973, The Great Railway Bazaar (travel) 1975, The Old Patagonian Express (travel) 1979, The Kingdom by the Sea (travel) 1983, Sailing through China (travel) 1983, Sunrise with Sea Monsters (travel) 1985, Riding the Iron Rooster: By Train Through China (travel) (Thomas Cook Prize for Best Literary Travel Book 1989) 1988, Travelling the World (travel) 1990, The Happy Isles of Oceania: Paddling the Pacific (travel) 1992, The Pillars of Hercules (travel) 1995, Sir Vidia's Shadow: A Friendship Across Five Continents (travel) 1998, Fresh-Air Fiend (travel) 1999, The Worst Journey in the World 2000, Nurse Wolf and Dr Sacks 2000, Dark Star Safari: Overland from Cairo to Cape Town (travel) 2002, Ghost Train to the Eastern Star (travel) 2008. *Honours:* Hon. DLitt (Tufts Univ., Trinity Univ.) 1983, (Univ. of Mass.) 1988; Playboy magazine Editorial Awards 1972, 1976, 1977, 1979. *Literary Agent:* Hamish Hamilton Ltd, 80 Strand, London, WC2, England; The Wylie Agency, 250 West 57th Street, New York NY 10107, USA.

THESEN, Sharon, BA, MA; Canadian poet, writer and editor; *Associate Professor of Creative Writing, University of British Columbia at Okanagan*; b. 1 Oct. 1946, Tisdale, Saskatchewan; d. of Clarence Norris Thesen and Dawn Marguerite Thesen. *Education:* Simon Fraser University. *Career:* teacher, Capilano College, Vancouver 1976–92; Poetry Ed., Capilano Review 1978–89, Ed. 2001–05; currently Assoc. Prof. of Creative Writing, Univ. of British Columbia at Okanagan; co-Ed., Lake (journal of arts and environment). *Publications:* Artemis Hates Romance 1980, Radio New France Radio 1981, Holding the Pose 1983, Confabulations: Poems for Malcolm Lowry 1984, The Beginning of the Long Dash 1987, The Pangs of Sunday 1990, The New Long Poems Anthology (ed.) 1991, Aurora 1995, A Pair of Scissors (Pat Lowther Memorial Award) 2000, The Good Bacteria 2006; contributions: various publications. *Address:* Department of Creative Studies, University of British Columbia, Arts Building, Room 131, 3333 University Way, Kelowna, BC V1V 1V7, Canada (office). *Telephone:* (250) 807-9417 (office). *Fax:* (250) 807-8027 (office). *E-mail:* sharon.thesen@ubc.ca (office). *Website:* web.ubc.ca/okanagan/creative/faculty/thesen (office).

THIBAUDEAU, Colleen, BA, MA; Canadian poet and writer; b. 29 Dec. 1925, Toronto, Ont.; m. James C. Reaney 1951 (died 2008); two s. one d. *Education:* St Thomas Collegiate Inst., Univ. Coll., Univ. of Toronto, Univ. Catholique de l'ouest, Angers. *Career:* mem. League of Canadian Poets 1997–; Life mem. New Democratic Party. *Publications include:* poetry: Ten Letters 1975, My Granddaughters Are Combing Out Their Long Hair 1977, The Martha Landscapes 1984, The Artemesia Book: Poems Selected and New 1991, The Patricia Album and Other Poems 1992; contribs include poems and stories in anthologies. *Address:* 276 Huron Street, London, ON N6A 2J9, Canada (home).

THIELE, Leslie Paul, BA, MA, PhD; Canadian academic and writer; *Professor of Political Science, University of Florida*; b. 27 Jan. 1959; m. Susan Wapner 1991; two s. *Education:* McGill Univ., Univ. of Calgary, Princeton Univ. *Career:* Asst Prof. of Political Science, Swarthmore Coll. 1989–91; Asst Prof., Univ. of Florida, Gainesville 1991–95, Assoc. Prof. 1995–98, Prof. of Political Science, Affiliated Faculty Mem., College of Natural Resources and the Environment 1997–, Head, Dept of Political Science 1997–2002. *Publications:* Friedrich Nietzsche and the Politics of the Soul: A Study of Heroic Individualism 1990, Timely Meditations: Martin Heidegger and Postmodern Politics 1995, Thinking Politics: Perspectives in Ancient, Modern, and Postmodern Political Theory 1997, Environmentalism for a New Millennium: The Challenge of Coevolution 1999, The Heart of Judgement: Practical Wisdom, Narrative and Neuroscience 2006; contributions: articles and reviews to periodicals including: Political Theory, Journal of Modern History, International Studies in Philosophy, Environmental Ethics, American Political Science Review. *Honours:* Grants, National Endowment for the Humanities 1990, 1991, Fellow, Social Science and Humanities Research Council of Canada 1991–93, Fellow, Social Science Research Council and MacArthur Foundation 1994–96. *Address:* Department of Political Science, 302 Anderson Hall, University of Florida, PO Box 117325, Gainesville, FL 32611-7325, USA (office). *Telephone:* (352) 273-2380 (office). *E-mail:* thiele@ufl.edu (office). *Website:* www.clas.ufl.edu/users/thiele (office).

THISELTON, Rev. Canon Anthony Charles, BD, MTh, PhD, DD, DD, FBA; British theologian and academic; *Professor of Christian Theology, University of Nottingham*; b. 13 July 1937, Woking, Surrey, England; s. of Eric Charles Thiselton and Hilda Winifred Thiselton (née Kevan); m. Rosemary Stella Harman 1963; two s. one d. *Education:* Univs of London, Sheffield and Durham, Archbishop of Canterbury at Lambeth, King's Coll., London British Acad. *Career:* Curate, Holy Trinity Church, Sydenham 1960–63; Lecturer and Tutor, Tyndale Hall, Bristol and Univ. of Bristol 1964–70; Lecturer in Biblical Studies, Univ. of Sheffield 1970–79, Sr Lecturer 1979–85; Prin. St John's Coll., Nottingham 1985–88; Prin. St John's Coll., Durham 1988–92; Prof. of Christian Theology and Head of Dept of Theology, Univ. of Nottingham 1992–2001, 2006–12, Prof. Emer. in Residence 2001–06; Canon Theologian of Leicester Cathedral 1993–, and of Southwell 2000–07; Prof. Emer. of Christian Theology, Chester Univ. Coll. 2003–; mem. Soc. for the Study of Theology (Pres. 1999, 2000), Crown Appointments Comm. 2001–07, Appointments Comm. 2005–10, Bd of Educ. 2005–10; external adviser to various univs and publrs; Fellow, King's Coll. London. *Publications:* 17 books, including The Two Horizons 1980, The Responsibility of Hermeneutics (with R. Lundin and C. Walhout) 1985, New Horizons in Hermeneutics 1992, Interpreting God and the Post-Modern Self 1995, The Promise of Hermeneutics (with R. Lundin and C. Walhout) 1999, I Corinthians: A Commentary on the Greek Text 2000, A Concise Encyclopedia of the Philosophy of Religion 2002, First Corinthians 2005, Thiselton on Hermeneutics: Collected Works and New Essays 2006, The Hermeneutics of Doctrine 2007, The Living Paul 2009; Hermeneutics 2009, 1 and 2 Thessalonians 2011, Life after Death: A New Approach to the Last Things 2012; contrib. to Journal of Theological Studies, New Testament Studies, Biblical Interpretation, Scottish Journal of Theology, approx. 80 research articles. *Honours:* British Acad. Research Award 1995–96, American Library Asscn Choice of Theology Books 1995. *Address:* 390 High Road, Chilwell, Nottingham, NG9 5EG, England (home). *Telephone:* (115) 917-6391 (home). *Fax:* (115) 917-6392 (home). *E-mail:* anthony.thiselton@ntlworld.com (home). *Website:* www.nottingham.ac.uk/theology (office).

THOM, James Alexander, AB; American novelist; b. 28 May 1933, Gosport, IN; m. Dark Rain 1990. *Education:* Butler Univ., Indianapolis. *Career:* reporter and columnist, The Indianapolis Star 1961–67; Lecturer in Journalism, Indiana Univ. 1978–80; mem. Authors' Guild. *Publications:* Spectator Sport 1978, Long Knife 1979, Follow the River 1981, From Sea to Shining Sea 1984, Staying Out of Hell 1985, Panther in the Sky 1989, The Children of First Man 1994, The Spirit of the Place 1995, Indiana II 1996, The Red Heart 1997, Sign-Talker 2000, Warrior Woman (with Dark Rain) 2003, St Patrick's Battalion 2006, The Art and Craft of Writing Historical Fiction 2010; contrib. to magazines. *Honours:* Hon. DHL (Butler Univ.) 1995. *Address:* 6276 W Stogsdill Road, Bloomington, IN 47404, USA (home).

THOMAS, Audrey Grace, MA; Canadian (b. American) writer; b. 17 Nov. 1935, Binghamton, New York; d. of Donald Earle and Frances Waldron (née Corbett) Callahan; m. Ian Thomas 1959 (divorced 1979); three d. *Education:* The Mary A. Burnham School (Northampton, MA), Smith Coll. and Univ. of British Columbia. *Career:* Teacher of English Language Univ. of Science and Tech., Ghana 1964–66; Visiting Lecturer Univ. of British Columbia 1975–76, Sr Lecturer 1981–82; Visiting Asst Prof. Concordia Univ., Montréal 1978, Visiting Prof. 1989–90; Visiting Prof. Univ. of Victoria 1978–79, 1988; Writer-in-Residence Simon Fraser Univ. 1982, David Thompson Univ. Centre, Nelson, BC 1984, Univ. of Ottawa 1987; Visiting Prof. Dartmouth Coll., Hanover, NH 1994; mem. Nat. Exec. Writers Union of Canada; mem. Canada Council Periodicals Cttee 1980–83, Editorial Collective, Women and Words Anthology 1984; mem. PEN, Amnesty Int.; Canada-Scotland Literary Fellow (Edinburgh) 1985–86; Dr hc (Simon Fraser Univ., Univ. of BC) 1994; Ethel Wilson Award 1985; Marian Engel Award 1987; Canada-Australia Literary Prize 1990. *Publications:* Ten Green Bottles 1967, Mrs Blood 1970, Muchmeyer and Prospero on the Island 1972, Songs My Mother Taught Me 1973, Blown Figures 1975, Ladies and Escorts 1977, Latakia 1979, Two in the Bush and Other Stories 1980, Real Mothers 1981, Intertidal Life (nominated Gov Gen's Award in Fiction) 1984, Goodbye Harold, Good Luck! 1986, The Wild Blue Yonder 1990, Graven Images 1993, Coming Down from Wa 1995, Isobel Gunn 1999, The Path of Totality 2001, Tattycoram 2005; Radio dramas include: Once Your Submarine Cable is Gone… 1973, The Milky Way 1984, The Woman in Black Velvet 1985, Rosa 1987, Shonadithit 1988, Sanctuary 1989, A Day in the Life of Medusa 1989; writer of several articles. *Address:* c/o Goose Lane Editions, 500 Beaverbrook Court, Suite 330, Fredericton, NB E3B 5X4, Canada (office). *E-mail:* info@gooselane.com (office). *Website:* gooselane .com (office).

THOMAS, Chantal; French essayist; *Director of Research, Centre National de la Recherche Scientifique (CNRS)*; b. 1945, Lyon. *Career:* specialist in eighteenth century history; biographical publs on Sade, Casanova, Thomas Berhard and Marie-Antoinette; debut novel Adieux à la Reine sold over 110,000 copies and translated into German, English, Korean, Greek, Italian, Japanese, Dutch and Portugese 2002; currently Dir of Research, CNRS. *Publications include:* Marquis de Sade: L'Oeil de la letter 1978, Casanova: Un Voyage libertine 1985, The Wicked Queen: The Origins of the Myth of Marie-Antoinette 2001, Coping with Freedom: Reflections on Ephemeral Happiness 2001, Adieux à la Reine (Farewell to the Queen, Prix Femina 2002) 2002, Le Lectrice-Adjointe 2003, Lîle flottante 2004, Apolline ou L'école de la Providence 2005, Le Palias de la Reine 2005, Chemins de sable 2006, Jardinière Arlequin 2006, Cafés de la Mémoire 2008. *Address:* CNRS Headquarters, 3, rue Michel-Ange, 75794 Paris cedex 16 (office); c/o Éditions du Seuil, 27 rue Jacob, 75006 Paris, France (office). *Telephone:* 1-44-96-40-00 (CRNS) (office); 1-40-46-50-50 (office). *Fax:* 1-44-96-53-90 (CRNS) (office); 1-40-46-43-00 (office). *E-mail:* contact@seuil.com (office). *Website:* www.cnrs.fr (office).

THOMAS, Donald Michael, MA; British novelist and poet; b. 27 Jan. 1935, Redruth, Cornwall, England; s. of Harold Redvers Thomas and Amy Thomas (née Moyle); m. Angela Thomas; two s. one d. *Education:* Redruth Grammar School, Univ. High School, Melbourne, New Coll., Oxford. *Career:* English teacher, Teignmouth, Devon 1959–63; Lecturer, Hereford Coll. of Educ. 1963–78; full-time author 1978–. *Play:* Hell Fire Corner 2004. *Publications:* Two Voices 1968, Logan Stone 1971, Love and Other Deaths 1975, Honeymoon Voyage 1978, The Flute-Player 1978, Birthstone 1980, The White Hotel 1981, Dreaming in Bronze 1981, Ararat 1983, Selected Poems 1983, Swallow 1984, Sphinx 1986, Summit 1987, Memories and Hallucinations 1988, Lying Together 1989, Flying in to Love 1992, The Puberty Tree (new and selected poems) 1992, Pictures at an Exhibition 1993, Eating Pavlova 1994, Lady with a Laptop 1996, Alexander Solzhenitsyn (biog.) 1998, Charlotte 2000, Dear Shadows 2003, Not Saying Everything 2006, Bleak Hotel 2008. *Honours:* Gollancz/Pan Fantasy Prize, PEN Fiction Prize, Cheltenham Prize, Los Angeles Times Fiction Prize, Cholmondeley Award for Poetry, Orwell Prize for Biography. *Address:* The Coach House, Rashleigh Vale, Truro, Cornwall, TR1 1TJ, England. *Telephone:* (1872) 261724. *E-mail:* dmthomas@btconnect.com. *Website:* www.dmthomasonline.com; www.don-whitehotel.blogspot.com.

THOMAS, Elizabeth Marshall, AB, MA; American author; b. 13 Sept. 1931, Boston, Mass; d. of Laurence K. Marshall and Lorna Jean McLean Marshall; m. Stephen M. Thomas 1956, one s. one d. *Education:* Radcliffe Coll., George Washington Univ. *Career:* mem. PEN, Soc. of Women Geographers. *Publications:* The Hill People 1953, The Harmless People 1959, Warrior Herdsmen 1966, Reindeer Moon 1987, The Animal Wife 1990, The Hidden Life of Dogs 1993, The Tribe of Tiger: Cats and Their Culture 1994, Certain Poor Shepherds 1996, The Social Lives of Dogs: The Grace of Canine Company 2000, The Old Way: A Story of the First People 2006, The Hidden Life of Deer 2009; contribs to journals. *Honours:* Hon. DLitt (Franklin Pierce Soc.) 1992; Brandeis Univ. Creative Arts Award 1968, PEN Hemingway Citation 1988, Radcliffe Coll. Alumni Recognition Award 1989. *Address:* 80 E Mountain Road, Peterborough, NH 03458-2318, USA (home). *Telephone:* (603) 924-3187 (office). *E-mail:* lizthomas@pobox.com (office).

THOMAS, Helen A., BA; American journalist; b. 4 Aug. 1920, Winchester, Ky; d. of George Thomas and Mary Thomas; m. Douglas B. Cornell. *Education:* Wayne State Univ., Detroit. *Career:* reporter, United Press Int. (UPI) 1943–74; White House Bureau Chief 1974–2000, Dean of the White House Press Corps 2000–10; columnist, Hearst Newspapers 2000–10; first woman mem. Gridiron Club 1975, apptd Pres. (first woman) 1992; mem. Women's Nat. Press Club, Pres. 1959–60; mem. American Newspaper Women's Club (fmr Vice-Pres.), White House Corresps Asscn (Pres. 1976). *Television:* Thank you, Mr. President (HBO documentary). *Publications:* Dateline White House 1975, Front Row at the White House: My Life and Times 2000, Thanks for the Memories, Mr. President: Wit and Wisdom from the Front Row at the White House 2003, Watchdogs of Democracy?: The Waning Washington Press Corps and How It Has Failed the Public 2006, The Great White House Breakout 2008, Listen Up, Mr President: Everything You Always Wanted Your President to Know and Do 2009. *Honours:* numerous hon. degrees, including Hon. LLD (Eastern Michigan State) 1972, (Ferris State Coll.) 1978, (Brown) 1986, (St Bonaventure) 1988, (Franklin Marshall) 1989, (Skidmore Coll., Mo.) 1992, (Susquehanna) 1993, (Sage Coll., Mo.) 1994, (Northwestern) 1995, (Franklin Coll.) 1995; Hon. LHD (Wayne State) 1974, (Detroit) 1979, (Siena Coll.) 2007; William Allen White Journalism Award, Women's Nat. Press Club, Woman of the Year Award, Ladies Home Journal 1975, Fourth Estate Award, Nat. Press Club 1984, Journalism Award, Univ. of Missouri 1990, Al Newharth Award 1990, Ralph McGill Award 1995, Lifetime Achievement Award, White House Corresps Asscn 1998, Nat. Newspaper Asscn Lifetime Award 2002, Intrepid Award, Nat. Org. for Women 2003. *Address:* c/o Nine Speakers Inc., 2501 Calvert Street, NW, Washington, DC 20008-2620, USA (office). *Telephone:* (202) 328-6861 (office). *E-mail:* ninespeakers@usa.net (office). *Website:* www.helenthomas.org.

THOMAS, Leslie, OBE; British writer; b. 22 March 1931, Newport, Wales; m. 1st; three c.; m. 2nd Diane Thomas; one s. *Career:* mil. service 1949–51; newspaper reporter; Vice-Pres. Barnardo's. *Publications:* novels: This Time Next Week 1964, The Virgin Soldiers 1966, Orange Wednesday 1967, The Love Beach 1968, Come to the War 1969, Arthur McCann and all his Women 1970, His Lordship 1970, Onward Virgin Soldiers 1971, The Man with the Power 1973, Bedtimes 1974, Tropic of Ruislip 1974, Stand Up Virgin Soldiers 1975, Dangerous Davies: The Last Detective 1976, Bare Nell 1977, That Old Gang of Mine 1979, Omerod's Landing 1979, The Magic Army 1981, The Dearest and the Best 1984, The Adventures of Goodnight and Loving 1986, Dangerous in Love 1987, Orders for New York 1989, The Loves and Journeys of Revolving Jones 1991, Arrivals and Departures 1992, Dangerous by Moonlight 1993, Running Away 1994, Kensington Heights 1996, Chloe's Song 1997, Dangerous Davies and the Lonely Hearts Detective Club 1998, Other Times 1999, Waiting for the Day 2003, Dover Beach 2005; non-fiction: Some Lovely Islands 1968, The Hidden Places of Britain 1983, This Time Next Week 1991, My World of Islands 1993, In My Wildest Dreams 2006. *Honours:* Hon. MA (Univ. of Wales), Dr hc (Univ. of Nottingham). *Address:* c/o Arrow Books, Random House UK, 20 Vauxhall Bridge Road, London, SW1V 2SA, England (office). *Website:* www.lesliethomas.co.uk.

THOMAS, Michael, BA, MFA; American writer; b. Boston; m.; three c. *Education:* Hunter Coll., Warren Wilson Coll. *Career:* Asst Prof. of English, Hunter Coll., New York 2005–. *Publication:* Man Gone Down (selected as a New York Times Notable Book of 2007, Int. IMPAC Dublin Literary Award 2009) 2007. *Address:* Department of English, Hunter College, Office 1203 HW, 695 Park Avenue, New York, NY 10065, USA (office). *Telephone:* (212) 772-5079 (office). *Fax:* (212) 772-5411 (office). *E-mail:* longasthesky@hotmail.com (office). *Website:* www.hunter.cuny.edu/english (office).

THOMAS, Richard; British composer and writer; b. 1965. *Education:* Univ. of Cambridge. *Career:* mem. of musical and comic duo Miles & Milner 1987–93; Co-founder and mem. Club Zarathustra 1993–98; Co-founder Kombat Opera 1996. *Compositions:* Jerry Springer: The Opera (music and lyrics, with Stewart Lee) (Evening Standard Theatre Award for Best New Musical 2004) 2001, Shoes (dance piece) 2010, Anna Nicole 2011. *Radio:* performer: The Miles & Milner Show (BBC Radio 4) 1991, Rainer Hersch's All Classical Music Explained (BBC Radio 4) 1998. *Television:* performer:

Beethoven's Not Dead (Spitting Image/BBC 2) 1992, This Morning With Richard Not Judy (BBC 2) 1998–99, Either/Or (PlayUK) 1999, Attention Scum (BBC Choice/BBC 2) 2001; Musical Dir The Frank Skinner Show (Avalon TV/BBC 1, later ITV) 1995–2001, This Morning With Richard Not Judy (BBC 2) 1998–99, Baddiel & Skinner Unplanned (Avalon TV/ITV) 2000–03, Jerry Springer: The Opera (BBC 2) 2004. *Address:* c/o Avalon, 4A Exmoor Street, London, W10 6BD, England. *Telephone:* (20) 7598-8000.

THOMAS, Victoria (see De Weese, Thomas Eugene (Gene))

THOMÉSE, P(ieter) F(rans), BA; Dutch writer; b. 23 Jan. 1958, Doetinchem; m.; three c. (one deceased). *Education:* Univ. of Amsterdam. *Publications:* Zuidland (AKO Literatuurprijs) 1991, Heldenjaren 1994, Haagse liefde en De vieze engel 1996, Het aesde bedriff 1999, Greatest Hits 2001, Schaduwkind 2003, Izak 2005, Vladiwostoki 2007, Nergensman 2008, Grillroom Jeruzalem 2011. *Address:* c/o Uitgeverij, Postbus 218, 1000 AE Amsterdam, Netherlands. *Website:* www.uitgeverijcontact.nl; www.thomese.nl.

THOMEY, Tedd, BA; American journalist and writer; b. 19 July 1920, Butte, MT; m. Patricia Natalie Bennett 1943, one d. *Education:* Univ. of California. *Career:* Publicity Dir, San Diego State Coll. 1941–42; reporter, San Diego Union-Tribune 1942; reporter, then Asst Editorial Promotion Man., San Francisco Chronicle 1942–43, 1945–48; News Ed. and columnist, Long Beach Press Telegram 1950–; creative writing instructor, Long Beach City Coll.; guest lecturer, Univ. of Southern California; consultant, 20th Century Fox Studios. *Publications:* And Dream of Evil 1954, Jet Pilot 1955, Killer in White 1956, Jet Ace 1958, I Want Out 1959, Flight to Takla-Ma 1961, The Loves of Errol Flynn 1961, The Sadist 1961, Doris Day (biog.) 1962, All the Way 1964, Hollywood Uncensored 1965, Hollywood Confidential 1967, The Comedians 1970, The Glorious Decade 1971, The Big Love (co-author) 1986, The Prodigy Plot 1987; plays: The Big Love (co-author) 1991, Immortal Images 1996; contrib. to many magazines. *Honours:* California Newspaper Publishers Award for Best Front Page. *Address:* 7228 Rosebay Street, Long Beach, CA 90808-4363, USA (home). *Telephone:* (562) 420-8435 (home).

THOMPSON, Ernest Victor, MBE; British writer; b. 14 July 1931, London, England; m. Celia Carole Burton 1972; two s. *Career:* mem. West Country Writers Club (Vice-Pres.), Mevagissey Male Choir (Vice-Patron), RSL, Cornish Literary Guild (Pres. 1998). *Publications:* Chase the Wind 1977, Harvest of the Sun 1978, The Music Makers 1979, Ben Retallick 1980, The Dream Traders 1981, Singing Spears 1982, The Restless Sea 1983, Cry Once Alone 1984, Polrudden 1985, The Stricken Land 1986, Becky 1988, God's Highlander 1988, Lottie Trago 1989, Cassie 1990, Wychwood 1991, Blue Dress Girl 1992, Mistress of Polrudden 1993, The Tolpuddle Woman 1994, Ruddlemoor 1995, Moontide 1996, Cast no Shadows 1997, Mud Huts and Missionaries 1997, Fires of Evening 1998, Somewhere a Bird is Singing 1999, Here, There and Yesterday 1999, Winds of Fortune 2000, Seek a New Dawn 2001, The Lost Years 2002, Paths of Destiny 2003, The Vagrant King 2005, Though the Heavens May Fall 2007, No Less Than the Journey 2008, Churchyard and Hawke 2009, Beyond the Storm 2010, Hawke's Tor 2011; also various books on Cornish and West Country subjects; contrib. of approx. 200 short stories to magazines. *Honours:* Best Historical Novel 1976. *Address:* Fourways, Trebartha, Launceston, Cornwall, PL15 7PD, England (home). *Telephone:* (1566) 782335 (office). *E-mail:* thompsonev@hotmail.com (home).

THOMPSON, Jean Louise, AB, MFA; American academic and writer; b. 1 Jan. 1950, Chicago, IL. *Education:* Univ. of Illinois, Bowling Green State Univ. *Career:* Prof. of English, Univ. of Illinois, Urbana 1973–; teacher, Warren Wilson Coll. MFA Program 1988, 1989, 1990; Distinguished Visiting Writer, Wichita State Univ. 1991; Assoc. Prof., San Francisco State Univ. 1992–93. *Publications:* The Gasoline Wars 1979, My Wisdom 1982, Little Faces and Other Stories 1984, The Woman Driver 1985, Who Do You Love? 1999, Wide Blue Yonder 2002, City Boy 2005, Throw Like a Girl 2007, Do Not Deny Me: Stories 2009; contrib. to various anthologies, journals and magazines. *Honours:* Illinois Arts Council Literary Awards 1976, 1996, NEA Fellowship 1977, Guggenheim Fellowship 1984, Pushcart Prize 1995. *Address:* c/o Simon & Schuster Inc., 1230 Avenue of the Americas, New York, NY 10020, USA (office). *Website:* www.jeanthompsononline.com.

THOMPSON, Judith Clare Francesca, BA; Canadian playwright; *Professor of Drama, University of Guelph*; b. 20 Sept. 1954, Montréal, PQ; d. of William and Mary (née Forde) Thompson; m. Gregor Campbell 1983; five c. *Education:* Queen's Univ. and Nat. Theatre School, Montréal. *Career:* numerous workshops 1980–90; Tutor in Playwriting, Univ. of Toronto 1983–84; mem. Playwright's Unit Tarragon Theatre 1984–86; Resident Instructor and Dir Univ. of New Brunswick 1989–90; Assoc. Prof. of Drama, Univ. of Guelph, Ont. 1991–; screenwriter. *Films include:* Lost and Delirious, Perfect Pie. *TV includes:* Turning to Stone (Prix Italia for Best Film Screenplay), Life with Billy (Best Screenplay, Golden Gate Awards, San Francisco) 1992. *Plays include:* The Crackwalker 1980, White Biting Dog (Gov.-Gen.'s Award) 1984, The Other Side of the Dark (Gov.-Gen.'s Award 1990), I Am Yours 1987, Lion in the Streets (an adaptation of 'Hedda Gabler') 1990, Sled 1997, Perfect Pie 2000, Habitat 2001, Capture Me 2004, The Pyramids 2005, Palace of the End 2007, Enoch Arden in the Hope Shelter 2007, Such Creatures 2010. *Radio includes:* Tornado (Nellie Award for Best Radio Drama), Sugarcane, White Sand, Thicket, A Big White Light, The Quickening. *Honours:* two Toronto Arts Awards, several Chalmer Awards, Canadian Author's Asscn B'nai Brith Award, Epilepsy Toronto Humanitarian Award, Walter Carsen Prize for Excellence in the Performing Arts 2007, Susan Smith Blackburn Prize 2008. *Address:* Creative Writing Department, College of Arts, University of Guelph, Guelph, Ontario, N1G 2W1, Canada (office). *E-mail:* cwmfa@uoguelph.ca (office). *Website:* arts.uoguelph.ca/creativewritingmfa (office).

THOMPSON, Kate, MA; British author; b. 1956, Halifax, Yorks., England; d. of E. P. Thompson and Dorothy Thompson; two d. *Education:* Univ. of Limerick, Ireland. *Career:* fmrly worked with racehorses; moved to Ireland 1981. *Publications:* There is Something (poems) 1992; novels for adults: Down Among the Gods 1997, Thin Air 1999, An Act of Worship 2000; novels for children: Switchers 1994, Midnight's Choice 1998, Wild Blood 1999, The Missing Link (aka Fourth World) 2000, Only Human 2001, The Beguilers (Children's Books Ireland (CBI) Bisto Children's Book of the Year 2001) 2001, The Alchemist's Apprentice (CBI Bisto Children's Book of the Year 2002) 2002, Origins 2003, Annan Water (CBI Bisto Children's Book of the Year 2004) 2004, The New Policeman (CBI Bisto Children's Book of the Year 2005, Whitbread Children's Book of the Year 2006, Guardian Children's Fiction Prize 2006, Dublin Airport Authority Children's Book of the Year 2006) 2005, The Fourth Horseman 2006, The Last of the High Kings 2007, Creature of the Night 2008, Highway Robbery 2008, The White Horse Trick 2009, Wanted (Most Wanted in USA) 2010, That Gallagher Girl 2011. *Literary Agent:* c/o Sophie Hicks, Ed Victor Ltd, 6 Bayley Street, Bedford Square, London, WC1B 3HE, England. *E-mail:* sophie@edvictor.com. *E-mail:* kate@katethompson.info (office). *Website:* www.katethompson.info.

THOMPSON, Samuel Richard Charles, BA (Hons), MA, PGCE; British teacher, poet and writer; *Teacher of English and Drama, Agora Portals International School, Majorca*; b. 9 Feb. 1968, London, England; m.; two d. *Education:* Univ. of Manchester, Charlotte Mason Coll. of Educ., Univ. of Lancaster. *Career:* Head of English, Fyling Hall School, N Yorks. 1993–95; Head of English and Drama, Int. School at Sotogrande, Spain 1997–99; Teacher of English and Drama and Head of Year, Guernsey Grammar School 1999–2007; Head of English, Bellver Int. Coll., Majorca 2007–09; Teacher of English and Drama, Agora Portals International School, Majorca 2009–; Ed. Muse magazine 1989, Que Me Cuentas 1997–99; Publishing Dir Saumarez Press 2002–; mem. Univ. of Manchester Poetry Soc., Chair. 1990. *Poetry performances:* Ambleside 1991, Ulverstone 1992, Manchester 1996, Guernsey annually 2001–07, Deia 2009–11. *Radio broadcasts of poetry:* Radio Guernsey 2002. *Television:* Channel Islands News 2004. *Publications:* poetry: What Am I Doing Here 1996, Where Home Was (also CD, with guitar accompaniment by Martin Spoelstra) 2002, Church Poems 2007; contrib. to anthologies, including Crossing the Bridge 2003, Parent to Child 2009, Martian Poems & Season Songs 2009; to journals, including Envoi, Exeter Flying Post, Fylingtales, Grammalogue, Guernsey Press, Hrafnhoh, In Touch, Island Ink, La Vista, Lynx, Majorca Daily Bulletin, Muse, Ore, Written, Canoe Focus. *Honours:* Thomas de Quincy Prize, Univ. of Manchester 1989. *Address:* Agora Portals International School, Portal Nous, 07181 Calvia, Majorca, Spain (office). *Telephone:* (971) 684042 (office); (971) 684042 (home). *E-mail:* samthompson@cwgsy.net (home).

THOMSON, David; British film critic; b. 1941, London; m.; two s. *Career:* fmrly taught film studies, Dartmouth Coll.; film critic, living in California, contributing to Film Comment, Film Criticism, The Independent, Movieline, The New Republic, New York Times, Sight and Sound, and others. *Publications include:* fiction: Warren Beatty and Desert Eye, Suspects 1985, Silver Light 1990; non-fiction: A Biographical Dictionary of Film (fourth edn as The New Biographical Dictionary of Film) 1975, Showman: The Life of David O. Selznick (biog.) 1993, Rosebud: The Story of Orson Welles (biog.) 1996, Beneath Mulholland: Thoughts on Hollywood and its Ghosts 1998, In Nevada: The Land, The People, God and Chance 1999, Hollywood: A Celebration 2001, Marlon Brando (biog.) 2003, Cinema Year by Year (revised edn, co-author) 2004, The Whole Equation: A History of Hollywood 2004, Nicole Kidman (biog.) 2006, Have You Seen? A Personal Introduction to 1,000 Films 2008, Try to Tell the Story (memoir) 2009, The Moment of Psycho 2009. *Address:* c/o Allen Lane, Penguin Publicity, 80 Strand, London, WC2R 0RL, England (office). *Website:* www.penguin.co.uk.

THOMSON, Derick Smith, (Ruaraidh MacThòmais), BA, MA, FBA, FRSE; British poet, writer and academic (retd); b. 5 Aug. 1921, Stornoway, Isle of Lewis, Scotland; m. Carol Galbraith 1952; five s. one d. *Education:* Univ. of Aberdeen, Emmanuel Coll., Cambridge. *Career:* Asst in Celtic, Univ. of Edinburgh 1948–49; Lecturer in Welsh, Univ. of Glasgow 1949–56, Prof. of Celtic 1963–91; Ed. Gairm Gaelic Literary Quarterly 1952–2002; Reader in Celtic, Univ. of Aberdeen 1956–63; mem. Glasgow Arts Club, Scottish Gaelic Texts Soc. (Hon. Pres.), Saltire Soc. (Hon. Pres. 1997), Scottish Poetry Library (Hon. Pres. 1999). *Publications:* An Dealbh Briste 1951, The Gaelic Sources of Macpherson's 'Ossian' 1952, Eadar Samhradh is Foghar 1967, An Rathad Cian 1970, The Far Road and Other Poems 1971, An Introduction to Gaelic Poetry 1974, Saorsa agus an Iolaire 1977, Creachadh na Clarsaich 1982, The Companion to Gaelic Scotland 1983, European Poetry in Gaelic Translation 1990, Smeur an Dochais 1992, Gaelic Poetry in the Eighteenth Century 1993, Meall Garbh/The Rugged Mountain 1995, Mac Mhaighstir Alasdair, Selected Poems 1996, Sùil air Fàire 2007; contrib. to books, journals and magazines. *Honours:* Hon. DLitt (Wales) 1987, (Aberdeen) 1994, (Glasgow) 2007; Scottish Arts Council Publication Awards 1971, 1992, FVS Foundation Ossian Prize, Hamburg 1974, Saltire Scottish Book of the Year Award 1983. *Address:* 15

Struan Road, Cathcart, Glasgow, G44 3AT, Scotland (home). *Telephone:* (141) 637-3704 (home).

THOMSON, Ian; British writer, journalist and editor. *Career:* currently Royal Literary Fund Fellow, Univ. Coll. London. *Publications:* Bonjour Blanc: A Journey through Haiti 1992, Primo Levi: A Biography (W.H. Heinemann Award 2003) 2002, The Dead Yard: A Story of Modern Jamaica (Royal Soc. of Literature Ondaatje Prize 2010, Dolman Travel Book of the Year 2010) 2009. *Literary Agent:* c/o James Gill, United Agents, 12–26 Lexington Street, London, W1F 0LE, England. *Telephone:* (20) 3214-0800. *Fax:* (20) 3214-0801. *E-mail:* info@unitedagents.co.uk. *Website:* unitedagents.co.uk.

THOMSON, June Valerie, BA; British writer; b. 24 June 1930, Kent; m. (divorced); two s. *Education:* Bedford Coll., London Univ. *Career:* mem. CWA (cttee mem.), Detection Club. *Publications:* Not One of Us, 1972; Deadly Relations, 1979; Sound Evidence, 1984; No Flowers By Request, 1987; The Spoils of Time, 1989; The Secret Files of Sherlock Holmes, 1990; The Secret Chronicles of Sherlock Holmes, 1992; Flowers for the Dead, 1992; The Secret Journals of Sherlock Holmes, 1993; A Study in Friendship, 1995; Burden of Innocence, 1996; The Secret Documents of Sherlock Holmes, 1997; The Unquiet Grave, 2000, Going Home 2006; contrib. several short stories to anthologies, including Ellery Queen Magazine, Winter's Crimes and CWA Anthology. *Honours:* Le Prix du Roman d'Aventures, 1983; Special Sherlock Award, 2000. *Address:* 177 Verulam Road, St Albans, Hertfordshire AL3 4DW, England (home). *E-mail:* junethomson1@aol.com (home).

THOMSON, Robert James; Australian journalist and newspaper editor; *Managing Editor, Wall Street Journal;* b. 11 March 1961, Torrumbarry; m. Ping Wang; two s. *Career:* financial and gen. affairs reporter, then Sydney Corresp. The Herald, Melbourne 1979–83; sr feature writer Sydney Morning Herald 1983–85; corresp. for the Financial Times, Beijing 1985–89, Tokyo 1989–94, Foreign News Ed., London 1994–96, Asst Ed. Financial Times and Ed. Weekend FT 1996–98, US Man. Ed. Financial Times 1998–2002; Ed. The Times (UK) 2002–07; Publisher, Wall Street Journal 2007–08, Managing Ed. 2008–; Ed.-in-Chief, Dow Jones 2008–; mem. Knight-Bagehot Fellowship Bd, Columbia Univ.; Dir and Chair. Arts International 2000–02. *Television:* regular appearances on ABC News, CNN, Fox News Channel. *Publications:* The Judges – A Portrait of the Australian Judiciary, The Chinese Army, True Fiction (ed.). *Honours:* Business Journalist of the Year, The Journalist and Financial Reporting Group (TJFR) 2001. *Address:* The Wall Street Journal, 200 Liberty Street, New York, NY 10281, USA (office). *Telephone:* (212) 416-2000 (office). *Website:* www.wsj.com (office).

THONGCHI, Yeshe Dorjee, BA, MA; Indian writer and civil servant; b. 1951, Jigaon, West Kameng Dist, Arunachal Pradesh. *Education:* Cotton Coll. Guwahati, Guwahati Univ. *Career:* Assamese writer; civil servant, Govt of Arunachal Pradesh. *Publications include:* Kameng Himantar, Sonam, Lingjhik, Papor Pukhuri (Kalaguru Bishnu Rava Prasad Award), Mouna Ounth Mukhar Hriday (Bhasha Bharati Puraskar Award 2005), Sav-Kata Manush, Boh Bhulor, Biskanyar Dehat, Mising. *Honours:* Sahitya Akademi Award 2005, Pulchand Khandewel Integrity Award.

THORNE, Ian (see May, Julian)

THORNE, Matt, MA, MLitt; British writer; b. 1974, Bristol, England; s. of David Thorne and Kaye Thorne; m. Lesley Thorne; one s. *Education:* Sidney Sussex Coll., Cambridge and St Andrews Univ. *Career:* reviewer, Independent, Independent on Sunday, Sunday Telegraph. *Publications:* Tourist 1998, Eight Minutes Idle (Encore Award 1999) 1999, Dreaming of Strangers 2000, All Hail the New Puritans (ed., anthology) 2000, Pictures of You 2001, Child Star 2003, Cherry 2004, Croatian Nights 2005; juvenile: Greengrove Castle 2004, Clearheart Castle 2005, The White Castle 2005. *Address:* 56A Windus Road, Stoke Newington, London, N16 6UP (home); c/o Weidenfeld & Nicholson, Orion House, 5 Upper St Martin's Lane, London, WC2H 9EA, England (office). *Telephone:* (20) 8442-4255 (home). *E-mail:* mdjthorne@aol.com (home).

THORNHILL, Arthur Horace, Jr, BA; American book publisher (retd); b. 1 Jan. 1924, Boston, Mass.; s. of Arthur Horace Thornhill and Mary J. Peterson; m. Dorothy M. Matheis 1944; one s. one d. *Education:* Englewood School for Boys and Princeton Univ. *Career:* joined Little, Brown & Co. 1948, Vice-Pres. 1955–58, Exec. Vice Pres. 1958–62, Pres. and CEO 1962–86, Chair. of Bd 1970–87; Pres. Little, Brown & Co. (Canada) 1955–84; Vice-Pres. Time Inc. 1968–87; Dir Bantam Books Inc. 1965–67, Conrac Corpn 1972–87; Treas. and Trustee, Princeton Univ. Press 1971–86; Dir Asscn of American Publrs. 1978–81; Trustee, Bennington Coll. 1969–76; Fellow Emer., Center for Creative Photography, Univ. of Ariz. *Honours:* Air Medal, USAF, Princeton Univ. Press Medal, Distinguished Alumnus Award, Dwight-Englewood School 1998. *Address:* 250 Pantops Mountain Road, Apartment 5303, Charlottesville, VA 22911-8703, USA (home).

THORNTON, Margaret (see Poole, Margaret Barbara)

THORPE, Adam, BA; British/French poet, novelist and dramatist; b. (Adam Naylor Thorpe), 5 Dec. 1956, Paris; s. of Benjamin Naylor Thorpe and Sheila Grace Thorpe; m. Joanna Wistreich; three c. *Education:* Magdalen Coll., Oxford. *Career:* founder Equinox Travelling Theatre; fmr teacher of mime, drama and English literature, London; resides in France. *Plays:* for BBC Radio: The Fen Story 1991, Offa's Daughter 1993, An Envied Place 2002; Himmler's Boy 2004, Devastated Areas 2006; for stage: Couch Grass and Ribbon 1996. *Publications:* poetry: Mornings in the Baltic 1988, Meeting Montaigne 1990, From the Neanderthal 1999, Nine Lessons from the Dark 2003, Birds with a Broken Wing 2007; novels: Ulverton (Winifred Holtby Memorial Prize) 1992, Still 1995, Pieces of Light 1998, Nineteen Twenty-One 2001, No Telling 2003, The Rules of Perspective 2005, Between Each Breath 2007, The Standing Pool 2008, Hodd 2009; short stories: Shifts 2000, Is This the Way You Said? 2006. *Honours:* Time Out Mime Street Entertainer of the Year 1984, Eric Gregory Award 1985, Winifred Holtby Memorial Prize 1992. *Literary Agent:* c/o Lucy Luck Associates, 20 Cowper Road, London, W3 6PZ, England. *Telephone:* (20) 7373-8672. *E-mail:* lucy@lucyluck.com. *Website:* www.lucyluck.com.

THORPE, David Richard, BA, MA; British political biographer; b. 12 March 1943, Huddersfield, England; s. of Cyril Thorpe and Mary Thorpe (née Avison). *Education:* Selwyn Coll., Cambridge. *Career:* Archive Fellow, Churchill Coll., Cambridge 1986; apptd official biographer of Lord Home of the Hirsel 1990; new authorized biographer of Sir Anthony Eden 1996; Alistair Horne Fellow, St Antony's Coll., Oxford 1997–98; Sr mem. Brasenose Coll., Oxford 1998–; mem. Johnson Club, Oxford and Cambridge Club. *Publications:* The Uncrowned Prime Ministers: A Study of Sir Austen Chamberlain, Lord Curzon and Lord Butler 1980, Selwyn Lloyd 1989, Alec Douglas-Home 1996, Eden: The Life and Times of Anthony Eden First Earl of Avon, 1897–1977 2003, Supermac: The Life of Harold Macmillan (Marsh Biography Award, Biennial English Speaking Union 2011) 2010; contrib. to The Blackwell Biographical Dictionary of British Political Life in the 20th Century 1990, Telling Lives: From W. B. Yeats to Bruce Chatwin 2000, The Oxford Dictionary of National Biography 2004 and online edn 2009–11, From New Jerusalem to New Labour: British Prime Ministers from Attlee to Blair 2010. *Address:* Brasenose College, Oxford, OX1 4AJ, England (office).

THORPE, Marie Louise, BA, HDLS; South African writer and teacher; *Teacher in special education, Westridge High School;* b. 1 Oct. 1949, East London, South Africa; m. James Thorpe. *Education:* Univ. of Natal. *Career:* demonstrator, then lecturer 1973–74, librarian 1975, teacher for the handicapped 1980–82; Principal School for Street Children 1995–2001; tutor at writing school; teacher in special educ., Westridge High School 2005–. *Publications:* Write from the Beginning 1987, From Gladiators to Clowns 1988, Aesop's Fables Retold 1988, Lucy's Games 1992, Limbo Land 1996, also reading series The Wordwise Project (organized by Human Sciences Research Council). *Honours:* Merit Awards for Best Student in Philosophy 1970, 1971, 1972, Notcut Prize for Best Student in Philosophy 1973, Emma Smith Queens Scholarship 1974, Sonlan Award for Youth Literature 1992, SA Writers' Circle Quill Award 1993. *Address:* 201 Premier Court, 200 Umbilo Road, Durban, South Africa (home). *Telephone:* 2024875 (home).

THORUP, Kirsten; Danish writer; b. (Kirsten Christensen), 9 Feb. 1942, Gelsted, Funen; d. of Svend Christensen and Jenny Christensen; one d. *Career:* mem. State Foundation for the Arts (literary cttee 1993–), Danish PEN (bd mem. 1995–). *Publications include:* Indenfor - udenfor 1967, I dagens anledning 1968, Love from Trieste (in trans.) 1969, Idag er det Daisy 1971, Baby (in trans.) 1973, Lille Jonna 1977, Den lange sommer 1979, Himmel og helvede 1982, Romantica: Skuespil 1983, Den yderste grænse 1987, Elskede ukendte 1994, Projekt paradis: En trilogi 1997, Digte 1967–71 2000, Bonsai 2000, Ingenmandsland 2003, Førkrigstid 2006. *Honours:* Lifetime Grant from Danish Art Foundation, Kt of the Dannebrog; Critics' Prize 1982, Danish Booksellers' Golden Laurels Award 1983, Danish Acad. Major Prize for Literature 2000, BG Prize 2004. *Address:* c/o Gyldendal, Klareboderne 3, 1001 Copenhagen, Denmark. *E-mail:* thorup.kirsten@gmail.com (office). *Website:* www.gyldendal.dk (office).

THUBRON, Colin Gerald Dryden, CBE, FRSL; British writer; *President, Royal Society of Literature;* b. 14 June 1939, London; s. of Brig. Gerald Ernest Thubron and Evelyn Kate Dryden; m. Margreta de Grazia 2011. *Education:* Eton Coll. *Career:* mem. editorial staff, Hutchinson & Co. Publishers Ltd 1959–62; freelance documentary film maker 1963–64; Production Ed., The Macmillan Co., USA 1964–65; freelance author 1965–; Vice-Pres., Royal Soc. of Literature 2003–10, Pres. 2010–; Fellow, Royal Asiatic Soc. 1991. *Scenario:* The Prince of the Pagodas (ballet at The Royal Opera House, Covent Garden). *Publications:* Mirror to Damascus, The Hills of Adonis, Jerusalem, Journey into Cyprus, Among the Russians, Behind the Wall, The Lost Heart of Asia, In Siberia, Shadow of the Silk Road 2006, To a Mountain in Tibet 2011; novels: The God in the Mountain, Emperor, A Cruel Madness, Falling, Turning Back the Sun, Distance, To the Last City. *Honours:* Hon. DLitt (Warwick) 2002; Silver Pen Award of PEN 1985, Thomas Cook Award 1988, Hawthornden Prize 1988, Mungo Park Medal, Royal Scottish Geographical Soc. 2000, Lawrence of Arabia Medal, Royal Soc. of Asian Affairs 2001, Soc. of Authors Travel Award 2008, Prix Bouvier 2010, Ness Award, Royal Geographical Soc. 2011. *Address:* 28 Upper Addison Gardens, London, W14 8AJ, England (home). *Telephone:* (20) 7602-2522 (home). *E-mail:* Thubron@hotmail.com (home).

THURLEY, Simon John, CBE, MA, PhD, FSA, FRHistS; British foundation executive and museum administrator; *Chief Executive, English Heritage;* b. 29 Aug. 1962, Huntingdon, Cambs., England; s. of the late Thomas Manley Thurley and Rachel Thurley (née House); m. 2nd Anna Keay 2008; one s. one d. *Education:* Kimbolton School, Cambs., Bedford Coll. and Courtauld Inst. of Art, London. *Career:* Insp. of Ancient Monuments, Crown Buildings and Monuments Group, English Heritage 1988–90; Curator Historic Royal

Palaces 1990–97; Dir Museum of London 1997–2002; CEO English Heritage 2002–; Chair. Cttee Soc. for Court Studies 1996–; Pres. City of London Archaeological Soc. 1997–2002, Huntingdonshire Local History Soc.; Visiting Prof. of Medieval History and Hon. Fellow, Royal Holloway Coll., Univ. of London; Visiting Prof. of Built Environment, Gresham Coll.; mem. Council St Paul's Cathedral. *Television:* Lost Buildings of Britain (Channel 4) 2004, The Buildings that Made Britain (Channel 5) 2006. *Publications:* Henry VIII: Images of a Tudor King (co-author) 1989, The Royal Palaces of Tudor England 1993, Whitehall Palace 2000, Lost Buildings of Britain 2004, Hampton Court 2004, Somerset House 2009; frequent contribs to historical pubs. *Honours:* Hon. mem. Royal Inst. of Chartered Surveyors; Hon. RIBA . *Address:* English Heritage, 1 Waterhouse Square, 138–142 Holborn, London, EC1N 2ST, England (office). *Telephone:* (20) 7973-3000 (office). *E-mail:* chief.executive@english-heritage.org.uk (office). *Website:* www.english-heritage.org.uk (office); www.simonthurley.com.

THWAITE, Ann, MA, DLitt, FRSL; British writer; b. 4 Oct. 1932, London; d. of Angus Harrop and Hilda Harrop (née Valentine); m. Anthony Thwaite 1955; four d. *Education:* Univ. of Oxford. *Career:* Visiting Prof., Tokyo Women's Univ.; occasional named lectures at Univ. of Southern Mississippi, Toronto Public Library, Skidmore Coll.; Contributing Ed., Editorial Bd, Cricket Magazine (USA); mem. Soc. of Authors, PEN. *Publications:* Waiting for the Party: A Life of Frances Hodgson Burnett 1974, re-issued as Frances Hodgson Burnett: Beyond the Secret Garden 2007, Edmund Gosse: A Literary Landscape 1984, A.A. Milne: His Life 1990, Emily Tennyson: The Poet's Wife 1996, Glimpses of the Wonderful: The Life of Philip Henry Gosse 2002, Passageways: the story of a New Zealand family 2009. *Honours:* Hon. Fellow, Univ. of Surrey 2001; Hon. DLitt (East Anglia) 2007; Leverhulme, Churchill and Gladys Krieble Delmas (British Library) Fellowships; Duff Cooper Prize 1985, Whitbread Biography Award 1990. *Address:* The Mill House, Low Tharston, Norwich, Norfolk, NR15 2YN, England (home). *Telephone:* (1508) 489569 (home). *Fax:* (1508) 489221 (home).

THWAITE, Anthony Simon, OBE, MA, DLitt, FRSL, FSA; British writer and poet; b. 23 June 1930, Chester, Cheshire; s. of Hartley Thwaite and Alice Thwaite (née Mallinson); m. Ann Barbara Thwaite (née Harrop) 1955; four d. *Education:* Kingswood School, Bath, Christ Church, Oxford. *Career:* Visiting Lecturer in English Literature, Univ. of Tokyo 1955–57; radio producer, BBC 1957–62; Literary Ed., The Listener 1962–65; Asst Prof. of English, Univ. of Libya, Benghazi 1965–67; Literary Ed., New Statesman 1968–72; Co-Ed., Encounter 1973–85; Editorial Dir, Editorial Consultant, André Deutsch 1986–95. *Publications:* poetry: Home Truths 1957, The Owl in the Tree 1963, The Stones of Emptiness 1967, Inscriptions 1973, New Confessions 1974, A Portion for Foxes 1977, Victorian Voices 1980, Poems 1953–1983 1984, revised edn as Poems 1953–1988 1989, Letter from Tokyo 1987, The Dust of the World 1994, Selected Poems 1956–1996 1997, A Different Country: New Poems 2000, A Move in the Weather 2003, The Ruins of Time (ed.) 2006, Collected Poems 2007, Late Poems 2010; other: Contemporary English Poetry 1959, The Penguin Book of Japanese Verse (co-ed. with Geoffrey Bownas) 1964, Japan (with Roloff Beny) 1968, The Deserts of Hesperides 1969, Poetry Today 1973, The English Poets (co-ed. with Peter Porter) 1974, In Italy (with Roloff Beny and Peter Porter) 1974, New Poetry 4 (co-ed. with Fleur Adcock) 1978, Twentieth Century English Poetry 1978, Odyssey: Mirror of the Mediterranean (with Roloff Beny) 1981, Larkin at Sixty (ed.) 1982, Poetry 1945 to 1980 (co-ed. with John Mole) 1983, Six Centuries of Verse 1984, Philip Larkin: Collected Poems (ed.) 1988, Selected Letters of Philip Larkin (ed.) 1992, Philip Larkin: Further Requirements (ed.) 2001, Poet to Poet: John Skelton 2008, Philip Larkin: Letters to Monica (ed.) 2010. *Honours:* Hon. Lay Canon, Norwich Cathedral 2005; Hon. DLitt (Hull) 1989, (East Anglia) 2007; Richard Hillary Memorial Prize 1968, Cholmondeley Award 1983. *Address:* The Mill House, Low Tharston, Norwich, Norfolk, NR15 2YN, England (home). *Telephone:* (1508) 489569 (home). *Fax:* (1508) 489221 (home).

THWAITES, (Stephen) Dane, BA; Australian poet, publisher and bookseller; b. 15 June 1950, Inverell, NSW; m.; one s. *Education:* University of Nebraska, Armidale. *Publications:* Winter Light 1983, South China 1994; contrib. to various publications. *Honours:* co-winner, Mattara Prize 1987. *Address:* c/o Hobo Poetry Magazine, PO Box 166, Hazelbrook, NSW 2779, Australia.

TIBBER, Robert (see Friedman, (Eve) Rosemary)

TIBBER, Rosemary (see Friedman, (Eve) Rosemary)

TIE, Ning; Chinese writer; *President, Chinese Writers Association*; b. 1957, Beijing; d. of Tie Yang and Xu Zhi-ying. *Career:* Council mem. Chinese Writers' Assen 1985–, Vice-Pres. 2001–06, Pres. (first woman) 2006–; Alt. mem. 16th CCP Cen. Cttee 2002–07. *Publications:* Path in the Night 1980, Xiangxue (Nat. Short Story Prize) 1982, Red Shirt With No Buttons (Nat. Fiction Prize) 1984, Rose Gate 1988, Cotton Stack 1988, Hay Stack (short stories) 1991, Women's White Night (non-fiction) 1991, Straw Ring (non-fiction) 1992, For Ever and Ever 1999, The Great Bather 2000. *Address:* 40-2-201 Luo Si-zhuang, Baoding City, Hebei Province, People's Republic of China (office). *Telephone:* (312) 34341 (office). *Website:* www.chinawriter.com.cn (office).

TIELSCH, Ilse, DPhil; Austrian (b. Czechoslovakian) writer; b. 20 March 1929, Czechoslovakia; d. of Fritz Felzmann and Marianne Felzmann (née Zamanek); m. Herr Tielsch 1950; two s. two d. *Education:* Univ. of Vienna. *Career:* resident in Austria 1945–; studied journalism before becoming a writer of poetry and prose; Vice-Pres. Austrian PEN-Club. *Publications include:* novels and stories: Ein Elefant in unserer Straße, Erinnerung mit Bäumen, Die Ahnenpyramide (trilogy) 1980, 1982, 1988, Heimatsuchen, Fremder Strand, Die Früchte der Tränen, Der Solitär; poetry: In meinem Orangengarten, Anrufung des Mondes, Regenzeit, Nicht beweisbar, Zwischenbericht, Lob der Freundheit. *Honours:* Austrian Medal of Honour for Science and Art, Andreas Gryphius-Preis 1989, Anton Wildgans-Preis 1990, Goldenes Ehrenzeichen für Verdienste um das Land Wien 1999 and other awards. *Address:* St-Michael-Gasse 68, 1210 Vienna, Austria (home). *E-mail:* tielschilse@utanet.at.

TIFFANY, Carrie, MA; Australian writer; b. 1965, Yorkshire, England. *Education:* RMIT Univ., Melbourne and Latrobe Univ. *Career:* park ranger, Uluru, Kata Tjuta Nat. Park aged 19; writer, Dept of Natural Resources; freelance agricultural journalist 1996–. *Publications include:* Dr Darnell's Cure (short story) (Australian Book Review Short Fiction Award) 2002, Everyman's Rules for Scientific Living (novel) (Victorian Premier's Prize for an unpublished manuscript by an emerging Victorian writer 2003) 2005; contrib. short stories to Australian journals, including Overland, Ulittara, New Australian Writing (Beijing Univ., China), and to Penguin Summer Stories 2002. *Honours:* The Age short story award, University of Canberra short story award, Judah Waten short story award, HQ Flamingo short story award, Victorian Ministry of the Arts New Work Arts Development Grant 2000, Australia Council Literature Board Grant for an Emerging Writer 2001, Varuna Writers' Centre NSW Emerging Writers' Fellowship 2002. *Address:* c/o Publicity Department, Pan Macmillan Australia, Level 25, 1 Market Street, Sydney, NSW 2000, Australia (office). *E-mail:* panpublicity@macmillan.com.au (office). *Website:* www.panmacmillan.com.au (office).

TIGHE, Carl, BA, MA, PDESL, PhD; British writer and dramatist; *Professor of Creative Writing, University of Derby*; b. 26 April 1950, Birmingham. *Education:* Univ. Coll., Swansea, Univ. of Leeds, Univ. of Manchester. *Career:* Prof. of Creatvie Writing, Univ. of Derb 1998–; mem. PEN, Welsh Acad., Writers Guild of Great Britain. *Publications:* Little Jack Horner 1985, Baku! 1986, Gdańsk: National Identity in the Polish-German Borderlands 1990, Rejoice! and Other Stories 1992, The Politics of Literature 1999, Pax: Variations 2000, Burning Worm 2001, KssssS 2004, Writing and Responsibility 2005; contrib. to anthologies, journals and radio broadcasts. *Honours:* Welsh Arts Council Literary Bursary 1983, All London Drama Prize 1987, British Council Travel Scholarship, Hungary 1990, City Life Writer of the Year 2000 Award, Authors' Club First Novel Award 2001. *Literary Agent:* c/o Simon Trewin, PFD Agency, Drury House, 34–43 Russell Street, London WC2B 5HA, England. *Telephone:* (20) 7344-1000. *E-mail:* postmaster@pfd.co.uk.

TIKHVINSKY, Sergej Leonidovich; Russian historian and academic; *President, National Committee of Russian Historians;* b. 1 Sept. 1918, Petrograd; s. of Leonid Tikhvinsky and Kira Tikhvinsky; m. Vera Nikitichna Tikhvinskaya 1940; one s. one d. *Education:* Oriental Inst., Moscow. *Career:* mem. CPSU 1941–91; diplomatic service in China, UK and Japan 1939–57; Head of Asian Dept of USSR State Cttee with Council of Ministers for Foreign Cultural Relations 1957–60; Prof., Moscow Univ. 1959; Dir USSR Acad. of Sciences Inst. of Sinology 1960–61; Deputy Dir of Acad. of Sciences Inst. of the Peoples of Asia 1961–63; Deputy Dir of Acad. of Sciences Inst. of World Socialist Economies 1963–65; Corresp. mem. of Acad. of Sciences 1968–81, mem. 1981–; Chief of History of Diplomacy Dept, Head of Asia Section in Foreign Policy Planning Dept USSR Ministry of Foreign Affairs 1965–80; Rector of Diplomatic Acad. of USSR Ministry of Foreign Affairs 1980–86; Academician-Sec. of Historical Section of USSR Acad. of Sciences 1982–88; Pres. Nat. Cttee of Soviet (now Russian) Historians 1980–; Chair. Scientific Council for The History of Russia's Foreign Policy and Int. Relations 1987–; Adviser to the Presidium of Acad. of Sciences 1988–. *Publications include:* The Reform Movement in China and K'ang Youwei 1959, Sun Yatsen Foreign Affairs Theories and Practice 1964, Manchu Rule in China 1966, History of China and Present Time 1976, The Reform Movements in China at the end of the 19th Century 1980, China and her Neighbours 1980, China and World History 1988, China: History through Personalities and Events 1991, China in My Life 1992, China's Road to Unity and Independence 1996, Eternal Sleep in China's Earth: Memorial Album 1996, Russia–Japan, Doomed to Good Neighbourhood 1996, My Return to Tiananmen Square 2002, The Age of Rapid Changes 2005, Selected Works (five vols) 2006; numerous articles on Soviet and Russian foreign policy and int. affairs. *Honours:* Hon. Chair. All-Russia Asscn of Sinologues 1988; Hon. mem. Accad. Fiorentina delle Arti 1984. *Address:* National Committee of Historians, Leninsky prosp. 32A, 117334 Moscow, Russia (office). *Telephone:* (495) 938-00-87 (office); (495) 124-07-24 (office); (495) 915-45-20 (home).

TILLER, Carl Frode, MA; Norwegian writer; b. 4 Jan. 1970, Namsos; s. of Jan Tiller and Skjoldvor Tiller; m. Marita Beate Rendal Ugseth, three d. *Career:* educated as a historian; writer of novels and plays. *Plays include:* Skråninga (Det Norske Teatret 2004), Folkehelsa (Trøndelag Teater) 2007, Portrett av en varulv (Det norske Teatret) 2011. *Publications:* novels: Skråninga (Tarjei Vesaas First Book Prize) 2001, Bipersonar (Bjørnson-stipendet 2004) 2003, Innsirkling (Brage Prize, Norwegian Critics Prize, Hunger Prize 2008, EU Prize for Literature 2009) 2007, Innsirkling 2 2010 (P2-lytternes romanpris, Liv Ullmann Prize); contrib. of short stories and prose to anthologies, magazines and newspapers. *Literary Agent:* c/o Aschehoug

Agency, Sehesteds gate 3, PO Box 363, Sentrum, 0102 Oslo, Norway. *Telephone:* 22-40-04-00. *E-mail:* christian.kjelstrup@aschehoug.com. *Telephone:* 47-87-41-82 (office). *E-mail:* carlfrodetiller@gmail.com (home). *Website:* www.cftiller.no.

TILLINGHAST, Richard Williford, BA, MA, PhD; American academic, poet and writer; b. 25 Nov. 1940, Memphis, Tenn.; m. 1st Nancy Walton Pringle 1965 (divorced 1970); m. 2nd Mary Graves 1973; one s. one d. *Education:* Univ. of the South, Harvard Univ. *Career:* Asst Prof. of English, Univ. of California, Berkeley 1968–73; Visiting Asst Prof., Univ. of the South 1979–80; Briggs-Copeland Lecturer, Harvard Univ. 1980–83; Assoc. Prof., Univ. of Michigan 1983–92, Prof. of English 1992–2005; Assoc., Michigan Inst. for the Humanities 1989–90, 1993–94; Bread Loaf Fellowship 1982, Millay Colony Residency 1985, Yaddo Writers' Retreat Residency 1986, Amy Lowell Travel Fellowship 1990–91, British Council Fellowship 1992. *Publications:* poetry: Sleep Watch 1969, The Knife and Other Poems 1980, Sewanee in Ruins 1981, Fossils, Metal, and the Blue Limit 1982, Our Flag Was Still There 1984, The Stonecutter's Hand 1994, Today in the Café Trieste 1997, Six Mile Mountain 2000, Dirty August 2009; Selected Poems 2009; other: A Quiet Pint in Kinvara 1991, Robert Lowell's Life and Work: Damaged Grandeur 1995, A Visit to the Gallery: The University of Michigan Museum of Art (ed.) 1997; contribs to newspapers, reviews, journals and magazines. *Honours:* National Endowment for the Humanities Grant 1980, Ann Stanford Prize for Poetry, University of Southern California 1992. *E-mail:* richardtillinghurst@eircom.net (home). *Website:* www-personal.umich.edu/~rwtill.

TILLMAN, Lynne, BA; American writer, film-maker and academic; *Professor and Writer in Residence, Department of English, The University at Albany*; b. New York; m. David Hofstra. *Education:* Hunter Coll. *Career:* writer of novels, stories and essays; Co-Head Writing Dept, MFA Program, Bard Coll. 1993–2003; Visiting Assoc. Prof. in Creative Writing, Brown Univ. 1998, Yale Graduate Arts Dept 1998, 2006, Columbia Univ. 1999; Lecturer in Creative Writing, Princeton Univ. 1999–2001; Assoc. Prof. and Writer in Residence, The Univ. at Albany 2002–; Co-Ed. Paranoids Anonymous Newsletter 1976–79; Contributing Ed. Bomb, Nest, New Observations; editorial advisor, Voice Literary Supplement Bd 1988–90; mem. Int. Advisory Bd Wexner Prize 1996–, Advisory Bd Fence magazine 2001–04, Fiction Ed. 2004–; mem. Bd Housing Works 2006–, PEN America 2008–. *Films:* Committed (co-dir, writer) 1984. *Publications include:* Living With Contradictions (with drawings by Jane Dickson) 1982, Weird Fucks 1982, Madame Realism (with drawings by Kiki Smith) 1984, Tagebuch einer Masochistin 1986, Haunted Houses 1987, Absence Makes The Heart 1990, Motion Sickness 1991, The Madame Realism Complex 1992, Cast in Doubt 1992, No Lease on Life 1998, Love Sentence 1999, This Is Not It 2002, American Genius: A Comedy 2006; non-fiction: Beyond Recognition: Representation, Power, Culture (co-ed. with Craig Owens) 1992, The Velvet Years: Warhol and the Factory 1965–1967 (photographs by Stephen Shore) 1995, The Broad Picture (essays) 1997, Bookstore: The Life and Times of Jeannette Watson and Books & Co. 1999; short stories and essays in anthologies, art catalogues, books and magazines. *Honours:* Jerome Foundation Grant 1988, New York Foundation for the Arts Grant 1989, New York State Council on the Arts Grant 1989, MacDowell Fellow 1991, 1995–96, 1997, 1999, 2000, 2001, Guggenheim Fellowship 2006. *Literary Agent:* c/o Joy Harris Literary Agency, 161 Fifth Avenue, Suite 617, New York, NY 10011, USA. *Telephone:* (212) 924-6269. *Address:* Peter Stuyvesant Station, POB 360, New York, NY 10009-0360, USA (home). *Telephone:* (212) 979-1739 (home). *E-mail:* tillwhen@aol.com (home).

TIMM, Uwe, DPhil; German writer; b. 1940, Hamburg. *Education:* Univ. of Munich, Univ. of Paris. *Publications include:* novels: Heisser Sommer 1974, Der Schlangenbaum 1980, Deutsche Kolonien 1981, Der Mann auf dem Hochrad 1984, The Train Mouse 1986, The Snake Tree 1988, Vogel, friss die Feige nicht 1989, Headhunter 1991, Kerbls Flucht 1991, The Invention of Curried Sausage 1993, Midsummer Night 1995, Johannisnacht 1996, Die Bubi Scholz story 1998, Nicht morgen, nicht gestern 1999, Eine Hand voll Gras 2000, Rot (trans. as Red) 2001, Morenga 2003, In My Brother's Shadow 2005, Der Freund und des Freunde 2005, Halbschatten 2008. *Honours:* Munich Literature Prize 1989, 2002, Grosser Literaturpreis der Bayerischen Akademie der Schönen Künste 2001, Jakob Wassermann Prize for Literature 2006. *Address:* c/o Deutscher Taschenbuch Verlag, Freidrichstrasse 1a, 80801 Munich, Germany (office). *E-mail:* verlag@dtv.de (office). *Website:* www.dtv.de (office); www.uwe-timm.com.

TINDALL, Gillian, MA, FRSL; British writer; b. 4 May 1938, London; d. of D.H. Tindall and U.M.D. Orange; m. Richard G. Lansdown 1963; one s. *Education:* Univ. of Oxford. *Career:* novelist, biographer, historian, freelance journalist, has worked on The Independent, The Times and other newspapers and periodicals and for BBC; JP, Inner London 1980–98; mem. Franco-British Council 1999–2005. *Publications:* novels: No Name in the Street 1959, The Water and the Sound 1961, The Edge of the Paper 1963, The Youngest 1967, Someone Else 1969, Fly Away Home (Somerset Maugham Award 1972) 1971, The Traveller and His Child 1975, The Intruder 1979, Looking Forward 1983, To The City 1987, Give Them All My Love 1989, Spirit Weddings 1992; short stories: Dances of Death 1973, The China Egg and Other Stories 1981, Journey of a Lifetime and Other Stories 1990; non-fiction: A Handbook on Witchcraft 1965, The Born Exile (biog. of George Gissing) 1974, The Fields Beneath 1977, City of Gold: The Biography of Bombay 1982, Rosamond Lehmann: An Appreciation 1985, Countries of the Mind: The Meaning of Places to Writers 1990, Célestine: Voices from a French Village (Franco-British Soc. Award 1995) 1995, The Journey of Martin Nadaud 1999, The Man Who Drew London (biog. of Wenceslaus Hollar) 2002, The House by the Thames and the People Who Lived There 2006, Footprints in Paris 2009. *Honours:* Chevalier des Arts et des Lettres 2001; Somerset Maugham Award 1972, Enid McLeod Prize 1985, Franco-British Soc. Award 1995. *Literary Agent:* c/o Gordon Wise, Curtis Brown Ltd, Haymarket House, 28–29 Haymarket, London, SW1Y 4SP, England. *Telephone:* (20) 7393-4400. *Fax:* (20) 7393-4401. *E-mail:* info@curtisbrown.co.uk. *Website:* www.curtisbrown.co.uk.

TIPTON, David John; British poet, writer, editor, translator and teacher; b. 28 April 1934, Birmingham; m. 1st Ena Hollis 1956; m. 2nd Glenys Tipton 1975; two s. three d. *Education:* Saltley Coll., Univ. of Essex. *Career:* Ed. Rivelin Press 1974–84, Redbeck Press 1984–. *Publications:* Peru: The New Poetry (trans.) 1970–76, Millstone Grit 1972, At Night the Cats, by Antonio Cisneros (trans.) 1985, Nomads and Settlers 1980, Wars of the Roses 1984, Crossing the Rimac 1995, Family Chronicle (poems) 1997, Path Through the Canefields (trans. of José Watanabe) 1997, Amulet Against the Evil Eye 1998, Paradise of Exiles (fiction) 1999, A Mountain Crowned by a Cemetery, by Tulio Mora (trans.) 2001, Nordic Barbarians (fiction) 2002, Medal for Malaya (fiction) 2002, A Sword in the Air (travel) 2003, Defying the Odds (poems) 2006, Blue Rondo (fiction) 2006, An Adventure in Existentialism (fiction) 2007, Passion and Prudence (fiction) 2008; contrib. to various publs. *Address:* 24 Aireville Road, Frizinghall, Bradford, BD9 4HH, England (home). *Telephone:* (1274) 498135 (home).

TIWANA, Dalip Kaur, PhD; Indian academic and writer; *Life Fellow, Punjabi University, Patiala*; b. 4 May 1935, Vill-Rabbon, Punjab; d. of Kaka Singh and Chand Kaur Tiwana; m. Bhupinder Singh 1972; one s. *Education:* Mohindra Coll. (Patiala), Punjab Univ. *Career:* mem. Senate, Syndicate, Acad. Council and Bd of Studies in Punjabi, Punjabi Univ., Patiala, Head of Dept of Foreign Languages, Head Nawab Sher Mohammad Khan Inst. of Advanced Studies in Urdu, Persian, Arabic and Malerkotla, fmrly Dean Faculty of Languages, Prof. and Head Dept of Punjabi 1981–, currently Life Fellow; works translated into many languages, several adapted for TV; Pres. Punjab Sahit Acad. Chandigarh, mem. Punjab Arts Council (Chandigarh), Punjabi Bd Sahitya Acad. (New Delhi), Language Advisory Cttee (Bhartiya Jnanpith), Language Advisory Cttee, K.K. Birla Foundation Samman; mem. Advisory Bd North Zone Cultural Centre; fmr mem. Advisory Bd Doordarshan; Vice-Pres. Kendri Lekhak Sabha; presided over Int. Punjabi Conference, London 1980; participant Int. Writing Together, Scotland 1990, Women 20th Century Conference, Glasgow 1990; UGC Nat. Lectureship. *Publications include:* Sadhana (Govt of Punjab Award for Short Stories 1960–61) 1961, Ehu Hamar Jeevna (Sahitya Acad. Award) 1972, Panchaan Vich Parmesar (Ministry of Educ. and Social Welfare Award for Children's Short Stories) 1975, Peele Patian Di Dastan (Nanak Singh Award, Govt of Punjab) 1980, Nange Pairan Da Safar (Gurmukh Singh Musafir Award for Autobiography, Govt of Punjab) 1982, Katha Kuknus Di (Nanjanagudu Thirumalamba Award) 1994, Duni Suhava Bagh (Vagdevi Award 1998), Katha Kaho Urvashi (Sarswati Samman, KK Birla Foundation Award) 2001. *Honours:* Canadian Int. Asscn of Punjabi Authors and Artists Award 1985, Shiromani Sahitkai Award, Govt of Punjab 1987, Praman Patar Award 1989, Dhaliwal Award, Punjabi Acad. (Ludhiana) 1991, Best Novelist of the Decade 1980–90 1993, Mata Sahib Kaur Award 1999, Kartar Singh Dhaliwal Award 2000, Giani Lal Singh Award 2003, Padma Shri 2004, Doordarshan Panj Pani Award 2005. *Address:* Punjabi University Campus, B-13, Patiala 147 002, India (office). *Telephone:* (175) 2282239 (office); (175) 2281229 (home). *E-mail:* DKTiwana@yahoo.com (office).

TLILI, Mustapha; Tunisian/American writer, political philosopher, diplomatist and academic; *Director, Center for Dialogues: Islamic World–US –The West, New York University*; b. 17 Oct. 1947, Fériana, Tunisia; one d. *Education:* Sorbonne, Univ. of Paris, France. *Career:* numerous posts with UN, including Special Adviser to Pres. of 66th session of UN Gen. Ass., Dir France Information Centre, Paris, Chief Namibia, Anti-Apartheid, Palestine and Decolonization programmes and Dir Communications Policy, Dept of Public Information, UN HQ, New York; fmr Sr Fellow and Dir UN Project, New School World Policy Inst.; fmr Adjunct Prof. of Int. Affairs, Columbia Univ.; currently Sr Fellow, Remarque Inst. and Research Scholar, New York Univ., Founder and Dir Center for Dialogues, Islamic World–US –The West; adviser, Americans for Informed Democracy; mem. Human Rights Watch Middle East and North Africa Advisory Cttee; UNITAR Adley Stevenson Fellow. *Publications:* fiction: La Rage aux tripes 1975, Le Bruit dort 1978, Gloire des sables 1982, La Montagne du lion 1988, Un après-midi dans le désert 2008; non-fiction: For Nelson Mandela (co-ed. with Jacques Derrida) 1987; contrib. to Sorbonne Revue de Métaphysique et de Morale, Le Monde diplomatique, World Policy Journal, The Philadelphia Inquirer. *Honours:* Chevalier des Arts et des Lettres; Prix Comar d'or (Tunisia). *Address:* Center for Dialogues: Islamic World–US –The West, New York University, 194 Mercer Street, Fourth Floor, New York, NY 10012, USA (office). *Telephone:* (212) 998-8693 (office). *Fax:* (212) 995-4091 (office). *E-mail:* tlili@centerfordialogues.org (office). *Website:* www.centerfordialogues.org (office).

TOBIA, Maguid, BSc; Egyptian writer; b. 25 March 1938, Minia. *Career:* teacher of math. 1960–68; mem. Higher Council of Arts and Literature 1969–78; mem. staff Ministry of Culture 1978–; mem. Writers' Union, Chamber of Cinema Industry, Soc. of Egyptian Film Critics, Fiction Cttee of Supreme Council of Culture. *Film scripts include:* Story of Our Country 1967,

Sons of Silence 1974, Stars' Maker 1978, Harem Cage 1981. *Play:* International Laugh Bank 2001. *Television:* Friendly Visit (series) 1980. *Publications:* (collections of short stories): Vostock Reaches the Moon 1967, Five Unread Papers 1970, The Coming Days 1972, The Companion 1978, The Accident Which Happens 1987, 23 Short Stories 2001; (novels): Circles of Impossibility 1972, The They 1973, Sons of Silence 1974, The Strange Deeds of Kings and the Intrigues of Banks 1976, The Room of Floor Chances 1978, The Music Kiosk 1980, Hanan 1981, West Virgin 1986, The Emigration to the North Country of Hathoot's Tribe (3 vols: To the North Country 1987, To the South Country 1992, To the Lakes Country 2005), The Story of Beautiful Reem 1991, The Great History of Donkeys 1996, Amosis Case 2005; contribs to Al Ahram and several Arabic magazines. *Honours:* Medal of Science and Arts (First Class); several literary prizes. *Address:* 15 El-Lewaa Abd El Aziz Aly, Heliopolis 11361, Cairo, Egypt (home). *Telephone:* 2917801 (home). *Fax:* 2917801 (home).

TODD, Emmanuel, PhD; French historian, political scientist and writer; b. 16 May 1951, Saint-Germain-en-Laye; s. of Olivier Todd. *Education:* Institut de Études Politiques, Univ. of Cambridge. *Career:* research officer, Institut National d'Études Démographiques, Paris. *Publications:* La Chute final: essais sur la décomposition de la sphére soviétique 1976, Le Fou et le prolétaire 1979, L'Invention de la France (with Hervé Le Bras) 1981, La Troisième planète: structures familiales et système idéologiques 1983, L'Enfance du monde: structures familiales et développement 1984, La Nouvelle France 1988, L'Invention de l'Europe 1990, Le Destin des immigrés: assimilation et ségrégation dans les démocraties occidentales 1994, L'Illusion économique: essai sur la stagnation des sociétés développées 1998, La Diversité du monde: structures familiales et modernité 1999, Après l'empire: essai sur la décomposition du système américain 2002, Le Rendex-vous des civilisations 2007, Après la démocratie 2008. *Address:* Institut National d'Études Démographiques, 133 boulevard Davout, Paris 75980, France (office). *Telephone:* 1-56-06-20-33 (office). *Fax:* 1-56-06-21-99 (office). *E-mail:* todd@ined.fr (office). *Website:* www.ined.fr (office).

TODD, Janet Margaret, BA, PhD; British academic, college president, author and editor; *President, Lucy Cavendish College, Cambridge*; b. 10 Sept. 1942, Llandrindod-Wells, Wales; m. 1st Aaron R. Todd 1966 (divorced 1984); one s. one d.; m. 2nd D. W. Hughes 2001. *Education:* Newnham Coll., Cambridge, Univ. of Leeds, Univ. of Florida, USA. *Career:* Lecturer in African and English Literature, Mfantsipim and Univ. of Cape Coast, Ghana 1964–67; Asst Prof. of English, Univ. of Puerto Rico, Mayaguez 1972–74; Asst, Assoc. and full Prof. of English, Rutgers Univ. 1974–83; Visiting Prof., Jawaharlal Nehru Univ. and Univ. of Rajastan 1980, Univ. of Southampton 1982–83; Fellow in English, Sidney Sussex Coll., Cambridge 1983–90; Prof. of English, Univ. of East Anglia 1990–2000; Francis Hutcheson Prof. of English, Univ. of Glasgow 2000–06; The Grierson Chair in English Literature, Univ. of Aberdeen 2006–09; Pres. Lucy Cavendish Coll., Univ. of Cambridge 2009–; mem. Arts and Humanities Research Bd, English panel 1999–2003, British Soc. for Eighteenth-Century Studies (Pres.) 2000–02. *Radio:* Women and the Enlightenment: Mary Wollstonecraft (BBC Radio 3) 2009, Requiem for a Garden of Eden (BBC Radio 3) 2009. *Publications:* In Adam's Garden: A Study of John Clare's Pre-Asylum Poetry 1973, Mary Wollstonecraft: An Annotated Bibliography 1976, Women's Friendship in Literature 1980, English Congregational Hymns in the Eighteenth Century: Their Purpose and Design (co-author) 1983, Mary Wollstonecraft (with M. Ferguson) 1984, Sensibility: An Introduction 1986, Feminist Literary History 1988, The Sign of Angellica: Woman, Writing and Fiction 1660–1800 1989, Gender, Art and Death 1993, The Secret Life of Aphra Behn 1996, The Critical Fortunes of Aphra Behn 1998, Mary Wollstonecraft: A Revolutionary Life 2000, Rebel Daughters: Ireland in Conflict 1798 2003, Death and the Maidens: Fanny Wollstonecraft and the Shelley Circle 2007, Cambridge Introduction to Jane Austen 2008; editor: Dictionary of British and American Women Writers 1660–1800 1985, The Complete Works of Mary Wollstonecraft, seven vols 1989, A Dictionary of British Women Writers 1989, The Complete Works of Aphra Behn, seven vols 1992–96, Female Education in the Age of Enlightenment, six vols 1996, Aphra Behn Studies 1996, The Collected Letters of Mary Wollstonecraft 2003, The Cambridge Edition of the Works of Jane Austen 2006–09, Jane Austen in Context 2007; contribs to scholarly books and journals. *Honours:* Hon. Fellow, Lucy Cavendish Coll. 1999–; Nat. Endowment for the Humanities Grant 1977–79, American Council of Learned Socs Fellowship 1978–79, Guggenheim Fellowship 1981–82, Helen Bing Fellowship, Huntingdon Library 1991, Leverhulme Institutional Grant 1991–93, Folger Shakespeare Library Fellowship 1993–94, Bye-Fellowship, Newnham Coll., Cambridge 1998. *Address:* Lucy Cavendish College, Lady Margaret Road, Cambridge, CB2 0BU, England (office). *Telephone:* (1223) 332192 (office). *Fax:* (1223) 332178 (office). *E-mail:* jt272@cam.ac.uk (office). *Website:* www.lucy-cav.cam.ac.uk (office).

TODD, Olivier René Louis, LèsL, MA; French writer; b. 19 June 1929, Neuilly; s. of Julius Oblatt and Helen Todd; m. 1st Anne-Marie Nizan 1948; m. 2nd France Huser 1982; two s. two d. *Education:* Sorbonne, Corpus Christi Coll., Cambridge. *Career:* teacher, Lycée Int. du Shape 1956–62; Univ. Asst, St-Cloud 1962–64; reporter, Nouvel Observateur 1964–69; Ed. TV Programme Panorama 1969–70; Asst Ed. Nouvel Observateur 1970–77; columnist and Man. Ed. L'Express 1977–81; worked for BBC (Europa, 24 Hours) and ORTF 1964–69. *Publications:* Une demi-campagne 1957, La traversée de la Manche 1960, Des trous dans le jardin 1969, L'année du Crabe 1972, Les canards de Ca Mao 1975, La marelle de Giscard 1977, Portraits 1979, Un fils rebelle 1981, Un cannibale très convenable 1982, Une légère gueule de bois 1983, La balade du chômeur 1986, Cruel Avril 1987, La négociation 1989, La Sanglière 1992, Albert Camus, une vie 1996, André Malraux, une vie 2001, Catre d'identités, souvenirs 2005. *Honours:* Chevalier, Légion d'honneur, Commdr, Ordre des Arts et des Lettres; Hon. PhD (Stirling, Bristol), Hon. DLitt (Edinburgh) 2005; Prix Cazes 1981, Prix France Télévision 1997, Prix du Mémorial 1997. *Address:* 8 rue du Pin, 83310 La Garde Freinet, France (home). *Telephone:* 4-94-43-63-34 (home).

TOEWS, Miriam, BA; Canadian writer and journalist; b. 1964, Steinbach, Manitoba. *Education:* Univ. of Manitoba, Univ. of King's Coll., Halifax. *Film:* as actor: Luz silenciosa 2007. *Publications:* novels: Summer of My Amazing Luck 1996, A Boy of Good Breeding (McNally Robinson Book of the Year Award) 1998, A Complicated Kindness (Margaret Laurence Award for Fiction, McNally Robinson Book of the Year, Canadian Booksellers Asscn Fiction Book of the Year 2005, Gov. Gen.'s Award for Fiction 2005) 2004, The Flying Troutmans (Rogers Writers' Trust Fiction Prize) 2008, Travails with an Aunt 2009; other: Swing Low: A Life (memoir) 2000. *Honours:* John Hirsch Award for Most Promising Manitoba Writer 1996, Gold Medal for Humour, Nat. Magazine Award 1999. *Literary Agent:* A M Heath & Company Limited, 6 Warwick Court, Holborn, London, WC1R 5DJ, England. *Telephone:* (20) 7242-2811. *Fax:* (20) 7242-2711. *E-mail:* euan.thorneycroft@amheath.com. *Website:* www.amheath.com. *Address:* c/o Author Mail, Random House of Canada Ltd., 1 Toronto Street, Unit 300, Toronto, Ontario, M5C 2V6, Canada (office).

TOFFLER, Alvin, BA; American writer; b. 4 Oct. 1928, New York, NY; m. Adelaide Elizabeth (Heidi) Toffler (née Farrell) 1950; one d. *Education:* New York Univ. *Career:* Assoc. Ed., Fortune Magazine 1959–61; Visiting Scholar, Russell Sage Foundation 1969–70; f. (with wife) Toffler Associates (consultancy) 1996; Fellow, AAAS; mem. American Soc. of Journalists and Authors, Int. Inst. for Strategic Studies, World Future Studies Federation. *Publications:* The Schoolhouse in the City 1968, The Eco-Spasm Report 1975; with Heidi Toffler: The Culture Consumers 1964, Future Shock 1970, The Futurists (ed.) 1972, Learning for Tomorrow (ed.) 1973, The Third Wave 1980, Previews and Premises 1983, The Adaptive Corporation 1984, Power Shift 1990, War and Anti-War 1993, Creating a New Civilization 1994–95, Revolutionary Wealth 2006; contrib. to newspapers, journals and periodicals. *Honours:* Officier, Ordre des Arts et Lettres hon. doctorates; American Soc. of Journalists and Authors Author of the Year, Prix de Meilleur Livre Étranger; Medal Pres. of Italy, Officer, Ordre des Arts et des Sciences. *Address:* Toffler Associates, 1775 Wiehle Avenue, Reston, VA 20190, USA (office). *Telephone:* (703) 674-5480 (office). *Fax:* (703) 674-5494 (office). *Website:* www.toffler.com (office).

TOFFLER, Adelaide Elizabeth (Heidi), BA; American writer and consultant; b. (Adelaide Elizabeth Farrell), 1 Aug. 1929, New York, NY; m. Alvin Toffler 1950; one d. *Education:* Long Island Univ. *Career:* Co-founder (with husband) Toffler Associates (consultancy) 1996. *Publications:* with Alvin Toffler: The Culture Consumers 1964, Future Shock 1970, The Futurists (ed.) 1972, Learning for Tomorrow (ed.) 1973, The Third Wave 1980, Previews and Premises 1983, The Adaptive Corporation 1984, Power Shift 1990, War and Anti-War 1993, Creating a New Civilization 1994–95, Revolutionary Wealth 2006; contrib. to newspapers, journals and periodicals. *Honours:* hon. doctorates; Pres. of Italy Medal. *Address:* Toffler Associates, 1775 Wiehle Avenue, Reston, VA 20190, USA (office). *Telephone:* (703) 674-5480 (office). *Fax:* (703) 674-5494 (office). *Website:* www.toffler.com (office).

TÓIBÍN, Colm; Irish journalist and writer; b. 1955, Enniscorthy, Co. Wexford; s. of Micheál Tóibín. *Education:* Christian Brothers School, Enniscorthy, Univ. Coll., Dublin. *Career:* in Spain 1975–78; Features Ed., In Dublin 1981–82; Ed. Magill (political and current affairs magazine) 1982–85; journalist and columnist, Dublin Sunday Independent 1985–. *Play:* Beauty in a Broken Place 2003. *Publications:* fiction: Infidelity (contrib.), The South (Irish Times First Novel Award 1991) 1990, The Heather Blazing (Encore Award) 1993, The Story of the Night 1996, The Blackwater Lightship 1999, Finbar's Hotel (contrib.) 1999, The Master (Int. IMPAC Dublin Literary Award 2006) 2004, Mothers and Sons 2006, Brooklyn (Costa Book Award for Best Novel) 2009, The Empty Family 2010; non-fiction: Seeing is Believing: Moving Statues in Ireland 1985, Walking Along the Border (with T. O'Shea) 1987, Homage to Barcelona 1990, Dubliners 1990, The Trial of the Generals: Selected Journalism 1980–90 1990, Bad Blood 1994, Sign of the Cross 1994, The Kilfenora Teaboy 1997, The Irish Famine 1999, Love in a Dark Time 2001, Lady Gregory's Toothbrush 2002; editor: SOHO Square VI: New Writing from Ireland 1993, Enniscorthy: History & Heritage 1998, Penguin Book of Irish Fiction 1999, The Modern Library 1999, New Writing II 2002; contrib. articles. *Honours:* American Acad. of Arts and Letters E. M. Forster Award 1995, Center for Scholars and Writers Fellowship, New York Public Library, Soc. of Authors Travelling Scholarship 2004. *Literary Agent:* c/o Rogers, Coleridge and White Ltd, 20 Powis Mews, London, W11 1JN, England. *Telephone:* (20) 7221-3717. *Fax:* (20) 7229-9084. *E-mail:* info@rcwlitagency.co.uk. *Website:* www.rcwlitagency.co.uk; www.colmtoibin.com.

TOKARCZUK, Olga; Polish writer; b. 1962, Sulechow. *Education:* Univ. of Warsaw. *Career:* fmr Head of Ruta publishing co. *Publications:* Podroz ludzi ksiegi (Journey of the People of the Book) (Polish Publishers' Asscn Prize) 1993, E.E. 1995, Prawiek i inne czasy (Prawiek and Other Times) 1996, Szafa (The Wardrobe) 1997, Dom dzienny, dom nocny (House of Day, House of Night) (Bruecke Berlin Literary Prize 2002) 1998, Opowiesci wigilijne

(Christmas Tales, with Jerzy Pilch and Andrzej Stasiuk) 2000, Lalka i perla (The Doll and the Pearl) 2001, Gra na wielu bębenkach (Playing on a Multitude of Drums, short stories) 2001, Ostatrie historie (The Lost Stories) 2004, Anna in w grobowcach swiata 2006, Bieguni (Runners) 2007 (Nike Award 2008), Prowadź swój pług przez kości umarły("Drive Your Plow Over the Bones of the Dead) 2009; contrib. to Granta journal. *Honours:* Koscielski Family Foundation Prize.

TOLLE, Eckhart; German spiritual teacher and writer; b. (Ulrich Tolle), 16 Feb. 1948. *Education:* Univ. of London and Univ. of Cambridge, UK. *Career:* emigrated to England in his early 20s, worked as counsellor and spiritual guide; based in Vancouver, Canada 1995–; lectures and tv appearances worldwide; A New Earth, ten-week internet event with Oprah Winfrey 2008. *Publications:* The Power of Now 1999, Practicing the Power of Now 2001, Stillness Speaks 2003, A New Earth 2005; numerous audio CDs including Stillness Amidst the World: Findhorn Retreat 2005, Through the Open Door: Journey to the Vastness of Your True Being 2006. *Address:* Eckhart Teachings, Inc., POB 93661, Nelson Park RPO, Vancouver, BC V6E 4L7, Canada (office). *Telephone:* (604) 893-8500 (home). *Fax:* (604) 893-8585 (office). *E-mail:* info@eckharttolle.com (office). *Website:* www.eckharttolle.com.

TOLSTAYA, Tatyana Nikitichna; Russian writer; b. 3 May 1951, Leningrad (now St Petersburg); d. of Mikhail Lozinsky; great-grandniece of Leo Tolstoy and granddaughter of Alexei Tolstoy; m. Andrey V. Lebedev; two s. *Education:* Univ. of Leningrad. *Career:* Ed. of Eastern Literature Nauka Publishing, Moscow 1987–89; fmr Assoc. Prof. of English, Skidmore Coll., NJ, USA; co-host The School for Scandal TV interview show (Telekanal Kultura). *Publications:* On the Golden Porch (short story) 1983, Sleepwalker in a Fog 1992, Night 1995, Day 1997, Kys 1998, Two of Them 2001, The Slynx 2007, White Walls 2007. *Honours:* Triumph Prize 2001. *Address:* c/o Telekanal Kultura (Television Channel Culture), 123995 Moscow, ul. M. Nikitskaya 24, Russia (office). *Telephone:* (495) 780-56-01 (office). *E-mail:* web@tv-culture.ru (office). *Website:* www.tvkultura.ru (office).

TOMALIN, Claire, MA, FRSL; British writer; b. 20 June 1933, London; d. of Emile Delavenay and Muriel Emily Herbert; m. 1st Nicholas Osborne Tomalin 1955 (died 1973); two s. three d. (one d. and one s. deceased); m. 2nd Michael Frayn (q.v.) 1993. *Education:* Hitchin Girls' Grammar School, Dartington Hall School, Newnham Coll., Cambridge. *Career:* publr's reader and Ed. 1955–67; Asst Literary Ed. New Statesman 1968–70, Literary Ed. 1974–77; Literary Ed. Sunday Times 1979–86; Vice-Pres. English PEN 1997, Royal Literary Fund 2000; mem. London Library Cttee 1997–2000, Advisory Cttee for the Arts, Humanities and Social Sciences, British Library 1997–2000, Council RSL 1997–2000; Trustee, Nat. Portrait Gallery 1992–2002, Wordsworth Trust 2004. *Exhibitions:* Mrs. Jordan, English Heritage Kenwood 1995, Hyenas in Petticoats: Mary Wollstonecraft and Mary Shelley, Wordsworth Trust and Nat. Portrait Gallery 1997–98. *Play:* The Winter Wife 1991. *Publications:* The Life and Death of Mary Wollstonecraft 1974, Shelley and his World 1980, Katherine Mansfield: A Secret Life 1987, The Invisible Woman 1990, The Winter Wife 1991, Mrs Jordan's Profession 1994, Jane Austen: A Life 1997, Maurice by Mary Shelley (ed.) 1998, Several Strangers: Writing from Three Decades 1999, Samuel Pepys: The Unequalled Self (Whitbread Awards for Book of the Year and Best Biog.) 2002, Thomas Hardy: The Time-Torn Man 2006, Selected Poems of Thomas Hardy 2006, Charles Dickens (Galaxy Nat. Book Award for Biography of the Year) 2011. *Honours:* Hon. Fellow, Lucy Cavendish Coll. Cambridge 2003, Newnham Coll. Cambridge 2003; Hon. DLitt (East Anglia) 2005, (Birmingham) 2005, (Greenwich) 2006, (Cambridge) 2007; Whitbread Prize 1974, James Tait Black Prize 1990, NCR Book Award 1991, Hawthornden Prize 1991, Samuel Pepys Award 2003, Rose Mary Crawshay Prize 2003. *Literary Agent:* c/o David Godwin, David Godwin Associates, 55 Monmouth Street, London, WC2H 9DG, England. *Telephone:* (20) 7240-9992. *Fax:* (20) 7395-6130. *E-mail:* assistant@davidgodwinassociates.co.uk. *Website:* www.davidgodwinassociates.co.uk.

TOMAZOS, Criton Plato, DipArch; British architect, artist, poet and playwright, writer, journalist and critic; *Co-ordinating Director, Theatre for Mankind*; b. 13 April 1940, Larnaca, Cyprus; s. of Plato Tomazos and Thessalia Tomazou. *Education:* The Polytechnic, Regent Street (now Univ. of Westminster), Croydon Coll. of Fine Art and Technology, London Acad. of Film and TV. *Career:* various positions in pvt and public architectural offices 1960–90; co-founder, Co-ordinating Dir Environmental Forum 1970–94; founder, resident playwright, designer, then Chair. Prometheus Theatre Co. 1982–84; Founder-Dir Theatre for Mankind Voluntary Org. 1985–; Ed., journalist, letters and arts page, Parikiaki 1995–98; currently Deputy Dir Gen. Int. Biographical Centre, Cambridge; mem. Writers' Guild, Poetry Soc., Writers' Forum, Theatre for Mankind, Theatre Writers' Union (Cttee mem.), New Playwrights' Trust (Man. Cttee mem.), Asscn of Greek Scientists/Professional People, Acad. Maison Internationale des Intellectuelles (by invitation) 1993–94; Trustee, Greek Diaspora Centre Trust; Fellow, ABI Bd of Research, Millennium Awards. *Art:* numerous paintings, 3-D works; one of three artists representing UK in first Int. Arts Biennale, Malta 1991, represented UK and Cyprus at Sixth Int. Arts Biennale, Florence, Italy 2007, Soulfabric Group Exhbn, London 2008, Surface Change (solo retrospective exhbn), London 2009, Open Art Exhbn to celebrate 50 years of Cyprus's independence (winner Third Prize) 2010, participant by invitation to 8th Int. Biennale of Contemporary Art, Florence 2011. *Plays:* Rehearsal, Maxim & Minnie (A Listener and the Playwright), Girl in a Dark Red Dress, The Shark, Tickets to No-Man's Land, Not Suitable for the National; in Greek: Certificate for an Insignificant Woman; bilingual: libretto for Fedeas (people's opera). *Radio:* five monologues by poet Yiannis Ritsos, LGR (London Greek Radio) co-production 2005. *Film scripts:* The Fraud, Daydreams Burn, Close Shave, Terra Incognita, Eyes Open at Midnight. *Television:* resented his poetry and that of others several times on Hellenic TV, London. *Publications:* poetry: Lovepoem 1965, Monologue of the Ancient Hero 1970, Relationships 1975, Poems of 1960–61 1976, He Who Left His Fingerprints 1979, Factory Backyard 1980, Diaphanies (Transparencies) (first prize for poetry EDON Int. Youth Festival) 1982, Letter to the Returning Astronaut 1982, The Song of Tefcros (first prize EDEN Youth Festival) 1983, Synora Mnemes (Boundaries of Memory) 1987–88, The Visit 1988, First Explorations 1989, The Story of Water & Night March 1990, Tora (Now) 1994; prose: The Meaning of Work in Contemporary Society (essay) 1977, Eugene Delacroix, the Painter, The Dramatic Work of Angelos Sikelianos; contrib. to numerous anthologies, including Our Poems 2004, to magazines, newspapers and journals, poems included in three poetry anthologies, following competition 2010. *Honours:* Dr hc (London Inst. of Applied Research, Acad. des Sciences Universelles, World Univ., Benson, USA); Millennium Award for project Wake Up to Your Environment 2003, numerous distinctions, gold, silver and bronze medals, hon. certificates and fellowships. *Address:* Theatre for Mankind, c/o 2 Park Terrace, Bell Lane, Enfield, Middx, EN3 5EU, England (office). *Telephone:* (20) 8443-4643 (home). *E-mail:* enform2003@yahoo.co.uk (office); tfmankind@hotmail.co.uk (office); ctomazos@btinterenet.co.uk (office). *Website:* www.freewebs.com/theatreformankind (office); www.freewebs.com/critontomazos.

TOMIOKA, Taeko; Japanese poet, novelist, critic, playwright and screenwriter; b. 1935, Ōsaka. *Education:* Ōsaka Women's Coll. *Career:* poetry debut 1957; turned to fiction 1970; author of novels, short stories, plays, screenplays, essays and criticism; has translated works of Gertrude Stein and Susan Sontag. *Films:* Shinjû: Ten no amijima (Double Suicide) 1969, Himiko 1974, Sakura no Mori no Mankai no Shita 1975, Yari no gonza (Gonza the Spearman) 1986. *Publications:* Oka ni mukatte hito wa narabu (Facing the Hills They Stand) 1971, Shokubutsusai (The Festival of Plants) (Tamura Toshiko Award) 1973, Meido no kazoku (Family in Hell) (Women Writers' Award) 1974, Tōsei bonjin den (Stories of Contemporary People) (Kawabata Yasunari Award) 1976, See You Soon: Poems of Taeko Tomioka 1979, Namiutsu tochi 1983, Saikaku no katari 1987, Fuji no koromo ni asa no fusuma, Koyujidai no shosetu 1989, Shinkazoku: Jisen Tanpenshu (New Family) 1990, Sakagami 1990, 'Katari' no Chihei 1990, Towazugatari 1990, Suijo teien 1991, Danryū bungakuron (co-author) (A Study of Male Literature) 1992, Naka Kansuke no koi (Naka Kansuke's Love) 1993, Hivernia to Kiko (Hivernia Islands Journal) (Noma Literary Prize) 1997, Shaku Choku note (Mainichi Publishing Culture Award) 2000, Saikaku no Kanjo (The Sentiment of Saikagu) (Osaragi Jiro Award) 2005, Mizuumi no minami (South of the Lake) 2007, Building Waves 2012.

TOMLINSON, (Alfred) Charles, CBE, BA, MA; British academic, poet, writer and translator; *Professor Emeritus and Senior Research Fellow, University of Bristol*; b. 8 Jan. 1927, Stoke-on-Trent, Staffordshire; m. 1948; two d. *Education:* Queens' Coll., Cambridge. *Career:* Lecturer, Univ. of Bristol 1956–68, Reader 1968–82, Prof. of English 1982–92, Prof. Emer. 1992–, Sr Research Fellow 1996–; Visiting Prof., Univ. of New Mexico, USA 1962–63; O'Connor Prof., Colgate Univ., New York 1967–68, 1989–90; Visiting Fellow of Humanities, Princeton Univ. 1981; Lamont Prof., Union Coll., New York 1987; mem. academic and literary orgs. *Publications:* poetry: Relations and Contraries 1951, The Necklace 1955, Seeing is Believing 1958, A Peopled Landscape 1963, American Scenes 1966, The Poem as Initiation 1968, The Way of a World 1969, Renga 1970, Written on Water 1972, The Way In 1974, The Shaft 1978, Selected Poems 1951–74 1978, The Flood 1981, Airborn: Hijos del aire 1981, Notes from New York 1984, Collected Poems 1985, The Return 1987, Nella pienezza del tempo 1987, Annunciations 1989, The Door in the Wall 1992, Poemas 1992, Gedichte 1994, La insistencia de las cosas 1994, In Italia 1995, Jubilation 1995, Portuguese Pieces 1996, The Fox Gallery 1996, Parole e Acqua 1997, Selected Poems 1955–97 1997, The Vineyard Above the Sea 1999, Luoghi Italiani 2000, Lugares y Relaciones 2003, Skywriting 2003, En la Plenitud del Tiempo 2005, Cracks in the Universe 2006, New Selected Poems 2009, Comme un rire de lumière 2009; other: In Black and White 1976, The Oxford Book of Verse in English Translation (ed.) 1980, Some Americans: A Literary Memoir 1981, Poetry and Metamorphosis 1983, Eros Englished: Erotic Poems from the Greek and Latin (ed.) 1991, American Essays: Making it New 2001, Metamorphoses: Poetry and Translation 2003, John Dryden: Poems Selected by Charles Tomlinson 2003; contrib. to books, professional journals and other publs. *Honours:* Hon. Fellow, Queens' Coll., Cambridge 1976–, Royal Holloway Coll., London 1991, Modern Language Asscn 2003; Hon. Foreign Fellow, American Acad. of Arts and Sciences 1998; hon. doctorates; Bess Hokin Prize 1968, Oscar Blumenthal Prize 1960, Inez Boulton Prize 1964, Frank O'Hara Prize 1968, Cheltenham Poetry Prize 1976, Cholmondeley Poetry Award 1979, Wilbur Award for Poetic Achievement 1982, Premio Europeo di Cittadella, Italy 1991, Bennett Award for Poetry 1992, Premio Intenazionale Flaiano 2001, The New Criterion Poetry Prize 2003, Premio Internazionale di Poesia 'Attilio Bertolucci' 2004. *Address:* Department of English, 3–5 Woodland Road, University of Bristol, Bristol, BS8 1TB, England (office). *Telephone:* (117) 928-7787 (office). *Fax:* (117) 928-8860 (office). *Website:* www.bris.ac.uk/english (office).

TOPOL, Jáchym; Czech poet, writer and journalist; b. 4 Aug. 1962, Prague; s. of Josef Topol; m.; two d. *Career:* prevented from univ. educ. because of father's dissident activities; imprisoned several times for publishing activities; signatory to Charter 77 human rights declaration; wrote lyrics for brother's rock band, Psí Vojáci 1970s–1980s; co-f. of samizdat (clandestinely copied and printed) magazines, Violit 1982, Revolver Revue 1985 (Ed.-in-Chief –1993); took part in Velvet Revolution in Czechoslovakia 1989; wrote, ed. and published Informační servis newsletter, which became investigative weekly magazine Respekt, reporter 1989–; published first collection of poetry in samizdat 1988; residency Ledig House, New York (USA) 1995. *Song lyrics:* for Monika Naceva: Monosti tu sou 1994, Nebe je rudý 1996, Mimoid 1998, Fontanela 2001, Mami 2007. *Publications:* poetry: Miluju tě k zbláznění (trans. as I Love You Madly) (Tom Stoppard Prize for Unofficial Literature, Charter 77 Foundation, Stockholm) 1988, V úterý bude válka (trans. as The War Will Be on Tuesday) 1993; prose: Výlet k nádraní hale (trans. as Trip to the Train Station) 1994, Sestra (trans. as City Sister Silver) (Egon Hostovský Prize, Czech Book of the Year) 1994, Anděl (trans. as Angel) 1995, Trnová divka (trans. as Thorn Girl) 1996, Nemůžu se zastavit: Rozhovory (trans. as I Can't Stand Still: Conversations) 2000, Noční práce (trans. as Night Works) 2001, Kloktat dehet (trans. as Gargling with Tar) 2005, Supermarket Sovětských Hrdinů (trans. as Supermarket of Soviet Heroes) 2007, Chladnou zemi 2009; contrib. in English to anthologies and reviews. *Literary Agent:* Pluh, Lange Vonder 90, 1035 Amsterdam, Netherlands. *Telephone:* (20) 3372676. *E-mail:* info@pluh.org. *Website:* www.pluh.org.

TOPOLSKI, Daniel, BA, MA, FRGS; British travel writer and sports broadcaster; b. 4 June 1945, London, England; m. Susan Gilbert; one s. two d. *Education:* New Coll., Oxford. *Career:* BBC sports commentator and journalist covering Olympic Games, World Rowing, Boat Race; rowed Boat Race 1967 (won), 1968 (lost), World Championships 1975 (silver medal), 1977 (gold medal); coached Oxford Boat Race crew 1973–87 (won 12), coached at Olympics 1980, 1984; consultant, Oxford Boat Race; motivational speaker; mem. Leander Club, London Rowing Club; Trustee, Topolski Century Museum; Churchill Fellow. *Film:* True Blue (based on his book). *Radio:* Topolski's Travels (BBC Radio 5 Live) 1994. *Publications:* Muzungu: One Man's Africa 1976, Travels with my Father: South America 1983, Boat Race: The Oxford Revival 1985, True Blue: The Oxford Mutiny 1988, Henley: The Regatta 1989; contribs to newspapers, periodicals, radio and TV. *Honours:* Sports Book of the Year 1990, Radio Travel Programme of the Year 1994. *Address:* 69 Randolph Avenue, London, W9 1DW, England. *Fax:* (20) 7266-1884. *E-mail:* dtopo35410@aol.com. *Website:* www.topolskicentury.org.uk.

TORON, Steve (see Stebel, Sidney Leo)

TORRANCE, Lee (see Sadgrove, Sidney Henry)

TOSCANA, David; Mexican writer; b. 1961, Monterrey, Nuevo León. *Education:* Instituto Tecnologico y de Estudios Superiores de Monterrey. *Career:* worked in Ciudad Juárez as an engineer; mem. Int. Writers Program, Univ. of Iowa, USA 1994, Berliner Künstler Program 2003; Guest of Writers-in-Residence Programme, Berlin 2003–04. *Publications include:* novels: Las bicicletas 1992, Estación Tula 1995, Santa María del Circo 1998, Duelo por Miguel Pruneda 2002, El último lector (Premio Nacional de Literatura José Fuentes Mares 2005) 2004, El ejército iluminado (Premio Casa de las Américas 2008) 2006, Los puentes de Königsberg 2009; stories: Historias de Lontananza 1997. *Address:* Santillana Ediciones Generales, S.A. de C.V., Av. Universidad 767, Col. Del Valle 03100 México DF, México. *Telephone:* (55) 5420-7530. *Website:* www.alfaguara.com/mx.

TOSCHES, Nick; American writer; b. 1949, Newark, NJ. *Career:* began writing in small music magazines; worked with Lester Bangs at Creem; has written liner notes for compilation albums by numerous artists, including Jerry Lee Lewis and Carl Perkins; collaborated with Hubert Selby, Jr; Contributing Ed., Vanity Fair. *Recordings:* albums: Blue Eyes and Exit Wounds (with Hubert Selby Jr) 1998, Nick & Homer (with Homer Henderson) 1998. *Publications include:* Country 1977, Hellfire (biog.) 1982, Unsung Heroes of Rock 'N' Roll 1984, Power on Earth 1986, Cut Numbers (novel) 1988, Dino: Living High in the Dirty Business of Dreams (Italian-American Literary Achievement Award for Distinction in Literature 1993) 1992, Trinities (novel) (New York Times Book Review Notable Book of the Year) 1994, Chaldea (poems) 1999, The Devil and Sonny Liston 2000, The Nick Tosches Reader (anthology) 2000, Where Dead Voices Gather 2001, The Last Opium Den 2002, In The Hand of Dante 2002, King of the Jews: The Arnold Rothstein Story 2006; contrib. poems to publications, including Contents, Esquire, GQ, Long Shot, Open City, Smokes Like a Fish. *E-mail:* webmaster@exitwounds.com (office). *Website:* www.nicktosches.com.

TÓTH, Krisztina; Hungarian poet and translator; b. 1967. *Career:* trans. of contemporary French literature. *Publications:* A beszélgetés fonala (The Thread of Conversation) 1994, Porhó (Snow) 2001, A Londoni mackók (London Teddy Bears) (Best Book of the Year award) 2003; contrib. to TLS, Hungarian Quarterly, crosspathculture.org. *Honours:* Graves Prize 1996, Déry Tibor Prize 1996, József Attila Prize 2000. *E-mail:* kriszta.toth@t-online.hu (office). *Website:* www.tothkrisztina.hu.

TOURNIER, Michel, LèsL, LenD, DPhil; French writer; b. 19 Dec. 1924, Paris; s. of Alphonse Tournier and Marie-Madeleine Tournier (née Fournier). *Education:* Saint-Germain-en-Laye, Univ. of Paris (Sorbonne), Univ. of Tübingen (Germany). *Career:* radio and TV production 1949–54; press attaché, Europe No. 1 1955–58; head of literary services, Editions Plon 1958–68; contrib. to Le Monde, Le Figaro; mem. Acad. Goncourt 1972–. *Publications:* fiction: Vendredi, ou les limbes du Pacifique (trans. as Friday) 1967 (Grand Prix de l'Acad. Française), Le Roi des Aulnes (trans. as The Ogre) (Prix Goncourt) 1970, Vendredi, ou la vie sauvage (trans. as Friday and Robinson: Life on Esperanza Island) 1971, Les Météores 1975, Le Coq de bruyère 1978, Pierrot, ou les secrets de la nuit 1979, Gaspard, Melchior et Balthazar (trans. as The Four Wise Men) 1980, Gilles et Jeanne 1983, Le Vagabond immobile 1984, Journal de voyage au Canada 1984, La Goutte d'or (trans. as The Golden Droplet) 1986, Le Médianioche amoureux (trans. as The Midnight Love Feast) 1989, La Couleuvrine 1994, Eléazar, ou la source et le buisson 1996, Barbedor 2003, La Famille Adam 2003, Telling Tales (contrib. to charity anthology) 2004, Journal extime 2004, Mephisto 2006, Vendredi ou la vie sauvage: D'après Vendredi ou les limbes du Pacifique 2007; non-fiction: Le Vent paraclet (trans. as The Wind Spirit: An Autobiography) 1977, Des clefs et des serrures 1979, Le Vol du vampire 1981, Le Tabor et le Sinaï 1989, Le Crépuscule des masques 1992, Le Miroir des idées 1994, Le Pied de la lettre 1994, Célébrations 1999, Les vertes lectures 2006, Le bonheur en Allemagne? 2004. *Honours:* Officier, Légion d'honneur, Commdr, Ordre nat. du Mérite; Dr hc (Univ. Coll. London) 1997; Goethe Medal 1993. *Address:* Le Presbytère, Choisel, 78460 Chevreuse, France (home). *Telephone:* 1-30-52-05-29 (home).

TOWER, Wells, BA, MFA; American writer and journalist; b. 14 April 1973, Vancouver, BC, Canada. *Education:* Wesleyan Univ., Columbia Univ. *Career:* mem. Hellbender punk band 1991–97; co-founder, Foodbox magazine 1993; fmr columnist, DoubleTake magazine; currently Lecturer in Creative Writing, Columbia University. *Publications:* short stories: Everything Burned, Everything Ravaged 2009; contribs to The New Yorker, Harper's, McSweeney's, The Paris Review, Anchor Book of New American Short Stories, Washington Post Magazine. *Honours:* two Pushcart Prizes, Plimpton Discovery Prize, The Paris Review. *Address:* c/o Farrar, Strauss & Giroux, 18 West 18th Street, New York, NY 10011, USA (office). *Website:* us.macmillan.com/fsg.aspx (office).

TOWNLEY, Roderick Carl, AB, PhD; American writer and poet; b. 7 June 1942, NJ; m. Wyatt Townley 1986; one s. one d. *Education:* Bard Coll., Rutgers Univ. *Career:* Prof. of English, Universidad de Concepcion, Chile 1978–79; Nat. Editorial Writer, TV Guide 1980–89; Sr Ed. US magazine 1989–90; Exec. Dir The Writers Place, Kansas City, Mo. 1995–96. *Publications:* poetry: Three Musicians 1978, Final Approach 1986; novels: Minor Gods 1977, The Great Good Thing 2001, Into the Labyrinth 2002, Sky 2004, The Constellation of Sylvie 2006, The Red Thread 2007; non-fiction: The Early Poetry of William Carlos Williams 1975, Night Errands: How Poets Use Dreams 1998; contrib. to newspapers, journals and anthologies. *Honours:* Acad. of American Poets Co-winner 1969, First Prize 1971, Fulbright Professorship, Chile 1978–79, Peregrine Prize in Short Fiction 1998, Kansas Arts Comm. Individual Artist grant 2000, Kansas Gov.'s Arts Award 2003, Thorpe Menn Award 2003. *Literary Agent:* c/o Writers House, 21 West 26 Street, New York, NY 10010, USA. *Telephone:* (212) 685-2405. *Address:* PO Box 13302, Shawnee Mission, KS 66282, USA (office). *E-mail:* rodericktownley@everestkc.net (office). *Website:* www.rodericktownley.com.

TOWNSEND, Susan (Sue) Lilian, FRSL; British writer; b. 2 April 1946, Leicester; m. (divorced); four c. *Career:* started writing professionally early 1980s; mem. Writers' Guild, PEN. *Plays:* Bazaar and Rummage 1984, Groping for Words 1984, Womberang 1984, The Great Celestial Cow 1985, Ten Tiny Fingers, Nine Tiny Toes 1990, The Secret Diary of Adrian Mole Aged 13$^{3}/_{4}$ 1992, Dayroom, The Ghost of Daniel Lambert, Captain Christmas and the Evil Adults, Are You Sitting Comfortably?. *Television:* Think of England (writer, narrator and presenter) 1991. *Publications:* The Secret Diary of Adrian Mole Aged 13$^{3}/_{4}$ 1982, The Growing Pains of Adrian Mole 1984, Rebuilding Coventry 1988, Mr Bevan's Dream 1989, True Confessions of Adrian Albert Mole, Margaret Hilda Roberts and Susan Lilian Townsend 1989, Adrian Mole from Minor to Major 1991, The Queen and I 1992, Adrian Mole: The Wilderness Years 1993, Adrian Mole, The Lost Years 1994, Ghost Children 1997, Adrian Mole, The Cappuccino Years 1999, The Public Confessions of a Middle-Aged Woman Aged 55$^{3}/_{4}$ 2001, Number 10 2002, Adrian Mole and the Weapons of Mass Destruction 2004, Queen Camilla 2006, The Lost Diaries of Adrian Mole 1999–2001 2008, Adrian Mole: The Prostrate Years 2009; contribs to London Times, New Statesman, Observer, Sainsbury's Magazine. *Honours:* Hon. MA (Leicester) 1991. *Literary Agent:* The Sale Agency, 11 Jubilee Place, London, SW3 3TD; Curtis Brown Group Ltd, 28–29 Haymarket, London, SW1Y 4SP, England. *Address:* c/o Reed Books, Michelin House, 81 Fulham Road, London, SW3 6RB, England (office). *E-mail:* kate50@fsmail.net (office).

TOWNSEND, Thomas (Tom) L.; American novelist; b. 1 Jan. 1944, Waukegan, Ill.; m. Janet L. Simpson 1965. *Education:* Arkansas Military Acad. *Films:* Ferret 101 (documentary) 2000, Military Motorpool (TV pilot) 2006. *Music:* The Ballad Of Ol' Hook 2008. *Publications include:* Texas Treasure Coast 1978, Where the Pirates Are 1985, Trader Wooly 1987, Trader Wooly and the Terrorists 1988, Queen of the Wind 1989, Battle of Galveston 1990, Trader Wooly and the Ghost in the Colonel's Jeep 1991, The Holligans 1991, Bubba's Truck 1992, The Ghost Flyers 1993, A Fair Wind to Glory 1994, The Trouble With An Elf 1995, Never trust A One-eyed Wizard 1996, The Dragon Trader 1997, Nadia Of the Night Witches 1998, Gypsy Prince War Horse 2000, Reichbahn Six-Nine, Shadow Kiss, The Ballad Of Ol'Hook, 2008, The Pirate Hunter Episode One 2009. *Honours:* Friend of American Writers Award 1986, Texas Blue Bonnet Master List 1986, Silver Award, Best Children's Video, Houston Int. Film Festival 1986, Silver Award Reel Dialogue screenplay competition 1999. *Address:* 3123 CR 2407, Rusk, TX

75785, USA (office). *Telephone:* (713) 502-4377 (office). *E-mail:* tom@tomtownsend-toyland.com (office). *Website:* www.tomtownsend-toyland.com (office).

TOYNBEE, Polly, (Mary Jenkins); British journalist, broadcaster and author; *Columnist, The Guardian*; b. 27 Dec. 1946, Isle of Wight, England; d. of the late Philip Toynbee and of Anne Powell; m. Peter Jenkins 1970 (died 1992); one s. three d. *Education:* Badminton School, Bristol, Holland Park Comprehensive, London and St Anne's Coll., Oxford. *Career:* feature writer, The Observer newspaper (UK) 1968–70, 1971–77; Ed. The Washington Monthly, USA 1970–71; columnist, The Guardian newspaper 1977–88, 1998–; SDP parl. cand. for Lewisham East 1983; Social Affairs Ed. BBC 1989–95; Assoc. Ed. and columnist, The Independent newspaper 1995–97; Gov. LSE 1988–99; mem. Dept of Health Advisory Cttee on the Ethics of Xenotransplantation 1996, Nat. Screening Cttee 1996–2005; Pres. Social Policy Asscn 2005–08; Chair. Brighton Dome and Festival 2005–; Dir Political Quarterly magazine; Visiting Fellow, Nuffield Coll., Oxford 2005–. *Publications:* Leftovers 1966, A Working Life 1970, Hospital 1976, Lost Children 1985, The Way We Live Now 1987, Did Things Get Better? (with David Walker) 2001, Hard Work: Life in Low Pay Britain 2003, Better or Worse? Has Labour Delivered? (with David Walker) 2005, Unjust Rewards (with David Walker) 2008, The Verdict: Did Labour Change Britain? (with David Walker) 2010. *Honours:* hon. degrees from Univs of Essex, Sussex, Kent, Leeds, Stafford, Loughborough, Univ. of the South Bank; Catherine Pakenham Award 1976, British Press Awards 1977, 1982, Columnist of the Year 1986, BBC What the Papers Say Award 1996, Magazine Writer of the Year, PPA 1996, George Orwell Prize 1997, Commentator of the Year, British Press Awards 1996. *Address:* The Guardian, Kings Place, 90 York Way, London, N1 9GU, England (office). *Telephone:* (20) 3353-2000 (office). *E-mail:* polly.toynbee@guardian.co.uk (office). *Website:* www.guardian.co.uk (office).

TRABOULSI, Yasmina; Lebanese writer; b. 1975. *Publication:* Les enfants de la Place (novel, trans. as Bahia Blues) 2002, Amers 2007. *Honours:* Young Francophone Writer's Award 2002, Prix du Premier Roman 2003. *Address:* c/o Editions Mercure de France, 26 rue de Condé, 75006 Paris, France (office). *Website:* www.mercuredefrance.fr (office).

TRACY, James D., BA, MA, PhD; American historian, academic and writer; *Professor Emeritus, Department of History, University of Minnesota*; b. 14 Feb. 1938, St Louis, Mo.; m. Nancy Ann McBride 1968; two s. one d. *Education:* St Louis Univ., Johns Hopkins Univ., Univ. of Notre Dame, Princeton Univ. *Career:* Instructor in History, Univ. of Michigan, 1964–66; Assoc. Prof. of History, Univ. of Minnesota 1966–77, Prof. of History 1977, now Prof. Emer.; Co-founder and fmr Man. Ed. Journal of Early Modern History. *Publications:* Erasmus: The Growth of a Mind, 1972; Early Modern European History, 1500–1715 (ed.), 1976; The Politics of Erasmus: A Pacifist Intellectual and His Political Milieu, 1979; True Ocean Found: Paludanus's Letters on Dutch Voyages to the Kara Sea, 1595–1596, 1980; A Financial Revolution in the Habsburg Netherlands: Renten and Renteniers in the Country of Holland, 1515–1565, 1985; Holland Under Habsburg Rule, 1506–1566: The Formation of a Body Politic, 1990; The Rise of Merchant Empires: Long-Distance Trade in the Early Modern World, 1350–1750 (ed.), 1990; The Political Economy of Merchant Empires: State Power and World Trade, 1350–1750 (ed.), 1991; Handbook of European History, 1400–1600: Late Middle Ages, Renaissance, and Reformation (ed. with Thomas A. Brady and Heiko A. Oberman), 1996; Erasmus of the Low Countries, 1996; Europe's Reformations, 1450–1650, 1999; City Wall: The Urban Enceinte in Global Perspective (ed.), 2000. Contributions: scholarly books and learned journals. *Address:* c/o Department of History, University of Minnesota, 1110 Heller Hall, Del. Code 7062, 271 19th Avenue South, Minneapolis, MN 55455, USA. *E-mail:* tracy001@umn.edu.

TRAN, Manh Hao; Vietnamese poet, writer and critic; b. 21 July 1949, Nam Dinh Prov. *Education:* Gorky Inst. of Literature, Moscow, USSR. *Career:* mem. Viet Nam Writers' Union. *Publications include:* poetry: Truong Son cua be (trans. as Baby's Truong Son) 1974, Giai Phong (trans. as Liberation) 1974, Tieng chim go cua (trans. as The Sound of the Bird Knocking at the Door) 1976, Van Nghe Giai Phong (trans. as Liberation and Arts) 1976, Hoa vua di vua no (trans. as The Flowers are Walking and Blooming at the Same Time) 1981, Mat troi trong long dat (trans. as The Underground Sun) 1981, Ba cap nui va mot hon nui le (trans. as Three Pairs of Mountains and One Standing-Alone Mountain) 1981, Tu chiec o troi cua me (trans. as From Mother's Heavenly Umbrella) 1987, Cuoc chien tranh khon nguoi (trans. as The Endless War) 1988, Minh anh trong mot the gioi (trans. as One You in One World) 1991, Dat nuoc hinh tia chop (trans. as Lightning-Shaped Country) 1994, Chuon chuon can ron (trans. as Dragonfly Biting the Navel) 1995, Tho tu tuyet (trans. as Four-Line Poems) 1995, Tho luc bat Tran Manh Hao (trans. as Tran Manh Hao's Six-Eight-Word-Metre Poetry) 2001; novels: Chia khoa cua moi nguoi (trans. as Everybody's Key) 1987, Trang mat (trans. as Honeymoon) 1989, Ly than (trans. as Separated) 1989, Sinh ra de yeu nhau (trans. as Born to Love Each Other) 1989; juvenile short stories: Cay trong vuon (trans. as Trees in the Garden) 1980, Chu heo dat (trans. as The Earthen Pig) 1981; criticism: Tho phan tho (trans. as Poetry against Poetry) 1995, Phe binh phan phe binh (trans. as Criticism against Criticism) 1996. *Honours:* Nat. Poetry Award for Children's Literature 1995, Nat. Poetry Awards 1996, 1999, Literary Arts Newspaper Award. *Address:* c/o Thanh Nien, 5 Ly Thuong Kiet, Hanoi, Viet Nam.

TRAN, Rev. Tam Tinh, (Hoang Tam), DUJ, PhD, FRSC; Vietnamese/Canadian archaeologist and academic; *Professor Emeritus of Classical Archaeology, Université Laval*; b. 16 April 1929, Nam Dinh. *Education:* Séminaire Pontifical, Università Laterano, Université de Fribourg, Ecole Pratique des Hautes Etudes, Paris, CNRS. *Career:* ordained priest 1956; excavations at Soli, Cyprus 1965–74, Pompeii and Herculaneum 1969–76; Co-founder Fraternité Vietnam 1976; Prof. of Classical Archaeology, Université Laval 1964–71, Sr Prof. 1971–94, Prof. Emer. 1994–. *Publications:* Le culte d'Isis à Pompéi 1964, Le culte des divinités orientales à Herculaneum 1971, Le culte des divinités orientales en Campanie 1972, Isis lactans 1973, Catalogue des peintures romaines au musée du Louvre 1974, Tôi vê Hanoi 1974, Tro vê nguôn 1974, I cattolici nella storia del Vietnam 1975, Dieu et César 1978, Sérapis debout 1983, Soloi I, La Basilique 1985, La casa dei Cervi à Herculaneum 1988, Corpus des lampes antiques conservées au Québec I 1991, Corpus des lampes à sujets asiatiques du musée gréco-romain d'Alexandrie 1993, Xin thay day con cau nguyen 2004, Loan bao tin mung 2004, Lay Cha 2004, Ong la ai? 2004; and numerous articles on classical iconography and religion. *Honours:* Tatiana Warscher Award for Archaeology, American Acad. at Rome 1973, Prix G. Mendel, Acad. des Inscriptions et Belles-Lettres, France 1978. *Address:* 2995 Maricourt, Suite 300, Québec, PQ G1W 4T8 (home); Université Laval, Cité Universitaire, Québec, PQ G1K 7P4, Canada (office). *Telephone:* (418) 653-3513 (office). *E-mail:* vinhsont2005@yahoo.ca (home). *Website:* www.ulaval.ca (office).

TRANSTRÖMER, Tomas Gösta; Swedish poet and psychologist; b. 15 April 1931, Stockholm; m. Monica Blach 1958; two d. *Education:* Univ. of Stockholm. *Career:* mem. Swedish Writers Union. *Publications include:* poetry: 17 dikter 1954, Hemligheter på vägen 1958, Den halvfärdiga himlen 1962, Klanger och spår 1966, Mörkerseende 1970, Stigar 1973, Östersjöar 1974, Sanningsbarriären 1978, Det vilda torget 1983, För levande och döda 1989, Sorgegondolen 1996, Den stora gåtan 2004, Samlade Dikter 1954–1996 2006; other: Minnena ser mig (memoir) 1993, Air Mail: 150 Brev 1964–1990 (collection of letters) 2001. *Honours:* Aftonbladets Literary Prize 1958, Bellman Prize 1966, Swedish Award, International Poetry Forum 1971, Oevralids Prize 1975, Boklotteriets Prize 1981, Petrarca Prize 1981, Nordic Council Literary Prize 1990, Griffin Poetry Prize Lifetime Recognition Award 2007, Nobel Prize for Literature 2011. *Address:* c/o Albert Bonniers Förlag, Box 3159, 103 63 Stockholm, Sweden (office). *E-mail:* info@abforlag.bonnier.se (office). *Website:* www.albertbonniersforlag.se (office).

TRAPIDO, Barbara Louise, DipEd, BA; British writer; b. (b. Barbara Louise Schuddeboom), 5 Nov. 1941, Cape Town, South Africa; d. of Frits Johan Schuddeboom and Annelise Jacobsen; m. Stanley Trapido 1963; one s. one d. *Education:* Univ. of Natal, Durban, S Africa, Univ. of London. *Career:* high school English teacher, London 1964–68, Lecturer in English Literature, Univ. of Durham 1968–70. *Publications:* Brother of the More Famous Jack 1982, Noah's Ark 1985, Temples of Delight 1990, Juggling 1994, The Travelling Horn Player 1998, Frankie and Stankie 2003, Sex and Stravinsky 2010; contrib. to Spectator, Sunday Telegraph, Sunday Times. *Honours:* Whitbread Award 1982. *Literary Agent:* c/o Victoria Hobbs, AM Heath & Co. Ltd, Authors' Agents, 6 Warwick Court, London, WC1R 5DJ, England. *Telephone:* (20) 7242-2811. *Fax:* (20) 7242-2711. *Website:* www.amheath.com. *Address:* c/o Bloomsbury Publishing, 38 Soho Square, London, W1D 3HB, England (office).

TRAVIS, Aaron (see Saylor, Steven Warren)

TRAWICK, Leonard Moses, BA, MA, PhD; American academic, poet, writer and editor; b. 4 July 1933, Decatur, Ala; m. Kerstin Ekfelt 1960; one s. one d. *Education:* Univ. of the South, Univ. of Chicago, Harvard Univ. *Career:* Instructor to Asst Prof. of English, Columbia Univ. 1961–69; Assoc. Prof., Cleveland State Univ. 1969–72, Prof. of English 1972–98, Prof. Emeritus 1998–, Principal Ed. Poetry Center 1971–98, Dir 1990–92; Founding Ed. The Gamut journal 1980, Co-Ed. 1983–92. *Publications:* Poetry: Beast Forms, 1971; Severed Parts, 1981; Beastmorfs, 1994. Opera Librettos: Spinoza, by Julius Drossin, 1982; The Enchanted Garden, by Klaus G. Roy, 1983; Mary Stuart: A Queen Betrayed, by Bain Murray, 1991. Other: Backgrounds of Romanticism: English Philosophical Prose of the Eighteenth Century, 1967; World, Self, Poem (ed.), 1990; German Literature of the Romantic Era and the Age of Goethe (co-ed. and principal trans.), 1993. Contributions: scholarly books and journals, and to anthologies and magazines. *Honours:* Dr hc (Cleveland State Univ.) 2011; Fulbright Scholarship, Univ. of Dijon, 1956–57, Individual Artist Award, Ohio Arts Council 1980, Award for Excellence in the Media, Northern Ohio Live 1990, James P. Barry Ohioana Award for Editorial Excellence (jtly) 1991, Ohioana Poetry Award for Lifetime Achievement in Poetry 1994. *Address:* c/o Department of English, Cleveland State University, 2121 Euclid Avenue, RT 1815, Cleveland, OH 44115-2214, USA. *E-mail:* L.TRAWICK@csuohio.edu.

TREANOR, Oliver, BA, PGCE, STB, STL, STD; Northern Irish priest, writer, theologian and academic; *Lecturer in Systematic Theology, St Patrick's College, Maynooth*; b. 1 May 1949, Warrenpoint. *Education:* Queen's Univ., Belfast, Pontifical Università Gregoriana, Rome, Italy. *Career:* ordained Roman Catholic Priest 1978; Lecturer in Systematic Theology, St Patrick's Coll., Maynooth, Ireland 1996–. *Publications:* Mother of the Redeemer, Mother of the Redeemed 1988, Seven Bells to Bethlehem: The O Antiphons 1995, This Is My Beloved Son: Aspects of The Passion 1997, The God Who Loved Stories 1999; contribs: Priests and People, Durham, England,

Osservatore Romano, Vatican City, Religious Life Review, Dublin, International Christian Digest, USA, The Furrow, Maynooth, Bible Alive, Stoke-on-Trent. *Address:* St Patrick's College, Maynooth, Ireland (office). *Telephone:* (1) 7083431 (office). *E-mail:* oliver.treanor@may.ie (office). *Website:* www.maynoothcollege.ie (office).

TREGLOWN, Jeremy Dickinson, BLitt, MA, PhD, FRSL; British academic, author and journalist; *Professor of English, University of Warwick;* b. 24 May 1946, Anglesey, N Wales; s. of the late Rev. G. L. Treglown and Beryl Treglown; m. 1st Rona Bower 1970 (divorced 1982); one s. two d.; m. 2nd Holly Eley (née Urquhart) 1984 (died 2010); one d. with Jennifer Lewis. *Education:* Bristol Grammar School, St Peter's Coll., Oxford. *Career:* Lecturer in English Literature, Lincoln Coll. Oxford 1973–76, Univ. Coll., London 1976–79; Asst Ed. The Times Literary Supplement 1979–81, Ed. 1982–90; Prof. of English, Univ. of Warwick 1993– (Chair. Dept of English and Comparative Literary Studies 1995–98); Chair. of Judges, Booker Prize 1991, Whitbread Book of the Year Award 1998; Co-Ed. Liber, a European Review of Books 1989; Contributing Ed., Grand Street magazine, New York 1991–98; Visiting Fellow, All Souls Coll., Oxford 1986; Fellow, Huntington Library 1988; Mellon Visiting Assoc., California Inst. of Tech. 1988; Ferris Visiting Prof., Princeton Univ. 1992; Jackson Brothers Fellow, Beinecke Library, Yale Univ. 1999; Leverhulme Research Fellow 2001–03; Margaret and Herman Sokol Fellow, Cullman Center for Scholars and Writers, New York Public Library 2002–03; Fellow in History, Bogliasco Foundation 2011; Fellow, Rockefeller Foundation, Bellagio 2011; mem. Council, RSL 2010–. *Publications:* The Letters of John Wilmot, Earl of Rochester (ed.) 1980, Spirit of Wit: Reconsiderations of Rochester (ed.) 1982, Roald Dahl: A Biography 1994, Grub Street and the Ivory Tower: Literary Journalism, and Literary Scholarship from Fielding to the Internet (co-ed. with Bridget Bennett) 1998, Romancing: The Life and Work of Henry Green 2000, VS Pritchett: a Working Life 2004, Essential Stories/V.S. Pritchett (ed.) 2005, Roald Dahl: Collected Stories (ed.) 2006; contrib. of introductions to recent edns of R. L. Stevenson's In the South Seas, Robert Louis Stevenson's The Lantern Bearers, the complete novels of Henry Green; various articles on poetry, drama and literary history. *Honours:* Hon. Research Fellow, Univ. Coll. London 1991–. *Address:* English and Comparative Literary Studies, Room H526, University of Warwick, Coventry, CV4 7AL, England (office). *Telephone:* (24) 7652-3323 (office). *Fax:* (24) 7652-4750 (office). *E-mail:* jeremy.treglown@warwick.ac.uk (office). *Website:* www2.warwick.ac.uk/fac/arts/english (office).

TREHEARNE, Elizabeth (see Maxwell, Patricia Anne)

TREISMAN, Deborah; British editor; *Fiction Editor, The New Yorker;* b. Oxford; m. Kenny Cummings; two d. *Education:* Univ. of California, Berkeley. *Career:* fmr ed. at The Threepenny Review; intern, Harper's Bazaar magazine; Ed. Grand Street (quarterly literary magazine); Deputy Fiction Ed., The New Yorker 1997–2002, Fiction Ed. 2003–; mem. Faculty, The Writers Inst., CUNY. *Publication:* 20 Under 40 2010. *Address:* The Mail, The New Yorker, 4 Times Square, New York, NY 10036, USA (office). *E-mail:* fiction@newyorker.com (office). *Website:* www.newyorker.com (office).

TRELFORD, Donald Gilchrist, MA, FRSA; British journalist; b. 9 Nov. 1937, Coventry; s. of T. S. Trelford and Doris Gilchrist; m. 1st Janice Ingram 1963 (divorced 1978); two s. one d.; m. 2nd Katherine Louise Mark 1978 (divorced 1998); one d.; m. 3rd Claire Elizabeth Bishop 2001. *Education:* Bablake School, Coventry, Selwyn Coll., Cambridge. *Career:* pilot officer, RAF 1956–58; worked on newspapers in Coventry and Sheffield 1961–63; Ed. Times of Malawi and corresp. in Africa, The Times, Observer, BBC 1963–66; joined Observer as Deputy News Ed. 1966, Asst Man. Ed. 1968, Deputy Ed. 1969–75, Dir and Ed. 1975–93, CEO 1992–93; Dir Optomen Television 1988–97, Observer Films 1989–93, Cen. Observer TV 1990–93; Dir, Prof., Dept of Journalism Studies, Univ. of Sheffield 1994–2000, Visiting Prof. 2001–, Prof. Emer. 2007–; Chair. Soc. of Gentlemen, Lovers of Musick 1996–2002, London Press Club 2002–07 (Pres. 2007–); mem. British Exec. Cttee, Int. Press Inst. 1976–, Asscn of British Eds 1984–, Guild of British Newspaper Eds 1985– (mem. Parl. and Legal Cttee 1987–91); Vice Pres. British Sports Trust 1988–2002; Ind. Assessor BBC TV Regional News 1997; mem. Council, Media Soc. 1981–2003 (Pres. 1999–2002), Judging Panel, British Press Awards 1981– (Chair. 2003–05), Scottish Press Awards 1985, Olivier Awards Cttee, SWET 1984–93, Defence, Press and Broadcasting Cttee 1986–93, Cttee, MCC 1988–91, Competition Comm.'s Newspaper Panel 1999–, Council Advertising Standards Authority 2002–; Vice-Pres. Newspaper Press Fund 1992– (Chair. Appeals Cttee 1991), Acting Ed. The Oldie 1994; Judge, Whitbread Literary Awards 1992, George Orwell Prize 1998; sports columnist Daily Telegraph 1993–; Dir St Cecilia Int. Festival of Music 1995–2002. *Radio:* presenter, LBC Breakfast News 1994; regular panellist, BBC Radio Five Live. *Television:* presenter sports and current affairs series, Channel 4 and BBC 2. *Publications:* Siege 1980, Snookered 1986, Child of Change (with Garry Kasparov) 1987, Saturday's Boys 1990, Fine Glances 1990; (contrib.) County Champions 1982, The Queen Observed 1986, Len Hutton Remembered 1992, World Chess Championships (with Daniel King) 1993, W. G. Grace 1998; Ed.: Sunday Best 1981, 1982, 1983, The Observer at 200 1992; contrib. to Animal Passions 1994. *Honours:* Freeman City of London 1988; Hon. DLitt (Sheffield); Granada Newspaper of the Year Award 1983, 1993; commended, Int. Ed. of the Year (World Press Review) 1984. *Address:* Flat 3, 6 River Terrace, Henley-on-Thames, RG9 1BG, England (home).

Telephone: (7850) 131742 (mobile) (home). *E-mail:* donaldtrelford@yahoo.co.uk (home).

TREMAIN, Rose, CBE, BA, FRSL; British writer; b. (Rosemary Jane Thomson), 2 Aug. 1943, London; d. of the late Keith Thomson and Viola Mabel Thomson; m. 1st Jon Tremain 1971; one d.; m. 2nd Jonathan Dudley 1982 (dissolved 1990); pnr Richard Holmes. *Education:* Sorbonne, Paris and Univ. of East Anglia. *Career:* novelist and playwright 1971–; part-time tutor Univ. of East Anglia 1988–95; mem. judging panel, Booker Prize 1988, 2000. *Plays for radio include:* Temporary Shelter 1985, Who Was Emily Davison? 1996, The End of Love 1999, One Night in Winter 2001. *Television:* A Room for the Winter 1979, Daylight Robbery 1982. *Publications:* fiction: Sadler's Birthday 1976, Letter to Sister Benedicta 1978, The Cupboard 1981, The Swimming Pool Season 1984, Restoration (Sunday Express Book of the Year Award) 1989, Sacred Country (James Tait Black Memorial Prize 1993, Prix Fémina Etranger 1994) 1992, The Way I Found Her 1997, Music and Silence (Whitbread Novel of the Year) 1999, The Colour 2003, The Road Home (Orange Broadband Prize for Fiction 2008) 2007, Trespass 2010; for children: Journey to the Volcano 1985; short story collections: The Colonel's Daughter (Dylan Thomas Short Story Prize 1984) 1982, The Garden of the Villa Mollini 1988, Evangelista's Fan 1994, Collected Short Stories 1996, The Darkness of Wallis Simpson and Other Stories 2005; non-fiction: The Fight for Freedom for Women 1971, Stalin: An Illustrated Biography 1974. *Honours:* Hon. DLitt (East Anglia) 2001, (Essex) 2005, (Open Univ.) 2010; Univ. of Essex Fellowship 1979–80; one of Granta's Best Young British Novelists 1983, Giles Cooper Award 1985, Angel Literary Award 1986, Sony Award 1996. *Address:* 2 High House, South Avenue, Thorpe St Andrew, Norwich, NR7 0EZ, England (home). *Telephone:* (1603) 439682 (home). *Fax:* (1603) 434234 (home).

TREMAYNE, Peter (see Ellis, Peter Berresford)

TREMBLAY, Gail Elizabeth, BA, MFA; American poet, artist and teacher; b. 15 Dec. 1945, Buffalo, NY. *Education:* Univ. of New Hampshire, Univ. of Oregon. *Career:* Lecturer, Keene State Coll., NH; Asst Prof., Univ. of Nebraska; currently faculty mem., Evergreen State Coll., Olympia, Washington; mem. Indian Youth of America, International Asscn of Art, UNESCO (US National Committee board mem.), Native American Writers Circle of the Americas, Woman's Caucus for Art, board mem., pres. *Works in collections:* The Portland Art Museum, Nat. Museum of the American Indian, Missoula Art Museum, Wallie Ford Museum, Dept of the Interior, Microsoft Collection. *Publications:* Night Gives Woman the Word 1979, Talking to the Grandfathers 1980, Indian Singing in 20th Century America 1990; contributions: reviews, quarterlies and journals. *Honours:* Alfred E. Richards Poetry Prize 1967, Pres.'s Award for Achievement in the Arts, Women's Caucus for Art 1993, Washington State Gov.'s Art Award 2001. *Address:* Evergreen State College, 2700 Evergreen Parkway NW, Olympia, WA 98505, USA (office). *Telephone:* (360) 867-6334 (office). *E-mail:* tremblay@evergreen.edu (office). *Website:* www.evergreen.edu (office).

TREMBLAY, Michel; Canadian writer; b. 25 June 1942, Montréal. *Education:* Graphic Arts Inst. of Québec. *Career:* worked as linotypist 1963–66. *Film scripts include:* Françoise Durocher, Waitress 1972, Il était une fois dans l'Est 1973, Parlez-nous d'amour 1976, Le Soleil se lève en retard 1977. *Plays include:* Les Belles sœurs 1968, En pièces detachées 1969, La Duchesse de Langeais 1969, Les Paons 1971, Hosanna 1973, Bonjour Là, bonjour 1974, Ste Carmen de la Main 1976, Damnée Manon, Sacrée Sandra 1977, L'Impromptu d'outremont 1980, Les Grandes vacances 1981, Les Anciennes odeurs 1981, Albertine en cinq temps 1984, Le Vrai monde? 1987, La Maison suspendue 1990, Nelligan (opera libretto, Opéra de Montréal) 1990, Marcel poursuivi par les chiens 1992, Messe solennelle pour une pleine lune d'été 1996, Encore une fois, si vous permettez 1998, L'État des lieux 2002, Le Passé antérieur 2003. *Radio plays include:* Le Cœur découvert 1986, Le Grand Jour 1988, Six Heures au plus tard 1988. *Television:* Le Cœur découvert 2000. *Publications:* Contes pour buveurs attardés 1966, La Cité dans l'oeuf 1969, C't'à ton tour, Laura Cadieux 1973, La Grosse femme d'à côté est enceinte 1973, Thérèse et Pierrette à l'école des Saints-Anges 1980, La Duchesse et le roturier 1982, Des Nouvelles d'Edouard 1984, Le Cœur découvert 1986, Le Premier quartier de la lune 1989, Les Vues animées 1991, Douze coups de théâtre 1992, Le Cœur éclaté 1995, Un Ange cornu avec des ailes de tôle 1996, L'Homme qui entendait siffler une bouilloire 2001, Bonbons assortis 2002, Le Cahier noir 2003, Le Cahier rouge 2004, Le Cahier Bleu 2005, Le Trou dans le mur 2006, La Traversée du continent 2007, La Traversée de la Ville 2008. *Honours:* Dr hc (Concordia, McGill, Stirling, Windsor); first prize for young writers sponsored by CBC (for play Le Train, written 1959) 1964, Gov.-Gen.'s Performing Arts Award 1999; Officier, Ordre des Arts et des Lettres, France. *Literary Agent:* Agence Goodwin, 839 rue Sherbrooke est, Suite 200, Montréal, QC H2L 1K6, Canada. *Telephone:* (514) 598-5252 (office). *Fax:* (514) 598-1878 (office). *E-mail:* artistes@goodwin.agent.ca (office). *Website:* www.agencegoodwin.com (office).

TREMLETT, George William, OBE; British author, journalist and bookseller; b. 5 Sept. 1939, England; m. Jane Mitchell 1971; three s. *Career:* mem. BBC Community Programme Unit, advisory panel 1985–. *Publications:* 17 biographies of rock musicians 1974–77, Living Cities 1979, Caitlin (with Mrs Caitlin Thomas) 1986, Clubmen 1987, Homeless, Story of St Mungo's 1989, Little Legs (with Roy Smith) 1989, Rock Gold 1990, Dylan Thomas: Book: In the Mercy of His Means 1991, Gadaffi: The Desert Mystic 1993, David Bowie 1994, The Death of Dylan Thomas (with James R. B. Nashold) 1997;

screenplay: The Map of Love 1998. *Literary Agent:* A.M. Heath and Co., 6 Warwick Court, London WC1R 5DJ, England. *Telephone:* (20) 7242-2811. *Fax:* (20) 7242-2711. *Website:* www.amheath.com.

TRENHAILE, John Stevens, BA, MA; British writer; b. 29 April 1949, Hertford, England. *Education:* Magdalen Coll., Oxford. *Career:* Ed. Taipei Review, Taiwan 1995–2001. *Publications:* Kyril 1981, A View from the Square 1983, Nocturne for the General 1985, The Mahjong Spies 1986, The Gates of Exquisite View 1987, The Scroll of Benevolence 1988, Kyrsalis 1989, Acts of Betrayal 1990, Blood Rules 1991, The Tiger of Desire 1992, A Means to Evil 1993, Against All Reason 1994. *Literary Agent:* Blake Friedmann Literary Agents, 122 Arlington Road, London, NW1 7HP, England.

TRETHEWEY, Natasha, AB, MA, MFA; American poet and academic; *Poet Laureate*; b. 26 April 1966, Gulfport, Miss.; d. of Eric Trethewey and the late Gwendolyn Ann Turnbough; m. Brett Gadsden. *Education:* Univ. of Georgia, Hollins Univ., Univ. of Massachusetts, Amherst. *Career:* Lehman Brady Jt Chair Prof. of Documentary and American Studies, Duke Univ. and Univ. of North Carolina 2005–06; currently Charles Howard Candler Prof. of English and Creative Writing, Emory Univ.; Louis D. Rubin Writer-in-Residence, Hollins Univ. 2012; Poet Laureate of Miss. 2012; US Poet Laureate 2012–; James Weldon Johnson Fellow in African American Studies, Beinecke Library, Yale Univ. 2009. *Publications:* Domestic Work (Cave Canem Foundation Poetry Prize 1999) 2000, Bellocq's Ophelia 2002, Native Guard (Pulitzer Prize for Poetry 2007) 2006, Beyond Katrina: A Meditation on the Mississippi Gulf Coast 2010, Thrall 2012. *Honours:* Dr hc (Delta State Univ.) 2007, (Hollins Univ.) 2010; Nat. Endowment for the Arts Literature Fellowship 1999, Bunting Fellowship for Radcliffe Inst. for Advanced Study, Harvard Univ. 2000, Lillian Smith Book Award 2001, 2007, Miss. Inst. of Arts and Letters Book Prizes 2001, 2003, 2007, John Simon Guggenheim Memorial Foundation Fellowship 2003, Rockefeller Foundation Fellowship 2004. *Literary Agent:* c/o Alison Granucci, Blue Flower Arts, PO Box 1361, Millbrook, NY 12545, USA. *Telephone:* (845) 677-8559. *Fax:* (845) 677-6446. *E-mail:* Alison@blueflowerarts.com. *Website:* www.blueflowerarts.com. *Address:* Creative Writing Program, N209 Callaway Center, Emory University, 537 Kilgo Circle, Atlanta, GA 30322, USA (office). *Telephone:* (404) 727-4683 (office). *Fax:* (404) 727-4672 (office). *E-mail:* creativewriting@emory.edu (office). *Website:* www.creativewriting.emory.edu/faculty/trethewey.html (office); www.loc.gov/poetry.

TRETYAKOV, Vitaly Toviyevich; Russian journalist; b. 2 Jan. 1953, Moscow; m.; one s. *Education:* Moscow State Univ. *Career:* jr ed. to Ed. Press Agency Novosti (APN) 1976–88; reviewer, political reviewer, Deputy Ed.-in-Chief Moskovskiye Novosti (weekly) 1988–90; f. Nesavisimaya Gazeta (newspaper) 1990, Ed.-in-Chief 1990–2000; Dir-Gen. Indpendent Publishing Group 2001–04; Ed.-in-Chief, Moskovskiye Novosti 2004–07; currently Ed.-in-Chief, Politicheskii Klass; mem. Exec. Bd Council on Foreign and Defence Policy. *Publications include:* Philanthropy in Soviet Society 1989, Gorbachev, Ligachev, Yeltsin: Political Portraits on the Perestroika Background 1990, Titus of Sovietologists: Their Struggle for Power: Essays on Idiotism of Russian Policy 1996; numerous articles on political problems. *Address:* Politicheskii Klass, 119002 Moscow, per. Sivtsev Vrazhek 29/16/415, Russia (office). *Telephone:* (495) 241-43-67 (office). *E-mail:* info@politklass.ru (office). *Website:* politklass.ru (office).

TREVELYAN, (Walter) Raleigh, FRSL; British writer; b. 6 July 1923, Port Blair, Andaman Islands; s. of Col W. R. F. Trevelyan and Olive Trevelyan (née Frost). *Education:* Winchester School. *Career:* publisher 1948–88; mem. Anglo-Italian Soc. for the Protection of Animals (pres.), PEN (vice-pres.). *Publications:* The Fortress 1956, A Hermit Disclosed 1960, Italian Short Stories: Penguin Parallel Texts (ed.) 1965, The Big Tomato 1966, Princes Under the Volcano 1972, The Shadow of Vesuvius 1976, A Pre-Raphaelite Circle 1978, Rome '44 1982, Shades of the Alhambra 1984, The Golden Oriole 1987, La Storia dei Whitaker 1989, Grand Dukes and Diamonds: The Wernhers of Luton Hoo 1991, A Clear Premonition 1995, The Companion Guide to Sicily 1996, Sir Walter Raleigh 2002; contributions: newspapers and journals. *Honours:* John Florio Prize for Trans. 1967. *Literary Agent:* A. M. Heath & Co Ltd, 6 Warwick Court, London WC1R 4DJ, England. *Telephone:* (20) 7242-2811. *Fax:* (20) 7242-2711. *Website:* www.amheath.com. *Address:* 18 Hertford Street, London, W1J 7RT (home); St Cadix, St Veep, Lostwithiel, Cornwall, PL22 0PB, England (home). *Telephone:* (20) 7629-5879 (home). *Fax:* (20) 7629-5879 (home).

TREVOR, William, CLit, BA; Irish writer; b. 24 May 1928, Mitchelstown, Co. Cork; s. of James William Cox and Gertrude Cox; m. Jane Ryan 1952; two s. *Education:* St Columba's Coll., Dublin, Trinity Coll., Dublin. *Career:* mem. Irish Acad. of Letters. *Publications:* The Old Boys 1964, The Boarding House 1965, The Love Department 1966, The Day We Got Drunk on Cake 1967, Mrs Eckdorf in O'Neill's Hotel 1968, Miss Gomez and the Brethren 1969, The Ballroom of Romance 1970, Elizabeth Alone 1972, Angels at the Ritz 1973, The Children of Dynmouth 1977, Lovers of Their Time 1979, Other People's Worlds 1980, Beyond the Pale 1981, Fools of Fortune 1983, A Writer's Ireland: Landscape in Literature 1984, The News from Ireland 1986, Nights at the Alexandra 1987, The Silence in the Garden 1988, Family Sins and Other Stories 1989, The Oxford Book of Irish Short Stories (ed.) 1989, Two Lives 1991, William Trevor: The Collected Stories 1992, Juliet's Story 1992, Excursions in the Real World (essays) 1993, Felicia's Journey 1994, Ireland: Selected Stories 1995, After Rain 1996, Cocktails at Doney's and Other Stories 1996, Death in Summer 1998, The Hill Bachelors 2000, The Story of Lucy Gault 2002, A Bit on the Side (short stories) 2004, Cheating at Canasta 2007, Love and Summer 2009, The Collected Stories 2009, Beyond the Pale and Other Stories 2010, Selected Stories 2011. *Honours:* Hon. KBE 2002; Hon. DLitt (Exeter) 1984, (Dublin) 1986, (Queen's Univ., Belfast) 1989, (Nat. Univ., Cork) 1990; Hawthornden Prize 1965, Royal Soc. of Literature Prize 1978, Whitbread Prize for Fiction 1978, Allied Irish Banks Award for Services to Literature 1978, Whitbread Prize for Fiction 1983, Whitbread Book of the Year 1994, Sunday Express Book of the Year Award 1994, David Cohen British Literature Prize 1999, PEN Prize for Short Stories 2001, Irish Times Prize for Irish Fiction 2001, Listowel Prize 2002, Int. Nonino Prize 2008. *Literary Agent:* PFD, Drury House, 34–43 Russell Street, London, WC2B 5HA, England. *Telephone:* (20) 7344-1000. *Fax:* (20) 7836-9543. *E-mail:* info@pfd.co.uk. *Website:* www.pfd.co.uk.

TREWIN, Ion Courtenay Gill; British journalist and publisher; *Literary Director, Man Booker Prizes*; b. 13 July 1943, London, England; s. of John Courtenay Trewin OBE and Wendy Elizabeth Trewin (née Monk); m. Susan Harriet Merry 1965; one s. one d. *Education:* Highgate School, London. *Career:* Literary Ed., The Times 1972–79; Sr Ed., then Editorial Dir, Hodder & Stoughton 1979–92; Publishing Dir, Man. Dir, then Ed.-in-Chief, Weidenfeld & Nicolson 1992–2006; London Ed., Publisher Weekly (USA); Ed. Drama Magazine 1990–92; Chair. Booker Prize judging panel 1974, mem. Advisory Cttee 1989; Chair. Cheltenham Booker Prize, Cheltenham Literature Festival 1996–2007; Deputy Admin. Man Booker Prizes 2004–06, Admin. 2006–08, Literary Dir 2008–; Special Prof. of Politics and Int. Relations, Univ. of Nottingham 2006–; Pres. Nat. Acad. of Writing 2009–. *Publications:* Journalism 1975, Norfolk Cottage 1977, Diaries: Into Politics, by Alan Clark (ed.) 2000, The Last Diaries: In and Out of the Wilderness, by Alan Clark (ed.) 2002, The Hugo Young Papers: Thirty Years of British Politics (Channel 4 Political Book of the Year) (ed.) 2008, Alan Clark: The Biography 2009. *Honours:* Ronald Politzer Award for Publishing Innovation 1975. *Literary Agent:* Man Booker Prizes, c/o Colman Getty, 28 Windmill Street, London W1T 2JJ, England. *Telephone:* (20) 7631-2666. *Address:* Flat 44, Cholmeley Lodge, Cholmeley Park, London, N6 5EN, England. *Telephone:* 7712-611922 (mobile). *E-mail:* itrewin@aol.com. *Website:* www.themanbookerprize.com; www.iontrewin.com.

TRIGELL, Jonathan, MA; British writer; b. 1974. *Education:* Manchester Univ. *Career:* lives in Chamonix, France; works in winter sports industry, as journalist and event organizer. *Publications:* Boy A (John Llewellyn Rhys Prize, Waverton Award, World Book Day Prize) 2004, Cham 2007, Genus 2011. *Address:* c/o Constable and Robinson Ltd, 55-56 Russell Square, London, WC1B 4HP, England (office).

TRILLARD, Marc; French journalist and writer; b. 1955, Baden-Baden, Germany. *Education:* Conservatoire régional d'art dramatique, Toulouse. *Career:* freelance journaliste 1987–94; writer for radio, TV and stage; founder and Dir Salon des littératures francophones, Balma; Dir Alliance Française de Buea, Cameroon 2006–09. *Publications:* Un exil 1988, Tête de cheval 1992, Cabotage: à l'écoute du chant des îles Cap-Vert 1994, Eldorado 51 (Prix Interallié) 1994, Coup de lame (Prix Louis Guilloux) 1997, Avène: au coeur du haut pays d'Oc (with Alain Aigoin) 1997, Journal cochinchinois: de Saïgon à Camau 1997, Madagascar 1999, Cuba, en attendant l'année prochaine 1999, Si j'avais quatre dromadaires 2000, Campagne dernière 2001, Entre Fosses et Cages 2001, Le Maître et la mort 2003, De Sabres et de Feu 2006, Rencontre avec un géant, récit de voyage 2006. *E-mail:* marc.trillard@yahoo.fr (office). *Website:* marctrillard.com.

TRILLIN, Calvin Marshall, BA; American journalist and writer; b. 5 Dec. 1935, Kansas City, Mo.; s. of Abe Trillin and Edyth Trillin; m. Alice Stewart 1965; two d. *Education:* Yale Univ. *Career:* served in US army; reporter, later writer, Time magazine 1960–63; staff writer, The New Yorker 1963–, including US Journal series 1967–82, American Chronicles series 1984–; columnist, The Nation 1978–85, now contributing weekly comic verse; syndicated columnist with King Features Syndicate 1986–, including Uncivil Liberties series. *Theatre includes:* Calvin Trillin's Uncle Sam (American Place Theatre, New York) 1988, Calvin Trillin's Words, No Music (American Place Theatre, New York) 1990. *Publications:* An Education in Georgia: Charlayne Hunter, Hamilton Holmes and the Integration of the University of Georgia 1964, Barnett Frummer is an Unbloomed Flower and Other Adventures of Barnett Frummer, Rosalie Mondle, Roland Magruder and Their Friends 1969, US Journal 1971, American Fried: Adventures of a Happy Eater 1974, Runestruck (novel) 1977, Alice, Let's Eat: Further Adventures of a Happy Eater 1978, Floater (novel) 1980, Uncivil Liberties (collected columns) 1982, Third Helpings 1983, Killings 1984, With All Disrespect: More Uncivil Liberties (collected columns) 1985, If You Can't Say Something Nice (collected columns) 1987, Travels with Alice 1989, Enough's Enough and Other Rules of Life (collected columns) 1990, American Stories (non-fiction) 1991, Remembering Denny 1993, Deadline Poet: My Life as a Doggerelist (poems from The Nation) 1994, Too Soon to Tell 1995, Messages from Father 1996, Family Man 1998, Tepper's Not Going Out (novel) 2002, Obliviously on he Sails: The Bush Administration in Rhyme 2004, About Alice 2007, Deciding the Next Decider: The 2008 Presidential Race in Rhyme 2008, Quite Enough of Calvin Trillin 2011. *Honours:* Dr hc (Beloit Coll.), (Albertus Magnus Coll.); Books-Across-the-Sea Amb. of Honor Citation, English-Speaking Union 1985. *Address:* c/New Yorker Magazine, 4 Times Square, New York, NY 10036, USA (office).

TRIPATHI, Amish; Indian author and fmr banker; b. 18 Oct. 1974, Mumbai; m. Preeti Vyas; one s. *Education:* Indian Inst. of Man., Kolkata. *Career:* Nat. Head, Marketing and Product Man., IDBI Federal Life Insurance –2011; cr. Shiva trilogy of novels 2010–. *Publications include:* Shiva Trilogy novels: The Immortals of Meluha 2010, The Secret of the Nagas 2011. *Address:* c/o Quercus Publishing, 55 Baker Street, 7th Floor, South Block, London, W1U 8EW, England (office). *Telephone:* (20) 7291-7200 (office). *E-mail:* enquiries@ quercusbooks.co.uk (office). *Website:* www.quercusbooks.co.uk (office); www .shivatrilogy.com.

TRIVERS, Robert L., BA, PhD; American evolutionary biologist and academic; *Professor of Anthropology and Biological Sciences, Rutgers University;* b. 19 Feb. 1943, Washington, DC; s. of Howard Trivers and Mildred Trivers; m. 1st Lorna Staples 1974 (divorced 1988); one s. three d.; m. 2nd Debra Dixon 1997 (divorced 2004); one s. *Education:* Phillips Acad., Andover and Harvard Univ. *Career:* Instructor in Anthropology, Harvard Univ. 1971–72, Asst Prof. of Biology 1973–75, Assoc. Prof. of Biology 1975–78, Visiting Prof. of Psychology 2005; Prof. of Biology, Univ. of California, Santa Cruz 1978–94; Prof. of Anthropology and Biological Sciences, Rutgers Univ. 1994–; Fellow, Inst. of Advanced Studies, Berlin 2008–09. *Publications:* Social Evolution 1985, Natural Selection and Social Theory: Selected Papers of Robert Trivers 2002, Genes in Conflict: The Biology of Selfish Genetic Elements (with Austin Burt) 2006; numerous papers in academic journals. *Honours:* Crafoord Prize, Royal Swedish Acad. of Sciences 2007. *Address:* Department of Anthropology, Rutgers University, 131 George Street, New Brunswick, NJ 08901-1414, USA (office). *Telephone:* (732) 979-8434 (office). *E-mail:* trivers@rci.rutgers.edu (office). *Website:* anthro.rutgers.edu/faculty/ trivers.shtml (office).

TROGDON, William Lewis (see Heat-Moon, William Least)

TROJANOW, Ilija; Bulgarian/German writer, publisher and translator; b. 23 Aug. 1965, Sofia. *Education:* Univ. of Munich. *Career:* left Bulgaria with family to seek exile in Germany 1971; lived in Nairobi, Kenya 1973–77, 1981–84, also lived in Paris, Mumbai, Vienna, Munich and Cape Town; f. Kyrill-und-Method-Verlag 1989 and Marino-Verlag 1992, publishing cos specializing in African literature; corresp. for Allgemeine Zeitung, Süddeutsche Zeitung and Neue Zürcher Zeitung while based in Mumbai; Lecturer in Poetry, Tübingen Univ. 2007–08; mem. PEN Germany 2002–; Guest Prof., Leipzig Univ. 2008–09; Lecturer in German Literature, Washington Univ., St Louis, Mo., USA 2012; jury mem. Lettre Ulysses Award for Reportage 2006–07. *Publications:* In Afrika (with Michael Martin) 1993, Hüter der Sonne (with Chenjerai Hove) (trans. as Guardians of the Soil) 1996, Die Welt ist groß und Rettung lauert überall 1996, Autopol 1997, Hundezeiten 1999, Der Sadhu an der Teufelswand 2001, An den inneren Ufern Indiens (trans. as Along the Ganges) 2003, Zu den heiligen Quellen des Islam 2004 (trans. as From Mumbai to Mecca), Der Weltensammler (trans. as The Collector of Worlds) (Leipzig Book Fair Prize) 2006, Gebrauchsanweisung für Indien (Int. Tourist Exchange Book Award 2007) 2006, Kampfabsage (with Ranjit Hoskoté) 2007 (trans. as Confluences), Der entfesselte Globus 2008, Angrif auf die Freiheit (with Juli Zeh) 2009, EisTau 2011. *Honours:* Bertelsmann Literature Prize 1995, Marburg Literature Prize 1996, Thomas Valentin Prize 1997, Adelbert von Chamisso Prize 2000, Berliner Literature Prize 2007, Mainzer Stadtschreiber Prize 2007, Würth Prize for European Literature 2011, Carl-Amery Award 2011. *Address:* c/o Carl Hanser Verlag GmbH & Co. KG, Postfach 86 04 20, 81631 Munich, Germany. *E-mail:* info@hanser.de. *Website:* www.hanser.de.

TROLLOPE, Joanna, (Caroline Harvey), OBE, MA, DL; British writer; b. 9 Dec. 1943, England; d. of Arthur Trollope and Rosemary Hodson; m. 1st David Potter 1966; two d.; m. 2nd Ian Curteis 1985 (divorced 2001); two step-s. *Education:* Reigate Co. School and St Hugh's Coll., Oxford. *Career:* Information and Research Dept Foreign Office 1965–67; various teaching posts, including Farnham Girl's Grammar School, Daneshill School 1967–79; Chair. Betty Trasker Prize for Soc. of Authors 1993, Advisory Cttee on Nat. Reading Initiative, Dept of Nat. Heritage 1996–97; mem. Advisory Cttee on Nat. Year of Reading, Dept of Educ. 1998, Council of Soc. of Authors 1997–, Campaign Bd St Hugh's Coll. Oxford, Council of West Country Writer's Asscn; Vice-Pres. Trollope Soc.; Judge, Costa Book Awards 2002, Chair. Advisory Bd 2007; mem. International PEN, Romantic Novelists' Asscn; Trustee, Joanna Trollope Charitable Trust 1995–; Patron County of Glos. Community Foundation 1994–2004, March Foundation, Mulberry Bush, For Dementia; Chair. Nat. Portrait Gallery Fund Raising Gala 2009; DL for Co. of Glos. 2002–08; Judge, The Melissa Nathan Awards 2005–11, The Sunday Times EFG Private Bank Short Story Award 2011–12; Chair. the Orange Prize 2012. *Publications:* as Caroline Harvey: Eliza Stanhope 1978, Parson Harding's Daughter (aka Mistaken Virtues) (Historical Novel of the Year Award, Romantic Novelists' Asscn 1979, Elizabeth Goudge Historical Award 1980) 1979, Leaves from the Valley 1980, The City of Gems 1981, The Steps of the Sun 1983, The Taverners' Place 1986, Legacy of Love 1992, A Second Legacy 1993, A Castle in Italy 1993, The Brass Dolphin 1997; as Joanna Trollope: Britannia's Daughters: A Study of Women in the British Empire 1983, The Choir 1988, A Village Affair 1989, A Passionate Man 1990, The Rector's Wife 1991, The Men and the Girls 1992, A Spanish Lover 1992, The Best of Friends 1992, The Country Habit: An Anthology (ed.) 1993, Next of Kin 1996, Faith 1996, Other People's Children 1998, Marrying the Mistress 2000, Girl from the South 2002, Brother and Sister 2004, Second Honeymoon 2006, The Book Boy 2006, Britannia's Daughters 2007, Friday Nights 2008, The Other Family 2010, Daughters in Law 2011; contribs to newspapers and magazines. *Honours:* Lifetime Achievement Award, Romantic Novelists' Asscn 2010. *Literary Agent:* c/o United Agents, 12–26 Lexington Street, London, W1F 0LE, England. *Telephone:* (20) 3214-0800. *Fax:* (20) 3214-0801. *E-mail:* info@ unitedagents.co.uk. *Website:* unitedagents.co.uk. *E-mail:* joanna@ joannatrollope.com (office). *Website:* www.joannatrollope.com.

TROUILLOT, Lyonel; Haitian author, poet and journalist; *President, Fondation Anne-Marie Morisset;* b. 31 Dec. 1956, Port-au-Prince. *Career:* Prof. of Literature, Ecole normale supérieure; Co-founder, Ed. and contrib. to journals, including Lakansyèl, Vivre en Haïti, Tèm, Langaj, Cahiers du Vendredi; Sec.-Gen. Asscn des écrivains haïtiens; Dir of the Cabinet under Sec. of State for Culture 2004–; Pres. Fondation Anne-Marie Morisset. *Publications:* novels: Depale (with Pierre Richard Narcisse) 1979, Zanj nan dlo 1995, Les fous de Saint-Antoine 1989, Le Livre de Marie 1993, Les dits du fou de l'île (novella) 1997, La Rue des pas perdus 1998, Thérèse en mille morceaux 2000, Les Enfants des héros 2002, Le Testament du mal de mer (short story in L'Odysée atlantique) 2002, Fait divers sur écran noir (short story in Paradis Brisé, nouvelles des Caraïbes) 2004, Bicentenaire 2004, L'Amour avant que j'oublie 2007; poetry: 'menm zwazo a mouri levi...' (poem in Conjonction 195, 54-5) July–Sept. 1992, La petite fille au regard d'île 1994. *Honours:* Chevalier des Arts et des Lettres; Prix Gouverneur de la Rosée du Livre et de la Littérature 2002, Prix TSR du roman 2005, Prix Louis Guilloux 2005, Prix des Amériques insulaires de la Guyane 2006, Prix Wepler 2009. *Address:* c/o Actes Sud, BP 90038, 13633 Arles, France (office). *Telephone:* 35-824950 (mobile, Haiti) (office). *E-mail:* contact@actes-sud.fr (office); lioneltrouillot@hotmail .com (office). *Website:* www.actes-sud.fr (office).

TROUPE, Quincy Thomas, Jr, AA, BA; American poet, writer and academic; b. 23 July 1943, New York, NY; m. Margaret Porter; four c. *Education:* Grambling Coll., Los Angeles City Coll. *Career:* instructor at various colls and univs; Instructor, UCLA 1967–68; Instructor, Ohio Univ. 1969–72; Visiting Prof., Lagos Univ., Nigeria 1971, University of Ghana 1971; Lecturer, Richmond Coll., Staten Island, New York 1971–76, Prof. 1989–94; Lecturer, Coll. of Staten Island 1976–79, Asst Prof. 1979–84, Assoc. Prof. 1984–89; Visiting Prof., California State Coll. 1978; Adjunct Prof., Graduate Division of Writing, Columbia Univ. 1985; Prof. Caribbean and American Literatures and Creative Writing, Univ. of California, San Diego 1991–2003; Poet Laureate of Calif. 2002 (resgnd); Ed. Black Renaissance Noire (journal) 2003–; Founding Editorial Dir Code Magazine 1999–2000; Ed.-at-Large The Green Magazine; mem. Poetry Society of America. *Publications:* Watts Poets: A Book of New Poetry and Essays (ed.) 1968, Embryo Poems 1967–1971 1972, Giant Talk: An Anthology of Third World Writings (ed. with Rainer Schulte) 1975, The Inside Story of TV's 'Roots' (ed. with David L. Wolper) 1978, Snake-back Solos: Selected Poems 1969–1977 1978, Skulls Along the River (poems) 1984, Soundings 1988, James Baldwin: The Legacy (ed.) 1989, Miles: The Autobiography (with Miles Davis) 1989, Weather Reports: New and Selected Poems 1991, Avalanche: Poems (Paterson Award for Sustained Literary Achievement 2007) 1996, Choruses: Poems 1999, Miles and Me 2000, Transcircularities; New and Selected Poems (Milt Kessler Award for Poetry 2003) 2002, The Architecture of Language 2006. *Honours:* National Endowment for the Arts Award in Poetry, 1978; American Book Awards, 1980, 1990; New York Foundation for the Arts Fellowship in Poetry, 1987, Stephen Henderson Poetry Award for Outstanding Achievement, African American Literature and Culture Society 2000, Odin Award, San Diego Writers/Editors Guild 2002, Distinguished Artist Award, Frederick Douglass Creative Arts Center 2002, American Book Award, Lifetime Achievement Award 2010. *Address:* c/o Margaret Porter Troupe Arts Projects, 1925 Seventh Avenue 7L, New York, NY 10026, USA. *E-mail:* mptroupe@yahoo.com. *Website:* www .quincytroupe.com.

TROWBRIDGE, William, BA, MA, PhD; American poet, editor and academic; *Lecturer, University of Nebraska;* b. 9 May 1941, Chicago, Ill.; m. Waneta Sue Downing 1963; two s. one d. *Education:* Univ. of Missouri at Columbia, Vanderbilt Univ. *Career:* instructor, Univ. of Missouri at Columbia 1966, Vanderbilt Univ. 1968–70; Asst Prof. to Distinguished Univ. Prof., Northwest Missouri State Univ. 1971–98, Distinguished Univ. Prof. Emer. 1998–; Co-Ed. The Laurel Review 1986–99, Assoc. Ed. 2001; Asst Ed. The Georgia Review 2000; Lecturer, Univ. of Missouri at Kansas City 2005; Lecturer, Low-Residency MFA Program, Univ. of Nebraska 2005–. *Publications:* The Book of Kong 1986, Enter Dark Stranger 1989, O Paradise 1995, Flickers 2000, The Four Seasons 2002, The Complete Book of Kong 2003, The Packing House Cantata 2006, Ship of Fool 2010; contrib. to Poetry, Georgia Review, Kenyon Review, Southern Review, Gettysburg Review and many others. *Honours:* Acad. of American Poets Prize 1970, Bread Loaf Writers' Conf. Scholarship 1981, MacDowell Colony Fellowship 1992, Yaddo Fellowship 1992, Ragdale Fellowship 1993, 1995, Camber Press Chapbook Prize 2005. *Address:* 224 SW Green Teal Street, Lee's Summit, MO 64082-4507, USA (home). *Telephone:* (816) 623-9036 (home). *E-mail:* willtrow@comcast.net (home). *Website:* williamtrowbridge.net.

TRUMAN, Jill, BA; British teacher, writer and dramatist; b. 12 June 1934, Enfield, Middx; m. Tony Truman 1956 (died 1975); one s. three d. *Career:* mem. Writers' Guild of GB. *Radio plays:* Letter to My Husband 1986, Gone Out-Back Soon 1988, Travels in West Africa 1990, For Lizzie 1994, Sounds of Silence 1998; plays for BBC Radio 4. *Theatre:* The Web (play) 1991, Flit (puppet play) 1992, Kings of the Night (musical) 1993; fringe theatre. *Publications:* Letter to My Husband 1988, On The Terrace (short story) 1998,

Full Moon (short story) 1998, In the Supermarket (short story) 1998; also memoirs, contribs to magazines. *Address:* 2 Ellesmere Road, Bow, London, E3 5QX, England (home). *Telephone:* (20) 8983-6414 (office). *E-mail:* jilltruman@mypostoffice.co.uk (office).

TRUSS, Lynne, BA, FRSL; British writer; b. 31 May 1955, Kingston, Surrey. *Education:* Univ. Coll. London. *Career:* copy ed., Radio Times; Literary Ed., The Listener 1986–90; writer and teacher at Arvon Foundation; contributor and presenter, BBC Radio 4; book reviewer, The Sunday Times; columnist, The Times, Woman's Journal; sports writer, The Times; Fellowship, Univ. Coll. London 2004. *Plays:* for BBC Radio 4: Acropolis Now (two series) 2000–01, A Certain Age 2002, Full Circle 2003, Inspector Steine 2007, 2008. *Publications:* novels: With One Lousy Free Packet of Seed 1994, Tennyson's Gift 1996, Going Loco 1999; non-fiction: Making the Cat Laugh 1995, Eats, Shoots and Leaves: The Zero Tolerance Approach to Punctuation (British Book Award Book of the Year 2004) 2003, Talk to the Hand 2005, A Certain Age: Twelve Monologues from the Classic Radio Series 2007, The Girl's Like Spaghetti 2007, Get Her Off the Pitch 2009. *Honours:* Dr hc (Brighton) 2005, (Open Univ.) 2006, (New York School of Visual Arts) 2006. *Address:* c/o David Higham Associates, 8 Lower John Street, Golden Square, London, W1R 4HA, England (office). *E-mail:* info@lynnetruss.com (office). *Website:* www.lynnetruss.com.

TSALOUMAS, Dimitris, BA, DipEd; Australian poet, editor, translator and teacher; b. 13 Oct. 1921, Leros, Greece; two s. two d. *Education:* Univ. of Melbourne. *Career:* teacher, Victoria schools 1958–82; writer-in-residence, University of Oxford, University of Melbourne, Queensland University, La Trobe University. *Publications:* Resurrection 1967, Triptych for a Second Coming 1974, Observations for a Hypochondriac 1974, The House with the Eucalyptus 1975, The Sick Barber and Other Characters 1979, The Book of Epigrams 1981, The Observatory: Selected Poems 1983, Falcon Drinking: The English Poems 1988, Portrait of a Dog 1991, The Barge 1993, Six Improvisations On the River 1995, The Harbour 1998, Stoneland Harvest 1999, New and Selected Poems 2000, Observations of a Hypochondriac 2003, Helen of Troy 2007, Thirst 2010. *Honours:* Australia Council Grant and Fellowship, National Book Council Award 1983, Wesley M. Wright Prize for Poetry 1994, Patrick White Award 1994, John Bray Poetry Award, Adelaide Festival 2000, Australia Council Emeritus Award 2002. *Address:* 72 Glenhuntly Road, Elwood, Vic. 3184, Australia (home). *Telephone:* (3) 9531-6605 (home).

TSE, David K. S.; British playwright, actor and director; b. 17 Nov. 1964, Hong Kong; s. of Tse Shin Kay and Tse Lai Oi Lin. *Education:* read law, trained as actor Rose Bruford Coll., as dir Leicester Haymarket, studied Beijing Opera movement with Lee Siu Wah and Jamie Guan. *Career:* Artistic Dir Yellow Earth touring theatre co. 1995–2009. *Plays as director:* for Yellow Earth: The Nightingale, Chinese Two-Step, Maritime Mysteries, 58, Lear's Daughters, Friends, The Butcher's Skin, Legend of Old Bawdy Town, Rashomon, Play to Win (Sainsbury's Checkout Award, with Soho Theatre), Behind the Takeaway, New Territories (Time Out Critics' Choice), Tibetan Inroads; at Leicester Haymarket: Dance and the Railroad, House of Sleeping Beauties, Pandavas in Leicester, The Pilgrims; other: Ballad of Mulan (NYMT), Kensuke's Kingdom (Polka Theatre). *Plays as actor:* Cross-mopolitan (Chung Ying, Hong Kong), Rashomon (YET), Whisper of a Leaf Falling (YET), New Territories (YET), Blue Remembered Hills (David Glass), Playstars (Soho), Cellarworks (LIFT/theatre-rites), The Tempest (Royal Nat. Theatre), The Changeling (Mark Rylance), The Magic Paintbrush (Polka Theatre), Yoshi and Teakettle (Fringe Award, Polka Theatre), Yellow Gentlemen (Sirius Arts), Under a Street Light (Royal Court). *Plays written:* for Yellow Earth: Play to Win 1997, New Territories 2000, The Nightingale; for Polka Theatre: The Snow Lion, The Magic Paintbrush. *Radio plays:* as actor: A Fire in the West, Breaking Jewel, The Searide Came out of a Van, Little Emperors, Tiananmen Square, Stream of Dragons, Nightwaves (BBC Radio 3), The Verb (BBC Radio 3), Trevor's World of Sport (BBC Radio 4); as presenter: Beyond the Takeaway (BBC Radio 4). *Radio plays as writer:* The Old Woman and the Beggar (BBC Radio 3). *Television appearances:* The Grid 2004, Down to Earth, Holby City, Hearts & Bones, Thieftakers, Cracker, Minder. *Film appearances:* Spy Game 2001, Tomb Raider 2001, Hermit of Amsterdam, Foreign Moon, Annnie 2, Soursweet. *Publication:* The Magic Paintbrush 1997. *Honours:* Sainsbury's Checkout Theatre Award 2000, Windrush Arts Achievement Award 2004, Pearl Creative Arts Award 2004. *Address:* c/o Yellow Earth Theatre, 18 Rupert Street, London, W1D 4TG, England (office).

TSIOLKAS, Christos, BA; Australian writer, playwright, essayist and screenwriter; b. 25 Oct. 1965, Melbourne. *Education:* Univ. of Melbourne. *Career:* Ed., student newspaper Farrago 1988. *Plays include:* Who's Afraid of the Working Class (Australian Writers' Guild Prize) (co-writer) 1999, Elektra AD 1999, Viewing Blue Poles 2000, Fever (co-writer) 2002, Dead Caucasians 2002, Non Parlo di Salo (co-writer) 2005. *Film screenplays:* Thug (co-writer) 1998, Saturn's Return 2000. *Publications:* novels: Loaded 1995, The Jesus Man 1999, Dead Europe (The Age Fiction Prize 2006, Melbourne Best Writing Award 2006) 2005, The Slap (Australian Literature Soc. Gold Medal 2008, Commonwealth Writers' Prizes for SE Asia & S Pacific region and Overall Best Book 2009) 2008; other: Jump Cuts: An Autobiography (co-writer) 1996, My Devil's Playground (non-fiction) 2002; short stories; contrib. essays, articles and reviews to newspapers and magazines. *Literary Agent:* Curtis Brown Literary Agents, POB 19, Paddington, NSW 2021, Australia. *Telephone:* (2) 9361-6161. *Fax:* (2) 9360-3935. *E-mail:* info@curtisbrown.com.au. *Website:* www.curtisbrown.com.au. *Address:* c/o Allen & Unwin, 406 Albert Street, East Melbourne, Vic. 3002, Australia (office). *E-mail:* info@allenandunwin.com (office).

TSUJI, Hitonari, (Jinsei Tsuji); Japanese novelist, scriptwriter and musician; b. 4 Oct. 1959, Tokyo; m. Nakayama Miho. *Career:* fmr singer rock band, Echoes; solo artist 1993–. *Recordings include:* albums: with Echoes: Welcome to the Lost Child Club 1985, Heart Edge 1986, Goodbye Gentle Land 1987, Hurts 1988, Foolish Game 1988, The History of Echoes 1985–89 1989, Dear Friend 1989, Eggs 1990, Gold Water 1990, Silver Bullet 1991, No Kiddin' 1994; solo: The Best of Jinsei Songs 1993, New Wall 1996, Best Wishes 1997, Echoes 2000. *Film scripts:* Tenshi no wakemae 1994, Sennen tabito 1999, Hotoke 2001, Filament 2001, Calmi Cuori Appassionati 2001, Mokka no koibito 2002. *Publications include:* novels: Pianishimo (Pianissimo) (Subaru Literature Prize) 1989, Kuraudi (Cloudy) 1989, Tabibito no ki (The Tree of the Traveller) 1992, Haha naru nagi to chichi naru shike (Motherly Calm, Fatherly Storm) 1993, Passajio 1994, Kaikyô no hikari (Lights in the Channel) (Akutagawa Prize) 1996, Hakubutsu (The White Buddha) (Prix Fémina Étranger 1999) 1997, Ai no Kumeni (Objective) 1997, Reisei to jônetsu no aida (with Ekuni Kaori) 2001, Antinoise 2005, Tokyo décibels 2005. *Literary Agent:* Lora Fountain and Associates, 7 rue de Belfort, 75011 Paris, France. *Telephone:* 1-43-56-21-96. *Fax:* 1-43-48-22-72. *E-mail:* agence@fountlit.com. *Website:* www.j-tsuji-h.com.

TSURUMI, Shunsuke, BS; Japanese writer; b. 25 June 1922, Tokyo; s. of Yusuke Tsurumi and Aiko Tsurumi; m. Sadako Yokoyama 1960; one s. *Education:* Harvard Coll. *Career:* f. The Science of Thought (philosophical journal) 1946; Asst Prof., Univ. of Kyoto 1949, Tokyo Inst. of Tech. 1954; Prof., Doshisha Univ. 1960; freelance author 1970–; Visiting Prof., El Colegio de México 1972–73, McGill Univ. 1979–80. *Publications:* Collected Works (five vols) 1974, An Intellectual History of Wartime Japan 1986, A History of Mass Culture in Postwar Japan 1987, Collected Works (12 vols) 1992, Conversation (ten vols) 1996, Further Collected Works (five vols) 2000. *Honours:* Takano Chóei Prize 1976, Osaragi Jiro Prize 1982, Mystery Writers' Soc. Prize 1989, Asahi Prize 1994. *Address:* 230-99 Nagatanicho, Iwakura, Sakyōku, Kyoto, Japan (home).

TSUTSUI, Yasutaka, BA; Japanese novelist and actor; b. 24 Sept. 1934, Osaka. *Education:* Doshisha Univ. *Career:* writer of science fiction, renowned for experimental, post-modern approach to fiction; co-f. Null (science fiction magazine) 1960; early short stories published in SF Magazine and Hoseki; refrained from publication as a protest against literary conservatism 1993–97, returned with novellas in Shincho and Bungaku-kai literary journals 1997; helped establish JALInet literary website 1996; publishes work online; mem. Science Fiction Writers' Asscn of Japan (Exec. Sec. 1980–83, Pres. 1984–85), Japan PEN. *Film appearances:* Bungakusho satsujin jiken: Oinaru jyoso 1989, Kowagaru hitobito 1994, Otokotachi no kaita e 1996, Ki no ue no sogyo 1997, Sôseiji 1999, Hakuchi 1999, Shisha no gakuensai 2000, Stacy 2001, Eli, Eli, rema, sabachthani? 2005, Yokubô 2005. *Television:* Gensou Midnight (writer and actor, series), Nanase futatabi (writer and actor, series), Meguriai (actor, series) 1998, Gakkou no kaidan (actor) 2000, Hojo Tokimune (actor, series) 2001. *Publications:* novels: Tokaido Senso (The Tokyo–Osaka War) 1964, Vietnam Kanko Kosha (The Vietnam Tourist Bureau) 1967, Dasso to Tsuiseki no Samba (The Samba for Runaways and Chasers) 1972, Kazoku Hakkei (What the Maid Saw: Eight Psychic Tales) 1972, Kyojin-tachi (Fictional Characters) (Izumi Kyoka Award 1981), Yumenokizaka-Bunkiten (The Yumenokizaka Intersection) (Tanizaki Jun'ichiro Award 1987), Yoppadani eno Koka (A Descent into the Yoppa Valley) (Kawabata Yasunari Award 1989), 48-oku no Mousou (4,800 Million Delusions), Afurika no Bakudan (The African Bomb), Toki wo Kakeru Shoujo (The Little Girl who Conquered Time), Fugou Keiji (The Millionaire Detective), Kyokou Sendan (The Fictional Fleet), Watashi no Guranpa (My Grandpa), Bungaku-bu Tadano Kyoju (Hitoshi Tadano the Professor of Literary Studies) 1990, Asa no Gasuparu (Gaspard of the Morning) (Nihon Science Fiction Taisho Award 1992) 1992, Paprika 1993, Tabi no Ragosu 1994, Zanzou ni Kuchibeni wo 1995, Teki 1998, Kyojintachi 1998, Engattsuio Shireitou 2000, Gyoran Kannonki 2000, Kyofu (Fear) 2001, Hell 2003, Ginrei no Hate (End of the Silver Age) 2006, Kyosen Bellas Letras (The Big Ship Bellas Letras) 2007; short stories: The Rumours About Me 1972, When the Shogun Awoke 1974, The Last of the Smokers 1974, How to Sleep 1979, The Wind 1984, The Dream Censor 1987, The Fish 1988, Standing Woman 1990, Polar King 1990, Porno Wakusei no Salmonella Ningen (Salmonella Men on Planet Porno) 2005; non-fiction: Kyoufu 2001, Gyorankannonki 2003. *Honours:* Chevalier, Ordre des Arts et des Lettres 1997. *Website:* www.jali.or.jp.

TSVETKOV, Aleksey, PhD; Russian poet and critic; b. 2 Feb. 1947, Stanislaw (now Ivano-Frankivsk), Ukraine; s. of Petr Tsvetkov and Bella Tsvetkov (née Tsyganov); m. Olga Samilenko 1978. *Education:* Odessa and Moscow Univs, Univ. of Michigan, USA. *Career:* journalist in Siberia and Kazakhstan; poetry recitals and participant in Volgin's Moscow Univ. literary soc. Luch 1970–75; emigrated to USA 1974; co-f Russkaya zhizn', San Francisco 1976–77; Prof. of Russian Language and Literature, Dickinson Coll., Pa 1981–85; broadcaster, Voice of America (to Germany and Czech Republic); poetry has appeared in Kontinent, Ekho, Vremya i my, Apollon, Glagol and elsewhere. *Publications include:* A Collection of Pieces for Life Solo 1978, Three Poets: Kuzminsky, Tsvetkov, Limonov 1981, Dream State 1981, Eden 1985, Simply Voice 1991. *Honours:* Dr hc (Univ. of Mich.) 1977.

TUCKER, Eva Marie, BA; German/British writer; b. 18 April 1929, Berlin, Germany; m. 1950 (died 1987); three d. *Education:* Univ. of London. *Career:* C. Day-Lewis Writing Fellow, Vauxhall Manor School, London 1978–79; Hawthornden Writing Fellowship 1991; Fellow, Royal Soc. of Literature 2009–; mem. English PEN. *Publications:* Contact (novel) 1966, Drowning (novel) 1969, Radetzkymarch by Joseph Roth (trans.) 1974, Dorothy Richardson: The Enchanted Guest of Spring and Summer, A Monograph 2003, Berlin Mosaic (novel) 2005, Becoming English 2009; contrib. to BBC Radio 3 and 4, Encounter, London Magazine, Woman's Journal, Vogue, Harper's, Spectator, Listener, PEN International, Times Literary Supplement. *Address:* 63B Belsize Park Gardens, London, NW3 4JN, England (home). *Telephone:* (20) 7722-9010 (home). *E-mail:* eva.tucker@btinternet.com (home).

TUCKER, Helen, BA; American author; b. 1 Nov. 1926, Raleigh, NC; m. William Beckwith. *Education:* Wake Forest Univ., Columbia Univ. *Career:* newspaper reporter and writer for radio, Burlington, North Carolina, Twin Falls and Boise, Idaho, Salt Lake City, Utah, Raleigh, North Carolina 1947–58; worked in editorial dept, Columbia Univ. Press 1959–60; Dir of Publs and Publicity, North Carolina Museum of Art, Raleigh 1967–70. *Publications:* The Sound of Summer Voices 1969, The Guilt of August Fielding 1972, No Need of Glory 1973, The Virgin of Lontano 1974, A Strange and Ill-Starred Marriage 1978, A Reason for Rivalry 1979, A Mistress to the Regent: An Infamous Attachment 1980, The Halverton Scandal 1980, A Wedding Day Deception 1981, The Double Dealers 1982, Season of Dishonor 1982, Ardent Vows 1983, Bound by Honor 1984, The Lady's Fancy 1991, Bold Impostor 1991; contrib. to Lady's Circle, Ellery Queen Mystery Magazine, Alfred Hitchcock Mystery Magazine, Ladies' Home Journal, Crescent Review, Montevallo Review, Redbook Magazine. *Honours:* Distinguished Alumni Award, Wake Forest Univ. 1971, Franklin County Artist of the Year Award 1992. *Address:* 501 East Whitaker Mill Road, Apartment 405-B, Raleigh, NC 27608, USA (home). *Telephone:* (919) 832-5461.

TUCKER, (Allan) James, (Bill James), BA, MA; British writer; b. 15 Aug. 1929, Cardiff, Wales; m. Marian Roberta Craig 1954; three s., one d. *Education:* Univ. of Wales, Cardiff. *Career:* mem. Authors' Guild, CWA, MWA. *Publications include:* Equal Partners 1960, The Alias Man 1968, The Novels of Anthony Powell 1976, The Lolita Man 1986, Baby Talk 1998, Lovely Mover 1998, The Tattoed Detective 1998, Bay City 2000, Kill Me 2000, Pay Days 2001, Split 2001, Double Jeopardy 2002, Middleman 2002, The Girl with the Long Back 2004, Easy Streets 2004, Wolves of Memory 2006, Girls 2006, Making Stuff Up 2006, The Sixth Man 2006, Pix 2007, Letters from Carthage 2007, In the Absence of Iles 2008; contributions: Punch, Spectator, New Statesman, New Review. *Address:* c/o Constable and Robinson, 3 The Lanchesters, 162 Fulham Palace Road, London W6 9ER, England (office). *Website:* www.constablerobinson.com (office).

TUCKER, Martin, BA, MA, PhD; American academic, writer and poet; *Editor, Confrontation*; b. 8 Feb. 1928, Philadelphia. *Education:* New York Univ., Univ. of Arizona. *Career:* Faculty mem., Long Island Univ. 1956–96, Prof. Emer. 1996–; Ed. Confrontation magazine 1970–; Distinguished Visiting Prof., Florida Int. Univ. 2000; mem. African Literature Asscn, African Studies Asscn, Authors' Guild, Modern Language Asscn, Nat. Book Critics Circle, PEN (mem. Exec. Bd 1973–96), Poetry Soc. of America (mem. Exec. Bd 1982–86). *Publications:* Modern British Literature, Vols I–IV (ed.) 1967–76, Africa in Modern Literature 1967, The Critical Temper, Vols I–V (ed.) 1970–89, Joseph Conrad 1976, Homes of Locks and Mysteries (poems) 1982, Literary Exile in the United States 1991, Sam Shepard 1992, Attention Spans (poems) 1997, Modern American Literature (ed.) 1997, While There is Time (poems) 2005, Love Among the Squabbles (plays) 2006, Plenty of Exits: New and Selected Poems 2008, Boundaries of Exile, Conditions of Hope (with Albert Russo) 2009; contrib. to professional journals and general periodicals. *Honours:* Nat. Endowment for the Arts/Co-ordinating Council and Literary Magazine Awards for Editorial Distinction 1976, 1984, English-Speaking Union Award 1982, Meritorious Service Award, New York Univ., Chancellor's Award, Long Island Univ. 2008. *Address:* Confrontation, English Department, C.W. Post of Long Island University, Brookville, NY 11548, USA (office). *Telephone:* (516) 299-2720 (office). *Fax:* (516) 299-2735 (office). *E-mail:* martin.tucker@liu.edu (office). *Website:* www.liu.edu (office).

TUDGE, Colin, MA (Cantab.); British science writer, journalist and author; b. 22 April 1943, London, England; m. 1st Rosemary Tudge; three c.; m. 2nd Ruth West. *Education:* Dulwich Coll., London, Peterhouse, Cambridge. *Career:* worked for World Medicine and Farmers' Weekly; Features Ed., New Scientist magazine 1980–85; worked as presenter of science programmes for BBC Radio 3 1985–1990; wrote annual scientific reports for British Govt's Agric. and Food Research Council 1987–1990; freelance writer 1990–; Visiting Research Fellow, Centre for Philosophy, LSE 1995–2005; Co-founder Land-Share 2008, The Campaign for Real Farming and The Coll. for Enlightened Agric. 2009; fmr Dir Food Ethics Council; fmr mem. Council, Zoological Soc. of London; Fellow, Linnean Soc. of London. *Radio:* presenter, Science on 3, Spectrum (BBC Radio 3). *Television:* writer and presenter, The Food Connection (BBC) 1985; made numerous documentaries; guest appearances on Horizon, Equinox, Newsnight, Open University, and others. *Publications:* Home Farm: Complete Food Self-Sufficiency (with Michael Allaby) 1977, The Famine Business 1977, Future Cook 1980, Food Crops for the Future: The Development of Plant Resources 1988, Global Ecology 1991, Last Animals at the Zoo 1991, The Engineer in the Garden 1993, The Day Before Yesterday 1995, The Food Connection: The BBC Guide to Healthy Eating 1995, Neanderthals, Bandits and Farmers: How Agriculture Really Began 1998, In Mendel's Footnotes 2000, The Second Creation: Dolly and the Age of Biological Control (with Keith Campbell and Ian Wilmut) 2000, The Variety of Life: A Survey and a Celebration of All the Creatures that Have Ever Lived 2000, So Shall We Reap 2003, The Secret Life of Trees 2005, Feeding People is Easy 2007, Consider the Birds: How They Live and Why They Matter 2008, The Link: Uncovering our Earliest Ancestor 2009; contrib. to newspapers and magazines, including The Independent, The Times, Natural History, Nature and New Statesman. *Literary Agent:* c/o Felicity Bryan, 2A North Parade, Banbury Road, Oxford, OX2 6LX, England. *Telephone:* (1865) 513816. *Fax:* (1865) 310055. *E-mail:* agency@felicitybryan.com. *Website:* www.felicitybryan.com. *Telephone:* (1865) 318997 (office). *E-mail:* colin@colintudge.co.uk (office). *Website:* www.campaignforrealfarming.org (office); www.colintudge.com.

TUDOR-CRAIG, Pamela Wynn, Lady Wedgwood, BA, PhD, FSA; British art historian and writer; b. 26 June 1928, London; m. 1st Algernon James Riccarton Tudor-Craig 1956 (died 1969); one d.; m. 2nd Sir John Wedgwood 1982 (died 1989). *Education:* Courtauld Inst. of Art, London. *Career:* lecturer at several US colls 1969–96; mem. Cathedrals Advisory Comm. 1975–90; mem. Architectural Advisory Panel, Westminster Abbey 1979–98; f. annual Harlaxton Symposium of English Medieval Studies 1984–, Cambridgeshire Historic Churches Trust 1982–; Chair. Friends of Sussex Historic Churches 2002–10; presenter, The Secret Life of Paintings (TV series) 1986; mem. English Speaking Union (Cultural Affairs Cttee 1990–2000) 1990–98, Soc. of Antiquaries (Council mem. 1989–92, currently Hon. Curator of Pictures). *Publications:* Richard III 1973, The Secret Life of Paintings (with R. Foster) 1986, Old St Paul's: the Society of Antiquaries Diptych 1616 2004; Contributions: Bells Guide to Westminster Abbey 1986, Exeter Cathedral 1991, Anglo-Saxon Wall Paintings 1991, The Regal Image of Richard II and the Wilton Diptych 1997, King Arthur's Round Table 2000, Art Reformed 2007; contrib. to books, exhibition catalogues, journals and learned journals, including Harlaxton Medieval Studies, Church Times, History Today, radio and television. *Honours:* Hon. DH (William Jewell Coll.) 1983. *Address:* 9 St Anne's Crescent, Lewes, East Sussex, BN7 1SB, England (home). *Telephone:* (1273) 479564 (home).

TULLI, Magdalena; Polish novelist; b. 1955; m.; two s. *Career:* has translated work of Marcel Proust and Italo Calvino into Polish. *Publications:* Sny i kamienie (Dreams and Stones) (Koscielski Foundation Prize 1995) 1995, W czerwieni (In Red) 1998, Tryby (novel) 2003, Skaza (Flaw) 2006. *Address:* c/o W.A.B. Publishers, ul. Lowicka 31, 02-502 Warsaw, Poland.

TULLY, Sir (William) Mark, Kt, KBE, MA; British journalist; b. 24 Oct. 1935, Calcutta, India; s. of William S. C. Tully and Patience T. Tully; m. Frances M. Butler 1960; two s. two d. *Education:* Marlborough Coll., Trinity Hall, Cambridge. *Career:* Regional Dir Abbeyfield Soc. 1960–64; Personnel Officer BBC 1964–65, Asst Rep. then Rep. (a.i.), BBC, Delhi 1965–69, Hindi Programme Organizer BBC External Services, London 1969–70, Chief Talks Writer 1970–71, Chief of Bureau BBC, Delhi 1971–93, BBC South Asia Corresp. 1993–94; freelance writer, broadcaster, journalist 1994–. *Radio:* series: Raj to Rajiv BBC 1987, Something Understood BBC 1995–, Indian Army in World War II 2007. *Television:* series: Lives of Jesus BBC 1996. *Publications:* Amritsar: Mrs Gandhi's Last Battle (jtly) 1985, Raj to Rajiv (jtly) 1988, No Full Stops in India 1991, The Heart of India 1995, The Lives of Jesus 1996, India in Slow Motion (with Gillian Wright) 2002, India's Unending Journey 2007, India: The Road Ahead 2011. *Honours:* Hon. Fellow, Trinity Hall, Cambridge 1994; Hon. DLitt (Strathclyde) 1997, Dr hc (Bradford Univ.) 2001, (York Univ.) 2008, (Open Univ.) 2009, (Queen's Univ., Belfast) 2011; Dimbleby Award (BAFTA) 1984, Padma Shri (India) 1992, Padma Bhushan (India) 2005. *Address:* B.26 Nizamuddin West, New Delhi 110 013, India (office). *Telephone:* (11) 41033839 (office). *E-mail:* markandgilly@gmail.com (office).

TUMWINE, James K., MBChB; M.Med; PhD; Ugandan writer and paediatrician; *Editor, African Health Sciences*; b. Kabale. *Education:* Makerere Univ. *Career:* Prof. of Paediatrics and Child Health, Makerere University College of Health Sciences; fmr health adviser for Africa region, Oxfam UK; Founder and Ed. African Health Sciences (journal) 2001–; mem. External Advisory Team, Resilience: Interdisciplinary Perspectives on Science and Humanitarianism (journal); Founder and Pres., Forum for African Medical Editors. *Publications include:* non-fiction: Drawers of Water: 30 Years of Change in Domestic Water Use and Environmental Health – Uganda County Case Study 2001. *Address:* African Health Sciences, Makerere University Medical School, PO Box 7072, Kampala, Uganda (office).

TUNNICLIFFE, Stephen, BA, MA; British poet and writer; b. 22 May 1925, Wakefield, Yorks.; m. Hilary Katharine Routh 1949; three s. (one deceased). *Education:* Univ. of London, Inst. of Education. *Career:* mem. Soc. of Authors. *Publications:* English in Practice (with Geoffrey Summerfield) 1971, Reading and Discrimination (with Denys Thompson) 1979, Poetry Experience: Teaching and Writing Poetry in Secondary Schools 1984, Building and Other Poems 1993, Uneasy Souls: A Forgotten Genius (novel) 1999, Some Poems 2003, Discovering Shakespeare (new edn) 2003, Dangers I Had Passed (novel) 2003, Money Makers (novel) 2009; other: Libretti for John Joubert: The Martyrdom of St Alban, The Raising of Lazarus, The Magus, The Prisoner, The Wayfarers, Wings of Faith, For Francis Routh: Circles; contrib. to reviews and journals. *Address:* Upper Clairmont, Kidd Lane, Clun, Shropshire, SY7 8LN, England (office). *Telephone:* (1588) 640398 (office). *E-mail:* s.tunnicliffe98@btinternet.com (home). *Website:* www.clairmontpress.co.uk (office).

TUOMEY, Nesta Catherine; Irish writer and dramatist; b. (Nesta O'Holohan), 21 Oct. 1941, Dublin; m. Laurence J. Tuomey; three s. one d. *Education:* Nat. Coll. of Art, Dublin. *Career:* mem. Soc. of Irish Playwrights (Chair. 1980–82), Irish PEN (Treasurer 2000–05, Sec. 2005–06), Writers' Union. *Plays:* two stage plays. *Radio:* two radio plays. *Television:* 18 documentaries. *Publications:* Up Up and Away 1995, Like One of the Family 1999; plays: The Same Again 1969, One of These Days 1977, Country Banking 1982, Whose Baby? 1996; 18 documentaries; contrib. to many magazines and journals. *Honours:* John Power Short Story at Listowel Award 1981, Image/Oil of Ulay Short Story 1994, O. Z. Whitehead Play Competition 1996. *Address:* Tully, Ballinteer Road, Dublin 16, Ireland (home). *Telephone:* (1) 2961158 (office). *Fax:* (1) 2961158 (office). *E-mail:* nesta@nestatuomey.com (home). *Website:* www.nestatuomey.com.

TURK, Frances Mary; British novelist; b. 14 April 1915, Huntingdon. *Career:* mem. Romantic Novelists Asscn; many other professional orgs. *Publications include:* Paddy O'Shea 1937, The Precious Hours 1938, Paradise Street 1939, Lovable Clown 1941, Angel Hill 1942, The Five Grey Geese 1944, Salutation 1949, The Small House at Ickley 1951, The Gentle Flowers 1952, The Dark Wood 1954, The Glory and the Dream 1955, Dinny Lightfoot 1956, No Through Road 1957, The White Swan 1958, A Temple of Fancy 1959, A Journey to Eternity 1960, A Time to Know 1960, The Secret Places, 1961, A Man Called Jeremy 1961, A Lamp From Murano 1963, The Guarded Heart 1964, The Sour-Sweet Days 1965, The Rectory at Hay 1966, Goddess of Threads 1966, Legacy of Love 1967, Lionel's Story 1967, The Flowering Field 1967, The Marion Window 1968, The Lesley Affair 1968, Fair Recompense 1969, Goddess of Threads 1975, A Visit to Marchmont 1977, Candle Corner 1986.

TURNER, Brian Lindsay, DLitt; New Zealand poet and writer; b. 4 March 1944, Dunedin; one s. *Career:* fmrly customs officer, rabbiter, sawmiller, ed. for Oxford University Press; Managing Ed., John McIndoe Ltd, Dunedin 1975–83, 1985–86; Writer-in-Residence, Univ. of Canterbury 1997; Te Mata Estate New Zealand Poet Laureate 2003–05; Robert Burns Fellow, Univ. of Otago 1984. *Publications:* poetry: Ladders of Rain (Commonwealth Poetry Prize) 1978, Ancestors 1981, Listening to the River 1983, Bones 1985, All That Blue Can Be 1989, Beyond (NZ Book Award for Poetry 1993) 1992, Taking Off 2001, Footfall 2005; other: Images of Coastal Otago 1982, New Zealand High Country: Four Seasons 1983, The Visitor's Guide to Fiordland, New Zealand 1983, Finger's Up? (play) (J.C. Reid Memorial Prize) 1985, Opening Up (with Glenn Turner) 1987, Lifting the Covers (with Glenn Turner) 1987, The Last River's Song 1989, Timeless Land (with Owen Marshall and Graham Sydney) 1992, The Guide to Trout Fishing in Otago 1994, On the Loose (biog., with Josh Kronfeld) 1998, New Zealand Photographers (with Scott Freeman) 2000, The Art of Grahame Sydney (essay contrib.) 2001, Meads (with Colin Meads) 2002, Somebodies and Nobodies (autobiog.) 2002, Inside (with Anton Oliver) 2005, Into the Wider World 2008, Just This (NZ Book Award for Poetry 2010) 2009; contrib. to National Business Review, Independent, poetry anthologies, literary sports anthologies, columns, reviews and articles to daily and weekly newspapers; TV scripts. *Honours:* New Zealand Journalists' Union Dulux Award for Sport Writing 1975, John Crowe Reid Memorial Prize 1985, Scholarship in Letters 1994, Arts Council Scholarship in Letters 1994–95, Prime Minister's Award for Literary Achievement in Poetry 2009, Lauris Edmond Memorial Award for distinguished contrib. to NZ poetry 2009. *Address:* 3363 Ida Valley-Omakau Road, Oturehua, Central Otago 9339, New Zealand.

TURNER, Frederick, BA, MA, BLitt; British academic, writer and poet; *Founders Professor of Arts and Humanities, University of Texas at Dallas*; b. 19 Nov. 1943, East Haddon, Northamptonshire, England; m. Mei Lin Chang 1966; two s. *Education:* Univ. of Oxford. *Career:* Asst Prof. of English, Univ. of California, Santa Barbara 1967–72; Assoc. Prof. of English, Kenyon Coll. 1972–85; Ed., Kenyon Review 1978–83; Visiting Prof. of English, Univ. of Exeter 1984–85; Founders Prof. of Arts and Humanities, Univ. of Texas at Dallas, Richardson 1985–; mem. PEN. *Publications:* Shakespeare and the Nature of Time 1971, Between Two Lives 1972, The Return 1979, The New World 1985, The Garden 1985, Natural Classicism 1986, Genesis: An Epic Poem 1988, Rebirth of Value 1991, Tempest, Flute and Oz 1991, April Wind 1991, Beauty 1991, Foamy Sky: The Major Poems of Miklos Radnoti (trans. with Zsuzanna Ozsváth) 1992, The Culture of Hope 1995, The Ballad of the Good Cowboy 1997, Hadean Eclogues 1999, Shakespeare's Twenty-First Century Economics: The Morality of Love and Money 1999, The Iron-Blue Vault: Selected Poems of Attila Jósef (trans. with Zsuzsanna Ozsváth) 1999; contrib. to journals and periodicals. *Honours:* Ohioana Prize for Editorial Excellence 1980, Djerassi Foundation Grant and Residency 1981, Levinson Poetry Prize 1983, Missouri Review Essay Prize 1986, PEN Golden Pen Award 1992, Milan Fust Prize 1996. *Address:* 2668 Aster Drive, Richardson, TX 75082, USA (home). *Telephone:* (972) 883-2777 (office). *E-mail:* frederickturner@comcast.net (office).

TUROW, Scott F., JD; American writer and lawyer; b. 12 April 1949, s. of David Turow and Rita Pastron. *Education:* Amherst Coll. and Stanford and Harvard Univs. *Career:* mem. Bar, Ill. 1978, US Dist Court. Ill. 1978, US Court of Appeals (7th Circuit) 1979; Assoc. Suffolk Co. Dist Attorney, Boston 1977–78; Asst US Attorney, US Dist Court, Ill., Chicago 1978–86; partner Sonnenschein, Nath & Rosenthal, Chicago 1986–; mem. Chicago Council of Lawyers. *Publications:* One L.: An Inside Account of Life in the First Year at Harvard Law School 1977, Presumed Innocent 1987, The Burden of Proof 1990, Pleading Guilty 1993, The Laws of our Fathers 1996, Personal Injuries 1999, Reversible Errors 2002, Ultimate Punishment: A Lawyer's Reflections on Dealing with the Death Penalty 2003, Ordinary Heroes 2006, The Best American Mystery Stories (ed.) 2006, Limitations 2007, Innocent 2010; contribs to professional journals. *Address:* Sonnenschein, Nath & Rosenthal, Sears Tower, Suite 8000, 233 South Wacker Drive, Chicago, IL 60606, USA (office). *Website:* www.scottturow.com.

TUSIANI, Joseph, DLitt; American (b. Italian) poet, translator and fmr academic; b. 14 Jan. 1924, Foggia, Italy. *Education:* Univ. of Naples. *Career:* Chair Italian Dept, Coll. of Mount St Vincent 1948–71; Lecturer in Italian, Hunter Coll., CUNY 1950–62; Visiting Assoc. Prof., New York Univ. 1956–64, CUNY 1971–83; NDEA Visiting Prof. of Italian, Connecticut State Coll. 1962; Prof., Lehman Coll., CUNY 1971–83; mem. Catholic Poetry Soc. of America, Poetry Soc. of America. *Publications:* Dante in Licenza 1952, Two Critical Essays on Emily Dickinson 1952, Melos Cordis (poems in Latin) 1955, Odi Sacre: Poems 1958, The Complete Poems of Michelangelo 1960, Lust and Liberty: The Poems of Machiavelli 1963, Tasso's Jerusalem Delivered (verse trans.) 1970, Italian Poets of the Renaissance 1971, The Age of Dante 1973, Tasso's Creation of the World 1982, Rosa Rosarum (poems in Latin) 1984, In Exilio Rerum (poems in Latin) 1985, La Parola Difficile (three vols) 1988, 1991, 1992, Carmina Latina 1994, Leopardi's Canti (trans.) 1994, Le Poesie Inglesi di G. A. Borgese 1995, Pulci's Morgante (verse trans.) 1998, Dante's Lyric Poems 1998, Radicitus (poems in Latin) 2000, Ethnicity 2000, Two Languages, Two Lands (proceedings of an int. convention on his work) 2000, Collected Poems 2004, Un Italiano in America (anthology) 2004, Le Lingue dell'Altrove 2004, In Nobis Caelum (poems in Latin) 2007, If Gold Should Rust (play in verse) 2009, Fragmenta ad Aemilium (poems in Latin) 2009, Proceedings of International Convention on his Latin Poetry 2010; contrib. to books and journals. *Honours:* Cavaliere Ufficiale, Italy 1973, Gold Medal from Gov. of Puglia 2004; Dr hc (Univ. of Foggia) 2004; Greenwood Prize for Poetry 1956, Leone di San Marco Award 1982, Joseph Tusiani Scholarship Fund founded in his honour, Lehman Coll., CUNY 1983, Congressional Medal of Merit 1984, Progresso Medal of Liberty 1986, American Asscn of Teachers of Italian Outstanding Teacher Award 1987, Renoir Literary Award 1988, Festschrift published in his honour 1995, Enrico Fermi Award 1995, Nat. Endowment for the Humanities Fellowship 1998, Fiorello La Guardia Award 1998, Governor's Award for Excellence 2000, Premio Puglia 2000, Premio Italiani nel Mondo 2004, fêted in Rome's Campidoglio 2004. *Address:* 308 E 72nd Street, New York, NY 10021, USA (home).

TUTTLE, Lisa, BA; American writer; b. 16 Sept. 1952, Houston, TX. *Education:* Syracuse Univ. *Publications:* Windhaven 1981, Familiar Spirit 1983, Catwitch 1983, Children's Literary Houses 1984, Encyclopedia of Feminism 1986, A Spaceship Built of Stone and Other Stories 1987, Heroines: Women Inspired by Women 1988, Lost Futures 1992, Memories of the Body 1992, Panther in Argyll 1996, The Pillow Friend 1996, Love On-line 1998, Mad House 1998, My Death 2004, The Mysteries 2005, The Silver Bough 2006; contributions: magazines. *Honours:* John W. Campbell Award 1974.

TWICHELL, Chase, BA, MFA; American poet, writer, teacher and publisher; b. 20 Aug. 1950, New Haven, Conn.; m. Russell Banks 1989. *Education:* Trinity Coll., Univ. of Iowa. *Career:* Ed., Pennyroyal Press 1976–85; Assoc. Prof., Univ. of Alabama 1985–88; Lecturer, Princeton Univ. 1990–2000; Assoc. Faculty, Goddard Coll. 1996–98, Warren Wilson Coll. 1999–; Ed., Ausable Press 1999–2009. *Publications:* Northern Spy 1981, The Odds 1986, Perdido 1991, The Practice of Poetry (co-ed.) 1992, The Ghost of Eden 1995, The Snow Watcher 1998, Dog Language 2005, Horses Where the Answers Should Have Been (Kingsley Tufts Poetry Award 2011) 2010; contribs: Antaeus, Field, Georgia Review, Nation, New England Review, New Yorker, Ohio Review, Ontario Review, Paris Review, Ploughshares, Poetry Review, Southern Review, Yale Review. *Honours:* Nat. Endowment for the Arts Fellowships 1987, 1993, Guggenheim Fellowship 1990, Artists Foundation Fellowship, Boston 1990, New Jersey State Council on the Arts Fellowship 1990, American Acad. of Arts and Letters Award 1994, Alice Fay Di Castagnola Award, Poetry Soc. of America 1997. *E-mail:* chasetwichell@mac.com (office).

TYLDESLEY, Joyce Ann, BA, DPhil; British archaeologist and researcher; *Lecturer in Egyptology, KNH Centre for Egyptology, University of Manchester*; b. 25 Feb. 1960, Bolton, England; m. Steven Ralph Snape 1985; one s. one d. *Education:* Univ. of Liverpool, St Anne's Coll., Oxford, St Cross Coll., Oxford. *Career:* Lecturer in Archaeology of the Eastern Mediterranean, Univ. of Liverpool 1986–87, Research Fellow, Inst. of Prehistoric Science and Archaeology 1987–91, Hon. Research Fellow, School of Archaeology, Classics and Oriental Studies 1993–; currently also Lecturer in Egyptology, KNH Centre for Biomedical Egyptology, Univ. of Manchester; mem. Egypt Exploration Soc. *Publications:* The Wolvercote Channel Handaxe Assemblage: A Comparative Study 1986, The Bout Coupe Biface: A Typological Problem 1987, Nazlet Tuna: An Archaeological Survey in Middle Egypt (co-author) 1988, Daughters of Isis: Women of Ancient Egypt 1994, Hatchepsut: The Female Pharaoh 1996, Nefertiti: The Sun Queen 1998, Pyramids: The Real Story Behind Egypt's Most Ancient Monuments 2003, Egypt: How a Lost Civilization was Rediscovered 2005, Chronicle of the Queens of Egypt 2006; contrib. articles and reviews to professional journals and popular magazines, including History Today, Focus, Popular Archaeology. *Honours:* British Acad. grant

1987. *Address:* KNH Centre for Biomedical Egyptology, University of Manchester, Floor F, Jackson's Mill, Sackville Street, PO Box 88, Manchester, M60 1QD, England (office). *E-mail:* joyce.tyldesley@manchester.ac.uk (office). *Website:* www.knhcentre.manchester.ac.uk (office).

TYLER, Anne, BA; American writer; b. 25 Oct. 1941, Minneapolis, Minn.; d. of Lloyd Parry Tyler and Phyllis (Mahon) Tyler; m. Taghi M. Modarressi 1963 (died 1997); two c. *Education:* Duke Univ., Columbia Univ. *Career:* mem. American Acad. of Arts and Letters, American Acad. of Arts and Sciences. *Publications:* If Morning Ever Comes 1964, The Tin Can Tree 1965, A Slipping-Down Life 1970, The Clock Winder 1972, Celestial Navigation 1974, Searching for Caleb 1976, Earthly Possessions 1977, Morgan's Passing 1980, Dinner at the Homesick Restaurant 1982, The Best American Short Stories (ed. with Shannon Ravenel) 1983, The Accidental Tourist (Nat. Book Critics Circle Award for Fiction) 1985, Breathing Lessons (Pulitzer Prize for Fiction 1989) 1988, Saint Maybe 1991, Tumble Tower (juvenile) 1993, Ladder of Years 1995, A Patchwork Planet 1998, Back When We Were Grown-ups 2001, The Amateur Marriage (Richard & Judy Book Club Choice 2005) 2004, Digging to America 2006, Noah's Compass 2010, The Beginner's Goodbye 2012; short stories in magazines. *Address:* 222 Tunbridge Road, Baltimore, MD 21212, USA (home). *E-mail:* atmBaltimore@aol.com (home).

TYSON, Harvey Wood; South African journalist; b. 27 Sept. 1928, Johannesburg; two s. one d. *Education:* Kingswood Coll., Rhodes Univ., Grahamstown. *Career:* Ed.-in-Chief The Star, Sunday Star, Johannesburg 1974–90; Dir Argus Holdings 1991–94, Argus Newspapers 1991–94, Sussens Mann Tyson Ogilvie & Mather, Omni Media Holdings 1994–. *Publication:* Editors Under Fire 1993. *Address:* c/o The Star, 47 Sauer Street, PO Box 1014, Johannesburg 2000, South Africa (office).

U

UGLOW, Jenny, OBE, BA, BLitt; British publisher (retd), biographer and writer; b. (Jenny Crowther), 28 March 1947, Wisbech, Cambs., England; m. Steve Uglow; four c. *Education:* Cheltenham Ladies' Coll., St Anne's Coll., Oxford. *Career:* Ed., Macmillan Press; Editorial Dir, Chatto and Windus 1996–2012. *Films:* historical consultant to films: Miss Potter, Pride and Prejudice, Jane Eyre. *Television:* historical consultant to classic serials: Tom Jones, Wives and Daughters, Vanity Fair, Daniel Deronda, The Way We Live Now, Bleak House, Sense and Sensibility, Diary of a Nobody, Cranford. *Publications:* George Eliot 1987, Elizabeth Gaskell: A Habit of Stories (British Acad. Prize) 1993, Henry Fielding 1995, Hogarth: A Life and a World 1997, Dr Johnson, his Club and Other Friends 1998, In a Green Shade 2002, The Lunar Men: The Friends Who Made the Future (James Tait Black Memorial Prize for Biography 2003) 2002, A Little History of British Gardening 2004, Nature's Engraver: A Life of Thomas Bewick 2006, Words and Pictures: Writers, Artists and a Peculiarly British Tradition 2008, A Gambling Man 2009, , The Pinecone 2012; editor: The Macmillan Biographical Dictionary of Women (fourth edn) 2005, Cultural Babbage: Technology Time and Invention (with Francis Spufford) 1996; contribs to The Guardian, Times Literary Supplement, Independent on Sunday, Sunday Times. *Honours:* Dr hc (Univs of Kent, Birmingham, Aston, Staffordshire, Central England); Hessell-Tiltman Prize for History, PEN International, Washington Arts Club Prize. *Literary Agent:* c/o Deborah Rogers, Rogers, Coleridge & White Literary Agency, 20 Powis Mews, London, W11 1JN, England. *Telephone:* (20) 7221-3717. *Fax:* (20) 7229-9084. *E-mail:* info@rcwlitagency.co.uk. *Website:* www.rcwlitagency.co.uk; www.jennyuglow.com.

UGRESIC, Dubravka, MA; Dutch (b. Croatian) novelist, essayist and literary scholar; b. 27 March 1949, Croatia. *Education:* Univ. of Zagreb. *Career:* Lecturer Inst. for Theory of Literature, Univ. of Zagreb 1974–93; Visiting Lecturer, Wesleyan Univ., USA 1989, 1992, Univ. of Amsterdam, Netherlands 1996–97, UCLA, USA 2001, Harvard Univ., USA 2002; Frey Foundation Distinguished Visiting Prof., Univ. of N Carolina, USA 1998–99; lives in Amsterdam, The Netherlands. *Publications:* Mali plamen (juvenile) 1971, Filip i Srecica (juvenile) 1976, Poza za prozu (short stories) 1978, Nova ruska proza (criticism) 1980, Stefica Cvek u raljama Zivota (short story, trans. as Steffie Speck in the Jaws of Life) 1981, Zivot je bajka (short stories, trans. as Life is a Fairy Tale) 1983, Forsiranje romana-reke (trans. as Fording the Stream of Consciousness) 1988, Kucni duhovi 1988, Americki fikcionar (non-fiction, trans. as Have a Nice Day) 1993, Kultura lazi (non-fiction, trans. as The Culture of Lies) 1996, Muzej bezuvjetne predaje (novel, trans. as The Museum of Unconditional Surrender) 1996, Zabranjeno citanje (non-fiction, trans. as Thank You for Not Reading) 2001, Ministarstvo Boli (novel, trans. as The Ministry of Pain) (English PEN Writers in Translation Award 2005) 2004, Nikog Nema Doma (trans. as Nobody's Home) 2005, Baba Jaga je snijela jaje (trans. as Baba Yaga Laid an Egg) 2008. *Honours:* Prix Européen de l'Essai Charles Veillon (Switzerland) 1996, Verzetsprijs (The Netherlands) 1997, SWF-Bestenliste Literature Prize (Germany) 1998, State Prize for European Literature (Austria) 1999, Heinrich Mann Award (Germany) 2000, Premio Feronia (Italy) 2004, Samuel Fischer Fellowship, Frei Universität 2006; several grants. *Literary Agent:* c/o The Susijn Agency Ltd, Third Floor, 64 Great Titchfield Street, London, W1W 7QH, England. *Telephone:* (20) 7580-6341. *Fax:* (20) 7580-8626. *E-mail:* info@thesusijnagency.com. *Website:* www.thesusijnagency.com; www.dubravkaugresic.com.

UHDE, Milan, PhD; Czech politician, journalist and playwright; b. 28 July 1936, Brno; m. Jitka Uhdeová; two c. *Education:* Masaryk Univ., Brno. *Career:* Ed. of literary monthly A Guest Is Coming 1958–70; signed Charter 77; published essays in unofficial periodicals and abroad; Reader, Faculty of Philosophy, Masaryk Univ., Brno Dec. 1989–; Ed.-in-chief, Atlantis Publishing House, Brno March–June 1990; Minister of Culture, Czech Repub. 1990–92; Pres. of Foundation for Preservation of Cultural Monuments 1991–; mem. Civic Democratic Party (ODS) 1991–98, Unie Svobody 1998; Deputy to Czech Nat. Council June 1992–; mem. Presidium; Pres. of Parl., Czech Repub. 1992–96; Chair. Civic Democratic Party in Parl. 1996–97; mem. State Radio Council 1999–. *Plays include:* in trans.: King Vávra 1964, The Tax-Collector 1965, Witnesses 1966, The Tart from the Town of Thebes 1967, The Gang 1969, Ballad for a Bandit 1975, Professional Woman 1975, A May Fairy Tale 1976, A Dentist's Temptation 1976, Lord of the Flames 1977, The Hour of Defence 1978, The Blue Angel 1979, Ave Maria played Softly 1981, The Annunciation 1986, The Bartered and the Bought 1987, Miracle in the Dark House (Alfred Radok Prize 2008) 2004, Depart in Peace 2004, Nana 2005. *Publications:* novels: Like Water off a Duck's Back 1961, A Mysterious Tower in B. 1967. *Honours:* Medal for Merit 2000; Czechoslovak Radio Prize 1966. *Literary Agent:* c/o Aura-Pont Agency, Radlická 99, 150 00 Prague, Czech Republic. *Telephone:* 251554938. *Fax:* 251550207. *E-mail:* aura-pont@aura-pont.cz. *Website:* www.aura-pont.cz. *Address:* Barvičova 59, 60200, Brno, Czech Republic (home). *Telephone:* 602366040 (home). *E-mail:* milan.uhde@seznam.cz (home).

UHRMAN, Celia, PhD; American artist and poet; b. 14 May 1927, New London, Conn.; d. of the late David Aaron Uhrman and Pauline Uhrman (née Schwartz). *Education:* Brooklyn Coll., Univ. of Gdańsk, Poland, City Univ. of New York, Brooklyn Museum Art School, Columbia Univ. *Career:* teacher, New York 1948–82; Pnr Uhrman Studio 1973–83; solo exhibitions include Leffert Jr High School, Brooklyn 1958, Connecticut Chamber of Commerce, New London 1962, Flatbush Chamber of Commerce, New York 1963; group exhibitions include Smithsonian Inst., Washington, DC 1958, Springfield Museum of Fine Arts, Mass 1959, Brooklyn Museum 1959, Old Mystic Art Center, Conn. 1959, Carnegie Endowment Int. Center, New York 1959, Lyman Allyn Museum, New London, Conn. 1960, Palacio de la Virrelna, Barcelona, Spain 1961, Soc. of 4 Arts, Palm Beach, Fla 1964, Premier Salon Int., Charleroi, Belgium 1968, Int. Arts Guild Shows, Monte Carlo 1969–88, Dibiux-Joan Miró Premi Int., Barcelona 1970, Ovar Museum, Portugal 1974; works in perm. collections of Brooklyn Coll. and Brooklyn Evangelical Church; Founding Fellow, World Literary Acad. and Int. Acad. of Poets 1985; Hon. Life mem. World Poetry Day Comm. Inc., Nat. Poetry Day Comm. 1977–. *Publications include:* Poetic Ponderances 1969, A Pause for Poetry 1970, Poetic Love Fancies 1970, A Pause for Poetry for Children 1973, The Chimps are Coming 1975, Love Fancies 1987. *Honours:* Order of Gandhi Award of Honour, Kt of Grand Cross 1972; George Washington Medal of Honor 1964, Diplôme d'Honneur, Palme d'Or des Beaux Arts Exhibition (Monaco) 1969, 1972, Gold Laurel Award, Exposition Int. d'Art Contemporain (Paris) 1974.

ULITSKAYA, Ludmila Yevgenyevna; Russian writer and screenwriter; b. 21 Feb. 1943, Davlekanovo, Bashkiria; m. Krasulin Andrei Nikolayevich; two s. *Education:* Moscow State Univ. *Career:* Head of Literary Div., Jewish Chamber Theatre 1979–89. *Plays:* Carmen, Jose and Death, My Grandchild Benjamin, Year of White Elephant (Best Stage Play Award, Moscow Culture Cttee) 2007. *Film scripts:* Sisters Liberty, A Woman for Everybody, It Is Easy to Die 1999. *Publications include:* One Hundred Buttons (juvenile) 1983, Sonechka (short stories) (Prix Médicis (France) 1996, Literature Prize Giuseppe Acerbi (Italy) 1998) 1992, Daughter of Bukhara 1993, Medea and her Children (Prix Medicis 1998, Giuseppe Acerbi Award 1998) 1996, The Funeral Party 1997, Kukotsky Case (Russian Booker Prize 2002, Penne Prize (Italy) 2006) 2001, Girls 2002, Women's Lies 2003, Sincerely Yours, Shurik (Novel of the Year Prize (Russia) 2004, Nat. Literature Prize (China) 2005, Grinzane Cavour Literary Award (Italy) 2008) 2003, Russian Marmalade 2005, All Our Lord's Men (Book of the Year Literary Prize (Russia) 2005) 2005, Daniel Stein, Translator (Nat. Literary Prize Big Book (Russia) 2007, Bolshaya Kniga Award 2007, Grinzane Cavour Award, Italy 2008, Father Alexander Men's Award (Germany/Russia) 2008) 2006, Dialogues with Ludmila Ulitskaya (GLOBE Annual Prize, Znamya monthly literature magazine (with Mikhail Khodorkovsky) 2010, Imago (Oleg Tabakov Prize (Russia) 2011) 2011; contrib. short stories to anthologies. *Honours:* Chevalier, Ordre des Palmes académiques 2003, Ordre des Arts et des Lettres 2004; Penne Prize (Italy) 1997, Best Writer of the Year Prize (Russia) 2004, Venetz (Crown) Literary Prize (Russia) 2006, Nat. Olympia Prize, Russian Acad. of Business 2007, Budapest Grand Prix (Hungary) 2009, Premio Bauer/Ca'Foscari (Italy) 2010, Gran Premio delle Lettrici ELLE (Italy) 2010, Prix Simone de Beauvoir pour la liberté des femmes (France) 2011. *Literary Agent:* c/o ELKOST International Literary Agency, C/Londres, 78, 6-1, 08036 Barcelona, Spain. *Telephone:* (93) 3221232. *E-mail:* rights@elkost.com. *Website:* www.elkost.com/authors/ulitskaya.

ULLMANN, Linn; Norwegian author, journalist and literary critic; b. (Karin Beate Ullmann), 9 Aug. 1966, Oslo; d. of the late Ingmar Bergman and of Liv Ullmann; m. Niels Fredrik Dahl. *Education:* New York Univ., USA. *Career:* columnist for Aftenposten newspaper; Co-founder and fmr Artistic Dir The Bergman Estate on Fårö (int. artist residency foundation) 2009; mem. jury for main competition, Cannes Film Festival 2011. *Publications:* Before You Sleep (Før du sovner) 1998, Stella Descending (Når jeg er hos deg) 2001, Grace (Nåde) (Norwegian Reader's Prize 2002, named one of the top ten novels by Weekendavisen newspaper, Denmark 2002, adapted for theatre and performed at Rikstreatret 2007) 2002, A Blessed Child (Et Velsignet Barn) (named Best Translated novel by The Independent newspaper, UK 2008) 2005; novels translated into 30 languages. *Honours:* Amalie Skram Award 2007, Gullpennen (Golden Pen) for her journalism, Aftenposten 2007. *Literary Agent:* c/o The Wylie Agency (UK) Ltd, 17 Bedford Square, London, WC1B 3JA, England. *Telephone:* (20) 7908-5900 (London). *Fax:* (20) 7908-5901 (London). *E-mail:* mail@wylieagency.co.uk. *Website:* www.wylieagency.co.uk. *Address:* c/o Forlaget Oktober AS, Postboks 6848, St Olavs plass, 0130 Oslo, Norway. *Telephone:* 23-35-46-20. *Fax:* 23-35-46-21. *E-mail:* oktober@oktober.no. *Website:* www.oktober.no; www.linnullmann.net.

UNDERHILL, Charles (see Hill, Reginald Charles)

UNDERWOOD, Elizabeth (see McConchie, Lyn)

UNGER, Barbara, BA, MA; American fmr academic, poet and writer; b. 2 Oct. 1932, New York, NY; m. 1st; two d.; m. 2nd Theodore Kiichiro Sakano 1987. *Education:* City Coll., CUNY. *Career:* Prof. of English and Creative Writing, Rockland Community Coll., SUNY from 1969 (now retired), then Adjunct Prof.; mem. Poetry Soc. of America. *Publications:* Basement Poems 1959–1961 1975, The Man Who Burned Money (poems) 1976, Inside the Wind (poems) 1986, Learning to Foxtrot (poems) 1989, Dying for Uncle Ray and Other Stories 1990, Blue Depression Glass (poems) (Goodman Award 1989, Anna Davidson Rosenberg Award for Poems on the Jewish Experience 1990) 1991,

Bronx Accent: A Literary and Pictorial History of the Borough (J. M. Kaplan Furthermore grant, New York Soc. Library Book Award for Borough History) 2000, Bittersweet Legacy 2001, Impulse Toward Flight (poetry) 2008. *Honours:* New York State Council on the Arts grant, NEA grant, Edna St Vincent Millay Colony for the Arts grant, Bread Loaf Scholar 1978, Nat. Poetry Competition Award 1982, Ragdale Foundation Fellowships 1985, 1986, Djerassi Foundation Literature Residency 1991, J. H. G. Roberts Writing Award in Poetry 1991. *Address:* c/o English Department, SUNY Rockland Community College, 145 College Road, Suffern, NY, USA (office).

UNGER, David, SL979854-portraitBA, MFA; American writer, poet and translator; b. (David Yarhi Unger), 6 Nov. 1950, Guatemala City, Guatemala; s. of the late Luis Unger and of Fortuna Yarhi Unger; m. Anne Gilman; two d. one step-d. *Education:* Univ. of Massachusetts at Amherst, Columbia Univ., New York. *Career:* US co-ordinator, Guadalajara Int. Book Fair; Dir City Coll. Publishing Certificate Program. *Publications include:* Neither Caterpillar or Butterfly (poetry), The Girl in the Treehouse, Life in the Damn Tropics (novel) 2002 (published in English, Spanish and Chinese), Ni chicha, ni limonada (stories) 2009, The Price of Escape (novel) 2011, Para mi eres divina 2011; translations: Antipoems: New and Selected, by Nicanor Parra 1985, Dead Leaves, by Bárbara Jacobs 1993, First Love and Look for my Obituary, by Elena Garro 1997, Popol Vuh, by Victor Montejo 1999, The Love You Promised Me, by Silvia Molina 1999, Girl from Chimel, by Rigoberta Menchu 2005, Letters to My Mother, by Teresa Cardenas 2006, Old Dog, by Teresa Cardenas 2007, others by Roque Dalton, Mario Benedetti, Sergio Ramirez, Luisa Valenzuela, José Agustin, Paco Igacio Taibo II, Vicente Aleixandre, Enrique Lihn. *Honours:* trans. grants from New York State Council on the Arts; Manhattan Borough Pres.'s Award for Excellence in the Arts 1991, Ivri-Nasawi Poetry Prize 1998. *Address:* Division of Humanities, NAC 5225, City College of New York, New York, NY 10031, USA (office). *Telephone:* (212) 650-7925 (office). *Fax:* (212) 650-7912 (office). *E-mail:* filny@aol.com (office).

UPCHURCH, Michael, BA; American writer; *Book Critic, Seattle Times*; b. 5 Feb. 1954, Rahway, NJ; pnr John Hartl 1992. *Education:* Univ. of Exeter, UK. *Career:* Book Critic, Seattle Times 1998–; mem. Nat. Book Critics' Circle. *Publications:* fiction: Jamboree 1981, Air 1986, The Flame Forest 1989, Passive Intruder 1995; contribs to periodicals including New York Times Book Review, Chicago Tribune, American Scholar, Washington Post Book World, San Francisco Chronicle, Seattle Times, The Oregonian. *Address:* 9725 Sand Point Way, NE, Seattle, WA 98115, USA (office). *Telephone:* (206) 525-2268 (office). *Fax:* (206) 525-0350 (office). *E-mail:* mupchurch@seattletimes.com (office).

UPTON, Andrew; Australian playwright, film-maker and director; m. Cate Blanchett 1997; three s. *Career:* Second Unit Dir, Big Sky (TV series); Dir, two Writers' Studios at the Australian Nat. Playwrights' Centre 1995–96; Co-Artistic Dir, Sydney Theatre Co. 2008–. *Plays:* as writer: Cyrano de Bergerac (adaptation) 1999, Don Juan (adaptation), Hanging Man 2002, Riflemind 2007; as dir: Dissident, Goes Without Saying 2006, Reunion 2007, Ruby Moon 2007. *Films:* Babe (asst ed.) 1995, Parklands (continuity) 1996, The Well 1997, Thank God he Met Lizzie 1997, A Little Bit of Soul 1998, Bangers (writer, prod., dir) 1999. *Literary Agent:* RGM Associates, PO Box 128, Surry Hills, NSW 2010, Australia. *Telephone:* (2) 9281-3911. *Fax:* (2) 9281-4705. *E-mail:* info@rgm.com.au. *Website:* www.rgm.com.au. *Address:* Sydney Theatre Company, PO Box 777, Millers Point, NSW 2000, Australia (office). *Telephone:* (2) 9250-1700 (office). *Fax:* (2) 9251-3687 (office). *E-mail:* mail@sydneytheatre .com.au (office). *Website:* www.sydneytheatre.com.au (office).

UPTON, Lee, BA, MFA, PhD; American academic, poet and writer; *Professor of English, Lafayette College*; b. 2 June 1953, St Johns, Mich.; d. of Charles Upton and Rose Upton; m. Eric Jozef Ziolkowski 1989; two d. *Education:* Michigan State Univ., Univ. of Massachusetts at Amherst, State Univ. of New York at Binghamton. *Career:* Visiting Asst Prof., Lafayette Coll. 1986–87, Asst Prof. of English 1988–92, Assoc. Prof. of English 1992–98, Prof. of English and Writer-in-Residence 1998–; Asst Prof., Grand Valley State Univ. 1987–88; mem. Modern Language Asscn, Nat. Council of Teachers of English, Poetry Soc. of America. *Publications:* poetry: The Invention of Kindness 1984, Sudden Distances 1988, No Mercy 1989, Approximate Darling 1996, Civilian Histories 2000, Undid in the Land of the Undone 2007; criticism: Jean Garrigue: A Poetics of Plenitude 1991, Obsession and Release: Rereading the Poetry of Louise Bogan 1996, The Muse of Abandonment: Origin, Identity and Mastery in Five American Poets 1998, Defensive Measures 2005; contribs to numerous reviews, quarterlies, journals and periodicals. *Honours:* Pushcart Prize 1988, Georgia Contemporary Poetry Series Award 1996, 2000, The Writer/Emily Dickinson Award 2005, Lyric Poetry Award 2005, Best American Poetry Award 2008. *Address:* Department of English, Lafayette College, Easton, PA 18042, USA (office). *Telephone:* (610) 330-5250 (office). *E-mail:* uptonlee@ lafayette.edu (office).

URASAWA, Naoki; Japanese writer and illustrator; b. 2 Jan. 1960, Fuchu, Tokyo. *Education:* Meisei Univ. *Career:* creator of numerous manga comic series; professional debut with Beta!! 1984. *Publications:* manga comics: Yawara!: A Fashionable Judo Girl (29 vols) (Shogakukan Manga Award 1990) 1986–93, Pineapple Army (10 vols, illustrator) 1986–88, Dancing Policeman 1987, Master Keaton (18 vols) 1988–94, Happy! (23 vols) 1993–99, Monster (18 vols) (Media Arts Festival Award for Excellence 1997, Asahi Newspaper Tezuka Osamu Award 1999) 1994–2001, 20th Century Boys (21 vols) (Media Arts Festival Award for Excellence 2002) 1999–, Pluto (two vols) (Tezuka Grand Prize 2005) 2003–09, Billy Bat 2008–; short story collections: NASA 1988, Jigoro! 1994. *Honours:* Shogakukan New Manga Artist Award 1982. *Address:* c/o Shogakukan Inc., 2-3-1, Hitotsubashi, Chiyoda-ku, Tokyo 101-8001, Japan. *Website:* www.shogakukan.co.jp.

URBAN, Jerzy; Polish journalist; *President, URMA Company Ltd*; b. 3 Aug. 1933, Łódź; s. of Jan Urban and Maria Urban; m. 1st 1957; one d.; m. 3rd Małgorzata Daniszewska 1986. *Education:* Warsaw Univ. *Career:* staff writer, weekly Po Prostu, Warsaw 1955–57; head of home section, weekly Polityka, Warsaw 1960–63, 1968–81; columnist of satirical weekly Szpilki, articles written under pen-names including Jan Rem and Jerzy Kibic; Govt Press Spokesman 1981–89; Minister without portfolio, Head Cttee for Radio and Television April–Sept. 1989; Dir and Ed.-in-Chief, Nat. Workers' Agency Nov. 1989–90; Dir and Ed.-in-Chief Unia-Press Feb.–May 1990; Pres. Kier Co. Ltd 1990–; Pres. URMA Co. Ltd, Warsaw 1991–; Ed.-in-Chief, political weekly Nie Oct. 1990–; participant Round Table debates, mem. group for mass media Feb.–April 1990; mem. Journalists' Asscn of Polish People's Repub. 1982–, Polish Writers' Union. *Screenplays include:* Sekret, Otello. *Publications:* Kolekcja Jerzego Kibica 1972, Impertynencje: Felietony z lat 1969–72 1974, Wszystkie nasze ciemne sprawy 1974, Grzechy chodzą po ludziach 1975, Gorączka 1981, Romanse 1981, Robak w jabłku 1982, Na odlew 1983, Samosądy 1 1984, Felietony dla cudzych zon 1984, Samosądy 2 1984, Z pieprzem i solą 1986, Jakim prawem 1988, Rozkosze podglądania 1988, Cały Urban 1989, Alfabet Urbana 1990, Jajakobyły 1991, Prima aprilis towarzysze 1992, Klątwa Urbana 1995, Druga Klątwa Urbana 2000. *Honours:* Ztoty KrzyżZastTugi, KrzyżKomandorski Polonia Restituta; Victor Prize (TV) 1987. *Address:* URMA Co. Ltd, ul. Słoneczna 25, 00 789 Warsaw, Poland (office). *Telephone:* (22) 8485290 (office). *Fax:* (22) 8497258 (office). *E-mail:* nie@ redakcja.nie.com.pl (office). *Website:* www.nie.com.pl (office).

URIAS, Alfonso Quijada, (Kijadurías); Salvadorean writer and poet; b. 8 Dec. 1940, Quezaltepeque. *Career:* fmr journalist. *Publications:* poetry: Poemas 1967, Los estados supernaturales y otros poemas 1971, Reunión 1992, De Este Tiempo 1994, Alteración del orden 1996, Obscuro 1997, Gotas sobre una hoja de loto 1997, La esfera imaginaria 1997, Es cara musa 1997, Toda razón dispersa 1998; fiction: Cuentos 1971, Otras historias famosas 1974, La fama infame del famoso a(pá)trida 1979, Para mirarte mejor 1987, Gravísima, altisonante, mínima, dulce e imaginada historia 1967–1991 1993, The Better to See You (short stories) 1994, Lujuria tropical 1996, Confusión y otros poemas (Premio de Poesía Instituto Cervantes) 2003. *Honours:* Winner, Poetry Prize, Juegos Florales de Quetzaltenango 1967.

URIBE, Kirmen; Spanish poet and columnist; b. 11 Oct. 1970, Ondarroa, Bizkaia. *Education:* Univ. of the Basque Country. *Career:* jailed for resisting universal compulsory mil. service 1995; worked as poet, teacher, columnist, translator, scriptwriter, multimedia, music collaborator; columnist, Egunkaria 1999, also Berria and Gara newspapers; scriptwriter ETB-1 (Basque-language public television station) 2003. *Publications:* poetry: Bar Puerto 2001, Zaharregia, txikiegia again 2001, Bitartean heldu eskutik (Spain's Premio de la Crítica) 2001, Bitartean heldu eskutik 2003, Mientras tanto dame la mano 2004, Meanwhile Take My Hand (English edition) (Critics' Prize) 2007; novel: Bilbao-New York-Bilbao (Premio Nacional de Narrativa 2009) 2008; essay: Lizardi eta erotismoa 1996; children's books: Garmendia eta zaldun beltza 2003, Ekidazu, lehoiek ez dakite biolina jotzen 2003, Ez naiz ilehoria, eta zer? 2004, Garmendia errege 2004, Garmendia eta Fannyren sekretua 2006; anthology: Portukoplak 2006. *Address:* Graywolf Press, 250 Third Avenue North, Suite 600, Minneapolis, MN 55401, USA. *Telephone:* (651) 641-0077. *Fax:* (651) 641-0036. *E-mail:* kirmenu@gmail.com (home); wolves@graywolfpress.org. *Website:* www.kirmenuribe.com/en; www .graywolfpress.org.

URIBE ARCE, Armando; Chilean writer, poet, lawyer and fmr diplomatist; b. 28 Oct. 1933, Santiago. *Career:* Amb. to China 1970–73; taught law at Universidad de Chile, Universidad Católica de Chile, Michigan State Univ., Univ., Sassari Univ., Italy, Univ. of Paris. *Publications:* El joven laurel 1953, Transeúnte pálido 1954, El engañoso laúd 1956, De los delitos calificados por el resultado 1957, Los obstáculos 1961, Una experiencia de la poesía 1962, Pound 1963, Repertorio de palabras de la ley penal chilena 1965, Posesión minera 1965, Los veinte años 1965, Léataud y el otro 1966, Dominio minero 1966, No hay lugar 1971, El libro negro de la intervención norteamericana en Chile 1974, Ces messieurs du Chili 1978, Por ser vos quien sois 1989, Alone, la sombra inquieta 1997, Odio lo que odio, Rabio como Rabio 1998, Las brujas de Uniforme 1998, Imágenes quebradas 1998, Los Ataúdes-Las Erratas 1999, El accidente Pinochet 1999, A Peor Vida 2000, Contra la voluntad 2000, El Fantasma de la sonrazón y el secreto de la poesía 2001, La inquietante extrañez 2001, Verso bruto 2002, Carta abierta a Agustín Edwards 2002, Memorias para Cecilia 2002, Caballeros de Chile 2003, Diario enamorado 2003, Cabeza de vaca 2003, El criollo en su destierro 2003, Obra reunida (1951–1989) 2004, Las críticas en crisis 2004, Qué debo hacer? 2004, De muerte 2004, Conversaciones en privado 2004, El viejo laurel 2004, Desdijo 2005, Insignificantes 2005, Ahorcón 2005, Te amo y de odio 2005, La fe el amor la estupidez 2006, De memoria. By Heart 2006, Coloquio del oro y del moro 2006, De nada, diario en verso 2006, Apocalipsis apócrifo 2006. *Honours:* Nat. Prize for Literature 2004. *Address:* c/o Editorial Norma, Avenida Providencia 1760, Of. 502, Providencia, Santiago, Chile (office). *E-mail:* ventasnorma@ carvajal.cl (office). *Website:* www.norma.com (office).

URQUHART, Jane, OC, BA; Canadian writer; b. 21 June 1949, Gerladton, Ont.; d. of Walter Andrew Carter and Marian Carter (née Quinn); m. Tony Urquhart 1976; one d. *Education:* Havergal Coll., Univ. of Guelph. *Career:* writer 1978–; Writer-in-Residence, Univ. of Ottawa 1990–, Memorial Univ. of Newfoundland 1992–, Massey Coll., Univ. of Toronto 1997–; mem. Writer's Union of Canada, PEN. *Publications:* poetry: False Shuffles 1981, I am Walking in the Garden of His Imaginary Palace 1981, The Little Flowers of Mme de Montespan 1984, Some Other Garden 2000; novels: The Whirlpool (aka Niagara) (Best Foreign Book Award, Paris 1992) 1986, Changing Heaven 1990, Away 1993, The Underpainter (Gov.-Gen.'s Award) 1997, The Stone Carvers 2001, A Map of Glass 2005, Sanctuary Line 2010; short stories: Storm Glass 1987. *Honours:* Hon. LLD (Waterloo) 1997, (St Thomas) 1998, (Newfoundland) 1999, (Guelph) 1999, (Toronto) 1999; Govt of Ont. Trillium Award (with Margaret Atwood) 1993, Marian Engel Award 1994. *Address:* c/o McClelland and Stewart Ltd., 75 Sherbourne Street, 5th Floor, Toronto, ON M5A 2P9, Canada (office). *Website:* www.mcclelland.com (office).

URSELL, Geoffrey, BA, MA, PhD; Canadian writer, dramatist, poet and publisher; b. 14 March 1943, Moose Jaw, Sask.; m. Barbara Sapergia 1967. *Education:* Univ. of Manitoba, Univ. of London. *Career:* Lecturer, Univ. of Regina 1975–79, Special Asst Prof. in English 1980–81, 1982–83; Co-founder and Pres. Coteau Books 1975–; Writer-in-Residence, Saskatoon Public Library 1984–85; mem. Writers Union of Canada, Asscn of Canadian Television and Radio Artists, Guild of Canadian Playwrights, Playwrights Canada. *Publications:* Number One Northern: Poetry from Saskatchewan (co-ed.) 1977, The Tenth Negative Pig (co-author) 1980, The Running of the Deer (play) (Clifford E. Lee Nat. Playwriting Award 1977) 1981, Saskatoon Pie! (Persephone Theatre Nat. Playwriting Award) 1981, Black Powder (musical) 1982, Saskatchewan Gold (ed.) 1982, Trap Lines (poems) 1982, Perdue, or, How the West Was Lost (novel) (WHSmith/Books in Canada First Novel Award) 1984, Sky High: Stories from Saskatchewan 1988, Way Out West (short stories) 1989, The Look-Out Tower (poems) 1989, Jumbo Gumbo (co-ed.) (Vicki Metcalfe Award) 1990, Due West (ed.) 1996; various unpublished stage plays and radio plays; contrib. to periodicals. *Honours:* several prizes and awards. *Address:* Coteau Books, 2517 Victoria Avenue, Regina, SK S4P 0T2, Canada. *Telephone:* (306) 777-0170. *Fax:* (306) 522-5152. *E-mail:* coteau@coteaubooks.com. *Website:* coteaubooks.com.

USHERWOOD, Elizabeth Ada; British writer and lecturer; b. 10 July 1923, London; d. of Walter Beavington and Annie Beavington (née Noonan); m. Stephen Usherwood 1970. *Career:* fmr Red Cross nurse; fmr int. banker; lectures on historical subjects. *Publications:* Visit Some London Catholic Churches (with Stephen Usherwood) 1982, The Counter-Armada 1596: The Journal of the 'Mary Rose' (with Stephen Usherwood) 1983, We Die for the Old Religion (with Stephen Usherwood) 1987, Women First 1989, A Saint in the Family (with Stephen Usherwood) 1992; contribs to periodicals. *Address:* 24 St Mary's Grove, Canonbury, London, N1 2NT, England (home). *Telephone:* (20) 7226-9813 (home). *E-mail:* eau@waitrose.com (home).

UTAMI, Ayu; Indonesian writer; b. 21 Nov. 1968, Bogor. *Publications:* novels: Saman 1998, Larung 2001, Bilangan Fu 2008; short stories: Buku lain: kumpulan kolom Si Parasit Lajang 2003. *Honours:* Best Novel, Jakarta Art Council 1998, Dutch Prince Clause Award 2000. *Address:* Jln. Utan Kayu, 68H, 13120 Jakarta, Indonesia (office). *Telephone:* (21) 8573388 (office). *Fax:* (21) 8573387 (office). *E-mail:* ayuutami@ayuutami.com (office).

UTLEY, Steven; American writer and poet; b. 10 Nov. 1948, Fort Knox, Ky. *Education:* Middle Tennessee State Univ., Murfreesboro. *Publications:* Lone Star Universe (anthology, ed. with Geo W. Proctor) 1976, Ghost Seas (short stories) 1997, This Impatient Ape (poems) 1998, Career Moves of the Gods (poems) 2000, The Beasts of Love (short stories) 2004, Where or When (short stories) 2005, Passing for Human (anthology, ed. with Michael Bishop) 2009, The 400-Million-Year Itch (short stories) 2012; contrib. to Asimov's Science Fiction, The Magazine of Fantasy and Science Fiction, Postscripts, Bewildering Stories. *Address:* 113 Kentwell Drive, Smyrna, TN 37167, USA (home). *E-mail:* impatientape@yahoo.com (office). *Website:* impatientape.livejournal.com.

UTTAMCHANDANI, Sundri Assandas, MA; Indian writer; b. 28 Sept. 1924, Hyderabad, Sind (now Pakistan); d. of Doolaram Ichatanmal Narwani; m. Assandas Uttamchandani 1947; two d. *Education:* Univs in Pakistan and India. *Career:* has acted on stage and in one film; co-ed. SATHI (women's magazine) 1946; Pres. Sindhu Women's Org. *Publications:* two novels and eight short story collections including Bhuri, To Jineeji Tat Bardhan, Travelogue (essays); has published translations of several novels; magazine articles and works for TV and radio. *Honours:* numerous awards including Soviet Land Nehru Peace Prize, Hindi Directorate Award, Sahitya Acad. Award 1986, Akhil B. B. Sabha Prize. *Address:* 12B-2 Jethi K., Sipahimalani Co-p Soc, Mahim, Mumbai 400 016, India (home). *Telephone:* (22) 24441130 (home).

UYS, Pieter-Dirk, BA; South African playwright, performer and producer; b. 28 Sept. 1945, Cape Town; s. of Helga Bassel and Hannes Uys. *Education:* Univ. of Cape Town, London Film School, UK. *Career:* joined Space Theatre, Cape Town 1973; f. Syrkel Theatre Co.; Dir P. D. Uys Productions, Bapetikosweti Marketing Enterprises; produced and performed 30 plays in revues throughout SA and in UK, USA, Australia, Canada, Netherlands; several videos and TV films and documentaries. *Theatre:* cr. Mrs Evita Bezuidenhout – the most famous white woman in South Africa. *Television:* Evita Live and Dangerous, weekly talk/satire show 1999. *Publications:* Die van Aardes van Grootoor 1979, Paradise is Closing Down 1980, God's Forgotten 1981, Karnaval 1982, Selle ou storie 1983, Farce about Uys 1984, Appassionata 1985, Skote! 1986, Paradise is Closing Down and Other Plays 1989, No one's Died Laughing 1986, P.W. Botha: In His Own Words 1987, A Part Hate, A Part Love 1990, Funigalore 1995, Elections and Erections 2002, Between the Devil and the Deep 2005. *Honours:* Hon. DLitt (Rhodes Univ.) 1997, (Univ. of Cape Town) 2003, (Univ. of the Witwatersrand) 2004; Hon. DEdu (Univ. of the Western Cape) 2003; Truth and Reconciliation Award 2001. *Address:* Evita SE Perron Theatre/Cafe/Bar Darling Station, Darling 7345 (office); 17 Station Road, Darling 7345, South Africa (home). *Telephone:* (22) 4922831 (office); (22) 4923208 (home). *Fax:* (22) 4923208 (home). *E-mail:* evita@evita.co.za (office). *Website:* www.evita.co.za; www.pdu.co.za.

V

VACHSS, Andrew Henry, BA, JD; American attorney, consultant and writer; b. 19 Oct. 1942, New York, NY; m. Alice Vachss. *Education:* Case Western Reserve University, New England School of Law. *Career:* called to the Bar, NY 1976, US Dist Court (S and E Dists), NY 1976; Program Rep., USPHS, Ohio 1965–66; Unit Supervisor, New York City Dept of Social Services 1966–69; Urban Co-ordinator, Community Devt Foundation, Norwalk, Conn. 1969–70; Dir Uptown Community Org., Chicago 1970–71; Deputy Dir Medfield (Mass)-Norfolk Prison Project 1971–72; Dir Intensive Treatment Unit ANDROS II, Roslindale, Mass 1972–73; Project Dir, Massachusetts Dept of Youth Services, Boston 1972–73; Dir Juvenile Justice Planning Project, New York 1975–85; pvt. practice, New York 1976–; Organizer and Co-ordinator Calumet (Ind.) Community Congress 1970; mem. Bd of Dirs Libra Inc., Cambridge, Mass, Advocacy Assocs, NY and NJ; Adunct Prof., Coll. New Resources, New York 1980–81; lecturer, trainer and speaker to numerous orgs; consultant on juvenile justice and child abuse to numerous orgs 1971–; mem. PEN American Center, Writers' Guild of America. *Publications:* novels: Flood 1985, Strega 1987, Blue Belle 1988, Hard Candy 1989, Blossom 1990, Sacrifice 1991, Shella 1993, Down in the Zero 1994, Another Chance to Get it Right 1995, Footsteps of the Hawk 1995, Batman: The Ultimate Evil 1995, False Allegations 1996, Safe House 1998, Choice of Evil 1999, Dead and Gone 2000, Pain Management 2001, Only Child 2002, The Getaway Man 2003, Down Here 2004, Two Trains Running 2005, Mask Market 2006, Terminal 2007, Another Life 2008, Haiku 2009, The Weight 2010; graphic novels: Hard Looks: Adapted Stories 1992, Predator: Race War 1995; other: The Life-Style Violent Juvenile: The Secure Treatment Approach (non-fiction) 1979, Proving It (audio book) 2001, Born Bad: Stories 1994, Everybody Pays: Stories 1999. *Honours:* John Hay Whitney Foundation Fellow 1976–77, Grand Prix de Littérature Policière 1988, Falcon Award, Maltese Falcon Soc. of Japan 1988, Deutschen Krimi Preis from Die Jury des Bochumer Krimi Archivs 1989, Raymond Chandler Award 2000. *Literary Agent:* c/o Ten Angry Pitbulls, Inc., 1658 N Milwaukee Avenue, Suite 535, Chicago, IL 60647, USA. *Telephone:* (773) 342-3407. *Website:* www.tenangrypitbulls.com. *Address:* 16 East 34th Street, FL16, New York, NY 10016-4359, USA (office). *Telephone:* (917) 816-2170 (office). *Fax:* (212) 949-8828 (office). *Website:* www.vachss.com.

VACULÍK, Ludvík; Czech writer, journalist and essayist; b. 23 July 1926, Brumov. *Career:* expelled from Communist Party 1967; publications banned by Communists 1968–89; signatory to Charter 77 human rights declaration; Ed. Literární Noviny, Rude Pravo; publisher of samizdat (clandestinely copied and printed) series, Edice Petlice 1973–79; columnist Lidové Noviny. *Publications include:* Na farmě mládeže 1958, Rušný dům 1963, Sekyra (trans. as The Axe) 1966, Morčata (trans. as The Guinea Pigs) 1970, Ceský Snář 1980, Milí spolužáci! 1986, Jaro je tady 1987, Srpnový rok 1990, Ach Stifter 1991, Stará dáma se baví 1991, Jak se dělá chlapec (trans. as How to Make a Boy) 1993, Poco rubato 1994, Nad jezerem škaredě hrát 1996, Nepaměti 1998, Cesta na Praděd 2001, Poslední slovo 2002, Loučeni k panně 2002, Vážený pane Mikule 2003, Polepšené pěsničky 2006, Hodiny klavíru 2007, Dřevená mysl 2008, Tisíce slov 2009. *E-mail:* info.vaculik@gmail.com (office). *Website:* www.ludvikvaculik.cz.

VAID, Krishna Baldev; Indian writer; b. 27 July 1927, Dinga, Punjab. *Career:* Hindi writer; taught at numerous univs in USA. *Publications include:* Us ka Bachpan (trans. as Steps of Darkness) 1957, Beech Ka Darwaza, Mera Dushman, Bimal Urf Jayen to Jayen Kahan (trans. as Bimal in Bog) 1974, Us ke Bayan, Nasreen, Dusra na koi (trans. as There is no Other) 1978, Dard la Dava, Meri Priya Kahanian, Guzara Hua Zamana (trans. as The Broken Mirror) 1981, Kala Kolaj, Pratinidhi Kahanian, Nar Naari, Bhookh Aag Hai, Mayalok (trans. as The World of Illusion) 1999, Hamaari Burhiya, Ek Naukrani ki Diary (trans. as The Diary of a Maidservant). *Address:* 1652, B-1, Vasant Kunj, New Delhi 110 070, India (home). *Telephone:* (11) 6895177 (home).

VAIZEY, Lady Marina, CBE, MA; British (b. American) art critic, lecturer and writer; b. 16 Jan. 1938, d. of Lyman Stansky and Ruth Stansky; m. Lord Vaizey 1961 (died 1984); two s. one d. *Education:* Brearley School, New York, Putney School, Vermont, Radcliffe Coll., Harvard Univ. and Girton Coll., Cambridge, UK. *Career:* Art Critic, Financial Times 1970–74, Sunday Times 1974–92; Dance Critic Now! 1979–81; mem. Art Panel Arts Council 1973–79, Deputy Chair. 1976–79; mem. Paintings for Hosps 1974–1990; mem. Advisory Cttee Dept of Environment 1975–81, mem. Art Working Group on Nat. Curriculum, Dept of Educ. and Science 1990–91; mem. Cttee Contemporary Arts Soc. 1975–79, 1980–94; Exec. Dir Mitchell Prize for the History of Art 1976–87; mem. History of Art and Complementary Studies Bd, CNAA 1978–82, Photography Bd 1979–81, Fine Arts Bd 1980–83, Cttee 20th Century Soc. 1995–98; Trustee, Nat. Museums and Galleries on Merseyside 1986–2001, Geffrye Museum, London 1990–2010, Imperial War Museum 1991–2003, Council of Friends of the Imperial War Museum 2003–; Chair. Council of Friends of the Victoria and Albert Museum 2007– (mem. 2002–); mem. Fine Arts Advisory Cttee British Council 1987–2005, Crafts Council 1988–94; mem. Int. Rescue Cttee UK 1998–2006; Editorial Dir Nat. Art Collections Fund 1991–94 (Consultant 1994–98); Gov. Camberwell Coll. of Arts and Crafts 1971–82, Bath Acad. of Art 1978–81, South Bank Centre 1993–2003, London Open House 1996–2007, Nat. Army Museum 2001–08; touring exhbn Painter as Photographer 1982–85; Judge, Turner Prize 1997. *Publications:* 100 Masterpieces of Art 1979, Andrew Wyeth 1980, The Artist as Photographer 1982, Peter Blake 1985, Christiane Kubrick 1990, Christo 1990, Sorensen 1994, Picasso's Ladies 1998, Sutton Taylor 1999, Felim Egan 1999, Great Women Collectors (with Charlotte Gere) 1999, Art, the Critics' Choice (ed.) 1999, Magdalene Odundo 2001, Wendy Ramshaw 2004, Andrew Logan 2008; articles in periodicals, anthologies and catalogues. *Address:* 41 Brackley Road, Chiswick, London, W4 2HW, England (home). *Telephone:* (20) 8994-7994 (home). *E-mail:* marina@vaizey.demon.co.uk.

VAKSBERG, Arkady Iosifovich, DJur; Russian writer, journalist and lawyer; b. 11 Nov. 1933, Novosibirsk; m.; one d. *Education:* Moscow State Univ. *Career:* barrister Moscow City Bd of Bar –1973; political observer in Paris, Literaturnaya Gazeta; Vice-Pres. Russian PEN Centre; mem. Russian Writer's Union, Journalist's Union, Union of Cinematography Workers, Int. Cttee of Writers in Prison. *Screenplays for films:* The Storm Warning, The Provincial Romance, In Broad Daylight. *Plays:* A Shot in the Dark, The Supreme Court, The Alarm. *TV work includes:* The Special Reporter (serial), A Dangerous Zone (actor and scriptwriter), Reprise (Grand-Prix and Best Screenplay, International Telefilm Festival), L'Asture et l'Amour (scriptwriter), Ils ont emporté avec eux la Russie (Grand-Prix, Int. Felices Documenteure 2009, Russie). *Publications:* three books and numerous articles on copyright law; over 40 works of fiction, collections of essays, biogs. and memoirs. *Honours:* Grand-Prix, the Eurasian Teleforum (Moscow). *Address:* Krasnoarmeiskaya str. 23, Apt 65, 125319 Moscow, Russia (home); 17 blvd Garibaldi, 75015 Paris, France (home). *Telephone:* (499) 151-33-69 (Moscow) (home); 1-45-66-45-31 (Paris) (home). *E-mail:* varkadi@yandex.ru (office).

VALENTINE, Alana, BA; Australian playwright; b. Redfern, NSW. *Education:* Univ. of Sydney. *Radio plays:* Screamers, The Word Salon, Oysters at the Paragon, Swallowing Communion. *Screenplays:* Mother Love 1994, The Witnesses 1995, Reef Dreaming 1997. *Plays:* The Story of Anger Lee Bredenza 1989, Southern Belle 1994, Swimming the Globe 1996, The Conjurers 1997, Spool Time 1998, Ozone 1998, Savage Grace 2001, Row of Tents 2001, The Prospectors 2001, The Mapmaker's Brother 2002, Titania's Boy 2003, Run Rabbit Run 2004, The Prospectors 2004, Covenant 2005, Crossing the Mountains 2005, Butterfly Dandy 2005, Parramatta Girls 2007. *Honours:* AWGIE Award, NSW State Literary Award, Churchill Fellowship, Rodney Seaborne Playwright's Award, ANPC/New Dramatist's Award, NSW Writer's Fellowship 2003, Queensland Premier's Literary Award 2004. *Literary Agent:* RGM Associates, PO Box 128, Surry Hills, NSW 2010, Australia. *Telephone:* (2) 9281-3911. *Fax:* (2) 9281-4705. *E-mail:* info@rgm.com.au. *Website:* www.rgm.com.au.

VALENZUELA, Luisa; Argentine writer and journalist; b. 26 Nov. 1938, Buenos Aires; d. of Luisa Mercedes Levinson and Pablo F. Valenzuela; m. Théodore Marjak 1958 (divorced); one d. *Education:* Belgrano Girls' School, Colegio Nacional Vicente Lopez, Buenos Aires. *Career:* lived in Paris, writing for Argentinian newspapers and for the RTF 1958–61; Asst Ed. La Nación Sunday Supplement, Buenos Aires 1964–69; writer, lecturer, freelance journalist in USA, Mexico, France, Spain 1970–73, Buenos Aires 1973–79; taught in Writing Div., Columbia Univ., New York 1980–83; conducted writers' workshops, English Dept, New York Univ. and seminars, Writing Div. 1984–89; returned to Buenos Aires 1989; Fulbright Grant 1969–70; Guggenheim Fellow 1983; Fellow, New York Inst. for the Humanities; mem. Acad. of Arts and Sciences, Puerto Rico. *Publications:* novels: Hay que sonreír 1966, El gato eficaz 1972, Como en la guerra 1977, Cambio de armas 1982, Cola de largartija 1983, Novela negra con argentinos 1990, Realidad Nacional desde la cama 1990, La travesía 2001, Trilogía de los bajos fondos 2004; short stories: Los heréticos 1967, Aquí pasan cosas raras 1976, Libro que no muerde 1980, Donde viven las águilas 1983, Simetrías (Cuentos de Hades) 1993, Antología Personal 1998, Cuentos Completos y Uno Más 1999, BREVS, microrrelatos completos hasta hoy 2004, Juego de villanos 2008, Tres por cinco 2008, Generosos inconvenientes 2008. *Honours:* Dr. hc (Knox Coll., Ill.) 1991; Machado de Assis Medal, Brazilian Acad. of Letters 1997. *Literary Agent:* c/o Amy Berkower, Writers House, 21 West 26th Street, New York, NY 10010, USA. *Telephone:* (212) 685-2400. *Fax:* (212) 685-1781. *E-mail:* aberkower@writershouse.com. *Website:* www.writershouse.com; www.luisavalenzuela.com.

VALERY, Anne; British scriptwriter, novelist and playwright; b. (Anne Catherine Firth), 24 Feb. 1926, London, England. *Education:* South Hampstead High School, Badminton School. *Career:* lecturer in writing for TV; TV producer for overseas stations; has presented more than 500 programmes on TV; mem. PEN International, Fawcett Soc. *Plays:* more than 40 plays for TV; Tenko (series) (BAFTA Award 1984), Crown Court. *Publications:* Baron Von Kodak, Shirley Temple and Me 1973, The Edge of a Smile 1974, The Passing Out Parade (theatre) 1979, Tenko Reunion 1984, Talking About the War... (non-fiction) 1991; contrib. to A Stately Homo, Radio Times and other publs. *Honours:* Telegraph Book of the Month. *Address:* Flat 3, 28 Arkwright Road, London, NW3 6BH, England (home). *Telephone:* (20) 7435-8663 (home).

VALGARDSON, William Dempsey, BA, BEd, MFA; Canadian writer, poet, dramatist and academic; b. 7 May 1939, Winnipeg, Manitoba; m. (divorced); one s. one d. *Education:* United Coll., Univ. of Manitoba, Univ. of Iowa. *Career:* Assoc. Prof., Univ. of Victoria, BC 1970–74, Prof. 1974–; Fiction Ed., Canadian Author 1996–. *Publications:* Bloodflowers 1973, God is Not a Fish Inspector 1975, In the Gutting Shed 1976, Red Dust 1978, Gentle Simmers 1980, The Carpenter of Dreams 1986, What Can't Be Changed Shouldn't Be Mourned 1990, The Girl With the Botticelli Face 1992, Thor 1994, Sarah and the People of Sand River 1996, Garbage Creek 1997, The Divorced Kids Club 1998, Frances 2002. *Honours:* Books in Canada First Novel Award 1980, Ethel Wilson Literary Prize 1992, Mr Christie Prize 1995, Vicky Metcalf Short Story Award 1998. *Address:* 1908 Waterloo Road, Victoria, BC V8P 1J3, Canada (home). *Telephone:* (250) 595-5648 (home).

VALLBONA, Rima Gretel Rothe, (Rima de Vallbona), BS, MA, DML; Costa Rican/American academic and writer; *Professor Emerita of Spanish, University of St Thomas*; b. 15 March 1931, San José, Costa Rica; d. of the late Ferdinand Hermann and Emilia (née Strassburger) Rothe; m. Carlos Vallbona 1956; four c. *Education:* Colegio Superior de Señoritas, San José, Univ. of Costa Rica, Middlebury Coll., VT, Univ. of Paris (Sorbonne), France and Univ. of Salamanca, Spain. *Career:* Liceo J. J. Vargas Calvo, Costa Rica 1955–56; Faculty mem. specializing in Latin American Literature Univ. of St Thomas, Houston, TX 1964–, Head then Chair. Spanish Dept 1966–71, Prof. of Spanish 1978–95, Chair. Modern Languages Dept 1978–81, Cullen Foundation Prof. of Spanish 1989–95, Prof. Emer. 1995–; Visiting Prof. Univ. of Houston 1975–76, Madrid 1980, Rice Univ. and Univ. of Houston 1981–83, 1995; mem. Nat. Writers Asscn, Latin American Writers Inst., Inst. of Hispanic Culture of Houston, Cultural Arts Council of Houston, Instituto Literario y Cultural Hispánico de Houston, Houston Hispanic Women in Leadership Org., South Central Org. of Latin American Studies, American Asscn of Teachers of Spanish and Portuguese, Soc. of Children's Book Writers and Illustrators, Texas Freelance Writers Asscn, Comunidad de Escritores Latinoamericanos de Costa Rica, Asociación de Literatura Femenina Hispánica, Instituto Internacional de Literatura Iberoamericana, Asociación de Licenciados y Doctores Españoles en Estados Unidos, Asociación Costarricense de Escritoras, Academia Norteamerican de la Lengua Española 1999–. *Publications:* literary studies: Yolanda Oreamuno 1971, La obra en prosa de Eunice Odio 1981, Vida i sucesos de la Monja Alférez 1992, La narrativa de Yolanda Oreamuno 1995; novels: Noche en vela 1968, Las sombras que perseguimos 1983, Mundo, demonio y mujer 1991; short stories: Polvo del camino 1973, La salamandra rosada 1979, Mujeres y agonias 1982, Baraja de soledades 1983, Cosecha de pecadores 1988, El arcángel del perdón 1990, Los infernos de la mujer y algo más... 1992, Flowering Inferno: Tales of Sinking Hearts 1992, Tormy, la gata prodigiosa de Donaldito (children's) 1997, Tejedoras de sueños versus realidad (short stories) 2003, A la deriva del tiempo y de la historia 2007. *Honours:* El Lazo de Dama de la Orden del Mérito Civil, Spain 1989; Nat. Novel Prize, Costa Rica 1968, Jorge Luis Borges Short Story Prize, Fundación Givré, Argentina 1977, Agripina Montes del Valle Latin American Novel Prize, Colombia 1978, Prof. Lilia Ramos Children's Poetry Prize, Uruguay 1978, Constantin Foundation Research Grants, Univ. of St Thomas 1981, Southwest Conf. of Latin American Studies Literary Prize 1982, Ancora Award for Best Book, Costa Rica 1983–84, Hispanic Women Hall Award 1993, Bay Area Writers' League Prize 2003. *Address:* 3706 Lake Street, Houston, TX 77098, USA (home). *Telephone:* (713) 528-6137 (home). *E-mail:* rvallbona@aol.com (home).

VALLEJO, Fernando; Colombian writer, screenwriter and film director; b. 1942, Medellín. *Education:* Universidad Nacional, Universidad de los Andes, Centro Sperimentale di Cinematografia, Rome, Italy. *Films:* Crónica roja (screenplay and dir) 1977, En la tormenta (screenplay and dir) 1980, Barrio de campeones (screenplay and dir) 1981. *Publications include:* Logoi (non-fiction) 1983, Barba Jacob el mensajero (biog.) 1983, Los días azules (vol. one of autobiog., El río del tiempo) 1984, El fuego secreto (vol. two of autobiog., El río del tiempo) 1985, Los caminos a Roma (vol. three of autobiog., El río del tiempo) 1986, Años de indulgencia (vol. four of autobiog., El río del tiempo) 1987, Entre fantasmas (vol. five of autobiog., El río del tiempo) 1992, La virgen de los sicarios (novel, trans. as Our Lady of the Assassins) 1994, Almas en pena chapolas negras (biog.) 1996, La tautología darwinista (essays) 1998, El desbarrancadero (Premio Internacional de Novela Rómulo Gallegos 2003) 2001, La rambla paralela 2002, Mi hermano el alcalde 2003, Manualito de imposturología física (essays) 2005, La Puta de Babilonia (essays) 2007. *Literary Agent:* Thomas Colchie, The Colchie Agency, 324 85th Street, Brooklyn, NY 11209, USA. *Telephone:* (718) 921-7468. *Fax:* (718) 921-7468. *E-mail:* colchieagency@gmail.com.

VALLGREN, Carl-Johan; Swedish writer and musician; b. 26 July 1964, Linköping. *Recordings:* albums: Klädpoker med Djävulen 1996, Easy listening för masochister 1998, Kärlek och andra katastrofer 2001, 2000 mil, 400 nätter 2003, I provinsen 2004, Livet 2007. *Publications:* novels: Nomaderna 1987, Längta bort 1988, Fågelkvinnan 1991, Berättelser om sömn och vaka 1994, Dokument rörande Spelaren Rubashov 1996, För herr Bachmanns broschyr 1998, Berlin på 8 kapitel 1999, Den vidunderliga kärlekens historia (Augustpriset 2002) 2002, Kunzelmann & Kunzelmann 2009. *Honours:* Årets bok-Månadens boks litterära pris 2002, Tylösandspriset 2004. *Address:* c/o Bonnier Books, PO Box 3159, 103 63 Stockholm, Sweden (office). *E-mail:* bonnierforlagen@bok.bonnier.se (office). *Website:* www.vallgren.nu.

VALLVEY, Ángela, BA; Spanish writer and poet; b. 1964, Ciudad Real. *Education:* Universidad de Granada. *Publications:* poetry: Capitales de tiniebla 1997, El tamaño del universo (Premio Jaén de Poesía) 1998, Extraños en el paraiso 2001, Nacida en cautividad 2006; novels: Kippel y la mirada electrónica 1995, Donde todos somos John Wayne 1997, Vida sentimental de Bugs Bunny 1997, A la caza del último hombre salvaje 2000, Vías de extinción 2000, Los estados carenciales (Premio Nadal) 2002, No lo llames amor 2003, La ciudad del diablo 2005, Todas las muñecas son carnívoras 2006, Muerte entre poetas 2008. *Honours:* Premio Ateneo de Sevilla de Poesía. *Literary Agent:* c/o Teresa Vilarrubla, MB Agencia Literaria, Casp 78, 3er 3a, 08010 Barcelona, Spain. *Telephone:* (93) 2659064. *Website:* www.angelavallvey.com.

VALTINOS, Thanassis; Greek writer; b. 16 Dec. 1932, Karatoula Kynourias; m.; one d. *Education:* Athens Univ. *Career:* Visiting Prof., War Research Inst., Frankfurt 1993–; Pres. Hellenic Authors' Soc. 1990–94, 2005–09; mem. European Acad. of Sciences and Arts, Int. Inst. of Theatre, Greek Soc. of Playwriters; mem. Greek Acad. 2008. *Publications include:* The Descent of the Nine 1963, The Book of Andreas Kordopatis 1964, Voyage to Kythira (film script) 1984, Data from the Decade of the Sixties (Nat. Book Award for Best Novel 1990) 2000, Accoutumance à la nicotine 2008. *Honours:* Scenario Award Cannes Festival 1984, Cavafy Prize 2001, Acad. of Athens Petros Haris Prize for lifetime achievement 2002, Gold Cross of Honour of the Pres. of the Greek Democracy 2003. *Address:* Hellenic Authors' Society, Kodrigtonos 8, 112 57 Athens (office); 66 Astidamantos Street, 116 34 Athens, Greece (home). *Telephone:* (210) 8231890 (office); (210) 7218793 (home). *Fax:* (210) 8232543 (office). *E-mail:* gwrisoc@otenet.gr (office). *Website:* www.dedalus.gr (office).

VAMÓS, Miklós, PhD; Hungarian writer and screenwriter; b. (Tibor Vamós), 29 Jan. 1950, Budapest; s. of Tibor Vámos and Erzsébet Ribárszky; m. 1st Judit Pataki; one d.; m. 2nd Dóra Esze; two s. *Education:* Univ. Eötvös Loránd, Budapest. *Career:* screenwriter, Objektív Filmstúdió 1975–92; fmr Eastern Europe correspondent, The Nation; Corresp., Washington Post online; taught creative writing and screenwriting at Yale and CUNY, USA 1988–90; host, TV talk shows Rögtön, Lehetetlen, 2 ember 1995–2003, Vámos Klub 2005–; mem. PEN. *Publications include:* novels: Borgisz 1976, Én és Én 1979, Hanyatthomlok 1983, Zenga zének 1983, Félnóta 1986, Jaj 1986, Ha én Bródy volnék 1994, Anya csak egy van 1995, Apák könyve (trans. as The Book of Fathers 2009) 2000, Sánta kutya 2003, Márkez meg én 2004, Utazások Erotikában (Ki a franc az a Goethe?) 2007; also short stories, plays, essays, articles. *Honours:* Honors of Merit of the Hungarian Republic 2004; József Attila-Award 1984, Award of the Unions for Lifetime Achievement 1996, Camera Hungaria 2000, Hungarian Libraries Award 2000, Pro Cultura Urbis 2002, Colombus Award 2003, Fulbright Fellowship 1988. *Literary Agent:* Susanna Lea Associates, 78 Rue Bonaparte, 75006 Paris, France. *Telephone:* 9-61-29-93-49. *E-mail:* info.vamosmiklos@gmail.com (office). *Website:* www.vamosmiklos.hu.

VAN BOOY, Simon, MFA; British writer; b. London; one d. *Education:* Southampton Coll. *Career:* Lecturer in Creative Writing, School of Visual Arts, New York; also teaches on Early Coll. Humanities Program, Rutgers Univ. *Publications:* short stories: The Secret Lives of People in Love 2007, Love Begins in Winter (Frank O'Connor Short Story Award) 2009; children's fiction: Pobble's Way 2010, as ed.: Why We Need Love 2010, Why We Fight 2010, Why Our Decisions Don't Matter 2010; contribs to The New York Times, The Daily Telegraph, The Times. *Honours:* H.R. Hays Poetry Prize 2002. *Literary Agent:* c/o Lucas Hunt, The Philip G. Spitzer Literary Agency Inc., 50 Talmage Farm Lane, East Hampton, NY 11937, USA. *Telephone:* (631) 329-3650. *E-mail:* luc.hunt@spitzeragency.com. *Website:* www.spitzeragency.com; www.simonvanbooy.com.

VAN DE LAAR, Waltherus Antonius Bernardinus, (Stella Napels, Victor Vroomkoning), MA; Dutch poet and writer; b. 6 Oct. 1938, Boxtel; s. of Wout van de Laar and Mathilde Lippens; one s. one d. *Education:* degrees in philosophy, Dutch linguistics and literature. *Career:* teacher, Interstudie Teachers' Training Coll., Arnhem 1977–83; Co-Ed., Kritisch Literatuur Lexicon 1981–; town poet, Nijmegen 2006–08; mem. Lira, Isengrimus, Mij der Nederlandse Letterkunde. *Publications:* De einders tegemoet 1983, De laatste dingen 1983, Circuit des souvenirs 1984, Klein museum 1987, Groesbeek Tijdrit 1989, Echo van een echo 1990, Oud zeer 1993, Een zucht als vluchtig eerbetoon 1995, Boxtel 1995, Lippendienst 1997, Ysbeerbestaan 1999, Verloren Spraak 2000, Bij verstek 2002, Het formaat van waterland 2004, Stapelen 2005, Dodemont 2006, Reislust 2008, Ommezien Gedichten 2008; contribs to magazines and periodicals. *Honours:* Pablo Neruda Prize 1983, Blanka Gyselen Prize 1995, Pieter Geert Buckinx Prize 2003, De Zilveren Kei 2004, Karel de Grote Prize 2006. *Address:* Aldenhof, 70-17, 6537 DZ Nijmegen, Netherlands (home). *Telephone:* (24) 3441694 (home). *E-mail:* vroomkoning@planet.nl (home). *Website:* www.victorvroomkoning.nl.

VAN DE RUIT, John Howard; South African writer, actor, playwright and producer; b. 20 April 1975, Durban. *Education:* Michaelhouse School, Univ. of Natal. *Career:* writer and performer with Ben Voss, satirical comedy shows Green Mamba 2002–05, Black Mamba 2005–. *Plays:* as actor: Hamlet, Master Harold ... and the Boys, Seeing Red, People are Living There; as writer: War Cry (FNB VITA Award for Best Script, Noupoort Award for New Writing), Crooked 2004. *Film:* actor: I Shot Lucy. *Television:* actor: Global Health. *Publications:* novels: Spud (Bookseller's Choice Award 2006) 2005, Spud: The Madness Continues 2007. *Honours:* Johannesburg Naledi Award for comedy performance (for Green Mamba) 2004, Durban Theatre Award for Best New Script (for Black Mamba) 2005. *Address:* c/o Penguin Group (South Africa), 24

Sturdee Avenue, Johannesburg 2196, South Africa. *E-mail:* info@za.penguingroup.com.

VAN DEN BOOGAARD, Oscar, (Emmanuel Lipp, Pearl Sweetlife); Dutch writer and playwright; b. 1964, Harderwijk. *Education:* Univs of Montpellier, Amsterdam and Brussels. *Career:* grew up in Suriname and the Netherlands; worked briefly in legal profession; full-time writer in Brussels 1990–; columnist, De Standaard. *Plays:* Verwantschappen (actor in theatre experiment) 2000, Lucia (writer) 2001, Nest (writer) 2004, Lucia Smelt 2004. *Publications:* Dentz 1990, Fremdkörper 1991, Bruno's optimisme 1993, De heerlijkheid van Julia 1995, Liefdesdood (trans. as Love's Death) 1999, Sensaties 2000, Een bed vol schuim 2002, Inspiration Point 2004, Het Verticale Strand 2005. *Address:* c/o De Standaard, Gossetlaan 28, 1702 Groot Bijgaarden, Netherlands (office). *E-mail:* oscarvdb@skynet.be (home). *Website:* www.oscarvandenboogaard.com.

VAN DER KISTE, John Patrick Guy; British author and library assistant; b. 15 Sept. 1954, Wendover, Bucks., England; s. of the late Wing Commdr R.E.G. Van der Kiste; m. Kim Graham (née Geldard) 2003. *Education:* Ealing Tech. Coll. School of Librarianship. *Career:* Library Asst, Plymouth Coll. of Further Educ. (now City Coll., Plymouth) 1978–. *Television:* King, Kaiser, Tsar (BBC) 2003. *Publications:* Frederick III 1981, Dearest Affie (with Bee Jordaan) 1984, Queen Victoria's Children 1986, Windsor and Habsburg 1987, Edward VII's Children 1989, Beyond the Summertime (with Derek Wadeson) 1990, Princess Victoria Melita 1991, George V's Children 1991, George III's Children 1992, Crowns in a Changing World 1993, Kings of the Hellenes 1994, Childhood at Court 1995, Northern Crowns 1996, King George II & Queen Caroline 1997, The Romanovs 1818–1959 1998, Kaiser Wilhelm II 1999, The Georgian Princesses 2000, Gilbert and Sullivan's Christmas 2000, Dearest Vicky, Darling Fritz 2001, Royal Visits to Devon and Cornwall 2002, Once a Grand Duchess (with Coryne Hall) 2002, William & Mary 2003, The Man on the Moor 2004, Emperor Francis Joseph 2005, Sons, Servants and Statements 2006, Devon Murders 2006, Divided Kingdom 2007, Devonshire's Own 2007, Cornish Murders (with Nicola Sly) 2008, A Grim Almanac of Devon 2008, Cornwall's Own 2008, Jonathan Wild 2009, Plymouth History and Guide 2009, A Grim Almanac of Cornwall 2009, West Country Murders (with Nicola Sly) 2009, Surrey Murders 2009, Durham Murders and Misdemeanours 2009, Berkshire Murders 2010, Ivybridge and South Brent Through Time (with Kim Van der Kiste) 2010, More Cornish Murders (with Nicola Sly) 2010, Dartmoor from Old Photographs 2010, More Somerset Murders (with Nicola Sly) 201, A Grim Almanac of Hampshire 2011, William John Wills 2011, A Mere Passing Shadow 2011, Plymouth Book of Days 2011, More Devon Murders 2011, Little Book of Devon 2011; contrib. to books, periodicals and CD booklets. *Address:* c/o The History Press, The Mill, Brinscombe Port, Stroud, Glos., GL5 2DQ, England.

VAN DER VALK, Sonja, PhD; Dutch drama critic and magazine editor; b. 8 Oct. 1952, Poeldijk; pnr Joost Sternheim (died 1992); two d. *Education:* Univ. of Utrecht. *Career:* theatre critic 1977–, writer for Toneel Teatraal, Serpentine (women's magazine), De groene Amsterdammer (weekly); apptd Ed. Toneel Theatraal 1990; teacher at theatre school, Amsterdam 1992–; Art Adviser to Amsterdamse Kunstraad 1992–; Lecturer, Amsterdamse Hogeschool voor de Kunsten 2001–05; Founder, Domein voor Kunstkritiek, Amsterdam. *Publications:* Een nieuwe generatie cultuurjournalisten 2004, State of the Art 2005, Het ligt in uw handen - de rol van de toeschouwer in hedendaags theater , een uitgave van het Domein ism Theaterschrift Lucifer 2008, Stroomopwaarts; De theatercriticus als creattief ondernemer 2010; contrib. articles on the theatre to magazines and newspapers. *Address:* Domein voor Kunstkritiek, Uithoornstraat 4-2, 1078 SX Amsterdam, Netherlands (office). *E-mail:* info@domeinvoorkunstkritiek.nl. *Website:* www.domeinvoorkunstkritiek.nl.

VAN DER VAT, Dan, BA; British writer and journalist; b. 28 Oct. 1939, Alkmaar, Netherlands; m. Christine Mary Ellis 1962; two d. *Education:* Univ. of Durham. *Career:* mem. Campaign for Freedom of Information, Soc. of Authors, Amnesty International, Liberty. *Publications:* The Grand Scuttle 1982, The Last Corsair 1983, Gentlemen of War 1984, The Ship That Changed the World 1985, The Atlantic Campaign, 1939–45 1988, The Pacific Campaign, 1941–45 1991, Freedom Was Never Like This: A Winter's Journey in East Germany 1991, Stealth at Sea: History of the Submarine 1994, The Riddle of the Titanic (with Robin Gardiner) 1995, The Good Nazi: The Life and Lies of Albert Speer 1997, Standard of Power: The Royal Navy in the 20th Century 2000, Pearl Harbor: The Day of Infamy: An Illustrated History 2001, D-Day: The Greatest Invasion, a People's History 2004; contrib. to newspapers, magazines, radio and television. *Honours:* Yorkshire Post Best First Work Award 1982, King George's Fund for Sailors Best Book of the Sea Award 1983, Publisher's Weekly Book of the Year 1997. *Literary Agent:* c/o Curtis Brown Ltd, Haymarket House, 28–29 Haymarket, London, SW1Y 4SP, England. *Telephone:* (20) 7393-4400. *Fax:* (20) 7393-4401. *E-mail:* info@curtisbrown.co.uk. *Website:* www.curtisbrown.co.uk.

VAN DIS, Adriaan; Dutch writer; b. 16 Dec. 1946, Bergen. *Education:* Univ. of Amsterdam. *Career:* fmr Ed. NRC Handelsblad newspaper. *Television:* presenter Here is... Adriaan van Dis 1983–92. *Play:* Tropenjaren 1986. *Publications:* Nathan Sid (novel) (Gouden Ezelsoor Award) 1984, Casablanca (short stories) 1986, De rat van Arras 1986, Komedie om geld 1986, Zoen 1987, Een barbaar in China 1987, Zilver, of Het verlies van de onschuld 1988, Een uur in de wind 1989, Het beloofde land 1990, In Afrika 1991, Waar twee olifanten vechten 1992, Noord Zuid 1994, Indische duinen (novel) (Gouden Uil Literature Prize 1995, Trouw Public Award 1995) 1994, Wij, koningin 1995, Palmwijn 1996, Een waarze sat 1997, Totok 1998, Een deken van herinnering 1998, Dubbelliefde (novel) 1999, Op oorlogspad in Japan (novel) 2000, Familieziek (novel) 2002, De Indische boeken 2002, De reisromans 2003, De karakterromans 2004, Onder het zink 2004, De wandelaar 2007, Leeftocht 2007, Weg uit Babylon 2008. *Honours:* Nipkowschijf prize for tv show 1986. *Address:* c/o Uitgeverij Augustus, Herengracht 481, 1017 BT Amsterdam, The Netherlands (office). *E-mail:* rblaakmeer@amsteluitgevers.nl (office). *Website:* www.adriaanvandis.nl.

VAN HENSBERGEN, Gijs; Dutch author and art critic. *Education:* trained as an architect. *Career:* lectures on architecture. *Publications:* A Taste of Castille (travel book, aka In the Kitchens of Castile) 1980, Art Deco 1986, Gaudí: A Biography 2001, Guernica: The Biography of a Twentieth-Century Icon 2004. *Literary Agent:* c/o Euan Thorneycroft, A.M. Heath & Company Ltd, 6 Warwick Court, Holborn, London, WC1R 5DJ, England. *Telephone:* (20) 7242-2811. *Fax:* (20) 242-2711. *E-mail:* euan.thorneycroft@amheath.com. *Website:* www.amheath.com.

VAN HERK, Aritha, BA, MA, FRSC; Canadian academic and writer; *Professor, University of Calgary;* b. 26 May 1954, Wetaskiwin, AB; m. Robert Sharp 1974. *Education:* Univ. of Alberta. *Career:* Asst Prof., Univ. of Calgary 1983–85, Assoc. Prof. 1985–91, Prof. 1991–. *Publications:* Judith 1978, More Stories from Western Canada (co-ed.) 1980, The Tent Peg 1981, West of Fiction (co-ed.) 1983, No Fixed Address 1986, Places Far From Ellesmere 1990, Alberta Rebound (ed.) 1990, In Visible Ink 1991, A Frozen Tongue 1992, Boundless Alberta (ed.) 1993, Due West 1996, Restlessness 1998, Mavericks: An Incorrigible History of Alberta 2001, Audacious and Adamant 2007, In This Place (with George Webber) 2011. *Honours:* Alberta Order of Excellence; mem. Order of the Univ. of Calgary 2008; Seal Books First Novel Award 1978, Alberta Achievement Award in Literature 1978, Grant MacEwan Author's Award 2002, Community Achievement Award, City of Calgary 2010, Golden Pen Award 2011, Calgary Public Library Champion Award 2011. *Address:* Department of English, University of Calgary, Social Sciences Tower, 11th Floor, 2500 University Drive NW, Calgary, AB T2N 1N4, Canada (office). *Telephone:* (403) 220-5481 (office). *Fax:* (403) 289-1123 (office). *E-mail:* vanherk@ucalgary.ca (office). *Website:* www.english.ucalgary.ca (office).

VAN NIEKERK, Marlene, MA; South African writer, poet and academic; *Associate Professor, Department of Afrikaans and Dutch, Stellenbosch University;* b. 10 Nov. 1954, Caledon, Western Cape. *Education:* Stellenbosch Univ. *Career:* studied theatre directing in Germany and philosophy in the Netherlands; fmr Lecturer in Philosophy, Univ. of Zululand and UNISA; fmr Lecturer in Afrikaans and Dutch, Univ. of the Witwatersrand; currently Assoc. Prof., Dept of Afrikaans and Dutch, Stellenbosch Univ. *Publications:* Sprokkelster (Eugène Marais Prize, Ingrid Jonker Prize) (poems) 1977, Groenstaar (poems) 1983, Die vrou wat haar verkyker vergeet het (short stories), Triomf (M-Net Prize, CNA Prize, Noma Prize) (novel) 1994, Agaat (trans. as The Way of the Women) (LitNet Dopper Joris-Oska, UJ Prize 2005, Hertzog Prize for Prose 2007, C.L. Engelbrecht Prize 2007, South African Sunday Times Literary Award 2007) (novel) 2004, Memorandum: 'N Verhaal met prente (novella, illustrated) 2006. *Honours:* Chancellor's Medal, Stellenbosch Univ. *Literary Agent:* c/o Isobel Dixon, Blake Friedmann Literary, Film & TV Agency, 122 Arlington Road, London, NW1 7HP, England. *Telephone:* (20) 7284-0408. *Fax:* (20) 7284-0442. *E-mail:* info@blakefriedmann.co.uk. *Website:* www.blakefriedmann.co.uk. *Address:* Department of Afrikaans and Dutch, Stellenbosch University, Room 679, Private Bag XI, Matieland 7602, South Africa (office). *Telephone:* (21) 808-2169 (office). *E-mail:* mvn4@sun.ac.za (office). *Website:* academic.sun.ac.za/afrndl (office).

VAN WINCKEL, Nance, BA, MA; American poet, writer and academic; b. 24 Oct. 1951, Roanoke, Va; m. Robert Fredrik Nelson 1985. *Education:* Univ. of Wisconsin, Milwaukee, Univ. of Denver. *Career:* Instructor in English, Marymount College, Salina, Kan. 1976–79; Assoc. Prof. of English and Dir, Writing Program, Lake Forest Coll., Ill. 1979–90; Assoc. Prof. to Prof. of English, Graduate Creative Writing Program, Eastern Washington Univ., Cheney 1990–, now Prof. Emer.; mem. Faculty, Vermont Coll. of Fine Art 2000–; Richard Hugo Poet-in-Residence, Univ. of Montana 2000; Poet-in-Residence, Univ. of North Dakota 2006; Poet-in-Residence, Westminster Coll., Salt Lake City 2008; Stadler Poet-in-Residence, Bucknell Univ. 2009; mem. Editorial Bd Eastern Washington University Press 1998–2007. *Publications:* poetry: Bad Girl, with Hawk 1988, The Dirt 1994, After a Spell (Washington State Gov's Award for Poetry) 1998, Beside Ourselves 2003, No Starling 2007; short stories: Limited Lifetime Warranty 1994, Quake 1997, Curtain Creek Farm 2000; contributions: many periodicals. *Honours:* Illinois Arts Council Fellowships 1983, 1985, 1987, 1989, National Endowment for the Arts Fellowships 1988, 2001, Society of Midland Authors Poetry Award 1989, Gordon Barber Award, Poetry Society of America 1989, Northwest Institute Grants 1991, 1993, 1994, Paterson Fiction Prize 1998, Washington State Artists Trust Literary Award in Fiction 1998, Pushcart Prize, Christopher Isherwood Fellowship 2005, People's Choice Award in Poetry from Prairie Schooner 2006, Washington State Artists Trust GAP Grant 2010. *Address:* 1515 South Garry, #4, Liberty Lake, WA 99019, USA. *E-mail:* nancev@sisna.com (office). *Website:* www.nancevanwinckel.com.

VAN WYK, Christopher; South African writer; b. 1957, Soweto; m. Kathy Van Wyk; two s. *Education:* Riverlea High School. *Career:* worked for SA Cttee for Higher Educ.; co-f. Wietie magazine with Fhazel Johennesse 1980; Ed.

Staffrider literary magazine 1981–86; mem. United Democratic Front (UDF) during 1980s. *Publications:* children's fiction: A Message in the Wind (Maskew Miller Longman Award) 1982, Petroleum and the Orphaned Ostrich 1988, Peppy 'n Them 1991; books for neo-literate adults: The Murder of Mrs Mohapi 1995, My Cousin Thabo 1995, Take a Chance 1995, My Name is Selina Mabiletsa 1996, Sergeant Dlamini Falls in Love 1996; other: It Is Time to Go Home (poems) (Olive Schreiner Prize 1980) 1979, The Year of the Tapeworm (novel) 1996, Now Listen Here: The Life and Times of Bill Jardine (biography) 2003, Freedom Fighters (biographies for young readers) 2003, Shirley, Goodness and Mercy (memoir) 2004, Freedom Fighters 2 2006, Eggs to Lay, Chickens to Hatch (memoir) 2010. *Honours:* Sanlam Prize for Best South African Short Story 1997. *Address:* c/o Pan Macmillan/Picador Africa, Private Bag X19, Northlands, 2116 Johannesburg, South Africa (office).

VANDERHAEGHE, Guy Clarence, OC, BA, MA, BEd, FRSC; Canadian writer, playwright and academic; b. 5 April 1951, Esterhazy, Sask.; s. of Clarence Earl Vanderhaeghe and Alma Beth Allen; m. Margaret Nagel 1972. *Education:* Univ. of Saskatchewan, Univ. of Regina. *Career:* St Thomas More Scholar, St Thomas More Coll., Univ. of Saskatchewan 1993–; Fellow, Pierre Eliott Trudeau Foundation 2007. *Publications:* novels: Man Descending (Gov. Gen. Literary Award for Fiction 1982, Geoffrey Faber Memorial Prize 1987) 1982, The Trouble With Heroes 1983, My Present Age 1984, Homesick (City of Toronto Book Award 1990) 1989, Things As They Are? 1992, The Englishman's Boy (Gov. Gen. Literary Award for Fiction) 1996, The Last Crossing 2004; plays: I Had a Job I Liked, Once (Canadian Authors' Asscn Award for Drama 1993) 1991, Dancock's Dance 1995. *Honours:* Saskatchewan Order of Merit 2004; Hon. DLitt (Saskatchewan) 1997; Gov.-Gen.'s Awards 1982, 1996, Canadian Authors' Asscn Award for Drama 1996, Saskatchewan Book Award 1996. *Address:* Department of English, St Thomas More College, University of Saskatchewan, 320 Arts Tower, 9 Campus Drive, Saskatoon, SK S7N 5A5, Canada (office). *Telephone:* (306) 966-5486 (office). *E-mail:* english@usask.ca (office). *Website:* www.usask.ca/english (office).

VANDERKAM, James Claire, AB, BD, PhD; American theologian, academic and author; *John A. O'Brien Professor of Theology, University of Notre Dame*; b. 15 Feb. 1946, Cadillac, Mich.; m. Mary Vander Molen 1967, two s. one d. *Education:* Calvin Coll., Calvin Theological Seminary, Harvard Univ. *Career:* currently John A. O'Brien Prof. of Theology, Univ. of Notre Dame; Gen. Ed. Journal of Biblical Literature. *Publications:* Textual and Historical Studies in the Book of Jubilees 1977, Enoch and the Growth of Apocalyptic Tradition 1984, The Book of Jubilees, two vols 1989, The Dead Sea Scrolls Today 1994 (2nd edn) 2010, Enoch: A Man for All Generations 1995, The Jewish Apocalyptic Heritage in Early Christianity (co-ed. with William Alder) 1996, Calenders in the Dead Sea Scrolls 1998, From Revelation to Canon 2000, An Introduction to Early Judaism 2001, The Book of Jubilees 2001, The Meaning of the Dead Sea Scrolls 2002, From Joshua to Caiaphas 2004, 1 Enoch: A New Translation (with George Nickelsburg) 2004, Presidential Voices: The Society of Biblical Literature in the Twentieth Century (co-ed. with Harold Attridge) 2006. *Honours:* Distinguished Research and Literary Publ. Award, Coll. of Humanities and Social Sciences, North Carolina State Univ. 1991, Biblical Archaeology Soc. Publ. Award for Best Popular Book on Archaeology 1995. *Address:* Department of Theology, University of Notre Dame, 837 Flanner Hall, Notre Dame, IN 46556, USA (office). *Telephone:* (574) 631-7811 (office). *E-mail:* vanderkam.1@nd.edu (office).

VANDO (HICKOK), Gloria, BA; American poet, publisher and editor; *Publisher and Editor, Helicon Nine Editions*; b. (Gloria Lucille Vando), 21 May 1936, New York, NY; d. of Erasmo Vando and Anita Velez-Mitchell; m. 1st Maurice Peress 1955; one s. two d.; m. 2nd William Harrison Hickok 1980. *Education:* New York Univ., Univ. of Amsterdam, Texas A & I Coll., Corpus Christi, Southampton Coll., Long Island Univ., NY. *Career:* Founding Publr and Ed. Helicon Nine Editions 1977–; Founder and Pres. Midwest Center for the Literary Arts, Inc. 1977– 96; Educational Consultant, Youth Diversion Project, Kansas 1977–79; Writer-in-Residence, various schools in Kansas City and St Louis 1987–96; Carolyn Benton Cockefair Chair, Univ. of Missouri-Kansas City (mem. Bd and Speakers Cttee) 1994–2005; Co-founder and mem. Bd The Writers' Place, Kansas City 1992–; Chair. Arts Cttee League of United Latin American Citizens 1987–90; Vice-Pres. Advisory Bd Missouri Center for the Book, State Library, Jefferson City, Mo. 1997–2000; mem. Bd Kansas City Arts Council 1984–86, Bd Soc. for Contemporary Photography 1985–87, Bd Educational Services Center 1986–88, Advisory Bd Midtown Arts Center, St Louis, Mo. 1993–98, Advisory Bd BkMk Press, Univ. of Missouri-Kansas City 1997–; mem. Alvin Ailey Dance Theatre, Judith Jamison Partners 1990–92, Council of Literary Magazines and Presses Literary Network 1993–; Founding mem. Nat. Museum of Women in the Arts 1985–90; Vice-Pres. Beyond Baroque Literary Center, Venice, Calif. 2011–; mem. Bd Venice Arts Council 2011–; mem. PEN International, Poetry Soc. of America, Acad. of American Poets; Trustee, N.W. Dible Foundation 1980–, Clearinghouse for Midcontinent Foundations 1985–95. *Play:* Moving Targets: Three Interpretations of Murder, produced by MultiStages at Sackett Group's Women's Work Festival 1999. *Publications:* books as author: Caprichos 1987, Promesas: Geography of the Impossible 1993, Shadows and Supposes: Poems 2002, Woven Voices: Three Generations of Puertorriqueñas Look at Their American Lives 2012; selected anthologies: The First Anthology of Missouri Women Writers 1987, Kansas City Out Loud II 1989, The Helicon Nine Reader 1990, Movieworks 1990, Looking for Home 1990, The Time of Our Lives 1993, In Other Words 1994, Daughters of the Fifth Sun 1995, Hispanic American Literature 1995, Anales 1995, Máscaras 1997, El Coro 1997, Fathers 1997, Verse and Universe: Poems about Science and Mathematics 1998, Touching the Fire: Fifteen Poets of Today's Latino Renaissance 1998, Writing Poems 2000, Memories & Memoirs 2000, American Diaspora 2001, Micro2: Fictions for the New Millennium 2002, 9mm: Poets Respond to Violence in America 2003, Wild and Whirling Words: A Poetic Conversation 2004, Poetry on Record: 98 Poets Read Their Work, 1888–2006 2006, Latino Boom 2006, Movable Nest 2007, Primera Página 2008, Poetic Voices Without Borders 2009, Storm Country 2011, Breaking Ground: Anthology of Puerto Rican Women Writers in New York 1980–2010; contrib. to Cottonwood Magazine (Gloria Vando Issue, Summer 1994), Kenyon Review, Western Humanities Review, Seattle Review, New Letters, Carolina Quarterly, Tar River Poetry, The Same, Cortland Review, Begin Again: 150 Kansas Poems, Spillway; editor: Helicon Nine Reader 1990, Spud Songs: Anthology of Potato Poems 1999, Chance of a Ghost 2005, In the Black/In the Red: Poems of Profit & Loss 2012. *Honours:* Poetry Fellowship, Kansas Arts Comm. 1989–91, Grant from Money for Women/Barbara Deming Memorial Fund, Inc. 1989, Billee Murray Denny Prize 1989, 1991, Kansas Gov.'s Arts Award 1991, Thorpe Menn Book Award 1994, River Styx Int. Poetry Award 1997, Alice Fay Di Castagnola Award, Poetry Soc. of America 1998, Latino Hall of Fame Best Poetry Book of the Year 2003, Torch Award for Excellence in Journalism, Greater Kansas City Women's Political Caucus 2004, Poetry Award, Inst. of Puerto Rican Culture 2009. *Address:* c/o Helicon Nine Editions, PO Box 22412, Kansas City, MO 64113, USA (office). *Telephone:* (816) 753-1095 (office). *Fax:* (816) 753-1016 (office). *E-mail:* vandog@heliconnine.com (office). *Website:* www.heliconnine.com (office).

VANIČEK, Zdeněk, (Alois Bocek), JUDr, PhD,; Czech diplomatist, academic, poet, writer and legal expert; *President, Czech Association of Electronic Communications*; b. 24 June 1947, Chlumec nad Cidlinou; s. of Bohuslav Vaniček and Ruzena Suchankova; m. Nadya Jankovska; two s. one d. *Education:* Charles Univ., Prague, Camden Univ., USA. *Career:* mem. Czechoslovak diplomatic service 1972–91; journalist and diplomatic adviser 1991–93; Prof. of Int. Relations and Law, Cyprus 1993–95; Asst Prof. in Tech. Law, Czech Tech. Univ., Prague 1995–; Pres. Czech Asscn of Electronic Communications 1999–; mem. Bd Cable Europe (ECCA) 2003; mem. various scientific councils and expert groups; mem. Poetry Soc. (UK), RSL; Fellow, American Biographical Inst. 2005. *Publications:* The Theory and the Practice of British Neo-Conservatism 1988, Amidst the Ruins of Memories 1990, To the Ends of the Earth 1992, On the Edge of Rain 1994, Under the Range of Mountains of Five Fingers 1996, Seven Thousand Years Chiselled in Limestone 1996, Amidst Memory's Ruins, Poems 1988–1997 1999, Whereupon He Was Arrested (short stories) 2004, To the Four Corners of the Earth 2005, 2007, La Haute Société (short stories) 2007, The Act on Electronic Communications – Legal Annotation 2008, The Legal Instruments Associated with the Act on Electronic Communications 2009, The Age of Closed Churches 2009, A Gentle Rain is Falling from the Dome (poetry) 2012, The Responsibility for the Transmitted Content in Electronic Communications (legal handbook) 2012; contrib. to newspapers and magazines. *Honours:* Hon. mem. 56 Group Wales (UK) 1986, American-Czechoslovak Soc. 1990, IBC Bd (UK) 1999; Order of Int. Ambs 2007; Bronze Medal for the Preparation of the World Postage Stamp Exhbn PRAGA 1988, Pontifical Medal 1990, Greek Olympic Cttee Commemorative Medal 1990, The 20th Century Award for Achievement (UK) 1993, Acad. of Arts Masaryk Award 1998, Karel Hynek Mácha Prize for Poetry 1998, The 21st Century Award for Achievement (UK) 2001, Emperor Rudolf II Prize for Poetry 2002, American Medal of Honour 2007, Master Diploma for Special Honours in Int. Law, World Acad. of Letters (USA) 2007, European Prize for Literature, European Union of Arts 2010, Franz Kafka Literary Award 2010, 500 Great Leaders (USA) 2010. *Address:* V Jame 699/1, Prague 1, Czech Republic (office). *Telephone:* 603-251838 (mobile) (office). *E-mail:* cacc@cacc.cz (office). *Website:* www.caek.cz (office).

VANNI, Carla, LLD; Italian journalist; b. 18 Feb. 1936, Leghorn (Livorno); m. Vincenzo Nisivoccia; two c. *Education:* Univ. of Milan. *Career:* joined Mondadori Publrs, working on fashion desk of Grazia magazine 1959, Head fashion desk 1964, Jt Ed.-in-Chief 1974, Ed.-in-Chief 1978–, responsible for launch of Marie Claire magazine in Italy 1987, Publishing Dir Marie Claire until 2002 and Cento Cose-Energy 1987–99, Donna Moderna 1995–, Flair 2003–, Easy Shop 2004–; has created several new supplements of Grazia: Grazia Bricolage, Grazia Blu and Grazia Int., Grazia Accessori and Grazia Uomo, Grazia Profumi e Balocchi and introduced coverage of social problems; also Ed.-in-Chief Grazia Casa; Head, Grazia Int. Network 2005–; mem. juries of several nat. and int. literary awards and many beauty competitions. *Honours:* Montenapoleone d'Oro (Best Journalist) 1970, The Oner (Journalist of the Year) 1987, Gullace (for coverage of women's interest issues) 1995, Letterario Castiglioncello costa degli Etruschi Award 2001, Milan Fashion Award 2003, Fondazione Marisa Bellisario Award 2003, Forte dei Marmi 'Dietro la bellezza' Award 2003, Premio Milano per la Moda 2003, Premio 'Dietro la bellezza', Ponte dei Nariù 2003, Premio Narisa Bellsario 2003. *Address:* Grazia, Arnoldi Mondadori Editore, Via Arnoldo Mondadori 1, 20090 Segrate, Milan, Italy (office). *Telephone:* (02) 754212390 (office). *Fax:* (02) 75422515 (office). *E-mail:* vanni@mondadori.it (office).

VARGAS, Fred; French novelist, historian and archaeologist; b. (Frédérique Audouin-Rouzeau), 1957, Paris; one s. *Career:* writes under pseudonym; currently archaeologist Inst. Pasteur. *Publications:* Les Jeux de l'amour et de la mort (Prix du festival de Cognac) 1986, Ceux qui vont mourir te saluent 1987, Debout les morts (Prix Mystère de la critique 1996) (trans. as The Three

Evangelists; Duncan Lawrie Int. Dagger Award 2006) 1995, Un Peu plus loin sur la droite 1996, L'Homme aux cercles bleus (trans. as The Chalk Circle Man) (CWA Int. Dagger Award 2009) 1996, Sans feu ni lieu 1997, L'Homme à l'envers (Grand Prix du roman noir de Cognac 2000) (trans. as Seeking Whom he May Devour) 1999, Les Quatre fleuves (Prix Alph-Art du meilleur scénario au festival d'Angoulême 2001) 2000, Pars vite et reviens tard (Prix des libraires 2001, Prix Européen des jeunes lecteurs 2005) (trans. as Have Mercy on Us All) 2001, Petit Traité de toutes vérités sur l'existence 2001, Coule la Seine (novellas) 2002, Salut et liberté 2004, Sous les vents de Neptune (trans. as Wash This Blood Clean from my Hand; Duncan Lawrie Int. Dagger Award 2007) 2004, La Vérité sur Césare Battisti 2004, Dans les bois éternels (trans. as The Eternal Forest) 2006, Un Lieu Incertain 2008. *Address:* c/o Éditions Viviane Hamy, Cour de la Maison Brülée, 89 rue du Faubourg-Saint-Antoine, 75011 Paris, France (office). *Website:* www.viviane-hamy.fr (office).

VARGAS LLOSA, (Jorge) Mario Pedro, PhD; Peruvian/Spanish writer and journalist; b. 28 March 1936, Arequipa, Peru; s. of Ernesto Vargas Maldonado and Dora Llosa de Vargas; m. 1st Julia Urquidi 1955 (divorced 1964); m. 2nd Patricia Llosa Urquidi 1965; two s. one d. *Education:* Colegio La Salle, Lima, Peru, Leoncio Prado Military Acad., Lima, Colegio Nacional San Miguel, Piura, Universidad Nacional Mayor de San Marcos, Lima and Universidad Complutense de Madrid, Spain. *Career:* journalist on local newspapers, Piura, Peru 1951, for magazines Turismo and Cultura Peruana and for Sunday supplement of El Comercio 1955; News Ed. Radio Panamericana, Lima 1955; Spanish teacher, Berlitz School 1959; journalist, Agence-France Presse 1959; broadcaster, Latin American services of Radiodiffusion Télévision Française 1959; Lecturer in Latin American Literature, Queen Mary Coll., Univ. of London, UK 1967, Prof. King's Coll. 1969; trans. UNESCO 1967; Visiting Prof., Washington State Univ., USA 1968, Univ. de Puerto Rico 1969, Columbia Univ., USA 1975; Prof., Univ. of Cambridge, UK 1977, Harvard Univ., USA 1992, Princeton Univ., USA 1993, Georgetown Univ., USA 1994, 1999; Writer-in-Residence, Woodrow Wilson Int. Center for Scholars, Smithsonian Inst., Washington, DC, USA 1980; Prof. and Chair., Dept of Ibero-American Literature and Culture, Georgetown Univ., Washington, DC 2001–06, Distinguished Writer-in-Residence 2003–06; Mentor, Literature Program of the Rolex Mentor and Protégé Arts Initative, Second Cycle 2004–05; Weidenfeld Visiting Prof. of European Comparative Literature, St Anne's Coll., Oxford, UK 2004; Distinguished Visitor, Program in Latin American Studies, Princeton Univ. 2010; f. Movimiento Libertad political party and co-f. Frente Democrático (FREDEMO) coalition 1988; cand. for Pres. of Peru 1990; Pres. Jury, Iberoamerican Film Festival, Huelva, Spain 1995, San Sebastian Int. Film Festival 2004; mem. Jury, ECHO Television and Radio Awards 1998, Miguel de Cervantes Prize 1998; Pres. PEN Club Int. 1976–79; mem. Acad. Peruana de la Lengua 1975, Real Acad. Española 1994 (incorporation 1996), Int. Acad. of Humanism 1996, Cervantes Inst. Foundation 1998; Neil Gunn Int. Fellow, Scottish Arts Council 1986; Fellow, Wissenschaftskolleg, Berlin 1991–92, Deutscher Akademischer Austauschdienst, Berlin 1997–98. *Films:* Co-Dir of film version of his novel Pantaleón y las visitadoras. *Television:* Dir La torre de Babel 1981. *Publications:* novels: La cuidad y los perros (Biblioteca Breve Prize) 1963, La casa verde (Premio Nacional de Novela, Peru 1967) 1966, Conversación en la catedral 1969, Pantaleón y las visitadoras 1973, La tía Julia y el escribidor (ILLA Prize, Italy 1982) 1977, La guerra del fin del mundo (Pablo Iglesias Literature Prize 1982) 1981, Historia de Mayta 1984, ¿Quién mató a Palomino Molero? 1986, El hablador 1987, Elogio de la madrastra 1988, Lituma en los Andes (Planeta Prize, Spain 1993, Archbishop Juan de San Clemente de Santiago de Compostella Literary Prize, Spain 1994, Int. Literary Prize, Chianti Ruffino Antico Fattore, Italy 1995) 1993, Los cuadernos de Don Rigoberto 1997, La fiesta del Chivo (first Book of the Year Prize, Union of Booksellers of Spain 2001, Readers of Crisol Libraries Prize, Spain 2001) 2000, El paraíso en la otra esquina (chosen for inclusion in "Books to Remember 2003" by cttee of librarians from The New York Public Library 2004) 2003, Travesuras de la niña mala 2006, El Sueño del Celta 2010; short stories: El desafío (Revue Française Prize) 1957, Los jefes (Leopoldo Alas Prize) 1959, Los cachorros 1967; anthologies: Contra viento y marea Vol. I (1962–72) 1986, Vol. II (1972–83) 1986, Vol. III (1983–90) 1990, Desafíos a la libertad 1994, Making Waves (Nat. Book Critics' Circle Award, New York 1998) 1996; plays: La huída del Inca 1952, La señorita de Tacna 1981, Kathie y el hipopótamo 1983, La Chunga 1986, El loco de los balcones 1993, Ojos bonitos, cuadros feos 1994, La verdad de las mentiras (II Bartolome March Prize for revised edn 2002) 1990; non-fiction: El pez en el agua (autobiog.) 1993, La orgía perpetua (criticism) 1975, La utopía arcaica 1978, Cartas a un joven novelista (literary essay) 1997, Nationalismus als neue Bedrohung (in German) 2000, El lenguaje de la pasión (selection of articles) 2001, L'Herne. Mario Vargas Llosa (essays etc.) 2003, Diario de Irak (essays) 2003, La tentación de lo imposible (essay on Les Miserables de Victor Hugo) 2004, Mario Vargas Llosa. Obras Completas, Vol. I Narraciones y novelas (1959–1967) and Vol. II, Novelas (1969–1977) 2004, Un demi-siècle avec Borges (interview and essays on Borges written between 1964 and 1999, in French) 2004; contrib. to El País (series Piedra de Toque), Letras Libres, Mexico (series Extemporaneos). *Honours:* Hon. Fellow, Hebrew Univ., Israel 1976, Modern Language Asscn of America 1986, American Acad. and Inst. of Arts and Letters 1986; Hon. Prof., Universidad de Ciencias Aplicadas, Lima 2001; Chevalier, Légion d'honneur, Commdr Ordre des Arts et des Lettres 1993, Medal Orden El Sol del Perú (Great Cross of Diamonds) 2001, Medalla de Honor en el Grado de Gran Cruz, Peru 2003; Hon. DHumLitt (Connecticut Coll.) 1991; Hon. DLitt (Warwick) 2004; Dr hc (Florida Int. Univ. of Miami) 1990, (Boston) 1992, (Geneva) 1992, (Dowling College) 1993, (Universidad Francisco Marroquin, Guatemala) 1993, (Georgetown) 1994, (Yale) 1994, (Rennes II) 1994, (Murcia) 1995, (Valladolid) 1995, (Lima) 1997, (Universidad Nacional de San Agustin, Peru) 1997, (Ben Gurion) 1998, (Univ. Coll. London) 1998, (Harvard) 1999, (Universidad Nacional Mayor de San Marcos, Lima) 2001, (Rome Tor Vergata) 2001, (Pau) 2001, (Universidad Nacional San Antonio Abad del Cusco) 2002, (Univ. of French Polynesia) 2002, (La Trobe Univ., Melbourne) 2002, (Skidmore Coll.) 2002, (Universidad Nacional de Piura) 2002, (Universidad Nacional Pedro Ruiz Gallo) 2002, (Catholic Univ. of Louvain) 2003, (Universidad Nacional de Ingenieria, Lima) 2003, (Oxford) 2003, (Universidad Pedagogica Nacional Francisco Morazan, Tegucigalpa, Honduras) 2003, (Universidad Católica Santa María, Arequipa) 2004; Diploma de Honor, Universidad Nacional Mayor de San Marcos 2000; Crítica Española Prize 1966, Premio de la Crítica, Argentina 1981, Ritz Paris Hemingway Prize 1985, Príncipe de Asturias Prize, Spain 1986, Castiglione de Sicilia Prize, Italy 1990, Miguel de Cervantes Prize, Spain 1994, Jerusalem Prize, Israel 1995, Congressional Medal of Honour, Peru 1982, T.S. Eliot Prize, Ingersoll Foundation of The Rockford Institute, USA 1991, Golden Palm Award, INTAR Hispanic American Arts Center, New York 1992, Miguel de Cervantes Prize, Ministry of Culture (Spain) 1994, Jerusalem Prize 1995, Peace Prize, German Publishers, Frankfurt Book Fair 1996, Pluma de Oro Award, Spain 1997, Medal and Diploma of Honour, Univ. Católica de Santa María, Arequipa, Peru 1997, Medal of the Univ. of Calif. 1999, Jorge Isaacs Award, Int. Festival of Art, Cali, Colombia 1999, Medal "Patrimonio Cultural de la Humanidad", Municipalidad de Arequipa 2000, Certificate of Recognition, Colegio de Abogados 2001, Crystal Award, World Econ. Forum, Davos, Switzerland 2001, Americas Award, Americas Foundation 2001, Son Latinos Festival Prize, Tenerife, Spain 2001, Caonabo de Oro Prize, Dominican Asscn of Journalsits and Writers, 2002, Golden Medal, City of Genoa (Italy) 2002, PEN Nabokov Award 2002, Int. Prize of Letters, Cristobal Gabarron Foundation 2002, Premio Ateneo Americano, on Xth Anniversary of Casa de America 2002, Medal of Honour, City of Trujillo, Peru 2003, Roger-Caillois PEN Club Prize 2003, Budapest Prize 2003, Presidential Medal of Hofstra Univ., New York 2003, Grinzane Cavour Prize: "A Life for Literature International Prize", Turin 2004, Konex Foundation Prize 2004, Medal of the Centenary of Pablo Neruda, Govt of Chile 2004, Medal of Honor of Peruvian Culture, Nat. Inst. of Culture 2004, Nobel Prize in Literature 2010. *Address:* Las Magnolias 295, 6° Piso, Barranco, Lima 4, Peru. *Telephone:* (1) 477-3868. *Fax:* (1) 477-3518. *Website:* www.mvargasllosa.com.

VARMA, Pavan Kumar, BA; Indian writer and diplomatist; *Ambassador to Bhutan*; b. 5 Nov. 1953; m. Renuka Varma. *Education:* St Stephen's Coll., New Delhi. *Career:* joined Indian Foreign Service 1976; fmr Press Sec. to Pres. of India, Spokesman, Ministry of External Affairs, Jt Sec. for Africa, High Commr to Cyprus, Dir, Nehru Centre, London, UK, Dir Gen. Indian Council for Cultural Relations, New Delhi, Amb. to Bhutan 2009–. *Publications:* Ghalib: The Man, The Times 1989, The Havelis of Old Delhi 1992, Krishna: The Playful Divine 1993, Yudhishtar and Draupadi 1993, The Great Indian Middle Class 1998, Widows of Vrindavan 2002, Being Indian: The Truth About Why the 21st Century will be India's 2004, Kama Sutra: The Art of Making Love to a Woman 2007, Becoming Indian: The Unfinished Revolution of Culture and Identity 2010. *Address:* India House, Thimphu, Bhutan (office). *Telephone:* (2) 322162 (office). *Fax:* (2) 323195 (office). *E-mail:* amb.thimphu@mea.gov.in (office); pavankvarma@hotmail.com (home). *Website:* www.indianembassythimphu.bt (office).

VARMUS, Harold Eliot, MA, MD; American microbiologist and academic; *President and CEO, Memorial Sloan-Kettering Cancer Center*; b. 18 Dec. 1939, Oceanside, NY; s. of Frank Varmus and Beatrice (née Barasch) Varmus; m. Constance Louise Casey 1969; two s. *Education:* Amherst Coll., Harvard Univ., Columbia Univ. *Career:* physician, Presbyterian Hosp., New York 1966–68; Clinical Assoc., NIH, Bethesda, Md 1968–70; lecturer, Dept of Microbiology, Univ. of Calif. at San Francisco 1970–72, Asst Prof. 1972–74, Assoc. Prof. 1974–79, Prof. 1979–83, American Cancer Soc. Research Prof. 1984–93; Dir NIH 1993–99; Pres. and CEO Memorial Sloan-Kettering Cancer Center 2000–; Consultant, Chiron Corp., Emoryville, Calif.; Assoc. Ed. Cell Journal; mem. Editorial Bd Cancer Surveys; mem. American Soc. of Virology, American Soc. of Microbiology, AAAS. *Publications:* Molecular Biology of Tumor Viruses (ed.) 1982, 1985, Readings in Tumor Virology (ed.) 1983, The Art and Politics of Science 2009. *Honours:* Calif. Acad. of Sciences Scientist of the Year 1982, Lasker Foundation Award 1982 (co-recipient), Passano Foundation Award 1983, Armand Hammer Cancer Prize 1984, Gen. Motors Alfred Sloan Award, Shubitz Cancer Prize (NAS) 1984, Nobel Prize 1989, Nat. Medal of Science 2001, Rave Award, Wired Magazine 2004. *Address:* Memorial Sloan-Kettering Cancer Center, 1275 York Avenue, New York, NY 10065, USA (office). *Telephone:* (212) 639-7317 (office); (212) 639-7227 (office). *Fax:* (212) 717-3125 (office). *E-mail:* varmus@mskcc.org (office). *Website:* www.mskcc.org (office).

VASILYEV, Boris Lvovich; Russian writer, dramatist and essayist; b. 21 May 1924, Smolensk; m. Zorya Albertovna Vasilyeva; two adopted s. *Education:* Mil. Acad. of Armoured Troops. *Career:* served in Red Army in World War II, seriously wounded; engineer with Acad. of Armoured Troops 1943–54; USSR People's Deputy 1989–91; mem. USSR Supreme Soviet 1991. *Publications include:* Dawns are Quiet Here 1969, Do Not Shoot the White Swans 1975, My Horses are Flying 1983, And Tomorrow was War (novel) 1984, The Burning Bush 1987, Regards from Baba Vera 1988, Absent from the

Casualty List (novel) 1988, There was Evening, There was Morning 1989, The Short Castling 1989, The Carnival (novel) 1990, The House Built by the Old Man 1991, Kahunk and Prince Prophetic Oleg (novel) 1996, Two Bananas in one Peel (novel) 1996, A Gambler and Rabid Duellist 1998; many screenplays. *Honours:* USSR State Prize 1975; Konstantin Simonov Prize; Dovzhenko Gold Medal. *Address:* Chasovaya Str. 58, Apt. 40, 125319 Moscow, Russia. *Telephone:* (495) 152-99-01.

VASILYEVA, Larisa Nikolayevna; Russian poet and writer; b. 23 Nov. 1935, Kharkov, Ukraine; d. of Nikolai Alekseyevich Kucherenko and Yekaterina Vasilievna Kucherenko; m. Oleg Vasiliyev 1957; one s. *Education:* Moscow Univ. *Career:* started publishing 1957; first collection of verse 1966; Sec. of Moscow Br. of Russian Union of Writers; Pres. Fed. of Russian Women Writers 1989–, Int. Publishing League Atlantida 1992–. *Publications include:* prose: Albion and the Secret of Time 1978, Novel About My Father 1983, Cloud of Fire 1988, Selected Works (two vols) 1989, The Kremlin Wives 1992, The Kremlin Children 1996, The Wives of the Russian Crown; poetry: Fire-fly 1969, The Swan 1970, Blue Twilight 1970, Encounter 1974, A Rainbow of Snow 1974, Meadows 1975, Fire in the Window 1978, Russian Names 1980, Foliage 1980, Fireflower 1981, Selected Poetry 1981, Grove 1984, Mirror 1985, Moskovorechie 1985, Lantern 1985, Waiting For You In The Sky 1986, A Strange Virtue 1991. *Honours:* Moscow Komsomol Prize 1971. *Address:* Usiyevicha str. 8, Apt. 86, 125319 Moscow, Russia. *Telephone:* (495) 155-74-86. *E-mail:* muzeiT-34@lobn.ru (office). *Website:* larisavasilyeva.ru.

VÁSQUEZ, Juan Gabriel; Colombian writer and columnist; b. 1973, Bogotá. *Education:* Univ. of Sorbonne, Paris. *Career:* lives in Barcelona; columnist, El Espectador magazine, Colombia. *Publications:* novels: Los informantes (trans. as The Informers) 2004, Historia secreta de Costaguana (trans. as The Secret History of Costaguana) (Qwerty Prize for Best Narrative Book in Spanish, Barcelona, Fundación Libros & Letras Best Fiction Award, Bogotá) 2007, Los amantes de todos los santos 2008; other: El hombre de ninguna parte (biog.) 2007, trans. works of John Hersey, Victor Hugo, E. M. Forster, and others; contrib. stories to anthologies world-wide. *Address:* c/o Alfaguara, Santillana Ediciones Generales, Calle Torrelaguna 60, 28043 Madrid, Spain (office). *E-mail:* alfaguara@santillana.es (office). *Website:* www.alfaguara.santillana.es (office).

VASSANJI, M(oyez) G(ulamhussein), CM, BS, PhD; Canadian writer; b. 30 May 1950, Nairobi, Kenya; m. Nurjehan Vassanji (née Aziz) 1979; two s. *Education:* Massachusetts Inst. of Tech. and Univ. of Pennsylvania. *Career:* grew up in Nairobi, Kenya, and Dar es Salaam, Tanzania; Post-doctoral Fellow, Atomic Energy of Canada Ltd 1978–80; Research Assoc., Univ. of Toronto 1980–89; first novel published 1989, full-time writer 1989–; Writer-in-Residence Int. Writing Program, Univ. of Iowa 1989; Fellow, Indian Inst. of Advanced Study 1996. *Publications:* The Gunny Sack (novel) (Commonwealth First Novel Award, Africa Region 1990) 1989, No New Land (novel) 1991, Uhuru Street (short stories) 1991, The Book of Secrets (novel) (Giller Prize for Best Novel 1994, F. G. Bressani Literary Prize 1994) 1994, Amriika (novel) 1999, The In-Between World of Vikram Lall (novel) (Giller Prize for Best Novel 2003) 2003, When She Was Queen (short stories) 2005, The Assassin's Song (novel) 2007, A Place Within: Rediscovering India (travel memoir) (Gov. Gen.'s Literary Award for Best Non-fiction 2009) 2008, Mordecai Richler (biog.) 2009. *Honours:* Hon. DLitt (York) 2005, (McMaster) 2006, (Old Dominion) 2007, (Toronto) 2009; Harbourfront Festival Prize 1994, Giller Prize 1994, 2003, Gov. Gen.'s Prize 2009. *Literary Agent:* c/o Doubleday Canada Ltd, 5900 Finch Avenue East, Scarborough, ON M1B 0A2; c/o Westwood Creative Artists, 94 Harbord Street, Toronto, ON M5S 1G6, Canada. *Telephone:* (416) 364-4449 (Toronto); (416) 964-3302 (Toronto). *Fax:* (416) 975-9209 (Toronto). *E-mail:* info@doubledaycanada.ca; info@wcaltd.com. *Website:* www.doubledaycanada.ca; www.wcaltd.com; www.mgvassanji.com.

VASSILIKOS, Vassilis; Greek writer; b. 18 Nov. 1934, Kavala; s. of Nikolaos Aikaterini; m. Vasso Papantoniou; one d. *Education:* Anatolia High School of Thessaloniki, Thessaloniki Law School, Yale Drama School, USA, School of Radio and Television, USA. *Career:* Dir-Gen. of Greek TV (public) 1981–85; Amb. to UNESCO 1996–2004; Pres. Hellenic Authors' Soc. 1999–2005; presenter of weekly TV show on books; mem. Int. Parl. of Writers, Athens Union of Daily Newspaper Journalists. *Publications include:* (in English trans.): The Plant, The Well, The Angel 1963, Z 1968, The Harpoon Gun 1972, Outside the Walls 1973, The Photographs 1974, The Monarch 1976, The Coroner's Assistant 1986, . . .And Dreams Are Dreams 1996, The Few Things I Know About Glafkos Thrassakis 2003. *Honours:* Dr hc (Univ. of Patra, Univ. of Thessaly); Commdr, Ordre des Arts et des Lettres 1999; Prize of 'The Twelve' 1961, Mediterraneo Prize 1971. *Address:* 5 Ambrosiou Moshonision, 17123 Athens, Greece (office). *Telephone:* (210) 363-4868 (office). *Fax:* (210) 362-0844 (office). *E-mail:* info@orama-opera.gr (office).

VATSUYEVA, Aset; Russian (Chechen) journalist; b. 1977, Grozny, Chechnya; one s. *Education:* St Petersburg Univ., Moscow State Univ. *Career:* corresp., Voice of the Chechen Repub. newspaper, Grozny 1997; fmr reporter, Obshaya Gazeta and Obyedinennaya Gazeta, Moscow; reporter, NTV Namedni 2002, Co-Host Strana i Mir (Russia and the World) programme, NTV 2003–04, resgnd and returned to Chechnya. *Honours:* Honoured Cultural Artist of Ingushetia 2004.

VÁZQUEZ DÍAZ, René; Cuban writer, poet and translator; b. 7 Sept. 1952, Caibarien. *Education:* Univ. of Łódź, Univ. of Lund. *Career:* living in exile in Sweden 1975–; review writer for Swedish journals; mem. Swedish Union of Writers; Swedish PEN Club. *Publications:* Hägringens tid 1986, Förrädarens sista vinter 1989, Kärleksblommans ö 1994, Fredrika i paradis 1996, Dårskap och kärlek 2003, Välkommen till Miami, dr Leal 2007, Florina 2008, Städer vid havet 2011; contributions: Sydsvendska Dagladet, Bonniers, El País, El Urogallo, Geo, El Nuevo Herald. *Honours:* Juan Rulfo Award 2005. *Address:* c/o Alhambra Publishing, PO Box 273, 24402 Furulund, Sweden. *E-mail:* alhambra@alhambra.se.

VELASCO, Xavier; Mexican journalist and writer; b. 7 Nov. 1964, Mexico City. *Career:* wrote for 16 years for Saturday supplement of Unomásuno (newspaper); columnist, Halla Deshoras y Penumbras 1995–2000, Epistolario 2000–04, El funámbulo errante 2000–03, Pronóstico del clímax 2004–. *Publications:* Una banda nombrada Caifanes 1990, Cecilia 1993, Los hijos de Ziggy Stardust 1995, Diablo Guardián (Premio Alfaguara) 2003, El materialismo histérico 2004, Luna llena en las rocas 2005, Éste que ves 2007, Puedo explicarlo todo 2010. *Address:* Santillana Ediciones Generales, S.A. de C.V., Av. Universidad 767, Col. Del Valle, 03100 México DF, México. *Telephone:* (55) 5420-7530. *Website:* www.xaviervelasco.com.

VELHO DA COSTA, Maria; Portuguese writer and teacher; b. 1938, Lisbon. *Education:* Univ. of Lisbon. *Career:* prominent mem. Portuguese feminist movement with Maria Isabel Barrero and Maria Teresa Horta; fmr secondary school teacher; Asst to Sec. of State for Culture 1979; Reader, Dept of Portuguese and Brazilian Studies, King's Coll., London 1980–87; Cultural Envoy to Cape Verde 1988–91; currently works for the Camões Institute; Pres. Portuguese Writers' Asscn 1973–78. *Publications:* O lugar comum 1966, Maina Mendes 1969, Novas cartas portuguesas (with Maria Isabel Barrero and Maria Teresa Horta) 1972, Ensino primário e ideologia 1972, Desescrita 1973, Cravo 1976, Português trabalhador, doente mental 1976, Casas pardas (Prémio Cidade de Lisboa) 1977, Da rosa fixa 1978, Corpo Verde 1979, Lúlialima (Prémio D. Dinis) 1983, O mapa cor da rosa 1984, Missa in albis 1988, Das Áfricas 1991, Dores (Grande Prémio de Conto Camilo Castelo Branco) 1994, Madame 1999, Irene ou o contralto social 2000, Inferno 2001, O amante do Crato 2002, O livro do meio 2006. *Honours:* Prémio Vergílio Ferreira 1997, Prémio Camões 2002. *Address:* c/o Editorial Caminho, Estrada de Paço de Arcos 66–A, 2735-336 Cacém, Portugal (office). *E-mail:* info@editorial-caminho.pt (office). *Website:* www.editorial-caminho.pt (office).

VENCLOVA, Tomas, PhD; Lithuanian/American linguist, academic, writer and poet; *Professor of Slavic Languages and Literatures, Yale University*; b. 11 Sept. 1937, Klaipeda, Lithuania; m. Tanya Milovidova 1990; one s. one d. *Education:* Univ. of Vilnius, Yale Univ. *Career:* Lecturer in Literature, Linguistics and Semiotics, Univ. of Vilnius 1966–73; Jr Fellow, Inst. of History, Lithuanian Acad. of Sciences 1974–76; Regents Prof. in Slavic Languages and Literatures, Univ. of California, Berkeley 1977; Lecturer in Slavic Languages and Literatures, UCLA 1977–80; Morton Prof. of Philosophy, Ohio Univ. 1978; Lecturer and Acting Instructor of Slavic Languages and Literatures, Yale Univ. 1980–85, Asst Prof. 1985–90, Assoc. Prof. 1990–93, Prof. 1993–; Fellow, New York Inst. for the Humanities 1981–84, Kennan Inst. for Advanced Russian Studies 1981; mem. Asscn for the Advancement of Baltic Studies (Pres. 1989–91), Int. PEN, PEN in Exile (mem. Exec. Bd 1982). *Publications include:* poetry: Kalbos zenklas 1972, 98 eilerasciai 1977, Pasnekesys ziema (partial trans. as Winter Dialogue) 1991, Szesc wierszy 1991, Cistost soli 1991, Mondjatok meg Fortinbrasnak 1992, Rinktine 1999, Vor der Tür das Ende der Welt 2000; prose: Tekstai apie tekstus 1985, Neustoichivoe ravnovesie: vosem russkikh poeticheskikh tekstov 1986, Vilties formos: Eseistika ir publistisika (partial trans. as Forms of Hope) 1991, Aleksander Wat: Life and Art of an Iconoclast 1996, Sobesedniki na piru 1997, Manau, kad. . . 2000, Ligi Lietuvos 10.000 kilometru 2003, Sankirta 2005, Kitaip 2006, The Junction 2008; translations: many works by major writers into Lithuanian; contrib. of articles to professional journals, including International Journal of Slavic Linguistics and Poetics, Russian Literature, Russian Review, World Literature Today, Journal of Baltic Studies, Comparative Civilizations Review, UCLA Slavic Studies. *Honours:* 1956 Hungarian Revolution Memorial Award 2006; Dr hc (Lublin) 1991, (Jagellonian Univ., Kraków) 2000; Vilenica Int. Literary Prize 1990, Lithuanian Nat. Prize 2000, Baltic Star 2008. *Address:* Department of Slavic Languages and Literatures, Yale University, New Haven, CT 06520 (office); 100 York Street, Apt 12 S, New Haven, CT 06511, USA (home). *E-mail:* tomas.venclova@yale.edu (office).

VENDLER, Helen Hennessy, AB, PhD; American academic and literary critic; *A. Kingsley Porter University Professor, Department of English, Harvard University*; b. (Helen Marie Hennessy), 30 April 1933, Boston, Mass; d. of George Hennessy and Helen Conway; m. Zeno Vendler (deceased); one s. *Education:* Emmanuel Coll. and Harvard Univ. *Career:* Instructor, Cornell Univ. 1960–63; Lecturer, Swarthmore Coll., Pa and Haverford Coll., Pa 1963–64; Asst Prof., Smith Coll. Northampton, Mass 1964–66; Assoc. Prof., Boston Univ. 1966–68, Prof. 1968–85; Visiting Prof., Harvard Univ. 1981–85, Kenan Prof. 1985–, Assoc. Acad. Dean 1987–92, A. Kingsley Porter Univ. Prof. 1990–; Sr Fellow, Harvard Soc. of Fellows 1981–92; poetry critic, New Yorker 1978–90; mem. Educ. Advisory Bd, Guggenheim Foundation, Pulitzer Prize Bd 1990–99; Fulbright Lecturer, Univ. of Bordeaux 1968–69; Overseas Fellow, Churchill Coll. Cambridge 1980; Parnell Fellow, Magdalene Coll., Cambridge 1986, Hon. Fellow 1996–; mem. American Acad. of Arts and Sciences, Norwegian Acad., American Philosophical Soc., American Acad. of Arts and Letters (Bd mem. 2006–09). *Publications include:* Yeats's Vision and the Later Plays 1963, On Extended Wings: Wallace Stevens' Longer Poems 1969, The Poetry of George Herbert 1975, Part of Nature, Part of Us 1980, The Odes of John Keats 1983, Wallace Stevens: Words Chosen Out of Desire 1985, Harvard Book of Contemporary American Poetry 1985, The Music of What Happens 1988, The Given and the Made 1995, The Breaking of Style 1995, Soul Says 1995, Poems, Poets, Poetry 1996, The Art of Shakespeare's Sonnets 1997, Seamus Heaney 1998, Coming of Age as a Poet: Milton, Keats, Eliot, Plath 2003, Poets Thinking: Pope, Whitman, Dickinson, Yeats 2005, Invisible Listeners: Lyric Intimacy in Herbert, Whitman, and Ashbery 2005, Our Secret Discipline 2007, Dickinson, Selected Poems with Commentaries 2010. *Honours:* 24 hon. degrees; Fulbright Fellow 1954, A.A.U.W. Fellow 1959, Lowell Prize 1969, Explicator Prize 1969, Guggenheim Fellow 1971–72, American Council of Learned Socs Fellow 1971–72, Nat. Inst. of Arts and Letters Award 1975, Nat. Book Critics Award 1980, Nat. Endowment for the Humanities (NEH) Fellow 1980, 1985, 1994, 2006, Wilson Fellow 1994, Newton Arvin Award, Jefferson Medal, Jefferson Lecturer, NEH, A.W. Mellon Lecturer in Fine Arts, Nat. Gallery of Art 2007, Siemens Fellow 2009. *Address:* Harvard University, Department of English, Barker Center 205, 12 Quincey Street, Cambridge, MA 02138 (office); 54 Trowbridge Street, Apt B, Cambridge, MA 02138, USA. *Telephone:* (617) 496-6028 (office). *Fax:* (617) 496-8737 (office). *E-mail:* vendler@fas.harvard.edu (office). *Website:* www.fas.harvard.edu/~english (office).

VENN, George Andrew Fyfe, BA, MFA; American academic, writer, poet, editor and literary historian; *Professor Emeritus of English, Eastern Oregon University*; b. (George Andrew Fyfe), 12 Oct. 1943, Tacoma, Wash.; s. of Ernest Fyfe and Beth Mayo Fyfe; m. 1st Elizabeth Cheney (divorced); one s. one d.; m. 2nd Marie Balaban 2007. *Education:* Coll. of Idaho, Univ. of Montana, Central Univ., Quito, Ecuador, Univ. of Salamanca, Spain, City Literary Inst., London, UK. *Career:* Instructor, US Information Agency Centro Ecuatoriano-Norteamericano, Quito, Equador 1963–64; Foreign Expert, Changsha Railway Univ. 1981–82; Gen. Ed. Oregon Literature Series Vols I–VI 1989–94; Faculty mem. Eastern Oregon Univ., Prof. Emer. 2002–; Pres. Oregon Council of Teachers of English 2001–03, Writer-on-Tour, Western States Arts Foundation; mem. Editorial Bd Oregon Historical Quarterly, Northwest Folklore; mem. Advisory Bd Fishtrap Writers' Conf., Exec. Bd Oregon Council of Teachers of English. *Film scripts:* Safe Havens: Oregon's New Ocean Protection Initiative, La Grande: Greenfire Productions for Oregon Ocean 2007. *Radio:* Honeycomb (novel in progress) performed on Nat. Public Radio, Utah State Univ., Facing West 1992. *Television:* 'C.E.S. Wood' and 'Oregon Experience' (Oregon Public Broadcasting) 2008. *Publications:* Sunday Afternoon: Grande Ronde 1975, Off the Main Road 1978, Marking the Magic Circle 1988, West of Paradise: New Poems 1999, Soldier to Advocate: C. E. S. Wood's 1877 Legacy 2006, Darkroom Soldier 2007; contrib. to Oregon Humanities, Writer's Northwest Handbook, North West Review, Northwest Reprint Series, Poetry Northwest, Willow Springs, Clearwater Journal, Oregon East, Portland Review, Worldviews and the American West (book), Idaho Yesterdays. *Honours:* Pushcart Prize 1980, Oregon Book Award 1988, Stewart Holbrook Award 1994, Northwest Writers Andres Berger Poetry Prize 1995, Distinguished Teaching Award, Eastern Oregon Univ. 2002. *Address:* Department of English, Eastern Oregon University, 702B Avenue, La Grande, OR 97850 (office); 702B Avenue, La Grande, OR 97850, USA (home). *Telephone:* (541) 962-0380 (home). *Fax:* (541) 663-9990 (home). *E-mail:* gvenn@eou.edu (office). *Website:* www.georgevenn.com.

VENTURI, Robert, AB, MFA, FAIA, Int. FRIBA; American architect; b. 25 June 1925, Philadelphia, Pa; s. of Robert C. Venturi and Vanna Lanzetta; m. Denise Scott Brown (née Lakofski) 1967; one s. *Education:* Princeton Univ. *Career:* Designer, Oskar Stonorov 1950, Eero Saarinen & Assoc. 1950–53; Rome Prize Fellow, American Acad. in Rome 1954–56; Designer, Louis I. Kahn 1957; Assoc. Prof., School of Fine Arts, Univ. of Pennsylvania 1957–65; Charlotte Shepherd Davenport Prof., Yale Univ. 1966–70; Prin., Venturi, Cope & Lippincott 1958–61, Venturi and Short 1961–64, Venturi and Rauch 1964–80, Venturi, Rauch and Scott Brown (architects and planners) 1980–89; Venturi, Scott Brown and Assocs June 1989–; Fellow, Accademia Nazionale di San Luca, American Acad. of Arts and Sciences; mem. Advisory Bd of Dirs Sir John Soane's Museum Foundation; mem. American Philosophical Soc. of Philadelphia, European Acad. of Sciences and Arts, Pennsylvania Soc. of Architects, American Acad. of Arts and Letters, Royal Soc. for the Encouragement of Arts, Manufacture & Commerce; mem. Bd of Overseers, School of Fine Arts, Univ. of Pennsylvania, 1985–2002. *Works include:* Vanna Venturi House, Phila, Pa 1961, Guild House, Phila 1961, Franklin Court, Phila 1972, Allen Memorial Art Museum Addition, Oberlin, Ohio 1973, Inst. for Scientific Information Corpn HQ, Phila 1978, Gordon Wu Hall, Princeton Univ., NJ 1980, Seattle Art Museum, Seattle, Wash. 1984, Clinical Research Bldg, Univ. of Pa 1985 (with Payette Assocs.), Nat. Gallery, Sainsbury Wing, London, UK 1986, Fisher-Bendheim Hall, Princeton Univ. 1986, Charles P. Stevenson Library, Bard Coll. 1989, Regional Govt Bldg, Toulouse, France 1992, Kirifuri Resort facilities, Nikko, Japan 1992, Univ. of Del. Student Center, Newark, Del. 1992, Memorial Hall Restoration and Addition, Harvard Univ. 1992, The Barnes Foundation Restoration and Renovation, Merion, Pa 1993, Disney Celebration Bank, Celebration, Fla 1993, Irvine Auditorium, Perelman Quadrangle, Univ. of Pa 1995, Princeton Campus Center, Princeton Univ. 1996, Congress Avenue Building, Yale Univ. School of Medicine 1998, Master Plan and Bldgs for Univ. of Michigan 1997–. *Publications:* Complexity and Contradiction in Architecture 1966, Learning from Las Vegas (with Denise Scott Brown and Steven Izenour) 1972, A View from the Campidoglio: Selected Essays, 1953–1984 (with Denise Scott Brown) 1984, Iconography and Electronics upon a Generic Architecture 1996, Architecture as Signs and Systems: for a Mannerist Time 2004; numerous articles in professional journals. *Honours:* Hon. Fellow, Royal Incorporation of Architects in Scotland, American Acad. and Inst. of Arts and Letters; Hon. Prof., Xi'an Acad. of Fine Arts; Hon. mem. Bund Deutscher Architekten; Commandeur, Ordre des Arts et Lettres 2000; Hon. DFA (Oberlin, Yale, Penn., Princeton, Phila Coll of Art); Hon. LHD (NJ Inst. of Tech.); Laurea hc (Univ. of Rome La Sapienza) 1994; Dr hc (Zhejiang Univ., Hangzhou, China) 2005; Wyck-Strickland Award, 1989, Pritzker Prize 1991, Nat. Medal of Arts 1992, Centennial Medal of American Acad. in Rome 1998, Vincent J. Scully Prize (jtly) 2002, Nat. Design Mind Award, Cooper-Hewitt, Nat. Design Museum (jtly) ,2007, The International Award, Soc. of American Registered Architects 2010, Anne d'Harnoncourt Award for Artistic Excellence, Arts and Business Council of Greater Philadelphia (jtly) 2010, and numerous other awards. *Address:* Venturi, Scott Brown and Associates, 4236 Main Street, Philadelphia, PA 19127-1696, USA (office). *Telephone:* (215) 487-0400 (office). *Fax:* (215) 487-2520 (office). *E-mail:* info@vsba.com (office). *Website:* www.vsba.com (office).

VERGHESE, Abraham, MFA, MD; Ethiopian writer; *Senior Associate Chair for the Theory and Practice of Medicine, Stanford University*; b. 1955; m.; two c. *Education:* Madras Medical Coll. India, East Tennessee State Univ., Boston Univ., Univ. of Iowa, USA. *Career:* specialist in HIV and AIDS research 1985–89; worked at Univ. of Iowa outpatient AIDS clinic 1990; Prof. of Medicine and Chief of Infectious Diseases, Texas Tech. Health Sciences Center, El Paso –2007; Sr Assoc. Chair. for the Theory and Practice of Medicine, Stanford Univ. 2007–. *Publications:* My Own Country: A Doctor's Story of a Town and its People in the Age of AIDS 1994, Soundings: A Doctor's Life in the Age of AIDS 1994, The Tennis Partner: A Doctor's Story of Friendship and Loss 1998, Short Stories 1999, Cutting for Stone 2009; contrib. to The New Yorker, North American Review, Granta, Sports Illustrated, Story, numerous medical journals. *Honours:* DS hc (Swarthmore Coll.) 2001, DHumLitt hc (Univ. of Northern Illinois) 2007; Boston Univ. Medical Center/Framington Fellowship 1985, East Tennessee State Univ. Fellowship 1988, Master, American Coll. of Physicians 2005, John P. McGovern Medal, Osler Soc., Montreal 2007. *Address:* Stanford University School of Medicine, 300 Pasteur Drive, S102C, MC 5109, Stanford, CA 94305, USA (office). *Telephone:* (650) 721-6966 (office). *Fax:* (650) 725-8381 (office). *E-mail:* abrahamv@stanford.edu (office). *Website:* med.stanford.edu (office).

VERHAEGHEN, Paul, PhD; Belgian psychologist and writer; *Associate Professor of Psychology, Georgia Institute of Technology.* *Education:* Univ. of Leuven. *Career:* cognitive psychologist specializing in the study of the ageing process; based in USA 1997–; currently Assoc. Prof. of Psychology, Ga Inst. of Tech. *Publications:* novels: Lichtenberg 1996, Omega Minor (Bordewijk Award, Flemish Government's Culture Award, Independent Foreign Fiction Prize 2008) 2005; numerous articles in journals including Psychological Bulletin, Psychology and Aging, Health Psychology. *Address:* School of Psychology, Georgia Institute of Technology, 654 Cherry Street, Atlanta, GA 30332-0170 (office). *Telephone:* (404) 894-0963 (office). *Fax:* (404) 894-8905 (office). *E-mail:* paul.verhaeghen@psych.gatech.edu (office). *Website:* www.psychology.gatech.edu (office).

VERHAGEN, Hans; Dutch poet and journalist; b. 1939, Vlissingen. *Career:* Ed., neo-realist periodical Gard Sivik, De Nieuwe Stijl 1962–66, and Haagse Post; fmr television producer, Hoepla, Het gat van Nederland. *Publications:* poetry collections: Rozen & motoren 1963, Sterren Cirkels Bellen 1968, Duizenden zonsondergangen 1971, Kouwe Voeten 1983, Autoriteit van de Emotie 1992, Echoput & Luchtkasteel 1995, Triomfantelijke Wandelingen 2000, Quasi-kamikaze 2002, Eeuwige Vlam 2003, Moeder is een rover 2004, Draak 2006, Zwarte gaten 2008, Automatische profeet. *Honours:* P.C. Hooft Prize 2008. *Address:* c/o Nijgh & Van Ditmar/Querido's uitgeverij BV, Singel 262, 1016 AC Amsterdam, Netherlands (office). *E-mail:* verkoop@querido.nl (office). *Website:* www.uitgeverijnijghenvanditmar.nl (office).

VERMES, Geza, MA, DTheol, DLitt, FBA; British academic and writer; *Editor, Journal of Jewish Studies*; b. 22 June 1924, Mako, Hungary; s. of Ernest Vermes and Terezia Riesz; m. 1st Pamela Hobson 1958 (died 1993); m. 2nd Margaret Unarska 1996. *Education:* Univ. of Budapest, Hungary, Univ. of Louvain, Belgium. *Career:* Licencié en Histoire et Philologie Orientales; Lecturer, later Sr Lecturer in Divinity, Univ. of Newcastle 1957–65; Reader in Jewish Studies, Univ. of Oxford 1965–89; Fellow, Wolfson Coll. 1965–91, Fellow Emer. 1991–, Prof. of Jewish Studies, Univ. of Oxford 1989–91, Prof. Emer. 1991–; Ed. Journal of Jewish Studies 1971–; Dir Oxford Forum for Qumran Research, Oxford Centre for Hebrew and Jewish Studies 1991–; Inaugural Lecturer, Geza Vermes Lectures in the History of Religions, Univ. of Leicester 1997; many visiting lectureships and professorships; mem. British Asscn for Jewish Studies, Pres. 1975, 1988; Pres. European Asscn for Jewish Studies 1981–84. *Publications:* Les manuscrits du désert de Juda 1953, Discovery in the Judean Desert 1956, Scripture and Tradition in Judaism 1961, The Dead Sea Scrolls in English 1962, Jesus the Jew 1973, History of the Jewish People in the Age of Jesus Christ, by E. Schürer I–III (co-reviser with F. Millar and M. Goodman) 1973–87, Post-Biblical Jewish Studies 1975, The Dead Sea Scrolls: Qumran in Perspective (with Pamela Vermes) 1977, The Gospel of Jesus the Jew 1981, Essays in Honour of Y. Yadin (co-ed.) 1982, Jesus and the World of Judaism 1983, The Essenes According to the Classical Sources (with M. D. Goodman) 1989, The Religion of Jesus the Jew 1993, The Complete Dead Sea Scrolls in English 1997, Providential Accidents: An

Autobiography 1998, Discoveries in the Judaean Desert XXVI: The Community Rule (with P. S. Alexander) 1998, An Introduction to the Complete Dead Sea Scrolls 1999, The Changing Faces of Jesus 2000, The Dead Sea Scrolls 2000, Jesus in His Jewish Context 2003, The Authentic Gospel of Jesus 2003, The Passion 2005, Who's Who in the Age of Jesus 2005, The Nativity 2006, The Resurrection 2008, Searching for the Real Jesus 2010, The Story of the Scrolls 2010, Jesus: Nativity-Passion-Resurrection 2010; contrib. to scholarly books and journals. *Honours:* Tribute of Recognition, US House of Reps 2009; Hon. DD (Edinburgh) 1989, (Durham) 1990; Hon. DLitt (Sheffield) 1994; Hon. DPhil (CEU Budapest) 2008; W. Bacher Medallist, Hungarian Acad. of Sciences 1996, Memorial Medal, City of Mako, Hungary 2008, awarded key to City of Monroe, La and Natchez, Mich., USA . *Address:* West Wood Cottage, Foxcombe Lane, Boars Hill, Oxford, OX1 5DH, England (home). *Telephone:* (1865) 735384 (office). *Fax:* (1865) 735034 (office). *E-mail:* geza.vermes@orinst.ox.ac.uk (office).

VERONESI, Sandro; Italian writer and publisher; b. 1959, Prato. *Education:* Univ. of Florence. *Career:* Co-founder Fandango Libri (publisher) 1989. *Publications include:* novels: Il Resto e il Cielo 1984, Per dore parte questo treno allegro 1988, Gli Sfiorati 1990, Venite venite B-52 1995, La forza del passato (trans. as The Force of the Past; Premio Viareggio L. Repaci, Premio Campiello) 2000, Ring City 2001, No Man's Land 2003, Caos Calmo (Premio Strega 2006) 2005, Brucia Troia 2007, XY 2010; non-fiction: Cronache Italiane 1991, Occhio per Occho 1992, Ritratti, sopralluoghi e collaudi 1996, Superalbo 2002. *Honours:* Campiello Prize. *Address:* Fandango Srl, Viale Gorizia 19, 00198 Rome, Italy (office). *E-mail:* info@fandango.it (office). *Website:* www.fandango.it (office); www.sandroveronesi.it.

VICKERS, Hugo Ralph; British writer and lecturer; *Chairman, Jubilee Walkway Trust*; b. 12 Nov. 1951, London, England; s. of the late Ralph Cecil Vickers, MC and Dulcie Vickers; m. Elizabeth Anne Blyth Vickers 1995; two s. one d. *Education:* Eton Coll., Univ. of Strasbourg, France. *Career:* radio and TV broadcaster 1973–; Dir Burkes Peerage 1974–79; mem. Historic Houses Asscn, RSL, Jubilee Walkway Trust (Trustee 2000–, Vice-Chair. 2001, Chair. 2002–); mem. Council of Man., Windsor Festival 1999–; Lay Steward, St George's Chapel, Windsor 1970–, Deputy Vice-Capt. Lay Stewards 1996–2011, Vice-Capt. 2011–; Golo Mann Distinguished Lecturer, Claremont McKenna Coll., Calif. 2007; DL Berks. 2010. *Play:* The Immortal Dropout 2008. *Film:* Historical Advisor, The King's Speech 2010. *Publications:* We Want the Queen 1977, Gladys, Duchess of Marlborough 1979, Debretts Book of the Royal Wedding 1981, Cocktails and Laughter (ed.) 1983, Cecil Beaton: The Authorised Biography 1985, Vivien Leigh 1988, Loving Garbo 1994, Royal Orders 1994, The Private World of the Duke and Duchess of Windsor 1995, The Kiss 1996, Alice, Princess Andrew of Greece 2000, The Unexpurgated Beaton (ed.) 2002, Beaton in the Sixties (ed.) 2003, Alexis – The Memoirs of the Baron de Redé (ed.) 2005, Elizabeth the Queen Mother 2005, Horses and Husbands (ed.) 2007, St George's Chapel 2008, Behind Closed Doors 2011; contrib. to books and periodicals. *Honours:* PEN Stern Prize for Non-Fiction 1996. *Literary Agent:* c/o Aitken Alexander Associates Ltd, 18–21 Cavaye Place, London, SW10 9PT, England. *Telephone:* (20) 7373-8672. *Fax:* (20) 7373-6002. *E-mail:* reception@aitkenalexander.co.uk. *Website:* www.aitkenalexander.co.uk. *Address:* Wyeford, Ramsdell, Hants., RG26 5QL, England (home). *Telephone:* (1256) 850044 (office). *Website:* www.hugovickers.co.uk.

VICKERS, Salley, MA (Cantab.); British university lecturer, psychoanalyst and writer; two c. *Education:* St Paul's Girls' School, Newnham Coll., Cambridge. *Career:* fmr univ. lecturer in English literature; lecturer on connections between literature, art, psychology and religion. *Play:* Where Three Roads Meet. *Publications:* Miss Garnet's Angel 2000 (screenplay in development), Instances of the Number 3 2001, Mr Golightly's Holiday 2003, The Other Side of You 2006, Where Three Roads Meet 2007, Dancing Backwards 2009, Aphrodite's Hat 2010, The Cleaner of Chartres 2012; regular contrib. to Guardian, Times and Observer newspapers. *Literary Agent:* c/o Curtis Brown Ltd, 28–29 Haymarket, London, SW1Y 4SP, England. *Telephone:* (20) 7393-4400. *Fax:* (20) 7393-4401. *E-mail:* info@curtisbrown.co.uk. *Website:* www.curtisbrown.co.uk. *Address:* c/o Viking Penguin, 80 Strand, London WC2R 0RL, England. *E-mail:* reception@salleyvickers.com (office). *Website:* www.salleyvickers.com.

VICTOR, Edward (Ed), MLitt; British literary agent; b. 9 Sept. 1939, New York, USA; s. of the late Jack Victor and the late Lydia Victor; m. 1st Michelene Dinah Samuels 1963 (divorced); two s.; m. 2nd Carol Lois Ryan; one s. *Education:* Dartmouth Coll., USA, Pembroke Coll., Cambridge. *Career:* Arts Book Ed., then Editorial Dir Weidenfeld & Nicolson 1964–67; Editorial Dir Jonathan Cape Ltd 1967–71; Sr Ed. Alfred A. Knopf Inc., New York 1972–73, literary agent and Dir John Farquharson Ltd 1974–76; Founding Ed. Victor Agency 1977; mem. Council Aids Crisis Trust 1986–98; Vice-Chair. Almeida Theatre 1994–2002 (Dir 1993–2002); Trustee, The Arts Foundation 1991–2004. *Publications include:* The Obvious Diet 2001. *Address:* Ed Victor Ltd, 6 Bayley Street, Bedford Square, London, WC1B 3HE (office); 10 Cambridge Gate, Regents Park, London, NW1 4JX, England (home). *Telephone:* (20) 7304-4100 (office); (20) 7224-3030 (home). *Fax:* (20) 7304-4111 (office); (20) 7935-3096 (home). *E-mail:* ed@edvictor.com. *Website:* www.edvictor.com (office).

VIDA, Vendela; American writer; b. 1971; m. Dave Eggers 2003. *Education:* Columbia Univ. *Career:* Co-Ed., The Believer literary magazine. *Publications:* Girls on the Verge 1999, And Now You Can Go 2003, Let the Northern Lights Erase Your Name 2007, The Lovers 2010. *Address:* 826 Valencia Street, San Francisco, CA 94110, USA (office). *E-mail:* letters@believermag.com (office). *Website:* www.believermag.com (office).

VIDAL, Gore; American writer; b. 3 Oct. 1925, West Point, New York; s. of Eugene L. Vidal and Nina Vidal (née Gore). *Education:* Phillips Acad., Exeter, NH. *Career:* served in US Army 1943–46; Drama Critic, Reporter (magazine) 1959, Democratic-Liberal Cand. for US Congress from New York 1960; mem. Pres. Kennedy's Advisory Council on the Arts 1961–63; Co-Chair. People's Party 1970–72; writes thrillers under pseudonym Edgar Box. *Film and television screenplays:* Wedding Breakfast, The Catered Affair 1956, The Left-Handed Gun 1958, I Accuse 1958, The Death of Billy the Kid (TV) 1958, Suddenly Last Summer 1959, The Best Man (Cannes Critics' Prize) 1964, Is Paris Burning? 1966, The Last of the Mobile Hotshots 1970, Dress Gray 1986. *Publications:* novels: Williwaw 1946, In a Yellow Wood 1947, The City and the Pillar 1948, The Season of Comfort 1949, A Search for the King 1950, Dark Green, Bright Red 1950, The Judgment of Paris 1952, Messiah 1954, Julian 1964, Washington, DC 1967, Myra Breckinridge 1968, Two Sisters 1970, Burr 1972, Myron 1974, 1876 1976, Kalki 1978, Creation (Prix Deauville) 1980, Duluth 1983, Lincoln 1984, Empire 1987, Hollywood 1990, Live from Golgotha 1992, With Honors 1994, Dark Green, Dark Red 1995, The Season of Conflict 1996, The Essential Vidal 1998, The Smithsonian Institution 1998, The Golden Age 2000; short stories: A Thirsty Evil 1956; plays: Visit to a Small Planet 1956, The Best Man 1960, Romulus 1962, Weekend 1968, An Evening with Richard Nixon 1972, Gore Vidal's Lincoln 1988, On the March to the Sea 2005; non-fiction: Rocking the Boat 1962, Reflections upon a Sinking Ship 1969, Homage to Daniel Shays 1972, Matters of Fact and Fiction 1977, The Second American Revolution 1982, Armageddon? 1987, At Home: Essays 1982–88 1988, A View from the Diners Club: Essays 1987–1991 1991, Screening History (memoir) 1992, United States: Essays 1952–1992 (Nat. Book Award) 1993, Palimpsest (memoir) 1995, Virgin Islands: A Dependency of United States Essays 1992–97 1997, The Last Empire: Essays 1992–2000 2001, Perpetual War for Perpetual Peace: How We Got So Hated 2002, Inventing a Nation: Washington, Adams, Jefferson 2003, Imperial America 2004, Point To Point Navigation (memoir) 2006; criticism in Partisan Review, The Nation, New York Review of Books, Times Literary Supplement. *Honours:* Hon. Citizen, Ravello, Italy 1983; Hon. Pres. American Humanist Asscn 2009–; Chevalier, Ordre Nat. des Arts et des Lettres; Edgar Allan Poe Award for Television 1955, Nat. Book Award for Distinguished Contrib. to American Letters 2009. *Address:* c/o Doubleday Publicity Department, 1745 Broadway, New York, NY 10019, USA (office). *Website:* doubleday.knopfdoubleday.com (office).

VIEIRA, Arménio; Cape Verde writer, poet and journalist; b. 24 Jan. 1941, Praia, Ilha de Santiago. *Career:* fmr Ed., Voz do Povo; has written pieces for newspapers and magazines including Boletim de Cabo Verde, Vértice, Raízes, Ponto & Vírgula, Fragmentos, Sopinha de Alfabeto. *Publications:* Poemas 1981, O eleito do sol 1990, No inferno 1999, MITOgrafias 2006. *Honours:* Prémio Camões 2009. *Address:* c/o Ministry of Culture, Praia, Santiago, Cape Verde (office).

VIEWEGH, Michal; Czech novelist and writer; b. 31 March 1931, Prague. *Education:* Charles Univ., Prague. *Career:* primary school teacher; Ed. Czech Writer publishing house 1993–95; Lecturer, Czech Acad. of Literature 1999–2004. *Publications:* Názory na vraždu 1990, Báječná léta pod psa (Jiří Orten Award 1993) 1992, Nápady laskavého čtenáře (parodies) 1993, Výchova dívek v Čechách (trans. as Bringing up Girls in Bohemia) 1994, Účastníci zájezdu 1996, Zapisovatelé otcovský lásky 1998, Povídky o manželství a sexu (short stories) 1999, Nové nápady laskavého čtenáře (parodies) 2000, Román pro ženy 2001, Báječná léta s Klausem 2002, Případ nevěrné Kláry 2003, Vybíjená 2004, Tři v háji (co-author) 2004, Lekce tvůrčího psaní 2005, Báječný rok (diary) 2006, Andělé všedního dne (novella) 2007, Krátké pohádky pro unavené rodiče (fairy tales) 2007, Román pro muže 2008; contrib. to newspapers and magazines. *Literary Agent:* Dana Blatná Literary Agency, Jinačovice 3, 66434 Kuřim, Czech Republic. *Telephone:* 608748157. *E-mail:* blatna@dbagency.cz. *Website:* www.dbagency.cz; www.viewegh.cz.

VIGÉE, Claude André, MA, PhD; French writer and poet; b. (Claude Strauss), 3 Jan. 1921, Bischwiller (Bas-Rhin); s. of Robert Strauss and Germaine Meyer; m. Evelyne Meyer 1947; two c. *Education:* Strasbourg Univ., Ohio State Univ. *Publications include* poetry: Claude Vigée, la Corne du grand pardon 1954, L'Été indien 1957, Moisson de Canaan 1967, Le Soleil sous la mer 1972, Du bec à l'oreille 1977, Pâque de la Parole 1978, Les Orties noires flambent dans le vent 1984, Heimat des Hauches 1985, Wénderôwefîr/Le Feu d'une nuit d'hiver 1989, Apprendre la nuit 1991, L'héritage du feu 1992, Aux portes du labyrinthe: poèmes du passage (1939–1996) 1996, La Double Voix 2010, Mon heure sur la terre: Poésies completes 1936–2008 2008; essays: Les Artistes de la faim 1960, Révoltes et Louanges 1962, La Lune d'hiver 1970, Délivrance du souffle 1977, L'Art et le Démonique 1978, L'Extase et l'Errance 1982, Le Parfum et la Cendre, entretiens sur trois continents 1984, Une voix dans le défilé, vivre à Jérusalem 1985, La Manne et la Rosée, fête de la Tora 1986, La Faille du regard 1987, Aux sources de la littérature moderne 1989, Vision et silence dans la poésie juive 1999, Demain la seule demeure 1999, Mélancolie solaire 2008, Le fin murmure de la lumière 2009; translations: Mon printemps viendra, poèmes de D. Seter 1965, Les yeux dans le rocher, poèmes de David Rokéah 1968, L'Herbe du songe, poèmes d'Yvan Goll 1971, Le vent du retour, poèmes de R. M. Rilke 1989, Quatre Quatuors, poèmes de T. S. Eliot 1992, Un abri pour nos têtes, poésie de Shirley Kaufman 2003; autobiography: Un panier de houblon 1995. *Honours:* Officier, Légion d'honneur, Chevalier, Ordre Nat. du Mérite, Chevalier, Ordre des Palmes Académiques; Prix Pierre de Régnier de l' Acad. française 1972, Univ. of Basle Prix Jacob-Burckhardt 1977, Prix Fémina-Vacaresco 1979, Prix Johann-Peter Hebel 1984, Grand Prix de la poésie de la Soc. des gens de lettres 1987, Prix des arts, des lettres et des sciences de la Fondation du judaïsme français 1994, Grand Prix de poésie de l' Acad. française 1996. *Address:* 12 rue Marronniers, 75016 Paris, France (home).

VIIDING, Elo, (Elo Vee); Estonian poet and writer; b. 20 March 1974, Tallinn; d. of Juhan Viiding; m. Jaanus Adamson. *Career:* mem. Estonian Writers' Union. *Publications:* poetry collections: 'Telg' Kassett '90 1990, Laeka lähedus 1993, Võlavalgel 1995, V 1998, Kaardipakk (poetry with Karl Martin Sinijärv, Jürgen Rooste, Triin Soomets, Asko Künnap) 2001, Esimene tahe 2002, Teatud erandid 2003, Selge jälg 2005, Kaardipakk Kaks (poetry with Asko Künnap, Karl Martin Sinijärv, Jürgen Rooste, Triin Soomets) 2006, , Meie paremas maailmas 2009, Kestmine 2011; prose collection: Ingelheim 1995; selection of poetry in Finnish: Paljastuksia (translated by Katja Meriluoto) 2000; selection of poetry in Swedish: För en stämma (translated by Peeter Puide) 2004; short story collections: Püha Maama 2008; in anthologies: prose: Välismaa naised (Foreign Women) (Best European Fiction 2010) (edited by Aleksandar Hemon, translated by Eric Dickens), poetry: Verden Finnes ikke på kartet (Poesi fra hele verden) (edited by Pedro Carmona-Alvarez and Gunnar Wærness, translated by Turid Farbregd) 2010, The Baltic Quintet: Poems from Estonia, Finland, Latvia, Lithuania and Sweden (edited by Edita Page, translated by Eric Dickens) 2008, New European Poets (edited by Wayne Miller and Kevin Prufer) (translated by Eric Dickens) 2008, Viie tunni tee. Five Hours Away (Poetry from Nordic Poetry Festival) 2001; in English: Vahur Afanasjev, Kristiina Ehin, Mehis Heinsaar, Aapo Ilves, Jan Kaus, Marko Kompus, Kalju Kruusa, Asko Künnap, Fagira D. Morti, Veiko Märka, Aare Pilv, Juku-Kalle Raid, Jürgen Rooste, Olavi Ruitlane, Francois Serpent, Karl-Martin Sinijärv, Lauri Sommer, Elo Viiding, Wimberg (edited by AcrossWords, translated by Tiina Laats, Acrosswords) 2001, Ajattelen koko ajan rahaa – Estonian Contemporary Poetry in Finnish: Jürgen Rooste, FS, Elo Viiding, Toomas Liiv, Aleksander Suuman, Kivisildnik, Kalev Keskküla, Asko Künnap, Kristiina Ehin, Triin Soomets, Mats Traat, Hasso Krull, Kalju Kruusa, Fagira D. Morti, Eeva Park, Karl Martin Sinijärv, Aare Pilv, Wimberg (edited by Harri Rinne, translated by Anu Laitila), Emadepäev (Mothers' Day) in Swedish literary magazine '00-tal' (English edn) (translated by Eric Dickens). *Honours:* Betti Alver's Bracelet given by Estonian poet Ave Alavainu 2009. *Address:* Koidula 17-4, Tallinn 10125, Estonia (home). *Telephone:* 5047784 (home). *E-mail:* eloviiding@hotmail.com (home). *Website:* www.lyrikline.com; elm.estinst.ee/issue/20/poetry-elo-viiding; nordicvoices.blogspot.com/2009/03/elo-viiding.html.

VILA-MATAS, Enrique; Spanish writer; b. 1948, Barcelona. *Career:* fmr journalist for Fotogramas magazine, Paris. *Publications include:* non-fiction: Al sur de los párpados 1980, Nunca voy al cine 1982, El viajero más lento 1992, Veneno en la boca, conversaciones con 18 escritores: Antón Castro 1994, Recuerdos inventados: primera antología personal 1994, El traje de los domingos 1995, Para acabar con los números redondos 1997, Desde la ciudad nerviosa 2000; fiction: La asesina ilustrada 1977, Impostura 1984, Historia abreviada de la literatura portátil 1985, Una casa para siempre 1988, Suicidios ejemplares 1991, Hijos sin hijos 1993, Lejos de Veracruz 1995, Extraña forma de vida 1997, El viaje vertical (Premio Rómulo Gallegos 2001) 1999, Bartleby y compañía 2000, El mal de Montano (trans. as Montano's Malady) 2002, París no se acaba nunca 2003, Doctor Pasavento (Premio de la Real Academia Española 2006, Internazionale Mondello Prize 2009) 2005, Exploradroes del abismo 2007, Dietario voluble 2008, Dublinesca (Bottari Lattes Grinzane Prize, Prix Jean Carriere, Leteo Award) 2010, Chet Baker pense à son art 2011, Aire de Dylan 2012. *Honours:* Chevalier, Légion d'honneur 2006; Premio Ciudad de Barcelona 2000, Prix au meilleur livre étranger 2000, Premio de la Crítica 2002, Premio Herralde 2002, Prix Médicis 2003. *Address:* c/o Editorial Anagrama SA, Pedró de la Creu 58, 08034 Barcelona, Spain (office). *E-mail:* anagrama@anagrama-ed.es (office). *Website:* www.enriquevilamatas.com.

VILIKOVSKÝ, Pavel; Slovak writer and translator; b. 27 June 1941, Palúdzka. *Publications:* Citova vychova v marci 1965, Prva veta spanku 1983, Kon na poschodi, Slepec vo Vrabloch, Vecne je zeleny 1989, Eskalacia citu 1989, Slovensky Casanova, Okno po erotickych snoch 1991, Pesi pribeh 1992, Kruty strojvodca 1996, Okridlena klietka 1998, Posledny kon Pompeji 2001, Vyznania naiveho milovnika 2004, Carovny papagai a ine gyce 2005, Silberputzen 2006. *Address:* POB 8, 90201 Pezinok, Slovakia.

VILLANUEVA, Tino, BA, MA, PhD; American writer, translator and poet; *Lecturer in Spanish, Boston University;* b. 11 Dec. 1941, San Marcos, Tex. *Education:* Southwest Texas State Univ., State Univ. of NY at Buffalo, Boston Univ. *Career:* Founder Imagine Publishers Inc.; Ed. Imagine: International Chicano Poetry Journal; currently Lecturer in Spanish, Boston Univ. *Exhibitions:* paintings exhibited in El Paso, Tex., Boston, Mass and at The Writer's Brush: Visual Art by Writers, Pierre Menard Gallery, Cambridge, Mass. *Publications:* Hay Otra Voz Poems 1972, Shaking off the Dark 1984, Crónica de Mis Años Peores 1987, Scene from the Movie GIANT (American Book Award, Before Columbus Foundation 1994) 1993, Primera Causa/First Cause 1999, Il Canto del Cronista 2002, Escena de la Película GIGANTE 2005; anthology: Chicanos: Antología Histórica y Literaria 1980; criticism: Tres Poetas de Posguerra: Celaya, González y Caballero Bonald (Estudio y Entrevistas) 1988. *Honours:* Distinguished Alumnus Award, Southwest Texas State Univ. 1995. *Address:* Department of Romance Studies, Boston University, Office 204B, 718 Commonwealth Avenue, Boston, MA 02215, USA (office). *Telephone:* (617) 353-6236 (VOX) (office). *Fax:* (617) 353-6246 (office). *E-mail:* tvillan@bu.edu (office). *Website:* www.bu.edu (office).

VILLASEÑOR, Victor; American writer; b. 11 May 1940, Carlsbad, CA. *Publications:* Macho! 1973, Jury: The People vs Juan Corona (non-fiction) 1977, Ballad of Gregorio Cortez (screenplay), Rain of Gold (memoir) 1991, Snow Goose: Global Thanksgiving (philosophy) 1993, Wild Steps of Heaven (memoir) 1996, Walking Stars (short stories) 1996, Thirteen Senses (memoir) 2001, Burro Genius (memoir) 2004, Crazyloco Love 2008; nine novels and 65 short stories. *Literary Agent:* Margret McBride Literary Agency, 7744 Fay Avenue, Suite 201, La Jolla, CA 92037, USA. *Telephone:* (760) 722-1463 (office). *E-mail:* victor@victorvillasenor.com (office). *Website:* www.victorvillasenor.com.

VILLEGAS, Paloma, BA; Mexican writer, editor and academic; *Research Scholar, Ontario Institute for Studies in Education;* b. 1951, Mexico City. *Education:* Universidad Nacional Autonoma de Mexico. *Career:* fmr Prof., Universidad Autónoma Metropolitana; mem. Editorial Bd Cuadernos Políticos; Ed. Ediciones Era 1988–; currently enrolled in doctoral program in Sociology and Equity Studies in Educ., Ontario Inst. for Studies in Educ., Univ. of Toronto, Canada. *Publication include:* poetry: Mapas 1981; novels: La luz oblicua 1995, Agosto y fuga (Premio Sor Juana Inés de la Cruz 2005) 2004. *Address:* Ontario Institute for Studies in Education, University of of Toronto, 252 Bloor Street West, Toronto, ON M5S 1V6, Canada (office). *Fax:* (416) 926-4751 (office). *Website:* www.oise.utoronto.ca/sese (office).

VILLORO, Juan; Mexican writer and journalist; b. 24 Sept. 1956, Mexico City. *Education:* Universidad Autónoma Metropolitana. *Career:* fmr magazine production ed. Pauta; Programme Dir El lado oscuro de la luna (radio programme) 1977–81; Cultural Attaché, Embassy in Berlin, Germany 1981–84; Dir La Jornada Semanal (cultural supplement) 1995–98. *Publications:* Vivir mata (screenplay), Madona de Guadalupe (short story), El mariscal de campo (short stories) 1978, La noche navegable (short stories) 1980, El cielo inferior (short stories) 1984, Las galosinas secretas (juvenile) 1985, Albercas (short stories) 1985, Tiempo transcurrido 1986, Las palmeras de la brisa rápida: un viaje a Yucatán (travel memoir) 1989, El disparo de Argón (novel) 1991, La alcoba dormida (short stories) 1992, El Profesor Ziper y la fabulosa guitarra eléctrica (juvenile) 1992, Los once de la Tribu (essay) 1995, Baterista numeroso (juvenile) 1997, Matéria dispuesta (novel) 1997, Autopista sanguijuela (juvenile) 1997, La casa pierde (short stories) (Premio Xavier Villarrutia) 1999, Efectos personales (essay) (Premio Mazatlán, Barcelona 2001) 2000, El té de tornillo del Profesor Ziper (juvenile) 2000, Entre amigos (short story) 2000, La voz del enemigo (short story) 2002, El testigo (novel) (Premio Herralde) 2004, Llamadas de Amsterdam (novel) 2007, Los culpables (short stories) (Priz Antonin-Artaud 2008) 2007; contrib. to newspapers, including Uno más uno, Diorama de la Cultura, El Gallo Ilustrado, Sábado. *Honours:* Premio Cuauhtémoc de traducción 1988. *Address:* c/o Interzona, República Arabe, Siria 3040, C1425EYJ, Buenos Aires, Argentina (office). *E-mail:* info@interzonaeditora.com (office). *Website:* www.interzonaeditora.com (office).

VINCENT, Rev. John James, DTheol; British theologian, broadcaster and writer; b. 29 Dec. 1929, Sunderland; s. of David Vincent and Beatrice Ethel Vincent (née Gadd); m. Grace Johnston Stafford 1958; two s. one d. *Education:* Manchester Grammar School, Richmond Coll., London Univ., Drew Univ., Madison, NJ, USA, Basel Univ., Switzerland. *Career:* ordained in Methodist Church 1956; Minister, Manchester and Salford Mission 1956–62; Supt Minister, Rochdale Mission 1962–69, Sheffield Inner City Ecumenical Mission 1970–77; Dir, Urban Theology Unit, Sheffield 1969–97, Dir Emer. and Doctoral Supervisor 1997–; Pres., Methodist Conf. 1989–90; Visiting Prof. of Theology, Boston School of Theology, USA 1969, New York Theological Seminary 1970, Theological School, Drew Univ. 1977; elected mem., Studiorum Novi Testamenti Societas 1961; Sec. Regional Working Party, WCC Faith and Order 1958–63; mem., British Council of Churches Comm. on Defence and Disarmament 1963–65, 1969–72; NW Vice-Pres., Campaign for Nuclear Disarmament 1957–69; Founding mem., Methodist Renewal Group 1961–70; Founding mem. and Leader, Ashram Community 1967–; Chair., Alliance of Radical Methodists 1971–74, Urban Mission Training Asscn of GB 1976–77, 1985–90; Co-ordinator, British Liberation Theology Project 1990–; mem. Bd, Int. Urban Ministry Network 1991–; presented Petition of Distress from the Cities to HM the Queen 1993; mem., Ind. Human Rights Del. to Colombia 1994, Partnership Bd Burngreave New Deal for Communities 2001–11; Chair., Methodist Report on The Cities 1997. *Publications:* Christ in a Nuclear World 1962, Christ and Methodism 1964, Here I Stand 1967, Secular Christ 1968, The Race Race 1970, The Jesus Thing 1973, Stirrings, Essays Christian and Radical 1975, Alternative Church 1976, Disciple and Lord 1976, Starting All Over Again 1981, Into the City 1982, O.K. Let's Be Methodists 1984, Radical Jesus 1986, Mark at Work 1986, Britain in the 90s 1989, Discipleship in the 90s 1991, Liberation Theology from the Inner City 1992, A Petition of Distress from the Cities 1993, A British Liberation Theology (ed.) 1995, The Cities: A Methodist Report 1997, Gospel from the City (ed.) 1997, Hope from the City 2000, Journey: Explorations in Discipleship 2001, Bible and Practice (ed.) 2001, Faithfulness in the City (ed.) 2003, Methodist and Radical (ed.) 2003, Outworkings: Gospel Practice and Interpretation 2005, Mark: Gospel of Action (ed.) 2006, A Lifestyle of Sharing 2009, The City in Biblical Perspective (jtly) 2009, The Drama of Mark (jtly) 2010, Christian Communities in the 21st Century (ed.) 2011, Stilling the Storm (ed.) 2011. *Honours:* Hon. Lecturer, Biblical Studies Dept, Univ. of Sheffield 1990–2011, Theology Dept, Univ. of Birmingham 2003–; Fellow, St Deiniol's Library 2003; Centenary Achievement Award, Univ. of Sheffield 2005. *Address:* 178 Abbeyfield Road, Sheffield, S4 7AY, England (home). *Telephone:* (114) 243-5342 (office); (114) 243-6688 (home). *Fax:* (114) 243-5356 (office).

VINCENZI, Penny; British writer; b. 10 April 1939, Bournemouth; m.; four c. *Career:* Sec., Vogue and Tatler magazines; staff, The Daily Mirror, Nova, Woman's Own; co-founder, Looking Good magazine; Contributing Ed., Cosmopolitan; Deputy Ed., Options. *Publications:* novels: Old Sins 1989, Free Sins 1990, Wicked Pleasures 1992, An Outrageous Affair 1993, Another Woman 1994, Forbidden Places 1995, The Dilemma 1996, The Glimpses 1996, Windfall 1997, Almost a Crime 1999, Into Temptation 2002, Sheer Abandon 2004, An Absolute Scandal 2007, The Best of Times 2009; non-fiction: The Compleat Liar 1977, Cosmopolitan Vital Health Guide 1982, There's One Born Every Minute: A Survival Guide for Parents 1984, Taking Stock: Over 75 Years of the Oxo Cube 1985. *Address:* c/o Hodder Headline, 338 Euston Road, London, NW1 3BH, England. *Website:* www.penny-vincenzi.com.

VINE, Barbara (see Rendell of Babergh, Ruth Barbara)

VINER, Katharine; British editor; *Deputy Editor, The Guardian*. *Education:* Univ. of Oxford. *Career:* Features Asst, then News and Careers Ed., Cosmopolitan magazine 1993–95; writer and Commissioning Ed., Sunday Times Magazine 1995–97; feature writer, Deputy Features Ed., Deputy Women's Ed., The Guardian newspaper 1997–98, Ed., the 'Weekend' magazine 1998–2006, Features Ed., currently Deputy Ed.; mem. Bd Royal Court Theatre, Women's Library. *Play:* My Name is Rachel Corrie, Playhouse Theatre, London (based on diaries and emails of Rachel Corrie, edited by Katharine Viner and Alan Rickman (dir), What's On Theatre Awards Best New Play 2006) 2006. *Publications:* contrib. chapter, The personal is still political, to On the Move: Feminism for a New Generation. *Honours:* Newspaper Magazine Editor of the Year 2001, 2002. *Address:* The Guardian, Kings Place, 90 York Way, London, N1 9GU, England (office). *E-mail:* katharine.viner@guardian.co.uk (office). *Website:* www.guardian.co.uk (office).

VINEY, Ethna, BSc, BA; Irish writer, television and film producer and director; b. 17 Jan. 1933, West Cavan; m. Michael Viney 1965; one d. *Education:* Coll. of Pharmacy, Dublin, University Coll., Dublin. *Career:* Independent Pharmacist 1956–61; Television Producer 1966–76; Freelance Journalist 1964–; Independent Television Film Producer and Dir 1990–. *Television documentaries:* Risen Women 1991, Shape of the Wind 1993, The Man Who Found léide 1995, Joclann na mBanta (series) 1997, Lé hecs an Tuath 1999, A Year's Turning (series) 2001. *Publications:* A Dozen Lips 1994, Survival or Salvation 1994, Dancing to Different Tunes 1996, 1997; A Wildlife Narrative 1999, Ireland's Ocean: A Natural History (with Michael Viney) 2008. *Honours:* Outstanding Academic Book of the Year, USA 1997. *Address:* Thallabawn, Carrownisky, County Mayo, Ireland (home). *Telephone:* (098) 68611 (home). *E-mail:* viney@anu.ie (home).

VINGE, Vernor Steffen, BS, MA, PhD; American mathematician and writer; b. 2 Oct. 1944, Waukesha, WI. *Education:* Michigan State Univ., Univ. of California at San Diego. *Career:* faculty, Dept of Mathematics, San Diego State University 1972–2000; mem. American Mathematical Soc., SFWA. *Publications:* Grimm's World, 1969, The Wilting 1976, The Peace War 1984, Marooned in Realtime 1986, A Fire Upon the Deep 1992, A Deepness in the Sky 1999, True Names and the Opening of Cyberspace Frontier (with James Frenkel) 2001, Rainbows End 2006; contributions: anthologies and periodicals. *Honours:* Hugo Award 1993. *Address:* 6439 Jackson Drive, San Diego, CA 92119-3306, USA (home).

VIRAG, Ibolya; Hungarian publisher, translator, editor and art consultant; *Publisher, Editions Ibolya Virag;* b. 7 Dec. 1950, Budapest; m. *Education:* Eötvös Coll., Eötvös Loránd Univ., Budapest, Univ. of the Sorbonne, Paris. *Career:* interpreter, Kolinda Group (world music and literature) 1970s; went into exile, France 1980; cr. Cen. Europe Editorial Collection (publishes works of Cen. European writers in French, including Sandor Marai, Peter Esterhazy, Josef Hirsal, Lajos Grendel, Hanna Krall, Ivan Matousek, Istvan Bibo, Jenö Szücs, Karel Capek, Jaroslav Hasek, Jaroslav Durych, Gyula Krudy, Dezsö Kosztolanyi, Antal Szerb, Sandor Weöres, Béla Marko, Otto Tolnai, Imre Oravecz), Paris 1983; joined Albin Michel Publrs 1989; Founder and Publr Editions Ibolya Virag, Paris 1996–; art consultant for MAGYart (Year of Hungarian Culture in France) 1999–2001; f. Dialogues France-Europe Centrale Asscn 2003, Festival of Hungarian Literature, Paris 2007. *Honours:* Chevalier des Arts et des Lettres 1993, Officier 2003. *Address:* Editions Ibolya Virag, 28 avenue de la Porte de Choisy, 75013 Paris, France (office). *Telephone:* 1-76-67-09-23 (office). *E-mail:* virageditions@gmail.com (office). *Website:* www.zazieweb.fr/site/editeur/pageediteurinfo.php?num=563 (office); europecentrale.asso-web.com (office).

VIRGO, Seán, BA; Canadian writer and poet; b. 1940, Mtarfa, Malta. *Education:* Univ. of Nottingham. *Career:* currently Lecturer in Writing, Univ. of Victoria; mem. League of Canadian Poets. *Publications:* fiction: White Lies and Other Fictions 1979, Through the Eyes of a Cat: Irish Stories 1983, Selakhi 1987, Wormwood 1989, White Lies... Plus Two 1990, Waking in Eden 1990, The Scream of the Butterfly 1996, A Traveller Came By 2000; poetry: Sea Change 1971, Pieces for the Old Earth Man 1973, Island (with Paul and Lutia Lauzon) 1975, Kiskatinaw Songs (with Susan Musgrave) 1977, Deathwatch on Skidegate Narrows 1979, Selected Poems 1992. *Address:* Department of Writing, University of Victoria, PO Box 1700, STN CSC, Victoria, BC V8W 2Y2, Canada (office). *Telephone:* (250) 721-7306 (office). *Fax:* (250) 721-6602 (office). *E-mail:* writing@finearts.uvic.ca (office). *Website:* finearts.uvic.ca/writing (office).

VIRILIO, Paul; French writer and artist; *Editorial Director, Editions Galilee;* b. 1932, Paris. *Education:* Ecole des Metiers d'Art, Paris, Univ. of the Sorbonne, Paris. *Career:* worked as artist in stained glass alongside Matisse in various churches in Paris; untrained architect; Chair. and Dir Ecole Spéciale d'Architecture, Paris 1968–98, Prof. Emer. 1998–; Ed. Espace Critique, Editions Galilee, Paris 1973–; Co-Founder and Programme Dir Collège Int. de Philosophie 1990–; mem. French Comm. concerned with housing for the poor (HCLD) 1992–; fmr mem. Editorial Bds Esprit, Cause Commune, Critiques, Traverses; has worked with Fondation Cartier pour l'art contemporain on several exhbns including Bunker Archeology, Pompidou Centre 1975, Speed, Jouy-en-Josas 1991, Unknown Quantity, Paris 2002. *Publications include:* Bunker Archeologie 1975, L'Insecurité du territoire 1976, Speed and Politics 1977, Popular Defense and Ecological Struggles 1978, L'Esthetique de la disparition 1980, Pure War (with Sylvère Lotringer) 1983, War and Cinema: The Logistics of Perception 1984, L'Espace critique 1984, Polar Inertia 1990, The Art of the Motor 1995, Politics of the Very Worst 1996, Open Sky 1997, The Information Bomb 1998, The Strategy of Deception 1999, A Landscape of Events 2000, Ground Zero 2002, Negative Horizon 2005, The Accident of Art 2005, City of Panic 2005, Art as Far as the Eye Can See 2007, The Original Accident 2007, Art as Far as the Eye Can See 2007, Strategy of Deception 2007, The University of Disaster 2009; numerous technical works. *Honours:* Grand Prix Nat. de la Critique 1987. *Address:* c/o Editions Galilee, 9 rue de Linné, 75005 Paris, France (office). *Telephone:* 1-47-07-85-11 (office). *Fax:* 1-45-35-53-68 (office). *E-mail:* editions.galilee@free.fr (office). *Website:* www.editions-galilee.fr (office).

VIRTUE, Noel; New Zealand author; b. 3 Jan. 1947, Wellington. *Education:* studied in New Zealand. *Publications:* The Redemption of Elsdon Bird 1987, Then Upon the Evil Season 1988, Among the Animals: A Zookeeper's Story (autobiog.) 1988, In the Country of Salvation 1990, Always the Islands of Memory 1991, The Eye of the Everlasting Angel 1993, Sandspit Crossing 1994, Once a Brethren Boy (autobiog.) 1995, Losing Alice 2000, Lady Jean 2001.

VITALE, Alberto; American publishing executive; b. 22 Dec. 1933, Vercelli, Piedmont, Italy; s. of Sergio Vitale and Elena Segre; m. Gemma G. Calori 1961; two s. *Education:* Turin Univ., IPSOA Business School and Wharton School, Univ. of Pa (Fulbright Scholar). *Career:* joined Olivetti 1958; moved to USA to assist in Olivetti's acquisition of Underwood 1959; Exec. IFI (Agnelli family holding co.) 1971; Exec. Vice-Pres. for Admin Bantam Books, New York 1975, Co-CEO 1985, sole CEO 1986; Pres. and CEO Bantam-Doubleday-Dell 1987; Chair., Pres. and CEO Random House Inc. 1989–96, Chair., CEO 1996–98; Chair. Supervisory Bd Random House Inc., New York 1998; mem. Bd of Dirs Transworld Publrs; mem. Bd of Trustees Mercy Coll. NY; mem. Nat. Advisory Council, Reading is Fundamental. *Honours:* Chevalier, Ordre des Arts et des Lettres 1996. *Address:* 135 Grace Trail, Palm Beach, FL 33480, USA (home). *E-mail:* aavitale1@aol.com (home).

VITALE, Ida; Uruguayan poet and writer; b. 1924, Montevideo; m. Enrique H. Fierro. *Career:* played part in Generación del 45 artistic movement in Uruguay 1945–50; lived in Mexico 1974–84, in Austin, Tex., USA 1989–; contrib. to El País, Marcha, Época, Jaque. *Publications include:* La Luz de esta Memoria 1949, Palabra Dada 1953, Cada uno en su noche 1960, Paso y Paso 1963, Oidor andante 1972, Fieles 1976, Jardín de sílice 1980, Elegías en otoño 1982, Entresaca 1984, Parvo Reino 1984, Sueños de la Constancia 1988, Serie del Sinsonte 1992, Procura de lo Imposible 1998, Un Invierno Equivocado 1999, Donde Vuela el Carnaleon 2000, Reducción del infinito 2002, Plantas y animales 2003, El ABC de Byobu 2005. *Honours:* Premio Internacional Octavio Paz de la Poesía 2009. *Address:* 1800 Lavaca Street, Apartment 514, Austin, TX 78701-1300, USA (home). *Telephone:* (512) 476-6774 (home).

VITALE, Serena, PhD; Italian writer and academic; *Professor of Russian Language and Literature, Catholic University of the Sacred Heart;* b. 1945, Brindisi. *Career:* Lecturer in Russian Language and Literature, Genoa Univ. 1972–77; Assoc. Prof., then Prof., Oriental Inst., Naples 1977–87; Prof., Pavia Univ. 1987–95, Catholic Univ. of the Sacred Heart, Milan 1997–; consultant on Russian literature, Mondadori publishing house 1997–; regular contrib., Il Domenicale supplement, Il Sole 24 ore 2001–. *Publications:* L'avanguardia russa 1979, Viktor Šklovskij. Testimone di un'epoca 1979, Il bottone di Puškin 1995, La casa di ghiaccio 2000, L'Imbroglio del turbante 2006; over 30 trans. into Italian from Russian, Czech and French. *Honours:* Biella-Poesia Int. Prize 1982, Mondello Prize 1985, Sabaudia-Circe Prize 1986, Premio Viareggio 1995, Premio della Presidenza del Consiglio 2000, Premio Bagutta 2000, Premio Grinzane-Cavour Prize 2005, 2006. *Address:* Department of Foreign Languages and Literature, Università Cattolica del Sacro Cuore, Via Necchi 9, 20123 Milan, Italy (office). *Telephone:* (02) 72342576 (office). *E-mail:* vitale@serenavitale.it (home); dip.linguestraniere@unicatt.it (office). *Website:* www.unicatt.it (office); www.serenavitale.it.

VITIELLO, Justin, BA, MA, PhD; American academic, poet and writer; b. 14 Feb. 1941, New York, NY; one s. *Education:* Brown Univ., Univ. of Michigan, Univ. of Madrid, Spain. *Career:* Teaching Fellow in Spanish, Univ. of Michigan 1964–69, Distinguished Teaching Fellow 1967, Lecturer in Romance Languages 1969–70, Asst Prof., Comparative Literature and Spanish 1969–73, Head, Residential College's Comparative Literature Program; Asst Prof., Temple Univ. 1974–80, Assoc. Prof. 1980–91, ATTIC Distinguished Teacher 1990, Prof. of Italian 1991–2006, Prof. Emer. 2006–; mem. MLA; American Italian Historical Assen, American Assen for Italian Studies; life mem. MELUS. *Publications:* poetry: Vanzetti's Fish Cart 1991, Subway Home 1994, Subway Home in Italian 1998, Suicide of an Ethnic Poet 2004, Poppies and Thistles 2006; other: Confessions of a Joe Rock 1992, Sicily Within 1992, Poetry and Literature of the Sicilian Diaspora: Studies in Oral History and Story Telling 1998, Labyrinths and Volcanoes: Windings Through Sicily 1999, Via Terra: Anthology of Neodialect Poetry 1999; Contributions: books and periodicals. *Honours:* Fulbright Scholar. *Website:* www.justinvitiello.net.

VITUKHNOVSKAYA, Alina Aleksandrovna; Russian poet, writer and journalist; b. 27 March 1973, Moscow. *Career:* first verses published late 1980s in periodicals; arrested on charge of drugs trafficking, freed Oct. 1995, arrested Nov. 1997; mem. Russian PEN Centre, Writers' Union; Pushkin Scholarship, Hamburg, Germany 1998. *Publications include:* Anomaly 1993, Children's Book of the Dead 1994, Pavlov's Dog (with K. Kedrov) 1996, The Last Old Woman Money-lender of Russian Literature (stories) 1996, Land of Zero 1996, Romance with Phenamine (novel) 1999, Day of Poetry (collaboration with French and Russian poets) 2001, Black Icon 2002. *Address:* Leningradskoye shosse 80, Apt. 89, 125565 Moscow, Russia (home). *Telephone:* (495) 452-15-31 (home).

VIZENOR, Gerald Robert, BA; American author, poet and academic; *Distinguished Professor of American Studies, University of New Mexico, Albuquerque*; b. 22 Oct. 1934, Minneapolis, Minn.; m. 1st Judith Helen Horns 1959 (divorced 1968); one s.; m. 2nd Laura Jane Hall 1981. *Education:* Univ. of Minnesota. *Career:* Lecturer, Univ. of California at Berkeley 1976–80, Prof. of Native American Literature 1985–2005, Richard and Rhoda Goldman Distinguished Prof. of American Studies 2000–02, Prof. Emer. of American Studies 2005–; Prof., Univ. of Minnesota 1980–85, Univ. of California at Santa Cruz 1987–90; Resident Scholar, School of American Research, Santa Fe, NM 1985–86; David Burr Chair of Letters and Prof., Univ. of Oklahoma 1990–91; Prof. of American Studies, Univ. of New Mexico, Albuquerque 2005–08, Distinguished Prof. of American Studies 2008–; Prin. Writer, Constitution of the White Earth Nation 2009. *Play:* Ishi and the Wood Ducks. *Film:* Harold of Orange (screenwriter). *Publications:* Thomas James White Hawk 1968, Summer in the Spring: Anishinaable Lyric Poems and Stories 1970, The Everlasting Sky: New Voices from the People Named the Chippewa 1972, Tribal Scenes and Ceremonies 1976, revised edn as Crossbloods: Bone Courts, Bingo, and Other Reports 1990, Darkness in Saint Louis Bearheart (novel) 1978, revised edn as Bearheart: The Heirship Chronicles 1990, Wordarrows: Indians and Whites in the New Fur Trade 1978, Earthdivers: Tribal Narratives on Mixed Descent 1983, The People Named the Chippewa: Narrative Histories 1983, Matsushima: Pine Islands (collected haiku poems) 1984, Griever: An American Monkey King in China (novel) 1986, Touchwood: A Collection of Ojibway Prose (ed.) 1987, The Trickster of Liberty: Tribal Heirs to a Wild Baronage (novel) 1988, Narrative Chance: Postmodern Discourse on Native American Literatures (ed.) 1989, Interior Landscapes: Autobiographical Myths and Metaphors 1990, Landfill Meditation (short stories) 1991, The Heirs of Columbus (novel) 1991, Dead Voices: Natural Agonies in the New World (novel) 1993, Manifest Manners: Postindian Warriors of Survivance (critical essays) 1994, Shadow Distance: A Gerald Vizenor Reader 1994, Native American Literature (ed.) 1995, Hotline Healers: An Almost Browne Novel 1997, Fugitive Poses: Native American Indian Scenes of Absence and Presence 1998, Postindian Conversations 1999, Cranes Arise (haiku). 1999, Raising the Moon Vines (haiku) 1999, Chancers (novel) 2000, Hiroshima Bugi: Atomu 57 (novel) 2003, Bear Island: The War at Sugar Point (narrative poem) 2006, Almost Ashore (selected poems) 2006, Literary Chance: Essays on Native American Survivance 2007, Father Meme (novel) 2008, Survivance: Narratives of Native Presence 2008, Interior Landscapes (autobiog. second edn), Native Liberty: Natural Reason and Cultural Survivance (essays) 2009, Father Meme (novel) 2010, Shrouds of White Earth (novel) 2010; contribs to numerous books, journals, and periodicals. *Honours:* Hon. DHumLitt (Macalester Coll.) 1999; New York Fiction Collective Award 1986, American Book Award 1988, California Arts Council Artists Fellowship in Literature 1989, Josephine Miles Awards, PEN Oakland 1990, 1996, Western Literature Distinguished Achievement Award 2005, MELUS Lifetime Achievement Award. *Address:* American Studies, 452 Humanities, University of New Mexico, Albuquerque, NM 87131, USA (office). *Telephone:* (505) 471-2190 (home), (239) 596-4335 (home). *Fax:* (505) 277-3929 (office). *E-mail:* vizenor@mac.com (home). *Website:* www.unm.edu/~amstudy (office).

VIZINCZEY, Stephen; Canadian/British writer; b. 1933, Kaloz, Hungary; m. 1963; three d. *Education:* Univ. of Budapest, Nat. Acad. of Theatre and Film Arts, Budapest. *Career:* Ed. Exchange Magazine 1960–61; Producer CBC 1962–65; mem. Soc. of Authors, Authors' Licensing and Collecting Soc. *Publications:* In Praise of Older Women 1965, The Rules of Chaos 1969, An Innocent Millionaire 1983, Truth and Lies in Literature 1986, El Hombre del Toque Magico 1994, Be Faithful unto Death (trans.) 1995. *Honours:* Premio Letterario Isola d'Elba 2004. *E-mail:* vizinczey@btinternet.com (home).

VLADISLAVIĆ, Ivan; South African writer and editor; b. 1957, Pretoria. *Education:* Univ. of the Witwatersrand. *Career:* fmr asst ed. Staffrider magazine; fmr fiction and social studies ed., Ravan Press. *Publications:* Missing Persons (Olive Schreiner Prize 1991) (short stories) 1989, The Folly (CNA Literary Award) (novel) 1993, Propaganda by Monuments (short stories) 1996, The Restless Supermarket (Sunday Times Fiction Prize 2002) (novel) 2001, The Exploded View (short stories) 2004, Willem Boshoff (biography) 2005, Portrait with Keys: The City of Johannesburg Unlocked (Sunday Times Alan Paton Award for Nonfiction 2007, Univ. of Johannesburg Prize 2007) (non-fiction) 2006; blank_Architecture: apartheid and after (co-ed.) 1998, T'kama-Adamastor (ed.) 2000. *Honours:* Thomas Pringle Prize 1994. *Address:* c/o Umuzi, POB 6810, Roggebaai 8012, South Africa (office). *E-mail:* umuzi@randomhouse.co.za (office). *Website:* www.umuzi-randomhouse.co.za (office).

VLAUTIN, Willy; American author, singer and songwriter; b. 1967, Reno, Nev. *Career:* Founder mem., guitarist, songwriter and lead singer, alternative country group Richmond Fontaine 1994–; novelist 2005–. *Recordings:* albums: with Richmond Fontaine: Safety 1996, Miles From 1997, Lost Son 1999, Winnemucca 2002, Post to Wire 2004, The Fitzgerald 2005, Obliteration by Time 2006, Thirteen Cities 2007, We Used to Think the Freeway Sounded Like a River 2009, The High Country 2011; solo: A Jockey's Christmas (spoken word) 2008. *Publications include:* novels: The Motel Life 2005, Northline 2008, Lean on Pete (Ken Kesey Award for Fiction , Ore. Book Awards 2011, Readers' Choice Award 2011) 2010. *Honours:* Nev. Writers Hall of Fame Silver Pen Award 2007. *Address:* c/o Decor Records, 19 Bryanstone Road, London, N8 8TN, England (office); Harper Perennial, HarperCollins, 10 East 53rd Street, New York, NY 10019, USA (office). *E-mail:* info@willyvlautin.com (home). *Website:* www.richmondfontaine.com; www.willyvlautin.com.

VOGEL, Paula Anne, ABD; American dramatist and teacher; *Eugene O'Neill Professor and Chair, Department of Playwriting, School of Drama, Yale University*; b. 16 Nov. 1951, Washington, DC; m. Anne Fausto Sterling. *Education:* Doctoral Program, Cornell Univ. *Career:* teaching asst, Cornell Univ. 1975–77, Instructor in Theatre Arts and Women's Studies 1977–78, 1982–82; Asst Prof., then Prof., Brown Univ. 1985–99, Prof.-at-Large 1999–2003, Adele Kellenberg Seaver Prof. in Creative Writing 2003–08; Eugene O'Neill Prof. and Chair., Dept of Playwriting, School of Drama, Yale Univ. 2008–; Fellow, American Acad. of Arts and Sciences 2006. *Plays:* The Long Christmas Ride Home, The Swan Song of Sir Henry 1974, Meg 1977, Apple-Brown Betty 1979, Desdemona, A Play About a Handkerchief 1979, The Last Pat Epstein Show Before the Reruns 1979, Bertha in Blue 1981, The Oldest Profession 1981, Heirlooms 1985, And Baby Makes Seven 1986, Lady in Black 1986, The Baltimore Waltz 1991, Hot 'n' Throbbing 1992, The Mineola Twins 1996, How I Learned to Drive 1997, A Civil War Christmas 2006. *Honours:* Dr hc (Univ. of Rhode Island) 2005; NEA Fellowships 1980, 1991, AT&T Award 1992, Obie Award 1992, 1997, Fund for New American Plays 1994, Guggenheim Fellowship 1995, Pew Charitable Trust Sr Artist Residency 1995–97, Lucille Lortel Award 1997, Pulitzer Prize for Drama 1998, Literature Prize, American Acad. of Arts and Letters 2005, Obies. *Literary Agent:* c/o Bruce Ostler, Bret Adams Ltd, 448 West 44th Street, New York, NY 10036, USA. *Telephone:* (212) 765-5630. *Fax:* (212) 265-2212. *E-mail:* bostler@bretadamsltd.com. *Address:* School of Drama, Yale University, PO Box 208244, New Haven, CT 06520-8244, USA (office). *Telephone:* (203) 432-2252 (office). *E-mail:* paula.vogel@yale.edu (office). *Website:* drama.yale.edu (office).

VOGELSANG, Arthur, BA, MA, MFA; American poet; b. 31 Jan. 1942, Baltimore, Md; m. Judith Ayers 1966. *Education:* Univ. of Maryland, Johns Hopkins Univ., Univ. of Iowa. *Career:* fmr Jt Ed. The American Poetry Review. *Publications:* A Planet 1983, Twentieth Century Women 1988, Cities and Towns 1996, The Body Electric: America's Best Poetry from The American Poetry Review (co-ed.) 2001, Left Wing of a Bird 2003, Expedition: New & Selected Poems 2011. *Honours:* Nat. Endowment for the Arts Fellowships in Poetry 1976, 1985, 1995, California Arts Council Grant 1995, Juniper Prize 1995. *Address:* 1730 N Vista Street, Los Angeles, CA 90046, USA (home). *Telephone:* (323) 874-2220 (home). *Fax:* (323) 874-2221 (home). *E-mail:* arthurv123@aol.com (office).

VOIGT, Ellen Bryant, BA, MFA; American poet and teacher; b. 9 May 1943, Danville, Va; m. Francis G. W. Voigt 1965, one s. one d. *Education:* Converse Coll., Spartanburg, SC, Univ. of Iowa. *Career:* Faculty mem., Iowa Wesleyan Coll. 1966–69, Goddard Coll. 1969–79, MIT 1979–82, Warren Wilson Coll. 1981–; Vermont State Poet 1999–2003; Chancellor, Acad. of American Poets 2003–09; Fellow, Fellowship of Southern Writers 2003. *Achievements include:* developed and directed first low-residency writing program in 1970s at Goddard Coll., then moved programme to Warren Wilson Coll. 1981. *Publications:* poetry: Claiming Kin 1976, The Forces of Plenty 1983, The Lotus Flowers 1987, Two Trees 1992, Kyrie 1996, The Flexible Lyric 2001, Shadow of Heaven 2002, Messenger: New and Selected Poems 1976–2006 2007; ed: Poets and Teaching Poets: Self and the World 1996, The Flexible Lyric 2001, A Gathering of Contemporary American Poets (with Heather McHugh) 2002; contribs: reviews, quarterlies, and journals. *Honours:* Hon. DLitt (Converse Coll.) 1989; National Endowment for the Arts Fellowship 1975, Guggenheim Fellowship 1978, Pushcart Prize 1983, 1987, Emily Clark

Balch Award 1987, Haines Award for Poetry, Fellowship of Southern Writers 1993, Acad. of American Poets Fellowship 2001. *Address:* Warren Wilson College MFA Program for Writers, PO Box 9000, Asheville, NC 28815-9000, USA (office). *Website:* www.warren-wilson.edu/~mfa/newwebsite/homepage.php (office).

VOLD, Jan Erik; Norwegian poet, essayist, translator, editor and poetry and jazz performer; b. 18 Oct. 1939, Oslo; s. of Ragnar Vold. *Music:* poetry and jazz albums: Briskeby blues (with Jan Garbarek) 1969, HAV 1971, ingentings bjeller 1977, Mor Godhjertas glade versjon. Ja 1968, kykelipi 1969, spor, snø 1970, Bok 8: Liv 1973, BusteR brenneR 1976, S 1978, sirkel, sirkel. Boken om prins Adrians reise 1979, Sorgen. Sangen. Veien 1987, En som het Abel Ek 1988, Elg 1989, Ikke. Skillingstrykk fra nittitallet 1993, En sirkel is 1994, Kalenderdikt 1995, Tolv meditasjoner (trans. as Twelve Meditations) 2002, Diktet minner om verden 2003, Drømmemakeren sa 2004, Store hvite bok å se 2011; essays: Entusiastiske essays 1976, Det norske syndromet 1980, Her. Her i denne verden 1984; Poetisk praksis 1990, Under Hauges ord 1994, Storytellers 1998, Mørkets sangerske 2000, Uten m anus 2001, P x 3 2003, God jul med Gertrude Stein 2005, Ruth Maiers dagbok 2007, Fem stemmer 2010; anthologies: Poesi 14 x 14 1971, Poesi Pluss 1974, Moderne norsk lyrikk. Frie vers 1890–1980 (with Kjell Heggelund) 1985; poetry translations: William Carlos Williams 1969; Robert Creeley 1972, Bob Dylan 1977, Samuel Beckett 1987, Tomas Tranströmer 1996, Richard Brautigan 2004, Wallace Stevens 2009. *Honours:* Hon. PhD (Oslo) 2000; Aschehougprisen 1981, Kulturrådets oversetterpris 1992, Brageprise 1993,1997, Gyldendalprisen 2000. *Address:* c/o Gyldendal Norsk Forlag, Postboks 6860, St Olavs plass, 0130 Oslo, Norway (office). *Website:* www.gyldendal.no (office).

VOLK, Patricia, BFA; American writer; b. 16 July 1943, New York; d. of Cecil Sussman Volk and Audrey Elayne Morgen Volk; m. Andrew Blitzer 1969; one s. one d. *Education:* Syracuse Univ., Acad. de la Grande Chaumière, Paris, School of Visual Arts, The New School, Columbia Univ. *Career:* Art Dir Appelbaum and Curtis 1964–65, Seventeen Magazine 1967–68; copy-writer, Assoc. Creative Dir, Sr Vice-Pres. Doyle Dane Bernbach Inc. (DDB Needham Worldwide Inc.) 1969–88; Adjunct Instructor of Fiction, Yeshiva Coll. 1991; columnist, Newsday, NY 1995–96; mem. PEN Authors Guild; Yaddo Fellow; MacDowell Fellow. *Publications include:* The Yellow Banana 1985, White Light 1987, All It Takes 1990, Stuffed: Adventures of a Restaurant Family 2001, To my Dearest Friends 2007; contribs to The New York Times Magazine, The Atlantic, Quarterly, Cosmopolitan, Family Circle, Mirabella, Playboy, 7 Days, Manhattan Inc., The New Yorker, New York Magazine, Red Book, Good Housekeeping, Allure; Anthologies: Stories About How Things Fall Apart and What's Left When They Do 1985, A Reader for Developing Writers 1990, Exploring Language 1992, Magazine and Feature Writing 1992, Hers 1993, Her Face in the Mirror 1994. *Honours:* Word Beat Fiction Book Award 1984 and numerous other awards. *Address:* c/o Gloria Loomis, 133 East 35th Street, New York, NY 10016, USA.

VOLKOV, Solomon; American musicologist; b. 17 April 1944, Ura-Tyube, Tajikistan. *Education:* Leningrad Conservatory. *Career:* Artistic Dir, Leningrad Experimental Studio of Chamber Opera 1965–70; staging of Fleischmann's Rothschild's Violin, completed by Shostakovich; conducted research at Russian Inst., Columbia Univ. 1976. *Publications:* Young Composers of Leningrad 1971, Remembrance of the 'Leningrad Spring' 1974, Testimony: The Memoirs of Dmitri Shostakovich (ed.) 1979, Scissors and Music: Music Censorship in the Soviet Union 1983, Balanchine's Tchaikovsky 1985, Yevgeny Mravinsky, Leningrad's Master Builder 1988, From Russia to the West: the Musical Memoirs of Nathan Milstein (with N. Milstein) 1990, St Petersburg: A Cultural History 1995, Conversations with Joseph Brodsky 1998, Shostakovich and Stalin 2004, The Magical Chorus 2008; contrib. articles in journals and newspapers 1959–. *Address:* c/o Knopf Publishing/ Author Mail, 1745 Broadway, New York, NY 10019, USA (office).

VOLLMANN, William T., BA; American writer; b. 28 July 1959, Santa Monica, CA; m.; one d. *Education:* Deep Springs Coll., Cornell Univ., Univ. of California at Berkeley. *Career:* Ella Lyman Cabot Trust Fellowship 1982, Regent's Fellow Univ. of California at Berkeley 1982–83. *Publications:* You Bright and Risen Angels (Whiting Writers' Award 1988) 1987, The Convict Bird: A Children's Poem 1987, The Tale of the Dying Lungs 1989, The Rainbow Stories 1989, Seven Dreams: A Book of North American Landscapes (seven vols, including so far The Ice Shirt 1990, Fathers and Crows 1992, The Rifles 1994, Argall: The True Story of Pocahontas and Captain John Smith 2001) 1990–, Whores for Gloria 1991, An Afghanistan Picture Show, or, How I Saved the World 1992, Thirteen Stories and Thirteen Epitaphs 1993, Butterfly Stories: A Novel 1993, The Atlas (PEN Center West Award 1997) 1996, The Students of Deep Springs College (with Michael A. Smith and L. Jackson Newell) 2000, The Royal Family (California Book Awards Silver Medal for Non-Fiction 2001) 2000, Expelled from Eden: A William T. Vollmann Reader 2003, Rising Up and Rising Down (seven vols) 2003, Europe Central (short stories) (Nat. Book Award for Fiction) 2005, Uncentering the Earth: Copernicus and the Revolutions of the Heavenly Spheres 2006, Poor People 2007, Riding Toward Everywhere 2008, Imperial 2009, Kissing the Mask 2010; contrib. to The New Yorker, Esquire, Spin, Gear, Granta. *Honours:* Ludwig Vogelstein Award 1987, Shiva Naipaul Memorial Prize 1989, American Acad. of Arts and Letters Award in Literature 2007. *Literary Agent:* Susan Golomb Literary Agency, 875 Avenue of the Americas, Suite 2302, New York, NY 10001, USA.

VOLPI, Jorge, LicenDer, DPhil; Mexican novelist and essayist; b. 1968, Mexico City. *Education:* Universidad Nacional Autónoma de México, Universidad de Salamanca. *Career:* fmr lawyer and lawyer's sec.; fmr Visiting Prof., Cornell Univ.; currently Dir, Centro Cultural Mexicano, Paris; Dir of public television channel Canal 22, Mexico 2007–; mem. Sistema Nacional de Creadores de México. *Publications:* fiction: A pesar del oscuro silencio (novel) 1993, Días de ira (novella) 1994, La paz de los sepulcros (novel) 1995, El temperamento melancólico (novel) 1996, Sanar tu piel amarga (novella) 1997, En busca de Klingsor (first novel of 'Trilogía del siglo XX') (Premio Biblioteca Breve 1999, Prix Deux Océans Grinzane Cavour, France 1999, Instituto Cervantes de Roma prize for best translation 2002) 1999, El juego del Apocalipsis (novella) 2000, El fin de la locura (second novel of 'Trilogía del siglo XX') 2003, No Será La Tierra 2006, La tejedora de sombras (Premio Iberoamericano Planeta-Casa de América de Narrativa 2012) 2011; non-fiction: La guerra y las palabras: una historia del alzamiento zapatista (essay), La imaginación y el poder. Una historia intelectual de 1968 (essay) 1998, Día de muertos (non-fiction) 2001. *Honours:* Guggenheim Foundation Fellowship. *Address:* c/o Agencia literaria Antonia Kerrigan, Travesía de Gracia 22, Barcelona 08021, Spain. *E-mail:* info@antoniakerrigan.com. *Website:* www.antoniakerrigan.com.

VOM VENN, Hubert; German writer and publisher; b. 12 Oct. 1953, Monschau/Eifel; m. Ingrid Peinhardt-Franke, one d. *Education:* studied journalism. *Career:* journalist 1974–; gag author 1984–91; TV writer 1988–93; radio comedian 1980–2002; radio speaker 1985–98; Chief Ed. Radio Station 1998–99; Theatre Dir 1995–; mem. Int. Fed. of Journalists, Deutscher Journalisten Verband. *Publications:* Bundesstrasse 258 1990, Zum Drehen und Wenden 1991, Die Schlacht um Monschau 1992, Meine Sorgen möchte ich haben 1994, Wir sind'n Volk 1995, Und Sonst – Wie Sonst 1996, Die Hand im Moor 1999, Kaisermord 2000, Mein Jahr in der Eifel 2001, Alles für die Katz 2002, Wer stirbt schon gern in Düsseldorf 2004, Sterne der Eifel 2005, Väter unser ... 2006, Gelogen wie gedruckt 2007, Kopflos in Reichenstein 2008, Den Letzten beißen die Werwölfe 2010; co-author: Hurra Deutschland 1991, Fritten fuer um hier zu essen (CD) 1997, Charly's Leute 1997, Der Tod klopft an 2000, Der Tod trifft ein 2001, Frühling, Sommer, Herbst und Mord 2003, The Best (CD) 2003, Die Sau ist tot (DVD) 2009. *Address:* Kalfstrasse 73A, Roetgen 52159, Germany (home). *E-mail:* hubert-vom-venn@t-online.de (home). *Website:* www.hubert-vom-venn.de.

VON DASSANOWSKY, Robert, (Robert Dassanowsky), BA, MA, PhD, FRHistS, FRSA; American/Austrian writer, academic and film producer; *Professor of German and Film and Director of Film Studies, University of Colorado at Colorado Springs*; b. 28 Jan. 1960, New York, NY; s. of the late Elfi von Dassanowsky. *Education:* American Acad. of Dramatic Arts, American Film Inst. Conservatory Program, Los Angeles, Univ. of California, Los Angeles. *Career:* Founding Ed. Rohweder: International Magazine of Literature and Art 1986–93; writer/researcher, Stone-Stanley Television Productions/Disney Channnel 1990–92; Corresp. Ed. Rampike 1991–; consultant/trans., J. Paul Getty Conservation Inst., Los Angeles 1991–92; Visiting Asst Prof. of German, UCLA 1992–93, Visiting Prof. of German 2007–08; Asst Prof. of German, Univ. of Colorado at Colorado Springs 1993–99, Dir of Film Studies 1997–, Assoc. Prof. of German and Film Studies 1999–2006, Prof. of German and Film Studies 2006–, Chair., Dept of Languages and Cultures 2001–07, Chair. Dept of Visual and Performing Arts 2001–02, 2010–11; Producer and CEO Belvedere Film, LLC 1999–; mem. Editorial Bd Osiris 1991–, Modern Austrian Literature/Journal of Austrian Studies 1997–2000, 2011–14, Ariadne Press 1999–, Poetry Salzburg Review 2002–; Dir, Elfi von Dassanowsky Foundation 2009–; mem. Bd Los Angeles Flickapalooza Film Festival 2001–03, TIE The Int. Experimental Cinema Exposition 2002–10; Co-founder and mem. Bd Int. Alexander Lernet-Holenia Soc. 1997–; Co-founder and Vice-Pres. Austrian American Film Asscn 1998–2009, Exec. Council, Modern Austrian Literature and Culture Asscn (MALCA) 2006–09, 2010–11 (Vice-Pres. Austrian Studies Asscn (fmrly MALCA) 2011–13, Pres. (2014–16)); External Reviewer, Fund for the Improvement of Postsecondary Educ. (FIPSE)/EC Directorate Gen. for Educ. and Culture Atlantis Project 2010–; mem. Modern Language Asscn, PEN/USA, Austrian PEN, Poet and Writers, Asscn of Austrian Film Producers, Film Independent LA, Soc. for Cinema and Media Studies, Screen Actors' Guild, German Studies Asscn, PEN Colorado (Founding Pres. 1994–99, 2001–02), Secession Museum Vienna, Wien Museum, Acad. of Austrian Film, European Acad. of Sciences and Arts 2001– (Cen. US Del. 2009–). *Films:* as producer, co-producer or exec. producer: Semmelweis 2001, Epicure 2001, The Nightmare Stumbles Past 2002, Believe 2002, Wilson Chance 2005, The Last Bogatyr 2009, The Retreat 2010, Vidas ambulante/The Troubadours 2011, Waking Eyes 2011, Felix Austria! (The Archduke and Herbert Hinkel) 2011, Dog Eat Dog 2012, Never Kissed by the Queen (The Black Countess from Bain Street) 2012. *Publications:* Phantom Empires: The Novels of Alexander Lernet-Holenia and the Question of Postimperial Austrian Identity 1996, Hans Raimund: Verses of a Marriage (trans.) 1996, Telegrams from the

Metropole: Selected Poetry 1999, Alexander Lernet-Holenia: Mars in Aries (trans.) 2003, Austrian Cinema: A History 2005, Soft Mayhem: Poetry 2010, New Austrian Cinema (co-ed.) 2011, The Nameable and the Unnameable: Hofmannsthal's 'Der Schwierige' Revisited (ed. and contrib.) 2011, Tarantino's Inglorious Basterds: Manipulations of Metacinema (ed.) 2012, World Film Locations: Vienna 2012, Screening Transcendence: Film under Austrofascism 2013; other: several plays and TV scripts; contribs: Contributing Ed., Gale Encyclopedia of Multicultural America 1999; mem. Editorial Bd and contrib. to International Dictionary of Films and Filmmakers 2000, Guest Co-Ed., Filmkunst 154, Special Issue: Austria's Hollywood/Hollywood's Austria 1997, Literatur der inneren Emigration in Österreich 1998, Thunder Rumbling at My Heels: Tracing Ingeborg Bachmann 1998, Alexander Lernet-Holenia: Poesie auf dem Boulevard 1999, Der BergFILM 1920–1940 2002, Harvard's Notable American Women, Vol. 5 2005, selected German poems, Landvermessung: Eine österreichische Bibliothek nach 1945, 2005, Greenwood Encyclopedia of World Popular Culture 2007, Cinema and the Swastika: The International Expansion of Third Reich Cinema 2007, Crime and Madness in Modern Austria: Myth, Metaphor and Cultural Realities 2008, Österreich 1918 und die Folgen 2008, European Academy of Sciences and Arts Twentieth Anniversary Festschrift 2009, Guest Ed., Modern Austrian Literature Special Issue: Michael Haneke, 43.2 2010, Women Film Pioneers Sourcebook, Vol. II 2011–12, selected poems in French trans., 12×2, ed. Teric Boucebci, Sexuality, Eroticism and Gender in Austrian Literature and Culture 2011, A New History of German Cinema 2011, Zeitenwende: Österreichische Literatur seit dem Millennium 2011, Nazisploitation! The History, Aesthetics, and Politics of the Nazi Image in Low-Brow Cinema 2011; numerous book chapters, and poetry and articles in periodicals and anthologies. *Honours:* Constantinian Order of St George, Order of Vitez (Hungary), Decoration of Honour in Silver (Austria); Academico hc (Academia Culturale d'Europa, Italy) 1989; Pres.'s Fund for the Humanities grants, Univ. of Colorado 1996, 2001, Outstanding Teaching Award, Univ. of Colorado at Colorado Springs 2001, Faculty Research Award, Coll. of Letters, Arts and Sciences, Univ. of Colorado at Colorado Springs 2002, US Prof. of the Year for Colorado, Carnegie Foundation/CASE 2004, Chancellor's Award, Univ. of Colorado at Colorado Springs 2006, Taft Center Lecturer, Univ. of Cincinnati 2011. *Address:* Department of Languages and Cultures, University of Colorado, 1420 Austin Bluffs Parkway, Colorado Springs, CO 80918, USA (office). *E-mail:* rvondass@uccs.edu (office). *Website:* www.belvederefilm.com (office); www.elfivondassanowsky.org (office).

VON LUCIUS, Wulf D., Dr rer. pol; German scientific publisher; *Publisher and President, Lucius & Lucius Verlag*; b. 29 Nov. 1938, Jena; s. of the late Tankred R. von Lucius and of Annelise Fischer; m. Akka Achelis 1967; three s. *Education:* Heidelberg, Berlin and Freiburg, Univ. of Hohenheim, Stuttgart. *Career:* mil. service 1958–60; Asst Inst. of Econometrics, Freiburg 1965–66; worked in several publishing houses and as public accountant 1966–69; Partner and Man. Dir Gustav Fischer Verlag 1969–95; mem. Bd of Exec. Officers, German Publrs Asscn (Börsenverein) 1976–86; mem. Bd C. Hanser Verlag 1984–; Publr and Pres. Lucius & Lucius Verlag, Stuttgart 1996–; Chair. Int. Publishers Copyright Council 1995–98, Asscn of Scientific Publrs in Germany 1994–2001, Wüstenrot Stiftung 2009–; mem. Exec. Cttee Int. Publrs Asscn Geneva 1996–2004; Bd German Nat. Library 1981–. *Exhibitions:* book exhbns from coll.. in Stuttgart, Frankfurt, Göttingen, Oldenburg. *Publications:* Bücherlust-Vom Sammeln 2000, Verlagswirtschaft 2005, Das Glück der Bücher 2012; numerous articles on publishing, copyright and book history. *Honours:* Hon. Prof. Univ. of Hohenheim, Stuttgart; Friedrich-Perthes-Medaille 1999, Antiquaria Preis 2001, Ludwig Erhard Preis 2004. *Address:* Gerokstrasse 51, 70184 Stuttgart, Germany (office). *Telephone:* (711) 242060 (office). *Fax:* (711) 242088 (office). *E-mail:* lucius@luciusverlag.com (office). *Website:* luciusverlag.com (office).

VON STAHLENBERG, Elisabeth (see Freeman, Gillian)

VONARBURG, Elisabeth, BA, MA, PhD; French/Canadian writer and translator; b. 5 Aug. 1947, Paris, France; m. Jean-Joel Vonarburg 1969 (divorced 1990). *Education:* Univ. of Dijon, Université de Laval. *Career:* Asst Lecturer in Literature, Université du Québec à Chicoutimi 1973–81; Asst Lecturer in Literature and Creative Writing, Université du Québec à Rimouski 1983–86; Teacher of Creative Writing in Science Fiction, Université Laval 1990; Science Fiction Columnist, Radio-Canada 1993–95; mem. Infini, France, International Asscn for the Fantastic in the Arts, SFWA, Science Fiction Canada, Science Fiction Research Asscn. *Publications:* L'Oeil de la nuit 1980, Le Silence de la Cité (trans. as The Silent City) 1981, Janus 1984, Comment Escrire des Histoires: Guide de l'explorateur 1986, Histoire de la Princesse et du Dragon 1990, Ailleurs et au Japon 1991, Chroniques de Pays des Meres (trans. as In the Mother's Land) 1992, Les Voyageurs maigre eux (trans. as Reluctant Voyagers) 1992, Les Contes de la Chatte Rouge 1993, Contes et Légendes de Tyranael 1994, La Maison au bord de la mer 2000, Le Jeu de Coquilles de Nautilus 2003. *Honours:* several Canadian and French science fictions awards. *E-mail:* evarburg@royaume.com (office). *Website:* www.sfwa.org/members/vonarburg.

VOYNOVICH, Vladimir Nikolayevich; Russian author, playwright and film scriptwriter; b. 26 Sept. 1932, Stalinabad (now Dushanbe), Tajikistan; s. of Nikolai Pavlovich Voinovich and Rosa Voinovich (née Goikhman); m. 1st Valentina Voinovich; one s. one d.; m. 2nd Irina Braude 1970; one d. *Career:* served in Soviet Army 1951–55; worked as carpenter 1956–57; studied Moscow Pedagogical Inst. 1958–59; started literary activity (and song writing for Moscow Radio) 1960; various dissident activities 1966–80; expelled from USSR Writers' Union 1974; elected mem. French PEN Centre 1974; emigrated from USSR 1980; USSR citizenship restored 1990; mem. Bavarian Acad. of Fine Arts. *Publications include:* The Life and Unusual Adventures of Private Ivan Chonkin (samizdat 1967) 1975 (English trans. 1977), Ivankiada 1976, By Way of Mutual Correspondence 1979, Pretender to the Throne 1981, Moscow–2042 1987, The Fur Hut 1989, The Zero Decision 1990, Case N3484 1992, The Conception 1994, Tales for Adults 1996, By Means of Mutual Correspondence 1998, Monumental Propaganda 2000, A Portrait Against the Background of a Myth 2002. *E-mail:* webmaster@voinovich.ru (office). *Website:* www.voinovich.ru.

VREELAND, Susan, BA, MA; American writer and teacher; b. 20 Jan. 1946, Racine, WI; m. Joseph C. Gray 1988. *Education:* San Diego State Univ. *Career:* taught English, San Diego City Schools 1969–99, and ceramics 1986–99; mem. California Asscn of Teachers of English. *Publications:* What Love Sees (novel) 1988, If I Had My Life to Live Over I Would Pick More Daisies (anthology) 1992, Family: A Celebration 1995, What English Teachers Want: A Student Handbook 1996, Generation to Generation 1998, Girl in Hyacinth Blue (novel) (Theodore Geisel Award Winner, Foreword Magazine Best Novel of the Year) 1999, The Passion of Artemisia (novel) (San Diego Book Awards Theodore Geisel Award, Best Novel of the Year) 2002, The Forest Lover (novel) 2004, Life Studies (novel) 2005, Luncheon of the Boating Party 2007, Clara and Mr Tiffany 2010; contrib. to Missouri Review, Dominion Review, Confrontation, Alaska Quarterly Review, Calyx, Crescent Review, West Wind Review, Ambergris, So To Speak, Phoebe, New England Review. *Honours:* Women's National Book Asscn First Place in Short Fiction 1991, Dominion Review First Prize for Essay 1996, New Millennium First Prize for Essay 1996, Inkwell Magazine Grand Prize for Fiction 1999. *E-mail:* susan@svreeland.com (office). *Website:* www.svreeland.com.

VROOMKONING, Victor (see Van De Laar, Waltherus Antonius Bernardinus)

W

WA THIONG'O, Ngugi, (James Thiong'o Ngugi), BA; Kenyan writer, dramatist, critic and academic; *Director of the International Center for Writing and Translation, University of California, Irvine*; b. 5 Jan. 1938, Limuru; m. 1st Nyambura 1961 (divorced 1982); m. 2nd Njeeri 1992; four s. two d. *Education:* Makerere Univ. Coll., Uganda and Univ. of Leeds, UK. *Career:* Lecturer in Literature, Univ. Nairobi 1967–69, Sr Lecturer, Assoc. Prof. and Chair Dept of Literature 1972–77; Fellow in Creative Writing, Makerere Univ. 1969–70; Visiting Assoc. Prof., Northwestern Univ., USA 1970–71; arrested and detained Dec. 1977, released Dec. 1978; in exile in London 1982–; Lecturer in Politics and Literature, Yale Univ.; currently Distinguished Prof of English and Comparative Literature and Dir, Int. Center for Writing and Translation, Univ. of California, Irvine. *Publications:* The Black Hermit (play) 1962, Weep Not, Child (novel) 1964, The River Between (novel) 1965, A Grain of Wheat (novel) 1967, This Time Tomorrow: Three Plays 1970, Homecoming: Essays on African and Caribbean Literature, Culture and Politics 1972, Secret Lives and Other Stories 1973, The Trial of Dedan Kimathi (with Micere Githae-Mugo) 1976, Petals of Blood (novel) 1977, Mtawa Mweusi 1978, Caitaani mutharaba-ini (trans. as Devil on the Cross) 1980, Writers in Politics: Essays 1981, Detained: A Writer's Prison Diary 1981, Njamba Nene na mbaathi i mathagu (trans. as Njamba Nene and the Flying Bus) 1982, Ngaahika Ndeena: Ithaako ria Ngerekano (play with Ngugi wa Mirii), (trans. as I Will Marry When I Want) 1982, Barrel of a Pen: Resistance to Repression in Neo-Colonial Kenya 1983, Bathitoora va Njamba Nene, 1984, English trans. as Njamba Nene's Pistol 1986, Decolonising the Mind: The Politics of Language in African Literature 1986, Writing Against Neo-colonialism 1986, Matigari ma Ngirũũngi (trans. as Matigari) 1986, Njambas Nene no Chiubu King'ang'i 1986, Moving the Centre: The Struggle for Cultural Freedoms 1992, Wizard of the Crow 2006, Dreams in a Time of War 2010. *Honours:* Foreign Hon. mem. American Academy of Arts and Letters; Hon. Llife Mem. Council for the Devt of Social Sciences Research in Africa 2003; Dr hc (Univ. of Leeds), (Univ. of Transkei); Fonlon-Nicholas Award 1996, Medal of the Presidency of the Italian Cabinet; Fourth Memorial Steve Biko Lecture 2003, Grinzane for Africa Heritage Prize 2008. *Address:* International Center for Writing and Translation, School of Humanities, 172 Humanities Instruction Building, University of California, Irvine, CA 92697-3380, USA (office). *Telephone:* (949) 824-1948 (office). *Fax:* (949) 824-9623 (office). *E-mail:* icwt@uci.edu (office). *Website:* www.humanities.uci.edu/icwt (office).

WABERI, Abdourahman A., BA, MA, DEA; Djibouti novelist, essayist, poet and academic; *Professor of French and Africana Studies, Claremont Colleges*; b. 20 July 1965, Djibouti City; two c. *Education:* Univ. of Caen, Univ. of Bourgogne, France. *Career:* moved to France 1985; English and French teacher, Lycée Clement Ader, Bernay, France 1996–99; Asst Lecturer, Univ. of Caen 1997–2002; English and French teacher, Lycée Paul Cornu, Lisieux 1999–2005; Writer-in-Residence, DAAD Berliner Künstlerprogramm 2006–07; Donald and Susan Newhouse Center Humanities Fellow, Wellesley Coll. 2007–08; William F. Podlich Distinguished Fellow and Africana Visiting Prof., Claremont McKenna Coll., USA 2009–10; Prof. of French and Africana Studies, Claremont Colleges, Calif. 2010–; Pensionnaire de l' Acad. de France à Rome – Villa Médicis, Rome, Italy 2010–11; fmr literary consultant, Editions Le Serpent à plumes, Paris; fmr literary critic, Le Monde Diplomatique, Paris; jury mem. Lettre Ulysses Award for the Art of Reportage, Berlin 2003, 2004, Impac Dublin Literary Award 2009–10; participant, Fabrica/Benetton Stock Exchange of Visions project 2007. *Publications:* Le Pays Sans Ombre 1994, Cahier nomade 1996, L'oeil nomade 1997, Balbala 1998, Les Nomades, mes frères vont boire à, la Grande Ourse 2000, Moisson de crânes 2000, Rift, routes, rails 2001, Transit 2003, Bouh et la vache magique 2002, Aux Etats Unis d'Afrique 2006, Passage des larmes 2009, Les Enfants de la balle (ed.) 2010. *Honours:* Grand Prix Littéraire de l'Afrique noire 1996, PEN Mandat pour la liberté Prize 1998, Stefan Georg Prize 2006. *Literary Agent:* c/o Pierre Astier et Associés, 4, rue Frédéric-Schneider, Hall 10, 75018 Paris, France. *Telephone:* 1-53-28-14-52. *E-mail:* pierre@pierreastier.com. *Website:* www.pierreastier.com; www.abdourahmanwaberi.com.

WADDELL, Martin, (Catherine Sefton); Northern Irish children's writer; b. 10 April 1941, Belfast. *Publications:* Little Dracula's First Bite 1976, Little Dracula's Christmas 1976, Ernie's Chemistry Set 1978, Ernie's Flying Trousers 1978, Napper Goes for Goal 1981, The Great Green Mouse Disaster 1981, Napper Strikes Again 1981, Harriet (series) 1982–, Going West 1984, The Mystery Squad (series) 1984–, Big Bad Bertie 1984, The House Under the Stairs 1984, School Reporter's Notebook 1985, Budgie Said Grrr! 1985, The Day it Rained Elephants 1986, Alice the Artist 1988, Tales from the Shop That Never Shuts 1988, Fred the Angel 1989, Judy the Bad Fairy 1989, We Love Them 1990, Amy Said 1990, My Great Grandpa 1990, Our Wild Weekend 1990, Rosie's Babies (Best Book for Babies Award) 1992, The Happy Hedgehog Band 1993, The Toymaker 1993, Squeak-A-Lot 1993, Owl Babies 1994, The Pig in the Pond 1994, Sailor Bear 1994, Farmer Duck (British Book Award for Children's Illustrated Book of the Year, Smarties Book Prize) 1995, When the Teddy Bears Came 1996, The Big Big Sea 1996, The Hollyhock Wall 2000, Starry Night (Other Award) 2000, Frankie's Story 2001, The Beat of the Drum 2001, A Kitten Called Moonlight 2001, What Use is a Moose? 2001, Cup Final Kid 2001, Once There Were Giants 2001, Herbie Monkey 2001, Night Night, Cuddly Bear 2001, I'll Tell You a Story and Other Story Poems 2001, Sam Vole and his Brothers 2002, The Tough Princess 2002, Tom Rabbit 2002, Webster J. Duck 2002, The Park in the Dark (Kurt Maschler Award) 2002, Going Up! 2003, Cup Run 2003, Snow Bears 2003, Hi, Harry! 2004, Shooting Star 2004, Well Done, Little Bear 2005, You and Me, Little Bear 2005, Let's Go Home, Little Bear 2005, Can't You Sleep, Little Bear? (Smarties Book Prize) 2005, Tiny's Big Adventure 2005, Who Do You Love? 2005, It's Quacking Time! 2005, Star Striker Titch 2005, Ernie and the Fishface Gang 2006, The Orchard Book of Goblins, Ghouls and Ghosts and Other Magical Stories (with Tony Ross) 2006, Gallow's Hill: And The Ghostly Penny (Tales of Ghostly Ghouls and Haunting Horrors) 2006, Room for a Little One 2008, Tiny's Big Adventure 2008. *Honours:* many awards including Hans Christian Andersen Award 2004. *Address:* c/o Walker Books, 87 Vauxhall Walk, London, SE11 5HJ, England. *E-mail:* editorial@walker.co.uk. *Website:* www.walker.co.uk/contributors/Martin-Waddell-1811.aspx.

WADDINGTON-FEATHER, John Joseph, BA, PGCE, FRSA; British writer, poet, Anglican priest and publisher; *Director, Feather Books*; b. 10 July 1933, Keighley, Yorkshire, England; m. Sheila Mary Booker 1960; three d. *Education:* Univs of Leeds and Keele. *Career:* prison visitor and Hon. Chaplain, HM Prisons 1969–2009; ordained priest 1977; Co-Ed. Orbis 1971–80; teacher, Shrewsbury Sixth Form Coll. 1981–83, Khartoum Univ. 1984–85; Chaplain, Prestfelde School 1985–96; Dir Feather Books; Ed. Poetry Church Magazine, Poetry Church Anthology 1997–; mem. Brontë Soc., Council mem. 1994–2000, Yorkshire Dialect Soc., J. B. Priestley Soc. (Chair. 1998–2004, Vice-Pres. 2004–). *Plays:* Garlic Lane 1972, Easy Street 1973, Bill Braithwaite's Miracle 2004, Limbo 2009, Bus Stop 2010, The German Martyrs Against Hitler 2010. *Publications:* Collection of Verse 1964, Of Mills, Moors and Men 1966, One Man's Road 1977, Quill's Adventures in the Great Beyond 1980, Tall Tales from Yukon 1983, Khartoum Trilogy and Other Poems 1985, Quill's Adventures in Wasteland 1986, Quill's Adventures in Grozzieland 1988, Six Christian Monologues 1990, Six More Christian Poems 1994, Shropshire 1994, Feather's Foibles 1995, Wild Tales from the West 1999, The Museum Mystery 1999, The Bradshaw Mystery 2000, The Marcham Mystery 2002, Yorkshire Dialect 2002, Legends of Americada 2002, Grundy and Feather Hymn Series (Part I) 2002, The Lollipop Man 2002, Chance-Child (Part I) 2003, Chance-Child (Part II) 2003, Sermonettes and Essays (Part I) 2003, Quill's Adventures in Mereful 2003, Legend Land 2004, Grundy and Feather Hymns and Songs for Seasons and Occasions 2004, Sermonettes and Essays (Part II) 2004, Grundy and Feather Hymns from the Classics 2005, Illingworth House 2005, Quill's Adventures in Human Folkland 2005, The Graveyard Mystery 2005, Judas 2009, Isaiah 2009, Magdalene 2010, Matthias 2010, Edward 2011, John the Baptist 2011; contrib. to journals and magazines. *Honours:* Brontë Soc. Prize 1966, Cyril Hodges Poetry Award 1974, Burton Prize 1999, William de Witt Romig Poetry Award 2002. *Address:* Fair View, Old Coppice, Lyth Bank, Shrewsbury, Shropshire, SY3 0BW (home); Feather Books, PO Box 438, Shewsbury, SY3 0WN, England (office). *Telephone:* (1743) 872177 (office). *Fax:* (1743) 872177 (office). *E-mail:* john@jjwfeather.uk.com (office).

WADE, David, BA; British writer; b. 2 Dec. 1929, Edinburgh, Scotland; m.; one s. one d. *Education:* Queens' College, Cambridge. *Career:* Radio Critic, The Listener, 1965–67, The Times, 1967–89; fmr Chair. Inst. for Cultural Research (educ. charity); mem. Society of Authors. *Radio drama:* Trying to Connect You, The Cooker, The Guthrie Process, The Gold Spinners, Three Blows in Anger, The Ogden File, The Carpet Maker of Samarkand, The Nightingale, Summer of 39, The Facts of Life, A Rather Nasty Crack, On Detachment, The Tree of Strife, Power of Attorney, Alexander. *Address:* Willow Cottage, Stockland Green Road, Southborough, Kent TN3 0TL, England (home). *Fax:* (1892) 521830 (home). *E-mail:* wadejp@aol.com (home).

WADLEY, Veronica; British journalist and editor; *London Chair, Arts Council England*; b. 28 Feb. 1952, London; d. of Neville John Wadley and Anne Hawise Colleton (née Browning); m. Tom Bower 1985; one s. one d. *Education:* Francis Holland School, London, Benenden. *Career:* journalist, Condé Nast Publs 1971–74, Sunday Telegraph Magazine 1978–81, Mail on Sunday 1982–86; Features Ed. Daily Telegraph 1986–89, Asst Ed. 1989–94, Deputy Ed. 1994–95; Assoc. Ed. Daily Mail 1995–98, Deputy Ed. (Features) 1998–2002; Ed. London Evening Standard 2002–09; London Chair., Arts Council England 2010–. *Address:* Arts Council England, 14 Great Peter Street, London, SW1P 3NQ, England (office). *Telephone:* (20) 7608-4100 (office). *Fax:* (20) 7973-6564 (office). *Website:* www.artscouncil.org.uk (office).

WAGNER-MARTIN, Linda, BA, MA, PhD; American academic, poet and writer; *Frank Borden Hanes Professor of English and Comparative Literature, University of North Carolina at Chapel Hill*; b. 18 Aug. 1936, St Marys, Ohio. *Education:* Bowling Green State Univ. *Career:* Instructor and Asst Prof., Bowling Green State Univ. 1961–66; Asst Prof., Wayne State Univ. 1966–68; Asst Prof. to Prof., Michigan State Univ. 1968–87; Frank Borden Hanes Prof. of English and Comparative Literature, Univ. of North Carolina at Chapel Hill 1988–; mem. Ellen Glasgow Society, pres. 1982–87, Ernest Hemingway Foundation and Society, pres. 1993–96, MLA, Society for the Study of Midwestern Literature, pres. 1974–76, Society for the Study of Narrative Technique, pres. 1988–89. *Publications:* The Poems of William Carlos

Williams: A Critical Study 1964, Denise Levertov 1967, Intaglios: Poems 1967, The Prose of William Carlos Williams 1970, Phyllis McGinley 1971, Hemingway and Faulkner: Inventors/Masters 1975, Ernest Hemingway: A Reference Guide 1977, William Carlos Williams: A Reference Guide 1978, Dos Passos: Artist as American 1979, American Modern: Selected Essays in Fiction and Poetry 1980, Songs for Isadora: Poems 1981, Ellen Glasgow; Beyond Convention 1982, Sylvia Plath: A Biography 1987, The Modern American Novel, 1914–1945 1989, Wharton's The House of Mirth: A Novel of Admonition 1990, Plath's the Bell Jar: A Novel of the Fifties 1992, Telling Women's Lives: The New Biography 1994, 'Favored Strangers': Gertrude Stein and Her Family 1995, Wharton's The Age of Innocence: A Novel of Ironic Nostalgia 1996, The Mid-Century American Novel, 1935–1965 1997, Sylvia Plath: A Literary Life 1999; editor: William Faulkner: Four Decades of Criticism 1973, Ernest Hemingway: Five Decades of Criticism 1974, T. S. Eliot 1976, 'Speaking Straight Ahead': Interviews with William Carlos Williams 1976, Robert Frost: The Critical Heritage 1977, Denise Levertov: In Her Own Province 1979, Joyce Carol Oates: Critical Essays 1979, Sylvia Plath: Critical Essays 1984, Ernest Hemingway: Six Decades of Criticism 1987, New Essays on Hemingway's The Sun Also Rises 1987, Sylvia Plath: The Critical Heritage 1988, Anne Sexton: Critical Essays 1989, Denise Levertov: Critical Essays 1991, The Oxford Companion to Women's Writing in the United States (with Cathy N. Davidson) 1995, The Oxford Book of Women's Writing in the United States 1995, New Essays to Faulkner's Go Down, Moses 1996, Ernest Hemingway: Seven Decades of Criticism 1998, Festchrift for Frederick Eckman (with David Adams) 1998, The Historical Guide to Ernest Hemingway 1999; contributions: scholarly books and journals. *Honours:* Guggenheim Fellowship 1975–76, Bunting Institute Fellow 1975–76, Rockefeller Foundation Fellow, Bellagio, Italy 1990, Fellow, Institute for the Arts and Humanities, Univ. of North Carolina 1992, National Endowment for the Humanities Senior Fellowship 1992–93, Teacher-Scholar Award, College English Asscn 1994, Visiting Distinguished Prof., Emory Univ. 1994, Citation for Exceptional Merit, House of Representatives, Ohio 1994, Brackenridge Distinguished Prof., Univ. of Texas at San Antonio 1998. *Address:* Department of English and Comparative Literature, University of North Carolina at Chapel Hill, Greenlaw Hall, CB #3520, Chapel Hill, NC 27599-3520, USA (office). *Telephone:* (919) 962-8765 (office). *E-mail:* wagnerl@prodigy.net (office). *Website:* english.unc.edu (office).

WAGONER, David Russell, MA; American writer and academic; *Professor Emeritus of English, University of Washington*; b. 5 June 1926, Massillon, Ohio; m. 1st Patricia Parrott 1961 (divorced 1982); m. 2nd Robin H. Seyfried 1982; two d. *Education:* Pennsylvania State Univ., Indiana Univ. *Career:* served in USN 1944–46; Instructor, DePauw Univ., Greencastle, Ind. 1949–50, Pennsylvania State Univ. 1950–54; Assoc. Prof., Univ. of Washington, Seattle 1954–66, Prof. of English 1966–2000, Prof. Emer. 2000–; Elliston Lecturer, Univ. of Cincinnati 1968; Ed. Poetry Northwest, Seattle 1966–2002, Ed. Princeton Univ. Press Contemporary Poetry Series 1977–81; Poetry Ed. Missouri Press 1983–2000; Guggenheim Fellowship 1956, Ford Fellowship 1964, American Acad. Grant 1967, Nat. Endowment for the Arts Grant 1969. *Short Stories:* Afternoon on the Ground 1978, Wild Goose Chase 1978, Mr. Wallender's Romance 1979, Cornet Solo 1979, The Water Strider 1979, Fly Boy 1980, The Bird Watcher 1980, Snake Hunt 1980. *Play:* An Eye for an Eye for an Eye 1973. *Verse:* Dry Sun, Dry Wind 1953, A Place to Stand 1958, Poems 1959, The Nesting Ground 1963, Five Poets of the Pacific Northwest (with others) 1964, Staying Alive 1966, New and Selected Poems 1969, Working Against Time 1970, Riverbed 1972, Sleeping in the Woods 1974, A Guide to Dungeness Spit 1975, Travelling Light 1976, Who Shall Be the Sun? Poems Based on the Lore, Legends and Myths of Northwest Coast and Plateau Indians 1978, In Broken Country 1979, Landfall 1981, First Light 1983, Through the Forest 1987, Walt Whitman Bathing 1996, Traveling Light: Collected and New Poems 1999, The House of Song 2002. *Novels:* The Man in the Middle 1955, Money, Money, Money 1955, Rock 1958, The Escape Artist 1965, Baby, Come On Inside 1968, Where is My Wandering Boy Tonight? 1970, The Road to Many a Wonder 1974, Tracker 1975, Whole Hog 1976, The Hanging Garden 1980. *Honours:* Morton Dauwen Zabel Prize (Poetry, Chicago) 1967, Ruth Lilly Prize 1991, Levinson Prize (Poetry, Chicago) 1994, Union League Prize (Poetry, Chicago) 1997; Pacific NW Booksellers Award 2000. *Address:* 5416 154th Place, SW, Edmonds, WA 98026-4348, USA (home). *Telephone:* (425) 745-6964 (home). *E-mail:* renogawd@aol.com (home).

WAH, Fred, MA; Canadian teacher and poet; *Parliamentary Poet Laureate*; b. 23 Jan. 1939, Swift Current, Sask.; m. Pauline Butling. *Education:* Univ. of British Columbia. *Career:* Co-founder and Ed. poetry newsletter TISH; f. writing program at DTUC and taught at Univ. of Calgary 1960–70s; ed. and contrib. to literary magazine Open Letter; co-ed online literary magazine SwiftCurrent; Writer-in-Residence, Simon Fraser Univ., Burnaby, BC 2006–07; Parl. Poet Laureate of Canada 2011–. *Publications:* 17 books of poetry including Lardeau 1965, Among 1972, Breathin' My Name With a Sigh 1981, Waiting For Saskatchewan (Gov.-Gen.'s Award) 1985, Music at the Heart of Thinking 1987, Limestone Lakes Utaniki 1989, So Far (Stephanson Award for Poetry) 1991, Alley Alley Home Free 1992, Isadora Blue 2005, Sentenced to Light 2008, is a door (Dorothy Livesay Poetry Prize, BC Book Awards 2010) 2009; other: Diamond Grill (Writers Guild of Alberta Howard O'Hagan Award for Short Fiction) 1996, Faking It: Poetics and Hybridity (critical writing) (Gabrielle Roy Prize) 2000. *Address:* c/o Talon Books, PO Box 2076, Vancouver, BC V6B 3S3, Canada (office). *E-mail:* info@talonbooks.com (office). *Website:* www.talonbooks.com (office).

WAINAINA, Binyavanga; Kenyan writer, journalist and academic; *Director and Bard Fellow, Chinua Achebe Center for African Writers and Artists, Bard College*; b. 18 Jan. 1971, Nakuru; s. of Job Muigai Wainaina and Rosemary Kankindi Wainaina. *Education:* Univ. of Transkei, South Africa, Univ. of East Anglia, UK. *Career:* Writer-in-Residence, Union Coll., Schenectady, NY, USA; Sterling Brown Prof., Williams Coll., Mass, USA 2008–; Dir and Bard Fellow, Chinua Achebe Center for African Writers and Artists, Bard Coll., Annandale-on-Hudson, NY, USA; Founding Ed., Kwani Trust; columnist, Mail and Guardian newspaper, South Africa. *Play:* Shine Your Eye 2010. *Publications:* An Affair to Dismember (short story), Discovering Home (short story) 2001, Discovering Home (memoir) 2006; contribs to Weekend Argus, Cape Town, Sunday Times, South Africa, Mail and Guardian, Y magazine, SL magazine, Pforward magazine, The Top of the Times (Cape Times weekend supplement), Adbusters, Granta, Tin House, Vanity Fair, National Geographic, New York Times, The Guardian, Die Zeit, Süddeutsche Zeitung. *Honours:* Caine Prize for African Writing 2002, Emily Clark Balch Award for short fiction (for Ships in High Transit) 2006. *Literary Agent:* c/o PO Box 7065, 20100 Nakuru, Kenya. *E-mail:* melissa@sikiliza-ink.com. *Website:* www.howtowriteaboutafrica.com. *Address:* Kwani Trust, PO Box 2895, Nairobi, Kenya (office). *Telephone:* (518) 6056215 (office). *Website:* www.binyavangawainaina.org.

WAINWRIGHT, Geoffrey, MA, DD (Cantab.), DrThéol; British ecclesiastic and academic; *Robert Earl Cushman Professor of Christian Theology, Divinity School, Duke University*; b. 16 July 1939, Yorks., England; s. of Willie Wainwright and Martha Burgess; m. Margaret H. Wiles 1965; one s. two d. *Education:* Gonville & Caius Coll. Cambridge and Univ. of Geneva. *Career:* Prof. of Dogmatics, Protestant Faculty of Theology, Yaoundé, Cameroon 1967–73; Lecturer in Bible and Systematic Theology, Queen's Coll. Birmingham 1973–79; Roosevelt Prof. of Systematic Theology, Union Theological Seminary, New York 1979–83; Robert Earl Cushman Prof. of Christian Theology, Duke Univ. 1983–; mem. Faith and Order Comm. WCC 1977–91; Pres. Soc. Liturgica 1985–87; Co-Chair. Jt Comm. between World Methodist Council and Roman Catholic Church 1986–2011; Sec. American Theological Soc. 1988–95, Pres. 1996–97; Leverhulme European Fellow 1966–67; Pew Evangelical Fellow 1996–97. *Publications include:* Christian Initiation 1969, Eucharist and Eschatology 1971, Doxology 1980, The Ecumenical Moment 1983, On Wesley and Calvin 1987, Methodists in Dialogue 1995, Worship With One Accord 1997, For Our Salvation: Two Approaches to the Work of Christ 1997, Is the Reformation Over? Protestants and Catholics at the Turn of the Millennia 2000, Lesslie Newbigin: A Theological Life 2000, Oxford History of Christian Worship 2006, Embracing Purpose: Essays on God, the World and the Church 2007. *Honours:* Hon. DD (North Park Univ.) 2001; Berakah Award, N American Acad. of Liturgy 1999, Festschrift: 'Ecumenical Theology in Worship, Doctrine and Life: Essays Presented to Geoffrey Wainwright on his Sixtieth Birthday' (ed. David Cunningham and others), Oxford Univ. Press 1999, Outstanding Ecumenist Award, Washington Theological Consortium 2003, Johannes Quasten Medal for excellence in theological scholarship, The Catholic University of America 2006. *Address:* The Divinity School, Box 90967, Duke University, Durham, NC 27708-0967 (office); 4011 W Cornwallis Road, Durham, NC 27705, USA (home). *Telephone:* (919) 660-3460 (office); (919) 489-2795 (home). *Fax:* (919) 660-3473 (office). *Website:* www.divinity.duke.edu/academics/faculty/geoffrey-wainwright (office).

WAINWRIGHT, Hilary, BA, BPhil; British journalist and editor; b. 1949, Leeds. *Education:* The Mount School, York, St Anne's Coll., Oxford and St Anthony's Coll., Oxford. *Career:* Research Asst, Sociology Dept, Durham Univ. 1973–75, Research Fellow 1975–78; Social Science Council Research Fellow, Open Univ. 1979–81; Founder, Asst Chief Econ. Advisor and Co-ordinator Popular Planning Unit, GLC (now GLA) 1982–86; freelance writer, lecturer and journalist, The New Statesman and The Guardian 1986–88; Fellow, Transnational Inst., Amsterdam 1988, now Research Dir New Politics Programme; Sr Simon Fellow, Sociology Dept, Univ. of Manchester 1989–90; Visiting Fellow, Center for Social Theory and Comparative History, UCLA 1991; Sr Research Fellow, Centre for Labour Studies, Univ. of Manchester 1992, now Hon. Fellow; Political Ed. Red Pepper Magazine 1994–95, Ed. 1995–; mem. Council Charter 88; frequent TV and radio appearances on UK discussion programmes including Question Time (BBC), Channel 4 News, Any Questions, Today Programme (BBC Radio 4) etc. *Publications:* The Workers' Report of Vickers (co-author) 1978, Beyond the Fragments (co-author) 1980, State Intervention in Industry: A Worker's Inquiry 1981, The Lucas Plan: A New Trades Unionism in the Making? 1982, A Taste of Power: The Politics of Local Economics (co-ed) 1986, Labour: A Tale of Two Parties 1987, After the Wall: Social Movements and Democratic Politics in the New Europe (ed) 1991, Arguments for a New Left: Answering the Free Market Right 1993, Reclaim the State: Adventures in Popular Democracy 2003; numerous essays and articles; regular articles in the Guardian. *Address:* Red Pepper Magazine, 1B Waterlow Road, London, N19 5NJ, England; c/o Transnational Institute, PO Box 14656, 1001 LD, Amsterdam, Netherlands. *Telephone:* (20) 7281-7024. *Fax:* (20) 7263-9345. *Website:* www.redpepper.org.uk; www.tni.org.

WAINWRIGHT, Jeffrey, BA, MA; British poet, dramatist, translator and academic; b. 19 Feb. 1944, Stoke on Trent, Staffs., England; m. Judith Batt 1967; one s. one d. *Education:* Univ. of Leeds. *Career:* Asst Lecturer, Lecturer, Univ. of Wales 1967–72; Visiting Instructor, Long Island Univ. 1970–71; Sr Lecturer, Manchester Metropolitan Univ. 1972–99, Prof. 1999–2008 (retd); Northern Theatre Critic, The Independent 1988–99. *Publications:* poetry: The

Important Man 1970, Heart's Desire 1978, Selected Poems 1985, The Red-Headed Pupil 1994, Out of the Air 1999, Clarity or Death! 2008; other: Poetry: The Basics (criticism) 2004, Acceptable Words: Essays on the Poetry of Geoffrey Hill (criticism) 2006, trans of various plays into English; contribs to various anthologies, BBC Radio and many periodicals. *Honours:* Judith E. Wilson Visiting Fellow 1985. *E-mail:* jeffrey.wainwright@btinternet.com (home). *Website:* www.jeffreywainwright.co.uk.

WAITE, Peter Busby, OC, BA, MA, PhD, FRSC; Canadian academic and writer; *Professor of History Emeritus, Dalhousie University;* b. 12 July 1922, Toronto, ON; m. Masha Maria Gropuzzo 1958; two d. *Education:* Univ. of British Columbia, Univ. of Toronto. *Career:* Lecturer 1951–55, Asst Prof. 1955–60, Assoc. Prof. 1960–61, Prof. of History 1961–88, Prof. Emeritus 1988–, Dalhousie Univ.; mem. Canadian Historical Asscn (pres. 1968–69), Humanities Research Council (chair. 1968–70), Aid to Publications Cttee Social Science Federation (chair. 1987–89). *Publications:* The Life and Times of Confederation, 1864–1867 1962, Canada 1874–1896 1971, John A. Macdonald, His Life and World 1975, The Man from Halifax: Sir John Thompson, Prime Minister 1985, Lord of Point Grey: Larry MacKenzie of UBC 1987, Between Three Oceans: Challenges of a Continental Destiny, 1840–1900, Chapter IV Illustrated History of Canada 1988, The Loner: The Personal Life and Ideas of R. B. Bennett 1870–1947 1992, The Lives of Dalhousie University: Vol. I Lord Dalhousie's College, 1818–1925 1994, Vol. II The Old College Transformed, 1925–1980 1998; contrib. some 55 articles to numerous magazines and journals. *Honours:* Hon. LLD (Dalhousie Univ.) 1991, Hon. DLitt (Univ. of New Brunswick) 1991, (Memorial Univ. of Newfoundland) 1991, (Carleton Univ.) 1993; Lieutenant-Governor's Medal, BC 1987. *Address:* 960 Ritchie Drive, Halifax, NS B3H 3P5, Canada (home). *E-mail:* peter.waite@dal.ca (home).

WAKEFIELD, Dan, BA; American writer and screenwriter; b. 21 May 1932, Indianapolis, IN. *Education:* Columbia Univ. *Career:* News Ed., Princeton Packet, NJ 1955; Staff Writer, The Nation magazine 1956–59; Staff, Bread Loaf Writers Conference 1964, 1966, 1968, 1970, 1986; Visiting Lecturer, Univ. of Massachusetts at Boston 1965–67, Univ. of Illinois 1968; Contributing Ed., The Atlantic Monthly 1969–80; Writer-in-Residence, Emerson Coll. 1989–92; Contributing Writer, GQ magazine 1992–94; Distinguished Visiting Writer, Florida International Univ. 1992; mem. Authors' Guild of America, National Writers Union, Writers Guild of America. *Publications:* Island of the City: The World of Spanish Harlem 1959, Revolt in the South 1961, An Anthology 1963, Between the Lines 1966, Supernation at Peace and War 1968, Going All the Way 1970, Starting Over 1973, All Her Children 1976, Home Free 1977, Under the Apple Tree 1982, Selling Out 1985, Returning: A Spiritual Journey 1988, The Story of Your Life: Writing a Spiritual Autobiography 1990, New York in the Fifties 1992, Expect a Miracle 1995, Creating from the Spirit 1996, How Do We Know When It's God? 1999; editor: The Addict: An Anthology 1963; television: James at 15 1977–78, The Seduction of Miss Leona 1980, Heartbeat 1988. *Honours:* Bernard DeVoto Fellow, Bread Loaf Writers Conference 1957, Rockefeller Foundation Grant 1968, Short Story Prize, National Council of the Arts 1968. *Literary Agent:* Janklow & Nesbit Associates, 445 Park Avenue, New York, NY 10022, USA. *Telephone:* (212) 421-1700. *Fax:* (212) 980-3671. *E-mail:* info@janklow.com. *Website:* www.janklowandnesbit.com. *E-mail:* wakespace@aol.com (office). *Website:* www.danwakefield.com.

WAKELING, Edward, BSc, MSc; British writer and editor; b. 31 Aug. 1946, Sutton Scotney, Hants., England. *Education:* Bishop Otter Coll., Chichester, Hatfield Polytechnic, Univ. of Oxford. *Career:* mem. Lewis Carroll Soc., Sec. 1976–79, Chair. 1982–85, Treas. 1986–89, Chair. Editorial Bd 1997–2002; organized first Int. Lewis Carroll Conf. 1989; contrib. to a variety of TV programmes. *Publications:* The Logic of Lewis Carroll 1978, The Cipher Alice 1990, Lewis Carroll's Games and Puzzles 1992, Lewis Carroll's Oxford Pamphlets 1993, Lewis Carroll's Diaries (ed.), 10 vols 1993–2007, Rediscovered Lewis Carroll Puzzles 1995, Alice in Escherland 1998, Lewis Carroll, Photographer (with Roger Taylor) 2002, Lewis Carroll and His Illustrators (with Morton N. Cohen) 2003, Lives of Victorian Literary Figures, Lewis Carroll 2008; contrib. to many reviews, quarterlies and journals. *Honours:* Hon. MA (Luton) 1996. *Address:* Yew Tree Cottage, Parks Road, Clifford, Herefords., HR3 5HQ, England (home). *E-mail:* edward@wakeling.demon.co.uk (home). *Website:* www.lewiscarroll-site.com (office).

WAKOSKI, Diane, BA; American poet and academic; *University Distinguished Professor, Department of English, Michigan State University;* b. 3 Aug. 1937, Whittier, Calif.; m. Robert J. Turney 1982. *Education:* Univ. of California, Berkeley. *Career:* began writing poetry in New York 1960–73; worked as book shop clerk, jr high school teacher and by giving poetry readings on coll. campuses; Poet-in-Residence and Prof. of English, Michigan State Univ. 1975–, Univ. Distinguished Prof. 1990–; mem. Authors' Guild, PEN, Poetry Soc. of America. *Publications:* Coins and Coffins 1962, Discrepancies and Apparitions 1966, The George Washington Poems 1967, Inside the Blood Factory 1968, The Magellanic Clouds 1970, The Motorcycle Betrayal Poems 1971, Smudging 1972, Dancing on the Grave of a Son of a Bitch 1973, Trilogy (reprint of first three collections) 1974, Virtuoso Literature for Two and Four Hands 1975, Waiting for the King of Spain 1976, The Man Who Shook Hands 1978, Cap of Darkness 1980, The Magician's Feastletters 1982, Norii Magellanici (collection of poems from various vols trans. into Romanian) 1982, The Collected Greed 1984, The Rings of Saturn 1986, Emerald Ice (selected poems 1962–87) (William Carlos Williams Prize 1989) 1988, The Archaeology of Movies and Books: Vol. I Medea The Sorceress 1991, Vol. II Jason The Sailor 1993, Vol. III The Emerald City of Las Vegas 1995, Vol. IV Argonaut Rose 1998, The Butcher's Apron: New and Selected Poems 2000; Towards A New Poetry (criticism) 1980. *Honours:* Cassandra Foundation Grant 1970, Guggenheim Fellowship 1972, Nat. Endowment for the Arts Grant 1973, Writer's Fulbright Award 1984, Mich. Arts Foundation Award 1989, Michigan Arts Foundation Distinguished Artist Award 1989, Michigan Library Asscn Author of the Year 2003. *Address:* 607 Division Street, East Lansing, MI 48823 (home); 207 Morrill Hall, East Lansing, MI 48824, USA (office). *Telephone:* (517) 355-0308 (office); (517) 332-3385 (home). *E-mail:* dwakoski@aol.com; wakoski@msu.edu (office). *Website:* www.english.msu.edu (office).

WALCOTT, Derek, OBE, BA, FRSL; Saint Lucia poet and playwright; b. 23 Jan. 1930, Castries; s. of Warwick Walcott and Alix Walcott; m. 1st Fay Moston 1954 (divorced 1959); one s.; m. 2nd Margaret R. Maillard 1962 (divorced); two d.; m. 3rd Norline Metivier 1982 (divorced 1993). *Education:* St Mary's Coll., Castries, Univ. of the West Indies, Jamaica. *Career:* teacher, St Mary's Coll., Castries 1947–50, 1954, Grenada Boys' Secondary School, St George's 1953–54, Jamaica Coll., Kingston 1955; feature writer, Public Opinion, Kingston 1956–57; founder-Dir, Little Carib Theatre Workshop, later Trinidad Theatre Workshop 1959–76; feature writer, Trinidad Guardian, Port-of-Spain 1960–62, drama critic 1963–68; Visiting Prof., Columbia Univ., USA 1981, Harvard Univ. 1982, 1987; Asst Prof. of Creative Writing, Brown Univ. 1981; Prof. of Creative Writing and Playwriting, Boston Univ. 1982–2008; Distinguished Scholar-in-Residence, Univ. of Alberta 2009–11; hon. mem. American Acad. of Arts and Letters; mem. Poetry Soc. (vice-pres.); Rockefeller Foundation grants 1957, 1966, and Fellowship 1958, Ingram Merrill Foundation grant 1962, Eugene O'Neill Foundation Fellowship 1969, Guggenheim Fellowship 1977, John D. and Catherine T. MacArthur Foundation Fellowship 1981. *Plays:* Cry for a Leader 1950, Henri Christophe: A Chronicle 1950, Robin and Andrea 1950, Senza Alcun Sospetto 1950, The Price of Mercy 1951, Three Assassins 1951, Harry Dernier 1952, The Charlatan 1954, Crossroads 1954, The Sea at Dauphin 1954, The Golden Lions 1956, The Wine of the Country 1956, Ione: A Play with Music 1957, Ti-Jear and his Brothers 1957, Drums and Colours 1958, Jourmard 1959, Malcochon 1959, Batai 1965, Dream on Monkey Mountain 1967, Franklin: A Tale of the Islands 1969, In a Fine Castle 1970, The Joker of Seville (with G. Mcdermott) 1974, O Babylon! 1976, Remembrance 1977, The Snow Queen 1977, Pantomime 1978, Marie Leveau (with G. Mcdermott) 1979, The Isle is Full of Noises 1982, Beef, No Chicken 1985, The Odyssey 1993, The Capeman (musical, jtly) 1997. *Publications:* poetry: 25 Poems 1948, Epitaph for the Young: XII Cantos 1949, Poems 1951, In a Green Night, Poems 1948–60 1962, Selected Poems 1964, The Castaway and Other Poems 1965, The Gulf and Other Poems 1969, Another Life 1973, Sea Grapes 1976, The Star-Apple Kingdom 1979, Selected Poetry 1981, The Fortunate Traveller 1981, The Caribbean Poetry of Derek Walcott, and the Art of Romare Bearden 1983, Midsummer 1984, Collected Poems 1948–1984 1986, The Arkansas Testament 1987, Omeros (epic poem) (WHSmith Literary Award 1991) 1989, Poems 1965–1980 1992, The Bounty 1997, Tiepolo's Hounds 2000, The Prodigal: A Poem 2005, Selected Poems 2007, White Egrets (TS Eliot prize 2010) 2010; non-fiction: The Antilles, Fragments of Epic Memory: The Nobel Lecture 1993, What the Twilight Says (essays) 1998, Homage to Robert Frost (jtly) 1998. *Honours:* Commdr des arts et des lettres 2007; Arts Advisory Council of Jamaica Prize 1960, Guinness Award 1961, Borestone Mountain Awards 1964, 1977, RSL Heinemann Awards 1966, 1983, Cholmondeley Award 1969, Gold Hummingbird Medal, Trinidad 1969, Obie Award 1971, Welsh Arts Council Int. Writers Prize 1980, Los Angeles Times Book Prize 1986, Queen's Gold Medal for Poetry 1988, Nobel Prize for Literature 1992, T.S. Eliot Prize 2011, Eugenio Montale Prize 2011, BOCA Prize 2011. *Address:* PO Box GM 926, Becune Point, Castries, Saint Lucia (home); c/o Faber & Faber, Bloomsbury House, 74–77 Great Russell Street, London, WC1B 3DA, England (office). *Telephone:* (758) 450-0559 (home). *Fax:* (758) 450-0935 (home).

WALDEN, (Alastair) Brian; British broadcaster, journalist and university lecturer; b. 8 July 1932, s. of W. F. Walden; m. Hazel Downes; one s. (and three s. from fmr marriages). *Education:* West Bromwich Grammar School, Queen's Coll. and Nuffield Coll., Oxford. *Career:* MP (Labour) for Birmingham All Saints 1964–74, Birmingham Ladywood 1974–77; TV presenter, Weekend World (London Weekend TV) 1977–86; mem. W Midland Bd, Cen. Ind. TV 1982–84; columnist London Standard 1983–86, Thomson Regional Newspapers 1983–86, The Sunday Times; presenter, The Walden Interview (London Weekend TV for ITV network) 1988, 1989, 1990–94, Walden on Labour Leaders (BBC) 1997, Walden on Heroes (BBC) 1998, Walden on Villains 1999, A Point of View (BBC Radio 4) 2005– ; Chair. Paragon 1994–, Ten Alps 2002–, Capital 2006–. *Publication:* The Walden Interviews 1990. *Honours:* Shell Int. Award 1982, BAFTA Richard Dimbleby Award 1985; Aims of Industry Special Free Enterprise Award 1990; ITV Personality of the Year 1991. *Address:* Landfall, Fort Road, St Peter Port, Guernsey, GY1 1ZU, United Kingdom. *Telephone:* (1481) 722860. *E-mail:* walden@guernsey.net.

WALDMAN, Anne, BA; American poet, lecturer, performer and editor; *Distinguished Professor of Poetry, Jack Kerouac School of Disembodied Poetics, Naropa University;* b. 2 April 1945, Millville, NJ. *Education:* Bennington Coll. *Career:* Ed., Angel Hair Magazine 1965–, The World 1966–78; Asst Dir, Poetry Project, St Mark's Church In-the-Bowery 1966–68; Dir, Poetry Project, New York City 1968–78; Founder-Dir, Jack

Kerouac School of Disembodied Poetics and Distinguished Prof. of Poetry, Naropa Univ., Boulder, CO; poetry readings and performance events worldwide; mem. Committee for International Poetry, PEN Poetry Society of America. *Publications include:* Journals and Dreams 1976, First Baby Poems 1983, Makeup on Empty Space 1984, Invention 1985, Skin Meat Bones 1985, Blue Mosque 1987, The Romance Thing 1987–88, Helping the Dreamer: New and Selected Poems 1966–1988, Iovis 1993, Troubairitz, Kill or Cure 1994, Iovis, Book II 1996; editor: The World Anthology 1969, Baby Breakdown 1970, Another World 1971, Fast Speaking Woman 1974, Helping the Dreamer: New and Selected Poems 1966–1988 1989, Nice to See You: Homage to Ted Berrigan 1991, In and Out of This World: An Anthology of the St Mark's Poetry Project 1992, Iovis: All is Full of Love 1993, Kill or Cure 1994, Marriage: A Sentence 2000, The Beat Book 1996, Vow to Poetry 2001, In the Room of Never Grieve: New and Selected Poems, 1985–2003 2003, Dark Arcana 2003, Outrider. Manatee/Humanity 2009; contributions: various publications. *Honours:* National Endowment for the Arts Grant 1980, Achievement in Poetry Award, Bennington Coll. Alumni 1981. *Address:* Jack Kerouac School of Disembodied Poetics, Naropa University, 2130 Arapahoe Avenue, Boulder, CO 80302, USA (office). *Telephone:* (303) 546-3540 (office). *Fax:* (303) 546-5297 (office). *E-mail:* writingandpoetics@naropa.edu (office). *Website:* www.naropa.edu (office).

WALDROP, Rosmarie, MA, PhD; American (b. German) poet, writer, translator, editor and publisher; b. 24 Aug. 1935, Kitzingen-am-Main; d. of Josef Sebald and Friederike Sebald (née Wohlgemuth); m. Keith Waldrop 1959. *Education:* Univ. of Würzburg, Univ. of Aix-Marseille, France, Univ. of Freiburg, Univ. of Michigan, USA. *Career:* Wesleyan Univ., Middletown, Conn., USA 1964–70; Co-Ed. and Co-Publr (with Keith Waldrop), Burning Desk Press 1968–; Visiting Assoc. Prof., Brown Univ., Providence, RI, USA 1977–78, 1983, 1990–91; Visiting Lecturer, Tufts Univ., Boston, Mass, USA 1979–81; Vice-Pres. Anyart Contemporary Arts Center; mem. PEN, American Acad. of Arts and Sciences 2006–. *Publications:* poetry: The Aggressive Ways of the Casual Stranger 1972, The Road is Everywhere or Stop This Body 1978, When They Have Senses 1980, Nothing Has Changed 1981, Differences for Four Hands 1984, Streets Enough to Welcome Snow 1986, The Reproduction of Profiles 1987, Shorter American Memory 1988, Peculiar Motions 1990, Lawn of Excluded Middle 1993, A Key Into the Language of America 1994, Another Language: Selected Poems 1997, Split Infinites 1998, Reluctant Gravities 1999, Blindsight 2003, Love, like Pronouns 2003, Splitting Image 2005, Curves to the Apple 2006, Driven to Abstraction 2010; fiction: The Hanky of Pippin's Daughter 1986, A Form/of Taking/it All 1990; essays: Against Language? 1971, The Ground is the Only Figure: Notebook Spring 1996, Lavish Absence: Recalling and Rereading Edmond Jabès 2002, Dissonance (If You are Interested): Collected Essays 2005, various poetry chapbooks and trans. *Honours:* Chevalier, Ordre des Arts et des Lettres 1999; Major Hopwood Award in Poetry 1963, Alexander von Humboldt Fellowships 1970–71, 1975–76, Howard Foundation Fellowship 1974–75, Trans. Center Award, Columbia Univ. 1978, Nat. Endowment for the Arts Fellowships 1980, 1984, Gov.'s Arts Award, RI 1988, Fund for Poetry Award 1990, PEN/Book-of-the-Month Club Citation in Trans. 1991, Deutscher Akademischer Austauschdienst Fellowship, Berlin 1993, Harold Morton Landon Trans. Award 1994, Lila Wallace-Reader's Digest Writer's Award 1999–2001, Foundation for Contemporary Performance Arts Award 2003, PEN Award for Poetry in Translation 2008. *Address:* 71 Elmgrove Avenue, Providence, RI 02906, USA (home). *E-mail:* krwaldrop@earthlink.net (home).

WALI, Najem, MA; Iraqi journalist and novelist; b. 20 Oct. 1956, Al-Amarah. *Education:* Baghdad Univ. *Career:* emigrated to Hamburg, Germany 1980 at outbreak of Iran–Iraq war; lived in Madrid, Spain 1987–90, later returning to Hamburg; currently freelance journalist, Cultural Corresp. Al-Hayat newspaper. *Publications:* novels: War in the Destruction of Pleasure 1989, The Least Night to Mary 1995, Place Names Kumait 1997, Tel Al Leham (trans. as The Mountain of Meet) 2001, Jussifs Gesichter 2008, Reise in das Herz des Feindes (Journey into the Heart of the Enemy) 2009, Mala'ika al-Junub (Angels of the South) 2009; short story collections: There in the Strange City 1990, Waltzing Matilda 2001. *Literary Agent:* c/o Literarische Agentur Simon, Eisenacher Str. 76, 10823 Berlin, Germany. *Telephone:* (30) 31518844. *Fax:* (30) 31518855. *E-mail:* info@agentursimon.com. *Website:* www.agentursimon.com.

WALKER, Alice Malsenior, BA; American writer; b. 9 Feb. 1944, Eatonton, Ga; d. of Willie L. Walker and Minnie Walker (née Grant); m. Melvyn R. Leventhal 1967 (divorced 1977); one d. *Education:* Sarah Lawrence Coll. *Publications:* Once 1968, The Third Life of George Copeland 1970, Five Poems 1972, In Love and Trouble 1973, Langston Hughes, American Poet 1973, Revolutionary Petunias 1974, Meridian 1976, I Love Myself When I am Laughing 1979, You Can't Keep a Good Woman Down 1981, Good Night Willi Lee, I'll See You in the Morning 1979, The Color Purple 1982, In Search of Our Mothers' Gardens 1983, Horses Make a Landscape Look More Beautiful 1984, To Hell with Dying 1988, Living By the Word 1988, The Temple of My Familiar 1989, Her Blue Body Everything We Know: Earthling Poems (1965–90) 1991, Finding the Green Stone 1991, Possessing the Secret of Joy 1992, Warrior Marks (with Pratibha Parmar) 1993, Double Stitch: Black Women Write About Mothers and Daughters (jtly) 1993, Everyday Use 1994, By the Light of my Father's Smile 1998, Alice Walker Banned 1996, Everything We Love Can Be Saved 1997, The Same River Twice 1997, The Way Forward is with a Broken Heart (ed.) 2000, Absolute Trust in the Goodness of the Earth: New Poems 2003, The Third Life of Grange Copeland 2003, Now is the Time to Open Your Heart 2004, We Are the Ones We Have Been Waiting For (essays) 2007, Overcoming Speechlessness 2010, The World Has Changed: Conversations with Alice Walker 2010, Hard Times Require Furious Dancing 2010. *Honours:* Hon. PhD (Russell Sage Univ.) 1972; Hon. DHL (Univ. of Mass.) 1983; Bread Loaf Writers Conf. Scholar 1966, Ingram Merrill Foundation Fellowship 1967, McDowell Colony Fellowships 1967, 1977–78, Nat. Endowment for the Arts Grants 1969, 1977, Richard and Hinda Rosenthal Pound Award, American Acad. and Inst. of Arts and Letters 1974, Lillian Smith Award 1974, Rosenthal Award, Nat. Inst. of Arts and Letters 1973, Guggenheim Foundation Award 1979, Nat. Book Award (for The Color Purple) 1983, Pulitzer Prize (for The Color Purple) 1983, O. Henry Award 1986, Nora Astorga Leadership Award 1989, Freedom to Write Award, PEN Center West 1990. *Literary Agent:* Wendy Weil Agency Inc, 232 Madison Avenue, Suite 1300, New York, NY 10016, USA. *Website:* www.wendyweil.com; www.alicewalkersgarden.com.

WALKER, George Frederick, CM; Canadian playwright; b. 23 Aug. 1947, Toronto, Ont. *Education:* Riverdale Coll., Toronto. *Career:* resident playwright, New York Shakespeare Festival 1981. *Publications:* The Prince of Naples 1971, Ambush at Tether's End 1971, Sacktown Rag 1972, Baghdad Saloon 1973, Beyond Mozambique 1974, Ramona and the White Slaves 1976, Gossip 1977, Zastrozzi: The Master of Discipline 1977, Filthy Rich 1979, Rumours of our Death (musical) 1980, Theatre of the Film Noir 1981, Science and Madness 1982, The Art of War: An Adventure 1983, Criminals in Love 1984, Better Living 1986, Beautiful City 1987, Nothing Sacred, after Turgenev 1988, Love and Anger 1990, Escape from Happiness 1991, Shared Anxiety 1994. *Honours:* Governor-General's Awards in Drama 1985, 1988, Toronto Arts Award for Drama 1994. *Literary Agent:* Great North Artists, Suite 500, 345 Adelaide Street West, Toronto, ON, MV5 1S4 Canada. *Telephone:* (416) 925-2051.

WALKER, Jeanne Murray, BA, MA, PhD; American academic, scholar, poet and playwright; *Professor of English, University of Delaware*; b. 27 May 1944, Parkers Prairie, Minn.; d. of John Gerald Murray and Erna Aderhold Murray; m. E. Daniel Larkin 1983; one s. one d. *Education:* Wheaton Coll., Ill., Loyola Univ., Chicago, Univ. of Pennsylvania. *Career:* Prof. of English, Univ. of Delaware; mem. Editorial Bd Shenandoah 1994–, Image 2006–; Poetry Ed. Christianity and Literature 1988–2004; Commonwealth Speaker, Pa 2004–08; Mentor, Seattle Pacific Univ. Master of Fine Arts Program 2005–; mem. Dramatists' Guild, Christianity and Literature, Poets and Writers, Asscn of Writers & Writing Programs. *Publications include:* poetry: Nailing Up the Home Sweet Home 1980, Fugitive Angels 1985, Coming into History 1990, Stranger Than Fiction 1992, Gaining Time 1997, A Deed to the Light 2004, New Tracks, Night Falling 2009, eight plays 1990–2003; poems appeared on trains and buses in asscn with Poetry in Motion, American Acad. of Poets, The Open Door: 100 Years, 100 Poems Published in Poetry 2012; numerous quarterlies, reviews, journals, anthologies and anniversary vols, including American Scholar, Arizona Quarterly, American Poetry Review, Aspen Anthology, Ariel, Poetry Miscellany, Jawbone, Carolina Quarterly, Chicago Tribune, Christian Science Monitor, Cimarron Review, Chariton Review, Critical Quarterly, Georgia Review, Southern Humanities Review, Iowa Review, Image, The Journal, Kenyon Review, Louisville Review, Lyric, Massachusetts Review, Milkweed Chronicle, Descant, Northwest Review, Christian Century, New England Review, Nantucket Review, Wascona Review, Poet and Critic, 2 Plus 2, Poetry Now, St Andrews Review, Pennsylvania Review, Kansas Quarterly, Seattle Review, Poetry, Shenandoah, Painted Bride Quarterly, Whetstone, Boulevard, Partisan Review, Prairie Schooner, The Nation. *Honours:* Delaware Humanities Council Grant 1979, Delaware Arts Council Grant 1981, eight Pennsylvania Council on the Arts Fellowships 1983–2007, Prairie Schooner/Strousse Award 1988, winner Washington Nat. Theatre Competition 1990, Colladay Award for Poetry 1992, Fellow, Center for Advanced Studies 1993, Nat. Endowment for the Arts Fellowship 1994, two Brigham Young Theatre Lewis Prizes for New Plays 1995, 1997, Pew Fellow in the Arts 1998, Stagetime Award 1998, Readers Choice Award for Poetry 2003, Glenna Luschi Prairie Prize for Poetry 2007. *Address:* Department of English, 131 Memorial Hall, University of Delaware, Newark, DE 19716, USA (office). *Telephone:* (610) 660-5230 (office). *E-mail:* jwalker@udel.edu (office). *Website:* www.jeannemurraywalker.com.

WALKER, Lou Ann, BA; American writer; b. 9 Dec. 1952, Hartford City, IN; m. Speed Vogel 1986; one d. *Education:* Ball State Univ., Univ. of Besançon, Harvard Univ. *Career:* reporter, Indianapolis News 1976; Asst to Exec. Ed., New York (magazine), New York 1976–77, Cosmopolitan, New York City 1979–80; Asst Ed., Esquire Magazine 1977–79; Assoc. Ed., Diversion (magazine), New York City 1980–81; Ed., Direct (magazine), New York City 1981–82; Sign Language Interpreter for New York Society for the Deaf; Consultant to Broadway's Theater Development Fund and sign language adviser on many Broadway shows 1984–; Contributing Ed., New York Woman 1990–92; mem. Authors' Guild. *Publications:* Amy: The Story of a Deaf Child 1985, A Loss for Words: The Story of Deafness in a Family (autobiog.) 1986, Hand, Heart and Mind 1994, Roy Lichtenstein: The Artist at Work 1994; contributions: New York Times Book Review, Chicago Sun-Times, Esquire, New York Times Magazine, New York Woman, Life. *Honours:* Rockefeller Foundation Humanities Fellowship 1982–83, Christopher Award 1987, National Endowment for the Arts Creative Writing Grant 1988.

WALKER, Martin, MA; British journalist, writer and broadcaster; *Senior Fellow, Global Business Policy Council, A.T. Kearney Inc.*; b. 23 Jan. 1947, Durham, England; m. Julia Watson 1978. *Education:* Balliol Coll., Oxford, Harvard Univ. *Career:* staff, The Guardian, Manchester 1972–, Moscow Bureau Chief 1983–88, US Bureau Chief 1989–98; Ed.-in-Chief United Press International 2004–07; Sr Fellow, Global Business Policy Council, A.T. Kearney Inc. 2007–; numerous radio and TV broadcasts; many lectures; Congressional Fellow, American Political Science Assen 1970–71; Public Policy Fellow, Woodrow Wilson Int. Center for Scholars 2000–01; Sr Fellow, World Policy Inst., New School Univ., New York; mem. Nat. Union of Journalists. *Television:* Martin Walker's Russia (BBC series) 1989. *Publications:* The National Front 1977, Daily Sketches: A History of Political Cartoons 1978, The Infiltrators (novel) 1978, A Mercenary Calling (novel) 1980, The Eastern Question (novel) 1981, Powers of the Press: A Comparative Study of the World's Leading Newspapers 1981, The Waking Giant: Gorbachev and Perestroika 1987, Martin Walker's Russia 1989, The Independent Traveller's Guide to the Soviet Union 1990, The Insight Guide to Washington, DC 1992, The Cold War: A History 1993, The President We Deserve: Bill Clinton: His Rise, Falls, and Comebacks 1996, America Reborn: A Twentieth-Century Narrative in Twenty-Six Lives 2000, The Iraq War 2003; contrib. to anthologies and periodicals. *Address:* Global Business Policy Council, A.T. Kearney, Inc., 8100 Boone Blvd, Suite 400, Vienna, VA 22182, USA (office). *Telephone:* (703) 891-5500 (office). *Website:* www.atkearney.com (office).

WALKER, Mary Willis, BA; American writer; b. 24 May 1942, Foxpoint, WI; m. (divorced); two d. *Education:* Duke Univ. *Career:* mem. Texas Inst. of Letters, MWA, Sisters in Crime. Int. Asscn of Crime Writers, Austin Writers' League. *Publications:* Zero at the Bone 1991, The Red Scream 1994, Under the Beetle's Cellar 1995, All the Dead Lie Down 1998, Mom's in Prison… Again (documentary script); contrib. essays to periodicals, including New York Times, Mostly Murder, book reviews to Mostly Murder, Austin American-Statesman. *Honours:* Agatha Award 1991, Mystery Readers Int. Macavity Award 1991, Int. Asscn of Crime Writers Hammett Award 1995, Anthony Award, Bouchercon 1995, MWA Edgar Award 1995. *Address:* POB 5612, Austin, TX 78763-5612 (office); Inkwell Management, 521 Fifth Avenue, New York, NY 10175, USA (office). *Fax:* (512) 323-0209 (office). *E-mail:* mwillis@austin.rr.com (office).

WALL, Ethan (see Holmes, Bryan John)

WALL, Geoffrey, (Geoffrey Chadwick), BA, BPhil; British academic, biographer and translator; *Reader in Modern French Literature, University of York*; b. 10 July 1950, Cheshire, England. *Education:* Univ. of Sussex, St Edmund Hall. *Career:* Lecturer, Dept of English and Related Literature, Univ. of York 1975–97, Sr Lecturer 1997–2002, Reader in Modern French Literature 2002–; Co-Ed. Cambridge Quarterly 1998–; mem. Asscn of Univ. Teachers. *Publications:* translator: Madame Bovary, by Gustave Flaubert 1992, The Dictionary of Received Ideas, by Gustave Flaubert 1994, Selected Letters, by Gustave Flaubert 1997, Flaubert: A Life 2001, Sentimental Education, by Gustave Flaubert 2004, Three Tales 2005; Modern Times: Selected Writings, by Jean-Paul Sartre (ed) 1999; contrib. to scholarly journals and newspapers. *Literary Agent:* c/o David Higham Associates Ltd, 5–8 Lower John Street, Golden Square, London, W1F 9HA, England. *Telephone:* (20) 7434-5900. *Fax:* (20) 7437-1072. *E-mail:* dha@davidhigham.co.uk. *Website:* www.davidhigham .co.uk. *Address:* Department of English and Related Literature, University of York, Heslington, York, YO10 5DD, England (office). *Telephone:* (1904) 323334 (office). *Fax:* (1904) 323372 (office). *E-mail:* geoffrey.wall@york.ac.uk (office). *Website:* www.york.ac.uk (office).

WALL, William, BA; Irish novelist and poet; b. 1955, Cork; m.; two c. *Education:* Univ. Coll. Cork. *Publications:* novels: Alice Falling 2000, Minding Children 2001, The Map of Tenderness 2003, This is the Country 2005; poetry: Mathematics and Other Poems 1997, Fahrenheit Says Nothing To Me 2004; short stories: No Paradiso 2006; contrib. to The Irish Press, The Sunday Tribune, Phoenix Irish Short Stories, Southword, Carve magazine, Faber Book of Best Irish Short Stories, RTÉ Radio. *Honours:* Patrick Kavanagh Award for Poetry 1995, American Ireland Fund/Listowel Writers' Week Award (Poetry) 1996, 1997, (Short Story) 1998, Seán O'Faoláin Award (Short Story) 2003. *E-mail:* kirwall@eircom.net (office). *Website:* www.williamwall .eu. *Literary Agent:* c/o Gill Coleridge, Rogers, Coleridge & White, 20 Powis Mews, London, WC11 1JN, England. *Telephone:* (20) 7221-3717. *Fax:* (20) 7229-9084. *E-mail:* gillc@rcwlitagency.co.uk. *Website:* www.rcwlitagency.co .uk.

WALLACE, Ian Robert; Canadian writer and illustrator; b. 31 March 1950, Niagara Falls, ON; m. Debra Wiedman. *Education:* Ontario College of Art. *Career:* mem. Canadian Children's Book Centre, Writer's Union of Canada. *Publications:* writer and illustrator: Julie News 1974, The Christmas Tree House 1976, Chin Chiang and the Dragon's Dance 1984, The Sparrow's Song 1986, Morgan the Magnificent 1987, Mr Kneebone's New Digs 1991, A Winter's Tale 1997, Boy of the Deeps 1999, Duncan's Way 2000, The True Story of Trapper Jack's Left Big Toe 2002, The Naked Lady 2002, The Man Who Walked the Earth 2003, Mavis and Merna 2005, The Huron Carol 2006, The Sleeping Porch 2008; illustrator: Seven books 1986–96; other: The Sandwich (with A. Wood) 1974. *Honours:* A. F. Howard Gibbons Award, Canadian Library Asscn 1984, IODE Book Award 1985, IBBY Honour List 1986, 2000, Mr Christie Book Award 1990, Aesop Accolade List 1994, Smithsonian Best Books of the Year List 2000. *E-mail:* ianwallacebooks@gmail.com (office). *Website:* www.ian-wallace.com.

WALLACE, Naomi French, BA, MFA; American poet and playwright; b. 17 Aug. 1960, Kentucky; m. Bruce McLeod; three d. *Education:* Hampshire Coll., Univ. of Iowa. *Career:* plays have been performed at theatres in UK and USA; teacher of play writing, Univ. of Iowa 1990–93; Playwright-in-Residence, Illinois State Univ. 1994. *Plays include:* In the Heart of America, Slaughter City (Mobil Prize) 1995, One Flea Spare (Obie Award for Best Play) 1997, Birdy 1997, Trestle at Pope Lick Creek 1999, Twenty One Positions: A Cartographic Dream of the Middle East (jtly) 2008, Things of Dry Hours 2009, One Short Sleepe 2009, The Hard Weather Boating Party 2010, And I and Silence 2011. *Films include:* Lawn Dogs 1997 (writer), War Boys 2009. *Publications include:* To Dance a Stony Field (poems) 1995; contrib. to reviews, journals and magazines. *Honours:* Susan Smith Blackburn Award, The Nation/Discovery Award, Fellowship of Southern Writers Award. *Literary Agent:* Charlotte Knight, Knight Hall Agency, Lower Ground Floor, 7 Mallow Street, London, EC1Y 8RQ, England. *E-mail:* office@knighthallagency.com.

WALLACE, Ronald William, BA, MA, PhD; American poet and academic; *Felix Pollak Professor of Poetry, University of Wisconsin, Madison*; b. 18 Feb. 1945, Cedar Rapids, Ia; m. Margaret Elizabeth McCreight 1968; two d. *Education:* Coll. of Wooster, Univ. of Michigan. *Career:* Dir of Creative Writing, Univ. of Wisconsin, Madison 1975–, , Halls-Bascom Prof. of English 1993–, Felix Pollak Prof. of Poetry 1999–; Series Ed., Brittingham Prize in Poetry 1985–; Dir Wisconsin Inst. for Creative Writing 1985–98; mem. Poets and Writers, Associated Writing Programs. *Publications:* Henry James and the Comic Form 1975, Installing the Bees 1977, Cucumbers 1977, The Last Laugh 1979, The Facts of Life 1979, Plums, Stones, Kisses and Hooks 1981, Tunes For Bears To Dance To 1983, God Be With the Clown 1984, The Owl in the Kitchen 1985, People and Dog in the Sun 1987, Vital Signs 1989, The Makings of Happiness 1991, Time's Fancy 1994, The Uses of Adversity 1998, Quick Bright Things 2000, Long for This World: New and Selected Poems 2003, For a Limited Time Only 2008; contrib. to New Yorker, Atlantic, Nation, Poetry, Southern Review, Poetry Northwest. *Honours:* Hopwood Award for Poetry 1970, Council for Wisconsin Writers Awards 1978, 1979, 1984, 1985, 1986, 1988, Helen Bullis Prize in Poetry 1985, Robert E. Gard Award for Excellence in Poetry 1990, Posner Poetry Prize 1992, 2004, Gerald A. Bartell Award in the Arts 1994, Wisconsin Library Association Notable Author 1994, Banta Award 1995, Hilldale Award 1998, Lynde and Harry Bradley Major (Lifetime) Achievement Award 1998, Alliant Energy/Underkoffler Distinguished Teaching Award 2002, George Garrett Award 2005. *Address:* Department of English, University of Wisconsin, 7195 Helen C. White Hall, 600 North Park Street, Madison, WI 53706, USA (office). *Telephone:* (608) 263-3705 (office). *Fax:* (608) 263-3709 (office). *E-mail:* rwallace@facstaffwisc.edu (office). *Website:* mendota.english.wisc.edu/~WALLACE (office).

WALLACE-CRABBE, Christopher Keith, MA, FAHA; Australian poet and critic; b. 6 May 1934, Melbourne, Vic.; s. of Kenneth Eyre Inverell Wallace-Crabbe and Phyllis Vera May Wallace-Crabbe (née Cock); m. 1st Helen Margaret Wiltshire 1957; one s. one d.; m. 2nd Marianne Sophie Feil 1979; two s.; m. 3rd Kristin Headlam. *Education:* Melbourne Univ., Yale Univ., USA. *Career:* cadet metallurgist 1951–52; then journalist, clerk, schoolteacher; Lockie Fellow in Australian Literature, Univ. of Melbourne 1962; Harkness Fellow, Yale Univ., USA 1965–67; Sr Lecturer in English, Univ. of Melbourne 1967, Reader 1976, Prof. 1987–, Personal Chair 1987–97; Prof. Emer. Australian Centre 1997–; Visiting Chair in Australian Studies, Harvard Univ., USA 1987–88; Chair. Australian Poetry Centre 2007. *Publications:* The Music of Division 1959, Selected Poems 1974, Melbourne or the Bush 1974, The Emotions are not Skilled Workers 1980, Toil and Spin: Two Directions in Modern Poetry 1980, Splinters (novel) 1981, The Amorous Cannibal 1985, I'm Deadly Serious 1988, Sangue è l'Acqua 1989, For Crying out Loud 1990, Falling into Language 1990, Poetry and Belief 1990, From the Republic of Conscience 1992, Rungs of Time 1993, Selected Poems 1956–94 1995, Whirling 1998, By and Large 2001, The Universe Looks Down 2005, Read It Again 2005, The Thing Itself 2007, Telling a Hawk from a Handsaw 2008. *Honours:* Hon. DLitt (Melbourne) 2006; Masefield Prize for Poetry 1957, Farmer's Poetry Prize 1964, Grace Leven Prize 1986, Dublin Prize 1987, Christopher Brennan Award 1990, Age Book of the Year Prize 1995, Philip Hodgins Memorial Medal 2002, Centenary Medal 2003. *Address:* The Australian Centre, University of Melbourne, Parkville, Vic. 3052 (office); 7 De Carle Street, Brunswick, Vic. 3056, Australia (home). *Telephone:* (3) 8344-6998 (office); (3) 9386-6938 (home). *Fax:* (3) 9347-7731 (office). *E-mail:* ckwc@unimelb.edu.au (office). *Website:* www.hlc.unimelb.edu.au/cwc (office).

WALLENSTEIN, Barry, BA, MA, PhD; American poet and academic; b. 13 Feb. 1940, New York, NY; m. Lorna Harbus 1978; one s. one d. *Education:* New York Univ. *Career:* Prof. of English, City College, CUNY 1965–2006, now Prof. Emer., Dir Poetry Outreach Center, coordinator of Annual Spring Poetry Festival; Exchange Prof., Univ. of Paris 1981, Polytechnic of North London, 1987–88; Assoc. Ed. American Book Review; Writer-in-Residence, Northern Michigan Univ. 1993; mem. Acad. of American Poets, Poets and Writers, Poets House. *Music collaborations:* albums: Tony's Blues, Pandemonium, Euphoria Ripens. *Publications:* Poetry: Beast is a Wolf with Brown Fire, 1977; Roller Coaster Kid, 1982; Love and Crush, 1991; The Short Life of the Five Minute Dancer, 1993; A Measure of Conduct, 1999. Criticism: Visions and Revisions: An Approach to Poetry, 1971. Contributions: anthologies, reviews, quarterlies, and journals. *Honours:* CUNY Research Fund Grant; MacDowell Colony Residency Fellowship. *Address:* c/o NYQ Books, The New York Quarterly, PO Box 2015, Old Chelsea Station, New York, NY 10113, USA.

WALLER, Robert James; American writer and musician; b. 1 Aug. 1939, s. of Robert Waller Sr and Ruth Waller; m. Georgia A. Wiedemeier 1961 (divorced 1997); one d. *Education:* Univ. of Northern Iowa, Indiana Univ. *Career:* Prof. of Man., Univ. of N Iowa 1968–91, Dean of Business School 1979–86 (retd); singer; guitarist; flautist. *Album:* The Ballads of Madison County 1993. *Publications:* Just Beyond the Firelight 1988, One Good Road is Enough 1990, Iowa: Perspectives on Today and Tomorrow 1991, The Bridges of Madison County 1992, Slow Waltz at Cedar Bend 1994, Old Songs in a New Café 1994, Selected Essays 1994, Border Music 1995, Puerto-Vallarta Squeeze 1995, A Thousand Country Roads 2002, High Plains Tango 2005, The Long Night of Winchell Dear 2006.

WALLEY, Byron (see Card, Orson Scott)

WALLIN, Raimo S.; Finnish novelist, playwright, poet and publisher; m. Terttu Wallin 1972. *Career:* fmr teacher; f. publishing co, Kustannus Sokrates. *Publications:* 100 Vuotta Kansakoulutoimintaa Vanajassa (with Uolevi Nurminen) 1965, Alttari (play) 1967, Matkan Loppu (short stories) 1967, Persialaisella Matolla 1972, Saul Ja Daavid 1972, Luova Kirjoitus 1973, Kansanruno-Kalevala (with Merja Totro, Terttu Wallin) 1979, Luova Kirjoitus 5 1982, Minä, Muut, Maailma 1982, Minä, Muut, Maailma 1983, Vapaat Kahleet 1986, Kaikki Tiet Käyvät Roomaan 1997, Luova Kirjoitus ABCD 1998. *Address:* c/o Kustannus Sokrates Ky, Ounasvaarantie 1 C 75, 00970 Helsinki, Finland.

WALSER, Martin, DPhil; German writer, playwright and poet; b. 24 March 1927, Wasserburg, Bodensee; s. of Martin Walser and Augusta Schmid; m. Käthe Jehle 1950; four d. *Education:* Theologisch-Philosophische Hochschule, Regensburg and Univ. of Tübingen. *Career:* writer 1951–. *Publications:* novels include: Ehen in Philippsburg 1957, Halbzeit 1960, Das Einhorn 1966, Fiction 1970, Die Gallistlische Krankheit 1972, Der Sturz 1973, Jenseits der Liebe 1976, Ein fliehendes Pferd 1978, Seelenarbeit 1979, Das Schwanenhaus 1980, Brief an Lord Liszt 1982, Brandung 1985, Dorle und Wolf 1987, Jagd 1988, Die Verteidigung der Kindheit 1991, Ohne einander 1993, Finks Krieg 1996, Ein springender Brunnen 1998, Der Lebenslauf der Liebe 2001, Tod eines Kritikers 2002, Der Augenblick der Liebe 2004, Die Verwaltung des Nichts 2004, Leben und Schreiben 2005, Angstblüte 2006, Der Lebensroman des Andreas Beck 2006, Das geschundene Tier 2007, Ein Liebender Mann 2008; short stories: Ein Flugzeug über dem Haus 1955, Lügengeschichten 1964; plays: Der Abstecher 1961, Eiche und Angora 1962, Überlebensgross Herr Krott 1963, Der schwarze Schwan 1964, Die Zimmerschlacht 1967, Ein Kinderspiel 1970, Das Sauspiel 1975, In Goethe's Hand 1982, Die Ohrfeige 1986, Das Sofa 1992, Kaschmir in Parching 1995; essays: Beschreibung einer Form, Versuch über Franz Kafka 1961, Erfahrungen und Leseerfahrungen 1965, Heimatkunde 1968, Wie und wovon handelt Literatur 1973, Wer ist ein Schriftsteller 1978, Selbstbewusstsein und Ironie 1981, Messmers Gedanken 1985, Über Deutschland reden 1988, Vormittag eines Schriftstellers 1994, Messmers Reisen 2003; poetry: Der Grund zur Freude 1978, Die Verwaltung des Nichts 2004. *Honours:* Grosses Bundesverdienstkreuz mit Stern 1997, Officier, L'Ordre des Arts et des Lettres; Group 47 Prize 1955, Hermann-Hesse Prize 1957, Gerhart-Hauptmann Prize 1962, Schiller Prize 1980, Büchner Prize 1981, Orden pour le mérite 1994, Friedenspreis des Deutschen Buchhandels 1998. *Address:* Zum Hecht 36, 88662 Überlingen-Nussdorf, Germany (home). *Telephone:* (7551) 4131 (home). *Fax:* (7551) 68494 (home). *E-mail:* nussdorf@t-online.de (home).

WALSH, (Mary) Noëlle, BA (Hons); British journalist; *Director, The Value for Money Co. Ltd;* b. 26 Dec. 1954, Birmingham, England; d. of Thomas Walsh and Mary Walsh (née Ferguson); m. David Heslam 1988; one s. one d. *Education:* Univ. of East Anglia. *Career:* Editorial Asst Public Relations Dept, St Dunstan's Org. for the War-Blinded 1977–79; News Ed. Cosmopolitan 1979–85; Ed. London Week 1985–86; freelance writer 1986–; Deputy Ed. Good Housekeeping 1986–87, Ed. 1987–91; Dir The Value For Money Co. Ltd 1992–. *Television:* Presenter, Consumer Issues, Channel 5 1998, contrib. to numerous news and money programmes 1992–. *Publications:* Hot Lips, the Ultimate Kiss and Tell Guide 1985, Ragtime to Wartime: the best of Good Housekeeping 1922–39 1986, The Home Front: the best of Good Housekeeping 1939–45 (co-ed) 1987, The Christmas Book: the best of Good Housekeeping at Christmas 1922–62 (co-ed) 1988, Food Glorious Food: eating and drinking with Good Housekeeping 1922–42 1990, Things My Mother Should Have Told Me 1991, Childhood Memories 1991, The Good Deal Directory 1992–, The Home Shopping Handbook 1995, Baby on a Budget 1995, Wonderful Wedding That Won't Cost a Fortune 1996, The Good Mail Order Guide 1996, The Good Deal Directory (annual) 1994–. *Address:* PO Box 4, Lechlade, Glos., GL7 3YB, England (office). *Telephone:* (1367) 860017 (office). *Fax:* (1367) 860177 (office). *E-mail:* nheslam@aol.com (office). *Website:* www.gooddealdirectory.co.uk; www.gooddealhouse.com; www.ukgrandsales.co.uk.

WALSHE, Aubrey Peter, BA, DPhil; British academic and writer; *Professor Emeritus of Political Science, University of Notre Dame;* b. 12 Jan. 1934, Johannesburg, South Africa; m. Catherine Ann Pettifer 1957; one s. three d. *Education:* Wadham Coll., Oxford, St Antony's Coll., Oxford. *Career:* Lecturer, Univ. of Lesotho 1959–62; Prof. of Political Science, Univ. of Notre Dame, USA 1967, now Prof. Emer., Fellow, Joan Kroc Inst. for Int. Peace Studies. *Publications:* The Rise of African Nationalism in South Africa 1971, Black Nationalism in South Africa 1974, Church Versus State in South Africa 1983, Prophetic Christianity and the Liberation Movement in South Africa 1996; contrib. to Cambridge History of Africa 1986, professional journals and newspapers. *Honours:* Notre Dame Grenville Clark Award for contributions to peace and human rights 1979, Kaneb Teaching Award 2000. *Address:* Kroc Institute for International Peace Studies 100 Hesburgh Center, University of Notre Dame, Notre Dame, IN 46556-5677, USA (office). *Fax:* (574) 631-6973 (office). *E-mail:* A.P.Walshe.1@nd.edu (office). *Website:* politicalscience.nd.edu (office).

WALT, Stephen Martin, BA, MA, PhD; American academic; *Professor of International Affairs, John F. Kennedy School of Government, Harvard University;* b. 2 July 1955; m.; two c. *Education:* Stanford Univ., Univ. of Calif. *Career:* part-time mem. Professional Staff Center for Naval Analyses 1980–82; Research Fellow, Center for Science and Int. Affairs, Harvard Univ. 1981–84, now Prof. of Int. Affairs, Academic Dean, John F. Kennedy School of Govt 2002–06; Asst Prof., Princeton Univ. 1984–89; Resident Assoc., Carnegie Endowment for Int. Peace 1986–87; Guest Scholar Brookings Inst. 1988; Assoc. Prof., Univ. of Chicago 1989–95, Prof. 1995–99, Master, Social Sciences Collegiate Div. and Deputy Dean, Div. of Social Sciences 1996–99; Visiting Prof., Nanyang Tech. Univ. Singapore 2000; mem. Editorial Bds Security Studies, Foreign Policy, Bulletin of the Atomic Scientists, Columbia Int. Affairs Online Service, Journal of Cold War Studies; Co-Ed. Cornell Studies in Security Affairs; mem. American Political Science Asscn, Int. Studies Asscn, Soc. of Historians of American Foreign Relations, IISS; Fellow, American Acad. of Arts and Sciences 2005. *Publications:* The Origins of Alliances 1987, Revolution and War 1996, Taming American Power: The Global Response to US Primacy 2006, The Israel Lobby and U.S. Foreign Policy (with John Mearsheimer) 2007; numerous articles and chapters in journals and books. *Honours:* Edgar S. Furniss Nat. Security Book Award 1988, Hugh Nott Best Article Prize 2002. *Address:* John F. Kennedy School of Government, Harvard University, 79 John F. Kennedy Street, Cambridge, MA 02138, USA (office). *Telephone:* (617) 495-5712 (office). *Fax:* (617) 495-8963 (office). *E-mail:* stephen_walt@harvard.edu (office). *Website:* www.hks.harvard.edu/fs/swalt (office); walt.foreignpolicy.com.

WALTERS, Minette, BA; British author; b. (Minette Jebb), 26 Sept. 1949, Bishop's, Stortford, Herts., England; d. of Capt. and Mrs S. H. D. Jebb; m. Alexander Walters 1978; two s. *Education:* Univ. of Durham. *Career:* patron of numerous charities. *Publications:* The Ice House (Crime Writers' Asscn (CWA) John Creasey Award for Best First Crime Novel) 1992, The Sculptress 1993, The Scold's Bridle (CWA Gold Dagger 1994) 1994, The Dark Room 1995, The Echo 1997, The Breaker 1998, The Tinder Box 1999, The Shape of Snakes (Pelle Rosekrantz Award, Denmark) 2000, Acid Row 2001, Fox Evil (CWA Gold Dagger 2003) 2002, Disordered Minds 2003, The Devil's Feather 2005, Chickenfeed 2006, The Chameleon's Shadow 2007. *Honours:* Hon. DLitt (Bournemouth) 2005, (Southampton Solent) 2006; John Creasey Award 1992, Macavity Award 1993, Edgar Allan Poe Award 1993, CWA Gold Dagger 1994, 2003, Pelle Rosenkrantz Prize 2000, Quick Reads Award 2006, Coventry Inspiration Award 2007. *Literary Agent:* c/o Gregory and Company Authors' Agents, 3 Barb Mews, London, W6 7PA, England. *Telephone:* (20) 7610-4676. *Fax:* (20) 7610-4686. *E-mail:* info@gregoryandcompany.co.uk. *Website:* www.gregoryandcompany.co.uk; www.minettewalters.co.uk.

WALTON, Jo; British/Canadian science fiction and fantasy author; b. 1 Dec. 1964, Aberdare, Wales; m. 1st Ken Walton 1990 (divorced 1997); one s.; m. 2nd Emmet A. O'Brien 2001; one s. *Education:* Aberdare Girls' Grammar School, Howell's School, Llandaff, Cardiff, Oswestry School, Shropshire, Univ. of Lancaster. *Career:* collaborations on role–playing game supplements with Ken Walton 1990s; moved to Montreal, Canada 2002. *Publications include:* novels: The King's Peace (John W. Campbell Award for Best New Writer 2002) 2000, The King's Name 2001, The Prize in the Game 2002, Tooth and Claw (World Fantasy Award 2004) 2003, Farthing 2006, Ha'penny (Jt Winner, Prometheus Award 2008) 2007, Half a Crown 2008, Lifelode (Mythopoeic Award 2010) 2009, Among Others (Nebula Award for Best Novel 2012) 2011; poetry chapbooks: Muses and Lurkers 2001, Sibyls and Spaceships 2009; various short stories, articles and poems. *Address:* c/o Tor Books, Tom Doherty Associates LLC, Pan Macmillan, 175 Fifth Avenue, New York, NY 10010, USA (office); c/o Tor UK, Pan Macmillan, 20 New Wharf Road, London, N1 9RR, England (office). *Telephone:* (20) 7014-6186 (office). *E-mail:* questions@tor.com (office); bluejo@gmail.com (home). *Website:* www.tor.com (office); www.torbooks.co.uk (office); papersky.livejournal.com (home).

WALVIN, James, OBE, BA, MA, DLitt, DPhil; British historian, academic and author; *Professor Emeritus, University of York;* b. 2 Jan. 1942, Manchester, England; m. Jennifer Walvin, two s. *Education:* Univ. of Keele, McMaster Univ., Canada. *Career:* Prof. Emer. of History, Univ. of York. *Publications:* A Jamaica Plantation: Worthy Park 1670–1870 (with M. Craton) 1970, The Black Presence: A Documentary of the Negro in Britain 1971, Black and White: The Negro and English Society 1555–1945 1973, The People's Game: A Social History of British Football 1975, Slavery, Abolition, and Emancipation (co-ed.) 1976, Beside the Seaside: A Social History of the Popular Seaside Holiday 1978, Leisure and Society 1830–1950 1978, Abolition of the Atlantic Slave Trade (co-ed.) 1981, A Child's World: A Social History of English Childhood 1800–1914 1982, Slavery and British Society 1776–1848 (ed.) 1982, English Radicals and Reformers 1776–1848 (with E. Royle) 1982, Slavery and the Slave Trade 1983, Black Personalities: Africans in Britain in the Era of Slavery 1983, Leisure in Britain Since 1800 (co-ed.) 1983, Urban England

1776–1851 1984, Manliness and Morality (co-ed.) 1985, Football and the Decline of Britain 1986, England, Slaves, and Freedom, 1776–1838 1986, Victorian Values 1987, Black Ivory: A History of British Slavery 1992, Slaves and Slavery 1992, The People's Game: The History of Football Revisited 1994, The Life and Times of Henry Clarke of Jamaica 1994, Questioning Slavery 1996, Fruits of Empire: Exotic Produce and British Taste 1660–1800 1997, The Quakers: Money and Morals 1997, An African Life 1998, Making the Black Atlantic 2000, The Only Game 2001, The Slavery Reader (ed. with Gad Heuman) 2003, The Trader, The Owner, The Slave 2007, A Short History of Slavery 2007. *Address:* c/o Department of History, University of York, Heslington, Yorks. YO1 5DD, England (office). *E-mail:* jameswalvin@aol.com (office).

WALWICZ, Ania, DipEd; poet, dramatist, writer, artist and academic; *Lecturer in Creative Writing, Royal Melbourne Institute of Technology*; b. 19 May 1951, Swidnica, Poland. *Education:* Univ. of Melbourne, Victorian Coll. of the Arts. *Career:* Writer-in-Residence, Deakin Univ. 1987–88, Murdoch Univ. 1988; Lecturer in Creative Writing, Victorian Coll. of the Arts, Melbourne Univ., Royal Melbourne Inst. of Tech. 1993–. *Composition:* Corruption (opera, commissioned by Ministry of Arts 2004, in devt by Chamber Made Opera, North Melbourne 2005–06). *Recording:* Body 1999. *Plays:* Girlboytalk 1986, Dissecting Mice 1989, Elegant 1990, Red Roses 1992, Telltale 1994, Scattergun Project (St Martin's Theatre, Melbourne) 2004. *Radio:* Voiceprints–Recordings 2007, 2009, Books and Writing Show — State Library of Victoria (recordings) 2009. *Television:* Overload Poetry 2010. *Publications:* Writing 1982, Boat 1989, Red Roses 1992; contrib. to over 200 anthologies. *Honours:* Australian Council Literature Board grants, and Fellowship 1990, Victorian Premier's Literary Awards New Writing Prize 1990. *Address:* School of Media and Communication, RMIT, GPO Box 2476V, Melbourne, Vic. 3001, Australia (office). *Telephone:* (3) 9925-4525 (office). *E-mail:* ania.walwicz@rmit.edu.au (office). *Website:* www.rmit.edu.au/mediacommunication (office).

WALZER, Michael, BA, PhD; American writer, academic and editor; b. 3 March 1935, New York, NY; m. Judith Borodovko 1956; two d. *Education:* Brandeis and Harvard Univs, Univ. of Cambridge, UK. *Career:* Asst Prof. of Politics, Princeton Univ., NJ 1962–66; Assoc. Prof., Harvard Univ. 1966–68, Prof. of Govt 1968–80; Ed. Dissent 1964–; Prof. of Social Science, School of Social Science, Inst. for Advanced Study, Princeton, NJ 1980, now Perm. Faculty Mem. Emer.; Fellow, Straus Inst. for the Advanced Study of Law and Justice, New York Univ. School of Law 2010–11; mem. Conf. on the Study of Political Thought, Soc. of Ethical and Legal Philosophy; mem. Editorial Bd Political Theory; Contributing Ed. The New Republic (weekly newsmagazine); mem. Bd of Govs Hebrew Univ. *Publications:* The Revolution of the Saints: A Study in the Origins of Radical Politics 1965, The Political Imagination in Literature (co-ed. with Philip Green) 1968, Obligations: Essays on Disobedience, War and Citizenship 1970, Political Action: A Practical Guide to Movement Politics 1971, Regicide and Revolution: Speeches at the Trial of Louis XVI (ed.) 1974, Just and Unjust Wars: A Moral Argument with Historical Illustrations 1977, Radical Principles: Reflections of an Unreconstructed Democrat 1977, Spheres of Justice: A Defense of Pluralism and Equality 1983, Exodus and Revolution 1985, Interpretation and Social Criticism 1987, The Company of Critics: Social Criticism and Political Commitment in the Twentieth Century 1988, Civil Society and American Democracy (selected essays in German) 1992, What it Means to be an American 1992, Thick and Thin: Moral Argument at Home and Abroad 1994, Pluralism, Justice and Equality (with David Miller) 1995, Toward a Global Civil Society (ed.) 1995, On Toleration 1997, Arguments from the Left (selected essays in Swedish) 1977, Pluralism and Democracy (selected essays in French) 1997, Reason, Politics and Pasion (The Horkheimer Lectures, in German) 1999, The Jewish Political Tradition, Vol. 1 Authority (co-ed with Menachem Lorberbaum, Noam Zohar and Yair Lorberbaum) 2000, Exilic Politics in the Hebrew Bible 2001, War, Politics, and Morality (selected essays in Spanish) 2001, The Thread of Politics: Democracy, Social Criticism, and World Government (selected essays in Italian) 2002, Erklärte Kriege—Kriegserklärungen (selected essays in German) 2003, Arguing About War (selected essays and articles) 2004, Politics and Passion 2004, Law, Politics, and Morality in Judaism 2006, Thinking Politically 2007; contribs to professional journals. *Honours:* Dr hc (Lawrence Univ.) 1980, (Brandeis Univ.) 1981, (Georgetown Univ.) 1992, (Kalamazoo Coll.) 1994, (Tel-Aviv Univ.) 2003, Brandeis Univ. Doctorate Alumni Award 2001; Fulbright Fellow, Univ. of Cambridge 1956–57, Harbison Award 1971, Spinoza Lens 2008. *Address:* School of Social Science, Institute for Advanced Study, Einstein Drive, Princeton, NJ 08540, USA (office). *Telephone:* (609) 734-8253 (office). *Fax:* (609) 951-4434 (office). *E-mail:* walzer@ias.edu (office). *Website:* www.sss.ias.edu (office).

WAMBAUGH, Joseph, MA; American writer; b. 22 Jan. 1937, East Pittsburgh, PA; s. of Joseph A. Wambaugh and Anne Malloy; m. Dee Allsup 1955; two s. (one deceased) one d. *Education:* Calif. State Coll., Los Angeles. *Career:* served US Marine Corps 1954–57; police officer, LA 1960–74; creator, TV series, Police Story 1973. *Publications:* The New Centurions 1971, The Blue Knight 1972, The Onion Field 1973, The Choirboys 1975, The Black Marble 1978, The Glitter Dome 1981, The Delta Star 1983, Lines and Shadows 1984, The Secrets of Harry Bright 1985, Echoes in the Darkness 1987, The Blooding 1989, The Golden Orange 1990, Fugitive Nights 1992, Finnegan's Week 1993, Floaters 1996, Fire Lover: A True Story 2002, Hollywood Station 2007, Hollywood Crows 2008, Hollywood Moon 2009, Hollywood Hills 2010. *Honours:* MWA Edgar Allan Poe Award 1974, Int. Asscn of Crime Writers Rodolfo Walsh Prize 1989. *Address:* c/o Little, Brown Book Group, 100 Victoria Embankment, London EC4Y 0DY, England (office). *Website:* www.littlebrown.co.uk (office); www.josephwambaugh.net.

WANDOR, Michelene Dinah, BA, LTCL, DipTCL, MA, MMus; British writer, poet, dramatist, critic and musician; b. 20 April 1940, London, England; m. Edward Victor 1963 (divorced); two s. *Education:* Newnham Coll., Cambridge, Univ. of Essex, Trinity Coll. of Music, London, Univ. of London. *Career:* Poetry Ed. Time Out Magazine 1971–82; Sr Lecturer in Creative Writing, London Metropolitan Univ. 1998–2006; Royal Literary Fund Fellowship 2004–09; mem. Soc. of Authors, RSL. *Play:* The Wandering Jew (Nat. Theatre) 1987, Pride and Prejudice (Watford Palace Theatre) 2008. *Radio:* Tulips in Winter (Radio 3) 2008. *Publications:* Cutlasses and Earrings (ed. and contrib.) 1977, Carry on Understudies 1981, Upbeat 1981, Touch Papers 1982, Five Plays 1984, Gardens of Eden 1984, Routledge 1986, Look Back in Gender 1987, Guests in the Body 1987, Drama 1970–1990 1993, Gardens of Eden Revisited 1999, Post-War British Drama: Looking Back in Gender 2000, False Relations 2004, Musica Transalpina (Poetry Book Soc. Recommendation) 2006, The Music of the Prophets 2007, The Author is Not Dead, Merely Somewhere Else 2008, The Art of Writing Drama 2008; contrib. to periodicals. *Honours:* Int. Emmy Award 1987. *Address:* 71 Belsize Lane, London, NW3 5AU, England (home). *Website:* www.mwandor.co.uk.

WANG, Anyi; Chinese writer and academic; *Professor, Department of Chinese Language and Literature, Fudan University*; b. 1954, Tong'an, Fujian Prov.; d. of Ru Zhijuan. *Education:* Xiangming Middle School. *Career:* joined as musician, Xuzhou Pref. Song and Dance Ensemble 1972; Ed. Children's Time 1978; currently Prof., Dept of Chinese Language and Literature, Fudan Univ., Shanghai; Vice-Chair. Shanghai Writers Asscn, Chair. 2001–; Vice-Pres. Writers' Asscn of China. *Publications:* Song of Eternal Hatred (Mao Dun Prize for Literature), Xiaobao Village, The Love of a Small Town, The Story of a School Principal, Self-selected Works of Wang Anyi (six vols), Lapse of Time, The Song of Everlasting Sorrow 2008. *Honours:* Outstanding Writer Award, Chinese Language Literary Media Awards 2008. *Address:* Department of Chinese Language and Literature, Fudan University, 220 Handan Road, Shanghai 200433, People's Republic of China (office).

WANG, Shuo; Chinese writer; b. 1958, Nanjing. *Career:* spent four years in navy, then worked at various jobs before becoming a full-time writer 1983; first novel Air Stewardesses published 1984; collected works banned by authorities in China 1996; has written over 20 novels with 10 million copies in print, has written scripts for TV and films including work for American Zeotrope, USA. *Film screenplays include:* The Trouble-Shooters 1989, I Love You 2002, Little Red Flowers 2006, Dreams May Come 2006. *Publications include:* Playing for Thrills (translated into English 1997), Please Don't Call Me Human (translated into English 1998), A Sigh 2000, A Conversation with Our Daughter 2008. *Address:* c/o No Exit Press, Oldcastle Books, PO Box 394, Harpenden, AL5 1XJ, England (office). *Website:* www.noexit.co.uk (office).

WARD, Jesmyn, MFA; American author and academic; *Assistant Professor of Creative Writing, University of South Alabama*; b. 1977, DeLisle, Miss. *Education:* Univ. of Michigan. *Career:* fmr Prof., Univ. of New Orleans; John and Renée Grisham Writer-in-Residence, Univ. of Mississippi 2010–11; Asst Prof. of Creative Writing, Univ. of Southern Alabama 2011–. *Publications include:* Where the Line Bleeds (Essence Book Club Selection 2009, Black Caucus of the American Library Asscn Honor Award 2009) 2008, Salvage the Bones (Nat. Book Award for Fiction 2011, Alex Award 2012) 2011; contrib. to literary magazines including: BOMB, The Oxford American, A Public Space. *Honours:* Stegner Fellowship, Stanford Univ. 2008–10. *Literary Agent:* c/o Jennifer Lyons Literary Agency LLC, West 19th Street, 3rd Floor, New York, NY 10011, USA. *Telephone:* (212) 368-2812. *E-mail:* jenniferhlyons@earthlink.net. *Website:* jenniferlyonsliteraryagency.com. *Address:* HUMB 259, University of South Alabama, Mobile, AL 36688-0002, USA (office). *Telephone:* (251) 460-7952 (office). *E-mail:* jward@usouthal.edu (office). *Website:* www.usouthal.edu (office); jesmimi.blogspot.co.uk (home).

WARD, Philip, FRGS, FRSA; British librarian and writer; b. 10 Feb. 1938, Harrow, England; m. 1964, two d. *Education:* University for Foreigners, Perugia, Coimbra University. *Career:* Hon. Ed. The Private Library 1958–64; Co-ordinator Library Services Tripoli, Libya 1963–71; Dir National Library Services 1973–74; mem. Private Libraries Asscn. *Publications:* The Oxford Companion to Spanish Literature 1978, A Dictionary of Common Fallacies 1978–80, Lost Songs 1981, A Lifetime's Reading 1983, Japanese Capitals 1985, Travels in Oman 1987, Sofia: Portrait of a City 1989, Wight Magic 1990, Bulgaria 1990, South India 1991, Western India 1991, Bulgarian Voices: Letting the People Speak. 1992, Bahrain 1993, Gujarat, Daman, Diu 1994, The Comfort of Women (novel) 2002, His Enamel Mug (poems) 2004. *Honours:* Guinness Poetry Award 1959, First Prize International Travel Writers Competition 1990. *Address:* c/o Oleander Press, 16 Orchard Street, Cambridge CB1 1JT, England (office).

WARDLE, (John) Irving, BA, ARCM; British drama critic and writer (retd); b. 20 July 1929, Bolton, Lancs.; m. 1st Joan Notkin 1958 (divorced); m. 2nd Fay Crowder 1963 (divorced); two s.; m. 3rd Elizabeth Grist 1975; one s. one d. *Education:* Wadham Coll., Oxford, Royal Coll. of Music, London. *Career:* sub-ed., Times Educational Supplement 1956; Deputy Theatre Critic, The Observer 1960; Drama Critic, The Times 1963–89; Ed. Gambit 1973–75; Theatre Critic, The Independent on Sunday 1989. *Plays produced:* The

Houseboy 1974, A Kurt Tucholsky Cabaret (Arcola Theatre, London) 2010. *Publications:* The Houseboy (Open Space Theatre) 1974, The Theatres of George Devine 1978, Theatre Criticism 1992. *Address:* 51 Richmond Road, New Barnet, Herts., EN5 1SF, England (home). *Telephone:* (20) 8440-3671 (home). *E-mail:* irvingwardle@gmail.com (home).

WARE, Armytage (see Barnett, Paul le Page)

WARKENTIN, Juliet, BA; Canadian magazine editor; *Content Director, WGSN*; b. 10 May 1961; m. Andrew Lamb 1991. *Education:* Univ. of Toronto and London Coll. of Fashion (UK). *Career:* Ed. Toronto Life Fashion, Draper's Record, UK 1993–96, Marie Claire (UK) 1996–98; Man. Dir Marketing and Internet Devt Arcadia Group PLC 1998–2000; Pnr The Fourth Room 2000–02; Editorial Dir Redwood Publishing 2002–07; Content Dir, WGSN (trend forecaster) 2007–; mem. Bd of Dirs EMAP ELAN 1999–2001; external assessor London Univ. of Arts MA in fashion journalism. *Honours:* Nat. Magazine Award, Canada 1989, PPA Business Ed. of the Year 1994. *Address:* WGSN, Greater London House, Hampstead Road, London, NW1 7EJ, England (office). *Telephone:* (20) 7728-5000 (office). *Fax:* (20) 7728-5001 (office). *Website:* www.wgsn.com (office).

WARNER, Alan, BA, MPhil; British novelist; b. 1964, Oban, Scotland; s. of Frank Warner and Patricia Bowman; m. Hollie Warner. *Education:* Oban High School, Ealing Coll., Univ. of Glasgow. *Film:* Morvern Callar (adaptation) 2003. *Publications:* Morvern Callar 1995, These Demented Lands 1997, The Sopranos 1998, The Man Who Walks 2002, The Worms Can Carry Me to Heaven 2006, The Stars in the Bright Sky 2010; contrib. to Children of Albion Rovers 1997, Disco Biscuits 1997. *Honours:* Somerset Maugham Award, Encore Award 1998, Saltire Prize. *Literary Agent:* David Godwin Associates, 55 Monmouth Street, London, WC2H 9DG, England. *Telephone:* (20) 7240-9992. *Fax:* (20) 7395-6110. *Website:* www.davidgodwinassociates.co.uk.

WARNER, Francis, MA, DLitt; British poet, dramatist and tutor; *Fellow Emeritus, St Peter's College, Oxford*; b. 21 Oct. 1937, Bishopthorpe, Yorks.; m. 1st Mary Hall 1958 (divorced 1972); two d.; m. 2nd Penelope Anne Davis 1983; one s. one d. *Education:* Christ's Hosp., London Coll. of Music, St Catharine's Coll., Cambridge. *Career:* Supervisor in English, St Catharine's Coll., Cambridge 1959–65, Hon. Fellow Residential 1999–; Staff Tutor in English, Univ. of Cambridge Bd of Extra-Mural Studies 1963–65; Fellow and Tutor 1965–99, Fellow Librarian 1966–76, Dean of Degrees 1984–2006, Vice-Master 1987–89, Fellow Emer. 1999–, St Peter's Coll., Oxford; Univ. Lecturer, Univ. of Oxford 1966–99, Pro-Proctor 1989–90, 1996–97, 1999–2000; Founder Elgar Centenary Choir and Orchestra 1957; Foreign Academician Acad. of Letters and Arts, Portugal 1993. *Recording:* conducted Honegger's King David, King's Coll. Chapel, Cambridge 1958, issued as an historic Landmark Recording by OxRecs Digital 2004. *Publications:* poetry: Perennia 1962, Early Poems 1964, Experimental Sonnets 1965, Madrigals 1967, The Poetry of Francis Warner (USA) 1970, Lucca Quartet 1975, Morning Vespers 1980, Spring Harvest 1981, Epithalamium 1983, Collected Poems 1960–84 1985, Nightingales: Poems 1985–96 1997, Cambridge 2001, Oxford 2002, By the Cam and the Isis 2005; plays: Maquettes: A Trilogy of One-Act Plays 1972, Requiem: Part 1 Lying Figures 1972, Part 2 Killing Time 1976, Part 3 Meeting Ends 1974, A Conception of Love 1978, Light Shadows 1980, Moving Reflections 1983, Living Creation 1985, Healing Nature: The Athens of Pericles 1988, Byzantium 1990, Virgil and Caesar 1993, Agora: An Epic 1994, King Francis First 1995, Goethe's Weimar 1997, Rembrandt's Mirror 1999; editor: Eleven Poems by Edmund Blunden 1965, Garland 1968, Studies in the Arts 1968, Beauty for Ashes (Selected Prose) 2012; contrib. to anthologies and journals. *Honours:* Benemerenti Silver Medal, Kts of St George, Constantinian Order, Italy 1990; Hon. DMus (William Jewell Coll., USA); Messing Int. Award for Literature 1972. *Telephone:* (1865) 511857 (home). *Address:* St Peter's College, Oxford, OX1 2DL (office); St Catharine's College, Cambridge, CB2 1RL, England. *Website:* www.franciswarner.com.

WARNER, Malcolm, BA, PhD; British writer, educator and museum curator; *Deputy Director, Kimbell Art Museum*; b. 17 May 1953, Aldershot, Hants., England; s. of Ronald Warner and Vera Warner; m. Sara Ryan 1988; one s. one d. *Education:* Courtauld Inst. of Art, London. *Career:* Visiting Asst Prof., Victoria Univ. of Manchester 1984–85; Research Curator, Dept of European Painting, Art Inst. of Chicago 1988–90; Curator, Prints and Drawings, San Diego Museum of Art 1990–96, European Art 1992–96; Ailsa Mellon Bruce Visiting Sr Fellowship, Center for Advanced Study in the Visual Arts, Nat. Gallery of Art 1994; Fellowship for Museum Professionals, Nat. Endowment for the Arts 1995; Sr Curator of Paintings and Sculpture, Yale Center for British Art 1996–2001; Assoc. Ed., New Dictionary of Nat. Biography 1997–2001; Sr Curator, Kimbell Art Museum, Fort Worth, Tex. 2002–07, Deputy Dir 2007–; mem. Print Council of America, Historians of British Art. *Exhibition:* commissioned and curated 'Butchers, Dragons, Gods & Skeletons' (one of TIME magazine's top 10 shows of 2009). *Publications:* Portrait Painting 1979, The Phaidon Companion to Art and Artists in the British Isles (co-author) 1980, Rainy Days at Brig o'Turk: The Highland Sketchbooks of John Everett Millais, 1853 (co-ed.) 1983, The Image of London: Views by Travellers and Emigrés, 1550–1920 1987, The Art of the Print: Glossary 1991, The Prints of Harry Sternberg 1994, French and British Paintings from 1600 to 1800 in the Art Institute of Chicago: A Catalogue of the Collection (co-author) 1996, The Victorians: British Painting, 1837–1901 1997, Millais: Portraits (co-ed.) 1999, James Tissot: Victorian Life/Modern Love (co-author) 1999, Great British Paintings from American Collections 2001, Stubbs and the Horse (co-author) 2004, The Mirror and the Mask: Portraiture in the Age of Picasso (co-author) 2007, Friendship and Loss in the Victorian Portrait: May Sartoris by Frederick Leighton 2009; contrib. to exhbn catalogues, articles and reviews to periodicals, including Apollo, Burlington Magazine, TLS, Pre-Raphaelite Review, Journal of the RSA, Huntington Library Quarterly. *Address:* Kimbell Art Museum, 3333 Camp Bowie Blvd, Fort Worth, TX 76107, USA (office). *Telephone:* (817) 332-8451 (office). *Fax:* (817) 877-1264 (office). *E-mail:* mwarner@kimbellmuseum.org (office). *Website:* www.kimbellart.org (office).

WARNER, Marina Sarah, CBE, MA, FBA, FRSL; British writer and academic; *Professor of Literature, Film and Theatre Studies, University of Essex*; b. 9 Nov. 1946, London, England; d. of Esmond Warner and Emilia Terzulli; m. 1st William Shawcross 1971; one s.; m. 2nd John Dewe Mathews 1981; pnr Graeme Segal FRS. *Education:* St Mary's Convent, Ascot and Lady Margaret Hall, Univ. of Oxford. *Career:* Getty Scholar, Getty Centre for the History of Art and the Humanities 1987–88; Tinbergen Prof., Erasmus Univ., Rotterdam 1990–91; Visiting Prof., Queen Mary and Westfield Coll., Univ. of London 1994, Univ. of Ulster 1994, Univ. of York 1996–, Birkbeck Coll., London; Tanner Lecturer, Yale Univ. 1999; Clarendon Lecturer, Oxford 2001; Prof. of Literature, Film and Theatre Studies, Univ. of Essex 2004–; Fellow Commonership, Trinity Coll. Cambridge 1998; Visiting Fellow, All Souls Coll. Oxford 2001, Univ. Paris XIII 2003; Fellow, Italian Acad., Columbia Univ., New York, 2003; Sr Fellow, Remarque Inst., New York Univ. 2006; Visiting Prof., Royal Coll. of Art 2008–; Distinguished Visiting Prof., Queen Mary, Univ. of London 2009–; mem. Exec. Cttee Charter 88 –1997, Literature Panel Arts Council of England –1997, Advisory Council British Library –1997, Man. Cttee Nat. Council for One-Parent Families, Bd Artangel, Cttee London Library, Cttee PEN; Trustee, Nat. Portrait Gallery. *Exhibitions include:* The Inner Eye (curator) 1996, Metamorphing: Transformation in Art, Science and Myth (curator) 2003, Only Make-Believe: Ways of Playing, Compton Verney 2005. *Radio:* short stories, criticism. *Publications:* Alone of All Her Sex: The Myth and the Cult of the Virgin Mary 1976, Joan of Arc 1982, Monuments and Maidens: The Allegory of the Female Form 1985, The Lost Father 1988, Indigo 1992, Mermaids in the Basement (short stories) 1993, Wonder Tales (ed.) 1994, Six Myths of Our Time – The 1994 Reith Lectures, From the Beast to the Blonde: On Fairy Tales and Their Tellers 1994, The Inner Eye: Art Beyond the Visible 1996, No Go the Bogeyman: On Scaring, Lulling and Making Mock 1998, The Leto Bundle 2001, Fantastic Metamorphoses, Other Worlds: The Clarendon Lectures 2002, Murderers I Have Known (short stories) 2002, Signs and Wonders: Essays on Literature and Culture 2003, Phantasmagoria: Spirit Visions, Metaphors, and Media 2006. *Honours:* Chevalier des Arts et des Lettres 2000, Commendatore dell'Ordine della Stella di Solidareità 2005; Hon. DLitt (Exeter) 1998, (Univ. of East London) 1999, (Kent) 2005, (Leicester) 2006, (Oxford) 2006; Dr hc (Sheffield Hallam, York, North London, St Andrews) 1998, (RCA) 2004, (King's Coll., London) 2009; Fawcett Prize 1986, Harvey Darton Award 1996, Mythopoeic Fantasy Award 1996, Katherine M. Briggs Award 1999, Rosemary Crawshay Prize, British Acad. 2000, Aby Warburg Prize 2004. *Literary Agent:* c/o Rogers, Coleridge & White, 20 Powis Mews, London, W11 1JN, England. *Telephone:* (20) 7221-3717. *Fax:* (20) 7229-9084. *E-mail:* info@rcwlitagency.com. *Website:* www.rcwlitagency.co.uk. *Address:* LIFTS, University of Essex, Colchester, CO4 3SQ, England (office). *Telephone:* (1206) 873073 (office). *E-mail:* mswarner@essex.ac.uk (office). *Website:* www.marinawarner.com.

WARNER, Val, BA, FRSL; British writer and poet; b. 15 Jan. 1946, Middx, England. *Education:* Somerville Coll., Oxford. *Career:* Writer-in-Residence, Univ. Coll. of Swansea 1977–78, Univ. of Dundee 1979–81; mem. PEN. *Publications:* These Yellow Photos 1971, Under the Penthouse 1973, The Centenary Corbiere (trans.) 1975, The Collected Poems and Prose of Charlotte Mew (ed.) 1981, Before Lunch 1986, The Collected Poems and Selected Prose of Charlotte Mew (ed.) 1997, Tooting Idyll 1998; contrib. to many journals and periodicals. *Honours:* Gregory Award for Poetry 1975, Third Prize, Lincolnshire Literature Festival Poetry Competition 1995. *Address:* c/o Carcanet Press, Alliance House, Cross Street, Manchester, M2 7AQ, England. *E-mail:* valwarner@etce.freeserve.co.uk (home).

WARNOCK, Baroness (Life Peer), cr. 1985, of Weeke in the City of Winchester; **(Helen) Mary Warnock,** DBE, FCP, FRSM; British philosopher and university administrator (retd); b. 14 April 1924, Winchester; d. of the late Archibald Edward Wilson and Ethel Schuster; m. Sir Geoffrey J. Warnock 1949 (died 1995); two s. three d. (one deceased). *Education:* St Swithun's, Winchester and Lady Margaret Hall, Oxford. *Career:* Tutor in Philosophy, St Hugh's Coll. Oxford 1949–66; Headmistress, Oxford High School 1966–72; Talbot Research Fellow, Lady Margaret Hall 1972–76; Sr Research Fellow, St Hugh's Coll. 1976–84; Mistress of Girton Coll. Cambridge 1985–91; Chair. Cttee of Inquiry into Special Educ. 1974–78, Advisory Cttee on Animal Experiments 1979–86, Cttee of Inquiry into Human Fertilization 1982–84, Educ. Cttee Girls' Day School Trust 1994–2001; mem. IBA 1973–81, Royal Comm. on Environmental Pollution 1979–84, Social Science Research Council 1981–85, UK Nat. Comm. for UNESCO 1981–85, Archbishop of Canterbury's Advisory Group on Medical Ethics 1992–2002; Fellow, Coll. of Teachers (fmrly Coll. of Preceptors). *Publications:* Ethics since 1900 1960, J.-P. Sartre 1963, Existentialist Ethics 1966, Existentialism 1970, Imagination 1976, Schools of Thought 1977, What Must We Teach? (with T. Devlin) 1977, Education: A Way Forward 1979, A Question of Life 1985, Teacher Teach Thyself (Dimbleby Lecture) 1985, Memory 1987, A Common Policy for Education 1989, Universities: Knowing Our Minds 1989, The Uses of Philosophy 1992, Imagination and Time 1994; Women Philosophers (ed.) 1996, An Intelligent Person's Guide to Ethics 1998, A Memoir: People and Places 2000, Making Babies 2002, Nature and Mortality 2003, Utilitariansim (ed.) 2003, Special Education: A New Look 2005, Easeful Death (with Elisabeth MacDonald) 2008, Dishonest to God – on keeping religion out of politics 2010. *Honours:* Hon. Master of the Bench, Gray's Inn 1986; Hon. Fellow, Imperial Coll. London 1986, Hertford Coll. Oxford 1997, Lady Margaret Hall Oxford, St Hugh's Coll. Oxford; Hon. FRCM; Hon. Fellow, Royal Soc. of Physicians, Scotland; Hon. FBA 2000; Hon. FRCP 2002; Hon. DUniv (Open Univ.) 1980, (St Andrews) 1992; Hon. LLD (Manchester) 1987, (Liverpool) 1991, (London) 1991; Hon. DLitt (Glasgow) 1988; Dr hc (Univ. of York) 1989; RSA Albert Medal 1998. *Address:* House of Lords, Westminster, London, SW1A 0PW (office); 2 Longdown Road, London, SE6 3SN, England (home). *Telephone:* (20) 7219-8619 (office); (20) 8461-3214 (home). *E-mail:* warnock@parliament.uk. *Website:* www.parliament.uk (office).

WARREN, Dianne, BFA; Canadian fiction writer and playwright; b. 28 Aug. 1950, Ottawa; m. Bruce Anderson; two s. *Education:* Univ. of Regina. *Plays include:* (premiered at Twenty-Fifth Street Theatre, Saskatoon) Serpent in the Night Sky 1992, Club Chernobyl 1994, The Last Journey of Captain Harte 1999. *Publications:* short story collections: The Wednesday Flower Man 1987, Bad Luck Dog (Saskatchewan Book of the Year Award) 1993, A Reckless Moon (a Globe and Mail Best Book of the Year) 2002; plays: Serpent in the Night Sky 1992, Club Chernobyl 1994, The Last Journey of Captain Harte 1999; Cool Water (novel) (Gov. Gen.'s Literary Award for Fiction) 2010. *Honours:* Western Magazine Award for Fiction (twice), City of Regina Writing Award (twice), Writers Trust Marian Engel Award (for a woman writer in mid-career) 2004, Nat. Magazine Gold Award for Fiction. *Literary Agent:* c/o The Cooke Agency, 278 Bloor Street East, Suite 305, Toronto, ON M4W 3M4, Canada. *Telephone:* (416) 406-3390. *Fax:* (416) 406-3389. *E-mail:* agents@cookeagency.ca. *Address:* c/o HarperCollins Canada, 2 Bloor Street East, 20th Floor, Toronto, ON M4W 1A8, Canada (office). *Telephone:* (416) 975-9334 (office).

WARREN, Rosanna, BA, MA; American academic, poet and writer; *Emma MacLachlan Metcalf Professor of the Humanities, Boston University*; b. 27 July 1953, Fairfield, Conn.; m. Stephen Scully 1981; two d. one step-s. *Education:* Yale Univ., Johns Hopkins Univ. *Career:* Asst Prof., Vanderbilt Univ. 1981–82; Visiting Asst Prof., Boston Univ. 1982–88, Asst Prof. 1989–95, Assoc. Prof. of English 1995–99, Emma MacLachlan Metcalf Prof. of the Humanities 1999–; Poetry Consultant and Contributing Ed., Partisan Review 1985–97; Poet-in-Residence, Robert Frost Farm 1990; mem. American Acad. of Arts and Sciences, Acad. of American Poets; board of chancellors 1999–2005, MLA, American Literary Trans Asscn, Asscn of Literary Scholars and Critics, PEN. *Publications include:* The Joey Story 1963, Snow Day 1981, Each Leaf Shines Separate 1984, The Art of Translation: Voices from the Field (ed.) 1989, Stained Glass 1993, Eugenio Montale's Cuttlefish Bones (ed.) 1993, Euripides' Suppliant Women (trans. with Stephen Scully) 1995, Eugenio Montale's Satura (ed.) 1998, Departure 2003, Fables of the Self: Studies in Lyric Poetry 2008; contributions: many journals and magazines. *Honours:* National Discovery Award in Poetry, 92nd Street YMHA-YWCA, New York City 1980, Yaddo Fellow 1980, Ingram Merrill Foundation Grants 1983, 1993, Guggenheim Fellowship 1985–86, ACLS Grant 1989–90, Lavan Younger Poets Prize 1992, Lamont Poetry Prize 1993, Acad. of American Poets; Lila Wallace Writers' Fund Award 1994, Witter Bynner Prize in Poetry, American Acad. of Arts and Letters 1994, May Sarton Award, New England Poetry Club 1995, Ellen Maris Gorrissen Berlin Prize, American Acad. in Berlin 2006. *Address:* c/o University Professors Program, Boston University, 745 Commonwealth Avenue, Boston, MA 02215, USA (office). *Telephone:* (617) 358-1782 (office). *E-mail:* scullywarren@yahoo.com (office). *Website:* www.bu.edu (office).

WARSH, Lewis, BA, MA; American poet, novelist, publisher and teacher; *Associate Professor, Long Island University*; b. 9 Nov. 1944, New York, NY; m. 1st Anne Waldman 1977; m. 2nd Bernadette Mayer 1975; one s. two d.; m. 3rd Katt Lissard 2001. *Education:* City Coll. of New York. *Career:* Co-founder and Jt Ed. Angel Hair magazine and Angel Hair Books, New York City 1966–77; Jt Ed. Boston Eagle, Mass 1973–75; teacher, St Mark's in the Bowery Poetry Project 1973–75; Co-founder and Publr, United Artists magazine and United Artists Books, New York 1977–; Lecturer, Naropa Univ., Boulder, Colo 1978, New England Coll. 1979–80, Queens Coll., CUNY 1984–86, Farleigh Dickinson Univ. 1987–; Assoc. Prof., Long Island Univ. 1987–, Dir MFA Program in Creative Writing 2007–. *Publications:* poetry: Moving Through Air 1968, Dreaming as One 1971, Long Distance 1971, Today 1974, Blue Heaven 1978, Methods of Birth Control 1982, The Corset 1986, Information from the Surface of Venus 1987, Avenue of Escape 1995, The Origin of the World 2001, Debtor's Prison (with Julie Harrison) 2001, Inseparable 2008; fiction: Agnes and Sally 1984, A Free Man 1991, Money Under the Table 1998, Touch of the Whip 2001, Ted's Favorite Skirt 2002, A Place in the Sun 2010; other: Part of My History (autobiog.) 1972, The Maharajah's Son (autobiog.) 1977. *Honours:* Poet's Foundation Award 1972, Creative Artists Public Service Award in Fiction 1977, National Endowment for the Arts Grant in Poetry 1979, Co-ordinating Council of Literary Magazines Ed.'s Fellowship 1981, Fund for Poetry Award 1987, James Shestack Prize American Poetry Review 1994. *Address:* Brooklyn Campus, Long Island University, 1 University Plaza, Brooklyn, NY 11201-8423 (office); 114 West 16th Street, 5C, New York, NY 10011, USA (home). *E-mail:* lwarsh@mindspring.com (home). *Website:* www.lewiswarsh.com.

WASSMO, Herbjørg; Norwegian writer and poet; b. 6 Dec. 1942, Myre i Vesteralen. *Publications:* fiction: Huset med den blinde glassveranda (trans. as The House With the Blind Glass Windows) 1981, Det stumme rommet 1983, Hudlos himmel 1986, Dinas bok (trans. as Dina's Book) 1989, Lykkens sonn 1992, Reiser: Fire Fortellinger 1995, Det sjuende mote 2000, Flukten fra Frank 2003, Et glass melk takk (Havmann Prize) 2006; poetry: Vingeslag 1976, Flotid 1977, Lite gront bilde i stor bla ramme 1991; contribs to periodicals. *Honours:* Norwegian Critics' Award 1982, Nordic Council Literature Prize 1987. *Address:* c/o Gyldendal Norsk Forlag, Postboks 6860, St Olavs Plass, 0130 Oslo, Norway (office). *E-mail:* gnf@gyldendal.no (office). *Website:* www.gyldendal.no (office).

WATADA, Terry, BA, BEd, MA; Canadian writer, dramatist, poet, editor and musician; b. 6 July 1951, Toronto, Ont.; s. of Matsujiro Watada and Chisato Watada; m. Tane Akamatsu 1989; one s. *Education:* Univ. of Toronto, York Univ. *Publications:* Asian Voices: Stories from Canada, Korea, China, Vietnam and Japan (ed.) 1992, The Tale of the Mask (play) 1995, Face Kao: Portraits of Japanese Canadians Interned During World War II (ed.) 1996, Bukkyo Tozen: A History of Jodo Shinshu Buddhism in Canada 1996, A Thousand Homes (poems) 1997, Daruma Days (short stories) 1997, Collected Voices: An Anthology of Asian North American Periodical Writing (ed.) 1997, Ten Thousand Views of Rain (poems) 2000, Obon, the Festival of the Dead (poems) 2006, Kuroshio: the Blood of Foxes (novel) 2007, The TBC: The Toronto Buddhist Church 1995–2010 (history) 2010; unpublished plays; contrib. to periodicals. *Honours:* City of Toronto William P. Hubbard Award for Race Relations 1991, League of Canadian Poets Gerald Lampert Memorial Award 1995, First Prize in Poetry, Moon Rabbit Review Fiction and Poetry Contest 1996. *Address:* 6 Wildwood Crescent, Toronto, ON M4L 2K7, Canada. *E-mail:* twatada@sympatico.ca.

WATANABE, Jun'ichi, MD; Japanese writer; b. 24 Oct. 1933, Hokkaido. *Education:* Sapporo Medical School. *Career:* practised as orthopaedic surgeon before becoming full-time writer 1969–. *Television:* Kurenai (series) 1998. *Films:* adaptations of his works include: Toki rakujitsu 1992, Shitsurakuen 1997, Ai no rukeichi 2007, Namida tsubo 2008. *Publications include:* over 130 novels and essays including Hikari to kage (Light and Shadows) (Naoki Prize 1970), Toki rakujitsu (The Distant Setting Sun) (Yoshikawa Eiji Prize 1979), Nagasaki roshia yujokan (Russian brothel in Nagasaki), Hitohira no yuki, Keshin, Wakarenu riyû, Shitsurakuen (trans. as A Lost Paradise) 2000, Kumo no kaidan, Kareinaru nenrin, Beyond the Blossoming Fields (in trans.), Ai no rukeichi, Namida tsubo. *Honours:* Hon. Chair., Japan-Iceland Soc.; Medal of Honour with Purple Ribbon (Japan) 2003; several Japanese literary prizes including Kikuchi Kan Prize 2003. *Address:* Udagawa-cho 2–1–901, Shibuya-ku, Tokyo 150–0042, Japan (office). *Telephone:* (3) 3476-0980 (office). *Fax:* (3) 3476-0406 (office). *E-mail:* junpei@jasmine.ocn.ne.jp (office).

WATERS, John Frederick, BS; American writer; b. 27 Oct. 1930, Somerville, MA. *Education:* Univ. of Massachusetts. *Career:* mem. Southeastern Massachusetts Creative Writers Club, Cape Cod Writers, 12 O'Clock Scholars, Society of Children's Book Writers, Authors' Guild. *Publications:* Marine Animal Collectors 1969, The Crab From Yesterday 1970, The Sea Farmers 1970, What Does An Oceanographer Do? 1970, Saltmarshes and Shifting Dunes 1970, Turtles 1971, Neighborhood Puddle 1971, Some Mammals Live in the Sea 1972, Green Turtle: Mysteries 1972, The Royal Potwasher 1972, Seal Harbour 1973, Hungry Sharks 1973, Giant Sea Creatures 1973, The Mysterious Eel 1973, Camels: Ships of the Desert 1974, Carnivorous Plants 1974, Exploring New England Shores 1974, The Continental Shelves 1975, Creatures of Darkness 1975, Victory Chimes 1976, Maritime Careers 1977, Fishing 1978, Summer of the Seals 1978, The Hatchlings 1979, Crime Labs 1979, A Jellyfish is Not a Fish 1979, Flood 1991, Watching Whales 1991, The Raindrop Journey 1991, Deep Sea Vents 1994, Night Raiders Along the Cape 1996, Mystery of the Horse Phoenix 1999, Murder on Seal Island 2000, Who Killed the Whale? 2001, Mystery of the Yellow Eyes 2001; contributions: Cape Cod Compass. *Honours:* Jr Literary Book Choice (twice), Outstanding Science Books for Children Award (seven times).

WATERS, Sarah, PhD; British writer; b. 1966, Neyland, Wales. *Education:* Univs of Kent, Lancaster and London. *Career:* fmr Assoc. Lecturer, Open Univ. *Publications:* Tipping the Velvet 1998, Affinity (Sunday Times Young Writer of the Year 2000, Somerset Maugham Award 2000) 1999, Fingersmith 2002, The Night Watch 2006, The Little Stranger 2009; contrib. of articles on lesbian and gay writing, cultural history. *Honours:* Betty Trask Award 1999, Mail on Sunday/John Llewellyn Rhys Prize 1999, CWA Ellis Peters Historical Dagger 2002, British Book Award for Author of the Year 2002. *Literary Agent:* c/o Greene & Heaton (Authors' Agents) Ltd, 37 Goldhawk Road, London, W12 8QQ, England. *Telephone:* (20) 8749-0315. *Website:* www.sarahwaters.com.

WATKINS, Clive, BL; British poet; *Associate Editor, The Waywiser Press*; b. 1945, Sheffield, S Yorks.; m.; three c. *Education:* educated in Liverpool. *Career:* fmr teacher, headteacher –1998 (retd); Assoc. Ed. The Waywiser Press; tutor for the Poetry School, London. *Publications:* Jigsaw (poetry collection) 2003; poems have appeared widely in magazines, including Agenda, Poetry Wales, The Hudson Review, The Malahat Review, The New Welsh Review, The Rialto and The Dark Horse; has also published papers on, inter alia, Conrad Aiken, Wallace Stevens, Edward Thomas, E. J. Scovell,

Michael Longley and on trans of Shakespeare and Montale. *Address:* The Waywiser Press, Bench House, 82 London Road, Chipping Norton, Oxon., OX7 5FN, England (office). *Telephone:* (1608) 644755 (office). *E-mail:* waywiserpress@aol.com (office). *Website:* waywiser-press.com (office).

WATKINS, Karen Christna, (Catrin Collier, Katherine John); British writer; b. 30 May 1948, Pontypridd, Wales; m. Trevor John Watkins 1968; two s. one d. *Education:* Swansea Coll. *Career:* mem. PEN, Soc. of Authors, CWA, Welsh Acad. *Publications:* Without Trace 1990, Hearts of Gold 1992, One Blue Moon 1993, Six Foot Under, A Silver Lining 1994, Murder of a Dead Man 1994, All That Glitters 1995, By Any Other Name 1995, Such Sweet Sorrow 1996, Past Remembering 1997, Broken Rainbows 1998, Spoils of War 2000, Swansea Girls 2001, Swansea Summer 2002, Beggars and Choosers 2003, Homecoming 2003, Winners and Losers 2004, Sinners and Shadows 2004, Finders and Keepers 2005, Winners & Losers 2005, Tiger Ragtime 2006, Midnight Murders 2006, Murder of a Dead Man 2006, Tiger Bay Blues 2006, Tiger Ragtime 2006, One Last Summer 2007, Magda's Daughter 2008, Black-eyed Devils 2009, Bobby's Girl 2011. *Address:* c/o Orion Publishing Group, Orion House, 5 Upper Saint Martin's Lane, London, WC2H 9EA, England. *E-mail:* author@catrincollier.com; catrincollier@aol.com. *Website:* www.catrincollier.co.uk.

WATKINS, Paul, BA; American writer; b. 23 Feb. 1964, Redwood City, CA; m. Cath Watkins; one d. *Education:* Eton Coll., Yale Univ., Syracuse Univ. *Publications:* fiction: Night over Day over Night 1988, Calm at Sunset, Calm at Dawn 1989, In the Blue Light of African Dreams 1990, The Promise of Light 1992, Archangel 1995, The Story of My Disappearance 1998, The Forger 2000, Thunder God 2004, The Fellowship of Ghosts 2004, The Ice Soldier 2005; non-fiction: Stand Before Your God 1994. *Honours:* Encore Award 1989. *Address:* c/o Faber and Faber Ltd, Bloomsbury House, 74–77 Great Russell Street, London, WC1B 3DA, England (office). *Website:* www.paulwatkins.com.

WATMOUGH, David Arthur; Canadian writer and novelist; b. 17 Aug. 1926, London, England; s. of Gerald Arthur Watmough and Ethel Bassett Watmough. *Education:* King's Coll., London. *Career:* mem. Writers' Union of Canada, Fed. of British Columbia Writers. *Publications:* Ashes for Easter (short stories) 1972, Love and the Waiting Game (short stories) 1975, From a Cornish Landscape (short stories) 1975, No More into the Garden (novel) 1978, Fury (short stories) 1984, The Connecticut Countess (short stories) 1984, The Unlikely Pioneer (opera) 1985, Vibrations in Time (short stories) 1986, The Year of Fears (novel) 1987, Thy Mother's Glass (novel) 1992, The Time of the Kingfishers (novel) 1994, Hunting with Diana (short stories) 1996, The Moor is Dark Beneath the Moon (novel) 2002, Vancouver Voices (novel) 2005; contrib. to Encounter, Spectator, New York Times Book Review, Saturday Night (Canada), Canadian Literature, Dalhousie Review, Connoisseur (New York), Malahat Review, Vancouver Step. *Honours:* Canada Council Sr Literary Arts Awards 1976, 1986, Winner, Best Novel of Year Award, Giovanni's Room, Philadelphia 1979. *Address:* Kernow, 175–65B Street, Delta, BC V4L 1M9, Canada (home). *Telephone:* (604) 948-2561 (home). *E-mail:* dwatmough@dccnet.com (home).

WATSON, John Richard, BA, MA, PhD; British academic, writer and poet; *Professor Emeritus of English, Durham University*; b. 15 June 1934, Ipswich, Suffolk, England; s. of Reginald Joseph Watson and Alice Mabel (née Tennant); m. Pauline Elizabeth Roberts 1962; one s. two d. *Education:* Magdalen Coll., Oxford, Univ. of Glasgow. *Career:* Asst, then Lecturer, Univ. of Glasgow 1962–66; Lecturer, then Sr Lecturer, Univ. of Leicester 1966–78; Prof. of English, Durham Univ. 1978–99, Prof. Emer. 1999–, Public Orator 1989–99; mem. Charles Wesley Soc., Int. Asscn of Univ. Profs of English (Pres. 1995–98), Modern Humanities Research Asscn, Charles Lamb Soc. (Pres. 2004–); Life Vice-Pres. Hymn Soc. of GB and Ireland 2011. *Publications:* A Leicester Calendar 1976, Everyman's Book of Victorian Verse (ed.) 1982, Wordsworth's Vital Soul 1982, Wordsworth 1983, English Poetry of the Romantic Period 1789–1830 1985, The Poetry of Gerard Manley Hopkins 1986, Companion to Hymns and Psalms 1988, A Handbook to English Romanticism 1992, The English Hymn 1997, An Annotated Anthology of Hymns 2002, Romanticism and War 2003, Awake My Soul 2005; contrib. to scholarly and literary journals. *Honours:* Hon. Fellow, Harris Manchester Coll., Oxford 2010; Univ. of Oxford Matthew Arnold Memorial Prize 1961, Univ. of Glasgow Ewing Prize 1962, Stroud Festival Prize 1971, Suffolk Poetry Soc. Prize 1975. *Address:* Stoneyhurst, 27 Albert Street, Western Hill, Durham, DH1 4RL, England (home). *E-mail:* j.r.watson@durham.ac.uk (office).

WATSON, Larry, BA, MA, PhD; American writer, poet and educator; *Visiting Professor, Marquette University*; b. 13 Sept. 1947, Rugby, ND; m. Susan Watson; two d. *Education:* Univ. of North Dakota, Univ. of Utah. *Career:* fmr teacher of writing and literature, Univ. of Wisconsin at Stevens Point; Visiting Prof., Marquette Univ. 2003–. *Publications:* In a Dark Time (novel) 1980, Leaving Dakota (poems) 1983, Montana 1948 (novel) 1993, Justice (short stories) 1995, White Crosses (novel) 1997, Laura (novel) 2000, Orchard (novel) 2003, Sundown, Yellow Moon (novel) 2007; contrib. to anthologies, including Essays for Contemporary Culture, Imagining Home, Off the Beaten Path, Baseball and the Game of Life, The Most Wonderful Books, These United States, Writing America; contrib. of short stories and poems to Gettysburg Review, New England Review, North American Review, Mississippi Review and other journals, essays and book reviews to Los Angeles Times, Washington Post, Chicago Sun-Times, Milwaukee Journal-Sentinel and other periodicals. *Honours:* Hon. Dr of Literature (Ripon Coll.); Nat. Educ. Asscn Creative Writing Fellowship 1987, NEA grants 1987, 2004, Milkweed Nat. Fiction Prize 1993, Wisconsin Arts Bd grant. *Address:* English Department, Marquette University, PO Box 1881, Milwaukee, WI 53201-1881, USA (office). *Telephone:* (414) 288-3474 (office). *E-mail:* readermail@larry-watson.com (office). *Website:* www.larry-watson.com.

WATSON, Lynn, BA, MFA; American teacher, writer and poet; b. 5 June 1948, Woodland, Calif. *Education:* Univ. of California, Berkeley, Sonoma State Univ., Univ. of Iowa. *Career:* teacher, Univ. of Iowa, Coll. of the Desert, Sonoma State Univ., Santa Rosa Jr Coll.; mem. California Poets-in-the-Schools. *Publications:* Alimony or Death of the Clock (novel) 1981, Amateur Blues (poems) 1990, Catching the Devil (poems) 1995; contrib. to journals and periodicals. *Honours:* first place Nat. Poetry Asscn 1990, honorable mention World of Poetry Contest 1991. *Address:* PO Box 1253, Occidental, CA 95465, USA (home). *E-mail:* petalumapoet@hotmail.com (home).

WATSON, Mary, MA; South African writer; b. 31 May 1975, Cape Town. *Education:* Univ. of Cape Town, Univ. of Bristol. *Career:* Lecturer in Film Studies, Univ. of Cape Town. *Publications:* Moss (short stories) 2004, Jungfrau (short story) (Caine Prize for African Writing) 2006. *Address:* University of Cape Town, Private Bag, Rondebosch 7701, Cape Town, South Africa (office).

WATSON, Richard Allan, MA, PhD, MS; American academic and writer; *Professor Emeritus of Philosophy, Washington University, St Louis*; b. 23 Feb. 1931, New Market, Ia; s. of Roscoe Richard Watson and Daisy Belle Watson (née Penwell); m. Patty Jo Andersen 1955; one d. *Education:* Univ. of Iowa, Univ. of Minnesota. *Career:* 1st Lt, USAF 1953–55; instructor, Univ. of Michigan 1961–64; Asst Prof., Washington Univ., St Louis, Mo. 1964–67, Assoc. Prof. 1967–74, Prof. of Philosophy 1974–2004, Prof. Emer. 2004–; Assoc. Philosophy Faculty Affiliate, Univ. of Montana 2004–; Ed. Classics in Speleology 1968–73, Speleologia 1974–81, Cave Books 1980–2002, Journal of the History of Philosophy 1983 (mem. Bd of Dirs 1982–2002, Pres. 1990–95), Journal of the History of Philosophy Monograph Series 1985–96, Journal of the History of Philosophy Book Series 2002; ACLS Fellow 1967–68; Center for Advanced Study in the Behavioral Sciences Fellowships 1967–68, 1981–82, 1991–92; Center for Int. Studies Fellow, Princeton Univ., NJ 1975–76; Camargo Foundation Fellow 1995; Bogliasco Foundation Fellow 1998; mem. Int. Writers' Center (mem. Bd of Dirs 1990–2002), Alpine Karst Foundation 2004–, AAAS, American Philosophical Asscn, Cave Research Foundation (mem. Bd of Dirs 1965–74, Pres. 1965–67), Authors' League of America, Nat. Parks and Conservation Asscn (Trustee 1969–81). *Play:* Secrets (one-act play). *Publications include:* The Mammoth Cave National Park Research Center (with Philip M. Smith) 1964, The Downfall of Cartesianism 1966, Man and Nature (with Patty Jo Watson) 1969, The Longest Cave (with Roger W. Brucker) 1976, Under Plowman's Floor (novel) 1978, The Runner (novel) 1981, The Philosopher's Diet (American Health Top 10 Book Award) 1985, The Breakdown of Cartesian Metaphysics 1987, The Philosopher's Joke 1990, Writing Philosophy 1992, Niagara (novel) 1993, Caving 1994, The Philosopher's Demise 1995, Representational Ideas From Plato to Patricia Churchland 1995, Good Teaching 1997, Cogito, Ergo Sum: The Life of René Descartes (NY Public Library 25 Books to Remember) 2002, 2007, In the Dark Cave, illustrated by Dean Norman (children's) 2005, Descartes' Ballet: His Doctrine of the Will and His Political Philosophy 2007; contribs to professional journals and literary quarterlies. *Honours:* Hon. Life mem. Spéléo Club de Paris, Nat. Speleological Soc.; Nat. Endowment for the Humanities grant 1975, Pushcart Prize 1990. *Address:* 2870 Mitten Mountain Road, Missoula, MT 59803, USA (home). *Telephone:* (406) 327-0098 (home). *E-mail:* rawatson@artsci.wustl.edu (home).

WATSON, (Margaret) Sophia Laura, BA, PGCE; British writer; b. 20 June 1962, London, England; m. Julian Watson 1986 (divorced 2000); four d. *Education:* Univ. of Durham, Univ. of Exeter. *Career:* Asst Ed., Quartet Books, London 1983–84; Ed., Fisher Publishing, London 1984–85, Hamish Hamilton, London 1985–87; feature writer, Mail on Sunday, London 1987, Daily Mail, London 1988–90. *Publications:* Winning Women: The Price of Success in a Man's World 1989, Marina: The Story of a Princess 1994, Her Husband's Children 1995, Strange and Well Bred 1996, The Perfect Treasure 1998, Only Pretending 2000. *Address:* Royal Oak House, Church Street, Wiveliscombe, Somerset TA4 2LR, England (home). *E-mail:* sophiawatson@watson545.fsnet.co.uk (home).

WATT-EVANS, Lawrence; American writer; b. 26 July 1954, Arlington, MA; m. Julie F. McKenna 1977, one s. one d. *Education:* Princeton University. *Career:* mem. Horror Writers Asscn. *Publications:* The Lure of the Basilisk 1980, The Seven Altars of Düsarra 1981, The Cyborg and the Sorcerers 1982, The Sword of Bheleu 1983, The Book of Silence 1984, The Chromosonal Code 1984, The Misenchanted Sword 1985, Shining Steel 1986, With a Single Spell 1987, The Wizard and the War Machine 1987, Denner's Wreck 1988, Nightside City 1989, The Unwilling Warlord 1989, The Nightmare People 1990, The Blood of a Dragon 1991, The Rebirth of Wonder 1992, Crosstime Traffic 1992, Taking Flight 1993, The Spell of the Black Dagger 1993, Split Heirs (with Esther Friesner) 1993, Out of This World 1994, In the Empire of Shadow 1995, The Reign of the Brown Magician 1996, Touched by the Gods 1997, Dragon Weather 1999, Night of Madness 2000, The Dragon Society 2001, The Wizard Lord 2006, The Ninth Talisman 2007, A Young Man Without Magic 2009; contributions: journals and magazines. *Honours:* Isaac

Asimov's Science Fiction Readers Poll Award 1987, Science Fiction Achievement Award (Hugo) for Best Short Story of 1987, 1988. *Literary Agent:* c/o Scovil Galen Literary Agency, 276 Fifth Avenue, Suite 708, New York, NY 10001, USA. *Telephone:* (212) 679-8686. *Fax:* (212) 679-6710. *E-mail:* russellgalen@scglit.com. *Website:* www.scglit.com. *E-mail:* lwe@sff.net (office). *Website:* www.watt-evans.com (office).

WATTS, Nigel John; British writer; b. 24 June 1957, Winchester, England; m. Sahera Chohan 1991. *Publications:* The Life Game 1989, Billy Bayswater 1990, We All Live in a House Called Innocence 1992, Twenty Twenty 1995, Teach Yourself Writing a Novel. *Honours:* Betty Trask Award 1989.

WAUGH, Alexander Evelyn Michael, MusB, DipMus; British writer and editor; b. 30 Dec. 1963, London, England; s. of Auberon Waugh and Lady Teresa (née Onslow); m. Eliza Chancellor; one s. two d. *Education:* Univ. of Manchester, Univ. of Surrey. *Career:* Dir, Manygate Management 1988–90; opera critic, Mail on Sunday 1990–91, Evening Standard 1991–96; Founder and Chief Exec. Travelman Publishing 1997–; Ind. Dir (non-exec.) Millennium & Copthorne Hotels PLC; Ed. The Complete Works of Evelyn Waugh, Oxford University Press 2009–. *Publications:* Opera on CD (with Julian Haylock) 1994, 1995, 1996, Classical Music on CD (with Julian Haylock) 1994, 1995, 1996, Classical Music, a New Way of Listening 1995, Opera, a New Way of Listening 1996, Time, from Microseconds to Millennia, a Search for the Right Time 1999, Bon Voyage! A Musical Farce (with Nathaniel Waugh) 2000, God: The Unauthorised Biography 2001, Fathers and Sons: The Autobiography of a Family 2004, The House of Wittgenstein 2008; contrib. to Literary Review, Spectator and others. *Honours:* Music Retailers Asscn Award 1994, Grand Prix du Disque 1995, Vivian Ellis Award for Best New Musical 1996, Design Council Millennium Award 2000. *Literary Agent:* c/o Aitken Alexander Associates Ltd, 18–21 Cavaye Place, London, SW10 9PT, England. *Telephone:* (20) 7373-8672. *Fax:* (20) 7373-6002. *E-mail:* reception@aitkenalexander.co.uk. *Website:* www.aitkenalexander.co.uk; www.alexanderwaugh.com.

WAUGH, Carol-Lynn Rössel, MA; American writer, artist and photographer; b. 5 Jan. 1947, Staten Island, NY; d. of Carl Rössel and Muriel Rössel (née Kiefer); m. Charles Waugh 1967 (divorced 2001); one s. one d. *Education:* State Univ. of New York at Binghamton, Harpur Coll., and Kent State Univ. *Career:* Instructor in Art History, Univ. of Maine 1977; freelance writer and artist 1973–; articles and lectures on teddy bears, dolls and antique toys; sculptor of original dolls 1973–; designer original teddy bears for House of Nisbet, UK 1987–, Effanbee Dolls 1989–, Ashton-Drake Galleries 1989–, Russ Berrie Ltd (USA and UK) 1991–; designer plates for Brimark Ltd 1986; numerous awards for watercolours, photography and designs; mem. Soc. of Children's Book Writers, Original Doll Artist Council of America, Mystery Writers of America, Maine Soc. of Doll and Bear Artists. *Publications include:* Petite Portraits 1982, My Friend Bear 1982, Teddy Bear Artists 1984, Contemporary Artist Dolls (jtly) 1986, The Official Guide to Antique and Modern Teddy Bears (jtly) 1990, Selling Your Dolls and Teddy Bears (jtly) 1996, Holmes for Christmas (jtly) 1996, Bear Making 101 1999, Heirloom Sewing for Teddy Bears and Dolls 2001; co-editor: The Twelve Crimes of Christmas 1981, Big Apple Mysteries 1982, Show Business Is Murder 1983, Murder on the Menu 1984, Manhattan Mysteries 1987, Hound Dunnit 1987, The Sport of Crime, Purr-fect Crime 1989, Senior Sleuths 1989, More Holmes for the Holidays 1999; contribs to professional magazines. *Address:* 5 Morrill Street, Winthrop, ME 04364, USA (home). *Telephone:* (207) 377-6769 (home). *Fax:* (207) 377-4158 (home). *E-mail:* CLWaugh@aol.com (home).

WAUGH, Sylvia, BA, DipEd; British writer and fmr teacher; b. (Sylvia Richardson), Co. Durham, England; m 1964; three c. *Education:* Univ. of Durham. *Career:* fmr English teacher. *Publications include:* The Mennyms (Guardian Children's Fiction Prize 1994) 1993, Mennyms in the Wilderness 1995, Mennyms Under Siege 1995, Mennyms Alive 1996, Mennyms Alone 1996, Space Race 2000, Earthborn 2002, Who Goes Home 2003. *Honours:* Kinderbuchpreis 2000. *Address:* c/o Publicity Department, Random House, 20 Vauxhall Bridge Road, London, SW1V 2SA, England.

WAUGH, Teresa Lorraine, BA; British writer; b. 26 Feb. 1940, London, England; m. Auberon Waugh 1961 (died 2001); two s. two d. *Education:* Univ. of Exeter. *Publications:* The Travels of Marco Polo: A Modern Translation (trans.) 1984, Painting Water (novel) 1984, Waterloo, Waterloo (novel) 1986, The Entertaining Book (co-author) 1986, An Intolerable Burden (novel) 1988, A Song at Twilight (novel) 1989, Sylvia's Lot (novel) 1994, The Gossips (novel) 1995, A Friend Like Harvey (novel) 1998, Alphonse de Custine (trans.) 1999, The House (novel) 2002.

WAYMAN, Thomas (Tom) Ethan, BA, MFA; Canadian poet, writer and essayist; *Associate Professor, University of Calgary*; b. 13 Aug. 1945, Hawkesbury, Ont. *Education:* Univ. of British Columbia, Univ. of California, Irvine. *Career:* Instructor, Colorado State Univ. 1968–69; Writer-in-Residence, Univ. of Windsor, Ont. 1975–76, Univ. of Alberta 1978–79, Simon Fraser Univ., Burnaby, BC 1983; Asst Prof., Wayne State Univ., Detroit 1976–77; mem. Faculty, David Thompson Univ. Centre, Nelson, BC 1980–82, Banff School of Fine Arts, Alberta 1980, 1982, Kwantlen Coll., Surrey, BC 1983, 1988–89, 1998–2000, Kootenay School of Writing, Vancouver 1984–87; Prof., Okanagan Univ. Coll., Kelowna, BC 1990–91, 1993–95; Faculty, Kootenay School of the Arts, Nelson, BC 1991–92, Co-Head, Writing Studio 1995–98; Presidential Writer-in-Residence, Univ. of Toronto 1996; Assoc. Prof., Univ. of Calgary 2002–; Fulbright Visiting Research Chair, Arizona State Univ. 2007; Ralph Gustafson Poetry Chair., Malaspina Univ.-Coll. 2007; mem. Asscn of Writers and Writing Programs, Fed. of British Columbia Writers, Alberta Writers' Guild. *Publications:* poetry: Waiting for Wayman 1973, For and Against the Moon 1974, Money and Rain 1975, Free Time 1977, A Planet Mostly Sea 1979, Living on the Ground 1980, Introducing Tom Wayman: Selected Poems 1973–80 1980, The Nobel Prize Acceptance Speech 1981, Counting the Hours 1983, The Face of Jack Munro 1986, In a Small House on the Outskirts of Heaven 1989, Did I Miss Anything?: Selected Poems 1973–1993 1993, The Astonishing Weight of the Dead 1994, I'll Be Right Back: New & Selected Poems 1980–1996 1997, The Colours of the Forest 1999, My Father's Cup 2002, High Speed Through Shoaling Water 2007; non-fiction: Inside Job: Essays on the New Work Writing 1983, A Country Not Considered: Canada, Culture, Work 1993; short fiction: Boundary Country 2007, A Vain Thing 2007; editor: Beaton Abbot's Got the Contract 1974, A Government Job at Last 1976, Going for Coffee 1981, East of Main: An Anthology of Poems from East Vancouver (with Calvin Wharton) 1989, Paperwork 1991, The Dominion of Love: An Anthology of Canadian Love Poems 2001; contrib. to anthologies and magazines. *Honours:* Helen Bullis Prize, Poetry Northwestern magazine 1972, Michigan State Univ. A. J. M. Smith Prize 1976, first prize Nat. Bicentennial Poetry Awards, San Jose 1976, several Canada Council Sr Arts grants. *Address:* PO Box 163, Winlaw, BC V0G 2J0, Canada (home). *Telephone:* (403) 220-4662 (office). *E-mail:* appledor@netidea.com (home). *Website:* www.library.utoronto.ca/canpoetry/wayman.

WAYS, C. R. (see Blount, Roy Alton, Jr)

WEARNE, Alan Richard, BA, DipEd; Australian poet, novelist and academic; *Senior Lecturer, Faculty of Creative Arts, University of Wollongong*; b. 23 July 1948, Melbourne, Vic. *Education:* Latrobe Univ. and Rusden. *Publications:* Public Relations 1972, New Devil, New Parish 1976, The Nightmarkets 1986, Out Here 1987, Kicking in Danger 1997, The Lovemakers, Book One 2001, The Lovemakers, Book Two 2004, The Australian Popular Songbook 2007. *Honours:* Nat. Book Council Award 1987, gold medal Asscn for the Study of Australian Literature 1987, New South Wales Premier's Prize for Poetry (Kenneth Slessor Award) 2002, New South Wales Premier's Prize Book of the Year 2002, Arts Queensland Judith Wright Calanthe Award for Australian Poetry 2002, Colin Roderick Award 2004. *Address:* POB 4399, University of Wollongong, Wollongong, NSW 2500, Australia (office). *Telephone:* (4) 2230-5780 (home); (2) 4221-4093 (office). *Fax:* (2) 4221-3301 (office). *E-mail:* awearne@uow.edu.au (office). *Website:* www.uow.edu.au/crearts (office); www.wikig.net.

WEBB, Phyllis, OC, BA; Canadian poet and writer; b. 8 April 1927, Victoria, BC; d. of Alfred Webb and Mary Webb (née Patton). *Education:* Univ. of BC and McGill Univ. *Career:* Teaching Asst, Univ. of BC 1960; mem. Public Affairs Dept CBC 1964; co-creator and Exec. Producer Ideas (radio programme) 1967; Writer-in-Residence, Univ. of Alberta 1980–81; Adjunct Prof., Creative Writing Dept, Univ. of Victoria 1989–91; mem. League of Canadian Poets. *Publications:* poetry: Trio (with G. Turnbull and Eli Mandel) 1954, Even Your Right Eye 1956, The Sea is Also a Garden 1962, Selected Poems 1954–1965 1971, Naked Poems 1965, Wilson's Bowl 1980, Sunday Water: Thirteen Anti Ghazals 1982, The Vision Tree: Selected Poems (Gov-Gen's Award for Poetry) 1982, Water and Light: Ghazals and Anti Ghazals 1984, Hanging Fire 1990; other: Talking (essays) 1982, Nothing But Brush Strokes: Selected Prose 1995. *Address:* Apt #207, 137 Blain Road, Salt Spring Island, BC, V8K 0A1, Canada (home). *Telephone:* (250) 537-5374 (home). *Fax:* (250) 537-5374 (home).

WEBER, Katharine; American critic, writer and teacher; *Adjunct Associate Professor of Creative Writing, Graduate School of the Arts, Columbia University*; b. (Katharine Swift Kaufman), 12 Nov. 1955, New York, NY; d. of Sidney Kaufman and Andrea Swift Kaufman; m. Nicholas Fox Weber 1976, two d. *Education:* New School for Social Research, New York and Yale Univ. *Career:* columnist, Sunday New Haven Register, Conn. 1985–87; reviewer, Publishers Weekly 1988–92; Visiting Writer-in-Residence, Connecticut Coll. 1996–97; Visiting Lecturer, Yale Univ. 1997, Lecturer 1998–2003; Writer-in-Residence, Paris Writers Workshop 2004–2006; currently Adjunct Assoc. Prof. of Creative Writing, Graduate School of the Arts, Columbia Univ.; mem. Authors' Guild, PEN, Nat. Book Critics Circle (Bd mem. 2001–03). *Film:* Sleeping 2008. *Publications:* Objects in Mirror are Closer Than They Appear 1995, The Music Lesson 1999, The Little Women 2003, Triangle 2006, True Confections 2010; contrib. to numerous anthologies and periodicals. *Honours:* Best Columnist of the Year, New England Women's Press Asscn 1986, Discover Award, New England Booksellers Asscn 1995, Granta Best Young American Novelist 1996, Connecticut Book Award for Fiction 2007. *Literary Agent:* 133 East 35th Street, New York, NY 10016, USA. *Telephone:* (212) 532-0080. *Address:* 108 Beacon Road, Bethany, CT 06524, USA (home). *E-mail:* katweber@snet.net (home). *Website:* www.katharineweber.com.

WEBSTER, John (Jack) Barron; British journalist and writer; b. 8 July 1931, Maud, Aberdeenshire; m. Eden Keith 1956; three s. *Education:* Maud School, Robert Gordon's Coll., Aberdeen. *Career:* reporter, Aberdeen Press and Journal 1950–60; feature writer, Scottish Daily Express 1960–80; columnist, Glasgow Herald 1986–2000. *Writing for television:* The Webster Trilogy 1992, John Brown: The Man Who Drew a Legend 1994, Walking Back to Happiness 1996. *Publications:* The Dons 1978, A Grain of Truth 1981, Gordon Strachan 1984, Another Grain of Truth 1988, Alistair MacLean: A Life 1991, Famous Ships of the Clyde 1993, The Flying Scots 1994, The Express Years 1994, In the Driving Seat 1996, The Herald Years 1996, Webster's World 1997, From

Dalí to Burrell 1997, Reo Stakis (biog.) 1999, The Auld Hoose 2005, Jack Webster's Aberdeen 2007, Writing for the Stage: The Life of Grassic Gibbon 2008, From Dali to Burrell 2010. *Honours:* Hon. DLitt (Robert Gordon Univ.) 2009, Hon. MUniv (Aberdeen) 2000; Bank of Scotland Columnist of the Year 1996, UK Speaker of the Year 1996, BAFTA Award 1996. *Address:* 58 Netherhill Avenue, Glasgow, G44 3XG, Scotland (home). *Telephone:* (141) 637-6437 (home).

WEDDE, Ian, MA; New Zealand writer, poet, dramatist and translator; *New Zealand Poet Laureate*; b. 17 Oct. 1946, Blenheim; m. Rosemary Beauchamp 1967; three s. *Education:* University of Auckland. *Career:* Poetry Reviewer, London magazine, 1970–71; Writer-in-Residence, Victoria University, Wellington, 1984; Art Critic, Wellington Evening Post, 1983–90; head of art and visual culture at Museum of New Zealand Te Papa Tongarewa 1994–2004; New Zealand Poet Laureate 2011–. *Publications include:* fiction: Dick Seddon's Great Drive 1976, The Shirt Factory and Other Stories 1981, Symmes Hole 1986, Survival Arts 1988, The Viewing Platform 2006; Poetry: Homage to Matisse 1971, Made Over 1974, Pathway to the Sea 1974, Earthly: Sonnets for Carlos 1975, Don't Listen 1977, Spells for Coming Out 1977, Castaly 1981, Tales of Gotham City 1984, Georgicon, 1984, Driving Into the Storm: Selected Poems 1988, Tendering 1988, The Drummer 1993, The Commonplace Odes 2001, Three Regrets and A Hymn to Beauty 2005; plays: Stations 1969, Pukeko 1972, Eyeball, Eyeball 1983, Double or Quit: The Life and Times of Percy TopLiss 1984; essays: Making Ends Meet: Essays & Talks 1992-2004 2005; Co-editor: The Penguin Book of New Zealand Verse (with Harvey McQueen), 1986; Now See Hear!: Art, Language, and Translation (with G. Burke), 1990. *Honours:* Arts Foundation Laureate Award 2006. *Address:* c/o Auckland University Press, Ground Floor/1-11 Short Street, Auckland 1010, New Zealand. *E-mail:* ian.wedde@paradise.net.nz. *Website:* nzpoetlaureate.natlib.govt.nz.

WEDGWOOD, Lady (see Tudor-Craig, Pamela Wynn)

WEI HUI (see Zhou, Wei Hui)

WEI, Jun-Yi; Chinese writer; b. Oct. 1917, Beijing; d. of Wei Hang; m. Yuang Shu; three c. *Education:* Tsinghua Univ., Beijing. *Career:* apptd Ed. and Pres. Renmin Wenxue Chubunshe (People's Literature Publishing House) 1950. *Publication:* Mother and Son 1982. *Honours:* Nat. Award for writing 1983. *Address:* People's Literature Publishing House, 166 Chaoyangmen Nei Dajie, Beijing 100705, People's Republic of China (office). *Telephone:* (10) 5138394 (office).

WEIDENFELD, Baron (Life Peer), cr. 1976, of Chelsea in Greater London; **Arthur George Weidenfeld,** Kt, GBE; British publisher; *Chairman, Weidenfeld and Nicholson Ltd*; b. 13 Sept. 1919, Vienna, Austria; s. of the late Max Weidenfeld and Rosa Weidenfeld; m. 1st Jane Sieff 1952; one d.; m. 2nd Barbara Skelton Connolly 1956 (divorced 1961); m. 3rd Sandra Payson Meyer 1966 (divorced 1976); m. 4th Annabelle Whitestone 1992. *Education:* Piaristen Gymnasium, Vienna, Univ. of Vienna and Konsular Akad. *Career:* came to UK 1938; BBC Monitoring Service 1939–42; BBC News Commentator on European Affairs on BBC Empire and N American service 1942–46; Foreign Affairs columnist, News Chronicle 1943–44; Political Adviser and Chief of Cabinet of Pres. Weizmann of Israel 1949–50; Founder of Contact Magazine 1945, George Weidenfeld & Nicolson Ltd 1948–; Chair. George Weidenfeld & Nicolson Ltd 1948–, Wheatland Corpn, New York 1985–90, Grove Press, New York 1985–90, Wheatland Foundation, San Francisco and New York 1985–92; Dir (non-exec.) Orion 1991–; Consultant Bertelsmann Foundation 1991–, Axel Springer AG Germany; Hon. Chair. Bd of Govs, Ben Gurion Univ. of the Negev 1996–; Gov. of Tel-Aviv Univ. 1980–, Weizmann Inst. of Science 1964–; Columnist Die Welt, Die Welt am Sonntag, Bild am Sonntag; mem., South Bank Bd 1986–99; mem. Bd ENO 1988–98, Herbert Quandt Foundation 1999–2008; Trustee, Royal Opera House 1974–87, Nat. Portrait Gallery 1988–95, Potsdam Einstein Forum, Jerusalem Foundation; Chair. Cheyne Capital 2000–10, Trialogue Educational Trust 1996–; mem. Governing Council, Inst. of Human Science, Vienna; Vice-Chair. Oxford Univ. Devt Programme 1994–99; Pres., Inst. for Strategic Dialogue 2006–. *Publications:* The Goebbels Experiment 1943, Remembering My Good Friends 1994. *Honours:* Freeman of the City of London; Honour of City of Vienna 2003; Hon. Senator, Bonn Univ. 1996; Hon. Fellow, St Peter's Coll. Oxford 1992, St Anne's Coll. Oxford 1993; Golden Kt's Cross of Order of Merit (Austria) 1989, Chevalier, Légion d'honneur 1990, Kt Commdr's Cross (Badge and Star) of Order of Merit (Germany) 1991, Cross of Honour First Class for Arts and Science (Austrian) 2003, Grand Officer, Order of Merit (Italy) 2005, Order of Merit of the Land Baden-Württemberg 2008; Hon. MA (Oxon.) 1992; Hon. PhD (Ben Gurion Univ.); Hon. DLitt (Exeter) 2001, (Oxford) 2010; Charlemagne Medal 2000, London Book Fair/Trilogy Lifetime Achievement Award 2007, Teddy Kollek Lifetime Achievement Award 2009. *Address:* Orion House, 5 Upper St Martin's Lane, London, WC2H 9EA (office); 9 Chelsea Embankment, London, SW3 4LE, England (home). *Telephone:* (20) 7520-4411 (office); (20) 7351-0042 (home). *Fax:* (20) 7379-1604 (office). *E-mail:* george.weidenfeld@orionbooks.co.uk (office).

WEIGEL, George, BA, MA; American theologian and writer; b. 17 April 1951, Baltimore, MD; m. Joan Balcombe 1975; one s. two d. *Education:* St Mary's Seminary and Univ., Baltimore, Univ. of St Michael's Coll., Toronto. *Career:* Fellow, Woodrow Wilson Int. Centre for Scholars 1984–85; Pres. Ethics and Public Policy Center 1989–96 (Sr Fellow 1996–); mem. Editorial Bd First Things, Orbis; mem. Catholic Theological Soc. of America, Council on Foreign Relations. *Publications:* Tranquillitas Ordinis: The Present Failure and Future Promise of American Catholic Thought on War and Peace 1987, Catholicism and the Renewal of American Democracy 1989, American Interests, American Purpose: Moral Reasoning and US Foreign Policy 1989, Freedom and Its Discontents 1991, Just War and the Gulf War (co-author) 1991, The Final Revolution: The Resistance Church and the Collapse of Communism 1992, Idealism Without Illusions: US Foreign Policy in the 1990s 1994, Soul of the World: Notes on the Future of Public Catholicism 1995, Witness to Hope: The Biography of Pope John Paul II 1999, The Truth of Catholicism: Ten Controversies Explored 2001, The Courage To Be Catholic: Crisis, Reform, and the Future of the Church 2002, Letters to a Young Catholic 2004, The Cube and the Cathedral: Europe, America and Politics Without God 2005, God's Choice: Pope Benedict XVI and the Future of the Catholic Church 2005, Faith, Reason and the War against Jihadism 2007, Against the Grain: Christianity and Democracy, War and Peace 2008; contrib. to numerous publications. *Honours:* Papal Cross Pro Ecclesia et Pontifice 2000; ten hon. doctorates; 'Gloria Artis' Gold Medal (Poland) 2006. *Literary Agent:* Loretta Barrett Books, 101 Fifth Avenue, New York, NY 10003, USA. *Telephone:* (212) 242-3420. *Address:* Ethics and Public Policy Center, 1015 15th Street NW, Suite 900, Washington, DC 20005, USA (office). *Telephone:* (202) 682-1200 (office). *Fax:* (202) 408-0632 (office).

WEIGL, Bruce Allan, BA, MA, PhD; academic, poet, writer, editor and translator; *Distinguished Professor, Lorain County Community College*; b. 27 Jan. 1949, Lorain, Ohio; s. of Albert L. Weigl and Dorathy Zora Weigl; m. Jean Kondo; one s. one d. *Education:* Oberlin Coll., Univ. of New Hampshire, Univ. of Utah. *Career:* instructor in English, Lorain County Community Coll. 1975–76, Distinguished Prof. 2000–; Asst Prof. of English, Univ. of Arkansas at Little Rock 1979–81, Old Dominion Univ., Norfolk, Va 1981–86; Assoc. Prof. to Prof. of English, Pennsylvania State Univ. at University Park 1986–2000. *Publications:* poetry: Like a Sack Full of Old Quarrels 1976, Executioner 1977, A Romance 1979, The Monkey Wars 1984, Song of Napalm 1988, What Saves Us 1992, Sweet Lorain 1996, Archeology of the Circle: New and Selected Poems 1999, After the Others, The Unravelling Strangeness, The Circle of Hanh: A Memoir 2000; editor: The Giver of Morning: On the Poetry of Dave Smith 1982, The Imagination as Glory: The Poetry of James Dickey (with T. R. Hummer) 1984, Charles Simic: Essays on the Poetry 1996, Writing Between the Lines: An Anthology on War and its Social Consequences (with Kevin Bowen) 1997, Mountain River: Vietnamese Poetry from the Wars, 1948–1993: A Bilingual Collection (with Kevin Bowen and Nguyan Ba Chung) 1998; other: Angel Riding the Beast (trans. from Romanian with author Lilliana Ursu), Poems from Captured Documents (trans. from Vietnamese with Nguyen); contrib. to anthologies, reviews, quarterlies and journals. *Honours:* Bronze Stud Vietnam Service 1967–68, American Acad. of Poets Prize 1979, Pushcart Prizes 1980, 1985, Bread Loaf Writers' Conf. Fellowship 1981, Nat. Endowment for the Arts grant 1988. *Address:* 41 Glenhurst Drive, Oberlin, OH 44074-1423, USA (home). *Telephone:* (440) 366-7141 (office); (440) 776-2041 (home). *E-mail:* bweigl@lorainccc.edu (office).

WEIN, Elizabeth Eve, (Elizabeth Gatland), BA, MA, PhD; American writer and folklorist; b. 2 Oct. 1964, New York, NY; d. of Norman Wein and Carol Flocken; m. Tim Gatland 1996; two c. *Education:* Yale Univ., Univ. of Pennsylvania. *Career:* mem. Authors' Guild, Science and Fiction Writers of America, Inc., Soc. of Children's Book Writers and Illustrators, Historical Writers' Asscn. *Publications:* The Winter Prince 1993, A Coalition of Lions 2003, The Sunbird 2004, The Mark of Solomon (in two parts, comprising Lion Hunter 2007 and The Empty Kingdom 2008), Code Name Verity 2012; contrib. to anthologies and encyclopaedias. *Honours:* Jacob K. Javits Fellow 1988–92, Alumna of the Year, Harrisburg Acad. 2008. *Literary Agent:* c/o Ginger Clark, Curtis Brown Ltd, 10 Astor Place, New York, NY 10003, USA. *Telephone:* (212) 473-5400. *Fax:* (212) 598-0917. *Website:* www.curtisbrown.com; eegatland.livejournal.com; www.elizabethwein.com.

WEINBERG, Gerhard Ludwig, BA, MA, PhD; American (b. German) academic and writer; *Professor Emeritus of History, University of North Carolina at Chapel Hill*; b. 1 Jan. 1928, Hanover, Germany; s. of Max B. Weinberg and Kate S. Weinberg; m. Janet I. White 1989; one s. *Education:* New York State Coll. for Teachers, Univ. of Chicago. *Career:* Prof. Emer. of History, Univ. of N Carolina at Chapel Hill; mem. American Historical Asscn, Conf. Group for Cen. European History, German Studies Asscn, World War II Studies Asscn. *Publications:* Germany and the Soviet Union 1939–41 1954, Hitlers Zweites Buch 1961, The Foreign Policy of Hitler's Germany 1933–36 1970, The Foreign Policy of Hitler's Germany 1937–39 1980, World in the Balance: Behind the Scenes of World War II 1981, A World at Arms: A Global History of World War II 1994, Germany, Hitler and World War II 1995, Hitler's Second Book: The Unpublished Sequel to Mein Kampf 2003, Visions of Victory: The Hopes of Eight World War II Leaders 2005; contrib. to professional journals. *Honours:* Service Cross, First Class (FRG); Hon. LHD 1989; Hon. DPhil 2001; Beer Prizes, American Historical Asscn 1971, 1994, Halverson Prize, German Studies Asscn 1981. *Address:* 1416 Mt Willing Road, Efland, NC 27243, USA (office). *Telephone:* (919) 563-4224 (office). *E-mail:* gweinber@email.unc.edu (office).

WEINBERG, Steven, PhD; American physicist and academic; *Jack S. Josey-Welch Foundation Chair in Science and Regental Professor and Director, Theory Research Group, Department of Physics, University of Texas*; b. 3 May 1933, New York; s. of Fred Weinberg and Eva Weinberg; m. Louise Goldwasser 1954; one d. *Education:* Cornell Univ., Univ. of Copenhagen and

Princeton Univ. *Career:* Columbia Univ. 1957–59; Lawrence Radiation Lab. 1959–60; Univ. of Calif. at Berkeley 1960–69; Prof. of Physics, MIT 1969–73; Higgins Prof. of Physics, Harvard Univ. 1973–83; Sr Scientist, Smithsonian Astrophysical Observatory 1973–83, Sr Consultant 1983–; Josey Chair and Regental Prof. of Science, Univ. of Texas, Austin 1982–, also Dir Theory Research Group; Co-Ed. Cambridge Univ. Press Monographs on Mathematical Physics 1978; Dir Jerusalem Winter School of Theoretical Physics 1983–, Headliners Foundation 1993–; mem. A.P. Sloan Foundation Science Book Cttee 1985–90, Einstein Archives Int. Advisory Bd 1988–, Scientific Policy Cttee, Supercollider Lab. 1989–93, American Acad. of Arts and Sciences 1968–, NAS 1972–, Council for Foreign Relations, President's Cttee on the Nat. Medal of Science 1979–80, Royal Soc. 1982–, American Philosophical Soc. 1983–; fmr mem. Council, American Physical Soc., Int. Astronomical Union, Philosophical Soc. of Tex. (Pres. 1994); Loeb Lecturer, Harvard Univ. and Visiting Prof. MIT 1966–69, Richtmeyer Lecturer of American Asscn of Physics Teachers 1974, Scott Lecturer, Cavendish Lab. 1975, Silliman Lecturer, Yale Univ. 1977, Lauritsen Lecturer, Calif. Inst. of Tech. 1979, Bethe Lecturer, Cornell Univ. 1979, Harris Lecturer, Northwestern Univ. 1982, Cherwell-Simon Lecturer, Oxford Univ. 1983, Bampton Lecturer, Columbia Univ. 1983, Hilldale Lecturer, Univ. of Wisconsin 1985, Brickweede Lecturer, Johns Hopkins Univ. 1986, Dirac Lecturer, Univ. of Cambridge 1986, Klein Lecturer, Univ. of Stockholm 1989, Sackler Lecturer, Univ. of Copenhagen 1994, Brittin Lecturer, Univ. of Colorado 1994, Gibbs Lecturer, American Math. Soc. 1996, Bochner Lecturer, Rice Univ. 1997, Sanchez Lecturer, Witherspoon Lecturer, Washington Univ. 2001. *Publications:* Gravitation and Cosmology 1972, The First Three Minutes 1977, The Discovery of Subatomic Particles 1982, Elementary Particles and the Laws of Physics (with R. P. Feynman) 1987, Dreams of a Final Theory 1993, The Quantum Theory of Fields (Vol. I) 1995, (Vol. II) 1996, (Vol. III) 2000, Facing Up 2001, Lake Views: This World and the Universe 2010, Lectures on Quantum Mechanics 2012; and over 250 articles. *Honours:* Hon. DSc (Knox Coll.) 1978, (Chicago, Yale, Rochester) 1979, (City Univ., New York) 1980, (Clark Univ.) 1982, (Dartmouth) 1984, (Weizmann Inst.) 1985, (Columbia) 1990, (Salamanca) 1992, (Padua) 1992, (Barcelona) 1996, (Bates Coll.) 2002, (McGill Univ.) 2003; Hon. DLitt (Washington Coll.) 1985; J. R. Oppenheimer Prize 1973, Dannie Heinemann Mathematical Physics Prize 1977, American Inst. of Physics-U.S. Steel Foundation Science Writing Award 1977, Elliott Cresson Medal, Franklin Inst. 1979, Joint Winner, Nobel Prize for Physics 1979, James Madison Medal (Princeton) 1991, Nat. Medal of Science 1991, Andrew Gemant Award 1997, Piazzi Prize 1998, Lewis Thomas Prize Honoring the Scientist as Poet 1999, Benjamin Franklin Medal, American Philosophical Soc. 2004. *Address:* Department of Physics, University of Texas, Theory Group, RLM 5.208 C1608, Austin, TX 78712-1081, USA. *Telephone:* (512) 471-4394 (office). *Fax:* (512) 471-4888 (office). *E-mail:* weinberg@physics.utexas.edu (office). *Website:* www.ph.utexas.edu/~weintech/weinberg.html (office).

WEINFIELD, Henry Michael, BA, MA, PhD; American (b. Canadian) academic, poet and writer; *Professor of Liberal Studies, Notre Dame University*; b. 3 Jan. 1949, Montreal; s. of Mortimer Weinfield and Susanne Weinfield; m. Joyce Block; one s. two d. *Education:* City Coll. of New York, State Univ. of NY (SUNY) at Binghamton, The Grad. Center of the CUNY. *Career:* Lecturer, SUNY at Binghamton 1973–74; Adjunct Lecturer, Lehman Coll. 1974–77, Baruch Coll. 1979–81, City Coll. 1982–83; Adjunct Lecturer, New Jersey Inst. of Tech. 1983–84, Special Lecturer 1984–91; Asst Prof., Univ. of Notre Dame 1991–96, Assoc. Prof. 1996–2003, Prof. of Liberal Studies 2003–. *Publications include:* poetry: The Carnival Cantata 1971, In the Sweetness of New Time 1980, Sonnets Elegiac and Satirical 1982, Without Mythologies: New and Selected Poems and Translations 2008; other: The Poet Without a Name: Gray's Elegy and the Problem of History 1991, The Collected Poems of Stéphane Mallarmé (trans. and commentator) 1995, The Sorrows of Eros and Other Poems 1999, Hesiod's Theogony and Works and Days (with Catherine Schlegel) 2006, Without Mythologies: New and Collected Poems and Translation 2008, The Music of Thought in the Poetry of George Oppen and William Brink 2009; contrib. of articles, poems, trans to numerous publs. *Honours:* Co-ordinating Council of Literary Magazines Award 1975, Nat. Endowment for the Humanities Fellowship 1989. *Address:* Program of Liberal Studies, University of Notre Dame, 215 O'Shaughnessy Hall, Notre Dame, IN 46556, USA (office). *Telephone:* (574) 631-7483 (office). *Fax:* (574) 631-8209 (office). *E-mail:* hweinfie@nd.edu (office). *Website:* pls.nd.edu/faculty/henry-weinfield (office).

WEINSTEIN, Michael Alan, BA, MA, PhD; American political philosopher, academic and author; *Professor of Political Science, Purdue University*; b. 24 Aug. 1942, New York, NY; m. Deena Schneiweiss 1964. *Education:* New York Univ., Western Reserve Univ. *Career:* Asst Prof., Western Reserve Univ. 1967, Virginia Polytechnic Inst. 1967–68; Prof. of Political Science, Purdue Univ. 1972–; Distinguished Prof. of Political Science, Univ. of Wyoming 1979. *Publications:* The Polarity of Mexican Thought: Instrumentalism and Finalism 1976, The Tragic Sense of Political Life 1977, Meaning and Appreciation: Time and Modern Political Life 1978, The Structure of Human Life: A Vitalist Ontology 1979, The Wilderness and the City: American Classical Philosophy as a Moral Quest 1982, Unity and Variety in the Philosophy of Samuel Alexander 1984, Finite Perfection: Reflections on Virtue 1985, Culture Critique: Fernand Dumont and the New Quebec Sociology 1985, Data Trash 1994, Culture/Flesh: Explorations of Postcivilized Modernity 1995, The Imaginative Prose of Oliver Wendell Holmes 2006; contribs to magazines and journals. *Honours:* Best Paper Prize, Midwest Political Science Asscn 1969, Guggenheim Fellowship 1974–75, Rockefeller Foundation Humanities Fellowship 1976. *Address:* Department of Political Science, Purdue University, BRNG 2216F, 100 N University Street, West Lafayette, IN 47907-2098, USA (office). *Telephone:* (765) 494-4173 (office). *E-mail:* weinstem@purdue.edu (office). *Website:* www.cla.purdue.edu/polsci (office).

WEINTRAUB, Stanley, BS, MA, PhD; American academic, writer and editor; *Professor Emeritus of Arts and Humanities, Pennsylvania State University*; b. 17 April 1929, Philadelphia, Pa; m. Rodelle Horwitz 1954; two s. one d. *Education:* West Chester State College, Temple Univ., Pennsylvania State Univ. *Career:* Instructor, Pennsylvania State Univ. 1953–59, Asst Prof. 1959–62, Assoc. Prof. 1962–65, Prof. of English 1965–70, Research Prof. 1970–86, Evan Pugh Prof. of Arts and Humanities 1986–2000, Prof. Emer. 2000–; Visiting Prof., UCLA 1963, Univ. of Hawaii 1973, Univ. of Malaya 1977, Nat. Univ. of Singapore 1982; Adjunct Prof., Univ. of Delaware 2002–. *Publications:* Private Shaw and Public Shaw: A Dual Portrait of Lawrence of Arabia and George Bernard Shaw 1963, The War in the Wards: Korea's Forgotten Battle 1964, The Art of William Golding (with B. S. Oldsey) 1965, Reggie: A Portrait of Reginald Turner 1965, Beardsley: A Biography 1967, The Last Great Cause: The Intellectuals and the Spanish Civil War 1968, Evolution of a Revolt: Early Postwar Writings of T. E. Lawrence (with R. Weintraub) 1968, Journey to Heartbreak: The Crucible Years of Bernard Shaw 1914–1918 1971, Whistler: A Biography 1974, Lawrence of Arabia: The Literary Impulse (with R. Weintraub) 1975, Aubrey Beardsley: Imp of the Perverse 1976, Four Rossettis: A Victorian Biography 1977, The London Yankees: Portraits of American Writers and Artists in England 1894–1914 1979, The Unexpected Shaw: Biographical Approaches to G. B. Shaw and his Work 1982, A Stillness Heard Round the World: The End of the Great War 1985, Victoria: An Intimate Biography 1987, Long Day's Journey into War: December 7, 1941 1991, Bernard Shaw: A Guide to Research 1992, Disraeli: A Biography 1993, The Last Great Victory: The End of World War II, July/August 1945 1995, Shaw's People, Victoria to Churchill 1996, Albert, Uncrowned King 1997, MacArthur's War: Korea and the Undoing of an American Hero 2000, The Importance of Being Edward: King in Waiting, 1841–1901 2000, Silent Night: The Remarkable 1914 Christmas Truce 2001, Charlotte and Lionel: A Rothschild Love Story 2003, General Washington's Christmas Farewell: A Mount Vernon Homecoming 1783 2003, Iron Tears: America's Battle for Freedom, Britain's Quagmire: 1775–1783 2005, 11 Days in December: Christmas at the Bulge 2006, 15 Stars: Eisenhower, MacArthur, Marshall: Three Generals Who Saved the American Century 2007, General Sherman's Christmas. Savannah, 1864 2009, Who's Afraid of Bernard Shaw? Some Personalities in Shaw's Plays 2011, Victorian Yankees at Queen Victoria's Court 2011, Pearl Harbor Christmas: A World at War, December 1941 2011,; ed. of over 20 vols; contrib. to professional journals, Oxford Dictionary of National Biography 2004. *Honours:* Guggenheim Fellowship 1968–69, Pennsylvania Humanities Council Distinguished Humanist Award 1985. *Address:* 4 Winterfield Court, Beech Hill, Newark, DE 19711-2957, USA (home). *Telephone:* (302) 235-2859 (office). *Fax:* (302) 235-2469 (office). *E-mail:* sqw4@comcast.net (home).

WEIR, Anne, BA, MEd; American writer; b. 9 Feb. 1942, Boston, MA; three d. *Education:* Smith Coll., Swarthmore Coll., Univ. of Maine. *Publications:* A Book of Certainties 1992, Marlowe: Being in the Life of the Mind 1996, The Color Book 1998.

WEIR, Hugh William Lindsay, DLitt; Irish writer and publisher; *Managing Director, Weir Publishing Group, Ballinakella Press*; b. 29 Aug. 1934; m. The Hon. Grania O'Brien 1973. *Education:* Trinity Coll., UIC, Trinity Coll., Dublin. *Career:* Managing Dir, Weir Publishing Group, Ballinakella Press and Bell'acards. *Publications:* Hall Craig – Words on an Irish House, Ennis – 750 Facts, O'Brien People and Places, Houses of Clare, Ireland – A Thousand Kings, O'Connor People and Places, The Clare Young Environmentalists, One of Our Own: Memoirs of Change, Brian Boru: High King of Ireland, 941–1014; short stories, academic articles/essays and topographical/historical contributions made to various anthologies and books; contrib. to The Other Clare, The Clare Champion, The Church of Ireland Gazette, The Catholic Twin Circle, English Digest. *Honours:* Oidhreacht Award. *Address:* Ballinakella Lodge, Whitegate, County Clare, Ireland (office). *Telephone:* (61) 927030 (office); (61) 927030 (home). *Fax:* (61) 927418 (office). *E-mail:* ballinakella@hotmail.com (office).

WEISSBORT, Daniel, BA, FRSL; British poet, translator, editor and academic; *Professor Emeritus, University of Iowa*; b. 1 May 1935, London. *Education:* Queens' Coll., Cambridge. *Career:* Co-founder (with Ted Hughes) Modern Poetry in Translation magazine 1966–83, Ed. relaunched version 1992–2004; Prof., Univ. of Iowa 1980, Prof. Emer. of the Translation Program. *Publications:* The Leaseholder 1971, In an Emergency 1972, Soundings 1977, Leaseholder: New and Collected Poems, 1965–85 1986, Inscription 1990, Lake 1993, Letters to Ted 2002, From Russia with Love 2004, Translation – Theory and Practice (co-author and co-ed.) 2006; translator: Far from Sodom: Selected Poems of Inna Lisnianskaya 2005, An Anthology of Russian Women Poets 2006, Selected Translations of Ted Hughes 2006, The Sum Total of Violation by Regina Derieva 2009, Ted Hughes and Translation 2010; ed. and translator of Russian literature. *Honours:* Hon. Research Fellow, Dept of English, King's Coll., London; Hon. Prof., Centre for Translation and Comparative Cultural Studies, Univ. of Warwick 2003; Arts Council Literature Award 1984.

Address: 3 Powis Gardens, London, NW11 8HH, England (home). *Telephone:* (20) 8458-2600 (home). *E-mail:* daniel.weissbort@ntlworld.com (home).

WELCH, Robert, BA, MA, PhD; Irish writer, poet, editor and academic; *Professor Emeritus of English, University of Ulster*; b. 25 Nov. 1947, Cork; m. Angela Welch 1970; four s. *Education:* National University of Ireland, University of Leeds. *Career:* Lecturer, University of Leeds 1971–73, 1974–84, University of Ife, Nigeria 1973–74; Visiting Lecturer, National University of Ireland, 1982; Prof. of English, University of Ulster 1984–2009, Head, Dept of English, Media and Theatre Studies 1984–94, Dir Centre for Irish Literature and Bibliography 1994, Prof. Emer. 2009–; Founder-General Ed., Ulster Editions and Monographs 1988–; Pres. Int. Asscn for the Study of Irish Literatures 1985–88; Visiting Fellow, St John's Coll., Oxford 1986; mem. Royal Irish Acad. 2008–. *Publications:* Irish Poetry from Moore to Yeats 1980, The Way Back: George Moore's The Untilled Field and The Lake (ed.) 1982, A History of Verse from the Irish 1789–1897 1988, Literature and the Art of Creation: Essays in Honour of A. N. Jeffares (co-ed.) 1988, Muskerry (poems) 1991, Irish Writers and Religion (ed.) 1991, Changing States: Transformations in Modern Irish Writing 1993, W. B. Yeats: Irish Folklore, Legend, and Myth (ed.) 1993, The Kilcolman Notebook (novel) 1994, The Oxford Companion to Irish Literature (ed.) 1996, Irish Myths 1996, Patrick Falvin: New and Selected Poems (co-ed.) 1996, Groundwork (novel) 1997, Secret Societies (poems) 1997, Tearmann (novel) 1997, The Blue Formica Table (poems) 1998, The Abbey Theatre 1899-1999: Form and Pressure 1999, Plays and Poems of J. M. Synge 1999, The Concise Oxford Companion to Irish Literature (ed.) 2000, Forty Four, Verse Translations of Dana Podracka 2005, Evergreen Road (poems) 2006, Constanza (poems) 2010; Co-Gen. Ed. Oxford History of the Irish Book. *Honours:* Oireachtas Prize 2003, O'Connor Literary Award 2009. *Address:* c/o Darton, Longman & Todd Ltd, 1 Spencer Court, 140-142 Wandsworth High Street, London, SW18 4JJ, England.

WELDON, Fay, CBE, MA, FRSA; British author and academic; *Professor of Creative Writing, Brunel University*; b. 22 Sept. 1931, Alvechurch, Worcs., England; d. of Frank T. Birkinshaw and Margaret J. Birkinshaw; m. 1st Ronald Weldon 1960 (divorced 1994); four s.; m. 2nd Nicholas Fox 1995. *Education:* Girls' High School, Christchurch, New Zealand, South Hampstead School for Girls and Univ. of St Andrews. *Career:* Chair. of Judges, Booker McConnell Prize 1983; Writer-in-Residence Savoy Hotel, London Oct.-Dec. 2002; Prof. of Creative Writing, Brunel Univ. 2006–; fmr mem. Arts Council Literary Panel; mem. Video Censorship Appeals Cttee. *Theatre plays:* Words of Advice 1974, Friends 1975, Moving House 1976, Mr Director 1977, Action Replay 1979, I Love My Love 1981, Woodworm 1981, Jane Eyre 1986, The Hole in the Top of the World 1987, Jane Eyre (adaptation), Playhouse Theatre, London 1995, The Four Alice Bakers, Birmingham Repertory 1999, Breakfast with Emma, Lyric Hammersmith 2003; more than 30 television plays, dramatizations and radio plays. *Television:* Big Women (series), Channel 4 1999. *Publications:* novels: The Fat Woman's Joke (aka And the Wife Ran Away) 1967, Down Among the Women 1972, Female Friends 1975, Remember Me 1976, Little Sisters (aka Words of Advice) 1977, Praxis 1978, Puffball 1980, The President's Child 1982, The Life and Loves of a She-Devil 1984, The Shrapnel Academy 1986, The Heart of the Country 1987, The Hearts and Lives of Men 1987, The Rules of Life (novella) 1987, Leader of the Band 1988, The Cloning of Joanna May 1989, Darcy's Utopia 1990, Growing Rich 1992, Life Force 1992, Affliction (aka Trouble) 1994, Splitting 1995, Worst Fears 1996, Big Women 1997, Rhode Island Blues 2000, Bulgari Connection 2001, She May Not Leave 2005, The Spa Decameron 2007, The Stepmother's Diary 2008, Chalcot Crescent 2009, Kehua 2010; children's books: Wolf the Mechanical Dog 1988, Party Puddle 1989, Nobody Likes Me! 1997; short story collections: Watching Me Watching You 1981, Polaris 1985, Moon Over Minneapolis 1991, Wicked Women 1995, Angel All Innocence and Other Stories 1995, A Hard Time to be a Father 1998, Nothing to Wear, Nowhere to Hide 2002; other: Letters to Alice 1984, Rebecca West 1985, Godless in Eden (essays) 2000, Auto da Fay (autobiography) 2002, Mantrapped (autobiography) 2004, What Makes Women Happy 2006. *Honours:* Fellow, City of Bath Coll. 1999; Hon. DLitt (Bath) 1989, (St Andrews) 1992, (Birmingham), (Univ. of Connecticut); Women in Publishing Pandora Award 1997. *Literary Agent:* c/o Capel Land, 29 Wardour Street, London, W1V 6HB, England. *Telephone:* (20) 7734-2414. *Address:* Brunel University, School of Arts, Uxbridge, Middx, UB8 3PH (office). *E-mail:* fay.weldon@brunel.ac.uk (office). *Website:* www.brunel.ac.uk/about/acad/sa (office).

WELLAND, Colin; British playwright and actor; b. (Colin Williams), 4 July 1934, Liverpool; s. of John Arthur Williams and Norah Williams; m. Patricia Sweeney 1962; one s. three d. *Education:* Newton-le-Willows Grammar School, Bretton Hall, Goldsmiths' Coll., London. *Career:* art teacher 1958–62; entered theatre 1962, Library Theatre, Manchester 1962–64; Fellow, Goldsmiths Coll., Univ. of London 2001. *Stage roles:* Waiting for Godot 1987, The Churchill Play, Man of Magic, Say Goodnight to Grandma, Ubu Roi. *Plays written:* Roomful of Holes 1972, Say Goodnight to Grandma 1973, Roll on Four O'Clock 1981. *Film roles:* Kes (BAFTA Award for Best Supporting Actor), Villain, Straw Dogs, Sweeney, The Secret Life of Ian Fleming, Dancing through the Dark. *Screenplays:* Yanks 1978, Chariots of Fire 1980 (Acad. Award), Twice in a Lifetime 1986, A Dry White Season, War of the Buttons 1994. *Television appearances:* Blue Remembered Hills, The Fix, United Kingdom. *Television plays include:* Kisses at 50, Leeds United, Your Man from Six Counties, Bambino Mio, Slattery's Mounted Foot, Jack Point, The Hallelujah Handshake, Roll on Four O'Clock (BAFTA Award for Best TV Screenplay). *Literary Agent:* United Agents, 12–26 Lexington Street, London, W1F 0LE, England. *Telephone:* (20) 3214-0800. *Fax:* (20) 3214-0801. *E-mail:* info@unitedagents.co.uk. *Website:* unitedagents.co.uk.

WELLS, Peter Frederick, (John Flint), MA, PhD; British/New Zealand academic and writer; b. 28 Feb. 1918, Cardiff, Wales; s. of Henry Wells and Eliza Bushell; m. 1st Jeanne Chiles 1945; three s.; m. 2nd Rita Davenport 1994. *Education:* Univ. of Wales, Genova Univ., Italy, Univ. of Paris-Sorbonne, France, Univs of Auckland and Waikato, New Zealand. *Career:* emigrated to New Zealand; Head of Language Studies Dept, Univ. of Waikato 1961–73; Dir Inst. of Modern Languages, James Cook Univ. of North Queensland 1974–84; mem. and Founder-Pres. New Zealand-Japan Soc., Hamilton. *Publications:* Let's Learn French 1963, Les Quatre Saisons 1966, Let's Learn Japanese 1968, Nihongo no Kakikata 1971, Anthology of Poems by Ishikawa Takuboku 1972, Phonetics and Orthography of French 1975, A Description of Kalaw Kawaw Ya 1976, French for Adult Beginners 1976, Three Loves and a Minesweeper: A Wartime Romance 1998, Myra Migrating 1999, One Night Between Fridays 2008, Three Piece Suite: Three Novellas 2009, Ghost and Other Stories 2009, Poison in Paradise 2010, My Name is Gareth: A Biography 2010, The Time Tumulus and Other Stories 2010; contrib. to Journal of Modern Languages and Literature, Bulletin de L'Asscn G. Budé, New Zealand Journal of French Studies, Education, LINQ, English Language and Literature Asscn. *Honours:* Order of the Sacred Treasure (Japan), Order of Merit (New Zealand). *Address:* 249 Bankwood Road, Chartwell, Hamilton, New Zealand. *E-mail:* peterfwells@hotmail.com.

WELLS, Robert; British poet and translator; b. 17 Aug. 1947, Oxford, England. *Education:* King's Coll., Cambridge. *Career:* teacher, Univ. of Leicester 1979–82. *Publications:* Shade Mariners (with Dick Davis and Clive Wilmer) 1970, The Winter's Task: Poems 1977, The Georgics, by Virgil (trans., four vols) 1981, Selected Poems 1986, The Idylls, by Theocritus (trans.) 1988, The Day and Other Poems 2006, Collected Poems and Translations 2009. *Address:* 6 Rue Robert Houdin, 41000, Blois, France (home). *Telephone:* 2-54-78-45-28 (home).

WELLS, Roger A. E., BA, DPhil; British academic and writer; b. 30 Jan. 1947, London, England; m. (divorced); one s. one d. *Education:* University of York. *Career:* Lecturer, University of Wales 1972–73, University of Exeter, 1973–75, University of York 1975–76; Senior Lecturer, University of Brighton 1976–95; apptd Prof. of History, Christ Church University College, Canterbury 1995; mem. Royal Historical Society. *Publications:* Dearth and Distress in Yorkshire, 1793–1801 1977, Riot and Political Disaffection in Nottinghamshire in the Age of Revolutions 1776–1803 1983, Insurrection: The British Experience 1795–1803 1983, Wretched Faces: Famine in Wartime England, 1793–1801 1988, Class, Conflict and Protest in the English Countryside (with M. Reed), 1700–1880 1990, Victorian Village 1992, Crime, Protest and Popular Politics in Southern England c. 1740–1850 (with J. Rule) 1997; contributions: Social History, Rural History, Southern History, Northern History, Policing and Society, Journal of Peasant Studies, Journal of Historical Geography, Local Historian, English Historical Review, Agricultural History Review, London Journal, Labour History Bulletin, Journal of Social Policy. *Address:* c/o The History Press, The Mill, Brimscombe Port, Stroud, Gloucestershire, GL5 2QG, England.

WELLS, Stanley William, CBE, BA, PhD; British writer and editor; *Professor Emeritus, University of Birmingham*; b. 21 May 1930, Hull, Humberside, England; s. of Stanley Cecil Wells and Doris Wells; m. Susan Hill; two d. *Education:* Univ. Coll., London, Univ. of Birmingham. *Career:* fmr Prof. of Shakespeare Studies, and Dir of the Shakespeare Inst., Univ. of Birmingham 1988–97, now Prof. Emer.; currently Chair. Shakespeare Birthplace Trust, Stratford; Fellow, Univ. Coll. London. *Publications:* Oxford Shakespeare Topics (co-gen. ed. with Peter Holland), Shakespeare: A Reading Guide 1969, Literature and Drama: With Special Reference to Shakespeare and his Contemporaries 1970, Shakespeare: Select Bibliographical Guides (ed.) 1974, Shakespeare: An Illustrated Dictionary (ed.) 1978, Royal Shakespeare: Four Major Productions at Stratford-upon-Avon 1977, Shakespeare 1978, Modernizing Shakespeare's Spelling: With Three Studies of the Text of Henry V (with Gary Taylor) 1979, Re-editing Shakespeare for the Modern Reader 1984, Twelfth Night: Critical Essays (ed.) 1986, The Cambridge Companion to Shakespeare (ed.) 1986, Shakespeare: A Bibliography 1989, Shakespeare and the Moving Image: The Plays on Film and Television (co-ed. with Anthony Davies) 1994, Shakespeare: A Dramatic Career 1994, Shakespeare – A Life in Drama 1995, Shakespeare in the Theatre: An Anthology of Criticism (ed.) 1997, Shakespeare: The Poet and His Plays 1997, Summerfolk: Essays Celebrating Shakespeare (ed.) 1997, A Dictionary of Shakespeare 1998, Shakespeare and Race (co-ed. with Catherine Alexander) 2000, Oxford Companion to Shakespeare (co-ed. with Michael Dobson) 2001, Shakespeare and Sexuality (co-ed. with Catherine M. S. Alexander) 2001, Shakespeare Surveys (co-ed. with others) 2002, Shakespeare: For All Time 2002, The Cambridge Companion to Shakespeare on Stage (co-ed. with Sarah Stanton) 2002, Shakespeare: An Oxford Guide (co-ed. with Lena Cowen Orlin) 2003, Looking for Sex in Shakespeare 2004, Shakespeare's Sonnets (with Paul Edmondson) 2004, Shakespeare & Co 2006, Thomas Middleton, John Fletcher and the Other Players in His Story 2007, Is It True What They Say About Shakespeare? 2007, Coffee with Shakespeare (with Paul Edmondson) 2008, Shakesepare, Sex, and Love 2010; gen. ed. or co-ed. numerous edns, anthologies and collections of Shakespeare's plays. *Honours:* Dr hc (Furman Univ., SC, USA, Univs of Hull, Durham and Warwick, Univ. of Munich,

Germany, Univ. of Craiova, Romania). *Literary Agent:* c/o Sheil Land Associates, 52 Doughty Street, London WC1N 2LS, England. *Telephone:* (20) 7405-9351. *Fax:* (20) 7831-2127. *E-mail:* info@sheilland.co.uk. *Website:* www.sheilland.co.uk. *Address:* The Shakespeare Centre, Henley Street, Stratford-upon-Avon, Warwicks., CV37 6QW, England (office). *Telephone:* (1789) 201828 (office). *E-mail:* stanley.wells@shakespeare.org.uk (office). *Website:* www.shakespeare.org.uk (office).

WELSH, Irvine, MBA; British writer; b. 1958, Edinburgh, Scotland. *Education:* Heriot-Watt Univ. *Career:* co-owner, 4 Way Productions film studio; Amb. for Unicef. *Publications:* Trainspotting (novel) 1993, The Acid House (short stories) 1994, Marabou Stork Nightmares: A Novel 1995, Ecstasy: Three Chemical Romances 1996, The Wedding (with Nick Waplington) 1996, You'll Have Had Your Hole (play) 1997, Filth: A Novel 1998, Glue (novel) 2000, Porno (novel) 2002, Soul Crew (screenplay, also dir) 2003, Meat Trade (screenplay) 2004, The Bedroom Secrets of the Master Chefs (novel) 2006, Babylon Heights (with Dean Cavanagh) 2006, If You Liked School, You'll Love Work (short stories) 2007, Crime (novel) 2008, Reheated Cabbage (short stories) 2009, Skagboys 2012; contrib. to newspapers; contrib. to anthologies, including Children of Albion Rovers 1996, Disco Biscuits 1996, Ahead of its Time 1997, The Weekenders 2002, One City 2006; contrib. to Loaded, Guardian, Daily Telegraph. *Address:* c/o Jonathan Cape, 20 Vauxhall Bridge Road, London, SW1V 2SA, England. *Website:* www.irvinewelsh.net.

WELSH, Louise, BA; British novelist; b. 1968, Edinburgh, Scotland. *Education:* Glasgow Univ., Univ. of Strathclyde. *Career:* bookshop owner. *Plays:* The Cutting Room (adaptation of novel) 2004. *Publications:* The Cutting Room 2002, Tamburlaine Must Die 2004, The Bullet Trick 2006, Naming the Bones 2010. *Honours:* CWA John Creasey Memorial Dagger, Saltire First Book Award (jt winner). *Address:* c/o Canongate Books, 14 High Street, Edinburgh, EH1 1TE, Scotland (office). *E-mail:* info@louisewelsh.com (office). *Website:* www.canongate.net (office); www.louisewelsh.com.

WELTNER, Peter Nissen, BA, PhD; American academic and writer; b. 12 May 1942, Plainfield, NJ; partner Atticus Carr. *Education:* Hamilton Coll., Indiana Univ. *Career:* Prof. of English, San Francisco State Univ. 1969–2006 (retd). *Publications:* Beachside Entries-Specific Ghosts (stories) 1989, Identity and Difference (novel) 1990, In a Time for Combat for the Angel (three short novels) 1991, The Risk of His Music (stories) 1997, How the Body Prays (novel) 1999, Laguna Beach: After Shelter (poetry chapbook) 2009, From a Lost Gospel of Mark (poetry chapbook) 2009, From a Lost Faust Book (poetry chapbook) 2009, News from the World at My Birth: A History (poetry) 2010, The One-Winged Body (poetry chapbook in collaboration with the artist Galen Garwood) 2011, The Outerlands (poetry) 2012. *Honours:* O. Henry Prizes 1993, 1998, Book of the Year Silver Award, ForeWord Magazine, Prick of the Spindle Grand Prize 2010. *Address:* 1587 47th Avenue, San Francisco, CA 94122-2910, USA (home). *Telephone:* (415) 665-2556 (home). *E-mail:* atticusandpeter@sbcglobal.net (office).

WELTON, Matthew; British poet and editor; b. 1969, Nottingham, England. *Career:* Ed. Stand Magazine; teacher of creative writing, University of Bolton; Hawthornden Fellow 2004. *Publications:* Slag Heap, The Book of Matthew (Jerwood-Aldeburgh Best First Collection Prize) 2003; contrib. to anthologies, including First Pressings, New Poetries 2. *Honours:* Eric Gregory Award 1997. *Address:* c/o Carcanet Press, 4th Floor, Alliance House, 30 Cross Street, Manchester, M2 7AQ, England (office).

WENDT, Albert; Samoan/New Zealand author; b. 1939, Apia; three c. *Education:* Ardmore Teachers' Coll., Victoria Univ. *Career:* fmr Prin., Samoa Coll.; Prof. of Pacific Literature and Pro-Vice Chancellor, Univ. of the South Pacific 1974–88; Prof. of New Zealand Literature, Auckland Univ. 1988–, now Prof. Emer.; Distinguished Writer-in-Residence, Univ. of Hawaii at Manoa 2004–08. *Play:* The Songmaker's Chair 2004. *Publications include:* novels: Sons for the Return Home 1973, Pouliuli 1977, Leaves of the Banyan Tree 1979, Ola 1991, Black Rainbow 1992, Mango's Kiss 2003, The Adventures of Vela (Commonwealth Writers' Prize for Best Book, South East Asia and Pacific Region 2010) 2009; short stories: Flying Fox in a Freedom Tree 1974, The Birth and Death of the Miracle Man 1986; poetry: Inside us the Dead: Poems 1961–1974 1976, Shaman of Visions 1984, Photographs 1995, The Book of the Black Star 2002. *Honours:* Order of Merit (Western Samoa), Companion, Order of Merit (New Zealand) 2000; Hon. PhD (Univ. de Bourgogne, France) 1993, Hon. DLit (Victoria Univ.) 2005; Hon. DHumLitt (Hawaii) 2009; Sr Pacific Islands Artist's Award 2003, Nikkei Asia Prize 2004. *Address:* Department of English, University of Auckland, Arts 1 Building, 14a Symonds Street, Level 4, Auckland 1, New Zealand (office). *Telephone:* (9) 373-7599 (office). *E-mail:* a.wendt@auckland.ac.nz (office). *Website:* www.arts.auckland.ac.nz (office).

WENER, Louise; British singer, songwriter and writer; b. 1966, Ilford, Essex, England; pnr Andy MacLure; one d. *Education:* Manchester Univ. *Career:* lead singer, Sleeper 1993–98; numerous tours, festival appearances; mem. PRS, MU, PAMRA; writer 2002–. *Recordings include:* albums: Smart 1995, It Girl 1996, Pleased To Meet You 1997. *Publications:* novels: Goodnight Steve McQueen 2002, The Big Blind (aka The Perfect Play) 2003, The Half Life of Stars 2006, Worldwide Adventures in Love 2008; memoir: Different for Girls: My True-Life Adventures in Pop 2010. *Address:* c/o Hodder & Stoughton, 338 Euston Road, London, NW1 3BH, England.

WENNER, Jann S.; American publisher; *Editor and Publisher, Rolling Stone;* b. 7 Jan. 1946, New York, NY; m. Jane Schindelheim (divorced); six c. *Career:* founder, Ed and Publisher, Rolling Stone magazine 1967–; TV appearances include Crime Story 1987–88; currently oversees Us and Men's Journal magazines; Chair., Wenner Media Inc. *Film appearances:* Up Your Legs Forever 1970, Perfect 1985, Jerry Maguire 1996, Almost Famous 2000. *Publications include:* Lennon Remembers (ed.) 1972, 20 Years of Rolling Stone: What a Long Strange Trip It's Been 1987, Rolling Stone Environmental Reader 1992, Gonzo: The Life of Hunter S. Thompson (with Corey Seymour) 2007, Fear and Loathing at Rolling Stone: The Essential Writing of Hunter S. Thompson (ed.) 2011. *Address:* Rolling Stone, Wenner Media Inc., 1290 Avenue of the Americas, New York, NY 10104-0298, USA (office). *Telephone:* (212) 484-1616 (office). *E-mail:* editors@rollingstone.com (office). *Website:* www.rollingstone.com (office).

WENTWORTH, Wendy (see Chaplin, Jenny)

WERBER, Bernard; French writer; b. Sept. 1961, Toulouse. *Education:* Ecole Supérieure de Journalisme de Paris. *Career:* scientific reviewer, Nouvel Observateur 1984–90. *Publications:* novels: Les Fourmis 1991, Le Jour des Fourmis 1992, Le Livre Secret des Fourmis 1993, Les Thanatonautes 1994, La Révolution des Fourmis 1996, Le Livre du Voyage 1997, Le Pére de Nos Péres 1998, L'Empire des Anges 2000, L'Ultime Secret 2001, L'Arbre des Possibles 2002, Nos Ames les Humains 2003, Nous les Dieux 2004, Le Souffle des Dieux 2005, Le Papillon des Étoiles 2006, Le Mystére des Dieux 2007, Nouvelle Encyclopédie du Savoir Relatif et Absolu 2008, Parades sur Mesure 2008, Le Miroir de Cassandre 2009. *Literary Agent:* Jacqueline Favero, 22 rue Huygens, Paris 75014, France. *Telephone:* 1-42-79-10-00. *E-mail:* bwerber@free.fr (office). *Website:* www.bernardwerber.com.

WERTENBAKER, Timberlake, FRSL; British playwright; *Artistic Director, Natural Perspective Theatre Company;* m. John Man; one d. *Career:* Resident Playwright, Royal Court Theatre 1984–85; Dir English Stage Co. 1991–99; mem. Exec. Cttee PEN 1999–2002; Royden B. Davis Visiting Prof. of Theatre, Georgetown Univ., Washington, DC 2005–06; Artistic Dir Natural Perspective Theatre Co. 2007–; Leverhulme Artist-in-Residence, Freud Museum, London 2011–; mem. Artistic Advisory Panel, Royal Acad. of Dramatic Art 2008–, Council of the Royal Soc. of Literature 2011–. *Plays include:* (for the Soho-Poly): Case to Answer 1980; (for the Women's Theatre Group): New Anatomies 1982; (for the Royal Court): Abel's Sister 1984, The Grace of Mary Traverse 1985, Our Country's Good 1988, Three Birds Alighting on a Field 1991, Credible Witness 2001; (for Out of Joint): The Break of Day 1995; (for RSC): The Love of the Nightingale 1988; (for Hampstead Theatre): After Darwin 1998; (for Birmingham Rep.): The Ash Girl 2000; (for Theatre Royal, Bath): Galileo's Daughter 2004; (for Arcola Theatre, London) The Line 2009; (for RSC): trans. Arianne Mnouchkine's Mephisto, trans. Sophocles' Thebans; (for San Francisco ACT): trans. Euripides' Hecuba; (for Peter Hall Co.): trans. Eduardo de Filippo's Filumena (Piccadilly Theatre) 1998, (for Chichester) Jean Anouilh's Wild Orchards 2002, trans. Gabriela Preissová's Jenufa (for Arcola Theatre, London) 2008; trans. Euripides' Hippolytus (Riverside Studios, London) 2009; trans. Racine's Phedre (Stratford, Ontario) 2009, (ACT, San Francisco) 2010, Sophocles' Elektra (Getty, Los Angeles) 2010; trans. Racine's Britannicus (Wilton's Music Hall) 2011; other trans. include Successful Strategies, False Admissions, La Dispute (Marivaux), Come tu mi vuoi (Pirandello), Pelleas and Mélisande (Maeterlinck). *Libretto:* The Love of the Nightingale (music by Richard Mills, Sydney Opera House) 2011. *Films:* The Children (Channel 4), Do Not Disturb (BBC TV). *Television:* Belle and the Beast (BBC). *Radio includes:* Credible Witness, Dianeira, Hecuba (trans. and adaptation), The H. File (adaptation of novel by Ismail Kadaré), Scenes of Seduction 2005, Divine Intervention 2006, What is the Custom of Your Grief? 2009, adaptation of A. S. Byatt's Possession 2011. *Publications:* Timberlake Wertenbaker: Plays 1 1996, The Break of Day 1996, After Darwin 1999, Filumena 1999, The Ash Girl 2000, Credible Witness 2001, Timberlake Wertenbaker: Plays 2 2002, Jenufa (Adaption) 2007, Hippolytus 2009, The Line 2009, Britannicus (trans.) 2011, Timberlake Wertenbaker: Teatro: Dopo Darwin, Testimone Credibile, Le Leggi del Moto 2011. *Honours:* Dr hc (Open Univ.); Plays and Players Most Promising Playwright (for The Grace of Mary Traverse) 1985, Evening Standard Most Promising Playwright, Olivier Play of the Year (for Our Country's Good) 1988, Eileen Anderson Drama Award (for The Love of the Nightingale) 1989, Critics' Circle Best West End Play 1991, Writers' Guild Best West End Play, Susan Smith Blackburn Award (for Three Birds Alighting on a Field) 1992, Mrs Giles Whiting Award (for gen. body of work) 1989, Guggenheim Fellowship 2004. *Literary Agent:* c/o The Agency, 24 Pottery Lane, Holland Park, London, W11 4LZ, England.

WESKER, Sir Arnold, Kt, FRSL; British playwright and director; b. 24 May 1932, Stepney, London, England; s. of Joseph Wesker and Leah Wesker (née Perlmutter); m. Doreen (Dusty) Cecile Bicker 1958; two s. one d. *Education:* mixed elementary schools and Upton House Central School, Hackney, London, London School of Film Technique. *Career:* left school 1948, worked as furniture maker's apprentice, carpenter's mate, bookseller's asst; RAF 1950–52 (ran drama group); plumber's mate, road labourer, farm labourer, seed sorter, kitchen porter and pastry-cook; Dir Centre 42 1961–70; Chair. British Centre of Int. Theatre Inst. 1978–82; Pres. Int. Cttee of Playwrights 1979–83; Arts Council Bursary 1959. *Film scripts:* The Master (free adaptation of An Unfortunate Incident by F. Dostoevsky) 1966, Madam Solario (from anonymous novel of same title) 1969, The Wesker Trilogy 1979, Lady Othello 1980, Homage to Catalonia (from George Orwell's autobiography) 1991,

Maudie (from Doris Lessing's novel Diary of a Good Neighbour) 1995, The Kitchen (for Italian film co.). *Opera librettos:* Caritas (music by Robert Saxton) 1988, Grief (one-woman opera commissioned by Japanese composer Shigeaki Saegusa) 2004. *Plays:* The Kitchen, Royal Court Theatre 1959, 1961, 1994, Chicken Soup with Barley, Roots, I'm Talking about Jerusalem (The Wesker Trilogy), Belgrade Theatre, Coventry 1958–60, Royal Court Theatre 1960, Chips with Everything, Royal Court 1962, Vaudeville 1962, Broadway 1963, The Four Seasons, Belgrade Theatre then The Saville Theatre 1965, Their Very Own and Golden City, Brussels and Royal Court 1966, The Friends (Stockholm and London) 1970, The Old Ones, Royal Court 1972, The Wedding Feast, Stockholm 1974, Leeds 1977, The Journalists, Coventry 1977, Germany 1981, The Merchant (later entitled Shylock), Stockholm and Århus 1976, Broadway 1977, Birmingham 1978, Love Letters on Blue Paper, Nat. Theatre 1978, Fatlips 1978, Caritas, Nat. Theatre 1981, Sullied Hand 1981, Edinburgh Festival and Finnish TV 1984, Four Portraits, Tokyo 1982, Edin. Festival 1984, Annie Wobbler, Birmingham 1983, Fortune Theatre 1984, New York 1986, One More Ride on the Merry-Go-Round, Leicester 1985, Yardsale, Edinburgh Festival and Stratford-on-Avon 1985, When God Wanted a Son, New End Theatre, London 1986, Whatever Happened to Betty Lemon, Yardsale, Lyric Studio, London 1987, Little Old Lady, Sweden 1988, The Mistress 1988, Beorhtel's Hill, Towngate, Basildon 1989, Three Women Talking (now Men Die Women Survive) 1990, Chicago 1992, Letter to a Daughter 1990, Blood Libel 1991, Wild Spring 1992, Tokyo 1994, Denial, Bristol Old Vic 2000, Groupie 2001 (based on radio play), Longitude 2002 (freely adapted from book by Dava Sobel), Letter To Myself 2004; 45-minute adaptations for Schools Shakespeare Festival of Much Ado About Nothing and Henry V 2006, Phoenix Phoenix Burning Bright 2006, The Rocking Horse Kid (adapted from radio play) 2008, Joy and Tyranny 2010. *Own plays directed:* The Four Seasons, Cuba 1968, world première of The Friends at Stadsteatern, Stockholm 1970, London 1970, The Old Ones, Munich, Their Very Own and Golden City, Århus 1974, Love Letters on Blue Paper, Nat. Theatre 1978, Oslo 1980, Annie Wobbler, Birmingham 1983, London 1984, Yardsale and Whatever Happened to Betty Lemon, London 1987, Shylock (workshop production), London 1989, The Kitchen, Univ. of Wis. 1990, The Mistress, Rome 1991, The Wedding Feast, Denison Univ., Ohio 1995, Letter to a Daughter, Edin. Festival 1998; also Dir Osborne's The Entertainer, Theatre Clwyd 1983, The Merry Wives of Windsor, Oslo 1989. *Radio includes:* Bluey (Cologne Radio) 1985, (BBC) 1985, Groupie (commissioned by BBC) 2001, adaptation of Shylock (commissioned by BBC Radio 3) 2006, The Rocking Horse (commissioned by BBC World Service) 2006. *Adaptations for TV:* Menace 1961, Thieves in the Night (Arthur Koestler) 1984–85, Diary of a Good Neighbour (Doris Lessing) 1989, Phoenix Phoenix Burning Bright (from own story, The Visit) 1992, Barabbas 2000. *Publications include:* plays: The Kitchen 1957, Chicken Soup with Barley 1958, Roots 1959, I'm Talking About Jerusalem 1960, Chips with Everything 1962, The Four Seasons 1965, Their Very Own and Golden City 1966, The Old Ones 1970, The Friends 1970, The Journalists 1972, The Wedding Feast 1974, Shylock (previously The Merchant) 1976, Love Letters on Blue Paper (TV play) 1976, (stage play) 1977, Words – As Definitions of Experience 1976, One More Ride on the Merry-Go-Round 1978, Fatlips 1980, Caritas 1980, Annie Wobbler 1982, Four Portraits – of Mothers 1982, Yardsale 1983, Cinders 1983, Bluey 1984, Whatever Happened to Betty Lemon 1986, When God Wanted a Son 1986, Badenheim 1939 1987, Shoeshine & Little Old Lady 1987, Lady Othello 1987, Beorhtel's Hill 1988, The Mistress 1988, Three Women Talking 1990, Letter to a Daughter 1990, Blood Libel 1991, Wild Spring 1992, Circles of Perception 1996, Break My Heart 1997, Denial 1997; essays, stories, etc.: Fears of Fragmentation 1971, Six Sundays in January 1971, Love Letters on Blue Paper 1974, Journey into Journalism 1977, Said the Old Man to the Young Man 1978, Distinctions 1985, As Much As I Dare (autobiog.) 1994, The Birth of Shylock and the Death of Zero Mostel (non-fiction) 1997, The King's Daughters 1998, The Wesker Trilogy 2001, One Woman Plays 2001; novels: Honey 2005, Longitude 2006; poetry: All Things Tire of Themselves 2009. *Honours:* Hon. Fellow, Queen Mary Coll. London 1995; Hon. DLitt (Univ. of E Anglia) 1989, Hon. DHumLitt (Denison Univ., Ohio) 1997; Evening Standard Award for Most Promising Playwright (for Roots) 1959, third prize Encyclopaedia Britannica Competition (for The Kitchen) 1961, Premio Marzotto Drama Prize (for Their Very Own and Golden City) 1964, Gold Medal, Premios el Espectador y la Critica (for The Kitchen) 1973, (for Chicken Soup with Barley) 1979, The Goldie Award (for Roots) 1986, Last Frontier Award for Lifetime Achievement, Valdez, Alaska 1999, Royal Literary Fund annual pension and award for lifetime achievement 2003. *Address:* Hay on Wye, Hereford, Herefords., HR3 5RJ, England (home). *Telephone:* (1497) 820473 (home). *E-mail:* wesker@compuserve.com (home). *Website:* www.arnoldwesker.com.

WEST, Cornel Ronald, AB, MA, PhD; American academic and writer; *Class of 1943 University Professor, Center for African American Studies, Princeton University*; b. 2 June 1953, Tulsa, Oklahoma; m. 1st (divorced); one s.; m. 2nd (divorced); m. 3rd Elleni West. *Education:* Harvard Univ., Princeton Univ. *Career:* Asst Prof. of the Philosophy of Religion, Union Theological Seminary, New York City 1977–83, 1988; Assoc., Yale Univ. Divinity School 1984–87, University of Paris 1987; Prof., Princeton Univ. 1989–94, Class of 1943 Univ. Prof., Center for African American Studies 2002–; Prof., Harvard Univ. 1994–2002. *Publications:* Theology in the Americas: Detroit II Conference Papers (ed. with Caridad Guidote and Margaret Coakley) 1982, Prophesy Deliverance!: An Afro-American Revolutionary Christianity 1982, Post-Analytic Philosophy (with John Rajchman) 1985, Prophetic Fragments 1988, The American Evasion of Philosophy: A Genealogy of Pragmatism 1989, Breaking Bread: Insurgent Black Intellectual Life (with Bell Hooks) 1991, The Ethical Dimensions of Marxist Thought 1991, Out There: Marginalization and Contemporary Cultures (co-ed.) 1991, Race Matters 1993, Keeping Faith: Philosophy and Race in America 1994, Beyond Eurocentrism and Multiculturalism 1993, The Future of the Race 1997, The Cornel West Reader 2000, The African American Century: How Black Americans Have Shaped Our Country (with Henry Louis Gates Jr) 2000, Democracy Matters 2004; contributions: newspapers and magazines. *Address:* Center for African American Studies, Princeton University, Stanhope Hall, Princeton, NJ 08544, USA (office). *Telephone:* (609) 258-0021 (office). *E-mail:* cwest@princeton.edu (office). *Website:* www.princeton.edu (office); www.cornelwest.com.

WEST, Ewan Donald, BA, MA, MBA, DPhil; British writer on music; b. 9 Aug. 1960, Cheltenham, Gloucestershire. *Education:* Exeter Coll., Oxford, Cranfield School of Management. *Career:* Lecturer on History of Music, Worcester Coll., Oxford 1986–94; Jr Research Fellow, Mansfield Coll., Oxford 1988–92; Dir of Studies in Music, Somerville Coll., Oxford 1989–94; Univ. of Oxford James Ingham Halstead Scholar 1985–87; mem. American Musicological Soc., Royal Musical Asscn. *Publications:* The Hamlyn Dictionary of Music 1982, The Oxford Dictionary of Opera (with John Warrack) 1992, The Concise Oxford Dictionary of Opera (third edn, with John Warrack) 1996; contrib. to Music and Letters, Austrian Studies. *Address:* 14 Moorhouse Road, London, W2 5DJ, England (office). *Telephone:* (20) 7221-6001 (home). *E-mail:* ewan_west@hotmail.com (home).

WEST, Kathleene, BA, MA, PhD; American academic, poet and editor; b. 28 Dec. 1947, Genoa, Neb. *Education:* Univ. of Nebraska, Univ. of Washington. *Career:* Assoc. Prof. of English, New Mexico State Univ. 1987–; Poetry Ed., Puerto del Sol 1995–; mem. Associated Writing Programs, Barbara Pym Society, PEN. *Publications:* Land Bound 1977, The Armadillo on the Rug 1978, The Garden Section 1982, Water Witching 1984, Plainswoman 1985, The Farmer's Daughter 1990, Death of a Regional Poet 1998, The Road to Mandalay, The Summer of the Sub-comandante; contributions: reviews, quarterlies and journals. *Honours:* Fulbright Scholar, Iceland 1983–85.

WEST, Nigel; British writer; b. 8 Nov. 1951, London, England; m. 1979 (divorced 1996); one s. one d. *Education:* Univs of Grenoble and Lille, France and Univ. of London. *Career:* worked for BBC TV 1977–82, The Centre for Counterintelligence & Security Studies 1997–2009. *Publications:* Spy 1980, A Matter of Trust: M15 1945–72 1982, Unreliable Witness 1984, Carbo M15 1981, M16 1983, 1985, GCHQ 1986, Molehunt 1986, The Friends 1987, Games of Intelligence 1990, Seven Spies Who Changed the World 1991, Secret War 1992, The Illegals 1993, Faber Book of Espionage 1993, Faber Book of Treachery 1995, Secret War for the Falklands 1997, Crown Jewels 1998, Counterfeit Spies 1998, Venona 1999, The Third Secret 2000, Mortal Crimes 2004, The Guy Liddell Diaries (ed.) 2005, Mask 2005, Historical Dictionary of British Intelligence 2005, At Her Majesty's Secret Service 2006, Historical Dictionary of World War II Intelligence 2007, Historical Dictionary of Cold War Counterintelligence 2007, TRIPLEX 2009; contrib. to The Times, Intelligence Quarterly. *Honours:* Observer The Expert's Expert 1989, US Asscn of Former Intelligence Officers' Lifetime Literature Award. *Address:* Westintel Research Ltd, 6 Burton Mews, London SW1W 9EP, England (office). *Telephone:* (20) 7352-1110 (office). *Fax:* (20) 7352-1111 (office). *E-mail:* nigel.west@cicentre.com (office). *Website:* www.nigelwest.com.

WEST, Owen (see Koontz, Dean Ray)

WEST, Paul, MA; American (b. British) author; b. 23 Feb. 1930, Eckington, Derbyshire, England; s. of Alfred West and Mildred Noden. *Education:* Univ. of Oxford, UK and Columbia Univ. *Career:* served with RAF 1954–57; Asst Prof. of English, Memorial Univ., Newfoundland 1957–58, Assoc. Prof. 1958–60; arrived in USA 1961, became naturalized 1971; contrib., Washington Post, New York Times 1962–95, also contributes to Harper's and GQ magazines, Paris Review; mem. of staff Pa State Univ. 1962, Prof. of English and Comparative Literature 1968–1995, Prof. Emer. 1995–; Crawshaw Prof., Colgate Univ. 1972; Melvin Hill Distinguished Visiting Prof., Hobart and William Smith Colls 1973; Distinguished Writer-in-Residence, Wichita State Univ. 1982; Writer-in-Residence, Univ. of Arizona 1984; Visiting Prof. of English, Cornell Univ. 1986, Brown Univ. 1992; Guggenheim Fellow 1962–63; Nat. Endowment for Arts Creative Writing Fellow 1979, 1984; mem. Author's Guild. *Publications include:* Byron and the Spoiler's Art 1960, I, Said the Sparrow 1963, The Snow Leopard 1965, Tenement of Clay 1965, The Wine of Absurdity 1966, I'm Expecting to Live Quite Soon 1970, Words for a Deaf Daughter 1970, Caliban's Filibuster 1971, Bela Lugosi's White Christmas 1972, Colonel Mint 1973, Gala 1976, The Very Rich Hours of Count von Stauffenberg 1980, Out of My Depths: A Swimmer in the Universe and Other Fictions 1988, The Place in Flowers Where Pollen Rests 1988, Lord Byron's Doctor 1989, Portable People, The Women of Whitechapel and Jack the Ripper 1991, James Ensor 1991, Love's Mansion 1992, A Stroke of Genius 1995, Sporting with Amaryllis 1996, Terrestrials 1997, Life with Swan 1999, O.K.: The Corral 2000, The Earps 2000, Doc Holliday 2000, The Dry Danube: A Hitler Forgery 2000, The Secret Lives of Words 2000, A Fifth of November 2001, Master Class 2001, Portable People 2001, Oxford Days 2002, Cheops: A Cupboard for the Sun 2002, The Immensity of the Here and Now: A Novel of 9.11 2003, My Father's War 2005, Tea with Osiris (poems) 2006, The Shadow Factory 2008. *Honours:* Chevalier, Ordre Arts et Lettres; Aga Khan Fiction Prize 1973, Hazlett Memorial Award for Excellence in Arts (Literature) 1981,

Literature Award, American Acad. and Inst. of Arts and Letters 1985, Pushcart Prize 1987, 1991, Best American Essays Award 1990, Grand Prix Halpérine Kaminsky Award 1992, Lannan Fiction Award 1993, Teaching Award NE Asscn of Grad. Schools 1994, Art of Fact Prize, State Univ. of NY 2000; Outstanding Achievement Medal, Pa State Univ. 1991. *Address:* c/o Lumen Books, 40 Camino Cielo, Santa Fe, NM 87506, USA.

WESTÖ, Kjell; Finnish writer and poet; b. 6 Aug. 1961, Helsinki. *Career:* writes mainly in Swedish and also in Finnish. *Play:* Det hjärta man har, Svenska Teatern i Helsingfors 2008. *Publications:* Tango Orange (poems) 1986, Epitaf över Mr Nacht (poems) 1988, Avig-Bön (poems, as Anders Hed) 1989, Utslag och andra noveller (short stories) 1989, Fallet Bruus (short stories) 1992, Drakarna över Helsingfors (novel) 1996, Vådan av vara Skrake (novel) 2000, Lang (novel) 2002, Lugna favoriter (short stories) 2004, Där vi en gång gått (novel) 2006, Gå inte ensam ut i natten (novel) 2009. *Honours:* Svenska Litteratursällskapet i Finland Literary Awards 1987, 1990, 1997, 2001, 2007, 2010, Nat. Prize for Literature 1990, Young Finland Prize 1996, Thank You for the Book Medallion 1997, Helsinki Medallion 2002, Svenska kulturfondens kulturpris 2004, Finlandia Prize 2006, Pro Finlandia Medallion 2008. *Address:* c/o Harvill Press, Random House, 20 Vauxhall Bridge Road, London, SW1V 2SA, England.

WESTON, Helen Gray (see Daniels, Dorothy)

WEVILL, David Anthony, BA, MA; Canadian academic and poet; b. 15 March 1935, Yokohama, Japan; m. Assia Gutman 1960. *Education:* Caius Coll., Cambridge. *Career:* Lecturer, Univ. of Texas, Austin, now Prof. Emer. *Publications:* Penguin Modern Poets 1963, Birth of a Spark 1964, A Christ of the Ice Floes 1966, Firebreak 1971, Where the Arrow Falls 1973, Other Names for the Heart: New and Selected Poems, 1964–84 1985, Figures of Eight 1987, Child Eating Snow 1993, Solo with Grazing Deer 2001, Departures: Selected Poems 2003, Asterisks 2007; translations of Hungarian poetry. *Address:* c/o Department of English, University of Texas at Austin, 1 University Station B5000, Austin, TX 78712-1164, USA (office). *E-mail:* wevill@mail.utexas.edu (office).

WEYERGANS, François; Belgian writer and critic; b. 9 Dec. 1941, Etterbeek. *Education:* Jesuit school, Brussels and Institut des Hautes Études Cinématographiques, Paris. *Career:* fmr film dir; literary and film critic, contributing to Cahiers du cinéma; mem. Académie Française 2009–. *Films:* Béjart (writer, dir) 1962, Hieronymus Bosch (writer, dir) 1963, Cinéma de notre temps: Robert Bresson - Ni vu, ni connu (TV film; dir) 1965, Beaudelaire est mort en été (dir) 1967, Aline (writer, dir) 1967, Un film sur quelqu'un (dir) 1972, Maladie mortelle (dir) 1977, Je t'aime, tu danses (writer, dir) 1977, Couleur chair (writer, dir) 1979, Une femme en Afrique (writer) 1985. *Publications:* novels: Le Pitre (Prix Roger Nimier) 1973, Berlin, mercredi 1979, Les Figurants (Prix de la Société des Gens de Lettres, Académie Royale de Langue et de Littérature françaises de Belgique Prix Sander Pierron) 1980, Macaire le Copte (Prix Rossel, Belgium, Prix des Deux Magots) 1981, Le Radeau de la méduse (Prix méridien des quatre jurys) 1983, La Vie d'un bébé 1986, Françaises, français 1988, Je suis écrivain 1989, Rire et pleurer 1990, La Démence du boxeur (Prix Renaudot) 1992, Franz et François (Grand prix de la langue Française) 1997, Salomé 2005, Trois jours chez ma mère (Prix Goncourt) 2005, La Démence du Boxeur 2008. *Address:* c/o Editions Gallimard, Folio, 5, rue Sébastian-Bottin, 75328 Paris, France (office). *Website:* www.folio-lesite.fr (office).

WHALLON, William, BA; American poet and writer; b. 24 Sept. 1928, Richmond, Ind. *Education:* McGill University. *Career:* Fellow, Center for Hellenic Studies 1962, Fulbright Prof. in Comparative Literature, Univ. of Bayreuth 1985. *Publications:* A Book of Time (poems) 1990, Giants in the Earth (ed.) 1991, The Oresteia/Apollo & Bacchus (scenarios) 1997.

WHEATCROFT, John Stewart, BA, MA, PhD; American academic, writer and poet; b. 24 July 1925, Philadelphia; m. 1st Joan Mitchell Osborne 1952 (divorced 1974); two s. one d.; m. 2nd Katherine Whaley Warner 1992. *Education:* Bucknell Univ., Rutgers Univ. *Publications:* poetry: Death of a Clown 1963, Prodigal Son 1967, A Voice from the Hump 1977, Ordering Demons 1981, The Stare on the Donkey's Face 1990, Random Necessities 1997, The Fugitive Self: New and Selected Poems 2009; fiction: Edie Tells 1975, Catherine, Her Book 1983, Slow Exposures (short stories) 1986, The Beholder's Eye 1987, Killer Swan 1992, Mother of All Loves 1994, Trio with Four Players 1995, The Education of Malcolm Palmer 1997, Answering Fire 2006; other: Our Other Voices (ed.) 1991; contrib. to New York Times, New York Times Book Review, Hartford Courant, Herald Tribune, Harper's Bazaar, Mademoiselle, Yankee, many literary magazines. *Honours:* Alcoa Playwriting Award 1966, Nat. Educational Television Award 1967, Yaddo Fellowships 1972, 1985, MacDowell Colony Fellowship 1973, Virginia Center for the Creative Arts Fellowship 1976, 1978, 1980, 1982. *Address:* 350 River Road, Lewisburg, PA 17837-8001, USA (home). *Telephone:* (717) 524-2617 (home). *E-mail:* jsw015@bucknell.edu (home).

WHEATCROFT, Baroness (Life Peer), cr. 2010, of Blackheath in the London Borough of Greenwich; **Patience Wheatcroft,** LLB; British journalist; b. 28 Sept. 1951, Chesterfield, Derbyshire, England; m. Tony Salter; three c. *Education:* Univ. of Birmingham. *Career:* launched with her husband, Retail Week 1988, Ed. 1988–92; has worked on financial sections of The Daily Mail, The Sunday Times and The Daily Telegraph; Deputy City Ed. Mail on Sunday –1997; Business and City Ed. The Times 1997–2006; Ed. The Sunday Telegraph 2006–07; Ed.-in-Chief The Wall Street Journal Europe 2009–10; mem. (Conservative) House of Lords 2010–; Dir (non-exec.) Barclays Bank 2007–09, Shaftesbury plc 2008–09; Head of Mayor of London's newly created Forensic Audit Panel 2008; mem. UK-India Round Table, Bd British Museum 2010–, Council of the Royal Albert Hall 2011–, Advisory Bd, British Olympic Asscn, Advisory Bd, Reuters Inst. for Study of Journalism; mem. (Conservative) House of Lords 2010–. *Honours:* Hon. Dr of Arts (City Univ.) 2011; Wincott Sr Journalist of the Year Award 2001, London Press Club Business Journalist of the Year 2003. *Address:* House of Lords, Westminster, London, SW1A 0PW, England (office). *Telephone:* (20) 7219-3107 (office); (20) 7219-1570 (office). *Website:* www.parliament.uk/biographies/patience-wheatcroft/57848 (office).

WHEELER, Katherine (Kate) Frazier, BA, MA; American teacher and writer; b. 27 July 1955, Tulsa, OK. *Education:* Rice Univ., Stanford Univ. *Career:* ordained Buddhist nun, Mahasi Sasana Yeiktha, Rangoon 1988; teacher of meditation; mem. Insight Meditation Soc. (bd mem.). *Publications:* Lo Esperado y lo vivado (co-trans.) 1984, In This Very Life: The Liberation Teachings of the Buddha (ed.) 1992, Not Where I Started From (short stories) 1993, When Mountains Walked 2000, Nixon Under the Bodhi Tree and other works of Buddhist Fiction 2004; contributions: periodicals. *Honours:* O. Henry Awards 1982, 1993, Pushcart Press Prize 1983–84, Best American Short Stories Prize, Houghton Mifflin Co 1992, National Education Asscn Grant 1994, Whiting Foundation Award 1994.

WHEELER, Sara, BA, MA, FRSL; British writer; partner; two s. *Education:* Univ. of Oxford. *Career:* mem. Council of the Royal Soc. of Literature 2000–05; Trustee, London Library 2006–09, Sibs 2009–; Contributing Ed., Literary Review 2010–. *Radio:* To Strive, To Seek (five-part series, BBC Radio 4) 2012. *Publications:* Evia: An Island Apart 1992, Travels in a Thin Country: A Journey Through Chile 1995, Terra Incognita: Travels in Antarctica 1997, Dear Daniel: Letters from Antarctica 1997, Amazonian: Penguin Book of Women's New Travel Writing (co-ed. with Dea Birkett) 1998, Cherry: A Life of Apsley Cherry-Garrard 2001, Too Close to the Sun: The Life and Times of Denys Finch Hatton 2006, The Magnetic North: Notes from the Arctic Circle 2009, Access All Areas: Selected Writings 2010; essays in various pubs worldwide. *Honours:* Hawthornden Fellow 2010. *Literary Agent:* c/o Aitken Alexander Associates Ltd, 18–21 Cavaye Place, London, SW10 9PT, England. *Telephone:* (20) 7373-8672. *E-mail:* reception@aitkenalexander.co.uk. *Website:* www.aitkenalexander.co.uk.

WHEELWRIGHT, Julie Diana, BA, MA; British writer and broadcaster; b. 2 June 1960, Farnborough, Kent, England. *Education:* Univ. of British Columbia, Univ. of Sussex. *Career:* reporter, Vancouver Sun 1980; Pres., Canadian Univ. Press 1981; Consultant, Open Univ. 1991; Course Dir, MA in Creative Writing (Non-fiction), City Univ., London 2007–; mem. Writers' Guild. *Publications:* Amazons and Military Maids 1989, The Fatal Lover 1992, A Stolen Child: The Story of Esther Wheelright; contributions: newspapers and journals. *Honours:* hon. research fellow Inst. of Historical Research, Royal Holloway, London; Canada Council Non-Fiction Writers' Grants 1990–91, 1994–95. *Address:* Department of Journalism, City University London, Northampton Square, London EC1V 0HB, England (office). *Telephone:* (20) 7040-8221 (office). *Website:* www.city.ac.uk/journalism (office).

WHELAN, Peter, BA; British playwright; b. 3 Oct. 1931, Newcastle-under-Lyme, Staffs.; s. of Thomas and Bertha Whelan; two s. one d. *Education:* Univ. of Keele, Staffs. *Career:* advertising copywriter and dir 1959–90. *Plays:* Double Edge (with Leslie Darbon, Vaudeville Theatre) 1975, Captain Swing (RSC) 1978, The Accrington Pals (RSC) 1981, Clay (RSC) 1982, The Bright and Bold Design (RSC) 1991, The School of Night (RSC) 1992, Shakespeare Country (Amateur Estival) 1993, Worlds Apart (RSC) 1993, The Tinderbox (New Vic) 1994, Divine Right (Birmingham Rep.) 1996, The Herbal Bed (RSC, West End and Broadway) 1996, Nativity (co-author, Birmingham Rep.) 1999, A Russian in the Woods (RSC) 2001, The Earthly Paradise (Almeida, London) 2004. *Television:* In Suspicious Circumstances (Granada) 1992, The Trial of Lord Lucan (Granada) 1994. *Honours:* Hon. Assoc. RSC 1995; Lloyds Private Banking Playwright of the Year 1996, TMA Regional Theatre Award for Best New Play 1996. *Literary Agent:* c/o The Agency, 24 Pottery Lane, Holland Park, London, W11 4LZ, England. *Telephone:* (20) 7727-1346. *E-mail:* info@theagency.co.uk. *Website:* www.theagency.co.uk.

WHICKER, Alan Donald, CBE, FRSA; British television broadcaster, journalist and author; b. 2 Aug. 1925, s. of the late Charles Henry Whicker and Anne Jane Cross. *Education:* Haberdashers' Aske's. *Career:* Dir Army Film and Photo Unit, with 8th Army and US 5th Army; war corresp., Korea; Foreign Corresp. Exchange Telegraph 1947–57, BBC TV 1957–68; Founder mem. Yorkshire TV 1968. *Radio includes:* Whicker's Wireless World (BBC Radio series) 1983; Around Whicker's World (six programmes for Radio 2) 1998, Whicker's New World (7 programmes for Radio 2) 1999, Whicker's World Down Under (6 programmes for Radio 2) 2000, Fabulous Fifties (4 programmes for Radio 2) 2000, It'll Never Last—The History of Television (6 programmes for Radio 2) 2001, Fifty Royal Years (6 programmes celebrating Queen's Golden Jubilee, Radio 2), Around Whicker's World (series of Radio 4 essays) 2002. *Television:* joined BBC TV 1957; regular appearances on 'Tonight' programme, then series Whicker's World 1959–60, Whicker Down Under 1961, Whicker in Sweden 1963, Whicker's World 1965–67; made 122 documentaries for Yorkshire TV including Whicker's New World Series, Whicker in Europe, World of Whicker; returned to BBC TV 1982; programmes include: Whicker's World – The First Million Miles! (four programmes) 1982, Whicker's World, A Fast Boat to China (four programmes) 1983, Whicker! (series talk shows) 1984, Whicker's World – Living with Uncle Sam (10 programmes) 1985, Whicker's World – Living with Waltzing Matilda (10 programmes) 1988, Whicker's World – Hong Kong (eight programmes) 1990, Whicker's World – A Taste of Spain (eight programmes) 1992, Around Whicker's World (four programmes, for ITV) 1992, Whicker's World – The Sultan of Brunei 1992, South Africa: Whicker's Miss World and Whicker's World – The Sun King 1993, South-East Asia: Whicker's World Aboard the Real Orient Express, Whicker's World – Pavarotti in Paradise 1994, Travel Channel (26 programmes) 1996, Whicker's Week, BBC Choice 1999; Travel Amb. on the Internet for AOL 2000; One on One 2002, Whicker's War Series (Channel 4) 2004, Comedy Map of Britain (series of 12 programmes) 2007, Comedy Map of Britain (four programmes) 2008, Whicker's World: Journey of a Lifetime (four programmes) 2009. *Publications:* Some Rise by Sin 1949, Away – With Alan Whicker 1963, Best of Everything 1980, Within Whicker's World (autobiog.) 1982, Whicker's Business Travellers Guide 1983, Whicker's New World 1985, Whicker's World Down Under 1988, Whicker's World – Take 2! 2000, Whicker's War 2005, Whicker's World: Journey of a Lifetime 2009. *Honours:* various awards, including Guild of TV Producers and Dirs., Personality of the Year 1964, Silver Medal, Royal TV Soc., Dimbleby Award, BAFTA 1978, TV Times Special Award 1978, first to be named in Royal Television Soc.'s new Hall of Fame for outstanding creative contrib. to British TV 1993, Travel Writers' Special Award, for truly outstanding achievement in travel journalism 1998, BAFTA Grierson Documentary Tribute Award 2001, Nat. Film Theatre tribute, sixth Television Festival 2002, Inaugural Star of Avenue of the Stars 2005, War Reporter of the Year 2006, OAG Airlines of the Year Lifetime Achievement Award 2006, Travel Press Award for Lifetime Contrib. to Travel 2010. *Address:* Trinity, Jersey, JE3 5BA, Channel Islands (home).

WHITBOURN, John, BA; British writer; b. 23 March 1958, Godalming, Surrey, England; m. Elizabeth Caroline Gale 1982; one s. two d. *Education:* Univ. Coll., Cardiff. *Publications:* Binscombe Tales 1989, Rollover Night 1990, A Dangerous Energy 1992, Popes and Phantoms 1993, To Build Jerusalem 1995, The Binscombe Tales (two vols) 1998–99, The Royal Changeling 1998, Downs-Lord Dawn 1999, Downs-Lord Day 2000, Downs-Lord Doomsday 2002. *Honours:* BBC-Gollancz First Fantasy Novel Prize 1991. *E-mail:* JAW@telinco.co.uk (office). *Website:* www.btinternet.com/~john.whitbourn.

WHITE, Edmund Valentine, III, BA; American writer and academic; *Professor of Creative Writing, Princeton University;* b. 13 Jan. 1940, Cincinnati, OH; s. of E. V. White and Delilah Teddlie. *Education:* Univ. of Michigan. *Career:* writer, Time-Life Books, New York 1962–70; Sr Ed. Saturday Review, New York 1972–73; Asst Prof. of Writing Seminars, Johns Hopkins Univ. 1977–79; Adjunct Prof., Columbia Univ. School of the Arts 1981–83; Exec. Dir New York Inst. for the Humanities 1982–83; Prof. of English, Brown Univ., Providence, RI 1990–92; Prof. of Humanities, Princeton Univ. 1999, now Prof. of Creative Writing in the Univ. Center for the Creative and Performing Arts; Guggenheim Fellowship; mem. Acad. of Arts and Letters 1998. *Play:* Terre Haute. *Publications:* fiction: Forgetting Elena 1973, Nocturnes for the King of Naples 1978, A Boy's Own Story 1982, Aphrodisiac (with others) 1984, Caracole 1985, The Darker Proof: Stories from a Crisis (with Adam Mars-Jones) 1987, The Beautiful Room is Empty 1988, Skinned Alive 1995, The Farewell Symphony 1997, The Married Man 2000, Fanny: A Fiction 2003, Chaos 2007, Hotel de Dream 2007; non-fiction: The Joy of Gay Sex: An Intimate Guide for Gay Men to the Pleasures of a Gay Lifestyle (with Charles Silverstein) 1977, States of Desire: Travels in Gay America 1980, The Faber Book of Gay Short Fiction (ed.) 1991, Genet: A Biography (Nat. Book Critics' Circle Award 1994) 1993, The Selected Writings of Jean Genet (ed.) 1993, The Burning Library (essays) 1994, Sketches from Memory 1994, Our Paris 1995, Proust 1998, The Flâneur 2001, My Lives (autobiog.) 2005, Rimbaud: The Double Life of a Rebel 2008, City Boy: My Life in New York during the 1960s and '70s 2009, Chaos 2010. *Honours:* Officier, Ordre des Arts et des Lettres 1999. *Literary Agent:* c/o Amanda Urban, ICM, 825 8th Avenue, New York, NY 10019, USA. *Telephone:* (212) 556-5764. *Address:* Room 224, 185 Nassau Street, Princeton, NJ 08544, USA (office). *Telephone:* (609) 258-5099 (office). *E-mail:* ewhite@princeton.edu (office). *Website:* www.princeton.edu/~visarts/cwr (office); www.edmundwhite.com.

WHITE, Howard; Canadian writer, poet, editor and publisher; b. 18 April 1945, Abbotsford, BC; m.; two s. *Career:* Founder, Ed. and Publisher, Peninsula Voice 1969–74; Ed., Raincoast Chronicles 1972–; Founder, Pres. and Publisher, Harbour Publishing 1974–; mem. Asscn of Book Publishers of British Columbia (Pres. 1988–90). *Publications:* Raincoast Chronicles (ed.) (five vols) 1975–94, A Hard Man to Beat: The Story of Bill White, Labour Leader, Historian, Shipyard Worker, Raconteur: An Oral History (co-author) 1983, The Men There Were Then 1983, The New Canadian Poets (ed.) 1985, Spilsbury's Coast: Pioneer Years in the Wet West (co-author) 1987, The Accidental Airline: Spilsbury's QCA 1988, Writing in the Rain (essays and poetry) (Stephen Leacock Medal for Humour) 1990, The Ghost in the Gears 1993, The Sunshine Coast: From Gibsons to Powell River 1996; contrib. to periodicals. *Honours:* Hon. DJur (Univ. of Victoria) 2003; Order of British Columbia 1997, Queen Elizabeth II 50th Jubilee Medal 2002; Eaton's British Columbia Book Award 1976, Career Award for Regional History, Canadian History Asscn 1989, Roderick Haig Brown Award 1995, James Douglas BC Publisher of the Year Award 2002. *Address:* PO Box 219, Madeira Park, BC V0N 2H0, Canada. *Website:* www.harbourpublishing.com.

WHITE, James Patrick, BA, MA, MA; American academic, writer, producer, dramatist and editor and translator; *Executive Director, Christopher Isherwood Foundation;* b. 28 Sept. 1940, Wichita Falls, Tex.; m. Janice Lou Turner 1961; one s. *Education:* Univ. of Texas at Austin, Vanderbilt Univ., Brown Univ. *Career:* Asst Prof., Univ. of Texas of the Permian Basin at Odessa 1973–74, Assoc. Prof. 1974–77; Ed., Sands literary review 1974–78; Visiting Prof., Univ. of Texas at Dallas 1977–78; Founder-Ed., Texas Books in Review 1977–79; Dir Masters in Professional Writing, Univ. of Southern California, Los Angeles 1979–82; mem. Int. Editorial Bd Translation Review 1980–; Dir of Creative Writing, Univ. of South Alabama 1982–87, Prof. 1987–2003; currently Exec. Univ. Christopher Isherwood Foundation; mem. Alabama Writer's Forum, Associated Writing Programs, Gulf Coast Asscn of Creative Writing Teachers (Founder-Pres. 1993), Texas Asscn of Creative Writing Teachers (Founder-Pres. 1974–78). *Film:* Chris and Don (producer) 2008. *Publications:* fiction: Birdsong 1977, The Ninth Car (with Anne Rooth) 1978, The Persian Oven 1985, Two Novellas: The Persian Oven and California Exit 1987, Clara's Call (in two short novels, with R. V. Cassill) 1992; poetry: Poetry 1979, The Great Depression (with Walter Feldman) 1997; non-fiction: I Am Everyone I Meet 2007, I Am Everyone I Meet (new edition) 2009, Observations Without Daddy 2010, Why Are You Telling Me This: Christopher Isherwood's Commonplace Book 2011; editor: Clarity: A Text on Writing (with Janice White) 1982, Where Joy Resides: A Christopher Isherwood Reader (with Don Bachardy) 1989, Black Alabama: An Anthology of Contemporary Black Alabama Fiction Writers 1998; contrib. to anthologies, reviews, quarterlies, journals, newspapers and magazines. *Honours:* Guggenheim Fellowship 1988–89, Dean's Lecturer, Univ. of South Alabama 1990, Alabama Writer's Fellowship. *Address:* Christopher Isherwood Foundation, 1223 Wilshire Boulevard, PMB 139, Santa Monica, CA 90403 (office); PO Box 428, Montrose, AL 36559, USA (home). *Telephone:* (251) 591-8982 (office). *E-mail:* jamespwhite@gmail.com (office). *Website:* americanartists.org (office).

WHITE, John Austin, LVO, BA, FRSA; British ecclesiastic, writer and poet; *Vice-Dean of Windsor;* b. 27 June 1942, England. *Education:* Univ. of Hull, Coll. of the Resurrection, Mirfield. *Career:* Asst Curate, St Aidan's Church, Leeds 1966–69; Asst Chaplain, Univ. of Leeds 1969–73; Asst Dir Post Ordination Training, Dioceses of Ripon 1970–73; Chaplain, Northern Ordination Course 1973–82; Canon of Windsor 1982–, Vice-Dean 2004–; Warden St George's House 2000–03; European Deputy for the Diocese of Mexico of the Anglican Church of Mexico 2003–. *Publications:* A Necessary End: Attitudes to Death (with Julia Neuberger) 1991, Nicholas Ferrar: Materials for a Life (with L.R. Muir) 1997, Phoenix in Flight (with Thetis Blacker); contrib. to various publications. *Address:* 4 The Cloisters, Windsor Castle, Berks., SL4 1NJ, England. *Telephone:* (1753) 848787 (office). *Fax:* (1753) 848752 (office). *E-mail:* precentor@stgeorges-windsor.org (office). *Website:* www.stgeorges-windsor.org (office).

WHITE, Jon Ewbank Manchip, MA; British writer, poet and academic (retd); b. 22 June 1924, Cardiff, Glamorganshire, Wales; m. Valerie Leighton (deceased); two d. *Education:* St Catharine's Coll., Cambridge. *Career:* story ed. BBC TV, London 1950–51; Sr Exec. Officer British Foreign Service 1952–56; author 1956–67, including a period as screenwriter for Samuel Bronston Productions, Paris and Madrid 1960–64; Prof. of English Univ. of Texas, El Paso 1967–77; Lindsay Young Prof. of English Univ. of Tennessee, Knoxville 1977–94; mem. Texas Inst. of Letters; Fellow Welsh Acad. *Publications:* fiction: Mask of Dust 1953, Build Us a Dam 1955, The Girl from Indiana 1956, No Home But Heaven 1957, The Mercenaries 1958, Hour of the Rat 1962, The Rose in the Brandy Glass 1965, Nightclimber 1968, The Game of Troy 1971, The Garden Game 1973, Send for Mr Robinson 1974, The Moscow Papers 1979, Death by Dreaming 1981, The Last Grand Master 1985, Whistling Past the Churchyard 1992, Echoes and Shadows 2003, Solo Goya 2007; poetry: Dragon and Other Poems 1943, Salamander and Other Poems 1945, The Rout of San Romano 1952, The Mountain Lion 1971; prose: Ancient Egypt 1952, Anthropology 1954, Marshal of France: The Life and Times of Maurice, Comte de Saxe 1962, Everyday Life in Ancient Egypt 1964, Diego Velázquez, Painter and Courtier 1969, The Land God Made in Anger: Reflections on a Journey Through South West Africa 1969, Cortés and the Downfall of the Aztec Empire 1971, A World Elsewhere: One Man's Fascination with the American Southwest 1975, Everyday Life of the North American Indians 1979, What to do When the Russians Come: A Survivors' Handbook (with Robert Conquest) 1984, The Journeying Boy: Scenes from a Welsh Childhood 1991. *Address:* 5620 Pinellas Drive, Knoxville, TN 37919, USA (home). *Telephone:* (865) 558-8578 (home). *E-mail:* salamanderjmw@man.com (home).

WHITE, Kenneth, MA, DèsL; British poet and writer; b. 28 April 1936, Glasgow, Scotland; m. Marie Claude Charlut. *Education:* Univ. of Glasgow, Univ. of Munich, Germany, Univ. of Paris, France. *Career:* Lecturer in French, Univ. of Glasgow 1963–67; Lecturer in English, Univ. of Paris VII 1969–83; Prof. of 20th Century Poetics, Univ. of Paris-Sorbonne 1983–96; Visiting Prof., Edinburgh Coll. of Art 1999–2002; Founder-Pres., Int. Inst. of Geopoetics 1989–. *Publications:* poetry: Wild Coal 1963, En Toute Candeur 1964, The Cold Wind of Dawn 1966, The Most Difficult Area 1968, A Walk Along the Shore 1977, Mahamudra 1979, Le Grand Rivage 1980, Terre de Diamant 1983, Atlantica: Mouvements et meditations 1986, The Bird Path: Collected Longer Poems 1989, Handbook for the Diamond Country: Collected

Shorter Poems 1990, Les Rives du Silence 1997, Limites et Marges 2000, Open World; Collected Poems 2003, Le Passage Extérieur 2005, Un Monde Ouvert 2007, Les Archives du littoral 2011; fiction: Letters from Gourgounel 1966, Les Limbes Incandescents 1978, Le Visage du Vent d'Est 1980, La Route Bleue 1983, Travels in the Drifting Dawn 1989, Les Cygnes Sauvages 1990, Pilgrim of the Void 1994, House of Tides 2000, Across the Territories 2004, La Maison des Marées 2005, Le Rôdeur des Confins 2006; essays: La Figure du Dehors 1982, L'Esprit Nomade 1987, Le Plateau de l'Albatros, an introduction to geopoetics 1994, On Scottish Ground 1998, The Wanderer and his Charts 2004, On the Atlantic Edge 2006, Les Finisterres de l'esprit 2007, Dialogue avex Deleuze 2007, Les Affinités extrêmes 2009; contrib. to various publs. *Honours:* Hon. mem. Royal Scottish Acad.; Officier des Arts et des Lettres 1993; Dr hc (Glasgow, Heriot-Watt, Open Univ.); Prix Médicis Etranger 1983, Grand Prix du Rayonnement, French Acad. 1985, Prix Alfred de Vigny 1987, Premio Aleramo 1996, Prix Roger Caillois 1998, Prix Edouard Glissant 2004, Prix Bretagne 2006, Premio Grinzane-Biamonti 2008, Prix Alain Bosquet 2011. *Address:* 9 chemin du Gwaker, 22560 Trébeurden, France. *Website:* www.kennethwhite.org.

WHITE, William Robinson, BA, MA; American writer and poet; b. 12 July 1928, Kodaikanal, South India; m. Marian Biesterfeld 1948 (died 1983); two s. one d. *Education:* Yale Univ., California State Polytechnic Univ. *Career:* Ed.-in-Chief, Per-Se International Quarterly, Stanford Univ. Press 1965–69; Instructor, Photojournalism, Mendocino Art Center 1973, Dir, Creative Writing Seminar 1984; Lecturer, Scripps Coll. 1984; Fiction Ed., West-word literary magazine 1985–90; Instructor, Univ. of California, Los Angeles 1985–; Research Reader, The Huntington Library 1985–86; Lecturer, Writing Programme and CompuWrite, California State Polytechnic Univ. 1985–93; Bread Loaf Fellow, Middlebury Coll. 1956; Stegner Creative Writing Fellow, Stanford Univ. 1956–57; mem. Authors' Guild, California State Poetry Society. *Publications:* House of Many Rooms 1958, Elephant Hill 1959, Men and Angels 1961, Foreign Soil 1962, All In Favor Say No 1964, His Own Kind 1967, Be Not Afraid 1972, The Special Child 1978, The Troll of Crazy Mule Camp 1979, Moses the Man 1981, The Winning Writer 1997; contributions: journals and magazines. *Honours:* Harper Prize 1959, O. Henry Prize 1960, Co-ordinating Council of Literary Magazines Award 1968, Distinguished Achievement Award, Educational Press 1974, Spring Harvest Poetry Awards 1992, 1994, 1995, Ed.'s Choice Awards, Poetry 1998, 2000, California State Polytechnic Univ. Golden Leaves Award 2000, New Century Writers Award 2000.

WHITEHEAD, Colson; American writer; b. 1969, New York City. *Education:* Harvard Coll. *Career:* fmr TV columnist, The Village Voice. *Publications:* The Intuitionist (Quality Paperback Book Club's New Voices Award) 1999, John Henry Days (Young Lions Fiction Award, Anisfield-Wolf Book Award) 2001, The Colossus of New York (essays) (New York Times Notable Book of the Year) 2003, Apex Hides the Hurt (PEN/Oakland Award) 2006, Sag Harbour 2009, Zone One 2011; contrib. reviews, essays and fiction to New York Times, The New Yorker, New York Magazine, Harper's, Granta and others. *Honours:* MacArthur Fellowship, Whiting Writers Award, Cullman Center for Scholars and Writers Fellowship. *E-mail:* ddaypub@randomhouse.com (office). *Website:* www.colsonwhitehead.com (home).

WHITEHOUSE, David, FRAS; British journalist, astronomer and writer. *Career:* fmr space scientist and astronomer, Mullard Space Science Lab., Univ. Coll., London and at Jodrell Bank radio observatory; Science Corresp. BBC 1988–98, Science Ed. BBC News Online 1998–2006; broadcasts regularly on TV and radio; presenter, science series (BBC TV); scientific adviser, Global Warming Policy Foundation; mem. Soc. for Popular Astronomy (fmr pres. *Publications:* non-fiction: The Moon: A Biography 2001, The Sun: A Biography 2004. One Small Step 2009, Renaissance Genius 2009; contrib. regularly to leading newspapers and magazines. *Honours:* two Glaxo science writing awards, five European Netmedia awards, including European Internet Journalist of the Year 2002–03, European Online Journalism award for science reporting. *E-mail:* david@davidwhitehouse.com (office). *Website:* www.davidwhitehouse.com.

WHITEHOUSE, David Bryn, BA, MA, PhD; British writer and editor; *Executive Director, The Corning Museum of Glass;* b. 15 Oct. 1941, Worksop, England. *Education:* Univ. of Cambridge. *Career:* Chief Curator Corning Museum of Glass, NY 1984, Deputy Dir Collections 1988, Dir 1992, Exec. Dir 1999–, also Curator of Ancient and Islamic Glass; Correspondent Archeologia Medievale; Ed. Journal of Glass Studies 1988–; Advisory Bd. American Early Medieval Studies 1991–; Advisory Bd Encyclopedia of Islamic Archaeology 1991; mem. Accademia Fiorentina delle Arti del Disegno, Int. Asscn for the History of Glass (pres. 1991–94), Keats-Shelley Memorial Asscn, Rome (pres. 1982–83), Pontificia Accademia Romana di Archeologia, RGS, Soc. of Antiquaries of London, Unione Internazionale degli Istituti di Archeologia, Storia e Storia dell'Arte in Roma (pres. 1980–81). *Publications:* Glass of the Roman Empire 1988, Glass: A Pocket Dictionary 1993, English Cameo Glass 1994, Roman Glass in the Corning Museum of Glass, Vol. 1 1997, Vol. 2 2001, Vol. 3 2003, Excavations at Ed-Dur, Vol. 1 The Glass Vessels 1998, The Corning Museum of Glass: A Decade of Glass Collecting 2000; co-author: Archaeological Atlas of the World 1975, Aspects of Medieval Lazio 1982, Mohammed, Charlemagne and the Origins of Europe 1983, Glass of the Caesars 1987, The Portland Vase 1990, Treasures from the Corning Museum of Glass 1992; contrib. to books, journals and other publications. *Address:* Corning Museum of Glass, One Museum Way, Corning, NY 14830-2253, USA (office). *Telephone:* (607) 974-8424 (office). *Fax:* (607) 974-8470 (office). *E-mail:* info@cmog.org (office). *Website:* www.cmog.org (office).

WHITEMAN, Robin, NDD, MA; British writer and filmmaker; b. 5 May 1944, King's Langley, Herts.; m.; three c. *Education:* City of Canterbury Coll. of Art and Royal Coll. of Art. *Career:* writer and Dir, United Motion Pictures, London 1968–70; Dir and Prod. Video Tracks Ltd, Royal Leamington Spa 1980–85; writer and Partner, Talbot Whiteman, Royal Leamington Spa 1985–2006. *Publications:* The Cotswolds 1987, Shakespeare's Avon: A Journey from Source to Severn 1989, The English Lakes 1989, Cadfael Country 1990, In the North of England: The Yorkshire Moors and Dales 1991, The Cadfael Companion 1991, The Benediction of Brother Cadfael 1992, The Heart of England 1992, The West Country 1993, Wessex 1994, The Garden of England: The Counties of Kent, Surrey and Sussex 1995, English Landscapes 1995, East Anglia and the Fens 1996, Brother Cadfael's Herb Garden 1996, The Peak District 1997, Lakeland Landscapes 1997, Northumbria: English Border Country 1998, Yorkshire Landscapes 1998, Cotswold Landscapes 1999, England 2000, Brother Cadfael's Book of Days 2000, A Family to Remember 2005, The Turners, A Family Chronicle 2011. *Honours:* Gold Award, British Film and Video Festival 1984, Border TV Prize 1998. *Address:* c/o Weidenfeld and Nicolson, Orion House, 5 Upper St Martin's Lane, London, WC2H 9EA, England. *Website:* www.orionbooks.co.uk.

WHITESIDE, Lesley, BA, DipEd, MA; Irish historian and writer; b. (Lesley Mathers), 13 May 1945, Co. Down, NI; d. of Arthur Mathers and Mabel Mathers (née Brice); m. Robert Whiteside 1968; one s. two d. *Education:* Trinity Coll., Dublin, Univ. of Liverpool. *Career:* Asst Keeper of Manuscripts, Trinity Coll., Dublin 1968–69; Archivist, The King's Hosp., Dublin 1969–. *Publications:* A History of The King's Hospital 1975, George Otto Simms: A Biography 1990, Through the Year with George Otto Simms (ed.) 1993, The Spirituality of St Patrick 1996, St Saviour's Church, Arklow 1997, In Search of Columba 1997, The Chapel of Trinity College, Dublin 1998, St Patrick in Stained Glass 1998, The Book of Saints 1998, The Stained Glass of Christ Church Cathedral, Dublin 1999, The Stained Glass of St Patrick's Cathedral, Dublin 2002, Music in the King's Hospital 1675–2003, Dublin 2003, Where Swift and Berkeley Learnt: A History of Kilkenny College, Dublin 2009, A Guide to the Stained Glass of Christ Church Cathedral, Dublin 2010. *Address:* The Meadows, Marlinstown, Mullingar, Co. Westmeath, Ireland (home). *Telephone:* (44) 9342994 (home).

WHITFIELD, Stephen Jack, BA, MA, PhD; American historian and academic; *Max Richter Chair of American Civilization, Brandeis University;* b. 3 Dec. 1942, Houston, Tex.; s. of Bert Whitfield and Joan Whitfield (née Schwarz); m. Lee Cone Hall 1984. *Education:* Tulane Univ., Yale Univ., Brandeis Univ. *Career:* instructor, Southern Univ. of New Orleans 1966–68; Asst Prof. 1972–75, Assoc. Prof. 1979–85, Prof. 1985–, Max Richter Chair of American Civilization, Dept of American Studies 1986–88, 1994–96, Brandeis Univ.; Fulbright Visiting Prof., Hebrew Univ. of Jerusalem 1983–84, Catholic Univ. of Louvain, Belgium 1993; Visiting Prof., Univ. of Paris IV 1994, 1998, Ludwig-Maximilian-Universität Munich 2004; mem. American Jewish Historical Soc. *Publications:* Scott Nearing: Apostle of American Radicalism 1974, Into the Dark: Hannah Arendt and Totalitarianism 1980, Voices of Jacob, Hands of Esau: Jews in American Life and Thought 1984, A Critical American: The Politics of Dwight Macdonald 1984, A Death in the Delta: The Story of Emmett Till 1988, American Space, Jewish Time 1988, The Culture of the Cold War 1991, In Search of American Jewish Culture 1999, A Companion to 20th Century America (ed.) 2004; contrib. to scholarly journals. *Honours:* Univ. of Colorado Kayden Prize 1981, Outstanding Academic Book Citation Choice 1985, Int. Center for Holocaust Studies of the Anti-Defamation League of B'nai B'rith Merit of Distinction 1987, Gustavus Myers Center for the Study of Human Rights Outstanding Book Citations 1989, 1992, Rockefeller Foundation Fellow, Bellagio, Italy 1991, Louis D. Brandeis Prize for Excellence in Teaching 1993, Brandeis Student Union Teaching Award 2008, Samuel Proctor Prize for Distinguished Scholarship in Southern Jewish History 2010. *Address:* Mailstop #005, American Studies Program, Brandeis University, 415 South Street, Waltham, MA 02454-9110, USA (office). *Telephone:* (781) 736-3035 (office). *Fax:* (781) 736-3040 (office). *E-mail:* swhitfie@brandeis.edu (office).

WHITTALL, Arnold, MA, PhD; British musicologist; b. 11 Nov. 1935, Shrewsbury, Shropshire. *Education:* Emmanuel Coll., Cambridge. *Career:* Lecturer, Univ. of Nottingham 1964–69; Sr Lecturer, Univ. Coll., Cardiff 1969–75; Reader, King's Coll., London 1976–81, Prof. of Musical Theory and Analysis 1981–96; Visiting Prof., Yale Univ. 1985. *Publications include:* Post-Twelve Note Analysis 1968, Stravinsky and Music Drama 1969, Schoenberg Chamber Music 1972, Music Since the First World War 1977, The Music of Britten and Tippett 1982, Romantic Music 1987, Wagner's Later Stage Works 1990, The Emancipation of Dissonance: Schoenberg and Stravinsky 1993, Musical Composition in the Twentieth Century 1999, Jonathon Harvey (biog.) 1999, Exploring Twentieth Century Music 2003.

WHITTAM SMITH, Andreas, CBE; British journalist; b. 13 June 1937, s. of Canon J. E. Smith; m. Valerie Catherine Sherry 1964; two s. *Education:* Keble Coll., Oxford. *Career:* with N. M. Rothschild 1960–62, Stock Exchange Gazette 1962–63, Financial Times 1963–64, The Times 1964–66; Deputy City Ed. The Telegraph 1966–69; City Ed. The Guardian 1969–70; Ed. Investors Chronicle, Stock Exchange Gazette and Dir Throgmorton Publs 1970–77; City Ed. Daily Telegraph 1977–85; Ed. The Independent 1986–94, Ed.-in-Chief Independent on Sunday 1991–94, Dir Newspaper Publishing PLC 1986–, CEO 1987–93, Chair. 1994–95; Chair., Publr Notting Hill 1995–, Sir Winston Churchill Archive Trust 1995–2000, Financial Ombudsman Service Ltd. 1999–2003; Pres. British Bd of Film Classification 1998–2002; First Church Estates Commr; Vice-Pres. Nat. Council for One Parent Families 1982–86, 1991–; currently commentator, The Independent. *Honours:* Hon. Fellow Keble Coll., Oxford, UMIST 1989, Liverpool John Moores 2001; Hon. DLitt (St Andrew's, Salford) 1989; Wincott Award 1975; Journalist of the Year 1987. *Address:* c/o The Independent, 2 Derry Street, London W8 5HF, England (office). *Website:* www.independent.co.uk (office).

WHITTEN, Leslie (Les) Hunter, Jr, BA; American writer, poet and journalist; b. 21 Feb. 1928, Jacksonville, Fla; m. Phyllis Webber 1951; three s. one d. *Education:* Lehigh Univ. *Career:* served in US Army 1946-48; worked as reporter for Radio Free Europe 1952–57, International News Service 1957–58, United Press International 1958, Washington Post 1958–63; reporter for Hearst Newspapers 1963–66, Asst Bureau Chief, Washington, DC 1966–69; Sr Investigator for Washington Merry-Go-Round column with Jack Anderson 1969–92; Visiting Assoc. Prof., Lehigh Univ. 1967–69; Adjunct Prof., Southern Illinois Univ. 1984. *Publications include:* Progeny of the Adder 1965, Moon of the Wolf 1967, Pinion, The Golden Eagle 1968, The Abyss 1970, F. Lee Bailey 1971, The Alchemist 1973, Conflict of Interest 1976, Washington Cycle (poems) 1979, Sometimes a Hero 1979, A Killing Pace 1983, A Day Without Sunshine 1985, The Lost Disciple 1989, The Fangs of Morning 1994, Sad Madrigals 1997, Moses: The Lost Book of the Bible 1999. *Honours:* Hon. DHumLitt (Lehigh Univ.) 1989; Edgerton Award, American Civil Liberties Union. *Address:* 114 Eastmoor Drive, Silver Spring, MD 20901-1507, USA (home). *Telephone:* (301) 593-5943 (home).

WHYTE, Kenneth; Canadian journalist, editor and publisher; *President, Rogers Publishing;* b. 1960, Winnipeg, Man.; m. Tina Leino-Whyte; one d. *Education:* Univ. of Alberta. *Career:* fmr janitor; sports reporter, Sherwood Park News; staff writer, then Exec. Ed. Alberta Report; Western Columnist, The Globe and Mail, Western Ed., then Ed. Saturday Night magazine; f. National Post 1998, Ed.-in-Chief 1998–2003; Publr Canadian Business, PROFIT & MoneySense 2009–10; Publr and Ed.-in-Chief Maclean's 2005–; Publr Chatelaine 2010–; Pres. Rogers Publishing 2010–. *Publication:* The Uncrowned King: The Sensational Rise of William Randolph Hearst 2009. *Address:* 1 Mount Pleasant Road, 7th Floor, Toronto, ON M4Y 2Y5, Canada (office). *Telephone:* (416) 764-1235 (office). *Fax:* (416) 764-1802 (office). *Website:* www.rogerspublishing.ca (office).

WICHTERICH, Christa, Dr rer. pol; German journalist, writer and academic; b. 4 March 1949, Brühl; m. Uwe Hoering 1979. *Education:* Univs of Bonn, Munich and Kassel. *Career:* Lecturer, Univ. of Gilan, Rasht, Iran 1978–79, Jawaharlal Nehru Univ., New Delhi 1979–82; Guest Lecturer, Univ. of Kassel 1983, Göttingen 1984, Münster 1986, Frankfurt/Main 1991, Bochum 1994; Foreign Corresp. for Africa for German newspapers and radio stations, Nairobi 1988–90; currently freelance journalist and writer; mem. WIDE (Women in Devt Europe): German Govt Award for Journalists working in the field of Devt Politics 1986. *Publications:* Stree Shakti, Frauen in Indien 1986, Kein Zustand dauert ewig, Afrika in den neunziger Jahren 1991, Die Erde bemuttern, Frauen und Ökologie nach dem Erdgipfel in Rio 1992, Menshen nach Maß, Bevölkerungspolitik in Nord und Süd 1994, Frauen der Welt, vom Fortschritt der Ungleichheit 1995, Wir sind das Wunder, Durch das wir Überleben, die Vierte Weltfrauenkonferenz in Peking 1996, The Globalised Woman 2000, Mythen globalen Umweltmanagements 2002. *Address:* c/o WIDE, rue Hobbema 59, 1000 Brussels, Belgium; Schloßtr 2, 53115 Bonn, Germany. *Telephone:* (228) 265032. *Fax:* (228) 265033. *E-mail:* info@wide-network.org. *Website:* www.wide-network.org.

WICKS, Susan Jane, BA, DPhil; British writer, poet and teacher; b. 24 Oct. 1947, Kent, England; m. John Collins 1973; two d. *Education:* Univ. of Hull, Univ. of Sussex. *Career:* Assoc. Lecturer in English, Univ. of Dijon 1974–76; Asst Lecturer in French, Univ. Coll., Dublin 1976–77; part-time Tutor in Comparative Literature, Univ. of Kent, Tonbridge 1983–2000, Lecturer, then Sr Lecturer in Creative Writing 2000–08, also Dir of the Centre for Creative Writing; mem. Soc. of Authors, Poetry Soc., Kent and Sussex Poetry Soc. *Publications:* Singing Underwater 1992, Open Diagnosis 1994, Driving My Father (memoir) 1995, The Clever Daughter 1996, The Key (novel) 1997, Little Thing (novel) 1998, Night Toad 2003, De-iced 2007, Roll Up for the Arabian Derby 2008, Past Away (trans. of Pas Revoir by Valerie Rouzeau) 2009; contrib. to TLS, Observer, LRB, Poetry Review, London Magazine, The Rialto, Ambit, Poetry London, Poetry Wales, Poetry Ireland Review, Magma, Smith's Knoll, Poetry East, Southern Review, Women's Review of Books, The New Yorker. *Honours:* MacDowell Colony residencies 1997, 2005, 2007, Aldeburgh Poetry Festival Prize 1992, Virginia Centre for the Creative Arts residency 1994–2005, Villa Mont-Noir residency 1999, 2003. *Website:* www.poetrypf.co.uk (office).

WICOMB, Zoe; South African writer; b. 23 Nov. 1948, Namaqualand. *Education:* Univ. of the Western Cape, Reading Univ., UK. *Career:* taught for three years in Dept of English, Univ. of the Western Cape; currently Prof., Dept of English Studies, Strathclyde Univ., Scotland; Visiting Prof., Extraordinaire Stellenbosch Univ. *Publications:* You Can't Get Lost in Cape Town (short stories) 1987, David's Story (novel) (M-Net Literary Award) 2002, Playing in the Light (novel) 2006, The One That Got Away (short stories) 2008; also literary criticism. *Address:* c/o Lyn Riesnik, Umuzi Publishers, PO Box 2002, Houghton 2041, South Africa (office). *Website:* www.umuzi-randomhouse.co.za (office).

WIDDECOMBE, Rt Hon. Ann Noreen, PC, MA; British writer and fmr politician; b. 4 Oct. 1947, Bath, Somerset; d. of the late James Murray Widdecombe and of Rita Noreen Plummer. *Education:* La Sainte Union Convent, Bath, Univ. of Birmingham, Lady Margaret Hall Oxford. *Career:* with Marketing Dept Unilever 1973–75; Sr Admin. Univ. of London 1975–87; contested Burnley 1979, Plymouth Devonport 1983; MP (Conservative) for Maidstone 1987–97, Maidstone and The Weald 1997–2010; Parl. Pvt. Sec. to Tristan Garel-Jones, MP 1990; Parl. Under-Sec. State Dept for Social Security 1990–93, Dept of Employment 1993–94; Minister for Employment 1994–95, Home Office 1995–97; Shadow Health Minister 1998–99, Shadow Home Sec. 1999–2001; columnist, Daily Express newspaper. *Publications:* Layman's Guide to Defence 1984, Inspired and Outspoken 1999, The Clematis Tree (novel) 2000, An Act of Treachery 2001, An Act of Peace 2005, Father Figure 2005. *Honours:* Spectator/Highland Park Minister of the Year 1996, Despatch Box Best Front Bencher 1998, Talk Radio Straight Talker of the Year 1998. *Address:* c/o United Agents, 12-26 Lexington St, London, London, W1F 0LE, England (office). *Website:* www.annwiddecombemp.com (office).

WIDDICOMBE, Gillian, ARAM; British music critic and journalist; b. 11 June 1943, Aldham, Suffolk, England; m. Sir Jeremy Isaacs 1988. *Education:* Royal Acad. of Music, Gloucester Cathedral. *Career:* with music division, BBC 1966; Glyndebourne Festival Opera 1969; critic and journalist on various publications, including Financial Times 1970–76, The Observer 1977–93; subtitles for television opera productions; Opera Consultant, Channel Four 1983–88; Arts Ed., The Observer 1988–93; Features Writer, The Independent 1993–95; Dir, Jeremy Isaacs Productions 1995–; Production Exec., Cold War 1998; Assoc. Prod., Millennium 1999; Prod., Artsworld TV Programmes, including Star Recitals with Paco Peña, Amanda Roocroft and Simon Preston 2000–; Poulenc, A Human Voice (for BBC 2). *Honours:* Prix Italia 1982, BP Award for Arts Journalism 1986. *Address:* 80 New Concordia Wharf, Mill Street, Bermondsey, London, SE1 2BB, England.

WIDEMAN, John Edgar, BA, BPhil; American writer and academic; *Asa Messer Professor and Professor of Africana Studies and English, Brown University;* b. 14 June 1941, Washington, DC; m.; three c. *Education:* Univ. of Pennsylvania, Univ. of Oxford, UK, Univ. of Iowa. *Career:* Prof. of English, Univ. of Wyoming 1974–85, Univ. of Massachusetts, Amherst 1986–2004; Asa Messer Prof. and Prof. of Africana Studies and English, Brown Univ. 2004–; mem. American Acad. of Arts and Sciences, American Acad. of Arts and Letters, American Asscn of Rhodes Scholars, MLA; John D. and Catherine T. MacArthur Foundation Fellowship 1993. *Publications:* A Glance Away 1967, Hurry Home 1969, The Lynchers 1973, Hiding Place 1981, Damballah 1981, Sent for You Yesterday 1983, Brothers and Keepers 1984, Reuben 1987, Fever 1989, Philadelphia Fire (PEN/Faulkner Awards for Fiction, American Book Award) 1990, The Homewood Books 1992, The Stories of John Edgar Wideman 1992, All Stories Are True 1993, Fatheralong 1994, The Cattle Killing 1996, Hoop Roots 2001, God's Gym 2005, Fanon 2008; contrib. to professional journals and general periodicals. *Honours:* Anisfield-Wolf Book Award for lifetime achievement 2011. *Address:* Department of Africana Studies, Brown University, Box 1904, 155 Angell Street, Providence, RI 02912, USA (office). *Telephone:* (401) 863-3137 (office). *E-mail:* John_Edgar_Wideman@brown.edu (office). *Website:* brown.edu/Departments/Africana_Studies (office).

WIEBE, Rudy Henry, OC, BA, MA, ThB; Canadian writer and academic; *Professor Emeritus of English and Creative Writing, University of Alberta;* b. 4 Oct. 1934, Fairholme, Sask.; m. Tena F. Isaak 1958, two s. one d. *Education:* Univ. of Alberta, Univ. of Tübingen, Mennonite Brethren Bible Coll., Univ. of Manitoba, Univ. of Iowa. *Career:* Asst and Assoc. Prof. of English, Goshen College, Ind. 1963–67; Asst Prof., Univ. of Alberta 1967–71, Assoc. Prof. 1971–77, Prof. of English and Creative Writing 1977–92, Prof. Emer. 1992–; mem. Writers Guild of Alberta (Founding Pres. 1980), Writers Union of Canada (Pres. 1986–87). *Publications:* fiction: Peace Shall Destroy Many 1962, First and Vital Candle 1966, The Blue Mountains of China 1970, The Temptations of Big Bear 1973, Where is the Voice Coming From? 1974, The Scorched-Wood People 1977, Alberta: A Celebration 1979, The Mad Trapper 1980, The Angel of the Tar Sands and Other Stories 1982, My Lovely Enemy 1983, A Chinook Christmas 1992, A Discovery of Strangers 1994, River of Stone: Fictions and Memories 1995, Sweeter Than All the World 2001; non-fiction (memoir): Of This Earth: A Mennonite Boyhood in the Boreal Forest 2006, Extraordinary Canadians: Big Bear 2008; play: Far as the Eye Can See 1977; essays: A Voice in the Land 1981, Playing Dead: A Contemplation Concerning the Arctic 1989, Place 2003; editor: The Story-Makers: A Selection of Modern Short Stories 1970, Stories from Western Canada 1971, Stories from Pacific and Arctic Canada (with Andreas Schroeder) 1974, Double Vision: Twentieth Century Stories in English 1976, Getting Here 1977, More Stories from Western Canada (with Aritha van Herk) 1980, West of Fiction (with Aritha van Herk and Leah Flater) 1983; numerous contribs to anthologies and periodicals. *Honours:* Hon. DLitt Univ. of Winnipeg 1986, Wilfred Laurier Univ. 1991, Brock Univ. 1991; Gov.-General's Awards for Fiction 1973, 1994, Lorne Pierce Medal, Royal Soc. of Canada 1987, Charles Taylor Prize for Literary Non-fiction 2007, Lt-Gov. of Alberta Distinguished Artist Award 2009. *Address:* c/o Penguin Group (Canada), 90 Eglinton Avenue East, Suite 700, Toronto, ON M4P 2Y3, Canada (office). *Website:* www.penguin.ca (office).

WIENER, Joel Howard, BA, PhD, FRHistS; American academic and writer; *Professor Emeritus of History, City University of New York*; b. 23 Aug. 1937, New York, NY; m. Suzanne Wolff 1961; one s. two d. *Education:* New York Univ., Univ. of Glasgow, Cornell Univ. *Career:* Asst Prof. of History, Skidmore Coll. 1964–66; Assoc. Prof. CUNY 1966–76, Prof. of History 1977–2000, Prof. Emeritus of History 2000–; mem. American Historical Asscn, American Journalism Historians Asscn, Conference on British Studies, Research Soc. for Victorian Periodicals (Pres.). *Publications:* The War of the Unstamped 1969, A Descriptive Finding List of Unstamped British Periodicals: 1830–1836 1970, Great Britain: Foreign Policy and the Span of Empire 1689–1970 (ed., four vols) 1972, Great Britain: The Lion at Home (four vols) 1974, Radicalism and Freethought in 19th Century Britain 1983, Innovators and Preachers: The Role of the Editor in Victorian England (ed.) 1985, Papers for the Millions: The New Journalism in Britain c. 1850s–1914 (ed.) 1988, William Lovett 1989, Dictionary of National Biography (assoc. ed.) 1999–2004; contrib. to scholarly books and journals. *Address:* 267 Glen Court, Teaneck, NJ 07666-6632, USA (home). *Telephone:* (201) 837-5452 (home). *Fax:* (201) 837-8658 (home). *E-mail:* jwiener267@aol.com (home).

WIER, Dara, (Phraz Barrois), BS, MFA; American poet and academic; *Professor, University of Massachusetts at Amherst*; b. 30 Dec. 1949, New Orleans, La; one s. one d. *Education:* Louisiana State Univ., Longwood Coll., Bowling Green State Univ. *Career:* Instructor, Univ. of Pittsburgh 1974–75; Instructor, Hollins Coll. 1975–76, Asst Prof. 1977–80; Assoc. Prof., Univ. of Alabama at Tuscaloosa 1980–85, Dir of Grad. Studies 1980–82, Dir of Writing Program 1983–84; Assoc. Prof. 1985–96, Prof. 1996–, Dir MFA programmes for writers and poets, Univ. of Massachusetts at Amherst 1985–91, 1992–94, 1997–98, 2004–07; visiting poet at various colls and univs; mem. Associated Writing Programs (Pres. 1981–82), Authors' Guild, Authors' League of America, PEN, Poetry Soc. of America. *Publications:* Blood, Hook, and Eye 1977, The 8-Step Grapevine 1981, All You Have in Common 1984, The Book of Knowledge 1988, Blue for the Plough 1992, Our Master Plan 1997, Voyages in English 2001, Hat on a Pond 2002, Reverse Rapture (American Poetry Archives/Poetry Center Book Award) 2005, Remnants of Hannah 2006, Selected Poems 2009; contrib. to anthologies and periodicals. *Honours:* Nat. Endowment for the Arts Fellowship 1980, Guggenheim Fellowship 1993–94, Jerome Shestack Award, American Poetry Review 2001, Pushcart Prize 2002. *Address:* 504 Montague Road, Amherst, MA 01002, USA (home). *Telephone:* (413) 549-1115 (home); (413) 545-0643 (office). *E-mail:* daraw@hfa.umass.edu (office).

WIESEL, Elie(zer), KBE; American author and academic; *University Professor, Andrew W. Mellon Professor in the Humanities and Professor of Philosophy and Religion, Boston University*; b. 30 Sept. 1928, Sighet, Romania; s. of Shlomo Wiesel and Sarah Wiesel (née Feig); m. Marion E. Wiesel 1969; one s. one step d. *Education:* Sorbonne, Paris. *Career:* naturalized US citizen 1963; Distinguished Prof., Coll. of City of New York 1972–76; Andrew Mellon Prof. in Humanities, Boston Univ. 1976–, Prof. of Philosophy and Religion 1988–; Founder The Elie Wiesel Foundation for Humanity 1986; mem. Bd Fund for the Holocaust 1997–; Founding Pres. Universal Acad. of Cultures, Paris 1993; mem. numerous bds of dirs, trustees, govs and advisers including Int. Rescue Cttee, American Jewish World Service, Yad Vashem, Mutual of America, AmeriCares, US Cttee for Refugees; mem. PEN, The Authors' Guild, Foreign Press Asscn, Writers and Artists for Peace in the Middle East, Council of Foreign Relations, American Acad. of Arts and Sciences, American Acad. of Arts and Letters (Dept of Literature), Jewish Acad. of Arts and Sciences, European Acad. of Arts, Sciences and Humanities, Royal Norwegian Soc. of Sciences and Letters. *Publications:* Night 1960, Dawn 1961, The Accident 1962, The Town Beyond the Wall 1964, The Gates of the Forest 1966, The Jews of Silence 1966, Legends of Our Time 1968, A Beggar in Jerusalem 1970, One Generation After 1971, Souls on Fire 1972, The Oath 1973, Ani Maamin, Cantata 1973, Zalmen or the Madness of God (play) 1975, Messengers of God 1976, A Jew Today 1978, Four Hasidic Masters 1978, The Trial of God 1979, One Generation After 1979, Le testament d'un poète juif assassiné 1980 (Prix Livre-Inter 1980, Prix des Bibliothéquaires 1981), The Testament 1980, Images from the Bible 1980, Five Biblical Portraits 1981, Somewhere a Master: Further Tales of the Hasidic Master 1982, Paroles d'étranger 1982, The Golem 1983, The Fifth Son (Grand Prix de la Littérature, Paris) 1985, Signes d'exode 1985, Against Silence 1985, A Song for Hope 1987, Job ou Dieu dans la tempête (with Josy Eisenberg) 1987, A Nobel Address 1987, Twilight (novel) 1988, The Six Days of Destruction (with Albert Friedlander) 1988, L'oublie 1989, Silences et mémoire d'hommes 1989, From the Kingdom of Memory, Reminiscences (essays) 1990, Evil and Exile 1990, A Journey of Faith 1990, Sages and Dreamers 1991, Célébration Talmudique 1991, The Forgotten 1992, A Passover Haggadah 1993, Se taire est impossible 1995, All Rivers Run to the Sea (Memoirs, Vol.I) 1995, Et la mer n'est pas remplie (Memoirs, Vol.II) 1996 (trans. as And the Sea Is Never Full 1999), Célébration prophétique 1998, King Solomon and His Magic Ring 2000, D'où viens-tu? 2001, The Judges 2002, After the Darkness 2002, Wise Men and Their Tales 2003, Et où vas-tu? 2004, The Time of the Uprooted 2005, Un Désir fou de Danser (trans. as A Mad Desire to Dance) 2006, Confronting Anti-Semitism (with Kofi Annan) 2006, Rashi 2009. *Honours:* Grand Officer, Légion d'honneur, Grand Cross of the Order of the Southern Cross, Brazil 1987, Grand Cross of the Order of Rio Branco, Brazil 2001, Grand Officer, The Order of the Star of Romania 2002, Commander's Cross, Order of Merit of Hungary 2004, King Hussein Award, Jordan 2005, Hon. KBE 2006; recipient of over 110 hon. degrees; Prix Rivarol 1964, Jewish Heritage Award 1965, Remembrance Award 1965, Prix Médicis 1968, Prix Bordin (Acad. Française) 1972, Eleanor Roosevelt Memorial Award 1972, American Liberties Medallion, American Jewish Comm. 1972, Martin Luther King Jr Award (Coll. of City of New York) 1973, Faculty Distinguished Scholar Award, Hofstra Univ. 1973–74, Congressional Gold Medal of Achievement 1985, Nobel Peace Prize 1986, Medal of Liberty Award 1986, Ellis Island Medal of Honor 1992, Presidential Medal of Freedom 1993, and numerous other awards. *Address:* Boston University, 147 Bay State Road, Boston, MA 02215, USA (office). *Telephone:* (617) 353-4561 (office). *Fax:* (617) 353-4024 (office). *E-mail:* jhoberer@bu.edu (office). *Website:* www.bu.edu/philo (office).

WIESENFARTH, Joseph John, BA, MA, PhD; American academic and author; *Professor Emeritus, University of Wisconsin at Madison*; b. 20 Aug. 1933, Brooklyn, NY; m. Louise Halpin 1971; one s. *Education:* Catholic Univ. of America, Washington, DC, Univ. of Detroit. *Career:* Asst Prof., La Salle Coll., Philadelphia 1962–64; Asst Prof. 1964–67, Assoc. Prof. 1967–70, Manhattan Coll., New York; Assoc. Prof. 1970–76, Prof. of English 1976–2000, Chair. Dept of English 1983–86, 1989–92, Assoc. Dean Grad. School 1995–96, Assoc. Dean Coll. of Letters and Science 1997, Prof. Emer. 2000–, Univ. of Wisconsin at Madison; Advisory Ed. George Eliot-George Henry Lewes Studies, Connotations, Renascence, Int. Ford Madox Ford Studies; Fellow, Nat. Endowment for the Humanities 1967–68; Inst. for Research in Humanities Fellow 1975; Fulbright Fellow 1981–82; Fellow, Istituto di Studi Avazati, Bologna 2004; mem. Modern Language Asscn, Jane Austen Soc. of N America, Henry James Soc., Katherine Anne Porter Soc., Ford Madox Ford Soc.; mem. Christian Gauss Prize Award Cttee 1986–88, 1989–90. *Publications:* Henry James and the Dramatic Analogy 1963, The Errand of Form: An Assay of Jane Austen's Art 1967, George Eliot's Mythmaking 1977, George Eliot: A Writer's Notebook 1854–1879 1981, Gothic Manners and the Classic English Novel 1988, Ford Madox Ford and the Arts 1989, Jane Austen's Jack and Alice 2001, History and Representation in Ford Madox Ford's Writings 2004, Jane Austen's The Three Sisters 2004, Ford Madox Ford and the Regiment of Women 2005, Ford Madox Ford's No More Parades (ed.) 2011; contrib. of numerous articles on British and American Fiction. *Address:* 5401 Greening Lane, Madison, WI 53705-1252, USA (home). *Fax:* (608) 233-2295 (home). *E-mail:* jjwiesen@wisc.edu (home).

WIGGINS, Marianne; American writer and academic; b. 8 Sept. 1947, Lancaster, Pa; m. Salman Rushdie 1988 (divorced 1993). *Education:* Manheim Township High School, Lancaster, Pa. *Career:* Prof. of English, Univ. of Southern Calif. 2005–. *Publications include:* Went South 1980, Separate Checks 1984, Herself in Love 1987, John Dollar (Janet Heidiger Kafka Prize 1990) 1989, Bet They'll Miss Us When We're Gone (short stories) 1991, Eveless Eden 1995, Almost Heaven 1998, Evidence of Things Unseen (Commonwealth Club Prize Gold Medal 2004) 2003, The Shadow Catcher 2007; two short story collections. *Honours:* Whiting Award 1989, Janet Heidiger Kafka Prize 1990. *Address:* Department of English, University of Southern California, THH 402H, 3501 Trousdale Parkway, Los Angeles, CA 90089-0354, USA (office). *Telephone:* (213) 740-3741 (office). *E-mail:* wigginsm@usc.edu (office). *Website:* www.usc.edu/schools/college/engl/home/index.shtml (office).

WIKSTRÖM, Jan-Erik, BA; Swedish politician and publisher; b. 11 Sept. 1932, St Skedvi, Dalarna; s. of Börje Wikström and Essy Wikström (née Lilja); m. Rev. Cecilia Wikström 1995; three s. one d. *Education:* Gothenberg Univ. *Career:* Man. Dir Gummessons Bokförlag Publishing House 1961–76; mem. Municipal Council, Stockholm 1962–70; mem. Riksdag (Parl.) 1970–73, 1976–92; Minister of Educ. and Cultural Affairs 1976–82; Gov. of Uppsala 1992–97; mem. Folkpartiet (Liberal Party). *Publications:* Röd och gul och vit och svart 1950, Skall kyrkan skiljas från staten 1958, Storm över Kongo 1961, Indien vid korsvägen 1962, Inför Herrens ansikte 1962, Politik och kristen tro 1964, Skall samhället utbilda präster? 1966, Liberala positioner 1969, Med frisinnat förtecken 1970, En bättre skola 1973, Möten med Mästaren 1975, I väntan på befrielsen 1977, Friket Mångfald Kvalitet 1978, Liberalism med frisinnat förtecken 1981. *Address:* Domkyrkoplan 1, 753 10 Uppsala, Sweden.

WILBER, Ken; American writer, philosopher and psychologist; b. (Kenneth Earl Wilber II), 1949, Oklahoma City, Okla. *Education:* Duke Univ. *Career:* Founder, Integral Institute 2000. *Publications include:* non-fiction: The Spectrum of Consciousness 1977, No Boundary: Eastern and Western Approaches to Personal Growth 1979, The Atman Project 1980, Up from Eden 1981, Holographic Paradigm and Other Paradoxes 1982, A Sociable God 1982, Eye to Eye: The Quest for the New Paradigm 1984, The Marriage of Sense and Soul 1988, Grace and Grit 1991, Sex, Ecology, Sprituality 1995, A Brief History of Everything 1995, The Eye of Spirit 1997, One Taste 1999, Integral Psychology: Consciousness Spirit, Psychology Therapy 2000, A Theory of Everything 2001, Boomeritis 2002, The Simple Feeling of Being 2004, Integral Sprituality: A Startling New Role for Religion in the Modern and Postmodern World 2006, The Integral Vision: A Very Short Introduction to the Revolutionary Integral Approach to Life, God, the Universe, and Everything 2007; editor: Quantum Questions: Mystical Writings of the World's Great Physicists 1984. *Address:* c/o Shambhala Publications, PO Box 308, Boston, MA 02117, USA (office). *Website:* www.shambhala.com; www.integralinstitute.org; www.integralnaked.org; www.kenwilber.com.

WILBUR, Richard Purdy, MA; American poet and academic; b. 1 March 1921, New York City; s. of Lawrence L. Wilbur and Helen Purdy Wilbur; m. Charlotte Ward 1942; three s. one d. *Education:* Amherst Coll. and Harvard

Univ. *Career:* Asst Prof. of English, Harvard Univ. 1950–54; Assoc. Prof. Wellesley Coll. 1954–57; Prof. Wesleyan Univ. 1957–77; Writer in Residence, Smith Coll., Northampton, Mass. 1977–86; mem. American Acad. of Arts and Sciences, Soc. of Fellows of Harvard Univ. 1947–50; Guggenheim Fellow 1952–53, 1963, Ford Fellow 1961; Chancellor, Acad. of American Poets 1961; Poet Laureate of USA 1987–88; mem. PEN; Pres. American Acad. of Arts and Letters 1974–76, Chancellor 1977–78; mem. Dramatists Guild. *Publications:* The Beautiful Changes and Other Poems 1947, Ceremony and Other Poems 1950, A Bestiary (anthology, with Alexander Calder) 1955, The Misanthrope (trans. from Molière) 1955, Things of This World (poems) 1956, Poems 1943–1956 1957, Candide (comic opera, with Lillian Hellman and others) 1957, (edition of his poems with introduction and notes) 1959, Advice to a Prophet (poems) 1961, Tartuffe (trans. from Molière) 1963, The Poems of Richard Wilbur 1963, Loudmouse (for children) 1963, Poems of Shakespeare (with Alfred Harbage) 1966, Walking to Sleep (new poems and translations) 1969, School for Wives (trans. from Molière) 1971, Opposites (children's verse, illustrated by the author) 1973, The Mind-Reader 1976, Responses: Prose Pieces 1953–1976 1976, The Learned Ladies (trans. from Molière) 1978, Selected Poems of Witter Bynner (editor) 1978, Seven Poems 1981, Andromache (trans. from Racine) 1982, The Whale (translations) 1982, Molière: Four Comedies (contains 4 plays translated previously listed) 1982, Phaedra (trans. from Racine) 1986, Lying and Other Poems 1987, New and Collected Poems 1988, More Opposites 1991, School for Husbands (trans. from Molière) 1992, The Imaginary Cuckold (trans. from Molière) 1993, A Game of Catch 1994, Amphitryon (trans. from Molière) 1995, The Catbird's Song (prose pieces) 1997, The Disappearing Alphabet (for children and others) 1998, Bone Key and Other Poems 1998, Mayflies (poems) 2000, Don Juan (trans. from Molière) 2000, The Bungler (trans. from Molière) 2000, Opposites, More Opposites and Some Differences (for children) 2000, The Pig in the Spigot (for children) 2000, Collected Poems 1953–2004 2004, Anterooms: New Poems and Translations 2010. *Honours:* Hon. Fellow, Modern Language Asscn 1986; Chevalier, Ordre des Palmes Académiques 1984; Harriet Monroe Prize 1948, Oscar Blumenthal Prize 1950, Prix de Rome from American Acad. of Arts and Letters 1954–55, Edna St Vincent Millay Memorial Award 1956, Nat. Book Award, Pulitzer Prize 1957, co-recipient Bollingen Translation Prize 1963, co-recipient Bollingen Prize in Poetry 1971, Prix Henri Desfeuilles 1971, Brandeis Creative Arts Award 1971, Shelley Memorial Prize 1973, Harriet Monroe Poetry Award 1978, Drama Desk Award 1983, PEN Translation Prize 1983, St Botolph's Foundation Award 1983, Aiken Taylor Award 1988, L.A. Times Book Award 1988, Pulitzer Prize 1989, Gold Medal for Poetry, American Acad. of Arts and Letters 1991, MacDowell Medal 1992, Nat. Arts Club Medal of Honour for Literature 1994, PEN/Manheim Medal for Translation 1994, Nat. Medal of Arts 1994, Milton Center Prize 1995, Robert Frost Medal, Poetry Soc. of America 1996, T. S. Eliot Award 1996, Wallace Stevens Award 2003, Theater Hall of Fame 2003, Ruth Lilly Prize for Poetry 2006. *Address:* 87 Dodwells Road, Cummington, MA 01026 (home); 715R Windsor Lane, Key West, FL 33040, USA (home). *Telephone:* (413) 634-2275 (home); (305) 296-7499 (home).

WILBY, Basil Leslie, (Gareth Knight), BA (Hons); British author and publisher; b. 3 April 1930, Colchester, Essex, England; s. of Leslie Bernard Wilby and Constance Mabel Sutherland; m. Roma Buckley Berryman; one s. one d. *Education:* Royal Holloway Coll., Univ. of London, Sheffield Hallam Univ. (Diploma in Imperialism and Culture). *Career:* Publr, Longman Group Ltd (retd). *Play:* The Pigeon Fancier, Leicester Phoenix Theatre 1969. *Publications:* A Practical Guide to Qabalistic Symbolism 1965, The New Dimensions Red Book 1968, The Practice of Ritual Magic 1969, Occult Exercises and Practices 1969, Meeting the Occult 1973, Experience of the Inner Worlds 1975, The Occult: An Introduction 1975, The Secret Tradition in Arthurian Legend 1983, The Rose Cross and the Goddess 1985, The Treasure House of Images 1986, The Magical World of the Inklings 1990, The Magical World of the Tarot 1991, Magic and the Western Mind 1991, Tarot and Magic 1991, Evoking the Goddess 1993, Dion Fortune's Magical Battle of Britain 1993, Introduction to Ritual Magic (with Dion Fortune) 1997, The Circuit of Force (with Dion Fortune) 1998, Magical Images and the Magical Imagination 1998, Principles of Hermetic Philosophy (with Dion Fortune) 1999, Merlin and the Grail Tradition 1999, Dion Fortune and the Inner Light 2000, Spiritualism and Occultism (with Dion Fortune) 2000, Pythoness, the Life and Work of Margaret Lumley Brown 2000, Esoteric Training in Everyday Life 2001, The Magical World of J. R. R. Tolkien 2001, The Magical World of C. S. Lewis 2001, The Magical World of Charles Williams 2002, The Magical World of Owen Barfield 2002, Practical Occultism (with Dion Fortune) 2002, The Abbey Papers 2002, Dion Fortune and the Threefold Way 2002, The Wells of Vision 2002, Granny's Magic Cards 2004, The Magical Fiction of Dion Fortune 2005, The Arthurian Formula (with Dion Fortune and Margaret Lumbley Brown) 2005, The Occult Fiction of Dion Fortune 2007, Magic and the Power of the Goddess 2008, The Faery Gates of Avalon 2009, Melusine of Lusignan and the Cult of the Faery Woman 2010, To the Heart of the Rainbow 2010, Yours Very Truly Gareth Knight (selected letters) 2010, The Romance of the Faery Melusine 2011, I Called it Magic (autobiog.) 2011; contrib. to Inner Light Journal 1993–. *Address:* c/o 38 Steeles Road, London, NW3 4RG, England. *E-mail:* garethknight.basil@gmail.com. *Website:* www.garethknight.net.

WILBY, Peter, BA (Hons); British journalist; b. 7 Nov. 1944, Leicester, England; m. Sandra James; two s. *Education:* Univ. of Sussex. *Career:* reporter, The Observer 1968–72, Educ. Corresp. 1972–75; Educ. Corresp. The New Statesman 1975–77, Ed. 1998–2005, now writes weekly column; Educ. Corresp. The Sunday Times 1977–86; Educ. Ed. The Independent 1986–89, Deputy Ed. 1991–95; Home Ed. Independent on Sunday 1989–91, Ed. 1995–96; Press Commentator, the Guardian newspaper 2007–09. *Publication:* Anthony Eden 2006. *Honours:* Hon. LLD (Leicester). *Address:* 51 Queens Road, Loughton, Essex, IG10 1RS, England. *E-mail:* peter.wilby@gmail.com.

WILCOX, James, BA; American author and academic; *MacCurdy Professor, Louisiana State University;* b. 4 April 1949, Hammond, La. *Education:* Yale Univ. *Career:* Robert Penn Warren Prof., Louisiana State Univ. 2004–11, MacCurdy Prof. 2011–; mem. Authors' Guild, PEN. *Publications:* novels: Modern Baptists 1983, North Gladiola 1985, Miss Undine's Living Room 1987, Sort of Rich 1989, Polite Sex 1991, Guest of a Sinner 1993, Plain and Normal 1998, Heavenly Days 2003, Hunk City 2007; contrib. to periodicals. *Honours:* Guggenheim Fellowship 1986, ATLAS 2007, Louisiana State Univ. Distinguished Faculty Award 2009, Distinguished Research Master of Arts, Humanities & Social Sciences 2008, Distinguished Faculty Award, Louisiana State Univ. 2009, Louisiana Writer Award 2011. *Address:* 211A Allen Hall, Department of English, Louisiana State University, Baton Rouge, LA 70803, USA (office). *Telephone:* (225) 578-3049 (office). *E-mail:* jwilcox1@lsu.edu (office). *Website:* www.lsu.edu/creativewriting (office).

WILDING, Michael, MA, DLitt; British/Australian writer and academic; *Professor Emeritus, University of Sydney;* b. 5 Jan. 1942, Worcester, England. *Education:* Lincoln Coll., Oxford. *Career:* Lecturer, Univ. of Sydney 1963–66, Sr Lecturer 1969–72, Reader 1972–92, Prof. 1993–2000, Prof. Emer. 2001–; Lecturer, Univ. of Birmingham 1967–68; Visiting Prof., Univ. of California, USA 1987. *Films:* The Phallic Forest 1972, Buying Jeans in Balmain, Belgrade Film School 1988. *Radio:* Frrried Potatoes Stories (BBC Radio, Morning Story) Aug. 1960, The Altar of the Family (Australian Broadcasting Corpn Sept.) 1975, Bye Bye Jack, See You Soon (ABC Radio) 1974, Her Most Bizarre Sexual Experience (New Poetry 24 i) 1976, (43 Radio Blue Danube, Vienna) 1990, (ABC 2CN) 1991, Reading the Signs (ABC 2BL) 1984, Gypsies (ABC) 1985, Welcome O Foreign Writer (ABC) 1985, Beach Report (ABC) 1985, For Trees (ABC) 1994, Singing Birds (2-SER-FM) 1990, (ABC) 2000. *Television:* Reading the Signs (documentary, Central TV) 1988, Michael Wilding interviewed by Don Graham Univ. of Sydney Television Service 1993. *Publications:* Australians Abroad (co-ed with Charles Higham) 1967, Milton's Paradise Lost 1969, Marvell: Modern Judgements 1969, Cultural Policy in Great Britain (with Michael Green) 1970, Aspects of the Dying Process 1972, Living Together 1974, The Short Story Embassy 1975, The West Midland Underground 1975, Scenic Drive 1976, Marcus Clarke 1977, The Radical Reader (co-ed with Stephen Knight) 1977, The Phallic Forest 1978, The Tabloid Story Pocket Book 1978, Political Fictions 1980, Pacific Highway 1982, Reading the Signs 1984, The Paraguyan Experiment 1985, The Man of Slow Feeling 1986, Dragons Teeth 1987, Under Saturn 1988, Great Climate 1990, Her Most Bizarre Sexual Experience 1991, Social Visions 1993, The Radical Tradition, Lawson, Furphy, Stead 1993, This is for You 1994, Book of the Reading 1994, The Oxford Book of Australian Short Stories 1994, Somewhere New 1996, Studies in Classical Australian Fiction 1997, Wildest Dreams 1998, Raising Spirits, Making Gold and Swapping Wives: The True Adventures of Dr John Dee and Sir Edward Kelly 1999, Academia Nuts 2002, Best Stories Under the Sun, Vols 1–3 (co-ed with David Myers) 2004–06, Wild Amazement 2006, National Treasure 2007, Superfluous Men 2009. *Honours:* Australia Council Literature Bd Sr Fellowship 1978. *Address:* c/o School of Letters, Arts and Media, University of Sydney, Sydney, NSW 2006, Australia (office). *E-mail:* books@michael-wilding.com (office). *Website:* www.michael-wilding.com.

WILENTZ, (Robert) Sean, BA, PhD; American historian and writer; *Sidney and Ruth Lapidus Professor in the American Revolutionary Era, Princeton University;* b. 20 Feb. 1951, New York; m. Mary Christine Stansell 1980, one s. one d. *Education:* Columbia Coll., Univ. of Oxford, Yale Univ. *Career:* currently Sidney and Ruth Lapidus Prof. in the American Revolutionary Era and Prof. of History, Princeton Univ.; mem. Soc. of American Historians. *Publications:* Chants Democratic 1984, Rites of Power 1985, The Key of Liberty 1993, The Kingdom of Matthias 1994, The Rise of American Democracy: Jefferson to Lincoln 2005, The Age of Reagan: A History, 1974–2008 2008, Bob Dylan in America 2010; contributions to New Republic, Dissent. *Honours:* Beveridge Award 1984, Turner Award 1985. *Address:* History Department, Princeton University, 134 Dickinson Hall, Princeton, NJ 08544-1017, USA (office). *Telephone:* (609) 258-4702 (office). *E-mail:* swilentz@princeton.edu (office). *Website:* www.princeton.edu/history (office).

WILFORD, John Noble, BS, MA; American journalist and writer; *Science Correspondent, New York Times;* b. 4 Oct. 1933, Murray, KY; m. Nancy Watts Paschall 1966; one d. *Education:* Univ. of Tennessee, Syracuse Univ., Columbia Univ. *Career:* science reporter 1965–73, 1979–, Asst Nat. Ed., New York Times 1973–75, Dir of Science News 1975–79, Science Correspondent 1979–; McGraw Distinguished Lecturer in Writing, Princeton Univ. 1985; Prof. of Science Journalism, Univ. of Tennessee 1989–90; American Acad. of Arts and Sciences Fellow 1998; mem. Century Club (New York), Nat. Asscn of Science Writers, American Geographical Soc. (council mem. 1994–). *Publications:* We Reach the Moon 1969, The Mapmakers 1981, The Riddle of the Dinosaur 1985, Mars Beckons 1990, The Mysterious History of Columbus 1991, Cosmic Dispatches 2000; contrib. to Nature, Wilson Quarterly, New York Times Magazine, Science Digest, Popular Science, National Geographic. *Honours:* Westinghouse-American Asscn for the Advancement of Science Writing Award 1983, Pulitzer Prizes for Nat. Reporting 1984, 1987 (jtly),

American Soc. of Mechanical Engineers Ralph Coats Roe Medal 1995, American Geological Inst. Award for Outstanding Contributions to Public Understanding of Geosciences 2001, Mayor's Award for Excellence in Science and Technology, New York 2001. *Address:* New York Times, 620 Eighth Avenue, New York, NY 10018, USA (office). *Telephone:* (212) 556-1234 (office). *E-mail:* public@nytimes.com (office). *Website:* www.nytimes.com (office).

WILHELM, Hans; American children's writer and illustrator; b. 21 Sept. 1945, Bremen, Germany; m. Judy Henderson. *Career:* lived in Africa for many years. *Publications include:* Waldo series: Waldo, Waldo and the Desert Island Adventure, Waldo at the Zoo, Waldo, One, Two, Three, Waldo, Tell me about Christ, Waldo, Tell me about Christmas, Waldo, Tell me about Dying, Waldo, Tell me about God, Waldo, Tell me about Guardian Angels, Waldo, Tell me about Me, Waldo, Tell me Where's Grandpa, Waldo's Christmas Surprise; Dinofours series: Let Me Play, I'm the Winner, It's Snowing, My Seeds Won't Grow, It's Thanksgiving, It's Class Picture Day, Bind Up, Our Holiday Show, I'm Sorry! I'm Sorry!, We Love Mud!; A Christmas Journey, A Cool Kid Like Me, A New Home A New Friend, All For The Best, Anook The Snow Princess, Bingo, Bunny Trouble, More Bunny Trouble, Bad Bad Bunny Trouble, Buzz Said the Bee, Don't Cut My Hair!, Franklin and the Messy Pigs, Friends are Forever, Hello Sun, Hiccups for Elephant, I am Lost!, I Can Help, I Hate Bullies!, I Hate My Bow, I Lost my Tooth!, I Love Colors!, I Love my Shadow, I Wouldn't Tell a Lie, I'll Always Love You, It's Too Windy!, Let's Be Friends Again, Mother Goose on the Loose, Never Lonely Again, No Kisses Please, Oh, What a Mess, Quacky Ducky's Easter Fun, Quacky Ducky's Easter Egg, Schnitzel is Lost, Schnitzel's First Christmas, Tales From the Land Under my Table, The Big Boasting Battle, The Boy Who Wasn't There, The Bremen Town Musicians, The Royal Raven, The Trapp Family Book, Tyrone the Horrible, Tyrone the Double Dirty Rotten Cheater, Tyrone and the Swamp Gang, Wake Up, Sun!, With Lots of Love. *Honours:* numerous int. awards. *Address:* PO Box 109, Westport, CT 06881, USA (home). *E-mail:* hans@hanswilhelm.com (home). *Website:* www.hanswilhelm.com.

WILKERSON, Cynthia (see Levinson, Leonard)

WILKINSON, Lisa Clare; Australian magazine editor and TV presenter; *Co-Host, Today Show*; b. 19 Dec. 1958, Wollongong, NSW; d. of the late Raymond William Wilkinson and of Beryl Jean Wilkinson; m. Peter FitzSimons 1992; three c. *Education:* Campbelltown High School, NSW. *Career:* Editorial Asst Dolly Magazine (magazine for girls) 1978, Asst Ed. 1979–80, apptd Ed. aged 21, youngest ever ed. of nat. women's magazine 1980, later Ed.-in-Chief; apptd Ed. Cleo (women's lifestyle magazine) magazine 1985, Int. Ed.-in-Chief Cleo's Int. edns in NZ, Singapore, Malaysia and Thailand; consultant Australian Consolidated Press; fmr Ed. Australian Women's Weekly; co-host Weekend Sunrise (Seven TV Network) 2005–07; co-host Today Show (Nine TV Network) 2007–. *Address:* Today Show, PO Box 27, Willoughby, NSW 2068, Australia (office). *Telephone:* (2) 9958-2899 (office). *Fax:* (2) 9436-1600 (office). *E-mail:* today@nine.com.au (office). *Website:* today.ninemsn.com.au (office).

WILL, Frederic, BA, PhD; American poet, academic, philosopher and translator; *Professor, School of Advanced Studies, University of Phoenix*; b. 4 Dec. 1928, New Haven, Conn.; m. Omotejohwo Ogaga 1995; four s. two d. *Education:* Indiana and Yale Univs. *Career:* Instructor in Classics, Dartmouth Coll. 1951–54; Asst Prof. of Classics, Pennsylvania State Univ. 1955–60, Univ. of Texas 1960–65; Assoc. Prof. of English and Comparative Literature 1964–66, Prof. of Comparative Literature 1966–71, Univ. of Iowa, Assoc. Dir Int. Writing Program 1983–85, Fellow, Inst. of Advanced Studies 1985–90; Prof. of Comparative Literature, Univ. of Massachusetts at Amherst 1971–83; Dir Bd of Overseers and Pres., Mellen Univ. 1991–2000; Fulbright Prof., Univ. of the Ivory Coast 2000–02; Prof. of American Studies, Hunan Normal Univ. 2003; Fulbright Sr Specialist, Univ. of N'djamena, Chad; Visiting Prof. of Greek, Deep Springs Coll. 2004–05; Professeur titulaire, École supérieure universitaire Robert de Sorbon 2004–06; Tutor en Filosofia, Instituto de Estudios Criticos, Mexico City 2007–; Prof., School of Advanced Studies, Univ. of Phoenix, Ariz. 2009–; poetry and scholarly readings at major US univs; Founding Ed. (with William Arrowsmith) Arion: A Journal of Classical Culture 1962–, Micromegas: A Journal of Poetry in Translation 1966–. *Publications:* Intelligible Beauty in Aesthetic Thought: From Winckelmann to Victor Cousin 1958, Mosaic and Other Poems 1959, A Wedge of Words (poems) 1962, Kostes Palamas: The Twelve Words of the Gypsy (trans.) 1964, Hereditas: Seven Essays on the Modern Experience of the Classical (ed.) 1964, Metaphrasis: An Anthology from the University of Iowa Trans. Workshop 1964–65 (ed.) 1965, Flumen Historicum: Victor Cousin's Aesthetic and Its Sources 1965, Literature Inside Out: Ten Speculative Essays 1966, Planets (poems) 1966, Kostes Palamas: The King's Flute (trans.) 1967, From a Year in Greece 1967, Archilochos 1969, Herondas 1972, Brandy in the Snow (poems) 1972, Theodor Adorno: The Jargon of Authenticity (trans. with Knut Tarnowski) 1973, The Knife in the Stone 1973, The Fact of Literature 1973, Guatemala 1973, Botulism (poems) 1975, The Generic Demands of Greek Literature 1976, Belphagor 1977, Epics of America (poems) 1977, Our Thousand Year Old Bodies: Selected Poems 1956–1976 1980, Shamans in Turtlenecks: Selected Essays 1984, The Sliced Dog 1984, Entering the Open Hole 1989, Recoveries 1993, Trips of the Psyche 1993, Textures, Spaces, Wonders 1993, Literature as Sheltering the Human 1993, Singing with Whitman's Thrush 1993, Adventure in Algiers 2002, Bill Ryerson's African Passion 2002, The Poppy Web 2002, By the Sweat of thy Brow 2002, Three North American Agricultural Communities 2002, Miroirs d'Eternité, une saison au Sahel 2002, Mellen University, Early Life and Times 2002, Flesh and the Color of Love 2002; contrib. of many poems and articles to various periodicals. *Honours:* Pfatteicher Prize 1946, Fulbright grants 1950–51, 1955, 1956–57, 1975–76, 1980–81, 2000–02, ACLS grant 1958, Texas Inst. of Letters Voertman Poetry Awards 1962, 1964, Bollingen Foundation grant 1963, Nat. Endowment for the Arts grant 1963, NEA and CCLM editorial grants 1965–73. *Address:* 617 7th Street NW, Mount Vernon, IA 52314, USA. *Telephone:* (319) 895-6159. *Fax:* (319) 895-6399. *E-mail:* samuelw981@aol.com. *Website:* www.phoenix.edu/colleges_divisions/doctoral.html (office).

WILL, George Frederick, BA, MA, PhD; American political columnist, broadcaster and writer; b. 4 May 1941, Champaign, IL. *Education:* Trinity College, Oxford, Princeton Univ. *Career:* Prof. of Political Philosophy, Michigan State University 1967–68, University of Toronto 1968–70; Ed., The National Review 1973–76; Syndicated Political Columnist, The Washington Post 1974–; Contributing Ed., Newsweek magazine 1976–; Television News Analyst, ABC-TV 1981–. *Publications:* The Pursuit of Happiness and Other Sobering Thoughts 1979, The Pursuit of Virtue and Other Tory Notions 1982, Statecraft as Soulcraft: What Government Does 1983, The Morning After: American Successes and Excesses 1986, The New Season: A Spectator's Guide to the 1988 Election 1987, Men at Work 1990, Suddenly: The American Idea at Home and Abroad, 1988–89 1990, Restoration: Congress, Term Limits and the Recovery of Deliberate Democracy 1992, The Leveling Wind: Politics, the Culture and Other News 1994, The Woven Figure: Conservatism and America's Fabric: 1994–97 1997, Bunts: Pete Rose, Curt Flood, Camden Yards and other reflections on baseball 1997, With a Happy Eye But...America and the World 1997–2002 2002, One Man's America: The Pleasures and Provocations of our Singular Nation 2008. *Honours:* Pulitzer Prize for Commentary 1977, Silurian Award 1990, 1991, Cronkie Award, Arizona State Univ. 1991, Madison Medal Award, Princeton Univ. 1992, William Allen White Award 1993, Walter B. Winston Lecture Award, Manhattan Inst. 2003, Champion of Liberty Award, Goldwater Inst. 2006. *Address:* The Washington Post, 1150 15th Street, NW, Washington, DC 20071, USA (office). *Telephone:* (202) 334-6000 (office). *Fax:* (202) 334-5693 (office). *Website:* www.postwritersgroup.com/will.htm (office).

WILLETTS, Sam; British poet; b. 1962. *Education:* Wadham Coll., Oxford. *Publications:* poetry collection: New Light for the Old Dark 2010; contrib. to TLS, London Review of Books, Granta, Poetry Review, Poetry magazine and others. *Address:* c/o Publicity Department, Random House, 20 Vauxhall Bridge Road, London, SW1V 2SA, England. *Website:* www.randomhouse.co.uk.

WILLIAMS, C(harles) K(enneth), BA; American poet and academic; *Lecturer, Creative Writing, Department of Comparative Literature, Princeton University*; b. 4 Nov. 1936, Newark, NJ; s. of Paul Bernard and Dossie (née Kasdin) Williams; m. 1st Sarah Dean Jones 1966 (divorced 1975); one d.; m. 2nd Catherine Justine Mauger 1975; one s. *Education:* Univ. of Pennsylvania. *Career:* Visiting Prof. of Literature, Beaver Coll., Jenkintown, Pa 1975, Drexel Univ., Philadelphia 1976, Franklin and Marshall Coll., Pa 1977, Univ. of Calif. at Irvine 1978, Boston Univ. 1979–80, Brooklyn Coll., CUNY 1982–83; Prof. of Writing, Columbia Univ. NY 1981–85; Prof. of Literature, George Mason Univ., Fairfax Va 1982–95; Halloway Lecturer Univ. of Calif. at Berkeley 1986; Lecturer, Creative Writing, Dept of Comparative Literature, Princeton Univ. 1995–; contributing Ed. American Poetry Review 1972–; Fellow, Guggenheim Foundation 1975–, Nat. Endowment for Arts 1985, 1993; mem. PEN, American Acad. of Arts and Sciences, American Acad. of Arts and Letters. *Publications:* A Day for Anne Frank 1968, Lies 1969, The Sensuous President 1972, I am the Bitter Name 1972, With Ignorance 1977, The Women of Trachis (co-trans.) 1978, The Lark, The Thrush, The Starling 1983, Tar 1983, Flesh and Blood 1987, Poems 1963–1983, 1988, The Bacchae of Euripides (trans.) 1990, Helen 1991, A Dream of Mind 1992, Selected Poems 1994, The Vigil 1997, Poetry and Consciousness (selected essays) 1998, Repair (poems) 1999, Misgivings: A Memoir 2000, Love About Love 2001, The Singing 2004, Pétain (1856–1951) 2005, Collected Poems 2006, Wait 2010, On Whitman 2010; contrib. to Akzent, Atlantic, Carleton Miscellany, Crazyhorse, Grand Street, Iowa Review, Madison Review, New England Review, New Yorker, Seneca Review, Transpacific Review, TriQuarterly, Yale Review, Threepenny Review. *Honours:* Pushcart Press Prizes 1982, 1983, 1987, Nat. Book Critics Circle Award for Poetry 1987, Morton Dauwen Zabel Prize, American Acad. of Arts and Letters 1989, Lila Wallace Writers Award 1993, Harriet Monroe Prize 1993, Berlin Prize, American Acad. in Berlin 1998, Voelcker Career Achievement Award, PEN 1998, Pulitzer Prize for Poetry 2000, LA Times Book Award 2000, Weathertop Prize 2000, Nat. Book Award 2003, Ruth Lilly Prize for Poetry 2005. *Address:* Lewis Center for the Arts, 185 Nassau Street, Princeton, NJ 08544, USA (office). *Telephone:* (609) 258-3176 (office). *E-mail:* ckwms@princeton.edu (office). *Website:* www.princeton.edu/arts (office).

WILLIAMS, David Larry, BA, MA, PhD; Canadian writer and academic; *Professor of English, University of Manitoba*; b. 22 June 1945, Souris, Man.; s. of Jack W. Williams, RCAF and Dorothy Williams (née Dahl); m. Darlene Olinyk 1967; two s. *Education:* Briercrest Bible Inst., Saskatchewan, Univ. of Saskatchewan, Univ. of Massachusetts, Amherst. *Career:* Lecturer in English, Univ. of Manitoba, Winnipeg 1972–73, Asst Prof. 1973–77, Assoc. Prof. 1977–83, Prof. of English 1983–; mem. Editorial Bd Canadian Review of American Studies 1976–86, Canadian Literature 2006–; Guest Prof., Indian Asscn for Canadian Studies, MS Univ. of Baroda 1992; Woodrow Wilson Fellow 1968–69; Canada Council Fellow 1969–72; mem. Writers' Union of

Canada, PEN Int., Asscn of Canadian Coll. and Univ. Teachers of English, Asscn for Canadian and Québec Literatures. *Publications:* The Burning Wood (novel) 1975, Faulkner's Women: The Myth and the Muse (criticism) 1977, The River Horsemen (novel) 1981, Eye of the Father (novel) 1985, To Run with Longboat: Twelve Stories of Indian Athletes in Canada (with Brenda Zeman) 1988, Confessional Fictions: A Portrait of the Artist in the Canadian Novel 1991, Imagined Nations: Reflections on Media in Canadian Fiction (criticism) (Asscn for Canadian and Québec Literatures Gabrielle Roy Prize) 2003, Media, Memory, and the First World War (criticism) 2009; contrib. to books and professional journals. *Honours:* Canada Council Arts grant 'B' 1977–78, 1981–82, Touring Writer in Scandinavia for External Affairs, Canada 1981, RH Inst. Award for Research in Humanities 1987, Olive Beatrice Stanton Award for Excellence in Teaching 1992, UM-UM Student Union Certificate of Teaching Excellence 1994. *Address:* Department of English, St Paul's College, University of Manitoba, Winnipeg, MB R3T 2M6, Canada (office). *Telephone:* (204) 474-8535 (office). *Fax:* (204) 474-7620 (office). *E-mail:* dwillms@cc.umanitoba.ca (office).

WILLIAMS, Gordon MacLean; British writer; b. 1934, Paisley, Renfrewshire, Scotland. *Career:* journalist, sportswriter. *Publications:* novels: The Last Day of Lincoln Charles 1965, The Camp 1966, The Man Who Had Power Over Women 1967, From Scenes Like These 1968, The Siege of Trencher's Farm (aka Straw Dogs) 1969, Upper Pleasure Garden 1970, Walk Don't Walk 1972, Big Morning Blues 1974, The Duellists 1977, The Microcolony 1979, Revolution of the Micronauts 1981, Pomeroy 1983, Pomeroy Unleashed 1986; co-writer of Hazell novels with Terry Venables. *Address:* c/o Bloomsbury Publishing PLC, 38 Soho Square, London, W1V 5DF, England. *Website:* www.bloomsbury.com.

WILLIAMS, Heathcote; British playwright and poet; b. 15 Nov. 1941, Helsby, Cheshire, England. *Career:* Assoc. Ed., Transatlantic Review, New York and London. *Publications:* The Local Stigmatic 1967, AC/DC 1970, Remember the Truth Dentist 1974, The Speakers 1974, Very Tasty: A Pantomime 1975, An Invitation to the Official Lynching of Abdul Malik 1975, Anatomy of a Space Rat 1976, Hancock's Last Half-Hour 1977, Playpen 1977, The Immortalist 1977, At It 1982, Whales 1986; poetry: Whale Nation 1988, Falling for a Dolphin 1988, Sacred Elephant 1989, Autogeddon 1991; other: The Speakers 1964, Manifestoes, Manifestern 1975, Severe Joy 1979, Elephants 1983. *Honours:* Evening Standard Award 1970.

WILLIAMS, Herbert Lloyd; British poet, author, novelist, biographer and scriptwriter and producer; b. 8 Sept. 1932, Aberystwyth, Wales; s. of Richard David Williams and Minnie Esther Williams; m. Dorothy Maud Edwards 1954; four s. one d. *Education:* Ardwyn Grammar School, Aberystwyth. *Career:* journalist with daily and weekly papers in Wales, England and Scotland; Editorial Officer, Wales Tourist Board; BBC radio producer; freelance writer of books, TV and radio plays and documentaries; part-time univ. tutor; mem. Soc. of Authors; Fellow, Welsh Acad. *Plays:* A Lethal Kind of Love (verse play commissioned by BBC), Bodyline (BBC Radio 4). *Radio:* Morning Story producer (BBC Radio 4) for several years; BBC productions include The Voice of Meadow Prospect (novelist, Gwyn Thomas) 1981, Time to Stand and Stare (poet, W. H. Davies) 1980, The Bracchis of Bardi 1980, People and Places 1981, Taylor Lloyd the Chemist 1982, Laughter Before Nightfall 1983, The Road to Llareggub (Dylan Thomas 1983, A Very Private View (Gwen John) 1983, A Shropshire Lass (Mary Webb) 1984; adaptations for Radio 4 of Dylan Thomas's A Child's Christmas in Wales 1994, A. J. Cronin's The Citadel 1997. *Television:* Taff Acre 1981, A Welsh Rarebit 1982, A Solitary Mister 1983, Alone in a Crowd 1984, Land of Milk and Money 1986, Davies the Ocean 1987, Calvert in Camera 1990, The Great Powys 1994, Arouse All Wales 1996; script consultant for prize-winning adaptation of A Child's Christmas in Wales by Atlantis Films, Canada. *Publications:* The Trophy 1967, A Lethal Kind of Love 1968, Battles in Wales 1975, Come Out Wherever You Are 1976, Stage Coaches in Wales 1977, The Welsh Quiz Book 1978, Railways in Wales 1981, The Pembrokeshire Coast National Park 1987, Stories of King Arthur 1990, Ghost Country 1991, Davies the Ocean 1991, The Stars in Their Courses 1992, John Cowper Powys 1997, Looking Through Time 1998, A Severe Case of Dandruff 1999, Voices of Wales 1999, The Woman in Back Row 2000, Punters 2002, Wrestling in Mud 2007, The Marionettes 2008, Tiger in the Park 2010; contrib. to reviews and journals. *Honours:* Bradbury Scholarship, Welsh Arts Council Short Story Prize 1972, and Bursary 1988, Aberystwyth Open Poetry Competition 1990, Hawthornden Poetry Fellowship 1992, Rhys Davies Short Story Award 1995, Harri Webb Poetry Award 2004, Cinnamon Press Novella Award 2007. *Address:* 63 Bwlch Road, Fairwater, Cardiff, CF5 3BX, Wales (home). *E-mail:* h.williams13@ntlworld.com (office). *Website:* www.herbert-williams.co.uk.

WILLIAMS, Hugo Mordaunt, FRSL; British poet and journalist; *Columnist, Times Literary Supplement*; b. 20 Feb. 1942, Windsor, Berks.; m. Hermine Demoriane 1966; one d. *Education:* Eton Coll. *Career:* Asst Ed., London Magazine 1961–70; TV critic 1983–88, Poetry Ed. New Statesman 1984–93; Theatre Critic, Sunday Correspondent 1989–91, writer of the Freelance Column in TLS 1988–; Film Critic, Harpers & Queen 1993–98. *Publications:* poetry: Symptoms of Loss 1965, Sugar Daddy 1970, Some Sweet Day 1975, Love Life 1979, Writing Home 1985, Selected Poems 1989, Self-Portrait with a Slide 1990, Dock Leaves 1994, Billy's Rain 1999, Curtain Call: 101 Portraits in Verse (ed.) 2001, Collected Poems 2002, Dear Room 2006, John Betjeman: Selected Poems (ed.) 2006, West End Final 2009; non-fiction: All the Time in the World 1966, No Particular Place to Go 1981, Freelancing: Adventures of a Poet 1993; contrib. to newspapers and periodicals. *Honours:* Eric Gregory Award 1965, Cholmondeley Award 1970, Geoffrey Faber Memorial Prize 1979, T. S. Eliot Prize 1999, Queen's Gold Medal for Poetry 2004. *Address:* 3 Raleigh Street, London, N1 8NW, England. *Telephone:* (20) 7226-1655 (office). *Fax:* (20) 7226-1655 (office).

WILLIAMS, Jeanne, (Megan Castell, Jeanne Crecy, Jeanne Foster, Kristin Michaels, Deirdre Rowan); American writer; b. 10 April 1930, Elkhart, KS. *Education:* Univ. of Oklahoma. *Career:* mem. Authors' Guild, Western Writers of America (Pres. 1974–75). *Publications:* To Buy a Dream 1958, Promise of Tomorrow 1959, Coyote Winter 1965, Beasts with Music 1967, Oil Patch Partners 1968, New Medicine 1971, Trails of Tears 1972, Freedom Trail 1973, Winter Wheat 1975, A Lady Bought with Rifles 1977, A Woman Clothed in Sun 1978, Bride of Thunder 1978, Daughter of the Sword 1979, The Valiant Women 1981, Harvest of Fury 1982, The Heaven Sword 1983, A Mating of Hawks 1984, The Cave Dreamers 1985, So Many Kingdoms 1986, Texas Pride 1987, Lady of No Man's Land 1988, No Roof but Heaven 1990, Home Mountain 1990, The Island Harp 1991, The Longest Road 1993, Daughter of the Storm 1994, The Unplowed Sky 1994, Home Station 1995, Wind Water 1997, The Underground River (Beneath the Burning Ground trilogy book one) 2004, The Hidden Valley (Beneath the Burning Ground trilogy book two) 2004, The Trampled Fields (Beneath the Burning Ground trilogy book three) 2005, All Ye Green and Growing Things 2007; as Megan Castell: The Queen of a Lonely Country 1980; as J. R. Williams: Mission in Mexico 1960, The Horsetalker 1961, The Confederate Fiddle 1962, River Guns 1962, Oh Susanna 1963, Tame the Wild Stallion 1967; as Jeanne Crecy: Hands of Terror (aka Lady Gift, The Lightning Tree) 1972, My Face Beneath Stone 1975, The Evil Among Us 1975, The Winter-Keeper 1975, The Night Hunters 1975; as Deirdre Rowan: Dragon's Mount 1973, Silver Wood 1974, Shadow of the Volcano 1975, Time of the Burning Mask 1976, Ravensgate 1976; as Kristin Michaels: To Begin with Love 1976, Enchanted Journey 1977, Song of the Heart 1977, Make Believe Love 1978, Magic Side of the Mo 1979, Shadow of Love 1979, Design for Love 1981; as Jeanne Foster: Deborah Leigh 1981, Eden Richards 1982, Woman of Three Worlds 1984; contrib. to journals. *Honours:* Texas Inst. of Letters Best Children's Book 1958, Four Western Writers of America Spur Awards, Best Novel of the West 1981, 1990, Levi Strauss Golden Saddleman Award for Lifetime Achievement 1988. *Address:* PO Box 16335, Portal, AZ 85632, USA (home). *Telephone:* (520) 558-2436 (home). *E-mail:* author@jeannewilliams.net (home). *Website:* www.jeannewilliams.net.

WILLIAMS, John Alfred, BA; American writer, journalist, poet and educator; *Professor Emeritus, Rutgers University*; b. 5 Dec. 1925, Jackson, Miss.; m. 1st Carolyn Clopton 1947 (divorced); two s.; m. 2nd Lorrain Isaac 1965, one s. *Education:* Syracuse University. *Career:* Foreign Corresp., Ebony, Jet, Newsweek 1950–63; Ed. and Publisher, Negro Market Newsletter 1956–57; Contributing Ed., Herald-Tribune Book Week 1963–65, American Journal 1972–74, Politicks 1977, Journal of African Civilizations 1980–88; Lecturer, College of the Virgin Islands 1968, City College, CUNY 1968–69; Visiting Prof., Macalester College 1970, University of Hawaii 1974, Boston University 1978–79, University of Houston 1994, Bard College 1994–95; Regents Lecturer, University of California, Santa Barbara 1972; Guest Writer, Sarah Lawrence College 1972–73; Distinguished Prof., LaGuardia Community College, CUNY 1973–79; Distinguished Prof., Cooper Union 1974–75; Distinguished Prof., Rutgers University 1979–93, Prof. Emer. 1993–; Exxon Visiting Prof., New York University 1986–87; mem. Authors' Guild, Poets and Writers, PEN. *Music:* Vanqui (libretto) 1999. *Play:* Last Flight from Ambo Bec 1983. *Publications:* fiction: The Angry Ones 1960, revised edn as One for New York, Night Song 1961, Sissie 1963, The Man Who Cried I Am 1967, Sons of Darkness, Sons of Light 1969, Captain Blackman 1972, Mothersill and the Foxes 1975, The Junior Bachelor Society 1976, Click Song 1982, The Berhama Account 1985, Jacob's Ladder 1987, Clifford's Blues 1999; poetry: Safari West 1998; non-fiction: Africa: Her History, Lands and People 1963, The Protectors (with Harry J. Anslinger) 1964, This Is My Country Too 1965, The Most Native of Sons: A Biography of Richard Wright 1970, The King God Didn't Save: Reflections on the Life and Death of Martin Luther King Jr. 1970, Flashbacks: A Twenty-Year Diary of Article Writing 1973, Minorities in the City 1975, If I Stop I'll Die: The Comedy and Tragedy of Richard Pryor (with Dennis A. Williams) 1991; ed. or co-ed.: The Angry Black 1962, revised edn as Beyond the Angry Black, Amistad 1 1970, Amistad 2 1971, Y'Bird 1978, Introduction to Literature 1985, Street Guide to African Americans in Paris 1992, Ways In: Approaches to Literature 1994, Bridges: Literature Across Cultures 1994, A Black Reader 2004, Dear Chester, Dear John: Letters between Chester Himes and John A. Williams 2008; contributions: anthologies, journals, magazines, newspapers. *Honours:* Hon. DLitt (Southeastern Mass Univ.) 1978, (Syracuse Univ.) 1995, (State Univ. of New York, Old Westbury) 2001; Hon. DHumLitt (Rochester Univ.) 2003; Nat. Inst. of Arts and Letters Award 1962, Centennial Medal 1970, Richard Wright-Jacques Roumain Award 1973, Nat. Endowment for the Arts Award 1977, Lindback Award for Distinguished Teaching, Rutgers Univ. 1982, American Book Award, Before Columbus Foundation 1983, 1998, New Jersey State Council on the Arts Award 1985, Michael Award, New Jersey Literary Hall of Fame 1987, Distinguished Writer Award, Middle Atlantic Writers 1987, J. A. Williams Archive established, Univ. of Rochester 1987, Carter G. Woodson Award, Mercy College 1989, Nat. Literary Hall of Fame 1998, John Oliver Killens Memorial Award for Fiction 2002. *Address:* 693 Forest Avenue, Teaneck, NJ 07666, USA (home).

WILLIAMS, John Hartley, BA, MPhil; British poet; b. 7 Feb. 1942, Cheadle, Cheshire, England; s. of Dafydd Ffrancon Williams and Sylvia Margaret Hartley; m. Gizella Horvat 1970; one d. *Education:* Univ. of Nottingham, Univ. Coll., London, Univ. of London. *Career:* teacher and lecturer, Univ. of Lille, France, INSA, Toulouse, France, Univ. of Novi Sad, Serbia, Fed. Univ. of Cameroon, Free Univ. of Berlin 1976–2007; Poet-in-Residence, The Wordsworth Trust, Grasmere; currently freelance writer. *Publications include:* Hidden Identities 1982, Bright River Yonder 1987, Cornerless People 1990, Double 1994, Ignoble Sentiments 1995, Teach Yourself Writing Poetry (with Matthew Sweeney) 1997, Canada 1997, The Scar in the Stone (contributing trans. to poems from Serbo-Croatian) 1998, Spending Time with Walter 2001, Marin Sorescu: Censored Poems (trans.) 2001, Mystery in Spiderville 2002, North Sea Improvisation, a fotopoem 2003, Blues 2004, The Ship 2007, Café des Artistes 2009, Outpost Theater 2009, A Poetry Inferno 2011, Hex Wheels 2011, Less of That W or I'll Z You! 2011; contrib. to anthologies, reviews and journals. *Honours:* First Prize, Arvon Int. Poetry Competition 1983, Poetry Book Recommendation 1987, 2004, Poetry Book Soc. Choice 1997. *Address:* 18 Jenbacherweg, 12209 Berlin, Germany (home). *Telephone:* (30) 7118307 (home). *E-mail:* johnhartleywilliams@t-online.de. *Website:* www.johnhartleywilliams.de.

WILLIAMS, Joy, MA, MFA; American writer; b. 11 Feb. 1944, Chelmsford, MA; m. Rust Hills, one c. *Education:* Marietta College, University of Iowa. *Career:* mem. American Acad. of Arts and Letters 2008–. *Publications:* State of Grace 1973, The Changeling 1978, Taking Care 1982, The Florida Keys: A History and Guide 1986, Breaking and Entering 1988, Escapes 1990, The Quick and the Dead 2000, Ill Nature 2001, Honored Guest (short stories) 2004; contrib. to anthologies. *Honours:* National Endowment for the Arts Grant 1973, Guggenheim Fellowship 1974, National Magazine Award 1980, American Acad. of Arts and Letters Literature Citation 1989, and Straus Living Award 1993–97, Rea Award 1999. *Literary Agent:* c/o International Creative Management, 40 W 57th Street, New York, NY 10019, USA.

WILLIAMS, Malcolm David, CertEd; Welsh writer; b. 9 April 1939, South Wales; m. (deceased); one d. *Education:* Birmingham Univ. Inst. of Education, Univ. of Durham. *Career:* Life Fellow World Literary Acad.; mem. Soc. of Authors, West Country Writers' Asscn, British Haiku Soc., Gloucestershire Wildlife Trust, Royal British Legion. *Publications:* Yesterday's Secret 1980, Poor Little Rich Girl 1981, Debt of Friendship 1981, Another Time, Another Place 1982, My Brother's Keeper 1982, The Stuart Affair 1983, The Cordillera Conspiracy 1983, The Girl from Derry's Bluff 1983, A Corner of Eden 1984, Sorrow's End 1984, A Stranger on Trust 1987, Shadows From the Past 1989, This Mask I Wear Today 1998, And the Dragons are Dead 2003, The Cotswold Male Voice Choir 2009; contrib. hundreds of serial stories, articles and short stories to numerous publications. *Honours:* James Hackett Int. Haiku Award 2006, 2008, 2009, first prizes in many short story and poetry competitions 1960–2005. *Address:* 19 Gilbert Ward Court, Croft Road, Charlton Kings, Cheltenham, Gloucestershire GL53 8ND, England (home). *Telephone:* (1242) 241476 (home).

WILLIAMS, Merryn, BA, PhD; British writer and poet; *Editor, The Interpreter's House;* b. 9 July 1944, Devon; m. John Hemp 1973; one s. one d. *Education:* Univ. of Cambridge. *Career:* Lecturer, Open Univ. 1970–71; Ed., The Interpreter's House 1996–; Ed., Wilfred Owen Asscn newsletter; mem. Open Univ. Poets, Welsh Acad. *Publications:* The Bloodstream 1989, Selected Poems of Federico García Lorca 1992, Wilfred Owen 1993, The Sun's Yellow Eye 1997, The Latin Master's Story 2000, In the Spirit of Wilfred Owen (ed., anthology) 2002, The Georgians 1901-1930, An Anthology (ed.) 2009; contrib. to reviews, quarterlies, journals and magazines. *Address:* Wolfson College, Oxford, OX2 6UD, England (office). *E-mail:* hemp@cranfield.ac.uk (office).

WILLIAMS, Miller, BS, MS; American academic, author and poet; *Professor, University of Arkansas;* b. 8 April 1930, Hoxie, Ark.; m. 1st Lucille Day 1951; one s. two d.; m. 2nd Jordan Hall 1969. *Education:* Arkansas State Coll., Univ. of Arkansas. *Career:* Founder-Ed. 1968–70, Advisory Ed. 1975–, New Orleans Review; Prof., Univ. of Arkansas 1971–, Dir, University of Arkansas Press 1980–97. *Publications:* A Circle of Stone 1964, Southern Writing in the Sixties (with J. W. Corrington, two vols) 1966, So Long at the Fair 1968, Chile: An Anthology of New Writing 1968, The Achievement of John Ciardi 1968, The Only World There Is 1968, The Poetry of John Crowe Ransom 1971, Contemporary Poetry in America 1972, Halfway from Hoxie: New and Selected Poems 1973, How Does a Poem Mean? (with John Ciardi) 1974, Railroad (with James Alan McPherson) 1976, Why God Permits Evil 1977, A Roman Collection 1980, Distraction 1981, Ozark, Ozark: A Hillside Reader 1981, The Boys on Their Bony Mules 1983, Living on the Surface: New and Selected Poems 1989, Adjusting to the Light 1992, Points of Departure 1995, The Ways We Touch (poems) 1997, Some Jazz a While: Collected Poems 1999, The Lives of Kelvin Fletcher: Stories Mostly Short 2002, Time and the Tilting Earth, Poems 2009; contrib. to various publs. *Honours:* Hon. DHum (Lander Coll.) 1983, Hon. LHD (Hendrix Coll.) 1995; Henry Bellaman Poetry Award 1957, Bread Loaf Fellowship in Poetry 1961, Fulbright Lecturer 1970, American Acad. of Arts and Letters Prix de Rome 1976, Nat. Poets Prize 1992, John William Corrington Award for Excellence in Literature, Centenary Coll., La 1994, American Acad. of Arts and Letters Award 1995, Inaugural Poet, Presidential Inauguration 1997. *Address:* 1111 Valley View Drive, Fayetteville, AR 72701, USA (home). *Telephone:* (479) 521-2934 (home). *E-mail:* mwms1000@aol.com (home).

WILLIAMS, Nigel, MA; British writer and television producer; b. 20 Jan. 1948, Cheshire; s. of the late David Ffrancon Williams; m. Suzan Harrison 1973; three s. *Education:* Highgate School, Oriel Coll., Oxford. *Career:* trainee BBC 1969–73, Producer/Dir Arts Dept 1973–85, Ed. Bookmark 1985–92, Omnibus 1992–96, writer and presenter 1997–2000. *Television includes:* Double Talk, Talking Blues, Real Live Audience 1977, Baby Love 1981, Breaking Up 1986, The Last Romantics 1992, Skallagrig (BAFTA Award) 1994. *Stage plays include:* Class Enemy 1978 (Plays and Players Award for Most Promising Playwright 1978), Trial Run 1980, Line 'Em 1980, Sugar & Spice 1980, My Brother's Keeper 1985, Country Dancing 1986, Nativity 1989, Harry & Me 1995, The Last Romantics 1997. *Publications:* novels: My Life Closed Twice 1977 (jt winner Somerset Maugham Award), Jack Be Nimble 1980, Star Turn 1985, Witchcraft 1987, The Wimbledon Poisoner 1990, They Came from SW19 1992, East of Wimbledon 1994, Scenes from a Poisoner's Life 1994, Stalking Fiona 1997, Fortysomething 1999, Hatchett and Lycett 2002; travel: Wimbledon to Waco 1995. *Address:* 18 Holmbush Road, Putney, London, SW15 3LE, England (home). *Telephone:* (20) 8964-8811 (home). *Fax:* (20) 8964-8966 (home).

WILLIAMS, Peter Fredric, BA, MusB, MA, PhD, LittD; British musicologist, organist and harpsichordist; b. 14 May 1937, Wolverhampton, Staffordshire; m. Rosemary Seymour 1982; three s. one d. *Education:* Birmingham Inst., St John's Coll., Cambridge. *Career:* Lecturer, Univ. of Edinburgh 1962–72, Reader 1972–82, Prof. 1982–85, Dean 1984; Dir, Russell Coll. of Harpsichords, Edinburgh 1969; Founder-Ed., The Organ Yearbook (Regensburg) 1969–; Arts and Sciences Distinguished Prof., Duke Univ., USA 1985–95, Dir, Graduate Center for Performance Practice Studies 1990–96; John Bird Prof., Univ. of Wales, Cardiff 1996–2002; Vice-Pres., Royal Coll. of Organists 2005; mem. British Inst. of Organ Studies (chair.). *Publications include:* The European Organ 1450–1850 1966, Figured Bass Accompaniment (two vols) 1970, Vente/Peeters' The Organ and its Music in the Netherlands (trans.) 1971, A New History of the Organ From the Greeks to the Present Day 1980, The Organ Music of J. S. Bach (three vols) 1980–84, Bach, Handel and Scarlatti: Tercentenary Essays (ed.) 1985, Playing the Works of Bach 1986, Playing the Organ Music of Bach 1988, Mozart: Perspectives in Performance (ed. with L. Todd) 1991, The Organ in Western Culture 750–1250 1992, The King of Instruments: How Do Churches Come to Have Organs? 1993, The Chromatic Fourth During Four Centuries of Music 1995, Cambridge Studies in Performance Practice (series ed., six vols) 1995, Music to Hear, or Fears for Higher Music Study 2001, The Life of Bach 2005 (expanded as JS Bach: A Life in Music 2007); several vols of keyboard music by Bach and Handel; contrib. to scholarly books and journals. *Honours:* Research Fellow, Cornell Univ., New York 1982, Hon. Fellow, Royal Coll. of Organists 1982, Royal Scottish Acad. of Art 1990, Curt Sachs Award, American Musical Instrument Soc. 1996; Hon. Prof. (Edinburgh) 1992. *Address:* c/o Department of Music, Corbett Road, University of Wales, Cardiff, CF10 3EB, Wales (office). *Telephone:* (1452) 831195 (home).

WILLIAMS, Most Rev., Rt Hon. Rowan Douglas, PC, MA, DPhil, DD, FRSL, FBA; British ecclesiastic and academic; *Archbishop of Canterbury;* b. 14 June 1950, Ystradgynlais, Swansea, Wales; s. of Aneurin Williams and Delphine (Del, Nancy) Morris; m. Jane Paul 1981; one s. one d. *Education:* Dynevor School, Swansea, Christ's Coll., Cambridge, Wadham Coll., Oxford. *Career:* lectured at Coll. of the Resurrection, Mirfield, W Yorks. 1975–77; deacon, Ely Cathedral 1977; priest 1978; tutor, Westcott House, Univ. of Cambridge 1977–80, Lecturer in Divinity 1980–1986, Dean and Chaplain, Clare Coll. 1984–86; Canon Theologian Leicester Cathedral 1981–82; Canon Residentiary, Christ Church, Oxford 1986–92; Lady Margaret Prof. of Theology, Oxford Univ. 1986–92; consecrated Bishop of Monmouth in the Church in Wales 1992–2002; Archbishop of Wales 2000–02; Archbishop of Canterbury, Metropolitan of the Prov. of Canterbury and Primate of All England 2002–12; Master of Magdalene Coll., Cambridge 2013–; inaugurated as first Chancellor of Canterbury Christ Church Univ. 2005; Visitor at King's Coll., London, Univ. of Kent, Keble Coll., Oxford; Gov. of Charterhouse School; Patron Peace Mala Youth Project for World Peace 2002–, Canterbury Open Centre run by Catching Lives; Founding Fellow, Learned Soc. of Wales 2010. *Television:* Conversations with Rowan Williams 2003. *Publications include:* The Wound of Knowledge 1979, Resurrection 1982, The Truce of God 1983, Arius: Heresy and Tradition 1987, Teresa of Avila 1991, Open to Judgement: Sermons and Addresses 1994, Sergei Bulgakov: towards a Russian political theory 1999, Christ on Trial: How the Gospel Unsettles our Judgement 2000, Lost Icons: Reflection on Cultural Bereavement 2000, On Christian Theology 2000, Love's Redeeming Work (ed.) 2001, Ponder These Things: Praying With Icons of the Virgin 2002, Writing in the Dust: Reflections on 11th September and its Aftermath 2002, Silence and Honey Cakes 2003, The Dwelling of the Light 2003, Anglican Identities 2004, Why Study the Past? 2005, Grace and Necessity 2006, Tokens of Trust: An Introduction to Christian Belief 2007, Wrestling with Angels: Conversations in Modern Theology 2007, Dostoevsky: Language, Faith and Fiction 2008; poetry: After Silent Centuries 1994, Remembering Jerusalem 2001, The Poems of Rowan Williams 2002, Headwaters 2008, Uncommon Gratitude (with Joan Chittister) 2010, Crisis and Recovery (with Larry Elliot) 2010. *Honours:* Hon. Student of Christ Church, Oxford; Hon. Curate, St George's, Chesterton, Cambridge 1980–83, Hon. Fellow, Univ. of Wales, Bangor 2003, Univ. of Wales, Swansea, Newport, Aberystwyth, Cardiff, Clare Coll., Cambridge, Christ Church, Oxford, Wadham Coll., Oxford, Christ's Coll., Cambridge; Order of Friendship (Russia) 2010; Hon. DD (Kent) 2003, (Univ. of Wales) 2003, (Cambridge)

2006, (Trinity Coll., Univ. of Toronto) 2007, (Wycliffe Coll., Univ. of Toronto) 2007, (Durham) 2007, (St Vladimir's Orthodox Theological Seminary) 2010, (Catholic Univ. of Louvain) 2011, (King's Coll., London) 2011; Hon. DrTheol (Evangelisch-Theologische Fakultät, Univ. of Bonn) 2004; Hon. DCL (Oxford) 2005; Dr hc (Erlangen, Nashoteh House, Exeter, Aberdeen, Open Univ., Roehampton). *Address:* Lambeth Palace, London, SE1 7JU, England (office). *Telephone:* (20) 7898-1200 (office). *Fax:* (20) 7401-9886 (office). *E-mail:* contact@lambethpalace.org.uk (office). *Website:* www.archbishopofcanterbury.org (office).

WILLIAMS, Roy, OBE; British playwright; b. 1968. *Education:* Rose Bruford Drama School. *Plays include:* No Boys Cricket Club 1996, Starstruck 1997, Lift Off 1999, The Gift 2000, Clubland 2001, Sing Yer Heart Out for the Lads 2002, Fallout 2003, Days of Significance 2007. *Publications include:* Plays 1 2002, Plays 2004. *Honours:* TAPS Writer of the Year Award 1996, Alfred Fagon Award 1998, John Whiting Award for Best New Play 1998–99, Evening Standard Most Promising Playwright Award 2001. *Literary Agent:* c/o Lisa Foster, Alan Brodie Representation Ltd, Paddock Suite, The Courtyard 55, Charterhouse Street, London, EC1M 6HA, England. *Address:* 45d Cambridge Gardens, London, W10 5UA, England.

WILLIAMS, Terry Tempest, BS, MEd; American author and ecologist; *Annie Clark Tanner Scholar in Environmental Humanities, University of Utah*; b. Sept. 1955, Salt Lake City, UT; d. of John Henry Tempest, III and Diane Dixon Tempest; m. Brooke Williams. *Education:* Univ. of Utah. *Career:* worked as 'a barefoot artist' in Rwanda; fmr Curator of Educ., later Naturalist-in-Residence, Utah Museum of Natural History; currently Annie Clark Tanner Scholar in Environmental Humanities, Univ. of Utah; fmr mem. Governing Council, The Wilderness Soc.; fmr mem. Western Team, Pres.'s Council for Sustainable Devt; Advisory Bd mem. Nat. Parks and Conservation Asscn; mem. Bd Round River Conservation Studies, Southern Utah Wilderness Alliance; mem. The Nature Conservancy; Advocate for America's Redrock Wilderness Act. *Publications:* Pieces of White Shell: A Journey to Navajoland 1984, Coyote's Canyon 1989, Refuge: An Unnatural History of Family and Place 1991, An Unspoken Hunger (essays) 1994, Desert Quartet: An Erotic Landscape 1995, Leap 2000, Red: Patience and Passion in the Desert 2001, The Open Space of Democracy 2004, Mosaic: Finding Beauty in a Broken World 2008; children's books: The Secret Language of Snow (with Ted Major) 1984, Between Cattails 1985; other: Great and Peculiar Beauty: A Utah Centennial Reader (co-ed. with Thomas J. Lyon) 1995, Testimony: Writers of the West Speak on Behalf of Utah Wilderness (co-ed. with Stephen Trimble) 1996, New Genesis: a Mormon Reader on Land and Community (co-ed. with William B. Smart, Gibbs M. Smith) 1998; contrib. to anthologies, journals and newspapers, including New Yorker, The Nation, Outside, Audubon, Orion, Iowa Review, New England Review. *Honours:* Hon. DH (Univ. of Utah) 2003; Hon. DHumLitt (Saint Mary-of-the-Woods Coll.) 2004; Inductee, Rachel Carson Honor Roll, Conservation Award for Special Achievement, Nat. Wildlife Fed., one of the Utne Reader's Utne 100 Visionaries, Guggenheim Memorial Foundation Fellow, Lannan Literary Fellowship in Creative Nonfiction, Distinguished Achievement Award, Western American Literature Asscn, Wallace Stegner Award, Center for the American West 2005, Robert Marshall Award, The Wilderness Soc. 2006. *Literary Agent:* c/o Steven Barclay Agency, 12 Western Avenue, Petaluma, CA 94952, USA. *Telephone:* (707) 773-0654. *Fax:* (707) 778-1868. *Website:* www.barclayagency.com. *Address:* TTW, PO Box 40, Moose, WY 83012, USA. *E-mail:* ttwcontact@frontier.com (office). *Website:* www.terrytempestwilliams.com; www.coyoteclan.com.

WILLIAMS-WITHERSPOON, Kimmika L. H., BA, MA, MFA, PhD; American playwright, poet and performance artist; *Assistant Professor of Theater History, Temple University*; b. 7 Jan. 1959, Pa; one s. two d. *Education:* Howard Univ., Temple Univ. *Career:* Future Faculty Fellow, Anthropology Dept, Temple Univ., currently Asst Prof. of Theater History; mem. Poets and Prophets; Poets and Writers. *Plays:* A Chained Foot Stumbling on a New World 1991, Nappy Truths 1993, By What Price Unity 1996, Dog Days 1998, Brown Ices: Chocolate Drops 1999, From Brillo Pads to Feminine Pads: Raw Abrasives 1999, Survival Strategies: A Tale of Faith 2003. *Publications:* God Made Men Brown 1982, It Ain't Easy To Be Different 1986, Halley's Comet 1988, Envisioning a Sea of Dry Bones 1990, Epic Memory: Places and Spaces I've Been 1995, Signs of the Times: Culture Gap 1999, The Secret Message in African American Theater: Hidden Meaning Embedded in Public Discourse, They never told me there'd be days like this 2002, Brother Love 2005; Contributions: Women's Words, Sunlight on the Moon. *Honours:* Playwrights Exchange Grants 1994, 1996, Daimler Chrysler Poetry Prize 1999, PEN Charitable Trusts Arts Grant 2000, Independence Grant 2001, Arts Initiative Grant, Temple Univ. 2003. *Address:* Department of Theater, Temple University, Tomlinson Theater 011-05, 1301 West Norris Street, Philadelphia, PA 19122, USA (office). *Telephone:* (215) 204-8414 (office). *Fax:* (215) 204-8566 (office). *E-mail:* kwilli01@temple.edu (office). *Website:* www.temple.edu/sct/theater (office).

WILLIAMSON, David Keith, AO, BE; Australian playwright and screenwriter; b. 24 Feb. 1942, Melbourne; s. of Edwin Keith David Williamson and Elvie May (née Armstrong) Williamson; m. Kristin Ingrid Lofven 1974; two s. one d. *Education:* Monash Univ., Melbourne Univ. *Career:* Design Engineer Gen. Motors-Holden's 1965; lecturer Swinbourne Tech. Coll. 1966–72; freelance writer 1972–. *Plays:* The Removalists 1972, Don's Party 1973, Three Plays 1974, The Department 1975, A Handful of Friends 1976, The Club 1977, Travelling North 1979, The Perfectionist 1981, Sons of Cain 1985, Emerald City 1987, Top Silk 1989, Siren 1990, Money and Friends 1992, Brilliant Lies 1993, Sanctuary 1994, Dead White Males 1995, Corporate Vibes 1999, Face to Face 1999, The Great Man 2000, Up for Grabs 2001, A Conversation 2001, Charitable Intent 2001, Soulmates 2002, Amigos 2004, Influence 2005, Scarlett O'Hara at the Crimson Parrot 2008. *Screenplays:* Gallipoli 1981, Phar Lap 1983, The Year of Living Dangerously 1983, Travelling North 1986, Emerald City 1988, The Four Minute Mile (2-part TV series) 1988, A Dangerous Life (6-hour TV series) 1988, Top Silk 1989, Siren 1990, Money and Friends 1992, Dead White Males 1995, Heretic 1996, Third World Blues 1997, After the Ball 1997, Brilliant Lies 1996, On the Beach 2000. *Honours:* Hon. DLitt (Sydney), (Monash), (Swinburne); numerous writing, TV and cinema awards. *Literary Agent:* Cameron Cresswell Management, Level 7, 61 Marlborough Street, Surry Hills, NSW 2010, Australia. *Telephone:* (2) 9319-7199. *Fax:* (2) 9319-6866. *E-mail:* info@cameronsmanagement.com.au. *Website:* www.cameronsmanagement.com.au.

WILLIAMSON, Joel R., AB, MA, PhD; American writer and academic (retd); b. 27 Oct. 1929, Anderson County, SC; m. Betty Anne Woodson 1986; one s. two d. *Education:* Univ. of South Carolina, Univ. of California, Berkeley. *Career:* instructor Dept of History, Univ. of North Carolina, Chapel Hill 1960–64, Asst Prof. 1964–66, Assoc. Prof. 1966–69, Prof. 1969–85, Linberger Prof. in Humanities 1985–2003; Fellow, Guggenheim Foundation 1970–71, Center for Advanced Study in Behavioral Sciences, Stanford 1977–78, summer 1979, 1980, 1981, NEH 1987–88, Charles Warren Center, Harvard Univ. 1981–82; mem. Soc. of American Historians, Southern Historical Asscn, Organization of American Historians, Southern Asscn for Women Historians, American Historical Asscn. *Publications:* After Slavery: The Negro in South Carolina During Reconstruction 1965, Origins of Segregation 1968, New People: Miscegenation and Mulattoes in the United States 1980, The Crucible of Race 1984, A Rage for Order 1986, William Faulkner and Southern History 1993; contrib. to various publications. *Honours:* Parkman, Emerson, Owsley, Kennedy, Mayflower Awards 1985, Mayflower Cup 1994. *Address:* 211 Hillsborough Street, Chapel Hill, NC 27514, USA (home). *Telephone:* (919) 929-6613 (home). *E-mail:* annaleoww@aol.com (home).

WILLIAMSON, Kristin Ingrid, BA,; Australian novelist and biographer; b. 16 Sept. 1940, Melbourne, Vic.; m. David Williamson 1974; three s. *Education:* Latrobe Univ., Trinity Coll., London. *Career:* Teacher of English, History and Drama, primary and high schools, Victoria 1960–70; Lecturer in Drama, Melbourne State Coll. 1970–72; freelance journalist 1973–79; journalist, columnist, National Times, Sydney 1979–87; writer 1987–. *Publications:* The Last Bastion 1984, Princess Kate (novel) 1988, Tanglewood (novel) 1992, The Jacaranda Years (novel) 1995, Brothers To Us (biog.) 1997, Treading on Dreams (novel) 1998, Women on the Rocks (novel) 2003, Behind the Scenes (biog.) 2009. *Literary Agent:* Curtis Brown Pty, PO Box 19, Paddington, NSW 2021, Australia. *Telephone:* (2) 9361-6161. *Fax:* (2) 9360-3935. *E-mail:* info@curtisbrown.com.au. *Website:* www.curtisbrown.com.au.

WILLIAMSON, Philip G., (Philip First, Joe Fish, Will Phillips); British writer; b. 4 Nov. 1955, Worcs., England. *Education:* Goldsmiths Coll., London. *Publications:* The Great Pervader (as Philip First) 1983, Paper Thin and Other Stories 1986, Dark Night (as Philip First) 1986, Dinbig of Khimmur 1991, The Legend of Shadd's Torment 1993, From Enchantery 1993, Moonblood 1993, Heart of Shadows 1994, Citadel 1995, Enchantment's Edge, three vols 1996–98, The Mates 2003, Killing Time 2003.

WILLIS, Connie; American science fiction writer; b. (Constance Elaine Trimmer), 31 Dec. 1945, Denver, Colo; m. Courtney Willis; one d. *Education:* Colorado State Coll. (now Univ. of Northern Colorado). *Publications include:* Even the Queen (short story) 1992, Lincoln's Dreams 1992, Doomsday Book (novel) 1993, Impossible Things 1993, Uncharted Territory 1994, Remake 1995, Bellwether 1997, To Say Nothing of the Dog 1998, Fire Watch 1998, Miracle and Other Christmas Stories 2000, Passage 2002, Roswell, Vegas and Area 51: Travels With Courtney 2002, D.A. 2007, Inside Job 2005, All Seated on the Ground 2008, Blackout/All Clear (Nebula Award for Best Novel) 2010. *Honours:* numerous awards including 10 World Science Fiction Convention Hugo Awards and seven Science Fiction Writers of America Nebula Awards. *Literary Agent:* c/o The Ralph Vicinanza Agency, 303 West 18th Street, New York, NY 10011-4400, USA. *Website:* www.sftv.org/cw; azsf.net/cwblog.

WILLIS, Meredith Sue, BA, MFA; American author and educator; *Special Lecturer, New York University*; b. 31 May 1946, WV; d. of Glenn E. Willis and Lucille Meredith Willis; m. Andrew B. Weinberger 1982; one s. *Education:* Barnard Coll., Columbia Univ., West Virginia Univ. *Career:* currently Special Lecturer, New York Univ.; also Consultant in Creative Writing, various schools and museums; featured at 25th Iron Mountain Review Festival of Authors 2006, featured author, Appalachian Heritage 2006. *Publications:* A Space Apart 1979, Higher Ground 1981, Only Great Changes 1985, Personal Fiction Writing 1984, Quilt Pieces 1990, Blazing Pencils 1990, Deep Revision 1993, The Secret Super Power of Marco 1994, In the Mountains of America 1994, Marco's Monster 1996, Trespassers 1997, Oradell at Sunset 2002, Dwight's House and Other Stories 2004, The City Built of Starships 2005, Billie of Fishhouse Lane 2006, Out of the Mountains: Appalachian Stories 2010. *Honours:* Hon. DHumLitt (West Virginia) 2004; Nat. Endowment for the Arts Fellowship 1978, New Jersey Arts Fellowship 1995, Honoree, Emory and Henry Literary Festival 1995. *Address:* 311 Prospect Street, South Orange,

NJ 07079, USA (home). *E-mail:* msuewillis@aol.com (home). *Website:* www.meredithsuewillis.com.

WILLMOTT, Hedley Paul, FRHistS, BA, MA, PhD; British lecturer and writer; b. 26 Dec. 1945, Bristol, England; m. Pauline Anne Burton 1978; one s. one d. *Education:* Univ. of Liverpool, Univ. of London. *Career:* Military Writer and Lecturer, Royal Military Acad., Sandhurst 1969–; Programme Writer, British Broadcasting Corporation World Service 1986–92; Visiting Lecturer, Temple University, Philadelphia 1989, Memphis State Univ., Tennessee 1989–90, National War College, Dept of Defense, Washington, DC 1992, Greenwich Maritime Inst. 2003–04; fmr Mark W. Clark Chair of Military History, The Citadel, Charleston, North Carolina. *Publications:* Warships 1975, B-17 Flying Fortress 1980, Sea Warfare: Weapons, Tactics and Strategy 1981, Empires in the Balance: Japanese and Allied Pacific Strategies to April 1942 1982, The Barrier and the Javelin: Japanese and Allied Pacific Strategies, February to June 1942 1983, Pearl Harbor 1983, Zero A6M 1983, June 1944 1984, The Great Crusade: A New Complete History of the Second World War 1989, Grave of a Dozen Schemes: British Naval Planning and the War against Japan, 1943–1945 1996, When Men Lost Faith in Reason 2002, Battleship 2003, The Second World War in the Far East 2004, A Gathering Darkness 2004, The Battle of Leyte Gulf 2005. *Honours:* Leman Award 1984.

WILLOUGHBY, Cass (see Olsen, Theodore Victor)

WILLS, Garry, BA, MA, PhD; American writer, journalist and academic; *Professor of History Emeritus, Northwestern University*; b. 22 May 1934, Atlanta, GA; m. Natalie Cavallo 1959; two s. one d. *Education:* St Louis Univ., Xavier Univ., Cincinnati and Yale Univ. *Career:* Fellow Center for Hellenic Studies 1961–62; Assoc. Prof. of Classics 1962–67, Adjunct Prof. 1968–80, Johns Hopkins Univ.; Newspaper Columnist Universal Press Syndicate 1970–; Henry R. Luce Prof. of American Culture and Public Policy 1980–88, Adjunct Prof., later Prof. of History Emeritus 1988–, Northwestern Univ.; mem. American Philosophical Soc., American Acad. of Arts and Letters, American Acad. of Arts and Sciences. *Publications:* Chesterton 1961, Politics and Catholic Freedom 1964, Roman Culture 1966, Jack Ruby 1967, Second Civil War 1968, Nixon Agonistes 1970, Bare Ruined Choirs 1972, Inventing America 1978, At Button's 1979, Confessions of a Conservative 1979, Explaining America 1980, The Kennedy Imprisonment 1982, Lead Time 1983, Cincinnatus 1984, Reagan's America 1987, Under God 1990, Lincoln at Gettysburg (Nat. Book Critics Circle Award 1993, Pulitzer Prize for General Non-Fiction 1993) 1992, Certain Trumpets: The Call of Leaders 1994, Witches and Jesuits: Shakespeare's Macbeth 1994, John Wayne's America 1997, Saint Augustine 1999, A Necessary Evil: A History of American Distrust of Government 1999, Papal Sin: Structures of Deceit 2000, Saint Augustine's Childhood 2001, Why I Am a Catholic 2002, President 2003, Saint Augustine's Sin 2004, Saint Augustine's Conversion 2004, Bush's Fringe Government 2006, Head and Heart: American Christianities 2007, What the Gospels Meant 2008, Martial's Epigrams (trans.) 2008, Bomb Power 2010, Outside Looking In: Adventures of an Observer 2010. *Honours:* various hon. doctorates; Nat. Humanities Medal 1998. *Address:* Department of History, Northwestern University, Harris Hall 202, 1881 Sheridan Road, Evanston, IL 60208, USA (office). *Telephone:* (847) 491-3406 (office). *Fax:* (847) 467-1393 (office). *E-mail:* g-wills@northwestern.edu (office). *Website:* www.history.northwestern.edu/faculty/wills.htm (office).

WILLUMSEN, Dorrit; Danish writer; b. 31 Aug. 1940. *Career:* received National Arts Foundation grant for life 1980. *Publications:* Komplikation 1963, Knagen 1965, Lukket Land 1966, Mycelium 1966, Stranden 1967, Da 1968, Min far binder sit kalvekrøs 1968, Kaffegaester 1969, The, keydderi, acryl, salaer, graeshopper 1970, Jomfru 1971, Besogstid 1972, Tingene 1972, Metamorfose 1973, Modellen Coppelia 1973, Svangerskab 1973, En vaertindes smil 1974, Min far binder sit kalvekrøs 1974, Neonhaven (trans. as Neon Park) 1976, Hvis det virk elig var en film 1978 (trans. as If It Really Were a Film), Marions forvandling 1978, Elektronatomalderen 1979, Nødvendigt opbrud 1979, Herman Bang 1980, Manden som påskud 1980, Skabelsen af Bianca 1980, Mutationen 1981, Et par 1982, Ni liv 1982, At ønske en pludselig forvandling 1983, Marie: A Novel about the Life of Madame Tussaud 1983, Umage par 1983, Dica elsker 1984, Glaeden ved at vide, man har rodder 1984, Puds ham, elskede 1984, År 2054 1984, Caroline 1985, Suk hjerte 1986, Efterskride 1987, Manden som påskud 1987, Glemslens forår (trans. as Seeds of Oblivion) 1988, Klaedt i purpur 1990, Sverige 1990, Herman Bang 1991, Den første sne 1995, Bang 1996 (Nordic Council Prize for Literature 1997), De kattens feriedage 1997, Koras stemme 2000, Postkort 2000, Tøs 2001, 2 dage før 12 1/2 år 2002, Bruden fra Gent 2003, Den dag jeg blev Honey Hotwing 2005. *Honours:* Danske Akademis Store Pris 1981, LOs Kulturpris 1991, Dansk Litteraturpris for Kvinder 1996. *Address:* c/o Gyldendal, Klareboderne 3, 1001 Copenhagen K, Denmark.

WILMER, Clive, BA, MA; British academic, writer, poet, translator and broadcaster; *Fellow in English, Sidney Sussex College, Cambridge*; b. 10 Feb. 1945, Harrogate, Yorks., England; s. of Eustace Wilmer and Kathleen Sybil Wilmer (née Rogers); m. Diane Redmond 1971 (divorced 1986); one s. one d. *Education:* King's Coll., Cambridge. *Career:* Visiting Instructor in Creative Writing, Univ. of California, Santa Barbara 1986; Ed. Numbers 1986–90; Presenter Poet of the Month series, BBC Radio 3 1989–92; Hon. Fellow, Anglia Polytechnic Univ. (now Anglia Ruskin Univ.) 1996–, Research Fellow and Poet-in-Residence 1998–; Assoc. Teaching Officer, Sidney Sussex and Fitzwilliam Colls, Cambridge 1999–, Fellow in English, Sidney Sussex Coll., Cambridge 2005–, Bye-Fellow, Fitzwilliam Coll., Cambridge 2004–, Affiliated Lecturer, Faculty of English, Univ. of Cambridge 2008–; mem. Organizing Cttee, Pound's Artists, Tate Gallery, London, Kettle's Yard Gallery, Cambridge 1985; mem. Companion of the Guild of St George 1995–, Dir 2004–, Master 2009–. *Publications:* poetry: The Dwelling Place 1977, Devotions 1982, Of Earthly Paradise 1992, Selected Poems 1995, The Falls 2000, Stigmata 2005, The Mystery of Things 2006, New and Collected Poems 2012; trans.: Forced March, by Miklós Radnóti (with G. Gömöri) 1979 (revised edn 2003), Night Song of the Personal Shadow, by György Petri (with G. Gömöri) 1991, My Manifold City, by George Gömöri 1996, Eternal Monday, by György Petri (with G. Gömöri) 1999, Polishing October, by George Gömöri 2008, Passio, by János Pilinszky 2011; ed.: Thom Gunn: The Occasions of Poetry 1982, John Ruskin: Unto This Last and Other Writings 1985, Dante Gabriel Rossetti: Selected Poems and Translations 1991, William Morris: News From Nowhere and Other Writings 1993, Poets Talking: The 'Poet of the Month' Interviews from BBC Radio 3 1994, Cambridge Observed: An Anthology (ed. with Charles Moseley) 1998, Donald Davie: With the Grain 1998, The Life and Work of Miklós Radnóti: Essays (ed. with George Gömöri) 1999, Donald Davie: Modernist Essays 2004; contribs to numerous books, reviews, newspapers, quarterlies and journals. *Honours:* Hon. Sr Scholar, King's Coll. Cambridge 1967; Hon. Patron William Morris Gallery, Walthamstow 2011; Chancellor's Medal for an English Poem, Univ. of Cambridge 1967, Writer's Grant, Arts Council of GB 1979, Author's Foundation Grant 1993, Mikimoto Memorial Ruskin Lecturer, Univ. of Lancaster 1996, Hungarian PEN Club Memorial Medal for Trans. 1998, Hungarian Ministry of Culture Medal 'Pro Cultura Hungarica' 2005. *Literary Agent:* c/o A.M. Heath & Co Ltd, 6 Warwick Court, London, WC1R 5DJ, England. *Address:* 57 Norwich Street, Cambridge, CB2 1ND, England (home). *Telephone:* (1223) 511975 (home). *E-mail:* cw291@cam.ac.uk (office).

WILMERS, Mary-Kay; British editor; *Editor, London Review of Books*; two s. *Career:* Ed. London Review of Books 1992–. *Publication:* The Eitingons: A Twentieth-Century Story 2009. *Address:* London Review of Books, 28 Little Russell Street, London, WC1A 2HN, England (office). *Telephone:* (20) 7209-1101 (office). *Fax:* (20) 7209-1102 (office). *E-mail:* edit@lrb.co.uk (office). *Website:* www.lrb.co.uk (office).

WILOCH, Thomas, BA; American poet, writer and editor; b. 3 Feb. 1953, Detroit, Mich.; m. Denise Gottis 1981. *Education:* Wayne State Univ. *Career:* associated with Gale Group 1977–2004; columnist, Retrofuturism 1991–93, Photo Static 1993–94; book reviewer, Anti-Matter Magazine 1992–94, Green Man Review 2002–04; Assoc. Ed. Sidereality Magazine 2004–05; mem. Asscn of Literary Scholars and Critics, Nat. Asscn for Self-Employed. *Publications:* Stigmata Junction 1985, Paper Mask 1988, The Mannikin Cypher 1989, Tales of Lord Shantih 1990, Decoded Factories of the Heart 1991, Night Rain 1991, Narcotic Signature 1992, Lyrical Brandy 1993, Mr Templeton's Toyshop 1995, Neon Trance 1997, Everything you need to know about protecting yourself and others from abduction 1997, Crime: A Serious American Problem 2004, National Security 2005, Prisons and Jails 2005, Screaming in Code 2006; contrib. to more than 200 magazines. *Honours:* Schoolcraft Coll. Poet Hunt Award 1985, Scantle Magazine Award 1986, Bohemian Chronicle Award 1994. *Address:* 42015 Ford Road, Suite #226, Canton, MI 48187, USA (office). *Fax:* (734) 468-0190 (office). *E-mail:* twiloch@wowway.com (office). *Website:* www.codeschaos.0catch.com.

WILSON, Andrew Norman (A. N.), MA, FRSL; British writer; b. 27 Oct. 1950, England; s. of the late N. Wilson and of Jean Dorothy Wilson (née Crowder); m. 1st Katherine Dorothea Duncan-Jones 1971 (divorced 1989); two d.; m. 2nd Ruth Guilding 1991; one d. *Education:* Rugby School and New Coll., Oxford. *Career:* Asst Master Merchant Taylors' School 1975–76; Lecturer, St Hugh's Coll. and New Coll., Oxford 1976–81; Literary Ed. Spectator 1981–83, Evening Standard 1990–97; columnist, The Daily Mail. *Publications:* fiction: The Sweets of Pimlico 1977, Unguarded Hours 1978, Kindly Light 1979, The Healing Art (Somerset Maugham Award) 1980, Who Was Oswald Fish? 1981, Wise Virgin (WHSmith Award) 1982, Scandal 1983, Gentleman in England 1985, Love Unknown 1986, Stray 1987, Incline Our Hearts 1988, A Bottle in the Smoke 1990, Daughters of Albion 1991, The Vicar of Sorrows 1993, Hearing Voices 1995, A Watch in the Night 1996, Hazel the Guinea-pig (for children) 1997, Dream Children 1998, My Name is Legion 2004, A Jealous Ghost 2005, Winnie and Wolf 2007; non-fiction: The Laird of Abbotsford 1980, A Life of John Milton 1983, Hilaire Belloc 1984, How Can We Know? An Essay on the Christian Religion 1985, The Church in Crisis (jtly) 1986, Landscape in France 1987, The Lion and the Honeycomb 1987, Penfriends from Porlock: Essays and Reviews 1977–86 1988, Tolstoy (Whitbread Award for Biography and Autobiography) 1988, Eminent Victorians 1989, John Henry Newman: prayers, poems, meditations (ed.) 1989, C.S. Lewis: A Biography 1990, Against Religion 1991, Jesus 1992, The Faber Book of Church and Clergy (ed.) 1992, The Rise and Fall of the House of Windsor 1993, The Faber Book of London (ed.) 1993, Paul: The Mind of the Apostle 1997, God's Funeral 1999, The Victorians 2003, Beautiful Shadow: A Life of Patricia Highsmith 2003, Iris Murdoch as I Knew Her 2004, London: A Short History 2004, After the Victorians 2005, Betjeman (biog.) 2006, Harold Robbins: The Man Who Invented Sex 2007, Our Times: The Age of Elizabeth II 2008, Dante in Love 2011, The Elizabethans 2011, Hitler: A Short Biography 2011. *Honours:* Hon. mem. American Acad. of Arts and Letters 1984; Chancellor's Essay Prize 1975, Ellerton Theological Prize 1975. *Address:* 5 Regent's Park Terrace, London, NW1 7EE, England.

WILSON, Charles; British journalist; b. 18 Aug. 1935, Glasgow, Scotland; s. of Adam Wilson and Ruth Wilson; m. 1st Anne Robinson 1968 (divorced 1973); one d.; m. 2nd Sally O'Sullivan 1980 (divorced 2001); one s. one d.; m. 3rd Rachel Pitkeathley 2001. *Education:* Eastbank Acad., Glasgow. *Career:* copy boy, The People 1951; later reporter with Bristol Evening World, News Chronicle and Daily Mail; Deputy Ed. Daily Mail (Manchester) 1971–74; Asst Ed. London Evening News 1974–76; Ed., Evening Times, Glasgow 1976; later Ed., Glasgow Herald; Ed. Sunday Standard, Glasgow 1981–82; Exec. Ed., The Times 1982, Jt Deputy Ed. 1984–85, Ed. 1985–90; Int. Devt Dir News Int. 1990–91; Ed.-in-Chief, Man. Dir The Sporting Life 1990–98; Editorial Dir Mirror Group Newspapers 1991–92, Group Man. Dir Mirror Group 1992–98; Acting Ed. The Independent 1995–96; Dir (non-exec.) Chelsea and Westminster Hosp. 1999–; mem. Newspaper Panel, Competition Comm. 1999–2007; mem. Jockey Club 1993–, Youth Justice Bd 1998–2004; Trustee World Wildlife Fund-UK 1997–2004, Royal Naval Museum 1999–. *Address:* Chairman's Office, Chelsea and Westminster Trust, 369 Fulham Road, London, SW10 9NH (office); 23 Campden Hill Square, London, W8 7JY, England. *Telephone:* (20) 7727-3366 (home). *E-mail:* wcampden@aol.com (home).

WILSON, Christopher, PhD; British novelist and semiotician; b. 18 Nov. 1949, London. *Education:* LSE. *Career:* fmr Lecturer, Goldsmiths' Coll., London; currently semiotician. *Publications:* novels: Gallimauf's Gospel 1986, Baa: A Novel 1987, Bluegrass 1990, Mischief 1991, Fou 1992, The Wurd 1995, The Ballad of Lee Cotton (aka Cotton) 2005. *Address:* c/o Little, Brown Book Group, 100 Victoria Embankment, London, EC4Y 0DY, England (office). *Website:* www.littlebrown.co.uk (office).

WILSON, Colin Henry; British writer; b. 26 June 1931, Leicester; s. of Arthur Wilson and Annetta Jones; m. 1st Dorothy Troop 1951; one s.; m. 2nd Joy Stewart 1960; two s. one d. *Education:* Gateway Secondary Technical School, Leicester. *Career:* laboratory asst 1948–49, civil servant (taxes) 1949–50; RAF 1950, discharged on medical grounds 1950; then navvy, boot and shoe operative, dish washer, plastic moulder; lived Strasbourg 1950, Paris 1953; later factory hand and dish washer; writer 1956–; Writer in Residence, Hollins Coll., Virginia, USA 1966–67; Visiting Prof., Univ. of Washington 1967–68, Dowling Coll., Majorca 1969, Rutgers Univ., NJ 1974. *Publications include: philosophy:* The Outsider 1956, Religion and the Rebel 1957, The Age of Defeat 1958, The Strength to Dream 1961, Origins of the Sexual Impulse 1963, Beyond the Outsider 1965, Introduction to the New Existentialism 1966; *other non-fiction:* Encyclopaedia of Murder 1960, Rasputin and the Fall of the Romanovs 1964, Brandy of the Damned (music essays) 1965, Eagle and Earwig (literary essays) 1965, Sex and the Intelligent Teenager 1966, Voyage to a Beginning (autobiog.) 1968, Shaw: A Reassessment 1969, A Casebook of Murder 1969, Poetry and Mysticism 1970, The Strange Genius of David Lindsay (with E. H. Visiak) 1970, The Occult 1971, New Pathways in Psychology 1972, Strange Powers 1973, A Book of Booze 1974, The Craft of the Novel 1975, The Geller Phenomenon 1977, Mysteries 1978, Beyond The Occult 1988; *novels:* Ritual in the Dark 1960, Adrift in Soho 1961, The World of Violence 1963, Man Without a Shadow 1963, Necessary Doubt 1964, The Glass Cage 1966, The Mind Parasites 1967, The Philosopher's Stone 1969, The Killer 1970, The God of the Labyrinth 1970, The Black Room 1970, The Schoolgirl Murder Case 1974, The Space Vampires 1976, Men of Strange Powers 1976, Enigmas and Mysteries 1977; *other works include:* The Quest for Wilhelm Reich 1979, The War Against Sleep: the Philosophy of Gurdjieff 1980, Starseekers 1980, Frankenstein's Castle 1980, The Directory of Possibilities (ed. with John Grant) 1981, Poltergeist! 1981, Access to Inner Worlds 1983, Encyclopaedia of Modern Murder (with Donald Seaman) 1983, The Psychic Detectives 1984, The Janus Murder Case 1984, The Personality Surgeon 1984, A Criminal History of Mankind 1984, Encyclopaedia of Scandal (with Donald Seaman) 1985, Afterlife 1985, Rudolf Steiner 1985, Strindberg (play) 1970, Spiderworld—The Tower 1987, Encyclopaedia of Unsolved Mysteries (with Damon Wilson) 1987, Aleister Crowley: the nature of the beast 1987, The Misfits 1988, Spiderworld—The Delta 1988, Written in Blood 1989, The Serial Killers 1990, Mozart's Journey to Prague (play) 1991, Spider World: the Magician 1992, The Strange Life of P. D. Ouspensky 1993, From Atlantis to the Sphinx 1996, Atlas of Sacred Sites and Holy Places 1996, Alien Dawn 1998, The Books in My Life 1998, The Devil's Party 2000, Atlantis Blueprint (with Rand Fle'math) 2000, Spiderworld—Shadowland 2003, Dreaming to Some Purpose (autobiography) 2004, Crimes of Passion (with Damon Wilson) 2006, Atlantis and the Neanderthals 2006, The Angry Years 2007, Super Consciousness 2009. *Address:* Tetherdown, Trewallock Lane, Gorran Haven, Cornwall, PL26 6NT, England (home). *Telephone:* (1726) 842708 (home).

WILSON, Edward Osborne, Jr, BS, MS, PhD; American biologist, academic and writer; *University Professor Emeritus and Honorary Curator of Entomology, Museum of Comparative Zoology, Harvard University*; b. 10 June 1929, Birmingham, Ala; s. of the late Edward Osborne Wilson, Sr and Linnette Freeman Huddleston; m. Irene Kelley 1955; one d. *Education:* Univ. of Alabama and Harvard Univ. *Career:* Jr Fellow, Soc. of Fellows, Harvard Univ. 1953–56, Prof. of Zoology 1964–76, F.B. Baird Prof. of Science 1976–94, Pellegrino Univ. Prof. 1994–97, Univ. Research Prof. 1997–2002, Prof. Emer. 2002–, Curator of Entomology, Museum of Comparative Zoology 1974–97, Hon. Curator of Entomology 1997–; Founder and mem. Bd Dirs E.O. Wilson Biodiversity Foundation; Fellow, Guggenheim Foundation 1977–78, Advisory Bd 1979–90, mem. Selection Cttee 1982–90; mem. Bd of Dirs World Wildlife Fund 1983–94, Org. for Tropical Studies 1984–91, American Museum of Natural History 1992–, American Acad. of Liberal Educ. 1993–2004, Nature Conservancy 1994–, Conservation Int. 1997–; Foreign mem. Royal Soc. 1990, Finnish Acad. of Science and Letters 1990, Russian Acad. of Natural Sciences 1994; Founding mem. Int. Centre of Insect Physiology and Ecology, Org. for Tropical Studies, Ecosystems Center of Marine Biological Lab.; mem. NAS 1969; Fellow, American Acad. of Arts and Sciences 1959, American Philosophical Soc. 1976, Animal Behavior Soc. 1976, Deutsche Akad. der Naturforscher Leopoldina 1977, Royal Soc. of Sciences of Uppsala 1989, World Econ. Forum 2000. *Achievement:* coined the term 'sociobiology'. *Publications include:* The Theory of Island Biogeography (with R. H. MacArthur) 1967, The Insect Societies 1971, Sociobiology: The New Synthesis 1975, On Human Nature (Pulitzer Prize for Gen. Non-Fiction 1979) 1978, Caste and Ecology in the Social Insects (with G. F. Oster) 1978, Genes, Mind and Culture (with C. J. Lumsden) 1981, Promethean Fire (with C. J. Lumsden) 1983, Biophilia 1984, Biodiversity (ed.) 1988, The Ants (with Bert Hölldobler) (Pulitzer Prize for Gen. Non-Fiction 1991) 1990, Success and Dominance in Ecosystems 1990, The Diversity of Life 1991, In Search of Nature (with Laura Simonds Southworth) 1996, Journey to the Ants (with Bert Hölldobler) 1994, Consilience: The Unity of Knowledge 1998, Biological Diversity: The Oldest Human Heritage 1999, Pheidole in the New World: A Dominant, Hyperdiverse Ant Genus 2002, From So Simple a Beginning: Darwin's Four Great Books 2005, The Creation: An Appeal to Save Life on Earth 2006, Nature Revealed: Selected Writings 1949–2006 2006, The Superorganism: The Beauty, Elegance, and Strangeness of Insect Societies (with Bert Hölldobler) 2009, Anthill: A Novel 2010; numerous articles on evolutionary biology, entomology and conservation. *Honours:* Hon. Life mem. American Genetic Asscn 1981, British Ecological Soc. 1983, Entomological Soc. of America 1987, Darwin Soc., Univ. of Bergen 1987, American Humanist Asscn 1989, Zoological Soc. of London 1992, Linnean Soc. of London 1994, Netherlands Entomological Soc. 1995, Asscn for Tropical Biology 1999, European Sociobiological Soc. 2000, Royal Entomological Soc. 2001; mem. Hon. Bd World Knowledge Dialogue and Scientist in Residence for symposium organized in Crans-Montana, Switzerland 2008; Silver Cross of Columbus (Dominican Repub.) 2003, Commdr (First Class), Royal Order of the Polar Star (Sweden) 2009; Hon. DHC (Univ. of Madrid Complutense) 1995; Hon. DPhil (Uppsala University) 1987; Hon. Dr rer. nat (Univ. of Wurzburg) 2000; Hon. DSc (Duke Univ.) 1978, (Grinnell Coll.) 1978, (Univ. of West Florida) 1979, (Muhlenberg Coll.) 1998, (Yale Univ.) 1998, (Cedar Crest Coll.) 1999, (State Univ. of NY, Albany) 1999; Hon. LHD (Univ. of Alabama) 1980, (Hofstra Univ.) 1986, (Pennsylvania State Univ.), (Lawrence Univ.) 1979, (Fitchburg State Coll.) 1989, (Macalester Coll.) 1990, (Univ. of Massachusetts) 1993, (Univ. of Oxford) 1993, (Ripon Coll.) 1994, (Univ. of Connecticut) 1995, (Bates Coll.) 1996, (Ohio Univ.) 1996, (Coll. of Wooster) 1997, Univ. of Guelph) 1997, (Univ. of Portland) 1997, (Bradford Coll.) 1997; Hon. LLD (Simon Fraser Univ.) 1982; Nat. Medal of Science 1976, Tyler Prize for Environmental Achievement 1983, Ingersoll Foundation Weaver Award for Scholarly Letters 1989, Crafoord Prize, Royal Swedish Acad. of Sciences 1990, Int. Prize for Biology, Govt of Japan 1993, Carl Sagan Award for Public Understanding of Science 1994, Audubon Soc. Medal 1995, Los Angeles Times Book Prize for Science 1995, Time Magazine's 25 Most Influential People in America 1995, Schubert Prize (Germany) 1996, German Ecological Foundation Book Award 1998, Franklin Prize for Science, American Philosophical Soc. 1999, Humanist of the Year, American Humanist Asscn 1999, Nonino Prize (Italy) 2000, Lewis Thomas Prize for Writing about Science 2000, King Faisal Int. Prize for Science (Saudi Arabia) 2000, Foundation for the Future Kistler Prize 2000, Nierenberg Prize 2001, Addison Emery Verrill Medal, Peabody Museum of Natural History 2007, TED (Tech. Entertainment Design) Prize (co-recipient) 2007, XIX Premi Internacional Catalunya 2007, and others. *Address:* Museum of Comparative Zoology, Harvard University, 26 Oxford Street, Cambridge, MA 02138-2902 (office); 1010 Waltham Street, A-208, Lexington, MA 02421-8062, USA (home). *Telephone:* (617) 495-2315 (office). *Fax:* (617) 495-1224 (office). *E-mail:* ewilson@oeb.harvard.edu (office). *Website:* www.mcz.harvard.edu/Departments/Entomology (office).

WILSON, Gina, MA; British children's writer and poet; b. 1 April 1943, Abergele, N Wales. *Education:* Univ. of Edinburgh, Mount Holyoke Coll., Mass, USA. *Career:* Asst Ed. Scottish Nat. Dictionary 1967–73, Dictionary of the Older Scottish Tongue 1972–73. *Publications:* Cora Ravenwing 1980, A Friendship of Equals 1981, The Whisper 1982, All Ends Up 1984, Family Feeling 1986, Just Us 1988, Polly Pipes Up 1989, I Hope You Know 1989, Jim Jam Pyjamas 1990, Wompus Galumpus 1990, Riding the Great White 1992, Prowlpuss 1994, Ignis 2001, Grandma's Bears 2004, Scissors Paper Stone 2010. *Honours:* Frogmore Poetry Prize 1997, Annual Lace Poetry Prize 1999. *Address:* 20 Davenant Road, Oxford, OX2 8BX, England (home).

WILSON, Jacqueline, DBE, OBE, FRSL; British writer, academic and university administrator; *Pro-Chancellor, Roehampton University*; b. 17 Dec. 1945, Bath, England; d. of the late Harry Aitken and of Margaret Aitken (née Clibbons); m. William Millar Wilson 1965 (divorced 2004); one d. *Education:* Coombe Girls' School. *Career:* journalist, D.C. Thomsons 1963–65; teenage magazine Jackie named after her; Amb. Reading is Fundamental, UK 1998–; mem. Cttee Children's Writers and Illustrators Group, Soc. of Authors 1997–; Advisory mem. Panel Costa (fmrly Whitbread) Book Awards 1997–; Judge, Rhône-Poulenc Prizes for Jr Science Books 1999, Orange Prize for Fiction 2006, Prince Maurice Award 2006; mem. Bd Children's Film and TV Foundation 2000–; Children's Laureate 2005–07; Visiting Prof. of Children's Literature, Roehampton Univ. 2010–, Pro-Chancellor Roehampton Univ.

2011–. *Plays:* books adapted for the stage include Lottie Project 1999, Double Act 2003, Bad Girls 2004, Midnight 2005, Tracy Beaker Gets Real 2006, Suitcase Kid 2007, Secrets 2008. *Television:* novels Girls in Love, Girls Under Pressure, Girls Out Late and Girls in Tears adapted into 13-part TV series, Granada 2003; The Story of Tracy Beaker adapted into five series on BBC children's TV; The Illustrated Mum adapted for Channel 4 children's TV (two BAFTA Awards, one Emmy Award). *Publications include:* fiction: Hide and Seek 1972, Truth or Dare 1973, Snap 1974, Let's Pretend 1975, Making Hate 1977; juvenile fiction: Nobody's Perfect 1982, Waiting for the Sky to Fall 1983, The Other Side 1984, Amber 1986, The Power of the Shade 1987, Stevie Day Series 1987, This Girl 1988, Is There Anybody There? 1990, Deep Blue 1993, Take a Good Look 1990, The Story of Tracy Beaker 1991, The Suitcase Kid (Children's Book of the Year Award 1993) 1992, Video Rose 1992, The Mum-minder 1993, The Werepuppy 1993, The Bed and the Breakfast Star (The Young Telegraph/Fully Booked Award 1995) 1994, Mark Spark in the Dark 1994, Twin Trouble 1995, Glubbslyme 1995, Jimmy Jelly 1995, The Dinosaur's Packed Lunch 1995, Cliffhanger 1995, Double Act (Children's Book of the Year Award, Smarties Prize) 1995, My Brother Bernadette 1995, Werepuppy on Holiday 1995, Bad Girls 1996, Mr Cool 1996, Monster Story-teller 1997, The Lottie Project 1997, Girls in Love 1997, Connie and the Water Babies 1997, Buried Alive! 1998, Girls Under Pressure 1998, How to Survive Summer Camp 1998, The Illustrated Mum (Guardian Children's Book of the Year Award, Children's Book of the Year Award 1999) 1999, Girls Out Late 1999, Lizzie Zipmouth 1999, The Dare Game 2000, Vicky Angel 2000, The Cat Mummy 2001, Sleepovers 2001, Dustbin Baby 2001, Secrets 2002, Girls in Tears 2002, The Worry Website 2002, Lola Rose 2003, Midnight 2004, The Diamond Girls 2004, Clean Break 2005, Love Lessons 2005, Best Friends (Red House Children's Book Award) 2005, Candyfloss 2006, Starring Tracy Beaker 2006, Kiss 2007, My Sister Jodie 2008, Cookie 2008, Hetty Feather 2009, Little Darlings 2010, The Longest Whale Song 2010, Lily Alone 2011, Sapphire Battersea: Hetty Feather 2 2011; other: Jacky Daydream (autobiog.) 2007, My Secret Diary (autobiog.) 2009. *Honours:* Hon. DLitt (Winchester) 2005, (Bath) 2005, (Roehampton) 2007; Hon. DEd (Kingston Univ.) 2006; Hon. LLD (Dundee) 2007; Oak Tree Award 1992, Sheffield Children's Book Award, WHSmith Children's Book of the Year 2002, BT Childline Award 2004, British Book Award for Services to Bookselling 2004. *Literary Agent:* c/o David Higham Associates, 5–8 Lower John Street, Golden Square, London, W1F 9HA, England. *Telephone:* (20) 7434-5900. *Website:* www.jacquelinewilson.co.uk.

WILSON, Keith, BS, MA; American poet and writer; b. 26 Dec. 1927, Clovis, NM; m. Heloise Brigham 1958; one s. four d. *Education:* US Naval Acad., University of New Mexico. *Career:* fmr Prof., New Mexico State Univ., now Prof. Emer.; National Endowment for the Arts Fellowship; Fulbright-Hays Fellowship; D. H. Lawrence Creative Writing Fellowship. *Publications:* Homestead 1969, Thantog: Songs of a Jaguar Priest 1977, While Dancing Feet Shatter the Earth 1977, The Streets of San Miguel 1979, Retablos 1981, Stone Roses: Poems from Transylvania 1983, Meeting at Jal (with Theodore Enslin) 1985, Lion's Gate: Selected Poems 1963–1986, 1988, The Wind of Pentecost 1991, Graves Registry 1992, The Way of the Dove 1994, Bosque Redondo: The Enclosed Grove 2000, The Priesthood Quartette 2002.

WILSON, Robert McLiam; British writer; b. 1964, Belfast, Northern Ireland; m. *Education:* Univ. of Cambridge. *Career:* several BBC TV documentaries. *Publications:* novels: Ripley Bogle 1989, Manfred's Pain 1992, Eureka Street 1996, The Extremists; non-fiction: The Dispossessed 1992. *Honours:* Rooney Prize 1989, Hughes Prize 1989, Betty Trask Prize 1990, Irish Book Award 1990. *Literary Agent:* Antony Harwood Ltd, 103 Walton Street, Oxford OX2 6EB, England. *Telephone:* (1865) 559615. *Fax:* (1865) 310660. *E-mail:* mail@antonyharwood.com. *Website:* www.antonyharwood.com.

WILSON, William Julius, BA, MA, PhD; American sociologist and academic; *Lewis P. and Linda L. Geyser University Professor, Harvard University*; b. 20 Dec. 1935, Derry Township, Pa; m. 1st Mildred Marie Hood 1957; two d.; m. 2nd Beverly Ann Huebner 1970; one s. one d.; m. 3rd Jittima Srikunnawin 2011. *Education:* Wilberforce Univ., Bowling Green State Univ., Washington State Univ. *Career:* Asst Prof., Univ. of Massachusetts, Amherst 1965–69, Assoc. Prof. of Sociology 1969–71; Visiting Assoc. Prof. and Research Scholar, Univ. of Chicago 1971–72, Assoc. Prof. of Sociology 1972–75, Prof. of Sociology 1975–80, Lucy Flower Prof. of Urban Sociology 1980–84, Lucy Flower Distinguished Service Prof. 1984–90, Lucy Flower Univ. Prof. of Sociology and Public Policy 1990–96; Visiting Assoc. Prof., Harvard Univ. 1972, Malcolm Wiener Prof. of Social Policy 1996–98, John F. Kennedy School of Govt, Lewis P. and Linda L. Geyser Univ. Prof. 1998–; mem. Social Science Research Council 1979–85, Domestic Strategic Group, Aspen Inst. 1992–2002, Pres.'s Cttee on the Nat. Medal of Science, NSF 1994–98, Pres.'s Comm. on White House Fellowships 1994–2001; Fellow, Center for Advanced Study in the Behavioral Sciences, Stanford, Calif. 1981–82; Andrew Dixon White Prof.-at-Large, Cornell Univ. 1994–98; Fellow, American Acad. of Arts and Sciences, American Acad. of Political and Social Science, AAAS, American Philosophical Soc., American Sociological Asscn (Pres. 1989–90), NAS, Nat. Acad. of Educ., British Acad., Inst. of Medicine, Russell Sage Foundation 1988–2002 (Chair. 1994–96), Sociological Research Asscn (Pres. 1987–88), Center for Advanced Study in the Behavioral Sciences 1989–2002 (Chair. 1999–2002), American Nat. Urban League 1995–98. *Publications include:* Power, Racism and Privilege: Race Relations in Theoretical and Socio-historical Perspectives 1973, Through Different Eyes: Black and White Perspectives on American Race Relations (co-ed. with Peter I Rose and Stanley Rothman) 1973, The Declining Significance of Race: Blacks and Changing American Institutions 1978, The Truly Disadvantaged: The Inner City, the Underclass, and Public Policy 1987, The Ghetto Underclass: Social Science Perspectives (ed.) 1989, Sociology and the Public Agenda (ed.) 1993, Poverty, Inequality and the Future of Social Policy: Western States in the New World Order (co-ed. with Katherine McFate and Roger Lawson) 1995, When Work Disappears: The World of the New Urban Poor 1996, The Bridge Over the Racial Divide: Rising Inequality and Coalition Politics 1999, Youth in Cities: A Cross-National Perspective (co-ed. with Marta Tienda) 2002, There Goes the Neighborhood: Racial, Ethnic, and Class Tensions in Four Chicago Neighborhoods and Their Meaning for America (with Richard Taub) 2006, Good Kids from Bad Neighborhoods: Successful Development in Social Context (with D. Elliott, S. Menard, A. C. Elliott, B. Rankin and D. Huizinga) 2006, More than Just Race: Being Black and Poor in the Inner City 2009; contribs to numerous scholarly books, journals and reviews, and to general periodicals. *Honours:* 44 hon. doctorates; ; mem. A. Philip Randolph Inst. 1981– John D. and Catherine T. MacArthur Foundation Fellowship 1987–92, New York Times Book Review Best Book Citations 1987, 1996, Washington Monthly Annual Book Award 1988, C. Wright Mills Award, Soc. for the Study of Social Problems 1988, Dubois, Johnson, Frazier Award, American Sociological Asscn 1990, Burton Gordon Feldman Award, Brandeis Univ. 1991, Frank E. Seidman Distinguished Award in Political Economy, Rhodes Coll. 1994, Martin Luther King Jr Nat. Award, Southern Christian Leadership Council, Los Angeles 1998, Lester F. Ward Distinguished Contribs to Applied Sociology Award 1998, Nat. Medal of Science 1998, Talcott Parsons Prize, American Acad. of Arts and Sciences 2003, Aaron Wildavsky Enduring Contrib. Award, American Political Science Asscn 2007, Walter Channing Cabot Fellow, Harvard Univ. 2009–10, Anisfield-Wolf Book Award 2010. *Address:* Harvard Kennedy School, Mailbox 103, 79 JFK Street, Cambridge, MA 02138, USA (office). *Telephone:* (617) 496-4514 (office). *Fax:* (617) 495-5834 (office). *E-mail:* bill_wilson@harvard.edu (office). *Website:* www.hks.harvard.edu (office).

WILTON-JONES, Anni, (Áine an Caipín), BA, PGCE, MA; British performance poet and learning development officer; b. 8 April 1949, Bromborough; two s. five d. *Education:* School of Radiography, Southampton, Open Univ., Univ. of Wales, Newport. *Career:* currently Chair. and Sec. Scriveners; offers workshops in creative writing and drama. *Publications:* Bridges 1999, This is... Salem (with Basil Griffiths, Claire Syder, Jeff Rees) 1999, Fresh Voices for Younger Listeners (with Mike Byrne) 2000, Winter Whiting 2009, War Poems (co-writer) 2009; contrib. to newspapers and journals. *Address:* Ty Beirdd, 53 Church Street, Ebbw Vale, NP23 6BG, Wales (home). *Telephone:* (1495) 305463 (home). *Fax:* (1495) 305463 (home). *E-mail:* scriveners@lycos.co.uk (office); anni@wiltonjones.fsnet.co.uk (home). *Website:* www.scriveners.supanet.com (office).

WIMAN, Christian; American poet and essayist; *Editor, Poetry*. *Career:* Editor, Poetry magazine 2003–. *Publications:* The Long Home (Nicholas Roerich Prize) 1998, Ambition and Survival: Essays on Poetry 2004, Hard Night 2005, Every Riven Thing 2010; contrib. to journals, including At Length, Atlantic Monthly, Harper's, LRB. *Address:* Poetry, 444 North Michigan Avenue, Suite 1850, Chicago, IL 60611, USA (office). *Telephone:* (312) 787-7070 (office). *Fax:* (312) 787-6650 (office). *E-mail:* editors@poetrymagazine.org (office). *Website:* www.poetrymagazine.org (office).

WINCH, Donald Norman, PhD, FBA, FRHistS; British academic; *Research Professor Emeritus, University of Sussex*; b. 15 April 1935, London, England; s. of Sidney Winch and Iris Winch; m. Doreen Lidster 1983. *Education:* Sutton Grammar School, London School of Econs, Princeton Univ. *Career:* Visiting Lecturer, Univ. of California 1959–60; Lecturer in Econs, Univ. of Edin. 1960–63; Univ. of Sussex 1963–66, Reader 1966–69, Prof. History of Econs 1969–, now Research Prof. Emer., Dean School of Social Sciences 1968–74, Pro-Vice-Chancellor (Arts and Social Studies) 1986–89; Vice-Pres. British Acad. 1993–94; Visiting Fellow, School of Social Science, Inst. of Advanced Study, Princeton 1974–75, King's Coll., Cambridge 1983, History of Ideas Unit, ANU 1983, St Catharine's Coll., Cambridge 1989, All Souls Coll., Oxford 1994; Visiting Prof., Tulane Univ. 1984; Carlyle Lecturer, Univ. of Oxford 1995, Publr Sec., Royal Econ. Soc. 1971–; Review Ed. The Economic Journal 1976–83. *Publications:* Classical Political Economy & Colonies 1965, James Mill, Selected Economic Writings 1966, Economics and Policy 1969, The Economic Advisory Council 1930–39 (with S. K. Howson) 1976, Adam Smith's Politics 1978, That Noble Science of Politics (with S. Collini and J. W. Burrow) 1983, Malthus 1987, Riches and Poverty 1996, Wealth and Life 2009. *Honours:* Hon. DLit (Sussex) 2005. *Address:* Arts B, University of Sussex, Brighton, East Sussex, BN1 9QN, England (office). *Telephone:* (1273) 678634 (office); (1273) 400635 (home). *E-mail:* d.winch@sussex.ac.uk (office). *Website:* www.economistspapers.org.uk (office).

WINCHESTER, Jack (see Freemantle, Brian Harry)

WINCHESTER, Simon; American writer; b. 1940. *Education:* Univ. of Oxford. *Publications:* Northern Ireland in Crisis 1975, American Heartbeat 1976, Their Noble Lordships 1978, Prison Diary, Argentina 1983, The Sun Never Sets: Travels to the Remaining Outposts of the British Empire 1986, The Rise and Fall of Travel 1989, Pacific Rising 1991, Pacific Nightmare: How Japan Starts World War III: A Future History 1992, The River at the Centre of the World 1996, The Surgeon of Crowthorne 1998, The Professor and the Madman 1998, The Fracture Zone: My Return to the Balkans 1999, The Map That Changed the World 2001, Tramping 2001, Outposts: Journeys to the Surviving Relics of the British Empire 2003, Krakatoa: The Day the World Exploded 2003, The Meaning of Everything: The Story of the Oxford English Dictionary 2003, Simon Winchester's Calcutta 2004, A Crack in the Edge of the World: The Great Earthquake of 1906 2005, The Man who Loved China 2008, Atlantic: A Vast Ocean of a Million Stories 2010; co-author: Small World: A Global Photographic Project 1995, America's Idea of a Good Time 2001; contrib. to Stories of Empire: Buildings of the Raj 1983, Conde Nast Traveller, Smithsonian, National Geographic. *E-mail:* simonwinchester@harpercollins.com (office). *Website:* www.simonwinchester.com.

WINDLEY, Carol; Canadian writer; b. 18 June 1947, Tofino, BC; m. Robert Windley 1971, one d. *Publications:* Visible Light (Bumbershoot-Weyerhauser Publication Award) 1993, City of Ladies 1998, Home Schooling (Ethel Wilson Fiction Prize 2007) 2006; contributions: anthologies and periodicals. *Honours:* Canada Council B. grants 1995, 1997. *Address:* 5989 Tweedsmuir Crescent, Nanaimo, BC V9T 5Y6, Canada (home). *Telephone:* (250) 756-0153 (home).

WINDSOR, Patricia, (Colin Daniel, Katonah Summertree); American writer, poet and academic; b. 21 Sept. 1938, New York, NY; one s. one d. *Career:* faculty mem., Institute of Children's Literature, Univ. of Maryland Writers Institute; Ed.-in-Chief, The Easterner, Washington, DC; Co-Dir, Wordspring Literary Consultants; Dir, Summertree Studios, Savannah; Instructor, Creative Writing, Armstrong Atlantic Univ., Savannah; mem. Authors' Guild, Children's Book Guild, International Writing Guild, MWA, Poetry Society of Georgia, Savannah Storytellers. *Publications:* The Summer Before 1973, Something's Waiting for You, Baker D 1974, Home is Where Your Feet Are Standing 1975, Driving for Roses 1976, Mad Martin 1976, Killing Time 1980, The Demon Tree 1982, The Sandman's Eyes 1985, The Hero 1986, How a Weirdo and a Ghost Can Change Your Entire Life 1986, Two Weirdos and a Ghost and A Very Weird and Moogly Christmas 1991, Just Like the Movies 1990, The Christmas Killer 1991, The Blooding 1996, The House of Death 1996, Nightwood 2006; contributions: anthologies and magazines. *Honours:* American Library Asscn Best Book Award 1973, Outstanding Book for Young Adults Citation, New York Times 1976, Edgar Allan Poe Award, MWA 1986. *Address:* PO Box 799, Severna Park, MD 21146, USA (office). *E-mail:* info@bornauthor.com (office). *Website:* www.bornauthor.com.

WINEGARTEN, Renee, BA, PhD; British literary critic and writer; b. 23 June 1922, London, England; m. Asher Winegarten (died 1946). *Education:* Girton Coll., Cambridge. *Career:* mem. George Sand Asscn, Soc. of Authors, Authors' Guild. *Publications:* French Lyric Poetry in the Age of Malherbe 1954, Writers and Revolution 1974, The Double Life of George Sand 1978, Madame de Staël 1985, Simone de Beauvoir: A Critical View 1988, Accursed Politics: Some French Women Writers and Political Life 1715–1850 2003, Germaine de Staël and Benjamin Constant 2008; contrib. to journals. *Address:* 12 Heather Walk, Edgware, HA8 9TS, England (home).

WINKLER, Josef; Austrian writer; b. 3 March 1953, Kamering, Kärnten. *Education:* Handelsakademie, Klagenfurt. *Career:* administrator, Univ. of Klagenfurt 1973–82, now teacher; publisher, literary magazine Schreibarbeiten 1979; freelance writer and novelist 1982–; writer in residence, Bergen 1994–95. *Publications include:* Das wilde Kärnten (trilogy): Menschenkind 1979, Der Ackermann aus Kärnten 1980, Muttersprache 1982, Die Verschleppung 1983, Der Leibeigene (trans. as The Serf) (novel) 1987, Friedhof der bitteren Orangen (novel) 1990, Das Zöglingsheft des Jean Genet (trans. as Flowers for Jean Genet) (essay) 1992, Das Wilde Kärnten 1995, Domra 1996, Wern es soweit ist 1998, Natura morta (novella) 2001, Leichnam, seine Familie belauernd 2003, Requiem für einen Vater 2004, Roppongi 2007, Ich eiss mir eine Wimper aus und stech dich damit tot 2008. *Honours:* Anton Wildgans Prize 1980, Theodor Körner Foundation Funds literary grant 1990, Robert Musil Scholarship 1990, German Literary Fund's Kranich mit dem Stein Prize 1990, Bettina von Arnim Prize 1994, Berlin Literature Prize 1996, Otto Stoessl Prize 2000, André-Gide Prize 2000, Alfred Döblin Prize 2001, George Saiko travel grant 2004, Franz Nabl Prize 2005, Georg Büchner Preis 2008. *Address:* c/o Suhrkamp Verlag, Postfach 101945, 60019 Frankfurt, Germany (office). *E-mail:* geschaeftsleitung@suhrkamp.de (office). *Website:* www.suhrkamp.de (office).

WINNER, Michael Robert, MA; British film producer and director and screenwriter; b. 30 Oct. 1935, London; s. of the late George Joseph Winner and Helen Winner. *Education:* Downing Coll. Cambridge. *Career:* Ed. and film critic of Cambridge Univ. paper; entered film industry as film critic and columnist for nat. newspapers and magazines 1951; wrote, produced and directed many documentary, TV and feature films for the Film Producers Guild, Anglo Amalgamated, United Artists 1955–61; Chair. Scimitar Films Ltd, Michael Winner Ltd, Motion Picture and Theatrical Investments Ltd 1957–; Columnist Sunday Times and News of the World; Chief Censorship Officer, Dirs. Guild of GB 1983, mem. Council and Trustee 1983–2007, Sr mem. 1991–2004; Founder and Chair. Police Memorial Trust 1984–; mem. Writers' Guild of Great Britain. *Films:* Play It Cool (dir) 1962, The Cool Mikado (dir, writer) 1962, West 11 (dir) 1963, The System (co-producer and dir) 1963–64, You Must Be Joking (producer, dir, writer) 1964–65, The Jokers (producer, dir, writer) 1966, I'll Never Forget What's 'is Name (producer, dir) 1967, Hannibal Brooks (producer, dir, writer) 1968, The Games (producer, dir) 1969, Lawman (producer, dir) 1970, The Nightcomers (producer, dir) 1971, Chato's Land (producer, dir) 1971, The Mechanic (dir) 1972, Scorpio (producer, dir) 1972, The Stone Killer (producer, dir) 1973, Death Wish (producer, dir) 1974, Won Ton Ton – The Dog Who Saved Hollywood (producer, dir) 1975, The Sentinel (producer, dir, writer) 1976, The Big Sleep (producer, dir, Writer) 1977, Firepower (producer, dir, writer) 1978, Death Wish II (producer, dir, writer) 1981, The Wicked Lady (producer, dir, writer) 1982, Scream For Help (producer, dir) 1983, Death Wish III (producer, dir) 1985, Appointment with Death (producer, dir, writer) 1988, A Chorus of Disapproval (producer, dir, co-writer) 1989, Bullseye! (producer, dir, co-writer) 1990, For the Greater Good (BBC film, actor, dir Danny Boyle) 1990, Decadence (actor, dir Steven Berkoff) 1993, Dirty Weekend (producer, jt screenplay writer) 1993, Parting Shots (producer, dir, writer) 1997. *Theatre:* The Silence of St Just (producer) 1971, The Tempest (producer) 1974, A Day in Hollywood, A Night in the Ukraine (producer) (Evening Standard Award for Best Comedy of the Year 1979). *Radio:* panellist, Any Questions (BBC Radio 4), The Flump (play) 2000. *Television appearances include:* Michael Winner's True Crimes (LWT), panellist, Question Time (BBC One), many variety show sketches, starring in and/or directing commercials for different cos 2003–. *Publications:* Winner's Dinners 1999, Winner Guide 2002, Winner Takes All: a Life of Sorts 2004, Michael Winner's Fat Pig Diet 2007; contrib. to Sunday Times, News of the World, Daily Mail. *Address:* 219 Kensington High Street, London, W8 6BD, England (office). *Telephone:* (20) 7734-8385 (office). *Fax:* (20) 7602-9217 (office).

WINNIFRITH, Thomas John, BA, MPhil, PhD; British writer; b. 5 April 1938, Dulwich, London, England; m. 1st Joanna Booker 1967; m. 2nd Helen Young 1988; one s. two d. *Education:* Christ Church, Oxford, Corpus Christi, Oxford, Univ. of Liverpool. *Career:* Asst Master Eton Coll. 1961–66, EK Chambers Student 1966–68, William Noble Fellow 1968–70; Lecturer, Sr Lecturer, Univ. of Warwick 1970–98; Visiting Fellow, All Souls Coll., Oxford 1984; Leverhulme Fellow Emer. 1999–2000. *Publications:* The Brontës and Their Background 1973, The Brontës 1977, Brontë Facts and Problems 1983, Nineteen Eighty Four and All's Well 1984, The Vlachs 1987, A New Life of Charlotte Brontë 1988, Charlotte and Emily Brontë 1989, Fallen Women in the Nineteenth Century Novel 1994, Shattered Eagles: Balkan Fragments 1996, Badlands Borderlands 2002. *Address:* 50 Sheep Street, Shipston on Stour, Warwicks., CV36 4AE, England (home). *Telephone:* (1608) 661244 (home). *Fax:* (1608) 661244 (home). *E-mail:* winnifrith@tiscali.co.uk (home).

WINOCK, Michel, LèsL, DèsL; French historian, academic, writer and publisher; *Professor, Institut d'Etudes politiques;* b. 19 March 1937, Paris; s. of Gaston Winock and Jeanne Winock (née Dussaule); m. Françoise Werner 1961; two s. *Education:* Sorbonne. *Career:* teacher, Lycée Joffre, Montpellier 1961–63, Lycée Hoche, Versailles 1963–66, Lycée Lakanal, Sceaux 1966–68; Lecturer, Sr Lecturer Univ. of Paris VIII-Vincennes à St-Denis 1968–78; Sr Lecturer, Institut d'Etudes politiques, Paris 1978–90, Prof. 1990–; Publr Editions du Seuil, Paris 1969–; radio producer, France-Inter 1983–85; Ed.-in-Chief L'Histoire magazine 1978–81, Editorial Adviser 1981–. *Publications include:* Histoire politique de la revue esprit 1930–1950 1975, La république se meurt 1978, Les grandes crises politiques 1971–1968 1986, La Fière hexagonale 1986, Nationalisme, antisemitisme et fascisme en France 1990, Le socialisme en France et en Europe XIXe–XXe siècle 1992, Le siècle des intellectuels (essays) 1997, La guerre de 1914–1918 racontée aux enfants 1998, La France politique XIXe–XXe siècle 1999, Les Voix de la liberté 2001, Les écrivains engagés au XIXe siècle 2001, La France et les juifs (Prix Montaigne de Bordeaux 2005) 2004, Pierre Mendès France 2005, Victor Hugo dans l'arène politique 2005, La Gauche au pouvoir: L'héritage du Front populaire 2006, La France antijuive de 1936: L'agression de Léon Blum à la Chambre des députés 2006, L'Agonie de la IVe République 2006, La Gauche en France 2006, La Mêlée présidentielle 2007, Clemenceau 2007, Madame De Stael (Prix Goncourt de la Biographie 2010) 2010. *Address:* Institut d'Etudes politiques, 25 Rue Gaston De Saporta, Aix En Provence, 13100 Paris, France (office). *Telephone:* 4-42-17-01-91 (office). *Fax:* 4-42-96-36-99 (office). *E-mail:* wimi@cybercable.fr; wimi@noos.fr.

WINSTON, Baron (Life Peer) cr. 1995, of Hammersmith in the London Borough of Hammersmith and Fulham; **Robert Maurice Lipson Winston,** MB, BS, DSc, FRCP, FRCOG, FRCPE, FRCPS, FMedSci, FIBiol, FRSA; British medical researcher; *Professor Emeritus of Reproductive Medicine, Imperial College London;* b. 15 July 1940, London, England; s. of the late Laurence Winston and of Ruth Winston-Fox; m. Lira Feigenbaum 1973; two s. one d. *Education:* St Paul's School, London and London Hosp. Medical Coll., Univ. of London. *Career:* Registrar and Sr Registrar, Hammersmith Hosp. 1970–74; Wellcome Research Sr Lecturer, Inst. of Obstetrics and Gynaecology 1974–78, Sr Lecturer 1978–81, Consultant Obstetrician and Gynaecologist 1978–2005; Prof. of Gynaecology, Univ. of Texas at San Antonio, USA 1980–81; Reader in Fertility Studies, Royal Postgraduate Medical School 1982–86, Prof. 1987–97; apptd Prof. of Fertility Studies, Imperial Coll. London 1997, now Prof. Emer. of Reproductive Medicine, Devt Cttee mem., Imperial Coll. London; Dir NHS Research and Devt, Hammersmith Hosps Trust 1998–2005; Chancellor Sheffield Hallam Univ. 2001–; Visiting Prof., Univ. of Leuven, Belgium 1976–77, Mount Sinai Hosp., New York, USA 1985; mem. (Labour) House of Lords 1995–, Chair. Select Cttee of Science and Tech. 1999–2002; Chair. Royal Coll. of Music 2008–; Vice-Chair. Parl. Office of Science and Tech. 2005–; Founder-mem. British Fertility Soc.; mem. Eng and Physical Sciences Research Council 2008–, Council mem. Surrey Univ. 2008–, Scottish Scientific Advisory Council; Trustee, Genesis (scientific research); numerous other professional appointments. *Director:* Each in his Own Way (Pirandello), Edinburgh Festival 1969. *Television:* Presenter, Your Life In Their Hands (BBC) 1979–87, Making Babies 1996, The Human Body 1998, The Secret Life of Twins 1999, Child of our Time (BBC) 2000, Superhuman 2000, Human Instinct 2002, 2003, Threads of Life (BBC) 2003, The Human Mind (BBC) 2004, Story of God (BBC) 2005, Child Against All Odds (BBC) 2006, Superdoctors 2008. *Radio:* Robert Winston's Musical Analysis 2009. *Publications:* Reversibility of Sterilization 1978, Tubal Infertility (jtly) 1981, Infertility: A Sympathetic Approach 1987, Getting Pregnant 1989, Making Babies 1996, The IVF Revolution 1999, Superman 2000, Human Instinct 2002, The Human Mind 2003, What Makes Me, Me? (Aventis Jr Prize, Royal Soc. 2005) 2004, Human (BMA Award for Best Popular Medicine Book) 2005, The Story of God 2005, Body 2005, A Child Against All Odds 2006, It's Elementary 2007, Evolution Revolution 2009; about 300 scientific articles on reproduction. *Honours:* Hon. Fellow, Queen Mary and Westfield Coll. 1996; Hon. FRCSE; Hon. Fellow, Royal Coll. of Physicians and Surgeons (Glasg); Hon. FIBiol; 20 hon. doctorates at British univs, including: Hon. DSc (Cranfield) 2001, (UMIST) 2001, (Oxford Brookes) 2001, (St Andrew's) 2003, (Exeter) 2004, (Trinity Coll. Dublin) 2005, (Univ. of Auckland) 2008; Victor Bonney Prize, Royal Coll. of Surgeons 1991–93, Chief Rabbinate Award for Contribution to Society 1992–93, Cedric Carter Medal, Clinical Genetics Soc. 1993, Gold Medal, Royal Soc. of Health 1998, Michael Faraday Award, Royal Soc. 1999, Wellcome Award for Science in the Media 2001, Edwin Stevens Medal, Royal Soc. of Medicine 2003, Gold Medal, North of England Zoological Soc. 2004, VLV Individual Award for Best contribs to UK Broadcasting 2004, Al Hammadi Medal, Royal Coll. of Surgeons, Edin. 2005. *Address:* Faculty Building, Imperial College, Exhibition Road, London, SW7 2AZ (office); House of Lords, Westminster, London, SW1A 0PW, England. *Telephone:* (20) 7594-5959 (office); (20) 7219-6020 (House of Lords). *Fax:* (20) 8458-4980 (home). *E-mail:* r.winston@imperial.ac.uk (office); info@robertwinston.org. *Website:* www.parliament.uk/biographies/lords/robert-winston/26716; www.robertwinston.org.uk.

WINSTON, Sarah; American writer; b. (Sarah E. Lorenz), 15 Dec. 1912, New York, NY; m. Keith Winston 1932; two s. *Education:* New York University, The Barnes Foundation. *Career:* mem. National League of American Pen Women. *Publications:* And Always Tomorrow 1963, Everything Happens for the Best 1969, Our Son, Ken 1969, Not Yet Spring (poems) 1976, V-Mail: Letters of the World War II Combat Medic 1985, Summer Conference 1990, Of Apples and Oranges 1993; contributions: journals. *Honours:* first prize National League of American Pen Women 1972, 1974.

WINTER, Kathleen; Canadian (b. British) writer and novelist; b. 1960, Bill Quay, NE England; m.; two d. *Career:* immigrated to Newfoundland as a child, now lives in Montreal; columnist, St John's Telegram 1993–. *Television includes:* scripts for Sesame Street and documentaries for CBC TV. *Publications include:* Where is Mario (novella) 1987, The Road Along the Shore (non-fiction) 1991, The Necklace of Occasional Dreams (non-fiction) 1996, boYs (short stories) (Metcalf-Rooke Award, Winterset Award 2008) 2007, Annabel (novel) (Thomas Head Raddall Atlantic Fiction Prize 2011) 2010; contrib. stories to literary journals. *Literary Agent:* c/o Shaun Bradley, 1603 Italy Cross Road, Petite Riviere, NS B4V 6R4, Canada. *Telephone:* (902) 693-2026. *E-mail:* shaun@tla1.com. *Address:* c/o House of Anansi Press, 110 Spadina Avenue, Suite 801, Toronto, ON M5V 2K4, Canada (office). *Telephone:* (416) 363-4343 (office). *Fax:* (416) 363-1017 (office). *E-mail:* poetrypizza@gmail.com (office). *Website:* sites.google.com/site/kathleenwinterauthor; kathleenwinter.livejournal.com.

WINTERSON, Jeanette, OBE, BA (Hons) (Oxon.); British writer; b. 27 Aug. 1959, Manchester; partner Susie Orbach. *Education:* Accrington Girls' Grammar School, St Catherine's Coll., Oxford. *Play:* The Power Book (Royal Nat. Theatre, London, Théâtre de Chaillot, Paris). *Screenplay:* Great Moments in Aviation 1992. *Television:* Oranges Are Not The Only Fruit (BBC) (BAFTA Award for Best Drama 1990, FIPA d'Argent Award for screenplay, Cannes Film Festival 1991) 1990, Orlando – Art That Shook the World (BBC) 2002, South Bank Show 2004, Ingenious (BBC) 2009. *Publications:* fiction: Oranges Are Not The Only Fruit (Whitbread Prize for Best First Novel 1985) 1985, Boating for Beginners 1985, The Passion 1987, Sexing the Cherry 1989, Written on the Body 1992, Art and Lies 1994, Gut Symmetries 1997, The World and Other Places (short stories) 1998, The Power Book 2000, The King of Capri (juvenile) 2003, Lighthousekeeping 2004, Weight: The Myth of Atlas and Heracles 2005, Tanglewreck (juvenile novel) 2006, The Stone Gods 2007, The Battle of the Sun (juvenile novel) 2009, The Lion, The Unicorn and Me (juvenile picture book) 2009; non-fiction: Fit for the Future 1986, Art Objects (essays) 1994, Why Be Happy When You Could Be Normal? (memoir) 2011; editor and contrib.: Midsummer Nights (short stories). *Honours:* Hon. Fellow, Royal Acad.; Whitbread Prize 1985, John Llewellyn Rhys Memorial Book Prize 1987, American Acad. of Arts and Letters E. M. Forster Award 1989, Golden Gate Award, San Francisco Int. Film Festival 1990, Best of Young British Novelists Award 1992, Int. Fiction Award, Festival Letteratura Mantua 1999. *Literary Agent:* c/o Caroline Michel, PFD, Drury House, 34–43 Russell Street, London, WC2B 5HA, England. *E-mail:* cmichel@pfd.co.uk. *Website:* www.jeanettewinterson.com.

WINTON, Timothy John; Australian writer; b. 4 Aug. 1960, nr Perth, WA; m. Denise Winton; two s. one d. *Education:* Western Australian Inst. of Tech. *Publications:* An Open Swimmer 1981, Shallows 1985, Scisson and Other Stories 1985, That Eye, The Sky 1986, Minimum of Two 1987, In the Winter Dark 1988, Jesse 1988, Lockie Leonard, Human Torpedo 1990, The Bugalugs Bum Thief 1991, Cloudstreet 1991, Lockie Leonard, Scumbuster 1993, Land's Edge (with Trish Ainslie and Roger Garwood) 1993, Local Colour: Travels in the Other Australia 1994, The Riders 1994, Lockie Leonard, Legend 1997, Blueback 1997, The Deep 1998, Down to Earth 1999, Dirt Music 2001, The Turning 2004, Breath (Miles Franklin Literary Award 2009) 2008. *Honours:* Vogel Literary Award 1981, Miles Franklin Award 1984, 1992, 2002, 2009, Western Australian Premier's Awards 1990, 1991, 2001, Deo Gloria Prize for Religious Writing 1991, Commonwealth Writers Prize 1995, NSF Premier's Awards Christina Stead Prize for Fiction 2002, 2005, Queensland Fiction Prize 2005. *Literary Agent:* c/o Jenny Darling & Associates, PO Box 413, Toorak, Vic. 3142, Australia. *Telephone:* (3) 9827-3883. *Fax:* (3) 9827-1270. *E-mail:* timwinton@jd-associates.com.au. *Website:* www.jd-associates.com.au; breath.timwinton.com.au.

WINTOUR, Anna, OBE; British editor; *Editor, Vogue;* b. 3 Nov. 1949, d. of the late Charles Wintour and Eleanor ('Nonie') Trego Baker; m. David Shaffer 1984 (divorced); one s. one d. *Education:* Queen's Coll. School, London, North London Collegiate School. *Career:* deputy fashion ed. Harpers & Queen 1970–76, Harper's Bazaar, New York 1976–77; fashion and beauty ed. Viva magazine 1977–78; contributing ed. for fashion and style, Savvy Magazine 1980–81; Sr Ed. New York Magazine 1981–83; Creative Dir US Vogue 1983–86; Ed.-in-Chief, UK Vogue 1986–87; Ed. House & Garden, New York 1987–88; Ed. Vogue (US) 1988–. *Honours:* ranked by Forbes magazine amongst The World's 100 Most Powerful Women (56th) 2010, (69th) 2011. *Address:* Vogue, 4 Times Square, 12th Floor, New York, NY 10036, USA (office). *Telephone:* (212) 286-2810 (office). *Fax:* (212) 286-8593 (office). *Website:* www.style.com/vogue (office).

WISSE, Ruth R., BA, MA, PhD; American academic, writer, editor and translator; *Martin Peretz Professor of Yiddish Literature and Professor of Comparative Literature, Harvard University;* b. (Ruth Roskies), 13 May 1936, Cernauti, Romania (now in Ukraine); d. of Leo Roskies and Masza Welczer; m. Leonard Wisse 1957; two s. one d. *Education:* McGill Univ., Columbia Univ. *Career:* Asst Prof., McGill Univ. 1968–71, Assoc. Prof. 1975, Chair., Dept of Jewish Studies 1976–79, Prof. 1978–92, Montréal Jewish Community Chair in Jewish Studies 1986–92; Sr Lecturer, Univ. of Tel-Aviv and Hebrew Univ., Tel-Aviv 1971–73; Visiting Prof., YIVO Inst. for Jewish Research 1975, mem. Academic Advisory Bd 2000–; Martin Peretz Prof. of Yiddish Literature and Prof. of Comparative Literature, Harvard Univ. 1993–, Dir Center for Jewish Studies 1993–96, College Prof. 2003–; mem. American Acad. for Jewish Research, Asscn for Jewish Studies (Pres. 1985–89), Bd of Academic Advisors Nat. Foundation for Jewish Culture 1979–82. *Publications:* The Schlemiel as Modern Hero 1970, A Shtetl and Other Yiddish Novellas (ed.) 1972, The Best of Sholem Aleichem (ed. with Irving Howe) 1979, The Penguin Book of Modern Yiddish Verse (ed. with Irving Howe and Khone Shmeruk) 1987, A Little Love in Big Manhattan 1988, The I. L. Peretz Reader (ed.) 1990, I. L. Peretz and the Making of Modern Jewish Culture 1991, If I Am Not for Myself: The Liberal Portrayal of the Jews 1992, The Modern Jewish Canon: A Journey Through Language and Culture 2000, Jews and Power 2007, The Glatstein Chronicles (ed.) 2010; contrib. to reference works and periodicals. *Honours:* Hon. DHumLitt (Yeshiva) 2004; J.I. Segal Awards for Literature 1971, 1989, Manger Prize for Yiddish Literature 1988, Moment Magazine Award in Jewish Scholarship 1989, Torch of Learning Award, Hebrew Univ., Tel-Aviv 1993, Maurice Stiller Prize, Baltimore Hebrew Univ. 1998, Jewish Cultural Achievement Award, Nat. Foundation for Jewish Culture 2001, Nat. Jewish Book Award 2001, Guardian of Zion Award of Rennert Center, Bar-Ilan Univ. 2003, Nat. Medal for the Humanities 2007. *Address:* Department of Near Eastern Languages and Civilizations, Harvard University, Cambridge, MA 02138, USA (office). *Telephone:* (617) 496-9050 (office). *E-mail:* wisse@fas.harvard.edu (office). *Website:* www.nelc.fas.harvard.edu (office).

WITHEROW, John Moore, BA (Hons), Dipl. in Journalism; British journalist; *Editor, The Sunday Times;* b. 20 Jan. 1952, Johannesburg, S. Africa; m. Sarah Linton 1985; two s. one d. *Education:* Bedford School, Univ. of York, Univ. of Cardiff. *Career:* voluntary service in Namibia (then SW Africa) after school; posted to Madrid for Reuters; covered Falklands War for The Times 1982; joined The Sunday Times 1984, successively Defence and Diplomatic Corresp., Focus Ed., Foreign Ed., Man. Ed. (news), Ed., The Sunday Times 1995–. *Publications:* The Winter War: The Falklands (with Patrick Bishop) 1982, The Gulf War 1993. *Address:* The Sunday Times, 1 Pennington Street, London, E98 1ST, England (office). *Telephone:* (20) 7782-5640 (office). *Fax:* (20) 7782-5420 (office). *Website:* www.thesundaytimes.co.uk (office).

WITKOWSKI, Michał, MA; Polish writer and journalist; b. 17 Jan. 1975, Wrocław. *Education:* Jagiellonian Univ. *Publications:* Copyright (short stories) 2001, Tekstylia: O rocznikach siedemdziesiątych (co-editor) 2002, Lubiewo (novel) (Gdynia Literary Award 2006) 2005, Fototapeta (short stories) 2006, Barbara Radziwiłłówna z Jaworzna-Szczakowej (novel) 2007, Margot (novel) 2009; contrib. to Ha!Art. *Honours:* Polityka Passport 2005. *Address:* c/o Portobello Books, 12 Addison Avenue, London, W11 4QR, England (office). *E-mail:* mail@portobellobooks.com (office); michal.witkowski@free.art.pl (home); witkoowski@wp.pl (home). *Website:* free.art.pl/michal.witkowski.

WITTICH, John Charles Bird, (Charles Bird), BA, FRSA; British fmr librarian, writer and lecturer; b. 18 Feb. 1929, London, England; m. June Rose Taylor 1954; one s. one d. *Career:* mem. Minor Order of Readers of the Church of England 1980–2005, Reader Emeritus 2005–; Liveryman Emeritus, Worshipful Co. of Woolmen of the City of London; Liveryman of the Worshipful Co. of Musicians, Master 1995–96; mem. Worshipful Co. of Parish Clerks of the City of London 1995–96, mem. Past Masters' Asscn 1996–; mem. Aldgate Ward Club, Samuel Pepys of London Nat. Art Fund Collection, Royal Photographic Soc., Ancient Monuments Soc. *Publications:* Off Beat Walks In London 1969, Discovering London Curiosities 1973, London Villages 1976, Discovering London Street Names 1977, Discovering London's Inns and Taverns 1978, History and Guide to St John the Evangelist Church, London W2 1980, Discovering London's Parks and Squares 1981, AA London Guide (contrib.) 1987, Catholic London 1988, Churches, Cathedrals and Chapels 1989, Guide to Bayswater 1989, Hidden World of Regent's Park 1992, Exploring Cathedrals 1992, London Villages 1992, History and Guide to St Magnus the Martyr's Church, London EC3 1994, Curiosities of Surrey 1994, Spot-It Guide to London (for children) 1995, Explorer's London 1995, Walks Around Haunted London 1996, London Bus Top Tourist 1997, History and Guide: St Vedast's Church, City of London 1999; as Charles Bird: Curiosities of the Cities of London and Westminster 2003; contrib. to periodicals and journals. *Address:* 88 Woodlawn Street, Whitstable, Kent, CT5 1HH, England (home). *Telephone:* (1227) 772619 (home). *E-mail:* johncwittich@yahoo.co.uk.

WOESSNER, Warren Dexter, BA, PhD, JD; American attorney, editor, poet and writer; b. 31 May 1944, Brunswick, NJ; m. Iris Freeman 1990. *Education:* Cornell Univ., Univ. of Wisconsin. *Career:* founder, Ed. and Publisher, Abraxas Magazine 1968–81, Sr Ed. 1981–; mem. of Bd of Dirs, Coffee House Press 1988–92, Pres. 1989–92; Contributing Ed., Pharmaceutical News. *Publications:* The Forest and the Trees 1968, Landing 1974, No Hiding Place 1979, Storm Lines 1987, Clear to Chukchi 1996, Iris Rising 1998, Chemistry 2002; contributions: anthologies, magazines and periodicals. *Honours:* National Endowment for the Arts Fellowship 1974, Wisconsin Arts Board Fellowships 1975, 1976, Loft-McKnight Fellow 1985, Minnesota Voices, Competition for Poetry 1986.

WOHMANN, Gabriele; German writer; b. 21 May 1932, Darmstadt; d. of Paul Guyot and Luise Guyot (née Lettermann); m. Reiner Wohmann 1953. *Education:* Univ. of Frankfurt/Main. *Career:* Teacher 1953–56; Writer-in-Residence, Gutenberg-Museum, Mainz (Literature Prize Zweites Deutsches Fernsehen ZDF/Mainz) 1984; mem. Berlin Akad. der Künste 1965–, Deutsche Akad. für Sprache und Dichtung 1980–; mem. PEN-Zentrum der Bundesrepublik Deutschland 1960–88. *Publications include:* novels: Jetzt und nie 1958, Abschied für länger 1965, Ernste Absicht 1970, Paulinchen war allein zu Haus 1974 (also TV play 1981), Ausflug mit der Mutter 1976, Ach wie gut, daß niemand weiß 1980, Das Glücksspiel 1981, Der Flötenton 1987, Bitte nicht sterben 1993, Das Handicap 1996, Schön und gut 2002, Hol mich einfach ab 2003; short stories: Mit einem Messer 1958, Trinken ist das Herrlichste 1963, Gegenangriff 1972, Dorothea Wörth 1975, Alles zu seiner Zeit 1976, Streit 1978, Wir sind eine Familie 1980, Stolze Zeiten 1981, Einsamkeit 1982, Der Kirschbaum 1984, Ein russischer Sommer 1988, Kassensturz 1989, Das Salz, bitte! 1992, Die Schönste im ganzen Land 1995, Scherben hütten Glück gebracht 2006, Schwarz und ohne alles 2008, Wann kommt die Liebe 2010; poetry: Grund zur Aufregung 1978, Komm lieber Mai 1981, Passau-Gleis 3 1984, Das könnte ich sein 1989; radio plays: Komm Donnerstag 1964, Norwegian Wood 1967, Kurerfolg 1970, Tod in Basel 1972, Wanda Lords Gespenster 1978, Ein gehorsamer Diener 1987, Es geht mir gut, ihr Kinder 1988, Drück mir die Daumen 1991, Der Mann am Fenster 1994, Besser als Liegen ist tot sein 1996, Café Caledonia 2006, Wir machen es morgen 2008; TV plays: Große Liebe 1966, Die Witwen 1972, Heiratskandidaten 1975, Unterwegs 1985, Schreiben müssen 1990. *Honours:* Hon. Fellow, American Asscn of Teachers of German 1994; Bundesverdienstkreuz (First Class) 1980; awards include Bremen Literature Prize 1971, Deutscher Schallplattenpreis 1981, J.H. Merck Honour, Darmstadt 1982, Hessischer Kulturpreis 1988, Adenauerpreis 1994, Montblanc Short Story Prize 1994, Grosses Bundesverdienstkreuz 1997. *Address:* Erbacher Str. 76A, 64287 Darmstadt, Germany. *Telephone:* (6151) 46801.

WOIWODE, Larry Alfred; American writer and poet; b. 30 Oct. 1941, Carrington, ND; m. Carole Ann Peterson 1965; four c. *Education:* Univ. of Illinois at Urbana-Champaign. *Career:* Writer-in-Residence, Univ. of Wisconsin at Madison 1973–74; Prof., Wheaton College 1981, 1984; Visiting Prof., SUNY at Binghamton 1983–85, Prof. and Dir of Creative Writing Program 1985–88; Poet Laureate of North Dakota 1995–; currently Writer-in-Residence, Jamestown College; Guggenheim Fellowship 1971–72; various workshops and readings at many colleges and universities. *Publications:* fiction: What I'm Going to Do, I Think 1969, Beyond the Bedroom Wall: A Family Album 1975, Poppa John 1981, Born Brothers 1988, The Neumiller Stories 1989, Indian Affairs: A Novel 1992, Silent Passengers: Stories 1993; poetry: Even Tide 1975; non-fiction: Acts 1993, The Aristocrat of the West: Biography of Harold Schafer 2000, What I Think I Did: A Season of Survival in Two Acts (autobiog.) 2000, A Step from Death (memoir) 2008, Words Made Fresh: Essays on Literature and Culture 2011; contributions: books, anthologies, reviews, periodicals, journals, etc. *Honours:* Dr hc (North Dakota State Univ.) 1977, (Geneva Coll.) 1997; Notable Book Award, American Library Asscn 1970, William Faulkner Foundation Award 1970, Fiction Award, Friends of American Writers 1976, Fiction Award 1980, Medal of Merit 1995, American Acad. of Arts and Letters, Aga Khan Literary Prize, Paris Review 1990, Book Award of Short Fiction, Louisiana State University/Southern Review 1990, John Dos Passos Prize 1991. *Address:* Jamestown College English and Theatre Arts Department, 6046 College Lane, Jamestown, ND 58405, USA (office). *E-mail:* woiwode@jc.edu (office). *Website:* www.jc.edu/english (office).

WOLF, Naomi, BA; American writer and feminist; b. 15 Nov. 1962, San Francisco, Calif.; d. of Leonard Wolf and Deborah Wolf; m. David Shipley 1993 (divorced 2005); one c. *Education:* Yale Univ., New Coll., Univ. of Oxford, UK. *Career:* Rhodes Scholar 1986; Co-founder Woodhull Inst. for Ethical Leadership 1997–, now Scholar in Residence and Woodhull Fellow; fmr columnist, George magazine; consultant, Al Gore Presidential campaign 2000. *Publications:* The Beauty Myth: How Images of Beauty Are Used Against Women 1990, Fire With Fire: The New Female Power and How It Will Change in the 21st Century 1993, Promiscuities: The Secret Struggle for Womanhood 1997, Misconceptions: Truth, Lies and the Unexpected on the Journey to Motherhood 2001, The Treehouse: Eccentric Wisdom from my Father on How to Live, Love and See 2006, The End of America: A Letter of Warning to a Young Patriot 2007, Give Me Liberty: A Handbook for American Revolutionaries 2008. *Address:* c/o The Woodhull Institute, 770 Broadway, 2nd Floor, New York, NY 10003; c/o Royce Carlton Inc., 866 UN Plaza, New York, NY 10017, USA. *Telephone:* (646) 495-6060 (Woodhull). *Fax:* (646) 495-6059 (Woodhull). *E-mail:* info@woodhull.org. *Website:* woodhull.org.

WOLFE, Christopher, BA, PhD; American political scientist, academic, institute director and author; *Co-Director, Thomas International Center*; b. 11 March 1949, Boston, Mass; s. of Walter Brewster Wolfe and Margaret Conway Wolfe; m. Anne McGowan 1972; five s. five d. *Education:* Univ. of Notre Dame, Ind., Boston Coll. *Career:* Instructor, Assumption Coll., Worcester, Mass 1975–78; Asst Prof., Marquette Univ., Milwaukee, Wis. 1978–84, Assoc. Prof. 1984–92, Prof. of Political Science 1992–2008, Prof. Emer. 2008–; Founder and Pres. American Public Philosophy Inst. 1989; Co-Dir Thomas Int. Center 2005–; mem. American Political Science Asscn, Federalist Soc., Fellowship of Catholic Scholars. *Publications:* The Rise of Modern Judicial Review: From Constitutional Interpretation to Judge-Made Law 1986, Faith and Liberal Democracy 1987, Judicial Activism: Bulwark of Freedom or Precarious Security? 1991, Liberalism at the Crossroads (ed. with John Hittinger) 1994, How to Interpret the Constitution 1996, The Family, Civil Society and the State (ed.) 1998, Homosexuality and American Public Life (ed.) 1999, Natural Law and Public Reason (ed. with Robert George) 2000, Same-Sex Matters (ed.) 2000, That Eminent Tribunal: Judicial Supremacy and the Constitution (ed.) 2004, Natural Law Liberalism 2006, The Naked Public Square Reconsidered (ed.) 2009; contrib. to professional journals and general periodicals. *Honours:* Woodrow Wilson Fellowship 1971, Inst. for Educational Affairs grants 1982, 1983, Bradley Foundation grant 1986, Benchmark Book of the Year Award 1987, Nat. Endowment for the Humanities Fellowship 1994, Templeton Honor Roll for Educ. in a Free Society 1997, Elmer Plischke Annual Faculty Research Award in Political Science, Marquette Univ. 2007. *Address:* Thomas International Center, 343 E Six Forks Road, Suite 370, Raleigh, NC 27609, USA (office). *Telephone:* (919) 995-3541 (office). *E-mail:* cwolfe@ticenter.net (office). *Website:* www.ticenter.net (office).

WOLFE, Peter, BA, MA, PhD; American academic and writer; *Curators' Professor of English, University of Missouri at St Louis*; b. 25 Aug. 1933, New York, NY; s. of Milton B. Wolfe and Mae Wolfe; m. 1st Marie Paley 1962 (divorced 1969); two s.; m. 2nd Retta Cardwell 1998. *Education:* City Coll. of New York, CUNY, Lehigh Univ., Univ. of Wisconsin. *Career:* Curators' Prof. of English, Univ. of Missouri at St Louis 2000–. *Publications:* books: The Disciplined Heart: Iris Murdoch 1966, Mary Renault 1969, Rebecca West, Artist and Thinker 1971, Graham Greene the Entertainer 1972, John Fowles: Magus and Moralist 1976, Dreamers Who Live Their Dreams: Ross Macdonald 1977, Jean Rhys 1980, Falling Beams: Dashiell Hammett 1980, Laden Choirs: Patrick White 1983, Something More Than Night: Raymond Chandler 1985, Corridors of Deceit: John le Carré 1987, Yukio Mishima 1989, Alarms and Epitaphs: Eric Ambler 1993, In the Zone: Rod Serling's Twilight Vision 1997, A Vision of His Own: William Gaddis 1997, Understanding Alan Bennett 1999, August Wilson 1999, Understanding Penelope Fitzgerald 2004, Like Hot Knives to the Brain: James Elroy's Search for Himself 2005, Havoc in the Hub: A Reading of George V. Higgins 2007; contrib. to Weekend Australian, Sydney Morning Herald, New Zealand Listener, Calcutta Statesman, New York Times Book Review, Chicago Tribune, Los Angeles Times, St Louis Post-Dispatch, St Louis Globe-Democrat, Washington Post, the Nation, Chicago Tribune. *Honours:* Fulbright Awards to India 1987, Poland 1991, Univ. of Missouri Pres.'s Award for Creativity and Research 1995. *Address:* Department of English, Office 465 Lucas Hall, University of Missouri at St Louis, 8001 Natural Bridge Road, St Louis, MO 63121-4499, USA (office). *Telephone:* (314) 516-5617 (office). *Fax:* (314) 516-5781 (office). *E-mail:* spwolfe@umsl.edu (office).

WOLFE, Thomas (Tom) Kennerly, Jr, AB, PhD; American author and journalist; b. 2 March 1930, Richmond, Va; s. of Thomas Kennerly and Helen Hughes; m. Sheila Berger; one s. one d. *Education:* Washington and Lee, and Yale Univs. *Career:* reporter, Springfield (Mass) Union 1956–59; reporter, Latin American Corresp., Washington Post 1959–62; reporter, magazine writer, New York Herald Tribune 1962–66; magazine writer, New York World Journal Tribune 1966–67; Contributing Ed. New York magazine 1968–76, Esquire Magazine 1977–; Contributing Artist, Harper's magazine 1978–81; exhibited one-man show of drawings, Maynard Walker Gallery, New York 1965, Tunnel Gallery, New York 1974; mem. American Acad. of Arts and Letters 1999. *Publications:* The Kandy-Kolored Tangerine-Flake Streamline

Baby 1965, The Electric Kool-Aid Acid Test 1968, The Pump House Gang 1968, Radical Chic and Mau-mauing the Flak Catchers 1970, The New Journalism 1973, The Painted Word 1975, Mauve Gloves and Madmen, Clutter and Vine 1976, The Right Stuff 1979, In Our Time 1980, From Bauhaus to Our House 1981, The Purple Decades: A Reader 1982, The Bonfire of the Vanities 1987, Ambush at Fort Bragg 1998, A Man in Full 1998, Hooking Up (essays and a novella) 2000, I Am Charlotte Simmons 2004. *Honours:* Hon. DFA (Minneapolis Coll. of Art) 1971; Hon. LittD (Washington and Lee) 1974; Hon. LHD (Virginia Commonwealth Univ.) 1983, (Southampton Coll., NY) 1984, (Johns Hopkins Univ.) 1990, (Boston Univ.) 2000, (Duke Univ.) 2002, Yale Univ.) 2004, (Trinity Coll.) 2007; Front Page Awards for Humour and Foreign News Reporting, Washington Newspaper Guild 1961, Award of Excellence, Soc. of Magazine Writers 1970, Frank Luther Mott Research Award 1973, Virginia Laureate for Literature 1977, Harold D. Vursell Memorial Award, American Acad. and Inst. of Arts and Letters 1980, American Book Award for Gen. Non-Fiction 1980, Columbia Journalism Award 1980, Citation for Art History, Nat. Sculpture Soc. 1980, John Dos Passos Award 1984, Gari Melchers Medal 1986, Benjamin Pierce Cheney Medal (E Washington Univ.) 1986, Washington Irving Medal (St Nicholas Soc.) 1986, Theodore Roosevelt Medal 1990, St Louis Literary Award 1990, Yale Graduate School Wilbur L. Cross Medal 1990, President's Humanities Medal 2001, Manhattan Inst. Alexander Hamilton Award 2006, Virginia Library Foundation Lifetime Achievement Award 2007, Nat. Book Awards Medal for Distinguished Contrib. to American Letters 2010. *Address:* c/o Janklow & Nesbit Associates, 445 Park Avenue, New York, NY 10022-2608, USA. *E-mail:* postmaster@janklow.com. *Website:* www.tomwolfe.com.

WOLFERS, Michael, BA, MA, MSc; British writer and translator; b. 28 Sept. 1938, London, England. *Education:* Wadham Coll., Oxford and South Bank Polytechnic. *Career:* journalist, The Times, London 1965–72; Visiting Sr Lecturer in African Politics and Government, Univ. of Juba 1979–82; mem. Royal Inst. of Int. Affairs, Gyosei Inst. of Management, Soc. of Authors, Translators' Asscn. *Publications:* Black Man's Burden Revisited 1974, Politics in the Organization of African Unity 1976, Luandino Vieira: The Real Life of Domingos Xavier 1978, Poems from Angola 1979, Samir Amin, Delinking: Towards a Polycentric World 1990, Hamlet and Cybernetics 1991, Thomas Hodgkin: Letters from Africa 2000, Thomas Hodgkin: Wandering Scholar 2007; contrib. to numerous publications. *Address:* 66 Roupell Street, London, SE1 8SS, England (home).

WOLFF, Christoph Johannes, PhD; German academic, writer and editor; *Adams University Professor, Harvard University*; b. 24 May 1940, Solingen; m. Barbara Mahrenholz 1964, three d. *Education:* Univ. of Berlin, Univ. of Freiburg im Breisgau, Univ. of Erlangen. *Career:* Lecturer, Univ. of Erlangen 1966–69; Asst Prof., Univ. of Toronto 1968–70; Assoc. Prof., Columbia Univ. 1970–73, Prof. of Musicology 1973–76; Visiting Prof. Princeton Univ. 1973, 1975; Ed. Bach-Jahrbuch 1974–; Prof. of Musicology, Harvard Univ. 1976–, Dept Chair. 1980–88, 1990–91, William Powell Mason Prof. 1985–, Acting Dir University Library 1991–92, Dean Graduate School of Arts and Sciences 1992–2000, Adams Univ. Prof. 2002–; Dir Bach Archive, Leipzig 2000–; mem. American Musicological Soc., Gesellschaft für Musikforschung, International Musicological Soc., American Philosophical Soc. *Publications:* Der stile antico in der Musik Johann Sebastian Bachs 1968, The String Quartets of Haydn, Mozart, and Beethoven: Studies of the Autograph Manuscripts (ed.) 1980, Bach Compendium: Analytisch-bibliographisches Repertorium der Werke Johann Sebastian Bachs (ed. with H.-J. Schulze), seven vols 1986–89, Bach: Essays on His Life and Music 1991, Mozart's Requiem: Historical and Analytical Studies, Documents, Score 1993, Wereld van de Bach-cantatas: The World of the Bach Canatatas 1997, The New Bach Reader (ed.) 1998, Driven Into Paradise: The Musical Migration from Nazi Germany to the United States (ed. with R. Brinkmann) 1999, Johann Sebastian Bach: The Learned Musician (Otto Kinkeldey Award) 2000; other: critical edns of works by Scheidt, Buxtehude, Bach, Mozart and Hindemith; contrib. to scholarly books and journals. *Honours:* Hon. Prof. University of Freiburg im Breisgau 1990–, Fellow American Acad. of Arts and Sciences 1982–; Dent Medal Royal Musical Asscn, London 1978, Humboldt Research Prize 1996, Bach Prize, Royal Acad. of Music 2006. *Address:* Department of Music, Harvard University, Music Building 204S, North Yard, Cambridge, MA 02138, USA (office). *Telephone:* (617) 495-2791 (office). *Fax:* (617) 496-8081 (office). *E-mail:* cwolff@fas.harvard.edu (office). *Website:* www.music.fas.harvard.edu (office).

WOLFF, Cynthia Griffin, BA, PhD; American academic and writer; b. 20 Aug. 1936, St Louis, MO; m. 1st Robert Paul Wolff 1962 (divorced 1986); two s.; m. 2nd Nicholas J. White 1988. *Education:* Radcliffe Coll., Harvard Univ. *Career:* Asst Prof. of English, Manhattanville Coll., Purchase, New York, 1968–70; Asst Prof., Univ. of Massachusetts, Amherst 1971–74, Assoc. Prof. 1974–76, Prof. of English 1976–80; Prof. of Humanities, MIT 1980–85, Class of 1922 Prof. of Literature and Writing 1985–, now Emer.; mem. American Studies Asscn. *Publications:* Samuel Richardson 1972, A Feast of Words: The Triumph of Edith Wharton 1977, Emily Dickinson 1986; contributions: scholarly journals. *Honours:* National Endowment for the Humanities Grants 1975–76, 1983–84, ACLS Grant 1984–85.

WOLFF, Geoffrey Ansell, BA; American academic and author; *Professor Emeritus of English and Creative Writing, University of California at Irvine*; b. 5 Nov. 1937, Los Angeles, CA; m. Priscilla Bradley Porter 1965, two s. *Education:* Eastbourne Coll., England, Princeton Univ., Churchill Coll., Cambridge. *Career:* Lecturer, Robert Coll., Istanbul 1961–63, Univ. of Istanbul 1962–63, Maryland Institute and College of Art 1965–69, Middlebury Coll., Vermont 1976–78; Book Ed., Washington Post 1964–69, Newsweek magazine 1969–71, New Times magazine 1974–79; Visiting Lecturer, Princeton Univ. 1970–71, Ferris Prof. 1980, 1992; Book Critic, Esquire magazine 1979–81; Visiting Lecturer, Columbia Univ. 1979, Boston Univ. 1981, Brown Univ. 1981, 1988; Writer-in-Residence, Brandeis Univ. 1982–95; Visiting Prof., Williams Coll. 1994; Prof. of English and Creative Writing, Univ. of California at Irvine 1995–, now Emer.; mem. PEN. *Publications:* Bad Debts 1969, The Sightseer 1974, Black Sun 1976, Inklings 1978, The Duke of Deception 1979, Providence 1986, Best American Essays (ed.) 1989, The Final Club 1990, A Day at the Beach 1992, The Age of Consent 1995, The Art of Burning Bridges: A Life of John O'Hara 2003, The Edge of Maine 2005, The Hard Way Round: The Passages of Joshua Slocum 2010; contributions: various publications. *Honours:* Woodrow Wilson Fellowship 1961–62, Fulbright Fellowship 1963–64, Guggenheim Fellowships 1972–73, 1977–78, National Endowment for the Humanities Senior Fellowship 1974–75, National Endowment for the Arts Fellowships 1979–80, 1986–87, ACLS Fellowship 1983–84, Governor's Arts Award, RI 1992, Lila Wallace Writing Fellowship 1992, American Acad. of Arts and Letters Award 1994. *Address:* c/o Department of English, University of California, 369 Humanities Instructional Building, Irvine, CA 92697, USA (office). *Telephone:* (949) 824-6712 (office). *E-mail:* gwolff@uci.edu (office).

WOLFF, Tobias Jonathan Ansell, BA, MA; American writer; *The Ward W. and Priscilla B. Woods Professor, Stanford University*; b. 19 June 1945, Birmingham, Ala; s. of Arthur S. Wolff and Rosemary Loftus; m. Catherine Dolores Spohn 1975; two s. one d. *Education:* The Hill School, Univ. of Oxford, UK, Stanford Univ., Calif. *Career:* served in US Army 1964–68; reporter, Washington Post 1972; Writing Fellow, Stanford Univ. 1975–78, Prof. of English and Creative Writing 1997–, currently The Ward W. and Priscilla B. Woods Prof.; Writer-in-Residence, Ariz. State Univ. 1978–80; Peck Prof. of English Syracuse Univ. 1980–97; Wallace Stegner Fellowship 1975–76, Nat. Endowment Fellow 1978, 1984; Arizona Council on the Arts and Humanities Fellowship 1980, Guggenheim Fellow 1983; mem. PEN; Fellow, American Acad. of Arts and Sciences 2009–. *Publications:* Ugly Rumours 1975, Hunters in the Snow 1981, The Barracks Thief (PEN/Faulkner Award for Fiction 1985) 1984, Back in the World 1985, A Doctor's Visit: The Short Stories of Anton Chekhov (ed.) 1987, The Stories of Tobias Wolff 1988, This Boy's Life 1989, The Picador Books of Contemporary American Stories (ed.) 1993, In Pharaoh's Army: Memories of a Lost War 1994, The Vintage Book of Contemporary American Short Stories 1994, The Best American Short Stories 1994, The Night in Question (short stories) 1996, Writers Harvest 3 (ed.) 2000, Old School 2003, Our Story Begins (short stories) 2008. *Honours:* Hon. Fellow, Hertford Coll., Oxford 2000; St Lawrence Award for Fiction 1982, Rea Award for Short Story 1989, Whiting Foundation Award 1989, LA Times Book Prize for Biography 1989, Amb. Book Award 1990, Lila Wallace/Reader's Digest Award 1993, Lyndhurst Foundation Award 1994, Esquire-Volvo-Waterstones Award for Non-Fiction 1994, Award of Merit, American Acad. of Arts and Letters 2001. *Address:* English Department, Building 460, Room 218, Stanford University, Stanford, CA 94305-2087, USA (office). *Telephone:* (650) 723-0504 (office). *Fax:* (650) 725-0755 (office). *E-mail:* twolff@stanford.edu (office). *Website:* english.stanford.edu (office).

WOLKSTEIN, Diane, BA, MA; American writer and storyteller; b. 11 Nov. 1942, New York, NY; one d. *Education:* Smith Coll., Bank Street Coll. of Education. *Career:* host of radio show Stories from Many Lands with Diane Wolkstein (WNYC-Radio), New York 1967–; Instructor, Bank Street Coll. 1970–; Dir of Storytelling at The Statue of Hans Christian Andersen in Central Park, New York 1972–; teacher, New York Univ. 1983–2003, Sarah Lawrence Coll. 1984, New School for Social Research, New York 1989; Founding mem. and Dir New York City Storytelling Center, New York 1983–90; Dir of CelebrateStory Festival, New York 2007–; researched and performed the Asian epic 'Journey to the West' in India, Taiwan, China, and Australia; leader of many storytelling workshops; has performed world-wide, including at the British Museum, London, American Museum of Natural History and Avery Fisher Hall, New York, The Smithsonian Inst., Washington, DC, and in Taiwan and Australia; described as "The greatest storyteller in the western world" by Joseph Campbell; 22 June 2007 named Diane Wolkstein Day by New York City Mayor Michael Bloomberg. *Publications:* 24 books, including 8,000 Stones 1972, The Cool Ride in the Sky: A Black-American Folk Tale 1973, The Visit 1974, Squirrel's Song: A Hopi-Indian Story 1975, Lazy Stories 1976, The Red Lion: A Persian Sufi Tale 1977, The Magic Orange Tree and Other Haitian Folk Tales 1978, White Wave: A Tao Tale 1979, The Banza: A Haitian Folk Tale 1980, Inanna, Queen of Heaven and Earth: Her Stories and Hymns from Summer (with Samuel Noah Kramer) 1983, The Magic Wings: A Chinese Tale 1983, The Legend of Sleepy Hollow 1987, The First Love Stories 1991, Oom Razoom 1991, Little Mouse's Painting 1992, Step by Step 1994, Esther's Story 1996, White Wave 1996, Bouki Dances the Kokioko 1997, The Magic Orange Tree and Other Haitian Folktales 1997, The Glass Mountain 1999, The Day Ocean Came to Visit 2001, Treasures of the Heart: Holiday Stories that Reveal the Soul of Judaism 2003, Sunmother Wakes the World 2004; contrib. to periodicals and recordings. *Honours:* three Parent's Choice Gold Awards, two storytelling world awards, Excellence in Storytelling Award, Nat. Storytelling Asscn, Women Who Make a Difference Centennial Award, Smith Coll. *Address:* 10 Patchin Place, New York, NY 10011, USA (home). *Telephone:* (212) 929-6871 (office). *E-mail:* wolkstein

.publicity@gmail.com (home). *Website:* www.dianewolkstein.com; www.monkeykingepic.com; www.celebratestory.org.

WOLSTENCROFT, David; British writer. *Career:* writer and creator of 'Spooks' (BBC, on A&E Network as MI-5). *Publications:* novels: Good News, Bad News 2004, Contact Zero 2006. *Literary Agent:* c/o Jonny Geller, Curtis Brown Ltd, Haymarket House, 28–29 Haymarket, London, SW1Y 4SP, England. *Telephone:* (20) 7393-4400. *Fax:* (20) 7393-4401. *E-mail:* info@curtisbrown.co.uk. *Website:* www.curtisbrown.co.uk. *E-mail:* david@davidwolstencroft.com (office). *Website:* www.davidwolstencroft.com.

WOMACK, Peter, BA, PhD; British academic and writer; *Professor of Literature, University of East Anglia*; b. 27 Jan. 1952, Surrey. *Education:* Univ. of Oxford, Univ. of Edinburgh. *Career:* Lecturer, Univ. of East Anglia 1988–96, Sr Lecturer 1996, now Prof. of Literature. *Publications:* Ben Jonson 1986, Improvement and Romance 1989, English Drama: A Cultural History (with Simon Shepherd) 1996, English Renaissance Drama 2006; contributions: scholarly books and journals. *Address:* School of Literature, University of East Anglia, Faculty of Arts and Humanities, Norwich, Norfolk NR4 7TJ, England (office). *Telephone:* (1603) 592296 (office). *Fax:* (1603) 250434 (office). *E-mail:* p.womack@uea.ac.uk (office). *Website:* www.uea.ac.uk/lit (office).

WONG, Betty; American journalist; *Global Managing Editor, Reuters*; b. 1964. *Education:* New York Univ. *Career:* worked at The Wall Street Journal 1984–89; joined Reuters 1989, has held various positions including Americas Equities Ed., US company news Ed., Sr Wall Street Corresp., Deputy Financial Copy Desk Ed., Global Equities Ed. –2004, Man. Ed. and Head of Editorial Operations, Reuters America 2004–08, Global Managing Ed. Reuters 2008–; Founding mem. Reuters Editorial Diversity Group; mem. Bd Overseas Press Club Foundation, Knight-Bagehot fellowship program; mem. jury, Pulitzer Prize, Soc. of American Business Eds and Writers Award, Loeb Award; mem. Asian-American Journalists Asscn. *Address:* Reuters, 11 Wall Street, New York, NY 10005-1905, USA (office). *Telephone:* (212) 742-2190 (office). *Website:* www.reuters.com (office).

WOOD, Adrian John Bickersteth, CBE, MA, MPA, PhD; British economist; *Professor Emeritus of International Development, University of Oxford*; b. 25 Jan. 1946, Woking, Surrey, England; s. of the late John H. F. Wood and of Mary E. B. Brain (née Ottley); m. Joyce M. Teitz 1971; two d. *Education:* Bryanston School, King's Coll., Cambridge, Harvard Univ., USA. *Career:* Fellow, King's Coll. Cambridge 1969–77; Asst Lecturer, Lecturer, Univ. of Cambridge 1973–77; Economist, Sr Economist, IBRD 1977–85; Professorial Fellow, Inst. of Devt Studies, Univ. of Sussex 1985–2000; Chief Economist Dept for Int. Devt 2000–05; Prof. of Int. Devt, Univ. of Oxford 2005–11, Prof. Emer. 2011–; Harkness Fellowship 1967–69. *Publications:* A Theory of Profits 1975, A Theory of Pay 1978, Poverty and Human Development (with others) 1981, China: Long-Term Development Issues and Options (with others) 1985, North-South Trade, Employment and Inequality 1994. *Address:* Queen Elizabeth House, 3 Mansfield Road, Oxford, OX1 3TB, England (office). *Telephone:* (1865) 281837 (office). *Fax:* (1865) 281801 (office). *E-mail:* adrian.wood@qeh.ox.ac.uk (office). *Website:* www.qeh.ox.ac.uk (office).

WOOD, Charles Gerald, FRSL; British playwright and scriptwriter; b. 6 Aug. 1932, St. Peter Port, Guernsey; s. of John Edward Wood and Catherine Mae Wood (née Harris); m. Valerie Elizabeth Newman 1954; one s. one d. *Education:* King Charles I School, Kidderminster and Birmingham Coll. of Art. *Career:* corporal, 17/21st Lancers 1950–55; factory worker 1955–57; Stage Man., scenic artist, cartoonist, advertising artist 1957–59; Bristol Evening Post 1959–62; mem. Drama Advisory Panel, South Western Arts 1972–73; consultant to Nat. Film Devt Fund 1980–82; mem. Council BAFTA 1991–93. *Plays include:* Prisoner and Escort, Spare, John Thomas 1963, Meals on Wheels 1965, Don't Make Me Laugh 1966, Fill the Stage with Happy Hours 1967, Dingo 1967, H 1969, Welfare 1971, Veterans 1972, Jingo 1975, Has 'Washington' Legs? 1978, Red Star 1984, Across from the Garden of Allah 1986; adapted Pirandello's Man, Beast and Virtue 1989, The Mountain Giants 1993, Alexandre Dumas's The Tower 1995. *TV plays include:* Prisoner and Escort, Drill Pig, A Bit of a Holiday, A Bit of an Adventure, Love Lies Bleeding, Dust to Dust. *Screenplays include:* The Knack 1965, Help! 1965, How I Won the War 1967, The Charge of the Light Brigade 1968, The Long Day's Dying 1969, Cuba 1980, Wagner 1983, Red Monarch 1983, Puccini 1984, Tumbledown 1988, Shooting the Hero 1991, An Awfully Big Adventure 1993, England my England (with John Osborne) 1995, The Ghost Road 1996, Mary Stuart 1996, Iris (with Richard Eyre) 1999, Snow White in New York 2001. *TV series:* Don't Forget to Write 1986, My Family and Other Animals 1987, The Settling of the Sun 1987, Sharpe's Company 1994, Sharpe's Regiment 1996, Mute of Malice (Kavanagh QC) 1997, Sharpe's Waterloo 1997, Monsignor Renard 1999. *Publications:* (plays): Cockade 1965, Fill the Stage with Happy Hours 1967, Dingo 1967, H 1970, Veterans 1972, Has 'Washington' Legs? 1978, Tumbledown 1987, Man, Beast and Virtue 1990, The Giants of the Mountain 1994, The Tower 1995, Iris 2002. *Honours:* Evening Standard Drama Award 1963 1972, Screenwriters Guild Award 1965, Royal TV Soc. Award 1988, BAFTA Award 1988, Prix Italia 1988, Humanitas Award 2002. *Literary Agent:* London Management, 2–4 Noel Street, London, W1V 3RB, England. *E-mail:* charles@wood4760.fsnet.co.uk (home).

WOOD, Gordon S., PhD; American historian, academic and author; *Alva O. Way University Professor Emeritus, Brown University*; b. 27 Nov. 1933, Concord, Mass; m. Louise Wood; one s. two d. *Education:* Tufts Univ., Harvard Univ. *Career:* taught at Harvard Univ. and Univ. of Michigan; Faculty mem. Brown Univ. 1969–, Alva O. Way Univ. Prof., now Prof. Emer.; Pitt Prof., Univ. of Cambridge, UK 1982–83; Chair. Bd of Advisors, Nat. Historical Soc. 1973–; mem. Advisory Bd Northeastern Univ. Press 1989–2003, Advisory Cttee for the Papers of Thomas Jefferson 1990–, Bd of Eds, International Journal of the Classical Tradition 1994–, Admin. Bd for the Papers of Benjamin Franklin 1995–, Bd of Eds Oxford History of the Enlightenment, Bd of Trustees, Nat. Council of History Educ. 1996–2006, Advisory Bd of Gilder-Lehrman Inst. of American History 1996–; mem. American Historical Asscn, American Antiquarian Soc.; Fellow, American Acad. of Arts and Sciences, American Philosophical Soc. *Publications:* The Creation of the American Republic, 1776–1787 (Bancroft Prize, John H. Dunning Prize 1970) 1969, The Radicalism of the American Revolution (Pulitzer Prize in History 1993, Ralph Waldo Emerson Prize 1993) 1992, The Americanization of Benjamin Franklin (Julia Ward Howe Prize, Boston Authors Club 2005) 2004, Revolutionary Characters: What Made the Founders Different 2006, The Purpose of the Past: Reflections on the Uses of History 2008, Empire of Liberty: A History of the Early Republic, 1789–1815 (American History Book Prize 2010, Soc. of Cincinnatus Prize 2010) 2009, The Idea of America: Reflections on the Birth of the United States 2011; contrib. of articles and reviews to journals and New York Review of Books, The New Republic. *Honours:* Hon. DLit (LaTrobe Univ., Australia) 2001, Hon. LLD (Providence Coll.) 2007, Hon. DHumLitt (Washington and Lee Univ.) 2010, (Tufts Univ.) 2010, Hon. DLitt (Brown Univ.) 2010; Distinguished Visitor Award, Australian-American Education Foundation 1976, Douglass Adair Award 1984, Fraunces Tavern Museum Book Award 1992, Rhode Island Heritage Hall of Fame 2000, Julia Ward Howe Prize, Boston Authors Club 2005, Prize for History, New York Historical Soc. 2010, Nat. Humanities Medal 2010, Schlesinger Award for History 2011; numerous fellowships and endowments. *Address:* Department of History, Box N, Brown University, 79 Brown Street, Providence, RI 02912, USA (office). *Telephone:* (401) 863-2820 (office). *Fax:* (401) 863-2131 (office). *E-mail:* gordon_wood@brown.edu (office). *Website:* research.brown.edu/research/profile.php?id=10107 (office).

WOOD, Michael, BA, MA, PhD; British academic and writer; *Charles Barnwell Straut Professor of English and Comparative Literature, Princeton University*; b. 19 Aug. 1936, Lincoln, England; m. Elena Uribe 1967; two s. one d. *Education:* St John's College, Cambridge. *Career:* Fellow in French, St John's College, Cambridge 1961–64; Instructor, Columbia University 1964–66, Asst Prof. of English 1968–71, Assoc. Prof. of English 1971–74, Prof. of English and Comparative Literature 1974–82; Visiting Prof., National University of Mexico 1981–82; Prof. of English Literature, University of Exeter 1982–95; Charles Barnwell Straut Prof. of English and Prof. of Comparative Literature, Princeton Univ. 1995–; Visitor, Institute for Advanced Study, Princeton Univ. 2001–02; mem. American Acad. of Arts and Sciences 2003–, American Philosophical Soc. 2004–. *Publications:* Stendahl 1971, America in the Movies 1975, García Márquez: One Hundred Years of Solitude 1990, The Magician's Doubts: Nabokov and the Risks of Fiction 1994, Children of Silence: On Contemporary Fiction 1998, Franz Kafka 1998, Belle de Jour 2001, The Road to Delphi: The Life and Afterlife of Oracles 2003, Literature and the Taste of Knowledge 2005; contributions: reviews, quarterlies and journals. *Honours:* Guggenheim Fellowship 1972–73, National Endowment for the Humanities Fellowship 1980–81, FRSL 1992–, Leverhulme Trust Fellow 1993, Fellow, New York Institute for the Humanities 1994–, Senior Fellow, Society of Fellows, Princeton University 1999–2001, Howard T. Behrman Award for Achievement in the Humanities, Princeton Univ. 2002, President's Award for Distinguished Teaching, Princeton Univ. 2005, Sr Fellow, Nat. Humanities Center 2009. *Address:* 26 Alexander Street, Princeton, NJ 08540, USA (home).

WOOD, Michael; British journalist, broadcaster, film-maker, historian and writer; b. Manchester; m.; two d. *Education:* Oriel Coll., Oxford. *Career:* writer and presenter, over 80 TV series and documentaries on history, travel, politics and cultural history. *Television:* Saddam's Killing Fields, Darshan, The Sacred Way, Great Railway Journeys of the World 1981, River Journeys 1985, In Search of the Trojan War (PBS) 1985, Art of the Western World 1989, Legacy: In Search of the Origins of Civilization 1992, In the Footsteps of Alexander the Great (BBC) 1997, Hitler's Search for the Holy Grail 1999, Conquistadors (BBC2) 2000, In Search of Shakespeare (BBC2) 2003, In Search of Myths and Heroes (BBC2) 2005, Gilbert White – The Nature Man 2006, The Story of India 2007, Christina: A Medieval Life 2008, In Search of Beowulf 2009, Michael Wood's Story of England 2010. *Publications:* In Search of the Dark Ages 1981, Great Railway Journeys of the World 1981, In Search of the Trojan War 1985, World Atlas of Archaeology (ed.) 1985, Domesday: A Search for the Roots of England 1986, Legacy: A Search for the Origins of Civilization 1992, The Smile of Murugan: A South Indian Journey 1995, In the Footsteps of Alexander the Great: A Journey from Greece to Asia 1997, In Search of England 1999, Conquistadors 2000, In Search of Shakespeare 2003, In Search of Myths and Heroes 2005, India: An Epic Journey Across the Subcontinent 2007, The Story of England 2010; contrib. reviews and articles in Daily Telegraph, Evening Standard, Literary Review, Times, Guardian, Daily Express, Independent, Daily Mail, Observer, Newsday, Dialogue magazine. *Address:* c/o Maya Vision International, 3rd Floor, Kinghorn Street, London, EC1A 7HW, England (office). *Telephone:* (20) 7796-4842 (office). *Fax:* (20) 7796-4580 (office). *E-mail:* info@mayavisionint.com (office). *Website:* www.mayavisionint.com (office).

WOOD, Victoria, CBE, BA; British writer and comedian; b. 19 May 1953, d. of the late Stanley Wood and of Helen Wood; m. Geoffrey Durham 1980 (divorced); one d. one s. *Education:* Univ. of Birmingham. *Career:* singer and performer on TV and radio 1974–78; first play Talent, at Crucible Theatre, Sheffield 1978, TV production won three Nat. Drama Awards 1980; numerous tours. *TV includes:* Screenplay (writer) 1979, Talent 1979, Nearly a Happy Ending (writer) 1981, Happy Since I Met You 1981, Wood and Walters (series with Julie Walters) 1981–82, Victoria Wood As Seen on TV (first series, Broadcasting Press Guilds Award, BAFTA Award for Best Light Entertainment Programme and Performance Awards) 1985, (second series, BAFTA Award for Best Light Entertainment Programme Award) 1986, (Special, BAFTA Award for Best Light Entertainment Programme Award) 1987, An Audience With Victoria Wood (BAFTA Award for Best Light Entertainment Programme and Performance Awards) 1988, Victoria Wood 1989 (series), Julie Walters and Friends 1991, Victoria Wood's All Day Breakfast 1992, Victoria Wood Live in Your Own Home 1995, Pat and Margaret 1995, Dinnerladies (two series) (British Comedy Award for Best TV Comedy 2000, Montreux Festival Press Prize for first series) 1998–2000, Don't Panic! The Dad's Army Story 2000, Victoria Wood with All the Trimmings 2000, Big Fat Documentary 2004, Victoria Wood: Moonwalking 2004, Housewife, 49 (BAFTA Awards for Best Actress, Best Single Drama 2007) 2006, Victoria's Empire 2007, Ballet Shoes 2007, Victoria Wood's Midlife Christmas 2009, Eric and Ernie 2010. *Stage appearances include:* Good Fun (writer, musical) 1980, Funny Turns 1982, Lucky Bag 1984, Victoria Wood 1987, Victoria Wood Up West 1990, Victoria Wood Live 1997, Victoria Wood – At It Again 2001, Acorn Antiques: The Musical, Haymarket 2005, nat. tour 2006. *Film:* The Wind in the Willows. *Publications:* Victoria Wood Song Book 1984, Up to You, Porky 1985, Barmy 1987, Mens Sana in Thingummy Doodah 1990, Chunky 1996, Victoria on Victoria 2007. *Honours:* Hon. DLitt (Lancaster) 1989, (Sunderland) 1994, (Bolton) 1995, (Birmingham) 1996; Variety Club BBC Personality of the Year 1987; Top Female Comedy Performer, British Comedy Awards 1996, BAFTA Tribute Award 2005. *Address:* c/o Phil McIntyre, 35 Soho Square, London, W1V 5DG, England. *Telephone:* (20) 7439-2270.

WOODEN, Rodney John; British playwright; b. 16 July 1945, London, England. *Career:* mem. PEN International. *Plays:* High Brave Boy 1990, Woyzeck (adaptation of Büchner's play) 1990, Your Home in the West 1991, Anti/Gone 1992, Medea Media 1993, Smoke 1993, Moby Dick 1993, One Hundred Feet 1993, Sorry Island 1995, Diamond 1996, Leviathan 1997, Chorus 1999, State of Coma 2000, The Leningrad Siege 2006. *Honours:* First Prize, Mobil International Playwriting Competition 1990, John Whiting Award 1991, Mobil Writer-in-Residence Bursary 1991–92. *Literary Agent:* Micheline Steinberg Associates, 104 Great Portland Street, London, W1W 6PE, England. *Telephone:* (20) 7631-1310. *Fax:* (20) 7631-1146. *E-mail:* info@steinplays.com. *Website:* www.steinplays.com.

WOODFORD, Peggy, MA; British writer; b. 19 Sept. 1937, Assam, India; s. of Ronald Curtis Woodford and Ruth Mahy Laine; m. Walter Aylen 1967; three d. *Education:* St Anne's Coll., Oxford. *Career:* mem. Soc. of Authors, RSL. *Publications:* Abraham's Legacy 1963, Please Don't Go 1972, Backwater War 1974, Mozart: His Life and Times 1977, Schubert: His Life and Times 1978, Rise of the Raj 1978, See You Tomorrow 1979, The Girl With a Voice 1981, Love Me, Love Rome 1984, Misfits 1984, Monster in Our Midst 1987, Out of the Sun 1990, Blood and Mortar 1994, Cupid's Tears 1995, On the Night 1997, Jane's Story 1998, One Son is Enough 2000. *Address:* 24 Fairmount Road, London, SW2 2BL, England. *Website:* www.peggywoodford.com.

WOODING, Chris, BA; British science fiction and fantasy writer; b. 1977, Leicester. *Education:* Univ. of Sheffield. *Publications include:* juvenile: Catchman 1998, Broken Sky series 1999, Kerosene 1999, Endgame 2000, The Haunting Of Alaizabel Cray (Smarties Book Prize) 2001, Poison 2003, Storm Thief 2006, The Fade 2008, Malice 2009, Havoc 2010; adult fiction: Braided Path trilogy: The Weavers of Saramyr 2003, The Skein of Lament 2004, The Ascendancy Veil 2005, Tale of Ketty Jay trilogy: Retribution Falls 2009, The Black Lung Captain 2010, The Iron Jackal 2011. *Address:* c/o Scholastic Children's Books, Euston House, 24 Eversholt Street, London, NW1 1DB, England. *E-mail:* scbenquiries@scholastic.co.uk. *Website:* www.chriswooding.com.

WOODRELL, Daniel, BA, MFA; American author; b. 4 March 1953, Springfield, Mo.; m. Katie Estill. *Education:* Univ. of Kansas, Iowa Writers' Workshop. *Career:* grew up in northern Mo.; dropped out of high school to join US Marines aged 17; spent a year on a Michener Fellowship. *Publications:* Under the Bright Lights 1986, Woe to Live On (adapted into a film Ride with the Devil by Ang Lee 1999) 1987, Muscle for the Wing 1988, The Ones You Do 1992, Give Us a Kiss: A Country Noir 1996, Tomato Red (PEN Center USA Award for Fiction 1999) 1998, The Death of Sweet Mister (Clifton Fadiman Medal, The Center for Fiction, Sponsored by Reba and Dave Williams 2011) 2001, Winter's Bone (adapted into an Oscar-nominated film of the same name 2010, Sundance Film Festival Award for top dramatic film 2010) 2006. *Address:* c/o Hachette Book Group, 3 Center Plaza, Suite G, Boston, MA 02108-2083, USA. *Telephone:* (617) 227-0730. *E-mail:* cs.international@hbgusa.com. *Website:* www.hachettebookgroup.com.

WOODWARD, Robert (Bob) Upshur, BA; American journalist and writer; *Associate Editor, The Washington Post;* b. 26 March 1943, Geneva, Ill.; s. of Alfred Woodward and Jane Upshur; m. Elsa Walsh 1989; two c. *Education:* Yale Univ. *Career:* reporter, Montgomery Co. (Md) Sentinel 1970–71; reporter, Washington Post 1971–78, Metropolitan Ed. 1979–81, Asst Man. Ed. 1981–2008, Assoc. Ed. 2008–. *Publications:* All the President's Men (with Carl Bernstein) 1973, The Final Days (with Carl Bernstein) 1976, The Brethren (with Scott Armstrong) 1979, Wired 1984, Veil: The Secret Wars of the CIA 1987, The Commanders 1991, The Man Who Would Be President (with David S. Broder) 1991, The Agenda: Inside the Clinton White House 1994, The Choice 1996, Shadow: Five Presidents and the Legacy of Watergate 1999, Maestro, Greenspan's Fed and the American Boom 2000, Bush at War... Inside the Bush White House 2002, Plan of Attack 2004, The Secret Man 2005, State of Denial: Bush at War, Part III 2006, The War Within: A Secret White House History 2006–2008 2008, Obama's Wars 2010. *Honours:* Pulitzer Prize (jtly) 1972. *Address:* The Washington Post, 1150 15th Street, NW, Washington, DC 20071, USA (office). *E-mail:* woodwardb@washpost.com (office).

WOODWARD, Gerard, MA; British poet and writer; b. Dec. 1961, London. *Education:* LSE, Manchester Univ. *Career:* creative writing lecturer, Bath Spa Univ. 2004–. *Publications:* poetry: Householder 1991, After the Deafening 1994, Island to Island 1999, Healing Fountain 2003, We Were Pedestrians 2005; fiction: August 2001, I'll Go to Bed at Noon 2004, A Curious Earth 2007, Caravan Thieves (short stories) 2008, Nourishment 2010. *Honours:* Somerset Maugham Award 1992. *Address:* c/o Chatto & Windus Ltd, 20 Vauxhall Bridge Road, London, SW1V 2SA, England (office).

WOODWORTH, Steven Edward, BA, PhD; American academic and writer; *Professor of History, Texas Christian University;* b. 28 Jan. 1961, Akron, Ohio; m. Leah Dawn Bunke 1983; seven c. *Education:* Southern Illinois Univ. at Carbondale, Univ. of Hamburg, Rice Univ. *Career:* Adjunct Instructor, Houston Community Coll. 1984–87; Instructor in History, Bartlesville Wesleyan Coll., Oklahoma 1987–89; Asst Prof. of History, Toccoa Falls Coll., Georgia 1989–97; Asst Prof. of History, Texas Christian Univ. 1997–2000, Assoc. Prof. 2000–05, Prof. of History 2005–; mem. Grady Mcwhiney Research Foundation, American Historical Asscn, Org. of American Historians, Southern Historical Asscn, Org. of Mil. Historians, Soc. of Civil War Historians. *Publications:* Jefferson Davis and His Generals: The Failure of Confederate Command in the West 1990, The Essentials of United States History, 1841 to 1877: Westward Expansion and the Civil War 1990, The Essentials of United States History, 1500 to 1789: From Colony to Republic 1990, The Advanced Placement Examination in United States History 1990, Davis and Lee at War 1995, Leadership and Command in the American Civil War (ed.), Vol. I 1995, The American Civil War: A Handbook of Literature and Research (ed.) 1996, Six Armies in Tennessee: The Chickamauga and Chattanooga Campaigns 1998, Civil War Generals in Defeat (ed.) 1999, No Band of Brothers: Problems in the Rebel High Command 1999, The Human Tradition in the Civil War and Reconstruction (ed.) 2000, Cultures in Conflict: The American Civil War 2000, A Scythe of Fire: The Civil War Story of the Eighth Georgia Regiment 2001, Grant's Lieutenants from Cairo to Vicksburg 2001, The Religious World of Civil War Soldiers 2001, Beneath a Northern Sky: A Short History of the Gettysburg Campaign 2003, The Oxford Atlas of Civil War 2004, Nothing but Victory: The Army of the Tennessee, 1861–1865 2005, Shiloh: A Battlefield Guide 2006, Decision in the Heartland 2008, Sherman 2009, Manifest Destinies: America's Westward Expansion and the Road to the Civil War 2010; contribs to books and professional journals. *Honours:* Fletcher Pratt Awards 1991, 1996, Grady McWhiney Award 2002. *Address:* History Department, Texas Christian University, Reed Hall 307, Fort Worth, TX 76129, USA (office). *Telephone:* (817) 257-6293 (office). *E-mail:* S.Woodworth@tcu.edu (office). *Website:* personal.tcu.edu/swoodworth (office).

WORSLEY, Dale; American writer and dramatist; b. 3 Nov. 1948, Baton Rouge, LA; m. Elizabeth Fox 1991. *Education:* Southwestern Univ., Memphis. *Career:* currently Adjunct Asst Prof. of Creative Writing, Columbia Univ.; mem. Dramatists' Guild. *Publications:* The Focus Changes of August Previco 1980, The Art of Science Writing 1989, Hoy 1992; plays: Cold Harbor 1983, The Last Living Newspaper 1993. *Honours:* NEA Fellowship in Fiction 1986, NEA Fellowship in Playwriting 1989. *Address:* 61 Eastern Parkway, Brooklyn, NY 11238, USA (home). *Telephone:* (718) 789-6200 (home).

WORSTHORNE, Sir Peregrine Gerard, Kt, MA; British journalist; b. 22 Dec. 1923, London; s. of Col A. Koch de Gooreynd and the late Baroness Norman; m. 1st Claudia Bertrand de Colasse 1950 (died 1990); one d. one steps.; m. 2nd Lady Lucinda Lambton 1991. *Education:* Stowe School, Peterhouse, Cambridge and Magdalen Coll., Oxford. *Career:* mem. editorial staff, Glasgow Herald 1946–48; mem. editorial staff, The Times 1948–50, Washington corresp. 1950–52, leader writer 1952–55; leader writer, Daily Telegraph 1955–61; Deputy Ed. Sunday Telegraph 1961–76, Assoc. Ed. 1976–86, Ed. 1986–89, Ed. Comment Section 1989–91; columnist, The Spectator 1997–, The New Statesman. *Publications:* The Socialist Myth 1972, Peregrinations 1980, By The Right 1987, Tricks of Memory (memoirs) 1993, In Defence of Aristocracy 2004. *Honours:* Granada TV Journalist of the Year 1981. *Address:* The Old Rectory, Hedgerley, Bucks., SL2 3UY, England (home). *Telephone:* (1753) 646167 (home). *Fax:* (1753) 646914 (home). *E-mail:* therectory.hedgerley@virgin.net (office).

WORTIS, Avi, (Avi), BA, MA, MS; American children's author; b. 23 Dec. 1937, New York, NY; m. 1st Joan Gabriner 1963 (divorced 1982); two s.; m. 2nd Coppelia Kahn 1983; one step-s. *Education:* Univ. of Wisconsin at Madison, Columbia Univ. *Career:* Librarian, New York Public Library 1962–70, Trenton State Coll., NJ 1970–86; conducted workshops and seminars with children, parents and educators; mem. Authors' Guild. *Publications:* Things That Sometimes Happen 1970, Snail Tale 1972, No More Magic 1975, Captain Grey 1977, Emily Upham's Revenge 1978, Night Journeys 1979, Man From the Sky 1980, History of Helpless Harry 1980, A Place Called Ugly 1981, Who Stole the Wizard of Oz? 1981, Sometimes I Think I Hear My Name 1982, Shadrach's Crossing 1983, Devil's Race 1984, SOR Losers 1984, The Fighting Ground 1984, Bright Shadow 1985, Wolf Rider 1986, Romeo and Juliet (Together and Alive!) At Last 1987, Something Upstairs 1988, The Man Who Was Poe 1989, True Confessions of Charlotte Doyle 1990, Windcatcher 1991, Nothing But the Truth 1991, Blue Heron 1992, Who Was That Masked Man, Anyway? 1992, Punch With Judy 1993, City of Light, City of Dark 1993, The Bird, the Frog, and the Light 1994, Smuggler's Island 1994, The Barn 1994, Tom, Babette & Simon 1995, Poppy 1995, Escape From Home 1996, Finding Providence 1996, Beyond the Western Sea 1996, Something Upstairs: A Tale of Ghosts 1997, What Do Fish Have to Do With Anything and Other Stories 1997, Finding Providence: The Story of Roger Williams 1997, Perloo the Bold 1998, Poppy and Rye: A Tale from Dimwood Forest 1998, Abigail Takes the Wheel 1999, Midnight Magic 1999, Ragweed 1999, Amanda Joins the Circus 1999, Second Sight 1999, Ereth's Birthday 2000, The Christmas Rat 2000, Don't You Know There's a War On? 2001, Prairie School 2001, The Good Dog 2001, The Secret School 2001, Crispin: The Cross of Lead 2002, Silent Movie 2003, The Mayor of Central Park 2003, Never Mind 2004, The End of the Beginning 2004, Poppy's Return 2005, The Book Without Words 2005, Strange Happenings 2006, Crispin: At the Edge of the World 2006, The Traitors' Gate 2007, Iron Thunder 2007, The Seer of Shadows 2008, A Beginning, a Middle and an End 2008, Poppy and Ereth 2009; contributions: Library Journal. *Honours:* American Library Asscn Notable Book Awards 1984, 1991, 1992, 1993, 1995, 1996, One of the Best Books of the Year Awards, Library of Congress 1989, 1990, Newbery Honor Book Awards 1991, 1992; many others. *Address:* 859 South York Street, Denver, CO 80207, USA (office). *Website:* www.avi-writer.com.

WOUK, Herman, AB; American writer and dramatist; b. 27 May 1915, New York, NY; s. of Abraham Isaac Wouk and Esther Levine; m. Betty Sarah Brown 1945; three s. (one deceased). *Education:* Columbia Univ. *Career:* radio scriptwriter for leading comedians, New York 1935–41; presidential consultant to US Treasury 1941; served in USNR 1942–46; Visiting Prof. of English, Yeshiva Univ., New York 1952–57; Trustee, Coll. of the Virgin Islands 1961–69; mem. Authors' Guild, USA, Authors' League, Center for Book Nat. Advisory Bd, Library of Congress, Advisory Council, Center for US –China Arts Exchange. *Publications:* fiction: The Man in the Trench Coat 1941, Aurora Dawn 1947, The City Boy 1948, Slattery's Hurricane 1949, The Caine Mutiny 1951, Marjorie Morningstar 1955, Slattery's Hurricane 1956, Youngblood Hawke 1961, Don't Stop the Carnival 1965, The Lomokome Papers 1968, The Winds of War (also TV screenplay) 1971, War and Remembrance (also TV screenplay) 1978, Inside, Outside 1985, The Hope 1993, The Glory 1994, A Hole in Texas 2004, The Language God Talks: On Science and Religion 2010; plays: The Traitor 1949, Modern Primitive 1951, The Caine Mutiny Court-Martial 1953, Nature's Way 1957; non-fiction: This is My God: The Jewish Way of Life 1959, The Will to Live on: The Resurgence of Jewish Heritage 2000. *Honours:* Hon. LHD (Yeshiva Univ.); Hon. DLitt (Clark Univ.), (George Washington Univ.) 2001; Hon. DLitt (American Int. Coll.) 1979; Hon. PhD (Bar Ilan) 1990, (Hebrew Univ.) 1997; Hon. DST (Trinity Coll.) 1998; Pulitzer Prize for Fiction 1952, Columbia Univ. Medal for Excellence, Alexander Hamilton Medal, Columbia Univ. 1980, Ralph Waldo Emerson Award, Int. Platform Asscn 1981, Univ. of Calif., Berkeley Medal 1984, Yad Vashem Kazetnik Award 1990, USN Memorial Foundation Lone Sailor Award 1987, Washingtonian Book Award (for Inside, Outside) 1986, American Acad. of Achievement Golden Plate Award 1986, Bar Ilan Univ. Guardian of Zion Award 1998, Univ. of California at San Diego Medal 1998, Jewish Book Council Lifetime Literary Achievement Award 2000. *Literary Agent:* BSW Literary Agency, 303 Crestview Drive, Palm Springs, CA 92264, USA.

WRIGHT, Alexis; Australian writer; m.; two d. *Education:* Univ. of Western Sydney. *Career:* Aboriginal writer and political activist and researcher from the Waanyi nation. *Publications:* fiction: Plains of Promise 2000, Carpentaria (Miles Franklin Award, Australian Literature Soc. Gold Medal, Victorian Premier's Award for Fiction, Queensland Premier's Award for Fiction, ABIA Literary Fiction Book of the Year 2007) 2006; non-fiction: Grog War. *Honours:* Yarramundi Research Scholarship, Univ. of Western Sydney. *Address:* c/o Giramondo Publishing Company, POB 752, Artarmon, NSW 1570, Australia (office). *E-mail:* books@giramondopublishing.com (office). *Website:* www.giramondopublishing.com (office).

WRIGHT, Amos Jasper, III, BA, MLS; American medical librarian, writer and poet; *Associate Professor of Anesthesiology, University of Alabama at Birmingham*; b. 3 March 1952, Gadsden, Ala; s. of Amos Jasper Wright Jr and Carolyn Shores Wright; m. Margaret Dianne Vargo 1980; one s. one d. *Education:* Auburn Univ., Univ. of Alabama. *Career:* Assoc. Prof. of Anesthesiology, Univ. of Alabama at Birmingham School of Medicine; mem. Anaesthesia History Asscn. *Publications:* Frozen Fruit (poems) 1978, Right Now I Feel Like Robert Johnson (poems) 1981, Criminal Activity in the Deep South, 1800–1930 1989; contribs to medical journals, anthologies, reviews, quarterlies, and magazines. *Address:* 119 Pintail Drive, Pelham, AL 35124 (home); University of Alabama at Birmingham School of Medicine, Department of Anesthesiology, Jefferson Tower 965, 619 South 19th Street, Birmingham, AL 35249-6810, USA (office). *Telephone:* (205) 975-0158 (office). *Fax:* (205) 975-5963 (office). *E-mail:* ajwright@uab.edu (office). *Website:* medicine.uab.edu/anesthesiology/education/35465 (office).

WRIGHT, Anthony David, BA, MA, DPhil, FRHistS; British academic and writer; *Professor of Ecclesiastical History, University of Leeds*; b. 9 June 1947, Oxford, England. *Education:* Merton Coll., Oxford, British School, Rome, Brasenose Coll., Oxford. *Career:* Lecturer, Univ. of Leeds 1974–92, Sr Lecturer in History 1992–2001, Reader in Ecclesiastical History 2001–11, Prof. of Ecclesiastical History 2011–; Visiting Fellow, Univ. of Edinburgh 1983, Jesuit Historical Inst., Rome 2002; mem. Accad. di San Carlo, Ecclesiastical History Soc. *Publications:* The Counter-Reformation: Catholic Europe and the Non-Christian World 1982 (revised edn 2005), Baronio Storico e la Controriforma (with Romeo De Maio, L. Gulia, and A. Mazzacane) 1982, Catholicism and Spanish Society Under the Reign of Philip II, 1555–1598, and Philip III, 1598–1621 1991, The Early Modern Papacy: From the Council of Trent to the French Revolution 1564–1789 2000, The Divisions of French Catholicism, 1629–1645 – 'The Parting of the Ways' 2011; contrib. to scholarly books and journals. *Address:* School of History, University of Leeds, Leeds, LS2 9JT, England (office). *Telephone:* (113) 343-3586 (office). *Fax:* (113) 234-2759 (office). *E-mail:* a.d.wright@leeds.ac.uk (office). *Website:* www.leeds.ac.uk/history (office).

WRIGHT, Carolyn D., BA, MFA; American poet and academic; *Professor of English and Creative Writing, Brown University*; b. 6 Jan. 1949, Mountain Home, Ark.; m. Forrest Gander 1983; one s. *Education:* Univ. of Memphis, Univ. of Arkansas. *Career:* Prof. of English and Creative Writing, Brown Univ. 1983–; State Poet of Rhode Island 1994–; mem. PEN, New England, Council Mem. *Publications:* Terrorism 1979, Translations of the Gospel Back Into Tongues 1981, Further Adventures with God 1986, String Light 1991, Just Whistle 1993, The Lost Roads Project: A Walk-in Book of Arkansas 1994, The Reader's Map of Arkansas 1994, Tremble 1996, Deepstep Come Shining 1998, Steal Away: Selected and New Poems 2002, One Big Self: Prisoners of Louisiana 2003, Cooling Time: An American Poetry Vigil 2005, Rising, Falling, Hovering (Griffin Poetry Prize 2009) 2008, 40 Watts 2009, One With Others 2010; contributions: American Letters and Commentary, BRICK, Conjunctions, Sulfur. *Honours:* National Endowment for the Arts Fellowships 1981, 1987, Witter Bynner Prize for Poetry 1986, Guggenheim Fellowship 1987, Mary Ingraham Bunting Fellowship 1987, General Electric Award for Younger Writers 1988, Whiting Writers Award 1989, Rhode Island Governor's Award for the Arts 1990, Lila Wallace/Reader's Digest Writers Award 1992, University of Arkansas Distinguished Alumni Award 1998, Lannan Literary Award 1999, Artist Award, Foundation for Contemporary Performance Art 1999, Lange-Taylor Prize, Center for Documentary Studies 2000, Macarthur Fellowship 2004. *Address:* 351 Nayatt Road, Barrington, RI 02806, USA (home). *E-mail:* carolyn_wright@brown.edu (office).

WRIGHT, Charles Penzel, BA, MFA; American poet, writer and academic; b. 25 Aug. 1935, Pickwick Dam, Tenn.; m. Holly McIntire 1969; one s. *Education:* Davidson Coll., Univ. of Iowa, Univ. of Rome. *Career:* mem. Faculty, Univ. of California, Irvine 1966–83, Univ. of Virginia 1983–; mem. Acad. of American Poets (mem. Bd of Chancellors 1999–2002), American Acad. of Arts and Letters, Fellowship of Southern Writers, American Acad. of Arts and Sciences, PEN American Centre. *Publications:* Grave of the Right Hand 1970, Hard Freight 1973, Bloodlines 1975, China Trace 1977, Southern Cross 1981, Country Music 1982, The Other Side of the River 1984, Zone Journals 1988, The World of the 10,000 Things 1990, Chickamauga 1995, Black Zodiac (Pulitzer Prize for Poetry 1998) 1997, Appalachia 1998, Negative Blue: Selected Later Poems 2000, A Short History of the Shadow, Snake Eyes 2004, Buffalo Years 2004, Scar Tissue 2006, Littlefoot 2007, Sestets 2009, Outtakes (with Eric Appleby) 2010, Bye-and-Bye: Selected Late Poems 2011; contrib. to numerous journals and magazines. *Honours:* Acad. of American Poets Edgar Allan Poe Award 1976, PEN Trans. Award 1979, Nat. Book Award for Poetry 1983, Brandeis Book Critics Circle Award 1998, Critics Award 1999, Artico Fattore Poetry Prize, Italy 1999, Griffin Int. Poetry Prize, Canada 2001, Leoncino d'Oro, Commune di Pistoia, Italy. *Address:* 940 Locust Avenue, Charlottesville, VA 22901, USA (home).

WRIGHT, Donald Richard, BA, MA, PhD; American historian and academic; *Distinguished Teaching Professor of History Emeritus, State University of New York at Cortland*; b. 3 Aug. 1944, Richmond, Ind.; s. of Richard Marion Wright and Wilma Sprong Wright; m. 1st Olwen Twyman 1969 (divorced 1987); two s.; m. 2nd Marilou Briggs 1990 (died 1997); m. 3rd Doris DeLuca 2004. *Education:* De Pauw Univ., Indiana Univ., Bloomington. *Career:* served as Capt., USAF 1968–72; Editorial Asst, American Historical Review 1975–76; Asst Prof., State Univ. of NY (SUNY) at Cortland 1976–79, Assoc. Prof. 1979–84, Dept Head 1983–85, Prof. 1984–90, Distinguished Teaching Prof. of History 1990–2007, Prof. Emer. 2007–; presenter, summer workshops 1980–95; Collector, Curator, Nat. Museum of the Gambia, Banjul 1982; Lead Scholar, Alabama Humanities Foundation Inst. 1994; Visiting Lecturer, History Dept, Univ. of Witwatersrand, Johannesburg, S Africa 2000; Scholar-in-Residence, Rockefeller Foundation Study and Conf. Center, Bellagio, Italy 2003; Mark W. Clark Distinguished Visiting Chair of History, The Citadel 2005–06; mem. American Historical Asscn, Mande Studies Asscn; Fellow, Nat. Endowment for the Humanities 1982–83. *Publications:* The Early History of Niumi: Settlement and Foundation of a Mandinka State on the Gambia River 1977, Oral Traditions from the Gambia, Vol. I: Mandinka Griots 1979, Vol. II: Family Elders 1980, Muslim Peoples (contrib.) 1984, What to Teach about Africa: A Guide for Secondary Teachers 1990, African Americans in the Colonial Era: From African Origins through the American Revolution 1990, 2000, 2010, African Americans in the Early Republic, 1789–1831 1993,

The World and a Very Small Place in Africa 1997, 2004, 2010, The Atlantic World: A History, 1400–1888 (co-author) 2007; contrib. to books, articles and reviews to journals, including Journal of American Ethnic History, American Heritage, Journal of General Education, African Economic History, Africana Journal, History in Africa, American Historical Review, Journal of Southern History. *Honours:* Air Force Commendation Medal; Fulbright Fellow 1974–75, SUNY Chancellor's Award for Excellence in Teaching 1989, SUNY Outstanding Research Fellow 2006. *Address:* 4355 Locust Avenue, Homer, NY 13077-9476, USA. *E-mail:* wrightd21@gmail.com.

WRIGHT, George Thaddeus, BA, MA, PhD; American academic, writer and poet; *Regents' Professor Emeritus, University of Minnesota*; b. 17 Dec. 1925, Staten Island, NY; m. Jerry Honeywell 1955. *Education:* Columbia Coll., Columbia Univ., Univ. of Geneva, Univ. of California. *Career:* teaching asst 1954–55, Lecturer 1956–57, Univ. of California; Visiting Asst Prof., New Mexico Highlands Univ. 1957; Instructor-Asst Prof., Univ. of Kentucky 1957–60; Asst Prof., San Francisco State Coll. 1960–61; Assoc. Prof., Univ. of Tennessee 1961–68; Fulbright Lecturer, Univ. of Aix-Marseilles 1964–66, Univ. of Thessaloniki 1977–78; Visiting Lecturer, Univ. of Nice 1965; Prof. 1968–89, Chair English Dept 1974–77, Regents' Prof. 1989–93, Regents' Prof. Emeritus 1993–, Univ. of Minnesota; mem. Minnesota Humanities Comission 1985–88, MLA, Shakespeare Asscn of America. *Publications:* The Poet in the Poem: The Personae of Eliot, Yeats and Pound 1960, W. H. Auden 1969, Shakespeare's Metrical Art 1988, Aimless Life: Poems 1961–1995 1999, Hearing the Measures: Shakespearean and Other Inflections 2002; editor: Seven American Literary Stylists from Poe to Mailer: An Introduction 1973; contrib. articles, reviews, poems and translations in many periodicals and books. *Honours:* Guggenheim Fellowship 1981–82, Nat. Endowment for the Humanities Fellowship 1984–85, MLA William Riley Parker Prizes 1974, 1981, Robert Fitzgerald Prosody Award 2002. *Address:* 2617 W Crown King Drive, Tucson, AZ 85741-2569, USA (home). *Telephone:* (520) 575-1130 (home). *E-mail:* twright@earthlink.net (home).

WRIGHT, Jay, MA; American poet and dramatist; b. 25 May 1934, Albuquerque, NM. *Education:* Univ. of California, Berkeley, Union Theological Seminary, New York, Rutgers Univ. *Career:* Hodder Fellow, Princeton Univ. 1970; Joseph Compton Creative Writing Fellow, Dundee Univ. 1972; Fellow, American Acad. of Arts and Sciences. *Publications:* The Homecoming Singer 1971, Soothsayers and Omens 1976, Dimensions of History 1976, The Double Invention of Komo 1980, Explications/Interpretations 1984, Selected Poems of Jay Wright 1987, Elaine's Book 1988, Boleros 1991, Transfigurations: Collected Poems 2000, Music's Mask and Measure 2007, The Guide Signs, Book One 2007, Book Two 2007, Polynomials and Pollen 2008, The Presentable Art of Reading Absence 2008. *Honours:* American Acad. and Inst. of Arts and Letters Award, Guggenheim Fellowship, MacArthur Fellowship, Ingram Merrill Foundation Award, NEA grant, Acad. of American Poets Fellowship 1996, Lannan Literary Award for Poetry 2000, L. L. Winship/PEN Award 2001, Anisfield-Wolf Lifetime Achievement Award 2002, Bollingen Prize for American Poetry 2005. *Address:* PO Box 381, Bradford, VT 05033, USA (home).

WRIGHT, Karen Jocelyn, MA, MBA, FRSA; American editor and journalist; b. 15 Nov. 1950, New York; d. of Louis David Wile and Grace Carlin Wile; m. 1981; two d. *Education:* Brandeis Univ., Univ. of Cambridge and London Grad. School of Business Studies, UK. *Career:* Founder and Owner Hobson Gallery, Cambridge 1981–87; co-f. (with Peter Fuller) Modern Painters magazine 1987, Ed. 1990–2006, Ed.-at-Large 2006–; co-f. (with David Bowie, Sir Timothy Sainsbury and Bernard Jacobson) 21 Publishing 1997; mem. Asscn Int. des Critiques d'Art. *Publications:* The Penguin Book of Art Writing (co-ed.) 1998, Colour for Kosovo (ed.) 1999, The Grove Book of Art Writing 2000, Colour 2003; contrib. to Independent on Sunday. *Address:* 21 Publishing, Unit 204, Buspace Studios, Conlan Street, London, W10 5AP (office); 39 Portland Road, London, W11 4LH, England (home). *Telephone:* (20) 8964-1113 (21 Publishing) (office). *Fax:* (20) 8964-9993 (21 Publishing) (office). *E-mail:* info@21publishing.com (office). *Website:* www.21publishing.com (office); www.modernpainters.co.uk (office).

WRIGHT, Nicholas; British playwright; b. 5 July 1940, Cape Town, South Africa. *Education:* London Acad. of Music and Dramatic Art. *Career:* Literary Man., Nat. Theatre, London 1987, Assoc. Dir 1992. *Publications:* Treetops 1978, The Gorky Brigade 1979, One Fine Day 1980, The Crimes of Vautrin (after Balzac) 1983, The Custom of the Country 1983, The Desert Air 1984, Six Characters in Search of an Author (after Pirandello) 1987, Mrs Klein 1988, Thérèse Raquin (after Zola) 1990, Essays 1992, Cressida 1999, Vincent in Brixton 2002, Changing Stages (with Richard Eyre) 2002, The Little Prince (libretto) 2003, His Dark Materials (after Philip Pullman) 2003, Three Sisters (after Chekhov) 2003, Man on the Moon (libretto) 2006, The Reporter 2007, He's Talking 2007, Rattigan's Nijinsky 2011, The Last of the Duchess 2011, Travelling Light 2012. *Address:* 2 St Charles Place, London, W10 6EG, England.

WRIGHT, Rt Rev. Nicholas Thomas, BA, MA, DPhil, DD; British theologian and Anglican bishop; *Bishop of Durham;* b. 1 Dec. 1948, Morpeth, Northumberland; s. of Nicholas Irwin Wright and Rosemary Wright (née Forman); m. Margaret Elizabeth Anne Fiske 1971; two s. two d. *Education:* Sedbergh School, Exeter Coll., Oxford, Wycliffe Hall, Oxford. *Career:* ordained deacon 1975, priest 1976; Jr Research Fellow, Merton Coll. Oxford 1975–78, Jr Chaplain 1976–78; Fellow and Chaplain Downing Coll. Cambridge 1978–81; Asst Prof. of New Testament Studies, McGill Univ., Montreal and Hon. Prof., Montreal Diocesan Theological Coll., Canada 1981–86; Lecturer in Theology, Univ. of Oxford and Fellow, Tutor and Chaplain, Worcester Coll. Oxford 1986–93; Dean of Lichfield 1994–99; Canon Theologian of Coventry Cathedral 1992–99; Canon Theologian of Westminster 2000–03; Bishop of Durham 2003–; Fellow Inst. for Christian Studies, Toronto 1992–; mem. Doctrine Comm., Church of England 1979–81, 1989–95, Lambeth Comm. 2004; regular broadcasts on TV and radio. *Publications include:* Small Faith, Great God 1978, The Work of John Frith 1983, The Epistles of Paul to the Colossians and to Philemon 1987, The Glory of Christ in the New Testament (co-ed.) 1987, The Interpretation of the New Testament 1861–1986 (co-author) 1988, The Climax of the Covenant 1991, New Tasks for a Renewed Church 1992, The Crown and the Fire 1992, The New Testament and the People of God 1992, Who Was Jesus? 1992, Following Jesus 1994, Jesus and the Victory of God 1996, The Lord and His Prayer 1996, What Saint Paul Really Said 1997, For All God's Worth 1997, Reflecting the Glory 1998, The Meaning of Jesus (co-author) 1999, The Myth of the Millennium 1999, Romans and the People of God (co-ed.) 1999, Holy Communion for Amateurs 1999, The Challenge of Jesus 2000, Twelve Months of Sundays, Year C 2000, Easter Oratorio (co-author) 2000, Twelve Months of Sundays, Year A 2001, Luke for Everyone 2001, Mark for Everyone 2001, Paul for Everyone: Galatians and Thessalonians 2002, John for Everyone 2002, Twelve Months of Sundays, Year B 2002, New Interpreter's Bible, Vol. X (contrib.) 2002, The Contemporary Quest for Jesus 2002, Paul for Everyone (The Prison Letters) 2002, Matthew for Everyone 2002, Paul for Everyone (I Corinthians 2003), Paul for Everyone (II Corinthians) 2003, Quiet Moments 2003, The Resurrection of the Son of God 2003, For All the Saints? 2003, Hebrews for Everyone 2003, Paul for Everyone (The Pastoral Letters) 2003, Paul for Everyone: Romans 2004, Scripture and the Authority of God 2005, Paul: Fresh Perspectives 2005, Simply Christian 2006, Evil and the Justice of God 2006, Judas and the Gospel of Jesus 2006, The Cross and the Colliery 2007, Surprised by Hope 2007, Acts for Everyone 2008, Jesus: the Final Days 2008, Anglican Evangelical Identity 2008, Justification 2009, For Everyone Bible Study Guides 2009, Lent for Everyone 2009, Virtue Reborn 2010. *Honours:* Hon. Fellow Downing Coll. Cambridge 2003, Merton Coll. Oxford 2004; Hon. DD (Aberdeen) 2000, (Nashotah House) 2006, (Wycliffe Coll., Toronto) 2006, (Durham) 2007; Hon. DHumLitt (Gordon Coll., Mass) 2003. *Address:* Bishop of Durham, Auckland Castle, Bishop Auckland, Co. Durham, DL14 7NR, England (office). *Telephone:* (1388) 602576 (office). *Fax:* (1388) 605264 (office). *E-mail:* bishops.office@durham.anglican.org (office). *Website:* www.durham.anglican.org (office); www.ntwrightpage.com.

WRIGHT, Richard Bruce, CM, BA; Canadian writer; b. 4 March 1937, Midland, Ont.; m. Phyllis Mary Cotton; two s. *Education:* Ryerson Polytechnic Inst., Toronto, Trent Univ., Peterborough. *Career:* fmr teacher of English, Ridley Coll., St Catharines, Ont. (now retd). *Publications:* Andrew Tolliver 1965, The Weekend Man 1970, In the Middle of a Life 1973, Farthing's Fortunes 1976, Final Things 1980, The Teacher's Daughter 1982, Tourists 1984, Sunset Manor 1990, The Age of Longing 1995, Clara Callan 2001, Adultery 2004, October 2007. *Honours:* Hon. DLitt (Brock Univ.) 2000, (Ryerson Univ.) 2002, (Trent Univ.) 2006; fellowships: City of Toronto Book Award 1973, Geoffrey Faber Memorial Prize, England 1975, Gov.-Gen.'s Award for Literature 2001, Giller Prize 2001, Trillium Award 2001. *Address:* 52 St Patrick Street, St Catharines, ON L2R 1K3; c/o HarperCollins Publishers, 2 Bloor Street East, 20th Floor, Toronto, ON M4W 1A8, Canada.

WRIGHT, Ronald, MA (Cantab.); British/Canadian author; b. 1948, Surrey, England. *Education:* Univ. of Cambridge. *Career:* Massey Lecturer 2004; mem. PEN Canada, Survival International. *Publications:* Cut Stones and Crossroads: A Journey in Peru 1984, On Fiji Islands 1986, Time Among the Maya 1989, Stolen Continents (history) (Gordon Montador Award 1993) 1992, Home and Away (essays) 1993, A Scientific Romance (novel) (David Higham Prize for Fiction 1998) 1997, Henderson's Spear (novel) 2001, A Short History of Progress (Libris Nonfiction Book of the Year 2005) 2004, What is America? A Short History of the New World Order (history) 2008; contrib. to TLS and other journals. *Honours:* Hon. LLD (Univ. of Calgary) 1996, (Bishop's Univ.) 2007; David Higham Prize for Fiction (UK) 1998, CBA Book of the Year (Canada) 2005. *Literary Agent:* c/o Dunow Carlson & Lerner Literary Agency, 27 West 20th Street, New York, NY 10011, USA. *Fax:* (212) 645-7606. *E-mail:* henry@dclagency.com. *Website:* www.ronaldwright.com.

WU, Duncan, BA, DPhil; British academic and author; *Professor of English, Georgetown University;* b. 3 Nov. 1961, Woking, Surrey, England; s. of Spencer Wu and Mary Sadler; divorced, remarried. *Education:* Univ. of Oxford. *Career:* Postdoctoral Fellow, British Acad. 1991–94; Reader in English Literature, Univ. of Glasgow 1995–99, Prof. of Romantic Studies 1999–2000; Univ. Lecturer in English Language and Literature, St Catherine's Coll. Oxford 2000–03, Prof. of English Language and Literature 2003–08; Prof. of English, Georgetown Univ., Washington, DC, USA 2008–; Trustee, Charles Lamb Soc., Keats-Shelley Memorial Asscn; mem. Editorial Bd Charles Lamb Bulletin, Wordsworth Circle, Romanticism on the Net; mem. The Hazlitt Soc. *Publications:* Wordsworth's Reading 1770–1799 1993, Romanticism: An Anthology 1994, William Wordsworth: A Selection 1994, Six Contemporary Dramatists 1994, Romanticism: A Critical Reader 1995, Wordsworth's Reading 1800–1815 1996, Romantic Women Poets: An Anthology 1997, A Companion to Romanticism 1998, Selected Writings of William Hazlitt 1998, Making Plays: Interviews with Contemporary British Playwrights and Directors 2000,

WUDUNN, Sheryl, MBA, MPA; American writer, journalist and campaigner; *President, TripleEdge;* b. 16 Nov. 1959, New York City; d. of David WuDunn and Alice WuDunn; m. Nicholas D. Kristof. *Education:* Cornell Univ., Harvard Business School, Woodrow Wilson School, Princeton Univ. *Career:* worked in editorial and management roles at The New York Times, foreign correspondent in Tokyo and Beijing; fmr Vice Pres. Investment Div., Goldman Sachs & Co.; fmr Commercial Loan Officer Bankers Trust; Pres. TripleEdge (social investing consultancy); Dir Mid-Market Securities; leads Half the Sky multimedia effort; mem. Bd of Trustees Cornell Univ., Chair. Acad. Affairs Cttee, mem. Finance Cttee. *Publications:* with Nicholas D. Kristof: China Wakes: The Struggle for the Soul of a Rising Power 1994, Thunder from the East 2000, Half the Sky: Turning Oppression into Opportunity for Women Worldwide (White House Project Beacon Award 2010) 2009. *Honours:* George Polk Award, Overseas Press Club Awards, Pulitzer Prize for coverage of China (co-winner) 1990, Dayton Literary Peace Prize for Lifetime Achievement (co-winner) 2009. *Address:* c/o Publicity Department, Knopf Publishers, 1745 Broadway, New York, NY 10019, USA (office). *Website:* knopf.knopfdoubleday.com (office).

WUNSCH, Josephine McLean, BA; American writer; b. 3 Feb. 1914, Detroit, MI; m. Edward Seward Wunsch 1940, one s. two d. *Education:* Univ. of Michigan. *Publications:* Flying Skis 1962, Passport to Russia 1965, Summer of Decision 1968, Lucky in Love 1970, The Aerie (as J. Sloan McLean with Virginia Gillett) 1974, Girl in the Rough 1981, Class Ring 1983, Free as a Bird 1984, Breaking Away 1985, The Perfect Ten 1986, Lucky in Love 1987, Between Us 1989.

WURLITZER, Rudolph; American author and screenwriter; b. 1937, Cincinnati, OH. *Education:* Columbia Univ., Univ. of Aix-en-Provence. *Films:* screenplays: Glen and Randa 1969, Two-Lane Blacktop (with Will Cory) 1971, Pat Garrett and Billy the Kid 1973, Walker 1987, Candy Mountain 1988, Voyager 1991, Wind 1992, Shadow of the Wolf 1992, Little Buddha 1993. *Publications:* Nog 1969, Flats 1971, Quake 1974, Slow Fade 1984, Walker 1989, Hard Travels to Sacred Places 1994, The Drop Edge of Yonder 2008; other: several screenplays; contributions: books and periodicals. *E-mail:* rudy@rudywurlitzer.com (office). *Website:* www.rudolphwurlitzer.com.

WURTS, Janny, BA; American writer; b. 10 Dec. 1953, Bryn Mawr, PA. *Education:* Hampshire College, Moore College of Art. *Career:* fantasy writer. *Publications:* Sorcerer's Legacy 1982, Stormwarden 1984, Daughter of the Empire (co-author) 1987, Keeper of the Keys 1988, Shadowfane 1988, Servant of the Empire (co-author) 1990, Mistress of the Empire (co-author) 1992, The Master of White Storm 1992, The Curse of the Mistwraith 1993, Ships of Merior 1995, Warhost of Vastmark 1995, That Way Lies Camelot 1996, Fugitive Prince 1997, Grand Conspiracy 1999, Peril's Gate 2001, To Ride Hell's Dream 2002, Traitor's Knot 2004, Stormed Fortress 2007. *E-mail:* jannywurts@paravia.com (office). *Website:* www.paravia.com/JannyWurts.

WYLD, Evelyn Rose Strange, BA, MA; British writer; b. 16 June 1980. *Education:* Bath Spa Univ., Goldsmiths Coll., London. *Career:* bookseller, Review bookshop, Peckham, London; Booktrust Online Writer-in-Residence 2010. *Publications:* After the Fire, a Still Small Voice (John Llewellyn Rhys Prize) 2009; short story contribs to Sea Stories, Granta, Vogue, 3:AM Magazine anthologies. *Honours:* Betty Trask Award 2010. *Literary Agent:* c/o Laetitia Rutherford, Mulcahy Conway Associates, 15 Canning Passage, Kensington, London, W8 5AA, England. *Website:* www.mca-agency.com. *E-mail:* evie@eviewyld.com (office). *Website:* www.eviewyld.com.

WYLIE, Andrew, BA; American literary agent; *President, The Wylie Agency;* b. 4 Nov. 1947; m. 1st Christina Meyer 1969; one s.; m. 2nd Camilla Carlini; two d. *Education:* St Paul's School, Harvard Coll. *Career:* founder and Pres. The Wylie Agency, New York 1980–, London 1996–, Madrid 1999–, with over 500 clients. *Address:* The Wylie Agency, 250 W 57th Street, Suite 2114, New York, NY 10107, USA. *Telephone:* (212) 246-0069. *Fax:* (212) 586-8953. *E-mail:* mail@wylieagency.com. *Website:* www.wylieagency.com.

WYLIE, Betty Jane, OC, BA, MA; Canadian writer, dramatist and poet; b. 21 Feb. 1931, Winnipeg, MB; m. William Tennent Wylie; two s. two d. *Education:* Univ. of Manitoba. *Career:* Bunting Fellow, Radcliffe College 1989–90; Writer-in-Residence, Metro Toronto Library, York Branch, 2001; Founding mem. Playwrights' Union of Canada; Chair. Writers' Union of Canada 1988–89. *Publications:* over 35 books including Beginnings: A Book for Widows; more than 35 plays; contrib. to periodicals.

WYNAND, Derk, BA, MA; Canadian academic, poet, writer, translator and editor; *Professor Emeritus, University of Victoria;* b. 1944, Bad Suderode, Germany; m. Eva Kortemme 1971. *Education:* Univ. of British Columbia. *Career:* Visiting Lecturer, Univ. of Victoria, BC 1969–73, Asst Prof. 1973–77, Prof. 1977–2004, Prof. Emer. 2004–, Chair. Dept of Creative Writing 1987–90, 1996–99; Ed. The Malahat Review (named Magazine of the Year 1995) 1992–98. *Radio:* Cyanide (CBC Playhouse) 1975. *Publications:* Locus 1971, Snowscapes 1974, Pointwise 1979, One Cook, Once Dreaming 1980, Second Person 1983, Fetishistic 1984, Heatwaves 1988, Airborne 1994, Door Slowly Closing 1995, Closer to Home 1997, Dead Man's Float 2002, Past Imperfect, Present Tense 2010; has published several trans of authors in book form, including H. C. Artmann, Erich Wolfgang Skwara, Dorothea Gruenzweig. *Honours:* hon. mention by Nichol Chapbook Award 1995. *Address:* 4243 Cedarglen Road, Victoria, BC V8N 4N7, Canada. *Telephone:* (250) 477-2267. *E-mail:* dwynand@shaw.ca.

X

XENAKIS, Françoise Marguerite Claude; French journalist and writer; b. 27 Sept. 1930, Blois; d. of Robert Gargouil and Suzanne Gargouil (née Richard); m. Yannis Xenakis 1953 (died 2001); one d. *Career:* journalist and literary critic Le Matin de Paris and L'Express, Paris 1987; TV journalist on Télématin, France 2. *Publications:* Des dimanches et des dimanches 1977, Moi, j'aime pas la mer, Le temps usé, La natte coupée, Zut, on a encore oublié Madame Freud 1985, Mouche-toi Cléopâtre 1986, Elle lui dirait dans l'île (play) 1987, La vie exemplaire de Rita Capuchon 1988, Chéri, tu viens pour la photo 1990, Attends moi (Prix des Libraires) 1993, Désolée mais ça ne se fait pas 1996, Maman, je veux pas être empereur 2001, Regarde, nos chemins se sont fermés 2002, Danielle Mitterrand: la petite fille qui voulait étre Antigone 2006, J'aurais dû épouser Marcel 2009. *Address:* 9 rue Chaptal, 75009 Paris, France (home).

XINRAN, Xue; Chinese radio journalist, writer and columnist; b. 19 July 1958, Beijing; m. 1st (divorced); one s.; m. 2nd Toby Eady 2002. *Education:* First Mil. Univ. of PLA. *Career:* writer under name, Xinran; radio producer, presenter, Words on the Night Breeze programme, Henhan Broadcasting and Jiangsu Broadcasting 1989–97; moved to London 1997; teacher, SOAS, London; Founder The Mothers' Bridge of Love charitable org. 2003; columnist, The Guardian. *Publications:* The Good Women of China (non-fiction) 2002, Sky Burial (non-fiction) 2004, What the Chinese Don't Eat 2006, Miss Chopsticks (novel) 2007, China Witness: Voices from a Silent Generation 2009, Message from an Unknown Chinese Mother: Stories of Loss and Love 2010; contribs to Western and Chinese newspapers and broadcasting journals. *Address:* The Mothers' Bridge of Love, 9 Orme Court, London, W2 4RL, England (office). *Telephone:* (20) 7034-0686 (office). *Fax:* (20) 7792-0879 (office). *E-mail:* xinran@motherbridge.org (office). *Website:* www.motherbridge.org (office).

XIRAU, Ramón; Mexican writer and poet; *Researcher Emeritus, Universidad Nacional Autónoma de México;* b. 20 Jan. 1924, Barcelona, Spain; s. of Joaquin Xirau. *Education:* Universidad Nacional Autónoma de México. *Career:* emigrated to Mexico 1939; teacher of Philosophy, Liceo Franco-Mexicano 1946–73; Prof. of Philosophy, later Head, Dept of Philosophy, Universidad de las Américas 1946–69; Prof. and Researcher, Faculty of Philosophy and Letters, Universidad Nacional Autónoma de México 1949–93, Researcher Emer. 1993–; founder and Ed., Diálogos magazine 1964–85; Visiting Prof. Univ. of Oxford 1963, 1966, Univ. of Bologna 1966, Yale Univ. 1974, Columbia Univ. 1974, Universidad Autónoma de Barcelona 1985, Universidad Central de Barcelona 1989–90, Institut d'Estudis Catalans, Barcelona 1991; mem. Mexican Acad. of Letters 1994–. *Publications:* over 40 books including Método y metafísica en la filosofía de Descartes 1946, Duración y existencia 1947, Diez Poemas 1951, Sentido de la Presencia 1953, L'espill soterrat 1955, El Péndulo y la Espiral 1959, Tres Poetas de la soledad 1959, Poetas de México y España 1961, Palabra y silencio 1964, Introducción a la historia de la filosofía 1964, Genio y figura de Sor Juana Inés de la Cruz 1967, The Nature of Man (with Erich Formm) 1968, Octavio Paz: el sentido de la palabra 1970, De Ideas y no Ideas 1974, Las Playas 1974, El desarrollo y la crisis de la filosofía en Occidente 1975, Poesía y Conocimiento 1979, Dos Poetas y lo Sagrado 1980, El Tiempo Vivido 1985, De Mística 1993, Memorial de Mascarones y otros ensayos 1995, Poesía Completa 1996, Naturalezas Vivas 1997, Obras Completas de Joaquin Xirau 1999. *Honours:* Chevalier, Ordre du Mérite, France 1964, Commendatore, Ordine al Merito, Italy 1971, Orden de Isabel la Católica, Spain 1979, Ordre des Palmes Académiques, France 1979, Chevalier, Ordre des Arts et des Lettres, France 1985, Légion d'Honneur, France 1991; Dr hc (Universidad de las Américas) 1970, (Universidad Autónoma de Barcelona) 1984; Rockefeller Foundation Grant 1950, 1955, 1956, Guggenheim Foundation Grant 1961, 1966, Premio Internacional Alfonso Reyes 1988, Premio Mazatlán 1990, Premio Nacionl de Ciencias y Artes 1995, Premio Internacional Octavio Paz de Ensayo 2009, PEN Mexico Prize 2010. *Address:* Instituto de Investigaciones Filosóficas, Universidad Nacional Autónoma de México, Ciudad Universitaria, Coyoacán, 04510 México, DF Mexico (office). *Telephone:* (55) 5622-7216 (office). *E-mail:* xirau@filosoficas.unam.mx (office). *Website:* www.filosoficas.unam.mx (office).

XONGERIN, Badai; Chinese Inner Mongolia administrator, writer and poet; b. 5 June 1930, Bayinguoltng Prefecture, Hejin Co., Xinjiang; s. of Honger Xongerin and Bayinchahan Xongerin; m. 1952; two s. two d. *Career:* Pres. Xinjiang Broadcasting and TV Univ. 1982–; Chair. Cttee of Xinjiang Uygur Autonomous Region of CPPCC 1989; mem. Standing Cttee CPPCC 1991. *Publications:* several books of prose, poetry and history in Mongol language and Chinese. *Address:* 15 South Beijing Road, Urumqi, Xinjiang, People's Republic of China. *Telephone:* (991) 2825701 (office); (991) 3839303 (home). *Fax:* (991) 2823443.

XU, Zhenshi; Chinese photographer, artist and publisher; b. 18 Aug. 1937, Songjiang Co., Shanghai; s. of Xu Weiqing and Jiang Wanying, step-s. of Cheng Shi-fa; m. Zhang Fuhe 1967; one d. *Education:* No. 1 High School, Songjiang Co., Zhejiang Acad. of Fine Arts. *Career:* moved to Beijing 1965; Ed. People's Fine Arts Publishing House 1965–86, Dir Picture Editorial Dept 1986–, Ed.-in-Chief 1992–; mem. China Artists' Asscn; Deputy Sec.-Gen. Spring Festival Pictures Research Centre, Publrs' Asscn of China; Deputy Sec.-Gen. and Assoc. Dir Photography Research Centre; mem. Selection Cttee 3rd, 4th and 5th Nat. Exhbns of Spring Festival Pictures and other exhbns; Assoc. Dir Standing Cttee Spring Festival Pictures; Sr Adviser, Office of East China–UN TIPS Nat. Exploit Bureau 1994–; exhbns in China, Japan, Korea, Hong Kong, Thailand; Vice-Ed.-in-Chief Gouache Vol. of Anthology of Contemporary Chinese Fine Arts 1996; Vice-Pres. Chinese Fan Art Soc. 1997; organized 1st Nat. Exhbn of Calligraphy and Paintings to Help the Poor 1998; Dir Foundation for Underdeveloped Regions in China 1998–; prepared 6th Nat. Exhbn of Spring Festival Pictures 1998; union art exhib., St Petersburg, Russia 2006. *Exhibitions include:* Taiyuan Shanxi Prov. 2003, Wei Fang Shandong Prov. 2004, Hangzhou 2005. *Publications:* China's Cultural Relics Unearthed during the Great Cultural Revolution 1973, Travel in China (four vols) 1979–80, Tibet 1981, Travel in Tibet 1981, Costumes of China's Minority Nationalities 1981, Travel in Guilin 1981, Travel Leisurely in China 1981, Travel in Yunnan 1982, China's Flowers in Four Seasons 1982, Poet Li Bai 1983, Native Places of Tang Dynasty Poems 1984, Travel along the Yangtse River 1985, Through the Moongate: A Guide to China's Famous Historical Sites 1986, Waters and Mountains in China 1986, Travel in Guangzhou 1986, China 1987, The Chinese Nation 1989, Poet Du Fu 1989, Selected Works of Xu Zhenshi 1990, 1993, Selected Paintings of Xu Zhenshi 1993, 1994, Boat on the Plateau 1998, Album of Xu Zhenshi's Sketches 1999, Love for China 2003; collection of Xu Zhenshi published in 2003, Love for China 2003; ed Olympic Games picture book 2008. *Honours:* numerous awards including Bronze Medal for albums of photographs, Leipzig Int. Book Exhbn 1987, Nat. Award 1993, Model Ed. Nat. Press and Publs System 1997, 1998, State Prize for Spring Festival Pictures 2001, two 6th Nat. Exhbn of Spring Festival Pictures Prizes (China) 1998, Chinese Contemporary Art Achievement Prize, Hong Kong, State Prize of Spring Festival Pictures 2001, Prize of A Brilliant Contrib. 2001, Outstanding People's Artist Award. *Address:* People's Fine Arts Publishing House, No. 32 Beizongbu Hutong, Beijing, People's Republic of China (office). *Telephone:* (10) 65244901 (office); (10) 65246353 (home).

Y

YAAD, (Muhammad) Mansha, MA; Pakistani fiction writer and playwright; b. 5 Sept. 1937, small village nr Farukabad, Shiakhupura Dist; s. of Haji Nazir Ahmed. *Education:* Diploma in Civil Eng, Punjab Univ., Lahore. *Career:* Deputy Dir/Civil Engineer, Capital Devt Authority, Islamabad 1960–97; Founder Halqa-e Arbab-e Zauq Islamabad literary forum 1972; writes in Urdu and Punjabi; numerous plays for Radio Pakistan and Pakistan TV. *Television:* serials: Janoon, Bandhan, Rahain (PTV Nat. Award), Pooray Chand ki Raat. *Publications:* short story collections: Band Muthi Main Jugnu (Firefly in the Fist) 1975, Mass Aur Mitti (Flesh and Clay) 1980, Khala Andar Khala (Space Within Space) 1983, Waqt Samundar (Time the Ocean) 1986, Mansha Yad Ke Muntkhib Afsany (Selected Stories) 1986, Wagda Pani (Running Water) 1987, Darakhat Adami (Tree the Man) 1990, Door Ki Awaz (A Distant Voice) 1994, Mansha Yad Ke Behtreen Afsany (Best Short Stories) 1994, Mansha Yad Ke Tees Muntakhib Afsany (Thirty Selected Short Stories) 1997, Tamasha (The Show) 1998; novel: Tanwan Tanwan Tara (Sparsely a Star) 1997, Khawb Saraiy (Lodge of Dreams). *Honours:* Waris Shah Adabi Awards, Pakistan Acad. of Letters for Punjabi books, Pres.'s Award 'Pride of Performance' for Literature 2004. *Address:* House No. 8, Seventh Avenue, Sector G-7/4, Islamabad 44000, Pakistan (home). *Telephone:* (51) 2277373 (home). *E-mail:* manshayaad@hotmail.com (home); afsananigar@yahoo.com (home). *Website:* www.manshayaad.com; manshayaad.tripod.com.

YAFFE, James, BA; American academic (retd), writer and dramatist; b. 31 March 1927, Chicago, IL; m. Elaine Gordon 1964; one s. two d. *Education:* Yale Univ. *Career:* Prof., Colorado Coll. 1980–2002, Prof. Emer. 2002–, Dir, General Studies 1982–99; mem. American Asscn of University Profs, Authors' League, Dramatists' Guild, MWA, PEN. *Publications:* Poor Cousin Evelyn 1951, The Good-for-Nothing 1953, What's the Big Hurry? 1954, Nothing But the Night 1959, Mister Margolies 1962, Nobody Does You Any Favors 1966, The American Jews 1968, The Voyage of the Franz Joseph 1970, So Sue Me! 1972, Saul and Morris, Worlds Apart 1982, A Nice Murder for Mom 1988, Mom Meets Her Maker 1990, Mom Doth Murder Sleep 1991, Mom Among the Liars 1992, My Mother, the Detective 1997; plays: The Deadly Game 1960, Ivory Tower (with Jerome Weidman) 1967, Cliffhanger 1983; other: television plays; contributions: various publications. *Honours:* National Arts Foundation Award 1968. *Address:* 12 West 72nd Street, Apartment 8D, New York, NY 10023-4264, USA (home). *Telephone:* (212) 724-9126 (home).

YAGUELLO, Marina; French linguist and writer; b. 1944, Paris. *Career:* Prof. Emer., Université de Paris VII (Denis Diderot). *Publications include:* Les Mots et les femmes: essai dapproche socio-linguistique de la condition féminine 1978, Alice au pays du langage (trans. as Language Through the Looking-Glass) 1981, Les Fous du langage: des langues imaginaires et de leurs inventeurs (trans. as Lunatic Lovers of Language: Imaginary Languages and their Inventors) 1984, Le Sexe des mots 1988, Catalogue des idées reçues sur la langue 1988, Histoire de Lettres 1990, En écoutant parler la langue 1991, Grammaire exploratoire de l'anglais 1991, J'apprends le wolof, Damay jang wolof (with Jean-Léopold Diouf) 1991, T'ar ta gueule à la récré! (with Nestor Salas) 1991, La Planète des langues 1993, Subjecthood and Subjectivity: Status of the Subject in Linguistic Theory 1994, Petits Faits de langue 1998, Le Grand livre de la langue française (with Claire-Blanche Benveniste, Jean-Paul Colin, Françoise Gadet et al) 2003, Les Langues Imaginaires 2006. *Address:* 68 rue Amelot, 75011 Paris, France (home). *Telephone:* 1-48-06-18-15 (home).

YAKHLEF, Yahya; Palestinian novelist, writer and fmr politician; b. 1944, Samakh. *Career:* Minister of Culture –2007. *Publications include:* novels: Najran tahta al-sifr 1975, Tuffah al-majanin 1982, Nashid al-hayah 1985, Tilka al-laylah al-tawilah 1992, Buhayrah Wara' al-Rih (trans. as A Lake Beyond the Wind 1999) 1997. *Address:* c/o Ministry of Culture, POB 147, Ramallah, Palestinian Autonomous Areas (office).

YAMADA, Amy (Eimi); Japanese writer; b. (Yamada Futaba), 8 Feb. 1959, Tokyo. *Career:* fmr cartoonist; novelist and short story writer 1980–. *Publications:* Beddo taimu aizu (Bedtime Eyes) (Kawade Literary Prize 1985, Bungei Prize for Literature 1987) 1985, Yubi no tawamure (Finger Play) 1986, Jeshii no sebone (Jessie's Spine) 1986, Chô-cho no tensoku (Binding the Butterfly's Feet) 1987, Harlem World 1987, Sōru myūjikku, rabaazu on rii (Soul Music: Lovers Only, novellas) (Naoki Prize) 1987, Fûsô no kyôshitsu (Classroom for the Abandoned Dead) (Hirabayashi Taiko Prize) 1988, Hôkago no kiinooto (After-School Music) 1989, Trash 1991, I Can't Study 1993, 120% Coool 1994, Animal Logic 1996, 4U 1997, Magnet 1999, A2Z (Yomiuri Literary Prize) 2003, Pay Day! 2003. *Address:* c/o Kodansha International Ltd, Otowa YK Building, 1-17-14 Otowa 1 chome, Bunkyo-ku, Tokyo 112-8652, Japan (office). *E-mail:* editorial@kodansha-intl.co.jp (office). *Website:* www.kodansha-intl.com (office).

YAMADA, Taichi; Japanese screenwriter, playwright and novelist; b. 1934, Tokyo. *Education:* Waseda Univ. *Career:* worked in Ofuna Studio Production Dept Shochiku Film Co. 1958–65. *Television writing includes:* Sorezore no Aki (Annual TV Award Grand Prize, Japan Screenwriters' Guild TV programme Award, New Talent Award) 1973, Kishibe no Arubamu 1977, Ensen Chizu 1979, Otoko tachi no Tabiji 1976, Omoide Zukuri 1981, Nagaraeba (Educ. Minister's Award) 1982, Fuzoroi no Ringo tachi 1983, Soushun Sukkechibukku 1983, Nihon no Omokage (Mukoda Kuniko Prize 1984, Kikuchi Kan Prize 1985) 1984, Omote dori e nukeru michi (Japanese Civilian Broadcasting Fed. Grand Prix Award) 1988, Kanashikute yarikirenai 1992, Aki no eki 1993, Setsunai Haru 1995, Shasin no ura 1995, Nara he ikumade 1998, Ichiban Kirei na toki 1999, And... Friend 2000, This Winter's Romance 2002, How to Walk a Maze 2002, The Fan of Hong Kong STAR 2002, The Following Days (Broadcasting Cultural Fund Award) 2004, Hoshi hitotsu no yoru 2007, Arifureta kiseki 2009. *Plays include:* Rabu, Jyampu, Suna no Ue no Dansu, Kawa no Mukou de Hito ga Yobu, Yonaka ni Okiteiru no wa. *Film screenplay:* Shonen Jidai (scenario) (Mainichi Film Competition, Japan Acad. Award, Japan Writers' Asscn Scenario Award, Japan Broadcast Writers' Asscn, Japan Scenario Writers' Asscn Mems) 1991. *Publications:* novels: Ai Yori Aoku (trans. as Deeper than Indigo) 1972, Kishiba no Album (trans. as The Album on the Shore) 1977, Ensen Chizu (trans. as Tokyo Suburbia) 1979, Owari ni Mita Machi (trans. as The Last Town we Saw-Apocalypse) 1981, Tobu Yume wo Shibaraku Minai (trans. as I Haven't Dreamed of Flying for a While) 1985, Ijintachi tono Natsu (trans. as Strangers) (Yamamoto Shugoro Prize) 1987, Oka no Ueno Himawari (trans. as Sunflower on the Hill) 1989, Tooku no Koe wo Sagashite (trans. as In Search of a Distant Voice) 1989, Kimi wo Miagete (trans. as Looking Up at You) 1990, Fuyu no Shinkiro (trans. as Winter Mirage) 1992, Mienai Kurayami (trans. as Invisible Darkness) 1994, Koi no Shisei (trans. as In Stance of Love) 1995, Minareta Machi ni Kaze ga Fuku (trans. as My Familiar Town in the Breeze) 1997, Yataro-san no Hanashi (trans. as Story of Yataro) 2001, Nihon no Omokage (trans. as Out of the East) 2002. *Literary Agent:* c/o Akiko Fujino, Frameworks Films Inc., 1120 S Robertson Boulevard, Suite 305, Los Angeles, CA 90035, USA. *Telephone:* (310) 858-8788. *Fax:* (323) 375-1391. *E-mail:* frameworksfilms@mac.com. *Website:* www.frameworksfilmsinc.com. *E-mail:* info@yamadataichi.com (office). *Website:* www.yamadataichi.com.

YAMASHITA, Karen Tei; American writer, dramatist and academic; *Professor of Literature, University of California at Santa Cruz;* b. 8 Jan. 1951, Oakland, Calif.; m. Ronaldo Yamashita; one s. one d. *Education:* Carleton Coll. *Career:* Asst Prof. of Literature, Univ. of California, Santa Cruz 1997–, later Assoc. Prof., then Prof.; mem. PEN Center West. *Publications:* Through the Arc of the Rain Forest 1990, Brazil-Moru 1992, Hannah Kusoh: An American Butoh 1995, Tropic of Orange 1997, Circle K Cycles 2001, I Hotel 2010; other: short stories, unpublished plays and screenplays; contributions: anthologies and periodicals. *Honours:* Rockefeller Playwright-in-Residence Fellow, East West Players, Los Angeles 1977–78, American Book Award 1991, 2011, Janet Heidinger Kafka Award 1992, City of Los Angeles Cultural Grant Award 1992–93, Japan Foundation Artist Fellowship 1997, Nat. Book Award 2010, California Book Award 2011. *Address:* Department of Literature, University of California at Santa Cruz, Humanities 1, Room 303, Santa Cruz, CA 95064, USA (office). *Telephone:* (831) 459-2167 (office). *E-mail:* ktyamash@ucsc.edu (office). *Website:* literature.ucsc.edu (office).

YAN, Lianke; Chinese author; b. 1958, Henan Prov. *Education:* Henan Univ. *Publications include:* novels: Xia Riluo 1994, Shouhuo (Joy of Living) (Lu Xun Award 2004, Lao She Award 2004) 2004, Serve the People 2005, The Dream of Ding Village 2006, Serve the People! 2008; also short stories. *Literary Agent:* c/o The Susijn Agency Ltd, Third Floor, 64 Great Titchfield Street, London, W1W 7QH, England. *Telephone:* (20) 7580-6341. *Fax:* (20) 7580-8626. *E-mail:* info@thesusijnagency.com. *Website:* www.thesusijnagency.com.

YANCEY, Philip David, BA, MA; American writer and editor; b. 4 Nov. 1949, Atlanta, GA; m. Janet Norwood 1970. *Education:* Columbia Bible Coll., Wheaton Coll., Univ. of Chicago. *Career:* Ed., Campus Life 1971–77; Ed.-at-Large, Christianity Today 1980–. *Publications:* After the Wedding 1976, Where is God When It Hurts? 1977, Unhappy Secrets of the Christian Life (with Tim Stafford) 1979, Fearfully and Wonderfully Made (with Paul Brand) 1980, Open Windows 1982, In His Image (with Paul Brand) 1984, The Student Bible (with Tim Stafford) 1988, Disappointment With God 1989, A Guided Tour of the Bible 1990, I Was Just Wondering 1990, Pain: The Gift Nobody Wants (with Paul Brand) 1993, Finding God in Unexpected Places 1995, The Jesus I Never Knew 1996, What's So Amazing About Grace? 1997, Church, Why Bother? 1998, The Bible Jesus Read 1999, Meet the Bible 2000, Reaching for the Invisible God 2000, Soul Survivor 2001, Rumors of Another World 2003, Prayer: Does It Make Any Difference? 2006; contrib. to numerous periodicals. *Honours:* many Evangelical Christian Publishers' Asscn Golden Medallion awards, two Book of the Year awards. *Address:* c/o Zondervan, 5300 Patterson Avenue SE, Grand Rapids, MI 49530, USA (office). *E-mail:* zauthor@zondervan.com (office). *Website:* www.philipyancey.com.

YANG, Lian; New Zealand/British poet and writer; *Artistic Director, Unique Mother Tone;* b. 22 Feb. 1955, Bern, Switzerland; m. Liu You Hong 1989. *Career:* grew up in Beijing; began writing when sent to countryside in 1970s; on return to Beijing was one of founders of 'Misty' school of contemporary Chinese poetry; known for poem sequences and long poems displaying understanding of classical Chinese poetry; poetry became well-known and influential both in China and abroad in 1980s, especially when 'Norilang' sequence was criticized by Chinese Govt during the 'Anti-Spiritual Pollution' movt; invited to visit Australia and NZ in 1988; became poet in exile after Tiananmen Square massacre; has continued to write and speak out in world literature, politics and culture; Artistic Dir Unique Mother Tongue (privately organized int. seminar series, London) 2005–; mem. Bd International PEN 2008–; has lived in London since 1997; writer-in-residence at numerous int. insts, including DAAD (Berlin programme), Amherst Coll., Bard Coll. (USA), Cove Park (UK), MEET (France), Univ. of Sydney (Australia), Univ. of Auckland (NZ); Pres. of Jury, The Crystal Vilenica Award 2008; mem. jury, Lettre Ulysses Award for the Art of Reportage (Germany), Int. Contest of Essays (Germany); adviser, Free The Word (Int. Literature Festival of PEN), Int. Literature Festival of Berlin, Poetry International Taipei and others. *Publications:* in Chinese: Lihun (Ritualization of the Soul) 1985, Huanghun (Desolate Soul) 1986, Huang (Yellow) 1989, Ren de zijue (Man's Self-Awakening) 1989, Mian ju yu e yu (trans. as Masks and Crocodile: A Contemporary Chinese Poet and his Poetry) 1990, Liu wang shi wo men huo de le shen me? (trans. as The Dead in Exile) 1990, Taiyang yu ren (The Sun and the People) 1991, Guihua (translated as Ghostspeak) 1994, Ren jing – Guihua (Human Scene – Ghostspeak) 1994, Yi 1994, Da hai ting zhi zhi chu (translated as Where the Sea Stands Still) (Poetry Book Soc. recommended trans. 1999) 1995, Yang Lian zuopin 1982–1997 (Yang Lian's Works 1982–1997) 1998, Si shi ren de cheng (trans. as City of Dead Poets) 2000, Yue shi de qi ge ban ye (Seven Half-Nights of Lunar Eclipse) 2002, Yang Lian Xin Zuo 1998–2002 (Yang Lian's New Works) 2003, Notes of a Blissful Ghost 2005, Whaur the Deep Sea Devauls (Where the Sea Stands Still) 2005, Tong xin yuan (Concentric Circles) 2005, Unreal City 2006; in English: Riding Pisces: Poems From Five Collections 2008, Lee Valley Poems – A Project of Poems and Translation 2009, A Tower Built Downward (essays) 2009, Anthology of Contemporary Chinese Poetry 1978–2008 (co-ed.) 2011; published four books of poems and prose in Taiwan 1994–2009; contrib. to anthologies and books, journals and periodicals, including Representations, Goldbatt, Xinwen ziyou daoji, Orientierungen, Australian Journal of Chinese Affairs, Canadian Review of Comparative Literature, Asian and African Studies, New Zealand Listener, PN Review, Renditions: A Chinese-English Translation Magazine, World Literature Today, Dushu, Zhongguo, TLS, New Left Review, Index on Censorship, The Guardian, Granta, Positions, Poetry London, OOTAL, Ezra Pound Magazine, Dove si ferma il mare, Kasel Documenta; works have been translated into more than 20 languages, including English, German, French, Italian, Spanish, Japanese and Eastern European languages. *Honours:* Chinese Poetry Reader's Choice 1986, Flaiano Int. Poetry Prize, Italy 1999. *Address:* 22 Carlton Mansions, Holmleigh Road, London, N16 5PX, England (home). *Telephone:* (20) 7503-6187 (office). *E-mail:* darkbluepoems@googlemail.com (home). *Website:* www.yanglian.net (home).

YANG, Namu; Chinese singer and writer; b. 1966, Zuosuo, Yunnan Prov. *Education:* Shanghai Music Conservatory. *Career:* from the Moso ethnic group, a matriarchal society near Burma; moved to Shanghai, later won singing competition and moved to Beijing 1982; performed in clubs and recorded six albums; went on to become music star and model. *Television includes:* autobiographical documentary for Chinese TV. *Publications include:* Leaving the Kingdom of Daughters 1997, Leaving Mother Lake: A Girlhood at the Edge of the World (with Christine Mathieu) 2003. *Address:* c/o Author Mail, Little, Brown & Company, 1271 Avenue of the Americas, New York, NY 10020, USA (office).

YANKOWITZ, Susan, BA, MFA; American writer and dramatist; b. 20 Feb. 1941, Newark, NJ; m. Herbert Leibowitz 1978, one s. *Education:* Sarah Lawrence Coll., Yale Drama School. *Career:* mem. Authors' Guild, Dramatists' Guild, New Dramatists, PEN, Writers' Guild of America. *Plays* Slaughterhouse Play 1971, Boxes 1973, Terminal 1975, Alarms 1988, Night Sky 1992, The Revenge, A Knife in the Heart, Phaedra in Delirium 2003, Chéri, Foreign Bodies,. *Film screenplay:* Portrait of a Scientist 1974. *Libretto:* Deronda (opera in three acts 1985–89, after George Eliot's Daniel Deronda). *Publications:* novel: Silent Witness 1977. *Honours:* Joseph Levine Fellowship in Screenwriting 1968, Vernon Rice Drama Desk Award for Most Promising Playwright 1969, Rockefeller Foundation grant 1973, and Award 1974, Guggenheim Fellowship 1975, MacDowell Colony Residencies 1975, 1984, 1987, 1990, NEA grants 1979, 1984, New York Foundation for the Arts grant 1989, McKnight Fellowship 1990. *E-mail:* syankowitz@aol.com (office); susan@susanyankowitz.com (office). *Website:* www.susanyankowitz.com.

YASUI, Kaoru, LLD; Japanese jurist and poet; b. 25 April 1907, Osaka; s. of Harumoto Yasui and Harue Yasui; m. Tazuko Kuki 1936; one s. one d. *Education:* Tokyo Univ. *Career:* Asst Prof., Tokyo Univ. 1932–42, Prof. 1942–48; Prof., Hosei Univ. 1952, Dean Faculty of Jurisprudence 1957–63, Dir 1963–66, Prof. Emer. 1978–; Leader (Chair. etc.) Japan Council Against Atomic and Hydrogen Bombs 1954–65; apptd Pres. Japanese Inst. for World Peace 1965; fmr Dir Maruki Gallery for Hiroshima Panels; apptd Chair. Japan–Korea (Democratic People's Repub.) Solidarity Cttee of Social Scientists 1972; apptd Dir-Gen. Int. Inst. of the Juche Idea 1978; mem. Lenin Peace Prize Cttee. *Publications include:* Outline of International Law 1939, Banning Weapons of Mass Destruction 1955, People and Peace 1955, Collection of Treaties 1960, My Way 1967, The Dialectical Method and the Science of International Law 1970, A Piece of Eternity (poems) 1977. *Honours:* Hon. mem. Japanese Asscn of Int. Law 1976–, Hon. DJur (San Gabriel Coll., USA); Lenin Peace Prize 1958, Gold Medal (Czechoslovakia) 1965. *Address:* Minami-Ogikubo 3-13-11, Suginami-ku, Tokyo, Japan.

YATROMANOLAKIS, Yoryis; Greek writer; b. 1940, Crete. *Career:* Prof. of Ancient Greek Literature, Univ. of Athens. *Publications include:* novels: Leimonario (trans. as The Spiritual Meadow) 1974, The History of a Vendetta 1991, A Report of a Murder 1995, Eroticon 1998, Spiritual Meadow 2000. *Honours:* First Greek National Prize for Literature, Nikos Kazantzakis Prize.

YEH, Jane, MA, MFA; American writer and poet; *Senior Lecturer in Creative Writing, Oxford Brookes University;* b. 1971. *Education:* Manchester Metropolitan Univ., Univ. of Iowa Writers' Workshop, Harvard Univ. *Career:* researcher, writer and Asst Ed., Let's Go Travel Guides (UK and USA) 1992–93; Research Asst, Univ. of Iowa Spine Research Center 1995–96; Asst Ed., The Village Voice, New York 1996–2001; freelance journalist and poet on various English-language publications 2001–05; writer-in-residence, Kingston Univ. 2003–05; Lecturer in Creative Writing 2003–05; Sr Lecturer in Creative Writing, Oxford Brookes Univ. 2005–. *Publications:* Teen Spies (chapbook) 2003, Marabou 2005; contrib. to numerous journals and newspapers, including TLS, The Village Voice, Time Out New York, and to anthologies. *Honours:* Harvard Univ. Acad. of American Poets Prize 1993, Univ. of Iowa Graduate Research Fellowship 1994–96, Prairie Lights Poetry Prize 1995, Scholarship to Bread Loaf Summer Writers' Conference 1996, Grolier Poetry Prize 1996, New York Foundation for the Arts Poetry Fellowship 2001. *Address:* Department of English, Oxford Brookes University, Gipsy Lane Campus, Headington, Oxford OX3 0BP, England (office). *Telephone:* (1865) 484329 (office). *E-mail:* jane@janeyeh3.com (office). *Website:* ah.brookes.ac.uk/english (office); janeyeh3.com.

YEHOSHUA, Abraham B., MA; Israeli writer and academic; *Professor of Comparative and Hebrew Literature, University of Haifa;* b. 9 Dec. 1936, Jerusalem; s. of Yakov Yehoshua and Malka Rosilio; m. Rivka Kirsninski 1960; two s. one d. *Career:* served in paratroopers unit 1954–57; Dir Israeli School in Paris 1964; Gen. Sec. World Union of Jewish Studies, Paris 1963–67; Dean of Students, Haifa Univ. 1967–72, Prof. of Comparative and Hebrew Literature 1972–; Visiting Prof., Harvard Univ., USA 1977, Univ. of Chicago 1988, 1997, 2000, Princeton Univ. 1992–; Co-Ed. Keshet 1965–72, Siman Kria 1973–, Tel Aviv Review 1987–; active mem. Israeli Peace Movt. *Film adaptations of novels and stories include:* The Lover, Facing the Forests, Continuing Silence, Mr Mani, Open Heart, A Voyage to the End of the Millennium, Early in the Summer of 1970. *Plays:* A Night in May 1969, Last Treatments 1973, Possessions 1992, The Night's Babies 1993. *Publications:* Death of the Old Man (short stories) 1963, Facing the Forest (short stories) 1968, Three Days and a Child (short stories) 1970, Early in the Summer of 1970 (novella) 1973, Two Plays 1975, The Lover (novel) 1977, Between Right and Right (essays) 1980, A Late Divorce (novel) (Flaiano Int. Poetry Prize, Italy 1996) 1982, Possessions 1986, Five Seasons (novel) (Nat. Jewish Book Award 1990, Cavour Prize, Italy 1994) 1988, The Wall and the Mountain (essays) 1988, Mister Mani (novel) (Israeli Booker Prize 1992, Nat. Jewish Book Award 1993, Wingate Prize, UK 1994) 1990, The Return from India 1994, Open Heart (novel) 1994, A Voyage to the End of the Millennium (novel) (Koret Prize) 1997, The Terrible Power of a Minor Guilt (essays) 1998, The Liberated Bride (novel) (Napoli Prize, Lampedusa Prize) 2001, The Mission of the Human Resource Man (novel) 2004, A Woman in Jerusalem (Los Angeles Times Book Prize for Fiction) 2006, Friendly Fire (novel) 2007. *Honours:* Dr hc (Hebrew Union Coll., Tel-Aviv Univ., Univ. of Turin, Bar Ilan Univ.); Brener Prize 1983, Alterman Prize 1986, Bialik Prize 1989, Booker Prize 1992, European B'nai B'rith Award 1993, Israel Prize 1995. *Address:* 33 Shoshanat Ha-Carmel, Haifa, 34322, Israel. *Telephone:* 4-8370001. *Fax:* 4-8375569. *E-mail:* bulli@research.haifa.ac.il (home).

YELIZAROV, Mikhail; Russian writer. *Publication:* The Librarian (novel) (Russian Booker Prize 2008) 2007. *Address:* c/o Ad Marginem Press, 5/7 1st Novokuznetsky per., 113184 Moscow, Russia (office). *E-mail:* ad_marg@livejournal.com (office). *Website:* www.ad-marginem.ru (office).

YELLAND, David, BA, AMP; British business executive and fmr journalist; *Partner, Brunswick Group LLP;* b. 14 May 1963, Harrogate, N Yorks., England; s. of John Michael Yelland and Patricia Ann McIntosh; m. 1st Tania Farrell 1996 (died 2006); one s.; m. 2nd Charlotte Elston 2010. *Education:* Brigg Grammar School, Lincs., Univ. of Coventry, Harvard Business School, USA. *Career:* grad. trainee, Westminster Press 1985; trainee reporter, Buckinghamshire Advertiser 1985–87; industrial reporter, Northern Echo 1987–88; gen. news and business reporter, North West Times and Sunday Times 1988–89; city reporter, Thomson Regional Newspapers 1989–90; joined News Corpn 1990; city reporter, then City Ed. The Sun 1990–92, New York Corresp. 1992–93, Ed. 1998–2003; Deputy Business Ed. Business Ed., then Deputy Ed. New York Post 1993–98; Sr Vice-Pres. News Corpn, New York 2003–04; Vice-Pres. Weber Shandwick Worldwide (public relations consultancy) 2004–06; Partner, Brunswick Group LLP 2006–. *Publication:* The Truth About Leo (novel) 2010. *Address:* Brunswick Group LLP, 16 Lincoln's Inn Fields, London, WC2A 3ED, England (office). *Telephone:* (20) 7404-5959 (office). *Fax:* (20) 7936-7730 (office). *E-mail:* dyelland@brunswickgroup.com (office). *Website:* www.brunswickgroup.com (office).

YEN MAH, Adeline, MD; Chinese physician and writer; b. 1937, Tianjin; m. Robert A. Mah; two c. *Career:* winner of int. playwriting competition aged 14; studied medicine at univ.; began career as anaesthetist, West Anaheim Community Hosp., Anaheim, Calif., became chief of anesthesia; autobiog. Falling Leaves became global bestseller with one million copies sold 1997; gave up career in medicine to write full-time 1997; mem. Cttee of One Hundred 1991–; Founder and Pres. Falling Leaves Return to their Roots Foundation, Huntington Beach, Calif. 1999–. *Publications include:* Falling Leaves 1997, Chinese Cinderella (autobiog. for children, Compelling Autobiography Award, Children's Literature Council 2001, Lamplighter Award, Nat. Christian School Asscn 2001) 2000, Watching the Tree 2000, A Thousand Pieces of Gold 2002, China, Land of Dragons and Emperors 2008. *Honours:* award for excellent service on Anesthesia Cttee, West Anaheim Community Hosp. 1985. *Address:* 16585 Ensign Circle, Huntington Beach, CA 92649, USA. *Website:* www.adelineyenmah.com.

YESSENIN-VOLPIN, Alexander Sergeyevich; Russian mathematician, philosopher and poet; b. 5 Dec. 1924, Leningrad (now St Petersburg); s. of poet Sergey Esenin and Nadiezhda Volpina; m. 1st V. B. Volpina; m. 2nd I. G. Kristi; m. 3rd 1994; one c. *Career:* studied at Faculty of Math., Moscow Univ. 1941–46; arrested for his poetry and committed to mental asylum 1949; in exile Karaganda, Kazakh SSR 1950; amnestied 1953; wrote numerous articles on logic and math. and translated extensively; worked at USSR Acad. of Sciences Inst. of Scientific and Tech. Information 1961–72; dissident activity 1959–; emigrated 1972. *Publications include:* A Free Philosophical Treatise 1959, A Leaf of Spring 1959, 1961, Open Letter to Solzhenitsyn 1970, Report on Committee on Rights of Man 1971, On the Logic of Moral Sciences (in English) 1988; numerous articles in Western and Russian scientific journals (after 1990s). *Honours:* Sakharov Prize. *Address:* 1513 North Shore Road, 2nd Floor, Revere, MA 02151, USA (home). *Telephone:* (781) 289-1072 (home). *Website:* yessenin-volpin.org.

YEVTUSHENKO, Yevgeniy Aleksandrovich; Russian poet and writer; b. 18 July 1933, Zima, Irkutsk Region; m. 1st Bella Akhmadulina 1954 (divorced); m. 2nd Galina Sokol 1962; one s.; m. 3rd Jan Butler 1978; two s.; m. 4th Maria Novikova 1986; two s. *Education:* Moscow Literary Inst. *Career:* geological expeditions with father to Kazakhstan 1948, the Altai 1949–50; literary work 1949–; mem. Editorial Bd of Yunost magazine 1962–69; People's Deputy of the USSR 1989–91; Sec. USSR Writers' Union 1986–91; Vice-Pres. Soviet PEN Cttee; moved to Tulsa, Okla, USA in mid-1990s, now teaches at Univ. of Tulsa; sometime Prof. Pittsburgh Univ. USA, Univ., Autónoma de Santo Domingo, Dominican Rep. *Films directed include:* Kindergarten 1983, Stalin's Funeral 1987; acted in Ascent (film on Tsiolkovsky). *Publications include:* poetry: Scouts of the Future (collected verse) 1952, The Third Snow (lyric verse) 1955, The Highway of Enthusiasts 1956, Zima Junction 1956, The Promise (collected verse) 1960, Moscow Goods Station, The Nihilist, The Apple 1960–61, Do the Russians Want War?, Babi Yar 1961, The Heirs of Stalin, Fears 1962, A Sweep of the Arm 1962, Tenderness 1962, A Precocious Autobiography 1963, The City of Yes and the City of No, Bratskaya Hydro-Electric Power Station 1964, Letter to Yesenin 1965, Italian Tears, A Boat of Communication, Poems Chosen by the Author 1966, Collection of Verses Yelabuga Nail, Cemetery of Whales 1967, That's What Is Happening to Me 1968, It's Snowing White 1969, Kazan University 1971, I am of Siberian Stock 1971, The Singing Domba 1972, Stolen Apples 1972, Under the Skin of the Statue of Liberty (play) 1972, Intimate Lyrics 1973, A Father's Hearing 1975, 1978, From Desire to Desire 1976, Love Poems 1977, People of the Morning 1978, Winter Station 1978, A Dove in Santiago: A Novella in Verse 1978, Heavy Soils 1979, The Face Behind the Face 1979, Ivan the Terrible and Ivan the Fool 1979, Berries (novel) 1981, Ardabiola (short story) 1981, Almost at the End (prose and verse) 1985, A Wind of Tomorrow (essays) 1987, Fatal Half Measures 1989, The Collected Poems 1952–90 1991, Farewell to Red Banner 1992, Twentieth Century Russian Poetry (compiler) 1994, Don't Die Before You're Dead (novel) 1996, My Very, Very... (poetry) 1996; photography: Divided Twins: Alaska and Siberia, Invisible Threads, Shadows and Faces. *Honours:* USSR Cttee for Defence of Peace Award 1965, Order of Red Banner of Labour, Badge of Honour, USSR State Prize 1984. *Address:* Kutuzovski Prospekt 2/1, Apt. 101, 121248 Moscow, Russia (home). *Telephone:* (495) 243-37-69 (home).

YI, Hoe-song (see RI Kai-sei)

YING, Diane, MA; Taiwanese journalist and publisher; *Editor-in-Chief and Publisher, CommonWealth;* b. Xian, People's Republic of China. *Education:* Nat. Cheng Kung Univ., Univ. of Iowa, USA. *Career:* emigrated with family from mainland China to Taiwan 1949; fmr reporter, The Philadelphia Inquirer, USA, Taiwan corresp. at various times for Asian Wall Street Journal, New York Times and United Press Int.; Co-founder, Chair., Ed.-in-Chief and Publr CommonWealth (monthly magazine) 1981–; fmr Lecturer (part-time) Chengchi Univ.; fmr Commr Nat. Unification Council; fmr advisor to Pres. Lee Tenghui. *Publications include:* Waiting for Heroes, People of the Pacific Century, The Decision Makers, Rediscovering Taiwan. *Honours:* Ramon Magsaysay Award for Journalism, Literature and Creative Communication (Philippines) 1987, Outstanding Alumnus Award, Nat. Cheng Kung Univ. 1987, Distinguished Alumni Award, Univ. of Iowa 1996. *Address:* CommonWealth, 11/F, Sec. 2, Nanking East Road, Taipei 10553, Taiwan (office). *Telephone:* (2) 26620332 (office). *Fax:* (2) 25082941 (office). *E-mail:* cwadmin@cw.com.tw (office). *Website:* www.cw.com.tw (office).

YING, Hong; Chinese writer; b. 1962, Chongqing; m. 1st Yiheng Zhao (divorced 2002), m. 2nd Adam Williams 2010; one d. *Publications include:* Far Goes the Girl 1994, Summer of Betrayal (in trans. 1997) 1995, Daughter of the River (autobiog., in trans. 1999) 1997, A Lipstick Called Red Pepper (short stories) 1999, K: The Art of Love (in trans. 2002) (Rome Prize) 1999, Ananda 2001, Peacock Cries (in trans. 2005) 2002, The Concubine of Shanghai (in trans. 2008) 2003, The Green Platye 2004, Death in Shanghai 2005, Good Children of the Flowers (autobiog.) 2009. *Literary Agent:* The Marsh Agency Ltd, 50 Albemarle Street, London, W1S 4BD, England. *Telephone:* (20) 7493-4361. *Fax:* (20) 7495-8961. *Website:* www.marsh-agency.co.uk. *Address:* c/o Marion Boyars Publishers, 26 Parke Road, London, SW13 9NG, England (office). *E-mail:* catheryn@marionboyars.com (office). *Website:* www.marionboyars.co.uk.

YOLEN, Jane, BA, MEd; American writer, poet, editor and storyteller; b. 11 Feb. 1939, New York, NY; m. David Wilber Stemple 1962; two s. one d. *Education:* Smith Coll., Univ. of Massachusetts. *Career:* mem. Authors' Guild, Children's Literature Asscn, MWA, SFWA (pres. 1986–88), Soc. of Children's Book Writers and Illustrators (bd of advisers 1970–). *Publications include:* adult books: Briar Rose, Cards of Grief, One-Armed Queen, Sister, Light, Sister Dark, White Jenna, The Books of Great Alta, Among Angels (poems), Dragonfield, Merlin's Booke, The Radiation Sonnets, Storyteller Nesfa, Tales of Wonder, Sister Emily's Lightship and Other Stories, The Whitethorn Wood and Other Magicks (chapbook), Except the Queen; children's poetry: Animal Fare, A Sip of Aesop, Best Witches, Bird Watch, Color Me a Rhyme, Dear Mother, Dear Daughter, Dinosaur Dances, Dragon Night, Horizons, How Beastly, O Jerusalem, Least Things, The Originals, Raining Cats & Dogs, Ring of Earth, Sacred Places, Sea Watch, Snow, Snow, Three Bears Holiday Rhyme Book, Three Bears Rhyme Book, Water Music, What Rhymes With Moon, Wild Wings; children's fiction: All in the Woodland Early, All Those Secrets of the World, An Invitation to the Butterfly Ball, Baby Bear's Bedtime Book, The Ballad of the Pirate Queens, Before the Storm, Beneath the Ghost Moon, Bird of Time, Boy Who Had Wings, Child of Faerie, Dove Isabeau, Eeny Meeny Miney Mole, Elfabet, Elsie's Bird, The Emperor & the Kite, Encounter, Fairy Holiday Book, Firebird, The Flying Witch, The Girl in the Golden Bower, The Girl Who Loved the Wind, Good Griselle, Grandad Bill's Song, Grandma's Hurrying Child, Greyling, Gwinellen: The Princess Who Could Not Sleep, Hands, Hannah Dreaming, Harvest Home, Honkers, Hoptoad, How Do Dinosaurs Get Well Soon?, How Do Dinosaurs Say Goodnight?, Isabel's Noel, It All Depends, King Longshanks, The Lady & the Merman, Letter From Phoenix Farm, Letting Swift River Go, Little Angel's Birthday, Little Mouse and Elephant, Little Spotted Fish, Longest Name on the Block, Meet the Monsters, Merlin & the Dragons, Milkweed Days, Minstrel & the Mountain, Miz Berlin Walks, Moonball, Mouse's Birthday, Musicians of Bremen, My Brothers' Flying Machine, My Uncle Emily, No Bath Tonight, Nocturne, Off We Go, Old Dame Counterpane, Owl Moon, Pegasus the Flying Horse, Picnic With Piggins, Piggins, Piggins & the Royal Wedding, Prince of Egypt, Rainbow Rider, Raising Yoder's Barn, The Scarecrow's Dance, Sea King, The Seeing Stick, See This Little Line, The Seventh Mandarin, The Simple Prince, Sky Dogs, Sleeping Beauty, Soft House, The Sultan's Perfect Tree, Tam Lin, Tea With an Old Dragon, Too Old For Naps, Traveler's Rose, Welcome to the Green House, Welcome to the Ice House, Welcome to the Sea of Sand, Welcome to the River of Grass, Where Have the Unicorns Gone?, Wings, The Witch Who Wasn't, Commander Toad in Space, Commander & the Big Black Hole, Commander Toad & the Intergalactic Spy, Commander Toad & the Space Pirates, Commander Toad & the Dis-Asteroid, Commander Toad & the Planet of the Grapes, Commander Toad & the Voyage Home, The Giants' Farm, The Giants Go Camping, Mice on Ice, Sleeping Ugly, Spider Jane, Spider Jane on the Move, Acorn Quest, Adventures of Eeka Mouse, And Twelve Chinese Acrobats, Boy Who Spoke Chimp, Boots & the Seven Leaguers, Disas-Tour, Brothers of the Wind, Hobo Toad & the Motorcycle Gang, Inway Investigators, The Magic Three of Solatia, The Mermaid's Three Wisdoms, Pay the Piper, Robot & Rebecca: The Case of the Code-Carrying Kids, Robot & Rebecca: The Mystery of the Missing Owser, The Seaman, Shirlick Holmes & The Case of the Wandering Wardrobe, Tartan Magic: The Pictish Child, Tartan Magic: The Wizard's Map, Tartan Magic: Bagpiper's Ghost, Transfigured Hart, Uncle Lemon's Spring, Wild Hunt, Wizard of Washington Square, Wizard's Hall, Young Heroes: Atalanta and The Arcadian Beast, Young Heroes: Hippolyta and the Curse of the Amazons, Young Heroes: Odysseus in the Serpent Maze, Young Heroes: Jason and the Gorgon's Blood, Passager, Hobby, Merlin, Armageddon Summer, Children of the Wolf, The Devil's Arithmetic, Dragon's Boy, The Gift of Sarah Barker, Dragon's Blood, Heart's Blood, A Sending of Dragons, Prince in the Heather, Queen's Own Fool, Rogue's Apprentice, Girl in a Cage, The Stone Silenus, Sword of the Rightful King, Trust a City Kid; non-fiction: Fairy Tale Feasts, Friend: The Story of George Fox & the Quakers, The Wolf Girls, Mary Celeste, Roanoke Colony, Salem Witch Trials, Amelia Earhart, House, House, My Brothers' Flying Machine, The Perfect Wizard: Hans Christian Andersen, Pirates in Petticoats, Ring Out: A Book of Bells, Simple Gifts: The Story of the Shakers, Wizard Islands, World on a String: The Story of Kites; other: short story collections, contrib. to anthologies, periodicals. *Honours:* Dr hc (Smith Coll., Northampton, MA), (Baypath Coll., Longmeadow, MA), (Keene State Coll., Keene, NH), (Our Lady of the Elms Coll., Chicopee, MA); Christopher Medals 1979, 2001, Mythopoeic Soc. Awards 1986, 1993, Smith Coll. Medal 1988, Caldecott Medal 1988, Regina Medal 1992, Keene State Coll. Children's Book Award 1995, Nebula Awards 1997, 1998, World Fantasy Award 1988. *Address:* Phoenix Farm, PO Box 27, Hatfield, MA 01038, USA (home). *E-mail:* janeyolen@aol.com (office). *Website:* www.janeyolen.com.

YOON, Prabda, BFA; Thai writer, artist and journalist; b. 1973, Bangkok. *Education:* Cooper Union School for the Advancement of Science and Art, New York, USA. *Career:* f. Typhoon Books publishing house 2005. *Screenplays:* Last Life in the Universe 2003, Invisible Waves 2006. *Publications include:* City of Right Angles (short stories) 1999, Probability (short stories) (SEA Write Award 2002) 2002, Chit-tak! (novel) 2002, Panda (novel) 2004, Lessons in Rain (novel) 2005, Under the Snow (novel) 2006; numerous essay collections and translations. *Honours:* SEA Write Award 2002. *E-mail:* typhoonbooks@yahoo.com (office). *Website:* www.typhoonbooks.com (office); prabdayoon.wordpress.com.

YORK, Alison (see Nicole, Christopher Robin)

YORK, Andrew (see Nicole, Christopher Robin)

YORKE, Margaret, (Margaret Beda Nicholson); British writer; b. 30 Jan. 1924, Surrey, England; m. Basil Nicholson 1945 (divorced 1957, deceased); one s. one d. *Career:* Asst Librarian St Hilda's Coll., Oxford 1959–60; Library Asst Christ Church, Oxford 1963–65; Chair. CWA 1979–80. *Publications:* Summer Flight 1957, Pray Love Remember 1958, Christopher 1959, Deceiving Mirror 1960, The China Doll 1961, Once a Stranger 1962, The Birthday 1963, Full Circle 1965, No Fury 1967, The Apricot Bed 1968, The Limbo Ladies 1969, Dead in the Morning 1970, Silent Witness 1972, Grave Matters 1973, No Medals for the Major 1974, Mortal Remains 1974, The Small Hours of the Morning 1975, Cast for Death 1976, The Cost of Silence 1977, The Point of Murder 1978, Death on Account 1979, The Scent of Fear 1980, The Hand of Death 1981, Devil's Work 1982, Find Me a Villain 1983, The Smooth Face of Evil 1984, Intimate Kill 1985, Safely to the Grave 1986, Evidence to Destroy 1987, Speak for the Dead 1988, Crime in Question 1989, Admit to Murder 1990, A Small Deceit 1991, Criminal Damage 1992, Dangerous to Know 1993, Almost the Truth 1994, Pieces of Justice 1994, Serious Intent 1995, A Question of Belief 1996, Act of Violence 1997, False Pretences 1998, The Price of Guilt 1999, A Case to Answer 2000, Cause for Concern 2001. *Honours:* Swedish Acad. of Detection Award 1982, CWA Cartier Diamond Dagger 1999. *Literary Agent:* Curtis Brown Ltd, Haymarket House, 28–29 Haymarket, London, SW1Y 4SP, England. *Telephone:* (20) 7393-4400. *Fax:* (20) 7393-4401. *E-mail:* info@curtisbrown.co.uk. *Website:* www.curtisbrown.co.uk.

YOSHIMASU, Gozo, BA; Japanese poet, essayist and lecturer; b. 22 Feb. 1939, Tokyo; m. Marilia 1973. *Education:* Keio Univ. *Career:* Chief Ed., Sansai Finer Arts magazine 1964–69; Fulbright Visiting Writer, Univ. of Iowa 1970–71; poet-in-residence, Oakland Univ., Rochester, MI 1979–81; Lecturer, Tama Art Univ. 1984–; visiting lecturer at various institutions; many poetry readings around the world; mem. Japan PEN Club, Japan Writers' Asscn. *Publications include:* Shuppatsu (Departure) 1964, A Thousand Steps and More: Selected Poems and Prose, 1964–1984 (in English trans.) 1987; contrib. to anthologies and periodicals. *Honours:* Takami Jun Prize 1971, Rekitei Prize 1979, Hanatsubaki Modern Poetry Prize 1984, Japan Govt Purple Ribbon Award 2003, Mainichi Art Award 2009. *Address:* c/o Japan Writers' Association, Shinkan 7F, Bungei-Shunju Building, 3-23, Kioi-Cho, Chiyoda-ku, Tokyo 102-8559, Japan.

YOSHIMOTO, Banana; Japanese writer; b. (Mahoko Yoshimoto), 24 July 1964, Tokyo; d. of Takaaki Yoshimoto. *Education:* Nihon Univ. *Career:* mem. Japan Writers' Asscn. *Publications include:* Mūn raito shadou (Moonlight Shadow) 1986, Kicchen (Kitchen) (Izumi Kyoka Literary Prize 1986, Kaien Magazine New Writer Prize 1987) 1987, Tugumi (Goodbye Tsugumi) (Yamamoto Shugoro Literary Prize 1989) 1988, Pineapple Pudding, N.P. 1990, Fruit Basket, Tokage (Lizard) 1993, Amrita (Murasaki-shikibu Prize 1995) 1994, Furin to nanbei (Asleep) (Bunkamura Duet Magot Literary Prize 2000) 2000, Hardboiled/Hard Luck 2005. *Honours:* Minister of Educ. Award for New Artists 1988, Scanno Prize 1993, Fendissime Literary Prize 1996, Maschera d'argento Prize 1999. *E-mail:* admin@yoshimotobanana.com (office). *Website:* www.yoshimotobanana.com.

YOUN, Monica, BA, JD, MPhil; American lawyer and poet. *Education:* Princeton Univ., Yale Law School, Oxford Univ., UK. *Career:* fmrly in private legal practice and law clerk to Judge John T. Noonan, Jr, US Court of Appeals for the Ninth Circuit; Sr Counsel, Brennan Center for Justice, New York Univ. School of Law; has taught creative writing at Columbia Univ. and Pratt Inst. *Publications:* poetry collections: Barter 2003, Ignatz 2010; contrib. poems to anthologies and journals and political commentary to Slate, Roll Call and The Huffington Post. *Honours:* Library of Congress Witter Bynner Fellowship, residencies from MacDowell Colony, Corpn of Yaddo and Rockefeller Foundation, New Leaders Council's Dipaola Foundation Democracy Rejuvenation Award and one of its 40 Under 40 for 2010. *Address:* c/o Four Way Books, PO Box 535, Village Station, New York, NY 10014, USA (office). *Telephone:* (212) 334-5430 (office). *E-mail:* editors@fourwaybooks.com (office).

YOUNG, Albert (Al) James, BA; American writer and poet; b. 31 May 1939, Ocean Springs, MS; m. Arline June Belch 1963; one s. *Education:* Univ. of Michigan, Stanford Univ., Univ. of California at Berkeley. *Career:* Edward B. Jones Lecturer in Creative Writing, Stanford Univ. 1969–76; writer-in-residence, Univ. of Washington, Seattle 1981–82; founder (with Ishmael Reed) and Ed., Quilt magazine 1981–; Mellon Distinguished Prof. of Humanities, Rice Univ. 1982; Lila Wallace-Readers Digest Fellowship Lecturer 1992–94; Woodrow Wilson Lecturer 1995–99; Rockefeller Distinguished Lecturer, Univ. of Arkansas at Pine Bluff 1995; Lurie Prof. of Creative Writing, San Jose State Univ. 2002; McGee Prof. in Writing, Davidson Coll., Davidson, NC 2003; Coffey Visiting Prof. of Creative Writing, Appalachian State Univ., Boone, NC 2003; Poet Laureate of California 2005–08; bd mem., California Council on Humanities 1987–91, Squaw Valley Community of Writers 1995–. *Screenplays:* Nigger 1972, Sparkle 1972, A Piece of the Action 1976, Bustin' Loose 1979, Personal Problems (TV pilot, with Ishmael Reed) 1982, The Stars and Their Courses 1983. *Publications:* poetry: Dancing 1969, The Song Turning Back into Itself 1971, Geography of the Near Past 1976, The Blues Don't Change: New and Selected Poems 1982, Heaven: Collected Poems 1956–1990 1992, Straight No Chaser (chapbook) 1994, Conjugal Visits (chapbook) 1996, The Sound of Dreams Remembered: Poems 1990–2000 (Before Columbus Foundation American Book Award, New York 2002) 2001, Coastal Nights and Inland Afternoons: Poems 2001–2006 2006; prose: Snakes (novel) (American Library Asscn Notable Book of the Year 1970) 1970, Yardbird Lives! (ed., with Ishmael Reed) 1972, Who is Angelina? (novel) 1976, Sitting Pretty (novel) 1976, Calafía: The California Poetry (co-ed.) 1979, Ask Me Now (novel) (New York Times Notable Book of the Year) 1980, Bodies and Soul (musical memoir) (American Book Award 1982) 1981, Kinds of Blue (musical memoir) 1984, Things Ain't What They Used to Be (musical memoir) 1987, Seduction by Light (novel) 1988, Mingus/Mingus: Two Memoirs (with Janet Coleman) 1989, Drowning in the Sea of Love (musical memoir) (PEN/USA Award for Best Non-Fiction Book of the Year 1996) 1995, African American Literature: A Brief Introduction and Anthology (ed.) 1996, The Literature of California (vols I and II, co-ed.) 2000, 2002. *Honours:* Wallace Stegner Writing Fellowship 1966, Nat. Arts Council Award for Magazine Editing (for Loveletter) 1969, Joseph Henry Jackson Award for Poetry 1969, CCLM Award for Poetry 1969, NEA Special Projects grant 1970, Guggenheim Fellowship 1974, NEA Writing Fellowship for Fiction 1975, Pushcart Prizes 1976, 1980, Key to the City of Detroit 1982, Detroit Bd of Education Outstanding Achievement Citation 1982, Fulbright Fellowship, Yugoslavia 1984, Ploughshares Rita and Mel Cohen Award for Poetry 1987, San Francisco Arts Commission Outstanding Artist Award 1987, Peninsula Book Club of California Outstanding Writer 1990, PEN/Library of Congress Award for Short Fiction 1991, Univ. of Michigan Martin Luther King Jr/César Chávez/Rosa Parks Award 1993. *E-mail:* alyoung@alyoung.org (office). *Website:* www.alyoung.org.

YOUNG, Dean, BA, MFA; American poet and academic; b. 1955, Columbia, Pa; m. Cornelia Nixon. *Education:* Indiana Univ. *Career:* Visiting Prof., Univ. of Wisconsin 1989; Visiting Distinguished Prof., St Mary's Coll. 2000; Asst Prof., Loyola Univ, Chicago 1989–95, Assoc. Prof. 1995–2000; Visiting Prof., Iowa Writers Workshop 1998, 2001–03, Assoc. Prof. 2003–06, Prof. 2006–08; William Livingston Chair of Poetry, Univ. of Texas 2008–; mem. faculty, Bread Loaf Writers Conf. 2003, 2004, 2008, Squaw Valley Writers Conf. 2004, 2006, 2008; Visiting Poet, Vermont Studio Center 2000, 2002, 2004; Virginia Butts Sturm Writer-in-Residence, Univ. of West Virginia 2002. *Publications include:* Design with X 1988, Beloved Infidel 1992, Strike Anywhere (Colorado Poetry Prize) 1995, First Course in Turbulence 1999, Skid 2002, Elegy on Toy Piano 2005, Embryoyo 2007, Primitive Mentor 2008, 7 Poets, 4 Days, 1 Book 2009, The Art of Recklessness: Poetry as Assertive Force and Contradiction 2010; contrib. to anthologies, including The Best American Poetry, and to journals, including Ploughshares, The Threepenny Review, Fence, American Letters & Commentary. *Honours:* Fine Arts Work Center, Provincetown fellowship, Stanford Univ. Stegner fellowship, two Nat. Endowment for the Arts fellowships, Guggenheim Fellowship 2002, American Acad. of Arts and Letters Award in Literature 2007. *Address:* Department of English, University of Texas, 1 University Station, B5000, Austin, TX 78712, USA (office). *Telephone:* (512) 471-8394. *E-mail:* deanyoung@mail.utexas.edu. *Website:* www.utexas.edu/cola/depts/english (office).

YOUNG, Ian George; British/Canadian poet, writer and editor; b. 5 Jan. 1945, London; s. of George Roland Young and Joan Margaret Patricia Young (née Morris); m. Wulf. *Career:* Dir Catalyst Press 1969–80, TMW Communications 1990–; Dir Ian Young Books 2001–, Sykes Press 2008–. *Publications:* poetry: White Garland 1969, Year of the Quiet Sun 1969, Double Exposure 1970, Cool Fire 1970, Lions in the Stream 1971, Some Green Moths 1972, The Male Muse 1973, Invisible Words 1974, Common-or-Garden Gods 1976, The Son of the Male Muse 1983, Sex Magick 1986; fiction: On the Line 1981; non-fiction: The Male Homosexual in Literature 1975, Overlooked and Underrated 1981, Gay Resistance 1985, The AIDS Dissidents 1993, The Stonewall Experiment 1995, The AIDS Cult 1997, The AIDS Dissidents: A Supplement 2001, Autobibliography 2001, The Beginnings of Gay Liberation in Canada 2004, Out in Paperback: A Visual History of Gay Pulps 2007. *Honours:* several Canada Council and Ont. Arts Council Awards. *Address:* 2483 Gerrard Street E, Scarborough, Ont. M1N 1W7, Canada (home). *E-mail:* iyoung@arvotek.net. *Website:* www.ianyoungbooks.com.

YOUNG OF HORNSEY, Baroness (Life Peer), cr. 2004, of Hornsey in the London Borough of Haringey; **Margaret Omolola (Lola) Young,** OBE, DipArts, BA, PhD, FRSA; British arts consultant and fmr government official and fmr academic; *Consultant, Cultural Brokers*; b. 1 June 1951; m. Barrie Birch 1984; one s. *Education:* Parliament Hill School for Girls, London, New Coll. of Speech and Drama, Middlesex Univ. *Career:* began career in arts devt promoting black arts and culture; residential social worker London Borough of Islington 1971–73; professional actor 1976–84; Co-Dir and Training and Devt Man. Haringey Arts Council 1985–89; freelance lecturer and arts consultant 1989–91; Lecturer in Media Studies Polytechnic of West London/Thames Valley Univ. 1990–92; Lecturer, Univ. of Middx, later Sr Lecturer, Principal Lecturer, Prof. of Cultural Studies 1992–2001; Head of Culture, GLA 2002–04; worked with METAL (arts centre) London; Project Dir Nat. Museum and Archives of Black History and Culture (NMABHC) 1997–2001; Commissioner Royal Commission on Historical Manuscripts 2000–01; fmr Chair. British Council Arts Advisory Cttee 2004; fmr Chair. Arts Council Cultural Diversity Panel; mem. Bd Dirs Royal Nat. Theatre 2000–03, South Bank Centre 2002–; currently arts, heritage and diversity consultant, Cultural Brokers; numerous radio and television broadcasts. *Publication:* Fear of the Dark: Race, Gender and Sexuality in Cinema 1996; numerous newspaper articles. *Address:* Cultural Brokers, Building D, Unit 208, The Chocolate Factory, London, N22 6XJ, England (office). *Telephone:* (20) 8888-8797 (office). *Fax:* (20) 8888-8797 (office). *E-mail:* culturalbrokers@btconnect.com (office). *Website:* www.culturalbrokers.com (office).

YOUNG, Rose (see Harris, Marion Rose)

YOUNG-EISENDRATH, Polly, BA, MA, MSW, PhD; American psychologist, psychoanalyst and author; *Clinical Associate Professor in Psychiatry, University of Vermont at Burlington;* b. (Pauline Young), 4 Feb. 1947, Akron, Ohio; single; two s. one d. *Education:* Ohio Univ., Institut de Touraine, France, Goddard Coll., Washington Univ., Inter-Regional Soc. of Jungian Analysts. *Career:* Chief Psychologist, Jungian analyst, Pres., Clinical Assocs West, P. C. Radnor 1986–94; ind. practice as psychologist and Jungian analyst, Burlington, Vt 1994–; Clinical Assoc. Prof. in Psychiatry, Medical Coll., Univ. of Vermont, Burlington 1996–, Clinical Assoc. Research Prof. in Psychology 2005–; Clinical Supervisor in Psychology, Norwich Univ. at Northfield 2005–; numerous lectures world-wide; mem. Int. Asscn for Analytical Psychology, American Psychological Asscn, Ind. Soc. for Analytical Psychology (Founding mem.). *Publications:* Jung's Self Psychology: A Constructivist Perspective 1991, You're Not What I Expected: Learning to Love the Opposite Sex 1993, The Gifts of Suffering: Finding Insight, Compassion and Renewal 1996, Gender and Desire: Uncursing Pandora 1997, A Cambridge Companion to Jung (co-ed.) 1997, Women and Desire: Beyond Wanting to be Wanted 1999, The Psychology of Mature Spirituality: Integrity, Wisdom, Transcendence 2000, Awakening and Insight: Zen Buddhism and Psychotherapy 2002, Subject to Change: Jung, Gender and Subjectivity in Psychoanalysis 2004, We Just Want You to Be Happy: Where American Parenting Went Wrong 2007, The Self-Esteem Trap 2008; contrib. to professional journals. *Honours:* Otto Weininger Award for Lifetime Achievement in Psychoanalysis, Canadian Psychological Asscn; various fellowships, assistantships and awards. *Address:* 195 Calais Road, Worcester, VT 05682, USA (office). *Telephone:* (802) 223-6223 (office). *E-mail:* pollye@comcast.net (office). *Website:* young-eisendrath.com.

YOUSSEF, Essam; Egyptian writer, film producer and business executive; *CEO, Montana Studios;* b. 21 Oct. 1965, Cairo; s. of Abdel Tawab Youssef and Notaila Rashed; m.; one s. two d. *Education:* Faculty of Arts, Univ. of Cairo. *Career:* Founder and CEO Montana Studios film production co. 2007–. *Publications:* A ¼ Gram (best selling novel in Egypt, 25 edns in two years) 2008. *Address:* Montana Studios, 10 El Refa'a Bek Street, off El Khalifa El Maamon, Apt 101, Heliopolis, Cairo, Egypt (office). *Telephone:* 24515570/80 (office). *Fax:* 24515590 (office). *E-mail:* info@montanastudios.tv (office). *Website:* www.montanastudios.tv (office).

YOUSSEF, Samir al-; Palestinian/British writer, essayist and reviewer; b. 1965, Rashidia, Lebanon. *Education:* Univ. of London. *Career:* regular contrib. to major Arab periodicals and London-based Arabic news services. *Publications include:* Domestic Affairs (short stories) 1994, Gaza Blues (short stories, with Etgar Keret) 2004, The Illusion of Return (novel) 2007, A Treaty of Love 2008. *Honours:* PEN Tucholsky Prize 2005. *Address:* c/o Halban Publishers Ltd, 22 Golden Square, London, W1F 9JW, England (office). *Website:* www.halbanpublishers.com (office).

YSÀS SOLANES, Pere, PhD; Spanish historian and academic; *Faculty Professor, Autonomous University of Barcelona;* b. 11 Feb. 1955, Rubi, Barcelona. *Education:* Universidad de Barcelona. *Career:* Prof., Dept of Modern and Contemporary History, Faculty of Philosophy and Literature, Autonomous Univ. of Barcelona 1986–, Prof., Faculty of Political Science and Sociology 1986–98; mem. Grup de Recerca sobre l'Època Franquista, Centre d'Estudis sobre les Epoques Franquista i Democratica (Dir). *Publications:* L'oposició antifeixista a Catalunya 1939–1950 (with Carme Molinero) 1981, 'Patria, Justicia y Pan'. Nivell de vida i condicions de treball a Catalunya 1939–1951 (with Carme Molinero) 1985, Els industrials catalans durant el franquisme (with Carme Molinero) 1991, El règim franquista. Feixisme, modernització i consens (with Carme Molinero) 1992, 2003, Productores disciplinados y minorías subversivas. Clase obrera y conflictividad laboral en la España franquista (with Carme Molinero) 1998, Catalunya durant el franquisme (with Carmen Molinero) 1999, Historia Política de españa 1939–2000 (with Carme Molinero and José M. Marin) 2001, Disidencia y subversión: La lucha del régimen franquista por su supervivencia 1960–1975 2004, La anatomía del franquismo. De la supervivencia a la agonía 1945–1977 (with Carme Molinero) 2008, Els anys del PSUC. El partit de l'antifranquisme (1956–1981) (with Carme Molinero) 2010; contrib. of chapters to numerous publs, articles to journals and newspapers, including Arraona, L'Avenç Revista d'Història, Avui, Ayer, Balma: Didàctica de les Ciencies Socials, Geografia i Historia, Cuadernos de Historia Contemporánea, Cuadernos de Relaciones Laborales, Historia Contemporánea, Storia e problemi contemporanei, Historia Social, Historia y Política, Nous Horitzons, El País, Realitat, Recerques, Revista de Historia Económica, Taula de Canvi, La Vanguardia, Veus Alternatives. *Address:* Departamento de Historia Moderna y Contemporánea, Edifici B, Universitat Autònoma de Barcelona, Campus Universitari, 08193 Bellaterra (Cerdanyola del Vallès), Barcelona (office); Calle Le Mola 3, 08912 Sant Quirze del Vallès, Barcelona, Spain (home). *Telephone:* (93) 581-23-18 (office). *Fax:* (93) 581-20-01 (office). *E-mail:* pere.ysas@uab.cat (office); pere.ysas@uab.es (office). *Website:* www.uab.cat/departament/historia-moderna-contemporania (office); www.cefid.uab.es/?q=es/membres#ysas (office).

YSTAD, Vigdis, DPhil; Norwegian academic; *Professor of Scandinavian Literature, University of Oslo;* b. 13 Jan. 1942, Verdal; d. of Ottar Ystad and Guri Todal; m. 1st Asbjørn Liland 1962; m. 2nd Daniel Haakonsen 1971; one s. one d. *Education:* Univs of Trondheim and Oslo. *Career:* lecturer, Univ. of Oslo 1974, Prof. of Scandinavian Literature 1979–, mem. Univ. Bd 1990–92; Chair. Council for Research in the Humanities 1985; Chair. Bd Centre for Advanced Study, Norwegian Acad. of Science and Letters 1992–93; Vice-Chair. Nat. Acad. of Dramatic Art 1993–96; mem. Norwegian Research Council 1979–85, Norwegian Govt Research Cttee 1982–84; mem. Norwegian Acad. of Science and Letters, Norwegian Acad. for Language and Literature, Royal Swedish Acad. of Letters, History and Antiquities 2004, Kungliga Vetenskaps-Societeten 2004; mem. Bd Nat. Acad. of Art 2000–02, Oslo Acad. of Art 2000–02, Nansenskolen, Lillehammer 2001–; Gen. Ed. Henrik Ibsens skrifter 1998–. *Publications:* Kristofer Uppdals Lyrikk 1978, Henrik Ibsens Dikt 1991, Sigrid Undsel: Et kvinneliv-'livets endeløse gåde' 1993, Ibsens dikt og drama 1996, Contemporary Approaches to Ibsen, Ibsen studies (ed.). *Address:* Centre for Ibsen Studies, Box 1116, Blindern, 0316 Oslo (office); Thomas Heftyes gt. 56b, 0267 Oslo, Norway (home). *Telephone:* 22-85-91-65 (office); 22-55-94-66 (home). *Fax:* 22-85-91-69 (office). *E-mail:* a.v.ystad@ibsen.uio.no (office).

YTURBIDE, Teresa Castelló, (Pascuala Corona); Mexican writer; b. 21 March 1917, Mexico City. *Education:* Escuela Nacional de Arte La Esmeralda. *Career:* contrib. to numerous magazines including El Rebozo, Artes de Mexico. *Publications include:* Cuentos mexicanos para niños 1945, Cuentos de rancho 1951, El traje indígena en México 1965, El Traje Indigena en Mexico Tomo II 1968, El Mueble Mexicano 1969, El Arte De La Cera En México 1974, Pita, pita, cedacero 1981, Tres colorantes prehispánicos (Premio White Ravens 1987) 1985, Presencia De La Comida Prehispanica 1986, Cuentos de Pascuala 1986, Sangalote 1987, La seda 1987, El niño dulcero 1987, Colorantes Naturales De Mexico 1988, Rebozos Y Sarapes De Mexico 1989, La Tejedora De Vida: Coleccion De Trajes Mexicanos De Banca Serfin 1989, Historia Y Arte De La Seda En Mexico: Siglos XVI–XX 1990, El pozo de los ratones 1992, El señor don gato 1992, La Seda (Coleccion Pinata Series) 1992, El Arte Plumaria En Mexico 1993, La frasterita 1996, Rebozos De La Coleccion Robert Everts 1997, La Chaquira En Mexico 1998, El morralito de ocelote (Premio Antoniorrobles 1993) 1998, Delicias De Antano: Historia Y Recetas De Los Conventos Mexicanos 2001, Baulito de cuentos contados por Pascuala Corona 2003, Leyenda de la china poblana 2005, Baulito De Cuentos 2005, Mi abuela Romualda 2006. *Honours:* Premio Bellas Artes de Cuento Infantil Juan de la Cabada 2010. *Address:* Ediciones Tecolote, Jose Ceballos 10, San Miguel Chapultepec, 11850 México DF, Mexico. *Telephone:* (25) 5272-8085. *Fax:* (25) 5272-8139. *Website:* www.edicionestecolote.com.

YU, Guangzhong; Taiwanese academic, poet, critic, translator and essayist; b. 9 Sept. 1928, Nanjing City, Jiangsu Prov.; m. Wo Chun Fan 1956; four d. *Education:* Iowa Univ., USA. *Career:* Chief Ed. of Blue Stars and Modern Literature; Prof., Taiwan Normal Univ., Chinese Univ. of Hong Kong; Kuang Hua Chair. Prof. of English, Nat. Sun Yat-sen Univ. 1998–; Pres. Taipei Chinese Centre, PEN Int. 1990–99. *Publications:* Elegy of Boatman, Stalactite, Blue Plume, Sirius, White Jade Bitter Gourd, A Tug of War with Eternity, Dream and Geography, Selected Poetry of Yu Guangzhong Vols I and II, The Child of Dogwood–A Life of Yu Guangzhong 1999, The Old Man and the Sea (trans.), The Importance of being Earnest (trans.), Lust for Life (trans.) Bartleby the Scrivener (trans.), Modern English and American Poetry (trans.), Ou Shen. *Honours:* Hon. Fellow Hong Kong Trans. Soc. 1991; Australian Cultural Award 1972; Best Books of the Year 1994, 1996, 1998, 2000 (Taiwan), 1998 (Hong Kong); Nat. Poetry Prize, Wu San-Lian Prose Prize and six others. *Address:* Foreign Literature Institute, Sun Yat-sen University, 135 Xingang Road, Guanzhou 510275, Guangdong Province, People's Republic of China. *Telephone:* (7) 5564908 (home); (20) 84112828. *Fax:* (20) 84039173. *E-mail:* adpo@zsu.edu.cn (office). *Website:* www.zsu.edu.cn (office).

YU, Hua, MA; Chinese writer; b. 3 April 1960, Gaotang, Shandong Prov.; m. Chen Hong; one s. *Career:* worked as a dentist for five years; writer 1983–. *Publications:* in trans: Leaving Home at Eighteen 1984, To Live (Grinzane Cavour Award, Italy) 1992, Chronicle of a Blood Merchant 1995, The Past and the Punishments 1996, Shouting in the Drizzle, Events of the World Are Like Smoke, One Kind of Reality, An Incident, Mistake at Riverside, Brothers 2005, China in Ten Words (essays) 2011. *Honours:* James Joyce Foundation Award 2002 (first Chinese to win award).

YŪ, Miri; South Korean (b. Japanese) writer, playwright and essayist; b. 22 June 1968, Kanagawa, Japan; one s. *Career:* fmr actress and Asst Dir Tokyo Kid Brothers theatre group; Co-founder Seishun Gogetsu To (The May Youth Group) theatre group 1986–. *Plays:* Sakana no matsuri (play, trans. as Fish Festival) 1993, Himawari no hitsugi (play, trans. as The Sunflowers' Coffin) 1993, Green Bench (play) 1993,. *Publications:* Ishi ni oyogu sakana (novel, trans. as Fish Swimming in Stone) 1994, Kazoku no hyōhon (essays, trans. as Family Disunity) 1995, Yū Miri no jisatsu (essays, trans. as Yū Miri's 'Suicide') 1995, Mado no aru shoten kara (essays, trans. as From the Bookshop with a Window) 1996, Full House (novel) 1996, Kazoku Shinema (novel, trans. as Family Cinema) (Akutegawa Prize) 1997, Mizube no yurikago 1997, Kaisetsu 1997, Kamen no kuni 1998, Gold Rush (novel) 1998, Inochi (memoir) 2000, Tamashii 2001, Ikiru 2001. *Honours:* Kishida Kunio Drama Prize, Izumi

Kyoka Prize, Noma Bungei Newcomer Literature Prize. *Website:* www.yu-miri.com.

YU, Nick Rongjun; Chinese playwright and director; b. July 1971, Anhui Prov. *Education:* Shanghai Theatre Acad. *Career:* Dir Shanghai Dramatic Arts Centre, Shanghai Univ. Theatre Festival 2004–, Shanghai Int. Contemporary Theatre Festival; versions of his plays have been performed in Singapore, Japan, Turkey, UK, Canada, South Korea, Germany, Italy and USA; has also translated several plays into Mandarin. *Plays:* The Insane Asylum is Next Door to Heaven, Last Winter 2000, www.com 2001, A Very Serious Matter 2002, The Salty Taste of Cappuccino 2002, Behind the Lie 2003, Perfume 2003, Midnight at Havana Club 2004, Dog's Face 2004, Activated Charcoal 2004, Love in a Fallen City 2005, A Winter Tale of Two Cities 2005, A Man Among Women 2005, Sighing 2006, Cry to Heaven 2007, The Angel in Wheelchair 2007, Drift 2007, The Dream of the Red Chamber 2007, Street Angel 2008, Dust to Dust 2008, Heartquake 2008, "1977" 2009, Das Kapital 2009, Boatmen 2010, Massage 2011, A Piano in the Factory 2011, Ballet Jane Eyre 2012; trans. into Mandarin include The Vagina Monologues (by Eve Ensler) 2006, I Love You, You're Perfect, Now Change (by Joe DiPietro and Jimmy Roberts) 2007. *Television:* Together For Life. *Address:* Shanghai Dramatic Arts Centre, 288 Anfu Lu, Xuhui, Shanghai 200031, People's Republic of China (office).

YU, Ying-shih, PhD; Chinese/American writer and academic; *Gordon Wu '58 Professor Emeritus of Chinese Studies, Princeton University;* b. 22 Jan. 1930, Tianjin; m. Monica Yu 1964; two d. *Education:* New Asia Coll., Hong Kong, Harvard Univ., USA. *Career:* moved to USA 1955; lecturer in various univs including Michigan, Harvard, Yale and Princeton; Pres. New Asia Coll. and Vice-Chancellor, Chinese Univ. of Hong Kong 1973–75; Prof., Harvard Univ. 1975–77, Yale Univ. 1977–87; Gordon Wu '58 Prof. of Chinese Studies, Princeton Univ. 1987–2001, Prof. Emer. 2001–; mem. Academia Sinica, Taiwan, American Philosophical Soc. *Publications include:* 30 books on various aspects of Chinese history including Trade and Expansion in Han China 1967, Anti-Intellectualism and the Tradition of Chinese Thought 1973, Modern Confucianist Theory (jtly) 1996, The Power of Culture: Studies in Chinese Cultural History (jtly). *Honours:* Kluge Prize (co-winner) 2006. *Address:* East Asian Studies Department, Princeton University, 211 Jones Hall, Princeton, NJ 08544, USA (office). *Telephone:* (609) 258-4276 (office). *E-mail:* ysyu@princeton.edu (office). *Website:* eastasia.princeton.edu (office).

YU, Youxian; Chinese publisher; b. 1937, Penglai Co., Shandong. *Education:* Nankai Univ. *Career:* joined CCP 1955; Teaching Asst, Chinese Language Dept, Nankai Univ. 1963, later becoming Head of Academic Research Section and Head of Teaching Reform Team; Ed. Henan People's Publishing House 1964, later Deputy Dir and Dir of Editorial Sub-Cttee, Asst Publr 1981, later Deputy Chief Ed., Publr, Chief Ed.; Deputy Head of Publicity, CCP Cttee, Henan Prov. 1984–86; Dir Educ. Comm., Henan Prov. 1986; Vice-Gov. Henan Prov. 1988–2000; Commr of State Admin of Press and Publs 1999; Commr, Nat. Copyright Admin of China 1999–; Pres. Publishers Asscn of China (now China Publication Asscn) –2011; mem. CCP Central Comm. for Discipline Inspection, 15th CCP Nat. Congress 1997; mem. Wisers China Advisory Bd 2008–. *Address:* c/o Press and Publications Administration, State Council, Beijing, People's Republic of China (office).

YUDKIN, Leon Israel, BA, MA, DLit; British academic and writer; b. 8 Sept. 1939, England; s. of Solomon and Ada Yudkin; m. Meirah Goss 1967. *Education:* Univ. of London. *Career:* Asst Lecturer, Lecturer, Univ. of Manchester 1966–; Lecturer, Univ. Coll. London 1996; Visiting Prof., Univ. of Paris VIII 2000; Visiting Prof., Charles Univ., Prague, Univ. of N Carolina, USA, Univ. of Paris 8 2004–. *Publications:* Isaac Lamdan: A Study in Twentieth-Century Hebrew Poetry 1971, Meetings with the Angel (co-ed.) 1973, Escape into Siege 1974, U. Z. Greenberg: On the Anvil of Hebrew Poetry 1980, Jewish Writing and Identity in the Twentieth Century 1982, 1948 and After: Aspects of Israeli Fiction 1984, Modern Hebrew Literature in English Translation (ed.) 1986, Agnon: Texts and Contexts in English Translation (ed.) 1988, Else Lasker-Schüler: A Study in German-Jewish Literature 1990, Beyond Sequence: Current Israeli Fiction and its Context 1992, The Israeli Writer and the Holocaust (ed.) 1993, The Other in Israeli Literature (ed.) 1993, A Home Within: Varieties of Jewish Expression in Modern Fiction 1996, Public Crisis and Literary Response: Modern Jewish Literature 2001, Literature in the Wake of the Holocaust 2003, Israel: A Vision of a State and its Literature 2006, In and Out: Bohemian Jewry and the Prague Circle 2010; contribs to various publs. *Telephone:* (20) 7794-6801 (office). *E-mail:* l.yudkin@ucl.ac.uk (office); yudk4@aol.com (home).

YUSON, Alfred, (Krip Yuson); Philippine writer; b. 1947. *Career:* fmr Henry Lee Irwin Professorial Chair, Ateneo de Manila Univ., now teaches fiction and poetry; literary confs, festivals and reading tours world-wide; columnist, The Philippine Star and Philippine Graphic magazine; Philippines Ed., MANOA: A Pacific Journal of International Writing (Univ. of Hawaii); founding mem., Philippine Literary Arts Council, Creative Writing Foundation, Inc., Manila Critics' Circle; Chair. UMPIL (Writers Union of the Philippines); bd mem. Movie and Television Ratings and Classification Bd. *Play:* Luto, Linis, Laba (Qbd Ink, The Writer's Center, Bethesda, USA) 2003. *Publications include:* 22 books, including three novels, short fiction, poetry and essay collections: Sea Serpent (poetry) 1980, Dream of Knives (poetry) 1986, The Great Philippine Jungle Energy Cafe (novel) (Palanca Grand Prize for the Novel) 1987, Confessions of a Q.C. house-husband and other privacies 1991, Trading in Mermaids (poetry) 1993, Voyeurs and Savages (novel) 1998, Mothers Like Elephants (poetry) 2000, Luto, Linis, Laba (play) (Carlos Palanca Memorial Awards for Literature 2000), The Word on Paradise (essays) 2001, The Philippines: Islands of Enchantment (non-fiction) 2002, Hairtrigger Loves: 50 Poems on Woman (poetry) 2002, Ang Walong Kuwento (short stories) 2002, The Music Child (novel) 2008. *Honours:* Rockefeller Foundation residency, Italy 2003, SEAWrite (SouthEast Asian Writers) Award for Lifetime Achievement 1992, Stalwart of Art & Culture Award 2003, Carlos Palanca Memorial Awards for Literature Hall of Fame, FAMAS Award, Catholic Mass Media Award. *Address:* c/o Anvil Publishing, 8007-B Pioneer Street, Bgy. Kapitolyo, 1603 Pasig City (office); c/o The Philippine Star, 13th Corner Railroad Street, Port Area, 1016 Manila, Philippines (office). *Telephone:* (2) 637-3621 (Anvil) (office); (2) 527-7901 (PhilStar) (office). *Fax:* (2) 637-6084 (Anvil) (office). *E-mail:* anvil.pubdept@yahoo.com (office); tmendoza@philstar.com.ph (office). *Website:* www.anvilpublishing.com (office).

YUSUF, Nova Riyanti; Indonesian novelist; b. 27 Nov. 1977. *Education:* Univ. of Indonesia. *Career:* trained as and fmrly worked as medical practitioner; mem. Dewan Perwakilan Rakyat (House of Reps) 2009–. *Publications:* Mahadewa Mahadewi (trans. as God, Goddess) 2003, Imipramine 2004, Jumal Prosa 4: Yang Jelita Yang Cerita 2004, 3some 2005, Garasi 2006. *Address:* c/o Dewan Perwakilan Rakyat (House of Representatives), Jalan Gatot Subroto 16, Jakarta, Indonesia (office). *E-mail:* humas@dpr.go.id (office). *Website:* www.dpr.go.id (office); noriyu.wordpress.com.

Z

ZABALETA, Marta Raquel, (Martita Criolla), BSc, MA, DPhil; British/Argentine economist, researcher, poet and writer; *Honorary Senior Visiting Lecturer in Latin American Studies, Middlesex University*; b. 26 June 1937, Alcorta, Santa Fe, Argentina; d. of the late Roque Zabaleta and Catalina Gerlo de Zabaleta; one s. one d. *Education:* Univ. del Litoral, Rosario, ESCOLATINA, Univ. de Chile and Inst. of Development Studies, Univ. of Sussex, UK. *Career:* Jr Fellow, CELADE UN, Chile 1965–66, ICIRA (FAO), Chile 1966–67; Assoc. Lecturer, then Prof., Univ. of Concepción, Chile 1968–73, Deputy Head, Dept of Econs 1973; expelled from Chile by Pinochet regime 1973; Researcher, Consejo Fed. de Inversiones, CFI Buenos Aires 1975; expelled from Argentina by Videla regime 1976; Lecturer, Middlesex Univ. (fmrly Middlesex Polytechnic) 1989–92, Sr Lecturer in Spanish and Latin American Studies, Culture and Gender, and Philosophy, Psychology and Sociology in Spanish 1992–2002, currently Hon. Visiting Sr Lecturer in Latin American Studies; Adviser, Change Int. UK 1980–2005; Co-ordinator Working Group on Gender and Women Studies, CEISAL 2001–, mem. int. jury of CEISAL Annual Prize 2002–06; Founder and Co-ordinator Int. Network 'Women and Words in the World' 1995–; mem. Exec. Cttee Latin American Women Rights' Service, UK 2005–07; organized several int. confs, simposia and round tables for Univ. of Middx, ICA and SLAS; corresp., FM Radio del Mar (Argentina) in London; mem. editorial bds of several scientific journals in Europe and Latin America and of Exiled Ink, UK; RESMES Rep. in UK. *Exhibition:* selected for her contribution to the culture and society of London, Be Longing Exhbn, Museum of London 2005. *Television:* featured in video and film documentaries, including Daughters of de Beauvoir (BBC) 1989. *Publications:* Reclaim the Earth: Women Speak Out for Life on Earth (contrib.) 1983, Daughters of de Beauvoir (contrib.) 1989, Women in Argentina: Realities, Myths and Dreams 1810–1992 1993, An Analysis of the Speeches of Eva Perón 1994, Feminine Stereotypes and Roles in Theory and Practice in Argentina Before and After the First Lady Eva Perón 2000, The Body Matters (ed.) 2002; numerous book chapters and conf. papers, in English, Spanish, Portuguese and Polish; numerous poems in Spanish, translated into Polish, Arabic, Catalan and English, including several anthologies. *Honours:* Govt of Argentina Presidential Decree of Recognition for work as First Class Social Scientist 1973, grants from several insts, including British Acad., British Council, German Acad., Soc. for the Protection of Science and Learning, Inst. of Devt Studies, Univ. of Sussex, Univ. of Warsaw, E.U. Socrates and numerous others. *Address:* Middlesex University, Trent Park Campus, Bramley Road, London, N14 4YZ, England (office). *Telephone:* (20) 8411-5000 (office). *E-mail:* m.zabaleta@mdx.ac.uk (office). *Website:* www.martazabaleta.com; www.martazabaleta.blogspot.com.

ZABUZHKO, Oksana, PhD; Ukrainian novelist and poet; b. 19 Sept. 1960, Lutsk; m. Rostyslav Luzhetsky. *Education:* Taras Shevchenko Univ. of Kiev. *Career:* fmr Assoc., Inst. of Philosophy, Nat. Acad. of Arts and Sciences, Kiev; Writer-in-Residence, Pennsylvania State Univ., USA 1992; Fulbright Scholar, Harvard Univ. and Univ. of Pittsburgh, USA 1994. *Publications:* poetry: Travnevyj Inij (translated as May Hoarfrost) 1985, Dyrygent Ostannyoji Svichky (translated as The Conductor of the Last Candle) 1990, Avtostop (translated as Hitchhiking) 1994, A Kingdom of Fallen Statues (poems and essays in trans.) 1996, Novyj Zakon Arkhimeda. Vybrani Virshi 1980–1998 (New Archimedes' Rule. Selected Poems 1980–1998) 2000, Druha Sproba (translated as The Second Try) 2005; fiction: Polyovi Doslidzhennia z Ukrajins'koho Seksu (novel, translated as Field Work in Ukrainian Sex) 1996, Kazka pro Kalynovu Sopilku (novella, translated as The Reedpipe Tale) 2000, Sestro, Sestro (short stories, translated as Sister, Sister) 2003, Knyha Buttia, Hlava Chetverta (novellas, translated as Book of Genesis, Chapter Four) 2008, Muzej Pokynutykh Sekretiv (novel, translated as The Museum of Abandoned Secrets) 2009; non-fiction: Shevchenkiv Mif Ukrajiny: Sproba Filosofs'koho Analizu (criticism, translated as Shevchenko's Myth of Ukraine: Toward a Philosophical Verification) 1997, Khroniky vid Fortinbrasa (translated as Chronicles of Fortinbras: the Selected Essays of the 1990s) 1999, Reportazh z 2000-ho Roku (essays, translated as News Report from the Year 2000) 2001, Let My People Go: 15 Textiv pro Ukrains'ku Revoluciju (Let My People Go: 15 Texts on Ukrainian Revolution) 2005, Notre Dame d'Ukraine: Ukrainka V Konflikti Mifolohij (criticism, translated as Notre Dame d'Ukraine: Ukrainka in the Clash of Mythologies) 2007; trans in fifteen countries; contrib. to Agni, Glas, Harvard Review, International Quarterly, Massachusetts Review, Mr Cogito, Nimrod, Partisan Review, Ploughshares, Poetry Miscellany, Slavic and East European Journal, Ukrainian Quarterly. *Honours:* Order of Princess Olha (Ukraine); Global Commitment Foundation Poetry Prize 1997, McArthur Grant 2002, The Most Important Ukrainian Book of the 15 Years of Independence Award 2006, Newsweek Ukraine's Top 100 Most Influential Ukrainians 2006, 2008, Antonovych Int. Foundation Award 2008. *Literary Agent:* c/o Galina Dursthoff Literarische Agentur, Marsiliusstr. 70, 50937 Cologne, Germany. *Telephone:* (221) 444254. *Fax:* (221) 4600053. *E-mail:* galina@dursthoff.de; gdursthoff@hotmail.com. *Website:* www.dursthoff.de; www.zabuzhko.com.

ZAGAJEWSKI, Adam, BA, MA; Polish writer, poet and academic; *Professor of Social Thought, University of Chicago*; b. 21 June 1945, Lvov; s. of Tadeusz Zagajewski and Ludwika Zagajewska; m. Maria Zagajewska. *Education:* Jagiellonian Univ., Kraków. *Career:* first published poetry and essays in literary reviews in 1960s; became well known as leading poet of 'Generation of 1968'; first collection of poems 1972; lived in France and joined staff of Zeszyty Literackie 1982–2002; Assoc. Prof. of English, Creative Writing Program, Univ. of Houston, USA 1988–2007; Prof. of Social Thought, Univ. of Chicago 2007–; mem. Polish Writers' Asscn, PEN Club; co-editor Zeszyty Literackie. *Publications include:* collections of poetry: Komunikat (Communique) 1972, Sklepy miesne (Meat Shops) 1975, Letter: An Ode to Multiplicity 1983, Jechac do Lwowa (Travelling to Lvov) 1985, Plotno (The Canvas) 1990, Ziemia ognista (The Fiery Land) 1994, Pragnienie (Desire) 2000, Powrót (Without End) 2003, Anteny 2005; novels: Cieplo, zimno (Warm and Cold) 1975, Cienka kreska (The Thin Line) 1983, Absolute Pitch (in German); short stories: Two Cities 1991; essays: Swiat nie przedstawiony (The Unpresented World, with Julian Kornhauser) 1974, Drugi oddech (Second Wind) 1978, Solidarnosc i samotnosc (Solidarity and Solitude) 1986, W cudzym pieknie (In the Beauty of Others) 1998, Obrona żarliwości (In Defence of Fervour) 2002, Poeta rozmawia z filozofem 2007. *Honours:* Koscielscy Foundation Award 1975, Andrzej Kijowski Award 1987, Alfred Jurzykowski Foundation Award 1989, Guggenheim Fellowship 1992, Int. Vilenica Prize (Slovenia) 1996, Tomas Transtromer Prize (Sweden) 2000, Neustadt Int. Prize for Fiction 2004. *Address:* Committee on Social Thought, Division of the Social Sciences, University of Chicago, 1130 East 59th Street, Chicago, IL 60637, USA (office). *Telephone:* (773) 702-8410 (office). *E-mail:* com-soc-tht@uchicago.edu (office). *Website:* socialthought.uchicago.edu (office).

ZAHIROVIĆ, Ajša Džemila, DLitt; Bosnia and Herzegovina writer, poet and lawyer; b. 21 March 1948, Sarajevo; d. of Ago Zahirović and Džemila Haćam; one d. *Education:* Faculty of Law, Sarajevo. *Career:* Adviser and Chef de Cabinet Cen. Cttee of Communist Party, Bosnia and Herzegovina 1970–78; Cultural Adviser and Chef de Cabinet Presidency of Bosnia and Herzegovina 1978–84; writer and poet 1984–; has published 15 books of poetry, works included in seven anthologies of women's poetry and several other anthologies; Co-Ed. Skylark Int. journal of poetry, India; mem. World Acad. of Arts and Culture, World Congress of Poets, Int. Women's Writing Guild, USA, Int. Poets' Acad., Madras (now Chennai), India, World Poetry Research Inst. Council of Dirs (Repub. of Korea), Poet–India Editorial Bd, Writers' Asscn of Bosnia and Herzegovina, Int. Writers and Artistics; many other literary orgs. *Publications include:* The Porch 1981, By The White Eye 1983, Terra Mare Amore 1983, Sapno Ki Chaya Me 1985, Vedeshi Mallige 1985, Another Moment 1987, At the Verge of the Road 1987, The Bridge Has Eyes 1988, Ak Aur Bazghashat 1989, Under the Crown (Australia Day Medallion) 1991, Selected Poems 1998, From Sarajevo to Ekashila 1998, Selected Poems 2002, Haiku From Sarajevo 2002, Selected Poems 2004; ed. of anthologies From Verse to Poem 1985, Special Yugoslav Women's Poetry Number of Skylark 1986, Special Bosnia and Herzegovina Poetry Number of Skylark 1987, Ombrela 1987, Pan Y Sueño – Anthologia de la Poesia Feminina Contemporanea Yugoslava 1989, Malaysia: Anthology of Contemporary Poetry 1990, The Poetic Voices of Women from all Meridians 1991, 1992, Skylark 1995, A Banqueting Table of Bosnian Beauty 2009; poems translated into languages including Italian, Hindi, English, Arabic, Urdu, Turkish, German, Greek, Spanish, Japanese, Punjabi, Bengali, French, Portuguese, Chinese, Malaysian, Thai, Korean, Gujrati, Telugu, Kashmiri, Tamil etc. *Honours:* Hon. mem. New Zealand PEN 1994; Hon. LittD (World Acad. of Arts and Culture) 1988; Int. Eminent Poet, Int. Poets' Acad., Madras, Robert Frost Award, Adult Literary Arts, San Mateo, USA 1990, World Award Gold Crown, World Poetry Research Inst. 1990, Silver Crown, Accad. Internazzionale di Pontzen, Italy 1991, Int. Prize for Poetry, Int. Soc. of Greek Writers 1994, Radio Corridor Golden Plate of Humanity, Sarajevo 1996, Poetry Day Australia Golden Medallion Dove in Peace 1996, Int. Poets' Acad. Poet of the Millennium, India –2000, World Acad. of Arts and Culture XX World Congress of Poets Prize, Thessaloniki, Greece 2000, World Award Mikis Theodorakis, Greece 2004, World Award Int. Asscn of Greek Writers and Int. Acad. of Literature and Arts Athens Goddess 2004, Int. Peace Prize 2005, United Cultural Convention 2005, Int. Poets Acad. Lifetime Achievement Award, Madras, India, ABI Gold Medal for Bosnia and Herzegovina, USA, XXIX World Congress of Poets Medal and Plaque, Budapest 2009, All India Intellectual Peace Acad. Int. Peace Award 2010, and other awards. *Address:* Str. Kranjčevićeva 41/3, 71000 Sarajevo, Bosnia and Herzegovina (home). *Telephone:* (33) 667578 (home). *Fax:* (33) 667578 (home). *E-mail:* ajsazahirovic@yahoo.com (home); ajsazahirovicc@hotmail.com (home).

ZAHNISER, Edward Defrance (Ed), BA (Magna cum laude); American writer, poet and editor; *Senior Writer and Editor, US National Park Service Publications Group*; b. 11 Dec. 1945, Washington, DC; s. of Howard Clinton Zahniser and Alice Bernita Hayden Zahniser; m. Ruth Christine Hope Duewel 1968; two s. *Education:* Greenville Coll., Ill., Defense Information School, Officer's Basic Course. *Career:* Poetry Ed., The Living Wilderness Magazine 1972–75; Founding Ed., Some of Us Press, Washington, DC 1972–75; Arts Ed., Good News Paper 1981–2002, Poetry Ed. 2002–; Ed., Artz and Kulchur of the Mountain State 1989–91; Assoc. Poetry Ed., Antietam Review 1992–; Poetry Ed., West Virginia Observer magazine 2009–10; Ed. and Writer, then Sr Writer and Ed., US Nat. Parks Service Publications Group 1977–. *Exhibitions:* Public Hanging (poetry as works on walls) 1994, Poetry Works on Walls 2007. *Publications:* The Ultimate Double Play (poems) 1974, I Live in a Small Town (with Justin Duewel-Zahniser) 1984, The Way to Heron Mountain (poems) 1986, Sheenjek and Denali (poems) 1990, Jonathan Edwards (artist book) 1991, Howard Zahniser: Where Wilderness Preservation Began: Adirondack Wilderness Writings (ed.) 1992, A Calendar of Worship and Other Poems 1995, Mall-Hopping with the Great I Am (poems) 2006; electronic chapbook; Ransacking Desire for that Seed of Contemplation 2007–08, Slow Down and Live (handmade chapbook) 2011; contrib. to numerous anthologies and more than 100 periodicals in USA and UK. *Honours:* Woodrow Wilson Fellow 1967, First and Second Prize in Poetry, West Virginia Writers' Annual Competitions 1989, 1991, 1992, 2004, Second Prize in Essay 1995. *Address:* c/o Atlantis Rising Communications, PO Box 955, Shepherdstown, WV 25443-0955, USA (office). *Telephone:* (304) 876-2442 (office). *E-mail:* eddzahniser@comcast.net (office).

ZAHRA, Trevor; Maltese writer and illustrator; b. 16 Dec. 1947, Zejtun; m. Stella Zahra (deceased); one s. one d. *Education:* Teachers' Coll. of Educ. *Career:* mem. Maltese Acad. of Writers; Council mem. Nat. Book Council. *Publications include:* Il-Pulena tad-Deheb (adventure story) 1971, Eden (poety) 1972, Il-Ghar tax-Xelter (adventure story) 1972, Dawra Durella (poetry for children) 1972, Dwal fil-Fortizza (adventure story) 1973, Is-Surmast (novel) 1973, Il-Praspar ta' Kuncett u Marinton (humorous short stories) 1974, Il-Kaxxa taz-Ziju (adventure story) 1974), Taht il-Weraq tal-Palm (novel) 1974, Praspar Ohra ta' Kuncett u Marinton (humorous short stories) 1975, Hdejn in-Nixxiegha (novel) 1975, Grajjiet in-Nannu Cens (humorous short stories) 1975), Qamar Ahdar (adventure story) 1976, Villa Siko-Sao 1977, Hmistax-il Numru 1977, Meta Jaqa' c-Cpar 1978, Il-Miraklu tal-Gizirana 1981, It-Tmien Kontinent 1981, Trid Kukkarda Hamra f'Gieh il-Biza'? 1982, Il-Praspar Kollha ta' Kuncett u Marinton 1983, Darba Kien Hemm Sultan 1984, LogHob Merill 1985, Qrempucu f'Belt il-Gobon 1985, Il-Ktieb tal-Fenek l-Ahmar 1986, Holm tal-Milied? 1987, Kliem ix-Xih 1988, Rigal tal-Milied 1989, Stella, Jien u HU 1990, Tlieta f'Wiehed 1994, Is-Surmast 1994, Fuklar Qadim u Bnadar Imcarrta 1995, Is-Seba' Trongiet Mewwija 1995, Hanut tal-Helu 1995, Lubien 1996, Taht Sema Kwiekeb 1997, Naqra Storja Zghra 1997, Sib it-Tezor 1999, Passiggata 1999, Mar id-Dawl 1999, Borma Minestra 1999, Koronata Traskurata 2000, Provenz 2000, Zvelajrin 2001, Mincott Hajt Iswed 2001, X'Tixtiequ Jaghmel il-Fenek? 2002, Din l-Art u Kull ma Fiha 2002, Il-Kotba ghat-Tfal 2002, Kieku Kieku 2005, Sfidi 2005, Kemm Naf Inpingi 2005, Ojnk Ojnk 2005, Krispella 2005, Il-Genn li jzommni f'Sikkti (autobiog.) 2008, Il-Hajja Sigrieta tan-Nanna Genoveffa (novel) 2008, Principessa 2009, Xi Jhobb jiekol id-Dragun 2009, 'Il Boghod mill-Habs 2009, Penumbra (short stories) 2010, Hadd Ma Jista' Jidhak (children's fiction) 2010; numerous translations and workbooks. *Honours:* Medal for Services to the Repub. (Malta) in recognition for commitment to children's literature 2004; First Prize, Book Club, Malta 1974, co-winner Rothmas Award 1975, Nat. Literary Award (eleven times). *Address:* 23 Qrempuc Street, Marsaskala MSK- 2205, Malta. *Telephone:* (356) 21632944. *E-mail:* zahratrevor@gmail.com. *Website:* www.trevorzahra.com.

ZAKARIA, Fareed, BA, PhD; American editor, academic, writer and television presenter; *Editor-at-Large, Time Magazine;* b. India; m. Paula Throckmorton Zakaria; one s. two d. *Education:* Yale and Harvard Univs. *Career:* Lecturer on Int. Politics and Econs. Harvard Univ., also Head of Project on the Changing Security Environment; Adjunct Prof., Columbia Univ., New York, Case Western Reserve Univ., Cleveland, OH; Man. Ed. Foreign Affairs journal 1992–2000; Ed. Newsweek Int. 2000–10, columnist, Newsweek (USA); Host and Man. Ed. Foreign Exchange with Fareed Zakaria (PBS Series) 2006–07; political commentator, ABC News 2006–07; host of Fareed Zakaria GPS, TV show on foreign affairs for CNN 2008–; Ed.-at-Large, Time Magazine 2010–; columnist, Washington Post 2001–; wine columnist for Slate (webzine); mem. Bd Trilateral Comm., IISS, Shakespeare and Co., The Century Asscn. *Publications include:* From Wealth to Power: The Unusual Origins of America's World Role, The American Encounter: The United States and the Making of the Modern World (co-ed.), The Future of Freedom 2003, The Post-American World 2008; contrib. to publs including The New York Times, The New Yorker and The Wall Street Journal. *Honours:* Overseas Press Club Award, Deadline Club Award, Edwin Hood Award, India Abroad Person of the Year 2009, Padma Bhushan 2010. *Address:* CNN, 1 Constitution Ave., Washington, DC 20002-5618, USA (office). *Website:* globalpublicsquare.blogs .cnn.com (office); www.fareedzakaria.com (office).

ZAKHAROV, Vladimir, PhD; Russian physicist, mathematician and poet; *Regent's Professor of Mathematics, University of Arizona;* b. (b. Vladimir Evgenyevich Zakharov), 1 Aug. 1939, Kazan; m. Svetlana Zakharova; three s. *Education:* Novosibirsk State Univ. *Career:* jr then sr researcher, Inst. of Nuclear Physics, Siberian Br., USSR (now Russian) Acad. of Sciences (RAN) 1966–73; Head of Plasma Theory Div., Landau Inst. of Theoretical Physics, RAN 1974–92, Dir 1992–2003; scientific supervisor lab. of nonlinear wave processes, Shirshov Inst. of Oceanology, RAN 1985–; Chair. Scientific Council on Nonlinear Dynamics, RAN 1988–; Dir Int. Centre on Nonlinear Studies 1990–; Prof. of Math., Univ. of Arizona, Tucson, USA 1991–2004, Regent's Prof. of Math. 2004–; Head of Dept of Math., P.N. Lebedev Inst. of Physics, Moscow 2004–; Ed.-in-Chief Journal of Nonlinear Science 1991–; mem. USSR Acad. of Sciences (Corresp. mem. 1984–91, Full mem. 1991–). *Publications:* more than 260 scientific works, including Theory of Solitons: The Method of the Inverse Scattering 1980, Kolmogorov Spectra of Wave Turbulence 1992; poetry: The Chorus in the Winter 1991, The Southern Autumn 1992, Before the Heavens 2005; contrib. to numerous periodicals. *Honours:* Order of Honours for the State 1989, Rank IV Order for Service to the Fatherland 1999; USSR State Prize 1987, Russian Fed. State Prize 1993, Dirac Medal 2003. *Address:* Mathematics Building, Room 518, Department of Mathematics, University of Arizona, 617 N Santa Rita Avenue, Tucson, AZ 85721, USA (office); ul. Profsoyuznaya 43/2, apt 479, 117420 Moscow, Russia (home). *Telephone:* (520) 621-4841 (office); (495) 331-5137 (home). *Fax:* (520) 621-8322 (office). *E-mail:* zakharov@math.arizona.edu (office). *Website:* math.arizona .edu/~zakharov (office).

ZALBEN, Jane Breskin, BA; American writer, artist and teacher; b. 21 April 1950, New York, NY; m. Steven Zalben 1969; two s. *Education:* Queens Coll., CUNY, Pratt Graphics Centre. *Career:* mem. Soc. of Children's Book Writers, Authors' Guild, PEN. *Publications:* Cecilia's Older Brother 1973, Lyle and Humus 1974, Basil and Hillary 1975, Penny and the Captain 1977, Norton's Nightime 1979, Will You Count the Stars Without Me 1979, All in the Woodland Early: An ABC by Jane Yolen 1979, Oliver and Alison's Week 1980, Oh Simple! 1981, Porcupine's Christmas Blues 1982, Maybe It Will Rain Tomorrow 1982, Here's Looking at You, Kid 1987, Water from the Moon 1987, Beni's First Chanukah 1988, Earth to Andrew O. Blechman 1989, Happy Passover, Rosie 1989, Leo and Blossom's Sukkah 1990, Goldie's Purim 1991, The Fortune Teller in 5B 1991, Beni's Little Library 1991, Buster Gets Braces 1992, Inner Chimes: Poems on Poetry 1992, Happy New Year, Beni 1993, Papa's Latkes 1994, Beni's First Chanukah 1994, Miss Violet's Shining Day 1995, Pearl Plants a Tree 1995, Beni's Family Cookbook 1996, Unfinished Dreams 1996, Papa's Latkes 1996, Pearl's Marigolds for Grandpa 1997, Beni's First Wedding 1998, Beni's Family Teasury 1998, Pearl's Eight Days of Chanukah 1998, To Every Season: A Family Cookbook 1999, Don't Go 2001, The Magic Menorah: A Modern Chanukah Tale 2001, Pearl's Passover 2002, Let There Be Light: Poems for Repairing the World 2002, Saturday Night at the Beastro (with Steven Zalben) 2004, Baby Babka, the Gorgeous Genius 2004, Hey, Mama Goose 2005, Paths to Peace: People who Changed the World 2006, Leap 2007; contrib. to journals and magazines. *Honours:* Sydney Taylor Honour Award 1989, and Silver Medal 2003, New York Public Library Best Books Citation 1991, Int. Reading Asscn Citation 1993, Parents' Choice Award 1995, ALA Notable Award 1996, CBC/Notable Social Studies Books 2003. *Address:* 70 South Road, Port Washington, NY 11050-2601, USA (home). *E-mail:* janezalben@hotmail.com (home). *Website:* www.janebreskinzalben .com.

ZAMA, Farahad; Indian author; b. 1966, Vizag; m.; two c. *Education:* Indian Inst. of Engineering, Kharagpur. *Career:* fmrly worked for investment bank, Mumbai; moved to New York, Zurich, Luxembourg, London. *Publications include:* novels: The Marriage Bureau for Rich People 2008, The Many Conditions of Love 2010, The Wedding Wallah 2011, Mrs Ali's Road to Happiness 2012. *Literary Agent:* c/o Janklow & Nesbit (UK) Limited, 13a Hillgate Street, London, W8 7SP, England. *Telephone:* (20) 7243-2975. *Fax:* (20) 7243-4339. *E-mail:* queries@janklow.co.uk. *Website:* www .janklowandnesbit.co.uk. *E-mail:* info@farahadzama.com. *Website:* www .farahadzama.com.

ZAMOYSKI, Adam, BA, MA, FSA, FRSA, FRSL; British/Polish historian and writer; b. 11 Jan. 1949, New York, NY, USA; s. of Count Stefan Zamoyski and Princess Elizabeth Czartoryska; m. Emma Sergeant 2001. *Education:* Univ. of Oxford. *Publications:* Chopin: A New Biography 1979, The Battle for the Marchlands 1981, Paderewski: A Biography 1982, The Polish Way 1987, The Last King of Poland 1992, The Forgotten Few 1995, Holy Madness 1999, Poland: A Traveller's Gazetteer 2001, 1812: Napoleon's Fatal March on Moscow 2004, Rites of Peace: The Fall of Napoleon and the Congress of Vienna 2007, Warsaw 1920: Lenin's failed conquest of Europe 2008, Poland: A History 2009, Chopin: Prince of the Romantics 2010. *Literary Agent:* Aitken Alexander Associates, 18–21 Cavaye Place, London, SW10 9PT, England. *Telephone:* (20) 7373-8672. *Fax:* (20) 7373-6002. *E-mail:* reception@aitkenalexander.co.uk. *Website:* www.aitkenalexander.co.uk. *Address:* 12 Avenue Studios, Sydney Close, London, SW3 6HW, England (home). *E-mail:* adam@adamzamoyski .com (office). *Website:* www.adamzamoyski.com.

ZANCANELLA, Don, BS, MA, PhD; American academic and writer; *Associate Professor of English Education, University of New Mexico;* b. 29 Oct. 1954, Rock Springs, WY; m. Dorene Kahl 1981; two c. *Education:* Univ. of Virginia, Univ. of Denver, Univ. of Missouri. *Career:* Assoc. Prof. of English Educ., Univ. of New Mexico, Albuquerque 1988–, now also Co-Dir Secondary English Language Arts Program. *Publications:* Western Electric (short stories) (Iowa Writers' Workshop John Simmons Short Fiction Award 1996) 1996, The Chimpanzees of Wyoming Territory (short story) 1998; contrib. to English Journal, Prairie Schooner, Alaska Quarterly Review, New Letters, Mid-American Review. *Honours:* O. Henry Award 1998. *Address:* Department of Language, Literacy and Sociocultural Studies, University of New Mexico, Hokona Hall 214, Albuquerque, NM 87131-0001, USA (office). *Telephone:* (505) 277-7782 (office). *E-mail:* zanc@unm.edu (office). *Website:* www.unm.edu (office).

ZANGANA, Haifa; British novelist, journalist and painter; b. 1950, Iraq. *Education:* Baghdad Univ. School of Pharmacy. *Career:* fmr prisoner of Saddam Hussein's Iraqi regime; moved to London 1976; weekly columnist for al-Quds newspaper and occasional commentator for the Guardian, Red Pepper and al-Ahram Weekly; lectures regularly on Iraqi culture, literature and women issues; Founding mem. International Association of Contemporary Iraqi Studies; mem. Advisory Bd Brussels Tribunal on Iraq. *Publications* include: Halabja (ed., collection of essays by Arab writers) 1989, Through the Vast Halls of Memory 1991, Bayt al-Namal (The Ant's Nest) 1996, Beyond What the Eye Sees 1997, The Presence of Others (short stories) 1999, Keys to the City 2000, Women on a Journey 2001; co-author: El Kalima, Aswat, Al Ightirab al Adabi. *Address:* c/o Verso Books, 6 Meard Street, London, W1F 0EG, England (home).

ZARIÂB, Spôjmaï; Afghan writer; b. 1949, Kabul; d. of Abdul Raouf and Zabeida Raouf; m. Rahnaward Zariâb; three d. *Education:* Faculty of Literature and Fine Arts, Univ. of Kabul, Université Paul-Valéry, France. *Career:* began writing stories in Dari (a variation of Persian) aged 17; trans., French Embassy in Kabul 1973–89; teacher of French and Dari languages, Kabul; published work in Iran, Pakistan and the Writer's Union (Afghanistan's only publisher and printer) during Soviet occupation; in exile, Montpellier and Paris, France 1991–. *Publications include:* Ringing the Bells (anthology of short stories) 1983, In Another Country 1988, Boots of Delirium (short story), Identity Card (short story), Portrait of a City on a Purple Background (adapted to theatre and performed at Avignon Off Festival 1991), These Walls That Listen to Us (novel) 2000, (adapted to theatre and performed at Avignon) 2003, The Plain of Cain (collection of short stories) 2001, Draw me a Rooster (short stories) 2003. *Honours:* Chevalier, Ordre des Arts et des Lettres 2001; Prix Literature, Germany 2003. *Address:* 85 rue Meaux, 75019 Paris, France (home). *Telephone:* 1-43-49-05-71 (home). *E-mail:* spojmaizariab@hotmail.fr (home).

ZAVALA, Iris M., PhD; Puerto Rican academic and writer; *Professor Emerita, Faculteit der Letteren, Rijksuniversiteit te Utrecht*; b. 27 Dec. 1936, Puerto Rico; one c. *Education:* Univs of Puerto Rico and Salamanca (Spain). *Career:* Asst Prof. Univ. of Puerto Rico 1962–64, Visiting Prof. 1978, 1981; Research Fellow El Colegio de México 1964–65, Visiting Prof. 1979; Visiting Lecturer Queen's Coll., New York 1966; Asst Prof. Hunter Coll., New York 1968–69; Assoc. Prof. State Univ. of New York at Stony Brook 1969–71, Prof. 1971–83, Jt Prof. of Comparative Literature 1976–83; Chair. of Hispanic Literatures Rijksuniversiteit te Utrecht, Netherlands 1983–, Prof. Emer. 1997–; Visiting Prof. Univ. di Calabria, Italy 1985, Univ. de les Illes Balears, Mallorca, Spain 1989; mem. Editorial Bd numerous journals including Third Woman 1982–, Anales de la Narrativa Española Contemporánea 1977–, Diálogos Hispánicos 1986–, La Torre 1986–, Journal of Interdisciplinary Studies 1988–; mem. Soc. for Spanish-Portuguese Historical Studies, American Asscn of Teachers of Spanish and Portuguese; has lectured on culture, literature and history in N and S America, E and W Europe, etc; Fellow American Philosophical Soc. 1966; Guggenheim Foundation Fellowship 1966–67; Dr hc (Univ. of Puerto Rico) 1996; Encomienda Lazo de Damad. la Orden de Mérito (Spain) 1988. *Publications include:* Unamuno y su teatro de conciencia (Nat. Literary Prize of Puerto Rico 1964) 1963, La Revolución de 1868: historia, pensamiento, literatura (co-ed.) 1970, Ideología y política en la novela española del siglo XIX (Nat. Literary Prize of Puerto Rico 1972) 1971, Escritura destada (ed.) 1974, Historia social de la literatura española 1979, Que nadie muera sin amar el mar 1983, Nocturna mas no funesta (Finalist Premio Herralde) 1987, Rubén Darío bajo el signo del cisne (Nat. Literary Prize 1990) 1989, Teorías de la modernidad 1991, Historia feminista de la literatura española (ed.) 1992, Nocturna mad no Funesta 2003; numerous articles. *Address:* Rijksuniversiteit te Utrecht, Faculteit der Letteren, Kromme Nieuwegracht 29, 3512 KD Utrecht, Netherlands. *Telephone:* (30) 253-6537. *Fax:* (30) 253-6167. *Website:* www2.let.uu.nl/solis (office).

ZAWODNY, Janusz Kazimierz, BS, MA, PhD; American (b. Polish) historian and academic (retd) and writer; b. 11 Dec. 1921, Warsaw, Poland; m. LaRae Jean Koppit 1971; one s. *Education:* Univ. of Iowa, Stanford Univ. *Career:* participant in Warsaw Uprising of 1944, fmr prisoner-of-war in Germany; instructor and Asst Prof., Princeton Univ. 1955–58; Fellow, Center for Advanced Study in the Behavioral Sciences, Stanford 1961–62; Assoc. Prof., Univ. of Pennsylvania 1962–63, Prof. of Political Science 1965–75; Prof. of Political Science, Washington Univ., St Louis 1963–65; Research Assoc., Center for Int. Affairs, Harvard Univ. 1968; Sr Assoc. Mem., St Antony's Coll., Oxford 1968–69; mem., Inst. for Advanced Study, Princeton 1971–72; Avery Prof. of Int. Relations, Claremont Graduate Univ. and Pomona Coll., Calif. 1975–82; consultant staff, Nat. Security Council, USA 1979–84. *Publications:* Death in the Forest: The Story of the Katyn Forest Massacre 1962, Guide to the Study of International Relations 1967, Man and International Relations: Contribution of the Social Sciences to the Study of Conflict and Integration (ed. and contrib., two vols) 1967, Nothing But Honour: The Story of the Uprising of Warsaw 1944 1978, Uczestnicy i Swiadkowie Powstania Warszawskiego 1994, Motyl na Sniegu 2004; contrib. to scholarly books and journals. *Honours:* Order of Virtuti Militari 1944, Order of Merit, Pres. of Poland 1994, Kustosz Pamieci Narodowej 2003; Hon. MA (Univ. of Pennsylvania) 1965, (Univ. of Oxford) 1968; Literary Award, Kultura, Paris 1981, Jurzykowski Foundation Citation and Award 1982, Research Awards, Polish Scientific Soc., London 1982, 1989, Scientific Soc. Book of the Year Award, Univ. of Lublin, Poland 1988, History Award, J. Pilsudski Inst., New York 1997. *Address:* 23703 NE Margaret Road, Brush Prairie, WA 98606, USA (home).

ZELDIN, Theodore, CBE, MA, DPhil, FBA, FRSL; British historian and philosopher; *President, The Oxford Muse*; b. 1933; m. Deirdre Wilson. *Education:* Birkbeck Coll., London, Christ Church, Oxford, St Antony's Coll., Oxford. *Career:* fmr Fellow and Dean, St Antony's Coll. Oxford, now Emer. Fellow; Assoc. Fellow, Green-Templeton Coll., Oxford; Assoc. Fellow, Said Business School, Oxford; fmr Visiting Prof., Harvard Univ., Univ. of Southern California; Pres. The Oxford Muse Foundation 2001–, Nord-Pas-de-Calais Future Comm.; mem. Comm. for Econ. Growth (France) 2008–10, Innovation Bd, Generali Italy, Visionaries Bd, Minatec Nanotechnology Lab., Grenoble, BBC Brains Trust; mem. Academia Europaea; Fellow, World Econ. Forum; Trustee, Amar Refugees Foundation, Wytham Hall Medical Charity for the Homeless; numerous radio talks and TV commentaries and debates. *Film:* Flirtations (dir Gideon Koppel). *Publications:* Political System of Napoleon III 1958, Emile Ollivier and the Liberal Empire 1963, Conflicts in French Society (ed.) 1971, France 1848–1945: (History of French Passions) Vol. 1 Ambition, Love and Politics 1973, Vol. 2 Intellect, Taste and Anxiety 1977, The French 1983, Happiness 1988, An Intimate History of Humanity 1994, Conversation 1998, Guide to an Unknown City (ed.) 2004, Guide to an Unknown University (ed.) 2006. *Honours:* Hon. Prof., École des Hautes Études Commerciales de Paris; Commdr des Arts et des Lettres; Wolfson Prize. *Address:* Tumbledown House, Cumnor, Oxford, OX2 9QE, England (home). *Telephone:* (1865) 862470 (office). *E-mail:* theodore.zeldin@sant.ox.ac.uk (office); info@oxfordmuse.com (office). *Website:* www.oxfordmuse.com (office).

ZELEZA, Paul Tiyambe, BA, MA, PhD; Malawi historian, literary critic, novelist, short-story writer and academic; *Professor and Head, Department of African-American Studies, University of Illinois at Chicago*; b. 25 May 1955, Salisbury, Rhodesia, now Harare, Zimbabwe; m.; one s. one d. *Education:* Univ. of Malawi, Univ. of London, UK, Dalhousie Univ., Halifax, NS, Canada. *Career:* Staff Assoc., Chancellor Coll., Univ. of Malawi 1976–77; Researcher, Univ. of Nairobi 1979–80; Lecturer, Univ. of the West Indies, Mona, Kingston, Jamaica 1982–84; Lecturer, Kenyatta Univ., Nairobi, Kenya 1984–87, Sr Lecturer 1987–90; worked on African econ. history research project at UN Econ. Comm. for Africa, Addis Ababa, Ethiopia, and at Dalhousie Univ. 1990; Asst Prof., Dept of History and Comparative Devt Studies, Trent Univ., Ont., Canada 1990–91, Assoc. Prof. 1991–95, Prof. 1995, Acting Dir Trent Int. Program 1994–95, Prin. Lady Eaton Coll. 1994–95; Prof. of History and African Studies and Dir Center for African Studies, Univ. of Illinois at Urbana-Champaign 1995–2003, Prof. and Head, Dept of African-American Studies, Univ. of Illinois at Chicago 2007–, Liberal Arts and Sciences Distinguished Prof. 2008–; Prof. of African Studies and History, Pennsylvania State Univ. 2003–06; fmr Ed. Odi journal, Umodzi magazine; Founder-mem. Malawian Writer's Series 1974; Co-Ed. Journal of Eastern African Studies; blogger at The Zeleza Post. *Publications:* fiction: Night of Darkness and Other Stories 1976, Smouldering Charcoal 1992, The Joys of Exile (short stories) 1994; non-fiction: Rethinking Africa's Globalization, Vol. 1: The Intellectual Challenges 2003, Imperialism and Labour: The International Relations of the Kenyan Labour Movement 1987, Labour, Unionization and Women's Participation in Kenya 1965–1987 1988, A Modern Economic History of Africa, Vol. 1: The Nineteenth Century (Noma Award for Publishing in Africa 1994) 1993, Vol. 2: The Twentieth Century, Maasai 1994, Akamba 1994, Mijikenda 1994, Manufacturing African Studies and Crises (Dakar Book Series) (Special Commendation of the Noma Award 1998) 1997, Science and Technology in Africa 2003, Leisure in Urban Africa (co-ed.) 2003, Rethinking Africa's Globalization –Vol. 1: The Intellectual Challenges 2003, Human Rights, the Rule of Law, and Development in Africa (co-ed.) 2004, African Universities in the Twenty-First Century –Vol. 1: Liberalisation and Internationalisation (ed.) 2004, Vol. 2: Knowledge and Society (ed.) 2004, Causes and Costs of African Conflicts 2007, Conflict Management and Resolution in Africa 2007, Africa and Its Diasporas: Dispersals and Linkages 2008; contrib. to numerous articles, chapters, reviews and short stories. *Honours:* Choice Outstanding Academic Title 2003, Hon. Mention, Conover-Porter Award 2004, Penn State Coll. of Liberal Arts Class of 1933 Distinction in the Humanities Award 2006; numerous grants from the Ford Foundation, Rockefeller Foundation, Carnegie Corpn of New York, Friedrich Ebert Foundation, US Dept of Educ. Title VI, Nat. Endowment for the Humanities, Canada Social Science and Humanities Research Council, Council for the Devt of Social Science Research in Africa. *Address:* Department of African-American Studies, Banner Dept: 2-363000, 1223 University Hall, M/C 069, 601 S Morgan Street, Chicago, IL 60607-7112, USA (office). *Telephone:* (312) 996-2950 (office). *Fax:* (312) 996-5799 (office). *E-mail:* zeleza@uic.edu (office). *Website:* www.uic.edu/las/afam/aasthome.html; www.zeleza.com; www.tandf.co.uk/journals/titles/17531055.asp.

ZELLER, Eva; German writer and poet; b. 25 Jan. 1923, Eberswalde; d. of Franz-Maria Feldhaus and Elisabeth Feldhaus (née Bertrand); m. Reimar Zeller 1951; one s. three d. *Education:* secondary school in Droyssig bei Zeitz, Univs of Greifswald, Marburg and Berlin. *Career:* left GDR for Namibia 1956; Guest Prof. of Poetry, Univ. of Mainz 1987; mem. Deutsche Akad. für Sprache und Dichtung, Akad. der Wissenschaften und der Literatur zu Mainz. *Publications:* novels: Der Sprung über den Schatten, Lampenfieber, Die Hauptfrau, Solange ich denken kann 1980, Nein und Amen 1985, Ein Stein aus Davids Hirtentasche 1992, Das versiegelte manuskript 1998, Stiftsgarten, Tübingen 2002; short stories: Die magische Rechnung, Ein Morgen Ende Mai, Der Turmbau 1975, Tod der Singschwäne; poetry: Der Sprung über den Schatten 1967, Ein Morgan Ende Mai 1969, Sage und schreibe 1971, Der Turmbau 1973, Lampenfieber 1974, Fliehkraft 1975, Die Hauptfrau 1977, Auf dem Wasser gehen 1980, Solange ich denken kann 1981, Tod der Singschwäne 1983, Unveränderliche kennzeichen 1983, Nein und Amen 1986, Heidelberger Novelle 1988, Stellprobe 1989, Das Sprungtuch 1991, Ein Stein aus Davids Hirtentasche 1992, Die Lutherin 1996, Das Versiegelte Manuskript 1998,

Dreisig Worte für Liebe 2002, Das unverschämte Glück 2006; editor: Dreißig deutsche Jahre: zum Generationsbruch heute; also radio plays, etc. *Honours:* Droste Preis 1975, Ida-Dehmel Preis 1986, Eichendorff-Preis 1991. *Address:* c/o Radius-Verlag, Alexanderstrasse 162, 70180 Stutrgart, Germany (office). *E-mail:* info@radius-verlag.de (office). *Website:* www.radius-verlag.de (office).

ZELLER, Florian; French novelist and playwright; b. 1979. *Career:* currently Lecturer in Literature, Institut d'études politiques de Paris (Sciences Po), also regular contrib. to Paris Match and Vogue. *Plays:* L'Autre (Théatre des Mathurins, Paris) 2004, Le Manège (Petit Montparnasse, Paris) 2004, Si tu mourais 2004, Elle t'attend 2008. *Publications:* novels: Neiges artificielles (trans. as Artificial Snow) (Prix de la Fondation Hachette) 2002, Les Amants du n'importe quoi (trans. as Lovers Or Something Like It) (Prix Prince Pierre de Monaco) 2003, La Fascination du pire (trans. as Fascination of Evil) (Prix Interallié) 2004, Julien Parme 2006. *Address:* c/o Pushkin Press, 12 Chester Terrace, London, NW1 4ND, England. *Telephone:* (20) 7730-0750. *E-mail:* books@pushkinpress.com. *Website:* www.pushkinpress.com.

ZEPHANIAH, Benjamin Obadiah Iqbal; British poet, writer, dramatist, musician and singer; *Professor of Poetry and Creative Writing, Brunel University*; b. 15 April 1958, Birmingham, England. *Education:* Deykin Avenue Primary School, Birmingham Ward End Hall Comprehensive School, Birmingham Broadway Comprehensive School, Birmingham Boreatton Park Approved School, Baschurch. *Career:* Writer-in-Residence, Africa Arts Collective, Liverpool 1989, Hay-on-Wye Literature Festival 1991, Memphis State Univ., TN 1991–95, Keats House, Hampstead 2011–; currently Prof. of Poetry and Creative Writing, Brunel Univ.; numerous radio performances, acting roles, appearances; mem. Musicians' Union, Equity, Performing Rights Soc., Authors' Licensing and Collecting Soc. *Recordings:* albums: Rasta 1983, Us and Dem 1990, Back To Our Roots 1995, Belly Of The Beast 1996, Heading For The Door 2000, Naked 2006; singles: Dub Ranting (EP) 1982, Big Boys Don't Make Girls Cry 1984, Free South Africa 1986, Crisis 1992, Naked 2004. *Compositions:* contrib. to Dancing Tribes (single, with Back To Base) 1999, Illegal (with Swayzak) 2000, What is in Between (With Mieko Shimizo) 2006, The Imagined Village 2007, The Police in Dub 2008, Skanny Skannky (Toddla T) 2009. *Plays:* Playing the Right Tune 1985, Job Rocking 1987, Delirium 1987, Streetwise 1990, The Trial of Mickey Tekka 1991; contrib. to periodicals, radio, TV and recordings, De Botty Business. *Radio plays:* Hurricane Dub 1988, Our Teacher's Gone Crazy 1990, Listen To Your Parents 2000, Face 2002. *Television play:* Dread Poets Society 1991. *Publications:* fiction: Face 1999, Refugee Boy 2001, Teacher's Dead 2007; poetry: Pen Rhythm 1980, The Dread Affair 1985, Inna Liverpool 1988, Rasta Time in Palestine 1990, City Psalms 1992, Talking Turkeys 1994, Funky Chickens 1996, Propa Propaganda 1996, School's Out 1997, We Are Britain 2002, Too Black, Too Strong 2002, The Little Book of Vegan Poems 2002, Gangsta Rap 2004, My Story 2011, When I Grow Up 2011, Kung Fu Trip 2011. *Honours:* Dr hc (Univ. of North London) 1998, (Univ. of West of England) 1999, (Staffordshire Univ.) 2001, (Oxford Brookes Univ.) 2002, (South Bank Univ., London) 2002, (Univ. of East London) 2003, (Univ. Coll. Northampton) 2003, (Open Univ.) 2004, (Univ. of Central England) 2005, Hon. DLitt (Westminster Univ.) 2006, (Univ. of Birmingham) 2008, (Univ. of Hull) 2010, (Univ. of Glamorgan) 2011; BBC Young Playwrights Festival Award 1988. *Literary Agent:* c/o United Agents, 12–26 Lexington Street, London, W1F 0LE, England. *Telephone:* (20) 3214-0800. *Fax:* (20) 3214-0801. *E-mail:* info@unitedagents.co.uk. *Website:* unitedagents.co.uk. *Address:* PO Box 1153, Spalding, Lincs. PE11 9BN, England (office). *Telephone:* (20) 7344-1000 (office). *Website:* www.benjaminzephaniah.com.

ZHANG, Wei; Chinese writer; b. 1956, Longkou, Shangdong Province. *Education:* Yantai Normal Inst. *Career:* fmrly apptd Vice-Mayor of Longkou city 1987; mem. Shandong Writers' Asscn (fmr assoc. chair.), Young Writers' Asscn (Shandong Province) (fmr assoc. chair.), Chinese Writers' Asscn. *Publications include:* Visiting the Bugler (long poem), The Ancient Ship (novel), Blending into the Untamed Land (essay), Voice (short story) (Chinese Writers' Asscn Award 1982), A Pool of Clear Water (short story) (Chinese Writers' Asscn Award 1984), The Autumn of Wrath (novella) (Novella Magazine Award 1986), Selected Writings of Zhang Wei (Shangdong Province Award for Best Book 1997), September's Fable (novel) (Chinese Writers' Asscn and China News Best Novel Award 1998). *Address:* c/o Chinese Writers' Association, No. 25 East Tucheng Road, Chaoyang District, Beijing 100013, People's Republic of China (office).

ZHANG, Xianliang; Chinese writer and poet; b. 1936, Jiangsu; m. Yan Huili; one d. *Career:* fmr teacher in Beijing and Ningxia; in political disgrace 1957–79; mem. editorial staff Shuofang literary magazine in late 1970s; Cttee mem. CPPCC 1983; mem. Chinese Writers' Asscn (Vice-Pres. 1986). *Publications:* Song of the Great Wind (poem) 1957, Soul and Flesh (aka A Herdsman's Story) 1981, Contemporary Chinese Short Stories (with Zhang Xian and others) 1984, Mimosa 1984, Prize-Winning Stories from China 1980–1981 (with others) 1985, Half of Man is Woman 1985, Yi Xiang Tian Kai (screenplay) 1986, Women Shi Shijie (screenplay) 1988, Getting Used to Dying 1989, Grass Soup 1992, My Bodhi Tree 1994. *Honours:* Best Novel of the Year Awards (China) 1981, 1983, 1984. *Address:* c/o Ningxia Writers' Association, Yinchuan City, People's Republic of China.

ZHANG, Yueran; Chinese writer; b. 1982, Jinan, Shangdong Prov. *Education:* Shangdong Univ., Nat. Univ. of Singapore. *Career:* first articles published when she was 14 years old. *Publications:* novels in Chinese: Sunflower Lost in 1890 2003, Cherry 2004, Did You Come to Take Care of My Wounds? 2004, Far Away Peaches, Red Shoes 2004, Daffodils Took Carp and Went Away 2005, Shiniao (Bird Under Oath) 2006. *Honours:* First Prize, Nat. New Concept Composition Competition. *Address:* c/o Chun Feng Literature and Art Publishing House, Liaoning Publishing Group, 25 Shiyiwei Road, Heping District, Shenyang, Liaoning 110003, People's Republic of China (office). *Telephone:* (24) 23284029 (office). *Fax:* (24) 23284391 (office).

ZHANG CHANGXIN, (Dongli Jiefu); Chinese writer; b. 30 Nov. 1940, Liaoning; m. Huang Fuju 1962; one s. one d. *Education:* China Siping Teachers' School. *Career:* mem. China Asscn of Writers, China Playwrights' Asscn. *Publications:* Changba Shan Hun (translated as Spirit of Changba Mountains) 1985, Aide San Yuan Se (translated as Three Colours of Love) 1987, East Madrid 1989, Zni Zhi Qiu (translated as Enjoyment in Autumn) 1991, Qingxi Lanxi (translated as Black and Blue) 1994, Chaoji Ai Qing Siwang (translated as The Death of Super Love) 1995. *Address:* c/o Jilin Writers' Association, Bldg 9, 167 Renmin Street, Changchun, Jilin, 130021, People's Republic of China.

ZHAO, Jia-Zi; Chinese musicologist; b. 30 Aug. 1934, Jiang-Su; m. Xu Si-Jie 1959; one s. one d. *Education:* Shanghai Conservatory of Music. *Career:* Research Scholar, Music Univ. of New Dheli, The Indian Art Centre, Chennai Ethonomusicology Research Inst. 1986–88; Head of Inst. Music Research of Shanghai Conservatory of Music; full-time Supervisor, Shanghai Conservatory of Music; Deputy Dir, World Ethnomusicological Asscn, Oriental Music Asscn; mem. Indian Musicological Soc., Singapore Asscn for Asian Studies, Chinese Writers' Asscn, Chinese Musicians' Asscn. *Publications:* The Music of Asia, Ethnic Music of Asian Countries, Collection of Writings on the Music of Shen Zhi-Bai, Indian Music Around the Period of Sui and Tang Dynasty, Rabindranath Tagore and his Music, Gamelan Music in Java and Bali, Comparative Study of Indian and Chinese Ancient Music, Comparative Study of Wu Dan-Qi Shen and Qi Tiao Bei. *Address:* c/o Trinity College, University of Melbourne, Royal Parade, Parkville 3052, Vic., Australia.

ZHAOYAN, Ye; Chinese writer; b. 1957, Nanjing. *Publications:* Tale of the Jujube Tree 1988, Nanjing 1937 – A Love Story 1996. *Address:* c/o Faber and Faber Ltd, Bloomsbury House, 74–77 Great Russell Street, London, WC1B 3DA, England (office). *Website:* www.faber.co.uk (office).

ZHENKAI, Zhao, (Bei Dao); Chinese poet and academic; *Professor of Humanities, Chinese University of Hong Kong*; b. (Zhao Zhenkai), 1949, Beijing; m. Shao Fei; one d. *Career:* Co-founder Jintian (literary magazine) 1978–80, 1990–; worked at Foreign Languages Press, Beijing; exiled 1989; McAndless Chair in Humanities, Eastern Michigan Univ. 1993; Visiting Artist/Writer, Int. Inst.; Visiting Scholar, Center for Chinese Studies; also taught at Univ. of California, Davis, Univ. of Alabama, Beloit Coll.; allowed to return to China 2006; Prof. of Humanities, Chinese Univ. of Hong Kong 2007–. *Publications include:* Taiyang cheng zhaji 1978, Huida (poetry) 1979, Notes from the City of the Sun (trans.) 1983, Bodong (novel, translated as Waves) 1985, Bei Dao shi xuan (poetry, translated as The August Sleepwalker) 1986, Bai ri meng (poetry) 1986, Bei Dao shi ji 1988, Old Snow (trans.) 1991, Forms of Distance (trans.) 1994, Landscape Over Zero 1996, Unlock 2000, Blue House 2000, At the Sky's Edge: Poems 1991–1996 2001, Midnight's Gate 2005, Rose of Time 2005; contribs to Shi Kan, Renditions, Bulletin of Concerned Asian Scholars, Contemporary Chinese Literature (anthology) 1985, numerous other anthologies. *Honours:* Hon. mem. American Acad. of Arts and Letters. *Address:* Centre for East Asian Studies, The Chinese University of Hong Kong, Sha Tin, NT, Hong Kong Special Administrative Region, People's Republic of China (office). *Telephone:* 3163-4392 (office). *Fax:* 2994-3105 (office). *E-mail:* ceas@cuhk.edu.hk (office). *Website:* www.cuhk.edu.hk/cea/Bei_Dao.html (office).

ZHOU, Wei Hui; Chinese writer; b. 1973, Ning Bo City. *Education:* Fudan Univ., Shanghai. *Career:* first year of coll. spent in mil. training; fifth novel Shanghai Baby banned in China 2001. *Publications include:* (titles in translation) The Shriek of the Butterfly, Virgin in the Water, Crazy Like Wei Hui, Desire Pistol, Shanghai Baby 1999, Marrying Buddha 2005. *Address:* c/o Joanne Wang, Constable & Robinson Ltd, 3 The Lanchester, 162 Fulham Road, London, W6 9ER, England (office). *E-mail:* enquiries@constablerobinson.com.

ZHU, Wen; Chinese writer, poet, film director and screenwriter; b. 1967, Fujian Prov. *Career:* worked in thermal power plant; full-time writer 1994–. *Films:* Wu shan yun yu (writer) 1996, Guo nian hui jia (writer) 1999, Hai xian (writer and dir, translated as Seafood) (Grand Jury Prize, Venice Film Festival) 2001, Yun de nan fang (dir, translated as South of the Clouds) 2003. *Publications include:* short stories: I Love Dollars 2007. *Address:* c/o Ministry of Culture, 10 Chaoyangmen Bei Jie, Dongcheng Qu, Beijing 100020, People's Republic of China (office).

ZHU, Yinghuang, MA; Chinese journalist, translator and academic; *Professor of Journalism and Communications, Tsinghua University*; b. 28 Dec. 1943, Shanghai; m. Yao Xiang 1972; one d. *Education:* Fudan Univ., Stanford Univ., USA. *Career:* teaching faculty, Shangdong Normal Univ. 1977; Ed.-in-Chief China Daily 1993–2004, Ed.-in-Chief Emer. 2004–; took part in translation work of Basic Law of Hong Kong Special Admin. Region 1987–88; Prof. of Journalism and Communications, Tsinghua Univ.; Doctoral tutor, China Communications Univ.; mem. CPPCC 2003–08; Vice-Chair. China Translation Asscn, China Pacific Econ. Cooperation Cttee. *Publications:* Translations:

Inside Stories of Macao and Singapore, The Memoirs of Dwight Whip, The Rich and Super Rich, Socialist Democratic Parties in Western Europe, Three Generations of a Newspaper Tycoon. *Honours:* Outstanding Journalist of China 1984. *Address:* China Daily, 15 Huixin Dongjie, Chao Yang Qu, Beijing 100029, People's Republic of China (office). *Telephone:* (10) 64995027 (office); (10) 64280990 (home). *Fax:* (10) 64918377 (office). *E-mail:* yhzhu@chinadaily.com.cn (office). *Website:* www.chinadaily.com.cn (office).

ZIEDAN, Youssef, PhD; Egyptian academic, writer and novelist; *Director, Centre and Museum of Manuscripts, Bibliotheca Alexandrina*; b. 30 June 1958; one s. two d. *Education:* Univ. of Alexandria. *Career:* Lecturer in Islamic Philosophy and History of Science, Damanhur Alexandria Univ. 1992–97; currently Dir Centre and Museum of Manuscripts, Bibliotheca Alexandrina; consultant to UNESCO, UN Econ. and Social Comm. for Western Asia (ESCWA), Arab League. *Publications:* Itiqa' al-Bahrin (essays in literary criticism), Zil al Af'a (novel), Azazel (novel) (Int. Prize for Arabic Fiction (Arabic Booker) 2009) 2008, Al-Nabati (The Nabataean) (novel) 2010, Arabic Theology 2010; more than 50 works of philosophy, history of medicine and information science. *Honours:* Kuwait Foundation for the Advancement of Science Prize 1994, 2005. *Address:* Bibliotheca Alexandrina, PO Box 138, El Shatby, Alexandria 21526 (office); c/o Dar El Shorouk, 8 Sibaweh El Masry Street, Nasr City, Egypt. *Telephone:* (3) 4839999 (ext. 1300) (Alexandria) (office); (2) 24023399 (Dar El Shorouk). *Fax:* (3) 4820461 (Alexandria) (office); (2) 24037567 (Dar El Shorouk). *E-mail:* youssef.ziedan@bibalex.org (home); secretariat@bibalex.org (office); dar@shorouk.com; ziedan@ziedan.com (home). *Website:* www.shorouk.com (office); www.ziedan.com.

ZIEGLER, Philip Sandeman, CVO, MA, FRHistS, FRSL; British writer; b. 24 Dec. 1929, Ringwood, Hants.; s. of Colin Louis Ziegler and Dora Ziegler (née Barnwell); m. 1st Sarah Collins 1960 (deceased); one s. one d.; m. 2nd Mary Clare Charrington 1971; one s. *Education:* Eton Coll., New Coll. Oxford. *Career:* joined Foreign Office 1952, served Vientiane, Paris, Pretoria, Bogotá; Editorial Dir Collins Publishers 1972, Ed.-in-Chief 1979–80, resgnd when apptd to write official biog. of the late Earl Mountbatten; Chair. London Library 1979–85, Soc. of Authors 1988–90, Public Lending Right Advisory Cttee 1993–96. *Publications include:* Duchess of Dino 1962, Addington 1965, The Black Death 1969, William IV 1971, Omdurman 1973, Melbourne 1976, Crown and People 1978, Diana Cooper 1981, Mountbatten 1985, Elizabeth's Britain 1926 to 1986 1986, The Sixth Great Power: Barings 1762–1929 1988, King Edward VIII, The Official Biography 1990, Wilson: The Authorized Life of Lord Wilson of Rievaulx 1993, London at War: 1939–45 1994, Osbert Sitwell 1998, Britain Then and Now 1999, Soldiers: Fighting Men's Lives 1901–2001 2001, Rupert Hart-Davis: Man of Letters 2004, Edward Heath: The Authorised Biography 2010; editor: The Diaries of Lord Louis Mountbatten 1920–1922 1987, Personal Diary of Admiral the Lord Louis Mountbatten 1943–1946 1988, From Shore to Shore: The Diaries of Earl Mountbatten of Burma 1953–1979 1989, Brooks's: A Social History (with Desmond Seward) 1991, Legacy: the Rhodes Trust and the Rhodes Scholarship 2008. *Honours:* Hon. DLitt (Westminster Coll., Mo., USA) 1987, (Univ. of Buckingham) 2000; Chancellor's Essay Prize 1950, Heinemann Award 1976. *Address:* 22 Cottesmore Gardens, London, W8 5PR, England (home). *Telephone:* (20) 7937-1903 (home). *Fax:* (20) 7937-5458 (home).

ZIFFRIN, Marilyn, BM, MA; American composer and writer; *Professor Emerita, New England College, Henniker*; b. 7 Aug. 1926, Moline, IL; d. of Harry B. Ziffrin and Betty S. Ziffrin. *Education:* Univ. of Wisconsin, Columbia Univ., Univ. of Chicago. *Career:* teacher, Chicago Public Schools 1952–56; Asst Prof. of Music Northeastern Ill. Univ. 1956–66; Assoc. Prof. of Music New England Coll., Henniker, NH 1957–83, Prof. Emer. 1983–; MacDowell Colony Fellowships 1961, 1963, 1971, 1977, 1980, 1989. *Compositions include:* solo: Theme and Variations for piano 1949, Suite for piano 1955, Toccata and Fugue for organ 1956, Three Songs for woman's voice 1957, Rhapsody for solo guitar 1958, Four Pieces for tuba 1973, Three Movements for guitar 1989, Themes and Variations for organ 1990, Three Songs of the Trobairitz 1991, Recurrences piano solo 1998, Moods piano solo 2003, Three Songs for D'Anna 2003, Piano Sonata 2005–06; chamber music: The Little Prince for clarinet and bassoon 1953, Make a Joyful Noise quintet for recorder 1966, In the Beginning for percussion ensemble 1968, XIII for chamber ensemble 1969, String Quartet 1970, Haiku for soprano, viola and harpsichord 1971, Movements for clarinet and percussion 1972, Sonata for organ and cello 1973, Trio for xylophone, soprano and tuba 1974, Trio for violin, cello and piano 1975, Quintet for oboe and string quartet 1976, Concerto for viola and woodwind quintet 1978, SONO for cello and piano 1980, White Lies (film score) 1983, Yankee Hooray piano duet 1984, Duo for alto recorders 1985, Conversations for double bass and harpsichord 1986, Tributum for clarinet, viola and double bass 1992, Flute Fun for two flutes 1995, Fantasy for two pianos 1995, Lines and Spaces for brass quintet 1996, For Love of Cynthia for baritone and classical accordion, or violin, horn and piano 1997, Two Songs for soprano, viola and piano 1998, String Quartet No. 2 1999, Two Movements for woodwind quintet 2000, Abbot's Duo for alto sax and violin 2001, Sonatina for trumpet and piano 2001, Trio for flute, clarinet and piano 2004, A Little Music for handbells 2006; choral: Jewish Prayer 1950, Death of Moses 1954, Prayer 1966, Drinking Song and Dance, from Captain Kidd 1971, Chorus from Alcestis 1990, Choruses from the Greeks 1992, New England Epitaphs 1994, Cantata for Freedom 2000, Almanack 1688 2002, Two Holiday Songs for chorus 2005; orchestral: Strings 1966, Soundscape 2000, Soundscape II 2002, Trio for flute, clarinet and piano 2004, Soundscape III 2005, Duo for Flute and Piano 2006, Lament for flute and string quartet 2009, Ten for woodwind quintet and string quartet 2009–10, Sonata for viola and piano 2011. *Publications:* Carl Ruggles: Composer, Painter and Storyteller 1994; contrib. to The New Grove Dictionary of Music and Musicians 1980, The New Grove Dictionary of American Music 1986. *Honours:* Special Mention Delius Composition Competition 1971, first prize Delius Composition Competition 1972, ASCAP Awards 1981–2007, Virginia Center for the Creative Arts Residency 1987, Music Fix Prize 1996, New Hampshire MTA Composer of the Year 1997, Laureate mem. 2006, Lotte Jacobi Living Treasure Award, New Hampshire Council on the Arts 2007. *Address:* PO Box 179, Bradford, NH 03221, USA (home).

ZIGAL, Thomas, BA, MA; American author; b. 20 Oct. 1948, Galveston, Tex. *Education:* Univ. of Texas, Stanford Univ. *Career:* mem. Texas Inst. of Letters 1995–, Mystery Writers of America, Authors Guild, Writers League of Texas. *Publications:* Playland 1982, Into Thin Air 1995, Hardrock Stiff 1996, Pariah 1999, The White League (Violet Crown Award 2005) 2005. *Honours:* Austin Book Award 1982, Texas Inst. of Letters Award for Short Fiction 1983, Violet Crown Award, Writers League of Texas 2005. *Literary Agent:* c/o Bill Contardi, Brandt and Hochman Literary Agents, 1501 Broadway, Suite 2310, New York, NY 10036, USA. *E-mail:* bill@billcontardi.com. *Website:* www.thomaszigal.com.

ZIMDAHL, Catherine; Australian playwright and screenwriter. *Education:* Australian Film, Television and Radio School. *Career:* writer of short features Sparks and Life on Earth as I Know It. *Plays:* Family Running for Mr Whippy 1995, Clark in Sarajevo 1998, The Wharf at Wooloomooloo, The Darling Loves 2005. *Honours:* Developing Writer's Grant, Literature Bd of the Australia Council; AFI Awards for Best Short Film, Best Short Screenplay 1990, Gold Plaque Award at the Chicago Int. Film Festival 1990, Le Prix Recherché at the Clermont Ferrand Film Festival 1990, Legal & General Umbrella Award for Best New Australian Writing 1998, Louis Esson Prize for Drama, Victorian Premier's Literary Awards 1999, ANPC/New Dramatists' Exchange to New York 1999. *Literary Agent:* RGM Associates, PO Box 128, Surry Hills, NSW 2010, Australia. *Telephone:* (2) 9281-3911. *Fax:* (2) 9281-4705. *E-mail:* info@rgm.com.au. *Website:* www.rgm.com.au.

ZIMLER, Richard, BA, MA; American/Portuguese journalist and writer; b. 1 Jan. 1956, Manhasset, Long Island, NY. *Education:* Duke Univ., Stanford Univ. *Career:* journalist 1982–90; teacher of journalism in Oporto, Portugal; reviewer for the LA Times and Literary Review. *Publications:* Unholy Ghosts 1996, The Last Kabbalist of Lisbon 1997, The Secret Life of Images by Al Berto (trans.) 1997, The Angelic Darkness 1998, Hunting Midnight 2003, Guardian of the Dawn 2005, The Search for Sana 2005, The Seventh Gate 2007, The Warsaw Anagrams 2011; ed: The Children's Hours (with Raša Sekulovic) 2008. *Honours:* National Endowment of the Arts Fellowship in Fiction 1994; Herodotus Award. *Literary Agent:* Cynthia Cannell, 833 Madison Avenue, New York, NY 10021, USA. *Telephone:* (212) 396-9595. *Fax:* (212) 396-9797. *E-mail:* cynthiacannell@aol.com. *E-mail:* rczimler@hotmail.com (home). *Website:* www.zimler.com.

ZIMMER, Carl; American writer and journalist; m. Grace Zimmer; two d. *Publications:* At the Water's Edge 1998, Parasite Rex 2000, Evolution: The Triumph of an Idea: From Darwin to DNA 2002, Soul Made Flesh 2004, Smithsonian Intimate Guide to Human Origins 2005, Evolution: The Triumph of an Idea 2006, The Descent of Man 2007, microcosm: E.coli and the New Science of Life 2008, Brain Cuttings 2010, Science Ink: Tattoos of the Science Obsessed 2011, A Planet of Viruses 2011; contrib. to Newsweek, Science, Discover, Sunday Telegraph, Popular Science, New York Newsday; monthly columnist for Natural History. *Honours:* Guggenheim Fellowship, AAAS Science Journalism Award, Pan-American Health Organization Award for Excellence in Int. Health Reporting, the American Institute Biological Sciences Media Award, Everett Clark Award for science writing, Nat. Academies Science Communication Award 2007. *E-mail:* mail@carlzimmer.com (office). *Website:* www.carlzimmer.com.

ZIMMERMAN, Franklin B., BLitt, PhD, FACLS; American musician, conductor and musicologist; b. 20 June 1923, Wanneta, Kan.; m. 1988; one s. five d. *Education:* Univ. of Southern California, Univ. of Oxford, UK, studied French Horn with Aubrey Brain, conducting with Ernest Read, orchestration with Leon Kirchner and Ingolf Dahl. *Career:* created Music SoundScapes, a three-dimensional, animated and colour-coded graphic musical notation; debut, London 1957; Founder and Dir, Pennsylvania Pro Musica playing over 5,200 concerts; mem. AMS, IMS. *Recordings include:* Handel L'Allegro ed Il Penseroso 1981. *Publications include:* Henry Purcell: Analytical Catalog 1963, Henry Purcell: Life and Times 1967, Henry Purcell: Thematic Index 1973, Words to Music 1965, Facsimile Editions: An Introduction to the Skill of Musick by John Playford (12th edn, corrected and amended by Henry Purcell, with index, introduction and glossary) 1972, Henry Purcell: a Guide to Research 1989, Henry Purcell (1659–1695): Analytical Essays on his Music 2001, Visible Music Sound-Scapes: A New Approach to Musical Notation and Understanding, Purcellian Melodies Indexed: A Thematic Index to the Complete Work of Henry Purcell; contrib. numerous articles and monographs. *Honours:* Arnold Bax Medal for Musicology 1958. *Address:* Visible Music SoundScapes Inc., Suite 1A, 225 S 42nd Street, Philadelphia, PA 19104, USA. *E-mail:* musica@dca.net. *Website:* www.visiblemusics.com/new.

ZINIK, Zinovy, BA; British (b. Russian) author, critic and broadcaster; b. (b. Zinovy (Zinik) Gluzberg), 16 June 1945, Moscow, USSR; m. Nina Gluzberg;

one s. one d. *Education:* Moscow School of Art, Moscow Univ. *Career:* emigrated to Israel 1975, worked as dir for a student theatre group in Jerusalem; moved to London to work for BBC 1976, based in London 1976–; columnist and presenter, BBC World Service 1976–2011; taught creative courses, Jerusalem Univ., Wesleyan Univ., Denver Univ., Columbia Univ.; Co-founder Safety Pin Soc. of UK; mem. The Colony Room Club, The Academy Club, London. *Radio:* Russian Service, BBC Radio 3 1984, After the Wall (with Claudia Sinnig) (Bronze Medal, New York Int. Radio Festival 2001), An A-Z of Kaliningrad, BBC Radio 3 2002, My Father's Leg, BBC Radio 3 2003, Artek, BBC Radio 3 2003, A Beep Heard Around The World, BBC Radio 3 2007, The Ghosts of Little Russia, BBC Radio 3 2009. *Television:* The Mushroom Picker (BBC) 1994. *Plays:* Out of a house walked a man (trans. and research) 1994, Here Comes the Tiger (writer) 1999, A Peripatetic Developer (writer) 2009. *Publications:* Une Personne Déplacée (novel) 1981, Service Russe (novel) 1984, Une Niche au Pantheon 1987, The Mushroom Picker (novel) 1988, One Way Ticket (short stories) 1989, The Lord and the Gamekeeper (novel) 1991, Vstrecha s Originalom (novel, in Russian) 1998, Mind the Doors (short stories) 2001, My Father's Leg (novella) 2005, At Home Abroad (short stories, in Russian) 2007, Letters from the Third Shore (short stories, in Russian) 2008, History Thieves 2011, Emigration as a Literary Device (essays); contrib. to Times Literary Supplement, Encounter, Guardian, Independent, Listener, New Yorker, Spectator, Eurozine. *Literary Agent:* c/o Anna Webber, United Agents, 12–26 Lexington Street, London, W1F 0LE, England. *Telephone:* (20) 3214-0800. *Fax:* (20) 3214-0801. *E-mail:* AWebber@unitedagents.co.uk. *Website:* unitedagents.co.uk. *E-mail:* zinovy.zinik@gmail.com (office).

ZIOLKOWSKI, Theodore Joseph, BA, MA, PhD; American academic and writer; *Professor Emeritus of German and Comparative Literature, Princeton University*; b. 30 Sept. 1932, Birmingham, Ala; s. of Miecislaw Ziolkowski and Cecilia J. Ziolkowski; m. Yetta Bart Goldstein 1951; two s. one d. *Education:* Duke Univ., Univ. of Innsbruck, Austria, Yale Univ. *Career:* instructor to Asst Prof., Yale Univ. 1956–62; Assoc. Prof., Columbia Univ. 1962–64; Prof. of Germanic Languages and Literature, Princeton Univ. 1964–69, Class of 1900 Prof. of Modern Languages 1969–2001, Prof. of Comparative Literature 1975–2001, Dean, Grad. School 1979–92, Prof. Emer. of German and Comparative Literature 2001–; various visiting lectureships and professorships; Resident Fellow, Bellagio Study Centre, Italy 1993; mem. Acad. of Literary Studies, American Acad. of Arts and Sciences, American Philosophical Soc., American Asscn of Teachers of German (Hon. Life Mem.), Asscn of Grad. Schools (Pres. 1990–91), Authors' Guild, Modern Language Asscn (Pres. 1985), Asscn of Literary Scholars and Critics, Int. Asscn of Germanists, German-American Academic Council, Austrian Acad. of Sciences, Göttingen Acad. of Sciences, Deutsche Akad. für Sprache und Dichtung, Darmstadt. *Publications:* Hermann Broch 1964, The Novels of Hermann Hesse 1965, Hermann Hesse 1966, Dimensions of the Modern Novel 1969, Fictional Transfigurations of Jesus 1972, Disenchanted Images 1977, Der Schriftsteller Hermann Hesse 1979, The Classical German Elegy 1980, Varieties of Literary Thematics 1983, German Romanticism and its Institutions 1990, Virgil and the Moderns 1993, The Mirror of Justice 1997, The View from the Tower 1998, Das Wunderjahr in Jena 1998, The Sin of Knowledge 2000, Berlin: Aufstieg einer Kulturmetropole um 1810 2002, Hesitant Heroes 2004, Clio the Romantic Muse 2004, Ovid and the Moderns 2005, Vorboten der Moderne: Kulturgeschichte der Fruehromantik 2006, Modes of Faith: Secular Surrogates for Lost Religious Faith 2007, Minos and the Moderns: Cretan Myth in Twentieth-Century Literature and Art 2008, Scandal on Stage: European Theater as Moral Trial 2009, Heidelberger Romantik 2009; editor: Hermann Hesse: Autobiographical Writings 1972, Hermann Hesse: Stories of Five Decades 1972, Hesse: A Collection of Critical Essays 1972, Hermann Hesse: My Belief: Essays on Life and Art 1974, Hermann Hesse: Pictor's Metamorphoses and Other Fantasies 1982, Hermann Hesse: Soul of the Age: Selected Letters 1891–1962 1991, Friedrich Duerrenmatt: Selected Fiction 2006; contrib. to books and professional journals. *Honours:* Commdr's Cross, Order of Merit (Germany) 2000; Hon. DPhil (Greifswald) 2001; Fulbright Research Grant 1958–59, American Philosophical Soc. Grant 1959, Guggenheim Fellowship 1964–65, American Council of Learned Socs Fellowships 1972, 1976, James Russell Lowell Prize for Criticism 1972, Yale Univ. Wilbur Lucius Cross Medal 1982, Goethe Inst. Gold Medal 1987, Henry Allen Moe Prize in Humanities 1988, Jacob und Wilhelm Grimm Prize 1998, Christian Gauss Award in Criticism 1998, Mellon Emer. Faculty Award 2004, Barricelli Prize 2004, Robert Motherwell Award 2005. *Address:* 36 Bainbridge Street, Princeton, NJ 08540, USA (home). *Telephone:* (609) 430-0209 (office). *E-mail:* tjziol@aol.com (home).

ŽIVKOVIĆ, Zoran, BA, MA, PhD; Serbian writer; b. 5 Oct. 1948, Belgrade; m. Mia; two s. (twins). *Education:* Univ. of Belgrade. *Career:* founder of imprint, Polaris 1982–; science-fiction writer and essayist. *Television:* Zvezdani ekran (The Starry Screen, series about sci-fi fiction cinema) 1984. *Publications:* fiction (titles in translation): The Fourth Circle (Milos Crnjanski Award 1994) 1993, Time Gifts 1997, The Writer 1998, The Book 1999, Impossible Encounters 2000, Seven Touches of Music 2001, The Library (World Fantasy Award for Best Novella 2003) 2002, Steps Through the Mist 2003, Hidden Camera 2003, Compartments 2004, Four Stories Till the End 2004, Twelve Collections and the Teashop 2005, The Bridge 2006, Miss Tamara 2006, Amarcord 2007, The Last Book 2007. *E-mail:* j.jarrold@btopenworld .com*E-mail:* zz@zoranzivkovic.com. *Website:* www.zoranzivkovic.com.

ZOLOTOW, Charlotte Shapiro; American publishing executive and writer; b. 26 June 1915, Norfolk, Va; d. of Louis J. Shapiro and Ella Shapiro (née Bernstein); m. Maurice Zolotow 1938 (divorced 1969, died 1991); one s. one d. *Education:* Univ. of Wisconsin. *Career:* Editorial Dir Junior Books Dept, Harper and Row 1938–44, Sr Ed. 1962–70; Vice-Pres. and Assoc. Publr Harper Jr Books 1976–81; Publr Emer., Adviser to Harper-Collins Jr Books 1991–99; Editorial Dir Charlotte Zolotow Books 1982–90; mem. PEN, Authors' League. *Publications include:* children's books: The Park Book 1944, The Storm Book 1952, Over and Over 1957, Do You Know What I'll Do? 1958, Big Brother 1960, The Three Funny Friends 1961, Mr Rabbit and the Lovely Present 1962, A Tiger Called Thomas 1963, The Quarreling Book 1963, The Sky Was Blue 1963, Someday (Outstanding Children's Book of 1964–65) 1965, When I Have a Little Girl 1965, Big Sister and Little Sister 1966, If It Weren't For You 1966, When I Have a Little Boy 1967, My Friend John 1968, The Hating Book 1969, A Father Like That 1971, Wake Up and Goodnight 1971, Hold My Hand 1972, William's Doll (Outstanding Children's Book of 1972) 1972, Janey 1973, The Summer Night 1974, My Grandson Lew (Christopher Award) 1974, The Unfriendly Book 1975, When the Wind Stops 1975, May I Visit? 1976, It's Not Fair 1976, Someone New 1978, If You Listen 1980, But Not Billy 1983, The Poodle Who Barked at the Wind 1987, A Rose, a Bridge and a Wild Black Horse 1987, Sleepy Book 1988, Something is Going to Happen, The Seashore Book 1992, Snippets 1992, This Quiet Lady 1992, The Moon was Best 1993, Peter and the Pigeons 1993, The Old Dog 1995, Who is Ben 1997; children's short stories: An Overpraised Season 1973, Early Sorrow 1986; poetry: Seasons 2002. *Honours:* Harper Gold Medal Award for Editorial Excellence 1974, Kerlan Award, Univ. of Minnesota 1986, Charlotte Zolotow Award cr. by Univ. of Wisconsin at Madison and given annually to honour the text of the previous year's most outstanding children's book. *Address:* 29 Elm Place, Hastings-on-Hudson, NY 10706, USA. *E-mail:* charlottesdaughter@ charlottezolotow.com (home). *Website:* www.charlottezolotow.com.

ZOLYNAS, Algirdas (Al) Richard Johann, BA, MA, PhD; American academic, poet and writer; *Professor of English, Alliant International University*; b. 1 June 1945, Dornbirn, Austria; m. 1967. *Education:* Univ. of Illinois, Univ. of Utah. *Career:* fmrly Instructor, Asst Prof. and writer-in-residence, Southwest State Univ., Marshall, MN; Lecturer, Weber State Coll., Ogden, UT and San Diego State Univ.; currently Prof. of English in the Dept of Global Liberal Studies, Alliant Int. Univ.; mem. Poets and Writers. *Publications:* The New Physics 1979, 4 Petunia Avenue 1987, Men of Our Time: An Anthology of Male Poetry in Contemporary America (ed. with Fred Moramarco) 1992, Under Ideal Conditions 1994, The Same Air 1997. *Honours:* San Diego Book Award for Best Poetry 1994. *Address:* Alliant International University, 10455 Pomerado Road, San Diego, CA 92131, USA (office). *E-mail:* azolynas@alliant.edu (office). *Website:* www.alliant.edu (office).

ZORIN, Leonid Genrikhovich; Russian playwright and writer; b. 3 Nov. 1924, Baku, Azerbaijan; s. of Genrikh Zorin and Polina Zorin; m. 1st 1951 (deceased); m. 2nd Tatjana Pospelova 1985; one s. *Education:* Azerbaijan State Univ., M. Gorky Inst. of Literature in Moscow. *Career:* literary Baku Russian Drama Theatre; later freelance, mem. USSR Union of Writers 1941–, Int. PEN Club, Russian PEN Centre, Russian Acad. of Cinema, Science and the Arts. *Plays:* more than 49 produced in 16 countries, including Decembrists, Kind Men, The Coronation, The Deck, Warsaw Melody, The Copper Grandmother, The Quotation, The Perished Plot, The Infidelity, The Carnival, The Moscow Nest, Lusgan, The Warsaw Melody 1997, Tsar's Hunt, Roman Comedy, The Invisibles 1999, The Maniac 2000, The Misprint 2001, The Outcome 2002, The Detectives 2003. *Film scripts:* 15 including A Man from Nowhere, The Law, Peace to the Newcomer, Grandmaster, Transit, The Friends and the Years, Pokrovskye Gates, Tsar's Hunt, Hard Sand 2002. *Publications:* (novels and short stories) Old Manuscript 1983, Wanderer 1987, The Topic of the Day 1992, Proscenium 1997, The Plots 1998, The Teetotaller (Banner Prize, Apollon Grigorjev Prize) 2001, The Auction (collection of novels and stories) 2001, Whip (Banner Prize) 2002, Jupiter 2002, Oblivion 2004; numerous essays; Theatre Fantasy (collection of plays) 1974, Selected Plays (2 vols) 1986, The Green Notebooks (collection of essays etc.), The Curtain of the Millennium (collection of later plays) 2002, The Sansara (novel) 2004, The Will of Yzand (humorous book) 2005, The Prose (collection of novels and short stories) in two vols, The Parting March (humorous book) 2005, The National Idea 2006, The Letters from Petersburg 2006. *Honours:* Grand Prix for the best film script Grandmaster (Festival in Kranje, Yugoslavia), Golden Medal for filmscript Peace to the Newcomer, Venice Film Festival 1961, Prize of All-Union Contest of Playwrights Revival of Russia (for Moscow Nest) 1995, (for Lusgan) 1997, Laureate of Apollon Igoziev-Price 2003, Prize of the Russian Authors Org. 2006. *Address:* Krasnoarmeyskaya str. 21, Apt. 73, 125319 Moscow, Russia. *Telephone:* (495) 151-43-33 (home).

ZUCKERMAN, Mortimer (Mort) Benjamin, BA, LLM, MBA; American (b. Canadian) real estate developer, publisher and editor; *Chairman and Editor-in-Chief, US News and World Report, L.P.*; b. 4 June 1937, Montreal, Québec; s. of Abraham Zuckerman and Esther Zuckerman. *Education:* McGill Univ., Pennsylvania Univ., Harvard Univ. *Career:* Sr Vice-Pres. Cabot, Cabot and Forbes 1965–69; Lecturer, then Assoc. Prof., Harvard Univ. Grad. School of Design 1966–74; Visiting Lecturer, Yale Univ. 1967–69; Chair. Boston Properties Co. 1970–; Dir RET Income Foundation 1976–79, Property Capital Trust Co. 1979–80; Pres., Chair. Atlantic Monthly Co., Boston 1980–; Chair. and Ed.-in-Chief US News and World Report 1984–; Propr, Chair. and Co-Publisher, New York Daily News. *Address:* US News and World Report L.P.,

450 West 33rd Street, 11th Floor, New York, NY 10001 (office); Boston Properties, 800 Boylston Street at the Prudential Center, Boston, MA 02199-8103, USA (office). *Telephone:* (212) 716-6800 (office). *Website:* www.usnews.com (office); www.bostonproperties.com (office).

ZUCKERT, Catherine H., BA, MA, PhD; American political scientist, author and editor; *Nancy Reeves Dreux Professor of Political Science, University of Notre Dame*; b. (Catherine Herdis Heldt), 20 Oct. 1942, Miami, Fla; d. of Henning Heldt and Agneta Dom Christensen; m. Michael Zuckert 1965; three d. *Education:* Cornell Univ., Univ. of Chicago. *Career:* Asst Prof., then Assoc. Prof., then William R. Kenan Jr Prof. of Political Philosophy, Carleton Coll. 1971–98; Nancy Reeves Dreux Prof. of Political Science, Univ. of Notre Dame 1998–; Ed.-in-Chief, The Review of Politics 2004–; mem. American Political Science Asscn, Soc. for the Study of Greek Thought, Midwest Political Science Asscn, Ancient Philosophy Soc. *Publications include:* Understanding the Political Spirit 1988, Natural Right and the American Imagination: Political Philosophy in Novel Form 1990, Postmodern Platos: Nietzsche, Heidegger, Gadamer, Strauss, Derrida 1996, The Truth Abour Leo Strauss: Politcal Philosophy in America (with Michael Zuckert) 2006, Plato's Philosophers: The Coherence of Dialogues (Best Book in Philosophy, Asscn of American Publrs 2009, CHOICE Outstanding Academic Title 2009) 2009. *Honours:* Fellowship, Nat. Endowment for the Humanities 2007–08, R.R. Hawkins Award for the Best Scholarly Book 2009, PROSE Awards for Excellence in the Humanities, Earhart Fellowship 2011–12. *Address:* Department of Political Science, 217 O'Shaughnessy Hall, University of Notre Dame, Notre Dame, IN 46556, USA (office). *Telephone:* (574) 631-6620 (office). *E-mail:* czuckert@nd.edu (office). *Website:* www.nd.edu/~czuckert (office).

ZURITA, Raúl; Chilean writer and poet; *Professor of Poetry, Universidad Diego Portales*; b. 10 Jan. 1950, Santiago; m. Paulina Wendt. *Education:* Universidad Frederico Santa Maria, Valparaiso, School of Tech. Engineering, Santiago. *Career:* fmr computer salesman; co-f. Colectivo de Accion de Arte protest group against Pinochet rule 1973; Visiting Prof., California State Univ. 1986, Tufts Univ. 2009; Cultural Attaché to Rome 1990; currently Prof. of Poetry, Universidad Diego Portales; sky-wrote passages from his poem, La Vida Nueva, over New York 1980; bulldozed the phrase 'Ni Pena Ni Miedo' (Without Pain Or Fear) into the Atacama Desert 1993 (because of its size, can only be seen from the sky). *Publications:* Purgatorio 1979, Anteparaiso 1982, El paraíso está vacio 1984, Canto a su amor desaparecido 1985, El amor de Chile 1987, Canto de los ríos que se aman 1993, La Vida Nueva 1994, El día más blanco 2000, Poemas Militantes 2000, INRI 2003, Los poemas muertos 2006, Los Países Muertos 2007, Cinco Fragmentos 2007, Las Ciudades de agua 2008, In Memoriam 2008, Sueños para Kurosawa 2009, Cuadernos de guerra 2009, Zurita 2011. *Honours:* Guggenheim scholarship 1984, Pablo Neruda Prize 1989, Pericle d'oro Prize (Italy) 1994, Nat. Prize for Literature 2000, Casa de América Prize (Cuba) 2006. *Address:* School of Creative Writing, Universidad Diego Portales, Avenida Vergara 240, Santiago, Chile (office). *Telephone:* (2) 6762398 (office). *Fax:* (2) 6762319 (office). *E-mail:* zurita_123@yahoo.com (office). *Website:* www.udp.cl (office).

ZUSAK, Markus; Australian writer; b. 1975, Sydney; m.; one d. *Publications:* The Underdog 1999, Fighting Ruben Wolfe 2001, Getting the Girl 2002, I Am the Messenger (Australia Children's Book Council Book of the Year 2003, Printz Honor 2006) 2002, The Book Thief 2006, Bridge of Clay 2009. *Literary Agent:* Curtis Brown (Australia) Pty Ltd, Post Office Box 19, Paddington, NSW 2021, Australia. *Telephone:* (2) 9331-5301. *Fax:* (2) 9360-3935. *E-mail:* info@curtisbrown.com.au. *Website:* www.curtisbrown.com.au; www.randomhouse.com/features/markuszusak.

ZWICKY, (Julia) Fay, BA; Australian poet and editor; b. 4 July 1933, Melbourne, Vic.; m. 1st Karl Zwicky 1957; one s. one d.; m. 2nd James Mackie 1990. *Education:* Univ. of Melbourne. *Career:* Sr Lecturer in English, Univ. of Western Australia 1972–87; Assoc. Ed., Westerly 1973–95. *Publications:* Isaac Babel's Fiddle 1975, Quarry: A Selection of Western Australian Poetry (ed.) 1981, Kaddish and Other Poems 1982, Journeys: Poems by Judith Wright, Rosemary Dobson, Gwen Harwood, Dorothy Hewett (ed.) 1982, Hostages and Other Stories 1983, The Lyre in the Pawnshop: Essays on Literature and Survival, 1974–84 1986, Procession: Youngstreet Poets 3 (ed.) 1987, Ask Me 1990, Poems 1970–1992 1993, The Gatekeeper's Wife 1997, Picnic 2006. *Honours:* New South Wales Premier's Award 1982, Western Australian Premier's Awards 1987, 1991, 1999, Patrick White Literary Award 2005, Christopher Brennan Award for Poetry 2005. *Address:* 30 Goldsmith Road, Claremont, WA 6010, Australia (home).

ZWICKY, Jan, BA, MA, PhD; Canadian poet and philosopher; b. 10 May 1955, Calgary, AB. *Education:* Univ. of Calgary, Univ. of Toronto. *Career:* teacher, Univ. of Waterloo 1981, 1984, 1985, Princeton Univ. 1982, Univ. of Western Ontario 1989, Univ. of Alberta 1992, Univ. of New Brunswick 1994, 1995; Prof., Univ. of Victoria 1996–2009, Prof. Emer. 2009–; Ed. Brick Books. *Publications include:* Wittgenstein Elegies 1986, The New Room 1989, Lyric Philosophy 1992, Songs for Relinquishing the Earth 1998, Wisdom & Metaphor 2003, Robinson's Crossing 2004, Thirty-seven Small Songs and Thirteen Silences 2005, Plato as Artist 2009, Forge 2011. *Honours:* Gov.-Gen.'s Award for Poetry 1999, Dorothy Livesay Poetry Prize 2004. *Address:* c/o Department of Philosophy, University of Victoria, PO Box 3045, Victoria, BC V8W 3P4, Canada.

ZWINGER, Ann Haymond, MA; American natural history writer, illustrator and academic; b. 12 March 1925, Muncie, Ind.; d. of William T. Haymond and Helen G. Haymond; m. Herman H. Zwinger 1952; three d. *Education:* Wellesley Coll., Indiana Univ. and Radcliffe Coll. *Career:* freelance natural history writer and illustrator 1969–; Outdoor Consultant for various river cos since 1975; apptd Dir American Electric Power 1977; Adjunct Prof., Southwest Studies and English, Colorado Coll. 1980–; Trustee Nature Conservancy 1984; endowed Chair. Hulbert Center for Southwest Studies 1991. *Publications:* Beyond the Aspen Grove 1970, Land Above the Trees 1972, Run, River Run 1975, Wind in the Rock 1978, A Desert Country Near the Sea 1983, The Mysterious Lands 1987, Shaped by Wind and Water: Reflections of a Naturalist 2000, Spanish Peaks: Land and Legends 2001, Fall Colors Across North America 2001, Yosemite: Valley of Thunder 2002, Grand Canyon: Little Things in a Big Place 2006; numerous further books and articles in magazines. *Honours:* Dr hc (Colorado Coll) 1976, (Carleton Coll) 1984; Burroughs Medal for Natural History Writing 1976, Wellesley Coll. Alumnae Award 1977, Stu Dodge Award, Palmer Land Trust 2007. *Address:* c/o Hulbert Center for Southwestern Studies, 14 East Cache la Poudre, Colorado Springs, CO 80903, USA (office). *Website:* www.coloradocollege.edu/Dept/SW (office).

Directory

APPENDIX A: LITERARY AWARDS AND PRIZES

J. R. Ackerley Prize for Autobiography: English Centre of International PEN, Free Word Centre, 60 Farringdon Road, London, EC1R 3GA, England. *Telephone:* (20) 7324-2535. *E-mail:* enquiries@englishpen.org. *Website:* www.englishpen.org. Annual award for literary autobiography, written in English and published in the preceding year. Short-listed titles are chosen by the Trustees of the J. R. Ackerley Foundation. Nominations are not accepted.

Jane Addams Children's Book Award: Jane Addams Peace Association, 777 United Nations Plaza, Sixth Floor, New York, NY 10017, USA. *Telephone:* (212) 682-8830. *Fax:* (212) 286-8211. *E-mail:* japa@igc.org. *Website:* www.janeaddamspeace.org. f. 1953. Annual award, in association with the Women's International League for Peace and Freedom, for a picture book and a longer book for children that best combine literary merit with themes promoting peace, social justice, world community and the equality of the sexes and all races. Open to books for pre-school through to high school age, including translations or titles published in English in other countries. Books may be submitted by the publishers or requested by the committee.

Akutagawa Ryûnosuke Shô (Akutagawa Prize): Association for the Promotion of Japanese Literature, Bungei-Shunjû Bldg, 3 Kioi-cho, Chiyoda-ku, Tokyo 102, Japan. Japan's top literary award for young writers. f. 1935 by Kikuchi Kan, the editor of Bungei Shunjû magazine, in memory of novelist Akutagawa Ryûnosuke. Awarded twice a year, in January and July, to the best literary short story published in a newspaper or magazine by a new author.

Alexander Prize: Royal Historical Society, University College London, Gower Street, London, WC1E 6BT, England. *Telephone:* (20) 7387-7532. *Fax:* (20) 7387-7532. *E-mail:* royalhistsoc@ucl.ac.uk. *Website:* www.royalhistoricalsociety.org. Offered for a published scholarly journal article or essay in a collective volume based on original historical research. Candidates must either be doctoral students in a UK institution, or be within two years of having completed a doctorate in history at a UK institution.

Alice Literary Award: Society of Women Writers (Australia), c/o Judy Bartosy, 73 Church Road, Carrum, Vic. 3197, Australia. *Website:* www.swwvic.net.au. Biennial award presented by the Society of Women Writers (Australia) for a distinguished and long-term contribution to literature by an Australian woman.

American Academy of Arts and Letters Gold Medal (Letters): American Academy of Arts and Letters, 633 West 155th Street, New York, NY 10032-1799, USA. *Telephone:* (212) 368-5900. *Fax:* (212) 491-4615. *E-mail:* academy@artsandletters.org. *Website:* www.artsandletters.org. A series of prestigious awards, which rotate between literary and artistic disciplines. Each discipline is awarded once every six years, with categories including poetry, belles lettres and criticism, history, drama, fiction, essays, music, and architecture.

Hans Christian Andersen Awards: International Board on Books for Young People (IBBY), Nonnenweg 12, Postfach, 4003 Basel, Switzerland. *Telephone:* (61) 272 29 17. *Fax:* (61) 272 27 57. *E-mail:* ibby@ibby.org. *Website:* www.ibby.org. f. 1956. Biennial awards to honour an author (Hans Christian Andersen Award for Writing), and an illustrator (Hans Christian Andersen Award for Illustration), whose work has made a lasting contribution to children's literature. Awards are open to living candidates from any country. Nominations are made by National Sections of IBBY.

Asham Award: Asham Literary Endowment Trust, The Town Hall, High Street, Lewes, East Sussex, BN7 2QS, England. *Website:* www.ashamaward.com. Biennial award for short stories (up to 4,000 words) by new women writers. Open to women aged over 18, resident in the UK, who have not yet had a novel or collection of short stories published. The entries must be in English and previously unpublished.

Augustpriset: Augustpriset, Svenska Förläggare AB, Drottninggatan 97, 113 60 Stockholm, Sweden. *Telephone:* (8) 736-19-40. *Fax:* (8) 736-19-44. *E-mail:* info@forlaggare.se. *Website:* www.augustpriset.info. f. 1989 by the Swedish Publishers' Association. Annual awards given in three categories: fiction, non-fiction and children's and young adult books, by a Swedish writer.

Australian Literature Society Gold Medal: Association for the Study of Australian Literature (ASAL) Ltd, Australia. *Website:* asaliterature.com. Annual award for an outstanding Australian literary work published in the preceding year, or occasionally awarded for outstanding services to Australian literature. Award was inaugurated by the ALS, which was incorporated in the Association for the Study of Australian Literature in 1982. No direct application is accepted. No nominations are required; instead ASAL members are invited to propose potential winners to the judging panel.

Australian Prime Minister's Literary Awards: Department of the Environment, Water, Heritage and the Arts, GPO Box 787, Canberra, ACT 2601, Australia. *Telephone:* (2) 6274-1111. *E-mail:* pmliteraryawards@environment.gov.au. *Website:* www.arts.gov.au/books/pmliteraryawards. Annual awards for fiction and non-fiction writers who contribute to Australia's cultural identity and economy. Entrants must be Australian citizens or permanent residents.

The Australian/Vogel Literary Award: Allen & Unwin Publishers, POB 8500, St Leonards, NSW 1590, Australia. *Telephone:* (2) 8425-0100. *Fax:* (2) 9906-2218. *Website:* www.allenandunwin.com. f. 1980. Annual award for an original unpublished manuscript of Australian history, fiction or biography. Entrants must normally be residents of Australia aged under 35. Manuscripts must be between 30,000 and 100,000 words and must not be under offer to any other publisher or award.

Authors' Club Best First Novel Award: Authors' Club, 40 Dover Street, London, W1S 4NP, England. *Telephone:* (20) 7499-8581. *Fax:* (20) 7409-0913. *Website:* www.theartsclub.co.uk. f. 1954. Annual award to the most promising first full-length novel of the year, published in the UK by a British author. The winner is selected from entries submitted by publishers.

BA/Nielsen Book Data Author of the Year Award: Minster House, 272 Vauxhall Bridge Road, London, SW1V 1BA, England. *Telephone:* (20) 7834-5477. *Fax:* (20) 7834-8812. *E-mail:* mail@booksellers.org.uk. *Website:* www.booksellers.org.uk. f. 1993. Annual award to the author judged to have had the most impact for booksellers in the year, as voted for by members of the Booksellers Association. The living author must be British or Irish.

Banipal Prize for Arabic Literary Translation: c/o The Banipal Trust, 1 Gough Square, London, EC4A 3DE, England. *Telephone:* (20) 7832-1350. *E-mail:* info@banipaltrust.org. *Website:* www.banipaltrust.org.uk/prize. f. 2006. Annual award to the translator of a full-length imaginative and creative work of literary merit published in English. Aims to raise the profile of contemporary Arabic literature and honour the work of translators.

BBC Samuel Johnson Prize for Non-Fiction: c/o Colman Getty Consultancy, 28 Windmill Street, London, W1T 2JJ, England. *E-mail:* hannah@colmangetty.co.uk. *Website:* www.thesamueljohnsonprize.co.uk. Formerly the AT&T Non-Fiction Award. Annual award to the best work of general non-fiction published by a British publisher in the previous year. Entries must be written in English by living writers from the British Commonwealth or the Republic of Ireland. Entries are submitted by publishers.

Benson Medal: The Royal Society of Literature, Strand, London, WC2R 1LA, England. *Telephone:* (20) 7845-4676. *Fax:* (20) 7845-4679. *E-mail:* info@rslit.org. *Website:* www.rslit.org/content/benson. f. 1916 by A. C. Benson, irregular periodical award recognizing a distinguished career in poetry, fiction or biography. Submissions are not accepted.

David Berry Prize: Royal Historical Society, University College London, Gower Street, London, WC1E 6BT, England. *Telephone:* (20) 7387-7532. *Fax:* (20) 7387-7532. *E-mail:* royalhistsoc@ucl.ac.uk. *Website:* www.royalhistoricalsociety.org. Annual award to the writer of the best essay on a subject dealing with Scottish history, of between 6,000 and 10,000 words. Previous winners may not reapply.

Besterman/McColvin Medals: The CILIP, 7 Ridgmount Street, London, WC1E 7AE, England. *Telephone:* (20) 7255-0500. *Fax:* (20) 7255-0501. *E-mail:* info@cilip.org.uk. *Website:* www.cilip.org.uk. Two medals are awarded annually for outstanding works of reference available in the UK: one for print and one for electronic formats. The awards are judged by a panel of members of the Information Services Group and the Multi-Media Information and Technology Group.

James Tait Black Memorial Prizes: Department of English Literature, University of Edinburgh, David Hume Tower, George Square, Edinburgh, EH8 9JX, Scotland. *Telephone:* (131) 650-3620. *Fax:* (131) 650-6898. *E-mail:* s.strathdee@ed.ac.uk. *Website:* www.englit.ed.ac.uk/jtbinfm.htm. f. 1918. Two annual awards for biographical and fictional work published in the preceding year. Works must be written in English and be published or co-published in the UK. Only publishers may apply.

The Blooker Prize: *E-mail:* peter@think-inc.co.uk. *Website:* lulublookerprize.typepad.com. f. 2006. Annual award, formerly the Lulu Blooker Prize. Awarded in three categories (fiction, non-fiction and comics) for 'blooks', or books with content originally in the form of a blog, web comic or website.

The Booker Prize: see Man Booker Prize for Fiction.

Boston Globe-Horn Book Award: The Horn Book, Inc., 56 Roland Street, Suite 200, Boston, MA 02129, USA. *E-mail:* info@hbook.com. *Website:* www.hbook.com/bghb. f. 1967 by The Boston Globe and The Horn Book Magazine. Annual award for books published in the USA within the previous year, in the categories of fiction, non-fiction and picture book.

Bremen Literatur Förderungspreis (City of Bremen Literary Encouragement Prize): c/o Stadtbibliothek Bremen, Am Wall 201 D-28195 Bremen, Germany. *Website:* www.rudolf-alexander-schroeder-stiftung.de. f. 1952 in honour of Rudolf Alexander Schröder, as the Literaturpreis der Freien Hansestadt Bremen. Annual award to a German-speaking writer or poet.

Bridport Prize: Bridport Arts Centre, PO Box 6910, Bridport, Dorset DT6 9BQ, England. *Telephone:* (1398) 428333. *E-mail:* frances@bridportprize.org.uk. *Website:* www.bridportprize.org.uk. f. 1973 by Peggy Chapman-Andrews. Annual award for original poems of not more than 42 lines, and short stories between 1,000 and 5,000 words. Open to previously unpublished works, written in English, not entered in any other competition.

Brit Writers' Awards: 63-65 Rea Street, Birmingham, West Midlands, B5 6BB, England. *Telephone:* (871) 237-4442. *E-mail:* enquiries@britwriters.co.uk. *Website:* www.britwriters.co.uk. f. 2010. Awards are given in eight categories: poetry, short stories, novels, non-fiction, children's stories, song-writing and to an unpublished writer from a black, minority or ethnic origin and to published writers. The winners then compete for the overall Book of the Year Award. The competition is open to all British citizens worldwide and people resident in the UK.

British Book Awards: c/o Midas Public Relations, 10-14 Old Court Place, London, W8 4PL, England. *Telephone:* (20) 7361-7860. *E-mail:* info@midaspr.co.uk. *Website:* www.galazybritishbookawards.com. f. 1989. Annual awards, known as 'Nibbies', in a range of categories, with various awards sponsored by different companies. Categories include Editor, Publisher, Author, Independent Bookseller and Children's Book.

British Columbia Book Prizes: West Coast Book Prize Society, Suite 901, 207 West Hastings Street, Vancouver, BC V6B 1H7, Canada. *Telephone:* (604) 687-2405. *Fax:* (604) 687-2435. *E-mail:* info@bcbookprizes.ca. *Website:* www.bcbookprizes.ca. f. 1985. Awards celebrating the achievements of British Columbian writers and publishers, presented in categories including fiction, non-fiction, poetry, regional writing, illustrated children's literature. Books must have been published during the preceding year; residency conditions for authors vary according to category.

British Fantasy Awards: British Fantasy Society, 23 Mayne Street, Hanford, Stoke on Trent, ST4 4RF, England. *E-mail:* info@britishfantasysociety.org.uk. *Website:* www.britishfantasysociety.org.uk. Set of awards presented by the British Fantasy Society at its annual conference, in categories including best novel (the August Derleth Award), best short story, and best anthology. The winners are selected by BFS members.

British Science Fiction Association Awards: British Science Fiction Association, 8 Century House, Armoury Road, London, SE8 4LH, England. *Telephone:* (20) 8469-3354. *E-mail:* awards@bsfa.co.uk. *Website:* www.bsfa.co.uk. f. 1966 to promote the best British (and other) science fiction novel, story, artwork, etc. Entries must have been first published in the UK in that year. No applications are permitted.

Bruntwood Playwriting Competition: Royal Exchange Theatre, St Ann's Square, Manchester, M2 7DH, England. *Telephone:* (161) 615 6765. *E-mail:* bruntwood@royalexchange.co.uk. *Website:* www.writeaplay.co.uk. f. 2005 by the Royal Exchange Theatre, Manchester. Annual competition to reward the best plays by writers across the UK and Ireland. Entries are judged anonymously and the competition is open to anyone over the age of 18 with a play not previously performed. The winner's play is staged at the Royal Exchange Theatre.

Georg-Büchner-Preis: Deutsche Akademie für Sprache und Dichtung, Glückert-Haus, Alexandraweg 23, 64287 Darmstadt, Germany. *Telephone:* (6151) 40920. *Fax:* (6151) 409299. *E-mail:* sekretariat@deutscheakademie.de. *Website:* www.deutscheakademie.de/preise_buechner.html. f. 1923. Annual award in recognition of the winner's special status and contribution to contemporary German culture. Awarded to a novelist or poet writing in German.

Caine Prize for African Writing: The Menier Gallery, Menier Chocolate Factory, 51 Southwark Street, London SE1 1RU, England. *Telephone:* (20) 7378-6234. *E-mail:* info@caineprize.com. *Website:* www.caineprize.com. f. 2000. Annual award to a short story or narrative poem (between 3,000 and 10,000 words) by an African writer, published in English anywhere in the world in the previous five years. Submissions should be made by publishers.

Randolph Caldecott Medal: Association for Library Service to Children, 50 East Huron Street, Chicago, IL 60611, USA. *E-mail:* alsc@ala.org. *Website:* www.ala.org/alsc. Annual award to an illustrator of the most distinguished American picture book for children published in the preceding year.

James Cameron Memorial Award: Department of Journalism, City University, Northampton Square, London, EC1 0HB, England. Annual award for journalism to a reporter of any nationality working for the British media. Nominations are not accepted.

Canadian Authors' Association Literary Awards: PO Box 581, St. Main, Orillia, ON L3V 6K5, Canada. *Telephone:* (705) 653-0323. *Fax:* (705) 653-0593. *E-mail:* admin@canauthors.org. *Website:* www.canauthors.org/awards. A series of annual awards from the Canadian Authors' Association and the Canada Council for the Arts, including fiction (CAA MOSAID Technology Inc. Award for Fiction), poetry (CAA Jack Chalmers Poetry Award), short story (CAA Jubilee Award for Short Stories), biography (CAA Birks Family Foundation Award for Biography), Canadian history (CAA Lela Common Award for Canadian History), drama (CAA Carol Bolt Drama Award), children's (CAA Children's Short Story Award), as well as a special award for a complete body of work. Awards are for full-length English-language literature by living authors who are Canadians or landed immigrants. All entries must have been first published during the preceding year, although publication may have taken place outside Canada. Previous winners are not eligible for awards they have won, but may be entered in the other categories.

Canadian Library Association Book of the Year for Children Award: Canadian Library Association, 328 Frank Street, Ottawa, ON K2P 0X8, Canada. *Telephone:* (613) 232-9625. *Fax:* (613) 563-9895. *E-mail:* info@cla.ca. *Website:* www.cla.ca. Annual award to an author of an outstanding children's book published in Canada during the previous year. The book must be suitable for children up to 14 years of age.

Carnegie Medal: The CILIP, 7 Ridgmount Street, London, WC1E 7AE, England. *Telephone:* (20) 7255-0650. *Fax:* (20) 7255-0651. *E-mail:* ckg@cilip.org.uk. *Website:* www.carnegiegreenaway.org.uk. Annual award for an outstanding book for children written in English and receiving its first publication in the UK during the preceding year.

Children's Book Award: Red House Children's Book Award, 2 Bridge Wood View, Horsforth, Leeds, West Yorkshire, LS18 5PE, England. *Website:* www.redhousechildrensbookaward.co.uk. Annual award, sponsored by Red House, judged by children. Winners announced at the Hay Festival. The three categories are picture books, shorter novels and longer novels, all of which are then considered for the Best Book of the Year award.

Children's Laureate: Education Department, Book Trust, Book House, 45 East Hill, London, SW18 2QZ, England. *E-mail:* childrenslaureate@booktrust.org.uk. *Website:* www.childrenslaureate.org.uk. f. 1999. Biennial award to honour a writer or illustrator of children's books for lifetime achievement. Nominees must be UK-based, have a significant body of work, and have attracted critical and popular success.

Arthur C. Clarke Award for Science Fiction: *E-mail:* chairofjudges.clarkeaward@gmail.com. *Website:* www.clarkeaward.com. f. 1987 to encourage science fiction in the UK. Annual award to the best science fiction novel published in the UK in the preceding year. The award is jointly administered and judged by the British Science Fiction Association, Science Fiction Foundation and the Science Museum.

David Cohen British Literature Prize: Arts Council of England, Literature Department, 14 Great Peter Street, London, SW1P 3NQ, England. *Telephone:* (20) 7973-6442. *Fax:* (20) 7973-6520. *E-mail:* info.literature@artscouncil.org.uk. *Website:* www.artscouncil.org.uk. f. 1980. Biennial award recognizing lifetime achievement of a living novelist, short story writer, essayist, biographer, poet, dramatist, travel writer or writer in any other literary genre.

Commonwealth Writers' Prize: The Commonwealth Writers' Prize, Commonwealth Foundation, Pall Mall, London, SW1Y 5HY, England. *Telephone:* (20) 7930-3783. *Fax:* (20) 7839-8157. *E-mail:* geninfo@commonwealth.int. *Website:* www.commonwealthfoundation.com. f. 1987. Annual award to reward excellence in Commonwealth literature, sponsored by the Commonwealth Foundation. For the purposes of the award the Commonwealth is divided into four regions: Africa, the Caribbean and Canada, Eurasia (which includes the UK), and Southeast Asia and the South Pacific. A shortlist is drawn up with a best book and a best first book for each region. Each year the award ceremony is held in a different Commonwealth country. Open to any work of prose fiction (drama and poetry are excluded). The work must have been written by a living citizen of the Commonwealth, must be of a reasonable length and be in English. It must have been first published during the previous calendar year. To be eligible for the best first published book category the entry must be the first work of fiction that the author has published.

Duff Cooper Prize: Box 22, 54 St Maur Road, London, SW6 4DP, England. *Telephone:* (20) 7736-3729. *Fax:* (20) 7731-7638. *E-mail:* info@theduffcooperprize.org. *Website:* www.theduffcooperprize.org. Annual award to a literary work in the field of history, biography, politics or poetry, published in the previous year.

Costa Book Awards: *E-mail:* amanda@amandajohnsonpr.com. *Website:* www.costabookawards.com. f. 1971 as the Whitbread Book Awards, changed sponsorship and name 2006. Annual awards to promote and increase British literature in each of five categories: novel, first novel, biography, children's novel and poetry. Entries are submitted by publishers and the authors must have been resident in the UK or Republic of Ireland for at least three years. One category winner is then voted Book of the Year by the panel of judges.

Crime Writers' Association (CWA) Awards: Crime Writers' Association, PO Box 273, Borehamwood, Hertfordshire WD6 2XA, England. *E-mail:* info@thecwa.co.uk. *Website:* www.thecwa.co.uk. The CWA gives a series of annual awards for outstanding works in the field of crime literature: Cartier Diamond Dagger for Fiction (for outstanding contribution to the genre), Gold Dagger for Fiction (for the best crime fiction of the year), Silver Dagger for Fiction, Gold Dagger for Non-Fiction (for the best non-fiction crime book), Short Story Dagger (for the best short story in the crime genre), Ian Fleming Steel Dagger (for the best thriller, adventure novel or spy fiction novel), John Creasey Memorial Dagger (for the best first crime novel by an author), Ellis Peters Historical Dagger (for the best historical crime novel), Dagger in the Library (for the author whose work has given the most pleasure to readers, judged by librarians), Début Dagger (for an unpublished writer of crime fiction).

Den Store Pris: Det Danske Akademi, Rungstedlund, Rungsted Strandvej 111, 2960 Rungsted Kyst, Denmark. *Telephone:* 33 13 11 12. *Fax:* 33 32 80 45. *Website:* www.danskeakademi.dk. f. 1961 by the Ministry of Culture. Biennial award for a complete body of work, with the recipient chosen by members of the Danish Academy. Open only to Danish authors. No direct applications are accepted.

Deutscher Buchpreis: Börsenverein des Deutschen Buchhandels eV, Grosser Hirschgraben 17–21 Buchhändlerhaus, 60311 Frankfurt am Main, Germany. *Telephone:* (69) 13 06 0. *Fax:* (69) 13 06 201. *E-mail:* info@boev.de. *Website:* deutscher-buchpreis.de. f. 2005 by the Börsenverein des Deutschen Buchhandels (German Publishers' & Booksellers' Association); annual award to promote literature written in German; open to any writer in German; the winner is announced at the Frankfurt Book Fair.

Encore Award: Society of Authors, 84 Drayton Gardens, London, SW10 9SB, England. *Telephone:* (20) 7373-6642. *Fax:* (20) 7373-5768. *E-mail:* info@societyofauthors.org. *Website:* www.societyofauthors.org. f. 1990. Annual award for a second published novel.

European Union Prize for Literature: FEE-FEP, Rue Montoyer, 31 - box 8, 1000 Brussels, Belgium. *Telephone:* (2) 770-11-10. *Fax:* (2) 771-20-71. *E-mail:* info@eupl.eu. *Website:* www.euprizeliterature.eu. f. 2008. Annual award for emerging writers of contemporary fiction. Entrants are selected by 11 or 12 of the 34 countries participating in the EU Culture Programme to represent their country.

Geoffrey Faber Memorial Prize: Faber and Faber Ltd, Bloomsbury House, 74-77 Great Russell Street, London, WC1B 3DA, England. *Telephone:* (20) 7927-3800. *Fax:* (20) 7927-3801. *Website:* www.faber.co.uk. f. 1963, in memory of the founder of the publishing firm Faber and Faber. Annual award, with prizes alternating between verse or fiction. Entrants must be under 40 years of age and a citizen of the UK and colonies, the Commonwealth, or the Republic of Ireland or South Africa. Entries must have been published in the two years preceding the year in which the award is given.

Eleanor Farjeon Award: *E-mail:* contact@childrensbookcircle.org.uk. *Website:* www.childrensbookcircle.org.uk. Awarded by the Children's Book Circle for distinguished service to children's books, both in the UK and overseas. Recipients include librarians, publishers, booksellers and authors and are chosen from nominations from members of the Children's Book Circle.

Sir Banister Fletcher Prize of the Authors' Club: Authors' Club, 40 Dover Street, London, W1X 3RB, England. *Telephone:* (20) 7499-8581. *Fax:* (20) 7409-0913. *Website:* www.theartsclub.co.uk. f. 1954 and named after the late Sir Banister Fletcher, a former President of both the Authors' Club and the Royal Institute of British Architects (RIBA), this annual prize is awarded for the most deserving book of the previous year on either architecture or the arts. Publishers only are invited to apply to the Club Secretary.

Miles Franklin Literary Award: Permanent Trustee Co. Ltd, Level 4, 35 Clarence Street, GPO Box 4270, Sydney, NSW 2001, Australia. *Telephone:* (2) 8295 8100. *Fax:* (2) 8295 8659. *E-mail:* trustawards@cauzgroup.com.au. *Website:* www.trust.com.au/awards/miles_franklin. f. 1957. Annual award for a novel or play of high literary merit, presenting aspects of Australian life, published in the previous year.

Giller Prize: see The Scotiabank Giller Prize.

Glenfiddich Food and Drink Awards: Wild Card PR, Brettenham House, 5 Savoy Street, London, WC2E 7AE, England. *Telephone:* (20) 7257-6470. *E-mail:* deck@wildcard.co.uk. *Website:* www.wildcard.co.uk. f. 1970. Annual awards recognizing the excellence in writing, publishing and broadcasting on the subjects of food and drink. Categories include best food book, best drinks book, best newspaper cookery writer, restaurant critic of the year and best drinks writer. Entries are accepted from publishers only.

Governor-General's Literary Awards: Canada Council, 350 Albert Street, PO Box 1047, Ottawa, ON K1P 5V8, Canada. *Telephone:* (613) 566-4305. *Website:* www.canadacouncil.ca/prizes/ggla. f. 1937. Annual awards, given by the Canada Council for the Arts, for Canadian authors writing both in English and French. Categories are: adult fiction, poetry, drama, non-fiction, children's literature (text), children's literature (illustrated), translation. Prizes in each language.

Gradam Litrochta Cló Iar-Chonnachta (Cló Iar-Chonnachta Literary Award): Cló Iar-Chonnachta Teo, Indreabhán, Connemara, County Galway, Ireland. *Telephone:* (91) 593307. *Fax:* (91) 593362. *E-mail:* cic@iol.ie. *Website:* www.cic.ie. f. 1995 by Micheal o Conghaile, writer and founder of Irish-language publisher Cló Iar-Chonnachta, to encourage Irish language writing. Annual award for a newly-written and unpublished work in the Irish language, a different type of work each year, either poetry, drama, novel or short story.

Grand Prix de la Francophonie (Grand Francophony Prize): Académie Française, Institut de France, 23 quai de Conti, 75006 Paris, France. *Telephone:* 1-44-41-43-00. *Fax:* 1-43-29-47-45. *E-mail:* contact@academie-francaise.fr. *Website:* www.academie-francaise.fr. f. 1986 at the suggestion of the Canadian government, with support from the governments of France, Monaco and Morocco and several private sponsors. Administered by the Académie Française, this annual award aims to promote the influence of French-language literature. Open to living authors of all ages; only published works may be submitted, and they must have appeared during the preceding year.

Kate Greenaway Medal: The CILIP, 7 Ridgmount Street, London, WC1E 7AE, England. *Telephone:* (20) 7255-0650. *Fax:* (20) 7255-0505. *E-mail:* ckg@cilip.org.uk. *Website:* www.carnegiegreenaway.org.uk. Annual award for an outstanding book in terms of illustration for children, published in the UK in the preceding year.

Guardian Children's Fiction Award: The Guardian, Kings Place, 90 York Way, London, N1 9GU, England. *Website:* www.guardian.co.uk. Annual award for an outstanding work of fiction for children by a Commonwealth or British author, first published in the UK in the previous year, excluding picture books and previous winners.

Guardian First Book Award: The Guardian, Kings Place, 90 York Way, London, N1 9GU, England. *Website:* www.guardian.co.uk. Annual award for a work of fiction by a British, Irish or Commonwealth writer and published in the UK. Submissions are not accepted.

Hammett Awards: International Association of Crime Writers, North American Branch, PO Box 8674, New York, NY 10116-8674, USA. *E-mail:* info@crimewritersna.org. *Website:* www.crimewritersna.org/hammett/index.htm. Annual award given by the North American branch of the Asociación Internacional de Escritores Policiacos, or International Association of Crime Writers, to reward excellence in the genre of crime literature. Open to US or Canadian writers.

Hawthornden Prize: 42a Hays Mews, Berkeley Square, London, W1X 7RU, England. f. 1919. Annual award to a British writer for a work of imaginative literature, published during the previous year. No direct applications are accepted.

William Hill Sports Book of the Year: *E-mail:* pressoffice@williamhill.co.uk. *Website:* www.williamhillmedia.com. Sponsored by bookmakers, William Hill. All books must be published in the UK during the previous year.

P. C. Hooft-prijs voor Letterkunde (P. C. Hooft Prize for Literature): Stichting P.C. Hooft-prijs voor Letterkunde, Postbus 90515, 2509 The Hague, The Netherlands. *Telephone:* (70) 3339666. *Fax:* (70) 3477941. *E-mail:* info@nlmd.nl. *Website:* www.pchooftprijs.nl. f. 1947. Annual award presented to a Dutch writer for lifetime achievement in literature. Works of prose, essay and poetry are all considered for the prize.

Independent Foreign Fiction Prize: Literature Department, Arts Council England, 14 Great Peter Street, London, SW1P 3NQ, England. *Telephone:* (20) 7333-0100. *Fax:* (20) 7973-6590. *E-mail:* info.literature@artscouncil.org.uk. *Website:* www.artscouncil.org.uk. f. 1990. Open to works of fiction by a living author, which have been translated into English from any other language and published in the UK during the previous year. The prize is shared between author and translator.

Institute of Historical Research Prize—IHR Prize: Institute of Historical Research, Senate House, London, WC1E 7HU, England. *Telephone:* (20) 7862-8756. *Website:* www.history.ac.uk. f. 2000. Biennial award to enable professional historians to write their first book for a general readership. Entrants must be previously unpublished professional historians (not including monographs, university press publications or academic imprints).

International IMPAC Dublin Literary Award: Dublin City Library and Archive, 138–144 Pearse Street, Dublin 2, Ireland. *Telephone:* (1) 674-4802. *Fax:* (1) 674-4879. *E-mail:* literaryaward@dublincity.ie. *Website:* www.impacdublinaward.ie. f. 1995 by Dublin City Council, in partnership with IMPAC, a productivity improvement company that operates worldwide. Annual award for the best work of fiction written in or translated into English. Books are nominated by selected libraries in capital and major cities around the world.

International Prize for Arabic Fiction: PO Box 280, Jounieh, Lebanon. *Telephone:* (9) 935333. *Fax:* (9) 935333. *E-mail:* info@arabicfiction.org. *Website:* www.arabicfiction.org. f. 2007 in Abu Dhabi, by the Booker Prize Foundation, the Emirates Foundation and the Weidenfeld Institute for Strategic Dialogue. Annual award for the best novel written in Arabic, published in the preceding year.

Jerusalem Prize: The Jerusalem International Book Fair, PO Box 775, Jerusalem 91007, Israel. *Website:* www.jerusalembookfair.com. Biennial award to a writer whose work expresses the idea of the freedom of the individual in society. Awarded at the Jerusalem International Book Fair.

Kalinga Prize: c/o UNESCO, 1 rue Miollis, 75015 Paris, France. *Telephone:* 1-45-68-39-17. *E-mail:* y.nur@unesco.org. *Website:* www.unesco.org. Annual award to popularizers of science with distinguished careers as writers, editors, lecturers, directors or producers. The winner is expected to have an understanding of science and technology and an awareness of the scientific work of the UN and UNESCO.

Keats–Shelley Prize: Keats–Shelley Memorial Association, Bedford House, 76a Bedford Street, Leamington Spa, Warwickshire CV32 5DT, England. *Fax:* (1926) 335133. *E-mail:* hello@keats-shelley.co.uk. *Website:* www.keats-shelley.co.uk. f. 1998. Previously sponsored by the Esmée Fairbairn Foundation, the John S. Cohen Foundation, Barclays Wealth, University of St Andrews and the Cowley Foundation. Annual award for an essay or poem on any aspect of Keats' or Shelley's work or life. Essays and poems must be in English and must be original and unpublished work; they must not have been submitted to a previous competition. Entries should be of 2,000–3,000 words, including quotations.

Kerala Sahitya Akademi Awards: Kerala Sahitya Akademi, Thrissur, Kerala 680020, India. *Telephone:* (487) 2331069. *Fax:* (487) 2331069. *Website:* www.keralasahityaakademi.org. Series of annual awards honouring writers of Malayalam language and literature. Prizes awarded in various categories including poetry, drama, short stories, biography, novels, literary criticism, essays, Vedic Literature, linguistics, humour and translation.

Kiriyama Pacific Rim Book Prize: c/o Jeannine Stronach, 300 Thrid Street, Suite 822, San Francisco, CA 94107, USA. *Telephone:* (415) 777-1628. *Fax:* (415) 777-1646. *E-mail:* jeannine@kiriyamaprize.org. *Website:* www.kiriyamaprize.org. f. 1996. Award in two categories, fiction and non-fiction, to promote books that will contribute to greater understanding and co-operation among the peoples and nations of the Pacific Rim.

John W. Kluge Prize: Office of Scholarly Programs, Library of Congress LJ 120, 101 Independence Avenue SE, Washington, DC 20540-4860, USA. *Telephone:* (202) 707-3302. *Fax:* (202) 707-3595. *E-mail:* scholarly@loc.gov. *Website:* www.loc.gov/loc/kluge/prize. f. 2003. Prize endowed by Library of Congress benefactor, John W. Kluge. The prize recognizes lifetime achievement in the human sciences (a wide range of disciplines, including history, philosophy, politics, anthropology, sociology, religion, criticism in the arts and humanities, and linguistics). The recipient may be of any nationality, the writing in any language.

Kossuth Prize: Kossuth Prize Committee, Mueveloedesi Miniszterium, Kossuth Lajos-Ter 1-3, 1055 Budapest, Hungary. Award presented by the Hungarian Government, recognizing lifetime achievement in literature, as well as being awarded for music, sculpture and scientific achievement. The prize is awarded at two levels: the Kossuth Prize for individuals, and the Grand Prix, for joint achievement.

Lannan Literary Awards: Lannan Foundation, 313 Read Street, Santa Fe, NM 87501-2628, USA. *Telephone:* (505) 986-8160. *Fax:* (505) 986-8195. *E-mail:* info@lannan.org. *Website:* www.lannan.org. f. 1989. Annual awards to honour established and new writers whose work is of exceptional quality. Recipients are chosen by the Foundation's Literary Committee, on recommendation from anonymous nominators. Awards are made in the areas of fiction, non-fiction and poetry for a body of work.

John Llewellyn Rhys Prize: Booktrust, Book House, 45 East Hill, London, SW18 2QZ, England. *Telephone:* (20) 8516-2977. *Fax:* (20) 8516-2978. *Website:* www.booktrust.org.uk. f. 1942. Annual award for works of fiction, non-fiction, drama or poetry written in English and published in the UK in the preceding calendar year. Writers must be under 35 years old at the time of publication, a citizen of the UK or Commonwealth. Previous winners are not eligible. Publishers are invited to submit entries.

Lloyds Private Banking Playwright of the Year Award: Tony Ball Association PLC, 174–78 North Gower Street, London, NW1 2NB, England. f. 1994. Award to encourage new and diverse writing for theatre, broadening support for the theatre and extending the links between Lloyds Private Banking and the arts. Playwrights should be British or Irish, whose new works have been performed in the UK or the Republic of Ireland for the first time in the previous year. Nominations by theatre critics form a short-list, with winners chosen by a panel of judges.

Longman/History Today Book of the Year Award: History Today, 20 Old Compton Street, London, W1V 4TW, England. *Telephone:* (20) 7534-8000. *Fax:* (20) 7534-8008. *Website:* www.historytoday.com. Annual award, administered by History Today, for an author's first or second non-fiction book on an historical subject, written in English.

Los Angeles Times Book Prizes: Los Angeles Times, 202 West First Street, Los Angeles, CA 90012, USA. *Website:* www.latimes.com. f. 1980. Prizes in nine single-title categories: biography, current interest, fiction, first fiction (the Art Seidenbaum Award, named after the founder of the Book Prize programme), history, mystery/thriller, poetry, science and technology, and young-adult fiction. In addition, the Robert Kirsch Award (named after a novelist and editor who was book critic for the LA Times) recognizes the body of work by a writer living in and/or writing on the American West. Entries must have been first published in English in the USA between January and December of the previous year. Translations are eligible and authors may be of any nationality. They should be alive at the time of their book's qualifying US publication, although eligibility is also extended to significant new translations of the work of deceased writers.

McKitterick Prize: Society of Authors, 84 Drayton Gardens, London, SW10 9SB, England. *Telephone:* (20) 7373-6642. *Fax:* (20) 7373-5768. *E-mail:* info@societyofauthors.org. *Website:* www.societyofauthors.org. Annual award for a full-length work written in English and first published in the UK or previously unpublished. Open to writers over 40 years old, who have had no previous work published other than that submitted.

Macmillan Writer's Prize for Africa: Macmillan Oxford, Between Towns Road, Oxford, OX4 3PP, England. *Telephone:* (1865) 405700. *Fax:* (1865) 405799. *Website:* www.writeforafrica.com. f. 2002. Biennial award for previously unpublished works of fiction in English, in three categories: Children's Literature (8–12 years old), Children's Literature (13–17 years old), and Most Promising New Children's Writer. Open to nationals or naturalized citizens of any African country.

Walter McRae Russell Award: *Website:* asaliterature.com. Biennial award by Association for the Study of Australian Literature for an outstanding work of literary scholarship on an Australian subject. No nominations are accepted.

The Man Booker International Prize: Colman Getty PR, 28 Windmill Street, London, W1T 2JJ, England. *Telephone:* (20) 7631-2666. *Fax:* (20) 7631-2699. *E-mail:* victoria@colmangetty.co.uk. *Website:* www.manbookerprize.com. f. 2005. Biennial award recognizing one writer's achievement in literature and their significant influence on writers and readers worldwide. It can be won by an author of any nationality, providing that his or her work is available in English.

The Man Booker International Prize for Translation: Colman Getty PR, 28 Windmill Street, London, W1T 2JJ, England. *Telephone:* (20) 7631-2666. *Fax:* (20) 7631-2699. *E-mail:* victoria@colmangetty.co.uk. *Website:* www.manbookerprize.com. f. 2005. Biennial award recognizing the role of translators in bringing fiction to an international audience.

The Man Booker Prize for Fiction: Colman Getty PR, 28 Windmill Street, London, W1T 2JJ, England. *Telephone:* (20) 7631-2666. *Fax:* (20) 7631-2699. *E-mail:* victoria@colmangetty.co.uk. *Website:* www.manbookerprize.com. Established 1968 by Booker Brothers (now Booker Prize Foundation) as The Booker Prize. It is judged by literary critics, editors, writers and academics: the judging panel changes every year and is selected by a management committee. The award is made to the judges' choice of the best novel of the year. Sponsored by Man Group, an alternative investment fund manager and broker. Writers must be citizens of the British Commonwealth or the Republic of Ireland. Only full-length novels written in English are considered. The prize may be awarded posthumously.

Marsh Award for Children's Literature in Translation: Marsh Christian Trust, Granville House, 132 Sloane Street, London, SW1X 9AX, England. *Telephone:* (20) 7730-2626. *Fax:* (20) 7823-5225. *Website:* www.marshchristiantrust.org. f. 1996. Biennial award to British translators of books for 4–16 year olds, published in the UK by a British publisher. The award is sponsored by the Marsh Christian Trust to encourage the translation of foreign children's books into English. No encyclopaedias, reference works or electronic books.

Marsh Biography Award: Marsh Christian Trust, Granville House, 132 Sloane Street, London, SW1X 9AX, England. *Telephone:* (20) 7730-2626. *Fax:* (20) 7823-5225. *Website:* www.marshchristiantrust.org. Formerly the Marsh Christian Trust Award. Biennial award for a significant biography by a British author, published in the UK in the two preceding years. Nominations are submitted by publishers.

Meyer-Whitworth Award: Playwright's Studio, Scotland, CCA, 350 Sauchiehall Street, Glasgow G2 3JD, Scotland. *Telephone:* (141) 332-4403. *Fax:* (141) 332-6352. *E-mail:* info@playwrightsstudio.co.uk. *Website:* www.playwrightsstudio.co.uk. Established to commemorate the Shakespeare Memorial National Theatre Committee of 1908, where the movement for a National Theatre joined forces with the movement to create a monument to William Shakespeare. Awarded to a playwright whose work displays promise of new talent, whose writing is of individual quality and whose work 'reveals the truth about the relationships of human beings with each other and the world at large' (Geoffrey Whitworth). Plays must be written in English and have been produced in the UK in the previous year.

Milner Award: *E-mail:* info@themilneraward.org. *Website:* themilneraward.org. Award to a living American author of children's books.

The Mitchell Prize for Art History/The Eric Mitchell Prize: c/o The Burlington Magazine, 14–16 Duke's Road, London, WC1H 9SZ, England. The Mitchell Prize is awarded for a book that has made an outstanding and original contribution to the understanding of the visual arts. The Eric Mitchell Prize is awarded for the best exhibition catalogue. Both must be on western art, written in English and published in the previous two years.

Naoki Prize: Association for the Promotion of Japanese Literature, Bungei-Shunju Building, 3 Kioi-cho, Chiyoda-ku, Tokyo 102, Japan. f. 1935, along with the Akutagawa Prize, for a work of popular fiction written by a more established writer. Awarded twice a year, in January and July.

National Book Awards: National Book Foundation, 95 Madison Avenue, Suite 709, New York, NY 10016, USA. *Telephone:* (212) 685-0261. *Fax:* (212) 213-6570. *E-mail:* nationalbook@nationalbook.org. *Website:* www.nationalbook.org. f. 1950. Annual awards to living American writers in four categories (fiction, non-fiction, poetry and young people's literature), and the Medal for Distinguished Contribution to American Letters.

National Book Critics Circle Awards: National Book Critics Circle, 360 Park Avenue South, New York, NY 10010, USA. *E-mail:* info@bookcritics.org. *Website:* www.bookcritics.org. Annual awards for excellence in works of fiction, general non-fiction, poetry, biography/autobiography and criticism by American authors, published for the first time in the previous year. Nominated by members. In addition the NBCC awards, the Ivan Sandrof Lifetime Achievement Award honours one member of the Circle with the Nona Balakian Citation for Excellence in Reviewing.

National Short Story Prize: Room 316, BBC Henry Wood House, 3 & 6 Langham Place, London, W1A 1AA, England. *Website:* www.theshortstory.org.uk/nssp. f. 2005. Annual award, funded by the BBC. The prize aims to celebrate the finest writers of short stories. It is open to authors with a previous record of publication, who are either UK nationals or residents. Entries may be stories published during the previous year, or previously unpublished.

Nebula Awards: Science Fiction and Fantasy Writers of America Inc., PO Box 877, Chestertown, MD 21620, USA. *Fax:* (410) 778-3052. *E-mail:* execdir@sfwa.org. *Website:* www.sfwa.org. f. 1965. Annual awards presented to the best science fiction novel, novella, novelette and short story.

Neustadt International Prize for Literature: World Literature Today, 630 Parrington Oval, Suite 110, Norman, OK 73019-4033, USA. *Telephone:* (405) 325-4531. *Fax:* (405) 325-7495. *E-mail:* rcdavis@ou.edu. *Website:* www.ou.edu/worldlit/neustadt.htm. f. 1969. Biennial award recognizing outstanding achievement of a living author, in fiction, poetry or drama. No applications are accepted.

New Zealand Post Book Awards: Booksellers New Zealand, PO Box 25033, Wellington 6146, New Zealand. *Telephone:* (4) 472-1908. *Fax:* (4) 472-1912. *E-mail:* info@booksellers.co.nz. *Website:* www.booksellers.co.nz/awards/new-zealand-post-book-awards. Annual awards to celebrate the best books written by New Zealanders in the preceding year. Awards are given in four categories: fiction, poetry, illustrated non-fiction and general non-fiction. The winners then compete for the overall Book of the Year Award. Awards are also presented for the Best First Book, the Best Maori Language Book and the Readers' Choice Award.

(John) Newbery Medal: Association for Library Service to Children, American Library Association, 50 East Huron Street, Chicago, IL 60611, USA. *Telephone:* (800) 545-2433. *E-mail:* ala@ala.org. *Website:* www.ala.org. Annual award to the author of the most distinguished contribution to literature for children, published in the USA during the preceding year. Writing of any form can be considered: fiction, non-fiction and poetry. The award may be made posthumously. Only original works are considered; reprints and compilations are not eligible. Authors must be citizens or residents of the USA and the work must not have been published originally outside the USA.

Nobelpriset i Litteratur (Nobel Prize in Literature): The Nobel Committee of the Swedish Academy, PO Box 2118, 103 13 Stockholm, Sweden. *Telephone:* (8) 555 125 54. *Fax:* (8) 555 125 49. *E-mail:* info@nobel.se. *Website:* www.nobel.se. One of several annual prizes for outstanding achievement in various fields, founded by the chemist Alfred Nobel. The prize in the field of literature has been awarded annually since 1901 in recognition of the literary merit of a distinguished writer in world letters. The Literature laureate is chosen from writers nominated by members of literary academies, academics, presidents of societies of authors, professors of literature and languages, and previous prize-winners, via the Nobel Committee. It is not possible to propose oneself as a candidate.

Nordic Council Literary Prize: The Nordic Council, Store Strandstraede 18, 1255 Copenhagen, Denmark. *Telephone:* 33-96-04-00. *Fax:* 33-11-18-70. *E-mail:* nordisk-rad@norden.org. *Website:* www.norden.org. Annual award for a work published in Danish, Norwegian or Swedish during the past two years, or other Nordic languages during the last four years.

Ondaatje Prize: Royal Society of Literature, Strand, London, WC2R 1LA, England. *Telephone:* (20) 7845-4676. *Fax:* (20) 7845-4679. *E-mail:* info@rslit.org. *Website:* www.rslit.org.uk. f. 2003. Sponsored by Sir Christopher Ondaatje, replacing the Winifred Holtby Memorial Prize. Annual award to a work of fiction or non-fiction with a strong sense of a particular place. Entries must have been written in the English language (translations are not eligible) by a living citizen of the UK, Republic of Ireland or Commonwealth, and published in the year preceding the year in which the award is presented.

Orange Prize for Fiction: Book Trust, Book House, 45 East Hill, London, SW18 2QZ, England. *Telephone:* (20) 8516-2972. *Fax:* (20) 8516-2978. *Website:* www.orangeprize.co.uk. f. 1996. Annual award founded by leading women in the publishing industry to help promote and reward female writers. Awarded for a full-length novel written in English by a woman of any nationality, which has been published in the UK by a UK publisher.

Orwell Prize: 5-7 Vernon Yard, Portobello Road, London W11 2DX, England. *Telephone:* (20) 7229-5722. *E-mail:* gavin.freeguard@mediastandardstrust.org. *Website:* www.theorwellprize.co.uk. f. 1993. Annual awards given by George Orwell Memorial Fund to encourage writing about politics, political thinking or public policy. The two categories are: book or pamphlet and newspaper and/or periodical article, feature or column, or sustained reportage on a theme. Writing must be in English and published in the preceding year in the UK or Ireland.

Pandora Award: *E-mail:* info@wipub.org.uk. *Website:* www.wipub.org.uk. Annual award from the Women in Publishing organization.

Francis Parkman Prize: Society of American Historians, Columbia University, 603 Fayerweather MC 2538, New York, NY 10027, USA. *E-mail:* amhistsociety@columbia.edu. *Website:* sah.columbia.edu. Awarded by the Society of American Historians to the best non-fiction book on an American theme published in the previous year.

PEN/Faulkner Award for Fiction: PEN/Faulkner Foundation, 201 East Capitol Street SE, Washington, DC 20003, USA. *Telephone:* (202) 898-9063. *Fax:* (202) 675-0345. *E-mail:* jneely@penfaulkner.org. *Website:* www.penfaulkner.org. f. 1981. Annual award for the best work of fiction by an American citizen published in the preceding year.

A. A. Phillips Award: Association for the Study of Australian Literature. *Website:* asaliterature.com. Occasional award to be made on the recommendation of the ASAL executive, when a work or the work of an author is considered to merit attention as an outstanding contribution to Australian literature or literary studies.

Edgar Allan Poe Awards: Mystery Writers of America, 1140 Broadway, Suite 1507, New York, NY 10001, USA. *Telephone:* (212) 888-8171. *Fax:* (212) 888-8107. *E-mail:* mwa@mysterywriters.org. *Website:* www.mysterywriters.org. f. 1954. These awards, sponsored by The Mystery Writers of America, honour the best in mystery fiction and non-fiction produced the previous year. The awards, known as the Edgars, are awarded to authors of distinguished work in various categories. Categories include short stories, novels, critical studies, juvenile and young adult fiction, television and motion picture screenplays, first novels, paperback originals, fact crime, and critical/biographical work. A Grand Master Award is also presented for lifetime achievement.

Premio Camões (Camões Prize): Avenida da Liberdade 270, 1250-149 Lisbon, Portugal. *Telephone:* (21) 3109100. *Fax:* (21) 3143987. *E-mail:* icgeral@instituto-camoes.pt. *Website:* www.instituto-camoes.pt. f. 1988 by the governments of Portugal and Brazil. Annual award by the governments of Portugal and Brazil for an author writing in Portuguese.

Premio Miguel de Cervantes (Cervantes Prize): Dirección General del Libro y Bibliotecas, Ministerio de Cultura, Plaza del Rey, 28004 Madrid, Spain. *Website:* www.mcu.es/premios/CervantesPresentacion.html. f. 1974. Annual award for the entire body of an author's output in Spanish.

Premio Internacional de Novela Rómulo Gallegos: Casa de Rómulo Gallegos, Avenida Luis Roche con 3ra Transversal, Altamira, Caracas, Veenzuela. *Telephone:* (212) 285-2721. *E-mail:* mcu@ministeriodelacultura.gob.ve. *Website:* www.celarg.ve.e. f. 1964 by the President of Venezuela, Raúl Leoni, in honour of the novelist and politican Rómulo Gallegos. Biennial award presented for the best novel written in Spanish. The winner can come from South America or Spain.

Premio Nadal: Ediciones Destino SA, Edificio Planeta,Diagonal, 662-664, 08034 Barcelona, Spain. *Website:* www.edestino.es. The oldest literary prize in Spain. Awarded annually for unpublished novels in Spanish, which have not won any prize previously.

Premio Octavio Paz de Poesía y Ensayo (Octavio Paz Poetry and Essay Prize): Fundación Octavio Paz, Francisco Sosa 383, Col. Barrio de Santa Catarina, 04000 México, DF, Mexico. *Telephone:* (5) 659-5797. *Fax:* (5) 554-9705. *E-mail:* correo@fundacionpaz.org.mx. *Website:* www.fundacionpaz.org.mx. Annual award for a poet or essayist with high artistic, intellectual and critical qualities, following in the modern tradition that Octavio Paz represented. Nominations are invited from official bodies and learned institutions.

Premio Planeta: Editorial Planeta, Diagonal 662-664, 08034 Barcelona, Spain. *Website:* www.editorial.planeta.es. Annual award for the best unpublished and original novel in Spanish.

Premio Príncipe de Asturias (Prince of Asturias Award for Letters): Fundación Príncipe de Asturias, General Yague 2, 33004 Oviedo, Spain. *Telephone:* (98) 5258755. *Website:* www.fpa.es/premios/letras. The prize is one of eight awarded by the Foundation, which were granted for the first time in 1981. (The others include Social Communication and Humanities, Arts, Sciences, Scientific Research and Technical Co-operation.) The prize is presented to a person, institution or group whose work represents an important contribution to the fields of linguistics and literature.

Premio Strega: Fundazione Maria e Goffredo Bellonci, Via Fratelli Ruspoli 2, 00198 Rome, Italy. *Telephone:* (06) 85358119. *Fax:* (06) 85358119. *E-mail:* info@fondazionebellonci.it. *Website:* www.fondazionebellonci.it. f. 1947. Annual award celebrating the best novel written in Italian in the preceding year. Sponsored by the Maria and Goffredo Bellonci Foundation.

Thomas Pringle Award: English Academy of Southern Africa, PO Box 124, Wits, 2050, South Africa. *Telephone:* (11) 717-9339. *Fax:* (11) 717-9339. *E-mail:* englishacademy@societies.wits.ac.za. *Website:* www.englishacademy.co.za. f. 1962. Annual award to honour achievements in five different categories: reviews, educational articles, literary articles, short stories or one act plays, and poetry. Three categories are honoured each year.

Prix Femina (Femina Prize): f. 1904 by 22 members of the periodical La Vie heureuse, in protest against the exclusion of women from the jury of the Prix Goncourt. It is awarded each year for a novel written in French. The winner is decided by an all-female jury. In 1986 the Prix Fémina Étranger, for foreign novels, was established, to provide an opportunity to recognize an outstanding work in the field of foreign novels.

Prix Goncourt (Goncourt Prize): Drouant, 18 Place Gaillon, 75002 Paris, France. *Telephone:* 1-45-20-27-21. *Website:* www.academie-goncourt.fr. The Académie (Société littéraire des Goncourt) was established in 1900, and comprises ten members, who hold a salon on the first Tuesday of every month above the restaurant Drouant in Paris. The first Prix Goncourt was awarded in 1903 and it has become regarded as France's most prestigious literary award. Prizes are awarded in the categories of novels, first novels, biography, children's book and poetry.

Prix Médicis (Médicis Prizes): 25 rue Dombasle, 75015 Paris, France. *Telephone:* 1-48-28-76-90. f. 1958. Annual awards in three categories: Prix Médicis (aims to reflect contemporary literary trends), Prix Médicis de l'Essai (awarded to an essay written in French), Prix Médicis Étranger (awarded to a novel which has been translated into French).

The Pulitzer Prizes: Columbia University, 709 Journalism Building, 2950 Broadway, New York, NY 10027, USA. *Telephone:* (212) 854-3841. *Fax:* (212) 854-3342. *E-mail:* pulitzer@pulitzer.org. *Website:* www.pulitzer.org. The Pulitzer Prizes were established in 1917 following a bequest from Joseph Pulitzer, a Hungarian-born journalist and pioneering publisher of American newspapers. The first Pulitzer Prizes were awarded as an incentive to excellence. There are now 21 prizes in total. In the category of 'Letters' (literature), awards are made in the fields of fiction, non-fiction and poetry, as well as biography/autobiography, drama and history. Entries must be published during the previous calendar year. Only US writers are considered except in the history category where author may be of any nationality as long as the book deals with American history. Fiction awards are made preferably to books dealing with American life.

Pushcart Prize: Best of the Small Presses: Pushcart Press, PO Box 380, Wainscott, NY 11975, USA. *Telephone:* (516) 324-9300. *Website:* www.pushcartprize.com. Annual award for work published by a small press or literary journal. Works are nominated by editors and then reviewed by judges. The winning works are published in a special anthology. Works of poetry, short fiction, essays, or self-contained extracts from books are eligible.

Rea Award for the Short Story: Dungannon Foundation, 53 West Church Hill Road, Washington, CT 06794, USA. *Website:* www.reaaward.org. f. 1986 by Michael M. Rea. Annual award to a writer who has made a significant contribution to the short story genre. US and Canadian writers are eligible. No applications are accepted.

Theodore Roethke Memorial Foundation Triennial Poetry Prize: Saginaw Valley State University, 7400 Bay Road, University Center, Saginaw, MI 48710, USA. *Telephone:* (989) 964-4000. Awarded for a book of poetry in English, not a collection. Selected by three judges, chosen by the Poet Laureate.

Romantic Novel of the Year: *E-mail:* pressofficer@rna-uk.org. *Website:* www.rna-uk.org. f. 1981. This annual award, administered by the Romantic Novelists' Association (RNA) is given to the best modern or historical (i.e. set before 1950) romantic novel of the year. Entries must be written in English and have been first published in the UK in the preceding year.

Rooney Prize for Irish Literature: Oscar Wilde Centre for Irish Writing, School of English, Trinity College Dublin, 21 Westland Row, Dublin 2, Ireland. *Telephone:* (1) 8962885. *Fax:* (1) 8962886. *E-mail:* oscar@tcd.ie. *Website:* www.tcd.ie/OWC/writers/rooney-prize.php. A non-competitive prize to reward and encourage young Irish talent. Writers must be Irish, under 40 years of age, and their work must be written in Irish or English. No applications are accepted, recipients are chosen by a panel of judges. Special awards are given on rare occasions where deemed of merit.

Royal Society Prizes for Science Books: The Royal Society, 6-9 Carlton House Terrace, London, SW1Y 5AG, England. *Telephone:* (20) 7451-2500. *Fax:* (20) 7930-2170. *E-mail:* info@royalsoc.ac.uk. *Website:* royalsociety.org. f. 1988 by COPUS—the Committee on the Public Understanding of Science of the Royal Society, the Royal Institution and the British Association for the Advancement of Science—and the Science Museum. Sponsored by the Aventis Foundation and known as the Aventis Prizes until 2006. General Prize and Junior Prize awarded to authors of popular non-fiction science or technology books, written in English, which are judged to contribute most to the public understanding of science.

Russian Booker Prize: Shubinsky per. 6, 121099 Moscow, Russia. *Telephone:* (495) 780-3360. *Fax:* (495) 780-3360. *E-mail:* post@russianbooker.org. *Website:* www.russianbooker.org. f. 1991, as the first independent literary prize in Russia, with the support of the British Booker Prize. From 2002-2005 general sponsorship of the prize was taken over by the regional charitable organization, Open Russia. The prize is awarded each year for the best novel written in the Russian language; it aims to encourage the creativity of authors writing in Russian, to arouse interest in contemporary Russian literature, and to assist the renaissance of the publishing industry and of translations from Russian into other languages. Works considered for the prize are put forward by Russian and foreign nominators appointed by the Russian Booker Committee, as well as by Russian publishing houses. After screening for conformity with the rules of the competition, these works comprise the Long List which is then judged by a jury consisting of professional literary critics, authors and other leading cultural figures. The jury delivers its short list of six finalists, before choosing the winner.

Sagittarius Prize: Society of Authors, 84 Drayton Gardens, London, SW10 9SB, England. *Telephone:* (20) 7373-6642. *Fax:* (20) 7373-5768. *Website:* www.societyofauthors.org. f. 1990. Award for a first published novel by an author over the age of 60.

Sahitya Akademi Award: Sahitya Akademi, Rabindra Bhavan, 35 Ferozeshah Road, New Delhi 110 001, India. *Telephone:* (11) 23386626. *Fax:* (11) 23382428. *E-mail:* secy@ndb.vsnl.net.in. *Website:* www.sahitya-akademi.gov.in. f. 1954. Annual award given by the Indian National Academy of Letters. The award honours excellence in Indian writing or new trends in one of twenty four major Indian languages..

Saltire Society Literary Awards: The Saltire Society, 9 Fountain Close, 22 High Street, Edinburgh, EH1 1TF, Scotland. *Telephone:* (131) 556-1836. *E-mail:* saltire@saltiresociety.org.uk. *Website:* www.saltiresociety.org.uk. f. 1936. Annual awards in four categories: Scottish Book of the Year (f. 1982), Scottish First Book of the Year (f. 1988), Scottish History Book of the Year (f. 1965), and Scottish Research Book of the Year. Open to any book by an author of Scottish descent or living in Scotland, or to any book which deals with the work or life of a Scot, or with a Scottish question, event or situation.

Saltire Society/Times Educational Supplement Scotland Prize for Educational Publications: The Saltire Society, 9 Fountain Close, 22 High Street, Edinburgh, EH1 1TF, Scotland. *E-mail:* saltire@saltiresociety.org.uk. *Website:* www.saltiresociety.org.uk. f. 1992 to enhance the teaching and learning of an aspect or aspects of the Scottish curriculum. Annual award open to published works of non-fiction, which must be relevant to Scottish schoolchildren aged 5–18, although not necessarily the product of a Scottish author or publisher. To be eligible, a work has to be a book or a package, the bulk of which comprises written words. Non-written elements such as videotapes or computer software may be included but must make up no more than 25% of the package.

Olive Schreiner Prize: English Academy of Southern Africa, PO Box 124, Wits, 2050, South Africa. *Telephone:* (11) 717-9339. *Fax:* (11) 717-9339. *E-mail:* englishacademy@societies.wits.ac.za. *Website:* www.englishacademy.co.za. f. 1964. Annual award to honour new talent for excellence in prose, poetry and drama. Open to works written in English by Southern African writers, published in South Africa. Winners are chosen by a panel of experts.

The Scotiabank Giller Prize: c/o Elana Rabinovitch, 576 Davenport Road, Toronto, ON M5R 1K9, Canada. *Telephone:* (416) 934-0755. *E-mail:* contact@scotiabankgillerprize.ca. *Website:* www.scotiabankgillerprize.ca. f. 1994 by Toronto businessman Jack Rabinovitch, in memory of his late wife, literary journalist Doris Giller. Annual award, co-sponsored by Scotiabank, for the best Canadian novel or short story collection published in English in the preceding year.

Scottish Arts Council Book of the Year Award: Scottish Arts Council, 12 Manor Place, Edinburgh, EH3 7DD, Scotland. *Telephone:* (131) 226-6051. *Website:* www.scottisharts.org.uk/bookawards. f. 2002 to replace the former Scottish Arts Council Book Awards and Children's Book Awards. One winner is chosen in each category of fiction, non-fiction, poetry and first book. One of these four is then awarded the overall title of Scottish Mortgage Investment Trust Book of the Year. Authors should be Scottish, resident in Scotland or have written works of Scottish interest. Applications from publishers only.

Somerset Maugham Awards: Somerset Maugham Trust Fund, Society of Authors, 84 Drayton Gardens, London, SW10 9SB, England. *Telephone:* (20) 7373-6642. *Fax:* (20) 7373-5768. *E-mail:* info@societyofauthors.org. *Website:* www.societyofauthors.org. Awarded annually to a British author under the age of 35 for a published piece of fiction, non-fiction or poetry.

Sunday Times Award for Literary Excellence: The Sunday Times, 1 Pennington Street, London, E98 1ST, England. f. 1987. Annual award to fiction and non-fiction writers. The winner is chosen by a panel of judges consisting of Sunday Times critics and awarded at the discretion of the Literary Editor.

Sunday Times Literary Awards: Sunday Times, POB 1742, Saxonwold 2132, South Africa. *Telephone:* (11) 2805155. *Fax:* (11) 2805111. *Website:* www.sundaytimes.co.za. f. 1989. Annual awards in two categories: Sunday Times Fiction Prize and the Alan Paton Award for Non-Fiction. Works must reflect South African identities and social concerns.

Sunday Times Young Writer of the Year Award: Society of Authors, 84 Drayton Gardens, London, SW10 9SB, England. *Telephone:* (20) 7373-6642. *Fax:* (20) 7373-5768. *E-mail:* info@societyofauthors.org. *Website:* www.societyofauthors.org. f. 1987. Annual award to a published writer of fiction, non-fiction or poetry, under the age of 35. The winner is chosen by a panel of judges consisting of Sunday Times critics.

Texas Institute of Letters Awards: Texas Institute of Letters, Literary Awards, PO Box 935, St Edward's University, Houston House, 217 Wook Street, Austin, TX 78704, USA. *Telephone:* (512) 448-8702. *Website:* texasinstituteofletters.org. A series of annual awards presented by the Texas Institute of Letters. Awards include Jesse H. Jones Award for Fiction, Best Book of Poetry Award, Helen C. Smith Poetry Award, Steven Turner Award for First Novel, John Bloom Humor Award, Soeurette Diehl Fraser Translation Award, O. Henry Award. Open to authors living in Texas or non-residents whose work concerns Texas; entries must have been published in the previous year.

Dylan Thomas Prize: Dylan Thomas Centre, Ty Llen, Somerset Place, Swansea, SA1 1RR, Wales. *Telephone:* (1792) 474051. *E-mail:* sian@dylanthomasprize.com. *Website:* www.thedylanthomasprize.com. f. 2004 (first award 2006); awarded to a piece of published writing in English by an author under the age of 30, from anywhere in the world.

Tir na n-Og Awards: Welsh Books Council, Castell Brychan, Aberystwyth, SY23 2JB, Wales. *Telephone:* (1970) 624151. *Fax:* (1970) 625385. *E-mail:* castellbrychan@wbc.org.uk. *Website:* www.cllc.org.uk. Annual awards in three categories: Best English-Language Book with authentic Welsh background, Best Welsh-Language Book for the primary school sector, and Best Welsh-Language Book for the secondary school sector.

Tom-Gallon Award: Society of Authors, 84 Drayton Gardens, London, SW10 9SB, England. *Telephone:* (20) 7373-6642. *Fax:* (20) 7373-5768. *E-mail:* info@societyofauthors.org. *Website:* www.societyofauthors.org. Biennial award for writers of limited means who have had at least one short story published.

Translators' Association Translation Prizes: Translators' Association, 84 Drayton Gardens, London, SW10 9SB, England. *Telephone:* (20) 7373-6642. *Fax:* (20) 7373-5768. *E-mail:* info@societyofauthors.org. Nine awards: John Florio Prize (biennial award for the best translation of a full-length 20th-century Italian literary work into English, published in the UK); Calouste Gulbenkian Prize (triennial award for translations into English of works from any period by a Portuguese national; the prize is also open to unpublished translations of works by Portuguese nationals); Hellenic Foundation for Culture Prize (triennial award for the best translation into English from modern Greek of a full-length work of imaginative literature); Scott Moncrieff Prize (annual award for the best translation into English of a full-length French literary work of the last 150 years, published in the UK); Sasakawa Prize (triennial award for the best translation into English of a full-length Japanese literary work, published in the UK); Schlegel-Tieck Prize (annual award for the best translation into English of a full-length German literary work of the last 100 years, published in the UK); Bernard Shaw Prize (triennial award for the best translation into English of a full-length Swedish work, published in the UK); Premio Valle Inclán (for the best translation into English of a full-length Spanish work from any period, published in the UK); Vondel Translation Prize (for the best translation of a Dutch or Flemish literary work into English, published in the UK or the USA).

Betty Trask Prize: Society of Authors, 84 Drayton Gardens, London, SW10 9SB, England. *Telephone:* (20) 7373-6642. *Fax:* (20) 7373-5768. *E-mail:* info@societyofauthors.org. *Website:* www.societyofauthors.org. Annual award for authors under 35 years old and Commonwealth citizens, for a first novel of a traditional or romantic nature.

Travelling Scholarship Fund: Society of Authors, 84 Drayton Gardens, London, SW10 9SB, England. *Telephone:* (20) 7373-6642. *Fax:* (20) 7373-5768. *E-mail:* info@societyofauthors.org. *Website:* www.societyofauthors.org. Non-competitive awards enabling British writers to travel abroad. No submissions accepted.

Wales Book of the Year Award: Welsh Academi, Third Floor, Mount Stuart House, Mount Stuart Square, Cardiff, CF10 5FQ, Wales. *Telephone:* (29) 2047-2266. *E-mail:* post@academi.org. *Website:* www.academi.org. f. 1992. Annual awards given for works of exceptional merit by Welsh authors (by birth or residence) published during the preceding year. Works may be in Welsh or in English, in the categories of creative writing and literary criticism. Non-fiction works must have subject matter that is concerned with Wales. Two First Prizes are given: one for works in Welsh, one in English.

Warwick Prize for Writing: Communications Office, University House, University of Warwick, Coventry CV4 8UW, England. *Telephone:* (2476) 150708. *E-mail:* prizeforwriting@warwick.ac.uk. *Website:* www2.warwick.ac.uk/fac/cross_fac/prizeforwriting. f. 2008. Biennual awards presented to authors of any nationality for a work of any genre written in English. Each prize will focus on a different theme.

Whitbread Book Awards: see Costa Book Awards.

Whitfield Prize: Royal Historical Society, University College London, Gower Street, London, WC1E 6BT, England. Award for an author's first book on British history, published in the UK in the previous three years. The winner is announced at the Royal Historical Society annual reception in July.

John Whiting Award: Drama Department, Arts Council England, 14 Great Peter Street, London, SW1P 3NQ, England. *Telephone:* (20) 7973-6431. *Fax:* (20) 7973-6983. *E-mail:* info.drama@artscouncil.org.uk. *Website:* www.artscouncil.org.uk. f. 1965. Award to commemorate the contribution of playwright John Whiting (member of the Drama Panel of the Arts Council 1955–63) to British post-war theatre. Writers who have received an award offer from the Arts Council Theatre Writing Scheme are eligible, as are those who have had a commission or premiere from a theatre company funded by the Arts Council or a Regional Arts Board.

Whiting Writers' Awards: Mrs Giles Whiting Foundation, Second Floor, 1133 Avenue of the Americas, New York, NY 10036, USA. *Website:* www.whitingfoundation.org. f. 1985. Annual awards presented to emergent writers in recognition of their writing achievement and future promise in four categories: fiction, poetry, non-fiction and drama. By internal nomination; applications are not accepted.

Yorkshire Post Book of the Year Award: c/o Margaret Brown, The Rectory, Ripley, Harrogate, North Yorkshire HG3 3AY, England. Annual award for a work of fiction or non-fiction by a British writer or one resident in the UK, published in the UK in the preceding year. Up to four books may be submitted by any one publisher for each imprint.

APPENDIX B: LITERARY ORGANIZATIONS

For organizations of particular interest to poets, please see Appendix B of the International Who's Who in Poetry.

Albania

Albanian PEN Centre: Rruga Ded Gjo Luli, Pallati 5, shk. 3/4, Tirana. *E-mail:* albania@aol2.albaniaonline.net.

Albanian Writers' and Artists' League: Rr. Kavajes Nr. 4, Tirana. *Telephone:* (42) 28229. *Fax:* (42) 27036.

Argentina

Argentine PEN Centre: Coronel Diaz 2089, 17°, 1425 Buenos Aires.

Salta PEN Centre: Biblioteca de Textos Universitarios, Universidad Católica de Salta, Pellegrini 790, Salta 4400.

Armenia

Armenian PEN Centre: Apt 8, 24 Papazian str., 375012 Yerevan. *E-mail:* armpen@arminco.com.

Australia

Australian Society of Authors: PO Box 1566, Strawberry Hills, NSW 2012. *Telephone:* (2) 9318-0877. *Fax:* (2) 9318-0530. *E-mail:* office@asauthors.org. *Website:* www.asauthors.org.

Australian Writers' Guild Ltd: 60 Kellett Street, Kings Cross, Sydney, NSW 2011. Professional association for writers in areas of television, radio, screen and stage to promote and protect professional interests.

Bibliographical Society of Australia and New Zealand: c/o Secretary/Treasurer, PO Box 1463, Wagga Wagga, NSW 2650. *Telephone:* (2) 6931-8669. *Fax:* (2) 6931-8669. *E-mail:* rsalmond@pobox.com. *Website:* www.csu.edu.au/community/BSANZ. Promotes research, largely through publishing, in all aspects of physical bibliography.

Canberra PEN Centre: PO Box 261, Dickson, ACT 2602. *Telephone:* (2) 6248-0912. *E-mail:* lawjs@ozemail.com.au. *Website:* www.pen.org.au.

Children's Book Council of Australia: (ACT Branch), PO Box 5548, Hughes, ACT 2605.

Melbourne PEN Centre: PO Box 2273, Caulfield Junction, Vic. 3161. *E-mail:* penmelbourne@optusnet.com.au. *Website:* www.pen.org.au.

PEN Australia North: PO Box 328, Annerley, Qld 4103. *Telephone:* (7) 3890-2089. *E-mail:* pen@plateaupress.com.au. *Website:* www.pen.org.au.

Perth PEN Centre: PO Box 1131, Subiaco, WA 6008. *Website:* www.pen.org.au.

Society of Editors: PO Box 176, Carlton South, Vic. 3053. Professional association of book editors. Organizes training seminars, monthly meetings and a newsletter.

Sydney PEN Centre: Faculty of Humanities and Social Sciences, University of Technology Sydney, PO Box 123, Broadway, NSW 2007. *Telephone:* (2) 9514-2738. *Fax:* (2) 9514-2778. *E-mail:* sydney@pen.org.au. *Website:* www.pen.org.au.

Austria

Austrian PEN Centre: Concordia Haus, Bankgasse 8, 1010 Vienna. *E-mail:* oepen.club@netway.at. *Website:* www.penclub.at.

Azerbaijan

Azerbaijani PEN Centre: ul. Bol'shaia Krepostnaia, 28, Baku.

Bangladesh

Bangladeshi PEN Centre: L'Espoir, 60/2, North Dhanmondi, Kalabagan, Dhaka-1205. *Telephone:* (2) 912-8965. *E-mail:* shajel123@hotmail.com.

Belarus

Belarusian PEN Centre: PO Box 218, Minsk 220050. *E-mail:* pen@pen.unibel.by. *Website:* www.pen.unibel.by.

Belgium

International PEN Club, Belgian Dutch-speaking Centre: Wiesbeek 25, 9255 Buggenhout. *E-mail:* penvl@skynet.be.

International PEN Club, Belgian French-speaking Centre: 10 avenue des Cerfs, 1950 Kraainem, Brussels. *E-mail:* huguette.db@skynet.be. Receptions of foreign writers, defence of the liberty of thought of all writers, participation at the worldwide congresses of PEN.

Koninklijke Vlaamse Academie van Belgie voor Wetenschappen en Kunsten (Royal Flemish Academy of Belgium for Science and the Arts): Paleis der Academien, Hertogsstraat 1, 1000 Brussels. *Telephone:* (2) 550-2323. *Fax:* (2) 550-2325. *E-mail:* info@kvab.be. *Website:* www.kvab.be.

Société de Langue et de Litterature Wallonnes: Université de Liège, 4000 Liège. Holds meetings, lectures, exhibitions, library, media, archives, publications.

Société Royale des Bibliophiles et Iconophiles de Belgique: 4 Boulevard de l'Empereur, 1000 Brussels. Publication of Le Livre et l'Estampe (Semestrial), exhibitions.

Society of Literary Writers: Rue du Prince Royal 87, 1050 Brussels. *Telephone:* (2) 551 0320. *Fax:* (2) 551 0325.

Benin

Benin PEN Centre: PO Box 03-2810, Cotonou.

Bolivia

Bolivian PEN Centre: PO Box 5920, Cochabamba. *E-mail:* gabyvall@supernet.com.bo.

Bosnia and Herzegovina

Association of Writers of Bosnia and Herzegovina: Ferhadija 19, 71000 Sarajevo.

PEN Centre of Bosnia and Herzegovina: Vrazova 1, Sarajevo 71 000. *E-mail:* krugpen@bih.net.ba.

Brazil

Academia Cearense de Letras: Palácio Senador Alencar, Rua São Paulo 51, 60000 Fortaleza CE. Cultivates and develops literature and scientific achievement. Meets monthly, annual publication.

Associação Brasileira de Imprensa (Brazilian Press Association): Rua Araújo Porto Alegre, 71 Centro, 20030, Rio de Janeiro, RJ. *Telephone:* (21) 2282-1292. *Website:* www.abi.org.br.

Brazilian PEN Centre: Praia do Flamengo 172, 11°, Rio de Janeiro, RJ.

Brazilian Translators' Union (SINTRA): Rua de Quitanda, 194 sala 1005, Centro, PO Box 20091, Rio de Janeiro, RJ.

Companhia Editora Nacional: Rua Joli 294, São Paulo, SP 03016-020.

Sindicato de Escritores de Rio de Janeiro: Avenida Heitor Beltrão 353, 20550, Rio de Janeiro, RJ.

Bulgaria

Bulgarian PEN Centre: Bull. Vassil Levsky 60, Sofia 1000. *E-mail:* alek@astratek.net.

Bulgarian Writers' Union: Anguel Kantchev 5, 1000 Sofia. *Telephone:* (2) 89 83 46.

Union of Bulgarian Writers: 2A Slaveikov Square, 1000 Sofia. *Telephone:* (2) 9880031.

Cameroon

Centre PEN du Cameroun (Cameroonian PEN Centre): PO Box 5329, Yaounde 1er.

Canada

Canada Council for the Arts—Conseil des Arts du Canada: 350 Albert Street, PO Box 1047, Ottawa, ON K1P 5V8. *Website:* www.canadacouncil.ca. Supports Canadian professional writers and book and magazine publishers to develop, produce and promote works of literary merit. Administers the annual Governor-General's Literary Awards.

Canadian Association of Journalists—L'Association Canadienne des Journalistes: Algonquin College, 1385 Woodroffe Avenue, B224, Ottawa, ON K2G 1V8. *Telephone:* (613) 526-8061. *Fax:* (613) 521-3904. *Website:* www.caj.ca.

Canadian Authors' Association: PO Box 419, Campbellford, ON K0L 1L0. *Telephone:* (705) 653-0323. *Fax:* (705) 653-0593. *E-mail:* info@canauthors.org. *Website:* www.canauthors.org. f. 1921.

Canadian PEN Centre: Suite 214, 24 Ryerson Avenue, Toronto, ON M5T 2P3. *E-mail:* pen@pencanada.ca. *Website:* www.pencanada.ca.

Canadian Science Writers' Association: PO Box 75, Station A, Toronto, ON M5W 2S9.

Canadian Society of Children's Authors, Illustrators and Performers (CANSCAIP): 104–140 Orchard View Boulevard, Lower Level Entrance, Toronto, ON M4R 1B9. *Telephone:* (416) 515-1559. *Fax:* (416) 515-7022. *E-mail:* office@canscaip.org. *Website:* www.canscaip.org.

Canadian Society of Magazine Editors: c/o Canadian Living, No. 100, 25 Sheppard Avenue West, North York, ON M2N 6S7.

Crime Writers of Canada: 3007 Kingston Road, PO Box 113, Scarborough, ON M1M 1P1.

Editors' Association of Canada: 27 Carlton Street, Suite 502, Toronto, ON M5B 1L2. *Telephone:* (416) 975-1379. *Fax:* (416) 975-1637. *E-mail:* info@editors.ca. *Website:* www.editors.ca.

Fédération internationale des écrivains de langue française: 3492 rue Laval, Montréal, QC H2X 3C8.

The Literary Consultancy International: PO Box 400, Station East, Toronto, ON M6H 4E3. *Telephone:* (403) 289-5859. *E-mail:* bethanyg.tlcc@sympatico.ca.

Periodical Writers' Association of Canada: 24 Ryerson Avenue, Toronto, ON M5T 2P3.

Quebecois PEN Centre: c/o La Maison des écrivains, 3492 rue Laval, Montréal, QC H2X 3C8. *E-mail:* penquebec@netscape.net.

Société des écrivains canadiens: 1195 rue Sherbrooke Ouest, Montréal, QC H3A 1H9.

Union des écrivaines et écrivains québecois: La Maison des écrivains, 3492 avenue Laval, Montréal, QC H2X 3C8.

Writers' Guild of Canada (WGC): 366 Adelaide Street West, Suite 401, Toronto, ON M5V 1R9. *Telephone:* (416) 979-7907. *Fax:* (416) 979-9273. *E-mail:* info@wgc.ca. *Website:* www.wgc.ca.

The Writers' Union of Canada (TWUC): 40 Wellington Street East, Third Floor, Toronto, ON M5E 1C7. *Telephone:* (416) 703-8982. *Fax:* (416) 504-7656. *E-mail:* info@writersunion.ca. *Website:* www.writersunion.ca. f. 1973.

The People's Republic of China

China PEN Centre: Chinese Writers' Activity Centre, 25 Dongtuchenglu, Beijing 10013.

The Chinese Writers' Association: No. 25, East Tucheng Road, Chaoyang District, Beijing 100013. *Telephone:* (10) 64221865. *Fax:* (10) 64222240. f. 1953. Publishes several magazines, including Chinese Writer, Folk Literature, People's Literature, Poetry, Newspaper of Art.

Guangzhou Chinese PEN Centre: 75 Wende Lu, Guangzhou.

Shanghai Chinese PEN Centre: 675 Julu Lu, Shanghai.

Colombia

Colombian PEN Centre: PO Box 101830, Zona 10, Bogotá. *E-mail:* pencolombia@hotmail.com. *Website:* quickbuilder.com/pencolombia.org/index.html.

Costa Rica

Costa Rican PEN Centre: Apdo 939-2050, Montes de Oca.

Côte d'Ivoire

Centre de PEN de Côte d'Ivoire (Côte d'Ivoire PEN Centre): 01 PO Box 269, Abidjan 01.

Croatia

Croatian PEN Centre: Trg bana Josipa Jelacica 7/II, 10000 Zagreb. *Telephone:* (1) 4816931. *Fax:* (1) 4861959.

Czech Republic

Czech Literary Foundation: Pod nuselskými schody 3, 120 00 Prague 2. *Telephone:* (2) 691 13 62. *Fax:* (2) 691 13 75.

Czech PEN Centre: 28, rijna 9, 110 00 Prague. *Telephone:* (2) 423-4343. *Fax:* (2) 422-1926. *E-mail:* centrum@pen.cz. *Website:* www.pen.cz.

Czech Writers' Guild: Narodni 11, 111 47 Prague 1. *Telephone:* (2) 232 09 24.

The Union of Czech Writers: Palaskova 1107/2, 18200 Prague CR. *Website:* www.volny.cz/uniecs.

Denmark

Association of Danish Authors: Strandgade 6, 1401 Copenhagen K. *Telephone:* 31-95-51-00. *Fax:* 31-54-01-15. *E-mail:* danskff@post6.tele.dk.

Danish PEN Centre: Dronningensgade 14, 1420 Copenhagen. *E-mail:* pen@pen.dk. *Website:* www.pen.dk.

Danish Writers of Fiction and Poetry: Ny Vestergade 1, 1471 Copenhagen. *Telephone:* 33-13-19-72. *Fax:* 33-12-15-33.

Dansk Fagpresse: Skindergade 7, 1159 Copenhagen K. *Telephone:* 33-97-40-00. *Fax:* 33-91-26-70. *E-mail:* df@danskfagpresse.dk. *Website:* www.danskfagpresse.dk.

Dansk Forfatterforening (Danish Writers' Association): Tordenskjolds gård, Strandgade 6, 1401 Copenhagen K. *E-mail:* danskforfatterforening@danskforfatterforening.dk. *Website:* www.danskforfatterforening.dk. Attends to social, artistic, professional and economic interests of Danish authors in Denmark and abroad.

Dansk Litteraturcenter (Danish Literature Centre): c/o The Agency of the Arts, Kongens Nytorv 3, PO Box 9012, 1022 Copenhagen K. *Telephone:* 33-74-45-00. *Fax:* 33-74-45-65. *E-mail:* danlit@danlit.dk. *Website:* www.danlit.dk.

Nyt Dansk Litteraturselskab: Hotelvej 9, 2640 Hedehusene. *Telephone:* 46-59-55-20. *Fax:* 46-59-55-21. *E-mail:* ndl@ndl.dk. *Website:* www.ndl.dk. Works for re-publishing of titles missing in public libraries, in co-operation with publishers.

Egypt

Egyptian PEN Centre: 5 Sayyid al-Bakri Street, (6ème étage, 63), Zamalek, Cairo.

Estonia

Estonian Authors' Union: Toompuiestee 7, Tallinn.

Estonian PEN Centre: 1–21 Harju Street, Tallinn 0001.

Faroe Islands

Rithövundafelag Föroya (Writers' Union of the Faroe Islands): PO Box 1124, 110 Tórshavn.

Finland

Finlands Svenska Författareförening r.f. (Society of Swedish Authors in Finland): Urho Kekkonens gata 8 B 14, 00100 Helsingfors.

Finnish PEN Centre: PO Box 84, 00131 Helsinki. *E-mail:* elisabeth.nordgren@pp.inet.fi.

Informationscentralen för Finlands Litterarur: PO Box 259, 00 171 Helsingfors. Information centre for Finnish literature and the State Literature Commission.

Kirjallisuudentutkijain Seura (Finnish Literary Research Society): Department of Finnish Literature, Fabianinkatu 33, 00014 Helsinki. *Website:* www.helsinki.fi/jarj/skts. Publications include Kirjallisuudentutkijain Seuran Vuosikirja (Yearbook of the Literary Research Society).

Suomalaisen Kirjallisuuden Seura: PO Box 259, 00170 Helsinki. *Telephone:* (9) 131231. *Fax:* (9) 13123220. *E-mail:* sks-fls@finlit.fi. *Website:* www.finlit.fi.

Suomen kääntäjien ja tulkkien liitto – Finlands översättar – och tolkförbund ry (Finnish Association of Translators and Interpreters): Museokatu 9 B 23, 00100 Helsinki. *Telephone:* (9) 445927. *Fax:* (9) 445937. *E-mail:* sktl@sktl.net. *Website:* www.sktl.net.

Suomen tietokirjailijat ry: Mariankatu 19 D 45, 00170 Helsinki. *Telephone:* (9) 45422550. *Fax:* (9) 45422551. *E-mail:* stik@suomentietokirjailijat.fi. *Website:* suomentietokirjailijat.fi.

Svenska Litteratursallskapet i Finland: Mariegatan 8, 00170 Helsinki. Publications include Skrifter (Writings).

Svenska Osterbottens Litteraturforening: Henriksgatan 7–9 4N, 65320 Vasa, Auroravagen 10, 65610 Smedsby. Co-owner of the publishers in Scriptum, publishing the journal Horisont. Organizes writers' seminars, programme evenings on lyrics, prose, music.

The Union of Finnish Writers: Runeberginkatu 32 C 28, 00100 Helsinki. *Telephone:* (9) 445 392. *Fax:* (9) 492 278. *E-mail:* suomen.kirjailijaliitto@cultnet.fi.

France

Centre National des Lettres: 53 rue de Verneuil, 75007 Paris. Upholds and encourages the work of French writers, gives financial help to writers, translators, publishers and public libraries and promotes translation into French.

Confédération Internationale des Sociétés d'Auteurs et Compositeurs (CISAC): CISAC Secretariat, 20–26 Boulevard du Parc, 92200 Neuilly-sur-Seine. *Telephone:* 1-55-62-08-50. *Fax:* 1-55-62-08-60. *E-mail:* cisac@cisac.org. *Website:* www.cisac.org. f. 1926; a non-governmental, non-profit organization working for increased recognition and protection of creators' rights.

PEN Club français: 6 rue François-Miron, 75004 Paris.

Société des Gens de Lettres: Hôtel de Massa, 38 rue du Faubourg Saint-Jacques, 75014 Paris. *Telephone:* 1-53-10-12-00. *Fax:* 1-53-10-12-12. *E-mail:* sgdlf@wanadoo.fr. *Website:* www.sgdl.org.

Georgia

Georgian PEN Centre: 13 Machabeli str., Tbilisi 380007.

Germany

Deutsche Akademie für Sprache und Dichtung: Alexandrakeg 23, 6100 Darmstadt.

Literarischer Verein in Stuttgart eV: PO Box 102251, 7000 Stuttgart 1.

PEN Zentrum Bundesrepublik Deutschland (German PEN Centre): Kasinostr. 3, 64293 Darmstadt. *E-mail:* pen-Germany@t-online.de.

Ghana

Ghanaian PEN Centre: PO Box 131, TUC, Accra. *E-mail:* mackay@ghana.com.

Greece

National Society of Greek Literary Writers: 63 Ippokratous st., 106 80 Athens. *Telephone:* (210) 36 08 239.

PEN Club Hellenique (Greek PEN Centre): 8 Karamanlaki st., 112-53 Athens.

Society of Greek Writers: 8 Kodrigtonos st., 112 57 Athens. *Telephone:* (210) 8231 890. *Fax:* (210) 8232 543.

Guinea

PEN International Centre de Guinée (Guinea PEN Centre): PO Box 4465, Conakry.

Hong Kong

Composers and Authors Society of Hong Kong Ltd: 18/F Universal Trade Centre, 3 Arbuthnot Road, Central, Hong Kong Special Administrative Region, People's Republic of China.

Hong Kong (Chinese-speaking) PEN Centre: Flat A, 22/F, Blk. 4, Cityone Shatin, Shatin NT, Hong Kong Special Administrative Region, People's Republic of China.

Hong Kong (English-speaking) PEN Centre: 1/F, West, Lok Yen Building, 23D Peak Road, Cheung Chau, Hong Kong Special Administrative Region, People's Republic of China. *E-mail:* hkpen_eng@yahoo.com.

Hungary

Artisjus—Agency for Literature and Theatre: PO Box 67, V, Vörösmarty ter 1, 1364 Budapest.

Hungarian PEN Centre: VII Kertész u. 36, 1073 Budapest.

Hungarian Writers' Society: Béthory u. 10, 1054 Budapest. *Telephone:* (1) 111 32 86.

Institute of Literary Studies of the Hungarian Academy of Sciences: Menesi ut 11–13, 1118 Budapest. Research of history of Hungarian literature, literary theory, literary criticism to influence contemporary literature; source publications on the history of Hungarian literature and editing of reference books and bibliographies.

National Association of Literary Authors: PO Box 15, 1363 Budapest. *Telephone:* (1) 111 04 89.

Iceland

Rithöfundasamband Íslands (Writers' Union of Iceland): Gunnarshusi, Dyngjuvegi 8, 104 Reykjavík. *Telephone:* 568-3190. *Fax:* 568-3192. *E-mail:* rsi@rsi.is. Union of Icelandic writers that guards copyrights, protects interests in the field of literature and book-publishing, drama, textbooks, radio and television scripts.

India

All-India PEN Centre: Theosophy Hall, 40 New Marine Lines, Mumbai 400 020. Publications include The Indian PEN (quarterly).

Sahitya Akademi: Rabindra Bhavan, 35 Ferozeshah Road, New Delhi 110 001. *Telephone:* (11) 23386626. *Fax:* (11) 23382428. *E-mail:* secy@ndb.vsnl.net.in. *Website:* www.sahitya-akademi.gov.in. National organization working for the development of Indian letters, to set high literary standards, foster and co-ordinate literary activities in the Indian languages, and promote through them the cultural unity of the country.

Indonesia

Indonesian PEN Centre: Jalan Camara 6, Jakarta Pusat.

Ireland

Irish Academy of Letters: School of Irish Studies, Thomas Prior House, Merrion Road, Dublin 4.

Irish PEN Centre: 26 Rosslyn, Killarney Road, Bray, County Wicklow.

Irish Writers' Centre: 19 Parnell Square, Dublin 1. *Telephone:* (1) 872-1302. *Fax:* (1) 872-6282. *E-mail:* info@writerscentre.ie. *Website:* www.writerscentre.ie.

Society of Irish Playwrights: Room 804, Liberty Hall, Dublin 1. Fosters interest in and promotes contemporary Irish drama. Guards the rights of Irish playwrights.

Israel

ACUM Ltd (Society of Authors, Composers and Music Publishers in Israel): 9 Tuval Street, PO Box 1704, Ramat-Gan 52117. *Telephone:* (3) 6113400. *Fax:* (3) 6122629. *E-mail:* info@acum.org.il. *Website:* www.acum.org.il.

Israeli PEN Centre: 6 Kaplan Street, Tel-Aviv, PO Box 7203, Code 61070. Meetings with members and receptions for guest writers. Publications include bulletin of information and translations of literature in European languages.

Italy

Independent Union of Italian Writers: Via IV Novembre 152, 00187 Rome. *Telephone:* (6) 67 84 96 4. *Fax:* (6) 67 82 92 4.

Italian PEN Centre: Via Daverio 7, 20122 Milan. *E-mail:* fmormando@planet.it.

National Union of Writers: Via Goito 39, 00185 Rome. *Telephone:* (6) 49 10 04. *Fax:* (6) 44 70 02 08.

Sardinian PEN Centre: c/o Facolta' di Lettere e Filosofia, Piazza Conte di Moriana 8, 07100 Sassari. *E-mail:* fch@ssmain.uniss.it. *Website:* www.uniss.it/fch/pen.

Societa' Italiana Autori Drammatici (SIAD): Via PO 10, 00198 Rome.

Societa' Italiana degli Autori et Editori (SIAE): Viale della Letteratura 30, 00144 Rome. *Telephone:* (6) 599 01. *Fax:* (6) 592 33 51.

Japan

English Literary Society of Japan: 501 Kenkyusha Building, 9 Surugadai 2-Chome, Kanda, Chiyoda-ku, Tokyo 101. Association of scholars in the fields of English and American literature and the English language. Publications include the journal, Studies in English Literature (two a year).

Japanese PEN Centre: 20-3 Kabuto-cho, Nihonbashi, Chuo-ku, Tokyo 103-0026. *E-mail:* secretariat03@japanpen.or.jp. *Website:* www.japanpen.or.jp.

Science Fiction Writers of Japan (SFWJ): *Website:* www.sfwj.or.jp. f. 1963. Awards the Nihon SF Taisho Award.

Kazakhstan

Kazakhstan PEN Centre: Tulebayeva 156, Apt 7, 480091 Almaty.

Kenya

Kenyan PEN Centre: PO Box 70147, Nairobi.

Kwani?: *E-mail:* editors@kwani.org. *Website:* www.kwani.org. Literary magazine founded by Binyavanga Wainaina.

Republic of Korea

Korean PEN Centre: Room 1105, Oseong B/D, 13-5 Youido-dong, Yong-dungpo-ku, Seoul 150-010. *E-mail:* penkon2001@yahoo.co.kr.

Kuwait

The Writers' Guild: PO Box 22070, Salmiya. *Fax:* 5720716. *E-mail:* msjohar@hotmail.com.

Latvia

Latvian PEN Centre: a.k. 506, 1010 Rīga. *E-mail:* juris.kronsbergs@swipnet.se.

Lebanon

Lebanese PEN Centre: Beit-Chahab, PO Box 86.

Liechtenstein

PEN Club Liechtenstein (Liechtenstein PEN Centre): PO Box 416, 9490 Vaduz.

Lithuania

Lithuanian PEN Centre: K. Sirvydo 6, 01101 Vilnius. *Telephone:* (5) 269-1977. *Fax:* (5) 261-9696. *E-mail:* platelis@takas.lt. *Website:* www.culture.lt/pen.

Luxembourg
Union of Luxembourg Writers: BP 250, 4003 Esch-Alzette, Luxembourg.

Macedonia
Macedonian PEN Centre: Str. Maksim Gorki 18, 1000 Skopje. *E-mail:* macedpen@unct.com.mk. *Website:* www.pen.org.mk.

Mexico
Mexican PEN Centre: Heriberto Frías 1452-407, Col. Del Valle, México, DF 03100. *E-mail:* maleona@hotmail.com.

PEN Centro Guadalajara (Guadalajaran PEN Centre): Circunvalación Agustin, Yanez 2839, Col. Arcos Vallarta, Guadalajara, Jal. 44100.

San Miguel de Allende PEN Centre: Apdo 287, San Miguel de Allende, México, DF 37700. *E-mail:* lucina@unisono.net.mx.

Moldova
Moldovan PEN Centre: Boulevard Stefan cel Mare 134, Post Office 12, PO Box 231, 2012 Chişinău. *E-mail:* contrafort@moldnet.md.

Monaco
Monaco PEN Centre: 27 Boulevard Albert 1er, 98000 Monte Carlo.

Morocco
Union des Écrivains du Maroc: 5 rue ab-Bakr Seddik, Rabat. *Website:* www.unecma.net.

Nepal
Nepal Journalists' Association: PO Box 285, Maitighar, Kathmandu.

Nepal PEN Centre: PO Box 8975, EPC 533, Kathmandu. *E-mail:* shaligrm@mos.com.np.

The Netherlands
Nederlandse Taalunie: Algemeen Secretariaat, Lange Voorhout 19, PO Box 10595, 2501 HN 's-Gravenhage. *Telephone:* (70) 346-9548. *Fax:* (70) 365-9818. *E-mail:* info@taalunie.org. *Website:* www.taalunieversum.org.

Netherlands PEN Centre: Graafseweg 3, 6512 BM Nijmegen.

Writers from the Former Yugoslavia PEN Centre: c/o AIDA Netherland, Van Ostadestraat 49a, 1072 SN Amsterdam.

New Zealand
Arts Council of New Zealand: Old Public Trust Building, 131–35 Lambton Quay, PO Box 3806, Wellington.

New Zealand Book Council: Floor 5, Old Wool House, 139–141 Featherston Street, Wellington. *Telephone:* (4) 499-1569. *Fax:* (4) 499-1424. *Website:* www.bookcouncil.org.nz.

New Zealand Society of Authors—NZSA (PEN NZ, Inc.): PO Box 67 013, Mount Eden, Auckland 3. *E-mail:* nzsa@clear.net.nz. *Website:* www.authors.org.nz. f. 1934. Promotes co-operation and mutual support among writers in all countries and encourages creative writing in New Zealand.

New Zealand Writers' Guild: 1/243 Ponsonby Road, PO Box 47 886, Ponsonby, Auckland. *Telephone:* (9) 360 1408. *Fax:* (9) 360 1409. *E-mail:* info@nzwritersguild.org.nz.

Nicaragua
Nicaraguan PEN Centre: Apdo RP24, Managua. *E-mail:* mquintana@uni.edu.ni.

Nigeria
West African Association for Commonwealth Literature and Language Studies: PO Box 622, Owerri, Imo State.

Norway
Den Norske Forfatterforening (Norwegian Authors' Union): PO Box 327 sentrum, Rådhusgate 7, 0103 Oslo. *Telephone:* 22 42 77. *Fax:* 22 42 11 07. *E-mail:* iehansen@online.no.

Det Norske Videnskaps-Akademi: Drammensveien 78, Oslo 2.

NORLA (Norwegian Literature Abroad—Fiction and Non-Fiction): Victoria Terr. 11, PO Box 2663 Solli, 0203 Oslo. *Telephone:* 2327-6350. *Fax:* 2327-6351. *E-mail:* firmapost@norla.no. *Website:* www.norla.no. Supports the translation of Norwegian fiction and non-fiction.

Norwegian PEN Centre: Urtegaten 50, 0187 Oslo. *E-mail:* pen@norskpen.no.

Panama
Panamanian PEN Centre: PO Box 1824, Panamá 1.

Peru
Peruvian PEN Centre: Avda Larco 1150, Piso 8, Oficina 804, Miraflores, Lima. *E-mail:* tumo13@hotmail.com.

The Philippines
Philippine PEN Centre: 531 Padre Faura, Ermita, Manila. *E-mail:* isaganicruz@yahoo.com.

Poland
Polish Authors' Association (SAP): ul. Madalinskiego 15m. 16, 02-513 Warsaw. *Telephone:* (22) 496 788. *Fax:* (22) 572 844.

Polish PEN Club: ul. Krakowskie Przedmieście 87/89, 00-079 Warsaw. *Telephone:* (22) 828 28 23. *Fax:* (22) 826 57 84. *E-mail:* penclub@ikp.atm.com.pl. *Website:* www.penclub.atomnet.pl.

Stowarzyszenie Autorów ZAiKS (Society of Authors): ul. Hipoteczna 2, 00-092 Warsaw. *Telephone:* (22) 827 6061. *Fax:* (22) 828 9204. *E-mail:* zaiks@zaiks.org.pl. *Website:* www.zaiks.org.pl.

Portugal
Portuguese PEN Centre: York House, Rua das Janelas Verdes 32, 1200 Lisbon. *E-mail:* penclube@mail.telepac.pt.

Portuguese Society of Authors: Avenida Duque de Loulé, 1069 Lisbon. *Telephone:* (21) 357 83 20. *Fax:* (21) 353 02 57.

Romania
Union of Writers: Calea Victoriei 133, Bucharest sector 1. *Telephone:* (21) 6507243. *Fax:* (21) 3129693.

Russia
Russian Authors' Society: ul. Bolshaya Bronnaya 6a, K-104, 103670 Moscow. *Telephone:* (495) 203 37 77. *Fax:* (495) 200 12 63. *E-mail:* rao@rao.ru. *Website:* www.rao.ru. Protects the rights and organizes legal protection for authors in Russia.

Russian PEN Centre: Neglinnaya Street, 18/1, Building 2, 103031 Moscow. *E-mail:* penrussia@hotmail.com. *Website:* www.penrussia.org.

Writers' Union of the Russian Federation: Komsomolskii prospekt 13, Moscow. *Telephone:* (495) 246 75 65. *Fax:* (495) 245 29 02.

Senegal
PEN Club du Sénégal (Senegal PEN Centre): Rue 1 Prolongée Pointe, Dakar.

Serbia
Serbian PEN Centre: Milutina Bojica 4, 11000 Belgrade. *E-mail:* pencent@bitsyu.net.

Slovakia
Autorská Spoločnost (LITA) (Society of Authors): Mozartova 9, 815 30 Bratislava 1. *Telephone:* (2) 62802248. *Fax:* (2) 62802246. *E-mail:* lita@lita.sk. *Website:* www.lita.sk.

Slovak PEN Centre: Laurinska 2, 815 08 Bratislava. *Telephone:* (2) 5443-4117. *Fax:* (2) 5443-4117. *E-mail:* info@scpen.sk. *Website:* www.scpen.sk.

Slovenia
Slovenian PEN Centre: Tomsiceva 12, 61000 Ljubljana. *Telephone:* (1) 125 23 40. *Fax:* (1) 214 144. *E-mail:* slopen@guest.arnes.si.

South Africa
English Academy of Southern Africa: PO Box 124, Wits, 2050. *E-mail:* englishacademy@societies.wits.ac.za. Concerned with all forms and functions of English in South Africa, and with all literature written in English. It promotes research and debate, organizes lectures, presents awards, and generally fosters the creative, critical and scholarly talents of users of English. It does this while respecting the multilingual heritage of Southern Africa.

Nasionale Afrikaanse Letterkundige Museum en Navorsingsentrum: Private Bag X20543, Bloemfontein 9300.

South African PEN Centre: 4 Bucksburn Road, Newlands 7700. *E-mail:* safpen@iafrica.com.

South African Union of Journalists: Office 512–13, Fifth Floor, Argon House, 87 Juta Street, Johannesburg 2017.

Spain

Asociació d'Escriptors en Llengua Catalana—AELC: Calle Canuda 6, 6è, Barcelona 08002. *Telephone:* (93) 302-7828. *Fax:* (93) 412-5873. *E-mail:* info@aelc.es. *Website:* www.escriptors.com. f. 1977.

Centre Català del PEN Club (Catalan PEN Centre): Calle Canuda, 6°, 08002 Barcelona. *Telephone:* (93) 318-3298. *Fax:* (93) 412-0666. *E-mail:* pen@pencatala.org. *Website:* www.pencatala.org.

Galician PEN Centre: Calle República El Salvador, 14, 1° izquierda, 15701 Santiago de Compostela. *E-mail:* pengalicia@mundo-r.com.

General Society of Spanish Authors: Calle Fernando VI 4, 28004 Madrid. *Telephone:* (91) 349 95 50.

Sri Lanka

Sri Lankan PEN Centre: Institute of Aesthetic Studies, 21 Albert Crescent, Colombo 7.

Sweden

Sveriges Författarförbund (Swedish Writers' Union): PO Box 3157, Drottninggatan 88B, 111 36 Stockholm. *Telephone:* (8) 791 22 80. *Fax:* (8) 791 22 85.

Swedish PEN Centre: Wollmar Yxkullsgatan 7, 118 50 Stockholm. *E-mail:* ljiljana.dufgran@pensweden.org. *Website:* www.pensweden.org.

Switzerland

Autorinnen und Autoren der Schweiz—Autrices et Auteurs de Suisse: Nordstrasse 9, 8035 Zürich. *Telephone:* (44) 350-0460. *Fax:* (44) 350-0461. *E-mail:* sekretariat@a-d-s.ch. *Website:* www.a-d-s.ch. Professional organization for the protection of writers' interests.

Suisse Romand PEN Centre: 14 rue Crespin, 1206 Geneva. *E-mail:* jakoutchoumow@bluewin.ch.

Swiss Italian and Reto-romansh PEN Centre: PO Box 107, 6903 Lugano. *E-mail:* penlugano@ticino.com. *Website:* www.writers-prison.org.

Swiss Society of Writers: Kirchgasse 25, Postfach, 8022 Zürich. *Telephone:* (44) 261 30 20. *Fax:* (44) 261 31 53.

Taiwan

Taipei Chinese PEN Centre: Fourth Floor, 4 Lane 68, When Chou Street, Taipei. *E-mail:* taipen@tpts5.seed.net.tw.

Tanzania

Journalists' Organization of Tanzania: PO Box 45526, Dar Es Salaam.

Thailand

The Siam Society: 131 Soi 21 (Asoke) Sukhumvit Road, Bangkok 10110. Promotes and tries to preserve artistic, scientific and other cultural affairs of Thailand and neighbouring countries. Publications include Journal of the Siam Society, Natural History Bulletin of the Siam Society.

Thai PEN Centre: PO Box 81, Dusit Post Office, Bangkok 10300. *E-mail:* wareeya@hotmail.com.

Turkey

Authors' Union of Turkey: Milli Müdafa Cad. No 10/13, Kizilay-Ankara. *Telephone:* (312) 417 45 70. *Fax:* (312) 417 45 70. *E-mail:* tyb@tyb.org.tr. *Website:* www.tyb.org.tr.

Ukraine

Ukrainian PEN Centre: Bankova St. 2, 01024 Kyiv. *Telephone:* (44) 293 45 86. *Fax:* (44) 293 45 86. *E-mail:* nspu@i.kiev.ua. *Website:* www.nspu.kiev.ua.

United Arab Emirates

Emirates Writers' and Litterateurs' Union: PO Box 11044, Ras al-Khaimah. *Telephone:* (7) 227-4344.

United Kingdom

Association for Scottish Literary Studies: Department of Scottish History, 9 University Gardens, University of Glasgow, Glasgow G12 8QH. *Telephone:* (141) 330-5309. *Fax:* (141) 330-5309. *E-mail:* office@asls.org.uk. *Website:* www.asls.org.uk. Promotes the teaching, study and writing of Scottish literature and languages, past and present.

Authors' Club: 40 Dover Street, London, W1X 3RB. Club for writers, publishers, critics, journalists and academics involved with literature. Administers several literary awards.

Book Trust: Book House, 45 East Hill, London, SW18 2QZ. Independent charitable trust promoting reading and the use of books. Administers several major literary awards, including the Man Booker Prize, and publishes reference and resource materials.

Book Trust Scotland: Scottish Book Centre, 137 Dundee Street, Edinburgh, EH11 1BG. Promotes reading and books in general, and provides a range of information and services on Scottish writers and books. Administers awards, including the Scottish Writer of the Year.

British Science Fiction Association: 52 Woodhill Drive, Grove, Wantage, Oxfordshire OX12 0DF. *Website:* www.bsfa.co.uk. Promotes the reading, writing and publishing of science fiction. Activities include literary criticism, news, reviews, serious articles, meetings, writers' workshops, lending library and magazine chain. Publications include Matrix (newsletter), Vector (journal), Focus (magazine).

Comhairle nan Leabhraichean (The Gaelic Books Council): 22 Mansfield Street, Glasgow, G11 5QP. *Telephone:* (141) 337-6211. *E-mail:* brath@gaelicbooks.net. *Website:* www.gaelicbooks.net. Offers publication grants to publishers for individual books and commission grants to writers, as well as advice and editorial services.

Crime Writers' Association—CWA: PO Box 273, Borehamwood, Hertfordshire WD6 2XA. *E-mail:* secretary@thecwa.co.uk. *Website:* www.thecwa.co.uk. Membership limited to professional crime writers, but associate membership is open to specialist publishers, agents and booksellers. Administers numerous annual awards. Publishes Red Herrings (monthly newsletter).

International Poets, Playwrights, Essayists, Editors and Novelists Association (PEN): 9–10 Charterhouse Buildings, Goswell Road, London, EC1M 7AT. *Telephone:* (20) 7253-4308. *Fax:* (20) 7253-5711. *E-mail:* intpen@dircon.co.uk. *Website:* www.internationalpen.org.uk. f. 1921. Branches worldwide.

Jewish Book Council: POB 38247, London, NW3 5YQ. *E-mail:* info@jewishbookweek.com. *Website:* www.jewishbookweek.com. f. 1947 to promote the reading of books on all aspects of Jewish thought and culture; produces Jewish Book Week UK literary festival; administers the TLS-Porjes Prize for Hebrew-English Translation; organizes poetry and creative writing competitions for younger people.

National Union of Journalists: Acorn House, 314 Gray's Inn Road, London, WC1X 8DP. Represents journalists in all sectors of publishing, providing advice and support on wages, conditions, and benefits. Publishes guides and magazines.

PEN English Centre: Free Word Centre, 60 Farringdon Road, London, EC1R 3GA. *Telephone:* (20) 7324-2535. *E-mail:* enquiries@englishpen.org. *Website:* www.englishpen.org. Publishes The Pen (two a year).

PEN Scottish Centre: 126 W Princes Street, Glasgow, G4 9DB, Scotland. *E-mail:* info@scottishpen.org. *Website:* www.scottishpen.org.

PEN Welsh Centre: 80 Plymouth Road, Penarth, CF64 5DL, Wales.

Romantic Novelists' Association: c/o RNA Hon. Membership Secretary, 38 Stanhope Road, Reading, Berkshire RG2 7HN. *Website:* www.rna-uk.org. Membership open to published writers of romantic novels, with associate membership open to agents, editors, publishers and booksellers. Administers two annual awards. Publishes RNA News.

Royal Society of Literature: Somerset House, Strand, London, WC2R 1LA. *Telephone:* (20) 7845-4676. *Fax:* (20) 7845-4679. *E-mail:* info@rslit.org. *Website:* www.rslit.org. Lectures, discussions, readings and publications. Adminsters awards, including the W. H. Heinemann Prize.

Seven Stories: 30 Lime Street, Newcastle upon Tyne, NE1 2PQ. *Fax:* (191) 276-4302. *E-mail:* info@sevenstories.org.uk. *Website:* www.sevenstories.org.uk. f. 2005. Seven Stories, the Centre for Children's Books is where the rich heritage of British children's books is collected, explored and celebrated. The centre is full of writers, artists, real and imaginary with all kinds of exhibitions, activities and events.

The Society of Authors: 84 Drayton Gardens, London, SW10 9SB. *Telephone:* (20) 7373-6642. *Fax:* (20) 7373-5768. *E-mail:* info@societyofauthors.org. *Website:* www.societyofauthors.org. f. 1884. Independent trade union which promotes and protects the interests of writers, and provides information and advice. Publishes The Author (quarterly journal) and numerous Quick Guides on the business aspects of the profession.

Translators' Association: 84 Drayton Gardens, London, SW10 9SB. *Telephone:* (20) 7373-6642. *Fax:* (20) 7373-5768. *E-mail:* info@societyofauthors.org. *Website:* www.societyofauthors.org. Subsidiary group within the Society of Authors dealing exclusively with literary translators into the English language.

Welsh Book Council (Cyngor Llyfrau Cymru): Castell Brychan, Aberystwyth, Ceredigion SY23 2JB, Wales. *Telephone:* (1970) 624151. *Website:* www.cllc.org.uk. Provides a focus for the publishing industry in Wales and distributes grants for books of Welsh interest in both Welsh and English.

Welsh Union of Writers: 13 Richmond Road, Roath, Cardiff, CF2 3AQ. Independent union for published Welsh writers.

Writer's Guild of Great Britain: 15 Britannia Street, London, WC1X 9JN. Represents professional writers in film, radio, television, theatre and publishing. Regularly provides assistance to members on items such as contracts and conditions of work.

United States of America

American Academy of Arts and Letters: 633 West 155th Street, New York, NY 10032. *Telephone:* (212) 368-5900. *Fax:* (212) 491-4615. *E-mail:* academy@artsandletters.org. *Website:* www.artsandletters.org.

American Literary Translators' Association: PO Box 830688, University of Texas, Richardson, TX 75083. Sponsors the biennial Gregory Rabassa Prize for the translation of fiction from any language into English, and the Richard Wilbur Prize for the translation of poetry from any language into English.

American Society of Composers, Authors and Publishers (ASCAP): 1 Lincoln Plaza, New York, NY 10023. *Website:* www.ascap.org. Performing rights society.

American Society of Journalists and Authors Inc. (ASJA): 1501 Broadway, Suite 302, New York, NY 10036. *Website:* www.asja.org. Service organization providing exchange of ideas and market information. Regular meetings with speakers from the industry. Annual writers conference. Medical plans available. Professional referral service, annual membership directory. First amendment advocacy group.

Asociación Internacional de Escritores Policiacos (AIEP—International Asscn of Crime Writers Inc.): *E-mail:* jeremiahealy@earthlink.net. *Website:* jmc.ou.edu/AIEP. f. 1986 by Paco Taibo II (Mexico) and the late Julian Semionov (Russia), has members in 22 countries. Sponsors the Hammett Awards.

Associated Writing Programs: George Mason University, Tallwood House, Mail Stop 1E3, Fairfax, VA 22030. National, non-profit organization of writers and teachers of writing.

Association of Literary Scholars and Critics: 2039 Shattuck Avenue, Suite 202, Berkeley, CA 94704. Professional society open to all individuals pursuing the study of literature.

Authors League of America: 330 West 42nd Street, 29th Floor, New York, NY 10036. Promotes the interests of authors and dramatists.

Children's Literature Association: PO Box 138, Battle Creek, MI 49016. *Website:* www.childlitassn.org. Promotes serious scholarship and criticism in the field of children's literature.

Dramatists' Guild: 1501 Broadway, Suite 701, New York, NY 10036. Promotes the interests of dramatists, lyricists and composers.

Horror Writers' Association: PO Box 50577, Palo Alto, CA 94303. *E-mail:* hwa@horror.org. *Website:* www.horror.org. Promotes horror and dark fantasy writing.

The MacDowell Colony: 100 High Street, Peterborough, NH 03458. *Telephone:* (603) 924-3886. *Fax:* (603) 924-9142. *E-mail:* info@macdowellcolony.org. *Website:* www.macdowellcolony.org. f. 1907 to provide creative artists with uninterrupted time and seclusion to work and enjoy the experience of living in a community of gifted artists. Residencies of up to eight weeks are available for writers, composers, film/video artists, visual artists, architects and interdisciplinary artists. Artists in residence receive room, board and exclusive use of a studio. Talent is the sole criterion for acceptance to the MacDowell Colony. Established artists as well as emerging artists are encouraged to apply. Committees of distinguished specialists donate their time to judge applications, which include work samples, references and a brief project description. There are no residency fees. Grants for travel to and from the Colony are available based on need. Financial aid for writers is available through a special grant from a foundation. An aid application will be mailed following acceptance. Deadlines for application are 15 Jan. (summer, May–Aug.), 15 April (autumn/winter, Sept.–Dec.), 15 Sept. (winter/spring, Jan.–April).

Ingram Merrill Foundation: 104 East 40th Street, Suite 302, New York, NY 10016.

Mystery Writers of America Inc.: 17 East 47th Street, Sixth Floor, New York, NY 10017. *Website:* www.mysterywriters.org. Supports and promotes mystery fiction. Sponsors the Edgar Allan Poe Awards.

National Book Critics Circle: 360 Park Avenue South, New York, NY 10010. *Website:* www.bookcritics.org. Gives annual awards for fiction, poetry, biography/autobiography, general non-fiction and criticism. Raises the standards of book criticism and enhances public appreciation of literature.

National League of American Pen Women: Pen Arts Building, 1300 17th Street NW, Washington, DC 20036.

National Press Club: 529 14th Street NW, Washington, DC 20045.

National Writers' Association: 3140 South Peoria Street, Suite 295PMB, Aurora, CO 80014. *Telephone:* (303) 841-0246. *Fax:* (303) 841-2607. *Website:* www.nationalwriters.com. Association for freelance writers.

National Writers' Union: 113 University Place, Sixth Floor, New York, NY 10003. *Website:* www.nwu.org. Union for the promotion of the interests of freelance writers.

PEN American Center: 568 Broadway, New York, NY 10012-3225. *Telephone:* (212) 334-1660. *Fax:* (212) 334-2181. *E-mail:* pen@pen.org. *Website:* www.pen.org. International organization of writers, poets, playwrights, essayists, editors, novelists and translators whose purpose is to bring about better understanding among writers of all nations.

PEN Center USA West: 672 South Lafayette Park Place, Suite 42, Los Angeles, CA 90057. *Telephone:* (213) 365-8500. *Fax:* (213) 365-9616. *E-mail:* pen@penusa.org. *Website:* www.penusa.org.

Romance Writers of America Inc.: 16000 Stuebner Airline Road, Suite 140, Spring, TX 77379. *Telephone:* (832) 717-5200. *Fax:* (832) 717-5201. *E-mail:* info@rwanational.org. *Website:* www.rwanational.org. Promotes the interests of writers of romance fiction.

Science Fiction and Fantasy Writers of America Inc.: PO Box 877, Chestertown, MD 21620. *Fax:* (410) 778-3052. *E-mail:* execdir@sfwa.org. *Website:* www.sfwa.org.

Sisters in Crime: PO Box 442124, Lawrence, KS 06044-8933. *Telephone:* (785) 842-1325. *Fax:* (785) 842-1034. *E-mail:* sistersincrime@juno.com. *Website:* www.sistersincrime.org. International organization promoting the work of female mystery writers.

Society of Children's Book Writers and Illustrators: 8271 Beverly Boulevard, Los Angeles, CA 90048. *Telephone:* (323) 782-1010. *Fax:* (323) 782-1892. *E-mail:* scbwi@scbwi.org. *Website:* www.scbwi.org. Professional society promoting the interests of children's book writers and illustrators.

Translation Center: 412 Dodge Hall, Columbia University, New York, NY 10027. Dedicated to finding and publishing the best translations of significant works of foreign contemporary literature. Publishes bi-annual magazine.

Writers' Guild of America East: 555 West 57th Street, New York, NY 10019. *Website:* www.wgae.org. Labour union representing professional writers in films, television and radio. Membership available only through the sale of literary material or employment for writing services in one of these areas.

Writers' Guild of America West: 7000 West Third Street, Los Angeles, CA 90048. *Website:* www.wga.org. Represents its membership in contract negotiation and compliance with the film and television industry.

Venezuela

Venezuelan PEN Centre: 10° Transversal con 7° Avenida, Residencias Villa Inés, 3°, Altamira, Caracas.

Zimbabwe

Zimbabwe PEN Centre: 10 Ashburton Avenue, Chadcombe, Harare.

APPENDIX C: LITERARY FESTIVALS

Amsterdam Literary Festival (ALF): Amsterdam, The Netherlands. *E-mail:* pip@amsterdamliteraryfestival.com. *Website:* www.amsterdamliteraryfestival.com. Annual festival, held in May.

Astonishing Travellers: Bamako, Mali. Held over a week and a half in December, to promote African writers and literacy.

Belfast Festival at Queen's: Culture and Arts Unit, Queen's University, 8 Fitzwilliam Street, Belfast, BT9 6AW, Northern Ireland. *Telephone:* (28) 9097-1034. *E-mail:* g.farrow@qub.ac.uk. *Website:* www.belfastfestival.com. Arts festival, held in October–November.

Cairo International Book Fair: Cairo, Egypt. *Telephone:* (2) 57 75 371. *Fax:* (2) 57 54 213. Held in January–February.

Calabash International Literature Festival: The Calabash International Literary Festival Trust, 14 Montego Freeport Center, Montego Bay, St James, Jamaica. *E-mail:* calabashfestival@hotmail.com. *Website:* www.calabashfestival.org. f. 2001; held annually in May, on Treasure Beach.

Cheltenham Literature Festival: Cheltenham Festivals, 109 Bath Road, Cheltenham, Gloucestershire, GL53 7LS, England. *Telephone:* (1242) 774400. *Website:* cheltenhamfestivals.com/literature. f. 1949; held annually in October.

Dubai International Poetry Festival: Mohammed bin Rashid Al Maktoum Foundation, P.O. Box 214444, Building 26, 7th Floor, Dubai Healthcare City, Dubai, United Arab Emirates. *Telephone:* (4) 3299999. *Fax:* (4) 3687777. *Website:* www.mbrfoundation.ae. f. 2009; held annually in March, at Madinat Jumeirah and the House of Poetry, Shindagha.

Edinburgh International Book Festival: 5a Charlotte Square, Edinburgh, EH2 4DR, Scotland. *Telephone:* (131) 718 5666. *Fax:* (131) 226 5335. *E-mail:* admin@edbookfest.co.uk. *Website:* www.edbookfest.co.uk. f. 1983; held in Charlotte Square Gardens, Edinburgh, in August.

Feria Internacional del Libro de Buenos Aires (Buenos Aires International Book Fair): Fundación El Libro, Hipólito Yrigoyen 1628, 5o Piso, C1089AAF Buenos Aires, Argentina. *Telephone:* (11) 4374-3288. *Fax:* (11) 4375-0268. *E-mail:* fundacion@el-libro.com.ar. *Website:* www.el-libro.com.ar. Held in April–May.

Feria Internacional del Libro de Guadalajara (Guadalajara International Book Fair): Avenida Alemania 1370, Colonia Moderna, Guadalajara, Jalisco 44190, Mexico. *Telephone:* (33) 3810-0331. *Fax:* (33) 3268-0921. *E-mail:* fil@fil.com.mx. *Website:* www.fil.com.mx. Held in November–December.

Feria Internacional del Libro de Santiago (Santiago International Book Fair): Cámara Chilena del Libro, Avenida Libertador Bernardo O'Higgins 1370, Oficina 501, Santiago de Chile, Chile. *E-mail:* prolibro@tie.cl. *Website:* www.camlibro.cl. Held in October–November.

Festival Spisovatelů Praha (Prague Writers' Festival): Platýz Národní 37/416, 110 00 Prague 1, Czech Republic. *Telephone:* 224 241 312. *Fax:* 224 241 312. *E-mail:* pwf@pwf.cz. *Website:* www.pwf.cz. Held in June.

Frankfurter Buchmesse (Frankfurt Book Fair): Ausstellungs- und Messe GmbH, Frankfurt Book Fair, Reineckstr. 3, 60313 Frankfurt am Main, Germany. *Telephone:* (69) 2102-0. *Fax:* (69) 2102-227. *E-mail:* info@book-fair.com. *Website:* www.frankfurt-book-fair.com. Held annually, in October.

Göteborg Book Fair: 412 94 Göteborg, Sweden. *Telephone:* (31) 708 84 00. *E-mail:* info@goteborg-bookfair.com. *Website:* www.bok-bibliotek.se. Held annually, in September, at the Swedish Exhibition Centre.

Grazerzählt (Tales of Graz): 8413 St Georgen an der Stiefing, Austria. *Telephone:* 3183-7423. *Fax:* 3183-7423 (ext 100). *E-mail:* grazerzaehlt@tegetthoff.at. *Website:* www.graz.tales.org. Held in June.

Harbourfront International Festival of Authors: 235 Queens Quay West, Toronto, ON M5J 2G8, Canada. *Telephone:* (416) 973-4600. *Fax:* (416) 973-6055. *E-mail:* info@harbourfrontcentre.com. *Website:* www.harbourfrontcentre.com. Annual festival, held in October at the Harbourfront Centre.

Hay Festival: The Drill Hall, 25 Lion Street, Hay-on-Wye, HR3 5AD, Wales. *Telephone:* (1497) 821299. *Fax:* (1497) 821066. *E-mail:* admin@hayfestival.co.uk. *Website:* www.hayfestival.co.uk. Held in May–June in Hay-on-Wye; now also held in Segovia, Spain in September, and in Cartagena, Colombia in January.

Het Andere Boek: Sint-Jacobsmarkt 82, Antwerp 2000, Belgium. *E-mail:* info@hetandereboek.com. *Website:* www.hetandereboek.com. Annual festival, held in October.

Ilkley Literature Festival: Manor House, 2 Castle Hill, Ilkley, West Yorkshire LS29 9DT, England. *Telephone:* (1943) 816714. *Fax:* (1943) 817079. *Website:* www.ilkleyliteraturefestival.org.uk. f. 1973; held annually in September–October.

Internationales Literaturfestival Berlin: Chausseestrasse 5, 10115 Berlin, Germany. *Telephone:* (30) 278786-20. *Fax:* (30) 278786-85. *E-mail:* info@literaturfestival.com. *Website:* www.literaturfestival.com. Held in May.

Istanbul Tanpinar Literature Festival: Kalem Literary Agency, Tunel Ensiz Sok No.2-3, Beyoglu, Istanbul, Turkey. *Telephone:* (212) 2454406. *Fax:* (212) 2454419. *E-mail:* info@itef.com.tr. *Website:* www.itef.com.tr. Held in May.

Jaipur Literature Festival: Teamwork Productions, 208-A/3 Savitri Nagar, New Delhi, 110 017, India. *Telephone:* (11) 26011430. *Website:* jaipurliteraturefestival.org. f. 2006; Annual festival held in January at the Diggi Palace Hotel.

Jerusalem International Book Fair: PO Box 775, Jerusalem 91007, Israel. *Telephone:* (2) 629 6415. *Fax:* (2) 624 0663. *E-mail:* grneta@jerusalem.muni.il. *Website:* www.jerusalembookfair.com. f. 1963; biennial event, held in February.

LIBER: Feria Internacional del Libro: *E-mail:* ifema@ifema.es. *Website:* www.liber.ifema.es. Annual festival, held in September, alternating between Barcelona and Madrid, Spain.

Los Angeles Times Festival of Books: Los Angeles Times Media Group, 202 West 1st Street, Los Angeles, CA 90012, USA. *Telephone:* (213) 237-5000. *Fax:* (213) 237-7679. *E-mail:* fobinfo@latimes.com. *Website:* events.latimes.com/festivalofbooks. Annual festival, held in April.

Man Hong Kong International Literary Festival: *E-mail:* info@festival.org.hk. *Website:* www.festival.org.hk. Held in March.

National Book Festival: c/o Library of Congress, 101 Independence Avenue SE, Washington, DC 20540-1400, USA. *E-mail:* bookfest@loc.gov. *Website:* www.loc.gov/bookfest. Held in September on the National Mall, Washington, DC.

National Eisteddfod of Wales: 33 Bridge Street, Newport, NP20 4BH, Wales. *E-mail:* de@eisteddfod.org.uk. *Website:* www.eisteddfod.org.uk. Welsh-language arts festival, held annually in August.

Nigeria International Book Fair: PMB 21068, Literamed Building, Plot 45 Oregun Industrial Estate, Alausa Bus-Stop, Ikeja, Nigeria. *E-mail:* info@nibf.org. *Website:* www.nibf.org. f. 1999; held in May.

Norsk Litteraturfestival (Norwegian Literary Festival): c/o Maihaugen, 2609 Lillehammer, Norway. *E-mail:* littfest@maihaugen.no. *Website:* www.litteraturfestival.no. Held in May–June.

PEN World Voices: The New York Festival of International Literature: PEN American Center, 588 Broadway, Suite 303, New York, NY 10012, USA. *E-mail:* pen@pen.org. *Website:* www.pen.org/festival. f. 2005; week-long festival.

Prague Writers' Festival: Platyz, Narodni 37/416, 110 00 Prague, Czech Republic. *Telephone:* 224241312. *Fax:* 224241312. *E-mail:* pwf@pwf.cz. *Website:* www.pwf.cz. Annual festival, held in June.

Salon du Livre: c/o Syndicat national de l'édition, 115 blvd Saint Germain, 75006 Paris, France. *E-mail:* livre@reedexpo.fr. *Website:* www.salondulivreparis.com. Held in March.

Shanghai International Literary Festival: M on the Bund, 7/F No.5 The Bund, Guangdong Lu, Shanghai 200002, People's Republic of China. *Telephone:* (21) 63509988. *Fax:* (21) 63220099. *Website:* www.m-restaurantgroup.com/mbund/literary-festival.html. Annual festival held in March at M on the Bund restaurant.

Singapore Writers' Festival: The Arts House, 1 Old Parliament Lane, Singapore 179429, Singapore. *Telephone:* 63326900. *Fax:* 63363021. *E-mail:* enquiries@toph.com.sg. *Website:* www.singaporewritersfestival.com. f. 1986; Biennial event held in October and November.

Sydney Writers' Festival: Ground Floor, 10 Hickson Road, The Rocks, NSW 2000, Australia. *Telephone:* (2) 9252-7729. *Fax:* (2) 9252-7735. *Website:* www.swf.org.au. Annual event held in May at various venues across Sydney and New South Wales.

Time of the Writer International Writers' Festival: c/o Centre for the Creative Arts, University of KwaZulu-Natal, Durban, South Africa. *E-mail:* cca@ukzn.ac.za. *Website:* www.nu.ac.za/cca/Time_of_the_writer.htm. Held in March.

Tokyo International Book Fair: TIBF Show Management, Reed Exhibitions Japan Ltd, 18F Shinjuku-Nomura Bldg, 1-26-2 Nishishinjuku, Shinjuku-ku, Tokyo 163-0570, Japan. *E-mail:* tibf-eng@reedexpo.co.jp. *Website:* www.reedexpo.co.jp/tibf. Held in July.

Tromso International Literature Festival: Postboks 539, 9256 Tromso, Norway. *Telephone:* 95-83-48-63. *E-mail:* festival@ordkalotten.no. *Website:* www.ordkalotten.no. Annual festival, held in September.

Vilenica International Literature Festival: c/o Društvo slovenskih pisateljev (Slovene Writers' Association), Tomšičeva 12, 1000 Ljubljana, Slovenia. *Telephone:* (1) 25 14 144. *Fax:* (1) 42 16 430. *E-mail:* barbara.subert@guest.arnes.si. *Website:* www.vilenica.si. f. 1986; held annually in various venues.

Word on the Street Festival: 6 Royal York Road, Suite 407, Toronto, ON M8V 2S7, Canada. *Telephone:* (416) 556-0812. *Website:* www.thewordonthestreet.ca. f. 1990; Annual festival of events, held in September in Halifax, Kitchener, Toronto and Vancouver.

APPENDIX D: NATIONAL LIBRARIES

Libraries are sorted alphabetically by country

Biblioteka Kombetare (National Library of Albania): Sheshi Skenderbej, Place Scanderbeg, Tirana, Albania. *Telephone:* (42) 23 843. *Fax:* (42) 23 843. *E-mail:* a_plasari@hotmail.com. *Website:* www.bksh.al.

Bibliothèque Nationale d'Algérie (National Library of Algeria): BP 127, al-Hamma, Algiers, Algeria. *Telephone:* (21) 67-57-81. *Fax:* (21) 68-23-00. *E-mail:* contact@biblionat.dz. *Website:* www.biblionat.dz.

Biblioteca Nacional (National Library of Andorra): Placeta de Sant Esteve s/n, 500 Andorra la Vella, Andorra. *Telephone:* 826445. *Fax:* 829445. *E-mail:* bncultura.gov@andorra.ad. *Website:* www.bibliotecanacional.ad.

Biblioteca Nacional de Angola (Angola National Library): Caixa Postal 2915, Luanda, Angola. *Telephone:* (2) 322 070. *Fax:* (2) 323 979.

Biblioteca Nacional (National Library of Argentina): Agüero 2502, (C1425EID), Buenos Aires, Argentina. *Telephone:* (11) 4808-6000. *E-mail:* bibnal@red.bibnal.edu.ar. *Website:* www.bibnal.edu.ar.

National Library of Armenia: 72 Terian Street, 375009, Yerevan, Armenia. *Telephone:* (10) 58-90-42. *Fax:* (10) 52-97-11. *Website:* www.nla.am.

Biblioteca Nacional Aruba (National Library of Aruba): George Madurostraat 13, Oranjestad, Aruba. *Telephone:* 582-1580. *Fax:* 582-5493. *E-mail:* info@bibliotecanacional.aw. *Website:* www.bibliotecanacional.aw.

National Library of Australia: Canberra, ACT 2600, Australia. *Telephone:* (2) 6262-1111. *Fax:* (2) 6257-1703. *Website:* www.nla.gov.au.

Österreichische Nationalbibliothek (Austrian National Library): Josefplatz 1, PO Box 308, 1015 Vienna, Austria. *Telephone:* (1) 534-100. *Fax:* (1) 534-102-80. *E-mail:* onb@onb.ac.at. *Website:* www.onb.ac.at.

M.F. Axundov adina Azerbaycan Milli Kitabxana (National Library of Azerbaijan): Xaqani küçesi 29, Baki 370601, Azerbaijan. *E-mail:* anl@aznet.org. *Website:* www.anl.aznet.org.

National Archives and National Library of Bangladesh: Department of Archives and Libraries, 32 Justice S. M. Morshed Sarani, Agargaon, Sher-e-Bangla Nagar, Dhaka 1207, Bangladesh. *Telephone:* (2) 9129992. *Fax:* (2) 9118704. *E-mail:* info@nanl.gov.bd. *Website:* www.nanl.gov.bd.

National Library Service of Barbados: Coleridge Street, Bridgetown, St Michael, Barbados. *Telephone:* 426 3981.

National Library of Belarus: Nezavisimosti Avenue 116, Minsk, Belarus. *Telephone:* (17) 293-29-50. *Website:* www.nlb.by.

Koninklijke Bibliotheek van België/Bibliothèque royale de Belgique (Royal Library of Belgium): Keizerslaan 4, Boulevard de l'Empereur 4, 1000 Brussels, Belgium. *Telephone:* (2) 519-53-11. *Fax:* (2) 519-55-33. *E-mail:* contacts@kbr.be. *Website:* www.kbr.be.

National Library Service of Belize: PO Box 287, Princess Margaret Drive, Belize City, Belize. *Telephone:* (2) 234248. *Fax:* (2) 234246. *E-mail:* nls@btl.net. *Website:* www.nlsbze.bz.

Bibliothèque Nationale du Bénin (National Library of Benin): BP 401, Porto-Novo, Benin. *Telephone:* 222585. *E-mail:* bn.benin@bj.refer.org. *Website:* www.bj.refer.org/benin_ct/tur/bnb.

Bermuda National Library: Par-la-ville, 13 Queen Street, Hamilton HM 11, Bermuda. *Telephone:* 295-3104. *Fax:* 292-8443. *E-mail:* libraryinfo@gov.bm. *Website:* www.bermudanationallibrary.bm.

National Library of Bhutan: GPO Box No.185, Thimphu, Bhutan. *Telephone:* (2) 324314. *Fax:* (2) 322693. *E-mail:* nlibrary@druknet.net.bt. *Website:* www.library.gov.bt.

Archivo y Biblioteca Nacionales de Bolivia (Bolivian National Archive and Library): Calle Dalence No. 4, Sucre, Bolivia. *Telephone:* (4) 6452246. *E-mail:* abnb@entelnet.bo. *Website:* www.archivoybibliotecanacionales.org.bo.

Nacionalna i univerzitetska biblioteka Bosne i Hercegovine (National and University Library of Bosnia and Herzegovina): PO Box 337, 71000 Sarajevo, Bosnia and Herzegovina. *Telephone:* (33) 275-312. *Fax:* (33) 218-431. *E-mail:* nubbih@nub.ba. *Website:* www.nub.ba.

Botswana National Library Service: PO Box OO36, Gaborone, Botswana. *Telephone:* 352-288. *Fax:* 301-149.

Fundação Biblioteca Nacional (National Library Foundation of Brazil): Avenida Rio Branco 219, Rio de Janeiro, CEP 20040-008, Brazil. *Telephone:* (21) 3095-3879. *Fax:* (21) 3095-3811. *E-mail:* gabinete@bn.br. *Website:* www.bn.br.

Dewan Bahasa dan Pustaka Library of Brunei: Jalan Elizabeth II, BS3510, Bandar Seri Begawan, Brunei. *Telephone:* (2) 235501. *E-mail:* chieflib@brunet.bn. *Website:* www.dbp.gov.bn/library_Info.

Narodna biblioteka Sv. Sv. Kiril i Metodii (St Cyril and St Methodius National Library of Bulgaria): 88 Vassil Levski Boulevard, 1037 Sofia, Bulgaria. *Telephone:* (2) 988-28-11. *Fax:* (2) 843-54-95. *E-mail:* nbkm@nationallibrary.bg. *Website:* www.nationallibrary.bg.

Bibliothèque Nationale du Burundi (National Library of Burundi): BP 1095, Bujumbura, Burundi. *Telephone:* 225051. *Fax:* 226231.

National Library of Cambodia: Street 92, Don Penh District, Phnom Phen, Cambodia.

Bibliothèque Nationale du Cameroun (National Library of Cameroon): BP 1O53, Yaoundé, Cameroon. *Telephone:* 237-002. *Fax:* 237-002.

Library and Archives Canada/Bibliothèque et Archives Canada: 395 Wellington Street, Ottawa, ON K1A 0N4, Canada. *Telephone:* (613) 996-5115. *Fax:* (613) 995-6274. *Website:* www.collectionscanada.ca.

Biblioteca Nacional de Chile (National Library of Chile): Avenida Libertador B. O'Higgins 651, Santiago 1400, Chile. *Telephone:* (2) 3605239. *Fax:* (2) 6380461. *Website:* www.bibliotecanacional.cl.

National Library of China: 33 Zhongguancun Nandajie, Beijing 100081, People's Republic of China. *Telephone:* (10) 6841-9260. *Fax:* (10) 6841-9271. *E-mail:* interco@nlc.gov.cn. *Website:* www.nlc.gov.cn.

Biblioteca Nacional de Colombia (National Library of Colombia): Calle 24 No. 5-60, Bogotá, Colombia. *Telephone:* (1) 3414029. *E-mail:* bnc@mincultura.gov.co. *Website:* www.bibliotecanacional.gov.co.

Bibliothèque Nationale Populaire (National Library of the Republic of the Congo): BP 1489, Brazzaville, Republic of the Congo. *Telephone:* 833 485.

National Library of the Cook Islands: c/o Ministry of Culture, Victoria Road, Tupapa Maraeenga, Rarotonga, Cook Islands. *Telephone:* 20725. *E-mail:* culture1@oyster.net.ck.

Biblioteca Nacional Miguel Obregón Lizano (National Miguel Obregón Lizano Library of Costa Rica): Calles 15 y 17, Avenida 3 y 3B, PO Box 10008, San José, Costa Rica. *Telephone:* 257-4814. *Fax:* 223-5510. *E-mail:* dibinacr@racsa.co.cr. *Website:* www.abinia.org/costarica.

Bibliothèque Nationale (National Library of Côte d'Ivoire): BP 180, Abidjan, Côte d'Ivoire. *Telephone:* 32 38 72.

Nacionalna i sveucilišna knjižnica u Zagrebu (National and University Library in Zagreb, Croatia): PO Box 550, 10000 Zagreb, Croatia. *Telephone:* (1) 616-4111. *Fax:* (1) 616-4186. *E-mail:* nsk@nsk.hr. *Website:* www.nsk.hr.

Biblioteca Nacional José Martí (National José Martí Library of Cuba): Avenida Independencia y 20 de Mayo, Plaza de la Revolución, Apdo Postal 6670, Havana, Cuba. *Telephone:* (7) 555442-49. *Fax:* (7) 816224. *E-mail:* publiweb@bnjm.cu. *Website:* www.bnjm.cu.

Kypriake Vivliotheke (Cyprus Library): Eleftherias Square, 1011 Nicosia, Cyprus. *Telephone:* (22) 303180. *Fax:* (22) 304532. *E-mail:* amaratheftis@hotmail.com.

Národní knihovna Ceské Republiky (National Library of the Czech Republic): Klementinum 190, 110 01 Prague 1, Czech Republic. *Telephone:* (2) 21663111. *Fax:* (2) 21663261. *E-mail:* sekret.ur@nkp.cz. *Website:* www.nkp.cz.

Det Kongelige Bibliotek (The Royal Library of Denmark): Postbox 2149, 1016 Copenhagen K, Denmark. *Telephone:* 33 47 47 47. *Fax:* 33 93 22 18. *E-mail:* kb@kb.dk. *Website:* www.kb.dk.

Biblioteca Nacional Pedro Henríquez Ureña (Pedro Henríquez Ureña National Library of the Dominican Republic): Avenida César Nicolás Penson No. 91, Apdo Postal 20711, Santo Domingo RD, Dominican Republic. *Telephone:* 688-4086. *Fax:* 685-8941. *E-mail:* webmaster@bnrd.gov.do. *Website:* www.bnrd.gov.do.

Biblioteca Nacional Eugenio Espejo (National Eugenio Espejo Library of Ecuador): 12 de Octubre 555, Apdo 67, Quito, Ecuador.

Library of Alexandria: PO Box 138, ash-Shatby, Alexandria 21526, Egypt. *Telephone:* (3) 4839999. *E-mail:* secretariat@bibalex.org. *Website:* www.bibalex.org.

National Library and Archives of Egypt: Corniche an-Nil, Ramlet Boulac, 11638 Cairo, Egypt. *Telephone:* (2) 5750886. *Fax:* (2)5765634. *E-mail:* info@darelkotob.org. *Website:* www.darelkotob.org.

Biblioteca Nacional de El Salvador (National Library of El Salvador): 4ta Calle Oriente y Avenida Mons. Oscar A. Romero No. 124, San Salvador, El Salvador. *Telephone:* 221-2099. *Fax:* 221-8847. *E-mail:* binaes@latinmail.com. *Website:* www.binaes.gob.sv.

Eesti Rahvusraamatukogu (National Library of Estonia): Tõnismägi 2, 15189 Tallinn, Estonia. *Telephone:* 630-7611. *Fax:* 631-1410. *E-mail:* nlib@nlib.ee. *Website:* www.nlib.ee.

National Archives and Library of Ethiopia: PO Box 717, Addis Ababa, Ethiopia. *Telephone:* (11) 5516532. *Fax:* (11) 5526411. *E-mail:* nale@telecom.net.et. *Website:* www.nale.gov.et.

Føroya landsbókasavn (National Library of the Faroe Islands): J. C. Svabosgøtu 16, PO Box 61, 110 Tórshavn, Faroe Islands. *Telephone:* 311626. *Fax:* 318895. *E-mail:* utlan@flb.fo. *Website:* www.flb.fo.

Helsingin Yliopiston Kirjasto – Suomen kansalliskirjasto (Helsinki University Library – The National Library of Finland): PO Box 15, 00014, Helsinki, Finland. *Telephone:* (9) 1912-3196. *Fax:* (9) 1912-2719. *E-mail:* hyk-palvelu@helsinki.fi. *Website:* www.lib.helsinki.fi.

Bibliothèque nationale de France (National Library of France): 8 rue Scribe, 75009 Paris, France. *Telephone:* 1-53-79-07-02. *Fax:* 1-42-65-10-16. *E-mail:* bib.opera@bnf.fr. *Website:* www.bnf.fr.

Bibliothèque Nationale Gabonais (National Library of Gabon): PO Box 1188, Libreville, Gabon. *Telephone:* 73 25 43.

Gambia National Library Service: PMB 552, Reg Pye Lane, Banjul, Gambia. *Telephone:* 22 64 91. *Fax:* 22 37 76. *E-mail:* national.library@qanet.gm.

National Parliamentary Ilia Chavchavadze Library of Georgia: 7 Gudiashvili Str., 0107 Tbilisi, Georgia. *Telephone:* (32) 98-75-48. *E-mail:* modzeli@nplg.gov.ge. *Website:* www.nplg.gov.ge.

Deutsche Nationalbibliothek (German National Library): Adickesallee 1, 60322 Frankfurt am Main, Germany. *Telephone:* (69) 1525-0. *Fax:* (69) 1525-1010. *E-mail:* info-f@d-nb.de. *Website:* www.d-nb.de.

Ghana Central Reference and Research Library: PO Box 1633, Accra, Ghana. *Telephone:* (21) 21 162.

Ethnike Bibliotheke tes Hellados (National Library of Greece): 32 Panepistimiou Street, 10679 Athens, Greece. *Telephone:* (210) 3382601. *Fax:* (210) 3382502. *E-mail:* nlg@nlg.gr. *Website:* www.nlg.gr.

Nunatta Atuagaateqarfia: Det Grønlandske Landsbibliotek (National Library of Greenland): Imaneq 26, Postboks 1011, 3900 Nuuk, Greenland. *Telephone:* 32 11 56. *Fax:* 32 39 43. *E-mail:* nalib@katak.gl. *Website:* www.katak.gl.

Biblioteca Nacional de Guatemala Luis Cardoza y Aragón (Luis Cardoza y Aragón National Library of Guatemala): 5a Avenida 7-26 zona 1, Ciudad de Guatemala, Guatemala. *Telephone:* (2) 2322443. *E-mail:* esthermdelima@yahoo.com.

Bibliothèque Nationale (National Library of Guinea): BP 139, Conakry, Guinea. *Telephone:* 30 45 10 66.

National Library of Guyana: 76–77 Church and Main Streets, Georgetown, Guyana. *Telephone:* (2) 227-4053. *Fax:* (2) 227-4053. *E-mail:* natlib@sdnp.org.gy. *Website:* www.natlib.gov.gy.

Bibliothèque Nationale d'Haiti (National Library of Haiti): 193 rue du Centre, Port-au-Prince, Haiti. *Telephone:* 232148. *Fax:* 226647.

Biblioteca Nacional de Honduras (National Library of Honduras): 6a Avenida Salvador Mendieta, Tegucigalpa, Honduras. *Telephone:* 228 577.

Országos Széchényi Könyvtár (National Széchényi Library of Hungary): Buda Royal Palace Wing F, 1827 Budapest, Hungary. *Telephone:* (1) 224-3700. *Fax:* (1) 202-0804. *E-mail:* inform@oszk.hu. *Website:* www.oszk.hu.

Landsbókasafn Islands – Háskólabókasafn (National and University Library of Iceland): Arngrimsgata 3, 107 Reykjavík, Iceland. *Telephone:* 525-5600. *Fax:* 525-5615. *E-mail:* lbs@bok.hi.is. *Website:* www.bok.hi.is.

National Library of India: Belvedere, Kolkata, West Bengal 700027, India. *Telephone:* (33) 2479-1381. *Fax:* (33) 2479-1462. *E-mail:* nldirector@rediffmail.com. *Website:* www.nlindia.org.

Perpustakaan Nasional (National Library of Indonesia): Jln. Salemba Raya No. 28A, Jakarta Pusat, PO Box 3624, Indonesia. *Telephone:* (21) 3154864. *Fax:* (21) 3103554. *E-mail:* pusjasa@rad.net.id. *Website:* www.pnri.go.id.

National Library of Iran: S.H. Bahonar Street, Tehran 19548, Iran. *Telephone:* (21) 8881966. *Fax:* (21) 8786859. *E-mail:* nli@nlai.ir. *Website:* www.nlai.ir.

Iraq National Library and Archive: Bab al-Muadam 14340, Baghdad, Iraq. *Telephone:* 4141303. *Fax:* 4141810. *E-mail:* info.nla@iraqnla.org. *Website:* www.iraqnla.org.

Leabharlann Náisiúnta na hÉireann/National Library of Ireland: Kildare Street, Dublin 2, Ireland. *Telephone:* (1) 6030200. *Fax:* (1) 6766690. *E-mail:* info@nli.ie. *Website:* www.nli.ie.

Jewish National and University Library of Israel: POB 39105, Jerusalem 91390, Israel. *Telephone:* (2) 6585004. *Fax:* (2) 6511771. *Website:* jnul.huji.ac.il.

Biblioteca Nazionale Centrale di Firenze (Central National Library of Florence, Italy): Piazza dei Cavalleggeri 1, 50122 Florence, Italy. *Telephone:* (55) 249191. *Fax:* (55) 2342482. *E-mail:* info@bncf.firenze.sbn.it. *Website:* www.bncf.firenze.sbn.it.

Biblioteca Nazionale Centrale di Roma (Central National Library of Rome, Italy): Viale Castro Pretorio 105, 00185 Rome, Italy. *Telephone:* (6) 49891. *Fax:* (6) 4457635. *E-mail:* bncrm@bnc.roma.sbn.it. *Website:* www.bncrm.librari.beniculturali.it.

National Library of Jamaica: 12 East Street, Kingston, Jamaica. *Telephone:* 967-1526. *Fax:* 922-5567. *E-mail:* nljresearch@cwjamaica.com. *Website:* www.nlj.org.jm.

National Diet (Parliament) Library of Japan: 1-10-1 Nagata-cho, Chiyodaku, Tokyo 100-8924, Japan. *Telephone:* (3) 3581-2331. *Fax:* (3) 3508-2934. *E-mail:* webmaster@ndl.go.jp. *Website:* www.ndl.go.jp.

Amman Public Library in Jordan: PO Box 182181, Amman, Jordan. *Telephone:* (6) 637 111.

National Library of Kazakhstan: Abai av. 14, Almaty 480013, Kazakhstan. *Telephone:* (3272) 69 65 86. *Fax:* (3272) 69 65 86. *E-mail:* nlrk@nursat.kz. *Website:* www.nlrk.kz.

Kenya National Library: PO Box 30573-00100, Ngong Road, Nairobi, Kenya. *Telephone:* (20) 2725550. *Fax:* (20) 2721749. *E-mail:* knls@nbnet.co.ke. *Website:* www.knls.or.ke.

National Library of Kiribati: PO Box 6, Bairiki, Tarawa, Kiribati. *Telephone:* 21337. *Fax:* 28222.

Grand People's Study House of the Democratic People's Republic of Korea: PO Box 200, Pyongyang, Central District, Democratic People's Republic of Korea. *Telephone:* (2) 344066.

National Library of the Republic of Korea: San 60-1, Banpo-dong, Seocho-gu, Seoul 137-702, Republic of Korea. *Telephone:* (2) 535-4142. *Fax:* (2) 590-0530. *Website:* www.nl.go.kr.

National Library of Kyrgyzstan: Ul. Ogonbaeva 242, 720873 Bishkek, Kyrgyzstan. *Telephone:* (312) 66-21-80. *Website:* www.nlkr.gov.kg.

National Library of Laos: PO Box 122, Vientiane, Laos. *Telephone:* (21) 212452. *Fax:* (21) 222485. *E-mail:* khaynll@pan-laos.net.la.

Latvijas Nacionâlâ Bibliotçka (National Library of Latvia): 14 K Barona Street, 1423 Rīga, Latvia. *Telephone:* 736-5250. *Fax:* 728-0851. *E-mail:* lnb@lnb.lv. *Website:* www.lnb.lv.

Bibliothèque Nationale du Liban: Place de l'Etoile, Beirut, Lebanon. *E-mail:* info@bnlb.org. *Website:* www.bnlb.org.

Lesotho National Library: PO Box 985, Maseru, Lesotho. *Telephone:* 323100. *Fax:* 310194.

National Library of Libya: PO Box 9127, Benghazi, Libya. *Telephone:* (61) 9097074. *Fax:* (61) 9097073. *E-mail:* nat_lib_libya@hotmail.com. *Website:* www.nll.8m.com.

Liechtensteinische Landesbibliothek (Liechtenstein National Library): PO Box 385, 9490 Vaduz, Liechtenstein. *Telephone:* 2366362. *Fax:* 2331419. *E-mail:* info@landesbibliothek.li. *Website:* www.lbfl.li.

Lietuvos Nacionaliné Martyno Mazvydo Biblioteka (Martynas Mazvydas National Library of Lithuania): Gedimino av. 51, 01504 Vilnius, Lithuania. *Telephone:* (5) 2497023. *Fax:* (5) 2496129. *E-mail:* biblio@lnb.lt. *Website:* www.lnb.lt.

Bibliothèque nationale de Luxembourg (National Library of Luxembourg): 37 boulevard F.-D. Roosevelt, 2450 Luxembourg. *Telephone:* 22 97 55 1. *Fax:* 47 56 72. *E-mail:* bib.nat@bi.etat.lu. *Website:* www.bnl.lu.

Narodna i univerzitetska biblioteka Sv. Kliment Ohridski (National and University St Kliment Ohridski Library of The former Yugoslav republic of Macedonia): Boulevard Goce Delcev 6, 91000, Skopje, The former Yugoslav republic of Macedonia. *Telephone:* (91) 226 846. *Fax:* (91) 226 846. *E-mail:* kliment@nubsk.edu.mk. *Website:* www.nubsk.edu.mk.

Bibliothèque Nationale (National Library of Madagascar): BP 257, Anosy, Antananarivo, Madagascar. *Telephone:* (2) 258 72.

National Library Service of Malawi: PO Box 30314, Lilongwe 3, Malawi. *Telephone:* (1) 773-700. *E-mail:* nls@malawi.net.

Perpustakaan Negara Malaysia (National Library of Malaysia): 232 Jalan Tun Razak, 50572 Kuala Lumpur, Malaysia. *Telephone:* (3) 26871700. *Fax:* (3) 26942490. *E-mail:* webmaster@pnm.my. *Website:* www.pnm.my.

National Library of Maldives: Billoorijehige, 59 Majeedi Magu, Galolhu Male 20-24, Maldives. *Telephone:* 323485.

Bibliothèque Nationale du Mali (National Library of Mali): BP 159, Avenue Kasse Keita, Bamako, Mali. *Telephone:* 22 49 63.

Bibljoteka Nazzjonali ta' Malta (National Library of Malta): 36 Old Treasury Street, CMR 02, Valletta, Malta. *Telephone:* (21) 236585. *Fax:* (21) 235992. *E-mail:* philip.borg@magnet.mt. *Website:* www.libraries-archives.gov.mt/nlm.

Bibliothèque Nationale (National Library of Mauritania): BP 20, Nouakchott, Mauritania. *Telephone:* 2435.

National Library of Mauritius: Second Floor, Fon Sing Building, 12 Edith Cavell Street, Port Louis, Mauritius. *Telephone:* 211-9891. *Fax:* 210-7173. *E-mail:* natlib@intnet.mu. *Website:* national-library.gov.mu.

Biblioteca Nacional de México (National Library of Mexico): Instituto de Investigaciones Bibliográficas, Centro Cultural Universitario, C. U., Delegación Coyoacán, México DF, CP 04510, Mexico. *Telephone:* (5) 622-6800. *Fax:* (5) 622-6899. *E-mail:* consulta@biblional.bibliog.unam.mx. *Website:* www.bibliog.unam.mx/bib/biblioteca.html.

Biblioteca Nationala a Republicii Moldova (National Library of Moldova): Str. 31 August 1989, 78A, MD 2012, Chișinău, Moldova. *Telephone:* 22-14-75. *Fax:* 22-14-75. *E-mail:* biblioteca@bnrm.md. *Website:* www.bnrm.md.

Bibliothèque Louis Notari (Louis Notari Library of Monaco): 8 rue Louis Notari, 98000 Monaco. *Telephone:* 93 15 29 40. *Fax:* 93 15 29 41.

Metropolitan Central Library of Ulaanbaatar (Ulan Bator), Mongolia: Seoul Street 7, Ulaanbaatar 28, Mongolia. *Telephone:* (11) 325593. *Fax:* (11) 329950. *E-mail:* mcl-ub@magicnet.mn. *Website:* www.mclibrary.edu.mn.

Central National Library of Montenegro: Bulevar Crnogorskih junaka 163, 81250 Cetinje, Montenegro. *Telephone:* (86) 231143. *Fax:* (86) 231726. *E-mail:* cnb@cg.yu.

Bibliothèque Générale et Archives (General Library and Archives of Morocco): BP 1003, Avenue Ibn Battouta, Rabat, Morocco. *Telephone:* (7) 71890.

Biblioteca Nacional de Moçambique (National Library of Mozambique): PO Box 141, Maputo, Mozambique. *Telephone:* (1) 425 676.

National Library of Myanmar: Strand Road, Yangon, Myanmar. *Telephone:* (1) 283332. *Fax:* (1) 212367.

National Library of Namibia: Private Bag 13301, Windhoek, Namibia. *Telephone:* (61) 2063874. *E-mail:* library@unam.na. *Website:* library.unam.na.

Nepal National Library: Harihar Bhawan, Pulchowk, PO Box 182, Lalitpur, Nepal. *Telephone:* (1) 5521132. *Fax:* (1) 5536461. *E-mail:* info@nnl.gov.np. *Website:* www.nnl.gov.np.

Koninklijke Bibliotheek (Royal Library of The Netherlands): PO Box 90407, 2509 LK The Hague, The Netherlands. *Telephone:* (70) 314-0911. *Fax:* (70) 314-0450. *Website:* www.kb.nl.

National Library of New Zealand/Te Puna Mātauranga o Aotearoa: PO Box 1467, Wellington 6140, New Zealand. *Telephone:* (4) 474 3000. *Fax:* (4) 474 3035. *E-mail:* information@natlib.govt.nz. *Website:* www.natlib.govt.nz.

Biblioteca Nacional Rubén Darío (National Rubén Darío Library of Nicaragua): Palacio Nacional de la Cultura, Apdo Postal 3514, Managua, Nicaragua. *Fax:* (2) 222722. *E-mail:* binanic@tmx.com.ni. *Website:* www.abinia.org/nicaragua.

National Library of Nigeria: 4 Wesley Street, PO Box 12626, Lagos, Nigeria. *Telephone:* (1) 2600220. *Fax:* (1) 631563.

Nasjonalbiblioteket (National Library of Norway): PO Box 2674 Solli, 0203 Oslo, Norway. *Telephone:* 23 27 60 00. *Fax:* 23 27 60 10. *E-mail:* nb@nb.no. *Website:* www.nb.no.

National Library of Pakistan: Constitution Avenue, Islamabad 44000, Pakistan. *Telephone:* (51) 9214523. *Fax:* (51) 9221375. *E-mail:* nlpiba@isb.paknet.com.pk. *Website:* www.nlp.gov.pk.

Biblioteca Nacional Ernesto J. Castillero R. (Ernesto J. Castillero R. National Library of Panama): Parque Omar. Vía Porras, Apdo Postal 0830-00547, Zona 9, Panama City, Panama. *Telephone:* 221-8360. *Fax:* 224-9988. *E-mail:* webmaster@binal.ac.pa. *Website:* www.binal.ac.pa.

National Library of Papua New Guinea: PO Box 734, Waigani NCD, Papua New Guinea. *Telephone:* 325 6200. *Fax:* 325 1331. *E-mail:* cla@datec.com.pg.

Biblioteca y Archivo Nacional (National Library and Archive of Paraguay): Mariscal Estigarriba 95, Asunción, Paraguay.

Biblioteca Nacional del Perú (National Library of Peru): Avenida de la Poesia 160, San Borja, Lima, Peru. *Telephone:* (1) 513-6900. *Fax:* (1) 513-7060. *E-mail:* bmperu@bnp.gob.pe. *Website:* www.bnp.gob.pe.

Pambansang Aklatan ng Pilipinas (National Library of The Philippines): T. M. Kalaw Street, Ermita, Manila 1000, The Philippines. *Telephone:* (2) 583252. *Fax:* (2) 502329. *E-mail:* nanie@nlp.gov.ph. *Website:* www.nlp.gov.ph.

Biblioteka Narodowa (National Library of Poland): al. Niepodleglosci 213, 02-086 Warsaw, Poland. *Telephone:* (22) 608-2999. *Fax:* (22) 825-5251. *E-mail:* biblnar@bn.org.pl. *Website:* www.bn.org.pl.

Biblioteca Nacional de Portugal (National Library of Portugal): Campo Grande 83, 1749-081 Lisbon, Portugal. *Telephone:* (21) 7982000. *Fax:* (21) 7982140. *E-mail:* bn@bn.pt. *Website:* www.bn.pt.

Qatar National Library: POB 205, Doha, Qatar. *Telephone:* 429955. *Fax:* 429976.

Biblioteca Naționalǎ a României (National Library of Romania): Str. Ion Ghica 4, sector 3, 79708 Bucharest, Romania. *Telephone:* (21) 314 24 34. *Fax:* (21) 312 33 81. *E-mail:* go@bibnat.ro. *Website:* www.bibnat.ro.

Rossiiskaya Gosudarstvennaya Biblioteka (Russian State Library): 3/5 Vozdvizhenka Street, 101000 Moscow, Russia. *Telephone:* (495) 202 73 71. *Fax:* (495) 290 60 62. *E-mail:* mbs@rsl.ru. *Website:* www.rsl.ru.

Rossiiskaya Natsionalnaya Biblioteka (Russian National Library): 18 Sadovaya Street, 191069 St Petersburg, Russia. *Telephone:* (812) 310 28 56. *Fax:* (812) 310 61 48. *E-mail:* office@nlr.ru. *Website:* www.nlr.ru.

Bibliothèque Nationale du Rwanda (National Library of Rwanda): PO Box 624, Kigali, Rwanda. *Telephone:* 72730.

Biblioteca di Stato (State Library of San Marino): Contrada Omerelli 13, Palazzo Valloni, 47890, San Marino. *Telephone:* 882248. *Fax:* 882295. *E-mail:* biblioteca@omniway.sm.

King Fahd National Library of Saudi Arabia: Riyadh, Saudi Arabia. *Website:* www.kfnl.org.sa.

Narodna Biblioteka Srbije (National Library of Serbia): Skerliceva 1, 11000 Belgrade, Serbia. *Telephone:* (11) 451750. *Fax:* (11) 451289. *E-mail:* nbs@nbs.bg.ac.yu. *Website:* www.nbs.bg.ac.yu.

Seychelles National Library: PO Box 45, Victoria, Mahe, Seychelles. *Telephone:* 32 13 33. *Fax:* 32 31 83. *E-mail:* natlib@seychelles.net. *Website:* www.national-library.edu.sc.

Lee Kong Chian Reference Library of Singapore: c/o National Library Board, 100 Victoria Street, 188064 Singapore. *Telephone:* 6332 3255. *Fax:* 6332 3395. *E-mail:* helpdesk@nlb.gov.sg. *Website:* www.nlb.gov.sg.

Slovenská národná knižnica (Slovak National Library): Námestie J. C. Hronského 1, 036 01 Martin, Slovakia. *Telephone:* (43) 413-1707. *Fax:* (43) 430-1802. *E-mail:* snk@snk.sk. *Website:* www.snk.sk.

Narodna in univerzitetna knjižnica (National and University Library of Slovenia): PO Box 259, 1000 Ljubljana, Slovenia. *Telephone:* (1) 2001110. *Fax:* (1) 4257293. *E-mail:* info@nuk.uni-lj.si. *Website:* www.nuk.uni-lj.si.

National Library of the Solomon Islands: PO Box 165, Honiara, Solomon Islands. *Telephone:* 21601. *Fax:* 25366.

National Library of Somalia: POB 1754, Mogadishu, Somalia. *Telephone:* (1) 22758.

National Library of South Africa: PO Box 397, 0001 Pretoria, South Africa. *Telephone:* (12) 321 8931. *Fax:* (12) 325 5984. *E-mail:* info@nlsa.ac.za. *Website:* www.nlsa.ac.za.

Biblioteca Nacional de España (National Library of Spain): Paseo de Recoletos 20, 28071 Madrid, Spain. *Telephone:* (91) 5807800. *Fax:* (91) 5775634. *E-mail:* info@bne.es. *Website:* www.bne.es.

National Library and Documentation Centre of Sri Lanka: 14 Independence Avenue, Colombo 07, Sri Lanka. *Telephone:* (11) 2698847. *Fax:* (11) 2685201. *E-mail:* nldsb@mail.natlib.lk. *Website:* www.natlib.lk.

Swaziland National Library Service: PO Box 1461, Mbabane, Swaziland. *Telephone:* 42633. *Fax:* 43863. *E-mail:* snlssz@snls.gov.sz.

Kungl. biblioteket, Sveriges nationalbibliotek (National Library of Sweden): PO Box 5039, 102 41 Stockholm, Sweden. *Telephone:* (8) 463 40 00. *Fax:* (8) 463 40 04. *E-mail:* kungl.biblioteket@kb.se. *Website:* www.kb.se.

Schweizerischen Landesbibliothek (Swiss National Library): Hallwylstrasse 15, 3003 Bern, Switzerland. *Telephone:* (31) 322 89 11. *Fax:* (31) 322 84 63. *E-mail:* slb-bns@slb.admin.ch. *Website:* www.snl.ch.

Al-Assad National Library of Syria: PO Box 3639, Malki Street, Damascus, Syria. *Telephone:* (11) 3320803. *Fax:* (11) 3320804. *E-mail:* contact@alassad-library.com. *Website:* www.alassad-library.gov.sy.

National Central Library of Taiwan: 20 Chungshan S. Road, Taipei 100-01, China (Taiwan). *Telephone:* (2) 2361-9132. *Website:* www.ncl.edu.tw.

Tajikistan National Library: Rudaki Avenue 26, Dushanbe, Tajikistan. *Telephone:* (372) 21 51 60. *E-mail:* toshev@yandex.ru.

Tanzania Library Service: PO Box 9283, Dar es Salaam, Tanzania. *Telephone:* (51) 26121.

National Library of Thailand: Samsen Road, Bangkok 10300, Thailand. *Telephone:* (2) 2810263. *Fax:* (2) 2815999. *Website:* www.nlt.go.th.

Bibliothèque Nationale du Togo (National Library of Togo): Avenue de la Victoire, PO Box 1002, Lomé, Togo. *Telephone:* 21 63 67. *Fax:* 22 19 67.

National Library and Information System of Trinidad and Tobago: National Library Building, Corner Hart and Abercromby Streets, Port of Spain, Trinidad and Tobago. *Telephone:* 624-4466. *E-mail:* adultlibrary@nalis.gov.tt. *Website:* www.nalis.gov.tt.

Bibliothèque Nationale (National Library of Tunisia): 20 Souk al-Attarine, 1008 Tunis, BP 42, Tunisia. *Telephone:* (71) 329903. *Fax:* (71) 200925. *E-mail:* Bibliotheque.Nationale@Email.ati.tn. *Website:* www.bibliotheque.nat.tn.

Millî Kütüphane (National Library of Turkey): Bahçelievler Son Durak, 06490 Ankara, Turkey. *Telephone:* (312) 2126200. *Fax:* (312) 2230451. *E-mail:* info@mkutup.gov.tr. *Website:* www.mkutup.gov.tr.

National Library of Turkmenistan: ul. Karl Marx, 744000 Aşgabat, Turkmenistan. *Telephone:* (12) 25 32 54.

National Library and Archives of Tuvalu: PO Box 36, Funafuti Island, Tuvalu. *Telephone:* 711.

National Library of Uganda: Plot 50 Buganda Road, PO Box 4262, Kampala, Uganda. *Telephone:* (41) 254661. *Fax:* (41) 348625. *E-mail:* info@nlu.go.ug. *Website:* www.nlu.go.ug.

Natsional'na biblioteka Ukraïny im. V. I. Vernadskoho (V. I. Vernadsky National Library of Ukraine): Pr. 40 richchia Zhovtnia, 03039 Kyiv, Ukraine. *Telephone:* (44) 265-81-04. *Fax:* (44) 264-33-98. *E-mail:* nlu@csl.freenet.kiev.ua. *Website:* www.nbuv.gov.ua.

Cultural Foundation National Library of the United Arab Emirates: Cultural Centre, PO Box 2380, Abu Dhabi, United Arab Emirates. *Telephone:* (2) 215300. *Fax:* (2) 217472. *Website:* www.cultural.org.ae.

The British Library: 96 Euston Road, London, NW1 2DB, England. *Telephone:* (20) 7412-7111. *E-mail:* press-and-pr@bl.uk. *Website:* www.bl.uk.

The National Library of Scotland: George IV Bridge, Edinburgh, EH1 1EW, Scotland. *Telephone:* (131) 6233700. *Fax:* (131) 6233701. *E-mail:* ils@nls.uk. *Website:* www.nls.uk.

Llyfrgell Genedlaethol Cymru/The National Library of Wales: Aberystwyth, Ceredigion, SY23 3BU, Wales. *Telephone:* (1970) 632800. *Fax:* (1970) 615709. *Website:* www.llgc.org.uk.

The US Library of Congress: 101 Independence Avenue SE, Washington, DC 20540, USA. *Telephone:* (202) 707-5000. *Website:* www.loc.gov.

Biblioteca Nacional (National Library of Uruguay): 18 de Julio 1790, Casilla 452, Montevideo, Uruguay. *E-mail:* bibna@adinet.com.uy. *Website:* www.bibna.gub.uy.

National Library of Uzbekistan: Horezm Street 51, 700047 Tashkent, Uzbekistan. *Telephone:* (71) 139-47-09. *Fax:* (71) 133-09-08. *E-mail:* navoi@tshtt.uz. *Website:* www.natlib.uz.

National Library of Vanuatu: PO Box 18, Vila, Vanuatu. *Telephone:* 2721. *Fax:* 2633. *Website:* www.vanuatuculture.org/library.

Biblioteca Apostolica Vaticana (Vatican City Library): Cortile del Belvedere, 00120 Città del Vaticano, Vatican City. *Telephone:* (6) 69879402. *Fax:* (6) 69884795. *E-mail:* bav@vatlib.it. *Website:* bav.vatican.va.

Biblioteca Nacional de Venezuela (National Library of Venezuela): PO Box 6525, Caracas 1010A, Venezuela. *Telephone:* (2) 922420. *Fax:* (2) 919545. *E-mail:* vbetanc@dlno.conicit.ve.

National Library of Viet Nam: 31 Tràng thi, 10000 Hanoi, Viet Nam. *Telephone:* (4) 8254927. *Fax:* (4) 8253357. *E-mail:* info@nlv.gov.vn. *Website:* www.nlv.gov.vn.

Zambia Library Service: PO Box 30802, Lusaka, Zambia.

National Library of Zimbabwe: PO Box 1773, Bulawayo, Zimbabwe. *Telephone:* (9) 69827. *Fax:* (9) 77662.